SCOTT

2024
STANDARD POSTAGE STAMP CATALOGUE

ONE HUNDRED AND EIGHTIETH EDITION IN SIX VOLUMES

Volume 4A
J-L

EDITOR-IN-CHIEF Jay Bigalke
EDITOR-AT-LARGE Donna Houseman
CONTRIBUTING EDITOR Charles Snee
EDITOR EMERITUS James E. Kloetzel
SENIOR EDITOR /NEW ISSUES AND VALUING Martin J. Frankevicz
ADMINISTRATIVE ASSISTANT/CATALOGUE LAYOUT Eric Wiessinger
SENIOR GRAPHIC DESIGNER Cinda McAlexander
SALES DIRECTOR David Pistello
SALES DIRECTOR Eric Roth
SALES DIRECTOR Brenda Wyen
SALES REPRESENTATIVE Julie Dahlstrom

Released July 2023
Includes New Stamp Listings through the May 2023 *Scott Stamp Monthly* Catalogue Update

AMOS MEDIA

1660 Campbell Road, Suite A, Sidney, OH 45365
Publishers of *Linn's Stamp News, Scott Stamp Monthly, Coin World* and *Coin World Monthly.*

Table of contents

See the following volumes for other country listings:
Volume 1A: United States, United Nations, Abu Dhabi-Australia; Volume 1B: Austria-B
Volume 2A: C-Cur; Volume 2B: Cyp-F
Volume 3B: H-I
Volume 4B: M
Volume 5A: N-Phil; Volume 5B: Pit-Sam
Volume 6A: San-Tete; Volume 6B: Thai-Z

Scott Catalogue Mission Statement

The Scott Catalogue Team exists to serve the recreational, educational and commercial hobby needs of stamp collectors and dealers.

We strive to set the industry standard for philatelic information and products by developing and providing goods that help collectors identify, value, organize and present their collections.

Quality customer service is, and will continue to be, our highest priority. We aspire toward achieving total customer satisfaction.

Copyright Notice

Trademark Notice

ISBN 978-0-89487-701-8

Library of Congress Card No. 2-3301

Acknowledgments

Our appreciation and gratitude go to the following individuals who have assisted us in preparing information included in this year's Scott catalogues. Some helpers prefer anonymity. These individuals have generously shared their stamp knowledge with others through the medium of the Scott catalogue.

Those who follow provided information that is in addition to the hundreds of dealer price lists and advertisements and scores of auction catalogues and realizations that were used in producing the catalogue values. It is from those noted here that we have been able to obtain information on items not normally seen in published lists and advertisements. Support from these people goes beyond data leading to catalogue values, for they also are key to editorial changes.

A special acknowledgment to Liane and Sergio Sismondo of The Classic Collector for their assistance and knowledge sharing that have aided in the preparation of this year's Standard and Classic Specialized Catalogues.

Clifford J. Alexander
(Carriers and Locals Society)
Roland Austin
Michael & Cecilia Ball (A To Z Stamps)
Jim Bardo (Bardo Stamps)
Brian M. Bleckwenn
(The Philatelic Foundation)
Les Bootman
Roger S. Brody
Tom Brougham
(Canal Zone Study Group)
Paul and Josh Buchsbayew
(Cherrystone Auctions, Inc.)
Timothy Bryan Burgess
Tina and John Carlson (JET Stamps)
Jay T. Carrigan
Carlson Chambliss
Bob Coale
Tony L. Crumbley
(Carolina Coin and Stamp, Inc.)
Christopher Dahle
Charles Deaton
Bob and Rita Dumaine
(Sam Houston Duck Co.)
Charles Epting (H.R. Harmer)
Mike Farrell
David Feldman International Auctioneers
Robert A. Fisher
Jeffrey M. Forster
Robert S. Freeman
Henry L. Gitner
(Henry Gitner Philatelists, Inc.)
Stan Goldfarb
Marc E. Gonzales
Daniel E. Grau
Bruce Hecht (Bruce L. Hecht Co.)
Eric Jackson
Michael Jaffe (Michael Jaffe Stamps, Inc.)
William A. (Bill) Jones
Allan Katz (Ventura Stamp Co.)
Patricia A. Kaufmann
(Civil War Philatelic Society)
Jon Kawaguchi
(Ryukyu Philatelic Specialist Society)
Han Ki Kim
Ingert Kuzych
Ulf Lindahl (Ethiopian Philatelic Society)
Ignacio Llach (Filatelia Llach, S.L.)
William K. McDaniel
Pat McElroy
Brian Metz
Mark S. Miller (India Study Circle)
Gary Morris (Pacific Midwest Co.)
Peter Mosiondz Jr.
Bruce M. Moyer
(Moyer Stamps & Collectables)
Scott Murphy
(Professional Stamp Experts)
Dr. Tiong Tak Ngo
Nik and Lisa Oquist
Don Peterson
(International Philippine Philatelic Society)
Todor Drumev Popov
Dr. Charles Posner
Peter W. W. Powell
Ed Reiser (Century Stamp Co.)
Ghassan D. Riachi
Robert G. Rufe
Theodosios D. Sampson Ph.D.
Dennis W. Schmidt
Joyce and Chuck Schmidt
Guy Shaw
(Mexico-Elmhurst Philatelic Society International)
J. Randall Shoemaker
(Philatelic Stamp Authentication and Grading, Inc.)
Sergio and Liane Sismondo
(The Classic Collector)
Jay Smith
Telah Smith
Mark Stelmacovich
Scott R. Trepel
(Robert A. Siegel Auction Galleries)
Dan Undersander
Steven Unkrich
Herbert R. Volin
Val Zabijaka (Zabijaka Auctions)

What's new for 2024 Scott Standard Volume 4

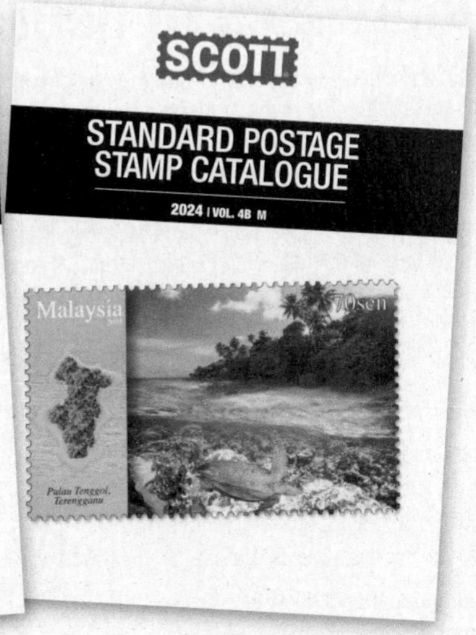

Another catalog season is upon us as we continue the journey of the 155-year history of the Scott catalogs. The 2024 volumes are the 180th edition of the Scott *Standard Postage Stamp Catalogue*.

Volume 4A includes listings for countries of the world Jamaica through Luxembourg. Listings for countries of the world Macao through Mozambique can be found in Vol. 4B.

Because Vol. 4B is a continuation of the first part of the Vol. 4 catalog, the introduction pages are not repeated in each volume.

This year's Vol. 4A cover features an 84-yen stamp (Scott 4402i) from Japan's 2020 pane of 10 Summer Greetings stamps (4402).

The Malaysia 2015 70-sen Pulau Tenggol, Trengganu stamp (Scott 1571a) from a pair of Islands stamps (1571) is shown on the Vol. 3B cover. The 2015 Islands issue (1571-1573) consists of two pairs of stamps and a souvenir sheet of one.

For the 2024 Scott catalog season, we continue a review of the Portuguese areas, which for Vol. 4 includes Lourenco Marques, Macao, Mozambique and Mozambique Company.

One important note for Macao needs to be emphasized. The values for unused stamps of all periods are for well-centered examples with original gum showing no traces of toning or disturbance. Any deviations would result in a substantial value decrease. For stamps issued without gum, the same condition standards still apply, except for the part about gum condition.

Approximately 2,900 value changes, mostly increases and very few decreases, were made for Macao. In the classic period, one example of an increase was for the 1892 30-real-on-200r surcharged stamp (Scott 45), which moved from $60 and $30 in unused and used condition to $120 and $55, respectively.

For a modern Macao issue, the 2013 block of six and souvenir sheet of the Chinese Calligraphy and Painting issue (Scott 1402-1403) increased from $5 and $7 in unused and used condition, respectively, to $11 and $25.

For both Mozambique and Mozambique Company, numerous value changes were made.

Mozambique had approximately 1,400 value changes with only a handful of decreases. Mozambique Company had more than 700 value changes, also with only a small number of decreases.

For Mozambique, the set of 13 1877-85 Portuguese Crown stamps (Scott 1-14) moved from $882.45 unused to $1,655.15. A large part of the jump was the 20r rose stamp (5) which increased substantially in value in unused condition. The value is now italicized to reflect an item that does not trade frequently.

For Mozambique Company, the set of 10 1919 Company Arms postage due stamps (Scott J31-J40) moved from $8.05 unused and used to $10.30 both ways.

Lourenco Marques was also reviewed, and almost every value changed. Most values increased slightly compared to values for the other countries already mentioned. For example, the 1899 50-real-on-75r rose stamp (Scott 57) increased from $6 and $2.50 in unused and used condition to $7.75 and $4.50, respectively.

Mexico was also extensively reviewed, and more than 4,000 value changes were recorded. Many of the changes were increases. One example was the first special delivery stamp, the 1919 20-centavo Motorcycle Postman (Scott E1), which advanced from $70 unused to $110.

Other reviewed countries include Japan, Jordan, Kuwait, Lebanon and Libya.

Many other countries received less extensive reviews that are not noted in this letter. We encourage you to pay special attention to the Number Additions, Deletions and Changes listing in this volume. We also suggest reading the catalog introduction, which includes an abundance of useful information.

A digital subscription is also available for the Scott catalogs, and information about the subscription can be found online at www.amosadvantage.com.

Approximately 1,000 images of stamps not pictured in the Vol. 4 print edition were added to this year's Vol. 4 digital catalog.

Best wishes in your collecting pursuits!

Jay

Jay Bigalke, Scott catalog editor-in-chief

Addresses, telephone numbers, web sites, email addresses of general and specialized philatelic societies

Collectors can contact the following groups for information about the philately of the areas within the scope of these societies, or inquire about membership in these groups. Aside from the general societies, we limit this list to groups that specialize in particular fields of philately, particular areas covered by the Scott *Standard Postage Stamp Catalogue*, and topical groups. Many more specialized philatelic society exist than those listed below. These addresses are updated yearly, and they are, to the best of our knowledge, correct and current. Groups should inform the editors of address changes whenever they occur. The editors also want to hear from other such specialized groups not listed.

Unless otherwise noted all website addresses begin with http://

General Societies

American Philatelic Society, 100 Match Factory Place, Bellefonte, PA 16823-1367; (814) 933-3803; https://stamps.org; apsinfo@stamps.org

International Society of Worldwide Stamp Collectors, Joanne Murphy, M.D., P.O. Box 19006, Sacramento, CA 95819; www.iswsc.org; executivedirector@iswsc.org

Royal Philatelic Society of Canada, P.O. Box 69080, St. Clair Post Office, Toronto, ON M4T 3A1 Canada; (888) 285-4143; www.rpsc.org; info@rpsc.org

Royal Philatelic Society London, 15 Abchurch Lane, London EX4N 7BW, United Kingdom; +44 (0) 20 7486 1044; www.rpsl.org.uk; secretary@rpsl.org.uk

Libraries, Museums, and Research Groups

American Philatelic Research Library, 100 Match Factory Place, Bellefonte, PA 16823; (814) 933-3803; www.stamplibrary.org; library@stamps.org.

V. G. Greene Philatelic Research Foundation, P.O. Box 69100, St. Clair Post Office, Toronto, ON M4T 3A1, Canada; (416) 921-2073; info@greenefoundation.ca

Aero/Astro Philately

American Air Mail Society, Stephen Reinhard, P.O. Box 110, Mineola, NY 11501; www.americanairmailsociety.org; sreinhard1@optonline.net

Postal History

Auxiliary Markings Club, Jerry Johnson, 6621 W. Victoria Ave., Kennewick, WA 99336; www.postal-markings.org; membership-2010@postal-markings.org

Postage Due Mail Study Group, Bob Medland, Camway Cottage, Nanny Hurn's Lane, Cameley, Bristol BS39 5AJ, United Kingdom; 01761 45959; www.postageduemail.org.uk; secretary.pdmsg@gmail.com

Postal History Society, Yamil Kouri, 405 Waltham St. #347, Lexington, MA 02421; www.postalhistorysociety.org; yhkouri@massmed.org

Post Mark Collectors Club, Bob Milligan, 7014 Woodland Oaks Drive, Magnolia, TX 77354; (281) 259-2735; www.postmarks.org; bob.milligan0@gmail.com

U.S. Cancellation Club, Roger Curran, 18 Tressler Blvd., Lewisburg, PA 17837; rdcnrc@ptd.net

Revenues and Cinderellas

American Revenue Association, Lyman Hensley, 473 E. Elm St., Sycamore, IL 60178-1934; www.revenuer.org; ilrno2@netzero.net

Christmas Seal and Charity Stamp Society, John Denune Jr., 234 E. Broadway, Granville, OH 43023; (740) 814-6031; www.seal-society.org

National Duck Stamp Collectors Society, Anthony J. Monico, P.O. Box 43, Harleysville, PA 19438-0043; www.ndscs.org; ndscs@ndscs.org

State Revenue Society, Kent Gray, P.O. Box 67842, Albuquerque, NM 87193; www.staterevenue.org; srssecretary@comcast.net

Thematic Philately

Americana Unit, Dennis Dengel, 17 Peckham Road, Poughkeepsie, NY 12603-2018; www.americanaunit.org; ddengel@americanaunit.org

American Topical Association, Jennifer Miller, P.O. Box 2143, Greer, SC 29652-2143; (618) 985-5100; americantopical.org; ata@americantopical.org

Astronomy Study Unit, Leonard Zehr, 1411 Chateau Ave., Windsor, ON N8P 1M2, Canada; (416) 833-9317; www.astronomystudyunit.net; lenzehr@gmail.com

Bicycle Stamps Club, Corey Hjalseth, 1102 Broadway, Suite 200, Tacoma, WA 98402; (253) 318-6222; www.bicyclestampsclub.org; coreyh@evergreenhomeloans.com

Biology Unit, Chris Dahle, 1401 Linmar Drive NE, Cedar Rapids, IA 52402-3724; www.biophilately.org; chris-dahle@biophilately.org

Bird Stamp Society, Mr. S. A. H. (Tony) Statham, Ashlyns Lodge, Chesham Road, Berkhamsted, Herts HP4 2ST United Kingdom; www.bird-stamps.org/bss; tony.statham@sky.com

Captain Cook Society, Jerry Yucht, 8427 Leale Ave., Stockton, CA 95212, www.captaincooksociety.com; us@captaincooksociety.com

The CartoPhilatelic Society, Marybeth Sulkowski, 2885 Sanford Ave., SW, #32361, Grandville, MI 49418-1342; www.mapsonstamps.org; secretary@mapsonstamps.org

Casey Jones Railroad Unit, Jeff Lough, 2612 Redbud Land, Apt. C, Lawrence, KS 66046; www.uqp.de/cjr; jeffydplaugh@gmail.com

Cats on Stamps Study Unit, Robert D. Jarvis, 2731 Teton Lane, Fairfield, CA 94533; www.catstamps.info; catmews1@yahoo.com

Chemistry and Physics on Stamps Study Unit, Dr. Roland Hirsch, 13830 Metcalf Ave., Apt. 15218, Overland Park, KS 66223-8017; (301) 792-6296; www.cpossu.org; rfhirsch@cpossu.org

Chess on Stamps Study Unit, Barry Keith, 511 First St. N., Apt. 106; Charlottesville, VA 22902; www.chessonstamps.org; keithfam@embarqmail.com

Cricket Philatelic Society, A. Melville-Brown, 11 Weppons, Ravens Road, Shoreham-by-Sea, West Sussex BN43 5AW, United Kingdom; www.cricketstamp.net; mel.cricket.100@googlemail.com

Earth's Physical Features Study Group, Fred Klein, 515 Magdalena Ave., Los Altos, CA 94024; http://epfsu.jeffhayward.com; epfsu@jeffhayward.com

Ebony Society of Philatelic Events and Reflections (ESPER), Don Neal, P.O. Box 5245, Somerset, NJ 08875-5245; www.esperstamps.org; esperdon@verizon.net

Europa Study Unit, Tonny E. Van Loij, 3002 S. Xanthia St.; Denver, CO 80231-4237; (303) 752-0189; www.europastudyunit.org; tvanloij@gmail.com

Fire Service in Philately, John Zaranek, 81 Hillpine Road, Cheektowaga, NY 14227-2259; (716) 668-3352; jczaranek@roadrunner.com

Gastronomy on Stamps Study Unit, David Wolfersburger, 5062 NW 35th Lane Road, Ocala, FL 34482; (314) 494-3795; www.gastronomystamps.org

Gay and Lesbian History on Stamps Club, Joe Petronie, P.O. Box 190842, Dallas, TX 75219-0842; www.glhsonline.org; glhsc@aol.com

Gems, Minerals and Jewelry Study Unit, Fred Haynes, 10 Country Club Drive, Rochester, NY 14618-3720; fredmhaynes55@gmail.com

Graphics Philately Association, Larry Rosenblum. 1030 E. El Camino Real, PMB 107, Sunnyvale, CA 94087-3759; www.graphics-stamps.org; larry@graphics-stamps.org

Journalists, Authors and Poets on Stamps, Christopher D. Cook, 7222 Hollywood Road, Berrien Springs, MI 49103; cdcook2@gmail.com

Lighthouse Stamp Society, www.lighthousestampsociety.org

Lions International Stamp Club, David McKirdy, s-Gravenwetering 248, 3062 SJ Rotterdam, Netherlands; 31(0) 10 212 0313; www.lisc.nl; davidmckirdy@aol.com

Masonic Study Unit, Gene Fricks, 25 Murray Way, Blackwood, NJ 08012-4400; genefricks@comcast.net

Medical Subjects Unit, Dr. Frederick C. Skvara, P.O. Box 6228, Bridgewater, NJ 08807; fcskvara@optonline.net

Napoleonic Age Philatelists, Ken Berry, 4117 NW 146th St., Oklahoma City, OK 73134-1746; (405) 748-8646; www.nap-stamps.org; krb4117@att.net

Old World Archaeological Study Unit, Caroline Scannell, 14 Dawn Drive, Smithtown, NY 11787-176; www.owasu.org; editor@owasu.org

Petroleum Philatelic Society International, Feitze Papa, 922 Meander Drive, Walnut Creek, CA 94598-4239; www.ppsi.org.uk; oildad@astound.net

Rotary on Stamps Fellowship, Gerald L. Fitzsimmons, 105 Calle Ricardo, Victoria, TX 77904; www.rotaryonstamps.org; glfitz@suddenlink.net

Scouts on Stamps Society International, Woodrow (Woody) Brooks, 498 Baldwin Road, Akron, OH 44312; (330) 612-1294; www.sossi.org; secretary@sossi.org

Ships on Stamps Unit, Erik Th. Matzinger, Voorste Haervelden 30, 4822 AL Breda, Netherlands; www.shipsonstamps.org; erikships@gmail.com

Space Topic Study Unit, David Blog, P.O. Box 174, Bergenfield, NJ 07621; www.space-unit.com; davidblognj@gmail.com

Stamps on Stamps Collectors Club, Michael Merritt, 73 Mountainside Road, Mendham, NJ 07945; www.stampsonstamps.org; michael@mischu.me

Windmill Study Unit, Walter J. Hallien, 607 N. Porter St., Watkins Glenn, NY 14891-1345; (607) 229-3541; www.windmillworld.com

Wine On Stamps Study Unit, David Wolfersburger, 5062 NW 35th Lane Road, Ocala, FL 34482; (314) 494-3795; www.wine-on-stamps.org;

United States

American Air Mail Society, Stephen Reinhard, P.O. Box 110, Mineola, NY 11501; www.americanairmailsociety.org; sreinhard1@optonline.net

American First Day Cover Society, P.O. Box 246, Colonial Beach VA 22443-0246; (520) 321-0880; www.afdcs.org; afdcs@afdcs.org

Auxiliary Markings Club, Jerry Johnson, 6621 W. Victoria Ave., Kennewick, WA 99336; www.postal-markings.org; membership-2010@postal-markings.org

American Plate Number Single Society, Rick Burdsall, APNSS Secretary, P.O. BOX 1023, Palatine, IL 60078-1023; www.apnss.org; apnss.sec@gmail.com

American Revenue Association, Lyman Hensley, 473 E. Elm St., Sycamore, IL 60178-1934; www.revenuer.org; ilrno2@netzero.net

American Society for Philatelic Pages and Panels, Ron Walenciak, P.O. Box 1042, Washington Township, NJ 07676; www.asppp.org; ron.walenciak@asppp.org

Canal Zone Study Group, Mike Drabik, P.O. Box 281, Bolton, MA 01740, www.canalzonestudygroup.com; czsgsecretary@gmail.com

Carriers and Locals Society, John Bowman, 14409 Pentridge Drive, Corpus Christi, TX 78410; (361) 933-0757; www.pennypost.org; jbowman@stx.rr.com

Christmas Seal & Charity Stamp Society, John Denune Jr., 234 E. Broadway, Granville, OH 43023; (740) 814-6031; www.seal-society.org; john@christmasseals.net

Civil War Philatelic Society, Patricia A. Kaufmann, 10194 N. Old State Road, Lincoln, DE 19960-3644; (302) 422-2656; www.civilwarphilatelicsociety.org; trishkauf@comcast.net

Error, Freaks, and Oddities Collectors Club, Scott Shaulis, P.O. Box 549, Murrysville, PA 15668-0549; (724) 733-4134; www.efocc.org; scott@shaulisstamps.com

National Duck Stamp Collectors Society, Anthony J. Monico, P.O. Box 43, Harleysville, PA 19438-0043; www.ndscs.org; ndscs@ndscs.org

Plate Number Coil Collectors Club (PNC3), Gene Trinks, 16415 W. Desert Wren Court, Surprise, AZ 85374; (623) 322-4619; www.pnc3.org; gctrinks@cox.net

Post Mark Collectors Club, Bob Milligan, 7014 Woodland Oaks Drive, Magnolia, TX 77354; (281) 259-2735; www.postmarks.org; bob.milligan0@gmail.com

Souvenir Card Collectors Society, William V. Kriebel, www.souvenircards.org; kriebewv@drexel.edu

United Postal Stationery Society, Dave Kandziolka, 404 Sundown Drive, Knoxville, TN 37934; www.upss.org; membership@upss.org

U.S. Cancellation Club, Roger Curran, 18 Tressler Blvd., Lewisburg, PA 17837; rdcnrc@ptd.net

U.S. Philatelic Classics Society, Rob Lund, 2913 Fulton St., Everett, WA 98201-3733; www.uspcs.org; membershipchairman@uspcs.org

US Possessions Philatelic Society, Daniel F. Ring, P.O. Box 113, Woodstock, IL 60098; http://uspps.tripod.com; danielfring@hotmail.com

United States Stamp Society, Rod Juell, P.O. Box 3508, Joliet, IL 60434-3508; www.usstamps.org; execsecretary@usstamps.org

Africa

Bechuanalands and Botswana Society, Otto Peetoom, Roos, East Yorkshire HU12 0LD, United Kingdom; 44(0)1964 670239; www.bechuanalandphilately.com; info@bechuanalandphilately.com

Egypt Study Circle, Mike Murphy, 11 Waterbank Road, Bellingham, London SE6 3DJ United Kingdom; (44) 0203 6737051; www.egyptstudycircle.org.uk; secretary@egyptstudycircle.org.uk

Ethiopian Philatelic Society, Ulf Lindahl, 21 Westview Place, Riverside, CT 06878; (203) 722-0769; https://ethiopianphilatelicsociety.weebly.com; ulindahl@optonline.net

Liberian Philatelic Society, P.O. Box 1570, Parker, CO 80134; www.liberiastamps.org; liberiastamps@comcast.net

Orange Free State Study Circle, J. R. Stroud, RDPSA, 24 Hooper Close, Burnham-on-sea, Somerset TA8 1JQ United Kingdom; 44 1278 782235; www.orangefreestatephilately.org.uk; richard@richardstroud.plus.com

Philatelic Society for Greater Southern Africa, David McNamee, 15 Woodland Drive, Alamo, CA 94507; www.psgsa.org; alan.hanks@sympatico.ca

Rhodesian Study Circle, William R. Wallace, P.O. Box 16381, San Francisco, CA 94116; (415) 564-6069; www.rhodesianstudycircle.org.uk; bwall8rscr@earthlink.net

Society for Moroccan and Tunisian Philately, S.P.L.M., 206, Bld Pereire, 75017 Paris, France; http://splm-philatelie.org; splm206@aol.com

South Sudan Philatelic Society, William Barclay, 1370 Spring Hill Road, South Londonderry, VT 05155; barclayphilatelics@gmail.com

Sudan Study Group, Andy Neal, Bank House, Coedway, Shrewsbury SY5 9AR United Kingdom; www.sudanstamps.org; andywneal@gmail.com

Transvaal Study Circle, c/o 9 Meadow Road, Gravesend, Kent DA11 7LR United Kingdom; www.transvaalstamps.org.uk; transvaalstudycircle@aol.co.uk

West Africa Study Circle, Martin Bratzel, 1233 Virginia Ave., Windsor, ON N8S 2Z1 Canada; www.wasc.org.uk; marty_bratzel@yahoo.ca

Asia

Aden & Somaliland Study Group, Malcom Lacey, 108 Dalestorth Road, Sutton-in-Ashfield, Nottinghamshire NG17 3AA, United Kingdom; www.stampdomain.com/aden; neil53williams@yahoo.co.uk

Burma (Myanmar) Philatelic Study Circle, Michael Whittaker, 1, Ecton Leys, Hillside, Rugby, Warwickshire CV22 5SL United Kingdom; https://burmamyanmarphilately.wordpress.com/burma-myanmar-philatelic-study-circle; manningham8@mypostoffice.co.uk

Ceylon Study Circle, Rodney W. P. Frost, 42 Lonsdale Road, Cannington, Bridgwater, Somerset TA5 2JS United Kingdom; 01278 652592; www.ceylonsc.org; rodney.frost@tiscali.co.uk

China Stamp Society, H. James Maxwell, 1050 W. Blue Ridge Blvd., Kansas City, MO 64145-1216; www.chinastampsociety.org; president@chinastampsociety.org

Hong Kong Philatelic Society, John Tang, G.P.O. Box 446, Hong Kong; www.hkpsociety.com; hkpsociety@outlook.com

Hong Kong Study Circle, Robert Newton, www.hongkongstudycircle.com/index.html; newtons100@gmail.com

India Study Circle, John Warren, P.O. Box 7326, Washington, DC 20044; (202) 488-7443; https://indiastudycircle.org; jw-kbw@earthlink.net

International Philippine Philatelic Society, James R. Larot, Jr., 4990 Bayleaf Court, Martinez, CA 94553; (925) 260-5425; www.theipps.info; jlarot@ccwater.com

International Society for Japanese Philately, P.O. Box 1283, Haddonfield NJ 08033; www.isjp.org; secretary@isjp.org

Iran Philatelic Study Circle, Nigel Gooch, Marchwood, 56, Wickham Ave., Bexhill-on-Sea, East Sussex TN39 3ER United Kingdom; www.iranphilately.org; nigelmgooch@gmail.com

Korea Stamp Society, Peter Corson, 1109 Gunnison Place, Raleigh, NC 27609; (919) 787-7611; koreastampsociety.org; pbcorson@aol.com

Nepal & Tibet Philatelic Study Circle, Colin Hepper, 12 Charnwood Close, Peterborough, Cambs PE2 9BZ United Kingdom; http://fuchs-online.com/ntpsc; ntpsc@fuchs-online.com

Pakistan Philatelic Study Circle, Jeff Siddiqui, P.O. Box 7002, Lynnwood, WA 98046; jeffsiddiqui@msn.com

Society of Indo-China Philatelists, Ron Bentley, 2600 N. 24th St., Arlington, VA 22207; (703) 524-1652; www.sicp-online.org; ron.bentley@verizon.net

Society of Israel Philatelists, Inc., Sarah Berezenko, 100 Match Factory Place, Bellefonte, PA 16823-1367; (814) 933-3803 ext. 212; www.israelstamps.com; israelstamps@gmail.com

Australasia and Oceania

Australian States Study Circle of the Royal Sydney Philatelic Club, Ben Palmer, G.P.O. 1751, Sydney, NSW 2001 Australia; http://club.philas.org.au/states

Fellowship of Samoa Specialists, Trevor Shimell, 18 Aspen Drive, Newton Abbot, Devon TQ12 4TN United Kingdom; www.samoaexpress.org; trevor.shimell@gmail.com

Malaya Study Group, Michael Waugh, 151 Roker Lane, Pudsey, Leeds LS28 9ND United Kingdom; http://malayastudygroup.com; mawpud43@gmail.com

New Zealand Society of Great Britain, Michael Wilkinson, 121 London Road, Sevenoaks, Kent TN13 1BH United Kingdom; 01732 456997; www.nzsgb.org.uk; mwilkin799@aol.com

Pacific Islands Study Circle, John Ray, 24 Woodvale Ave., London SE25 4AE United Kingdom; www.pisc.org.uk; secretary@pisc.org.uk

Papuan Philatelic Society, Steven Zirinsky, P.O. Box 49, Ansonia Station, New York, NY 10023; (718) 706-0616; www.papuanphilatelicsociety.com; szirinsky@cs.com

Pitcairn Islands Study Group, Dr. Everett L. Parker, 207 Corinth Road, Hudson, ME 04449-3057; (207) 573-1686; www.pisg.net; eparker@hughes.net

Ryukyu Philatelic Specialist Society, Laura Edmonds, P.O. Box 240177, Charlotte, NC 28224-0177; (336) 509-3739; www.ryukyustamps.org; secretary@ryukyustamps.org

Society of Australasian Specialists / Oceania, Steve Zirinsky, P.O. Box 230049, New York, NY 10023-0049; www.sasoceania.org; president@sosoceania.org

Sarawak Specialists' Society, Stephen Schumann, 2417 Cabrallo Drive, Hayward, CA 94545; (510) 785-4794; www.britborneostamps.org.uk; vpnam@s-s-s.org.uk

Western Australia Study Group, Brian Pope, P.O. Box 423, Claremont, WA 6910 Australia; (61) 419 843 943; www.wastudygroup.com; wastudygroup@hotmail.com

Europe

American Helvetia Philatelic Society, Richard T. Hall, P.O. Box 15053, Asheville, NC 28813-0053; www.swiss-stamps.org; secretary2@swiss-stamps.org

American Society for Netherlands Philately, Hans Kremer, 50 Rockport Court, Danville, CA 94526; (925) 820-5841; www.asnp1975.com; hkremer@usa.net

Andorran Philatelic Study Circle, David Hope, 17 Hawthorn Drive, Stalybridge, Cheshire SK15 1UE United Kingdom; www.andorranpsc.org.uk; andorranpsc@btinternet.com

Austria Philatelic Society, Ralph Schneider, P.O. Box 978, Iowa Park, TX 76376; (940) 213-5004; www.austriaphilatelicsociety.com; rschneiderstamps@gmail.com

Channel Islands Specialists Society, Richard Flemming, Burbage, 64 Falconers Green, Hinckley, Leicestershire, LE102SX, United Kingdom; www.ciss.uk; secretary@ciss.uk

Cyprus Study Circle, Rob Wheeler, 47 Drayton Ave., London W13 0LE United Kingdom; www.cyprusstudycircle.org; robwheeler47@aol.com

Danish West Indies Study Unit of Scandinavian Collectors Club, Arnold Sorensen, 7666 Edgedale Drive, Newburgh, IN 47630; (812) 480-6532; www.scc-online.org; valbydwi@hotmail.com

Eire Philatelic Association, John B. Sharkey, 1559 Grouse Lane, Mountainside, NJ 07092-1340; www.eirephilatelicassoc.org; jsharkeyepa@me.com

Faroe Islands Study Circle, Norman Hudson, 40 Queen's Road, Vicar's Cross, Chester CH3 5HB United Kingdom; www.faroeislandssc.org; jntropics@hotmail.com

France & Colonies Philatelic Society, Edward Grabowski, 111 Prospect St., 4C, Westfield, NJ 07090; (908) 233-9318; www.franceandcolsps.org; edjjg@alum.mit.edu

Germany Philatelic Society, P.O. Box 6547, Chesterfield, MO 63006-6547; www.germanyphilatelicusa.org; info@germanyphilatelicsocietyusa.org

Gibraltar Study Circle, Susan Dare, 22, Byways Park, Strode Road, Clevedon, North Somerset BS21 6UR United Kingdom; www.gibraltarstudycircle.wordpress.com; smldare@yahoo.co.uk

International Society for Portuguese Philately, Clyde Homen, 1491 Bonnie View Road, Hollister, CA 95023-5117; www.portugalstamps.com; ispp1962@sbcglobal.net

Italy and Colonies Study Circle, Richard Harlow, 7 Duncombe House, 8 Manor Road, Teddington, Middlesex TW118BE United Kingdom; 44 208 977 8737; www.icsc-uk.com; richardharlow@outlook.com

Liechtenstudy USA, Paul Tremaine, 410 SW Ninth St., Dundee, OR 97115-9731; (503) 538-4500; www.liechtenstudy.org; tremaine@liechtenstudy.org

Lithuania Philatelic Society, Audrius Brazdeikis, 9915 Murray Landing, Missouri City, TX 77459; (281) 450-6224; www.lithuanianphilately.com/lps; audrius@lithuanianphilately.com

Luxembourg Collectors Club, Gary B. Little, 7319 Beau Road, Sechelt, BC V0N 3A8 Canada; (604) 885-7241; http://lcc.luxcentral.com; gary@luxcentral.com

Plebiscite-Memel-Saar Study Group of the German Philatelic Society, Clayton Wallace, 100 Lark Court, Alamo, CA 94507; claytonwallace@comcast.net

Polonus Polish Philatelic Society, Daniel Lubelski, P.O. Box 2212, Benicia, CA 94510; (419) 410-9115; www.polonus.org; info@polonus.org

Rossica Society of Russian Philately, Alexander Kolchinsky, 1506 Country Lake Drive, Champaign, IL 61821-6428; www.rossica.org; alexander.kolchinsky@rossica.org

Scandinavian Collectors Club, Alan Warren, Scandinavian Collectors Club, P.O. Box 39, Exton PA 19341-0039; (612) 810-8640; www.scc-online.org; alanwar@att.net

Society for Czechoslovak Philately, Tom Cossaboom, P.O. Box 4124, Prescott, AZ 86302; (928) 771-9097; www.csphilately.org; klfck1@aol.com

Society for Hungarian Philately, Alan Bauer, P.O. Box 4028, Vineyard Haven, MA 02568; (617) 645-4045; www.hungarianphilately.org; alan@hungarianstamps.com

Spanish Study Circle, Edith Knight, www.spaincircle.wixsite.com/spainstudycircle; spaincircle@gmail.com

Ukrainian Philatelic & Numismatic Society, Martin B. Tatuch, 5117 8th Road N., Arlington, VA 22205-1201; www.upns.org; treasurer@upns.org

Vatican Philatelic Society, Dennis Brady, 4897 Ledyard Drive, Manlius NY 13104-1514; www.vaticanphilately.org; dbrady7534@gmail.com

Yugoslavia Study Group, Michael Chant, 1514 N. Third Ave., Wausau, WI 54401; 208-748-9919; www.yugosg.org; membership@yugosg.org

Interregional Societies

American Society of Polar Philatelists, Alan Warren, P.O. Box 39, Exton, PA 19341-0039; (610) 321-0740; www.polarphilatelists.org; alanwar@att.net

First Issues Collector's Club, Kurt Streepy, 3128 E. Mattatha Drive, Bloomington, IN 47401; www.firstissues.org; secretary@firstissues.org

Former French Colonies Specialist Society, Col.fra, BP 628, 75367 Paris, France; www.colfra.org; postmaster@colfra.org

France & Colonies Philatelic Society, Edward Grabowski, 111 Prospect St., 4C, Westfield, NJ 07090; (908) 233-9318, www.franceandcolsps.org; edjjg@alum.mit.edu

Joint Stamp Issues Society, Richard Zimmermann, 29A, Rue Des Eviats, 67220 Lalaye, France; www.philarz.net; richard.zimmermann@club-internet.fr

The King George VI Collectors Society, Brian Livingstone, 21 York Mansions, Prince of Wales Drive, London SW11 4DL United Kingdom; www.kg6.info; livingstone484@btinternet.com

International Society of Reply Coupon Collectors, Peter Robin, P.O. Box 353, Bala Cynwyd, PA 19004; peterrobin@verizon.net

Italy and Colonies Study Circle, Richard Harlow, 7 Duncombe House, 8 Manor Road, Teddington, Middlesex TW118BE United Kingdom; 44 208 977 8737; www.icsc-uk.com; richardharlow@outlook.com

St. Helena, Ascension & Tristan Da Cunha Philatelic Society, Dr. Everett L. Parker, 207 Corinth Road, Hudson, ME 04449-3057; (207) 573-1686; www.shatps.org; eparker@hughes.net

United Nations Philatelists, Blanton Clement, Jr., P.O. Box 146, Morrisville, PA 19067-0146; www.unpi.com; bclemjunior@gmail.com

Latin America

Asociación Filatélica de Panamá, Edward D. Vianna B. ASOFILPA, 0819-03400, El Dorado, Panama; http://asociacionfilatelicadepanama.blogspot.com; asofilpa@gmail.com

Asociacion Mexicana de Filatelia (AMEXFIL), Alejandro Grossmann, Jose Maria Rico, 129, Col. Del Valle, 3100 Mexico City, DF Mexico; www.amexfil.mx; amexfil@gmail.com

Associated Collectors of El Salvador, Pierre Cahen, Vipsal 1342, P.O. Box 02-5364, Miami FL 33102; www.elsalvadorphilately.org; sfes-aces@elsalvadorphilately.org

Association Filatelic de Costa Rica, Giana Wayman (McCarty), #SJO 4935, P.O. Box 025723, Miami, FL 33102-5723; 011-506-2-228-1947; scotland@racsa.co.cr

Brazil Philatelic Association, William V. Kriebel, www.brazilphilatelic.org, info@brazilphilatelic.org

Canal Zone Study Group, Mike Drabik, P.O. Box 281, Bolton, MA 01740; www.canalzonestudygroup.com; czsgsecretary@gmail.com

Colombia-Panama Philatelic Study Group, Allan Harris, 26997 Hemmingway Ct, Hayward CA 94542-2349; www.copaphil.org; copaphilusa@aol.com

Falkland Islands Philatelic Study Groups, Morva White, 42 Colton Road, Shrivenham, Swindon SN6 8AZ United Kingdom; 44(0) 1793 783245; www.fipsg.org.uk; morawhite@supanet.com

Federacion Filatelica de la Republica de Honduras, Mauricio Mejia, Apartado Postal 1465, Tegucigalpa, D.C. Honduras; 504 3399-7227; www.facebook.com/filateliadehonduras; ffrh@hotmail.com

International Cuban Philatelic Society (ICPS), Ernesto Cuesta, P.O. Box 34434, Bethesda, MD 20827; (301) 564-3099; www.cubafil.org; ecuesta@philat.com

International Society of Guatemala Collectors, Jaime Marckwordt, 449 St. Francis Blvd., Daly City, CA 94015-2136; (415) 997-0295; www.guatemalastamps.com; president@guatamalastamps.com

Mexico-Elmhurst Philatelic Society International, Eric Stovner, P.O. Box 10097, Santa Ana, CA 92711-0097; www.mepsi.org; treasurer@mepsi.org

Nicaragua Study Group, Erick Rodriguez, 11817 S. W. 11th St., Miami, FL 33184-2501; nsgsec@yahoo.com

North America (excluding United States)

British Caribbean Philatelic Study Group, Bob Stewart, 7 West Dune Lane, Long Beach Township, NJ 08008; (941) 379-4108; www.bcpsg.com; bcpsg@comcast.net

British North America Philatelic Society, Andy Ellwood, 10 Doris Ave., Gloucester, ON K1T 3W8 Canada; www.bnaps.org; secretary@bnaps.org

British West Indies Study Circle, Steve Jarvis, 5 Redbridge Drive, Andover, Hants SP10 2LF United Kingdom; 01264 358065; www.bwisc.org; info@bwisc.org

Bermuda Collectors Society, John Pare, 405 Perimeter St., Mount Horeb, WI 53572; (608) 852-7358; www.bermudacollectorssociety.com; pare16@mhtc.net

Haiti Philatelic Society, Ubaldo Del Toro, 5709 Marble Archway, Alexandria, VA 22315; www.haitiphilately.org; u007ubi@aol.com

Hawaiian Philatelic Society, Gannon Sugimura, P.O. Box 10115, Honolulu, HI 96816-0115, www.hpshawaii.com; hiphilsoc@gmail.com

Stamp Dealer Associations

American Stamp Dealers Association, Inc., P.O. Box 513, Centre Hall PA 16828; (800) 369-8207; www.americanstampdealer.com; asda@americanstampdealer.com

National Stamp Dealers Association, Sheldon Ruckens, President, 3643 Private Road 18, Pinckneyville, IL 62274-3426; (618) 357-5497; www.nsdainc.org; nsda@nsdainc.org

Youth Philately

Young Stamp Collectors of America, 100 Match Factory Place, Bellefonte, PA 16823; (814) 933-3803; https://stamps.org/learn/youth-in-philately; ysca@stamps.org

Expertizing services

The following organizations will, for a fee, provide expert opinions about stamps submitted to them. Collectors should contact these organizations to find out about their fees and requirements before submitting philatelic material to them. The listing of these groups here is not intended as an endorsement by Amos Media Co.

General Expertizing Services

American Philatelic Expertizing Service (a service of the American Philatelic Society)
100 Match Factory Place
Bellefonte PA 16823-1367
(814) 237-3803
www.stamps.org/stamp-authentication
apex@stamps.org
Areas of Expertise: Worldwide

BPA Expertising, Ltd.
P.O. Box 1141
Guildford, Surrey, GU5 0WR
United Kingdom
www.bpaexpertising.com
sec@bpaexpertising.org
Areas of Expertise: British Commonwealth, Great Britain, Classics of Europe, South America and the Far East

Philatelic Foundation
353 Lexington Avenue, Suite 804
New York NY 10016
(212) 221-6555
www.philatelicfoundation.org
philatelicfoundation@verizon.net
Areas of Expertise: U.S. & Worldwide

Philatelic Stamp Authentication and Grading, Inc.
P.O. Box 41-0880
Melbourne FL 32941-0880
(305) 345-9864
www.psaginc.com
info@psaginc.com
Areas of Expertise: U.S., Canal Zone, Hawaii, Philippines, Canada & Provinces

Professional Stamp Experts
P.O. Box 539309
Henderson NV 89053-9309
(702) 776-6522
www.gradingmatters.com
www.psestamp.com
info@gradingmatters.com
Areas of Expertise: Stamps and Covers of U.S., U.S. Possessions, British Commonwealth

Royal Philatelic Society London Expert Committee
15 Abchurch Lane
London, EX4N 7BW
United Kingdom
www.rpsl.limited/experts.aspx
experts@rpsl.limited
Areas of Expertise: Worldwide
Expertizing Services Covering Specific Fields or Countries

China Stamp Society Expertizing Service
1050 W. Blue Ridge Blvd.
Kansas City MO 64145
(816) 942-6300
hjmesq@aol.com
Areas of Expertise: China

Civil War Philatelic Society Authentication Service
C/O Stefan T. Jaronski
P.O. Box 232
Sidney, MT 59270-0232
www.civilwarphilatelicsociety.org/authentication/
authentication@civilwarphilatelicsociety.org
Areas of Expertise: Confederate stamps and postal history

Errors, Freaks and Oddities Collectors Club Expertizing Service
138 East Lakemont Drive
Kingsland GA 31548
(912) 729-1573
Areas of Expertise: U.S. errors, freaks and oddities

Hawaiian Philatelic Society Expertizing Service
P.O. Box 10115
Honolulu HI 96816-0115
www.stampshows.com/hps.html
hiphilsoc@gmail.com
Areas of Expertise: Hawaii

Hong Kong Stamp Society Expertizing Service
P.O. Box 206
Glenside PA 19038
Areas of Expertise: Hong Kong

International Association of Philatelic Experts United States Associate members:
Paul Buchsbayew
300 Frank W. Burr Blvd. - Second Floor
Box 35
Teaneck, NJ 07666.
(212) 977-7734
Areas of Expertise: Russia, Soviet Union

William T. Crowe
P.O. Box 2090
Danbury CT 06813-2090
wtcrowe@aol.com
Areas of Expertise: United States

International Society for Japanese Philately Expertizing Committee
132 North Pine Terrace
Staten Island NY 10312-4052
(718) 227-5229
Areas of Expertise: Japan and related areas, except WWII Japanese Occupation issues

International Society for Portuguese Philately Expertizing Service
P.O. Box 43146
Philadelphia PA 19129-3146
(215) 843-2106
s.s.washburne@worldnet.att.net
Areas of Expertise: Portugal and Colonies

Mexico-Elmhurst Philatelic Society International Expert Committee
Expert Committee Administrator
Marc E. Gonzales
P.O. Box 29040
Denver CO 80229-0040
www.mepsi.org/expert_committeee.htm
expertizations@mepsi.org
Areas of Expertise: Mexico

Ukrainian Philatelic & Numismatic Society Expertizing Service
30552 Dell Lane
Warren MI 48092-1862
Areas of Expertise: Ukraine, Western Ukraine

V. G. Greene Philatelic Research Foundation
P.O. Box 69100
St. Clair Post Office
Toronto, ON M4T 3A1
Canada
(416) 921-2073
www.greenefoundation.ca
info@greenefoundation.ca
Areas of Expertise: British North America

Information on catalogue values, grade and condition

Catalogue value

The Scott Catalogue value is a retail value; that is, an amount you could expect to pay for a stamp in the grade of Very Fine with no faults. Any exceptions to the grade valued will be noted in the text. The general introduction on the following pages and the individual section introductions further explain the type of material that is valued. The value listed for any given stamp is a reference that reflects recent actual dealer selling prices for that item.

Dealer retail price lists, public auction results, published prices in advertising and individual solicitation of retail prices from dealers, collectors and specialty organizations have been used in establishing the values found in this catalogue. Amos Media Co. values stamps, but Amos Media is not a company engaged in the business of buying and selling stamps as a dealer.

Use this catalogue as a guide for buying and selling. The actual price you pay for a stamp may be higher or lower than the catalogue value because of many different factors, including the amount of personal service a dealer offers, or increased or decreased interest in the country or topic represented by a stamp or set. An item may occasionally be offered at a lower price as a "loss leader," or as part of a special sale. You also may obtain an item inexpensively at public auction because of little interest at that time or as part of a large lot.

Stamps that are of a lesser grade than Very Fine, or those with condition problems, generally trade at lower prices than those given in this catalogue. Stamps of exceptional quality in both grade and condition often command higher prices than those listed.

Values for pre-1900 unused issues are for stamps with approximately half or more of their original gum. Stamps with most or all of their original gum may be expected to sell for more, and stamps with less than half of their original gum may be expected to sell for somewhat less than the values listed. On rarer stamps, it may be expected that the original gum will be somewhat more disturbed than it will be on more common issues. Post-1900 unused issues are assumed to have full original gum. From breakpoints in most countries' listings, stamps are valued as never hinged, due to the wide availability of stamps in that condition. These notations are prominently placed in the listings and in the country information preceding the listings. Some countries also feature listings with dual values for hinged and never-hinged stamps.

Grade

A stamp's grade and condition are crucial to its value. The accompanying illustrations show examples of Very Fine stamps from different time periods, along with examples of stamps in Fine to Very Fine and Extremely Fine grades as points of reference. When a stamp seller offers a stamp in any grade from fine to superb without further qualifying statements, that stamp should not only have the centering grade as defined, but it also should be free of faults or other condition problems.

FINE stamps (illustrations not shown) have designs that are quite off center, with the perforations on one or two sides very close to the design but not quite touching it. There is white space between the perforations and the design that is minimal but evident to the unaided eye. Imperforate stamps may have small margins, and earlier issues may show the design just touching one edge of the stamp design. Very early perforated issues normally will have the perforations slightly cutting into the design. Used stamps may have heavier than usual cancellations.

FINE-VERY FINE stamps will be somewhat off center on one side, or slightly off center on two sides. Imperforate stamps will have two margins of at least normal size, and the design will not touch any edge. For perforated stamps, the perfs are well clear of the design, but are still noticeably off center. *However, early issues of a country may be printed in such a way that the design naturally is very close to the edges. In these cases, the perforations may cut into the design very slightly.* Used stamps will not have a cancellation that detracts from the design.

VERY FINE stamps will be just slightly off center on one or two sides, but the design will be well clear of the edge. The stamp will present a nice, balanced appearance. Imperforate stamps will be well centered within normal-sized margins. *However, early issues of many countries may be printed in such a way that the perforations may touch the design on one or more sides. Where this is the case, a boxed note will be found defining the centering and margins of the stamps being valued.* Used stamps will have light or otherwise neat cancellations. This is the grade used to establish Scott Catalogue values.

EXTREMELY FINE stamps are close to being perfectly centered. Imperforate stamps will have even margins that are slightly larger than normal. Even the earliest perforated issues will have perforations clear of the design on all sides.

Amos Media Co. recognizes that there is no formally enforced grading scheme for postage stamps, and that the final price you pay or obtain for a stamp will be determined by individual agreement at the time of transaction.

Condition

Grade addresses only centering and (for used stamps) cancellation. *Condition* refers to factors other than grade that affect a stamp's desirability.

Factors that can increase the value of a stamp include exceptionally wide margins, particularly fresh color, the presence of selvage, and plate or die varieties. Unusual cancels on used stamps (particularly those of the 19th century) can greatly enhance their value as well.

Factors other than faults that decrease the value of a stamp include loss of original gum, regumming, a hinge remnant or foreign object adhering to the gum, natural inclusions, straight edges, and markings or notations applied by collectors or dealers.

Faults include missing pieces, tears, pin or other holes, surface scuffs, thin spots, creases, toning, short or pulled perforations, clipped perforations, oxidation or other forms of color changelings, soiling, stains, and such man-made changes as reperforations or the chemical removal or lightening of a cancellation.

Grading illustrations

On the following two pages are illustrations of various stamps from countries appearing in this volume. These stamps are arranged by country, and they represent early or important issues that are often found in widely different grades in the marketplace. The editors believe the illustrations will prove useful in showing the margin size and centering that will be seen on the various issues.

In addition to the matters of margin size and centering, collectors are reminded that the very fine stamps valued in the Scott catalogues also will possess fresh color and intact perforations, and they will be free from defects.

Examples shown are computer-manipulated images made from single digitized master illustrations.

Stamp illustrations used in the catalogue

It is important to note that the stamp images used for identification purposes in this catalogue may not be indicative of the grade of stamp being valued. Refer to the written discussion of grades on this page and to the grading illustrations on the following two pages for grading information.

Fine-Very Fine →

SCOTT CATALOGUES VALUE STAMPS IN THIS GRADE

Very Fine →

Extremely Fine →

Fine-Very Fine →

SCOTT CATALOGUES VALUE STAMPS IN THIS GRADE

Very Fine →

Extremely Fine →

Fine-Very Fine →

SCOTT CATALOGUES VALUE STAMPS IN THIS GRADE

Very Fine →

Extremely Fine →

Fine-Very Fine →

SCOTT CATALOGUES VALUE STAMPS IN THIS GRADE

Very Fine →

Extremely Fine →

Gum Conditions

For purposes of helping to determine the gum condition and value of an unused stamp, Scott presents the following chart which details different gum conditions and indicates how the conditions correlate with the Scott values for unused stamps. Used together, the Illustrated Grading Chart on the previous pages and this Illustrated Gum Chart should allow catalogue users to better understand the grade and gum condition of stamps valued in the Scott catalogues.

Never Hinged (NH; ★★): A never-hinged stamp will have full original gum that will have no hinge mark or disturbance. The presence of an expertizer's mark does not disqualify a stamp from this designation.

Original Gum (OG; ★): Pre-1900 stamps should have approximately half or more of their original gum. On rarer stamps, it may be expected that the original gum will be somewhat more disturbed than it will be on more common issues. Post-1900 stamps should have full original gum. Original gum will show some disturbance caused by a previous hinge(s) which may be present or entirely removed. The actual value of a post-1900 stamp will be affected by the degree of hinging of the full original gum.

Disturbed Original Gum: Gum showing noticeable effects of humidity, climate or hinging over more than half of the gum. The significance of gum disturbance in valuing a stamp in any of the Original Gum categories depends on the degree of disturbance, the rarity and normal gum condition of the issue and other variables affecting quality.

Regummed (RG; (★)): A regummed stamp is a stamp without gum that has had some type of gum privately applied at a time after it was issued. This normally is done to deceive collectors and/or dealers into thinking that the stamp has original gum and therefore has a higher value. A regummed stamp is considered the same as a stamp with none of its original gum for purposes of grading.

Gum Categories:	MINT N.H.	ORIGINAL GUM (O.G.)				NO GUM
	 **Mint Never Hinged** *Free from any disturbance*	 **Lightly Hinged** *Faint impression of a removed hinge over a small area*	 **Hinge Mark or Remnant** *Prominent hinged spot with part or all of the hinge remaining*	 **Large part o.g.** *Approximately half or more of the gum intact*	 **Small part o.g.** Approximately less than half of the gum intact	 **No gum** *Only if issued with gum*
Commonly Used Symbol:	★★	★	★	★	★	(★)
Pre-1900 Issues (Pre-1881 for U.S.)	*Very fine pre-1900 stamps in these categories trade at a premium over Scott value*			Scott Value for "Unused"		Scott "No Gum" listings for selected unused classic stamps
From 1900 to breakpoints for listings of never-hinged stamps	Scott "Never Hinged" listings for selected unused stamps	Scott Value for "Unused" (Actual value will be affected by the degree of hinging of the full o.g.)				
From breakpoints noted for many countries	Scott Value for "Unused"					

Catalogue listing policy

It is the intent of Amos Media Co. to list all postage stamps of the world in the Scott *Standard Postage Stamp Catalogue*. The only strict criteria for listing is that stamps be decreed legal for postage by the issuing country and that the issuing country actually have an operating postal system. Whether the primary intent of issuing a given stamp or set was for sale to postal patrons or to stamp collectors is not part of our listing criteria. Scott's role is to provide basic comprehensive postage stamp information. It is up to each stamp collector to choose which items to include in a collection.

It is Scott's objective to seek reasons why a stamp should be listed, rather than why it should not. Nevertheless, there are certain types of items that will not be listed. These include the following:

1. Unissued items that are not officially distributed or released by the issuing postal authority. If such items are officially issued at a later date by the country, they will be listed. Unissued items consist of those that have been printed and then held from sale for reasons such as change in government, errors found on stamps or something deemed objectionable about a stamp subject or design.

2. Stamps "issued" by non-existent postal entities or fantasy countries, such as Nagaland, Occusi-Ambeno, Staffa, Sedang, Torres Straits and others. Also, stamps "issued" in the names of legitimate, stamp-issuing countries that are not authorized by those countries.

3. Semi-official or unofficial items not required for postage. Examples include items issued by private agencies for their own express services. When such items are required for delivery, or are valid as prepayment of postage, they are listed.

4. Local stamps issued for local use only. Postage stamps issued by governments specifically for "domestic" use, such as Haiti Scott 219-228, or the United States nondenominated stamps, are not considered to be locals, since they are valid for postage throughout the country of origin.

5. Items not valid for postal use. For example, a few countries have issued souvenir sheets that are not valid for postage. This area also includes a number of worldwide charity labels (some denominated) that do not pay postage.

6. Egregiously exploitative issues such as stamps sold for far more than face value, stamps purposefully issued in artificially small quantities or only against advance orders, stamps awarded only to a selected audience such as a philatelic bureau's standing order customers, or stamps sold only in conjunction with other products. All of these kinds of items are usually controlled issues and/or are intended for speculation. These items normally will be included in a footnote.

7. Items distributed by the issuing government only to a limited group, club, philatelic exhibition or a single stamp dealer or other private company. These items normally will be included in a footnote.

8. Stamps not available to collectors. These generally are rare items, all of which are held by public institutions such as museums. The existence of such items often will be cited in footnotes.

The fact that a stamp has been used successfully as postage, even on international mail, is not in itself sufficient proof that it was legitimately issued. Numerous examples of so-called stamps from non-existent countries are known to have been used to post letters that have successfully passed through the international mail system.

There are certain items that are subject to interpretation. When a stamp falls outside our specifications, it may be listed along with a cautionary footnote.

A number of factors are considered in our approach to analyzing how a stamp is listed. The following list of factors is presented to share with you, the catalogue user, the complexity of the listing process.

Additional printings — "Additional printings" of a previously issued stamp may range from an item that is totally different to cases where it is impossible to differentiate from the original. At least a minor number (a small-letter suffix) is assigned if there is a distinct change in stamp shade, noticeably redrawn design, or a significantly different perforation measurement. A major number (numeral or numeral and capital-letter combination) is assigned if the editors feel the "additional printing" is sufficiently different from the original that it constitutes a different issue.

Commemoratives — Where practical, commemoratives with the same theme are placed in a set. For example, the U.S. Civil War Centennial set of 1961-65 and the Constitution Bicentennial series of 1989-90 appear as sets. Countries such as Japan and Korea issue such material on a regular basis, with an announced, or at least predictable, number of stamps known in advance. Occasionally, however, stamp sets that were released over a period of years have been separated. Appropriately placed footnotes will guide you to each set's continuation.

Definitive sets — Blocks of numbers generally have been reserved for definitive sets, based on previous experience with any given country. If a few more stamps were issued in a set than originally expected, they often have been inserted into the original set with a capital-letter suffix, such as U.S. Scott 1059A. If it appears that many more stamps than the originally allotted block will be released before the set is completed, a new block of numbers will be reserved, with the original one being closed off. In some cases, such as the U.S. Transportation and Great Americans series, several blocks of numbers exist. Appropriately placed footnotes will guide you to each set's continuation.

New country — Membership in the Universal Postal Union is not a consideration for listing status or order of placement within the catalogue. The index will tell you in what volume or page number the listings begin.

"No release date" items — The amount of information available for any given stamp issue varies greatly from country to country and even from time to time. Extremely comprehensive information about new stamps is available from some countries well before the stamps are released. By contrast some countries do not provide information about stamps or release dates. Most countries, however, fall between these extremes. A country may provide denominations or subjects of stamps from upcoming issues that are not issued as planned. Sometimes, philatelic agencies, those private firms hired to represent countries, add these later-issued items to sets well after the formal release date. This time period can range from weeks to years. If these items were officially released by the country, they will be added to the appropriate spot in the set. In many cases, the specific release date of a stamp or set of stamps may never be known.

Overprints — The color of an overprint is always noted if it is other than black. Where more than one color of ink has been used on overprints of a single set, the color used is noted. Early overprint and surcharge illustrations were altered to prevent their use by forgers.

Personalized Stamps — Since 1999, the special service of personalizing stamp vignettes, or labels attached to stamps, has been offered to customers by postal administrations of many countries. Sheets of these stamps are sold, singly or in quantity, only through special orders made by mail, in person, or through a sale on a computer website with the postal administrations or their agents for which an extra fee is charged, though some countries offer to collectors at face value personalized stamps having generic images in the vignettes or on the attached labels. It is impossible for any catalogue to know what images have been chosen by customers. Images can be 1) owned or created by the customer, 2) a generic image, or 3) an image pulled from a library of stock images on the stamp creation website. It is also impossible to know the quantity printed for any stamp having a particular image. So from a valuing standpoint, any image is equivalent to any other image for any personalized stamp having the same catalogue number. Illustrations of personalized stamps in the catalogue are not always those of stamps having generic images.

Personalized items are listed with some exceptions. These include:

1. Stamps or sheets that have attached labels that the customer cannot personalize, but which are nonetheless marketed as "personalized," and are sold for far more than the franking value.

2. Stamps or sheets that can be personalized by the customer, but where a portion of the print run must be ceded to the issuing country for sale to other customers.

3. Stamps or sheets that are created exclusively for a particular commercial client, or clients, including stamps that differ from any similar stamp that has been made available to the public.

4. Stamps or sheets that are deliberately conceived by the issuing authority that have been, or are likely to be, created with an excessive number of different face values, sizes, or other features that are changeable.

5. Stamps or sheets that are created by postal administrations using the same system of stamp personalization that has been put in place for use by the public that are printed in limited quantities and sold above face value.

6. Stamps or sheets that are created by licensees not directly affiliated or controlled by a postal administration.

Excluded items may or may not be footnoted.

Se-tenants — Connected stamps of differing features (se-tenants) will be listed in the format most commonly collected. This includes pairs, blocks or larger multiples. Se-tenant units are not always symmetrical. An example is Australia Scott 508, which is a block of seven stamps. If the stamps are primarily collected as a unit, the major number may be assigned to the multiple, with minors going to each component stamp. In cases where continuous-design or other unit se-tenants will receive significant postal use, each stamp is given a major Scott number listing. This includes issues from the United States, Canada, Germany and Great Britain, for example.

Understanding the listings

On the opposite page is an enlarged "typical" listing from this catalogue. Below are detailed explanations of each of the highlighted parts of the listing.

1 Scott number — Scott catalogue numbers are used to identify specific items when buying, selling or trading stamps. Each listed postage stamp from every country has a unique Scott catalogue number. Therefore, Germany Scott 99, for example, can only refer to a single stamp. Although the Scott catalogue usually lists stamps in chronological order by date of issue, there are exceptions. When a country has issued a set of stamps over a period of time, those stamps within the set are kept together without regard to date of issue. This follows the normal collecting approach of keeping stamps in their natural sets.

When a country issues a set of stamps over a period of time, a group of consecutive catalogue numbers is reserved for the stamps in that set, as issued. If that group of numbers proves to be too few, capital-letter suffixes, such as "A" or "B," may be added to existing numbers to create enough catalogue numbers to cover all items in the set. A capital-letter suffix indicates a major Scott catalogue number listing. Scott generally uses a suffix letter only once. Therefore, a catalogue number listing with a capital-letter suffix will seldom be found with the same letter (lower case) used as a minor-letter listing. If there is a Scott 16A in a set, for example, there will seldom be a Scott 16a. However, a minor-letter "a" listing may be added to a major number containing an "A" suffix (Scott 16Aa, for example).

Suffix letters are cumulative. A minor "b" variety of Scott 16A would be Scott 16Ab, not Scott 16b.

There are times when a reserved block of Scott catalogue numbers is too large for a set, leaving some numbers unused. Such gaps in the numbering sequence also occur when the catalogue editors move an item's listing elsewhere or have removed it entirely from the catalogue. Scott does not attempt to account for every possible number, but rather attempts to assure that each stamp is assigned its own number.

Scott numbers designating regular postage normally are only numerals. Scott numbers for other types of stamps, such as air post, semi-postal, postal tax, postage due, occupation and others have a prefix consisting of one or more capital letters or a combination of numerals and capital letters.

2 Illustration number — Illustration or design-type numbers are used to identify each catalogue illustration. For most sets, the lowest face-value stamp is shown. It then serves as an example of the basic design approach for other stamps not illustrated. Where more than one stamp use the same illustration number, but have differences in design, the design paragraph or the description line clearly indicates the design on each stamp not illustrated. Where there are both vertical and horizontal designs in a set, a single illustration may be used, with the exceptions noted in the design paragraph or description line.

When an illustration is followed by a lower-case letter in parentheses, such as "A2(b)," the trailing letter indicates which overprint or surcharge illustration applies.

Illustrations normally are 70 percent of the original size of the stamp. Oversized stamps, blocks and souvenir sheets are reduced even more. Overprints and surcharges are shown at 100 percent of their original size if shown alone, but are 70 percent of original size if shown on stamps. In some cases, the illustration will be placed above the set, between listings or omitted completely. Overprint and surcharge illustrations are not placed in this catalogue for purposes of expertizing stamps.

3 Paper color — The color of a stamp's paper is noted in italic type when the paper used is not white.

4 Listing styles — There are two principal types of catalogue listings: major and minor.

Major listings are in a larger type style than minor listings. The catalogue number is a numeral that can be found with or without a capital-letter suffix, and with or without a prefix.

Minor listings are in a smaller type style and have a small-letter suffix or (if the listing immediately follows that of the major number) may show only the letter. These listings identify a variety of the major item. Examples include perforation and shade differences, multiples (some souvenir sheets, booklet panes and se-tenant combinations), and singles of multiples.

Examples of major number listings include 16, 28A, B97, C13A, 10N5, and 10N6A. Examples of minor numbers are 16a and C13Ab.

5 Basic information about a stamp or set — Introducing each stamp issue is a small section (usually a line listing) of basic information about a stamp or set. This section normally includes the date of issue, method of printing, perforation, watermark and, sometimes, some additional information of note. *Printing method, perforation and watermark apply to the following sets until a change is noted.* Stamps created by overprinting or surcharging previous issues are assumed to have the same perforation, watermark, printing method and other production characteristics as the original. Dates of issue are as precise as Scott is able to confirm and often reflect the dates on first-day covers, rather than the actual date of release.

6 Denomination — This normally refers to the face value of the stamp; that is, the cost of the unused stamp at the post office at the time of issue. When a denomination is shown in parentheses, it does not appear on the stamp. This includes the nondenominated stamps of the United States, Brazil and Great Britain, for example.

7 Color or other description — This area provides information to solidify identification of a stamp. In many recent cases, a description of the stamp design appears in this space, rather than a listing of colors.

8 Year of issue — In stamp sets that have been released in a period that spans more than a year, the number shown in parentheses is the year that stamp first appeared. Stamps without a date appeared during the first year of the issue. Dates are not always given for minor varieties.

9 Value unused and Value used — The Scott catalogue values are based on stamps that are in a grade of Very Fine unless stated otherwise. Unused values refer to items that have not seen postal, revenue or any other duty for which they were intended. Pre-1900 unused stamps that were issued with gum must have at least most of their original gum. Later issues are assumed to have full original gum. From breakpoints specified in most countries' listings, stamps are valued as never hinged. Stamps issued without gum are noted. Modern issues with PVA or other synthetic adhesives may appear ungummed. Unused self-adhesive stamps are valued as appearing undisturbed on their original backing paper. Values for used self-adhesive stamps are for examples either on piece or off piece. For a more detailed explanation of these values, please see the "Catalogue Value," "Condition" and "Understanding Valuing Notations" sections elsewhere in this introduction.

In some cases, where used stamps are more valuable than unused stamps, the value is for an example with a contemporaneous cancel, rather than a modern cancel or a smudge or other unclear marking. For those stamps that were released for postal and fiscal purposes, the used value represents a postally used stamp. Stamps with revenue cancels generally sell for less.

Stamps separated from a complete se-tenant multiple usually will be worth less than a pro-rated portion of the se-tenant multiple, and stamps lacking the attached labels that are noted in the listings will be worth less than the values shown.

10 Changes in basic set information — Bold type is used to show any changes in the basic data given for a set of stamps. These basic data categories include perforation gauge measurement, paper type, printing method and watermark.

11 Total value of a set — The total value of sets of three or more stamps issued after 1900 are shown. The set line also notes the range of Scott numbers and total number of stamps included in the grouping. The actual value of a set consisting predominantly of stamps having the minimum value of 25 cents may be less than the total value shown. Similarly, the actual value or catalogue value of se-tenant pairs or of blocks consisting of stamps having the minimum value of 25 cents may be less than the catalogue values of the component parts.

A6

King George VI
A7

1938-44 Engr. Perf. 12½

54	A6	½p	green	.25	*2.00*
54A	A6	½p	dk brown ('42)	.25	*2.25*
55	A6	1p	dark brown	2.50	.35
55A	A6	1p	green ('42)	.25	*1.75*
56	A6	1½p	dark carmine	5.00	*6.00*
56A	A6	1½p	gray ('42)	.25	*5.75*
57	A6	2p	gray	5.00	1.25
57A	A6	2p	dark car ('42)	.25	*2.00*
58	A6	3p	blue	.60	1.00
59	A6	4p	rose lilac	1.75	2.00
60	A6	6p	dark violet	2.00	2.00
61	A6	9p	olive bister	2.00	*5.25*
62	A6	1sh	orange & blk	2.10	*3.25*

Typo.
Perf. 14
Chalky Paper

63	A7	2sh	ultra & dl vio, *bl*	7.00	*17.50*
64	A7	2sh6p	red & blk, *bl*	9.00	*24.00*
65	A7	5sh	red & grn, *yel*	35.00	30.00
a.		5sh	dk red & dp grn, *yel* ('44)	55.00	*140.00*
66	A7	10sh	red & grn, *grn*	35.00	*70.00*

Wmk. 3

67	A7	£1	blk & vio, *red*	30.00	*52.50*
			Nos. 54-67 (18)	138.20	*228.85*
			Set, never hinged	220.00	

1 SCOTT NUMBER

2 ILLUS. NUMBER

3 PAPER COLOR

4 LISTING STYLES — MAJORS — MINORS

5 BASIC INFORMATION ON STAMP OR SET

6 DENOMINATION

7 COLOR OR OTHER DESCRIPTION

8 YEAR OF ISSUE

9 CATALOGUE VALUES — UNUSED — USED

10 CHANGES IN BASIC SET INFORMATION

11 TOTAL VALUE OF SET

Special notices

Classification of stamps

The Scott Standard Postage Stamp Catalogue lists stamps by country of issue. The next level of organization is a listing by section on the basis of the function of the stamps. The principal sections cover regular postage, semi-postal, air post, special delivery, registration, postage due and other categories. Except for regular postage, catalogue numbers for all sections include a prefix letter (or number-letter combination) denoting the class to which a given stamp belongs. When some countries issue sets containing stamps from more than one category, the catalogue will at times list all of the stamps in one category (such as air post stamps listed as part of a postage set).

The following is a listing of the most commonly used catalogue prefixes.

Prefix.......Category
C..........Air Post
M ....Military
P..........Newspaper
N..........Occupation - Regular Issues
O..........Official
Q..........Parcel Post
J ....Postage Due
RA ....Postal Tax
B..........Semi-Postal
E..........Special Delivery
MR.......War Tax

Other prefixes used by more than one country include the following:
H..........Acknowledgment of Receipt
I ....Late Fee
CO ....Air Post Official
CQ.......Air Post Parcel Post
RAC.....Air Post Postal Tax
CF........Air Post Registration
CB ....Air Post Semi-Postal
CBO ....Air Post Semi-Postal Official
CE ....Air Post Special Delivery
EY........Authorized Delivery
S..........Franchise
G..........Insured Letter
GY ....Marine Insurance
MC.......Military Air Post
MQ ......Military Parcel Post
NC ....Occupation - Air Post
NO ....Occupation - Official
NJ........Occupation - Postage Due
NRA.....Occupation - Postal Tax
NB ....Occupation - Semi-Postal
NE ....Occupation - Special Delivery
QY ....Parcel Post Authorized Delivery
AR ....Postal-fiscal
RAJ......Postal Tax Due
RAB.....Postal Tax Semi-Postal
F ....Registration
EB........Semi-Postal Special Delivery
EO ....Special Delivery Official
QE ....Special Handling

New issue listings

Updates to this catalogue appear each month in the *Linn's Stamp News* monthly magazine. Included in this update are additions to the listings of countries found in the Scott *Standard Postage Stamp Catalogue* and the *Specialized Catalogue of United States Stamps and Covers,* as well as corrections and updates to current editions of this catalogue.

From time to time there will be changes in the final listings of stamps from the *Linn's Stamp News* magazine to the next edition of the catalogue. This occurs as more information about certain stamps or sets becomes available.

The catalogue update section of the *Linn's Stamp News* magazine is the most timely presentation of this material available. Annual subscriptions to *Linn's Stamp News* are available from Linn's Stamp News, Box 4129, Sidney, OH 45365-4129.

Number additions, deletions and changes

A listing of catalogue number additions, deletions and changes from the previous edition of the catalogue appears in each volume. See Catalogue Number Additions, Deletions & Changes in the table of contents for the location of this list.

Understanding valuing notations

The *minimum catalogue value* of an individual stamp or set is 25 cents. This represents a portion of the cost incurred by a dealer when he prepares an individual stamp for resale. As a point of philatelic-economic fact, the lower the value shown for an item in this catalogue, the greater the percentage of that value is attributed to dealer mark up and profit margin. In many cases, such as the 25-cent minimum value, that price does not cover the labor or other costs involved with stocking it as an individual stamp. The sum of minimum values in a set does not properly represent the value of a complete set primarily composed of a number of minimum-value stamps, nor does the sum represent the actual value of a packet made up of minimum-value stamps. Thus a packet of 1,000 different common stamps — each of which has a catalogue value of 25 cents — normally sells for considerably less than $250!

The *absence of a retail value* for a stamp does not necessarily suggest that a stamp is scarce or rare. A dash in the value column means that the stamp is known in a stated form or variety, but information is either lacking or insufficient for purposes of establishing a usable catalogue value.

Stamp values in *italics* generally refer to items that are difficult to value accurately. For expensive items, such as those priced at $1,000 or higher, a value in italics indicates that the affected item trades very seldom. For inexpensive items, a value in italics represents a warning. One example is a "blocked" issue where the issuing postal administration may have controlled one stamp in a set in an attempt to make the whole set more valuable. Another example is an item that sold at an extreme multiple of face value in the marketplace at the time of its issue.

One type of warning to collectors that appears in the catalogue is illustrated by a stamp that is valued considerably higher in used condition than it is as unused. In this case, collectors are cautioned to be certain the used version has a genuine and contemporaneous cancellation. The type of cancellation on a stamp can be an important factor in determining its sale price. Catalogue values do not apply to fiscal, telegraph or non-contemporaneous postal cancels, unless otherwise noted.

Some countries have released back issues of stamps in canceled-to-order form, sometimes covering as much as a 10-year period. The Scott Catalogue values for used stamps reflect canceled-to-order material when such stamps are found to predominate in the marketplace for the issue involved. Notes frequently appear in the stamp listings to specify which items are valued as canceled-to-order, or if there is a premium for postally used examples.

Many countries sell canceled-to-order stamps at a marked reduction of face value. Countries that sell or have sold canceled-to-order stamps at *full* face value include United Nations, Australia, Netherlands, France and Switzerland. It may be almost impossible to identify such stamps if the gum has been removed, because official government canceling devices are used. Postally used examples of these items on cover, however, are usually worth more than the canceled-to-order stamps with original gum.

Abbreviations

Scott uses a consistent set of abbreviations throughout this catalogue to conserve space, while still providing necessary information.

Color Abbreviations

amb.......... amber	crim.........crimson	ol................. olive
anil .... aniline	cr.............. cream	olvn........... olivine
ap...............apple	dk................ dark	org .... orange
aqua..aquamarine	dl....................dull	pck.........peacock
az ....azure	dp .... deep	pnksh pinkish
bis............. bister	db .... drab	Prus ....Prussian
bl..................blue	emer....... emerald	pur .... purple
bld............. blood	gldn.......... golden	redsh........reddish
blk...............black	grysh........grayish	res............reseda
bril...........brilliant	grn .... green	ros.............rosine
brn .... brown	grnsh......greenish	ryl................royal
brnsh ....brownish	hel....... heliotrope	sal ....salmon
brnz.......... bronze	hn..............henna	saph.......sapphire
brt .... bright	ind.............indigo	scar...........scarlet
brnt .... burnt	int............intense	sep.............sepia
car..........carmine	lav ....lavender	sien .... sienna
cer.............cerise	lem............lemon	sil .... silver
chlky .... chalky	lil .... lilac	sl ....slate
cham......chamois	lt...................light	stl ....steel
chnt........chestnut	mag....... magenta	turq ...... turquoise
choc.....chocolate	man...........manila	ultra... ultramarine
chr.......... chrome	mar .... maroon	Ven.........Venetian
cit.............. citron	mv............mauve	ver.........vermilion
cl ....claret	multi..multicolored	vio ....violet
cob........... cobalt	mlky .... milky	yel .... yellow
cop.......... copper	myr............myrtle	yelsh .....yellowish

When no color is given for an overprint or surcharge, black is the color used. Abbreviations for colors used for overprints and surcharges include: "(B)" or "(Blk)," black; "(Bl)," blue; "(R)," red; and "(G)," green.

Additional abbreviations in this catalogue are shown below:

Adm. ....Administration
AFL ....American Federation of Labor
Anniv. ....Anniversary
APS...............American Philatelic Society
Assoc............Association
ASSR. ....Autonomous Soviet Socialist Republic
b....................Born
BEP...............Bureau of Engraving and Printing
Bicent. ....Bicentennial
Bklt. ....Booklet
Brit. ....British
btwn.............Between
Bur. ....Bureau
c. or ca. ....Circa
Cat. ....Catalogue
Cent. ....Centennial, century, centenary
CIO ....Congress of Industrial Organizations
Conf. ....Conference
Cong. ....Congress
Cpl. ....Corporal
CTO ....Canceled to order
d....................Died
Dbl. ....Double
EDU ....Earliest documented use
Engr...............Engraved
Exhib.............Exhibition
Expo. ....Exposition
Fed................Federation
GB ....Great Britain
Gen. ....General
GPO..............General post office
Horiz. ....Horizontal
Imperf. ....Imperforate
Impt. ....Imprint
Intl.................International
Invtd..............Inverted
L....................Left
Lieut., lt.........Lieutenant
Litho..............Lithographed
LL..................Lower left
LR ....Lower right
mm ....Millimeter
Ms.................Manuscript
Natl. ....National
No. ....Number
NY.................New York
NYC ....New York City
Ovpt..............Overprint
Ovptd............Overprinted
P ....Plate number
Perf. ....Perforated, perforation
Phil.................Philatelic
Photo. ....Photogravure
PO.................Post office
Pr. ....Pair
P.R. ....Puerto Rico
Prec. ....Precancel, precanceled
Pres. ....President
PTT ....Post, Telephone and Telegraph
R ....Right
Rio ....Rio de Janeiro
Sgt. ....Sergeant
Soc. ....Society
Souv..............Souvenir
SSR...............Soviet Socialist Republic, see ASSR
St. ....Saint, street
Surch. ....Surcharge
Typo. ....Typographed
UL ....Upper left
Unwmkd. ....Unwatermarked
UPU ....Universal Postal Union
UR.................Upper Right
US.................United States
USPOD ....United States Post Office Department
USSR............Union of Soviet Socialist Republics
Vert. ....Vertical
VP ....Vice president
Wmk. ....Watermark
Wmkd. ....Watermarked
WWI ....World War I
WWII ....World War II

Examination

Amos Media Co. will not comment upon the genuineness, grade or condition of stamps, because of the time and responsibility involved. Rather, there are several expertizing groups that undertake this work for both collectors and dealers. Neither will Amos Media Co. appraise or identify philatelic material. The company cannot take responsibility for unsolicited stamps or covers sent by individuals.

All letters, emails, etc. are read attentively, but they are not always answered because of time considerations.

How to order from your dealer

When ordering stamps from a dealer, it is not necessary to write the full description of a stamp as listed in this catalogue. All you need is the name of the country, the Scott catalogue number and whether the desired item is unused or used. For example, "Japan Scott 422 unused" is sufficient to identify the unused stamp of Japan listed as "422 A206 5y brown."

Basic stamp information

A stamp collector's knowledge of the combined elements that make a given stamp issue unique determines his or her ability to identify stamps. These elements include paper, watermark, method of separation, printing, design and gum. On the following pages each of these important areas is briefly described.

Paper

Paper is an organic material composed of a compacted weave of cellulose fibers and generally formed into sheets. Paper used to print stamps may be manufactured in sheets, or it may have been part of a large roll (called a web) before being cut to size. The fibers most often used to create paper on which stamps are printed include bark, wood, straw and certain grasses. In many cases, linen or cotton rags have been added for greater strength and durability. Grinding, bleaching, cooking and rinsing these raw fibers reduces them to a slushy pulp, referred to by paper makers as "stuff." Sizing and, sometimes, coloring matter is added to the pulp to make different types of finished paper.

After the stuff is prepared, it is poured onto sieve-like frames that allow the water to run off, while retaining the matted pulp. As fibers fall onto the screen and are held by gravity, they form a natural weave that will later hold the paper together. If the screen has metal bits that are formed into letters or images attached, it leaves slightly thinned areas on the paper. These are called watermarks.

When the stuff is almost dry, it is passed under pressure through smooth or engraved rollers — dandy rolls — or placed between cloth in a press to be flattened and dried.

Wove **Laid** **Granite**

Quadrille **Oblong Quadrille** **Laid Batonne**

Stamp paper falls broadly into two types: wove and laid. The nature of the surface of the frame onto which the pulp is first deposited causes the differences in appearance between the two. If the surface is smooth and even, the paper will be of fairly uniform texture throughout. This is known as wove paper. Early papermaking machines poured the pulp onto a continuously circulating web of felt, but modern machines feed the pulp onto a cloth-like screen made of closely interwoven fine wires. This paper, when held to a light, will show little dots or points very close together. The proper name for this is "wire wove," but the type is still considered wove. Any U.S. or British stamp printed after 1880 will serve as an example of wire wove paper.

Closely spaced parallel wires, with cross wires at wider intervals, make up the frames used for what is known as laid paper. A greater thickness of the pulp will settle between the wires. The paper, when held to a light, will show alternate light and dark lines. The spacing and the thickness of the lines may vary, but on any one sheet of paper they are all alike. See Russia Scott 31-38 for examples of laid paper.

Batonne, from the French word meaning "a staff," is a term used if the lines in the paper are spaced quite far apart, like the printed ruling on a writing tablet. Batonne paper may be either wove or laid. If laid, fine laid lines can be seen between the batons.

Quadrille is the term used when the lines in the paper form little squares. Oblong quadrille is the term used when rectangles, rather than squares, are formed. Grid patterns vary from distinct to extremely faint. See Mexico-Guadalajara Scott 35-37 for examples of oblong quadrille paper.

Paper also is classified as thick or thin, hard or soft, and by color. Such colors may include yellowish, greenish, bluish and reddish.

Brief explanations of other types of paper used for printing stamps, as well as examples, follow.

Colored — Colored paper is created by the addition of dye in the paper-making process. Such colors may include shades of yellow, green, blue and red. Surface-colored papers, most commonly used for British colonial issues in 1913-14, are created when coloring is added only to the surface during the finishing process. Stamps printed on surface-colored paper have white or uncolored backs, while true colored papers are colored through. See Jamaica Scott 71-73.

Pelure — Pelure paper is a very thin, hard and often brittle paper that is sometimes bluish or grayish in appearance. See Serbia Scott 169-170.

Native — This is a term applied to handmade papers used to produce some of the early stamps of the Indian states. Stamps printed on native paper may be expected to display various natural inclusions that are normal and do not negatively affect value. Japanese paper, originally made of mulberry fibers and rice flour, is part of this group. See Japan Scott 1-18.

Manila — This type of paper is often used to make stamped envelopes and wrappers. It is a coarse-textured stock, usually smooth on one side and rough on the other. A variety of colors of manila paper exist, but the most common range is yellowish-brown.

Silk — Introduced by the British in 1847 as a safeguard against counterfeiting, silk paper contains bits of colored silk thread scattered throughout. The density of these fibers varies greatly and can include as few as one fiber per stamp or hundreds. U.S. revenue Scott R152 is a good example of an easy-to-identify silk paper stamp.

Silk-thread paper has uninterrupted threads of colored silk arranged so that one or more threads run through the stamp or postal stationery. See Great Britain Scott 5-6 and Switzerland Scott 14-19.

Granite — Filled with minute cloth or colored paper fibers of various colors and lengths, granite paper should not be confused with either type of silk paper. Austria Scott 172-175 and a number of Swiss stamps are examples of granite paper.

Chalky — A chalk-like substance coats the surface of chalky paper to discourage the cleaning and reuse of canceled stamps, as well as to provide a smoother, more acceptable printing surface. Because the designs of stamps printed on chalky paper are imprinted on what is often a water-soluble coating, any attempt to remove a cancellation will destroy the stamp. Do not soak these stamps in any fluid. To remove a stamp printed on chalky paper from an envelope, wet the paper from underneath the stamp until the gum dissolves enough to release the stamp from the paper. See St. Kitts-Nevis Scott 89-90 for examples of stamps printed on this type of chalky paper.

India — Another name for this paper, originally introduced from China about 1750, is "China Paper." It is a thin, opaque paper often used for plate and die proofs by many countries.

Double — In philately, the term double paper has two distinct meanings. The first is a two-ply paper, usually a combination of a thick and a thin sheet, joined during manufacture. This type was used experimentally as a means to discourage the reuse of stamps.

The design is printed on the thin paper. Any attempt to remove a cancellation would destroy the design. U.S. Scott 158 and other Banknote-era stamps exist on this form of double paper.

The second type of double paper occurs on a rotary press, when the end of one paper roll, or web, is affixed to the next roll to save time feeding the paper through the press. Stamp designs are printed over the joined paper and, if overlooked by inspectors, may get into post office stocks.

Goldbeater's Skin — This type of paper was used for the 1866 issue of Prussia, and was a tough, translucent paper. The design was printed in reverse on the back of the stamp, and the gum applied over the printing. It is impossible to remove stamps printed on this type of paper from the paper to which they are affixed without destroying the design.

Ribbed — Ribbed paper has an uneven, corrugated surface made by passing the paper through ridged rollers. This type exists on some copies of U.S. Scott 156-165.

Various other substances, or substrates, have been used for stamp manufacture, including wood, aluminum, copper, silver and gold foil, plastic, and silk and cotton fabrics.

Watermarks

Watermarks are an integral part of some papers. They are formed in the process of paper manufacture. Watermarks consist of small designs, formed of wire or cut from metal and soldered to the surface of the mold or, sometimes, on the dandy roll. The designs may be in the form of crowns, stars, anchors, letters or other characters or symbols. These pieces of metal — known in the paper-making industry as "bits" — impress a design into the paper. The design sometimes may be seen by holding the stamp to the light. Some are more easily seen with a watermark detector. This important tool is a small black tray into which a stamp is placed face down and dampened with a fast-evaporating watermark detection fluid that brings up the watermark image in the form of dark lines against a lighter background. These dark lines are the thinner areas of the paper known as the watermark. Some watermarks are extremely difficult to locate, due to either a faint impression, watermark location or the color of the stamp. There also are electric watermark detectors that come with plastic filter disks of various colors. The disks neutralize the color of the stamp, permitting the watermark to be seen more easily.

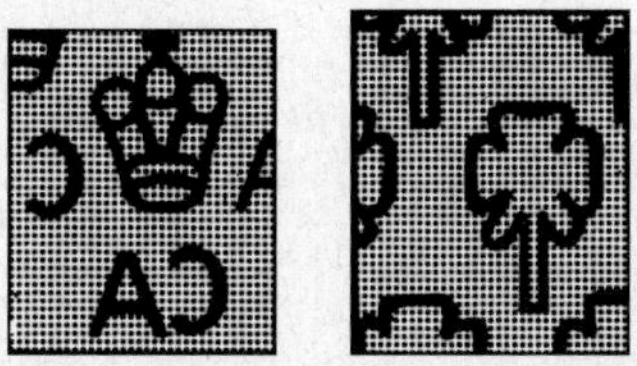

Multiple watermarks of Crown Agents and Burma

Watermarks of Uruguay, Vatican City and Jamaica

WARNING: Some inks used in the photogravure process dissolve in watermark fluids (Please see the section on Soluble Printing Inks). Also, see "chalky paper."

Watermarks may be found normal, reversed, inverted, reversed and inverted, sideways or diagonal, as seen from the back of the stamp. The relationship of watermark to stamp design depends on the position of the printing plates or how paper is fed through the press. On machine-made paper, watermarks normally are read from right to left. The design is repeated closely throughout the sheet in a "multiple-watermark design." In a "sheet watermark," the design appears only once on the sheet, but extends over many stamps. Individual stamps may carry only a small fraction or none of the watermark.

"Marginal watermarks" occur in the margins of sheets or panes of stamps. They occur on the outside border of paper (ostensibly outside the area where stamps are to be printed). A large row of letters may spell the name of the country or the manufacturer of the paper, or a border of lines may appear. Careless press feeding may cause parts of these letters and/or lines to show on stamps of the outer row of a pane.

Soluble printing inks

WARNING: Most stamp colors are permanent; that is, they are not seriously affected by short-term exposure to light or water. Many colors, especially of modern inks, fade from excessive exposure to light. There are stamps printed with inks that dissolve easily in water or in fluids used to detect watermarks. Use of these inks was intentional to prevent the removal of cancellations. Water affects all aniline inks, those on so-called safety paper and some photogravure printings - all such inks are known as fugitive colors. Removal from paper of such stamps requires care and alternatives to traditional soaking.

Separation

"Separation" is the general term used to describe methods used to separate stamps. The three standard forms currently in use are perforating, rouletting and die-cutting. These methods are done during the stamp production process, after printing. Sometimes these methods are done on-press or sometimes as a separate step. The earliest issues, such as the 1840 Penny Black of Great Britain (Scott 1), did not have any means provided for separation. It was expected the stamps would be cut apart with scissors or folded and torn. These are examples of imperforate stamps. Many stamps were first issued in imperforate formats and were later issued with perforations. Therefore, care must be observed in buying single imperforate stamps to be certain they were issued imperforate and are not perforated copies that have been altered by having the perforations trimmed away. Stamps issued imperforate usually are valued as singles. However, imperforate varieties of normally perforated stamps should be collected in pairs or larger pieces as indisputable evidence of their imperforate character.

PERFORATION

The chief style of separation of stamps, and the one that is in almost universal use today, is perforating. By this process, paper between the stamps is cut away in a line of holes, usually round, leaving little bridges of paper between the stamps to hold them together. Some types of perforation, such as hyphen-hole perfs, can be confused with roulettes, but a close visual inspection reveals that paper has been removed. The little perforation bridges, which project from the stamp when it is torn from the pane, are called the teeth of the perforation.

As the size of the perforation is sometimes the only way to differentiate between two otherwise identical stamps, it is necessary to be able to accurately measure and describe them. This is done with a perforation gauge, usually a ruler-like device that has dots or graduated lines to show how many perforations may be counted in the space of two centimeters. Two centimeters is the space universally adopted in which to measure perforations.

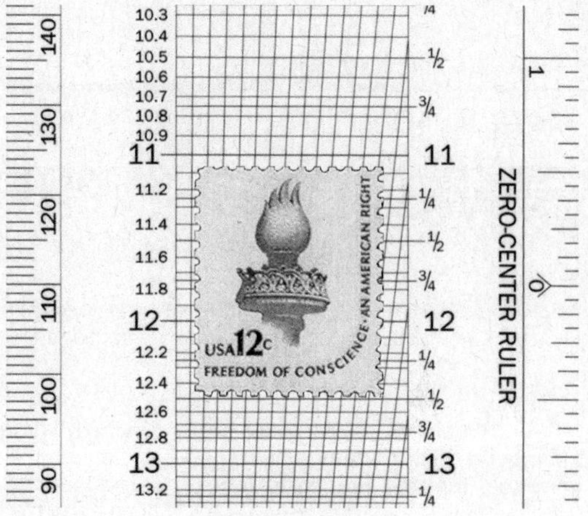

Perforation gauge

To measure a stamp, run it along the gauge until the dots on it fit exactly into the perforations of the stamp. If you are using a graduated-line perforation gauge, simply slide the stamp along the surface until the lines on the gauge perfectly project from the center of the bridges or holes. The number to the side of the line of dots or lines that fit the stamp's perforation is the measurement. For example, an "11" means that 11 perforations fit between two centimeters. The description of the stamp therefore is "perf. 11." If the gauge of the perforations on the top and bottom of a stamp differs from that on the sides, the result is what is known as compound perforations. In measuring compound perforations, the gauge at top and bottom is always given first, then the sides. Thus, a stamp that measures 11 at top and bottom and 10½ at the sides is "perf. 11 x 10½." See U.S. Scott 632-642 for examples of compound perforations.

Stamps also are known with perforations different on three or all four sides. Descriptions of such items are clockwise, beginning with the top of the stamp.

A perforation with small holes and teeth close together is a "fine perforation." One with large holes and teeth far apart is a "coarse perforation." Holes that are jagged, rather than clean-cut, are "rough perforations." *Blind perforations* are the slight impressions left by the perforating pins if they fail to puncture the paper. Multiples of stamps showing blind perforations may command a slight premium over normally perforated stamps.

The term *syncopated perfs* describes intentional irregularities in the perforations. The earliest form was used by the Netherlands from 1925-33, where holes were omitted to create distinctive patterns. Beginning in 1992, Great Britain has used an oval perforation to help prevent counterfeiting. Several other countries have started using the oval perfs or other syncopated perf patterns.

A new type of perforation, still primarily used for postal stationery, is known as microperfs. Microperfs are tiny perforations (in some cases hundreds of holes per two centimeters) that allows items to be intentionally separated very easily, while not accidentally breaking apart as easily as standard perforations. These are not currently measured or differentiated by size, as are standard perforations.

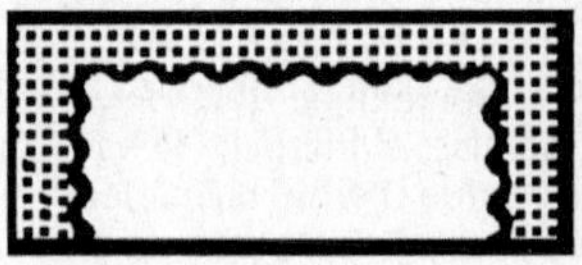

perce en arc

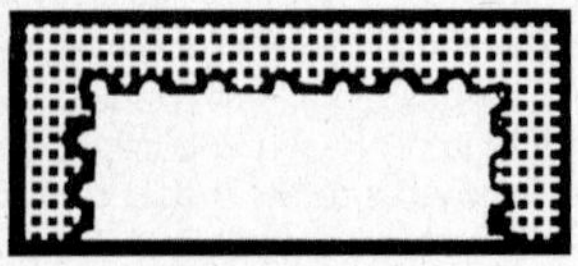

perce en lignes

perce en points

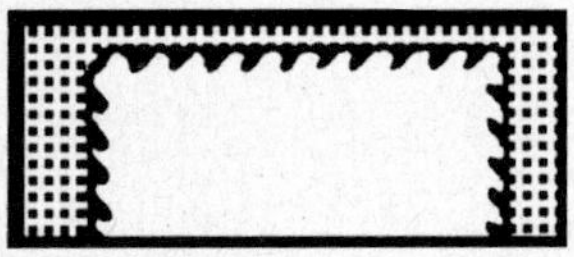

oblique roulette

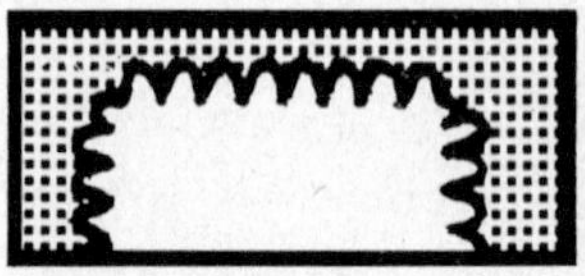

perce en scie

perce serpentin

ROULETTING

In rouletting, the stamp paper is cut partly or wholly through, with no paper removed. In perforating, some paper is removed. Rouletting derives its name from the French roulette, a spur-like wheel. As the wheel is rolled over the paper, each point makes a small cut. The number of cuts made in a two-centimeter space determines the gauge of the roulette, just as the number of perforations in two centimeters determines the gauge of the perforation.

The shape and arrangement of the teeth on the wheels varies. Various roulette types generally carry French names:

Perce en lignes — rouletted in lines. The paper receives short, straight cuts in lines. This is the most common type of rouletting. See Mexico Scott 500.

Perce en points — pin-rouletted or pin-perfed. This differs from a small perforation because no paper is removed, although round, equidistant holes are pricked through the paper. See Mexico Scott 242-256.

Perce en arc and perce en scie — pierced in an arc or saw-toothed designs, forming half circles or small triangles. See Hanover (German States) Scott 25-29.

Perce en serpentin — serpentine roulettes. The cuts form a serpentine or wavy line. See Brunswick (German States) Scott 13-18.

Once again, no paper is removed by these processes, leaving the stamps easily separated, but closely attached.

DIE-CUTTING

The third major form of stamp separation is die-cutting. This is a method where a die in the pattern of separation is created that later cuts the stamp paper in a stroke motion. Although some standard stamps bear die-cut perforations, this process is primarily used for self-adhesive postage stamps. Die-cutting can appear in straight lines, such as U.S. Scott 2522, shapes, such as U.S. Scott 1551, or imitating the appearance of perforations, such as New Zealand Scott 935A and 935B.

Printing processes

ENGRAVING (Intaglio, Line-engraving, Etching)

Master die — The initial operation in the process of line engraving is making the master die. The die is a small, flat block of softened steel upon which the stamp design is recess engraved in reverse.

Photographic reduction of the original art is made to the appropriate size. It then serves as a tracing guide for the initial outline of the design. The engraver lightly traces the design on the steel with his graver, then slowly works the design until it is completed. At various points during the engraving process, the engraver hand-inks the die and makes an impression to check his progress. These are known as progressive die proofs. After completion of the engraving, the die is hardened to withstand the stress and pressures of later transfer operations.

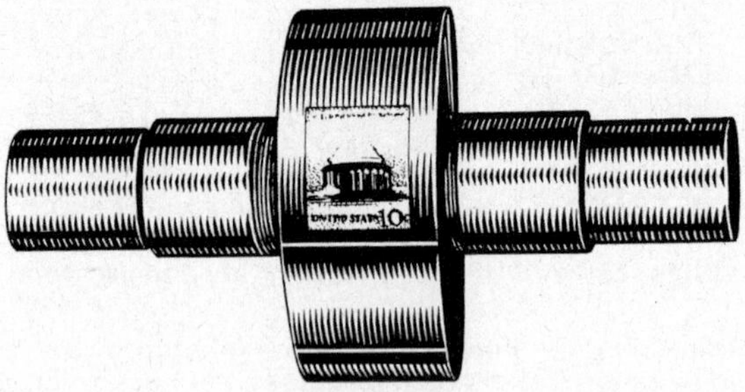

Transfer roll

Transfer roll — Next is production of the transfer roll that, as the name implies, is the medium used to transfer the subject from the master die to the printing plate. A blank roll of soft steel, mounted on a mandrel, is placed under the bearers of the transfer press to allow it to roll freely on its axis. The hardened die is placed on the bed of the press and the face of the transfer roll is applied to the die, under pressure. The bed or the roll is then rocked back and forth under increasing pressure, until the soft steel of the roll is forced into every engraved line of the die. The resulting impression on the roll is known as a "relief" or a "relief transfer." The engraved image is now positive in appearance and stands out from the steel. After the required number of reliefs are "rocked in," the soft steel transfer roll is hardened.

Different flaws may occur during the relief process. A defective relief may occur during the rocking in process because of a minute piece of foreign material lodging on the die, or some other cause. Imperfections in the steel of the transfer roll may result in a breaking away of parts of the design. This is known as a relief break, which will show up on finished stamps as small, unprinted areas. If a damaged relief remains in use, it will transfer a repeating defect to the plate. Deliberate alterations of reliefs sometimes occur. "Altered reliefs" designate these changed conditions.

Plate — The final step in pre-printing production is the making of the printing plate. A flat piece of soft steel replaces the die on the bed of the transfer press. One of the reliefs on the transfer roll is positioned over this soft steel. Position, or layout, dots determine the correct position on the plate. The dots have been lightly marked on the plate in advance. After the correct position of the relief is determined, the design is rocked in by following the same method used in making the transfer roll. The difference is that this time the image is being transferred from the transfer roll, rather than to it. Once the design is entered on the plate, it appears in reverse and is recessed. There are as many transfers entered on the plate as there are subjects printed on the sheet of stamps. It is during this process that double and shifted transfers occur, as well as re-entries. These are the result of improperly entered images that have not been properly burnished out prior to rocking in a new image.

Modern siderography processes, such as those used by the U.S. Bureau of Engraving and Printing, involve an automated form of rocking designs in on preformed cylindrical printing sleeves. The same process also allows for easier removal and re-entry of worn images right on the sleeve.

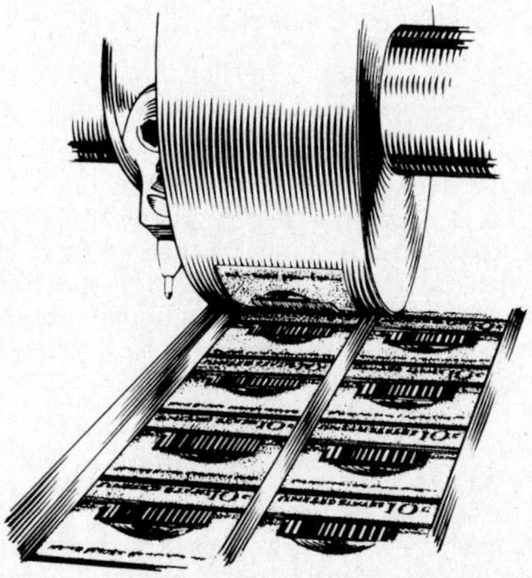

Transferring the design to the plate

Following the entering of the required transfers on the plate, the position dots, layout dots and lines, scratches and other markings generally are burnished out. Added at this time by the siderographer are any required guide lines, plate numbers or other marginal markings. The plate is then hand-inked and a proof impression is taken. This is known as a plate proof. If the impression is approved, the plate is machined for fitting onto the press, is hardened and sent to the plate vault ready for use.

On press, the plate is inked and the surface is automatically wiped clean, leaving ink only in the recessed lines. Paper is then forced under pressure into the engraved recessed lines, thereby receiving the ink. Thus, the ink lines on engraved stamps are slightly raised, and slight depressions (debossing) occur on the back of the stamp. Prior to the advent of modern high-speed presses and more advanced ink formulations, paper had to be dampened before receiving the ink. This sometimes led to uneven shrinkage by the time the stamps were perforated, resulting in improperly perforated stamps, or misperfs. Newer presses use drier paper, thus both *wet and dry printings* exist on some stamps.

Rotary Press — Until 1914, only flat plates were used to print engraved stamps. Rotary press printing was introduced in 1914, and slowly spread. Some countries still use flat-plate printing.

After approval of the plate proof, older rotary press plates require additional machining. They are curved to fit the press cylinder. "Gripper slots" are cut into the back of each plate to receive the "grippers," which hold the plate securely on the press. The plate is then hardened. Stamps printed from these bent rotary press plates are longer or wider than the same stamps printed from flat-plate presses. The stretching of the plate during the curving process is what causes this distortion.

Re-entry — To execute a re-entry on a flat plate, the transfer roll is re-applied to the plate, often at some time after its first use on the press. Worn-out designs can be resharpened by carefully burnishing out the original image and re-entering it from the transfer roll. If the original impression has not been sufficiently removed and the transfer roll is not precisely in line with the remaining impression, the resulting double transfer will make the re-entry obvious. If the registration is true, a re-entry may be difficult or impossible to distinguish. Sometimes a stamp printed from a successful re-entry is identified by having a much sharper and clearer impression than its neighbors. With the advent of rotary presses, post-press re-entries were not possible. After a plate was curved for the rotary press, it was impossible to make a re-entry. This is because the plate had already been bent once (with the design distorted).

However, with the introduction of the previously mentioned modern-style siderography machines, entries are made to the preformed cylindrical printing sleeve. Such sleeves are dechromed and softened. This allows individual images to be burnished out and re-entered on the curved sleeve. The sleeve is then rechromed, resulting in longer press life.

Double Transfer — This is a description of the condition of a transfer on a plate that shows evidence of a duplication of all, or a portion of the design. It usually is the result of the changing of the registration between the transfer roll and the plate during the rocking in of the original entry. Double transfers also occur when only a portion of the design has been rocked in and improper positioning is noted. If the worker elected not to burnish out the partial or completed design, a strong double transfer will occur for part or all of the design.

It sometimes is necessary to remove the original transfer from a plate and repeat the process a second time. If the finished re-worked image shows traces of the original impression, attributable to incomplete burnishing, the result is a partial double transfer.

With the modern automatic machines mentioned previously, double transfers are all but impossible to create. Those partially doubled images on stamps printed from such sleeves are more than likely re-entries, rather than true double transfers.

Re-engraved — Alterations to a stamp design are sometimes necessary after some stamps have been printed. In some cases, either the original die or the actual printing plate may have its "temper" drawn (softened), and the design will be re-cut. The resulting impressions from such a re-engraved die or plate may differ slightly from the original issue, and are known as "re-engraved." If the alteration was made to the master die, all future printings will be consistently different from the original. If alterations were made to the printing plate, each altered stamp on the plate will be slightly different from each other, allowing specialists to reconstruct a complete printing plate.

Dropped Transfers — If an impression from the transfer roll has not been properly placed, a dropped transfer may occur. The final stamp image will appear obviously out of line with its neighbors.

Short Transfer — Sometimes a transfer roll is not rocked its entire length when entering a transfer onto a plate. As a result, the finished transfer on the plate fails to show the complete design, and the finished stamp will have an incomplete design printed. This is known as a "short transfer." U.S. Scott No. 8 is a good example of a short transfer.

TYPOGRAPHY (Letterpress, Surface Printing, Flexography, Dry Offset, High Etch)

Although the word "Typography" is obsolete as a term describing a printing method, it was the accepted term throughout the first century of postage stamps. Therefore, appropriate Scott listings in this catalogue refer to typographed stamps. The current term for this form of printing, however, is "letterpress."

As it relates to the production of postage stamps, letterpress printing is the reverse of engraving. Rather than having recessed areas trap the ink and deposit it on paper, only the raised areas of the design are inked. This is comparable to the type of printing seen by inking and using an ordinary rubber stamp. Letterpress includes all printing where the design is above the surface area, whether it is wood, metal or, in some instances, hardened rubber or polymer plastic.

For most letterpress-printed stamps, the engraved master is made in much the same manner as for engraved stamps. In this instance, however, an additional step is needed. The design is transferred to another surface before being transferred to the transfer roll. In this way, the transfer roll has a recessed stamp design, rather than one done in relief. This makes the printing areas on the final plate raised, or relief areas.

For less-detailed stamps of the 19th century, the area on the die not used as a printing surface was cut away, leaving the surface area raised. The original die was then reproduced by stereotyping or electrotyping. The resulting electrotypes were assembled in the required number and format of the desired sheet of stamps. The plate used in printing the stamps was an electroplate of these assembled electrotypes.

Once the final letterpress plates are created, ink is applied to the raised surface and the pressure of the press transfers the ink impression to the paper. In contrast to engraving, the fine lines of letterpress are impressed on the surface of the stamp, leaving a debossed surface. When viewed from the back (as on a typewritten page), the corresponding line work on the stamp will be raised slightly (embossed) above the surface.

PHOTOGRAVURE (Gravure, Rotogravure, Heliogravure)

In this process, the basic principles of photography are applied to a chemically sensitized metal plate, rather than photographic paper. The design is transferred photographically to the plate through a halftone, or dot-matrix screen, breaking the reproduction into tiny dots. The plate is treated chemically and the dots form depressions, called cells, of varying depths and diameters, depending on the degrees of shade in the design. Then, like engraving, ink is applied to the plate and the surface is wiped clean. This leaves ink in the tiny cells that is lifted out and deposited on the paper when it is pressed against the plate.

Gravure is most often used for multicolored stamps, generally using the three primary colors (red, yellow and blue) and black. By varying the dot matrix pattern and density of these colors, virtually any color can be reproduced. A typical full-color gravure stamp will be created from four printing cylinders (one for each color). The original multicolored image will have been photographically separated into its component colors.

Modern gravure printing may use computer-generated dot-matrix screens, and modern plates may be of various types including metal-coated plastic. The catalogue designation of Photogravure (or "Photo") covers any of these older and more modern gravure methods of printing.

For examples of the first photogravure stamps printed (1914), see Bavaria Scott 94-114.

LITHOGRAPHY (Offset Lithography, Stone Lithography, Dilitho, Planography, Collotype)

The principle that oil and water do not mix is the basis for lithography. The stamp design is drawn by hand or transferred from engraving to the surface of a lithographic stone or metal plate in a greasy (oily) substance. This oily substance holds the ink, which will later be transferred to the paper. The stone (or plate) is wet with an acid fluid, causing it to repel the printing ink in all areas not covered by the greasy substance.

Transfer paper is used to transfer the design from the original stone or plate. A series of duplicate transfers are grouped and, in turn, transferred to the final printing plate.

Photolithography — The application of photographic processes to lithography. This process allows greater flexibility of design, related to use of halftone screens combined with line work. Unlike photogravure or engraving, this process can allow large, solid areas to be printed.

Offset — A refinement of the lithographic process. A rubber-covered blanket cylinder takes the impression from the inked lithographic plate. From the "blanket" the impression is offset or transferred to the paper. Greater flexibility and speed are the principal reasons offset printing has largely displaced lithography. The term "lithography" covers both processes, and results are almost identical.

EMBOSSED (Relief) Printing

Embossing, not considered one of the four main printing types, is a method in which the design first is sunk into the metal of the die. Printing is done against a yielding platen, such as leather or linoleum. The platen is forced into the depression of the die, thus forming the design on the paper in relief. This process is often used for metallic inks.

Embossing may be done without color (see Sardinia Scott 4-6); with color printed around the embossed area (see Great Britain Scott 5 and most U.S. envelopes); and with color in exact registration with the embossed subject (see Canada Scott 656-657).

HOLOGRAMS

For objects to appear as holograms on stamps, a model exactly the same size as it is to appear on the hologram must be created. Rather than using photographic film to capture the image, holography records an image on a photoresist material. In processing, chemicals eat away at certain exposed areas, leaving a pattern of constructive and destructive interference. When the photoresist is developed, the result is a pattern of uneven ridges that acts as a mold. This mold is then coated with metal, and the resulting form is used to press copies in much the same way phonograph records are produced.

A typical reflective hologram used for stamps consists of a reproduction of the uneven patterns on a plastic film that is applied to a reflective background, usually a silver or gold foil. Light is reflected off the background through the film, making the pattern present on the film visible. Because of the uneven pattern of the film, the viewer will perceive the objects in their proper three-dimensional relationships with appropriate brightness. The first hologram on a stamp was produced by Austria in 1988 (Scott 1441).

FOIL APPLICATION

A modern technique of applying color to stamps involves the application of metallic foil to the stamp paper. A pattern of foil is applied to the stamp paper by use of a stamping die. The foil usually is flat, but it may be textured. Canada Scott 1735 has three different foil applications in pearl, bronze and gold. The gold foil was textured using a chemical-etch copper embossing die. The printing of this stamp also involved two-color offset lithography plus embossing.

THERMOGRAPHY

In the 1990s stamps began to be enhanced with thermographic printing. In this process, a powdered polymer is applied over a sheet that has just been printed. The powder adheres to ink that lacks drying or hardening agents and does not adhere to areas where the ink has these agents. The excess powder is removed and the sheet is briefly heated to melt the powder. The melted powder solidifies after cooling, producing a raised, shiny effect on the stamps. See Scott New Caledonia C239-C240.

COMBINATION PRINTINGS

Sometimes two or even three printing methods are combined in producing stamps. In these cases, such as Austria Scott 933 or Canada 1735 (described in the preceding paragraph), the multiple-printing technique can be determined by studying the individual characteristics of each printing type. A few stamps, such as Singapore Scott 684-684A, combine as many as three of the four major printing types (lithography, engraving and typography). When this is done it often indicates the incorporation of security devices against counterfeiting.

INK COLORS

Inks or colored papers used in stamp printing often are of mineral origin, although there are numerous examples of organic-based pigments. As a general rule, organic-based pigments are far more subject to varieties and change than those of mineral-based origin.

The appearance of any given color on a stamp may be affected by many aspects, including printing variations, light, color of paper, aging and chemical alterations.

Numerous printing variations may be observed. Heavier pressure or inking will cause a more intense color, while slight interruptions in the ink feed or lighter impressions will cause a lighter appearance. Stamps printed in the same color by water-based and solvent-based inks can differ significantly in appearance. This affects several stamps in the U.S. Prominent Americans series. Hand-mixed ink formulas (primarily from the 19th century) produced under different conditions (humidity and temperature) account for notable color variations in early printings of the same stamp (see U.S. Scott 248-250, 279B, for example). Different sources of pigment can also result in significant differences in color.

Light exposure and aging are closely related in the way they affect stamp color. Both eventually break down the ink and fade colors, so that a carefully kept stamp may differ significantly in color from an identical copy that has been exposed to light. If stamps are exposed to light either intentionally or accidentally, their colors can be faded or completely changed in some cases.

Papers of different quality and consistency used for the same stamp printing may affect color appearance. Most pelure papers, for example, show a richer color when compared with wove or laid papers. See Russia Scott 181a, for an example of this effect.

The very nature of the printing processes can cause a variety of differences in shades or hues of the same stamp. Some of these shades are scarcer than others, and are of particular interest to the advanced collector.

Luminescence

All forms of tagged stamps fall under the general category of luminescence. Within this broad category is fluorescence, dealing with forms of tagging visible under longwave ultraviolet light, and phosphorescence, which deals with tagging visible only under shortwave light. Phosphorescence leaves an afterglow and fluorescence does not. These treated stamps show up in a range of different colors when exposed to UV light. The differing wavelengths of the light activates the tagging material, making it glow in various colors that usually serve different mail processing purposes.

Intentional tagging is a post-World War II phenomenon, brought about by the increased literacy rate and rapidly growing mail volume. It was one of several answers to the problem of the need for more automated mail processes. Early tagged stamps served the purpose of triggering machines to separate different types of mail. A natural outgrowth was to also use the signal to trigger machines that faced all envelopes the same way and canceled them.

Tagged stamps come in many different forms. Some tagged stamps have luminescent shapes or images imprinted on them as a form of security device. Others have blocks (United States), stripes, frames (South Africa and Canada), overall coatings (United States), bars (Great Britain and Canada) and many other types. Some types of tagging are even mixed in with the pigmented printing ink (Australia Scott 366, Netherlands Scott 478 and U.S. Scott 1359 and 2443).

The means of applying taggant to stamps differs as much as the intended purposes for the stamps. The most common form of tagging is a coating applied to the surface of the printed stamp. Since the taggant ink is frequently invisible except under UV light, it does not interfere with the appearance of the stamp. Another common application is the use of phosphored papers. In this case the paper itself either has a coating of taggant applied before the stamp is printed, has taggant applied during the papermaking process (incorporating it into the fibers), or has the taggant mixed into the coating of the paper. The latter method, among others, is currently in use in the United States.

Many countries now use tagging in various forms to either expedite mail handling or to serve as a printing security device against counterfeiting. Following the introduction of tagged stamps for public use in 1959 by Great Britain, other countries have steadily joined the parade. Among those are Germany (1961); Canada and Denmark (1962); United States, Australia, France and Switzerland (1963); Belgium and Japan (1966); Sweden and Norway (1967); Italy (1968); and Russia (1969). Since then, many other countries have begun using forms of tagging, including Brazil, China, Czechoslovakia, Hong Kong, Guatemala, Indonesia, Israel, Lithuania, Luxembourg, Netherlands, Penrhyn Islands, Portugal, St. Vincent, Singapore, South Africa, Spain and Sweden to name a few.

In some cases, including United States, Canada, Great Britain and Switzerland, stamps were released both with and without tagging. Many of these were released during each country's experimental period. Tagged and untagged versions are listed for the aforementioned countries and are noted in some other countries' listings. For at least a few stamps, the experimentally tagged version is worth far more than its untagged counterpart, such as the 1963 experimental tagged version of France Scott 1024.

In some cases, luminescent varieties of stamps were inadvertently created. Several Russian stamps, for example, sport highly fluorescent ink that was not intended as a form of tagging. Older stamps, such as early U.S. postage dues, can be positively identified by the use of UV light, since the organic ink used has become slightly fluorescent over time. Other stamps, such as Austria Scott 70a-82a (varnish bars) and Obock Scott 46-64 (printed quadrille lines), have become fluorescent over time.

Various fluorescent substances have been added to paper to make it appear brighter. These optical brightners, as they are known, greatly affect the appearance of the stamp under UV light. The brightest of these is known as Hi-Brite paper. These paper varieties are beyond the scope of the Scott Catalogue.

Shortwave UV light also is used extensively in expertizing, since each form of paper has its own fluorescent characteristics that are impossible to perfectly match. It is therefore a simple matter to detect filled thins, added perforation teeth and other alterations that involve the addition of paper. UV light also is used to examine stamps that have had cancels chemically removed and for other purposes as well.

Gum

The Illustrated Gum Chart in the first part of this introduction shows and defines various types of gum condition. Because gum condition has an important impact on the value of unused stamps, we recommend studying this chart and the accompanying text carefully.

The gum on the back of a stamp may be shiny, dull, smooth, rough, dark, white, colored or tinted. Most stamp gumming adhesives use gum arabic or dextrine as a base. Certain polymers such as polyvinyl alcohol (PVA) have been used extensively since World War II.

The *Scott Standard Postage Stamp Catalogue* does not list items by types of gum. The *Scott Specialized Catalogue of United States Stamps and Covers* does differentiate among some types of gum for certain issues.

Reprints of stamps may have gum differing from the original issues. In addition, some countries have used different gum formulas for different seasons. These adhesives have different properties that may become more apparent over time.

Many stamps have been issued without gum, and the catalogue will note this fact. See, for example, United States Scott 40-47. Sometimes, gum may have been removed to preserve the stamp. Germany Scott B68, for example, has a highly acidic gum that eventually destroys the stamps. This item is valued in the catalogue with gum removed.

Reprints and reissues

These are impressions of stamps (usually obsolete) made from the original plates or stones. If they are valid for postage and reproduce obsolete issues (such as U.S. Scott 102-111), the stamps are reissues. If they are from current issues, they are designated as *second, third,* etc., *printing*. If designated for a particular purpose, they are called *special printings*.

When special printings are not valid for postage, but are made from original dies and plates by authorized persons, they are *official reprints*. *Private reprints* are made from the original plates and dies by private hands. An example of a private reprint is that of the 1871-1932 reprints made from the original die of the 1845 New Haven, Conn., postmaster's provisional. *Official reproductions* or imitations are made from new dies and plates by government authorization. Scott will list those reissues that are valid for postage if they differ significantly from the original printing.

The U.S. government made special printings of its first postage stamps in 1875. Produced were official imitations of the first two stamps (listed as Scott 3-4), reprints of the demonetized pre-1861 issues (Scott 40-47) and reissues of the 1861 stamps, the 1869 stamps and the then-current 1875 denominations. Even though the official imitations and the reprints were not valid for postage, Scott lists all of these U.S. special printings.

Most reprints or reissues differ slightly from the original stamp in some characteristic, such as gum, paper, perforation, color or watermark. Sometimes the details are followed so meticulously that only a student of that specific stamp is able to distinguish the reprint or reissue from the original.

Remainders and canceled to order

Some countries sell their stock of old stamps when a new issue replaces them. To avoid postal use, the remainders usually are canceled with a punch hole, a heavy line or bar, or a more-or-less regular-looking cancellation. The most famous merchant of remainders was Nicholas F. Seebeck. In the 1880s and 1890s, he arranged printing contracts between the Hamilton Bank Note Co., of which he was a director, and several Central and South American countries. The contracts provided that the plates and all remainders of the yearly issues became the property of Hamilton. Seebeck saw to it that ample stock remained. The "Seebecks," both remainders and reprints, were standard packet fillers for decades.

Some countries also issue stamps *canceled-to-order (CTO)*, either in sheets with original gum or stuck onto pieces of paper or envelopes and canceled. Such CTO items generally are worth less than postally used stamps. In cases where the CTO material is far more prevalent in the marketplace than postally used examples, the catalogue value relates to the CTO examples, with postally used examples noted as premium items. Most CTOs can be detected by the presence of gum. However, as the CTO practice goes back at least to 1885, the gum inevitably has been soaked off some stamps so they could pass as postally used. The normally applied postmarks usually differ slightly from standard postmarks, and specialists are able to tell the difference. When applied individually to envelopes by philatelically minded persons, CTO material is known as *favor canceled* and generally sells at large discounts.

Cinderellas and facsimiles

Cinderella is a catch-all term used by stamp collectors to describe phantoms, fantasies, bogus items, municipal issues, exhibition seals, local revenues, transportation stamps, labels, poster stamps and many other types of items. Some cinderella collectors include in their collections local postage issues, telegraph stamps, essays and proofs, forgeries and counterfeits.

A *fantasy* is an adhesive created for a nonexistent stamp-issuing authority. Fantasy items range from imaginary countries (Occusi-Ambeno, Kingdom of Sedang, Principality of Trinidad or Torres Straits), to non-existent locals (Winans City Post), or nonexistent transportation lines (McRobish & Co.'s Acapulco-San Francisco Line).

On the other hand, if the entity exists and could have issued stamps (but did not) or was known to have issued other stamps, the items are considered bogus stamps. These would include the Mormon postage stamps of Utah, S. Allan Taylor's Guatemala and Paraguay inventions, the propaganda issues for the South Moluccas and the adhesives of the Page & Keyes local post of Boston.

Phantoms is another term for both fantasy and bogus issues.

Facsimiles are copies or imitations made to represent original stamps, but which do not pretend to be originals. A catalogue illustration is such a facsimile. Illustrations from the Moens catalogue of the last century were occasionally colored and passed off as stamps. Since the beginning of stamp collecting, facsimiles have been made for collectors as space fillers or for reference. They often carry the word "facsimile," "falsch" (German), "sanko" or "mozo" (Japanese), or "faux" (French) overprinted on the face or stamped on the back. Unfortunately, over the years a number of these items have had fake cancels applied over the facsimile notation and have been passed off as genuine.

Forgeries and counterfeits

Forgeries and counterfeits have been with philately virtually from the beginning of stamp production. Over time, the terminology for the two has been used interchangeably. Although both forgeries and counterfeits are reproductions of stamps, the purposes behind their creation differ considerably.

Among specialists there is an increasing movement to more specifically define such items. Although there is no universally accepted terminology, we feel the following definitions most closely mirror the items and their purposes as they are currently defined.

Forgeries (also often referred to as Counterfeits) are reproductions of genuine stamps that have been created to defraud collectors. Such spurious items first appeared on the market around 1860, and most old-time collections contain one or more. Many are crude and easily spotted, but some can deceive experts.

An important supplier of these early philatelic forgeries was the Hamburg printer Gebruder Spiro. Many others with reputations in this craft included S. Allan Taylor, George Hussey, James Chute, George Forune, Benjamin & Sarpy, Julius Goldner, E. Oneglia and L.H. Mercier. Among the noted 20th-century forgers were Francois Fournier, Jean Sperati and the prolific Raoul DeThuin.

Forgeries may be complete replications, or they may be genuine stamps altered to resemble a scarcer (and more valuable) type. Most forgeries, particularly those of rare stamps, are worth only a small fraction of the value of a genuine example, but a few types, created by some of the most notable forgers, such as Sperati, can be worth as much or more than the genuine. Fraudulently produced copies are known of most classic rarities and many medium-priced stamps.

In addition to rare stamps, large numbers of common 19th- and early 20th-century stamps were forged to supply stamps to the early packet trade. Many can still be easily found. Few new philatelic forgeries have appeared in recent decades. Successful imitation of well-engraved work is virtually impossible. It has proven far easier to produce a fake by altering a genuine stamp than to duplicate a stamp completely.

Counterfeit (also often referred to as Postal Counterfeit or Postal Forgery) is the term generally applied to reproductions of stamps that have been created to defraud the government of revenue. Such items usually are created at the time a stamp is current and, in some cases, are hard to detect. Because most counterfeits are seized when the perpetrator is captured, postal counterfeits, particularly used on cover, are usually worth much more than a genuine example to specialists. The first postal counterfeit was of Spain's 4-cuarto carmine of 1854 (the real one is Scott 25). Apparently, the counterfeiters were not satisfied with their first version, which is now very scarce, and they soon created an engraved counterfeit, which is common. Postal counterfeits quickly followed in Austria, Naples, Sardinia and the Roman States. They have since been created in many other countries as well, including the United States.

An infamous counterfeit to defraud the government is the 1-shilling Great Britain "Stock Exchange" forgery of 1872, used on telegraph forms at the exchange that year. The stamp escaped detection until a stamp dealer noticed it in 1898.

Fakes

Fakes are genuine stamps altered in some way to make them more desirable. One student of this part of stamp collecting has estimated that by the 1950s more than 30,000 varieties of fakes were known. That number has grown greatly since then. The widespread existence of fakes makes it important for stamp collectors to study their philatelic holdings and use relevant literature. Likewise, collectors should buy from reputable dealers who guarantee their stamps and make full and prompt refunds should a purchased item be declared faked or altered by some mutually agreed-upon authority. Because fakes always have some genuine characteristics, it is not always possible to obtain unanimous agreement among experts regarding specific items. These students may change their opinions as philatelic knowledge increases. More than 80 percent of all fakes on the philatelic market today are regummed, reperforated (or perforated for the first time), or bear forged overprints, surcharges or cancellations.

Stamps can be chemically treated to alter or eliminate colors. For example, a pale rose stamp can be re-colored to resemble a blue shade of high market value. In other cases, treated stamps can be made to resemble missing color varieties. Designs may be changed by painting, or a stroke or a dot added or bleached out to turn an ordinary variety into a seemingly scarcer stamp. Part of a stamp can be bleached and reprinted in a different version, achieving an inverted center or frame. Margins can be added or repairs done so deceptively that the stamps move from the "repaired" into the "fake" category.

Fakers have not left the backs of the stamps untouched either. They may create false watermarks, add fake grills or press out genuine grills. A thin India paper proof may be glued onto a thicker backing to create the appearance an issued stamp, or a proof printed on cardboard may be shaved down and perforated to resemble a stamp. Silk threads are impressed into paper and stamps have been split so that a rare paper variety is added to an otherwise inexpensive stamp. The most common treatment to the back of a stamp, however, is regumming.

Some in the business of faking stamps have openly advertised fool-proof application of "original gum" to stamps that lack it, although most publications now ban such ads from their pages. It is believed that very few early stamps have survived without being hinged. The large number of never-hinged examples of such earlier material offered for sale thus suggests the widespread extent of regumming activity. Regumming also may be used to hide repairs or thin spots. Dipping the stamp into watermark fluid, or examining it under longwave ultraviolet light often will reveal these flaws.

Fakers also tamper with separations. Ingenious ways to add margins are known. Perforated wide-margin stamps may be falsely represented as imperforate when trimmed. Reperforating is commonly done to create scarce coil or perforation varieties, and to eliminate the naturally occurring straight-edge stamps found in sheet margin positions of many earlier issues. Custom has made straight-edged stamps less desirable. Fakers have obliged by perforating straight-edged stamps so that many are now uncommon, if not rare.

Another fertile field for the faker is that of overprints, surcharges and cancellations. The forging of rare surcharges or overprints began in the 1880s or 1890s. These forgeries are sometimes difficult to detect, but experts have identified almost all. Occasionally, overprints or cancellations are removed to create non-overprinted stamps or seemingly unused items. This is most commonly done by removing a manuscript cancel to make a stamp resemble an unused example. "SPECIMEN" overprints may be removed by scraping and repainting to create non-overprinted varieties. Fakers use inexpensive revenues or pen-canceled stamps to generate unused stamps for further faking by adding other markings. The quartz lamp or UV lamp and a high-powered magnifying glass help to easily detect removed cancellations.

The bigger problem, however, is the addition of overprints, surcharges or cancellations — many with such precision that they are very difficult to ascertain. Plating of the stamps or the overprint can be an important method of detection.

Fake postmarks may range from many spurious fancy cancellations to a host of markings applied to transatlantic covers, to adding normally appearing postmarks to definitives of some countries with stamps that are valued far higher used than unused. With the increased popularity of cover collecting, and the widespread interest in postal history, a fertile new field for fakers has come about. Some have tried to create entire covers. Others specialize in adding stamps, tied by fake cancellations, to genuine stampless covers, or replacing less expensive or damaged stamps with more valuable ones. Detailed study of postal rates in effect at the time a cover in question was mailed, including the analysis of each handstamp used during the period, ink analysis and similar techniques, usually will unmask the fraud.

Restoration and repairs

Scott bases its catalogue values on stamps that are free of defects and otherwise meet the standards set forth earlier in this introduction. Most stamp collectors desire to have the finest copy of an item possible. Even within given grading categories there are variances. This leads to a controversial practice that is not defined in any universal manner: stamp *restoration*.

There are broad differences of opinion about what is permissible when it comes to restoration. Carefully applying a soft eraser to a stamp or cover to remove light soiling is one form of restoration, as is washing a stamp in mild soap and water to clean it. These are fairly accepted forms of restoration. More severe forms of restoration include pressing out creases or removing stains caused by tape. To what degree each of these is acceptable is dependent upon the individual situation. Further along the spectrum is the freshening of a stamp's color by removing oxide build-up or the effects of wax paper left next to stamps shipped to the tropics.

At some point in this spectrum the concept of *repair* replaces that of restoration. Repairs include filling thin spots, mending tears by reweaving or adding a missing perforation tooth. Regumming stamps may have been acceptable as a restoration or repair technique many decades ago, but today it is considered a form of fakery.

Restored stamps may or may not sell at a discount, and it is possible that the value of individual restored items may be enhanced over that of their pre-restoration state. Specific situations dictate the resultant value of such an item. Repaired stamps sell at substantial discounts from the value of sound stamps.

Terminology

Booklets — Many countries have issued stamps in small booklets for the convenience of users. This idea continues to become increasingly popular in many countries. Booklets have been issued in many sizes and forms, often with advertising on the covers, the panes of stamps or on the interleaving.

The panes used in booklets may be printed from special plates or made from regular sheets. All panes from booklets issued by the United States and many from those of other countries contain stamps that are straight edged on the sides, but perforated between. Others are distinguished by orientation of watermark or other identifying features. Any stamp-like unit in the pane, either printed or blank, that is not a postage stamp, is considered to be a *label* in the catalogue listings.

Scott lists and values booklet panes. Modern complete booklets also are listed and valued. Individual booklet panes are listed only when they are not fashioned from existing sheet stamps and, therefore, are identifiable from their sheet stamp counterparts.

Panes usually do not have a used value assigned to them because there is little market activity for used booklet panes, even though many exist used and there is some demand for them.

Cancellations — The marks or obliterations put on stamps by postal authorities to show that they have performed service and to prevent their reuse are known as cancellations. If the marking is made with a pen, it is considered a "pen cancel." When the location of the post office appears in the marking, it is a "town cancellation." A "postmark" is technically any postal marking, but in practice the term generally is applied to a town cancellation with a date. When calling attention to a cause or celebration, the marking is known as a "slogan cancellation." Many other types and styles of cancellations exist, such as duplex, numerals, targets, fancy and others. See also "precancels," below.

Coil Stamps — These are stamps that are issued in rolls for use in dispensers, affixing and vending machines. Those coils of the United States, Canada, Sweden and some other countries are perforated horizontally or vertically only, with the outer edges imperforate. Coil stamps of some countries, such as Great Britain and Germany, are perforated on all four sides and may in some cases be distinguished from their sheet stamp counterparts by watermarks, counting numbers on the reverse or other means.

Covers — Entire envelopes, with or without adhesive postage stamps, that have passed through the mail and bear postal or other markings of philatelic interest are known as covers. Before the introduction of envelopes in about 1840, people folded letters and wrote the address on the outside. Some people covered their letters with an extra sheet of paper on the outside for the address, producing the term "cover." Used airletter sheets, stamped envelopes and other items of postal stationery also are considered covers.

Errors — Stamps that have some major, consistent, unintentional deviation from the normal are considered errors. Errors include, but are not limited to, missing or wrong colors, wrong paper, wrong watermarks, inverted centers or frames on multicolor printing, inverted or missing surcharges or overprints, double impressions, missing perforations, unintentionally omitted tagging and others. Factually wrong or misspelled information, if it appears on all examples of a stamp, are not considered errors in the true sense of the word. They are errors of design. Inconsistent or randomly appearing items, such as misperfs or color shifts, are classified as freaks.

Color-Omitted Errors — This term refers to stamps where a missing color is caused by the complete failure of the printing plate to deliver ink to the stamp paper or any other paper. Generally, this is caused by the printing plate not being engaged on the press or the ink station running dry of ink during printing.

Color-Missing Errors — This term refers to stamps where a color or colors were printed somewhere but do not appear on the finished stamp. There are four different classes of color-missing errors, and the catalog indicates with a two-letter code appended to each such listing what caused the color to be missing. These codes are used only for the United States' color-missing error listings.

FO = A *foldover* of the stamp sheet during printing may block ink from appearing on the face of a stamp. Instead, the color will appear on the back of the foldover (where it might fall on the back of the selvage or perhaps a bit on the back of the stamp or on the back of another stamp. FO also will be used in the case of foldunders, where the paper may fold underneath the other stamp paper and the color will print on the platen.

EP = When the extraneous paper is removed, an unprinted area of stamp paper remains and may show a color or colors to be totally missing on the finished stamp.

CM = A misregistration of the printing plates during printing will result in a *color misregistration*, and such a misregistraion may result in a color not appearing on the finished stamp.

PS = *A perforation shift* after printing may remove a color from the finished stamp. Normally, this will occur on a row of stamps at the edge of the stamp pane.

Measurements – When measurements are given in the Scott catalogues for stamp size, grill size or any other reason, the first measurement given is always for the top and bottom dimension, while the second measurement will be for the sides (just as perforation gauges are measured). Thus, a stamp size of 15mm x 21mm will indicate a vertically oriented stamp 15mm wide at top and bottom, and 21mm tall at the sides. The same principle holds for measuring or counting items such as U.S. grills. A grill count of 22x18 points (B grill) indicates that there are 22 grill points across by 18 grill points down.

Overprints and Surcharges — Overprinting involves applying wording or design elements over an already existing stamp. Overprints can be used to alter the place of use (such as "Canal Zone" on U.S. stamps), to adapt them for a special purpose ("Porto" on Denmark's 1913-20 regular issues for use as postage due stamps, Scott J1-J7) or to commemorate a special occasion (United States Scott 647-648).

A *surcharge* is a form of overprint that changes or restates the face value of a stamp or piece of postal stationery.

Surcharges and overprints may be handstamped, typeset or, occasionally, lithographed or engraved. A few hand-written overprints and surcharges are known.

Personalized Stamps — In 1999, Australia issued stamps with se-tenant labels that could be personalized with pictures of the customer's choice. Other countries quickly followed suit, with some offering to print the selected picture on the stamp itself within a frame that was used exclusively for personalized issues. As the picture used on these stamps or labels vary, listings for such stamps are for any picture within the common frame (or any picture on a se-tenant label), be it a "generic" image or one produced especially for a customer, almost invariably at a premium price.

Precancels — Stamps that are canceled before they are placed in the mail are known as precancels. Precanceling usually is done to expedite the handling of large mailings and generally allow the affected mail pieces to skip certain phases of mail handling.

In the United States, precancellations generally identified the point of origin; that is, the city and state. This information appeared across the face of the stamp, usually centered between parallel lines. More recently, bureau precancels retained the parallel lines, but the city and state designations were dropped. Recent coils have a service inscription that is present on the original printing plate. These show the mail service paid for by the stamp. Since these stamps are not intended to receive further cancellations when used as intended, they are considered precancels. Such items often do not have parallel lines as part of the precancellation.

In France, the abbreviation *Affranchts* in a semicircle together with the word *Postes* is the general form of precancel in use. Belgian precancellations usually appear in a box in which the name of the city appears. Netherlands precancels have the name of the city enclosed between concentric circles, sometimes called a "lifesaver." Precancellations of other countries usually follow these patterns, but may be any arrangement of bars, boxes and city names.

Precancels are listed in the Scott catalogues only if the precancel changes the denomination (Belgium Scott 477-478); if the precanceled stamp is different from the non-precanceled version (such as untagged U.S. precancels); or if the stamp exists only precanceled (France Scott 1096-1099, U.S. Scott 2265).

Proofs and Essays — Proofs are impressions taken from an approved die, plate or stone in which the design and color are the same as the stamp issued to the public. Trial color proofs are impressions taken from approved dies, plates or stones in colors that vary from the final version. An essay is the impression of a design that differs in some way from the issued stamp. "Progressive die proofs" generally are considered to be essays.

Provisionals — These are stamps that are issued on short notice and intended for temporary use pending the arrival of regular issues. They usually are issued to meet such contingencies as changes in government or currency, shortage of necessary postage values or military occupation.

During the 1840s, postmasters in certain American cities issued stamps that were valid only at specific post offices. In 1861, postmasters of the Confederate States also issued stamps with limited validity. Both of these examples are known as "postmaster's provisionals."

Se-tenant — This term refers to an unsevered pair, strip or block of stamps that differ in design, denomination or overprint.

Unless the se-tenant item has a continuous design (see U.S. Scott 1451a, 1694a) the stamps do not have to be in the same order as shown in the catalogue (see U.S. Scott 2158a).

Specimens — The Universal Postal Union required member nations to send samples of all stamps they released into service to the International Bureau in Switzerland. Member nations of the UPU received these specimens as samples of what stamps were valid for postage. Many are overprinted, handstamped or initial-perforated "Specimen," "Canceled" or "Muestra." Some are marked with bars across the denominations (China-Taiwan), punched holes (Czechoslovakia) or back inscriptions (Mongolia).

Stamps distributed to government officials or for publicity purposes, and stamps submitted by private security printers for official approval, also may receive such defacements.

The previously described defacement markings prevent postal use, and all such items generally are known as "specimens."

Tete-Beche — This term describes a pair of stamps in which one is upside down in relation to the other. Some of these are the result of intentional sheet arrangements, such as Morocco Scott B10-B11. Others occurred when one or more electrotypes accidentally were placed upside down on the plate, such as Colombia Scott 57a. Separation of the tete-beche stamps, of course, destroys the tete beche variety.

Carson Products

MicroMini 20x LED Microscope
Item No. MSMM-2800
$9.99 *AA* price*
$14.00 Retail

Pop-Up Keychain Magnifier
Item No. MGGN-70
$6.99 *AA* price*
$10.00 Retail

ZPix Digital Microscope
Item No. MCPIX
$99.99 *AA* price*
$129.99 Retail

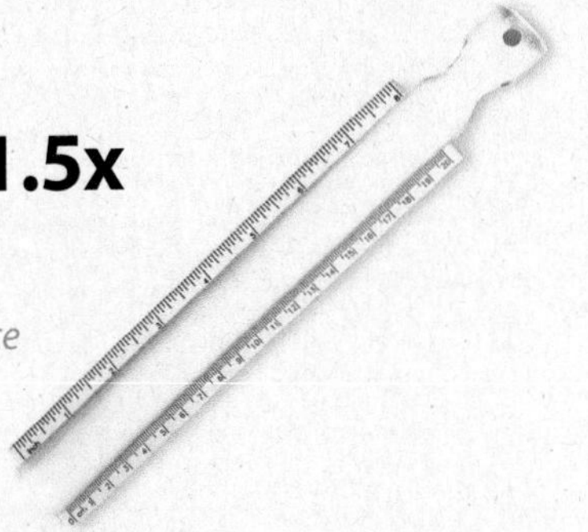

Bar Ruler Magnifier 1.5x
Item No. MGMR-65
$9.99 *AA* price*
$13.00 Retail

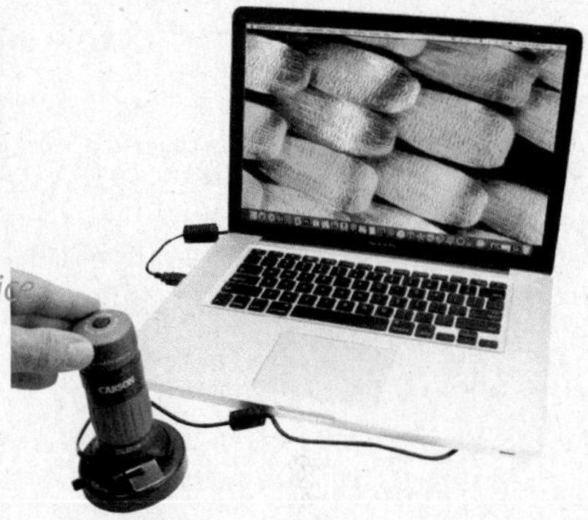

SAVE 33%

zOrb Digital Microscope
Item No. MCZORB2
$50.99 *AA* price*
$74.99 Retail

ON SALE

MicroFlip Phone Scope
Item No. MCFLIP
$21.99 *AA* price*
$27.99 Retail

MicroPen Pocket Microscope
Item No. MCPEN
$12.99 *AA* price*
$14.99 Retail

SmartPhone Microscope
Item No. MCSCOPE
$119.99 *AA* price*
$164.99 Retail

SAVE $45

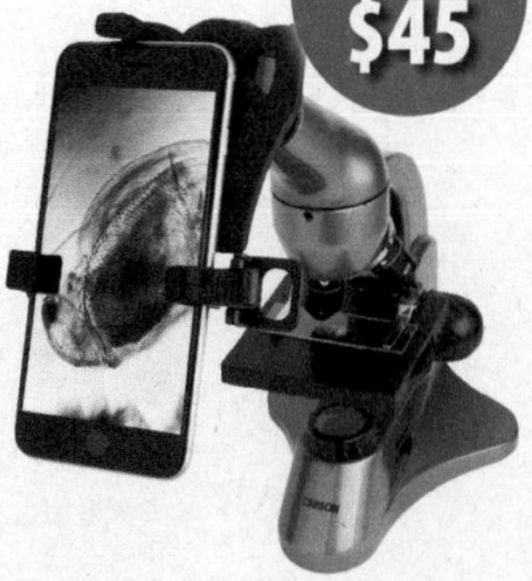

FREE SHIPPING! on orders $75 or more

AmosAdvantage.com | 1-800-572-6885

ORDERING INFORMATION: *AA prices apply to paid subscribers of Amos Media titles, or for orders placed online. Prices, terms and product availability subject to change. **SHIPPING & HANDLING:** U.S.: Orders total $0-$10.00 charged $4.99 shipping. U.S. Order total $10.01-$74.99 charged $9.99 shipping. Orders totaling $75+ will ship FREE! Taxes will apply in CA, OH, & IL. Canada: 20% of order total. Minimum charge $19.99 Maximum charge $200.00. Foreign orders are shipped via FedEx Intl. or USPS and billed actual freight.

Pronunciation Symbols

ə .... **b**a**n**a**n**a, **c**o**ll**ide, **a**but

ˈə, ˌə .... hum**dr**u**m**, ab**u**t

ə .... immediately preceding \l\, \n\, \m\, \ŋ\, as in battle, mitten, eaten, and sometimes open \ˈō-pᵊm\, lock **and** key \-ᵊŋ-\; immediately following \l\, \m\, \r\, as often in French table, prisme, titre

ər .... **fur**th**er**, m**er**g**er**, b**ir**d

ˈər- / ˈə-r .... as in two different pronunciations of hurry \ˈhər-ē, ˈhə-rē\

a .... m**a**t, m**a**p, m**a**d, g**a**g, sn**a**p, p**a**tch

ā .... d**ay**, f**a**de, d**a**te, **a**orta, dr**a**pe, c**a**pe

ä .... b**o**ther, c**o**t, and, with most American speakers, f**a**ther, c**a**rt

ȧ .... f**a**ther as pronounced by speakers who do not rhyme it with *bother*; French p**a**tte

aů .... n**ow**, l**ou**d, **ou**t

b .... **b**a**b**y, ri**b**

ch .... **ch**in, na**t**ure \ˈnā-chər\

d .... **d**i**d**, a**dd**er

e .... b**e**t, b**e**d, p**e**ck

ˈē, ˌē .... b**ea**t, nosebl**ee**d, **e**venly, **ea**sy

ē .... eas**y**, meal**y**

f .... **f**i**f**ty, cu**ff**

g .... **g**o, bi**g**, **g**ift

h .... **h**at, a**h**ead

hw .... **wh**ale as pronounced by those who do not have the same pronunciation for both *whale* and *wail*

i .... t**i**p, ban**i**sh, act**i**ve

ī .... s**i**te, s**i**de, b**uy**, tr**i**pe

j .... **j**ob, **g**em, e**dge**, **j**oin, **j**u**dge**

k .... **k**in, **c**oo**k**, a**che**

<u>k</u> .... German i**ch**, Bu**ch**; one pronunciation of lo**ch**

l .... **l**i**l**y, poo**l**

m .... **m**ur**m**ur, di**m**, ny**m**ph

n .... **n**o, ow**n**

ⁿ .... indicates that a preceding vowel or diphthong is pronounced with the nasal passages open, as in French *un bon vin blanc* \œⁿ -bōⁿ -vaⁿ -bläⁿ\

ŋ .... si**ng** \ˈsiŋ\, si**ng**er \ˈsiŋ-ər\, fi**ng**er \ˈfiŋ-gər\, i**n**k \ˈiŋk \

ō .... b**o**ne, kn**ow**, b**eau**

ȯ .... s**aw**, **a**ll, gn**aw**, c**au**ght

œ .... French b**oeu**f, German H**ö**lle

œ̄ .... French f**eu**, German H**ö**hle

ȯi .... c**oi**n, destr**oy**

p .... **p**e**pp**er, li**p**

r .... **r**ed, ca**r**, **r**a**r**ity

s .... **s**our**c**e, le**ss**

sh .... as in **sh**y, mi**ss**ion, ma**ch**ine, spe**ci**al (actually, this is a single sound, not two); with a hyphen between, two sounds as in *grasshopper* \ˈgras-ˌhä-pər\

t .... **t**ie, a**tt**ack, la**t**e, la**t**er, la**tt**er

th .... as in **th**in, e**th**er (actually, this is a single sound, not two); with a hyphen between, two sounds as in *knighthood* \ˈnīt-ˌhu̇d\

<u>th</u> .... **th**en, ei**th**er, **th**is (actually, this is a single sound, not two)

ü .... r**u**le, y**ou**th, union \ˈyün-yən\, few \ˈfyü\

u̇ .... p**u**ll, w**oo**d, b**oo**k, curable \ˈkyu̇r-ə-bəl\, fury \ˈfyu̇r-ē\

ue .... German f**ü**llen, h**ü**bsch

ūe .... French r**ue**, German f**üh**len

v .... **v**i**v**id, gi**ve**

w .... **w**e, a**w**ay

y .... **y**ard, **y**oung, cue \ˈkyü\, mute \ˈmyüt\, union \ˈyün-yən\

ʸ .... indicates that during the articulation of the sound represented by the preceding character the front of the tongue has substantially the position it has for the articulation of the first sound of *yard*, as in French *digne* \dēnʸ\

z .... **z**one, rai**se**

zh .... as in vi**si**on, azure \ˈa-zhər\ (actually, this is a single sound, not two); with a hyphen between, two sounds as in *hogshead* \ˈhȯgz-ˌhed, ˈhägz-\

\ .... slant line used in pairs to mark the beginning and end of a transcription: \ˈpen\

ˈ .... mark preceding a syllable with primary (strongest) stress: \ˈpen-mən-ˌship\

ˌ .... mark preceding a syllable with secondary (medium) stress: \ˈpen-mən-ˌship\

\- .... mark of syllable division

( ) .... indicate that what is symbolized between is present in some utterances but not in others: *factory* \ˈfak-t(ə-)rē\

÷ .... indicates that many regard as unacceptable the pronunciation variant immediately following: *cupola* \ˈkyü-pə-lə, ÷-ˌlō\

Currency conversion

Country	Dollar	Pound	S Franc	Yen	HK $	Euro	Cdn $	Aus $
Australia	1.4750	1.7808	1.5770	0.0109	0.1879	1.5767	1.0848	—
Canada	1.3597	1.6416	1.4538	0.0100	0.1732	1.4534	—	0.9218
European Union	0.9355	1.1294	1.0002	0.0069	0.1192	—	0.6880	0.6342
Hong Kong	7.8496	9.4770	8.3962	0.0579	—	8.3908	5.7730	5.3218
Japan	135.59	163.70	144.97	—	17.273	144.94	99.721	91.925
Switzerland	0.9353	1.1292	—	0.0069	0.1192	0.9998	0.6879	0.6341
United Kingdom	0.8283	—	0.8856	0.0061	0.1055	0.8854	0.6092	0.5616
United States	—	1.2073	1.0692	0.0074	0.1274	1.0689	0.7355	0.6780

Country	Currency	U.S. $ Equiv.
Jamaica	dollar	.0065
Japan	yen	.0074
Jordan	dinar	1.4104
Kazakhstan	tenge	.0023
Kenya	shilling	.0079
Kiribati	Australian dollar	.6780
Korea (South)	won	.0008
Korea (North)	won	.0011
Kosovo	euro	1.0689
Kuwait	dinar	3.2595
Kyrgyzstan	som	.0114
Laos	kip	.0001
Latvia	euro	1.0689
Lebanon	pound	.0001
Lesotho	maloti	.0551
Liberia	dollar	.0063
Libya	dinar	.2067
Liechtenstein	Swiss franc	1.0692
Lithuania	euro	1.0689
Luxembourg	euro	1.0689
Macao	pataca	.1237
Macedonia	denar	.0173
Malagasy Republic	ariary	.0002
Malawi	kwacha	.0010
Malaysia	ringgit (dollar)	.2236
Maldive Islands	rafiyaa	.0649
Mali	Community of French Africa (CFA) franc	.0016
Malta	euro	1.0689
Marshall Islands	U.S. dollar	1.000
Mauritania	ouguiya	.0275
Mauritius	rupee	.0216
Mexico	peso	.0548
Micronesia	U.S. dollar	1.000
Moldova	leu	.0529
Monaco	euro	1.0689
Mongolia	tugrik	.0003
Montenegro	euro	1.0689
Montserrat	East Caribbean dollar	.3704
Morocco	dirham	.0966
Mozambique	metical	.0156

Source: xe.com Mar. 1, 2023. Figures reflect values as of Mar. 1, 2023.

COMMON DESIGN TYPES

Pictured in this section are issues where one illustration has been used for a number of countries in the Catalogue. Not included in this section are overprinted stamps or those issues which are illustrated in each country. Because the location of Never Hinged breakpoints varies from country to country, some of the values in the listings below will be for unused stamps that were previously hinged.

EUROPA

Europa, 1956

The design symbolizing the cooperation among the six countries comprising the Coal and Steel Community is illustrated in each country.

Belgium	*496-497*
France	*805-806*
Germany	*748-749*
Italy	*715-716*
Luxembourg	*318-320*
Netherlands	*368-369*

Nos. 496-497 (2)	9.00	.50
Nos. 805-806 (2)	5.25	1.00
Nos. 748-749 (2)	7.40	1.10
Nos. 715-716 (2)	9.25	1.25
Nos. 318-320 (3)	65.50	42.00
Nos. 368-369 (2)	25.75	1.50
Set total (13) Stamps	122.15	47.35

Europa, 1958

"E" and Dove — CD1

European Postal Union at the service of European integration.

1958, Sept. 13

Belgium	527-528
France	889-890
Germany	790-791
Italy	750-751
Luxembourg	341-343
Netherlands	375-376
Saar	317-318

Nos. 527-528 (2)	3.75	.60
Nos. 889-890 (2)	1.65	.55
Nos. 790-791 (2)	2.95	.60
Nos. 750-751 (2)	1.05	.60
Nos. 341-343 (3)	1.35	.90
Nos. 375-376 (2)	1.25	.75
Nos. 317-318 (2)	1.05	2.30
Set total (15) Stamps	13.05	6.30

Europa, 1959

6-Link Enless Chain — CD2

1959, Sept. 19

Belgium	536-537
France	929-930
Germany	805-806
Italy	791-792
Luxembourg	354-355
Netherlands	379-380

Nos. 536-537 (2)	1.55	.60
Nos. 929-930 (2)	1.40	.80
Nos. 805-806 (2)	1.35	.60
Nos. 791-792 (2)	.80	.50
Nos. 354-355 (2)	2.65	1.00
Nos. 379-380 (2)	2.10	1.85
Set total (12) Stamps	9.85	5.35

Europa, 1960

19-Spoke Wheel CD3

First anniverary of the establishment of C.E.P.T. (Conference Europeenne des Administrations des Postes et des Telecommunications.) The spokes symbolize the 19 founding members of the Conference.

1960, Sept.

Belgium	553-554
Denmark	379
Finland	376-377
France	970-971
Germany	818-820
Great Britain	377-378
Greece	688
Iceland	327-328
Ireland	175-176
Italy	809-810
Luxembourg	374-375
Netherlands	385-386
Norway	387
Portugal	866-867
Spain	941-942
Sweden	562-563
Switzerland	400-401
Turkey	1493-1494

Nos. 553-554 (2)	1.25	.55
No. 379 (1)	.55	.50
Nos. 376-377 (2)	1.80	1.40
Nos. 970-971 (2)	.50	.50
Nos. 818-820 (3)	1.90	1.35
Nos. 377-378 (2)	7.00	2.75
No. 688 (1)	4.25	1.75
Nos. 327-328 (2)	1.30	1.85
Nos. 175-176 (2)	47.50	27.50
Nos. 809-810 (2)	.50	.50
Nos. 374-375 (2)	1.00	.80
Nos. 385-386 (2)	2.00	2.00
No. 387 (1)	1.00	.80
Nos. 866-867 (2)	3.00	1.75
Nos. 941-942 (2)	1.50	.75
Nos. 562-563 (2)	1.05	.55
Nos. 400-401 (2)	1.75	.75
Nos. 1493-1494 (2)	2.10	1.35
Set total (34) Stamps	79.95	47.40

Europa, 1961

19 Doves Flying as One — CD4

The 19 doves represent the 19 members of the Conference of European Postal and Telecommunications Administrations C.E.P.T.

1961-62

Belgium	572-573
Cyprus	201-203
France	1005-1006
Germany	844-845
Great Britain	382-384
Greece	718-719
Iceland	340-341
Italy	845-846
Luxembourg	382-383
Netherlands	387-388
Spain	1010-1011
Switzerland	410-411
Turkey	1518-1520

Nos. 572-573 (2)	.75	.50
Nos. 201-203 (3)	*2.10*	*1.20*
Nos. 1005-1006 (2)	.50	.50
Nos. 844-845 (2)	.60	.75
Nos. 382-384 (3)	.75	.75
Nos. 718-719 (2)	.80	.50
Nos. 340-341 (2)	1.10	1.60
Nos. 845-846 (2)	.50	.50
Nos. 382-383 (2)	.55	.55
Nos. 387-388 (2)	.50	.50
Nos. 1010-1011 (2)	.60	.50
Nos. 410-411 (2)	1.90	.60
Nos. 1518-1520 (3)	1.55	.90
Set total (29) Stamps	12.20	9.35

Europa, 1962

Young Tree with 19 Leaves CD5

The 19 leaves represent the 19 original members of C.E.P.T.

1962-63

Belgium	582-583
Cyprus	219-221
France	1045-1046
Germany	852-853
Greece	739-740
Iceland	348-349
Ireland	184-185
Italy	860-861
Luxembourg	386-387
Netherlands	394-395
Norway	414-415
Switzerland	416-417
Turkey	1553-1555

Nos. 582-583 (2)	.65	.65
Nos. 219-221 (3)	*76.25*	*6.75*
Nos. 1045-1046 (2)	.60	.50
Nos. 852-853 (2)	.65	.75
Nos. 739-740 (2)	2.00	1.15
Nos. 348-349 (2)	.85	.85
Nos. 184-185 (2)	2.00	.50
Nos. 860-861 (2)	1.00	.55
Nos. 386-387 (2)	.75	.55
Nos. 394-395 (2)	1.35	.90
Nos. 414-415 (2)	1.75	1.70
Nos. 416-417 (2)	1.65	1.00
Nos. 1553-1555 (3)	*2.05*	1.10
Set total (28) Stamps	91.55	16.95

Europa, 1963

Stylized Links, Symbolizing Unity — CD6

1963, Sept.

Belgium	598-599
Cyprus	229-231
Finland	419
France	1074-1075
Germany	867-868
Greece	768-769
Iceland	357-358
Ireland	188-189
Italy	880-881
Luxembourg	403-404
Netherlands	416-417
Norway	441-442
Switzerland	429
Turkey	1602-1603

Nos. 598-599 (2)	1.60	.55
Nos. 229-231 (3)	*64.00*	*9.40*
No. 419 (1)	1.25	.55
Nos. 1074-1075 (2)	.60	.50
Nos. 867-868 (2)	.50	.55
Nos. 768-769 (2)	4.65	1.65
Nos. 357-358 (2)	1.20	1.20
Nos. 188-189 (2)	4.75	3.25
Nos. 880-881 (2)	.50	.50
Nos. 403-404 (2)	.75	.55
Nos. 416-417 (2)	1.30	1.00
Nos. 441-442 (2)	2.60	2.40
No. 429 (1)	.90	.60
Nos. 1602-1603 (2)	1.20	.50
Set total (27) Stamps	85.80	23.20

Europa, 1964

Symbolic Daisy — CD7

5th anniversary of the establishment of C.E.P.T. The 22 petals of the flower symbolize the 22 members of the Conference.

1964, Sept.

Austria	738
Belgium	614-615
Cyprus	244-246
France	1109-1110
Germany	897-898
Greece	801-802
Iceland	367-368
Ireland	196-197
Italy	894-895
Luxembourg	411-412
Monaco	590-591
Netherlands	428-429
Norway	458
Portugal	931-933
Spain	1262-1263
Switzerland	438-439
Turkey	1628-1629

No. 738 (1)	1.10	.25
Nos. 614-615 (2)	1.40	.60
Nos. 244-246 (3)	*32.25*	*5.10*
Nos. 1109-1110 (2)	.50	.50
Nos. 897-898 (2)	.50	.50
Nos. 801-802 (2)	4.15	1.55
Nos. 367-368 (2)	1.40	1.15
Nos. 196-197 (2)	17.00	4.25
Nos. 894-895 (2)	.50	.50
Nos. 411-412 (2)	.75	.55
Nos. 590-591 (2)	2.50	.70
Nos. 428-429 (2)	.75	.60
No. 458 (1)	3.50	3.50
Nos. 931-933 (3)	*10.00*	*2.00*
Nos. 1262-1263 (2)	1.15	.80
Nos. 438-439 (2)	1.65	.50
Nos. 1628-1629 (2)	2.00	.80
Set total (34) Stamps	81.10	23.85

Europa, 1965

Leaves and "Fruit" CD8

1965

Belgium	636-637
Cyprus	262-264
Finland	437
France	1131-1132
Germany	934-935
Greece	833-834
Iceland	375-376
Ireland	204-205
Italy	915-916
Luxembourg	432-433
Monaco	616-617
Netherlands	438-439
Norway	475-476
Portugal	958-960
Switzerland	469
Turkey	1665-1666

Nos. 636-637 (2)	.50	.50
Nos. 262-264 (3)	*25.35*	*6.00*
No. 437 (1)	1.25	.55
Nos. 1131-1132 (2)	.70	.55
Nos. 934-935 (2)	.50	.50
Nos. 833-834 (2)	2.25	1.15
Nos. 375-376 (2)	2.50	1.75
Nos. 204-205 (2)	16.00	3.35
Nos. 915-916 (2)	.50	.50
Nos. 432-433 (2)	.75	.55
Nos. 616-617 (2)	3.25	1.65
Nos. 438-439 (2)	.55	.50
Nos. 475-476 (2)	2.40	1.90
Nos. 958-960 (3)	*10.00*	*2.75*
No. 469 (1)	1.15	.50
Nos. 1665-1666 (2)	2.00	1.25
Set total (32) Stamps	69.65	23.95

Europa, 1966

Symbolic Sailboat — CD9

1966, Sept.

Andorra, French	172
Belgium	675-676
Cyprus	275-277
France	1163-1164
Germany	963-964

Greece	862-863
Iceland	384-385
Ireland	216-217
Italy	942-943
Liechtenstein	415
Luxembourg	440-441
Monaco	639-640
Netherlands	441-442
Norway	496-497
Portugal	980-982
Switzerland	477-478
Turkey	1718-1719

No. 172 (1)	3.00	3.00
Nos. 675-676 (2)	.80	.50
Nos. 275-277 (3)	*4.75*	*2.75*
Nos. 1163-1164 (2)	.55	.50
Nos. 963-964 (2)	.50	.55
Nos. 862-863 (2)	2.10	1.05
Nos. 384-385 (2)	4.50	3.50
Nos. 216-217 (2)	6.75	2.00
Nos. 942-943 (2)	.50	.50
No. 415 (1)	.40	.35
Nos. 440-441 (2)	.70	.55
Nos. 639-640 (2)	2.00	.65
Nos. 441-442 (2)	.85	.50
Nos. 496-497 (2)	2.35	2.15
Nos. 980-982 (3)	*9.75*	2.25
Nos. 477-478 (2)	1.40	.60
Nos. 1718-1719 (2)	3.35	1.75
Set total (34) Stamps	44.25	23.15

Europa, 1967

Cogwheels
CD10

1967

Andorra, French	174-175
Belgium	688-689
Cyprus	297-299
France	1178-1179
Germany	969-970
Greece	891-892
Iceland	389-390
Ireland	232-233
Italy	951-952
Liechtenstein	420
Luxembourg	449-450
Monaco	669-670
Netherlands	444-447
Norway	504-505
Portugal	994-996
Spain	1465-1466
Switzerland	482
Turkey	B120-B121

Nos. 174-175 (2)	10.75	6.25
Nos. 688-689 (2)	1.05	.55
Nos. 297-299 (3)	*4.25*	*2.50*
Nos. 1178-1179 (2)	.55	.50
Nos. 969-970 (2)	.55	.55
Nos. 891-892 (2)	3.05	.85
Nos. 389-390 (2)	3.00	2.00
Nos. 232-233 (2)	5.90	2.30
Nos. 951-952 (2)	.60	.50
No. 420 (1)	.45	.40
Nos. 449-450 (2)	1.00	.70
Nos. 669-670 (2)	2.75	.70
Nos. 444-447 (4)	2.70	2.05
Nos. 504-505 (2)	2.00	1.80
Nos. 994-996 (3)	*9.50*	1.85
Nos. 1465-1466 (2)	.50	.50
No. 482 (1)	.60	.30
Nos. B120-B121 (2)	2.50	2.00
Set total (38) Stamps	51.70	26.30

Europa, 1968

Golden Key
with
C.E.P.T.
Emblem
CD11

1968

Andorra, French	182-183
Belgium	705-706
Cyprus	314-316
France	1209-1210
Germany	983-984
Greece	916-917
Iceland	395-396
Ireland	242-243
Italy	979-980
Liechtenstein	442
Luxembourg	466-467
Monaco	689-691
Netherlands	452-453
Portugal	1019-1021
San Marino	687
Spain	1526
Switzerland	488
Turkey	1775-1776

Nos. 182-183 (2)	16.50	10.00
Nos. 705-706 (2)	1.25	.50
Nos. 314-316 (3)	*2.90*	*2.50*
Nos. 1209-1210 (2)	.85	.55
Nos. 983-984 (2)	.50	.55
Nos. 916-917 (2)	3.10	1.45
Nos. 395-396 (2)	3.00	2.20
Nos. 242-243 (2)	3.30	2.25
Nos. 979-980 (2)	.50	.50
No. 442 (1)	.45	.40
Nos. 466-467 (2)	.80	.70
Nos. 689-691 (3)	*5.40*	.95
Nos. 452-453 (2)	1.05	.70
Nos. 1019-1021 (3)	*9.75*	2.10
No. 687 (1)	.55	.35
No. 1526 (1)	.25	.25
No. 488 (1)	.40	.25
Nos. 1775-1776 (2)	2.50	1.25
Set total (35) Stamps	53.05	27.45

Europa, 1969

"EUROPA"
and "CEPT"
CD12

Tenth anniversary of C.E.P.T.

1969

Andorra, French	188-189
Austria	837
Belgium	718-719
Cyprus	326-328
Denmark	458
Finland	483
France	1245-1246
Germany	996-997
Great Britain	585
Greece	947-948
Iceland	406-407
Ireland	270-271
Italy	1000-1001
Liechtenstein	453
Luxembourg	475-476
Monaco	722-724
Netherlands	475-476
Norway	533-534
Portugal	1038-1040
San Marino	701-702
Spain	1567
Sweden	814-816
Switzerland	500-501
Turkey	1799-1800
Vatican	470-472
Yugoslavia	1003-1004

Nos. 188-189 (2)	18.50	12.00
No. 837 (1)	.55	.25
Nos. 718-719 (2)	.75	.50
Nos. 326-328 (3)	*3.00*	*2.25*
No. 458 (1)	.75	.75
No. 483 (1)	2.50	.60
Nos. 1245-1246 (2)	.55	.50
Nos. 996-997 (2)	.70	.50
No. 585 (1)	.25	.25
Nos. 947-948 (2)	4.00	1.25
Nos. 406-407 (2)	4.20	2.40
Nos. 270-271 (2)	3.50	2.00
Nos. 1000-1001 (2)	.50	.50
No. 453 (1)	.45	.45
Nos. 475-476 (2)	.95	.50
Nos. 722-724 (3)	*10.50*	2.00
Nos. 475-476 (2)	1.35	1.00
Nos. 533-534 (2)	2.20	1.95
Nos. 1038-1040 (3)	17.75	2.40
Nos. 701-702 (2)	.90	.90
No. 1567 (1)	.25	.25
Nos. 814-816 (3)	4.00	2.85
Nos. 500-501 (2)	1.85	1.00
Nos. 1799-1800 (2)	2.50	1.65
Nos. 470-472 (3)	.75	.75
Nos. 1003-1004 (2)	4.00	4.00
Set total (51) Stamps	87.20	43.45

Europa, 1970

Interwoven
Threads
CD13

1970

Andorra, French	196-197
Belgium	741-742
Cyprus	340-342
France	1271-1272
Germany	1018-1019
Greece	985, 987
Iceland	420-421
Ireland	279-281
Italy	1013-1014
Liechtenstein	470
Luxembourg	489-490
Monaco	768-770
Netherlands	483-484
Portugal	1060-1062
San Marino	729-730
Spain	1607
Switzerland	515-516
Turkey	1848-1849
Yugoslavia	1024-1025

Nos. 196-197 (2)	20.00	8.50
Nos. 741-742 (2)	1.10	.55
Nos. 340-342 (3)	*2.70*	*2.75*
Nos. 1271-1272 (2)	.65	.50
Nos. 1018-1019 (2)	.60	.50
Nos. 985,987 (2)	6.35	1.60
Nos. 420-421 (2)	6.00	4.00
Nos. 279-281 (3)	7.50	2.50
Nos. 1013-1014 (2)	.50	.50
No. 470 (1)	.45	.45
Nos. 489-490 (2)	.80	.55
Nos. 768-770 (3)	*6.35*	2.10
Nos. 483-484 (2)	1.30	1.15
Nos. 1060-1062 (3)	*9.75*	2.35
Nos. 729-730 (2)	.90	.55
No. 1607 (1)	.25	.25
Nos. 515-516 (2)	1.85	.70
Nos. 1848-1849 (2)	2.50	1.50
Nos. 1024-1025 (2)	.80	.80
Set total (40) Stamps	70.35	31.80

Europa, 1971

"Fraternity,
Cooperation,
Common
Effort"
CD14

1971

Andorra, French	205-206
Belgium	803-804
Cyprus	365-367
Finland	504
France	1304
Germany	1064-1065
Greece	1029-1030
Iceland	429-430
Ireland	305-306
Italy	1038-1039
Liechtenstein	485
Luxembourg	500-501
Malta	425-427
Monaco	797-799
Netherlands	488-489
Portugal	1094-1096
San Marino	749-750
Spain	1675-1676
Switzerland	531-532
Turkey	1876-1877
Yugoslavia	1052-1053

Nos. 205-206 (2)	20.00	7.75
Nos. 803-804 (2)	1.30	.55
Nos. 365-367 (3)	*2.60*	*3.25*
No. 504 (1)	2.50	.50
No. 1304 (1)	.45	.40
Nos. 1064-1065 (2)	.60	.50
Nos. 1029-1030 (2)	4.00	1.80
Nos. 429-430 (2)	5.00	3.75
Nos. 305-306 (2)	4.50	1.50
Nos. 1038-1039 (2)	.65	.50
No. 485 (1)	.45	.45
Nos. 500-501 (2)	1.00	.65
Nos. 425-427 (3)	*.80*	*.80*
Nos. 797-799 (3)	*15.00*	2.80
Nos. 488-489 (2)	1.20	.95
Nos. 1094-1096 (3)	*9.75*	1.75
Nos. 749-750 (2)	.65	.55
Nos. 1675-1676 (2)	.75	.55
Nos. 531-532 (2)	1.85	.65
Nos. 1876-1877 (2)	2.50	1.25
Nos. 1052-1053 (2)	.50	.50
Set total (43) Stamps	76.05	31.40

Europa, 1972

Sparkles, Symbolic
of Communications
CD15

1972

Andorra, French	210-211
Andorra, Spanish	62
Belgium	825-826
Cyprus	380-382
Finland	512-513
France	1341
Germany	1089-1090
Greece	1049-1050
Iceland	439-440
Ireland	316-317
Italy	1065-1066
Liechtenstein	504
Luxembourg	512-513
Malta	450-453
Monaco	831-832
Netherlands	494-495
Portugal	1141-1143
San Marino	771-772
Spain	1718
Switzerland	544-545
Turkey	1907-1908
Yugoslavia	1100-1101

Nos. 210-211 (2)	21.00	7.00
No. 62 (1)	60.00	60.00
Nos. 825-826 (2)	.95	.55
Nos. 380-382 (3)	*5.95*	*4.25*
Nos. 512-513 (2)	4.00	1.00
No. 1341 (1)	.50	.35
Nos. 1089-1090 (2)	1.10	.50
Nos. 1049-1050 (2)	2.00	1.55
Nos. 439-440 (2)	2.90	2.65
Nos. 316-317 (2)	13.00	4.50
Nos. 1065-1066 (2)	.55	.50
No. 504 (1)	.45	.45
Nos. 512-513 (2)	.95	.65
Nos. 450-453 (4)	1.05	1.40
Nos. 831-832 (2)	5.00	1.40
Nos. 494-495 (2)	1.20	.90
Nos. 1141-1143 (3)	*9.75*	1.50
Nos. 771-772 (2)	.70	.50
No. 1718 (1)	.50	.40
Nos. 544-545 (2)	1.65	.60
Nos. 1907-1908 (2)	4.00	2.00
Nos. 1100-1101 (2)	1.20	1.20
Set total (44) Stamps	138.40	93.85

Europa, 1973

Post Horn
and Arrows
CD16

1973

Andorra, French	219-220
Andorra, Spanish	76
Belgium	839-840
Cyprus	396-398
Finland	526
France	1367
Germany	1114-1115
Greece	1090-1092
Iceland	447-448
Ireland	329-330
Italy	1108-1109
Liechtenstein	528-529
Luxembourg	523-524
Malta	469-471
Monaco	866-867
Netherlands	504-505
Norway	604-605
Portugal	1170-1172
San Marino	802-803
Spain	1753
Switzerland	580-581
Turkey	1935-1936
Yugoslavia	1138-1139

Nos. 219-220 (2)	20.00	11.00
No. 76 (1)	1.25	.85
Nos. 839-840 (2)	1.00	.65
Nos. 396-398 (3)	*4.25*	*3.85*
No. 526 (1)	1.25	.55
No. 1367 (1)	1.25	.75
Nos. 1114-1115 (2)	.85	.50
Nos. 1090-1092 (3)	2.10	1.40
Nos. 447-448 (2)	6.65	3.35

Nos. 329-330 (2)	5.25	2.00
Nos. 1108-1109 (2)	.50	.50
Nos. 528-529 (2)	.60	.60
Nos. 523-524 (2)	.90	.75
Nos. 469-471 (3)	.90	1.20
Nos. 866-867 (2)	15.00	2.40
Nos. 504-505 (2)	1.20	.95
Nos. 604-605 (2)	4.00	1.80
Nos. 1170-1172 (3)	*13.00*	2.15
Nos. 802-803 (2)	*1.00*	.60
No. 1753 (1)	.35	.25
Nos. 580-581 (2)	1.55	.60
Nos. 1935-1936 (2)	4.15	2.25
Nos. 1138-1139 (2)	1.15	1.10
Set total (46) Stamps	88.15	40.05

Europa, 2000

CD17

2000

Albania	2621-2622
Andorra, French	522
Andorra, Spanish	262
Armenia	610-611
Austria	1814
Azerbaijan	698-699
Belarus	350
Belgium	1818
Bosnia & Herzegovina (Moslem)	358
Bosnia & Herzegovina (Serb)	111-112
Croatia	428-429
Cyprus	959
Czech Republic	3120
Denmark	1189
Estonia	394
Faroe Islands	376
Finland	1129
Aland Islands	166
France	2771
Georgia	228-229
Germany	2086-2087
Gibraltar	837-840
Great Britain (Jersey)	935-936
Great Britain (Isle of Man)	883
Greece	1959
Greenland	363
Hungary	3699-3700
Iceland	910
Ireland	1230-1231
Italy	2349
Latvia	504
Liechtenstein	1178
Lithuania	668
Luxembourg	1035
Macedonia	187
Malta	1011-1012
Moldova	355
Monaco	2161-2162
Poland	3519
Portugal	2358
Portugal (Azores)	455
Portugal (Madeira)	208
Romania	4370
Russia	6589
San Marino	1480
Slovakia	355
Slovenia	424
Spain	3036
Sweden	2394
Switzerland	1074
Turkey	2762
Turkish Rep. of Northern Cyprus	500
Ukraine	379
Vatican City	1152

Nos. 2621-2622 (2)	9.50	9.50
No. 522 (1)	2.00	1.00
No. 262 (1)	1.75	.80
Nos. 610-611 (2)	4.75	4.75
No. 1814 (1)	1.25	1.25
Nos. 698-699 (2)	6.00	6.00
No. 350 (1)	1.75	1.75
No. 1818 (1)	1.40	.60
No. 358 (1)	4.75	4.75
Nos. 111-112 (2)	110.00	110.00
Nos. 428-429 (2)	6.25	6.25
No. 959 (1)	2.10	1.40
No. 3120 (1)	1.20	.40
No. 1189 (1)	3.50	2.25
No. 394 (1)	1.25	1.25
No. 376 (1)	2.40	2.40
No. 1129 (1)	2.00	.60
No. 166 (1)	1.10	1.20
No. 2771 (1)	1.25	.40
Nos. 228-229 (2)	9.00	9.00
Nos. 2086-2087 (2)	4.35	2.10
Nos. 837-840 (4)	5.50	5.30
Nos. 935-936 (2)	2.40	2.40
No. 883 (1)	1.75	1.75
No. 363 (1)	1.90	1.90
Nos. 3699-3700 (2)	6.50	2.50
No. 910 (1)	1.60	1.60
Nos. 1230-1231 (2)	4.35	4.35
No. 2349 (1)	1.50	.40
No. 504 (1)	5.00	2.40
No. 1178 (1)	2.25	1.75
No. 668 (1)	1.50	1.50
No. 1035 (1)	1.40	.85
No. 187 (1)	3.00	3.00
Nos. 1011-1012 (2)	4.35	4.35
No. 355 (1)	3.50	3.50
Nos. 2161-2162 (2)	2.80	1.40
No. 3519 (1)	1.25	.75
No. 2358 (1)	1.25	.65
No. 455 (1)	1.25	.50
No. 208 (1)	1.25	.50
No. 4370 (1)	2.50	1.25
No. 6589 (1)	4.00	.85
No. 1480 (1)	1.00	1.00
No. 355 (1)	1.60	.80
No. 424 (1)	3.25	3.25
No. 3036 (1)	1.00	.40
No. 2394 (1)	3.00	1.50
No. 1074 (1)	2.10	1.05
No. 2762 (1)	2.75	2.00
No. 500 (1)	2.50	2.50
No. 379 (1)	4.50	3.00
No. 1152 (1)	1.75	1.75
Set total (68) Stamps	261.80	228.35

The Gibraltar stamps are similar to the stamp illustrated, but none have the design shown above. All other sets listed above include at least one stamp with the design shown, but some include stamps with entirely different designs. Bulgaria Nos. 4131-4132, Guernsey Nos. 802-803 and Yugoslavia Nos. 2485-2486 are Europa stamps with completely different designs.

PORTUGAL & COLONIES
Vasco da Gama

Fleet Departing CD20

Fleet Arriving at Calicut — CD21

Embarking at Rastello CD22

Muse of History CD23

San Gabriel, da Gama and Camoens CD24

Archangel Gabriel, the Patron Saint CD25

Flagship San Gabriel — CD26

Vasco da Gama — CD27

Fourth centenary of Vasco da Gama's discovery of the route to India.

1898

Azores	93-100
Macao	67-74
Madeira	37-44
Portugal	147-154
Port. Africa	1-8
Port. Congo	75-98
Port. India	189-196
St. Thomas & Prince Islands	170-193
Timor	45-52

Nos. 93-100 (8)	113.50	73.50
Nos. 67-74 (8)	250.25	170.25
Nos. 37-44 (8)	60.55	37.25
Nos. 147-154 (8)	155.00	50.25
Nos. 1-8 (8)	44.00	29.25
Nos. 75-98 (24)	78.50	64.65
Nos. 189-196 (8)	25.25	15.50
Nos. 170-193 (24)	56.30	43.00
Nos. 45-52 (8)	33.50	23.25
Set total (104) Stamps	816.85	506.90

Pombal
POSTAL TAX
POSTAL TAX DUES

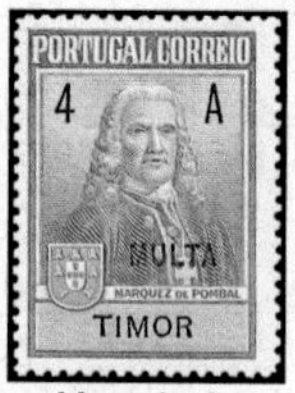

Marquis de Pombal — CD28

Planning Reconstruction of Lisbon, 1755 — CD29

Pombal Monument, Lisbon — CD30

Sebastiao Jose de Carvalho e Mello, Marquis de Pombal (1699-1782), statesman, rebuilt Lisbon after earthquake of 1755. Tax was for the erection of Pombal monument. Obligatory on all mail on certain days throughout the year. Postal Tax Dues are inscribed "Multa."

1925

Angola	RA1-RA3, RAJ1-RAJ3
Azores	RA9-RA11, RAJ2-RAJ4
Cape Verde	RA1-RA3, RAJ1-RAJ3
Macao	RA1-RA3, RAJ1-RAJ3
Madeira	RA1-RA3, RAJ1-RAJ3
Mozambique	RA1-RA3, RAJ1-RAJ3
Nyassa	RA1-RA3, RAJ1-RAJ3
Portugal	RA11-RA13, RAJ2-RAJ4
Port. Guinea	RA1-RA3, RAJ1-RAJ3
Port. India	RA1-RA3, RAJ1-RAJ3
St. Thomas & Prince Islands	RA1-RA3, RAJ1-RAJ3
Timor	RA1-RA3, RAJ1-RAJ3

Nos. RA1-RA3,RAJ1-RAJ3 (6)	6.60	6.60
Nos. RA9-RA11,RAJ2-RAJ4 (6)	6.60	6.60
Nos. RA1-RA3,RAJ1-RAJ3 (6)	7.80	7.65
Nos. RA1-RA3,RAJ1-RAJ3 (6)	36.50	17.25
Nos. RA1-RA3,RAJ1-RAJ3 (6)	7.95	*14.70*
Nos. RA1-RA3,RAJ1-RAJ3 (6)	3.75	3.60
Nos. RA1-RA3,RAJ1-RAJ3 (6)	85.50	76.50
Nos. RA11-RA13,RAJ2-RAJ4 (6)	5.95	5.20
Nos. RA1-RA3,RAJ1-RAJ3 (6)	5.10	4.65
Nos. RA1-RA3,RAJ1-RAJ3 (6)	3.45	3.45
Nos. RA1-RA3,RAJ1-RAJ3 (6)	4.50	4.50
Nos. RA1-RA3,RAJ1-RAJ3 (6)	3.90	3.45
Set total (72) Stamps	177.60	154.15

Vasco da Gama CD34

Mousinho de Albuquerque CD35

Dam CD36

Prince Henry the Navigator CD37

Affonso de Albuquerque CD38

Plane over Globe CD39

1938-39

Angola	274-291, C1-C9
Cape Verde	234-251, C1-C9
Macao	289-305, C7-C15
Mozambique	270-287, C1-C9
Port. Guinea	233-250. C1-C9
Port. India	439-453, C1-C8
St. Thomas & Prince Islands	302-319, 323-340, C1-C18
Timor	223-239, C1-C9

Nos. 274-291,C1-C9 (27)	129.40	22.85
Nos. 234-251,C1-C9 (27)	122.40	38.30
Nos. 289-305,C7-C15 (26)	889.60	338.55
Nos. 270-287,C1-C9 (27)	95.71	15.95
Nos. 233-250,C1-C9 (27)	130.20	49.15
Nos. 439-453,C1-C8 (23)	82.75	30.95
Nos. 302-319,323-340,C1-C18 (54)	467.70	244.80
Nos. 223-239,C1-C9 (26)	213.85	104.90
Set total (237) Stamps	2,132.	845.45

Lady of Fatima

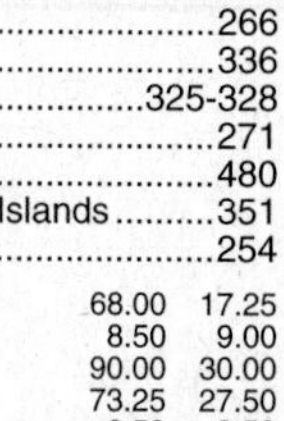

Our Lady of the Rosary, Fatima, Portugal — CD40

1948-49

Angola	315-318
Cape Verde	266
Macao	336
Mozambique	325-328
Port. Guinea	271
Port. India	480
St. Thomas & Prince Islands	351
Timor	254

Nos. 315-318 (4)	68.00	17.25
No. 266 (1)	8.50	9.00
No. 336 (1)	90.00	30.00
Nos. 325-328 (4)	73.25	27.50
No. 271 (1)	6.50	3.50
No. 480 (1)	4.50	3.00
No. 351 (1)	8.50	7.00
No. 254 (1)	6.00	12.50
Set total (14) Stamps	265.25	109.75

A souvenir sheet of 9 stamps was issued in 1951 to mark the extension of the 1950 Holy Year. The sheet contains: Angola No. 316, Cape Verde No. 266, Macao No. 336, Mozambique No. 325, Portuguese Guinea No. 271, Portuguese India Nos. 480, 485, St. Thomas & Prince Islands No. 351, Timor No. 254. The sheet also contains a portrait of Pope Pius XII and is inscribed "Encerramento do

Ano Santo, Fatima 1951." It was sold for 11 escudos.

Holy Year

Church Bells and Dove
CD41

Angel Holding Candelabra
CD42

Holy Year, 1950.

1950-51

Angola	331-332
Cape Verde	268-269
Macao	339-340
Mozambique	330-331
Port. Guinea	273-274
Port. India	490-491, 496-503
St. Thomas & Prince Islands	353-354
Timor	258-259

Nos. 331-332 (2)	7.60	1.35
Nos. 268-269 (2)	7.35	4.75
Nos. 339-340 (2)	110.00	34.00
Nos. 330-331 (2)	3.00	1.60
Nos. 273-274 (2)	11.25	3.50
Nos. 490-491,496-503 (10)	10.40	4.95
Nos. 353-354 (2)	7.75	4.90
Nos. 258-259 (2)	8.75	5.00
Set total (24) Stamps	166.10	60.05

A souvenir sheet of 8 stamps was issued in 1951 to mark the extension of the Holy Year. The sheet contains: Angola No. 331, Cape Verde No. 269, Macao No. 340, Mozambique No. 331, Portuguese Guinea No. 275, Portuguese India No. 490, St. Thomas & Prince Islands No. 354, Timor No. 258, some with colors changed. The sheet contains doves and is inscribed 'Encerramento do Ano Santo, Fatima 1951.' It was sold for 17 escudos.

Holy Year Conclusion

Our Lady of Fatima — CD43

Conclusion of Holy Year. Sheets contain alternate vertical rows of stamps and labels bearing quotation from Pope Pius XII, different for each colony.

1951

Angola	357
Cape Verde	270
Macao	352
Mozambique	356
Port. Guinea	275
Port. India	506
St. Thomas & Prince Islands	355
Timor	270

No. 357 (1)	5.25	1.50
No. 270 (1)	1.75	1.25
No. 352 (1)	110.00	23.00
No. 356 (1)	3.25	1.75
No. 275 (1)	1.75	.90
No. 506 (1)	2.50	1.00
No. 355 (1)	3.00	2.00
No. 270 (1)	3.75	2.75
Set total (8) Stamps	131.25	34.15

Medical Congress

CD44

First National Congress of Tropical Medicine, Lisbon, 1952. Each stamp has a different design.

1952

Angola	358
Cape Verde	287
Macao	364
Mozambique	359
Port. Guinea	276
Port. India	516
St. Thomas & Prince Islands	356
Timor	271

No. 358 (1)	1.50	.50
No. 287 (1)	.95	.75
No. 364 (1)	20.00	7.00
No. 359 (1)	1.90	.90
No. 276 (1)	1.00	.45
No. 516 (1)	5.50	2.00
No. 356 (1)	.35	.30
No. 271 (1)	2.00	1.60
Set total (8) Stamps	33.20	13.50

Postage Due Stamps

CD45

1952

Angola	J37-J42
Cape Verde	J31-J36
Macao	J53-J58
Mozambique	J51-J56
Port. Guinea	J40-J45
Port. India	J47-J52
St. Thomas & Prince Islands	J52-J57
Timor	J31-J36

Nos. J37-J42 (6)	4.30	2.55
Nos. J31-J36 (6)	2.80	2.30
Nos. J53-J58 (6)	27.80	12.05
Nos. J51-J56 (6)	2.40	1.95
Nos. J40-J45 (6)	2.55	2.55
Nos. J47-J52 (6)	6.10	6.10
Nos. J52-J57 (6)	3.85	3.85
Nos. J31-J36 (6)	4.00	2.35
Set total (48) Stamps	53.80	33.70

Sao Paulo

Father Manuel da Nobrega and View of Sao Paulo — CD46

Founding of Sao Paulo, Brazil, 400th anniv.

1954

Angola	385
Cape Verde	297
Macao	382
Mozambique	395
Port. Guinea	291
Port. India	530
St. Thomas & Prince Islands	369
Timor	279

No. 385 (1)	.80	.50
No. 297 (1)	.95	.80
No. 382 (1)	30.00	6.00
No. 395 (1)	.75	.30
No. 291 (1)	.35	.25
No. 530 (1)	.80	.40
No. 369 (1)	.70	.50
No. 279 (1)	2.00	1.40
Set total (8) Stamps	36.35	10.15

Tropical Medicine Congress

CD47

Sixth International Congress for Tropical Medicine and Malaria, Lisbon, Sept. 1958. Each stamp shows a different plant.

1958

Angola	409
Cape Verde	303
Macao	392
Mozambique	404
Port. Guinea	295
Port. India	569
St. Thomas & Prince Islands	371
Timor	289

No. 409 (1)	3.50	1.10
No. 303 (1)	6.75	3.25
No. 392 (1)	13.00	6.00
No. 404 (1)	3.50	1.50
No. 295 (1)	3.00	1.10
No. 569 (1)	1.75	.75
No. 371 (1)	2.75	2.00
No. 289 (1)	5.50	4.25
Set total (8) Stamps	39.75	19.95

Sports

CD48

Each stamp shows a different sport.

1962

Angola	433-438
Cape Verde	320-325
Macao	394-399
Mozambique	424-429
Port. Guinea	299-304
St. Thomas & Prince Islands	374-379
Timor	313-318

Nos. 433-438 (6)	5.50	3.20
Nos. 320-325 (6)	16.05	7.40
Nos. 394-399 (6)	129.85	28.95
Nos. 424-429 (6)	6.55	2.45
Nos. 299-304 (6)	6.00	3.00
Nos. 374-379 (6)	6.75	3.20
Nos. 313-318 (6)	11.65	5.90
Set total (42) Stamps	182.35	54.10

Anti-Malaria

Anopheles Funestus and Malaria Eradication Symbol — CD49

World Health Organization drive to eradicate malaria.

1962

Angola	439
Cape Verde	326
Macao	400
Mozambique	430
Port. Guinea	305
St. Thomas & Prince Islands	380
Timor	319

No. 439 (1)	1.75	.90
No. 326 (1)	1.90	1.60
No. 400 (1)	12.00	4.00
No. 430 (1)	2.00	.50
No. 305 (1)	1.25	.45
No. 380 (1)	2.25	1.25
No. 319 (1)	2.25	1.40
Set total (7) Stamps	23.40	10.10

Airline Anniversary

Map of Africa, Super Constellation and Jet Liner — CD50

Tenth anniversary of Transportes Aereos Portugueses (TAP).

1963

Angola	490
Cape Verde	327
Mozambique	434
Port. Guinea	318
St. Thomas & Prince Islands	381

No. 490 (1)	1.00	.35
No. 327 (1)	1.50	1.10
No. 434 (1)	.55	.25
No. 318 (1)	.65	.35
No. 381 (1)	.80	.50
Set total (5) Stamps	4.50	2.55

National Overseas Bank

Antonio Teixeira de Sousa — CD51

Centenary of the National Overseas Bank of Portugal.

1964, May 16

Angola	509
Cape Verde	328
Port. Guinea	319
St. Thomas & Prince Islands	382
Timor	320

No. 509 (1)	.90	.30
No. 328 (1)	1.50	1.30
No. 319 (1)	.65	.40
No. 382 (1)	.70	.50
No. 320 (1)	1.50	1.30
Set total (5) Stamps	5.25	3.80

ITU

ITU Emblem and the Archangel Gabriel — CD52

International Communications Union, Cent.

1965, May 17

Angola	511
Cape Verde	329
Macao	402
Mozambique	464
Port. Guinea	320
St. Thomas & Prince Islands	383
Timor	321

No. 511 (1)	1.25	.65
No. 329 (1)	2.90	2.25
No. 402 (1)	9.00	3.00
No. 464 (1)	.65	.25
No. 320 (1)	1.90	.75
No. 383 (1)	2.00	1.00
No. 321 (1)	2.20	1.40
Set total (7) Stamps	19.90	9.30

National Revolution

CD53

40th anniv. of the National Revolution. Different buildings on each stamp.

1966, May 28

Angola	525
Cape Verde	338
Macao	403
Mozambique	465
Port. Guinea	329
St. Thomas & Prince Islands	392
Timor	322

No. 525 (1)	.50	.25
No. 338 (1)	.85	.75
No. 403 (1)	9.00	3.75
No. 465 (1)	.65	.30
No. 329 (1)	.55	.35
No. 392 (1)	.80	.50
No. 322 (1)	2.40	1.40
Set total (7) Stamps	14.75	7.30

Navy Club

CD54

Centenary of Portugal's Navy Club. Each stamp has a different design.

1967, Jan. 31

Angola	527-528
Cape Verde	339-340
Macao	412-413
Mozambique	478-479
Port. Guinea	330-331
St. Thomas & Prince Islands	393-394
Timor	323-324

Nos. 527-528 (2)	1.75	.75
Nos. 339-340 (2)	2.70	2.30
Nos. 412-413 (2)	18.00	4.70
Nos. 478-479 (2)	1.75	.65
Nos. 330-331 (2)	1.20	.90
Nos. 393-394 (2)	3.30	1.30
Nos. 323-324 (2)	4.25	2.40
Set total (14) Stamps	32.95	13.00

Admiral Coutinho

CD55

Centenary of the birth of Admiral Carlos Viegas Gago Coutinho (1869-1959), explorer and aviation pioneer. Each stamp has a different design.

1969, Feb. 17

Angola	547
Cape Verde	355
Macao	417
Mozambique	484
Port. Guinea	335
St. Thomas & Prince Islands	397
Timor	335

No. 547 (1)	.85	.35
No. 355 (1)	.60	.25
No. 417 (1)	7.50	2.25
No. 484 (1)	.30	.25
No. 335 (1)	.35	.25
No. 397 (1)	.60	.35
No. 335 (1)	2.50	1.40
Set total (7) Stamps	12.70	5.10

Administration Reform

Luiz Augusto Rebello da Silva — CD56

Centenary of the administration reforms of the overseas territories.

1969, Sept. 25

Angola	549
Cape Verde	357
Macao	419
Mozambique	491
Port. Guinea	337
St. Thomas & Prince Islands	399
Timor	338

No. 549 (1)	.35	.25
No. 357 (1)	.65	.40
No. 419 (1)	12.50	2.00
No. 491 (1)	.30	.25
No. 337 (1)	.25	.25
No. 399 (1)	.45	.45
No. 338 (1)	1.40	.70
Set total (7) Stamps	15.90	4.30

Marshal Carmona

CD57

Birth centenary of Marshal Antonio Oscar Carmona de Fragoso (1869-1951), President of Portugal. Each stamp has a different design.

1970, Nov. 15

Angola	563
Cape Verde	359
Macao	422
Mozambique	493
Port. Guinea	340
St. Thomas & Prince Islands	403
Timor	341

No. 563 (1)	.45	.25
No. 359 (1)	.70	.50
No. 422 (1)	5.00	1.75
No. 493 (1)	.40	.25
No. 340 (1)	.35	.25
No. 403 (1)	.75	.40
No. 341 (1)	1.00	.50
Set total (7) Stamps	8.65	3.90

Olympic Games

CD59

20th Olympic Games, Munich, Aug. 26-Sept. 11. Each stamp shows a different sport.

1972, June 20

Angola	569
Cape Verde	361
Macao	426
Mozambique	504
Port. Guinea	342
St. Thomas & Prince Islands	408
Timor	343

No. 569 (1)	.65	.25
No. 361 (1)	.85	.40
No. 426 (1)	2.50	1.50
No. 504 (1)	.30	.25
No. 342 (1)	.45	.25
No. 408 (1)	.45	.25
No. 343 (1)	1.60	.80
Set total (7) Stamps	6.80	3.70

Lisbon-Rio de Janeiro Flight

CD60

50th anniversary of the Lisbon to Rio de Janeiro flight by Arturo de Sacadura and Coutinho, March 30-June 5, 1922. Each stamp shows a different stage of the flight.

1972, Sept. 20

Angola	570
Cape Verde	362
Macao	427
Mozambique	505
Port. Guinea	343
St. Thomas & Prince Islands	409
Timor	344

No. 570 (1)	.35	.25
No. 362 (1)	.85	.40
No. 427 (1)	40.00	12.00
No. 505 (1)	.30	.25
No. 343 (1)	.25	.25
No. 409 (1)	.50	.25
No. 344 (1)	1.25	.90
Set total (7) Stamps	43.50	14.30

WMO Centenary

WMO Emblem — CD61

Centenary of international meterological cooperation.

1973, Dec. 15

Angola	571
Cape Verde	363
Macao	429
Mozambique	509
Port. Guinea	344
St. Thomas & Prince Islands	410
Timor	345

No. 571 (1)	.45	.25
No. 363 (1)	.85	.40
No. 429 (1)	15.00	2.50
No. 509 (1)	.40	.25
No. 344 (1)	.45	.35
No. 410 (1)	.60	.50
No. 345 (1)	3.75	2.75
Set total (7) Stamps	21.50	7.00

FRENCH COMMUNITY

Upper Volta can be found under Burkina Faso in Vol. 1

Madagascar can be found under Malagasy in Vol. 3

Colonial Exposition

People of French Empire CD70

Women's Heads CD71

France Showing Way to Civilization CD72

"Colonial Commerce" CD73

International Colonial Exposition, Paris.

1931

Cameroun	213-216
Chad	60-63
Dahomey	97-100
Fr. Guiana	152-155
Fr. Guinea	116-119
Fr. India	100-103
Fr. Polynesia	76-79
Fr. Sudan	102-105
Gabon	120-123
Guadeloupe	138-141
Indo-China	140-142
Ivory Coast	92-95
Madagascar	169-172
Martinique	129-132
Mauritania	65-68
Middle Congo	61-64
New Caledonia	176-179
Niger	73-76
Reunion	122-125
St. Pierre & Miquelon	132-135
Senegal	138-141
Somali Coast	135-138
Togo	254-257
Ubangi-Shari	82-85
Upper Volta	66-69
Wallis & Futuna Isls.	85-88

Nos. 213-216 (4)	23.00	18.25
Nos. 60-63 (4)	22.00	22.00
Nos. 97-100 (4)	26.00	26.00
Nos. 152-155 (4)	22.00	22.00
Nos. 116-119 (4)	19.75	19.75
Nos. 100-103 (4)	18.00	*18.00*
Nos. 76-79 (4)	30.00	30.00
Nos. 102-105 (4)	19.00	19.00
Nos. 120-123 (4)	17.50	17.50
Nos. 138-141 (4)	19.00	19.00
Nos. 140-142 (3)	12.00	11.50
Nos. 92-95 (4)	22.50	22.50
Nos. 169-172 (4)	9.25	6.50
Nos. 129-132 (4)	21.00	21.00
Nos. 65-68 (4)	22.00	22.00
Nos. 61-64 (4)	20.00	18.50
Nos. 176-179 (4)	24.00	24.00
Nos. 73-76 (4)	20.50	20.50
Nos. 122-125 (4)	22.00	22.00
Nos. 132-135 (4)	24.00	24.00
Nos. 138-141 (4)	20.00	20.00
Nos. 135-138 (4)	22.00	22.00
Nos. 254-257 (4)	22.00	22.00
Nos. 82-85 (4)	21.00	21.00
Nos. 66-69 (4)	19.00	19.00
Nos. 85-88 (4)	31.00	35.00
Set total (103) Stamps	548.50	543.00

Paris International Exposition Colonial Arts Exposition

"Colonial Resources" CD74 CD77

Overseas Commerce CD75

Exposition Building and Women CD76

"France and the Empire" CD78

Cultural Treasures of the Colonies CD79

Souvenir sheets contain one imperf. stamp.

1937

Cameroun	217-222A
Dahomey	101-107
Fr. Equatorial Africa	27-32, 73
Fr. Guiana	162-168
Fr. Guinea	120-126
Fr. India	104-110
Fr. Polynesia	117-123
Fr. Sudan	106-112
Guadeloupe	148-154
Indo-China	193-199
Inini	41
Ivory Coast	152-158
Kwangchowan	132
Madagascar	191-197
Martinique	179-185
Mauritania	69-75
New Caledonia	208-214
Niger	77-83
Reunion	167-173
St. Pierre & Miquelon	165-171
Senegal	172-178
Somali Coast	139-145
Togo	258-264
Wallis & Futuna Isls.	89

Nos. 217-222A (7)	18.80	20.30
Nos. 101-107 (7)	23.60	27.60
Nos. 27-32, 73 (7)	28.10	32.10
Nos. 162-168 (7)	22.50	24.50
Nos. 120-126 (7)	24.00	28.00
Nos. 104-110 (7)	21.15	36.50
Nos. 117-123 (7)	58.50	75.00
Nos. 106-112 (7)	23.60	27.60
Nos. 148-154 (7)	19.55	21.05
Nos. 193-199 (7)	17.70	19.70
No. 41 (1)	21.00	27.50
Nos. 152-158 (7)	22.20	26.20
No. 132 (1)	9.25	11.00
Nos. 191-197 (7)	19.25	21.75
Nos. 179-185 (7)	19.95	21.70
Nos. 69-75 (7)	20.50	24.50
Nos. 208-214 (7)	39.00	50.50
Nos. 73-83 (11)	40.60	45.10
Nos. 167-173 (7)	21.70	23.20
Nos. 165-171 (7)	49.60	64.00
Nos. 172-178 (7)	21.00	23.80
Nos. 139-145 (7)	25.60	32.60
Nos. 258-264 (7)	20.40	20.40
No. 89 (1)	19.00	37.50
Set total (154) Stamps	606.55	742.10

Curie

Pierre and Marie Curie CD80

40th anniversary of the discovery of radium. The surtax was for the benefit of the Intl. Union for the Control of Cancer.

1938

Cameroun	B1
Cuba	B1-B2
Dahomey	B2
France	B76
Fr. Equatorial Africa	B1
Fr. Guiana	B3
Fr. Guinea	B2
Fr. India	B6
Fr. Polynesia	B5
Fr. Sudan	B1
Guadeloupe	B3
Indo-China	B14
Ivory Coast	B2
Madagascar	B2
Martinique	B2
Mauritania	B3
New Caledonia	B4
Niger	B1
Reunion	B4
St. Pierre & Miquelon	B3
Senegal	B3
Somali Coast	B2
Togo	B1

No. B1 (1)	10.00	10.00
Nos. B1-B2 (2)	12.00	3.35
No. B2 (1)	9.50	9.50
No. B76 (1)	21.00	12.50
No. B1 (1)	24.00	24.00
No. B3 (1)	13.50	13.50
No. B2 (1)	8.75	8.75
No. B6 (1)	10.00	10.00
No. B5 (1)	20.00	20.00
No. B1 (1)	12.50	12.50
No. B3 (1)	11.00	10.50
No. B14 (1)	12.00	12.00
No. B2 (1)	11.00	7.50
No. B2 (1)	11.00	11.00
No. B2 (1)	13.00	13.00
No. B3 (1)	7.75	7.75
No. B4 (1)	16.50	17.50
No. B1 (1)	16.50	16.50
No. B4 (1)	14.00	14.00
No. B3 (1)	21.00	22.50
No. B3 (1)	10.50	10.50
No. B2 (1)	7.75	7.75
No. B1 (1)	20.00	20.00
Set total (24) Stamps	313.25	294.60

Caillie

Rene Caillie and Map of Northwestern Africa — CD81

Death centenary of Rene Caillie (1799-1838), French explorer. All three denominations exist with colony name omitted.

1939

Dahomey	108-110
Fr. Guinea	161-163
Fr. Sudan	113-115
Ivory Coast	160-162
Mauritania	109-111
Niger	84-86
Senegal	188-190
Togo	265-267

Nos. 108-110 (3)	1.20	3.60
Nos. 161-163 (3)	1.20	3.20
Nos. 113-115 (3)	1.20	3.20
Nos. 160-162 (3)	1.05	2.55
Nos. 109-111 (3)	1.05	3.80
Nos. 84-86 (3)	2.35	2.35
Nos. 188-190 (3)	1.05	2.90
Nos. 265-267 (3)	1.05	3.30
Set total (24) Stamps	10.15	24.90

New York World's Fair

Natives and New York Skyline CD82

1939

Cameroun	223-224
Dahomey	111-112
Fr. Equatorial Africa	78-79
Fr. Guiana	169-170
Fr. Guinea	164-165
Fr. India	111-112
Fr. Polynesia	124-125
Fr. Sudan	116-117
Guadeloupe	155-156
Indo-China	203-204
Inini	42-43
Ivory Coast	163-164
Kwangchowan	133-134
Madagascar	209-210
Martinique	186-187
Mauritania	112-113
New Caledonia	215-216
Niger	87-88
Reunion	174-175
St. Pierre & Miquelon	205-206
Senegal	191-192
Somali Coast	179-180
Togo	268-269
Wallis & Futuna Isls.	90-91

Nos. 223-224 (2)	2.80	2.40
Nos. 111-112 (2)	1.60	3.20
Nos. 78-79 (2)	1.60	3.20
Nos. 169-170 (2)	2.60	2.60
Nos. 164-165 (2)	1.60	3.20
Nos. 111-112 (2)	3.00	*8.00*
Nos. 124-125 (2)	4.80	4.80
Nos. 116-117 (2)	1.60	3.20
Nos. 155-156 (2)	2.50	2.50
Nos. 203-204 (2)	2.05	2.05
Nos. 42-43 (2)	7.50	9.00
Nos. 163-164 (2)	1.50	3.00
Nos. 133-134 (2)	2.50	2.50
Nos. 209-210 (2)	1.50	2.50
Nos. 186-187 (2)	2.35	2.35
Nos. 112-113 (2)	1.40	2.80
Nos. 215-216 (2)	3.35	3.35
Nos. 87-88 (2)	1.60	2.80
Nos. 174-175 (2)	2.80	2.80
Nos. 205-206 (2)	4.80	6.00
Nos. 191-192 (2)	1.40	2.80
Nos. 179-180 (2)	1.40	2.80
Nos. 268-269 (2)	1.40	2.80
Nos. 90-91 (2)	5.00	6.00
Set total (48) Stamps	62.65	86.65

French Revolution

Storming of the Bastille CD83

French Revolution, 150th anniv. The surtax was for the defense of the colonies.

1939

Cameroun	B2-B6
Dahomey	B3-B7
Fr. Equatorial Africa	B4-B8, CB1
Fr. Guiana	B4-B8, CB1
Fr. Guinea	B3-B7
Fr. India	B7-B11
Fr. Polynesia	B6-B10, CB1
Fr. Sudan	B2-B6
Guadeloupe	B4-B8
Indo-China	B15-B19, CB1
Inini	B1-B5
Ivory Coast	B3-B7
Kwangchowan	B1-B5
Madagascar	B3-B7, CB1
Martinique	B3-B7
Mauritania	B4-B8
New Caledonia	B5-B9, CB1
Niger	B2-B6
Reunion	B5-B9, CB1
St. Pierre & Miquelon	B4-B8
Senegal	B4-B8, CB1
Somali Coast	B3-B7
Togo	B2-B6
Wallis & Futuna Isls.	B1-B5

Nos. B2-B6 (5)	60.00	60.00
Nos. B3-B7 (5)	47.50	47.50
Nos. B4-B8,CB1 (6)	120.00	120.00
Nos. B4-B8,CB1 (6)	79.50	79.50
Nos. B3-B7 (5)	47.50	47.50
Nos. B7-B11 (5)	28.75	*32.50*
Nos. B6-B10,CB1 (6)	122.50	122.50
Nos. B2-B6 (5)	50.00	50.00
Nos. B4-B8 (5)	50.00	50.00
Nos. B15-B19,CB1 (6)	85.00	85.00
Nos. B1-B5 (5)	80.00	100.00
Nos. B3-B7 (5)	43.75	43.75
Nos. B1-B5 (5)	46.25	46.25
Nos. B3-B7,CB1 (6)	65.50	65.50
Nos. B3-B7 (5)	52.50	52.50
Nos. B4-B8 (5)	42.50	42.50
Nos. B5-B9,CB1 (6)	101.50	101.50
Nos. B2-B6 (5)	60.00	60.00
Nos. B5-B9,CB1 (6)	87.50	87.50
Nos. B4-B8 (5)	67.50	72.50
Nos. B4-B8,CB1 (6)	56.50	56.50
Nos. B3-B7 (5)	45.00	45.00
Nos. B2-B6 (5)	42.50	42.50
Nos. B1-B5 (5)	80.00	110.00
Set total (128) Stamps	1,562.	1,621.

Plane over Coastal Area CD85

All five denominations exist with colony name omitted.

1940

Dahomey	C1-C5
Fr. Guinea	C1-C5
Fr. Sudan	C1-C5
Ivory Coast	C1-C5
Mauritania	C1-C5
Niger	C1-C5
Senegal	C12-C16
Togo	C1-C5

Nos. C1-C5 (5)	4.00	4.00
Nos. C1-C5 (5)	4.00	4.00
Nos. C1-C5 (5)	4.00	4.00
Nos. C1-C5 (5)	3.80	3.80
Nos. C1-C5 (5)	3.50	3.50
Nos. C1-C5 (5)	3.50	3.50
Nos. C12-C16 (5)	3.50	3.50
Nos. C1-C5 (5)	3.15	3.15
Set total (40) Stamps	29.45	29.45

Defense of the Empire

Colonial Infantryman — CD86

1941

Cameroun	B13B
Dahomey	B13
Fr. Equatorial Africa	B8B
Fr. Guiana	B10
Fr. Guinea	B13
Fr. India	B13
Fr. Polynesia	B12
Fr. Sudan	B12
Guadeloupe	B10
Indo-China	B19B
Inini	B7
Ivory Coast	B13
Kwangchowan	B7
Madagascar	B9
Martinique	B9
Mauritania	B14
New Caledonia	B11
Niger	B12
Reunion	B11
St. Pierre & Miquelon	B8B
Senegal	B14
Somali Coast	B9
Togo	B10B
Wallis & Futuna Isls.	B7

No. B13B (1)	1.60
No. B13 (1)	1.20
No. B8B (1)	3.50
No. B10 (1)	1.40
No. B13 (1)	1.40
No. B13 (1)	1.25
No. B12 (1)	3.50
No. B12 (1)	1.40
No. B10 (1)	1.00
No. B19B (1)	3.00
No. B7 (1)	1.75
No. B13 (1)	1.25
No. B7 (1)	.85
No. B9 (1)	1.50
No. B9 (1)	1.40
No. B14 (1)	.95
No. B12 (1)	1.40
No. B11 (1)	1.60
No. B8B (1)	4.50
No. B14 (1)	1.25
No. B9 (1)	1.60
No. B10B (1)	1.10
No. B7 (1)	1.75
Set total (23) Stamps	40.15

Each of the CD86 stamps listed above is part of a set of three stamps. The designs of the other two stamps in the set vary from country to country. Only the values of the Common Design stamps are listed here.

Colonial Education Fund

CD86a

1942

Cameroun	CB3
Dahomey	CB4
Fr. Equatorial Africa	CB5
Fr. Guiana	CB4
Fr. Guinea	CB4
Fr. India	CB3
Fr. Polynesia	CB4
Fr. Sudan	CB4
Guadeloupe	CB3
Indo-China	CB5
Inini	CB3
Ivory Coast	CB4
Kwangchowan	CB4
Malagasy	CB5
Martinique	CB3
Mauritania	CB4
New Caledonia	CB4
Niger	CB4
Reunion	CB4
St. Pierre & Miquelon	CB3
Senegal	CB5
Somali Coast	CB3
Togo	CB3
Wallis & Futuna	CB3

No. CB3 (1)	1.10	
No. CB4 (1)	.80	5.50
No. CB5 (1)	.80	
No. CB4 (1)	1.10	
No. CB4 (1)	.40	5.50
No. CB3 (1)	.90	
No. CB4 (1)	2.00	
No. CB4 (1)	.40	5.50
No. CB3 (1)	1.10	
No. CB5 (1)	2.00	
No. CB3 (1)	1.25	
No. CB4 (1)	1.00	5.50
No. CB4 (1)	1.00	
No. CB5 (1)	.65	
No. CB3 (1)	1.00	
No. CB4 (1)	.80	
No. CB4 (1)	2.25	
No. CB4 (1)	.35	
No. CB4 (1)	.90	
No. CB3 (1)	7.00	
No. CB5 (1)	.80	6.50
No. CB3 (1)	.70	
No. CB3 (1)	.35	
No. CB3 (1)	2.00	
Set total (24) Stamps	30.65	28.50

Cross of Lorraine & Four-motor Plane CD87

1941-5

Cameroun	C1-C7
Fr. Equatorial Africa	C17-C23
Fr. Guiana	C9-C10
Fr. India	C1-C6
Fr. Polynesia	C3-C9
Fr. West Africa	C1-C3
Guadeloupe	C1-C2
Madagascar	C37-C43

Martinique.. C1-C2
New Caledonia................................ C7-C13
Reunion.. C18-C24
St. Pierre & Miquelon.................. C1-C7
Somali Coast................................. C1-C7

Nos. C1-C7 (7)	6.30	6.30
Nos. C17-C23 (7)	10.40	6.35
Nos. C9-C10 (2)	3.80	3.10
Nos. C1-C6 (6)	9.30	*15.00*
Nos. C3-C9 (7)	13.75	10.00
Nos. C1-C3 (3)	9.50	3.90
Nos. C1-C2 (2)	3.75	2.50
Nos. C37-C43 (7)	5.60	3.80
Nos. C1-C2 (2)	3.00	1.60
Nos. C7-C13 (7)	8.85	7.30
Nos. C18-C24 (7)	7.05	5.00
Nos. C1-C7 (7)	11.60	9.40
Nos. C1-C7 (7)	13.95	11.10
Set total (71) Stamps	106.85	85.35

Somali Coast stamps are inscribed "Djibouti".

Transport Plane CD88

Caravan and Plane CD89

1942

Dahomey.. C6-C13
Fr. Guinea..................................... C6-C13
Fr. Sudan....................................... C6-C13
Ivory Coast.................................... C6-C13
Mauritania...................................... C6-C13
Niger... C6-C13
Senegal.. C17-C25
Togo.. C6-C13

Nos. C6-C13 (8)	7.15
Nos. C6-C13 (8)	5.75
Nos. C6-C13 (8)	8.00
Nos. C6-C13 (8)	11.15
Nos. C6-C13 (8)	9.75
Nos. C6-C13 (8)	6.20
Nos. C17-C25 (9)	9.45
Nos. C6-C13 (8)	6.75
Set total (65) Stamps	64.20

Red Cross

Marianne CD90

The surtax was for the French Red Cross and national relief.

1944

Cameroun....................................... B28
Fr. Equatorial Africa...................... B38
Fr. Guiana...................................... B12
Fr. India... B14
Fr. Polynesia.................................. B13
Fr. West Africa................................ B1
Guadeloupe.................................... B12
Madagascar.................................... B15
Martinique...................................... B11
New Caledonia................................ B13
Reunion.. B15
St. Pierre & Miquelon.................... B13
Somali Coast.................................. B13
Wallis & Futuna Isls....................... B9

No. B28 (1)	2.00	1.60
No. B38 (1)	1.60	1.20
No. B12 (1)	1.75	1.25
No. B14 (1)	1.50	1.25
No. B13 (1)	2.00	1.60
No. B1 (1)	6.50	4.75
No. B12 (1)	1.40	1.00
No. B15 (1)	.90	.90
No. B11 (1)	1.20	1.20
No. B13 (1)	1.50	1.50
No. B15 (1)	1.60	1.10
No. B13 (1)	2.60	2.60
No. B13 (1)	1.75	2.00
No. B9 (1)	3.00	3.00
Set total (14) Stamps	29.30	24.95

Eboue

CD91

Felix Eboue, first French colonial administrator to proclaim resistance to Germany after French surrender in World War II.

1945

Cameroun...................................... 296-297
Fr. Equatorial Africa.................... 156-157
Fr. Guiana..................................... 171-172
Fr. India.. 210-211
Fr. Polynesia.................................. 150-151
Fr. West Africa................................ 15-16
Guadeloupe................................... 187-188
Madagascar................................... 259-260
Martinique..................................... 196-197
New Caledonia.............................. 274-275
Reunion... 238-239
St. Pierre & Miquelon................... 322-323
Somali Coast................................. 238-239

Nos. 296-297 (2)	2.40	1.95
Nos. 156-157 (2)	2.55	2.00
Nos. 171-172 (2)	2.45	2.00
Nos. 210-211 (2)	2.20	1.95
Nos. 150-151 (2)	3.60	2.85
Nos. 15-16 (2)	2.40	2.40
Nos. 187-188 (2)	2.05	1.60
Nos. 259-260 (2)	2.00	1.45
Nos. 196-197 (2)	2.05	1.55
Nos. 274-275 (2)	3.40	3.00
Nos. 238-239 (2)	2.40	2.00
Nos. 322-323 (2)	4.40	3.45
Nos. 238-239 (2)	2.45	2.10
Set total (26) Stamps	34.35	28.30

Victory

Victory — CD92

European victory of the Allied Nations in World War II.

1946, May 8

Cameroun.. C8
Fr. Equatorial Africa...................... C24
Fr. Guiana...................................... C11
Fr. India.. C7
Fr. Polynesia.................................. C10
Fr. West Africa................................ C4
Guadeloupe..................................... C3
Indo-China..................................... C19
Madagascar.................................... C44
Martinique....................................... C3
New Caledonia............................... C14
Reunion.. C25
St. Pierre & Miquelon..................... C8
Somali Coast................................... C8
Wallis & Futuna Isls........................ C1

No. C8 (1)	1.60	1.20
No. C24 (1)	1.60	1.25
No. C11 (1)	1.75	1.25
No. C7 (1)	1.00	4.00
No. C10 (1)	2.75	2.00
No. C4 (1)	1.60	1.20
No. C3 (1)	1.25	1.00
No. C19 (1)	1.00	.55
No. C44 (1)	1.00	.35
No. C3 (1)	1.30	1.00
No. C14 (1)	1.50	1.25
No. C25 (1)	1.10	.90
No. C8 (1)	2.10	2.10
No. C8 (1)	1.75	1.40
No. C1 (1)	2.25	1.90
Set total (15) Stamps	23.55	21.35

Chad to Rhine

Leclerc's Departure from Chad — CD93

Battle at Cufra Oasis — CD94

Tanks in Action, Mareth — CD95

Normandy Invasion — CD96

Entering Paris — CD97

Liberation of Strasbourg — CD98

"Chad to the Rhine" march, 1942-44, by Gen. Jacques Leclerc's column, later French 2nd Armored Division.

1946, June 6

Cameroun................................ C9-C14
Fr. Equatorial Africa............... C25-C30
Fr. Guiana.............................. C12-C17
Fr. India.................................. C8-C13
Fr. Polynesia.......................... C11-C16
Fr. West Africa........................ C5-C10
Guadeloupe.............................. C4-C9
Indo-China............................. C20-C25
Madagascar............................ C45-C50
Martinique................................ C4-C9
New Caledonia...................... C15-C20
Reunion.................................. C26-C31
St. Pierre & Miquelon.............. C9-C14
Somali Coast........................... C9-C14
Wallis & Futuna Isls................. C2-C7

Nos. C9-C14 (6)	12.05	9.70
Nos. C25-C30 (6)	14.70	10.80
Nos. C12-C17 (6)	12.65	10.35
Nos. C8-C13 (6)	12.80	*15.00*
Nos. C11-C16 (6)	17.55	13.40
Nos. C5-C10 (6)	16.05	11.95
Nos. C4-C9 (6)	12.00	9.60
Nos. C20-C25 (6)	6.40	6.40
Nos. C45-C50 (6)	10.30	8.40
Nos. C4-C9 (6)	8.85	7.30
Nos. C15-C20 (6)	13.40	11.90
Nos. C26-C31 (6)	10.25	6.55
Nos. C9-C14 (6)	17.30	14.35
Nos. C9-C14 (6)	18.10	12.65
Nos. C2-C7 (6)	13.75	10.45
Set total (90) Stamps	196.15	158.80

UPU

French Colonials, Globe and Plane — CD99

Universal Postal Union, 75th anniv.

1949, July 4

Cameroun.. C29
Fr. Equatorial Africa...................... C34
Fr. India.. C17
Fr. Polynesia.................................. C20
Fr. West Africa............................... C15
Indo-China..................................... C26
Madagascar.................................... C55
New Caledonia............................... C24
St. Pierre & Miquelon.................... C18
Somali Coast.................................. C18
Togo... C18
Wallis & Futuna Isls....................... C10

No. C29 (1)	8.00	4.75
No. C34 (1)	16.00	12.00
No. C17 (1)	11.50	8.75
No. C20 (1)	20.00	15.00
No. C15 (1)	12.00	8.75
No. C26 (1)	4.75	4.00
No. C55 (1)	4.00	2.75
No. C24 (1)	7.50	5.00
No. C18 (1)	20.00	12.00
No. C18 (1)	14.00	10.50
No. C18 (1)	8.50	7.00
No. C10 (1)	11.00	8.25
Set total (12) Stamps	137.25	98.75

Tropical Medicine

Doctor Treating Infant CD100

The surtax was for charitable work.

1950

Cameroun.. B29
Fr. Equatorial Africa...................... B39
Fr. India.. B15
Fr. Polynesia.................................. B14
Fr. West Africa................................ B3
Madagascar.................................... B17
New Caledonia............................... B14
St. Pierre & Miquelon.................... B14
Somali Coast.................................. B14
Togo... B11

No. B29 (1)	7.25	5.50
No. B39 (1)	7.25	5.50
No. B15 (1)	6.00	4.00
No. B14 (1)	10.50	8.00
No. B3 (1)	9.50	7.25
No. B17 (1)	5.50	5.50
No. B14 (1)	6.75	5.25
No. B14 (1)	16.00	15.00
No. B14 (1)	7.75	6.25
No. B11 (1)	5.00	3.50
Set total (10) Stamps	81.50	65.75

Military Medal

Medal, Early Marine and Colonial Soldier — CD101

Centenary of the creation of the French Military Medal.

1952

Cameroun.. 322
Comoro Isls....................................... 39
Fr. Equatorial Africa....................... 186

Fr. India	233
Fr. Polynesia	179
Fr. West Africa	57
Madagascar	286
New Caledonia	295
St. Pierre & Miquelon	345
Somali Coast	267
Togo	327
Wallis & Futuna Isls.	149

No. 322 (1)	7.25	3.25
No. 39 (1)	45.00	37.50
No. 186 (1)	8.00	5.50
No. 233 (1)	5.50	7.00
No. 179 (1)	13.50	10.00
No. 57 (1)	8.75	6.50
No. 286 (1)	3.75	2.50
No. 295 (1)	6.50	6.00
No. 345 (1)	16.00	15.00
No. 267 (1)	9.00	8.00
No. 327 (1)	5.50	4.75
No. 149 (1)	7.25	7.25
Set total (12) Stamps	136.00	113.25

Liberation

Allied Landing, Victory Sign and Cross of Lorraine — CD102

Liberation of France, 10th anniv.

1954, June 6

Cameroun	C32
Comoro Isls.	C4
Fr. Equatorial Africa	C38
Fr. India	C18
Fr. Polynesia	C22
Fr. West Africa	C17
Madagascar	C57
New Caledonia	C25
St. Pierre & Miquelon	C19
Somali Coast	C19
Togo	C19
Wallis & Futuna Isls.	C11

No. C32 (1)	7.25	4.75
No. C4 (1)	32.50	19.00
No. C38 (1)	12.00	8.00
No. C18 (1)	11.00	8.00
No. C22 (1)	10.00	8.00
No. C17 (1)	12.00	5.50
No. C57 (1)	3.25	2.00
No. C25 (1)	7.50	5.00
No. C19 (1)	19.00	12.00
No. C19 (1)	10.50	8.50
No. C19 (1)	7.00	5.50
No. C11 (1)	11.00	8.25
Set total (12) Stamps	143.00	94.50

FIDES

Plowmen CD103

Efforts of FIDES, the Economic and Social Development Fund for Overseas Possessions (Fonds d' Investissement pour le Developpement Economique et Social). Each stamp has a different design.

1956

Cameroun	326-329
Comoro Isls.	43
Fr. Equatorial Africa	189-192
Fr. Polynesia	181
Fr. West Africa	65-72
Madagascar	292-295
New Caledonia	303
St. Pierre & Miquelon	350
Somali Coast	268-269
Togo	331

Nos. 326-329 (4)	6.90	3.20
No. 43 (1)	2.25	1.60
Nos. 189-192 (4)	3.20	1.65
No. 181 (1)	4.00	2.00
Nos. 65-72 (8)	16.00	6.35
Nos. 292-295 (4)	2.25	1.20
No. 303 (1)	1.90	1.10
No. 350 (1)	6.00	4.00
Nos. 268-269 (2)	5.35	3.15
No. 331 (1)	4.25	2.10
Set total (27) Stamps	52.10	26.35

Flower

CD104

Each stamp shows a different flower.

1958-9

Cameroun	333
Comoro Isls.	45
Fr. Equatorial Africa	200-201
Fr. Polynesia	192
Fr. So. & Antarctic Terr.	11
Fr. West Africa	79-83
Madagascar	301-302
New Caledonia	304-305
St. Pierre & Miquelon	357
Somali Coast	270
Togo	348-349
Wallis & Futuna Isls.	152

No. 333 (1)	1.60	.80
No. 45 (1)	5.25	4.25
Nos. 200-201 (2)	3.60	1.60
No. 192 (1)	6.50	4.00
No. 11 (1)	8.75	7.50
Nos. 79-83 (5)	10.45	5.60
Nos. 301-302 (2)	1.60	.60
Nos. 304-305 (2)	8.00	3.00
No. 357 (1)	4.50	2.25
No. 270 (1)	4.25	1.40
Nos. 348-349 (2)	1.10	.50
No. 152 (1)	3.25	3.25
Set total (20) Stamps	58.85	34.75

Human Rights

Sun, Dove and U.N. Emblem CD105

10th anniversary of the signing of the Universal Declaration of Human Rights.

1958

Comoro Isls.	44
Fr. Equatorial Africa	202
Fr. Polynesia	191
Fr. West Africa	85
Madagascar	300
New Caledonia	306
St. Pierre & Miquelon	356
Somali Coast	274
Wallis & Futuna Isls.	153

No. 44 (1)	9.00	9.00
No. 202 (1)	2.40	1.25
No. 191 (1)	13.00	8.75
No. 85 (1)	2.40	2.00
No. 300 (1)	.80	.40
No. 306 (1)	2.00	1.50
No. 356 (1)	3.50	2.50
No. 274 (1)	3.50	2.10
No. 153 (1)	4.50	4.50
Set total (9) Stamps	41.10	32.00

C.C.T.A.

CD106

Commission for Technical Cooperation in Africa south of the Sahara, 10th anniv.

1960

Cameroun	339
Cent. Africa	3
Chad	66
Congo, P.R.	90
Dahomey	138
Gabon	150
Ivory Coast	180
Madagascar	317
Mali	9
Mauritania	117
Niger	104
Upper Volta	89

No. 339 (1)	1.60	.75
No. 3 (1)	1.60	.75
No. 66 (1)	1.75	.50
No. 90 (1)	1.00	1.00
No. 138 (1)	.50	.25
No. 150 (1)	1.25	1.10
No. 180 (1)	1.10	.50
No. 317 (1)	.60	.30
No. 9 (1)	1.20	.50
No. 117 (1)	.75	.40
No. 104 (1)	.85	.45
No. 89 (1)	.65	.40
Set total (12) Stamps	12.85	6.90

Air Afrique, 1961

Modern and Ancient Africa, Map and Planes — CD107

Founding of Air Afrique (African Airlines).

1961-62

Cameroun	C37
Cent. Africa	C5
Chad	C7
Congo, P.R.	C5
Dahomey	C17
Gabon	C5
Ivory Coast	C18
Mauritania	C17
Niger	C22
Senegal	C31
Upper Volta	C4

No. C37 (1)	1.00	.50
No. C5 (1)	1.00	.65
No. C7 (1)	1.00	.25
No. C5 (1)	1.75	.90
No. C17 (1)	.80	.40
No. C5 (1)	11.00	6.00
No. C18 (1)	2.00	1.25
No. C17 (1)	2.40	1.25
No. C22 (1)	1.75	.90
No. C31 (1)	.80	.30
No. C4 (1)	3.50	1.75
Set total (11) Stamps	27.00	14.15

Anti-Malaria

CD108

World Health Organization drive to eradicate malaria.

1962, Apr. 7

Cameroun	B36
Cent. Africa	B1
Chad	B1
Comoro Isls.	B1
Congo, P.R.	B3
Dahomey	B15
Gabon	B4
Ivory Coast	B15
Madagascar	B19
Mali	B1
Mauritania	B16
Niger	B14
Senegal	B16
Somali Coast	B15
Upper Volta	B1

No. B36 (1)	1.00	.45
No. B1 (1)	1.40	1.40
No. B1 (1)	1.00	.50
No. B1 (1)	3.50	3.50
No. B3 (1)	1.40	1.00
No. B15 (1)	.75	.75
No. B4 (1)	1.00	1.00
No. B15 (1)	1.25	1.25
No. B19 (1)	.75	.50
No. B1 (1)	1.25	.60
No. B16 (1)	.50	.50
No. B14 (1)	.75	.75
No. B16 (1)	1.10	.65
No. B15 (1)	7.00	7.00
No. B1 (1)	.75	.70
Set total (15) Stamps	23.40	20.55

Abidjan Games

CD109

Abidjan Games, Ivory Coast, Dec. 24-31, 1961. Each stamp shows a different sport.

1962

Cent. Africa	19-20, C6
Chad	83-84, C8
Congo, P.R.	103-104, C7
Gabon	163-164, C6
Niger	109-111
Upper Volta	103-105

Nos. 19-20,C6 (3)	4.15	2.85
Nos. 83-84,C8 (3)	5.80	1.55
Nos. 103-104,C7 (3)	3.85	1.80
Nos. 163-164,C6 (3)	5.00	3.00
Nos. 109-111 (3)	2.60	1.25
Nos. 103-105 (3)	2.80	1.75
Set total (18) Stamps	24.20	12.20

African and Malagasy Union

Flag of Union CD110

First anniversary of the Union.

1962, Sept. 8

Cameroun	373
Cent. Africa	21
Chad	85
Congo, P.R.	105
Dahomey	155
Gabon	165
Ivory Coast	198
Madagascar	332
Mauritania	170
Niger	112
Senegal	211
Upper Volta	106

No. 373 (1)	2.00	.75
No. 21 (1)	1.25	.75
No. 85 (1)	1.25	.25
No. 105 (1)	1.50	.50
No. 155 (1)	1.25	.90
No. 165 (1)	1.60	1.25
No. 198 (1)	2.10	.75
No. 332 (1)	.80	.80
No. 170 (1)	.75	.50
No. 112 (1)	.80	.50
No. 211 (1)	.80	.50
No. 106 (1)	1.10	.75
Set total (12) Stamps	15.20	8.20

Telstar

Telstar and Globe Showing Andover and Pleumeur-Bodou — CD111

First television connection of the United States and Europe through the Telstar satellite, July 11-12, 1962.

1962-63

Andorra, French	154
Comoro Isls.	C7
Fr. Polynesia	C29
Fr. So. & Antarctic Terr.	C5
New Caledonia	C33
St. Pierre & Miquelon	C26
Somali Coast	C31
Wallis & Futuna Isls.	C17

No. 154 (1)	2.00	1.60
No. C7 (1)	4.50	2.75
No. C29 (1)	11.50	8.00

No. C5 (1)	29.00	21.00
No. C33 (1)	25.00	18.50
No. C26 (1)	7.25	4.50
No. C31 (1)	1.00	1.00
No. C17 (1)	3.75	3.75
Set total (8) Stamps	84.00	61.10

Freedom From Hunger

World Map and Wheat Emblem CD112

U.N. Food and Agriculture Organization's "Freedom from Hunger" campaign.

1963, Mar. 21

Cameroun	B37-B38
Cent. Africa	B2
Chad	B2
Congo, P.R.	B4
Dahomey	B16
Gabon	B5
Ivory Coast	B16
Madagascar	B21
Mauritania	B17
Niger	B15
Senegal	B17
Upper Volta	B2

Nos. B37-B38 (2)	2.25	.75
No. B2 (1)	1.25	1.25
No. B2 (1)	1.10	.50
No. B4 (1)	1.40	1.00
No. B16 (1)	.80	.80
No. B5 (1)	1.00	1.00
No. B16 (1)	1.50	1.50
No. B21 (1)	.60	.45
No. B17 (1)	.60	.60
No. B15 (1)	.75	.75
No. B17 (1)	.80	.50
No. B2 (1)	.75	.70
Set total (13) Stamps	12.80	9.80

Red Cross Centenary

CD113

Centenary of the International Red Cross.

1963, Sept. 2

Comoro Isls.	55
Fr. Polynesia	205
New Caledonia	328
St. Pierre & Miquelon	367
Somali Coast	297
Wallis & Futuna Isls.	165

No. 55 (1)	7.50	6.00
No. 205 (1)	15.00	12.00
No. 328 (1)	8.00	6.75
No. 367 (1)	12.00	5.50
No. 297 (1)	6.25	6.25
No. 165 (1)	4.00	4.00
Set total (6) Stamps	52.75	40.50

African Postal Union, 1963

UAMPT Emblem, Radio Masts, Plane and Mail CD114

Establishment of the African and Malagasy Posts and Telecommunications Union.

1963, Sept. 8

Cameroun	C47
Cent. Africa	C10
Chad	C9
Congo, P.R.	C13
Dahomey	C19
Gabon	C13
Ivory Coast	C25
Madagascar	C75
Mauritania	C22
Niger	C27
Rwanda	36
Senegal	C32
Upper Volta	C9

No. C47 (1)	2.25	1.00
No. C10 (1)	1.90	.90
No. C9 (1)	1.80	.60
No. C13 (1)	1.40	.75
No. C19 (1)	.75	.25
No. C13 (1)	1.90	.80
No. C25 (1)	2.50	1.50
No. C75 (1)	1.25	.80
No. C22 (1)	1.50	.60
No. C27 (1)	1.25	.60
No. 36 (1)	1.10	.75
No. C32 (1)	1.75	.50
No. C9 (1)	1.50	.75
Set total (13) Stamps	20.85	9.80

Air Afrique, 1963

Symbols of Flight — CD115

First anniversary of Air Afrique and inauguration of DC-8 service.

1963, Nov. 19

Cameroun	C48
Chad	C10
Congo, P.R.	C14
Gabon	C18
Ivory Coast	C26
Mauritania	C26
Niger	C35
Senegal	C33

No. C48 (1)	1.25	.40
No. C10 (1)	1.80	.60
No. C14 (1)	1.60	.60
No. C18 (1)	1.25	.65
No. C26 (1)	1.00	.50
No. C26 (1)	.70	.25
No. C35 (1)	1.00	.55
No. C33 (1)	2.00	.65
Set total (8) Stamps	10.60	4.20

Europafrica

Europe and Africa Linked — CD116

Signing of an economic agreement between the European Economic Community and the African and Malagasy Union, Yaounde, Cameroun, July 20, 1963.

1963-64

Cameroun	402
Cent. Africa	C12
Chad	C11
Congo, P.R.	C16
Gabon	C19
Ivory Coast	217
Niger	C43
Upper Volta	C11

No. 402 (1)	2.25	.60
No. C12 (1)	2.50	1.75
No. C11 (1)	1.60	.50
No. C16 (1)	1.60	1.00
No. C19 (1)	1.25	.75
No. 217 (1)	1.10	.35
No. C43 (1)	.85	.50
No. C11 (1)	1.50	.80
Set total (8) Stamps	12.65	6.25

Human Rights

Scales of Justice and Globe CD117

15th anniversary of the Universal Declaration of Human Rights.

1963, Dec. 10

Comoro Isls.	56
Fr. Polynesia	206
New Caledonia	329
St. Pierre & Miquelon	368
Somali Coast	300
Wallis & Futuna Isls.	166

No. 56 (1)	7.50	6.00
No. 205 (1)	15.00	12.00
No. 329 (1)	7.00	6.00
No. 368 (1)	7.00	3.50
No. 300 (1)	8.50	8.50
No. 166 (1)	7.00	7.00
Set total (6) Stamps	52.00	43.00

PHILATEC

Stamp Album, Champs Elysees Palace and Horses of Marly CD118

Intl. Philatelic and Postal Techniques Exhibition, Paris, June 5-21, 1964.

1963-64

Comoro Isls.	60
France	1078
Fr. Polynesia	207
New Caledonia	341
St. Pierre & Miquelon	369
Somali Coast	301
Wallis & Futuna Isls.	167

No. 60 (1)	4.00	3.50
No. 1078 (1)	.25	.25
No. 206 (1)	15.00	10.00
No. 341 (1)	6.50	6.50
No. 369 (1)	11.00	8.00
No. 301 (1)	7.75	7.75
No. 167 (1)	3.00	3.00
Set total (7) Stamps	47.50	39.00

Cooperation

CD119

Cooperation between France and the French-speaking countries of Africa and Madagascar.

1964

Cameroun	409-410
Cent. Africa	39
Chad	103
Congo, P.R.	121
Dahomey	193
France	1111
Gabon	175
Ivory Coast	221
Madagascar	360
Mauritania	181
Niger	143
Senegal	236
Togo	495

Nos. 409-410 (2)	2.50	.50
No. 39 (1)	.90	.50
No. 103 (1)	1.00	.25
No. 121 (1)	.90	.35
No. 193 (1)	.80	.35
No. 1111 (1)	.25	.25
No. 175 (1)	.90	.60
No. 221 (1)	1.10	.35
No. 360 (1)	.60	.25
No. 181 (1)	.60	.35
No. 143 (1)	.80	.40
No. 236 (1)	1.60	.85
No. 495 (1)	.70	.25
Set total (14) Stamps	12.65	5.25

ITU

Telegraph, Syncom Satellite and ITU Emblem CD120

Intl. Telecommunication Union, Cent.

1965, May 17

Comoro Isls.	C14
Fr. Polynesia	C33
Fr. So. & Antarctic Terr.	C8
New Caledonia	C40
New Hebrides	124-125
St. Pierre & Miquelon	C29
Somali Coast	C36
Wallis & Futuna Isls.	C20

No. C14 (1)	18.00	9.00
No. C33 (1)	80.00	52.50
No. C8 (1)	200.00	160.00
No. C40 (1)	10.00	8.00
Nos. 124-125 (2)	32.25	27.25
No. C29 (1)	24.00	11.50
No. C36 (1)	15.00	9.00
No. C20 (1)	16.00	16.00
Set total (9) Stamps	395.25	293.25

French Satellite A-1

Diamant Rocket and Launching Installation — CD121

Launching of France's first satellite, Nov. 26, 1965.

1965-66

Comoro Isls.	C16a
France	1138a
Reunion	359a
Fr. Polynesia	C41a
Fr. So. & Antarctic Terr.	C10a
New Caledonia	C45a
St. Pierre & Miquelon	C31a
Somali Coast	C40a
Wallis & Futuna Isls.	C23a

No. C16a (1)	9.00	9.00
No. 1138a (1)	.65	.65
No. 359a (1)	3.50	3.00
No. C41a (1)	14.00	14.00
No. C10a (1)	29.00	24.00
No. C45a (1)	7.00	7.00
No. C31a (1)	14.50	14.50
No. C40a (1)	7.00	7.00
No. C23a (1)	8.50	8.50
Set total (9) Stamps	93.15	87.65

French Satellite D-1

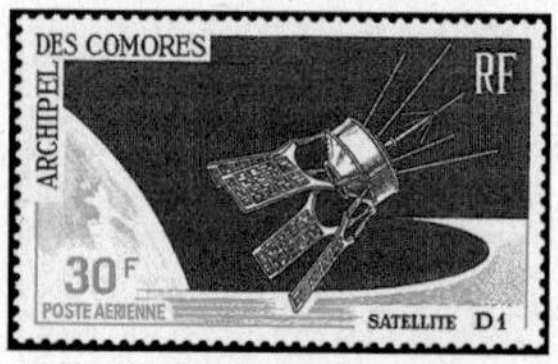

D-1 Satellite in Orbit — CD122

Launching of the D-1 satellite at Hammaguir, Algeria, Feb. 17, 1966.

1966

Comoro Isls.	C17
France	1148

Fr. Polynesia C42
Fr. So. & Antarctic Terr. C11
New Caledonia C46
St. Pierre & Miquelon C32
Somali Coast C49
Wallis & Futuna Isls. C24

No. C17 (1)	4.00	4.00
No. 1148 (1)	.25	.25
No. C42 (1)	7.00	4.75
No. C11 (1)	57.50	40.00
No. C46 (1)	2.25	2.00
No. C32 (1)	9.00	6.00
No. C49 (1)	4.25	2.75
No. C24 (1)	3.50	3.50
Set total (8) Stamps	87.75	63.25

Air Afrique, 1966

Planes and Air Afrique Emblem — CD123

Introduction of DC-8F planes by Air Afrique.

1966

Cameroun C79
Cent. Africa C35
Chad C26
Congo, P.R. C42
Dahomey C42
Gabon C47
Ivory Coast C32
Mauritania C57
Niger C63
Senegal C47
Togo C54
Upper Volta C31

No. C79 (1)	.80	.25
No. C35 (1)	1.00	.50
No. C26 (1)	.85	.25
No. C42 (1)	1.00	.25
No. C42 (1)	.75	.25
No. C47 (1)	.90	.35
No. C32 (1)	1.00	.60
No. C57 (1)	.60	.30
No. C63 (1)	.70	.35
No. C47 (1)	.80	.30
No. C54 (1)	.80	.25
No. C31 (1)	.75	.50
Set total (12) Stamps	9.95	4.15

African Postal Union, 1967

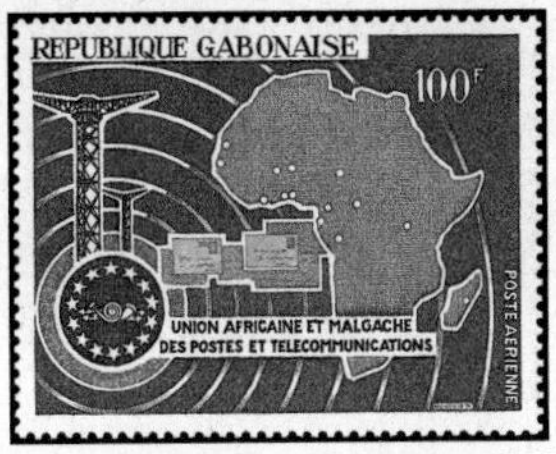

Telecommunications Symbols and Map of Africa — CD124

Fifth anniversary of the establishment of the African and Malagasy Union of Posts and Telecommunications, UAMPT.

1967

Cameroun C90
Cent. Africa C46
Chad C37
Congo, P.R. C57
Dahomey C61
Gabon C58
Ivory Coast C34
Madagascar C85
Mauritania C65
Niger C75
Rwanda C1-C3
Senegal C60
Togo C81
Upper Volta C50

No. C90 (1)	2.40	.65
No. C46 (1)	2.25	.85
No. C37 (1)	2.00	.60
No. C57 (1)	1.60	.60
No. C61 (1)	1.75	.95
No. C58 (1)	2.00	.85
No. C34 (1)	3.50	1.50
No. C85 (1)	1.25	.60
No. C65 (1)	1.25	.60
No. C75 (1)	1.40	.60
Nos. C1-C3 (3)	2.05	1.25
No. C60 (1)	1.75	.50
No. C81 (1)	1.90	.30
No. C50 (1)	1.80	.70
Set total (16) Stamps	26.90	10.55

Monetary Union

Gold Token of the Ashantis, 17-18th Centuries — CD125

West African Monetary Union, 5th anniv.

1967, Nov. 4

Dahomey 244
Ivory Coast 259
Mauritania 238
Niger 204
Senegal 294
Togo 623
Upper Volta 181

No. 244 (1)	.65	.65
No. 259 (1)	.85	.40
No. 238 (1)	.45	.25
No. 204 (1)	.55	.25
No. 294 (1)	.60	.25
No. 623 (1)	.60	.25
No. 181 (1)	.65	.35
Set total (7) Stamps	4.35	2.40

WHO Anniversary

Sun, Flowers and WHO Emblem CD126

World Health Organization, 20th anniv.

1968, May 4

Afars & Issas 317
Comoro Isls. 73
Fr. Polynesia 241-242
Fr. So. & Antarctic Terr. 31
New Caledonia 367
St. Pierre & Miquelon 377
Wallis & Futuna Isls. 169

No. 317 (1)	3.00	3.00
No. 73 (1)	2.40	1.75
Nos. 241-242 (2)	22.00	12.75
No. 31 (1)	62.50	47.50
No. 367 (1)	4.00	2.25
No. 377 (1)	12.00	9.00
No. 169 (1)	5.75	5.75
Set total (8) Stamps	111.65	82.00

Human Rights Year

Human Rights Flame — CD127

1968, Aug. 10

Afars & Issas 322-323
Comoro Isls. 76
Fr. Polynesia 243-244
Fr. So. & Antarctic Terr. 32
New Caledonia 369
St. Pierre & Miquelon 382
Wallis & Futuna Isls. 170

Nos. 322-323 (2)	6.75	4.00
No. 76 (1)	3.25	3.25
Nos. 243-244 (2)	24.00	14.00
No. 32 (1)	55.00	47.50
No. 369 (1)	2.75	1.50
No. 382 (1)	8.00	5.50
No. 170 (1)	3.25	3.25
Set total (9) Stamps	103.00	79.00

2nd PHILEXAFRIQUE

CD128

Opening of PHILEXAFRIQUE, Abidjan, Feb. 14. Each stamp shows a local scene and stamp.

1969, Feb. 14

Cameroun C118
Cent. Africa C65
Chad C48
Congo, P.R. C77
Dahomey C94
Gabon C82
Ivory Coast C38-C40
Madagascar C92
Mali C65
Mauritania C80
Niger C104
Senegal C68
Togo C104
Upper Volta C62

No. C118 (1)	3.25	1.25
No. C65 (1)	1.75	1.75
No. C48 (1)	2.40	1.00
No. C77 (1)	2.00	1.75
No. C94 (1)	2.25	2.25
No. C82 (1)	2.00	2.00
Nos. C38-C40 (3)	14.50	14.50
No. C92 (1)	1.75	.85
No. C65 (1)	1.75	1.00
No. C80 (1)	1.90	.75
No. C104 (1)	3.00	1.90
No. C68 (1)	2.00	1.40
No. C104 (1)	2.25	.45
No. C62 (1)	4.00	3.25
Set total (16) Stamps	44.80	34.10

Concorde

Concorde in Flight CD129

First flight of the prototype Concorde supersonic plane at Toulouse, Mar. 1, 1969.

1969

Afars & Issas C56
Comoro Isls. C29
France C42
Fr. Polynesia C50
Fr. So. & Antarctic Terr. C18
New Caledonia C63
St. Pierre & Miquelon C40
Wallis & Futuna Isls. C30

No. C56 (1)	26.00	16.00
No. C29 (1)	18.00	12.00
No. C42 (1)	.75	.35
No. C50 (1)	55.00	35.00
No. C18 (1)	55.00	37.50
No. C63 (1)	27.50	20.00
No. C40 (1)	32.50	11.00
No. C30 (1)	15.00	10.00
Set total (8) Stamps	229.75	141.85

Development Bank

Bank Emblem — CD130

African Development Bank, fifth anniv.

1969

Cameroun 499
Chad 217
Congo, P.R. 181-182
Ivory Coast 281
Mali 127-128
Mauritania 267
Niger 220
Senegal 317-318
Upper Volta 201

No. 499 (1)	.80	.25
No. 217 (1)	.90	.25
Nos. 181-182 (2)	1.00	.50
No. 281 (1)	.70	.40
Nos. 127-128 (2)	1.00	.50
No. 267 (1)	.60	.25
No. 220 (1)	.70	.30
Nos. 317-318 (2)	1.55	.50
No. 201 (1)	.65	.30
Set total (12) Stamps	7.90	3.25

ILO

ILO Headquarters, Geneva, and Emblem — CD131

Intl. Labor Organization, 50th anniv.

1969-70

Afars & Issas 337
Comoro Isls. 83
Fr. Polynesia 251-252
Fr. So. & Antarctic Terr. 35
New Caledonia 379
St. Pierre & Miquelon 396
Wallis & Futuna Isls. 172

No. 337 (1)	2.75	2.00
No. 83 (1)	1.25	.75
Nos. 251-252 (2)	24.00	12.50
No. 35 (1)	15.00	10.00
No. 379 (1)	2.25	1.10
No. 396 (1)	10.00	5.50
No. 172 (1)	2.75	2.75
Set total (8) Stamps	58.00	34.60

ASECNA

Map of Africa, Plane and Airport CD132

10th anniversary of the Agency for the Security of Aerial Navigation in Africa and Madagascar (ASECNA, Agence pour la Securite de la Navigation Aerienne en Afrique et a Madagascar).

1969-70

Cameroun 500
Cent. Africa 119
Chad 222
Congo, P.R. 197
Dahomey 269
Gabon 260
Ivory Coast 287
Mali 130
Niger 221
Senegal 321
Upper Volta 204

No. 500 (1)	2.00	.60
No. 119 (1)	2.00	.80
No. 222 (1)	1.00	.25
No. 197 (1)	2.00	.40
No. 269 (1)	.90	.55
No. 260 (1)	1.75	.75
No. 287 (1)	.90	.40
No. 130 (1)	.90	.40
No. 221 (1)	1.40	.70
No. 321 (1)	1.60	.50
No. 204 (1)	1.75	1.00
Set total (11) Stamps	16.20	6.35

U.P.U. Headquarters

CD133

New Universal Postal Union headquarters, Bern, Switzerland.

1970

Afars & Issas	342
Algeria	443
Cameroun	503-504
Cent. Africa	125
Chad	225
Comoro Isls.	84
Congo, P.R.	216
Fr. Polynesia	261-262
Fr. So. & Antarctic Terr.	36
Gabon	258
Ivory Coast	295
Madagascar	444
Mali	134-135
Mauritania	283
New Caledonia	382
Niger	231-232
St. Pierre & Miquelon	397-398
Senegal	328-329
Tunisia	535
Wallis & Futuna Isls.	173

No. 342 (1)	2.50	1.40
No. 443 (1)	1.10	.40
Nos. 503-504 (2)	2.60	.55
No. 125 (1)	1.75	.70
No. 225 (1)	1.20	.25
No. 84 (1)	5.50	2.00
No. 216 (1)	1.00	.25
Nos. 261-262 (2)	20.00	10.00
No. 36 (1)	40.00	27.50
No. 258 (1)	.90	.55
No. 295 (1)	1.10	.50
No. 444 (1)	.55	.25
Nos. 134-135 (2)	1.05	.50
No. 283 (1)	.60	.30
No. 382 (1)	3.00	1.50
Nos. 231-232 (2)	1.50	.60
Nos. 397-398 (2)	34.00	16.25
Nos. 328-329 (2)	1.55	.55
No. 535 (1)	.60	.25
No. 173 (1)	3.25	3.25
Set total (26) Stamps	123.75	67.55

De Gaulle

CD134

First anniversary of the death of Charles de Gaulle, (1890-1970), President of France.

1971-72

Afars & Issas	356-357
Comoro Isls.	104-105
France	1325a
Fr. Polynesia	270-271
Fr. So. & Antarctic Terr.	52-53
New Caledonia	393-394
Reunion	380a
St. Pierre & Miquelon	417-418
Wallis & Futuna Isls.	177-178

Nos. 356-357 (2)	12.50	7.50
Nos. 104-105 (2)	9.00	5.75
No. 1325a (1)	3.00	2.50
Nos. 270-271 (2)	51.50	29.50
Nos. 52-53 (2)	40.00	29.50
Nos. 393-394 (2)	23.00	11.75
No. 380a (1)	9.25	8.00
Nos. 417-418 (2)	56.50	31.00
Nos. 177-178 (2)	20.00	16.25
Set total (16) Stamps	224.75	141.75

African Postal Union, 1971

UAMPT Building, Brazzaville, Congo — CD135

10th anniversary of the establishment of the African and Malagasy Posts and Telecommunications Union, UAMPT. Each stamp has a different native design.

1971, Nov. 13

Cameroun	C177
Cent. Africa	C89
Chad	C94
Congo, P.R.	C136
Dahomey	C146
Gabon	C120
Ivory Coast	C47
Mauritania	C113
Niger	C164
Rwanda	C8
Senegal	C105
Togo	C166
Upper Volta	C97

No. C177 (1)	2.00	.50
No. C89 (1)	2.25	.85
No. C94 (1)	1.50	.50
No. C136 (1)	1.60	.75
No. C146 (1)	1.75	.80
No. C120 (1)	1.75	.70
No. C47 (1)	2.00	1.00
No. C113 (1)	1.10	.65
No. C164 (1)	1.25	.60
No. C8 (1)	2.75	2.50
No. C105 (1)	1.60	.50
No. C166 (1)	1.25	.40
No. C97 (1)	1.50	.70
Set total (13) Stamps	22.30	10.45

West African Monetary Union

African Couple, City, Village and Commemorative Coin — CD136

West African Monetary Union, 10th anniv.

1972, Nov. 2

Dahomey	300
Ivory Coast	331
Mauritania	299
Niger	258
Senegal	374
Togo	825
Upper Volta	280

No. 300 (1)	.65	.25
No. 331 (1)	1.00	.50
No. 299 (1)	.75	.25
No. 258 (1)	.65	.30
No. 374 (1)	.50	.30
No. 825 (1)	.60	.25
No. 280 (1)	.60	.25
Set total (7) Stamps	4.75	2.10

African Postal Union, 1973

Telecommunications Symbols and Map of Africa — CD137

11th anniversary of the African and Malagasy Posts and Telecommunications Union (UAMPT).

1973, Sept. 12

Cameroun	574
Cent. Africa	194
Chad	294
Congo, P.R.	289
Dahomey	311
Gabon	320
Ivory Coast	361
Madagascar	500
Mauritania	304
Niger	287
Rwanda	540
Senegal	393
Togo	849
Upper Volta	297

No. 574 (1)	1.75	.40
No. 194 (1)	1.25	.75
No. 294 (1)	1.75	.40
No. 289 (1)	1.60	.50
No. 311 (1)	1.25	.55
No. 320 (1)	1.40	.75
No. 361 (1)	2.50	1.00
No. 500 (1)	1.10	.35
No. 304 (1)	1.10	.40
No. 287 (1)	.90	.60
No. 540 (1)	3.00	2.00
No. 393 (1)	1.60	.50
No. 849 (1)	1.00	.35
No. 297 (1)	1.25	.70
Set total (14) Stamps	21.45	9.25

Philexafrique II — Essen

CD138

CD139

Designs: Indigenous fauna, local and German stamps. Types CD138-CD139 printed horizontally and vertically se-tenant in sheets of 10 (2x5). Label between horizontal pairs alternately commemoratives Philexafrique II, Libreville, Gabon, June 1978, and 2nd International Stamp Fair, Essen, Germany, Nov. 1-5.

1978-1979

Benin	C286a
Central Africa	C201a
Chad	C239a
Congo Republic	C246a
Djibouti	C122a
Gabon	C216a
Ivory Coast	C65a
Mali	C357a
Mauritania	C186a
Niger	C292a
Rwanda	C13a
Senegal	C147a
Togo	C364a

No. C286a (1)	9.00	8.50
No. C201a (1)	7.50	7.50
No. C239a (1)	7.50	4.00
No. C246a (1)	7.00	7.00
No. C122a (1)	6.50	6.50
No. C216a (1)	6.50	4.00
No. C65a (1)	9.00	9.00
No. C357a (1)	5.00	3.00
No. C186a (1)	5.50	5.00
No. C292a (1)	6.00	6.00
No. C13a (1)	4.00	4.00
No. C147a (1)	10.00	4.00
No. C364a (1)	3.00	1.50
Set total (13) Stamps	86.50	70.00

BRITISH COMMONWEALTH OF NATIONS

The listings follow established trade practices when these issues are offered as units by dealers. The Peace issue, for example, includes only one stamp from the Indian state of Hyderabad. The U.P.U. issue includes the Egypt set. Pairs are included for those varieties issued with bilingual designs se-tenant.

Silver Jubilee

Windsor Castle and King George V CD301

Reign of King George V, 25th anniv.

1935

Antigua	77-80
Ascension	33-36
Bahamas	92-95
Barbados	186-189
Basutoland	11-14
Bechuanaland Protectorate	117-120
Bermuda	100-103
British Guiana	223-226
British Honduras	108-111
Cayman Islands	81-84
Ceylon	260-263
Cyprus	136-139
Dominica	90-93
Falkland Islands	77-80
Fiji	110-113
Gambia	125-128
Gibraltar	100-103
Gilbert & Ellice Islands	33-36
Gold Coast	108-111
Grenada	124-127
Hong Kong	147-150
Jamaica	109-112
Kenya, Uganda, Tanzania	42-45
Leeward Islands	96-99
Malta	184-187
Mauritius	204-207
Montserrat	85-88
Newfoundland	226-229
Nigeria	34-37
Northern Rhodesia	18-21
Nyasaland Protectorate	47-50
St. Helena	111-114
St. Kitts-Nevis	72-75
St. Lucia	91-94
St. Vincent	134-137
Seychelles	118-121
Sierra Leone	166-169
Solomon Islands	60-63
Somaliland Protectorate	77-80
Straits Settlements	213-216
Swaziland	20-23
Trinidad & Tobago	43-46
Turks & Caicos Islands	71-74
Virgin Islands	69-72

The following have different designs but are included in the omnibus set:

Great Britain	226-229
Offices in Morocco (Sp. Curr.)	67-70
Offices in Morocco (Br. Curr.)	226-229
Offices in Morocco (Fr. Curr.)	422-425
Offices in Morocco (Tangier)	508-510
Australia	152-154
Canada	211-216
Cook Islands	98-100
India	142-148
Nauru	31-34
New Guinea	46-47
New Zealand	199-201
Niue	67-69
Papua	114-117
Samoa	163-165
South Africa	68-71
Southern Rhodesia	33-36
South-West Africa	121-124

Nos. 77-80 (4)	20.25	23.25
Nos. 33-36 (4)	58.50	127.50
Nos. 92-95 (4)	25.00	46.00
Nos. 186-189 (4)	30.00	50.30
Nos. 11-14 (4)	11.60	21.25
Nos. 117-120 (4)	15.75	36.00
Nos. 100-103 (4)	16.80	58.50
Nos. 223-226 (4)	22.35	35.50
Nos. 108-111 (4)	15.25	16.35
Nos. 81-84 (4)	21.60	24.50
Nos. 260-263 (4)	10.40	21.60
Nos. 136-139 (4)	39.75	34.40
Nos. 90-93 (4)	18.85	19.85
Nos. 77-80 (4)	55.00	14.75
Nos. 110-113 (4)	20.25	34.00
Nos. 125-128 (4)	13.05	25.25
Nos. 100-103 (4)	28.75	42.75
Nos. 33-36 (4)	36.80	67.00
Nos. 108-111 (4)	25.75	78.10
Nos. 124-127 (4)	16.70	40.60
Nos. 147-150 (4)	73.75	20.75
Nos. 109-112 (4)	24.20	50.50
Nos. 42-45 (4)	10.25	11.75
Nos. 96-99 (4)	35.75	49.60
Nos. 184-187 (4)	22.00	33.70
Nos. 204-207 (4)	44.60	58.25
Nos. 85-88 (4)	10.25	30.25
Nos. 226-229 (4)	17.50	12.05
Nos. 34-37 (4)	17.50	73.00
Nos. 18-21 (4)	17.00	15.00
Nos. 47-50 (4)	43.50	82.50
Nos. 111-114 (4)	31.15	36.50
Nos. 72-75 (4)	11.80	18.65
Nos. 91-94 (4)	16.00	20.80
Nos. 134-137 (4)	9.45	21.25
Nos. 118-121 (4)	15.75	40.00
Nos. 166-169 (4)	23.60	50.35
Nos. 60-63 (4)	29.00	38.00
Nos. 77-80 (4)	17.00	48.25
Nos. 213-216 (4)	15.00	25.10
Nos. 20-23 (4)	6.80	18.25
Nos. 43-46 (4)	18.60	37.50
Nos. 71-74 (4)	9.90	14.50
Nos. 69-72 (4)	25.00	55.25
Nos. 226-229 (4)	5.15	9.90

Nos. 67-70 (4)	13.60	*30.70*
Nos. 226-229 (4)	16.30	*56.00*
Nos. 422-425 (4)	9.35	3.95
Nos. 508-510 (3)	26.00	*33.50*
Nos. 152-154 (3)	49.50	45.35
Nos. 211-216 (6)	23.85	13.35
Nos. 98-100 (3)	9.65	*12.00*
Nos. 142-148 (7)	28.85	14.00
Nos. 31-34 (4)	12.35	*13.15*
Nos. 46-47 (2)	4.35	1.70
Nos. 199-201 (3)	23.00	*28.50*
Nos. 67-69 (3)	19.25	*31.00*
Nos. 114-117 (4)	9.20	*17.50*
Nos. 163-165 (3)	4.40	6.50
Nos. 68-71 (4)	57.50	*153.00*
Nos. 33-36 (4)	27.75	*45.25*
Nos. 121-124 (4)	13.00	*36.10*
Set total (245) Stamps	1,401.	2,231.

Coronation

Queen Elizabeth and King George VI
CD302

1937

Aden ...13-15
Antigua ...81-83
Ascension ...37-39
Bahamas ...97-99
Barbados ...190-192
Basutoland...15-17
Bechuanaland Protectorate...121-123
Bermuda...115-117
British Guiana...227-229
British Honduras...112-114
Cayman Islands...97-99
Ceylon ...275-277
Cyprus ...140-142
Dominica...94-96
Falkland Islands ...81-83
Fiji...114-116
Gambia...129-131
Gibraltar...104-106
Gilbert & Ellice Islands...37-39
Gold Coast ...112-114
Grenada...128-130
Hong Kong ...151-153
Jamaica ...113-115
Kenya, Uganda, Tanzania ...60-62
Leeward Islands ...100-102
Malta...188-190
Mauritius...208-210
Montserrat ...89-91
Newfoundland...230-232
Nigeria ...50-52
Northern Rhodesia...22-24
Nyasaland Protectorate...51-53
St. Helena ...115-117
St. Kitts-Nevis...76-78
St. Lucia ...107-109
St. Vincent...138-140
Seychelles ...122-124
Sierra Leone...170-172
Solomon Islands...64-66
Somaliland Protectorate...81-83
Straits Settlements ...235-237
Swaziland ...24-26
Trinidad & Tobago ...47-49
Turks & Caicos Islands ...75-77
Virgin Islands...73-75

The following have different designs but are included in the omnibus set:

Great Britain ...234
Offices in Morocco (Sp. Curr.)...82
Offices in Morocco (Fr. Curr.) ...439
Offices in Morocco (Tangier)...514
Canada...237
Cook Islands ...109-111
Nauru...35-38
Newfoundland...233-243
New Guinea...48-51
New Zealand ...223-225
Niue ...70-72
Papua ...118-121
South Africa...74-78
Southern Rhodesia ...38-41
South-West Africa ...125-132

Nos. 13-15 (3)	2.70	*5.65*
Nos. 81-83 (3)	1.85	*8.00*
Nos. 37-39 (3)	2.75	*2.75*
Nos. 97-99 (3)	1.05	*3.05*
Nos. 190-192 (3)	1.10	1.95
Nos. 15-17 (3)	1.15	*3.00*
Nos. 121-123 (3)	.95	3.35
Nos. 115-117 (3)	1.25	5.00
Nos. 227-229 (3)	1.45	3.05
Nos. 112-114 (3)	1.20	2.40
Nos. 97-99 (3)	1.10	2.70
Nos. 275-277 (3)	8.25	10.35
Nos. 140-142 (3)	3.75	6.50
Nos. 94-96 (3)	.85	2.40
Nos. 81-83 (3)	2.90	*2.30*
Nos. 114-116 (3)	1.35	*5.75*
Nos. 129-131 (3)	.95	3.95
Nos. 104-106 (3)	2.25	6.45
Nos. 37-39 (3)	.85	*2.15*
Nos. 112-114 (3)	3.10	*10.00*
Nos. 128-130 (3)	1.00	.85
Nos. 151-153 (3)	17.00	17.75
Nos. 113-115 (3)	1.25	1.25
Nos. 60-62 (3)	1.25	2.35
Nos. 100-102 (3)	1.55	4.00
Nos. 188-190 (3)	1.25	1.60
Nos. 208-210 (3)	1.75	3.50
Nos. 89-91 (3)	1.00	3.35
Nos. 230-232 (3)	7.00	2.80
Nos. 50-52 (3)	3.25	8.50
Nos. 22-24 (3)	.95	2.25
Nos. 51-53 (3)	1.05	1.30
Nos. 115-117 (3)	1.45	2.05
Nos. 76-78 (3)	.95	2.15
Nos. 107-109 (3)	1.05	2.05
Nos. 138-140 (3)	.80	*4.75*
Nos. 122-124 (3)	1.20	*1.90*
Nos. 170-172 (3)	1.95	5.65
Nos. 64-66 (3)	.90	2.00
Nos. 81-83 (3)	1.10	*3.50*
Nos. 235-237 (3)	3.25	1.60
Nos. 24-26 (3)	.75	2.70
Nos. 47-49 (3)	1.10	3.20
Nos. 75-77 (3)	1.25	.95
Nos. 73-75 (3)	2.20	6.90

No. 234 (1)	.30	.25
No. 82 (1)	.80	.60
No. 439 (1)	.50	.25
No. 514 (1)	1.25	.50
No. 237 (1)	.35	.25
Nos. 109-111 (3)	.85	.80
Nos. 35-38 (4)	1.25	*5.50*
Nos. 233-243 (11)	41.90	30.40
Nos. 48-51 (4)	1.40	*7.90*
Nos. 223-225 (3)	1.75	*2.25*
Nos. 70-72 (3)	.90	*2.05*
Nos. 118-121 (4)	1.60	*5.25*
Nos. 74-78 (5)	7.60	9.35
Nos. 38-41 (4)	3.55	15.50
Nos. 125-132 (8)	5.00	8.40
Set total (189) Stamps	166.05	268.90

Peace

King George VI and Parliament Buildings, London
CD303

Return to peace at the close of World War II.

1945-46

Aden ...28-29
Antigua ...96-97
Ascension...50-51
Bahamas ...130-131
Barbados ...207-208
Bermuda...131-132
British Guiana...242-243
British Honduras...127-128
Cayman Islands...112-113
Ceylon ...293-294
Cyprus ...156-157
Dominica...112-113
Falkland Islands ...97-98
Falkland Islands Dep...1L9-1L10
Fiji...137-138
Gambia...144-145
Gibraltar...119-120
Gilbert & Ellice Islands...52-53
Gold Coast ...128-129
Grenada...143-144
Jamaica ...136-137
Kenya, Uganda, Tanzania ...90-91
Leeward Islands ...116-117
Malta...206-207
Mauritius...223-224
Montserrat ...104-105
Nigeria ...71-72
Northern Rhodesia...46-47
Nyasaland Protectorate...82-83
Pitcairn Islands...9-10
St. Helena ...128-129
St. Kitts-Nevis...91-92
St. Lucia ...127-128
St. Vincent...152-153
Seychelles ...149-150
Sierra Leone...186-187
Solomon Islands...80-81
Somaliland Protectorate...108-109
Trinidad & Tobago ...62-63
Turks & Caicos Islands ...90-91
Virgin Islands...88-89

The following have different designs but are included in the omnibus set:

Great Britain ...264-265
Offices in Morocco (Tangier)...523-524
Aden
Kathiri State of Seiyun...12-13
Qu'aiti State of Shihr and Mukalla ...
...12-13
Australia...200-202
Basutoland...29-31
Bechuanaland Protectorate...137-139
Burma...66-69
Cook Islands ...127-130
Hong Kong ...174-175
India...195-198
Hyderabad ...51-53
New Zealand ...247-257
Niue ...90-93
Pakistan-Bahawalpur...O16
Samoa ...191-194
South Africa...100-102
Southern Rhodesia ...67-70
South-West Africa ...153-155
Swaziland ...38-40
Zanzibar...222-223

Nos. 28-29 (2)	.95	2.50
Nos. 96-97 (2)	.50	*.80*
Nos. 50-51 (2)	.80	*2.00*
Nos. 130-131 (2)	.50	1.40
Nos. 207-208 (2)	.50	1.10
Nos. 131-132 (2)	.55	.55
Nos. 242-243 (2)	1.05	*1.40*
Nos. 127-128 (2)	.50	.50
Nos. 112-113 (2)	.80	.80
Nos. 293-294 (2)	.60	*2.10*
Nos. 156-157 (2)	.90	.70
Nos. 112-113 (2)	.50	.50
Nos. 97-98 (2)	.90	1.35
Nos. 1L9-1L10 (2)	1.30	1.00
Nos. 137-138 (2)	.75	*1.75*
Nos. 144-145 (2)	.60	.95
Nos. 119-120 (2)	.75	*1.00*
Nos. 52-53 (2)	.50	*1.10*
Nos. 128-129 (2)	1.85	*3.75*
Nos. 143-144 (2)	.50	*.95*
Nos. 136-137 (2)	2.00	*13.50*
Nos. 90-91 (2)	.65	.85
Nos. 116-117 (2)	.50	1.50
Nos. 206-207 (2)	.65	2.00
Nos. 223-224 (2)	.50	1.05
Nos. 104-105 (2)	.50	.50
Nos. 71-72 (2)	.70	*2.75*
Nos. 46-47 (2)	1.25	*2.00*
Nos. 82-83 (2)	.55	.60
Nos. 9-10 (2)	1.40	.60
Nos. 128-129 (2)	.65	.70
Nos. 91-92 (2)	.50	.50
Nos. 127-128 (2)	.50	.60
Nos. 152-153 (2)	.50	.50
Nos. 149-150 (2)	.55	.50
Nos. 186-187 (2)	.50	.50
Nos. 80-81 (2)	.50	1.50
Nos. 108-109 (2)	.70	.50
Nos. 62-63 (2)	.75	1.85
Nos. 90-91 (2)	.50	.50
Nos. 88-89 (2)	.50	.50

Nos. 264-265 (2)	.50	.50
Nos. 523-524 (2)	2.00	2.55
Nos. 12-13 (2)	.50	.90
Nos. 12-13 (2)	.50	*1.25*
Nos. 200-202 (3)	1.60	*1.25*
Nos. 29-31 (3)	2.10	2.60
Nos. 137-139 (3)	2.05	*4.75*
Nos. 66-69 (4)	1.50	1.25
Nos. 127-130 (4)	2.00	1.85
Nos. 174-175 (2)	6.75	2.75
Nos. 195-198 (4)	5.60	5.50
Nos. 51-53 (3)	1.50	1.70
Nos. 247-257 (11)	3.35	3.65
Nos. 90-93 (4)	1.70	*2.20*
No. O16 (1)	15.00	*10.00*
Nos. 191-194 (4)	2.05	1.00
Nos. 100-102 (3)	1.00	3.25
Nos. 67-70 (4)	1.40	1.75
Nos. 153-155 (3)	1.85	3.25
Nos. 38-40 (3)	2.40	*5.50*
Nos. 222-223 (2)	.65	1.00
Set total (151) Stamps	86.15	118.15

Silver Wedding

King George VI and Queen Elizabeth
CD304 CD305

1948-49

Aden ...30-31
Kathiri State of Seiyun...14-15
Qu'aiti State of Shihr and Mukalla ...
...14-15
Antigua ...98-99
Ascension...52-53
Bahamas ...148-149
Barbados ...210-211
Basutoland...39-40
Bechuanaland Protectorate...147-148
Bermuda...133-134
British Guiana...244-245
British Honduras...129-130
Cayman Islands...116-117
Cyprus ...158-159
Dominica...114-115
Falkland Islands ...99-100
Falkland Islands Dep...1L11-1L12
Fiji...139-140
Gambia...146-147
Gibraltar...121-122
Gilbert & Ellice Islands...54-55
Gold Coast ...142-143
Grenada...145-146
Hong Kong ...178-179
Jamaica ...138-139
Kenya, Uganda, Tanzania ...92-93
Leeward Islands ...118-119
Malaya
Johore ...128-129
Kedah...55-56
Kelantan...44-45
Malacca...1-2
Negri Sembilan ...36-37
Pahang...44-45
Penang...1-2
Perak...99-100
Perlis ...1-2
Selangor...74-75
Trengganu ...47-48
Malta...223-224
Mauritius...229-230
Montserrat ...106-107
Nigeria ...73-74
North Borneo...238-239
Northern Rhodesia...48-49
Nyasaland Protectorate...85-86
Pitcairn Islands...11-12
St. Helena ...130-131
St. Kitts-Nevis...93-94
St. Lucia ...129-130
St. Vincent...154-155
Sarawak...174-175
Seychelles ...151-152
Sierra Leone...188-189
Singapore ...21-22
Solomon Islands...82-83
Somaliland Protectorate...110-111
Swaziland ...48-49
Trinidad & Tobago ...64-65
Turks & Caicos Islands ...92-93
Virgin Islands...90-91
Zanzibar...224-225

The following have different designs but are included in the omnibus set:

Great Britain ...267-268
Offices in Morocco (Sp. Curr.) ...93-94
Offices in Morocco (Tangier) ...525-526
Bahrain ...62-63
Kuwait...82-83
Oman...25-26
South Africa...106
South-West Africa ...159

Nos. 30-31 (2)	40.40	56.50
Nos. 14-15 (2)	17.85	*16.00*
Nos. 14-15 (2)	18.55	*12.50*
Nos. 98-99 (2)	13.55	*15.75*
Nos. 52-53 (2)	55.55	50.45
Nos. 148-149 (2)	45.25	40.30
Nos. 210-211 (2)	18.35	13.55
Nos. 39-40 (2)	52.80	*55.25*
Nos. 147-148 (2)	42.85	*47.75*
Nos. 133-134 (2)	47.75	*55.25*
Nos. 244-245 (2)	24.25	*28.45*
Nos. 129-130 (2)	25.25	*53.20*
Nos. 116-117 (2)	25.25	*33.50*
Nos. 158-159 (2)	58.50	*78.05*
Nos. 114-115 (2)	25.25	*32.75*
Nos. 99-100 (2)	112.10	76.10
Nos. 1L11-1L12 (2)	4.25	6.00
Nos. 139-140 (2)	18.20	11.50
Nos. 146-147 (2)	21.30	21.25
Nos. 121-122 (2)	61.00	*78.00*
Nos. 54-55 (2)	14.25	*26.25*
Nos. 142-143 (2)	35.25	48.20
Nos. 145-146 (2)	21.75	21.75
Nos. 178-179 (2)	329.00	106.75
Nos. 138-139 (2)	30.35	*75.25*
Nos. 92-93 (2)	51.00	*68.00*
Nos. 118-119 (2)	7.00	8.25
Nos. 128-129 (2)	29.25	*53.25*
Nos. 55-56 (2)	35.25	*50.25*
Nos. 44-45 (2)	35.75	*62.75*
Nos. 1-2 (2)	35.40	*49.75*
Nos. 36-37 (2)	28.10	*38.20*
Nos. 44-45 (2)	28.00	*38.05*
Nos. 1-2 (2)	40.50	37.80

Nos. 99-100 (2)	27.80	37.75
Nos. 1-2 (2)	33.50	58.00
Nos. 74-75 (2)	30.25	25.30
Nos. 47-48 (2)	32.75	61.75
Nos. 223-224 (2)	40.55	45.25
Nos. 229-230 (2)	19.25	45.25
Nos. 106-107 (2)	8.75	17.25
Nos. 73-74 (2)	17.85	22.80
Nos. 238-239 (2)	35.30	45.75
Nos. 48-49 (2)	100.30	90.25
Nos. 85-86 (2)	18.25	35.25
Nos. 11-12 (2)	44.50	54.00
Nos. 130-131 (2)	32.80	42.80
Nos. 93-94 (2)	13.25	10.50
Nos. 129-130 (2)	22.25	40.25
Nos. 154-155 (2)	27.75	30.25
Nos. 174-175 (2)	52.80	67.80
Nos. 151-152 (2)	16.25	48.25
Nos. 188-189 (2)	25.25	29.75
Nos. 21-22 (2)	116.00	45.40
Nos. 82-83 (2)	13.40	13.40
Nos. 110-111 (2)	8.40	8.75
Nos. 48-49 (2)	40.30	47.75
Nos. 64-65 (2)	31.80	50.25
Nos. 92-93 (2)	16.25	22.75
Nos. 90-91 (2)	16.25	22.25
Nos. 224-225 (2)	29.60	38.00
Nos. 267-268 (2)	30.40	25.25
Nos. 93-94 (2)	17.10	25.75
Nos. 525-526 (2)	22.90	32.75
Nos. 62-63 (2)	38.50	57.75
Nos. 82-83 (2)	69.50	45.50
Nos. 25-26 (2)	41.00	42.50
No. 106 (1)	.80	1.00
No. 159 (1)	1.10	.35
Set total (136) Stamps	2,542.	2,754.

U.P.U.

Mercury and Symbols of Communications — CD306

Plane, Ship and Hemispheres — CD307

Mercury Scattering Letters over Globe CD308

U.P.U. Monument, Bern CD309

Universal Postal Union, 75th anniversary.

1949

Aden 32-35
Kathiri State of Seiyun 16-19
Qu'aiti State of Shihr and Mukalla 16-19
Antigua 100-103
Ascension 57-60
Bahamas 150-153
Barbados 212-215
Basutoland 41-44
Bechuanaland Protectorate 149-152
Bermuda 138-141
British Guiana 246-249
British Honduras 137-140
Brunei 79-82
Cayman Islands 118-121
Cyprus 160-163
Dominica 116-119
Falkland Islands 103-106
Falkland Islands Dep. 1L14-1L17
Fiji 141-144
Gambia 148-151
Gibraltar 123-126
Gilbert & Ellice Islands 56-59
Gold Coast 144-147
Grenada 147-150
Hong Kong 180-183
Jamaica 142-145
Kenya, Uganda, Tanzania 94-97
Leeward Islands 126-129
Malaya
Johore 151-154
Kedah 57-60
Kelantan 46-49
Malacca 18-21
Negri Sembilan 59-62
Pahang 46-49
Penang 23-26
Perak 101-104
Perlis 3-6
Selangor 76-79
Trengganu 49-52
Malta 225-228
Mauritius 231-234
Montserrat 108-111
New Hebrides, British 62-65
New Hebrides, French 79-82
Nigeria 75-78
North Borneo 240-243
Northern Rhodesia 50-53
Nyasaland Protectorate 87-90
Pitcairn Islands 13-16
St. Helena 132-135
St. Kitts-Nevis 95-98
St. Lucia 131-134
St. Vincent 170-173
Sarawak 176-179
Seychelles 153-156
Sierra Leone 190-193
Singapore 23-26
Solomon Islands 84-87
Somaliland Protectorate 112-115
Southern Rhodesia 71-72
Swaziland 50-53
Tonga 87-90
Trinidad & Tobago 66-69
Turks & Caicos Islands 101-104
Virgin Islands 92-95
Zanzibar 226-229

The following have different designs but are included in the omnibus set:

Great Britain 276-279
Offices in Morocco (Tangier) 546-549
Australia 223
Bahrain 68-71
Burma 116-121
Ceylon 304-306
Egypt 281-283
India 223-226
Kuwait 89-92
Oman 31-34
Pakistan-Bahawalpur 26-29, O25-O28
South Africa 109-111
South-West Africa 160-162

Nos. 32-35 (4)	5.85	8.45
Nos. 16-19 (4)	2.75	16.00
Nos. 16-19 (4)	2.60	8.00
Nos. 100-103 (4)	3.60	7.70
Nos. 57-60 (4)	11.10	9.00
Nos. 150-153 (4)	5.35	9.30
Nos. 212-215 (4)	4.40	14.85
Nos. 41-44 (4)	4.75	10.00
Nos. 149-152 (4)	3.35	7.25
Nos. 138-141 (4)	4.75	6.15
Nos. 246-249 (4)	2.75	4.20
Nos. 137-140 (4)	3.30	6.35
Nos. 79-82 (4)	9.50	8.45
Nos. 118-121 (4)	3.60	7.25
Nos. 160-163 (4)	4.60	10.70
Nos. 116-119 (4)	2.30	5.65
Nos. 103-106 (4)	14.00	17.10
Nos. 1L14-1L17 (4)	14.60	14.50
Nos. 141-144 (4)	3.35	15.75
Nos. 148-151 (4)	2.75	7.10
Nos. 123-126 (4)	5.90	8.75
Nos. 56-59 (4)	4.30	13.00
Nos. 144-147 (4)	2.55	10.35
Nos. 147-150 (4)	2.15	3.55
Nos. 180-183 (4)	66.75	19.95
Nos. 142-145 (4)	2.50	2.45
Nos. 94-97 (4)	2.90	4.00
Nos. 126-129 (4)	3.05	9.60
Nos. 151-154 (4)	4.70	8.90
Nos. 57-60 (4)	4.80	12.00
Nos. 46-49 (4)	4.25	12.65
Nos. 18-21 (4)	4.25	17.30
Nos. 59-62 (4)	3.50	10.75
Nos. 46-49 (4)	3.00	7.25
Nos. 23-26 (4)	5.10	11.75
Nos. 101-104 (4)	3.65	10.75
Nos. 3-6 (4)	3.95	14.25
Nos. 76-79 (4)	4.90	12.30
Nos. 49-52 (4)	5.55	12.25
Nos. 225-228 (4)	4.50	4.85
Nos. 231-234 (4)	3.70	7.05
Nos. 108-111 (4)	3.30	4.35
Nos. 62-65 (4)	1.60	4.25
Nos. 79-82 (4)	15.40	22.00
Nos. 75-78 (4)	2.80	9.25
Nos. 240-243 (4)	7.15	6.50
Nos. 50-53 (4)	5.00	6.50
Nos. 87-90 (4)	4.55	6.60
Nos. 13-16 (4)	15.05	14.25
Nos. 132-135 (4)	4.85	7.10
Nos. 95-98 (4)	4.35	5.55
Nos. 131-134 (4)	2.55	3.85
Nos. 170-173 (4)	2.20	5.05
Nos. 176-179 (4)	13.40	13.35
Nos. 153-156 (4)	3.00	5.15
Nos. 190-193 (4)	2.90	9.15
Nos. 23-26 (4)	19.00	13.70
Nos. 84-87 (4)	4.05	4.90
Nos. 112-115 (4)	3.95	9.95
Nos. 71-72 (2)	1.95	2.25
Nos. 50-53 (4)	2.80	4.65
Nos. 87-90 (4)	3.00	5.25
Nos. 66-69 (4)	3.55	6.80
Nos. 101-104 (4)	3.05	8.90
Nos. 92-95 (4)	2.60	5.90
Nos. 226-229 (4)	4.95	13.50
Nos. 276-279 (4)	1.35	1.00
Nos. 546-549 (4)	2.60	16.00
No. 223 (1)	.40	.40
Nos. 68-71 (4)	4.75	16.50
Nos. 116-121 (6)	7.30	5.35
Nos. 304-306 (3)	3.35	4.25
Nos. 281-283 (3)	5.75	2.70
Nos. 223-226 (4)	27.25	10.50
Nos. 89-92 (4)	6.10	10.25
Nos. 31-34 (4)	8.00	17.50
Nos. 26-29,O25-O28 (8)	2.40	44.00
Nos. 109-111 (3)	2.00	2.70
Nos. 160-162 (3)	3.00	5.50
Set total (313) Stamps	466.45	742.80

University

Arms of University College CD310

Alice, Princess of Athlone CD311

1948 opening of University College of the West Indies at Jamaica.

1951

Antigua 104-105
Barbados 228-229
British Guiana 250-251
British Honduras 141-142
Dominica 120-121
Grenada 164-165
Jamaica 146-147
Leeward Islands 130-131
Montserrat 112-113
St. Kitts-Nevis 105-106
St. Lucia 149-150
St. Vincent 174-175
Trinidad & Tobago 70-71
Virgin Islands 96-97

Nos. 104-105 (2)	1.35	3.75
Nos. 228-229 (2)	1.75	2.65
Nos. 250-251 (2)	1.10	1.25
Nos. 141-142 (2)	1.40	2.20
Nos. 120-121 (2)	1.40	1.75
Nos. 164-165 (2)	1.20	1.60
Nos. 146-147 (2)	1.05	.70
Nos. 130-131 (2)	1.35	4.00
Nos. 112-113 (2)	.85	2.00
Nos. 105-106 (2)	1.40	2.25
Nos. 149-150 (2)	1.40	1.50
Nos. 174-175 (2)	1.00	2.15
Nos. 70-71 (2)	1.00	4.20
Nos. 96-97 (2)	1.50	3.75
Set total (28) Stamps	17.75	33.75

Coronation

Queen Elizabeth II — CD312

1953

Aden 47
Kathiri State of Seiyun 28
Qu'aiti State of Shihr and Mukalla 28
Antigua 106
Ascension 61
Bahamas 157
Barbados 234
Basutoland 45
Bechuanaland Protectorate 153
Bermuda 142
British Guiana 252
British Honduras 143
Cayman Islands 150
Cyprus 167
Dominica 141
Falkland Islands 121
Falkland Islands Dependencies 1L18
Fiji 145
Gambia 152
Gibraltar 131
Gilbert & Ellice Islands 60
Gold Coast 160
Grenada 170
Hong Kong 184
Jamaica 153
Kenya, Uganda, Tanzania 101
Leeward Islands 132
Malaya
Johore 155
Kedah 82
Kelantan 71
Malacca 27
Negri Sembilan 63
Pahang 71
Penang 27
Perak 126
Perlis 28
Selangor 101
Trengganu 74
Malta 241
Mauritius 250
Montserrat 127
New Hebrides, British 77
Nigeria 79
North Borneo 260
Northern Rhodesia 60
Nyasaland Protectorate 96
Pitcairn Islands 19
St. Helena 139
St. Kitts-Nevis 119
St. Lucia 156
St. Vincent 185
Sarawak 196
Seychelles 172
Sierra Leone 194
Singapore 27
Solomon Islands 88
Somaliland Protectorate 127
Swaziland 54
Trinidad & Tobago 84
Tristan da Cunha 13
Turks & Caicos Islands 118
Virgin Islands 114

The following have different designs but are included in the omnibus set:

Great Britain 313-316
Offices in Morocco (Tangier) 579-582
Australia 259-261
Bahrain 92-95
Canada 330
Ceylon 317
Cook Islands 145-146
Kuwait 113-116
New Zealand 280-284
Niue 104-105
Oman 52-55
Samoa 214-215
South Africa 192
Southern Rhodesia 80
South-West Africa 244-248
Tokelau Islands 4

No. 47 (1)	1.25	1.25
No. 28 (1)	.75	1.50
No. 28 (1)	1.10	.60
No. 106 (1)	.40	.75
No. 61 (1)	1.25	2.75
No. 157 (1)	1.40	.75
No. 234 (1)	1.00	.25
No. 45 (1)	.50	.60
No. 153 (1)	.50	.35
No. 142 (1)	.85	.50
No. 252 (1)	.45	.25
No. 143 (1)	.60	.40
No. 150 (1)	.40	1.75
No. 167 (1)	1.60	.75
No. 141 (1)	.40	.40
No. 121 (1)	.90	1.50
No. 1L18 (1)	1.80	1.40
No. 145 (1)	1.00	.60
No. 152 (1)	.50	.50
No. 131 (1)	.50	.50
No. 60 (1)	.65	2.25
No. 160 (1)	1.00	.25

No. 170 (1)	.30	.25
No. 184 (1)	3.00	.30
No. 153 (1)	.70	.25
No. 101 (1)	.40	.25
No. 132 (1)	1.00	*2.25*
No. 155 (1)	1.40	.30
No. 82 (1)	2.25	.60
No. 71 (1)	1.60	1.60
No. 27 (1)	1.10	*1.50*
No. 63 (1)	1.40	.65
No. 71 (1)	2.25	.25
No. 27 (1)	1.75	.30
No. 126 (1)	1.60	.25
No. 28 (1)	1.75	*4.00*
No. 101 (1)	1.75	.25
No. 74 (1)	1.50	1.00
No. 241 (1)	.50	.25
No. 250 (1)	1.10	.25
No. 127 (1)	.60	.45
No. 77 (1)	.75	.60
No. 79 (1)	.40	.25
No. 260 (1)	1.75	1.00
No. 60 (1)	.70	.25
No. 96 (1)	.75	.75
No. 19 (1)	2.00	3.50
No. 139 (1)	1.25	1.25
No. 119 (1)	.35	.25
No. 156 (1)	.70	.35
No. 185 (1)	.50	.30
No. 196 (1)	1.75	*1.75*
No. 172 (1)	.80	.80
No. 194 (1)	.40	.40
No. 27 (1)	2.50	.40
No. 88 (1)	1.00	1.00
No. 127 (1)	.40	.25
No. 54 (1)	.30	.25
No. 84 (1)	.30	.25
No. 13 (1)	1.00	1.75
No. 118 (1)	.40	*1.10*
No. 114 (1)	.40	*1.00*
Nos. 313-316 (4)	11.40	4.05
Nos. 579-582 (4)	10.90	5.30
Nos. 259-261 (3)	3.60	2.75
Nos. 92-95 (4)	15.25	12.75
No. 330 (1)	.30	.25
No. 317 (1)	1.40	.25
Nos. 145-146 (2)	2.65	2.65
Nos. 113-116 (4)	16.00	8.50
Nos. 280-284 (5)	3.30	*4.55*
Nos. 104-105 (2)	2.25	1.50
Nos. 52-55 (4)	14.25	6.50
Nos. 214-215 (2)	2.50	.80
No. 192 (1)	.45	.30
No. 80 (1)	7.25	7.25
Nos. 244-248 (5)	3.00	2.35
No. 4 (1)	2.75	2.75
Set total (106) Stamps	160.40	114.75

Separate designs for each country for the visit of Queen Elizabeth II and the Duke of Edinburgh.

Royal Visit 1953

1953

Aden 62
Australia 267-269
Bermuda 163
Ceylon 318
Fiji 146
Gibraltar 146
Jamaica 154
Kenya, Uganda, Tanzania 102
Malta 242
New Zealand 286-287

No. 62 (1)	.65	4.00
Nos. 267-269 (3)	2.75	2.05
No. 163 (1)	.50	.25
No. 318 (1)	1.00	.25
No. 146 (1)	.65	.35
No. 146 (1)	.50	.30
No. 154 (1)	.50	.25
No. 102 (1)	.50	.25
No. 242 (1)	.35	.25
Nos. 286-287 (2)	.50	.50
Set total (13) Stamps	7.90	8.45

West Indies Federation

Map of the Caribbean
CD313

Federation of the West Indies, April 22, 1958.

1958

Antigua 122-124
Barbados 248-250
Dominica 161-163
Grenada 184-186
Jamaica 175-177
Montserrat 143-145
St. Kitts-Nevis 136-138
St. Lucia 170-172
St. Vincent 198-200
Trinidad & Tobago 86-88

Nos. 122-124 (3)	5.80	3.80
Nos. 248-250 (3)	1.60	*2.90*
Nos. 161-163 (3)	1.95	1.85
Nos. 184-186 (3)	1.50	1.20
Nos. 175-177 (3)	2.65	3.45
Nos. 143-145 (3)	2.35	1.35
Nos. 136-138 (3)	3.00	3.10
Nos. 170-172 (3)	2.05	2.80
Nos. 198-200 (3)	1.50	1.75
Nos. 86-88 (3)	2.40	2.35
Set total (30) Stamps	24.80	24.55

Freedom from Hunger

Protein Food
CD314

U.N. Food and Agricultural Organization's "Freedom from Hunger" campaign.

1963

Aden 65
Antigua 133
Ascension 89
Bahamas 180
Basutoland 83
Bechuanaland Protectorate 194
Bermuda 192
British Guiana 271
British Honduras 179
Brunei 100
Cayman Islands 168
Dominica 181
Falkland Islands 146
Fiji 198
Gambia 172
Gibraltar 161
Gilbert & Ellice Islands 76
Grenada 190
Hong Kong 218
Malta 291
Mauritius 270
Montserrat 150
New Hebrides, British 93
North Borneo 296
Pitcairn Islands 35
St. Helena 173
St. Lucia 179
St. Vincent 201
Sarawak 212
Seychelles 213
Solomon Islands 109
Swaziland 108
Tonga 127
Tristan da Cunha 68
Turks & Caicos Islands 138
Virgin Islands 140
Zanzibar 280

No. 65 (1)	1.50	1.75
No. 133 (1)	.35	.35
No. 89 (1)	1.00	.50
No. 180 (1)	.65	.65
No. 83 (1)	.50	.25
No. 194 (1)	.50	.50
No. 192 (1)	1.00	.50
No. 271 (1)	.45	.25
No. 179 (1)	.60	.25
No. 100 (1)	3.25	2.25
No. 168 (1)	.55	.30
No. 181 (1)	.30	.30
No. 146 (1)	10.50	2.50
No. 198 (1)	3.50	2.25
No. 172 (1)	.50	.25
No. 161 (1)	4.00	2.25
No. 76 (1)	1.40	.40
No. 190 (1)	.30	.25
No. 218 (1)	37.50	5.00
No. 291 (1)	2.00	2.00
No. 270 (1)	.45	.25
No. 150 (1)	.55	.35
No. 93 (1)	.60	.25
No. 296 (1)	1.90	.75
No. 35 (1)	3.50	1.50
No. 173 (1)	2.25	1.10
No. 179 (1)	.40	.40
No. 201 (1)	.90	.50
No. 212 (1)	1.60	*1.00*
No. 213 (1)	.85	.35
No. 109 (1)	3.00	.85
No. 108 (1)	.50	.50
No. 127 (1)	.60	.35
No. 68 (1)	.75	.35
No. 138 (1)	.30	.25
No. 140 (1)	.50	.50
No. 280 (1)	1.50	.80
Set total (37) Stamps	90.50	32.80

Red Cross Centenary

Red Cross and Elizabeth II
CD315

1963

Antigua 134-135
Ascension 90-91
Bahamas 183-184
Basutoland 84-85
Bechuanaland Protectorate 195-196
Bermuda 193-194
British Guiana 272-273
British Honduras 180-181
Cayman Islands 169-170
Dominica 182-183
Falkland Islands 147-148
Fiji 203-204
Gambia 173-174
Gibraltar 162-163
Gilbert & Ellice Islands 77-78
Grenada 191-192
Hong Kong 219-220
Jamaica 203-204
Malta 292-293
Mauritius 271-272
Montserrat 151-152
New Hebrides, British 94-95
Pitcairn Islands 36-37
St. Helena 174-175
St. Kitts-Nevis 143-144
St. Lucia 180-181
St. Vincent 202-203
Seychelles 214-215
Solomon Islands 110-111
South Arabia 1-2
Swaziland 109-110
Tonga 134-135
Tristan da Cunha 69-70
Turks & Caicos Islands 139-140
Virgin Islands 141-142

Nos. 134-135 (2)	1.00	*2.00*
Nos. 90-91 (2)	6.75	3.35
Nos. 183-184 (2)	2.30	2.80
Nos. 84-85 (2)	1.20	.90
Nos. 195-196 (2)	.95	.85
Nos. 193-194 (2)	3.00	2.80
Nos. 272-273 (2)	.85	.60
Nos. 180-181 (2)	1.00	2.50
Nos. 169-170 (2)	1.10	*3.00*
Nos. 182-183 (2)	.70	*1.05*
Nos. 147-148 (2)	18.00	5.50
Nos. 203-204 (2)	3.25	2.80
Nos. 173-174 (2)	.80	1.00
Nos. 162-163 (2)	6.25	5.40
Nos. 77-78 (2)	2.00	*3.50*
Nos. 191-192 (2)	.80	.50
Nos. 219-220 (2)	18.75	7.35
Nos. 203-204 (2)	.75	*1.65*
Nos. 292-293 (2)	2.50	4.75
Nos. 271-272 (2)	.85	.50
Nos. 151-152 (2)	1.00	.75
Nos. 94-95 (2)	1.00	.50
Nos. 36-37 (2)	2.50	4.00
Nos. 174-175 (2)	1.70	2.30
Nos. 143-144 (2)	.90	.90
Nos. 180-181 (2)	1.25	1.25
Nos. 202-203 (2)	.90	.90
Nos. 214-215 (2)	1.00	1.50
Nos. 110-111 (2)	1.25	1.15
Nos. 1-2 (2)	1.25	1.25
Nos. 109-110 (2)	1.10	1.10
Nos. 134-135 (2)	1.00	1.25
Nos. 69-70 (2)	1.15	.80
Nos. 139-140 (2)	.55	1.00
Nos. 141-142 (2)	.80	1.25
Set total (70) Stamps	90.15	72.70

Shakespeare

Shakespeare Memorial Theatre, Stratford-on-Avon — CD316

400th anniversary of the birth of William Shakespeare.

1964

Antigua 151
Bahamas 201
Bechuanaland Protectorate 197
Cayman Islands 171
Dominica 184
Falkland Islands 149
Gambia 192
Gibraltar 164
Montserrat 153
St. Lucia 196
Turks & Caicos Islands 141
Virgin Islands 143

No. 151 (1)	.35	.25
No. 201 (1)	.60	.35
No. 197 (1)	.35	.35
No. 171 (1)	.35	.30
No. 184 (1)	.35	.35
No. 149 (1)	1.60	.50
No. 192 (1)	.35	.25
No. 164 (1)	.65	.55
No. 153 (1)	.35	.25
No. 196 (1)	.45	.25
No. 141 (1)	.30	.25
No. 143 (1)	.45	.45
Set total (12) Stamps	6.15	4.10

ITU

ITU Emblem
CD317

Intl. Telecommunication Union, cent.

1965

Antigua 153-154
Ascension 92-93
Bahamas 219-220
Barbados 265-266
Basutoland 101-102
Bechuanaland Protectorate 202-203
Bermuda 196-197
British Guiana 293-294
British Honduras 187-188
Brunei 116-117
Cayman Islands 172-173
Dominica 185-186
Falkland Islands 154-155
Fiji 211-212
Gibraltar 167-168
Gilbert & Ellice Islands 87-88
Grenada 205-206
Hong Kong 221-222
Mauritius 291-292
Montserrat 157-158
New Hebrides, British 108-109
Pitcairn Islands 52-53
St. Helena 180-181
St. Kitts-Nevis 163-164
St. Lucia 197-198
St. Vincent 224-225
Seychelles 218-219
Solomon Islands 126-127
Swaziland 115-116
Tristan da Cunha 85-86
Turks & Caicos Islands 142-143
Virgin Islands 159-160

Nos. 153-154 (2)	1.45	1.35
Nos. 92-93 (2)	1.90	1.30
Nos. 219-220 (2)	1.35	1.50
Nos. 265-266 (2)	1.50	1.25
Nos. 101-102 (2)	.85	.65
Nos. 202-203 (2)	1.10	.75
Nos. 196-197 (2)	2.15	*2.25*
Nos. 293-294 (2)	.50	.50
Nos. 187-188 (2)	.75	.75
Nos. 116-117 (2)	1.75	1.75
Nos. 172-173 (2)	1.00	.85
Nos. 185-186 (2)	.55	.55
Nos. 154-155 (2)	6.75	3.15
Nos. 211-212 (2)	2.00	1.05
Nos. 167-168 (2)	9.00	5.95
Nos. 87-88 (2)	.85	.60
Nos. 205-206 (2)	.50	.50
Nos. 221-222 (2)	10.50	4.75
Nos. 291-292 (2)	1.10	.50
Nos. 157-158 (2)	1.05	1.15
Nos. 108-109 (2)	.65	.50
Nos. 52-53 (2)	1.65	1.90
Nos. 180-181 (2)	.80	.60
Nos. 163-164 (2)	.60	.60
Nos. 197-198 (2)	1.25	1.25
Nos. 224-225 (2)	.80	.90
Nos. 218-219 (2)	.75	.60
Nos. 126-127 (2)	.70	.55
Nos. 115-116 (2)	.70	.70
Nos. 85-86 (2)	1.00	.65
Nos. 142-143 (2)	.50	.50
Nos. 159-160 (2)	.85	.85
Set total (64) Stamps	56.85	40.70

Intl. Cooperation Year

ICY Emblem
CD318

1965

Antigua	155-156
Ascension	94-95
Bahamas	222-223
Basutoland	103-104
Bechuanaland Protectorate	204-205
Bermuda	199-200
British Guiana	295-296
British Honduras	189-190
Brunei	118-119
Cayman Islands	174-175
Dominica	187-188
Falkland Islands	156-157
Fiji	213-214
Gibraltar	169-170
Gilbert & Ellice Islands	104-105
Grenada	207-208
Hong Kong	223-224
Mauritius	293-294
Montserrat	176-177
New Hebrides, British	110-111
New Hebrides, French	126-127
Pitcairn Islands	54-55
St. Helena	182-183
St. Kitts-Nevis	165-166
St. Lucia	199-200
Seychelles	220-221
Solomon Islands	143-144
South Arabia	17-18
Swaziland	117-118
Tristan da Cunha	87-88
Turks & Caicos Islands	144-145
Virgin Islands	161-162

Nos. 155-156 (2)	.55	.50
Nos. 94-95 (2)	1.30	1.40
Nos. 222-223 (2)	.65	1.90
Nos. 103-104 (2)	.75	.85
Nos. 204-205 (2)	.85	1.00
Nos. 199-200 (2)	2.05	1.25
Nos. 295-296 (2)	.55	.50
Nos. 189-190 (2)	.60	.55
Nos. 118-119 (2)	.85	.85
Nos. 174-175 (2)	1.00	.75
Nos. 187-188 (2)	.55	.55
Nos. 156-157 (2)	6.00	1.65
Nos. 213-214 (2)	1.95	1.25
Nos. 169-170 (2)	1.25	*2.75*
Nos. 104-105 (2)	.85	.60
Nos. 207-208 (2)	.50	.50
Nos. 223-224 (2)	11.00	3.50
Nos. 293-294 (2)	.65	.50
Nos. 176-177 (2)	.80	.65
Nos. 110-111 (2)	.50	.50
Nos. 126-127 (2)	12.00	12.00
Nos. 54-55 (2)	1.60	1.85
Nos. 182-183 (2)	.95	.50
Nos. 165-166 (2)	.80	.60
Nos. 199-200 (2)	.55	.55
Nos. 220-221 (2)	.80	.60
Nos. 143-144 (2)	.70	.60
Nos. 17-18 (2)	1.20	.50
Nos. 117-118 (2)	.75	.75
Nos. 87-88 (2)	1.05	.65
Nos. 144-145 (2)	.50	.50
Nos. 161-162 (2)	.65	.50
Set total (64) Stamps	54.75	41.60

Churchill Memorial

Winston Churchill and St. Paul's, London, During Air Attack
CD319

1966

Antigua	157-160
Ascension	96-99
Bahamas	224-227
Barbados	281-284
Basutoland	105-108
Bechuanaland Protectorate	206-209
Bermuda	201-204
British Antarctic Territory	16-19
British Honduras	191-194
Brunei	120-123
Cayman Islands	176-179
Dominica	189-192
Falkland Islands	158-161
Fiji	215-218
Gibraltar	171-174
Gilbert & Ellice Islands	106-109
Grenada	209-212
Hong Kong	225-228
Mauritius	295-298
Montserrat	178-181
New Hebrides, British	112-115
New Hebrides, French	128-131
Pitcairn Islands	56-59
St. Helena	184-187
St. Kitts-Nevis	167-170
St. Lucia	201-204
St. Vincent	241-244
Seychelles	222-225
Solomon Islands	145-148
South Arabia	19-22
Swaziland	119-122
Tristan da Cunha	89-92
Turks & Caicos Islands	146-149
Virgin Islands	163-166

Nos. 157-160 (4)	3.05	3.05
Nos. 96-99 (4)	10.00	6.40
Nos. 224-227 (4)	2.30	*3.20*
Nos. 281-284 (4)	3.00	4.95
Nos. 105-108 (4)	2.80	3.25
Nos. 206-209 (4)	2.50	2.50
Nos. 201-204 (4)	4.00	*4.75*
Nos. 16-19 (4)	41.20	18.00
Nos. 191-194 (4)	2.45	1.30
Nos. 120-123 (4)	7.65	6.55
Nos. 176-179 (4)	3.10	3.65
Nos. 189-192 (4)	1.15	1.15
Nos. 158-161 (4)	12.75	9.55
Nos. 215-218 (4)	4.40	3.00
Nos. 171-174 (4)	3.05	5.30
Nos. 106-109 (4)	1.50	1.30
Nos. 209-212 (4)	1.10	1.10
Nos. 225-228 (4)	52.50	11.40
Nos. 295-298 (4)	3.70	3.75
Nos. 178-181 (4)	1.60	1.55
Nos. 112-115 (4)	2.30	1.00
Nos. 128-131 (4)	8.35	8.35
Nos. 56-59 (4)	4.45	6.10
Nos. 184-187 (4)	1.85	1.95
Nos. 167-170 (4)	1.50	1.70
Nos. 201-204 (4)	1.50	1.50
Nos. 241-244 (4)	1.50	1.75
Nos. 222-225 (4)	3.20	4.35
Nos. 145-148 (4)	1.50	1.60
Nos. 19-22 (4)	2.95	2.20
Nos. 119-122 (4)	1.70	2.55
Nos. 89-92 (4)	5.95	2.70
Nos. 146-149 (4)	1.60	1.75
Nos. 163-166 (4)	1.90	1.90
Set total (136) Stamps	204.05	135.10

Royal Visit, 1966

Queen Elizabeth II and Prince Philip
CD320

Caribbean visit, Feb. 4 - Mar. 6, 1966.

1966

Antigua	161-162
Bahamas	228-229
Barbados	285-286
British Guiana	299-300
Cayman Islands	180-181
Dominica	193-194
Grenada	213-214
Montserrat	182-183
St. Kitts-Nevis	171-172
St. Lucia	205-206
St. Vincent	245-246
Turks & Caicos Islands	150-151
Virgin Islands	167-168

Nos. 161-162 (2)	3.50	2.60
Nos. 228-229 (2)	3.05	3.05
Nos. 285-286 (2)	3.00	2.00
Nos. 299-300 (2)	2.35	.85
Nos. 180-181 (2)	3.45	1.80
Nos. 193-194 (2)	3.00	.60
Nos. 213-214 (2)	.80	.50
Nos. 182-183 (2)	2.00	1.00
Nos. 171-172 (2)	.90	.75
Nos. 205-206 (2)	1.50	1.35
Nos. 245-246 (2)	2.75	1.35
Nos. 150-151 (2)	1.00	.50
Nos. 167-168 (2)	1.75	1.75
Set total (26) Stamps	29.05	18.10

World Cup Soccer

Soccer Player and Jules Rimet Cup
CD321

World Cup Soccer Championship, Wembley, England, July 11-30.

1966

Antigua	163-164
Ascension	100-101
Bahamas	245-246
Bermuda	205-206
Brunei	124-125
Cayman Islands	182-183
Dominica	195-196
Fiji	219-220
Gibraltar	175-176
Gilbert & Ellice Islands	125-126
Grenada	230-231
New Hebrides, British	116-117
New Hebrides, French	132-133
Pitcairn Islands	60-61
St. Helena	188-189
St. Kitts-Nevis	173-174
St. Lucia	207-208
Seychelles	226-227
Solomon Islands	167-168
South Arabia	23-24
Tristan da Cunha	93-94

Nos. 163-164 (2)	.80	.85
Nos. 100-101 (2)	2.50	2.00
Nos. 245-246 (2)	.65	.65
Nos. 205-206 (2)	1.75	1.75
Nos. 124-125 (2)	1.30	1.25
Nos. 182-183 (2)	.75	.65
Nos. 195-196 (2)	1.20	.75
Nos. 219-220 (2)	1.70	.60
Nos. 175-176 (2)	1.85	1.75
Nos. 125-126 (2)	.70	.60
Nos. 230-231 (2)	.65	*.95*
Nos. 116-117 (2)	1.00	1.00
Nos. 132-133 (2)	7.00	7.00
Nos. 60-61 (2)	2.00	2.00
Nos. 188-189 (2)	1.25	.60
Nos. 173-174 (2)	.85	.80
Nos. 207-208 (2)	1.15	.90
Nos. 226-227 (2)	.85	.75
Nos. 167-168 (2)	1.10	1.10
Nos. 23-24 (2)	1.90	.55
Nos. 93-94 (2)	1.25	.80
Set total (42) Stamps	32.20	27.30

WHO Headquarters

World Health Organization Headquarters, Geneva — CD322

1966

Antigua	165-166
Ascension	102-103
Bahamas	247-248
Brunei	126-127
Cayman Islands	184-185
Dominica	197-198
Fiji	224-225
Gibraltar	180-181
Gilbert & Ellice Islands	127-128
Grenada	232-233
Hong Kong	229-230
Montserrat	184-185
New Hebrides, British	118-119
New Hebrides, French	134-135
Pitcairn Islands	62-63
St. Helena	190-191
St. Kitts-Nevis	177-178
St. Lucia	209-210
St. Vincent	247-248
Seychelles	228-229
Solomon Islands	169-170
South Arabia	25-26
Tristan da Cunha	99-100

Nos. 165-166 (2)	1.15	.55
Nos. 102-103 (2)	6.60	3.35
Nos. 247-248 (2)	.80	.80
Nos. 126-127 (2)	1.35	1.35
Nos. 184-185 (2)	2.25	1.20
Nos. 197-198 (2)	.75	.75
Nos. 224-225 (2)	4.70	3.30
Nos. 180-181 (2)	6.50	4.50
Nos. 127-128 (2)	.80	.70
Nos. 232-233 (2)	.80	.50
Nos. 229-230 (2)	11.25	2.30
Nos. 184-185 (2)	1.00	1.00
Nos. 118-119 (2)	.75	.50
Nos. 134-135 (2)	8.50	8.50
Nos. 62-63 (2)	5.50	7.00
Nos. 190-191 (2)	3.50	1.50
Nos. 177-178 (2)	.60	.60
Nos. 209-210 (2)	.80	.80
Nos. 247-248 (2)	1.15	1.05
Nos. 228-229 (2)	1.25	.65
Nos. 169-170 (2)	.95	.80
Nos. 25-26 (2)	2.10	.70
Nos. 99-100 (2)	1.90	1.25
Set total (46) Stamps	64.95	43.65

UNESCO Anniversary

"Education" — CD323

"Science" (Wheat ears & flask enclosing globe). "Culture" (lyre & columns). 20th anniversary of the UNESCO.

1966-67

Antigua	183-185
Ascension	108-110
Bahamas	249-251
Barbados	287-289
Bermuda	207-209
Brunei	128-130
Cayman Islands	186-188
Dominica	199-201
Gibraltar	183-185
Gilbert & Ellice Islands	129-131
Grenada	234-236
Hong Kong	231-233
Mauritius	299-301
Montserrat	186-188
New Hebrides, British	120-122
New Hebrides, French	136-138
Pitcairn Islands	64-66
St. Helena	192-194
St. Kitts-Nevis	179-181
St. Lucia	211-213
St. Vincent	249-251
Seychelles	230-232
Solomon Islands	171-173
South Arabia	27-29
Swaziland	123-125
Tristan da Cunha	101-103
Turks & Caicos Islands	155-157
Virgin Islands	176-178

Nos. 183-185 (3)	1.90	*2.50*
Nos. 108-110 (3)	11.00	5.80
Nos. 249-251 (3)	2.35	2.35
Nos. 287-289 (3)	2.35	2.15
Nos. 207-209 (3)	3.80	*3.90*
Nos. 128-130 (3)	4.65	5.40
Nos. 186-188 (3)	2.50	1.50
Nos. 199-201 (3)	1.60	.75
Nos. 183-185 (3)	6.50	3.25
Nos. 129-131 (3)	2.50	*2.45*
Nos. 234-236 (3)	1.10	1.20
Nos. 231-233 (3)	49.50	24.00
Nos. 299-301 (3)	2.10	1.50
Nos. 186-188 (3)	2.40	2.40
Nos. 120-122 (3)	1.90	1.90
Nos. 136-138 (3)	7.75	7.75
Nos. 64-66 (3)	4.05	4.00
Nos. 192-194 (3)	5.25	3.65
Nos. 179-181 (3)	.90	.90
Nos. 211-213 (3)	1.15	1.15
Nos. 249-251 (3)	2.30	1.35
Nos. 230-232 (3)	2.40	2.40
Nos. 171-173 (3)	2.00	1.50
Nos. 27-29 (3)	5.50	5.50
Nos. 123-125 (3)	1.40	1.40
Nos. 101-103 (3)	2.00	1.40
Nos. 155-157 (3)	1.15	1.20
Nos. 176-178 (3)	1.40	1.30
Set total (84) Stamps	133.40	94.55

Silver Wedding, 1972

Queen Elizabeth II and Prince Philip — CD324

Designs: borders differ for each country.

1972

Anguilla	161-162
Antigua	295-296
Ascension	164-165
Bahamas	344-345
Bermuda	296-297
British Antarctic Territory	43-44
British Honduras	306-307
British Indian Ocean Territory	48-49

Brunei	186-187
Cayman Islands	304-305
Dominica	352-353
Falkland Islands	223-224
Fiji	328-329
Gibraltar	292-293
Gilbert & Ellice Islands	206-207
Grenada	466-467
Hong Kong	271-272
Montserrat	286-287
New Hebrides, British	169-170
New Hebrides, French	188-189
Pitcairn Islands	127-128
St. Helena	271-272
St. Kitts-Nevis	257-258
St. Lucia	328-329
St.Vincent	344-345
Seychelles	309-310
Solomon Islands	248-249
South Georgia	35-36
Tristan da Cunha	178-179
Turks & Caicos Islands	257-258
Virgin Islands	241-242

Nos. 161-162 (2)	1.10	*1.50*
Nos. 295-296 (2)	.50	.50
Nos. 164-165 (2)	.70	.70
Nos. 344-345 (2)	.60	.60
Nos. 296-297 (2)	.50	*.65*
Nos. 43-44 (2)	6.50	5.65
Nos. 306-307 (2)	.80	.80
Nos. 48-49 (2)	2.00	1.00
Nos. 186-187 (2)	.70	.70
Nos. 304-305 (2)	.75	.75
Nos. 352-353 (2)	.65	.65
Nos. 223-224 (2)	1.00	1.15
Nos. 328-329 (2)	.70	.70
Nos. 292-293 (2)	.50	.50
Nos. 206-207 (2)	.50	.50
Nos. 466-467 (2)	.70	.70
Nos. 271-272 (2)	1.70	1.50
Nos. 286-287 (2)	.50	.50
Nos. 169-170 (2)	.50	.50
Nos. 188-189 (2)	1.25	1.25
Nos. 127-128 (2)	.90	.85
Nos. 271-272 (2)	.60	1.20
Nos. 257-258 (2)	.65	.50
Nos. 328-329 (2)	.75	.75
Nos. 344-345 (2)	.55	.55
Nos. 309-310 (2)	.90	.90
Nos. 248-249 (2)	.50	.50
Nos. 35-36 (2)	1.40	1.40
Nos. 178-179 (2)	.70	.70
Nos. 257-258 (2)	.50	.50
Nos. 241-242 (2)	.50	.50
Set total (62) Stamps	30.10	29.15

Princess Anne's Wedding

Princess Anne and Mark Phillips — CD325

Wedding of Princess Anne and Mark Phillips, Nov. 14, 1973.

1973

Anguilla	179-180
Ascension	177-178
Belize	325-326
Bermuda	302-303
British Antarctic Territory	60-61
Cayman Islands	320-321
Falkland Islands	225-226
Gibraltar	305-306
Gilbert & Ellice Islands	216-217
Hong Kong	289-290
Montserrat	300-301
Pitcairn Islands	135-136
St. Helena	277-278
St. Kitts-Nevis	274-275
St. Lucia	349-350
St. Vincent	358-359
St. Vincent Grenadines	1-2
Seychelles	311-312
Solomon Islands	259-260
South Georgia	37-38
Tristan da Cunha	189-190
Turks & Caicos Islands	286-287
Virgin Islands	260-261

Nos. 179-180 (2)	.55	.55
Nos. 177-178 (2)	.60	.60
Nos. 325-326 (2)	1.10	.50
Nos. 302-303 (2)	.50	.50
Nos. 60-61 (2)	1.10	1.10
Nos. 320-321 (2)	.50	.50
Nos. 225-226 (2)	.70	.60
Nos. 305-306 (2)	.55	.55
Nos. 216-217 (2)	.50	.50
Nos. 289-290 (2)	2.65	2.00
Nos. 300-301 (2)	.55	.55
Nos. 135-136 (2)	.70	.60
Nos. 277-278 (2)	.50	.50
Nos. 274-275 (2)	.50	.50
Nos. 349-350 (2)	.50	.50
Nos. 358-359 (2)	.50	.50
Nos. 1-2 (2)	.50	.50
Nos. 311-312 (2)	.65	.65
Nos. 259-260 (2)	.70	.70
Nos. 37-38 (2)	.75	.75
Nos. 189-190 (2)	.50	.50
Nos. 286-287 (2)	.50	.50
Nos. 260-261 (2)	.50	.50
Set total (46) Stamps	16.10	14.65

Elizabeth II Coronation Anniv.

CD326

CD327

CD328

Designs: Royal and local beasts in heraldic form and simulated stonework. Portrait of Elizabeth II by Peter Grugeon. 25th anniversary of coronation of Queen Elizabeth II.

1978

Ascension	229
Barbados	474
Belize	397
British Antarctic Territory	71
Cayman Islands	404
Christmas Island	87
Falkland Islands	275
Fiji	384
Gambia	380
Gilbert Islands	312
Mauritius	464
New Hebrides, British	258
New Hebrides, French	278
St. Helena	317
St. Kitts-Nevis	354
Samoa	472
Solomon Islands	368
South Georgia	51
Swaziland	302
Tristan da Cunha	238
Virgin Islands	337

No. 229 (1)	2.00	2.00
No. 474 (1)	1.35	1.35
No. 397 (1)	4.50	5.00
No. 71 (1)	6.00	6.00
No. 404 (1)	2.00	2.00
No. 87 (1)	3.50	*4.00*
No. 275 (1)	4.00	5.50
No. 384 (1)	1.75	1.75
No. 380 (1)	1.50	1.50
No. 312 (1)	1.25	1.25
No. 464 (1)	2.10	2.10
No. 258 (1)	1.75	1.75
No. 278 (1)	3.50	3.50
No. 317 (1)	1.75	1.75
No. 354 (1)	1.00	1.00
No. 472 (1)	2.10	2.10
No. 368 (1)	2.50	2.50
No. 51 (1)	3.00	3.00
No. 302 (1)	1.60	1.60
No. 238 (1)	1.50	1.50
No. 337 (1)	1.80	1.80
Set total (21) Stamps	50.45	52.95

Queen Mother Elizabeth's 80th Birthday

CD330

Designs: Photographs of Queen Mother Elizabeth. Falkland Islands issued in sheets of 50; others in sheets of 9.

1980

Ascension	261
Bermuda	401
Cayman Islands	443
Falkland Islands	305
Gambia	412
Gibraltar	393
Hong Kong	364
Pitcairn Islands	193
St. Helena	341
Samoa	532
Solomon Islands	426
Tristan da Cunha	277

No. 261 (1)	.40	.40
No. 401 (1)	.45	.75
No. 443 (1)	.40	.40
No. 305 (1)	.40	.40
No. 412 (1)	.40	.50
No. 393 (1)	.35	.35
No. 364 (1)	1.10	1.25
No. 193 (1)	.60	.60
No. 341 (1)	.50	.50
No. 532 (1)	.55	.55
No. 426 (1)	.50	.50
No. 277 (1)	.45	.45
Set total (12) Stamps	6.10	6.65

Royal Wedding, 1981

Prince Charles and Lady Diana — CD331

CD331a

Wedding of Charles, Prince of Wales, and Lady Diana Spencer, St. Paul's Cathedral, London, July 29, 1981.

1981

Antigua	623-627
Ascension	294-296
Barbados	547-549
Barbuda	497-501
Bermuda	412-414
Brunei	268-270
Cayman Islands	471-473
Dominica	701-705
Falkland Islands	324-326
Falkland Islands Dep.	1L59-1L61
Fiji	442-444
Gambia	426-428
Ghana	759-764
Grenada	1051-1055
Grenada Grenadines	440-443
Hong Kong	373-375
Jamaica	500-503
Lesotho	335-337
Maldive Islands	906-909
Mauritius	520-522
Norfolk Island	280-282
Pitcairn Islands	206-208
St. Helena	353-355
St. Lucia	543-549
Samoa	558-560
Sierra Leone	509-518
Solomon Islands	450-452
Swaziland	382-384
Tristan da Cunha	294-296
Turks & Caicos Islands	486-489
Caicos Island	8-11
Uganda	314-317
Vanuatu	308-310
Virgin Islands	406-408

Nos. 623-627 (5)	6.55	2.55
Nos. 294-296 (3)	1.00	1.00
Nos. 547-549 (3)	.90	.90
Nos. 497-501 (5)	10.95	10.95
Nos. 412-414 (3)	2.00	2.00
Nos. 268-270 (3)	2.15	*4.50*
Nos. 471-473 (3)	1.20	1.30
Nos. 701-705 (5)	8.35	2.35
Nos. 324-326 (3)	1.65	1.70
Nos. 1L59-1L61 (3)	1.45	1.45
Nos. 442-444 (3)	1.35	1.35
Nos. 426-428 (3)	.90	.80
Nos. 759-764 (9)	6.20	6.20
Nos. 1051-1055 (5)	9.85	1.85
Nos. 440-443 (4)	2.35	2.35
Nos. 373-375 (3)	3.10	2.85
Nos. 500-503 (4)	1.45	1.35
Nos. 335-337 (3)	.90	.90
Nos. 906-909 (4)	1.55	1.55
Nos. 520-522 (3)	2.15	2.15
Nos. 280-282 (3)	1.75	1.75
Nos. 206-208 (3)	1.20	1.10
Nos. 353-355 (3)	.85	.85
Nos. 543-549 (5)	7.00	7.00
Nos. 558-560 (3)	.85	.85
Nos. 509-518 (10)	15.50	15.50
Nos. 450-452 (3)	1.25	1.25
Nos. 382-384 (3)	1.30	1.25
Nos. 294-296 (3)	.90	.90
Nos. 486-489 (4)	2.20	2.20
Nos. 8-11 (4)	5.00	5.00
Nos. 314-317 (4)	3.10	3.00
Nos. 308-310 (3)	1.15	1.15
Nos. 406-408 (3)	1.10	1.10
Set total (131) Stamps	109.15	92.95

Princess Diana

CD332

CD333

Designs: Photographs and portrait of Princess Diana, wedding or honeymoon photographs, royal residences, arms of issuing country. Portrait photograph by Clive Friend. Souvenir sheet margins show family tree, various people related to the princess. 21st birthday of Princess Diana of Wales, July 1.

1982

Antigua	663-666
Ascension	313-316
Bahamas	510-513
Barbados	585-588
Barbuda	544-547
British Antarctic Territory	92-95
Cayman Islands	486-489
Dominica	773-776
Falkland Islands	348-351
Falkland Islands Dep.	1L72-1L75
Fiji	470-473
Gambia	447-450
Grenada	1101A-1105
Grenada Grenadines	485-491
Lesotho	372-375
Maldive Islands	952-955
Mauritius	548-551
Pitcairn Islands	213-216
St. Helena	372-375
St. Lucia	591-594
Sierra Leone	531-534
Solomon Islands	471-474
Swaziland	406-409
Tristan da Cunha	310-313
Turks and Caicos Islands	531-534
Virgin Islands	430-433

Nos. 663-666 (4)	8.25	7.35
Nos. 313-316 (4)	3.50	3.50
Nos. 510-513 (4)	6.00	3.85
Nos. 585-588 (4)	3.40	3.25
Nos. 544-547 (4)	9.75	7.70
Nos. 92-95 (4)	4.25	3.45
Nos. 486-489 (4)	*4.75*	*2.70*
Nos. 773-776 (4)	7.05	7.05
Nos. 348-351 (4)	2.95	2.95
Nos. 1L72-1L75 (4)	2.50	2.60
Nos. 470-473 (4)	3.25	2.95
Nos. 447-450 (4)	2.90	2.85
Nos. 1101A-1105 (7)	16.05	15.55

Nos. 485-491 (7)	17.65	17.65
Nos. 372-375 (4)	4.00	4.00
Nos. 952-955 (4)	5.50	3.90
Nos. 548-551 (4)	5.00	5.00
Nos. 213-216 (4)	1.90	1.85
Nos. 372-375 (4)	2.00	2.00
Nos. 591-594 (4)	8.70	8.70
Nos. 531-534 (4)	7.20	7.20
Nos. 471-474 (4)	2.90	2.90
Nos. 406-409 (4)	3.85	2.25
Nos. 310-313 (4)	3.65	1.45
Nos. 486-489 (4)	2.20	2.20
Nos. 430-433 (4)	3.00	3.00
Set total (110) Stamps	142.15	127.85

250th anniv. of first edition of Lloyd's List (shipping news publication) & of Lloyd's marine insurance.

CD335

Designs: First page of early edition of the list; historical ships, modern transportation or harbor scenes.

1984

Ascension	351-354
Bahamas	555-558
Barbados	627-630
Cayes of Belize	10-13
Cayman Islands	522-526
Falkland Islands	404-407
Fiji	509-512
Gambia	519-522
Mauritius	587-590
Nauru	280-283
St. Helena	412-415
Samoa	624-627
Seychelles	538-541
Solomon Islands	521-524
Vanuatu	368-371
Virgin Islands	466-469

Nos. 351-354 (4)	2.90	2.55
Nos. 555-558 (4)	4.15	2.95
Nos. 627-630 (4)	6.10	5.15
Nos. 10-13 (4)	4.85	4.85
Nos. 522-526 (5)	9.30	8.45
Nos. 404-407 (4)	3.50	3.65
Nos. 509-512 (4)	5.30	4.90
Nos. 519-522 (4)	4.20	4.30
Nos. 587-590 (4)	9.40	9.40
Nos. 280-283 (4)	2.40	2.35
Nos. 412-415 (4)	2.40	2.40
Nos. 624-627 (4)	2.55	2.35
Nos. 538-541 (4)	5.00	5.00
Nos. 521-524 (4)	4.65	3.95
Nos. 368-371 (4)	1.85	1.85
Nos. 466-469 (4)	4.25	4.25
Set total (65) Stamps	72.80	68.35

Queen Mother 85th Birthday

CD336

Designs: Photographs tracing the life of the Queen Mother, Elizabeth. The high value in each set pictures the same photograph taken of the Queen Mother holding the infant Prince Henry.

1985

Ascension	372-376
Bahamas	580-584
Barbados	660-664
Bermuda	469-473
Falkland Islands	420-424
Falkland Islands Dep.	1L92-1L96
Fiji	531-535
Hong Kong	447-450
Jamaica	599-603
Mauritius	604-608
Norfolk Island	364-368
Pitcairn Islands	253-257
St. Helena	428-432
Samoa	649-653
Seychelles	567-571
Zil Elwannyen Sesel	101-105
Solomon Islands	543-547
Swaziland	476-480
Tristan da Cunha	372-376
Vanuatu	392-396

Nos. 372-376 (5)	4.65	4.65
Nos. 580-584 (5)	7.70	6.45
Nos. 660-664 (5)	8.00	6.70
Nos. 469-473 (5)	9.40	9.40
Nos. 420-424 (5)	7.35	6.65
Nos. 1L92-1L96 (5)	8.00	8.00
Nos. 531-535 (5)	6.15	6.15
Nos. 447-450 (4)	9.50	8.50
Nos. 599-603 (5)	6.15	7.00
Nos. 604-608 (5)	11.30	11.30
Nos. 364-368 (5)	5.00	5.00
Nos. 253-257 (5)	5.30	5.95
Nos. 428-432 (5)	5.25	5.25
Nos. 649-653 (5)	8.40	7.55
Nos. 567-571 (5)	8.70	8.70
Nos. 101-105 (5)	6.60	6.60
Nos. 543-547 (5)	3.95	3.95
Nos. 476-480 (5)	7.75	7.25
Nos. 372-376 (5)	5.40	5.40
Nos. 392-396 (5)	5.25	5.25
Set total (99) Stamps	139.80	135.70

Queen Elizabeth II, 60th Birthday

CD337

1986, April 21

Ascension	389-393
Bahamas	592-596
Barbados	675-679
Bermuda	499-503
Cayman Islands	555-559
Falkland Islands	441-445
Fiji	544-548
Hong Kong	465-469
Jamaica	620-624
Kiribati	470-474
Mauritius	629-633
Papua New Guinea	640-644
Pitcairn Islands	270-274
St. Helena	451-455
Samoa	670-674
Seychelles	592-596
Zil Elwannyen Sesel	114-118
Solomon Islands	562-566
South Georgia	101-105
Swaziland	490-494
Tristan da Cunha	388-392
Vanuatu	414-418
Zambia	343-347

Nos. 389-393 (5)	2.80	3.30
Nos. 592-596 (5)	2.75	*3.70*
Nos. 675-679 (5)	3.25	3.10
Nos. 499-503 (5)	4.65	*5.15*
Nos. 555-559 (5)	4.55	5.60
Nos. 441-445 (5)	3.95	*4.95*
Nos. 544-548 (5)	3.00	3.00
Nos. 465-469 (5)	8.75	6.75
Nos. 620-624 (5)	2.75	2.70
Nos. 470-474 (5)	2.25	2.10
Nos. 629-633 (5)	3.50	3.50
Nos. 640-644 (5)	4.10	4.10
Nos. 270-274 (5)	2.80	2.70
Nos. 451-455 (5)	2.50	3.05
Nos. 670-674 (5)	2.55	2.55
Nos. 592-596 (5)	2.70	2.70
Nos. 114-118 (5)	2.15	2.15
Nos. 562-566 (5)	2.90	2.90
Nos. 101-105 (5)	3.30	3.65
Nos. 490-494 (5)	2.15	2.15
Nos. 388-392 (5)	3.00	3.00
Nos. 414-418 (5)	3.10	3.10
Nos. 343-347 (5)	1.65	1.60
Set total (115) Stamps	75.10	77.50

Royal Wedding

Marriage of Prince Andrew and Sarah Ferguson CD338

1986, July 23

Ascension	399-400
Bahamas	602-603
Barbados	687-688
Cayman Islands	560-561
Jamaica	629-630
Pitcairn Islands	275-276
St. Helena	460-461
St. Kitts	181-182
Seychelles	602-603
Zil Elwannyen Sesel	119-120
Solomon Islands	567-568
Tristan da Cunha	397-398
Zambia	348-349

Nos. 399-400 (2)	1.60	1.60
Nos. 602-603 (2)	2.75	2.75
Nos. 687-688 (2)	2.00	1.25
Nos. 560-561 (2)	1.70	*2.35*
Nos. 629-630 (2)	1.35	1.35
Nos. 275-276 (2)	2.40	2.40
Nos. 460-461 (2)	1.05	1.05
Nos. 181-182 (2)	1.50	2.25
Nos. 602-603 (2)	2.50	2.50
Nos. 119-120 (2)	2.30	2.30
Nos. 567-568 (2)	1.00	1.00
Nos. 397-398 (2)	1.40	1.40
Nos. 348-349 (2)	1.10	1.30
Set total (26) Stamps	22.65	23.50

Queen Elizabeth II, 60th Birthday

Queen Elizabeth II & Prince Philip, 1947 Wedding Portrait — CD339

Designs: Photographs tracing the life of Queen Elizabeth II.

1986

Anguilla	674-677
Antigua	925-928
Barbuda	783-786
Dominica	950-953
Gambia	611-614
Grenada	1371-1374
Grenada Grenadines	749-752
Lesotho	531-534
Maldive Islands	1172-1175
Sierra Leone	760-763
Uganda	495-498

Nos. 674-677 (4)	8.00	8.00
Nos. 925-928 (4)	5.50	6.20
Nos. 783-786 (4)	23.15	23.15
Nos. 950-953 (4)	7.25	7.25
Nos. 611-614 (4)	8.25	7.90
Nos. 1371-1374 (4)	6.80	6.80
Nos. 749-752 (4)	6.75	6.75
Nos. 531-534 (4)	5.25	5.25
Nos. 1172-1175 (4)	6.25	6.25
Nos. 760-763 (4)	5.25	5.25
Nos. 495-498 (4)	8.50	8.50
Set total (44) Stamps	90.95	91.30

Royal Wedding, 1986

CD340

Designs: Photographs of Prince Andrew and Sarah Ferguson during courtship, engagement and marriage.

1986

Antigua	939-942
Barbuda	809-812
Dominica	970-973
Gambia	635-638
Grenada	1385-1388
Grenada Grenadines	758-761
Lesotho	545-548
Maldive Islands	1181-1184
Sierra Leone	769-772
Uganda	510-513

Nos. 939-942 (4)	7.00	*8.75*
Nos. 809-812 (4)	14.55	14.55
Nos. 970-973 (4)	7.25	7.25
Nos. 635-638 (4)	7.80	7.80
Nos. 1385-1388 (4)	8.30	8.30
Nos. 758-761 (4)	9.00	9.00
Nos. 545-548 (4)	7.45	7.45
Nos. 1181-1184 (4)	8.45	8.45
Nos. 769-772 (4)	5.35	5.35
Nos. 510-513 (4)	9.25	10.00
Set total (40) Stamps	84.40	86.90

Lloyds of London, 300th Anniv.

CD341

Designs: 17th century aspects of Lloyds, representations of each country's individual connections with Lloyds and publicized disasters insured by the organization.

1986

Ascension	454-457
Bahamas	655-658
Barbados	731-734
Bermuda	541-544
Falkland Islands	481-484
Liberia	1101-1104
Malawi	534-537
Nevis	571-574
St. Helena	501-504
St. Lucia	923-926
Seychelles	649-652
Zil Elwannyen Sesel	146-149
Solomon Islands	627-630
South Georgia	131-134
Trinidad & Tobago	484-487
Tristan da Cunha	439-442
Vanuatu	485-488

Nos. 454-457 (4)	5.00	5.00
Nos. 655-658 (4)	8.90	4.95
Nos. 731-734 (4)	12.50	8.35
Nos. 541-544 (4)	8.00	*6.60*
Nos. 481-484 (4)	5.45	3.85
Nos. 1101-1104 (4)	4.25	4.25
Nos. 534-537 (4)	11.00	7.85
Nos. 571-574 (4)	8.35	8.35
Nos. 501-504 (4)	8.70	7.15
Nos. 923-926 (4)	8.80	8.80
Nos. 649-652 (4)	12.85	12.85
Nos. 146-149 (4)	11.25	11.25
Nos. 627-630 (4)	7.00	4.45
Nos. 131-134 (4)	6.30	3.70
Nos. 484-487 (4)	10.25	6.35
Nos. 439-442 (4)	7.60	7.60
Nos. 485-488 (4)	4.85	4.85
Set total (68) Stamps	141.05	116.20

Moon Landing, 20th Anniv.

CD342

Designs: Equipment, crew photographs, spacecraft, official emblems and report profiles created for the Apollo Missions. Two stamps in each set are square in format rather than like the stamp shown; see individual country listings for more information.

1989

Ascension	468-472
Bahamas	674-678
Belize	916-920
Kiribati	517-521
Liberia	1125-1129
Nevis	586-590
St. Kitts	248-252
Samoa	760-764
Seychelles	676-680
Zil Elwannyen Sesel	154-158
Solomon Islands	643-647
Vanuatu	507-511

Nos. 468-472 (5)	9.40	8.60
Nos. 674-678 (5)	23.00	19.70
Nos. 916-920 (5)	29.25	21.60
Nos. 517-521 (5)	12.50	12.50
Nos. 1125-1129 (5)	8.50	8.50
Nos. 586-590 (5)	7.50	7.50

Nos. 248-252 (5)	8.00	8.25
Nos. 760-764 (5)	9.85	9.30
Nos. 676-680 (5)	16.05	16.05
Nos. 154-158 (5)	26.85	26.85
Nos. 643-647 (5)	9.00	6.75
Nos. 507-511 (5)	8.60	8.60
Set total (60) Stamps	168.50	154.20

Queen Mother, 90th Birthday

CD343

CD344

Designs: Portraits of Queen Elizabeth, the Queen Mother. See individual country listings for more information.

1990

Ascension....................................491-492
Bahamas......................................698-699
Barbados.....................................782-783
British Antarctic Territory..........170-171
British Indian Ocean Territory........106-107
Cayman Islands............................622-623
Falkland Islands..........................524-525
Kenya..527-528
Kiribati.......................................555-556
Liberia......................................1145-1146
Pitcairn Islands............................336-337
St. Helena...................................532-533
St. Lucia.....................................969-970
Seychelles...................................710-711
Zil Elwannyen Sesel.............171-172
Solomon Islands..........................671-672
South Georgia..............................143-144
Swaziland....................................565-566
Tristan da Cunha.........................480-481

Nos. 491-492 (2)	4.75	4.75
Nos. 698-699 (2)	5.25	5.25
Nos. 782-783 (2)	4.00	3.70
Nos. 170-171 (2)	6.00	6.00
Nos. 106-107 (2)	18.00	18.50
Nos. 622-623 (2)	4.00	*5.50*
Nos. 524-525 (2)	4.75	4.75
Nos. 527-528 (2)	6.05	6.05
Nos. 555-556 (2)	4.75	4.75
Nos. 1145-1146 (2)	3.25	3.25
Nos. 336-337 (2)	4.25	4.25
Nos. 532-533 (2)	5.25	5.25
Nos. 969-970 (2)	4.60	4.60
Nos. 710-711 (2)	6.60	6.60
Nos. 171-172 (2)	8.25	8.25
Nos. 671-672 (2)	5.00	*5.30*
Nos. 143-144 (2)	5.50	6.50
Nos. 565-566 (2)	4.10	4.10
Nos. 480-481 (2)	5.60	5.60
Set total (38) Stamps	109.95	112.95

Queen Elizabeth II, 65th Birthday, and Prince Philip, 70th Birthday

CD345

CD346

Designs: Portraits of Queen Elizabeth II and Prince Philip differ for each country. Printed in sheets of 10 + 5 labels (3 different) between. Stamps alternate, producing 5 different triptychs.

1991

Ascension...506a
Bahamas...731a
Belize..970a
Bermuda...618a
Kiribati..572a
Mauritius..734a
Pitcairn Islands...................................349a
St. Helena..555a
St. Kitts..319a
Samoa..791a
Seychelles..724a
Zil Elwannyen Sesel..........................178a
Solomon Islands..................................689a
South Georgia.....................................150a
Swaziland...587a
Vanuatu..541a

No. 506a (1)	3.50	3.75
No. 731a (1)	4.00	4.00
No. 970a (1)	4.25	4.25
No. 618a (1)	3.50	*4.00*
No. 572a (1)	4.00	4.00
No. 734a (1)	4.00	4.00
No. 349a (1)	3.25	3.25
No. 555a (1)	2.75	2.75
No. 319a (1)	3.00	3.00
No. 791a (1)	3.75	3.75
No. 724a (1)	5.00	5.00
No. 178a (1)	6.25	6.25
No. 689a (1)	3.75	3.75
No. 150a (1)	4.75	7.00
No. 587a (1)	4.00	4.00
No. 541a (1)	2.50	2.50
Set total (16) Stamps	62.25	65.25

Royal Family Birthday, Anniversary

CD347

Queen Elizabeth II, 65th birthday, Charles and Diana, 10th wedding anniversary: Various photographs of Queen Elizabeth II, Prince Philip, Prince Charles, Princess Diana and their sons William and Henry.

1991

Antigua..1446-1455
Barbuda...1229-1238
Dominica..1328-1337
Gambia..1080-1089
Grenada...2006-2015
Grenada Grenadines.......................1331-1340
Guyana..2440-2451
Lesotho..871-875
Maldive Islands..............................1533-1542
Nevis..666-675
St. Vincent.....................................1485-1494
St. Vincent Grenadines....................769-778
Sierra Leone..................................1387-1396
Turks & Caicos Islands....................913-922
Uganda...918-927

Nos. 1446-1455 (10)	21.70	20.05
Nos. 1229-1238 (10)	125.00	119.50
Nos. 1328-1337 (10)	30.20	30.20
Nos. 1080-1089 (10)	24.65	24.40
Nos. 2006-2015 (10)	25.45	22.10
Nos. 1331-1340 (10)	23.85	23.35
Nos. 2440-2451 (12)	21.40	21.15
Nos. 871-875 (5)	13.55	13.55
Nos. 1533-1542 (10)	28.10	28.10
Nos. 666-675 (10)	23.65	23.65
Nos. 1485-1494 (10)	26.75	25.90
Nos. 769-778 (10)	25.40	25.40
Nos. 1387-1396 (10)	26.35	26.35
Nos. 913-922 (10)	27.50	25.30
Nos. 918-927 (10)	17.65	17.65
Set total (147) Stamps	461.20	446.65

Queen Elizabeth II's Accession to the Throne, 40th Anniv.

CD348

Various photographs of Queen Elizabeth II with local Scenes.

1992

Antigua..1513-1518
Barbuda...1306-1311
Dominica..1414-1419
Gambia..1172-1177
Grenada...2047-2052
Grenada Grenadines.......................1368-1373
Lesotho..881-885
Maldive Islands..............................1637-1642
Nevis..702-707
St. Vincent.....................................1582-1587
St. Vincent Grenadines....................829-834
Sierra Leone..................................1482-1487
Turks and Caicos Islands.................978-987
Uganda...990-995
Virgin Islands....................................742-746

Nos. 1513-1518 (6)	15.00	*15.10*
Nos. 1306-1311 (6)	125.25	83.65
Nos. 1414-1419 (6)	12.50	12.50
Nos. 1172-1177 (6)	15.00	14.85
Nos. 2047-2052 (6)	15.95	15.95
Nos. 1368-1373 (6)	17.00	15.35
Nos. 881-885 (5)	11.90	11.90
Nos. 1637-1642 (6)	17.55	17.55
Nos. 702-707 (6)	13.55	13.55
Nos. 1582-1587 (6)	14.40	14.40
Nos. 829-834 (6)	19.65	19.65
Nos. 1482-1487 (6)	22.50	22.50
Nos. 913-922 (10)	27.50	25.30
Nos. 990-995 (6)	19.50	19.50
Nos. 742-746 (5)	15.50	15.50
Set total (92) Stamps	362.75	317.25

CD349

1992

Ascension...531-535
Bahamas...744-748
Bermuda...623-627
British Indian Ocean Territory........119-123
Cayman Islands....................................648-652
Falkland Islands..................................549-553
Gibraltar..605-609
Hong Kong..619-623
Kenya..563-567
Kiribati...582-586
Pitcairn Islands....................................362-366
St. Helena...570-574
St. Kitts..332-336
Samoa...805-809
Seychelles...734-738
Zil Elwannyen Sesel...........................183-187
Solomon Islands..................................708-712
South Georgia.....................................157-161
Tristan da Cunha.................................508-512
Vanuatu...555-559
Zambia..561-565

Nos. 531-535 (5)	6.10	6.10
Nos. 744-748 (5)	6.90	4.70
Nos. 623-627 (5)	7.40	*7.55*
Nos. 119-123 (5)	22.75	19.25
Nos. 648-652 (5)	7.60	6.60
Nos. 549-553 (5)	5.95	5.90
Nos. 605-609 (5)	5.15	*5.50*
Nos. 619-623 (5)	5.10	5.25
Nos. 563-567 (5)	7.80	7.75
Nos. 582-586 (5)	3.85	3.85
Nos. 362-366 (5)	5.35	5.35
Nos. 570-574 (5)	5.70	5.70
Nos. 332-336 (5)	6.60	5.50
Nos. 805-809 (5)	7.85	5.90
Nos. 734-738 (5)	10.55	10.55
Nos. 183-187 (5)	9.40	9.40
Nos. 708-712 (5)	5.00	5.30
Nos. 157-161 (5)	5.60	5.90
Nos. 508-512 (5)	8.75	8.30
Nos. 555-559 (5)	3.10	3.10
Nos. 561-565 (5)	5.20	5.15
Set total (105) Stamps	151.70	142.60

Royal Air Force, 75th Anniversary

CD350

1993

Ascension...557-561
Bahamas...771-775
Barbados...842-846
Belize...1003-1008
Bermuda...648-651
British Indian Ocean Territory........136-140
Falkland Is..573-577
Fiji...687-691
Montserrat..830-834
St. Kitts..351-355

Nos. 557-561 (5)	15.60	14.60
Nos. 771-775 (5)	24.65	21.45
Nos. 842-846 (5)	14.15	12.85
Nos. 1003-1008 (6)	21.15	16.50
Nos. 648-651 (4)	9.65	*10.45*
Nos. 136-140 (5)	16.10	16.10
Nos. 573-577 (5)	10.85	10.85
Nos. 687-691 (5)	17.75	17.40
Nos. 830-834 (5)	14.10	14.10
Nos. 351-355 (5)	22.80	23.55
Set total (50) Stamps	166.80	157.85

Royal Air Force, 80th Anniv.

Design CD350 Re-inscribed

1998

Ascension...697-701
Bahamas...907-911
British Indian Ocean Terr.........198-202
Cayman Islands....................................754-758
Fiji...814-818
Gibraltar..755-759
Samoa...957-961
Turks & Caicos Islands.....................1258-1265
Tuvalu...763-767
Virgin Islands.....................................879-883

Nos. 697-701 (5)	16.10	16.10
Nos. 907-911 (5)	13.60	12.65
Nos. 136-140 (5)	16.10	16.10
Nos. 754-758 (5)	15.25	15.25
Nos. 814-818 (5)	14.00	12.75
Nos. 755-759 (5)	9.70	9.70
Nos. 957-961 (5)	15.70	14.90
Nos. 1258-1265 (2)	27.50	27.50
Nos. 763-767 (5)	7.75	7.75
Nos. 879-883 (5)	15.00	15.00
Set total (47) Stamps	150.70	147.70

End of World War II, 50th Anniv.

CD351

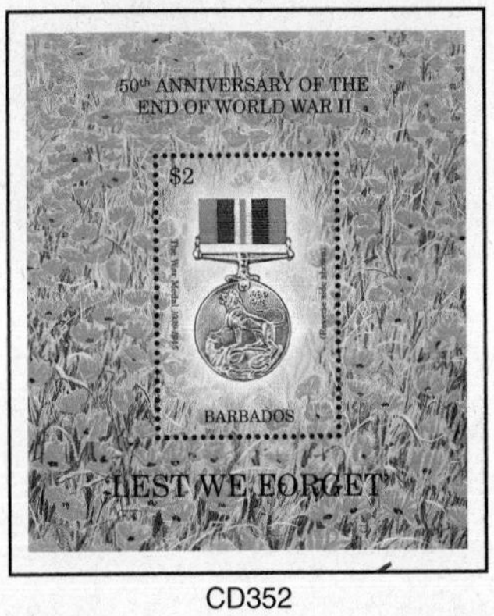

CD352

1995

Ascension...613-617
Bahamas...824-828
Barbados...891-895
Belize...1047-1050
British Indian Ocean Territory........163-167
Cayman Islands....................................704-708
Falkland Islands..................................634-638
Fiji...720-724
Kiribati...662-668
Liberia...1175-1179
Mauritius..803-805
St. Helena...646-654
St. Kitts..389-393
St. Lucia..1018-1022
Samoa...890-894
Solomon Islands..................................799-803
South Georgia.....................................198-200
Tristan da Cunha.................................562-566

Nos. 613-617 (5)	21.50	21.50

Nos. 824-828 (5)	22.00	18.70
Nos. 891-895 (5)	14.20	11.90
Nos. 1047-1050 (4)	8.25	5.90
Nos. 163-167 (5)	16.25	16.25
Nos. 704-708 (5)	17.65	13.95
Nos. 634-638 (5)	18.65	17.15
Nos. 720-724 (5)	17.50	14.50
Nos. 662-668 (7)	12.55	12.55
Nos. 1175-1179 (5)	15.25	11.15
Nos. 803-805 (3)	7.50	7.50
Nos. 646-654 (9)	26.10	26.10
Nos. 389-393 (5)	16.40	16.40
Nos. 1018-1022 (5)	12.25	10.15
Nos. 890-894 (5)	15.25	14.50
Nos. 799-803 (5)	14.75	14.75
Nos. 198-200 (3)	14.50	15.50
Nos. 562-566 (5)	20.10	20.10
Set total (91) Stamps	290.65	268.55

UN, 50th Anniv.

CD353

1995

Bahamas	839-842
Barbados	901-904
Belize	1055-1058
Jamaica	847-851
Liberia	1187-1190
Mauritius	813-816
Pitcairn Islands	436-439
St. Kitts	398-401
St. Lucia	1023-1026
Samoa	900-903
Tristan da Cunha	568-571
Virgin Islands	807-810

Nos. 839-842 (4)	7.15	6.40
Nos. 901-904 (4)	7.00	5.75
Nos. 1055-1058 (4)	6.80	4.70
Nos. 847-851 (5)	5.40	5.45
Nos. 1187-1190 (4)	10.90	10.90
Nos. 813-816 (4)	4.55	4.55
Nos. 436-439 (4)	8.15	8.15
Nos. 398-401 (4)	6.15	7.15
Nos. 1023-1026 (4)	7.50	7.25
Nos. 900-903 (4)	9.35	8.20
Nos. 568-571 (4)	13.50	13.50
Nos. 807-810 (4)	7.45	7.45
Set total (49) Stamps	93.90	89.45

Queen Elizabeth, 70th Birthday

CD354

1996

Ascension	632-635
British Antarctic Territory	240-243
British Indian Ocean Territory	176-180
Falkland Islands	653-657
Pitcairn Islands	446-449
St. Helena	672-676
Samoa	912-916
Tokelau	223-227
Tristan da Cunha	576-579
Virgin Islands	824-828

Nos. 632-635 (4)	5.30	5.30
Nos. 240-243 (4)	9.45	8.15
Nos. 176-180 (5)	11.50	11.50
Nos. 653-657 (5)	13.55	11.20
Nos. 446-449 (4)	8.60	8.60
Nos. 672-676 (5)	12.45	12.70
Nos. 912-916 (5)	10.50	10.50
Nos. 223-227 (5)	10.50	10.50
Nos. 576-579 (4)	8.35	8.35
Nos. 824-828 (5)	11.30	11.30
Set total (46) Stamps	101.50	98.10

Diana, Princess of Wales (1961-97)

CD355

1998

Ascension	696
Bahamas	901A-902
Barbados	950
Belize	1091
Bermuda	753
Botswana	659-663
British Antarctic Territory	258
British Indian Ocean Terr.	197
Cayman Islands	752A-753
Falkland Islands	694
Fiji	819-820
Gibraltar	754
Kiribati	719A-720
Namibia	909
Niue	706
Norfolk Island	644-645
Papua New Guinea	937
Pitcairn Islands	487
St. Helena	711
St. Kitts	437A-438
Samoa	955A-956
Seycelles	802
Solomon Islands	866-867
South Georgia	220
Tokelau	252B-253
Tonga	980
Niuafo'ou	201
Tristan da Cunha	618
Tuvalu	762
Vanuatu	718A-719
Virgin Islands	878

No. 696 (1)	5.25	5.25
Nos. 901A-902 (2)	5.30	5.30
No. 950 (1)	6.25	6.25
No. 1091 (1)	10.00	10.00
No. 753 (1)	5.00	5.00
Nos. 659-663 (5)	8.25	8.80
No. 258 (1)	5.50	5.50
No. 197 (1)	5.50	5.50
Nos. 752A-753 (3)	7.40	7.40
No. 694 (1)	5.00	5.00
Nos. 819-820 (2)	5.25	5.25
No. 754 (1)	4.75	4.75
Nos. 719A-720 (2)	4.60	4.60
No. 909 (1)	1.75	1.75
No. 706 (1)	5.50	5.50
Nos. 644-645 (2)	5.60	5.60
No. 937 (1)	6.25	6.25
No. 487 (1)	4.75	4.75
No. 711 (1)	4.25	4.25
Nos. 437A-438 (2)	5.15	5.15
Nos. 955A-956 (2)	7.00	7.00
No. 802 (1)	6.25	6.25
Nos. 866-867 (2)	5.40	5.40
No. 220 (1)	4.50	5.00
Nos. 252B-253 (2)	6.00	6.00
No. 980 (1)	4.00	4.00
No. 201 (1)	6.50	6.50
No. 618 (1)	5.00	5.00
No. 762 (1)	3.50	3.50
Nos. 718A-719 (2)	8.00	8.00
No. 878 (1)	4.50	4.50
Set total (46) Stamps	171.95	173.00

Wedding of Prince Edward and Sophie Rhys-Jones

CD356

1999

Ascension	729-730
Cayman Islands	775-776
Falkland Islands	729-730
Pitcairn Islands	505-506
St. Helena	733-734
Samoa	971-972
Tristan da Cunha	636-637
Virgin Islands	908-909

Nos. 729-730 (2)	4.50	4.50
Nos. 775-776 (2)	4.95	4.95
Nos. 729-730 (2)	14.00	14.00
Nos. 505-506 (2)	7.00	7.00
Nos. 733-734 (2)	5.00	5.00
Nos. 971-972 (2)	5.00	5.00
Nos. 636-637 (2)	7.50	7.50
Nos. 908-909 (2)	7.50	7.50
Set total (16) Stamps	55.45	55.45

1st Manned Moon Landing, 30th Anniv.

CD357

1999

Ascension	731-735
Bahamas	942-946
Barbados	967-971
Bermuda	778
Cayman Islands	777-781
Fiji	853-857
Jamaica	889-893
Kirbati	746-750
Nauru	465-469
St. Kitts	460-464
Samoa	973-977
Solomon Islands	875-879
Tuvalu	800-804
Virgin Islands	910-914

Nos. 731-735 (5)	12.80	12.80
Nos. 942-946 (5)	14.10	14.10
Nos. 967-971 (5)	9.45	8.25
No. 778 (1)	9.00	9.00
Nos. 777-781 (5)	9.25	9.25
Nos. 853-857 (5)	9.25	8.45
Nos. 889-893 (5)	8.30	7.18
Nos. 746-750 (5)	8.60	8.60
Nos. 465-469 (5)	7.55	7.10
Nos. 460-464 (5)	11.35	11.65
Nos. 973-977 (5)	12.60	12.45
Nos. 875-879 (5)	7.50	7.50
Nos. 800-804 (5)	6.75	6.75
Nos. 910-914 (5)	11.75	11.75
Set total (66) Stamps	138.25	134.83

Queen Mother's Century

CD358

1999

Ascension	736-740
Bahamas	951-955
Cayman Islands	782-786
Falkland Islands	734-738
Fiji	858-862
Norfolk Island	688-692
St. Helena	740-744
Samoa	978-982
Solomon Islands	880-884
South Georgia	231-235
Tristan da Cunha	638-642
Tuvalu	805-809

Nos. 736-740 (5)	15.50	15.50
Nos. 951-955 (5)	13.75	12.65
Nos. 782-786 (5)	8.35	8.35
Nos. 734-738 (5)	30.00	28.25
Nos. 858-862 (5)	12.80	13.25
Nos. 688-692 (5)	9.50	9.50
Nos. 740-744 (5)	16.15	16.15
Nos. 978-982 (5)	12.50	12.10
Nos. 880-884 (5)	7.50	7.00
Nos. 231-235 (5)	29.75	30.00
Nos. 638-642 (5)	18.00	18.00
Nos. 805-809 (5)	7.00	7.00
Set total (60) Stamps	180.80	177.75

Prince William, 18th Birthday

CD359

2000

Ascension	755-759
Cayman Islands	797-801
Falkland Islands	762-766
Fiji	889-893
South Georgia	257-261
Tristan da Cunha	664-668
Virgin Islands	925-929

Nos. 755-759 (5)	15.50	15.50
Nos. 797-801 (5)	11.15	10.90
Nos. 762-766 (5)	24.60	22.50
Nos. 889-893 (5)	12.90	12.90
Nos. 257-261 (5)	29.00	28.75
Nos. 664-668 (5)	21.50	21.50
Nos. 925-929 (5)	14.50	14.50
Set total (35) Stamps	129.15	126.55

Reign of Queen Elizabeth II, 50th Anniv.

CD360

2002

Ascension	790-794
Bahamas	1033-1037
Barbados	1019-1023
Belize	1152-1156
Bermuda	822-826
British Antarctic Territory	307-311
British Indian Ocean Territory	239-243
Cayman Islands	844-848
Falkland Islands	804-808
Gibraltar	896-900
Jamaica	952-956
Nauru	491-495
Norfolk Island	758-762
Papua New Guinea	1019-1023
Pitcairn Islands	552
St. Helena	788-792
St. Lucia	1146-1150
Solomon Islands	931-935
South Georgia	274-278
Swaziland	706-710
Tokelau	302-306
Tonga	1059
Niuafo'ou	239
Tristan da Cunha	706-710
Virgin Islands	967-971

Nos. 790-794 (5)	14.10	14.10
Nos. 1033-1037 (5)	15.25	15.25
Nos. 1019-1023 (5)	12.90	12.90
Nos. 1152-1156 (5)	17.10	15.10
Nos. 822-826 (5)	18.00	18.00
Nos. 307-311 (5)	23.00	23.00
Nos. 239-243 (5)	19.40	19.40
Nos. 844-848 (5)	13.25	13.25
Nos. 804-808 (5)	23.00	22.00
Nos. 896-900 (5)	6.65	6.65
Nos. 952-956 (5)	16.65	16.65
Nos. 491-495 (5)	17.75	17.75
Nos. 758-762 (5)	15.90	15.90
Nos. 1019-1023 (5)	14.50	14.50
No. 552 (1)	8.50	8.50
Nos. 788-792 (5)	19.75	19.75
Nos. 1146-1150 (5)	12.25	12.25
Nos. 931-935 (5)	12.40	12.40
Nos. 274-278 (5)	28.00	28.50
Nos. 706-710 (5)	12.50	12.50
Nos. 302-306 (5)	14.50	14.50
No. 1059 (1)	8.00	8.00
No. 239 (1)	8.75	8.75
Nos. 706-710 (5)	18.50	18.50
Nos. 967-971 (5)	16.50	16.50
Set total (113) Stamps	387.10	384.60

Queen Mother Elizabeth (1900-2002)

CD361

2002

Ascension 799-801
Bahamas 1044-1046
Bermuda......................................834-836
British Antarctic Territory..........312-314
British Indian Ocean Territory 245-247
Cayman Islands..........................857-861
Falkland Islands 812-816
Nauru..499-501
Pitcairn Islands...........................561-565
St. Helena 808-812
St. Lucia 1155-1159
Seychelles 830
Solomon Islands.........................945-947
South Georgia 281-285
Tokelau 312-314
Tristan da Cunha........................715-717
Virgin Islands..............................979-983

Nos. 799-801 (3)	8.85	8.85
Nos. 1044-1046 (3)	9.10	9.10
Nos. 834-836 (3)	12.25	12.25
Nos. 312-314 (3)	18.75	18.75
Nos. 245-247 (3)	17.35	17.35
Nos. 857-861 (5)	15.00	15.00
Nos. 812-816 (5)	28.50	28.50
Nos. 499-501 (3)	14.00	14.00
Nos. 561-565 (5)	15.25	15.25
Nos. 808-812 (5)	12.00	12.00
Nos. 1155-1159 (5)	12.00	12.00
No. 830 (1)	6.50	6.50
Nos. 945-947 (3)	9.25	9.25
Nos. 281-285 (5)	19.50	19.50
Nos. 312-314 (3)	11.85	11.85
Nos. 715-717 (3)	16.25	16.25
Nos. 979-983 (5)	23.50	23.50
Set total (63) Stamps	249.90	249.90

Head of Queen Elizabeth II

CD362

2003

Ascension 822
Bermuda...865
British Antarctic Territory..................322
British Indian Ocean Territory 261
Cayman Islands..................................878
Falkland Islands 828
St. Helena 820
South Georgia 294
Tristan da Cunha................................731
Virgin Islands....................................1003

No. 822 (1)	12.50	12.50
No. 865 (1)	50.00	50.00
No. 322 (1)	9.50	9.50
No. 261 (1)	11.00	11.00
No. 878 (1)	14.00	14.00
No. 828 (1)	9.00	9.00
No. 820 (1)	9.00	9.00
No. 294 (1)	8.50	8.50
No. 731 (1)	10.00	10.00
No. 1003 (1)	10.00	10.00
Set total (10) Stamps	143.50	143.50

Coronation of Queen Elizabeth II, 50th Anniv.

CD363

2003

Ascension 823-825
Bahamas 1073-1075
Bermuda......................................866-868
British Antarctic Territory..........323-325
British Indian Ocean Territory 262-264
Cayman Islands..........................879-881
Jamaica 970-972
Kiribati 825-827
Pitcairn Islands...........................577-581
St. Helena 821-823
St. Lucia 1171-1173
Tokelau 320-322
Tristan da Cunha........................732-734
Virgin Islands..........................1004-1006

Nos. 823-825 (3)	12.50	12.50
Nos. 1073-1075 (3)	13.00	13.00
Nos. 866-868 (2)	14.25	14.25
Nos. 323-325 (3)	23.00	23.00
Nos. 262-264 (3)	28.00	28.00
Nos. 879-881 (3)	19.25	19.25
Nos. 970-972 (3)	10.00	10.00
Nos. 825-827 (3)	13.00	13.00
Nos. 577-581 (5)	14.40	14.40
Nos. 821-823 (3)	7.25	7.25
Nos. 1171-1173 (3)	8.75	8.75
Nos. 320-322 (3)	17.25	17.25
Nos. 732-734 (3)	16.75	16.75
Nos. 1004-1006 (3)	25.00	25.00
Set total (43) Stamps	222.40	222.40

Prince William, 21st Birthday

CD364

2003

Ascension 826
British Indian Ocean Territory 265
Cayman Islands..........................882-884
Falkland Islands 829
South Georgia 295
Tokelau 323
Tristan da Cunha................................735
Virgin Islands..........................1007-1009

No. 826 (1)	7.25	7.25
No. 265 (1)	8.00	8.00
Nos. 882-884 (3)	6.95	6.95
No. 829 (1)	13.50	13.50
No. 295 (1)	8.50	8.50
No. 323 (1)	7.25	7.25
No. 735 (1)	6.00	6.00
Nos. 1007-1009 (3)	10.00	10.00
Set total (12) Stamps	67.45	67.45

British Commonwealth of Nations

Dominions, Colonies, Territories, Offices and Independent Members

Comprising stamps of the British Commonwealth and associated nations.

A strict observance of technicalities would bar some or all of the stamps listed under Burma, Ireland, Kuwait, Nepal, New Republic, Orange Free State, Samoa, South Africa, South-West Africa, Stellaland, Sudan, Swaziland, the two Transvaal Republics and others but these are included for the convenience of collectors.

1. Great Britain

Great Britain: Including England, Scotland, Wales and Northern Ireland.

2. The Dominions, Present and Past

AUSTRALIA

The Commonwealth of Australia was proclaimed on Jan. 1, 1901. It consists of six former colonies as follows:

New South Wales
Queensland
South Australia
Victoria
Tasmania
Western Australia

The following islands and territories are, or have been, administered by Australia: Australian Antarctic Territory, Christmas Island, Cocos (Keeling) Islands, Nauru, New Guinea, Norfolk Island, Papua.

CANADA

The Dominion of Canada was created by the British North America Act in 1867. The following provinces were former separate colonies and issued postage stamps:

British Columbia and Vancouver Island
New Brunswick
Newfoundland
Nova Scotia
Prince Edward Island

FIJI

The colony of Fiji became an independent nation with dominion status on Oct. 10, 1970.

GHANA

This state came into existence March 6, 1957, with dominion status. It consists of the former colony of the Gold Coast and the Trusteeship Territory of Togoland. Ghana became a republic July 1, 1960.

INDIA

The Republic of India was inaugurated on Jan. 26, 1950. It succeeded the Dominion of India which was proclaimed Aug. 15, 1947, when the former Empire of India was divided into Pakistan and the Union of India. The Republic is composed of about 40 predominantly Hindu states of three classes: governor's provinces, chief commissioner's provinces and princely states. India also has various territories, such as the Andaman and Nicobar Islands.

The old Empire of India was a federation of British India and the native states. The more important princely states were autonomous. Of the more than 700 Indian states, these 43 are familiar names to philatelists because of their postage stamps.

CONVENTION STATES

Chamba
Faridkot
Gwalior
Jhind
Nabha
Patiala

FEUDATORY STATES

Alwar
Bahawalpur
Bamra
Barwani
Bhopal
Bhor
Bijawar
Bundi
Bussahir
Charkhari
Cochin
Dhar
Dungarpur
Duttia
Faridkot (1879-85)
Hyderabad
Idar
Indore
Jaipur
Jammu
Jammu and Kashmir
Jasdan
Jhalawar
Jhind (1875-76)
Kashmir
Kishangarh
Kotah
Las Bela
Morvi
Nandgaon
Nowanuggur
Orchha
Poonch
Rajasthan
Rajpeepla
Sirmur
Soruth
Tonk
Travancore
Wadhwan

NEW ZEALAND

Became a dominion on Sept. 26, 1907. The following islands and territories are, or have been, administered by New Zealand:

Aitutaki
Cook Islands (Rarotonga)
Niue
Penrhyn
Ross Dependency
Samoa (Western Samoa)
Tokelau Islands

PAKISTAN

The Republic of Pakistan was proclaimed March 23, 1956. It succeeded the Dominion which was proclaimed Aug. 15, 1947. It is made up of all or part of several Moslem provinces and various districts of the former Empire of India, including Bahawalpur and Las Bela. Pakistan withdrew from the Commonwealth in 1972.

SOUTH AFRICA

Under the terms of the South African Act (1909) the self-governing colonies of Cape of Good Hope, Natal, Orange River Colony and Transvaal united on May 31, 1910, to form the Union of South Africa. It became an independent republic May 3, 1961.

Under the terms of the Treaty of Versailles, South-West Africa, formerly German South-West Africa, was mandated to the Union of South Africa.

SRI LANKA (CEYLON)

The Dominion of Ceylon was proclaimed Feb. 4, 1948. The island had been a Crown Colony from 1802 until then. On May 22, 1972, Ceylon became the Republic of Sri Lanka.

3. Colonies, Past and Present; Controlled Territory and Independent Members of the Commonwealth

Abu Dhabi
Aden
Aitutaki
Alderney
Anguilla
Antigua
Ascension
Australia
Bahamas
Bahrain
Bangladesh
Barbados
Barbuda
Basutoland
Batum
Bechuanaland
Bechuanaland Prot.
Belize
Bermuda
Botswana
British Antarctic Territory
British Central Africa
British Columbia and Vancouver Island

British East Africa
British Guiana
British Honduras
British Indian Ocean Territory
British New Guinea
British Solomon Islands
British Somaliland
Brunei
Burma
Bushire
Cameroons
Canada
Cape of Good Hope
Cayman Islands
Christmas Island
Cocos (Keeling) Islands
Cook Islands
Crete,
  British Administration
Cyprus
Dominica
East Africa & Uganda
  Protectorates
Egypt
Falkland Islands
Fiji
Gambia
German East Africa
Ghana
Gibraltar
Gilbert Islands
Gilbert & Ellice Islands
Gold Coast
Grenada
Griqualand West
Guernsey
Guyana
Heligoland
Hong Kong
Indian Native States
  (see India)
Ionian Islands
Jamaica
Jersey
Jordan
Kenya
Kenya, Uganda & Tanzania
Kiribati
Kuwait
Labuan
Lagos
Leeward Islands
Lesotho
Madagascar
Malawi
Malaya
  Federated Malay States
  Johore
  Kedah
  Kelantan
  Malacca
  Negri Sembilan
  Pahang
  Penang
  Perak
  Perlis
  Selangor
  Singapore
  Sungei Ujong
  Trengganu
Malaysia
Maldive Islands
Malta
Man, Isle of
Mauritius
Mesopotamia
Montserrat
Mozambique
Muscat
Namibia
Natal
Nauru
Nevis
New Britain
New Brunswick
Newfoundland
New Guinea
New Hebrides
New Republic
New South Wales
New Zealand
Niger Coast Protectorate
Nigeria
Niue
Norfolk Island
North Borneo
Northern Nigeria
Northern Rhodesia
North West Pacific Islands
Nova Scotia
Nyasaland Protectorate
Oman
Orange River Colony
Pakistan
Palestine
Papua New Guinea
Penrhyn Island
Pitcairn Islands
Prince Edward Island
Qatar
Queensland
Rhodesia
Rhodesia & Nyasaland
Ross Dependency
Rwanda
Sabah
St. Christopher
St. Helena
St. Kitts
St. Kitts-Nevis-Anguilla
St. Lucia
St. Vincent
Samoa
Sarawak
Seychelles
Sierra Leone
Singapore
Solomon Islands
Somaliland Protectorate
South Africa
South Arabia
South Australia
South Georgia
Southern Nigeria
Southern Rhodesia
South-West Africa
Sri Lanka
Stellaland
Straits Settlements
Sudan
Swaziland
Tanganyika
Tanzania
Tasmania
Tobago
Togo
Tokelau Islands
Tonga
Transvaal
Trinidad
Trinidad and Tobago
Tristan da Cunha
Trucial States
Turks and Caicos
Turks Islands
Tuvalu
Uganda
United Arab Emirates
Vanuatu
Victoria
Virgin Islands
Western Australia
Zambia
Zanzibar
Zimbabwe
Zululand

POST OFFICES IN FOREIGN COUNTRIES

Africa
  East Africa Forces
  Middle East Forces
Bangkok
China
Morocco
Turkish Empire

Colonies, former colonies, offices, territories controlled by parent states

Belgium

Belgian Congo
Ruanda-Urundi

Denmark

Danish West Indies
Faroe Islands
Greenland
Iceland

Finland

Aland Islands

France

COLONIES PAST AND PRESENT, CONTROLLED TERRITORIES

Afars & Issas, Territory of
Alaouites
Alexandretta
Algeria
Alsace & Lorraine
Anjouan
Annam & Tonkin
Benin
Cambodia (Khmer)
Cameroun
Castellorizo
Chad
Cilicia
Cochin China
Comoro Islands
Dahomey
Diego Suarez
Djibouti (Somali Coast)
Fezzan
French Congo
French Equatorial Africa
French Guiana
French Guinea
French India
French Morocco
French Polynesia (Oceania)
French Southern & Antarctic Territories
French Sudan
French West Africa
Gabon
Germany
Ghadames
Grand Comoro
Guadeloupe
Indo-China
Inini
Ivory Coast
Laos
Latakia
Lebanon
Madagascar
Martinique
Mauritania
Mayotte
Memel
Middle Congo
Moheli
New Caledonia
New Hebrides
Niger Territory
Nossi-Be
Obock
Reunion
Rouad, Ile
Ste.-Marie de Madagascar
St. Pierre & Miquelon
Senegal
Senegambia & Niger
Somali Coast
Syria
Tahiti
Togo
Tunisia
Ubangi-Shari
Upper Senegal & Niger
Upper Volta
Viet Nam
Wallis & Futuna Islands

POST OFFICES IN FOREIGN COUNTRIES

China
Crete
Egypt
Turkish Empire
Zanzibar

Germany

EARLY STATES

Baden
Bavaria
Bergedorf
Bremen
Brunswick
Hamburg
Hanover
Lubeck
Mecklenburg-Schwerin
Mecklenburg-Strelitz
Oldenburg
Prussia
Saxony
Schleswig-Holstein
Wurttemberg

FORMER COLONIES

Cameroun (Kamerun)
Caroline Islands
German East Africa
German New Guinea
German South-West Africa
Kiauchau
Mariana Islands
Marshall Islands
Samoa
Togo

Italy

EARLY STATES

Modena
Parma
Romagna
Roman States
Sardinia
Tuscany
Two Sicilies
  Naples
  Neapolitan Provinces
  Sicily

FORMER COLONIES, CONTROLLED TERRITORIES, OCCUPATION AREAS

Aegean Islands
  Calimno (Calino)
  Caso
  Cos (Coo)
  Karki (Carchi)
  Leros (Lero)
  Lipso
  Nisiros (Nisiro)
  Patmos (Patmo)
  Piscopi
  Rodi (Rhodes)
  Scarpanto
  Simi
  Stampalia
Castellorizo
Corfu
Cyrenaica
Eritrea
Ethiopia (Abyssinia)
Fiume
Ionian Islands
  Cephalonia
  Ithaca
  Paxos
Italian East Africa
Libya
Oltre Giuba
Saseno
Somalia (Italian Somaliland)
Tripolitania

POST OFFICES IN FOREIGN COUNTRIES

"ESTERO"*
Austria
China
  Peking
  Tientsin
Crete
Tripoli
Turkish Empire
  Constantinople
  Durazzo
  Janina
Jerusalem
Salonika
Scutari
Smyrna
Valona

**Stamps overprinted "ESTERO" were used in various parts of the world.*

Netherlands

Aruba
Caribbean Netherlands
Curacao
Netherlands Antilles (Curacao)
Netherlands Indies
Netherlands New Guinea
St. Martin
Surinam (Dutch Guiana)

Portugal

COLONIES PAST AND PRESENT, CONTROLLED TERRITORIES

Angola
Angra
Azores
Cape Verde
Funchal
Horta
Inhambane
Kionga
Lourenco Marques
Macao
Madeira
Mozambique
Mozambique Co.
Nyassa
Ponta Delgada
Portuguese Africa
Portuguese Congo
Portuguese Guinea
Portuguese India
Quelimane
St. Thomas & Prince Islands
Tete
Timor
Zambezia

Russia

ALLIED TERRITORIES AND REPUBLICS, OCCUPATION AREAS

Armenia
Aunus (Olonets)
Azerbaijan
Batum
Estonia
Far Eastern Republic
Georgia
Karelia
Latvia
Lithuania
North Ingermanland
Ostland
Russian Turkestan
Siberia
South Russia
Tannu Tuva
Transcaucasian Fed. Republics
Ukraine
Wenden (Livonia)
Western Ukraine

Spain

COLONIES PAST AND PRESENT, CONTROLLED TERRITORIES

Aguera, La
Cape Juby
Cuba
Elobey, Annobon & Corisco
Fernando Po
Ifni
Mariana Islands
Philippines
Puerto Rico
Rio de Oro
Rio Muni
Spanish Guinea
Spanish Morocco
Spanish Sahara
Spanish West Africa

POST OFFICES IN FOREIGN COUNTRIES

Morocco
Tangier
Tetuan

Dies of British colonial stamps

DIE A:

1. The lines in the groundwork vary in thickness and are not uniformly straight.

2. The seventh and eighth lines from the top, in the groundwork, converge where they meet the head.

3. There is a small dash in the upper part of the second jewel in the band of the crown.

4. The vertical color line in front of the throat stops at the sixth line of shading on the neck.

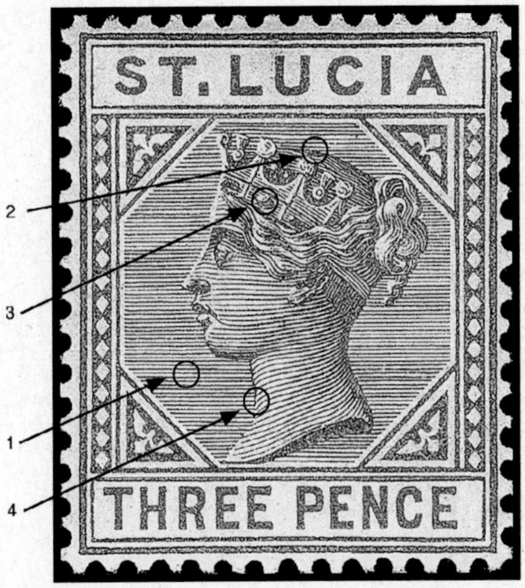

DIE B:

1. The lines in the groundwork are all thin and straight.

2. All the lines of the background are parallel.

3. There is no dash in the upper part of the second jewel in the band of the crown.

4. The vertical color line in front of the throat stops at the eighth line of shading on the neck.

DIE I:

1. The base of the crown is well below the level of the inner white line around the vignette.

2. The labels inscribed "POSTAGE" and "REVENUE" are cut square at the top.

3. There is a white "bud" on the outer side of the main stem of the curved ornaments in each lower corner.

4. The second (thick) line below the country name has the ends next to the crown cut diagonally.

DIE Ia.	DIE Ib.
1 as die II.	1 and 3 as die II.
2 and 3 as die I.	2 as die I.

DIE II:

1. The base of the crown is aligned with the underside of the white line around the vignette.

2. The labels curve inward at the top inner corners.

3. The "bud" has been removed from the outer curve of the ornaments in each corner.

4. The second line below the country name has the ends next to the crown cut vertically.

Wmk. 1
Crown and C C

Wmk. 2
Crown and C A

Wmk. 3
Multiple Crown and C A

Wmk. 4
Multiple Crown and Script C A

Wmk. 4a

Wmk. 46

Wmk. 314
St. Edward's Crown and C A Multiple

Wmk. 373

Wmk. 384

Wmk. 406

British Colonial and Crown Agents watermarks

Watermarks 1 to 4, 314, 373, 384 and 406, common to many British territories, are illustrated here to avoid duplication.

The letters "CC" of Wmk. 1 identify the paper as having been made for the use of the Crown Colonies, while the letters "CA" of the others stand for "Crown Agents." Both Wmks. 1 and 2 were used on stamps printed by De La Rue & Co.

Wmk. 3 was adopted in 1904; Wmk. 4 in 1921; Wmk. 46 in 1879; Wmk. 314 in 1957; Wmk. 373 in 1974; Wmk. 384 in 1985; Wmk 406 in 2008.

In Wmk. 4a, a non-matching crown of the general St. Edwards type (bulging on both sides at top) was substituted for one of the Wmk. 4 crowns which fell off the dandy roll. The non-matching crown occurs in 1950-52 printings in a horizontal row of crowns on certain regular stamps of Johore and Seychelles, and on various postage due stamps of Barbados, Basutoland, British Guiana, Gold Coast, Grenada, Northern Rhodesia, St. Lucia, Swaziland and Trinidad and Tobago. A variation of Wmk. 4a, with the non-matching crown in a horizontal row of crown-CA-crown, occurs on regular stamps of Bahamas, St. Kitts-Nevis and Singapore.

Wmk. 314 was intentionally used sideways, starting in 1966. When a stamp was issued with Wmk. 314 both upright and sideways, the sideways varieties usually are listed also — with minor numbers. In many of the later issues, Wmk. 314 is slightly visible.

Wmk. 373 is usually only faintly visible.

JAMAICA

jə-'mā-kə

LOCATION — Caribbean Sea, about 90 miles south of Cuba
GOVT. — Independent state in the British Commonwealth
AREA — 4,411 sq. mi.
POP. — 2,652,443 (1999 est.)
CAPITAL — Kingston

Jamaica became an independent state in the British Commonwealth in August 1962. As a colony, it administered two dependencies: Cayman Islands and Turks and Caicos Islands.

12 Pence = 1 Shilling
20 Shillings = 1 Pound
100 Cents = 1 Dollar (1969)

Catalogue values for unused stamps in this country are for Never Hinged items, beginning with Scott 129 in the regular postage section and Scott B4 in the semi-postal section.

Watermarks

Wmk. 45 — Pineapple

Wmk. 352 — J and Pineapple, Multiple

Values for unused stamps are for examples with original gum as defined in the catalogue introduction. Very fine examples of Nos. 1-12 will have perforations touching the design on at least one side due to the narrow spacing of the stamps on the plates. Stamps with perfs clear on all four sides are scarce and will command higher prices.

Queen Victoria
A1 A2

A3

A4

A5

A6

1860-63 Typo. Wmk. 45 *Perf. 14*

1	A1 1p blue	75.00	16.00
a.	Diagonal half used as ½p on cover		650.00
b.	1p deep blue	145.00	37.50
c.	1p pale blue	77.50	20.00
d.	1p pale greenish blue	115.00	21.00
2	A2 2p rose	225.00	60.00
a.	2p deep rose	170.00	60.00
3	A3 3p green ('63)	170.00	32.50
4	A4 4p brown org	275.00	62.50
a.	4p orange	225.00	50.00
5	A5 6p lilac	240.00	25.00
a.	6p deep lilac	1,000.	60.00
b.	6p gray lilac	300.00	40.00
6	A6 1sh brown	230.00	30.00
a.	1sh lilac brown	750.00	25.00
b.	1sh yellow brown	525.00	27.50

All except No. 3 exist imperforate.

1870-73 Wmk. 1

7	A1 1p blue	100.00	.90
8	A2 2p rose	100.00	.85
a.	2p brownish rose	110.00	1.10
9	A3 3p green	160.00	11.50
10	A4 4p brown org ('72)	350.00	13.50
a.	4p red orange	425.00	6.50
11	A5 6p lilac ('71)	100.00	6.00
12	A6 1sh brown ('73)	27.50	9.50
	Nos. 7-12 (6)	837.50	42.25

The 1p and 4p exist imperf.
See Nos. 17-23, 28, 40, 43, 47-53.

A7

1872, Oct. 29

13	A7 ½p claret	24.50	4.00
a.	½p deep claret	30.00	6.00

Exists imperf. See No. 16.

A8

A9

1875, Aug. 27 *Perf. 12½*

14	A8 2sh red brown	50.00	40.00
15	A9 5sh violet	125.00	*175.00*

Exist imperf.
See Nos. 29-30, 44, 54.

1883-90 Wmk. 2 *Perf. 14*

16	A7 ½p blue green ('85)	12.00	1.50
a.	½p gray green	3.75	.25
17	A1 1p blue ('84)	325.00	8.50
18	A1 1p carmine ('86)	72.50	1.10
a.	1p rose ('85)	82.50	2.25
19	A2 2p rose ('84)	230.00	5.75
20	A2 2p slate ('86)	110.00	.70
a.	2p gray ('85)	160.00	9.00
21	A3 3p ol green	2.75	3.00
22	A4 4p red brown	2.25	.40
a.	4p orange brown	450.00	25.00
23	A5 6p orange yel ('90)	5.00	4.00
a.	6p yellow	40.00	8.50
	Nos. 16-23 (8)	759.50	24.95

Nos. 18 and 20 exist imperf. Perf. 12 stamps are considered to be proofs.
For surcharge, see No. 27.

A10

1889-91

24	A10 1p lilac & red vio	14.00	.25
25	A10 2p deep green	26.00	9.00
a.	2p green	42.50	7.50
26	A10 2½p lilac & ultra ('91)	11.00	.75
	Nos. 24-26 (3)	51.00	*10.00*

No. 22 Surcharged in Black

1890, June

27	A4 2½p on 4p red brn	40.00	17.50
b.	Double surcharge	330.00	250.00
d.	"PFNNY"	100.00	70.00
f.	As "d," double surcharge		—

Three settings of surcharge.

1897

28	A6 1sh brown	11.00	6.50
29	A8 2sh red brown	35.00	40.00
30	A9 5sh violet	70.00	*100.00*
	Nos. 28-30 (3)	116.00	*146.50*

The 2sh exists imperf.

Llandovery Falls — A12

1900, May 1 Engr. Wmk. 1

31	A12 1p red	15.00	.25

1901, Sept. 25

32	A12 1p red & black	14.00	.25
a.	Pair, imperf. horiz.	25,000.	
b.	Bluish paper	115.00	110.00

Arms of Jamaica — A13

1903-04 Typo. Wmk. 2

33	A13 ½p gray & dull grn	2.60	.40
b.	"SERv ET" for "SERVIET"	45.00	*50.00*
34	A13 1p gray & car ('04)	4.75	.25
b.	"SERv ET" for "SERVIET"	35.00	40.00
35	A13 2½p gray & ultra	9.50	.45
a.	"SERv ET" for "SERVIET"	65.00	*75.00*
36	A13 5p gray & yel ('04)	20.00	*26.00*
a.	"SERv ET" for "SERVIET"	875.00	*1,100.*
	Nos. 33-36 (4)	36.85	*27.10*

1905-11 Chalky Paper Wmk. 3

37	A13 ½p gray & dull grn	3.00	.25
b.	"SERv ET" for "SERVIET"	27.50	*42.50*
38	A13 1p gray & car	20.00	2.00
39	A13 2½p gray & ultra ('07)	7.50	*9.25*
39A	A3 3p vio, *yel* ('10)	2.25	1.50
40	A4 4p blk, *yel* ('10)	20.00	*60.00*
41	A13 5p gray & org yel ('07)	67.50	*82.50*
a.	"SERv ET" for "SERVIET"	1,425.	*1,600.*
42	A13 6p red vio & vio ('11)	16.00	*24.00*
42A	A5 6p purple ('10)	11.50	*37.50*
43	A6 1sh blk, *grn* ('10)	15.00	*10.00*
a.	"$" for "S" in "SHILLING"	1,100.	*1,400.*
44	A8 2sh vio, *blue* ('10)	17.00	8.50
45	A13 5sh gray & vio	57.50	65.00
	Nos. 37-45 (11)	237.25	300.50

1905-11 Ordinary Paper

46a	A3 2½p deep ultra	2.75	1.90
47	A3 3p sage grn ('07)	8.00	3.50
a.	3p olive green ('05)	13.00	4.75
48	A3 3p pale pur, *yel* ('10)	12.00	3.75
49	A4 4p red brn ('08)	77.50	*82.50*
50	A4 4p red, *yel* ('11)	1.75	*4.00*
51	A5 6p dull vio ('09)	35.00	*62.50*
52	A5 6p org yel ('09)	45.00	*70.00*
a.	6p orange ('06)	18.00	27.50
53	A6 1sh brown ('06)	27.50	*52.50*
a.	1sh deep brown	42.50	*62.50*
54	A8 2sh red brn ('08)	140.00	*175.00*
	Nos. 46-54 (8)	346.75	*453.75*

A14

A15

1906

58	A14 ½p green	4.00	.25
a.	Booklet pane of 6	—	
59	A15 1p carmine	1.60	.25
a.	Booklet pane of 6	—	

For overprints see Nos. MR1, MR4, MR7, MR10.

Edward VII — A16

1911, Feb. 3

60	A16 2p gray	10.00	*15.00*

George V — A17

1912-20

61	A17 1p scarlet ('16)	10.00	.80
a.	1p carmine ('12)	1.75	.25
b.	Booklet pane of 6	—	
62	A17 1½p brn org ('16)	2.25	.70
a.	1½p yellow orange	18.50	1.50
63	A17 2p gray	2.50	*2.00*
64	A17 2½p dp br blue	.90	*1.25*
a.	2½p ultra ('13)	2.00	.25

Chalky Paper

65	A17 3p violet, *yel*	.60	.50
66	A17 4p scar & blk, *yel* ('13)	.60	*3.00*
67	A17 6p red vio & dl vio	1.90	1.60
68	A17 1sh black, *green*	2.60	2.25
a.	1sh blk, *bl grn*, olive back ('20)	5.50	*12.50*
69	A17 2sh ultra & vio, *blue* ('19)	27.50	*45.00*
70	A17 5sh scar & grn, *yel* ('19)	82.50	*105.00*

Surface-colored Paper

71	A17 3p violet, *yel* ('13)	.60	.45
72	A17 4p scar & blk, *yel* ('14)	.85	*3.50*
73	A17 1sh blk, *grn* ('15)	7.50	*5.00*
	Nos. 61-73 (13)	140.30	*171.05*

See Nos. 101-102. For overprints see Nos. MR2-MR3, MR5-MR6, MR8-MR9, MR11.

Exhibition Buildings of 1891
A18

Arawak Woman Preparing Cassava
A19

World War I Contingent Embarking for Overseas Duty
A20

King's House, Spanish Town
A21

Return of Overseas Contingent, 1919
A22

Columbus Landing in Jamaica
A23

Cathedral in Spanish Town
A24

Statue of Queen Victoria
A26

Memorial to Admiral Rodney
A27

Monument to Sir Charles Metcalfe
A28

Woodland Scene — A29

King George V — A30

1919-21 Typo. Wmk. 3 *Perf. 14*
Chalky Paper

75	A18 ½p ol grn & dk grn ('20)	1.10	1.10

76 A19 1p org & car ('21) 2.00 2.00

Engr.

Ordinary Paper

77 A20 1½p green .45 *1.10*
78 A21 2p grn & bl ('21) 1.25 *4.50*
79 A22 2½p blue blk & blue 3.00 2.00
- *a.* 2½p blue & dark blue ('21) 15.00 3.50
- *b.* "C" of "CA" missing from watermark *350.00 300.00*
- *c.* "A" of "CA" missing from watermark *350.00*

80 A23 3p blue & grn ('21) 7.50 *2.75*
81 A24 4p grn & dk brn ('21) 4.00 *10.00*
83 A26 1sh brt org & org ('20) 5.00 *5.75*
- *a.* Frame inverted *40,000. 25,000.*
  As "a," revenue cancel *2,500.*
- *b.* "C" of "CA" missing from watermark *1,100.*
- *c.* "A" of "CA" missing from watermark *1,800. 1,000.*

84 A27 2sh brn & bl ('20) 12.50 *37.50*
- *b.* "C" of "CA" missing from watermark *800.00*
- *c.* "A" of "CA" missing from watermark

85 A28 3sh org & vio ('20) 27.50 *135.00*
- *a.* "C" of "CA" missing from watermark *1,200.*

86 A29 5sh ocher & blue ('21) 60.00 *100.00*
87 A30 10sh dk myr grn ('20) 85.00 *160.00*
Nos. 75-87 (12) 209.30 *461.70*

See note after No. 100. Watermark varieties exist and sell for much higher values.

A 6p stamp depicting the abolition of slavery was sent to the Colony but was not issued. "Specimen" examples exist with wmk. 3 or 4. Value $875 each.

Without "Specimen," values: wmk. 3, $60,000; wmk. 4, $40,000.

Port Royal in 1853 — A31

1921-23 Typo. Wmk. 4 *Perf. 14*

Chalky Paper

88 A18 ½p ol grn & dk grn ('22) .60 .60
- *a.* Booklet pane of 4 *150.00*

89 A19 1p org & car ('22) 2.00 .25
- *a.* Booklet pane of 6 *225.00*

Engr.

Ordinary Paper

90 A20 1½p green 4.00 .55
91 A21 2p grn & blue 8.50 .90
92 A22 2½p bl & dk bl 6.50 2.00
93 A23 3p bl & grn ('22) 7.00 .80
94 A24 4p grn & dk brn 1.50 .40
95 A31 6p bl & blk ('22) 17.00 1.75
96 A26 1sh brn org & dl org 2.50 .90
97 A27 2sh brn & bl ('22) 3.75 1.00
98 A28 3sh org & violet 20.00 11.00
99 A29 5sh ocher & bl ('23) 35.00 29.00
- *a.* 5sh orange & blue 82.50 *82.50*

100 A30 10sh dk myr grn ('22) 60.00 80.00
Nos. 88-100 (13) 168.35 129.15
Set, never hinged 380.00

No. 89 differs from No. 76 in having the words "Postage and Revenue" at the bottom.

On No. 79 the horizontal bar of the flag at the left has a broad white line below the colored line. On No. 92 this has been corrected and the broad white line placed above the colored line.

Watermark is sideways on Nos. 76-77, 87, 89-90. Watermark varieties other than these and normal are scarce and sell for much higher values.

Type of 1912-19 Issue

1921-27 Typo. Wmk. 4

101 A17 ½p green ('27) 4.00 .25
- *a.* Booklet pane of 6

102 A17 6p red vio & dl vio 18.50 4.50

No. 102 is on chalky paper.

A32

Type I

Type II

Type II — Cross shading beneath "Jamaica."

1929-32 Engr. *Perf. 13½x14, 14*

103 A32 1p red, type I 16.50 .25
- *a.* 1p red, type II ('32) 16.50 .25
- *b.* Booklet pane of 6, type II

104 A32 1½p brown 10.00 .25
105 A32 9p violet brown 10.00 1.25
Nos. 103-105 (3) 36.50 1.75
Set, never hinged 42.50

The frames on Nos. 103 to 105 differ.

Coco Palms at Columbus Cove A33

Scene near Castleton, St. Andrew A34

Priestman's River, Portland Parish — A35

1932 *Perf. 12½*

106 A33 2p grn & gray blk 40.00 4.50
- *a.* Vertical pair, imperf. between *22,500.*

107 A34 2½p ultra & sl bl 6.75 2.00
- *a.* Vertical pair, imperf. between *25,000. 25,000.*

108 A35 6p red vio & gray blk 37.50 6.00
Nos. 106-108 (3) 84.25 12.50
Set, never hinged 125.00

Common Design Types pictured following the introduction.

Silver Jubilee Issue

Common Design Type

1935, May 6 *Perf. 11x12*

109 CD301 1p car & blue .45 .25
- *a.* Booklet pane of 6 *175.00*

110 CD301 1½p black & ultra .75 *1.75*
111 CD301 6p indigo & grn 14.00 *22.50*
112 CD301 1sh brn vio & ind 9.00 *26.00*
Nos. 109-112 (4) 24.20 50.50
Set, never hinged 35.00

Coronation Issue

Common Design Type

1937, May 12 *Perf. 13½x14*

113 CD302 1p carmine .25 .25
114 CD302 1½p gray black .40 .30
115 CD302 2½p bright ultra .60 *.70*
Nos. 113-115 (3) 1.25 1.25
Set, never hinged 2.00

King George VI — A36

Coco Palms at Columbus Cove — A37

Scene near Castleton, St. Andrew A38

Bananas A39

Citrus Grove — A40

Priestman's River, Portland Parish — A41

Kingston Harbor — A42

Sugar Industry — A43

Bamboo Walk — A44

Woodland Scene — A45

King George VI — A46

1938-51 *Perf. 13½x14*

116 A36 ½p dk blue grn 1.25 .25
- *a.* Booklet pane of 6 8.00
- *b.* Wmkd. sideways — *9,000.*

117 A36 1p carmine .85 .25
- *a.* Booklet pane of 6 12.00

118 A36 1½p brown .85 .25

Perf. 12½, 13x13½, 13½x13, 12½x13

119 A37 2p grn & gray blk, perf. 12½ .85 .85
- *a.* Perf. 13x13½ ('39) 1.90 .50
- *b.* Perf. 12½x13 ('51) .85 .25

120 A38 2½p ultra & sl bl 5.75 *2.75*
121 A39 3p grn & lt ultra .75 *1.50*
122 A40 4p grn & yel brn .60 .25
123 A41 6p red vio & gray blk, perf. 13½x13 ('50) 2.00 .25
- *a.* Perf. 12½ 5.75 .30
- *b.* As "a," double impression of gray blk —

124 A42 9p rose lake .60 .50
125 A43 1sh dk brn & brt grn 10.00 .25
126 A44 2sh brn & brt bl 21.00 1.00

Perf. 13, 14

127 A45 5sh ocher & bl, perf. 13 ('50) 7.25 3.75
- *a.* Bluish paper, perf. 13 ('49) 7.25 3.00
- *b.* Perf. 14 12.00 3.25

128 A46 10sh dk myr grn, perf. 14 6.75 *11.50*
- *a.* Perf. 13x13½ ('50) 11.00 *7.50*

Nos. 116-128 (13) 58.50 23.35
Set, never hinged 125.00

See Nos. 140, 148, 149, 152.

Catalogue values for unused stamps in this section, from this point to the end of the section, are for Never Hinged items.

Courthouse, Falmouth A47

Kings Charles II and George VI A48

House of Assembly, 1762-1869 A50

Institute of Jamaica A49

Allegory of Labor and Learning A51

Constitution and Flag of Jamaica A52

Perf. 12½

1945, Aug. 20 Engr. Wmk. 4

129 A47 1½p brown .30 .30
- *a.* Booklet pane of 4 37.50
- *b.* Perf. 12½x13½ ('46) 18.00 1.75

130 A48 2p dp grn, perf. 12½x13½ .40 *.50*
- *a.* Perf. 12½ 18.00 2.25

131 A49 3p bright ultra .25 *.50*
- *a.* Perf. 13 ('46) 4.00 *2.50*

132 A50 4½p slate black 1.50 .45
- *a.* Perf. 13 ('46) 6.50 *6.50*

133 A51 2sh chocolate 2.25 .50
134 A52 5sh deep blue 4.50 2.00
135 A49 10sh green 3.50 *2.00*
Nos. 129-135 (7) 12.70 *6.25*

Granting of a new Constitution in 1944.

Peace Issue

Common Design Type

1946, Oct. 14 Wmk. 4 *Perf. 13½*

136 CD303 1½p black brown 1.00 *4.50*
- *a.* Perf. 13½x14 3.00 .25

Perf. 13½x14

137 CD303 3p deep blue 1.00 9.00
- *a.* Perf. 13½ 10.00 *4.00*

Silver Wedding Issue

Common Design Types

1948, Dec. 1 Photo. *Perf. 14x14½*

138 CD304 1½p red brown .35 .25

Engr.; Name Typo.

Perf. 11½x11

139 CD305 £1 red 30.00 *75.00*

Type of 1938 and

Tobacco Industry — A53

1949, Aug. 15 Engr. *Perf. 12½*

140 A39 3p ultra & slate blue 4.50 1.25
141 A53 £1 violet & dk brn 60.00 40.00

In 1956, a stamp matching the design of No. 141, but with Queen Elizabeth II, was prepared but not issued.

UPU Issue

Common Design Types

Perf. 13½, 11x11½

1949, Oct. 10 Wmk. 4

142 CD306 1½p red brown .25 .25
- *a.* "A" of "CA" missing from watermark *700.00*

143 CD307 2p dark green 1.25 1.00
144 CD308 3p indigo .50 *.50*
145 CD309 6p rose violet .50 *.70*
Nos. 142-145 (4) 2.50 2.45

University Issue

Common Design Types

1951, Feb. 16 *Perf. 14x14½*

146 CD310 2p brown & gray blk .35 .40
147 CD311 6p rose lil & gray blk .70 .30

George VI Type of 1938

1951, Oct. 25 *Perf. 13½x14*

148 A36 ½p orange 3.25 .30
- *a.* Booklet pane of 6 23.00

149 A36 1p blue green 4.75 .25
- *a.* Booklet pane of 6 34.00

Boy Scout Emblem with Map — A54

Map and Emblem — A55

Perf. 13½x13, 13x13½

1952, Mar. 5 Typo. Wmk. 4

150 A54 2p blk, yel grn & blue .30 .25
151 A55 6p blk, yel grn & dk red .70 .70

1st Caribbean Boy Scout Jamboree, 1952.

Banana Type of 1938

1952, July 1 Engr. *Perf. 12½*

152 A39 3p rose red & green 6.00 .30

Coronation Issue

Common Design Type

1953, June 2 *Perf. 13½x13*

153 CD312 2p dk green & black .70 .25

Type of 1938 with Portrait of Queen Elizabeth II

Inscription: "ROYAL VISIT 1953"

1953, Nov. 25 *Perf. 13*

154 A37 2p green & gray black .50 .25

Visit of Queen Elizabeth II and the Duke of Edinburgh, 1953.

Warship off Port Royal — A56

Designs: 2½p, Old Montego Bay. 3p, Old Kingston. 6p, Proclaiming abolition of slavery.

1955, May 10 Engr. *Perf. 12x12½*
Center in Black

155 A56 2p olive green .50 .25
156 A56 2½p light ultra .25 .30
157 A56 3p deep plum .25 .30
158 A56 6p rose red .25 .25
Nos. 155-158 (4) 1.25 1.10

300th anniv. of Jamaica's establishment as a British territory.

Palm Trees — A57

Blue Mountain Peak — A58

Arms of Jamaica A59

Arms of Jamaica A60

1p, Sugar cane. 2p, Pineapple. 2½p, Bananas. 3p, Mahoe flower. 4p, Breadfruit. 5p, Ackee fruit. 6p, Streamer (hummingbird). 1sh, Royal Botanic Gardens, Hope. 1sh6p, Rafting on the Rio Grande. 2sh, Fort Charles.

1956 Wmk. 4 *Perf. 12½*

159 A57 ½p org ver & blk .25 .25
a. Booklet pane of 6 .30
160 A57 1p emer & blk .25 .25
a. Booklet pane of 6 .50
161 A57 2p rose red & blk .25 .25
a. Booklet pane of 6 .85
162 A57 2½p lt ultra & black 1.00 .50
a. Booklet pane of 6 6.00
163 A57 3p brn & grn .25 .25
164 A57 4p dk blue & ol grn .50 .25
165 A57 5p ol green & car 1.00 *2.00*
166 A57 6p car & blk 3.25 .25

Perf. 13½

167 A58 8p red org & brt ultra 1.75 .25
168 A58 1sh blue & yel grn 1.75 .25
169 A58 1sh6p dp cl & ultra 1.00 .25
170 A58 2sh ol grn & ultra 13.50 2.50

Perf. 11½

171 A59 3sh blue & black 2.75 *3.25*
172 A59 5sh carmine & blk 4.00 *6.00*
173 A60 10sh blue grn & blk 27.50 *14.00*
174 A60 £1 purple & blk 27.50 *14.00*
Nos. 159-174 (16) 86.50 44.50

For overprints see Nos. 185-196. For types overprinted see Nos. 208-216.

West Indies Federation

Common Design Type

Perf. 11½x11

1958, Apr. 22 Engr. Wmk. 314

175 CD313 2p green .70 .25
176 CD313 5p blue .95 *2.75*
177 CD313 6p carmine rose 1.00 .45
Nos. 175-177 (3) 2.65 3.45

Britannia Plane over 1860 Packet Boat — A61

1sh Stamps of 1860 and 1956 — A62

6p, Victorian post cart and mail truck.

1960, Jan. 4 *Perf. 13x13½*

178 A61 2p lilac & blue .50 .25
179 A61 6p ol grn & car rose .50 .45

Perf. 13

180 A62 1sh blue, yel grn & brn .60 .50
Nos. 178-180 (3) 1.60 1.20

Centenary of Jamaican postal service.

Independent State

Zouave Bugler and Map of Jamaica — A63

1sh6p, Gordon House (Legislature) & hands of three races holding banner. 5sh, Map & symbols of agriculture & industry.

1962, Aug. 8 Photo. *Perf. 13*

181 A63 2p multicolored 1.40 .25
182 A63 4p multicolored 1.00 .25
a. Yellow omitted
183 A63 1sh6p red, black & brn 3.00 .80
184 A63 5sh multicolored 4.25 5.50
Nos. 181-184 (4) 9.65 6.80

Issue of 1956 Overprinted

a

b

Perf. 12½

1962, Aug. 8 Wmk. 4 Engr.

185 A57(a) ½p org ver & blk .25 *.80*
186 A57(a) 1p emer & blk .25 .25
187 A57(a) 2½p lt ultra & blk .25 *.80*
188 A57(b) 3p brn & grn .25 .25
189 A57(b) 5p ol grn & car .25 *.55*
190 A57(b) 6p car & black 2.25 .25

Perf. 13½

191 A58(b) 8p red org & brt ultra .25 .25
192 A58(b) 1sh bl & yel grn .30 .25
193 A58(b) 2sh ol green & ultra 1.00 *1.25*

Perf. 11½

194 A59(a) 3sh blue & blk 1.00 *1.50*
195 A60(a) 10sh bl grn & blk 3.75 *3.50*
196 A60(a) £1 pur & black 4.00 *4.25*
Nos. 185-196 (12) 13.80 *13.90*

Nos. 181-196 issued to commemorate Jamaica's independence.

"Independence" measures 17½x1½mm on Nos. 185-187; 18x1mm on Nos. 194-196.

See Nos. 208-216.

Weight Lifting, Soccer, Boxing and Cycling — A64

Designs: 6p, Various water sports. 8p, Running and jumping. 2sh, Arms and runner.

Perf. 14½x14

1962, Aug. 11 Photo. Wmk. 314

197 A64 1p car & dk brown .25 .25
198 A64 6p blue & brown .25 .25
199 A64 8p olive & dk brown .25 .25
200 A64 2sh multicolored .30 *.70*
Nos. 197-200 (4) 1.05 1.45

IX Central American and Caribbean Games, Kingston, Aug. 11-25.

A souvenir sheet containing one each of Nos. 197-200, imperf., was sold exclusively by National Sports, Ltd., at 5sh (face 3sh3p). The Jamaican Post Office sold the entire issue of this sheet to National Sports at face value, plus the printing cost. The stamps are postally valid. The sheet has marginal inscriptions and simulated perforations in ultramarine. Value $14.

Freedom from Hunger Issue

Man Planting Mango Tree and Produce — A65

Perf. 12½

1963, June 4 Unwmk. Litho.

201 A65 1p blue & multi .25 .25
202 A65 8p rose & multi .80 .60

See note after CD314, Common Design section.

Red Cross Centenary Issue

Common Design Type

1963, Sept. 2 Wmk. 314 *Perf. 13*

203 CD315 2p black & red .25 .25
204 CD315 1sh6p ultra & red .50 *1.40*

Carole Joan Crawford — A66

Unwmk.

1964, Feb. 14 Photo. *Perf. 13*

205 A66 3p multicolored .25 .25
206 A66 1sh olive & multi .30 .25
207 A66 1sh6p multicolored .40 .40
a. Souvenir sheet of 3 1.50 1.50
Nos. 205-207 (3) .95 .90

Carole Joan Crawford, Miss World, 1963.

No. 207a contains one each of Nos. 205-207 with simulated perforations. Issued May 25. Sold for 4sh.

Types of 1956 Overprinted like 1962 Independence Issue

Wmk. 314

1963-64 Engr. *Perf. 12½*

208 A57(a) ½p org ver & blk .25 .25
209 A57(a) 1p emer & blk ('64) .25 *1.25*
210 A57(a) 2½p lt ultra & blk ('64) .25 *2.00*
211 A57(b) 3p brn & grn .25 .25
212 A57(b) 5p ol grn & car ('64) .40 *2.00*

Perf. 13½

213 A58(b) 8p red org & brt ultra ('64) .30 *.75*
214 A58(b) 1sh bl & yel grn .35 .75
215 A58(b) 2sh ol grn & ultra ('64) .60 *6.00*

Perf. 11½

216 A59(a) 3sh bl & blk ('64) 2.75 *4.50*
Nos. 208-216 (9) 5.40 17.75

Overprint is at bottom on Nos. 214-215, at top on Nos. 192-193.

Lignum Vitae, National Flower, and Map — A67

1½p, Ackee, national fruit, and map. 2p, Blue Mahoe, national tree, and map, vert. 2½p, Land shells (snails). 3p, Flag over map. 4p, Murex antillarum, sea shell. 6p, Papilio homerus. 8p, Doctor bird (Trochilus polytmus). 9p, Gypsum industry. 1sh, Stadium and statue of runner. 1sh6p, Palisadoes International Airport. 2sh, Bauxite mining. 3sh, Blue marlin and boat. 5sh, Port Royal exploration of sunken city, map, ship and artifacts. 10sh, Coat of arms, vert. £1, Flag and Queen Elizabeth II.

Perf. 14½, 14x14½

1964, May 4 Photo. Wmk. 352
Size: 26x22mm, 22x26mm

217 A67 1p bis, vio bl & grn .25 .25
a. Booklet pane of 6 .40
218 A67 1½p multicolored .25 .25
219 A67 2p multicolored .25 .25
a. Booklet pane of 6 .90
220 A67 2½p multicolored .90 .50
221 A67 3p emer, yel & black .25 .25
a. Booklet pane of 6 3.00
222 A67 4p violet & buff .50 .25
223 A67 6p multicolored 1.90 .25
a. Ultramarine omitted 95.00
b. Denomination omitted *2,200.*
224 A67 8p multicolored 2.00 1.25
a. Red omitted 200.00

Perf. 14½x14, 13½x14½, 14x14½
Size: 32x26mm, 26x32mm

225 A67 9p blue & yel 1.25 .25
226 A67 1sh yel brn & blk .25 .25
a. Yellow brown omitted 3,000. 3,000.
b. Black omitted 2,200.
c. Denomination (only) omitted 1,600.
227 A67 1sh6p sl, buff & bl 3.00 .25
228 A67 2sh bl, brn red & black 2.25 .25
229 A67 3sh grn, saph & dk bl, perf. 14½x14 .35 *.60*
a. Perf. 14x14½ 1.00 1.00
230 A67 5sh bl, blk & bis 1.00 1.00
231 A67 10sh multicolored 1.25 1.10
a. Blue ("Jamaica" etc.) omitted 450.00
232 A67 £1 multicolored 2.75 1.00
Nos. 217-232 (16) 18.40 7.95

See Nos. 306-318. For overprints & surcharges see Nos. 248-251, 279-291, 305.

Scout Hat, Globe, Neckerchief — A68

Scout Emblem, American Crocodile — A69

Design: 3p, Scout belt buckle.

Perf. 14½x14, 14

1964, Aug. 27 Wmk. 352

233 A68 3p pink, black & red .25 .25
234 A68 8p ultra, black & olive .25 *.25*
235 A69 1sh ultra & gold .25 *.45*
Nos. 233-235 (3) .75 *.95*

6th Inter-American Scout Conference, Kingston, Aug. 25-29.

Gordon House, Kingston, and Commonwealth Parliamentary Association Emblem — A70

6p, Headquarters House, Kingston. 1sh6p, House of Assembly, Spanish Town.

1964, Nov. 16 Photo. *Perf. 14½x14*

236 A70 3p yel green & blk .25 .25
237 A70 6p red & black .30 .25
238 A70 1sh6p ultra & black .40 .25
Nos. 236-238 (3) .95 .75

10th Commonwealth Parliamentary Conf.

Eleanor Roosevelt — A71

1964, Dec. 10 **Wmk. 352**
239 A71 1sh lt green, blk & red .25 .25

Eleanor Roosevelt (1884-1962) on the 16th anniv. of the Universal Declaration of Human Rights.

Map of Jamaica and Girl Guide Emblem — A72

Girl Guide Emblems A73

Perf. 14x14½, 14
1965, May 17 **Photo.** **Wmk. 352**
240 A72 3p lt blue, yel & yel grn .25 .25
241 A73 1sh lt yel grn, blk & bis .25 .30

50th anniv. of the Girl Guides of Jamaica.

Salvation Army Cap — A74

1sh6p, Flag bearer, drummer, globe, vert.

Perf. 14x14½, 14½x14
1965, Aug. 23 **Photo.** **Wmk. 352**
242 A74 3p dp blue, yel, mar & blk .25 .25
243 A74 1sh6p emerald & multi .50 .40

Centenary of the Salvation Army.

Paul Bogle, William Gordon and Morant Bay Court House — A75

1965, Dec. 29 **Unwmk.** ***Perf. 14x13***
244 A75 3p vio blue, blk & brn .25 .25
245 A75 1sh6p yel grn, blk & brn .25 .25
246 A75 3sh pink & brown .30 *.80*
Nos. 244-246 (3) .80 1.30

Cent. of the Morant Bay rebellion against governor John Eyre.

ITU Emblem, Telstar, Telegraph Key and Man Blowing Horn — A76

Perf. 14x14½
1965, Dec. 29 **Photo.** **Wmk. 352**
247 A76 1sh gray, black & red .50 .25

Cent. of the ITU.

Nos. 221, 223, 226-227 Overprinted

Perf. 14½, 14½x14
1966, Mar. 3 **Photo.** **Wmk. 352**
Size: 26x22mm
248 A67 3p emer, yel & black .30 .25
249 A67 6p multicolored 2.00 .40

Size: 32x26mm
250 A67 1sh yel brown & blk .65 .25
251 A67 1sh6p slate, buff & blue 3.25 2.50
Nos. 248-251 (4) 6.20 3.40

See note after Antigua No. 162.

Winston Churchill — A77

1966, Apr. 18 ***Perf. 14, 14x14½***
252 A77 6p olive green & gray .55 .35
253 A77 1sh violet & sepia .80 .95

Sir Winston Leonard Spencer Churchill (1874-1965), statesman and WWII leader.

Runner, Flags of Jamaica, Great Britain and Games' Emblem — A78

Designs: 6p, Bicyclists and waterfall. 1sh, Stadium. 3sh, Games' Emblem.

Perf. 14½x14
1966, Aug. 4 **Photo.** **Wmk. 352**
254 A78 3p multicolored .25 .25
255 A78 6p multicolored .35 .25
256 A78 1sh multicolored .25 .25
257 A78 3sh gold & dk vio blue .35 .40
a. Souvenir sheet of 4 5.00 5.00
Nos. 254-257 (4) 1.20 1.15

8th British Empire and Commonwealth Games, Aug. 4-13, 1966.

No. 257a contains 4 imperf. stamps with simulated perforations similar to Nos. 254-257. Issued Aug. 25, 1966.

Bolivar Statue, Kingston, Flags of Jamaica and Venezuela — A79

1966, Dec. 5 ***Perf. 14x14½***
258 A79 8p multicolored .35 .25

150th anniv. of the "Bolivar Letter," written by Simon Bolivar, while in exile in Jamaica.

Jamaican Pavilion — A80

1967, Apr. 28 ***Perf. 14½x14***
259 A80 6p multicolored .25 .25
260 A80 1sh multicolored .25 .25

EXPO '67 Intl. Exhibition, Montreal, Apr. 28-Oct. 27.

Donald Burns Sangster — A81

Perf. 13x13½
1967, Aug. 28 **Unwmk.**
261 A81 3p multicolored .25 .25
262 A81 1sh6p multicolored .25 .25

Sir Donald Burns Sangster (1911-1967), Prime Minister.

Traffic Police and Post Office — A82

Designs: 1sh, Officers representing various branches of police force in front of Police Headquarters. 1sh6p, Constable, 1867, Old House of Assembly, and 1967 constable with New House of Assembly.

Perf. 13½x14
1967, Nov. 28 **Photo.** **Wmk. 352**
Size: 42x25mm
263 A82 3p red brown & multi .40 .25

Size: 56½x20½mm
Perf. 13½x14½
264 A82 1sh yellow & multi .40 .25

Size: 42x25mm
Perf. 13½x14
265 A82 1sh6p gray & multi .70 *.75*
Nos. 263-265 (3) 1.50 1.25

Centenary of the Constabulary Force.

A Human Rights set of three (3p, 1sh, 3sh) was prepared and announced for release on Jan. 2, 1968. The Crown Agents distributed sample sets, but the stamps were not issued. On Dec. 3, Nos. 271-273 were issued instead. Designs of the unissued set show bowls of food, an abacus and praying hands. Value, $175.

Wicketkeeper, Emblem of West Indies Cricket Team — A82a

Designs: No. 266, Wicketkeeper and emblem of West Indies Cricket Team. No. 267, Batsman and emblem of Marylebone Cricket Club. No. 268, Bowler and emblem of West Indies Cricket Team.

1968, Feb. 8 **Photo.** ***Perf. 14***
266 A82a 6p multicolored .35 *.35*
267 A82a 6p multicolored .35 *.35*
268 A82a 6p multicolored .35 *.35*
a. Horiz. strip of 3, #266-268 1.75 *1.75*
Nos. 266-268 (3) 1.05 *1.05*

Visit of the Marylebone Cricket Club to the West Indies, Jan.-Feb. 1968. Miniature sheet of 3 of No 268a. Value, $5.75.

Sir Alexander and Lady Bustamante A83

1968, May 23 ***Perf. 14½***
269 A83 3p brt rose & black .25 .25
270 A83 1sh olive green & black .25 .25

Labor Day, May 23, 1968.

Human Rights Flame and Map of Jamaica — A84

Designs: 1sh, Hands shielding Human Rights flame, vert. 3sh, Man kneeling on Map of Jamaica, and Human Rights flame.

1968, Dec. 3 **Wmk. 352** ***Perf. 14½***
271 A84 3p multicolored .25 .25
a. Gold (flame) omitted 150.00
272 A84 1sh multicolored .25 .25
273 A84 3sh multicolored .40 *.80*
a. Gold (flame) omitted 175.00
Nos. 271-273 (3) .90 1.30

International Human Rights Year.

ILO Emblem — A85

Unwmk.
1969, May 23 **Litho.** ***Perf. 14***
274 A85 6p black & orange yel .25 .25
275 A85 3sh black & brt green .30 .30

50th anniv. of the ILO.

WHO Emblem, Children and Nurse — A86

Designs: 1sh, Malaria eradication, horiz. 3sh, Student nurses.

1969, May 30 **Photo.** ***Perf. 14***
276 A86 6p org, black & brown .25 .25
277 A86 1sh blue grn, blk & brn .25 .25
278 A86 3sh ultra, black & brn .25 *.80*
Nos. 276-278 (3) .75 1.30

WHO, 20th anniv.

Nos. 217-219, 221-223, 225-232 Surcharged

1969, Sept. 8 **Wmk. 352** ***Perf. 14½***
Size: 26x22mm, 22x26mm
279 A67 1c on 1p multi .25 .25
280 A67 2c on 2p multi .25 .25
281 A67 3c on 3p multi .25 .25
282 A67 4c on 4p multi 1.00 .25
283 A67 5c on 6p multi 1.00 .25
a. Blue (wing dots) omitted *100.00*

Perf. 14½x14, 13½x14½, 14x14½
Size: 32x26mm, 26x32mm
284 A67 8c on 9p multi .25 .25
285 A67 10c on 1sh multi .25 .25
286 A67 15c on 1sh6p multi .40 *.50*
287 A67 20c on 2sh multi 1.10 *.90*
288 A67 30c on 3sh multi 2.00 *1.50*
289 A67 50c on 5sh multi 1.00 *2.00*
290 A67 $1 on 10sh multi 1.00 *4.00*
291 A67 $2 on £1 multi 2.00 *5.00*
Nos. 279-291 (13) 10.75 15.65

Introduction of decimal currency.

The old denomination is obliterated by groups of small rectangles on the 1c and 3c, and with a square on the 2c, 4c and 8c; old denominations not obliterated on others.

Madonna and Child with St. John, by Raphael — A87

Christmas (Paintings): 2c, The Adoration of the Kings, by Vincenzo Foppa. 8c, The Adoration of the Kings, by Dosso Dossi.

1969, Oct. 25 **Litho.** ***Perf. 13***
292 A87 2c vermilion & multi .25 .35
293 A87 5c multicolored .25 .35
294 A87 8c orange & multi .25 .35
Nos. 292-294 (3) .75 1.05

First Jamaica Penny — A88

Design: 3c, First Jamaica halfpenny.

1969, Oct. 27 ***Perf. 12x12½***
295 A88 3c brt pink, blk & silver .25 .25
296 A88 15c emerald, blk & silver .25 .25

Centenary of the first Jamaican coinage.

George William Gordon — A89

Portraits: 3c, Sir Alexander Bustamante (1884-1977). 5c, Norman W. Manley (1893-1969). 10c, Marcus M. Garvey (1887-1940). 15c, Paul Bogle (1820-1865).

Perf. 12x12½

1970, Mar. 11 Photo. Unwmk.

297	A89	1c lt violet & multi	.25	.25
298	A89	3c lt blue & multi	.25	.25
299	A89	5c lt gray & multi	.25	.25
300	A89	10c pale rose & multi	.25	.25
301	A89	15c pale green & multi	.25	.25
		Nos. 297-301 (5)	1.25	1.25

National heroes connected with Jamaica's independence.

Crucifixion, by Antonello da Messina — A90

Easter: 3c, Christ Appearing to St. Peter, by Annibale Carracci. 20c, Easter lily.

1970, Mar. 23

302	A90	3c pink & multi	.25	.25
303	A90	10c gray green & multi	.25	.25
304	A90	20c gray & multi	.25	*.55*
		Nos. 302-304 (3)	.75	1.05

No. 219 Surcharged

1970, July 16 Wmk. 352 *Perf. 14½*

305	A67	2c on 2p multicolored	.30	.25

Type of Regular Issue, 1964

Values in Cents and Dollars

Designs: 1c, Lignum vitae and map. 2c, Blue mahoe and map, vert. 3c, Flag over map. 4c, Murex antillarum, sea shell. 5c, Papilio homerus. 8c, Gypsum industry. 10c, Stadium and statue of runner. 15c, Palisadoes International Airport. 20c, Bauxite mining. 30c, Blue marlin and boat. 50c, Port Royal exploration of sunken city, map, ship and artifacts. $1, Coat of arms, vert. $2, Flag and Queen Elizabeth II.

1970 Wmk. 352 Photo. *Perf. 14½*

Size: 26x22mm, 22x26mm

306	A67	1c bister & multi	.65	*1.00*
307	A67	2c gray grn & multi	.30	.25
308	A67	3c emer, yel & black	.50	*.80*
309	A67	4c violet & buff	2.25	.30
310	A67	5c green & multi	2.25	.50

Perf. 14½x14, 13½x14½, 14x14½

Size: 32x26mm, 26x32mm

311	A67	8c blue & yellow	1.50	.25
312	A67	10c yel brn & black	.50	.25
313	A67	15c multicolored	2.00	1.50
314	A67	20c multicolored	1.00	*1.50*
315	A67	30c multicolored	3.00	*4.50*
316	A67	50c multicolored	1.25	*3.50*
317	A67	$1 multicolored	1.00	*5.00*
318	A67	$2 multicolored	1.50	*4.00*
		Nos. 306-318 (13)	17.70	23.35

Issued: Nos. 306-312, 9/7; Nos. 313-318, 11/2.

Bright's Cable Gear on "Dacia" — A91

Designs: 3c, Telegraph cable ship "Dacia." 50c, Double current Morse key, 1870, and map of Jamaica.

1970, Oct. 12 Litho. *Perf. 14½*

319	A91	3c red orange & multi	.25	.25
320	A91	10c blue green & multi	.25	.25
321	A91	50c emerald & multi	.75	.75
		Nos. 319-321 (3)	1.25	1.25

Centenary of telegraph service.

Bananas, Citrus Fruit, Sugar Cane and Tobacco — A92

1970, Nov. 2 Wmk. 352 *Perf. 14*

322	A92	2c brown & multi	.25	.30
323	A92	10c black & multi	.35	.25

Jamaica Agricultural Society, 75th anniv.

"The Projector," 1845 — A93

Locomotives: 15c, Engine 54, 1944. 50c, Engine 102, 1967.

1970, Nov. 21 Litho. *Perf. 13½*

324	A93	3c green & multi	.25	.25
325	A93	15c org brown & multi	.80	.80
326	A93	50c multicolored	2.00	2.00
		Nos. 324-326 (3)	3.05	3.05

125th anniv. of the Jamaican railroad.

Kingston Cathedral — A94

30c, Arms of Jamaica Bishopric. 10c, 20c, like 3c.

1971, Feb. 22 *Perf. 14½*

327	A94	3c lt green & multi	.25	.25
328	A94	10c dull orange & multi	.25	.25
329	A94	20c ultra & multi	.30	.30
330	A94	30c gray & multi	.30	*.60*
		Nos. 327-330 (4)	1.10	1.40

Centenary of the disestablishment of the Church of England.

Henry Morgan, Ships in Port Royal Harbor — A95

Designs: 15c, Mary Read, Anne Bonny and pamphlet on their trial. 30c, 18th century merchantman surrendering to pirate schooner.

1971, May 10 Litho. Wmk. 352

331	A95	3c red brown & multi	1.00	.25
332	A95	15c gray & multi	1.25	.35
333	A95	30c lilac & multi	1.60	1.25
		Nos. 331-333 (3)	3.85	1.85

Pirates and buccaneers.

Dummer Packet Letter, 1705 — A96

Designs: 5c, Stampless cover, 1793. 8c, Post office, Kingston, 1820. 10c, Modern date cancellation on No. 312. 20c, Cover with stamps of Great Britain and Jamaica cancellations, 1859. 50c, Jamaica No. 83a, vert.

1971, Oct. 30 *Perf. 13½*

334	A96	3c dk carmine & black	.25	.25
335	A96	5c lt ol grn & black	.25	.25
336	A96	8c purple & black	.25	.25
337	A96	10c slate, black & brn	.25	.25
338	A96	20c multicolored	.30	.30
339	A96	50c dk gray, blk & org	.50	.60
		Nos. 334-339 (6)	1.80	1.90

Tercentenary of Jamaica Post Office.

Earth Station and Satellite — A97

1972, Feb. 17 *Perf. 14x13½*

340	A97	3c red & multi	.25	.25
341	A97	15c gray & multi	.30	.25
342	A97	50c multicolored	.65	*1.00*
		Nos. 340-342 (3)	1.20	1.50

Jamaica's earth satellite station.

Bauxite Industry A98

National Stadium A99

1c, Pimento, vert. 2c, Red ginger, vert. 4c, Kingston harbor. 5c, Oil refinery. 6c, Senate Building, Univ. of the West Indies. 9c, Devon House, Hope Road. 10c, Stewardess and Air Jamaica plane. 15c, Old Iron Bridge, vert. 20c, College of Arts, Science & Technology. 30c, Dunn's River Falls, vert. 50c, River raft. $1, Jamaica House. $2, Kings House. $5, Map and arms of Jamaica ('79).

Perf. 14½x14, 14x14½

1972-79 Litho. Wmk. 352

343	A98	1c multicolored	.25	.25
344	A98	2c multicolored	.25	.25
345	A98	3c shown	.25	.25
346	A98	4c multicolored	.25	.25
347	A98	5c multicolored	.25	.25
348	A98	6c multicolored	.25	.25

Perf. 13½

349	A99	8c shown	.25	.25
350	A99	9c multicolored	.25	.25
351	A99	10c multicolored	.25	.25
352	A99	15c multicolored	1.25	.25
353	A99	20c multicolored	.30	.25
354	A99	30c multicolored	.55	.25
355	A99	50c multicolored	1.10	.35
356	A99	$1 multicolored	.60	*1.00*
357	A99	$2 multicolored	.80	*1.25*

Perf. 14½x14

Size: 37x26½mm

358	A99	$5 multicolored	1.50	*1.75*
		Nos. 343-358 (16)	8.35	7.35

For overprints see Nos. 360-362, 451.

Nos. 345, 351, 355 Overprinted

1972, Aug. 8 *Perf. 14½x14, 13½*

360	A98	3c multicolored	.30	.30
361	A99	10c multicolored	.30	.25
362	A99	50c multicolored	.55	*1.40*
		Nos. 360-362 (3)	1.15	1.95

Arms of Kingston A100

Design: 5c, 30c, Arms of Kingston, vert.

1972, Dec. 4 *Perf. 13½x14, 14x13½*

363	A100	5c pink & multi	.25	.25
364	A100	30c lemon & multi	.30	.25
365	A100	50c lt blue & multi	.50	*1.50*
		Nos. 363-365 (3)	1.05	2.00

Centenary of Kingston as capital.

Mongoose and Map of Jamaica — A101

40c, Mongoose & rat. 60c, Mongoose & chicken.

Perf. 14x14½

1973, Apr. 9 Litho. Wmk. 352

366	A101	8c yel green & blk	.25	.25
367	A101	40c blue & black	.35	.35
368	A101	60c salmon & black	.65	*1.00*
a.		Souvenir sheet of 3, #366-368	1.75	1.75
		Nos. 366-368 (3)	1.25	1.60

Centenary of the introduction of the mongoose to Jamaica.

Euphorbia Punicea — A102

Flowers: 6c, Hylocereus triangularis. 9c, Columnea argentea. 15c, Portlandia grandiflora. 30c, Samyda pubescens. 50c, Cordia sebestena.

1973, July 9 *Perf. 14*

369	A102	1c dp green & multi	.25	.25
370	A102	6c vio blue & multi	.25	.25
371	A102	9c orange & multi	.25	.25
372	A102	15c brown & multi	.25	.25
373	A102	30c olive & multi	.50	.50
374	A102	50c multicolored	.75	*1.10*
		Nos. 369-374 (6)	2.25	2.60

Broughtonia Sanguinea A103

Orchids: 10c, Arpophyllum jamaicense, vert. 20c, Oncidium pulchellum, vert. $1, Brassia maculata.

1973, Oct. 8 *Perf. 14x13½, 13½x14*

375	A103	5c multicolored	.45	.25
376	A103	10c multicolored	.60	.25
377	A103	20c slate & multi	1.25	.30
378	A103	$1 ultra & multi	3.00	*3.25*
a.		Souv. sheet of 4, #375-378, perf 12	5.00	5.00
		Nos. 375-378 (4)	5.30	4.05

Mailboat "Mary" (1808-1815) A104

Mailboats: 10c, "Queensbury" (1814-27). 15c, "Sheldrake" (1829-34). 50c, "Thames" (1842).

Perf. 13½ (5c, 50c), 14½ (10c, 15c)

1974, Apr. 8 Wmk. 352

379	A104	5c shown	.80	.25
a.		Perf. 14½	1.75	*2.50*
380	A104	10c multicolored	.80	.25
381	A104	15c multicolored	1.10	.50
382	A104	50c multicolored	2.00	2.00
a.		Souv. sheet of 4, #379-382, perf 13½	5.00	5.00
		Nos. 379-382 (4)	4.70	3.00

Jamaican Dancers — A105

Designs: Dancers.

1974, Aug. 1 Litho. *Perf. 13½*

383	A105	5c green & multi	.25	.25
384	A105	10c black & multi	.25	.25
385	A105	30c brown & multi	.30	.30

386 A105 50c lilac & multi .45 .45
a. Souvenir sheet of 4, #383-386 2.00 2.00
Nos. 383-386 (4) 1.25 1.25

National Dance Theatre.

Globe, Letter, UPU Emblem — A106

1974, Oct. 9 ***Perf. 14***
387 A106 5c plum & multi .25 .25
388 A106 9c olive & multi .25 .25
389 A106 50c multicolored .30 .30
Nos. 387-389 (3) .80 .80

Centenary of Universal Postal Union.

Senate Building and Sir Hugh Wooding — A107

10c, 50c, Chapel & Princess Alice. 30c, like 5c.

1975, Jan. 13 **Wmk. 352**
390 A107 5c yellow & multi .25 .25
391 A107 10c salmon & multi .25 .25
392 A107 30c dull orange & multi .25 .25
393 A107 50c multicolored .30 .30
Nos. 390-393 (4) 1.05 1.05

University College of the West Indies, 25th anniversary.

Commonwealth Symbol — A108

Commonwealth Symbol and: 10c, Arms of Jamaica. 30c, Dove of peace. 50c, Jamaican flag.

1975, Apr. 29 **Litho.** ***Perf. 13½***
394 A108 5c buff & multi .25 .25
395 A108 10c rose & multi .25 .25
396 A108 30c violet blue & multi .25 .25
397 A108 50c multicolored .25 .25
Nos. 394-397 (4) 1.00 1.00

Commonwealth Heads of Government Conference, Jamaica, Apr.-May.

Graphium Marcellinus — A109

Butterflies: 20c, Papilio thoas melonius. 25c, Papilio thersites. 30c, Papilio homerus.

1975, Aug. 25 **Litho.** ***Perf. 14***
398 A109 10c lt green & multi 1.00 .25
399 A109 20c lt green & multi 1.40 .70
400 A109 25c lt green & multi 1.50 *1.75*
401 A109 30c lt green & multi 2.00 *2.25*
a. Souvenir sheet of 4, #398-401 8.00 8.00
Nos. 398-401 (4) 5.90 *4.95*

See Nos. 423-426, 435-438.

Koo Koo, "Actor-boy" — A110

Christmas: 10c, Red "set-girls." 20c, French "set-girls." 50c, Jawbone or "House John Canoe." Festival dancers drawn by I. M. Belisario in Kingston, 1837.

1975, Nov. 3 **Litho.** **Wmk. 352**
402 A110 8c multicolored .25 .25
403 A110 10c olive & multi .25 .25
404 A110 20c ultra & multi .40 .40
405 A110 50c multicolored .80 .80
a. Souv. sheet of 4, #402-405, perf. 13½ 2.25 2.25
Nos. 402-405 (4) 1.70 1.70

See Nos. 416-418.

Map of Jamaica, by Benedetto Bordone, 1528 — A111

Maps of Jamaica by: 20c, Tommaso Porcacchi, 1576. 30c, Theodor DeBry, 1594. 50c, Barent Langenes, 1598.

1976, Mar. 12 ***Perf. 13½x14***
406 A111 10c brown, buff & red .30 .25
407 A111 20c bister & multi .45 .25
408 A111 30c lt blue & multi .75 .75
409 A111 50c multicolored 1.00 *1.25*
Nos. 406-409 (4) 2.50 2.50

See Nos. 419-422.

Olympic Rings — A112

1976, June 14 **Litho.** ***Perf. 13½x14***
410 A112 10c black & multi .25 .25
411 A112 20c blue & multi .30 .25
412 A112 25c red & multi .30 .25
413 A112 50c green & multi .45 *1.00*
Nos. 410-413 (4) 1.30 1.75

21st Olympic Games, Montreal, Canada, July 17-Aug. 1.

Map of West Indies, Bats, Wicket and Ball — A112a

Prudential Cup — A112b

1976, Aug. 9 **Unwmk.** ***Perf. 14***
414 A112a 10c lt blue & multi .35 .30
415 A112b 25c lilac rose & blk .65 *1.10*

World Cricket Cup, won by West Indies Team, 1975.

Christmas Type of 1975

Belisario Prints, 1837: 10c, Queen of the "set-girls." 20c, Band of Jawbone John Canoe. 50c, Koo Koo, "actor-boy."

1976, Nov. 8 **Wmk. 352** ***Perf. 13½***
416 A110 10c brick red & multi .25 .25
417 A110 20c bister & multi .25 .25
418 A110 50c tan & multi .40 .60
a. Souv. sheet of 3, #416-418, perf. 14 1.25 1.25
Nos. 416-418 (3) .90 1.10

Christmas.

Map Type of 1976

Maps of Jamaica by: 9c, Edmund Hickeringill, 1661. 10c, John Ogilby, 1671. 25c, House of Visscher, 1680. 40c, John Thornton, 1689.

1977, Feb. 28 **Litho.** ***Perf. 13***
419 A111 9c lt blue & multi .30 *.40*
420 A111 10c buff & multi .40 .25
421 A111 25c multicolored .70 .55
422 A111 40c multicolored .85 *1.40*
Nos. 419-422 (4) 2.25 2.60

Butterfly Type of 1975

10c, Eurema elathea. 20c, Dynamine egaea. 25c, Atlantea pantoni. 40c, Hypolimnas misippus.

1977, May 9 **Wmk. 352** ***Perf. 13½***
423 A109 10c black & multi .40 .25
424 A109 20c black & multi .80 .50
425 A109 25c black & multi 1.25 1.25
426 A109 40c black & multi 2.25 *3.50*
a. Souv. sheet of 4, #423-426, perf. 14½ 7.00 7.00
Nos. 423-426 (4) 4.70 5.50

Scout Emblem, Doctor Bird, Outline of Jamaica — A113

1977, Aug. 5 **Litho.** ***Perf. 14***
427 A113 10c multicolored .65 .25
428 A113 20c multicolored .90 .25
429 A113 25c multicolored 1.00 .35
430 A113 50c multicolored 1.50 1.50
Nos. 427-430 (4) 4.05 2.35

6th Caribbean Jamboree, Hope Gardens, Kingston, Aug. 3-17.

Trumpeter A114

10c, 2 clarinetists and oboist. 20c, kettle drummer and oboist, vert. 25c, Cellist and trumpeter, vert.

1977, Dec. 19 **Litho.** ***Perf. 14***
431 A114 9c multicolored .25 .25
432 A114 10c multicolored .25 .25
433 A114 20c multicolored .40 .30
434 A114 25c multicolored .50 .60
a. Souvenir sheet of 4, #431-434 3.00 3.00
Nos. 431-434 (4) 1.40 1.40

Jamaica Military Band, 50th anniversary.

Butterfly Type of 1975

Butterflies: 10c, Callophrys crethona. 20c, Siproeta stelenes. 25c, Urbanus proteus. 50c, Anaea troglodyta.

1978, Apr. 17 **Litho.** ***Perf. 14½***
435 A109 10c black & multi .55 .25
436 A109 20c black & multi 1.00 .25
437 A109 25c black & multi 1.25 .60
438 A109 50c black & multi 2.25 *2.75*
a. Souvenir sheet of 4, #435-438 5.75 5.75
Nos. 435-438 (4) 5.05 3.85

Half Figure with Canopy — A115

Arawak Artifacts, found 1792: 20c, Standing figure. 50c, Birdman.

1978, July 10 **Litho.** ***Perf. 13½x13***
439 A115 10c multicolored .25 .25
440 A115 20c multicolored .25 .25
441 A115 50c multicolored .35 .35
a. Souv. sheet of 3, #439-441, perf. 14 1.00 1.00
Nos. 439-441 (3) .85 .85

Norman Manley Statue — A116

Designs: 20c, Alexander Bustamante statue. 25c, Kingston coat of arms. 40c, Gordon House Chamber, House of Representatives.

1978, Sept. 25 **Litho.** **Wmk. 352**
442 A116 10c multicolored .25 .25
443 A116 20c multicolored .25 .25
444 A116 25c multicolored .25 .25
445 A116 40c multicolored .30 *.35*
Nos. 442-445 (4) 1.05 1.10

24th Commonwealth Parliamentary Conf.

Salvation Army Band — A117

Designs: 20c, Trumpeter. 25c, "S" and Cross entwined on pole of Army flag. 50c, William Booth and Salvation Army shield.

1978, Dec. 4 ***Perf. 14***
446 A117 10c multicolored .30 .25
447 A117 20c multicolored .35 .25
448 A117 25c multicolored .35 .30
449 A117 50c multicolored .50 *.75*
Nos. 446-449 (4) 1.50 1.55

Christmas; Salvation Army centenary.

"Negro Aroused," by Edna Manley — A118

1978, Dec. 11 ***Perf. 13***
450 A118 10c multicolored .35 .25

International Anti-Apartheid Year.

No. 351 Overprinted

1979, Apr. 2 **Litho.** ***Perf. 13½***
451 A99 10c multicolored .45 .45

Arawak Grinding Stone, c. 400 B.C. — A119

Arawak Artifacts (all A.D.): 10c, Stone implements, c. 500, horiz. 20c, Cooking pot, c. 300, horiz. 25c, Serving boat, c. 300, horiz. 50c, Storage jar fragment, c. 300.

1979, Apr. 23 ***Perf. 14***
452 A119 5c multicolored .25 .25
453 A119 10c multicolored .25 .25
454 A119 20c multicolored .25 .25
455 A119 25c multicolored .25 .25
456 A119 50c multicolored .25 .25
Nos. 452-456 (5) 1.25 1.25

Jamaica No. 183, Hill Statue — A120

Hill Statue and Stamps of Jamaica: 20c, No. 83a. 25c, No. 5. 50c, No. 271.

1979, Aug. 13 **Litho.** ***Perf. 14***
457 A120 10c multicolored .25 .25
458 A120 20c multicolored .25 .25
a. Souvenir sheet of 1 .55 .55
459 A120 25c multicolored .25 .25
460 A120 50c multicolored .25 *.50*
Nos. 457-460 (4) 1.00 1.25

Sir Rowland Hill (1795-1879), originator of penny postage.

Children, IYC Emblem — A121

International Year of the Child: 20c, Doll, vert. 25c, "The Family." 25c, "House on the Hill." 25c, 50c are children's drawings.

1979, Oct. 1

461	A121	10c multicolored	.25	.25
462	A121	20c multicolored	.25	.25
463	A121	25c multicolored	.25	.25
464	A121	50c multicolored	.25	.25
		Nos. 461-464 (4)	1.00	1.00

Tennis, Montego Bay — A122

Jamaican Tody — A123

Designs: 2c, Golfing, Tryall Hanover. 4c, Horseback riding, Negril Beach. 5c, Old Waterwheel, Tryall Hanover. 6c, Fern Gully, Ocho Rios. 7c, Dunn's River Falls, Ocho Rios. 10c, Doctorbird. 12c, Yellow-billed parrot. 15c, Hummingbird. 35c, White-chinned thrush. 50c, Jamaican woodpecker. 65c, Rafting Martha Brae Trelawny. 75c, Blue marlin fishing, Port Antonio. $1, Scuba diving. Ocho Rios. $2, Sail boats, Montego Bay.

Wmk. 352

1979-80 Litho. *Perf. 13½*

465	A122	1c multicolored	.70	*.90*
466	A122	2c multicolored	2.00	*2.50*
467	A122	4c multicolored	1.00	*2.00*
468	A122	5c multicolored	1.25	.30
469	A122	6c multicolored	1.25	*2.25*
470	A122	7c multicolored	.50	.30
472	A123	8c multicolored	1.00	1.00
473	A123	10c multicolored	1.00	.25
474	A123	12c multicolored	1.00	*1.50*
475	A123	15c multicolored	1.00	.30
476	A123	35c multicolored	1.50	.35
477	A123	50c multicolored	2.00	.35
478	A122	65c multicolored	2.00	*2.50*
479	A122	75c multicolored	2.25	2.25
480	A122	$1 multicolored	2.25	2.25
481	A122	$2 multicolored	2.25	1.00
		Nos. 465-481 (16)	22.95	20.00

Issued: Nos. 465-470, 11/26/79; Nos. 472-481, 5/80.

For surcharges see Nos. 581-582, 665-666.

Institute of Jamaica Centenary A124

15c, Institute building, 1980. 35c, "The Ascension" on microfilm reader, vert. 50c, Hawksbill and green turtles. 75c, Jamaican owl, vert.

1980, Feb. 25 Litho. *Perf. 13½*

484	A124	5c shown	.25	.25
485	A124	15c multicolored	.25	.25
486	A124	35c multicolored	.25	.25
487	A124	50c multicolored	.30	.30
488	A124	75c multicolored	1.50	1.50
		Nos. 484-488 (5)	2.55	2.55

Don Quarrie, 1976 Gold Medalist, 200-Meter Race, Moscow '80 Emblem — A125

1952 4x400-meter Relay Team: a, Arthur Wint. b, Leslie Laing. c, Herbert McKenley. d, George Rhoden.

1980, July 21 Litho. *Perf. 13*

489	A125	15c shown	.40	.25
490		Strip of 4	2.00	2.00
a.-d.	A125	35c any single	.45	.40

22nd Summer Olympic Games, Moscow, July 19-Aug. 3.

Parish Church, Kingston — A126

20c, Coke Memorial. 25c, Church of the Redeemer. $5, Holy Trinity Cathedral.

1980, Nov. 24 Litho. *Perf. 14*

491	A126	15c shown	.25	.25
492	A126	20c multicolored	.25	.25
493	A126	25c multicolored	.25	.25
494	A126	$5 multicolored	1.00	1.00
a.		Souvenir sheet of 4, #491-494	2.00	2.00
		Nos. 491-494 (4)	1.75	1.75

Christmas.

Tube Sponge — A127

20c, Blood cup sponge, vert. 60c, Black coral, vert. 75c, Tire reef.

1981, Feb. 27 Wmk. 352 *Perf. 14*

495	A127	20c multicolored	.25	.25
496	A127	45c shown	.35	.35
497	A127	60c multicolored	.45	.45
498	A127	75c multicolored	.55	.55
		Nos. 495-498 (4)	1.60	1.60

See Nos. 523-527.

Indian Coney — A128

Designs: b, Facing left. c, Eating. d, Family.

1981, May 25 Wmk. 352 *Perf. 14*

499		Strip of 4	1.25	1.25
a.-d.	A128	20c any single	.25	.25

Royal Wedding Issue

Common Design Type

20c, White orchid. 45c, Royal coach. 60c, Couple. $5, St. James' Palace.

1981, July 29 Litho. *Perf. 15*

500	CD331	20c multicolored	.25	.25
501	CD331	45c multicolored	.25	.25
502	CD331	60c multicolored	.25	.25

Perf. 13½

503	CD331	$5 multicolored	.70	.60
a.		Souvenir sheet of 1	.90	.90
b.		Bklt. pane of 4, perf 14x14½	1.60	
		Nos. 500-503 (4)	1.45	1.35

Also issued in sheets of 5 + label, perf. 13½.

Intl. Year of the Disabled — A129

20c, Blind weaver. 45c, Artist. 60c, Learning sign language. $1.50, Basketball players.

1981, Sept. 14 Wmk. 352 *Perf. 13½*

504	A129	20c multicolored	.25	.25
505	A129	45c multicolored	.35	.35
506	A129	60c multicolored	.45	.45
507	A129	$1.50 multicolored	1.75	1.75
		Nos. 504-507 (4)	2.80	2.80

World Food Day — A130

Perf. 13x13½, 13½x13

1981, Oct. 16 Litho. Wmk. 352

508	A130	20c No. 218	.40	.25
509	A130	45c No. 76, vert.	.70	.40
510	A130	$2 No. 121	1.75	1.25
511	A130	$4 No. 125	2.75	2.25
		Nos. 508-511 (4)	5.60	4.15

Bob Marley (1945-1981), Reggae Musician — A131

Portraits of Bob Marley and song titles.

1981, Oct. 20 Wmk. 373 *Perf. 14½*

512	A131	1c multicolored	.60	*.90*
513	A131	2c multicolored	.60	*.90*
514	A131	3c multicolored	.60	*.90*
515	A131	15c multicolored	2.50	.30
516	A131	20c multicolored	2.50	.30
517	A131	60c multicolored	3.50	2.50
518	A131	$3 multicolored	5.25	*9.50*
		Nos. 512-518 (7)	15.55	15.30

Souvenir Sheet

519	A131	$5.25 multicolored	6.75	6.75

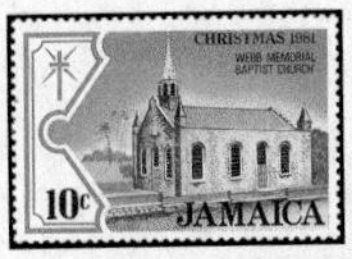

Christmas A132

10c, Webb Memorial Baptist Church. 45c, Church of God. $5, Bryce United Church.

1981, Dec. 11 Wmk. 352 *Perf. 14*

520	A132	10c multicolored	.30	.25
521	A132	45c multicolored	.50	.25
522	A132	$5 multicolored	1.40	*2.00*
a.		Souvenir sheet of 3, #520-522, perf. 12½x12	3.50	3.50
		Nos. 520-522 (3)	2.20	2.50

See Nos. 547-549.

Marine Life Type of 1981

20c, Gorgonian coral, vert. 45c, Hard sponge. 60c, Sea cow. 75c, Plume worm. $3, Coral-banded shrimp.

1982, Feb. 22 Litho. *Perf. 14*

523	A127	20c multicolored	.50	.25
524	A127	45c multicolored	.70	.25
525	A127	60c multicolored	.80	.40
526	A127	75c multicolored	.90	.50
527	A127	$3 multicolored	2.25	1.50
		Nos. 523-527 (5)	5.15	2.90

Scouting Year — A133

20c, 45c, 60c, Various scouts. $2, Baden-Powell.

1982, July 12 Litho. *Perf. 13½*

528	A133	20c multicolored	.50	.25
529	A133	45c multicolored	.75	.30
530	A133	60c multicolored	1.00	.65
531	A133	$2 multicolored	1.90	1.90
a.		Souvenir sheet of 4, #528-531	5.75	5.75
		Nos. 528-531 (4)	4.15	3.10

Princess Diana, 21st Birthday — A134

20c, Lignum vitae. 45c, Couple in coach. 60c, Wedding portrait. 75c, Saxifraga longifolia. $2, Diana. $3, Viola gracilis major. $5, Honeymoon.

1982, Sept. 1 *Perf. 14½*

532	A134	20c multicolored	.35	.25
533	A134	45c multicolored	.55	.35
534	A134	60c multicolored	.65	.45
a.		Booklet pane of 3, #532-534	1.75	
535	A134	75c multicolored	1.00	*1.25*
536	A134	$2 multicolored	1.50	1.50
537	A134	$3 multicolored	1.75	*2.50*
a.		Booklet pane of 3, #535-537	7.00	
		Nos. 532-537 (6)	5.80	6.30

Souvenir Sheet

538	A134	$5 multicolored	3.25	3.25

Nos. 535, 537 in sheets of 5.

Nos. 532-538 Overprinted

1982, Sept. 13

539	A134	20c multicolored	.30	.25
540	A134	45c multicolored	.35	.35
541	A134	60c multicolored	.45	.45
a.		Booklet pane of 3, #539-541	1.75	
542	A134	75c multicolored	.70	*1.25*
543	A134	$2 multicolored	1.00	1.00
544	A134	$3 multicolored	1.25	*1.75*
a.		Booklet pane of 3, #542-544	6.00	
		Nos. 539-544 (6)	4.05	5.05

Souvenir Sheet

545	A134	$5 multicolored	2.75	2.75

Birth of Prince William of Wales, June 21.

Lizard Cuckoo Capturing Prey — A135

Designs: b, Searching for prey. c, Calling. d, Landing. e, Flying.

1982, Oct. 25

546		Strip of 5	8.00	8.00
a.-e.	A135	$1 any single	1.25	1.25

Christmas Type of 1981

20c, United Pentecostal Church. 45c, Disciples of Christ Church. 75c, Open Bible Church.

Perf. 13x13½

1982, Dec. 8 Wmk. 352

547	A132	20c multicolored	.60	.25
548	A132	45c multicolored	.75	.25
549	A132	75c multicolored	1.60	*2.00*
		Nos. 547-549 (3)	2.95	2.50

Visit of Queen Elizabeth II — A136

1983, Feb. 14 Litho. *Perf. 14*

550	A136	$2 Queen Elizabeth II	3.00	3.25
551	A136	$3 Arms	4.00	*5.75*

A136a

1983, Mar. 14 Litho. Wmk. 352

552	A136a	20c Dancers	.25	.25
553	A136a	45c Bauxite mining	.35	.35
554	A136a	75c Map	.50	.50
555	A136a	$2 Arms, citizens	1.00	*1.25*
		Nos. 552-555 (4)	2.10	2.35

Commonwealth Day.

25th Anniv. of Intl. Maritime Org. — A137

15c, Cargo ship. 20c, Cruise liner. 45c, Container vessel. $1, Intl. Seabed Headquarters.

1983, Mar. 17 Litho. *Perf. 14*

556	A137	15c multi	1.00	.30
557	A137	20c multi	1.50	.35
558	A137	45c multi	2.00	.75
559	A137	$1 multi	3.00	*4.00*
		Nos. 556-559 (4)	7.50	5.40

21st Anniv. of Independence — A138

Prime Ministers Alexander Bustamante and Norman Washington Manley.

1983, July 25	**Litho.**	***Perf. 14***		
560 A138	15c blue & multi		.25	.25
561 A138	20c lt green & multi		.25	.25
562 A138	45c yellow & multi		.30	.30
	Nos. 560-562 (3)		.80	.80

World Communications Year — A139

20c, Ship-to-shore radio. 45c, Postal services. 75c, Telephone communication. $1, TV satellite.

1983, Oct. 18	**Wmk. 352**	***Perf. 14***		
563 A139	20c multi		.60	.25
564 A139	45c multi		1.25	.35
565 A139	75c multi		1.50	*2.00*
566 A139	$1 multi		1.75	*2.50*
	Nos. 563-566 (4)		5.10	5.10

Christmas 1983 — A140

Paintings: 15c, Racing at Caymanas, by Sidney McLaren. 20c, Seated Figures, by Karl Parboosingh. 75c, The Petitioner, by Henry Daley, vert. $2, Banana Plantation, by John Dunkley, vert.

1983, Dec. 12	**Litho.**	***Perf. 13½***		
567 A140	15c multicolored		.25	.25
568 A140	20c multicolored		.25	.25
569 A140	75c multicolored		.40	.55
570 A140	$2 multicolored		1.25	*2.00*
	Nos. 567-570 (4)		2.15	3.05

Alexander Bustamante (1884-1977), First Prime Minister — A141

1984, Feb. 24	**Litho.**	***Perf. 14***		
571	20c Portrait		.85	.85
572	20c Blenheim (birthplace)		.85	.85
a.	A141 Pair, #571-572		2.00	*2.00*

Sea Planes — A142

25c, Gypsy Moth. 55c, Consolidated Commodore. $1.50, Sikorsky S-38. $3, Sikorsky S-40.

1984, June 11	**Litho.**	***Perf. 14***		
573 A142	25c multi		1.50	.30
574 A142	55c multi		2.00	.75
575 A142	$1.50 multi		3.00	3.50
576 A142	$3 multi		4.25	5.00
	Nos. 573-576 (4)		10.75	9.55

1984 Summer Olympics A143

25c, Bicycling. 55c, Relay race. $1.50, Running. $3, Women's running.

1984, July 11				
577 A143	25c multi		1.75	.50
578 A143	55c multi		.75	.30
579 A143	$1.50 multi		1.60	*3.25*
580 A143	$3 multi		2.25	*3.50*
a.	Souvenir sheet of 4, #577-580		6.25	6.25
	Nos. 577-580 (4)		6.35	7.55

Nos. 469, 474 Surcharged

1984, Aug. 7	**Litho.**	***Perf. 13½***		
581 A122	5c on 6c #469		.40	.40
582 A123	10c on 12c #474		1.25	.55

Early Steam Engines A144

25c, Enterprise, 1845. 55c, Tank Locomotive, 1880. $1.50, Kitson-Meyer Tank, 1904. $3, Superheater, 1916.

1984, Nov. 16	**Litho.**	***Perf. 13½***		
583 A144	25c multicolored		1.40	.30
584 A144	55c multicolored		2.00	.60
585 A144	$1.50 multicolored		3.00	3.00
586 A144	$3 multicolored		3.75	*5.00*
	Nos. 583-586 (4)		10.15	8.90

See Nos. 608-611.

Christmas — A145

Local sculptures: 20c, Accompong Madonna, by Namba Roy. 25c, Head, by Alvin Marriott. 55c, Moon, by Edna Manley. $1.50, All Women are Five Women, by Mallica Reynolds.

1984, Dec. 6	**Wmk. 352**	***Perf. 14***		
587 A145	20c multicolored		.30	.25
588 A145	25c multicolored		.35	.25
589 A145	55c multicolored		1.00	.50
590 A145	$1.50 multicolored		1.90	*2.25*
	Nos. 587-590 (4)		3.55	3.25

Jamaican Boas — A146

25c, Head of boa. 55c, Boa over water. 70c, Boa with young. $1, Boa on branch.

1984, Oct. 22	**Litho.**	***Perf. 14½***		
591 A146	25c multi		*9.50*	.60
592 A146	55c multi		*10.00*	*1.25*
593 A146	70c multi		*11.50*	*4.25*
594 A146	$1 multi		*14.50*	*4.75*
a.	Souv. sheet of 4, #591-594		*11.00*	*11.00*
	Nos. 591-594 (4)		*45.50*	*10.85*

Stamps in No. 594a do not have WWF emblem.

Brown Pelicans — A147

1985, Apr. 15	**Wmk. 352**	***Perf. 13***		
595 A147	20c multicolored		1.00	.25
596 A147	55c multicolored		1.50	.40
597 A147	$2 multicolored		2.25	2.75
598 A147	$5 multicolored		3.00	*4.75*
a.	Souvenir sheet of 4, #595-598		8.00	8.00
	Nos. 595-598 (4)		7.75	8.15

Birth bicentenary of artist and naturalist John J. Audubon (1785-1851).

Queen Mother 85th Birthday

Common Design Type

25c, Holding photograph album, 1963. 55c, With Prince Charles, Windsor Castle, 1983. $1.50, At Belfast University. $3, Holding Prince Henry. $5, With limousine.

1985, June 7	**Litho.**	***Perf. 14½x14***		
599 CD336	25c multicolored		.30	.25
600 CD336	55c multicolored		.55	.25
601 CD336	$1.50 multicolored		.80	*1.25*
602 CD336	$3 multicolored		1.50	*2.25*
	Nos. 599-602 (4)		3.15	4.00

Souvenir Sheet

603 CD336	$5 multicolored		3.00	3.00

Maps of Americas and Jamaica, IYY and Jamboree Emblems A148

1985, July 30	**Litho.**	***Perf. 14***		
604 A148	25c multicolored		.85	.25
605 A148	55c multicolored		1.10	.30
606 A148	70c multicolored		1.60	1.25
607 A148	$4 multicolored		3.25	*5.00*
	Nos. 604-607 (4)		6.80	6.80

Intl. Youth Year and 5th Pan-American Scouting Jamboree.

Locomotives Type of 1984

1985, Sept. 30		**Size: 39x25mm**		
608 A144	25c Baldwin		1.40	.30
609 A144	55c Rogers		1.75	.50
610 A144	$1.50 Projector		2.75	2.75
611 A144	$4 Diesel		3.50	*5.00*
	Nos. 608-611 (4)		9.40	8.55

The Old Settlement, by Ralph Campbell A149

Christmas (Paintings by local artists): 55c, The Vendor, by Albert Hiue, vert. 75c, Road Menders, by Gaston Tabois. $4, Woman, Must I Not Be About My Father's Business? by Carl Abrahams, vert.

1985, Dec. 9				
612 A149	20c multicolored		.25	.25
613 A149	55c multicolored		.25	.25
614 A149	75c multicolored		.25	.25
615 A149	$4 multicolored		1.00	1.00
	Nos. 612-615 (4)		1.75	1.75

Birds — A150

25c, Chestnut-bellied cuckoo. 55c, Jamaican becard. $1.50, White-eyed thrush. $5, Rufous-tailed flycatcher.

1986, Feb. 10	**Litho.**	***Perf. 14***		
616 A150	25c multicolored		.55	.25
617 A150	55c multicolored		.75	.30
618 A150	$1.50 multicolored		1.00	1.00
619 A150	$5 multicolored		1.75	*3.50*
	Nos. 616-619 (4)		4.05	5.05

Queen Elizabeth II 60th Birthday

Common Design Type

Designs: 20c, With Princess Margaret, 1939. 25c, Leaving Liverpool Street Station for Sandringham with Princes Charles and Andrew, 1962. 70c, Visiting the Montego Bay war memorial, Jamaica, 1983. $3, State visit to Luxembourg, 1976. $5, Visiting Crown Agents' offices, 1983.

1986, Apr. 21		***Perf. 14½***		
620 CD337	20c scar, blk & sil		.35	.25
621 CD337	25c ultra & multi		.35	.25
622 CD337	70c green & multi		.40	.30
623 CD337	$3 violet & multi		.65	.65
624 CD337	$5 rose vio & multi		1.00	*1.25*
	Nos. 620-624 (5)		2.75	2.70

A151

AMERIPEX '86: 25c, Bustamante Childrens Hospital. 55c, Vacation cities. $3, Norman Manley Law School. $5, Exports.

1986, May 19				
625 A151	25c multicolored		.60	.25
626 A151	55c multicolored		1.75	.40
627 A151	$3 multicolored		1.10	*2.00*
628 A151	$5 multicolored		5.75	5.75
a.	Souvenir sheet of 4, #625-628		9.75	9.75
	Nos. 625-628 (4)		9.20	8.40

Royal Wedding Issue, 1986

Common Design Type

Designs: 20c, At the races. $5, Andrew addressing the press.

Perf. 14½x14

1986, July 23		**Wmk. 352**		
629 CD338	20c multicolored		.25	.25
630 CD338	$5 multicolored		1.10	1.10

Boxing Champions — A152

Champions: 45c, Richard "Shrimpy" Clarke, 1986 Commonwealth flyweight. 70c, Michael McCallum, 1984 WBA junior middleweight. $2, Trevor Berbick, 1986 WBC heavyweight. $4, Clarke, McCallum and Berbick.

1986, Oct. 27	**Litho.**	***Perf. 14***		
631 A152	45c multicolored		.25	.25
632 A152	70c multicolored		.35	.30
633 A152	$2 multicolored		.75	*1.00*
634 A152	$4 multicolored		1.60	*2.00*
	Nos. 631-634 (4)		2.95	3.55

Flowers — A153

20c, Heliconia wagneriana, vert. 25c, Heliconia psittacorum. 55c, Heliconia rostrata, vert. $5, Strelitzia reginae.

1986, Dec. 1		***Perf. 14***		
635 A153	20c multicolored		.25	.25
636 A153	25c multicolored		.25	.25
637 A153	55c multicolored		.25	.25
638 A153	$5 multicolored		1.60	*3.00*
	Nos. 635-638 (4)		2.35	3.75

Christmas. See Nos. 675-678, 706-709.

Shells — A154

1987, Feb. 23	**Litho.**	***Perf. 15***		
639 A154	35c Crown cone		.55	.25
640 A154	75c Measled cowrie		.75	.55
641 A154	$1 Trumpet triton		.85	*.85*
642 A154	$5 Rooster-tail conch		1.25	*2.50*
	Nos. 639-642 (4)		3.40	4.15

Prime Ministers A155

Natl. Coat of Arms A156

Designs: 1c-9c, 55c, Norman Washington Manley. 10c-50c, 60c-90c, Sir Alexander Bustamante.

1987-94 ***Perf. 12½x13***

No inscription below design unless noted

643 A155 1c dull red .25 *.85*
644 A155 2c rose pink .25 *.85*
645 A155 3c light olive .25 *.85*
646 A155 4c dull green .25 *.85*
647 A155 5c slate blue .45 *.75*
a. Inscribed "1988" .60 .75
648 A155 6c ultramarine .30 *.75*
649 A155 7c dull magenta .60 .75
650 A155 8c red lilac .30 .25
651 A155 9c brown olive .70 .25
652 A155 10c deep rose 2.00 *.75*
a. Inscribed "1993" 1.25 .75
b. Inscribed "1994" 2.75 .75
653 A155 20c bright org .40 .40
a. Inscribed "1988" .50 .25
b. Inscribed "1989" .50 .25
c. Inscribed "1992" .55 .25
d. Inscribed "1993" .55 .25
e. Inscribed "1994" .40 .40
654 A155 30c emerald .50 .25
a. Inscribed "1994" 1.25 *1.75*
655 A155 40c lt blue green 1.00 *1.25*
a. Inscribed "1991" 1.25 .85
b. Inscribed "1992" 1.00 *1.25*
c. Inscribed "1994" .85 *.85*
656 A155 50c gray olive 1.00 .85
a. Inscribed "1991" 2.00 1.00
b. Inscribed "1992" .85 *1.00*
c. Inscribed "1993" .85 *.85*
d. Inscribed "1994" .85 *.85*
656A A155 55c ol brn, inscr. "1994" 1.50 1.50
657 A155 60c light ultra .40 .35
658 A155 70c pale violet .40 .30
659 A155 80c violet .55 .45
660 A155 90c light brown 1.25 *1.50*
a. Inscribed "1992" 2.75 1.00
b. Inscribed "1993" 1.25 *1.50*
661 A156 $1 dull brn & buff .55 .40
a. Inscribed "1991" .65 .50
b. Inscribed "1992" .75 .50
c. Inscribed "1993" .75 .50
d. Inscribed "1997" .50 .40
661A A156 $1.10 dl brn & buff, inscr. "1994" 1.00 1.00
662 A156 $2 orange .85 *.95*
a. Inscribed "1997" *1.50* 1.25
663 A156 $5 gray ol & grnsh buff .95 *1.25*
a. Inscribed "1997" 1.50 1.50
664 A156 $10 royal bl & pale bl *.90* *1.75*

Perf. 13x13½

664A A156 $25 vio & pale vio, inscr. "1991" 3.00 2.00
664B A156 $50 lil & pale lil, inscr. "1991" 5.75 3.25
Nos. 643-664B (26) 25.35 24.35

Issued: $25, $50 (dated "1991"), 10/9/91; 55c, $1.10 (dated "1994"), 10/10/94; others (undated), 5/18/87.

Reprints issued: No. 647a, 653a, 6/6/88; 653b, 1989; 645a, 656a, 2/12/91; 661a, 6/6/91; 661b, 1992; 653c, 655b, 656b, 660a, 5/92; 653d, 656c, 660b, 661c, 1993; 652a, 11/93; 654d, 655c, 656c, 1994; 652b, 654a, 10/10/94; 661d, 662a, 663a, 4/30/97.

Nos. 477-478 Surcharged

1986, Nov. 3 ***Perf. 13½***
665 A123 5c on 50c multi 3.25 3.25
666 A122 10c on 65c multi 1.75 1.75

A157

Wmk. 352

1987, July 27 **Litho.** ***Perf. 14***
667 A157 55c Flag, sunset 1.60 .60
668 A157 70c Flag, horiz. 1.60 *2.25*

Natl. Independence, 25th anniv.

A158

1987, Aug. 17
669 25c Portrait 1.25 *1.25*
670 25c Statue 1.25 *1.25*
a. A158 Pair, #669-670 3.75 *3.75*

Marcus Mosiah Garvey (1887-1940), natl. hero. No. 670a has a continuous design.

Salvation Army in Jamaica, Cent. — A159

Designs: 25c, School for the Blind. 55c, Col. Mary Booth, Bramwell-Booth Memorial Hall. $3, "War Chariot," 1929. $5, Arrival of col. Abram Davey on the S.S. Alene, 1887.

1987, Oct. 8 ***Perf. 13***
671 A159 25c multicolored 1.50 .35
672 A159 55c multicolored 1.50 .35
673 A159 $3 multicolored 3.50 3.50
674 A159 $5 multicolored 5.25 *7.50*
a. Souvenir sheet of 4, #671-674 17.50 17.50
Nos. 671-674 (4) 11.75 11.70

Flower Type of 1986

20c, Hibiscus hybrid. 25c, Hibiscus elatus. $4, Hibiscus cannabinus. $5, Hibiscus rosa sinensis.

1987, Nov. 30 **Litho.** ***Perf. 14½***
675 A153 20c multicolored .25 .25
676 A153 25c multicolored .25 .25
677 A153 $4 multicolored 2.75 2.50
678 A153 $5 multicolored 3.00 3.00
Nos. 675-678 (4) 6.25 6.00

Christmas. Nos. 675-678 vert.

Birds A160

Designs: No. 679, Chestnut-bellied cuckoo, black-billed parrot, Jamaican euphonia. No. 680, Jamaican white-eyed vireo, rufous-throated solitaire, yellow-crowned elaenia. No. 681, Snowy plover, little blue heron, great white heron. No. 682, Common stilt, snowy egret, black-crowned night heron.

1988, Jan. 22 **Litho.** ***Perf. 14***
679 45c multicolored 1.50 1.50
680 45c multicolored 1.50 1.50
a. A160 Pair, #679-680 4.75 *4.75*
681 $5 multicolored 4.00 *4.00*
682 $5 multicolored 4.00 *4.00*
a. A160 Pair, #681-682 10.00 *11.50*
Nos. 679-682 (4) 11.00 11.00

Nos. 680a, 682a have continuous designs.

Marine Mammals A161

20c, Blue whales. 25c, Gervais's whales. 55c, Killer whales. $5, Common dolphins.

1988, Apr. 14 **Litho.** ***Perf. 14***
683 A161 20c multicolored 1.50 .75
684 A161 25c multicolored 2.00 .75
685 A161 55c multicolored 3.50 .85
686 A161 $5 multicolored 6.00 *7.00*
Nos. 683-686 (4) 13.00 9.35

Cricket — A162

Bat, wicket posts, ball, 18th cent. belt buckle and batsmen: 25c, Jackie Hendriks. 55c, George Headley. $2, Michael Holding. $3, R.K. Nunes. $4, Allan Rae.

1988, June 6 **Litho.** ***Perf. 14***
687 A162 25c multicolored 1.60 .45
688 A162 55c multicolored 1.75 .45
689 A162 $2 multicolored 3.00 3.00
690 A162 $3 multicolored 3.25 3.25
691 A162 $4 multicolored 4.50 4.50
Nos. 687-691 (5) 14.10 11.65

Intl. Red Cross and Red Crescent Organizations, 125th Annivs. — A163

Anniversary emblem, Jamaica Red Cross emblem and: 55c, Ambulances. $5, Jean-Henri Dunant, 1828-1910, treating the wounded after the Battle of Solferino, 1859.

1988, Aug. 8 **Litho.** ***Perf. 14½***
692 A163 55c multicolored .75 .30
693 A163 $5 multicolored 2.75 2.75

1988 Summer Olympics, Seoul — A164

1988, Aug. 24 **Wmk. 352** ***Perf. 14***
694 A164 25c Boxing .45 .25
695 A164 45c Cycling 2.00 .65
696 A164 $4 Women's running 2.50 2.50
697 A164 $5 Hurdling 2.75 2.75
a. Souvenir sheet of 4, #694-697 7.50 7.50
Nos. 694-697 (4) 7.70 6.15

No. 697a sold for $9.90. For surcharges see Nos. B4-B7.

Natl. Olympic Bobsled Team — A165

No. 698, Team members. No. 699, Two-man bobsled. No. 700, Team members, diff. No. 701, Four-man bobsled.

1988, Nov. 4 **Litho.** ***Perf. 14***
698 A165 25c multi .50 .50
699 A165 25c multi .50 .50
a. Pair, #698-699 2.50 *3.00*
700 A165 $5 multi 2.00 2.00
701 A165 $5 multi 2.00 2.00
a. Pair, #700-701 6.00 *7.50*
Nos. 698-701 (4) 5.00 5.00

Nos. 699a, 701a have continuous designs.

Labor Year — A166

25c, Medicine, fire fighting. 55c, Handicrafts. $3, Garment industry. $5, Fishing.

Perf. 14½x14

1988, Nov. 24 **Wmk. 352**
702 A166 25c multicolored 1.25 .45
703 A166 55c multicolored .55 .45
704 A166 $3 multicolored 1.50 1.25
705 A166 $5 multicolored 1.75 1.75
Nos. 702-705 (4) 5.05 3.90

Flower Type of 1986

25c, Euphorbia pulcherrima, vert. 55c, Spathodea campanulata. $3, Hylocereus triangularis, vert. $4, Broughtonia sanguinea.

1988, Dec. 15
706 A153 25c multicolored .65 .25
707 A153 55c multicolored .80 .25
708 A153 $3 multicolored 1.75 1.75
709 A153 $4 multicolored 2.25 2.25
Nos. 706-709 (4) 5.45 4.50

Christmas.

Methodist Church in Jamaica, Bicent. — A167

25c, Old York Castle School. 45c, Parade Chapel, Kingston, Rev. Thomas Coke. $5, Fr. Hugh Sherlock, St. John's Church.

1989, Jan. 19 ***Perf. 13½***
710 A167 25c multicolored .30 .25
711 A167 45c multicolored .35 .25
712 A167 $5 multicolored 2.50 2.50
Nos. 710-712 (3) 3.15 3.00

Indigenous Moths — A168

25c, Syntomidopsis variegata. 55c, Himantoides undata-perkinsi. $3, Hypercompe nigriplaga. $5, Sthenognatha toddi.

Wmk. 352

1989, Aug. 30 **Litho.** ***Perf. 14***
713 A168 25c multicolored .75 .25
714 A168 55c multicolored 1.25 .30
715 A168 $3 multicolored 2.00 2.00
716 A168 $5 multicolored 3.50 3.50
Nos. 713-716 (4) 7.50 6.05

See Nos. 725-728, 752-755. For surcharges & overprints see Nos. 729-732, 756-759.

A169

Discovery of America, 500th Anniv. (in 1992): 25c, Arawak spear fisherman. 70c, Smoking tobacco. $5, Ferdinand and Isabella inspecting caravels. $10, Columbus studying chart.

1989, Dec. 22 ***Perf. 13½***
717 A169 25c multicolored .25 .25
718 A169 70c multicolored .50 .30
719 A169 $5 multicolored 2.00 2.00
720 A169 $10 multicolored 5.75 *5.75*
a. Souvenir sheet of 4, #717-720, perf. 12½ 17.50 17.50
Nos. 717-720 (4) 8.50 8.30

No. 720a exists imperf. Value $25.

A171

Wmk. 352

1990, June 28 **Litho.** ***Perf. 14***
721 A171 45c multicolored 1.25 .30
722 A171 55c multi, diff. 1.25 .30
723 A171 $5 multi, diff. 5.50 *7.00*
Nos. 721-723 (3) 8.00 7.60

Girl Guides of Jamaica, 75th anniv.

Indigenous Moths Type of 1989

25c, Eunomia rubripunctata. 55c, Perigonia jamaicensis. $4, Uraga haemorrhoa. $5, Empyreuma pugione.

Wmk. 352

1990, Sept. 12 **Litho.** ***Perf. 14***
725 A168 25c multicolored 1.00 .30
726 A168 55c multicolored 1.60 .30
727 A168 $4 multicolored 2.75 3.00
728 A168 $5 multicolored 3.00 3.00
Nos. 725-728 (4) 8.35 6.60

Nos. 725-728 Ovptd. in Black

1990, Sept. 12

729 A168 25c No. 725 .80 .35
730 A168 55c No. 726 1.25 .35
731 A168 $4 No. 727 2.75 2.75
732 A168 $5 No. 728 3.25 3.25
Nos. 729-732 (4) 8.05 6.70

Expo '90, International Garden and Greenery Exposition, Osaka, Japan.

Intl. Literacy Year — A172

Design: $5, Mathematics class.

Wmk. 352

1990, Oct. 10 Litho. *Perf. 14*

733 A172 55c multi .75 .30
734 A172 $5 multi 5.00 *6.00*

Christmas A173

Children's art — 20c, To the market. 25c, Untitled (houses). 55c, Jack and Jill. 70c, Untitled (market). $1.50, Lonely (beach). $5, Market woman, vert.

Perf. 13½x14

1990, Dec. 7 Litho. Wmk. 352

735 A173 20c multicolored .50 .25
736 A173 25c multicolored .60 .25
737 A173 55c multicolored .70 .25
738 A173 70c multicolored 1.00 .40
739 A173 $1.50 multicolored 1.75 1.75
740 A173 $5 multicolored 2.25 *4.25*
Nos. 735-740 (6) 6.80 7.15

See Nos. 760-763.

Discovery of America, 500th Anniv. (in 1992) — A174

Maps of Columbus' voyages.

1990, Dec. 19 *Perf. 14*

741 A174 25c First, 1492 1.00 .40
742 A174 45c Second, 1493 1.25 .40
743 A174 $5 Third, 1498 3.75 3.75
744 A174 $10 Fourth, 1502 6.50 *8.00*
Nos. 741-744 (4) 12.50 12.55

Souvenir Sheet

745 Sheet of 4 13.00 13.00
a. A174 25c Cuba, Jamaica 1.00 1.00
b. A174 45c Hispaniola, Puerto Rico 1.10 1.10
c. A174 $5 Central America 3.00 3.00
d. A174 $10 Venezuela 5.00 5.00

Souvenir sheet also exists imperf. Value, $20.

See Nos. 764-767.

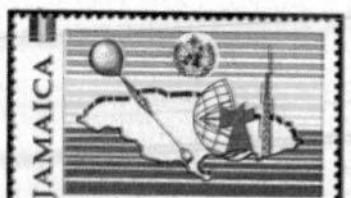

Natl. Meteorological Service — A175

1991, May 20 Litho. Wmk. 352

746 A175 50c multicolored .55 .25
747 A175 $10 multicolored 6.00 6.00

11th World Meteorological Congress.

Intl. Council of Nurses Council of Natl. Representatives, Jamaica — A176

50c, Mary Seacole. $1.10, Mary Seacole House. $8, Hospital at Scutari.

Wmk. 352

1991, June 24 Litho. *Perf. 13½*

748 A176 50c multicolored 1.00 .35
749 A176 $1.10 multicolored 1.75 1.75

Souvenir Sheet

750 A176 $8 multicolored 4.00 4.00

Cyclura Collei (Jamaican Iguana) — A177

Designs: a, Head pointed to UR. b, Facing right. c, Climbing rock. d, Facing left. e, Head pointed to UL.

Wmk. 352

1991, July 29 Litho. *Perf. 13*

751 A177 $1.10 Strip of 5, #a.-e. 4.50 4.50

Natural History Soc. of Jamaica, 50th anniv.

Moths Type of 1989

50c, Urania sloanus. $1.10, Phoenicoprocta jamaicensis. $1.40, Horama grotei. $8, Amplypterus gannascus.

1991, Aug. 12 *Perf. 14*

752 A168 50c multicolored 1.00 .25
753 A168 $1.10 multicolored 1.10 .50
754 A168 $1.40 multicolored 1.25 1.00
755 A168 $8 multicolored 3.25 3.25
Nos. 752-755 (4) 6.60 5.00

Nos. 752-755 Overprinted

1991, Sept. 23

756 A168 50c on No. 752 1.00 .25
757 A168 $1.10 on No. 753 1.25 .65
758 A168 $1.40 on No. 754 1.50 1.10
759 A168 $8 on No. 755 4.50 *6.50*
Nos. 756-759 (4) 8.25 8.50

Children's Christmas Art Type

Children's drawings.

1991, Nov. 27 *Perf. 14x15*

760 A173 50c Doctor bird .70 .25
761 A173 $1.10 Road scene 1.00 .30
762 A173 $5 House, people 3.00 3.00
763 A173 $10 Cows grazing 6.00 *8.00*
Nos. 760-763 (4) 10.70 11.55

Christmas.

Discovery of America Type of 1990

Designs: 50c, Explorers did not land at Santa Gloria because of hostile Indians. $1.10, Fierce dog used to subdue the Indians. $1.40, Indians brought gifts of fruit. $25, Columbus describes Jamaica with crumpled paper.

1991, Dec. 16 *Perf. 13½x14*

764 A174 50c multicolored .65 .25
765 A174 $1.10 multicolored .85 .30
766 A174 $1.40 multicolored .95 .30
767 A174 $25 multicolored 6.25 *8.00*
a. Souvenir sheet of 4, #764-767 9.00 9.00
Nos. 764-767 (4) 8.70 8.85

Souvenir sheet also exists imperf. Same value as perf.

First Provincial Grand Master of English Freemasonry in Jamaica, 250th Anniv. — A178

Masonic symbols: 50c, Square and compass. $1.10, Stained glass window. $1.40, Square and compass on Bible. $25, Seeing eye.

1992, May 1 *Perf. 13½*

768 A178 50c multicolored .85 .30
769 A178 $1.10 multicolored 1.00 .40
770 A178 $1.40 multicolored 1.25 .45
771 A178 $25 multicolored 10.00 10.00
a. Souvenir sheet of 4, #768-771 18.00 18.00
Nos. 768-771 (4) 13.10 11.15

Destruction of Port Royal by Earthquake, 300th Anniv. — A179

Scenes of destruction: 50c, Ship in harbor. $1.10, Homes, church. $1.40, Homes toppling. $5, Port Royal from contemporary broadsheet. $25, Fissure in street.

1992, June 7 *Perf. 14x13½*

772 A179 50c multicolored .50 .40
773 A179 $1.10 multicolored .60 .45
774 A179 $1.40 multicolored .75 .50
775 A179 $25 multicolored 7.75 *8.75*
Nos. 772-775 (4) 9.60 10.10

Souvenir Sheet

Perf. 13x12

776 A179 $5 multicolored 5.75 5.75

No. 776 inscribed on reverse.

Independence, 30th Anniv. — A180

1992, Aug. 6 *Perf. 13½*

777 A180 50c black & multi .25 .25
778 A180 $1.10 green & multi .35 .35
779 A180 $25 yellow & multi 3.00 3.00
Nos. 777-779 (3) 3.60 3.60

Credit Union Movement in Jamaica, 50th Anniv. A181

50c, Emblem. $1.40, Emblem, O'Hare Hall.

1992, Aug. 24 *Perf. 14x15*

780 A181 50c multi 1.00 .50
781 A181 $1.40 multi 2.00 1.75

Pottery — A182

Designs: 50c, "Rainbow" vase, by Cecil Baugh O.D. $1.10, "Yabba Pot," by Louisa Jones (MaLou) O.D. $1.40, "Sculptured Vase," by Gene Pearson. $25, "Lidded Form," by Norma Rodney Harrack.

1993, Apr. 26 *Perf. 13½*

782 A182 50c multicolored .25 .25
783 A182 $1.10 multicolored .35 .25
784 A182 $1.40 multicolored .40 .25
785 A182 $25 multicolored 3.75 3.75
Nos. 782-785 (4) 4.75 4.50

Girls' Brigade, Cent. — A183

50c, Parade. $1.10, Brigade members.

1993, Aug. 9 *Perf. 14x13½*

786 A183 50c multicolored 1.00 .50
787 A183 $1.10 multicolored 1.25 1.25

Jamaica Combined Cadet Force, 50th Anniv. — A184

Designs: 50c, Tank, cadet, vert. $1.10, Airplane, female cadet. $1.40, Ships, female cadet, vert. $3, Cap badge, cadet.

1993, Nov. 8 *Perf. 14*

788 A184 50c multicolored .35 .25
789 A184 $1.10 multicolored .45 .40
790 A184 $1.40 multicolored .55 .40
791 A184 $3 multicolored 1.10 *1.25*
Nos. 788-791 (4) 2.45 2.30

Golf Courses — A185

50c, $1.10, Constant Spring. $1.40, $2, Half Moon. $3, $10, Jamaica Jamaica. $25, Tryall, vert.

1993-94 Litho. Wmk. 352 *Perf. 14*

792 A185 50c yellow & multi .40 .25
793 A185 $1.10 blue & multi .45 .25
794 A185 $1.40 brn org & multi .60 .25
795 A185 $2 lilac & multi .90 .90
796 A185 $3 dark blue & multi 1.00 1.00
797 A185 $10 tan & multi 2.00 2.00
Nos. 792-797 (6) 5.35 4.65

Souvenir Sheets

798 A185 $25 green & multi 5.50 5.50
799 A185 $25 #798 inscribed with Hong Kong '94 emblem 5.50 5.50

Issued: Nos. 792-797, 12/21/93; No. 798, 12/16/93; No. 799, 2/18/94.

A186

1994, Jan. 12 *Perf. 14x15*

800 $25 Portrait 2.50 2.50
801 $50 Portrait, diff. 3.00 3.00
a. A186 Pair, #800-801 8.25 *10.00*

Norman Washington Manley, birth cent.

A187

Royal Visit: $1.10, Jamaican, United Kingdom flags. $1.40, Royal yacht Britannia. $25, Queen Elizabeth II. $50, Prince Philip, Queen.

1994, Mar. 1 *Perf. 14*

802 A187 $1.10 multicolored .75 .25
803 A187 $1.40 multicolored 1.60 .40
804 A187 $25 multicolored 3.25 3.25
805 A187 $50 multicolored 5.25 *6.50*
Nos. 802-805 (4) 10.85 10.40

Air Jamaica, 25th Anniv. A188

Wmk. 352

1994, Apr. 26 Litho. *Perf. 14*

806 A188 50c Douglas DC9 .30 .25
807 A188 $1.10 Douglas DC8 .35 .25
808 A188 $5 Boeing 727 .75 .75
809 A188 $50 Airbus A300 3.75 3.75
Nos. 806-809 (4) 5.15 5.00

Giant Swallowtail — A189

Various views of the butterfly.

Perf. 14x13½

1994, Aug. 18 Litho. Wmk. 352

810 A189	50c	multicolored	.50	.30
811 A189	$1.10	multicolored	.50	.30
812 A189	$10	multicolored	2.00	2.00
813 A189	$25	multicolored	3.75	3.75
		Nos. 810-813 (4)	6.75	6.35

Souvenir Sheet

814 189	$50	multicolored	9.50	9.50

A190

Tourism — A191

Designs: 50c, Royal Botanical Gardens, by Sidney McClaren. $1.10, Blue Mountains, coffee beans, leaves. $5, Woman in hammock, waterfalls.

Tourist poster: No. 818a, Flowers, birds (c). b, Diver (d). c, Vegetation, coastline (a, d). d, Guide, tourists on raft.

Wmk. 352

1994, Sept. 7 Litho. *Perf. 14*

815 A190	50c	multicolored	.40	.25
816 A190	$1.10	multicolored	.65	.30
817 A190	$5	multicolored	3.00	3.00
		Nos. 815-817 (3)	4.05	3.55

Souvenir Sheet

818 A191	$25	Sheet of 4, #a.-d.	6.50	6.50

Caribbean Tourism Conf. (No. 818).

Red Poll Cattle — A192

1994, Nov. 16 *Perf. 14x13½*

819 A192	50c	Calf	.25	.25
820 A192	$1.10	Heifer	.25	.25
821 A192	$25	Cow	1.50	1.50
822 A192	$50	Bull	3.75	3.75
		Nos. 819-822 (4)	5.75	5.75

Christmas A193

Paintings by Children: 50c, Clean-up crew. 90c, Hospital Room. $1.10, House. $50, Meadow.

1994, Dec. 1 *Perf. 14x14½*

823 A193	50c	multicolored	.25	.25
824 A193	90c	multicolored	.25	.25
825 A193	$1.10	multicolored	1.00	.25
826 A193	$50	multicolored	2.00	*3.75*
		Nos. 823-826 (4)	3.50	4.50

Birds — A194

50c, Ring-tailed pigeon. 90c, Yellow-billed parrot. $1.10, Black-billed parrot. No. 830, Brown owl.

No. 831, Streamertail.

Wmk. 384

1995, Apr. 24 Litho. *Perf. 14*

827 A194	50c	multicolored	.70	.35
828 A194	90c	multicolored	.80	.35
829 A194	$1.10	multicolored	.80	.35
830 A194	$50	multicolored	5.50	*7.00*
		Nos. 827-830 (4)	7.80	8.05

Souvenir Sheet

831 A194	$50	multicolored	7.50	7.50
a.		Ovptd. in sheet margin	6.00	6.00

No. 831 is a continuous design.

No. 831a ovptd. with Singapore '95 emblem. Issued: 9/1/95.

Caribbean Development Bank, 25th Anniv. — A195

Anniversary emblem and: 50c, $1, Jamaican flag, graph, vert. $1.10, Industries, agriculture. $50, Bank notes, coins.

Wmk. 352

1995, May 11 Litho. *Perf. 13½*

832 A195	50c	green & multi	.25	.25
833 A195	$1	black & multi	.25	.25
834 A195	$1.10	multicolored	.25	.25
835 A195	$50	multicolored	3.50	*4.00*
		Nos. 832-835 (4)	4.25	4.75

Bob Marley (1945-81), Reggae Musician — A196

Marley performing songs: 50c, Songs of Freedom, by Adrian Boot. $1.10, Fire, by Neville Garrick. $1.40, Time Will Tell, by Peter Murphy. $3, Natural Mystic, by Boot. $10, Live at Lyceum, by Boot.

$100, Legend, by Boot.

Wmk. 352

1995, July 31 Litho. *Perf. 14*

836 A196	50c	multicolored	.35	.25
837 A196	$1.10	multicolored	.55	.25
838 A196	$1.40	multicolored	.60	.35
839 A196	$3	multicolored	.90	.90
840 A196	$10	multicolored	1.75	1.75
		Nos. 836-840 (5)	4.15	3.50

Souvenir Sheet

841 A196	$100	multicolored	7.50	7.50

Souvenir Sheet

Queen Mother, 95th Birthday A197

1995, Aug. 4 *Perf. 14x13½*

842 A197	$75	multicolored	5.25	5.25

Order of the Caribbean Community A198

Designs: 50c, Michael Manley, former prime minister, Jamaica. $1.10, Sir Alister McIntyre, Vice Chancellor, UWI, Jamaica. $1.40, P. Telford Georges, former Chief Justice, Bahamas. $50, Dame Nita Barrow, Governor General, Barbados.

1995, Aug. 23 *Perf. 14x14½*

843 A198	50c	multicolored	.25	.25
844 A198	$1.10	multicolored	.25	.25
845 A198	$1.40	multicolored	.30	.25
846 A198	$50	multicolored	3.25	*5.00*
		Nos. 843-846 (4)	4.05	5.75

UN, 50th Anniv.

Common Design Type

Designs: 50c, Signals Land Rover. $1.10, Antonov AN-32. $3, Bedford Articulated Tanker. $5, Fairchild DC-119 Flying Boxcar. $50, Observation vehicles.

Wmk. 352

1995, Oct. 24 Litho. *Perf. 14*

847 CD353	50c	multicolored	.30	.25
848 CD353	$1.10	multicolored	.50	.25
849 CD353	$3	multicolored	.70	.70
850 CD353	$5	multicolored	.90	*1.25*
		Nos. 847-850 (4)	2.40	2.45

Souvenir Sheet

851 CD353	$50	multicolored	3.00	3.00

No. 851 has continuous design.

Arrival of East Indians in Jamaica, 150th Anniv. — A199

$2.50, Coming ashore. $10, Musicians, dancers.

Wmk. 352

1996, May 22 Litho. *Perf. 14*

852 A199	$2.50	multicolored	.25	.25
853 A199	$10	multicolored	.75	.75

UNICEF, 50th Anniv. — A200

1996, Sept. 2 *Perf. 14½x14*

854 A200	$2.50	multicolored	.60	.60
855 A200	$8	multicolored	1.10	1.10
856 A200	$10	multicolored	1.50	1.50
		Nos. 854-856 (3)	3.20	3.20

Jamaican Hutia (Indian Coney) — A201

$2.50, Two in den. $10, One on ledge. $12.50, Mother, young. $25, One up close.

1996, Sept. 23 *Perf. 13½x14*

857 A201	$2.50	multicolored	.30	.25
858 A201	$10	multicolored	.65	.25
859 A201	$12.50	multicolored	.80	.80
860 A201	$25	multicolored	1.40	*2.50*
		Nos. 857-860 (4)	3.15	3.80

World Wildlife Fund.

Kingston Parish Church of St. Thomas the Apostle, 300th Anniv. — A202

$2, High altar. $8, Exterior view. $12.50, Carving, "The Angel," by Edna Manley, vert. $60, Exterior view at sunset.

Unwmk.

1997, Feb. 7 Litho. *Perf. 14*

861 A202	$2	multicolored	.40	.25
862 A202	$8	multicolored	1.00	1.00
863 A202	$12.50	multicolored	1.50	1.50
		Nos. 861-863 (3)	2.90	2.75

Souvenir Sheet

864 A202	$60	multicolored	3.50	3.50

No. 864 contains one 42x56mm stamp.

Chernobyl's Children A203

Perf. 13½x14

1997, Apr. 7 Litho. Unwmk.

865 A203	$55	multicolored	4.00	4.00

Caribbean Integration, 50th Anniv. — A203a

$2.50, Map of Caribbean. $8, $10, View of coastline.

Wmk. 352

1997, June 30 Litho. *Perf. 14*

865A A203a	$2.50	multi	*8.00*	*7.00*
865B A203a	$8	multi	*9.00*	*3.25*
865C A203a	$10	multi	*10.00*	*3.25*
		Nos. 865A-865C (3)	*27.00*	*13.50*

Orchids — A204

$1, Coelia triptera. $2, Oncidium pulchellum. $2.50, Oncidium triquetrum. $3, Broughtonia negrilensis. $5, Enclyclia frangrans.

Wmk. 352

1997, Oct. 6 Litho. *Perf. 14*

866 A204	$1	multi, vert.	.30	.25
867 A204	$2	multi	.35	.25
868 A204	$2.50	multi, vert.	.40	.25
869 A204	$3	multi, vert.	.45	.25
870 A204	$5	multi	.50	.35
		Nos. 866-870 (5)	2.00	1.35

See Nos. 873-877.

Diana, Princess of Wales (1961-97) — A205

Unwmk.

1998, Feb. 24 Litho. *Perf. 14*

871 A205	$20	Portrait	1.25	1.25

Souvenir Sheet

872 A205	$80	With Mother Teresa	6.00	6.00

No. 871 was issued in sheets of 6. No. 872 contains one 42x56mm stamp.

Orchid Type of 1997

Designs: $4.50, Oncidium gauntlettii. $8, Broughtonia sanguinea. $12, Phaius tankervilleae, vert. $25, Cochleanthes flabelliformis. $50, Broughtonia sanguinea (3 varieties).

Wmk. 352

1997, Dec. 1 Litho. *Perf. 14*

873 A204	$4.50	multicolored	.60	.60
874 A204	$8	multicolored	.85	.85
875 A204	$12	multicolored	1.00	1.00
876 A204	$25	multicolored	2.00	2.00
a.		Inscribed "1999"	*2.00*	*2.00*
877 A204	$50	multicolored	2.00	2.00
		Nos. 873-877 (5)	6.45	6.45

CARICOM, 25th Anniv. — A206

Perf. 13½

1998, Sept. 17 Litho. Unwmk.

878 A206	$30	multicolored	3.00	3.00

University of the West Indies, Mona, 50th Anniv. — A207

$8, Chapel. $10, Philip Sherlock Centre for the Creative Arts. $50, University arms.

1998, July 31 Wmk. 352

879 A207	$8	multi	.50	.50
880 A207	$10	multi	.50	.50
881 A207	$50	multi, vert.	2.25	2.25
		Nos. 879-881 (3)	3.25	3.25

1998 World Cup Soccer Championships, France, Jamaica's Debut in Tournament
A208

Wmk. 373

1998, Sept. 28 Litho. ***Perf. 13½***

882 A208 $10 Player, vert. .50 .35
883 A208 $25 Team picture 1.40 1.25
884 A208 $100 Team picture, diff. 4.50 *5.50*
Nos. 882-884 (3) 6.40 7.10

Intl. Year of the Ocean — A209

Designs: $10, Underwater scene. $30, Fishermen, Negril. $50, Long spiny black urchin. $100, Design elements from Nos. 885-887, vert.

Wmk. 352

1998, Dec. 23 Litho. ***Perf. 14***

885 A209 $10 multicolored 1.50 .40
886 A209 $30 multicolored 2.75 1.50
887 A209 $50 multicolored 4.00 4.00

Size: 28x42mm

888 A209 $100 multicolored 7.50 *10.00*
Nos. 885-888 (4) 15.75 15.90

Christmas.

1st Manned Moon Landing, 30th Anniv.

Common Design Type

Designs: $7, Michael Collins. $10, Service module reverses to dock with lunar module. $25, Aldrin walks on lunar surface. $30, Command module back in earth orbit.
$100, Looking at earth from moon.

Perf. 14x13¾

1999, July 20 Litho. Wmk. 352

889 CD357 $7 multicolored .50 .50
890 CD357 $10 multicolored .65 .65
891 CD357 $25 multicolored 1.25 .125
892 CD357 $30 multicolored 1.40 1.40
Nos. 889-892 (4) 3.80 2.68

Souvenir Sheet

Perf. 14

893 CD357 $100 multicolored 4.50 4.50

No. 893 contains one 40mm circular stamp.

Athletes — A210

Designs: $5, Polo player Lesley Ann Masterton Fong-Yee. $10, Men's cricketers Collie Smith, Lawrence Rowe and Alfred Valentine. $20, Women's cricketer Vivalyn Latty-Scott, vert. $25, Soccer player Lindy Delapenha, vert. $30, Netball player Joy Grant-Charles, vert. $50, Boxers Percy Hayles, Gerald Gray and Bunny Grant.
$100, Delapenha and Grant-Charles.

Perf. 13¼x13¾, 13¾x13¼

1999, Aug. 3 Litho. Wmk. 352

894 A210 $5 multicolored .75 .45
895 A210 $10 multicolored 1.00 .55
896 A210 $20 multicolored 1.25 1.25
897 A210 $25 multicolored 1.50 1.50
898 A210 $30 multicolored 1.60 1.60
899 A210 $50 multicolored 1.75 *2.50*
Nos. 894-899 (6) 7.85 7.85

Souvenir Sheet

900 A210 $100 multicolored 6.50 6.50

No. 900 contains one 52x38mm stamp.

UPU, 125th Anniv. — A211

Designs: $7, Mail ship "Spey." $10, Mail ship "Jamaica Planter." $25, Lockheed Constellation. $30, Airbus A-310.

Wmk. 352

1999, Oct. 8 Litho. ***Perf. 14***

901 A211 $7 multicolored 1.00 .40
902 A211 $10 multicolored 1.25 .50
903 A211 $25 multicolored 2.00 2.00
904 A211 $30 multicolored 2.25 *2.75*
Nos. 901-904 (4) 6.50 5.65

Air Jamaica, 30th Anniv. — A212

Wmk. 352

1999, Nov. 1 Litho. ***Perf. 14***

905 A212 $10 A-310 .75 .50
906 A212 $25 A-320 1.25 1.25
907 A212 $30 A-340 1.75 *2.25*
Nos. 905-907 (3) 3.75 4.00

Dogs — A213

1999, Nov. 25 ***Perf. 14¼***

908 A213 $7 Shih tzu 1.25 .75
909 A213 $10 German shepherd 1.75 .75
910 A213 $30 Doberman pinscher 3.00 *3.25*
Nos. 908-910 (3) 6.00 4.75

Parks — A214

Designs: $7, Nelson Mandela Park. $10, St. William Grant Park. $25, Seaview Park. $30, Holruth Park.

1999, Dec. 15 ***Perf. 14***

911 A214 $7 multi .40 .35
912 A214 $10 multi .50 .40
913 A214 $25 multi 1.10 1.00
914 A214 $30 multi 1.40 1.40
Nos. 911-914 (4) 3.40 3.15

Edna Manley (1900-87), Sculptor — A215

Designs: $10, The Prophet, 1935. $25, Horse of the Morning, 1943. $30, The Angel, 1970. $100, Portrait of Manley.

2000, Mar. 1 Litho. ***Perf. 13¾***

915 A215 $10 multi .65 .65
916 A215 $25 multi 1.50 1.50
917 A215 $30 multi 1.75 1.75
918 A215 $100 multi 5.00 5.00
a. Souvenir sheet, #915-918 9.00 9.00
Nos. 915-918 (4) 8.90 8.90

Lennox Lewis, Heavyweight Boxing Champion of the World — A216

a, $10, With belt & Empire State Building. b, $10, Holding up arm. c, $10, Holding up belt. d, $25, In ring with opponent. e, $25, Close-up. f, $25, In ring with referee. g, $30, Holding up belt, diff. h, $30, Holding 4 belts. i, $30, Holding belts in front of buildings.

Wmk. 352

2000, Mar. 24 Litho. ***Perf. 14***

919 A216 Sheet of 9, #a.-i. 9.00 9.00

Ferrari Automobiles A217

Unwmk.

2000, May 26 Litho. ***Perf. 14***

920 A217 $10 1947 125S .75 .75
921 A217 $10 1950 375F1 .75 .75
922 A217 $10 1966 312F1 .75 .75
923 A217 $25 1965 Dino 166P 1.50 1.50
924 A217 $25 1971 312P 1.50 1.50
925 A217 $25 1990 F190 1.50 1.50
Nos. 920-925 (6) 6.75 6.75

Queen Mother, 100th Birthday — A218

Various photos.

2000, Aug. 4 Wmk. 352

926 A218 $10 multi .60 .60
927 A218 $25 multi 1.00 1.00
928 A218 $30 multi 1.50 1.50
929 A218 $50 multi 3.25 3.25
Nos. 926-929 (4) 6.35 6.35

2000 Summer Olympics, Sydney — A219

Jamaican flag and various views of sculpture, "The Runner," by Alvin Marriott. Denominations, $10, $25, $30, vert., $50, vert.

Wmk. 352

2000, Sept. 1 Litho. ***Perf. 14***

930-933 A219 Set of 4 6.75 6.75

Trees — A220

Designs: $10, Bull thatch palm. $25, Blue mahoe. $30, Silk cotton. $50, Yellow pout.
$100, Lignum vitae, horiz.

2000, Oct. 6

934-937 A220 Set of 4 7.75 7.75

Souvenir Sheet

938 A220 $100 multi 8.00 8.00

Christmas A221

Designs: $10, Madonna and Child, by Osmond Watson, vert. $20, Boy in the Temple, by Carl Abrahams. $25, Ascension, by Abrahams, vert. $30, Jah Lives, by Watson.

Wmk. 352

2000, Dec. 6 Litho. ***Perf. 13¾***

939-942 A221 Set of 4 4.25 4.25

Commonwealth Day, 25th Anniv. — A222

Wmk. 352

2001, Mar. 12 Litho. ***Perf. 12½***

943 A222 $30 multi 2.00 2.00

Father Andrew Duffus Mowatt, Founder of Jamaica Burial Scheme Society — A223

Wmk. 352

2001, Oct. 12 Litho. ***Perf. 13¼***

944 A223 $15 multi 1.50 1.50

Lithographs of Daguerrotypes by Adolphe Duperly (1801-64) — A224

Designs: $15, The Market, Falmouth. $40, Ferry Inn, Spanish Town Road. $45, Coke Chapel. $60, King Street, Kingston.

2001, Nov. 14 ***Perf. 13***

945-948 A224 Set of 4 9.25 9.25
a. Souvenir sheet, #945-948 8.75 8.75

Christmas — A225

Poinsettias with background colors of: $15, Light blue. $30, Pink. $40, Pale orange.

2001, Dec. 10 ***Perf. 13¼***

949-951 A225 Set of 3 6.00 6.00

Reign Of Queen Elizabeth II, 50th Anniv. Issue

Common Design Type

Designs: Nos. 952, 956a, $15, Princess Elizabeth. Nos. 953, 953b, $40, Wearing striped dress. Nos. 954, 956c, $45, In 1953. Nos. 955, 956d, $60, In 1995. No. 956e, $30, 1955 portrait by Annigoni (38x50mm).

Perf. 14¼x14½, 13¾ (#956e)

2002, Feb. 6 Litho. Wmk. 373

With Gold Frames

952	CD360 $15 multicolored	.65	.65
953	CD360 $40 multicolored	2.00	2.00
954	CD360 $45 multicolored	2.25	2.25
955	CD360 $60 multicolored	3.25	3.25
	Nos. 952-955 (4)	8.15	8.15

Souvenir Sheet

Without Gold Frames

956 CD360 Sheet of 5, #a-e 8.50 8.50

Visit of Queen Elizabeth II and Prince Philip, Feb. 18-20 — A226

Designs: $15, Queen and Prince in 1983, flag of the Royal Standard. $45, Queen in 1983, Jamaican arms.

Perf. 13¼x13¾

2002, Feb. 18 Litho. Wmk. 352

957-958 A226 Set of 2 5.75 5.75

Sir Philip Sherlock (1902-2000), Educator — A227

2002, Mar. 11 ***Perf. 13¾***

959 A227 $40 multi 2.00 2.00

Pan-American Health Organization, Cent. — A228

Wmk. 352

2002, Dec. 2 Litho. ***Perf. 13¾***

960 A228 $40 multi 2.25 2.25

Christmas A229

Art: $15, Masquerade, by Osmond Watson, vert. $40, John Canoe in Guanaboa Vale, by Gaston Tabois. $45, Mother and Child, sculpture, by Kapo, vert. $60, Hills of Papine, sculpture by Edna Manley.

2002, Dec. 6

961-964 A229 Set of 4 6.75 6.75

Natl. Dance Theater Company, 40th Anniv. — A230

2002, Dec. 27 ***Perf. 14***

965 A230 $15 multi 1.75 1.75

Independence, 40th Anniv. — A231

Flag and: $15, Natl. Dance Theater Company performers. $40, Sir Alexander Bustamante, Michael Manley. $60, Factory workers.

2002, Dec. 27

966-968 A231 Set of 3 7.25 7.25

Kingston, Bicent. — A232

Historical views of Kingston and panel colors of: a, Brown. b, Olive green. c, Indigo.

2002, Dec. 31 ***Perf. 13¾***

969 A232 Horiz. strip of 3 3.75 3.75
a.-c. $15 Any single 1.00 1.00

Coronation of Queen Elizabeth II, 50th Anniv.

Common Design Type

Designs: Nos. 970, $15, 972b, $100, Queen in chair awaiting crown. Nos. 971, $45, 972a, $50, Queen and Prince Philip in carriage.

Perf. 14¼x14½

2003, June 2 Litho. Wmk. 352

Vignettes Framed, Red Background

970	CD363 $15 multicolored	1.00	1.00
971	CD363 $45 multicolored	3.00	3.00

Souvenir Sheet

Vignettes Without Frame, Purple Panel

972 CD363 Sheet of 2, #a-b 6.00 6.00

Caribbean Community (CARICOM), 30th Anniv. — A233

Wmk. 352

2003, July 4 Litho. ***Perf. 14***

973 A233 $40 multi 3.25 3.25

Bird Life International A234

Designs: $15, Jamaican stripe-headed tanager, vert. $40, Crested quail dove. $45, Jamaican tody. $60, Blue Mountain vireo.

No. 978 — Jamaican blackbird: a, With beak open (35x30mm). b, Chicks in nest (35x30mm). c, In palm fronds, vert. (30x35mm). d, With beak open, vert. (30x35mm) e, With insect in beak (35x30mm).

2003, Sept. 19 ***Perf. 14***

974-977 A234 Set of 4 8.50 8.50

Souvenir Sheet

Perf. 14¼x14½, 14½x14¼

978 A234 $30 Sheet of 5, #a-e 9.00 9.00

Maritime Heritage — A235

No. 979: a, Map, sailing ships. b, Sailing ships, ship with passengers. c, The Sugar Refiner and barges.

2003, Sept. 25 ***Perf. 14x14¾***

979 A235 Horiz. strip of 3 8.00 8.00
a.-c. $40 Any single 2.00 2.00

Christmas A236

Flowers and: $15, Adoration of the Magi. $30, Christ child. $60, Holy Family.

2003, Dec. ***Perf. 13¼***

980-982 A236 Set of 3 6.00 6.00

Haitian Revolution, Bicent. — A237

Wmk. 352

2004, Jan. 30 Litho. ***Perf. 13½***

983 A237 $40 multi 2.75 2.75

Caribbean Bird Festival — A238

No. 984: a, Yellow-billed amazon. b, Jamaican oriole. c, Orangequit. d, Yellow-shouldered grassquit. e, Jamaican woodpecker. f, Red-billed streamertail. g, Jamaican mango. h, White-eyed thrush. i, Jamaican lizard cuckoo. j, Arrow-headed warbler.

Wmk. 352

2004, May 17 Litho. ***Perf. 13¾***

984 Block of 10 10.00 10.00
a.-j. A238 $10 Any single .80 .60

Miniature Sheet

World Environment Day — A239

No. 985: a, $10, Water lilies. b, $10, Hawksbill turtle. c, $10, Tube sponge. d, $10, Boater on Parattee Pond. e, $40, Vase sponge, star coral. f, $40, Sea fan, black and white crinoid. g, $40, Glassy sweepers. h, $40, Giant sea anemone.

Unwmk.

2004, June 4 Litho. ***Perf. 14***

985 A239 Sheet of 8, #a-h 9.50 9.50

2004 Summer Olympics, Athens — A240

Jamaican athletes: $30, Women's hurdles. $60, Running. $70, Swimming. $90, Rifle shooting, women's badminton.

Wmk. 352

2004, Aug. 10 Litho. ***Perf. 14***

986-989 A240 Set of 4 9.50 9.50

FIFA (Fédération Internationale de Football Association), Cent. — A241

FIFA emblem and various soccer players: $10, $30, $45, $50.

Wmk. 352

2004, Oct. 13 Litho. ***Perf. 14***

990-993 A241 Set of 4 6.75 6.75

Jamaica Hotels Law, Cent. — A242

Designs: No. 994, Ralph Lauren, Doctors Cave Beach, Montego Bay.

No. 995 — Ambassador John Pringle, Round Hill Hotel and: a, Pink panel. b, Lilac panel.

No. 996 — Tower Isle Hotel and: a, Abe Issa, yellow green panels. b, John Issa, green panels. c, Abe Issa, red panels. d, John Issa, yellow green panels. e, Abe Issa, green panels. f, John Issa, red panels.

2004 Unwmk. ***Perf. 13¼x13½***

994	A242 $40 multi	6.00	6.00
995	A242 $40 Pair, #a-b	8.00	8.00
996	A242 $40 Sheet of 6, #a-f	10.00	10.00
	Nos. 994-996 (3)	24.00	24.00

Issued: No. 994, 11/19; Nos. 995-996, 11/12. No. 994 printed in sheets of six; No. 995 printed in sheets containing three pairs. Value, set of three sheets $45.

Christmas — A243

White sorrel stalks: $10, $20, $50, $60. $50 and $60 are horiz.

Wmk. 352

2004, Nov. 22 Litho. ***Perf. 14¼***

997-1000 A243 Set of 4 7.50 7.50

Founding of Moravian Church in Jamaica, 250th Anniv. — A244

Designs: 90c, Mary Morris Knibb, Mizpah Moravian Church. $10, Rev. W. O'Meally, Mizpah Moravian Church. $50, Bishop S. U. Hastings, Redeemer Moravian Church.

2004, Dec. 14

1001-1003 A244 Set of 3 4.00 4.00

Buildings — A245

Designs: 90c, Rose Hall Great House, St. James. $5, Holy Trinity Cathedral. $30, National Commercial Bank, New Kingston. $60, Court House, Falmouth.

2005, Jan. 13 Wmk. 352 ***Perf. 13¼***

1004	A245 90c multi	.25	.25
1004A	A245 $5 multi	.30	.25
1005	A245 $30 multi	1.50	1.10
a.	Dated 2006 at bottom	2.00	1.50
b.	Dated 2008 at bottom	1.00	.75
1006	A245 $60 multi	3.00	2.75
a.	Dated 2008 at bottom	2.00	1.50
	Nos. 1004-1006 (4)	5.05	4.35

Self-Adhesive

Serpentine Die Cut 12¼x12½

Unwmk.

1008	A245 $5 multi	.40	.25
1008A	A245 $30 multi	1.50	1.50
b.	Booklet pane of 10	15.00	
	Complete booklet, #1008Ab	15.00	
c.	Dated 2006 at right	2.00	2.00
1009	A245 $60 multi	3.50	3.50

See Nos. 1038-1053.

Chinese in Jamaica, 150th Anniv. — A246

Flags of People's Republic of China and Jamaica and: $30, Food and fruits from China and Jamaica. $60, Chinatown. $90, Chinese Benevolent Association Building.

2005, Feb. 5 Wmk. 352 ***Perf. 14¼***

1010-1012 A246 Set of 3 9.00 9.00

European Philatelic Cooperation, 50th Anniv. (in 2006) — A247

Designs: $60, Green square. $70, Yellow diamond. $100 Blue square.

Perf. 13½

2005, June 1 Litho. Unwmk.

1013-1015	A247 Set of 3	8.00	8.00
1015a	Souvenir sheet, #1013-1015	8.00	8.00

Europa stamps, 50th anniv. (in 2006).

Battle of Trafalgar, Bicent. A248

Designs: $20, Gun captain holding powder cartridge. $30, Admiral Horatio Nelson, vert. $50, British 12-pounder cannon. $60, HMS Africa, vert. $70, HMS Leviathan being attacked by the Intrepide, vert. $90, HMS Victory.

$200, HMS Africa at Port Royal, Jamaica.

Wmk. 352, Unwmkd. ($90)

2005, June 23 Litho. ***Perf. 13¼***

1016-1021 A248 Set of 6 12.00 12.00

Souvenir Sheet

Perf. 13½

1022 A248 $200 multi 10.00 10.00

No. 1021 has particles of wood from the HMS Victory embedded in areas covered by a thermographic process that produces a raised, shiny effect. No. 1022 contains one 44x44mm stamp.

Rotary International, Cent. — A249

2005, June 30 Wmk. 352 ***Perf. 13¾***

1023 A249 $30 multi 2.00 2.00

Pope John Paul II (1920-2005) — A250

Unwmk.

2005, Aug. 18 Litho. ***Perf. 14***

1024 A250 $30 multi 1.75 1.75

Battle of Trafalgar, Bicent. — A251

Designs: $50, HMS Victory. $90, Ships in battle, horiz. $100, Admiral Horatio Nelson.

Perf. 13¼

2005, Oct. 18 Litho. Unwmk.

1025-1027 A251 Set of 3 12.50 12.50

Mary Seacole (1805-81), Nurse — A252

Seacole and: $30, Herbal remedies and medicines. $50, Seacole Hall, University of the West Indies. $60, Crimean War soldiers. $70, Medals.

Wmk. 352

2005, Nov. 21 Litho. ***Perf. 13½***

1028-1031 A252 Set of 4 7.50 7.50

World AIDS Day — A253

2005, Dec. 1 ***Perf. 14¾x14***

1032 A253 $30 multi 1.50 1.50

Christmas — A254

Star of Bethlehem and poinsettia with various frame designs: $20, $30, $50, $80.

2005, Dec. 1

1033-1036 A254 Set of 4 6.75 6.75

Jessie Ripoll (Sister Mary Peter Claver), Founder of Alpha Schools — A255

2005, Dec. 12 ***Perf. 13½***

1037 A255 $30 multi 1.25 1.25

Alpha Schools, 125th anniv.

Buildings Type of 2005

Designs: $10, Court House, Morant Bay. $15, Spanish Town Square, St. Catherine. $20, Mico College. $25, Simms Building, Jamaica College. $50, Devon House, St. Andrew. $70, Ward Theater, Kingston. $90, Vale Royal, St. Andrew. $100, Falmouth Post Office.

Perf. 14x13¼

2006, May 12 Litho. Wmk. 352

No date inscription below design

1038	A245	$10 multi	.70	.40
a.		Inscribed "2008"	.35	.35
1039	A245	$15 multi	.60	.50
1040	A245	$20 multi	1.25	1.00
a.		Inscribed "2008"	.70	.65
1041	A245	$25 multi	.90	.80
1042	A245	$50 multi	2.75	1.75
a.		Inscribed "2008"	1.75	1.00
1043	A245	$70 multi	3.25	3.25
a.		Inscribed "2008"	2.25	1.75
1044	A245	$90 multi	4.50	4.50
a.		Inscribed "2008"	2.75	2.25
1045	A245	$100 multi	3.25	3.25
		Nos. 1038-1045 (8)	17.20	15.45

Self-Adhesive

Unwmk.

Serpentine Die Cut 13¼x14

1046	A245	$10 multi	.40	.40
1047	A245	$15 multi	.65	.65
1048	A245	$20 multi	.75	.75
1049	A245	$25 multi	.90	.90
1050	A245	$50 multi	2.00	2.00
1051	A245	$70 multi	2.50	2.50
1052	A245	$90 multi	3.00	3.00
1053	A245	$100 multi	3.25	3.25
		Nos. 1046-1053 (8)	13.45	13.45

Worldwide Fund for Nature (WWF) — A256

Black-billed Amazon parrot: $5, Chicks. $10, Head of adult bird. $30, Bird on branch. $50, Two birds.

Perf. 13¼x13½

2006, Nov. 30 Litho. Wmk. 352

1054-1057 A256 Set of 4 *7.00 7.00*

1057a Sheet, 4 each #1054-1057 *28.00 28.00*

Christmas A257

Flowers: $20, Cup and saucer. $30, Lignum vitae. $50, Neocogniauxia monophylla, vert. $60, Ghost orchid, vert.

Perf. 13¼x13¾, 13¾x13¼

2006, Nov. 30

1058-1061 A257 Set of 4 7.00 7.00

2007 ICC Cricket World Cup, West Indies — A258

Designs: No. 1062, $30, Courtney Walsh. No. 1063, $30, Collie Smith. $40, New Sabrina Park, horiz. $50, Like #1062. $60, Trelawney Multi-purpose Sports Complex, horiz.

$200, ICC Cricket World Cup.

Wmk. 352

2007, Feb. 28 Litho. ***Perf. 14***

1062-1066 A258 Set of 5 11.00 11.00

Souvenir Sheet

1067 A258 $200 multi 10.00 10.00

British Abolition of the Slave Trade, Bicent. — A259

Wmk. 352

2007, June 7 Litho. ***Perf. 14***

1068 A259 $30 multi 1.50 1.50

Scouting, Cent. — A260

Designs: $5, Boy scout, Jamaican flag, Scout salute. $10, Scouts, compass. $30, Scouts, lashed poles. $70, Scouts handling Jamaican flag, Scout making craft.

No. 1073, vert.: a, $50, Scouts on parade. b, $100, Lord Robert Baden-Powell blowing kudu horn.

2007, July 9 ***Perf. 13¾***

1069-1072 A260 Set of 4 5.00 5.00

Souvenir Sheet

1073 A260 Sheet of 2, #a-b 8.00 8.00

Christmas — A261

Flowers: $20, Tolumnia triquetra. $30, Broughtonia negrilensis, horiz. $50, Broughtonia sanguinea, horiz. $60, Spathelia sorbifolia.

Wmk. 352

2007, Nov. 9 Litho. ***Perf. 14***

1074-1077 A261 Set of 4 7.00 7.00

2008 Summer Olympics, Beijing — A262

Designs: $20, Fish, Asafa Powell. $60, Lanterns, Veronica Campbell-Brown.

No. 1079: a, Bamboo, Aleen Bailey, Veronica Campbell-Brown. b, Sherone Simpson, Tayna Lawrence, dragon.

Wmk. 352

2008, Apr. 30 Litho. ***Perf. 13¼***

1078	A262	$20 multi	1.00	1.00
1079	A262	$30 Horiz. pair, #a-b	3.00	3.00
1080	A262	$60 multi	3.00	3.00
		Nos. 1078-1080 (3)	7.00	7.00

University of Technology, 50th Anniv. — A263

2008, May 26 Litho. ***Perf. 14***

1081 A263 $30 multi 2.00 2.00

a. Souvenir sheet of 1 2.10 2.10

Associated Board of the Royal Schools of Music in Jamaica, Cent. — A264

Map of Jamaica and: $30, Piano keyboard. $70, Violin.

Wmk. 352

2008, Oct. 30 Litho. ***Perf. 14***

1082-1083 A264 Set of 2 5.00 5.00

Christmas — A265

Various ferns: $20, $30, $50, $60.

Wmk. 352

2008, Nov. 21 Litho. ***Perf. 13¾***

1084-1087 A265 Set of 4 7.00 7.00

George Headley (1909-83), Cricket Player — A266

Designs: $10, Head of Headley. $30, Headley in front of wickets. $200, Statue of Headley.

$250, Statue of Headley, Sabina Park, Kingston.

Wmk. 352

2009, Sept. 25 Litho. ***Perf. 14***

1088-1090 A266 Set of 3 *8.00* 8.00

Souvenir Sheet

Perf. 14¼x14

1091 A266 $250 multi 8.50 8.50

No. 1091 contains one 43x57mm stamp.

Christmas — A267

Paintings by Juanita Isabel Ramos: $20, Guardian Angel. $30, Madonna and Child. $50, Madonna and Flowers, horiz.

Wmk. 352

2009, Nov. 20 Litho. ***Perf. 13½***

1092-1094 A267 Set of 3 3.50 3.50

Christmas — A268

Musical groups: $40, NDTC Singers. $60, Kingston College Chapel Choir. $120, The University Singers. $160, The Jamaican Folk Singers.

Wmk. 352

2010, Dec. 13 Litho. *Perf. 13¾*
1095-1098 A268 Set of 4 11.00 11.00

Souvenir Sheet

Wedding of Prince William and Catherine Middleton — A269

2011, Apr. 29 *Perf. 14¾x14¼*
1099 A269 $400 multi 11.00 11.00

Lighthouses A270

Designs: $20, Negril Lighthouse. $50, Morant Point Lighthouse. $60, Lover's Leap Lighthouse, vert. $200, Galina Lighthouse, vert.

2011, July 4 *Perf. 14*
1100 A270 $20 multi .50 .50
a. Dated "2012" .50 .50
b. Dated "2013" .40 .40
c. Dated "2015" .35 .35
1101 A270 $50 multi 1.25 1.25
a. Dated "2012" 1.25 1.25
b. Dated "2013" 1.00 1.00
c. Dated "2015" .85 .85
1102 A270 $60 multi 1.40 1.40
a. Dated "2012" 1.40 1.40
b. Dated "2013" 1.25 1.25
c. Dated "2015" 1.00 1.00
d. Perf. 13½x13¼, dated "2018" .95 .95
1103 A270 $200 multi 4.75 4.75
a. Dated "2012" 4.75 4.75
b. Dated "2013" 4.00 4.00
c. Dated "2015" 3.25 3.25
Nos. 1100-1103 (4) 7.90 7.90

Issued: Nos. 1100a, 1101a, 1102a, 1103a, 3/23/12. Nos. 1100b, 1101b, 1102b, 1103b, 6/13/13. Nos. 1100c, 1101c, 112c, 1103c, 3/14/16.

See Nos. 1122-1125.

Independence, 50th Anniv. — A271

Designs: $60, Fiftieth anniversary emblem. $120, Coat of arms, vert.

Perf. 14x14¾, 14¾x14

2012, Aug. 31
1104-1105 A271 Set of 2 4.25 4.25

Medalists at 2008 Summer Olympics — A272

Designs: No. 1106, $60, Usain Bolt, Men's 100-meter and 200-meter gold medalist (orange panel). No. 1107, $60, Melaine Walker, Women's 400-meter hurdles gold medalist (red panel). No. 1108, $60, Veronica Campbell-Brown, women's 200-meter gold medalist (blue panel). No. 1109, $60, Men's 4x100-meter relay team (Bolt, Michael Frater, Nesta Carter, Asafa Powell) (green panel). No. 1110, $60, Shelly-Ann Fraser, gold medalist, Sherone Simpson and Kerron Stewart, silver medalists in women's 100-meter (black panel).

2013, May 3 *Perf. 13¼*
1106-1110 A272 Set of 5 6.25 6.25

Christmas — A273

Bells and: $20, Night-blooming cereus. $60, Coffee berries and flowers. $120, Century palm. $160, Cactus flower.

Wmk. 352

2013, Dec. 6 Litho. *Perf. 13¼*
1111-1114 A273 Set of 4 7.50 7.50

St. Andrew Parish Church, 350th Anniv. A274

Various views of church's exterior: $20, $60, $120.

$200, Stained-glass windows, vert.

Perf. 14¼x14¾

2014, Dec. 11 Litho.
1115-1117 A274 Set of 3 3.50 3.50

Souvenir Sheet

Perf. 14¾x14¼

1118 A274 $200 multi 3.50 3.50

2016 Summer Olympics, Rio de Janeiro — A275

No. 1119: a, Shelly-Ann Fraser-Price with medal. b, Usain Bolt with medal.

$120, Fraser-Price and Bolt in track uniforms. $300, Fraser-Price and Bolt with medal ribbons around necks.

Wmk. 352

2016, July 3 Litho. *Perf. 14*
1119 Horiz. pair 1.90 1.90
a.-b. A275 $60 Either single .95 .95
c. Souvenir sheet of 2, #1119a-1119b 1.90 1.90
1120 A275 $120 multi 1.90 1.90
1121 A275 $300 multi 4.75 4.75
Nos. 1119-1121 (3) 8.55 8.55

Lighthouses Type of 2011

Designs: $40, Folly Lighthouse, vert. $140, Rosehall Lighthouse. $180, Plumb Point Lighthouse, vert. $300, Portland Point Lighthouse.

2016 Litho. Wmk. 352 *Perf. 14*
1122 A270 $40 multi .65 .65
1123 A270 $140 multi 2.25 2.25
1124 A270 $180 multi 2.75 2.75
1125 A270 $300 multi 4.75 4.75
Nos. 1122-1125 (4) 10.40 10.40

Dated 2015.

Butterflies — A276

No. 1126: a, Giant swallowtail. b, Monarch.

Perf. 13¼

2016, Oct. 28 Litho. Unwmk.
1126 A276 $60 Horiz. pair, #a-b 1.90 1.90

See Mexico Nos. 3029-3030.

Jamaica Civil Service Association, Cent. — A277

Denominations: $60, $120, $140, $180, $200.

Perf. 13¼x13½

2019, May 6 Litho. Unwmk.
1127-1131 A277 Set of 5 10.50 10.50

Louise "Miss Lou" Bennett-Coverley (1919-2006), Poet — A278

Various photographs of Bennett-Coverley: $20, $50, $60, $500.

Perf. 13¼x13½

2020, Sept. 7 Litho. Unwmk.
1132-1135 A278 Set of 4 9.00 9.00
1135a Souvenir sheet of 4, #1132-1135 9.00 9.00

Jamaica Post Office, 350th Anniv. A279

No. 1136: a, Cross Road Post Office, 1920. b, Central Sorting Office Headquarters, Kingston, 2020. c, Mobile Post and mail delivery vans. d, Postmen at General Post Office, Kingston. e, Gordon Town Post Office, 2020. f, Ocho Rios Post Office, 2019. g, Royal mail van delivery. h, Spanish Town Post Office, 2020. i, Postmen on motorbikes. j, Mail dispatch, Constant Spring Post Office, 1930s. k, Mail sorting. l, Port Royal Post Office, 2020. m, Airmail arrival in Jamaica. n, Stonehenge Post Office. o, Mobile Post van. p, Falmouth Post Office, 1815. q, Mail delivery at the Mona Housing Estate, Kingston, 1961. r, Black River Post Office, 2020.

$350, 350th anniv. emblem.

Wmk. 352

2021, Oct. 29 Litho. *Perf. 14*
1136 A279 Sheet of 18 65.00 65.00
a.-c. $60 Any single .75 .75
d.-f. $100 Any single 1.30 1.30
g.-i. $120 Any single 1.60 1.60
j.-l. $180 Any single 2.40 2.40
m.-o. $200 Any single 2.60 2.60
p.-r. $1000 Any single 13.00 13.00
s. Souvenir sheet of 6, #1136d, 1136g, 1136i, 1136j, 1136m, 1136o 12.50 12.50

Souvenir Sheet

1137 A279 $350 multi 4.50 4.50

No. 1137 contains one 50x30mm stamp in the shape of a parallelogram.

Independence, 60th Anniv. — A280

Panel color: $60, Bister. $120, Green.

Perf. 13¼x13½

2022, July 21 Litho. Wmk. 352
1138-1139 A280 Set of 2 2.40 2.40

SEMI-POSTAL STAMPS

Native Girl — SP1

Native Boy — SP2

Native Boy and Girl — SP3

1923, Nov. 1 Engr. *Perf. 12*
B1 SP1 ½p green & black 1.25 *6.00*
B2 SP2 1p car & black 4.00 *13.50*
B3 SP3 2½p blue & black 22.50 *22.00*
Nos. B1-B3 (3) 27.75 *41.50*

Each stamp was sold for ½p over face value. The surtax benefited the Child Saving League of Jamaica.

Catalogue values for unused stamps in this section, from this point to the end of the section, are for Never Hinged items.

Nos. 694-697 Surcharged in Black

Wmk. 352

1988, Nov. 11 Litho. *Perf. 14*
B4 A164 25c +25c multi .30 .25
B5 A164 45c +45c multi .40 .25
B6 A164 $4 +$4 multi 2.25 *3.00*
B7 A164 $5 +$5 multi 2.50 *3.00*
Nos. B4-B7 (4) 5.45 6.50

Red Surcharge

B4a A164 25c + 25c .30 .25
B5a A164 45c + 45c .40 .25
B6a A164 $4 + $4 2.25 *3.00*
B7a A164 $5 + $5 2.50 *3.00*
Nos. B4a-B7a (4) 5.45 6.50

WAR TAX STAMPS

Regular Issues of 1906-19 Overprinted

1916 Wmk. 3 *Perf. 14*
MR1 A14 ½p green 1.00 .75
a. Without period 20.00 *27.50*
b. Double overprint 140.00 *160.00*
c. Inverted overprint 130.00 *150.00*
d. As "c," without period 350.00
MR2 A17 3p violet, *yel* 4.50 *25.00*
a. Without period 45.00 *100.00*

Surface-colored Paper

MR3 A17 3p violet, *yel* 37.50 *52.50*
Nos. MR1-MR3 (3) 43.00 *78.25*

Regular Issues of 1906-18 Overprinted

MR4 A14 ½p green .25 .30
a. Without period 22.50 *57.50*
b. Pair, one without ovpt. 6,500. 5,250.
c. "R" inserted by hand 1,800. 1,500.
d. "WAR" only 125.00
MR5 A17 1½p orange .75 .35
a. Without period 7.50 *8.50*
b. "TAMP" 250.00 *240.00*
c. "S" inserted by hand 450.00 450.00
d. "R" omitted 3,600. 3,100.
e. "R" inserted by hand 1,550. 1,250.
MR6 A17 3p violet, *yel* 10.00 1.50
a. Without period 75.00 *75.00*
b. "TAMP" 1,000. 1,000.
c. "S" inserted by hand 225.00 225.00

d.	Inverted overprint	325.00	250.00
e.	As "a," inverted		
	Nos. MR4-MR6 (3)	11.00	2.15

Regular Issues of 1906-19 Overprinted

1917, Mar.

MR7	A14 ½p green	3.00	.35
a.	Without period	18.50	*30.00*
b.	Overprinted on back instead of face	290.00	
c.	Inverted overprint	27.50	57.50
MR8	A17 1½p orange	1.00	.25
a.	Without period	5.00	*20.00*
b.	Double overprint	85.00	*100.00*
c.	Inverted overprint	85.00	85.00
d.	As "a," inverted	*400.00*	
MR9	A17 3p violet, *yel*	3.50	*1.75*
a.	Without period	30.00	*52.50*
b.	Vertical overprint	425.00	425.00
c.	Inverted overprint	160.00	190.00
d.	As "a," inverted	*450.00*	
e.	Pair, overprint omitted on one	5,000.	
	Nos. MR7-MR9 (3)	7.50	2.35

There are many minor varieties of Nos. MR1-MR9.

Regular Issues of 1906-19 Overprinted in Red

1919, Oct. 4

MR10	A14 ½p green	1.00	1.00
MR11	A17 3p violet, *yel*	15.00	4.00
a.	3p pale pur, *buff*	8.00	2.00

OFFICIAL STAMPS

No. 16 Overprinted in Black

Type I — Word 15 to 16mm long.
Type II — Word 17 to 17½mm long.

1890 **Wmk. 2** ***Perf. 14***

O1	A7 ½p green (II)	18.50	2.50
a.	Type I	47.50	30.00
b.	Inverted overprint (II)	110.00	*120.00*
c.	Double overprint (II)	110.00	*120.00*
d.	Dbl. ovpt., one invtd. (II)	575.00	575.00
e.	Dbl. ovpt., one vert. (II)	1,100.	
f.	Double overprint (I)	825.00	

Missing "O," "L" or one or both "I's" known.

No. 16 and Type of 1889 Overprinted

1890-91

O2	A7 ½p green ('91)	10.00	1.80
O3	A10 1p carmine rose	8.50	2.00
O4	A10 2p slate	32.50	2.00
	Nos. O2-O4 (3)	51.00	5.80

JAPAN

jə-'pan

LOCATION — North Pacific Ocean, east of China
GOVT. — Constitutional monarchy
AREA — 142,726 sq. mi.
POP. — 126,182,077 (1999 est.)
CAPITAL — Tokyo

1000 Mon = 10 Sen
100 Sen = 1 Yen (or En)
10 Rin = 1 Sen

Catalogue values for unused stamps in this country are for Never Hinged items, beginning with Scott 375 in the regular postage section, Scott B8 in the semi-postal section, and Scott C9 in the airpost section.

Watermarks

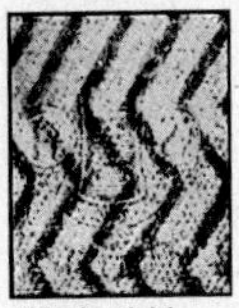

Wmk. 141 — Zigzag Lines

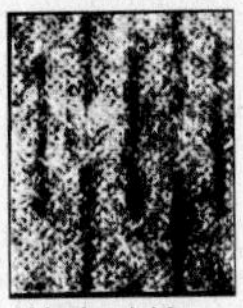

Wmk. 142 — Parallel Lines

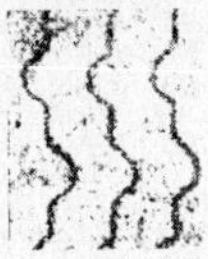

Wmk. 257 — Curved Wavy Lines

After 1945, Wmk. 257 exists also in a narrow spacing on a small number of issues.

Counterfeits of Nos. 1-71 are plentiful. Some are excellent and deceive many collectors.

Nos. 1-54A were printed from plates of 40 with individually engraved subjects. Each stamp in the sheet is slightly different.

Pair of Dragons Facing Characters of Value — A1

Plate I

Plate II

48 mon:
Plate I — Solid dots in inner border.
Plate II — Tiny circles replace dots.

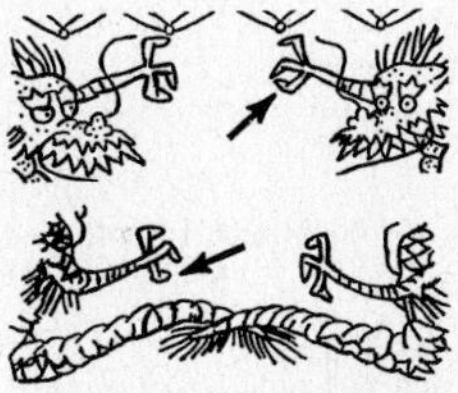

Plate I

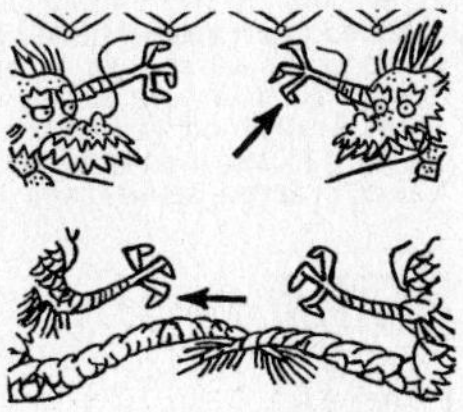

Plate II

100 mon:
Plate I — Lowest dragon claw at upper right and at lower left point upward.
Plate II — Same two claws point downward.

Plate I

Plate II

200 mon:
Plate I — Dot in upper left corner.
Plate II — No dot. (Some Plate I copies show dot faintly; these can be mistaken for Plate II.)

Plate I

Plate II

500 mon:
Plate I — Lower right corner of Greek-type border incomplete
Plate II — Short horizontal line completes corner border pattern.

Unwmk.

1871, Apr. 20 Engr. ***Imperf.***

Native Laid Paper Without Gum

Denomination in Black

1	A1	48m brown (I)	225.	225.
a.		48m red brown (I)	375.	375.
b.		Wove paper (I)	300.	300.
c.		48m brown (II)	325.	325.
d.		Wove paper (II)	400.	400.
2	A1	100m blue (I)	225.	225.
a.		Wove paper (I)	350.	350.
b.		Plate II	550.	550.
c.		Wove paper (II)	800.	800.
3	A1	200m ver (I)	350.	325.
a.		Wove paper (I)	500.	425.
b.		Plate II	2,500.	2,000.
c.		Wove paper (II)		*4,000.*
4	A1	500m bl grn (I)	575.	550.
a.		500m greenish blue (I)	650.	625.
b.		500m green (I)	2,000.	1,400.
c.		500m yellow green (I)	3,500.	1,500.
d.		Wove paper (I)	725.	625.
e.		500m blue green (II)	750.	*4,000.*
f.		500m greenish blue (II)	750.	*4,000.*
g.		Wove paper (II)	2,750.	*5,000.*
h.		Denomination inverted (I)		*175,000.*

Perforations, Nos. 5-8

Perforations on Nos. 5-8 generally are rough and irregular due to the perforating equipment used and the quality of the paper. Values are for stamps with rough perfs that touch the frameline on one or more sides.

Dragons and Denomination — A1a

½ sen:
Plate I — Same as 48m Plate II. Measures not less than 19.8x19.8mm. Some subjects on this plate measure 20.3x20.2mm.
Plate II — Same as 48m Plate II. Measures not more than 19.7x19.7mm. Some subjects measure 19.3x18.7mm.

Plate I & II

Plate III

1 sen:
Plate I — Same as 100m Plate I. Narrow space between frameline and Greek-type border.
Plate II — Same as 100m Plate II. Same narrow space between frameline and border.
Plate III — Space between frameline and border is much wider. Frameline thinner. Shading on dragon heads heavier than on Plates I and II.

Native Laid Paper
With or Without Gum

1872 ***Perf. 9-12 & compound***

Denomination in Black

5	A1a	½s brown (II)	110.00	100.00
a.		½s red brown (II)	125.00	110.00
b.		½s gray brown (II)	125.00	110.00
c.		Wove paper (II)	725.00	675.00
d.		½s brown (I)	200.00	200.00
e.		½s red brown (I)	200.00	200.00
f.		½s gray brown (I)	200.00	200.00
g.		Wove paper (I)	275.00	275.00
6	A1a	1s blue (II)	375.00	325.00
a.		Wove paper (II)	675.00	675.00
b.		Plate I	1,400.	*3,000.*
c.		Wove paper (I)	*7,000.*	
d.		Plate III	*15,000.*	2,500.
e.		Wove paper (III)		*7,500.*
7	A1a	2s vermilion	500.00	475.00
a.		Wove paper	625.00	575.00
8	A1a	5s blue green	800.00	725.00
a.		5s yellow green	850.00	800.00
b.		Wove paper	900.00	900.00

In 1896 the government made imperforate imitations of Nos. 6-7 to include in a presentation book.

Beginning with No. 9, Japanese stamps intended for distribution outside the Postal Ministry were overprinted with three characters, as shown above, reading "Mihon" (specimen). These specimens were included in ministry announcements detailing forthcoming issues and were in presentation booklets given to government officials, foreign governments, etc.

Expect perforations on Nos. 9-71 to be rough and irregular.

Imperial Crest and Branches of Kiri Tree — A2

Dragons and Chrysanthemum Crest — A3

Imperial Chrysanthemum Crest — A4

Imperial Crest and Branches of Kiri Tree — A5

Perf. 9 to 13 and Compound

1872-73

Native Wove or Laid Paper of Varying Thickness

9	A2	½s brn, *hard wove*	25.00	20.00
a.		Upper character in left label has 2 diagonal top strokes missing	2,100.	1,250.
b.		Laid paper	80.00	—
c.		As "a," laid paper	2,200.	—
d.		½s gray brown, *soft porous native wove*	80.00	—

Nos. 9, 9a are on stiff, brittle wove paper. Nos. 9b, 9c and 9d on a soft, fibrous paper. Nos. 9b, 9c and 9d probably were never put in use, though genuine used examples do exist.

10	A2	1s blue, *wove*	50.00	26.00
a.		Laid paper	52.50	29.00
11	A2	2s ver, *wove*	100.00	50.00
12	A2	2s dull rose, *laid*	75.00	35.00
a.		Wove paper	100.00	50.00
13	A2	2s yel, *laid* ('73)	75.00	21.00
a.		Wove paper ('73)	175.00	26.00
14	A2	4s rose, *laid* ('73)	67.50	26.00
a.		Wove paper ('73)	210.00	32.00
15	A3	10s blue grn, *wove*	250.00	150.00
16	A3	10s yel grn, *laid*	400.00	275.00
a.		Wove paper ('73)	1,150.	500.00
17	A4	20s lilac, *wove*	600.00	350.00
a.		20s violet, *wove*	750.00	350.00
b.		20s red violet, *laid*		—
18	A5	30s gray, *wove*	625.00	375.00

See Nos. 24-25, 30-31, 37-39, 51-52.

1874 **Foreign Wove Paper**

24	A2	4s rose	650.	300.
25	A5	30s gray	*30,000.*	*7,500.*

A6

A7

A8

Design A6 differs from A2 by the addition of a syllabic character in a box covering crossed kiri branches above SEN. Stamps of design A6 differ for each value in border and spandrel designs.

In design A7, the syllabic character appears just below the buckle. In design A8, it appears in an oval frame at bottom center below SE of SEN. Design A3 and A4 have a syllabic character immediately below the central design, above the 'S' of 'SEN'.

With Syllabic Characters

イロハニホヘトチ
i ro ha ni ho he to chi
1 2 3 4 5 6 7 8

リヌルヲワカヨタ
ri nu ru wo wa ka yo ta
9 10 11 12 13 14 15 16

レソツ子ナラム
re so tsu ne na ra mu
17 18 19 20 21 22 23

Perf. 9½ to 12½ and Compound

1874 Native Laid or Wove Paper

28	A6	2s yel (Syll. 1)	27,000.	400.00
		Syllabic 16	425.00	
29	A7	6s vio brn (Syll. 1)	1,700.	475.00
		Syllabic 2	1,900.	500.00
		Syllabic 3	20,000.	1,100.
		Syllabic 4	20,000.	600.00
		Syllabic 5	20,000.	600.00
		Syllabic 6	20,000.	700.00
		Syllabic 7	25,000.	550.00
		Syllabic 8	25,000.	550.00
		Syllabic 9	20,000.	700.00
		Syllabic 10		3,500.
		Syllabic 11		3,000.
		Syllabic 12	20,000.	1,900.
30	A4	20s red vio (Syll. 3)	10,000.	
		Syllabic 1	150,000.	
		Syllabic 2	10,000.	
31	A5	30s gray (Syll. 1)	3,000.	3,000.
a.		Very thin laid paper	3,000.	3,000.

No. 30, syll. 1, comes only with small, eliptical specimen dot (*Sumiten*, "secret mark").

Perf. 11 to 12½ and Compound

1874 Foreign Wove Paper

32	A6	½s brn (Syll. 1)	25.00	20.00
		Syllabic 2	40.00	40.00
33	A6	1s blue (Syll. 4)	160.00	40.00
		Syllabic 1	150.00	35.00
		Syllabic 2	225.00	40.00
		Syllabic 3	200.00	40.00
		Syllabic 5	650.00	150.00
		Syllabic 6, 9	150.00	45.00
		Syllabic 7	350.00	50.00
		Syllabic 8	150.00	40.00
		Syllabic 10	225.00	70.00
		Syllabic 11	215.00	60.00
		Syllabic 12	250.00	65.00
34	A6	2s yel (Syll. 2-4, 15, 17, 20)	175.00	30.00
		Syllabic 1	400.00	35.00
		Syllabic 5	450.00	30.00
		Syllabic 6	2,000.	50.00
		Syllabic 7	2,000.	30.00
		Syllabic 8	200.00	55.00
		Syllabic 9	200.00	35.00
		Syllabic 10	2,750.	50.00
		Syllabic 11	200.00	30.00
		Syllabic 12,22	2,650.	30.00
		Syllabic 13	2,500.	30.00
		Syllabic 14	2,650.	45.00
		Syllabic 16	2,500.	35.00
		Syllabic 18,19	200.00	30.00
		Syllabic 21	250.00	30.00
		Syllabic 23	265.00	30.00
35	A6	4s rose (Syll. 1)	3,500.	475.00
36	A7	6s vio brn (Syll. 16)	175.00	65.00
		Syllabic 10	650.00	650.00
		Syllabic 11	500.00	
		Syllabic 13	14,000.	5,000.
		Syllabic 14	300.00	275.00
		Syllabic 15	25,000.	3,000.
		Syllabic 17	225.00	80.00
		Syllabic 18	325.00	110.00
37	A3	10s yel grn (Syll. 2)	200.00	65.00
		Syllabic 1	525.00	80.00
		Syllabic 3	1,000.	300.00
38	A4	20s violet (Syll. 5)	425.00	90.00
		Syllabic 4	450.00	95.00
39	A5	30s gray (Syll. 1)	475.00	95.00

1875 ***Perf. 9 to 13 and Compound***

40	A6	½s gray (Syll. 2, 3)	25.00	20.00
		Syllabic 4	30.00	1,000.
41	A6	1s brn (Syll. 15)	35.00	22.50
		Syllabic 5	375.00	50.00
		Syllabic 7	2,250.	275.00
		Syllabic 8	32,500.	275.00
		Syllabic 12	1,300.	225.00
		Syllabic 13	50.00	22.50
		Syllabic 14	50.00	22.50
		Syllabic 16-17	45.00	25.00
42	A6	4s grn (Syll. 1)	130.00	29.00
		Syllabic 2	200.00	29.00
		Syllabic 3	130.00	29.00
43	A7	6s org (Syll. 16,17)	90.00	27.50
		Syllabic 10	175.00	55.00
		Syllabic 11	150.00	50.00
		Syllabic 13	325.00	45.00
		Syllabic 14	160.00	32.50
		Syllabic 15		162,500.
44	A8	6s org (Syll. 20)	110.00	27.50
		Syllabic 19	125.00	27.50
		Syllabic 21	100.00	27.50
		Syllabic 22	4,250.	1,750.

Dragons
A9

Wild Goose
A10

Wagtail — A11

Imperial Crest — A11a

Kiri Branches — A11b

Goshawk — A12

45	A9	10s ultra (Syll. 4)	180.00	30.00
		Syllabic 5	4,250.	375.00
46	A10	12s rose (Syll. 1)	375.00	160.00
		Syllabic 2	500.00	185.00
		Syllabic 3	3,500.	500.00
47	A11	15s lilac (Syll. 1)	350.00	160.00
		Syllabic 2	400.00	175.00
		Syllabic 3	350.00	190.00
48	A11a	20s rose (Syll. 8)	140.00	22.50
		Syllabic 9		—
49	A11b	30s vio (Syll. 2-4)	175.00	70.00
50	A12	45s lake (Syll. 1)	500.00	240.00
		Syllabic 2	1,250.	550.00
		Syllabic 3	1,200.	425.00

Issued: No. 46, syll. 2, 1882; No. 46, syll. 3, 1883; others, 1875.

The 1s brown on laid paper, type A6, formerly listed as No. 50A, is one of several stamps of the preceding issue which exist on a laid type paper. They are difficult to identify and mainly of interest to specialists.

1875 Without Syllabic Characters

51	A2	1s brown	7,500.	675.00
52	A2	4s dark gray green	375.00	100.00

Branches of Kiri Tree Tied with Ribbon
A13

Imperial Crest and Kiri Branches
A14

1875-76

53	A13	1s brown	75.00	18.00
54	A13	2s yellow	110.00	18.00
54A	A14	5s green ('76)	220.00	110.00
		Nos. 53-54A (3)	405.00	146.00

Postal Cancellations

Bota Cancel

Postal Cancel

Telegraph Cancellation

Nos. 58, 61-62, 64-65, 71-84 are found with telegraph or telephone office cancellations. These sell at considerably lower prices than postally used examples. Examples with bota cancels are valued the same as postally used examples.

A15

A16

Imperial Crest, Star and Kiri Branches
A17

Sun, Kikumon and Kiri Branches
A18

Perf. 8 to 14 and Compound

1876-77 Typo.

55	A15	5r slate	25.00	15.00
56	A16	1s black	50.00	4.75
a.		Horiz. pair, imperf. btwn.		
57	A16	2s brown ol	90.00	4.50
58	A16	4s blue grn	50.00	4.00
a.		4s green	50.00	4.00
59	A17	5s brown	65.00	20.00
60	A17	6s orange ('77)	200.00	85.00
61	A17	8s vio brn ('77)	75.00	5.50
62	A17	10s blue ('77)	55.00	2.50
63	A17	12s rose ('77)	240.00	160.00
64	A18	15s yel grn ('77)	150.00	2.50
65	A18	20s dk blue ('77)	160.00	15.00
66	A18	30s violet ('77)	250.00	110.00
a.		30s red violet	275.00	110.00
67	A18	45s carmine ('77)	700.00	600.00

1879

68	A16	1s maroon	17.50	1.25
69	A16	2s dk violet	70.00	2.50
70	A16	3s orange	75.00	30.00
71	A18	50s carmine	250.00	17.50
		Nos. 68-71 (4)	412.50	51.25

1883

72	A16	1s green	11.00	1.25
73	A16	2s car rose	16.00	.30
74	A17	5s ultra	27.50	1.10
		Nos. 72-74 (3)	54.50	2.65

Imperial Crest and Kiri Branches
A19

Kikumon
A20

1888-92

75	A15	5r gray blk ('89)	6.00	.85
76	A16	3s lilac rose ('92)	22.50	.75
77	A16	4s olive bis	17.50	.75
78	A17	8s blue lilac	35.00	2.50
79	A17	10s brown org	25.00	.75
80	A18	15s purple	60.00	1.00
81	A18	20s orange	75.00	3.00
a.		20s yellow	75.00	3.00
82	A19	25s blue green	110.00	3.25
83	A18	50s brown	120.00	5.75
84	A20	1y carmine	160.00	6.25
		Nos. 75-84 (10)	631.00	24.85

Stamps of types A16-A18 differ for each value, in backgrounds and ornaments.

Cranes and Imperial Crest — A21

Perf. 11½ to 13 and Compound

1894, Mar. 9

85	A21	2s carmine	19.00	3.00
86	A21	5s ultra	30.00	14.00

25th wedding anniv. of Emperor Meiji (Mutsuhito) and Empress Haru.

Gen. Yoshihisa Kitashirakawa
A22 A23

Field Marshal Akihito Arisugawa
A24 A25

1896, Aug. 1 Engr.

87	A22	2s rose	22.50	4.75
88	A23	5s deep ultra	45.00	4.75
89	A24	2s rose	22.50	4.75
90	A25	5s deep ultra	45.00	4.75
		Nos. 87-90 (4)	135.00	19.00

Victory in Chinese-Japanese War (1894-95).

A26

A27

A28

A29

Perf. 11½ to 14 and Compound

1899-1907 Typo.

91	A26	5r gray	14.00	2.25
92	A26	½s gray ('01)	7.50	.25
93	A26	1s lt red brn	10.00	.30
94	A26	1½s ultra ('00)	28.00	1.75
95	A26	1½s violet ('06)	20.00	.55
a.		Booklet pane of 6	500.00	
96	A26	2s lt green	20.00	.30
a.		Booklet pane of 6	130.00	
97	A26	3s violet brn	20.00	.35
a.		Double impression		
98	A26	3s rose ('06)	12.00	.30
a.		Booklet pane of 6	500.00	
99	A26	4s rose	14.00	2.25
a.		4s pink ('06)	37.50	4.25
b.		As No. 99, booklet pane of 6	125.00	
100	A26	5s orange yel	27.50	.40
101	A27	6s maroon ('07)	50.00	5.00
a.		Booklet pane of 6	500.00	
102	A27	8s olive grn	60.00	7.50
103	A27	10s deep blue	24.00	.30
a.		Booklet pane of 6	200.00	
104	A27	15s purple	80.00	3.50
105	A27	20s red orange	47.50	.30
106	A28	25s blue green	80.00	1.50
107	A28	50s red brown	90.00	2.25
108	A29	1y carmine	140.00	3.25
		Nos. 91-108 (18)	744.50	32.30

For overprints see Nos. M1, Offices in China, 1-18, Offices in Korea, 1-14.

Boxes for Rice Cakes and Marriage Certificates — A30

Perf. 11½ to 12½ and Compound

1900, May 10

109	A30	3s carmine	30.00	1.50

Wedding of the Crown Prince Yoshihito and Princess Sadako.

For overprints see Offices in China No. 19, Offices in Korea No. 15.

Symbols of Korea and Japan — A31

1905, July 1

110	A31	3s rose red	110.00	25.00

Issued to commemorate the amalgamation of the postal services of Japan and Korea. Korean stamps were withdrawn from sale June 30, 1905, but remained valid until Aug. 31. No. 110 was used in the Korea and China Offices of Japan, as well as in Japan proper.

Field-piece and Japanese Flag — A32

1906, Apr. 29

111 A32 1½s blue 40.00 6.50
112 A32 3s carmine rose 85.00 25.00

Triumphal military review following the Russo-Japanese War.

Empress Jingo — A33

1908 **Engr.**

113 A33 5y green 1,200. 11.00
114 A33 10y dark violet 1,750. 15.00

The frame of No. 114 differs slightly from the illustration.
See Nos. 146-147.
For overprints see Offices in China Nos. 20-21, 48-49.

A34

A35

A36

Perf. 12, 12x13, 13x13½

1913 **Typo.** **Unwmk.**

115 A34 ½s brown 9.00 1.50
116 A34 1s orange 17.50 1.50
117 A34 1½s lt blue 25.00 2.50
a. Booklet pane of 6 600.00
118 A34 2s green 27.50 1.50
a. Booklet pane of 6 1,200.
119 A34 3s rose 35.00 1.50
a. Booklet pane of 6 750.00
120 A35 4s red 40.00 17.50
a. Booklet pane of 6 350.00
121 A35 5s violet 47.50 3.00
122 A35 10s deep blue 120.00 2.00
a. Booklet pane of 6 750.00
123 A35 20s claret 150.00 3.50
124 A35 25s olive green 140.00 6.00
125 A36 1y yel grn & mar 650.00 40.00
Nos. 115-125 (11) 1,262. 80.50

1914-25 **Wmk. 141** **Granite Paper**
Size: 19x22½mm ("Old Die")

127 A34 ½s brown 4.50 .25
128 A34 1s orange 5.00 .25
129 A34 1½s blue 5.50 .25
a. Booklet pane of 6 100.00
d. As "a," imperf.
130 A34 2s green 7.50 .30
a. Booklet pane of 6 150.00
131 A34 3s rose 4.00 .30
a. Booklet pane of 6 100.00
132 A35 4s red 25.00 2.25
a. Booklet pane of 6 160.00
133 A35 5s violet 17.50 .75
134 A35 6s brown ('19) 37.50 7.00
136 A35 8s gray ('19) 32.50 17.50
137 A35 10s deep blue 22.50 .30
a. Booklet pane of 6 200.00
138 A35 13s olive brn ('25) 40.00 6.00
139 A35 20s claret 120.00 2.00
140 A35 25s olive grn 22.50 2.00
141 A36 30s org brn ('19) 30.00 1.50
143 A36 50s dk brown ('19) 50.00 2.25
145 A36 1y yel grn & mar 150.00 2.50
b. Imperf., pair
146 A33 5y green 400.00 6.00
147 A33 10y violet 600.00 11.00
Nos. 127-147 (18) 1,574. 62.40

"New Die" Size: 18½x22mm (Flat Plate) or 18½x22½mm (Rotary)

1924-33

127a A34 ½s brown 3.75 2.25
128a A34 1s orange 3.75 2.25
129b A34 1½s blue 4.25 .30
c. Bklt. pane of 6 ('30) 40.00
131b A34 3s rose 3.50 .30
c. Bklt. pane of 6 ('28) 40.00
133a A35 5s violet 35.00 .30
135 A35 7s red org ('30) 18.00 .40
138a A35 13s bister brn ('25) 13.00 .40
140a A35 25s olive green 100.00 1.25
142 A36 30s org & grn ('29) 40.00 .60
144 A36 50s yel brn & dk bl ('29) 17.50 .90
145a A36 1y yel grn & mar 140.00 1.10
Nos. 127a-145a (11) 378.75 10.05

See Nos. 212-213, 239-241, 243, 245, 249-252, 255. For overprints see Nos. C1-C2, M2-M5, Offices in China, 22-47.

Ceremonial Cap — A37

Imperial Throne — A38

Enthronement Hall, Kyoto — A39

Perf. 12½

1915, Nov. 10 **Typo.** **Unwmk.**

148 A37 1½s red & blk 4.00 .80
149 A38 3s orange & vio 5.50 1.25

Engr.

Perf. 12x12½

150 A39 4s carmine rose 22.50 14.00
151 A39 10s ultra 42.50 18.00
Nos. 148-151 (4) 74.50 34.05

Enthronement of Emperor Yoshihito.

Mandarin Duck — A40

Ceremonial Cap — A41

1916, Nov. 3 **Typo.** ***Perf. 12½***

152 A40 1½s grn, red & yel 4.25 1.75
153 A40 3s red & yellow 8.00 2.00
154 A41 10s ultra & dk bl 800.00 300.00

Nomination of the Prince Heir Apparent, later Emperor Hirohito.

A42

Dove and Olive Branch — A43

Perf. 12, 12½, 13½x13

1919, July 1 **Engr.**

155 A42 1½s dark brown 3.00 1.25
156 A43 3s gray green 3.25 2.00
157 A42 4s rose 9.00 6.50
158 A43 10s dark blue 25.00 17.50
Nos. 155-158 (4) 40.25 27.25

Restoration of peace after World War I.

Census Officer, A.D. 652 — A44

Perf. 12½

1920, Sept. 25 **Typo.** **Unwmk.**

159 A44 1½s red violet 7.50 5.50
160 A44 3s vermilion 9.00 6.00

Taking of the 1st modern census in Japan. Not available for foreign postage except to China.

Meiji Shrine, Tokyo — A45

1920, Nov. 1 **Engr.**

161 A45 1½s dull violet 3.75 1.75
162 A45 3s rose 3.75 1.75

Dedication of the Meiji Shrine. Not available for foreign postage except to China.

National and Postal Flags — A46

Ministry of Communications Building, Tokyo — A47

Typographed (A46), Engraved (A47)

1921, Apr. 20 ***Perf. 12½, 13x13½***

163 A46 1½s gray grn & red 3.25 1.75
164 A47 3s violet brn 4.00 2.25
165 A46 4s rose & red 47.50 37.50
166 A47 10s dark blue 275.00 185.00
Nos. 163-166 (4) 329.75 226.50

50th anniv. of the establishment of postal service and Japanese postage stamps.

Battleships "Katori" and "Kashima" — A48

1921, Sept. 3 **Litho.** ***Perf. 12½***

167 A48 1½s violet 3.25 1.75
168 A48 3s olive green 3.00 1.75
169 A48 4s rose red 35.00 20.00
170 A48 10s deep blue 47.50 27.50
Nos. 167-170 (4) 88.75 51.00

Return of Crown Prince Hirohito from his European visit.

Mount Fuji — A49

Granite Paper
Size: 18½x22mm ("New Die")

Perf. 13x13½

1930-37 **Typo.** **Wmk. 141**

171 A49 4s green ('37) 4.25 .80
172 A49 4s orange 12.00 .50
174 A49 8s olive green 19.00 .45
175a A49 20s blue ('37) 30.00 30.00
176 A49 20s brown violet 85.00 .50
Nos. 171-176 (5) 150.25 32.25

1922-29
Size: 19x22½mm ("Old Die")

171a A49 4s green 12.00 3.00
172a A49 4s orange ('29) 110.00 11.00
173 A49 8s rose 22.50 7.50
174a A49 8s olive green ('29) 275.00 90.00

175 A49 20s deep blue 35.00 1.00
176a A49 20s brown vio ('29) 110.00 2.25
Nos. 171a-176a (6) 564.50 114.75

See Nos. 242, 246, 248.

Mt. Niitaka, Taiwan — A50

Perf. 12½

1923, Apr. 16 **Unwmk.** **Engr.**

177 A50 1½s orange 12.50 9.50
178 A50 3s dark violet 17.50 8.50

1st visit of Crown Prince Hirohito to Taiwan. The stamps were sold only in Taiwan, but were valid throughout the empire.

Cherry Blossoms A51

Sun and Dragonflies A52

Without Gum; Granite Paper

1923 **Wmk. 142** **Litho.** ***Imperf.***

179 A51 ½s gray 4.50 4.25
180 A51 1½s lt blue 6.75 2.00
181 A51 2s red brown 8.00 2.00
182 A51 3s brt rose 3.75 1.25
183 A51 4s gray green 40.00 32.50
184 A51 5s dull violet 17.50 2.00
185 A51 8s red orange 65.00 45.00
186 A52 10s deep brown 40.00 2.00
187 A52 20s deep blue 60.00 2.50
Nos. 179-187 (9) 245.50 93.50

Nos. 179-187 exist rouletted and with various perforations. These were made privately.

Empress Jingo — A53

Granite Paper

Perf. 12, 13x13½

1924 **Engr.** **Wmk. 141**

188 A53 5y gray green 275.00 4.00
189 A53 10y dull violet 450.00 3.25

See Nos. 253-254.

Cranes
A54

Phoenix
A55

Perf. 10½ to 13½ and Compound

1925, May 10 Litho. Unwmk.

190	A54	1½s gray violet	2.25	1.75
191	A55	3s silver & brn org	7.50	3.75
a.		Vert. pair, imperf. btwn.	425.00	
192	A54	8s light red	30.00	19.00
193	A55	20s sil & gray grn	67.50	57.50
		Nos. 190-193 (4)	107.25	82.00

25th wedding anniv. of the Emperor Yoshihito (Taisho) and Empress Sadako.

Mt. Fuji
A56

Yomei Gate, Nikko
A57

Nagoya Castle — A58

Granite Paper

Perf. 13½x13

1926-37 Typo. Wmk. 141

194	A56	2s green	3.25	.25
195	A57	6s carmine	15.00	.60
196	A58	10s dark blue	15.00	.25
197	A58	10s carmine ('37)	12.00	*20.00*
		Nos. 194-197 (4)	45.25	21.10

See Nos. 244, 247. For surcharges see People's Republic of China No. 2L5-2L6.

Baron Hisoka Maeshima
A59

Map of World on Mollweide's Projection
A60

Perf. 12½, 13x13½

1927, June 20 Unwmk.

198	A59	1½s lilac	3.75	2.00
199	A59	3s olive green	3.75	2.00
200	A60	6s carmine rose	62.50	55.00
201	A60	10s blue	80.00	55.00
		Nos. 198-201 (4)	150.00	114.00

50th anniv. of Japan's joining the UPU. Baron Maeshima (1835-1919) organized Japan's modern postal system and was postmaster general.

Phoenix — A61

Enthronement Hall, Kyoto — A62

Yellow Paper

1928, Nov. 10 Engr. *Perf. 12½*

202	A61	1½s deep green	1.25	.85
203	A62	3s red violet	1.25	.95
204	A61	6s carmine rose	5.50	3.25
205	A62	10s deep blue	6.00	3.75
		Nos. 202-205 (4)	14.00	8.80

Enthronement of Emperor Hirohito.

Great Shrines of Ise — A63

1929, Oct. 2 *Perf. 12½*

206	A63	1½s gray violet	2.25	1.50
207	A63	3s carmine	2.75	2.10

58th rebuilding of the Ise Shrines.

Map of Japanese Empire — A64

1930, Sept. 25 Unwmk.

208	A64	1½s deep violet	3.50	1.75
209	A64	3s deep red	4.00	2.50

2nd census in the Japanese Empire.

Meiji Shrine — A65

1930, Nov. 1 Litho.

210	A65	1½s green	2.75	2.25
211	A65	3s brown org	3.75	2.75

10th anniv. of dedication of Meiji Shrine.

Coil Stamps

Wmk. Zigzag Lines (141)

1933 Typo. *Perf. 13 Horiz.*

212	A34	1½s light blue	22.50	22.50
213	A34	3s rose	34.00	34.00

Japanese Red Cross Badge
A66

Red Cross Building, Tokyo
A67

Perf. 12½

1934, Oct. 1 Engr. Unwmk.

214	A66	1½s green & red	2.25	1.90
215	A67	3s dull vio & red	2.50	2.50
216	A66	6s dk car & red	13.50	10.00
217	A67	10s blue & red	16.50	8.00
		Nos. 214-217 (4)	34.75	22.40

15th International Red Cross Congress. Sheets of 20 with commemorative marginal inscription. One side of sheet is perf. 13.

White Tower of Liaoyang and Warship "Hiei" — A68

Akasaka Detached Palace, Tokyo — A69

1935, Apr. 2

218	A68	1½s olive green	1.75	1.50
219	A69	3s red brown	3.25	1.75
220	A68	6s carmine	11.00	8.00
221	A69	10s blue	14.50	10.00
		Nos. 218-221 (4)	30.50	21.25

Visit of Emperor Kang Teh of Manchukuo (Henry Pu-yi) to Tokyo, April 6, 1935. Four sheets of 20 each with commemorative marginal inscription. One side of sheet is perf. 13. Value, set of 4, $900.

Mt. Fuji — A70

Granite Paper

1935 Typo. *Perf. 13x13½*

222	A70	1½s rose carmine	11.50	.75
a.		Miniature sheet of 20	700.00	500.00

Issued to pay postage on New Year's cards from Dec. 1-31, 1935. After Jan. 1, 1936, used for ordinary letter postage. No. 222 was issued in sheets of 100.

Mt. Fuji — A71

Fuji from Lake Ashi — A72

Fuji from Lake Kawaguchi
A73

Fuji from Mishima — A74

Granite Paper

1936, July 10 Photo. Wmk. 141

223	A71	1½s red brown	3.75	3.50
224	A72	3s dark green	4.75	4.25
225	A73	6s carmine rose	12.50	11.00
226	A74	10s dark blue	13.50	13.00
		Nos. 223-226 (4)	34.50	31.75

Fuji-Hakone National Park.

Dove, Map of Manchuria and Kwantung
A75

Shinto Shrine, Port Arthur
A76

Headquarters of Kwantung Government — A77

Granite Paper

1936, Sept. 1 Litho. *Perf. 12½*

227	A75	1½s gray violet	17.50	17.50
228	A76	3s red brown	21.00	20.00
229	A77	10s dull green	190.00	160.00
		Nos. 227-229 (3)	228.50	197.50

30th anniv. of Japanese administration of Kwantung Leased Territory and the South Manchuria Railway Zone.

Imperial Diet Building — A78

Grand Staircase — A79

1936, Nov. 7 Engr. *Perf. 13*

230	A78	1½s green	2.25	2.00
231	A79	3s brown vio	2.75	2.25
232	A79	6s carmine	7.50	6.50
233	A78	10s blue	14.00	10.00
		Nos. 230-233 (4)	26.50	20.75

Opening of the new Diet Building, Tokyo.

"Wedded Rocks," Futamigaura — A80

1936, Dec. 10 Photo.

234	A80	1½s rose carmine	4.00	.40

Issued to pay postage on New Year's greeting cards.

Types of 1913-26

Perf. 13½x13, 13x13½

1937 Typo. Wmk. 257

239	A34	½s brown	3.75	2.75
240	A34	1s orange yel	7.00	4.50
241	A34	3s rose	3.25	.55
242	A49	4s green	8.00	.40
243	A35	5s violet	11.00	.40
244	A57	6s crimson	14.50	2.75
245	A35	7s red org	12.50	.40
246	A49	8s olive bister	18.50	2.00
247	A58	10s carmine	12.50	.40
248	A49	20s blue	20.00	.60
249	A35	25s olive grn	80.00	3.75
250	A36	30s org & grn	50.00	1.00
251	A36	50s brn org & dk bl	250.00	2.75
252	A36	1y yel grn & mar	140.00	1.50
		Nos. 239-252 (14)	631.00	23.75

Engr.

253	A53	5y gray green	400.00	12.50
254	A53	10y dull violet	550.00	10.00

For overprint see People's Republic of China No. 2L6.

Coil Stamps

1938 Typo. *Perf. 13 Horiz.*

255	A34	3s rose	7.50	7.50

New Year's Decoration — A81

1937, Dec. 15 Photo. *Perf. 13*

256	A81	2s scarlet	7.00	.50

Issued to pay postage on New Year's cards, later for ordinary use.

Trading Ship
A82

Harvesting
A83

Gen. Maresuke Nogi
A84

Power Plant
A85

Admiral Heihachiro Togo
A86

Mount Hodaka
A87

Garambi Lighthouse, Taiwan
A88

Diamond Mountains, Korea
A89

Meiji Shrine, Tokyo A90

Yomei Gate, Nikko A91

Plane and Map of Japan A92

Kasuga Shrine, Nara A93

Mount Fuji and Cherry Blossoms A94

Horyu Temple, Nara A95

Miyajima Torii, Itsukushima Shrine A96

Golden Pavilion, Kyoto A97

Great Buddha, Kamakura A98

Kamatari Fujiwara A99

Plum Blossoms — A100

Typographed or Engraved

1937-45 Wmk. 257 *Perf. 13*

257	A82	½s purple	1.25	.75
258	A83	1s fawn	3.50	.65
259	A84	2s crimson	1.00	.25
a.		Booklet pane of 20	75.00	
b.		2s pink, perf. 12 ('45)	17.50	12.00
c.		2s vermilion ('44)	6.50	5.00
260	A85	3s green ('39)	1.00	.30
261	A86	4s dark green	1.75	.25
a.		Booklet pane of 20	22.50	
262	A87	5s dark ultra ('39)	2.25	.25
263	A88	6s orange ('39)	4.75	2.00
264	A89	7s deep green ('39)	1.25	.50
265	A90	8s dk pur & pale vio ('39)	1.50	.65
266	A91	10s lake ('38)	7.00	.35
267	A92	12s indigo ('39)	1.25	1.00
268	A93	14s rose lake & pale rose ('38)	1.40	.50
269	A94	20s ultra ('40)	1.75	.25
270	A95	25s dk brn & pale brn ('38)	1.25	.35
271	A96	30s pck blue ('39)	3.25	.30
a.		Imperf., pair	*900.00*	
272	A97	50s ol & pale ol ('39)	1.75	.30
a.		Pale olive (forest) omitted	*750.00*	*600.00*
273	A98	1y brn & pale brn ('39)	6.50	1.00
274	A99	5y dp gray grn ('39)	35.00	3.25
275	A100	10y dk brn vio ('39)	32.50	2.00
		Nos. 257-275 (19)	109.90	14.90

Nos. 257-261, 265, 268, 270, 272- 273 are typographed; the others are engraved.

Coil Stamps

1938-39 Typo. *Perf. 13 Horiz.*

276	A82	½s purple ('39)	7.00	7.00
277	A84	2s crimson	7.25	7.25
278	A86	4s dark green	7.75	7.75
279	A93	14s rose lake & pale rose	150.00	125.00
		Nos. 276-279 (4)	172.00	147.00

See Nos. 329, 331, 333, 341, 351, 360 and 361. For surcharges see Nos. B4-B5, Burma 2N4-2N27, China-Taiwan, 8-9, People's Republic of China 2L3, 2L7, 2L9-2L10, 2L39, Korea 55-56. For overprints see Ryukyu Islands (Scott US Specialized catalogue) Nos. 2X1-2X2, 2X4-2X7, 2X10, 2X13-2X14, 2X17, 2X20, 2X23, 2X27, 2X29, 2X33-2X34, 3X2-3X7, 3X10-3X11, 3X14, 3X17, 3X19, 3X21, 3X23, 3X26-3X30, 5X1-5X3, 5X5-5X8, 5X10.

Mount Nantai A101

Kegon Falls A102

Sacred Bridge, Nikko — A103

Mount Hiuchi — A104

Unwmk.

1938, Dec. 25 Photo. *Perf. 13*

280	A101	2s brown orange	1.00	1.00
281	A102	4s olive green	1.00	1.00
282	A103	10s deep rose	10.00	7.50
283	A104	20s dark blue	10.00	7.50
a.		Souvenir sheet of 4, #280-283	90.00	80.00
		Never hinged	140.00	
		Nos. 280-283 (4)	22.00	17.00
		Set, never hinged	40.00	

Nikko National Park. No. 283a sold for 50s.

Many souvenir sheets were sold in folders. Values are for sheets without folders.

Mount Daisen — A106

Yashima Plateau, Inland Sea — A107

Abuto Kwannon Temple — A108

Tomo Bay, Inland Sea — A109

1939, Apr. 20

285	A106	2s lt brown	1.00	1.00
286	A107	4s yellow grn	3.75	2.75
287	A108	10s dull rose	8.75	8.00
288	A109	20s blue	9.00	9.00
a.		Souvenir sheet of 4, #285-288	47.50	40.00
		Never hinged	65.00	
		Nos. 285-288 (4)	22.50	20.75
		Set, never hinged	37.50	

Daisen and Inland Sea National Parks. No. 288a sold for 50s.

View from Kuju Village, Kyushu — A111

Mount Naka — A112

Crater of Mount Naka — A113

Volcanic Cones of Mt. Aso — A114

1939, Aug. 15

290	A111	2s olive brown	1.00	1.00
291	A112	4s yellow green	3.75	3.75
292	A113	10s carmine	20.00	17.50
293	A114	20s sapphire	25.00	22.50
a.		Souvenir sheet of 4, #290-293	145.00	145.00
		Never hinged	210.00	
		Nos. 290-293 (4)	49.75	44.75
		Set, never hinged	95.00	

Aso National Park. No. 293a sold for 50s.

Globe A116

Tsunetami Sano A117

1939, Nov. 15 *Perf. 12½*

Cross in Carmine

295	A116	2s brown	1.90	1.75
296	A117	4s yellow green	2.25	2.25
297	A116	10s crimson	9.00	8.50
298	A117	20s sapphire	9.00	8.50
		Nos. 295-298 (4)	22.15	21.00
		Set, never hinged	37.50	

Intl. Red Cross Society founding, 75th anniv.

Sacred Golden Kite A118

Mount Takachiho A119

Five Ayu Fish and Sake Jar A120

Kashiwara Shrine A121

1940 Engr. *Perf. 12*

299	A118	2s brown orange	1.00	1.00
300	A119	4s dark green	.60	.60
301	A120	10s dark carmine	4.50	4.50
302	A121	20s dark ultra	1.75	1.75
		Nos. 299-302 (4)	7.85	7.85
		Set, never hinged	12.50	

2,600th anniv. of the legendary date of the founding of Japan.

Mt. Hokuchin, Hokkaido A122

Mt. Asahi, Hokkaido A123

Sounkyo Gorge A124

Tokachi Mountain Range — A125

1940, Apr. 20 Photo. *Perf. 13*

303	A122	2s brown	1.00	1.00
304	A123	4s yellow green	3.00	3.00
305	A124	10s carmine	10.00	10.00
306	A125	20s sapphire	12.50	12.50
a.		Souvenir sheet of 4, #303-306	185.00	175.00
		Never hinged	350.00	
		Nos. 303-306 (4)	26.50	26.50
		Set, never hinged	55.00	

Daisetsuzan National Park. No. 306a sold for 50s.

Mt. Karakuni, Kyushu — A127

Mt. Takachiho A128

Torii of Kirishima Shrine — A129

Lake of the Six Kwannon A130

1940, Aug. 21

308	A127	2s brown	1.00	1.00
309	A128	4s green	1.25	1.25
310	A129	10s carmine	10.00	10.00
311	A130	20s deep ultra	13.00	13.00
a.		Souvenir sheet of 4, #308-311	240.00	225.00
		Never hinged	360.00	
		Nos. 308-311 (4)	25.25	25.25
		Set, never hinged	55.00	

Kirishima National Park. No. 311a sold for 50s.

Education Minister with Rescript on Education A132

Characters Signifying Loyalty and Filial Piety A133

1940, Oct. 25 Engr. *Perf. 12½*

313	A132	2s purple	1.00	1.00
314	A133	4s green	1.40	1.40
		Set, never hinged	4.00	

50th anniv. of the imperial rescript on education, given by Emperor Meiji to clarify Japan's educational policy.

Mt. Daiton, Taiwan — A134

Central Peak of Mt. Niitaka — A135

Buddhist Temple on Mt. Kwannon A136

View from Mt. Niitaka — A137

1941, Mar. 10 Photo. *Perf. 13*

315	A134	2s brown	1.25	1.25
316	A135	4s brt green	2.50	2.50
317	A136	10s rose red	7.00	7.00
318	A137	20s brilliant ultra	9.00	9.00
a.		Souv. sheet of 4, #315-318	125.00	125.00
		Never hinged	175.00	
		Nos. 315-318 (4)	19.75	19.75
		Set, never hinged	47.50	

Daiton and Niitaka-Arisan National Parks.

No. 318a sold with No. 323a in same folder for 90s.

Seisui Precipice, East Taiwan Coast A139

Taroko Gorge A141

Mt. Tsugitaka A140

Upper River Takkiri District — A142

1941, Mar. 10

320	A139	2s brown	1.25	1.25
321	A140	4s lt green	2.50	2.50
322	A141	10s rose red	7.00	7.00
323	A142	20s brt ultra	9.00	9.00
a.		Souv. sheet of 4, #320-323	125.00	125.00
		Never hinged	175.00	
		Nos. 320-323 (4)	19.75	19.75
		Set, never hinged	42.50	

Tsugitaka-Taroko National Park.

See note after No. 318.

War Factory Girl A144

Building of Wooden Ship A145

Hyuga Monument and Mt. Fuji A146

War Worker and Planes A147

Palms and Map of "Greater East Asia" A148

"Enemy Country Surrender" A149

Aviator Saluting and Japanese Flag A150

Torii of Yasukuni Shrine A151

Mt. Fuji and Cherry Blossoms A152

Torii of Miyajima A153

Garambi Lighthouse, Taiwan — A154

Typographed; Engraved

1942-45 Wmk. 257 *Perf. 13*

325	A144	1s org brn ('43)	.50	.40
328	A145	2s green	.70	.70
329	A84	3s brown ('44)	1.50	.70
330	A146	4s emerald	.45	.30
331	A86	5s brown lake	.50	.40
332	A147	6s lt ultra ('44)	.75	.60
a.		Imperf., pair		
333	A86	7s org ver ('44)	.50	.40
334	A148	10s crim & dl rose	1.00	.25
a.		Dull rose (map) omitted	475.00	475.00
335	A149	10s lt gray ('45)	5.25	5.25
336	A150	15s dull blue	3.50	2.00
337	A151	17s gray vio ('43)	1.00	.60
338	A152	20s blue ('44)	1.10	.30
339	A151	27s rose brn ('45)	1.00	1.00
340	A153	30s bluish grn ('44)	3.25	2.00
341	A88	40s dull violet	2.00	.30
342	A154	40s dk violet ('44)	2.75	2.50
		Nos. 325,328-342 (16)	25.75	17.70

Nos. 325-335, 337-340 and 342 are typo. Nos. 336 and 341 are engr.

Nos. 329, 331, 333-334, 342 issued with and without gum. No. 335 issued only without gum. These are valued without gum.

Nos. 328, 342 exist with watermark sideways. No. 328 exists printed on gummed side.

Most stamps of the above series exist in numerous shades.

For overprints and surcharges see North Borneo Nos. N34, N37, N41-N42, People's Republic of China 2L4, 2L8, Korea 57-60, Ryukyu Islands (US Specialized) Nos. 2X3, 2X9, 2X12, 2X15-2X16, 2X18-2X19, 2X21-2X22, 2X24-2X26, 2X28, 3X1, 3X8-3X9, 3X12-3X13, 3X15-3X16, 3X18, 3X20, 3X25, 3X31, 4X1-4X2, 5X4.

Kenkoku Shrine, Hsinking — A155

Boys of Japan and Manchukuo A156

Orchid Crest of Manchukuo A157

1942 Unwmk. Engr. *Perf. 12*

343	A155	2s brown	.85	.85
344	A156	5s olive	1.00	1.00
345	A155	10s red	1.75	1.75
346	A157	20s dark blue	3.25	*5.00*
		Nos. 343-346 (4)	6.85	8.60
		Set, never hinged	11.50	

The 2s and 10s were issued Mar. 1 for the 10th anniv. of the creation of Manchukuo; 5s and 20s on Sept. 15 for the 10th anniv. of Japanese diplomatic recognition of Manchukuo.

C-59 Locomotive — A158

1942, Oct. 14 Photo.

347	A158	5s Prus green	4.00	*6.00*
		Never hinged	9.00	

70th anniv. of Japan's 1st railway.

Yasukuni Shrine, Tokyo — A159

1944, June 29 *Perf. 13*

348	A159	7s Prus green	.85	.85
		Never hinged	2.00	

75th anniversary of Yasukuni Shrine.

Kwantung Shrine and Map of Kwantung Peninsula — A160

1944, Oct. 1

349	A160	3s red brown	4.00	*10.00*
350	A160	7s gray violet	4.50	*10.00*
		Set, never hinged	14.00	

Dedication of Kwantung Shrine, Port Arthur.

Sun and Cherry Blossoms A161

Sunrise at Sea and Plane A162

Coal Miners A163

Yasukuni Shrine A164

Lithographed, Typographed

1945-47 Wmk. 257 *Imperf.*

Without Gum

351	A84	2s rose red	.90	.90
352	A161	3s rose carmine	.50	.50
353	A162	5s green	.60	.40
a.		5s blue	11.00	7.50
354	A149	10s lt gray	11.50	11.50
354A	A149	10s blue	29.00	
355	A152	10s red orange	.60	.30
356	A152	20s ultra ('46)	.65	.35
357	A153	30s brt blue ('46)	2.50	1.25
358	A163	50s dk brn ('46)	.75	.30
a.		Souvenir sheet of 5 ('47)	11.00	*12.50*
359	A164	1y dp ol grn ('46)	2.00	2.00
360	A99	5y dp gray grn	7.25	1.50
361	A100	10y dk brown vio	40.00	1.60
		Nos. 351-361 (12)	96.25	
		Nos. 351-354,355-361 (11)		20.60

Nos. 351 and 354 are typographed. The other stamps in this set are printed by offset lithography.

No. 358a was issued with marginal inscriptions to commemorate the Sapporo (Hokkaido) Philatelic Exhibition, Nov., 1947.

Nos. 351 to 361 are on grayish paper, and Nos. 355 to 361 also exist on white paper.

Most stamps of the above series exist in numerous shades and with private perforation or roulette.

Beware of forgeries of Nos. 352, 353, 355-357 and 360 on unwatermarked paper.

See No. 404. For overprints see Ryukyu Islands (US Specialized) Nos. 2X8, 2X11, 2X30, 3X22, 4X3, 5X9.

Baron Hisoka Maeshima A165

Horyu Temple Pagoda A166

"Thunderstorm below Fuji," by Hokusai A167

"First Geese," Print by Hokusai A168

Kintai Bridge, Iwakuni A169

Kiyomizu Temple, Kyoto A170

Goldfish A171

Noh Mask A172

Plum Blossoms — A173

Characters Read Right to Left

1946-47 Wmk. 257 Litho. *Imperf.*

Without Gum

362	A165	15s dark green	.70	.70
363	A166	30s dull lilac	1.50	.55
364	A167	1y ultra	3.00	.35
a.		1y deep ultramarine	5.00	.35
b.		1y light blue	2.75	.35
365	A168	1.30y olive bister	4.00	1.25
366	A169	1.50y dark gray	4.50	1.00
367	A170	2y vermilion ('47)	3.75	.40
a.		Souvenir sheet of 5 ('47)	35.00	*55.00*
368	A171	5y lilac rose	9.50	1.25
		Nos. 362-368 (7)	26.95	5.50

Engr.

369	A172	50y bister brn	87.50	2.00
370	A173	100y brn car ('47)	87.50	2.00

Perf. 13

371	A172	50y bis brn, with gum ('47)	87.50	1.25
372	A173	100y brn car, with gum ('47)	87.50	1.25

Litho.

Perf. 13x13½, 12, 12x12½

373	A166	30s dull lilac	4.25	3.50

Rouletted in Colored Lines

Typo. Unwmk.

With Gum

374	A166	30s deep lilac	2.50	*2.75*

Nos. 363, 368, 373 exist with and without gum, valued without gum, as are Nos. 371-372, 374.

No. 367a for the "Know Your Stamps" exhibition, Kyoto, Aug. 19-24, 1947. Size: 113x71mm

Nos. 362, 369 exist with watermark horizontal. Values, $27.50, $100, respectively.

Beware of Nos. 362-364, 364a, 364b, 365 and 367 on unwatermarked paper.

See Nos. 384-387, 512A. For overprints see Ryukyu Islands (US Specialized) Nos. 2X32, 3X24, 4X4.

Catalogue values for unused stamps in this section, from this point to the end of the section, are for Never Hinged items.

Medieval Postman's Bell A175

Baron Hisoka Maeshima A176

Design of First Japanese Stamp A177

Communication Symbols A178

Perf. 12½, 13½x13

1946, Dec. 12 Engr. Unwmk.

375 A175 15s orange 5.50 5.00
376 A176 30s deep green 7.00 6.00
377 A177 50s carmine 3.50 3.00
378 A178 1y deep blue 3.50 3.00
a. Souvenir sheet of 4, #375-378, imperf. 200.00 200.00
Hinged 125.00
Nos. 375-378 (4) 19.50 17.00

Government postal service in Japan, 75th anniv.

No. 378a measures 180-183x125-127mm and is ungummed. There were 2 printings: I — The 4 colors were printed simultaneously. Arched top inscription and other inscriptions in high relief (no more than 2,000 sheets). II — Stamps were printed in one step, sheet inscriptions and 15s orange stamp in another. Lines of top inscription and inscriptions at lower left and lower right (flanking the 1y blue stamp) are much flatter (less raised) than the lines of the green, carmine and blue stamps, almost level with paper's surface (about 49,000 sheets). 1st printing value $800.

Mother and Child, Diet Building A180

Bouquet of Japanese May Flowers A181

Wmk. 257

1947, May 3 Litho. *Perf. 12½*
Without Gum

380 A180 50s rose brown .75 .50
381 A181 1y brt ultra 1.25 1.00
a. Souv. sheet of 2, #380-381, imperf, without gum 14.00 14.00
b. As "a," 50s stamp omitted 800.00
c. As "a," 1y stamp omitted 800.00

Inauguration of the constitution of May 3, 1947.

A182

1947, Aug. 15 Photo. *Perf. 12½*

382 A182 1.20y brown 3.00 2.25
383 A182 4y brt ultra 6.00 1.40

Reopening of foreign trade on a private basis.

The ornaments on No. 383 differ from those shown in the illustration.

Types of 1946 Redrawn
Characters Read Left to Right

1947-48 Wmk. 257 Typo. *Perf. 13*

384 A166 30s deep lilac 5.75 2.00
385 A166 1.20y lt olive grn 2.75 .50
a. Souvenir sheet of 15 225.00 225.00
386 A170 2y vermilion ('48) 12.50 1.50
387 A168 4y lt ultra 8.50 .40
Nos. 384-387 (4) 29.50 4.40

No. 385a was issued with marginal inscriptions to commemorate the "Know Your Stamps" Exhibition, Tokyo, May, 1947.

On No. 386, the chrysanthemum crest has been eliminated and the top inscription centered.

Plum Blossoms — A183

1947 Typo. *Imperf.*
Without Gum

388 A183 10y dk brown vio 50.00 1.75

This stamp is similar to type A100 but with new inscription "Nippon Yubin" (Japan Post), reading from left to right. The characters for the denomination are likewise transposed.

A184

A185

Baron Hisoka Maejima A186

Whaling A187

National Art, Imperial Treasure House, Nara — A188

1947 Typo. *Perf. 13x13½*

389 A184 35s green 1.25 1.00

Litho.

390 A185 45s lilac rose 1.60 1.40
a. Imperf., pair 1,500.
b. Perf. 11x13½ 12.00 10.00
391 A186 1y dull brown 6.50 1.00

Typo.

392 A187 5y blue 11.50 .30
a. Imperf., pair 650.00
b. Perf. 11x13½ 32.50 4.75

Engr.

Perf. 13½x13

393 A188 10y lilac 15.00 .25
a. Imperf., pair *3,000.*
Nos. 389-393 (5) 35.85 3.95

No. 389 was produced on both rotary and flat press. Sheets of the rotary press printing have a border. Those of the flat press printing have none.

Lily of the Valley — A188a

1947, Sept. 13 Unwmk. *Perf. 12½*

394 A188a 2y dk Prus green 6.00 3.25

Relief of Ex-convicts Day, Sept. 13, 1947.

Souvenir Sheet

A189

1947 Wmk. 257 Litho. *Imperf.*
Without Gum

395 A189 Sheet of 5, ultra 4.75 4.75

Stamp Hobby Week, Nov. 1-7, 1947. Sheet size: 113½x71½mm, on white or grayish paper.

For overprint, see No. 408.

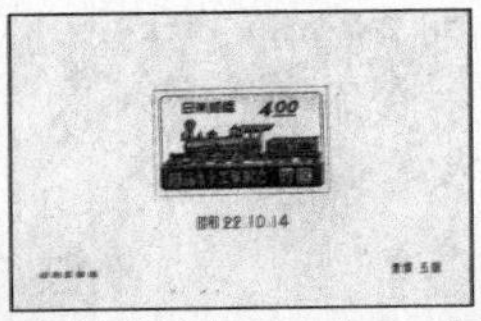
"Benkei," 1880 Locomotive — A190

1947, Oct. 14 Unwmk. Engr.
Without Gum

396 A190 4y deep ultra 20.00 20.00

75th anniv. of railway service in Japan.

Hurdling A191

Diving A192

Discus Throwing A193

Volleyball A194

1947, Oct. 25 Photo. *Perf. 12½*

397 A191 1.20y red violet 8.50 7.50
398 A192 1.20y red violet 8.50 7.50
399 A193 1.20y red violet 8.50 7.50
400 A194 1.20y red violet 8.50 7.50
a. Block of 4, #397-400 50.00 50.00

2nd Natl. Athletic Meet, held in Kanazawa, Oct. 30-Nov. 3.

Souvenir Sheets

A195

1948 Wmk. 257 Litho. *Imperf.*
Without Gum

401 A195 Sheet of 2, As #368, rose carmine 17.50 *17.50*

Same, Inscribed with Three instead of Two Japanese Characters at Bottom Center

402 A195 Sheet of 2, #368 20.00 *20.00*

Philatelic exhibitions at Osaka (No. 401) and Nagoya (No. 402).

For Nos. 401-402 overprinted in green, see Nos. 407, 407b.

Stylized Tree — A196

Perf. 12½

1948, Apr. 1 Unwmk. Photo.

403 A196 1.20y dp yellow grn 1.40 1.25

Forestation movement. Sheets of 30, marginal inscription.

Coal Miners Type of 1946 and

National Art Treasure, Nara — A197

Perf. 13x13½

1948 Wmk. 257 Litho.

404 A163 50s dark brown 1.60 1.25

Typo.

Perf. 13x13½

405 A197 10y rose violet 15.00 .30
a. Imperf., pair

See No. 515A.

School Children — A198

Perf. 12½

1948, May 3 Unwmk. Photo.

406 A198 1.20y dark carmine 1.40 1.25

Reorganization of Japan's educational system. Sheets of 30, marginal inscription.

No. 402 Overprinted at Top, Bottom and Sides with Japanese Characters and Flowers in Green

1948, Apr. 3 Souvenir Sheets

407 A195 Sheet of 2 75.00 40.00
a. Overprint inverted 150.00 150.00
b. Overprint on No. 401 125.00 125.00

Mishima Philatelic Exhibition, Apr. 3-9.

No. 395 Overprinted at Top and Bottom With Japanese Characters in Plum

1948, Apr. 18

408 A189 Sheet of 5, ultra 27.50 27.50

Centenary of the death of Katsushika Hokusai, painter.

Sampans on Inland Sea, Near Suma — A199

Engr. & Litho.

1948, Apr. 22 Unwmk. *Imperf.*
Without Gum

409 A199 Sheet of 2, grn & rose car 16.00 11.00

Communications Exhib., Tokyo, Apr. 27-May 3, 1948. Sheet contains two 2y deep carmine stamps.

Sheet exists with green border omitted.

1948, May 20 Without Gum

410 A199 Sheet of 2, ultra & rose car 20.00 18.00

Aomori Newspaper and Stamp Exhibition. Border design of apples and apple blossoms.

Type A199 With Altered Border and Inscriptions

1948, May 23 Without Gum

411 A199 Sheet of 2, blue & rose car 20.00 18.00

Fukushima Stamp Exhibition. Border design of cherries and crossed lines.

Horse Race — A200

1948, June 6 Photo. *Perf. 12½*

412 A200 5y brown 3.50 1.75

25th anniv. of the enforcement of Japan's horse racing laws. Each sheet contains 30 stamps and 2 labels, with marginal inscription.

Stamps with labels are worth more than values listed.

A201

A202

Wmk. 257

1948, Sept. 10 Litho. *Perf. 13*

413	A201	1.50y blue	4.00	.80
414	A202	3.80y lt brown	11.50	5.25

Souvenir Sheet
Without Gum
Imperf

415	Sheet of 4	35.00	35.00

Kumamoto Stamp Exhibition, Sept. 20. Souvenir sheet, issued Sept. 20, contains two each of 1.50y deep blue (A201) and 3.80y brown (A202).

Rectifying Tower — A203

Perf. 12½

1948, Sept. 14 Photo. Unwmk.

416	A203	5y dark olive bister	4.50	2.75

Government alcohol monopoly.

Swimmer A204

Runner A205

Designs: No. 419, High jumper. No. 420, Baseball players. No. 421, Bicycle racers.

1948

417	A204	5y blue	4.50	1.25
418	A205	5y green	11.00	5.50
419	A205	5y green	11.00	5.50
420	A205	5y green	11.00	5.50
421	A205	5y green	11.00	5.50
a.		Block of 4, #418-421	60.00	60.00
		Nos. 417-421 (5)	48.50	23.25

3rd Natl. Athletic Meet. Swimming matches held at Yawata, Sept. 16-19, field events, Fukuoka, Oct. 29-Nov. 3.

No. 417 was issued in sheets of 50 with labels. Stamps with labels, value, $13.

"Beauty Looking Back," Print by Moronobu — A206

1948, Nov. 29 *Perf. 13*

422	A206	5y brown	25.00	40.00
a.		Sheet of 5	350.00	300.00
		Sheet, hinged	250.00	—

Philatelic Week, Nov. 29-Dec. 5.
See Nos. 2418-2419.

Souvenir Sheets

1948, Dec. 3 Without Gum *Imperf.*

423	A206	5y brown, sheet of 1	45.00	40.00

Kanazawa and Takaoka stamp exhibitions.

Child Playing Hanetsuki — A207

1948, Dec. 13 Litho. *Perf. 13*

424	A207	2y scarlet	6.00	5.00

Issued to pay postage on New Year's cards, later for ordinary use.

Farm Woman A208

Whaling A209

Miner A210

Tea Picking A211

Girl Printer A212

Factory Girl with Cotton Bobbin A213

Mt. Hodaka A214

Planting A215

Postman A216

Blast Furnace A217

Locomotive Assembly — A218

Typographed, Engraved

1948-49 Wmk. 257 *Perf. 13x13½*

425	A208	2y green	3.50	.25
a.		Overprinted with 4 characters in frame	1.40	1.00
b.		As "a," overprint inverted	*125.00*	
426	A209	3y lt grnsh bl ('49)	7.50	.30
427	A210	5y olive bis	22.50	1.50
a.		Booklet pane of 20	475.00	*15.00*
		Hinged	175.00	
428	A211	5y blue grn ('49)	60.00	9.50
429	A212	6y red org ('49)	12.50	.25
430	A210	8y brn org ('49)	14.00	.25
a.		Booklet pane of 20	*325.00*	*10.00*
		Hinged	175.00	
431	A213	15y blue	4.50	.25
432	A214	16y ultra ('49)	15.00	7.00
433	A215	20y dk grn ('49)	52.50	.25
434	A216	30y violet bl ('49)	62.50	.25
435	A217	100y car lake ('49)	600.00	4.50
436	A218	500y dp blue ('49)	550.00	7.00
		Nos. 425-436 (12)	1,405.	31.30
		Set, hinged	550.00	

No. 425a has a red control overprint of four characters ("Senkyo Jimu," or "Election Business") arranged vertically in a rectangular frame. Each candidate received 1,000 copies.

Nos. 432, 435-436 are engraved.

See Nos. 442, 511-512, 514-515, 518, 520, 521A-521B.

Souvenir Sheets

Typo. and Litho.

1948, Oct. 16 *Imperf.*

437	A213	15y blue, sheet of 1	50.00	45.00

Nagano Stamp Exhibition, Oct. 16.

1948, Nov. 2 *Imperf.*

438	A210	5y ol bis, sheet of 2	60.00	45.00

Shikoku Traveling Stamp Exhib., Nov. 1948.

Sampans on Inland Sea — A219

Perf. 13x13½

1949 Wmk. 257 Engr.

439	A219	10y rose lake	30.00	20.00
440	A219	10y car rose	22.50	17.50
441	A219	10y orange ver	45.00	25.00
442	A214	16y brt blue	11.00	6.25
		Nos. 439-442 (4)	108.50	68.75
		Set, hinged	60.00	

Issued in sheets of 20 stamps with marginal inscription publicizing expositions at Takamatsu (No. 439), Okayama (No. 440) and Matsuyama (No. 441), Nagano Peace Exposition, Apr. 1-May 31, 1949 (No. 442).

Ice Skater A221

Ski Jumper A222

1949 Unwmk. Photo. *Perf. 12*

444	A221	5y violet	3.25	2.25
445	A222	5y ultra	4.00	2.25

Winter events of the 4th Natl. Athletic Meet: skating at Suwa Jan. 27-30, skiing at Sapporo Mar. 3-6. Issued: No. 444, 1/27; No. 445, 3/3.

Steamer in Beppu Bay — A223

1949, Mar. 10 Engr. *Perf. 13x13½*

446	A223	2y carmine & ultra	1.50	1.25
447	A223	5y green & ultra	5.75	1.75

Scene at Fair — A224

1949, Mar. 15 Photo. *Imperf.*

448	A224	5y brt rose	2.50	1.75
a.		Perf. 13	4.00	2.50
b.		Sheet of 20, imperf.	65.00	45.00

Issued to publicize the Japan Foreign Trade Fair, Yokohama, 1949.

No. 448a was printed in sheets of 50 (10x5); No. 448 in sheets of 20 (4x5) with marginal inscriptions (No. 448b).

Stylized Trees — A225

1949, Apr. 1 Unwmk. *Perf. 12*

449	A225	5y bright green	12.00	2.50

Issued to publicize the forestation movement.

Lion Rock — A226

Daiho-zan (Mt. Ohmine) A227

Doro Gorge — A228

Bridge Pier Rocks — A229

1949, Apr. 10 Photo. *Perf. 13*

450	A226	2y brown	1.50	1.00
451	A227	5y yellow grn	5.00	1.75
452	A228	10y scarlet	22.00	14.00
453	A229	16y blue	10.00	8.50
a.		Souv. sheet of 4, #450-453, no gum	50.00	37.50
b.		As "a," 10y stamp omitted		
		Nos. 450-453 (4)	38.50	25.25

Yoshino-Kumano National Park.
No. 453a sold for 40y.

Boy — A230

1949, May 5 *Perf. 12*

455	A230	5y rose brn & org	7.50	2.57
a.		Orange omitted	275.00	

Children's Day, May 5, 1949.

Souvenir Sheets

1949, May 5 *Imperf.*

456	A230	5y rose brn & org, sheet of 10	450.00	300.00
		Hinged	275.00	

Children's Exhib., Inuyama, Apr. 1-May 31.

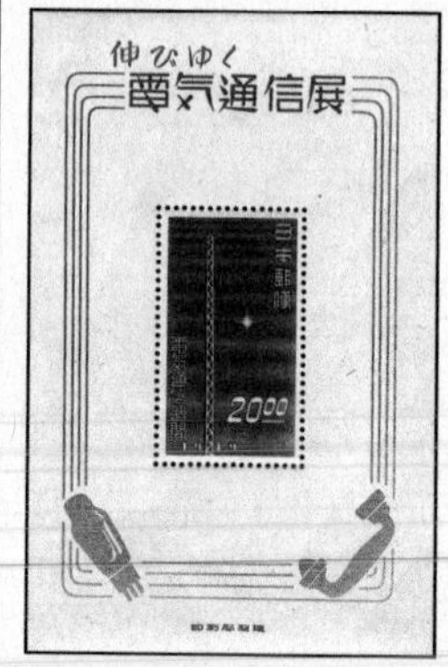
Radio Tower and Star A231

1949, May 11 *Perf. 13*

457	A231	20y dp blue	140.00	120.00
		Hinged	75.00	

Electrical Communication Week, May 11-18.

Symbols of Communication — A232

Wmk. 257

1949, June 1 Engr. *Perf. 12*

458	A232	8y brt ultra	4.50	2.25

Establishment of the Post Ministry and the Ministry of Electricity and Communication.

Central Meteorological Observatory, Tokyo — A233

1949, June 1 **Unwmk.** ***Perf. 12½***
459 A233 8y deep green 4.50 2.25

75th anniv. of the establishment of the Central Meteorological Observatory.

Mt. Fuji in Autumn — A234

Lake Kawaguchi A235

Mt. Fuji from Mt. Shichimen A236

Shinobuno Village and Mt. Fuji — A237

1949, July 15 **Photo.** ***Perf. 13***
460 A234 2y yellow brown 4.50 1.00
461 A235 8y yellow green 5.00 1.75
462 A236 14y carmine lake 2.50 .75
463 A237 24y blue 9.00 1.00
a. Souv. sheet of 4, #460-463 47.50 47.50
Nos. 460-463 (4) 21.00 4.50

Fuji-Hakone National Park.
No. 463a sold for 55y.

Allegory of Peace A238

Doves over Nagasaki A239

Perf. 13x13½, 13½x13
1949 **Photo.** **Unwmk.**
465 A238 8y yellow brown 11.00 3.00
466 A239 8y green 6.50 3.00

Establishment of Hiroshima as the City of Eternal Peace and of Nagasaki as the International City of Culture. Issued: No. 465, 8/6; No. 466, 8/9.

Boy Scout — A240

1949, Sept. 22 ***Perf. 13x13½***
467 A240 8y brown 9.00 3.00

Natl. Boy Scout Jamboree.

Pen Nib of Newspaper Stereotype Matrix — A241

1949, Oct. 1 ***Perf. 13½x13***
468 A241 8y deep blue 7.00 3.00

Nátl. Newspaper Week.

Racing Swimmer Poised for Dive A242

Javelin Thrower A243

1949 ***Perf. 13½***
469 A242 8y dull blue 6.00 2.25

Perf. 12
470 A243 8y shown 8.00 3.00
471 A243 8y Yacht Racing 8.00 3.00
472 A243 8y Relay Race 8.00 3.00
473 A243 8y Tennis 8.00 3.00
a. Block of 4, #470-473 40.00 *55.00*
Nos. 469-473 (5) 38.00 14.25

4th Natl. Athletic Meet. The swimming matches were held at Yokohama, Sept. 15-18 and the fall events at Tokyo, Oct. 30.
Issued: No. 469, 9/15; Nos. 470-473, 10/30.
Nos. 470-473 exist perf 12½. Values 50 percent above those of perf 12 copies.
No. 469 was issued in sheets with labels. Value, stamp with label, $22.50.

Map and Envelopes Forming "75" — A244

Symbols of UPU — A245

1949, Oct. 10 **Engr.** ***Perf. 12, 13½***
474 A244 2y dull green 4.00 2.25
475 A245 8y maroon 5.00 2.25
a. Souv. sheet of 2, #474-475, imperf. 7.00 7.00
476 A244 14y carmine 13.00 9.00
477 A245 24y aqua 19.00 11.00
a. Imperf., pair
Nos. 474-477 (4) 41.00 24.50

75th anniv. of the UPU.
No 475a was issued without gum.

Floating Zenith Telescope — A246

1949, Oct. 30 **Photo.** ***Perf. 12***
478 A246 8y dk blue grn 5.50 2.25

50th anniv. of the Mizusawa Latitudinal Observatory.

"Moon and Geese," Print by Hiroshige — A247

1949, Nov. 1 ***Perf. 13x13½***
479 A247 8y purple 150.00 55.00
a. Sheet of 5 800.00 450.00
Sheet, hinged 240.00

Postal Week, Nov. 1-7. See Nos. 2420-2421.

Dr. Hideyo Noguchi A248

Yukichi Fukuzawa A249

Soseki Natsume A250

Shoyo Tsubouchi A251

Danjuro Ichikawa A252

Joseph Hardy Niijima A253

Hogai Kano A254

Kanzo Uchimura A255

Ichiyo Higuchi A256

Ogai Mori A257

Shiki Masaoka A258

Shunso Hishida A259

Amane Nishi A260

Kenjiro Ume A261

Hisashi Kimura A262

Inazo Nitobe A263

Torahiko Terada A264

Tenshin Okakura A265

1949-52 **Unwmk.** **Engr.** ***Perf. 12½***
480 A248 8y green 10.00 1.25
a. Imperf., pair
481 A249 8y deep olive ('50) 5.00 1.25
a. Imperf., pair
482 A250 8y dk Prus grn ('50) 5.00 1.25
483 A251 8y Prus grn ('50) 4.50 1.25
a. Imperf., pair
484 A252 8y dk violet ('50) 12.00 4.00
485 A253 8y vio brn ('50) 4.00 1.25
486 A254 8y dk green ('51) 11.00 3.00
487 A255 8y dp purple ('51) 11.00 3.00
488 A256 8y carmine ('51) 17.50 3.00
489 A257 8y vio brn ('51) 30.00 4.00
490 A258 8y choc ('51) 17.50 4.00
491 A259 8y dk blue ('51) 14.00 4.00
492 A260 10y dk green ('52) 65.00 5.00
493 A261 10y brn vio ('52) 12.50 2.00
494 A262 10y carmine ('52) 4.00 2.00
495 A263 10y dk grn ('52) 5.50 2.00
496 A264 10y choc ('52) 5.00 2.00
497 A265 10y dk blue ('52) 5.50 2.00
Nos. 480-497 (18) 239.00 46.25
Set, hinged 100.00

Tiger — A266

1950, Feb. 1 **Photo.** ***Perf. 12***
498 A266 2y dark red 11.00 3.00

New Year, 1950. 6th prize (lottery), sheet of 5, value $225.

Microphones of 1925 and 1950 — A267

1950, Mar. 21 ***Perf. 13***
499 A267 8y ultra 6.00 2.50

25th anniversary of broadcasting in Japan. Sheets of 20 with marginal inscription.

Dove and Olive Twig on Letter Box — A268

1950, Apr. 20 ***Perf. 12***
500 A268 8y dp yellow grn 5.00 2.50

Day of Posts, Apr. 20.

Lake Akan and Mt. Akan — A269

Lake Kutcharo, Hokkaido A270

Mt. Akan-Fuji A271

Lake Mashu — A272

1950, July 15 **Unwmk.** ***Perf. 13***
501 A269 2y yellow brn 2.50 1.25
502 A270 8y dp yellow grn 3.50 1.75
503 A271 14y rose car 16.00 7.00
504 A272 24y brt blue 18.00 7.75
a. Souv. sheet of 4, #501-504 55.00 40.00
Nos. 501-504 (4) 40.00 17.75

Akan National Park.
No. 504a sold for 55y.

Gymnast on Rings — A273

Designs: No. 506, Pole vault. No. 507, Soccer. No. 508, Equestrian.

1950, Oct. 28 ***Perf. 13½x13***
505 A273 8y rose brown 40.00 17.50
506 A273 8y rose brown 40.00 17.50
507 A273 8y rose brown 40.00 17.50

508 A273 8y rose brown 40.00 17.50
a. Strip of 4, #505-508 175.00 *140.00*
b. Block of 4, #505-508 190.00 *150.00*
As "b," hinged 85.00

5th National Athletic Meet. Sheets of 20 stamps in which each horizontal row contains all four designs. Value, sheet $850.

Types of 1947-49 and

Ishiyama-dera Pagoda A274

Hisoka Maeshima A275

Long-tailed Cock of Tosa A276

Goddess Kannon A277

Himeji Castle A278

Nyoirin Kannon of Chuguji A280

Phoenix Hall, Byodoin Temple — A279

Perf. 13x13½, 13½x13 (14y)

1950-52 Typo. Unwmk.

509 A274 80s carmine ('51) 2.75 2.25
a. Sheet of 1 11.00 *13.00*

Photo.

510 A275 1y dk brn ('51) 5.00 1.00
a. Souvenir sheet of 4 22.50 17.50

Typo.

511 A208 2y green ('51) 2.50 .25
512 A209 3y lt grnsh bl ('51) 67.50 2.25
512A A168 4y lt ultra ('52) 45.00 4.00
513 A276 5y dp grn & org brn ('51) 7.50 .25
a. Orange brown omitted 425.00
514 A212 6y red org ('51) 9.00 .75
515 A210 8y dk org brn ('51) 45.00 1.00
515A A197 10y rose vio ('51) 77.50 6.50
516 A277 10y red brn & lil ('51) 27.50 .25

Engr.

517 A278 14y brn & car ('51) 65.00 42.50
a. Sheet of 1 80.00 75.00

Typo.

518 A215 20y dk green ('51) 70.00 2.50

Engr.

519 A279 24y dp ultra 52.50 22.50
a. Sheet of 1 65.00 45.00

Typo.

520 A216 30y vio bl ('52) 225.00 3.00

Photo.

521 A280 50y dk brn ('51) 175.00 2.50
Hinged 85.00
c. Sheet of 1 375.00 375.00
Hinged 175.00

Engr.

521A A217 100y car lake ('52) 500.00 3.25
521B A218 500y dp blue ('52) 450.00 3.75
Nos. 509-521B (17) 1,827. 98.50

No. 510a for the 80th anniv. of Japan's postal service. On No. 512A, characters read from left to right.

Compare designs: A274 with A314c; A275 with A314a, A447, A563a, A5174; A277 with A332a; A278 with A373a; A279 with A385a; A280 with A314b and A565f.

Girl and Rabbit — A281

1951, Jan. 1 Photo. *Perf. 12*

522 A281 2y rose pink 8.00 1.25

New Year Greetings 1951. 9th prize (lottery), sheet of 5, value $50.

See No. 2655a.

Scenic Spots Issue

Skiers on Mt. Zao
A282 A283

1951, Feb. 15 *Perf. 13*

523 A282 8y olive 15.00 2.50
524 A283 24y blue 17.00 6.00

Tea Picking A284

Mt. Fuji Seen from Nihon Plateau A285

Nihon-daira Plateau.

1951, Apr. 2

525 A284 8y olive green 12.00 2.75
526 A285 24y bright blue 90.00 25.00

Hot Springs, Hakone A286

Lake Ashi, Hakone A287

1951, May 25

527 A286 8y chestnut brown 10.00 2.50
528 A287 24y deep blue 8.00 3.50

Senju Waterfall A288

Ninai Waterfall A289

Akame 48 Waterfalls.

1951, June 1

529 A288 8y deep green 12.50 2.75
530 A289 24y deep blue 12.50 4.00

Pavilion, Wakanoura Bay — A290

Wakanoura Bay — A291

Wakanoura & Tomogashima.

1951, June 25

531 A290 8y brown 9.00 2.75
532 A291 24y brt blue 9.00 4.00

Uji River A292

View from Uji Bridge A293

Perf. 13x13½, 13½x13

1951, Aug. 1 Engr.

533 A292 8y brown 8.50 2.75
534 A293 24y deep blue 8.00 3.50

Oura Catholic Church, Nagasaki A294

Sofuku Temple A295

1951, Sept. 15 Photo. *Perf. 13½*

535 A294 8y carmine rose 11.00 2.75
536 A295 24y dull blue 10.00 3.50

Marunuma A296

Sugenuma A297

1951, Oct. 1

537 A296 8y rose violet 12.50 2.75
a. Imperf., pair
538 A297 24y dull blue grn 7.50 4.00

Kakuenpo (peak) A298

Nagatoro Bridge A299

Shosenkyo Gorge.

1951, Oct. 15

539 A298 8y brown red 11.00 2.75
540 A299 24y dp Prus grn 12.00 4.00
Nos. 523-540 (18) 275.50 81.75

Boy's Head and Seedling — A300

1951, May 5 *Perf. 13½*

541 A300 8y orange brown 22.50 3.00

Issued to publicize Children's Day, May 5, 1951.

Oirase River — A301

Lake Towada — A302

View from Kankodai A303

Mt. Hakkoda from Mt. Yokodake A304

1951, July 20 Photo. *Perf. 13x13½*

542 A301 2y brown 2.50 .95
543 A302 8y green 10.00 1.40
544 A303 14y dark red 11.50 4.75
545 A304 24y blue 12.00 5.50
a. Souv. sheet of 4, #542-545 45.00 45.00
Nos. 542-545 (4) 36.00 12.60

Towada Natl. Park. No. 545a sold for 55y.

Chrysanthemum A305

National Flag A306

1951, Sept. 9 *Perf. 13½*

546 A305 2y orange brown 2.25 1.10
547 A306 8y slate blue & red 6.75 2.75
548 A305 24y blue green 20.00 7.00
Nos. 546-548 (3) 29.00 10.85

Signing of the peace treaty of 1951.

Putting the Shot A307

Hockey A308

1951, Oct. 27

549 A307 2y orange brown 3.50 1.75
550 A308 2y gray blue 3.50 1.75
a. Pair, #549-550 10.00 8.00

6th Natl. Athletic Meet, Hiroshima, 10/27-31.

Okina Mask — A309

1952, Jan. 16 Photo. *Perf. 13½x13*

551 A309 5y crimson rose 14.00 1.25

New Year Greetings 1952

Sheets reproducing four of these stamps with Japanese inscriptions and floral ornament at left were awarded as sixth prize in the national lottery. Value $150.

Southern Cross from Ship A310

Earth and Big Dipper A311

1952, Feb. 19

552 A310 5y purple 6.00 1.25
553 A311 10y dark green 17.50 3.00

75th anniv. of Japan's admission to the UPU.

Red Cross and Lilies
A312

Red Cross Nurse
A313

1952, May 1

554 A312 5y rose red & dk red 4.25 .95
555 A313 10y dk green & red 10.00 2.00
a. Red cross omitted *500.00*
b. Imperf., pair *75.00*

75th anniv. of the formation of the Japanese Red Cross Society.

Goldfish — A314

A314a

A314b

A314c

1952 ***Perf. 13x13½***
556 A314 35y red orange 10.00 .25
a. Imperf., pair

Types of 1951 Redrawn; Zeros Omitted
Unwmk.

557 A314a 1y dark brown .55 .25
558 A314b 50y org brn 5.00 .25

Typo.

559 A314c 4y dp cl & pale rose 1.50 .25
a. Background (pale rose) omitted

Ornamental frame and background added, denomination at upper left, Japanese characters at upper right.

Japanese Serow — A315

Photo.

560 A315 8y brown .30 .25
Nos. 556-560 (5) 17.35 1.25

Mt. Yari
A316

Kurobe Valley
A317

Mt. Shirouma
A318

Mt. Norikura — A319

1952, July 5 ***Perf. 13½x13, 13x13½***
561 A316 5y red brn 6.00 1.00
562 A317 10y blue green 27.50 3.50
563 A318 14y bright red 7.50 7.00
564 A319 24y bright blue 12.50 7.00
a. Souv. sheet of 4, #561-564, imperf. 100.00 75.00
Nos. 561-564 (4) 53.50 18.50

Japan Alps (Chubu-Sangaku) National Park. No. 564a sold for 60y.

Yasuda Hall, Tokyo University — A320

1952, Oct. 1 **Engr.** ***Perf. 13***
565 A320 10y green 18.00 2.50

75th anniversary of the founding of Tokyo University.

Yomei Gate, Nikko — A321

1952, Oct. 15 **Photo.** ***Perf. 13x13½***
566 A321 45y blue 4.50 .25

Mountain Climber — A322

1952, Oct. 18 **Dated "1952"**
567 A322 5y shown 7.50 2.00
568 A322 5y Wrestlers 7.50 2.00
a. Pair, #567-568 17.50 9.00

7th Nat.l Athletic Meet, Fukushima, 10/18-22.

Mt. Azuma — A323

Mt. Asahi — A324

Mt. Bandai — A325

Mt. Gatsun — A326

Unwmk.

1952, Oct. 18 **Photo.** ***Perf. 13***
569 A323 5y org brn 3.75 .60
570 A324 10y olive grn 11.50 1.50
571 A325 14y rose red 4.50 2.25
572 A326 24y Prus blue 10.00 4.00
a. Souv. sheet of 4, #569-572, imperf. 80.00 60.00
Nos. 569-572 (4) 29.75 8.35

Bandai-Asahi National Park. No. 572a sold for 60y.

Kirin
A327

Flag of Crown Prince
A328

Engr. and Photo.

1952, Nov. 10 ***Perf. 13½***
573 A327 5y red org & pur 2.25 1.00
574 A327 10y red org & dk grn 2.50 1.50
575 A328 24y deep blue 16.00 8.00
a. Souv. sheet of 3, #573-575, imperf. 80.00 *90.00*
Nos. 573-575 (3) 20.75 10.50

Issued to commemorate the nomination of Crown Prince Akihito as Heir Apparent.

No. 575a measures 130x129mm, and has a background design of phoenix and clouds in violet brown and blue. Sold for 50y.

Sambaso Doll — A329

Perf. 13½x13
1953, Jan, 1 **Photo.** **Unwmk.**
576 A329 5y carmine 9.50 1.00

For postage on New Year's cards, later for ordinary use.

Sheets of 4 were awarded as 6th prize in the natl. lottery. Value $100.

First Electric Lamp in Japan — A330

1953, Mar. 25
577 A330 10y brown 8.00 2.25

75th anniv. of electric lighting in Japan.

"Kintai Bridge," Print by Hiroshige — A331

Kintai Bridge as Rebuilt in 1953 — A332

1953, May 3 ***Perf. 13***
578 A331 10y chestnut 8.00 2.50
579 A332 24y blue 8.00 4.00

Kannon Type of 1951 Redrawn; Zeros Omitted

A332a

1953-54 **Typo.**
580 A332a 10y red brn & lil 4.00 .25
a. Booklet pane 10 + 2 labels (souvenir) ('54) 150.00 140.00
b. Bklt. pane 10 + 2 labels ('54) 67.50 60.00

No. 580a was issued in honor of Philatelic Week 1954. The inscriptions on the two labels are arranged in two columns of boldface characters.

On No. 580b, the left-hand label inscriptions are arranged in three columns of mixed heavy and thin characters.

See Nos. 611a-611b and 672.

Lake Shikotsu, Hokkaido
A333

Mt. Yotei — A334

1953, July 25 **Photo.** ***Perf. 13***
581 A333 5y ultra 2.00 .55
582 A334 10y green 5.00 1.10
a. Souv. sheet of 2, #581-582, imperf., no gum 45.00 35.00

Shikotsu-Toya National Park. No. 582a sold for 20 yen.

Akita Dog
A335

Cormorant Fishing
A336

1953 **Unwmk.**
583 A335 2y gray .30 .25

Engr.

584 A336 100y dark red 35.00 .25
a. Imperf., pair *2,750.*

See No. 1622.

Futamigaura Beach — A337

Namikiri Coast — A338

1953, Oct. 2 **Photo.**
585 A337 5y red 2.50 .75
586 A338 10y blue 6.00 1.50
a. Souv. sheet of 2, #585-586, imperf., no gum 25.00 20.00

Ise-Shima National Park.

Phoenix — A339

Design: 10y, Japanese crane in flight.

1953, Oct. 12 **Engr.** ***Perf. 12½***
587 A339 5y brown carmine 3.50 1.50

Photo.

588 A339 10y dark blue 7.50 2.50

Nos. 587-588 were issued on the occasion of the return of Crown Prince Akihito from his visit to Europe and America. Issued in sheets of 20 with marginal inscription.

Rugby Match — A340

Judo — A341

1953, Oct. 22 ***Perf. 13½***
589 A340 5y black 5.75 1.25
590 A341 5y blue green 5.75 1.25
a. Pair, #589-590 13.50 7.50

8th Natl. Athletic Meet, Matsuyama, Oct. 22-26.

Sky and Top of Observatory — A342

1953, Oct. 29
591 A342 10y dk gray blue 12.00 2.50

75th anniversary of the Tokyo Astronomical Observatory.

Mt. Unzen from Golf Course — A343

Mt. Unzen from Chijiwa Beach — A344

1953, Nov. 20 ***Perf. 13***

592 A343 5y red 2.00 .75
593 A344 10y blue 6.00 1.50
a. Souv. sheet of 2, #592-593, imperf., no gum 25.00 20.00

Unzen National Park.

Toy Horse — A345

1953, Dec. 25 ***Perf. 13½x13***

594 A345 5y rose 7.50 .80

New Year Greetings 1953
Issued to pay postage on New Year's cards, later for ordinary use. A sheet reproducing four of these stamps was awarded as sixth prize in the national lottery. Value, $47.50.

Racing Skaters — A346

1954, Jan. 16

595 A346 10y blue 6.00 2.00

World Speed Skating Matches for Men, Sapporo City, Jan. 16-17, 1954.

Golden Hall, Chusonji Temple — A347

1954, Jan. 20

596 A347 20y olive green 1.25 .25

Thread, Pearls, Gears, Buttons and Globe — A348

1954, Apr. 10

597 A348 10y dark red 6.00 2.00

International Trade Fair, Osaka, Apr. 10-23.

Little Cuckoo — A349

1954, May 10 ***Perf. 13x13½***

598 A349 3y blue green .30 .25
a. Imperf., pair *500.00*

For stamp inscribed "NIPPON," see No. 1067.

Wrestlers — A350

1954, May 22 **Engr.**

599 A350 10y deep green 3.50 1.75

World Free Style Wrestling Championship Matches, Tokyo, 1954.

Mt. Asama — A351

Mt. Tanikawa A352

1954, June 25 ***Perf. 13***

600 A351 5y dk gray brn 2.50 .75
601 A352 10y dk blue grn 5.00 1.50
a. Souvenir sheet of 2, #600-601, no gum 25.00 20.00

Jo-Shin-etsu National Park.

Table Tennis A353

Archery A354

1954, Aug. 22 **Engr.** ***Perf. 12***

602 A353 5y dull brown 4.50 1.00
603 A354 5y gray green 4.50 1.00
a. Pair, #602-603 10.00 5.75

9th Natl. Athletic Meet, Sapporo, Aug. 22-26.

Morse Telegraph Instrument A355

ITU Monument A356

1954, Oct. 13 ***Perf. 13x13½, 13½x13***

604 A355 5y dark purple brown 2.00 1.00
605 A356 10y deep blue 6.00 2.00

75th anniv. of Japanese membership in the ITU.

Daruma Doll — A357

1954, Dec. 20 **Photo.** ***Perf. 13½x13***

606 A357 5y black & red 6.00 .75

Sheets reproducing four of these stamps with Japanese inscriptions and ornaments were awarded as fifth prize in the national lottery. Value $45.

Mountain Stream, Tama Gorge A358

Chichibu Mountains A359

1955, Mar. 1 **Engr.** ***Perf. 13***

607 A358 5y blue 1.75 .75
608 A359 10y red brown 2.25 1.00
a. Souv. sheet of 2, #607-608, imperf., no gum 25.00 20.00

Chichibu-Tama National Park.

Bridge and Iris — A360

1955, Mar. 15 ***Perf. 13x13½***

609 A360 500y brown purple 60.00 .25

Paper Carp as Flown on Boys' Day — A361

Unwmk.

1955, May 16 **Photo.** ***Perf. 13***

610 A361 10y multicolored 6.00 2.00

15th congress of the International Chamber of Commerce, Tokyo, May 16-21, 1955.

Mandarin Ducks — A362

1955-64

611 A362 5y lt bl & red brn .30 .25
a. Bklt. pane, 4 #611, 8 #580 ('59) *50.00*
b. Bklt. pane, 4 #611, 8 #725 ('63) *35.00* 17.00
c. Bklt. pane of 4 ('64) 4.25 2.75
d. Imperf., pair 1,400.

See Nos. 738, 881d, 914b.

Benten Cape A363

Jodo Beach A364

1955, Sept. 30

612 A363 5y deep green 1.50 .60
613 A364 10y rose lake 2.00 1.00
a. Souv. sheet of 2, #612-613, imperf., no gum 25.00 20.00

Rikuchu-Kaigan National Park.
No. 613a sold for 20y.

Gymnastics A365

Runners A366

1955, Oct. 30 **Engr.**

614 A365 5y brown lake 1.75 .75
615 A366 5y bluish black 1.75 .75
a. Pair, #614-615 6.50 5.00

10th National Athletic Meet, Kanagawa Prefecture.
See Nos. 639-640, 657.

"A Girl Blowing Glass Toy," by Utamaro — A367

1955, Nov. 1 **Photo.**

616 A367 10y multicolored 10.00 7.50

150th anniv. of the death of Utamaro, wood-cut artist, and to publicize Philatelic Week, Nov. 1955. Issued in sheets of 10.

Kokeshi Dolls — A368

1955, Dec. 30 **Unwmk.** ***Perf. 13***

617 A368 5y olive grn & red 2.50 .35

New Year Greetings 1956
Sheets reproducing four of these stamps, were awarded as fifth prize in the New Year's lottery. Value, $35.

Table Tennis — A369

1956, Apr. 2 ***Perf. 13x13½***

618 A369 10y red brown 2.00 .75

Intl. Table Tennis Championship, Tokyo, 4/2-11.

Judo — A370

1956, May 2 ***Perf. 13***

619 A370 10y green & brn pur 2.00 .75

Issued to publicize the first World Judo Championship Meet, Tokyo, May 3, 1956.

Boy and Girl with Paper Carp — A371

1956, May 5

620 A371 5y lt blue & blk 1.50 .75

Establishment of World Children's Day, 5/5/56.

Water Plants, Lake Akan A372

Big Purple Butterfly A373

1956 **Unwmk.** ***Perf. 13***

621 A372 55y lt blue, grn & blk 12.50 .55
622 A373 75y multicolored 8.00 .55

See Nos. 887A, 917.

Castle Type of 1951
Redrawn; Zeros Omitted

A373a

1956 **Engr.** ***Perf. 13½x13***

623 A373a 14y gray olive 6.00 2.00

Osezaki Promontory A374

Kujuku Island — A375

1956, Oct. 1 **Photo.**

624 A374 5y red brown 1.00 .45

Engr. & Photo.

625 A375 10y lt blue & indigo 1.50 1.00
a. Souv. sheet of 2, #624-625, imperf., no gum 20.00 17.50

Saikai National Park.
No. 625a sold for 20y.

Palace Moat and Modern Tokyo — A376

1956, Oct. 1 **Engr.**

626 A376 10y dull purple 2.50 1.00

500th anniv. of the founding of Tokyo.

Sakuma Dam — A377

1956, Oct. 15 Unwmk. *Perf. 13*
627 A377 10y dark blue 2.25 1.00

Completion of Sakuma Dam.

Long Jump A378 — Basketball A379

1956, Oct. 28 *Perf. 13½x13*
628 A378 5y brown violet 1.00 .75
629 A379 5y steel blue 1.00 .75
a. Pair, #628-629 3.00 3.00

11th Natl. Athletic Meet, Hyogo Prefecture. See No. 658.

Kabuki Actor Ebizo Ichikawa by Sharaku — A380

1956, Nov. 1 Photo. *Perf. 13*
630 A380 10y multicolored 10.00 7.50

Stamp Week. Sheets of 10.

Mount Manaslu — A381

1956, Nov. 3
631 A381 10y multicolored 4.00 2.00

Japanese expedition which climbed Mount Manaslu in the Himalayas on May 9 and 11, 1956.

Electric Locomotive and Hiroshige's "Yui Stage" — A382

1956, Nov. 19 Unwmk. *Perf. 13*
632 A382 10y dk ol bis, blk & grn 6.00 2.00

Electrification of Tokaido Line.

Cogwheel, Vacuum Tube and Ship — A383

1956, Dec. 18 Engr.
633 A383 10y ultra 1.00 .75

Japanese Machinery Floating Fair.

Toy Whale — A384

1956, Dec. 20 Photo.
634 A384 5y multicolored 1.50 .35
a. Imperf., pair

Sheets reproducing four of these stamps, with inscriptions and ornaments, were awarded as sixth prize in the national lottery. Value $13.50.

United Nations Emblem — A385

Photogravure and Engraved

1957, Mar. 8 Unwmk. *Perf. 13½x13*
635 A385 10y lt blue & dk car .70 .55

Japan's admission to the UN, Dec. 18, 1956.

Temple Type of 1950 Redrawn; Zeros Omitted

A385a

1957-59 Engr. *Perf. 13x13½*
636 A385a 24y violet 17.50 3.00
636A A385a 30y rose lil ('59) 45.00 .90
b. Imperf., pair *6,000.* 2,000.

IGY Emblem, Penguin and "Soya" — A386

1957, July 1 Photo. *Perf. 13*
637 A386 10y blue, yel & blk 1.00 .50

International Geophysical Year.

Atomic Reactor — A387

1957, Sept. 18 Engr. *Perf. 13*
638 A387 10y dark purple .45 .25

Completion of Japan's atomic reactor at Tokai-Mura, Ibaraki Prefecture.

Sports Type of 1955

No. 639, Girl on parallel bars. No. 640, Boxers.

1957, Oct. 26 Unwmk. *Perf. 13*
639 A366 5y ultra .35 .25
640 A366 5y dark red .35 .25
a. Pair, #639-640 1.00 .75

12th Natl. Athletic Meet, Shizuoka Prefecture.

"Girl Bouncing Ball," by Suzuki Harunobu — A388

1957, Nov. 1 Photo.
641 A388 10y multicolored 1.75 1.50

1957 Stamp Week. Issued in sheets of 10. See Nos. 646, 671, 728, 757.

Lake Okutama and Ogochi Dam — A389

1957, Nov. 26 Engr. *Perf. 13½*
642 A389 10y ultra .40 .25

Completion of Ogochi Dam, part of the Tokyo water supply system.

Modern and First Japanese Blast Furnaces — A390

1957, Dec. 1 Photo. Unwmk.
643 A390 10y orange & dk pur .40 .25

Centenary of Japan's iron industry.

Toy Dog (Inu-hariko) — A391

1957, Dec. 20 *Perf. 13½x13*
644 A391 5y multicolored .50 .40

New Year 1958. Sheets reproducing 4 No. 644, with inscriptions and ornaments, were awarded as 5th prize in the New Year lottery. Value $7.50.

Shimonoseki-Moji Tunnel — A392

1958, Mar. 9 *Perf. 13x13½*
645 A392 10y multicolored .25 .25

Completion of the Kan-Mon Underwater Highway connecting Honshu and Kyushu Islands.

Stamp Week Type of 1957

Design: 10y, Woman with Umbrella, woodcut by Kiyonaga.

1958, Apr. 20 Unwmk. *Perf. 13*
646 A388 10y multicolored .65 .25

Stamp Week, 1958. Sheets of 10.

Statue of Ii Naosuke and Harbor — A393

Unwmk.

1958, May 10 Engr. *Perf. 13*
647 A393 10y gray blue & car .30 .25

Cent. of the opening of the ports of Yokohama, Nagasaki and Hakodate to foreign powers.

National Stadium — A394

3rd Asian Games, Tokyo: 10y, Torch and emblem. 14y, Runner. 24y, Woman diver.

1958, May 24 Photo.
648 A394 5y bl grn, bis & pink .30 .25
649 A394 10y multicolored .30 .30
650 A394 14y multicolored .30 .25
651 A394 24y multicolored .35 .30
Nos. 648-651 (4) 1.25 1.10

Kasato Maru, Map and Brazilian Flag — A395

1958, June 18
652 A395 10y multicolored .30 .25

50 years of Japanese emigration to Brazil.

Sado Island and Local Dancer — A396 — Mt. Yahiko and Echigo Plain — A397

1958, Aug. 20 Unwmk. *Perf. 13*
653 A396 10y multicolored .70 .25
654 A397 10y multicolored .55 .25

Sado-Yahiko Quasi-National Park.

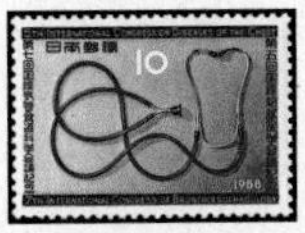
Stethoscope A398

1958, Sept. 7 Photo. *Perf. 13*
655 A398 10y Prussian green .30 .25

5th Intl. Cong. on Diseases of the Chest and the 7th Intl. Cong. of Bronchoesophagology.

"Kyoto" (Sanjo Bridge), Print by Hiroshige — A399

1958, Oct. 5
656 A399 24y multicolored 2.50 .70

Issued for International Letter Writing Week, Oct. 5-11. See No. 679.

Sports Types of 1955-56

Designs: No. 657, Weight lifter. No. 658, Girl badminton player.

1958, Oct. 19 Engr.
657 A365 5y gray blue .30 .25
658 A379 5y claret .30 .25
a. Pair, #657-658 1.00 *2.00*

13th Natl. Athletic Meet, Toyama Prefecture.

Keio University and Yukichi Fukuzawa — A400

1958, Nov. 8 Engr. *Perf. 13½*
659 A400 10y magenta .35 .25

Centenary of Keio University.

Globe and Playing Children — A401

1958, Nov. 23 Photo. *Perf. 13*
660 A401 10y deep green .30 .25

9th Intl. Conf. of Social Work and the 2nd Intl. Study Conf. on Child Welfare.

Flame: Symbol of Human Rights — A402

1958, Dec. 10 Unwmk. *Perf. 13*
661 A402 10y multicolored .30 .25

10th anniv. of the signing of the Universal Declaration of Human Rights.

Toy of Takamatsu (Tai-Ebisu) — A403

1958, Dec. 20 *Perf. 13½*

662 A403 5y multicolored .50 .30

New Year 1959. Sheets reproducing 4 No. 662, with inscriptions and ornaments, were awarded as prizes in the New Year lottery. Size: 103x89mm. Value $7.50.

Tractor and Map of Kojima Bay — A404

1959, Feb. 1 *Perf. 12½*

663 A404 10y claret & bister brn .30 .25

Completion of the embankment closing Kojima Bay for reclamation.

Karst Plateau A405

Akiyoshi Cave A406

1959, Mar. 16 Photo. *Perf. 13½*

664 A405 10y green, bl & ocher .90 .25
665 A406 10y multicolored 1.50 .25

Akiyoshidai Quasi-National Park.

Map of Southeast Asia — A407

1959, Mar. 27

666 A407 10y deep carmine .30 .25

Asian Cultural Cong., Tokyo, Mar. 27-31, marking the 2,500th anniv. of the death of Buddha.

Ceremonial Fan — A408

Prince Akihito and Princess Michiko — A409

Photogravure; Portraits Engraved

1959, Apr. 10

667 A408 5y magenta & violet .30 .25
668 A409 10y red brn & dull pur .50 .25
a. Souv. sheet of 2, #667-668, imperf. 6.00 6.00
669 A408 20y org brn & brn .85 .25
670 A409 30y yel grn & dk grn 2.50 .30
Nos. 667-670 (4) 4.15 1.05

Wedding of Crown Prince Akihito and Princess Michiko, Apr. 10, 1959.

Type of 1957

Women Reading Poetry, print by Eishi Fujiwara.

1959, May 20 Photo. *Perf. 13*

671 A388 10y multicolored 2.10 .90

Stamp Week. Issued in sheets of 10.

Redrawn Kannon Type of 1953

Coil Stamp

Perf. 13 Horiz.

1959, Jan. 20 Typo. Unwmk.

672 A332a 10y red brn & lilac 18.00 *20.00*

Measuring Glass, Tape Measure and Scales — A410

1959, June 5 Photo. *Perf. 13*

673 A410 10y lt blue & blk .30 .25

Adoption of the metric system.

Nurses Carrying Stretcher — A411

1959, June 24

674 A411 10y olive grn & red .30 .25

Centenary of the Red Cross idea.

Mt. Fuji and Lake Motosu — A412

1959, July 21 Engr. *Perf. 13*

675 A412 10y green, bl & sepia .50 .25

Establishment of Natural Park Day and 1st Natural Park Convention, Yumoto, Nikko, July 21, 1959.

Ao Cave Area of Yabakei A413

Hita, Mt. Hiko and Great Cormorant A414

1959, Sept. 25 Photo. *Perf. 13*

676 A413 10y multicolored .90 .25
677 A414 10y multicolored .90 .25

Yaba-Hita-Hiko Quasi National Park.

Golden Dolphin, Nagoya Castle — A415

1959, Oct. 1

678 A415 10y brt bl, gold & blk .50 .25

350th anniversary of Nagoya.

Hiroshige Type of 1958

Design: 30y, "Kuwana," the 7-ri Crossing Point, print by Hiroshige.

1959, Oct. 4 Unwmk.

679 A399 30y multicolored 7.50 1.50

Intl. Letter Writing Week, Oct. 4-10. See listing of No. 4448 for image of the Hiroshige print.

Japanese Crane, IATA Emblem — A416

1959, Oct. 12 Engr.

680 A416 10y brt grnsh blue .35 .25

15th General Meeting of the International Air Transport Association.

Shoin Yoshida and PTA Symbol — A417

1959, Oct. 27 Photo. *Perf. 13*

681 A417 10y brown .30 .25

Centenary of the death of Shoin Yoshida, educator, and in connection with the Parent-Teachers Association convention.

Throwing the Hammer — A418

Design: No. 683, Woman Fencer.

1959, Oct. 25 Engr.

682 A418 5y gray blue .35 .25
683 A418 5y olive bister .35 .25
a. Pair, #682-683 1.00 1.00

14th National Athletic Meet, Tokyo.

Globes — A419

1959, Nov. 2 Photo.

684 A419 10y brown red .30 .25

15th session of GATT (General Agreement on Tariffs & Trade), Tokyo, Oct. 12-Nov. 21.

Toy Mouse of Kanazawa — A420

1959, Dec. 19 Unwmk. *Perf. 13½*

685 A420 5y gold, red, grn & blk .60 .25

New Year 1960. Sheets reproducing 4 No. 685, with marginal inscription and ornaments, were awarded as prizes in natl. lottery. Value $7.50.

Yukio Ozaki and Clock Tower, Ozaki Memorial Hall — A421

1960, Feb. 25 Photo. *Perf. 13½*

686 A421 10y red brn & dk brn .30 .25

Completion of Ozaki Memorial Hall, erected in memory of Yukio Ozaki (1858-1954), statesman.

Nara Period Artwork, Shosoin Treasure House — A422

1960, Mar. 10

687 A422 10y olive gray .40 .25

Transfer of the capital to Nara, 1250th anniv.

Scenic Trio Issue

Bay of Matsushima A423

Ama-no-hashidate (Heavenly Bridge) — A424

Miyajima from the Sea — A425

1960 Engr.

688 A423 10y maroon & bl grn 1.25 .45
689 A424 10y green & lt bl 1.60 .45
690 A425 10y vio blk & bl grn 1.60 .45
Nos. 688-690 (3) 4.45 1.35

Issued: No. 688, 3/15; No. 689, 7/15; No. 690, 11/15.

Takeshima, off Gamagori — A426

1960, Mar. 20 Photo. *Perf. 13½*

691 A426 10y multicolored .95 .25

Mikawa Bay Quasi-National Park.

Poetess Isé, 13th Century Painting A427

1960, Apr. 20 Unwmk. *Perf. 13*

692 A427 10y multicolored 2.25 2.25

Stamp Week, 1960.

Kanrin Maru — A428

Design: 30y, Pres. Buchanan receiving first Japanese diplomatic mission.

1960, May 17 Engr.

693 A428 10y bl grn & brn .40 .25
694 A428 30y car & indigo 1.50 .40

Cent. of the Japan-US Treaty of Amity and Commerce. Nos. 694 and 693 form pages of an open book when placed next to each other. Souvenir sheet is No. 703.

Crested Ibis (Toki) — A429

1960, May 24 Photo. *Perf. 13½*

695 A429 10y gray, pink & red .55 .45

12th Intl. Congress for Bird Preservation.

Radio Waves Encircling Globe — A430

1960, June 1 Engr.

696 A430 10y carmine rose .30 .25

25th anniv. of the Intl. Radio Program by the Japanese Broadcasting Corporation.

Flower Garden (Gensei Kaen) — A431

1960, June 15 Photo.

697 A431 10y multicolored 1.00 .40

Abashiri Quasi-National Park.

Cape Ashizuri — A432

1960, Aug. 1 **Unwmk.**
698 A432 10y multicolored .65 .40

Ashizuri Quasi-National Park.

Rainbow Spanning Pacific, Cherry Blossoms and Pineapples — A433

1960, Aug. 20 ***Perf. 13½***
699 A433 10y multicolored .60 .25

75th anniversary of Japanese contract emigration to Hawaii.

Henri Farman's Biplane and Jet — A434

1960, Sept. 20 ***Perf. 13***
700 A434 10y brn & chlky bl .35 .25

50th anniversary of Japanese aviation.

Seat Plan of Diet A435

"Red Fuji" by Hokusai and Diet Building A436

1960, Sept. 27
701 A435 5y indigo & org .30 .25
702 A436 10y blue & red brn .50 .25

49th Inter-Parliamentary Conference.

Souvenir Sheet

1960, Sept. 27 **Engr.**
703 A428 Sheet of 2, #693-694 27.50 27.50

Visit of Prince Akihito and Princess Michiko to the US.

"Night Snow at Kambara," by Hiroshige — A437

1960, Oct. 9 **Photo.**
704 A437 30y multicolored 15.00 5.00

Issued for International Letter Writing Week, Oct. 9-15. See Nos. 735, 769.

Japanese Fencing (Kendo) — A438

No. 706, Girl gymnast and vaulting horse.

1960, Oct. 23 **Engr.** ***Perf. 13½***
705 A438 5y dull blue .40 .30
706 A438 5y rose violet .40 .30
a. Pair, #705-706 1.50 1.50

15th National Athletic Meet, Kumamoto.

Okayama Astrophysical Observatory A439

1960, Oct. 19
707 A439 10y brt violet .50 .25

Opening of the Okayama Astrophysical Observatory.

Lt. Naoshi Shirase and Map of Antarctica — A440

1960, Nov. 29 **Photo.**
708 A440 10y fawn & black .55 .25

50th anniv. of the 1st Japanese Antarctic expedition.

Little Red Calf of Aizu, Gold Calf of Iwate — A441

1960, Dec. 20 **Unwmk.** ***Perf. 13½***
709 A441 5y multicolored .80 .30

New Year 1961. Sheets reproducing 4 No. 709 were awarded as prizes in the New Year lottery. Size: 102x89mm. Value $8.50.

Diet Building at Night A442

Opening of First Session A443

1960, Dec. 24 **Photo.; Engr. (10y)**
710 A442 5y gray & dk bl .35 .25
711 A443 10y carmine .45 .25

70th anniversary of the Japanese Diet.

Narcissus — A444

No. 713, Plum blossoms. No. 714, Camellia japonica. No. 715, Cherry blossoms. No. 716, Peony. No. 717, Iris. No. 718, Lily. No. 719, Morning glory. No. 720, Bellflower. No. 721, Gentian. No. 722, Chrysanthemum. No. 723, Camellia sasanqua.

1961 **Photo.** ***Perf. 13½***
712 A444 10y lilac, yel & grn 3.75 .80
713 A444 10y brown, grn & yel 1.60 .80
714 A444 10y lem, grn, pink & yel 1.40 .80
715 A444 10y gray, brn, pink, yel & blk 1.40 .80
716 A444 10y blk, grn, pink & yel 1.00 .80
717 A444 10y gray, pur, grn & yel .65 .50
718 A444 10y gray grn, yel & brn .50 .40
719 A444 10y lt bl, grn & lil .50 .40
720 A444 10y lt yel grn, vio & grn .50 .40
721 A444 10y org, vio bl & grn .50 .40
722 A444 10y blue, yel & grn .50 .40
723 A444 10y sl, pink, yel & grn .50 .40
Nos. 712-723 (12) 12.80 6.90

Nojima Cape Lighthouse and Fisherwomen A445

1961, Mar. 15
724 A445 10y multicolored .55 .25

South Boso Quasi-National Park.

Cherry Blossoms — A446

Unwmk.

1961, Apr. 1 **Photo.** ***Perf. 13***
725 A446 10y lilac rose & gray .30 .25
a. Lilac rose omitted 300.00
b. Imperf., pair 1,100.
c. Booklet pane of 4 5.50 2.25
d. Gray omitted 200.00

See No. 611b.

Coil Stamp

1961, Apr. 25 ***Perf. 13 Horiz.***
726 A446 10y lil rose & gray 5.00 2.50

Hisoka Maeshima — A447

1961, Apr. 20 ***Perf. 13***
727 A447 10y olive & black 1.10 .25

90th anniv. of Japan's modern postal service from Tokyo to Osaka, inaugurated by Deputy Postmaster General Hisoka Maeshima.

Type of 1957

"Dancing Girl" from a "Screen of Dancers."

1961, Apr. 20 ***Perf. 13½***
728 A388 10y multicolored 1.25 1.00

Stamp Week, 1961. Sheets of 10 (5x2).

Lake Biwa — A448

1961, Apr. 25
729 A448 10y blk, dk bl & yel grn .55 .25

Lake Biwa Quasi-National Park.

Rotary Emblem and People of Various Races — A449

1961, May 29 **Engr.** ***Perf. 13***
730 A449 10y gray & orange .30 .25

52nd convention of Rotary Intl., Tokyo, May 29-June 1, 1961.

Faucet, Wheat, Insulator & Cogwheel — A450

1961, July 7 **Photo.** ***Perf. 13½***
731 A450 10y violet & aqua .30 .25

Aichi irrigation system, Kiso river.

Sun, Earth and Meridian — A451

1961, July 12
732 A451 10y yellow, red & blk .30 .25

75th anniv. of Japanese standard time.

Parasol Dance on Dunes of Tottori — A452

1961, Aug. 15
733 A452 10y multicolored .55 .25

San'in Kaigan Quasi-National Park.

Onuma Lake and Komagatake Volcano — A453

1961, Sept. 15
734 A453 10y grn, red brn & bl .60 .25

Onuma Quasi-National Park.

Hiroshige Type of 1960

Design: 30y, "Hakone," print by Hiroshige from the 53 Stages of the Tokaido.

1961, Oct. 8 ***Perf. 13***
735 A437 30y multicolored 7.50 6.00

Intl. Letter Writing Week, Oct. 8-14. See listing of No. 4448 for image of the Hiroshige print.

Gymnast on Horizontal Bar — A454

Design: No. 737, Women rowing.

1961, Oct. 8 **Engr.** ***Perf. 13½***
736 A454 5y blue green .30 .25
737 A454 5y ultra .30 .25
a. Pair, #736-737 1.00 1.00

16th National Athletic Meet, Akita. See Nos. 770-771, 816-817, 852-853.

Duck Type of 1955
Coil Stamp

1961, Oct. 2 **Photo.** ***Perf. 13 Horiz.***
738 A362 5y lt bl & red brn 2.50 2.00

National Diet Library and Book — A455

1961, Nov. 1 ***Perf. 13½***
739 A455 10y dp ultra & gold .30 .25

Opening of the new Natl. Diet Library, Tokyo.

Paper Mâché Tiger — A456

1961, Dec. 15 ***Perf. 13½***
740 A456 5y multicolored .35 .25

New Year 1962. Sheets reproducing 4 No. 740 were awarded as 5th prize in the New Year lottery. Size: 102x90, Value $9.

Mt. Fuji from Lake Ashi — A457

Minokake-Iwa at Irozaki — A458

Mt. Fuji from Mitsu Pass — A459

Mt. Fuji from Cape of Ose — A460

1962, Jan. 16 Unwmk. Photo.

741 A457	5y deep green	.40	.25
742 A458	5y dark blue	.40	.25
743 A459	10y red brown	1.10	.25
744 A460	10y black	1.10	.30
	Nos. 741-744 (4)	3.00	1.05

Fuji-Hakone-Izu National Park.

Omishima — A461

1962, Feb. 15 ***Perf. 13½***

745 A461 10y ultra, red & yel .55 .25

Kitanagato-Kaigan Quasi-National Park.

Perotrochus Hirasei A462

Sacred Bamboo A463

Shari-den of Engakuji A464

Yomei Gate, Nikko A465

Noh Mask — A466

Copper Pheasant A466a

Wind God, Fujin, by Sotatsu A467

Japanese Crane A468

Mythical Winged Woman, Chusonji A469

1962-65 Unwmk. ***Perf. 13***

746 A462	4y dk brn & red ('63)	.30	.25
747 A463	6y gray grn & car	.30	.25
748 A464	30y violet black	5.00	.25
749 A465	40y rose red	6.00	.25
750 A466	70y yel brn & blk ('65)	2.25	.25
751 A466a	80y crim & brn ('65)	1.25	.25
752 A467	90y brt blue grn	26.00	.35
753 A468	100y pink & blk ('63)	10.00	.25
754 A469	120y purple	10.00	.65
	Nos. 746-754 (9)	61.10	2.75

See Nos. 888, 888A, 1076, 1079, 1257.

Coil Stamp

Perf. 13 Horiz.

755 A464 30y dull violet ('63) 4.50 3.00

Hinamatsuri, Doll Festival — A470

1962, Mar. 3 ***Perf. 13½***

756 A470 10y brn, blk, bl & car 1.00 .50

The Doll Festival is celebrated Mar. 3 in honor of young girls.

Type of 1957

Design: Dancer from "Flower Viewing Party" by Naganobu Kano.

1962, Apr. 20 Photo. ***Perf. 13½***

757 A388 10y multicolored 1.00 .75

Stamp Week, 1962. Sheets of 10.

Sakurajima Volcano and Kagoshima Bay — A471

1962, Apr. 30

758 A471 10y multicolored .35 .25

Kinkowan Quasi-National Park.

Mount Kongo — A472

1962, May 15 ***Perf. 13½***

759 A472 10y gray bl, dk grn & sal .35 .25

Kongo-Ikoma Quasi-National Park.

Suigo Park Scene and Iris — A473

1962, June 1 ***Perf. 13½***

760 A473 10y multicolored .35 .25

Suigo Quasi-National Park.

Train Emerging from Hokuriku Tunnel — A474

1962, June 10 Photo.

761 A474 10y olive gray .85 .40

Opening of Hokuriku Tunnel between Tsuruga and Imajo, Fukui Prefecture.

Star Festival (Tanabata Matsuri) — A475

1962, July 7 Unwmk. ***Perf. 13½***

762 A475 10y multicolored .30 .25

The Tanabata festival is celebrated on the evening of July 7.

Boy Scout Hat on Map of Southeast Asia — A476

1962, Aug. 3

763 A476 10y red org, blk & bis .30 .25

Asian Boy Scout Jamboree, Mt. Fuji, Aug. 3-7.

Ozegahara Swampland and Mt. Shibutsu — A477

Fumes on Mt. Chausu, Nasu — A478

Lake Chuzenji and Mt. Nantai — A479

Senryu-kyo Narrows, Shiobara — A480

1962, Sept. 1

764 A477	5y greenish blue	.35	.30
765 A478	5y maroon	.35	.30
766 A479	10y purple	.45	.30
767 A480	10y olive	.45	.30
	Nos. 764-767 (4)	1.60	1.20

Nikko National Park.

Wakato Suspension Bridge — A481

Perf. 13½x13

1962, Sept. 26 Engr. Unwmk.

768 A481 10y rose red .65 .25

Opening of Wakato Bridge over Dokai Bay in North Kyushu.

Hiroshige Type of 1960

Design: 40y, "Nihonbashi," print by Hiroshige from the 53 Stages of the Tokaido.

1962, Oct. 7 Photo. ***Perf. 13***

769 A437 40y multicolored 5.00 4.00

Intl. Letter Writing Week, Oct. 7-13. See listing of No. 4448 for image of the Hiroshige print.

Sports Type of 1961

Design: No. 770, Woman softball pitcher. No. 771, Rifle shooting.

1962, Oct. 21 Engr. ***Perf. 13½***

770 A454	5y bluish black	.30	.25
771 A454	5y brown violet	.30	.25
a.	Pair, #770-771	.85	.85

17th National Athletic Meeting, Okayama.

Shichi-go-san Festival — A482

1962, Nov. 15 Photo. ***Perf. 13½***

772 A482 10y multicolored .30 .25

This festival for 7 and 3-year-old girls and 5-year-old boys is celebrated on Nov. 15.

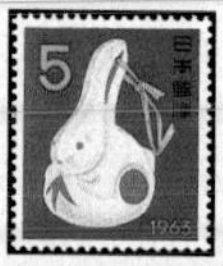

Rabbit Bell — A483

1962, Dec. 15

773 A483 5y multicolored .35 .25

New Year 1963. Sheets reproducing 4 No. 773 were awarded as prizes in the New Year lottery. Value $7.50.
See No. 2655b.

Mt. Ishizuchi — A484

1963, Jan. 11 Unwmk. ***Perf. 13½***

774 A484 10y multicolored .35 .25

Ishizuchi Quasi-National Park.

Setsubun, Spring Festival, Bean Scattering Ceremony — A485

1963, Feb. 3 Photo.

775 A485 10y multicolored .30 .25

Map of City, Birds, Ship and Factory — A486

1963, Feb. 10

776 A486 10y chocolate .30 .25

Consolidation of the communities of Moji, Kokura, Wakamatsu, Yawata and Tobata into Kita-Kyushu City.

"Frost Flowers" on Mt. Fugen — A487

Amakusa Island and Mt. Unzen — A488

1963, Feb. 15

777 A487	5y gray blue	.30	.25
778 A488	10y carmine rose	.35	.25

Unzen-Amakusa National Park.

Green Pond, Midorigaike A489

Hakusan Range A490

Perf. 13½

1963, Mar. 1 Unwmk. Photo.

779 A489	5y violet brown	.30	.25
780 A490	10y dark green	.35	.25

Hakusan National Park.

Keya-no-Oto Rock — A491

1963, Mar. 15

781 A491 10y multicolored .30 .25

Genkai Quasi-National Park.

Wheat Emblem and Globe — A492

1963, Mar. 21

782 A492 10y dark green .30 .25

FAO "Freedom from Hunger" campaign.

"Girl Reading Letter," Yedo Screen — A493

1963, Apr. 20 ***Perf. 13½***

783 A493 10y multicolored .45 .45

Issued to publicize Stamp Week, 1963.

World Map and Centenary Emblem — A494

1963, May 8
784 A494 10y multicolored .30 .25

Centenary of the International Red Cross.

Globe and Leaf with Symbolic River System — A495

1963, May 15 **Photo.**
785 A495 10y blue .30 .25

5th Congress of the Intl. Commission on Irrigation and Drainage.

Ito-dake, Asahi Range — A496

Lake Hibara and Mt. Bandai — A497

1963, May 25 **Unwmk.** ***Perf. 13½***
786 A496 5y green .30 .25
787 A497 10y red brown .35 .25

Bandai-Asahi National Park.

Lidth's Jay — A498

No. 789, Rock ptarmigan. No. 790, Eastern turtle dove. No. 791, Japanese white stork. No. 792, Bush warbler. No. 792A, Meadow bunting.

1963-64 ***Perf. 13½***

Design and Inscription

788	A498	10y	lt green	.75	.45
789	A498	10y	blue	.30	.25
790	A498	10y	pale yellow	.30	.25
791	A498	10y	grnsh blue ('64)	.30	.25
792	A498	10y	green ('64)	.30	.25
792A	A498	10y	lt rose brn ('64)	.30	.25
	Nos. 788-792A (6)			2.25	1.70

Intersection at Ritto, Shiga — A499

1963, July 15 **Unwmk.** ***Perf. 13½***
793 A499 10y bl grn, blk & org .30 .25

Opening of the Nagoya-Kobe expressway, linking Nagoya with Kyoto, Osaka and Kobe.

Girl Scout and Flag — A500

1963, Aug. 1 **Photo.**
794 A500 10y multicolored .30 .25

Asian Girl Scout and Girl Guides Camp, Togakushi Heights, Nagano, Aug. 1-7.

View of Nashu — A501

Whirlpool at Naruto — A502

1963, Aug. 20
795 A501 5y olive bister .30 .25
796 A502 10y dark green .35 .25

Inland Sea National Park.

Lake Shikaribetsu, Hokkaido — A503

Mt. Kurodake from Sounkyo Valley — A504

1963, Sept. 1 **Unwmk.** ***Perf. 13½***
797 A503 5y deep Prus blue .30 .25
798 A504 10y rose violet .35 .25

Daisetsuzan National Park.

Parabolic Antenna for Space Communications — A505

1963, Sept. 9 **Photo.**
799 A505 10y multicolored .30 .25

14th General Assembly of the International Scientific Radio Union, Tokyo.

"Great Wave off Kanagawa," by Hokusai — A506

1963, Oct. 10 ***Perf. 13***
800 A506 40y gray, dk bl & yel 4.00 1.50

Issued for International Letter Writing Week, Oct. 6-12. Design from Hokusai's "36 Views of Fuji." Printed in sheets of 10 (5x2).

Diver, Pole Vaulter and Relay Runner — A507

1963, Oct. 11 ***Perf. 13½***
801 A507 10y bl, ocher, blk & red .30 .25

Tokyo Intl. (Pre-Olympic) Sports Meet, Tokyo, Oct. 11-16.

Woman Gymnast — A508

No. 803, Japanese wrestling (sumo).

Perf. 13½

1963, Oct. 27 **Unwmk.** **Engr.**
802 A508 5y slate green .30 .25
803 A508 5y brown .30 .25
a. Pair, #802-803 .60 *.85*

18th National Athletic Meet, Yamaguchi.

Phoenix Tree and Hachijo Island — A509

1963, Dec. 10 **Photo.**
804 A509 10y multicolored .30 .25

Izu Islands Quasi-National Park.

Toy Dragons of Tottori and Yamanashi — A510

1963, Dec. 16
805 A510 5y gold, pink, aqua, ind & red .30 .25
a. Aqua omitted

New Year 1964. Sheets containing 4 No. 805 were awarded as 5th prize in the New Year lottery. Value $4.75.

Wakasa-Fuji from Takahama — A511

1964, Jan 25 ***Perf. 13½***
806 A511 10y multicolored .30 .25

Wakasa Bay Quasi-National Park.

Agave and View from Horikiri Pass — A512

1964, Feb. 20 **Unwmk.**
807 A512 10y multicolored .30 .25

Nichinan-Kaigan Quasi-National Park.

Uji Bridge — A513

View of Toba — A514

1964, Mar. 15 **Photo.**
808 A513 5y sepia .30 .25
809 A514 10y red lilac .35 .25

Ise-Shima National Park.

Takayama Festival Float and Mt. Norikura — A515

No. 811, Yamaboko floats & Gion Shrine, Kyoto.

1964 **Photo.** ***Perf. 13½***
810 A515 10y lt green & multi .30 .25
811 A515 10y grnsh blue & multi .30 .25

No. 810 issued for the annual Takayama spring and autumn festivals, Takayama City, Gifu Prefecture. No. 811 for the annual Gion festival of Kyoto, July 10-30.
Issue dates: No. 810, 4/15. No. 811, 7/15.

Yadorigi Scene from Genji Monogatari Scroll A516

1964, Apr. 20
814 A516 10y multicolored .35 .25

Stamp Week, 1964. Sheets of 10 (2x5).

Himeji Castle — A517

1964, June 1 ***Perf. 13½***
815 A517 10y dark brown .30 .25

Restoration of Himeji Castle.

Sports Type of 1961

1964, June 6 ***Perf. 13½***
816 A454 5y Handball .30 .25
817 A454 5y Woman on beam .30 .25
a. Pair, #816-817 .65 .65

19th National Athletic Meeting, Niigata.

Cable Cross Section, Map of Pacific Ocean — A518

1964, June 19
818 A518 10y gray grn, dp mag & yel .30 .25

Opening of the transpacific cable.

Tokyo Expressway Crossing Nihonbashi — A519

1964, Aug. 1 **Photo.**
819 A519 10y green, silver & blk .30 .25

Opening of the Tokyo Expressway.

Coin-like Emblems — A520

1964, Sept. 7 **Unwmk.** ***Perf. 13½***
820 A520 10y scarlet, gold & blk .30 .25

Annual general meeting of the Intl. Monetary Fund, Intl. Bank for Reconstruction and Development, Intl. Financial Corporation and the Intl. Development Assoc., Tokyo, Sept. 7-11.

Athletes, Olympic Flame and Rings A521

National Stadium, Tokyo A522

30y, Nippon Bodokan (fencing hall). 40y, Natl. Gymnasium. 50y, Komazawa Gymnasium.

1964

821	A521	5y	multicolored	.30	.25
822	A522	10y	multicolored	.30	.25
823	A522	30y	multicolored	.45	.25
824	A522	40y	multicolored	.55	.25
825	A522	50y	multicolored	.65	.25
a.	Souvenir sheet of 5, #821-825			5.00	6.00
	Nos. 821-825 (5)			2.25	1.25

18th Olympic Games, Tokyo, Oct. 10-25.
Issue dates: 5y, Sept. 9. Others, Oct. 10.

Hand with Grain, Cow and Fruit — A523

1964, Sept. 15 ***Perf. 13½***
826 A523 10y violet brn & gold .30 .25

Draining of Hachirogata Lagoon, providing new farmland for the future.

Express Train — A524

1964, Oct. 1
827 A524 10y blue & black .35 .25

Opening of the new Tokaido railroad line.

Mt. Fuji Seen from Tokaido, by Hokusai — A525

1964, Oct. 4 ***Perf. 13***
828 A525 40y multicolored 1.00 .50

Issued for International Letter Writing Week, Oct. 4-10. Issued in sheets of 10 (5x2). See Nos. 850, 896, 932, 971, 1016.

"Straw Snake" Mascot — A526

1964, Dec. 15 Photo. ***Perf. 13½***
829 A526 5y crimson, blk & yel .30 .30

New Year 1965. Sheets containing 4 No. 829 were awarded as prizes in the New Year lottery (issued Jan. 20, 1965). Value $2.75.

Mt. Daisen — A527

Paradise Cove, Oki Islands — A528

1965, Jan. 20 Unwmk. ***Perf. 13½***
830 A527 5y dark blue .30 .25
831 A528 10y brown orange .35 .25

Daisen-Oki National Park.

Niseko-Annupuri A529

1965, Feb. 15 **Photo.**
832 A529 10y multicolored .30 .25

Niseko-Shakotan-Otarukaigan Quasi-Natl. Park.

Meteorological Radar Station on Mt. Fuji — A530

1965, Mar. 10 Photo. ***Perf. 13½***
833 A530 10y multicolored .30 .25

Completion of the Meteorological Radar Station on Kengamine Heights of Mt. Fuji.

Kiyotsu Gorge A531

Lake Nojiri and Mt. Myoko A532

1965, Mar. 15
834 A531 5y brown .30 .25
835 A532 10y magenta .35 .25

Jo-Shin-etsu Kogen National Park.

Communications Museum, Tokyo — A533

1965, Mar. 25 Unwmk. ***Perf. 13½***
836 A533 10y green .30 .25

Philatelic Exhibition celebrating the completion of the Communications Museum.

"The Prelude" by Shoen Uemura — A534

1965, Apr. 20 **Photo.**
837 A534 10y gray & multi .35 .30

Issued for Stamp Week, 1965.

Playing Children, Cows and Swan — A535

1965, May 5 Unwmk. ***Perf. 13½***
838 A535 10y pink & multi .30 .25

Opening of the National Garden for Children, Tokyo-Yokohama.

Stylized Tree and Sun — A536

1965, May 9
839 A536 10y multicolored .30 .25

Issued to publicize the forestation movement and the forestation ceremony, Tottori Prefecture.

Globe, Old and New Communication Equipment — A537

1965, May 17
840 A537 10y brt blue, yel & blk .30 .25

Cent. of the ITU.

Crater of Mt. Naka, Kyushu — A538

Five Central Peaks of Aso and Mountain Road — A539

1965, June 15 Photo. ***Perf. 13½***
841 A538 5y carmine rose .30 .25
842 A539 10y deep green .35 .25

Aso National Park.

ICY Emblem and Doves — A540

1965, June 26 **Unwmk.**
843 A540 40y multicolored .65 .30

Intl. Cooperation Year, 1965, and 20th anniv. of the UN.

Horse Chase, Soma — A541

Chichibu Festival Scene — A542

1965 Photo. ***Perf. 13x13½***
844 A541 10y multicolored .30 .25
845 A542 10y multicolored .30 .25

No. 844 issued to publicize the ancient Soma Nomaoi Festival, Fukushima Prefecture; No. 845, to publicize the festival dedicated to the Chichibu Myoken Shrine (built 1584).
Issue dates: No. 844, 7/16; No. 845, 12/3.

Meiji Maru, Black-tailed Gulls — A543

1965, July 20 ***Perf. 13½***
846 A543 10y grn, gray, blk & yel .30 .25

25th Maritime Day, July 20.

Drop of Blood, Girl's Face and Bloodmobile A544

1965, Sept. 1 ***Perf. 13½***
847 A544 10y yel, grn, blk & red .30 .25

Issued to publicize the national campaign for blood donations, Sept. 1-30.

Tokai Atomic Power Station and Structure of Alpha Uranium — A545

1965, Sept. 21 **Photo.**
848 A545 10y multicolored .30 .25

9th General Conf. of the Intl. Atomic Energy Agency, IAEA, Tokyo, Sept. 21-30.

People and Flag — A546

1965, Oct. 1
849 A546 10y multicolored .30 .25

Tenth national census.

Hokusai Type of 1964

Design: No. 850, "Waters at Misaka" by Hokusai (Mt. Fuji seen across Lake Kawaguchi).

1965, Oct. 6 Unwmk. ***Perf. 13***
850 A525 40y multicolored 1.00 .60

Issued for International Letter Writing Week, Oct. 6-12. Issued in sheets of 10 (5x2).

Emblems and Diagram of Seats in National Diet — A547

1965, Oct. 15 ***Perf. 13½***
851 A547 10y multicolored .30 .25

75th anniv. of natl. suffrage, 40th anniv. of universal suffrage and 20th anniv. of women's suffrage.

Sports Type of 1961

Designs: No. 852, Gymnast on vaulting horse. No. 853, Walking race.

1965, Oct. 24 Engr. ***Perf. 13½***
852 A454 5y red brown .30 .25
853 A454 5y yellow green .30 .25
a. Pair, #852-853 .65 *.65*

20th National Athletic Meeting, Gifu.

Profile and Infant — A548

1965, Oct. 30 Photo. ***Perf. 13***
854 A548 30y car lake, yel & lt bl .45 .25

8th Intl. Conf. of Otorhinolaryngology and the 11th Intl. Conf. of Pediatrics.

Mt. Iwo from Shari Coast, Hokkaido A549

Rausu Lake and Mt. Rausu A550

1965, Nov. 15 ***Perf. 13½***
855 A549 5y Prus green .30 .25
856 A550 10y bright blue .35 .25

Shiretoko National Park.

Aurora Australis, Map of Antarctica and "Fuji" — A551

1965, Nov. 20
857 A551 10y bl, yel & dk bl .30 .25

Issued to publicize the Antarctic expedition, which left on the observation ship "Fuji," Nov. 20, 1965.

"Secret Horse" Straw Toy, Iwate Prefecture — A552

1965, Dec. 10
858 A552 5y lt blue & multi .30 .25

Issued for New Year 1966. Sheets containing four of No. 858 were awarded as prizes in the New Year lottery (issued Jan. 20, 1966). Value $2.50.

Telephone Dial and 1890 Switchboard — A553

1965, Dec. 16
859 A553 10y multicolored .30 .25

75th anniversary of telephone service in Japan.

Japanese Spiny Lobster — A554

Carp — A555

Bream — A555a

Skipjack Tuna — A555b

Three Ayu — A555c

Eel — A555d

Jack Mackeral — A555e

Chum Salmon — A555f

Yellowtail A555g

Tiger Puffer A555h

Squid — A555i

Turbo Cornutus — A555j

1966-67 Photo. *Perf. 13*

Multicolored; Background in Colors Indicated

860	A554	10y green & ultra	.30	.25
861	A555	10y blue green	.30	.25
862	A555a	10y dk blue	.30	.25
863	A555b	10y dk ultra	.30	.25
864	A555c	10y bis & dk grn	.30	.25
865	A555d	15y grnsh bl & yel	.30	.25
866	A555e	15y brt grn	.30	.25
867	A555f	15y brt grn & bl	.30	.25
868	A555g	15y lt bl grn ('67)	.30	.25
869	A555h	15y brt grn ('67)	.30	.25
870	A555i	15y ultra & grn ('67)	.30	.25
871	A555j	15y chlky bl ('67)	.30	.25
		Nos. 860-871 (12)	3.60	3.00

Famous Gardens Issue

A556

A557

A558

10y, Kobuntei Pavilion and plum blossoms, Kairakuen Garden, Ibaraki. No. 873, Japanese cranes and Okayama Castle, Korakuen Garden, Okayama. No. 874, Kenrokuen Garden in the snow.

1966-67 *Perf. 13½*

872	A556	10y gold, blk & grn	.30	.25
873	A557	15y blue, blk & mag	.35	.25
874	A558	15y silver, grn & dk brn	.35	.25
		Nos. 872-874 (3)	1.00	.75

Issued: 10y, 2/25; No. 873, 11/3; No. 874, 1/25/67.

Crater Lake, Zao — A559

1966, Mar. 15

875 A559 10y multicolored .30 .25

Zao Quasi-National Park.

Muroto Cape A560

Senba Cliffs, Anan Coast A561

1966, Mar. 22 *Perf. 13½*

876	A560	10y multicolored	.30	.25
877	A561	10y multicolored	.30	.25

Muroto-Anan Coast Quasi-National Park.

AIPPI Emblem — A562

1966, Apr. 11 *Perf. 13*

878 A562 40y multicolored .75 .25

26th General Assembly of the Intl. Association for the Protection of Industrial Properties, Tokyo, Apr. 11-16.

"Butterflies" by Takeji Fujishima A563

Photogravure and Engraved

1966, Apr. 20 *Perf. 13½*

879 A563 10y gray & multi .30 .25

Stamp Week, 1966. Sheets of 10 (2x5). See No. 907.

Hisoka Maeshima — A563a

Goldfish — A564

Chrysanthemums A565

Wisteria A565a

Hydrangea A565b

Golden Hall, Chusonji A565c

Yomei Gate, Nikko A565d

Nyoirin Kannon of Chuguji — A565f

Central Hall, Enryakuji Temple A566

Ancient Clay Horse (Haniwa) A567

A567a

A567b

A567c

Katsura Palace Garden — A568

A569

Bodhisattva Playing Flute (from Todaiji Lantern) — A570

Designs: 20y, Wisteria. 25y, Hydrangea. 35y, Luminescent squid. 45y, Lysichiton camtschatsense (white flowers). 500y, Deva King statue, South Gate, Todaiji.

1966-69 Photo. *Perf. 13*

879A	A563a	1y olive bis ('68)	.30	.25
880	A564	7y ol & dp org	1.50	.25
881	A565	15y bl & yel (bl "15")	.95	.25
b.		Bklt. pane of 2 + label ('67)	3.25	
c.		Bklt. pane of 4 ('67)	2.25	
d.		Bklt. pane of 4 (2 #881 + 2 #611) ('67)	6.00	
e.		Imperf., pair	400.00	
881A	A565a	20y vio & multi ('67)	2.25	*2.50*
882	A565b	25y grn & lt ultra	.50	.25
882A	A565c	30y dp ultra & gold ('68)	.55	.25
883	A564	35y blue, gray & blk	1.50	.25
883A	A565d	40y bl grn & brn ('68)	.60	.25
884	A565	45y blue & multi ('67)	.55	.25
885	A565f	50y dk car rose	7.50	.25
		Engr.		
886	A566	60y slate green	1.25	.25
		Photo.		
887	A567	65y orange brown	9.00	.25
887A	A567a	75y rose, blk, yel & pur	1.10	.25
888	A567b	90y gold & brn	2.00	.25
888A	A567c	100y ver & blk ('68)	1.90	.25
		Engr.		
889	A568	110y brown	1.90	.25
890	A569	120y red	2.50	.25
891	A570	200y Prus grn (22x33mm)	4.00	.25
891A	A570	500y dull pur ('69)	9.50	.25
		Nos. 879A-891A (19)	49.35	7.00

Nos. 880-881 were also issued with fluorescent frame on July 18, 1966.

Compare type A563a with type A2682.

See Nos. 913-916, 918, 926, 1072, 1079, 1081, 1244, 1256.

UNESCO Emblem — A571

1966, July 2 Photo. *Perf. 13*

892 A571 15y multicolored .30 .25

20th anniv. of UNESCO.

Map of Pacific Ocean — A572

1966, Aug. 22 *Perf. 13*

893 A572 15y bis brn, dl bl & rose .30 .25

11th Pacific Science Congress, Tokyo, Aug. 22-Sept. 10.

Amakusa Bridges, Kyushu — A573

1966, Sept. 24 Photo. *Perf. 13*

894 A573 15y multicolored .30 .25

Completion of five bridges linking Misumi Harbor, Kyushu, with Amakusa islands.

Emblem of Post Office Life Insurance and Family — A574

1966, Oct. 1

895 A574 15y yellow grn & multi .30 .25

Post office life insurance service, 50th anniv.

Hokusai Type of 1964

50y, "Sekiya on the Sumida" (horseback riders and Mt. Fuji) from Hokusai's "36 Views of Fuji."

1966, Oct. 6

896 A525 50y multicolored 1.25 .70

Intl. Letter Writing Week, Oct. 6-12. Printed in sheets of 10 (5x2).

Sharpshooter — A575

Design: No. 898, Hop, skip and jump.

1966, Oct. 23 Engr. *Perf. 13½*

897	A575	7y ultra	.30	.25
898	A575	7y carmine rose	.30	.25
a.		Pair, #897-898	.55	.55

21st Natl. Athletic Meet, Oita, Oct. 23-28.

National Theater — A576

Kabuki Scene A577

Bunraku Puppet Show — A578

1966, Nov. 1 *Perf. 13, 13½*

899	A576	15y multicolored	.30	.25
900	A577	25y multicolored	.45	.30
901	A578	50y multicolored	.85	.45
		Nos. 899-901 (3)	1.60	1.00

Inauguration of first National Theater in Japan. Nos. 900-901 issued in sheets of 10.

Rice Year Emblem — A579

1966, Nov. 21 *Perf. 13½*

902 A579 15y red, blk & ocher .30 .25

FAO International Rice Year.

Ittobori Carved Sheep, Nara Prefecture — A580

1966, Dec. 10 Photo. *Perf. 13½*
903 A580 7y bl, gold, blk & pink .30 .25

New Year 1967. Sheets containing 4 No. 903 were awarded as prizes in the New Year lottery. Value $2.

International Communications Satellite, Lani Bird 2 — A581

1967, Jan. 27 *Perf. 13½*
904 A581 15y dk Prus bl & sepia .30 .25

Inauguration in Japan of Intl. commercial communications service via satellite.

Around the World Air Route and Jet Plane — A582

1967, Mar. 6 Photo. *Perf. 13½*
905 A582 15y multicolored .30 .25

Issued to publicize the inauguration of Japan Air Lines Tokyo-London service via New York, which completes the around the world air route.

Library of Modern Japanese Literature — A583

1967, Apr. 11
906 A583 15y grnsh bl, lt & dk brn .30 .25

Opening of the Library of Modern Japanese Literature, Komaba Park, Meguro-ku, Tokyo.

Painting Type of 1966

Design: 15y, Lakeside (seated woman), by Seiki (Kiyoteru) Kuroda.

1967, Apr. 20
907 A563 15y multicolored .40 .25

Stamp Week, 1967. Sheets of 10 (2x5).

Kobe Harbor — A584

1967, May 8 Photo. *Perf. 13x13½*
908 A584 50y multicolored .95 .25

5th Cong. of the Intl. Association of Ports and Harbors, Tokyo, May 8-13.

Welfare Commissioner's Emblem — A585

1967, May 12 *Perf. 13½*
909 A585 15y dk brown & gold .30 .25

50th anniversary of the Welfare Commissioner System.

Traffic Light, Automobile and Children — A586

1967, May 22 *Perf. 13x13½*
910 A586 15y emer, red, blk & yel .30 .25

Issued to publicize traffic safety.

Kita and Kai-Koma Mountains A587

Akaishi and Hijiri Mountains A588

1967, July 10
911 A587 7y Prus blue .30 .25
912 A588 15y rose lilac .35 .25

South Japan Alps National Park.

Types of 1966-69 Redrawn and

A588a

Original - No. 881A

Redrawn - No. 915

On No. 915 the wisteria leaves do not touch frame at left and top. On No. 881A they do.

1967-69 Photo. *Perf. 13*
913 A564 7y brt yel grn & dp org .30 .25
914 A565 15y bl & yel (white "15") .30 .25
a. Pane of 10 (5x2) ('68) 2.75
b. Bklt. panes of 4 with gutter (6 #914 + 2 #611) ('68) 7.00
c. Imperf., pair 500.00
d. Blue shading omitted
e. Bklt. panes of 2 & 4 with gutter ('68) 45.00 45.00
915 A565a 20y vio & multi ('69) 1.10 .25
916 A565f 50y brt carmine .90 .25
917 A588a 55y lt bl, grn & blk ('69) .85 .25
918 A567 65y deep orange 1.10 .25
Nos. 913-918 (6) 4.55 1.50

Issued for use in facer-canceling machines. Issue dates: 7y, Aug. 1; 15y, 50y, July 1; 65y, July 20, 1967; 20y, Apr. 1, 1969; 55y, Sept. 1, 1969.

On No. 913 the background has been lightened and a frame line of shading added at top and right side.

No. 914a is imperf. on four sides.

The two panes of Nos. 914b and 914e are connected by a vertical creased gutter 21mm wide. The left pane of No. 914b consists of 2 No. 914 and 2 No. 611; the right pane, 4 of No. 914. The left pane of 2 of No. 914e includes a 4-line inscription.

Coil Stamp

1968, Jan. 9 *Perf. 13 Horiz.*
926 A565 15y bl & yel (white "15") .55 .30

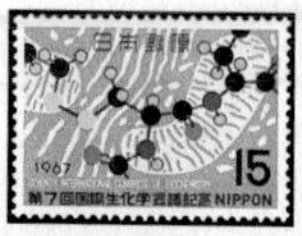

Mitochondria and Protein Model — A589

1967, Aug. 19 Photo. *Perf. 13*
927 A589 15y gray & multi .30 .25

7th Intl. Biochemistry Cong., Tokyo, Aug. 19-25.

Gymnast on Horizontal Bar A590

Universiade Emblem A591

1967, Aug. 26
928 A590 15y red & multi .30 .25
929 A591 50y yellow & multi .95 .25

World University Games, Universiade 1967, Tokyo, Aug. 26-Sept. 4.

Paper Lantern, ITY Emblem — A592

"Sacred Mt. Fuji" by Taikan Yokoyama A593

1967, Oct. 2 Photo. *Perf. 13*
930 A592 15y ultra & multi .30 .25
931 A593 50y multicolored 1.25 1.00

International Tourist Year, 1967. No. 931 issued in sheets of 10.

Hokusai Type of 1964

50y, "Kajikazawa, Koshu" (fisherman and waves) from Hokusai's "36 Views of Fuji."

1967, Oct. 6
932 A525 50y multicolored 1.25 .55

Issued for International Letter Writing Week, Oct. 6-12. Sheets of 10 (5x2).

Athlete, Wild Primrose and Chichibu Mountains — A594

1967, Oct. 22 Photo. *Perf. 13*
933 A594 15y gold & multi .30 .25

22nd Natl. Athletic Meet, Saitama, 10/22-27.

Miroku Bosatsu, Koryuji Temple, Kyoto — A595

Kudara Kannon, Horyuji Temple, Nara — A596

Golden Hall and Pagoda, Horyuji Temple, Nara — A597

1967, Nov. 1 Photo.
934 A595 15y multicolored .30 .25

Engr.
935 A596 15y pale grn, blk & red .30 .25

Photo. & Engr.
936 A597 50y multicolored 1.25 .75
Nos. 934-936 (3) 1.85 1.25

National treasures of Asuka Period (6th-7th centuries). No. 936 issued in sheets of 10.

Highway and Congress Emblem — A598

1967, Nov. 5 Photo. *Perf. 13*
937 A598 50y multicolored .95 .25

13th World Road Cong., Tokyo, Nov. 5-11.

Mt. Kumotori — A599

Lake Chichibu — A600

1967, Nov. 27
938 A599 7y olive .30 .25
939 A600 15y red lilac .35 .25

Chichibu-Tama National Park

Climbing Monkey Toy (Noborizaru), Miyazaki Prefecture — A601

1967, Dec. 11 Photo. *Perf. 13*
940 A601 7y multicolored .30 .25

New Year 1968. Sheets containing 4 No. 940 were awarded as prizes in the New Year lottery. Value $1.75.

Mt. Sobo — A602

Takachiho Gorge — A603

1967, Dec. 20
941 A602 15y multicolored .30 .25
942 A603 15y multicolored .30 .25

Sobo Katamuki Quasi-National Park.

Girl, Boy and Sakura Maru — A604

1968, Jan. 19 Photo. *Perf. 13*
943 A604 15y ultra, ocher & blk .30 .25

Cent. of the Meiji Era, and 1st Japanese Youth Good Will Cruise in celebration of the centenary.

Ashura, Kofukuji Temple, Nara — A605

Gakko Bosatsu, Todaiji Temple, Nara — A606

Kichijo Ten, Yakushiji Temple, Nara — A607

1968, Feb. 1 Engr. *Perf. 13*
944 A605 15y sepia & car .30 .25

Engr. & Photo.
945 A606 15y dk brn, pale grn & org .30 .25

Photo.
946 A607 50y multicolored 1.25 1.25
Nos. 944-946 (3) 1.85 1.75

Issued to show National Treasures of the Nara Period (710-784).

Grazing Cows and Mt. Yatsugatake A608

Mt. Tateshina A609

1968, Mar. 21 **Photo.** ***Perf. 13***

947 A608 15y multicolored .30 .25
948 A609 15y multicolored .30 .25

Yatsugatake-Chushin-Kogen Quasi-Natl. Park.

Young Dancer (Maiko) in Tenjuan Garden, by Bakusen Tsuchida — A610

1968, Apr. 20 **Photo.** ***Perf. 13***

949 A610 15y multicolored .30 .25

Stamp Week, 1968. Sheets of 10 (5x2).

Rishiri Isl. Seen from Rebun Isl. — A611

1968, May 10 **Photo.** ***Perf. 13***

950 A611 15y multicolored .30 .25

Rishiri-Rebun Quasi-National Park.

Gold Lacquer and Mother-of-Pearl Box — A612

"The Origin of Shigisan" Painting from Chogo-sonshiji, Nara — A613

Bodhisattva Samantabhadra A614

1968, June 1 **Engr. & Photo.**

951 A612 15y lt blue & multi .30 .25

Photo.

952 A613 15y tan & multi .30 .25
953 A614 50y sepia & multi 1.75 1.50
Nos. 951-953 (3) 2.35 2.00

Issued to show national treasures of the Heian Period (8-12th centuries).

Memorial Tower and Badge of Hokkaido — A615

1968, June 14

954 A615 15y grn, vio bl, bis & red .30 .25

Centenary of development of Hokkaido.

Sunrise over Pacific and Fan Palms — A616

1968, June 26 **Photo.** ***Perf. 13***

955 A616 15y blk, org & red org .30 .25

Return of Bonin Islands to Japan by US.

Map of Japan Showing Postal Codes — A617

Two types of inscription:

Type I (enlarged)

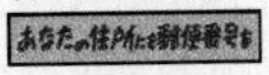

"Postal code also on your address"

Type II (enlarged)

"Don't omit postal code on the address"

1968, July 1

956 A617 7y yel grn & red (I) 2.00 .25
957 A617 7y yel grn & red (II) 2.00 .25
a. Pair, #956-957 5.00 1.50
958 A617 15y sky bl & car (I) .60 .25
a. Bklt. panes of 4 with gutter (4 #958 + 2 #959 + 2 #611) 80.00 80.00
959 A617 15y sky bl & car (II) .60 .25
d. Pair, #958-959 1.75 1.25
Nos. 956-959 (4) 5.20 1.00

Introduction of the postal code system.

The double booklet pane, No. 958a, comes in two forms, the positions of the Postal Code types being transposed.

Coil Stamps

Perf. 13 Horiz.

959A A617 15y sky blue & car (I) 1.50 .85
959B A617 15y sky blue & car (II) 1.50 .85
c. Pair, #959A-959B 4.00 4.00

Kiso River A618

Inuyama Castle A619

1968, July 20 ***Perf. 13½***

960 A618 15y multicolored .30 .25
961 A619 15y multicolored .30 .25

Hida-Kisogawa Quasi-National Park.

Youth Hostel Emblem, Trees and Sun — A620

1968, Aug. 6 **Photo.** ***Perf. 13***

962 A620 15y citron & multi .30 .25

27th Intl. Youth Hostel Cong., Tokyo, 8/6-20.

Boys Forming Tournament Emblem — A621

Pitcher and Tournament Flag — A622

1968, Aug. 9

963 A621 15y yel grn, yel, blk & red .30 .25
964 A622 15y red, yellow & blk .30 .25
a. Pair, #963-964 .65 .60

50th All-Japan High School Baseball Championship Tournament, Koshi-en Baseball Grounds, Aug. 9. Nos. 963-964 printed checkerwise.

Minamoto Yoritomo, Jingoji, Kyoto — A623

Heiji Monogatari Scroll Painting A624

Red-threaded Armor, Kasuga Shrine, Nara — A625

1968, Sept. 16 **Photo.** ***Perf. 13***

965 A623 15y black & multi .35 .25
966 A624 15y tan & multi .35 .25

Photo. & Engr.

967 A625 50y multicolored 1.25 1.25
Nos. 965-967 (3) 1.95 1.75

National treasures of Kamakura period (1180-1192 to 1333).

Mt. Iwate, seen from Hachimantai A626

Lake Towada, seen from Mt. Ohanabe A627

1968, Sept. 16 **Photo.**

968 A626 7y red brown .30 .25
969 A627 15y green .35 .25

Towada-Hachimantai National Park.

Gymnast, Tojimbo Cliff and Narcissus — A628

1968, Oct. 1 **Photo.** ***Perf. 13***

970 A628 15y multicolored .30 .25

23rd National Athletic Meet, Fukui Prefecture, Oct. 1-6.

Hokusai Type of 1964

Design: 50y, "Fujimihara in Owari Province" (cooper working on a barrel) from Hokusai's "36 Views of Fuji."

1968, Oct. 7

971 A525 50y multicolored 1.00 1.00

Issued for International Letter Writing Week, Oct. 7-13. Sheets of 10 (5x2).

Centenary Emblem, Sun and First Western Style Warship A629

Imperial Carriage Arriving in Tokyo (1868), by Tomote Kobori A630

1968, Oct. 23

972 A629 15y vio bl, red, gold & gray .30 .25
973 A630 15y multicolored .30 .25
a. Imperf., pair

Meiji Centenary Festival.

Old and New Lighthouses — A631

1968, Nov. 1 **Photo.** ***Perf. 13***

974 A631 15y multicolored .30 .25

Centenary of the first western style lighthouse in Japan.

Ryo'o Court Dance and State Hall, Imperial Palace A632

1968, Nov. 14

975 A632 15y multicolored .30 .25

Completion of the new Imperial Palace.

Mt. Takachiho A633

Mt. Motobu, Yaku Island A634

1968, Nov. 20

976 A633 7y purple .30 .25
977 A634 15y orange .35 .25

Kirishima-Yaku National Park.

Carved Toy Cock of Yonezawa, Yamagata Prefecture — A635

1968, Dec. 5 **Photo.** ***Perf. 13***

978 A635 7y lt blue & multi .30 .25

New Year 1969. Sheets containing 4 No. 978 were awarded as prizes in the New Year lottery. Value $1.75.

Human Rights Flame, Dancing Children and Globe — A636

1968, Dec. 10

979 A636 50y orange & multi .95 .25

International Human Rights Year.

Striped Squirrel — A637

1968, Dec. 14

980 A637 15y emerald & blk .30 .25

Issued to promote saving.

Kochomon Cave and Road — A638

1969, Jan. 27 **Photo.**

981 A638 15y multicolored .30 .25

Echizen-Kaga-Kaigan Quasi-National Park.

Silver Pavilion, Jishoji Temple, Kyoto A639

Pagoda, Anrakuji Temple, Nagano A640

Winter Landscape by Sesshu — A641

1969, Feb. 10 Photo. *Perf. 13*
982 A639 15y multicolored .30 .25

Photo. & Engr.
983 A640 15y lt green & multi .30 .25

Photo.
984 A641 50y tan, blk & ver 1.25 1.00
Nos. 982-984 (3) 1.85 1.50

Issued to show national treasures of the Muromachi Period (1333-1572).

Mt. Chokai, seen from Tobishima Island — A642

1969, Feb. 25 Photo.
985 A642 15y brt blue & multi .30 .25

Chokai Quasi-National Park.

Mt. Koya Seen from Jinnogamine A643

Mt. Gomadan and Rhododendron A644

1969, Mar. 25 Photo. *Perf. 13*
986 A643 15y multicolored .30 .25
987 A644 15y multicolored .30 .25

Koya-Ryujin Quasi-National Park.

Hair (Kami), by Kokei Kobayashi — A645

1969, Apr. 20 Photo. *Perf. 13*
988 A645 15y multicolored .30 .25

Issued for Philatelic Week.

Mother, Son Crossing Street — A646

1969, May 10 Photo. *Perf. 13*
989 A646 15y lt blue, red & grn .30 .25

National traffic safety campaign.

Tokyo-Nagoya Expressway and Sakawagawa Bridge — A647

1969, May 26
990 A647 15y multicolored .30 .25

Completion of Tokyo-Nagoya Expressway.

Nuclear Ship Mutsu and Atom Diagram — A648

1969, June 12
991 A648 15y gray, blk, pink & bl .30 .25

Issued to publicize the launching of the first Japanese nuclear ship, Mutsu.

Museum of Modern Art and Palette — A649

1969, June 11 Photo. *Perf. 13½*
992 A649 15y lt bl, brn, yel & blk .30 .25

Opening of the new National Museum of Modern Art, Tokyo.

Cable Ship KKD Maru and Map of Japan Sea — A650

1969, June 25
993 A650 15y lt bl, blk & ocher .30 .25

Completion of the Japan sea cable between Naoetsu, Japan, and Nakhodka, Russia.

Postcards, Postal Code Symbol A651

Mailbox, Postal Code Symbol A652

1969, July 1 Photo. *Perf. 13*
997 A651 7y yellow grn & car .30 .25
998 A652 15y sky blue & car .30 .25

1st anniv. of the postal code system and to promote its use.

Lions Emblem and Rose — A653

1969, July 2
999 A653 15y bl, blk, rose & gold .30 .25

52nd Convention of Lions Intl., Tokyo, July 2-5.

Hotoke-ga-ura on Shimokita Peninsula, Northern Honshu — A654

1969, July 15
1000 A654 15y multicolored .30 .25

Shimokita Hanto Quasi-National Park.

Himeji Castle, Hyogo Prefecture A655

"Pine Forest" (Detail), by Tohaku Hasegawa A656

"Cypresses," Attributed to Eitoku Kano A657

1969, July 21 Photo. & Engr.
1001 A655 15y lt blue & multi .30 .25

Photo.
1002 A656 15y pale brown & blk .30 .25
1003 A657 50y gold & multi 1.10 .60
Nos. 1001-1003 (3) 1.70 1.10

Issued to show national treasures of the Momoyama period (1573-1614). The 50y is in sheets of 10 (2x5); Nos. 1001-1002 in sheets of 20 (5x4).

Harano-fudo Waterfall A658

Mt. Nagisan A659

1969, Aug. 20
1004 A658 15y multicolored .30 .25
1005 A659 15y multicolored .30 .25

Hyobosen-Ushiroyama-Nagisan Quasi-Natl. Park.

Mt. O-akan, Hokkaido A660

Mt. Iwo A661

1969, Aug. 25 Photo. *Perf. 13*
1006 A660 7y bright blue .30 .25
1007 A661 15y sepia .30 .25

Akan National Park.

Angling, by Taiga Ikeno — A662

The Red Plum, by Korin Ogata — A663

Pheasant-shaped Incense Burner — A664

No. 1010, The White Plum, by Korin Ogata.

1969, Sept. 25 Photo. *Perf. 13x13½*
1008 A662 15y multicolored .30 .25

Perf. 13
1009 A663 15y gold & multi .30 .25
1010 A663 15y gold & multi .30 .25
a. Pair, #1009-1010 .75 .75

Photo. & Engr.
1011 A664 50y multicolored 1.00 .65
Nos. 1008-1011 (4) 1.90 1.40

Natl. treasures, Edo Period (1615-1867).

Birds Circling Globe and UPU Congress Emblem — A665

Woman Reading Letter, by Utamaro — A666

Designs (UPU Congress Emblem and): 50y, Two Women Reading a Letter, by Harunobu. 60y, Man Reading a Letter (Miyako Dennai), by Sharaku.

1969, Oct. 1 Photo. *Perf. 13*
1012 A665 15y red & multi .30 .25
1013 A666 30y multicolored .60 .40
1014 A666 50y multicolored 1.00 .50
1015 A666 60y multicolored 1.25 .75
Nos. 1012-1015 (4) 3.15 1.90

16th UPU Congress, Tokyo, 10/1-11/16. 15y issued in sheets of 20, others in sheets of 10.

Hokusai Type of 1964

Design: 50y, "Passing through Koshu down to Mishima" from Hokusai's 36 Views of Fuji.

1969, Oct. 7 Photo. *Perf. 13*
1016 A525 50y multicolored 1.25 .65

Issued for International Letter Writing Week Oct. 7-13. Sheets of 10 (5x2).

Rugby Player, Camellia and Oura Catholic Church — A667

1969, Oct. 26
1017 A667 15y lt ultra & multi .30 .25

24th Natl. Athletic Meet, Nagasaki, 10/26-31.

Cape Kitayama A668

Goishi Coast A669

1969, Nov. 20 Photo. *Perf. 13*
1018 A668 7y gray & dk blue .30 .25
1019 A669 15y salmon & dk red .30 .25

Rikuchu Coast National Park.

Worker in Hard Hat — A670

1969, Nov. 26
1020 A670 15y ultra, blk yel & brn .30 .25

50th anniv. of the ILO.

Dog Amulet, Hokkeji, Nara — A671

1969, Dec. 10

1021 A671 7y orange & multi .30 .25

New Year 1970. Sheets containing 4 No. 1021 were awarded as prizes in the New Year lottery. Value $1.50.

Aso Bay and Tsutsu Women with Horse — A672

1970, Feb. 25 Photo. *Perf. 13*

1022 A672 15y multicolored .30 .25

Iki-Tsushima Quasi-National Park.

Fireworks over EXPO '70 A673

Cherry Blossoms Around Globe A674

Irises, by Korin Ogata (1658-1716) A675

1970, Mar. 14 Photo. *Perf. 13*

1023 A673 7y red & multi .30 .25
1024 A674 15y gold & multi .30 .25
1025 A675 50y gold & multi .90 .45
a. Souv. sheet of 3, #1023-1025 1.75 1.75
b. Bklt. pane of 4 & 3 with gutter 3.00
Nos. 1023-1025 (3) 1.50 .95

EXPO '70 Intl. Exposition, Senri, Osaka, Mar. 15-Sept. 13.

No. 1025b contains a pane of 4 No. 1023 and a pane with Nos. 1023-1025. A 35mm gutter separates the panes.

Woman with Hand Drum, by Saburosuke Okada — A676

1970, Apr. 20 Photo. *Perf. 13*

1026 A676 15y multicolored .45 .25

Issued for Stamp Week, Apr. 20-26.

Mt. Yoshino A677

Nachi Waterfall A678

1970, Apr. 30 Photo. *Perf. 13*

1027 A677 7y gray & pink .30 .25
1028 A678 15y pale blue & grn .30 .25

Yoshino-Kumano National Park.

Pole Lanterns at EXPO A679

View of EXPO Within Globe A680

Grass in Autumn Wind, by Hoitsu Sakai (1761-1828) A681

1970, June 15 Photo. *Perf. 13*

1029 A679 7y red & multi .30 .25
1030 A680 15y blue & multi .30 .25
1031 A681 50y silver & multi .75 .30
a. Souv. sheet of 3, #1029-1031 2.00
b. Bklt. panes of 4 & 3 with gutter 2.50
Nos. 1029-1031 (3) 1.35 .80

EXPO '70, 2nd issue.

No. 1031b contains a pane of 4 No. 1029 and a pane with Nos. 1029-1031. A 35mm gutter separates the panes.

Buildings and Postal Code Symbol — A682

1970, July 1 Photo. *Perf. 13*

1032 A682 7y emerald & vio .30 .25
1033 A682 15y brt blue & choc .40 .25

Postal code system.

"Maiden at Dojo Temple" A683

Scene from "Sukeroku" A684

"The Subscription List" (Kanjincho) A685

1970, July 10

1034 A683 15y multicolored .30 .25
1035 A684 15y multicolored .30 .25
1036 A685 50y multicolored .90 .30
Nos. 1034-1036 (3) 1.50 .80

Issued to publicize the Kabuki Theater.

Girl Scout — A686

1970, July 26

1037 A686 15y multicolored .30 .25

50th anniversary of Japanese Girl Scouts.

Kinoura Coast and Festival Drum — A687

Tate Mountains Seen from Himi Coast — A688

1970, Aug. 1

1038 A687 15y multicolored .30 .25
1039 A688 15y multicolored .30 .25

Noto Hanto Quasi-National Park.

Sunflower and UN Emblem — A689

1970, Aug. 17

1040 A689 15y lt blue & multi .30 .25

Issued to publicize the 4th United Nations Congress on the Prevention of Crime and the Treatment of Offenders, Kyoto, Aug. 17-26.

Mt. Myogi — A690

Mt. Arafune — A691

1970, Sept. 11 Photo. *Perf. 13*

1041 A690 15y multicolored .30 .25
1042 A691 15y multicolored .30 .25

Myogi-Arafune-Sakukogen Quasi-Natl. Park.

G.P.O., Tokyo, by Hiroshige III — A692

1970, Oct. 6

1043 A692 50y multicolored .75 .30

Intl. Letter Writing Week, Oct. 6-12. Sheets of 10 (5x2). Design from wood block series, "Noted Places in Tokyo."

Equestrian, Mt. Iwate and Paulownia — A693

1970, Oct. 10 Photo. *Perf. 13*

1044 A693 15y silver & multi .30 .25

25th Natl. Athletic Meet, Morioka, 10/10-16.

Hodogaya Stage, by Hiroshige III — A694

1970, Oct. 20

1045 A694 15y silver & multi .30 .25

Centenary of telegraph service in Japan.

Tree and UN Emblem — A695

50y, UN emblem and Headquarters with flags.

1970, Oct. 24

1046 A695 15y olive, ap grn & gold .30 .25
1047 A695 50y multicolored .65 .25

25th anniversary of United Nations.

Vocational Training Competition Emblem — A696

1970, Nov. 10 Photo. *Perf. 13*

1048 A696 15y multicolored .30 .25

The 19th International Vocational Training Competition, Chiba City, Nov. 10-19.

Diet Building and Doves — A697

1970, Nov. 29

1049 A697 15y multicolored .30 .25

80th anniversary of Japanese Diet.

Wild Boar, Folk Art, Arai City, Niigata Prefecture — A698

1970, Dec. 10

1050 A698 7y multicolored .30 .25

New Year 1971. Sheets containing 4 No. 1050 were awarded as prizes in the New Year lottery. Value $1.60.

Gen-jo-raku A699

Ko-cho A700

Tai-hei-raku A701

1971, Apr. 1 Photo. *Perf. 13*

1051 A699 15y multicolored .30 .25
1052 A700 15y multicolored .30 .25
1053 A701 50y multicolored .75 .25
Nos. 1051-1053 (3) 1.35 .75

Gagaku, classical Japanese court entertainment.

Woman Voter and Parliament — A702

1971, Apr. 10 Photo. *Perf. 13*

1054 A702 15y orange & multi .30 .25

25th anniversary of woman suffrage.

Pines and Maple Leaves — A703

1971, Apr. 18

1055 A703 7y emerald & violet .30 .25

National forestation campaign.

Woman of Tokyo, by Kiyokata Kaburagi — A704

1971, Apr. 19
1056 A704 15y gray & multi .35 .25

Philatelic Week, Apr. 19-25.

Mailman A705

Mailbox A706

Railroad Post Office — A707

1971, Apr. 20
1057 A705 15y blk & org brn .30 .25
1058 A706 15y multicolored .30 .25
1059 A707 15y multicolored .30 .25
Nos. 1057-1059 (3) .90 .75

Centenary of Japanese postage stamps.

Titmouse — A708

1971, May 10 Photo. *Perf. 13*
1060 A708 15y emer, blk & bis .30 .25

25th Bird Week.

Penguins — A709

1971, June 23 Photo. *Perf. 13*
1061 A709 15y dk blue, yel & grn .30 .25

Antarctic Treaty pledging peaceful uses of and scientific co-operation in Antarctica, 10th anniv.

Goto Wakamatsu Seto Region A710

Kujukushima ("99 Islands"), Kyushu A711

1971, June 26 Photo. *Perf. 13*
1062 A710 7y dark green .30 .25
1063 A711 15y deep brown .30 .25

Saikai National Park.

Arabic Numerals and Postal Code Symbol — A712

1971, July 1
1064 A712 7y emerald & red .30 .25
1065 A712 15y blue & carmine .30 .25

Promotion for postal code system.

Types of 1962-67 and

Little Cuckoo A713

Mute Swan A714

Sika Deer A715

Beetle A716

Pine — A717

Noh Mask A717a

Pheasant A717b

Golden Eagle — A717c

Bronze Phoenix, Uji — A718

Burial Statue of Warrior, Ota A718a

Buddha, Sculpture, 685 A718b

Tentoki Sculpture, 11th Century A718c

Bazara-Taisho, c. 710-794 A718d

Goddess Kissho — A718e

Inscribed "NIPPON"

Photo., Engr. (No. 1087)

1971-75 *Perf. 13*
1067 A713 3y emerald .30 .25
a. Bklt. pane of 20 ('72) 2.00
1068 A714 5y bright blue .30 .25
1069 A715 10y yel grn & sep ('72) .30 .25
a. Bklt. pane of 6 (2 #1069, 4 #1071 with gutter btwn.) ('72) 2.50
1070 A716 12y deep brown .30 .25
1071 A717 20y grn & sep ('72) .30 .25
a. Pane of 10 (5x2) ('72) 4.00
1072 A565b 25y emer & lt ultra ('72) .40 .25
1074 A717a 70y dp org & blk 1.00 .25
1075 A717b 80y crim & brn 1.25 .25
1076 A467 90y org & dk brn 1.50 .25
1077 A717c 90y org & brn ('73) 1.50 .25
1079 A569 120y dk brn & lt grn ('72) 1.75 .25
1080 A718 150y lt & dk grn 2.50 .25
1081 A570 200y dp car (18x22mm; '72) 3.50 .25
1082 A718a 200y red brn ('74) 3.50 .30
1083 A718b 300y dk blue ('74) 5.50 .25
1084 A718c 400y car rose ('74) 7.00 .25
1085 A718d 500y green ('74) 9.00 .35
1087 A718e 1000y multi ('75) 15.00 .75
a. Miniature sheet of 1 20.00 15.00
Nos. 1067-1087 (18) 54.90 5.15

No. 1071a is imperf. on four sides.
Compare type A718a with types A1207 and A2686. Compare types A713, A714 and A718d with types A2683, A2684 and A2687.
See Nos. 1249-1250, 1254.

Coil Stamp

Perf. 13 Horiz.
1088 A717 20y green & sep ('72) .45 .30

Boy Scout Bugler — A719

1971, Aug. 2
1090 A719 15y lt blue & multi .30 .25

13th World Boy Scout Jamboree, Asagiri Plain, Aug. 2-10.

Rose and Rings — A720

1971, Oct. 1
1091 A720 15y ultra & multi .30 .25

50th anniv. of Japanese Conciliation System.

Tokyo Horsedrawn Streetcar, by Yoshimura — A721

1971, Oct. 6
1092 A721 50y multicolored .95 .30

Intl. Letter Writing Week. Sheets of 10 (5x2).

Emperor's Flag, Chrysanthemums and Phoenix — A722

"Beyond the Sea," by Empress Nagako — A723

1971, Oct. 14
1093 A722 15y gold, vio, red & bl .30 .25
1094 A723 15y gold, vio, red & bl .30 .25
a. Souv. sheet of 2, #1093-1094, imperf. .85 .85
b. Pair, #1093-1094 .60 .25

European trip of Emperor Hirohito and Empress Nagako, Sept. 28-Oct. 15. No. 1094a has violet map of Asia, Africa and Europe in background.

Tennis, Cape Shionomisaki, Plum Blossoms — A724

1971, Oct. 24 Photo. *Perf. 13*
1095 A724 15y orange & multi .30 .25

26th National Athletic Meet, Wakayama Prefecture, Oct. 24-29.

Child's Face and "100" — A725

1971, Oct. 27
1096 A725 15y pink, car & blk .30 .25

Centenary of Japanese Family Registration System.

Tiger, by Gaho Hashimoto — A726

Design: No. 1098, Dragon, from "Dragon and Tiger," by Gaho Hashimoto.

1971, Nov. 1 Engr. *Perf. 13*
1097 A726 15y olive & multi .30 .25
1098 A726 15y olive & multi .30 .25
a. Pair, #1097-1098 .75 .65

Centenary of Government Printing Works. Nos. 1097-1098 printed checkerwise.

Mt. Yotei from Lake Toya A727

Mt. Showa-Shinzan A728

1971, Dec. 6
1099 A727 7y slate grn & yel .30 .25
1100 A728 15y pink & vio bl .30 .25

Shikotsu-Toya National Park.

Treasure Ship — A729

1971-72
1101 A729 7y emerald, gold & org .35 .30
1102 A729 10y lt blue, org & gold .35 .30

New Year 1972. Sheets containing 3 No. 1102 were awarded as prizes in the New Year lottery. Value $1.50.
Issued: 7y, 12/10; 10y, 1/11/72.

Downhill Skiing — A730

No. 1104, Bobsledding. 50y, Figure skating, pairs.

1972, Feb. 3 Photo. *Perf. 13*

Size: 24x34mm
1103 A730 20y ultra & multi .30 .25
1104 A730 20y ultra & multi .30 .25

Size: 49x34mm
1105 A730 50y ultra & multi .65 .25
a. Souv. sheet of 3, #1103-1105 1.60 1.60
Nos. 1103-1105 (3) 1.25 .75

11th Winter Olympic Games, Sapporo, Feb. 3-13. No. 1105a has continuous design extending into margin.

Bunraku, Ningyo Jyoruri Puppet Theater
A731 A732

A733

1972, Mar. 1 Photo. ***Perf. 13½***
1106 A731 20y gray & multi .30 .25

Perf. 12½x13

1107 A732 20y multicolored .30 .25

Lithographed and Engraved

Perf. 13½x13

1108 A733 50y multicolored .75 .25
Nos. 1106-1108 (3) 1.35 .75

Japanese classical entertainment.

Express Train on New Sanyo Line — A734

1972, Mar. 15 Photo. ***Perf. 13***
1109 A734 20y multicolored .30 .25

Centenary of first Japanese railroad.

Taishaku-kyo Valley A735

Hiba Mountains Seen from Mt. Dogo A736

1972, Mar. 24
1110 A735 20y gray & multi .30 .25
1111 A736 20y green & multi .30 .25

Hiba-Dogo-Taishaku Quasi-National Park.

Heart and UN Emblem — A737

1972, Apr. 15
1112 A737 20y gray, red & black .30 .25

"Your heart is your health," World Health Day.

"A Balloon Rising," by Gakuryo Nakamura — A738

1972, Apr. 20
1113 A738 20y violet bl & multi .30 .25

Philatelic Week, Apr. 20-26.

Shurei Gate, Okinawa — A739

1972, May 15
1114 A739 20y ultra & multi .30 .25

Ratification of the Reversion Agreement with US under which the Ryukyu Islands were returned to Japan.

Camellia — A740

1972, May 20
1115 A740 20y brt grn, vio bl & yel .30 .25

National forestation campaign and 23rd Arbor Day, May 21.

Mt. Kurikoma and Kijiyama Kokeshi Doll — A741

Naruko-kyo Gorge and Naruko Kokeshi Doll — A742

1972, June 20 Photo. ***Perf. 13***
1116 A741 20y blue & multi .30 .25
1117 A742 20y red & multi .30 .25

Kurikoma Quasi-National Park.

Envelope, Postal Code Symbol A743

Mailbox, Postal Code Symbol A744

1972, July 1
1118 A743 10y blue, blk & gray .30 .25
1119 A744 20y emerald & org .30 .25

Publicity for the postal code system.

Mt. Hodaka — A745

Mt. Tate — A746

1972, Aug. 10 Photo. ***Perf. 13***
1120 A745 10y rose & violet .30 .25
1121 A746 20y blue & buff .30 .25

Chubu Sangaku National Park.

Ghost in "Tamura" A747

Lady Rokujo in "Lady Hollyhock" A748

"Hagoromo" (Feather Robe) A749

1972, Sept. 20 Engr.
1122 A747 20y multicolored .30 .25

Photo.

1123 A748 20y multicolored .30 .25

Perf. 13½x13

1124 A749 50y multicolored .85 .25
Nos. 1122-1124 (3) 1.45 .75

Noh, classical public entertainment.

School Children — A750

1972, Oct. 5 Photo. ***Perf. 13***
1125 A750 20y lt ultra, vio bl & car .30 .25

Centenary of modern education system.

Eitai Bridge, Tokyo, by Hiroshige III — A751

1972, Oct. 9
1126 A751 50y multicolored .90 .25

Intl. Letter Writing Week, Oct. 9-15.

Inauguration of Railway Service, by Hiroshige III — A752

Locomotive, Class C62 — A753

1972, Oct. 14
1127 A752 20y multicolored .40 .25
1128 A753 20y multicolored .40 .25

Centenary of Japanese railroad system.

Kendo (Fencing) and Sakurajima Volcano — A754

1972, Oct. 22
1129 A754 10y yellow & multi .30 .25

27th National Athletic Meet, Kagoshima Prefecture, Oct. 22-27.

Boy Scout Shaking Hand of Cub Scout — A755

1972, Nov. 4
1130 A755 20y yellow & multi .30 .25

50th anniversary of the Boy Scouts of Japan.

US Ship, Yokohama Harbor — A756

1972, Nov. 28 Photo. ***Perf. 13***
1131 A756 20y multicolored .30 .25

Centenary of Japanese customs. Wood block by Hiroshige III (d. 1896).

"Clay Plate with Plum Blossoms" — A757

1972, Dec. 11
1132 A757 10y blue & multi .30 .25

New Year 1973. Art work by Kenzan Ogata (1663-1743). Sheets containing 3 No. 1132 were awarded as prizes in the New Year lottery. Value $1.60.

Mt. Tsurugi — A758

Oboke Valley — A759

1973, Feb. 20 Photo. ***Perf. 13***
1133 A758 20y multicolored .30 .25
1134 A759 20y multicolored .30 .25

Mt. Tsurugi Quasi-National Park.

Mt. Takao A760

Minoo Falls A761

1973, Mar. 12 Photo. ***Perf. 13***
1135 A760 20y multicolored .30 .25
1136 A761 20y multicolored .30 .25

Meiji Forests Quasi-National Park.

Phoenix Tree — A762

1973, Apr. 7 Photo. ***Perf. 13***
1137 A762 20y brt grn, yel & dk bl .30 .25

National forestation campaign.

Sumiyoshi Shrine Visitor — A763

1973, Apr. 20
1138 A763 20y multicolored .30 .25

Philatelic Week, Apr. 20-26. Design from painting by Ryusei Kishida (1891-1929) of his daughter, "A Portrait of Reiko Visiting Sumiyoshi Shrine."

Mt. Kamagatake A764

Mt. Haguro A765

1973, May 25 Photo. ***Perf. 13***
1139 A764 20y multicolored .30 .25
1140 A765 20y multicolored .30 .25

Suzuka Quasi-National Park.

Chichijima Beach — A766

Coral Reef on Minami Island — A767

1973, June 26
1141 A766 10y grnsh bl & Prus bl .30 .25
1142 A767 20y lilac & dk pur .30 .25

Ogasawara National Park.
5th anniversary of the return of the Bonin (Ogasawara Islands) to Japan.

Tree, Postal Code Symbol A768

Mailman, Postal Code Symbol A769

1973, July 1 **Photo.** ***Perf. 13***

1143 A768 10y brt green & gold .30 .25
1144 A769 20y blue, purple & car .30 .25

Postal code system, 5th anniversary.

Sandan Gorge A770

Mt. Shinnyu A771

1973, Aug. 28 **Photo.** ***Perf. 13***

1145 A770 20y multicolored .30 .25
1146 A771 20y multicolored .30 .25

Nishi-Chugoku-Sanchi Quasi-National Park.

Tenryu Valley A772

Mt. Horaiji A773

1973, Sept. 18 **Photo.** ***Perf. 13***

1147 A772 20y lilac & multi .30 .25
1148 A773 20y vio bl, lt bl & sil .30 .25

Tenryu-Okumikawa Quasi-National Park.

Cock, by Jakuchu Ito (1716-1800) — A774

1973, Oct. 6

1149 A774 50y gold & multi .90 .25

International Letter Writing Week, Oct. 7-13. Sheets of 10.

Woman Runner at Start — A775

1973, Oct. 14

1150 A775 10y silver & multi .30 .25

28th National Athletic Meet, Chiba Prefecture, Oct. 14-19.

Kan Mon Bridge — A776

1973, Nov. 14 **Engr.** ***Perf. 13***

1151 A776 20y black, rose & yel .30 .25

Opening of Kan Mon Bridge connecting Honshu and Kyushu.

Old Man and Dog — A777

Designs: No. 1153, Old man and wife pounding rice mortar, which yields gold. No. 1154, Old man sitting in tree and landlord admiring tree.

1973, Nov. 20 **Photo.**

1152 A777 20y multicolored .30 .25
1153 A777 20y multicolored .30 .25
1154 A777 20y multicolored .30 .25
Nos. 1152-1154 (3) .90 .75

Folk tale "Hanasaka-jiiji" (The Old Man Who Made Trees Bloom).

Bronze Lantern, Muromachi Period — A778

1973, Dec. 10

1155 A778 10y emerald, blk & org .30 .25

New Year 1974. Sheets containing 3 No. 1155 were awarded as prizes in the New Year lottery. Value $1.75.

Nijubashi, Tokyo — A779

Imperial Palace, Tokyo — A780

1974, Jan. 26 **Photo.** ***Perf. 13***

1156 A779 20y gold & multi .30 .25
1157 A780 20y gold & multi .30 .25
a. Souv. sheet of 2, #1156-1157 1.10 1.10

50th anniversary of the wedding of Emperor Hirohito and Empress Nagako.

Young Wife — A781

Crane Weaving — A782

Cranes in Flight — A783

1974, Feb. 20 **Photo.** ***Perf. 13***

1158 A781 20y multicolored .30 .25
1159 A782 20y multicolored .30 .25
1160 A783 20y multicolored .30 .25
Nos. 1158-1160 (3) .90 .75

Folk tale "Tsuru-nyobo" (Crane becomes wife of peasant).

Marudu Falls A784

Marine Scene A785

1974, Mar. 15

1161 A784 20y multicolored .30 .25
1162 A785 20y multicolored .30 .25

Iriomote National Park.

"Finger," by Ito Shinsui — A786

1974, Apr. 20 **Photo.** ***Perf. 13***

1163 A786 20y multicolored .30 .25

Philatelic Week, Apr. 20-27.

Nambu Red Pine Sapling & Mt. Iwate — A787

1974, May 18

1164 A787 20y multicolored .30 .25

National forestation campaign.

Supreme Court Building — A788

1974, May 23 **Engr.**

1165 A788 20y redsh brown .30 .25

Completion of Supreme Court Building, Tokyo.

Midget Using Bowl as Boat — A789

Designs: No. 1167, Midget fighting demon. No. 1168, Princess and midget changed into prince with magic hammer.

1974, June 10 **Photo.** ***Perf. 13***

1166 A789 20y yellow & multi .30 .25
1167 A789 20y bister & multi .30 .25
1168 A789 20y bister & multi .30 .25
Nos. 1166-1168 (3) .90 .75

Folk tale "Issun Hoschi" (The Story of the Mini-mini Boy).

"Police," by Kunimasa Baido — A790

1974, June 17 ***Perf. 13***

1169 A790 20y multicolored .30 .25

Centenary of the Tokyo Metropolitan Police Department.

Japanese Otter — A791

No. 1170, Mayailurus iriomotensis. No. 1172, Pentalagus furnessi. No. 1173, Pteropus pselaphon.

Litho. and Engr.; Photo. and Engr. (Nos. 1172-1173)

1974

1170 A791 20y multicolored .30 .25
1171 A791 20y multicolored .30 .25
1172 A791 20y multicolored .30 .25
1173 A791 20y multicolored .30 .25
Nos. 1170-1173 (4) 1.20 1.00

Nature conservation.

Issue dates: No. 1170, 3/25; No. 1171, 6/25; No. 1172, 8/30; No. 1173, 11/15.

Transfusion Bottle, Globe, Doves — A794

1974, July 1 **Photo.**

1174 A794 20y brt blue & multi .30 .25

Intl. Red Cross Blood Donations Year.

Discovery of Kaguya Hime in Shining Bamboo — A795

Kaguya Hime as Grown-up Beauty — A796

Kaguya Hime and Escorts Returning to Moon — A797

1974, July 29 **Photo.** ***Perf. 13***

1175 A795 20y multicolored .30 .25
1176 A796 20y multicolored .30 .25
1177 A797 20y multicolored .30 .25
Nos. 1175-1177 (3) .90 .75

Folk tale "Kaguya Hime" or "Tale of the Bamboo Cutter."

Rich and Poor Men with Wens — A798

Poor Man Dancing With Spirits — A798a

Design: No. 1180, Rich man with two wens, poor man without wen, spirits.

1974, Sept. 9 **Photo.** ***Perf. 13***

1178 A798 20y multicolored .30 .25
1179 A798a 20y multicolored .30 .25
1180 A798 20y multicolored .30 .25
Nos. 1178-1180 (3) .90 .75

Folk tale "Kobutori Jiisan," or "The Old Man who had his Wen Taken by Spirits."

Goode's Projection and Diet — A799

"Aizen" by Ryushi Kawabata A800

1974, Oct. 1 **Photo.** ***Perf. 13***

1181 A799 20y multicolored .30 .25
1182 A800 50y multicolored .90 .25

Interparliamentary Union, 61st Meeting, Tokyo, Nov. 2-11.

Pine and Hawk, by Sesson — A801

1974, Oct. 7
1183 A801 50y sepia, blk & dk brn .85 .25

Intl. Letter Writing Week, Oct. 6-12.

UPU Emblem A802

Tending Cow, Fan by Sotatsu Tawaraya A803

1974, Oct. 9
1184 A802 20y multicolored .30 .25
1185 A803 50y multicolored .85 .25

Centenary of Universal Postal Union.

Soccer Players and Sailboat — A804

1974, Oct. 20 **Photo.**
1186 A804 10y multicolored .30 .25

29th National Athletic Meet, Ibaraki Prefecture, Oct. 20-25.

Various Mushrooms — A805

1974, Nov. 2
1187 A805 20y multicolored .30 .25

9th International Congress on the Cultivation of Edible Fungi, Japan, Nov. 4-13.

Steam Locomotive Class D51 — A806

Class C57 — A807

Designs: Steam locomotives.

1974, Nov. 26 **Photo.** ***Perf. 13***
1188 A806 20y shown .45 .25
1189 A807 20y shown .45 .25
a. Pair, #1188-1189 .95 .60

1975, Feb. 25
1190 A806 20y Class D52 .45 .25
1191 A807 20y Class C58 .45 .25
a. Pair, #1190-1191 .95 .60

Class 8620 — A808

Class C11 — A809

1975, Apr. 3
1192 A808 20y shown .30 .25
1193 A809 20y shown .30 .25
a. Pair, #1192-1193 .95 .60

1975, May 15
1194 A806 20y Class 9600 .30 .25
1195 A807 20y Class C51 .30 .25
a. Pair, #1194-1195 .95 .60

1975, June 10 **Photo. & Engr.**
1196 A806 20y Class 7100 .30 .25
1197 A806 20y Class 150 .30 .25
a. Pair, #1196-1197 .95 .60
Nos. 1188-1197 (10) 3.60 2.50

Japanese National Railways.

Ornamental Nail Cover, Katsura Palace — A810

1974, Dec. 10
1198 A810 10y blue & multi .30 .25

New Year 1975. Sheets containing 3 No. 1198 were awarded as prizes in the New Year Lottery. Value $1.60.

Short-tailed Albatrosses A811

Bonin Island Honey-eater A812

Temminck's Robin — A813

Ryukyu-Yamagame Tortoise — A814

Design: No. 1200, Japanese cranes.

1975-76 **Photo. & Engr.** ***Perf. 13***
1199 A811 20y multicolored .30 .25
1200 A811 20y multicolored .30 .25
1201 A812 20y multicolored .30 .25
1202 A813 50y multicolored .75 .25
1203 A814 50y multicolored .75 .25
Nos. 1199-1203 (5) 2.40 1.25

Nature conservation.

Issued: No. 1199, 1/16; No. 1200, 2/13; No. 1201, 8/8; No. 1202, 2/27/76; No. 1203, 3/25/76.

Taro Urashima Releasing Turtle — A815

Palace of the Sea God and Fish — A816

Smoke from Casket Making Taro an Old Man — A817

1975, Jan. 28 **Photo.** ***Perf. 13***
1204 A815 20y multicolored .30 .25
1205 A816 20y multicolored .30 .25
1206 A817 20y multicolored .30 .25
Nos. 1204-1206 (3) .90 .75

Folk tale "Legend of Taro Urashima."

Kan-mon-sho (Seeing and Hearing), by Shiko Munakata — A818

1975, Mar. 20 **Photo.** ***Perf. 13***
1207 A818 20y brown & multi .30 .25

Japan Broadcasting Corp., 50th anniv.

Old Man Feeding Mouse A819

Man Following Mouse Underground A820

Mice Entertaining and Bringing Gifts — A821

1975, Apr. 15 **Photo.** ***Perf. 13***
1208 A819 20y multicolored .30 .25
1209 A820 20y multicolored .30 .25
1210 A821 20y multicolored .30 .25
Nos. 1208-1210 (3) .90 .75

Folk tale "Paradise for the Mice."

Matsuura Screen (detail), 16th Century A822

1975, Apr. 21
1211 20y denomination at LL .30 .25
1212 20y denomination at LR .30 .25
a. A822 Pair, #1211-1212 .80 .65

Philatelic Week, Apr. 21-27.

Oil Derricks, Congress Emblem — A824

1975, May 10 **Photo.** ***Perf. 13***
1213 A824 20y multicolored .30 .25

9th World Petroleum Cong., Tokyo, May 11-16.

Trees and River — A825

1975, May 24
1214 A825 20y green & multi .30 .25

National forestation campaign.

IWY Emblem, Sun and Woman — A826

1975, June 23
1215 A826 20y orange & multi .30 .25

International Women's Year 1975.

Okinawan Dancer, EXPO 75 Emblem A827

Birds in Flight (Bingata) A828

Aquapolis and Globe A829

1975, July 19 **Photo.** ***Perf. 13***
1216 A827 20y ultra & multi .30 .25
1217 A828 30y blue grn & multi .50 .25
1218 A829 50y ultra & multi .80 .25
a. Souv. sheet of 3, #1216-1218 1.75 1.75
Nos. 1216-1218 (3) 1.60 .75

Oceanexpo 75, 1st Intl. Ocean Exposition, Okinawa, July 20, 1975-Jan. 18, 1976.

Historic Ship Issue

Kentoshi-sen 7th-9th Centuries — A830

Ships: No. 1220, Kenmin-sen, 7th-9th cent. No. 1221, Goshuin-sen, merchant ship, 16th-17th cent. No. 1222, Tenchi-maru, state barge, built 1630. No. 1223, Sengoku-bune (cargo ship) and fishing vessel. No. 1224, Shoheimaru, 1852, European-type sailing ship. No. 1225, Taisei-maru, four-mast bark training ship, 1903. No. 1226, Tenyomaru, first Japanese passenger liner, 1907. No. 1227, Asama-maru, passenger liner. No. 1228, Kinai-maru, transpacific freighter and Statue of Liberty. No. 1229, Container ship. No. 1230, Tanker.

1975-76 **Engr.** ***Perf. 13***
1219 A830 20y rose red .30 .25
1220 A830 20y sepia .30 .25
a. Pair, #1219-1220 .75 .75
1221 A830 20y lt olive .30 .25
1222 A830 20y dark blue .30 .25
a. Pair, #1221-1222 .75 .75
1223 A830 50y violet blue .65 .25
1224 A830 50y lilac .65 .25
a. Pair, #1223-1224 1.50 .75
1225 A830 50y gray .65 .25
1226 A830 50y dark brown .65 .25
a. Pair, #1225-1226 1.50 .75
1227 A830 50y olive green .65 .25
1228 A830 50y olive brown .65 .25
a. Pair, #1227-1228 1.50 .75
1229 A830 50y ultra .65 .25
1230 A830 50y violet blue .65 .25
a. Pair, #1229-1230 1.50 .75
Nos. 1219-1230 (12) 6.40 3.00

Printed checkerwise in sheets of 20.

Issued: Nos. 1219-1220, 8/30; Nos. 1221-1222, 9/25; Nos. 1223-1224, 3/11/76; Nos. 1225-1226, 4/12/76; Nos. 1227-1228, 6/1/76; Nos. 1229-1230, 8/18/76.

Apple and Apple Tree — A831

1975, Sept. 17 **Photo.** ***Perf. 13***
1231 A831 20y gray, black & red .30 .25

Centenary of apple cultivation in Japan.

Peacock, by Korin Ogata — A832

1975, Oct. 6 **Photo.** ***Perf. 13***
1232 A832 50y gold & multi .80 .25

Intl. Letter Writing Week, Oct. 6-12.

American Flag and Cherry Blossoms — A833

Japanese Flag and Dogwood — A834

1975, Oct. 14

1233 A833 20y ultra & multi .30 .25
1234 A834 20y green & multi .30 .25
a. Souv. sheet of 2, #1233-1234 .80 .60

Visit of Emperor Hirohito and Empress Nagako to the United States, Oct. 1-14.

Savings Box and Coins — A835

1975, Oct. 24

1235 A835 20y multicolored .30 .25

Japan's Postal Savings System, centenary.

Weight Lifter — A836

1975, Oct. 25

1236 A836 10y multicolored .30 .25

30th National Athletic Meet, Mie Prefecture, Oct. 26-31.

Papier-mache Dragon, Fukushima Prefecture — A837

1975, Dec. 13 Photo. *Perf. 13*

1237 A837 10y multicolored .30 .25

New Year 1976. Sheets containing 3 No. 1237 were awarded as prizes in the New Year Lottery. Value $1.60.

Types of 1963-74 and

Japanese Narcissus A841

Noh Mask, Old Man A843

Guardian Dog, Katori Shrine A845

Sho-Kannon, Yakushiji Temple A846

Inscribed "NIPPON"

Designs: 50y, Nyoirin Kannon, Chuguji Temple. 150y, Bronze phoenix, Uji. 200y, Clay burial figure of warrior, Ota.

1976-79 Photo. *Perf. 13*

1244 A565f 50y emerald .80 .25
a. Bklt. panes of 2 & 4 with gutter 5.00
1245 A841 60y multicolored 1.10 .25
1248 A843 140y lil rose & lil 2.25 .25
1249 A718 150y red org & brn 2.25 .25
1250 A718a 200y red orange 3.00 .25
1251 A845 250y blue 3.00 .25
1253 A846 350y dk violet brn 5.50 .25
Nos. 1244-1253 (7) 17.90 1.75

Coil Stamps

Perf. 13 Horiz.

1254 A715 10y yel grn & sep ('79) .30 .25
1256 A565f 50y emerald .90 .25
1257 A567c 100y ver & blk ('79) 1.50 .30
Nos. 1254-1257 (3) 2.70 .80

See No. 1631.

Hikone Folding Screen (detail), 17th Century A850

1976, Apr. 20 Photo. *Perf. 13*

1258 50y denomination at LR .55 .25
1259 50y denomination at UR .55 .25
a. A850 Pair, #1258-1259 1.25 .75

Philatelic Week, Apr. 20-26.

Plum Blossoms, Cedars, Mt. Tsukuba — A852

1976, May 22

1260 A852 50y multicolored .55 .25

National forestation campaign.

Green Tree Frog — A853

Bitterlings — A854

Sticklebacks A855

1976 Photo. & Engr. *Perf. 13*

1261 A853 50y multicolored .75 .25
1262 A854 50y multicolored .75 .25
1263 A855 50y multicolored .75 .25
Nos. 1261-1263 (3) 2.25 .75

Nature conservation.

Issued: No. 1261, 7/20; No. 1262, 8/26; No. 1263, 9/16.

Crows, by Yosa Buson — A856

1976, Oct. 6 Photo. *Perf. 13*

1264 A856 100y gray, blk & buff 1.25 .25

Intl. Letter Writing Week, Oct. 6-12.

Gymnasts and Stadium — A857

1976, Oct. 23 Photo. *Perf. 13*

1265 A857 20y multicolored .30 .25

31st National Athletic Meet, Saga Prefecture, Oct. 24-29.

Cable, Cable Ship, Map of East China Sea — A858

1976, Oct. 25

1266 A858 50y blue, blk & silver .90 .25

Opening of Sino-Japanese cable between Shanghai and Reihoku-cho, Kumamoto Prefecture.

Classical Court Dance — A859

Imperial Coach — A860

1976, Nov. 10 Photo. *Perf. 13*

1267 A859 50y multicolored .40 .25
1268 A860 50y multicolored .40 .25
a. Souv. sheet of 2, #1267-1268 .90 .65

Emperor Hirohito's accession to the throne, 50th anniversary.

Kindergarten Class — A861

1976, Nov. 16

1269 A861 50y multicolored .55 .25

Centenary of first kindergarten in Japan.

Healthy Family — A862

1976, Nov. 24

1270 A862 50y multicolored .55 .25

Natl. Health Insurance, 50th anniv.

Bamboo Toy Snake — A863

1976, Dec. 1 Photo. *Perf. 13*

1271 A863 20y multicolored .30 .25

New Year 1977. Sheets containing 2 No. 1271 were awarded as prizes in the New Year lottery. Value $1.50.

National Treasures

East Pagoda, Yakushiji Temple, c. 730 — A864

Deva King in Armor Holding Spear, Nara Period — A865

1976, Dec. 9 Photo. *Perf. 13*

1272 A864 50y multicolored .75 .25

Engr.

1273 A865 100y green & multi 1.50 .30

Golden Pavilion, Toshodai-ji Temple, 8th Century A866

Praying Women, from Heike Nokyo Sutra, 12th Century — A867

Photogravure and Engraved

1977, Jan. 20 *Perf. 13*

1274 A866 50y multicolored .75 .25

Photo.

1275 A867 100y multicolored 1.50 .30

Comic Picture Scroll, Attributed to Toba Sojo Kakuyu (1053-1140) A868

Saint on Cloud, 11th Century Wood Carving, Byodoin Temple — A869

1977, Mar. 25 Photo. *Perf. 13*

1276 A868 50y multicolored .75 .25

Engr.

1277 A869 100y multicolored 1.50 .30

Noblemen on Way to Court, from Picture Scroll, Heian Period A870

Statue of Seitaka-doji, Messenger, Kamakura Period — A871

1977, June 27 Photo. *Perf. 13*

1278 A870 50y multicolored .75 .25

Engr.

1279 A871 100y multicolored 1.50 .30

The Recluse Han Shan, 14th Century Painting — A872

Tower, Matsumoto Castle, 16th Century A873

1977, Aug. 25 Photo. *Perf. 13*

1280 A872 50y multicolored .75 .25

Photogravure and Engraved

1281 A873 100y black & multi 1.50 .30

Pine and Flowers, Chishakuin Temple, Kyoto, 1591 A874

Main Hall, Kiyomizu Temple, 1633 A875

1977, Nov. 16 Photo. *Perf. 13*

1282 A874 50y multicolored .75 .25

Engr.

1283 A875 100y multicolored 1.50 .30

Scene from Tale of Genji, by Sotatsu Tawaraya A876

Inkstone Case, by Koetsu Honami A877

1978, Jan. 26 Photo. *Perf. 13*

1284 A876 50y multicolored .75 .25

Photogravure and Engraved

1285 A877 100y black & multi 1.50 .30

Family Enjoying Cool Evening, by Morikage Kusumi A878

Yomeimon, Toshogu Shrine, 1636 A879

1978, Mar. 3 Photo. *Perf. 13*

1286 A878 50y gray & multi .75 .25

Photogravure and Engraved

1287 A879 100y multicolored 1.50 .30

Horseshoe Crabs A884

Graphium Doson Albidum A885

Firefly A886

Cicada A887

Dragonfly — A888

1977 Photo. *Perf. 13*

1292 A884 50y multicolored .75 .25

Photogravure and Engraved

1293 A885 50y multicolored .75 .25
1294 A886 50y multicolored .75 .25
1295 A887 50y multicolored .75 .25

Photo.

1296 A888 50y multicolored .75 .25
Nos. 1292-1296 (5) 3.75 1.25

Issued: No. 1292, 2/18; No. 1293, 5/18; No. 1294, 7/22; No. 1295, 8/15; No. 1296, 9/14.

Figure Skating A889

Figure Skating Pair A890

1977, Mar. 1

1297 A889 50y silver & multi .55 .25
1298 A890 50y silver & multi .55 .25

World Figure Skating Championships, National Yoyogi Stadium, March 1-6.

Sun Shining on Forest — A891

1977, Apr. 16 Photo. *Perf. 13*

1299 A891 50y green & multi .55 .25

National forestation campaign.

Weavers and Dyers (Detail from Folding Screen) A892

1977, Apr. 20

1300 50y denomination at LL .55 .25
1301 50y denomination at UL .55 .25
a. A892 Pair, #1300-1301 1.10 .60

Philatelic Week, Apr. 20-26.

Nurses — A894

1977, May 30 Photo. *Perf. 13*

1302 A894 50y multicolored .55 .25

16th Quadrennial Congress of the Intl. Council of Nurses, Tokyo, May 30-June 3.

Fast Breeder Reactor, Central Part — A895

1977, June 6

1303 A895 50y multicolored .55 .25

Experimental fast breeder reactor "Joyo," which began operating Apr. 24, 1977.

Workers and Safety Emblems A896

Work on High-rise Buildings A897

Cargo Unloading A898

Machinery Work A899

1977, July 1

1304 A896 50y multicolored .55 .25
1305 A897 50y multicolored .55 .25
1306 A898 50y multicolored .55 .25
1307 A899 50y multicolored .55 .25
a. Block or strip of 4, #1304-1307 3.50 1.25

National Safety Week, July 1-July 7.

Carrier Pigeons, Mail Box, UPU Emblem — A900

UPU Emblem, Postal Service Flag of Meiji Era, world Map — A900a

1977, June 20 Photo. *Perf. 13*

1308 A900 50y multicolored .55 .25
1309 A900a 100y multicolored 1.50 .30
a. Souv. sheet of 2, #1308-1309 2.25 2.00

Cent. of Japan's admission to the UPU.

Surgeon in Operating Room — A901

1977, Sept. 3 Photo. *Perf. 13*

1310 A901 50y multicolored .55 .25

27th Cong. of the Intl. Surgeon's Society on the 75th anniv. of its founding, Kyoto, 9/3-8.

Child Using Telephone, Map of New Cable Route — A902

1977, Aug. 26

1311 A902 50y multicolored .55 .25

Inauguration of underwater telephone cable linking Okinawa, Luzon and Hong Kong.

Early Speaker, Waves and Telegraph Key — A903

1977, Sept. 24 Photo. *Perf. 13*

1312 A903 50y multicolored .55 .25

50th anniversary of amateur radio in Japan.

Bicyclist, Mt. Iwaki and Iwaki River — A904

1977, Oct. 1

1313 A904 20y multicolored .30 .25

32nd National Athletic Meet, Aomori Prefecture, Oct. 2-7.

Flowers and Ducks, Attributed to Hasegawa Tohaku — A905

1977, Oct. 6

1314 A905 100y multicolored 1.50 .30

Intl. Letter Writing Week, Oct. 6-12.

Dinosaur, Stars, Museum — A906

1977, Nov. 2 Photo. *Perf. 13*

1315 A906 50y multicolored .75 .25

Centenary of National Science Museum.

Decorated Horse, Fushimi Toy — A907

1977, Dec. 1 Photo. *Perf. 13*

1316 A907 20y multicolored .30 .25

New Year 1978. Sheets containing 2 No. 1316 were awarded as prizes in the New Year lottery. Value $1.60.

Tokyo Subway, 1927 — A908

1977, Dec. 6

1317 50y shown .75 .25
1318 50y Subway, 1977 .75 .25
a. A908 Pair, #1317-1318 1.60 .60

Tokyo Subway, 50th anniversary.

Primrose A909

Pinguicula Ramosa A910

Dicentra — A911

1978 Photo. & Engr. *Perf. 13*

1319 A909 50y multicolored	.75	.25
1320 A910 50y multicolored	.75	.25
1321 A911 50y multicolored	.75	.25
Nos. 1319-1321 (3)	2.25	.75

Nature protection.

Issued: No. 1319, 4/12; No. 1320, 6/8; No. 1321, 7/25.

Kanbun Bijinzu Folding Screen, Edo Period A912

1978, Apr. 20 Photo. *Perf. 13*

1322 50y inscribed at left	.55	.25
1323 50y inscribed at right	1.40	.25
a. A912 Pair, #1322-1323	2.10	.65

Philatelic Week, Apr. 16-22.

Rotary Emblem, Mt. Fuji — A914

1978, May 13 Photo. *Perf. 13*

1324 A914 50y multicolored .75 .25

69th Rotary International Convention, Tokyo, May 14-18.

Congress Emblem, by Taro Okamoto — A915

1978, May 15

1325 A915 50y multicolored .55 .25

23rd International Ophthalmological Congress, Kyoto, May 14-20.

Narita International Airport, Tokyo — A916

1978, May 20

1326 A916 50y multicolored .65 .25

Opening of Tokyo International Airport.

Rainbow, Japanese Cedars, Cape Ashizuri — A917

1978, May 20

1327 A917 50y multicolored .55 .25

National forestation campaign.

Lion, by Sotatsu Tawaraya, Lions Emblem — A918

1978, June 21 Photo. *Perf. 13*

1328 A918 50y multicolored .75 .25

61st Lions Intl. Convention, Tokyo, 6/21-24.

Sumo Print Issues

Grand Champion Hidenoyama with Sword Bearer and Herald, by Kunisada I (Toyokuni III) — A919

Ekoin Drum Tower, Ryogoku, by Hiroshige — A921

Photogravure and Engraved

1978, July 1 *Perf. 13*

1329 50y multicolored	.55	.25
1330 50y multicolored	.55	.25
a. A919 Pair, #1329-1330	1.25	.75

Photo.

1331 A921 50y multicolored	.55	.25
Nos. 1329-1331 (3)	1.65	.75

Champions Tanikaze and Onogawa in Ring-entry Ceremony, 1782, by Shunsho — A922

Jimmaku, Raiden and Referee Shonosuke, 1791 Bout, by Shun'ei — A924

Photogravure and Engraved

1978, Sept. 9 *Perf. 13*

1332 50y multicolored	.55	.25
1333 50y multicolored	.55	.25
a. A922 Pair, #1332-1333	1.25	.75
1334 A924 50y multicolored	.55	.25
Nos. 1332-1334 (3)	1.65	.75

Referee Shonosuke and Champion Onomatsu, by Kunisada I — A925

Children's Sumo Play, by Utamaro — A927

1978, Nov. 11 *Perf. 13*

1335 50y multicolored	.55	.25
1336 50y multicolored	.55	.25
a. A925 Pair, #1335-1336	1.25	.75
1337 A927 50y multicolored	.55	.25
Nos. 1335-1337 (3)	1.65	.75

Wrestlers on Ryogoku Bridge, by Kunisada I — A928

Bow-receiving Ceremony at Tournament, by Kunisada II — A930

1979, Jan. 13 *Perf. 13*

1338 50y multicolored	.55	.25
1339 50y multicolored	.55	.25
a. A928 Pair, #1338-1339	1.25	.75
1340 A930 50y multicolored	.55	.25
Nos. 1338-1340 (3)	1.65	.75

Takekuma and Iwamigata (Hidenoyama) Wrestling, by Kuniyoshi — A931

Daidozan (Great Child Mountain) in Ring-entry Ceremony, by Sharaku — A933

1979, Mar. 10 *Perf. 13*

1341 50y multicolored	.55	.25
1342 50y multicolored	.55	.25
a. A931 Pair, #1341-1342	1.25	.75
1343 A933 50y multicolored	.55	.25
Nos. 1341-1343 (3)	1.65	.75

Radio Gymnastics Emblem — A934

1978, Aug. 1 Photo. *Perf. 13*

1344 A934 50y multicolored .75 .25

Radio gymnastics program exercises, 50th anniversary.

Chamber of Commerce and Industry — A935

1978, Aug. 28 Photo. *Perf. 13*

1345 A935 50y multicolored .55 .25

Tokyo Chamber of Commerce, centenary.

Symbolic Sculptures, Tokyo Stock Exchange — A936

1978, Sept. 14 Engr. *Perf. 13*

1346 A936 50y lilac, grn & brn .55 .25

Centenary of the Tokyo and Osaka Stock Exchanges.

Flowering Plum with Pheasant, from Screen, Tenkyuin Temple — A937

1978, Oct. 6 Photo. *Perf. 13*

1347 A937 100y multicolored 1.50 .30

Intl. Letter Writing Week, Oct. 6-12.

Softball and Mt. Yarigatake — A938

1978, Oct. 14

1348 A938 20y multicolored .30 .25

33rd National Athletic Meet, Nagano Prefecture, Oct. 15-20.

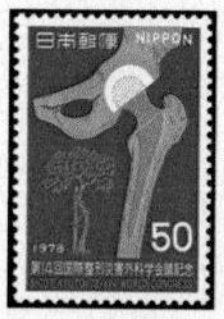

Artificial Hip, Orthopedists' Emblem — A939

1978, Oct. 16

1349 A939 50y multicolored .55 .25

14th World Cong. of Intl. Soc. of Orthopedic Surgeons (50th anniv.), Kyoto, Oct. 15-20.

Telescope and Stars — A940

1978, Dec. 1 Photo.

1350 A940 50y multicolored .55 .25

Tokyo Astronomical Observatory, cent.

Sheep Bell, Nakayama Toy — A941

1978, Dec. 4

1351 A941 20y multicolored .30 .25

New Year 1979. Sheets containing 2 No. 1351 were awarded as prizes in the New Year Lottery. Value $1.60.

Family, Human Rights Emblem — A942

1978, Dec. 4

1352 A942 50y multicolored .55 .25

Human Rights Week, Dec. 4-10.

Hands Shielding Children — A943

1979, Feb. 16 Photo. *Perf. 13*

1353 A943 50y multicolored .55 .25

Education of the handicapped, centenary.

Telephone Dials — A944

1979, Mar. 14 Photo. *Perf. 13*

1354 A944 50y multicolored .55 .25

Nation-wide telephone automatization completion.

Sketch of Man, by Leonardo da Vinci — A945

Photogravure and Engraved

1979, Apr. 7 *Perf. 13*
1355 A945 50y multicolored .55 .25

Centenary of promulgation of State Medical Act, initiating modern medicine.

Standing Beauties, Middle Edo Period A946

1979, Apr. 20 **Photo.**
1356 50y multicolored .55 .25
1357 50y multicolored .55 .25
a. A946 Pair, #1356-1357 1.25 .65

Philatelic Week, Apr. 16-22.

Mt. Horaiji and Maple — A948

1979, May 26 **Photo.** *Perf. 13*
1358 A948 50y multicolored .55 .25

National forestation campaign.

Modern Japanese Art Issue

Merciful Mother Goddess, by Kano Hogai A949

Sea God's Princess, by Aoki Shigeru A950

1979, May 30 **Photo.** *Perf. 13*
1359 A949 50y multicolored .75 .25
1360 A950 50y multicolored .75 .25

Fire Dance, by Gyoshu Hayami A951

Leaning Figure, by Tetsugoro Yorozu A952

1979, June 25 **Photo.** *Perf. 13*
1361 A951 50y red & multi .75 .25

Photogravure and Engraved

1362 A952 50y red & multi .75 .25

The Black Cat, by Shunso Hishida A953

Kinyo, by Sotaro Yasui A954

1979, Sept. 21 **Photo.** *Perf. 13*
1363 A953 50y multicolored .75 .25
1364 A954 50y multicolored .75 .25

Nude, by Kagaku Murakami — A955

Harvest, by Asai Chu — A956

Photogravure and Engraved

1979, Nov. 22 *Perf. 13*
1365 A955 50y multicolored .75 .25
1366 A956 50y multicolored .75 .25

Salmon, by Yuichi Takahashi A956a

Hall of the Supreme Buddha, by Kokei Kabayashi A956b

Photogravure and Engraved

1980, Feb. 22 *Perf. 13½*
1367 A956a 50y multicolored .75 .25

Photo.

1368 A956b 50y multicolored .75 .25

Quarantine Officers, Ships, Plane, Microscope — A957

1979, July 14 **Photo.**
1369 A957 50y multicolored .65 .25

Centenary of Japanese Quarantine system.

Girl Mailing Letter A958

Hakata Doll with Letter-paper Roll A959

1979, July 23
1370 A958 20y multicolored .30 .25
1371 A959 50y multicolored .55 .25

Letter Writing Day.

Pitcher, Baseball with Black Lion Emblem — A960

1979, July 27
1372 A960 50y multicolored .55 .25

50th National Inter-city Amateur Baseball Tournament, Tokyo, August.

Girl Floating in Space — A961

Design: No. 1374, Boy floating in space.

1979, Aug. 1
1373 A961 50y magenta & multi .75 .25
1374 A961 50y blue & multi .75 .25
a. Souv. sheet of 2, #1373-1374 1.60 1.10

International Year of the Child.

Japanese Song Issue

Moon over Castle, by Rentaro Taki A962

Evening Glow, by Shin Kusakawa A963

1979, Aug. 24 **Photo. & Engr.**
1375 A962 50y multicolored .55 .25
1376 A963 50y multicolored .55 .25

Maple Leaves, by Teiichi Okano A964

The Birthplace, by Teiichi Okano A965

1979, Nov. 26
1377 A964 50y multicolored .55 .25
1378 A965 50y multicolored .55 .25

Winter Landscape A966

Mt. Fuji A967

1980, Jan. 28 *Perf. 13*
1379 A966 50y multicolored .55 .25
1380 A967 50y multicolored .55 .25

Spring Brook A968

Cherry Blossoms A969

1980, Mar. 21
1381 A968 50y multicolored .55 .25
1382 A969 50y multicolored .55 .25
Nos. 1375-1382 (8) 4.40 2.00

Great Owl, by Okyo Maruyama — A970

1979, Oct. 8 **Photo.** *Perf. 13*
1383 A970 100y multicolored 1.50 .30

Intl. Letter Writing Week, Oct. 8-14.

Runner — A971

1979, Oct. 13
1384 A971 20y multicolored .30 .25

34th National Athletic Meet, Miyazaki, Oct. 4-19.

"ITU," Globe — A972

1979, Oct. 13 **Litho.** *Perf. 13½*
1385 A972 50y multicolored .55 .25

Admission to ITU, cent.

Woman and Fetus — A973

1979, Nov. 12 **Photo.**
1386 A973 50y multicolored .55 .25

9th World Congress of Gynecology and Obstetrics, Tokyo, Oct. 25-31.

Happy Monkeys, Osaka Toy — A974

1979, Dec. 1 **Photo.** *Perf. 13x13½*
1387 A974 20y multicolored .30 .25

New Year 1980. Sheets of 2 No. 1387 were New Year Lottery prizes. Value $1.60.

Government Auditing Centenary — A975

1980, Mar. 5 **Photo.** *Perf. 13½*
1388 A975 50y multicolored .55 .25

Scenes of Outdoor Play in Spring, by Sukenobu Nishikawa — A976

1980, Apr. 21 **Photo.** *Perf. 13½*
1389 50y multicolored .55 .25
1390 50y multicolored .55 .25
a. A976 Pair, #1389-1390 1.25 .65

Philatelic Week, Apr. 21-27. Sheets of 10.

Japanese Song Issue

The Sea
A978

The Night of the Hazy Moon
A979

Memories of Summer
A981

The Sun Flag
A980

1980 Photo. & Engr. *Perf. 13*

1391 A978 50y multicolored .55 .25
1392 A979 50y multicolored .55 .25
1393 A980 50y multicolored .55 .25
1394 A981 50y multicolored .55 .25
Nos. 1391-1394 (4) 2.20 1.00

Issued: Nos. 1391-1392, 4/28; Nos. 1393-1394, 6/16.

The Red Dragonfly
A982

Song by the Sea
A983

1980, Sept. 18 *Perf. 13*

1395 A982 50y multicolored .55 .25
1396 A983 50y multicolored .55 .25

Lullaby
A984

Coconut, by Toraji Ohnaka
A985

1981, Feb. 9 *Perf. 13*

1397 A984 60y multicolored .75 .25
1398 A985 60y multicolored .75 .25

Spring Has Come, by Tatsuyuki Takano
A986

Cherry Blossoms, by Hagoromo Takeshima
A987

1981, Mar. 10 *Perf. 13*

1399 A986 60y multicolored .75 .25
1400 A987 60y multicolored .75 .25

Modern Japanese Art Issue

Dancers, by Seiki Kuroda
A988

Mother and Child, by Shoen Uemura
A989

1980, May 12 Photo. *Perf. 13½*

1401 A988 50y multicolored .75 .25
1402 A989 50y multicolored .75 .25

The Black Fan, by Takeji Fujishima
A990

Dear Me . . . It's a Shower, by Seiho Takeuchi
A991

1980, July 7 Photo. *Perf. 13½*

1403 A990 50y multicolored .55 .25
1404 A991 50y multicolored .55 .25

Woman, by Morie Ogiwara
A992

Kurofuneya, by Yumeji Takehisa
A993

1980, Oct. 27 Photo. *Perf. 13½*

1405 A992 50y multicolored .55 .25
1406 A993 50y multicolored .55 .25

Nippon Maru, Institute Emblem — A994

1980, May 17

1407 A994 50y multicolored .75 .25

Institute for Nautical Training, training ships Nippon Maru and Kaio Maru, 50th anniversary.

Mt. Gozaisho-dake, Cedars, Flowers — A995

1980, May 24 *Perf. 13x13½*

1408 A995 50y multicolored .75 .25

National forestation campaign.

Yayosu Fire Brigade Review, by Hiroshige III — A996

1980, May 31

1409 A996 50y multicolored .75 .25

Fire fighting centenary.

A997

A997a

Letter Writing Day: 20y, Teddy Bear holding letter. 50y, Folded and tied letter of good wishes, horiz.

1980, July 23 *Perf. 13x13½, 13½x13*

1410 A997 20y multicolored .30 .25
1411 A997a 50y multicolored .75 .25

Lühdorfla Japonica — A998

1980, Aug. 2 *Perf. 13½*

1412 A998 50y multicolored .75 .25

16th Intl. Cong. of Entomology, Kyoto, Aug. 3-9.

Three-dimensional World Map — A999

1980, Aug. 25 Photo.

1413 A999 50y multicolored .75 .25

24th Intl. Geographic Cong. and 10th Intl. Cartographic Conf., Tokyo, August.

Integrated Circuit — A1000

1980, Sept. 29

1414 A1000 50y multicolored .75 .25

Intl. Federation for Information Processing Cong. '80, Tokyo, Oct. 6-9 and World Conf. on Medical Informatics '80, Tokyo, 9/29-10/4.

Camellia — A1001

40y, Rape flower, cabbage butterflies. 50y, Cherry blossoms.

1980, Oct. 1

1415 A1001 30y shown .30 .25
1416 A1001 40y multicolored .55 .25
1417 A1001 50y multicolored .75 .25
Nos. 1415-1417 (3) 1.60 .75

See No. 1437.

Cranes, by Motooki Watanabe — A1002

1980, Oct. 6 *Perf. 13*

1418 A1002 100y multicolored 1.25 .30

24th Intl. Letter Writing Week, Oct. 6-12.

Archery, Mt. Nantai — A1003

1980, Oct. 11

1419 A1003 20y multicolored .30 .25

35th Natonal Athletic Meet, Tochigi, Oct.

Globe, Jaycee Emblem — A1004

1980, Nov. 8 *Perf. 13*

1420 A1004 50y multicolored .65 .25

35th Jaycee (Intl. Junior Chamber of Commerce) World Congress, Osaka, Nov. 9-15.

Diet Building and Doves — A1005

1980, Nov. 29 *Perf. 13½*

1421 A1005 50y multicolored .65 .25

90th anniversary of Japanese Diet.

Type of 1980 and

Amur Adonis
A1006

White Trumpet Lily
A1007

Hanging Bell, Byodoin Temple
A1008

Bronze Buddhist Ornament, 7th Century
A1009

Writing Box Cover
A1010

Mirror with Figures
A1011

Heart-shaped Figurine
A1012

Silver Crane
A1013

Maitreya, Horyuji Temple
A1014

Ichiji Kinrin, Chusonji Temple
A1015

Komokuten, Todaiji Temple A1016

Lady Maya A1017

Enamel Jar, by Ninsei Nonomura A1018

Miroku Bosatsu, Koryuji Temple A1019

1980-82 Photo. *Perf. 13x13½*

1422 A1006	10y multicolored	.30	.25
1423 A1007	20y multicolored	.30	.25
1424 A1008	60y multicolored	.65	.25
a.	Bklt. pane (#1424, 4 #1424 with gutter btwn.) ('81)	5.00	
1425 A1009	70y multicolored	1.25	.30
1426 A1010	70y multicolored	1.25	.25
1427 A1011	80y multicolored	1.50	.25
1428 A1012	90y multicolored	1.75	.25
1429 A1013	100y multicolored	1.75	.25
1430 A1014	170y multicolored	2.00	.25
1431 A1015	260y multicolored	4.00	.30
1432 A1016	310y multicolored	5.00	.30
1433 A1017	410y multicolored	7.50	.60
1434 A1018	410y multicolored	6.50	.40
1435 A1019	600y multicolored	9.00	.60
	Nos. 1422-1435 (14)	42.75	4.50

Coil Stamps

Perf. 13 Horiz.

1436 A1006	10y multi ('82)	.30	.25
1437 A1001	40y as #1416	.75	.30
1438 A1008	60y multi ('82)	.90	.30
1439 A1013	100y multi ('82)	1.75	.35
	Nos. 1436-1439 (4)	3.70	1.20

Compare type A1013 with type A2685. See Nos. 1627-1628.

Clay Chicken, Folk Toy — A1026

1980, Dec. 1 *Perf. 13 Horiz.*

1442 A1026 20y multicolored .30 .25

New Year 1981.
Sheets of two were New Year Lottery Prizes. Value $1.60.

Modern Japanese Art Issue

Snow-Covered Power Station, by Shikanosuke Oka — A1027

NuKada-no-Ohkimi and Nara in Spring, by Yukihiko Yasuda — A1028

1981, Feb. 26 *Perf. 13½*

1443 A1027 60y multicolored .75 .25

Photo.

1444 A1028 60y multicolored .75 .25

Artist's Family, by Narashige Koide A1029

Bamboo Shoots, by Heihachiro Fukuda — A1030

Photo. & Engr., Photo.

1981, June 18 *Perf. 13½*

1445 A1029 60y multicolored .75 .25
1446 A1030 60y multicolored .75 .25

Portrait of Ichiyo, by Kiyokata Kaburagi (1878-1972) A1031

Portrait of Reiko, by Ryusei Kishida (1891-1929) A1032

Photo., Photo. and Engr.

1981, Nov. 27 Engr. *Perf. 13½*

1447 A1031 60y multicolored .75 .25
1448 A1032 60y multicolored .75 .25

Yoritomo in a Cave, by Seison Maeda A1033

Advertisement of a Terrace, by Yuzo Saeki — A1034

1982, Feb. 25 Photo. *Perf. 13½*

1449 A1033 60y multicolored .75 .25
1450 A1034 60y multicolored .75 .25

Emblem, Port Island — A1035

1981, Mar. 20 *Perf. 13*

1451 A1035 60y multicolored .90 .25

Portopia '81, Kobe Port Island Exhibition, Mar. 20-Sept. 15.

Agriculture, Forestry and Fishery Promotion Centenary — A1036

1981, Apr. 7

1452 A1036 60y multicolored 1.00 .25

Moonflower, by Harunobu Suzuki — A1037

1981, Apr. 20 Photo. *Perf. 13½*

1453	60y multicolored	.75	.25
1454	60y multicolored	.75	.25
a.	A1037 Pair, #1453-1454	1.75	1.25

Philatelic Week, Apr. 21-27.

Cherry Blossoms — A1039

1981, May 23 Photo. *Perf. 13x13½*

1455 A1039 60y multicolored .90 .25

Cargo Ship and Crane — A1040

1981, May 25 *Perf. 13*

1456 A1040 60y multicolored .90 .25

International Port and Harbor Association, 12th Convention, Nagoya, May 23-30.

Land Erosion Control Cent. — A1041

1981, June 27 *Perf. 13½*

1457 A1041 60y multicolored .90 .25

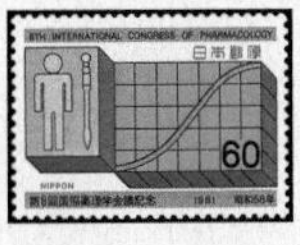
Stylized Man and Spinal Cord Dose Response Curve — A1042

1981, July 18 Photo. *Perf. 13*

1458 A1042 60y multicolored .90 .25

8th Intl. Pharmacology Cong., Tokyo, July 19-24.

Girl Writing Letter — A1043

1981, July 23

1459 A1043 40y shown .65 .25
1460 A1043 60y Boy, stamp .90 .25

Letter Writing Day (23rd of each month).

Japanese Crested Ibis — A1044

1981, July 27 Litho.

1461 A1044 60y multicolored 1.00 .25

Plug, faucet A1044a

Plugs A1045

1981, Aug. 1 Photo.

1462 A1044a 40y multicolored .65 .25
1463 A1045 60y multicolored .90 .25

Energy conservation.

Western Architecture Issue

Oura Cathedral A1046

Hyokei Hall, Tokyo A1047

Photogravure and Engraved

1981, Aug. 22

1464 A1046 60y multicolored .90 .25
1465 A1047 60y multicolored .90 .25

Old Kaichi School, Nagano — A1048

Doshisha University Chapel, Kyoto — A1049

1981, Nov. 9 *Perf. 13*

1466 A1048 60y multicolored .90 .25
1467 A1049 60y multicolored .90 .25

St. John's Church, Meiji-mura A1050

Military Exercise Hall (Former Sapporo Agricultural School), Sapporo A1051

1982, Jan. 29 *Perf. 13*

1468 A1050 60y multicolored .90 .25
1469 A1051 60y multicolored .90 .25

Former Kyoto Branch of Bank of Japan A1052

Main Building, Former Saiseikan Hospital A1053

1982, Mar. 10 *Perf. 13*

1470 A1052 60y multicolored .90 .25
1471 A1053 60y multicolored .90 .25

Oyama Shrine Gate, Kanazawa A1054

Former Iwasaki Family Residence, Tokyo A1055

1982, June 12 *Perf. 13*

1472 A1054 60y multicolored .90 .25
1473 A1055 60y multicolored .90 .25

Hokkaido Prefectural Govt. Building, Sapporo — A1056

Former Residence of Tsugumichi Saigo — A1057

1982, Sept. 10 *Perf. 13*
1474 A1056 60y multicolored .90 .25
1475 A1057 60y multicolored .90 .25

Old Mutsuzawa School — A1058

Sakuranomiya Public Hall — A1059

1983, Feb. 15
1476 A1058 60y multicolored .90 .25
1477 A1059 60y multicolored .90 .25

Globe on Brain — A1060

1981, Sept. 12 **Photo.**
1478 A1060 60y multicolored .80 .25

Intl. medical conferences, Kyoto: 12th Neurology, Sept. 20-25; 10th Brainwaves and Clinical Neurophysiology, Sept. 13-17; 1981 Intl. Epilepsy Conference, Sept. 17-21.

Congress Emblem — A1061

1981, Sept. 16
1479 A1061 60y multicolored .90 .25

24th World PTTI (Post, Telegraph and Telephone Intl. Labor Federation) Cong., Tokyo, Sept. 16-22.

Plum Trees and Fowl, by Sanraku Kano — A1062

1981, Oct. 6 **Photo.**
1480 A1062 130y multicolored 1.75 .30

25th Intl. Letter Writing Week, Oct. 6-12.

A1063

1981, Oct. 9 **Photo. & Engr.**
1481 A1063 60y No. 1 .75 .25
1482 A1063 60y No. 2 .75 .25
1483 A1063 60y No. 3 .75 .25
1484 A1063 60y No. 4 .75 .25
a. Strip or block of 4, #1481-1484 3.50 3.50

Philatokyo '81 Intl. Stamp Exhibition,Tokyo, Oct. 9-18.

A1064

1981, Oct. 13 **Photo.**
1485 A1064 40y multicolored .75 .25

36th Natl. Athletic Meet, Oct. 13-18.

A1065

1981, Dec. 1 **Photo.** *Perf. 13x13½*
1486 A1065 40y multicolored .65 .30

New Year of 1982 (Year of the Dog). Sheets of 2 were lottery prizes. Value $1.60.

A1066

Ueno Zoo Centenary: a, Gorilla, flamingo. b, Penguins, lion. c, Panda, elephants. d, Zebras, giraffe.

1982, Mar. 20 **Photo.**
1487 A1066 Strip of 4 4.00 1.50
a.-d. 60y any single .90 .30

Views of the Snow on Matsuchiyama, by Kiyonaga Torii — A1067

1982, Apr. 20 **Photo.** *Perf. 13½*
1488 60y multicolored .90 .30
1489 60y multicolored .90 .30
a. A1067 Pair, #1488-1489 2.00 1.25

Philatelic Week.

Shisa (Lion-shaped Guard Dog) — A1069

1982, May 15 **Photo.**
1490 A1069 60y multicolored .90 .30

10th anniv. of Reversion Agreement returning Ryukyu Islands.

Natl. Forestation Campaign — A1070

1982, May 22 *Perf. 13x13½*
1491 A1070 60y multicolored .90 .25

16th Intl. Dermatology Conference Tokyo, May 23-28 — A1071

1982, May 24 *Perf. 13*
1492 A1071 60y Noh mask .90 .25

Tohoku-Shinkansen Railroad Line Opening — A1072

1982, June 23
1493 60y Diesel locomotive .90 .30
1494 60y Steam model 1290 .90 .30
a. A1072 Pair, #1493-1494 2.00 1.25

Letter Writing Day — A1073

1982, July 23 *Perf. 13x13½, 13½x13*
1495 A1073 40y Sea gull, letter .75 .25
1496 A1073 60y Fairy, letter, horiz. 1.00 .30

Modern Japanese Art Issue

Kimono Patterned with Irises, by Saburosuke Okada (1869-1939) A1074

Bodhisattva Kuan-yin on Potalaka Island, by Tessai Tomioka (1837-1924) A1075

1982, Aug. 5 **Photo.** *Perf. 13½*
1497 A1074 60y multicolored .90 .30
1498 A1075 60y multicolored .90 .30

The Sarasvati, by Shiko Munakata (1903-1975) A1076

Saltimbanque, by Seiji Togo (1897-1978) A1077

1982, Nov. 24
1499 A1076 60y multicolored .90 .30
1500 A1077 60y multicolored .90 .30

Snowstorm, by Shinsui Ito A1078

Spiraeas and Callas with Persian Pot, by Zenzaburo Kojima A1079

1983, Jan. 24 **Photo.**
1501 A1078 60y multicolored .90 .30
1502 A1079 60y multicolored .90 .30

Innocence, by Taikan Yokoyama (1868-1958) A1080

Roen, by Koun Takamura (1852-1934) A1081

Photo., Photo. and Engr.

1983, Mar. 10 *Perf. 13½*
1503 A1080 60y multicolored .90 .30
1504 A1081 60y multicolored .90 .30

A1082

A1083

A1084

1982, Aug. 23 *Perf. 13x13½*
1505 A1082 60y Wreath .90 .35
1506 A1083 60y Crane .90 .35
1507 A1084 70y Tortoise 1.00 .35
Nos. 1505-1507 (3) 2.80 1.05

For use on greeting (Nos. 1506-1507) and condolence (No. 1505) cards.

See Nos. 1555-1556, 1836-1839, 2227-2230 and footnotes after Nos. 1708, 1765.

400th Anniv. of Boys' Delegation to Europe, Tensho Era — A1085

60y, 16th cent. ship, map.

1982, Sept. 20 **Photo.** *Perf. 13*
1508 A1085 60y multicolored 1.00 .25

10th Anniv. of Japanese-Chinese Relations Normalization A1086

Design: Hall of Prayer for Good Harvests, Temple of Heaven, Peking, by Ryuzaburo Umehara.

1982, Sept. 29
1509 A1086 60y multicolored .90 .30

Table Tennis — A1087

1982, Oct. 2
1510 A1087 40y multicolored .75 .25

37th Natl. Athletic Meet, Matsue, Oct. 3-8.

"Amusement," Doll by Goyo Hirata — A1088

1982, Oct. 6
1511 A1088 130y multicolored 1.75 .45

Intl. Letter Writing Week, Oct. 6-12.

Central Bank System Centenary — A1089

Design: The Bank of Japan near Eitaibashi in Snow, by Yasuji Inoue.

Photogravure and Engraved

1982, Oct. 12 *Perf. 13½*
1512 A1089 60y multicolored 1.00 .25

Opening of Joetsu Shinkansen Railroad Line — A1090

1982, Nov. 15
1513 60y Locomotive, 1982 .90 .30
1514 60y Locomotive, 1931 .90 .30
a. A1090 Pair, #1513-1514 2.00 1.25

New Year 1983 — A1092

40y, Kintaro on Wild Boar.

1982, Dec. 1 *Perf. 13x13½*
1515 A1092 40y multicolored .80 .30

Sheets of 2 were lottery prizes. Value, $1.50.

Natl. Museum of History and Folklore Opening — A1093

1983, Mar. 16 Photo. *Perf. 13½x13*
1516 A1093 60y multicolored 1.00 .25

Women Working in the Kitchen, by Utamaro Kitagawa (1753-1806) — A1094

1983, Apr. 20 Photo. *Perf. 13*
1517 60y multicolored .90 .30
1518 60y multicolored .90 .30
a. A1094 Pair, #1517-1518 2.00 1.25

Philatelic Week.

Natl. Forestation Campaign — A1096

Hakusan Mountains, black lily, forest.

1983, May 21 *Perf. 13*
1519 A1096 60y multicolored 1.00 .25

50th Nippon Derby — A1097

1983, May 28
1520 A1097 60y Colt, racing horse 1.00 .25

Islands Cleanup Campaign — A1098

1983, June 13 Photo. *Perf. 13½*
1521 A1098 60y multicolored 1.00 .25

Western Architecture Series

Hohei Hall Sapporo A1099

Old Glover House, Nagasaki A1100

Photogravure and Engraved

1983, June 23 *Perf. 13*
1522 A1099 60y multicolored 1.00 .30
1523 A1100 60y multicolored 1.00 .30

Gojyuku Bank, Hirosaki — A1101

Gakushuin Elementary School, Tokyo — A1102

1983, Aug. 15
1524 A1101 60y multicolored 1.00 .30
1525 A1102 60y multicolored 1.00 .30

Bank of Japan, Tokyo — A1103

Old Hunter House, Kobe — A1104

1984, Feb. 16
1526 A1103 60y multicolored 1.00 .30
1527 A1104 60y multicolored 1.00 .30
Nos. 1522-1527 (6) 6.00 1.80

Official Gazette Centenary — A1107

Design: First issue, Drawing of the Government Bulletin Board at Nihonbashi, by Hiroshige Ando III.

1983, July 2 Photo.
1530 A1107 60y multicolored 1.00 .25

Letter Writing Day — A1108

40y, Boy writing letter. 60y, Fairy bringing letter, horiz.

1983, July 23 *Perf. 13x13½, 13½x13*
1531 A1108 40y multicolored .70 .25
1532 A1108 60y multicolored 1.00 .30

Opening of Natl. Noh Theater, Tokyo — A1109

60y, Masked actor, theater.

1983, Sept. 14 Photo. *Perf. 13*
1533 A1109 60y multicolored 1.00 .25

Endangered Birds Issue

Rallus Okinawae A1110

Ketupa Blakistoni A1111

Photo. and Engr., Photo.

1983, Sept. 22 *Perf. 13*
1534 A1110 60y multicolored 1.00 .30
1535 A1111 60y multicolored 1.00 .30

No. 1536, Sapheopipo noguchii. No. 1537, Branta canadensis leucopareia.

Photo., Photo. & Engr.

1983, Nov. 25
1536 A1110 60y multicolored 1.00 .30
1537 A1111 60y multicolored 1.00 .30

No. 1538, Megalurus pryeri pryeri. No. 1539, Spilornis cheela perplexus.

Photo., Photo. and Engr.

1984, Jan. 26
1538 A1111 60y multicolored 1.00 .30
1539 A1110 60y multicolored 1.00 .30

No. 1540, Columba janthina nitens. No. 1541, Tringa guttifer.

1984, Mar. 15 Photo.
1540 A1110 60y multicolored 1.00 .30
1541 A1111 60y multicolored 1.00 .30

No. 1542, Falco peregrinus frutti. No. 1543, Dendrocopus leucutus austoni.

1984, June 22
1542 A1110 60y multicolored 1.00 .30

Photo. and Engr.

1543 A1111 60y multicolored 1.00 .30
Nos. 1534-1543 (10) 10.00 3.00

Souvenir Sheet

1984, Dec. 10 Photo. & Engr.
1544 Sheet of 3 3.50 3.50
a. A1111 60y Prus grn, engr., #1535 1.00 .30
b. A1110 60y vio brn, engr., #1539 1.00 .30
c. A1110 60y ol blk, engr., #1542 1.00 .30

Intl. Letter Writing Week — A1124

Chikyu Doll by Juzo Kagoshima (1898-1982).

1983, Oct. 6 Photo. *Perf. 13*
1548 A1124 130y multicolored 1.90 .40

38th Natl. Athletic Meet — A1125

1983, Oct. 15 *Perf. 13*
1549 A1125 40y Naginata event .75 .25

A1126

World Communications Year — A1127

1983, Oct. 17 Photo. *Perf. 13*
1550 A1126 60y multicolored 1.00 .25
1551 A1127 60y multicolored 1.00 .25

Showa Memorial National Park Opening — A1128

1983, Oct. 26 Photo. *Perf. 13*
1552 A1128 60y multicolored 1.00 .30

A1129

1983, Nov. 14 Photo.
1553 A1129 60y multicolored 1.00 .25

71st World Dentistry Congress.

A1130

1983, Nov. 14 Photo. *Perf. 13*
1554 A1130 60y multicolored 1.00 .30

Shirase, Antarctic observation ship, maiden voyage.

Type of 1982

1983, Nov. 22 Photo. *Perf. 12½*
1555 A1082 40y Wreath .75 .25
1556 A1083 40y Crane .75 .25

For use on condolence and greeting cards.

New Year 1984 — A1131

40y, Rat riding hammer.

1983, Dec. 1 Photo. *Perf. 13x13½*
1557 A1131 40y multicolored .80 .30

Sheets of 2 were lottery prizes. Value, $1.90.

Emblem — A1132

1983, Dec. 5 Photo. *Perf. 13½*
1558 A1132 60y multicolored 1.00 .25

Universal Declaration of Human Rights, 35th anniv.

20th Grand Confectionery Fair, Tokyo, Feb. 24-Mar. 12 — A1133

60y, Confection, tea whisk.

1984, Feb. 24 **Photo.**
1559 A1133 60y multicolored 1.00 .25

Natl. Bunraku Theater Opening, Osaka — A1134

60y, Bunraku puppet.

1984, Apr. 6 **Photo.** ***Perf. 13***
1560 A1134 60y multicolored 1.00 .25

A1135

Philatelic Week (Sharaku Prints): No. 1561, Hanshiro Iwai IV (facing right) Playing Shigenoi. No. 1562, Oniji Otani (facing left) Playing Edobe.

Photogravure and Engraved

1984, Apr. 20 ***Perf. 13½***
1561 60y multicolored 1.00 .30
1562 60y multicolored 1.00 .30
a. A1135 Pair, #1561-1562 2.25 .90

Natl. Forestation Campaign — A1137

60y, Cedar Forest, Sakurajima.

1984, May 19 **Photo.**
1563 A1137 60y multicolored 1.00 .25

Weather Forecasting Centenary — A1138

60y, Himawari satellite, map.

1984, June 1 ***Perf. 13x13½***
1564 A1138 60y multicolored 1.00 .30

UNESCO Emblem, Doves — A1139

1984, July 16 **Photo.**
1565 A1139 60y multicolored 1.00 .25

UNESCO Clubs and Associations World Congress, July 16-24.

Letter Writing Day — A1140

40y, Birds in tree. 60y, Bird holding letter, horiz.

1984, July 23 ***Perf. 13x13½, 13½x13***
1566 A1140 40y multicolored .75 .25
1567 A1140 60y multicolored 1.00 .30

Disaster Relief — A1141

40y, Fire, wind. 60y, Mother, child, vert.

Perf. 13x12½, 12½x13

1984, Aug. 23 **Photo.**
1568 A1141 40y multicolored .75 .25
1569 A1141 60y multicolored 1.00 .30

Alpine Plant Series

Leontopodium Fauriei A1142

Lagotis Glauca A1143

Photogravure and Engraved
Perf. 12½x13, 13x12½

1984, Aug. 27
1570 A1142 60y multicolored 1.00 .30
1571 A1143 60y multicolored 1.00 .30

Trollius Riederianus A1144

Primula Cuneifolia A1145

1984, Sept. 21 ***Perf. 13***
1572 A1144 60y multicolored 1.00 .30
1573 A1145 60y multicolored 1.00 .30

Rhododendron Aureum A1146

Oxytropis Nigrescens Var. Japonica A1147

1985, Jan. 25 ***Perf. 13***
1574 A1146 60y multicolored 1.00 .30
1575 A1147 60y multicolored 1.00 .30

Draba Japonica A1148

Dryas Octopetala A1149

1985, Feb. 28
1576 A1148 60y multicolored 1.00 .30
1577 A1149 60y multicolored 1.00 .30

Callianthemum Insigne Var. Miyabeanum A1150

Gentiana Nipponica A1151

1985, July 31 ***Perf. 13***
1578 A1150 60y multicolored 1.00 .30
1579 A1151 60y multicolored 1.00 .30

Campanula Chamissonis A1152

Viola Crassa A1153

1985, Sept. 27
1580 A1152 60y multicolored 1.00 .30
1581 A1153 60y multicolored 1.00 .30

Diapensia Lapponica A1154

Pedicularis Apodochila A1155

1986, Feb. 13 ***Perf. 13***
1582 A1154 60y multicolored 1.00 .30
1583 A1155 60y multicolored 1.00 .30

Basho's Street, Sendai — A1156

1984, Sept. 1 **Photo.** ***Perf. 13***
1584 A1156 60y multicolored 1.00 .25

Intl. Microbiological Association's 6th Intl. Congress of Virology, Sendai, Sept. 1-7.

Electronic Mail — A1157

1984, Oct. 1 **Photo.**
1585 A1157 500y multicolored 9.50 4.50

28th Intl. Letter Writing Week, Oct. 6-12 — A1158

1984, Oct. 6
1586 A1158 130y Wooden doll 2.00 .50

17th Intl. Internal Medicine Congress, Kyoto, Oct. 7-12 — A1159

1984, Oct. 8
1587 A1159 60y Ginkakuji Temple 1.00 .25

39th Natl. Athletic Meet, Nara City, Oct. 12-17 — A1160

1984, Oct. 12
1588 A1160 40y Field hockey .75 .25

Traditional Crafts Series

Kutaniyaki Plates A1161

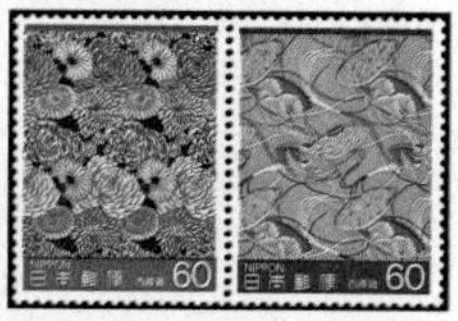

Nishijinori Weavings A1163

1984, Nov. 2 **Photo.** ***Perf. 12½x13***
1589 60y Birds 1.00 .30
1590 60y Flowers 1.00 .30
a. A1161 Pair, #1589-1590 2.25 .90
1591 60y Flowers 1.00 .30
1592 60y Leaves 1.00 .30
a. A1163 Pair, #1591-1592 2.25 .90

Edokimekomi Dolls — A1165

Ryukyubingata Cloth — A1167

1985, Feb. 15 **Photo.** ***Perf. 13***
1593 60y Adult figures 1.00 .30
1594 60y Child and pet 1.00 .30
a. A1165 Pair, #1593-1594 2.25 .90
1595 60y Bird and branch 1.00 .30
1596 60y Birds 1.00 .30
a. A1167 Pair, #1595-1596 2.25 .90

Ichii-ittobori Carved Birds — A1169

Imariyaki & Aritayaki Ceramic Ware A1171

1985, May 23 **Photo.** ***Perf. 13***
1597 60y Bird 1.00 .30
1598 60y Birds 1.00 .30
a. A1169 Pair, #1597-1598 2.25 .90
1599 60y Bowl 1.00 .30
1600 60y Plate 1.00 .30
a. A1171 Pair, #1599-1600 2.25 .90

Kamakurabori Wood Carvings — A1173

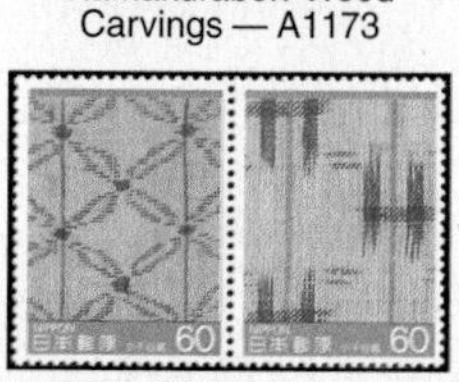

Ojiyachijimi Weavings — A1175

1985, June 24 Photo. & Engr.

1601 60y Bird and flower panel 1.00 .30
1602 60y Round flower panel 1.00 .30
a. A1173 Pair, #1601-1602 2.25 .90

Litho.

1603 60y Hemp star pattern 1.00 .30
1604 60y Hemp linear pattern 1.00 .30
a. A1175 Pair, #1603-1604 2.25 .90

Hakata Ningyo Clay Figures A1177

Nanbu Tekki Iron Ware A1179

1985, Aug. 8 Photo.

1605 60y Man 1.00 .30
1606 60y Woman and child 1.00 .30
a. A1177 Pair, #1605-1606 2.25 .90

Photogravure and Engraved

1607 60y Silver kettle 1.00 .30
1608 60y Black kettle 1.00 .30
a. A1179 Pair, #1607-1608 2.25 .90

Wajimanuri Lacquerware — A1181

Izumo-ishidoro Sandstone Sculptures — A1183

Photo., Photo. & Engr. (#1611-1612)
1985, Nov. 15

1609 60y Bowl on table 1.00 .30
1610 60y Bowl 1.00 .30
a. A1181 Pair, #1609-1610 2.25 .90
1611 60y Columnar lantern 1.00 .30
1612 60y Lantern on four legs 1.00 .30
a. A1183 Pair, #1611-1612 2.25 .90

Kyo-sensu Silk Fans A1185

Tobeyaki Porcelain A1187

1986, Mar. 13 Photo. *Perf. 13*

1613 60y Flower bouquets 1.00 .30
1614 60y Sun and trees 1.00 .30
a. A1185 Pair, #1613-1614 2.25 .90
1615 60y Jug 1.00 .30
1616 60y Jar 1.00 .30
a. A1187 Pair, #1615-1616 2.25 .90
Nos. 1613-1616 (4) 4.00 1.20

Japanese Professional Baseball, 50th Anniv. — A1189

1984, Nov. 15 *Perf. 13½*

1617 60y Pitcher 1.00 .30
1618 60y Batter 1.00 .30
a. A1189 Pair, #1617-1618 2.25 .90
1619 A1189 60y Matsutaro Shoriki 1.00 .30
Nos. 1617-1619 (3) 3.00 .90

Industrial Education Centenary — A1190

1984, Nov. 20 *Perf. 13x12½*

1620 A1190 60y Workers, symbols 1.00 .25

New Year 1985 — A1191

40y, Sakushu Cattle Folk Toy.

1984, Dec. 1 Photo. *Perf. 13½x13*

1621 A1191 40y .80 .30

Sheets of 2 were lottery prizes. Value, $1.90.

A1200 Akita | A1201 Ivory Shell

A1202 Hiougi-gai (Bivalve) | A1203 Rinbo Shell

A1204 | A1205

A1206 | A1207

A1208 | A1209

Photo., Engr. (300y)
1984-89 *Perf. 13x13½*

1622 A1200 2y turq blue ('89) .30 .25
1623 A1201 40y multi ('88) .70 .25
1624 A1202 41y multi ('89) .70 .25
1624B A1202 41y Imperf., self-adhesive .80 .25
1625 A1203 60y multi ('88) 1.00 .25
a. Bklt. pane, 5 each #1623, 1625 10.00
1626 A1204 62y multi ('89) 1.10 .25
a. Bklt. pane, 2 #1624, 4 #1626 6.00
1626B A1204 62y Imperf., self-adhesive 1.10 .25
c. Bklt. pane, 2 #1624B, 4 #1626B ('89) 6.00
1627 A1205 72y dark vio, blk & org yel ('89) 1.10 .25
1628 A1206 175y multi ('89) 2.75 .25
1629 A1207 210y multi ('89) 3.25 .30
1630 A1208 300y dk red brown 5.00 .35
1631 A1209 360y dull pink & brn ('89) 6.00 .35
Nos. 1622-1631 (12) 23.80 3.25

Coil Stamps
Perf. 13 Horiz.

1636 A1202 41y multi ('89) .70 .25
1637 A1204 62y multi ('89) 1.10 .25

No. 1622 inscribed "Nippon," unlike No. 583.

No. 1626Bc is adhered to the booklet cover, made of peelable paper, folded in half and rouletted down the center fold.

Issued: 40y, 60y, 4/1; 300y, 4/3; 2y, 72y, 4/1; 42y, Nos. 1626, 1626a, 41y, No. 1637, 3/24; 175y, 210y, 360y, 6/1; No.1626d, 7/3.

A1210

EXPO '85 — A1211

1985, Mar. 16 Photo. *Perf. 13*

1640 A1210 40y multicolored .75 .25
1641 A1211 60y multicolored 1.00 .30
a. Souv. sheet of 2, #1640-1641 2.50 2.50

University of the Air — A1212

60y, University broadcast tower.

1985, Apr. 1 Photo. *Perf. 13½*

1642 A1212 60y multicolored 1.00 .30

Inauguration of adult education through broadcasting.

Nippon Telegraph & Telephone Co. — A1213

1985, Apr. 1

1643 A1213 60y Satellite receiver 1.00 .25

Inauguration of Japan's new telecommunications system.

World Import Fair, Nagoya — A1214

60y, 16th century map of Japan.

1985, Apr. 5 Photo. *Perf. 13*

1644 A1214 60y multicolored 1.00 .25

Industrial Proprietary System Cent. — A1215

Design: Portrait of Korekiyo Takashashi, system promulgator, inscriptions in English.

1985, Apr. 18 Photo. *Perf. 13½*

1645 A1215 60y multicolored 1.00 .25

Winter in the North A1216

To the Morning Light A1217

Paintings by Yumeji Takehisa (1884-1934).

1985, Apr. 20 *Perf. 13*

1646 A1216 60y multicolored 1.00 .30
1647 A1217 60y multicolored 1.00 .30
a. Pair, #1646-1647 2.25 .90

Philatelic Week. Printed in sheets of 10.

Natl. Land Forestation Project — A1218

Intl. Year of the Forest: Autumn bellflower, camphor tree, cattle and Mt. Aso.

1985, May 10 *Perf. 13½*

1648 A1218 60y multicolored 1.00 .25

Radio Japan, 50th Anniv. A1219

Painting: Cherry Blossoms at Night, by Taikan Yokoyama.

1985, June 1 Photo. *Perf. 13*

1649 60y multi (Left) 1.00 .30
1650 60y multi (Right) 1.00 .30
a. A1219 Pair, #1649-1650 2.25 .90

Hisoka Maejima, 1st Postmaster General — A1220

60y, Portrait, former P.O. building.

1985, June 5 Photo. *Perf. 13*

1651 A1220 60y multicolored 1.00 .30

Oonaruto Bridge Opening — A1221

1985, June 7 *Perf. 13½*

1652 A1221 60y multicolored 1.00 .25

Intl. Youth Year — A1222

60y, Emblem, silhouette.

1985, July 20 Photo. *Perf. 13*

1653 A1222 60y multicolored 1.00 .25

Owl Carrying Letter — A1223

60y, Girl, cat, bird, letter.

Perf. 13½x13, 13x13½

1985, July 23 **Photo.**

1654 A1223 40y shown .75 .25
1655 A1223 60y multicolored 1.00 .30

Letter Writing Day (23rd of each month).

Electronic Mail — A1224

1985, Aug. 1 Photo. ***Perf. 13x13½***

1656 A1224 500y multicolored 9.50 2.75

Meson Theory, 50th Anniv. — A1225

60y, Portrait, nuclear particles.

1985, Aug. 15 Photo. ***Perf. 13***

1657 A1225 60y multicolored 1.00 .25

Dr. Hideki Yukawa was presented the Nobel Prize for Physics for the Meson Theory in 1949, which is the foundation for high-energy physics.

A1226

60y, Gymnast, horse.

1985, Aug. 24 Photo. ***Perf. 13½***

1658 A1226 60y multicolored 1.00 .25

Universiade 1985, Kobe.

A1227

40y, Emblem, competitor.

1985, Sept. 13 **Photo.**

1659 A1227 40y multicolored .75 .25

28th Intl. Vocational Training Competition, Oct. 21-27.

Normalization of Diplomatic Relations Between Japan and the Republic of Korea, 20th Anniv. — A1228

1985, Sept. 18

1660 A1228 60y Rose of Sharon 1.00 .30

Kan-Etsu Tunnel Opening — A1229

60y, Mountains, diagram, cross sections.

1985, Oct. 2 ***Perf. 13***

1661 A1229 60y multicolored 1.00 .25

Seisen Doll by Goyo Hirata (1903-1981) — A1230

1985, Oct. 7

1662 A1230 130y multicolored 2.00 .50

Intl. Letter Writing Week, Oct. 6-12.

30th Intl. Apicultural Congress, Oct. 10-16, Nagoya — A1231

60y, Honeybee, strawberry plants.

1985, Oct. 9

1663 A1231 60y multicolored 1.00 .25

Japanese Overseas Cooperation Volunteers, 20th Anniv. — A1232

1985, Oct. 9 **Litho.**

1664 A1232 60y Planting crop 1.00 .30

40th Natl. Athletic Meet, Oct. 20-25, Tottori City Sports Arena — A1233

40y, Handball player, Mt. Daisen.

1985, Oct. 19 **Photo.**

1665 A1233 40y multicolored .75 .25

New Year 1986 — A1234

40y, Shinno papier-mache tiger.

1985, Dec. 2 Photo. ***Perf. 13x13½***

1666 A1234 40y multicolored .80 .30

Sheets of 2 were lottery prizes. Value, $1.90.

Natl. Ministerial System of Government, Cent. — A1235

60y, Official seal, Cabinet emblem.

1985, Dec. 20 Litho. ***Perf. 13½***

1667 A1235 60y multicolored 1.00 .25

Building Institute, Cent. — A1236

1986, Apr. 9 Photo. ***Perf. 13***

1668 A1236 60y multicolored 1.00 .25

Philately Week A1237

Southern Hateroma (details), by Keigetsu Kikuchi.

1986, Apr. 15

1669 60y Woman standing 1.00 .30
1670 60y Seated woman 1.00 .30
a. A1237 Pair, #1669-1670 2.25 .90

Kyoto Imperial Palace, Phoenix — A1238

No. 1672, Imperial chrysanthemum crest & partridges.

1986, Apr. 28

1671 A1238 60y multicolored 1.00 .30
1672 A1238 60y multicolored 1.00 .30
a. Souv. sheet of 2, #1671-1672 2.40 2.40

Reign of Emperor Hirohito, 60th anniv.

6th Intl. Summit, Tokyo — A1239

1986, May 2

1673 A1239 60y Mt. Fuji 1.00 .30

Shrike on Reed, Emperor Nintoku's Mausoleum — A1240

1986, May 9 ***Perf. 13½***

1674 A1240 60y multicolored 1.00 .30

Natl. Land Afforestation Campaign.

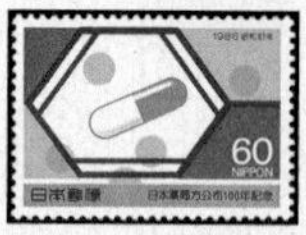
Japanese Pharmaceutical Regulatory Syst., Cent. — A1241

1986, June 25 Photo. ***Perf. 13½***

1675 A1241 60y multicolored 1.00 .30

Japanese Standard Time, Cent. — A1242

1986, July 11 Litho. ***Perf. 13***

1676 A1242 60y Meridian, clock 1.00 .30

Letter Writing Day — A1243

1986, July 23 Photo. ***Perf. 13x13½***

1677 A1243 40y Bird .75 .25
1678 A1243 60y Girl, rabbit, birds 1.00 .30
a. Bklt. pane, 5 each #1677-1678 9.25

Sheets of 2 were lottery prizes. Value, *$60.*

Merchant Marine Education, 110th Anniv. — A1244

Training ship Nihonmaru & navigation training institute founders Makoto Kondo, Yataro Iwasaki.

1986, July 26 ***Perf. 13***

1679 A1244 60y multicolored 1.00 .30

CTO's exist for Nos. 1680-1681, 1684-1685, 1688-1689, 1694-1695, 1696-1697. They read "Japan" between two arcs in a corner.

Insects

A1245

No. 1680, Parnassius eversmanni. No. 1681, Poecilocoris lewisi. No. 1682, Rasalia batesi. No. 1683, Epiophlebia superstes.

Photogravure and Engraved

1986, July 30 ***Perf. 13***

1680 60y multicolored 1.00 .35
1681 60y multicolored 1.00 .35
a. A1245 Pair, #1680-1681 2.25 1.00
1682 60y multicolored 1.00 .35
1683 60y multicolored 1.00 .35
a. A1245 Pair, #1682-1683 2.25 1.00

No. 1684, Dorcus hopei. No. 1685, Thermozephyrus ataxus. No. 1686, Sympetrum pedemontanum. No. 1687, Damaster blaptoides.

1986, Sept. 26

1684 60y multicolored 1.00 .35
1685 60y multicolored 1.00 .35
a. A1245 Pair, #1684-1685 2.25 1.00
1686 60y multicolored 1.00 .35
1687 60y multicolored 1.00 .35
a. A1245 Pair, #1686-1687 2.25 1.00

No. 1688, Elcysma westwoodii. No. 1689, Rhyothemis variegata. No. 1690, Tibicen japonicus. No. 1691, Chrysochroa holstii.

1986, Nov. 21

1688 60y multicolored 1.00 .35
1689 60y multicolored 1.00 .35
a. A1245 Pair, #1688-1689 2.25 1.00
1690 60y multicolored 1.00 .35
1691 60y multicolored 1.00 .35
a. A1245 Pair, #1690-1691 2.25 1.00

No. 1692, Parantica sita. No. 1693, Cheirotonus jambar. No. 1694, Lucanus maculifemoratus. No. 1695, Anotogaster sieboldii.

1987, Jan. 23

1692 60y multicolored 1.00 .35
1693 60y multicolored 1.00 .35
a. A1245 Pair, #1692-1693 2.25 1.00
1694 60y multicolored 1.00 .35
1695 60y multicolored 1.00 .35
a. A1245 Pair, #1694-1695 2.25 1.00

No. 1696, Ascaraphus ramburi. No. 1697, Polyphylla laticollis. No. 1698, Kallima inachus. No. 1699, Calopteryx cornelia.

1987, Mar. 12

1696 60y multicolored 1.00 .35
1697 60y multicolored 1.00 .35
a. A1245 Pair, #1696-1697 2.25 1.00
1698 60y multicolored 1.00 .35
1699 60y multicolored 1.00 .35
f. A1245 Pair, #1698-1699 2.25 1.00
Nos. 1680-1699 (20) 20.00 7.00

Miniature Sheet

1699A Sheet of 4 (#1680, 1692, 1699b-1699c) 5.00 5.00
b. 40y Anthocaris cardamines .75 .35
c. 40y Sasakia charonda .75 .35
d. Bklt. pane, 5 #1680, 5 #1699b 9.25
e. Bklt. pane, 5 #1692, 5 #1699c 9.25
g. A1245 Pair, #1699b, 1680 1.90
h. A1245 Pair, #1699c, 1692 1.90

Booklet panes are perf. 13x13½ on 2 or 3 sides.

Folkways in Twelve Months (Detail), by Shunsho Katsukawa — A1265

1986, Aug. 23 Photo. ***Perf. 13***

1700 A1265 60y multicolored 1.00 .30

52nd conference of the Intl. Federation of Library Associations, Tokyo, Aug. 24-29.

Electron Microscope — A1266

1986, Aug. 30
1701 A1266 60y multicolored 1.00 .30

11th Int. Congress of Electron Microscopy, Kyoto, Aug. 31-Sept. 7.

23rd Intl. Conference on Social Welfare, Tokyo, Aug. 31-Sept. 5 — A1267

1986, Aug. 30 **Litho.**
1702 A1267 60y multicolored 1.00 .25

Ohmorimiyage Doll, by Juzoh Kagoshima — A1268

1986, Oct. 6 **Photo.**
1703 A1268 130y multicolored 2.00 .60

Intl. Letter Writing Week.

41st Natl. Athletic Meet, Oct. 12-17, Kofu — A1269

1986, Oct. 9
1704 A1269 40y multicolored .75 .25

5th World Ikebana Convention A1270

Painting: Flower in Autumn and a Girl in Rakuhoku.

1986, Oct. 17 **Photo.** ***Perf. 13½x13***
1705 A1270 60y multicolored 1.00 .30

A1271

Intl. Peace Year — A1272

Lithographed, Photogravure (#1707)
1986, Nov. 28
1706 A1271 40y multicolored .75 .25
1707 A1272 60y multicolored 1.00 .30

New Year 1987 (Year of the Hare) — A1273

Design: A Couple of Rabbits Making Rice Cake, Nagoya clay figurine.

1986, Dec. 1 **Photo.** ***Perf. 13x13½***
1708 A1273 40y multicolored .80 .30

Sheets of two containing Nos. 1506 and 1708 were lottery prizes. Value, $2.25.
See No. 2655c.

Real Estate Registry System, Cent. — A1274

1987, Jan. 30 **Photo.** ***Perf. 13½***
1709 A1274 60y multicolored 1.00 .25

Basho Series, Part I

A1275

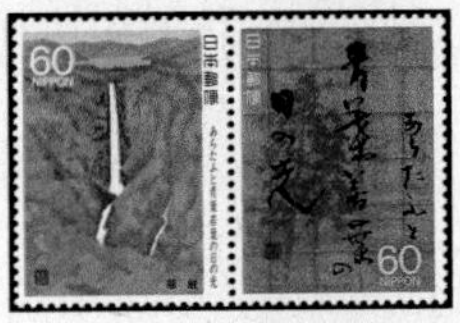
A1277

A1279

A1281

A1283

A1285

A1287

A1289

A1291

A1293

No. 1710, Basho. No. 1711, Basho's haiku. No. 1712, Kegon Falls. No. 1713, Haiku. No. 1714, Cuckoo. No. 1715, Horse and haiku. No. 1716, Willow Tree. No. 1717, Rice Paddy and haiku. No. 1718, Chestnut Tree in Bloom. No. 1719, Chestnut Leaves and haiku. No. 1720, Planting Rice Paddy. No. 1721, Fern Leaves and haiku. No. 1722, Sweetflags. No. 1723, Sweetflags and haiku. No. 1724, Prosperous Man, 17th Cent. No. 1725, Summer Grass and haiku. No. 1726, Safflowers in Bloom. No. 1727, Haiku. No. 1728, Yamadera (Temple). No. 1729, Forest and haiku.

1987-89 **Photo.** ***Perf. 13x13½***
1710 60y multicolored 1.00 .35
1711 60y multicolored 1.00 .35
a. Sheet of 2, #1710-1711, imperf. ('89) 2.50 2.50
b. A1275 Pair, #1710-1711 2.25 1.00
1712 60y multicolored 1.00 .35
1713 60y multicolored 1.00 .35
a. Sheet of 2, #1712-1713, imperf. ('89) 2.50 2.50
b. A1277 Pair, #1712-1713 2.25 1.00
1714 60y multicolored 1.00 .35
1715 60y multicolored 1.00 .35
a. Sheet of 2, #1714-1715, imperf. ('89) 2.50 2.50
b. A1279 Pair, #1714-1715 2.25 1.00
1716 60y multicolored 1.00 .35
1717 60y multicolored 1.00 .35
a. Sheet of 2, #1716-1717, imperf. ('89) 2.50 2.50
b. A1281 Pair, #1716-1717 2.25 1.00
1718 60y multicolored 1.00 .35
1719 60y multicolored 1.00 .35
a. Sheet of 2, #1718-1719, imperf. ('89) 2.50 2.50
b. A1283 Pair, #1718-1719 2.25 1.00
1720 60y multicolored 1.00 .35
1721 60y multicolored 1.00 .35
a. Sheet of 2, #1720-1721, imperf. ('89) 2.50 2.50
b. A1285 Pair, #1720-1721 2.25 1.00
1722 60y multi ('88) 1.00 .35
1723 60y multi ('88) 1.00 .35
a. Sheet of 2, #1722-1723, imperf. ('89) 2.50 2.50
b. A1287 Pair, #1722-1723 2.25 1.00
1724 60y multi ('88) 1.00 .35
1725 60y multi ('88) 1.00 .35
a. Sheet of 2, #1724-1725, imperf. ('89) 2.50 2.50
b. A1289 Pair, #1724-1725 2.25 1.00
1726 60y multi ('88) 1.00 .35
1727 60y multi ('88) 1.00 .35
a. Sheet of 2, #1726-1727, imperf. ('89) 2.50 2.50
b. A1291 Pair, #1726-1727 2.25 1.00
1728 60y multi ('88) 1.00 .35
1729 60y multi ('88) 1.00 .35
a. Sheet of 2, #1728-1729, imperf. ('89) 2.50 2.50
b. A1293 Pair, #1728-1729 2.25 1.00
Nos. 1710-1729 (20) 20.00 7.00

Issued to commemorate the 300th anniversary of a trip from Edo (now Tokyo) to northern Japan by the famous haiku poet Matsuo Munefusa "Basho" (1644-1694). His prose account of the journey, *Oku no hosomichi* (*Narrow Road to a Far Province*), contains numerous 17-syllable poems (*haiku*), which are shown on the stamps.

In each setenant pair, a complete *haiku* by Basho is inscribed vertically at right on the left stamp and in the center of the right stamp. The same poem appears on both stamps in each pair.

Issued: Nos. 1710-1713, 2/26; Nos. 1714-1717, 6/23; Nos. 1718-1721, 8/25; Nos. 1722-1725, 1/3; Nos. 1726-1729, 3/26.

See Nos. 1775-1794.

12th World Orchid Congress, Tokyo
A1295 A1296

1987, Mar. 19 **Photo.** ***Perf. 13***
1730 A1295 60y multicolored 1.00 .30
1731 A1296 60y multicolored 1.00 .30

Railway Post Office Termination, Oct. 1, 1986 — A1297

1987, Mar. 26 **Litho.** ***Perf. 13½***
1732 60y Mail car 1.00 .30
1733 60y Loading mail on car 1.00 .30
a. A1297 Pair, #1732-1733 2.25 1.00

Privatization of Japan Railways — A1298

No. 1734, Locomotive No. 137, c. 1900. No. 1735, Linear induction train, 1987.

1987, Apr. 1 **Photo.** ***Perf. 13½***
1734 A1298 60y multicolored 1.00 .35
1735 A1298 60y multicolored 1.00 .35

Natl. Marine Biology Research, Cent. — A1299

1987, Apr. 2 ***Perf. 13***
1736 A1299 60y Sea slugs 1.00 .25

Paintings by Hashiguchi Goyo (1880-1921) — A1300

1987, Apr. 14
1737 60y denomination at UR 1.00 .30
1738 60y denomination at LL 1.00 .30
a. A1300 Pair, #1737-1738 2.25 1.00

Philately Week.

Map of Asia and Oceania — A1302

1987, Apr. 27 **Photo.** ***Perf. 13½***
1739 A1302 60y multicolored 1.00 .25

20th annual meeting of the Asian Development Bank.

Nat'l. Land Afforestation Campaign — A1303

60y, Magpie, seashore.

1987, May 23
1740 A1303 60y multicolored 1.00 .25

National Treasures Series

A1304

A1305

Designs: No. 1741, Yatsuhashi gold inkstone box, by Kohrin Ogata. No. 1742, Donjon of Hikone Castle, c. 1573-1592.

1987, May 26 **Photo.** ***Perf. 13***
1741 A1304 60y multicolored 1.00 .35

Photo. & Engr.
Perf. 13½
1742 A1305 110y multicolored 1.90 .50

Golden Turtle Sharito A1306

Imuyama Castle Donjon, 1469 A1307

1987, July 17 Photo. *Perf. 13*

1743 A1306 60y multicolored 1.00 .35

Photo. & Engr.

Perf. 13½

1744 A1307 110y multicolored 1.90 .50

Kongo Sanmai in Tahotoh Temple, Kamakura Era — A1308

Wood Ekoh-Dohji Statue in the Likeness of Kongobuji Fudodo, Kamakura Era, by Unkei — A1309

1988, Feb. 12 Photo. *Perf. 13*

1745 A1308 60y multicolored 1.00 .35

Photo. & Engr.

Perf. 13½

1746 A1309 110y multicolored 1.90 .50

Itsukushima Shrine, Heian Period — A1310

Kozakura-gawa, Braided Armor Worn by Minamoto-no-Yoshimitsu, Heian Period War Lord, Kai Province — A1311

1988, June 23 Photo. *Perf. 13*

1747 A1310 60y multicolored 1.00 .35

Photo. & Engr.

Perf. 13½

1748 A1311 100y multicolored 1.75 .50

Statue of *Nakatsu-hime-no-mikoto,* a Hachiman Goddess, Heian Period, Yakushiji Temple — A1312

Murou-ji Temple Pagoda, 9th Cent. — A1313

1988, Sept. 26 Photo. *Perf. 13*

1749 A1312 60y multicolored 1.00 .35

Photo. & Engr.

Perf. 13½

1750 A1313 100y multicolored 1.75 .50

Nos. 1741-1750 (10) 14.20 4.25

Letter Writing Day — A1314

40y, Flowers, envelope. 60y, Elephant.

1987, July 23 Photo. *Perf. 13x13½*

1751 A1314 40y multicolored .75 .30

1752 A1314 60y multicolored 1.00 .30

a. Bklt. pane, 5 ea #1751-1752 5.00 10.00

Sheets of 2, Nos. 1751-1752, were lottery prizes. Value, $5.

Kiso Three Rivers Flood Control, Cent. — A1315

60y, Kiso, Nagara and Ibi Rivers.

1987, Aug. 7 Photo. *Perf. 13½*

1753 A1315 60y multicolored 1.00 .25

Japan — Thailand Diplomatic Relations, Cent. — A1316

Design: Temple of the Emerald Buddha and cherry blossoms.

1987, Sept. 26 *Perf. 13*

1754 A1316 60y multicolored 1.00 .30

Intl. Letter Writing Week — A1317

Dolls by Goyo Hirata: 130y, Gensho Kanto, by Royojo Hori (1898-1984). 150y, Utage-no-Hana (Fair Woman at the Party).

1987, Oct. 6 Photo. *Perf. 13*

1755 A1317 130y multicolored 2.00 .50

1756 A1317 150y multicolored 2.25 .60

13th World Congress of Certified Public Accountants, Tokyo, Oct. 11-15 — A1318

Design: Three Beauties (adaptation), by Toyokuni Utagawa (1769-1825).

1987, Oct. 9 *Perf. 13*

1757 A1318 60y multicolored 1.00 .35

Modern Waterworks, Cent. — A1319

Design: Lion's head public fountain, 1887, Waterworks Museum, Yokohama.

1987, Oct. 16 Engr.

1758 A1319 60y multicolored 1.00 .25

Shurei Gate, Okinawa, Basketball Players — A1320

1987, Oct. 24 Photo.

1759 A1320 40y multicolored .75 .25

42nd Natl. Athletic Meet, Okinawa.

6th World Cong. on Smoking & Health, Nov. 9-12, Tokyo — A1321

1987, Nov. 9

1760 A1321 60y multicolored 1.00 .25

World Telecommunications Conf., Nov. 15-18, Tokyo — A1322

Design: Microwave dish antenna at Kashima Station Radio Research Laboratory.

1987, Nov. 13 *Perf. 13½*

1761 A1322 60y multicolored 1.00 .25

World Conference on Large Historic Cities, Nov. 18-21, Kyoto — A1323

Design: Nijo Castle guardhouse roof and Ninomaru Hall, 17th cent.

1987, Nov. 18 *Perf. 13*

1762 A1323 60y multicolored 1.00 .30

Intl. Year of Shelter for the Homeless — A1324

Prize-winning illustrations by: 40y, Takahiro Nahahama. 60y, Yoko Sasaki.

1987, Nov. 25

1763 A1324 40y multicolored .75 .30

1764 A1324 60y multicolored 1.00 .30

New Year 1988 (Year of the Dragon) — A1325

Design: Kurashiki papier-mache dragon, 1869, by Tajuro Omizu.

1987, Dec. 1 *Perf. 13x13½*

1765 A1325 40y multicolored .80 .30

Sheets of 2, Nos. 1506, 1765, were lottery prizes. Value, $2.40.

Seikan Tunnel Opening — A1326

60y, ED 79 locomotive, map.

1988, Mar. 11 Photo. *Perf. 13¼*

1766 A1326 60y multicolored 1.00 .30

a. Booklet pane of 10 10.00 8.00

Opening of Seto-Oohashi Bridge

Kagawa Side

A1327 A1328

Okayama Side

A1329 A1330

1988, Apr. 8 Engr. *Perf. 13½*

1767 A1327 60y multicolored 1.00 .35

1768 A1328 60y multicolored 1.00 .35

1769 A1329 60y multicolored 1.00 .35

1770 A1330 60y multicolored 1.00 .35

a. Strip of 4, #1767-1770 4.50 2.00

Nos. 1767-1768 and 1769-1770 have continuous designs.

Philately Week A1331

Prints by Kotondo Torii (1900-76): No. 1771, Long Undergarment. No. 1772, Kimono Sash.

1988, Apr. 19 Photo. *Perf. 13*

1771 60y denomination at LR 1.00 .35

1772 60y denomination at UL 1.00 .35

a. A1331 Pair, #1771-1772 2.50 1.50

Souv. sheet of 2 exists. Value $6.

Silk Road Exposition, Apr. 24-Oct. 23, Nara — A1333

Design: Plectrum guard playing the biwa, detail of Raden-Shitan-no-Gogen-Biwa, a five-panel work of gold lacquer nacre on sandalwood preserved at Shosoin.

1988, Apr. 23 Photo. & Engr.

1773 A1333 60y multicolored 1.00 .30

Natl. Afforestation Campaign — A1334

Design: Yahsima, site of the Genji-Heike war, and cuckoo on olive tree branch.

1988, May 20 Photo. *Perf. 13½*

1774 A1334 60y multicolored 1.00 .25

Basho Series, Part II

A1335

A1337

No. 1775, Mogami River. No. 1776, Haiku and flower. No. 1777, Mt. Gassan. No. 1778, Haiku and mountain.

1988, May 30 Photo. *Perf. 13x13½*

1775	60y multicolored	1.00	.35
1776	60y multicolored	1.00	.35
a.	Souv. sheet of 2, #1775-1776, imperf. ('89)	2.50	2.50
b.	A1335 Pair, #1775-1776	2.25	1.00
1777	60y multicolored	1.00	.35
1778	60y multicolored	1.00	.35
a.	Souv. sheet of 2, #1777-1778, imperf. ('89)	2.50	2.50
b.	A1337 Pair, #1777-1778	2.25	1.00

A1339

A1341

No. 1779, Mimosa in bloom. No. 1780, Verse, birds, Kisagata Inlet. No. 1781, Ocean waves. No. 1782, Verse and current.

1988, Aug. 23

1779	60y multicolored	1.00	.35
1780	60y multicolored	1.00	.35
a.	Souv. sheet of 2, #1779-1780, imperf ('89)	2.50	2.50
b.	A1339 Pair, #1779-1780	2.25	1.00
1781	60y multicolored	1.00	.35
1782	60y multicolored	1.00	.35
a.	Souv. sheet of 2, #1781-1782, imperf. ('89)	2.50	2.50
b.	A1341 Pair, #1781-1782	2.25	1.00

A1343

A1345

No. 1783, Rice. No. 1784, Birds in flight, haiku. No. 1785, Sun glow. No. 1786, Rice, haiku.

1988, Nov. 11

1783	60y multicolored	1.00	.35
1784	60y multicolored	1.00	.35
a.	Souv. sheet of 2, #1783-1784, imperf. ('89)	2.50	2.50
b.	A1343 Pair, #1783-1784	2.25	1.00
1785	60y multicolored	1.00	.35
1786	60y multicolored	1.00	.35
a.	Souv. sheet of 2, #1785-1786, imperf. ('89)	2.50	2.50
b.	A1345 Pair, #1785-1786	2.25	1.00

A1347

A1349

No. 1787, Nata-dera Temple. No. 1788, Haiku, white grass. No. 1789, Trees. No. 1790, Haiku, moonlit forest.

1989, Feb. 13

1787	60y multicolored	1.00	.35
1788	60y multicolored	1.00	.35
a.	Souv. sheet of 2, #1787-1788, imperf.	2.50	2.50
b.	A1347 Pair, #1787-1788	2.25	1.00
1789	60y multicolored	1.00	.35
1790	60y multicolored	1.00	.35
a.	Souv. sheet of 2, #1789-1790, imperf.	2.50	2.50
b.	A1349 Pair, #1789-1790	2.25	1.00

A1351

A1353

No. 1791, Autumn on the beach. No. 1792, Haiku. No. 1793, Clams. No. 1794, Haiku.

1989, May 12

1791	62y multicolored	1.00	.35
1792	62y multicolored	1.00	.35
a.	Souv. sheet of 2, #1791-1792, imperf.	2.50	2.50
b.	A1351 Pair, #1791-1792	2.25	1.00
1793	62y multicolored	1.00	.35
1794	62y multicolored	1.00	.35
a.	Souv. sheet of 2, #1793-1794, imperf.	2.50	2.50
b.	A1353 Pair, #1793-1794	2.25	1.00

Haiku from *Oku-no-hosomichi,* "*Narrow Road to a Far Province,*" 1694, a travel description written by Matsuo Munefusa (1644-94), a haiku poet best known by his pen-name Basho.

In each setenant pair, a complete *haiku* by Basho is inscribed vertically at right on the left stamp and in the center of the right stamp. The same poem appears on both stamps in each pair.

Issued: Nos. 1776a-1794a, Aug. 1, 1989.

Intl. Conference on Volcanoes, Kagoshima
A1355

1988, July 19 Photo. *Perf. 14*

1795	A1355 60y multicolored	1.00	.30

A1356

A1357

A1358

Letter Writing Day, 10th Anniv. — A1359

Designs and contest-winning children's drawings: No. 1796, Cat and letter. No. 1797, *Crab and Letter,* by Katsuyuki Yamada. No. 1798, Fairy and letter. No. 1799, *Girl and Letter,* by Takashi Ukai.

Photo., Litho. (Nos. 1797, 1799)

1988, July 23 *Perf. 13x13½*

1796	A1356 40y multicolored	.75	.30
1796A	A1356 40y Imperf., self-adhesive	.75	.30
1797	A1357 40y multicolored	.75	.30
1798	A1358 60y multicolored	1.00	.30
a.	Bklt. pane, 5 each #1796, 1798	10.00	10.00
1798B	A1358 60y Imperf., self-adhesive	1.00	.30
c.	Bklt. pane, 3 each #1796A, 1798B	7.50	
1799	A1359 60y multicolored	1.00	.30
	Nos. 1796-1799 (6)	5.25	1.80

No. 1798c is adhered to the booklet cover, made of peelable paper, folded in half and rouletted down the center fold, with No. 1796a at left and No. 1798b at right of the roulette.

Sheets of 2 containing Nos. 1796, 1798 were lottery prizes. Value, $5.

15th World Puppetry Festival, July 27-Aug. 11 — A1360

Puppets: No. 1800, *Ohana,* string puppet from the film *Spring and Fall in the Meiji Era,* by Kinosuke Takeda (1923-1979), Japan. No. 1801, Girl, stick puppet from the Natl. Radost Puppet Theater, Brno, Czechoslovakia. No. 1802, Woman, shadow puppet from China. No. 1803, Knight, a marionette from Sicily.

1988, July 27 Photo. *Perf. 13*

1800	60y multicolored	1.00	.35
1801	60y multicolored	1.00	.35
1802	60y multicolored	1.00	.35
1803	60y multicolored	1.00	.35
a.	A1360 Block or strip of 4, #1800-1803	4.50	1.75

Japan-China Treaty, 10th Anniv. — A1364

1988, Aug. 12 Photo.

1804	60y Peony	1.00	.35
1805	60y Panda	1.00	.35
a.	A1364 Pair, #1804-1805	2.25	1.00

18th World Poultry Congress, Nagoya, Sept. 4-9 — A1366

1988, Sept. 3 *Perf. 13½*

1806	A1366 60y multicolored	1.00	.30

Rehabilitation Intl. 16th World Congress, Tokyo, Sept. 5-9 — A1367

Photo. & Embossed

1988, Sept. 5 *Perf. 13*

1807	A1367 60y multicolored	1.00	.25

Intl. Letter-Writing Week — A1368

Prints: 80y, *Kumesaburo Iwai as Chiyo,* by Kunimasa Utagawa (1773-1810), late Edo Period. 120y, *Komazo Ichikawa III as Ganryu Sasaki,* by Toyokuni Utagawa (1769-1825).

1988, Oct. 6 Photo.

1808	A1368 80y multicolored	1.25	.40
1809	A1368 120y multicolored	2.00	.50

43rd Natl. Athletic Meet, Kyoto — A1369

Design: Gymnast on parallel bars and "Kinkakuji," Temple of the Golden Pavilion.

1988, Oct. 14

1810	A1369 40y multicolored	.75	.25

Japan-Mexico Trade Agreement, Cent. — A1370

1988, Nov. 30 Photo.

1811	A1370 60y multicolored	1.00	.30

New Year 1989 (Year of the Snake) — A1371

Clay bell snake by Masanobu Ogawa.

1988, Dec. 1

1812	A1371 40y multicolored	.90	.35

Sheets of two containing Nos. 1506, 1812 were lottery prizes. Value, $2.50.

UN Declaration of Human Rights, 40th Anniv. — A1372

1988, Dec. 5 Litho. *Perf. 13½*

1813	A1372 60y multicolored	1.00	.25

National Treasures Series

Votive Silver Lidded Bowl Used in Todai-ji Temple Ground-Breaking Ceremony, 8th Cent. — A1373

Bronze Yakushi-nyorai Buddha, Asuka Period, 7th Cent. — A1374

Photo., Photo & Engr. (100y)

1989, Jan. 20 *Perf. 13, 13½ (100y)*

1814	A1373 60y multicolored	1.00	.35
1815	A1374 100y multicolored	1.75	.50

Kondo-Sukashibori-Kurakanagu, Bronze Saddle from Ohjin Imperial Mausoleum — A1375

Tamamushi-no-Zushi, Buddhist Altar in Lacquered Cypress from the Asuka Era — A1376

1989, June 30

1816 A1375 62y multicolored 1.10 .35
1817 A1376 100y multicolored 1.75 .50

Kin-in, a Gokan Era Gold Seal Given to the King of Na by Emperor Kobutei — A1377

Shinninshaba-gazokyo, a 5th Cent. European Bronze Mirror Back — A1378

1989, Aug. 15

1818 A1377 62y multicolored 1.10 .35
1819 A1378 100y multicolored 1.75 .50
Nos. 1814-1819 (6) 8.45 2.55

Asian-Pacific Expo, Fukuoka, Mar. 17-Sept. 3 — A1383

1989 Photo. *Perf. 13*

1822 A1383 60y multicolored 1.00 .30
1823 A1383 62y multicolored 1.75 .50

Issue dates: 60y, Mar. 16; 62y, Apr. 18.

Yokohama Exposition (Space and Children), Yokohama City, Mar. 25 to Oct. 1 — A1384

Design: Detail of *Russian Lady Sight-seeing at the Port,* by Yoshitora, and entrance to the Yokohama City Art Museum.

1989, Mar. 24 Litho.

1824 A1384 60y multicolored 1.00 .30
1825 A1384 62y multicolored 1.75 .50

World Bonsai Convention, Omiya, Apr. 6-9 — A1385

1989, Apr. 6 Photo. *Perf. 13*

1826 A1385 62y multicolored 1.10 .35

Awa-odori, by Tsunetomi Kitano (b. 1880) A1386

1989, Apr. 18 *Perf. 13*

1827 62y multicolored 1.10 .35
1828 62y multicolored 1.10 .35
a. A1386 Pair, #1827-1828 2.25 1.00

Philately Week. Sheets of 2 containing Nos. 1827-1828 were lottery prizes. Value, $5.

Holland Festival 1989 — A1388

1989, Apr. 19 *Perf. 13½*

1829 A1388 62y Ship 1.10 .30

Fiber-optic Cable, the 3rd Transpacific Line Relay Linking Japan and the US — A1389

62y, Station tower, map.

1989, May 10 *Perf. 13½x13*

1830 A1389 62y multicolored 1.10 .30

Natl. Afforestation Campaign — A1390

62y, Bayberry, lime, Mt. Tsurugi.

1989, May 19 *Perf. 13½*

1831 A1390 62y multicolored 1.10 .30

World Design Exposition, Nagoya, July 15-Nov. 26
A1391 A1392

1989, July 14

1832 A1391 41y multicolored .80 .35
1833 A1392 62y multicolored 1.10 .35

Letter Writing Day
A1393 A1394

1989, July 21 *Perf. 13x13½*

1834 A1393 41y multicolored .80 .30
1835 A1394 62y multicolored 1.10 .30
a. Bklt. pane, 5 each #1834-1835 9.50

Sheets of 2 containing Nos. 1834-1835 were lottery prizes. Value, $3.

Congratulations and Condolences Types of 1982

1989, Aug. 10 Photo. *Perf. 13x13½*

1836 A1082 41y Wreath .80 .25
1837 A1083 41y Crane .80 .30
1838 A1083 62y Crane 1.10 .30
1839 A1084 72y Tortoise 1.30 .35
Nos. 1836-1839 (4) 4.00 1.20

6th Interflora World Congress, Tokyo, Aug. 27-30 — A1395

1989, Aug. 25 Photo. *Perf. 13½*

1840 A1395 62y multicolored 1.10 .35

Prefecture Issues

Nos. 1841-1990 have been changed to Nos. Z1-Z150. The listings can be found in the section immediately following the postage section and preceding the semi-postal listings.

A1546

1989, Sept. 14 Photo. *Perf. 13½*

1991 A1546 62y multicolored 1.10 .30

Far East and South Pacific Games for the Disabled (FESPIC), Kobe, Sept. 15-20.

Okuni Kabuki Screen
A1547 A1548

1989, Sept. 18 *Perf. 13*

1992 A1547 62y multicolored 1.10 .35
1993 A1548 70y multicolored 1.25 .40

EUROPALIA '89, Japan.

A1549

A1550

Scenes from the Yadorigi and Takekawa Chapters of the Tales of the Genji picture scroll, attributed to Fujiwara-no-Takeyoshi, late Heian Period (897-1185).

1989, Oct. 6 Photo. *Perf. 13½*

1994 A1549 80y multicolored 1.40 .45
1995 A1550 120y multicolored 2.00 .55

Intl. Letter Writing Day.

Intl. Conference on Irrigation and Drainage — A1551

1989, Oct. 13

1996 A1551 62y Rice 1.10 .30

100th Tenno Sho Horse Race — A1552

62y, Jockey riding Shinzan.

1989, Oct. 27 *Perf. 13*

1997 A1552 62y multicolored 1.10 .30

9th Hot Air Balloon World Championships, Saga — A1553

1989, Nov. 17 Photo. *Perf. 13x13½*

1998 A1553 62y multicolored 1.10 .35

Copyright Control System, 50th Anniv. — A1554

1989, Nov. 17 *Perf. 13*

1999 A1554 62y Conductor 1.10 .30

New Year 1990 (Year of the Horse)
A1555 A1556

41y, *Yawata-Uma* festival horse. 62y, *Kazari-Uma,* Meiji Period.

1989, Dec. 1 *Perf. 13x13½, 13½*

2000 A1555 41y multicolored .85 .30
2001 A1556 62y multicolored 1.25 .35

No. 2001 was sold through Jan. 10, 1990, serving as a lottery ticket.

Sheets of two containing Nos. 1838, 2000 were lottery prizes. Value, $2.50.

Electric Locomotives

10,000 — A1557

Photo. & Engr., Photo.

1990 *Perf. 13*

2002 A1557 62y shown 1.10 .35
2003 A1557 62y EF58 1.10 .35
2004 A1557 62y ED40 1.10 .35
2005 A1557 62y EH10 1.10 .35
2006 A1557 62y EF53 1.10 .35
2007 A1557 62y ED70 1.10 .35
2008 A1557 62y EF55 1.10 .35
2009 A1557 62y ED61 1.10 .35
2010 A1557 62y EF57 1.10 .35
2011 A1557 62y EF30 1.10 .35
Nos. 2002-2011 (10) 11.00 3.50

Issued two stamps at a time, the first photo. & engr., the second photo.

Issued: Nos. 2002-2003, 1/31; Nos. 2004-2005, 2/28; Nos. 2006-2007, 4/23; Nos. 2008-2009, 5/23; Nos. 2010-2011, 7/18.

Intl. Garden and Greenery Exposition, Osaka — A1558

1990, Mar. 30 Photo. *Perf. 13*

2021 A1558 62y multicolored 1.10 .30

See No. B45.

Philately Week — A1559

Painting: *Women Gazing at the Stars,* by Chou Ohta.

1990, Apr. 20 Photo. *Perf. 13*

2022 A1559 62y multicolored 1.10 .30
a. Souvenir sheet of 1 1.25 1.25

A1560

62y, Azalea, Mt. Unzen.

1990, May 18 Photo. *Perf. 13½*
2023 A1560 62y multicolored 1.10 .30

Natl. Land Afforestation Campaign.

Flower, Butterfly — A1561

Abstract Art — A1561a

1990, June 1 Photo. *Perf. 13*
2024 A1561 62y multicolored 1.10 .35
2025 A1561a 70y multicolored 1.25 .35

Japan-Turkey Relations, Cent. — A1562

1990, June 13
2026 A1562 62y multicolored 1.10 .30

Horses Series

Horses at Stable from Umaya-zu Byobu — A1563

Foals — A1564

Lacquered Saddle, 16th Cent. — A1565

Lacquered Stirrups, 16th Cent. A1566

Horse by S. Nishiyama A1567

Kettei A1568

"Kamo-Kurabeuma-Monyo-Kosode" A1569

Perf. 13x13½, 13
1990 Litho. & Engr.

Color of Horse

2027 62y red brown 1.10 .35
2028 62y gray 1.10 .35
2029 62y beige 1.10 .35
2030 62y tan 1.10 .35
2031 62y mottled 1.10 .35
a. A1563 Strip of 5, #2027-2031 6.75 2.75

Photo.

2032 A1564 62y shown 1.10 .35

Photo. & Engr.

2033 A1565 62y shown 1.10 .35
2034 A1566 62y shown 1.10 .35
a. Pair, #2033-2034 2.75 1.00

Photo.

2035 A1567 62y multicolored 1.10 .35
2036 A1568 62y multicolored 1.10 .35
2037 A1569 62y multicolored 1.10 .35

Postal Carriages A1569a

Inkstone Case "Sano-no-Watashi" A1570

"Bushu-Senju-zu" by Hokusai A1571

"Shudan" by Kogetsu Saigo — A1571a

Photo. & Engr., Photo. (#2040, 2042)
1991 *Perf. 12½x13*
2038 62y one horse 1.10 .35
2039 62y two horses 1.10 .35
a. A1569a Pair, #2038-2039 2.75 1.00

Perf. 13½x13

2040 A1570 62y multicolored 1.10 .35
2041 A1571 62y multicolored 1.10 .35
2042 A1571a 62y multicolored 1.10 .35
Nos. 2027-2042 (16) 17.60 5.60

Issued: Nos. 2027-2032, 6/20; Nos. 2033-2035, 7/31; Nos. 2036-2037, 9/27; Nos. 2038-2040, 1/31. Nos. 2041-2042, 2/28.

38th Intl. Youth Hostel Fed. Conference — A1573

1990, June 25 Litho. *Perf. 13*
2057 A1573 62y multicolored 1.10 .30

Letter Writing Day
A1574 A1575

1990, July 23 Photo. *Perf. 13½*
2058 A1574 41y multicolored .80 .35
2059 A1575 62y multicolored 1.10 .40
a. Souv. sheet of 1 1.25 1.25
b. Bklt. pane, 5 ea #2058-2059 9.50

See No. 2117.

21st Intl. Congress of Mathematicians A1576

1990, Aug. 17 Photo. *Perf. 13*
2060 A1576 62y multicolored 1.10 .30

World Cycling Championships — A1577

1990, Aug. 20 Litho. *Perf. 13½*
2061 A1577 62y multicolored 1.10 .30

Ogai Mori, Educator — A1578

1990, Aug. 27 Photo.
2062 A1578 62y multicolored 1.10 .30

Intl. Assoc. for Germanic Studies (IVG), 8th Congress.

Character "Ji" in Shape of Rosetta Stone — A1579

1990, Sept. 7 *Perf. 13*
2063 A1579 62y multicolored 1.10 .30

Intl. Literacy Year.

Decade for Natural Disaster Reduction — A1580

1990, Sept. 27 Photo.
2064 A1580 62y multicolored 1.10 .30

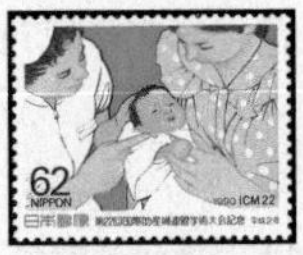
Intl. Confederation of Midwives, 22nd Congress — A1581

1990, Oct. 5 Photo.
2065 A1581 62y multicolored 1.10 .30

A1582

"Choju-Jinbutsu-Giga" — A1583

Photo. & Engr.
1990, Oct. 5 *Perf. 13½*
2066 A1582 80y multicolored 1.40 .45
2067 A1583 120y multicolored 2.00 .55

Intl. Letter Writing Week.

"Fumizukai-zu" by Harunobu Suiendo — A1584

1990, Oct. 16 Photo.
2068 A1584 100y multicolored 1.75 .55
a. Souv. sheet of 1 2.00 2.00

No. 2068a exists with surcharge which paid admission to PHILANIPPON '91. These were not sold by the post office.

Court System, Cent. — A1585

1990, Nov. 1 Photo. *Perf. 13x13½*
2069 A1585 62y "Justice" 1.10 .35

Japanese Braille, Cent. — A1586

Photo & Embossed
1990, Nov. 1 *Perf. 13½*
2070 A1586 62y multicolored 1.10 .30

Enthronement of Akihito — A1587

No. 2071, Chinese phoenix depicted on Emperor's chair. No. 2072, Diamond pattern for costume worn at banquet ceremony.

1990, Nov. 9 Photo. *Perf. 13*
2071 A1587 62y multicolored 1.10 .35
2072 A1587 62y multicolored 1.10 .35
a. Souv. sheet of 2, #2071-2072 2.50 2.50

Japanese Diet, Cent. — A1588

1990, Nov. 29 Litho.
2073 A1588 62y multicolored 1.10 .35

New Year 1991 (Year of the Sheep)
A1589 A1590

1990, Dec. 3 Photo. *Perf. 13x13½*
2074 A1589 41y multicolored .75 .30

Photo. & Engr.
Perf. 13½

2075 A1590 41y multicolored .90 .35
2076 A1590 62y multi, diff. 1.40 .40
Nos. 2074-2076 (3) 3.05 1.05

Sheets of 2 No. 2074 were lottery prizes. Value, $2.

Dr. Yoshio Nishina, Physicist — A1591

1990, Dec. 6 Photo. *Perf. 13*
2077 A1591 62y multicolored 1.10 .30

Use of radio isotopes in Japan, 50th anniv.

Telephone Service, Cent. — A1592

1990, Dec. 14

2078 A1592 62y multicolored 1.10 .30

A1593

41y, Figure skating. 62y, Speed skating, horiz.

1991, Mar. 1 Photo. *Perf. 13½*

2079 A1593 41y multi .80 .30

Perf. 13½x13

2080 A1593 62y multi 1.10 .30

1991 Winter Universiade.

A1594

1991, Apr. 1 Photo. *Perf. 13*

2081 A1594 62y multicolored 1.10 .30

Postal Life Insurance System.

Philately Week

A1595 A1596

No. 2082, Beauty Looking Back by Moronobu. No. 2083, Opening Dance by Shuho Yamakawa.

1991, Apr. 19

2082 A1595 62y multicolored 1.10 .35

2083 A1596 62y multicolored 1.10 .35

a. Souv. sheet of 2, #2082-2083 2.50 2.50

b. Pair, #2082-2083 2.50 2.50

Postal Service, 120th anniv.

Pairs of Nos. 2082-2083 with label between are available from sheets of 20.

A1597

1991, Apr. 19 *Perf. 13½*

2084 A1597 62y multicolored 1.10 .30

Ceramic World Shigaraki '91.

A1598

1991, May 24 Photo. *Perf. 13½*

2085 A1598 41y multicolored .80 .30

Natl. Land Afforestation Campaign.

Standard Datum of Leveling, Cent. — A1599

1991, May 30 Photo. *Perf. 13*

2086 A1599m 62y mutlicolored 1.10 .35

Int'l Stamp Design Contest Winning Entries

Flowers A1600

Couple in Ethnic Dress A1601

World Peace — A1601a

Butterfly — A1601b

1991, May 31 Photo. *Perf. 13*

2087 A1600 41y multi .80 .30

2088 A1601 62y multi 1.10 .30

2089 A1601a 70y multi 1.25 .40

2090 A1601b 100y multi 1.75 .50

Nos. 2087-2090 (4) 4.90 1.50

Int'l. Stamp Design Contest winning entries.

Kabuki Series

Kagamijishi A1602

Yaegakihime A1603

Koshiro Matsumoto VII A1604

Danjuro Ichikawa XI A1605

Baigyoku Nakamura III A1606

Ganjiro Nakamura II A1607

Kichiemon Nakamura I — A1608

Nizaemon Kataoka XIII — A1609

Enjaku Jitsukawa II A1610

Hakuo Matsumoto I A1611

Fuji-Musume A1612

Kotobuki-Soganotaimen A1613

Perf. 13 (62y), 13½ (100y)

1991-92 Photo.

2091 A1602 62y dp bl grn & gold 1.10 .35

2092 A1603 100y multicolored 1.75 .55

2093 A1604 62y multicolored 1.10 .35

2094 A1605 100y multicolored 1.75 .55

2095 A1606 62y multicolored 1.10 .35

2096 A1607 100y multicolored 1.75 .55

2097 A1608 62y multicolored 1.10 .35

2098 A1609 100y multicolored 1.75 .55

2099 A1610 62y multicolored 1.10 .35

2100 A1611 100y multicolored 1.75 .55

2101 A1612 62y multicolored 1.10 .35

2102 A1613 100y multicolored 1.75 .55

Nos. 2091-2102 (12) 17.10 5.40

Issued: Nos. 2091-2092, 6/28; Nos. 2093-2094, 9/27; Nos. 2095-2096, 11/20; Nos. 2097-2098, 2/20/92; Nos. 2099-2100, 4/10/92; Nos. 2101-2102, 6/30/92.

Waterbird Series

Gallinago Hardwickii (Latham's Snipe) — A1614

No. 2104, Sula leucogaster. No. 2105, Larus crassirostris. No. 2106, Podiceps ruficollis. No. 2107, Lunda cirrhata. No. 2108, Grus monacha. No. 2109, Cygnus cygnus. No. 2110, Rostratula benghalensis. No. 2111, Calonectris leucomelas. No. 2112, Halcyon coromanda. No. 2113, Alcedo atthis. No. 2114, Bubulcus ibis.

1991-93 Photo. *Perf. 13½*

2103 A1614 62y multicolored 1.10 .35

2104 A1614 62y multicolored 1.10 .35

2105 A1614 62y multicolored 1.10 .35

2106 A1614 62y multicolored 1.10 .35

2107 A1614 62y multicolored 1.10 .35

2108 A1614 62y multicolored 1.10 .35

2109 A1614 62y multicolored 1.10 .35

2110 A1614 62y multicolored 1.10 .35

2111 A1614 62y multicolored 1.10 .35

2112 A1614 62y multicolored 1.10 .35

2113 A1614 62y multicolored 1.10 .35

2114 A1614 62y multicolored 1.10 .35

Nos. 2103-2114 (12) 13.20 4.20

Nos. 2103-2104 printed in blocks of 12 with gutter between in sheet of 24.

Issued: Nos. 2103-2104, 6/28; Nos. 2105-2106, 9/27; Nos. 2107-2108, 1/30/92; Nos. 2109-2110, 3/25/92; Nos. 2111-2112, 8/31/92; Nos. 2113-2114, 1/29/93.

See Nos. 2192-2195.

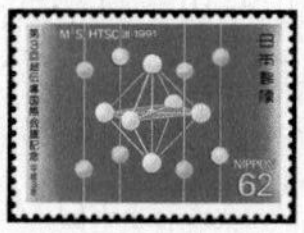

Intl. Conf. on Superconductivity A1620

1991, July 19 Litho. *Perf. 13½*

2115 A1620 62y multicolored 1.10 .30

Type of Letter Writing Day of 1990 and

A1621

1991, July 23 Photo. *Perf. 13x13½*

2116 A1621 41y multicolored .80 .35

2117 A1575 62y multicolored 1.10 .35

a. Souvenir sheet of 1 1.25 1.25

b. Bklt. pane, 5 each #2116-2117 9.50

Nos. 2117, 2117a have light blue frameline and inscription and violet denomination.

3rd IAAF World Track & Field Championships, Tokyo — A1622

1991, Aug. 23 *Perf. 13*

2118 A1622 41y High jump .80 .30

2119 A1622 62y Shot put 1.10 .30

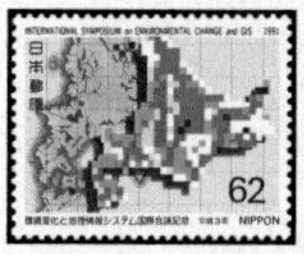

Intl. Symposium on Environmental Change and Geographical Information Systems — A1623

1991, Aug. 23

2120 A1623 62y multicolored 1.10 .30

Intl. Letter Writing Week — A1624

Bandainagon-emaki picture scroll probably by Mitsunaga Tokiwa: 80y, Crowd of people. 120y, People, house.

Photo. & Engr.

1991, Oct. 7 *Perf. 13½*

2121 A1624 80y multicolored 1.40 .45

2122 A1624 120y multicolored 2.00 .55

A1625

62y, Breezy Fine Weather by Hokusai.

1991, Oct. 8 Photo. *Perf. 13*

2123 A1625 62y multicolored 1.10 .35

Summit Conf. on Earthquake and Natural Disasters Countermeasures.

A1626

1991, Oct. 31 Litho. *Perf. 13*

2124 A1626 62y multicolored 1.10 .35

Japanese Green Tea, 800th anniv.

A1627

Koshaku-Musume by Kunisada Utagawa.

Photo. & Engr.

1991, Nov. 15 *Perf. 13*

2125 A1627 62y multicolored 1.10 .35
a. Sheet of 2 3.50 3.50

World Stamp Exhibition, Nippon '91.

A1628

1991, Nov. 20 **Photo.**

2126 A1628 62y multicolored 1.10 .30

Administrative Counselors System, 30th anniv.

A1629

A1630

New Year 1992 (Year of the Monkey)
A1631 A1632

1991, Dec. 2 **Photo.** *Perf. 13½*

2127 A1629 41y multicolored .75 .30
2128 A1630 62y multicolored 1.10 .40
2129 A1631 41y +3y, multi .90 .40
2130 A1632 62y +3y, multi 1.25 .40
Nos. 2127-2130 (4) 4.00 1.50

Sheets of 2 No. 2127 were lottery prizes. Value, $2.10.

8th Conference on Intl. Trade in Endangered Species (CITES) — A1633

1992, Mar. 2 **Photo.** *Perf. 13*

2131 A1633 62y multicolored 1.10 .30

Philately Week — A1634

Flowers on the Chair, by Hoshun Yamaguchi.

1992, Apr. 20

2132 A1634 62y multicolored 1.10 .30

A1635

1992, May 15

2133 A1635 62y multicolored 1.10 .35

Return of Ryukyu Islands to Japan, 20th anniv.

Intl. Space Year A1636

No. 2134, Satellite at left. No. 2135, Space station upper right.

1992, July 7 **Photo.** *Perf. 13*

2134 62y multicolored 1.10 .35
2135 62y multicolored 1.10 .35
a. A1636 Pair, #2134-2135 2.25 1.25

Letter Writing Day
A1638 A1639

1992, July 23 *Perf. 13x13½*

2136 A1638 41y multicolored .80 .35

Perf. 13½

2137 A1639 62y multicolored 1.10 .35
a. Souvenir sheet of 1 1.25 1.25
b. Bklt. pane, 5 each #2136-2137 9.50

29th Intl. Geological Congress, Kyoto — A1640

1992, Aug. 24 **Photo.** *Perf. 13½x13*

2138 A1640 62y multicolored 1.10 .30

47th Natl. Athletic Meet, Yamagata Prefecture — A1641

1992, Sept. 4 *Perf. 13½*

2139 A1641 41y multicolored .80 .30

Normalization of Japanese-Chinese Relations, 20th Anniv. — A1642

Photo. & Engr.

1992, Sept. 29 *Perf. 13*

2140 62y jug 1.10 .35
2141 62y long-neck jar 1.10 .35
a. A1642 Pair, #2140-2141 2.25 1.00

Intl. Letter Writing Week — A1644

Heiji picture scroll: 80y, Nobles, servants in carriages by Taikenmon gate. 120y, Fujiwara-no Nobuyori seated before samurai.

Photo. & Engr.

1992, Oct. 6 *Perf. 13½*

2142 A1644 80y multicolored 1.40 .45
2143 A1644 120y multicolored 2.00 .55

Cat and Birds — A1644a

Design: 70y, Santa Claus, snow scene, vert.

Perf. 13½x13, 13x13½

1992, Oct. 9 **Photo.**

2144 A1644a 62y multicolored 1.10 .30
2145 A1644a 70y multicolored 1.25 .30

Winners of Third Postage Stamp Design contest.

30th Congress of Intl. Cooperative Alliance, Tokyo — A1644b

1992, Oct. 27 *Perf. 13x13½*

2146 A1644b 62y multicolored 1.10 .30

A1645

Cultural Pioneers: No. 2147, Takakazu Seki (1642?-1708), mathematician. No. 2148, Akiko Yosano (1878-1942), poet.

Photo. & Engr.

1992, Nov. 4 *Perf. 13*

2147 A1645 62y multicolored 1.10 .30
2148 A1645 62y multicolored 1.10 .30

See Nos. 2217-2219, 2434-2435, 2642, 2717-2718.

A1646

1992, Nov. 9 **Photo.** *Perf. 13x13½*

2149 A1646 62y multicolored 1.10 .30

Certified Public Tax Accountant System, 50th anniv.

A1647

A1648

New Year 1993 (Year of the Rooster)
A1649 A1650

1992, Nov. 16 *Perf. 13x13½*

2150 A1647 41y multicolored .75 .30
2151 A1648 62y multicolored 1.10 .40
a. Souvenir sheet of 2, #2150-2151 2.40 2.40

Perf. 13½

2152 A1649 41y +3y multi .90 .40
2153 A1650 62y +3y multi 1.25 .40
Nos. 2150-2153 (4) 4.00 1.50

Surtax on Nos. 2152-2153 for lottery. No. 2151a also was a lottery prize.

Flora and Fauna — A1651

9y, Dragonfly. 15y, Swallowtail. 18y, Ladybug. 41y, Mandarin duck. No. 2158, 50y, Japanese white-eye. No. 2159, 62y, Rufous turtle dove. 72y, Varied tit. 80y, Pied kingfisher. 90y, Spotbill duck. 130y, Bullfinch. 190y, Fringed orchid. 270y, Wild pink. 350y, Adder's tongue lily. 420y, Japanese iris. 430y, Violet.

1992-94 **Photo.** *Perf. 13x13½*

2154 A1651 9y multi .30 .25
2155 A1651 15y multi .30 .25
2156 A1651 18y multi .40 .25
2157 A1651 41y multi 1.10 .35
2158 A1651 50y multi 1.10 .25
2159 A1651 62y multi 1.50 .25
a. Bklt. pane, 5 ea #2157, 2159 13.00
b. Booklet pane of 10 15.00
2160 A1651 72y multi 2.25 .25
2161 A1651 80y multi 1.75 .25
a. Miniature sheet, 5 #2158, 10 #2161 + 3 labels *45.00*
2162 A1651 90y multi 2.00 .25
2163 A1651 130y multi 3.00 .25
2164 A1651 190y multi 4.00 .25
2165 A1651 270y multi 6.00 .25
2166 A1651 350y multi 7.00 .25
2167 A1651 420y multi 9.00 .25
2167A A1651 430y multi 9.00 .25
Nos. 2154-2167A (15) 48.70 3.85

Coil Stamps

Perf. 13 Horiz.

2168 A1651 50y like #2158 1.25 .25
2169 A1651 80y like #2161 2.00 .25

Booklet Stamps

Self-Adhesive

Die Cut

2170 A1651 41y like #2157 1.10 .35
2171 A1651 50y like #2158 1.10 .45
2172 A1651 62y like #2159 1.50 .50
a. Bklt. pane, 2 #2170, 4 #2172 8.50
2173 A1651 80y like #2161 1.75 .70
a. Bklt. pane, 4 #2171, 4 #2173 14.00

Issued: 41y, 62y, 72y, 11/30/92; 9y, 18y, Nos. 2158, 2161, 90y, 1/13/94; 270y, 350y, 420y, 1/24/94; 15y, 130y, 190y, 430y, 4/25/94.

Nos. 2172a, 2173a are adhered to the booklet cover, made of peelable paper, folded in half and rouletted down the center fold.

See Nos. 2475-2483, 2486-2488. Compare No. 2166 with No. 3446.

World Alpine Skiing Championships, Morioka-Shizukuishi A1657

1993, Feb. 3 **Photo.** *Perf. 13*

2174 A1657 41y shown .80 .40
2175 A1657 62y Skier, diff. 1.10 .55

Seasonal Flowers Series

Poppy
A1658

Cherry Blossoms
A1659

Lily
A1660

Thistle
A1661

Chinese Bellflowers
A1662

Chrysanthemums
A1663

Plum Blossom
A1664

Winter Camellia
A1665

Perf. 13½ (41y, 50y), 13 (62y, 80y)

1993-94 **Photo.**

2176 A1658 41y multicolored .80 .35

Perf. 13

2177 A1659 62y multicolored 1.10 .35
2178 A1660 41y multicolored .80 .35

Perf. 13

2179 A1661 62y multicolored 1.10 .35
2180 A1662 41y multicolored .80 .35
2181 A1663 62y multicolored 1.10 .35
2182 A1664 50y multicolored .90 .35
2183 A1665 80y multicolored 1.40 .55
Nos. 2176-2183 (8) 8.00 3.00

Issued: Nos. 2176-2177, 3/12; Nos. 2178-2179, 6/18; Nos. 2180-2181, 9/16; Nos. 2182-2183, 1/28/94.

Waterbird Type

1993 **Photo.** ***Perf. 13½***

2192 A1614 62y Grus vipio 1.10 .35
2193 A1614 62y Ansner albifrons 1.10 .35
2194 A1614 62y Anas formosa 1.10 .35
2195 A1614 62y Haliaeetus albicilla 1.10 .35
Nos. 2192-2195 (4) 4.40 1.40

Issued: Nos. 2192-2193, 3/31; Nos. 2194-2195, 5/25.

Philately Week — A1674

Painting: In the Studio, by Nampu Katayama.

1993, Apr. 20 **Photo.** ***Perf. 13***

2196 A1674 62y multicolored 1.10 .30

Natl. Land Afforestation Campaign — A1675

1993, Apr. 23 ***Perf. 13½***

2197 A1675 41y multicolored .80 .30

Mandarin Duck in the Nest
A1676

Gardenia in the Nest
A1677

Design: 70y, Mandarin Duck and Gardenia emblems, horiz.

1993, June 8 **Photo.** ***Perf. 13***

2198 A1676 62y multicolored 1.10 .35
2199 A1677 62y multicolored 1.10 .35
a. Pair, #2198-2199 2.25 1.25
2200 A1676 70y multicolored 1.25 .40
Nos. 2198-2200 (3) 3.45 1.10

Royal Wedding of Crown Prince Naruhito and Masako Owada.

5th Meeting of Signatories to Ramsar, Iran Convention on Wetlands and Waterfowl Habitats — A1678

No. 2201, Crane with young. No. 2202, Crane's head.

1993, June 10 **Photo.** ***Perf. 13½***

2201 A1678 62y multicolored 1.10 .35
2202 A1678 62y multicolored 1.10 .35
a. Pair, #2201-2202 2.50 2.00

Commercial Registration System, Cent. — A1679

1993, July 1 **Photo.** ***Perf. 13x13½***

2203 A1679 62y multicolored 1.10 .30

Letter Writing Day
A1680 A1681

1993, July 23 ***Perf. 13x13½***

2204 A1680 41y multicolored .80 .35

Perf. 13½x13

2205 A1681 62y multicolored 1.10 .35
a. Souvenir sheet of 1 1.25 1.25
b. Booklet pane, 5 each #2204-2205 10.00

15th Intl. Botanical Congress, Tokyo — A1682

Designs: No. 2206, Glaucidium palmatum. No. 2207, Sciadopitys verticillata.

1993, Aug. 23 **Photo.** ***Perf. 13½x13***

2206 62y multicolored 1.10 .35
2207 62y multicolored 1.10 .35
a. A1682 Pair, #2206-2207 2.50 1.25

World Federation for Mental Health Congress, Chiba City — A1683

1993, Aug. 23 ***Perf. 13½x13***

2208 A1683 62y multicolored 1.10 .30

A1684

1993, Sept. 3 **Photo.** ***Perf. 13½***

2209 41y Swimming .80 .30
2210 41y Karate .80 .30
a. A1684 Pair, #2209-2210 1.75 1.00

48th natl. athletic meet, Kagawa Prefecture.

A1685

Japanese-Portuguese Relations, 450th Anniv.: No. 2211, Arrival of Portuguese, folding screen, c. 1560-1630. No. 2212, Mother-of-Pearl Host Box, Jesuit symbols and grape motif.

1993, Sept. 22 **Photo.** ***Perf. 13***

2211 62y multicolored 1.10 .35
2212 62y multicolored 1.10 .35
a. A1685 Pair, #2211-2212 2.50 1.25

Intl. Letter Writing Week — A1686

Portraits from Picture Scrolls of the Thirty-Six Immortal Poets: 80y, Ki no Tsurayuki. 120y, Kodai no Kimi.

1993, Oct. 6 ***Perf. 13½***

2213 A1686 80y multicolored 1.40 .40
2214 A1686 120y multicolored 2.00 .50

10th World Veterans' Track and Field Championships, Miyazaki Prefecture — A1687

1993, Oct. 7 ***Perf. 14***

2215 A1687 62y multicolored 1.10 .30

Souvenir Sheet

Wedding of Crown Prince Naruhito and Princess Masako — A1688

1993, Oct. 13 **Photo.** ***Perf. 13½***

2216 A1688 62y multicolored 1.25 1.25

Cultural Pioneers Type of 1992

No. 2217, Kazan Watanabe (1793-1841), artist. No. 2218, Umetaro Suzuki (1874-1943), chemist. No. 2219, Toson Shimazaki (1872-1943), poet.

1993, Nov. 4 **Photo.** ***Perf. 13***

2217 A1645 62y multicolored 1.10 .30

Photo. & Engr.

2218 A1645 62y multicolored 1.10 .30
2219 A1645 62y multicolored 1.10 .30
Nos. 2217-2219 (3) 3.30 .90

Agricultural Research Center, Cent. — A1689

1993, Nov. 17 ***Perf. 13½***

2220 A1689 62y multicolored 1.10 .30

A1690

A1691

New Year 1994 (Year of the Dog)
A1692 A1693

1993, Nov. 17 ***Perf. 13x13½***

2221 A1690 41y multicolored .75 .30
2222 A1691 62y multicolored 1.10 .40

Perf. 13½

2223 A1692 41y +3y multi .90 .40
2224 A1693 62y +3y multi 1.25 .40
Nos. 2221-2224 (4) 4.00 1.50

Sheets of 2, Nos. 2221-2222, were lottery prizes. Value, $2.40.

Declaration of Human Rights, 45th Anniv. — A1694

Designs: 62y, Man with bird perched on head. 70y, Globe, dove, person breaking chains, peace symbol.

1993, Dec. 10 **Photo.** ***Perf. 13***

2225 A1694 62y multicolored 1.10 .30
2226 A1694 70y multicolored 1.25 .40

Congratulations and Condolences Types of 1982

1994, Mar. 10 **Photo.** ***Perf. 13x13½***

2227 A1082 50y Wreath .90 .35
2228 A1083 50y Crane .90 .35
2229 A1083 80y Crane 1.40 .40
2230 A1084 90y Tortoise 1.60 .40
Nos. 2227-2230 (4) 4.80 1.50

For use on condolence and greeting cards.

1994 World Figure Skating Championships, Tokyo — A1695

No. 2231, Ice dancing. No. 2232, Women's singles. No. 2233, Men's singles, vert. No. 2234, Pairs, vert.

1994, Mar. 17 **Photo.** ***Perf. 13***

2231 A1695 50y multicolored .90 .35
2232 A1695 50y multicolored .90 .35
a. Pair, #2231-2232 2.25 1.25
2233 A1695 80y multicolored 1.40 .40
2234 A1695 80y multicolored 1.40 .40
a. Pair, #2233-2234 3.00 1.50
Nos. 2231-2234 (4) 4.60 1.50

Philately Week — A1696

1994, Apr. 20 Photo. *Perf. 13*

2235	A1696	80y	Irises	1.50	.40

Intl. Year of the Family — A1697

Designs: No. 2236, "Love" spelled by people. No. 2237, Faces in flowers. No. 2238, Sun shining on people, homes. No. 2239, Family flying inside bird.

1994, May 13 Photo. *Perf. 13*

2236	A1697	50y	multicolored	.90	.30
2237	A1697	50y	multicolored	.90	.30
2238	A1697	80y	multicolored	1.40	.35
a.			Pair, #2236, 2238	2.50	1.25
2239	A1697	80y	multicolored	1.40	.35
a.			Pair, #2237, 2239	2.50	1.25
			Nos. 2236-2239 (4)	4.60	1.30

Natl. Land Afforestation Campaign — A1698

1994, May 20

2240	A1698	50y	multicolored	1.00	.35

Intl. Conference on Natural Disaster Reduction — A1699

1994, May 23

2241	A1699	80y	multicolored	1.50	.35

No. 2241 printed in sheets of 16 with 4 labels.

A1700

1994, May 24

2242	A1700	80y	multicolored	1.50	.35

Prototype Fast Breeder Reactor, Monju.

Environment Day — A1701

1994, June 3 Photo. *Perf. 13*

2243	A1701	80y	multicolored	1.50	.40

Letter Writing Day
A1702 A1703

1994, July 22

2244	A1702	50y	multicolored	1.00	.35
2245	A1703	80y	multicolored	1.50	.40
a.			Souvenir sheet of 1	1.75	1.75
b.			Bklt. pane, 5 each #2244-2245	12.50	

Prefecture Issues

Nos. 2246-2400B have been changed to #Z151-Z307. The listings can be found in a new section immediately following the postage section and preceding the semi-postal listings.

10th Intl. Conference on AIDS, Yokohama — A1859

1994, Aug. 5 Photo. *Perf. 13*

2401	A1859	80y	multicolored	1.50	.35

Postal History Series

A1860

First Japanese stamps (Baron Hisoka Maeshima and): No. 2402, #1. No. 2403, #2. No. 2404, #3. No. 2405, #4.

CTO's exist for Nos. 2402-2405. They read "Japan" between two arcs in a corner.

Photo. & Engr.

1994, Aug. 10 *Perf. 13*

2402	A1860	80y	brown & black	1.40	.40
2403	A1860	80y	blue & black	1.40	.40
2404	A1860	80y	ver & black	1.40	.40
2405	A1860	80y	olive grn & blk	1.40	.40
a.			Strip of 4, #2402-2405	6.00	6.00

A1861

Early Japanese stamps (Edoardo Chiossone and): No. 2406, #55. No. 2407, Type A16. No. 2408, #63. No. 2409, #65.

1994, Nov. 18 *Perf. 13½*

2406	A1861	80y	buff, slate & blk	1.40	.40
2407	A1861	80y	gray & dk brown	1.40	.40
2408	A1861	80y	gray lilac & rose	1.40	.40
2409	A1861	80y	lt blue & dk blue	1.40	.40
a.			Strip of 4, #2406-2409	6.00	6.00

A1862

Designs: No. 2410, #85, transporting mail by ricksha. No. 2411, #86, transporting mail by horse-drawn carriage.

1995, Jan. 25

2410	A1862	80y	multicolored	1.40	.40
2411	A1862	80y	multicolored	1.40	.40
			Nos. 2402-2411 (10)	14.00	4.00

A1863

Designs: No. 2412, #C3, First Osaka-Tokyo airmail flight. No. 2413, #C6, Workers loading freight onto airplane.

Photo. & Engr.

1995, May 25 *Perf. 13½*

2412	A1863	110y	multicolored	2.00	.50
2413	A1863	110y	multicolored	2.00	.50

Nos. 2412-2413 printed in blocks of 10 with gutter between in sheets of 20.

A1864

No. 2414, Light mail van, #436. No. 2415, Cherub commemorative mail box, #428. No. 2416, Mail box, #435. No. 2417, Van, #433.

Photo. & Engr.

1995, Sept. 19 *Perf. 13½*

2414	A1864	80y	multicolored	1.40	.40
2415	A1864	80y	multicolored	1.40	.40
2416	A1864	80y	multicolored	1.40	.40
2417	A1864	80y	multicolored	1.40	.40
a.			Block of 4, #2414-2417	6.00	6.00

Postal History Series
Types of 1948-49 With "NIPPON" Inscribed at Bottom
Size: 22x47mm

Photo. & Engr.

1996, June 3 *Perf. 13½*

2418	A206	80y	like #422, brown	1.40	.40
2419	A206	80y	like #422, multi	1.40	.40
2420	A247	80y	like #479, purple	1.40	.40
2421	A247	80y	like #479, multi	1.40	.40
a.			Strip of 4, #2418-2421	6.00	6.00

Opening of Kansai Intl. Airport — A1877

Designs: No. 2422, Airport, part of plane's vertical stabilizer. No. 2423, Aft section of airplane. No. 2424, Airport, jet.

1994, Sept. 2 Photo. *Perf. 13*

2422	A1877	80y	multicolored	1.40	.35
2423	A1877	80y	multicolored	1.40	.35
a.			Vert. pair, #2422-2423	3.00	3.00
b.			Vert. strip of 3, #2422-2424	4.50	4.50
2424	A1877	80y	multicolored	1.40	.35
			Nos. 2422-2424 (3)	4.20	1.05

A1878

1994, Sept. 19

2425	A1878	80y	multicolored	1.50	.35

ITU Plenipotentiary Conference, Kyoto.

12th Asian Games, Hiroshima — A1879

No. 2426, Kick volleyball. No. 2427, Steeplechase. No. 2428, Synchronized swimming

1994, Sept. 30

2426	A1879	50y	multicolored	1.00	.30
2427	A1879	80y	multicolored	1.40	.35
2428	A1879	80y	multicolored	1.40	.35
a.			Pair, #2427-2428	3.00	1.75
			Nos. 2426-2428 (3)	3.80	1.00

Intl. Letter Writing Week — A1880

Screen paintings of popular indoor games, Momoyama, Edo periods: 90y, Sugoroku. 110y, Japanese chess. 130y, Go.

1994, Oct. 6 Photo. *Perf. 13x13½*

2429	A1880	90y	multicolored	1.75	.45
2430	A1880	110y	multicolored	2.25	.55
2431	A1880	130y	multicolored	2.50	.55
			Nos. 2429-2431 (3)	6.50	1.55

49th Natl. Athletic Meet, Aichi Prefecture — A1881

1994, Oct. 28 *Perf. 13½*

2432	A1881	50y	multicolored	1.00	.30

A1882

1994, Nov. 4 Photo. *Perf. 13*

2433	A1882	80y	multicolored	1.50	.35

Intl. Diabetes Federation, 15th Congress, Kobe.

Cultural Pioneers Type of 1992

Cultural pioneers: No. 2434, Michio Miyagi (1894-1956), Musician. No. 2435, Gyoshu Hayami (1894-1935), artist.

1994, Nov. 4 Photo. & Engr.

2434	A1645	80y	multicolored	1.40	.35
2435	A1645	80y	multicolored	1.40	.35

A1884

Heiankyo (Kyoto), 1200th Anniv. — A1885

Kanpuzu, by Hideyori Kano, Momoyama period depicts autumn scene on Kiyotakigawa River: No. 2436, People seated, white birds. No. 2437, Bridge, people. No. 2438, Bridge, birds flying. No. 2439, People, Jingoji Temple, Atago-Jinja Shrine. No. 2440, People seated, tree.

No. 2441, Painting of Dry Garden (Sekitei), Ryoanji Temple, by Eizo Kato. No. 2442, Painting of artificial pond, Shugakuin Rikyu, by Kanji Kawai, horiz.

1994, Nov. 8 Photo. *Perf. 13x13½*

2436		80y	multicolored	1.40	.40
2437		80y	multicolored	1.40	.40
2438		80y	multicolored	1.40	.40
2439		80y	multicolored	1.40	.40
2440		80y	multicolored	1.40	.40
a.	A1884		Strip of 5, #2436-2440	8.50	8.50
2441	A1885	80y	multicolored	1.40	.40

Perf. 13½x13

2442	A1885	80y	multicolored	1.40	.40
			Nos. 2436-2442 (7)	9.80	2.80

A1886

A1887

New Year 1995 (Year of the Boar)
A1888 A1889

1994, Nov. 15 *Perf. 13x13½*

2443	A1886	50y multicolored		1.00	.30
2444	A1887	80y multicolored		1.50	.40

Perf. 13½

2445	A1888	50y +3y multi		1.25	.40
2446	A1889	80y +3y multi		1.75	.40
		Nos. 2443-2446 (4)		5.50	1.50

Sheets of two containing Nos. 2443-2444 were lottery prizes. Value $2.75.

World Heritage Series

Himeji Castle
A1890 A1891

1994, Dec. 14 **Photo.** *Perf. 13*

2447	A1890	80y multicolored	1.50	.40
2448	A1891	80y multicolored	1.50	.40

A1892

Horyuji Temple — A1893

Designs: 80y, Goddess Kannon from inner temple wall. 110y, Temple exterior.

1995, Feb. 22

2449	A1892	80y multicolored	1.50	.40
2450	A1893	110y multicolored	2.25	.55

Cryptomeria Japonica
A1894

Cervus Nippon Yakushimae
A1895

1995, July 28

2451	A1894	80y multicolored	1.50	.40
2452	A1895	80y multicolored	1.50	.40

Virgin Beech Forest
A1896

Black Woodpecker
A1897

1995, Nov. 21

2453	A1896	80y multicolored	1.50	.40
2454	A1897	80y multicolored	1.50	.40
		Nos. 2447-2454 (8)	12.75	3.35

Japan-Brazil Friendship, Cent. — A1898

Designs: No. 2455, Natl. emblems, flowers. No. 2456, Soccer players.

1995, Mar. 3 **Photo.** *Perf. 13½*

2455	A1898	80y multicolored	1.40	.35
2456	A1898	80y multicolored	1.40	.35

A1899

Fujiwara-Kyo Palace, 1300th Anniv. — A1900

Designs: 50y, Unebiyama, Nijozan Mountains, roofing tile from palace. 80y, Portrait of a Woman, in Asuka and Hakuho era style, by Okada, 1925.

1995, Mar. 28

2457	A1899	50y multicolored	1.00	.35
2458	A1900	80y multicolored	1.50	.40

Modern Anatomical Education — A1901

1995, Mar. 31 *Perf. 13*

2459	A1901	80y multicolored	1.50	.35

1995 Census — A1902

1995, Apr. 12 **Photo.** *Perf. 13*

2460	A1902	80y multicolored	1.50	.40

A1903

1995, Apr. 20

2461	A1903	80y multicolored	1.50	.40

Japanese Overseas Cooperation Volunteers, 30th anniv.

A1904 A1905

A1906 A1907

A1908

1995, Apr. 25 *Perf. 13x13½*

2462	A1904	50y multicolored	1.00	.30
2463	A1905	50y multicolored	1.00	.30
2464	A1906	80y multicolored	1.50	.35
2465	A1907	80y multicolored	1.50	.35
2466	A1908	90y multicolored	1.75	.55
		Nos. 2462-2466 (5)	6.75	1.85

For use on condolence and greeting cards.

A1909

1995, May 19 **Photo.** *Perf. 13½x13*

2467	A1909	50y multicolored	1.00	.30

Natl. land afforestation campaign.

A1910

Greetings: No. 2468, Rainbow, hearts. No. 2469, Girl holding heart-shaped balloon. No. 2470, Flower holding pencil, sign. No. 2471, Star, sun, moon as flowers, fauna. No. 2472, Person, dog with flowers, butterfly in hair.

Self-Adhesive

1995, June 1 *Die Cut Perf. 13½*

2468	A1910	80y multicolored	1.50	.40
2469	A1910	80y multicolored	1.50	.40
2470	A1910	80y multicolored	1.50	.40
2471	A1910	80y multicolored	1.50	.40
2472	A1910	80y multicolored	1.50	.40
a.		Miniature sheet, #2468-2472 + 5 labels	8.50	8.50

Letter Writing Day
A1911 A1912

1995, July 21 **Photo.** *Perf. 13½*

2473	A1911	50y multicolored	1.00	.30
2474	A1912	80y multicolored	1.50	.35
a.		Souvenir sheet of 1	1.75	1.75
b.		Bklt. pane, 5 ea #2473-2474	12.50	
		Complete booklet, #2474b	13.00	

Flora & Fauna Type of 1992 and

Shikikacho-zu — A1926

Matsutaka-Zu A1926a

10y, Scarab, dandelions. 20y, Honey bee, flower. 30y, Hairstreak, flowers. 70y, Great tit. 110y, Plover. 120y, Shrike. 140y, Japanese grosbeak. 160y, Jay. 390y, Dayflower.

1995-98 **Photo.** *Perf. 13½*

2475	A1651	10y multi	.30	.25
2476	A1651	20y multi	.40	.25
2477	A1651	30y multi	.60	.25
2478	A1651	70y multi	1.60	.25
2479	A1651	110y multi	2.25	.25
2480	A1651	120y multi	2.50	.25
2481	A1651	140y multi	3.00	.25
2482	A1651	160y multi	3.25	.25

Perf. 13x13½

2483	A1651	390y multi	8.00	.25

Perf. 13½

2484	A1926	700y multi	21.00	1.00

Photo. & Engr.

2485	A1926a	1000y multi	19.00	.50
a.		Imperf. (3799b)	30.00	30.00

Self-Adhesive

Die Cut Perf. 13x13½

2486	A1651	50y Like #2158	1.10	.25
2487	A1651	80y Like #2161	1.75	.25

Coil Stamp

Perf. 13 Horiz.

2488	A1651	10y like #2475	.25	.25
		Nos. 2475-2488 (14)	65.00	4.50

Issued: 700y, 7/4/95; 390y, 1000y, 3/28/96; 70y, 110y, 7/22/97; No. 2475, 20y, 30y, 11/28/97; 120y, 140y, 2/16/98 160y, 2/23/98; No. 2488, 9/11/98. Nos. 2486-2487, 3/25/02. No. 2485a, 2/2/15.

Nos. 2486 and 2487 were issued in panes of 10.

End of World War II, 50th Anniv.
A1937 A1938

Design: No. 2491, Children holding hands behind stained glass window, peace dove, earth from space.

1995, Aug. 1 **Photo.** *Perf. 13*

2489	A1937	50y multicolored	1.00	.30
2490	A1938	80y multicolored	1.50	.35
2491	A1938	80y multicolored	1.50	.35
		Nos. 2489-2491 (3)	4.00	1.00

18th Universiade, Fukuoka — A1939

1995, Aug. 23

2492	A1939	80y multicolored	1.50	.35

A1940

50y, Radio controlled plane, transmitter. 80y, Radio controlled helicopter, competitor, assistant.

1995, Aug. 25

2493	A1940	50y multicolored	1.00	.30
2494	A1940	80y multicolored	1.50	.35

1995 Aeromodel World Championships, Okayama Prefecture.

World Veterinary Congress, Yokohama — A1941

80y, Dog, cow & horse.

1995, Sept. 1 **Photo.** *Perf. 13*

2495	A1941	80y multicolored	1.50	.35

World Sports Championships
A1942

No. 2496, 1995 World Judo Championships, Chiba Prefecture. No. 2497, 1995 World Gymnastics Championships, Sabae, Fukui Prefecture.

1995, Sept. 28

2496 A1942 80y multicolored 1.50 .35
2497 A1942 80y multicolored 1.50 .35

Letter Writing Week — A1943

Screen paintings: 90y, Shell-matching game. 110y, Battledore and shuttlecock. 130y, Playing cards.

1995, Oct. 6 ***Perf. 13½***

2498 A1943 90y multicolored 1.75 .45
2499 A1943 110y multicolored 2.25 .55
2500 A1943 130y multicolored 2.50 .55
Nos. 2498-2500 (3) 6.50 1.55

A1944

1995, Oct. 13 ***Perf. 13x13½***

2501 A1944 50y multicolored 1.00 .30

50th Natl. athletic meet, Fukushima prefecture.

UN, UNESCO, 50th Anniv. — A1945

No. 2502, UN, hearts. No. 2503, UNESCO, children.

1995, Oct. 24 ***Perf. 13***

2502 A1945 80y multi 1.50 .35
2503 A1945 80y multi 1.50 .35

Cultural Pioneers Type of 1992

No. 2504, Tadataka Ino (1745-1818), cartographer. No. 2505, Kitaro Nishida (1870-1945), philosopher.

Photo. & Engr.

1995, Nov. 6 ***Perf. 13***

2504 A1645 80y multicolored 1.50 .40
2505 A1645 80y multicolored 1.50 .40

A1947

A1948

New Year 1996 (Year of the Rat)
A1949 A1950

1995, Oct. 15 Photo. ***Perf. 13x13½***

2506 A1947 50y multicolored 1.00 .30
2507 A1948 80y multicolored 1.50 .40

Perf. 13½

2508 A1949 50y +3y multi 1.25 .40
2509 A1950 80y +3y multi 1.75 .40
Nos. 2506-2509 (4) 5.50 1.50

Sheets of two containing Nos. 2506-2507 were lottery prizes. Value $2.75.

Japanese-Korean Diplomatic Relations, 30th Anniv. — A1951

1995, Dec. 18 ***Perf. 13***

2510 A1951 80y multicolored 1.50 .35

Nos. 2511-2512 are unassigned.

A1952

1996, Feb. 16 Photo. ***Perf. 13***

2513 A1952 80y multicolored 1.50 .35

Philipp Franz von Siebold (1796-1866), naturalist.

A1953

1996, Mar. 1

2514 A1953 80y multicolored 1.50 .35

Labor Relations Commissions, 50th anniv.

Senior Citizens — A1954

1996, Mar. 21 ***Perf. 13½***

2515 A1954 80y multicolored 1.50 .35

No. 2515 issued in sheets of 5.

50th Postwar Memorial Year
A1955 A1956

No. 2516, Crowd, Emperor's limosine approaching Diet. No. 2517, Prime Minister Yoshida signing Peace Treaty, San Francisco, 9/8/51. No. 2518, Women performing traditional Okinawan dance.

1996, Apr. 1 Photo. ***Perf. 13***

2516 A1955 80y multicolored 1.25 .40
2517 A1955 80y multicolored 1.25 .40
a. Pair, Nos. 2516-2517 3.00 2.25
2518 A1956 80y multicolored 1.50 .40
Nos. 2516-2518 (3) 4.00 1.20

Promulgation of the the Constitution, 11/7/46 (No. 2517a). Return of Okinawa, 5/15/72 (No. 2518).

Woman Suffrage, 50th Anniv. — A1957

1996, Apr. 10 ***Perf. 13½***

2519 A1957 80y multicolored 1.50 .35

Philately Week — A1958

1996, Apr. 19 ***Perf. 13***

2520 A1958 80y multicolored 1.50 .40

UNICEF, 50th Anniv. — A1959

1996, May 1 Photo. ***Perf. 13***

2521 A1959 80y multicolored 1.50 .35

Child Welfare Week, 50th Anniv. — A1960

1996, May 1

2522 A1960 80y multicolored 1.50 .35

Bird Week, 50th Anniv. A1961

1996, May 10

2523 80y Birds 1.25 .40
2524 80y Field Glasses 1.25 .40
a. A1961 Pair, #2523-2524 3.00 1.75

Natl. Afforestation Campaign — A1963

1996, May 17

2525 A1963 50y multicolored 1.00 .30

50th Postwar Memorial Year
A1964 A1965

1996, June 24 Photo. ***Perf. 13***

2526 A1964 80y multicolored 1.50 .40
2527 A1965 80y multicolored 1.50 .40

River Administration System, Cent. — A1966

1996, July 5 Photo. ***Perf. 13½***

2528 80y denomination lower right 1.25 .40
2529 80y denomination lower left 1.25 .40
a. A1966 Pair, #2528-2529 3.25 1.75

A1968

Marine Day's Establishment — A1969

1996, July 19

2530 A1968 50y multicolored 1.00 .35
2531 A1969 80y multicolored 1.50 .40

Letter Writing Day
A1970 A1971

1996, July 23

2532 A1970 50y multicolored 1.00 .35
2533 A1971 80y multicolored 1.50 .40
a. Souvenir sheet of 1 1.75 1.75
b. Bklt. pane, 5 ea #2532-2533 12.00
Complete booklet 13.00

Cultural Pioneers Type of 1992

No. 2534, Kenji Miyazaw (1896-1933). No. 2535, Hokiichi Hanawa (1746-1821).

Photo. & Engr.

1996, Aug. 27 ***Perf. 13***

2534 A1645 80y multicolored 1.50 .35
2535 A1645 80y multicolored 1.50 .35

A1974 A1975

Designs: No. 2536, Advances of women in society, diffusion of home electrical products. No. 2537, Modern highway, railway systems.

1996, Aug. 27 Photo. ***Perf. 13***

2536 A1974 80y multicolored 1.50 .40
2537 A1975 80y multicolored 1.50 .40

51st Natl. Athletic Meet — A1976

1996, Sept. 6 Photo. ***Perf. 13½***

2538 A1976 50y Archery 1.00 .30

Community Chest, 50th Anniv. — A1977

1996, Sept. 30

2539 A1977 80y multicolored 1.50 .35

Intl. Music Day — A1978

1996, Oct. 1 ***Perf. 13***

2540 A1978 80y multicolored 1.50 .35

A1979

A1980

A1980a

Intl. Letter Writing Week — A1980b

Paintings: No. 2541, Water wheel, Mt. Fuji. No. 2543, Mt. Fuji in Clear Weather (Red Fuji), by Hokusai. No. 2545, Mt. Fuji, lake.

1996, Oct. 7 ***Perf. 13½***

2541	A1979	90y multicolored	1.75	.50
2542	A1980	90y multicolored	1.75	.50
a.		Pair, #2541-2542	3.75	1.75
2543	A1979	110y multicolored	2.25	.55
2544	A1980a	110y multicolored	2.25	.55
a.		Pair, #2543-2544	4.50	2.00
2545	A1979	130y multicolored	2.50	.60
2546	A1980b	130y multicolored	2.50	.60
a.		Pair, #2545-2546	5.50	2.25
		Nos. 2541-2546 (6)	13.00	3.30

18th World Congress of Savings Banks — A1981

1996, Oct. 23 ***Perf. 13***

2547 A1981 80y multicolored 1.50 .35

50th Postwar Memorial Year
A1982 A1983

No. 2548, Earth from space. No. 2549, Cellular telephone, fiber optic cable, satellite in orbit.

1996, Nov. 8 Photo. ***Perf. 13***

2548	A1982	80y multicolored	1.50	.40
2549	A1983	80y multicolored	1.50	.40

A1984 A1985

New Year 1997 (Year of the Ox)
A1986 A1987

1996, Nov. 15 Photo. ***Perf. 13x13½***

2550	A1984	50y multicolored	1.00	.30
2551	A1985	80y multicolored	1.50	.40

Perf. 13½

2552	A1986	50y +3y multi	1.25	.40
2553	A1987	80y +3y multi	1.75	.40
		Nos. 2550-2553 (4)	5.50	1.50

Sheets of 2 containing Nos. 2550-2551 were lottery prizes. Value $2.75.

Yujiro Ishihara, Actor — A1988

Hibari Misora, Entertainer — A1990

Osamu Tezuka, Cartoonist — A1992

1997, Jan. 28 Photo. ***Perf. 13***

2554		80y multicolored	1.25	.40
2555		80y multicolored	1.25	.40
a.	A1988	Pair, #2554-2555	3.50	1.75
2556		80y multicolored	1.25	.40
2557		80y multicolored	1.25	.40
a.	A1990	Pair, #2556-2557	3.50	1.75
2558		80y multicolored	1.25	.45
2559		80y multicolored	1.25	.45
a.	A1992	Pair, #2558-2559	3.50	2.00
		Nos. 2554-2559 (6)	7.50	2.50

Sparrow, Rice Plant, Camellia
A1994

Sparrow, Maple, Camellia
A1995

Perf. 14 Horiz. Syncopated Type A

1997, Apr. 10 Photo.

2560	A1994	50y multi	1.50	.50
2560A	A1994	80y multi	2.25	.50
2560B	A1994	90y multi	2.50	.60
2560C	A1994	120y multi	3.25	.65
2560D	A1994	130y multi	*28.00*	7.00
2561	A1995	270y multi	7.00	1.25
		Nos. 2560-2561 (6)	44.50	10.50

Denominations of Nos. 2560-2561 were printed by machine at point of sale, and were limited to the denominations listed.

Daigo, by Okumura Dogyu (1889-1990)
A1996

1997, Apr. 18 Litho. ***Perf. 13½***

2562 A1996 80y multicolored 1.60 .35

Philately Week.

Supreme Court, 50th Anniv. — A1997

1997, May 2 Photo. ***Perf. 13***

2563 A1997 80y Main court room 1.50 .35

Doraemon — A1998

Designs: No. 2564, Shown. No. 2565, With envelope. No. 2566, Standing on hand. No. 2567, With propeller. No. 2568, In love.

Booklet Stamps

Serpentine Die Cut 13½

1997, May 2 Self-Adhesive

2564	A1998	80y multicolored	1.50	.40
2565	A1998	80y multicolored	1.50	.40
2566	A1998	80y multicolored	1.50	.40
2567	A1998	80y multicolored	1.50	.40
2568	A1998	80y multicolored	1.50	.40
a.		Pane of 5, #2564-2568	8.00	*8.00*

Japanese Migration to Mexico, Cent. — A1999

1997, May 12 ***Perf. 13***

2569 A1999 80y multicolored 1.50 .35

See Mexico No. 2035.

Natl. Afforestation Campaign — A2000

50y, Miyagi bush clover.

1997, May 16 ***Perf. 13½***

2570 A2000 50y multicolored 1.00 .30

Natl. Diet — A2001

1997, May 20 ***Perf. 13***

2571 A2001 80y multicolored 1.50 .35

Natl. House of Councilors, 50th anniv.

Letter Writing Day

A2002

A2003

A2004

A2005

1997, July 23 Photo. ***Perf. 13***

2572	A2002	50y multicolored	1.00	.30
2573	A2003	70y multicolored	1.25	.35
2574	A2004	80y multicolored	1.50	.35
a.		Souvenir sheet of 1	1.75	1.75
b.		Bklt. pane, 5 ea #2572, 2574	13.00	
		Complete booklet, #2574b	13.00	
2575	A2005	90y multicolored	1.75	.45
		Nos. 2572-2575 (4)	5.50	1.45

A2006

1997, Aug. 11 Photo. ***Perf. 13***

2576 A2006 50y multicolored 1.00 .30

Part-time and correspondence education at upper secondary schools, 50th anniv.

Labor Standards Law, 50th Anniv. — A2007

1997, Sept. 1

2577 A2007 80y multicolored 1.50 .35

Friendship Between Japan and Chile, Cent. — A2008

1997, Sept. 1 ***Perf. 13½***

2578 A2008 80y multicolored 1.50 .35

See Chile No. 1217.

52nd Natl. Sports Festival — A2009

1997, Sept. 12

2579 A2009 50y multicolored 1.00 .30

A2010

A2010a

A2010b

Intl. Letter Writing Week — A2010c

Paintings of Tokaido's 53 Stations by Hiroshige: No. 2580, Hodogaya (bridge over waterway). No. 2582, Kameyama snow-covered mountain slope).

No. 2584, Sumida Riverbank Snowscape (woman in traditional attire beside river), by Hiroshige
From Scrolls of Flowers and Birds of the Four Seasons by Hoitsu Sakai: No. 2581, Bird on tree. No. 2583, Leaves and berries. No. 2585, Bird on tree branch of blossoms.

1997, Oct. 6 Photo. *Perf. 13½*
2580 A2010 90y multicolored 1.75 .45
2581 A2010a 90y multicolored 1.75 .45
a. Pair, #2580-2581 3.75 2.00
2582 A2010 110y multicolored 2.25 .50
2583 A2010b 110y multicolored 2.25 .50
a. Pair, #2582-2583 4.75 2.00
2584 A2010 130y multicolored 2.50 .55
2585 A2010c 130y multicolored 2.50 .55
a. Pair, #2584-2585 5.25 2.25
Nos. 2580-2585 (6) 13.00 3.00

Grand Opening of the Natl. Theater of Tokyo — A2011

1997, Oct. 9 *Perf. 13*
2586 A2011 80y multicolored 1.50 .35

Favorite Songs
A2012 A2013

50y Departure on a Fine Day, by Tanimura Shinji. 80y, Desert Under the Moon, by Kato Masao & Sakasi Suguru.

1997, Oct. 24
2587 A2012 50y multicolored 1.00 .30
2588 A2013 80y multicolored 1.50 .40

Cultural Pioneers Type of 1992

No. 2589, Rohan Kouda (1867-1947), writer. No. 2590, Ando Hiroshige (1797-1858), artist.

1997, Nov. 4
2589 A1645 80y multicolored 1.50 .35
2590 A1645 80y multicolored 1.50 .35

A2016

A2017

New Year 1997 (Year of the Tiger)
A2018 A2019

1997, Nov. 14 *Perf. 13x13½*
2591 A2016 50y multicolored 1.00 .30
2592 A2017 80y multicolored 1.50 .40

Perf. 13½
2593 A2018 50y +3y multi 1.25 .40
2594 A2019 80y +3y multi 1.75 .40

Sheets of two containing Nos. 2591-2592 were lottery prizes. Value $2.75.

Return of Okinawa to Japan, 25th Anniv. — A2020

1997, Nov. 21 *Perf. 13*
2595 A2020 80y multicolored 1.50 .35

Shibuya Family's House — A2021

Tomizawa Family's House — A2022

Photo. & Engr.
1997, Nov. 28 *Perf. 13½*
2596 A2021 80y multicolored 1.50 .45
2597 A2022 80y multicolored 1.50 .45

A2023

Woodprints: No. 2598, Mother Sea. No. 2599, Mother Earth.

1997, Dec. 1 Photo. *Perf. 13*
2598 A2023 80y multicolored 1.50 .35
2599 A2023 80y multicolored 1.50 .35
a. Pair, #2598-2599 3.00 2.00

3rd Conference of the Parties to the UN Framework Convention on Climate Change, Kyoto.

A2024

1997, Dec. 2
2600 A2024 80y multicolored 1.50 .35

Agricultural Insurance System, 50th anniv.

Favorite Songs

Sunayama
A2025

Jingle Bells
A2026

1997, Dec. 8
2601 A2025 50y multicolored 1.00 .30
2602 A2026 80y multicolored 1.50 .35

Shabondama
A2027

Kitaguni no Haru
A2028

1998, Jan. 26 Photo. *Perf. 13*
2603 A2027 50y multicolored 1.00 .30
2604 A2028 80y multicolored 1.50 .35

1998 Winter Olympic & Paralympic Games, Nagano
A2029 A2030

Paralympic logo and: No. 2605, Glaucidium palmatum. No. 2606, Ice hockey.
Olympic rings and: No. 2607: a, Gentiana nipponica. b, Caltha palustris. c, Fritillaria camtschatcensis. d, Paeonia japonica. e, Erythronium japonicum. f, Snowboarding. g, Curling. h, Speed skating. i, Cross-country skiing. j, Downhill skiing.

1998, Feb. 5
2605 A2029 50y multicolored .75 .30
2606 A2030 80y multicolored 1.25 .35
a. Pair, #2605-2606 2.50 1.00
2607 Sheet of 10 12.50 12.50
a.-e. A2029 50y Any single .75 .30
f.-j. A2030 80y Any single 1.25 .35

Historic Houses

A2031

A2032

Photo. & Engr.
1998, Feb. 23 *Perf. 13½*
2608 A2031 80y multicolored 1.50 .45
2609 A2032 80y multicolored 1.50 .45

Japanese Fire Service, 50th Anniv. — A2033

1998, Mar. 6 Photo. *Perf. 13*
2610 80y multicolored 1.50 .40
2611 80y multicolored 1.50 .40
a. A2033 Pair, #2610-2611 3.50 3.50

Favorite Songs
A2035 A2036

50y, Medaka-no-Gakko. 80y, Aoi Sanmyaku.

1998 Photo. *Perf. 13*
2612 A2035 50y multicolored 1.00 .30
2613 A2036 80y multicolored 1.50 .35

Issued: 50y, 3/23; 80y, 3/16.

Greetings Stamps A2037

Designs: a, Puppy. b, Kitten. c, Parakeets. d, Pansies. e, Bunny.

1998, Mar. 13 Photo. *Die Cut*
Self-Adhesive
2614 Sheet of 5 9.00 9.00
a.-e. A2037 80y any single 1.25 .75

Philately Week — A2038

"Poppies," by Kokei Kobayashi (1883-1957).

1998, Apr. 17 *Perf. 13½*
2615 A2038 80y multicolored 1.50 .35

1998 Year of France in Japan — A2039

"Liberty Leading the People," by Delacroix.

1998, Apr. 28 *Perf. 13½*
2616 A2039 110y multicolored 2.25 .55

Natl. Afforestation Campaign — A2040

50y, Trout, Renge azalea.

1998, May 8
2617 A2040 50y multicolored 1.00 .30

Favorite Songs

A2041 A2042

Designs: 50y, "Wild Roses," by Franz Schubert. 80y, "Hill Abloom with Tangerine Flowers," by Minoru Uminuma and Shogo Kato.

1998, May 25 *Perf. 13*
2618 A2041 50y multicolored 1.00 .30
2619 A2042 80y multicolored 1.50 .35

Historic Houses

Kowata Residence
A2043

Kamihaga Residence
A2044

Photo. & Engr.
1998, June 22 *Perf. 13½*
2620 A2043 80y multicolored 1.50 .45
2621 A2044 80y multicolored 1.50 .45

Favorite Songs

A2045 A2046

50y, Kono Michi, "This Road." 80y, Ware Wa Umino Ko, "I'm a Boy of the Sea."

1998, July 6 Photo. *Perf. 13*
2622 A2045 50y multicolored 1.00 .30
2623 A2046 80y multicolored 1.50 .35

Letter Writing Day — A2047

Stylized drawings of children: No. 2624, Child writing letter. No. 2625, Child wearing glasses, letter on table. No. 2626, Child with ink pen, flowers overhead. No. 2627, Child with ink pen, dove overhead. No. 2628, Children holding letters, envelopes.

1998, July 23 *Perf. 13*
2624 A2047 50y multi .75 .30
2625 A2047 50y multi .75 .30
a. Pair, #2624-2625 2.00 1.10
2626 A2047 80y multi 1.25 .35
2627 A2047 80y multi 1.25 .35

2628 A2047 80y multi, horiz. 1.25 .35
a. Souvenir sheet of 1 1.75 1.75
b. Sheet, 4 each #2626-2627, 2 #2628 17.50 17.50
c. Bklt. pane, 2 ea #2624-2628 14.00 14.00
Complete booklet, #2628c 15.00

See Nos. 2682-2686, 2738-2742, 2779-2783, 2824-2828. See Nos. 2733h-2733j for self-adhesive stamps.

Historic Houses

Kamio Residence A2048

Nakamura Residence A2049

Photo. & Engr.

1998, Aug. 24 ***Perf. 13½***
2629 A2048 80y multicolored 1.50 .45
2630 A2049 80y multicolored 1.50 .45

53rd Natl. Sports Festival, Kanagawa — A2050

1998, Sept. 11 **Photo.** ***Perf. 13½***
2631 A2050 50y multicolored 1.00 .30

A2051

A2051a

A2051b

Intl. Letter Writing Week, Greetings — A2051c

Details or complete paintings by Jakuchu Ito: No. 2632, "Birds & Autumn Maple." No. 2633, "Parakeet in Oak Tree." No. 2634, "Mandarin Ducks in the Snow." No. 2635, "Golden Pheasant & Bamboo in Snow." No. 2636, "Leafy Peonies & Butterflies." No. 2637, "Parakeet in Rose Bush."

1998, Oct. 6 **Photo.** ***Perf. 13½***
2632 A2051 90y multicolored 1.75 .45
2633 A2051a 90y multicolored 1.75 .45
a. Pair, #2632-2633 3.75 1.50
2634 A2051 110y multicolored 2.25 .55
2635 A2051b 110y multicolored 2.25 .55
a. Pair, #2634-2635 5.00 1.75
2636 A2051 130y multicolored 2.50 .65
2637 A2051c 130y multicolored 2.50 .65
a. Pair, #2636-2637 5.50 1.75
Nos. 2632-2637 (6) 13.00 3.30

Nos. 2632, 2634, 2636 are from "Plants and Animals" and are inscribed for Intl. Letter Writing Week. Nos. 2633, 2635, 2637 are from "Painted Woodcuts of Flowers and Birds."

1998 World Volleyball Championships for Men and Women, Japan — A2052

1998, Nov. 2 ***Perf. 13***
2638 A2052 80y Serve 1.25 .35
2639 A2052 80y Receive 1.25 .35
2640 A2052 80y Set & spike 1.25 .35
2641 A2052 80y Block 1.25 .35
a. Strip of 4, #2638-2641 6.00 6.00

Cultural Pioneer Type of 1992 and

Yoshie Fujiwara(1898-1976) — A2053

No. 2642, Bakin Takizawa (1767-1848).

Photo. & Engr.

1998, Nov. 4 ***Perf. 13***
2642 A1645 80y multicolored 1.50 .35
2643 A2053 80y multicolored 1.50 .35

See Nos. 2719, 2747-2748, 2839-2840.

A2054

A2055

New Year 1999 (Year of the Rabbit)
A2056 A2057

1998, Nov. 13 **Photo.** ***Perf. 13x13½***
2644 A2054 50y multicolored 1.00 .30
2645 A2055 80y multicolored 1.50 .40

Perf. 13½x13

2646 A2056 50y +3y multi 1.25 .40
2647 A2057 80y +3y multi 1.75 .40
Nos. 2644-2647 (4) 5.50 1.50

Sheets of two containing Nos. 2644-2645 were lottery prizes. Value $2.75.
See No. 2655.

Favorite Songs

A2058

A2059

50y, The Apple Song. 80y, Toys Cha-Cha-Cha at Night.

1998, Nov. 24 ***Perf. 13x13½***
2648 A2058 50y multicolored 1.00 .30
2649 A2059 80y multicolored 1.50 .35

Japan-Argentina Friendship Treaty, Cent. — A2060

1998, Dec. 2 **Photo.** ***Perf. 13***
2650 A2060 80y multicolored 1.50 .35

A2061

A2062

Universal Declaration of Human Rights, 50th Anniv.
A2063 A2064

1998, Dec. 10
2651 A2061 50y multicolored 1.00 .35
2652 A2062 70y multicolored 1.25 .40
2653 A2063 80y multicolored 1.50 .35
2654 A2064 90y multicolored 1.75 .45
Nos. 2651-2654 (4) 5.50 1.55

Greetings Types of 1951, 1962, 1986 and 1998

1998, Dec. 15 **Photo.** ***Perf. 13x13½***
2655 50y Sheet of 8, 2 each #a.-c., 2644 8.00 8.00
a. A281 rose pink, like #522 .75 .30
b. A483 multi, like #773 .75 .30
c. A1273 multi, like #1708 .75 .30

Favorite Songs

A2065

A2066

50y, Flowing Like a River. 80y, Song of the Four Seasons.

1999, Jan. 26 **Photo.** ***Perf. 13***
2656 A2065 50y multicolored 1.00 .30
2657 A2066 80y multicolored 1.50 .35

Traditional Houses

Iwase Family House, Gokayama District — A2067

Gassho-Zukuri Houses, Shirakawa-mura District — A2068

Gassho-Zukuri House — A2069

Photo. & Engr.

1999, Feb. 16 ***Perf. 13½***
2658 A2067 80y multicolored 1.50 .45
2659 A2068 80y multicolored 1.25 .45
2660 A2069 80y multicolored 1.25 .45
a. Pair, #2659-2660 3.00 1.50
Nos. 2658-2660 (3) 4.00 1.35

Rakugo (Comic Storytellers) Stamps

Kokontei Shinshou V — A2070

Katsura Bunraku VIII — A2071

Sanyutei Enshou VI — A2072

Yanagiya Kosan V — A2073

Katsura Beichou III — A2074

1999, Mar. 12 **Photo.** ***Perf. 13***
2661 A2070 80y multicolored 1.25 .50
2662 A2071 80y multicolored 1.25 .50
2663 A2072 80y multicolored 1.25 .50
2664 A2073 80y multicolored 1.25 .50
2665 A2074 80y multicolored 1.25 .50
a. Sheet, 2 each #2661-2665 16.00 16.00

Favorite Songs

Sukiyaki Song A2075

Soushunfu A2076

1999, Mar. 16
2666 A2075 50y multicolored 1.00 .30
2667 A2076 80y multicolored 1.50 .35

Greetings Stamps A2077

a, Kitten, daisies. b, Checks, flowers, roses. c, Tartan, puppy. d, Flowers, brown rabbit. e, Gray and white rabbit, moon and stars.

1999, Mar. 23 ***Die Cut***

Self-Adhesive

2668 Sheet of 5 7.50 7.50
a.-e. A2077 80y Any single 1.25 .75

25th General Assembly of Japan Medical Congress — A2078

1999, Apr. 2 ***Perf. 13***
2669 A2078 80y multicolored 1.50 .35

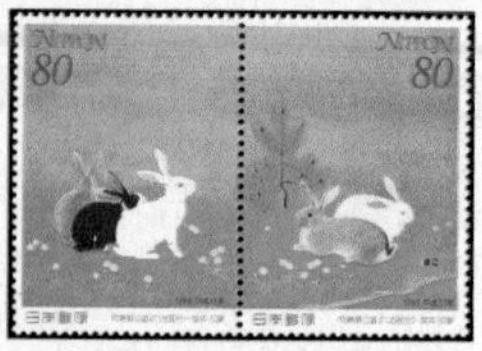
Philately Week A2079

Rabbits Playing in the Field in Spring, by Doumoto Inshou (1891-1975): No. 2670, Three rabbits. No. 2671, Two rabbits.

1999, Apr. 20 ***Perf. 13½***
2670 80y Three rabbits 1.25 .40
2671 80y Two rabbits 1.25 .40
a. A2079 Pair, #2670-2671 3.00 1.50

No. 2671a is a continuous design. No. 2671a also exists as a strip of two with central label. Value, $6.50.

A2080

1999, May 18 Photo. *Perf. 13*

2672	A2080 80y multicolored		1.50	.35

Japanese migration to Peru, cent.

Natl. Afforestation Campaign — A2081

1999, May 28 *Perf. 13¼*

2673	A2081 50y multicolored		1.00	.30

A2082

Painting: Ruins of Tholos, by Masayuki Murai.

1999, June 1 Photo. *Perf. 13*

2674	A2082 80y multicolored		1.50	.35

Japanese-Greek Treaty of Commerce & Navigation, cent.

A2083

1999, June 3

2675	A2083 80y multicolored		1.50	.35

Japanese emigration to Bolivia, cent.

Land Improvement System, 50th Anniv. — A2084

1999, June 4

2676	A2084 80y multicolored		1.50	.35

Family Court, 50th Anniv. — A2085

1999, June 16

2677	A2085 80y multicolored		1.50	.35

Patent Attorney System in Japan, Cent. — A2086

1999, July 1 Photo. *Perf. 13*

2678	A2086 80y multicolored		1.50	.35

A2087

1999, July 1

2679	A2087 80y multicolored		1.50	.35

Japanese Community-Based Treatment of Offenders System, 50th anniv.

A2088

Enforcement of Civil and Commercial Codes, Cent.: Masaakira Tomii (1858-1935), Kenjiro Ume (1860-1910) and Nobushige Hozumi (1856-1926), drafters of Civil and Commerical Codes.

1999, July 19

2680	A2088 80y multicolored		1.50	.35

Copyright System in Japan, Cent. — A2089

1999, July 22

2681	A2089 80y multicolored		1.50	.35

Letter Writing Day Type of 1998

Stylized drawings of children and toys: No. 2682, Boy and clown, letter. No. 2683, Teddy bear seated on pencil. No. 2684, Girl, ink pen. No. 2685, Clown with yellow hat, jumping up out of envelope.

No. 2686: a, Giraffes. b, Kite, bird, horiz. c, Boy holding kite string. d, Girl with pencil and paper. e, Bunny and bear. f, Boy blowing trumpet. g, Girl playing cello. h, Girl in red. i, Girl in yellow holding envelope. j, Three ducks.

1999, July 23 Photo. *Perf. 13*

2682	A2047 50y multicolored	.75	.30
2683	A2047 50y multicolored	.75	.30
2684	A2047 50y multicolored	.75	.30
2685	A2047 50y multicolored	.75	.30
a.	Strip of 4, #2682-2685	4.00	3.50
2686	Sheet of 10	16.00	16.00
a.-j.	A2047 80y any single	1.25	.35
k.	Booklet pane, #2682-2685, 2 each #2686c, 2686g, 2686i	14.00	
	Complete booklet, #2686k	15.00	
l.	Sheet of 2, #2682, 2686g	2.75	2.75

Nos. 2686a is 53x27mm. Nos. 2686d, 2686h, 2686j are 30mm in diameter. No. 2686f is 38x39mm. Sheet numbers are in center of rectangles at top of sheets.

The 20th Century — A2090

1900-10 (Sheet 1) — No. 2687: a, 50y, 1905-06 Serialized novel "Wagahai wa Neko de aru," by Soseki Natsume (stamp 7). b, 50y, 1906 Novel "Bochan," by Natsume (stamp 8). c, 80y, 1901 Collection of poems "Midaregami," by Akiko Yosano (stamp 1). d, 80y, Opening of Denkikan movie theater in Asakusa, 1903 (stamp 2). e, 80y, Electrification of streetcars, 1903 (stamp 3). f, 80y, Otojirou Kawakami & Sadayakko, actors (stamp 4). g, 80y, Westernization of fashion (stamp 9). h, 80y, Completion of Ryogoku Kokugikan sumo arena, 1909 (stamp 10). i, 80y, Russo-Japanese War soldiers on horseback (stamp 5). j, 80y, Russo-Japanese War soldiers in tent (stamp 6).

A2090a

1910-13 (Sheet 2) — No. 2688: a, 50y, 1st Japanese-produced airship, tail of 1st Japanese airplane (stamp 3). b, 50y, Front of 1st Japanese airplane (stamp 4). c, 80y, Elementary school song book published by Education ministry, 1910 (stamp 1). d, 80y, Antarctic expedition led by Nobu Shirase, 1910 (stamp 2). e, 80y, Dr. Hideyo Noguchi (stamp 5). f, 80y, Extinction of Japanese wolves (stamp 6). g, 80y, Runner Shizo Kanaguri at 1st participation in Olympic Games, 1912 (stamp 7). h, Takarazuka Musical Review founded, 1913 (stamp 8). i, 80y, "Song of Kachusha," by Sumako Matsui & Hogetsu Shimamura (stamp 9). j, 80y, 1st sale of caramels, 1913 (stamp 10).

A2090b

1914-20 (Sheet 3) — No. 2689: a, 50y, Painting of couple in boat by Yumeji Takehisa (stamp 9). b, 50y, Takehisa, painting of flowers (stamp 10). c, 80y, 1914 Opening of Tokyo train station (blimp in sky) (stamp 1). d, 80y, Tokyo train station main entrance (stamp 2). e, 80y, Japanese WWI seamen (stamp 3). f, 80y, Western-style women's hair styles (stamp 4). g, 80y, 1915 Poetry book "Rashomon," by Ryunosuke Akutagawa (stamp 5). h, 80y, 1916 Start of postal life insurance (goddess in clouds) (stamp 6). i, 80y, Sakuzo Yoshino, political scientist & democracy advocate, & tree (stamp 7). j, 80y, 1918 Rice riots (painting, photo of crowds) (stamp 8).

A2090c

1920-25 (Sheet 4) — No. 2690: a, 50y, Silent film star Matsunosuke Onoe (denomination at UR) (stamp 8). b, 50y, Silent film star Tsumasaburo Bandoh (denomination at UL) (stamp 9). c, 80y, 1st Hakone Relay Marathon, 1920 (stamp 1). d, 80y, Popularity of "Gondola Song" recording, spread of phonographs (stamp 2). e, 80y, Ruins from 1923 Kanto earthquake (stamp 3). f, "Nonki na Tosan" comic strip (man with dog) (stamp 4). g, 80y, "Adventures of Sho-chan" comic strip (man with vulture). h, 80y, Japanese crane nears extinction (stamp 6). i, 80y, 1924 Opening of Koshien Stadium (stamp 7). j, 80y, Man, woman in Western-style clothing (stamp 10).

A2090d

1927-28 (Sheet 5) — No. 2691: a, 50y, 1927 Opening of Tokyo subway (close-up of car) (stamp 2). b, 50y, Subway car approaching station (stamp 3). c, 80y, Movie "Kurama Tengu" (Samurai) (stamp 1). d, 80y, Radio broadcast of "National Health Gymnastics" exercise program (stamp 4). e, 80y, Yoshiyuki Tsuruta, 1928 Olympic swimming champion (stamp 5). f, 80y, Mikio Oda, 1928 Olympic triple jump champion (stamp 6). g, 80y, Olympic Games program (stamp 7). h, 80y, Runner Kinue Hitomi, 1st female Japanese Olympic medalist (stamp 8). i, 80y, Man in Western clothing, cafe (stamp 9). j, 1928 Publishing of "Horoki," by Fumiko Hayashi (stamp 10).

A2090e

1929-32 (Sheet 6) — No. 2692: a, 50y, Mass production of Japanese automobiles (green 1932 Datsun Model 10) (stamp 4). b, 50y, Black 1936 Toyota Model AA (stamp 5). c, 80y, Volcano, Mt. Asama (stamp 1). d, 80y, Takiji Kobayashi, writer of "Kani-kosen," crane, smokestacks (stamp 2). e, 80y, Man with shirt with open collar, woman with handbag (stamp 3). f, 80y, "Norakuro" comic strip (cat, brick wall) (stamp 6). g, 80y, 1932 Nippon Derby winner Wakataka & jockey (stamp 7). h, 80y, Nippon Derby winner Kabutoyama (stamp 8). i, 80y, Song "Longing for Your Shadow" (woman with closed eyes) (stamp 9). j, 80y, 1932, 1936 Political assassinations (soldiers, truck, building) (stamp 10).

A2090f

1932-36 (Sheet 7) — No. 2693: a, 50y, Front of D51 steam locomotive (stamp 8). b, 50y, Rear of D51 (stamp 9). c, 80y, Fumihiko

Otsuki, lexicographer (Otsuki, geometric design) (stamp 1). d, 80y, Song "Tokyo Ondo" (woman, buildings) (stamp 2). e, 80y, Keinichi Enomoto, comic actor, with feather (stamp 3). f, 80y, Formation of Japanese Baseball League (catcher, umpire) (stamp 4). g, 80y, Batter (stamp 5). h, 80y, Hachiko, dog that waited for dead owner, statue of Hachiko (stamp 6). i, 80y, Eiji Yoshikawa, author of "Miyamoto Musashi." (stamp 7). j, Extinct species Okinawan pigeon (stamp 10).

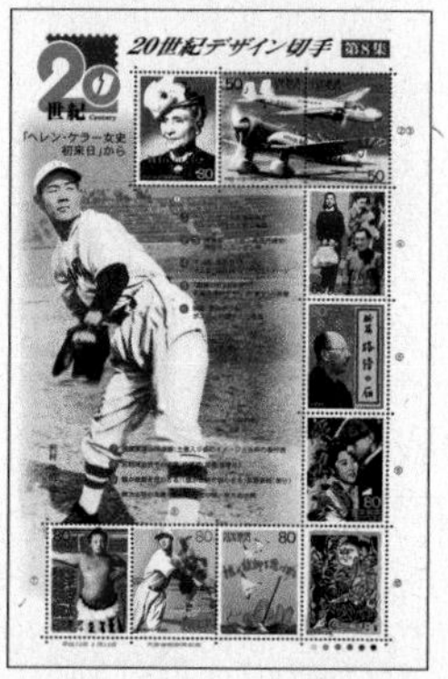

A2090g

1937-40 (Sheet 8) — No. 2694: a, 50y, Nose of Kamikaze plane, tail of Nippon cargo plane (stamp 2). b, 50y, Nose of Nippon cargo plain, tail of Kamikaze plane (stamp 3). c, 80y, Helen Keller's 1st trip to Japan (stamp 1). d, 80y, Women with senninbari cloths, monpe work pants, man with kokumin-fuku uniform (stamp 4). e, 80y, Yuzo Yamamoto, author of "Robo No Ishi" (stamp 5). f, 80y, Woman & man embracing in movie, "Aizenkatsura" (stamp 6). g, 80y, Sumo wrestler Yokozuna Futabayama, winner of 69 consecutive matches (stamp 7). h, 80y, Baseball pitcher Eiji Sawamura (stamp 8). i, 80y, Song, "Dareka Kokyo" (ducks in flight) (stamp 9). j, 80y, Woodblock art of Shiko Munakata (stamp 10).

A2090h

1940-45 (Sheet 9) — No. 2695: a, 50y, "Ohgon Bat," cartoon by Ichiro Suzuki (character without hat) (stamp 9). b, 50y, "Ohgon Bat" character wearing hat (stamp 10). c, 80y, Chiune Sugihara, vice-consul in Lithuania who saved Jews from Holocaust (stamp 1). d, 80y, Start of Kokumin Gakko school system (children exercising) (stamp 2). e, 80y, Airplane in attack on Pearl Harbor (stamp 3). f, 80y, Kotaro Takamura, poet, winner of 1st Imperial Art Academy prize, & Japanese characters (stamp 4). g, 80y, Eruption of Mt. Showashinzan (stamp 5). h, 80y, Atomic Bomb Memorial Dome (stamp 6). i, 80y, Statue at Nagasaki Atomic Bomb Museum (stamp 7). j, Signing of World War II surrender documents on USS Missouri (stamp 8).

A2090i

1945-52 (Sheet 10) — No. 2696: a, 50y, "Captain Atom" cartoon by Osamu Tezuka (stamp 7). b, 50y, "Astro Boy," cartoon by Tezuka (stamp 8). c, 80y, Song, "Ringo No Uta" (Apple Song) (stamp 1). d, 80y, "Sazae San," cartoon by Machiko Hasegawa (stamp 2). e, 80y, Promulgation of Japanese Constitution (woman, child, buildings) (stamp 3). f, 80y, Swimming records by Hironoshin Furuhashi (stamp 4). g, 80y, Dr. Hideki Yukawa, Nobel laureate for Physics (stamp 5). h, 80y, New Year's Eve radio program "Kohaku Uta Gassen" on NHK (stamp 6). i, 80y, Radio soap opera "Kimino Na Wa" (woman and man) (stamp 9). j, 80y, Novel "Nijyu-Yon No Hitomi," by Sakae Tsuboi (stamp 10).

A2090j

1953-58 (Sheet 11) — No. 2697: a, 50y, Tokyo Tower (olive green panel) (stamp 9). b, 50y, Tokyo Tower from ground (stamp 10). c, 80y, Popularity of radio and television (stamp 1). d, 80y, Director Akira Kurosawa, camera, two Samurai from "Shinchinin No Samurai." (stamp 2). e, 80y, Five Samurai from "Shinchinin No Samurai." (stamp 3). f, 80y, Sumo wrestler Rikidozan and championship belt (stamp 4). g, 80y, Rikidozan in action (stamp 5). h, 80y, Movie "Godzilla" (stamp 6). i, 80y, Taiyozoku fashions (man, woman at seaside) (stamp 7), j, 80y, Portrait of Shotokutaishi from 10,000-yen bank note (stamp 8, 31x42mm oval stamp).

A2090k

1959-64 (Sheet 12) — No. 2698: a, 50y, Dog Taro, survivor of abandonment in Antarctica, ship's stern (stamp 1). b, 50y, Dog Giro, survivor of abandonment in Antarctic, ship's bow (stamp 2). c, 80y, Commemorative cake box from Wedding of Crown Prince Akihito (stamp 3). d, 80y, Weather map of Isewan Typhoon (stamp 4). e, 80y, "Sukiyaki Song," by Rokusuke Ei (stamp 5). f, 80y, Novelist Ryotaro Shiba and cover from "Ryomaga Yuku," depicting Ryoma Sakamoto (stamp 6). g, 80y, Baby doll, and song "Konnichiwa Akachan," by Ei (stamp 7). h, 80y, Inauguration of Bullet Train (stamp 8). i, 80y, Poster depicting swimmer from Tokyo Olympics (stamp 9). j, 80y, Poster depicting torchbearer from Tokyo Olympics (stamp 10).

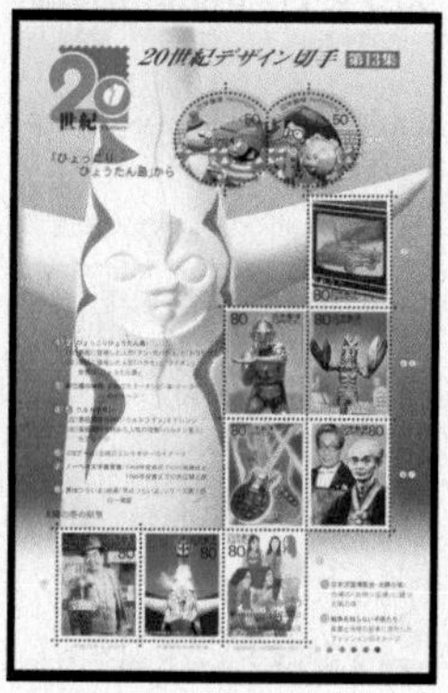

A2090l

1964-71 (Sheet 13) — No. 2699: a, 50y, TV show puppets Don Gabacho and Torahige (stamp 1, 31x30mm semi-oval stamp with straight side at right). b, 50y, TV show puppets Hakase and Lion (stamp 2, 31x30mm semi-oval stamp with straight side at left). c, 80y, Color television, automobile and air conditioner (stamp 3). d, 80y, TV character, Ultraman (stamp 4). e, 80y, Baltan Seijin, character from Ultraman TV series (stamp 5). f, 80y, Electric guitars (stamp 6). g, 80y, Yasunari Kawabata and Kenzaburo Oe, Nobel laureates for Literature (stamp 7). h, 80y, Scene from movie "Otokowa Tsuraiyo" (man holding basket) (stamp 8). i, 80y, Tower from Expo '70, Osaka (stamp 9). j, 80y, Youth fashions and song "Senso O Shiranai Kodomotachi" (stamp 10).

A2090m

1972-74 (Sheet 14) — No. 2700: a, 50y, Baseball player Sadaharu Oh (leg in air) (stamp 7). b, 50y, Baseball player Shigeo Nagashima (Tokyo uniform) (stamp 8). c, 80y, Two men from Takamatsu Zuka wall paintings, Asuka (stamp 1). d, 80y, Four women from Takamatsu Zuka wall paintings (stamp 2). e, 80y, Pandas Kankan and Ranran, gift from China (stamp 3). f, Shureimon, Return of Okinawa to Japanese control (stamp 4). g, 80y, Oscar, from cartoon "Roses of Versailles," by Riyoko Ikeda (stamp 5). h, 80y, Conductor Seiji Ozawa (stamp 6). i, 80y, Erimo Cape, and song "Erimo Misaki" (stamp 9). j, 80y, Space battleship Yamato from cartoon "Uchu Senkan Yamato," by Reiji Matsumoto (stamp 10).

A2090n

1975-83 (Sheet 15) — No. 2701: a, 50y, Gundam and Zaku, from TV cartoon series "Kidosenshi Gundam" (blue background) (stamp 7). b, 50y, Amuro and Gundam, from "Kidonsenshi Gundam" (orange background) (stamp 8). c, 80y, Guitar, and song "Jidai" (stamp 1). d, 80y, Fish character Taiyaki Kun, from children's song "Oyoge! Taiyaki Kun" (stamp 2). e, 80y, Musical notes and microphones (popularity of karaoke) (stamp 3). f, 80y, Flower, and song "Cosmos" (stamp 4). g, 80y, UFO, and song "UFO" (stamp 5). h, 80y, Students from TV series, "San Nen B Gumi Kinpachi Sensei" (stamp 6). i, 80y, Musical notes and electronic synthesizer (stamp 9). j, 80y, Oshin, from TV series "Oshin" (stamp 10).

A2090o

1986-93 (Sheet 16) — No. 2702: a, 50y, Character from cartoon show "Soreike! Anpanman" (stamp 3). b, 50y, Four characters from "Soreike! Anpanman" (stamp 4). c, 80y, Return of Halley's Comet (stamp 1, pentagonal). d, 80y, Opening of Seikan Railroad Tunnel (stamp 2). e, 80y, Watchtower excavated at Yoshinogari Iseki ruins (stamp 5). f, 80y, Singer Hibari Misora, National Medal of Honor recipient (stamp 6). g, 80y, Mascot of J-League Soccer Games (stamp 7, 34x28mm semi-oval stamp with straight side at bottom). h, 80y, Soccer ball (stamp 8, 34x28mm stamp with straight side at top). i, 80y, Selection of Dunjuang as World Heritage Site (Cliffside, stamp 9). j, 80y, Selection of Horyuji Temple as World Heritage Site (Temple and sun, stamp 10).

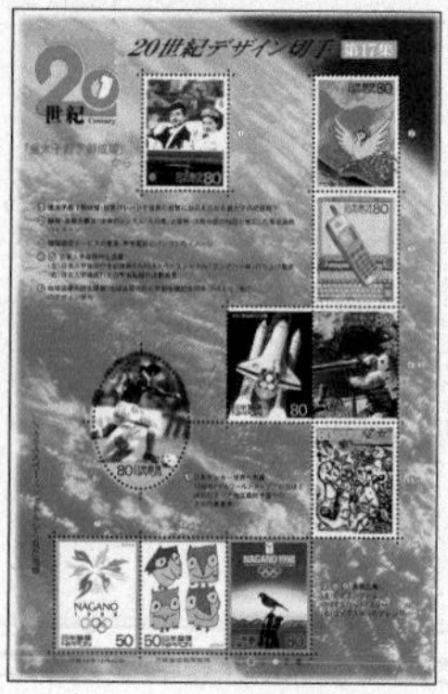

A2090p

1993-98 (Sheet 17) — No. 2703: a, 50y, Nagano Winter Olympics emblem (stamp 7). b, 50y, Four owl mascots of Nagano Winter Olympics (stamp 8). c, 80y, Wedding of Crown Prince Naruhito and Masako Owada (stamp 1). d, 80y, Phoenix and damage from Hanshin-Awaji earthquake (stamp 2). e, 80y, Cellular phone and computer (stamp 3). f, 80y, Launch of Japanese astronaut aboard Space Shuttle Endeavor (stamp 4). g, 80y, Astronaut Mamoru Mohri in space (stamp 5). h, 80y, Details from Kyoto Climate Change Conf. stamps, #2598-2599 (stamp 6). i, 80y, Poster for Nagano Winter Olympics (stamp 9). j, Soccer player at 1998 World Cup Championships (stamp 10, 42x31mm elliptical stamp).

Illustrations reduced.

1999-2000 Photo. *Perf. 13x13¼*

Sheets of 10

2687	A2090	#a.-j.	15.00	15.00
a.-b.	50y any single		.75	.50
c.-j.	80y any single		1.25	.50
2688	A2090a	#a.-j.	15.00	15.00
a.-b.	50y any single		.75	.50
c.-j.	80y any single		1.25	.50
2689	A2090b	#a.-j.	15.00	15.00
a.-b.	50y any single		.75	.50
c.-j.	80y any single		1.25	.50
2690	A2090c	#a.-j.	15.00	15.00
a.-b.	50y any single		.75	.50
c.-j.	80y any single		1.25	.50
2691	A2090d	#a.-j.	15.00	15.00
a.-b.	50y any single		.75	.50
c.-j.	80y any single		1.25	.50
2692	A2090e	#a.-j.	15.00	15.00
a.-b.	50y any single		.75	.50
c.-j.	80y any single		1.25	.50

2693	A2090f	#a.-j.	15.00	15.00
a.-b.		50y any single	.75	.50
c.-j.		80y any single	1.25	.50
2694	A2090g	#a-j	15.00	15.00
a.-b.		50y Any single	.75	.50
c.-j.		80y Any single	1.25	.50
2695	A2090h	#a-j	15.00	15.00
a.-b.		50y Any single	.75	.50
c.-j.		80y Any single	1.25	.50
2696	A2090i	#a-j	15.00	15.00
a.-b.		50y Any single	.75	.50
c.-j.		80y Any single	1.25	.50
2697	A2090j	#a-j	15.00	15.00
a.-b.		50y Any single	.75	.50
c.-j.		80y Any single	1.25	.50
2698	A2090k	#a-j	15.00	15.00
a.-b.		50y Any single	.75	.50
c.-j.		80y Any single	1.25	.50
2699	A2090l	#a-j	15.00	15.00
a.-b.		50y Any single	.75	.50
c.-j.		80y Any single	1.25	.50
2700	A2090m	#a-j	15.00	15.00
a.-b.		50y Any single	.75	.50
c.-j.		80y Any single	1.25	.50
2701	A2090n	#a-j	15.00	15.00
a.-b.		50y Any single	.75	.50
c.-j.		80y Any single	1.25	.50
2702	A2090o	#a-j	15.00	15.00
a.-b.		50y Any single	.75	.50
c.-j.		80y Any single	1.25	.50
2703	A2090p	#a-j	15.00	15.00
a.-b.		50y Any single	.75	.50
c.-j.		80y Any single	1.25	.50
		Nos. 2687-2703 (17)	255.00	255.00

Sheet numbers are in UR corner of sheets or in center of rectangles at top of sheet. Stamp numbers are in sheet margin.

Issued: No. 2687, 8/23; No. 2688, 9/22; No. 2689, 10/22; No. 2690, 12/22; No. 2691, 1/21/00; No. 2692, 2/9/00; No. 2693, 2/23/00; No. 2694, 3/23/00; No. 2695, 4/21/00; No. 2696, 5/23/00; No. 2697, 6/23/00; No. 2698, 7/21/00; No. 2699, 8/23/00; No. 2700, 9/22/00; No. 2701, 10/23/00; No. 2702, 11/22; No. 2703, 12/22.

Hearts and Doves A2092

Celebration A2093

Red-crowned Crane — A2094

1999, Aug. 16 **Photo.** ***Perf. 13¼***

2704	A2092	50y multi	1.00	.30
2705	A2093	80y multi	1.75	.35
2706	A2094	90y multi	2.00	.40
		Nos. 2704-2706 (3)	4.75	1.05

54th Natl. Sports Festival — A2095

1999, Sept. 10

2707	A2095	50y multi	1.00	.30

A2096

1999, Oct. 1 ***Perf. 12¾x13***

2708	A2096	80y multi	1.50	.35

Intl. Year of Older Persons.

A2097

A2098

A2099

Intl. Letter Writing Week — A2100

Hokusai Paintings: No. 2709, Sea Route in Kazusa Area. No. 2710, Roses & a Sparrow. No. 2711, Rain Beneath the Mountaintop. No. 2712, Chrysanthemums & a Horsefly. No. 2713, Under the Fukagawa Bridge. No. 2714, Peonies & a Butterfly.

1999, Oct. 6 ***Perf. 13¼***

2709	A2097	90y multi	1.75	.45
2710	A2098	90y multi	1.75	.45
a.		Pair, #2709-2710	3.50	1.75
2711	A2097	110y multi	2.25	.55
2712	A2099	110y multi	2.25	.55
a.		Pair, #2711-2712	4.50	1.75
2713	A2097	130y multi	2.50	.60
2714	A2100	130y multi	2.50	.60
a.		Pair, #2713-2714	5.25	1.75
		Nos. 2709-2714 (6)	13.00	3.20

Central and Pacific Baseball Leagues, 50th Anniv. A2101

Mascots wearing uniforms of: a, Yokohama Bay Stars. b, Chunichi Dragons. c, Seibu Lions. d, Nippon Ham Fighters. e, Yomiuri Giants. f, Yakult Swallows g, Orix Blue Wave. h, Fukuoka Daiei Hawks. i, Hiroshima Toyo Carp. j, Hanshin Tigers. k, Kintetsu Buffaloes. l, Chiba Lotte Marines.

1999, Oct. 22 ***Die Cut***

Self-Adhesive

2715	A2101	Sheet of 12	18.00	18.00
a.-l.		80y any single	1.40	.35

Natl. Science Council, 50th Anniv. — A2102

1999, Oct. 28 ***Perf. 13x13¼***

2716	A2102	80y multi	1.50	.35

Cultural Pioneers Types of 1992-98

No. 2717, Hokusai (1760-1849), painter. No. 2718: Yasunari Kawabata (1899-1972), writer. No. 2719, Shoen Uemura (1875-1949), painter.

1999, Nov. 4 **Photo.** ***Perf. 12¾x13***

2717	A1645	80y multi	1.50	.35

Photo. & Engr.

Perf. 13

2718	A1645	80y multi	1.50	.35
2719	A2053	80y multi	1.50	.35
		Nos. 2717-2719 (3)	4.50	1.05

Reign of Emperor Akihito, 10th Anniv. — A2103

Designs: No. 2720, Paulownia and bamboo crest. No. 2721, Phoenix crest.

1999, Nov. 12 **Photo.** ***Perf. 12¼***

2720	A2103	80y red & multi	1.75	.35
2721	A2103	80y yel & multi	1.75	.35
a.		Souvenir sheet, #2720-2721	3.50	3.00

A2104

A2105

New Year 2000 (Year of the Dragon)
A2106 A2107

1999, Nov. 15 ***Perf. 13x13¼***

2722	A2104	50y multi	1.00	.30
2723	A2105	80y multi	1.50	.40

Perf. 13¼

2724	A2106	50y +3y multi	1.25	.40
2725	A2107	80y +3y multi	1.75	.40

Sheets of 2 containing Nos. 2722-2723 were lottery prizes. Value $2.75.

Children's Book Day — A2108

a, Flower with child reading, bird in flight. b, Flower with child reading, bird perched. c, Child, left half of new Intl. Library of Children's Literature. d, Child, right half of library. e, Butterfly with child's head. f, Two children, library.

Perf. 12¾x13¼

2000, Mar. 31 **Photo.**

2726	A2108	Sheet of 10, #e-f, 2 each #a-d	16.00	16.00
a.-f.		80y any single	1.25	.35

Seishu Hanaoka (1760-1835), Physician, and Flower — A2109

2000, Apr. 11 ***Perf. 12¾x13***

2727	A2109	80y multi	1.50	.35

Japan Surgical Society, 100th congress.

Japan-Netherlands Relations, 400th Anniv. — A2110

2000, Apr. 19 ***Perf. 13***

2728		80y multi	1.25	.35
2729		80y multi	1.25	.35
a.	A2110	Pair, #2728-2729	3.00	1.50

Dragon and Tiger by Gaho Hashimoto — A2112

2000, Apr. 20 ***Perf. 13¼***

2730		80y multi	1.25	.40
2731		80y multi	1.25	.40
a.	A2112	Pair, #2730-2731	3.00	1.50

Philately week.

Natl. Land Afforestation Campaign — A2114

2000, Apr. 21 ***Perf. 13¼***

2732	A2114	50y multi	1.00	.40

Phila Nippon 2001, Tokyo A2115

Designs: a, Wild goose (dull green frame background). b, Wagtail (dull violet frame background). c, Goshawk (dull rose frame background). d, A Girl Blowing Glass Toy, by Utamaro. e, Kabuki Actor Ebizo Ichikawa, by Sharaku. f, Flowers. g, Dog and cat. h, Children with pen and envelope (blue background). i, Child with clown. j, Children with pen and envelope (red background).

2000, May 19 **Photo.** ***Die Cut***

Self-Adhesive

2733	A2115	Sheet of 10, #a-j	16.00	16.00
a.-j.		80y any single	1.25	.55

Kyushu-Okinawa Summit — A2116

2000, June 21 **Photo.** ***Perf. 12¾x13***

2734		80y multi	1.25	.35
2735		80y multi	1.25	.35
a.	A2116	Pair, #2734-2735	3.00	1.50

A2117

2000, June 30

2736		80y Three flowers	1.25	.35
2737		80y Two flowers	1.25	.35
a.	A2117	Pair, #2736-2737	3.00	1.50

Crime Prevention Campaign, 50th anniv.

Letter Writing Day Type of 1998

Designs: No. 2738, Girl with bows in hair, pen. No. 2739, Birds, house, letter. No. 2740, Clown with red hat, open envelope. No. 2741, Boy reading letter, puppy.

No. 2742: a, Child, dog, in basket. b, Apple tree, flower (circular stamp). c, Parrots holding envelope (elliptical stamp). d, Bicycle, rabbit, flower (oval stamp). e, Boy, girl, dove. f, Girl, letter, snail, porcupine (oval stamp). g, Child playing harp. h, Child playing recorder. i, Child playing bass (semicircular stamp). j, Girl with blue hat, pen, birds holding envelope.

2000, July 21 ***Perf. 12¾x13¼***

2738	A2047	50y multi	.80	.35
2739	A2047	50y multi	.80	.35
2740	A2047	50y multi	.80	.35

2741	A2047 50y multi		.80	.35
a.	Strip of 4, #2738-2741		4.00	4.00
2742	Sheet of 10		16.00	16.00
a.-j.	A2047 80y Any single		1.25	.40
k.	Booklet pane, #2738-2741, 2742g, 2742h, 2 #2742e, 2742j		13.00	13.00
	Booklet, #2742k		15.00	
l.	Souvenir sheet, #2739, 2742e		2.75	2.75

No. 2742b is 30mm in diameter, No. 2742c is 23x34mm, Nos. 2742d, 2742f are 28x40mm, and No. 2742i is 24x40mm.

Women's Private Higher Education, Cent. — A2118

2000, Sept. 22 Photo. *Perf. 13*

2743	A2118 80y multi	1.50	.35

Intl. Letter Writing Week — A2119

Artwork by Hiroshige: 90y, Okabe. 110y, Maisaka. 130y, Okazaki.

2000, Oct. 6 *Perf. 13¼*

2744	A2119 90y multi	1.75	.50
2745	A2119 110y multi	2.25	.60
2746	A2119 130y multi	2.50	.65
	Nos. 2744-2746 (3)	6.50	1.75

See Nos. 2791-2793, 2835-2837, 2865-2867, 2904-2906, 2938-2940, 2999-3001, 3064-3066. See listing of No. 4448 for images of each Hiroshige print.

Cultural Pioneers Type of 1998 and

Ukichiro Nakaya (1900-62), Snow Crystal Researcher — A2120

Designs: No. 2747, Hantaro Nagaoka (1865-1950), physicist. No. 2748, Teijo Nakamura (1900-88), poet.

Photo. & Engr.

2000, Nov. 6 *Perf. 13*

2747	A2053 80y multi	1.50	.35
2748	A2053 80y multi	1.50	.35
2749	A2120 80y multi	1.50	.35
	Nos. 2747-2749 (3)	4.50	1.05

See No. 2841.

A2121

A2122

New Year 2001 (Year of the Snake)

A2123 A2124

2000, Nov. 15 Photo. *Perf. 13x13¼*

2750	A2121 50y multi	1.00	.30
2751	A2122 80y multi	1.50	.40

Perf. 13¼x13½

2752	A2123 50y +3y multi	1.25	.40
2753	A2124 80y +3y multi	1.75	.40
	Nos. 2750-2753 (4)	5.50	1.50

Sheets of 2, Nos. 2750-2751, were lottery prizes. Value, $2.75.

Diet, 110th Anniv. — A2125

2000, Nov. 29 *Perf. 13*

2754	A2125 80y multi	1.50	.35

Internet Expo 2001 A2126

2001, Jan. 5 *Perf. 13x13¼*

2755	80y Denom. at L	1.25	.35
2756	80y Denom. at R	1.25	.35
a.	A2126 Pair, #2755-2756	3.00	1.50

Intl. Volunteers Year — A2127

2001, Jan. 17 *Perf. 13½x13¼*

2757	A2127 80y multi	1.50	.35

Administrative Scriveners System, 50th Anniv. — A2128

2001, Feb. 22 Photo. *Perf. 13¼*

2758	A2128 80y multi	1.50	.35

World Heritage Sites

Sheet 1 A2129

Sheet 2 A2130

Sheet 3 A2131

Sheet 4 A2132

Sheet 5 A2133

Sheet 6 A2134

No. 2759 — Nikko: a, Bridge (stamp 1). b, Shrine with pillars in foreground (stamp 2). c, Temple gate (stamp 3). d, Dragon (stamp 4). e, Peacock (stamp 5). f, Cat (stamp 6). g, Statue of blue green figure (stamp 7). h, Statue of red figure (stamp 8). i, Shrine (stamp 9). j, Shrine and walkways (stamp 10).

No. 2760 — Itsukushima: a, Marodo Jinjya and pillar in water (stamp 1). b, Marodo Jinjya (stamp 2). c, Honsha (shrine entrance with steps, stamp 3). d, Koma-inu (lion statue, stamp 4). e, Marodo Jinjya and Gojyuno-tou (stamp 5). f, Bugakumen (sculpture with blue water background, stamp 6). g, Kazari-uma (horse statue, stamp 7). h, Noubutai (building with brown eaves, stamp 8). i, Tahoutou (building with cherry blossoms, stamp 9). j, Oomoto Jinjya (building with red fence, stamp 10).

No. 2761 — Kyoto: a, Hosodono Hall, Maidono Hall and Tsuchinoya Hall, Kamowakeikazuchi Shrine (buildings with cones in foreground, stamp 1). b, Romon Gate, Kamowakeikazuchi Shrine (building with stream, stamp 2). c, East Main Hall, Kamomioya Shrine (building with guardian dog statue on landing, stamp 3). d, Guardian dog statue, Kamomioya Shrine (stamp 4). e, South Great Gate and 5-Story Pagoda (deep blue sky, stamp 5). f, Fukuu Joju Nyorai Statue, Toji Temple (gold statue, stamp 6). g, Nyoirin Kannon, Toji Temple (painting, stamp 7). h, Daiitoku Myoo Statue, Toji Temple (stone statue, stamp 8). i, West Gate, 3-Story Pagoda, Kiyomizudera Temple (red gate and temple, stamp 9). j, Main Hall, Kiyomizudera Temple (building with cherry bloosoms, stamp 10).

No. 2762 — Kyoto: a, Konpon Chudo Hall, Enryakuji Temple (roof, stamp 1). b, Eternal Flame, Enryakuji Temple (stamp 2). c, Ninaido Hall, Enryakuji Temple (building with large trees in foreground, stamp 3). d, Sanbo-in Temple Garden, Daigoji Temple (building, one end of small bridge, stamp 4). e, Sanbo-in Temple Garden (end of bridge, trees, stamp 5). f, 5-Story Pagoda, Daigoji Temple (white sky, stamp 6). g, Goten, Ninnaji Temple (buildings with walkways, stamp 7). h, 5-Story Pagoda (cherry trees in foreground, stamp 8). i, Phoenix Hall, Byodoin Temple (black sky, stamp 9). j, Wooden carving of Bodhisattvas Floating on Clouds, Byodoin Temple (stamp 10).

No. 2763 — Kyoto: a, Ujikami Shrine (low fence around shrine with denomination at UL, stamp 1). b, Kaeru Mata, Ujikami Shrine (thin, crossing diagonal strips, stamp 2). c, Front approach to Kozanji Temple (walkway of square panels, stamp 3). d, Sekisuiin, Kozanji Temple (yellow tree blossoms in front of temple, stamp 4). e, Kasumijima Garden, Saihoji Temple (moss-covered bridge, stamp 5) f, Kojokan Garden, Saihoji Temple (Stone stairs and rocks, stamp 6). g, View of garden and pond from under roof, Tenryuji Temple (denomination at left, stamp 7). h, View of garden and pond from under roof, Tenryuji Temple (denomination at right, stamp 8). i, Rokuonji Temple in autumn (Building on lake, green leaves on trees, stamp 9). j, Rokuonji Temple in winter (snow covered roofs and trees, stamp 10).

No. 2764 — Kyoto: a, Snow-covered Silver Pavilion, Jishoji Temple (stamp 1). b, Silver Pavilion without snow (stamp 2). c, Moss-covered rock, Hojo Garden, Ryoanji Temple (stamp 3). d, Rock and snow, Hojo Garden (stamp 4). e, Karamon, Honganji Temple (gate with curved roof, stamp 5). f, Hiunkaku, Honganji Temple (building near pond, stamp 6). g, Shoin, Honganji Temple (wall with landscape, stamp 7). h, Ninomaur Palace, Nijo Castle (roof with chrysanthemum crest at peak, stamp 8). i, Detail from "Hawks on Pine," Nijo Castle (hawk looking left, stamp 9). j, Detail from "Hawks on Pine," Nijo Castle (hawk looking down, stamp 10).

2001 Photo. *Perf. 13x13¼*

2759	A2129	Sheet of 10	16.00	16.00
a.-j.		80y Any single	1.25	.55
2760	A2130	Sheet of 10	16.00	16.00
a.-j.		80y Any single	1.25	.55
2761	A2131	Sheet of 10	16.00	16.00
a.-j.		80y Any single	1.25	.55
2762	A2132	Sheet of 10	16.00	16.00
a.-j.		80y Any single	1.25	.55
2763	A2133	Sheet of 10	16.00	16.00
a.-j.		80y Any single	1.25	.55
2764	A2134	Sheet of 10	16.00	16.00
a.-j.		80y Any single	1.25	.55
		Nos. 2759-2764 (6)	96.00	96.00

Issued: No. 2759, 2/23; No. 2760, 3/23; No. 2761, 6/22; No. 2762, 8/23. No. 2763, 12/21. No. 2764, 2/22/02.

Sheet numbers are in center of colored rectangles at top of sheet. Stamp numbers are in sheet margins.

Exhibit of Italian Art at Museum of Western Art, Tokyo — A2135

Designs: 80y, Show emblem. No. 2766, Angel, from The Annunciation, by Botticelli. No. 2767, Virgin Mary, from The Annunciation.

2001, Mar. 19 Photo. *Perf. 13*

2765	A2135 80y multi	1.50	.35

Size: 33x44mm

Perf. 13¼

2766	A2135 110y multi	1.75	.55
2767	A2135 110y multi	1.75	.55
a.	Pair, #2766-2767	4.50	3.00
	Nos. 2765-2767 (3)	5.00	1.45

Japanese Dermatological Association, 100th Annual Meeting — A2136

2001, Apr. 6 *Perf. 13¼*

Color of Triangle Behind "0" in Denomination

2768	A2136 80y pink		1.25	.35
2769	A2136 80y orange		1.25	.35
2770	A2136 80y yellow		1.25	.35
2771	A2136 80y green		1.25	.35
2772	A2136 80y blue		1.25	.35
a.	Vert. strip of 5, #2768-2772		8.00	5.00

Depositing Mail, by Senseki Nakamura — A2137

2001, Apr. 20 *Perf. 13x13¼*

2773	A2137 80y multi	1.50	.35

Philately Week, Cent. of red cylindrical mailboxes.

Membership in UNESCO, 50th Anniv. — A2138

2001, July 2 *Perf. 13¼*

2774	A2138 80y multi	1.50	.35

9th FINA World Swimming Championships, Fukuoka — A2139

Designs: No. 2775, Swimming race. No. 2776, Synchronized swimming. No. 2777, Diving. No. 2778, Water polo.

2001, July 16 *Perf. 13x13¼*

2775	A2139 80y multi	1.25	.35
2776	A2139 80y multi	1.25	.35
2777	A2139 80y multi	1.25	.35
2778	A2139 80y multi	1.25	.35
a.	Horiz. strip of 4, #2775-2778	6.00	6.00

Letter Writing Day Type of 1998

Designs: No. 2779, Three rabbits, tulip background. No. 2780, Girl with pencil, pencil background. No. 2781, Boy with envelope, bird background. No. 2782, Girl, flower background.

No. 2783: a, Girl with rabbit, bird, flower (oval stamp). b, Bird in tree (circular stamp). c, Boy with pen behind back. d, Girl with envelope and dog. e, Girl on bicycle, flowers (semi-circular stamp). f, Flowers, bird with envelope, insect (circular stamp). g, Bird flying, bird on roof. h, Chicken, chicks, pig (oval stamp). i, Rabbit, flowers (elliptical stamp). j, Boy with hat, rabbit (oval stamp).

2001, July 23 *Perf. 13x13¼*

2779	A2047 50y multi	.80	.30
2780	A2047 50y multi	.80	.30
2781	A2047 50y multi	.80	.30
2782	A2047 50y multi	.80	.30
a.	Horiz. strip of 4, #2779-2782	4.00	4.00
2783	Sheet of 10	16.00	16.00
a.-j.	A2047 80y Any single	1.25	.35
k.	Booklet pane, #2779-2782, 2 each #2783c, 2783d, 2783g	13.50	
	Booklet, #2783k	15.00	
l.	Souvenir sheet, #2780, 2783g	2.75	2.75

Phila Nippon '01 (Nos. 2783, 2783l). Nos. 2783a and 2783e are 35x29mm; Nos. 2783b and 2783f are 29mm in diameter; No. 2783h is 40x28mm; No. 2783i is 35x23mm; No. 2783j is 34x28mm.

On No. 2783e, the bicycle appears in the selvage below the stamp.

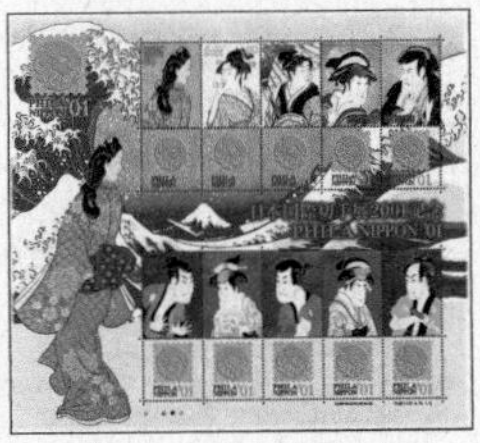

Phila Nippon '01 A2140

Art: a, Oniji Otani as Edobei (striped kimono), by Sharaku. b, Hanshiro Iwai as Shigenoi (flowered kimono, facing left), by Sharaku. c, Hangoro Sakata as Mizuemon Fujikawa (brown kimono), by Sharaku. d, Kikunojo Segawa as Oshizu, Bunzo Tanabe's Wife (kimono with stars), by Sharaku. e, Omezo Ichikawa as Ippei Yakko (with sword), by Sharaku. f, Beauty Looking Back (flowered kimono), by Moronobu Hishikawa. g, A Girl Whistling a Vidro (checkered kimono), by Utamaro. h, Nishiki Fuzoku Higashino Returning From a Bathhouse in the Rain (with umbrella), by Kiyonaga Torii. i, Kumesaburo Iwai as Chiyo (blue background), by Kunimasa Utagawa. j, Komazo Ichikawa as Ganryu Sasaki (with sword), by Toyokuni Utagawa.

2001, Aug. 1 *Perf. 13*

2784	A2140 Sheet of 10+10 labels	12.50	12.50
a.-e.	50y Any single	.80	.50
f.-j.	80y Any single	1.25	.50

Labels could be personalized by customers at Phila Nippon stamp exhibition.

2001 World Games, Akita — A2141

Designs: No. 2785, Fishing, Frisbee throwing. No. 2786, Aerobics, billiards. No. 2787, Life saving, water skiing. No. 2788, Body building, tug-of-war.

2001, Aug. 16 *Perf. 13*

2785	A2141 50y multi	.80	.30
2786	A2141 50y multi	.80	.30
a.	Pair, #2785-2786	2.00	1.00
2787	A2141 80y multi	1.25	.35
2788	A2141 80y multi	1.25	.35
a.	Pair, #2787-2788	3.25	1.50
	Nos. 2785-2788 (4)	4.10	1.30

Phila Nippon '01 A2142

Designs: a, Hanshiro Iwai as Shigenoi (figure with stick in hair), by Sharaku. b, Oniji Otani as Edobei (figure with fingers splayed), by Sharaku. c, Mandarin duck in water. d, White-eye on branch. e, Children with letters. f, Kumesaburo Iwai as Chiyo (lilac background), by Kunimasa Utagawa. g, Komazo Ichikawa as Ganryu Sasaki (brown background), by Toyokuni Utagawa. h, Turtledove (blue background). i, Greater pied kingfisher (green background). j, Japan #1.

2001, Aug. 1 **Photo.** *Die Cut*

Self-Adhesive

2789	A2142 Sheet of 10	12.00	12.00
a.-e.	50y Any single	.80	.30
f.-j.	80y Any single	1.25	.35

San Francisco Peace Treaty, 50th Anniv. — A2143

2001, Sept. 7 *Perf. 13*

2790	A2143 80y multi	1.50	.35

Intl. Letter Writing Week Type of 2000

Hiroshige paintings from 53 Stations of the Tokaido: 90y, Hara. 110y, Oiso. 130y, Sakanoshita.

2001, Oct. 5 *Perf. 13¼*

2791	A2119 90y multi	1.75	.50
2792	A2119 110y multi	2.25	.55
2793	A2119 130y multi	2.50	.60
	Nos. 2791-2793 (3)	6.50	1.65

See listing of No. 4448 for images of each Hiroshige print.

Town Safety Campaign A2144

Designs: No. 2794, Boy, duck chicks, owl, frogs, insects. No. 2795, Girl, dogs, cats, birds, insects.

2001, Oct. 11 *Perf. 13x13¼*

2794	80y multi	1.25	.35
2795	80y multi	1.25	.35
a.	A2144 Horiz. pair, #2794-2795	3.25	1.50

1st National Games for the Disabled A2145

Designs: No. 2796, Disc throwing. No. 2797, Wheelchair race.

2001, Oct. 26 *Perf. 12¾x13*

2796	80y multi	1.25	.35
2797	80y multi	1.25	.35
a.	A2145 Horiz. pair, #2796-2797	3.00	1.50

Norinaga Motoori (1730-1801), Physician, Scholar A2146

Gidayu Takemoto (1651-1714), Joruri Chanter A2147

Photo. & Engr.

2001, Nov. 5 *Perf. 12¾x13*

2798	A2146 80y multi	1.50	.35
2799	A2147 80y multi	1.50	.35

Commercial Broadcasting, 50th Anniv. — A2148

2001, Nov. 15 **Photo.**

2800	A2148 80y multi	1.50	.35

A2149

A2150

New Year 2002 (Year of the Horse)

A2151 A2152

2001, Nov. 15 *Perf. 13x13¼*

2801	A2149 50y multi	1.00	.30
2802	A2150 80y multi	1.50	.40

Perf. 13¼x13½

2803	A2151 50y +3y multi	1.25	.40
2804	A2152 80y +3y multi	1.75	.40
	Nos. 2801-2804 (4)	5.50	1.50

Sheets of two containing Nos. 2801-2802 were lottery prizes. Value, $3.

Legal Aid System, 50th Anniv. — A2153

2002, Jan. 24 *Perf. 12¾x13*

2805	A2153 80y multi	1.50	.35

Japan — Mongolia Diplomatic Relations, 30th Anniv. — A2154

2002, Feb. 15

2806	A2154 80y multi	1.50	.35

Lions Clubs in Japan, 50th Anniv. — A2155

2002, Mar. 1 **Photo.** *Perf. 13x13¼*

2807	A2155 80y multi	1.50	.35

2002 World Figure Skating Championships, Nagano — A2156

2002, Mar. 8

2808	80y Men's Singles	1.25	.90
2809	80y Pairs	1.25	.90
a.	A2156 Horiz. pair, #2808-2809	3.00	1.90

Diplomatic Relations Anniversaries — A2157

Designs: No. 2810, Taj Mahal, India. No. 2811, Sculpture of "Priest King," Mohenjo Daro excavations, Pakistan. No. 2812, Sigiriya goddess, Lion's Rock, Sri Lanka. No. 2813, Carving from Buddhist Vihara, Paharpur, Bangladesh.

2002, Apr. 12

2810	A2157 80y multi	1.50	.40
2811	A2157 80y multi	1.50	.40
2812	A2157 80y multi	1.50	.40
2813	A2157 80y multi	1.50	.40
	Nos. 2810-2813 (4)	6.00	1.60

Japanese diplomatic relations with India, 50th anniv. (No. 2810); Pakistan, 50th anniv.

(No. 2811). Sri Lanka, 50th anniv. (No. 2812), and Bangladesh, 30th anniv. (No. 2813).

Philately Week A2158

Folding screen panels depicting horse racing scenes: No. 2814, Denomination at bottom. No. 2815, Denomination at top.

2002, Apr. 19 *Perf. 13¼*

2814	80y multi		1.25	.40
2815	80y multi		1.25	.40
a.	A2158 Horiz. pair, #2814-2815		3.00	1.75

Fulbright Exchange Program, 50th Anniv. — A2159

2002, May 8 *Perf. 12¾x13*

2816	A2159 80y multi	1.50	.35

Return of Okinawa, 30th Anniv. — A2160

2002, May 15 *Perf. 13x13¼*

2817	A2160 80y multi	1.50	.35

2002 World Cup Soccer Championships, Japan and Korea — A2161

2002, May 24

2818	80y Soccer field	1.25	.35
2819	80y World Cup	1.25	.35
a.	A2161 Horiz. pair, #2818-2819	3.00	1.75

Nos. 2818-2819 were issued in sheets of 10 stamps, containing five of each. Thirteen different sheet margins exist.

World Heritage Sites

Sheet 7 A2162

No. 2820 — Todaiji and Koufukuji Temples, Nara: a, Great Buddha Hall, Todaiji Temple (stamp 1). b, Underside of roof of Nandaimon Gate, Todaiji Temple (stamp 2). c, Engraving on lotus petal, Todaiji Temple (stamp 3). d, Head of Koumokuten, Todaiji Temple (stamp 4). e, Hokkedo Hall and steps, Todaiji Temple (stamp 5). f, Five-story pagoda, Koufukuji Temple (stamp 6). g, Hokuendo Hall (with roof ornament), Koufukuji Temple (stamp 7). h, Ashura (statue with four arms), Koufukuji Temple (stamp 8). i, Head of Buddha, Koufukuji Temple (stamp 9). j, Ogre under dragon lantern, Koufukuji Temple (stamp 10).

2002 **Photo.** *Perf. 13x13¼*

2820	A2162	Sheet of 10	16.00	16.00
a.-j.	80y Any single		1.25	.55

Issued: No. 2820, 6/21.

Sheet numbers are in center of colored rectangle at top of sheet. Stamp numbers are in sheet margins.

World Heritage Series

Sheet 8 A2163

Sheet 9 A2164

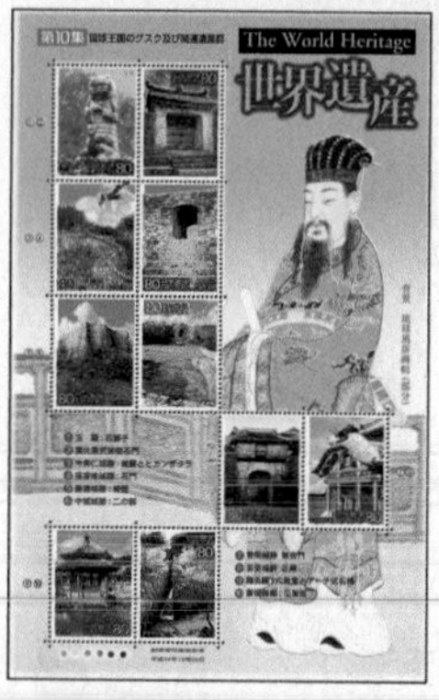

Sheet 10 A2165

No. 2821 — Nara: a, Covered passageway, Kasuga Taisha Shrine (stamp 1). b, Chumon, Kasuga Taisha Shrine (stamp 2). c, Deer in Kasuga-yama Primeval Forest (stamp 3). d, Gokurakubo Zenshitsu and Gokurakubo Hondo, Gango-ji Temple (stamp 4). e, Gokurakubo Five-story Pagoda, Gango-ji Temple (stamp 5). f, East and West Pagodas, Yakushi-ji Temple (stamp 6). g, Yakushi Nyorai (seated Buddha), Yakushi-ji Temple (stamp 7). h, Golden Hall, Toshodai-ji Temple (stamp 8). i, Senju Kannon Ryu-zo (standing image with hands together of Thousand-handed Goddess of Mercy), Toshodai-ji Temple (stamp 9). j, Suzakumon Gate, Heijo Imperial Palace (stamp 10).

No. 2822 — Villages of Shirakawa-go and Gokayama: a, House with large tree at left, Ogimachi (stamp 1). b, Two houses, trees in fall colors Ogimachi (stamp 2). c, House with flowers, Ogimachi (stamp 3). d, Myozen-ji Temple and house, Ogimachi (stamp 4). e, Two houses covered in snow at night, Ogimachi (stamp 5). f, Neighborhood of houses, Ainokura (stamp 6). g, Sonen-ji Temple with stone wall, Ainokura (stamp 7). h, Two houses, Ainokura (stamp 8). i, House with shrub in front, Suganuma (stamp 9). j, House covered in snow, Suganuma (stamp 10).

No. 2823 — Gusuku Sites of the Ryukyu Kingdom: a, Stone lion at royal mausoleum (stamp 1). b, Three steps and stone gate to Sonohyan'utaki Sanctuary (stamp 2). c, Cherry blossoms and ruins of Nakijinjou Castle (stamp 3). d, Steps and stone gate at ruins of Zakimijou Castle (stamp 4). e, Ruins of Katsurenjou Castle walls (stamp 5). f, Ruins of Nakagusukujou Castle citadel (walls with gate, stamp 6). g, Kankaimon, main gate of Shurijou Castle (stamp 7). h, Main hall of Shurijou Castle (red building, stamp 8). i, Shikina'en, royal garden (stamp 9). j, Seifautaki Sanctuary (niche in rocks, stamp 10).

2002 **Photo.** *Perf. 13x13¼*

2821	A2163	Sheet of 10	16.00	16.00
a.-j.	80y Any single		1.25	.55
2822	A2164	Sheet of 10	16.00	16.00
a.-j.	80y Any single		1.25	.55
2823	A2165	Sheet of 10	16.00	16.00
a.-j.	80y Any single		1.25	.55

Issued: No. 2821, 7/23; No. 2822, 9/20; No. 2823, 12/20. Sheet numbers are in center of colored rectangle at top of sheet. Stamp numbers are in sheet margins.

Letter Writing Day Type of 1998

Designs: No. 2824, Girl with bows in hair holding envelope. No. 2825, Monkey in tree holding envelope. No. 2826, House and flowers. No. 2827, Boy with arms raised, fence.

No. 2828: a, Cow and bird (triangular stamp). b, Boy and sheep (elliptical stamp). c, Caterpillar and ladybug under magnifying glass (round stamp). d, Girl with bows in hair, flowers (oval stamp). e, Boy with soccer ball. f, Girl with tennis racquet and ball. g, Man on bicycle. h, Girl with flower in vase (round stamp). i, Truck and automobile. j, Woman holding gift and coat, boy holding envelope

Perf. 13x13¼, 13 (#2828a)

2002, July 23 **Photo.**

2824	A2047 50y multi	.80	.40
2825	A2047 50y multi	.80	.40
2826	A2047 50y multi	.80	.40
2827	A2047 50y multi	.80	.40
a.	Strip of 4, #2824-2827	4.00	2.75
2828	Sheet of 10	16.00	16.00
a.-j.	A2047 80y Any single	1.40	.45
k.	Booklet pane, #2824-2827, 3 each #2828g, 2828j	16.00	—
	Booklet, #2828k	16.00	
l.	Souvenir sheet, #2825, 2828j	2.75	2.75

No. 2828a is 34x28mm; No. 2828b is 29x26mm; No. 2828c is 29mm in diameter; No. 2828d is 28x40mm; Nos. 2828e and 2828f are 22x36mm; No. 2828h is 28mm in diameter; No. 2828i is 25x25mm.

12th World Congress of Psychiatry, Yokohama — A2166

2002, Aug. 1 **Photo.** *Perf. 12¾x13*

2829	A2166 80y multi	1.50	.35

World Wheelchair Basketball Championships, Kitakyushu — A2167

2002, Aug. 9

2830	A2167 80y multi	1.50	.35

Civil Aviation, 50th Anniv. — A2168

2002, Sept. 6

2831	A2168 80y multi	1.50	.35

Normalization of Diplomatic Relations Between Japan and People's Republic of China, 30th Anniv. — A2169

Designs: No. 2832, Purple wisteria flowers. No. 2833, Goldfish and cherry blossoms.

2002, Sept. 13 *Perf. 13x13¼*

2832	80y multi	1.25	.55
2833	80y multi	1.25	.55
a.	A2169 Horiz. pair, #2832-2833	3.00	2.50

Intl. Fleet Review, Tokyo Bay — A2170

2002, Oct. 1

2834	A2170 80y multi	1.50	.40

Letter Writing Week Type of 2000

Hiroshige paintings from 53 Stations of the Tokaido Highway: 90y, Yui. 110y, Shono. 130y, Tozuka.

2002, Oct. 7 *Perf. 13¼*

2835	A2119 90y multi	1.75	.50
2836	A2119 110y multi	2.25	.55
2837	A2119 130y multi	2.50	.60
	Nos. 2835-2837 (3)	6.50	1.65

See listing of No. 4448 for images of each Hiroshige print.

Asian and Pacific Decade of Disabled Persons — A2171

2002, Oct. 10 *Perf. 12¾x13*

2838	A2171 80y multi	1.50	.40

Cultural Pioneers Types of 1998-2000

Designs: No. 2839, Shiki Masaoka (1867-1902), poet. No. 2840, Ookawabata Yusuzumi-zu, by Kiyonaga Torii (1752-1815), artist. No. 2841, Aikitu Tanakadate (1856-1952), physicist.

Photo. & Engr., Photo. (#2840)

2002, Nov. 5 *Perf. 13*

2839	A2053 80y multi	1.50	.40
2840	A2053 80y multi	1.50	.40
2841	A2120 80y multi	1.50	.40
	Nos. 2839-2841 (3)	4.50	1.20

A2172

A2173

New Year 2003 (Year of the Ram)

A2174 A2175

2002, Nov. 15 **Photo.** *Perf. 13x13¼*

2842	A2172 50y multi	1.00	.30
2843	A2173 80y multi	1.50	.40

Perf. 13½x13¼

2844	A2174 50y +3y multi	1.25	.40
2845	A2175 80y +3y multi	1.75	.40
	Nos. 2842-2845 (4)	5.50	1.50

Sheets of two containing Nos. 2842-2843 were lottery prizes. Value, $2.75.

Kabuki, 400th Anniv. A2176

Designs: No. 2846, Shibaraku and Tsuchigumo. No. 2847, Okuni Kabuki-zu, detail from painted screen.

2003, Jan. 15 Photo. *Perf. 13x13¼*

2846 80y multi 1.25 .50
2847 80y multi 1.25 .50
a. A2176 Horiz. pair, #2846-2847 3.50 2.00

Japanese Television, 50th Anniv.
A2177 A2178

2003, Jan. 31

2848 A2177 80y multi 1.50 .40
2849 A2178 80y multi 1.50 .40

A2179

Greetings — A2180

No. 2850: a, Roses. b, Reindeer. c, Cat and butterfly. d, Rabbits in automobile. e, White flowers.

No. 2851: a, Heart and flower. b, Dog with noisemaker. c, Bird and snowman. d, Bird and strawberries. e, Cranes and turtle.

2003, Feb. 10 *Die Cut Perf. 13½*
Self-Adhesive

2850 A2179 Pane of 5 + 5 labels 7.00 7.00
a.-e. 80y Any single 1.25 .75
2851 A2180 Pane of 5 + 5 labels 7.00 7.00
a.-e. 80y Any single 1.25 .75

See Nos. 2855A-2855J.

World Heritage Series

Sheet 11
A2181

No. 2852 — Hiroshima buildings and stamps on theme of "Peace": a, Atomic Bomb Dome (stamp 1). b, Hiroshima Prefectural Commercial Exhibit Hall (stamp 2). c, Dove over Atomic Bomb Dome, yellow denomination (stamp 3). d, Child's drawing of person with flower (stamp 4). e, Dove over Atomic Bomb Dome, blue denomination (stamp 5). f, Dove over Atomic Bomb Dome, red denomination (stamp 6). g, Doves, stylized person holding child (stamp 7). h, People on hill (stamp 8). i, Bird (stamp 9). j, Rabbit, butterflies and flowers (stamp 10).

2003, Mar. 20 Photo. *Perf. 13x13¼*

2852 A2181 Sheet of 10 16.00 16.00
a.-j. 80y Any single 1.25 .55

Sheet numbers are in center of colored rectangle at top of sheet. Stamp numbers are in sheet margin.

Inauguration of Japan Post — A2182

No. 2853 — Flowers: a, Adonis (yellow flowers). b, Primrose (pink flowers). c, Violets and Japanese quince (violet and red flowers). d, Field horsetail (flowerless). e, Japanese wisteria (white hanging flowers). f, Weeping cherry tree (pink buds and flowers) and swallow. g, Hydrangea (lilac flowers). h, Japanese magnolia (white and pink flowers). i, Candock (yellow flower) and moorhen. j, Peony (pink flower and bud) and butterfly.

2003, Apr. 1 *Die Cut Perf. 13¼*
Self-Adhesive

2853 A2182 Sheet of 10 16.00 16.00
a.-j. 80y Any single 1.25 .55

Japan Post Mascots A2183

Designs: a, Aichan (squirrel with pink bow). b, Male Kanchan (with heart on shorts). c, Posuton (with hands extended). d, Yuchan (squirrel with cap). e, Female Kanchan (with flower). f, Posuton (with letter). g, Posuton (with letter). h, Aichan (with pink bow), diff. i, Female Kanchan (with flower), diff. j, Posuton (with hands extended), diff. k, Yuchan (with cap), diff. l, Male Kanchan (waving).

2003, Apr. 1 *Die Cut Perf. 13¼*
Self-Adhesive

2854 A2183 Sheet of 12 16.00 16.00
a.-f. 50y Any single 1.25 .40
g.-l. 80y Any single 1.50 .55

Ram and Tree Batik Screen Design — A2184

2003, Apr. 18 *Perf. 13¼*

2855 A2184 80y multi 1.50 .40

Philately Week.

Greetings Type of 2003

2003 Photo. *Perf. 13*

2855A A2180 80y Like No. 2851a + label —
2855B A2179 80y Like No. 2850d + label —
2855D A2179 80y Like No. 2850e + label —
2855E A2180 80y Like No. 2851b + label —
2855F A2180 80y Like No. 2851c + label —
2855H A2180 80y Like No. 2851e + label —
2855I A2179 80y Like No. 2850b + label —
2855J A2179 80y Like No. 2850c + label —

Issued: Nos. 2855A, 2855B, 2855D, 4/19; Nos. 2855E, 2855F, 2855H, 2855I, 2855j, 6/11. Below each stamp was a label that could be personalized. Two additional stamps were issued in this set. The editors would like to examine any examples.

Edo Shogunate, 400th Anniv.

Screen Depicting Edo A2185

Wall Decoration, Edo Castle A2186

Armor of Ieyasu Tokugawa A2187

Detail from Writing Box A2188

Noh Mask and Costume — A2189

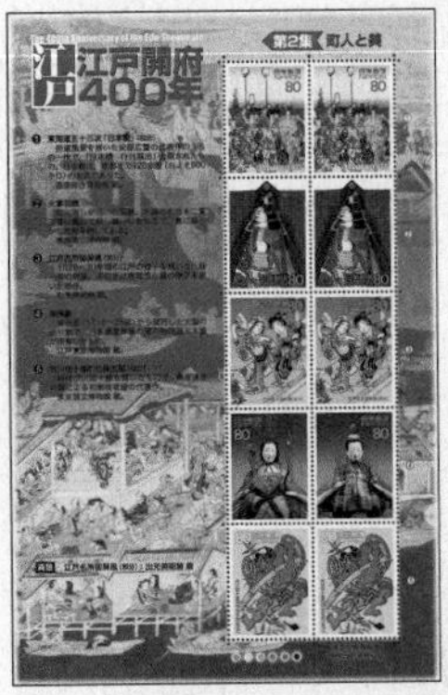

Sheet 2
A2190

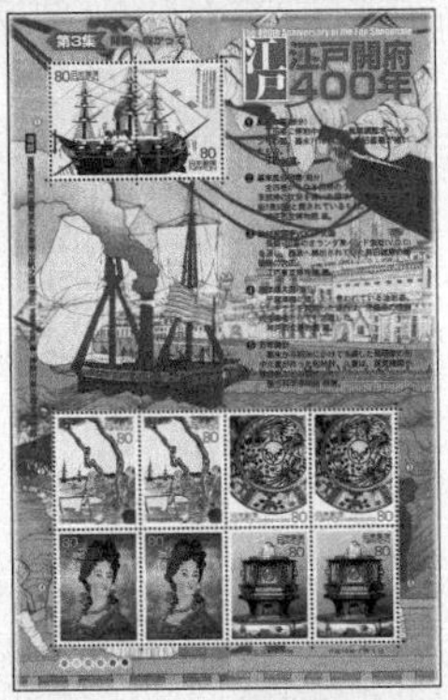

A2191

No. 2857 — Sheet 2: a, Nihonbashi, from 53 Stations of the Tokaido Road, by Hiroshige (stamp 1). b, Fireman's coat (stamp 2). c, Screen depicting Kabuki theater (stamp 3). d, Hina-matsuri fesitval doll of empress (no number). e, Hina-matsuri festival doll of emperor (stamp 4). f, Danjurou Ichikawa playing role of Goro Takenuki (stamp 5).

No. 2858 — Sheet 3: a, Stern of USS Powhatan (stamp 1). b, Bow of USS Powhatan (no number). c, Screen art depicting return of Commodore Perry's fleet to Japan (stamp 2). d, Ceramic platter for export to Europe (stamp 3). e, Portrait of a European Woman, probably by Gennai Hiraga (stamp 4). f, Perpetual clock (stamp 5).

2003 *Perf. 13x13¼*

2856 Vert. strip of 5 7.00 7.00
a. A2185 80y multi 1.25 .55
b. A2186 80y multi 1.25 .55
c. A2187 80y multi 1.25 .55
d. A2188 80y multi 1.25 .55
e. A2189 80y multi 1.25 .55
Sheet, 2 #2856 (Sheet 1) 16.50 16.50
2857 A2190 Sheet of 10, #2857d-2857e, 2 each #2857a-2857c, 2857f 16.50 16.50
a.-f. 80y Any single 1.25 .55
2858 A2191 Sheet of 10, #2858a-2858b, 2 each #2858c-2858f 16.50 16.50
a.-f. 80y Any single 1.25 .55

Issued: No. 2856, 5/23; No. 2857, 6/12; No. 2858, 7/1. Sheet numbers are in center of arrows at top of sheet. Stamp numbers are in sheet margins.

ASEAN — Japan Exchange Year — A2192

No. 2859: a, Omar Ali Saifuddien Mosque, Brunei (stamp 1). b, Angkor Wat, Cambodia (stamp 2). c, Borobudur Temple, Indonesia (stamp 3). d, That Luang, Laos (stamp 4). e, Sultan Abdul Samad Building, Malaysia (stamp 5). f, Shwedagon Pagoda, Myanmar (stamp 6). g, Rice terraces, Philippines (stamp 7). h, Merlion Statue, Singapore (stamp 8). i, Wat Phra Kaeo, Thailand (stamp 9). j, Van Mieu, Viet Nam (stamp 10).

2003, June 16 Photo. *Perf. 13x13¼*

2859 A2192 Sheet of 10 16.50 16.50
a.-j. 80y Any single 1.25 .55

Letter Writing Day — A2193

Designs: No. 2860, Bear with guitar, bird. No. 2861, Monkey with letter. No. 2862, Crocodile with accordion, bird. No. 2863, Cat with camera, letter.

No. 2864: a, Hippopotamus with umbrella, flowers, birds (oval stamp). b, Parakeet with letter. c, Owl (round stamp). d, Bear with letter, bird (oval stamp). e, Elephant with flowers. f, Giraffe with letter (oval stamp). g, Rabbit with letter, flowers (semi-circular stamp). h, Lion with letter, lantern. i, Goat with letter. j, Gorilla with koala, bird and owl.

2003, July 23 Photo. *Perf. 13x13¼*

2860 A2193 50y multi .80 .35
2861 A2193 50y multi .80 .35
2862 A2193 50y multi .80 .35
2863 A2193 50y multi .80 .35
a. Horiz. strip of 4, #2860-2863 4.00 2.25
2864 Sheet of 10 16.50 16.50
a.-j. A2193 80y Any single 1.25 .55
k. Booklet pane of 10, #2860-2863, 2 each #2864b, 2864h, 2864i 13.00 13.00
Complete booklet, #2864k 15.00
l. Souvenir sheet, #2860, #2864b 2.75 2.75

Nos. 2864a, 2864d and 2864f are 28x40mm; No. 2864c is 30mm in diameter; No. 2864g is 40x24mm.

Intl. Letter Writing Week Type of 2000

Hiroshige paintings from 53 Stations of the Tokaido Highway: 90y, Kawasaki. 110y, Miya. 130y, Otsu.

2003, Oct. 6 *Perf. 13¼*

2865 A2119 90y multi 1.75 .45
2866 A2119 110y multi 2.25 .55
2867 A2119 130y multi 2.50 .65
Nos. 2865-2867 (3) 6.50 1.65

See listing of No. 4448 for images of each Hiroshige print.

Cultural Pioneers — A2194

Designs: No. 2868, Mokichi Saito (1882-1953), poet. No. 2869, Shibasaburo Kitasato (1853-1931), bacteriologist.

Photo. & Engr.

2003, Nov. 4 ***Perf. 13***

2868	A2194	80y multi	1.40	.40
2869	A2194	80y multi	1.40	.40

See Nos. 2907-2909.

Reversion of the Amami Islands to Japanese Control, 50th Anniv. — A2195

2003, Nov. 7 **Photo.**

2870	A2195	80y multi	1.50	.40

A2196 A2197

New Year 2004 (Year of the Monkey)
A2198 A2199

2003, Nov. 14 ***Perf. 13x13¼***

2871	A2196	50y multi	1.00	.30
2872	A2197	80y multi	1.50	.40

Photo. & Litho.

Perf. 13½x13¼

2873	A2198	50y +3y multi	1.25	.40
2874	A2199	80y +3y multi	1.75	.40
		Nos. 2871-2874 (4)	5.50	1.50

Sheets of two containing Nos. 2871-2872 were lottery prizes. Value, $2.75.

Happy Face — A2199a

Sky — A2199b

Serpentine Die Cut 9¼x9

2003, Dec. 1 **Photo.**

Self-Adhesive

2874A	A2199a	80y multi + label	2.00	1.25

Serpentine Die Cut 6½x5½

Stamp + Label

Color of Japanese Inscription

2874B	A2199b	80y blue	2.00	1.25
2874C	A2199b	80y red orange	2.00	1.25
2874D	A2199a	80y white	—	—
		Nos. 2874A-2874C (3)	6.00	3.75

Stamps and labels are separated by a line of rouletting on Nos. 2874B-2874D. Labels could be personalized. No. 2874A was printed in sheets of 4 stamps and 4 labels that sold for 500y, and sheets of 10 stamps and 10 labels that sold for 1000y. Nos. 2874B-2874C were printed in sheets containing five of each stamp and 10 labels that sold for 1000y. No. 2874D was printed in sheets of 10 and 10 labels and sold for 1000y.

Bubbles — A2199c Bubbles — A2199d

Rose — A2199e

Serpentine Die Cut 6

2004, Jan. 23 **Photo.**

Self-Adhesive

2874E	A2199c	50y multi + label	1.75	1.25
2874F	A2199d	50y multi + label	1.75	1.25
2874G	A2199e	90y multi + label	*2.50*	1.50
		Nos. 2874E-2874G (3)	6.00	4.00

Stamps and labels are separated by a line of rouletting. Labels could be personalized. Nos. 2874E-2874F were printed in sheets containing ten of each stamp and 20 labels that sold for 1200y. No. 2874G was printed in a sheet of 20 stamps and 20 labels that sold for 2000y.

Science, Technology and Animation

Astro Boy — A2200

Bowman Doll — A2201

Hantaro Nagaoka A2202

H-II Rocket A2203

Morph 3 — A2204

Astro Boy — A2205

Astro Boy — A2206

Astro Boy — A2207

Super Jetter A2208

Japanese Clock A2209

Otomo A2210

KAZ A2211

Stratospheric Platform Airship A2212

Super Jetter A2213

Super Jetter A2214

Super Jetter A2215

2003-2004 **Photo.** ***Perf. 13x13¼***

2875	Vert. strip of 5	8.00	8.00
a.	A2200 80y multi	1.25	.50
b.	A2201 80y multi	1.25	.50
c.	A2202 80y multi	1.25	.50
d.	A2203 80y multi	1.25	.50
e.	A2204 80y multi	1.25	.50
	Sheet, 2 #2875	17.50	17.50
2876	Sheet, #2875b-2875e, 2 each #2876a-2876c	17.50	17.50
a.	A2205 80y multi	1.25	.50
b.	A2206 80y multi	1.25	.50
c.	A2207 80y multi	1.25	.50
2877	Vert. strip of 5	8.00	8.00
a.	A2208 80y multi	1.25	.50
b.	A2209 80y multi	1.25	.50
c.	A2210 80y multi	1.25	.50
d.	A2211 80y multi	1.25	.50
e.	A2212 80y multi	1.25	.50
	Sheet, 2 #2875	17.50	17.50
2878	Sheet, #2877b-2877e, 2 each #2878a-2878c	17.50	17.50
a.	A2213 80y multi	1.25	.50
b.	A2214 80y multi	1.25	.50
c.	A2215 80y multi	1.25	.50

Issued: Nos. 2875-2876, 12/16/03; Nos. 2877-2878, 1/23/04.

Science, Technology and Animation

Marvelous Melmo and Baby A2216

Seishu Hanaoka (1760-1835), Surgeon A2217

Wooden Microscope A2218

Jokichi Takamine (1854-1922), Chemist A2219

Drug Delivery System A2220

Marvelous Melmo with Mother A2221

Marvelous Melmo with Man A2222

Marvelous Melmo and Others in Bottle A2223

Science Ninja Team Gatchaman A2224

Proposed Perpetual Motion Machine of Michitaka Kume A2225

OHSUMI Satellite A2226

Conducting Polymer A2227

Tissue and Organ Reproduction A2228

Science Ninja Team Gatchaman A2229

Science Ninja Team Gatchaman A2230

Science Ninja Team Gatchaman A2231

2004 **Photo.** ***Perf. 13x13¼***

2879	Vert. strip of 5	8.00	8.00
a.	A2216 80y multi	1.25	.50
b.	A2217 80y multi	1.25	.50
c.	A2218 80y multi	1.25	.50
d.	A2219 80y multi	1.25	.50
e.	A2220 80y multi	1.25	.50
	Sheet, 2 #2879	17.50	17.50
2880	Sheet, #2879b-2879e, 2 each #2880a-2880c	17.50	17.50
a.	A2221 80y multi	1.25	.50
b.	A2222 80y multi	1.25	.50
c.	A2223 80y multi	1.25	.50
2881	Vert. strip of 5	8.00	8.00
a.	A2224 80y multi	1.25	.50
b.	A2225 80y multi	1.25	.50
c.	A2226 80y multi	1.25	.50
d.	A2227 80y multi	1.25	.50
e.	A2228 80y multi	1.25	.50
	Sheet, 2 #2881	17.50	17.50

2882	Sheet, #2881b-2881e, 2 each #2882a-2882c	17.50	17.50
a.	A2229 80y multi	1.25	.50
b.	A2230 80y multi	1.25	.50
c.	A2231 80y multi	1.25	.50

Issued: Nos. 2879-2880, 2/23/04. Nos. 2881-2882, 3/23/04.

A2232

Hello Kitty A2233

No. 2883: a, Red, white and blue flowers under chin. b, Red flower under chin, beige background. c, No flower under chin. d, Blue and red flowers under chin. e, Red flower under chin. f, Two blue flowers under chin. g, White flowers with green leaves under chin. h, Two pink flowers under chin. i, One blue flower under chin. j, Pink, yellow and green flower under chin.

No. 2884 — Head of Kitty with: a, Cherries. b, Bow. c, Strawberries. d, Blue flower. e, Spray of flowers.

Die Cut Perf. 13¼

2004, Feb. 6 **Litho.**

Self-Adhesive

2883	A2232 Sheet of 10	9.50	9.50
a.-j.	50y Any single	.80	.80
2884	A2233 Sheet of 5	7.00	7.00
a.-e.	80y Any single	1.25	.80

Uchu-no Sakura Gohiki-no Saru-zu, by Sosen Mori — A2234

Perf. 12½x12¾ Syncopated

2004, Apr. 20 **Photo.**

2885	A2234 80y multi	1.50	.45

Philatelic Week.

Japanese Racing Association, 50th Anniv. — A2235

Designs: No. 2886, Ten Point and Tosho Boy, 22nd Armia Memorial Stakes. No. 2887, Narita Brian, 61st Tolyo Yushun.

2004, May 28 ***Perf. 13x13¼***

2886	80y green & multi	1.25	.45
2887	80y blue & multi	1.25	.45
a.	A2235 Horiz. pair, #2886-2887	3.00	2.25

Police Law, 50th Anniv. A2236

2004, June 21 ***Perf. 13***

2888	80y Police car	1.25	.45
2889	80y Police motorcycle	1.25	.45
a.	A2236 Horiz. pair, #2888-2889	3.00	2.25

Letter Writing Day — A2237

Designs: No. 2890, Donkichi with pencil. No. 2891, Hime (woman with letter). No. 2892, Shouchan (man with ski cap). No. 2893, Owl with letter.

No. 2894: a, Dove with letter, rainbow. b, Squirrel with wings, rainbow. c, Stork (round stamp). d, Hime with wings (oval stamp). e, Donkichi with wings, letter. f, Kuriko (elf in pink) with wings. g, Megami (woman in white) (oval stamp). h, Shouchan with wings. i, Squirrel with flowers, letter. j, Rabbit (round stamp).

2004, July 23 **Photo.** ***Perf. 13x13¼***

2890	A2237 50y multi	.80	.25
2891	A2237 50y multi	.80	.25
2892	A2237 50y multi	.80	.25
2893	A2237 50y multi	.80	.25
a.	Horiz. strip of 4, #2890-2893	4.00	2.75
2894	Sheet of 10	16.50	16.50
a.-j.	A2237 80y Any single	1.25	.55
k.	Booklet pane of 10, #2890-2893, 2 each #2894b, 2894e, 2894f	14.00	—
	Complete booklet, #2894k	15.00	
l.	Souvenir sheet, #2890, #2894f	2.75	2.75

Nos. 2894c, 2894j are 30mm in diameter; No. 2894d is 28x37mm; No. 2894g is 28x40mm; No. 2894i is 28x29mm.

2004 Summer Olympics, Athens A2238

Olympic rings and: No. 2895, Olympic Flame, Olympia. No. 2896, 2004 Athens Olympics emblem.

2004, Aug. 6 ***Perf. 13***

2895	80y multi	1.25	.45
2896	80y multi	1.25	.45
a.	A2238 Horiz. pair, #2895-2896	3.00	2.25

Science, Technology and Animation

Mazinger-Z A2239

Steam Locomotive A2240

New KS Steel A2241

Shinkai 6500 Research Submarine A2242

Fuel Cell A2243

Mazinger-Z A2244

Mazinger-Z A2245

Mazinger-Z A2246

2004, Aug. 23 **Photo.** ***Perf. 13x13¼***

2897	Vert. strip of 5	8.00	8.00
a.	A2239 80y multi	1.25	.40
b.	A2240 80y multi	1.25	.40
c.	A2241 80y multi	1.25	.40
d.	A2242 80y multi	1.25	.40
e.	A2243 80y multi	1.25	.40
	Sheet, 2 #2897	17.50	17.50
2898	Sheet, #2897b-2897e, 2 each #2898a-2898c	17.50	17.50
a.	A2244 80y multi	1.25	.40
b.	A2245 80y multi	1.25	.40
c.	A2246 80y multi	1.25	.40

Science, Technology and Animation

Doraemon A2247

Gennai Hiraga A2248

Mechanical Netsuke A2249

Television A2250

Optical Fiber A2251

Doraemon A2252

Doraemon A2253

Doraemon A2254

2004, Nov. 22 **Photo.** ***Perf. 13x13¼***

2899	Vert. strip of 5	8.00	8.00
a.	A2247 80y multi	1.25	.40
b.	A2248 80y multi	1.25	.40
c.	A2249 80y multi	1.25	.40
d.	A2250 80y multi	1.25	.40
e.	A2251 80y multi	1.25	.40
	Sheet, 2, #2899	17.50	17.50
2900	Sheet, #2899b-2899e, 2 each #2900a-2900c	17.50	17.50
a.	A2252 80y multi	1.25	.40
b.	A2253 80y multi	1.25	.40
c.	A2254 80y multi	1.25	.40

Japan — United States Relationships, 150th Anniv. — A2255

Designs: No. 2901, Mt. Fuji, by Frederick Harris. No. 2902, Cafe, by Yasuo Kuniyoshi.

2004, Sept. 22 ***Perf. 13***

2901	80y multi	1.25	.50
2902	80y multi	1.25	.50
a.	A2255 Horiz. pair, #2901-2902	3.00	2.25

World Medical Association General Assembly, Tokyo — A2256

2004, Oct. 6 ***Perf. 12¾x13***

2903	A2256 80y multi	1.50	.40

International Letter Writing Week Type of 2000

Hiroshige paintings from 53 Stations of the Tokaido Highway: 90y, Hiratsuka. 110y, Yokkaichi. 130y, Tsuchiyama.

2004, Oct. 8 ***Perf. 13¼***

2904	A2119 90y multi	1.75	.45
2905	A2119 110y multi	2.25	.55
2906	A2119 130y multi	2.50	.65
	Nos. 2904-2906 (3)	6.50	1.65

See listing of No. 4448 for images of each Hiroshige print.

Cultural Pioneers Type of 2003

Designs: No. 2907, Lafcadio Hearn (1850-1904), writer. No. 2908, Isamu Noguchi (1904-88), sculptor. No. 2909, Masao Koga (1904-78), composer.

Litho. & Engr.

2004, Nov. 4 ***Perf. 12¾x13***

2907	A2194 80y multi	1.50	.40
2908	A2194 80y multi	1.50	.40
2909	A2194 80y multi	1.50	.40
	Nos. 2907-2909 (3)	4.50	1.20

A2257

A2258

New Year 2005 (Year of the Cock)
A2259 A2260

2004, Nov. 15 Photo. *Perf. 13x13¼*

2910	A2257	50y multi	1.00	.30
2911	A2258	80y multi	1.50	.40

Photo. & Typo.

Perf. 13½x13¼

2912	A2259	50y +3y multi	1.25	.40
2913	A2260	80y +3y multi	1.75	.40
		Nos. 2910-2913 (4)	5.50	1.50

Sheets of two containing Nos. 2910-2911 were lottery prizes. Value, $2.75.

Miniature Sheet

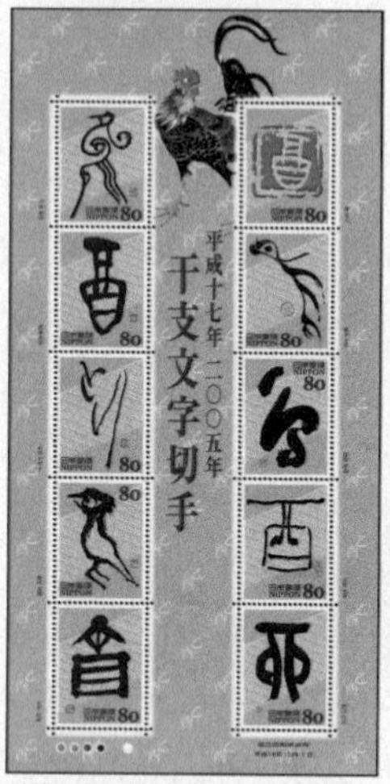

Eto Calligraphy — A2261

Word "tori" in: a, Tensho style. b, Kinbun style (red). c, Kinbun style (black). d, Pictographic tensho style. e, Kana style. f, Sousho style. g, Kobun style (denomination at UR). h, Reisho style. i, Koukotsumoji style. j, Kobun style (denomination at LR).

Photo. & Embossed

2004, Dec. 1 *Perf. 13*

2914	A2261	Sheet of 10	25.00	20.00
a.-j.		80y Any single	1.25	.50

"Japan Post" — A2261a

A2261b

A2261c

Rose — A2261d

A2261e

A2261f

Die Cut Perf. 12½

2004, Dec. 15 Photo.

Stamp + Label

Denomination Color

2914K	A2261a 80y rose	*3.00*	1.25
2914L	A2261a 80y blue	*3.00*	1.25
2914M	A2261b 80y lilac	*3.00*	2.00
2914N	A2261c 80y green	*3.00*	2.00
2914O	A2261d 80y rose	*3.00*	2.00
2914P	A2261e 80y gray	*3.00*	2.00
2914Q	A2261f 80y rose	*3.00*	2.00
	Nos. 2914K-2914Q (7)	21.00	12.50

Stamps and labels are separated by a line of rouletting. Labels could be personalized. Nos. 2914K-2914L were printed in sheets containing five of each stamp and 10 labels that sold for 1000y. Nos. 2914M-2914Q were printed in sheets of two of each stamp and 10 labels that sold for 1000y.

World Conference on Disaster Reduction — A2262

2005, Jan. 11 Photo. *Perf. 13*

2915	A2262	80y multi	1.50	.40

Opening of Chubu Natl. Airport — A2263

2005, Feb. 1

2916	A2263	80y multi	1.50	.40

Science, Technology and Animation

Time Bokan
A2264

Circular Loom
A2265

Bullet Train
A2266

Micromachines
A2267

International Space Station
A2268

Time Bokan
A2269

Time Bokan
A2270

Time Bokan
A2271

2005, Mar. 23 Photo. *Perf. 13x13¼*

2917	Vert. strip of 5	8.00	8.00
a.	A2264 80y multi	1.25	.50
b.	A2265 80y multi	1.25	.50
c.	A2266 80y multi	1.25	.50
d.	A2267 80y multi	1.25	.50
e.	A2268 80y multi	1.25	.50
	Sheet, 2 #2917	17.50	17.50
2918	Sheet, #2917b-2917e, 2 each #2918a-2918c	17.50	17.50
a.	A2269 80y multi	1.25	.50
b.	A2270 80y multi	1.25	.50
c.	A2271 80y multi	1.25	.50

Pokémon

Gonbe
A2272

Rayquaza
A2273

Mew
A2274

Rizadon
A2275

Pikachu — A2276

2005, June 23 Litho. *Perf. 13x13¼*

2919	Vert. strip of 5	6.50	6.50
a.	A2272 50y multi	.80	.50
b.	A2273 50y multi	.80	.50
c.	A2274 80y multi	1.25	.50
d.	A2275 80y multi	1.25	.50
e.	A2276 80y multi	1.25	.50
	Sheet, 2 #2919	22.00	20.00

Self-Adhesive

Booklet Stamps

2919F	A2272 50y multi	1.00	.50
i.	Booklet pane of 2	2.75	2.75
2919G	A2276 80y multi	1.25	.50
2919H	A2274 80y multi	1.25	.50
j.	Booklet pane, #2919G-2919H	3.00	3.00
	Complete booklet, #2919Fi, 2919Hj + 8 postal cards	14.00	

Complete booklet sold for 1000y.

Mobile Suit Gundam

Freedom Gundam and Kira Yamato
A2277

Justice Gundam and Athrun Zala
A2278

Gundam W — A2279

Hiiro — A2280

Kamille Bidan
A2281

Z Gundam
A2282

Zaku
A2283

Char Aznable
A2284

Amuro Ray
A2285

Gundam
A2286

2005, Aug. 1

2920	Sheet of 10	22.00	22.00
a.	A2277 50y multi	.80	.50
b.	A2278 50y multi	.80	.50
c.	A2279 50y multi	.80	.50
d.	A2280 50y multi	.80	.50
e.	A2281 80y multi	1.25	.50
f.	A2282 80y multi	1.25	.50
g.	A2283 80y multi	1.25	.50
h.	A2284 80y multi	1.25	.50
i.	A2285 80y multi	1.25	.50
j.	A2286 80y multi	1.25	.50

Expo 2005, Aichi
A2287

Designs: No. 2921, Earth and mammoth skull and tusks. No. 2922, Earth and mammoth.

2005, Mar. 25 Photo. *Perf. 13x13¼*

2921	80y multi	1.25	.45
2922	80y multi	1.25	.45
a.	A2287 Horiz. pair, #2921-2922	3.00	2.25

Daikei-shiyu-zu, by Jakuchu Itou — A2288

Perf. 12½x12¾ Syncopated

2005, Apr. 20

2923	A2288	80y multi	1.50	.45

Philately Week.

Rotary International, Cent. — A2289

2005, Apr. 28 Litho. *Perf. 12¾x13*

2924	A2289	80y multi	1.50	.40

Hodakadake
A2290

Hakusan-ichige
A2291

Yarigatake
A2292

Miyama-odamaki
A2293

2005, May 2 *Perf. 13¼*

2925	A2290 50y multi		.80	.30
2926	A2291 50y multi		.80	.30
2927	A2292 50y multi		.80	.30
2928	A2293 50y multi		.80	.30
a.	Horiz. strip of 4, #2925-2928		4.00	2.00

Japanese Alpine Club, cent.

Letter Writing Day — A2294

Designs: No. 2929, Owl on branch with envelope. No. 2930, Kuriko with letter. No. 2931, Squirrel with acorn. No. 2932, Rabbit and flowers.

No. 2933: a, Pigeon with pink letter. b, Donkichi in tree (round stamp). c, Castle and rainbow (oval stamp). d, Shochan with blue ski cap. e, Rabbit with pink letter (round stamp). f, Kuriko with flute on horse. g, Hime with bows in hair. h, Squirrel. i, Fox with letter (round stamp). j, Violets (oval stamp).

2005, July 22 **Photo.** *Perf. 13x13¼*

2929	A2294 50y multi	.80	.30
2930	A2294 50y multi	.80	.30
2931	A2294 50y multi	.80	.30
2932	A2294 50y multi	.80	.30
a.	Horiz. strip of 4, #2929-2932	4.00	2.00
2933	Sheet of 10	13.00	13.00
a.-j.	A2294 80y Any single	1.25	.50
k.	Booklet pane of 10, #2929-2932, 2 each #2933d, 2933f, 2933g	13.00	—
	Complete booklet, #2933k	14.00	
l.	Souvenir sheet, #2932, #2933d	2.75	2.75

Nos. 2933a, 2933h are 28x29mm, Nos. 2933b, 2933e, 2933i are 30mm in diameter; No. 2933c, 2933j are 28x40mm.

Poetry Collections — A2295

Poets: No. 2934, Ono no Komachi. No. 2935, Fujiwara no Teika.

2005, Sept. 1 **Litho.** *Perf. 12¾x13*

2934	80y multi	1.25	.45
2935	80y multi	1.25	.45
a.	A2295 Horiz. pair, #2934-2935	3.00	2.25

Kokin Wakashu, 1100th anniv. (No. 2934), Shinkokin Wakashu, 800th anniv. (No. 2935).

Intl Astronautics Congress, Fukuoka — A2296

Designs: No. 2936, Himawari-6 satellite. No. 2937, H-IIA rocket launch.

2005, Oct. 3

2936	80y multi	1.25	.50
2937	80y multi	1.25	.50
a.	A2296 Horiz. pair, #2934-2935	3.00	2.25

Intl. Letter Writing Week Type of 2000

Hiroshige paintings from 53 Stations of the Tokaido Highway: 90y, Mariko. 110y, Minakuchi. 130y, Shinagawa.

2005, Oct. 7 **Photo.** *Perf. 13¼*

2938	A2119 90y multi	1.75	.50
2939	A2119 110y multi	2.25	.50
2940	A2119 130y multi	2.50	.50
	Nos. 2938-2940 (3)	6.50	1.50

See listing of No. 4448 for images of each Hiroshige print.

Souvenir Sheets

A2297

Greetings Stamps — A2298

No. 2941: a, Cyclamen. b, Elf and flower. c, Bear and bird. d, Owl, gorilla playing banjo. e, Snowman.

No. 2942: a, Santa Claus. b, Poinsettias and candle. c, Angel with gift. d, Hamster and strawberries. e, Owl, cat playing drums.

Litho. With Foil Application
Serpentine Die Cut 13¼

2005, Oct. 21 **Self-Adhesive**

2941	A2297	Sheet of 5	6.00	6.00
a.-e.	50y Any single		.80	.80

Serpentine Die Cut 13¼x13½

2942	A2298	Sheet of 5	10.00	10.00
a.-e.	80y Any single		1.25	.80

A2299

A2300

New Year 2006 (Year of the Dog)
A2301 A2302

2005, Nov. 15 **Photo.** *Perf. 13x13¼*

2943	A2299 50y multi	1.00	.30
2944	A2300 80y multi	1.50	.40

Photo. & Typo.
Perf. 13¼

2945	A2301 50y +3y multi	1.25	.40
2946	A2302 80y +3y multi	1.75	.40
	Nos. 2943-2946 (4)	5.50	1.50

Sheets of two containing Nos. 2943-2944 were lottery prizes. Value, $2.75.

Miniature Sheet

Germany — Japan Exchange Year — A2303

No. 2947: a, Ludwig van Beethoven. b, Benz automobile. c, Meissen porcelain figurine of Japanese man playing drum. d, Meissen porcelain figurine of female musician. e, Meissen porcelain figurine of woman on circus horse. f, Meissen porcelain figurine of a harlequin.

2005, Dec. 1 **Photo.** *Perf. 13*

2947	A2303	Sheet of 10, #a-b, 2 each #c-f	16.00	16.00
a.-f.	80y Any single		1.25	.50

Miniature Sheet

Eto Calligraphy — A2304

Word "inu" in: a, Tensho style (connected lines). b, Kinbun style (on brown red panel). c, Pictograph (denomination at UL). d, Phonetic letters (2 lines unconnected, denomination at LR). e, Tensho style (2 red chops). f, Tensho style (blue half-circle). g, Symbolic characters (red). h, Semi-cursive style (red chop at L, denomination at LL). i, Semi-cursive style (oval chop in red at L). j, Koukotsumoji style (denomination at L, red chop at R).

Photo. & Embossed

2005, Dec. 1 *Perf. 13x13¼*

2948	A2304	Sheet of 10	16.00	16.00
a.-j.	80y Any single		1.25	.50

Animation

Galaxy Express 999
A2305

No. 2949: a, Tetsuro and Galaxy Express 999 in flight. b, Matael and passenger cars. c, Claire holding book. d, The Conductor. e, Freija and Matael. f, Tetsuro and Moriki Yutaka. g, Emeraldas and Count Mecha. h, Herlock. i, Matael and galaxy. j, Galaxy Express 999.

2006, Feb. 1 **Litho.** *Perf. 13x13¼*

2949	A2305	Sheet of 10	27.50	20.00
a.-j.	80y Any single		1.25	.50

Detective Conan
A2306

No. 2950: a, Conan in green jacket. b, Conan wearing glasses, with woman in light blue jacket. c, With Shinichi, scratching chins. d, Ran holding letter. e, Dr. Agasa, Ayumi, front of car. f, Mitushiko, Genta, rear of car. g, Haibara Ai. h, Conan with backpack. i, Mysterious Thief Kid. j, Shinichi and Conan, city in background.

2006, Apr. 3 **Litho.** *Perf. 13x13¼*

2950	A2306	Sheet of 10	22.50	20.00
a.-j.	80y Any single		1.25	.50

International Exchanges and Friendships — A2307

Designs: No. 2951, Rabbit and flowers. No. 2952, Children kissing. No. 2953, Bears and caught fish. No. 2954, Children's drawing of two animals. No. 2955, Chick, cat, dog, rabbit, squirrel and rocket.

2006, Mar. 1 **Photo.** *Perf. 13*

2951	A2307 80y multi	1.25	.50
2952	A2307 80y multi	1.25	.50
2953	A2307 80y multi	1.25	.50
2954	A2307 80y multi	1.25	.50
2955	A2307 80y multi	1.25	.50
a.	Vert. strip of 5, #2951-2955	8.50	5.00
	Sheet, 2 each #2951-2955	17.50	17.50

Morning Glories and Puppies, Door Painting by Okyu Maruyama — A2308

Designs: No. 2956, Morning glories. No. 2957, Puppies.

Perf. 13½x13 Syncopated

2006, Apr. 20 **Photo.**

2956	80y multi	1.25	.50
2957	80y multi	1.25	.50
a.	A2308 Horiz. pair, #2956-2957	4.00	2.00

Philately Week.

Miniature Sheet

Australia-Japan Year of Exchange — A2309

No. 2958: a, Australian flag, Ayers Rock. b, Kangaroo and Ayers Rock. c, Sydney Opera House. d, Australian flag and Sydney Opera House. e, Fish of Great Barrier Reef. f, Heart Reef. g, Golden wattle flowers. h, Bottlebrush flowers. i, Koalas. j, Kookaburra.

2006, May 23 Photo. *Perf. 13*

2958 A2309 Sheet of 10 16.00 16.00
a.-j. 80y Any single 1.25 .50

Miniature Sheet

Sacred Sites and Pilgrimage Routes of the Kii Mountains World Heritage Site — A2310

No. 2959: a, Kumano Hongu-Taisha Shrine Building 3 (brown roof, part of stairs seen at bottom). b, Kumano Hongu-Taisha Shrine Building 4 (brown roof, full set of stairs at LR). c, Great Waterfall of Nachi. d, Overhead view of Kumano Nachi-Taisha Shrine (denomination at LL). e, Nachi Fire Festival. f, Seigantoji Temple (dark blue roof). g, Kongobuji Temple (blue green roof). h, Wooden Kongara-Doji-Ryuzo (statue, denomination at UL). i, Kinpusenji Temple (gray roof). j, Wooden Zao-Gongen-Ryuzo (statue, denomination at LL).

2006, June 23 *Perf. 13x13¼*

2959 A2310 Sheet of 10 17.50 17.50
a.-j. 80y Any single 1.25 .50

Miniature Sheets

A2311

Greetings Stamps — A2312

No. 2960: a, Fairy and flower. b, Church bell. c, Flower bouquet and ribbons. d, Dolphin. e, Hibiscus and hummingbird.

No. 2961: a, Pink cattleya orchid. b, Fairy, flowers and trees. c, Flower and oranges. d, Parrot and flowers. e, Fairy with pail and orange flowers.

Litho. With Foil Application
Serpentine Die Cut 13¼

2006, June 30 Self-Adhesive

2960 A2311 Sheet of 5 6.00 6.00
a.-e. 50y Any single .80 .80

Serpentine Die Cut 13½

2961 A2312 Sheet of 5 10.00 10.00
a.-e. 80y Any single 1.25 .80

No. 2960 sold for 300y; No. 2961 for 500y.

Taifu Iseno, Poet A2313

Sadaijin Gotokudaijino, Poet A2314

Mitsune Ooshikochino, Poet A2315

Akahito Yamabeno, Poet A2316

Naishi Suono, Poet — A2317

Poets and Poetry A2318

No. 2963: a, Double Cherry Blossoms, by Yasuko Koyama. b, Iseno and poetry. c, Pale Morning Moon, by Keiso Mitsuoka. d, Gotokudaijino and poetry. e, White Chrysanthemum, by Shiko Miyazaki. f, Ooshikochino and poetry. g, Mt. Fuji, by Eiko Matsumoto. h, Yamabeno and poetry. i, Spring Night, by Soshu Miyake. j, Suono and poetry.

2006, July 21 Photo. *Perf. 13¼*

2962 Vert. strip of 5 5.00 3.50
a. A2313 50y multi .80 .30
b. A2314 50y multi .80 .30
c. A2315 50y multi .80 .30
d. A2316 50y multi .80 .30
e. A2317 50y multi .80 .30
Sheet, 2 #2962 13.00 13.00

Perf. 13

2963 A2318 Sheet of 10 16.00 16.00
a.-j. 80y Any single 1.25 .50

Letter Writing Day.

Horizontal Lines and Colored Circles — A2318a

Die Cut Perf. 13¼

2006, Sept. 1 Litho.

Self-Adhesive

2963K A2318a 80y multi 1.50 .50

Printed in sheets of 10 that sold for 1000y. Value, $22.50. The image portion could be personalized. The image shown is a generic image.

Blue Flowers — A2318b

Pink Flowers — A2318c

Die Cut Perf. 13¼

2006, Sept. 1 Litho.

Self-Adhesive

2963L A2318b 80y multi 1.25 .50
2963M A2318c 80y multi 1.25 .50

Nos. 2963L-2963M were printed in sheets of 10, containing five of each stamp, that sold for 1000y. Value, $22.50. The image portions could be personalized. The images shown are generic images.

Accession to the United Nations, 50th Anniv. A2319

Paintings by Toshiro Sawanuki: 90y, Glorious World To Come. 110y, Eternity.

2006, Sept. 29 Litho. *Perf. 13¾x14*

2964 A2319 90y multi 1.75 .50
2965 A2319 110y multi 2.25 .50

Miniature Sheet

Greetings — A2320

No. 2966: a, Mokara Lion's Gold orchid. b, Renanthera Singaporean orchid. c, Vanda Miss Joaquim orchid. d, Vanda Mimi Palmer orchid. e, Hollyhocks and Egret, by Hoitsu Sakai, horiz. f, Irises and Moorhens, by Sakai, horiz.

Litho. With Foil Application

2006, Oct. 3 *Die Cut Perf. 13½x13¾*

Self-Adhesive

2966 A2320 Sheet of 6 10.00 *10.00*
a.-b. 50y Either single .80 .80
c.-d. 80y Either single 1.25 .80
e. 90y multi 1.40 .80
f. 110y multi 1.75 .80

Roulettes separate adjacent 50y and 80y stamps. No. 2966 sold for 500y. See Singapore Nos. 1225-1231.

Miniature Sheets

A2321

Scenes From Japanese Movies — A2322

No. 2967: a, Tange Sazen (scarred samurai, green). b, Carmen Kokyo-Ni-Kaeru (women waving, lilac). c, Ugetsu Monogatari (man and woman, maroon). d, Tokyo Monogatari (man and woman, brown). e, Shichinin-No-Samurai (helmeted samurai, deep green). f, Hawaii-No-Yoru (man and woman, olive green). g, Nemuri Kyoshiro (samurai, blue green). h, Guitar-Wo-Motta-Wataridori (man with guitar, blue). i, Miyamoto Musashi (swordsman, blue gray). j, Cupola-No-Aru-Machi (girl, brown).

No. 2968: a, Sailor-Fuku-To-Kikanju (woman with gun). b, Otoko-Ha-Tsuraiyo (man in light blue kimono). c, Kamata Koshin Kyoku (Three people). d, Yomigaeru Kinro (man in chair). e, Setouchi-Shonen-Yakyu-Dan (woman with baseball glove). f, HANA-BI (man standing). g, Shitsurakuen (Woman hugging man). h, Gamera (monster, denomination at UL). i, Tasogare Seibei (woman grooming man). j, Godzilla (monster, denomination at UR).

2006, Oct. 10 Photo. *Perf. 13*

2967 A2321 Sheet of 10 17.50 17.50
a.-j. 80y Any single 1.25 .50
2968 A2322 Sheet of 10 17.50 17.50
a.-j. 80y Any single 1.25 .50

Ikebana International Ninth World Convention A2323

2006, Oct. 23 Litho. *Perf. 13x13¼*

Background Colors

2969 80y grn & lt grn 1.25 .50
2970 80y red & yel 1.25 .50
a. A2323 Pair, #2969-2970 3.00 2.00

A2324

A2325

New Year 2007 (Year of the Pig)
A2326 A2327

2006, Nov. 1 Photo. *Perf. 13x13¼*

2971	A2324	50y multi	1.00	.30
2972	A2325	80y multi	1.50	.40

Photo. & Typo.

Perf. 13¼

2973	A2326	50y +3y multi	1.25	.40
2974	A2327	80y +3y multi	1.75	.40
		Nos. 2971-2974 (4)	5.50	1.50

Sheets of two containing Nos. 2971-2972 were lottery prizes. Value, $3.

New Year Greetings — A2327a

Inscribed "'07 New Year" Stamp + Label Panel Color

2006, Nov. 1 Photo. *Perf. 13¼*

2974A	A2327a	50y blue	1.50	1.50
2974B	A2327a	50y red violet	1.50	1.50
c.		Pair, #2974A-2974B + 2 labels	3.50	3.50

Labels could be personalized.
See Nos. 3010P-3010Q, 3074-3075.

Miniature Sheets

A2328

Greetings Stamps — A2329

No. 2975: a, Squirrel in mug. b, Bell with flowers. c, Clown with flower. d, Skating polar bear. e, Bear in Santa Claus suit, guitar, birds.

No. 2976: a, Cat in Santa Claus suit ringing bell. b, Fairy and cyclamen. c, Snowman with gift. d, Reindeer and star. e, Floral wreath.

Litho. with Foil Application
Die Cut Perf. 13½x13¼

2006, Nov. 24 Self-Adhesive

2975	A2328	Sheet of 5	6.00	6.00
a.-e.		50y Any single	.80	.80

Die Cut Perf. 13

2976	A2329	Sheet of 5	10.00	10.00
a.-e.		80y Any single	.80	.80

No. 2975 sold for 300y; No. 2976 for 500y.

Miniature Sheet

Eto Calligraphy — A2330

No. 2977: a, Semicursive style (white background, red chop at lower left). b, Kinbun style (blue background). c, Reisho style (red background). d, Japanese cursive syllabary (white background, red chop at lower right, character with small arc at top). e, Kinbun style (white background, red chop at lower right, character with funnel-shaped line at top). f, Kinbun style (red character). g, Kinbun style (white background, red chop at lower left, character with flat line at top. h, Kinbun style (white background. red chop at lower right, character with large blotch at top). i, Tensho style (white background, red chop at lower left, character with long curved arc and circle at top) j, Reisho style (white background, red chop at lower right, character with dot and straight line at top).

Litho. & Embossed

2006, Dec. 1 *Perf. 13x13¼*

2977	A2330	Sheet of 10	17.50	17.50
a.-j.		80y Any single	1.25	.50

Miniature Sheet

A2331

Japanese Antarctic Research Expeditions, 50th Anniv. — A2332

No. 2978: a, Observation ship Fuji. b, Spotter plane. c, Adult emperor penguin and chick. d, Adult emperor penguins and five chicks. e, Observation ship Soya and Adelie penguins. f, Adult Adelie penguins and chick. g, Dog, Jiro, in snow, dog team. h, Dog, Taro, standing, dog sled. i, Scientist, observation ship Shirase. j, Snowmobile with cabin.

No. 2979: a, Snowmobile with cabin (26x28mm). b, Spotter plane (28mm diameter). c, Soya and dog sled (34x26mm). d, Weddell seal (28x23mm ellipse). e, Head of emperor penguin (26x37mm oval). f, Two Adelie penguins (26x28mm). g, Dog, Taro, standing with mouth open (28mm diameter). h, Emperor penguin chicks (28mm diameter). i, Adult emperor penguin and chick (26x28mm). j, Dog, Jiro, in snow (26x37mm oval).

2007, Jan. 23 Litho. *Perf. 13*

2978	A2331	Sheet of 10	16.50	16.50
a.-j.		80y Any single	1.25	.40

Self-Adhesive

Die Cut Perf. 13¾x13½

2979	A2332	Sheet of 10	20.00	20.00
a.-j.		80y Any single	1.25	.55

Animation
Miniature Sheet

Neon Genesis Evangelion — A2333

No. 2980: a, Evangelion Unit 01. b, Shinji Ikari. c, Rei Ayanami. d, Evangelion Unit 00. e, Soryu Asuka Langley. f, Evangelion Unit 02. g, Rei Ayanami and Soryu Asuka Langley. h, Misato Katsuragi. i, Kawora Nagisa. j, Sachiel, the third angel.

2007, Feb. 23 *Perf. 13x13¼*

2980	A2333	Sheet of 10	22.50	22.50
a.-j.		80y Any single	1.25	.50

Animation
Miniature Sheet

Future Boy Conan A2334

No. 2981: a, Conan (with name). b, Lana (with name). c, Lana (without name). d, Conan (without name). e, Monsley and airplane. f, Lepka. g, Jimsy and Umaso. h, Dyce on running robot. i, Dr. Lao and hovering craft. j, Grandpa.

2007, June 22 Litho. *Perf. 13x13¼*

2981	A2334	Sheet of 10	16.50	16.50
a.-j.		80y Any single	1.25	.50

World Heritage Sites
Miniature Sheet

Sacred Sites and Pilgrimage Routes of the Kii Mountains World Heritage Site — A2335

No. 2982: a, Yoshino Mikumari Shrine, cherry blossoms at left. b, Pictoral and rope decoration at Yoshino Mikumari shrine. c, Omine-Okugake-Michi trail. d, Kumano Hayatama-Taisha Shrine (black-roofed building with red trim). e, Kumano Hayatama-Taisha Shrine, diff. f, Wooden icon of Kumano-Fusumino-Okami-Zazo. g, Cherry trees in bloom at Kumano Sankei-Michi Nakahechi. h, Stone sculpture of Emperor Kazan riding ox and horse. i, Kongo-Sanmaiin Temple. j, Steps to Kong-Sanmaiin Temple.

2007, Mar. 23 Photo. *Perf. 13x13¼*

2982	A2335	Sheet of 10	16.50	16.50
a.-j.		80y Any single	1.25	.50

World Heritage Sites
Miniature Sheet

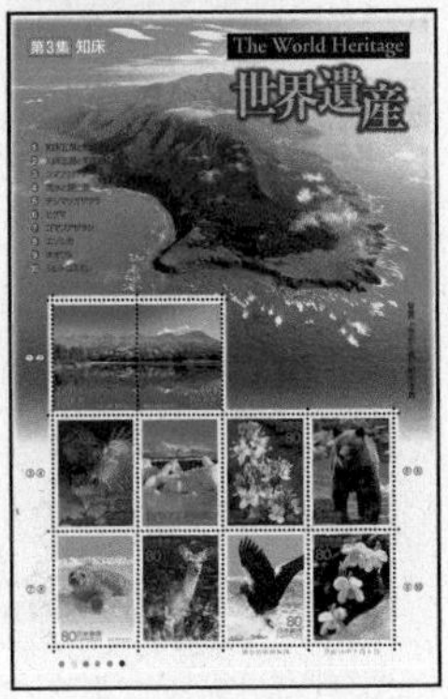

Shiretoko World Heritage Site A2336

No. 2983: a, Lake and mountain, cloudless sky. b, Lake and mountain, cloud in sky. c, Blakiston's fish owl. d, Sea ice, Mt. Rausu. e, Cherry blossoms. f, Brown bear. g, Harbor seal. h, Ezo deer. i, Sea eagle. j, Shiretoko violets (white and yellow flowers).

2007, July 6 Photo. *Perf. 13x13¼*

2983	A2336	Sheet of 10	16.50	16.50
a.-j.		80y Any single	1.25	.50

Sleeping Boar, by Ippo Mori — A2337

Boar Loping Across Fields, by Mori — A2338

Sparrow, by Mori — A2339

Cherry Blossoms, by Mori — A2340

Bird Flock, by Mori — A2341

Great Tits Sitting In a Japanese Bush Clover, by Mori — A2342

Perf. 13¼x13 Syncopated

2007, Apr. 20 **Photo.**

2984	A2337 80y multi		1.25	.50
2985	A2338 80y multi		1.25	.50
a.	Horiz. pair, #2984-2985		3.00	2.00
	Sheet, 5 #2985a		16.00	16.00
2986	A2339 80y multi		1.25	.50
2987	A2340 80y multi		1.25	.50
2988	A2341 80y multi		1.25	.50
2989	A2342 80y multi		1.25	.50
a.	Vert. strip of 4, #2986-2989		7.50	4.00
	Sheet, 2 each #2985-2989		16.00	16.00
	Nos. 2984-2989 (6)		7.50	3.00

Miniature Sheet

Japan - India Friendship Year — A2343

No. 2990: a, Taj Mahal. b, Taj Mahal and camels. c, Bengal tiger. d, Peacock. e, Buddhist monastery, Sanchi, India. f, Statue of goddess, Sanchi. g, Painting of Indian woman facing left. h, Calico print of Indian facing right. i, Indian folk dancer. j, Character from Kathakali, Indian dance drama.

2007, May 23 ***Perf. 13***

2990	A2343	Sheet of 10	16.00	16.00
a.-j.		80y Any single	1.25	.50

Tsurayuki Kino, Poet — A2344

Empress Jito, Poet — A2345

Dayu Sarumaru, Poet — A2346

Kanemasa Minamotono, Poet — A2347

Sanuki Nijoinno, Poet — A2348

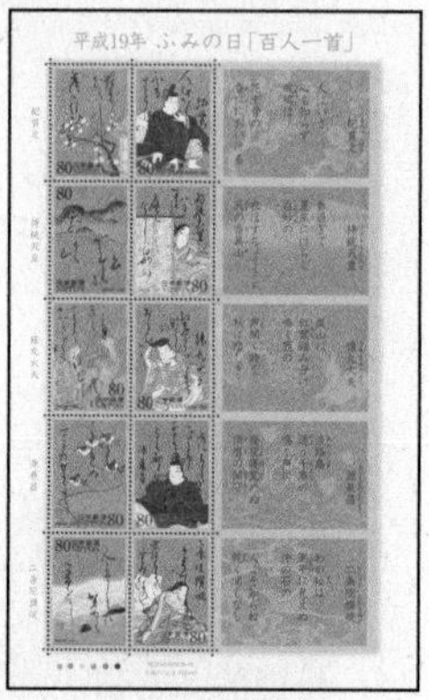

Poetry A2349

No. 2996 — Poetry in Japanese calligraphy and: a, Plum blossoms. b, Tsurayuki Kino. c, Mount Kagu. d, Empress Jito. e, Deer. f, Dayu Sarumaru. g, Plovers. h, Kanemasa Minamotono. i, Stone in sea. j, Sanuki Nijoinno.

2007, July 23 **Photo.** ***Perf. 13½***

2991	A2344 50y multi		.80	.30
2992	A2345 50y multi		.80	.30
2993	A2346 50y multi		.80	.30
2994	A2347 50y multi		.80	.30
2995	A2348 50y multi		.80	.30
a.	Vert. strip of 5, #2991-2995		5.75	4.00

Perf. 13

2996	A2349	Sheet of 10	16.50	16.50
a.-j.		80y Any single	1.25	.50

Letter Writing Day.

Miniature Sheet

11th World Track and Field Championships, Osaka — A2350

No. 2997: a, Dai Tamesue (athlete 545), hurdler. b, Kumiko Ikeda (athlete 426), sprinter. c, Yuzo Kanemaru (athlete 300), runner. d, Shingo Suetsugu (athlete 526), runner. e, Kayoko Fukushi (athlete 422), runner. f, Masato Naito running over hurdle. g, Naoyuki Daigo high jumping. h, Kenji Narisako (athlete 531), hurdler. i, Daichi Sawano pole vaulting. j, Koji Murofushi (athlete 774), hammer throw.

2007, Aug. 23 **Litho.** ***Perf. 13x13¼***

2997	A2350	Sheet of 10	16.50	16.50
a.-j.		80y Any single	1.25	.50

Miniature Sheet

Diplomatic Relations Between Japan and Thailand, 120th Anniv. — A2351

No. 2998: a, Maple leaves, bamboo. b, Cherry blossoms. c, Ratchaphruek (yellow flower) blossom. d, Rhynchostylis gigantea (purple and white orchids). e, Mother-of-pearl elephant. f, Mother-of-pearl flower. g, Thai dancer. h, Statue, Wat Phra Keo. i, Elephant with head at left, from Toshogu Shrine, Japan, horiz. j, Elephant with head at right, from Toshogu Shrine, horiz.

Die Cut Perf. and Serpentine Die Cut

2007, Sept. 26 **Litho.**

Self-Adhesive

2998	A2351	Sheet of 10	16.50	16.50
a.-j.		80y Any single	1.25	.50

Vertical stamps are die cut perf. 13 at top and bottom, serpentine die cut 10¼ on side adjacent to another stamp, and die cut perf. 12½ on remaining side. Horizontal stamps are die cut perf. 13 at top and bottom, serpentine die cut 10¼ on side adjacent to another stamp, and die cut perf. 12¾ on remaining side.

See Thailand No. 2316.

International Letter Writing Week Type of 2000

Hiroshige paintings from 53 Stations of the Tokaido Highway: 90y, Hodogaya. 110y, Arai. 130y, Kusatsu.

2007, Sept. 28 **Litho.** ***Perf. 14***

2999	A2119 90y multi		1.75	.50
3000	A2119 110y multi		2.25	.50
3001	A2119 130y multi		2.50	.50
	Nos. 2999-3001 (3)		6.50	1.50

See listing of No. 4448 for images of each Hiroshige print.

Mandarin Duck A2352

Eastern Turtle Dove A2353

2007, Oct. 1 **Photo.** ***Perf. 13x13½***

3002	A2352 50y multi		1.50	.30
3003	A2353 80y multi		1.60	.30

See No. 3281.

Miniature Sheets

A2354

Establishment of Japan Post Corporation — A2355

No. 3004: a, Baron Hisoka Maejima (red panels). b, Japan #2 (red panels). c, Post office counter (orange panels). d, Postal workers loading mail coach (dark red panels). e, Postal saving counter (green panels). f, People at post office counters (blue panels).

No. 3005 — Paintings of flowers: a, Sunflower, by Hoitsu Sakai. b, Confederate Roses, by Sakai. c, Chrysanthemums, by Sakai. d, Maple Leaves, by Kiitsu Suzuki (showing branch). e, Maple Leaves, by Suzuki (no branch). f, Camellia, by Sakai. g, Cherry Tree, by Sakai (bird in tree). h, Tree Peony, by Sakai. i, Iris, by Sakai, j, Hydrangeas, by Sakai.

2007, Oct. 1 **Photo.** ***Perf. 13¼***

3004	A2354	Sheet of 10, #a-b, 2 each #c-f	16.50	16.50
a.-f.		80y Any single	1.25	.50
3005	A2355	Sheet of 10	16.50	16.50
a.-j.		80y Any single	1.25	.50

Miniature Sheet

Intl. Skills Festival For All A2356

No. 3006: a, Computer operator and robot. b, Computer operator. c, Plasterer and Geisha. d, Plasterer and pillar. e, Pastry chef and cake. f, Pastry chef and bowls. g, Flower arranger and flowers. h, Flower arranger holding scissors. i, Sheet metal worker and automobile. j, Sheet metal worker hammering metal.

2007, Oct. 23 **Litho.** ***Perf. 13***

3006	A2356	Sheet of 10	16.00	16.00
a.-j.		80y Any single	1.25	.50

A2357

A2358

New Year 2008 (Year of the Rat)

A2359 A2360

2007, Nov. 1 **Photo.** ***Perf. 13x13½***

3007	A2357 50y multi		1.00	.30
3008	A2358 80y multi		1.50	.40

Photo. & Typo.

Perf. 13¼

3009	A2359 50y +3y multi		1.25	.40
3010	A2360 80y +3y multi		1.40	.40
	Nos. 3007-3010 (4)		5.15	1.50

Sheets of two containing stamps similar to Nos. 3009-3010 were lottery prizes. Value, $4.

Diamonds — A2360a

Diamonds — A2360b

Diamonds — A2360c

Diamonds — A2360d

Die Cut Perf. 13¼

2007, Nov. 1 Litho.

Self-Adhesive

Green Diamonds

Color of Country Name

3010A	A2360a	50y	blue	*3.50*	*3.50*
3010B	A2360a	50y	green	*3.50*	*3.50*
3010C	A2360a	50y	red	*3.50*	*3.50*
3010D	A2360a	50y	purple	*3.50*	*3.50*
3010E	A2360a	50y	black	*3.50*	*3.50*

Blue Diamonds

3010F	A2360a	80y	blue	*4.00*	*4.00*
3010G	A2360a	80y	green	*4.00*	*4.00*
3010H	A2360a	80y	red	*4.00*	*4.00*
3010I	A2360a	80y	purple	*4.00*	*4.00*
3010J	A2360a	80y	black	*4.00*	*4.00*

Blue Diamonds

Color of Country Name

3010L	A2360b	80y	dk blue	—	—
3010M	A2360b	80y	brt grn	—	—
3010N	A2360b	80y	orange	—	—
3010O	A2360b	80y	red violet	—	—
3010S	A2360c	80y	blue, country name at LR	—	—
3010T	A2360d	80y	blue, country name at LL	—	—
u.	Sheet of 10, #3010S, 3010T, 2 each #3010L-3010O			—	

Nos. 3010A-3010E were printed in sheets of 10, containing two of each stamp, that sold for 900y. Nos. 3010F-3010J were printed in sheets of 10, containing two of each stamp, that sold for 1200y. The image portion could be personalized. The image shown is a generic image.

The image portions of Nos. 3010L-3010o, 3010S-3010T could be personalized.

New Year Greetings Type of 2006 Inscribed "'08 New Year" Stamp + Label Panel Color

2007, Nov. 1 Photo. *Perf. 13¼*

3010P	A2327a	50y	red violet	1.50	1.00
3010Q	A2327a	50y	orange	1.50	1.00
r.	Pair, #3010P-3010Q + 2 labels			4.00	4.00

Labels could be personalized.

Miniature Sheets

A2361

Greetings Stamps — A2362

No. 3011: a, White buildings. b, Fairies on flying swans. c, Santa Claus. d, Flowers and snow-covered trees. e, Cat and candy cane.

No. 3012: a, Santa Claus and reindeer. b, Fairy and flowers. c, Snowman with green cap. d, Strawberries. e, Snowman and flying reindeer.

2007, Nov. 26 Litho. *Die Cut Perf.*

Self-Adhesive

3011	A2361 Sheet of 5		6.00	6.00
a.-e.	50y Any single		.80	.80

Die Cut Perf. 13

3012	A2362 Sheet of 5		10.00	10.00
a.-e.	80y Any single		1.25	.80

Miniature Sheet

Edo Calligraphy — A2363

No. 3013 — Charcters for "rat": a, In Kinbun style (red character). b, Black character with three long vertical lines at top, with red chop at LR. c, In Tensho style (gold character on red and brown background). d, In Reisho style (black character resembling a "3" with line through it, with red chop at LR). e, In Shoden style (gold character on blue and pink background). f, In Kana style (black characters resembling "12" with a check mark, with red chop at LR). g, In Reisho style (black characters, with red chop at LL). h, In Sosho style (black character with pink lines, with red chop at LL). i, Black character resembling stick figure with raised arms, with red chop at LR. j, In Kinbun style (black character with five short vertical lines at top, red chop at LL).

Litho. & Embossed

2007, Dec. 3 *Perf. 13*

3013	A2363 Sheet of 10		16.00	16.00
a.-j.	80y Any single		1.25	.50

Mt. Fuji — A2364

Mt. Fuji — A2365

Mt. Fuji — A2366

Mt. Fuji — A2367

Mt. Fuji — A2368

Bamboo A2369

Someiyoshino Blossoms A2370

Hydrangea Blossoms A2371

Maple Leaves A2372

Narcissuses A2373

2008, Jan. 23 Litho. *Perf. 13¾x14*

3014	Sheet of 10	17.50	17.50
a.	A2364 80y multi	1.25	.50
b.	A2365 80y multi	1.25	.50
c.	A2366 80y multi	1.25	.50
d.	A2367 80y multi	1.25	.50
e.	A2368 80y multi	1.25	.50
f.	A2369 80y multi	1.25	.50
g.	A2370 80y multi	1.25	.50
h.	A2371 80y multi	1.25	.50
i.	A2372 80y multi	1.25	.50
j.	A2373 80y multi	1.25	.50

Yokoso! Japan Weeks.

Souvenir Sheet

New Year 2008 (Year of the Rat) A2374

No. 3015: a, Two rats. b, One rat.

2008, Jan. 28 Photo. *Perf. 13*

3015	A2374 Sheet of 2	2.50	2.50
a.	50y multi	.90	.45
b.	80y multi	1.25	.50

Miniature Sheet

Animated Folktales — A2375

No. 3016: a, Man on horse, cherry trees, pagoda. b, Man in cherry tree. c, Moon Princess in bamboo stump, woodsman with ax. d, Moon Princess, flying horse and wagon, archers. e, Four statues in snow. f, Two statues in snow, man with basket. g, Boy in ship. h, Demons. i, Woman carrying roll of cloth. j, Man, woman, crane.

2008, Feb. 22 Litho. *Perf. 13*

3016	A2375 Sheet of 10	16.00	16.00
a.-j.	80y Any single	1.25	.50

Folktales "The Old Man Who Made Cherry Trees Blossom" (No. 3016a-3016b), "The Moon Princess" (Nos. 3016c-3016d), "Six Little Statues" (Nos. 3016e-3016f), "The Peach Boy" (NOs. 3016g-3016h), "The Grateful Crane" (Nos. 3016i-3016j).

Miniature Sheet

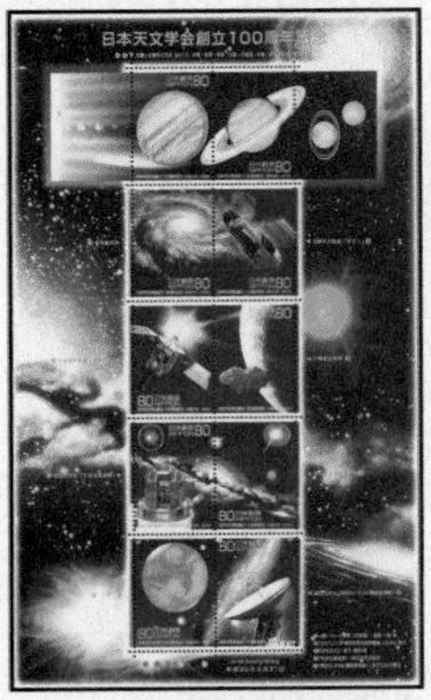
Astronomical Society of Japan, Cent. — A2376

No. 3017: a, Jupiter. b, Saturn. c, Spiral galaxy. d, Suzaku X-ray satellite. e, Hayabusa probe. f, Asteroids and Earth. g, Subaru Telescope. h, Stars. i, Mars. j, Nobeyama Radio Telescope.

2008, Mar. 21

3017	A2376 Sheet of 10	17.50	17.50
a.-j.	80y Any single	1.25	.50

Miniature Sheet

Diplomatic Relations Between Japan and Indonesia, 50th Anniv. — A2377

No. 3018: a, Kelimutu Volcano, Indonesia. b, Mt. Fuji, Japan, and cherry blossoms. c, Borobudur, Indonesia. d, Toji Temple, Kyoto. e, Rafflesia arnoldii. f, Cherry blossoms. g, Angklung (Indonesian musical instrument). h, Gaku biwa (Japanese musical instrument). i, Red arowana fish, horiz. j, Three koi, horiz.

2008, June 23 Photo. *Perf. 13*

3018	A2377 Sheet of 10	15.00	15.00
a.-j.	80y Any single	1.25	.50

See Indonesia Nos. 2135-2139.

Small Bird in Cherry Blossom, by Seitei Watanabe A2378

Butterfly in Peony Branch, by Watanabe A2379

Egrets in the Rain Beneath Willow Trees, by Watanabe A2380

Grapes, by Watanabe A2381

Sea Birds on a Rocky Crag, by Watanabe — A2382

Perf. 13½x13 Syncopated

2008, Apr. 18				**Photo.**	
3019	A2378	80y	multi	1.25	.50
3020	A2379	80y	multi	1.25	.50
3021	A2380	80y	multi	1.25	.50
3022	A2381	80y	multi	1.25	.50
3023	A2382	80y	multi	1.25	.50
a.	Vert. strip of 5, #3019-3023			7.50	7.50
	Sheet, 2 #3023a			15.00	15.00

Philately Week.

See note after No. Z827 in the Prefecture Stamp listings.

Miniature Sheet

Home Towns A2383

No. 3024 — Paintings by Taiji Harada of views of towns: a, Water Shield (Yamamoto District, Akita prefecture). b, Bell of Time (Kawago, Saitama prefecture). c, Enjoying the Evening Cool (Gujo, Gifu prefecture). d, The Little Electric Train (Choshi, Chiba prefecture). e, Sea of the Heart (Shozu District, Kagawa prefecture). f, Lake in the Evening Sun (Gamo District, Shiga prefecture). g, Tanabata Dolls (Matsumoto, Nagano prefecture). h, Town of Outdoor Warehouses (Ise, Mie prefecture). i, The Farm Clock (Aki, Kochi prefecture). j, Late Summer Heat in the Street (Hakusan, Ishikawa prefecture).

2008, May 2		**Photo.**	***Perf. 13***	
3024	A2383	Sheet of 10	16.00	16.00
a.-j.	80y Any single		1.25	.50

Hideyo Noguchi Africa Prize A2384

2008, May 23		**Litho.**	***Perf. 13***	
3025	80y	Noguchi	1.25	.50
3026	80y	Map of Africa	1.25	.50
a.	A2384	Horiz. pair, #3025-3026	3.00	2.00

Miniature Sheet

National Afforestation Campaign — A2385

No. 3027 — Scenes from Akita prefecture: a, Aleutian avens and Mt. Moriyoshi, denomination at UL. b, Aleutian avens and Mt. Moriyoshi, denomination at UR. c, Fringed galax flowers, denomination at LL. d, Fringed galax flowers, denomination at LR. e, Autumn leaves, denomination at LL. f, Autumn leaves, denomination at UR. g, Beech forest in autumn, denomination in UL. h, Beech forest in autumn, denomination in UR. i, Weigela. j, Waterfall.

2008, June 13		**Photo.**	***Perf. 13***	
3027	A2385	Sheet of 10	8.00	5.00
a.-j.	50y Any single		.80	.40

Miniature Sheet

Year of Exchange Between Japan and Brazil — A2386

No. 3028: a, Roasted coffee beans, seal of Brazilian vice-consulate in Kobe. b, Coffee cherries, ship. c, Christ the Redeemer Statue, Rio de Janeiro. d, Sugarloaf Mountain, Rio de Janeiro. e, Iguaçu Falls, denomination at UL. f, Iguaçu Falls, denomination at UR. g, Houses, denomination at LL. h, Houses, denomination at LR. i, Butterflies. j, Toucan.

2008, June 18		**Litho.**	***Perf. 13***	
3028	A2386	Sheet of 10	16.00	16.00
a.-j.	80y Any single		1.25	.50

See Brazil No. 3051.

Miniature Sheet

Publication of *Anne of Green Gables,* by Lucy Maud Montgomery, Cent. — A2387

No. 3029: a, Anne holding buttercups. b, Green Gables House. c, Matthew Cuthbert, wearing hat, vert. d, Marilla Cuthbert, wearing hat, vert. e, Anne, Diana Barry holding hands, vert. f, Diana, vert. g, Anne in black dress, vert. h, Anne and Gilbert Blythe, vert. i, Matthew Cuthbert, without hat, vert. j, Anne, Marilla Cuthbert, vert.

Perf. 13¼x13 (#3029a-3029b), 13x13¼

2008, June 20				
3029	A2387	Sheet of 10	12.00	12.00
a.-j.	80y Any single		1.25	.50

See Canada Nos. 2276-2278.

Lily A2388

Rugosa Rose A2389

Rhododendron A2390

Safflower A2391

Gentian A2392

Lily A2393

Rugosa Rose A2394

Rhododendron A2395

Safflower A2396

Gentian A2397

2008, July 1		**Photo.**		***Perf. 13¼***	
3030	A2388	50y	multi	.80	.40
3031	A2389	50y	multi	.80	.40
3032	A2390	50y	multi	.80	.40
3033	A2391	50y	multi	.80	.40
3034	A2392	50y	multi	.80	.40
a.	Vert. strip of 5, #3030-3034			4.50	3.00
3035	A2393	80y	multi	1.25	.60
3036	A2394	80y	multi	1.25	.60
3037	A2395	80y	multi	1.25	.60
3038	A2396	80y	multi	1.25	.60
3039	A2397	80y	multi	1.25	.60
a.	Vert. strip of 5, #3035-3039			6.50	4.00
	Nos. 3030-3039 (10)			10.25	5.00

Flowers of Kanagawa, Hokkaido, Fukushima, Yamagata and Nagano prefectures.

Miniature Sheet

Hokkaido Local Autonomy Law, 60th Anniv. — A2398

No. 3040: a, Lake Toya, cranes (32x39mm). b, Goryokaku Fortress (28x33mm). c, Hills around Biei (28x33mm). d, Sea angel (28x33mm). e, Otaru Canal (28x33mm).

2008, July 1	***Perf. 13¼ (#3040a), 13***			
3040	A2398	Sheet of 5	6.50	3.50
a.-e.	80y Any single		1.25	.55

Miniature Sheet

G8 Summit, Toyako A2399

No. 3041: a, Mt. Yotei (stamp 1). b, Showa Shinzan (stamp 2). c, Mt. Yotei and Lake Toya (stamp 3). d, Mt. Yotei and Fukidashi Park (stamp 4). e, Mt. Eniwa and Lake Shikotsu (stamp 5). f, Pink Japanese wood poppies (stamp 6). g, Squirrel (stamp 7). h, Beardtongue flowers (stamp 8). i, Mountain ash leaves and berries (stamp 9). j, Northern fox (stamp 10).

2008, July 7		**Litho.**	***Perf. 13¾x14***	
3041	A2399	Sheet of 10	16.00	16.00
a.-j.	80y Any single		1.25	.50

Lady Shikibu Murasaki, Poet A2400

Sanekata Fujiwara, Poet A2401

Lady Shonagon Sei, Poet A2402

Kinto Dainagon, Poet A2403

Lady Shikibu Izumi, Poet — A2404

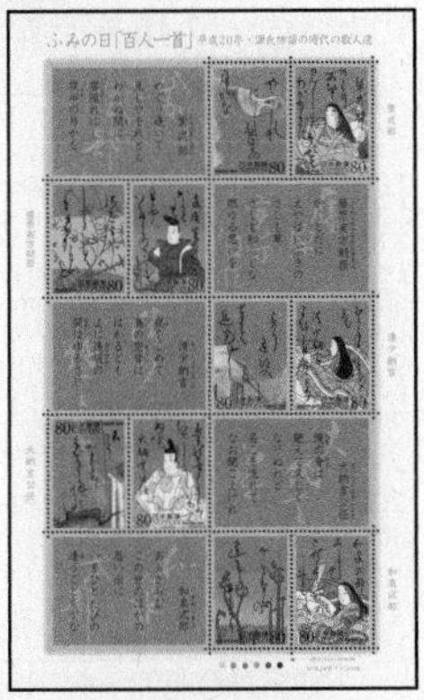
Poetry A2405

No. 3047 — Poetry in Japanese calligraphy and: a, Moon behind cloud. b, Lady Shikibu Murasaki. c, Mugwort. d, Sanekata Fujiwara. e, Waterfall. f, Lady Shonagon Sei. g, Barrier. h, Kinto Dainagon. i, Bare branches. j, Lady Shikibu Izumi.

2008, July 23 Photo. *Perf. 13¼*

3042	A2400	50y multi	.80	.30
3043	A2401	50y multi	.80	.30
3044	A2402	50y multi	.80	.30
3045	A2403	50y multi	.80	.30
3046	A2404	50y multi	.80	.30
a.		Vert. strip of 5, #3042-3046	5.00	5.00

Perf. 12¾x13

3047	A2405	Sheet of 10	16.00	16.00
a.-j.		80y Any single	1.25	.55

Letter Writing Day.

Miniature Sheets

A2406

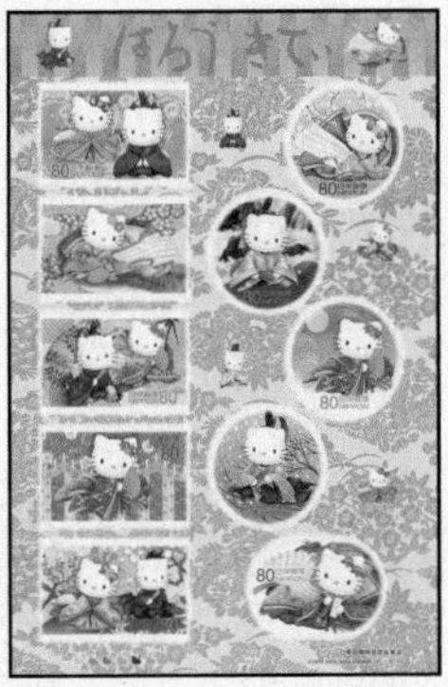
Hello Kitty A2407

No. 3048 — Hello Kitty characters with: a, Gold denomination at UR. b, Green denomination at UR. c, Yellow denomination at UL, Kitty with pink flowers on head. d, Yellow denomination at UR, Kitty wearing green patterned kimono. e, Green denomination at UL, Kitty wearing black kimono. f, Green denomination at UL, Kitty with pink and blue flowers on head. g, Green denomination at UL, Kitty with bow and flowers on head. h, Yellow denomination at UL, Kitty wearing dark green kimono. i, Green denomination at UL, Kitty wearing brown kimono. j, Green denomination at UL, Kitty with purple and green flowers on head.

No. 3049 — Hello Kitty characters with: a, Green denomination at LL (41x27mm). b, Gold denomination at LR, one Kitty with two pink flowers on head (41x27mm). c, Gold denomination at LR, Kitty at right with purple and green flowers on head (41x27mm). d, Green denomination at UR (41x27mm). e, Gold denomination at LR, Kitty at left with bow and flower on head (41x27mm). f, Blue denomination (34mm diameter). g, Gold denomination, Kitty wearing gray kimono (34mm diameter). h, Gold denomination, Kitty holding fan (34mm diameter). i, Gold denomination, Kitty with snowflakes in background (34mm diameter). j, Blue denomination (40x28mm oval stamp).

Die Cut Perf. and Serpentine Die Cut (see note)

2008, July 23 Litho.

Self-Adhesive

3048	A2406	Sheet of 10	9.50	9.50
a.-j.		50y Any single	.80	.80

Die Cut Perf. 13x13¼ (#3049a-3049e), Die Cut Perf.

3049	A2407	Sheet of 10	12.50	12.50
a.-j.		80y Any single	1.25	.80

Stamps on No. 3048 are arranged in five rows of se-tenant pairs. Each pair is die cut perf. 13¾ at top and bottom, die cut perf. 13½ on the outer sides, and serpentine die cut 11¼ between the stamps in the pair.

Love That Meets the Night, by Utamaro A2408

Yatsumi Bridge, by Hiroshige A2409

Mannen Bridge, Fukagawa, by Hiroshige A2410

Koshiro Matsumoto IV as Gorobe Sakanaya of San'ya, by Sharaku A2411

Hanazuma From Hyogoya, by Utamaro A2412

Ayase River at Kanegafuchi, by Hiroshige A2413

Tsukiji Hongan-ji Temple, Teppozu, by Hiroshige A2414

Hikosaburo Bando III as Sanai Sagisaka, by Sharaku A2415

Roko of Tatsumi, by Utamaro A2416

Kameido Plum Gardens, by Hiroshige A2417

2008, Aug. 1 Litho. *Perf. 13¼*

3050		Sheet of 10	16.00	16.00
a.	A2408	80y multi	1.25	.50
b.	A2409	80y multi	1.25	.50
c.	A2410	80y multi	1.25	.50
d.	A2411	80y multi	1.25	.50
e.	A2412	80y multi	1.25	.50
f.	A2413	80y multi	1.25	.50
g.	A2414	80y multi	1.25	.50
h.	A2415	80y multi	1.25	.50
i.	A2416	80y multi	1.25	.50
j.	A2417	80y multi	1.25	.50

Life in Edo (Tokyo).

Miniature Sheet

Hometown Festivals — A2418

No. 3051: a, Streamers for Sendai Tanabata Festival, Miyagi prefecture (light green background, denomination at UR). b, Streamers for Sendai Tanabata Festival (light green background, denomination at UL). c, Portable shrine for Kanda Festival, Tokyo prefecture (yellow background, denomination in red at LL). d, Portable shrine for Kanda Festival (yellow background, denomination in blue at UR). e, Dancers from Awa Dance Festival, Tokushima prefecture (pink background, denomination at LR). f, Dancers from Awa Dance Festival (pink background, denomination at UR). g, Participants and lanterns for Hakata Gion Yamakasa Festival, Fukuoka prefecture (light blue background, denomination at UL). h, Participants and float for Hakata Gion Yamakasa Festival (light blue background, denomination at UR). i, Drummers for Eisa Festival, Okinawa prefecture (yellow background, denomination in red at LR). j, Drummers for Eisa Festival (yellow background, denomination in blue at UR).

2008, Aug. 1 Photo. *Perf. 13½x13¼*

3051	A2418	Sheet of 10	8.00	8.00
a.-j.		50y Any single	.80	.40

Miniature Sheet

Treaty of Peace and Friendship Between Japan and People's Republic of China, 30th Anniv. — A2419

No. 3052: a, Temple of Heaven, Beijing. b, Huangshan Mountains, China. c, Mogao Cave Shrines, China. d, Temple of the Flourishing Law, Ikaruga, Japan. e, Female mandarin duck. f, Male mandarin duck. g, Panel from painting by Wang Chuanfeng depicting three stylized fish and red Japanese apricot flower. h, Panel from painting by Wang Chuanfeng depicting two stylized fish and water lily. i, Panel from painting by Wang Chuanfeng depicting one stylized fish and autumn leaves. j, Panel from painting by Wang Chuanfeng depicting two staylized fish and white and red narcissi. Nos. 3052a-3052d, 3052g-3052j are 28x49mm; Nos. 3052e-3052f, 32x49mm.

2008, Aug. 12 Photo. *Perf. 13*

3052	A2419	Sheet of 10	16.00	16.00
a.-j.		80y Any single	1.25	.50

Animation

Miniature Sheet

Patlabor A2420

No. 3053: a, Ingram Model 1 robot. b, Noa Izumimn, with "2" on sleeve patch. c, Isao Ota, with crossed arms. d, Ingram Model 2 robot. e, Shinobu Nagumo, with long hair. f, Ingram Model 3 robot. g, Robot, diff. h, Asumo Shinohara, with hand on head. i, Ingram Model 1 robot and eight characters. j, Ingram Model 2 robot and three characters.

2008, Aug. 22 Litho. *Perf. 13x13¼*

3053	A2420	Sheet of 10	16.00	16.00
a.-j.		80y Any single	1.25	.50

Miniature Sheet

Home Towns A2421

No. 3054 — Paintings by Taiji Harada of views of towns: a, Idyllic Village (Farmhouses, Tonami, Toyama prefecture). b, Blessing (Wedding at Yamate Catholic Church, Yokohama, Kanagawa prefecture). c, Approaching Winter (Lake Nojiri, Kamiminochi District, Nagano prefecture). d, Konjac Field (Farmers planting, Numata, Gunma prefecture). e, Vespers (Family in garden near houses, Nara, Nara prefecture). f, Cosmos (Flowers, boats and boathouses, Mikatakaminaka District, Fukui prefecture). g, Voices of Excited Children (Farmhouse and hill, Haga District, Tochigi prefecture). h, Autumn Colors Everywhere (Farmhouse and train car, Namegata, Ibaraki prefecture). i, Small Market (Family at roadside market, Asakura District, Fukuoka prefecture). j, Lullaby Village (Village and bridge, Kuma District, Kumamoto prefecture).

2008, Sept. 1 Photo. *Perf. 13*

3054 A2421 Sheet of 10 12.50 12.50
a.-j. 80y Any single 1.25 .55

Miniature Sheet

Kyoto Travel Scenes A2422

No. 3055: a, Otagi Nebutsu Temple and stone sculptures (stamp 1). b, Toriimoto (stamp 2). c, Adashino Nenbutsu Temple (stamp 3). d, Gio Temple (stamp 4). e, Buddha sculptures, Nison Temple (stamp 5). f, Hut of Fallen Persimmons, persimmons on tree (stamp 6). g, Jojakko Temple (stamp 7). h, Sagano Scenic Railway bridge and trains (stamp 8). i, Rowboats on Hozu River (stamp 9). j, Togetsu Bridge (stamp 10).

2008, Sept. 1 Litho. *Perf. 13x13¼*

3055 A2422 Sheet of 10 12.50 12.50
a.-j. 80y Any single 1.25 .55

Personalized Stamp — A2423

Die Cut Perf. 12¾ Syncopated

2008, Aug. 7 Litho.

Self-Adhesive

Color of Denomination

3056 A2423 80y blue *2.00 2.00*
3057 A2423 80y red *2.00 2.00*
3058 A2423 80y orange *2.00 2.00*
3059 A2423 80y green *2.00 2.00*
3060 A2423 80y black *2.00 2.00*
Nos. 3056-3060 (5) 10.00 10.00

Nos. 3056-3060 were printed in sheets of 10 containing 2 of each stamp that sold for 1200y. The image portion could be personalized. The image shown is a generic image.

A2424

A2425

A2426

A2427

A2428

A2429

A2430

A2431

A2432

The Tale of Genji, by Shikibu Murasaki A2433

2008, Sept. 22 Photo. *Perf. 13¼*

3061 Sheet of 10 16.00 16.00
a. A2424 80y multi 1.25 .50
b. A2425 80y multi 1.25 .50
c. A2426 80y multi 1.25 .50
d. A2427 80y multi 1.25 .50
e. A2428 80y multi 1.25 .50
f. A2429 80y multi 1.25 .50
g. A2430 80y multi 1.25 .50
h. A2431 80y multi 1.25 .50
i. A2432 80y multi 1.25 .50
j. A2433 80y multi 1.25 .50

Kyushu Oil Dome, Oita Sports Park A2435

Fencing A2436

Hurdler A2437

Kayaker A2438

2008, Sept. 26 *Perf. 13x13¼*

3062 Sheet of 10, 2 each #3062a, 3062b, 3062d, 4 #3062c 9.50 9.50
a. A2435 50y multi .90 .50
b. A2436 50y multi .90 .50
c. A2437 50y multi .90 .50
d. A2438 50y multi .90 .50

Miniature Sheet

Travel Scenes A2439

No. 3063: a, Sanjunoto Pagoda (stamp 1). b, Kiyomizudera Temple (stamp 2). c, Detail from painted sliding partition showing flowers from Chishaku Temple, denomination at LL (stamp 3). d, Like "c," denomination at LR (stamp 4). e, Kodai Temple (stamp 5). f, Temple garden (stamp 6). g, Sannei Hill (stamp 7). h, Yasaka Pagoda (stamp 8). i, Apprentice geisha (stamp 9). j, Kamo River and waterfront (stamp 10).

2008, Oct. 1 Litho. *Perf. 13x13¼*

3063 A2439 Sheet of 10 12.50 12.50
a.-j. 80y Any single 1.25 .55

International Letter Writing Week Type of 2000

Hiroshige paintings from 53 Stations of the Tokaido Highway: 90y, Kanagawa. 110y, Mishima. 130y, Ishibe.

2008, Oct. 9 Photo. *Perf. 13¼x13½*

3064 A2119 90y multi 1.75 .50
3065 A2119 110y multi 2.25 .50
3066 A2119 130y multi 2.50 .50
Nos. 3064-3066 (3) 6.50 1.50

See listing of No. 4448 for images of each Hiroshige print.

World Heritage Sites

Miniature Sheet

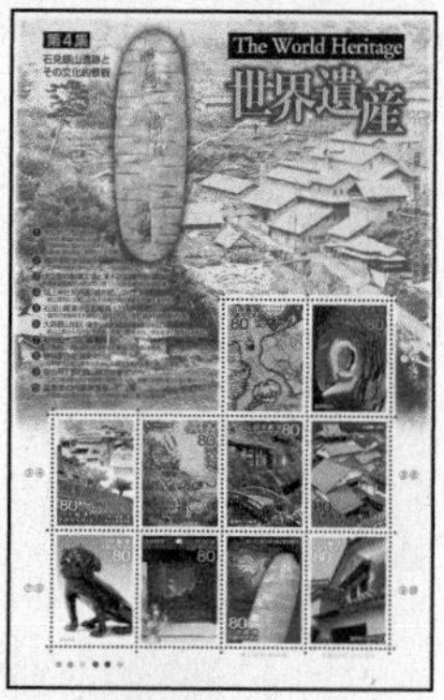

Iwami Silver Mine World Heritage Site A2440

No. 3067: a, Map of Tartary by Abraham Ortelius (stamp 1). b, Ryugenji mine shaft (stamp 2). c, Smelting plant and ruins of Shimizudani smelting works (stamp 3). d, Painting of dragon, ceiling of Kigami Shinto shrine (stamp 4). e, Rakanji Temple (stamp 5). f, Omori silver mine district (stamp 6). g, Silver guardian dog (stamp 7). h, Interior of Kumagai family residence (stamp 8). i, Silver coin for official use and picture scroll (stamp 9). j, Naito Mansion, Yunotsu (stamp 10).

2008, Oct. 23 *Perf. 13x13¼*

3067 A2440 Sheet of 10 16.00 16.00
a.-j. 80y Any single 1.25 .50

Miniature Sheet

Kyoto Prefecture Local Autonomy Law, 60th Anniv. — A2441

No. 3068: a, Scene from The Tale of Genji, by Shikibu Murasaki (33x39mm). b, Cherry blossoms, Kyoto Prefectural Botanical Garden (28x33mm). c, Thatched-roof house, Nantan (28x33mm). d, Kaijusen Pagoda, Wazuka tea plantation (28x33mm). e, Amanohashidate Sandbar (28x33mm).

Perf. 13¼ (#3068a), 13x13¼

2008, Oct. 27 Photo.

3068 A2441 Sheet of 5 7.50 7.50
a.-e. 80y Any single 1.25 .50

Miniature Sheet

Home Towns A2442

No. 3069 — Paintings by Taiji Harada of views of towns: a, Stove Train (train, Kitatsugaru District, Aomori prefecture). b, New Year (buildings with snow-covered roofs, man shoveling snow, Nishimurayama District, Yamagata prefecture). c, Seaside Station (train station and telephone pole, Abashiri, Hokkaido prefecture). d, Incense Waterwheel (mill with waterwheel, Tsuyama, Okayama prefecture). e, Harness Straps (horse dragging log, Kurayoshi, Tottori prefecture). f, Life in the Snow Country (postman delivering mail to people at snow-covered house, Waga District, Iwate prefecture). g, Good Friends (people on town street in snowfall, Aizu Wakamatsu, Fukushima prefecture). h, Community of Stone Walls (people walking by stone wall, Minamiuwa District, Ehime prefecture). i, Village on Steep Slope (houses on mountainside, Miyoshi, Toskushima prefecture). j, Sedge-woven Hat (woman standing outside of building in snowstorm, Nakauonuma District, Niigata prefecture).

2008, Nov. 4 ***Perf. 13***

3069 A2442 Sheet of 10 12.50 12.50
a.-j. 80y Any single 1.25 .50

A2443 A2444

New Year 2009 (Year of the Ox)
A2445 A2446

2008, Nov. 4 **Photo.** ***Perf. 13x13¼***

3070	A2443 50y multi		1.00	.30
3071	A2444 80y multi		1.50	.40

Perf. 13¼

3072	A2445 50y +3y multi	1.25	.40
3073	A2446 80y +3y multi	1.75	.40
	Nos. 3070-3073 (4)	5.50	1.50

Sheets of two containing Nos. 3070-3071 were lottery prizes. Value, $3.25.

New Year Greetings Type of 2006 Inscribed "'09 New Year" Stamp + Label Panel Color

2008, Nov. 4 **Photo.** ***Perf. 13¼***

3074	A2327a 50y blue green	1.50	1.50
3075	A2327a 50y red	1.50	1.50
a.	Pair, #3074-3075 + 2 labels	3.00	3.00

Labels could be personalized.

Miniature Sheet

Keio University, 150th Anniv. — A2447

No. 3076: a, Yukichi Fukuzawa (1835-1901), founder (stamp 1). b, University emblem (stamp 2). c, Old Library, denomination at LL (stamp 3). d, Old Library, denomination at LR (stamp 4). e, Keio and Waseda University rugby players (stamp 5). f, Keio and Waseda University baseball players (stamp 6). g, Stained-glass window depicting horse's head (stamp 7). h, Stained-glass window depicting goddess with upraised arm (stamp 8). i, Stained-glass window depicting feudal warrior (stamp 9). j, Stained-glass window with Latin inscription "Calamus Gladio Fortior" (stamp 10).

2008, Nov. 7 ***Perf. 13***

3076 A2447 Sheet of 10 16.00 16.00
a.-j. 80y Any single 1.25 .50

Miniature Sheet

Edo Calligraphy — A2448

No. 3077 — Characters for "ox": a, Depiction of ox head (Kinbun style) with red chop at LL. b, Blue character on lilac background, in Kokotsubun style. c, Character with three horizontal lines and two vertical lines, in standard script, with red chop at LR. d, Red character in Kinbun style. e, Character with two horizontal lines and one vertical line, in standard script, with red chop at left center. f, Character in Tensho style with red chop at right center. g, Character with arc and crossed lines in Tensho style, with red chop at LR. h, Character with two crossing curves in Kokotsubun style, with red chop in center. i, Character with two components in Reisho style, with red chop at left. j, Character with dot above sinuous line in Hiragana style, with red chop at LR.

Litho. & Embossed

2008, Nov. 21 ***Perf. 13x13¼***

3077 A2448 Sheet of 10 16.00 16.00
a.-j. 80y Any single 1.25 .50

A2449

A2450

A2451

A2452

A2453

Iron and Steel Industry, 150th Anniv. — A2454

2008, Dec. 1 **Photo.** ***Perf. 12¾x13***

3078 Sheet of 10, #3078a, 3078b, 2 each #3078c-3078f 16.00 16.00

a.	A2449 80y multi	1.25	.50
b.	A2450 80y multi	1.25	.50
c.	A2451 80y multi	1.25	.50
d.	A2452 80y multi	1.25	.50
e.	A2453 80y multi	1.25	.50
f.	A2454 80y multi	1.25	.50

Daffodils
A2455

Plum Blossoms
A2456

Fuki
A2457

Plum Blossoms
A2458

Weeping Cherry Blossoms
A2459

Daffodils
A2460

Plum Blossoms
A2461

Fuki
A2462

Plum Blossoms
A2463

Weeping Cherry Blossoms
A2464

2008, Dec. 1 **Photo.** ***Perf. 13¼***

3079	A2455 50y multi	.80	.40
3080	A2456 50y multi	.80	.40
3081	A2457 50y multi	.80	.40
3082	A2458 50y multi	.80	.40
3083	A2459 50y multi	.80	.40
a.	Vert. strip of 5, #3079-3083	4.50	3.50
3084	A2460 80y multi	1.25	.55
3085	A2461 80y multi	1.25	.55
3086	A2462 80y multi	1.25	.55
3087	A2463 80y multi	1.25	.55
3088	A2464 80y multi	1.25	.55
a.	Vert. strip of 5, #3084-3088	7.00	5.00
	Nos. 3079-3088 (10)	10.25	4.75

Flowers of Fukui, Wakayama, Akita, Fukuoka and Kyoto prefectures.

Miniature Sheets

A2465

Greetings Stamps — A2466

No. 3089: a, Santa Claus holding star (26x30mm). b, Stylized man, woman as bell (26x30mm). c, Kittens (26x30mm). d, Teddy bears and gift box (26x30mm). e, Chick, flowers (29mm diameter).

No. 3090: a, Kittens (34x28mm oval). b, Elf with bag of roses (25x34mm). c, Bluebirds in bouquet of roses (25x34mm). d, Santa Claus with horn (25x34mm). e, Fruit and flowers (25x34mm).

Die Cut Perf. 13¼

2008, Dec. 8 **Litho.**

3089 A2465 Sheet of 5 5.00 5.00
a.-e. 50y Any single .80 .80

Die Cut Perf. 13

3090 A2466 Sheet of 5 7.50 7.50
a.-e. 80y Any single 1.25 .80

Miniature Sheet

Shimane Prefecture Local Autonomy Law, 60th Anniv. — A2467

No. 3091: a, Tree peony, silver coin for official use (33x39mm). b, Kuniga Coast (28x33mm). c, Matsue Castle (28x33mm). d, Tsuwano (28x33mm). e, Bronze bell (28x33mm).

Perf. 13¼ (#3091a), 13x13¼

2008, Dec. 8 **Photo.**

3091 A2467 Sheet of 5 6.50 6.50
a.-e. 80y Any single 1.25 .40

Miniature Sheet

Travel Scenes
A2468

No. 3092: a, Dragon from Shuri Castle Main Hall (stamp 1). b, Shuri Castle Main Hall (stamp 2). c, Ryukyuan dancer with arm raised at left (stamp 3). d, Ryukyuan dancer with arm raised at right (stamp 4). e, Shurei Gate (stamp 5). f, Zuisen Gate and Rokoku Gate, Shuri Castle (stamp 6). g, Shikina Garden (stamp 7). h, Stone pavement, Kinjo (stamp 8). i, Guardian lion, International Street, Naha (stamp 9). j, Yui Monorail, Naha (stamp 10).

2009, Jan. 23 **Litho.** ***Perf. 13x13¼***

3092 A2468 Sheet of 10 12.50 12.50
a.-j. 80y Any single 1.25 .60

Miniature Sheet

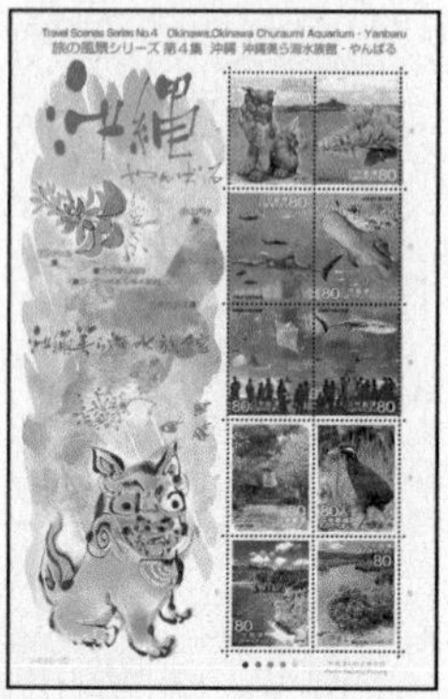
Travel Scenes A2469

No. 3093: a, Guardian Lion (stamp 1). b, Indian coral tree, Iejima (stamp 2). c, Fish in Okinawa Churaumi Aquarium, denomination at UR (stamp 3). d, As "c," denomination at LL (stamp 4). e, People watching fish in Okinawa Churaumi Aquarium, denomination at LL (stamp 5). f, As "e," denomination at LR (stamp 6). g, Nakijin Castle ruins (stamp 7). h, Okinawa rail (stamp 8). i, Cape Hedo, Okinawa (stamp 9). j, Mangroves, Gesashi Inlet (stamp 10).

2009, Feb. 2

3093	A2469	Sheet of 10	12.50	12.50
a.-j.		80y Any single	1.25	.60

Yoshino Cherry Blossoms A2470

Azaleas A2471

Tulips A2472

Rhododendron A2473

Nara Cherry Blossoms A2474

Yoshino Cherry Blossoms A2475

Azaleas A2476

Tulips A2477

Rhododendrons A2478

Nara Cherry Blossoms A2479

2009, Feb. 2 Photo. *Perf. 13¼*

3094	A2470	50y multi	.80	.40
3095	A2471	50y multi	.80	.40
3096	A2472	50y multi	.80	.40
3097	A2473	50y multi	.80	.40
3098	A2474	50y multi	.80	.40
a.		Vert. strip of 5, #3094-3098	5.00	3.75
3099	A2475	80y multi	1.25	.60
3100	A2476	80y multi	1.25	.60
3101	A2477	80y multi	1.25	.60
3102	A2478	80y multi	1.25	.60
3103	A2479	80y multi	1.25	.60
a.		Vert. strip of 5, #3099-3103	6.50	3.50
		Nos. 3094-3103 (10)	10.25	5.00

Flowers of Tokyo, Tochigi, Niigata, Shiga and Nara prefectures.

Animation
Miniature Sheet

GeGeGe no Kitaro A2480

No. 3104: a, Kitaro and Otoko Nezumi. b, Daddy Eyeball in bowl. c, Kitaro kicking. d, Kitaro in fire. e, Villain with elongated head, villain with blades for arms. f, Villains with red face, villain with snake. g, Kitaro and mermaid. h, Musume Neko. i, Otoko Nezumi, Musume Neko, Babaa Sunakake and Nurikabe. j, Kitaro, Daddy Eyeball, Jijii Konaki, Momen Ittan.

2009, Feb. 23 Litho. *Perf. 13x13¼*

3104	A2480	Sheet of 10	16.00	16.00
a.-j.		80y Any single	1.25	.50

Miniature Sheet

Travel Scenes A2481

No. 3105: a, Todai Temple (stamp 1). b, Buddha, Todai Temple (stamp 2). c, Asura, Kofuku Temple (stamp 3). d, Nara National Museum (stamp 4). e, Kasuga Taisha Shrine (stamp 5). f, Roof of Kasuga Taisha Shrine and overhanging roof (stamp 6). g, Japanese deer, Wakakusa Hill (stamp 7). h, Inanuishi family residence (stamp 8). i, Gazebo, Nara Park (stamp 9). j, Bridge to gazebo, Nara Park (stamp 10).

2009, Mar. 2

3105	A2481	Sheet of 10	12.50	12.50
a.-j.		80y Any single	1.25	.60

Miniature Sheet

Home Towns A2482

No. 3106 — Paintings by Taiji Harada of views of towns: a, Cultivating (farmer in field, Nishitama District, Tokyo prefecture). b, Children Planting Rice (children in rice paddy, Katta District, Miyagi prefecture). c, I'm Home (child running up hill to farmhouse, Yamagata District, Hiroshima prefecture). d, Northern Springtime (farmer and wheelbarrow in field of yellow flowers, Iwanai District, Hokkaido prefecture). e, Chinese Milk Vetch Field (people near farmhouse, Kyoto, Kyoto prefecture). f, Water Mortar (farmer near water mortar, Hita, Oita prefecture). g, Short Rest (woman resting on bench in front of building, Numazu, Shizuoka prefecture). h, Red Train (street scene with train in background, Izumo, Shimane prefecture). i, Oven-shaped Thatch Roofs (woman, children with toy car in front of farm house, Kishima District, Saga prefecture). j, Little Post Office (people outside of post office, Hosu District, Ishikawa prefecture).

2009, Mar. 2 Photo. *Perf. 13*

3106	A2482	Sheet of 10	12.50	12.50
a.-j.		80y Any single	1.25	.60

Miniature Sheets

A2483

Weekly Comic Books For Boys, 50th Anniv A2484

No. 3107: a, Osomatsu-kun (boy's face, green panel at top). b, Makoto Chan (boy with broom). c, Kamui Gaiden (swordsman with black hair). d, Gambare Genki (boxer, dark blue background). e, Paman (three characters with masks and capes). f, Urusei Yatsura (boy in cap, girl in bikini). g, Dame Oyaji (man holding radish and knife). h, Saibogu 009 (characters with galaxy in background). i, Purogorufa Saru (golfer). j, Tacchi (boy and girl looking over their shoulders).

No. 3108: a, Eitoman (android with "8" on chest). b, Taiga Masuku (caped man with tiger mask). c, Kyojin no Hoshi (Yomiuri Giants pitcher). d, Karate Baka Ichidai (karate master with green hair). e, GeGeGe no Kitaro (Kitaro, Daddy Eyeball and Otoko Nezumi). f, Ai to Makoto (girl with orange hair, boy with green hair). g, Tensai Bakabon (woman with yellow hair bow, screaming man). h, Tsurikichi Sanpei (boy holding fish). i, Ashita no Jo (boxer, pale blue background). j, Tonda Kappuru (boy, girl with green dress and orange bow).

2009, Mar. 17 Litho. *Perf. 13*

3107	A2483	Sheet of 10	12.50	12.50
a.-j.		80y Any single	1.25	.60
3108	A2484	Sheet of 10	12.50	12.50
a.-j.		80y Any single	1.25	.60

Wedding of Emperor Akihito and Empress Michiko, 50th Anniv. — A2485

Designs: No. 3109, Confectionery box. No. 3110, Fan.

2009, Apr. 10 Photo. *Perf. 13¼*

3109		80y multi	1.50	.60
3110		80y multi	1.50	.60
a.	A2485	Pair, #3109-3110	3.20	2.50
b.		Souvenir sheet, #3109-3110	3.50	3.50

Animation
Miniature Sheet

Detective Conan A2486

No. 3111: a, Ai Haibara and Conan and brick wall. b, Mitsuhiko Tsuburaya, Ayumi Yoshida, and Genta Kojima and brick wall. c, Heiji Hattori and cherry blossoms. d, Kazuha Toyama and cherry blossoms. e, Conan and night sky. f, Gin and night sky. g, Conan and fence. h, Ran Mori and fence. i, Kiddo Kaito holding Christmas gift. j, Conan, Moon and hang-glider.

2009, Apr. 17 Litho. *Perf. 13x13¼*

3111	A2486	Sheet of 10	16.00	16.00
a.-j.		80y Any single	1.25	.50

Peonies, by Yu Fei'an — A2487

Peonies, by Ren Bonian — A2488

Peonies, by Keika Kanashima A2489

Peonies, by Keika Kanashima A2490

Peonies, by Keika Kanashima A2491

Peonies, by Keika Kanashima A2492

2009, Apr. 20 Photo. *Perf. 13¼*

3112	Sheet of 10, #3112c-3112f, 3 each, #3112a-3112b	16.00	16.00
a.	A2487 80y multi	1.20	.60
b.	A2488 80y multi	1.20	.60
c.	A2489 80y multi	1.20	.60
d.	A2490 80y multi	1.20	.60
e.	A2491 80y multi	1.20	.60
f.	A2492 80y multi	1.20	.60

Philately Week.

Red Cross, 150th Anniv. A2493

Designs: No. 3113, Henri Dunant (1828-1910), founder of Red Cross. No. 3114, Japanese Red Cross Day poster, 1933.

2009, May 8 Litho. *Perf. 13*

3113	80y multi	1.25	.50
3114	80y multi	1.25	.50
a.	A2493 Pair, #3113-3114	3.00	2.50

Miniature Sheet

Nagano Prefecture Local Autonomy Law, 60th Anniv. — A2494

No. 3115: a, Kappa Bridge, Azusa River, Mt. Hodaka (33x39mm). b, Nanohana Park and Chikuma River, Iiyama City (28x33mm). c, Anraku Temple (28x33mm). d, Matsumoto Castle (28x33mm). e, Manji Buddha statue (28x33mm).

Perf. 13¼ (#3115a), 13x13¼

2009, May 14 Photo.

3115	A2494	Sheet of 5	6.50	6.50
a.-e.		80y Any single	1.25	.60

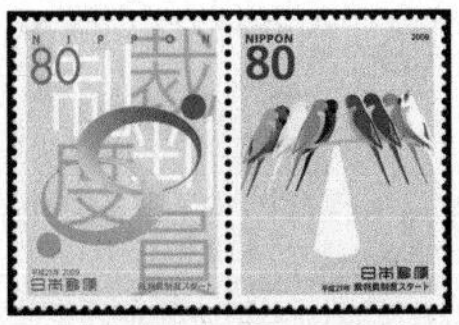

Inauguration of Lay Judge System — A2495

Designs: No. 3116, Lay Judge System emblem. No. 3117, Birds on scale.

2009, May 21 Litho. *Perf. 13x13¼*

3116	80y multi	1.25	.50
3117	80y multi	1.25	.50
a.	A2495 Pair, #3116-3117	3.00	2.50

Miniature Sheets

A2496

Weekly Comic Books For Boys, 50th Anniv A2497

No. 3118: a, Gu-Gu Ganmo (child and chicken-like alien). b, Major (baseball player with bat, ball and glove). c, Patlabor Mobile Police (man standing on robot). d, Rekka no Hono (boy with gloved hand raised). e, Ushio to Tora (monster and boy holding torch). f, ARMS (boy with extended hand and slash marks in background). g, GS Mikami Gakuraku Daisakusen (woman with long red hair). h, Kekkaishi (magician pointing finger forward). i, Detective Conan (boy pointing forward wearing glasses and bow tie). j, Hayate no Gotoku (girl, boy and tower).

No. 3119: a, 1, 2 no Sanshiro (judo fighter with flame in background). b, Hajime no Ippo (boxer). c, Kabocha Wain (boy and tall girl). d, Kindaichi Shonen no Jikenbo (two boys and girl). e, Kotaro Makari Tooru (boy and girl in white clothes). f, GTO (boy with GTO tattoo). g, Bari Bari Densetsu (motorcyclist). h, RAVE (swordsman and other characters). i, Misuta Ajikko (chef). j, Daiya no A (baseball pitcher).

2009, May 22 Litho. *Perf. 13*

3118	A2496	Sheet of 10	16.00	16.00
a.-j.		80y Any single	1.25	.50
3119	A2497	Sheet of 10	16.00	16.00
a.-j.		80y Any single	1.25	.50

Opening of Japanese Ports, 150th Anniv.

Miniature Sheets

Nagasaki A2498

Yokohama — A2499

Hakodate — A2500

No. 3120: a, 19th century woodblock print of Nagasaki Port (denomination at left in black). b, 19th century woodblock print of Nagasaki Port (denomination at right in black). c, Nagasaki Port at night (denomination at UL in white). d, Nagasaki Port at night (denomination at UR in black). e, Drawing of boats and ships (denomination at UL in black). f, Drawing of boats and ships (denomination at LR in white). g, Nagasaki Port at night (denomination at LL in white). h, Oura Catholic Church. i, Goddess Great Bridge, Nippon Maru cruise ship. j, Glover Garden, Nagasaki Port (lamppost in foreground).

No. 3121: a, Woodblock print of Yokohama Port, 1871 (denomination at LL in black). b, Woodblock print of Yokohama Port, 1871 (denomination at LR in black). c, Yokohama Port at night (denomination at UL in white, tall building at right). d, Yokohama Port at night (denomination at LR in white). e, Yokohama Bay Bridge. f, Yokohama City Port Opening Memorial Hall. g, Sailing ship Nippon Maru. h, Yokohama International Passenger Boat Terminal and cruise ship.

No. 3122: a, Woodblock print of Hakodate Port, 1882 (denomination at LL in black). b, Woodblock print of Hakodate Port, 1882 (denomination at UL in black). c, Hakodate Port at night (denomination at UR in white). d, Hakodate Port at night (denomination at UL in white). e, Street on Hachiman Slope, Hakodate Port at night. f, Hakodate Orthodox Christian Church. g, Ship, lamppost at Old Pier at night. h, Hakodate Park, Hakodate Port (denomination at UL in black).

2009, June 2 Litho. *Perf. 13*

3120	A2498	Sheet of 10	16.00	16.00
a.-j.		80y Any single	1.25	.50
3121	A2499	Sheet of 10, #3120e-3120f, 3121a-3121h	16.00	16.00
a.-h.		80y Any single	1.25	.50
3122	A2500	Sheet of 10, #3120e-3120f, 3122a-3122h	16.00	16.00
a.-h.		80y Any single	1.25	.50
		Nos. 3120-3122 (3)	48.00	48.00

Miniature Sheet

National Afforestation Campaign — A2501

No. 3123 — Flora from Fukui Prefecture: a, Weeping cherry blossoms. b, Japanese zelkova tree. c, Japanese red pine tree. d, Japanese bird cherry tree. e, Magnolia blossoms. f, Camellia. g, Japanese horse chestnut tree. h, Kousa dogwood blossoms. i, Narcissi (denomination at UL). j, Narcissi (denomination at UR).

2009, June 5 Litho. *Perf. 13*

3123	A2501	Sheet of 10	8.00	8.00
a.-j.		50y Any single	.80	.40

Miniature Sheet

Home Towns A2502

No. 3124 — Paintings by Taiji Harada of views of towns: a, Flowers Blooming in the Rain (mother and daughter under umbrellas on path by flower field, Tone District, Gumma prefecture). b, Potato Blossoms (train car near potato field, Nakagawa District, Hokkaido prefecture). c, High Country Flowers (people in flower field, Suwa, Nagano prefecture). d, Memories on the Wind (farmer with wheelbarrow on path near farmhouse, Hagi, Yamaguchi prefecture). e, Tranquility (people near stone wall in front of house, Sumoto, Hyogo prefecture). f, Sunset Skies (adult and child on hillside path near house, Nishiusuki District, Miyazaki prefecture). g, Island Post Office (people standing in front of post office, Yaeyama District, Okinawa prefecture). h, Lotus Blossoms (field of lotus with house and large tree in background, Hakusan, Ishikawa prefecture). i, Flower Garden (two women picking flowers with house and telephone pole in background, Minamiboso, Chiba prefecture). j, Peach Blossoms (adult and child picnicking under trees, Fuefuki, Yamanashi prefecture).

2009, June 23 Photo. *Perf. 13*

3124	A2502	Sheet of 10	12.50	12.50
a.-j.		80y Any single	1.25	.60

Miniature Sheet

Intl. Polar Year A2503

No. 3125: a, Polar bears. b, Weddell seal. c, Arctic fox. d, Adélie penguin.

Litho. With Hologram Affixed

2009, June 30 *Die Cut Perf. 13*

Self-Adhesive

3125	A2503	Sheet of 4	7.00	7.00
a.-d.		80y Any single	1.25	.60

Gentian A2504

Chrysanthemums A2505

Miyagi Bush Clover A2506

Black Lilies A2507

Japanese Maple A2508

Gentian A2509

Chrysanthemums A2510

Miyagi Bush Clover A2511

Black Lilies A2512

Japanese Maple A2513

2009, July 1 Photo. *Perf. 13¼*

3126	A2504 50y multi		.80	.40
3127	A2505 50y multi		.80	.40
3128	A2506 50y multi		.80	.40
3129	A2507 50y multi		.80	.40
3130	A2508 50y multi		.80	.40
a.	Vert. strip of 5, #3126-3130		4.50	4.00
3131	A2509 80y multi		1.25	.60
3132	A2510 80y multi		1.25	.60
3133	A2511 80y multi		1.25	.60
3134	A2512 80y multi		1.25	.60
3135	A2513 80y multi		1.25	.60
a.	Vert. strip of 5, #3131-3135		6.50	6.50
	Nos. 3126-3135 (10)		10.25	5.00

Flora of Kumamoto, Hyogo, Miyagi, Ishikawa and Hiroshima prefectures.

Miniature Sheet

Niigata Prefecture Local Autonomy Law, 60th Anniv. — A2514

No. 3136: a, Japanese crested ibis over Sado Island (33x39mm). b, Cherry blossoms, Takada Castle (28x33mm). c, Fireworks over Nagaoka (28x33mm). d, Imori Pond, Mt. Myoko (28x33mm). e, Fireworks at Tokamichi Snow Festival (28x33mm).

Perf. 13¼ (#3136a), 13x13¼

2009, July 8 Photo.

3136	A2514	Sheet of 5	6.50	6.50
a.-e.		80y Any single	1.25	.60

Statue of Eki Doji — A2515

2009, July 23 Photo. *Perf. 13x13½*

3137	A2515 300y multi	8.00	.30

Ono no Komachi, Poet A2516

Ietaka Junii, Poet A2517

Hoshi Jakuren, Poet A2518

Sakanoue no Korenori, Poet A2519

Daini no Sanmi, Poet — A2520

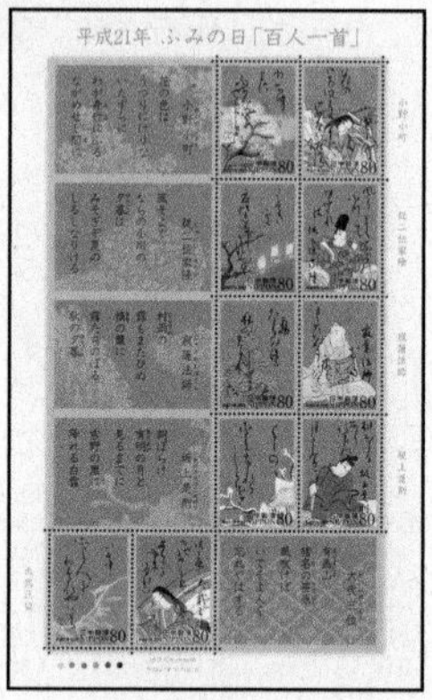

Poetry A2521

No. 3143 — Poetry in Japanese calligraphy and: a, Tree with white blossoms. b, Ono no Komachi. c, Tree near pond. d, Ietaka Junii. e, Tree with green leaves. f, Hoshi Jakuren. g, House. h, Sakanoue no Korenori. i, Leaves. j, Daini no Sanmi.

2009, July 23 Photo. *Perf. 13¼*

3138	A2516 50y multi	.80	.30
3139	A2517 50y multi	.80	.30
3140	A2518 50y multi	.80	.30
3141	A2519 50y multi	.80	.30
3142	A2520 50y multi	.80	.30
a.	Vert. strip of 5, #3138-3142	5.00	3.50

Perf. 12¾x13

3143	A2521	Sheet of 10	16.00	16.00
a.-j.		80y Any single	1.25	.50

Letter Writing Day.

Miniature Sheets

A2522

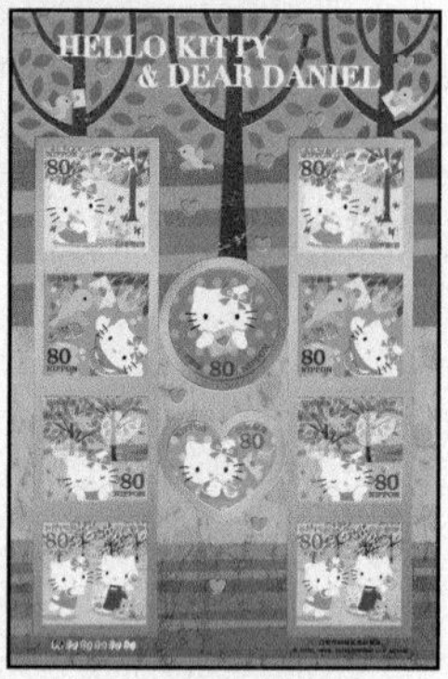

Hello Kitty and Dear Daniel A2523

No. 3144: a, Hello Kitty with envelope. b, Hello Kitty, Dear Daniel, birds in pond. c, Hello Kitty, Dear Daniel, two trees. d, Hello Kitty and Dear Daniel with envelopes. e, Hello Kitty, Dear Daniel, three trees.

No. 3145: a, Hello Kitty with envelope (35mm diameter). b, Hello Kitty, two birds (35x28mm, heart-shaped). c, Hello Kitty, tree, three birds. d, Bird carrying envelope flying over Hello Kitty. e, Hello Kitty, bird, two trees. f, Hello Kitty, Dear Daniel, bird, squirrel and rabbit.

Die Cut Perf. 13½

2009, July 23 Litho.

3144	A2522	Sheet of 10, 2 each #a-e	9.00	9.00
a.-e.		50y Any single	.80	.80

Die Cut Perf. (#3145a-3145b), Die Cut Perf. 13½

3145	A2523	Sheet of 10, #a-b, 2 each #c-f	13.00	13.00
a.-f.		80y Any single	1.25	.80

Suwa Bluff, Nippori, by Hiroshige A2524

Pensive Love, by Utamaro A2525

Tokuji Otani as Yakko Sodesuke, by Sharaku A2526

Kumano Junisha Shrine, by Hiroshige A2527

Moon Promontory, by Hiroshige A2528

Woman Reading a Letter, by Utamaro A2529

Wadaemon Nakajima as Bodara Chozaemon and Konozo Nakamura as Funayado Kanagaway no Gon, by Sharaku A2530

Pagoda at Zojo Temple, by Hiroshige A2531

Clear Weather After Snowfall at Japan Bridge, by Hiroshige A2532

Kameikichi of Sodegaura, by Utamaro A2533

2009, Aug. 3 Litho. *Perf. 13¼*

3146	Sheet of 10	13.00	13.00
a.	A2524 80y multi	1.25	.60
b.	A2525 80y multi	1.25	.60
c.	A2526 80y multi	1.25	.60
d.	A2527 80y multi	1.25	.60
e.	A2528 80y multi	1.25	.60
f.	A2529 80y multi	1.25	.60
g.	A2530 80y multi	1.25	.60
h.	A2531 80y multi	1.25	.60
i.	A2532 80y multi	1.25	.60
j.	A2533 80y multi	1.25	.60

Life in Edo (Tokyo).

Gujo Dance (Gifu) A2534

Fukagawa Hachiman Festival (Tokyo) A2535

Denomination at: No. 3147, Right. No. 3148, Left. No. 3149, Right. No. 3150, Left.

2009, Aug. 10

3147	50y multi	.80	.40
3148	50y multi	.80	.40
a.	A2534 Horiz. pair, #3147-3148	1.75	1.25
3149	50y multi	.80	.40
3150	50y multi	.80	.40
a.	A2535 Horiz. pair, #3149-3150	1.75	1.25
	Nos. 3147-3150 (4)	3.20	1.60

Miniature Sheet

Travel Scenes A2536

No. 3151: a, Asuka, denomination at LL (stamp 1). b, Asuka, denomination at LR (stamp 2). c, Tachibana Temple, denomination at LL (stamp 3). d, Tachibana Temple, denomination at LR (stamp 4). e, Sculpture, Asuka Historical Museum (stamp 5). f, Stone burial mound (stamp 6). g, Tanzan Shrine, denomination at UR (stamp 7). h, Tanzan Shrine, denomination at UL (stamp 8). i, Picture scroll, denomination at UL (stamp 9). j, Picture scroll, denomination at LL (stamp 10).

2009, Aug. 21 *Perf. 13x13¼*

3151	A2536 Sheet of 10	13.00	13.00
a.-j.	80y Any single	1.25	.60

Persimmons and Haiku by Shiki Masaoka A2537

Roofs of Dogo Onsen and Haiku by Shiki Masaoka A2538

Mountain, Field and Haiku by Kyoshi Takahama A2539

House and Haiku by Soseki Natsume A2540

Cherry Blossoms and Haiku by Hekigoto Kawahigashi — A2541

2009, Sept. 1 Litho.

3152	A2537 80y multi	1.25	.40
3153	A2538 80y multi	1.25	.40
3154	A2539 80y multi	1.25	.40
3155	A2540 80y multi	1.25	.40
3156	A2541 80y multi	1.25	.40
a.	Vert. strip of 5, #3152-3156	6.50	6.50

Miniature Sheet

National Athletic Meet (Niigata) A2542

No. 3157: a, Tohoku Electric Power Big Swan Stadium. b, Soccer player. c, Boxer. d, Basketball player.

2009, Sept. 25 *Perf. 13x13¼*

3157	A2542 Sheet of 10, 2 each #3157a-3157c, 4 #3157d	8.00	8.00
a.-d.	50y Any single	.80	.40

Takayama Festival (Gifu) A2543

Hakone Feudal Lord's Procession (Kanagawa) A2544

Designs: No. 3158, Crowd at Night Festival. No. 3159, Shakkyo float puppet. No. 3160, Three men and box. No. 3161, Three men.

2009, Oct. 1 *Perf. 13¼*

3158	50y multi	.80	.40
3159	50y multi	.80	.40
a.	A2543 Pair, #3158-3159	1.75	1.25
3160	50y multi	.80	.40
3161	50y multi	.80	.40
a.	A2544 Horiz. pair, #3160-3161	1.75	1.25
	Nos. 3158-3161 (4)	3.20	1.60

Miniature Sheet

Home Towns A2545

No. 3162 — Paintings by Taiji Harada of views of towns: a, Nagasaki Kunchi (palanquin in parade, Nagasaki, Nagasaki prefecture). b, Rice Paddy Spirit Festival (people in rice paddy, Satsumasendai, Kagoshima prefecture). c, Carp Streamers (people making carp streamers, Iwakura, Aichi prefecture). d, Doll Send-off (winter parade, Waga District, Iwate prefecture). e, Deer Dance (musicians, people in blue, white, red and yellow costumes holding poles with banners, Kitauwa District, Ehime prefecture). f, Business Success Festival (crowd in front of Ebisu Shrine, Naniwa Ward, Osaka prefecture). g, Amahage Festival (masked man visiting children and parents, Akumi District, Yamagata prefecture). h, Lion Dance (large crowd surrounding float with dancers on tower, Wakayama, Wakayama prefecture). i, Floating Doll Festival (women dropping dolls into Sendai River, Tottori, Tottori prefecture). j, Gruel Doll Festival (children at table near Kama River, Tano District, Gumma prefecture).

2009, Oct. 8 Photo. *Perf. 13*

3162	A2545 Sheet of 10	13.00	13.00
a.-j.	80y Any single	1.25	.60

International Letter Writing Week Type of 2000

Hiroshige paintings from 53 Stations of the Tokaido Highway: 90y, Fujisawa. 110y, Okitsu. 130y, Chiryu.

2009, Oct. 9 Photo. *Perf. 13¼*

3163	A2119 90y multi	1.75	.50
3164	A2119 110y multi	2.25	.50
3165	A2119 130y multi	2.50	.50
	Nos. 3163-3165 (3)	6.50	1.50

See listing of No. 4448 for images of each Hiroshige print.

Miniature Sheet

Diplomatic Relations Between Japan and Austria, 140th Anniv. — A2546

No. 3166: a, Portrait of Emilie Flöge, by Gustav Klimt (45x30mm). b, Autumn Clothing, by Shoen Uemura (45x30mm). c, Vienna Art History Museum and fountain (39x30mm). d, Empress Elizabeth of Austria, by Franz Winterhalter (39x30mm). e, Melk Abbey (steeple at right), Austria (39x30mm). f, Melk Abbey (steeple at left, 39x30mm). g, Wolfgang Amadeus Mozart and Salzburg (39x30mm). h, Salzburg (39x30mm). i, Hallstatt waterfront (39x30mm). j, Mountainside buildings, Hallstatt (39x30mm).

2009, Oct. 16 Litho. *Perf. 13¼x13*

3166	A2546 Sheet of 10	16.00	16.00
a.-j.	80y Any single	1.25	.50

See Austria No. 2227.

Miniature Sheet

Diplomatic Relations Between Japan and Hungary, 140th Anniv. — A2547

No. 3167: a, Hungarian flask. b, Mount Fuji, horiz. c, Jar from Japanese tea service. d, Hungarian Parliament (flag above building). e, Hungarian Parliament (building with dome). f, Matyo folk embroidery, Hungary. g, Elizabeth Bridge, Hungary, horiz. h, Crane and leaves fabric pattern from Japanese kimono. i, Herend porcelain figurine (Hussar examining sword blade). j, Herend porcelain vase.

Perf. 13x13¼, 13¼x13

2009, Oct. 16 Litho.

3167 A2547 Sheet of 10 16.00 16.00
a.-j. 80y Any single 1.25 .50

See Hungary No. 4141.

Animation

Miniature Sheet

Naruto: Hurricane Chronicles — A2548

No. 3168: a, Naruto Uzumaki (yellow hair, black and orange shirt). b, Sasuke Uchiha (with open shirt). c, Sakura Haruno (girl with pink hair). d, Kakashi Hatake (with red spiral on sleeve). e, Sai (with sword). f, Shikamaru Nara (clasping hands). g, Deidara (girl with yellow hair and raised hand). h, Itachi Uchiha (with black hair and black and red robe). i, Jiraiya (with white hair). j, Fourth Hokage (yellow hair, white, gray and red robe).

2009, Oct. 23 Litho. *Perf. 13x13¼*

3168 A2548 Sheet of 10 16.00 16.00
a.-j. 80y Any single 1.25 .50

Miniature Sheet

Ibaraki Prefecture Local Autonomy Law, 60th Anniv. — A2549

No. 3169: a, H-2 rocket, Mt. Tsukuba (33x39mm). b, Fukuroda Falls (28x33mm). c, Mitsukuni Tokugawa (1628-1700), Mito daimyo (28x33mm). d, Boat on Kasumigaura (28x33mm). e, Fireworks over Tsuchiura (28x33mm).

Perf. 13¼ (#3169a), 13x13¼

2009, Nov. 4 Photo.

3169 A2549 Sheet of 5 7.50 7.50
a.-e. 80y Any single 1.25 .60

A2550 A2551

New Year 2010 (Year of the Tiger)

A2552 A2553

2009, Nov. 11 Photo. *Perf. 13x13½*

3170 A2550 50y multi 1.00 .30
3171 A2551 80y multi 1.50 .40

Perf. 13¼

3172 A2552 50y +3y multi 1.25 .40
3173 A2553 80y +3y multi 1.75 .40
Nos. 3170-3173 (4) 5.50 1.50

Sheets of two containing Nos. 3170-3171 were lottery prizes. Value, $4.

Phoenix A2554

Kirin Facing Right — A2555

Kirin Facing Left — A2556

2009, Nov. 12 Photo. *Perf. 13¼*

3174 A2554 80y multi 1.25 .50
3175 A2555 80y multi 1.25 .50
3176 A2556 80y multi 1.25 .50
a. Souvenir sheet, #3175-3176 3.50 3.50
Nos. 3174-3176 (3) 3.75 1.50

Enthronement of Emperor Akihito, 20th anniv. Nos. 3174-3176 were printed in sheets containing two each of Nos. 3175 and 3176 and six of No. 3174.

Miniature Sheet

Calligraphy — A2557

No. 3177 — Characters for "tiger" by calligraphers: a, Chikusei Hayashi (character in running script with red background). b, Chosho Kneko (character in clerical style, with denomination at LR, and large red chop at LL). c, Gakufu Toriyama (character in kinbun style in gold with blue green background). d, Hosen Takeuchi (character in kinbun style with denomination at LL, red chop at LR). e, Shiko Miyazaki (character in hiragana script with denomination above Japanese characters and "Nippon" at LL). f, Setsuzan Kitano (character in kokotsubun style with denomination and red chop at LL). g, Masato Seki (character in kinbun style in red). h, Junichi Yanagida (characters in running script with denomination at LL above Japanese characters and "Nippon" at LR). i, Kukoku Tamura (character in clerical script in blue with light blue and white background). j, Bokushun Kito (character in kinbun style with denomination at LR and small red chop at LL).

Litho. & Embossed

2009, Nov. 20 *Perf. 13x13¼*

3177 A2557 Sheet of 10 16.00 16.00
a.-j. 80y Any single 1.25 .50

Miniature Sheets

A2558

Greetings Stamps — A2559

No. 3178: a, Girl and apples. b, Snowman and stars. c, Angel holding toy rabbit. d, Apple, ribbon, ring of roses. e, Figures with blue and pink faces, horiz.

No. 3179: a, Christmas wreath. b, Santa Claus playing violin on chimney. c, Oil lamp and flowers. d, Angel with gift. e, Figure made of fir branches, candle.

Die Cut Perf. 12¾x13, 13x12¾

2009, Nov. 24 Litho.

Self-Adhesive

3178 A2558 Sheet of 5 5.00 5.00
a.-e. 50y Any single .80 .80

Die Cut Perf. 12¾x13

3179 A2559 Sheet of 5 7.00 7.00
a.-e. 80y Any single 1.25 .80

Peach Blossoms A2560

Rape Blossoms A2561

Plum Blossoms and Primrose A2562

Bayberry A2563

Bungo Plum Blossoms A2564

Peach Blossoms A2565

Rape Blossoms A2566

Plum Blossoms and Primrose A2567

Bayberry A2568

Bungo Plum Blossoms A2569

2009, Dec. 1 Photo. *Perf. 13¼*

3180 A2560 50y multi .80 .40
3181 A2561 50y multi .80 .40
3182 A2562 50y multi .80 .40
3183 A2563 50y multi .80 .40
3184 A2564 50y multi .80 .40
a. Vert. strip of 5, #3180-3184 4.50 4.50
3185 A2565 80y multi 1.25 .60
3186 A2566 80y multi 1.25 .60
3187 A2567 80y multi 1.25 .60
3188 A2568 80y multi 1.25 .60
3189 A2569 80y multi 1.25 .60
a. Vert. strip of 5, #3185-3189 6.50 6.50
Nos. 3180-3189 (10) 10.25 5.00

Flowers of Okayama, Chiba, Osaka, Kochi and Oita prefectures.

Prefecture Types of 1991-2007

Designs as before.

Die Cut Perf. 13¼ at T, L and R, Serpentine Die Cut 11¾ at B

2009 Litho. Self-Adhesive

3189B ZA684 50y multi .90 .50

Serpentine Die Cut 11¾ at T and B, Die Cut Perf. 13¼ at L and R

3189C ZA685 50y multi .90 .50
3189D ZA686 50y multi .90 .50
3189E ZA687 50y multi .90 .50

Serpentine Die Cut 11¾ at T, Die Cut Perf. 13¼ at L, R and B

3189F ZA688 50y multi .90 .50
j. Vert. strip of 5, #3189B-3189F 5.50

Serpentine Die Cut 11½ at T, Die Cut Perf. 13½ at L, R and B

3189G ZA115 80y multi 1.40 .90

Serpentine Die Cut 11¾

3189H 80y Katsura Beach 1.40 .90
3189I 80y Sakamoto Ryoma 1.40 .90
k. ZA352 Horiz. pair, #3189H-3189I 3.50
Nos. 3189B-3189I (8) 8.70 5.20

Issued: Nos. 3189B-3189F, Oct.; No. 3189G, 3/19; Nos. 3189H-3189I, Nov.

Animation

Miniature Sheet

Sergeant Keroro A2570

No. 3190: a, Sergeant Keroro, wearing helmet, holding post card. b, Fuyuki Hinata holding post card. c, Natsumi Hinata holding gift. d, Corporal Giroro, wearing helmet, with arms crossed. e, Private Tamama holding gift above head. f, Momoka Nishizawa holding letter. g, Saburo holding stamps. h, Sergeant Major Kururu with stamp on forehead. i, Lance Corporal Dororo, with white helmet, holding scroll. j, Koyuki Azumaya, holding scroll.

2010, Jan. 22 Litho. *Perf. 13*

3190 A2570 Sheet of 10 16.00 16.00
a.-j. 80y Any single 1.25 .50

Miniature Sheets

A2571

Greetings Stamps — A2572

No. 3191: a, Fairy with watering can. b, Fairy giving letter to bird. c, Fairies holding flower basket. d, Fairy with horn on back of flying bird. e, Fairy with violin on flower leaf.

No. 3192: a, Flower bouquet in red wrapping paper, butterflies. b, Woman with flute. c, Flower bouquet in white wrapping paper, butterflies. d, Flowers, G clef. e, Flowers, rabbit.

Die Cut Perf. 12¾x13

2010, Jan. 25 **Litho.**

Self-Adhesive

3191	A2571	Sheet of 5	5.00	5.00
a.-e.		50y Any single	.80	.80
3192	A2572	Sheet of 5	7.00	7.00
a.-e.		80y Any single	1.25	.80

Miniature Sheet

Travel Scenes A2573

No. 3193: a, Matsushima, denomination at LL (stamp 1). b, Matsushima, denomination at LR (stamp 2). c, Sendai Castle ruins (stamp 3). d, Suit of armor and crested helmet (stamp 4). e, Sendai tourist bus (stamp 5). f, A Bathing Woman, sculpture by Venanzo Crocetti, Sendai (stamp 6). g, Tanabata Festival, Sendai (stamp 7). h, Zuihoden Mausoleum (stamp 8). i, Rinno Temple, denomination at LL (stamp 9). j, Garden and pond at Rinno Temple (stamp 10).

2010, Jan. 29 **Litho.** ***Perf. 13***

3193	A2573	Sheet of 10	13.00	13.00
a.-j.		80y Any single	1.25	.50

Tulips A2574

Chinese Milk Vetch A2575

Nijisseiki Pear Blossoms A2576

Coral Tree Blossoms A2577

Fuji Cherry Blossoms A2578

Tulips A2579

Chinese Milk Vetch A2580

Nijisseiki Pear Blossoms A2581

Coral Tree Blossoms A2582

Fuji Cherry Blossoms A2583

2010, Feb. 1 **Photo.** ***Perf. 13¼***

3194	A2574 50y multi		.80	.40
3195	A2575 50y multi		.80	.40
3196	A2576 50y multi		.80	.40
3197	A2577 50y multi		.80	.40
3198	A2578 50y multi		.80	.40
a.	Vert. strip of 5, #3194-3198		4.50	3.00
3199	A2579 80y multi		1.25	.60
3200	A2580 80y multi		1.25	.60
3201	A2581 80y multi		1.25	.60
3202	A2582 80y multi		1.25	.60
3203	A2583 80y multi		1.25	.60
a.	Vert. strip of 5, #3199-3203		6.50	4.50
	Nos. 3194-3203 (10)		10.25	5.00

Flowers of Toyama, Gifu, Tottori, Okinawa and Yamanashi prefectures.

Miniature Sheet

Nara Prefecture Local Autonomy Law, 60th Anniv. — A2584

No. 3204: a, Great Hall of State, cherry blossoms, kemari players (33x39mm). b, Hase Temple, peonies (28x33mm). c, Ukimodo during Nara Candlelight Festival (28x33mm). d, Muro Temple pagoda (28x33mm). e, Mt. Yoshino and cherry blossoms (28x33mm).

Perf. 13¼ (#3204a), 13x13¼

2010, Feb. 8 **Photo.**

3204	A2584	Sheet of 5	6.50	6.50
a.-e.		80y Any single	1.25	.60

Miniature Sheet

Travel Scenes A2585

No. 3205: a, Kurashiki District buildings, denomination at LL (stamp 1). b, Kurashiki District buildings, swans, denomination at UR (stamp 2). c, Ohara Museum of Art (stamp 3). d, Belgian Girl in Kimono, painting by Torajiro Kojima (stamp 4). e, Seto Great Bridge, from distance (stamp 5). f, Arches and roadway of Seto Great Bridge (stamp 6). g, Kotohira Shrine (stamp 7). h, Mt. Iino (stamp 8). i, Bridge, Ritsurin Park, Takamatsu, denomination at LL (stamp 9). j, Bridge, Ritsurin Park, and cherry blossoms, denomination at UR (stamp 10).

2010, Mar. 1 **Litho.** ***Perf. 13***

3205	A2585	Sheet of 10	13.00	13.00
a.-j.		80y Any single	1.25	.60

Miniature Sheet

Characters From Peanuts Comic Strip — A2586

No. 3206: a, Snoopy reading letter (33x32mm). b, Woodstock reading letter under lamp (33x32mm). c, Peppermint Patty reading letter (33x32mm). d, Snoopy hugging Woodstock (35mm diameter). e, Sally reading letter (33x32mm). f, Snoopy and Woodstock on doghouse (35x29mm heart-shaped). g, Snoopy giving letter to Woodstock (33x32mm). h, Charlie Brown writing letter (33x32mm).

Die Cut Perf. 13½

2010, Mar. 3 **Litho.**

Self-Adhesive

3206	A2586	Sheet of 10, #3206c-3206h, 2 each #3206a-3206b	13.00	13.00
a.-h.		80y Any single	1.25	.80

Peony A2587

Sudachi Flowers A2588

Unzen Azalea Flowers A2589

Kakitsubata Irises A2590

Camphor Blossoms A2591

Peonies A2592

Sudachi Flowers A2593

Unzen Azalea Flowers A2594

Kakitsubata Irises A2595

Camphor Blossoms A2596

2010, Mar. 8 **Photo.** ***Perf. 13¼***

3207	A2587 50y multi		.80	.40
3208	A2588 50y multi		.80	.40
3209	A2589 50y multi		.80	.40
3210	A2590 50y multi		.80	.40
3211	A2591 50y multi		.80	.40
a.	Vert. strip of 5, #3207-3211		4.50	3.00
3212	A2592 80y multi		1.25	.60
3213	A2593 80y multi		1.25	.60
3214	A2594 80y multi		1.25	.60
3215	A2595 80y multi		1.25	.60
3216	A2596 80y multi		1.25	.60
a.	Vert. strip of 5, #3212-3216		6.50	4.50
	Nos. 3207-3216 (10)		10.25	5.00

Flowers of Shimane, Tokushima, Nagasaki, Aichi and Saga prefectures.

Miniature Sheet

Friendship With San Marino — A2597

No. 3217: a, La Repubblica, statue by Vittorio Pocchini, San Marino (stamp 1). b, First Tower, San Marino (stamp 2). c, Saint Marinus, angel and crowd from Appearance of Saint Marinus to His People, mural by Emilio Retrosi (stamp 3). d, Angel and crowd from Appearance of Saint Marinus to His People (stamp 4). e, Statue of Liberty, San Marino Government Building (stamp 5). f, Basilica of Saint Marinus (stamp 6). g, Second Tower, San Marino (stamp 7). h, Bell tower, First Tower (stamp 8). i, St. Mary Magdalene, painting by Francesco Menzocchi (stamp 9). j, St. Marinus, painting by unknown artist (stamp 10).

2010, Mar. 23 **Litho.** ***Perf. 13***

3217	A2597	Sheet of 10	16.00	16.00
a.-j.		80y Any single	1.25	.50

See San Marino No. 1818.

Miniature Sheet

Hometown Festival — A2598

No. 3218 — Suwa Grand Shrine Sacred Pillar Festival, Nagano Prefecture: a, Honmiya Shrine, denomination in yellow. b, Maemiya Shrine, denomination in pink. c, Akimiya Shrine, denomination in greenish black. d, Harumiya Shrine, denomination in light blue. e, Men dragging logs to Miya River, denomination in pink. f, Nagamochi, denomination in black. g, Men dragging log down hill, denomination in blue.

2010, Apr. 1 Litho. *Perf. 13¼*

Self-Adhesive

3218 A2598 Sheet of 10, #3218a-3218d, 2 each #3218e-3218g 9.00 9.00
a.-g. 50y Any single .80 .40

Philately Week A2599

No. 3219: a, Tiger from screen painting by Gaho Hashimoto, denomination at UL. b, Peonies from screen painting by Hashimoto, denomination at LL. c, Peonies and birds from screen painting by Hashimoto, denomination at UL. d, Tiger, by Zhang Shanzi, denomination at LR.

Perf. 12¾x12½ Syncopated

2010, Apr. 20 Photo.

3219 A2599 Block of 4 6.00 6.00
a.-d. 80y Any single 1.25 .50

Miniature Sheet

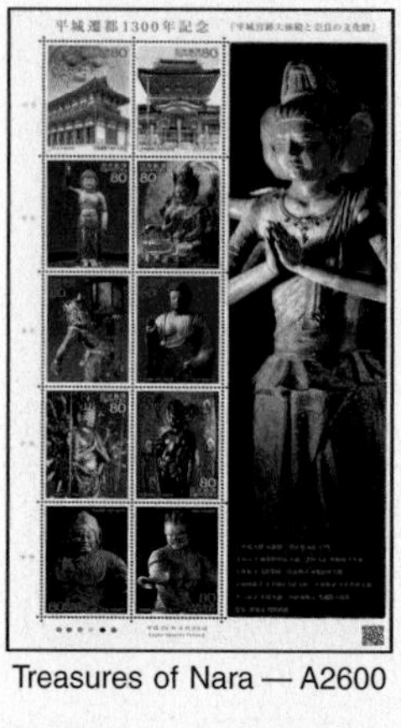

Treasures of Nara — A2600

No. 3220: a, Restored Heijo Palace (stamp 1). b, Inner gate, Kasuga Grand Shrine (stamp 2). c, Tanjo Shaka statue, denomination in white at UR (stamp 3). d, Aizen Myo-o statue, denomination in white at UL (stamp 4). e, Tentoki holding lantern, denomination in gold at UL (stamp 5). f, Buddha Yakushi, denomination in gold at UL (stamp 6). g, Thousand-armed Kannon statue, denomination in white at UR (stamp 7). h, Standing Bodhisattva statue, denomination in white at LR (stamp 8). i, Tamonten statue, denomination in gold at LL (stamp 9). j, Basara Taisho statue, denomination in gold at LR (stamp 10).

2010, Apr. 23 Litho. *Perf. 14x13¾*

3220 A2600 Sheet of 10 16.00 16.00
a.-j. 80y Any single 1.25 .50

Move of Imperial capital to Nara, 1300th anniv.

Hanashobu Iris A2601

Olive Blossoms A2602

Azalea Flowers A2603

Paulownia Blossoms A2604

Crinum Flowers A2605

Hanashobu Irises A2606

Olive Blossoms A2607

Azalea Flowers A2608

Paulownia Blossoms A2609

Crinum Flowers A2610

2010, Mar. 8 Photo. *Perf. 13¼*

3221	A2601	50y multi		.80	.40
3222	A2602	50y multi		.80	.40
3223	A2603	50y multi		.80	.40
3224	A2604	50y multi		.80	.40
3225	A2605	50y multi		.80	.40
a.		Vert. strip of 5, #3221-3225		4.50	3.00
3226	A2606	80y multi		1.25	.60
3227	A2607	80y multi		1.25	.60
3228	A2608	80y multi		1.25	.60
3229	A2609	80y multi		1.25	.60
3230	A2610	80y multi		1.25	.60
a.		Vert. strip of 5, #3226-3230		6.50	4.00
		Nos. 3221-3230 (10)		10.25	5.00

Flowers of Mie, Kagawa, Gumma, Iwate and Miyazaki prefectures.

Kobe-Awaji Expressway Prefecture Type of 1998

Serpentine Die Cut 11½

2010, Aug. Self-Adhesive Litho.

3230B ZA229 80y Like No. Z237 — 2.50
3230C ZA229 80y Like No. Z238 — 2.50
d. Horiz. pair, #3230B-3230C —

Miniature Sheet

A2611

Hello Kitty A2612

No. 3231 — Hello Kitty: a, With butterflies and flowers (28x31mm heart-shaped). b, In kimono, flowers (28x31mm heart-shaped). c, With dragon (28x28mm). d, With mountain (28x28mm). e, With peonies (28x28mm). f, With origami cranes (28x28mm).

No. 3232 — Hello Kitty: a, And Shanghai skyline (30x32mm). b, And pagoda in Shanghai (30x32mm). c, And Tiger (30x32mm). d, With peonies (31x28mm heart-shaped). e, Holding fan (31mm diameter).

Die Cut Perf. 13½

2010, May 6 Litho.

Self-Adhesive

3231 A2611 Sheet of 10, #3231a-3231b, 2 each #3231c-3231f 9.00 9.00
a.-f. 50y Any single .80 .80

Die Cut Perf. 12½

3232 A2612 Sheet of 10, 2 each #3232a-3232e 13.00 13.00
a.-e. 80y Any single 1.25 .80

Miniature Sheet

Kochi Prefecture Local Autonomy Law, 60th Anniv. — A2613

No. 3233: a, Ryoma Sakamoto (1836-67), samurai, and Katsura Beach (33x39mm). b, Farmhouse clock, Aki (28x33mm). c, Harimaya Bridge, streetcar (28x33mm). d, Paper carp streamers (28x33mm). e, Cape Ashizuri Lighthouse (28x33mm).

Perf. 13¼ (#3233a), 13x13¼

2010, May 14 Photo.

3233 A2613 Sheet of 5 7.00 7.00
a.-e. 80y Any single 1.25 .60

Miniature Sheet

Kanagawa Prefecture Afforestation — A2614

No. 3234: a, Pinks. b, Japanese cedar. c, Sawtooth oak. d, Japanese maple. e, Golden-rayed lilies. f, Evergreen oak. g, Japanese chinquapin. h, Ginkgo. i, Beech. j, Gentians.

2010, May 21 Litho. *Perf. 13*

3234 A2614 Sheet of 10 10.00 10.00
a.-j. 50y Any single .80 .40

Miniature Sheets

A2615

2010 World Cup Soccer Championships, South Africa — A2616

No. 3235: a, Soccer ball, African animals (33x39mm). b, World Cup trophy (29x38mm). c, Poster for 2010 World Cup tournament (29x38mm). d, Emblem of 2010 World Cup (29x38mm). e, Emblem of Japan Soccer Association (29x38mm).

No. 3236 — Posters for World Cup tournaments of: a, 1930. b, 1934. c, 1938. d, 1950. e, 1954. f, 1958. g, 1962. h, 1970. i, 1978. j, 1986. k, 1990. l, 1994. m, 1998. n, 2002. o, 2006. p, Jules Rimet Cup. q, Jules Rimet Cup and hand.

Litho., Litho. & Embossed (#3235a)

Perf. 13, 14x13½ (#3235a)

2010, May 31

3235 A2615 Sheet of 5 8.00 8.00
a.-e. 80y Any single 1.25 .50

Litho.

Perf. 13

3236 A2616 Sheet of 20, #3236a-3236o, 3 #3236p, 2 #3236q 35.00 35.00
a.-q. 80y Any single 1.25 .50

Miniature Sheet

Asia-Pacific Economic Cooperation Economic Leader's Meeting, Yokohama — A2617

No. 3237: a, Flowers at top and left, denomination at LR. b, Flowers at top and right, denomination at LL. c, Purple flower at center right, denomination at UR. d, Purple flower at center left, denomination at UL. e, Pink rose at center right, denomination at LL. f, Pink rose at center left, denomination at LR. g, White flowers at center right, denomination at UR. h, White flowers at center left, denomination at UL. i, Flowers at bottom and left, red flowers at LR, denomination at UR. j, Flowers at bottom and right, red flowers at LL, denomination at UL.

2010, June 4 **Litho.** ***Perf. 13***

3237 A2617 Sheet of 10 16.00 16.00
a.-j. 80y Any single 1.25 .50

Emblem of Japan Academy A2618

Certificate and Photograph of First Awards Ceremony A2619

Venue of First Awards Ceremony A2620

Former Japan Academy Hall A2621

Rooster — A2622

2010, June 7 **Litho.** ***Perf. 13***

3238 A2618 80y multi 1.25 .50
3239 A2619 80y multi 1.25 .50
3240 A2620 80y multi 1.25 .50
3241 A2621 80y multi 1.25 .50
3242 A2622 80y multi 1.25 .50
a. Vert. strip of 5, #3238-3242 7.50 7.50
Nos. 3238-3242 (5) 6.25 2.50

Japan Academy Prizes, cent.

Animation

Miniature Sheet

Full Metal Alchemist — A2623

No. 3243: a, Edward Elric (with yellow hair and hand on his shoulder). b, Alphonse Elric (in black armor). c, Riza Hawkeye (holding gun). d, Roy Mustang with symbol on back of hand. e, Xiao Mei (panda). f, May Chang (with braided hair). g, Ling Yao holding sword. h, Lan Fan holding dagger. i, Winry Rockbell (girl in tank top). j, Edward Elric with dog, Den.

2010, June 14 **Litho.** ***Perf. 13x13¼***

3243 A2623 Sheet of 10 16.00 16.00
a.-j. 80y Any single 1.25 .50

Miniature Sheet

Gifu Local Autonomy Law, 60th Anniv. — A2624

No. 3244: a, Cormorant fishing on Nagara River (32x39mm). b, Gifu Castle (28x33mm). c, Yokokura Temple (28x33mm). d, Art exhibition, Mino (28x33mm). e, Restored buildings, Magome (28x33mm).

Perf. 13¼ (#3244a), 13x13¼

2010, June 18 **Photo.**

3244 A2624 Sheet of 5 7.00 7.00
a.-e. 80y Any single 1.25 .60

Revision of Japan-United States Security Treaty, 50th Anniv. — A2625

Designs: No. 3245, Flags of U.S. and Japan, Japanese Prime Minister Nobusuke Kishi and U.S. President Dwight D. Eisenhower. No. 3246, Japanese Diet and U.S. Capitol.

2010, June 23 **Litho.** ***Perf. 13***

3245 80y multi 1.25 .50
3246 80y multi 1.25 .50
a. A2625 Pair, #3245-3246 3.00 1.50

Miniature Sheet

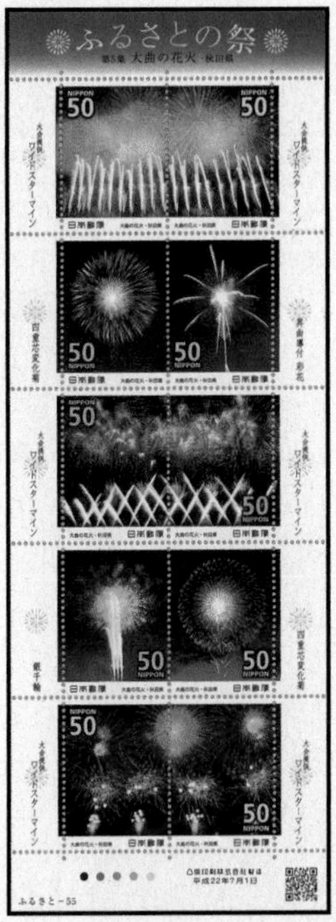

National Fireworks Competition, Omagari, Akita Prefecture — A2626

No. 3247 — Various fireworks with denomination in: a, Yellow green at UL, country name in Japanese characters at LL. b, Yellow green at UR. c, Pale orange at LL. d, Blue at LL. e, Rose at UL. f, Rose at LR, country name in Japanese characters at LR. g, Rose at LR, country name in Japanese characters at LL. h, Blue green at LR. i, Yellow green at UL, country name in Japanese characters at LR. j, Yellow green at LR.

2010, July 1 **Litho.** ***Perf. 13¼***

3247 A2626 Sheet of 10 10.00 10.00
a.-j. 50y Any single .80 .40

Miniature Sheet

Travel Scenes A2627

No. 3248: a, Kurushima-Kaikyo Great Bridge, denomination at LL (stamp 1). b, Kurushima-Kaikyo Great Bridge, denomination at LR (stamp 2). c, Jodo Temple, denomination at UR (stamp 3). d, Jodo Temple, denomination at UL (stamp 4). e, Bridge, sculptures on Mt. Shirataki (stamp 5). f, Kojoji three-story pagoda (stamp 6). g, Oyamazumi Shrine (stamp 7). h, Omishima Bridge, boat (stamp 8). i, Building with red window shutters at Imabari Castle (stamp 9). j, Six-story donjon at Imabari Castle (stamp 10).

2010, July 8 **Litho.** ***Perf. 13x13¼***

3248 A2627 Sheet of 10 13.00 13.00
a.-j. 80y Any single 1.25 .60

Emperor Koko, Poet A2628

Lady Ise, Poet A2629

Saki no Daisojo Gyoson, Poet A2630

Yushi Naishinno-ke no Kii, Poet A2631

Sutoku In, Poet — A2632

Poetry A2633

No. 3254 — Poetry in Japanese calligraphy and: a, Purple flowers. b, Emperor Koko. c, Pond. d, Lady Ise. e, Hill and flowering trees. f, Saki no Daisojo Gyoson. g, Ocean waves. h, Yushi Naishinno-ke no Kii. i, Waterfall. j, Sutoku In.

2010, July 23 Photo. *Perf. 13¼*

3249	A2628	50y multi	.80	.30
3250	A2629	50y multi	.80	.30
3251	A2630	50y multi	.80	.30
3252	A2631	50y multi	.80	.30
3253	A2632	50y multi	.80	.30
a.		Vert. strip of 5, #3249-3253	5.00	3.50

Perf. 12¾x13

3254	A2633	Sheet of 10	16.00	16.00
a.-j.		80y Any single	1.25	.50

Letter Writing Day.

Suruga Street, by Hiroshige A2634

Woman Reading a Letter, by Utamaro A2635

Dyer's Quarters, Kanda, by Hiroshige A2636

Sojuro Sawamura II as Kurando Ogishi, by Sharaku A2637

Asakusa Ricefields and Torinomachi Festival, by Hiroshige A2638

White Uchikake, by Utamaro A2639

Takinogawa, Oji, by Hiroshige A2640

Torazo Tanimura as Yaheiji Washizuka, by Sharaku A2641

Yamashita Park, Ueno, by Hiroshige A2642

Glass Goblet, by Utamaro A2643

2010, Aug. 2 Litho. *Perf. 13¼*

3255		Sheet of 10	13.00	13.00
a.	A2634	80y multi	1.25	.60
b.	A2635	80y multi	1.25	.60
c.	A2636	80y multi	1.25	.60
d.	A2637	80y multi	1.25	.60
e.	A2638	80y multi	1.25	.60
f.	A2639	80y multi	1.25	.60
g.	A2640	80y multi	1.25	.60
h.	A2641	80y multi	1.25	.60
i.	A2642	80y multi	1.25	.60
j.	A2643	80y multi	1.25	.60

Life in Edo (Tokyo).

Miniature Sheet

Fukui Local Autonomy Law, 60th Anniv. — A2644

No. 3256: a, Dinosaur at Tojimbo (32x39mm). b, Narcissus (28x33mm). c, Lake and flowers (28x33mm). d, Ichijodani ruins, cherry tree (28x33mm). e, Crab, Echizen-Kaga Kaigan Quasi-National Park (28x33mm).

Perf. 13¼ (#3256a), 13x13¼

2010, Aug. 9 Photo.

3256	A2644	Sheet of 5	7.00	7.00
a.-e.		80y Any single	1.25	.60

Miniature Sheet

Home Towns A2645

No. 3257 — Paintings by Taiji Harada of views of Hokkaido prefecture towns: a, Shiranuka Line (Farmhouses, haystack, two cows, Shiranuka). b, Shiranuka Line (Train, three cows, Shiranuka). c, Red-crowned Cranes (Building near forest in snow, Tsurui). d, Red-crowned Cranes (Woman feeding cranes, Tsurui). e, Flowers of the Land (Houses, trees hills, Biei). f, Flowers of the Land (Tractor, hills, trees, Biei). g, Farm (Farm buildings, mail box cows, Ishikari). h, Farm (Farm buildings, silo, farmer tending cow, Ishikari). i, Hibernation (Building in snow, fishing boats, Wakkanai). j, Canal in Spring (Boats in canal, Otaru).

2010, Sept. 10 Photo. *Perf. 13*

3257	A2645	Sheet of 10	16.00	16.00
a.-j.		80y Any single	1.25	.60

Biplane of Henri Farman — A2646

Aeronautical Research Plane — A2647

Asuka — A2648

Boeing 747-400 — A2649

Mitsubishi Regional Jet — A2650

Monoplane of Hans Grade — A2651

YS-11 — A2652

Kawasaki T-4 — A2653

US-2 — A2654

Supersonic Plane — A2655

2010, Sept. 21 Litho. *Perf. 13*

3258		Sheet of 10	16.00	16.00
a.	A2646	80y multi	1.25	.50
b.	A2647	80y multi	1.25	.50
c.	A2648	80y multi	1.25	.50
d.	A2649	80y multi	1.25	.50
e.	A2650	80y multi	1.25	.50
f.	A2651	80y multi	1.25	.50
g.	A2652	80y multi	1.25	.50
h.	A2653	80y multi	1.25	.50
i.	A2654	80y multi	1.25	.50
j.	A2655	80y multi	1.25	.50

Aviation in Japan, cent.

Animation

Miniature Sheet

Chibi Maruko-chan — A2656

No. 3259: a, Sakura family members, Maruko, Sakiko, and mother Sumire (denomination in red at UL). b, Sakura family members father Hiroshi, grandfather Tomozo, and grandmother Kotake (denomination in white at LL). c, Maruko blowing bubbles (holding gun). d, Tomozo and bubbles. e, Hiroshi and Maruko with glow worm. f, Sakiko with glow worm. g, Sumire preparing food. h, Maruko and Kotake preparing food. i, Hamaji and Butaro (boys and snowflakes). j, Maruko and Tama-chan (and snowflakes).

2010, Sept. 22 Litho. *Perf. 13x13¼*

3259	A2656	Sheet of 10	16.00	16.00
a.-j.		80y Any single	1.25	.50

Chiba Central Sports Center and Chiba Marine Stadium A2657

Hammer Throw A2658

Equestrian A2659

Rock Climbing A2660

Pole Vault — A2661

2010, Sept. 24 Litho. *Perf. 13x13¼*

3260		Sheet of 10, 2 each #a-e	10.00	10.00
a.	A2657	50y multi	.80	.40
b.	A2658	50y multi	.80	.40
c.	A2659	50y multi	.80	.40
d.	A2660	50y multi	.80	.40
e.	A2661	50y multi	.80	.40

65th National Athletics Meet, Chiba.

Miniature Sheet

Travel Scenes A2662

No. 3261: a, Akashi Strait Great Bridge, denomination in blue at UL (stamp 1). b, Akashi Strait Great Bridge, Sun Yat-sen Memorial Hall, Kobe, denomination at UR (stamp 2). c, Flowers, Awaji Island, denomination at UR to right of "Nippon" (stamp 3). d, Flowers, Awaji Island, denomination at UR below "Nippon" (stamp 4). e, Awaji puppet theater, denomination at UR (stamp 5). f, Awaji puppet theater, denomination at UL (stamp 6). g, Onaruto Bridge, denomination in white at LL (stamp 7). h, Onaruto Bridge, denomination in white at UR(stamp 8). i, Bridge, Naruto Whirlpools (stamp 9). j, Esaki Lighthouse (stamp 10).

2010, Oct. 1 Litho. *Perf. 13x13¼*

3261 A2662 Sheet of 10 13.00 13.00
a.-j. 80y Any single 1.25 .60

Miniature Sheet

Aichi Local Autonomy Law, 60th Anniv. — A2663

No. 3262: a, Golden dolphin sculpture at Nagoya Castle, irises, Atsumi Peninsula (32x39mm). b, Eurasian scops owl (28x33mm). c, Ginkgo leaves (28x33mm). d, Seto ceramic jar (28x33mm). e, Cherry blossoms (28x33mm).

Perf. 13¼ (#3262a), 13x13¼

2010, Oct. 4 Photo.

3262 A2663 Sheet of 5 7.00 7.00
a.-e. 80y Any single 1.25 .60

Intl. Letter Writing Week — A2664

Painting details: 90y, Michitose, by Shinsui Ito. 110y, Nozaki Village, by Kiyokata Kaburagi. 130y, Botanyuki, by Shoen Uemura, horiz.

2010, Oct. 8 Photo. *Perf. 13¼*

3263 A2664 90y multi 1.75 .50
3264 A2664 110y multi 2.25 .50
3265 A2664 130y multi 2.50 .50
Nos. 3263-3265 (3) 8.25 6.25

Miniature Sheet

Tenth Conference of Parties to the Convention on Biological Diversity, Nagoya — A2665

No. 3266: a, Lake Mashu, frost-covered trees. b, Spotted seal. c, Mt. Tsurugi. d, Japanese antelope. e, Buildings in mountains. f, Common tree frog and flowers. g, Banks of Shimanto River. h, Common kingfisher. i, Flowers at Cape Tamatori. j, False clownfish and sea anemone.

2010, Oct. 18 Litho. *Perf. 13x13¼*

3266 A2665 Sheet of 10 16.00 16.00
a.-j. 80y Any single 1.25 .50

Miniature Sheet

Friendship Between Japan and Portugal, 150th Anniv. — A2666

No. 3267: a, Japanese screen painting depicting bow of Portuguese ship, denomination at LL (30x45mm, stamp 1). b, Japanese screen painting depicting stern of Portuguese ship, denomination at LR (30x45mm, stamp 2). c, Belém Tower, Lisbon (30x43mm, stamp 3). d, Statue of St. Vincent (30x43mm, stamp 4). e, Monastery of the Hieronymites, Lisbon (30x43mm, stamp 5). f, Ruins of Roman Temple of Evora, Portugal (30x43mm, stamp 6). g, Oporto, Portugal, and boat (30x43mm, stamp 7). h, Batalha Monastery, Batalha, Portugal (30x43mm, stamp 8). i, Portuguese decorative tiles (30x43mm, stamp 9). j, Puppet of St. Isabel of Portugal (30x43mm, stamp 10).

2010, Oct. 22 Litho. *Perf. 13¼x13*

3267 A2666 Sheet of 10 16.00 16.00
a.-j. 80y Any single 1.25 .50

See Portugal No. 3271.

Seven People A2667

Eight People A2668

Congress Emblem A2669

Peace Statute, Nagasaki A2670

2010, Nov. 5 Photo. *Perf. 13*

3268 Sheet of 10, 2 each #3268a-3268c, 4 #3268d 16.00 16.00
a. A2667 80y multi 1.25 .50
b. A2668 80y multi 1.25 .50
c. A2669 80y multi 1.25 .50
d. A2670 80y multi 1.25 .50

Third UNI Global Union World Congress, Nagasaki.

Miniature Sheets

A2671

A2672

Greetings — A2673

No. 3269: a, Star and Santa Claus with sack. b, Poinsettias, ribbon and bell. c, Sleigh of Santa Claus over church, horiz. d, Heart-shaped wreath. e, Reindeer and Aurora Borealis.

No. 3270: a, Santa Claus. b, Christmas tree. c, Sleigh of Santa Claus over mountain, horiz. d, Wreath with pine cones. e, Reindeer and Aurora Borealis, diff.

No. 3271: a, Fairy with horn flying above town. b, Snowman juggling snowballs. c, Children singing, horiz. d, Rose in box. e, Cakes.

Die Cut Perf. 13

2010, Nov. 8 Litho.

Self-Adhesive

3269 A2671 Sheet of 5 5.00 5.00
a.-e. 50y Any single .80 .80
3270 A2672 Sheet of 5 7.00 7.00
a.-e. 80y Any single 1.25 .80
3271 A2673 Sheet of 5 9.00 9.00
a.-e. 90y Any single 1.40 .80

A2674 A2675

New Year 2011 (Year of the Rabbit)

A2676 A2677

2010, Nov. 10 Photo. *Perf. 13x13½*

3272 A2674 50y multi 1.00 .30
3273 A2675 80y multi 1.50 .40

Photo. & Typo.

Perf. 13¼

3274 A2676 50y +3y multi 1.25 .40
3275 A2677 80y +3y multi 1.75 .40
Nos. 3272-3275 (4) 6.75 5.15

Sheets of two containing Nos. 3272-3273 were lottery prizes. Value, $3.25.

Miniature Sheet

Aomori Local Autonomy Law, 60th Anniv. — A2678

No. 3276: a, Apples, Nebuta Festival floats (32x39mm). b, Hirosaki Castle and cherry blossoms (28x33mm). c, Three Shrines Festival, Hachinohe (28x33mm). d, Lake Towada (28x33mm). e, Horse and Shiriyazaki Lighthouse (28x33mm).

Perf. 13¼ (#3276a), 13x13¼

2010, Nov. 15 Photo.

3276 A2678 Sheet of 5 7.00 7.00
a.-e. 80y Any single 1.25 .60

Miniature Sheet

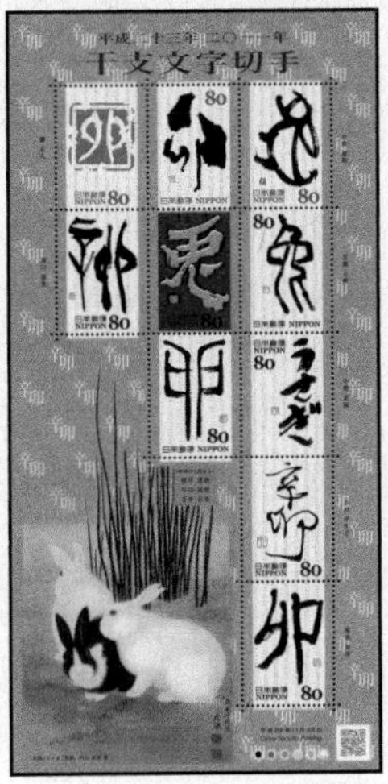

Edo Calligraphy — A2679

No. 3277 — Charcters for "rabbit": a, In Kinbun style (red character). b, In Six Dynasties style standard script (heavy black characters with red chop at LL, denomination at UR. c, In oracle bone script (single black character resembling animal with legs and tail, denomination at LR). d, In oracle bone script (three characters having horizontal line at UL, with red chop at LR, denomination at LR). e, In clerical script (silver character on green background). f, In small seal script (denomination at UL, "Nippon" at LR). g, In seal script (two black characters, with red chop, denomination and "Nippon" at LR). h, In Hirigana style (black character with denomination and "Nippon" at UL, red chop near center). i, In running script (black character with small dot at top, with denomination at LR and "Nippon" at LL). j, In standard script (two black characters with red chop and denomination at LR, "Nippon" at LL).

Litho. & Embossed

2010, Dec. 3 *Perf. 13x13¼*

3277 A2679 Sheet of 10 16.00 16.00
a.-j. 80y Any single 1.25 .50

Japanese Diet, 120th Anniv. A2680

Stained-glass window from Central Hall, old and new Diet buildings with entranceway of: No. 3278, New Diet. No. 3279, Old Diet.

2010, Nov. 29 Litho. *Perf. 13*

3278	80y multi		1.25	.50
3279	80y multi		1.25	.50
a.	A2680 Horiz. pair, #3278-3279		3.00	1.50

Miniature Sheet

Home Towns A2681

No. 3280 — Paintings by Taiji Harada of views of Tohuku region towns: a, Paulownia Village (Cyclist near house, Mishima, Fukushima prefecture). b, Paulownia Village (Farmers and tree near water, Mishima). c, Bonnet Bus (White bus, Hiraizumi, Iwate prefecture). d, Bonnet Bus (Houses, people under umbrella, Hiraizumi). e, Bent House by the Sea (Mother with children near sea, Yurihonjo, Akita prefecture). f, After the Snowfall (Person and houses in snow, Akita, Akita prefecture). g, Railbus (Railbus and station, Kamikita District, Aomori prefecture). h, Railbus (People at station, Kamikita District). i, Dear Home (People on path near house, Tsuruoka, Yamagata prefecture). j, Kokeshi Doll (Children and adults near doll vendor's stall, Shiroishi, Miyagi prefecture).

2010, Dec. 1 Photo. *Perf. 13*

3280	A2681	Sheet of 10	13.00	13.00
a.-j.		80y Any single	1.25	.60

Mandarin Duck Type of 2007

Perf. 13¾x13½ Syncopated

2010, Jan. Litho.

3281	A2352	50y multi	.90	.50

Prefecture Type of 1990 Redrawn and Prefecture Types of 1991-96

Designs as before.

Serpentine Die Cut 10¾x11½

2010 Litho. Self-Adhesive

3282	ZA85	80y multi	1.25	.60
3283	ZA86	80y multi	1.25	.60
3284	ZA87	80y multi	1.25	.60
3285	ZA88	80y multi	1.25	.60
a.		Horiz. strip of 4, #3282-3285	6.00	6.00
3286	ZA97	80y multi	1.25	.60
3287	ZA98	80y multi	1.25	.60
3288	ZA99	80y multi	1.25	.60
3289	ZA100	80y multi	1.25	.60
a.		Horiz. strip of 4, #3286-3289	6.00	6.00

Serpentine Die Cut 11½x11¾

3290	ZA186	80y multi	1.25	.60
		Nos. 3282-3290 (9)	11.25	5.40

Issued: Nos. 3282-3289, Mar.; No. 3290, Apr.

Hisoka Maeshima (1835-1919), Founder of Japanese Postal Service A2682

Little Cuckoo A2683

Mute Swan A2684

Silver Crane A2685

Burial Statue of Warrior, Ota A2686

Bazara-Taisho, c. 710-794 A2687

2010-11 Photo. *Perf. 13x13½*

3293	A2682	1y brown	.30	.25
3294	A2683	3y green	.30	.25
3295	A2684	5y blue & lt bl	.30	.25
3296	A2685	100y multi	2.50	.40
3297	A2686	200y vermilion	5.00	.40
3298	A2687	500y dark green	14.00	.50
		Nos. 3293-3298 (6)	22.40	2.05

Issued: 1y, 1/7/11; 3y, 12/8; 5y, 12/6; 100y, 12/27; 200y, 2/10/11; 500y, 12/15. Compare type A2682 with types A563a and A3348, types A2683-A2687 with types A713, A714, A718a, A718d, A1013 and A1207.

Miniature Sheet

Saga Local Autonomy Law, 60th Anniv. — A2688

No. 3299: a, Shigenobu Okuma (1838-1922), politician, and Arita porcelain (32x39mm). b, Yoshinogari ruins (28x33mm). c, Yutoku Inari shrine and bridge (28x33mm). d, Hot-air balloons, Saga International Balloon Festival (28x33mm). e, Sea bream float, Karatsu Festival (28x33mm).

Perf. 13¼ (#3299a), 13x13¼

2011, Jan. 14 Photo.

3299	A2688	Sheet of 5	7.00	7.00
a.-e.		80y Any single	1.25	.60

Miniature Sheet

Phila Nippon'11, Yokohama — A2689

No. 3300: a, Mighty Atom (blue background, 28x48mm). b, Doraemon (green background, 28x48mm). c, Pikachu (purple background, 28x48mm), d, Hello Kitty (red background, 28x48mm). e, Rabbit riding donkey from 11th cent. scroll (28x48mm). f, Mighty Atom, diff. (28x32mm). g, Doraemon, diff. (28x32mm). h, Pikachu, diff. (28x32mm). i, Hello Kitty, diff. (28x32mm). j, Rabbit riding donkey, diff. (28x32mm).

Die Cut Perf. 12¾x13

2011, Jan. 21 Litho.

Self-Adhesive

3300	A2689	Sheet of 10	16.00	16.00
a.-j.		80y Any single	1.50	.60

Miniature Sheet

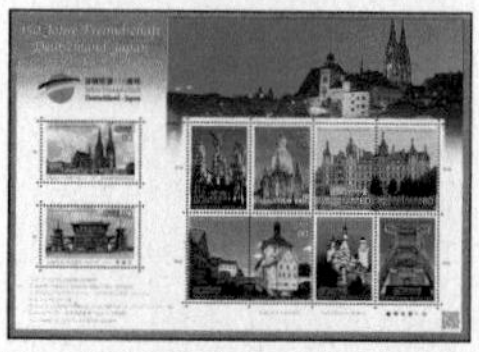

Friendship Between Japan and Germany, 150th Anniv. — A2690

No. 3301 — UNESCO World Heritage Sites and other landmarks: a, Old Town, Regensburg, horiz. (45x26mm, stamp 1). b, Yakushi-ji, Historic Monuments of Ancient Nara, Japan, horiz. (45x26mm, stamp 2). c, Quadriga of Brandenburg Gate, Berlin (27x38mm, stamp 3). d, Frauenkirche, Dresden (27x38mm, stamp 4). e, Schwerin Castle (two tall spires, 27x38mm, stamp 5). f, Schwerin Castle (three tall spires, 27x38mm, stamp 6). g, Old Town, Bamberg (bridge at right, 27x38mm, stamp 7). h, Old Town, Bamberg (bridge at left, 27x38mm, stamp 8). i, Neuschwanstein Castle (27x38mm, stamp 9). j, Tower at Zollverein Coal Mine Industrial Complex, Essen (27x38mm, stamp 10).

2011, Jan. 24 Litho. *Perf. 13*

3301	A2690	Sheet of 10	16.00	16.00
a.-j.		80y Any single	1.25	.50

Miniature Sheet

Travel Scenes A2691

No. 3302: a, Snow sculpture of Frauenkirche of Dresden, Germany at Sapporo Snow Festival, German and Japanese flags (stamp 1). b, Penguins walking at Asahiyama Zoo (stamp 2). c, Lamp post along canal at Otaru Snow Light Path (stamp 3). d, Building along canal in Otaru (stamp 4). e, Lake Toya in winter (stamp 5). f, Hakodate Orthodox Christian Church (stamp 6). g, Lake and snow-capped mountains at Shiretoko UNESCO World Heritage Site, denomination at LL (stamp 7). h, Lake and snow-capped mountains at Shiretoko UNESCO World Heritage Site, denomination at LR (stamp 8). i, Red-crowned cranes (stamp 9). j, Ice on Sea of Okhotsk near Abashiri (stamp 10).

2011, Feb. 1 Litho. *Perf. 13x13¼*

3302	A2691	Sheet of 10	13.00	13.00
a.-j.		80y Any single	1.25	.60

Miniature Sheets

A2692

Greetings Stamps — A2693

No. 3303: a, Fawn, yellow crocuses. b, Bluebird, blue lilies. c, Rose, butterfly made of pink violets. d, Swans, blue roses. e, Hares, strawberries and flowers.

No. 3304: a, Flowers trailing from fairy's hat. b, Fairy blowing horn in daffodils. c, Fairy on back of bird delivering mail, horiz. d, Fairy with letter on rainbow. e, Fairy writing in purple flowers.

2011, Feb. 4 Litho. *Die Cut Perf.*

Self-Adhesive

3303	A2692	Sheet of 5	5.00	5.00
a.-e.		50y Any single	.80	.80

Die Cut Perf. 13

3304	A2693	Sheet of 5	7.00	7.00
a.-e.		80y Any single	1.25	.80

Rose A2694

Apple Blossoms A2695

Primroses A2696

Japanese Grapefruit Blossoms A2697

Kyushu Azalea Flowers A2698

Roses A2699

Apple Blossoms A2700

Primroses A2701

Japanese Grapefruit Blossoms A2702

Kyushu Azalea Flowers A2703

2011, Feb. 8 Photo. *Perf. 13¼*

3305	A2694	50y multi	.80	.40
3306	A2695	50y multi	.80	.40
3307	A2696	50y multi	.80	.40
3308	A2697	50y multi	.80	.40
3309	A2698	50y multi	.80	.40
a.		Vert. strip of 5, #3305-3309	4.50	3.00
3310	A2699	80y multi	1.25	.60
3311	A2700	80y multi	1.25	.60
3312	A2701	80y multi	1.25	.60
3313	A2702	80y multi	1.25	.60
3314	A2703	80y multi	1.25	.60
a.		Vert. strip of 5, #3310-3314	7.50	4.50
		Nos. 3305-3314 (10)	10.25	5.00

Flowers of Ibaraki, Aomori, Saitama, Yamaguchi and Kagoshima prefectures.

Miniature Sheet

Home Towns A2704

No. 3315 — Paintings by Taiji Harada of views of towns of Kanto region: a, Rice Nursery (farmers in rice field, Hitachi, Ibaraka prefecture, denomination at UL). b, Rice Nursery (farmers in rice field, Hitachi, denomination at LL). c, Spring Breeze (woman and child near farmhouse, Kumagaya, Saitama prefecture, denomination at LL). d, Spring Breeze (farm buildings, trees in bloom in orchard, Kumagaya, denomination at UL). e,Spring Garden (tall tree, farmer with pole near shed, Tone District, Gumma prefecture). f, Spring Garden (boy with dog near mailbox near farmhouse, Tone District). g, Wheat Field (farmer and dog in field, Haga District, Tochigi prefecture). h, Home Inside a Tree Grove (house amidst trees, Kisarazu, Chiba prefecture). i, Roadside Zelkova Trees (city street with trees, Shibuya Ward, Tokyo prefecture). j, Westernized Building (building with lamp post, Yokohama, Kanagawa prefecture).

2011, Mar. 1 Photo. *Perf. 13*

3315	A2704	Sheet of 10	13.00	13.00
a.-j.		80y Any single	1.25	.60

Miniature Sheets

Characters From Children's Stories by Beatrix Potter — A2705

Scenes From *The Tale of Peter Rabbit*, by Beatrix Potter A2706

No. 3316: a, Peter Rabbit running. b, Mouse of Gloucester. c, Peter Rabbit standing. d, Benjamin Bunny. e, Pigling Bland. f, Old Mr. Brown and Nutkin. g, Mrs. Tiggy-winkle. h, Jemima Puddle-duck. i, Squirrel Nutkin. j, Tom Kitten.

No. 3317: a, Rabbit family's home under fir tree. b, Mother and younger sisters (27x37mm oval). c, Peter Rabbit and back of sisters. d, Mother dressing Peter (29mm diameter) e, Mother holding basket. f, Peter near pots in garden, robin. g, Peter going under garden fence (27x37mm oval). h, Peter eating vegetables. i, Peter encountering Mr. McGregor (29mm diameter). j, Peter running from Mr. McGregor (29mm diameter).

2011, Mar. 3 Litho. *Die Cut Perf.*
Self-Adhesive

3316	A2705	Sheet of 10	11.00	11.00
a.-j.		50y Any single	.80	.80

Die Cut Perf. 13¼x13¾, Die Cut Perf.

3317	A2706	Sheet of 10	13.00	13.00
a.-j.		80y Any single	1.25	.80

Animation
Miniature Sheet

One Piece A2707

No. 3318: a, Monkey D. Luffy wearing hat and red shirt. b, Chopper wearing large top hat. c, Sanji wearing blue shirt. d, Zoro wearing white shirt. e, Robin wearing red striped blouse. f, Nami wearing beige shirt. g, Usopp and Brook. h, Franky with chain on chest. i, D Successor 1 with fire coming from hand. j, D Successor 2 with clouds.

2011, Mar. 23 Litho. *Perf. 13x13¼*

3318	A2707	Sheet of 10	16.00	16.00
a.-j.		80y Any single	1.25	.50

Samisen Player A2708

Samisen Player and Children A2709

Matsubashi Parade Participants, Decorated Bamboo A2710

Matsubashi Parade A2711

2011, Apr. 4 Litho. *Perf. 13¼*

3319		Block of 6, #3319c-3319d, 2 each #3319a-3319b	6.00	6.00
a.	A2708	50y green & multi	.80	.40
b.	A2709	50y red violet & multi	.80	.40
c.	A2710	50y blue & multi	.80	.40
d.	A2711	50y blue & multi	.80	.40

Hakata Dontaku Port Festival, Fukuoka, Fukuoka prefecture. Printed in sheets of 10 containing Nos. 3319c-3319d and 4 each Nos. #3319a-3319b.

Administrative Counselors System, 50th Anniv. — A2712

2011, Apr. 15 *Perf. 13*

3320		80y Denomination at LL	1.25	.50
3321		80y Denomination at LR	1.25	.50
a.	A2712	Horiz. pair, #3320-3321	3.00	2.00

Digital Television Broadcasting Towers — A2713

Designs: No. 3322, Tokyo Sky Tree, emblem at LR. No. 3323, Tokyo Tower, emblem at LL.

2011, Apr. 15 *Perf. 14x14¼*

3322		80y multi	1.25	.50
3323		80y multi	1.25	.50
a.	A2713	Pair, #3322-3323	3.00	2.00

Kabuki Actor Kikugoro Onoe V as Postman, by Kunichika Toyohara — A2714

Yokkaichi Postal Communications Bureau, by Hiroshige III — A2715

A Quick Primer on Modernization, by Kunimasa Baido — A2716

Perf. 12½x12¾ Syncopated
2011, Apr. 20 Photo.

3324	A2714	80y multi	1.25	.50
3325	A2715	80y multi	1.25	.50
3326	A2716	80y multi	1.25	.50
a.		Vert. strip of 3, #3324-3326	5.00	3.50

Philately Week. Printed in sheets of 10 containing 4 No. 3325 and 3 each Nos. 3324, 3326.

Azalea Flowers A2717

Satsuma Orange Blossoms A2718

Azalea Flowers A2719

Satsuma Orange Blossoms A2720

2011, May 2 Photo. *Perf. 13¼*

3327	A2717	50y multi	.80	.40
3328	A2718	50y multi	.80	.40
a.		Horiz. pair, #3327-3328	2.00	1.25
b.		Sheet of 47 + label (see contents below)	50.00	50.00
3329	A2719	80y multi	1.25	.60
3330	A2720	80y multi	1.25	.60
a.		Horiz. pair, #3329-3330	3.00	2.00
b.		Sheet of 47 + label (see contents below)	80.00	80.00
		Nos. 3327-3330 (4)	4.10	2.00

Flowers of Shizuoka and Ehime prefectures.
Issued: Nos. 3328b, 3330b, 7/15.

No. 3328b contains Nos. 3030-3034, 3079-3083, 3094-3098, 3126-3130, 3180-3184, 3194-3198, 3207-3211, 3221-3225, 3305-3309, 3327-3328 + label.

No. 3330b, contains Nos. 3035-3039, 3084-3088, 3099-3103, 3131-3135, 3185-3189, 3199-3203, 3212-3216, 3226-3230, 3310-3314, 3329-3330 + label.

Miniature Sheet

Kumamoto Local Autonomy Law, 60th Anniv. — A2721

No. 3331: a, Mt. Azo (32x39mm). b, Kumamoto Castle (28x33mm). c, Kikuchi Castle (octagonal tower, 28x33mm). d, Utasebune (sailboat, 28x33mm). e, Matsushima and Maejima Bridges (28x33mm).

Perf. 13¼ (#3331a), 13x13¼
2011, May 13 Photo.

3331	A2721	Sheet of 5	7.00	7.00
a.-e.		80y Any single	1.25	.60

Miniature Sheet

Intl. Year of Forests A2722

No. 3332: a, Japanese cypress (denomination in white at LL, Japanese text in green, date at UR). b, Cherry blossoms (denomination in white at UR, Japanese text in blue, date at LL). c, Persea thunbergii (denomination in white at LL, Japanese text in blue, date at LR). d, Japanese umbrella pine (denomination in blue at UR, Japanese text in green, date at UL). e, Plum blossoms (denomination in white at UR, Japanese text in green, date at LL). f, Boat oak (denomination in white at UR, Japanese text in blue, date at LL). g, Nageia nagi (denomination in white at LL, Japanese text in blue, date at UL). h, Michelia compressa blossom (denomination in white at UR, Japanese text in green, date at UL). i, Japanese Douglas fir (denomination in white at UL, Japanese text in green, date at LL). j, Intl. Year of Forests emblem.

2011, May 20 Litho. ***Perf. 13***

3332	A2722	Sheet of 10	10.00	10.00
a.-j.		50y Any single	.80	.40

Miniature Sheet

Travel Scenes A2723

No. 3333: a, Spotted seal (stamp 1). b, Wheat field, Biei (stamp 2). c, Lavender field, Furano, denomination at LR (stamp 3). d, Lavender field, Furano, denomination at LL (stamp 4). e, Statue of Dr. William Smith Clark, Hitsujigaoka (stamp 5). f, Cattle in pasture, Kamishihoro (stamp 6). g, Rugosa roses, Mt. Rishiri, denomination at UL (stamp 7). h, Rugosa roses, Mt. Rishiri, denomination at UR (stamp 8). i, Trees on hill at Higashimokoto Moss Pink Park, denomination at UL (stamp 9). j, Trees on hill at Higashimokoto Moss Pink Park, denomination at UR (stamp 10).

2011, May 30 Litho. ***Perf. 13x13¼***

3333	A2723	Sheet of 10	13.00	13.00
a.-j.		80y Any single	1.25	.60

Animation

Miniature Sheet

Rose of Versailles — A2724

No. 3334: a, Marie Antoinette holding rose (blue denomination at LL). b, Oscar François de Jarjayes holding sword (blue denomination at LR). c, André Grandier (pink denomination at LL). d, Jarjayes wearing green shirt (pink denomination at UR). e, Hans Axel von Fersen in brown cape (trees in background, blue denomination at LL). f, Marie Antoinette (pink denomination at LR). g, Von Fersen (bubbles in background, blue denomination at LL). h, Jarjayes in blue dress (bubbles in background, blue denomination at IR) i, Rosalie Lamorlière in pink dress (blue denomination at UL). j, Jeanne de Valois-Saint Rémy (pink denomination at UR).

2011, June 10 ***Perf. 13x13¼***

3334	A2724	Sheet of 10	16.00	16.00
a.-j.		80y Any single	1.25	.50

Miniature Sheet

Toyama Local Autonomy Law, 60th Anniv. — A2725

No. 3335: a, Tateyama Mountains (32x39mm). b, Kurobe Dam (28x33mm). c, Japanese rock ptarmigan (28x33mm). d, Zuiryu Temple (28x33mm). e, Gokayama farmhouse (28x33mm).

Perf. 13¼ (#3335a), 13x13¼

2011, June 15 Photo.

3335	A2725	Sheet of 5	7.00	7.00
a.-e.		80y Any single	1.25	.60

A2726

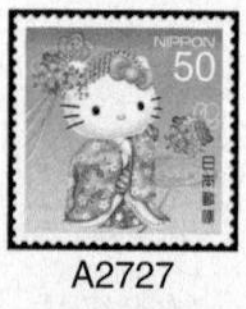

A2727

A2728

A2729

A2730

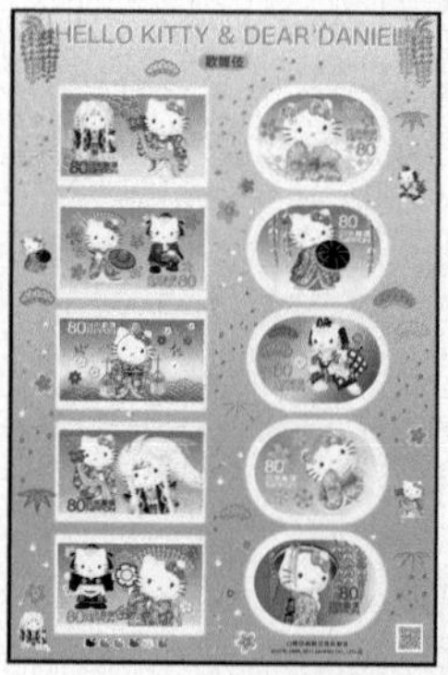

Hello Kitty A2731

No. 3341: a, Dear Daniel at left, and Hello Kitty, rectangular stamp with green background, denomination in green at LL. b, Hello Kitty and Dear Daniel, rectangular stamp with pink background. c, Hello Kitty, rectangular stamp with blue gray background, denomination in white at UL. d, Hello Kitty and Dear Daniel, rectangular stamp with green background, denomination in purple at LL. e, Dear Daniel and Hello Kitty, rectangular stamp with purple background, denomination in gold at LL. f, Hello Kitty, oval stamp with pink background and gold denomination at right. g, Hello Kitty, oval stamp with blue gray background, denomination in white at UR. h, Dear Daniel, oval stamp with green background. i, Hello Kitty, oval stamp with pink background and white denomination at left. j, Hello Kitty, oval stamp with purple background, denomination in purple at LR.

Die Cut Perf. 13½

2011, June 22 Litho.

Self-Adhesive

3336	A2726	50y multi	.80	.80
3337	A2727	50y multi	.80	.80
3338	A2728	50y multi	.80	.80
3339	A2729	50y multi	.80	.80
3340	A2730	50y multi	.80	.80
a.		Vert. strip of 5, #3336-3340	4.50	4.50

Die Cut Perf. 11½x13¼ (#3341a-3341e), 12 (#3341f-3341j)

3341	A2731	Sheet of 10	13.00	13.00
a.-j.		80y Any single	1.25	.80

Nos. 3336-3340 were printed in sheets containing 2 of each stamp.

Adélie Penguin A2732

Chinstrap Penguin A2733

Gentoo Penguin A2734

Emperor Penguin A2735

Macaroni Penguin A2736

Map of Antarctica and Snowflakes A2737

2011, June 23 ***Perf. 13***

3342		Sheet of 10, #3342a-3342e, 5 #3342f	16.00	16.00
a.	A2732	80y multi	1.25	.50
b.	A2733	80y multi	1.25	.50
c.	A2734	80y multi	1.25	.50
d.	A2735	80y multi	1.25	.50
e.	A2736	80y multi	1.25	.50
f.	A2737	80y multi	1.25	.50

Antarctic Treaty, 50th Anniv.

Miniature Sheet

Constellations — A2738

No. 3343: a, Libra (scales). b, Scorpius (scorpion). c, Sagittarius (archer). d, Lyra (lyre). e, Aquila (eagle). f, Cygnus (swan). g, Hercules. h, Ophiuchus and Serpens (man and snake). i, Delphinus (dolphin). j, Fishhook asterism.

Litho. With Foil Application

2011, July 7 ***Die Cut Perf. 13***

Self-Adhesive

3343	A2738	Sheet of 10	22.00	22.00
a.-j.		80y Any single	1.50	.80

Miniature Sheet

Japan Sports Association, Cent. — A2739

No. 3344: a, Jigoro Kano (1860-1938), and Seiichi Kishi (1867-1933), presidents of Japan Amateur Sports Association (stamp 1). b, Athletes in parade at 1912 Stockholm Olympics (stamp 2). c, Women's volleyball, horse jumping, and emblem of National Athletic Meet (stamp 3). d, Hironoshin Furuhashi (1928-2009), swimmer (stamp 4). e, Baseball players and boy with martial arts stick (stamp 5). f, Weight lifter, gymnast and women's volleyball team members from 1964 Tokyo Summer Olympics (stamp 6). g, Skiers from 1972 Sapporo Winter Olympics (stamp 7). h, Skier and skater from 1998 Nagano Winter Olympics (stamp 8). i, Emblem of Sports Masters Japan Tournament (stamp 9). j, Woman wrestler, swimmer and women's softball team members from 2008 Beijing Summer Olympics (stamp 10).

2011, July 8 Litho. ***Perf. 13***

3344	A2739	Sheet of 10	16.00	16.00
a.-j.		80y Any single	1.25	.50

A2740

A2741

PhilaNippon 2011 Intl. Philatelic Exhibition, Yokohama — A2742

No. 3345 — Woodblock prints by Hokusai depicting Mt. Fuji: a, Shower Below the Summit (Mt. Fuji and clouds, denomination in gold at LL). b, Fujimigahara in Owari Province (cooper making cask). c, Hodogaya on the Tokaido (people on road near Mt. Fuji). d, Mishima Pass in Kai Province (large tree and Mt. Fuji). e, The Surface of the Water at Misaka (boat and reflection of Mt. Fuji in lake). f, Clear Day with a Southern Breeze (Mt. Fuji and clouds, denomination in white at LR). g, The Village of Sekiya on the Sumida River (horsemen on road). h, Sea Route to Kazusa (sailing ship). i, Hongan Temple at Asakusa (kite and temple roof). j, Senju in Musashi Province (fishermen, man with horse).

No. 3346: a, Writing box depicting rabbit, bamboo and chrysanthemum. b, Japan #1.

No. 3347: a, Astro Boy (32x47mm). b, Doraemon (cat, 28x47mm). c, Pikachu (28x47mm). d, Hello Kitty (28x47mm). e, Emblem of PhilaNippon 2011, Mt. Fuji (28x47mm). f, Astro Boy, diff. (28x32mm). g, Doraemon, diff. (28x32mm). h, Pikachu, diff. (28x32mm). i, Hello Kitty, diff. (28x 32mm). j, Emblem, diff. (28x32mm).

2011, July 28 Litho. *Perf. 13*

3345	A2740	Sheet of 10 + 10 labels	21.00	21.00
a.-j.		80y Any single + label	1.25	.50

Souvenir Sheet

Litho. & Embossed With Foil Application

Perf. 14x13¾

3346	A2741	Sheet of 2	32.50	32.50
a.-b.		500y Either single	9.50	9.50

Self-Adhesive

Litho. With Foil Application

Die Cut Perf. 13

3347	A2742	Sheet of 10	21.00	21.00
a.-j.		80y Any single	1.50	.80

No. 3346 sold for 1200y inside a folder that was sealed in plastic.

Sazae Hall, by Hiroshige A2743

Kisegawa of Matsubaya, by Utamaro A2744

Tanabata Festival in a Prospering City, by Hiroshige A2745

Komazo Ishikawa III as Daishichi Shiga, by Sharaku A2746

Plum Garden at Kamata, by Hiroshige A2747

Three Beauties of the Present Day, by Utamaro A2748

Yatsukoji, Inside Sujikai Gate, by Hiroshige A2749

Tomisaburo Segawa II as Yadorigi, by Sharaku A2750

Old Man's Tea House, Meguro, by Hiroshige A2751

Hanaogi of Ogiya, by Utamaro A2752

2011, Aug. 1 Litho. *Perf. 13¼*

3348		Sheet of 10	15.00	15.00
a.	A2743	80y multi	1.25	.60
b.	A2744	80y multi	1.25	.60
c.	A2745	80y multi	1.25	.60
d.	A2746	80y multi	1.25	.60
e.	A2747	80y multi	1.25	.60
f.	A2748	80y multi	1.25	.60
g.	A2749	80y multi	1.25	.60
h.	A2750	80y multi	1.25	.60
i.	A2751	80y multi	1.25	.60
j.	A2752	80y multi	1.25	.60

Life in Edo (Tokyo).

A2753

A2754

A2755

A2756

A2757

Lantern Float Festival, Aomori — A2758

2011, Aug. 2

3349		Sheet of 10, #3349a-3349b, 3349e-3349f, 3 each #3349c-3349d	10.00	10.00
a.	A2753	50y multi	.80	.40
b.	A2754	50y multi	.80	.40
c.	A2755	50y multi	.80	.40
d.	A2756	50y multi	.80	.40
e.	A2757	50y multi	.80	.40
f.	A2758	50y multi	.80	.40

Miniature Sheet

Tottori Local Autonomy Law, 60th Anniv. — A2759

No. 3350: a, Tottori Sand Dunes and San'in Coast (32x39mm). b, Japanese pear (28x33mm). c, Kirin lion mask (28x33mm). d, Nageire Hall, Sanbutsu Temple (28x33mm). e, Mt. Daisen (28x33mm).

Perf. 13¼ (#3350a), 13x13¼

2011, Aug. 15 Photo.

3350	A2759	Sheet of 5	7.00	7.00
a.-e.		80y Any single	1.25	.60

Tsushima Leopard Cat — A2760

Saunders's Gull — A2761

Rebun Large-flowered Cypripedium A2762

Green Sea Turtle A2763

Shijimiaeoides Divinus — A2764

2011, Aug. 23 *Perf. 13¼*

3351	A2760	80y multi	1.25	.50
3352	A2761	80y multi	1.25	.50
3353	A2762	80y multi	1.25	.50
3354	A2763	80y multi	1.25	.50
3355	A2764	80y multi	1.25	.50
a.		Vert strip of 5, #3351-3355	7.50	5.00

Endangered species. Nos. 3351-3355 printed in sheets containing two vertical strips.

Airplane and Old Control Tower A2765

Airplane and New Control Tower A2766

Airplane and Map of Airport A2767

Airplane and New Control Tower A2768

2011, Aug. 25 Litho. *Perf. 13*

3356	A2765	80y multi	1.25	.60
3357	A2766	80y multi	1.25	.60
3358	A2767	80y multi	1.25	.60
3359	A2768	80y multi	1.25	.60
a.		Block of 4, #3356-3359	6.50	4.00
		Nos. 3356-3359 (4)	5.00	2.40

Nos. 3356-3359 were printed in a sheet of 10 containing Nos. 3356-3357, and 4 each Nos. 3358-3359.

Bellflower A2769

Pink A2770

Sweet Olive Flowers A2771

Cosmos A2772

Bush Clover A2773

Bellflowers A2774

Pinks A2775

Sweet Olive Flowers A2776

Cosmos A2777

Bush Clover A2778

2011, Sept. 1 Photo. *Perf. 13¼*

3360	A2769	50y multi	.80	.40
3361	A2770	50y multi	.80	.40
3362	A2771	50y multi	.80	.40
3363	A2772	50y multi	.80	.40
3364	A2773	50y multi	.80	.40
a.		Vert. strip of 5, #3360-3364	4.50	3.00
3365	A2774	80y multi	1.25	.60
3366	A2775	80y multi	1.25	.60
3367	A2776	80y multi	1.25	.60

3368 A2777 80y multi 1.25 .60
3369 A2778 80y multi 1.25 .60
a. Vert. strip of 5, #3365-3369 6.50 4.00
Nos. 3360-3369 (10) 10.25 5.00

Miniature Sheet

Travel Scenes A2779

No. 3370: a, Midori Swamp, denomination at LL (stamp 1). b, Lake Mashu in autumn, denomination at LR (stamp 2). c, Old Hokkaido Central Government Building, denomination at UR (stamp 3). d, Sapporo Clock Tower, denomination at LR (stamp 4). e, Lake Toya, Nakajima and tree top in autumn, denomination at LL (stamp 5). f, Lake Toya, Nakajima and tree in autumn, denomination at LR (stamp 6). g, Hagoromo Falls (stamp 7). h, Glasswort in Lake Notoro (red plants in lake) (stamp 8). i, Ezo sable, denomination at UR (stamp 9). j, Ezo flying squirrel, denomination at UL (stamp 10).

2011, Sept. 9 Litho. *Perf. 13x13¼*
3370 A2779 Sheet of 10 13.00 13.00
a.-j. 80y Any single 1.25 .60

Mt. Fuji — A2780

Mt. Bandai — A2781

Hakusan A2782

Mt. Hiei A2783

Mt. Ishizuchi — A2784

Mt. Iwate — A2785

Mt. Tanigawa A2786

Mt. Akaishi A2787

Hiruzen — A2788

Mt. Aso — A2789

2011, Sept. 22 *Perf. 13*
3371 Sheet of 10 16.00 16.00
a. A2780 80y multi 1.25 .50
b. A2781 80y multi 1.25 .50
c. A2782 80y multi 1.25 .50
d. A2783 80y multi 1.25 .50
e. A2784 80y multi 1.25 .50
f. A2785 80y multi 1.25 .50
g. A2786 80y multi 1.25 .50
h. A2787 80y multi 1.25 .50
i. A2788 80y multi 1.25 .50
j. A2789 80y multi 1.25 .50

66th National Athletic Meet — A2790

2011, Sept. 30
3372 A2790 50y Sailing .80 .40
3373 A2790 50y Wrestling .80 .40
3374 A2790 50y Rock climbing .80 .40
3375 A2790 50y Handball .80 .40
3376 A2790 50y Softball .80 .40
a. Vert. strip of 5, #3372-3376 4.50 3.00

2011 Artistic Gymnastics World Championships, Tokyo — A2791

Designs: No. 3377, Female gymnast. No. 3378, Male gymnast.

2011, Oct. 6 Litho. *Perf. 13*
3377 A2791 80y red vio & multi 1.25 .50
3378 A2791 80y blue & multi 1.25 .50
a. Horiz. pair, #3377-3378 3.00 1.50

Intl. Letter Writing Week — A2792

Designs: 90y, Sound of the Tsuzumi, by Shoen Uemura. 110y, Backstage, by Shinsui Ito. 130y, Midori, Heroine of Takekurabe, by Kiyokata Kaburagi.

2011, Oct. 7 Photo. *Perf. 13¼*
3379 A2792 90y multi 1.75 .50
3380 A2792 110y multi 2.25 .50
3381 A2792 130y multi 2.50 .50
Nos. 3379-3381 (3) 6.50 1.50

Miniature Sheet

Shiga Local Autonomy Law, 60th Anniv. — A2793

No. 3382: a, Ukimido Temple, grebes on Lake Biwa (32x39mm). b, Boats in canal, Omihachiman (28x33mm). c, Boat tied to tree limb (28x33mm). d, Ishiyama Temple, Japanese red maples (28x33mm). e, Hikone Castle in winter (28x33mm).

Perf. 13¼ (#3382a), 13x13¼
2011, Oct. 14 Photo.
3382 A2793 Sheet of 5 7.00 7.00
a.-e. 80y Any single 1.25 .60

Miniature Sheet

Travel Scenes A2794

No. 3383: a, Yoyogi National Gymnasium, denomination at UR (stamp 1). b, Bench in Yoyogi Park, denomination at LR (stamp 2). c, Illumination of Omotesando trees at left, denomination at LL (stamp 3). d, Illumination of Otmotesando, trees at right, denomination at LR (stamp 4). e, Sidewalk and buildings along Omotesando, denomination at UL (stamp 5). f, Meiji Memorial Picture Gallery, denomination at UL (stamp 6). g, Ginkgo trees in Meiji Shrine Outer Garden, trees at left, denomination in blue at UL (stamp 7). h, Ginkgo trees in Meiji Shrine Outer Garden, trees at right, denomination in blue at UR (stamp 8). i, Nezu Museum, denomination at UL (stamp 9). j, Irises, painted screen, by Korin Ogata, denomination at LR (stamp 10).

2011, Oct. 21 Litho. *Perf. 13x13¼*
3383 A2794 Sheet of 10 13.00 13.00
a.-j. 80y Any single 1.25 .60

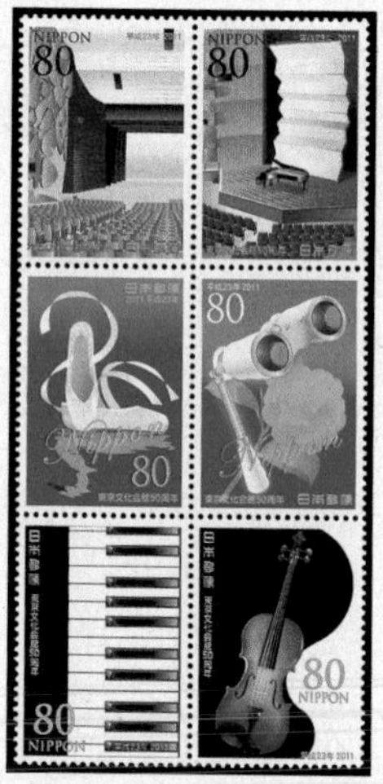

Tokyo Metropolitan Festival Hall, 50th Anniv. — A2795

No. 3384: a, Stage and seating of Main Hall. b, Piano on stage of Small Hall. c, Ballet slippers, reflection of swan. d, Opera glasses, camellia. e, Piano keyboard. f, Violin.

2011, Oct. 31 Litho. *Perf. 13*
3384 A2795 Block of 6 8.00 8.00
a.-f. 80y Any single 1.25 .50

No. 3384 was pritned in a sheet of 10 containing Nos. 3384a, 3384b and 2 each Nos. 3384c-3384f.

Miniature Sheets

A2796

A2797

Greetings — A2798

No. 3385: a, Wreath and dog (29mm diameter). b, Children and three Christmas trees (28x36mm). c, Christmas tree (28x38mm, Christmas tree-shaped). d, Santa Claus (28x36mm). e, Wreath and cat (29mm diameter).

No. 3386: a, Children starting to decorate Christmas tree. b, Children and decorated Christmas tree. c, Santa Claus, Christmas tree, children in bed. d, Santa Claus at Christmas tree. e, Children with Christmas presents.

No. 3387: a, Dog in snow (28x34mm oval). b, Flower bouquet (28x34mm oval). c, Snowman and animals on child's hat (38x28mm). d, Fairy and flowers (28x34mm oval). e, Children and cat looking at rabbit in snow (28x34mm oval).

2011, Nov. 10 *Die Cut Perf. 13*
Self-Adhesive
3385 A2796 Sheet of 5 5.00 5.00
a.-e. 50y Any single .80 .80
3386 A2797 Sheet of 5 7.00 7.00
a.-e. 80y Any single 1.25 .80
3387 A2798 Sheet of 5 9.00 9.00
a.-e. 90y Any single 1.40 .80

A2799

A2800

New Year 2012 (Year of the Dragon)
A2801 A2802

2011, Nov. 11 Photo. *Perf. 13x13½*
3388 A2799 50y multi 1.00 .30
3389 A2800 80y multi 1.50 .40

Photo. & Typo.
Perf. 13¼
3390 A2801 50y +3y multi 1.25 .40
3391 A2802 80y +3y multi 1.75 .40
Nos. 3388-3391 (4) 5.50 1.50

Sheets of two containing Nos. 3388-3389 were lottery prizes. Value, $3.

Miniature Sheet

Iwate Local Autonomy Law, 60th Anniv. — A2803

No. 3392: a, Golden Hall, Chuson-ji, lotus flower (32x39mm). b, Cherry trees in bloom (28x33mm). c, Hayachine Kagura folk performers (28x33mm). d, Rocks at Jodogahama (28x33mm). e, Joboji lacquer trees (28x33mm).

Perf. 13¼ (#3392a), 13x13¼
2011, Nov. 15 Photo.
3392 A2803 Sheet of 5 7.00 7.00
a.-e. 80y Any single 1.25 .60

Miniature Sheet

Edo Calligraphy — A2804

No. 3393 — Characters for "dragon": a, In running script (black chracter with small red chop at LR). b, In Kinbun style (blue background). c, In Kinbun style (red background). d, In Sosho cursive style (black character with large dot, red chop at LL). e, In Kana (black character with five lines not touching each other, red chop at left). f, In Reisho script (complex black character, red chop of right angle and circle at lower left). g, In Reisho script (black character with thick diagonal line over denomination, red chop at left). h, In seal script form (black character with two thick parallel horizontal lines at top, red chop at LL). i, In Tensho seal style (in red). j, In Kana black character with thin curved line well above rest of character, red chop at left).

Litho. & Embossed

2011, Nov. 21 *Perf. 13x13¼*

3393	A2804	Sheet of 10	16.00	16.00
a.-j.		80y Any single	1.25	.50

Ministry of Agriculture, Forestry and Fisheries Festival, 50th Anniv. — A2805

Designs: No. 3394, Rice, chickens, tomatoes, fruit trees. No. 3395, Rice and fish.

2011, Nov. 22 **Litho.** *Perf. 13*

3394	80y	multi	1.25	.50
3395	80y	multi	1.25	.50
a.	A2805	Horiz. pair, #3394-3395	3.00	1.50

Miniature Sheet

Home Towns A2806

No. 3396 — Paintings by Taiji Harada of views of towns of Shinetsu region: a, Excursion (children, farmhouse, field of flowers, Iiyama, Nagano prefecture, denomination at LL). b, Excursion (children, hosue, river, field of flowers, Iiyama, denomination at UL). c, Kite Flying (three children near houses, Oshino Hakkai, Yamanashi prefecture, denomination at UL). d, Kite Flying (women and children, kites in air, Oshino Hakkai, denomination at UL). e, Riverbank Homes (person with dog in front of house, Kashiwazaki, Niigata prefecture). f, Riverbank Homes (man on scooter in front of house, Kashiwazaki). g, Yamakoshi in Springtime (koi breeding pool and building, Nagaoka, Niigata prefecture, denomination at LL). h, Yamakoshi in Springtime (building, man along path beside breeding pool, Nagaoka, denomination at UR). i, Town with a View of Fuji (adult and child, building, Mount Fuji, Yamanashi, Yamanashi prefecture). j, Snow Removal (adults cleaning snow, children playing, Naganao, Nagano prefecture).

2011, Dec. 1 **Photo.** *Perf. 13*

3396	A2806	Sheet of 10	13.00	13.00
a.-j.		80y Any single	1.25	.60

Miniature Sheet

Akita Local Autonomy Law, 60th Anniv. — A2807

No. 3397: a, Nobu Shirase (1861-1946), Antarctic explorer, and two namahage (32x39mm). b, Korakukan Theater, Kosaka (28x33mm). c, Weeping cherry trees, Kakunodate (28x33mm). d, Statue of Tatsuko, Lake Tazawa (28x33mm). e, Kamakura Snow Festival, Yokote (28x33mm).

Perf. 13¼ (#3397a), 13x13¼

2012, Jan. 13

3397	A2807	Sheet of 5	7.00	7.00
a.-e.		80y Any single	1.25	.60

Animation

Miniature Sheet

Dragon Ball Kai A2808

No. 3398: a, Vegeta on rock (white denomination at UL). b, Son Goku (purple denomination at LL). c, Son Gohan (red denomination at LL). d, Piccolo (purple denomination at LR). e, Trunks facing left(white denomination at LL). f, Vegeta facing right (white denomination at UR). g, Son Goku with fist extended(red denomination at LR). h, Piccolo flying (white denomination at LR) i, Son Gohan with white cape (white denomination at LL). j, Son Goku with brown tunic (white denomination at LR).

2012, Jan. 23 **Litho.** *Perf. 13x13¼*

3398	A2808	Sheet of 10	16.00	16.00
a.-j.		80y Any single	1.25	.50

Miniature Sheets

A2809

Greetings Stamps — A2810

No. 3399: a, Child on bird. b, Child with boxes and pail, cat, flowers. c, Tree, bear, rabbit, bird, flowers. d, Swan, flower bouquet. e, Children on cherry blossom petals.

No. 3400: a, Cat and flowers in box. b, Dog, falling cherry blossom petals. c, Bouquet of cherry blossoms. d, Birds in basket of flowers. e, Girl with letter, mailbox.

Die Cut Perf. 13¼x13½

2012, Feb. 1 **Litho.**

Self-Adhesive

3399	A2809	Sheet of 5	5.00	5.00
a.-e.		50y Any single	.80	.80

Die Cut Perf. 13

3400	A2810	Sheet of 5	7.00	7.00
a.-e.		80y Any single	1.25	.80

Violets A2811

Rose A2812

Flowering Dogwood A2813

Muscari A2814

Poppy A2815

Violets A2816

Roses A2817

Flowering Dogwood A2818

Muscari A2819

Poppies A2820

2012, Mar. 1 **Photo.** *Perf. 13¼*

3401	A2811	50y multi	.80	.40
3402	A2812	50y multi	.80	.40
3403	A2813	50y multi	.80	.40
3404	A2814	50y multi	.80	.40
3405	A2815	50y multi	.80	.40
a.		Vert. strip of 5, #3401-3405	4.50	3.00
3406	A2816	80y multi	1.25	.60
3407	A2817	80y multi	1.25	.60
3408	A2818	80y multi	1.25	.60
3409	A2819	80y multi	1.25	.60
3410	A2820	80y multi	1.25	.60
a.		Vert. strip of 5, #3406-3410	6.50	4.00
		Nos. 3401-3410 (10)	10.25	5.00

Miniature Sheets

A2821

Disney Characters — A2822

No. 3411: a, Mickey and Minnie Mouse holding each other with arms extended (36x29mm heart-shaped stamp). b, Mickey with arm raised (27x28mm). c, Minnie with arms at side (27x28mm). d, Mickey with arms behind back (27x28mm). e, Minnie winking (27x28mm). f, Mickey with hands on hips (27x28mm). g, Minnie and Mickey, Minnie at left (36x29mm heart-shaped stamp). h, Mickey and Minnie not touching, Mickey's arm extended (36x29mm heart-shaped stamp). i, Mickey and Minnie, tails crossing (36x29mm heart-shaped stamp). j, Mickey and Minnie, Minnie's arms extended (36x29mm heart-shaped stamp).

No. 3412: a, Mickey (yellow background, 28mm diameter). b, Minnie (yellow background, 28mm diameter). c, Mickey, Minnie, Goofy, Pluto, Daisy Duck, Donald Duck (yellow background, 37mm diameter). d, Minnie and Daisy (pink background, 28mm diameter). e, Daisy (pink background, 28mm diameter). f, Donald (blue background, 28mm diameter). g, Mickey and Pluto (blue background, 28mm diameter). h, Mickey with arms raised (white, beige and blue background, oval). i, Goofy, Mickey and Donald (pink background, 37mm diameter). j, Minnie, Pluto and Mickey (blue background, 37mm diameter).

Die Cut Perf., Die Cut Perf. 13¼x13½ (#3411b-3411f)

2012, Mar. 2 **Litho.**

Self-Adhesive

3411	A2821	Sheet of 10	10.00	10.00
a.-j.		50y Any single	.80	.80
3412	A2822	Sheet of 10	13.00	13.00
a.-j.		80y Any single	1.25	.80

Miniature Sheet

U.S. Cherry Blossom Centennial — A2823

No. 3413: a, Cherry trees in bloom, Washington Monument. b, Cherry trees in bloom, Jefferson Memorial. c, Cherry blossoms, bright blue background. d, Cherry blossoms, dark green background. e, Cherry blossoms, gray blue background. f, Cherry blossoms, olive brown background. g, Cherry blossoms, pink background.

2012, Mar. 27 *Perf. 13*

3413	A2823	Sheet of 10, #3413a-3413f, 4 #3413g	16.00	16.00
a.-g.		80y Any single	1.25	.50

See U.S. Nos. 4651-4652.

Miniature Sheet

Okinawa Local Autonomy Law, 60th Anniv. — A2824

No. 3414: a, Shuri Castle and Kumiodori dancer (32x39mm). b, Shurei Gate, Shuri Castle (28x33mm). c, Ryukyuan bingata (28x33mm). d, Ryukyuan dancers (28x33mm). e, Coral tree blossoms (28x33mm).

Perf. 13¼ (#3414a), 13x13¼

2012, Apr. 13 **Photo.**

3414	A2824	Sheet of 5	7.00	7.00
a.-e.		80y Any single	1.25	.60

Fence with Grasses and Flowers, From Paper Partition by Unknown Artist — A2825

Dragon, From Screen by Sanraku Kano — A2826

Peonies, From Screen by Eino Kano — A2827

Perf. 12¾ Syncopated

2012, Apr. 20 **Photo.**

3415	A2825	80y multi	1.25	.50
3416	A2826	80y multi	1.25	.50
3417	A2827	80y multi	1.25	.50
	Nos. 3415-3417 (3)		3.75	1.50

Philately Week. Nos. 3415-3417 were printed in a sheet of 10 containing 3 each Nos. 3415 and 3417 and 4 No. 3416.

Miniature Sheet

Travel Scenes A2828

No. 3418: a, Giant panda with open mouth (stamp 1). b, Giant panda with closed mouth (stamp 2). c, Shinobazo Pond, Ueno Park, Tokyo, denomination at UL (stamp 3). d, Shinobazo Pond, Ueno Park and Tokyo Buildings in distance, denomination at UR (stamp 4). e, Thunder Gate, Senso-ji Temple, denomination at LL (stamp 5). f, Senso-ji pagodas, denomination at UL (stamp 6). g, Boat on Sumida River. buildings, denomination at UR (stamp 7). h, Asahi Beer Buildings along Sumida River, denomination at UR (stamp 8). i, Cherry blossoms, Sumida Park, denomination at UL (stamp 9). j, Fireworks display alomg Sumida River, denomination at LR (stamp 10).

2012, Apr. 23 **Litho.** ***Perf. 13x13¼***

3418	A2828	Sheet of 10	13.00	13.00
a.-j.		80y Any single	1.25	.60

Japanese Bush Cranberry — A2829

Yellow-flowered Toad Lily — A2830

Phedimus Sikokianus A2831

Japanese Wild Orchid A2832

Stigmatodactylus Sikokianus — A2833

2012, Apr. 24 ***Perf. 12¾x13***

3419	A2829	80y multi	1.25	.50
3420	A2830	80y multi	1.25	.50
3421	A2831	80y multi	1.25	.50
3422	A2832	80y multi	1.25	.50
3423	A2833	80y multi	1.25	.50
a.		Vert. strip of 5, #3419-3423	8.00	8.00
	Nos. 3419-3423 (5)		6.25	2.50

Plant illustrations by Tomitaro Makino (1862-1957), botanist.

Miniature Sheet

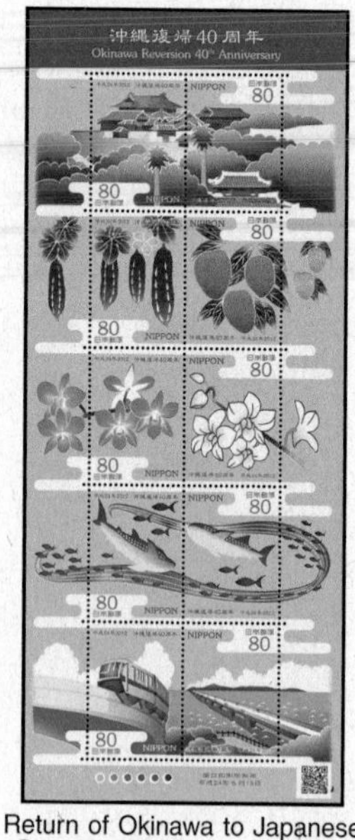

Return of Okinawa to Japanese Control, 40th Anniv. — A2834

No. 3424: a, Shuri Castle, denomination at LL. b, Shuri Castle, denomination at UR. c, Bitter melon, denomination at LL. d, Mangos, denomination at UR. e, Pink and white orchids, denomination at LL. f, White orchids, denomination at UR. g, Whale shark and fish, denomination at LL. h, Whale shark and fish, denomination at UR. i, Okinawa Urban Monorail, denomination at LL. j, Bridge between islands, denomination at UR.

2012, May 15 **Photo.** ***Perf. 13***

3424	A2834	Sheet of 10	16.00	16.00
a.-j.		80y Any single	1.25	.50

Miniature Sheet

Yamaguchi Prefecture Afforestation — A2835

No. 3425: a, Camphor tree, denomination at UR. b, Japanese maple, denomination at LR in yellow. c, Ginkgo (yellow leaves on branch), denomination at LL in yellow. d, Wild camellia, denomination at UR. e, Citrus natsudaiidai (single white flower), denomination at UR. f, Japanese red pine, denomination at UR in green. g, Rape blossoms (yellow flowers), denomination at LR in yellow. h, Japanese cypress, denomination at LL. i, Boat oak, denomination at LL in green . j, Cherry blossoms, denomination at LL.

2012, May 25 **Litho.**

3425	A2835	Sheet of 10	9.00	9.00
a.-j.		50y Any single	.80	.40

A2836

A2837

A2838

A2839

A2840

A2841

A2842

A2843

A2844

Ikebana, 550th Anniv. — A2845

2012, May 31

3426		Sheet of 10	16.00	16.00
a.	A2836	80y multi	1.25	.50
b.	A2837	80y multi	1.25	.50
c.	A2838	80y multi	1.25	.50
d.	A2839	80y multi	1.25	.50
e.	A2840	80y multi	1.25	.50
f.	A2841	80y multi	1.25	.50
g.	A2842	80y multi	1.25	.50
h.	A2843	80y multi	1.25	.50
i.	A2844	80y multi	1.25	.50
j.	A2845	80y multi	1.25	.50

Miniature Sheet

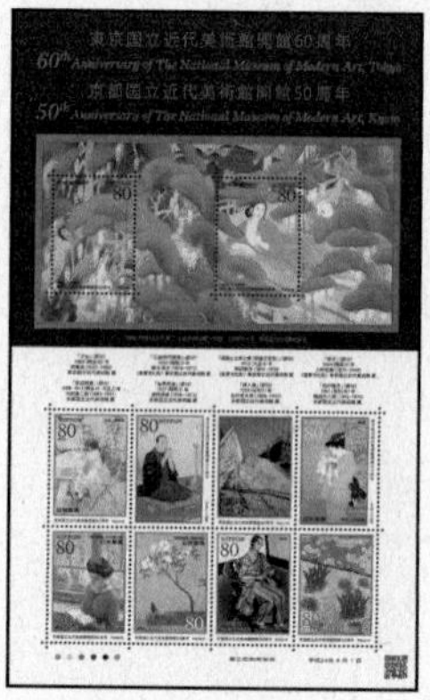

Modern Art A2846

No. 3427: a, Bathhouse Girls, by Bakusen Tsuchida (detail of bird in tree). b, Bathouse Girls, by Tsuchida (detail of girl). c, Young Girl, by Kunzo Minami (girl at table writing). d, Portrait of Encho San'yutei, by Kiyokata Kaburagi (man kneeling on mat). e, Road, Cut Bank and Fence, by Ryusei Kishida. f, Mother and Child, by Shoen Uemura. g, Reading by the Window, by Kijiro Ota (woman reading book). h, Back Garden After the Rain, by Shinsen Tokuoka (bird under flowering bush). i, Portrait of a Lady, by Sotaro Yasui (woman seated in chair). j, Study of Flowers, by Heihachiro Fukuda (pond with iris shoots and fallen cherry blossoms).

2012, June 1 **Photo.** ***Perf. 13***

3427	A2846	Sheet of 10	16.00	16.00
a.-j.		80y Any single	1.25	.50

Wisteria A2847

Lily of the Valley A2848

Hydrangea A2849

Sunflower A2850

Morning Glories A2851

Wisteria A2852

Lily of the Valley A2853

Hydrangea A2854

Sunflowers A2855

Morning Glories A2856

2012, June 7 Photo. *Perf. 13¼*

3428	A2847	50y multi		.80	.40
3429	A2848	50y multi		.80	.40
3430	A2849	50y multi		.80	.40
3431	A2850	50y multi		.80	.40
3432	A2851	50y multi		.80	.40
a.		Vert. strip of 5, #3428-3432		4.50	3.00
3433	A2852	80y multi		1.25	.60
3434	A2853	80y multi		1.25	.60
3435	A2854	80y multi		1.25	.60
3436	A2855	80y multi		1.25	.60
3437	A2856	80y multi		1.25	.60
a.		Vert. strip of 5, #3433-3437		6.50	4.00
		Nos. 3428-3437 (10)		10.25	5.00

Tenjin Festival (Osaka) A2857

2012, June 15 Litho. *Perf. 13¼*

3438		50y Denomination at UR	.80	.50
3439		50y Denomination at UL	.80	.50
a.	A2857	Horiz. pair, #3438-3439	1.75	1.25

Japanese Forces in United Nations Peacekeeping Operations, 20th Anniv. — A2858

2012, June 19 *Perf. 13*

3440		80y pink & multi	1.25	.50
3441		80y blue & multi	1.25	.50
a.	A2858	Pair, #3440-3441	3.00	1.50

Miniature Sheet

Ogaswara Islands UNESCO World Heritage Site — A2859

No. 3442: a, Bonin white-eye, denomination at UL (stamp 1). b, Bonin peonies, denomination at LR (stamp 2). c, Heart Rock, denomination at UL (stamp 3). d, Snail on leaf, denomination at LL (stamp 4). e, Ogi Pond and rock arch, denomination at LL (stamp 5). f, Semi-fossilized shells, denomination at UL (stamp 6). g, Bonin camellia, denomination at LL (stamp 7). h, Chichijima Forests, denomination at LR (stamp 8). i, Southern bottlenose dolphins, denomination at UR (stamp 9). j, Pandanus boninensis, denomination at UR (stamp 10).

2012, June 20 Photo. *Perf. 13x13¼*

3442	A2859	Sheet of 10	16.00	16.00
a.-j.		80y Any single	1.25	.50

Miniature Sheets

A2860

Hello Kitty A2861

No. 3443: a, Hello Kitty and Dear Daniel (25x38mm fan-shaped stamp). b, Hello Kitty (25x38mm fan-shaped stamp). c, Hello Kitty, pink panel (25x25mm). d, Hello Kitty, lilac panel (25x25mm). e, Hello Kitty, yellow panel (25x25mm).

No. 3444: a, Hello Kitty and Dear Daniel (42x27mm rectangular stamp). b, Hello Kitty, rabbit, building with blue roof (40x29mm building-shaped stamp). c, Hello Kitty, denomination in red at R (29mm diameter). d, Hello Kitty, bear, building with red roof (40x29mm building shaped stamp). e, Hello Kitty, white denomination at L (29mm diameter). f, Hello Kitty and Dear Daniel, building with orange roof (40x29mm building-shaped stamp). g, Hello Kitty and Dear Daniel, fireworks overhead (28x38mm oval stamp). h, Hello Kitty and Dear Daniel holding fans (28x38mm oval stamp).

Die Cut Perf. 13¼ (#3443a-3443b), Die Cut Perf. 13¼x13½ (#3443c-3443e)

2012, June 22 Litho.

Self-Adhesive

3443	A2860	Sheet of 10, 2 each #3443a-3443e	12.50	12.50
a.-e.		50y Any single	1.25	.80

Die Cut Perf. 13½

3444	A2861	Sheet of 10, #3444a-3444f, 2 each #3444g-3444h	16.00	16.00
a.-h.		80y Any single	1.25	.80

Miniature Sheet

Hiraizumi UNESCO World Heritage Site — A2862

No. 3445: a, Golden Hall, Chuson-ji, denomination at LR in gold (stamp 1). b, Hanging ornament, denomination at LL (stamp 2). c, Kyozo buildings, Chuson-ji, denomination at UL (stamp 3). d, People under umbrellas at Motsuji, denomination at LL (stamp 4). e, Motsuji Jodo Garden and pond, denomination at UL (stamp 5). f, Motsuji Jodo Garden and pond, denomination at UR (stamp 6). g, Kanjizaio-in temple garden and pond, denomination at LR (stamp 7). h, Kanjizaio-in temple garden and pond, denomination at LL (stamp 8). i, Muryoko-in ruins, trees and mountain, denomination at LR (stamp 9). j, Lotus blossoms, denomination at LL (stamp 10).

2012, June 29 Photo. *Perf. 13x13¼*

3445	A2862	Sheet of 10	16.00	16.00
a.-j.		80y Any single	1.25	.80

Adder's Tongue Lily A2863

Bazara-Taisho (c. 710-794) A2864

2012, July 2 Photo. *Perf. 13x13¼*

3446	A2863	350y multi	9.00	.50
3447	A2864	500y multi	11.00	.50

No. 3446 has a vignette different from No. 2166.

Miniature Sheet

Season's Memories in My Heart — A2865

No. 3448: a, Woman on bench near water, denomination at UL (stamp 1). b, Street vendor booths at festival, denomination at LR in gold (stamp 2). c, Child running stick against fence posts, denomination at UR (stamp 3). d, Children and animals in fog, denomination at UR (stamp 4). e, Girl with flower, boy with fishing pole and bucket, denomination at UL (stamp 5). f, Children on steps near sea, denomination at LR (stamp 6). g, Children, boats on shore, flying gull, denomination at UL (stamp 7). h, Children on hill looking at boat, denomination at UL in gold (stamp 8). i, Boat on shore, children looking at jellyfish, denomination at UL (stamp 9). j, Cricket with leaf cello, child, bottle, denomination at UL in gold (stamp 10).

2012, July 3 Photo. *Perf. 13*

3448	A2865	Sheet of 10	16.00	16.00
a.-j.		80y Any single	1.25	.50

Miniature Sheet

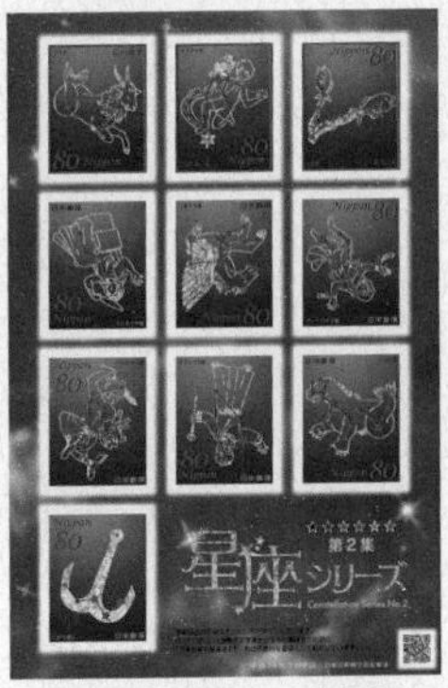

Constellations — A2866

No. 3449: a, Capricornus (goat). b, Aquarius (water bearer). c, Pisces (fish). d, Cassiopeia (woman in chair). e, Pegasus. f, Andromeda (woman in chains). g, Perseus (swordsman). h, Cepheus (king with scepter). i, Cetus (creature with two front legs and tail). j, Cassiopeia (anchor).

Litho. With Foil Application

2012, July 6 *Die Cut Perf. 13*

Self-Adhesive

3449	A2866	Sheet of 10	16.00	16.00
a.-j.		80y Any single	1.50	.80

Miniature Sheet

Kanagawa Local Autonomy Law, 60th Anniv. — A2867

No. 3450: a, Tsurugaoka Hachimangu, Kamakura, and mounted archer (32x39mm). b, Minato Mirai 21 buildings, Yokohama (28x33mm). c, Jogashima Lighthouse (28x33mm). d, Tanzawa Mountains and Lake Miyagase (28x33mm). e, Lake Ashi (28x33mm).

Perf. 13¼ (#3450a), 13x13¼

2012, July 13			**Photo.**	
3450	A2867	Sheet of 5	7.00	7.00
a.-e.		80y Any single	1.25	.60

Susanoo, Shinto God of the Sea A2868

Legendary Princess Inada A2869

Legendary Princess Konohanasakuya A2870

Legendary Prince Yamatotakeru A2871

2012, July 20		**Litho.**	***Perf. 13***	
3451	A2868	80y multi	1.25	.50
3452	A2869	80y multi	1.25	.50
3453	A2870	80y multi	1.25	.50
3454	A2871	80y multi	1.25	.50
a.		Block of 4, #3451-3454	7.00	7.00
		Nos. 3451-3454 (4)	5.00	2.00

Nos. 3451-3454 were printed in sheets of 10 containing 3 each Nos. 3451-3452 and 2 each Nos. 3453-3454.

Inpumon In no Taifu, Poet A2872

Fujiwara no Toshiyuki Ason, Poet A2873

Shune-hoshi, Poet A2874

Kokamon In no Betto, Poet A2875

Sone no Yoshitada, Poet — A2876

Poetry A2877

No. 3460 — Poetry in Japanese calligraphy and: a, Boat in lake, denomination at LL. b, Inpumon In no Taifu. c, Hill near water, denomination at UL. d, Fujiwara no Toshiyuki Ason. e, Building and tree. f, Shune-hoshi. g, Eddies in river, denomination at UR. h, Kokamon In no Betto. i, Man rowing boat. j, Sone no Yoshitada.

2012, July 23		**Photo.**	***Perf. 13¼***	
3455	A2872	50y multi	.80	.30
3456	A2873	50y multi	.80	.30
3457	A2874	50y multi	.80	.30
3458	A2875	50y multi	.80	.30
3459	A2876	50y multi	.80	.30
a.		Vert. strip of 5, #3455-3459	5.00	5.00
		Nos. 3455-3459 (5)	4.00	1.50

Perf. 12¾x13

3460	A2877	Sheet of 10	16.00	16.00
a.-j.		80y Any single	1.25	.50

Hanaogi of the Ogi Establishment Going Elsewhere, by Eisho Chokosai A2878

The Moon Crossing Bridge at Arashiyama in Yamashiro Province, by Hiroshige A2879

Tosei Onna Fuzuoku Tsuu Hokkoku no Keisei, by Utamaro A2880

The Brocade Bridge at Iwakuni in Suo Province, by Hiroshige A2881

Furyu Setsugekka Tsuki, by Eizan Kikukawa A2882

Mt. Kyodai and the Moon Reflected in the Rice Fields at Sarashina in Shinano Province, by Hiroshige A2883

Ogiya Uchi Hanaogi Yoshino Tatsuta, by Utamaro A2884

Rough Sea at Naruto in Awa Province, by Hiroshige A2885

Furyu Mutamagawa Chofu no Tamagawa, by Eizan Kikukawa A2886

The Monkey Bridge in Kai Province, by Hiroshige A2887

2012, Aug. 1	**Litho.**	***Perf. 13***	
3461	Sheet of 10	16.00	16.00
a.	A2878 80y multi	1.25	.50
b.	A2879 80y multi	1.25	.50
c.	A2880 80y multi	1.25	.50
d.	A2881 80y multi	1.25	.50
e.	A2882 80y multi	1.25	.50
f.	A2883 80y multi	1.25	.50
g.	A2884 80y multi	1.25	.50
h.	A2885 80y multi	1.25	.50
i.	A2886 80y multi	1.25	.50
j.	A2887 80y multi	1.25	.50

Miniature Sheet

Miyazaki Local Autonomy Law, 60th Anniv. — A2888

No. 3462: a, Miyazaki Prefectural Office and dancer (32x39mm). b, Koibitono-oka (hill with gazebo) (28x33mm). c, Yellow flowers, Saitobaru Burial Grounds (28x33mm). d, Pink flowers, Ebino-kogen Highlands (28x33mm). e, Terraced rice fields (28x33mm).

Perf. 13¼ (#3462a), 13x13¼

2012, Aug. 15			**Photo.**	
3462	A2888	Sheet of 5	7.00	7.00
a.-e.		80y Any single	1.25	.60

Sorex Minutissimus A2889

Aquila Chrysaetos A2890

Paeonia Obovata — A2891

Oryzias Latipes — A2892

Tachypleus Tridentatus A2893

2012, Aug. 23			***Perf. 13¼***	
3463	A2889	80y multi	1.25	.50
3464	A2890	80y multi	1.25	.50
3465	A2891	80y multi	1.25	.50
3466	A2892	80y multi	1.25	.50
3467	A2893	80y multi	1.25	.50
a.		Vert. strip of 5, #3463-3467	7.50	5.00
		Nos. 3463-3467 (5)	6.25	2.50

Normalization of Diplomatic Relations Between Japan and People's Republic of China, 40th Anniv. — A2894

2012, Sept. 4			***Perf. 13***	
3468	A2894	80y multi	1.50	.50

Miniature Sheet

Travel Scenes A2895

No. 3469 — Sites in Nagasaki: a, Urakami Cathedral, denomination at UR (stamp 1). b, Peace Statue, Nagasaki (stamp 2). c, Megane Bridge, denomination at LL (stamp 3). d, Megane Bridge, denomination at LR (stamp 4). e, Lantern Festival, denomination at UL below country name (stamp 5). f, Sofuku Temple, denomination at UL, to left of country name (stamp 6). g, Glover House, Glover Gardens, denomination at UR (stamp 7). h, Glover House, Glover Gardens, denomination at LR (stamp 8). i, People carrying dragon at Kunchi Festival, denomination at LL (stamp 9). j, Tall Ships Festival, denomination at UR (stamp 10).

2012, Sept. 11		**Litho.**	***Perf. 13x13¼***	
3469	A2895	Sheet of 10	13.00	13.00
a.-j.		80y Any single	1.25	.60

Miniature Sheets

A2896

Teddy Bears A2897

No. 3470 — Teddy bear with: a, Blue cap, pink background, red bow at top (28x28mm). b, Blue cap, light blue background, blue bow at top (28x28mm). c, Blue and white box with red ribbon, pink background, pink bow at top (28x28mm). d, Gold box with yellow ribbon, yellow background, yellow bow at top (28x28mm). e, Card with red ribbon, lilac background, red bow at top(28x28mm). f, Card with blue ribbon, light green background, gray green bow at top (28x28mm). g, Red box with white ribbon, plaid bow around neck (26x30mm). h, Blue box with red ribbon, dark blue bow around neck (26x30mm). i, Card with red ribbon, green bow around neck (26x30mm). j, Blue and white box with red ribbon, blue bow around neck (26x30mm).

No. 3471: a, Bear with blue and white box with yellow ribbon (26x38mm). b, Bear with green box with red ribbon (26x38mm). c, Bear with card with red ribbon (26x38mm). d, Two bears, lilac denomination (42x27mm). e, Two bears, blue denomination (27x38mm oval). f, Two bears, red denomination (27x38mm oval). g, Bear with black and brown bow around neck, red denomination (27x38mm oval). h, Bear with card with red ribbon, red denomination (27x38mm oval). i, Bear with flower (27x38mm oval). j, Bear with cap, two boxes (42x27mm).

Die Cut Perf. 14, Die Cut Perf. (#3470g-3470j)

2012, Sept. 21 **Litho.**

Self-Adhesive

3470	A2896	Sheet of 10	10.00	10.00
a.-j.		50y Any single	.80	.80

Die Cut Perf. 14½x14 (#3471a-3471c), 11¼x13½ (#3471d, 3471j), 13¾

3471	A2897	Sheet of 10	13.00	13.00
a.-j.		80y Any single	1.25	.80

Badminton A2898

Rhythmic Gymnastics A2899

Rowing A2900

Cycling A2901

Field Hockey — A2902

2012, Sept. 28 **Litho.** ***Perf. 13***

3472	A2898	50y multi	.80	.40
3473	A2899	50y multi	.80	.40
3474	A2900	50y multi	.80	.40
3475	A2901	50y multi	.80	.40
3476	A2902	50y multi	.80	.40
a.		Vert. strip of 5, #3472-3476	4.50	3.00

67th National Athletic Meet, Gifu. Compare with type A2790.

Miniature Sheet

Horse Racing in Japan, 150th Anniv. — A2903

No. 3477: a, Orfevre (horse #9, jockey with green helmet). b, Apapane (horse #9, jockey with yellow helmet, blue and yellow silks). c, Deep Impact (horse #5, jockey with red helmet, yellow and gray silks). d, Still in Love (horse #9, jockey with yellow helmet, red and blue silks). e, Narita Brian (horse #4, jockey with red helmet). f, Mejiro I'Amone (horse #13). g, Symboli Rudolf (horse #5, jockey with red helmet, blue and red silks). h, Mr. C.B. (horse #12, jockey with green and white silks). i, Shinzan (horse #4, jockey with brown helmet). j, Saint Lite (horse #12, black-and-white photograph).

2012, Oct. 2 **Photo.** ***Perf. 13***

3477	A2903	Sheet of 10	16.00	16.00
a.-j.		80y Any single	1.40	.90

Intl. Letter Writing Week — A2904

Designs: 90y, Hatsugochi, by Kiyokata Kaburaki. 110y, Shunpo, by Shoen Uemura. 130y, Hubuki, by Shinsui Ito.

2012, Oct. 9 **Photo.** ***Perf. 13¼***

3478	A2904	90y multi	1.75	.50
3479	A2904	110y multi	2.25	.50
3480	A2904	130y multi	2.50	.50
		Nos. 3478-3480 (3)	6.50	1.50

Miniature Sheet

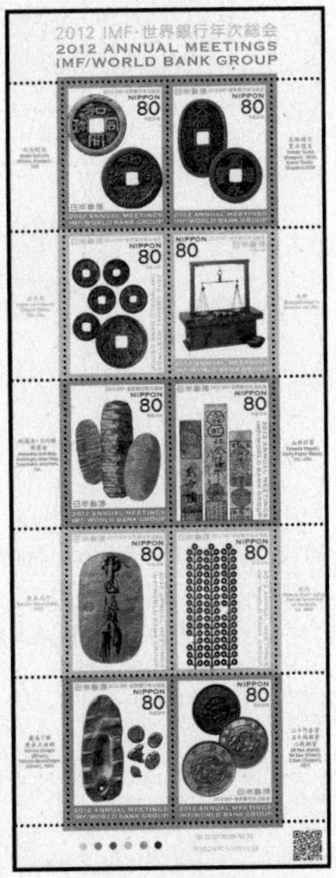

Annual Meeting of Intl. Monetary Fund and World Bank Group, Tokyo A2905

No. 3481: a, Silver and copper Wado Kaichin coins, 708 (gold frame). b, Oval copper Tempo Tsuho coin, 1835, round Kanei Tsuho coin, 1636 (gold frame). c, Six round Chinese copper coins, 12th-15th cent. (silver frame) d, Moneychanger's balance, 19th cent. (silver frame). e, Hirumokin gold slug, Sekishugin silver slug, Yuzurihakin gold plate, 16th cent. (gold frame). f, Yamada Hagaki paper money, 17th-19th cent. (gold frame). g, Gold Keicho Oban, 1601 (silver frame). h, Molded coins attached to sprues, c. 1863 (silver frame). i, Silver Keicho Chogin coin and five Silver Keicho Mameitagin coins, 1601 (silver frame). j, 1871 gold 20-yen, silver 50-yen and copper 2-sen coins (gold frame).

2012, Oct. 12 **Photo.** ***Perf. 13***

3481	A2905	Sheet of 10	16.00	16.00
a.-j.		80y Any single	1.25	.60

Miniature Sheet

Tochigi Local Autonomy Law, 60th Anniv. — A2906

No. 3482: a, Yomei Gate, Toshogu Shrine (32x39mm). b, Gate at Ashikaga School (28x33mm). c, Carp amulets on sticks (28x33mm). d, Moka Railway steam locomotive and flowers (28x33mm). e, Cherry blossoms and mountain, Nasu Kogen (28x33mm).

Perf. 13¼ (#3482a), 13x13¼

2012, Oct. 15 **Photo.**

3482	A2906	Sheet of 5	7.00	7.00
a.-e.		80y Any single	1.25	.60

Animation

Miniature Sheet

Rascal A2907

No. 3483: a, Rascal the Raccoon on tree (white denomination at UR). b, Sterling and Alice (white denomination at UL). c, Rascal with book and lamp (white denomination at UL). d, Sterling and book (white denomination at UR). e, Three raccoon babies, butterflies (black denomination at UL). f, Rascal facing left (black denomination at UR). g, Rascal drinking from bottle (white denomination at UL). h, Sterling drinking from bottle (white denomination at UL). i, Rascal, Rascal in canoe (black denomination at UR). j, Sterling, Sterling in canoe (white denomination at UR).

2012, Oct. 23 **Litho.** ***Perf. 13x13¼***

3483	A2907	Sheet of 10	16.00	16.00
a.-j.		80y Any single	1.25	.50

Miniature Sheet

Traditional Crafts — A2908

No. 3484: a, Hakata doll depicting man holding fan (Fukuoka Prefecture). b, Black rectangular inkstone and lid (Miyagi Prefecture). c, Banana-fiber handbag (Okinawa Prefecture). d, Container and two cups (Fukushima Prefecture). e, Two lacquerware bowls (Aomori Prefecture). f, Folding fan (Kyoto Prefecture). g, Kaga dyed screen (Ishikawa Prefecture). h, Decorated Kutani plate (Ishikawa Prefecture). i, Cast-iron kettle (Iwate Prefecture). j, Tsuboya ceramic urn with handles (Okinawa Prefecture).

2012, Oct. 25 **Photo.** ***Perf. 13½***

3484	A2908	Sheet of 10	16.00	16.00
a.-j.		80y Any single	1.25	.60

Miniature Sheets

A2909

A2910

Greetings — A2911

No. 3485: a, Star, Santa Clauses, gift (29x39mm). b, Kitten in stocking (26x34mm). c, Wreath, children, squirrel (29mm diameter). d, Puppy in stocking (26x34mm). e, Christmas tree and cardinal (29x39mm).

No. 3486: a, Santa Claus and reindeer on building roof. b, Fireplace, Christmas tree, two children, cat and bird. c, Fireplace, three children, bird. d, Fireplace, Christmas tree, two children, two cats, bird. e, Fireplace, two children, Christmas tree being decorated, bird.

No. 3487: a, Cat on roof, envelope in night sky (37x28mm). b, Angel with violin, bird carrying letter (35x28mm ellipse). c, Snowman, squirrel, mailbox, child (28x37mm). d, Roses and open letter (35x28mm ellipse). e, three children in pajamas, candles (37x28mm).

Self-Adhesive

Die Cut Perf. 13

2012, Nov. 9 **Litho.**

3485	A2909	Sheet of 5	5.00	5.00
a.-e.		50y Any single	.80	.80
3486	A2910	Sheet of 5	7.00	7.00
a.-e.		80y Any single	1.25	.80
3487	A2911	Sheet of 5	8.00	8.00
a.-e.		90y Any single	1.50	.80

A2912 A2913

New Year 2013 (Year of the Snake)
A2914 A2915

2012, Nov. 12 **Photo.** ***Perf. 13x13½***

3488	A2912	50y multi	1.00	.30
3489	A2913	80y multi	1.50	.40

Photo. & Typo.

Perf. 13¼

3490	A2914	50y +3y multi	1.25	.40
3491	A2915	80y +3y multi	1.75	.40
		Nos. 3488-3491 (4)	5.50	1.50

Sheets of two containing Nos. 3488-3489 were lottery prizes. Value, $4.

Miniature Sheet

Oita Local Autonomy Law, 60th Anniv. — A2916

No. 3492: a, Usa Jingu Shrine, Oita, Futabayama (1912-68), sumo wrestler (32x39mm). b, Plum blossoms, Japanese white-eye (28x33mm). c, Fukiji Temple (28x33mm). d, Hita Gion Festival (28x33mm). e, Sunrise at Bungofutamigaura (28x33mm).

Perf. 13¼ (#3492a), 13x13¼

2012, Nov. 15 **Photo.**

3492	A2916	Sheet of 5	7.00	7.00
a.-e.		80y Any single	1.25	.60

Miniature Sheets

A2917

Disney Characters — A2918

No. 3493: a, Winnie the Pooh (27x27mm). b, Piglet (27x27mm). c, Alice in Wonderland (27x38mm oval). d, Donald Duck (26x34mm). e, Daisy Duck (26x34mm). f, Cinderella (27x38mm oval). g, Dumbo (29mm diameter). h, Marie the Cat (26x34mm). i, Goofy (26x34mm). j, Three Dalmatians (29mm diameter).

No. 3494: a, Tinker Bell (27x27mm). b, Mickey Mouse (27x38mm oval). c, Minnie Mouse (27x38mm oval). d, Bambi (27x27mm). e, Pinocchio (27x35mm). f, Snow White (27x38mm oval). g, Pluto (27x35mm). h, Ariel (35x27mm). i, Stitch (29mm diameter). j, Three Little Pigs (35x27mm).

Die Cut Perf. 13½, Die Cut Perf. 13 (#3493d, 3493e, 3493h, 3493i), Die Cut Perf. 13¼x13¾ (#3494e, 3494g), Die Cut Perf. 13¾x13¼ (#3494h, 3494j) Die Cut Perf. (#3493g, 3493j, 3494i)

2012, Nov. 20 **Litho.**

Self-Adhesive

3493	A2917	Sheet of 10	10.00	10.00
a.-j.		50y Any single	.80	.80
3494	A2918	Sheet of 10	13.00	13.00
a.-j.		80y Any single	1.25	.80

Miniature Sheet

Edo Calligraphy — A2919

No. 3495 — Characters for "snake": a, In Gyosho style (red background). b, In Reisho style (black character with red chop at bottom center). c, From Qing Dynaasty seal (black curved character with circle with small red chop at left). d, In Reisho style (pink background, red chop at bottom center). e, In Kana (black character similar to "3", red chop at LR). f, In Kaisho script (black character, red chop at LL). g, In Sosho stylet (black character with thick line similar to "2" and thin curved line, red chop at LR). h, In Gyosho style (green background). i, In small seal cutting (character in red). j, In Kinbun style (character in gold, brown background).

Litho. & Embossed

2012, Nov. 21 ***Perf. 13x13¼***

3495	A2919	Sheet of 10	16.00	16.00
a.-j.		80y Any single	1.25	.50

Camellia
A2920

Plum Blossom
A2921

Adonis Flower
A2922

Cyclamen
A2923

Hellebore
A2924

Camellia
A2925

Plum Blossoms
A2926

Adonis Flowers
A2927

Cyclamen
A2928

Hellebores
A2929

2012, Dec. 3 **Photo.** ***Perf. 13¼***

3496	A2920	50y multi	.80	.40
3497	A2921	50y multi	.80	.40
3498	A2922	50y multi	.80	.40
3499	A2923	50y multi	.80	.40
3500	A2924	50y multi	.80	.40
a.		Vert. strip of 5, #3496-3500	4.50	3.00
3501	A2925	80y multi	1.25	.60
3502	A2926	80y multi	1.25	.60
3503	A2927	80y multi	1.25	.60
3504	A2928	80y multi	1.25	.60
3505	A2929	80y multi	1.25	.60
a.		Vert. strip of 5, #3501-3505	6.50	4.00
		Nos. 3496-3505 (10)	10.25	5.00

Miniature Sheet

Hyogo Local Autonomy Law, 60th Anniv. — A2930

No. 3506: a, Flying crane, Himeji Castle (32x39mm). b, Meriken Park, Kobe, and waterfront buildings (28x33mm). c, Shinkoro Tower, Izushi (28x33mm). d, Shinmaiko Beach (28x33mm). e, Narcissuses, Awaji-shima (28x33mm).

Perf. 13¼ (#3506a), 13x13¼

2013, Jan. 15

3506	A2930	Sheet of 5	7.00	7.00
a.-e.		80y Any single	1.25	.60

Animation

Miniature Sheet

Heidi, Girl of the Alps A2931

No. 3507: a, Lamb and flowers. b, Heidi picking flowers). c, Dog and chalet. d, Heidi and chalet. e, Heidi's grandfather. f, Heidi pointing. g, Heidi and Peter on sled. h, Rabbits. i, Heidi running, mountain in background. j, Clara in blue dress.

2013, Jan. 23 Litho. ***Perf. 13x13¼***

3507	A2931	Sheet of 10	16.00	16.00
a.-j.		80y Any single	1.25	.50

Miniature Sheets

A2932

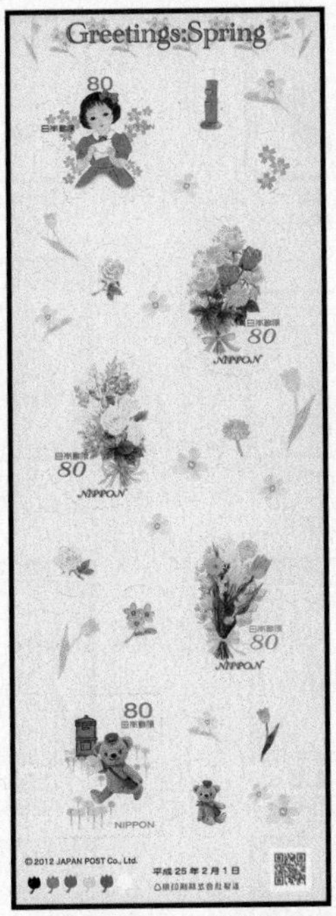

Greetings — A2933

No. 3508: a, Cherry blossom, boy, birds with letter (30x29mm flower-shaped stamp). b, Wreath with strawberries (29mm diameter). c, Boy, girl, cat, wreath of cherry blossoms (29mm diameterl). d, Tulips, cats and rabbit (28x28mm). e, Girl carrying potted plant up stairs, cat with broom (28x28mm).

No. 3509: a, Gril with letter, cherry blossoms (30x29mm flower shaped stamp). b, Bouquet of red and pink flowerst (24x34mm oval). c, Bouquet of blue and white flowers (24x34mm oval). d, Bouquet of yellow and orange flowers (24x34mm oval). e, Teddy bear with letter and mail bag, mail box (23x30mm).

Die Cut Perf., Die Cut Perf 13¼ (#3508d, 3508e, 3509b-3509d), Die Cut Perf. 13¼x12¾ (#3509e)

2013, Feb. 1

Self-Adhesive

3508	A2932	Sheet of 5	5.00	5.00
a.-e.		50y Any single	.80	.80
3509	A2933	Sheet of 5	7.00	7.00
a.-e.		80y Any single	1.25	.80

Dianthus Caryophyllus A2934

Tulip A2935

Cherry Blossoms A2936

Gerbera Daisy A2937

Myosotis Scorpioides A2938

Dianthus Caryophyllus A2939

Tulip A2940

Cherry Blossoms A2941

Gerbera Daisy A2942

Myosotis Scorpioides A2943

2013, Feb. 8 Photo. ***Perf. 13¼***

3510	A2934	50y multi	.80	.40
3511	A2935	50y multi	.80	.40
3512	A2936	50y multi	.80	.40
3513	A2937	50y multi	.80	.40
3514	A2938	50y multi	.80	.40
a.		Vert. strip of 5, #3510-3514	4.50	3.00
3515	A2939	80y multi	1.25	.60
3516	A2940	80y multi	1.25	.60
3517	A2941	80y multi	1.25	.60
3518	A2942	80y multi	1.25	.60
3519	A2943	80y multi	1.25	.60
a.		Vert. strip of 5, #3515-3519	6.50	4.00
		Nos. 3510-3519 (10)	14.25	11.25

Mt. Fuji A2944

Mt. Tsukuba A2945

Mt. Kasa — A2946

Mt. Ibuki — A2947

Mt. Iino — A2948

Mt. Zao — A2949

Mt. Gassan A2950

Mt. Ryokami A2951

Mt. Nijo — A2952

Mt. Kuju — A2953

2013, Feb. 22 Litho. ***Perf. 13¼x13***

3520	Sheet of 10	16.00	16.00
a.	A2944 80y multi	1.25	.50
b.	A2945 80y multi	1.25	.50
c.	A2946 80y multi	1.25	.50
d.	A2947 80y multi	1.25	.50
e.	A2948 80y multi	1.25	.50
f.	A2949 80y multi	1.25	.50
g.	A2950 80y multi	1.25	.50
h.	A2951 80y multi	1.25	.50
i.	A2952 80y multi	1.25	.50
j.	A2953 80y multi	1.25	.50

A2954

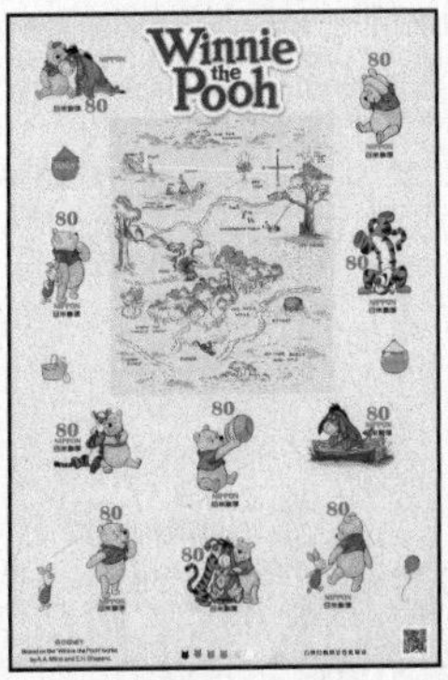

Winnie the Pooh A2955

No. 3521: a, Winnie, Piglet, two beamed sixteenth notes in blue, eighth note in black. b, Winnie, sixteenth notes in black and green. c, Winnie, staff in pink, two beamed eighth notes in black. d, Tigger, staff in pink, eighth note in black. e, Winnie, staff in yellow, black and red sixteenth notes. f, Tigger, staff in yellow, two beamed eighth notes in black, eighth note in blue. g, Piglet, staff in yellow, three beamed sixteenth notes, eighth notes in black and pink, half note. h, Eeyore, staff in yellow, sixteenth note and two beamed sixteenth notes in black, eighth note in lilac. i, Winnie, staff in pink, sixteenth note and two beamed sixteenth notes in black. j, Winnie, staff in pink, eighth note, sixteenth note and two beamed sixteenth notes in black.

No. 3522, oval stamps: a, Winnie and Eeyore. b, Winnie seated, touching his nose and with arm wrapped over his head, vert. c, Winnie and Piglet standing, vert. d, Tigger, vert. e, Winnie and Tigger. f, Winnie and honey jar, vert. g, Eeyore and log. h, Winnie standing with arm near mouth. i, Tigger, Eeyore and Winnie. j, Winnie and Piglet walking, vert.

2013, Mar. 1 ***Die Cut Perf. 13x12¾***

Self-Adhesive

3521	A2954	Sheet of 10	9.00	9.00
a.-j.		50y Any single	.80	.80

Die Cut Perf. 13

3522	A2955	Sheet of 10	13.00	13.00
a.-j.		80y Any single	1.25	.80

Grand Canyon, United States — A2956

Pyramids, Egypt — A2957

Mont-Saint-Michel, France — A2958

Macchu Picchu, Peru A2959

Angkor Wat, Cambodia A2960

2013, Mar. 14 *Perf. 13¼x13*

3523 A2956 80y multi	1.25	.50
3524 A2957 80y multi	1.25	.50
3525 A2958 80y multi	1.25	.50
3526 A2959 80y multi	1.25	.50
3527 A2960 80y multi	1.25	.50
a. Horiz. strip of 5, #3523-3527	7.50	4.00
Nos. 3523-3527 (5)	6.25	2.50

Foreign UNESCO World Heritage Sites.

Hirosaki Cherry Blossom Festival (Aomori) A2961

Designs: No. 3528, Weeping cherry branch, Mt. Iwaki (denomination in green). No. 3529, Yoshino cherry blossoms, Hirosaki Castle (denomination in lilac).

2013, Mar. 22 *Perf. 13¼*

3528 50y multi	.80	.40
3529 50y multi	.80	.40
a. A2961 Horiz. pair, #3528-3529	1.75	1.25

Miniature Sheet

Season's Memories in My Heart — A2962

No. 3530: a, Girl in yellow dress staring at cherry blossom petals (stamp 1). b, Two children and flower cart (stamp 2). c, Three children, falling cherry blossom petals (stamp 3). d, Girl holding fiddlehead fern in field (stamp 4). e, Girl and flowers (stamp 5). f, Boy and girl looking at flowers (stamp 6). g, Boy in tulips, cat (stamp 7). h, Boy playing flute, girl reading book, flowers (stamp 8). i, Girl with doll, girl with dog, flowers (stamp 9). j, Girls playing house with doll, lawn chair (stamp 10).

2013, Apr. 3 **Photo.** *Perf. 13*

3530 A2962 Sheet of 10	16.00	16.00
a.-j. 80y Any single	1.25	.50

Miniature Sheet

Travel Scenes A2963

No. 3531 — Sites in Tateyama and Kurobe areas of Toyama: a, Ptarmigan (stamp 1). b, Bus and tourists in Great Snow Valley (stamp 2). c, Shomyo Falls (stamp 3). d, Tateyama gentians, denomination at LL (stamp 4). e, Midagahara Wetlands, denomination at UL (stamp 5). f, Midagahara Wetlands, denomination at UR (stamp 6). g, Murodo Highland, yellow lily flowers (stamp 7). h, Stoat (stamp 8). i, Aleutian avens flowers, denomination at LR (stamp 9). j, Cable car at Daikanbo (stamp 10).

2013, Apr. 16 **Litho.** *Perf. 13x13¼*

3531 A2963 Sheet of 10	13.00	13.00
a.-j. 80y Any single	1.25	.60

A2964

A2965

A2966

A2967

A2968

A2969

A2970

A2971

Sections of Painted Screen by Motonobu Kano (1476-1559)
A2972 A2973

2013, Apr. 19 **Photo.** *Perf. 13¼*

3532 Sheet of 10	16.00	16.00
a. A2964 80y multi	1.25	.50
b. A2965 80y multi	1.25	.50
c. A2966 80y multi	1.25	.50
d. A2967 80y multi	1.25	.50
e. A2968 80y multi	1.25	.50
f. A2969 80y multi	1.25	.50
g. A2970 80y multi	1.25	.50
h. A2971 80y multi	1.25	.50
i. A2972 80y multi	1.25	.50
j. A2973 80y multi	1.25	.50

Philately Week.

Lily A2974

Day Lily A2975

Lilac A2976

Clematis A2977

Skunk Cabbage A2978

Lilies A2979

Day Lilies A2980

Lilac A2981

Clematis A2982

Skunk Cabbages A2983

2013, Apr. 24 *Perf. 13¼*

3533 A2974 50y multi	.80	.40
3534 A2975 50y multi	.80	.40
3535 A2976 50y multi	.80	.40
3536 A2977 50y multi	.80	.40
3537 A2978 50y multi	.80	.40
a. Vert. strip of 5, #3533-3537	4.50	3.00
3538 A2979 80y multi	1.25	.60
3539 A2980 80y multi	1.25	.60
3540 A2981 80y multi	1.25	.60
3541 A2982 80y multi	1.25	.60
3542 A2983 80y multi	1.25	.60
a. Vert. strip of 5, #3538-3542	6.50	4.00

Miniature Sheet

Miyagi Local Autonomy Law, 60th Anniv. — A2984

No. 3543: a, Statue of Masamune Date, replica of Date Maru ship (32x39mm). b, Mt. Kurikoma and cherry tree (28x33mm). c, Sendai Tanabata Festival (28x33mm). d, Bridge, Narukokyo Gorge (28x33mm). e, Sendai Pageant of Starlight (28x33mm).

Perf. 13¼ (#3543a), 13x13¼

2013, May 15 **Photo.**

3543 A2984 Sheet of 5	7.00	7.00
a.-e. 80y Any single	1.25	.60

Martes Zibellina Brachyura A2985

Luscinia Komadori Namiyei A2986

Primula Kisoana Miquel — A2987

Neolucanus Insulicola Donan — A2988

Meretrix Lusoria — A2989

2013, May 23 *Perf. 13¼*

3544 A2985 80y multi	1.25	.50
3545 A2986 80y multi	1.25	.50
3546 A2987 80y multi	1.25	.50
3547 A2988 80y multi	1.25	.50
3548 A2989 80y multi	1.25	.50
a. Vert. strip of 5, #3544-3548	7.50	4.00
Nos. 3544-3548 (5)	6.25	2.50

Miniature Sheet

Tottori Prefecture Afforestation — A2990

No. 3549: a, Quercus serrata (tree), denomination at LL. b, Lilium japonicum (pink flower), denomination at LL. c, Prunus jamasakura (cherry blossoms), denomination at LR. d, Taxus cuspidata (Japanese yew with red arils), denomination at LR. e, Castanopsis sieboldii (tree), denomination at UR. f, Iris sanguinea (purple flowers), denomination at UL. g, Nijisseiki pear tree blossoms, denomination at LR. h, Japanese persimmons on branch, denomination at LR. i, Castanea crenata (Japanese chestnut), denomination at UR. j, Magnolia obovata flower, denomination at LL.

2013, May 24 **Litho.** *Perf. 13*

3549 A2990 Sheet of 10	10.00	10.00
a.-j. 50y Any single	.80	.40

Second Hideyo Noguchi Africa Prize A2991

Noguchi (1876-1928), bacteriologist, and: No. 3550, Microscope and flowers. No. 3551, Globe.

2013, May 31 **Photo.**

3550		80y multicolored	1.25	.50
3551		80y multicolored	1.25	.50
a.	A2991	Horiz. pair, #3550-3551	3.00	1.50

Animation

Doraemon — A2992

No. 3552: a, Doraemon with wings, two children with wings. b, Three children with wings. c, Doraemon paddling raft. d, Children on fish. e, Doraemon, machine, woman near doorway carrying tray with bottles and glasses. f, Man and boy in indoor fountain. g, Three children with helicopter rotor on head flying. h, Doraemon and child with helicopter rotor on head flying. i, Boy and girl on orse, boy with smokestack on head, boy with umbrella in flight. j, Doraemon and cat on flying seahorses.

2013, June 4 **Litho.** ***Perf. 13x13¼***

3552	A2992	Sheet of 10	16.00	16.00
a.-j.		80y Any single	1.25	.50

Miniature Sheet

Hiroshima Local Autonomy Law, 60th Anniv. — A2993

No. 3553: a, Itsukushima Shrine, Bugaku dancer, maple leaves (32x39mm). b, Mibo no Hana Taue rice-planting ritual (28x33mm). c, Taishakukyo Valley (28x33mm). d, Lemons (28x33mm). e, Lighthouse and street, Tomonoura (28x33mm).

Perf. 13¼ (#3553a), 13x13¼

2013, June 14 **Photo.**

3553	A2993	Sheet of 5	7.00	7.00
a.-e.		80y Any single	1.25	.60

Japan Women's Association for Rehabilitation Aid, 50th Anniv. — A2994

Designs: No. 3554, Two women. No. 3555, Three women.

2013, June 18 **Litho.** ***Perf. 13***

3554		80y multicolored	1.25	.50
3555		80y multicolored	1.25	.50
a.	A2994	Horiz. pair, #3554-3555	3.00	1.50

Miniature Sheets

A2995

Greetings — A2996

No. 3556: a, Hello Kitty reading book (30x27mm heart-shaped stamp). b, Hello Kitty and house (27x30mm house-shaped stamp). c, Mimmy riding tricycle (23x23mm). d, Dear Daniel with letter at mailbox (22x30mm oval stamp). e, My Melody receiving kiss from mouse on tree stump (28mm diameter). f, Hello Kitty watering flowers (27x21mm). g, My Melody, bird in mailbox holding letter (21x27mm). h, My Melody and mouse jumping (30x27mm heart-shaped stamp). i, Little Twin Stars on crescent moon (28mm diameter). j, Little Twin Stars with music book and harp (23x23mm).

No. 3557: a, Little Twin Stars on cloud (27x21mm). b, Little Twin Stars, stars (24x28mm). c, Hello Kitty in airplane (28mm diameter). d, Hello Kitty holding teddy bear and letter (23x23mm). e, Hello Kitty on back of envelope (27x21mm). f, Hello Kitty and Mimmy on tricycles (27x21mm). g, Dear Daniel reaching to insert letter in mailbox (26x29mm). h, Hello Kitty holding apple (29x27mm heart-shaped stamp). i, My Melody receiving letter from bird in mailbox (29x26mm). j, My Melody receiving kiss from mouse (30x27mm oval stamp).

Die Cut Perf. 13¼, Die Cut Perf. 14 (#3556c, 3556j, 3557d), Die Cut Perf. 13¼x14 (#3556f, 3557a, 3557e, 3557f), Die Cut Perf. 14x13¾ (#3556g), Die Cut Perf. (#3556e, 3556i, 3557b, 3557c)

2013, June 21 **Litho.**

Self-Adhesive

3556	A2995	Sheet of 10	9.00	9.00
a.-j.		50y Any single	.80	.80
3557	A2996	Sheet of 10	13.00	13.00
a.-j.		80y Any single	1.25	.80

Miniature Sheet

Travel Scenes A2997

No. 3558 — Sites in Chiba: a, Narita-san Temple (stamp 1). b, Tourists in boat, flowers at Suigo Sarawa Aquatic Botanical Gardens (stamp 2). c, Chiba Port Tower (stamp 3). d, Nokogiriyama Cable Car (stamp 4). e, Yellow and red Kominato Railway train car (stamp 5). f, Waterfall, Yoro-keikoku Valley (stamp 6). g, Tsuki-no-Sabaku Statues, Onjuku Beach (stamp 7). h, Yellow and green Isumi Railway train car (stamp 8). i, Light green Choshi Electric Railway train car (stamp 9). j, Inubosaki Lighthouse (stamp 10).

2013, June 25 **Litho.** ***Perf. 13x13¼***

3558	A2997	Sheet of 10	13.00	13.00
a.-j.		80y Any single	1.25	.60

Gion Festival, Kyoto A2998

Various festival scenes with denomination in purple at: No. 3559, UL. No. 3560, UR. No. 3561, LL. No. 3562, LR.

2013, July 1 ***Perf. 13¼***

3559		50y multi	.80	.40
3560		50y multi	.80	.40
3561		50y multi	.80	.40
3562		50y multi	.80	.40
a.	A2998	Block of 4, #3559-3562	3.50	2.50
		Nos. 3559-3562 (4)	3.20	1.60

Miniature Sheet

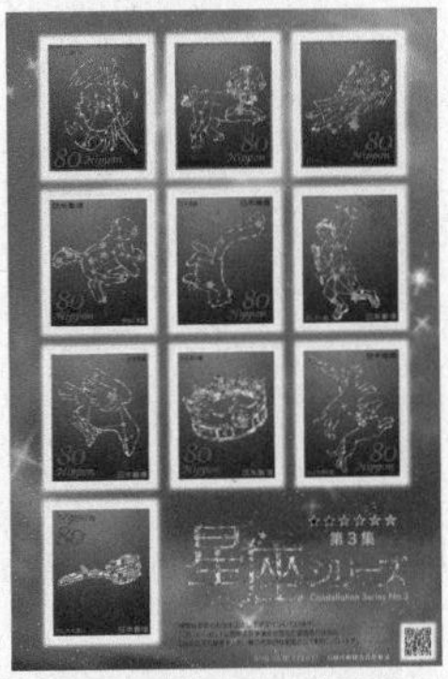

Constellations — A2999

No. 3563: a, Cancer (crab). b, Leo (lion). c, Virgo (virgin). d, Ursa Major (large bear, tail at left). e, Ursa Minor (small bear, tail at top). f, Boötes (herdsman). g, Corvus (crow). h, Corona Borealis (crown). i, Canes Venatici (hunting dogs). j, Big Dipper asterism.

Litho. With Foil Application

2013, July 5 ***Die Cut Perf. 13***

Self-Adhesive

3563	A2999	Sheet of 10	16.00	16.00
a.-j.		80y Any single	1.50	.60

Miniature Sheet

Gunma Local Autonomy Law, 60th Anniv. — A3000

No. 3564: a, Tomioka Silk Mill, woman (32x39mm). b, Red rhododendrons (28x33mm). c, Usui Railway Bridge (28x33mm). d, Fukiware Falls (28x33mm). e, Yellow day lilies (28x33mm).

Perf. 13¼ (#3564a), 13x13¼

2013, July 12 **Photo.**

3564	A3000	Sheet of 5	7.00	7.00
a.-e.		80y Any single	1.25	.60

Boy Writing Postcard A3001

Goldfish in Bowl A3002

Mailbox, Dragonfly, Net A3003

Japanese Morning Glories and Trellis A3004

Cucumbers, Eggplants, and Tomatoes — A3005

A3006

No. 3570: a, Girl writing a letter. b, Mailbox, dragonfly, net, diff. c, Beans and bowl of rice. d, Tea kettle and glasses. e, Corn. f, Japanese morning glories and trellis, diff. g, Postal truck on bridge. h, Spiral mosquito repellent coils. i, Bowls of noodles and sauce. j, Tomatoes.

2013, July 23 ***Perf. 13¼***

3565	A3001	50y multi	.80	.30
3566	A3002	50y multi	.80	.30
3567	A3003	50y multi	.80	.30
3568	A3004	50y multi	.80	.30
3569	A3005	50y multi	.80	.30
a.		Vert strip of 5, #3565-3569	4.50	3.00
		Nos. 3565-3569 (5)	4.00	1.50

Perf. 13

3570	A3006	Sheet of 10	16.00	16.00
a.-j.		80y Any single	1.25	.50

Letter Writing Day.

Kisegawa of Matsubaya, by Eishi Chobunsai
A3007

Pine Grove at Miho, by Hiroshige
A3008

Midorigi of the Wakamatsu House, by Eisho Chokosai
A3009

Oyashirazu, by Hiroshige
A3010

Woman Holding an Umbrella, by Eizan Kikukawa
A3011

Waka Bay, by Hiroshige
A3012

Koito of Itoya, by Utamaro
A3013

Festival at the Itsukushima Shrine, by Hiroshige
A3014

Geisha of Tachibana Street, by Kiyonaga Torii
A3015

Amanohashidate, by Hiroshige
A3016

2013, Aug. 1 **Litho.** ***Perf. 13***

3571	Sheet of 10	16.00	16.00
a.	A3007 80y multi	1.25	.50
b.	A3008 80y multi	1.25	.50
c.	A3009 80y multi	1.25	.50
d.	A3010 80y multi	1.25	.50
e.	A3011 80y multi	1.25	.50
f.	A3012 80y multi	1.25	.50
g.	A3013 80y multi	1.25	.50
h.	A3014 80y multi	1.25	.50
i.	A3015 80y multi	1.25	.50
j.	A3016 80y multi	1.25	.50

Miniature Sheets

A3017

Disney Characters — A3018

No. 3572: a, Mickey Mouse on blue box. b, Minnie Mouse on pink box. c, Donald Duck on blue box. d, Daisy Duck on pink box. e, Tinker Bell on pink box. f, Marie the Cat on blue box. g, Buzz Lightyear and Woody on pink box. h, Lightning McQueen on blue box. i, Winnie the Pooh on blue box. j, Alice on pink box.

No. 3573: a, Tinker Bell (29mm diameter). b, Winnie the Pooh and Piglet in balloon gondola (21x30mm oval). c, Alice in balloon gondola (29mm diameter). d, Marie the Cat in balloon gondola (21x30mm oval). e, Oswald the Rabbit in balloon gondola (23x23mm). f, Mike Wazowski and James P. Sullivan in balloon gondola (21x30mm oval). g, Goofy, Chip, Donald Duck, Pluto, Mickey Mouse, Minnie Mouse, Daisy Duck in balloon gondola (44x35mm). h, Woody and Buzz Lightyear in balloon gondola (21x30mm oval). i, Snow White, Rapunzel and Cinderella in balloon gondola (29mm diameter). j, Dumbo (30x21mm oval).

Die Cut Perf. 13¼

2013, Aug. 8 **Litho.**

Self-Adhesive

3572	A3017	Sheet of 10	9.00	9.00
a.-j.		50y Any single	.80	.80

Die Cut Perf., Die Cut Perf. 13¼ (oval stamps), Die Cut Perf. 14 (#3573e), Die Cut Perf. 13½ (#3573g)

3573	A3018	Sheet of 10	13.00	13.00
a.-j.		80y Any single	1.25	.80

Kayak on Tama River
A3019

Sailboats Near Tokyo Gate Bridge
A3020

Bonin Islands
A3021

Tokyo Skyline
A3022

Tokyo Stadium — A3023

2013, Aug. 25 **Litho.** ***Perf. 13***

3574	A3019	80y multi	1.25	.60
3575	A3020	80y multi	1.25	.60
3576	A3021	80y multi	1.25	.60
3577	A3022	80y multi	1.25	.60
3578	A3023	80y multi	1.25	.60
a.		Vert. strip of 5, #3574-3578	6.50	4.00
		Nos. 3574-3578 (5)	6.25	3.00

68th National Athletic Meet, Tokyo.

Persimmon
A3024

Bok Choy
A3025

Chestnut
A3026

Sweet Potato
A3027

Pear
A3028

Apple
A3029

Taro Roots
A3030

Japanese Pears
A3031

Turnip Greens
A3032

Grapes
A3033

Die Cut Perf. 13x13¼, 13¼x13

2013, Aug. 30 **Photo.**

Self-Adhesive

3579	Sheet of 10, 2 each #3579a-3579e	10.00	10.00
a.	A3024 50y multi	1.00	.75
b.	A3025 50y multi	1.00	.75
c.	A3026 50y multi	1.00	.75
d.	A3027 50y multi	1.00	.75
e.	A3028 50y multi	1.00	.75
3580	Sheet of 10, 2 each #3580a-3580e	16.00	16.00
a.	A3029 80y multi	1.60	.80
b.	A3030 80y multi	1.60	.80
c.	A3031 80y multi	1.60	.80
d.	A3032 80y multi	1.60	.80
e.	A3033 80y multi	1.60	.80

Dahlia
A3034

Chrysanthemum
A3035

Cockscomb
A3036

Asiatic Dayflower
A3037

Rose
A3038

Dahlias
A3039

Chrysanthemums
A3040

Cockscombs
A3041

Asiatic Dayflowers
A3042

Roses
A3043

2013, Sept. 13 **Photo.** ***Perf. 13¼***

3581	A3034	50y multi	.80	.40
3582	A3035	50y multi	.80	.40
3583	A3036	50y multi	.80	.40
3584	A3037	50y multi	.80	.40
3585	A3038	50y multi	.80	.40
a.		Vert. strip of 5, #3581-3585	4.50	3.00
3586	A3039	80y multi	1.25	.60
3587	A3040	80y multi	1.25	.60
3588	A3041	80y multi	1.25	.60
3589	A3042	80y multi	1.25	.60
3590	A3043	80y multi	1.25	.60
a.		Vert. strip of 5, #3586-3590	6.50	4.00
		Nos. 3581-3590 (10)	10.25	5.00

Ambulance Service Legislation, 50th Anniv. — A3044

2013, Sept. 9 Litho. *Perf. 13*

3591		80y Helicopter ambulance	1.25	.50
3592		80y Ambulance	1.25	.50
a.	A3044	Horiz. pair, #3591-3592	3.00	1.50

Miniature Sheets

A3045

Greetings — A3046

No. 3593 — Teddy bear wearing postman's cap: a, In bed (21x30mm oval). b, Alone at table (21x30mm oval). c, At right of pillar box (23x23mm). d, At left of pillar box (23x23mm). e, Delivering letter to large teddy bear (23x23mm). f, Delivering gift to large teddy bear (23x23mm). g, Holding flower bouquet with light blue ribbon (27x30mm). h, Holding flower bouquet with yellow ribbon (27x30mm). i, With two other teddy bears at table (21x30mm oval). j, Reading book in bed (21x30mm oval).

No. 3594: a, Teddy bear delivering letter to large teddy bear (27x21mm). b, Teddy bear walking on path, holding letter (21x30mm oval). c, Teddy bear delivering gift to large teddy bear (27x21mm). d, Teddy bear delivering letter to bird (21x30mm oval). e, Teddy bear on bicycle (27x21mm). f, Teddy bear delivering letter to bear with pail and fishing pole (27x21mm). g, Small teddy bear without cap holding letter near pillar box (21x30mm oval). h, Teddy bear with cap, small teddy bear with flower bouquet (27x21mm). i, Teddy bear with cap lifting small teddy bear to slot of pillar box (21x27mm). j, Small teddy bear behind teddy bear with cap (29mm diameter).

Die Cut Perf. 13¼ (oval stamps), Die Cut Perf. 14 (square stamps), Die Cut Perf. (#3593g, 3593h)

2013, Sept. 19 Litho.

Self-Adhesive

3593	A3045	Sheet of 10	9.00	9.00
a.-j.		50y Any single	.80	.80

Die Cut Perf. 13¼x13¾, Die Cut Perf. 13¼ (oval stamps), Die Cut Perf. 13¾x13¼ (#3594i), Die Cut Perf. (#3594j)

3594	A3046	Sheet of 10	13.00	13.00
a.-j.		80y Any single	1.25	.80

Baby Elephant A3047

Baby and Adult Killer Whales A3048

Black-tailed Prairie Dog A3049

Adult and Juvenile Gentoo Penguins A3050

Kangaroo A3051

Amur Tiger Cub A3052

Timber Wolf Pups — A3053

Ring-tailed Lemurs — A3054

Polar Bear A3055

White Oryx A3056

Die Cut Perf. 13¼

2013, Sept. 20 Litho.

Self-Adhesive

3595		Sheet of 10, 2 each #3595a-3595e	10.00	10.00
a.	A3047	50y multi	1.00	.75
b.	A3048	50y multi	1.00	.75
c.	A3049	50y multi	1.00	.75
d.	A3050	50y multi	1.00	.75
e.	A3051	50y multi	1.00	.75
3596		Sheet of 10, 2 each #3596a-3596e	16.00	16.00
a.	A3052	80y multi	1.60	.75
b.	A3053	80y multi	1.60	.75
c.	A3054	80y multi	1.60	.75
d.	A3055	80y multi	1.60	.75
e.	A3056	80y multi	1.60	.75

Miniature Sheet

Diplomatic Relations Between Japan and Spain, 400th Anniv. — A3057

No. 3597: a, Potted geraniums on decorative shelf. b, Japanese bush clover. c, Guggenheim Museum, Bilbao, Spain (white denomination at UR, numeral to right of "Nippon.") d, Santiago de Compostela Cathedral (gold denomination at UR). e, Museum of Contemporary Art, León, Spain (white denomination at UR, numeral below "Nippon."). f, Alcazar of Segovia (castle with spires). g, Royal Palace, Madrid (building with dome). h, Arches and columns, Córdoba Cathedral, Spain. i, Courtyard and archway, Palace of Generalife, Granada, Spain. j, Field of sunflowers.

2013, Oct. 1 Litho. *Perf. 13*

3597	A3057	Sheet of 10	16.00	16.00
a.-j.		80y Any single	1.25	.50

See Spain No. 3944.

Miniature Sheet

Okayama Local Autonomy Law, 60th Anniv. — A3058

No. 3598: a, Korakuen Gardens, Momotaro with animals (32x39mm). b, Bridge and buildings, Kurashiki Bikan (28x33mm). c, Shizutani School (28x33mm). d, Cattle grazing, Hiruzenkogen Highlands (28x33mm). e, Tsuyama Castle and cherry blossoms (28x33mm).

Perf. 13¼ (#3598a), 13x13¼

2013, Oct. 4 Photo.

3598	A3058	Sheet of 5	7.00	7.00
a.-e.		80y Any single	1.25	.60

Intl. Letter Writing Week — A3059

Posting stations from The Fifty-three Stations of the Tokaido, by Hiroshige: 70y, Shirasuka. 90y, Odawara. 110y, Hamamatsu. 130y, Ishiyakushi.

2013, Oct. 9 Photo. *Perf. 13*

3599	A3059	70y multi	1.25	.50
3600	A3059	90y multi	1.75	.50
3601	A3059	110y multi	2.25	.50
3602	A3059	130y multi	2.60	.50
		Nos. 3599-3602 (4)	7.85	2.00

See listing of No. 4448 for images of each Hiroshige print.

Tokyo Railroad Station A3060

Odakyu 3000 Series Locomotive A3061

JNR 151 Series Locomotive A3062

Kintetsu 10100 Series Locomotive A3063

JNR Kiha 81 Series Locomotive A3064

Meitetsu 7000 Series Locomotive A3065

Kintetsu 20100 Series Locomotive A3066

Odakyu 3100 Series Locomotive A3067

JNR Shinkansen 0 Series Locomotive A3068

Shinkansen E5 Series Locomotive A3069

2013, Oct. 11 Photo. *Perf. 13¼x13*

3603		Sheet of 10	16.00	16.00
a.	A3060	80y multi	1.25	.50
b.	A3061	80y multi	1.25	.50
c.	A3062	80y multi	1.25	.50
d.	A3063	80y multi	1.25	.50
e.	A3064	80y multi	1.25	.50
f.	A3065	80y multi	1.25	.50
g.	A3066	80y multi	1.25	.50
h.	A3067	80y multi	1.25	.50
i.	A3068	80y multi	1.25	.50
j.	A3069	80y multi	1.25	.50

Miniature Sheet

Shizuoka Local Autonomy Law, 60th Anniv. — A3070

No. 3604: a, Mount Fuji and clouds (32x39mm). b, Mount Fuji and yellow flowers (28x33mm). c, Mount Fuji reflected in Lake Tanuki (28x33mm). d, Mount Fuji and trees (28x33mm). e, Mount Fuji, ships and coastal rocks (28x33mm).

Perf. 13¼ (#3604a), 13x13¼

2013, Oct. 15 **Photo.**

3604	A3070	Sheet of 5		7.00	7.00
a.-e.		80y Any single		1.25	.60

Tortoise on Galapagos Islands, Ecuador A3071

Taj Mahal, India A3072

Venice, Italy A3073

Victoria Falls, Zambia and Zimbabwe A3074

Cologne Cathedral, Germany — A3075

2013, Oct. 23 **Litho.** ***Perf. 13¼x13***

3605	A3071	80y multi	1.25	.50
3606	A3072	80y multi	1.25	.50
3607	A3073	80y multi	1.25	.50
3608	A3074	80y multi	1.25	.50
3609	A3075	80y multi	1.25	.50
a.		Horiz. strip of 5, #3605-3609	7.50	4.50
		Nos. 3605-3609 (5)	6.25	2.50

Foreign UNESCO World Heritage Sites.

Miniature Sheet

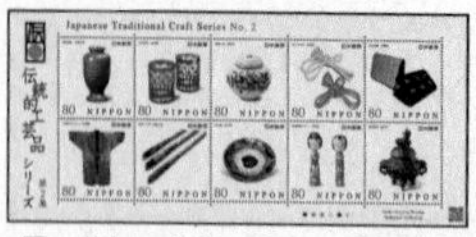

Traditional Crafts — A3076

No. 3610: a, Kishu lacquerware vase (Wakayama Prefecture). b, Two Edo Kiriko glasses (Tokyo Prefecture). c, Owari Shippo porcelain bowl with lid (Aichi Prefecture). d, Two Kyo Kumihimo braids (Kyoto Prefecture). e, Chibana Okinawa weavings (Okinawa Prefecture). f, Ainu ceremonial costume (Hokkaido Prefecture). g, Kishu lacquered utensil handles (Wakayama Prefecture). h, Mashiko-yaki pottery bowl (Tochigi Prefecture). i, Kokeshi dolls (Miyagi Prefecture). j, Takaoka copper vessel (Toyama Prefecture).

2013, Oct. 25 **Litho.** ***Perf. 13½***

3610	A3076	Sheet of 10	16.00	16.00
a.-j.		80y Any single	1.25	.50

A3077

A3078

New Year 2014 (Year of the Horse)
A3079 A3080

2013, Nov. 1 **Photo.** ***Perf. 13x13½***

3611	A3077	50y multi	1.00	.30
3612	A3078	80y multi	1.50	.40

Photo. & Typo.

Perf. 13¼

3613	A3079	50y +3y multi	1.25	.40
3614	A3080	80y +3y multi	1.75	.40
		Nos. 3611-3614 (4)	5.50	1.50

Sheets of two containing Nos. 3611-3612 were lottery prizes. Value, $3.

Miniature Sheet

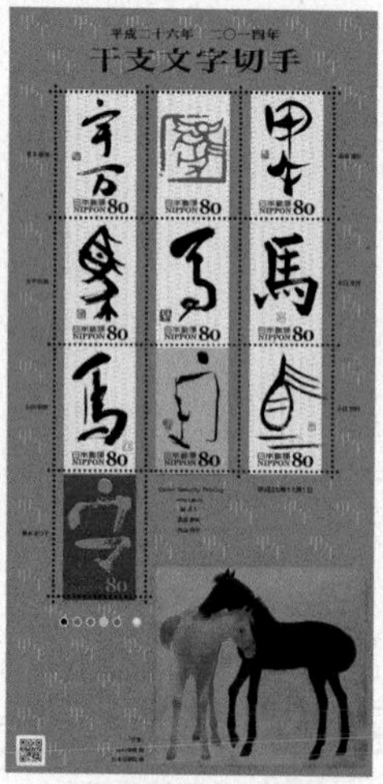

Edo Calligraphy — A3081

No. 3615 — Characters for "horse": a, In Manyo-kana style (black character with dot at top, red chop at center left). b, In oracle bone script (red character). c, In Qin Dynasty bamboo roll calligraphy (black character with curved arc crossing center line, red chop at center left). d, In Western Zhou Dynasty Kinbun style (black character with teardrop shaped top with dot in center, red chop at LL). e, In Sosho style (black character of one continuous curved line, red chop at LL). f, In Kaisho style (black character, red chop at bottom center). g, In Gyosho style (black character with red chop at LR. h, In Kana (black character with lilac background). i, In Seal style calligraphy (black character with two horizontal lines at bottom, red chop at center right). j, In Katakana (gold character on blue violet background).

Litho. & Embossed

2013, Nov. 1 ***Perf. 13x13¼***

3615	A3081	Sheet of 10	16.00	16.00
a.-j.		80y Any single	1.25	.50

Two Snowmen A3082

Snowman With Broom A3083

Three Snowmen A3084

Snowman With Gift A3085

Snowman on Skis A3086

Snowflake Jewelry With Sapphires A3087

Snowflake Jewelry With Emeralds A3088

Snowflake Jewelry With Aquamarines A3089

Snowflake Jewelry With Peridots A3090

Snowflake Jewelry With Rubies A3091

Two Wine Glasses A3092

Two Candles A3093

Two Champagne Flutes A3094

Candle A3095

Two Martini Glasses — A3096

Die Cut Perf. 13¼

2013, Nov. 7 **Litho.**

Self-Adhesive

3616		Sheet of 10, 2 each #3616a-3616e	9.00	9.00
a.	A3082	50y multi	.80	.80
b.	A3083	50y multi	.80	.80
c.	A3084	50y multi	.80	.80
d.	A3085	50y multi	.80	.80
e.	A3086	50y multi	.80	.80
3617		Sheet of 10	13.00	13.00
a.	A3087	80y multi	1.25	.80
b.	A3088	80y multi	1.25	.80
c.	A3089	80y multi	1.25	.80
d.	A3090	80y multi	1.25	.80
e.	A3091	80y multi	1.25	.80
f.	A3092	80y multi	1.25	.80
g.	A3093	80y multi	1.25	.80
h.	A3094	80y multi	1.25	.80
i.	A3095	80y multi	1.25	.80
j.	A3096	80y multi	1.25	.80

Miniature Sheet

Yamanashi Local Autonomy Law, 60th Anniv. — A3097

No. 3618: a, Mount Fuji, grapes, and maglev test train (32x39mm). b, Shosenkyo Gorges (28x33mm). c, Nishizawa Valley waterfalls (28x33mm). d, Pagoda and cherry blossoms (28x33mm). e, Saruhashi Bridge (28x33mm).

Perf. 13¼ (#3618a), 13x13¼

2013, Nov. 15 **Photo.**

3618	A3097	Sheet of 5	7.00	7.00
a.-e.		80y Any single	1.25	.60

Mt. Iwakisan A3098

Mt. Tsurugidake A3099

Mt. Hirugatake A3100

Mt. Gozaishodake A3101

Mt. Daisen A3102

Mt. Myokosan A3103

Mt. Aobasan A3104

Mt. Kaikomagatake A3105

Mt. Oodaigahara A3106

Mt. Tenzan A3107

2013, Nov. 19 **Litho.** ***Perf. 13¼x13***

3619		Sheet of 10	16.00	16.00
a.	A3098	80y multi	1.25	.50
b.	A3099	80y multi	1.25	.50
c.	A3100	80y multi	1.25	.50
d.	A3101	80y multi	1.25	.50
e.	A3102	80y multi	1.25	.50
f.	A3103	80y multi	1.25	.50
g.	A3104	80y multi	1.25	.50
h.	A3105	80y multi	1.25	.50
i.	A3106	80y multi	1.25	.50
j.	A3107	80y multi	1.25	.50

Volunteer Fire Service, 120th Anniv. A3108

Paintings by Kunichida Toyohara of Kabuki actors wearing costumes of fire fighters: No. 3620, Jyuzaburo Nakamura (denomination at right). No. 3621, Hikosaburo Bando (denomination at left).

2013, Nov. 25 Litho. *Perf. 13*

3620		80y multi	1.25	.50
3621		80y multi	1.25	.50
a.	A3108	Horiz. pair, #3620-3621	3.00	1.50

Japanese Allspice A3109

Snowdrop A3110

Christmas Camellia A3111

Narcissus A3112

Leopard Plant Flowers A3113

Japanese Allspice A3114

Snowdrops A3115

Christmas Camellias A3116

Narcissi A3117

Leopard Plant Flowers A3118

2013, Dec. 3 Photo. *Perf. 13¼*

3622	A3109	50y multi	.80	.40
3623	A3110	50y multi	.80	.40
3624	A3111	50y multi	.80	.40
3625	A3112	50y multi	.80	.40
3626	A3113	50y multi	.80	.40
a.		Vert. strip of 5, #3622-3626	4.50	3.00
3627	A3114	80y multi	1.25	.60
3628	A3115	80y multi	1.25	.60
3629	A3116	80y multi	1.25	.60
3630	A3117	80y multi	1.25	.60
3631	A3118	80y multi	1.25	.60
a.		Vert. strip of 5, #3627-3631	6.50	4.00
		Nos. 3622-3631 (10)	10.25	5.00

Miniature Sheet

Constellations — A3119

No. 3632: a, Aries (ram). b, Taurus (bull). c, Gemini (twins). d, Orion (hunter with shield). e, Auriga (man holding goat). f, Canis Major (dog on hind legs). g, Canis Minor (dog on four legs). h, Lepus (rabbit). i, Monoceros (unicorn). j, Tsuzumiboshi (Japanese drum, Japanese version of Orion).

Litho. With Foil Application

2013, Dec. 4 *Die Cut Perf. 13*

Self-Adhesive

3632	A3119	Sheet of 10	16.00	16.00
a.-j.		80y Any single	1.50	.80

Wakamatsu Castle A3120

Odawara Castle A3121

Hikone Castle A3122

Nijo Castle A3123

Okayama Castle — A3124

2013, Dec. 10 Litho. *Perf. 13*

3633	A3120	80y multi	1.25	.50
3634	A3121	80y multi	1.25	.50
3635	A3122	80y multi	1.25	.50
3636	A3123	80y multi	1.25	.50
3637	A3124	80y multi	1.25	.50
a.		Vert. strip of 5, #3633-3637	8.00	4.00
		Nos. 3633-3637 (5)	6.25	2.50

Diplomatic Relations Between Japan and Kenya, 50th Anniv. — A3125

African wildlife: No. 3638, Giraffes. No. 3639, Cheetahs. No. 3640, Elephants. No. 3641, Zebras. No. 3642, Lion.

2013, Dec. 12 Litho. *Perf. 13¼x13*

3638	A3125	80y multi	1.25	.50
3639	A3125	80y multi	1.25	.50
3640	A3125	80y multi	1.25	.50
3641	A3125	80y multi	1.25	.50
3642	A3125	80y multi	1.25	.50
a.		Horiz. strip of 5, #3638-3642	8.00	4.00
		Nos. 3638-3642 (5)	6.25	2.50

Miniature Sheet

Kagoshima Local Autonomy Law, 60th Anniv. — A3126

No. 3643: a, Jomon Sugi tree, rhododendrons (32x39mm). b, Sakurajima Volcano (28x33mm). c, Kaimondake Volcano and coastal rocks (28x33mm). d, Flowers on Kirishima Mountains (28x33mm). e, Cranes (28x33mm).

Perf. 13¼ (#3643a), 13x13¼

2013, Dec. 13 Photo.

3643	A3126	Sheet of 5	7.00	7.00
a.-e.		80y Any single	1.25	.60

Teddy Bear, Gift and Dog A3127

Boy, Gift, Birds With Ribbon A3128

Girl With Broom, Squirrel and Turtle A3129

Animals, Gift, Flowers and Strawberries A3130

Roses A3131

Cherry Blossoms A3132

Mt. Fuji and Cherry Blossoms A3133

Rose Bouquet A3134

Tulips and Girl With Letter and Flower Bouquet A3135

Teddy Bears, Flowers and Mailbox A3136

Die Cut Perf., Die Cut Perf. 13 (#3644d, 3644e, 3645e)

2014, Jan. 16 Litho.

Self-Adhesive

3644		Sheet of 10, 2 each #3644a-3644e	9.00	9.00
a.	A3127	50y multi	.80	.80
b.	A3128	50y multi	.80	.80
c.	A3129	50y multi	.80	.80
d.	A3130	50y multi	.80	.80
e.	A3131	50y multi	.80	.80
3645		Sheet of 10, 2 each #3645a-3645e	12.00	12.00
a.	A3132	80y multi	1.25	.80
b.	A3133	80y multi	1.25	.80
c.	A3134	80y multi	1.25	.80
d.	A3135	80y multi	1.25	.80
e.	A3136	80y multi	1.25	.80

Miniature Sheet

Diplomatic Relations Between Japan and Switzerland, 150th Anniv. — A3137

No. 3646: a, Swiss mountains in spring. b, Mount Fuji and cherry blossoms. c, Aletsch Glacier, Switzerland. d, Bern, Switzerland. e, Lavaux Vineyard Terraces. f, Rhaetian Railway train on bridge. g, Jungfrau Railway train, flowers and mountains. h, Narcissus Path, Les Avants, Switzerland. i, Fluhalp Mountain Lodge. j, Meadow in Bernina Alps.

2014, Feb. 6 Litho. *Perf. 13*

3646	A3137	Sheet of 10	16.00	16.00
a.-j.		80y Any single	1.25	.50

See Switzerland Nos. 1507-1508.

Hokkaido Mountain Hare A3138

Cherry Blossoms A3139

Plum Blossoms A3140

Violets A3141

Cedar Tree A3142

Nachi Falls A3143

Rishiri Island — A3144

2014, Mar. 3 Photo. *Perf. 13x13¼*

3647	A3138	2y multi	.30	.25
3648	A3139	52y multi	1.00	.75
3649	A3140	82y multi	1.60	1.25
3650	A3141	92y multi	1.90	1.40
3651	A3142	205y multi	4.00	3.00
3652	A3143	280y multi	5.50	4.25
3653	A3144	310y multi	6.00	4.50
		Nos. 3647-3653 (7)	20.30	15.40

Flowers For Mourning — A3145

2014, Mar. 3 Photo. *Perf. 13x13¼*

3654	A3145	52y multi	1.00	.75

See No. 4106.

Fan With Plum Blossoms A3146

Fan With Bamboo A3147

Fan With Tree Branches — A3148

2014, Mar. 3 Photo. *Perf. 13x13¼*

3655	A3146	52y multi	1.00	.75
3656	A3147	82y multi	1.60	1.25
3657	A3148	92y multi	1.90	1.40
	Nos. 3655-3657 (3)		4.50	3.40

Compare with type A3914.

A3149 A3150

A3151 A3152

A3153 A3154

A3155 A3156

A3157 Takarazuka Revue, 100th Anniv. — A3158

2014, Apr. 1 Litho. *Perf. 13*

3658		Sheet of 10	16.00	16.00
a.	A3149	82c multi	1.25	.50
b.	A3150	82c multi	1.25	.50
c.	A3151	82c multi	1.25	.50
d.	A3152	82c multi	1.25	.50
e.	A3153	82c multi	1.25	.50
f.	A3154	82c multi	1.25	.50
g.	A3155	82c multi	1.25	.50
h.	A3156	82c multi	1.25	.50
i.	A3157	82c multi	1.25	.50
j.	A3158	82c multi	1.25	.50

Organization for Economic Cooperation, 50th Anniv. — A3159

Designs: No. 3659, Emblem, Organization Headquarters, Paris. No. 3660, Symbols for cooperation and development.

2014, Apr. 2 Litho. *Perf. 13*

3659		82y multi	1.25	.50
3660		82y multi	1.25	.50
a.	A3159	Pair, #3659-3660	3.00	1.50

Daisy and Sweet Peas A3160

Lily A3161

Cherry Blossoms A3162

Water Lily A3163

Poppies and Ranunculus A3164

Peony A3165

Roses A3166

Magnolias A3167

2014, Apr. 3 Litho. *Perf. 14x14¼*

3661	A3160	52y multi	.80	.30
3662	A3161	52y multi	.80	.30
3663	A3162	52y multi	.80	.30
3664	A3163	52y multi	.80	.30
a.		Horiz. strip of 4, #3661-3664	4.00	2.00
3665	A3164	82y multi	1.25	.50
3666	A3165	82y multi	1.25	.50
3667	A3166	82y multi	1.25	.50
3668	A3167	82y multi	1.25	.50
a.		Horiz. strip of 4, #3665-3668	6.00	3.00
	Nos. 3661-3668 (8)		8.20	3.20

Miniature Sheet

Ehime Local Autonomy Law, 60th Anniv. — A3168

No. 3669: a, Oranges, Dogo Hot Springs Building (32x39mm). b, Matsuyama Castle (28x33mm). c, Mount Ichizuchi (28x33mm). d, Terraced fields, Yusumizugaura (28x33mm). e, Sadamisaki Lighthouse (28x33mm).

Perf. 13¼ (#3669a), 13x13¼

2014, Apr. 17 Photo.

3669	A3168	Sheet of 5	7.00	7.00
a.-e.		82y Any single	1.25	.60

Philatelic Week A3169

Details from folding screens by Eishuku Kano: No. 3670, Seven small birds near tree. No. 3671, Two birds below tree branch. No. 3672, Three adult and three juvenile cranes, white and yellow flowers. No. 3673, Adult cranes and flowers.

2014, Apr. 18 Photo. *Perf. 13¼*

3670		82y multi	1.25	.50
3671		82y multi	1.25	.50
3672		82y multi	1.25	.50
3673		82y multi	1.25	.50
a.	A3169	Block of 4, #3670-3673	6.00	3.00
	Nos. 3670-3673 (4)		5.00	2.00

Nos. 3670-3673 were printed in sheets of 10 containing 3 each of Nos. 3670-3671 and 2 each of Nos. 3672-3673.

Mount Akita-Komagatake A3170

Mount Iyo A3171

Mount Oku-Hotakadake A3172

Mount Fuji A3173

Mount Rokko — A3174

Mount Mikura — A3175

Mount Tsurugi — A3176

Mount Unzen — A3177

Mount Okue — A3178

Mount Tama — A3179

2014, May 1 Litho. *Perf. 13¼x13*

3674		Sheet of 10	16.00	16.00
a.	A3170	82y multi	1.25	.50
b.	A3171	82y multi	1.25	.50
c.	A3172	82y multi	1.25	.50
d.	A3173	82y multi	1.25	.50
e.	A3174	82y multi	1.25	.50
f.	A3175	82y multi	1.25	.50
g.	A3176	82y multi	1.25	.50
h.	A3177	82y multi	1.25	.50
i.	A3178	82y multi	1.25	.50
j.	A3179	82y multi	1.25	.50

Souvenir Sheets

A3180

A3181

2014 World Cup Soccer Championships, Brazil — A3182

No. 3675 — Trophy with: a, Denomination at UL, "Nippon" at UR. b, Denomination at LR. c, Denomination and "Nippon" at UL.

No. 3676: a, Emblem. b, Emblem, design with stylized soccer player dribbling ball at left. c, Emblem, design with stylized goalie making save at right.

No. 3677 — Mascot: a, Carrying flag. b, Holding soccer ball. c, Dribbling soccer ball.

2014, May 12 Litho. *Perf. 13*

3675	A3180	Sheet of 3	5.00	5.00
a.-c.		82y Any single	1.25	.50
3676	A3181	Sheet of 3	5.00	5.00
a.-c.		82y Any single	1.25	.50
3677	A3182	Sheet of 3	5.00	5.00
a.-c.		82y Any single	1.25	.50
	Nos. 3675-3677 (3)		15.00	15.00

Miniature Sheet

Yamagata Local Autonomy Law, 60th Anniv. — A3183

No. 3678: a, Mogami River and cherries (32x39mm). b, Mt. Haguro five-story pagoda (28x33mm). c, Kubo cherry tree blossoming (28x33mm). d, Hayashi Family court dancer (28x33mm). e, Shinjo Festival (28x33mm).

Perf. 13¼ (#3678a), 13x13¼

2014, May 14 Photo.

3678	A3183	Sheet of 5	8.00	8.00
a.-e.		82y Any single	1.25	.60

Pentalagus Furnessi A3184

Lagopus Muta Japonica A3185

Polemonium Kiushianum A3186

Tanakia Tanago A3187

Cuora Flavomarginata Evelynae — A3188

2014, May 15 **Litho.** ***Perf. 13¼***

3679	A3184 82y multi	1.25	.50
3680	A3185 82y multi	1.25	.50
3681	A3186 82y multi	1.25	.50
3682	A3187 82y multi	1.25	.50
3683	A3188 82y multi	1.25	.50
a.	Vert. strip of 5, #3679-3683	8.00	4.00
	Nos. 3679-3683 (5)	6.25	2.50

Miniature Sheets

A3189

Characters From Disney Animated Films — A3190

No. 3684: a, Snow White and bird. b, Sleeping Beauty. c, Cinderella. d, Peter Pan with Wendy, John and Michael Darling. e, March Hare, Alice and Mad Hatter. f, Dumbo and Timothy. g, Thumper, Bambi and Flower. h, Lady and the Tramp. i, 101 Dalmatians. j, Geppetto and Pinocchio.

No. 3685: a, Winnie the Pooh seated, looking in honey jar. b, Winnie standing, looking in honey jar. c, Winnie and Eeyore. d, Winnie and Tigger. e, Winnie, Kanga and Roo. f, Winnie and Piglet. g, Winnie holding note. h, Winnie reaching for honey jar. i, Winnie turning over honey jar. j, Winnie standing in large honey pot.

Die Cut Perf. 14

2014, May 23 **Litho.**

Self-Adhesive

3684	A3189	Sheet of 10	10.00	10.00
a.-j.		52y Any single	1.00	.75
3685	A3190	Sheet of 10	16.00	16.00
a.-j.		82y Any single	1.25	.80

Miniature Sheet

National Afforestation — A3191

No. 3686: a, Tulipa gesneria. b, Magnolia salicifolia flowers. c, Magnolia obovata flowers. d, Erythronium japonicum. e, Fagus crenata leaves. f, Camellia rusticana. g, Maple leaves on branches. h, Hepatica nobilis. i, Narcissus tazetta. j, Azalea flowers.

2014, May 30 **Litho.** ***Perf. 13***

3686	A3191	Sheet of 10	10.00	10.00
a.-j.		52y Any single	1.00	.75

Palace of Versailles, France — A3192

Thebes, Egypt — A3193

Roman Colosseum, Italy A3194

Great Barrier Reef, Australia A3195

La Pedrera, Barcelona, Spain — A3196

2014, June 3 **Litho.** ***Perf. 13¼x13***

3687	A3192 82y multi	1.25	.50
3688	A3193 82y multi	1.25	.50
3689	A3194 82y multi	1.25	.50
3690	A3195 82y multi	1.25	.50
3691	A3196 82y multi	1.25	.50
a.	Horiz. strip of 5, #3687-3691	8.00	4.00
	Nos. 3687-3691 (5)	6.25	2.50

UNESCO World Heritage sites.

Cherries A3197

Bell Peppers A3198

Japanese Plums A3199

Corn A3200

Watermelons A3201

Tomato A3202

Japanese Apricots A3203

Eggplants A3204

Cucumbers A3205

Peach A3206

Die Cut Perf. 13x13¼, 13¼x13

2014, June 4 **Litho.**

Self-Adhesive

3692		Sheet of 10, 2 each #3692a-3692e	10.00	10.00
a.	A3197 52y multi		.80	.80
b.	A3198 52y multi		.80	.80
c.	A3199 52y multi		.80	.80
d.	A3200 52y multi		.80	.80
e.	A3201 52y multi		.80	.80
3693		Sheet of 10, 2 each #3693a-3693e	16.00	16.00
a.	A3202 82y multi		1.25	.80
b.	A3203 82y multi		1.25	.80
c.	A3204 82y multi		1.25	.80
d.	A3205 82y multi		1.25	.80
e.	A3206 82y multi		1.25	.80

Miniature Sheet

Mie Local Autonomy Law, 60th Anniv. — A3207

No. 3694: a, Uji Bridge and Isuzu River (32x39mm). b, Iris ensata (28x33mm). c, Wedded Rocks, Ise-Shima National Park (28x33mm). d, Lion Rock and fireworks (28x33mm). e, Ago Bay (28x33mm).

Perf. 13¼ (#3694a), 13x13¼

2014, June 19 **Photo.**

3694	A3207	Sheet of 5	8.00	8.00
a.-e.		82y Any single	1.25	.60

Miniature Sheets

A3208

Sanrio Cartoon Characters — A3209

No. 3695: a, Hello Kitty on bicycle (29x26mm heart-shaped stamp). b, Hello Kitty on elephant (29mm diameter). c, Hello Kitty and Mimmy on telephone (23x23mm). d, Hello Kitty and Mimmy on see-saw (22x30mm oval stamp). e, Hello Kitty in airplane (23x23mm). f, Hello Kitty on scale (27x22mm). g, My Melody on swing with squirrel, Blanco (22x27mm). h, My Melody on ground with mouse, Flat (29x26mm heart-shaped stamp). i, Pompompurin and Macaroon (29mm diameter). j, Pompompurin and stuffed toys (23x23mm).

No. 3696: a, Hello Kitty, umbrella, cherries, pencils and candy bag (22x27mm). b, Hello Kitty with balloon (29x26mm heart-shaped stamp). c, Hello Kitty and Mimmy on telephone with apples (29mm diameter). d, Hello Kitty with watering can (27x22mm). e, Hello Kitty and Mimmy in go-karts (23x23mm). f, Hello Kitty with hair brush (22x30mm oval stamp). g, My Melody at mailbox (27x22mm). h, My Melody reading letter (30x22mm oval stamp). i, Pompompurin and Muffin (29x26mm heart-shaped stamp). j, Pompompurin and "PURIN" (27x22mm).

Die Cut Perf. 14 (square stamps), 13¼x13¾, 13¾x13¼ (rectangular stamps), 13¼ (oval stamps), Die Cut Perf.

2014, June 23 Litho.

Self-Adhesive

3695	A3208	Sheet of 10	10.00	10.00
a.-j.		52y Any single	1.00	.75
3696	A3209	Sheet of 10	16.00	16.00
a.-j.		82y Any single	1.25	.75

Miniature Sheet

Mount Fuji UNESCO World Heritage Site — A3210

No. 3697 — Various views of Mount Fuji: a, Clouds above mountain, denomination at LL. b, Clouds obscuring base, denomination at LR. c, Framed by cherry trees in bloom, denomination at UL. d, With farm fields below, denomination at LL. e, With cherry blossoms at top, denomination at UL. f, In winter, with hills below, denomination at LL. g, With lake below, denomination at UL. h, With clouds and forest below, denomination at LL. i, With forest and waterfall below, denomination at LL. j, With swan on lake below, denomination at UR.

2014, June 26 Photo. *Perf. 13x13¼*

3697	A3210	Sheet of 10	16.00	16.00
a.-j.		82y Any single	1.25	.50

Miniature Sheet

Constellations — A3211

No. 3698: a, Cancer. b, Leo. c, Virgo. d, Vega (without white frame).

Litho. With Foil Application

2014, July 7 *Die Cut Perf. 13x13¼*

Self-Adhesive

3698	A3211	Sheet of 10, 3 each #3698a-3698c, 1 #3698d	16.00	16.00
a.-d.		82y Any single	1.25	.80

Matsumae Castle A3212

Inuyama Castle A3213

Matsue Castle A3214

Takamatsu Castle A3215

Kumamoto Castle — A3216

2014, July 15 Litho. *Perf. 13*

3699	A3212	82y multi	1.25	.50
3700	A3213	82y multi	1.25	.50
3701	A3214	82y multi	1.25	.50
3702	A3215	82y multi	1.25	.50
3703	A3216	82y multi	1.25	.50
a.		Vert. strip of 5, #3699-3703	8.00	4.00
		Nos. 3699-3703 (5)	6.25	2.50

Irises A3217

Goldfish A3218

Flowers A3219

Rabbits A3220

Birds in Plum Tree A3221

Raspberries A3222

Morning Glories A3223

Gourds A3224

Cranes A3225

Cherry Blossoms and Water Wheels A3226

Geometric Pattern A3227

Poppies A3228

Grapevines A3229

Flowers A3230

Rape Blossoms A3231

Loquats A3232

Morning Glory and Fan A3233

Leaves and Nuts A3234

Pine Trees A3235

Cherry Blossoms A3236

Die Cut Perf. 13x13½

2014, July 23 Litho.

Booklet Stamps

Self-Adhesive

3704	A3217	52y multi	.80	.75
3705	A3218	52y multi	.80	.75
3706	A3219	52y multi	.80	.75
3707	A3220	52y multi	.80	.75
3708	A3221	52y multi	.80	.75
3709	A3222	52y multi	.80	.75
3710	A3223	52y multi	.80	.75
3711	A3224	52y multi	.80	.75
3712	A3225	52y multi	.80	.75
3713	A3226	52y multi	.80	.75
a.		Booklet pane of 10, #3704-3713	10.00	10.00
3714	A3227	82y multi	1.25	.80
3715	A3228	82y multi	1.25	.80
3716	A3229	82y multi	1.25	.80
3717	A3230	82y multi	1.25	.80
3718	A3231	82y multi	1.25	.80
3719	A3232	82y multi	1.25	.80
3720	A3233	82y multi	1.25	.80
3721	A3234	82y multi	1.25	.80
3722	A3235	82y multi	1.25	.80
3723	A3236	82y multi	1.25	.80
a.		Booklet pane of 10, #3714-3723	16.00	16.00
		Nos. 3704-3723 (20)	20.50	15.50

The Ide Tama River: Karuta of the Choji-ya, by Eizan Kikukawa A3237

Karokoyama, by Hiroshige Utagawa A3238

Hitomoto of the Mojiro, by Utamaro Kitagawa A3239

Fishing Boats Netting Flounder, by Hiroshige Utagawa A3240

Washing and Starching Fabric, by Eizan Kikukawa A3241

Tsushima Tenno Festival, by Hiroshige Utagawa A3242

Girl with a Fan, by Utamaro Kitagawa A3243

Cherry Island, by Hiroshige Utagawa A3244

The Doll Festival, by Eisho Chokosai A3245

Basket Ferry, by Hiroshige Utagawa A3246

2014, Aug. 1 Litho. *Perf. 13½*

3724	Sheet of 10	16.00	16.00
a.	A3237 82y multi	1.25	.50
b.	A3238 82y multi	1.25	.50
c.	A3239 82y multi	1.25	.50
d.	A3240 82y multi	1.25	.50
e.	A3241 82y multi	1.25	.50
f.	A3242 82y multi	1.25	.50
g.	A3243 82y multi	1.25	.50
h.	A3244 82y multi	1.25	.50
i.	A3245 82y multi	1.25	.50
j.	A3246 82y multi	1.25	.50

Mount Asahi — A3247

Mount Sanbe — A3248

Mount Nantai — A3249

Mount Tokusa — A3250

Mount Takao — A3251

Mount Hiko — A3252

Mount Mitsuse-Myojin A3253

Mount Miune A3254

Kumano Kodo A3255

Mount Shinmoe A3256

2014, Aug. 11 Litho. *Perf. 13¼x13*

3725	Sheet of 10	16.00	16.00
a.	A3247 82y multi	1.25	.50
b.	A3248 82y multi	1.25	.50
c.	A3249 82y multi	1.25	.50
d.	A3250 82y multi	1.25	.50
e.	A3251 82y multi	1.25	.50
f.	A3252 82y multi	1.25	.50
g.	A3253 82y multi	1.25	.50
h.	A3254 82y multi	1.25	.50
i.	A3255 82y multi	1.25	.50
j.	A3256 82y multi	1.25	.50

Miniature Sheets

A3257

Characters From Peanuts Comic Strip — A3258

No. 3726: a, Sally, Woodstock and Snoopy drawing (26x22mm). b, Snoopy and heart (26x25mm). c, Snoopy holding slice of bread, Woodstock near mug (26x22mm). d, Snoopy, Linus, Woodstock and cookies (26x22mm). e, Snoopy on Charlie Brown's head, woodstock on books (26x22mm). f, Sally and Snoopy eating (26x22mm). g, Snoopy, Lucy and Woodstock with flowers (26x22mm). h, Woodstock flying, Snoopy attempting to fly (26x22mm). i, Snoopy and Woodstock on dog house roof (29x36mm). j, Snoopy, Woodstock, umbrella and musical notes (26x22mm).

No. 3727: a, Snoopy and Woodstock with letters, bird flying (22x27mm). b, Charlie Brown with letter near mailbox (22x27mm). c, Snoopy wearing mailman's uniform (22x27mm). d, Snoopy with nose in mailbox (22x27mm). e, Snoopy reading letter near mailbox (27x22mm). f, Snoopy and Woodstock at typewriter (27x22mm). g, Snoopy watching Sally write letter (27x22mm). h, Snoopy sitting and reading letter with Woodstock (27x22mm). i, Charlie Brown and stream of letters in mailbox (27x22mm). j, Charlie Brown and Sally looking at letter (27x22mm).

Die Cut Perf. 14, 12¼ (#3726b, 3726i)

2014, Aug. 19 Litho.

Self-Adhesive

3726	A3257	Sheet of 10	10.00	10.00
a.-j.		52y Any single	1.00	.75

Die Cut Perf. 14x13½, 13½x14

3727	A3258	Sheet of 10	16.00	16.00
a.-j.		52y Any single	1.25	.75

Miniature Sheet

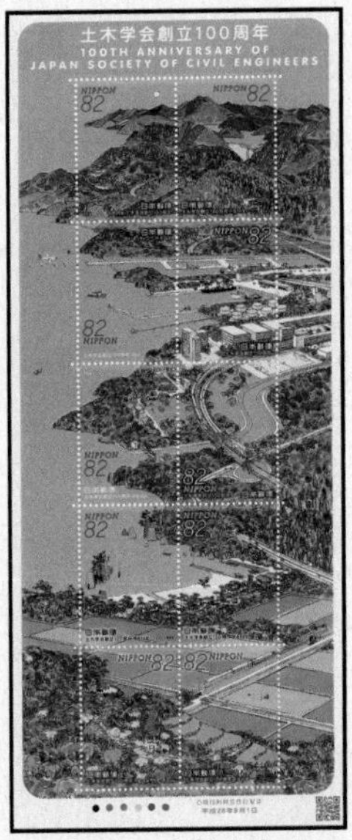

Japan Society of Civil Engineers, Cent. — A3259

No. 3728: a, Tunnel, sun over mountains. b, Dam. c, Ships and jetties, airport runway. d, Harbor and airport. e, Floodgate ar mouth of river. f, Bridges over river and interchange. g, Farm fields near coast, rocks in water. h, Small harbor and highway tunnel. i, Terraces and irrigation canal. j, Train and irrigation canal.

2014, Sept. 1 Litho. *Perf. 13*

3728	A3259	Sheet of 10	16.00	16.00
a.-j.		82y Any single	1.25	.50

Miniature Sheet

Season's Memories in My Heart — A3260

No. 3729: a, Houses near water, denomination in black at LL. b, Farm houses, denomination in white at LR. c, Farm house near river, denomination in white at UL. d, Sunset, denomination in white at UL. e, Village in mist, denomination in white at LL. f, Cars near church and building, denomination in black at UR. g, Church at end of path, denomination in white at left. h, Large cloud over church, flowers in air, denomination in white at UL. i, House near water, denomination in black at UR. j, Houses and path, denomination in black at UR.

2014, Sept. 2 Photo. *Perf. 13*

3729	A3260	Sheet of 10	16.00	16.00
a.-j.		82y Any single	1.25	.50

A3261

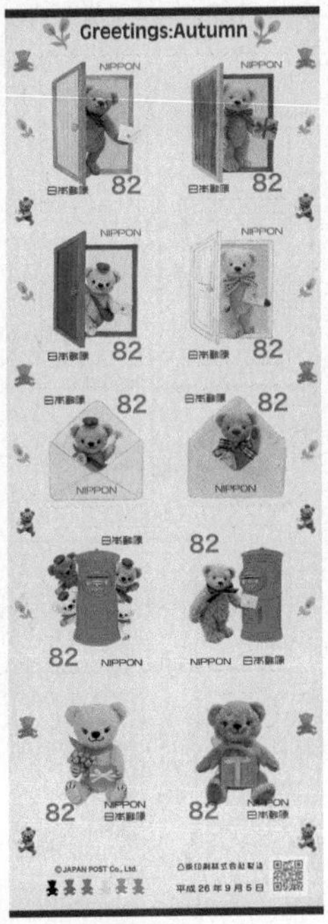

Teddy Bears A3262

No. 3730: a, Bear with gray fur and pearl necklace, pink rose (22x30mm). b, Bear with brown fur and red ribbon, yellow flowers (22x30mm). c, Bear with light brown fur and blue bow tie, red rose (22x30mm). d, Bear with beige fur and yellow bow tie, pink flower (22x30mm). e, Bear with light brown fur, wearing cap and red ribbon, with flower bouquet (22x30mm). f, Bear with light brown fur and green ribbon, with pink lily (22x30mm). g, Three bears wearing caps, pink flowers (28x28mm). h, Five bears and yellow flowers (28x28mm). i, Two bears, pink flowers, red ribbon at top (28x28mm). j, Two bears, pink flowers, blue ribbon at top (28x28mm).

No. 3731: a, Bear with letter, yellow door (23x30mm). b, Bear with gift, green door (23x30mm). c, Bear with cap, mail bag and letter, blue door (23x30mm). d, Bear with letter, white door (23x30mm). e, Bear with cap in yellow envelope (25x25mm). f, Bear in light blue envelope (25x25mm). g, Four bears and mail box (23x30mm). h, Bear with letter at mail box (23x30mm). i, Pink bear with pink gift (27x30mm). j, Bear with blue gift (27x30mm).

Die Cut Perf. 13¼x13¾, 13¾x13½

2014, Sept. 5 Litho.

Self-Adhesive

3730	A3261	Sheet of 10	10.00	10.00
a.-j.		52y Any single	1.00	.75

Die Cut Perf. 13x12¾, 13 (#3731e, 3731f)

3731 A3262 Sheet of 10 15.00 15.00
a.-j. 82y Any single 1.25 .75

Miniature Sheet

Kagawa Local Autonomy Law, 60th Anniv. — A3263

No. 3732: a, Ritsurin Koen Park (32x39mm). b, Gennai Hiraga and his electrostatic generator (28x33mm). c, Marugame Castle (28x33mm). d, Kotohiki Park (28x33mm). e, Olives (28x33mm).

Perf. 13¼ (#3732a), 13x13¼

2014, Sept. 10 Photo.

3732 A3263 Sheet of 5 7.50 7.50
a.-e. 82y Any single 1.50 .60

Intl. Congress on Child Abuse and Neglect, Nagoya — A3264

2014, Sept. 12 Litho. *Perf. 13*

3733 A3264 82y multi 1.50 .50

Miniature Sheet

69th National Sports Festival A3265

No. 3734: a, Gymnast on rings. b, Blue hydrangeas. c, Runner in starting blocks. d, Pink rhododendrons. e, Archer. f, Pink day lily. g, Soccer players. h, Lilac pink rhododendrons. i, Kendoka. j, Red camellias.

2014, Sept. 12 Litho. *Perf. 13*

3734 A3265 82y Sheet of 10 16.00 16.00
a.-j. 82y Any single 1.25 .50

Tortoise A3266

Spotted Seals A3267

Tapir A3268

Giraffes A3269

Orangutans A3270

Koalas A3271

Giant Pandas A3272

Capybara A3273

Lion A3274

Fennec Fox A3275

Die Cut Perf. 13x13¼

2014, Sept. 19 Litho.

Self-Adhesive

3735 Sheet of 10, 2 each #3735a-3735e 10.00 10.00
a. A3266 52y multi .80 .75
b. A3267 52y multi .80 .75
c. A3268 52y multi .80 .75
d. A3269 52y multi .80 .75
e. A3270 52y multi .80 .75

Die Cut Perf. 13¼

3736 Sheet of 10, 2 each #3736a-3736e 15.00 15.00
a. A3271 82y multi 1.25 .75
b. A3272 82y multi 1.25 .75
c. A3273 82y multi 1.25 .75
d. A3274 82y multi 1.25 .75
e. A3275 82y multi 1.25 .75

Miniature Sheet

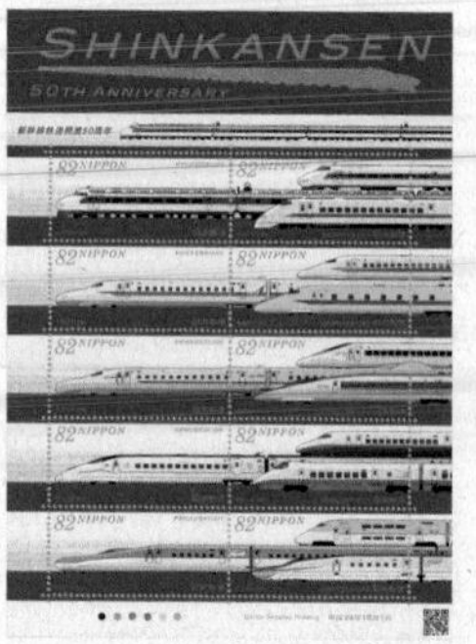

Shinkansen High-Speed Rail Lines, 50th Anniv. — A3276

No. 3737: a, Train with thick blue stripe (Tokaido and Sanyo 0 series). b, Three trains (Tokaido and Sanyo 100, 0 and 300 series), top train with thick blue stripe above thin blue stripe, bottom train with thin blue strip over thick blue stripe. c, Train with two thin blue stripes (Tokaido and Sanyo N700A). d, Three trains (Tokaido and Sanyo 700 series, N700A, and T4 model), top train with two thin blue stripes, bottom train yellow with two blue stripes. e, Light blue train with one blue stripe (Sanyo and Kyushu N700). f, Three trains (Sanyo 700 series Rail Star, Sanyo and Kyushu N700, Sanyo 500 series), top train with gray and yellow stripes along windows. g, Train with red stripe (Kyushu New 800 series). h, Three trains (Tohuku E2 series, Kyushu New 800 series, Yamagata 400 series), top train with red stripe under window above blue along bottom of train. i, Train with blue green top and red stripe (Tohuku E5 series). j, Three trains (Joetsu E1 series, Tohuku E5 series, Akita E6 series, light blue top train with blue green stripe.

2014, Oct. 1 Litho. *Perf. 13½x13¼*

3737 A3276 Sheet of 10 16.00 16.00
a.-j. 82y Any single 1.25 .50

Miniature Sheet

Saitama Local Autonomy Law, 60th Anniv. — A3277

No. 3738: a, Eiichi Shibusawa, industrialist, Bell of Time (32x39mm). b, Saitama Stadium (28x33mm). c, Chichibu Night Festival (28x33mm). d, Shoden Hall, Kangi Temple (28x33mm). e, Stairway at Sakitama ancient tomb complex (28x33mm).

Perf. 13¼ (#3738a), 13x13¼

2014, Oct. 8 Photo.

3738 A3277 Sheet of 5 7.50 7.50
a.-e. 82y Any single 1.25 .60

A3278

International Letter Writing Week — A3279

Paintings by Hiroshige: 70y, Sparrows and Camellia in the Snow. 90y, The Fifty-three Stations of the Tokaido: Ejiri. 110y, The Fifty-three Stations of the Tokaido: Kanaya. 130y, The Fifty-three Stations of the Tokaido: Fukuroi.

2014, Oct. 9 Photo. *Perf. 13¼*

3739 A3278 70y multi 1.25 .50

Perf. 13

3740 A3279 90y multi 1.75 .50
3741 A3279 110y multi 2.25 .50
3742 A3279 130y multi 2.75 .50
Nos. 3739-3742 (4) 8.00 2.00

See listing of No. 4448 for images of each Hiroshige print.

Fronts of Five Passenger Train Cars A3280

Nagoya Railroad KiHa 8000 Series Locomotive A3281

Kintetsu 18200 Series Locomotive A3282

Japan National Railways 581 Series Locomotive A3283

Japan National Railways Class EF66 Locomotive A3284

Seibu Railways 5000 Series Locomotive A3285

Japan National Railways 14 Series Sleeping Car A3286

East Japan Railway E259 Series Locomotive A3287

Keisei Electric Railway AE Series Locomotive A3288

Tokyo Underground Railway 1000 Series Train A3289

2014, Oct. 10 Photo. *Perf. 13¼x13*

3743 Sheet of 10 16.00 16.00
a. A3280 82y multi 1.25 .50
b. A3281 82y multi 1.25 .50
c. A3282 82y multi 1.25 .50
d. A3283 82y multi 1.25 .50
e. A3284 82y multi 1.25 .50
f. A3285 82y multi 1.25 .50
g. A3286 82y multi 1.25 .50
h. A3287 82y multi 1.25 .50
i. A3288 82y multi 1.25 .50
j. A3289 82y multi 1.25 .50

Sandalwood Go Game Board and Pieces A3290

Gold and Silver Inlaid Lacquered Kin A3291

Glass Goblet A3292

Decorated Catapult Sticks A3293

Sandalwood Lute — A3294

2014, Oct. 17 Photo. *Perf. 13*

3744 A3290 82y multi 1.25 .50
3745 A3291 82y multi 1.25 .50
3746 A3292 82y multi 1.25 .50
3747 A3293 82y multi 1.25 .50
3748 A3294 82y multi 1.25 .50
a. Vert. strip of 5, #3744-3748 7.50 4.00
Nos. 3744-3748 (5) 6.25 2.50

Treasures of the Shosoin.

Fish
A3295

"Happy" and Stars
A3296

2014, Oct. 23 Litho. *Perf. 13x13¼*

3749	A3295 52y multi		1.00	.30

Background Color

3750	A3296 52y rose lilac		.90	.30
3751	A3296 52y orange		.90	.30
a.	Vert. pair, #3750-3751		1.80	1.00
	Nos. 3749-3751 (3)		2.80	.90

Miniature Sheet

Traditional Crafts — A3297

No. 3752: a, Imari-Arita ceramic ware (Saga Prefecture). b, Inshu hand-made paper (Tottori Prefecture). c, Echizen chest of drawers (Fukui Prefecture). d, Chichibu-meisen silk textiles (Saitama Prefecture). e, Kagawa lacquered container (Kagawa Prefecture). f, Ise katagami paper stencils (Mie Prefecture). g, Yamaga lantern (Kumamoto Prefecture). h, Koshu carved crystal (Yamanashi Prefecture). i, Hakone parquet containers (Kanagawa Prefecture). j. Arimatsu-Narumi tie-dyed fabrics (Aichi Prefecture).

2014, Oct. 24 Litho. *Perf. 13½*

3752	A3297 Sheet of 10	16.00	16.00
a.-j.	82y Any single	1.25	.50

Miniature Sheet

Edo Calligraphy — A3298

No. 3753 — Characters for "sheep": a, In Kobun style (blue character). b, In Han Dynasty document style (character in black with two red chops at left). c, In small seal script (character in black with thick lines, small red chop at LR. d, In cursive script (character in black with small red chop at LL). e, In running script (Black character on brown red background). f, In Kana characters (surved black character with dots with large red chop at LR). g, In oracle bone script (black character with curved and straight lines, large red chop at LR). h, In Chou Dyansty bronze vessel style (character in thick black lines with small red chop at LL). i, In seal script (character in red). j, In clerical script (character in thick black lines with large red chop at LL).

Litho. & Embossed

2014, Oct. 30 *Perf. 13x13¼*

3753	A3298 Sheet of 10	16.00	16.00
a.-j.	82y Any single	1.25	.80

New Year 2014 Japanese Foods
A3299

Designs: No. 3754, Sushi (denomination at LL). No. 3755, Tempura (denomination at LR).

2014, Oct. 30 Litho. *Perf. 13¼x13*

3754	18y multi	.35	.30
3755	18y multi	.35	.30
a.	A3299 Horiz. pair, #3754-3755	.90	.90

A3300

A3301

New Year 2015 (Year of the Ram)
A3302 A3303

2014, Oct. 30 Photo. *Perf. 13x13¼*

3756	A3300 52y multi	1.00	.30
3757	A3301 82y multi	1.50	.40

Photo. & Typo.

Perf. 13¼

3758	A3302 52y +3y multi	1.25	.40
3759	A3303 82y +3y multi	1.75	.40
	Nos. 3756-3759 (4)	5.50	1.50

Sheets of two containing Nos. 3756-3757 were lottery prizes. Value, $4.

Lady Shikibu Murasaki Scroll and Books
A3304

Flower Arrangement and Go Players
A3305

Noh and Bunraku Theater
A3306

Lute Player and Entertainers
A3307

Tale of the Genji Scroll — A3308

2014, Oct. 31 Litho. *Perf. 13*

3760	A3304 82y multi	1.25	.50
3761	A3305 82y multi	1.25	.50
3762	A3306 82y multi	1.25	.50
3763	A3307 82y multi	1.25	.50
3764	A3308 82y multi	1.25	.50
a.	Vert. strip of 5, #3760-3764	7.50	4.00
	Nos. 3760-3764 (5)	6.25	2.50

Classics Day.

Narcissus
A3309

Plum Blossoms
A3310

Adonis Ramosa
A3311

Cyclamen
A3312

Matthiola Incana
A3313

Camellia Japonica
A3314

Brassica Oleracea
A3315

Poinsettia
A3316

2014, Nov. 6 Litho. *Perf. 14x14¼*

3765	A3309 52y multi	.80	.30
3766	A3310 52y multi	.80	.30
3767	A3311 52y multi	.80	.30
3768	A3312 52y multi	.80	.30
a.	Horiz. strip of 4, #3765-3768	4.00	2.00
3769	A3313 82y multi	1.25	.50
3770	A3314 82y multi	1.25	.50
3771	A3315 82y multi	1.25	.50
3772	A3316 82y multi	1.25	.50
a.	Horiz. strip of 4, #3769-3772	6.00	3.50
	Nos. 3765-3772 (8)	8.20	3.20

Miniature Sheets

A3317

Winter Greetings — A3318

No. 3773: a, Cookie with snowman design. b, Cookies in shape of man and woman. c, Cookie with mailbox design. d, Cookie with polar bear design. e, Cookie in shape of rabbit. f, Cookie with Christmas tree design. g, Cookie in shape of horse. h, Cookie in shape of woman. i, Cookie with poinsettia design. j, Cookie in shape of man.

No. 3774 — Needlepoint designs: a, House with brown door standing in front of trees. b, Post office with red mailbox at left. c, House with red door. d, House with brown door and shrubbery. e, Automobile. f, Snowman. g, One sheep. h, Two sheep. i, Boy and dog. j, Mailbox and fence.

Die Cut Perf. 13x13¼

2014, Nov. 7 Litho.

Self-Adhesive

3773	A3317 Sheet of 10	10.00	10.00
a.-j.	52y Any single	.90	.70
3774	A3318 Sheet of 10	15.00	15.00
a.-j.	82y Any single	1.25	.80

Miniature Sheet

Season's Memories in My Heart — A3319

No. 3775 — Illustrations from children's book *Guri and Gura,* by Yuriko Yamawaki: a, Guri, Gura and rabbits on sled. b, Child looking out of window. c, Guri and Gura making snowman. d, Guri and Gura reading near fireplace. e, Guri picking strawberries. f, Guri cooking. g, Gura looking at head-shaped cake. h, Guri and Gura holding basket. i, Stove and various animals. j, Guri, Gura, various animals and table.

2014, Nov. 20 Litho. *Perf. 13½*

3775	A3319 Sheet of 10	16.00	16.00
a.-j.	82y Any single	1.25	.50

Miniature Sheet

Ishikawa Local Autonomy Law, 60th Anniv. — A3320

No. 3776: a, Stone lantern, trees in Kenrokuen Garden (32x39mm). b, Terraced rice fields at sunset (28x33mm). c, Mitsukejima (28x33mm). d, Mount Hakusan (28x33mm). e, Fritillaria cantschatcensis (28x33mm).

Perf. 13¼ (#3776a), 13x13¼

2014, Nov. 26 Photo.

3776	A3320 Sheet of 5	8.00	8.00
a.-e.	82y Any single	1.25	.60

Matsumoto Castle
A3321

Takeda Castle
A3322

Nagoya Castle — A3323

Bitchu-Matsuyama Castle — A3324

Shuri Castle — A3325

2014, Dec. 10 Litho. *Perf. 12¾x13*

3777	A3321 82y multi	1.25	.50
3778	A3322 82y multi	1.25	.50
3779	A3323 82y multi	1.25	.50
3780	A3324 82y multi	1.25	.50
3781	A3325 82y multi	1.25	.50
a.	Vert. strip of 5, #3777-3781	7.50	4.00
	Nos. 3777-3781 (5)	6.25	2.50

Miniature Sheets

A3326

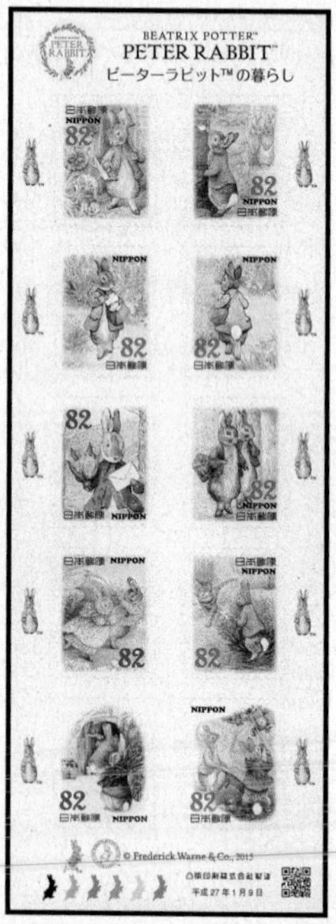

Illustrations From *Peter Rabbit,* by Beatrix Potter — A3327

No. 3782: a, Jemima Puddleduck. b, Peter Rabbit holding placard. c, Squirrel Nutkin. d, Owl reading "Squirrel Nutkin" book. e, Tom Kitten. f, Benjamin Bunny. g, Peter holding shovel. h, Peter and Benjamin Bunny. i, Mother Rabbit and young. j, Rabbits holding towel.

No. 3783: a, Peter with shovel and flower box. b, Peter posting letter. c, Rabbit with mail bag, facing forward. d, Rabbit with mail bag, facing backward. e, Rabbit holding letter and cauliflower. f, Rabbits with basket. g, Peter and female rabbit on windy day. h, Cat, Peter with daffodil. i, Peter and Benjamin carrying sticks. j, Peter and Benjamin harvesting apples.

2015, Jan. 9 Litho. *Die Cut Perf. 14*

Self-Adhesive

3782 A3326 Sheet of 10 10.00 10.00
a.-j. 52y Any single .90 .70

Die Cut Perf. 14x13¼

3783 A3327 Sheet of 10 15.00 15.00
a.-j. 82y Any single 1.25 .75

Flowers, Musical Notes, Clef and Staff
A3328

Flowers in Music Box
A3329

Four Teddy Bears
A3330

Musicians and Bird
A3331

Animals With Musical Instruments
A3332

Cherry Blossoms and Bird
A3333

Roses
A3334

Violas
A3335

Girl and Carnations
A3336

Teddy Bear and Flowers
A3337

Die Cut Perf. 14

2015, Jan. 16 Litho.

Self-Adhesive

3784 Sheet of 10, 2 each #3784a-3784e 10.00 10.00
a. A3328 52y multi .90 .70
b. A3329 52y multi .90 .70
c. A3330 52y multi .90 .70
d. A3331 52y multi .90 .70
e. A3332 52y multi .90 .70

Die Cut Perf. 14x13¼, 13¼x14

3785 Sheet of 10, 2 each #3785a-3785e 15.00 15.00
a. A3333 82y multi 1.25 .80
b. A3334 82y multi 1.25 .80
c. A3335 82y multi 1.25 .80
d. A3336 82y multi 1.25 .80
e. A3337 82y multi 1.25 .80

Wombats
A3338

Lamb
A3339

Baby Rhinoceros
A3340

Chick
A3341

Porcupines
A3342

Red Pandas
A3343

Puppy
A3344

Japanese Macaque
A3345

Snow Leopard
A3346

California Sea Lions
A3347

Die Cut Perf. 13¼

2015, Jan. 23 Litho.

Self-Adhesive

3786 Sheet of 10, 2 each #3786a-3786e 10.00 10.00
a. A3338 52y multi .90 .70
b. A3339 52y multi .90 .70
c. A3340 52y multi .90 .70
d. A3341 52y multi .90 .70
e. A3342 52y multi .90 .70
3787 Sheet of 10, 2 each #3787a-3787e 16.00 16.00
a. A3343 82y multi 1.25 .80
b. A3344 82y multi 1.25 .80
c. A3345 82y multi 1.25 .80
d. A3346 82y multi 1.25 .80
e. A3347 82y multi 1.25 .80

Hisoka Maejima (1835-1919), Founder of Japanese Postal Service
A3348

Siberian Chipmunk
A3349

Japanese Macaque
A3350

Crested Ibis
A3351

Sika Deer
A3352

Red Fox
A3353

Japanese Serow
A3354

Japanese Primrose
A3355

Japanese Wisteria
A3356

Kerria Japonica
A3357

Stream, Towada-Hachimantai National Park — A3358

Mt. Fuji, by Chikuden Tanomura — A3359

2015, Feb. 2 Photo. *Perf. 13x13¼*

3788 A3348 1y brown .30 .25
3789 A3349 3y multi .30 .25
a. Souvenir sheet of 2, #3648, 3789 .50 .50
3790 A3350 5y multi .30 .25
3791 A3351 10y multi .30 .25
3792 A3352 20y multi .35 .25
3793 A3353 30y multi .50 .40
3794 A3354 50y multi .55 .45
3795 A3355 100y multi 1.10 .50
3796 A3356 120y multi 1.40 .50
3797 A3357 140y multi 1.60 .50
3798 A3358 500y multi 6.50 1.00

Photo. & Engr.

Perf. 13¼

3799 A3359 1000y multi 13.00 5.00
a. Imperf. 30.00 30.00
b. Souvenir sheet of 2, #2485a, 3799a 60.00 60.00
Nos. 3788-3799 (12) 26.20 9.60

Compare type A3348 with types A563a and A2682.

Cabbage
A3360

Satsuma Orange
A3361

Peas
A3362

Mango
A3363

Onion
A3364

Oranges
A3365

Asparagus
A3366

Strawberries
A3367

Lettuce
A3368

Pineapple
A3369

Die Cut Perf. 13¼x13, 13x13¼

2015, Feb. 23 Litho.

Self-Adhesive

3800 Sheet of 10, 2 each #3800a-3800e 10.00 10.00
a. A3360 52y multi .80 .70
b. A3361 52y multi .80 .70
c. A3362 52y multi .80 .70
d. A3363 52y multi .80 .70
e. A3364 52y multi .80 .70
3801 Sheet of 10, 2 each #3801a-3801e 16.00 16.00
a. A3365 82y multi 1.25 .80
b. A3366 82y multi 1.25 .80
c. A3367 82y multi 1.25 .80
d. A3368 82y multi 1.25 .80
e. A3369 82y multi 1.25 .80

A3370

No. 3802 — Arcs of color and map of Japan made of flowers, with denomination in: a, Orange. b, Carmine. c, Purple. d, Blue. e, Turquoise green.

Perf. 13½x13¼

2015, Mar. 13 **Photo.**

3802	Horiz. strip of 5	7.00	5.00
a.-e.	A3370 82y Any single	1.25	.50

United Nations World Conference on disaster risk reduction, Sendai.

Kanazawa Railroad Station — A3371

Tateyama Mountain Range — A3372

Takada Park — A3373

Zenkoji Temple — A3374

Marunouchi Railroad Station, Tokyo — A3375

Series W7, E2 and E7 Trains — A3376

Series W7 Train — A3377

Series E7 Train — A3378

2015, Mar. 13 **Litho.** ***Perf. 13¼x13***

3803	Sheet of 10, #3803a-3803f, 2 each #3803g-3803h	16.00	16.00
a.	A3371 82y multi	1.25	.50
b.	A3372 82y multi	1.25	.50
c.	A3373 82y multi	1.25	.50
d.	A3374 82y multi	1.25	.50
e.	A3375 82y multi	1.25	.50
f.	A3376 82y multi	1.25	.50
g.	A3377 82y multi	1.25	.50
h.	A3378 82y multi	1.25	.50

Canadian Rocky Mountain Parks — A3379

Historic Areas of Istanbul, Turkey — A3380

Stonehenge, Great Britain A3381

Historic Center of Prague, Czech Republic A3382

Ha Long Bay, Viet Nam — A3383

2015, Mar. 26 **Litho.** ***Perf. 13¼x13***

3804	A3379 82y multi	1.25	.50
3805	A3380 82y multi	1.25	.50
3806	A3381 82y multi	1.25	.50
3807	A3382 82y multi	1.25	.50
3808	A3383 82y multi	1.25	.50
a.	Horiz. strip of 5, #3804-3808	7.00	4.50
	Nos. 3804-3808 (5)	6.25	2.50

UNESCO World Heritage Sites.

Hirosaki Castle A3384

Kanazawa Castle A3385

Himeji Castle A3386

Fukuyama Castle A3387

Fukuoka Castle — A3388

2015, Apr. 3 **Litho.** ***Perf. 13***

3809	A3384 82y multi	1.25	.50
3810	A3385 82y multi	1.25	.50
3811	A3386 82y multi	1.25	.50
3812	A3387 82y multi	1.25	.50
3813	A3388 82y multi	1.25	.50
a.	Vert. strip of 5, #3809-3813	7.50	3.00
	Nos. 3809-3813 (5)	6.25	2.50

Japanese Diet, Tokyo, and Cherry Blossoms A3389

Clock Tower, Tokyo, and Dogwood Blossoms A3390

Lincoln Memorial and Cherry Blossoms A3391

U. S. Capitol and Dogwood Blossoms A3392

White Dogwood Blossoms A3393

Cherry Blossoms A3394

Red Dogwood Blossoms A3395

2015, Apr. 10 **Photo.** ***Perf. 13x12¾***

3814	Sheet of 10, #3814a-3814d, 2 each #3814e-3814g	16.00	16.00
a.	A3389 82y multi	1.25	.50
b.	A3390 82y multi	1.25	.50
c.	A3391 82y multi	1.25	.50
d.	A3392 82y multi	1.25	.50
e.	A3393 82y multi	1.25	.50
f.	A3394 82y multi	1.25	.50
g.	A3395 82y multi	1.25	.50

See United States Nos. 4982-4985.

Mount Rishiri — A3396

Mount Adatara — A3397

Mount Shibutu — A3398

Shirouma Sanzan — A3399

Mount Tateyama A3400

Yarigatake A3401

Yatsugatake A3402

Mount Fuji A3403

Kitadake A3404

Miyanouradake A3405

2015, Apr. 17 **Litho.** ***Perf. 13¼x13***

3815	Sheet of 10	16.00	16.00
a.	A3396 82y multi	1.25	.50
b.	A3397 82y multi	1.25	.50
c.	A3398 82y multi	1.25	.50
d.	A3399 82y multi	1.25	.50
e.	A3400 82y multi	1.25	.50
f.	A3401 82y multi	1.25	.50
g.	A3402 82y multi	1.25	.50
h.	A3403 82y multi	1.25	.50
i.	A3404 82y multi	1.25	.50
j.	A3405 82y multi	1.25	.50

Japan Overseas Cooperation Volunteers, 50th Anniv. — A3406

2015, Apr. 20 **Litho.** ***Perf. 13***

Denomination Color

3816	82y blue	1.25	.50
3817	82y crimson	1.25	.50
a.	A3406 Horiz. pair, #3816-3817	3.00	1.50

Phoenixes by Pawlonia Trees, Screen Painting by Kano Tan'yu — A3407

Designs: No. 3818, White phoenix facing left, denomination at LL. No. 3819, Phoenix facing left, denomination at UR. No. 3820, White phoenix facing right, denomination at UR. No. 3821, Phoenix with tail raised facing right, denomination at LL.

2015, Apr. 20 **Photo.** ***Perf. 13¼***

3818	82y multi	1.25	.50
3819	82y multi	1.25	.50
3820	82y multi	1.25	.50
3821	82y multi	1.25	.50
a.	A3407 Block of 4, #3818-3821	5.60	3.50
	Nos. 3818-3821 (4)	5.00	2.00

Philatelic Week.

Miniature Sheets

A3408

Moomins A3409

No. 3822: a, Moomin standing, bright blue background. b, Little My, red background. c, Moomin, yellow background. d, Snufkin, green background. e, Moomin, red violet background. f, Moominpappa, dark blue background. g, Moomin running, bright blue background. h, Moominmamma, pink background. i, Moomin, yellow brown background. j, Snork Maiden, rose background.

No. 3823: a, Moomin characters, Snufkin with accordion. b, Moomin and Snufkin (29mm diameter). c, Moomin, Snork Maiden, ship, flowers. d, Moomin characters, Little My at left. e, Moomin characters and hammock. f, Moomin characters hugging. g, Little My in teapot. h, Moomin, Snork Maiden and Little My. i, Moominmamma and Moominpappa. j, Hattifatteners and top hat.

2015, May 1 **Litho.** ***Die Cut Perf. 14***

3822	A3408 Sheet of 10	10.00	10.00
a.-j.	52y Any single	.90	.70

Die Cut Perf. 13¼x13¾

3823	A3409 Sheet of 10	15.00	15.00
a.-j.	82y Any single	1.25	.80

Miniature Sheet

Yamaguchi Local Autonomy Law, 60th Anniv. — A3410

No. 3824: a, Kintaikyo Bridge, Akiyoshidai (32x39mm). b, Goldfish lantern and buildings (28x33mm). c, Hooded crane (28x33mm). d, Shokasonjuku Academy and citrons (28x33mm). e, Misuzu Street (28x33mm).

Perf. 13¼ (#3824a), 13x13¼

2015, May 12 **Photo.**

3824	A3410	Sheet of 5	7.00	7.00
a.-e.		82y Any single	1.25	.60

Miniature Sheet

National Afforestation — A3411

No. 3825: a, Crepe myrtle blossoms. b, Ate cypress. c, Horse chestnut blossoms. d, Freesia. e, Japanese black pine. f, Plum blossoms. g, Wild cherry blossoms. h, Azalea blossoms. i, Zelkova tree. j, Chocolate lily.

2015, May 15 **Litho.** ***Perf. 13***

3825	A3411	Sheet of 10	10.00	10.00
a.-j.		52y Any single	1.00	.40

Crepe Myrtle A3412

Sunflowers A3413

Southern Stars A3414

Eustomas A3415

Gladiolus A3416

Marigolds A3417

Salvia A3418

Hydrangeas A3419

Gymnaster Savatieri A3420

Delphinium and Calla Lily A3421

Die Cut Perf. 14

2015, May 29 **Litho.**

Self-Adhesive

3826		Sheet of 10, 2 each #3826a-3826e	10.00	10.00
a.	A3412	52y multi	.85	.65
b.	A3413	52y multi	.85	.65
c.	A3414	52y multi	.85	.65
d.	A3415	52y multi	.85	.65
e.	A3416	52y multi	.85	.65
3827		Sheet of 10, 2 each #3827a-3827e	16.00	16.00
a.	A3417	82y multi	1.25	.80
b.	A3418	82y multi	1.25	.80
c.	A3419	82y multi	1.25	.80
d.	A3420	82y multi	1.25	.80
e.	A3421	82y multi	1.25	.80

Miniature Sheet

Tokushima Local Autonomy Law, 60th Anniv. — A3422

No. 3828: a, Naruto Whirlpools, Naruto Bridge, Awa Dance Festival dancer, sudachi flower (32x39mm). b, Awa Puppet Theater (28x33mm). c, Yoshino River and Mount Bizan (28x33mm). d, Vine bridges in Iya Valley (28x33mm). e, Sea turtle on Ohama Beach (28x33mm).

Perf. 13¼ (#3828a), 13x13¼

2015, June 2 **Photo.**

3828	A3422	Sheet of 5	7.00	7.00
a.-e.		82y Any single	1.25	.60

Shells — A3423

No. 3829: a, Conus ammiralis (23x35mm). b, Mimachlamys nobilis (23x30mm). c, Terebridae (22x29mm). d, Babelomurex gemmatus (22x26mm). e, Scutarcopagia linguafelis (27x23mm).

No. 3830: a, Columbarium pagoda (22x36mm). b, Phalium flammiferum (22x30mm). c, Neocancilla papilio (22x30mm). d, Spondylus sanguineus (24x27mm). e, Architectonica perspectiva (29x25mm).

Die Cut Perf. 13x13¼, 13¼x13 (#3829e, 3830e)

2015, June 5 **Litho.**

3829		Sheet of 10, 2 each #3829a-3829e	10.00	10.00
a.-e.	A3423	52y Any single	.85	.65
3830		Sheet of 10, 2 each #3830a-3830e	16.00	16.00
a.-e.	A3423	82y Any single	1.25	.80

Miniature Sheet

Fukuoka Local Autonomy Law, 60th Anniv. — A3424

No. 3831: a, Okinoshima Island, Munakata Taisha Shrine, gold ring (32x39mm). b, Kokura Castle (28x33mm). c, Triple water wheel, Asakura (28x33mm). d, Boat on Yanagawa River (28x33mm). e, Kane-no Torii and steps (28x33mm).

Perf. 13¼ (#3831a), 13x13¼

2015, June 16 **Photo.**

3831	A3424	Sheet of 5	7.00	7.00
a.-e.		82y Any single	1.25	.60

Normalization of Diplomatic Relations Between Japan and South Korea, 50th Anniv. — A3425

Designs: No. 3832, Japanese woman in kimono, Korean woman in hanbok. No. 3833, Rose of Sharon and cherry blossoms.

2015, June 22 **Litho.** ***Perf. 13½***

3832		82y multi	1.25	.50
3833		82y multi	1.25	.50
a.	A3425	Vert. pair, #3832-3833	3.00	1.50

Miniature Sheet

Tomioka Silk Mill UNESCO World Heritage Site — A3426

No. 3834: a, Joshu Tomioka Silk Mill, woodblock print by Kuniteru Ichiyosai, denomination at UR (stamp 1). b, Joshu Tomioka Silk Mill, denomination at UL (stamp 2). c, The Diligence of Women Workers at Tomioka Spinning Mill, woodblock print by Asataka, denomination at LR (stamp 3). d, East Cocoon Warehouse, denomination at UL (stamp 4). e, Silk-reeling mill, denomination at UL (stamp 5). f, Illustration from Tomioka Diary, denomination at LL (stamp 6). g, Tajima Yahei Sericulture Farm, denomination at UR (stamp 7). h, Takayama-sha Sericulture School, denomination at LL (stamp 8). i, Arafune Cold Storage, denomination at LL (stamp 9). j, Keystone of Tomioka Silk Mill, denomination at UL (stamp 10).

2015, June 25 **Photo.** ***Perf. 13x13¼***

3834	A3426	Sheet of 10	16.00	16.00
a.-j.		82y Any single	1.25	.50

Yosemite National Park, United States — A3427

Acropolis, Athens, Greece — A3428

Chichen Itza, Mexico — A3429

Saint Petersburg, Russia — A3430

Borobudur Temple Compounds, Indonesia — A3431

2015, July 10 **Litho.** ***Perf. 13¼x13***

3835	A3427	82y multi	1.25	.50
3836	A3428	82y multi	1.25	.50
3837	A3429	82y multi	1.25	.50
3838	A3430	82y multi	1.25	.50
3839	A3431	82y multi	1.25	.50
a.		Horiz. strip of 5, #3835-3839	7.00	4.50
		Nos. 3835-3839 (5)	6.25	2.50

UNESCO World Heritage Sites.

Boy With Pencil and Postcard A3432

Penguins A3433

Squashes A3434

Snow on Camellias A3435

Cherry Blossoms and Birds A3436

Boy Putting Letter in Mailbox A3437

Hollyhocks A3438

Sparrows A3439

Chrysanthemums and Noshi — A3440

Carp Streamer A3441

Child Swimming A3442

Hydrangeas A3443

Flowers A3444

Crane A3445

Cranes, Turtle and Flowers A3446

Child, Coins, Letter and Stamp A3447

Paper Balloons A3448

Dried Persimmons A3449

Ume Blossoms A3450

Horsetails — A3451

Die Cut Perf. 13x13½

2015, July 23 Litho.

Booklet Stamps Self-Adhesive

3840	A3432 52y multi		.85	.65
3841	A3433 52y multi		.85	.65
3842	A3434 52y multi		.85	.65
3843	A3435 52y multi		.85	.65
3844	A3436 52y multi		.85	.65
3845	A3437 52y multi		.85	.65
3846	A3438 52y multi		.85	.65
3847	A3439 52y multi		.85	.65
3848	A3440 52y multi		.85	.65
3849	A3441 52y multi		.85	.65
a.	Booklet pane of 10, #3840-3849		10.00	10.00
3850	A3442 82y multi		1.25	.80
3851	A3443 82y multi		1.25	.80
3852	A3444 82y multi		1.25	.80
3853	A3445 82y multi		1.25	.80
3854	A3446 82y multi		1.25	.80
3855	A3447 82y multi		1.25	.80
3856	A3448 82y multi		1.25	.80
3857	A3449 82y multi		1.25	.80
3858	A3450 82y multi		1.25	.80
3859	A3451 82y multi		1.25	.80
a.	Booklet pane of 10, #3850-3859		16.00	16.00
	Nos. 3840-3859 (20)		21.00	14.50

Letter Writing Day.

23rd World Scout Jamboree, Kirarahama — A3452

Designs: No. 3860, Three scouts, denomination at UL. No. 3861, Three scouts, denomination at UR. No. 3862, Male scout, denomination at UL. No. 3863, Female scout, denomination at UR.

2015, July 28 Litho. *Perf. 13¾x13½*

3860	82y multi	1.25	.50
3861	82y multi	1.25	.50
3862	82y multi	1.25	.50
3863	82y multi	1.25	.50
a.	A3452 Block of 4, #3860-3863	6.00	3.50
	Nos. 3860-3863 (4)	5.00	2.00

Roses A3453

Chrysanthemums A3454

Gerbera Daisies A3455

Ranunculus A3456

Freesias A3457

Cosmos and Dahlias A3458

Lilies and Baby's Breath A3459

Pansies A3460

Moth Orchids A3461

Christmas Cactus A3462

Die Cut Perf. 14

2015, July 31 Litho.

Self-Adhesive

3864	Sheet of 10, 2 each #3864a-3864e	10.00	10.00
a.	A3453 52y multi	.85	.65
b.	A3454 52y multi	.85	.65
c.	A3455 52y multi	.85	.65
d.	A3456 52y multi	.85	.65
e.	A3457 52y multi	.85	.65
3865	Sheet of 10, 2 each #3865a-3865e	16.00	16.00
a.	A3458 82y multi	1.25	.80
b.	A3459 82y multi	1.25	.80
c.	A3460 82y multi	1.25	.80
d.	A3461 82y multi	1.25	.80
e.	A3462 82y multi	1.25	.80

Edo Castle A3463

Maruoka Castle A3464

Hiroshima Castle A3465

Kochi Castle A3466

Uwajima Castle — A3467

2015, Aug. 7 Litho. *Perf. 13*

3866	A3463 82y multi	1.25	.50
3867	A3464 82y multi	1.25	.50
3868	A3465 82y multi	1.25	.50
3869	A3466 82y multi	1.25	.50
3870	A3467 82y multi	1.25	.50
a.	Vert. strip of 5, #3866-3870	7.00	4.50
	Nos. 3866-3870 (5)	6.25	2.50

Nagano Flora Prefecture Type of 2003

Designs: No. 3871, Dogtooth violet (pink flowers) and mountain. No. 3872, Skunk cabbage (white flower). No. 3873, Nikko daylily (yellow flower). No. 3874, Cosmos (white, pink and red flowers).

2015, Aug. 21 Photo. *Perf. 13¼*

3871	82y multi	1.25	.50
3872	82y multi	1.25	.50
3873	82y multi	1.25	.50
3874	82y multi	1.25	.50
a.	ZA510 Horiz. strip of 4, #3871-3874	6.50	3.50
	Nos. 3871-3874 (4)	5.00	2.00

Owara Wind Festival Prefecture Type of 2007

No. 3875, Night Light. No. 3876, Lattice Door. No. 3877, Saotome Dancers. No. 3878, Limelight. No. 3879, Moonlight Night.

2015, Aug. 21 Litho. *Perf. 13¼*

3875	ZA710 82y multi	1.25	.50
3876	ZA711 82y multi	1.25	.50
3877	ZA712 82y multi	1.25	.50
3878	ZA713 82y multi	1.25	.50
3879	ZA714 82y multi	1.25	.50
a.	Vert. strip of 5, #3875-3879	6.50	3.50

See Nos. Z807-Z811.

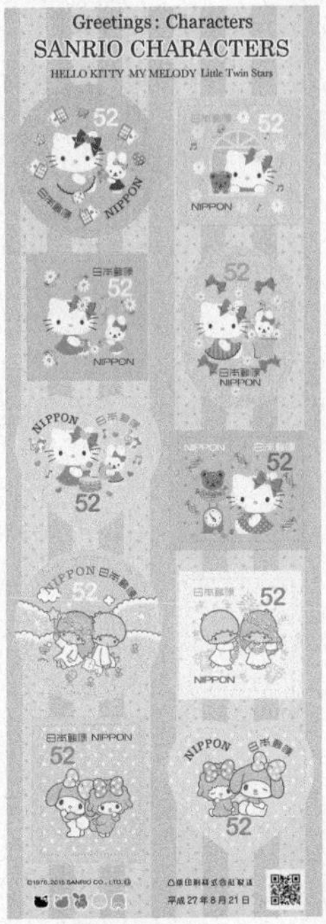

A3468

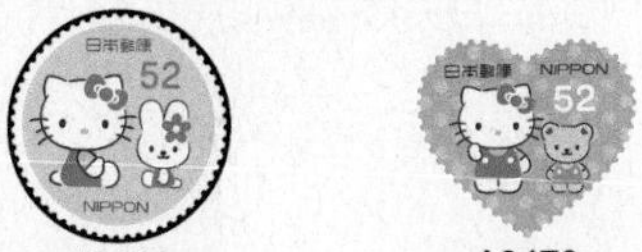
A3469 A3470

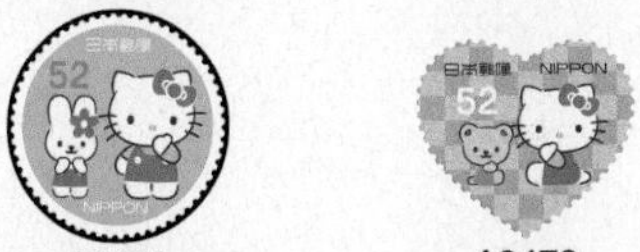
A3471 A3472

A3473 A3474

A3475 A3476

A3477 A3478

A3479 A3480

A3481 A3482

A3483 A3484

A3485

A3486

A3487

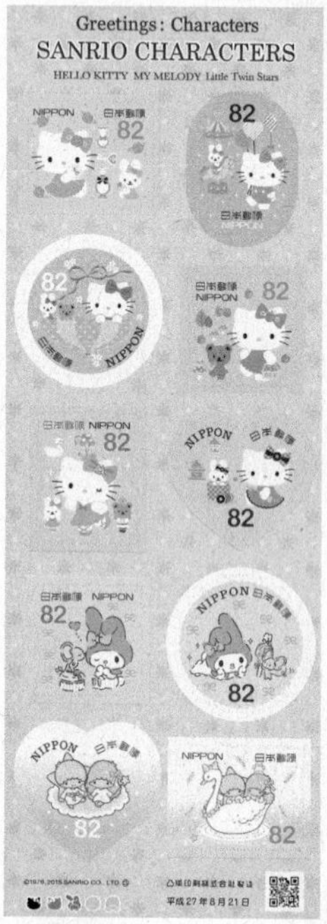

A3488

A3489

A3490

A3491

A3492

A3493

A3494

A3495

A3496

A3497

A3498

A3499

A3500

A3501

A3502

A3503

A3504

A3505

A3506

Sanrio Characters — A3507

No. 3880: a, Hello Kitty, Mimmy, playing cards, pink background (29mm diameter). b, Hello Kitty, Teddy bear in window, blue background (23x23mm). c, Hello Kitty, Mimmy, flowers, green background (23x23mm). d, Hello Kitty, Mimmy, bucket, flowers, bows, pink background (22x30mm oval). e, Hello Kitty, Mimmy, drum, cymbals, musical symbols, yellow background (29x26mm heart). f, Hello Kitty, Teddy bear, scale, blue background (27x22mm). g, Little Twin Stars, cat, blue & pink background (29mm diameter). h, Little Twin Stars, cream background (23x23mm). i, My Melody and Piano, yellow brown background with polka dots (22x27mm). j, My Melody and Piano, blue background with polka dots (29x26mm heart).

No. 3894: a, Hello Kitty, Mimmy, flowers, yellow background (27x22mm). b, Hello Kitty, Mimmy on carousel, pink background (22x30mm oval). c, Hello Kitty, Mimmy, Teddy bear in umbrella, pale lilac background (29mm diameter). d, Hello Kitty, Teddy bear, bird, berries and mushrooms, buff background (23x23mm). e, Hello Kitty, Mimmy, Teddy bear, swan, blue background (22x27mm). f, Hello Kitty, Mimmy in coffee mug, light green background (29x26mm heart). g, My Melody and mouse, pale sage green background (23x23mm). h, My Melody and mouse, pink background (29mm diameter). i, Little Twin Stars, white & rose background (29x26mm heart). j, Little Twin Stars on swan, blue & rose background (27x22mm).

Die Cut Perf. 14 (#3880b, 3880c, 3880d, 3880h), Die Cut Perf. 13½x13¾ (#3880f), Die Cut Perf. 13¾x13½ (#3880i), Die Cut Perf.

2015, Aug. 21 Litho.

Self-Adhesive

3880	A3468	Sheet of 10	10.00	10.00
a.-j.		52y Any single	.90	.70

Die Cut Perf. (A3469-A3474), Die Cut Perf. 13 (A3475-A3487)

3881	Sheet of 10, #3881a-3881f, 4 #3881g	10.00	10.00
a.	A3469 52y multi	.90	.70
b.	A3470 52y multi	.90	.70
c.	A3471 52y multi	.90	.70
d.	A3472 52y multi	.90	.70
e.	A3473 52y multi	.90	.70
f.	A3474 52y multi	.90	.70
g.	A3475 52y multi	.90	.70
3882	Sheet of 10, #3881a-3881f, 4 #3882a	10.00	10.00
a.	A3476 52y multi	.90	.70
3883	Sheet of 10, #3881a-3881f, 4 #3883a	10.00	10.00
a.	A3477 52y multi	.90	.70
3884	Sheet of 10, #3881a-3881f, 4 #3884a	10.00	10.00
a.	A3478 52y multi	.90	.70
3885	Sheet of 10, #3881a-3881f, 4 #3885a	10.00	10.00
a.	A3479 52y multi	.90	.70
3886	Sheet of 10, #3881a-3881f, 4 #3886a	10.00	10.00
a.	A3480 52y multi	.90	.70
3887	Sheet of 10, #3881a-3881f, 4 #3887a	10.00	10.00
a.	A3481 52y multi	.90	.70
3888	Sheet of 10, #3881a-3881f, 4 #3888a	10.00	10.00
a.	A3482 52y multi	.90	.70
3889	Sheet of 10, #3881a-3881f, 4 #3889a	10.00	10.00
a.	A3483 52y multi	.90	.70
3890	Sheet of 10, #3881a-3881f, 4 #3890a	10.00	10.00
a.	A3484 52y multi	.90	.70
3891	Sheet of 10, #3881a-3881f, 4 #3891a	10.00	10.00
a.	A3485 52y multi	.90	.70
3892	Sheet of 10, #3881a-3881f, 4 #3892a	10.00	10.00
a.	A3486 52y multi	.90	.70
3893	Sheet of 10, #3881a-3881f, 4 #3893a	10.00	10.00
a.	A3487 52y multi	.90	.70

Die Cut Perf. 13½x13¾ (#3894a, 3894j), Die Cut Perf. 14 (#3894b, #3894d, 3894g), Die Cut Perf. 13¾x13½ (#3894e), Die Cut Perf.

3894	A3488	Sheet of 10	15.00	15.00
a.-j.		82y Any single	1.40	.80

Die Cut Perf. 14 (A3489-A3494), Die Cut Perf. 13½x13¾ (A3495-A3507)

3895	Sheet of 10, #3895a-3895f, 4 #3895g	15.00	15.00
a.	A3489 82y multi	1.40	.80
b.	A3490 82y multi	1.40	.80
c.	A3491 82y multi	1.40	.80
d.	A3492 82y multi	1.40	.80
e.	A3493 82y multi	1.40	.80
f.	A3494 82y multi	1.40	.80
g.	A3495 82y multi	1.40	.80
3896	Sheet of 10, #3895a-3985f, 4 #3896a	15.00	15.00
a.	A3496 82y multi	1.40	.80
3897	Sheet of 10, #3895a-3985f, 4 #3897a	15.00	15.00
a.	A3497 82y multi	1.40	.80
3898	Sheet of 10, #3895a-3985f, 4 #3898a	15.00	15.00
a.	A3498 82y multi	1.40	.80
3899	Sheet of 10, #3895a-3985f, 4 #3899a	15.00	15.00
a.	A3499 82y multi	1.40	.80
3900	Sheet of 10, #3895a-3985f, 4 #3900a	15.00	15.00
a.	A3500 82y multi	1.40	.80
3901	Sheet of 10, #3895a-3985f, 4 #3901a	15.00	15.00
a.	A3501 82y multi	1.40	.80
3902	Sheet of 10, #3895a-3985f, 4 #3902a	15.00	15.00
a.	A3502 82y multi	1.40	.80
3903	Sheet of 10, #3895a-3985f, 4 #3903a	15.00	15.00
a.	A3503 82y multi	1.40	.80
3904	Sheet of 10, #3895a-3985f, 4 #3904a	15.00	15.00
a.	A3504 82y multi	1.40	.80
3905	Sheet of 10, #3895a-3985f, 4 #3905a	15.00	15.00
a.	A3505 82y multi	1.40	.80
3906	Sheet of 10, #3895a-3985f, 4 #3906a	15.00	15.00
a.	A3506 82y multi	1.40	.80
3907	Sheet of 10, #3895a-3985f, 4 #3907a	15.00	15.00
a.	A3507 82y multi	1.40	.80
	Nos. 3880-3907 (28)	350.00	

Miniature Sheet

70th National Sports Festival, Wakayama — A3508

No. 3908: a, Kayaking. b, Sailing. c, Basketball. d, Field hockey. e, Cycling. f, Gymnastics. g, Fencing. h, Soccer. i, Naginata. j, Volleyball.

2015, Aug. 28 Litho. *Perf. 13*

3908	A3508	Sheet of 10	16.00	16.00
a.-j.		82y Any single	1.25	.60

Niigata Flowers Prefecture Type of 2002

Designs: No. 3909, Red camellias, Kamoyama Kouen Park. No. 3910, Yellow daylilies, Oonogame. No. 3911, Irises, Ijimino Kouen Park. No. 3912, Pink iwakagami flowers, Mt. Myoukousan.

2015, Aug. 28 Photo. *Perf. 13¼*

3909	82y multi	1.25	.50
3910	82y multi	1.25	.50
3911	82y multi	1.25	.50
3912	82y multi	1.25	.50
a.	ZA488 Horiz. strip of 4, #3909-3912	6.00	3.50
	Nos. 3909-3912 (4)	5.00	2.00

Hokkaido Flowers Prefecture Type of 1991

Designs as before.

2015, Aug. 28 Photo. *Perf. 13*

3913	ZA97 82y multi	1.25	.50
3914	ZA98 82y multi	1.25	.50
3915	ZA99 82y multi	1.25	.50
3916	ZA100 82y multi	1.25	.50
a.	Horiz. strip of 4, #3913-3916	6.00	3.50
	Nos. 3913-3916 (4)	5.00	2.00

Hokkaido Flowers Prefecture Type of 2005

Designs as before.

2015, Aug. 28 Photo. *Perf. 13¼*

3917	ZA569 82y multi	1.25	.50
3918	ZA570 82y multi	1.25	.50
3919	ZA571 82y multi	1.25	.50
3920	ZA572 82y multi	1.25	.50
a.	Horiz. strip of 4, #3917-3920	6.00	3.50
	Nos. 3917-3920 (4)	5.00	2.00

Plums A3509

Lemon and Lime A3510

Okra A3511

Olives A3512

Mustard Spinach A3513

Celery A3514

Lotus Root A3515

Loquats A3516

Soybeans A3517

Fig A3518

Die Cut Perf. 13¼x13, 13x13¼

2015, Aug. 31 Litho.

Self-Adhesive

3921	Sheet of 10, 2 each #3921a-3921e	10.00	10.00
a.	A3509 52y multi	.90	.70
b.	A3510 52y multi	.90	.70
c.	A3511 52y multi	.90	.70
d.	A3512 52y multi	.90	.70
e.	A3513 52y multi	.90	.70
3922	Sheet of 10, 2 each #3922a-3922e	15.00	15.00
a.	A3514 82y multi	1.25	.80
b.	A3515 82y multi	1.25	.80

c.	A3516 82y multi		1.25	.80
d.	A3517 82y multi		1.25	.80
e.	A3518 82y multi		1.25	.80

Miniature Sheets

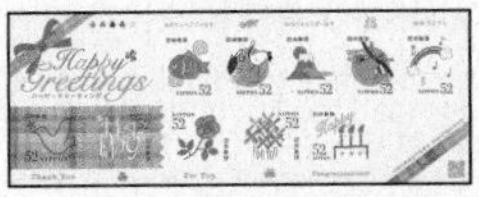

A3519

A3520

Greetings — A3521

No. 3923: a, Sea bream. b, Turtle and crane. c, Mount Fuji. d, Noshi. e, Clouds, rainbow and musical notes. f, Dove, horiz. g, "Happy" and shamrocks, horiz. h, Rose, horiz. i, Flowers and "For You," horiz. j, "Happy," birthday cake and candles, horiz.

No. 3924: a, Sea bream, diff. b, Gourds. c, Gift box with bow. d, Pine, bamboo and plum. e, Party hat, streamers and confetti. f, Bird, horiz. g, "Happy" and shamrocks, diff., horiz. h, Two roses, horiz. i, Bow and "For You," horiz. j, "Happy" and slice of birthday cake, horiz.

No. 3925: a, Sea bream, diff. b, Fans. c, Mount Fuji, diff. d, Mallet of luck. e, "Happy," heart with bow. f, Bird, diff., horiz. g, "Happy" and shamrocks, diff., horiz. h, Five roses, horiz. i, Envelope, "For You," feather, horiz. j, "Happy" and cup, horiz.

Die Cut Perf. 13x13¼, 13¼x13

2015, Sept. 4 — Litho.

Self-Adhesive

3923	A3519	Sheet of 10	10.00	10.00
a.-j.		52y Any single	.90	.70
3924	A3520	Sheet of 10	15.00	15.00
a.-j.		82y Any single	1.25	.80
3925	A3521	Sheet of 10	17.00	17.00
a.-j.		92y Any single	1.25	.80
		Nos. 3923-3925 (3)	42.00	

Miniature Sheet

Wakayama Local Autonomy Law, 60th Anniv. — A3522

No. 3926: a, Koyasan Danjo Garan (32x39mm). b, Wakayama Castle (28x33mm). c, Shirahama and beach (28x33mm). d, Hashikuiiwa Rocks (28x33mm). e, Nachi Waterfall and pagoda (28x33mm).

Perf. 13¼ (#3926a), 13x13¼

2015, Sept. 8 — Photo.

3926	A3522	Sheet of 5	7.00	7.00
a.-e.		82y Any single	1.25	.60

Miniature Sheets

A3523

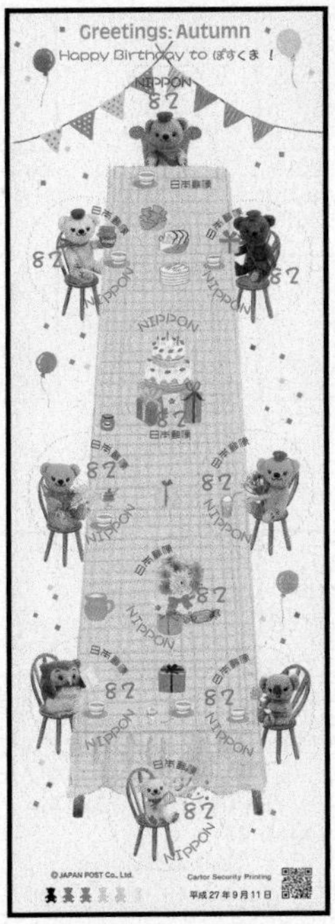

Greetings — A3524

No. 3927: a, Koala bear on tree (23x23mm). b, Bird with letter (23x23mm). c, Bees holding heart (23x23mm). d, Owl holding letter (23x23mm). e, Brown Teddy bear with mail bag and flowers (22x30mm oval). f, White Teddy bear with mail bag and gift box (22x30mm oval). g, Pink Teddy bear with flowers (22x30mm oval). h, Dark brown Teddy bear with mail bag and gift box (22x30mm oval). i, Light green Teddy bear with mail bag and flowers (22x30mm oval). j, Teddy bear with envelope (25x22mm heart).

No. 3928: a, Teddy bear, cup on table (26x29mm). b, Teddy bear holding honey jar (25mm diameter). c, Teddy bear holding gift box (25mm diameter). d, Birthday cake, gifts and envelope (22x30mm oval). e, Pink Teddy bear holding flowers, cup and dessert bowl on table (25mm diameter). f, Light greenTeddy bear holding flowers, drinking glass with straw on table (25mm diameter). g, Flowers, gifts and envelope (25mm diameter). h, Owl (25mm diameter). i, Gray Teddy bear holding lollipop (25mm diameter). j, Teddy bear with party hat, streamers and confetti (25mm diameter).

Die Cut Perf. 14

2015, Sept. 11 — Litho.

Self-Adhesive

3927	A3523	Sheet of 10	10.00	10.00
a.-j.		52y Any single	.90	.70
3928	A3524	Sheet of 10	15.00	15.00
a.-j.		82y Any single	1.25	.80

Okinawa Fish Prefecture Type of 2007

Designs as before.

2015, Sept. 16 — Litho. — *Perf. 13¼*

3929	ZA704	82y multi	1.25	.60
3930	ZA705	82y multi	1.25	.60
3931	ZA706	82y multi	1.25	.60
3932	ZA707	82y multi	1.25	.60
3933	ZA708	82y multi	1.25	.60
a.		Horiz. strip of 5, #3929-3933	7.00	4.50
		Nos. 3929-3933 (5)	6.25	3.00

Miniature Sheet

Children A3525

No. 3934: a, Mother, girl and balloon. b, Girl and balloon. c, Child holding flowers. d, Boy with drum. e, Girl in raincoat looking at snail. f, Girl on beach. g, Children reading book. h, Child playing with blocks. i, Child in angel costume. j, Child sleeping with stuffed animal.

2015, Sept. 18 — Photo. — *Perf. 13*

3934	A3525	Sheet of 10	16.00	16.00
a.-j.		82y Any single	1.25	.50

A sheet of five 82y self-adhesive stamps depicting Hello Kitty characters was printed in limited quantities and sold only in a package containing stationery. Value, $20.

Astronomy — A3526

No. 3935: a, Moon (25x34mm). b, Libra and scales (22x25mm). c, Scorpio and scorpion (22x25mm). d, Sagittarius, bow and arrow (22x25mm).

Litho. With Foil Application

Die Cut Perf. 13x13¼

2015, Sept. 25 — Self-Adhesive

3935	A3526	Sheet of 10, #3935a, 3 each #3935b-3935d	16.00	16.00
a.-d.		82y Any single	1.25	.80

Miniature Sheet

Osaka Local Autonomy Law, 60th Anniv. — A3527

No. 3936: a, Bunraku puppet, Osaka Castle (32x39mm). b, Interior of Osaka Prefectural Government Building (28x33mm). c, Tower of the Sun (28x33mm). d, Jinai-machi Town, Tondabayashi (28x33mm). e, Eggplant (28x33mm).

Perf. 13¼ (#3936a), 13x13¼

2015, Oct. 6 — Photo.

3936	A3527	Sheet of 5	7.00	7.00
a.-e.		82y Any single	1.25	.80

A3528

International Letter Writing Week — A3529

Paintings by Hiroshige: 70y, Thoroughwort and Pink. 90y, The Fifty-three Stations of the Tokaido: Yoshiwara. 110y, The Fifty-three Stations of the Tokaido: Yoshida. 130y, The Fifty-three Stations of the Tokaido: Fujikawa.

2015, Oct. 9 — Photo. — *Perf. 13¼*

3937	A3528	70y multi	1.25	.50

Perf. 13

3938	A3529	90y multi	1.75	.50
3939	A3529	110y multi	2.25	.50
3940	A3529	130y multi	2.50	.50
		Nos. 3937-3940 (4)	7.75	2.00

See listing of No. 4448 for images of each Hiroshige print.

Front Ends of Tokaido Shinkansen Rail Cars A3530

Japan National Railways 183 Series Locomotive A3531

Keisei Class AE Locomotive A3532

Hankyu 6300 Series Locomotive A3533

Meitetsu 6000 Series Locomotive A3534

Kintetsu 12400 Series Locomotive A3535

Japan Railways West 500 Series Locomotive A3536

Japan Railways Tokai and Japan Railways West N700 Series Locomotive A3537

Odakyu 60000 Series Locomotive A3538

Kintetsu 50000 Series Locomotive A3539

Front Ends of Tokaido Shinkansen Rail Cars A3540

Kintetsu 12400 Series Locomotive A3541

Japan National Railways 183 Series Locomotive A3542

Japan Railways West 500 Series Locomotive A3543

Keisei Class AE Locomotive A3544

Japan Railways Tokai and Japan Railways West N700 Series Locomotive A3545

Hankyu 6300 Series Locomotive A3546

Odakyu 60000 Series Locomotive A3547

Meitetsu 6000 Series Locomotive A3548

Kintetsu 50000 Series Locomotive A3549

2015, Oct. 9 Photo. *Perf. 13¼x13*

3941	Sheet of 10	16.00	16.00
a.	A3530 82y multi	1.25	.50
b.	A3531 82y multi	1.25	.50
c.	A3532 82y multi	1.25	.50
d.	A3533 82y multi	1.25	.50
e.	A3534 82y multi	1.25	.50
f.	A3535 82y multi	1.25	.50
g.	A3536 82y multi	1.25	.50
h.	A3537 82y multi	1.25	.50
i.	A3538 82y multi	1.25	.50
j.	A3539 82y multi	1.25	.50

Perf. 13x13¼

3942	Sheet of 10 + 10 labels	16.00	16.00
a.	A3540 82y multi	1.25	.50
b.	A3541 82y multi	1.25	.50
c.	A3542 82y multi	1.25	.50
d.	A3543 82y multi	1.25	.50
e.	A3544 82y multi	1.25	.50
f.	A3545 82y multi	1.25	.50
g.	A3546 82y multi	1.25	.50
h.	A3547 82y multi	1.25	.50
i.	A3548 82y multi	1.25	.50
j.	A3549 82y multi	1.25	.50

Chinese Style Sword A3550

Folding Screen Depicting Lady of the Court A3551

Circular Mirror With Inlaid Decorations A3552

Batik Folding Screen A3553

Lacquer Ewer — A3554

2015, Oct. 16 Photo. *Perf. 13*

3943	A3550	82y multi	1.25	.50
3944	A3551	82y multi	1.25	.50
3945	A3552	82y multi	1.25	.50
3946	A3553	82y multi	1.25	.50
3947	A3554	82y multi	1.25	.50
a.		Vert. strip of 5, #3943-3947	7.00	4.50
		Nos. 3943-3947 (5)	6.25	2.50

Treasures of the Shosoin.

Chihuahua A3555

Shiba A3556

Yorkshire Terrier A3557

French Bulldog A3558

Cavalier King Charles Spaniel A3559

Jack Russell Terriers A3560

Papillon A3561

Golden Retriever A3562

Beagles A3563

American Cocker Spaniel A3564

Toy Poodles A3565

Dachshund A3566

Pomeranians A3567

Maltese A3568

Miniature Schnauzer A3569

Shih Tzu A3570

Pembroke Welsh Corgi A3571

Pug A3572

Miniature Pinscher A3573

Bichon Frise A3574

Die Cut Perf. 13x13¼

2015, Oct. 23 Litho.

Self-Adhesive

3948	Sheet of 10	10.00	10.00
a.	A3555 52y multi	.90	.70
b.	A3556 52y multi	.90	.70
c.	A3557 52y multi	.90	.70
d.	A3558 52y multi	.90	.70
e.	A3559 52y multi	.90	.70
f.	A3560 52y multi	.90	.70
g.	A3561 52y multi	.90	.70
h.	A3562 52y multi	.90	.70
i.	A3563 52y multi	.90	.70
j.	A3564 52y multi	.90	.70
3949	Sheet of 10	16.00	16.00
a.	A3565 82y multi	1.25	.80
b.	A3566 82y multi	1.25	.80
c.	A3567 82y multi	1.25	.80
d.	A3568 82y multi	1.25	.80
e.	A3569 82y multi	1.25	.80
f.	A3570 82y multi	1.25	.80
g.	A3571 82y multi	1.25	.80
h.	A3572 82y multi	1.25	.80
i.	A3573 82y multi	1.25	.80
j.	A3574 82y multi	1.25	.80

Miniature Sheet

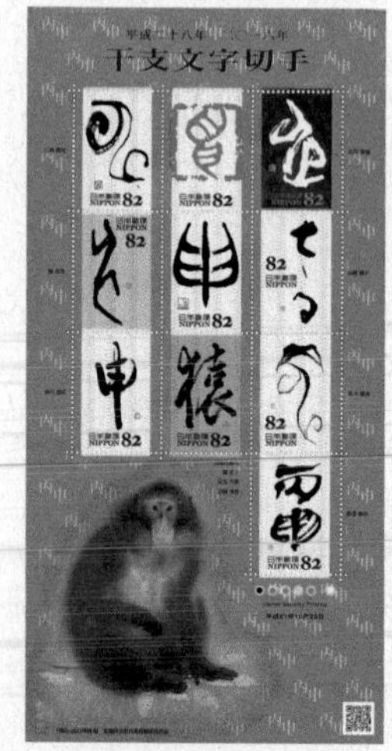
Edo Calligraphy — A3575

No. 3950 — Characters for "monkey": a, In Kinbun style of Western Zhou period (character with large red chop at LL). b, In Kinbuntai seal engraving style (red character). c, In Yin Dynasty oracle bone script style (white character with purple and black background). d, In Yin Dynasty oracle bone script style (character in black with light green background). e, In Shoten style (Black character with large central vertical line and large red chop at LL). f, In Hiragana style (black character, denomination at center left). g, In Gyosho style (black character with large central vertical line, small red chop at LR). h, In Gyosho style (black character with salmon pink background). i, In oracle bone script (black character with curved lines, small red chop at LL above denomination). j, In Tenreitai style (three-part black character with small red chop at LL).

Litho. & Embossed

2015, Oct. 29 *Perf. 13x13¼*

3950	A3575	Sheet of 10	16.00	16.00
a.-j.		82y Any single	1.125	.80

Japanese Foods A3576

Designs: No. 3951, Ramen noodles (denomination at LL). No. 3952, Sukiyaki (denomination at UL).

2015, Oct. 29 Photo. *Perf. 13¼x13*

3951	18y multi	.30	.25
3952	18y multi	.30	.25
a.	A3576 Horiz. pair, #3951-3952	.60	.45

A3577 A3578

New Year 2016 (Year of the Monkey)
A3579 A3580

2015, Oct. 29 Photo. *Perf. 13x13¼*

3953	A3577	52y multi	1.00	.30
3954	A3578	82y multi	1.50	.40

Photo. & Typo.

Perf. 13¼

3955	A3579	52y +3y multi	1.25	.40
3956	A3580	82y +3y multi	1.75	.40
		Nos. 3953-3956 (4)	5.50	1.50

Sheets of two containing Nos. 3953-3954 were lottery prizes. Value, $3.50.

Establishment of Tsunami Preparedness Day — A3581

2015, Nov. 5 Litho. *Perf. 13*

3957	A3581	82y multi	1.40	.50

Miniature Sheet

Traditional Crafts — A3582

No. 3758: a, Takaoka Shikki lacquer box (Toyama Prefecture). b, Makabe Ishidoro stone lantern (Ibaraki Prefecture). c, Edo glassware (Tokyo Prefecture). d, Tokoname Yaki pottery (Aichi Prefecture). e, Mino Washi Japanese paper (Gifu Prefecture). f, Kyo Yuzen dyed fabric (Kyoto Prefecture). g, Osaka Naniwa Suzuki tin container (Osaka Prefecture). h, Kumano Fude brushes (Hiroshima Prefecture). i, Awa Sho-ai Shijira-ori weaving (Tokushima Prefecture). j. Beppu Takesaiku bamboo basket (Oita Prefecture).

2015, Nov. 5 Litho. *Perf. 13½*

3958	A3582	Sheet of 10	16.00	16.00
a.-j.		82y Any single	1.40	.50

Miniature Sheets

A3583

Disney Characters — A3584

No. 3959: a, Winnie the Pooh, honey jar at his side. b, Winnie the pooh sticking snout in honey jar. c, Winnie the Pooh standing with head stuck in honey jar. d, Winnie the Pooh writing list. e, Winnie the Pooh in grass carrying honey jar. f, Winnie the Pooh scratching. g, Winnie the Pooh and Piglet. h, Christopher Robin draggin Winnie the Pooh down stairs. i, Winnie the Pooh next to Christopher Robin putting boots on feet. j, Christopher Robin and Winnie the Pooh reading sign.

No. 3960: a, Princess Aurora and pink roses (22x27mm). b, Princess Aurora and pink roses (27x22mm). c, Cinderella and lilies (22x27mm). d, Cinderella and lilies (27x22mm). e, Snow White and pink roses (22x27mm). f, Snow White, animals and pink roses (27x22mm). g, Ariel and red flowers (22x27mm). h, Rapunzel, lizard and pink flowers (27x22mm). i, Belle and pink rose (22x27mm). j, Jasmine and white flowers (27x22mm).

Die Cut Perf. 11¼

2015, Nov. 6 **Litho.**

Self-Adhesive

3959 A3583 Sheet of 10 10.00 10.00

Die Cut Perf. 14x13½, 13½x14

a.-j. 52y Any single 1.00 .80

3960 A3584 Sheet of 10 16.00 16.00

a.-j. 82y Any single 1.25 .80

Miniature Sheet

Nagasaki Local Autonomy Law, 60th Anniv. — A3585

No. 3961: a, Oura Church and camellias (32x39mm). b, Nagasaki Kunchi Festival (28x33mm). c, Hashima (28x33mm). d, Mount Heisei-shinzan (28x33mm). e, Golden tiger lily (28x33mm).

Perf. 13¼ (#3961a), 13x13¼

2015, Nov. 17 **Photo.**

3961 A3585 Sheet of 5 7.00 7.00

a.-e. 82y Any single 1.25 .60

Iyokan Orange A3586

Carrot A3587

Yuzus A3588

Daikon Radish A3589

Green Onions A3590

Chinese Cabbage A3591

Broccoli A3592

Tangerines A3593

Spinach A3594

Kiwi A3595

Die Cut Perf. 13¼

2015, Nov. 20 **Litho.**

Self-Adhesive

3962 Sheet of 10, 2 each #3962a-3962e 10.00 10.00

a. A3586 52y multi .85 .65

b. A3587 52y multi .85 .65

c. A3588 52y multi .85 .65

d. A3589 52y multi .85 .65

e. A3590 52y multi .85 .65

3963 Sheet of 10, 2 each #3963a-3963e 16.00 16.00

a. A3591 82y multi 1.25 .80

b. A3592 82y multi 1.25 .80

c. A3593 82y multi 1.25 .80

d. A3594 82y multi 1.25 .80

e. A3595 82y multi 1.25 .80

Miniature Sheet

Japanese Foods — A3596

No. 3964: a, Chestnuts and rice. b, Miso soup. c, Shrimp tempura. d, Rice and Narazuke pickles. e, Miso soup and simmered seaweed. f, Steamed egg custard. g, Dried mackerel. h, Rice and Nukazuke pickles. i, Vegetable soup. j, Simmered pumpkin and cold tofu.

2015, Nov. 24 **Litho.** ***Perf. 13½***

3964 A3596 Sheet of 10 16.00 16.00

a.-j. 82y Any single 1.25 .50

Miniature Sheet

Japan at Night A3597

No. 3965: a, Hakucho Bridge (stamp 1). b, Streetlight and buildings at Otaru Canal (stamp 2). c, Lighted trees at Hakodate Winter Festival, denomination at LR (stamp 3). d, Port of Akita and highway (stamp 4). e, Mount Iwate (stamp 5). f, Ginzan Onsen (stamp 6). g, Sendai Pageant of Starlight, denomination at UR (stamp 7). h, Nakayam Setsugekka (stamp 8). i, Center of Mutsu City (stamp 9). j, Mutsu City and harbor (stamp 10).

2015, Nov. 27 **Litho.** ***Perf. 13***

3965 A3597 Sheet of 10 16.00 16.00

a.-j. 82y Any single 1.25 .50

Miniature Sheet

Chiba Local Autonomy Law, 60th Anniv. — A3598

No. 3966: a, Tokyo Bay Aqua-line, rape blossoms (32x39mm). b, Character from Nanso Satomi Hakkenden (28x33mm). c, Inubosaki Lighthouse (28x33mm). d, Narita International Airport (28x33mm). e, Suigo Sawara Aquatic Botanical Garden (28x33mm).

Perf. 13¼ (#3966a), 13x13¼

2015, Dec. 8 **Photo.**

3966 A3598 Sheet of 5 7.00 7.00

a.-e. 82y Any single 1.25 .60

A3599

A3600

A3601

A3602

A3603

A3604

A3605

A3606

A3607

A3608

Candles A3609

Girl Looking at Frosted Window A3610

Snowglobe A3611

House and Snowflakes A3612

Snow-covered Trees A3613

Bird in Cage A3614

Poinsettia A3615

Polar Bear A3616

Reindeer in Forest A3617

Ice Skater A3618

Die Cut Perf. 13x13¼

2015, Dec. 11 **Litho.**

Self-Adhesive

3967		Sheet of 10	10.00	10.00
a.	A3599	52y multi	.90	.70
b.	A3600	52y multi	.90	.70
c.	A3601	52y multi	.90	.70
d.	A3602	52y multi	.90	.70
e.	A3603	52y multi	.90	.70
f.	A3604	52y multi	.90	.70
g.	A3605	52y multi	.90	.70
h.	A3606	52y multi	.90	.70
i.	A3607	52y multi	.90	.70
j.	A3608	52y multi	.90	.70
3968		Sheet of 10	15.00	15.00
a.	A3609	82y multi	1.25	.80
b.	A3610	82y multi	1.25	.80
c.	A3611	82y multi	1.25	.80
d.	A3612	82y multi	1.25	.80
e.	A3613	82y multi	1.25	.80
f.	A3614	82y multi	1.25	.80
g.	A3615	82y multi	1.25	.80
h.	A3616	82y multi	1.25	.80
i.	A3617	82y multi	1.25	.80
j.	A3618	82y multi	1.25	.80

Phoenix Hall, Kyoto — A3619

State Guest House, Tokyo — A3620

Photo. & Engr.

2016, Jan. 8 ***Perf. 13¼***

3969	A3619	82y multi	1.25	.50
3970	A3620	82y multi	1.25	.50
a.		Vert. pair, #3969-3970	3.00	1.50

Miniature Sheet

Astronomy — A3621

No. 3971: a, Morning star (26x36mm). b, Aries and ram (22x25mm). c, Taurus and bull (22x25mm). d, Gemini and twins (22x25mm).

Die Cut Perf. 11 (#3971a), Die Cut Perf. 13x13¼

Litho. With Foil Application

2016, Jan. 22 **Self-Adhesive**

3971	A3621	Sheet of 10, #3971a, 3 each #3971b-3971d	16.00	16.00
a.-d.		82y Any single	1.25	.60

Souvenir Sheets

Red Fuji, by Hokusai A3622

Great Wave of Kanagawa, by Hokusai — A3623

No. 3972: a, Detail of Mount Fuji. b, Entire print.

No. 3973: a, Detail of wave. b, Entire print.

Litho. & Embossed With Foil Application

2016, Jan. 29 ***Perf. 13¾x14***

3972	A3622	Sheet of 2	70.00	70.00
a.-b.		1000y Either single	25.00	5.00
3973	A3623	Sheet of 2	70.00	70.00
a.-b.		1000y Either single	25.00	5.00

Nos. 3972-3973 were only sold mounted in a booklet that sold for 8000y.

Miniature Sheet

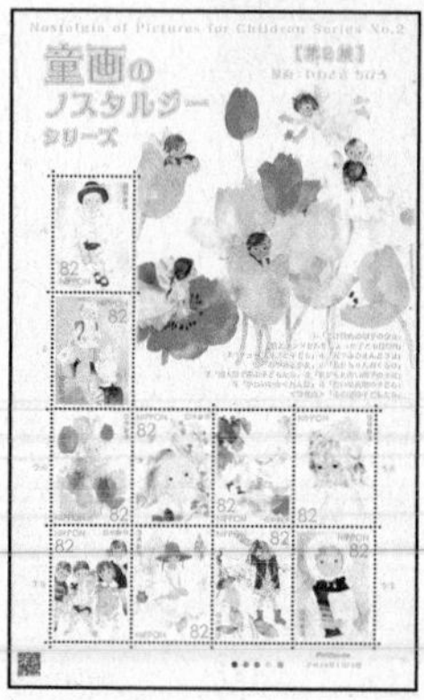
Children A3624

No. 3974: a, Girl wearing dark brown hat. b, Cat and girl with red backpack. c, Child and tulips. d, Girl, peas and pea plant. e, Girl and irises. f, Child wearing blue bonnet. g, Four children with puppets. h, Girl wearing red hat, sea shells. i, Girl wearing red boots, hide and seek. j, Child wearing scarf and white knitted hat.

2016, Jan. 29 **Litho.** ***Perf. 13***

3974	A3624	Sheet of 10	16.00	16.00
a.-j.		82y Any single	1.25	.60

Miniature Sheets

A3625

Miffy A3626

No. 3975: a, Miffy and Auntie Alice, plate of food (29x26mm). b, Miffy on bicycle (24x24mm). c, Miffy with hat over ears (23x29mm). d, Miffy with uncovered ears (23x29mm). e, Miffy and parents in car (24x24mm). f, Miffy writing letter (25mm diameter). g, Miffy and toys (24x24mm). h, Miffy and parent on chair (25mm diameter). i, Miffy holding plate of food (24x24mm). j, Miffy and other rabbits (35x20mm).

No. 3976: a, Miffy wearing orange dress (25x48mm). b, Miffy's father watering flowers (27x27mm). c, Miffy's mother with basket (27x27mm). d, Miffy wearing flowered dress (25mm diameter). e, Three rabbits and ball (25mm diameter). f, Angel (25mm diameter). g, Miffy wearing orange dress (25mm diameter). h, Miffy and father at dinner table (27x27mm). i, Miffy holding teddy bear (27x27mm). j, Miffy wearing flowered dress (25x48mm).

Die Cut Perf. 12½ (#3975a, 3975j), Die Cut Perf. (3975c, 3975d, 3975f, 3975h), Die Cut Perf. 13¼x12½ (square stamps)

2016, Feb. 12 **Litho.**

Self-Adhesive

3975	A3625	Sheet of 10	10.00	10.00
a.-j.		52y Any single	.95	.70

Die Cut Perf. 12¼ (#3976a, 3976f), Die Cut Perf. (round stamps), Die Cut Perf. 13¼ (square stamps)

3976	A3626	Sheet of 10	15.00	15.00
a.-j.		82y Any single	1.25	.80

Kototsuru of Nishizuchiya in Shinmachi, by Kiyonaga Torii A3627

Idemi Beach at Sumiyoshi, Settsu Province, by Hiroshige Utagawa A3628

Karakoto of the Chojiya, by Utamaro Kitagawa A3629

Urami Waterfall at Nikko, Shimotsuke Province, by Hiroshige Utagawa A3630

Eight Views of Genji: Komurasaki of the Tamaya, by Eizan Kikukawa A3631

Cave Entrance at Enoshima, Sagami Province, by Hiroshige Utagawa A3632

Hinazuru of Keizetsuro House, by Utamaro Kitagawa A3633

Gokanosho, Higo Province, by Hiroshige Utagawa A3634

Collection of Elegant Beauties: Mirror Stand, by Eizan Kikukawa A3635

Maiko Beach, Harima Province, by Hiroshige Utagawa A3636

2016, Feb. 26 **Litho.** ***Perf. 13***

3977		Sheet of 10	16.00	16.00
a.	A3627	82y multi	1.25	.50
b.	A3628	82y multi	1.25	.50
c.	A3629	82y multi	1.25	.50
d.	A3630	82y multi	1.25	.50
e.	A3631	82y multi	1.25	.50
f.	A3632	82y multi	1.25	.50
g.	A3633	82y multi	1.25	.50
h.	A3634	82y multi	1.25	.50
i.	A3635	82y multi	1.25	.50
j.	A3636	82y multi	1.25	.50

Cherry Blossom A3637

Dumplings on Stick A3638

Blackberries and Blueberries A3639

Blueberries and Raspberries A3640

Teddy Bears A3641

Cherry Blossom A3642

Peach Blossoms A3643

Letters and Bird A3644

Strawberries A3645

Owl and Teddy Bears A3646

Die Cut Perf. (#3978a), Die Cut Perf. 13 (#3978b); Die Cut Perf. 14

2016, Mar. 3 **Litho.**

Self-Adhesive

3978		Sheet of 10, 2 each #3978a-3978e	10.00	10.00
a.	A3637	52y multi	.95	.70
b.	A3638	52y multi	.95	.70
c.	A3639	52y multi	.95	.70
d.	A3640	52y multi	.95	.70
e.	A3641	52y multi	.95	.70

Die Cut Perf. (#3979a, 3979b, 3979d), Die Cut Perf. 14x13¼ (#3979c)

3979		Sheet of 10, 2 each #3979a-3979e	15.00	15.00
a.	A3642	82y multi	1.25	.80
b.	A3643	82y multi	1.25	.80
c.	A3644	82y multi	1.25	.80
d.	A3645	82y multi	1.25	.80
e.	A3646	82y multi	1.25	.80

Hokkaido Shinkansen Train Facing Left — A3647

Port of Aomori, Hokkaido Shinkansen Train — A3648

Hirosaki Castle, Hokkaido Shinkansen Train — A3649

Cape Tappi, Hokkaido Shinkansen Train — A3650

Hokkaido Shinkansen Train Facing Right — A3651

Matsumae Castle, Hokkaido Shinkansen Train — A3652

Moss Phlox on Mt. Yakushi, Hokkaido Shinkansen Train — A3653

Tree-Lined Road and Trappist Monastery, Hokkaido Shinkansen Train — A3654

Hakodate, Hokkaido Shinkansen Train — A3655

Onuma Quasi-National Park, Hokkaido Shinkansen Train — A3656

Perf. 13¼x12¾

2016, Mar. 25 **Litho.**

3980	Sheet of 10	16.00	16.00
a.	A3647 82y multi	1.25	.50
b.	A3648 82y multi	1.25	.50
c.	A3649 82y multi	1.25	.50
d.	A3650 82y multi	1.25	.50
e.	A3651 82y multi	1.25	.50
f.	A3652 82y multi	1.25	.50
g.	A3653 82y multi	1.25	.50
h.	A3654 82y multi	1.25	.50
i.	A3655 82y multi	1.25	.50
j.	A3656 82y multi	1.25	.50

Opening of Hokkaido Shinkansen Line From Aomori to Hakodate

Columbines A3657

Scabiosa A3658

Moss Phlox A3659

Cymbidium A3660

Irises A3661

Agapanthus A3662

Carnations A3663

Reeve's Spirea A3664

Peruvian Lilies A3665

Clematis A3666

Die Cut Perf. 14x14¼

2016, Apr. 1 **Litho.**

Self-Adhesive

3981	Sheet of 10, 2 each #3981a-3981e	10.00	10.00
a.	A3657 52y multi	.95	.70
b.	A3658 52y multi	.95	.70
c.	A3659 52y multi	.95	.70
d.	A3660 52y multi	.95	.70
e.	A3661 52y multi	.95	.70
3982	Sheet of 10, 2 each #3982a-3982e	16.00	16.00
a.	A3662 82y multi	1.25	.80
b.	A3663 82y multi	1.25	.80
c.	A3664 82y multi	1.25	.80
d.	A3665 82y multi	1.25	.80
e.	A3666 82y multi	1.25	.80

Miniature Sheet

Castles A3667

No. 3983: a, Goryokaku. b, Matsumoto Castle. c, Ueda Castle. d, Inuyama Castle. e, Osaka Castle. f, Hikone Castle. g, Marugame Castle. h, Himeji Castle. i, Matsuyama Castle. j, Matsue Castle.

2016, Apr. 8 **Litho.** ***Perf. 13***

3983	A3667 Sheet of 10	16.00	16.00
a.-j.	82y Any single	1.25	.50

Miniature Sheet

2016 G-7 Summit Ministers Meeting A3668

No. 3984: a, Hiroshima Peace Memorial, Hiroshima. b, Shinano River and Bandai Bridge, Niigata. c, Ritsurin Garden, Takamatsu. d, Moji Port. e, Kurashiki Bikan Historical Quarter. f, Toyama Castle. g, Tsukuba Space Center. h, Equestrian statue, Sendai Castle Ruins. i, Port of Kobe. j, Shiraito Falls.

2016, Apr. 8 **Photo.** ***Perf. 13***

3984	A3668 Sheet of 10	18.00	18.00
a.-j.	82y Any single	1.25	.60

Miniature Sheet

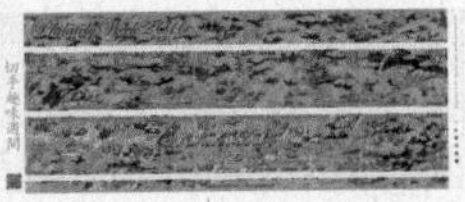
Philately Week A3669

No. 3985 — Various details of 16th century folding screen depicting Kyoto, by Eitoku Kano.

2016, Apr. 20 **Photo.** ***Perf. 13¼***

3985	A3669 Sheet of 10	16.00	16.00
a.-j.	82y Any single	1.25	.50

Miniature Sheets

A3670

Cats A3671

No. 3986: a, Scottish Fold cat (30x27mm). b, Russian Blue cat (22x26mm). c, Maine Coon cat (22x26mm). d, Abyssinian cat (22x26mm). e, Ragdoll cat (22x26mm). f, Ocicat (22x26mm). g, Munchkin cat (22x26mm). h, Persian cat (22x26mm). i, Two Tonkinese cats (22x26mm). j, American curl cat (22x26mm).

No. 3987: a, American shorthair cat (30x27mm). b, British shorthair cat (22x26mm). c, Norwegian Forest cat (22x26mm). d, Himalayan cat (22x26mm). e, Bengal cat (22x26mm). f, Singapura cats (22x26mm). g, Somali cat (22x26mm). h, Chartreux cat (22x26mm). i, Ragamuffin cat (22x26mm). j, Siamese cat (22x26mm).

Die Cut Perf. (#3986a, 3987a), Die Cut Perf. 13x13¼

2016, Apr. 22 **Litho.**

Self-Adhesive

3986	A3670 Sheet of 10	10.00	10.00
a.-j.	52y Any single	1.00	.75
3987	A3671 Sheet of 10	16.00	16.00
a.-j.	82y Any single	1.25	.80

Miniature Sheet

2016 G-7 Summit A3672

No. 3988: a, Pearls and Ago Bay, denomination at UL. b, Pearls and Ago Bay, denomination at UR. c, Snowy plover. d, Uji Bridge. e, Uji Bridge and Isuzu River. f, Japanese iris. g, Japanese spiny lobster. h, Wedded Rocks, Ise-Shima National Park. i, Cape Daio Lighthouse. j, Ise katagami and Iga kumihimo fabric crafting.

2016, Apr. 26 **Photo.** ***Perf. 13½***

3988	A3672 Sheet of 10	16.00	16.00
a.-j.	82y Any single	1.25	.50

99th Lions Club International Convention, Fukuoka — A3673

2016, May 6 **Litho.** ***Perf. 13***

3989	A3673 82y multi	1.50	.50

Miniature Sheet

Fukushima Local Autonomy Law, 60th Anniv. — A3674

No. 3990: a, Hideyo Noguchi (1876-1928), bacteriologist, Mt. Bandai, Lake Inawashiro (32x39mm). b, Red cow and Okiagari-koboshi dolls (28x33mm). c, Waterfall cherry tree, Miharu (28x33mm). d, Obori Soma pottery (28x33mm). e, Aquamarine Fukushima (28x33mm).

Perf. 13¼ (#3990a), 13x13¼

2016, May 11 **Litho.**

3990	A3674 Sheet of 5	7.50	7.50
a.-e.	82y Any single	1.50	.60

Miniature Sheets

A3675

Sanrio Characters — A3676

No. 3991: a, Hello Kitty, lavender gray stripes (29x26mm heart). b, Hello Kitty, pale blue stripes (23x23mm). c, Hello Kitty, rose pink stripes (27x22mm). d, Hello Kitty, doily (29mm diameter). e, My Melody (22x30mm oval). f, My Melody, rose pink background (23x23mm). g, Little Twin Stars (22x28mm). h, Little Twin Stars, diff, (29x26mm heart). i, Pompompurin, rose pink background (29mm diameter). j, Pompompurin, pale blue background (23x23mm).

No. 3992: a, Hello Kitty, pale blue stripes (22x28mm). b, Hello Kitty, rose pink stripes (22x30mm oval). c, Hello Kitty, rose red background (29x26mm heart). d, Hello Kitty, rose pink stripes and pale blue circle (29mm diameter). e, My Melody, rose pink stripes (23x23mm). f, My Melody (29x26mm heart). g, Little Twin Stars, (27x22mm). h, Little Twin Stars (23x23mm). i, Pompompurin (29mm diameter). j, Pompompurin, pale orange stripes (27x22mm).

Die Cut Perf. (#3991a, 3991c, 3991h, 3991i), Die Cut Perf. 14 (#3991b, 3991f, 3991j), Die Cut Perf. 12¼x11¾ (#3991c), Die Cut Perf. 13 (#3991e), Die Cut Perf12¾x13¼ (#3991g)

2016, May 13 Litho.

Self-Adhesive

3991	A3675	Sheet of 10	10.00	10.00
a.-j.		52y Any single	.95	.70

Die Cut Perf. 13¼x12¾ (#3992a), Die Cut Perf. 13 (#3992b), Die Cut Perf. 14 (#3992e), Die Cut Perf. 13¼x14 (#3992g, 3992j), Die Cut Perf. 13½ (#3992h), Die Cut Perf.

3992	A3676	Sheet of 10	15.00	15.00
a.-j.		82y Any single	1.25	.80

Tangerine A3677

Japanese Ginger A3678

Perilla Leaf A3679

Ginkgo Nuts A3680

Potato A3681

Kabocha Squash A3682

Red and Yellow Peppers A3683

Fava Beans A3684

Kumquats A3685

Blueberries A3686

Die Cut Perf. 13¼x13 (#3993a, 3994a, 3994b), Die Cut Perf. 13x13¼

2016, May 20 Litho.

Self-Adhesive

3993		Sheet of 10, 2 each #3993a-3993e	10.00	10.00
a.	A3677	52y multi	.95	.70
b.	A3678	52y multi	.95	.70
c.	A3679	52y multi	.95	.70
d.	A3680	52y multi	.95	.70
e.	A3681	52y multi	.95	.70
3994		Sheet of 10, 2 each #3994a-3994e	16.00	16.00
a.	A3682	82y multi	1.25	.80
b.	A3683	82y multi	1.25	.80
c.	A3684	82y multi	1.25	.80
d.	A3685	82y multi	1.25	.80
e.	A3686	82y multi	1.25	.80

Souvenir Sheet

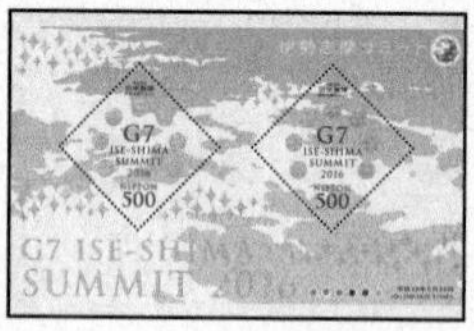

2016 G-7 Summit A3687

No. 3995 — Pearls and Ago Bay with denomination over: a, White area, b, Colored area.

Litho. With Foil Application

2016, May 26 ***Perf. 14¼***

Printed on Silk

3995	A3687	Sheet of 2	40.00	40.00
a.-b.		500y Either single	10.00	10.00

No. 3995 sold for 1300y.

Miniature Sheet

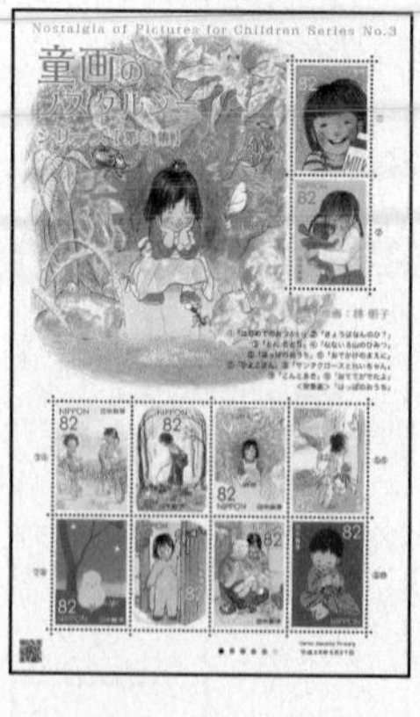

Children A3688

No. 3996: a, Child with milk container. b, Girl hugging puppy. c, Children on bicycles with training wheels. d, Child poking mushrooms with stick. e, Girl crouched in foliage. f, Child holding doll opening curtain. g, Chick under tree. h, Child opening door. i, Grandmother repairing teddy bear for girl. j, Child in too-large orange kimono.

2016, May 27 Litho. ***Perf. 12¾x13***

3996	A3688	Sheet of 10	16.00	16.00
a.-j.		82y Any single	1.25	.50

Miniature Sheet

National Afforestation — A3689

No. 3825: a, Takato winter-flowering cherry blossoms. b, Nikko fir. c, Chestnut. d, Gentian. e, Lisianthus. f, Japanese rowan. g, Japanese larch. h, Japanese white birch trees. i, Rape blossoms. j, Apple blossoms.

2016, June 3 Litho. ***Perf. 13***

3997	A3689	Sheet of 10	10.00	10.00
a.-j.		52y Any single	1.00	.75

Miniature Sheet

Tokyo Local Autonomy Law, 60th Anniv. — A3690

No. 3998: a, Tokyo Tower, Rainbow Bridge and gulls (32x39mm). b, Eastern Sea Road 53 Stations, Morning Scene at Nihonbashi, by Hiroshige (28x33mm). c, Mt. Takao Yakuoin Izuna Gongen Hall (28x33mm). d, Camellia, Mt. Mihara (28x33mm). e, Ogasawara Islands and Ogi Pond (28x33mm).

Perf. 13¼ (#3998a), 13x13¼

2016, June 7 Litho.

3998	A3690	Sheet of 5	8.00	8.00
a.-e.		82y Any single	1.60	1.25

White Frangipani Flower A3695

White and Red Frangipani Flowers A3696

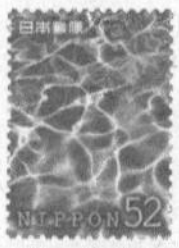

Sunlight Reflected Off Water A3697

Palm Trees A3698

Hibiscus A3699

Sunflower A3700

Two Seashells A3701

Seashell A3702

Drink in Glass A3703

Palm Trees A3704

Hibiscus A3705

Clouds A3706

Die Cut Perf. 13¼, Die Cut Perf. 12 (#4000e, 4000f, 4001a, 4001b)

2016, June 10 Litho.

Self-Adhesive

4000		Sheet of 10, 2 each #4000a-4000d, 1 each #4000e, 4000f	10.00	10.00
a.	A3695	52y multi	1.00	.75
b.	A3696	52y multi	1.00	.75
c.	A3697	52y multi	1.00	.75
d.	A3698	52y multi	1.00	.75
e.	A3699	52y multi	1.00	.75
f.	A3700	52y multi	1.00	.75
4001		Sheet of 10, 1 each #4001a, 4001b, 2 each #4001c-4001f	16.00	16.00
a.	A3701	82y multi	1.25	.80
b.	A3702	82y multi	1.25	.80
c.	A3703	82y multi	1.25	.80
d.	A3704	82y multi	1.25	.80
e.	A3705	82y multi	1.25	.80
f.	A3706	82y multi	1.25	.80

Miniature Sheets

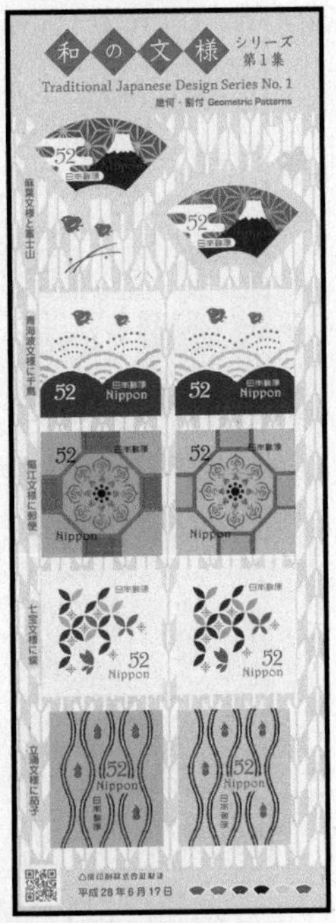

A3707

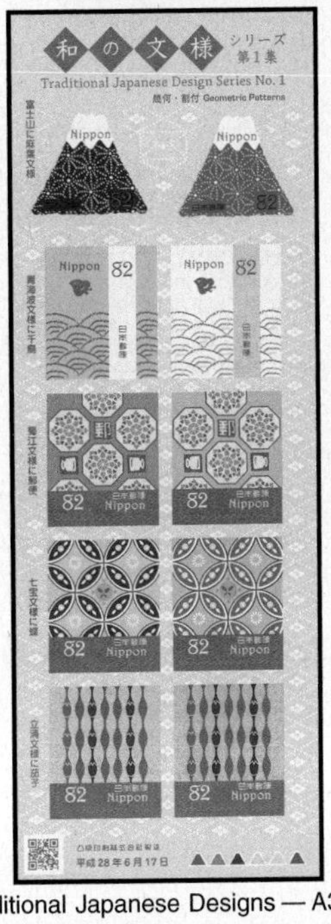

Traditional Japanese Designs — A3708

No. 4002: a, Fan with Mt. Fuji, dull green background (33x19mm). b, As "a", light purple background (33x19mm). c, Birds and waves, blue bottom panel (23x23mm). d, As "c," purple bottom panel (23x23mm). e, Octagon, apple green background (23x23mm). f, As "e," pale peach background (23x23mm). g, Flowers, blue green, light blue and gold petals (23x23mm). h, As "g," blue green, rose pink and gold petals (23x23mm). i, Eggplants and wavy lines, light blue background (22x26mm). j, As "i," lilac background (22x26mm).

No. 4003: a, Dark blue Mt. Fuji (30x25mm). b, Bright blue Mt. Fuji (30x25mm). c, Bird and waves, light blue background (22x26mm). d, As "c," pink panel (22x26mm). e, Octagons, sage green background (22x26mm). f, As "e," pink background (22x26mm). g, Interlocking circles, beige background (22x26mm). h, As "g," light blue background (22x26mm). i, Eggplants and wavy lines, pink background (22x26mm). j, As "i," orange yellow background (22x26mm).

Die Cut Perf. 12¾ (#4002a, 4002b), Die Cut Perf. 14, Die Cut Perf. 13¼ (#4002i, 4002j)

2016, June 17 **Litho.**

Self-Adhesive

4002	A3707	Sheet of 10	10.00	10.00
a.-j.		52y Any single	1.00	.75

Die Cut Perf. 13 (#4003a, 4003b), Die Cut Perf. 13x13¼

4003	A3708	Sheet of 10	16.00	16.00
a.-j.		82y Any single	1.25	.80

Miniature Sheets

A3709

Doraemon Characters — A3710

No. 4004: a, Doraemon carrying mailbox (19x27mm oval). b, Doraemon holding stamp (20x23mm). c, Doraemon delivering letter (20x24mm). d, Dorami, yellow background with white polka dots (25mm diameter). e, Doraemon, Nobita and Shizuka (31x31mm). f, Doraemon eating (20x23mm). g, Dorami winking (20x23mm). h, Nobita writing letter (20x23mm). i, Shizuka reading letter (20x23mm). j, Doraemon licking lips (19x27mm oval).

No. 4005: a, Doraemon with bamboo helicopter on head (21x29mm oval). b, Doraemon and tree cloth (21x29mm oval). c, Doraemon in pass-through loop (22x26mm). d, Doraemon shining light on Nobita (22x26mm). e, Doraemon and Nobita on time machine (31x28mm). f, Doraemon in Anywhere Door (30x37mm). g, Doraemon with open mouth (25mm diameter). h, Doraemon with closed mouth (25mm diameter). i, Doraemon with raised paws (25mm diameter). j, Doraemon licking lips (25mm diameter).

Die Cut Perf. 13 (#4004a, 4004j), Die Cut Perf. 14¼x14½, Die Cut Perf. 12½ (#4004c, 4004e), Die Cut Perf. (#4004d)

2016, July 1 **Litho.**

Self-Adhesive

4004	A3709	Sheet of 10	10.00	10.00
a.-j.		52y Any single	1.00	.75

Die Cut Perf. 13¾ (#4005a, 4005b), Die Cut Perf. 13x13¼ (#4005c, 4005d), Die Cut Perf. 13 (#4005e), Die Cut Perf. 12¾x13 (#4005f), Die Cut Perf.

4005	A3710	Sheet of 10	16.00	16.00
a.-j.		82y Any single	1.25	.80

Personalized Stamp — A3710a

Die Cut Perf. 13¼x12¾ Syncopated

2016, July 1 **Litho.**

Self-Adhesive

4005K A3710a 82y gldn brn + label *5.50 5.50*

No. 4005K was printed in sheets of 5 that sold for 1400y. The labels, separated from the stamp by a row of rouletting, could be personalized. The image shown on the label above is a generic image. Six additional stamps were issued in this set. The editors would like to examine any examples.

Miniature Sheet

Japan's Meiji Industrial Revolution Iron, Steel, Shipbuilding and Coal Mining UNESCO World Heritage Site — A3711

No. 4006: a, Former office of Yawata Steel Works, denomination at UR (stamp 1). b, Onga River Pumping Station, denomination at LL (stamp 2). c, Hagi Reverberatory Furnace, denomination at UL (stamp 3). d, Shuseikan Industrial Comples, denomination at LL (stamp 4). e, Nirayama Reverberatory Furnace, denomination at UR (stamp 5). f, Hashino Iron Mining and Smelting Site, denomination at UR (stamp 6). g, Mietsu Naval Dock Ruins, denomination at LL (stamp 7). h, Kosuge Slip Dock, denomination at LL (stamp 8). i, Misumi West Port, denomination at UL (stamp 9). j, Aerial view of Miike Port, denomination at UR (stamp 10).

2016, July 8 **Litho.** ***Perf. 13***

4006	A3711	Sheet of 10	16.00	16.00
a.-j.		82y Any single	1.25	.50

Amaryllises A3712

Narcissi A3713

Pine Tree, Sarcandra Glabra, and Ornamental Kale A3714

Statice and Dendrobium Orchids A3715

Dahlias A3716

Roses A3717

Cockscombs A3718

Hyacinths A3719

Chrysanthemums A3720

Nerines A3721

Die Cut Perf. 14

2016, July 15 **Litho.**

Self-Adhesive

4007	Sheet of 10, 2 each #4007a-4007e	10.00	10.00
a.	A3712 52y multi	1.00	.75
b.	A3713 52y multi	1.00	.75
c.	A3714 52y multi	1.00	.75
d.	A3715 52y multi	1.00	.75
e.	A3716 52y multi	1.00	.75
4008	Sheet of 10, 2 each #4008a-4008e	16.00	16.00
a.	A3717 82y multi	1.25	.80
b.	A3718 82y multi	1.25	.80
c.	A3719 82y multi	1.25	.80
d.	A3720 82y multi	1.25	.80
e.	A3721 82y multi	1.25	.80

Letter Writing Day — A3722

Designs: No. 4009, Pen nibs. No. 4010, Tape rolls and strips. No. 4011, Erasers. No. 4012, Pencils. No. 4013, Paper clips. No. 4014, Three envelopes. No. 4015, Crayons. No. 4016, Fountain pens. No. 4017, Colored pencils. No. 4018, Two long envelopes.

Die Cut Perf. 13x13¼

2016, July 22 **Litho.**

Booklet Stamps

Self-Adhesive

4009	A3722 52y multi	1.00	.75
4010	A3722 52y multi	1.00	.75
4011	A3722 52y multi	1.00	.75
4012	A3722 52y multi	1.00	.75
4013	A3722 52y multi	1.00	.75
a.	Booklet pane of 10, 2 each #4009-4013	10.00	10.00
4014	A3722 82y multi	1.25	.80
4015	A3722 82y multi	1.25	.80
4016	A3722 82y multi	1.25	.80
4017	A3722 82y multi	1.25	.80
4018	A3722 82y multi	1.25	.80
a.	Booklet pane of 10, 2 each #4014-4018	16.00	16.00
	Nos. 4009-4018 (10)	11.25	7.75

Toji of the Ogiya, Kamuro, Satoji and Uraji, by Kiyonaga Torii A3723

Mt. Otoko at Hirakata, Kawachi Province, by Hiroshige Utagawa A3724

The Maiden at the Dojo Temple, by Yukimaro Kitagawa A3725

Bonito Fishing at Sea, Tosa Province, by Hiroshige Utagawa A3726

The Brine Maidens, by Kiyonaga Torii A3727

Mt. Asama, Teahouse on the Mountain Pass, Ise Province, by Hiroshige Utagawa A3728

Tsukioka of the Hyogo House, by Eisui Ichirakutei
A3729

The Takuhi Shrine, Oki Province, by Hiroshige Utagawa
A3730

Good Relations Between Siblings, by Utamaro Kitagawa
A3731

The Weir in the Shallows, Chikugo Province, by Hiroshige Utagawa
A3732

2016, July 29 **Litho.** ***Perf. 13***

4019	Sheet of 10	16.00	16.00
a.	A3723 82y multi	1.25	.50
b.	A3724 82y multi	1.25	.50
c.	A3725 82y multi	1.25	.50
d.	A3726 82y multi	1.25	.50
e.	A3727 82y multi	1.25	.50
f.	A3728 82y multi	1.25	.50
g.	A3729 82y multi	1.25	.50
h.	A3730 82y multi	1.25	.50
i.	A3731 82y multi	1.25	.50
j.	A3732 82y multi	1.25	.50

Miniature Sheet

Diplomatic Relations Between Japan and Belgium, 150th Anniv. — A3733

No. 4006: a, Grand Place, Brussels, at night, denomination at LL. b, Grand Place, at night, denomination at LR. c, Cut diamond. d, Begonia. e, Notre Dame Cathedral, Tournai, Belgium, denomination at LL. f, Notre Dame Cathedral, Tournai, denomination at UR. g, Belgian waffles. h, Beer. i, Historic Center of Bruges, denomination at LL. j, Historic Center of Bruges, denomination at LR.

2016, Aug. 1 **Litho.** ***Perf. 13***

4020	A3733	Sheet of 10	16.00	16.00
a.-j.		82y Any single	1.25	.50

Miniature Sheets

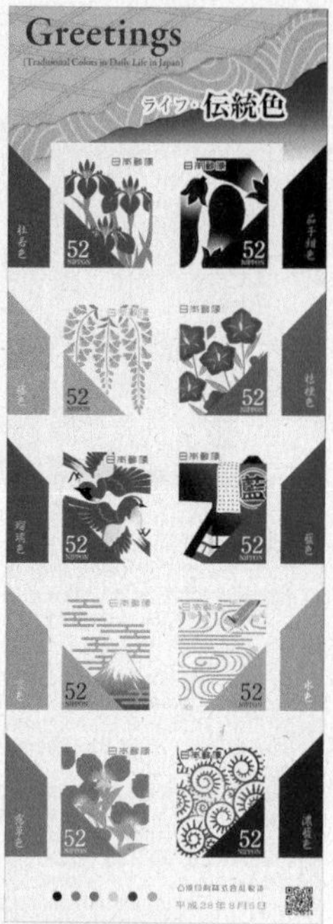

A3734

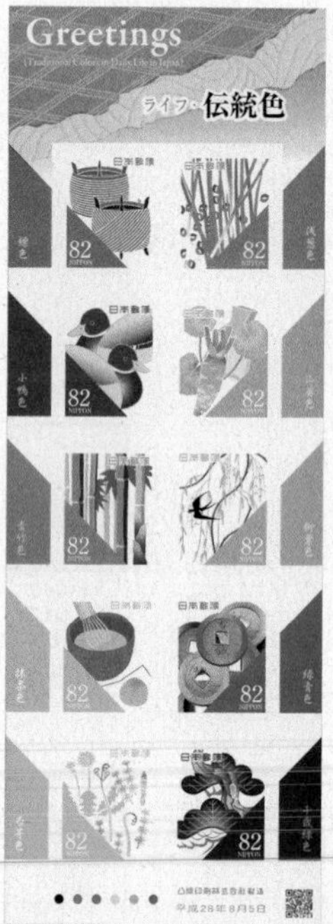

Colors in Daily Life
A3735

No. 4021: a, Japanese irises. b, Eggplants. c, Wisteria. d, Bellflowers. e, Blue birds. f, Hanten (short coat). g, Mt. Fuji. h, Bamboo boat and cherry blossoms in water. i, Asiatic dayflower. j, Octopus arabesque pattern.

No. 4022: a, Yarn on holders. b, Green onions. c, Mallards. d, Wasabi and grater. e, Bamboo. f, Bird and willow tree. g, Green tea and confection. h, Old Japanese coins. i, Dandelions, fiddleheads and horsetails. j, Pine tree.

Die Cut Perf. 13x13¼

2016, Aug. 5 **Litho.**

Self-Adhesive

4021	A3734	Sheet of 10	10.00	10.00
a.-j.		52y Any single	1.00	.75
4022	A3735	Sheet of 10	16.00	16.00
a.-j.		82y Any single	1.25	.80

Miniature Sheet

Mountain Day
A3736

No. 4023: a, Daisetsuzan. b, Hokkaido crying rabbit. c, Mt. Iwate. d, Komakusa flowers. e, Mt. Yari. f, Yarigatake Eastern Blue butterfly. g, Daisen. h, Daisen yellow violet. i, Kuju Mountain Range. j, Hooaka bird.

2016, Aug. 10 **Litho.** ***Perf. 13x13¼***

4023	A3736	Sheet of 10	16.00	16.00
a.-j.		82y Any single	1.25	.50

Miniature Sheets

A3737

Kyoto Area Tourist Attractions — A3738

No. 4024: a, Kiyomizudera, denomination in white at LL. b, Kiyomizudera, denominaiton in white at LR, horiz. c, Sannenzaka, denomination in orange red at LL, horiz. d, Sannenzaka, denomination in white at LR, horiz. e, Nanzen-ji interior, denomination in pink at UR. f, Nanzen-ji exterior, denomination at LL, horiz. g, Shisen-do sands, denomination in magenta at LR, horiz. h, Shisen-do, denomination in yellow green at LR. i, Hanamikoji Dori, denomination in black at LL. j, Hanamikoji Dori at night, denomination in white at LL.

No. 4025: a, Togetsu-kyo, denomination in white at LR, horiz. b, Togetsu-kyo, denominaiton in white at UL. c, Daigo-ji statue of Buddha, denomination in white at LR. d, Daigo-ji hall, denomination in rose at LL, horiz. e, Sanzen-in, denomination in white at UR. f, Sanzen-in, denomination in white at LL, horiz. g, Nakagyo Post Office doorway, denomination in red at LR, horiz. h, Nakagyo Post Office, denomination in red at UR, horiz. i, Shoden-ji at night, denomination in azure at right, horiz. j, Shoden-ji, denomination in red at UL.

Die Cut Perf. 13x13¼ (vert. stamps), Die Cut Perf. 13¼x13

2016, Aug. 19 **Litho.**

Self-Adhesive

4024	A3737	Sheet of 10	10.00	10.00
a.-j.		52y Any single	1.00	.75
4025	A3738	Sheet of 10	16.00	16.00
a.-j.		82y Any single	1.25	.80

Miniature Sheet

Diplomatic Relations Between Japan and Italy, 150th Anniv. — A3739

No. 4026: a, Silkworm cocoons on mulberry leaves. b, Red silk. c, Madonna of the Yarnwinder, by Leonardo da Vinci. d, Maria de'Medici, by Agnolo Bronzino. e, Basil leaves and mozzarella cheese. f, Mozzarella cheese and tomatoes. g, Madonna of the Book, by Sandro Botticelli. h, Boy with a Basket of Fruit, by Caravaggio. i, Val d'Orcia, Trulli of Alberobello. j, Trulli of Alberobello, Florence Cathedral.

2016, Aug. 25 **Litho.** ***Perf. 13***

4026	A3739	Sheet of 10	16.00	16.00
a.-j.		82y Any single	1.25	.50

Fish A3740

Crane and Tortoise A3741

Mt. Fuji in Blue A3742

Fish A3743

Owl A3744

Mt. Fuji in Gold A3745

Bird and Flowers A3746

Balloons A3747

Bird of Ribbon A3748

G Clef, Notes and Stars A3749

Rose A3750

Flower Bouquet A3751

Bells A3752

Lilies and Ribbon A3753

Die Cut Perf. 14, Die Cut Perf. (#4030a, 4030c)

2016, Aug. 26 **Litho.**

Self-Adhesive

4027	Sheet of 10, 4 each #4027a-4027b, 2 #4027c	10.00	10.00
a.	A3740 52y multi	1.00	.75
b.	A3741 52y multi	1.00	.75
c.	A3742 52y multi	1.00	.75
4028	Sheet of 10, 4 each #4028a-4028b, 2 #4028c	16.00	16.00
a.	A3743 82y multi	1.25	.80
b.	A3744 82y multi	1.25	.80
c.	A3745 82y multi	1.25	.80
4029	Sheet of 10, 4 #4029b, 2 each #4029a, 4029c, 4029d	16.00	16.00
a.	A3746 82y multi	1.25	.80
b.	A3747 82y multi	1.25	.80
c.	A3748 82y multi	1.25	.80
d.	A3749 82y multi	1.25	.80
4030	Sheet of 10, 4 #4030a, 2 each #4030b, 4030c, 4030d	17.00	17.00
a.	A3750 92y multi	1.40	.80
b.	A3751 92y multi	1.40	.80
c.	A3752 92y multi	1.40	.80
d.	A3753 92y multi	1.40	.80

Miniature Sheet

71st National Athletic Meet, Iwate A3754

No. 4026: a, Rugby. b, Field hockey. c, Triathlon. d, Wrestling. e, Naginatajutsu. f, Boxing. g, Soccer. h, Tennis. i, Basketball. j, Baseball.

2016, Sept. 1 **Litho.** ***Perf. 13***

4031	A3754	Sheet of 10	16.00	16.00
a.-j.		82y Any single	1.25	.50

Flower Pots on Trellis A3755

Potted Tree and Flowers A3756

Trellis, Potted Plants, Watering Can A3757

Seeds, Lantern, Gardening Tools A3758

Watering Can, Plant Labels, Shovel, Gloves A3759

Roses, Pastry Carrier, Tea Cup A3760

Hanging Flower Basket A3761

Garden A3762

Rose Trellis A3763

Potted Tree and Roses A3764

Die Cut Perf. 14, Die Cut Perf. (#4033a, 4033b)

2016, Sept. 9 **Litho.**

Self-Adhesive

4032	Sheet of 10, 2 each #4032a-4032e	10.00	10.00
a.	A3755 52y multi	1.00	.75
b.	A3756 52y multi	1.00	.75
c.	A3757 52y multi	1.00	.75
d.	A3758 52y multi	1.00	.75
e.	A3759 52y multi	1.00	.75
4033	Sheet of 10, 2 each #4033a-4033e	16.00	16.00
a.	A3760 82y multi	1.25	.80
b.	A3761 82y multi	1.25	.80
c.	A3762 82y multi	1.25	.80
d.	A3763 82y multi	1.25	.80
e.	A3764 82y multi	1.25	.80

Teddy Bear Postman Delivering Letter A3765

Teddy Bear Holding Letter A3766

Owl at Table A3767

Teddy Bear at Table A3768

Two Teddy Bears A3769

Beige Teddy Bear A3770

Gray Teddy Bear A3771

Brown Teddy Bear A3772

Blue Teddy Bear A3773

Teddy Bears and Mailbox A3774

Die Cut Perf. 12, Die Cut Perf. (#4034e)

2016, Sept. 16 **Litho.**

Self-Adhesive

4034	Sheet of 10, 2 each #4034a-4034e	10.00	10.00
a.	A3765 52y multi	1.00	.75
b.	A3766 52y multi	1.00	.75
c.	A3767 52y multi	1.00	.75
d.	A3768 52y multi	1.00	.75
e.	A3769 52y multi	1.00	.75

Die Cut Perf. 12½, Die Cut Perf. 12x11¾ (#4035e)

4035	Sheet of 10, 2 each #4035a-4035e	16.00	16.00
a.	A3770 82y multi	1.25	.80
b.	A3771 82y multi	1.25	.80
c.	A3772 82y multi	1.25	.80
d.	A3773 82y multi	1.25	.80
e.	A3774 82y multi	1.25	.80

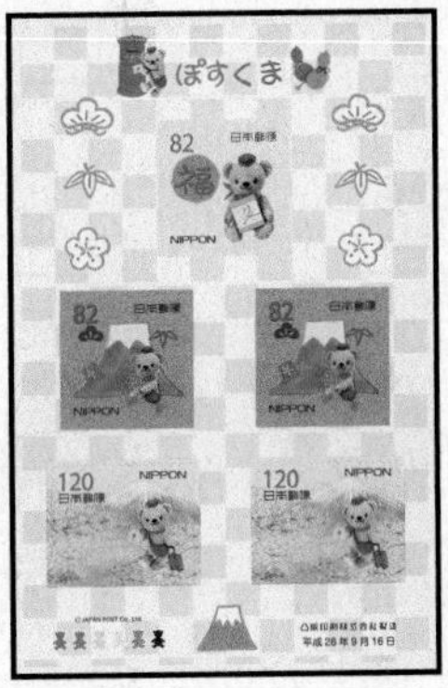

A sheet of five self-adhesive stamps depicting teddy bears (three denominated 82y and two denominated 120y) was printed in limited quantities and sold only in a package containing stationery. Value, $20.

Miniature Sheet

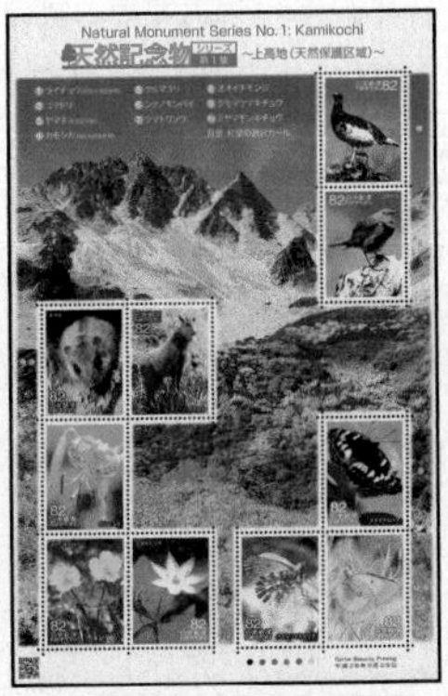

Kamikochi Natural Monument — A3775

No. 4036: a, Japanese rock ptarmigan (stamp 1). b, Japanese robin (stamp 2). c, Japanese dormouse (stamp 3). d, Japanese serow (stamp 4). e, Lilium medeoloides (stamp 5). f, Trollius riederianus var. japonicus (stamp 6). g, Chickweed wintergreen (stamp 7). h, Poplar admiral butterfly (stamp 8). i, Orange tip butterfly (stamp 9). j, Moorland clouded yellow butterfly (stamp 10).

2016, Sept. 23 Litho. *Perf. 13*

4036 A3775 Sheet of 10 16.00 16.00
a.-j. 82y Any single 1.25 .50

Miniature Sheet

Postal Life Insurance Service, Cent. — A3776

No. 4037 — Heart-shaped flowers: a, Blue denomination, pink flower at bottom. b, Blue denomination, pink flower at top. c, Blue denomination, pink flower left of center. d, Blue denomination, pink flower at center. e, Blue denomination, pink flower at right. f, White denomination, pink flower at LL. below dark blue flower. g, White denomination, pink flower at bottom to right of white flower. h, White denomination, pink flower partly covered by dark blue flower. i, White denomination, pink flower at UR. j, White denomination, pink flower at LR.

2016, Sept. 30 Photo. *Perf. 13*

4037 A3776 Sheet of 10 16.00 16.00
a.-j. 82y Any single 1.25 .50

Fox A3777

Purple Grapes A3778

Rabbit A3779

Akebia A3780

Moose A3781

Bear A3782

Snake Gourds A3783

Squirrel A3784

White Grapes A3785

Japanese Raccoon Dog A3786

Die Cut Perf. 13x13¼, Die Cut Perf. (#4038e, 4039e)

2016, Oct. 3 Litho.

Self-Adhesive

4038 Sheet of 10, 2 each #4038a-4038e 10.00 10.00
a. A3777 52y multi 1.00 .75
b. A3778 52y multi 1.00 .75
c. A3779 52y multi 1.00 .75
d. A3780 52y multi 1.00 .75
e. A3781 52y multi 1.00 .75

4039 Sheet of 10, 2 each #4039a-4039e 16.00 16.00
a. A3782 82y multi 1.25 .80
b. A3783 82y multi 1.25 .80
c. A3784 82y multi 1.25 .80
d. A3785 82y multi 1.25 .80
e. A3786 82y multi 1.25 .80

Map and Trains of Hokuriku Shinkansen Line A3787

Kintetsu 30000 Series Locomotive A3788

Enoden 1000 Series Locomotive A3789

Odakyu Electric Railway 7000 Series Locomotive A3790

Hakone Tozan 1000 Series Locomotive A3791

Keikyu 2000 Series Locomotive A3792

Nankai Electric Railway 5000 Series Locomotive A3793

East Japan Railway E26 Series Locomotive A3794

Kyushu Railway 885 Series Locomotive A3795

Toyama Light Rail TLR0600 Series Train A3796

Hokuriku Shinkansen Line Locomotives A3797

Keikyu 2000 Series Locomotive A3798

Kintetsu 30000 Series Locomotive A3799

Nankai Electric Railway 5000 Series Locomotive A3800

Enoden 1000 Series Locomotive A3801

East Japan Railway E26 Series Locomotive A3802

Odakyu Electric Railway 7000 Series Locomotive A3803

Kyushu Railway 885 Series Locomotive A3804

Hakone Tozan 1000 Series Locomotive A3805

Toyama Light Rail TLR0600 Series Train A3806

2016, Oct. 7 Litho. *Perf. 13¼x12¾*

4040 Sheet of 10 16.00 16.00
a. A3787 82y multi 1.25 .50
b. A3788 82y multi 1.25 .50
c. A3789 82y multi 1.25 .50
d. A3790 82y multi 1.25 .50
e. A3791 82y multi 1.25 .50
f. A3792 82y multi 1.25 .50
g. A3793 82y multi 1.25 .50
h. A3794 82y multi 1.25 .50
i. A3795 82y multi 1.25 .50
j. A3796 82y multi 1.25 .50

Perf. 12¾x13¼

4041 Sheet of 10 16.00 16.00
a. A3797 82y multi 1.25 .50
b. A3798 82y multi 1.25 .50
c. A3799 82y multi 1.25 .50
d. A3800 82y multi 1.25 .50
e. A3801 82y multi 1.25 .50
f. A3802 82y multi 1.25 .50
g. A3803 82y multi 1.25 .50
h. A3804 82y multi 1.25 .50
i. A3805 82y multi 1.25 .50
j. A3806 82y multi 1.25 .50

A3807

International Letter Writing Week — A3808

Paintings by Hiroshige: 70y, Wild Duck Among Snow-Covered Reeds. 90y, Travelers Walking Towards Numazu. 110y, Changing of Horses and Porters at Fujieda Relay Station. 130y, Futagawa Station.

2016, Oct. 7 Photo. *Perf. 13¼*

4042 A3807 70y multi 1.40 .50

Perf. 13

4043 A3808 90y multi 1.75 .50
4044 A3808 110y multi 2.25 .50
4045 A3808 130y multi 2.50 .50
Nos. 4042-4045 (4) 7.90 2.00

See listing of No. 4448 for images of each Hiroshige print.

Miniature Sheet

Japan at Night A3809

No. 4046: a, Rainbow Bridge (stamp 1). b, Tokyo Sky Tree (stamp 2). c, Tokyo tower (stamp 3). d, Yokohama Minata Mirai 21 (stamp 4). e, Kanto Plain (stamp 5). f, Chichibu Night Festival (stamp 6). g, Gunman Flower Park (stamp 7). h, Ashikaga Flower Park (stamp 8). i, Tokyo German Village (stamp 9). j, Fuefukigawa Fruit Park (stamp 10).

2016, Oct. 14 Litho. *Perf. 13*

4046 A3809 Sheet of 10 16.00 16.00
a.-j. 82y Any single 1.25 .50

Banner Decoration A3810

Silver Platter A3811

Incense Burner A3812

Lacquered Wooden Box A3813

Detail of Incense Burner — A3814

2016, Oct. 21 Photo. *Perf. 13*

4047 A3810 82y multi 1.25 .50
4048 A3811 82y multi 1.25 .50
4049 A3812 82y multi 1.25 .50
4050 A3813 82y multi 1.60 .50
4051 A3814 82y multi 1.25 .50
a. Vert. strip of 5, #4047-4051 8.00 6.25
Nos. 4047-4051 (5) 6.60 2.50

Miniature Sheet

Japanese Foods — A3815

No. 4052: a, Rice cake in ceremonial display. b, Tray of New Year foods. c, Box of beans, hiirage and sardine heads. d, Dolls and crackers. e, Mochi wrapped in cherry leaves. f, Rice in bamboo leaves. g, Noodles. h, Tsukimi dumplings. i, Chrysanthemum petal in saki. j, Kabocha squash and yuzu.

2016, Oct. 24 Litho. *Perf. 13½*

4052 A3815 Sheet of 10 16.00 16.00
a.-j. 82y Any single 1.25 .50

Miniature Sheet

Astronomy — A3816

No. 4053: a, Saturn (35x30mm). b, Capricorn and goat (22x25mm). c, Aquarius and water urn (22x25mm). d, Pisces and fish (22x25mm).

Die Cut Perf. 9¾x10 (#4053a), Die Cut Perf. 13x13¼
Litho. With Foil Application

2016, Oct. 28 **Self-Adhesive**

4053 A3816 Sheet of 10, #4053a, 3 each #4053b-4053d 16.00 16.00
a.-d. 82y Any single 1.25 .80

Japanese Foods A3817

Designs: No. 4054, Soba noodles on square plate. No. 4055, Oyakodon soup in bowl.

2016, Nov. 1 **Litho.** ***Perf. 13¼x13***

4054 18y multi .25 .25
4055 18y multi .25 .25
a. A3817 Horiz. pair, #4054-4055 .55 .45

A3818 A3819

New Year 2017 (Year of the Rooster)
A3820 A3821

2016, Nov. 1 **Photo.** ***Perf. 13x13¼***

4056 A3818 52y multi 1.00 .30
4057 A3819 82y multi 1.50 .40

Photo. & Typo.
Perf. 13¼

4058 A3820 52y +3y multi 1.25 .40
4059 A3821 82y +3y multi 1.75 .40
Nos. 4056-4059 (4) 5.50 1.50

Miniature Sheet

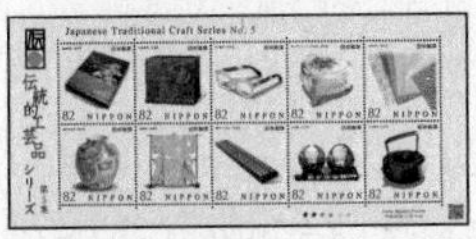

Traditional Crafts — A3822

No. 4060: a, Echizen lacquerware (Fukui Prefecture). b, Sendai storage cabinet (Miyagi Prefecture). c, Edo tortoiseshell eyeglasses (Tokyo Prefecture). d, Tokyo antimony jewelry box (Tokyo Prefecture). e, Tosa paper (Kochi Prefecture). f, Seto underglazed pottery (Aichi Prefecture). g, Nishijin textiles (Kyoto Prefecture). h, Banshu abacus (Hyogo Prefecture). i, Ouchi lacquerware (Yamaguchi Prefecture). j, Yamagata metal cast kettle (Yamagata Prefecture).

2016, Nov. 4 **Litho.** ***Perf. 13¼***

4060 A3822 Sheet of 10 16.00 16.00
a.-j. 82y Any single 1.25 .50

Miniature Sheet

World Tsunami Awareness Day — A3823

No. 4061: a, Earth and ocean. b, Man running from tsunami. c, Burning rice sheaves, man with torch. d, Miracle Pine of Rikuzentakata. e, Winning children's art in tsunami awareness poster contest.

2016, Nov. 4 **Litho.** ***Perf. 13***

4061 A3823 Sheet of 10, 2 each #4053a-4053e 16.00 16.00
a.-e. 82y Any single 1.25 .50

Miniature Sheets

A3824

Animals A3825

No. 4062: a, Netherland Dwarf rabbit (30x28mm heart). b, Flying squirrel (22x26mm). c, Hamster (22x26mm). d, Chipmunk (22x26mm). e, Guinea pig (22x26mm). f, White birds on fence (30x28mm heart). g, Zebra finches (22x26mm). h, Cockatiel (22x26mm). i, Canaries (22x26mm). j, Parakeets (22x26mm).

No. 4063: a, Hedgehogs (30x28mm heart). b, Djungarian hamster (22x26mm). c, Lop-eared rabbit (22x26mm). d, Ferret (22x26mm). e, Chinchilla (22x26mm). f, Budgerigars (30x28mm heart). g, Rosy-faced lovebirds (22x26mm). h, Society finches (22x26mm). i, Sulphur-crested cockatoo (22x26mm). j, Java sparrows (22x26mm).

Die Cut Perf. 11¼x11, Die Cut Perf. (#4062a, 4062f, 4063a, 4063f)

2016, Nov. 11 **Litho.**
Self-Adhesive

4062 A3824 Sheet of 10 10.00 10.00
a.-j. 52y Any single .95 .70
4063 A3825 Sheet of 10 16.00 16.00
a.-j. 82y Any single 1.25 .80

Miniature Sheet

Illustrations From Children's Books by Mitsumasa Anno — A3826

No. 4064: a, People and horses on path (stamp 1). b, People gathered near buildings, man near tricycle, man with delivery bicycle (stamp 2). c, Anno's Counting house (stamp 3). d, Anno's medieval world (stamp 4). e, Anno's flea market (stamp 5). f, Anno's Aesop: A book of fables by Aesop & Mr. Fox (stamp 6). g, Anno's Journey, scene 15 (stamp 7). h, Anno's Journey III, scene 10 (stamp 8). i, Anno's Journey IV, scene 11 (stamp 9). j, Anno's Journey VIII, scene 2 (stamp 10).

2016, Nov. 25 **Photo.** ***Perf. 13***

4064 A3826 Sheet of 10 16.00 16.00
a.-j. 82y Any single 1.25 .50

Miniature Sheet

Diplomatic Relations Between Japan and Singapore, 50th Anniv. — A3827

No. 4065: a, Three Singaporean pots with handle. b, Two Japanese bowls. c, Merlion, Singapore. d, Gardens by the Bay, Singapore. e, Singapore at night. f, Singapore Art Museum. g, Plate of chili crab. h, Marina Bay at dusk. i, Orchid. j, Singapore Flyer Ferris Wheel and ArtScience Museum at night.

2016, Nov. 29 **Litho.** ***Perf. 13***

4065 A3827 Sheet of 10 16.00 16.00
a.-j. 82y Any single 1.25 .50

See Singapore Nos. 1812-1813.

Fireplace A3828

Stew Pot and Bowl A3829

Snow-Covered House A3830

Snowman and Mailbox A3831

Child Rolling Large Snowball A3832

Trees A3833

Concert, Bows on Instruments A3834

Piano A3835

Trees With Lights at Night A3836

Shoppers With Packages A3837

Concert, Bows Raised A3838

Window and Door in Winter A3839

Die Cut Perf. 11¼x11¾, Die Cut Perf. 11½x11 (#4066c)

2016, Dec. 2 **Litho.**
Self-Adhesive

4066 Sheet of 10, 2 each #4066a-4066d, 1 each #4066e, 4066f 10.00 10.00
a. A3828 52y multi .95 .70
b. A3829 52y multi .95 .70
c. A3830 52y multi .95 .70
d. A3831 52y multi .95 .70
e. A3832 52y multi .95 .70
f. A3833 52y multi .95 .70
4067 Sheet of 10, #4067a, 4067e, 2 each #4067b-4067d, 4067f 16.00 16.00
a. A3834 82y multi 1.25 .80
b. A3835 82y multi 1.25 .80
c. A3836 82y multi 1.25 .80
d. A3837 82y multi 1.25 .80
e. A3838 82y multi 1.25 .80
f. A3839 82y multi 1.25 .80

A3840

A3841

A3842

A3843

A3844

A3845

A3846

A3847

A3848

A3849

A3850

A3851

A3852

A3853

Flowers — A3854

Die Cut Perf. 13x13¼

2016, Dec. 9 Litho.

Self-Adhesive

4068		Sheet of 10	10.00	10.00
a.	A3840	52y multi	.90	.70
b.	A3841	52y multi	.90	.70
c.	A3842	52y multi	.90	.70
d.	A3843	52y multi	.90	.70
e.	A3844	52y multi	.90	.70
f.	A3845	52y multi	.90	.70
g.	A3846	52y multi	.90	.70
h.	A3847	52y multi	.90	.70
i.	A3848	52y multi	.90	.70
j.	A3849	52y multi	.90	.70
4069		Sheet of 10, 2 each #4069a-4069e	16.00	16.00
a.	A3850	82y multi	1.25	.80
b.	A3851	82y multi	1.25	.80
c.	A3852	82y multi	1.25	.80
d.	A3853	82y multi	1.25	.80
e.	A3854	82y multi	1.25	.80

Five-Story Pagoda at Kyo-o-gokoku-ji Temple, Kyoto — A3855

Tokyo Tower — A3856

Photo. & Engr.

2017, Jan. 6 ***Perf. 13¼***

4070	A3855	82y multi	1.25	.50
4071	A3856	82y multi	1.25	.50
a.		Horiz. pair, #4070-4071	3.00	2.25

Monocolor (green, red, orange brown and blue) engraved examples of Nos. 4070-4071 were printed in two sheets of ten that were in booklets produced in limited quantities that sold for 2500y.

Miniature Sheets

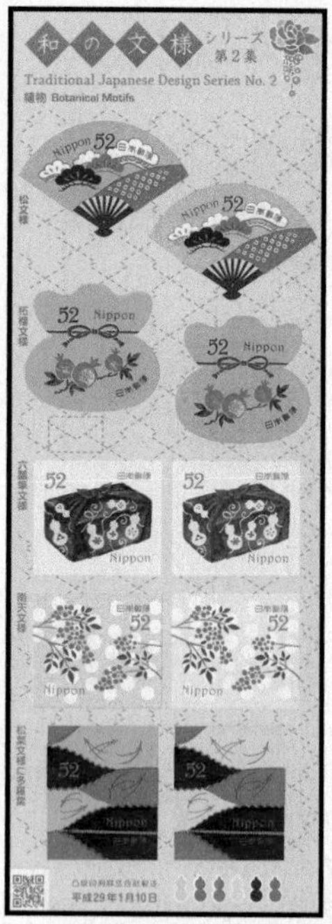

A3857

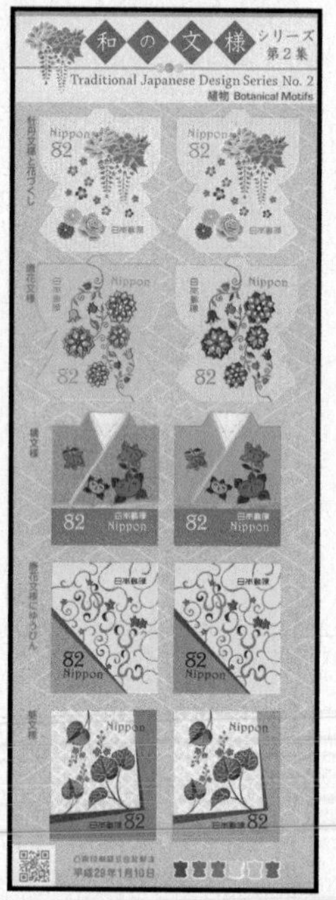

Traditional Japanese Designs — A3858

No. 4072: a, Fan with pine trees, lilac background (30x21mm). b, As "a," buff background (30x21mm). c, Pomegranates and tied rope, dull green background (27x24mm). d, As "c," rose background (27x24mm). e, Blue box with gourd pattern and bow (26x22mm), f, As "e," red violet box (26x22mm). g, Nandina berries, pink background (26x22mm). h, As "g," pale yellow background (26x22mm). i, Pine needles, dull green background (22x26mm). j, As "i," light yellow background (22x26mm).

No. 4073: a, Peonies, pink background (26x27mm). b, As "a," pale orange background (26x27mm). c, Flowers, yellow orange background (26x27mm). d, As "c," light blue background (26x27mm). e, Flowers on salmon kimono (22x23mm). f, As "e," pale green kimono (22x23mm). g, Flowers, mauve triangular panel (22x26mm). h, As "g," turquoise blue triangular panel (22x26mm). i, Flowers and leaves, light green background (22x26mm). j, As "i," lilac background (22x26mm).

Die Cut Perf. 11 (#4072a, 4072b), Die Cut Perf. (#4072c, 4072d), Die Cut Perf. 11½x11, Die Cut Perf. 11¼x11¾ (#4072i, 4072j)

2017, Jan. 10 Litho.

Self-Adhesive

4072	A3857	Sheet of 10	10.00	10.00
a.-j.		52y Any single	.95	.70
4073	A3858	Sheet of 10	16.00	16.00
a.-j.		82y Any single	1.25	.80

Souvenir Sheet

New Year 2017 (Year of the Rooster) A3859

No. 4074 — Rooster facing: a, Right. b, Left.

2017, Jan. 16 Litho. ***Perf. 13x13¼***

4074	A3859	Sheet of 2	2.75	2.75
a.		52y multi	1.00	.30
b.		82y multi	1.50	.40

No. 4074 was sold to customers as well as being a lottery prize.

Skiing A3860

Biathlon A3861

Skating A3862

Ice Hockey A3863

Curling — A3864

2017, Jan. 19 Photo. ***Perf. 13***

4075	A3860	82y multi	1.50	.50
4076	A3861	82y multi	1.50	.50
4077	A3862	82y multi	1.50	.50
4078	A3863	82y multi	1.50	.50
4079	A3864	82y multi	1.50	.50
a.		Horiz. strip of 5, #4075-4079	7.50	5.50
		Nos. 4075-4079 (5)	7.50	2.50

2017 Sapporo Asian Winter Games.

A sheet of six heart-shaped self-adhesive stamps (three denominated 52y and three denominatied 82y) was printed in limited quantities and sold only in a package containing stationery that sold for 1200y.

Miniature Sheets

A3865

Disney Characters — A3866

No. 4080: a, Mickey Mouse, orange yellow background (23x23mm). b, Minnie Mouse, orange yellow background (23x23mm). c, Mickey Mouse, apple green background (23x23mm). d, Minnie Mouse, apple green background (23x23mm). e, Mickey Mouse, lilac background (23x23mm). f, Minnie Mouse, lilac background (23x23mm). g, Mickey Mouse, rose background (22x26mm). h, Minnie Mouse, rose background (22x26mm). i, Mickey Mouse, light blue background (22x26mm). j, Minnie Mouse, light blue background (22x26mm).

No. 4081: a, Winnie the Pooh and Piglet looking at book (23x23mm). b, Winnie the Pooh in light blue frame (23x23mm). c, Winnie the Pooh and Piglet reading books (23x23mm). d, Piglet and Winnie the Pooh holding butterfly (23x23mm). e, Piglet with Winnie the Pooh holding "A," "B" and "C" (23x23mm). f, Piglet sitting on Winnie the Pooh's leg (23x23mm). g, Winnie the Pooh and letter "P" (23x23mm). h, Winnie the Pooh and Tigger (23x23mm). i, Tigger, Winnie the Pooh and Eeyore sleeping (25x22mm). j Winnie the Pooh with toys and honey pot (22x25mm).

Die Cut Perf. 14

2017, Feb. 9 **Litho.**

Self-Adhesive

4080	A3865	Sheet of 10	16.00	16.00
a.-j.		82y Any single	1.25	.80
4081	A3866	Sheet of 10	16.00	16.00
a.-j.		82y Any single	1.25	.80

Cherry Blossoms A3867

Plum Blossoms A3868

Pansies and Sweet Alyssum A3869

Snapdragons A3870

Lupines A3871

Cherry Blossoms A3872

Mimosa Blossoms A3873

Bellflowers A3874

Ornithogalum A3875

Anemones A3876

Die Cut Perf. 14

2017, Feb. 15 **Litho.**

Self-Adhesive

4082		Sheet of 10, 2 each #4082a-4082e	10.00	10.00
a.	A3867	52y multi	.95	.70
b.	A3868	52y multi	.95	.70
c.	A3869	52y multi	.95	.70
d.	A3870	52y multi	.95	.70
e.	A3871	52y multi	.95	.70
4083		Sheet of 10, 2 each #4083a-4083e	16.00	16.00
a.	A3872	82y multi	1.25	.80
b.	A3873	82y multi	1.25	.80
c.	A3874	82y multi	1.25	.80
d.	A3875	82y multi	1.25	.80
e.	A3876	82y multi	1.25	.80

Cherry Blossoms A3877

Dandelions and Clover A3878

Vegetables in Basket A3879

Bamboo Shoots A3880

Cherry Blossoms A3881

Strawberries and Mailbox A3882

Field Mustard A3883

Wreath of Flowers A3884

Die Cut Perf. (#4085a-4085b, 4086a, 4086b), Die Cut Perf. 14

2017, Feb. 24 **Litho.**

Self-Adhesive

4084		Sheet of 10, 4 #4084a, 2 each #4084b-4084d	10.00	10.00
a.	A3877	52y multi	.95	.70
b.	A3878	52y multi	.95	.70
c.	A3879	52y multi	.95	.70
d.	A3880	52y multi	.95	.70
4085		Sheet of 10, 4 #4085a, 2 each #4085b-4085d	16.00	16.00
a.	A3881	82y multi	1.25	.80
b.	A3882	82y multi	1.25	.80
c.	A3883	82y multi	1.25	.80
d.	A3884	82y multi	1.25	.80

Miniature Sheet

Southern Hemisphere Constellations — A3885

No. 4086: a, Grus and goose. b, Telescopium and telescope. c, Centaurus and centaur. d, Tucana and toucan. e, Pavo and peacock. f, Crux and cross. g, Volans and flying fish. h, Dorado and dolphinfish. i, Chamaeleon and chameleon. j, Carina and ship.

Litho. With Foil Application

2017, Mar. 3 ***Die Cut Perf. 13x13¼***

Self-Adhesive

4086	A3885	Sheet of 10	16.00	16.00
a.-j.		82y Any single	1.25	.80

This self-adhesive sheet depicting Zodiac constellations, issued Mar. 3, 2017, was printed in limited quantities and was mounted in a booklet, which was only sold together with writing paper and envelopes for 1500y.

Hydrangea A3890

Daisies A3891

Peony A3892

Lantana A3893

Hibiscus A3894

Hydrangea A3895

Sunflowers and Roses A3896

Carnations A3897

Gardenias A3898

Tulips A3899

Die Cut Perf. 10¼

2017, Apr. 4 **Litho.**

Self-Adhesive

4091		Sheet of 10, 2 each #4091a-4091e	10.00	10.00
a.	A3890	52y multi	.95	.70
b.	A3891	52y multi	.95	.70
c.	A3892	52y multi	.95	.70
d.	A3893	52y multi	.95	.70
e.	A3894	52y multi	.95	.70
4092		Sheet of 10, 2 each #4092a-4092e	16.00	16.00
a.	A3895	82y multi	1.25	.80
b.	A3896	82y multi	1.25	.80
c.	A3897	82y multi	1.25	.80
d.	A3898	82y multi	1.25	.80
e.	A3899	82y multi	1.25	.80

Miniature Sheets

A3900

My Journey A3901

No. 4093: a, Enoshima Lighthouse and sea gulls (27x26mm). b, Electric train (27x22mm). c, Enoshima (27x22mm). d, Electric train in station (27x22mm). e, Drink with lime and kiwifruit (22x26mm). f, Hamburger (22x26mm). g, Girl on beach, three sailboats (27x22mm). h, Dog on surfboard (27x22mm). i, Enoshima at night and shooting star (22x26mm). j, Rocky beach at sunset (27x22mm).

No. 4094: a, Great Buddha at Kamakura (25x31mm). b, Bicycle on sidewalk (26x22mm). c, Archer on horseback (26x22mm). d, Vegetables (25mm diameter). e, Mailbox and hydrangeas (25mm diameter). f, Hydrangeas (26x22mm). g, Bamboo grove (26x22mm). h, Bowl of anmitsu (26x22mm). i, Electric train and railroad crossing sign (26x22mm). j, Girl at Gokurakuji railroad station (26x22mm).

Die Cut Perf. 10¾ (#4093a), Die Cut Perf. (#4093f), Die Cut Perf. 10¼

2017, Apr. 14 **Litho.**

Self-Adhesive

4093	A3900	Sheet of 10	10.00	10.00
a.-j.		52y Any single	.95	.70

Die Cut Perf. (#4094a, 4094d, 4094e), Die Cut Perf. 10¼

4094	A3901	Sheet of 10	16.00	16.00
a.-j.		82y Any single	1.25	.80

A sheet of seven self-adhesive stamps (five denominated 82y and two denominated 120y) was printed in limited quantities and sold only in a package containing stationery that sold for 1200y. Value, 22.50.

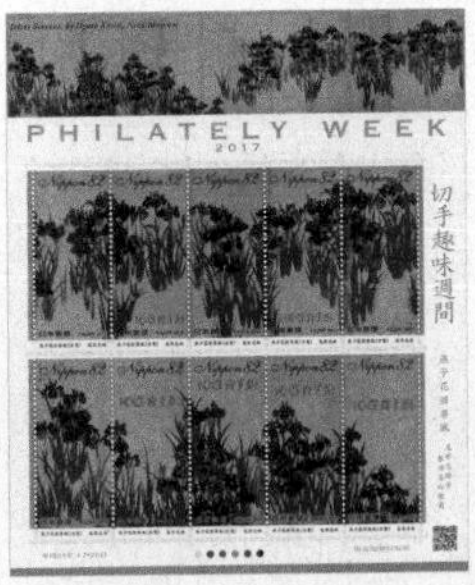

Irises, by Korin Ogata A3902

Various details of the screen painting, as shown.

2017, Apr. 20 **Photo.** ***Perf. 13x13¼***

4095	A3902	Sheet of 10	16.00	16.00
a.-j.		82y Any single	1.25	.80

Philately Week.

Products of Institute of Physical and Chemical Research
A3903

K Supercomputer
A3904

Discovery of Element 113 (Nihonium) — A3905

Photomicrographs of Plant and Animal Tissue — A3906

Cherry Blossom Mutations From Heavy Ion Beam Breeding Technique — A3907

2017, Apr. 26 Photo. ***Perf. 13¼***

4096 A3903 82y multi		1.25	.50
4097 A3904 82y multi		1.25	.50
4098 A3905 82y multi		1.25	.50
4099 A3906 82y multi		1.25	.50
4100 A3907 82y multi		1.25	.50
a.	Horiz. strip of 5, #4096-4100	7.50	5.50
	Nos. 4096-4100 (5)	6.25	2.50

Institute of Physical and Chemical Research (RIKEN), cent.

Miniature Sheet

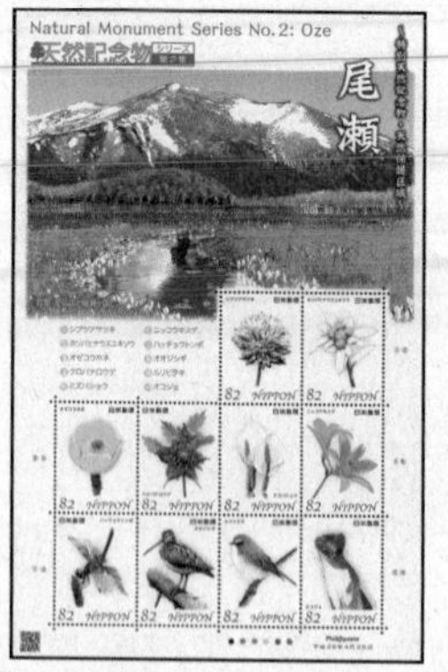

Flora and Fauna of Oze Natural Monument — A3908

No. 4101: a, Allium schoenoprasum var. shibutuense (purple flower, stamp 1). b, Leontopodium fauriei var. angustifolium (white flower, stamp 2). c, Nuphar pumilum var. ozeense (yellow flower, stamp 3). d, Potentilla palustris (red flower, stamp 4). e, Lysichiton camtschatcense (two white flowers, stamp 5). f, Hemerocallis dumortieri (orange flower, stamp 6). g, Dragonfly (stamp 7). h, Latham's snipe on thick branch (stamp 8). i, Red-flanked bluetail on thin branch (stamp 9). j, Stoat (stamp 10).

2017, Apr. 28 Litho. ***Perf. 13***

4101 A3908	Sheet of 10	16.00	16.00
a.-j.	82y Any single	1.25	.80

Miniature Sheet

Diplomatic Relations Between Japan and Denmark, 150th Anniv. — A3909

No. 4102: a, Nyhavn, Copenhagen with red boat. b, Nyhavn with green boat. c, Tivoli Gardens and swans. d, Pigs and vegetables. e, Cyclists. f, Wind generators. g, Ship and Little Mermaid. h, Thumbelina in flower. i, Kronborg Castle. j, Amalienborg and guards.

2017, May 2 Litho. ***Perf. 13***

4102 A3909	Sheet of 10	16.00	16.00
a.-j.	82y Any single	1.25	.50

Miniature Sheets

A3910

Characters From *Peanuts* Comic Strip — A3911

No. 4103: a, Snoopy with blue box (29mm diameter). b, Snoopy driving truck facing left (24x26mm). c, Snoopy in gift box (26x25mm). d, Snoopy driving truck facing right (28x23mm). e, Charlie Brown and Snoopy exchanging gifts (26x22mm). f, Snoopy pushing gift on cart (26x22mm). g, Snoopy and Woodstock carrying boxes (26x22mm). h, Snoopy with red box (23x25mm). i, Snoopy on dog house (28x36mm). j, Snoopy holding red heart (25x30mm).

No. 4104: a, Snoopy reading Valentine's Day card (29x26mm). b, Snoopy holding yellow envelope (29mm diameter). c, Snoopy dancing (32x25mm). d, Woodstock and birds in hot air balloon (24x28mm). e, Woodstock on bicycle (26x24mm). f, Snoopy, Charlie Brown and mailbox (27x23mm). g, Snoopy, Woodstock and bird with umbrellas (22x26mm). h, Woodstock and Snoopy at mailbox (26x26mm). i, Snoopy typing (26x27mm). j, Snoopy delivering letter (22x26mm).

Die Cut Perf. (#4103a), Die Cut Perf. 12¾x13 (#4103b, 4103h), Die Cut Perf. 13x12¾ (#4103c), Die Cut Perf. 13 (#4103d), Die Cut Perf. 14 (#4103e, 4103f, 4103g), Die Cut Perf. 12 (#4103i, 4103j)

2017, May 10 Litho.

Self-Adhesive

4103 A3910	Sheet of 10	16.00	16.00
a.-j.	82y Any single	1.25	.80

Die Cut Perf. 12½ (#4104a, 4104h), Die Cut Perf, (#4104b, 4104d), Die Cut Perf. 12¾x12 (#4104c), Die Cut Perf 12½x12¼ (#4104e), Die Cut Perf. 13½x13 (#4104f), Die Cut Perf. 13¾x14 (#4104g), Die Cut Perf. 12¾ (#4104i), Die Cut Perf. 13¾x13½ (#4104j)

4104 A3911	Sheet of 10	16.00	16.00
a.-j.	82y Any single	1.25	.80

Volunteer Welfare Commisioners System, Cent. — A3912

2017, May 12 Litho. ***Perf. 13***

4105 A3912 82y multi 1.50 .50

Flowers For Mourning Type of 2014 and

Cherry Blossoms
A3913

Fan With Apricot Blossoms
A3914

2017, May 15 Photo. ***Perf. 13x13¼***

4106 A3145 62y multi		1.10	.40
4107 A3913 62y multi		1.10	.40
4108 A3914 62y multi		1.10	.40
	Nos. 4106-4108 (3)	3.30	1.20

Compare type A3914 with types A3146-A3148.

"82" — A3915

Die Cut Perf. 13x13¼

2017, May 17 Litho.

Self-Adhesive

4109 A3915 82y multi 1.25 .80

A3916

A3917

A3918

A3919

Lions Clubs International, Cent. — A3920

Design: No. 4110, Logo of Lions Club International. No. 4111, Engaging our youth. No. 4112, Sharing the vision. No. 4113, Relieving the hunger. No. 4114, Protecting our environment.

2017, May 24 Litho. ***Perf. 13***

4110 A3916 82y multi		1.50	.50
4111 A3917 82y multi		1.50	.50
4112 A3918 82y multi		1.50	.50
4113 A3919 82y multi		1.50	.50
4114 A3920 82y multi		1.50	.50
a.	Vert. strip of 5, #4110-4114	7.50	5.50
	Nos. 4110-4114 (5)	7.50	2.50

Miniature Sheet

National Afforestation — A3921

No. 4115: a, Cherry blossoms. b, North Kobushi magnolia flower. c, Gentian. d, Tulips. e, Japanese bigleaf magnolia. f, Cherry blossoms, diff. g, Adder's tongue lilies. h, Kanoko lily. i, Japanese bay tree, j, Tateyama cedar tree.

2017, May 26 **Litho.** ***Perf. 13***

4115	A3921	Sheet of 10	11.00	11.00
a.-j.		62y Any single	.85	.40

Clouds A3922

Shells and Ramune Bottles A3923

Water Balloons A3924

Sunflowers A3925

Sunflowers A3926

Goldfish in Bowl A3927

Bowl of Shaved Ice A3928

Beach A3929

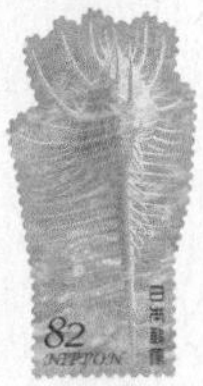

Shell A3930

Shell A3931

Marbles A3932

Watermelon Slice A3933

Die Cut Perf. 13x13¼, Die Cut Perf. 13¼x13 (#4116d, 4116e), Die Cut Perf. (#4116f)

2017, June 2 **Litho.**

Self-Adhesive

4116	Sheet of 10, #4116d, 4116e, 2 each #4116a-4116c, 4116f	12.00	12.00
a.	A3922 62y multi	1.10	.85
b.	A3923 62y multi	1.10	.85
c.	A3924 62y multi	1.10	.85
d.	A3925 62y multi	1.10	.85
e.	A3926 62y multi	1.10	.85
f.	A3927 62y multi	1.10	.85

Die Cut Perf. 13x13¼ (#4117a, 4117b), Die Cut Perf. 13 (#4117c, 4117d, 4117f), Die Cut Perf. 13¼ (#4117e)

4117	Sheet of 10, #4117c, 4117d, 2 each #4117a-4117b, 4117e-4117f	16.00	16.00
a.	A3928 82y multi	1.25	.85
b.	A3929 82y multi	1.25	.85
c.	A3930 82y multi	1.25	.85
d.	A3931 82y multi	1.25	.85
e.	A3932 82y multi	1.25	.85
f.	A3933 82y multi	1.25	.85

Miniature Sheet

Paintings A3934

No. 4118: a, Sunflowers, by Chinami Nakajima (stamp 5, 32x39mm). b, Morning Glories, by Nakajima (stamp 6, 32x28mm). c, Chinese Bellflowers, by Fumiko Hori (stamp 7, 30x32mm). d, The Flow of Mountain Seasons, by Hori (stamp 8, 32x39mm). e, Angela and the Blue Sky II, by Koji Kinutani (stamp 1, 32x28mm). f, Celebration - Flying Dragon, Sacred Gateway of Fuji, by Kinutani (stamp 2, 32x39mm). g, Early Summer, by Rieko Morita (stamp 9, 32x39mm). h, Autumn Flowers, by Morita (stamp 10, 32x28mm). i, Nachi Waterfall in the Moonlight, by Yuji Tezuka (stamp 3, 32x39mm). j, Beautiful Sky, by Tezuka (stamp 4, 32x32mm).

Die Cut Perf. 12½x13, Die Cut Perf. 13x12 (#4118b, 4118e, 4118h), Die Cut Perf. 12½ (#4118c, 4118j)

2017, June 7 **Litho.**

Self-Adhesive

4118	A3934	Sheet of 10	16.00	16.00
a.-j.		82y Any single	1.25	.80

Miniature Sheet

Japan at Night A3935

No. 4119: a, Sky Gate Bridge R, Osaka Prefecture (stamp 1). b, Meriken Park, Hyogo Prefecture (stamp 2). c, Kodaiji in autumn, Kyoto Prefecture (stamp 3). d, Nagoya Television Tower, Aichi Prefecture (stamp 4). e, Gifu Castle and Gifu, Gifu Prefecture (stamp 5). f, Shimizu Port and Mount Fuji, Shizuoka Prefecture (stamp 6). g, Lake Suwa Fireworks Festival, Nagano Prefecture (stamp 7). h, Ishiyama-dera Autumn Moon Viewing Festival, Shiga Prefecture (stamp 8). i, Echigo Hillside National Government Park, Niigata Prefecture (stamp 9). j, Seki-juku, Mie Prefecture (stamp 10).

2017, June 9 **Litho.** ***Perf. 13***

4119	A3935	Sheet of 10	16.00	16.00
a.-j.		82y Any single	1.25	.50

Dragées A3936

Jordan Almonds A3937

Dragées A3938

Macarons A3939

Dragées A3940

Konpeito Candy A3941

Die Cut Perf. 13x13¼

2017, June 23 **Photo.**

Self-Adhesive

4120	Sheet of 10, 5 each #4120a-4120b	12.00	12.00
a.	A3936 62y multi	1.25	.85
b.	A3937 62y multi	1.25	.85
4121	Sheet of 10, 5 each #4121a-4121b	16.00	16.00
a.	A3938 82y multi	1.25	.85
b.	A3939 82y multi	1.25	.85
4122	Sheet of 10, 5 each #4122a-4122b	17.50	17.50
a.	A3940 92y multi	1.40	.80
b.	A3941 92y multi	1.40	.80
	Nos. 4120-4122 (3)	45.50	45.50

Miniature Sheet

Characters From *Super Mario* Video Games — A3942

No. 4123: a, Mario with fist and leg raised (22x33mm). b, Mario mailing letter (24x25mm). c, Mario seated, reading letter (24x27mm). d, Princess Peach writing letter (23x25mm). e, Mario on Yoshi (25x23mm). f, Luigi removing letter from mailbox (23x25mm). g, Toad with mail bag (25x23mm). h, Mario pointing (24x24mm). i, Mario and Princess Peach (26x25mm). j, Princess Peach (24x24mm).

Die Cut Perf. 11¾ (#4123a), Die Cut Perf. 11 (#4123b, 4123c), Die Cut Perf. 11½x11 (#4123d, 4123f, 4123i), Die Cut Perf. 11x11½ (#4123e, 4123g), Die Cut Perf. 11½ (#4123h, 4123j)

2017, June 28 **Litho.**

Self-Adhesive

4123	A3942	Sheet of 10	16.00	16.00
a.-j.		82y Any single	1.25	.80

A3943

A3944

A3945

A3946

A3947

A3948

A3949

A3950

A3951

Penguins — A3952

Litho. With Foil Application

2017, July 5 ***Die Cut Perf. 10¼***

Self-Adhesive

4124	Sheet of 10	16.00	16.00
a.	A3943 82y multi	1.25	.80
b.	A3944 82y multi	1.25	.80
c.	A3945 82y multi	1.25	.80
d.	A3946 82y multi	1.25	.80
e.	A3947 82y multi	1.25	.80
f.	A3948 82y multi	1.25	.80
g.	A3949 82y multi	1.25	.80
h.	A3950 82y multi	1.25	.80
i.	A3951 82y multi	1.25	.80
j.	A3952 82y multi	1.25	.80

Miniature Sheet

National Museum of Western Art UNESCO World Heritage Site — A3953

No. 4125: a, Entrance to Main building (stamp 1). b, 19th Century Hall (stamp 2). c, Aerial view of Main building (stamp 3). d, Main building's second-floor exhibition room (stamp 4). e, Entrance to Main building, diff (stamp 5). f, The Thinker, statue by Auguste Rodin (stamp 6). g, Roses, by Vincent van Gogh (stamp 7). h, Boy in Flowers (Jacques Hoschedé), by Edouard Manet (stamp 8). i, The Port of Saint-Tropez, by Paul Signac (stamp 9). j, Water Lilies, by Claude Monet (stamp 10).

2017, July 14 **Litho.** ***Perf. 13¾x14¼***

4125	A3953	Sheet of 10	16.00	16.00
a.-j.		82y Any single	1.25	.50

Flowers and "Thank You" A3954 — Cupcake A3955

Tea Cup and Tea Pot A3956 — Stars A3957

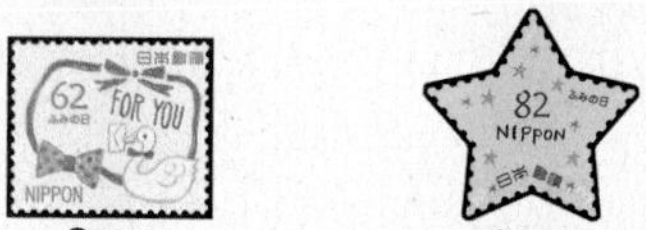

Swan Holding Letter A3958 — Stars A3959

Dots and "Thank You" A3960 — Elephant and Flower A3961

Gift A3962 — Ribbon With Bow A3963

Die Cut Perf. 13x13¼ (#4126), Die Cut Perf. 13x12¾ (#4127, 4129, 4132, 4134), Die Cut Perf. 13½x13¼ (#4128, 4130, 4133, 4135), Die Cut Perf. 10¾ (#4131)

2017, July 21 **Litho.**

Booklet Stamps Self-Adhesive

4126	A3954 62y multi	1.10	.80
4127	A3955 62y multi	1.10	.80
4128	A3956 62y multi	1.10	.80
4129	A3957 62y multi	1.10	.80
4130	A3958 62y multi	1.10	.80
a.	Booklet pane of 5, #4126-4130	6.00	6.00
4131	A3959 82y multi	1.25	.80
4132	A3960 82y multi	1.25	.80
4133	A3961 82y multi	1.25	.80
4134	A3962 82y multi	1.25	.80
4135	A3963 82y multi	1.25	.80
a.	Booklet pane of 5, #4131-4135	8.00	8.00
	Nos. 4126-4135 (10)	11.75	8.00

Letter Writing Day.

Rilakkuma A3964 — Kiiroitori and Korilakkuma A3965

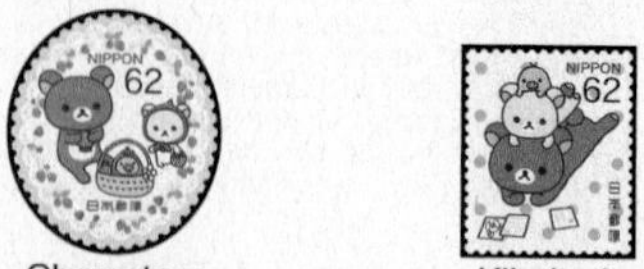

Characters Picking Strawberries A3966 — Kiiroitori, Korilakkuma and Rilakkuma A3967

Characters With Flowers A3968 — Characters and Skerwered Dumplings A3969

Characters in Tub A3970 — Characters and Lemon A3971

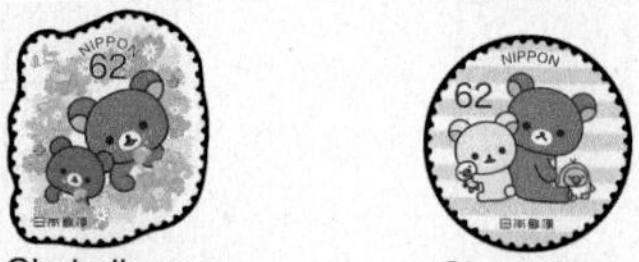

Chairoikoguma and Rilakkuma A3972 — Characters With Toy A3973

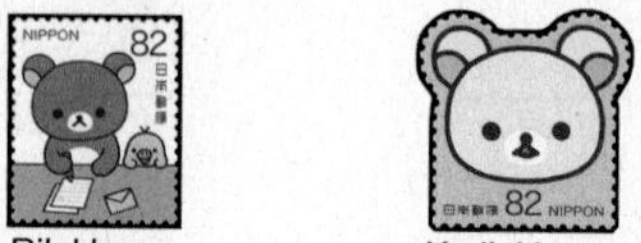

Rilakkuma and Kiiroitori A3974 — Korilakkuma A3975

Kiiroitori A3976 — Rilakkuma A3977

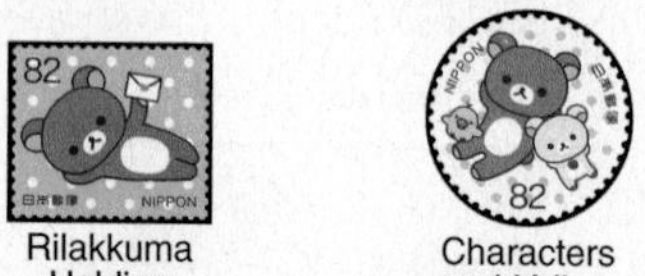

Rilakkuma Holding Letter A3978 — Characters and Yellow Dots A3979

Rilakkuma Eating A3980 — Korilakkuma and Toys A3981

Rilakkuma and Kiiroitori A3982 — Rilakkuma A3983

Die Cut Perf. 13x13¼ (#4136a, 4136b, 4136d, 4136e), Die Cut Perf. (#4136c, 4136i, 4136j), Die Cut Perf. 11½x11¼ (#4136f), Die Cut Perf. 11½ (#4136g), Die Cut Perf. 13¼x13 (#4136h)

2017, July 26 **Litho.**

Self-Adhesive

4136	Sheet of 10	12.00	12.00
a.	A3964 62y multi	1.10	.80
b.	A3965 62y multi	1.10	.80
c.	A3966 62y multi	1.10	.80
d.	A3967 62y multi	1.10	.80
e.	A3968 62y multi	1.10	.80
f.	A3969 62y multi	1.10	.80
g.	A3970 62y multi	1.10	.80
h.	A3971 62y multi	1.10	.80
i.	A3972 62y multi	1.10	.80
j.	A3973 62y multi	1.10	.80

Die Cut Perf. 13x13¼ (#4137a, 4137g, 4137h, 4137i), Die Cut Perf 11¾ (#4137b, 4137d), Die Cut Perf. 11 (#4132c), Die Cut Perf. 13¼x13 (#4137e, 4137j), Die Cut Perf. (#4137f)

4137	Sheet of 10	16.00	16.00
a.	A3974 82y multi	1.25	.80
b.	A3975 82y multi	1.25	.80
c.	A3976 82y multi	1.25	.80
d.	A3977 82y multi	1.25	.80
e.	A3978 82y multi	1.25	.80
f.	A3979 82y multi	1.25	.80
g.	A3980 82y multi	1.25	.80
h.	A3981 82y multi	1.25	.80
i.	A3982 82y multi	1.25	.80
j.	A3983 82y multi	1.25	.80

Miniature Sheet

Kimonos A3984

No. 4138: a, Green and red kimono (26x27mm). b, Woman in Heian era kimono (light green background, 22x28mm). c, Beige and brown kimono (26x27mm). d, Woman in Muromachi era kimono (light brown and brown background, 22x28mm). e, Beige and brown kimono with checkerboard pattern and flowers (26x27mm). f, Woman in Azuchi-Momoyama era kimono (pale orange background, 22x28mm). g, Blue and red kimono with flowers (26x27mm). h, Woman in Edo era kimono (light blue background, 22x28mm). i, Purple kimono with flowers and cart (26x27mm). j, Modern kimono (buff background, 22x28mm).

Die Cut Perf. 11x10¼ (#4138a, 4138c, 4138e, 4138g, 4138i), Die Cut Perf. 11¾x11½ (#4138b, 4138d, 4138f, 4138h, 4138j)

2017, Aug. 4 **Litho.**

Self-Adhesive

4138	A3984	Sheet of 10	16.00	16.00
a.-j.		82y Any single	1.25	.80

A3985

A3986

A3987

A3988

A3989

A3990

A3991

A3992

A3993

Women's Fashion — A3994

Die Cut Perf. 11¼x11

2017, Aug. 9 **Litho.**

Self-Adhesive

4139	Sheet of 10	16.00	16.00
a.	A3985 82y multi	1.25	.80
b.	A3986 82y multi	1.25	.80
c.	A3987 82y multi	1.25	.80
d.	A3988 82y multi	1.25	.80
e.	A3989 82y multi	1.25	.80
f.	A3990 82y multi	1.25	.80
g.	A3991 82y multi	1.25	.80
h.	A3992 82y multi	1.25	.80
i.	A3993 82y multi	1.25	.80
j.	A3994 82y multi	1.25	.80

Butterflies A3995

Deer A3996

Rabbits A3997

Horses A3998

Dragonflies A3999

Peacock and Peony A4000

Geese and Clover A4001

Mandarin Ducks A4002

Egrets A4003

Plovers A4004

Die Cut Perf. (#4140a), Die Cut Perf. 11¼x11¾ (#4140b, 4140e, 4141b, 4141d, 4141e), Die Cut Perf. 11¾x11¼ (#4140c, 4140d, 4141c), Die Cut Perf. 11¼ (#4141a)

2017, Aug. 18 **Litho.**

Self-Adhesive

4140	Sheet of 10, 2 each #4140a-4140e	12.00	12.00
a.	A3995 62y multi	1.00	.80
b.	A3996 62y multi	1.00	.80
c.	A3997 62y multi	1.00	.80
d.	A3998 62y multi	1.00	.80
e.	A3999 62y multi	1.00	.80
4141	Sheet of 10, 2 each #4141a-4141e	16.00	16.00
a.	A4000 82y multi	1.25	.80
b.	A4001 82y multi	1.25	.80
c.	A4002 82y multi	1.25	.80
d.	A4003 82y multi	1.50	.80
e.	A4004 82y multi	1.25	.80

Mailbox in Autumn A4005

Girl and Mushrooms A4006

Chestnuts A4007

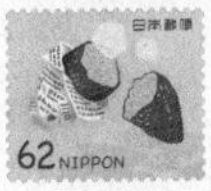
Baked Sweet Potato A4008

Girl Raking Leaves A4009

House and Trees A4010

Rabbits Pounding Rice A4011

Child Reading in Moonlight A4012

Mushrooms on Brazier A4013

Girl in Library A4014

Dragonflies Over Rice Field A4015

Mailbox in Autumn A4016

Fish on Brazier — A4017

Die Cut Perf. 13x13¼ (#4142a, 4142b, 4142e, 4142f, 4143b, 4143d, 4143f), Die Cut Perf. (#4142c, 4143a, 4143c), Die Cut Perf. 13¼x13 (#4142d, 4143e), Die Cut Perf. 12 (#4143g)

2017, Aug. 23 **Litho.**

Self-Adhesive

4142	Sheet of 10, #4142a, 4142b, 2 each #4142c-4142f	12.50	12.50
a.	A4005 62y multi	1.00	.80
b.	A4006 62y multi	1.00	.80
c.	A4007 62y multi	1.00	.80
d.	A4008 62y multi	1.00	.80
e.	A4009 62y multi	1.00	.80
f.	A4010 62y multi	1.00	.80
4143	Sheet of 10, #4143a, 4143c, 4143f, 4143g, 2 each #4143b, 4143d, 4143e	16.00	16.00
a.	A4011 82y multi	1.25	.80
b.	A4012 82y multi	1.25	.80
c.	A4013 82y multi	1.25	.80
d.	A4014 82y multi	1.25	.80
e.	A4015 82y multi	1.25	.80
f.	A4016 82y multi	1.25	.80
g.	A4017 82y multi	1.25	.80

Miniature Sheet

72nd National Athletic Meet, Ehime A4018

No. 4144: a, Kendo. b, Mount Ishizuchi. c, Rowing. d, Shimanami Kaido and bridge. e, Weight lifting. f, Bathhouse at Dogo Onsen Hot Springs. g, Archery. h, Mikan oranges. i, Basketball. j, Red seabream.

2017, Aug. 30 **Litho.** ***Perf. 13½***

4144	A4018	Sheet of 10	16.00	16.00
a.-j.		82y Any single	1.25	.80

The Koya Tama River, Kii Province, by Eizan Kikukawa A4019

Mount Hiyori and Toba Bay, Shima Province, by Hiroshige Utagawa A4020

Yosooi and Matsumura of the Matsubaya, by Utamaro Kitagawa A4021

Mount Inasa at Nagasaki, Hizen Province, by Hiroshige Utagawa A4022

Kisegawa of the Matsubaya, by Utamaro Kitagawa A4023

Daijingu Shrine at Kashima, Hitachi Province, by Hiroshige Utagawa A4024

Beauty with Ball and Fan, by Utamaro Kitagawa A4025

Kanegasaka, Tanba Province, by Hiroshige Utagawa A4026

Hanaogi of the Ogiya, by Eishi Chobunsai A4027

Clear Evening on the Coast, Tsushima Province, by Hiroshige Utagawa A4028

2017, Sept. 6 **Litho.** ***Perf. 13½***

4145	Sheet of 10	16.00	16.00
a.	A4019 82y multi	1.25	.80
b.	A4020 82y multi	1.25	.80
c.	A4021 82y multi	1.25	.80
d.	A4022 82y multi	1.25	.80
e.	A4023 82y multi	1.25	.80
f.	A4024 82y multi	1.25	.80
g.	A4025 82y multi	1.25	.80
h.	A4026 82y multi	1.25	.80
i.	A4027 82y multi	1.25	.80
j.	A4028 82y multi	1.25	.80

Miniature Sheets

A4029

Posukuma and Friends — A4030

No. 4146: a Two bears near mailbox. b, Two bears, one with letter, near mailbox. c, Three bears. d, Large bear delivering letter to small bear. e, Bear and flowers. f, Two bears, tree, letter in mailbox. g, Bear with violin. h, Mailbox, bear licking envelope. i, Two bears on swings. j, Crying bear and letter.

No. 4147 — Tree and: a, Two bears with raised arms, two beamed yellow sixteenth notes. b, Bear and owl, red orange eighth note. c, Two bears, one with mail bag, with arms crossed, green eighth note. d, Two bears, one with crossed arms, two beamed yellow sixteenth notes. e, Two bears waving, red orange eighth note. f, Two bears with mail bags waving, red eighth note. g, Two bears, one with mail bag, sitting, red eighth note. h, Two bears sitting, green eighth note. i, Two bears waving, two beamed blue sixteenth notes. j, Seven bears and owl, red orange eighth note and two beamed blue sixteenth notes.

Die Cut Perf. 13½x13¼

2017, Sept. 15 **Litho.**

Self-Adhesive

4146	A4029	Sheet of 10	12.00	12.00
a.-j.		62y Any single	1.00	.80
4147	A4030	Sheet of 10	16.00	16.00
a.-j.		82y Any single	1.25	.80

Fringed Pinks A4031

Gentian Flowers A4032

Mandarin Oranges A4033

Straw Sandals A4034

Grapes A4035

Patrinia Flowers A4036

Morning Glories A4037

Dragonflies A4038

Rough Horsetails A4039

Fallen Leaves A4040

Red Maple Leaves A4041

Moon, Rabbit and Flowers A4042

Mouse, Rice and Rice Bags A4043

Chestnuts A4044

Bush Clover A4045

Hen and Chicks A4046

Persimmon A4047

Walnuts A4048

Grass A4049

Eurasian Siskin A4050

Die Cut Perf. 13x13¼

2017, Sept. 20 **Litho.**

Self-Adhesive

4148	Sheet of 10	12.00	12.00
a.	A4031 62y multi	1.00	.80
b.	A4032 62y multi	1.00	.80
c.	A4033 62y multi	1.00	.80
d.	A4034 62y multi	1.00	.80
e.	A4035 62y multi	1.00	.80
f.	A4036 62y multi	1.00	.80
g.	A4037 62y multi	1.00	.80
h.	A4038 62y multi	1.00	.80
i.	A4039 62y multi	1.00	.80
j.	A4040 62y multi	1.00	.80
4149	Sheet of 10	16.00	16.00
a.	A4041 82y multi	1.25	.80
b.	A4042 82y multi	1.25	.80
c.	A4043 82y multi	1.25	.80
d.	A4044 82y multi	1.25	.80
e.	A4045 82y multi	1.25	.80
f.	A4046 82y multi	1.25	.80
g.	A4047 82y multi	1.25	.80
h.	A4048 82y multi	1.25	.80
i.	A4049 82y multi	1.25	.80
j.	A4050 82y multi	1.25	.80

Miniature Sheet

Japan at Night A4051

No. 4150: a, Kobe and Osaka Bay (stamp 1). b, Kobe and Osaka Bay, diff (stamp 2). c, Fireworks at Grass Burning Festival (stamp 3). d, Nabana no Sato (stamp 4). e, Hashigui Rocks (stamp 5). f, Unazzuki Onsen (stamp 6). g, Laguna Ten Bosch Amusement Park (stamp 7). h, Shiroyone Senmaida (stamp 8). i, Echizen City and Sabae (stamp 9). j, Gakunan electric train at station (stamp 10).

2017, Sept. 29 **Litho.** ***Perf. 13***

4150	A4051 Sheet of 10	16.00	16.00
a.-j.	82y Any single	1.25	.80

Kyoto Railway Museum, Class 230 Steam Locomotive A4052

Japan National Railways 14-700 Series Locomotive A4053

Nagoya Railroad 8800 Panorama DX Series Locomotive A4054

Izukyu 2100 Series Locomotive A4055

Hokkaido Railway Company KiHa 84/83 Series Locomotive A4056

Odakyu Electric Railway 10000 Series Locomotive A4057

Tobu Railway 100 Series Locomotive A4058

Kyushu Railway 787 Series Locomotive A4059

Central and West Japan Railways 285 Series Locomotive A4060

Hanshin 5700 Series Locomotive A4061

Class 230 Steam Locomotive A4062

Odakyu Electric Railway 10000 Series Locomotive A4063

Japan National Railways 14-700 Series Locomotive A4064

Tobu Railway 100 Series Locomotive A4065

Nagoya Railroad 8800 Panorama DX Series Locomotive A4066

Kyushu Railway 787 Series Locomotive A4067

Izukyu 2100 Series Locomotive A4068

Central and West Japan Railways 285 Series Locomotive A4069

Hokkaido Railway Company KiHa 84/83 Series Locomotive A4070

Hanshin 5700 Series Locomotive A4071

2017, Oct. 4 **Litho.** ***Perf. 13***

4151	Sheet of 10	16.00	16.00
a.	A4052 82y multi	1.25	.50
b.	A4053 82y multi	1.25	.50
c.	A4054 82y multi	1.25	.50
d.	A4055 82y multi	1.25	.50
e.	A4056 82y multi	1.25	.50
f.	A4057 82y multi	1.25	.50
g.	A4058 82y multi	1.25	.50
h.	A4059 82y multi	1.25	.50
i.	A4060 82y multi	1.25	.50
j.	A4061 82y multi	1.25	.50
4152	Sheet of 10	16.00	16.00
a.	A4062 82y multi	1.25	.50
b.	A4063 82y multi	1.25	.50
c.	A4064 82y multi	1.25	.50
d.	A4065 82y multi	1.25	.50
e.	A4066 82y multi	1.25	.50
f.	A4067 82y multi	1.25	.50
g.	A4068 82y multi	1.25	.50
h.	A4069 82y multi	1.25	.50
i.	A4070 82y multi	1.25	.50
j.	A4071 82y multi	1.25	.50

A4072

International Letter Writing Week — A4073

Art by Hirogshige: No. 4153, Drooping Cherry Tree with Small Bird (upper half, denomination at UR). b, Drooping Cherry Trees with Small Bird (lower half, denomination at LL).

90y, Travelers Crossing the Abe River West of the Fuchu Station. 110y, Goyu Station at Nightfall. 130y, Travelers at the Oi River.

2017, Oct. 6 **Litho.** ***Perf. 14x14¼***

4153	70y multi	1.10	.50
4154	70y multi	1.10	.50
a.	A4072 Vert. pair, #4153-4154	2.50	1.90
	Perf. 13		
4155	A4073 90y multi	1.75	.50
4156	A4073 110y multi	2.25	.50
4157	A4073 130y multi	2.50	.50
	Nos. 4153-4157 (5)	8.70	2.50

See listing of No. 4448 for images of each Hiroshige print.

Miniature Sheets

Puppies A4074

Adult Dogs A4075

Nos. 4158 and 4159: a, Labrador retriever. b, Bernese Mountain dog. c, Akita. d, Old English sheepdog. e, Chow chow. f, German shepherd. g, Border collie. h, Siberian husky. i, Bulldog. j, Dalmatian.

Die Cut Perf. 11

2017, Oct. 11 **Litho.**

Self-Adhesive

4158	A4074 Sheet of 10	12.00	12.00
a.-j.	62y Any single	1.00	.80
4159	A4075 Sheet of 10	16.00	16.00
a.-j.	82y Any single	1.25	.80

A4076 A4077

Flowers
A4078 A4079

A4080 A4081

Lace Flowers
A4082 A4083

Die Cut Perf. 13x13¼ (#4160a-4160b), Die Cut Perf. 13 (#4161a-4161c), Die Cut Perf. (#4160c-4160d, 4161d)

2017, Oct. 20 **Litho.**

Self-Adhesive

4160	Sheet of 10, 3 each #4160a-4160b, 2 each #4160c-4160d	12.00	12.00
a.	A4076 62y multi	1.00	.80
b.	A4077 62y multi	1.00	.80
c.	A4078 62y multi	1.00	.80
d.	A4079 62y multi	1.00	.80
4161	Sheet of 10, 3 each #4161a-4161b, 2 each #4161c-4161d	16.00	16.00
a.	A4080 82y multi	1.25	.80
b.	A4081 82y multi	1.25	.80
c.	A4082 82y multi	1.25	.80
d.	A4083 82y multi	1.25	.80

Rice Balls and Sushi A4084

No. 4162: a, Futomaki sushi (27mm diameter). b, Rice ball with kelp (30x27mm). c, Rice ball with pickled plum (30x27mm). d, Rice ball with salmon (30x27mm). e, Rice ball with baby sardines (33x20mm). f, Tofu pockets with sushi rice (33x20mm). g, Rice ball with red beans (30x27mm). h, Tempura rice ball (30x28mm). i, Rice ball with sesame seeds and salt (30x27mm). j, Rice ball with edamame beans (30mm diameter).

Die Cut Perf. 12¾ (#4162b-4162d, 4162g-4162i), Die Cut Perf. 12½ (#4162e-4162f), Die Cut Perf. (#4162a, 4162j)

2017, Oct. 24 **Litho.**

Self-Adhesive

4162	A4084	Booklet pane of 10	16.00	16.00
a.-j.		82y Any single	1.25	.80

Japanese Foods A4085

Designs: No. 4163, Dango (dumplings on skewers). No. 4164, Taiyaki (fish-shaped bean paste cake).

2017, Nov. 1 **Litho.** ***Perf. 13¼x13***

4163	18y multi	.35	.25
4164	18y multi	.35	.25
a.	A4085 Horiz. pair, #4163-4164	.70	.55

A4086

A4087

New Year 2018 (Year of the Dog)

A4088 A4089

2017, Nov. 1 **Litho.** ***Perf. 13x13¼***

4165	A4086	52y gold & multi	.95	.30
4166	A4087	82y gold & multi	1.50	.40

Photo. & Typo.

Perf. 13¼

4167	A4088	52y +3y multi	1.25	.40
4168	A4089	82y +3y gold & multi	1.75	.40
		Nos. 4165-4168 (4)	5.45	1.50

The stamps shown above were printed in a sheet offered as a prize for the 2018 New Year lottery. This sheet was not sold to the public.

Miniature Sheets

A4090

Gifts From the Forest A4091

No. 4169: a, Bird in tree. b, Hardwood trees (trees with yellowed leaves in foreground). c, Conifers. d, Conifer branch with cones. e, Hardwood trees with conifers in background. f, Conifers with hardwood tree in background. g, Purple berries on tree. h, Man preparing to chop down tree. i, Flying squirrel and trees. j, Conifers in fog.

No. 4170: a, Three trees (22x26mm). b, Bird and tree (22x26mm). c, Two birds on tree branches (22x26mm). d, Hawk in flight (30x30mm). e, Magnolia blossom (30x30mm). f, Woodpecker (22x26mm). g, Yew tree branches and berries (22x26mm). h, Flying squirrel (22x26mm). i, Tree in winter (30x30mm). j, Maple samaras (30x30mm).

Die Cut Perf. 13x13¼ (#4169a-4169j, 4170a-4170c, 4170f-4170h), Die Cut Perf. 13¼ (#4170d-4170e, 4170i-4170j)

2017, Nov. 8 **Litho.**

Self-Adhesive

4169	A4090	Sheet of 10	12.00	12.00
a.-j.		62y Any single	1.00	.80
4170	A4091	Sheet of 10	16.00	16.00
a.-j.		82y Any single	1.25	.80

Miniature Sheet

Diplomatic Relations Between Japan and the Maldive Islands, 50th Anniv. — A4092

No. 4171: a, Atolls. b, Shadows of palm trees. c, Beach at tourist resort. d, Clouds over island. e, Palm tree on beach. f, Maldives anemonefish. g, Manta ray. i, Aerial view of Malé. j, Coconuts. k, Palm trees and ocean with sun approaching horizon.

2017, Nov. 14 **Litho.** ***Perf. 13***

4171	A4092	Sheet of 10	16.00	16.00
a.-j.		82y Any single	1.25	.80

Miniature Sheets

A4093

A4094

Greetings — A4095

No. 4172: a, Sun with circle of blue diamonds. b, Sun with circle of orange diamonds. c, Girl, cat, shooting star, horiz. d, Girl, guitar and cat. e, Girl and cat at table, rainbow. f, Dove carrying letter.

No. 4173: a, Gifts, letters on blue pennants, horiz. b, Gifts, letters on pink pennants, horiz. c, Birthday cake. d, Dog wearing birthday hat. e, Balloons. f, Cracker and streamers, horiz.

No. 4174: a, Tuxedo and tie (22x26mm). b, Gown and necklace (22x26mm). c, Champagne bottle and flutes (22x26mm). d, Cut jewel (22x26mm). e, Tray of canapés (22x26mm). f, Flowers in vase (22x32mm).

Die Cut Perf. 13x13¼, 13¼x13, Die Cut Perf. 13 (#4174f)

2017, Nov. 22 **Litho.**

Self-Adhesive

4172	A4093	Sheet of 10, #4172a-4172b, 2 each #4172c-4172f	12.00	12.00
a.-f.		62y Any single	1.00	.80
4173	A4094	Sheet of 10, #4173a-4173b, 2 each #4173c-4173f	16.00	16.00
a.-f.		82y Any single	1.25	.80
4174	A4095	Sheet of 10, #4174a-4174b, 2 each #4174c-4174f	17.00	17.00
a.-f.		92y Any single	1.40	.80
		Nos. 4172-4174 (3)	45.00	

Miniature Sheets

A4096

Winter Greetings — A4097

No. 4175: a, Buildings in snow (22x26mm). b, Boy holding hot drink in snow (22x26mm). c, Cup of coffee with cream snowman (22x24mm). d, Wood stove (22x26mm). e, Woman holding shopping bag (22x26mm). f, Street lamps in snow (22x26mm).

No. 4176: a, Rabbit facing left (22x26mm). b, Rabbit facing right (22x26mm). c, Snowman with stick hands and shovel (22x26mm). d, Snowman with mitten on stick hand and shovel (22x26mm). e, Snow-covered house (22x26mm). f, Child with telescope, mountains in background (22x26mm). g, Snow globe (23x22mm). h, Child and starry night (22x26mm).

Die Cut Perf. 13x13¼, Die Cut Perf. (#4175c, 4176g)

2017, Dec. 1 **Litho.**

Self-Adhesive

4175	A4096	Sheet of 10, #4175a-4175b, 2 each #4175c-4175f	12.00	12.00
a.-f.		62y Any single	1.00	.80
4176	A4097	Sheet of 10, #4176a-4176f, 2 each #4176g-4176h	16.00	16.00
a.-h.		82y Any single	1.25	.80

Thunberg Spirea A4098

Ranunculus A4099

Freesia and Leucocoryne A4100

Camellias A4101

Plum Blossoms A4102

Forsythia A4103

Cyclamen A4104

Violas A4105

Camellias A4106

Plum Blossoms A4107

Die Cut Perf. 13x13¼

2017, Dec. 13 **Litho.**

Self-Adhesive

4177	Sheet of 10, 2 each #4177a-4177e	12.00	12.00
a.	A4098 62y multi	1.00	.80
b.	A4099 62y multi	1.00	.80
c.	A4100 62y multi	1.00	.80
d.	A4101 62y multi	1.00	.80
e.	A4102 62y multi	1.00	.80
4178	Sheet of 10, 2 each #4178a-4178e	16.00	16.00
a.	A4103 82y multi	1.25	.80
b.	A4104 82y multi	1.25	.80
c.	A4105 82y multi	1.25	.80
d.	A4106 82y multi	1.25	.80
e.	A4107 82y multi	1.25	.80

Miniature Sheet

Illustrations from Children's Book, *Where's the Fish?* by Taro Gomi — A4108

No. 4179: a, Three fish (33mm diameter). b, Fish facing left (32x24mm). c, Fish facing right (32x24mm). d, Fish in water facing right (29x23mm). e, Fish on television screen (30x30mm). f, Fish and children's toys (30x30mm). g, Fish on curtain (30x30mm). h, Fish on flower stem (28x30mm). i, Fish in candy jar (23x30mm). j, Fish in fruit bowl (30x30mm).

Die Cut Perf. (#4179a-4179d), Die Cut Perf. 13¼x13½ (#4169e-4169g, 4169j), Die Cut Perf. 13x12¾ (#4169h)

2017, Dec. 20 **Litho.**

Self-Adhesive

4179	A4108	Sheet of 10	16.00	16.00
a.-j.		82y Any single	1.25	.80

Kangi Temple Shoden Hall, Kumagaya
A4109

Main Hall of Tsukiji Hongan-ji, Tokyo — A4110

Photo. & Engr.

2018, Jan. 5 ***Perf. 13¼***

4180 A4109 82y multi		1.25	.50
4181 A4110 82y multi		1.25	.50
a.	Vert. pair, #4180-4181	3.00	2.25

Miniature Sheets

A4111

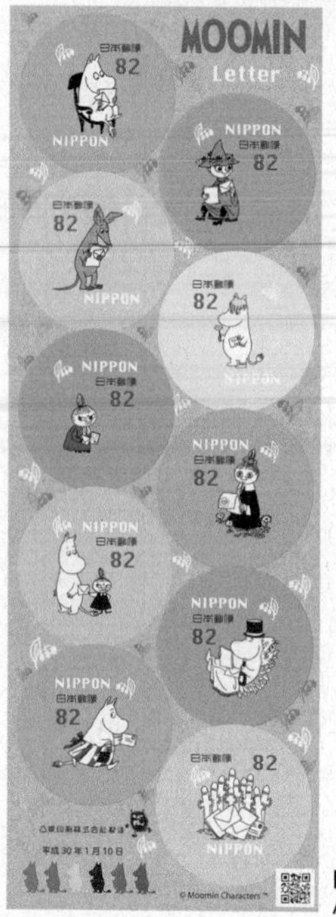

Moomins
A4112

No. 4182: a, Moominpappa at typewwriter. b, Moominmamma cooking. c, Snork Maiden knitting. d, Hemulen with stamp album. e, Too-Ticky with hammer. f, Snufkin with shell at ear. g, Little My and eyeglasses. h, Moomin with pencil and drawing. i, Moomin and Snufkin in tree. j, Moomin family creating picture.

No. 4183: a, Moomin in chair reading letter. b, Snufkin reading letter. c, Sniff reading letter. d, Snork Maiden holding flower and letter. e, Little My holding letter. f, Mymble sitting near flowers reading letter. g, Little My handing letter to Moomin. h, Moominpappa holding letter and bottle. i, Moominmamma holding letter and handbag. j, Hattifatteners with letters.

2018, Jan. 10 Litho. ***Die Cut Perf.***
Self-Adhesive

4182 A4111	Sheet of 10	12.00	12.00
a.-j.	62y Any single	1.00	.80

Die Cut Perf. 13x13¼

4183 A4112	Sheet of 10	16.00	16.00
a.-j.	82y Any single	1.25	.80

A4113

A4114

A4115

A4116

A4117

A4118

A4119

A4120

A4121

Traditional Japanese Designs — A4122

Die Cut Perf. 13

2018, Jan. 23 **Litho.**

Self-Adhesive

4184	Sheet of 10, 2 each #4184a-4184e	12.00	12.00
a.	A4113 62y multi	1.00	.80
b.	A4114 62y multi	1.00	.80
c.	A4115 62y multi	1.00	.80
d.	A4116 62y multi	1.00	.80
e.	A4117 62y multi	1.00	.80

Die Cut Perf. 12x12¼

4185	Sheet of 10, 2 each #4185a-4185e	16.00	16.00
a.	A4118 82y multi	1.25	.80
b.	A4119 82y multi	1.25	.80
c.	A4120 82y multi	1.25	.80
d.	A4121 82y multi	1.25	.80
e.	A4122 82y multi	1.25	.80

Miniature Sheet

Heavenly Bodies
A4123

No. 4186: a, Horsehead Nebula (22x27mm). b, Orion Nebula (Messier 42) (22x27mm). c, Pillars of Creation in Eagle Nebula (22x27mm). d, S106 star-forming region (22x27mm). e, Orion Nebula, diff. (22x27mm). f, Iota Orionis star cluster (22x27mm). g, Hale-Bopp Comet (26x30mm oval). h, Sun and solar flare (22x27mm). i, Mercury (22x27mm). j, Venus (22x27mm).

Die Cut Perf. (#4186g), Die Cut Perf. 13x13¼

Litho. With Holographic Foil Affixed

2018, Feb. 7 **Self-Adhesive**

4186 A4123	Sheet of 10	16.00	16.00
a.-j.	82y Any single	1.25	.80

Cat
A4124

Cat on Roof
A4125

Cat
A4126

Cat's Paw Prints
A4127

Cat on Tree
A4128

Cat's Tail
A4129

Cat
A4130

Cat
A4131

Cat in Tree
A4132

Cat and Kitten
A4133

Sleeping Cat
A4134

Cat
A4135

Cat Under Chair
A4136

Cat in Bag
A4137

Cat and Cards
A4138

Kittens in Bowl
A4139

Sleeping Cat
A4140

Cat and Flowers
A4141

Sleeping Cat
A4142

Cat's Paw
A4143

Die Cut Perf. 13¼x13 (horiz. stamps), Die Cut Perf. 13x13¼ (vert. stamps), Die Cut Perf. (#4187f, 4188j)

2018, Feb. 22 **Litho.**

Self-Adhesive

4187	Sheet of 10	12.50	12.50
a.	A4124 62y multi	1.00	.80
b.	A4125 62y multi	1.00	.80
c.	A4126 62y multi	1.00	.80
d.	A4127 62y multi	1.00	.80
e.	A4128 62y multi	1.00	.80
f.	A4129 62y multi	1.00	.80
g.	A4130 62y multi	1.00	.80
h.	A4131 62y multi	1.00	.80
i.	A4132 62y multi	1.00	.80
j.	A4133 62y multi	1.00	.80
4188	Sheet of 10	16.00	16.00
a.	A4134 82y multi	1.25	.80
b.	A4135 82y multi	1.25	.80
c.	A4136 82y multi	1.25	.80
d.	A4137 82y multi	1.25	.80
e.	A4138 82y multi	1.25	.80
f.	A4139 82y multi	1.25	.80
g.	A4140 82y multi	1.25	.80
h.	A4141 82y multi	1.25	.80
i.	A4142 82y multi	1.25	.80
j.	A4143 82y multi	1.25	.80

Miniature Sheets

A4144

My Journey
A4145

No. 4189: a, Nagoya Castle, vert. b, Shinkansen train and Mt. Fuji. c, Cherry blossoms and Mt. Fuji. d, Terraced tea fields and Mt. Fuji. e, Tea service. f, Pine tree and Mt. Fuji. g, Shrine and cherry blossoms. h, Torii and Mt. Fuji. i, Waterfall. j, Cattle in pasture and Mt. Fuji.

No. 4190: a, Cherry blossoms and Mt. Fuji (22x30mm). b, Peach tree and Mt. Fuji (26x22mm). c, Peach blossoms (26x22mm). d, Grapes (22x26mm). e, Table with food and wine, Mt. Fuji (22x26mm). f, Hot spring and Mt. Fuji (22x26mm). g, Sun over Mt. Fuji and Lake Tanuki (22x26mm). h, Temples by pond, Mt. Fuji (22x26mm). i, Swan Lake Ferry on Lake Yamanaka, Mt. Fuji (22x26mm). j, Phlox flowers near lake, Mt. Fuji (22x26mm)

Die Cut Perf. 13¼ (#4189a), Die Cut Perf. 13x13¼ (#4190a, 4190d), Die Cut Perf. 13¼x13

2018, Mar. 2 **Photo.**

Self-Adhesive

4189 A4144 Sheet of 10 12.50 12.50
a.-j. 62y Any single 1.00 .80
4190 A4145 Sheet of 10 16.00 16.00
a.-j. 82y Any single 1.25 .80

Cherry Blossoms
A4146

Plants
A4147

Tulips
A4148

Rape Blossoms
A4149

Strawberry Plant and Flowers
A4150

Cherry Blossoms
A4151

Flowers
A4152

Dandelions
A4153

Strawberries
A4154

Sprout
A4155

Die Cut Perf. (#4191a-4191b, 4192a-4192b), Die Cut Perf. 13x13¼

2018, Mar. 9 **Litho.**

Self-Adhesive

4191 Sheet of 10, 2 each #4191a-4191e 12.50 12.50
a. A4146 62y gold & multi 1.00 .80
b. A4147 62y gold & multi 1.00 .80
c. A4148 62y gold & multi 1.00 .80
d. A4149 62y gold & multi 1.00 .80
e. A4150 62y gold & multi 1.00 .80
4192 Sheet of 10, 2 each #4192a-4192e 16.00 16.00
a. A4151 82y gold & multi 1.25 .80
b. A4152 82y gold & multi 1.25 .80
c. A4153 82y gold & multi 1.25 .80
d. A4154 82y gold & multi 1.25 .80
e. A4155 82y gold & multi 1.25 .80

Roses
A4156

Roses
A4157

Hydrangea
A4158

Hollyhocks
A4159

Curcuma and Bouvardia Bouquet
A4160

Roses
A4161

Pink Rose
A4162

Hydrangea Bouquet
A4163

Carnations
A4164

Chinese Bellflowers
A4165

Die Cut Perf. 13x13¼

2018, Apr. 2 **Litho.**

Self-Adhesive

4193 Sheet of 10, 2 each #4193a-4193e 12.50 12.50
a. A4156 62y multi 1.00 .80
b. A4157 62y multi 1.00 .80
c. A4158 62y multi 1.00 .80
d. A4159 62y multi 1.00 .80
e. A4160 62y multi 1.00 .80
4194 Sheet of 10, 2 each #4194a-4194e 16.00 16.00
a. A4161 82y multi 1.25 .80
b. A4162 82y multi 1.25 .80
c. A4163 82y multi 1.25 .80
d. A4164 82y multi 1.25 .80
e. A4165 82y multi 1.25 .80

Miniature Sheet

Flora and Fauna of Daisetsuzan National Park — A4166

No. 4195: a, Northern fox (32x28mm). b, Hokkaido chipmunk (32x28mm). c, Hokkaido Crying Rabbit (32x28mm). d, Hokkaido flying squirrel (32mm diameter). e, Purple mountain heather (23x26mm). f, Primula flowers (23x26mm). g, Mountain avens (23x26mm). h, Mountain avens, diff. (23x26mm). i, Arctic gentians (23x26mm). j, Aleutian bellflowers (23x26mm).

Die Cut Perf. 13x12¼ (#4195a-4195c), Die Cut Perf. (#4195d), Die Cut Perf. 13x13¼

2018, Apr. 11 **Litho.**

Self-Adhesive

4195 A4166 Sheet of 10 16.00 16.00
a.-j. 82y Any single 1.25 .80

Philately Week — A4167

Screen art by Tawaraya Sotatsu (c. 1570-c.1640): No. 4196, Raijin (Thunder God). No. 4197, Fujin (Wind God).

Photo. & Engr.

2018, Apr. 20 ***Perf. 13¼***

4196 82y gold & multi 1.25 .50
4197 82y gold & multi 1.25 .50
a. A4167 Vert. pair, #4196-4197 3.00 2.20

A4168

A4169

A4170

A4171

A4172

A4173

A4174

A4175

Greetings — A4176

Die Cut Perf. 13¼, Die Cut Perf. (#4198a), Die Cut Perf. 13 (#4199a, 4200a),

Litho. With Foil Application

2018, Apr. 23 **Self-Adhesive**

4198 Sheet of 10, #4198a, 5 #4198b, 4 #4198c, + 3 stickers 12.00 12.00
a. A4168 62y gold & multi 1.00 .80
b. A4169 62y gold & multi 1.00 .80
c. A4170 62y gold & multi 1.00 .80
4199 Sheet of 10, #4199a, 5 #4199b, 4 #4199c, + 3 stickers 16.00 16.00
a. A4171 82y gold & multi 1.25 .80
b. A4172 82y gold & multi 1.25 .80
c. A4173 82y gold & multi 1.25 .80
4200 Sheet of 10, #4200a, 5 #4200b, 4 #4200c, + 3 stickers 17.50 17.50
a. A4174 92y gold & multi 1.40 .80
b. A4175 92y gold & multi 1.40 .80
c. A4176 92y gold & multi 1.40 .80
Nos. 4198-4200 (3) 45.50

Envelopes — A4177

Die Cut Perf. 13x13¼

2018, May 7 **Litho.**

Self-Adhesive

4201 A4177 82y sil & multi 1.25 .80

Miniature Sheets

A4178

Kabuki
A4179

No. 4202: a, Dancer from *The Wisteria Maiden* (lilac background color). b, Character from *Sugawara and the Secrets of Calligraphy* (pink background color). c, Face makeup (green panel at bottom). d, Character from *The Fight of the Carriage* (rose pink background color). e, Character from *Tales of the Licensed Quarter* (pale green background color). f, Character from *The Gion Festival Chronicle of Faith* (light blue background color). g, Face makeup (pink panel at bottom. h, Character from *Sugawara and the Secrets of Calligraphy* (blue green background color). i, Face makeup (red panel at bottom). j, Character from *Kotobuki Soga no Taimen* (buff background).

No. 4203: a, Character with umbrella from *The Flower of Edo* (32x43mm). b, Courtesan character from *The Flower of Edo* (26x48mm). c, Face makeup (purple panels at top and left) (28x36mm). d, Face makeup (striped panel at left) (28x36mm). e, Character from *Yoshitsune and the Thousand Cherry Trees* (31x38mm). f, Character from *Twenty-four Paragons of Filial Piety in This Land* (31x39mm). g, Face makeup (dark red panels at top and sides) (28x36mm). h, Two characters from *The Pair of Lions* (39x33mm). i, Face makeup (light gray panels at top and sides (28x36mm). j, Princess character from *Twenty-four Paragons of Filial Piety in This Land* (28x51mm).

Die Cut Perf. 13x13¼

2018, May 9 **Litho.**

Self-Adhesive

4202 A4178 Sheet of 10 12.00 12.00
a.-j. 62y Any single 1.00 .80

Die Cut Perf. 13

4203 A4179 Sheet of 10 16.00 16.00
a.-j. 62y Any single 1.25 .80

Flowers
A4180

Designs: No. 4204, Daisies and rhododendrons, white, red and blue ribbon. No. 4205, Chrysanthemums and cherry blossoms, red and white polka-dotted ribbon.

2018, May 16 **Litho.** ***Perf. 13x13¼***

4204 82y multi 1.25 .80
4205 82y multi 1.25 .80
a. A4180 Horiz. pair, #4204-4205 3.00 2.20

Japan-Russia Exchange Year. See Russia No. 7923.

Miniature Sheets

A4181

Hello Kitty
A4182

No. 4206 — Hello Kitty: a, With tray of cookies (29x26mm). b, In airplane (26x25mm). c, Holding opened stamped letter (23x25mm). d, Blowing up blue balloon (27x24mm). e, Holding red balloon (22x32mm). f, With Mimmy in basket (30x24mm). g, At easel (27x23mm). h, On elephant (24x28mm). i, On apple (23x27mm). j, Holding teddy bear (23x29mm).

No. 4207 — Hello Kitty: a, At mailbox (27x23mm). b, Holding sealed letter (24x26mm). c, With Mimmy reading letter (26x24mm). d, Holding gift (22x27mm). e, Holding letter and fountain pen (23x28mm). f, Writing letter with quill pen (23x24mm). g, Holding letter and quill pen (26x24mm). h, With mouse, Joey (25x26mm). i, Holding large stamp (23x27mm). j, With bird holding letter (22x26mm).

Die Cut Perf. 12¼, Die Cut Perf. 11¾ (#4207f)

2018, May 23 **Litho.**

Self-Adhesive

4206	A4181	Sheet of 10	12.00	12.00
a.-j.		62y Any single	1.00	.80
4207	A4182	Sheet of 10	16.00	16.00
a.-j.		82y Any single	1.25	.80

Fish in Bowl
A4183

Wind Chimes
A4184

Electric Fan Blades
A4185

Mosquito Coil
A4186

Watermelon
A4187

Fan
A4188

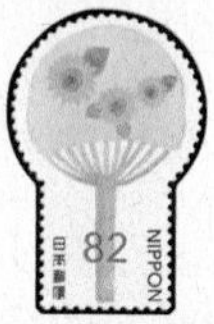

Fan
A4189

Yukata, Morning Glory Design
A4190

Yukata, Goldfish Design
A4191

Fireworks
A4192

Water Balloons
A4193

Boats, Crabs, Beach Umbrella and Chair
A4194

2018, June 1 **Litho.** ***Die Cut Perf.***

Self-Adhesive

4208	Sheet of 10, 2 each #4208a-4208e	12.00	12.00
a.	A4183 62y multi	1.00	.80
b.	A4184 62y multi	1.00	.80
c.	A4185 62y multi	1.00	.80
d.	A4186 62y multi	1.00	.80
e.	A4187 62y multi	1.00	.80

Die Cut Perf. 13x13¼ (#4209a-4209b), 12¼ (#4209c-4209d), 12¾x13 (#4209e-4209g)

4209	Sheet of 10, #4209a-4209d, 2 each #4209e-4209g	16.00	16.00
a.	A4188 82y multi	1.25	.80
b.	A4189 82y multi	1.25	.80
c.	A4190 82y multi	1.25	.80
d.	A4191 82y multi	1.25	.80
e.	A4192 82y multi	1.25	.80
f.	A4193 82y multi	1.25	.80
g.	A4194 82y multi	1.25	.80

Miniature Sheet

National Afforestation — A4195

No. 4210: a, Rhododendrons. b, Day lilies. c, Peach blossoms. d, Heartleaf false pickerelweed. e, Japanese black pine. f, Mountain cherry blossoms. g, Wheeping cherry blossoms. h, Castanopsis sieboldii. i, Japanese zelkova. j, Rhaphiolepis umbellata.

2018, June 6 **Litho.** ***Perf. 13¼***

4210	A4195	Sheet of 10	12.00	12.00
a.-j.		62y Any single	1.00	.80

Miniature Sheets

A4196

Greetings — A4197

No. 4211: a, Large red flower, stem and leaves at UR. b, Two small orange and pink flowers, striped pink flower. c, Two small orange flowers, d, Two violet flowers. e, Two small orange flowers, one violet flower. f, Large red flower stem and leaves at left. g, Pink flower and small orange and pink flower. h, Violet flower, pink striped flower, small orange flower. i, Pink flower, small orange flower, violet flower, stem and leaves at top. j, Dark pink flower, stem and flowers at top.

No. 4212: a, Large orange flower, small yellow flower. b, Two small yellow flowers. c, Large yellow flower and pale blue flower. d, Small peach flower and two pale blue flowers. e, Two small yellow flowers and part of large yellow flower. f, Pale blue flower and large red flower. g, Small yellow flower and pale blue flower. h, Three yellow flowers. i, Two peach flowers at left and part of large violet blue flower at right. j, Large violet blue flower at left, two small yellow flowers at right.

Die Cut Perf. 13

2018, June 13 **Litho.**

Self-Adhesive

4211	A4196	Sheet of 10	12.00	12.00
a.-j.		62y Any single	1.00	.80
4212	A4197	Sheet of 10	16.00	16.00
a.-j.		82y Any single	1.25	.80

Miniature Sheet

100th National High School Baseball Championship — A4198

No. 4213: a, Cap, bat, glove, home plate. b, Base and baseball. c, Batter holding bat. d, Pitcher. e, Batter swinging at ball. f, Cheerleaders. g, Recording statistics in dugout. h, Player sliding home. i, Scoreboard. j, Fielder diving for ball.

2018, June 15 **Litho.** ***Perf. 13***

4213	A4198	Sheet of 10	16.00	16.00
a.-j.		82y Any single	1.25	.80

Miniature Sheet

Return of Ogasawara (Bonin) Islands to Japan, 50th Anniv. — A4199

No. 4214: a, Military at return ceremony, tower in background. b, Military at return ceremony, Japanese flag on pole. c, Man, girl and boy on beach. d, Two women and girl on beach. e, People waving at boats, man at left. f, People waving at boats, woman at left. g, Two Meguro birds on branch. h, One Meguro bird on branch. i, Palm tree and Sun. j, Outrigger canoe and palm tree.

2018, June 26 Litho. *Perf. 13*

4214 A4199 Sheet of 10 16.00 16.00
a.-j. 82y Any single 1.25 .80

Miniature Sheet

Jellyfish
A4200

No. 4215 — Various unnamed jellyfish as shown. Nos. 4215d, 4215e and 4215j are horiz.

Litho. & Embossed

2018, July 4 *Die Cut Perf. 13¼*

Self-Adhesive

4215 A4200 Sheet of 10 15.00 15.00
a.-j. 82y Any single 1.50 1.10

Miniature Sheet

Okinoshima UNESCO World Heritage Sites — A4201

No. 4216: a, Aerial view of northwest coast of Fukuoka Prefecture, denomination at UL (stamp 1). b, Aerial view of northwest coast of Fukuoka Prefecture, denomination at UR (stamp 2). c, Okitsu-miya of Munakata Grand Shrine (stamp 3). d, Nakatsu-miya of Munakata Grand Shrine (stamp 4). e, Hetsu-miya of Munataka Grand Shrine (stamp 5). f, Shinbaru-Nuyama Mounded Tomb Group (stamp 6). g, Gold ring (stamp 7). h, Gilt-bronze dragon's head (stamp 8). i, Nara style jar (stamp 9). j, Deity and beast mirror (stamp 10).

2018, July 11 Litho. *Perf. 13*

4216 A4201 Sheet of 10 15.00 15.00
a.-j. 82y Any single 1.50 1.10

Miniature Sheet

Hokkaido, 150th Anniv. — A4202

No. 4217: a, Hokkaido Naming Place Monument. b, Nibutani Attush. c, Clock Tower, Sapporo. d, Former Hokkaido Central Government Building, Sapporo. e, Hanada Family Fisherman's Lodge. f, Former Branch Office of NYK Shipping Line, Otaru. g, Old Public Hall, Hakodate Ward. h, Former Court of Appeals, Sapporo. i, Aerial view of Shiretoko Peninsula. j, Hokkaido Shinkansen train leaving tunnel.

2018, July 13 Litho. *Perf. 12¾x13*

4217 A4202 Sheet of 10 15.00 15.00
a.-j. 82y Any single 1.50 1.10

Leaves
A4203

Blue Bird Holding Letter
A4204

Green Bird Holding Letter Near Pillar Box
A4205

Birds Flying to Left With Letter
A4206

Birds Flying to Right With Letter
A4207

Yellow Bird With Letter and Mail Bag
A4208

Open Letter and Flowers
A4209

Owl, Letter and Open Mailbox
A4210

Flowers, Letter, Pen and Ink Bottle
A4211

Envelopes, Gift, Ribbons and Cat
A4212

Die Cut Perf. 13x13¼

2018, July 23 Litho.

Self-Adhesive

4218 Booklet pane of 5 5.50
a. A4203 62y multi 1.10 .85
b. A4204 62y multi 1.10 .85
c. A4205 62y multi 1.10 .85
d. A4206 62y multi 1.10 .85
e. A4207 62y multi 1.10 .85
4219 Sheet of 10, 2 each #4219a-4219e 15.00
a. A4208 82y multi 1.50 1.10
b. A4209 82y multi 1.50 1.10
c. A4210 82y multi 1.50 1.10
d. A4211 82y multi 1.50 1.10
e. A4212 82y multi 1.50 1.10

Miniature Sheets

A4213

Animals
A4214

No. 4220: a, Deer (22x26mm). b, Flamingo (22x32mm). c, Hedgehog (23x26mm oval). d, Chipmunk (23x26mm oval). e, Snakes (22x32mm). f, Turtle (22x26mm). g, Crocodiles (25x26mm). h, Zebra (25x26mm). i, Frog (23x26mm oval). j, Birds and two capybaras (25x26mm).

No. 4221: a, Elephant (30x30mm). b, Panda (30mm diameter). c, Adult and juvenile pandas (36x36mm). d, Adult and juvenile koalas (30x30mm). e, Giraffe (19x40mm). f, Shoebill (19x40mm). g, Seal (26mm diameter). h, Chameleon (26mm diameter). i, Adult and juvenile otter (22x26mm). j, Lion (30x30mm).

Die Cut Perf. 12¼x12½ (#4220a, 4220f), 12¼x12 (#4220b, 4220c), 12x12½ (#4220g, 4220h, 4220j), Die Cut Perf. (#4220c, 4220d, 4220i)

2018, July 27 Litho.

Self-Adhesive

4220 A4213 Sheet of 10 11.00
a.-j. 62y Any single 1.10 .85

Die Cut Perf. 12 (#4221a, 4221d, 4221j), 11½x12½ (#4221e, 4221f), 12x12½ (#4221i), Die Cut Perf. (#4221b, 4221c, 4221g, 4221h)

4221 A4214 Sheet of 10 15.00
a.-j. 82y Any single 1.50 1.10

Miniature Sheet

Diplomatic Relations Between Japan and Sweden, 150th Anniv. — A4215

No. 4222: a, City Hall, Stockholm. b, Mt. Fuji and cherry blossoms. c, Swedish people in traditional costumes. d, Japanese people in traditional costumes. e, Swedish house and twinflowers. f, Japanese house. g, Coffee and fika, Sweden. h, Tea, tea whisk and yokan, Japan. i, Houses, Gamlestaden, Sweden. j, Bridge and poetry line by Basho, Japan.

2018, Aug. 2 Litho. *Perf. 12¾x13*

4222 A4215 Sheet of 10 15.00 15.00
a.-j. 82y Any single 1.50 1.10

Miniature Sheets

A4216

Disney Characters — A4217

No. 4223 — Winnie the Pooh characters: a, Winnie and dripping honey (30x26mm hexagonal). b, Winnie and Tigger at pond (30x26mm hexagonal). c, Winnie sitting on honey pot (30x26mm hexagonal), d, Tigger on Winnie (30x26mm hexagonal). e, Winnie and Piglet (30x26mm hexagonal). f, Winnie and Eeyore (30x26mm hexagonal). g, Winnie, Piglet and ducklings (30x26mm hexagonal). h, Winnie and Christopher Robin (30x26mm hexagonal). i, Tigger and Piglet (23x26mm). j, Winnie, with trumpet, and Eeyore (26x23mm).

No. 4224 — Mickey Mouse characters: a, Mickey at ship's wheel, in *Steamboat Willie* (26x22mm). b, Minnie Mouse, in *Steamboat Willie* (26x22mm). c, Mickey (22x26mm). d, Minnie running (22x26mm). e, Mickey wearing brown pants (26x22mm). f, Minnie touching bow (26x22mm). g, Mickey holding hat (22x26mm). h, Minnie holding umbrella (22x26mm). i, Mickey wearing wizard's hat (26x22mm). j, Minnie wearing red bow (26x22mm).

Die Cut Perf. 13¼ (hexagonal stamps), 13x13¼ (#4223i), 13¼x13 (#4223j)

2018, Aug. 8 **Litho.**

Self-Adhesive

4223 A4216 Sheet of 10 11.00
a.-j. 62y Any single 1.10 .85

Die Cut Perf. 13¼x13 (#4224a, 4224b, 4224e, 4224f, 4224i, 4224j), 13x13¼ (#4224c, 4224d, 4224g, 4224h)

4224 A4217 Sheet of 10 15.00
a.-j. 82y Any single 1.50 1.10

Red Maple Leaves A4218

Leaves in Rocky Stream A4219

Grapes A4220

Blossoms on Tree Branch A4221

Mushrooms A4222

Leaves Changing Color A4223

Red, Yellow and Orange Leaves A4224

Flowers and Leaves A4225

Wreath A4226

Acorns A4227

Chipmunk and Mushrooms A4228

Red Maple Tree A4229

Flowers A4230

Fallen Leaves and Mushrooms A4231

Bird Holding Berry A4232

Leaves A4233

Chestnuts A4234

Pumpkin Soup A4235

Gourds A4236

Flowers A4237

Die Cut Perf. 13¼x13 (#4225a, 4225d), 13x13¼ (#4225f, 4225c, 4225f, 4225g, 4225h, 4225i), Die Cut Perf. (#4225e, 4225j)

2018, Aug. 23 **Litho.**

Self-Adhesive

4225		Sheet of 10	11.00	
a.	A4218	62y multi	1.10	.85
b.	A4219	62y multi	1.10	.85
c.	A4220	62y multi	1.10	.85
d.	A4221	62y multi	1.10	.85
e.	A4222	62y multi	1.10	.85
f.	A4223	62y multi	1.10	.85
g.	A4224	62y multi	1.10	.85
h.	A4225	62y multi	1.10	.85
i.	A4226	62y multi	1.10	.85
j.	A4227	62y multi	1.10	.85

Die Cut Perf. (#4226a, 4226d), Die Cut Perf. 13x13¼ (#4226b, 4226c, 4226f, 4226g, 4226h, 4226i), 13¼x13 (#4226e, 4226j)

4226		Sheet of 10	15.00	
a.	A4228	82y multi	1.50	1.10
b.	A4229	82y multi	1.50	1.10
c.	A4230	82y multi	1.50	1.10
d.	A4231	82y multi	1.50	1.10
e.	A4232	82y multi	1.50	1.10
f.	A4233	82y multi	1.50	1.10
g.	A4234	82y multi	1.50	1.10
h.	A4235	82y multi	1.50	1.10
i.	A4236	82y multi	1.50	1.10
j.	A4237	82y multi	1.50	1.10

Miniature Sheet

73rd National Athletic Meet, Fukui Prefecture — A4238

No. 4227: a, Gymnast on rings. b, Snow crabs. c, Wall climbing. d, Eyeglass frames. e, Cyclist. f, Narcissi. g, Field hockey. h, Mikata Five Lakes. i, Rowing. j, Tojinbo Cliffs.

2018, Aug. 29 **Photo.** ***Perf. 12¾x13***

4227 A4238 Sheet of 10 15.00 15.00
a.-j. 82y Any single 1.50 1.10

Cape Kannon Lighthouse A4239

Mikomotoshima Lighthouse A4240

Cape Muroto Lighthouse A4241

Hesaki Lighthouse A4242

Original Cape Kannon Lighthouse — A4243

2018, Sept. 3 **Litho.** ***Perf. 13½***

4228	A4239	82y multi	1.50	1.10
4229	A4240	82y multi	1.50	1.10
4230	A4241	82y multi	1.50	1.10
4231	A4242	82y multi	1.50	1.10
4232	A4243	82y multi	1.50	1.10
a.		Horiz. strip of 5, #4228-4232	7.50	5.50
		Nos. 4228-4232 (5)	7.50	5.50

Japanese lighthouses, 150th anniv.

Nos. 4228-4232 comes in sheets of 10, 2 horiz. strips of 5.

A4244

My Journey A4245

No. 4233: a, Nishi-Oyama Railroad Station (26x22mm). b, Sakurajima (26x22mm). c, Bowl of shaved ice with condensed milk and fruit (26x22mm). d, Pillar box at Nishi-Oyama Railroad Station (26x22mm). e, Boat in Takachiho Gorge (26x22mm). f, Takachiho Gorge (22x26mm). g, Mangos (26x22mm). h, Japanese macaques, Mt. Takasaki (26x22mm). i, Lake Kinrin (26x22mm). j, Steam rising from Hells of Beppu hot spring (26x22mm).

No. 4234: a, Tenman-gu Shrine, Dazaifu (26x22mm). b, Mentaiko (pollock roe) and rice (22x26mm). c, Bowl of Hakata ramen noodles (26x22mm). d, Karatsu Castle (26x22mm). e, Arita ware plate on stand (25x26mm). f, Nagasaki at night (26x22mm). g, Glover House, Nagasaki (26x22mm). h, Oura Catholic Church (22x30mm). i, Kokin Denju no Ma Teahouse, Kumamoto (26x22mm). j, Mt. Aso (26x24mm).

Die Cut Perf. 13¼x13, 13x13¼ (#4233f)

2018, Sept. 5 **Litho.**

Self-Adhesive

4233 A4244 Sheet of 10 11.00
a.-j. 62y Any single 1.10 .85

Die Cut Perf. 13¼x13 (#4234a, 4234c, 4234d, 4234f, 4234g, 4234i),

13x13¼ (#4234b, 4324h), 12½ (#4234e), 13¼x12 (#4234j)

4234	A4245	Sheet of 10	15.00	
a.-j.		82y Any single	1.50	1.10

This sheet of four 62y stamps, four 82y stamps and two 120y stamps, issued Sept. 5, 2018, was printed in limited quantities and sold only with a set of stationery, postcards and envelopes for 2000y.

Miniature Sheets

A4246

Posukuma and Kumamon — A4247

No. 4235 — Teddy bear mascot of Japan Post wearing cap and black bear mascot of Kumamoto Prefecture: a, Facing each other. b, Waving. c, With musical notes. d, Jumping. e, With one paw raised. f, With cherry blossoms. g, Holding tags on tree. h, Sitting on bench. i, Ice skating. j, With hearts.

No. 4236: a, Head of Japan Post mascot in thought bubble. b, Head of Kumamoto Prefecture mascot in thought bubble, Japan Post mascot with paws crossed. c, Japan Post mascot and pillar box in thought bubble. d, Head of Kumamoto Prefecture mascot in thought bubble, Japan Post mascot with one paw raised. e, Japan Post mascot carrying letter in thought bubble. f, Kumamoto Prefecture mascot leaning in thought bubble. g, Kumamoto Prefecture mascot writing, Japan Post mascot sitting in thought bubble. h, Japan Post mascot at table with envelopes, Kumamoto Prefecture mascot in thought bubble. i, Kumamoto Prefecture mascot presenting letter to Japan Post mascot. j, Japan Post mascot presenting letter to Kumamoto Prefecture mascot.

Die Cut Perf. 12½x13

2018, Sept. 14 **Litho.**

Self-Adhesive

4235	A4246	Sheet of 10	11.00	
a.-j.		62y Any single	1.10	.85
4236	A4247	Sheet of 10	15.00	
a.-j.		82y Any single	1.50	1.10

This sheet of three 82y stamps and two 120y stamps + 23 stickers depicting the teddy bear mascot of Japan Post, issued Sept. 14, 2018, was printed in limited quantities and sold only with a set of envelopes and cards for 1200y.

Fashion
A4248

No. 4237: a, Six eyeglass frames, hat and pair of gloves (28mm diameter). b, Four t-shirts, blue green background (22x26mm). c, Four blouses, blue background (22x26mm). d, Four jackets, purple background (22x26mm). e, Six handbags (28mm diameter). f, Lipsticks, necklaces and make-up (28mm diameter). g, Four pairs of jeans and pair of shorts (22x26mm). h, Three dresses (22x26mm). i, Scarf, winter cap and three sweaters (22x26mm). j, Four pairs of high-heeled shoes (28mm diameter).

Die Cut Perf. (circular stamps), Die Cut Perf. 13x13¼ (rectangular stamps)

2018, Sept. 19 **Litho.**

Self-Adhesive

4237	A4248	Booklet pane of 10	15.00	
a.-j.		82y Any single	1.50	1.10

Miniature Sheet

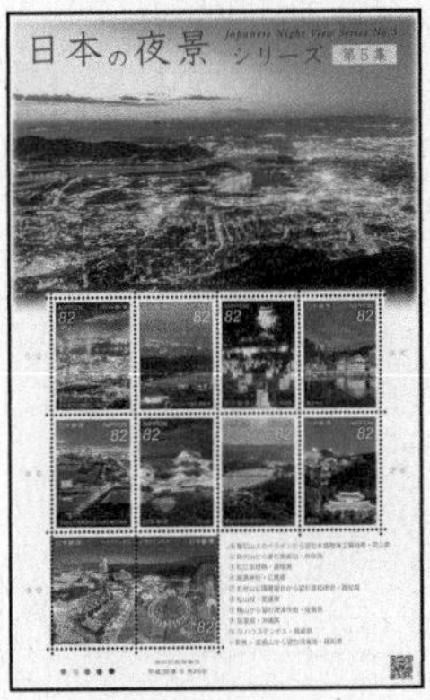

Japan at Night
A4249

No. 4238: a, Mizushima Coastal Industrial Area, Okayama Prefecture (stamp 1). b, Lake Togo area, Tottori Prefecture (stamp 2). c, Matsue water lanterns, Shimane Prefecture (stamp 3). d, Itsukushima Shrine, Hiroshima Prefecture (stamp 4). e, Kochi City, Kochi Prefecture (stamp 5). f, Matsuyama Castle, Ehime Prefecture (stamp 6). g, Karatsu, Saga Prefecture (stamp 7). h, Shuri Castle, Okinawa Prefecture (stamp 8). i, Huis Ten Bosch Theme Park (denomination at LL), Nagasaki Prefecture (stamp 9), j, Huis Ten Bosch Theme Park (denomination at LR), Nagasaki Prefecture (stamp 10).

2018, Sept. 26 **Photo.** ***Perf. 13***

4238	A4249	Sheet of 10	15.00	15.00
a.-j.		82y Any single	1.50	1.10

Tokyo Metro Cars
A4250

Kintetsu 21000 and 21020 Series Locomotives
A4251

East Japan Railways 651 Series Locomotive
A4252

Odakyu Electric Railway 20000 Series Locomotive
A4253

Kyushu Railway 883 Series Locomotive
A4254

East Japan Railways E257 Series Locomotive
A4255

Shikoku Railway 5100 Series Locomotive
A4256

Japan Freight Railway M250 Series Locomotive
A4257

Odakyu Electric Railway 50000 Series Locomotive
A4258

Kyushu Railway BEC819 Series Locomotive
A4259

Tokyo Metro Car
A4260

East Japan Railways E257 Series Locomotive
A4261

Kintetsu 21000 and 21020 Series Locomotives
A4262

Shikoku Railway 5100 Series Locomotive
A4263

East Japan Railways 651 Series Locomotive
A4264

Japan Freight Railway M250 Series Locomotive
A4265

Odakyu Electric Railway 20000 Series Locomotive
A4266

Odakyu Electric Railway 50000 Series Locomotive
A4267

Kyushu Railway 883 Series Locomotive A4268

Kyushu Railway BEC819 Series Locomotive A4269

2018, Oct. 4 Litho. *Perf. 13x12¾*

4239	Sheet of 10	15.00	15.00
a.	A4250 82y multi	1.50	1.10
b.	A4251 82y multi	1.50	1.10
c.	A4252 82y multi	1.50	1.10
d.	A4253 82y multi	1.50	1.10
e.	A4254 82y multi	1.50	1.10
f.	A4255 82y multi	1.50	1.10
g.	A4256 82y multi	1.50	1.10
h.	A4257 82y multi	1.50	1.10
i.	A4258 82y multi	1.50	1.10
j.	A4259 82y multi	1.50	1.10

Perf. 12¾x13

4240	Sheet of 10	15.00	15.00
a.	A4260 82y multi	1.50	1.10
b.	A4261 82y multi	1.50	1.10
c.	A4262 82y multi	1.50	1.10
d.	A4263 82y multi	1.50	1.10
e.	A4264 82y multi	1.50	1.10
f.	A4265 82y multi	1.50	1.10
g.	A4266 82y multi	1.50	1.10
h.	A4267 82y multi	1.50	1.10
i.	A4268 82y multi	1.50	1.10
j.	A4269 82y multi	1.50	1.10

A4270

A4271

International Letter Writing Week — A4272

Art by Hiroshige (1797-1858): 8y, Hawk at Sunrise. No. 4242, Camellia from Camellias with Small Birds. No. 4243, Camellia and bird from Camellias with Small Birds. 90y, Travelers on Bridge Over Kake River Near the Tokaido Station. 110y, Sandbank in the Tenryu River Near the Mitsuke Station. 130y, Travelers and Hostesses at an Inn.

2018, Oct. 9 Litho. *Perf. 14*

4241	A4270 8y multi	.30	.25
4242	70y multi	1.25	.95
4243	70y multi	1.25	.95
a.	A4271 Vert. pair, #4242-4243	2.50	1.90

Perf. 12¾x13

4244	A4272 90y multi	1.60	1.25
4245	A4272 110y multi	2.00	1.50
4246	A4272 130y multi	2.40	1.75
	Nos. 4241-4246 (6)	8.80	6.65

See listing of No. 4448 for images of each Hiroshige print.

Miniature Sheets

A4273

Gifts From the Forest A4274

No. 4247: a, Fruit hanging from tree (22x26mm). b, Faces of flying squirrels (22x26mm). c, Berries on stem and leaves (22x26mm). d. Flowers (22x26mm). e, Two birds (34x34mm diamond-shaped). f, Tree bark (22x26mm). g, Birds and bird house (22x26mm). h, Vine (22x26mm). i, Animal climbing tree (22x26mm). j, Deer (34x34mm diamond-shaped).

No. 4248: a, Red flowers (22x26mm). b, Pink flowers (22x26mm). c, Two stylized birds (22x26mm). d, Tree, flowers, and leaves (27mm diameter). e, Monkey in tree (27mm diameter). f, Insect (22x26mm). g, Vine, diff. (22x26mm). h, Leaves and fruit clusters (22x26mm). i, Fruits (27mm diameter). j, Berries on stem (27mm diameter).

Die Cut Perf. 13x13¼, 13¼ (#4247e, 4247j)

2018, Oct. 17 Litho.

Self-Adhesive

4247	A4273 Sheet of 10	11.00	
a.-j.	62y Any single	1.10	.85

Die Cut Perf. 13x13¼, Die Cut Perf. (circular stamps)

4248	A4274 Sheet of 10	15.00	
a.-j.	82y Any single	1.50	1.10

Miniature Sheet

Start of Meiji Era, 150th Anniv. A4275

No. 4249 — Woodblock prints: a, View of Waiting Room at the Shiodome Railway Station (ceiling lamp in foreground), by Hiroshige III. b, As "a," (steam locomotive). c, View of the Opening Ceremonies of the Yokohama Post Office (one flag), by Hiroshige III. d, As "c," (four flags). e, Prominent Sights in Tokyo: Cherry Blossoms in Full Bloom at Ueno Park (women with blue umbrellas), by Hiroshige III. f, As "e," (women with beige umbrellas). g, Prominent Sights in Tokyo: Brick Buildings Along Ginza Street, Horse-Drawn Trams (horses), by Hiroshige III. h, As "g," (no horses). i, View of a European-style Musical Concert (four musicians with string instruments), by Chikanobu Yoshu. j, As "i," (pianist).

2018, Oct. 23 Litho. *Perf. 12¾x13*

4249	A4275 Sheet of 10	15.00	15.00
a.-j.	82y Any single	1.50	1.10

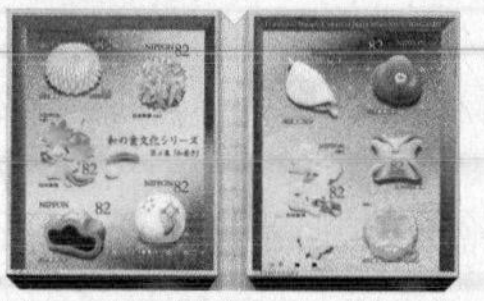

Japanese Cuisine — A4276

No. 4250 — Confections: a, Jonamagashi (chrysanthemum shaped) (32x27mm). b, Kinton (shredded sweet potato) (27x32mm). c, Flower petal mochi (white folded rice cake) (27x32mm). d, Jonamagashi (red and white, flower-shaped) (27x32mm). e, Higashi (red maple, ginkgo leaves and mushroom-shaped) (27x32mm). f, Higashi (butterfly, plants and knot-shaped) (27x32mm). g, Jonamagashi (pink folded square) (26x26mm). h, Jonamagashi (green, white and dark brown) (32x27mm). i, Oribe manju (white filled bun with brown and green decorations (27x32mm). j, Jonamagashi (cherry blossom shaped) (26x26mm).

Die Cut Perf. 12½x12¾ (#4250a, 4250h), 12¾x12½ (#4250b-4250f, 4250i), 12¾ (#4250g, 4250j)

2018, Oct. 24 Litho.

Self-Adhesive

4250	A4276 Booklet pane of 10	15.00	
a.-j.	82y Any single	1.50	1.10

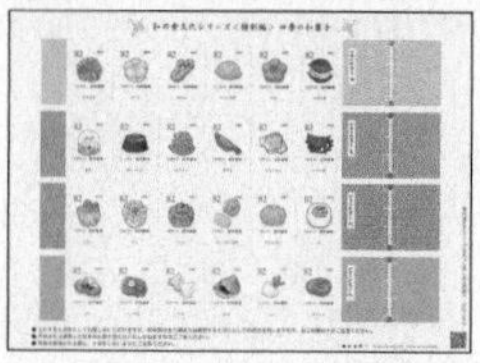

This sheet of 24 82y stamps, depicting various confections, issued Oct. 24, 2018, was printed in limited quantities and sold only with a set of stationery and envelopes for 2500y. Value, $30.

Great Wave of Kanagawa, by Hokusai A4277

Red Fuji, by Hokusai A4278

2018, Nov. 1 Litho. *Perf. 13¼x13*

4251	A4277 8y multi	.30	.25
4252	A4278 8y multi	.30	.25
a.	Horiz. pair, #4251-4252	.35	.25

A4279

A4280

New Year 2019 (Year of the Pig)

A4281 A4282

2018, Nov. 1 Litho. *Perf. 13x13¼*

4253	A4279 62y multi	1.10	.85
4254	A4280 82y multi	1.50	1.10

Litho. & Typo.

Perf. 13¼

4255	A4281 62y+3y multi	1.25	.95
4256	A4282 82y+3y multi	1.50	1.10
	Nos. 4253-4256 (4)	5.35	4.00

A4283

A4284

A4285

A4286

A4287

A4288

A4289

A4290

A4291

A4292

A4293

A4294

A4295

A4296

A4297

A4298

A4299

A4300

A4301

Plants and Fruits in Glass Jars — A4302

Die Cut Perf. 13x13¼

2018, Nov. 14 Photo.

Self-Adhesive

4257	Sheet of 10	11.00	
a.	A4283 62y multi	1.10	.85
b.	A4284 62y multi	1.10	.85
c.	A4285 62y multi	1.10	.85
d.	A4286 62y multi	1.10	.85
e.	A4287 62y multi	1.10	.85
f.	A4288 62y multi	1.10	.85
g.	A4289 62y multi	1.10	.85
h.	A4290 62y multi	1.10	.85
i.	A4291 62y multi	1.10	.85
j.	A4292 62y multi	1.10	.85

Die Cut Perf. 13x13¼ (#4258a-4258e, 4258j), 13¼x13 (#4258f-4258i)

4258	Sheet of 10	15.00	
a.	A4293 82y multi	1.50	1.10
b.	A4294 82y multi	1.50	1.10
c.	A4295 82y multi	1.50	1.10
d.	A4296 82y multi	1.50	1.10
e.	A4297 82y multi	1.50	1.10
f.	A4298 82y multi	1.50	1.10
g.	A4299 82y multi	1.50	1.10
h.	A4300 82y multi	1.50	1.10
i.	A4301 82y multi	1.50	1.10
j.	A4302 82y multi	1.50	1.10

Labor and Social Security Attorney System, 50th Anniv. — A4303

Designs: No. 4259, Flowers. No. 4260, Bird carrying heart-shaped balloons.

2018, Nov. 28 Litho. *Perf. 13*

4259	82y multi	1.50	1.10
4260	82y multi	1.50	1.10
a.	A4303 Vert. pair, #4259-4260	3.00	2.20

Miniature Sheet

Illustrations From *The Very Hungry Caterpillar*, by Eric Carle — A4304

No. 4261: a, Butterfly (41x24mm). b, Caterpillar ("Nippon" at bottom) (30mm diameter). c, Caterpillar ("Arigato" at bottom) (30mm diameter). d, Caterpillar and two pears (30x30mm). e, Caterpillar and three plums (30x30mm). f, Caterpillar and five oranges (30x30mm). g, Moon and egg (32x23mm). h, Sun, caterpillar on leaf (30x30mm). i, Sun and caterpillar (30x30mm). j, Caterpillar (30x30mm).

Die Cut Perf. (#4261a-4261c), Die Cut Perf. 13¼ (#4261d-4261f, 4261h-4261j), 11¼ (#4261g)

2018, Nov. 30 Litho.

Self-Adhesive

4261	A4304	Sheet of 10 + 16 stickers	15.00	
a.-j.		82y Any single	1.50	1.10

Harp and Harpist A4305

Bassoon and Bassoonist A4306

Trumpet and Trumpeter A4307

Cymbals and Percussionist A4308

Violin and Violinist — A4309

Musical Instruments — A4310

No. 4263: a, Harp (22x30mm). b, Celesta (22x30mm). c, Trombone (30x22mm). d, French horn (24x28mm). e, Timpani (22x28mm). f, Violin (22x26mm). g, Flute and piccolo (30x22mm). h, Clarinet (22x30mm). i, Cello, pink F-clef (22x30mm). j, Bass, gray F-clef (22x33mm).

Die Cut Perf. 13x13¼ (#4262a, 4262d), 13½x13¼ (#4262b), 14¾x13 (#4262c), 12½x13¼ (#4262e)

2018, Dec. 6 Litho.

Self-Adhesive

4262	Sheet of 10, 2 each #4262a-4262e		11.00	
a.	A4305 62y multi		1.10	.85
b.	A4306 62y multi		1.10	.85
c.	A4307 62y multi		1.10	.85
d.	A4308 62y multi		1.10	.85
e.	A4309 62y multi		1.10	.85

Die Cut Perf. 13x13¼ (#4263a, 4263b, 4263f, 4263h, 4263i, 4263j), 13¼x13 (#4263c, 4263g), 12x12¼ (#4263d), 13x12¼ (#4263e)

4263	A4310	Sheet of 10	15.00	
a.-j.		82y Any single	1.50	1.10

Circles of Dots A4311

Triangles A4312

Squares and Parallel Lines A4313

Squares A4314

Lines and Dots A4315

Flowers A4316

Flowers A4317

Flowers A4318

Flowers A4319

Flowers A4320

A4321

A4322

A4323

A4324

A4325

Litho. With Foil Application

2018, Dec. 10 ***Die Cut Perf. 13***

Self-Adhesive

4264	Sheet of 10, 2 each #4264a-4264e	11.00	
a.	A4311 62y gold & multi	1.10	.85
b.	A4312 62y gold & multi	1.10	.85
c.	A4313 62y gold & multi	1.10	.85
d.	A4314 62y gold & multi	1.10	.85
e.	A4315 62y gold & multi	1.10	.85

Die Cut Perf. 13¼

4265	Sheet of 10, 2 each #4265a-4265e	15.00	
a.	A4316 82y gold & multi	1.50	1.10
b.	A4317 82y gold & multi	1.50	1.10
c.	A4318 82y gold & multi	1.50	1.10
d.	A4319 82y gold & multi	1.50	1.10
e.	A4320 82y gold & multi	1.50	1.10
4266	Sheet of 10, 2 each #4266a-4266e	17.50	
a.	A4321 92y silver & multi	1.75	1.40
b.	A4322 92y silver & multi	1.75	1.40
c.	A4323 92y silver & multi	1.75	1.40
d.	A4324 92y silver & multi	1.75	1.40
e.	A4325 92y silver & multi	1.75	1.40
	Nos. 4264-4266 (3)	43.50	

Background colors differ on the two examples on the sheet of Nos. 4264a-4264e and 4266a-4266e.

Tulips and Sweet Peas A4326

Roses A4327

Narcssi A4328

Adonis Flowers A4329

Snowdrops A4330

Cherry Blossoms A4331

Roses A4332

Fuchsias A4333

Nemophila A4334

Christmas Roses A4335

Die Cut Perf. 13x13¼

2018, Dec. 14 Litho.

Self-Adhesive

4267	Sheet of 10, 2 each #4267a-4267e	11.00	
a.	A4326 62y multi	1.10	.85
b.	A4327 62y multi	1.10	.85
c.	A4328 62y multi	1.10	.85
d.	A4329 62y multi	1.10	.85
e.	A4330 62y multi	1.10	.85
4268	Sheet of 10, 2 each #4268a-4268e	15.00	
a.	A4331 82y multi	1.50	1.10
b.	A4332 82y multi	1.50	1.10
c.	A4333 82y multi	1.50	1.10
d.	A4334 82y multi	1.50	1.10
e.	A4335 82y multi	1.50	1.10

A4336

Gaspard and Lisa, Children's Book Characters by Anne Gutman and Georg Hallensleben — A4337

No. 4269: a, Lisa (white animal) and red balloon (30x35mm). b, Gaspard (black animal) and yellow balloon (32x32mm). c, Gaspard and Lisa with ice cream sundaes (24x24mm). d, Gaspard and Lisa with sushi plates and chopsticks (24x24mm). e, Gaspard in bed (24x24mm). f, Lisa in bed (24x24mm). g, Gaspard and Lisa on slide (24x24mm). h, Gaspard and Lisa on scooters (24x24mm). i, Gaspard and Lisa at desk with open books (24x24mm). j, Gaspard and Lisa with backpacks (24x24mm).

No. 4270: a, Lisa with dessert bowl (28x37mm). b, Gaspard with dessert bowl (28x37mm). c, Gaspard and Lisa at Eiffel Tower (24x24mm). d, Gaspard and Lisa on bridge over River Seine (24x24mm). e, Gaspard and Lisa picnicking (24x24mm). f, Gaspard and Lisa in gondola of hot air balloon (24x24mm). g, Gaspard and Lisa with puppy and kitten (24x24mm). h, Gaspard and Lisa on balcony (24x24mm). i, Gaspard and Lisa rollerblading (24x24mm). j, Gaspard and Lisa sitting on benches (24x24mm).

Die Cut Perf. 13¼, Die Cut Perf. (#4269a, 4269b), Die Cut Perf. 13½x13¼ (#4270a, 4270b)

2019, Jan. 16 Litho.

Self-Adhesive

4269	A4336	Sheet of 10	11.00	
a.-j.		62y Any single	1.10	.85
4270	A4337	Sheet of 10	15.00	
a.-j.		82y Any single	1.50	1.10

Souvenir Sheet

New Year 2019 A4338

No. 4271: a, Cat holding postcard. b, Cat holding envelope.

2019, Jan. 21 Litho. ***Perf. 13x13¼***

4271	A4338	Sheet of 2	2.60	2.60
a.		62y multi	1.10	.85
b.		82y multi	1.50	1.10

No. 4271 was also a prize in the New Year lottery.

Rolled Cookies A4339 — Sandwich Cookies A4340

Rice Dumplings A4341 — Filled Wheat Cakes A4342

Lemon Cakes A4343 — Filled Rice Dumplings A4344

Canelés A4345 — Strawberry Shortcake A4346

Layered Cake Roll Slices A4347 — Fruit Sandwiches A4348

Desserts A4349

No. 4273: a, Sweet bean paste on toast (23x23mm). b, Strawberry parfait (23x27mm). c, Bowl of fruit and syrup (28x22mm). d, Pancake (28x21mm oval). e, Bowl of coffee jelly (24x27mm). f, Fruit tart (25x22mm oval). g, Chantilly cream (30x20mm oval). h, Custard with whipped cream, syrup and fruit (28x23mm oval). i, Rice dumplings (29x22mm oval). j, Slice of cheesecake (30x22mm oval).

Die Cut Perf. 12½

2019, Feb. 1 Litho.

Self-Adhesive

4272		Sheet of 10	11.00	
	a.	A4339 62y multi	1.10	.85
	b.	A4340 62y multi	1.10	.85
	c.	A4341 62y multi	1.10	.85
	d.	A4342 62y multi	1.10	.85
	e.	A4343 62y multi	1.10	.85
	f.	A4344 62y multi	1.10	.85
	g.	A4345 62y multi	1.10	.85
	h.	A4346 62y multi	1.10	.85
	i.	A4347 62y multi	1.10	.85
	j.	A4348 62y multi	1.10	.85

Die Cut Perf., Die Cut Perf. 14 (#4273a), Die Cut Perf. 13¼ (#4273c)

4273		A4349 Sheet of 10	15.00	
	a.-j.	82y Any single	1.50	1.10

Miniature Sheet

Astronomy — A4350

No. 4247: a, Star cluster (red at right, 32mm diameter). b, Pleaides (32mm diameter). c, Mars (denomination at LR, 22x26mm). d, Ceres (denomination at UL, 22x26mm). e, Sirius (denomination at LL, 22x26mm). f, Moon (denomination at UL, 22x26mm). g, Io (denomination at UL, 22x26mm). h, Europa and Jupiter denomination at LL, 22x26mm). i, Earth (43mm diameter). j, Great Red Spot of Jupiter (32mm diameter).

Die Cut Perf. 13x13¼, Die Cut Perf. (round stamps)

Litho. With Hologram Affixed

2019, Feb. 6 Self-Adhesive

4274		A4350 Sheet of 10	15.00	
	a.-j.	82y Any single	1.50	1.10

Cherry Blossoms A4351 — Bird A4352

Flowers and Butterfly A4353 — Poppies A4354

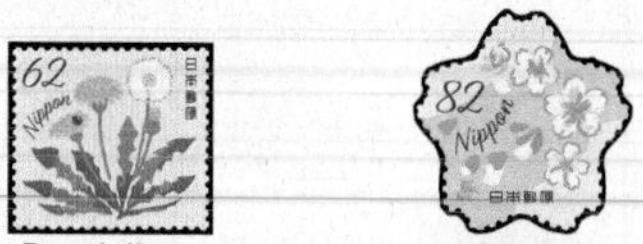

Dandelions A4355 — Cherry Blossoms A4356

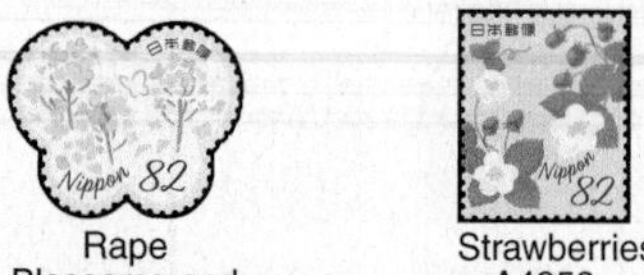

Rape Blossoms and Butterfly A4357 — Strawberries A4358

Clover Flowers and Leaves A4359 — Tulips A4360

Die Cut Perf., Die Cut Perf. 13x13¼ (#4275c, 4275d, 4276c, 4276e), Die Cut Perf. 13¼x13¾ (#4275e), Die Cut Perf. 13¼ (#4276e)

2019, Feb. 20 Litho.

Self-Adhesive

4275		Sheet of 10, 2 each #4275a-4275e	11.00	
	a.	A4351 62y multi	1.10	.85
	b.	A4352 62y multi	1.10	.85
	c.	A4353 62y multi	1.10	.85
	d.	A4354 62y multi	1.10	.85
	e.	A4355 62y multi	1.10	.85
4276		Sheet of 10, 2 each #4276a-4276e	11.00	
	a.	A4356 82y multi	1.50	1.10
	b.	A4357 82y multi	1.50	1.10
	c.	A4358 82y multi	1.50	1.10
	d.	A4359 82y multi	1.50	1.10
	e.	A4360 82y multi	1.50	1.10

Crane and Tortoise A4361 — Chrysanthemums A4362

2019, Feb. 22 Photo. *Perf. 13¼*

4277		A4361 82y multi	1.50	1.10
4278		A4362 82y multi	1.50	1.10
	a.	Pair, #4277-4278	3.00	2.20

Reign of Emperor Akihito, 30th anniv.

Dandelions A4363 — Water Wheels A4364

Wisteria A4365 — Rape Blossoms A4366

Tadpoles A4367 — Azaleas A4368

Daffodils A4369 — Leaves A4370

Peach and Peach Blossoms A4371 — Seaweed A4372

Bush Warblers A4373 — Bluets A4374

Violets A4375 — Sea Shells A4376

Parasol A4377 — Rice Seedlings A4378

Cherry Blossoms A4379 — Kerria Flowers A4380

Mountains A4381 — Pussy Willows A4382

Die Cut Perf. 13x13¼

2019, Mar. 6 Litho.

Self-Adhesive

4279		Sheet of 10	11.00	
	a.	A4363 62y multi	1.10	.85
	b.	A4364 62y multi	1.10	.85
	c.	A4365 62y multi	1.10	.85
	d.	A4366 62y multi	1.10	.85
	e.	A4367 62y multi	1.10	.85
	f.	A4368 62y multi	1.10	.85
	g.	A4369 62y multi	1.10	.85
	h.	A4370 62y multi	1.10	.85
	i.	A4371 62y multi	1.10	.85
	j.	A4372 62y multi	1.10	.85
4280		Sheet of 10	15.00	
	a.	A4373 82y multi	1.50	1.10
	b.	A4374 82y multi	1.50	1.10
	c.	A4375 82y multi	1.50	1.10
	d.	A4376 82y multi	1.50	1.10
	e.	A4377 82y multi	1.50	1.10
	f.	A4378 82y multi	1.50	1.10
	g.	A4379 82y multi	1.50	1.10
	h.	A4380 82y multi	1.50	1.10
	i.	A4381 82y multi	1.50	1.10
	j.	A4382 82y multi	1.50	1.10

Dahlias and Cosmos A4383 — Apple Blossoms A4384

Roses A4385 — Osmanthus A4386

Petunias A4387 — Carnations and Roses A4388

Queen of the Night A4389 — Roses A4390

Sunflowers and Cockscombs
A4391

Irises
A4392

Die Cut Perf. 13x13¼

2019, Apr. 1 — Litho.

Self-Adhesive

4281 Sheet of 10, 2 each #4281a-4281e — 11.00
- *a.* A4383 62y multi — 1.10 .85
- *b.* A4384 62y multi — 1.10 .85
- *c.* A4385 62y multi — 1.10 .85
- *d.* A4386 62y multi — 1.10 .85
- *e.* A4387 62y multi — 1.10 .85

4282 Sheet of 10, 2 each #4282a-4282e — 15.00
- *a.* A4388 82y multi — 1.50 1.10
- *b.* A4389 82y multi — 1.50 1.10
- *c.* A4390 82y multi — 1.50 1.10
- *d.* A4391 82y multi — 1.50 1.10
- *e.* A4392 82y multi — 1.50 1.10

Miniature Sheet

Flora and Fauna of Kurobe Gorge
A4393

No. 4283: a, Red-flanked bluetail (28x32mm). b, Japanese rowan (22x26mm). c, Japanese serow (28x32mm). d, Blue-and-white flycatcher (28x32mm). e, Tiger lily (22x26mm). f, Hosta flowers (22x26mm). g, Japanese macaque (32x28mm). h, Potentilla dickinsii (22x26mm). i, White-spotted char (32mm diameter). j, Alpine accentor (32x28mm).

Die Cut Perf. 12¼x13 (#4283a, 4283c, 4283d); Die Cut Perf. 13x13¼ (#4283b, 4283e, 4283f, 4283h); Die Cut Perf. 13x12¼ (#4283g, 4283j); Die Cut Perf. (#4283h)

2019, Apr. 12 — Litho.

Self-Adhesive

4283 A4393 Sheet of 10 — 15.00
- *a.-j.* 82y Any single — 1.50 1.10

A4394 A4395

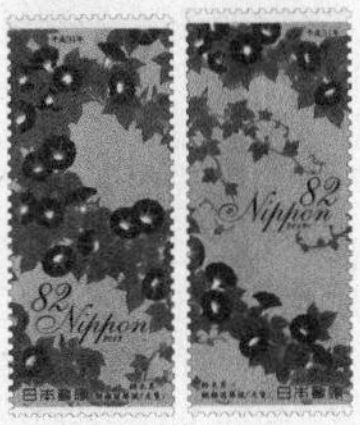
A4396 A4397

A4398 A4399

A4400 A4401

Morning Glories, by Kiitsu Suzuki (1796-1858)
A4402 A4403

Photo. & Engr.

2019, Apr. 19 — *Perf. 13x13¼*

4284 Sheet of 10 — 15.00 15.00
- *a.* A4394 82y multi — 1.50 1.10
- *b.* A4395 82y multi — 1.50 1.10
- *c.* A4396 82y multi — 1.50 1.10
- *d.* A4397 82y multi — 1.50 1.10
- *e.* A4398 82y multi — 1.50 1.10
- *f.* A4399 82y multi — 1.50 1.10
- *g.* A4400 82y multi — 1.50 1.10
- *h.* A4401 82y multi — 1.50 1.10
- *i.* A4402 82y multi — 1.50 1.10
- *j.* A4403 82y multi — 1.50 1.10

Philately Week.

A4404

A4405

A4406

A4407

Jewelry
A4408 A4409

Litho. With Foil Application

Die Cut Perf. 12¾x13½

2019, Apr. 23 — Self-Adhesive

4285 Sheet of 10, 5 each #4285a-4285b — 11.00
- *a.* A4404 62y multi — 1.10 .85
- *b.* A4405 62y multi — 1.10 .85

4286 Sheet of 10, 5 each #4286a-4286b — 15.00
- *a.* A4406 82y multi — 1.50 1.10
- *b.* A4407 82y multi — 1.50 1.10

4287 Sheet of 10, 5 each #4287a-4287b — 17.50
- *a.* A4408 92y multi — 1.75 1.40
- *b.* A4409 92y multi — 1.75 1.40

Nos. 4285-4287 (3) — 43.50

Simple — A4410

Die Cut Perf. 13x13¼

2019, May 8 — Litho.

Self-Adhesive

4288 A4410 82y multi — 1.50 1.10

Greeting Stamp.

Souvenir Sheet

Paintings of Mount Fuji
A4411

No. 4289: a, The Sacred Peak in the Morning Sun, by Taikan Yokoyama (1868-1958) (denomination at LR). b, The Bay at Tago no Ura, by Yoshimatsu Goseda (1855-1925) (denomination at UR).

2019, May 20 — Photo. — *Perf. 13¼*

Without Serial Number

4289 A4411 Sheet of 2 — 18.50 18.50
- *a.-b.* 500y Either single — 9.25 7.00

In the sheet margins of No. 4289 there are holographic images of two birds.

Sheets with serial numbers were prizes for lottery held Jan. 20, 2019.

Miniature Sheet

Diplomatic Relations Between Japan and Finland, Cent. — A4412

No. 4290: a, People chopping logs near log cabin. b, Sauna. c, Boy fishing at lake. d, Children swimming in lake. e, Children gathering berries, kayak on shore. f, Kayakers and bicyclists. g, Children gathering mushrooms, bears. h, People, reindeer, Santa Claus. i, Woman bringing food to table. j, Table, child in hammock.

2019, May 24 — Litho. — *Perf. 13*

4290 A4412 Sheet of 10 — 15.00 15.00
- *a.-j.* 82y Any single — 1.50 1.10

Japanese Cypress
A4413

Star Magnolia
A4414

Mongolian Oak
A4415

Chinese Fringe Tree
A4416

Japanese Irises — A4417

2019, May 28 — Litho. — *Perf. 13¼*

4291 A4413 62y multi — 1.25 .95
4292 A4414 62y multi — 1.25 .95
4293 A4415 62y multi — 1.25 .95
4294 A4416 62y multi — 1.25 .95
4295 A4417 62y multi — 1.25 .95
- *a.* Vert. strip of 5, #4291-4295 — 6.25 4.75

Nos. 4291-4295 (5) — 6.25 4.75

Sun
A4418

Starfish and Shells
A4419

Pineapple and Lemons
A4420

Fish
A4421

Hibiscus Flower
A4422

Morning Glories
A4423

Fireworks
A4424

Wind Chimes
A4425

Watermelons
A4426

Goldfish
A4427

Die Cut Perf. 13x13¼

2019, May 30 — Litho.

Self-Adhesive

4296 Sheet of 10, 2 each #4296a-4296e — 12.50
- *a.* A4418 62y multi — 1.25 .95
- *b.* A4419 62y multi — 1.25 .95
- *c.* A4420 62y multi — 1.25 .95
- *d.* A4421 62y multi — 1.25 .95
- *e.* A4422 62y multi — 1.25 .95

4297 Sheet of 10, 2 each #4297a-4297e — 15.00
- *a.* A4423 82y multi — 1.50 1.10
- *b.* A4424 82y multi — 1.50 1.10
- *c.* A4425 82y multi — 1.50 1.10
- *d.* A4426 82y multi — 1.50 1.10
- *e.* A4427 82y multi — 1.50 1.10

Ishioka Geodetic Station — A4428

Survey Airplane — A4429

Mountain Summit Triangulation With Global Navigational Satellite System — A4430

Surveyors Leveling — A4431

Japanese Sea Level Reference Point — A4432

Surveyor Using Drone — A4433

Digital Plotting A4434

Analog Stereoplotting A4435

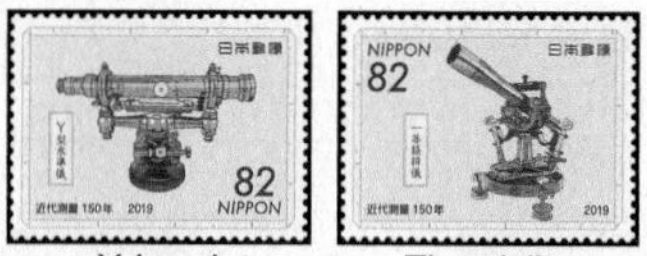

Y Level A4436

Theodolite A4437

2019, June 3 Litho. *Perf. 13x12¾*

4298	Sheet of 10	15.00	15.00
a.	A4428 82y multi	1.50	1.10
b.	A4429 82y multi	1.50	1.10
c.	A4430 82y multi	1.50	1.10
d.	A4431 82y multi	1.50	1.10
e.	A4432 82y multi	1.50	1.10
f.	A4433 82y multi	1.50	1.10
g.	A4434 82y multi	1.50	1.10
h.	A4435 82y multi	1.50	1.10
i.	A4436 82y multi	1.50	1.10
j.	A4437 82y multi	1.50	1.10

Modern surveying in Japan, 150th anniv.

Plum Knot and Umeda Sky Building, Osaka A4438

Plum Knot and Osaka Castle A4439

Plum Knot and International Exhibition Center, Osaka A4440

Plum Knot and Osaka Central City Public Hall A4441

Plum Knot and Tsutenkaku Tower, Osaka — A4442

2019, June 14 Litho. *Perf. 12¾x13*

4299	A4438 82y multi	1.50	1.10
4300	A4439 82y multi	1.50	1.10
4301	A4440 82y multi	1.50	1.10
4302	A4441 82y multi	1.50	1.10
4303	A4442 82y multi	1.50	1.10
a.	Horiz. strip of 5, #4299-4303	7.50	5.50
	Nos. 4299-4303 (5)	7.50	5.50

G20 Summit, Osaka.

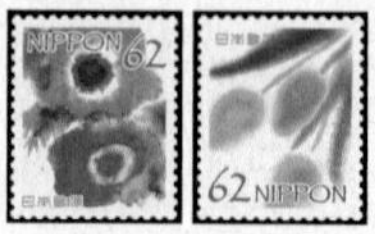

A4443 A4444

A4445 A4446

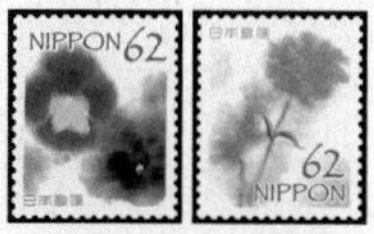

A4447 A4448

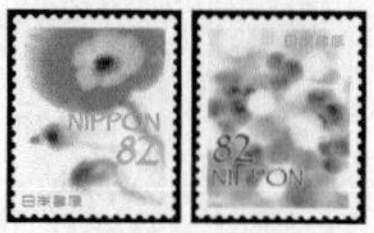

A4449 A4450

A4451 A4452

Flowers

A4453 A4454

Die Cut Perf. 13x13¼

2019, June 19 Litho.

Self-Adhesive

4304	Sheet of 10, #4304c, 4304f, 2 each #4304a-4304b, 4304d-4304e	12.50	
a.	A4443 62y multi	1.25	.95
b.	A4444 62y multi	1.25	.95
c.	A4445 62y multi	1.25	.95
d.	A4446 62y multi	1.25	.95
e.	A4447 62y multi	1.25	.95
f.	A4448 62y multi	1.25	.95
4305	Sheet of 10, #4305c, 4305f, 2 each #4305a-4305b, 4305d-4305e	15.00	
a.	A4449 82y multi	1.50	1.10
b.	A4450 82y multi	1.50	1.10
c.	A4451 82y multi	1.50	1.10
d.	A4452 82y multi	1.50	1.10
e.	A4453 82y multi	1.50	1.10
f.	A4454 82y multi	1.50	1.10

Miniature Sheet

International Labor Organization, Cent. — A4455

No. 4306: a, People, factory, wind generators. b, Farm and fishing boat. c, Cargo ship, hospital, ambulance, police car and fire engine. d, City, train, bus, bicyclist. e, Workers at construction site. f, Gears, test tubes, knife sharpener, hand, microscope beaker, can of fish, sewing machine. g, Frying pan, kitchen utensils, chef's toque, coffee pot, cutting board, corkscrew, goblet, meal on plate. h, Medical and dental items. i, Makeup, lipstick, shaver, socks, eyeglasses, scissors, comb, shirt, bag, groceries, shopping basket, cash register. j, Carpenter's square, triangle, compass, file, chisel, hammer, pencil, hard hat, camera, tape measure, paint brush and roller.

2019, June 27 Litho. *Perf. 14*

4306	A4455 Sheet of 10	15.00	15.00
a.-j.	82y Any single	1.50	1.10

A4457 A4458

A4459 A4460

A4461 A4462

A4463 A4464

A4465

Dolphins — A4466

Die Cut Perf. 13x13¼, 13¼x13 (horiz. stamps)

2019, July 3 Litho.

Self-Adhesive

4307	Sheet of 10	15.00	
a.	A4457 82y multi	1.50	1.10
b.	A4458 82y multi	1.50	1.10
c.	A4459 82y multi	1.50	1.10
d.	A4460 82y multi	1.50	1.10
e.	A4461 82y multi	1.50	1.10
f.	A4462 82y multi	1.50	1.10
g.	A4463 82y multi	1.50	1.10
h.	A4464 82y multi	1.50	1.10
i.	A4465 82y multi	1.50	1.10
j.	A4466 82y multi	1.50	1.10

Miniature Sheet

Hidden Christian Sites in the Nagasaki Region UNESCO World Heritage Sites — A4467

No. 4308: a, Aerial view of Hara Castle ruins. b, Kasugu, terraced fields and Mount Yasuman, Hirado Island. c, Nakano Island. d, Wooden church and village of Sakitsu, Amakusa Islands. e, Church and bell tower, Sotome. f, Church and statue, Ono. g, Ruins of village on Nozaki Island. h, Village and pier on Kashiraga Island. i, Church and stone wall, Hisaka Island. i, Church with blue shutters, Egami, Naru Island.

2019, July 12 Litho. *Perf. 13¼x13*

4308	A4467 Sheet of 10	15.00	15.00
a.-j.	82y Any single	1.50	1.10

Child Mailing Letter A4468

Potted Plant A4469

Squash and Flowers A4470

Bicycle A4471

Books, Lamp, Cup, Saucer, Pen and Ink Bottle A4472

Woman Writing Letter A4473

Pigeon With Letter A4474

Sunflowers A4475

Ice Cream Soda A4476

Cat and Mailbox A4477

Die Cut Perf. 13x13¼

2019, July 23 Litho.

Self-Adhesive

4309	Sheet of 10, 2 each #4309a-4309e	12.50	
a.	A4468 62y multi	1.25	.95
b.	A4469 62y multi	1.25	.95
c.	A4470 62y multi	1.25	.95
d.	A4471 62y multi	1.25	.95
e.	A4472 62y multi	1.25	.95
4310	Sheet of 10, 2 each #4310a-4310e	15.00	
a.	A4473 82y multi	1.50	1.10
b.	A4474 82y multi	1.50	1.10
c.	A4475 82y multi	1.50	1.10
d.	A4476 82y multi	1.50	1.10
e.	A4477 82y multi	1.50	1.10

Letter Writing Day.

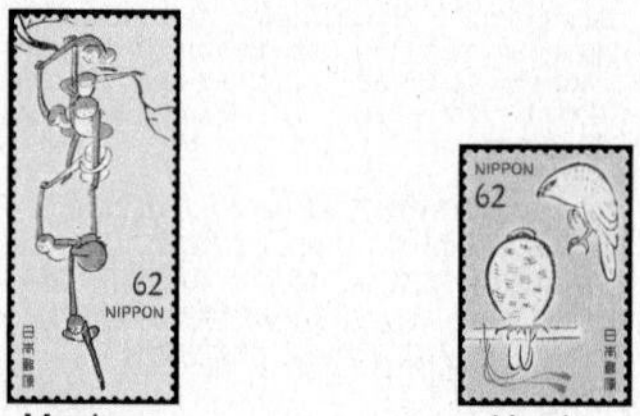

Monkeys A4478

Hawks A4479

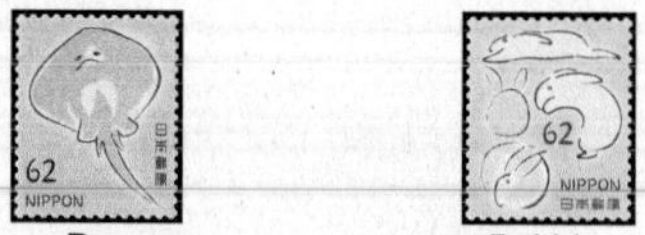

Ray A4480

Rabbits A4481

Japanese Raccoon Dogs A4482

Sparrows A4483

Frogs A4484

Mole A4485

Quails A4486

Foxes A4487

Ducks and Geese A4488

Owl A4489

Cats A4490

Squirrel A4491

Geese A4492

Deer A4493

Tigers A4494

Tilefish A4495

Cranes A4496

Elephants A4497

Die Cut Perf. 13x13¼ (#4311a, 4311c, 4311d); Die Cut Perf. 13x12¾ (#4311b, 4311e); Die Cut Perf. 13¼x13 (#4311f, 4311h); Die Cut Perf. (#4311g, 4311i), Die Cut Perf. 12¾ (#4311j)

2019, July 30 **Litho.**

Self-Adhesive

4311	Sheet of 10	12.50	
a.	A4478 62y multi	1.25	.85
b.	A4479 62y multi	1.25	.85
c.	A4480 62y multi	1.25	.85
d.	A4481 62y multi	1.25	.85
e.	A4482 62y multi	1.25	.85
f.	A4483 62y multi	1.25	.85
g.	A4484 62y multi	1.25	.85
h.	A4485 62y multi	1.25	.85
i.	A4486 62y multi	1.25	.85
j.	A4487 62y multi	1.25	.85

Die Cut Perf. 13 (#4312a, 4312e); Die Cut Perf. (#4312b, 4312d); Die Cut Perf. 13¼ (#4312c); Die Cut Perf. 12¾ (#4312f, 43121j); Die Cut Perf. 12¾x13 (#4312g, 4312i); Die Cut Perf. 13¼x13 (#4312h)

4312	Sheet of 10	15.00	
a.	A4488 82y multi	1.50	1.10
b.	A4489 82y multi	1.50	1.10
c.	A4490 82y multi	1.50	1.10
d.	A4491 82y multi	1.50	1.10
e.	A4492 82y multi	1.50	1.10
f.	A4493 82y multi	1.50	1.10
g.	A4494 82y multi	1.50	1.10
h.	A4495 82y multi	1.50	1.10
i.	A4496 82y multi	1.50	1.10
j.	A4497 82y multi	1.50	1.10

Hybrid Cherry Blossoms A4498

Plum Blossoms A4499

Violets — A4500

Iriomote-Ishigaki National Park — A4501

Nikko National Park A4502

Seto Inland Sea National Park A4503

2019, Aug. 20 **Photo.** ***Perf. 13x13¼***

4313	A4498	63y multi	1.25	.95
4314	A4499	84y multi	1.60	1.25
4315	A4500	94y multi	1.75	1.40
4316	A4501	210y multi	4.00	3.00
4317	A4502	290y multi	5.50	4.25
4318	A4503	320y multi	6.00	4.50
	Nos. 4313-4318 (6)		20.10	15.35

A4504

Red-crowned Cranes
A4505 A4506

2019, Aug. 20 **Photo.** ***Perf. 13x13¼***

4319	A4504	63y multi	1.25	.95
4320	A4505	84y multi	1.60	1.25
4321	A4506	94y multi	1.75	1.40
	Nos. 4319-4321 (3)		4.60	3.60

Flowers — A4507

2019, Aug. 20 **Photo.** ***Perf. 13x13¼***

4322	A4507	63y multi	1.25	.95

Miniature Sheets

A4508

Miffy A4509

No. 4323 — Miffy: a, In house (25x35mm). b, On bicyle (26x31mm). c, With pilot in airplane (25x25mm). d, Viewing heads of rabbits on wall (25x25mm). e, On swing (25x25mm). f, With three elephants (25x25mm). g, Wearing yellow headdress (25x25mm). h, In tree (25x25mm). i, With paint brushes (25x25mm). j, With chicks (25x25mm).

No. 4324: a, Miffy writing letter (26x30mm). b, Head of Miffy (23x33mm). c, Miffy wearing red dress (26x26mm). d, Miffy and flowers (26x26mm). e, Miffy holding teddy bear (26x26mm). f, Miffy and pen (26x26mm). g, Miffy and five other rabbits (26x26mm). h, Miffy, other rabbit and beach ball (26x26mm). i, Miffy and stuffed animals (26x26mm). j, Miffy and pig wearing rabbit ears (26x26mm).

Die Cut Perf. 14½; Die Cut Perf. 13 (#4323a); Die Cut Perf. (#4323b)

2019, Aug. 20 **Litho.**

Self-Adhesive

4323	A4508	Sheet of 10 + 5 stickers	12.50	
a.-j.		63y Any single	1.25	.95

Die Cut Perf. 14; Die Cut Perf. 13 (#4324a, 4324b)

4324	A4509	Sheet of 10 + 6 stickers	16.00	
a.-j.		84y Any single	1.60	1.25

Miniature Sheets

A4510

Autumn Greetings — A4511

No. 4325: a, Squirrel with acorn. b, Walnut. c, Pine cone (denomination at right in white and brown). d, Bird, walnut and pine cone. e, Pine cones (green denomination). f, Pine cones (denomination at UL in white and red). g, Yew aril and pine cone. h, Squirrel and pine cone. i, Bird and acorn. j, Cedar rose pine cones (denomination at LL in white and brown).

No. 4326: a, Mushrooms. b, Cardinal and apple. c, Flowers. d, Grapes and melon. e, Autumn leaves and berries. f, Squirrel, squash and berries. g, Carrots, squash and berries. h, Apples, flowers and pumpkin. i, Mouse and beet. j, Mouse and pumpkin.

Die Cut Perf. 13x13¼

2019, Aug. 23 **Litho.**

Self-Adhesive

4325	A4510	Sheet of 10	12.50	
a.-j.		63y Any single	1.25	.95
4326	A4511	Sheet of 10	16.00	
a.-j.		84y Any single	1.60	1.25

Miniature Sheet

74th National Athletic Meet, Ibaraki Prefecture — A4512

No. 4327: a, Golf. b, Kairaku-en Gardens, Mito. c, Sailboats. d, Mount Tsukuba. e, Show jumping. f, Hitachi Seaside Park. g, Wall climbing. h, Fukuroda Falls. i, Rifle shooting. j, Ryujin Gorge.

2019, Aug. 28 **Litho.** ***Perf. 13***

4327	A4512	Sheet of 10	16.00	16.00
a.-j.		84y Any single	1.60	1.25

Souvenir Sheet

Moon and Plum Blossoms — A4513

No. 4328: a, Moon. b, Plum blossoms.

2019, Sept. 3 **Litho.** ***Perf. 13x13¼***

4328	A4513	Sheet of 2	3.00	3.00
a.		63y multi	1.25	.95
b.		84y multi	1.60	1.25

No. 4328 was sold to the public, but also was awarded as a lottery prize.

Miniature Sheets

A4514

My Journey
A4515

No. 4329: a, Lantern, Kenroku-en Garden (23x19mm). b, Illuminated trees at night, Kenroku-en Garden (19x24mm). c, Higasahi Chaya District at twilight, Kanazawa (23x19mm). d, Plum knot (26x25mm). e, Kutani porcelain plate (26mm diameter). f, Shima Teahouse, Higashi Chaya District (23x19mm). g, Exterior of houses, Nagamachi Samurai House District (23x19mm). h, Confections (23x19mm). i, Dyed textile with floral design (19x23mm). j, Stream near Samurai house (23x19mm).

No. 4330: a, Oyama Shrine, Kanazawa (19x23mm). b, Tsuzumi Gate (23x19mm). c, Lanterns, Kenroku-en Garden (23x19mm). d, Illuminated trees in daylight, Kenroku-en Garden (23x19mm). e, Higashi Chaya District in daylight (23x19mm). f, Doll (23x25mm). g, Temari ball (24mm diameter). h, Kanazawa Castle (23x19mm). i, Bridge, Gyokusen-in Garden (23x19mm). j, Shrimp and rice bowl (25mm diameter).

Die Cut Perf. 13¼x13; Die Cut Perf. 13x12¾ (#4329b); Die Cut Perf. (#4329d, 4329e, 4330f, 4330g, 4330j); Die Cut Perf. 13x13¼ (#4329i, 4330a)

2019, Sept. 4 Litho.

Self-Adhesive

4329	A4514	Sheet of 10	12.50	
a.-j.		63y Any single	1.25	.95
4330	A4515	Sheet of 10	16.00	
a.-j.		84y Any single	1.60	1.25

Miniature Sheet

2019 Rugby World Cup, Japan
A4516

No. 4331 — Emblem or flag of teams from: a, Ireland, New Zealand. b, Scotland, South Africa. c, Japan, Italy. d, Russia, Namibia. e, Samoa, Canada. f, England, Australia. g, France, Wales. h, Argentina, Georgia. i, United States, Fiji. j, Tonga, Uruguay.

2019, Sept. 6 Litho. *Perf. 14¼*

4331	A4516	Sheet of 10	16.00	16.00
a.-j.		84y Any single	1.60	1.25

Miniature Sheets

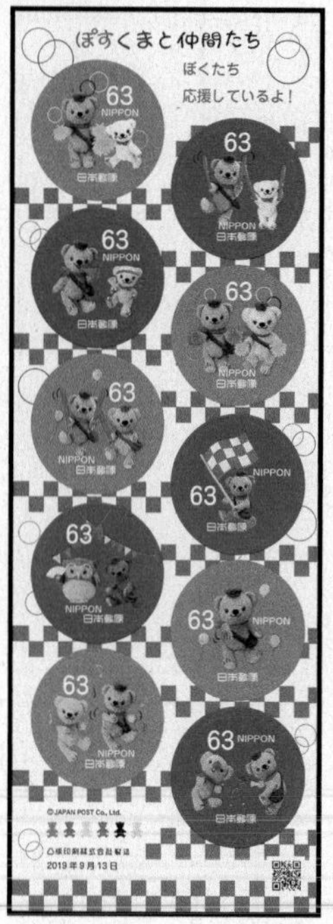

A4517

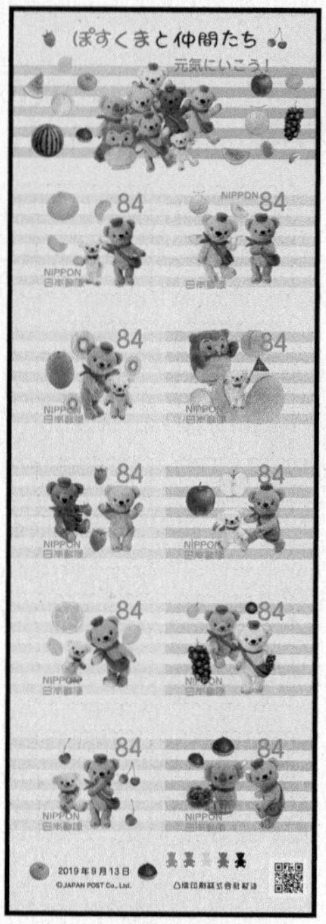

Posukuma — A4518

No. 4332 — Japan Post teddy bear mascot with: a. Other teddy bear, yellow pom-poms. b, Other teddy bear, red batons. c, Other teddy bear, megaphones. d, Other teddy bear, blue and yellow pom-poms. e, Other teddy bear, blue batons. f, Checkered flag. g, Owl. h, Balloons. i, Other teddy bear, musical notes. j, Streamers and confetti.

No. 4333 — Stuffed animals and: a, Oranges. b, Honeydew melons. c, Kiwis. d, Peaches. e, Strawberries. f, Apples. g, Lemons. h, Grapes. i, Cherries. j, Chestnuts.

2019, Sept. 13 Litho. *Die Cut Perf.*

Self-Adhesive

4332	A4517	Sheet of 10	12.50	
a.-j.		63y Any single	1.25	.95

Die Cut Perf. 10¼x12¼

4333	A4518	Sheet of 10	16.00	
a.-j.		84y Any single	1.60	1.25

Miniature Sheet

Japan Art Academy, Cent. — A4519

No. 4334 — Paintings: a, The Charcoal Kiln, by Somei Yuki (stamp #1). b, The White Horse, by Kayo Yamaguchi (stamp #2). c, Evening Glow, by Kaii Higashiyama (stamp #3). d, Silence, by Manyo Ito (stamp #4). e, By the Window, by Gakuryo Nakamura (stamp #5). f, Forest Light, by Kan Hamada (stamp #6). g, Portrait of a Lady, by Keizo Koyama (stamp #7). h, Wall on the Rue St. Jacques, by Shinichi Nishiyama (stamp #8). i, Clematis, by Chikuma Suzuki (stamp #9). j, Interior with Female Figure, by Takanori Kinoshita (stamp #10).

2019, Sept. 20 Litho. *Perf. 13*

4334	A4519	Sheet of 10	16.00	16.00
a.-j.		84y Any single	1.60	1.25

Stars
A4520

Leaves
A4521

Birds — A4522

Die Cut Perf. 13x13¼

2019, Sept. 25 Litho.

Self-Adhesive

4335	A4520	63y multi	1.25	.95
4336	A4521	84y multi	1.60	1.25
4337	A4522	94y multi	1.75	1.40
		Nos. 4335-4337 (3)	4.60	3.60

Miniature Sheet

Chugoku Region, Honshu, at Night
A4523

No. 4338: a, Bridge over Kanmon Straits (stamp #1). b, Breakwater Lighthouse, Takamatsu (stamp #2). c, Tokushima (stamp #3). d, Moji (stamp #4). e, Beppu Hot Springs (stamp #5). f, Nobeoka (stamp #6). g, Kumamoto Castle (stamp #7). h, Sakurajima (stamp #8). i, Onomichi Channel, denomination at UL. j, Onomichi Channel, denomination at UR.

2019, Sept. 27 Litho. *Perf. 13*

4338	A4523	Sheet of 10	16.00	16.00
a.-j.		84y Any single	1.60	1.25

Origami Pinwheel
A4524

Origami Dove
A4525

Origami Swallow
A4526

Origami Houses
A4527

Origami Dahlia
A4528

Origami Airplane
A4529

Origami Birds
A4530

Origami Goldfish
A4531

Origami Crane and Tortoise
A4532

Origami Camellia
A4533

Playthings — A4534

No. 4340: a, Paper balloon (30mm diameter). b, Kite (42x38mm). c, Party favors (30x30mm). d, Paddle and shuttlecock (25x42mm). e, Stick helicopter (30x30mm). f, Boats (30x30mm). g, Shogi piece (30x35mm). h, Top (30x39mm oval). i, Marbles (30x30mm). j, Ball and cup (24x44mm).

Die Cut Perf. 13¼

2019, Oct. 2 **Litho.**

Self-Adhesive

4339		Sheet of 10	12.50	
a.	A4524 63y multi		1.25	.95
b.	A4525 63y multi		1.25	.95
c.	A4526 63y multi		1.25	.95
d.	A4527 63y multi		1.25	.95
e.	A4528 63y multi		1.25	.95
f.	A4529 63y multi		1.25	.95
g.	A4530 63y multi		1.25	.95
h.	A4531 63y multi		1.25	.95
i.	A4532 63y multi		1.25	.95
j.	A4533 63y multi		1.25	.95

Die Cut Perf. 12½; Die Cut Perf. 12¼ (#4340b, 4340d, 4340j), Die Cut Perf. (#4340a, 4340h)

4340	A4534	Sheet of 10	16.00	
a.-j.		84y Any single	1.60	1.25

A4535

A4536

International Letter Writing Week — A4537

Art by Hiroshige: 7y, Mandarin Duck. No. 4342, Flowering Apple Tree with Small Birds (apple tree). No. 4343, Flowering Apple Tree with Small Birds (bird). 90y, Travelers to Nissaka Near Night Weeping Stone. 110y, Travelers in Narumi. 130y, Seki, Early Departure from the Headquarters Inn.

2019, Oct. 9 **Litho.** ***Perf. 13x13¼***

4341	A4535	7y multi	.25	.25
4342		70y multi	1.30	1.00
4343		70y multi	1.30	1.00
a.	A4536	Vert. pair, #4342-4343	2.60	2.00
4344	A4537	90y multi	1.75	1.40
4345	A4537	110y multi	2.10	1.60
4346	A4537	130y multi	2.40	1.75
		Nos. 4341-4346 (6)	9.10	7.00

See listing of No. 4448 for images of each Hiroshige print.

Miniature Sheet

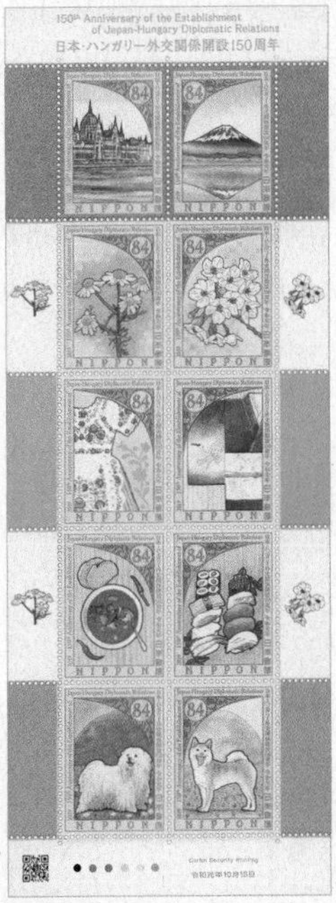

Diplomatic Relations Between Japan and Hungary, 150th Anniv. — A4538

No. 4347: a, Hungarian Parliament Building. b, Mount Fuji. c, White and yellow chamomile flowers. d, Pink and white cherry blossoms. e, Hungarian woman's traditional costume from Kalocsa. f, Japanese kimono. g, Pot of Hungarian goulash. h, Sushi. i, Puli (white dog). j, Shiba (brown dog).

2019, Oct. 15 **Litho.** ***Perf. 13***

4347	A4538	Sheet of 10	16.00	16.00
a.-j.		84y Any single	1.60	1.25

See Hungary No. 4535.

Miniature Sheet

Diplomatic Relations Between Japan and Austria, 150th Anniv. — A4539

No. 4348: a, Hofburg Palace, Vienna. b, St. Stephen's Cathedral, Vienna. c, Schönbrunn Palace, Vienna. d, Christmas Market at Vienna City Hall. e, Wolfgang Amadeus Mozart (1756-91), composer. f, The Kiss, by Gustav Klimt (1862-1918). g, Sachertorte and coffee. h, Alps. i, Vienna Philharmonic Orchestra. j, Vienna Boys' Choir.

2019, Oct. 16 **Litho.** ***Perf. 13***

4348	A4539	Sheet of 10	16.00	16.00
a.-j.		84y Any single	1.60	1.25

Phoenix
A4540

Floral Arabesque
A4541

2019, Oct. 18 **Photo.** ***Perf. 13¼***

4349	A4540	84y multi	1.60	1.25
4350	A4541	84y multi	1.60	1.25
a.		Pair, #4349-4350	3.20	2.50

Enthronement of Emperor Naruhito. Printed in sheet that contains 5 of No. 4350a.

Mushrooms
A4542

Nuts and Pine Cone
A4543

Ladybugs
A4544

Animal Tracks
A4545

Moss-covered Rocks
A4546

Leaves
A4547

Japanese Raccoon Dog
A4548

Leaves and Bears
A4549

Pinecone Detail
A4550

Fish
A4551

Acorns, Nuts and Seeds
A4552

Pine Needles
A4553

Flowers
A4554

Animals
A4555

Squirrel
A4556

Leaves
A4557

Mushrooms
A4558

Tree Growth Rings
A4559

Rabbit
A4560

Animals
A4561

Die Cut Perf. 13x13¼; Die Cut Perf. 13¼ (#4352d, 4352e, 4352i, 4352j)

2019, Oct. 23 **Litho.**

Self-Adhesive

4351	Sheet of 10	12.50	
a.	A4542 63y multi	1.25	.95
b.	A4543 63y multi	1.25	.95
c.	A4544 63y multi	1.25	.95
d.	A4545 63y multi	1.25	.95
e.	A4546 63y multi	1.25	.95
f.	A4547 63y multi	1.25	.95
g.	A4548 63y multi	1.25	.95
h.	A4549 63y multi	1.25	.95
i.	A4550 63y multi	1.25	.95
j.	A4551 63y multi	1.25	.95
4352	Sheet of 10	16.00	
a.	A4552 84y multi	1.60	1.25
b.	A4553 84y multi	1.60	1.25
c.	A4554 84y multi	1.60	1.25
d.	A4555 84y multi	1.60	1.25
e.	A4556 84y multi	1.60	1.25
f.	A4557 84y multi	1.60	1.25
g.	A4558 84y multi	1.60	1.25
h.	A4559 84y multi	1.60	1.25
i.	A4560 84y multi	1.60	1.25
j.	A4561 84y multi	1.60	1.25

A4562

A4563

New Year 2020 (Year of the Rat)
A4564 A4565

2019, Nov. 1 **Litho.** ***Perf. 13x13¼***

4353	A4562	63y multi	1.25	.95
4354	A4563	84y multi	1.60	1.25

Litho. & Typo.

Perf. 13¼

4355	A4564	63y+3y multi	1.25	.95
4356	A4565	84y+3y multi	1.60	1.25
		Nos. 4353-4356 (4)	5.70	4.40

Plants
A4566

Cast Iron Teapot
A4567

Salmon
A4568

Pine Branches
A4569

New Year's Decoration
A4570

Bobblehead Cat Doll
A4571

Lobster
A4572

Mice With Gold Coins
A4573

Red-crowned Cranes
A4574

Sparrows
A4575

Plum Blossoms
A4576

Charcoal
A4577

Decorative Carrot Slices
A4578

Igloo
A4579

Bean Soup
A4580

Yu Instrument
A4581

Mountain
A4582

Pine Needles
A4583

Comb and Hair Stick
A4584

Rolled Omelet
A4585

Die Cut Perf. 13x13¼

2019, Nov. 6 **Litho.**

Self-Adhesive

4357 Sheet of 10 12.50
a. A4566 63y multi 1.25 .95
b. A4567 63y multi 1.25 .95
c. A4568 63y multi 1.25 .95
d. A4569 63y multi 1.25 .95
e. A4570 63y multi 1.25 .95
f. A4571 63y multi 1.25 .95
g. A4572 63y multi 1.25 .95
h. A4573 63y multi 1.25 .95
i. A4574 63y multi 1.25 .95
j. A4575 63y multi 1.25 .95
4358 Sheet of 10 16.00
a. A4576 84y multi 1.60 1.25
b. A4577 84y multi 1.60 1.25
c. A4578 84y multi 1.60 1.25
d. A4579 84y multi 1.60 1.25
e. A4580 84y multi 1.60 1.25
f. A4581 84y multi 1.60 1.25
g. A4582 84y multi 1.60 1.25
h. A4583 84y multi 1.60 1.25
i. A4584 84y multi 1.60 1.25
j. A4585 84y multi 1.60 1.25

Miniature Sheets

A4586

Winter Greetings — A4587

No. 4359: a, Candles and snow globe (24x24mm). b, Cat and flower vase (24x24mm). c, Books, eyeglasses, unfinished woolen sock (24x24mm). d, Fruit bowl, teapot and cup (24x24mm). e, Mouse in yarn basket (24x24mm). f, Cat and sweater (26x24mm). g, Mice, mitten and sock (24x24mm). h, Knitted sweater and knitting needles (25x26mm). i, Cat and mitten (24x24mm). j, Cat and ball of yarn (27mm diameter).

No. 4360: a, Chair lift (30x21mm). b, Skiers (21x30mm). c, Deer, fox and trees (27x27mm). d, House (30x21mm). e, Snowman, rabbit and dog (27x27mm). f, People making snowman (27x27mm). g, Man pulling children on sled (30x21mm). h, Ice skater (21x30mm). i, Two ice skaters (21x30mm). j, Ice fisherman (27x27mm).

Die Cut Perf. 13¼; Die Cut Perf. (#4359h, 4359j)

2019, Nov. 22 **Litho. & Embossed**

Self-Adhesive

4359 A4586 Sheet of 10 + 2 stickers 12.50
a.-j. 63y Any single 1.25 .95

Die Cut Perf. 13¼x13 (#4360a, 4360d, 4360g); Die Cut Perf. 13x13¼ (#4360b, 4360h, 4360i); Die Cut Perf. 13¼ (#4360c, 4360e, 4360f, 4360j)

4360 A4587 Sheet of 10 + 5 stickers 16.00
a.-j. 84y Any single 1.60 1.25

Miniature Sheet

Guri and Gura, Children's Book Characters by Rieko Nakagawa — A4588

No. 4361: a, Guri and Gura with backpacks (34x29mm). b, Guri and Gura on log with other animals (38x28mm). c, Guri and Gura in cracked egg car (38x28mm). d, Guri whisking food in bowl (32x27mm). e, Gura lifting lid of frying pan (38x28mm). f, Guri and Gura writing (34x29mm). g, Guri and Gura carrying basket (28x28mm). h, Guri and Gura lifting egg (39x31mm oval). i, Guri and Gura on log (39x31mm oval). j, Guri lifting lid on frying pan (27x32mm).

Die Cut Perf. 13x13¼ (#4361a, 4361d, 4361f); Die Cut Perf. 13¼x13 (#4361b, 4361e, 4361j); Die Cut Perf. 13 (#4361c, 4361g); Die Cut Perf. (#4361h, 4361i)

2019, Nov. 28 **Litho.**

Self-Adhesive

4361 A4588 Sheet of 10 + 4 stickers 16.00
a.-j. 84y Any single 1.60 1.25

Upright Piano
A4589

Bass Drum
A4590

Banjo
A4591

Sousaphone
A4592

Trumpet — A4593

Musical Instruments — A4594

No. 4363: a, Vibraphone (28x23mm). b, Drum set (32x22mm). c, Electric guitar (30x25mm). d, Two trumpets (28x23mm). e, Three trombones (32x32mm). f, Grand piano (26x33mm). g, Bass (23x32mm). h, Alto saxophone (22x30mm). i, Tenor saxophone (21x32mm). j, Baritone saxophone (21x42mm).

Die Cut Perf. 13x12¾ (#4362a), 13¼x13 (#4362b), 13¾x13¼ (#43623c), 13 (#4362d), 13x13¾ (#4362e)

2019, Dec. 6 **Litho.**

Self-Adhesive

4362 Sheet of 10, 2 each #4362a-4362e 12.50
a. A4589 63y multi 1.25 .95
b. A4590 63y multi 1.25 .95
c. A4591 63y multi 1.25 .95
d. A4592 63y multi 1.25 .95
e. A4593 63y multi 1.25 .95

Die Cut Perf. 12¾x12½ (#4363a), 12¾x13 (#4363b), 13 (#4363c), 12¾x12¼ (#4363d, 4363h),13¼x13 (#4363e, 4363i), 13x13¼ (#4363f), 13½ (#4363g), 13¼ (#4363j)

4363 A4594 Sheet of 10 16.00
a.-j. 84y Any single 1.60 1.25

A4595

A4596

A4597

A4598

A4599

The Little Prince, by Antoine de Saint-Exupery (1900-44) — A4600

No. 4365 — The Little Prince: a, With sword (37x41mm). b, Standing near two flowers (24x45mm). c, With shovel (28x27mm). d, Carried by birds (28x38mm). e, Under star (28x38mm). f, Standing near flower bushes (38x27mm). g, On ground, looking at flowers (27x27mm). h, Looking at fox (38x27mm). i, At well (27x27mm). j, Bending backwards (27x27mm).

Die Cut Perf. (#4364a, 4364e), Die Cut Perf. 13¼ (#4364b-4364d, 4365b-4365c, 4365f-4365j), 13 (#4365a), 13x13¼ (#4365d-4365e)

2019, Dec. 11 **Litho.**

Self-Adhesive

4364 Sheet of 10, 2 each #4364a-4364e 12.50
a. A4595 63y multi 1.25 .95
b. A4596 63y multi 1.25 .95
c. A4597 63y multi 1.25 .95
d. A4598 63y multi 1.25 .95
e. A4599 63y multi 1.25 .95
4365 A4600 Sheet of 10 16.00
a.-j. 84y Any single 1.60 1.25

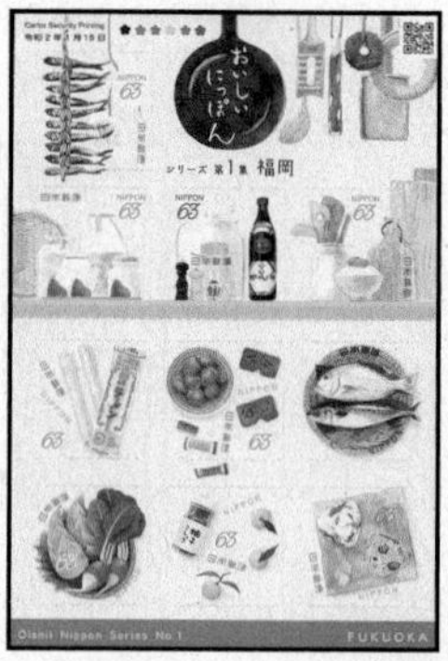
A4601

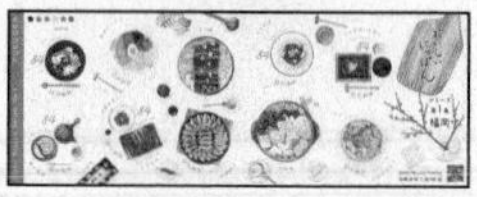
Food
A4602

No. 4366: a, Dried fish and garlic bulbs. b, Steamed buns shaped like chicks, jars. c, Bottle of soy sauce, salt shaker and pepper mill. d, Bowl of rice with pollock roe, kitchen utensils. e, Package of ramen noodles. f, Rice crackers and bowl of strawberries. g, Sea bream and mackerel on plate. h, Vegetables. i, Bottle of pepper and lemons. j, Rice balls.

No. 4367: a, Bowl of soup with rice cakes and vegetables. b, Plate of pork, egg, vegetables and ramen noodles. c, Hot pot with vegetables. d, Dish of raw mackerel with soy sauce and vegetables. e, Rectangular plate with steamed eel. f, Rice cake, tea pot and tea cup. g, Bowl of seaweed, plate of chicken strips on skewers. h, Dumplings in pan. i, Hot pot with chicken and vegetables. j, Bowl of burdock root tempura noodle soup.

Die Cut Perf. 13¼

2020, Jan. 15 **Litho.**

Self-Adhesive

4366 A4601 Booklet pane of 10, #4366a-4366j 12.50
a.-j. 63y Any single 1.25 .95
4367 A4602 Booklet pane of 10, #4367a-4367j 16.00
a.-j. 84y Any single 1.60 1.25

Souvenir Sheet

New Year 2020 (Year of the Rat)
A4603

No. 4368: a, Rat, flower and Japanese character for "good fortune." b, Flower and Japanese character for "best wishes."

2020, Jan. 20 Photo. *Perf. 13x13¼*

4368	A4603	Sheet of 2	3.00	3.00
a.		63y multi	1.25	.95
b.		84y multi	1.60	1.25

No. 4368 was sold to the public, but also was awarded as a lottery prize.

Roses
A4604

Roses
A4605

Flowers
A4606

Flowers
A4607

Orchids
A4608

Orchids
A4609

Die Cut Perf. 12¾x13 (#4369a), 13 (#4370a, 4371a), Die Cut Perf. (#4369b, 4370b, 4371b)
Litho. With Foil Application
2020, Jan. 23
Self-Adhesive

4369	Sheet of 10, 5 each #4369a-4369b	12.50	
a.	A4604 63y gold & multi	1.25	.95
b.	A4605 63y gold & multi	1.25	.95
4370	Sheet of 10, 5 each #4370a-4370b	16.00	
a.	A4606 84y gold & multi	1.60	1.25
b.	A4607 84y gold & multi	1.60	1.25
4371	Sheet of 10, 5 each #4371a-4371b	17.50	
a.	A4608 94y gold & multi	1.75	1.40
b.	A4609 94y gold & multi	1.75	1.40
	Nos. 4369-4371 (3)	46.00	

Miniature Sheet

National Parks
A4610

No. 4372: a, Akan-Mashu National Park. b, Oze National Park. c, Chibu Sangaku National Park. d, San'in Kaigan National Park. e, Unzen-Amakusa National Park. f, Sanriku Fukko National Park. g, Dolphins at Ogasawara National Park. h, Yoshino-Kumano National Park. i, Amami Gunto National Park. j, Fish at Kerama Shoto National Park.

2020, Jan. 28 Litho. *Perf. 12¾x13*

4372	A4610	Sheet of 10	16.00	16.00
a.-j.		84y Any single	1.60	1.25

Miniature Sheet

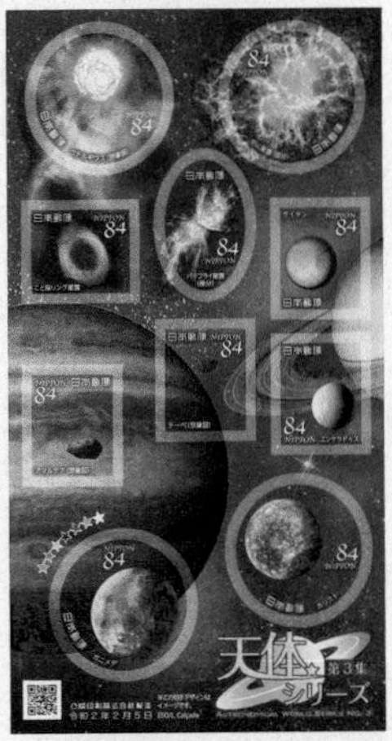

Astronomy — A4611

No. 4373: a, Star cluster (32mm diameter). b, Crab Nebula (32mm diameter. c, Ring Nebula (26x22mm). d, Butterfly Nebula (21x32mm oval). e, Titan (22x26mm). f, Amalthea (22x26mm). g, Thebe (22x26mm). h, Enceladus (22x26mm). i, Ganymede (32mm diameter). j, Callisto (32mm diameter).

Die Cut Perf. (#4373a-4373b, 4373d, 4373i-4373j), Die Cut Perf. 13¼x13 (#4373c); 13x13¼ (#4373e-4373h)
Litho. With Holographic Foil Affixed
2020, Feb. 5
Self-Adhesive

4373	A4611	Sheet of 10	16.00	
a.-j.		84y Any single	1.60	1.25

Miniature Sheets

Hakodate Tourist Attractions — A4612

Miyakojima Tourist Attractions — A4613

No. 4374: a, Hakodate Orthodox Christian Church (28x28mm). b, Old Public Hall (38x28mm). c, Tram (32mm diameter). d, Goryokaku Tower (32x31mm pentagonal), e, Red brick warehouses (38x28mm).

No. 4375: a, Guardian lion (28x28mm). b, Ruddy kingfisher (38x28mm). c, Hibiscus (32mm diameter). d, Clownfish (28x28mm). e, Green sea turtle (38x28mm).

Die Cut Perf. 13x13½ (#4374a, 4375a, 4375d), 13¼ (#4374b, 4374e, 4375b, 4375e), 13 (4374d); Die Cut Perf. (4374c, 4375c)
2020, Feb. 7 Litho.
Self-Adhesive

4374	A4612	Sheet of 5	8.00	
a.-e.		84y Any single	1.60	1.25
4375	A4613	Sheet of 5	8.00	
a.-e.		84y Any single	1.60	1.25

Miniature Sheets

A4614

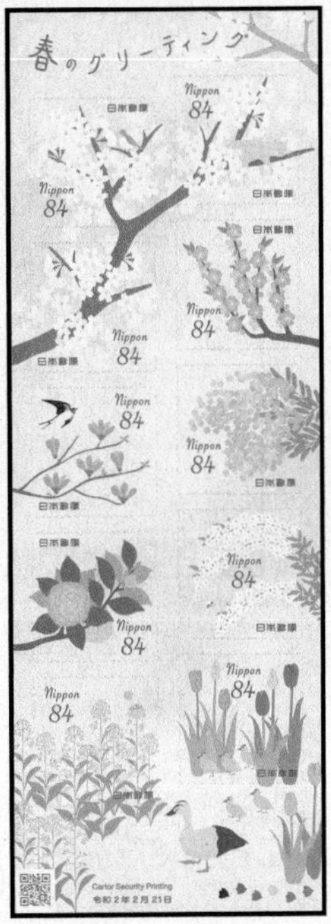

Flowers
A4615

No. 4376: a, Dandelions. b, Nemophila. c, Strawberries. d, Primroses. e, Daisies and ladybug. f, Winter daphnes and bee. g, Peonies. h, Poppies. i, Pansies, j, Clover and cat.

No. 4377: a, White cherry blossoms and cat. b, White cherry blossoms and bird. c, Pink peach blossoms. d, White cherry blossoms. e, Mimosa. f, Rose of Sharon and swallow. g, Spirea and bee. h, Camellia. i, Tulips and ducklings. j, Rape blossoms.

2020, Feb. 21 Litho. *Die Cut Perf.*
Self-Adhesive

4376	A4614	Sheet of 10	12.50	
a.-j.		63y Any single	1.25	.95

Die Cut Perf. 13¼

4377	A4615	Sheet of 10	16.00	
a.-j.		84y Any single	1.60	1.25

Cherry Blossoms
A4616

Asian Fawnlily
A4617

Safflower
A4618

Hydrangea
A4619

Japanese Irises
A4620

Citrus Blossoms
A4621

Tulips
A4622

Cherry Blossoms
A4623

Hydrangea
A4624

Carnations
A4625

Die Cut Perf. 13x13¼
2020, Mar. 3 Litho.
Self-Adhesive

4378	Sheet of 10, 2 each #4378a-4378e	12.50	
a.	A4616 63y multi	1.25	.95
b.	A4617 63y multi	1.25	.95
c.	A4618 63y multi	1.25	.95
d.	A4619 63y multi	1.25	.95
e.	A4620 63y multi	1.25	.95
4379	Sheet of 10, 2 each #4379a-4379e	16.00	
a.	A4621 84y multi	1.60	1.25
b.	A4622 84y multi	1.60	1.25
c.	A4623 84y multi	1.60	1.25
d.	A4624 84y multi	1.60	1.25
e.	A4625 84y multi	1.60	1.25

Torch and Torch Bearer for 2020 Summer Olympics, Tokyo — A4626

Torch, torch bearer and: No. 4380, Olympic rings. No. 4381, Paralympics emblem.

2020, Mar. 10 Litho. *Perf. 14*

4380	84y multi	1.60	1.25
4381	84y multi	1.60	1.25
a.	A4626 Vert. pair, #4380-4381	3.20	2.50

The 2020 Summer Olympics and Paralympics were postponed until 2021 because of the coronavirus pandemic.

Miniature Sheets

A4627

Art A4628

No. 4382: a, Rabbits and flowers from Edo period porcelain plate (27x28mm). b, Irises from Scroll of Flowers and Plants of the Four Seasons, by Hoitsu Sakai (1761-1829) (27x28mm). c, Fisherman from Kajikazawa in Kai Provimce, by Hokusai Katsushika (1760-1849) (27x28mm). d, Woman Waiting for the Moon to Rise, by Shoen Uemura (1875-1949) (25x26mm). e, Hydrangea from Cloisonné vase, by Yasuyuki Namikawai (1845-1927) (22x30mm). f, The Lakeside, by Seiki Kuroda (1866-1924) (25x30mm). g, Mount Fuji Above the Clouds, by Taikan Yokoyama (1868-1958) (31x25mm). h, Pegasus, by Odilon Redon (1840-1916) (22x30mm). i, Portrait of Valentine Tessier, by Marie Laurencin (1883-1956) (22x30mm). j, Water Lilies, by Claude Monet (1846-1926) (27x25mm).

No. 4383: a, Rabbits and flowers from Edo period porcelain plate (31x35mm). b, Irises from Scroll of Flowers and Plants of the Four Seasons, by Sakai (36x30mm). c, Fisherman from Kajikazawa in Kai Provimce, by Hokusai (36x30mm). d, Oh, an Evening Shower, by Seiho Takeuchi (1864-1942) (23x45mm). e, The Lakeside, by Kuroda (33x32mm). f, Mount Fuji Above the Clouds, by Yokoyama (36x30mm). g, Grand Bouquet, by Redon (33x39mm). h, Portrait of Valentine Tessier, by Laurencin (28x39mm). i, Water Lilies, by Monet (33x395mm). j, Cloisonné vase depicting hydrangeas, by Namikawai (23x45mm).

Die Cut Perf. 12¾ (#4382a, 4382b, 4382c, 4382j), 12¾x13 (#4382d), 13x13¼ (#4382e, 4382f), 13x12½ (#4382g), 13 (#4382h, 4382i)

2020, Mar. 19 Litho.

Self-Adhesive

4382 A4627 Sheet of 10 12.50
a.-j. 63y Any single 1.25 .95

Die Cut Perf. 13x12¾ (#4383a), 13x13¼ (#4383b, 4383c, 4383d, 4383e, 4383f, 4383j), 13 (#4383g, 4383h, 4383i)

4383 A4628 Sheet of 10 16.00
a.-j. 84y Any single 1.60 1.25

White Roses A4629

Pink Roses A4630

Purple Roses A4631

Orange Roses A4632

Red Roses A4633

Pink Roses A4634

Pale Orange Roses A4635

Magenta Roses A4636

Peach Roses A4637

White Roses A4638

Die Cut Perf. 13½x13, 13½ (#4385e)

2020, Apr. 1 Litho.

Self-Adhesive

4384 Sheet of 10, 2 each #4384a-4384e 12.50
a. A4629 63y multi 1.25 .95
b. A4630 63y multi 1.25 .95
c. A4631 63y multi 1.25 .95
d. A4632 63y multi 1.25 .95
e. A4633 63y multi 1.25 .95

4385 Sheet of 10, 2 each #4385a-4385e 16.00
a. A4634 84y multi 1.60 1.25
b. A4635 84y multi 1.60 1.25
c. A4636 84y multi 1.60 1.25
d. A4637 84y multi 1.60 1.25
e. A4638 84y multi 1.60 1.25

Miniature Sheet

14th United Nations Congress on Crime Prevention and Criminal Justice, Kyoto — A4639

No. 4386: a, Birds and feathers. b, Congress emblem depicting cherry blossoms. c, Golden Pavilion, Kyoto. d, Kyoto Congress Youth Forum emblem depicting crane. e, Homes, woman and child. f, Buildings, four people.

2020, Apr. 6 Litho. *Perf. 13½*

4386 A4639 Sheet of 10, #4386e, 4386f, 2 each #4386a-4386d 16.00 16.00
a.-f. 84y Any single 1.60 1.25

Stylized Tree A4640

Stylized Tree A4641

Stylized Tree — A4642

Die Cut Perf. 13x13¼

2020, Apr. 15 Litho.

Self-Adhesive

4387 A4640 63y blue & multi 1.25 .95
4388 A4641 84y emerald & multi 1.60 1.25
4389 A4642 94y red violet & multi 1.75 1.40
Nos. 4387-4389 (3) 4.60 3.60

Red and White Plum Blossoms, Screen Painting by Korin Ogata (1658-1716) — A4643

Plum tree with: No. 4390, White blossoms. No. 4391, Red blossoms.

Photo. & Engr.

2020, Apr. 20 *Perf. 13¼*

4390 84y gold & black 1.60 1.25
4391 84y gold & black 1.60 1.25
a. A4643 Horiz. pair, #4390-4391 3.20 2.50

Philatelic Week.
No. 4391a was printed in sheets of 5 pairs.

Miniature Sheet

Upopoy National Ainu Musuem and Park A4644

No. 4392: a, Sheathed knives. b, Square carved wood trays. c, Idiophones. d, Sword and sword belt. e, Pink and blue elm bark robe. f, Necklaces with medallions. g, Tonkoris (stringed instruments). h, Three Ainu dancers. i, Sake paddle and cup. j, Black, white, green and red ruunpe (garment).

2020, Apr. 21 Litho. *Perf. 14¼x13¾*

4392 A4644 Sheet of 10 16.00 16.00
a.-j. 84y Any single 1.60 1.25

A4645

Sumo Wresting A4646

No. 4393: a, Two wrestlers in Yorikiri move (22x26mm). b, Two wrestlers and referee (22x26mm). c, Wrestler squatting with one arm extended (32x26mm), d, Wrestler squatting with both arms extended (33x26mm). e, Wrestler receiving prize money from referee (22x26mm). f, Two wrestlers in Uwatenage move (22x26mm). g, Two wrestlers in Harimanage move (22x26mm). h, Three wrestlers standing wearing ceremonial ropes and aprons (34x30mm). i, Two wresiters with arms extended in ring with referee (34x30mm). j, Two wrestlers in Tsuridashi move (22x26mm).

No. 4394 — Edo era woodblock prints of sumo wrestlers: a, Dohyoiri at a Sumo Match with the Emperor in the Audience (three wrestlers, referee and spectators), by Toyonobu Utagawa (1859-86) (32x34mm). b, A Benefit Match (wrestlers in action in ring, referee and spectators in background and ringside), by Kunitoshi Utagawa (1847-99) (32x34mm). c, The Yokozuna Reigoro Hidenoyama Performing Dohyoiri (wrestler with arms extended), by Toyokuni Utagawa III (1786-1865) (30x35mm). d, A Mirror of Japan's Great Sumo Wrestlers (group of wrestlers, denomination at LL), by Yoshiiku Ochiai (1833-1904) (26x30mm). e, A Mirror of Japan's Great Sumo Wrestlers (different group of wrestlers, denomination at LR), by Ochiai (26x30mm). f, A Benefit O-zumo Match Featuring Rikishi Koyanagi and Arauma (two wrestlers in and referee in ring, three ringside spectators), by Toyokuni Utagawa III (34x35mm). g, Group of wrestlers from A Benefit O-zumo Match Featuring Rikishi Koyanagi and Arauma (23x27mm). h, Two wrestlers in ring bent over with heads touching, from A Benefit O-zumo Match Featuring Rikishi Koyanagi and Arauma (22x26mm). i, Dohyoiri from the East League (four wrestlers, denomination at UL), by Toyokuni Utagawa III (28x36mm). j, Four different wrestlers from Dohyoiri from the East League (denominiation at top center) (28x36mm).

Die Cut Perf. 13x13¼ (#4393a, 4393b, 4393e, 4393f, 4393g, 4393j), 13 (#4393c, 4393d), 13½ (#4393h, 4393i)

2020, May 8 Litho.

Self-Adhesive

4393 A4645 Sheet of 10 12.50
a.-j. 63y Any single 1.25 .95

Die Cut Perf. 13¼x13 (#4394a, 4394b, 4394c), 13¼ (#4394d, 4394e), 13 (#4394f), 13x13¼ (#4394g, 4394h), 12¾x13 (#4394i, 4394j)

4394 A4646 Sheet of 10 16.00
a.-j. 84y Any single 1.60 1.25

Snail Shell A4647

Shell Spiral A4648

Starfish A4649

Conch Shell A4650

Scallop Shell A4651

Flowers A4652

Flowers A4653

Flowers A4654

Flowers A4655

Flowers A4656

Flowers A4657

Flowers A4658

Litho. With Foil Application

2020, May 14 *Die Cut Perf. 13¼*

Self-Adhesive

4395 Sheet of 10, 2 each #4395a-4395e 12.50
a. A4647 63y multi 1.25 .95
b. A4648 63y multi 1.25 .95
c. A4649 63y multi 1.25 .95
d. A4650 63y multi 1.25 .95
e. A4651 63y multi 1.25 .95

4396 Sheet of 10, 2 each #4396a-4396e 16.00
a. A4652 84y multi 1.60 1.25
b. A4653 84y multi 1.60 1.25
c. A4654 84y multi 1.60 1.25
d. A4655 84y multi 1.60 1.25
e. A4656 84y multi 1.60 1.25

4397 Sheet of 10, 5 each #4397a-4397b 17.50
a. A4657 94y multi 1.75 1.40
b. A4658 94y multi 1.75 1.40
Nos. 4395-4397 (3) 46.00

Doraemon at Festival A4659

Doraemon Fishing A4660

Doraemon and Mount Fuji A4661

Doraemon and Bridge A4662

Doraemon on Picnic A4663

Doraemon Harvesting Rice A4664

Doraemon as Japanese Mailman A4665

Doraemon Picking Tea Leaves A4666

Doraemon Under Umbrella A4667

Doraemon and Bamboo A4668

Doraemon — A4669

No. 4399 — Doraemon: a, Standing and smiling (27x30mm). b, In desk drawer (30x30mm). c, Eating (27x30mm). d, Flying with Nobita Nobi (30x30mm). e, Walking with Nobita Nobi (30x30mm). f, On telephone (27x30mm). g, Unfurling time kerchief (30x30mm). h, Laughing with arm and leg raised (27x30mm). i, Seated in time machine (30x30mm). j, Dancing with Nobita Nobi (27x30mm).

Die Cut Perf. 12¾x12½

2020, May 20 **Litho.**

Self-Adhesive

4398 Booklet pane of 10 12.50
a. A4659 63y multi 1.25 .95
b. A4660 63y multi 1.25 .95
c. A4661 63y multi 1.25 .95
d. A4662 63y multi 1.25 .95
e. A4663 63y multi 1.25 .95
f. A4664 63y multi 1.25 .95
g. A4665 63y multi 1.25 .95
h. A4666 63y multi 1.25 .95
i. A4667 63y multi 1.25 .95
j. A4668 63y multi 1.25 .95

4399 A4669 Sheet of 10 16.00
a.-j. 84y Any single 1.60 1.25

Miniature Sheets

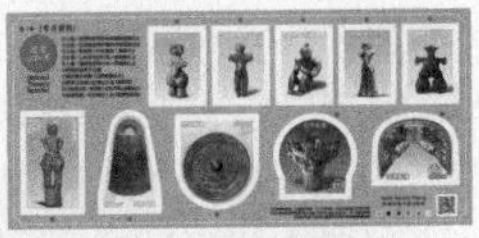
A4670

National Treasures — A4671

No. 4400: a, Jomon Venus (pink background, 22x30mm). b, Hollow Dogu (orange background, 22x30mm). c, Gassho Dogu (yellow background, 22x30mm). d, Jomon Goddess (green background, 22x30mm). e, Masked Goddess (blue background, 22x30mm). f, Haniwa Armored Male statue (tan background, 24x39mm). g, Bronze ritual bell (lt blue background, 24x39mm). h, Bronze mirror (pink background, 32x36mm). i, Flame-shpaed piece of pottery (dark red background, 32x32mm). j, Saddle fittings (gray background, 39x28mm).

No. 4401: a, Engaku-ji Reliquary Hall (two roofs and steps, 39x28mm). b, Todai-ji Belfry (with one roof, 39x33mm). c, Daigo-ji Five-story Pagoda (24x45mm). d, Chuson-ji Golden Hall at night (39x28mm). e, Ishiyamadera Tahoto (with two roofs, 39x33mm). f, Kofuku-ji Octagonal Hall (39x33mm). g, Mt. Haguro Five-story Pagoda (24x45mm). h, Mt. Mitoku Sanbutsu-ji Nageiredo on rock face (39x33mm). i, Jodo-ji Treasure Tahoto (denomination at UL, 39x33mm). j, Shosoin Repository (one roof, 39x28mm).

Die Cut Perf. 14 (#4400a, 4400b, 4400c, 4400d, 4400e), 13¼ (#4400f), 13¼x13½ (#4400g), 13¾x13¼ (#4400h), 13x13¼ (#4400i), 13 (#4400j)

2020, May 29 **Litho.**

Self-Adhesive

4400 A4670 Sheet of 10 12.50
a.-j. 63y Any single 1.25 .95

Die Cut Perf. 12½x13 (#4401a, 4401d, 4401j), 13 (#4401b, 4401e, 4401f, 4401h, 4401i), 13¼ (#4401c, 4401g)

4401 A4671 Sheet of 10 16.00
a.-j. 84y Any single 1.60 1.25

Miniature Sheets

A4672

Summer Greetings — A4673

No. 4402: a, Red ginger flower (22x30mm). b, Palm tree, pink sky (22x26mm). c, Palm tree, lilac sky (22x26mm). d, Papaya (23x27mm). e, Sunflower (22x30mm). f, Bird-of-paradise flower (22x36mm). g, Hibiscus flower (22x26mm). h, Frangipani flower (27x23mm). i, Sea shell (29x22mm). j, Hibiscus flowers (29x22mm).

No. 4403: a, Palm tree reflected in drink glass (22x26mm). b, Red frangipani flowers (22x26mm). c, Palm tree, blue sky (22x26mm). d, Cloud (22x26mm). e, Red ginger flower, diff. (22x26mm). f, Seagull (29x22mm). g, White frangipani flowers (28x23mm). h, People at beach (23x27mm). i, Shadow of palm tree (22x26mm). j, Lei (29x22mm).

Die Cut Perf. 13x13¼ (#4402a, 4402b, 4402c, 4402e, 4402f, 4402g), 13¼ (#4402d), 13¼x13 (#4402h, 4402i, 4402j)

2020, June 1 **Litho.**

Self-Adhesive

4402 A4672 Sheet of 10 12.50
a.-j. 63y Any single 1.25 .95

Die Cut Perf. 13x13¼ (#4403a, 4403b, 4403c, 4403d, 4403e, 4403h, 4403i), 13¼x13 (#4403f, 4403g, 4403j)

4403 A4673 Sheet of 10 16.00
a.-j. 84y Any single 1.60 1.25

Miniature Sheet

Flora and Fauna of Iriomote Island A4674

No. 4404: a, Crested serpent eagle (29x36mm). b, Ruddy kingfisher (29x33mm). c, Ryukyu scops owl (28x32mm). d, Iriomote wild cat (29x36mm). e, Chinese box turtle (32mm diameter). f, Large tree nymph butterfly (22x26mm). g, Bamboo orchid (22x26mm). h, Screw pine cone (22x26mm). i, Powder-puff tree (22x26mm). j, Loop-root mangrove (29x36mm).

Die Cut Perf. 13¼ (#4404a, 4404d, 4404j), 12x13 (#4404b, 4404c), 13x13¼ (#4404f, 4404g, 4404h, 4404i), Die Cut Perf. (#4404e)

2020, June 10 **Litho.**

Self-Adhesive

4404 A4674 Sheet of 10 16.00
a.-j. 84y Any single 1.60 1.25

Miniature Sheets

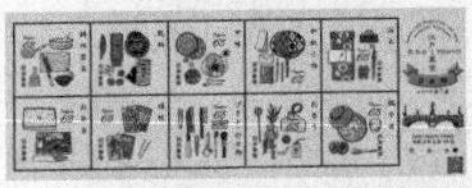
A4675

Items of Nihonbashi Business District of Tokyo — A4676

No. 4405: a, Kitchen utensils, b, Dried seaweed, fish and mushrooms. c, Fork, spoon and desserts. d, Calligraphy brush, fan and paper products. e, Kimono, sandals, umbrella and handbag. f, Lunch food and chopsticks. g, Toothpicks and toothpick boxes. h, Brushes, sewing scissors, tongs and knife. i, Tags, coin and shrine gifts. j, Bowl of rice with chicken and egg, spoon, dish and glass.

No. 4406: a, Entrance of Mitsukoshi-Isetan Department Store (denomination at LR, 27x27mm). b, Woman drinking from cup, pot and dried food (27x27mm). c, Entrance to specialty brush shop (denomination at UL, 27x27mm). d, Entrance to specialty knife shop (24x30mm). e, Bridge (30x21mm). f, Tamahide chicken restaurant (30x21mm). g, Fans and items on stationery store shelves (27x27mm). h, Postman, letter, stamp, pen, stationery, bust of Hisoka Maeshima (1835-1919), founder of Japanese Postal Service (27x27mm). i, Festival participants (27x27mm). j, People at Koami Shrine (27x27mm).

Die Cut Perf. 13¼

2020, June 16 **Litho.**

Self-Adhesive

4405 A4675 Sheet of 10 12.50
a.-j. 63y Any single 1.25 .95
4406 A4676 Sheet of 10 16.00
a.-j. 84y Any single 1.60 1.25

Mulberries A4677

Bitter Melon A4678

Soft Drink Bottle A4679

Two Goldfish A4680

Bowl of Flavored Shaved Ice A4681

Bowl of Ice Cream A4682

Pea Pod A4683

Kingfisher A4684

Dianthus Flowers A4685

Roses A4686

Glass and Bottle A4687

Fan A4688

Bowl of Curry A4689

Straw Hat A4690

Fishing With Cormorants A4691

Jellyfish A4692

Cloud, Airplane and Flowers A4693

Ear of Corn A4694

Sunflowers A4695

Beetles A4696

Die Cut Perf. 13x13¼

2020, June 19 **Litho.**

Self-Adhesive

4407 Sheet of 10 12.50
a. A4677 63y multi 1.25 .95
b. A4678 63y multi 1.25 .95
c. A4679 63y multi 1.25 .95
d. A4680 63y multi 1.25 .95
e. A4681 63y multi 1.25 .95
f. A4682 63y multi 1.25 .95
g. A4683 63y multi 1.25 .95
h. A4684 63y multi 1.25 .95
i. A4685 63y multi 1.25 .95
j. A4686 63y multi 1.25 .95

4408 Sheet of 10 16.00
a. A4687 84y multi 1.60 1.25
b. A4688 84y multi 1.60 1.25
c. A4689 84y multi 1.60 1.25
d. A4690 84y multi 1.60 1.25
e. A4691 84y multi 1.60 1.25
f. A4692 84y multi 1.60 1.25
g. A4693 84y multi 1.60 1.25
h. A4694 84y multi 1.60 1.25
i. A4695 84y multi 1.60 1.25
j. A4696 84y multi 1.60 1.25

Miniature Sheet

Fish
A4697

No. 4409: a, Pacific double-saddle butterflyfish, Moorish idol, Blue-green chromis. b, Two Blue devils, Blue-green chromis. c, Blue tang. d, Shepard's angelfish, Yellow tang, Blue-green chromis, coral. e, Two Moorish idols. f, Two Forceps butterflyfish. g, Two fire gobies, horiz. h, Saddle butterflyfish, Yellow boxfish. i, Clownfish, horiz. j, Two Clowhfish in anemone, horiz.

Die Cut Perf. 13x13¼ (vert. stamps), 13¼x13 (horiz. stamps)

2020, July 1 **Litho.**

Self-Adhesive

4409 A4697 Sheet of 10 16.00
a.-j. 84y Any single 1.60 1.25

Emperor Ninkoku Kofun — A4698

Emperor Richu Kofun — A4699

Haniwa Helmet from Itasuke Kofun — A4700

Itasuke Kofun — A4701

Gobyoyama Kofun — A4702

Emperor Ojin Kofun — A4703

Nakatsuhime-no-Mikoto Kofun — A4704

Waterfowl-shaped Haniwas from Tsudo Shiroyama Kofun — A4705

Emperor Chuai Kofun — A4706

Hakuchoryo Kofun — A4707

2020, July 8 **Litho.** ***Perf. 13¾x14¼***

4410 Sheet of 10 16.00 16.00
a. A4698 84y multi 1.60 1.25
b. A4699 84y multi 1.60 1.25
c. A4700 84y multi 1.60 1.25
d. A4701 84y multi 1.60 1.25
e. A4702 84y multi 1.60 1.25
f. A4703 84y multi 1.60 1.25
g. A4704 84y multi 1.60 1.25
h. A4705 84y multi 1.60 1.25
i. A4706 84y multi 1.60 1.25
j. A4707 84y multi 1.60 1.25

Mozo-Furuichi Kofun Group UNESCO World Heritage Site.

Miniature Sheet

Protection of Historic Sites and Natural Monuments — A4708

No. 4411: a, Goryokaku. b, Nakijin Castle ruins. c, East Palace Garden of Heijo Palace. d, Yohinogari Archaeological Site. e, Kamikochi Valley (Japanese inscription at UR). f, Kamikochi Valley (Japanese inscription at UL). g, Kenroku-en. h, Amanohashidate. i, Japanese serow. j, Oriental white storks.

2020, July 17 **Litho.** ***Perf. 13***

4411 A4708 Sheet of 10 16.00 16.00
a.-j. 84y Any single 1.60 1.25

First Japanese Natural Monument, cent.

House, Mailbox and Van A4709

Fruit Basket A4710

House and Clothes Drying on Line A4711

Chicken and Goat A4712

Child Reading Letter Near Mailbox A4713

Child Writing Letter A4714

Jar of Fruit A4715

Iron and Folded Clothes A4716

Sandwiches, Jars and Utensils A4717

Child Mailing Letter A4718

Die Cut Perf. 13x13¼

2020, July 22 **Litho.**

Booklet Stamps

Self-Adhesive

4412 A4709 63y multi 1.25 .95
4413 A4710 63y multi 1.25 .95
4414 A4711 63y multi 1.25 .95
4415 A4712 63y multi 1.25 .95
4416 A4713 63y multi 1.25 .95
a. Booklet pane of 10, 2 each #4412-4416 12.50
4417 A4714 84y multi 1.60 1.25
4418 A4715 84y multi 1.60 1.25
4419 A4716 84y multi 1.60 1.25
4420 A4717 84y multi 1.60 1.25
4421 A4718 84y multi 1.60 1.25
a. Booklet pane of 10, 2 each #4417-4421 16.00
Nos. 4412-4421 (10) 14.25 11.00

Letter Writing Day.

Miniature Sheet

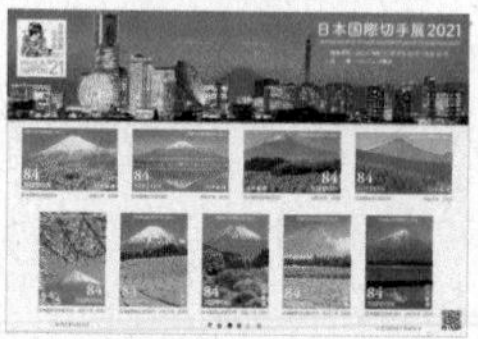

Philanippon 2021 World Stamp Championship Exhibition, Yokohama — A4719

No. 4422 — Mount Fuji and: a, Yokohama buildings at night. b, Cherry blossoms. c, Lake Yamanaka. d, Kochia and cosmos flowers. e, Larch forest. f, Cherry blossoms, vert. g, Tea plantation, vert. h, Azalea garden, vert. i, Small building and cosmos flower field, vert. j, Lake Kawaguchi, vert.

Die Cut Perf. 13¼

2020, Aug. 3 **Litho.**

Self-Adhesive

4422 A4719 Sheet of 10 16.00
a.-j. 84y Any single 1.60 1.25

Ginkgo Branch and Leaves A4720

Dahlia and Cosmos Flowers A4721

Gentian Flowers A4722

Chrysanthemums A4723

Roses A4724

Maple Branch and Leaves A4725

Dahlia and Cosmos Flowers A4726

Chinese Bellflowers A4727

Cockscomb Flowers A4728

Roses A4729

Die Cut Perf. 13x13¼

2020, Aug. 18 **Litho.**

Self-Adhesive

4423 Sheet of 10, 2 each #4423a-4423e 12.50
a. A4720 63y multi 1.25 .95
b. A4721 63y multi 1.25 .95
c. A4722 63y multi 1.25 .95
d. A4723 63y multi 1.25 .95
e. A4724 63y multi 1.25 .95
4424 Sheet of 10, 2 each #4424a-4424e 16.00
a. A4725 84y multi 1.60 1.25
b. A4726 84y multi 1.60 1.25
c. A4727 84y multi 1.60 1.25
d. A4728 84y multi 1.60 1.25
e. A4729 84y multi 1.60 1.25

Miniature Sheets

A4730

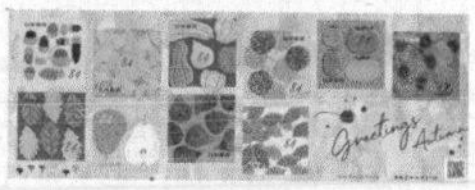

Autumn Greetings — A4731

No. 4425: a, Maple leaf (33x33mm). b, Pine cone (27x29mm). c, Pear (27x33mm). d, Red leaf (33x30mm). e, Oak leaf (32x31mm). f, Persimmon (28x28mm). g, Pumpkin (27x33mm). h, Orange leaf (27x27mm). i, Acorns (28x31mm). j, Fig (25x31mm).

No. 4426: a, Acorns. b, Ginkgo leaves. c, Squashes. d, Pine cones. e, Persimmons, f, Rambutans. g, Six leaves. h, Pears. i, Figs. j, Red and brown leaves.

2020, Aug. 21 **Litho.** ***Die Cut Perf.***

Self-Adhesive

4425 A4730 Sheet of 10 + 2 stickers 12.50
a.-j. 63y Any single 1.25 .95

Die Cut Perf. 13¼

4426 A4731 Sheet of 10 16.00
a.-j. 84y Any single 1.60 1.25

People of 1920 and Bar Graphs A4732

Woman and Tabulating Machine A4733

Japanese Statistics Bureau, Koji Sugi (1828-1917), Statistician and Prime Ministers Shigenobu Okuma (1838-1922) and Takashi Hara (1856-1921)
A4734

Woman Providing Data by Smartphone
A4735

People of 2020 and Bar Graphs — A4736

2020, Sept. 1 **Litho.** ***Perf. 13***

4427	A4732 84y multi		1.60	1.25
4428	A4733 84y multi		1.60	1.25
4429	A4734 84y multi		1.60	1.25
4430	A4735 84y multi		1.60	1.25
4431	A4736 84y multi		1.60	1.25
a.	Vert. strip of 5, #4427-4431		8.00	6.25
	Nos. 4427-4431 (5)		8.00	6.25

Miniature Sheets

A4737

Japan Post Teddy Bears
A4738

No. 4432 — Teddy bear: a, With cup of tea (26x23mm). b, With three other teddy bears (22x33mm). c, With cat (26x23mm). d, With owl (34x21mm fan-shaped stamp). e, With two other teddy bears (27mm diameter).

No. 4433 — Teddy bear: a, With knotted cord (22x23mm). b, With other teddy bear, owl and mountain (23x45mm). c, On paper lantern (27mm diameter). d, Coming through curtain (26x22mm). e, With koala in hot spring (26x22mm).

Die Cut Perf. 13¼x13 (#4432a, 4432c, 4433d, 4433e), Die Cut Perf. 13¼ (4432b, 4432d), Die Cut Perf. (#4432e, 4433c), Die Cut Perf. 13½x13 (#4433a), 13x13½ (#4433b)

2020, Sept. 15 **Litho.**

Self-Adhesive

4432	A4737	Sheet of 10, 2 each #4432a-4432e	12.50	
a.-e.		63y Any single	1.25	.95
4433	A4738	Sheet of 10, 2 each #4433a-4433e	16.00	
a.-e.		84y Any single	1.60	1.25

First Rotary Club in Japan, Cent. — A4739

"Rotary," Rotary International emblem and: No. 4434, Dove. No. 4435, Stethoscopes. No. 4436, Water droplets. No. 4437, Stylized mother and child. No. 4438, Open books.

2020, Sept. 18 **Photo.** ***Perf. 13***

Denomination Color

4434	A4739 84y magenta	1.60	1.25
4435	A4739 84y dk brown	1.60	1.25
4436	A4739 84y blue	1.60	1.25
4437	A4739 84y orange	1.60	1.25
4438	A4739 84y emerald	1.60	1.25
a.	Horiz. strip of 5, #4434-4438	8.00	6.25
	Nos. 4434-4438 (5)	8.00	6.25

Sofa Cushion
A4740

Sofa Cushion
A4741

Mirror
A4742

Perfume Bottles
A4743

Tiles
A4744

Tiles
A4745

Tiles
A4746

Tiles
A4747

Tiles — A4748

Litho. & Embossed

2020, Sept. 25 ***Die Cut Perf. 11***

Self-Adhesive

4439	Sheet of 10, 2 each #4439a-4439e	12.50	
a.	A4740 63y lt blue sofa cushion	1.25	.85
b.	A4741 63y lt brown sofa cushion	1.25	.85
c.	A4740 63y green sofa cushion	1.25	.85
d.	A4741 63y claret sofa cushion	1.25	.85
e.	A4740 63y blue green sofa cushion	1.25	.85

Litho. With Foil Application

4440	Sheet of 10, 5 each #4440a-4440b	16.00	
a.	A4742 84y gold & multi	1.60	1.25
b.	A4743 84y gold & multi	1.60	1.25

Litho.

4441	Sheet of 10, 2 each #4441a-4441e	17.50	
a.	A4744 94y multi	1.75	1.40
b.	A4745 94y multi	1.75	1.40
c.	A4746 94y multi	1.75	1.40
d.	A4747 94y multi	1.75	1.40
e.	A4748 94y multi	1.75	1.40
	Nos. 4439-4441 (3)	46.00	

Miniature Sheet

International Year of Plant Health — A4749

No. 4442: a, Airport baggage carousel opening and red suitcase. b, Baggage claim sign, baggage carousel with green and light blue suitcases. c, Child near baggage carousel, red, yellow and blue suitcases. d, Man and woman near baggage carousel with retrieved suitcases. e, Woman with red suitcase at customs counter. f, Man with green suitcase at customs counter. g, Male customs agent inspecting fruit. h, Female customs agent inspecting flowers. i, Man and girl with fruit. j, Woman and child with flowers.

2020, Oct. 5 **Photo.** ***Perf. 13***

4442	A4749	Sheet of 10	16.00	16.00
a.-j.		84y Any single	1.60	1.25

Peonies and Canary, Detail of Print by Hokusai (1760-1849)
A4750

Peonies and Canary, Detail of Print by Hokusai
A4751

Fuji from Ushibori in Hitachi Province, Print by Hokusai — A4752

In the Mountains of Totomi Province, Print by Hokusai — A4753

Nihonbashi in Edo, Print by Hokusai — A4754

2020, Oct. 9 **Litho.** ***Perf. 13x13¼***

4443	A4750 7y multi	.30	.25
4444	A4751 70y multi	1.40	1.10

Perf. 13

4445	A4752 90y multi	1.75	1.40
4446	A4753 110y multi	2.10	1.60
4447	A4754 130y multi	2.50	1.90
	Nos. 4443-4447 (5)	8.05	6.25

International Letter Writing Week.

Nihonbashi (Print Shown on No. 769) — A4755

Shinagawa (Print Shown on No. 2940) — A4756

Kawasaki (Print Shown on No. 2865) — A4757

Kanagawa (Print Shown on No. 3064) — A4758

Hodogaya (Print Shown on No. 2999) — A4759

Totsuka (Print Shown on No. 2837) — A4760

Fujisawa (Print Shown on No. 3163) — A4761

Hirutsuka (Print Shown on No. 2904) — A4762

Oiso (Print Shown on No. 2792) — A4763

Odawara (Print Shown on No. 3600) — A4764

Hakone (Print Shown on No. 735) — A4765

Mishima (Print Shown on No. 3065) — A4766

Numazu (Print Shown on No. 4043) — A4767

Hara (Print Shown on No. 2791) — A4768

Yoshiwara (Print Shown on No. 3938) — A4769

Kanbara (Print Shown on No. 704) — A4770

Yui (Print Shown on No. 2835) — A4771

Okitsu (Print Shown on No. 3164) — A4772

Ejiri (Print Shown on No. 3740) — A4773

Fuchu (Print Shown on No. 4155) — A4774

Mariko (Print Shown on No. 2938) — A4775

Okabe (Print Shown on No. 2744) — A4776

Fujieda (Print Shown on No. 4044) — A4777

Shimada (Print Shown on No. 4157) — A4778

Kanaya (Print Shown on No. 3741) — A4779

Nissaka (Print Shown on No. 4344) — A4780

Kakegawa (Print Shown on No. 4244) — A4781

Fukuroi (Print Shown on No. 3742) — A4782

Mitsuke (Print Shown on No. 4245) — A4783

Hamamatsu (Print Shown on No. 3601) — A4784

Maisaka (Print Shown on No. 2745) — A4785

Arai (Print Shown on No. 3000) — A4786

Shirasuka (Print Shown on No. 3599) — A4787

Futagawa (Print Shown on No. 4045) — A4788

Yoshida (Print Shown on No. 3939) — A4789

Goyu (Print Shown on No. 4156) — A4790

Akasaka (Print Shown on No. 4246) — A4791

Fujikawa (Print Shown on No. 3940) — A4792

Okazaki (Print Shown on No. 2746) — A4793

Chiryu (Print Shown on No. 3165) — A4794

Narumi (Print Shown on No. 4345) — A4795

Atsuta (Print Shown on No. 2866) — A4796

Kuwana (Print Shown on No. 679) — A4797

Yokkaichi (Print Shown on No. 2905) — A4798

Ishiyakushi (Print Shown on No. 3602) — A4799

Shono (Print Shown on No. 2836) — A4800

Kameyama (Print Shown on No. 2582) — A4801

Seki (Print Shown on No. 4346) — A4802

Sakanoshita (Print Shown on No. 2793) — A4803

Tsuchiyama (Print Shown on No. 2906) — A4804

Minakuchi (Print Shown on No. 2939) — A4805

Ishibe (Print Shown on No. 3066) — A4806

Kusatsu (Print Shown on No. 3001) — A4807

Otsu (Print Shown on No. 2867) — A4808

Kyoto (Print Shown on No. 656) — A4809

2020, Oct. 9 Litho. *Perf. 13*

4448		Sheet of 55	105.00	105.00
a.	A4755	70y multi	1.90	1.90
b.	A4756	70y multi	1.90	1.90
c.	A4757	70y multi	1.90	1.90
d.	A4758	70y multi	1.90	1.90
e.	A4759	70y multi	1.90	1.90
f.	A4760	70y multi	1.90	1.90
g.	A4761	70y multi	1.90	1.90
h.	A4762	70y multi	1.90	1.90
i.	A4763	70y multi	1.90	1.90
j.	A4764	70y multi	1.90	1.90
k.	A4765	70y multi	1.90	1.90
l.	A4766	70y multi	1.90	1.90
m.	A4767	70y multi	1.90	1.90
n.	A4768	70y multi	1.90	1.90
o.	A4769	70y multi	1.90	1.90
p.	A4770	70y multi	1.90	1.90
q.	A4771	70y multi	1.90	1.90
r.	A4772	70y multi	1.90	1.90
s.	A4773	70y multi	1.90	1.90
t.	A4774	70y multi	1.90	1.90
u.	A4775	70y multi	1.90	1.90
v.	A4776	70y multi	1.90	1.90
w.	A4777	70y multi	1.90	1.90
x.	A4778	70y multi	1.90	1.90
y.	A4779	70y multi	1.90	1.90
z.	A4780	70y multi	1.90	1.90
aa.	A4781	70y multi	1.90	1.90
ab.	A4782	70y multi	1.90	1.90
ac.	A4783	70y multi	1.90	1.90
ad.	A4784	70y multi	1.90	1.90
ae.	A4785	70y multi	1.90	1.90
af.	A4786	70y multi	1.90	1.90
ag.	A4787	70y multi	1.90	1.90
ah.	A4788	70y multi	1.90	1.90
ai.	A4789	70y multi	1.90	1.90
aj.	A4790	70y multi	1.90	1.90
ak.	A4791	70y multi	1.90	1.90
al.	A4792	70y multi	1.90	1.90
am.	A4793	70y multi	1.90	1.90
an.	A4794	70y multi	1.90	1.90
ao.	A4795	70y multi	1.90	1.90
ap.	A4796	70y multi	1.90	1.90
aq.	A4797	70y multi	1.90	1.90
ar.	A4798	70y multi	1.90	1.90
as.	A4799	70y multi	1.90	1.90
at.	A4800	70y multi	1.90	1.90
au.	A4801	70y multi	1.90	1.90
av.	A4802	70y multi	1.90	1.90
aw.	A4803	70y multi	1.90	1.90
ax.	A4804	70y multi	1.90	1.90
ay.	A4805	70y multi	1.90	1.90
az.	A4806	70y multi	1.90	1.90
ba.	A4807	70y multi	1.90	1.90
bb.	A4808	70y multi	1.90	1.90
bc.	A4809	70y multi	1.90	1.90

Completion of depicting each of the prints from Hiroshige's "The Fifty-three Stations of the Tokaido" on International Letter Writing Week stamps, 1st anniv. Nos. 4448a and 4448bc depict prints by Hiroshige of the Eastern (Nihonbashi) and Western (Kyoto) terminals of the Tokaido route. No. 4448 sold for 5000y.

Miniature Sheets

A4810

Art A4811

No. 4449: a, Detail of 17th century overglazed enamel tea jar with Moon and plum branches design, by Ninsei Nonomura (25x28mm). b, Devotion, detail of painting by Ryushi Kawabata (1885-1966) (27x26mm). c, The Sound of the Hand Drum, painting by Shoen Uemura (1875-1949) (27x27mm). d, Dusk at the Ferry Crossing, painting by Eisaku Wada (1874-1959) (31x26mm). e, Peony and swallow fabric design from 19th century cotton robe (22x32mm). f, Thirty-six Views of Fuji, South Wind and Clear Skies, detail of woodblock print by Hokusai (1760-1849) (24x34mm). g, Birds and Flowers of the Four Seasons, Autumn, painting by Jippo Araki (1872-1944) (23x34mm). h, Girl with Braids, detail of painting by Amadeo Modigliani (1884-1920) (25x30mm). i, La France, painting by Henri Matisse (1869-1954) (24x33mm). j, Peony Garden, painting by Claude Monet (1840-1926) (30x26mm).

No. 4450: a, 17th century overglazed enamel tea jar with Moon and plum branches design, by Nonomura (28x35mm). b, Devotion, by Kawabata (35x29mm). c, The Prelude, painting by Uemura (31x38mm). d, Salmon, painting by Yuichi Takahashi (1828-94) (23x45mm). e, Thirty-six Views of Fuji, South Wind and Clear Skies, by Hokusai (36x30mm). f, Fire Dance, painting by Gyoshu Hayami (1894-1935) (27x43mm). g, Girl with Braids, by Modigliani (26x39mm). h, Haystacks at Giverny, Sunset, painting by Monet (36x31mm). i, The Lute, painting by Matisse (34x31mm). j, 19th century cotton robe with peony and swallow design (32x42mm).

Die Cut Perf. 12¾ (#4449a), Die Cut Perf. 13¼x13¾ (#4449b), Die Cut Perf. 13¼ (#4449c, 4449d, 4449j, 4450b), Die Cut Perf. 12x12½ (#4449e, 4450f), Die Cut Perf. 12x13 (#4449f, 4449i), Die Cut Perf. 12½x13 (#4449g), Die Cut Perf. 13x12¾ (#4449h, 4450d, 4450h), Die Cut Perf. 12¼ (#4450a), Die Cut Perf. 13x12 (#4450c), Die Cut Perf. 13x13½ (#4450e), Die Cut Perf. 13¼x13 (#4450g), Die Cut Perf. 12¼x12¾ (#4450i), Die Cut Perf. 12½x11½ (#4450j)

2020, Oct. 16 Litho.

Self-Adhesive

4449	A4810	Sheet of 10	12.50	
a.-j.		63y Any single	1.25	.95
4450	A4811	Sheet of 10	16.00	
a.-j.		84y Any single	1.60	1.25

Souvenir Sheet

Summer Greetings — A4812

No. 4451: a, Boy writing postcard. b, Mailbox, insect and net.

2020, Oct. 23 Litho. *Perf. 13x13¼*

4451	A4812	Sheet of 2	3.00	3.00
a.		63y multi	1.25	.95
b.		84y multi	1.60	1.25

No. 4451 was sold to the public, but also was awarded as a lottery prize.

A4813 A4814

New Year 2021 (Year of the Ox)

A4815 A4816

2020, Oct. 29 Litho. *Perf. 13x13¼*

4452	A4813	63y multi	1.25	.95
4453	A4814	84y multi	1.60	1.25

Photo. & Typo.
Perf. 13¼

4454 A4815 63y+3y multi 1.25 .95
4455 A4816 84y+3y multi 1.75 1.30
Nos. 4452-4455 (4) 5.85 4.45

Coffee Grinder, Cup and Pot
A4817

Sliced Melon and Blue Honeysuckle
A4818

Carved Bear and Ice Cream Cone
A4819

Gyoza Curry
A4820

Cheesecake and Cup of Coffee — A4821

Packaged Cookies and Chocolate-Covered Potato Chips — A4822

Milk Bottle and Stuffed Rolls
A4823

Cheese Board and Butter
A4824

Grilled Corn and Potato
A4825

Stir-fried Yakisoba Noodles
A4826

Rice with Sea Urchin and Salmon Roe
A4827

Ramen with Miso
A4828

Mutton and Vegetables
A4829

Dried Mackerel
A4830

Grilled Scallop
A4831

Curry Soup
A4832

Salmon Hot Pot
A4833

Salmon Soup with Vegetables
A4834

Fried Chicken
A4835

Squid Sashimi and Ramen Salad
A4836

Die Cut Perf. 13¼
2020, Nov. 11 **Litho.**
Self-Adhesive

4456 Sheet of 10 12.50
a. A4817 63y multi 1.25 .95
b. A4818 63y multi 1.25 .95
c. A4819 63y multi 1.25 .95
d. A4820 63y multi 1.25 .95
e. A4821 63y multi 1.25 .95
f. A4822 63y multi 1.25 .95
g. A4823 63y multi 1.25 .95
h. A4824 63y multi 1.25 .95
i. A4825 63y multi 1.25 .95
j. A4826 63y multi 1.25 .95

Die Cut Perf.

4457 Sheet of 10 16.00
a. A4827 84y multi 1.60 1.25
b. A4828 84y multi 1.60 1.25
c. A4829 84y multi 1.60 1.25
d. A4830 84y multi 1.60 1.25
e. A4831 84y multi 1.60 1.25
f. A4832 84y multi 1.60 1.25
g. A4833 84y multi 1.60 1.25
h. A4834 84y multi 1.60 1.25
i. A4835 84y multi 1.60 1.25
j. A4836 84y multi 1.60 1.25

Miniature Sheets

Juvenile Animals
A4837

Adult and Juvenile Animals
A4838

No. 4458: a, Kitten (26x25mm). b, Chicks (26x23mm oval). c, Rabbit kit (23x26mm oval). d, Hedgehog pup with adult (26x23mm oval). e, Puppy (26x25mm). f, Chipmunk (22x26mm). g, Piglets (26x22mm). h, Long-tailed tit (26x22mm). i, Wild piglets (26x22mm). j, Hamster pup (22x26mm).

No. 4459: a, Elephant and calf (37x24mm). b, Panda and cub (37x26mm). c, Koala and joey (30x24mm). d, Polar bear and cub (28x37mm). e, Penguin and chick (25x36mm). f, Zebra and foal (28x23mm). g, Indian spot-billed duck and ducklings (26x22mm). h, Kangaroo and joey (28x37mm). i, Deer and fawn (28x23mm). j, Macaque and infant (22x32mm).

Die Cut Perf. 12¾ (#4458a, 4458e, 4459e), Die Cut Perf. (#4458b, 4458c, 4458d), Die Cut Perf. 13x13¼ (#4458f, #4458j), Die Cut Perf. 13¼x13 (#4458g, 4458h, 4458i), Die Cut Perf. 13x12½ (#4459a, 4459j), Die Cut Perf. 13 (#4459b), Die Cut Perf. 12½ (#4459c), Die Cut Perf. 12¾x13 (#4459d, 4459f, 4459h, 4459i), Die Cut Perf. 13½x13 (#4459g)

2020, Nov. 16 **Litho.**
Self-Adhesive

4458 A4837 Sheet of 10 12.50
a.-j. 63y Any single 1.25 .95
4459 A4838 Sheet of 10 16.00
a.-j. 84y Any single 1.60 1.25

Snowflakes
A4839

Tree, Buildings and Snowflakes
A4840

Snowflakes
A4841

Buildings, Tree and Snowflakes
A4842

Trees and Snowflakes
A4843

Snowflakes
A4844

Snowflakes and Trees
A4845

Snow-covered House and Tree
A4846

Fox and Snow-covered Trees
A4847

Deer and Snow-covered Trees
A4848

Snowflakes
A4849

Rabbits and Snow-covered Trees
A4850

Squirrel and Snow-covered Trees
A4851

Owl and Snow-covered Trees
A4852

Robin and Snow-covered Trees — A4853

Litho. With Foil Application
2020, Nov. 20 ***Die Cut Perf. 13x13½***
Self-Adhesive

4460 Sheet of 10, 2 each #4460a-4460e, + 4 stickers 12.50
a. A4839 63y sil & multi 1.25 .95
b. A4840 63y sil & multi 1.25 .95
c. A4841 63y sil & multi 1.25 .95
d. A4842 63y sil & multi 1.25 .95
e. A4843 63y sil & multi 1.25 .95

Die Cut Perf. 13¼ (#4461a-4461f), Die Cut Perf. 12¾x13 (#4461g-4461j)

4461 Sheet of 10 + 2 stickers 16.00
a. A4844 84y sil & multi 1.60 1.25
b. A4845 84y sil & multi 1.60 1.25
c. A4846 84y sil & multi 1.60 1.25
d. A4847 84y sil & multi 1.60 1.25
e. A4848 84y sil & multi 1.60 1.25
f. A4849 84y sil & multi 1.60 1.25
g. A4850 84y sil & multi 1.60 1.25
h. A4851 84y sil & multi 1.60 1.25
i. A4852 84y sil & multi 1.60 1.25
j. A4853 84y sil & multi 1.60 1.25

Miniature Sheet

Children's Book Illustrations by Leo Lionni (1910-99) — A4854

No. 4462: a, Black fish, rocks and seaweed (38x28mm). b, Black fish approaching school of fish (38x28mm). c, Black fish as eye of fish-shaped school of fish (38x28mm). d, Close-up of head of fish-shaped school (38x28mm). e, Five mice (38x28mm). f, Mouse, wind-up mouse, bird and teddy bear (38x28mm). g, Mouse holding flower (32x37mm). h, Mouse, wind-up mouse and nesting doll (32x37mm). i, Mouse in boot (32x37mm). j, Mouse, box containing gifts and wind-up mouse (32x37mm).

Die Cut Perf. 13¼x13½
2020, Nov. 27 **Litho.**
Self-Adhesive

4462 A4854 Sheet of 10 16.00
a.-j. 84y Any single 1.60 1.25

Miniature Sheets

A4855

Japanese Musical Instruments — A4856

No. 4463: a, Satsuma biwa (light green background, 22x26mm). b, Sanshin (yellow background, 22x26mm). c, Man beating odaiko (light blue background, 26x27mm). d, Surigane and shinobue (light blue background, 22x26mm). e, Shimedaiko (light brown background, 22x26mm). f, Otsuzumi (light brown background, 26x22mm). g, Nokan and kotsuzumi (tan and pale orange background, 22x26mm). h, Woman playing so (orange yellow and rose background, 29x23mm). i, Samisen (orange yellow and rose background, 22x26mm). j, Shakuhachi (orange yellow and rose background, 21x29mm).

No. 4464: a, Furitsuzumi (22x31mm, denomination at LR above country name). b, Man playing gakuso (24x27mm). c, Hichiriki and ryuteki (22x30mm, denomination at UL). d, Sho (22x32mm, denomination at LR). e, Man holding and playing gakubiwa (27x26mm, denomination at UR under country name). f, Dadaiko (30x40mm). g, Shoko (22x32mm, denomination at UR above country name). h, Gakudaiko (24x32mm, denomination at UR above country name). i, Kakko (26x29mm, denomination at UL). j, San no Tsuzumi and Ikko (26x28mm, denomination at LR above country name).

Die Cut Perf. 13x13¼ (#4463a-4463e, 4463g, 4463i, 4464c, 4464d, 4464g) Die Cut Perf. 13¼x13 (#4463f, 4464i, 4464j), Die Cut Perf. 12½x13 (#4463h), Die Cut Perf. 13x12½ (#4463j), Die Cut Perf. 13 (#4464a, 4464f), Die Cut Perf. 12¾ (#4464b), Die Cut Perf. 12¾x13 (#4464e), Die Cut Perf. 13¼ (#4464h)

2020, Dec. 4 **Litho.**
Self-Adhesive

4463 A4855 Sheet of 10 12.50
a.-j. 63y Any single 1.25 .95
4464 A4856 Sheet of 10 16.00
a.-j. 84y Any single 1.60 1.25

Forsythia
A4857

Anemones
A4858

Coralberry A4859 — Narcissi A4860

Roses A4861 — Magnolia A4862

Poppies A4863 — Plum Blossoms A4864

Cherry Blossoms A4865 — Rapeseed and Peach Blossoms A4866

Die Cut Perf. 13x13¼

2020, Dec. 14 **Litho.**

Self-Adhesive

4465	Sheet of 10, 2 each #4465a-4465e	12.50	
a.	A4857 63y multi	1.25	.95
b.	A4858 63y multi	1.25	.95
c.	A4859 63y multi	1.25	.95
d.	A4860 63y multi	1.25	.95
e.	A4861 63y multi	1.25	.95
4466	Sheet of 10, 2 each #4466a-4466e	16.00	
a.	A4862 84y multi	1.60	1.25
b.	A4863 84y multi	1.60	1.25
c.	A4864 84y multi	1.60	1.25
d.	A4865 84y multi	1.60	1.25
e.	A4866 84y multi	1.60	1.25

Sunrise on Mitsukejima A4867 — Sun and Clouds Over Kujuku Islands A4868

Cherry Tree in Bloom, Maniwa A4869 — Cherry Blossoms on Water A4870

Frost Flowers on Ice A4871 — Nomizo Falls, Kameiwa Cave A4872

Naruto Strait Whirlpool A4873 — Frozen Kiyotaki Waterfall A4874

Rainstorm, Amaharashi Beach A4875 — Hornfels on Susa Bay A4876

Clouds Over Mount Fuji A4877 — Fog Near Takeda Castle Ruins A4878

Cherry Blossoms on Mt. Yoshino A4879 — Tree and Nemophila Flowers, Hitachi Seaside Park A4880

Frost-covered Trees on Mt. Zao A4881 — Inazumi Underwater Cave A4882

Flukes of Humpback Whale A4883 — Snow on Trees, Okutama A4884

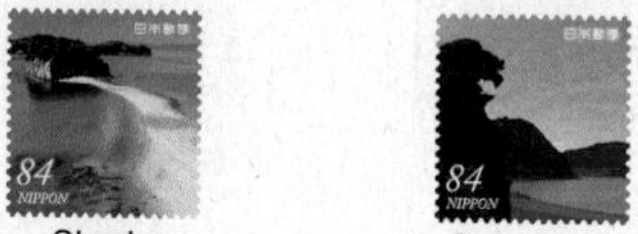

Shodo Island Angel Road A4885 — Sunrise at Shishi-Iwa A4886

Die Cut Perf. 13¼

2021, Jan. 12 **Litho.**

Self-Adhesive

4467	Sheet of 10	12.50	
a.	A4867 63y multi	1.25	.95
b.	A4868 63y multi	1.25	.95
c.	A4869 63y multi	1.25	.95
d.	A4870 63y multi	1.25	.95
e.	A4871 63y multi	1.25	.95
f.	A4872 63y multi	1.25	.95
g.	A4873 63y multi	1.25	.95
h.	A4874 63y multi	1.25	.95
i.	A4875 63y multi	1.25	.95
j.	A4876 63y multi	1.25	.95
4468	Sheet of 10	16.00	
a.	A4877 84y multi	1.60	1.25
b.	A4878 84y multi	1.60	1.25
c.	A4879 84y multi	1.60	1.25
d.	A4880 84y multi	1.60	1.25
e.	A4881 84y multi	1.60	1.25
f.	A4882 84y multi	1.60	1.25
g.	A4883 84y multi	1.60	1.25
h.	A4884 84y multi	1.60	1.25
i.	A4885 84y multi	1.60	1.25
j.	A4886 84y multi	1.60	1.25

Snork Maiden, Mymble, Little My A4887 — Little My, Moomin, Snork Maiden A4888

Moominmamma, Moominpappa, Little My — A4889

Moominmamma, Little My — A4890

Snufkin, Little My, Moomin A4891 — Moomin, Little My, Stinky A4892

Little My Spraying Hattifatteners A4893 — Little My With Large Eyeglasses A4894

Little My, Shadow on Floating Box of Seeds A4895 — Moominpappa, Little My, Moominmamma A4896

Stinky, Sniff A4897 — Little My on Tree Branch A4898

Moominmamma, Too-Ticky Planting Seedling — A4899

Moominpappa, and Plate of Fruit — A4900

Moominhouse A4901 — Mymble Reading A4902

Snufkin With Accordion A4903 — Moomin Picking Flowers A4904

Snork Maiden in Flowers A4905 — Police Inspector Watering Flowers A4906

Die Cut Perf. 13¼

2021, Jan. 15 **Litho.**

Self-Adhesive

4469	Sheet of 10	12.50	
a.	A4887 63y multi	1.25	.95
b.	A4888 63y multi	1.25	.95
c.	A4889 63y multi	1.25	.95
d.	A4890 63y multi	1.25	.95
e.	A4891 63y multi	1.25	.95
f.	A4892 63y multi	1.25	.95
g.	A4893 63y multi	1.25	.95
h.	A4894 63y multi	1.25	.95
i.	A4895 63y multi	1.25	.95
j.	A4896 63y multi	1.25	.95
4470	Sheet of 10	16.00	
a.	A4897 84y multi	1.60	1.25
b.	A4898 84y multi	1.60	1.25
c.	A4899 84y multi	1.60	1.25
d.	A4900 84y multi	1.60	1.25
e.	A4901 84y multi	1.60	1.25
f.	A4902 84y multi	1.60	1.25
g.	A4903 84y multi	1.60	1.25
h.	A4904 84y multi	1.60	1.25
i.	A4905 84y multi	1.60	1.25
j.	A4906 84y multi	1.60	1.25

Souvenir Sheet

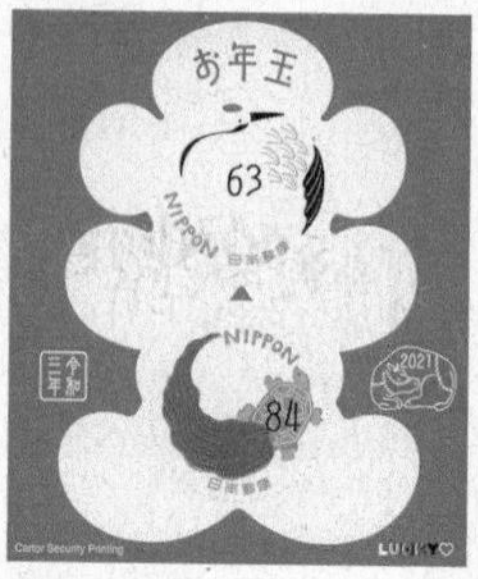

New Year 2021 A4907

No. 4471: a, Red-crowned crane. b, Turtle.

2021, Jan. 18 **Photo.** ***Die Cut Perf.***

Self-Adhesive

4471	A4907 Sheet of 2	3.00	
a.	63y gold & multi	1.25	.95
b.	84y gold & multi	1.60	1.25

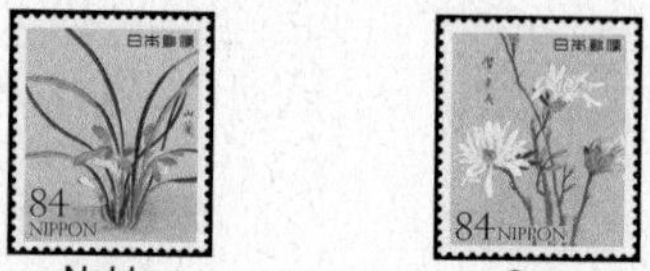

Noble Orchids A4908 — Star Magnolias A4909

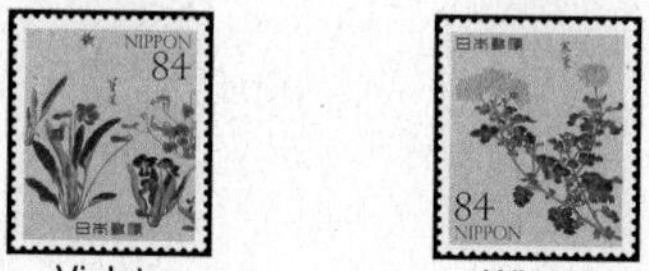

Violets A4910 — Winter Chrysanthemums A4911

Narcissi A4912 — Hydrangea A4913

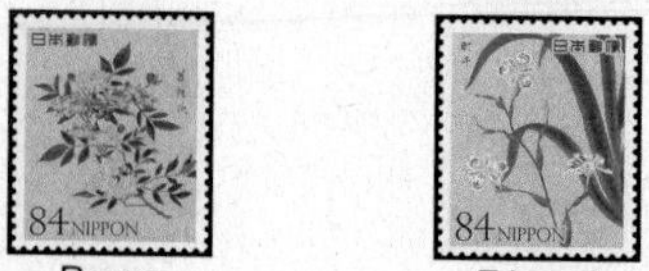

Roses A4914 — Fringed Irises A4915

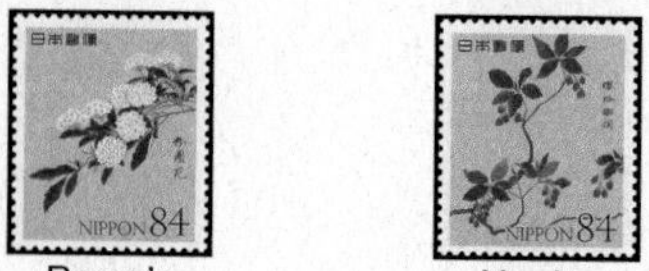

Reeve's Spiraea A4916 — Yoraku Azalea A4917

Die Cut Perf. 13¼

2021, Jan. 22 **Litho.**

Self-Adhesive

4472	Sheet of 10	16.00	
a.	A4908 84y multi	1.60	1.25
b.	A4909 84y multi	1.60	1.25
c.	A4910 84y multi	1.60	1.25
d.	A4911 84y multi	1.60	1.25
e.	A4912 84y multi	1.60	1.25
f.	A4913 84y multi	1.60	1.25
g.	A4914 84y multi	1.60	1.25
h.	A4915 84y multi	1.60	1.25
i.	A4916 84y multi	1.60	1.25
j.	A4917 84y multi	1.60	1.25

Miniature Sheeta

A4918

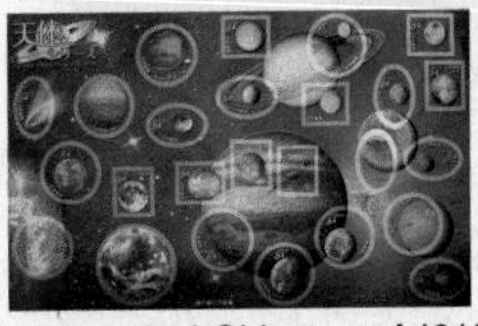

Astronomical Objects — A4919

No. 4473: a, Neutron star (22x26mm). b, Black hole (26x22mm). c, Oumuamua (22x26mm). d, Saturn and its moon, Mimas (44x32mm irregular shape). e, 486958 Arrokoth (26x22mm). f, Saturn's moon, Rhea (32x22mm oval). g, Pluto (32mm diameter). h, Uranus and its moon, Miranda (32mm diameter). i, Neptune (22x32mm oval). j, Neptune's moon, Triton (22x32mm oval).

No. 4474: a, Mars (32mm diameter). b, Saturn's moon, Titan (26x22mm). c, Saturn and its moon, Mimas (32mm diameter). d, Pluto's moon, Charon (22x26mm). e, Hale-Bopp Comet (22x32mm oval). f, Venus (32mm diameter). g, Dwarf planet Ceres (32x22mm oval). h, Saturn's rings and its moon, Enceladus (32x22mm oval). i, Saturn's moon, Rhea (26x22mm). j, Uranus's moon, Titania (22x32mm oval). k, Pluto (22x26mm). l, Mercury (32mm diameter). m, Moon (22x26mm). n, Jupiter's moon, Io (26x22mm). o, Jupiter's moon, Europa (22x26mm). p, Jupiter's moons, Thebe and Amalthea (22x26mm). q, Uranus (22x32mm oval). r, Uranus's moon, Miranda (32x22mm oval). s, Sun (32mm diameter), t, Earth (43mm diameter). u, Great Red Spot of Jupiter (32mm diameter). v, Jupiter's moon, Ganymede (32mm diameter). w, Jupiter's moon, Callisto (32mm diameter). x, Neptune (32mm diameter). y, Neptune's moon, Triton (32x22mm oval).

Die Cut Perf. 13x13¼ (#4473a, 4473c, 4474k, 4474m, 4474o, 4474p), Die Cut Perf. 13¼x13 (#4473b, 4473e, 4474b, 4474d, 4474i, 4474n), Die Cut Perf. (others)

Litho. With Hologram Affixed

2021, Feb. 3

Self-Adhesive

4473	A4918 Sheet of 10	16.00	
a.-j.	84y Any single	1.60	1.25

Litho With Silver Foil Application

4474	A4919 Sheet of 25	57.00	
a.-y.	84y Any single	*2.25*	*2.25*

No. 4474 sold for 3000y.

Fiddlehead Ferns A4920

Poppies A4921

Bee and Rape Blossoms A4922

Strawberries A4923

Rabbits A4924

Cat, Flowers and Butterfly A4925

Tulips A4926

Dandelions A4927

Wisteria A4928

Pansies A4929

Camellias and Birds A4930

Dog and Cherry Blossoms A4931

Die Cut Perf. 13x13¼

2021, Feb. 19 **Photo.**

Self-Adhesive

4475	Sheet of 10, #4475c, 4475f, 2 each #4475a-4475b, 4475d-4475e	12.50	
a.	A4920 63y multi	1.25	.95
b.	A4921 63y multi	1.25	.95
c.	A4922 63y multi	1.25	.95
d.	A4923 63y multi	1.25	.95
e.	A4924 63y multi	1.25	.95
f.	A4925 63y multi	1.25	.95
4476	Sheet of 10, #4476c, 4476f, 2 each #4476a-4476b, 4476d-4476e	16.00	
a.	A4926 84y multi	1.60	1.25
b.	A4927 84y multi	1.60	1.25
c.	A4928 84y multi	1.60	1.25
d.	A4929 84y multi	1.60	1.25
e.	A4930 84y multi	1.60	1.25
f.	A4931 84y multi	1.60	1.25

Miniature Sheets

A4932

My Journey A4933

No. 4477: a, Hirosaki Park, Hirosaki (26x22mm). b, Lake Towada (26x22mm). c, Bowl of Kiritanpo (22x26mm). d, Namahage (26x22mm). e, Nambu iron kettle (23x27 oval). f, Cherries (25mm diameter). g, Plate of beef tongue (22x26mm). h, Matsushima (26x22mm). i, Red cow toys with bobbling heads (23x27mm oval). j, Weeping cherry tree, Miharu (26x22mm).

No. 4478: a, Lake Inawashiro and Mt. Bandai (26x22mm). b, Crane Castle, Wakamatsu (26x22mm). c, Statue of Masamune Date (1567-1636), warrior, Sendai (22x26mm). d, Kokeshi dolls (23x27mm oval). e, Game pieces for Shogi (23x28mm pentagonal). f, Yamagata Prefectural Local History Museum (26x22mm). g, Jodogahama Beach (26x22mm). h, Soba bowls (26x22mm). i, Akita dog (23x27mm oval). j, Forest in Shirakami Mountain Range (22x27mm).

Die Cut Perf. 13¼x13 (#4477a, 4477b, 4477d, 4477h, 4477j, 4478a, 4478b, 4478f, 4478g, 4478h), Die Cut Perf. 13x13¼ (#4477c, 4477g, 4478c), Die Cut Perf 13x12¾ (#4478e), Die Cut Perf. (others)

2021, Mar. 9 **Litho.**

Self-Adhesive

4477	A4932 Sheet of 10	12.50	
a.-j.	63y Any single	1.25	.95
4478	A4933 Sheet of 10	15.00	
a.-j.	84y Any single	1.50	1.10

This sheet of self-adhesive stamps containing four 63y, four 84y and two 120y stamps was produced in limited quantities and sold in a package with post cards, envelopes and stationery for 2000y.

Survey Ship Kasuba and First Japanese Nautical Chart A4934

Echo Sounding Survey of Sea Bottom A4935

Nautical Chart and Naval Surveying Tools A4936

Airplane Conducting Laser Survey of Sea Bottom A4937

Japanese Coast Guard Ship Heiyo and Nautical Chart of Kamaishi Bay — A4938

2021, Mar. 12 Litho. *Perf. 13½*

4479	A4934	84y multi		1.50	1.10
4480	A4935	84y multi		1.50	1.10
4481	A4936	84y multi		1.50	1.10
4482	A4937	84y multi		1.50	1.10
4483	A4938	84y multi		1.50	1.10
a.		Horiz. strip of 5, #4479-4483		7.50	5.50
		Nos. 4479-4483 (5)		7.50	5.50

Nautical chart production in Japan, 150th anniv.

Hostas A4939 — Sunflowers A4940

Blue Passionflowers A4941 — Hydrangea and Roses A4942

Gloriosas A4943 — Jasmines A4944

Marigolds A4945 — Delphiniums and Carnations A4946

Peonies A4947 — Roses A4948

Die Cut Perf. 13x13¼

2021, Apr. 1 Litho.

Self-Adhesive

4484		Sheet of 10, 2 each #4484a-4484e	12.50	
a.	A4939	63y multi	1.25	.95
b.	A4940	63y multi	1.25	.95
c.	A4941	63y multi	1.25	.95
d.	A4942	63y multi	1.25	.95
e.	A4943	63y multi	1.25	.95
4485		Sheet of 10, 2 each #4485a-4485e	15.00	
a.	A4944	84y multi	1.50	1.10
b.	A4945	84y multi	1.50	1.10
c.	A4946	84y multi	1.50	1.10
d.	A4947	84y multi	1.50	1.10
e.	A4948	84y multi	1.50	1.10

Flowers Types of 2015, Violets Type of 2019 and

Oze National Park — A4949

2021 Photo. *Perf. 13x13¼*

With Iridescent Security Images Overprinted at UR and LL

4486	A4500	94y multi	1.75	1.30
4487	A3355	100y multi	1.90	1.40
4488	A3356	120y multi	2.25	1.75
4489	A3357	140y multi	2.60	2.00
4490	A4949	260y multi	4.75	3.75
		Nos. 4486-4490 (5)	13.25	10.20

Issued: Nos. 4486-4489, 4/13; 260y, 9/1. The security image at the upper right is a Japanese character that looks like a capital "T" with a line above it. The security image at the lower left is a five-petaled cherry blossom.

Posukuma Teddy Bear A4950 — Numeral in Rectangle A4951

Die Cut Perf. 13x13¼

2021, Apr. 14 Litho.

Self-Adhesive

4491	A4950	1y multi	.25	.25
4492	A4951	84y multi	1.60	1.25

A4952 A4953

A4954 A4955

A4956 A4957

A4958 A4959

A4960

Scenes From *The Postal Operations Picture Scrolls,* Silk Paintings by Shinsai Shibata (1858-95)
A4961

Photo. & Engr.

2021, Apr. 20 *Perf. 13*

4493		Sheet of 10	16.00	16.00
a.	A4952	84y gold & multi	1.60	1.25
b.	A4953	84y gold & multi	1.60	1.25
c.	A4954	84y gold & multi	1.60	1.25
d.	A4955	84y gold & multi	1.60	1.25
e.	A4956	84y gold & multi	1.60	1.25
f.	A4957	84y gold & multi	1.60	1.25
g.	A4958	84y gold & multi	1.60	1.25
h.	A4959	84y gold & multi	1.60	1.25
i.	A4960	84y gold & multi	1.60	1.25
j.	A4961	84y gold & multi	1.60	1.25

Hummingbird and Flowers A4962 — Bird on Branch A4963

Bird and Flora A4964 — Bird and Wreath A4965

Peacock A4966 — Peacock A4967

Litho. With Foil Application

2021, Apr. 23 Self-Adhesive

Die Cut Perf. 12¾x13 (#4494a, 4494b), 13¼x13½ (#4495a, 4496a), Die Cut Perf. (#4495b, 4496b)

4494		Sheet of 10, 5 each #4494a-4494b + sticker	12.50	
a.	A4962	63y gold & multi	1.25	.95
b.	A4963	63y gold & multi	1.25	.95
4495		Sheet of 10, 5 each #4495a-4495b + sticker	16.00	
a.	A4964	84y gold & multi	1.60	1.25
b.	A4965	84y gold & multi	1.60	1.25
4496		Sheet of 10, 5 each #4496a-4496b + sticker	17.50	
a.	A4966	94y gold & multi	1.75	1.30
b.	A4967	94y gold & multi	1.75	1.30
		Nos. 4494-4496 (3)	46.00	

Miniature Sheet

Flora, Fauna and Scenery of Lake Towada and Oirase Gorge A4968

No. 4497: a, Ruddy kingfisher facing left (28x32mm). b, Gray wagtail facing right (32x28mm). c, Narcissus flycatcher facing left (32x28mm). d, Japanese dwarf flying squirrel (22x26mm). e, Flaccid anemone (22x26mm). f, Japanese serow (32mm diameter). g, Anemone pseudoaltaica (22x26mm). h, Oirase River and feather moss (29x36mm). i, Blue-and-white flycatcher (32x28mm). j, Japanese marten (29x36mm).

Die Cut Perf. 12¼x13 (#4497a), 13x12¼ (#4497b, 4497c, 4497i), 13x13¼ (#4497d, 4497e, 4497g), 13¼ (#4497h, 4497j), Die Cut Perf. (#4497f)

2021, May 10 Litho.

Self-Adhesive

4497	A4968	Sheet of 10	16.00	
a.-j.		84y Any single	1.60	1.25

A4969 A4970

A4971 A4972

A4973 A4974

A4975 A4976

A4977 A4978

A4979 A4980

A4981 A4982

A4983 A4984

A4985 A4986

Flowers and Plants
A4987 A4988

Die Cut Perf. 13¼x13 (#4498j, 4499g, 4499h), 13x13¼ (others)

2021, May 17 Litho.

Self-Adhesive

4498		Sheet of 10	12.50	
a.	A4969	63y multi	1.25	.95
b.	A4970	63y multi	1.25	.95
c.	A4971	63y multi	1.25	.95
d.	A4972	63y multi	1.25	.95
e.	A4973	63y multi	1.25	.95
f.	A4974	63y multi	1.25	.95
g.	A4975	63y multi	1.25	.95
h.	A4976	63y multi	1.25	.95
i.	A4977	63y multi	1.25	.95
j.	A4978	63y multi	1.25	.95
4499		Sheet of 10	16.00	
a.	A4979	84y multi	1.60	1.25
b.	A4980	84y multi	1.60	1.25
c.	A4981	84y multi	1.60	1.25
d.	A4982	84y multi	1.60	1.25
e.	A4983	84y multi	1.60	1.25
f.	A4984	84y multi	1.60	1.25
g.	A4985	84y multi	1.60	1.25
h.	A4986	84y multi	1.60	1.25
i.	A4987	84y multi	1.60	1.25
j.	A4988	84y multi	1.60	1.25

A4989 A4990

A4991 A4992

A4993 A4994

A4995 A4996

Fabric Designs for Kimonos
A4997 A4998

Kimonos and Fabric Designs
A4999

No. 4501: a, Kimono with black and white background colors and plum blossom design (30x42mm). b, Blue and white kimono with flower garden design (30x42mm). c, Red kimono with fans and flowers design (30x42mm). d, White and pink kimono with tree and dandelions design (30x42mm). e, Yellow kimono with picture frames design (30x42mm). f, Fabric design of yellow and red flowers on arbor (30x36mm). g, Fabric designs of water and flowers (30x36mm). h, Fabric design of pine trees and flowers (30mm diameter). i, Fabric design of palace decorations and ornate fence (30x36mm). j, Fabric desgin of peonies and waterfalls (30x36mm).

Die Cut Perf. 13¼

2021, May 21 **Litho.**

Self-Adhesive

4500		Sheet of 10	12.50	
a.	A4989	63y gold & multi	1.25	.95
b.	A4990	63y gold & multi	1.25	.95
c.	A4991	63y gold & multi	1.25	.95
d.	A4992	63y gold & multi	1.25	.95
e.	A4993	63y gold & multi	1.25	.95
f.	A4994	63y gold & multi	1.25	.95
g.	A4995	63y gold & multi	1.25	.95
h.	A4996	63y gold & multi	1.25	.95
i.	A4997	63y gold & multi	1.25	.95
j.	A4998	63y gold & multi	1.25	.95

Die Cut Perf. 13¼ (#4501a-4501e), 13¼x13 (#4501f, 4501g, 4501i, 4501j), Die Cut Perf. (#4501h)

4501	A4999	Sheet of 10	16.00	
a.-j.		84y Any single	1.60	1.25

A5000 A5001

A5002 A5003

National Afforestation (Shimane) — A5004

2021, May 26 **Litho.** ***Perf. 13½x14***

4502	A5000	84y multi	1.60	1.25
4503	A5001	84y multi	1.60	1.25
4504	A5002	84y multi	1.60	1.25
4505	A5003	84y multi	1.60	1.25
4506	A5004	84y multi	1.60	1.25
a.		Vert. strip of 5, #4502-4506	8.00	6.25
		Nos. 4502-4506 (5)	8.00	6.25

Ice Cream Cone and Bar
A5005

Food on Cutting Board
A5006

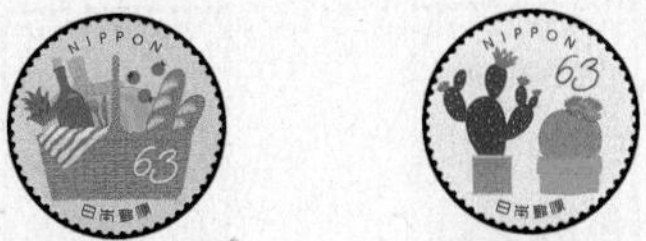

Food Basket
A5007

Cacti
A5008

Sandals and Crab
A5009

Starfish, Shells and Coral
A5010

Sunglasses
A5011

Fish and Seahorse
A5012

Avocado, Tomato and Banana
A5013

Lemon Drink
A5014

Bowl of Shaved Ice
A5015

Fireworks
A5016

Fan and Mosquito Coil
A5017

Bitter Melons
A5018

Japanese Rice Fish
A5019

Watermelon Slice and Beetle
A5020

Plums
A5021

Ginger, Perilla and Japanese Ginger
A5022

Ramune Bottles
A5023

Beans and Corn
A5024

2021, June 1 **Litho.** ***Die Cut Perf.***

Self-Adhesive

4507		Sheet of 10	12.50	
a.	A5005	63y multi	1.25	.95
b.	A5006	63y multi	1.25	.95
c.	A5007	63y multi	1.25	.95
d.	A5008	63y multi	1.25	.95
e.	A5009	63y multi	1.25	.95
f.	A5010	63y multi	1.25	.95
g.	A5011	63y multi	1.25	.95
h.	A5012	63y multi	1.25	.95
i.	A5013	63y multi	1.25	.95
j.	A5014	63y multi	1.25	.95

Die Cut Perf. 13¼

4508		Sheet of 10	16.00	
a.	A5015	84y multi	1.60	1.25
b.	A5016	84y multi	1.60	1.25
c.	A5017	84y multi	1.60	1.25
d.	A5018	84y multi	1.60	1.25
e.	A5019	84y multi	1.60	1.25
f.	A5020	84y multi	1.60	1.25
g.	A5021	84y multi	1.60	1.25
h.	A5022	84y multi	1.60	1.25
i.	A5023	84y multi	1.60	1.25
j.	A5024	84y multi	1.60	1.25

Merrymaking Under the Cherry Blossoms (Detail), Screen Painting by Naganobu Kano (1577-1654)
A5025

Merrymaking Under the Cherry Blossoms (Detail), Screen Painting by Naganobu
A5026

Thunder God Raijin (Detail), Screen Painting by Tawaraya Sotatsu (c. 1570-c.1640)
A5027

Wind God Fujin (Detail), Screen Painting by Sotatsu
A5028

Viewing Maple Leaves (Detail), Screen Painting by Hideyori Kano (fl. 16th Cent)
A5029

Heian Period Sutra Box
A5030

Kamakura Period Gilt Copper Reliquary
A5031

17th Cent. Tea Jar, by Ninsei Nonmura
A5032

12th-13 Cent. Tea Bowl
A5033

Heian Period Leather Ornament
A5034

Negoro-ji Daito, Iwade — A5035

Tamaudun Royal Mausoleum, Shuri — A5036

Flying Cloud Pavilion, Kyoto
A5037

Ruriko-ji Five-Story Pagoda, Yamaguchi
A5038

Osaki Hachimangu Shrine, Sendai — A5039

Matsue Castle, Matsue — A5040

Ninna-ji Temple, Kyoto
A5041

Kunozan Tosho-ga Shrine, Shizuoka
A5042

Iwashimizu Hachimangu Main Shrine, Yawata
A5043

Siofuku-ji Temple Main Hall, Nagasaki
A5044

Die Cut Perf. 13¼

2021, June 16 **Litho.**

Self-Adhesive

4509		Sheet of 10	12.50	
a.	A5025	63y multi	1.25	.95
b.	A5026	63y multi	1.25	.95
c.	A5027	63y multi	1.25	.95
d.	A5028	63y multi	1.25	.95
e.	A5029	63y multi	1.25	.95
f.	A5030	63y multi	1.25	.95
g.	A5031	63y multi	1.25	.95
h.	A5032	63y multi	1.25	.95
i.	A5033	63y multi	1.25	.95
j	A5034	63y multi	1.25	.95

Die Cut Perf. 13 (#4510a, 4510b, 4510e-4510j), 12½x13 (#4510c), 13¼ (#4510d)

4510		Sheet of 10	15.00	
a.	A5035	84y multi	1.50	1.10
b.	A5036	84y multi	1.50	1.10
c.	A5037	84y multi	1.50	1.10
d.	A5038	84y multi	1.50	1.10
e.	A5039	84y multi	1.50	1.10
f.	A5040	84y multi	1.50	1.10
g.	A5041	84y multi	1.50	1.10
h.	A5042	84y multi	1.50	1.10
i.	A5043	84y multi	1.50	1.10
j.	A5044	84y multi	1.50	1.10

3-on-3 Basketball
A5045

Archery
A5046

Gymnastics
A5047

Artistic
Swimming
A5048

Track and
Field
A5049

Badminton
A5050

Baseball
A5051

Softball
A5052

Basketball
A5053

Beach
Volleyball
A5054

Boxing
A5055

Canoe
Slalom
A5056

Canoe Sprint
A5057

BMX
Freestyle
Bicycling
A5058

BMX Racing
A5059

Mountain
Biking
A5060

Road Cycling
A5061

Track Cycling
A5062

Diving
A5063

Equestrian
Dressage
A5064

Equestrian
Eventing
A5065

Equestrian
Jumping
A5066

Fencing
A5067

Soccer
A5068

Golf — A5069

Handball
A5070

Field Hockey
A5071

Judo
A5072

Karate Kata
A5073

Karate
Kumite
A5074

Marathon
Swimming
A5075

Modern
Pentathlon
A5076

Rhythmic
Gymnastics
A5077

Rowing
A5078

Rugby
A5079

Sailing
A5080

Shooting
A5081

Skateboarding
A5082

Sport
Climbing
A5083

Surfing
A5084

Swimming
A5085

Table Tennis
A5086

Taekwondo
A5087

Tennis
A5088

Trampolining
A5089

Triathlon
A5090

Volleyball
A5091

Water Polo
A5092

Weight Lifting
A5093

Wrestling — A5094

Paralympics
Archery
A5095

Paralympics
Track and
Field
A5096

Paralympics
Badminton
A5097

Paralympics
Bocce
A5098

Paralympics
Canoeing
A5099

Paralympics
Road Cycling
A5100

Paralympics
Track Cycling
A5101

Paralympics
Equestrian
A5102

Paralympics
5-on-5
Soccer
A5103

Paralympics
Goalball
A5104

Paralympics
Judo
A5105

Emblem of
2020
Summer
Paralympics
A5106

Paralympics
Powerlifting
A5107

Paralympics
Rowing
A5108

Paralympics
Shooting
A5109

Paralympics
Sitting
Volleyball
A5110

Paralympics Swimming A5111

Paralympics Table Tennis A5112

Paralympics Taekwondo A5113

Paralympics Triathlon A5114

Paralympics Wheelchair Basketball A5115

Paralympics Wheelchair Fencing A5116

Paralympics Wheelchair Rugby A5117

Paralympics Wheelchair Tennis A5118

2021, June 23 Litho. *Perf. 13*

4511 Sheet of 25 37.50 37.50
a. A5045 84y multi 1.50 1.10
b. A5046 84y multi 1.50 1.10
c. A5047 84y multi 1.50 1.10
d. A5048 84y multi 1.50 1.10
e. A5049 84y multi 1.50 1.10
f. A5050 84y multi 1.50 1.10
g. A5051 84y multi 1.50 1.10
h. A5052 84y multi 1.50 1.10
i. A5053 84y multi 1.50 1.10
j. A5054 84y multi 1.50 1.10
k. A5055 84y multi 1.50 1.10
l. A5056 84y multi 1.50 1.10
m. A5057 84y multi 1.50 1.10
n. A5058 84y multi 1.50 1.10
o. A5059 84y multi 1.50 1.10
p. A5060 84y multi 1.50 1.10
q. A5061 84y multi 1.50 1.10
r. A5062 84y multi 1.50 1.10
s. A5063 84y multi 1.50 1.10
t. A5064 84y multi 1.50 1.10
u. A5065 84y multi 1.50 1.10
v. A5066 84y multi 1.50 1.10
w. A5067 84y multi 1.50 1.10
x. A5068 84y multi 1.50 1.10
y. A5069 84y multi 1.50 1.10

4512 Sheet of 25 37.50 37.50
a. A5070 84y multi 1.50 1.10
b. A5071 84y multi 1.50 1.10
c. A5072 84y multi 1.50 1.10
d. A5073 84y multi 1.50 1.10
e. A5074 84y multi 1.50 1.10
f. A5075 84y multi 1.50 1.10
g. A5076 84y multi 1.50 1.10
h. A5077 84y multi 1.50 1.10
i. A5078 84y multi 1.50 1.10
j. A5079 84y multi 1.50 1.10
k. A5080 84y multi 1.50 1.10
l. A5081 84y multi 1.50 1.10
m. A5082 84y multi 1.50 1.10
n. A5083 84y multi 1.50 1.10
o. A5084 84y multi 1.50 1.10
p. A5085 84y multi 1.50 1.10
q. A5086 84y multi 1.50 1.10
r. A5087 84y multi 1.50 1.10
s. A5088 84y multi 1.50 1.10
t. A5089 84y multi 1.50 1.10
u. A5090 84y multi 1.50 1.10
v. A5091 84y multi 1.50 1.10
w. A5092 84y multi 1.50 1.10
x. A5093 84y multi 1.50 1.10
y. A5094 84y multi 1.50 1.10

4513 Sheet of 25, #4513a-4513k, 4513l-4513x, 2 #4513l 37.50 37.50
a. A5095 84y multi 1.50 1.10
b. A5096 84y multi 1.50 1.10
c. A5097 84y multi 1.50 1.10
d. A5098 84y multi 1.50 1.10
e. A5099 84y multi 1.50 1.10
f. A5100 84y multi 1.50 1.10
g. A5101 84y multi 1.50 1.10
h. A5102 84y multi 1.50 1.10
i. A5103 84y multi 1.50 1.10
j. A5104 84y multi 1.50 1.10
k. A5105 84y multi 1.50 1.10
l. A5106 84y multi 1.50 1.10
m. A5107 84y multi 1.50 1.10
n. A5108 84y multi 1.50 1.10
o. A5109 84y multi 1.50 1.10
p. A5110 84y multi 1.50 1.10
q. A5111 84y multi 1.50 1.10
r. A5112 84y multi 1.50 1.10
s. A5113 84y multi 1.50 1.10
t. A5114 84y multi 1.50 1.10
u. A5115 84y multi 1.50 1.10
v. A5116 84y multi 1.50 1.10
w. A5117 84y multi 1.50 1.10
x. A5118 84y multi 1.50 1.10
Nos. 4511-4513 (3) 112.50 112.50

Sports of the 2020 Summer Olympics and Paralympics, Tokyo. The 2020 Summer Olympics and Paralympics were postponed until 2021 because of the COVID-19 pandemic.

Souvenir Sheet

Japan National Stadium, Tokyo A5119

2021, June 23 Photo. *Perf. 13¼*
4514 A5119 500y multi *75.00 75.00*

2020 Summer Olympics and Paralympics, which were postponed until 2021 because of the COVID-19 pandemic.

No. 4514 was included in a booklet that also contained Nos. 4511-4513, which sold for 10,000y.

Japan Mint Gas Lamps A5120

Early Coinage Press A5121

Original Entrance to Japan Mint A5122

Balance Scale A5123

Shigenobu Okuma (1838-1922), Prime Minister A5124

Coin Commemorating 150th Anniv. of Modern Currency System A5125

Silver 1-yen Coin — A5126

Gold 1-yen Coin — A5127

Copper 1-yen Coin A5128

Wadokaichin Coin, c. 7th-10th Cent. A5129

2021, June 25 Litho. *Die Cut Perf.*
Self-Adhesive

4515 Sheet of 10 15.00
a. A5120 84y sil & multi 1.50 1.10
b. A5121 84y sil & multi 1.50 1.10
c. A5122 84y sil & multi 1.50 1.10
d. A5123 84y sil & multi 1.50 1.10
e. A5124 84y sil & multi 1.50 1.10
f. A5125 84y sil & multi 1.50 1.10
g. A5126 84y sil & multi 1.50 1.10
h. A5127 84y sil & multi 1.50 1.10
i. A5128 84y sil & multi 1.50 1.10
j. A5129 84y sil & multi 1.50 1.10

Modern currency system, 150th anniv.

Reef Manta Ray A5130

Spotted Eagle Ray A5131

Double-lined Fusilier A5132

Devil Ray and Double-lined Fusiliers A5133

Whale Shark and Remora A5134

Head of Whale Shark and Three Golden Trevallies A5135

Gills of Whale Shark A5136

Two Golden Trevallies and Fin of Whale Shark A5137

Giant Trevallies A5138

Whale Shark A5139

Die Cut Perf. 13¼x13 (#4516a, 4516c, 4516e, 4516f, 4516g, 4516j), 13x13¼ (#4516b, 4516d, 4516h, 4516i)

2021, July 1 Litho.
Self-Adhesive

4516 Sheet of 10 15.00
a. A5130 84y multi 1.50 1.10
b. A5131 84y multi 1.50 1.10
c. A5132 84y multi 1.50 1.10
d. A5133 84y multi 1.50 1.10
e. A5134 84y multi 1.50 1.10
f. A5135 84y multi 1.50 1.10
g. A5136 84y multi 1.50 1.10
h. A5137 84y multi 1.50 1.10
i. A5138 84y multi 1.50 1.10
j. A5139 84y multi 1.50 1.10

Sand was applied to parts of the designs of Nos. 4516a-4516j.

Pokémon Game Card Depicting Butterfree A5140

Pokémon Game Card Depicting Aceburn A5141

Pokémon Game Card Depicting Magikarp A5142

Back of Pokémon Game Card A5143

Pokémon Game Card Depicting Pikachu A5144

Pokémon Game Card Depicting Eevee A5145

Pokémon Game Card Depicting Mewtwo A5146

Pokémon Game Card Depicting Lucario A5147

Pokémon Game Card Depicting Liepard A5148

Pokémon Game Card Depicting Jirachi A5149

Various Pokémon Characters — A5150

No. 4518 — Pikachu and other Pokémon characters: a: Running on hilltop with streamer in air (26x27mm). b, With cherry blossoms in background (29x30mm). c, With Pikachu holding fishing rod (26x27mm). d, Taking shelter from the rain (26x26mm). e, At beach (26x27mm). f, With pile of fruits (26x29mm). g, Sleeping on hilltop (26x27mm). h, Soaking in natural pool (26x27mm). i, Running near tree in autumn (26x27mm). j, By fire in cave (22x26mm).

Die Cut Perf. 13¼

2021, July 7 Litho.
Self-Adhesive

4517 Sheet of 10 12.50
a. A5140 63y multi 1.25 .95
b. A5141 63y multi 1.25 .95
c. A5142 63y multi 1.25 .95
d. A5143 63y multi 1.25 .95
e. A5144 63y multi 1.25 .95
f. A5145 63y multi 1.25 .95
g. A5146 63y multi 1.25 .95
h. A5147 63y multi 1.25 .95
i. A5148 63y multi 1.25 .95
j. A5149 63y multi 1.25 .95

Die Cut Perf. 13½ (#4518j), 13¼ (others)

4518 A5150 Sheet of 10 16.00
a.-j. 84y Any single 1.60 1.25

Child Mailing Letter A5151

Cyclist A5152

House and Mail Van A5153

Motorcyclist A5154

Mail Van Passing Farm Field A5155

Store A5156

Barbershop A5157

Coffeeshop A5158

Cyclist Near Public Bathhouse A5159

House, Mailbox and Delivery Bike A5160

Die Cut Perf. 13¼

2021, July 21 **Litho.**

Booklet Stamps
Self-Adhesive

4519	A5151 63y multi		1.25	.95
4520	A5152 63y multi		1.25	.95
4521	A5153 63y multi		1.25	.95
4522	A5154 63y multi		1.25	.95
4523	A5155 63y multi		1.25	.95
a.	Booklet pane of 10, 2 each #4519-4523		12.50	
4524	A5156 84y multi		1.60	1.25
4525	A5157 84y multi		1.60	1.25
4526	A5158 84y multi		1.60	1.25
4527	A5159 84y multi		1.60	1.25
4528	A5160 84y multi		1.60	1.25
a.	Booklet pane of 10, 2 each #4524-4528		16.00	
	Nos. 4519-4528 (10)		14.25	11.00

Letter Writing Day.

A5161

A5162

A5163

A5164

A5165

A5166

A5167

A5168

A5169

Flowers — A5170

Die Cut Perf. 12¾x13

2021, Aug. 16 **Litho.**

Self-Adhesive

4529	Sheet of 10, 2 each #4529a-4529e	12.50	
a.	A5161 63y multi	1.25	.95
b.	A5162 63y multi	1.25	.95
c.	A5163 63y multi	1.25	.95
d.	A5164 63y multi	1.25	.95
e.	A5165 63y multi	1.25	.95
4530	Sheet of 10, 2 each #4530a-4530e	16.00	
a.	A5166 84y multi	1.60	1.25
b.	A5167 84y multi	1.60	1.25
c.	A5168 84y multi	1.60	1.25
d.	A5169 84y multi	1.60	1.25
e.	A5170 84y multi	1.60	1.25

Miniature Sheet

Phila Nippon 21 Philatelic Exhibition, Yokohama — A5171

No. 4531: a, Love that Meets Each Night, print by Utamaro Kitigawa (c. 1753-1806) (30x49mm). b, Kabuki Actor Jingoro Hidari Holding Cup, print by Kunichika Toyohara (1835-1900) (30x40mm). c, Satemo Migoto Nadai No Horimono Kabuki Actor Wearing White Kimono with Irises, print by Kunichika (28x40mm). d, Kabuki Actor Kikugoro Onoe V as Postman, print by Kunichika (28x40mm). e, The Courtesan Hanaogi of Ogiya, print by Utamaro (30x42mm). f, Woman Holding Scroll, print by Eisen Keisai (1790-1848) (28x36mm). g, Two Women Reading a Letter, print by Harunobu Suzuki (c. 1725-70) (30x42mm). h, A Mirror of the Ages (three women), print by Chikanobu Yoshu (1838-1912) (30x42mm). i, A Sigh of Amazement at the Prosperity of Great Edo, Where 3,000 Ryo Changes Hands Every Day (detail of woman looking upwards), print by Kunisawa Utagawa (1786-1865) (24x30mm). j, A Sigh of Amazement at the Prosperity of Great Edo, Where 3,000 Ryo Changes Hands Every Day (detail of woman looking downwards), print by Utagawa (1786-1865) (35mm diameter).

Die Cut Perf. 13¼ (#4531a, 4531e, 4531g, 4531h, 4531i), 12¾x13 (#4531b, 4531c, 4531d), 12¾x13¼ (#4531f), Die Cut Perf. (#4531j)

2021, Aug. 25 **Litho.**

Self-Adhesive

4531	A5171	Sheet of 10	16.00	
a.-j.		84y Any single	1.60	1.25

Souvenir Sheets

A5172

A5173

Modern Postal Service of Japan, 150th Anniv. A5174

No. 4532: a, Beauty Looking Back, print by Moronobu Hishikawa (1618-94). b, Moon and Geese, print by Hiroshige Utagawa (1797-1858).

No. 4533: a, Koshaku-Musume, print by Kunisada Utagawa (1786-1865). b, View of the Opening Ceremonies of the Yokohama Post Office, print by Hiroshige II (c. 1842-94), horiz.

No. 4534 — Hisoka Maeshima (1835-1919), founder of Japanese postal service, in: a, Red. b, Green, c, Blue. d, Purple. e, Red violet. f, Orange.

Die Cut Perf. 13¼

2021, Aug. 25 **Photo.**

Self-Adhesive

4532	A5172	Sheet of 2	27.50	
a.-b.		500y Either single	13.50	13.50

Die Cut Perf. 13¼ (#4533a), 13¼x13 (#4533b)

4533	A5173	Sheet of 2	23.00	
a.-b.		500y Either single	11.50	11.50

Die Cut Perf. 13

4534	A5174	Sheet of 6	68.00	
a.-b.		500y Any single	11.00	11.00

No. 4532 was sold in a folder for 1500y. Nos. 4533 and 4534 were sold together in a folder for 5000y. Nos. 4532-4534 were printed on a machine made paper that mimics traditional Japanese hand-crafted paper.

On Aug. 25, 2021, a sheet of 10 stamps (eight 84y stamps depicting Pokémon game cards and two 120y stamps depicting the artwork depicted on Nos. 4532a and 4532b) was offered for sale in a package that contained the sheet, a Pokémon game and other promotional material at a price of 4000y. The sheet was not offered for sale without the other contents of the package.

Miniature Sheets

A5175

Jspanese Art Using Green Shades — A5176

No. 4535: a, Detail of 7th cent. glazed lidded jar with plum blossom design (25x28mm). b, Detail from folding screen from Amanosan Kongoji Termple depicting Moon over valley (25x28mm). c, Detail of folding screen by Kiitsu Suzuki (1796-1858) depicting mountain stream (25x28mm). d, Road, painting by Kaii Higashiyama (1908-99) (27x27mm). e, Detail of celadon incense burner (22x32mm). f, Brindled Cat, detail of painting by Seiho Takeuchi (1864-1942) (23x32mm). g, A Tour of Waterfalls Around the Country — Oku-Amida Falls on the Kiso Road, detail of print by Hokusai Katsushika (1760-1849) (23x32mm). h, Needlework, painting by Seiki Kuroda (1866-1924) (23x32mm). i, Daubigny's Garden, detail of painting by Vincent van Gogh (1853-90) (23x33mm). j, Eve in the Garden of Eden, painting by Henri Rousseau (1844-1910 (29x27mm))

No. 4536: a, Entire 7th cent. glazed lidded jar with plum blossom design (28x36mm). b, Detail from folding screen from Amanosan Kongoji Termple depicting Moon over valley, diff. (39x26mm). c, Detail of folding screen by Kiitsu depicting mountain stream, diff. (37x27mm). d, Echoes of Green, painting by Kaii (34x31mm). e, A Tour of Waterfalls Around the Country — Oku-Amida Falls on the Kiso Road, detail of print by Hokusai , diff. (32x36mm). f, Brindled Cat, detail of painting by Seiho (34x36mm). g, Ducklings, painting by John Everett Millais (1829-96) (31x38mm). h, Daubigny's Garden, detail of painting by van Gogh, diff. (39x27mm). i, Water Lily Pond, painting by Claude Monet (1840-1926) (30x35mm). j, Entire celadon incense burner (32x33mm).

Die Cut Perf. 12¾x13 (#4535a, 4536f), 12¾ (#4535b, 4535c, 4535d), 12¾x12½ (#4535e, 4536a, 4536h), 12¼x12½ (#4535f), 12x12¾ (#4535g), 13 (#4535h, 4536d), 12¼x12¾ (#4535i), 12½ (#4535j, 4536g), 13x12½ (#4536b), 13x13¼ (#4536c), 12½x12¾ (#4536e), 13¼x12¾ (#4536i), 13¼ (#4536j)

2021, Sept. 8 **Litho.**

Self-Adhesive

4535	A5175	Sheet of 10	12.50	
a.-j.		63y Any single	1.25	.95
4536	A5176	Sheet of 10	15.00	
a.-j.		84y Any single	1.50	1.10

Miniature Sheets

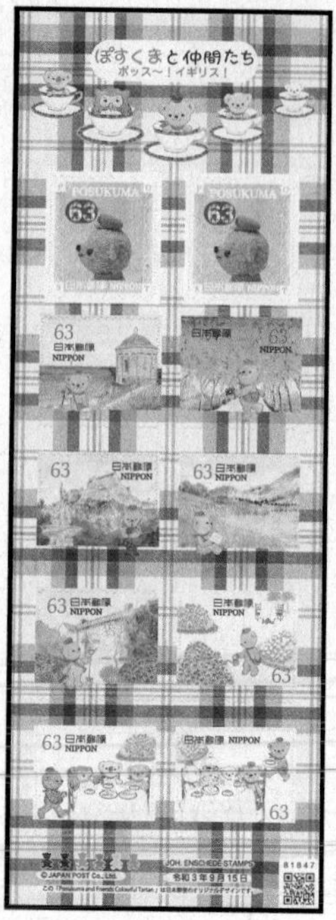

A5177

Teddy Bear Mascot of Japan Post
A5178

No. 4537: a, Head of mascot. b, Mascot with fishing rod and bucket, horiz. c, Mascot holding camera, horiz. d, Mascot playing bagpipes, horiz. e, Mascot holding airmail letter, horiz. f, Mascot holding shovel, horiz. g, Mascot watering flowers, horiz. h, Mascot, owl, koala, another teddy bear, table, horiz. h, Mascot, other teddy bears, table, horiz.

No. 4538: a, Head of mascot, diff. b, Teddy bears crossing street, horiz. c, Mascot and another teddy bear holding letters, horiz. d, Mascot and double-decker bus. e, Mascot holding magnifying glass at British House of Parliament, horiz. f, Mascot holding honey pot, horiz. g, Mascot holding bowl, another teddy bear near statue, horiz. h, Teddy bear holding basket of flowers, horiz. i, Mascot with wheeled suitcase, horiz.

Die Cut Perf. 13x13¼ (#4537a, 4538a), 13¼x13 (others)

2021, Sept. 15 **Litho.**

Self-Adhesive

4537	A5177	Sheet of 10, #4537b-4537i, 2 #4537a	12.50	
a.-i.		63y Any single	1.25	.95
4538	A5178	Sheet of 10, #4538b-4538i, 2 #4538a	15.00	
a.-i.		84y Any single	1.50	1.10

A5179 A5180

A5181 A5182

A5183 A5184

A5185 A5186

Gift Boxes with Ribbons
A5187 A5188

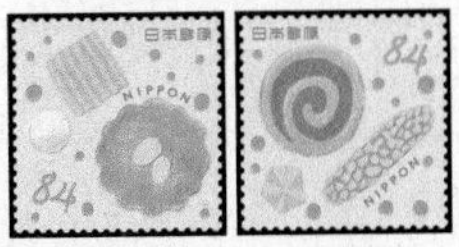

A5189 A5190

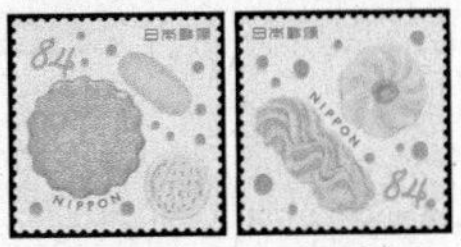

A5191 A5192

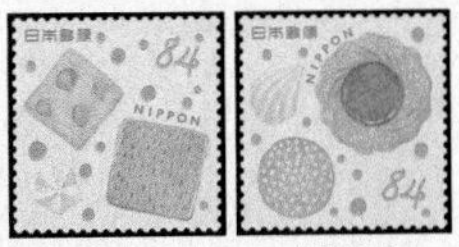

A5193 A5194

A5195 A5196

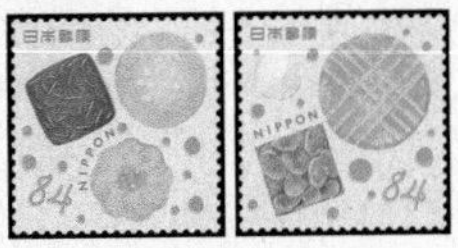

Cookies
A5197 A5198

A5199 A5200

A5201 A5202

A5203 A5204

A5205 A5206

A5207

Flowers — A5208

Litho. With Foil Application

2021, Sept. 22 ***Die Cut Perf. 13¼***

Self-Adhesive

4539	Sheet of 10	12.50	
a.	A5179 63y gold & multi	1.25	.95
b.	A5180 63y gold & multi	1.25	.95
c.	A5181 63y gold & multi	1.25	.95
d.	A5182 63y gold & multi	1.25	.95
e.	A5183 63y gold & multi	1.25	.95
f.	A5184 63y gold & multi	1.25	.95
g.	A5185 63y gold & multi	1.25	.95
h.	A5186 63y gold & multi	1.25	.95
i.	A5187 63y gold & multi	1.25	.95
j.	A5188 63y gold & multi	1.25	.95
4540	Sheet of 10	15.00	
a.	A5189 84y gold & multi	1.50	1.10
b.	A5190 84y gold & multi	1.50	1.10
c.	A5191 84y gold & multi	1.50	1.10
d.	A5192 84y gold & multi	1.50	1.10
e.	A5193 84y gold & multi	1.50	1.10
f.	A5194 84y gold & multi	1.50	1.10
g.	A5195 84y gold & multi	1.50	1.10
h.	A5196 84y gold & multi	1.50	1.10
i.	A5197 84y gold & multi	1.50	1.10
j.	A5198 84y gold & multi	1.50	1.10
4541	Sheet of 10	17.50	
a.	A5199 94y gold & multi	1.75	1.30
b.	A5200 94y gold & multi	1.75	1.30
c.	A5201 94y gold & multi	1.75	1.30
d.	A5202 94y gold & multi	1.75	1.30
e.	A5203 94y gold & multi	1.75	1.30
f.	A5204 94y gold & multi	1.75	1.30
g.	A5205 94y gold & multi	1.75	1.30
h.	A5206 94y gold & multi	1.75	1.30
i.	A5207 94y gold & multi	1.75	1.30
j.	A5208 94y gold & multi	1.75	1.30
	Nos. 4539-4541 (3)	45.00	

Miniature Sheet

Diplomatic Relations Between Japan and Uruguay, Cent. — A5209

No. 4542: a, Salvo Palace, Montevideo, Uruguay (30x36mm). b, Piriápolis, Uruguay waterfront (40x26mm). c, Casapueblo and its swimming pool, Punta Ballena, Uruguay (38x28mm). d, Buildings, Colonia del Sacramento, Uruguay (38x28mm). e, Maté pot and cups (24x32mm). f, Southern lapwing (24x32mm). g, Cows grazing (24x32mm). h, Carnival drummers (24x32mm). i, Gaucho with flag of Uruguay (24c32mm). j, Children playing soccer (24x32mm).

Die Cut Perf. 13¼x12¾ (#4542c, 4542d), 13½x13¼ (others)

2021, Sept. 24 **Litho.**

Self-Adhesive

4542	A5209	Sheet of 10	15.00	
a.-j.		84y Any single	1.50	1.10

Support Ships Natsushima and Yokosuka
A5210

Drilling Vessel Chikyu
A5211

Research Submarine Shinkai 2000
A5212

Underwater Vehicles Jinbei and Yumeiruka
A5213

Research Submarine Shinkai 6500 — A5214

Die Cut Perf. 13¼x11 (#4543a), 13¼x10¾ (#4543b), Die Cut Perf. (circular stamps)

2021, Oct. 1 **Litho.**

Self-Adhesive

4543	Sheet of 10, 2 each #4543a-4543e, + 3 stickers	15.00	
a.	A5210 84y multi	1.50	1.10
b.	A5211 84y multi	1.50	1.10
c.	A5212 84y multi	1.50	1.10
d.	A5213 84y multi	1.50	1.10
e.	A5214 84y multi	1.50	1.10

Japan Agency for Marine-Earth Science and Technology, 50th anniv.

Hawfinch
A5215

Marvel-of-Peru
A5216

Hongan Temple at Asakusa in Edo
A5217

Honjo Tatekawa
A5218

Sunset Across the Ryogoku Bridge From the Bank of the Sumida Riverat Onmya Embankment
A5219

2021, Oct. 8 **Photo.** ***Perf. 13x13¼***

4544	A5215	7y multi	.25	.25
4545	A5216	70y multi	1.25	.95

Perf. 13

4546	A5217	90y multi	1.60	1.25
4547	A5218	110y multi	2.00	1.50
4548	A5219	130y multi	2.25	1.75
		Nos. 4544-4548 (5)	7.35	5.70

Details from prints by Hokusai (1760-1849), International Letter-Writing Week.

Mailboxes — A5220

Designs: No. 4549, Yellow mailbox of France. No. 4550, Red mailbox of Japan.

2021, Oct. 8 **Litho.** ***Perf. 13***

4549	70y multi	1.25	.95
4550	70y multi	1.25	.95
a.	A5220 Pair, #4549-4550	2.50	1.90

Joint issue between Japan and France. See France Nos. 6101-6102.

International Letter-Writing Week.

Landscape, Shiga Prefecture
A5221

Clouds from Waterfall, Niigata Prefecture
A5222

Field in Kanagawa Prefecture
A5223

Hamarikyu Gardens, Tokyo Prefecture
A5224

Nabegataki Falls, Kumamoto Prefecture A5225

Senjugahama Beach and Lake Chuzenji, Tochigi Prefecture A5226

Yodo River, Aichi Prefecture A5227

Rocks Off Jodogahama Beach, Iwate Prefecture A5228

Sunset Over Sukumo Bay, Kochi Prefecture A5229

Trees and Islands, Hokkaido Prefecture A5230

Die Cut Perf. 13¼

2021, Oct. 13 **Litho.**

Self-Adhesive

4551	Sheet of 10	15.00	
a.	A5221 84y multi	1.50	1.10
b.	A5222 84y multi	1.50	1.10
c.	A5223 84y multi	1.50	1.10
d.	A5224 84y multi	1.50	1.10
e.	A5225 84y multi	1.50	1.10
f.	A5226 84y multi	1.50	1.10
g.	A5227 84y multi	1.50	1.10
h.	A5228 84y multi	1.50	1.10
i.	A5229 84y multi	1.50	1.10
j.	A5230 84y multi	1.50	1.10

Plum Blossoms A5231

Chrysanthemums A5232

Camellias A5233

Narcissi A5234

Roses A5235

Violas A5236

Cyclamen A5237

Mitsumata Blossoms A5238

Poinsettias A5239

Roses A5240

Die Cut Perf. 13x13¼

2021, Oct. 20 **Litho.**

Self-Adhesive

4552	Sheet of 10, 2 each #4552a-4552e	11.00	
a.	A5231 63y multi	1.10	.85
b.	A5232 63y multi	1.10	.85
c.	A5233 63y multi	1.10	.85
d.	A5234 63y multi	1.10	.85
e.	A5235 63y multi	1.10	.85
4553	Sheet of 10, 2 each #4553a-4553e	15.00	
a.	A5236 84y multi	1.50	1.10
b.	A5237 84y multi	1.50	1.10
c.	A5238 84y multi	1.50	1.10
d.	A5239 84y multi	1.50	1.10
e.	A5240 84y multi	1.50	1.10

A5241

A5242 A5243

New Year 2022 (Year of the Tiger) — A5244

2021, Nov. 1 **Litho.** ***Perf. 13x13¼***

4554	A5241	84y gold & multi	1.50	1.10

Litho. & Typo.

Perf. 13¼

4555	A5242	63y+3y gold & multi	1.25	.95
4556	A5243	84y+3y gold & multi	1.60	1.25
		Nos. 4554-4556 (3)	4.35	3.30

Litho.

Self-Adhesive

Die Cut Perf. 13x13¼

4557	A5244	63y gold & multi	1.10	.85

Numerals — A5245

Die Cut Perf. 13x13¼

2021, Nov. 5 **Litho.**

Self-Adhesive

4558	A5245	84y multi	1.50	1.10

Fried Shrimp Sandwich A5246

Spaghetti A5247

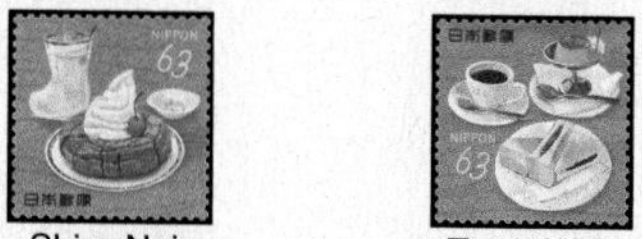

Shiro-Noir A5248

Toast With Bean Spread and Pudding A5249

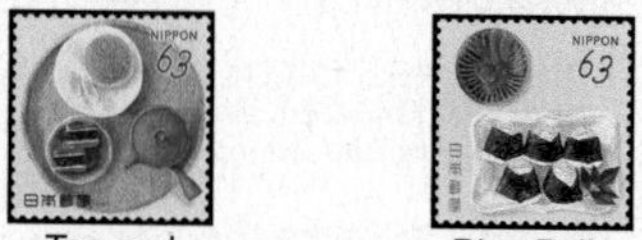

Tea and Cookies A5250

Rice Balls With Nori, Pickled Radishes A5251

Ramen Noodles and Red Bean Soup A5252

Rice Flour Cake and Devil's Food Cake A5253

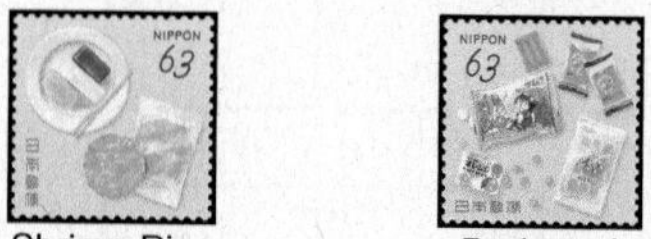

Shrimp Rice Crackers and Steamed Rice Flour Cakes A5254

Packaged Food and Candies A5255

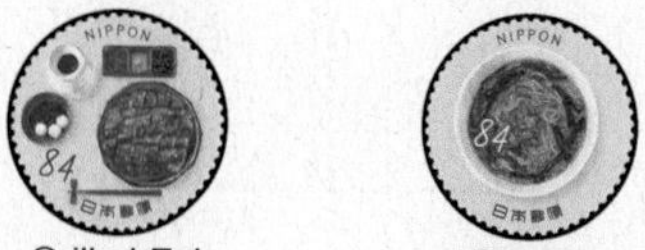

Grilled Eel on Rice A5256

Ramen Noodles With Pork and Onions A5257

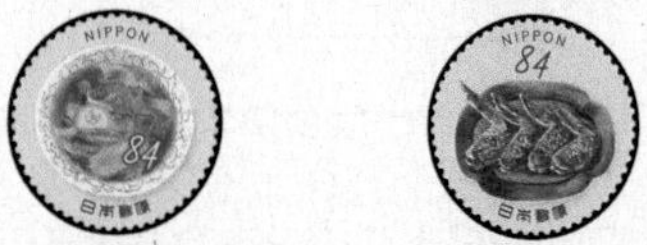

Noodles A5258

Chicken Wings A5259

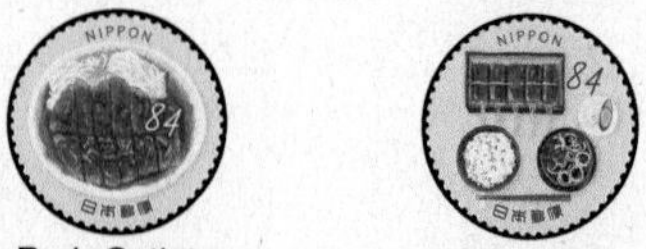

Pork Cutlets and Miso Sauce A5260

Rice With Vegetables and Red Miso Tofu A5261

Udon Noodle Soup A5262

Chicken Hot Pot A5263

Beef Stewed in Miso A5264

Miso Stew A5265

Die Cut Perf. 13¼

2021, Nov. 11 **Litho.**

Self-Adhesive

4559	Sheet of 10	11.00	
a.	A5246 63y multi	1.10	.85
b.	A5247 63y multi	1.10	.85
c.	A5248 63y multi	1.10	.85
d.	A5249 63y multi	1.10	.85
e.	A5250 63y multi	1.10	.85
f.	A5251 63y multi	1.10	.85
g.	A5252 63y multi	1.10	.85
h.	A5253 63y multi	1.10	.85
i.	A5254 63y multi	1.10	.85
j.	A5255 63y multi	1.10	.85

Die Cut Perf.

4560	Sheet of 10	15.00	
a.	A5256 84y multi	1.50	1.10
b.	A5257 84y multi	1.50	1.10
c.	A5258 84y multi	1.50	1.10
d.	A5259 84y multi	1.50	1.10
e.	A5260 84y multi	1.50	1.10
f.	A5261 84y multi	1.50	1.10
g.	A5262 84y multi	1.50	1.10
h.	A5263 84y multi	1.50	1.10
i.	A5264 84y multi	1.50	1.10
j.	A5265 84y multi	1.50	1.10

Candle Stand A5266

Sleigh A5267

Wolf A5268

Gift Bag A5269

Reindeer A5270

Bird A5271

Lanterns A5272

Poinsettia A5273

Quill Pen and Envelope A5274

Apple A5275

Litho. With Foil Application

2021, Nov. 19 ***Die Cut Perf. 13x13¼***

Self-Adhesive

4561	Sheet of 10, 2 each #4561a-4561e	11.00	
a.	A5266 63y met bl & pale bl	1.10	.85
b.	A5267 63y met bl & pale bl	1.10	.85
c.	A5268 63y met bl & pale bl	1.10	.85
d.	A5269 63y met bl & pale bl	1.10	.85
e.	A5270 63y met bl & pale bl	1.10	.85
4562	Sheet of 10, 2 each #4562a-4562e	15.00	
a.	A5271 84y met red & pink	1.50	1.10
b.	A5272 84y met red & pink	1.50	1.10
c.	A5273 84y met red & pink	1.50	1.10
d.	A5274 84y met red & pink	1.50	1.10
e.	A5275 84y met red & pink	1.50	1.10

A5276 A5277

A5278 A5279

A5280 A5281

A5282 A5283

A5284

Children's Book Illustrations by Ken Wakayama (1930-2015) — A5285

Die Cut Perf. 13x13¼

2021, Nov. 26 **Litho.**

Self-Adhesive

4563	Sheet of 10 + 9 stickers	15.00	
a.	A5276 84y multi	1.50	1.10
b.	A5277 84y multi	1.50	1.10
c.	A5278 84y multi	1.50	1.10
d.	A5279 84y multi	1.50	1.10
e.	A5280 84y multi	1.50	1.10
f.	A5281 84y multi	1.50	1.10
g.	A5282 84y multi	1.50	1.10
h.	A5283 84y multi	1.50	1.10
i.	A5284 84y multi	1.50	1.10
j.	A5285 84y multi	1.50	1.10

Nezuko Kamado A5286

Tanjiro Kamado A5287

Inosuke Hashibira A5288

Zenitsu Agatsuma A5289

Tanjiro Kamado — A5290

Giyu Tomioka A5291

Shinobu Kocho — A5292

Kyojuro Rengoku A5293

Mitsuri Kanroji A5294

Tengen Uzui — A5295

Kyojuro Rengoku A5296

Sanemi Shinazugsawa A5297

Obanai Iguro — A5298

Muichiro Tokito — A5299

Gyomei Himejima A5300

Die Cut Perf. 11¾

2021, Dec. 6 **Litho.**

Self-Adhesive

4564	Sheet of 15	22.50	
a.	A5286 84y multi	1.50	1.10
b.	A5287 84y multi	1.50	1.10
c.	A5288 84y multi	1.50	1.10
d.	A5289 84y multi	1.50	1.10
e.	A5290 84y multi	1.50	1.10
f.	A5291 84y multi	1.50	1.10
g.	A5292 84y multi	1.50	1.10
h.	A5293 84y multi	1.50	1.10
i.	A5294 84y multi	1.50	1.10
j.	A5295 84y multi	1.50	1.10
k.	A5296 84y multi	1.50	1.10
l.	A5297 84y multi	1.50	1.10
m.	A5298 84y multi	1.50	1.10
n.	A5299 84y multi	1.50	1.10
o.	A5300 84y multi	1.50	1.10

Characters from *Demon Slayer: Kimetsu no Yaiba,* manga by Koyoharu Gotouge.

Miniature Sheet

Fruits and Vegetables With Rabbits from *Peter Rabbit,* by Beatrix Potter (1866-1943) — A5301

No. 4565 — Various rabbits and: a, Lemons (22x30mm). b, Pepper (22x30mm). c, Apple (22x26mm). d, Grapes (22x26mm). e, Oranges (22x36mm). f, Strawberry (22x30mm). g, Grapefruit (22x30mm). h, Fruit and vegetable basket (32mm diameter). i, Mushrooms (22x36mm). j, Blueberries (22x36mm).

Die Cut Perf. (#4565h), Die Cut Perf. 13x13¼ (others)

2021, Dec. 10 **Litho.**

Self-Adhesive

4565	A5301	Sheet of 10	15.00	
a.-j.		84y Any single	1.50	1.10

Miniature Sheets

A5302

My Journey A5303

No. 4566: a, Tenneiji Temple pagoda (26x22mm). b, Onomichi Channel (26x22mm). c, Bowl of Onomichi ramen (23x25mm). d, Setoda Sunset Beach (26x22mm). e, Innoshima Suigun Castle (22x27mm). f, Building and bridge, Kurashiki Bikan Historical Quarter (26x22mm). g, Waterfront trees and buildings, Kurashiki Bikan Historical Quarter (26x22mm). h, Peach and muscat grapes (22x27mm). i, Pair of blue jeans (22x30mm). j, Great Seto Bridge (26x22mm).

No. 4567: a, Drawing of houses, Kurashiki Bikan Historical Quarter (30x24mm). b, Fruit parfait and cookie (22x28mm). c, Kurashiki Ivy Square (26x22mm). d, Bridge and building, Kurashiki Bikan Historical Quarter, diff. (26x22mm). e, Okayama Barazushi (dish with shrimp) (23x25mm). f, Senkoji Temple aerial tramway (26x22mm). g, Senko-ji Temple (22x29mm). h, Cat on steps (22x27mm). i, Lemons and jar of lemon curd (22x27mm). j, Lemon orchard, Tatara Bridge (22x27mm).

Die Cut Perf. 13¼x13 (#4566a, 4566b, 4566d, 4566e, 4566f, 4566g, 4566j, 4567c, 4567d, 4567f), 12½x13 (#4566c, 4566h), 12 (#4566i, 4567b), 12¾x12½ (#4567a), 12¼x12¾ (#4567e), 13 (#4567g, 4567j), 12¼x13 (#4567h, 4567i)

2022, Jan. 14 **Litho.**

Self-Adhesive

4566	A5302	Sheet of 10	11.00	
a.-j.		63y Any single	1.10	.85
4567	A5303	Sheet of 10	15.00	
a.-j.		84y Any single	1.50	1.10

Souvenir Sheet

New Year 2022 (Year of the Tiger) A5304

No. 4568 — Tiger with: a, Scroll (24x40mm). b, Envelope (29x33mm).

2022, Jan. 17 **Litho.** ***Die Cut Perf.***

Self-Adhesive

4568	A5304	Sheet of 2	2.60	
a.		63y multi	1.10	.85
b.		84y multi	1.50	1.10

Blue-and-White Flycatcher A5305

Ruddy and Common Kingfishers A5306

Java Sparrow A5307

Great Spotted Woodpecker A5308

Green Peacock A5309

Horned Owl A5310

Yellow-Crested Cockatoo A5311

Bantam Chicken A5312

White's Thrush A5313

Mandarin Duck A5314

Die Cut Perf. 13¼, 13¼x13 (#4569e)

2022, Jan. 24 **Litho.**

Self-Adhesive

4569	Sheet of 10	15.00	
a.	A5305 84y multi	1.50	1.10
b.	A5306 84y multi	1.50	1.10
c.	A5307 84y multi	1.50	1.10
d.	A5308 84y multi	1.50	1.10
e.	A5309 84y multi	1.50	1.10
f.	A5310 84y multi	1.50	1.10

g.	A5311 84y multi	1.50	1.10
h.	A5312 84y multi	1.50	1.10
i.	A5313 84y multi	1.50	1.10
j.	A5314 84y multi	1.50	1.10

Miniature Sheets

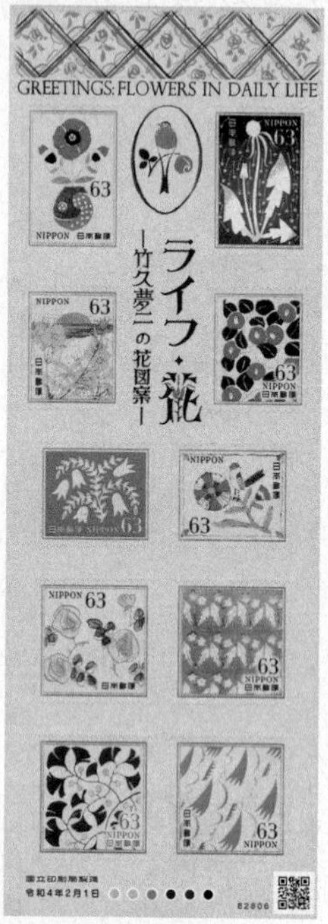

A5315

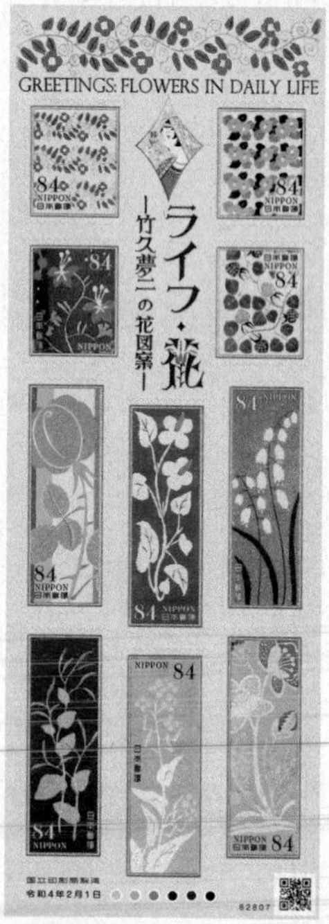

Flora
A5316

No. 4570: a, Dahlias (22x31mm). b, Dandelions (22x31mm). c, Evening primrose and Sun (22x26mm). d, Camellia (22x26mm). e, White flowers on red orange background (26x22mm). f, Flowers and bird (26x22mm). g, Roses (26x26mm). h, Primroses (26x26mm). i, Ginkgo tree leaves (26x26mm). j, Asiatic dayflower (26x26mm).

No. 4571: a, Flowers on vines (22x26mm). b, Camellias (22x26mm). c, Red flowers (22x26mm). d, Strawberries (22x26mm). e, Rose (19x48mm). f, Chameleon plant, light blue background (19x48mm). g, Lily of the valley, light green background (19x48mm). h, Oriental lady's thumb, dark green background (19x48mm). i, Rape blossoms, pink background (19x48mm). j, Flowers, yellow background (19x48mm).

Die Cut Perf. 13x13¼ (#4570a, 4570b, 4570c, 4570d), 13¼x13 (#4570e, 4570f), 13¼ (#4570g, 4570h, 4570i, 4570j)

2022, Feb. 1 **Litho.**

Self-Adhesive

4570 A5315 Sheet of 10		11.00	
a.-j. 63y Any single		1.10	.85

Die Cut Perf. 13x13¼

4571 A5316 Sheet of 10		15.00	
a.-j. 84y Any single		1.50	1.10

Pink Flowers
A5317

Yellow Flowers
A5318

Pink and White Flowers
A5319

Light Purple Flowers
A5320

Pink Flowers
A5321

Orange and Yellow Flowers
A5322

White, Pink and Purple Flowers
A5323

Pink Flowers
A5324

Red Violet Flowers
A5325

Blue Flowers
A5326

Die Cut Perf. 12¾x13 (#4572a, 4572c); 13x12¾ (#4572b, 4572d, 4572e)

2022, Feb. 15 **Litho.**

Self-Adhesive

4572	Sheet of 10, 2 each #4572a-4572e	11.00	
a.	A5317 63y multi	1.10	.85
b.	A5318 63y multi	1.10	.85
c.	A5319 63y multi	1.10	.85
d.	A5320 63y multi	1.10	.85
e.	A5321 63y multi	1.10	.85

Die Cut Perf. 13

4573	Sheet of 10, 2 each #4573a-4573e	15.00	
a.	A5322 84y multi	1.50	1.10
b.	A5323 84y multi	1.50	1.10
c.	A5324 84y multi	1.50	1.10
d.	A5325 84y multi	1.50	1.10
e.	A5326 84y multi	1.50	1.10

Miniature Sheets

A5327

Gems and Minerals
A5328

No. 4574 — Unprocessed gems: a, Red beryl. b, Tanzanite. c, Emerald. d, Citrine. e, Pearl, horiz. f, Mandarin garnet, horiz. g, Fluorite. h, Rhodochrosite. i, Aquamarine. j, Tourmaline.

No. 4575 — Cut gems: a, Fire opal (26x23mm). b, Blue sapphire (23x26mm). c, Diamond (26x27mm). d, Ruby (23x26mm). e, Jadeite (26x23mm). f, Peridot (25x26mm). g, Pink spinel (23x26mm). h, Paraiba tourmaline (24x26mm). i, Amethyst (25x26mm). j, Imperial topaz (22x27mm).

Die Cut Perf. 13x13¼, 13¼x13 (#4574e, 4574f)

2022, Feb. 22 **Litho.**

Self-Adhesive

4574 A5327 Sheet of 10		11.00	
a.-j. 63y Any single		1.10	.85

Die Cut Perf. 13¼x13 (#4575a, 4575c, 4575e), 13 (others)

4575 A5328 Sheet of 10		15.00	
a.-j. 84y Any single		1.50	1.10

Names of gems are found in margin below stamps on No. 4574, and above stamps on No. 4575.

Miniature Sheets

A5329

Sites, Scenes and Items From Asakusa District of Edo and Tokyo
A5330

No. 4576: a, Wooden spice bottle (27x25mm). b, Bowl of soba noodles and tempura (32x22mm). c, Folding fan (29x22mm). d, Animal-shaped toy (23x30mm). e, Cut glass (23x26mm). f, Puffed millet candy (29x26mm). g, Covered bowl with sweet bean paste and millet (28x26mm). h, Braided cord (26x26mm). i, Socks (25x28mm). j, Tortoise-shell hair pin (25x26mm).

No. 4577: a, Kitchen Supply District buildings (21x30mm). b, Theater entrance (27x27mm). c, Panda sculpture at entrance to flower garden (27x27mm). d, Sensoji Temple pagoda (21x30mm). e, Maneki-neko (beckoning cat) at Imado pottery factory building (27x27mm). f, Paper lanterns (30x21mm). g, Teapot, cup and dessert dish (27x27mm). h, Thunder Gate of Sensoji (30x21mm). i, Hot pot of loach soup, chopsticks, boxes (27x27mm). j, Bridge over Sumida River (27x27mm).

2022, Mar. 3 **Litho.** ***Die Cut Perf.***

Self-Adhesive

4576 A5329 Sheet of 10		11.00	
a.-j. 63y Any single		1.10	.85

Die Cut Perf. 13¼

4577 A5330 Sheet of 10		14.00	
a.-j. 84y Any single		1.40	1.10

A5331

A5332

A5333

A5334

2022 **Litho.** ***Die Cut Perf. 13x13¼***

Self-Adhesive

4578 A5331 84y multi		1.30	1.00
4579 A5332 94y multi		1.50	1.10
4580 A5333 120y multi		2.00	1.50
4581 A5334 140y multi		2.40	1.75
Nos. 4578-4581 (4)		7.20	5.35

Issued: Nos. 4578-4579, 5/18; Nos. 4580-4581, 3/17.

Carnations
A5335

Begonias
A5336

Bougainvillea
A5337

Columbines
A5338

Roses
A5339

Carnations and Baby's Breath
A5340

Sunflowers
A5341

Handkerchief Tree Flowers
A5342

Azaleas
A5343

Roses
A5344

Die Cut Perf. 13x13¼

2022, Apr. 6 **Litho.**

Self-Adhesive

4582	Sheet of 10, 2 each #4582a-4582e	10.00	
a.	A5335 63y multi	1.00	.75
b.	A5336 63y multi	1.00	.75
c.	A5337 63y multi	1.00	.75
d.	A5338 63y multi	1.00	.75
e.	A5339 63y multi	1.00	.75
4583	Sheet of 10, 2 each #4583a-4583e	13.00	
a.	A5340 84y multi	1.30	1.00
b.	A5341 84y multi	1.30	1.00
c.	A5342 84y multi	1.30	1.00
d.	A5343 84y multi	1.30	1.00
e.	A5344 84y multi	1.30	1.00

Flowers
A5345

Owl
A5346

Flowers
A5347

Dove
A5348

Flowers
A5349

Rabbit
A5350

Die Cut Perf. 13¼ (#4584a, 4585a, 4586a), Die Cut Perf. (#4584b, 4585b, 4586b)

Litho. With Foil Application

2022, Apr. 13

Self-Adhesive

4584	Sheet of 10, 6 #4584a, 4 #4584b	10.00	
a.	A5345 63y multi	1.00	.75
b.	A5346 63y multi	1.00	.75

4585 Sheet of 10, 6 #4585a, 4 #4585b 13.00
a. A5347 84y multi 1.30 1.00
b. A5348 84y multi 1.30 1.00
4586 Sheet of 10, 6 #4586a, 4 #4586b 15.00
a. A5349 94y multi 1.50 1.10
b. A5350 94y multi 1.50 1.10
Nos. 4584-4586 (3) 38.00

Beauty Blowing a Biidoro, by Utamaro (1753-1806) A5351

Ebizo Ichikawa (1741-1806), Actor, by Sharaku A5352

Playing With a Temari Ball, by Harunobu Suzuki (c. 1725-70) — A5353

Litho. & Engr.

2022, Apr. 20 ***Perf. 13½***
4587 Horiz. strip of 3 3.90 3.00
a. A5351 84y multi 1.30 1.00
b. A5352 84y multi 1.30 1.00
c. A5353 84y multi 1.30 1.00

Philately Week. Printed in sheets of 10 containing 4 each Nos. 4587a-4587b and 2 No. 4587c.

Bitter Melon, Fish and Pottery Flask A5354

Drums and Lion Dance Costume A5355

Phoenix and Shuri Castle A5356

Okinawa Rail, Hibiscus Flower and Indian Coral Tree A5357

Airplane, Whale Shark and Irabu Bridge — A5358

Die Cut Perf. 12¾x13¼

2022, May 13 **Litho.**

Self-Adhesive

4588 Sheet of 10, 2 each #4588a-4588e 13.00
a. A5354 84y multi 1.30 1.00
b. A5355 84y multi 1.30 1.00
c. A5356 84y multi 1.30 1.00
d. A5357 84y multi 1.30 1.00
e. A5358 84y multi 1.30 1.00

Return to Japan of Ryukyu Islands, 50th anniv.

Horse Chestnut Tree A5359

Japanese Maple Tree A5360

Black Pine Tree and Lake Biwa A5361

Rhododendrons A5362

Japanese Evergreen Oak Tree — A5363

2022, May 25 **Litho.** ***Perf. 13¼x14***
4589 A5359 84y multi 1.30 1.00
4590 A5360 84y multi 1.30 1.00
4591 A5361 84y multi 1.30 1.00
4592 A5362 84y multi 1.30 1.00
4593 A5363 84y multi 1.30 1.00
a. Vert. strip of 5, #4589-4593 6.50 5.00
Nos. 4589-4593 (5) 6.50 5.00

National Afforestation (Shiga).

Hydrangea A5364
Lavender A5365

Morning Glories A5366
Day Lilies and Rainbow A5367

Oriental Lily A5368
Sunflowers A5369

Goldfish A5370
Watermelon and Beverage A5371

Bowl of Shaved Ice A5372
Wind Chimes A5373

Beach A5374
Coral and Fish A5375

Fish in Sea Anemone A5376

Bindweed A5377

Morning Glories A5378

Frog A5379

Cloud and Rainbow A5380

Sunflowers A5381

Lily A5382

Fireworks A5383

Die Cut Perf. 13x13¼

2022, June 1 **Litho.**

Self-Adhesive

4594 Sheet of 10 10.00
a. A5364 63y multi 1.00 .75
b. A5365 63y multi 1.00 .75
c. A5366 63y multi 1.00 .75
d. A5367 63y multi 1.00 .75
e. A5368 63y multi 1.00 .75
f. A5369 63y multi 1.00 .75
g. A5370 63y multi 1.00 .75
h. A5371 63y multi 1.00 .75
i. A5372 63y multi 1.00 .75
j. A5373 63y multi 1.00 .75
4595 Sheet of 10 13.00
a. A5374 84y multi 1.30 1.00
b. A5375 84y multi 1.30 1.00
c. A5376 84y multi 1.30 1.00
d. A5377 84y multi 1.30 1.00
e. A5378 84y multi 1.30 1.00
f. A5379 84y multi 1.30 1.00
g. A5380 84y multi 1.30 1.00
h. A5381 84y multi 1.30 1.00
i. A5382 84y multi 1.30 1.00
j. A5383 84y multi 1.30 1.00

A5384 A5385

A5386 A5387

A5388 A5389

A5390 A5391

A5392 A5393

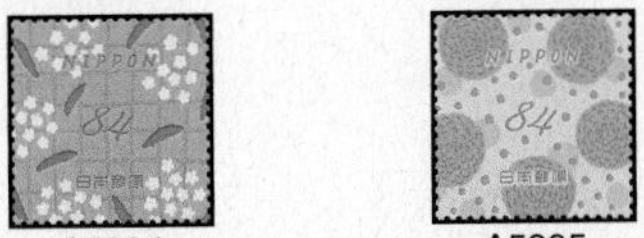
A5394 A5395

A5396 A5397

A5398 A5399

A5400 A5401

A5402

Flowers — A5403

Die Cut Perf. 13¼

2022, June 8 **Litho.**

Self-Adhesive

4596 Sheet of 10 9.50
a. A5384 63y multi .95 .75
b. A5385 63y multi .95 .75
c. A5386 63y multi .95 .75
d. A5387 63y multi .95 .75
e. A5388 63y multi .95 .75
f. A5389 63y multi .95 .75
g. A5390 63y multi .95 .75
h. A5391 63y multi .95 .75
i. A5392 63y multi .95 .75
j. A5393 63y multi .95 .75
4597 Sheet of 10 12.50
a. A5394 84y multi 1.25 .95
b. A5395 84y multi 1.25 .95
c. A5396 84y multi 1.25 .95
d. A5397 84y multi 1.25 .95
e. A5398 84y multi 1.25 .95
f. A5399 84y multi 1.25 .95
g. A5400 84y multi 1.25 .95
h. A5401 84y multi 1.25 .95
i. A5402 84y multi 1.25 .95
j. A5403 84y multi 1.25 .95

Miniature Sheet

Diplomatic Relations Between Japan and Mongolia, 50th Anniv. — A5404

No. 4598: a, Altai Tavan Bogd National Park, Mongolia (40x32mm). b, Hunter with eagle (33x38mm). c, Reindeer (40x32mm). d, Eurasian wolf (38x31mm). e, Pincushion flowers (38x31mm). f, Yurt (41x30mm pentagonal). g, Taimen (42x26mm). h, Shepherd on horseback, grazing sheep (40x32mm). i, Rider on Bactrian camel (40x32mm). j, Saurolophus (42x31mm).

Die Cut Perf. 13 (#4598a, 4598d, 4598e, 4598h, 4598i, 4598j), 13¼ (#4598b, 4598f), 13x13¼ (#4598c), 12¾x13 (#4598g)

2022, June 15 **Litho.**

Self-Adhesive

4598 A5404 Sheet of 10 12.50
a.-j. 84y Any single 1.25 .95

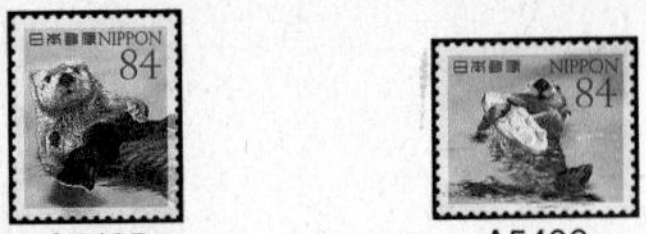
A5405 A5406

A5407

A5408

A5409

A5410

A5411

A5412

A5413

Sea Otters — A5414

Die Cut Perf. 13x13¼ (vert. stamps), 13¼x13 (horiz. stamps)

2022, June 22 Litho. & Engr.

Self-Adhesive

4599	Sheet of 10	12.50	
a.	A5405 84y multi	1.25	.95
b.	A5406 84y multi	1.25	.95
c.	A5407 84y multi	1.25	.95
d.	A5408 84y multi	1.25	.95
e.	A5409 84y multi	1.25	.95
f.	A5410 84y multi	1.25	.95
g.	A5411 84y multi	1.25	.95
h.	A5412 84y multi	1.25	.95
i.	A5413 84y multi	1.25	.95
j.	A5414 84y multi	1.25	.95

Miniature Sheets

A5415

Characters From *Toy Story* Movies — A5416

No. 4600: a, Buzz Lightyear. b, Jessie, vert. c, Woody, vert. d, Bo Peep, vert. e, Rex, vert. f, Hamm. g, Aliens. h, Mr. Potato Head. i, Mrs. Potato Head. j, Slinky Dog.

No. 4601 — Envelopes and: a, Woody. b, Buzz Lightyear, vert. c, Woody and Buzz Lightyear. d, Bo Peep, vert. e, Hamm. f, Aliens. g, Jessie, vert. h, Mr. and Mrs. Potato Head. i, Rex, vert. j, Slinky Dog.

Die Cut Perf. 13

2022, July 13 Litho.

Self-Adhesive

4600	A5415 Sheet of 10	9.50	
a.-j.	63y Any single	.95	.75
4601	A5416 Sheet of 10	13.00	
a.-j.	84y Any single	1.30	1.00

A5417

A5418

A5419

Letter Writing Day — A5420

Die Cut Perf. 12¾

2022, July 22 Litho.

Self-Adhesive

4602	Sheet of 10, 5 each #4602a-4602b	9.50	
a.	A5417 63y multi	.95	.75
b.	A5418 63y multi	.95	.75
4603	Sheet of 10, 5 each #4603a-4603b	13.00	
a.	A5419 84y multi	1.30	1.00
b.	A5420 84y multi	1.30	1.00

Scout's Hat A5421

Scouts Saluting A5422

Boy Scout Tent — A5423

Scout's Mess Kit — A5424

Scouts Around Campfire — A5425

Die Cut Perf. 13

2022, July 27 Litho.

Self-Adhesive

4604	Sheet of 10, 2 each #4604a-4604e	13.00	
a.	A5421 84y multi	1.30	1.00
b.	A5422 84y multi	1.30	1.00
c.	A5423 84y multi	1.30	1.00
d.	A5424 84y multi	1.30	1.00
e.	A5425 84y multi	1.30	1.00

Scouting in Japan, cent.

Ko-Kutani Bowl Decorated With Peonies A5426

Muromachi Period Folding Screen Depicting Beach and Pines A5427

Beautiful Vessel, Painting by Yuki Ogura (1895-2000) A5428

Sunflowers, Painting by Kiitsu Suzuki (1796-1858) A5429

Writing Box Cover Depicting Deer A5430

Folding Screen With Dragon and Tiger, by Gaho Hashimoto (1835-1908) A5431

A Tour of Bridges Around the Country - Rope Bridge on the Hietsu Border, Print by Hokusai (1760-1849) A5432

Morning at Etretat, Painting by Claude Monet (1840-1926) A5433

Portrait of Eugenia Primavesi, Painting by Gustav Klimt (1862-1918) A5434

Sunflowers, Painting by Vincent van Gogh (1853-90) A5435

Ko-Kutani Bowl Decorated With Peonies A5436

Muromachi Period Folding Screen Depicting Beach and Pines A5437

The Path, Painting by Ogura A5438

Sunflowers, by Suzuki A5439

Folding Screen With Dragon and Tiger, by Hashimoto A5440

A Tour of Bridges Around the Country - Rope Bridge on the Hietsu Border, by Hokusai A5441

Sunflowers, by van Gogh — A5442

Life is a Struggle (Golden Knight), Painting by Klimt — A5443

Yellow Irises, Painting by Monet A5444

Writing Box Cover Depicting Deer A5445

Die Cut Perf. 13 (#4605a, 4605c), 13x12¼ (#4605b), 13¼x12¼ (#4605d), 12¾x12½ (#4605e, 4605f, 4605g), 12¾ (#4605h), 13x12½ (#4605i), 12½x12¾ (#4605j)

2022, Aug. 3 Litho.

Self-Adhesive

4605	Sheet of 10	9.00	
a.	A5426 63y multi	.90	.70
b.	A5427 63y multi	.90	.70
c.	A5428 63y multi	.90	.70
d.	A5429 63y multi	.90	.70
e.	A5430 63y multi	.90	.70
f.	A5431 63y multi	.90	.70
g.	A5432 63y multi	.90	.70
h.	A5433 63y multi	.90	.70
i.	A5434 63y multi	.90	.70
j.	A5435 63y multi	.90	.70

Die Cut Perf. 13 (#4606a), 13½x13 (#4606b), 13x12½ (#4606c, 4606i), 12½x13 (#4606d), 13¼x13 (#4606e, 4606f), 13½x12¾ (#4306g), 13½x13¼ (#4606h), 12¾x12¼ (#4606j)

4606	Sheet of 10	12.50	
a.	A5436 84y multi	1.25	.95
b.	A5437 84y multi	1.25	.95
c.	A5438 84y multi	1.25	.95
d.	A5439 84y multi	1.25	.95
e.	A5440 84y multi	1.25	.95
f.	A5441 84y multi	1.25	.95
g.	A5442 84y multi	1.25	.95
h.	A5443 84y multi	1.25	.95
i.	A5444 84y multi	1.25	.95
j.	A5445 84y multi	1.25	.95

Miniature Sheet

Flora and Fauna of Amami-Oshima Island, Tokunoshima Island, Northern Part of Okinawa Island and Iriomote Island UNESCO World Heritage Site — A5446

No. 4607: a, Amami rabbit (37x28mm). b, Crested serpent eagle (28x37mm). c, Yanbaru long-armed scarab beetle (28x37mm). d, Amami violet (28x37mm). e, Lidth's jay (28mm diameter). f, Okinawa rail (28mm diameter). g, Yaeyama Chinese box turtle (28mm diameter). h, Amami Ishikawa's frog (28x37mm). i, Iriomote cat (28x37mm). j, Banded ground gecko (28x37mm).

Die Cut Perf. 13x12¾ (#4607a), 12¾x13 (#4607b, 4607c, 4607d, 4607h, 4607i, 4607j), Die Cut Perf. (#4607e, 4607f, 4607g)

2022, Aug. 10 Litho.

Self-Adhesive

4607	A5446 Sheet of 10	12.50	
a.-j.	84y Any single	1.25	.95

Miniature Sheet

Items From Jomon Prehistoric Sites in Northern Japan UNESCO World Heritage Site — A5447

No. 4608: a, Clay figurine with large eyes (28x37mm). b, Lacquered spouted earthenware vessel (28x37mm). c, Bowl with ornamental projections (28x37mm). d, Daigi pottery (28x37mm). e, Triangular flat stones (28x37mm). f, Clay figurine with open mouth (28x37mm). g, Deer-horn comb (37x28mm). h, Obsidian spearheads (37x28mm). i, Jade bead (37x28mm). j, Ceremonial spoons (37x28mm).

Die Cut Perf. 12¾x13 (vert. stamps), 13x12¾ (horiz. stamps)

2022, Aug. 17 **Litho.**

Self-Adhesive

4608 A5447 Sheet of 10 12.50
a.-j. 84y Any single 1.25 .95

Ginkgo Tree Branch A5448

Persimmons on Tree A5449

Dahlias A5450

Cosmos A5451

Chrysanthemums A5452

Japanese Maple Tree Branch A5453

Konara Acorns A5454

Wild Grapes A5455

Winter Cosmos A5456

Marigolds A5457

Die Cut Perf. 13x12¾

2022, Aug. 24 **Litho.**

Self-Adhesive

4609 Sheet of 10, 2 each #4609a-4609e 9.00
a. A5448 63y multi .90 .70
b. A5449 63y multi .90 .70
c. A5450 63y multi .90 .70
d. A5451 63y multi .90 .70
e. A5452 63y multi .90 .70

4610 Sheet of 10, 2 each #4610a-4610e 12.50
a. A5453 84y multi 1.25 .95
b. A5454 84y multi 1.25 .95
c. A5455 84y multi 1.25 .95
d. A5456 84y multi 1.25 .95
e. A5457 84y multi 1.25 .95

Miniature Sheet

77th National Athletic Meet, Tochigi A5458

No. 4611: a, Field hockey. b, Kegon Falls. c, Equestrian. d, Mt. Chausu. e, Diving. f, Plate of gyoza (potstickers). g, Softball. h, Ashikaga Flower Park. i, Climbing. j, Moka Railway.

2022, Sept. 1 **Litho.** ***Perf. 12¾x13***

4611 A5458 Sheet of 10 12.50 12.50
a.-j. 84y Any single 1.25 .95

Miniature Sheets

A5459

Posukuma and Friends — A5460

No. 4612: a, Small teddy bear reading letter in bed. b, Small teddy bear waving in window. c, Posukuma holding mail bag and waving. d, Posukuma, pillar box, small teddy bear with envelope. e, Posukuma, two other teddy bears with mailbags, house. f, Posukuma, three other teddy bears, owl. g, Posukuma, small teddy bear, near pillar box with statue of Posukuma. h, Posukuma, six other teddy bears, owl. i, Posukuma carrying tray of food. j, Posukuma waving, Parliament Building, London in background.

No. 4613: a, Posukuma delivering letter to penguins (33x23mm). b, Posukuma in space, delivering letter to planet (33x23mm). c, Posukuma and other teddy bears watching fireworks display (23x33mm). d, Posukuma bathing in hot spring (33x23mm). e, Posukuma on merry-go-round (25x23mm). f, Posukuma and small teddy bear on roller coaster (25x23mm). g, Posukuma and small teddy bear at tea ceremony (25x23mm). h, Posukuma and buttered bread (25x23mm). i, Posukuma making meal (25x23mm). j, Posukuma and friends around 10th anniversary cake (25x23mm).

Litho. With Foil Application

2022, Sept. 14 ***Die Cut Perf.***

Self-Adhesive

4612 A5459 Sheet of 10 + 23 stickers 9.00
a.-j. 63y Any single .90 .70

Die Cut Perf. 13x13¼ (#4613c), 13¼x13 (others)

4613 A5460 Sheet of 10 + 15 stickers 12.50
a.-j. 84y Any single 1.25 .95

This sheet of three 120y stamps + 6 stickers, issued Sept. 14, 2022, was printed in limited quantities and sold only with a set of postcards for 1000y.

Locomotive No. 1 — A5461

Tokyo Subway 1000 Series Car 1001 — A5462

Type C62 Locomotive A5463

Odakyu 3000 Series Express Train A5464

Japan National Railways 101 Series Train — A5465

Japan National Railways 151 Series Train — A5466

Japan National Railways KiHa58 Series Diesel Train — A5467

Japan National Railways / Japan Railways ED75 Series Locomotive and KoKi 5500 Series Freight Cars — A5468

0 Series Shinkansen Train A5469

Japan Railways Sleeper Express "Hokutosei" A5470

Die Cut Perf. 13¼

2022, Sept. 21 **Litho.**

Self-Adhesive

4614 Sheet of 10 12.50
a. A5461 84y multi 1.25 .95
b. A5462 84y multi 1.25 .95
c. A5463 84y multi 1.25 .95
d. A5464 84y multi 1.25 .95
e. A5465 84y multi 1.25 .95
f. A5466 84y multi 1.25 .95
g. A5467 84y multi 1.25 .95
h. A5468 84y multi 1.25 .95
i. A5469 84y multi 1.25 .95
j. A5470 84y multi 1.25 .95

Railways in Japan, 150th anniv.

A5471

Normalization of Diplomatic Relations Between Japan and People's Republic of China, 50th Anniv. — A5472

Die Cut Perf. 12¾x13

2022, Sept. 29 **Litho.**

Self-Adhesive

4615 Sheet of 10, 5 each #4615a-4615b 12.50
a. A5471 84y multi 1.25 .95
b. A5472 84y multi 1.25 .95

Factory and Trees A5473

Calculator, Piggy Bank, Currency, Change Purse A5474

Family and House A5475

Tree and House A5476

Bicyclist, Scooter Rider and Automobiles — A5477

2022, Oct. 3 **Litho.** ***Die Cut Perf. 13***

Self-Adhesive

4616 Sheet of 10, 2 each #4616a-4616e 12.50
a. A5473 84y multi 1.25 .95
b. A5474 84y multi 1.25 .95
c. A5475 84y multi 1.25 .95
d. A5476 84y multi 1.25 .95
e. A5477 84y multi 1.25 .95

Conciliation system in Japan, cent.

Black-naped Oriole and Shrubby Chinese Rose, Detail of Print by Hokusai (1760-1849) A5478

Black-naped Oriole and Shrubby Chinese Rose, Detail of Print by Hokusai A5479

Snowy Morning in Koishikawa, Print by Hokusai — A5480

Fuji From Palace Hill, Shinagawa, Tokaido, Print by Hokusai — A5481

Inume Pass in Kai Province, Print by Hokusai — A5482

2022, Oct. 7 Photo. *Perf. 13x13¼*

4617	A5478	7y multi	.30	.30
4618	A5479	70y multi	.95	.70

Perf. 13

4619	A5480	90y multi	1.25	.85
4620	A5481	110y multi	1.50	1.10
4621	A5482	130y multi	1.75	1.30
		Nos. 4617-4621 (5)	5.75	4.25

International Letter Writing Week.

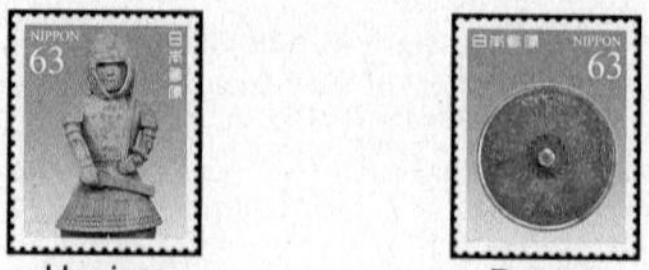

Haniwa Armored Man Clay Figurine, c. 6th Cent. A5483

Bronze Mirror with Beach Scene Decoration, c. 8th Cent. A5484

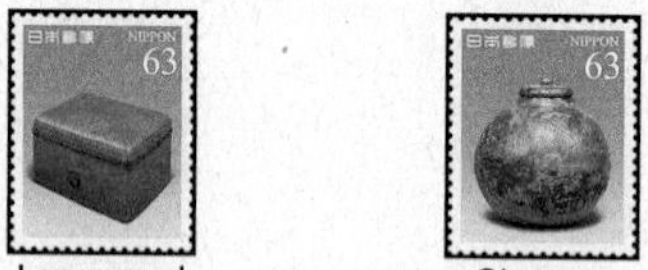

Lacquered Wooden Box With Mother of Pearl Inlay, 13th Cent. A5485

Cinerary Urn, 8th Cent. A5486

Ewer With Dragon Head Spout, 7th Cent. A5487

Autumn Landscape, Painting on Silk by Toyo Sesshu (1420-c. 1506) A5488

Detail of Painted Folding Screen by Eitoku Kano (1543-90) A5489

Detail of Painted Folding Screen by Eitoku Kano A5490

Red and White Cotton Roses, Painting on Silk by Li Di (c. 1100-c. 1197) — A5491

Red and White Cotton Roses, Painting on Silk by Li Di — A5492

16 Arhats, Ninth Arhat (Svaka), Painting on Silk, 11th Cent. A5493

Image of Bodhisattva Akasagarbha, Painting on Silk, 12th Cent. A5494

Snow Landscape, Painting on Silk by Liang Kai (c. 1140-c.1210) A5495

Sakyamuni Coming Down From the Mountain, Painting on Silk by Liang Kai A5496

Snow Landscape, Painting on Silk by Liang Kai A5497

Portrait of Senseki Takami, Painting on Silk by Kazan Watanabe (1793-1841) A5498

Image of Mahamayuri-vidya-rajni, Painting on Silk, 12th Cent. — A5499

Screen Painting Depicting Kyoto City Scenes, 17th Cent. A5500

Screen Painting Depicting Kyoto City Scenes, 17th Cent. A5501

Detail From Heiji Monogatari Scroll, 13th Cent. — A5502

Die Cut Perf. 13¼ (#4622a, 4622b, 4622c, 4622d, 4622e, 4622i, 4622j), 13 (#4622f, 4622g, 4622h)

2022, Oct. 12 Litho.

Self-Adhesive

4622		Sheet of 10	8.50	
a.	A5483	63y multi	.85	.65
b.	A5484	63y multi	.85	.65
c.	A5485	63y multi	.85	.65
d.	A5486	63y multi	.85	.65
e.	A5487	63y multi	.85	.65
f.	A5488	63y multi	.85	.65
g.	A5489	63y multi	.85	.65
h.	A5490	63y multi	.85	.65
i.	A5491	63y multi	.85	.65
j.	A5492	63y multi	.85	.65

Die Cut Perf. 13¼ (#4623a, 4623b, 4623c, 4623d, 4623e, 4623h, 4623i), 13 (#4623f, 4623g, 4623j)

4623		Sheet of 10	11.00	
a.	A5493	84y multi	1.10	.85
b.	A5494	84y multi	1.10	.85
c.	A5495	84y multi	1.10	.85
d.	A5496	84y multi	1.10	.85
e.	A5497	84y multi	1.10	.85
f.	A5498	84y multi	1.10	.85
g.	A5499	84y multi	1.10	.85
h.	A5500	84y multi	1.10	.85
i.	A5501	84y multi	1.10	.85
j.	A5502	84y multi	1.10	.85

Tokyo National Museum, 150th anniv.

Japanese Apricot Blossoms A5503

Narcissi A5504

Sarcandra A5505

Tulips and Pansies A5506

Roses A5507

Christmas Roses A5508

Pieris A5509

Roses A5510

Rosemary A5511

Ornamental Cabbages A5512

Die Cut Perf. 13x13¼

2022, Oct. 26 Litho.

Self-Adhesive

4624		Sheet of 10, 2 each #4624a-4624e	8.50	
a.	A5503	63y multi	.85	.65
b.	A5504	63y multi	.85	.65
c.	A5505	63y multi	.85	.65
d.	A5506	63y multi	.85	.65
e.	A5507	63y multi	.85	.65
4625		Sheet of 10, 2 each #4625a-4625e	11.00	
a.	A5508	84y multi	1.10	.85
b.	A5509	84y multi	1.10	.85
c.	A5510	84y multi	1.10	.85
d.	A5511	84y multi	1.10	.85
e.	A5512	84y multi	1.10	.85

A5513

A5514

A5515

New Year 2023 (Year of the Rabbit) — A5516

2022, Nov. 1 Photo. *Perf. 13x13¼*

4626	A5513	84y multi	1.10	.85

Photo. & Typo.

Perf. 13¼

4627	A5514	63y+3y multi	.90	.70
4628	A5515	84y+3y multi	1.25	.95
		Nos. 4626-4628 (3)	3.25	2.50

Photo.

Die Cut Perf. 13x13¼

Self-Adhesive

4629	A5516	63y multi	.85	.65

Child and Dog Near Pond A5517

Cup of Cocoa A5518

House in Winter A5519

Heater and Cat A5520

Snowman A5521

House in Snow Globe A5522

Child Carrying Gifts in Snow Globe A5523

Deer and Rabbit in Snow Globe A5524

Child Making Snowman in Snow Globe A5525

Child Looking at Star in Snow Globe A5526

Die Cut Perf. 13x12½

2022, Nov. 16 **Litho.**

Self-Adhesive

4630	Sheet of 10, 2 each #4630a-4630e	9.00	
a.	A5517 63y multi	.90	.70
b.	A5518 63y multi	.90	.70
c.	A5519 63y multi	.90	.70
d.	A5520 63y multi	.90	.70
e.	A5521 63y multi	.90	.70
4631	Sheet of 10, 2 each #4631a-4631e	12.50	
a.	A5522 84y multi	1.25	.95
b.	A5523 84y multi	1.25	.95
c.	A5524 84y multi	1.25	.95
d.	A5525 84y multi	1.25	.95
e.	A5526 84y multi	1.25	.95

PREFECTURE ISSUES

Japan has 47 prefectures (political subdivisions) and 13 postal regions (12 until 2004). Since 1989, the national postal ministry has issued stamps to publicize each prefecture. These prefectural stamps are valid throughout Japan and were issued not only in the prefecture named on the stamp but in all other prefectures in the postal region, and in one or more post offices in the other 11 or 12 postal regions. Prefectural stamps are distinguishable from other Japanese stamps by the style of the ideographic characters of "Nippon yubin" on each stamp:

日本郵便

Inscr. on National Stamps since 1948

日本郵便

Inscr. on Prefectural Stamps

Monkeys (Nagano) ZA1

Cherries on Tree (Yamagata) ZA2

Shurei-mon, Gate of Courtesy (Okinawa) ZA3

Dogo Hot Spa (Ehime) ZA4

Blue-eyed Doll (Kanagawa) — ZA5

Seto Inland Sea (Hiroshima) — ZA6

Memorial Hall and Mandai Bridge (Niigata) ZA8

Nagoya Castle and *Shachihoko* (Aichi) ZA9

Mt. Takasaki Monkey Holding Perilla Leaf, Fruit (Oita) ZA10

City Hall, 1888 (Hokkaido) ZA11

Runner, Flower (Hokkaido) ZA12

Kumamoto Castle (Kumamoto) ZA13

Stone Lantern, Kenroku-en Park (Ishikawa) ZA14

Bunraku Puppets and Theater (Osaka) ZA15

Shigaraki Ware Raccoon Dog and Lake Biwa (Shiga) ZA16

Apples and Blossoms (Aomori) ZA17

Raccoon Dogs Dancing (Chiba) ZA18

Blowfish Lanterns (Yamaguchi) ZA19

Tokyo Station (Tokyo) ZA20

2nd Asian Winter Olympics (Hokkaido) ZA21

Waterfalls (Toyama) — ZA22

Perf. 13, 13½ (#Z4, Z11, Z20), 13x13½ (#Z12-Z19)

1989-90 **Photo., Litho. (#Z16-Z17)**

Z1	ZA1	62y multicolored		1.10	.70
Z2	ZA2	62y multicolored		1.10	.70
Z3	ZA3	62y multicolored		1.10	.70
Z4	ZA4	62y multicolored		1.10	.70
Z5	ZA5	62y multicolored		1.10	.70
Z6		62y sampan, bridge		1.10	.70
Z7		62y islands, stairs, starbursts		1.10	.70
a.	ZA6	Pair, #Z6-Z7		2.25	2.25
Z8	ZA8	62y multicolored		1.10	.70
Z9	ZA9	62y multicolored		1.10	.70
Z10	ZA10	62y multicolored		1.10	.70
Z11	ZA11	62y multicolored		1.10	.70
Z12	ZA12	62y multicolored		1.10	.70
Z13	ZA13	62y multicolored		1.10	.70
Z14	ZA14	62y multicolored		1.10	.70
Z15	ZA15	62y multicolored		1.10	.70
Z16	ZA16	62y multicolored		1.10	.70
Z17	ZA17	62y multicolored		1.10	.70
Z18	ZA18	62y multicolored		1.10	.70
Z19	ZA19	62y multicolored		1.10	.70
Z20	ZA20	62y multicolored		1.10	.70
Z21	ZA21	62y multicolored		1.10	.70
Z22	ZA22	62y multicolored		1.10	.70
		Nos. Z1-Z22 (22)		24.20	15.40

Sheets containing 4 Nos. Z1, Z2, Z4, Z11 or 3 No. Z14 + label, 3 No. Z19 + label were lottery prizes.

Issued: Nos. Z1-Z2, 4/1; No. Z3, 5/15; No. Z4, 6/1; No. Z5, 6/2; NOs. Z6-Z7, 7/7; No. Z8, 7/14; No. Z9, 8/1; Nos. Z10-Z11, 8/15; No. Z12, 9/1; No. Z13, 9/29; Nos. Z14-Z17, 10/2; No. Z18, 10/27; Nos. Z19-Z20, 11/1; No. Z21, 3/1/90; No. Z22, 4/18/90.

See Nos. Z263, Z285, Z363.

Nos. Z23-Z69 were issued as one set. It is broken into sections for ease of reference. See No. Z69a for sheet containing all 47 stamps.

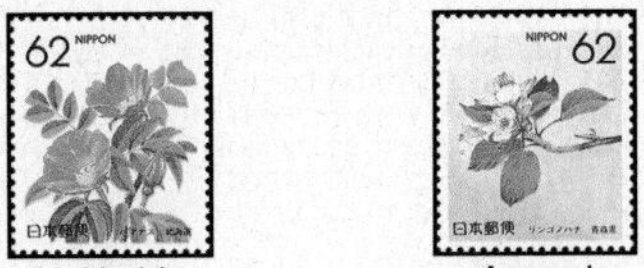

Hokkaido ZA23 — Aomori ZA24

Iwate ZA25 — Miyagi ZA26

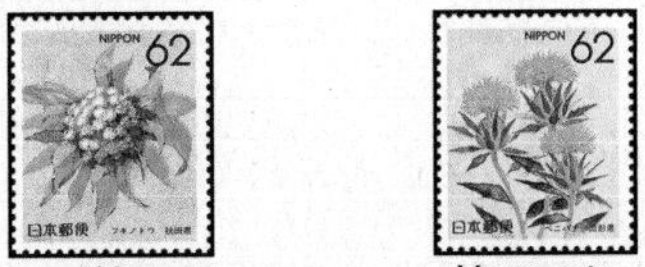

Akita ZA27 — Yamagata ZA28

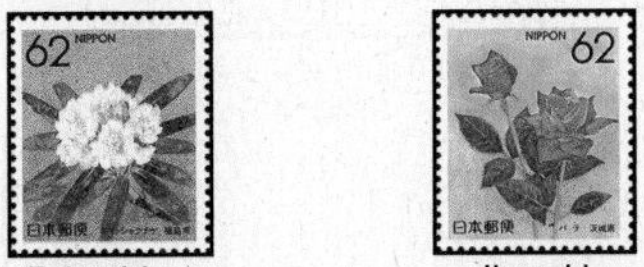

Fukushima ZA29 — Ibaraki ZA30

Flowers of the Prefectures: No. Z23, Sweet briar. No. Z24, Apple blossom. No. Z25, Paulowina. No. Z26, Japanese bush clover. No. Z27, Butterbur flower. No. Z28, Safflower. No. Z29, Alpine rose. No. Z30, Rose.

1990, Apr. 27 **Litho.** ***Perf. 13½***

Z23	ZA23	62y multicolored	3.50	.70
Z24	ZA24	62y multicolored	1.25	.70
Z25	ZA25	62y multicolored	1.25	.70
Z26	ZA26	62y multicolored	1.25	.70
Z27	ZA27	62y multicolored	1.25	.70
Z28	ZA28	62y multicolored	1.25	.70
Z29	ZA29	62y multicolored	1.25	.70
Z30	ZA30	62y multicolored	1.25	.70
		Nos. Z23-Z30 (8)	12.25	5.60

See Nos. Z190, Z614-Z619.

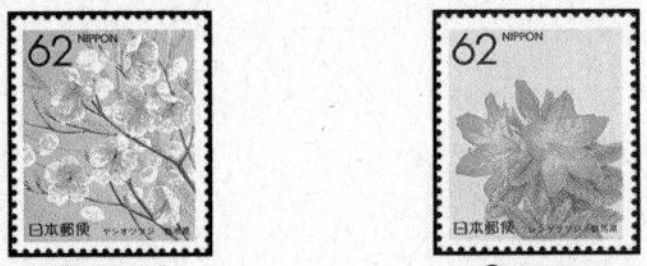

Tochigi ZA31 — Gunma ZA32

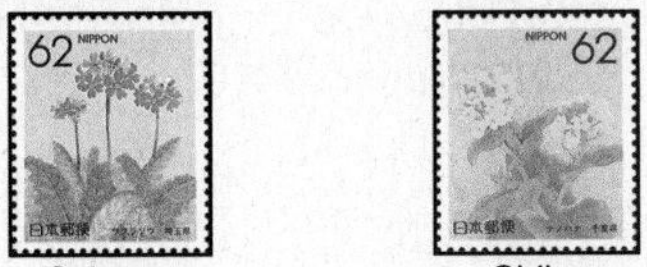

Saitama ZA33 — Chiba ZA34

Tokyo ZA35 — Kanagawa ZA36

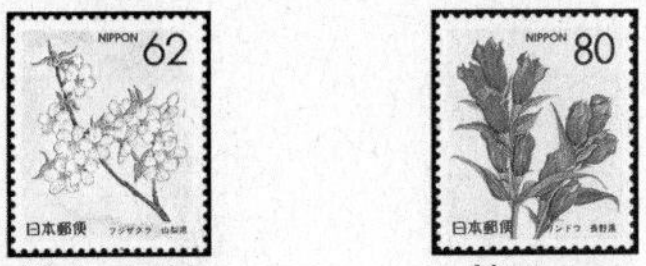

Yamanashi ZA37 — Nagano ZA38

Niigata ZA39 — Toyama ZA40

No. Z31, Yashio azalea. No. Z32, Japanese azalea. No. Z33, Primrose. No. Z34, Rape blossom. No. Z35, Cherry blossom. No. Z36, Gold-banded lily. No. Z37, Cherry blossom. No. Z38, Autumn bellflower. No. Z39, Tulip. No. Z40, Tulip.

Z31	ZA31	62y multicolored	1.25	.70
Z32	ZA32	62y multicolored	1.25	.70
Z33	ZA33	62y multicolored	1.25	.70
Z34	ZA34	62y multicolored	1.25	.70
Z35	ZA35	62y multicolored	1.25	.70
Z36	ZA36	62y multicolored	1.25	.70
Z37	ZA37	62y multicolored	1.25	.70
Z38	ZA38	62y multicolored	3.50	.70
Z39	ZA39	62y multicolored	1.25	.70
Z40	ZA40	62y multicolored	1.25	.70
		Nos. Z31-Z40 (10)	14.75	7.00

See No. Z197.

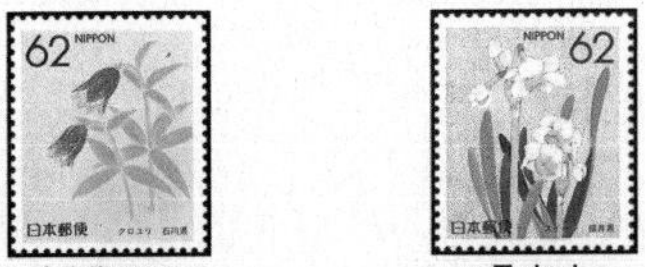

Ishikawa ZA41 — Fukui ZA42

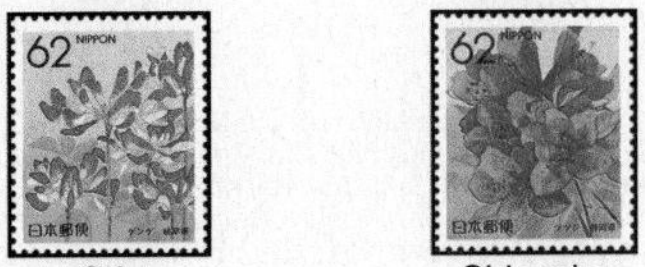

Gifu ZA43 — Shizuoka ZA44

Aichi ZA45 — Mie ZA46

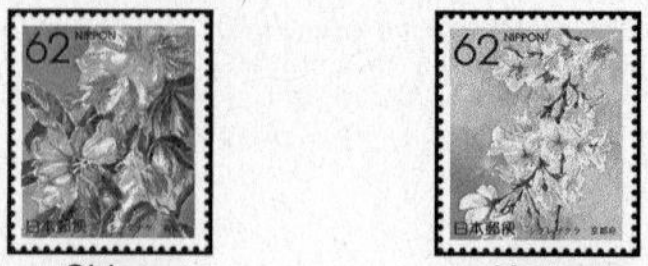

Shiga ZA47 — Kyoto ZA48

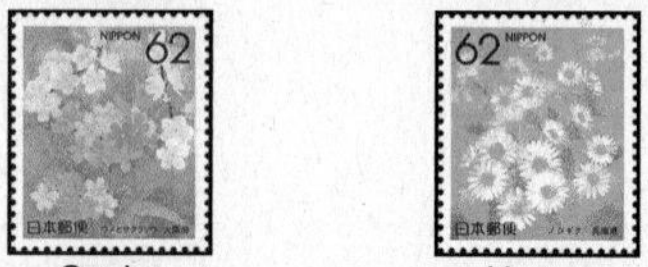

Osaka ZA49 — Hyogo ZA50

No. Z41, Black lily. No. Z42, Daffodil. No. Z43, Chinese milk vetch. No. Z44, Azalea. No. Z45, Rabbit-ear iris. No. Z46, Iris. No. Z47, Alpine rose. No. Z48, Drooping cherry blossom. No. Z49, Japanese apricot and primrose. No. Z50, Chrysanthemum.

Z41	ZA41	62y	multicolored	1.25	.70
Z42	ZA42	62y	multicolored	1.25	.70
Z43	ZA43	62y	multicolored	1.50	.70
Z44	ZA44	62y	multicolored	2.00	.70
Z45	ZA45	62y	multicolored	1.25	.70
Z46	ZA46	62y	multicolored	1.25	.70
Z47	ZA47	62y	multicolored	3.00	.70
Z48	ZA48	62y	multicolored	3.00	.70
Z49	ZA49	62y	multicolored	1.25	.70
Z50	ZA50	62y	multicolored	1.25	.70
	Nos. Z41-Z50 (10)			17.00	7.00

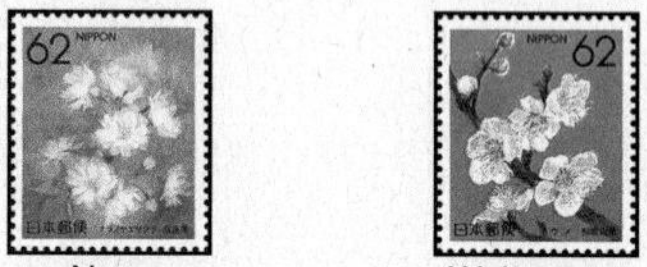

Nara ZA51 — Wakayama ZA52

Tottori ZA53 — Shimane ZA54

Okayama ZA55 — Hiroshima ZA56

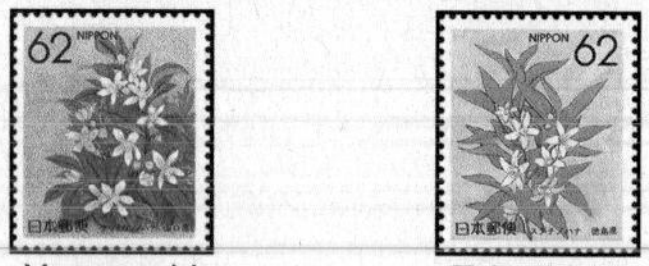

Yamaguchi ZA57 — Tokushima ZA58

Kagawa ZA59 — Ehime ZA60

No. Z51, Double cherry blossom. No. Z52, Japanese apricot. No. Z53, Pear blossom. No. Z54, Peony. No. Z55, Peach blossom. No. Z56, Japanese Maple. No. Z57, Summer orange blossom. No. Z58, Sudachi orange blossom. No. Z59, Olive blossom. No. Z60, Mandarin orange blossom.

Z51	ZA51	62y	multicolored	2.00	.70
Z52	ZA52	62y	multicolored	1.50	.70
Z53	ZA53	62y	multicolored	1.25	.70
Z54	ZA54	62y	multicolored	1.25	.70
Z55	ZA55	62y	multicolored	1.25	.70
Z56	ZA56	62y	multicolored	1.25	.70
Z57	ZA57	62y	multicolored	1.25	.70
Z58	ZA58	62y	multicolored	1.50	.70
Z59	ZA59	62y	multicolored	5.00	.70
Z60	ZA60	62y	multicolored	2.50	.70
	Nos. Z51-Z60 (10)			18.75	7.00

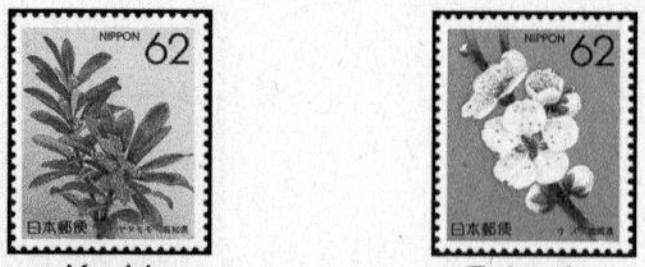

Kochi ZA61 — Fukuoka ZA62

Saga ZA63 — Nagasaki ZA64

Kumamoto ZA65 — Oita ZA66

Miyazaki ZA67 — Kagoshima ZA68

Okinawa — ZA69

No. Z61, Myrica. No. Z62, Japanese apricot. No. Z63, Laurel. No. Z64, Unzen azalea. No. Z65, Autumn bellflower. No. Z66, Japanese apricot of bungo. No. Z67, Crinum. No. Z68, Rosebay. No. Z69, Coral tree.

Z61	ZA61	62y	multicolored	2.00	.70
Z62	ZA62	62y	multicolored	1.25	.70
Z63	ZA63	62y	multicolored	1.25	.70
Z64	ZA64	62y	multicolored	1.25	.70
Z65	ZA65	62y	multicolored	1.25	.70
Z66	ZA66	62y	multicolored	1.25	.70
Z67	ZA67	62y	multicolored	1.25	.70
Z68	ZA68	62y	multicolored	1.25	.70
Z69	ZA69	62y	multicolored	1.25	.70
a.	Sheet of 47 + 3 labels, #Z23-Z69			110.00	
	Nos. Z61-Z69 (9)			12.00	6.30

Nos. Z23-Z69 were issued in sheets of 20.
No. Z69a was released in all prefectures.

Seven Baby Crows (Ibaraki) — ZA70

Inns of Tsumago & Magome (Nagano)
ZA71 ZA72

Mt. Fuji and Tea Picking (Shizuoka) ZA73 — Two Peaches (Fukushima) ZA74

Mt. Sakurajima (Kagoshima) ZA75 — Fireworks Festival of Omagari (Akita) ZA76

Travel Expo '90, Nagasaki (Nagasaki) ZA77 — Tokyo Shin Post Office (Tokyo) ZA78

Yasukibushi Folk Song (Shimane) ZA79 — Ryukyu Dancer (Okinawa) ZA80

Litho., Litho. & Engr. (#Z70-Z71)

1990 ***Perf. 13***

Z70	ZA70	62y	multicolored	1.10	.70
Z71	ZA71	62y	blk & buff	1.10	.70
Z72	ZA72	62y	blk & pale grn	1.10	.70
a.	Pair, #Z71-Z72			2.25	2.25
Z73	ZA73	62y	multicolored	1.10	.70
Z74	ZA74	62y	multicolored	1.10	.70
Z75	ZA75	62y	multicolored	1.10	.70
Z76	ZA76	62y	multicolored	1.10	.70
Z77	ZA77	62y	multicolored	1.10	.70
Z78	ZA78	62y	multicolored	1.10	.70
Z79	ZA79	62y	multicolored	1.10	.70
Z80	ZA80	62y	multicolored	1.10	.70
	Nos. Z70-Z80 (11)			12.10	7.70

Issued: Nos. Z70-Z72, 5/1; No. Z73, 5/2; No. Z74, 6/1; Nos. Z75-Z76, 7/2; No. Z77, 8/1; No. Z78, 8/6; Nos. Z79-Z80, 8/15.

Sheets of 3 + label of Nos. Z70, Z73, Z80 were lottery prizes. Value, each $3.25.

See Nos. Z332-Z333.

Dancing Girl (Kyoto) ZA81 — Old Path of Kumano (Wakayama) ZA82

45th Natl. Athletic Meet (Fukuoka) ZA83 — Izu Swamp, Swans (Miyagi) ZA84

Spring (Gifu) ZA85 — Summer (Gifu) ZA86

Autumn (Gifu) ZA87 — Winter (Gifu) ZA88

Nursery Rhyme, Toryanse (Saitama) ZA89 — Japanese Cranes (Hokkaido) ZA90

1990

Z81	ZA81	62y	multicolored	1.10	.70
Z82	ZA82	62y	multicolored	1.10	.70
Z83	ZA83	62y	multicolored	1.10	.70
Z84	ZA84	62y	multicolored	1.10	.70
Z85	ZA85	62y	multicolored	1.10	.70
Z86	ZA86	62y	multicolored	1.10	.70
Z87	ZA87	62y	multicolored	1.10	.70
Z88	ZA88	62y	multicolored	1.10	.70
a.	Strip of 4, #Z85-Z88			4.50	4.50
Z89	ZA89	62y	multicolored	1.10	.70
Z90	ZA90	62y	multicolored	1.10	.70
	Nos. Z81-Z90 (10)			11.00	7.00

Issued: Nos. Z81-Z83, 9/3; No. Z84, 10/1; Nos. Z85-Z88, 10/9; No. Z89, 10/12; No. Z90, 10/30.

Sheets of 3 No. Z82 + label were lottery prizes. Value, $3.25.

See Nos. 3282-3285, Z171-Z174.

Bizen Ware (Okayama) — ZA92

Battle of Yashima (Kagawa) ZA91 — Yoshinogari Ruins (Saga) ZA94

Bride Under Cherry Blossoms (Yamanashi) ZA95 — Carp (Niigata) ZA96

Lily of the Valley (Hokkaido) ZA97 — Lilac (Hokkaido) ZA98

Daylily (Hokkaido) ZA99

Rowanberry (Hokkaido) ZA100

Litho., Photo. (#Z94-Z95)

1991 *Perf. 13*

Z91	ZA91	62y multicolored	1.10	.70
Z92		62y pedestal	1.10	.70
Z93		62y bowl	1.10	.70
a.		ZA92 Pair, #Z92-Z93	2.25	2.25
Z94	ZA94	62y multicolored	1.10	.70
Z95	ZA95	62y multicolored	1.10	.70
Z96	ZA96	62y multicolored	1.10	.70
Z97	ZA97	62y multicolored	1.10	.70
Z98	ZA98	62y multicolored	1.10	.70
Z99	ZA99	62y multicolored	1.10	.70
Z100	ZA100	62y multicolored	1.10	.70
a.		Strip of 4, #Z97-Z100	4.50	4.50
		Nos. Z91-Z100 (10)	11.00	7.00

Issued: No. Z91, 2/19; Nos. Z92-Z93, 4/5; No. Z94, 4/12; No. Z95, 4/18; No. Z96, 5/1; Nos. Z97-Z100, 5/31.

See Nos. 3286-3289, 3913-3916, Z304-Z307.

Nikkou Mountains (Tochigi) ZA101

Mt. Iwate by Yaoji Hashimoto (Iwate) ZA102

Wooden Puppet (Tokushima) ZA103

Whales (Kochi) ZA104

Fringed Orchids (Tokyo) ZA105

Cape Toi, Horses (Miyazaki) ZA106

Black Pearls of Kabira Bay (Okinawa) ZA107

Japanese Pears (Tottori) ZA108

Tsujun-kyo Bridge (Kumamoto) ZA109

1991 **Photo.**

Z101	ZA101	62y multicolored	1.10	.70
Z102	ZA102	62y multicolored	1.10	.70
a.		Booklet pane of 10	11.00	
		Complete booklet, #Z102a	11.00	
Z103	ZA103	62y multicolored	1.10	.70
a.		Pane of 10	11.00	
Z104	ZA104	62y multicolored	1.10	.70
a.		Pane of 10	11.00	
Z105	ZA105	41y multicolored	2.50	1.00
a.		Booklet pane of 10	15.00	
		Complete booklet, #Z105a	15.00	
Z106	ZA106	62y multicolored	1.10	.70
a.		Booklet pane of 10	15.00	
		Complete booklet, #Z106a	15.00	
Z107	ZA107	41y multicolored	.80	.50
Z108	ZA108	62y multicolored	1.10	.70
Z109	ZA109	62y multicolored	1.10	.70
a.		Booklet pane of 10	15.00	
		Complete booklet, #Z108a	15.00	
		Nos. Z101-Z109 (9)	11.00	6.40

Issued: No. Z101, 5/29; No. Z102, 6/10; Nos. Z103-Z104, 6/26; Nos. Z105-Z106, 7/1; Nos. Z107-Z108, 8/1; No. Z109, 8/26.

Sheets of 3 No. Z106 + label were lottery prizes. Value, $3.

Ninja, Iga Ueno Castle (Mie) ZA111

46th Natl. Athletic Meet (Ishikawa) ZA110

Eyeglass Industry (Fukui) ZA112

Nursery Rhyme, Tortoise and the Hare ZA113

Kobe City Weathervane (Hyogo) ZA114

Spring (Nara) ZA115

Autumn (Nara, Gunma) — ZA116

Litho., Photo. (#Z110, Z112)

1991 *Perf. 13, 13½ (#Z110)*

Z110	ZA110	41y multicolored	.80	.50
a.		Pane of 10	8.00	
Z111	ZA111	62y multicolored	1.10	.70
a.		Booklet pane of 10	14.00	
		Complete booklet, #Z111a	14.00	
Z112	ZA112	62y multicolored	1.10	.70
a.		Booklet pane of 10	14.00	
		Complete booklet, #Z112a	14.00	
Z113	ZA113	62y multicolored	1.10	.70
a.		Booklet pane of 10	14.00	
		Complete booklet, #Z113a	14.00	
Z114	ZA114	62y multicolored	1.10	.70
a.		Booklet pane of 10	14.00	
		Complete booklet, #Z114a	14.00	
Z115	ZA115	62y multicolored	1.10	.70
Z116	ZA116	62y multicolored	1.10	.70
a.		Pair, #Z115-Z116	2.25	2.25
b.		Booklet pane, 5 #Z116a	14.00	
		Complete booklet, #Z116b	14.00	
		Nos. Z110-Z116 (7)	7.40	4.70

Issued: No. Z110, 9/2; No. Z111, 9/10; No. Z112, 10/1; No. Z113, 10/23; Nos. Z114-Z116, 10/25.

See Nos. 3189G, Z177-Z178.

Gogo-An Temple, Sea of Japan (Niigata) ZA117

Natl. Land Afforestation Campaign (Fukuoka) ZA118

Arctic Fox (Hokkaido) ZA119

Tateyama Mountain Range (Toyama) ZA120

Rikuchu Coast (Iwate) ZA121

Kurushima Strait (Ehime) ZA122

Tsurusaki Dance (Oita) ZA123

Tanabata Lantern Festival (Yamaguchi) ZA124

Shasui-no-taki Waterfall (Kanagawa) ZA125

Kurodabushi Dance (Fukuoka) ZA126

Boat Race (Okinawa) ZA127

Osaka Castle, Business Park (Osaka) ZA128

Owl, Mt. Horaiji (Aichi) — ZA129

1992 **Litho.** *Perf. 13½*

Z117	ZA117	41y multicolored	.80	.50
a.		Pane of 10	8.00	

Photo.

Z118	ZA118	41y multicolored	.80	.50
Z119	ZA119	62y multicolored	1.10	.70
a.		Souvenir sheet of 3	3.50	3.50

Litho.

Z120	ZA120	62y multicolored	1.10	.70
a.		Pane of 10	11.00	

Photo.

Z121	ZA121	62y multicolored	1.10	.70
a.		Pane of 10	11.00	
Z122	ZA122	62y multicolored	1.10	.70
a.		Pane of 10	11.00	
Z123	ZA123	62y multicolored	1.10	.70
Z124	ZA124	62y multicolored	1.10	.70
Z125	ZA125	62y multicolored	1.10	.70
a.		Pane of 10	11.00	
b.		Souvenir sheet of 3	3.50	3.50

Litho.

Z126	ZA126	62y multicolored	1.10	.70
Z127	ZA127	62y multicolored	1.10	.70
Z128	ZA128	41y multicolored	.80	.60

Photo.

Z129	ZA129	62y multicolored	1.10	.70
a.		Souvenir sheet of 3	3.50	3.50
b.		Pane of 10	11.00	
		Nos. Z117-Z129 (13)	13.40	8.60

Issued: No. Z117, 5/1; No. Z118, 5/8; No. Z119, 5/29; No. Z120, 6/10; Nos. Z121-Z122, 6/23; No. Z124, 7/7; No. Z123, 7/23; No. Z125, 7/24; No. Z126, 8/3; No. Z127, 8/17; No. Z129, 10/15.

See also No. Z320.

Oga Peninsula (Akita) ZA130

Fukuroda Waterfall (Ibaraki) ZA131

Notojima Bridge, Nanao Bay (Ishikawa) ZA132

Tama District Mountains (Metropolitan Tokyo) ZA133

Harbor Seal (Hokkaido) ZA134

Peace Statue (Kagawa) ZA135

Hana Ta'ue Rice Planting Festival (Hiroshima) ZA136

Paradise Flycatcher and Mt. Fuji (Shizuoka) ZA137

Sailboats on Lake Biwa (Shiga) ZA138

Matumoto Castle & Japan Alps (Nagano) ZA139

Ohara Festival (Kagoshima) ZA140

Oirase Mountain Stream (Aomori) ZA141

Yourou Valley (Chiba) — ZA142

1993 **Litho.** *Perf. 13½*

Z130	ZA130	41y multicolored	.80	.50
a.		Pane of 10	8.00	

Z131 ZA131 62y multicolored 1.10 .70
a. Pane of 10 11.00

Photo.

Z132 ZA132 62y multicolored 1.10 .70
a. Pane of 10 11.50
Z133 ZA133 62y multicolored 1.10 .70
a. Booklet pane of 10 11.50
Complete booklet, #Z133a 11.50
Z134 ZA134 62y multicolored 1.10 .70
Z135 ZA135 62y multicolored 1.10 .70
a. Pane of 10 11.50
Z136 ZA136 62y multicolored 1.25 .70
Z137 ZA137 41y multicolored .80 .50
a. Pane of 10 12.00
Z138 ZA138 62y multicolored 1.25 .70
a. Pane of 10 12.00
Z139 ZA139 62y multicolored 1.25 .70
a. Pane of 10 12.00
Z140 ZA140 41y multicolored .80 .50
a. Pane of 10 8.00

Perf. 13x13½

Z141 ZA141 62y multicolored 1.10 .70
a. Pane of 10 11.00

Perf. 13½

Z142 ZA142 41y multicolored .80 .50
a. Pane of 10 8.00
Nos. Z130-Z142 (13) 13.55 8.30

Issued: No. Z130, 2/12; No. Z131, 3/26; No. Z132, 4/2; No. Z133, 4/23; No. Z134, 5/17; No. Z135, 5/21; No. Z136, 6/4; No. Z137, 6/23; No. Z138, 7/1; No. Z139, 7/16; No. Z140, 9/1; No. Z141, 9/22; No. Z142, 10/1.

See also No. Z321.

Dream Bridge (Metropolitan Tokyo) ZA143

Kurobe Canyon & Dam (Toyama) ZA144

Haiku, Storehouse of Poet Issa (1763-1827) (Nagano) ZA145

Okuni, Izumo Great Shrine, Taisha (Shimane) ZA146

Fukiwari Falls (Gunma) ZA147

Ezoshika (Hokkaido) ZA148

Watch Tower, Festival in Tajima (Hyogo) ZA149

Wakura Coast (Wakayama) ZA150

1994 Photo. *Perf. 13*

Z143 ZA143 50y multicolored .90 .50
a. Pane of 10 9.50
Z144 ZA144 80y multicolored 1.40 .90
a. Pane of 10 15.00
Z145 ZA145 80y multicolored 1.40 .90
a. Pane of 10 15.00
Z146 ZA146 80y multicolored 1.40 .90
a. Pane of 10 15.00

Litho.

Z147 ZA147 80y multicolored 1.40 .90
a. Pane of 10 15.00
Z148 ZA148 50y multicolored .90 .50
a. Pane of 10 10.00
Z149 ZA149 50y multicolored .90 .50
a. Pane of 10 10.00
Z150 ZA150 80y multicolored 1.40 .90
a. Pane of 10 15.00
Nos. Z143-Z150 (8) 9.70 6.00

Issued: No. Z143, 3/23; No. Z144, 4/25; Nos. Z145-Z146, 5/2; No. Z147, 6/6; No. Z148, 6/7; No. Z149, 6/23; No. Z150, 7/15.

Kentish Plovers (Mie) ZA151

Awaodori Dance (Tokushima) ZA152

Tug-of-War (Okinawa) ZA153

Kehi Pine Wood (Fukui) ZA154

Matsushima (Miyagi) ZA155

Kunchi Festival (Nagasaki) ZA156

1994 Photo. *Perf. 13*

Z151 ZA151 80y multicolored 1.40 .90
a. Pane of 10 15.00
Z152 ZA152 50y multicolored .90 .50
a. Pane of 10 10.00
Z153 ZA153 50y multicolored .90 .50
Z154 ZA154 50y multicolored .90 .50
a. Pane of 10 10.00
Z155 ZA155 80y multicolored 1.40 .90
a. Pane of 10 16.50
Z156 ZA156 80y multicolored 1.40 .90
a. Pane of 10 16.50
Nos. Z151-Z156 (6) 6.90 4.20

Issued: No. Z151, 7/22; Nos. Z152-Z153, 8/1; No. Z154, 9/1; No. Z155, 9/20; No. Z156, 10/3.

Hokkaido Chipmunks (Hokkaido) ZA157

Ushiwakamaru and Benkei (Kyoto) ZA158

Utopia Flower (Gifu) ZA159

Jade Bead, Gyofu Soma (1883-1950), Lyricist (Niigata) ZA160

Cape Ashizuri-Misaki Lighthouse (Kochi) ZA161

Ishikawamon Gate, Kanazawa Castle (Ishikawa) ZA162

Akamon Gate, University of Tokyo (Tokyo) ZA163

Three Waterfalls, Kuroyama (Saitama) ZA164

Lady's Slipper, Rebun Island (Hokkaido) ZA165

Street with Zelkova Trees (Miyagi) ZA166

Eisa Festival (Okinawa) — ZA167

1995 Photo. *Perf. 13*

Z157 ZA157 80y multicolored 1.40 .90
a. Pane of 10 19.00

Perf. 13½

Z158 ZA158 80y multicolored 1.40 .90
a. Pane of 10 19.00
Z159 ZA159 80y multicolored 1.40 .90
a. Pane of 10 19.00
Z160 ZA160 80y multicolored 1.40 .90
a. Pane of 10 19.00
Z161 ZA161 80y multicolored 1.40 .90
a. Pane of 10 19.00
Z162 ZA162 80y multicolored 1.40 .90
a. Pane of 10 19.00
Z163 ZA163 50y multicolored .90 .50
a. Pane of 10 11.00
Z164 ZA164 80y multicolored 1.40 .90
a. Pane of 10 17.50
Z165 ZA165 80y multicolored 1.40 .90
a. Pane of 10 17.50
Z166 ZA166 50y multicolored .90 .50
a. Pane of 10 10.00
Z167 ZA167 80y multicolored 1.40 .90
Nos. Z157-Z167 (11) 14.40 9.10

Issued: No. Z157, 3/3; No. Z158, 4/3; No. Z159, 4/26; No. Z160, 5/1; Nos. Z161-Z162, 6/1; Nos. Z163-Z165, 7/7; Nos. Z166-Z167, 8/1.

Seasons Types of 1990-91 Redrawn and

Kishiwada Danjiri Festival (Osaka) ZA168

Yamadera Temple (Yamagata) ZA169

Karatsu Kunchi Festival (Saga) ZA170

Niimi-No-Shou Festival (Okayama) ZA171

Kirifuri Waterfall (Tochigi) ZA172

10th All-Japan Holstein Show (Chiba) ZA173

Nos. Z171-Z174: (Gifu). No. Z177, (Nara). No. Z178, (Nara, Gunma).

1995 Photo. *Perf. 13½*

Z168 ZA168 80y multicolored 1.40 .90
a. Pane of 10 16.00
Z169 ZA169 80y multicolored 1.40 .90
a. Pane of 10 16.00
Z170 ZA170 80y multicolored 1.40 .90
a. Pane of 10 16.00

Perf. 13

Z171 ZA85 80y Spring 1.40 .90
Z172 ZA86 80y Summer 1.40 .90
Z173 ZA87 80y Autumn 1.40 .90
Z174 ZA88 80y Winter 1.40 .90
a. Strip of 4, #Z171-Z174 6.50 6.50

Perf. 13½

Z175 ZA171 80y multicolored 1.40 .90
Z176 ZA172 50y multicolored .90 .50
a. Pane of 10 10.00
Z177 ZA115 80y Spring 1.40 .90
Z178 ZA116 80y Autumn 1.40 .90
a. Pair, #Z177-Z178 3.00 3.00
Z179 ZA173 80y multicolored 1.40 .90
a. Pane of 10 15.00
Nos. Z168-Z179 (12) 16.30 10.40

Issued: No. Z168, 9/1; No. Z169, 9/15; Nos. Z170-Z174, 10/2; No. Z175, 10/13; No. Z176, 10/27; Nos. Z177-Z178, 11/6; No. Z179, 11/21.

For self-adhesives, see Nos. 3282-3285.

Clione Limancia (Hokkaido) ZA174

Ushibuka Haiya Festival (Kumamoto) ZA175

Peony of Sukagawa (Fukushima) ZA176

Hamayu (Mie) ZA177

Ama Divers (Mie) ZA178

World Ceramics Expo '96 (Saga) ZA179

Shosenkyo Gorge (Yamanashi) ZA180

Murasaki Shikibu of Takefu (Fukui) ZA181

1996 Litho. *Perf. 13½x13*

Z180 ZA174 80y multicolored 1.40 .90
a. Pane of 10 11.50

Photo.

No.	Description		
Z181	ZA175 80y multicolored	1.40	.90
a.	Pane of 10	15.00	
Z182	ZA176 80y multicolored	1.40	.90
a.	Pane of 10	15.00	
Z183	ZA177 80y multicolored	1.40	.90
Z184	ZA178 80y multicolored	1.40	.90
a.	Pair, #Z183-Z184	3.00	3.00
b.	Pane, 5 #Z184a	15.00	
Z185	ZA179 80y multicolored	1.40	.90
	Perf. 13½		
Z186	ZA180 50y multicolored	.90	.50
a.	Pane of 10	9.50	
Z187	ZA181 80y multicolored	1.40	.90
a.	Pane of 10	15.00	
	Nos. Z180-Z187 (8)	10.70	6.80

Issued: No. Z180, 2/6; No. Z181, 4/1; No. Z182, 4/26; Nos. Z183-Z184, 5/1; No. Z185, 5/17; No. Z186, 6/3; No. Z187, 6/24.

Flower Types of 1990 and

Ancient Trees, Kompon-chudo of Mt. Hiei (Shiga) ZA182

Nishiumi Marine Park (Ehime) ZA183

Nebuta Festival (Aomori) ZA184

Main Palace, Shuri Castle (Okinawa) ZA186

Shimozuru Usudaiko Odori Folk Dance (Miyazaki) ZA185

Asakusa Kaminarimon Gate (Metropolitan Tokyo) ZA187

Tottori Shanshan Festival (Tottori) ZA188

Saito Kinen Festival Matsumoto (Nagano) ZA189

No. Z190, (Hokkaido). No. Z197, (Nagano).

1996	Photo.	*Perf. 13½*	
Z188	ZA182 80y multicolored	1.40	.90
a.	Pane of 10	15.00	
Z189	ZA183 80y multicolored	1.40	.90
a.	Pane of 10	15.00	
Z190	ZA23 80y Sweetbriar	1.40	.90
Z191	ZA184 80y multicolored	1.40	.90
a.	Pane of 10	15.00	
Z192	ZA185 80y multicolored	1.40	.90
a.	Pane of 10	15.00	
Z193	ZA186 80y multicolored	1.40	.90
Z194	ZA187 80y multicolored	1.40	.90
a.	Pane of 10	15.00	
Z195	ZA188 80y multicolored	1.40	.90
Z196	ZA189 80y multicolored	1.40	.90
a.	Pane of 10	15.00	
Z197	ZA38 80y Autumn bell-flower	1.40	.90
	Nos. Z188-Z197 (10)	14.00	9.00

Issued: Nos. Z188-Z189, 7/1; No. Z190, 7/5; No. Z191, 7/23; Nos. Z192-Z193, 8/1; No. Z194, 8/8; No. Z195, 8/16; Nos. Z196-Z197, 8/22.

For self-adhesive, see No. 3290.

Sengokubara Marsh (Kanagawa) ZA190

Nagoya Festival (Aichi) ZA191

Grass-burning Rite on Mt. Wakakusa (Nara) ZA193

1997 Men's Handball World Championships (Kumamoto) ZA194

Tea Picking (Shizuoka) ZA195

Dahurian Rhododendron (Hokkaido) ZA196

Mt. Fuji (Shizuoka) ZA197

1996-97	Photo.	*Perf. 13½*	
Z198	ZA190 80y multicolored	1.40	.90
a.	Pane of 10	15.00	
Z199	80y horse, rider	1.40	.90
Z200	80y two floats	1.40	.90
a.	ZA191 Pair, #Z199-Z200	3.00	3.00
b.	Pane, 5 #Z200a	15.00	
Z201	ZA193 50y multicolored	.90	.50
a.	Pane of 10	9.50	
Z202	ZA194 80y multicolored	1.40	.90
a.	Pane of 10	15.00	
Z203	ZA195 50y multicolored	.90	.50
a.	Pane of 10	9.50	
Z204	ZA196 80y multicolored	1.40	.90
a.	Pane of 10	15.00	
Z205	80y cattle	1.40	.90
Z206	80y orange grasses	1.40	.90
a.	ZA197 Pair, #Z205-Z206	2.50	2.50
b.	Pane, 5 #Z206a	12.50	
	Nos. Z198-Z206 (9)	11.60	7.30

Issued: No. Z198, 9/6; Nos. Z199-Z200, 10/1; No. Z201, 11/15; No. Z202, 4/17/97; Nos. Z203-Z206, 4/25/97.

Marugame Castle (Kagawa) ZA199

Hokkaido Ermine (Hokkaido) ZA200

Okayama Castle (Okayama) ZA201

Okinawan Fruits (Okinawa) ZA202

ZA204 ZA205

ZA206 ZA207

Nagasaki Kaido Highway (Nagasaki, Saga, Fukuoka)

Fukiya Koji's Hanayome Ningyo, Doll of Bride (Niigata) ZA208

The Clock Tower of Kyoto University (Kyoto) ZA209

1997	Photo.	*Perf. 13½*	
Z207	ZA199 80y multicolored	1.40	.90
a.	Pane of 10	15.00	
Z208	ZA200 50y multicolored	.90	.50
a.	Pane of 10	9.50	
Z209	ZA201 80y multicolored	1.40	.90
a.	Pane of 10	15.00	
Z210	ZA202 50y pineapple	.90	.50
Z211	ZA202 50y mango	.90	.50
a.	Pair, #Z210-Z211	1.90	1.90
Z212	ZA204 80y multicolored	1.40	.90
Z213	ZA205 80y multicolored	1.40	.90
Z214	ZA206 80y multicolored	1.40	.90
Z215	ZA207 80y multicolored	1.40	.90
a.	Strip of 4, #Z212-Z215	6.00	6.00
Z216	ZA208 50y multicolored	.90	.50
a.	Pane of 10	9.50	
Z217	ZA209 80y multicolored	1.40	.90
a.	Pane of 10	15.00	
	Nos. Z207-Z217 (11)	13.40	8.30

Issued: No. Z207, 5/15; Nos. Z208-Z209, 5/30; Nos. Z210-Z211, 6/2; Nos. Z212-Z215, 6/3; Nos. Z216-Z217, 6/18.

Kanto Festival (Akita) ZA210

San-in Yume Minato Exposition (Tottori) ZA211

Waterwheel Plant, Hozoji-numa Pond (Saitama) ZA212

Lake Kasumigaura (Ibaraki) ZA215

Bon Wind Festival, Owara (Toyama) ZA213

Tokyo Big Site (Tokyo) ZA216

Telecom Center (Tokyo) ZA217

Rainbow Bridge (Tokyo) ZA218

Intl. Forum (Tokyo) ZA219

Tokyo Museum (Tokyo) ZA220

First World Walking Festival (Saitama) — ZA221

1997	Photo.	*Perf. 13½*	
Z218	ZA210 80y multicolored	1.40	.90
a.	Pane of 10	15.00	
Z219	ZA211 80y multicolored	1.40	.90
a.	Pane of 10	15.00	
Z220	ZA212 50y multicolored	.90	.50
a.	Pane of 10	9.50	
Z221	80y woman	1.40	.90
Z222	80y man	1.40	.90
a.	ZA213 Pair, #Z221-Z222	3.00	3.00
b.	Pane, 5 #Z222a	15.00	
Z223	ZA215 80y multicolored	1.40	.90
a.	Pane of 10	15.00	
Z224	ZA216 80y multicolored	1.40	.90
Z225	ZA217 80y multicolored	1.40	.90
Z226	ZA218 80y multicolored	1.40	.90
Z227	ZA219 80y multicolored	1.40	.90
Z228	ZA220 80y multicolored	1.40	.70
a.	Strip of 5, #Z224-Z228	7.50	7.50
b.	Pane, 2 #Z228a	15.00	
Z229	ZA221 80y multicolored	1.40	.70
a.	Pane of 10	15.00	
	Nos. Z218-Z229 (12)	16.30	10.00

Issued: No. Z218, 7/7; No. Z219, 7/11; No. Z220, 8/1; Nos. Z221-Z222, 8/20; No. Z223, 9/1; Nos. Z224-Z228, 10/1; No. Z229, 10/28.

Kanagawa-Chiba Bridge Tunnel (Chiba, Kanagawa) ZA222

Snow-Covered Tree (Hokkaido) ZA224

Flower in a Dream (Hokkaido) ZA225

Hiyoshi Dam (Kyoto) ZA226

Sanshin (Okinawa) ZA227

Okoshi Daiko (Gifu) ZA228

Kobe-Awaji Expressway (Tokushima, Hyogo) ZA229

1997-98 Litho. *Perf. 13½*

Z230 80y denomination upper right 1.40 .90
Z231 80y denomination lower left 1.40 .90
a. ZA222 Pair, #Z230-Z231 3.00 3.00
b. Pane, 5 #Z231a 15.00
Z232 ZA224 80y multicolored 1.40 .90
Z233 ZA225 80y multicolored 1.40 .90
a. Pair, #Z232-Z233 3.00 3.00
b. Pane, 5 #Z233a 15.00

Photo.

Perf. 13

Z234 ZA226 80y multicolored 1.40 .90
a. Pane of 10 15.00

Perf. 13½

Z235 ZA227 80y multicolored 1.40 .90
a. Pane of 10 15.00
Z236 ZA228 80y multicolored 1.40 .90
a. Pane of 10 15.00
Z237 80y bridge, whirlpool 1.40 .90
Z238 80y bridge, flowers 1.40 .90
a. ZA229 Pair, #Z237-Z238 3.00 3.00
b. Pane, 5 #Z238a 15.00

Issued: Nos. Z230-Z231, 12/18; Nos. Z232-Z233, 2/5/98; No. Z234, 3/2/98; No. Z235, 3/4/98; No. Z236, 3/19/98; Nos. Z237-Z238, 3/20/98.

See Nos. 3230B-3230C.

Jomon Figurine (Nagano) ZA231

Chaguchagu Umakko, Mt. Iwate (Iwate) ZA232

Tokyo '98 Business Show (Tokyo) ZA233

Mt. Heisei Shinzan (Nagasaki) ZA234

Oze (Gunma) ZA235

Hanagasa Matsuri (Yamagata) ZA237

9th Women's World Softball Championships (Shizuoka) ZA238

1998 Photo. *Perf. 13½*

Z239 ZA231 80y multicolored 1.40 .90
a. Pane of 10 15.00
Z240 ZA232 80y multicolored 1.40 .90
a. Pane of 10 15.00
Z241 ZA233 80y multicolored 1.40 .90
a. Pane of 10 15.00
Z242 ZA234 80y multicolored 1.40 .90
a. Pane of 10 15.00
Z243 80y blue & multi 1.40 .90
Z244 80y brown & multi 1.40 .90
a. ZA235 Pair, #Z243-Z244 3.00 3.00
b. Pane, 5 #Z244a 15.00
Z245 ZA237 50y multicolored .90 .50
a. Pane of 10 9.50
Z246 ZA238 80y multicolored 1.40 .90
a. Pane of 10 15.00
Nos. Z239-Z246 (8) 10.70 6.80

Issued: No. Z239, 4/1; No. Z240, 4/24; No. Z241, 5/19; No. Z242, 5/20/98; Nos. Z243-Z244, 5/21; No. Z245, 6/5; No. Z246, 6/22.

Mt. Hakusan (Ishikawa) ZA239

Hita Gion (Ohita) ZA240

World Puppetry Festival (Nagano) ZA241

Views of Seto (Hiroshima) ZA243

First Postage Stamps of Ryukyu Islands, 50th Anniv. (Ryukyu Islands) ZA245

1998 Photo. *Perf. 13½*

Z247 ZA239 50y multicolored .90 .50
a. Pane of 10 9.50
Z248 ZA240 50y multicolored .90 .50
a. Pane of 10 9.50
Z249 50y stage left .90 .50
Z250 50y stage right .90 .50
a. ZA241 Pair, #Z249-Z250 1.90 1.90
b. Pane, 5 #Z250a 9.50
Z251 80y harbor 1.40 .90
Z252 80y highway 1.40 .90
a. ZA243 Pair, #Z251-Z252 3.00 3.00
b. Pane, 5 #Z252a 15.00
Z253 80y Ryukyu Islands #1 1.40 .90
Z254 80y Ryukyu Islands #228 1.40 .90
a. ZA245 Pair, #Z253-Z254 3.00 3.00
Nos. Z247-Z254 (8) 9.20 5.60

Issued: Nos. Z247-Z248, 7/1; Nos. Z249-Z252, 7/17; Nos. Z253-Z254, 7/23.

Satsuma Pottery, 400th Anniv. (Kogoshima) ZA247

Seto Ohashi Bridge (Kagawa) ZA249

Kobe Luminaries (Hyogo) ZA250

Apples (Aomori) ZA251

Kumano Path (Wakayama) ZA252

Tama Monorail (Tokyo) — ZA253

1998 Photo. *Perf. 13½*

Z255 80y bowl 1.40 .90
Z256 80y vase 1.40 .90
a. ZA247 Pair, #Z255-Z256 3.00 3.00
b. Pane, 5 #Z256a 15.00
Z257 ZA249 80y multicolored 1.40 .90
a. Pane of 10 15.00
Z258 ZA250 80y multicolored 1.40 .90
a. Pane of 10 15.00

Perf. 13

Z259 ZA251 80y multicolored 1.40 .90
a. Pane of 10 15.00
Z260 ZA252 80y multicolored 1.40 .90

Perf. 13½

Z261 ZA253 80y multicolored 1.40 .90
a. Pane of 10 15.00
Nos. Z255-Z261 (7) 9.80 6.30

Issued: Nos. Z255-Z256, 10/1; Nos. Z257-Z258, 11/9; Nos. Z259-Z260, 11/13; No. Z261, 11/26.

Dogo Hot Spa (Ehime) Type of 1989 and

Ibara Line (Okayama, Hiroshima) — ZA254

ZA255

Ao-no-Domon (Oita) — ZA256

ZA257

ZA258

Snow World (Hokkaido) ZA259 ZA260

Tokamachi Snow Festival (Niigata) ZA261

Orchids (Tokyo) ZA262

Dinosaurs (Fukui) ZA264

1999 Photo. *Perf. 13½*

Z262 ZA254 80y multicolored 1.40 .70
a. Pane of 10 15.00
Z263 ZA4 80y multicolored 1.40 .70
Z264 ZA255 80y multicolored 1.40 .70
Z265 ZA256 80y multicolored 1.40 .70
a. Vert. pair, #Z264-Z265 3.00 3.00
b. Pane, 5 #Z265a 15.00
Z266 ZA257 50y multicolored .90 .50
Z267 ZA258 50y multicolored .90 .50
Z268 ZA259 80y multicolored 1.40 .70
Z269 ZA260 80y multicolored 1.40 .70
a. Strip of 4, #Z266-Z269 5.00 3.50
Z270 ZA261 80y multicolored 1.40 .70
a. Pane of 10 15.00
Z271 80y white flowers 1.40 .70
Z272 80y purple flowers 1.40 .70
a. ZA262 Pair, #Z271-Z272 3.00 3.00
b. Pane, 5 #Z272a 15.00
Z273 80y denomination upper left 1.40 .70
Z274 80y denomination lower left 1.40 .70
a. ZA264 Pair, #Z273-Z274 3.00 3.00
b. Pane, 5 #Z274a 15.00
Nos. Z262-Z274 (13) 17.20 8.70

Issued: No. Z262, 1/1; Nos. Z263-Z265, 2/1; Nos. Z266-Z269, 2/5; Nos. Z270-Z272, 2/12; Nos. Z273-Z274, 2/22.

Lake Chuzenji (Tochigi) ZA266

Renowned Cherry Tree (Gifu) ZA268

Kiso Observatory, Mt. Ontake (Nagano) ZA271

Postal Service in Okinawa, 125th Anniv. (Okinawa) — ZA269

ZA272

ZA273

ZA274

The Old Path for Kumano (Mie) — ZA275

No. Z275, Spring. No. Z276, Fall. No. Z278, Traditional costume. No. Z279, Laughing lions. No. Z281, Tsuzurato Pass. No. Z282, Matsumoto Pass. No. Z283, Umagoshi Pass. No. Z284, Touri Pass.

1999 Photo. *Perf. 13½*

Z275 80y multicolored 1.40 .90
Z276 80y multicolored 1.40 .90
a. ZA266 Pair, #Z275-Z276 3.00 3.00
b. Pane, 5 #Z276a 15.00
Z277 ZA268 80y multicolored 1.40 .90
a. Pane of 10 15.00
Z278 80y multicolored 1.40 .90
Z279 80y multicolored 1.40 .90
a. ZA269 Pair, #Z278-Z279 3.00 3.00
b. Pane, 5 #Z279a 15.00
Z280 ZA271 80y multicolored 1.40 .90
a. Pane of 10 15.00
Z281 ZA272 80y multicolored 1.40 .70
Z282 ZA273 80y multicolored 1.40 .70
Z283 ZA274 80y multicolored 1.40 .70
Z284 ZA275 80y multicolored 1.40 .70
a. Strip of 4, #Z281-Z284 6.00 6.00
Nos. Z275-Z284 (10) 14.00 8.20

Issued: Nos. Z275-Z276, 3/1. No. Z277, 3/16. Nos. Z278-Z279, 3/23. No. Z280, 4/9. Nos. Z281-Z284, 4/16.

Cherries (Yamagata) Type of 1989 and

Taiko-Mon Gate, Matsumoto Castle (Nagano)
ZA276

Firefly Squid (Toyama)
ZA277

ZA278 ZA279

Four Seasons, Kenrokuen Garden (Ishikawa)
ZA280 ZA281

No. Z288, Kaisekitou Pagoda, Spring. No. Z289, Fountain, Summer. No. Z290, Kinjou-reitaku spring, Autumn. No. Z291, Kotoji stone lantern and yukitsuri, Winter.

1999, Apr. 26 Photo. *Perf. 13*

Z285	ZA2	80y like #Z2		1.40	.90

Perf. 13½

Z286	ZA276	80y multicolored		1.40	.90
a.		Pane of 10		15.00	
Z287	ZA277	80y multicolored		1.40	.90
a.		Pane of 10		15.00	
Z288	ZA278	80y multicolored		1.40	.90
Z289	ZA279	80y multicolored		1.40	.90
Z290	ZA280	80y multicolored		1.40	.90
Z291	ZA281	80y multicolored		1.40	.90
a.		Strip of 4, #Z288-Z291		6.00	6.00
b.		Souvenir sheet, #Z288-Z291		6.00	6.00
		Nos. Z285-Z291 (7)		9.80	6.30

ZA282 ZA283

ZA284 ZA285

ZA286 ZA287

ZA288 ZA289

Opening of Shimanami Seaside Highway (Hiroshima & Ehime)
ZA290 ZA291

Designs: No. Z292, Onomichi-suido Channel. No. Z293, Kurushima-kaikyo Straits. No. Z294, Old, new Onomichi-oohashi Bridges. No. Z295, Kurushima-kaikyo-oohashi Bridge. No. Z296, Innoshima-oohashi Bridge. No. Z297, Kurushima-kaikyo-oohashi Bridge, diff. No. Z298, Ikuchibashi Bridge. No. Z299, Hakatabashi, Ooshima-oohashi Bridges. No. Z300, Tatara-oohashi Bridge. No. Z301, Oomishimabashi Bridge.

1999, Apr. 26 Photo. *Perf. 13½*

Z292	ZA282	80y multicolored	1.40	.90
Z293	ZA283	80y multicolored	1.40	.90
Z294	ZA284	80y multicolored	1.40	.90
Z295	ZA285	80y multicolored	1.40	.90
Z296	ZA286	80y multicolored	1.40	.90
Z297	ZA287	80y multicolored	1.40	.90
Z298	ZA288	80y multicolored	1.40	.90
Z299	ZA289	80y multicolored	1.40	.90
Z300	ZA290	80y multicolored	1.40	.90
Z301	ZA291	80y multicolored	1.40	.90
a.		Block of 10, #Z292-Z301	15.00	15.00
b.		Sheet of 8, # Z294-Z301	12.00	12.00

Flora (Hokkaido) Type of 1991 and

Southern Kii Peninsula (Wakayama)
ZA292

Designs: No. Z302, Nachi-no-taki Falls. No. Z303, Engetsutou Island.

1999, Apr. 28 Photo. *Perf. 13½*

Z302		80y multicolored	1.40	.90
Z303		80y multicolored	1.40	.90
a.	ZA292	Pair, #Z302-Z303	3.00	3.00
b.		Pane, 5 #Z303a	15.00	

Perf. 13

Z304	ZA97	80y Lily bell	1.40	.90
Z305	ZA98	80y Lilac	1.40	.90
Z306	ZA99	80y Daylily	1.40	.90
Z307	ZA100	80y Rowanberry	1.40	.90
a.		Strip of 4, #Z304-Z307	6.00	6.00

Sendai Tanabata Festival (Miyagi)
ZA294

Souma Nomaoi Festival (Fukushima)
ZA295

1999, May 14 Photo. *Perf. 13½*

Z310	ZA294	80y multicolored	1.40	.90
Z311	ZA295	80y multicolored	1.40	.90
a.		Pair, #Z310-Z311	3.00	3.00
b.		Pane, 5 #Z311a	15.00	

Ryukyu Dance (Okinawa) — ZA296

1999, May 14

Z312	ZA296	80y multicolored	1.40	.90
a.		Pane of 10	15.00	

ZA297

Northern Paradise (Hokkaido) — ZA298

1999, May 25

Z313	ZA297	50y Lavender field	.90	.50
Z314	ZA298	80y Wheat field	1.40	.90

Kurashiki Sightseeing District (Okayama) — ZA299

1999, May 25 Photo. *Perf. 13½*

Z316	ZA299	80y multicolored	1.40	.90
a.		Pane of 10	15.00	

Shirone Big Kite Battle (Niigata)
ZA300 ZA301

1999, June 1 Litho. *Perf. 13½*

Z317	ZA300	80y multicolored	1.40	.90
Z318	ZA301	80y multicolored	1.40	.90
a.		Pair, #Z317-Z318	3.00	3.00
b.		Pane, 5 #Z318a	15.00	

Noto Kiriko Festival (Ishikawa) — ZA302

1999, June 11

Z319	ZA302	80y multicolored	1.40	.90
a.		Pane of 10	15.00	

Hokkaido Types of 1992-93

1999, June 25 Photo. *Perf. 13½*

Z320	ZA119	80y Arctic fox	1.40	.90

Litho.

Z321	ZA134	80y Largha seals	1.40	.90

ZA303

Tokyo: No. Z323, morning glories. No. Z324, starburst fireworks over Sumida River. No. Z325, flower burst fireworks.

1999, July 1 Photo. *Perf. 13½*

Z323		80y multicolored	1.40	.90
Z324		80y multicolored	1.40	.90
Z325		80y multicolored	1.40	.90
a.	ZA303	Block of 3, #Z323-Z325	4.50	4.50
b.		Souv. sheet of 2, #Z324-Z325	3.00	3.00

Hakata Gion Yamagasa Festival (Fukuoka) — ZA306

1999, July 1 Litho.

Z326	ZA306	80y multicolored	1.40	.90
a.		Pane of 10	15.00	

ZA307 ZA308

ZA309 ZA310

Five Fuji Lakes (Yamanashi) — ZA311

1999, July 1

Z327	ZA307	80y Yamanakako	1.40	.90
Z328	ZA308	80y Kawaguchiko	1.40	.90
Z329	ZA309	80y Saiko	1.40	.90
Z330	ZA310	80y Shoujiko	1.40	.90
Z331	ZA311	80y Motosuko	1.40	.90
a.		Strip of 5, #Z327-Z331	7.70	7.50
b.		Pane, 2 #Z331a	15.00	

Inns of Tsumago, Magome Types of 1990

Photo. & Engr.

1999, July 16 *Perf. 13*

Z332	ZA71	80y like #Z71	1.40	.90
Z333	ZA72	80y like #Z72	1.40	.90
a.		Pair, #Z332-Z333	3.00	3.00

ZA312

Toki (Japanese Crested Ibis) (Niigata) — ZA313

No. Z334, Youyou, Yangyang. No. Z335, Kin.

1999, July 16 Litho. *Perf. 13½*

Z334	ZA312	80y multicolored	1.40	.90
Z335	ZA313	80y multicolored	1.40	.90
a.		Pair, #Z334-Z335	3.00	3.00
b.		Pane, 5 #Z335a	15.00	

ZA314

Design: Amanohashidate sandbar, Miyatsu Bay (Kyoto).

1999, July 16

Z336	ZA314	80y multicolored	1.40	.90

ZA315

Design: Ooga lotus (Chiba).

1999, July 16

Z337	ZA315	80y multicolored	1.40	.90
a.		Pane of 10	15.00	

ZA316

ZA317

ZA318

ZA319

Birds (Hokkaido): No. Z338, Steller's sea-eagle. No. Z339, Tufted puffin. No. Z340, Blakiston's fish owl. No. Z341, Red-crowned crane.

1999, July 23 Photo. *Perf. 13½*

Z338	ZA316 50y multicolored	.90	.50
Z339	ZA317 50y multicolored	.90	.50
Z340	ZA318 50y multicolored	.90	.50
Z341	ZA319 50y multicolored	.90	.50
a.	Strip of 4, #Z337-Z340	4.00	4.00

Hill on Ie Island, Sabani Boat (Okinawa) — ZA320

1999, July 23 Litho. *Perf. 13¼*

Z343	ZA320 80y multicolored	1.40	.90
a.	Pane of 10	15.00	

National Treasures (Wakayama) ZA321

No. Z344, Kouyasan, Buddhist monastic complex. No. Z345, Natl. treasure, Kongara-douji.

1999, July 26 *Perf. 13½*

Z344	80y multicolored	1.40	.90
Z345	80y multicolored	1.40	.90
a.	ZA321 Pair, #Z344-Z345	3.00	3.00
b.	Pane, 5 #Z345a	15.00	

Autumn Bellflowers (Iwate) — ZA323

1999, July 30

Z346	ZA323 50y multicolored	.90	.50
a.	Pane of 10	9.50	

Shimizu Port, Cent. (Shizuoka) ZA324

Fishing Boat (Kumamoto) ZA325

1999, Aug. 2 Litho. *Perf. 13¼*

Z347	ZA324 80y multi	1.40	.90
a.	Pane of 10	15.00	
Z348	ZA325 80y multi	1.40	.90
a.	Pane of 10	15.00	

Ritsurin Park (Kagawa) — ZA326

1999, Aug. 2 *Perf. 13¼*

Z349	ZA326 80y multi	1.40	.90
a.	Pane of 10	15.00	

Artificial Island, Dejima (Nagasaki) — ZA327

1999, Sept. 1 Photo.

Z350	ZA327 80y multi	1.40	.90
a.	Pane of 10	15.00	

Yoritomo Minamotono (1174-99), Shogun (Kanagawa) — ZA328

1999, Sept. 2 Litho.

Z351	ZA328 80y multi	1.40	.90
a.	Pane of 10	15.00	

Shirakami Mountains (Aomori) — ZA329

1999, Sept. 6

Z352	ZA329 80y multi	1.40	.90
a.	Pane of 10	15.00	

Gassho-zukuri Farmhouses and Kokiriko Dance (Toyama) — ZA330

1999, Sept. 14 Photo.

Z353	ZA330 80y multi	1.40	.90
a.	Pane of 10	15.00	

Corn (Hokkaido) ZA331

Potatoes (Hokkaido) ZA332

Asparagus (Hokkaido) ZA333

Muskmelon (Hokkaido) ZA334

1999, Sept. 17 Litho.

Z354	ZA331 50y multi	.90	.50
Z355	ZA332 50y multi	.90	.50
Z356	ZA333 50y multi	.90	.50
Z357	ZA334 50y multi	.90	.50
a.	Strip, #Z354-Z357	4.00	4.00

(Gumma) — ZA335

1999, Sept. 17 *Perf. 13¼*

Z358	ZA335 80y multi	1.40	.90
a.	Pane of 10	15.00	

Iwajuku Paleolithic Site Excavations, 50th anniv.

(Osaka) — ZA336

1999, Sept. 27

Z359	ZA336 80y multi	1.40	.90

23rd Rhythmic Gymnastics World Championships.

Nihonmatsu Chrysanthemum Exhibition (Fukushima) — ZA337

1999, Oct. 1

Z360	ZA337 80y multi	1.40	.90

Town of Obi (Miyazaki) ZA338

Designs: No. Z361, Taihei dance, front gate of Obi Castle. No. Z362, Shintokudou School, Komura Jutarou (1855-1911).

1999, Oct. 1 *Perf. 13¼*

Z361	80y multi	1.40	.90
Z362	80y multi	1.40	.90
a.	ZA338 Pair, #Z361-Z362	3.00	3.00
b.	Pane, 5 #Z362a	15.00	

Nagano Monkey Type of 1989

1999, Oct. 13 Photo. *Perf. 12¾x13*

Z363	ZA1 80y multi	1.50	.75

(Aichi) ZA340

No. Z364, Ichiei Sato. No. Z365, "Beautiful Yamato."

1999, Oct. 13 Photo. *Perf. 13¼*

Z364	80y multi	1.40	.90
Z365	80y multi	1.40	.90
a.	ZA340 Pair, #Z364-Z365	3.00	3.00
b.	Pane, 5 #Z365a	15.00	

ZA342

No. Z366, Hagi (Yamaguchi). No. Z367, Tsuwano (Shimane).

1999, Oct. 13

Z366	80y multi	1.40	.90
Z367	80y multi	1.40	.90
a.	ZA342 Vert. pair, #Z366-Z367	3.00	3.00
b.	Pane, 5 #Z367a	15.00	

(Nara) ZA344

No. Z368, Yamato Three Mountains. No. Z369, Ishibutai Tomb.

1999, Oct. 28 Litho. *Perf. 13¼*

Z368	80y multi	1.40	.90
Z369	80y multi	1.40	.90
a.	ZA344 Pair, #Z368-Z369	3.00	3.00
b.	Pane, 5 #Z369a	15.00	

Shikina-en Garden (Okinawa) ZA346

1999, Oct. 28

Z370	50y multi	.90	.50
Z371	50y multi	.90	.50
a.	ZA346 Pair, #Z370-Z371	1.90	1.90
b.	Pane, 5 #Z371a	9.50	

(Fukui) ZA348

No. Z372, Echizen Crab. No. Z373, Tojinbou Cliff.

1999, Nov. 4

Z372	80y multi	1.40	.90
Z373	80y multi	1.40	.90
a.	ZA348 Pair, #Z372-Z373	3.00	3.00
b.	Pane, 5 #Z373a	15.00	

Children in Santa's Sleigh (Hokkaido) ZA350

Yoshinogari Dig Site (Saga) ZA351

1999, Nov. 11 *Perf. 13¼*

Z374	ZA350 80y multi	1.40	.90
a.	Pane of 10	15.00	
Z375	ZA351 80y multi	1.40	.90
a.	Pane of 10	15.00	

(Kochi) ZA352

No. Z376, Katsura Beach. No. Z377, Sakamoto Ryoma.

1999, Nov. 15 Photo.

Z376	80y multi	1.40	.90
Z377	80y multi	1.40	.90
a.	ZA352 Pair, #Z376-Z377	3.00	3.00
b.	Pane, 5 #Z377a	15.00	

For self-adhesives, see Nos. 3189H-3189I.

Samurai House, Kakunodate (Akita) — ZA354

1999, Dec. 17 Litho. *Perf. 13¼*

Z378	ZA354 80y multi	1.40	.90
a.	Pane of 10	15.00	

ZA355

ZA356

ZA357

ZA358

Tokyo Scenes (Tokyo) — ZA359

2000, Jan. 12 Litho. *Perf. 13¼*

Z379 ZA355 50y multi .90 .50
Z380 ZA356 50y multi .90 .50
Z381 ZA357 50y multi .90 .50
Z382 ZA358 50y multi .90 .50
Z383 ZA359 50y multi .90 .50
a. Horiz. strip, #Z379-Z383 4.75 4.75
b. Pane, 2 each #Z379-Z383 9.50

ZA360 ZA361

ZA362 ZA363
Snow World (Hokkaido)

2000, Feb. 7 Photo.

Z384 ZA360 80y multi 1.40 .90
Z385 ZA361 80y multi 1.40 .90
Z386 ZA362 80y multi 1.40 .90
Z387 ZA363 80y multi 1.40 .90
a. Strip, #Z384-Z387 6.00 6.00

ZA364

Japan Flora 2000 (Hyogo) — ZA365

2000, Mar. 1 Litho. *Perf. 13¼*

Z388 ZA364 50y multi .90 .50
Z389 ZA365 80y multi 1.40 .90
a. Pane, 5 each #Z388-Z389 12.50

ZA366 ZA367

ZA368 ZA369
Korakuen Gardens, 300th Anniv. (Okayama)

2000, Mar. 2 Photo.

Z390 ZA366 80y multi 1.40 .70
Z391 ZA367 80y multi 1.40 .70
Z392 ZA368 80y multi 1.40 .70
Z393 ZA369 80y multi 1.40 .70
a. Strip, #Z390-Z393 6.00 6.00
b. Souvenir sheet, #Z390-Z393 6.00 6.00

Cherry Blossoms in Takato (Nagano) — ZA370

2000, Mar. 3

Z394 ZA370 80y multi 1.40 .90
a. Pane of 10 15.00

Dyed Fabrics (Okinawa) — ZA371

2000, Mar. 17 Litho.

Z395 ZA371 50y multi .90 .50
a. Pane of 10 9.50

Azumino (Nagano) — ZA372

2000, Mar. 23 Photo.

Z396 ZA372 80y multi 1.40 .90
a. Pane of 10 15.00

Cherry Blossoms (Aomori) ZA373

Cherry Blossoms (Fukushima) ZA374

Cherry Blossoms (Iwate) ZA375

Cherry Blossoms (Miyagi) ZA376

Cherry Blossoms (Akita) ZA377

Cherry Blossoms (Yamagata) ZA378

2000, Apr. 3 Litho.

Z397 ZA373 80y multi 1.40 .90
a. Pair, #Z397, Z399 3.00 3.00
b. Pair, #Z397, Z400 3.00 3.00
c. Pair, #Z397, Z401 3.00 3.00
d. Pair, #Z397, Z402 3.00 3.00
Z398 ZA374 80y multi 1.40 .90
a. Pair, #Z398, Z399 3.00 3.00
b. Pair, #Z398, Z400 3.00 3.00
c. Pair, #Z398, Z401 3.00 3.00
d. Pair, #Z398, Z402 3.00 3.00
Z399 ZA375 80y multi 1.40 .90
Z400 ZA376 80y multi 1.40 .90
Z401 ZA377 80y multi 1.40 .90
Z402 ZA378 80y multi 1.40 .90
a. Vert. strip, #Z399-Z402 6.00 6.00
Nos. Z397-Z402 (6) 8.40 5.40

Printed in sheets containing one column of four stamps of Nos. Z397 and Z398 at left and right respectively with 3 No. Z402a between.

Tulips (Toyama) ZA379

2000, Apr. 28 Photo. *Perf. 13¼*

Z403 50y multi .90 .50
Z404 80y multi 1.40 .90
a. ZA379 Pair, #Z403-Z404 2.50 2.50
b. Pane, 5 #Z404a 12.50

Uwajima Castle (Ehime) — ZA381

2000, Apr. 28 *Perf. 13½x13¼*

Z405 ZA381 80y multi 1.40 .90

New Urban Center (Saitama) ZA382

2000, May 1 *Perf. 13¼*

Z406 50y multi .90 .50
Z407 50y multi .90 .50
a. ZA382 Pair, #Z406-Z407 1.90 1.90
b. Pane, 5 #Z407a 9.50

Flowers of the Chugoku Region

(Tottori) ZA384

(Shimane) ZA385

(Okayama) ZA386

(Hiroshima) ZA387

(Yamaguchi) — ZA388

2000, May 1 Litho. *Perf. 13¼*

Z408 ZA384 50y multi .90 .50
Z409 ZA385 50y multi .90 .50
Z410 ZA386 50y multi .90 .50
Z411 ZA387 50y multi .90 .50
Z412 ZA388 50y multi .90 .50
a. Vert. strip, #Z408-Z412 4.75 4.75
b. Pane, 2# Z412a 9.50

Cosmos (Tokyo) ZA389

Roses (Tokyo) ZA390

Bird of Paradise Flowers (Tokyo) ZA391

Sasanquas (Tokyo) ZA392

Freesias (Tokyo) — ZA393

2000, June 1 Photo. *Perf. 13¼*

Z413 ZA389 50y multi .90 .50
Z414 ZA390 50y multi .90 .50
Z415 ZA391 50y multi .90 .50
Z416 ZA392 50y multi .90 .50
Z417 ZA393 50y multi .90 .50
a. Vert. strip of 5, #Z413-Z417 4.75 4.75
b. Pane, 2 #Z417a 9.50

Shonan Hiratsuka Tanabata Festival (Kanagawa) ZA394

2000, June 2 Litho.

Z418 50y multi .90 .50
Z419 50y multi .90 .50
a. ZA394 Pair, #Z418-Z419 1.90 1.90
b. Pane, 5 #Z419a 9.50

Bankoku Shinryokan (Okinawa) — ZA396

2000, June 21 Photo. *Perf. 13¼*

Z420 ZA396 80y multi 1.40 .90
a. Pane of 10 15.00

World Performing Arts Festival (Osaka) — ZA397

2000, June 28 Litho.

Z421 ZA397 80y multi 1.40 .90
a. Pane of 10 15.00

Kujuku Islands (Akita) — ZA398

2000, July 7 Photo.

Z422 ZA398 80y multi 1.40 .90
a. Pane of 10 15.00

Potato Field (Hokkaido) ZA399

Hillside and Hay Rolls (Hokkaido) ZA400

2000, July 19

Z423 50y Flowers, barn .90 .50
Z424 50y Barn, silo .90 .50
a. ZA399 Pair, #Z423-Z424 1.90 1.90
Z425 80y + 20y Hayrolls, houses 1.90 1.00
Z426 80y + 20y Hayrolls, barns 1.90 1.00
a. ZA400 Pair, #Z425-Z426 4.00 4.00
Nos. Z423-Z426 (4) 5.60 3.00

Surtax on Nos. Z425-Z426 for refugees of eruption of Mt. Usu.

Awa-odori (Tokushima) — ZA401

2000, July 31 **Litho.**
Z427 ZA401 80y multi 1.40 .90
a. Pane of 10 15.00

Golden Hall of Chusonji Temple (Iwate) — ZA402

2000, Aug. 1
Z428 ZA402 80y multi 1.40 .90
a. Pane of 10 15.00

Hakata Doll (Fukuoka) — ZA403

2000, Aug. 2
Z429 ZA403 80y multi 1.40 .90
a. Pane of 10 15.00

55th Natl. Athletic Meet (Toyama) — ZA404

2000, Sept. 1 **Photo.**
Z430 ZA404 50y multi .90 .50
a. Pane of 10 9.50

25th World Parachuting Championships (Mie) — ZA405

No. Z431, 2 skydivers. No. Z432, 3 skydivers.

2000, Sept. 13
Z431 80y multicolored 1.40 .90
Z432 80y multicolored 1.40 .90
a. ZA405 Pair, #Z431-Z432 3.00 3.00
b. Pane, 5 #Z432a 15.00

Friendly Tokyo (Tokyo) — ZA406

2000, Sept. 29 **Litho.**
Z433 ZA406 80y multi 1.40 .90
a. Pane of 10 15.00

Iwakuni Kintaikyo Bridge (Yamaguchi) — ZA407

2000, Oct. 10
Z434 ZA407 80y multi 1.40 .90
a. Pane of 10 15.00

Intl. Wheelchair Marathon (Oita) — ZA408

2000, Oct. 11
Z435 ZA408 80y multi 1.40 .90
a. Pane of 10 15.00

Willow and Frog (Aichi) — ZA409

2000, Oct. 20 **Photo.**
Z436 ZA409 80y multi 1.40 .90
a. Pane of 10 15.00

ZA410 ZA411

ZA412 ZA413

Four Seasons (Kyoto)

2000, Oct. 20 **Litho.**
Z437 ZA410 80y multi 1.40 .90
Z438 ZA411 80y multi 1.40 .90
a. Pane, 5 each #Z437-Z438 15.00
Z439 ZA412 80y multi 1.40 .90
Z440 ZA413 80y multi 1.40 .90
a. Horiz. strip, #Z437-Z440 6.00 3.50
b. Pane, 5 each #Z439-Z440 15.00

Odawarajo Castle (Kanagawa) ZA414

2000, Oct. 27 ***Perf. 13¼***
Z441 50y multi .90 .50
Z442 50y multi .90 .50
a. ZA414 Pair, #Z441-Z442 1.90 1.90
b. Pane, 5 #Z442a 9.50

Intl. Balloon Festival (Saga) — ZA415

2000, Nov. 1 **Litho.** ***Perf. 13¼***
Z443 ZA415 80y multi 1.40 .90
a. Pane of 10 15.00

Chichibu Night Festival (Saitama) ZA416

2000, Nov. 1 **Photo.**
Z444 80y Yatai, fireworks 1.40 .90
Z445 80y Kasahoko 1.40 .90
a. ZA416 Pair, #Z444-Z445 3.00 3.00
b. Pane, 5 #Z445a 15.00

Scenic Izu (Shizuoka) ZA417

2000, Nov. 29 **Litho.**
Z446 50y Garden .90 .50
Z447 50y Waterfall .90 .50
a. ZA417 Pair, #Z446-Z447 1.90 1.90
b. Pane, 5 #Z447a 9.50

Hata Festival, Kohata (Fukushima) — ZA418

2000, Dec. 1 **Photo.**
Z448 ZA418 80y multi 1.40 .90
a. Pane of 10 15.00

Sekino'o-taki Falls and Kirishima (Miyazaki) ZA419

2000, Dec. 12 **Photo.**
Z449 80y Waterfall 1.40 .90
Z450 80y Mountain 1.40 .90
a. ZA419 Pair, #Z449-Z450 3.00 3.00
b. Pane, 5 #Z450a 15.00

Megane-bashi Bridge (Gunma) — ZA420

2000, Dec. 15 **Litho.**
Z451 50y Bridge .90 .50
Z452 50y Transformer substation .90 .50
a. ZA420 Pair, #Z451-Z452 1.90 1.90

Song "Shinano-no Kuni" (Nagano) ZA421

2000, Dec. 15 **Photo.**
Z453 50y Denom. at L .90 .50
Z454 50y Denom. at R .90 .50
a. ZA421 Pair, #Z453-Z454 1.90 1.90

Kobe Earthquake Restoration (Hyogo) ZA422

2001, Jan. 17 **Photo.** ***Perf. 13¼***
Z455 50y Pandas .90 .50
Z456 80y Kobe Port 1.40 .90
a. ZA422 Pair, #Z455-Z456 2.50 2.50
b. Pane, 5 #Z456a 12.50

Ooe Kouwaka-mai (Fukuoka) — ZA423

2001, Jan. 19 **Litho.**
Z457 ZA423 80y multi 1.40 .90
a. Pane of 10 15.00

Kairakuen Garden (Ibaraki) — ZA424

Designs: No. Z458, Koubuntei Pavilion, tree blossoms. No. Z459, Path, Chumon Gate. No. Z460, Togyokusen Spring, path. No. Z461, Koubuntei Pavilion in winter.

2001, Feb. 1 **Photo.**
Z458 50y multi .90 .50
Z459 50y multi .90 .50
Z460 50y multi .90 .50
Z461 50y multi .90 .50
a. ZA424 Horiz. strip, #Z458-Z461 4.00 4.00
b. Souvenir sheet, #Z461a 4.00 4.00

Ezo Sable (Hokkaido) — ZA425

2001, Feb. 6 **Litho.**
Z462 ZA425 80y multi 1.40 .90
a. Pane of 10 15.00
b. Horiz. pair, #Z321, Z462 3.00 3.00

Issued: No. Z462b, Sept. 2007.

Kochi Castle and Sunday Market (Kochi) ZA426

2001, Mar. 1 **Photo.** ***Perf. 13¼***
Z463 80y multi 1.40 .90
Z464 80y multi 1.40 .90
a. ZA426 Pair, #Z463-Z464 3.00 3.00
b. Pane, 5 #Z464a 15.00

Takarazuka Revue Dancers (Hyogo) ZA427

Violets (Hyogo) ZA428

2001, Mar. 21 **Litho.**
Z465 ZA427 80y multi 1.40 .90
Z466 ZA428 80y multi 1.40 .90
a. Pane, 5 each #Z465-Z466 15.00

Matsue Castle and Meimei-an Teahouse (Shimane) ZA429

2001, Mar. 21
Z467 80y multi 1.40 .90
Z468 80y multi 1.40 .90
a. ZA429 Pair, #Z467-Z468 3.00 3.00
b. Pane, 5 #Z468a 15.00

Grapes, Jewelry and Mt. Fuji (Yamanashi) — ZA430

2001, Mar. 30 **Photo.**
Z469 ZA430 80y multi 1.40 .90
a. Pane of 10 15.00

Sports Paradise (Osaka) ZA431

Designs: No. Z470, Thunder god (red) playing table tennis. No. Z471, Wing god (green) playing table tennis. No. Z472, Bowling. No. Z473, Taekwondo.

2001, Apr. 3

Z470	50y multi	.90	.50
Z471	50y multi	.90	.50
Z472	50y multi	.90	.50
Z473	50y multi	.90	.50
a.	ZA431 Horiz. strip, #Z470-Z473	4.00	4.00

Beautiful Fukushima Future Expo (Fukushima) — ZA432

2001, Apr. 10

Z474	ZA432 80y multi	1.40	.90
a.	Pane of 10	15.00	

Cherry Blossoms at Takada Castle (Niigata) — ZA433

2001, Apr. 10 **Litho.**

Z475	ZA433 80y multi	1.40	.90
a.	Pane of 10	15.00	

Hamamatsu Festival (Shizuoka) — ZA434

Designs: No. Z476, Palace Festival. No. Z477, Kite fighting.

2001, May 1

Z476	80y multi	1.40	.90
Z477	80y multi	1.40	.90
a.	ZA434 Pair, #Z476-Z477	3.00	3.00
b.	Pane, 5 #Z477a	15.00	

Ashikaga School Gate (Tochigi) ZA435

Ashikaga School (Tochigi) ZA436

2001, May 11 **Photo.**

Z478	ZA435 80y multi	1.40	.90
Z479	ZA436 50y multi	1.40	.90
a.	Pane, 5 each #Z478-Z479	15.00	

Natl. Afforestation Campaign (Yamanashi) — ZA437

2001, May 18

Z480	ZA437 50y multi	.90	.50
a.	Pane of 10	9.50	

Sendai, 400th Anniv. (Miyagi) — ZA438

2001, May 18 **Litho.**

Z481	ZA438 80y multi	1.40	.90
a.	Pane of 10	15.00	

Zenkoji Temple and Mt. Iizunayama (Nagano) ZA439

2001, May 23

Z482	80y multi	1.40	.90
Z483	80y multi	1.40	.90
a.	ZA439 Pair, #Z482-Z483	3.00	3.00
b.	Pane, 5 #Z483a	15.00	

Ducks (Yamaguchi) ZA440

Kirara Band, Japan Expo Site (Yamaguchi) ZA441

2001, May 25

Z484	ZA440 50y multi	.90	.50
Z485	ZA441 80y multi	1.40	.90
a.	Pane, 5 each #Z484-Z485	12.25	

Cherry Blossoms (Tokyo) ZA442

Hydrangea (Tokyo) ZA443

Salvia (Tokyo) — ZA444

Chrysanthemums (Tokyo) — ZA445

Camellias (Tokyo) — ZA446

2001, June 1 **Photo.**

Z486	ZA442 50y multi	.90	.50
Z487	ZA443 50y multi	.90	.50
Z488	ZA444 50y multi	.90	.50
Z489	ZA445 50y multi	.90	.50
Z490	ZA446 50y multi	.90	.50
a.	Vert. strip, #Z486-Z490	4.75	4.75
b.	Pane, 2 #Z490a	9.50	

ZA447

Sites (Tottori) ZA448

Designs: No. Z491, Snow crab, Uradome Coast. No. Z492, Tottori Dunes. No. Z493, Paper Hina dolls in river. No. Z494, Mt. Daisen. No. Z495, Nageiredo Hall. No. Z496, Mukibanda Yayoi Period.

Illustration ZA447 reduced.

2001, June 1

Z491	50y multi	.90	.50
Z492	50y multi	.90	.50
Z493	50y multi	.90	.50
Z494	50y multi	.90	.50
a.	ZA447 Horiz. strip, #Z491-Z494	4.00	4.00
Z495	80y multi	1.40	.90
Z496	80y multi	1.40	.90
a.	ZA448 Horiz. pair, #Z495-Z496	3.00	3.00
	Nos. Z491-Z496 (6)	6.40	3.80

Prosperity in Kaga (Ishikawa) — ZA449

2001, June 4 **Litho.**

Z497	ZA449 80y multi	1.40	.90
a.	Pane of 10	15.00	

Poppies (Hokkaido) ZA450

Calanthe (Hokkaido) ZA451

2001, June 22 **Litho.**

Z498	ZA450 50y multi	.90	.50
a.	Pane of 10	9.50	
Z499	ZA451 50y multi	.90	.50
a.	Pane of 10	9.50	

Cornerstone of Peace (Okinawa) — ZA452

2001, June 22 **Photo.**

Z500	ZA452 80y multi	1.40	.90

Peach Blossoms, Shirane-sanzan Mountains (Yamanashi) ZA453

Irises, Mt. Kitadake (Yamanashi) ZA454

Horses. Mt. Yatsugatake (Yamanashi) ZA455

Oshino-hakkai Pond (Yamanashi) ZA456

Cherry Blossoms, Minobu (Yamanashi) — ZA457

2001, July 2

Z501	ZA453 50y multi	.90	.50
Z502	ZA454 50y multi	.90	.50
Z503	ZA455 50y multi	.90	.50
Z504	ZA456 50y multi	.90	.50
Z505	ZA457 50y multi	.90	.50
a.	Vert. strip, #Z501-Z505	4.75	4.75
b.	Pane, 2 #Z505a	9.50	

Automobile City, Toyota (Aichi) ZA458

Designs: No. Z506, Toyota-oohashi Bridge. No. Z507, Toyota Stadium.

2001, July 2

Z506	50y multi	.90	.50
Z507	50y multi	.90	.50
a.	ZA458 Pair, #Z506-Z507	1.90	1.90
b.	Pane, 5 #Z507a	9.50	

Kitakyushu Expo Festival (Fukuoka) — ZA459

2001, July 4

Z508	ZA459 80y multi	1.40	.90
a.	Pane of 10	15.00	

World Trade Organization, 14th General Assembly (Osaka) — ZA460

Designs: No. Z509, Namdaemun, Seoul, and Doton-bori, Osaka. No. Z510, Bunraku, Nong-ak.

2001, July 6 **Litho.**

Z509	80y multi	1.40	.90
Z510	80y multi	1.40	.90
a.	ZA460 Pair, #Z509-Z510	3.00	3.00

Grand Fireworks of Nagaoka (Niigata) ZA461

2001, July 23

Z511	50y yel & multi	.90	.50
Z512	50y pink & multi	.90	.50
a.	ZA461 Pair, #Z511-Z512	1.90	1.90
b.	Pane, 5 #Z512a	9.50	

Poplars (Hokkaido) ZA462

Statue, Sheep (Hokkaido) ZA463

2001, Sept. 3 **Litho.** ***Perf. 13¼***

Z513	ZA462 80y multi	1.40	.90
Z514	ZA463 80y multi	1.40	.90
a.	Pane, 5 each #Z513-Z514	15.00	

56th Natl. Athletic Meets (Miyagi) — ZA464

2001, Sept. 7 **Photo.**

Z515	ZA464 50y multi	.90	.50
a.	Pane of 10	9.50	

Matsuyama Castle, Masaoki Shiki (1867-1902), Poet (Ehime) ZA465

2001, Sept. 12

Z516 50y Castle .90 .50
Z517 50y Poet .90 .50
a. ZA465 Horiz. pair, #Z516-Z517 1.90 1.90

Ibi Traditions (Gifu) ZA466

Designs: No. Z518, Tanigumi-Odori dance. No. Z519, Train, persimmons.

2001, Sept. 28 Photo. *Perf. 13¼*

Z518 50y multi .90 .50
Z519 50y multi .90 .50
a. ZA466 Horiz. pair, #Z518-Z519 1.90 1.90
b. Pane, 5 #Z519a 9.50

Kamakura Igloo (Akita) — ZA467

2001, Oct. 1 Litho.

Z520 ZA467 80y multi 1.40 .90
a. Pane of 10 15.00

9th Intl. Conference on Lake Conservation & Management (Shiga) — ZA468

2001, Oct. 1

Z521 ZA468 50y multi .90 .50
a. Pane of 10 9.50

World Indoor Cycling Championships (Kagoshima) — ZA469

2001, Oct. 1

Z522 ZA469 80y multi 1.40 .90

Okuma Auditorium, Waseda University (Tokyo) — ZA470

2001, Oct. 19

Z523 ZA470 80y multi 1.40 .90
a. Pane of 10 15.00

Wild Narcissi (Fukui) ZA471

Echizen Coast and Wild Narcissi (Fukui) ZA472

2001, Nov. 6

Z524 ZA471 50y multi .90 .50
a. Pane of 10 9.50
Z525 ZA472 80y multi 1.40 .90
a. Pane of 10 15.00

Tokyo Millenalio (Tokyo) — ZA473

2001, Dec. 3 Photo.

Z526 ZA473 80y multi 1.40 .90
a. Pane of 10 15.00

Ezo Flying Squirrels (Hokkaido) — ZA474

2002, Feb. 5

Z527 ZA474 80y multi 1.40 .90

Scenes North of Hiroshima (Hiroshima) ZA475

Designs: No. Z528, Nukui Dam. No. Z529, On-bashi Bridge.

2002, Feb. 22 Litho.

Z528 80y multi 1.40 .90
Z529 80y multi 1.40 .90
a. ZA475 Horiz. pair, #Z528-Z529 3.00 3.00

Azaleas (Wakayama) — ZA476

2002, Mar. 1 Photo. *Perf. 13¼*

Z530 ZA476 80y multi 1.40 .90

Glover Garden (Nagasaki) ZA477

Designs: No. Z531, Houses, fountain, roses. No. Z532, House, tulips.

2002, Mar. 1 Litho.

Z531 50y multi .90 .50
Z532 50y multi .90 .50
a. ZA477 Horiz. pair, #Z531-Z532 1.90 1.90

Cherry Blossoms, Hiikawa River (Shimane) ZA478

Cherry Blossoms, Bicchu-Kokubunji Temple (Okayama) ZA479

2002, Mar. 18

Z533 ZA478 50y multi .90 .50
Z534 ZA479 50y multi .90 .50
a. Horiz. pair, #Z533-Z534 1.90 1.90
b. Pane, 5 #Z534a 9.50 —

Tangerine, Sata Cape (Ehime) ZA480

Citrus Fruit, Mt. Tsurugisan (Tokushima) ZA481

Bayberry, Tengu Highlands (Kochi) ZA482

Olives, Shodo Island (Kagawa) ZA483

2002, Mar. 20 Photo.

Z535 ZA480 50y multi .90 .50
Z536 ZA481 50y multi .90 .50
Z537 ZA482 50y multi .90 .50
Z538 ZA483 50y multi .90 .50
a. Horiz. strip of 4, #Z535-Z538 4.00 4.00

Flowers (Hokkaido) ZA484

No. Z539, Tulips, windmills. No. Z540, Sunflowers, field.

2002, Apr. 25 Litho.

Z539 80y multicolored 1.40 .90
Z540 80y multicolored 1.40 .90
a. ZA484 Horiz. pair, #Z539-Z540 3.00 3.00

54th Intl. Whaling Commission (Yamaguchi) — ZA485

2002, Apr. 25

Z541 ZA485 80y multi 1.40 .90

Bonsai Village (Saitama) — ZA486

2002, Apr. 26 Photo.

Z542 ZA486 80y multi 1.40 .90

Yokohama (Kanagawa) ZA487

Designs: No. Z543, Sailing ships. No. Z544, Modern ship, skyline, woman.

2002, May 1

Z543 50y multi .90 .50
Z544 50y multi .90 .50
a. ZA487 Horiz. pair, #Z543-Z544 1.90 1.90
b. Pane, 5 #Z544a 9.50

Flowers (Niigata) ZA488

Designs: No. Z545, Red camellias. No. Z546, Yellow daylilies. No. Z547, Purple and pink irises. No. Z548, Pink iwakagami flowers.

2002, May 1 Litho.

Z545 50y multi .90 .50
Z546 50y multi .90 .50
Z547 50y multi .90 .50
Z548 50y multi .90 .50
a. ZA488 Horiz. strip of 4, #Z545-Z548 4.00 4.00

See Nos. 3909-3912.

Natl. Afforestation Campaign (Yamagata) — ZA489

2002, May 31 Photo.

Z549 ZA489 50y multi .90 .50
a. Pane of 10 9.50 —

Oze (Fukushima) ZA490

Designs: No. Z550, Flowers, bare trees, walkway. No. Z551, Flowers, evergreens.

2002, June 28 Litho.

Z550 50y multi .90 .50
Z551 50y multi .90 .50
a. ZA490 Horiz. pair, #Z550-Z551 1.90 1.90

Mt. Tanigawadake (Gunma) ZA491

Mountains and: No. Z552, Rhododendrons. No. Z553, Trees in autumn.

2002, June 28

Z552 80y multi 1.40 .90
Z553 80y multi 1.40 .90
a. ZA491 Horiz. pair, #Z552-Z553 3.00 3.00

Tokyo Fair and Market (Tokyo) ZA492

Designs: No. Z554, Morning Glory Fair. No. Z555, Hozuki Fair.

2002, June 28 Photo.

Z554 80y multi 1.40 .90
Z555 80y multi 1.40 .90
a. ZA492 Horiz. pair, #Z554-Z555 3.00 3.00

Alpine Flora (Ishikawa) — ZA493

2002, July 1 Flower Color

Z556 50y Purple .90 .50
Z557 50y Brown .90 .50
Z558 50y Bright pink .90 .50
Z559 50y White .90 .50
a. ZA493 Horiz. strip of 4, #Z556-Z559 4.00 4.00

Gujou-odori Dance (Gifu) — ZA494

2002, July 1

Z560 ZA494 50y multi .90 .50

85th Lions Club Intl. Convention (Osaka) — ZA495

2002, July 1
Z561 ZA495 80y multi 1.40 .90

23rd Asia-Pacific Scout Jamboree (Osaka) — ZA496

2002, July 15
Z562 ZA496 50y multi .90 .50

Yachiyoza Theater (Kumamoto) — ZA497

2002, July 15 **Litho.**
Z563 ZA497 80y multi 1.40 .90

Hikan-zakura, Iejima (Okinawa) ZA498

Hibiscus, Kaichudouro Highway (Okinawa) ZA499

Bougainvillea, House in Tsuboya (Okinawa) ZA500

Lily, Higashihennazaki (Okinawa) ZA501

Seishika Flower, Seishika Bridge (Okinawa) — ZA502

2002, Aug. 23 **Photo.** ***Perf. 13¼***
Z564 ZA498 50y multi .90 .50
Z565 ZA499 50y multi .90 .50
Z566 ZA500 50y multi .90 .50
Z567 ZA501 50y multi .90 .50
Z568 ZA502 50y multi .90 .50
a. Vert. strip of 5, #Z564-Z568 4.75 4.75

Printed in sheets containing two No. Z568a.

Flora (Tokyo) ZA503

Designs: No. Z569, Azalea (pink flower, blue denomination). No. Z570, Lily. No. Z571, Crape myrtle (pink flower and denomination). No. Z572, Ginkgo leaves.

2002, Sept. 2
Z569 50y multi .90 .50
Z570 50y multi .90 .50
Z571 50y multi .90 .50
Z572 50y multi .90 .50
a. ZA503 Horiz. strip of 4, #Z569-Z572 4.00 4.00

57th Natl. Athletic Meet (Kochi) — ZA504

2002, Sept. 5
Z573 ZA504 50y multi .90 .50

Iga-Ueno (Mie) ZA505

Designs: No. Z574, Basho Matsuo, Iga-Ueno Castle. No. Z575, Iga-Ueno Castle, Haisei-den Hall.

2002, Sept. 10 **Litho.**
Z574 80y multi 1.40 .90
Z575 80y multi 1.40 .90
a. ZA505 Horiz. pair, #Z574-Z575 3.00 3.00

Tohoku's Four Season Story (Aomori) — ZA506

2002, Oct. 23 **Photo.** ***Perf. 13¼***
Z576 ZA506 80y multi 1.40 .90

Fifth Winter Asian Games (Aomori) — ZA507

2003, Jan. 24 **Photo.** ***Perf. 13¼***
Z577 ZA507 50y multi 1.40 .90

Nobeoka, City of Noh Theater (Miyazaki) ZA508

Designs: No. Z578, Actor on stage, audience. No. Z579, Actor with red kimono.

2003, Feb. 3
Z578 80y multi 1.40 .90
Z579 80y multi 1.40 .90
a. ZA508 Horiz. pair, #Z578-Z579 3.00 3.00

Hokkaido Heritage (Hokkaido) ZA509

2003, Feb. 5 **Photo.** ***Perf. 13¼***
Z580 80y Ainu design 1.40 .90
Z581 80y Lake Mashuko 1.40 .90
a. ZA509 Horiz. pair, #Z580-Z581 3.00 3.00

Flora (Nagano) ZA510

Designs: No. Z582, Dogtooth violet (pink flowers) and mountain. No. Z583, Skunk cabbage (white flower). No. Z584, Nikko day lily (yellow flower. No. Z585, Cosmos (white, pink and red flowers).

2003, Mar. 5 **Photo.** ***Perf. 13¼***
Z582 50y multi .85 .50
Z583 50y multi .85 .50
Z584 50y multi .85 .50
Z585 50y multi .85 .50
a. ZA510 Horiz. strip of 4, #Z582-Z585 3.50 3.50

See Nos. 3871-3874.

Kibitsu Shrine (Okayama) — ZA511

2003, Mar. 5
Z586 ZA511 80y multi 1.40 .90

Kompira-Ohshibai Theater (Kagawa) — ZA512

2003, Mar. 24 **Litho.**
Z587 ZA512 80y multi 1.40 .90

Imari-Arita Ceramics (Saga) — ZA513

2003, Apr. 10
Z588 ZA513 80y multi 1.40 .90

Kaneko Misuzu and Poem "Tairyo" (Yamaguchi) ZA514

2003, Apr. 11 **Photo.**
Z589 80y Misuzu 1.40 .90
Z590 80y Poem 1.40 .90
a. ZA514 Horiz. pair, #Z589-Z590 2.80 2.80

Cormorant Fishing and Gifu Castle (Gifu) ZA515

2003, May 1 ***Perf. 13¼***
Z591 50y Fishermen .85 .50
Z592 50y Castle .85 .50
a. ZA515 Horiz. pair, #Z591-Z592 1.75 1.75

Traditional Events (Kyoto) — ZA516

Designs: No. Z593, Aoi-matsuri (wagon decorated with flowers). No. Z594, Gion-matsuri festival float (tower on wheels). No. Z595, Okuribi (fire on mountain). No. Z596, Jidai-matsuri (parade procession).

2003, May 1 **Litho.**
Z593 50y multi .85 .50
Z594 50y multi .85 .50
Z595 50y multi .85 .50
Z596 50y multi .85 .50
a. ZA516 Horiz. strip of 4, #Z593-Z596 3.50 3.50

Natl. Afforestation Campaign (Chiba) — ZA517

2003, May 16 **Photo.**
Z597 ZA517 50y multi .85 .50

Mt. Tsukuba and Iris (Ibaraki) — ZA518

2003, May 20 **Litho.**
Z598 ZA518 80y multi 1.40 .90

Tsurugajou Castle, Persimmons (Fukushima) — ZA519

2003, July 1 **Photo.** ***Perf. 13¼***
Z599 ZA519 80y multi 1.40 .90

Kyuya Fukada, Mountineer, Birth Cent. (Ishikawa) — ZA520

2003, July 1 **Litho.**
Z600 ZA520 80y multi 1.40 .90

Okinawa Urban Monorail (Okinawa) ZA521

2003, Aug. 8
Z601 50y Shurijo Castle .85 .50
Z602 50y Naha Airport .85 .50
a. ZA521 Horiz. pair, #Z601-Z602 1.75 1.75

58th Natl. Athletics Meets (Shizuoka) — ZA522

2003, Aug. 29 **Photo.**
Z603 ZA522 50y multi .85 .65

Sweet Briar (Tokyo) ZA523

Wisterias (Tokyo) ZA524

Irises (Tokyo) ZA525

Tea Blossoms (Tokyo) ZA526

2003, Sept. 1
Z604 ZA523 50y multi .85 .50
Z605 ZA524 50y multi .85 .50
Z606 ZA525 50y multi .85 .50
Z607 ZA526 50y multi .85 .50
a. Horiz. strip, #Z604-Z607 3.50 3.50

Chiyojo, Haiku Poet (Ishikawa) ZA527

2003, Oct. 3 **Litho.**

Z608 80y Haiku text 1.40 .90
Z609 80y Chiyojo 1.40 .90
a. ZA527 Horiz. pair, #Z608-Z609 3.00 3.00

Yasujiro Ozu (1903-63), Film Director (Mie) — ZA528

2003, Oct. 23 **Photo.**

Z610 ZA528 80y multi 1.40 .90

Kiritappu Wetland and Wakka Primeval Garden (Hokkaido) ZA529

2004, Feb. 5 **Litho.** ***Perf. 13¼***

Z611 80y Yellow flowers 1.40 .90
Z612 80y Orange flowers 1.40 .90
a. ZA529 Horiz. pair, #Z611-Z612 3.00 3.00

Kyushu Bullet Train (Kagoshima) ZA530

2004, Mar. 12 **Photo.** ***Perf. 13¼***

Z613 ZA530 50y multi .90 .65

Flower Types of 1990

Designs as before.

2004, Mar. 19

Z614 ZA24 50y multi .90 .50
Z615 ZA25 50y multi .90 .50
Z616 ZA26 50y multi .90 .50
Z617 ZA27 50y multi .90 .50
Z618 ZA28 50y multi .90 .50
Z619 ZA29 50y multi .90 .50
Nos. Z614-Z619 (6) 5.40 3.00

Zuiryuji Temple (Toyama) — ZA531

2004, Mar. 19 **Litho.**

Z620 ZA531 80y multi 1.40 .90

Hana-Kairou Flower Park (Tottori) — ZA532

2004, Mar. 23

Z621 ZA532 80y multi 1.40 .90

Gerbera (Shizuoka) ZA533

Carnation (Shizuoka) ZA534

Rose (Shizuoka) ZA535

Lisianthus (Shizuoka) ZA536

2004, Apr. 8

Z622 ZA533 80y multi 1.40 .90
Z623 ZA534 80y multi 1.40 .90
Z624 ZA535 80y multi 1.40 .90
Z625 ZA536 80y multi 1.40 .90
a. Horiz. strip of 4, #Z622-Z625 6.00 6.00

Pacific Flora 2004.

National Afforestation Campaign (Miyazaki) — ZA537

2004, Mar. 23 **Photo.**

Z626 ZA537 50y multi .90 .50

Murouji's Five Story Pagoda (Nara) — ZA538

2004, Apr. 26

Z627 ZA538 80y multi 1.40 .90

Rotary International Convention (Osaka) — ZA539

2004, May 21

Z628 ZA539 80y multi 1.40 .90

Ice Breaker Garinko-go, Steller's Sea Eagle (Hokkaido) — ZA540

2004, May 28

Z629 ZA540 80y multi 1.40 .90

Kanto Festival Performer, Namahage (Akita) ZA541

2004, June 1 **Litho.**

Z630 50y blue & multi .90 .50
Z631 50y red & multi .90 .50
a. ZA541 Horiz. pair, #Z630-Z631 1.80 1.80

Akita City, 400th anniv.

Magnolia (Tokyo) ZA542

Azalea (Tokyo) ZA543

Wildflower (Tokyo) ZA544

Bush Clover (Tokyo) ZA545

2004, June 1 **Photo.**

Z632 ZA542 50y multi .90 .50
Z633 ZA543 50y multi .90 .50
Z634 ZA544 50y multi .90 .50
Z635 ZA545 50y multi .90 .50
a. Horiz. strip of 4, #Z632-Z635 3.75 3.75

Roses and Buildings (Kanagawa) ZA546

Gold-banded Lily and Buildings (Kanagawa) ZA547

Wisteria and Enoshima Island (Kanagawa) ZA548

Hydrangea and Lake Ashinoko (Kanagawa) ZA549

2004, June 1

Z636 ZA546 50y multi .90 .50
Z637 ZA547 50y multi .90 .50
Z638 ZA548 50y multi .90 .50
Z639 ZA549 50y multi .90 .50
a. Horiz. strip of 4, #Z636-Z639 3.75 3.75

Daimyo Processions of Lord Takachika Mouri (Yamaguchi) ZA550

2004, June 21 **Litho.**

Z640 80y red & multi 1.40 .90
Z641 80y green & multi 1.40 .90
a. ZA550 Horiz. pair, #Z640-Z641 3.00 3.00

Rose, Mt. Tsukubasan (Ibaraki) ZA551

Yashio-tsutsuji and Lake Chuzenjiko (Tochigi) ZA552

Renge-tsutsuji and Mt. Akagisan (Gunma) ZA553

Primrose and Tajimagahara Native Primrose Field (Saitama) ZA554

Rape Blossoms and Nojimazaki Lighthouse (Chiba) — ZA555

2004, June 23 **Photo.**

Z642 ZA551 50y multi .90 .50
Z643 ZA552 50y multi .90 .50
Z644 ZA553 50y multi .90 .50
Z645 ZA554 50y multi .90 .50
Z646 ZA555 50y multi .90 .50
a. Vert. strip of 5, #Z642-Z646 4.75 4.75

Owara Dance (Toyama) ZA556

Designs: No. Z647, Children. No. Z648, Dancers in pink kimonos. No. Z649, Dancers in black clothes. No. Z650, Dancers in blue kimonos.

2004, Aug. 20 **Litho.**

Z647 50y multi .90 .50
Z648 50y multi .90 .50
Z649 50y multi .90 .50
Z650 50y multi .90 .50
a. ZA556 Horiz. strip of 4, #Z647-Z650 3.75 3.75

59th National Athletic Meets (Saitama) — ZA557

2004, Sept. 10 **Photo.** ***Perf. 13¼***

Z651 ZA557 50y multi .90 .50

Miniature Sheet

88 Temples (Shikoku) ZA558

No. Z652: a, Ryozenji (Temple 1). b, Gokurakuji (Temple 2). c, Konsenji (Temple 3). d, Dainchiji (Temple 4). e, Tatsueji (Temple 19). f, Kakurinji (Temple 20). g, Tairyuji (Temple 21). h, Byoudouji (Temple 22). i, Iwamotoji (Temple 37). j, Kongoufukuji (Temple 38). k, Enkouji (Temple 39). l, Kanjizaiji (Temple 40). m, Nankoubou (Temple 55). n, Taizanji (Temple 56). o, Eifukuji (Temple 57). p, Senyuji (Temple 58). q, Shusshakaji (Temple 73). r, Kouyamaji (Temple 74). s, Zentsuji (Temple 75). t, Kouzouji (Temple 76).

2004, Nov. 5

Z652 ZA558 Sheet of 20 30.00 30.00
a.-t. 80y Any single 1.40 .90

Temple numbers are found in the first group of small Japanese characters on each stamp. The numbers used are the same as those found under "China" in the Illustrated Identifier at the back of the book. The left and right Japanese characters in this first group of small characters, which ranges from 3 to 5 characters in length, are the same on each stamp. The characters between these two constant characters represent the temple number. As there is no character for zero, the number "20" will show the character for "2" (=) to the left of the character for "10" (+). Numbers 11-19 will have the unit's character to the right of the character for "10." Thus, the numbers "12" and "20" will have the same characters, just in a different order. Two-digit numbers beginning with 21 that are not divisible by 10 will be three characters long. Number 21, as an example, will show the characters for "2," "10," and "1" reading from left to right (= + -).

National Theater (Okinawa) — ZA559

2005, Jan. 21 **Litho.** ***Perf. 13¼***

Z653 ZA559 50y multi .90 .50

Apple Blossoms (Nagano) ZA560

Renge Azalea (Nagano) ZA561

Lily of the Valley (Nagano) ZA562

Gentian (Nagano) ZA563

2005, Apr. 1 **Litho.** ***Perf. 13¼***

Z654	ZA560	50y multi	.90	.50
Z655	ZA561	50y multi	.90	.50
Z656	ZA562	50y multi	.90	.50
Z657	ZA563	50y multi	.90	.50
a.		Horiz. strip of 4, #Z654-Z657	3.75	3.75

Tulip (Toyama, Ishikawa, Fukui) ZA564

Hydrangea (Toyama, Ishikawa, Fukui) ZA565

Rhododendron (Toyama, Ishikawa, Fukui) ZA566

Lily (Toyama, Ishikawa, Fukui) ZA567

2005, Apr. 1

Z658	ZA564	50y multi	.90	.50
Z659	ZA565	50y multi	.90	.50
Z660	ZA566	50y multi	.90	.50
Z661	ZA567	50y multi	.90	.50
a.		Horiz. strip of 4, #Z658-Z661	3.75	3.75

Peace Memorial Park (Hiroshima) ZA568

Designs: No. Z662, Birds, Cenotaph for Atomic Bomb Victims. No. Z663, Fountains, Hiroshima Peace Memorial Museum.

2005, Apr. 22

Z662		50y multi	.90	.50
Z663		50y multi	.90	.50
a.	ZA568	Horiz. pair, #Z662-Z663	1.90	1.90

Sweetbrier (Hokkaido) ZA569

Lavender (Hokkaido) ZA570

Cowslip (Hokkaido) ZA571

Lily of the Valley (Hokkaido) ZA572

2005, Apr. 26

Z664	ZA569	50y multi	.90	.50
Z665	ZA570	50y multi	.90	.50
Z666	ZA571	50y multi	.90	.50
Z667	ZA572	50y multi	.90	.50
a.		Horiz. strip of 4, #Z664-Z667	3.75	3.75

See Nos. 3917-3920.

Momordica Charantia (Okinawa) — ZA573

2005, May 6

Z668	ZA573	50y multi	.90	.50

Sunflower, Mt. Yatsugatake (Yamanashi) ZA574

Gentian, Mt. Kitadake (Yamanashi) ZA575

Evening Primrose, Mt. Fuji (Yamanashi) ZA576

Lady's Slipper, Mt. Fuji (Yamanashi) ZA577

2005, May 16 **Litho.** ***Perf. 13¼***

Z669	ZA574	80y multi	1.40	.90
Z670	ZA575	80y multi	1.40	.90
Z671	ZA576	80y multi	1.40	.90
Z672	ZA577	80y multi	1.40	.90
a.		Horiz. strip of 4, #Z669-Z672	6.00	6.00

National Afforestation Campaign (Ibaraki) — ZA578

2005, May 27 **Photo.**

Z673	ZA578	50y multi	.90	.50

Orchid (Tokyo) ZA579

Crinum (Tokyo) ZA580

Kerria (Tokyo) ZA581

Azalea (Tokyo) ZA582

2005, June 1

Z674	ZA579	50y multi	.90	.50
Z675	ZA580	50y multi	.90	.50
Z676	ZA581	50y multi	.90	.50
Z677	ZA582	50y multi	.90	.50
a.		Horiz. strip of 4, #Z674-Z677	3.75	3.75

Une, Dazaifu-Tenmangu (Fukuoka) ZA583

Cherry Blossoms, Kanmon Bridge (Fukuoka) ZA584

Camphor Blossoms, Ariake Sea (Saga) ZA585

Azaleas, Mt. Fugendake (Nagasaki) ZA586

Tulips, Huis Ten Bosch (Nagasaki) ZA587

Gentians, Mt. Aso (Kumamoto) ZA588

Bungo-ume, Mt. Takasaki (Oita) ZA589

Crinums, Nichinan Beach (Miyazaki) ZA590

Azaleas, Kirishima Mountains (Kagoshima) ZA591

Hibiscus, Screw Pine (Kagoshima) ZA592

2005, June 1

Z678	ZA583	50y multi	.90	.50
Z679	ZA584	50y multi	.90	.50
Z680	ZA585	50y multi	.90	.50
Z681	ZA586	50y multi	.90	.50
Z682	ZA587	50y multi	.90	.50
Z683	ZA588	50y multi	.90	.50
Z684	ZA589	50y multi	.90	.50
Z685	ZA590	50y multi	.90	.50
Z686	ZA591	50y multi	.90	.50
Z687	ZA592	50y multi	.90	.50
a.		Block of 10, #Z678-Z687	9.50	9.50

Reintroduction of Oriental White Stork (Hyogo) — ZA593

2005, June 6 **Litho.**

Z688	ZA593	80y multi	1.40	.90

Azaleas, Tsutsujigaoka Park (Gunma) ZA594

Nikko Day Lily, Kirifuri Heights (Tochigi) ZA595

Sunflowers, Hana-hotaru (Chiba) ZA596

Bush Clover, Kairakuen Garden (Ibaraki) ZA597

Allspice, Mt. Bukosan (Saitama) — ZA598

2005, June 23

Z689	ZA594	50y multi	.90	.50
Z690	ZA595	50y multi	.90	.50
Z691	ZA596	50y multi	.90	.50
Z692	ZA597	50y multi	.90	.50
Z693	ZA598	50y multi	.90	.50
a.		Vert. strip of 5, #Z689-Z693	4.50	4.50

Apples (Aomori) ZA599

Apples (Iwate) ZA600

Cherries (Yamagata) ZA601

Peaches (Fukushima) ZA602

2005, June 28 **Litho.**

Z694	ZA599	50y multi	.90	.50
Z695	ZA600	50y multi	.90	.50
Z696	ZA601	50y multi	.90	.50
Z697	ZA602	50y multi	.90	.50
a.		Horiz. strip of 4, #Z694-Z697	3.75	3.75

Miniature Sheet

88 Temples (Shikoku) ZA603

No. Z698: a, Zizouji (Temple 5). b, Anrakuji (Temple 6). c, Juurakuji (Temple 7). d, Kumadaniji (Temple 8). e, Yakuooji (Temple 23). f, Hotsumisakiji (Temple 24). g, Shinjouji (Temple 25). h, Kongouchouji (Temple 26). i, Ryukouji (Temple 41). j, Butsumokuji (Temple 42). k, Meisekiji (Temple 43). l, Daihouji (Temple 44). m, Kokubunji (Temple 59). n, Yokomineji (Temple 60). o, Kouonji (Temple 61). p, Houjuji (Temple 62). q, Douryuji (Temple 77). r, Goushouji (Temple 78). s, Tennouji (Temple 79). t, Kokubunji (Temple 80).

2005, July 8 **Photo.**

Z698	ZA603	Sheet of 20	30.00	30.00
a.-t.		80y Any single	1.40	.90

See note under No. Z652 for information on identifying temple numbers.

Swwtbriar, Old Shana Post Office (Hokkaido) ZA604

Sea Otter (Hokkaido) ZA605

Cherry Blossoms (Hokkaido) ZA606

Tufted Puffins (Hokkaido) ZA607

2005, Aug. 22

Z699	ZA604	80y multi		1.40	.90
Z700	ZA605	80y multi		1.40	.90
Z701	ZA606	80y multi		1.40	.90
Z702	ZA607	80y multi		1.40	.90
a.	Horiz. strip of 4, #Z699-Z702			6.00	6.00

60th Natl. Athletic Meets (Okayama) — ZA608

2005, Sept. 1

Z703	ZA608	50y multi	.90	.50

Kobe Luminarie (Hyogo) ZA609

2005, Dec. 9 **Litho.**

Z704		50y Yellow denomination	.85	.50
Z705		50y Blue denomination	.85	.50
a.	ZA609	Horiz. pair, #Z704-Z705	1.75	1.75

Kawazu Cherry Blossoms (Shizuoka) ZA610

2006, Feb. 1 **Photo.** ***Perf. 13¼***

Z706		50y With bird	.85	.50
Z707		50y Without bird	.85	.50
a.	ZA610	Horiz. pair, #Z706-Z707	1.75	1.75

Japanese Characters (Fukui) ZA611

Maruoka Castle, Hills (Fukui) ZA612

Maruoka Castle, Clouds (Fukui) ZA613

Maruoka Castle, Sun (Fukui) ZA614

Maruoka Castle, Moon (Fukui) — ZA615

2006, Apr. 3 **Litho.**

Z708	ZA611	80y multi	1.40	.90
Z709	ZA612	80y multi	1.40	.90
Z710	ZA613	80y multi	1.40	.90
Z711	ZA614	80y multi	1.40	.90
Z712	ZA615	80y multi	1.40	.90
a.		Horiz. strip of 4, #Z709-Z712	5.75	5.75
		Nos. Z708-Z712 (5)	7.00	4.50

Printed in sheets of 20 consisting of 12 No. ZA708, and 2 each Nos. Z709-Z712.

Primroses (Osaka) ZA616

Cherry Blossoms (Nara) ZA617

Wild Chrysanthemums (Hyogo) ZA618

Rhododendrons (Shiga) ZA619

Ume Blossoms (Wakayama) ZA620

Weeping Cherry Blossoms (Kyoto) ZA621

2006, Apr. 3

Z713	ZA616	50y multi	.85	.50
Z714	ZA617	50y multi	.85	.50
Z715	ZA618	50y multi	.85	.50
Z716	ZA619	50y multi	.85	.50
Z717	ZA620	50y multi	.85	.50
a.		Horiz. strip of 4, #Z714-Z717	3.50	3.50
Z718	ZA621	50y multi	.85	.50
		Nos. Z713-Z718 (6)	5.10	3.00

Printed in sheets containing 4 each nos. Z713, Z718, 3 each Nos. Z714-Z717.

Pear Blossoms, Yumigahama Beach (Tottori) ZA622

Peonies, Hinomisaki Lighthouse (Shimane) ZA623

Peach Blossoms, Seto-oohashi Bridge (Okayama) ZA624

Scarlet Maple Leaves, Miyajima Shrine (Hiroshima) ZA625

Citron Blossoms, Oomi Island (Yamaguchi) — ZA626

2006, May 1 **Photo.**

Z719	ZA622	50y multi	.90	.50
Z720	ZA623	50y multi	.90	.50
Z721	ZA624	50y multi	.90	.50
Z722	ZA625	50y multi	.90	.50
Z723	ZA626	50y multi	.90	.50
a.		Vert. strip of 5, #Z719-Z723!	4.50	4.50
		Nos. Z719-Z723 (5)	4.50	2.50

National Afforestation Campaign (Gifu) — ZA627

2006, May 19

Z724	ZA627	50y multi	.90	.50

Mt. Echigo (Niigata, Nagano) ZA628

Sankayou Flowers (Niigata, Nagano) ZA629

Mt. Asama (Niigata, Nagano) ZA630

Sakurasou Flowers (Niigata, Nagano) ZA631

2006, June 1 **Litho.**

Z725	ZA628	80y multi	1.40	.90
Z726	ZA629	80y multi	1.40	.90
Z727	ZA630	80y multi	1.40	.90
Z728	ZA631	80y multi	1.40	.90
a.		Horiz. strip of 4, #Z725-Z728	6.00	6.00
		Nos. Z725-Z728 (4)	5.60	3.60

Daffodils, Nokonoshima Island (Fukuoka) ZA632

Bellflowers, Hirodai (Fukuoka) ZA633

Hydrangeas, Mikaerinotaki Falls (Saga) ZA634

Cosmos, Kujukushima Islands (Nagasaki) ZA635

Camellias, Amakusa Bridges (Kumamoto) ZA636

Flowers, Mt. Aso (Kumamoto) ZA637

Primroses, Mt. Yufudake (Oita) ZA638

Lavender, Kujurenzan (Oita) ZA639

Poppies, Mt. Hinamoridake (Miyazaki) ZA640

Nanohana, Mt. Kaimondake (Kagoshima) ZA641

2006, June 1 **Photo.**

Z729	ZA632	80y multi	1.40	.90
Z730	ZA633	80y multi	1.40	.90
Z731	ZA634	80y multi	1.40	.90
Z732	ZA635	80y multi	1.40	.90
Z733	ZA636	80y multi	1.40	.90
Z734	ZA637	80y multi	1.40	.90
Z735	ZA638	80y multi	1.40	.90
Z736	ZA639	80y multi	1.40	.90
Z737	ZA640	80y multi	1.40	.90
Z738	ZA641	80y multi	1.40	.90
a.		Block of 10, #Z729-Z738	15.00	15.00
		Nos. Z729-Z738 (10)	14.00	9.00

Fox (Hokkaido) ZA642

Bears (Hokkaido) ZA643

Squirrel (Hokkaido) ZA644

Owl (Hokkaido) ZA645

2006, June 3

Z739	ZA642	50y multi	.90	.50
Z740	ZA643	50y multi	.90	.50
Z741	ZA644	50y multi	.90	.50
Z742	ZA645	50y multi	.90	.50
a.		Horiz. strip of 4, #Z739-Z742	3.75	3.75
		Nos. Z739-Z742 (4)	3.60	2.00

Aomori Nebuta Festival (Aomori) ZA646

Akita Kanto Festival (Akita) ZA647

Yamagata Hanagasa Festival (Yamagata) ZA648

Sendai Tanabata Festival (Miyagi) ZA649

2006, June 3 **Litho.**

Z743	ZA646 80y multi	1.40	.90
Z744	ZA647 80y multi	1.40	.90
Z745	ZA648 80y multi	1.40	.90
Z746	ZA649 80y multi	1.40	.90
a.	Horiz. strip of 4, #Z743-Z746	5.75	5.75
	Nos. Z743-Z746 (4)	5.60	3.60

Azaleas, Eboshi-iwa, Mt. Fuji (Kanagawa) ZA650

Daffodils, Sakawagawa River (Kanagawa) ZA651

Pinks, Tanzawa Mountains (Kanagawa) ZA652

Balloon Flowers, Mt. Fuji (Kanagawa) ZA653

2006, Aug. 1 **Photo.**

Z747	ZA650 80y multi	1.40	.90
Z748	ZA651 80y multi	1.40	.90
Z749	ZA652 80y multi	1.40	.90
Z750	ZA653 80y multi	1.40	.90
a.	Horiz. strip of 4, #Z747-Z750	5.75	5.75
	Nos. Z747-Z750 (4)	5.60	3.60

Miniature Sheet

88 Temples (Shikoku) ZA654

No. Z751: a, Hourinji (Temple 9). b, Kirihata (Temple 10). c, Fujiidera (Temple 11). d, Shouzanji (Temple 12). e, Kounomineji (Temple 27). f, Dainichiji (Temple 28). g, Kokubunji (Temple 29). h, Zenrakuji (Temple 30). i, Iwayaji (Temple 45). j, Joururiji (Temple 46). k, Yasakaji (Temple 47). l, Sairinji (Temple 48). m, Kichijouji (Temple 63). n, Maegamiji (Temple 64). o, Sankakuji (Temple 65). p, Unbenji (Temple 66). q, Shiromineji (Temple 81). r, Negoroji (Temple 82). s, Ichinomiyaji (Temple 83). t, Yashimaji (Temple 84).

2006, Aug. 1

Z751	ZA654 Sheet of 20	28.00	28.00
a.-t.	80y Any single	1.40	.90

See note under No. Z652 for information on identifying temple numbers.

61st National Athletic Meets (Hyogo) — ZA655

2006, Sept. 1

Z752	ZA655 50y multi	.85	.50

Loquats, Byobugaura (Chiba) ZA656

Umes, Fukuroda Waterfall (Ibaraki) ZA657

Apples, Oze (Gunma) ZA658

Japanese Pears, Nagatoro (Saitama) ZA659

Strawberries, Kegon Waterfall (Tochigi) — ZA660

2006, Sept. 1

Z753	ZA656 80y multi	1.40	.90
Z754	ZA657 80y multi	1.40	.90
Z755	ZA658 80y multi	1.40	.90
Z756	ZA659 80y multi	1.40	.90
Z757	ZA660 80y multi	1.40	.90
a.	Vert. strip of 5, #Z753-Z757	7.00	7.00
	Nos. Z753-Z757 (5)	7.00	4.50

Roses (Aichi) — ZA661

Chrysanthemums (Aichi) — ZA662

Orchids (Aichi) ZA663

Cyclamen (Aichi) ZA664

2006, Oct. 2 **Litho.**

Z758	ZA661 50y multi	.85	.50
Z759	ZA662 50y multi	.85	.50
Z760	ZA663 50y multi	.85	.50
Z761	ZA664 50y multi	.85	.50
a.	Horiz. strip of 4, #Z758-Z761	3.50	3.50
	Nos. Z758-Z761 (4)	3.40	2.00

Cherry Blossoms, Chidorigafuchi (Tokyo) ZA665

Roses, Akasaka Palace (Tokyo) ZA666

Cosmos, Shouwa Kinen Park (Tokyo) ZA667

Japanese Apricot Blossoms, Yushima Tenjin Shrine (Tokyo) ZA668

2006, Oct. 2 **Photo.**

Z762	ZA665 80y multi	1.40	.90
Z763	ZA666 80y multi	1.40	.90
Z764	ZA667 80y multi	1.40	.90
Z765	ZA668 80y multi	1.40	.90
a.	Horiz. strip of 4, #Z762-Z765	5.75	5.75
	Nos. Z762-Z765 (4)	5.60	3.60

Iris, Takeshima (Aichi, Mie, Gifu, Shizuoka) ZA669

Chinese Milk Vetch, Shirakawa Village (Aichi, Mie, Gifu, Shizuoka) ZA670

Lily, Nagoya Castle (Aichi, Mie, Gifu, Shizuoka) ZA671

Japanese Iris, Couple Rock (Aichi, Mie, Gifu, Shizuoka) ZA672

Azalea, Jogasaki Coast (Aichi, Mie, Gifu, Shizuoka) — ZA673

2007, Apr. 2 **Photo.** ***Perf. 13¼***

Z766	ZA669 80y multi	1.40	.90
Z767	ZA670 80y multi	1.40	.90
Z768	ZA671 80y multi	1.40	.90
Z769	ZA672 80y multi	1.40	.90
Z770	ZA673 80y multi	1.40	.90
a.	Vert. strip of 5, #Z766-Z770	7.00	7.00

Cherry Blossom, Yatsugatake (Yamanashi) ZA674

Grapes, Katsunuma Vineyard (Yamanashi) ZA675

Azalea, Syosenkyo (Yamanashi) ZA676

Lavender, Mt. Fuji (Yamanashi) ZA677

Peaches, Southern Japanese Alps (Yamanashi) — ZA678

2007, Apr. 2

Z771	ZA674 80y multi	1.40	.90
Z772	ZA675 80y multi	1.40	.90
Z773	ZA676 80y multi	1.40	.90
Z774	ZA677 80y multi	1.40	.90
Z775	ZA678 80y multi	1.40	.90
a.	Vert. strip of 5, #Z771-Z775	7.00	7.00

Tulips (Niigata) ZA679

Rice (Niigata) ZA680

Pears (Niigata) ZA681

Mealy Primrose (Niigata) ZA682

Iris (Niigata) — ZA683

2007, Apr. 2 **Litho.**

Z776	ZA679 80y multi	1.40	.90
Z777	ZA680 80y multi	1.40	.90
Z778	ZA681 80y multi	1.40	.90
Z779	ZA682 80y multi	1.40	.90
Z780	ZA683 80y multi	1.40	.90
a.	Vert. strip of 5, #Z776-Z780	7.00	7.00

Cherry Blossom (Saitama) ZA684

Japanese Rose (Ibaraki) ZA685

Skunk Cabbage (Gunma) ZA686

Adder's Tongue Lily (Tochigi) ZA687

Poppies (Chiba) — ZA688

2007, May 1 **Photo.** ***Perf. 13¼***

Z781	ZA684	50y multi	.85	.50
Z782	ZA685	50y multi	.85	.50
Z783	ZA686	50y multi	.85	.50
Z784	ZA687	50y multi	.85	.50
Z785	ZA688	50y multi	.85	.50
a.	Vert. strip of 5, #Z781-Z785		4.25	4.25

For self-adhesives, see Nos. 3189B-3189F.

Mandarin Ducks (Tottori) ZA689

Swans (Shimane) ZA690

Pheasants (Okayama) ZA691

Red-throated Loons (Hiroshima) ZA692

Hooded Cranes (Yamaguchi) — ZA693

2007, May 1 **Litho.**

Z786	ZA689	80y multi	1.40	.90
Z787	ZA690	80y multi	1.40	.90
Z788	ZA691	80y multi	1.40	.90
Z789	ZA692	80y multi	1.40	.90
Z790	ZA693	80y multi	1.40	.90
a.	Vert. strip of 5, #Z786-Z790		7.00	7.00

Japanese Cranes (Hokkaido) ZA694

Hokkaido Mountain Hares (Hokkaido) ZA695

Flying Squirrels (Hokkaido) ZA696

Hokkaido Deer (Hokkaido) ZA697

Spotted Seals (Hokkaido) — ZA698

2007, May 1 **Litho.**

Z791	ZA694	80y multi	1.40	.90
Z792	ZA695	80y multi	1.40	.90
Z793	ZA696	80y multi	1.40	.90
Z794	ZA697	80y multi	1.40	.90
Z795	ZA698	80y multi	1.40	.90
a.	Horiz. strip of 5, #Z791-Z795		7.00	7.00

Koriyama Castle (Nara) ZA699

Hikone Castle (Shiga) ZA700

Himeji Castle (Hyogo) ZA701

Osaka Castle (Osaka) ZA702

Wakayama Castle (Wakayama) — ZA703

2007, June 1 **Photo.**

Z796	ZA699	50y multi	.85	.50
Z797	ZA700	50y multi	.85	.50
Z798	ZA701	50y multi	.85	.50
Z799	ZA702	50y multi	.85	.50
Z800	ZA703	50y multi	.85	.50
a.	Vert. strip of 5, #Z796-Z800		4.25	4.25

Whale Shark (Okinawa) ZA704

Longfin Bannerfish (Okinawa) ZA705

False Clownfish (Okinawa) ZA706

Blue Damselfish (Okinawa) ZA707

Manta Ray (Okinawa) — ZA708

2007, June 1 **Photo.**

Z801	ZA704	80y multi	1.40	.90
Z802	ZA705	80y multi	1.40	.90
Z803	ZA706	80y multi	1.40	.90
Z804	ZA707	80y multi	1.40	.90
Z805	ZA708	80y multi	1.40	.90
a.	Horiz. strip of 5, #Z801-Z805		7.00	7.00

See Nos. 3929-3933.

National Afforestation Campaign (Hokkaido) — ZA709

2007, June 22 ***Perf. 12½x12¾***

Z806	ZA709	50y multi	.85	.60

Dancers, Owara Wind Festival (Toyama) ZA710

Dancers, Owara Wind Festival (Toyama) ZA711

Dancers, Owara Wind Festival (Toyama) ZA712

Dancers, Owara Wind Festival (Toyama) ZA713

Dancers, Owara Wind Festival (Toyama) — ZA714

2007, July 2 **Litho.** ***Perf. 13¼***

Z807	ZA710	80y multi	1.40	.90
Z808	ZA711	80y multi	1.40	.90
Z809	ZA712	80y multi	1.40	.90
Z810	ZA713	80y multi	1.40	.90
Z811	ZA714	80y multi	1.40	.90
a.	Vert. strip of 5, #Z807-Z811		7.00	7.00

See Nos. 3875-3879.

Tokyo Tower, Japanese Allspice (Tokyo) ZA715

Double Bridge, Chinese Violet Cress (Tokyo) ZA716

Meiji shrine Outer Garden, Sweet Olive (Tokyo) ZA717

Lake Okutama, Gentian (Tokyo) ZA718

Japan Bridge, Camellia (Tokyo) — ZA719

2007, July 2 **Photo.**

Z812	ZA715	80y multi	1.40	.90
Z813	ZA716	80y multi	1.40	.90
Z814	ZA717	80y multi	1.40	.90
Z815	ZA718	80y multi	1.40	.90
Z816	ZA719	80y multi	1.40	.90
a.	Vert. strip of 5, #Z812-Z8161		7.00	7.00

Oirase Mountain Stream (Aomori) ZA720

Hirosaki Castle (Aomori) ZA721

Chuson Temple (Iwate) ZA722

Jodogahama (Iwate) ZA723

Matsushima (Miyagi) ZA724

Mt. Zao Crater Lake (Miyagi, Yamagata) ZA725

Oga Peninsula (Akita) ZA726

Mt. Chokai (Akita, Yamagata) ZA727

Oze (Fukushima) ZA728

Gassan Volcano (Yamagata) ZA729

2007, July 2

Z817	Sheet of 10		14.00	14.00
a.	ZA720	80y multi	1.40	.90
b.	ZA721	80y multi	1.40	.90
c.	ZA722	80y multi	1.40	.90
d.	ZA723	80y multi	1.40	.90
e.	ZA724	80y multi	1.40	.90
f.	ZA725	80y multi	1.40	.90
g.	ZA726	80y multi	1.40	.90
h.	ZA727	80y multi	1.40	.90
i.	ZA728	80y multi	1.40	.90
j.	ZA729	80y multi	1.40	.90

Main Tower, Kumamoto Castle, Cherry Blossoms (Kumamoto) ZA730

Uto Turret, Kumamoto Castle, in Summer (Kumamoto) ZA731

Main Tower, Kumamoto Castle, Gingko Trees (Kumamoto) ZA732

Uto Turret, Kumamoto Castle, in Winter (Kumamoto) ZA733

Three Towers, Kumamoto Castle (Kumamoto) — ZA734

2007, Aug. 1 **Litho.**

Z818	ZA730	80y multi	1.40	.90
Z819	ZA731	80y multi	1.40	.90
Z820	ZA732	80y multi	1.40	.90
Z821	ZA733	80y multi	1.40	.90
Z822	ZA734	80y multi	1.40	.90
a.	Vert. strip of 5, #Z818-Z822		7.00	7.00

Edo Bridge from Japan Bridge, by Hiroshige (Tokyo) ZA735

Ohisa Takashima, by Utamaro (Tokyo) ZA736

Yaozo Ichikawa II as Bunzo Tanabe, by Sharaku (Tokyo) ZA737

Horikiri Irises, by Hiroshige (Tokyo) ZA738

Kinryuzan Temple, by Hiroshige (Tokyo) ZA739

Seven Women Applying Makeup Using a Full Length Mirror, by Utamaro (Tokyo) ZA740

Ryuzo Arashi II as Kinkichi Ishibe, Moneylender, by Sharaku (Tokyo) ZA741

Suido Bridge and Surugadai, by Hiroshige (Tokyo) ZA742

Moon Pine, Ueno Temple, by Hiroshige (Tokyo) ZA743

Hanaogi from Ogiya, No. 1 District, Edo Town, by Utamaro (Tokyo) ZA744

2007, Aug. 1

Z823	Sheet of 10	14.00	14.00
a.	ZA735 80y multi	1.40	.90
b.	ZA736 80y multi	1.40	.90
c.	ZA737 80y multi	1.40	.90
d.	ZA738 80y multi	1.40	.90
e.	ZA739 80y multi	1.40	.90
f.	ZA740 80y multi	1.40	.90
g.	ZA741 80y multi	1.40	.90
h.	ZA742 80y multi	1.40	.90
i.	ZA743 80y multi	1.40	.90
j.	ZA744 80y multi	1.40	.90

ZA745

88 Temples (Shikoku) ZA746

No. Z824: a, Dainchiji (Temple 13). b, Jorakuji (Temple 14). c, Kokubunji (Temple 15). d, Kanonji (Temple 16). e, Chikurinji (Temple 31). f, Zenjibuji (Temple 32). g, Sekkeiji (Temple 33). h, Tanemaji (Temple 34). i, Jodoji (Temple 49). j, Hantaji (Temple 50). k, Ishiteji (Temple 51). l, Taisanji (Temple 52). m, Daikoji (Temple 67). n, Jinnein (Temple 68). o, Kannonji (Temple 69). p, Motoyamaji (Temple 70). q, Yakuriji (Temple 85). r, Shidoji (Temple 86). s, Nagaoji (Temple 87). t, Okuboji (Temple 88).

No. Z825: a, Idoji (Temple 17). b, Onzanji (Temple 18). c, Kiyotakiji (Temple 35). d, Shoryuji (Temple 36). e, Emmyoji (Temple 53). f, Emmeiji (Temple 54). g, Iyadaniji (Temple 71). h, Mandaraji (Temple 72). i, Deities Cave (no temple number). j, Painting of Daishi Kobo (no temple number).

2007, Aug. 1 Photo. *Perf. 13¼*

Z824	ZA745	Sheet of 20	28.00	28.00
a.-t.		80y Any single	1.40	.90
Z825	ZA746	Sheet of 10	14.00	14.00
a.-j.		80y Any single	1.40	.90

See note under No. Z652 for information on identifying temple numbers.

62nd National Athletic Meet (Akita) — ZA747

2007, Sept. 3 Litho.

Z826 ZA747 50y multi .90 .50

Miniature Sheet

Nagoya Port (Aichi) ZA748

No. Z827: a, Hibiscus and Antarctic survey. b, Hibiscus and Port Tower. c, Azaleas, killer whale at Nagoya Aquarium. d, Azaleas, dolphins at Nagoya Aquarium. e, Yellow chrysanthemums, Meiko Triton Bridge. f, Orange and yellow chrysanthemums, two bridges. g, Snapdragons and fireworks. h, Sailing ship and snapdragons. i, Azaleas, bridge, Nagoya Aquarium and half of Ferris wheel. j, Azaleas, Port Tower, Nagoya Castle, and half of Ferris wheel.

2007, Nov. 5 Litho. *Perf. 13¼*

Z827	ZA748	Sheet of 10	15.00	15.00
a.-j.		80y Any single	1.40	.90

Beginning in 2008 the planning and design of prefecture stamps, previously done by regional postal authorities, was taken over by national postal authorities. The national authorities planned issues for 2008 that would be available in more of postal regions, thus making prefectural issues more nationwide and less local in scope. Additionally, the style of the "Nippon yubin" ideographic characters that had been used solely for prefecture stamps reverted to the style used on the national issues for most issues. Because of these changes, prefecture stamps will be listed in the regular postage listings starting with the 2008 issues.

PREFECTURE SEMI-POSTAL STAMPS

Earthquake and Volcano Eruption Refugee Relief (Tokyo) ZSP1

2000, Nov. 15 Photo.

ZB1	80y +20y Pink ribbon	1.75	1.25
ZB2	80y +20y Blue ribbon	1.75	1.25
a.	ZSP1 Pair, #ZB1-ZB2	4.00	4.00

SEMI-POSTAL STAMPS

Douglas Plane over Japan Alps — SP1

Wmk. Zigzag Lines (141)

1937, June 1 Photo. *Perf. 13*

B1	SP1 2s + 2s rose carmine	2.50	1.50
B2	SP1 3s + 2s purple	2.50	2.00
B3	SP1 4s + 2s green	3.00	1.50
	Nos. B1-B3 (3)	8.00	5.00
	Set, never hinged	13.00	

The surtax was for the Patriotic Aviation Fund to build civil airports.

Nos. 259 and 261 Surcharged in Blue or Red

1942, Feb. 16 Wmk. 257 *Perf. 13*

B4	A84 2s +1s crimson (Bl)	1.25	2.50
B5	A86 4s +2s dk grn (R)	1.25	2.50
	Set, never hinged	4.25	

Fall of Singapore to Japanese forces.

Tank Corps Attack, Bataan — SP2

Pearl Harbor Under Japanese Attack — SP3

Unwmk.

1942, Dec. 8 Photo. *Perf. 12*

B6	SP2 2s +1s rose brown	2.00	2.00
B7	SP3 5s +2s sapphire	2.25	3.50
	Set, never hinged	7.00	

1st anniv. of the "Greater East Asia War." The surtax was for national defense.

Catalogue values for unused stamps in this section, from this point to the end of the section, are for Never Hinged items.

SP4

1947, Nov. 25 Wmk. 257 *Perf. 12½*

B8 SP4 1.20y + 80s dk rose red 2.00 2.00

Japan's 1st Community Chest drive. The surtax was for charitable purposes.

Nurse SP5

Bird Feeding Young SP6

1948, Oct. 1 Unwmk. *Perf. 12½*

B9	SP5 5y + 2.50y bright red	12.00	15.00
B10	SP6 5y + 2.50y emerald	12.00	17.00

Souvenir Sheet

Wmk. 257

Imperf

Without Gum

B11 Sheet of 2 65.00 *65.00*

The surtax on Nos. B9-B11 was divided between the Red Cross and Community Chest organizations.

No. B11 contains Nos. B9-B10, imperf.

Javelin Thrower — SP8

No. B13, Wrestlers. No. B14, Diver. No. B15, Water polo. No. B16, Woman gymnast. No. B17, Judo. No. B18, Fencing. No. B19, Basketball. No. B20, Rowing. No. B21, Sailing. No. B22, Boxing. No. B23, Volleyball. No. B24, Bicyclist. No. B25, Equestrian. No. B26, Field hockey. No. B27, Pistol shooting. No. B28, Modern pentathlon. No. B29, Weight lifter. No. B30, Women's kayak doubles. No. B31, Soccer.

Perf. 13½

1961, Oct. 11 Unwmk. Engr.

B12 SP8 5y + 5y bister 1.00 1.50
B13 SP8 5y + 5y dk green 1.00 1.50
B14 SP8 5y + 5y carmine 1.00 1.50
a. Souvenir sheet of 3 ('64) 6.00 7.00

1962, June 23

B15 SP8 5y + 5y green .65 1.25
B16 SP8 5y + 5y dk purple .65 1.25
B17 SP8 5y + 5y dk carmine .65 1.25
a. Souvenir sheet of 3 ('64) 4.00 5.00

1962, Oct. 10

B18 SP8 5y + 5y brick red .55 .65
B19 SP8 5y + 5y slate grn .55 .65
B20 SP8 5y + 5y violet .55 .65
a. Souvenir sheet of 3 ('64) 3.00 4.00

1963, June 23

B21 SP8 5y + 5y blue .55 .65
B22 SP8 5y + 5y dk brown .55 .65
B23 SP8 5y + 5y brown .55 .65
a. Souvenir sheet of 3 ('64) 6.50 7.50

1963, Nov. 11

B24 SP8 5y + 5y dk blue .50 .50
B25 SP8 5y + 5y olive .50 .50
B26 SP8 5y + 5y black .50 .50
B27 SP8 5y + 5y claret .50 .50
a. Souvenir sheet of 4 ('64) 6.50 7.50

1964, June 23

B28 SP8 5y + 5y bluish vio .40 .40
B29 SP8 5y + 5y dp olive .40 .40
B30 SP8 5y + 5y grnsh blue .40 .40
B31 SP8 5y + 5y rose claret .40 .40
a. Souvenir sheet of 4 ('64) 6.50 7.50
Nos. B12-B31 (20) 11.85 15.75

Issued to raise funds for the 1964 Olympic Games in Tokyo.

The souvenir sheets were issued Aug. 20, 1964. Each contains one each of the stamps in the set it follows. Nos. B14a, B20a, B23a and B27a, exist imperf.

Cobalt Treatment Unit SP9

Early Cancer Detection with X-rays SP10

1966, Oct. 21 Photo. *Perf. 13*

B32 SP9 7y + 3y yel org & blk .25 .25
B33 SP10 15y + 5y multicolored .40 .25

9th Intl. Anticancer Congress, Tokyo, Oct. 23-29. The surtax was for the fight against cancer and for research.

EXPO '70 Emblem and Globe SP11

Cherry Blossoms, Screen, Chishakuin Temple SP12

1969, Mar. 15 Photo. *Perf. 13*

B34 SP11 15y + 5y bl, ocher & ver .60 .60
B35 SP12 50y + 10y gold, brn & grn 1.25 1.25

Issued to publicize EXPO '70, International Exhibition, Osaka, 1970.

Ice Hockey, Sapporo Olympic Emblem — SP13

Design: No. B37, Ski jump and Sapporo Olympic Games emblem, vert.

1971, Feb. 6 Photo. *Perf. 13*

B36 SP13 15y + 5y multi .40 .25
B37 SP13 15y + 5y multi .40 .25

To promote the 11th Winter Olympic Games, Sapporo, Japan, 1972.

Blue Dragon, East Wall — SP14

Murals from ancient tomb mound: No. B39, Two men, east wall, vert. 50y+10y, Four women, west wall, vert.

1973, Mar. 26 Photo. *Perf. 13*

Size: 48x27mm, 27x48mm

B38 SP14 20y + 5y multi .50 .40
B39 SP14 20y + 5y multi .50 .40

Photogravure and Engraved

Size: 33x48mm

B40 SP14 50y + 10y multi 1.10 1.10
Nos. B38-B40 (3) 2.10 1.90

Surtax was for restoration work on the murals of the Takamatsu-zuka tomb mound, discovered in March, 1972, and excavated in Nara Prefecture.

Reefs, by Hyakusui Hirafuku SP15

1974, Mar. 2 Photo. *Perf. 13*

B41 SP15 20y + 5y multi .50 .30

The surtax was for the International Ocean Exposition, Okinawa, 1975.

Intl. Year of the Disabled — SP16

Photogravure and Embossed

1981, Sept. 1 *Perf. 13½*

B42 SP16 60y + 10y multi 1.00 .35

Surtax was for education of the disabled.

TSUKUB'85 Intl. Exposition, Mar. 17-Sept. 16, 1985 — SP17

1984, Feb. 19 Photo. *Perf. 13½*

B43 SP17 60y + 10y multi 1.00 .35

Intl. Garden and Greenery Exposition, Osaka — SP18

1989, June 1 Photo. *Perf. 13*

B44 SP18 62y +10y multi 1.40 .40

Surtax for the preparation and management of the exposition.

Intl. Garden and Greenery Exposition, Osaka — SP19

1990, Mar. 30

B45 SP19 41y +4y multi .75 .25

SP20

1991, July 5 Photo. *Perf. 13*

B46 SP20 62y +10y multi 1.25 .40

11th World Congress of the World Federation of the Deaf.

SP21

1995, Apr. 20 Photo. *Perf. 13*

B47 SP21 80y +20y multi 2.00 .60

Philately week. Surtax for benefit of victims of Kobe earthquake.

1998 Winter Olympic Games, Nagano SP22

1997, Feb. 7 Photo. *Perf. 13*

B48 80y +10y Emblem 1.75 .60
B49 80y +10y Stylized owls 1.75 .60
a. SP22 Pair, #B48-B49 3.50 2.25

2002 Soccer World Cup, Japan and Korea — SP23

Colors of mascots: No. B50, Purple, yellow and blue. No. B51, Purple. No. B52, Blue.

2001, May 31 Photo. *Perf. 13x13¼*

B50 SP23 80y +10y multi 1.75 .50
B51 SP23 80y +10y multi 1.75 .50
B52 SP23 80y +10y multi 1.75 .50
a. Horiz. pair, #B51-B52 3.50 2.20

Wall Paintings, Kitora Tumulus, Asuka SP24

Designs: No. B53, White Tiger of the West. No. B54, Red Bird fo the South.

2003, Oct. 15 Photo. *Perf. 13*

B53 80y +10y multi 1.50 .60
B54 80y +10y multi 1.50 .60
a. SP24 Horiz. pair, #B53-B54 3.50 2.50

2005 World Exposition, Aichi — SP25

Exposition mascots and: No. B55, Earth. No. B56, Cherry blossoms.

2004, Mar. 25 Photo. *Perf. 13x13¼*

B55 80y +10y multi 1.75 1.25
B56 80y +10y multi 1.75 1.25
a. SP25 Horiz. pair, #B55-B56 3.50 3.50

Miniature Sheet

Be Kind to Animals Week SP26

No. B57: a, Dog, flower background. b, White cat, red background. c, White Yorkshire terrier, green curtain. d, Cat, bubbles in background. e, Black Labrador retriever puppy sitting. f, Cat, brown striped background. g, Shiba puppy standing. h, Scottish Fold cat, dots and stripes in background. i, Dog in doorway. j, Cat, crescent moon.

2009, Sept. 18 Litho. *Perf. 13¼*

B57 SP26 Sheet of 10 11.00 11.00
a.-j. 50y+5y Any single 1.00 .40

Surtax for animal welfare organizations.

SP27

SP28

SP29

SP30

Mar. 11, 2011 Earthquake and Tsunami Relief — SP31

2011, June 21 Photo. *Perf. 13*

B58 SP27 80y+20y multi 1.50 .60
B59 SP28 80y+20y multi 1.50 .60
B60 SP29 80y+20y multi 1.50 .60
B61 SP30 80y+20y multi 1.50 .60
B62 SP31 80y+20y multi 1.50 .60
a. Vert. strip of 5, #B58-B62 12.50 12.50

Nos. B58-B62 were printed in sheets containing two strips.

Miniature Sheet

2019 Rugby World Cup, Japan SP32

No. B63: a, Mount Fuji in blue rugby ball. b, Mount Fuji in red rugby ball. c, Mount Fuji in yellow rugby ball. d, Mount Fuji in purple rugby ball. e, World Cup. f, Rugby World Cup emblem in rugby ball. g, Mascots.

2018, Aug. 20 Litho. *Perf. 13½*

B63	SP32 Sheet of 10, #B63a-B63d, 2 each #B63e-B63g	17.50	17.50
a.-g.	82y+10y Any single	1.75	1.75

Surtax for preparation and management of 2019 Rugby World Cup.

Miniature Sheet

2020 Summer Olympics and Paralympics, Tokyo — SP33

No. B64: a, Dark blue mascot with raised fist. b, Dark blue 2020 Olympics emblem (circular) and Olympic rings in color. c, Aerial view of New National Stadium, Tokyo. d, Dark blue 2020 Paralympics emblem (crescent) and Paralympics crescents in color. e, Magenta mascot with arm extended. f, Dark blue mascot with arms extended. g, Red 2020 Olympics emblem and Olympic rings in magenta. h, Yoyogi Nation Stadium exterior, Tokyo. i, Carmine 2020 Paralympics emblem and carmine Paralympics crescents. j, Magenta mascot with fists raised.

Litho., Litho. & Embossed (#B64b, B64d, B64g, B64i)

2019, Mar. 12 *Perf. 13½*

B64	SP33 Sheet of 10	17.50	17.50
a.-j.	82y+10y Any single	1.75	1.75

Surtax for preparation and management of 2020 Summer Olympics and Paralympics. The 2020 Summer Olympics and Paralympics were postponed to 2021 due to the Coronovirus pandemic.

Miniature Sheet

2020 Summer Olympics and Paralympics, Tokyo — SP34

No. B65: a, Circular 2020 Olympics emblem, Olympic rings, silver background. b, As "a," gold background. c, As "a," bronze background. d, Crescent-shaped 2020 Paralympics emblem, Paralympics crescents, silver background. e, As "e," gold background. f, As "e," bronze background. g, Dark blue 2020 Olympics emblem and Olympic rings in color. h, Dark blue 2020 Paralympics emblem and Paralympics crescents in color.

Litho. & Embossed

2019, Aug. 26 *Perf. 13½*

B65	SP34 Sheet of 10, #B65a-B65f, 2 each #B65g-B65h	17.50	17.50
a.-h.	84y+10y Any single	1.75	1.75

Surtax for preparation and management of 2020 Summer Olympics and Paralympics. The 2020 Summer Olympics and Paralympics were postponed to 2021 due to the Coronovirus pandemic.

AIR POST STAMPS

Regular Issue of 1914 Overprinted in Red or Blue

Wmk. Zigzag Lines (141)

1919, Oct. 3 *Perf. 13x13½*

Granite Paper

C1	A34	1½s blue (R)	400.00	150.00
C2	A34	3s rose (Bl)	900.00	500.00

Excellent counterfeits exist.

Passenger Plane over Lake Ashi — AP1

Granite Paper

1929-34 Engr. *Perf. 13½x13*

C3	AP1	8½s orange brn	45.00	45.00
C4	AP1	9½s rose	15.00	10.00
C5	AP1	16½s yellow grn	20.00	20.00
C6	AP1	18s ultra	25.00	10.00
C7	AP1	33s gray	45.00	10.00
		Nos. C3-C7 (5)	150.00	95.00
		Set, never hinged	225.00	

Souvenir Sheet

C8	AP1	Sheet of 4, #C4-C7	1,300.	1,300.
		Never hinged	2,000.	

Issued: 9½s, 3/1/34; No. C8, 4/20/34; others, 10/6/29. No. C8 for Communications Commemoration Day (1st observance of establishment of the postal service and issuance of #1-4). Sold only at Phil. Exhib. p.o., Tokyo, 4/20-27. Size: 110x100mm.

Catalogue values for unused stamps in this section, from this point to the end of the section, are for Never Hinged items.

Southern Green Pheasant — AP3

Perf. 13x13½

1950, Jan. 10 Engr. Unwmk.

C9	AP3	16y gray	35.00	10.00
C10	AP3	34y brown violet	60.00	12.00
C11	AP3	59y carmine	80.00	7.00
C12	AP3	103y orange yellow	55.00	20.00
C13	AP3	144y olive	65.00	22.50
		Nos. C9-C13 (5)	295.00	71.50
		Set, hinged	125.00	

Pagoda and Plane AP4

Plane and Mt. Tsurugi-dake AP5

1951-52 Photo.

C14	AP4	15y purple	5.00	4.00
C15	AP4	20y blue	35.00	3.00
C16	AP4	25y yellow grn	35.00	.45
C17	AP4	30y brown red	25.00	.45
C18	AP4	40y gray blk	9.00	.55
C19	AP5	55y brt blue	230.00	40.00
C20	AP5	75y brnsh red	175.00	25.00
C21	AP5	80y magenta	30.00	3.00
C22	AP5	85y black	50.00	10.00
C23	AP5	125y olive bis	15.00	5.00
C24	AP5	160y Prus green	40.00	5.00
		Nos. C14-C24 (11)	649.00	96.45
		Set, hinged	300.00	

Issue dates: 25y, 30y, Dec. 20; 15y, 20y, 40y, Sept. 1; 55y-160y, Feb. 11, 1952.

Redrawn; Underlined Zeros Omitted

1952-62

C25	AP4	15y purple ('62)	2.50	.90
C26	AP4	20y blue	75.00	6.00
C27	AP4	25y yel grn ('53)	1.25	.30
C28	AP4	30y brown red	6.00	.30
C29	AP4	40y gray blk ('53)	5.25	.40
C30	AP5	55y brt blue	70.00	4.00
C32	AP5	75y brnsh red	160.00	15.00
C33	AP5	80y magenta	120.00	4.00
C34	AP5	85y black	5.50	3.00
C36	AP5	125y olive bis	12.50	3.00
C38	AP5	160y Prus green	40.00	4.00
		Nos. C25-C38 (11)	498.00	40.90
		Set, hinged	185.00	

See No. C43.

Great Buddha of Kamakura — AP6

1953, Aug. 15 *Perf. 13½*

C39	AP6	70y red brown	3.50	.25
C40	AP6	80y blue	5.00	.25
C41	AP6	115y olive green	3.00	.40
C42	AP6	145y Prus green	20.00	2.50
		Nos. C39-C42 (4)	31.50	3.40

Redrawn Type of 1952-62

Coil Stamp

1961, Oct. 2 *Perf. 13 Horiz.*

C43	AP4	30y brown red	40.00	27.50

MILITARY STAMPS

Nos. 98, 119, 131 Overprinted

1910-14 Unwmk. *Perf. 11½ to 13½*

M1	A26	3s rose	200.00	35.00
M2	A34	3s rose ('13)	325.00	140.00

Wmk. 141

M3	A34	3s rose ('14)	30.00	16.00
		Nos. M1-M3 (3)	555.00	191.00

Nos. M1-M3 overprint type I has 3.85mm between characters; type II, 4-4.5mm (movable type).

1921 On Offices in China No. 37

M4	A34	3s rose	*5,750.*	*4,750.*

No. M4 is a provisional military stamp issued at the Japanese Post Office, Tsingtao, China. The overprint differs from the illustration, being 12mm high with thicker characters. Counterfeits are plentiful.

Overprint 16mm High

1924 On No. 131

M5	A34	3s rose	90.00	72.50
a.		3s rose (#131b)	90.00	75.00

Excellent forgeries exist of Nos. M1-M5.

JAPANESE OFFICES ABROAD

Offices in China

1899-1907 Regular Issues of Japan Overprinted in Red or Black

Perf. 11½, 12, 12½, 13½, 13x13½

1900-06 Unwmk.

1	A26	5r gray (R)	3.25	2.50
2	A26	½s gray (R) ('01)	2.00	.70
3	A26	1s lt red brn (R)	2.00	.70
4	A26	1½s ultra	9.00	2.00
5	A26	1½s vio ('06)	5.00	.95
6	A26	2s lt grn (R)	5.00	.70
7	A26	3s violet brn	5.50	.70
8	A26	3s rose ('06)	4.00	.50
9	A26	4s rose	4.50	1.25
10	A26	5s org yel (R)	9.00	1.25
11	A27	6s maroon ('06)	16.00	11.00
12	A27	8s ol grn (R)	9.00	5.50
13	A27	10s deep blue	9.00	1.00
14	A27	15s purple	18.00	1.75
15	A27	20s red org	16.00	1.00
16	A28	25s blue grn (R)	32.50	3.50
17	A28	50s red brown	35.00	2.50
18	A29	1y carmine	55.00	2.50
		Nos. 1-18 (18)	239.75	40.00

No. 6 with black overprint is bogus.

Nos. 5, 6, 8, 9 and 13 exist as booklet panes of 6, made from sheet stamps. They are rare.

1900

19	A30	3s carmine	25.00	15.00

Wedding of Crown Prince Yoshihito and Princess Sadako.

Japan Nos. 113 & 114 Overprinted

1908

20	A33	5y green	400.00	47.50
21	A33	10y dark violet	700.00	110.00

On #20-21 the space between characters of the overprint is 6½mm instead of 1½mm.

Stamps of 1913-33 Issues Overprinted

1913 *Perf. 12, 12x13, 13x13½*

22	A34	½s brown	14.00	14.00
23	A34	1s orange	15.00	15.00
24	A34	1½s lt blue	40.00	18.00
25	A34	2s green	45.00	20.00
26	A34	3s rose	22.50	8.00
27	A35	4s red	62.50	62.50
28	A35	5s violet	62.50	50.00
29	A35	10s deep blue	62.50	21.00
30	A35	20s claret	250.00	140.00
31	A35	25s olive green	90.00	21.00
32	A36	1y yel grn & mar	750.00	500.00
		Nos. 22-32 (11)	1,414.	869.50

Nos. 24, 25, 26, 27 and 29 exist in booklet panes of 6, made from sheet stamps. The No. 26 pane is very rare.

Japan Nos. 127-137, 139-147 Overprinted

1914-21 Wmk. 141

Granite Paper

33	A34	½s brown	3.25	.80
34	A34	1s orange	3.75	.80
35	A34	1½s blue	4.25	.80
36	A34	2s green	2.75	.95
37	A34	3s rose	2.40	.80
38	A35	4s red	10.00	4.75
39	A35	5s violet	17.50	1.75
40	A35	6s brown ('20)	30.00	18.00
41	A35	8s gray ('20)	37.50	20.00
42	A35	10s dp blue	12.00	1.25
43	A35	20s claret	42.50	3.25
44	A35	25s olive grn	50.00	3.50
45	A36	30s org brn ('20)	75.00	27.50
46	A36	50s dk brn ('20)	90.00	30.00
47	A36	1y yel grn & mar ('18)	130.00	6.75
48	A33	5y green	1,850.	525.00
49	A33	10y violet ('21)	2,650.	1,600.
		Nos. 33-49 (17)	5,011.	2,246.

On Nos. 48-49 the space between characters of overprint is 4½mm, instead of 6½mm on Nos. 20-21 and 1½mm on all lower values. See No. M4.

No. 42 exists as a booklet pane of 6, made from sheet stamps. It is very rare.

Counterfeit overprints exist of Nos. 1-49.

Offices in Korea

Regular Issue of Japan Overprinted in Red or Black

1900 Unwmk. *Perf. 11½, 12, 12½*

1	A26	5r gray (R)	19.00	8.75
2	A26	1s lt red brn (R)	20.00	5.00
3	A26	1½s ultra	250.00	130.00
4	A26	2s lt green (R)	19.00	10.00
5	A26	3s violet brn	17.00	4.75
6	A26	4s rose	65.00	27.50
7	A26	5s org yel (R)	67.50	27.50
8	A27	8s ol grn (R)	250.00	120.00
9	A27	10s deep blue	35.00	9.00
10	A27	15s purple	62.50	6.00
11	A27	20s red orange	62.50	5.00
12	A28	25s blue grn (R)	220.00	55.00

13	A28	50s red brown	175.00	18.00
14	A29	1y carmine	475.00	14.00
		Nos. 1-14 (14)	1,738.	440.50

1900

15	A30	3s carmine	125.00	55.00

Wedding of Crown Prince Yoshihito and Princess Sadako.

Counterfeit overprints exist of Nos. 1-15.

Taiwan (Formosa)

Numeral of Value and Imperial Crest — A1

1945 Unwmk. Litho. *Imperf.*
Without Gum

1	A1	3s carmine	30.00	30.00
2	A1	5s blue green	24.00	24.00
3	A1	10s pale blue	35.00	35.00
		Nos. 1-3 (3)	89.00	89.00

Additional values, prepared, but not issued, were: 30s, 40s, 50s, 1y, 5y and 10y. The entire set of nine was overprinted by Chinese authorities after World War II and issued for use in Taiwan.

For overprints see China-Taiwan Nos. 1-7.

JORDAN

'jor-dən

Trans-Jordan

LOCATION — In the Near East, separated from the Mediterranean Sea by Israel
GOVT. — Kingdom
AREA — 38,400 sq. mi.
POP. — 4,561,147 (1999 est.)
CAPITAL — Amman

The former Turkish territory was mandated to Great Britain following World War I. It became an independent state in 1946.

10 Milliemes = 1 Piaster
1000 Mils = 1 Palestine Pound (1930)
1000 Fils = 100 piasters = 1 Jordan Dinar (1951)

Catalogue values for unused stamps in this country are for Never Hinged items, beginning with Scott 221 in the regular postage section, Scott B13 in the semi-postal section, Scott C1 in the air post section, Scott J47 in the postage due section, Scott RA1 in the postal tax section, Scott N1 in the occupation section, Scott NJ1 in the occupation postage due section, and Scott NRA1 in the occupation postal tax section.

Watermarks

Wmk. 305 — Roman and Arabic Initials

Wmk. 328 — UAR

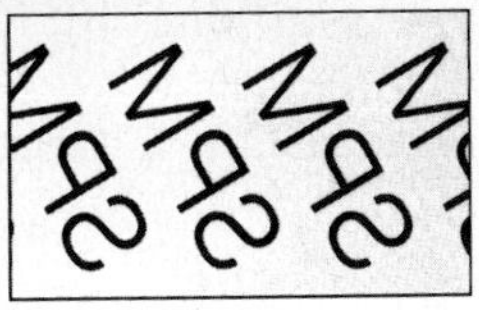
Wmk. 388 — Multiple "SPM"

British Mandate

Stamps and Type of Palestine 1918 Overprinted in Black or Silver

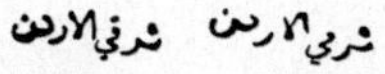
Type I Type II

1920, Nov. Wmk. 33 *Perf. 15x14*

1 A1 1m dark brown 3.75 6.00
a. Inverted overprint 150.00 300.00
2 A1 2m blue green 25.00 27.50
3 A1 3m light brown (I) 3.75 4.75
a. Overprint type II 1,200.
4 A1 4m scarlet 4.50 4.50
a. Arabic "40" 82.50
5 A1 5m orange 10.00 3.50
6 A1 1pi dark blue (S) 2,200.
7 A1 2pi olive green (I) 14.00 16.00
a. Overprint type II 950.00
8 A1 5pi plum 55.00 82.50
a. Overprint type II 1,500.
9 A1 9pi bister 100.00 120.00
Nos. 1-9 (9) 2,416. 264.75

Perf. 14

1B A1 1m dark brown 1.40 5.00
a. Inverted overprint 190.00
2B A1 2m blue green 3.00 4.50
a. Silver overprint 625.00 675.00
3B A1 3m light brown 22.50 30.00
4B A1 4m scarlet 19.00 50.00
a. Arabic "40" 160.00
5B A1 5m orange 2.75 3.50
6B A1 1pi dark blue (S) 3.75 4.25
7B A1 2pi olive green 13.00 13.00
8B A1 5pi plum 8.00 16.00
9B A1 9pi bister 8.00 55.00
10 A1 10pi ultramarine 22.50 60.00
11 A1 20pi gray 25.00 100.00
Nos. 1B-11 (11) 128.90 341.25

The overprint reads "Sharqi al-ardan" (East of Jordan).
For overprints see Nos. 12-73, 83A.

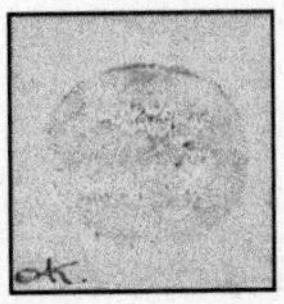
Moab District Seal

1920, Nov. Handstamped *Imperf.*

12 A2 (1p) pale blue 4,000. 4,500.

No. 12 was issued at Kerak by the political officer for the Moab District and was used until March 1921 pending the arrival of Nos. 1//11.

Stamps of 1920 Issue Handstamp Surcharged "Ashir el qirsh" (tenth of piaster) and numeral in Black, Red or Violet

On Nos. 1-9 (Perf. 15x14)

1922, Nov.

13 A1 1/10pi on 1m dk brn 32.50 *55.00*
14 A1 1/10pi on 1m dk brn (R) 77.50 77.50
15 A1 1/10pi on 1m dk brn (V) 77.50 77.50
16 A1 2/10pi on 2m bl grn 37.50 37.50
a. 3/10pi on 2m bl grn (error) 140.00 120.00
17 A1 2/10pi on 2m bl grn (R) 87.50 87.50
18 A1 2/10pi on 2m bl grn (V) 110.00 110.00
19 A1 3/10pi on 3m lt brn 16.00 16.00
a. Pair, one without surcharge 925.00
b. On #3a (type II) 1,400. 1,400.
20 A1 3/10pi on 3m lt brn (V) 160.00 160.00
a. On #3a (type II) 3,000.
21 A1 4/10pi on 4m scar 65.00 70.00
22 A1 5/10pi on 5m org 200.00 110.00
23 A1 5/10pi on 5m dp org (V) 275.00 275.00

Handstamp Surcharged "El qirsh" (piaster) and numeral in Black, Red or Violet

24 A1 2pi on 2pi ol grn 275.00 82.50
a. On #7a (type II) 1,500.
25 A1 2pi on 2pi ol grn (R) 350.00 87.50
26 A1 2pi on 2pi ol grn (V) 325.00 100.00
27 A1 5pi on 5pi plum 70.00 87.50
a. On #8a (type II) 1,750.
28 A1 9pi on 9pi bister 325.00 375.00
29 A1 9pi on 9pi bister (R) 140.00 150.00

For overprint see No. 83B.

On Nos. 1B-11 (Perf. 14)

13C A1 1/10pi on 1m dk brn 27.50 32.50
a. Pair, one without surcharge 1,700.
14C A1 1/10pi on 1m dk brn (R) 65.00 65.00
15C A1 1/10pi on 1m dk brn (V) 275.00 325.00
16C A1 2/10pi on 2m bl grn 32.50 32.50
a. Pair, one without surcharge 1,700.
b. 3/10pi on 2m bl grn (error) 120.00 120.00
17C A1 2/10pi on 2m bl grn (R) 87.50 87.50
18C A1 2/10pi on 2m bl grn (V) 87.50 87.50
22C A1 5/10pi on 5m org 250.00 110.00
a. Pair, one without surcharge 2,350.
23C A1 5/10pi on 5m org (V) 300.00
23D A1 1pi on 1pi dk blue (R) 225.00 65.00
a. Pair, one without surcharge 2,000.
23E A1 1pi on 1pi dk blue 450.00
29C A1 9pi on 9pi bister 600.00 600.00
31 A1 10pi on 10pi ultra 925.00 1,100.
32 A1 20pi on 20pi gray 700.00 825.00
33 A1 20pi on 20pi gray (V) 1,000. 1,050.

Surcharge in Black on Palestine Nos. 13-14

34 A1 10pi on 10pi ultra 2,000. 2,750.
35 A1 20pi on 20pi gray 2,750. 3,250.

Nos. 13-35 are handstamped, and the overprints exist double on most values. They have been extensively forged. Values above are for expertized examples.

Stamps of 1920 Handstamped in Violet, Black or Red

1922, Dec. *Perf. 14*
On Nos. 1-5, 7-9 (Perf. 15x14)

36 A1 1m dk brn (R) 32.50 32.50
37 A1 1m dk brn (V) 32.50 37.50
38 A1 1m dk brn (Blk) 27.50 27.50
39 A1 2m bl grn (R) 30.00 30.00
40 A1 2m bl grn (V) 26.00 26.00
41 A1 2m bl grn (Blk) 25.00 25.00
42 A1 3m lt brn (R) 52.50 *52.50*
a. On #3a (type II) 1,750.
43 A1 3m lt brn (V) 10.00 10.00
a. Pair, one without surcharge 1,500.
b. On #3a (type II) 1,600. 1,600.
44 A1 3m lt brn (Blk) 11.00 11.00
45 A1 4m scar (R) 65.00 70.00
46 A1 4m scar (V) 65.00 70.00
47 A1 4m scar (Blk) 65.00 70.00
48 A1 5m orange (R) 50.00 13.00
49 A1 5m orange (V) 20.00 13.00
50 A1 2pi ol grn (R) 65.00 50.00
a. On #7a (type II) 1,600.
52 A1 2pi ol grn (V) 27.50 20.00
a. On #7a (type II) 1,600. 1,400.
53 A1 2pi ol grn (Blk) 18.00 13.00
54 A1 5pi plum (R) 110.00 130.00
a. Pair, one without surcharge 1,750.
55 A1 5pi plum (V) 70.00 90.00
56 A1 9pi bister (R) 450.00 500.00
57 A1 9pi bister (V) 225.00 275.00
a. Type II overprint 2,500.
58 A1 9pi bister (Blk) 75.00 90.00

On #1B//11 (Perf. 14)

36C A1 1m dk brn (R) 17.50 22.00
a. Pair, one without ovpt. 1,500.
37C A1 1m dk brn (V) 27.50 25.00
38C A1 1m dk brn (Blk) 25.00 25.00
39C A1 2m bl grn (R) 35.00 35.00
40C A1 2m bl grn (V) 11.00 11.00
41C A1 2m bl grn (Blk) 17.50 17.50
43C A1 3m lt brn (V) 850.00 375.00
48C A1 5m orange (R) 325.00 80.00
49C A1 5m orange (V) 35.00 25.00
51 A1 1pi dark blue (R) 40.00 19.00
51C A1 1pi dark blue (V) 25.00 12.50
52C A1 2pi ol grn (V) 85.00 90.00
54C A1 5pi plum (R) 110.00 120.00
55C A1 5pi plum (V) 110.00 130.00
57C A1 9pi bister (V) 1,000. 1,100.
59 A1 10pi ultra (R) 2,000. 2,100.
60 A1 10pi ultra (V) 1,200. 1,750.
61 A1 20pi gray (R) 1,750. 2,200.
62 A1 20pi gray (V) 1,200. 2,000.

The overprint reads "Hukumat al Sharqi al Arabia" (Arab Government of the East) and date, 1923. The surcharges or overprints on Nos. 12 to 61 inclusive are handstamped and, as usual, are found inverted and double.
Ink pads of several colors were in use at the same time and the surcharges and overprints frequently show a mixture of two colors.
For overprints see Nos. 84, 87, 89, 92-93, 95-96.

Stamps of 1920 Overprinted in Gold or Black

1923, Mar. 1 *Perf. 15x14*

63 A1 1m dark brn (G) 1,600. 1,900.
64 A1 2m blue grn (G) 25.00 27.50
65 A1 3m lt brn (G) 19.00 20.00
a. Double overprint 550.00
b. Inverted overprint 600.00
c. Black overprint 87.50 100.00
66 A1 4m scarlet (Blk) 22.50 20.00
67 A1 5m orange (Blk) 65.00 55.00
a. Original ovpt. albino 1,300. 1,500.
69 A1 2pi ol grn (G) 25.00 22.50
a. On #7a (type II) 1,300. 1,100.
b. Black overprint 275.00 275.00
70 A1 5pi plum (G) 80.00 110.00
a. Inverted overprint 240.00
b. On #8a (type II) 2,200.
c. As "b," inverted ovpt. 2,750.
d. Black overprint inverted 1,600.

Perf. 14

63E A1 1m dark brn (G) 21.00 35.00
a. Inverted overprint 800.00
64E A1 2m blue grn (G) 20.00 22.50
a. Double overprint 325.00
b. Inverted overprint 375.00 375.00
c. Black overprint 325.00
d. As "c," inverted overprint 1,600.
67E A1 5m orange (Blk) 15.00 15.00
68 A1 1pi dk blue (G) 15.00 20.00
a. Double overprint 550.00 *600.00*
b. Black overprint 850.00 *900.00*
71 A1 9pi bister (Blk) 100.00 *140.00*
a. Gold overprint 3,250.
72 A1 10pi ultra (G) 90.00 140.00
73 A1 20pi gray (G) 90.00 140.00
a. Inverted overprint 400.00
b. Double overprint 500.00
c. Double ovpt., one inverted 500.00
d. Double ovpt., one inverted, one gold, one black, black ovpt. inverted 800.00
e. Triple overprint, one inverted 1,200.
f. Black overprint 900.00
g. As "f," inverted overprint 1,200.
h. As "f," double overprint, one inverted 1,400.

The overprint reads "Hukumat al Sharqi al Arabia, Nissan Sanat 921" (Arab Government of the East, April, 1921).
For overprints see Nos. 85, 99, 100, 102.

Stamps of Hejaz, 1922, Overprinted in Black

Coat of Arms (Hejaz A7)

1923, Apr. Unwmk. *Perf. 11½*

74A A7 1/8pi orange brn 5.75 *4.50*
a. Double overprint 225.00
b. Inverted overprint 120.00
74B A7 1/2pi red 5.75 4.50
a. Inverted overprint *125.00*
74C A7 1pi dark blue 4.50 1.50
a. Inverted overprint 140.00 140.00
74D A7 1 1/2pi violet 4.75 *2.75*
a. Double overprint 160.00
b. Pair, one without overprint 250.00
c. Pair, imperf. between 175.00
74E A7 2pi orange 6.00 *8.50*
74F A7 3pi olive brn 15.00 *20.00*
a. Inverted overprint 250.00
b. Double overprint 250.00 250.00
c. Pair, one without overprint *400.00*
74G A7 5pi olive green 35.00 *47.50*
Nos. 64-70 (7) 76.75 *89.25*

The overprint is similar to that on the preceding group but is differently arranged. There are numerous varieties in the Arabic letters.
For overprints see Nos. 71-72, 91, J1-J5.

With Additional Surcharge of New Value in Arabic

a

b

74H A7(a) 1/4pi on 1/8pi 16.00 *11.00*
a. Inverted surcharge 175.00
b. Surcharge doubled — 200.00
c. Inverted surch. & ovpt. 425.00
74I A7(b) 10pi on 5pi 37.50 *42.50*

Independence Issue

Palestine Stamps and Type of 1918 Overprinted Vertically in Black or Gold

1923, May Wmk. 33 *Perf. 15x14*

74J A1 1m dark brn (Bk) 24.00 *24.00*
a. Double ovpt., one reversed 725.00 650.00
74K A1 1m dark brn (G) 175.00 175.00
c. Double ovpt., one reversed 1,000.
74 A1 2m blue grn 42.50 *50.00*
75 A1 3m lt brown 14.00 *17.50*
76 A1 4m scarlet 14.00 *17.50*
77 A1 5m orange 70.00 *80.00*
78 A1 1pi dk blue (G) 95.00 *110.00*
a. Double overprint *750.00* *850.00*
79 A1 2pi olive grn 70.00 *90.00*
80 A1 5pi plum (G) 80.00 *90.00*
a. Double overprint (G) *725.00*
b. Double overprint (Bk) *1,500.*
81 A1 9pi bis, perf. 14 70.00 *85.00*
82 A1 10pi ultra, perf. 14 80.00 *100.00*
83 A1 20pi gray 85.00 *110.00*
Nos. 73-83 (12) 819.50 949.00

The overprint reads, "Arab Government of the East (abbreviated), Souvenir of Independence, 25th, May, 1923 ('923')."
There were printed 480 complete sets and a larger number of the 1, 2, 3 and 4m. A large number of these sets were distributed to high officials. The overprint was in a setting of twenty-four and the error "933" instead of "923" occurs once in the setting. Value about five times the "923" stamps.

The overprint exists reading downward on all values, as illustrated, and reading upward on all except the 5m and 2pi.
Forged overprints exist.
For overprint see No. 101.

Stamps of Preceding Issues, Handstamp Surcharged

83A	A1	2½/ 10ths pi on 5m dp org	240.00	240.00
83B	A1	5/10pi on 3m (#17)	—	120.00
84	A1	5/10pi on 3m (#36)	100.00	60.00
85	A1	5/10pi on 3m (#55)	27.50	40.00
86	A1	5/10pi on 5pi (#23)	85.00	100.00
87	A1	5/10pi on 5pi (#48)	10.00	17.50
88	A1	1pi on 5pi (#23)	75.00	140.00
89	A1	1pi on 5pi (#48)	2,500.	2,750.

Same Surcharge on Palestine Stamp of 1918

90	A1	5/10pi on 3m lt brn	17,000.	

No. 90 is valued in the grade of fine-very fine. Very fine examples are not known.
As is usual with handstamped surcharges these are found double, inverted, etc.

No. 67 Surcharged by Handstamp

Unwmk. ***Perf. 11½***

91	A7	½pi on 1½pi vio	12.00	14.00
a.		Surcharge typographed	55.00	55.00
b.		As "a," inverted surcharge	150.00	
c.		As "a," double surcharge	180.00	
d.		As "a," pair, one with surcharge	500.00	

The surcharge reads: "Nusf el qirsh" (half piastre). See note after No. 90.
Handstamped surcharge exists double; inverted; double, one inverted, etc.

Stamps of Preceding Issues Surcharged by Handstamp

No. 92

Perf. 14, 15x14

1923, Nov. **Wmk. 33**

92	A1	½pi on 2pi (#45)	70.00	85.00
93	A1	½pi on 2pi (#47)	110.00	125.00
94	A1	½pi on 5pi (#23)	75.00	85.00
95	A1	½pi on 5pi (#48)	3,000.	2,000.
96	A1	½pi on 5pi (#49)	2,000.	2,750.
97	A1	½pi on 9pi (#24)	6,500.	
98	A1	½pi on 9pi (#25)	95.00	160.00
99	A1	½pi on 9pi (#61)	200.00	160.00

Surcharged by Handstamp

No. 102

100	A1	1pi on 10pi (#62)	2,250.	2,500.
101	A1	1pi on 10pi (#82)	3,000.	3,000.
102	A1	2pi on 20pi (#63)	70.00	95.00

Of the 25 examples of No. 100, a few were handstamped in violet. Value, unused $2,750.

Stamp of Hejaz, 1922, Overprinted by Handstamp

1923, Dec. **Unwmk.** ***Perf. 11½***

103	A7	½pi red	9.00	5.00

Two settings of No. 103 exist. They differ in the spacing of the characters and the position of the bottom line of the overprint, either to the left or centered.
Nos. 92-103 handstamps exist inverted, doubled, etc.

Stamp of Hejaz, 1922, Overprinted

1924 **Typo.**

104	A7	½pi red	14.00	16.00

King Hussein Issue

Stamps of Hejaz, 1922, Overprinted

1924 **Gold Overprint**

105	A7	½pi red	4.00	4.00
106	A7	1pi dark blue	4.25	3.25
107	A7	1½pi violet	5.00	4.50
108	A7	2pi orange	12.00	13.00

Black Overprint

109	A7	½pi red	3.00	3.00
110	A7	1pi dark blue	3.75	3.75
111	A7	1½pi violet	5.50	5.50
112	A7	2pi orange	13.00	13.00
		Nos. 105-112 (8)	50.50	50.00

The overprint reads: "Arab Government of the East. In commemoration of the visit of H. M. the King of the Arabs, 11 Jemad el Than i 1342 (17th Jan. 1924)." The overprint was in a setting of thirty-six and the error "432" instead of "342" occurs once in the setting and is found on all values. Value, $75 each.

Stamps of Hejaz, 1922-24, Overprinted in Black or Red

Coat of Arms (Hejaz A8)

1924

113	A7	1/8pi red brown	2.00	1.75
a.		Inverted overprint	130.00	—
114	A7	1/4pi yellow green	2.00	1.00
a.		Tête bêche pair	15.00	35.00
b.		As "a," one overprint inverted	300.00	—
c.		Inverted overprint	85.00	—
115	A7	½pi red	2.00	.90
116	A7	1pi dark blue	11.00	1.50
a.		Inverted overprint	—	—
117	A7	1½pi violet	7.00	7.00
118	A7	2pi orange	5.00	3.50
a.		Double overprint	—	—
119	A7	3pi red brown	5.00	5.00
a.		Double overprint	100.00	—
b.		Inverted overprint	100.00	—
120	A7	5pi olive green	7.00	7.00
121	A8	10pi vio & dk brn (R)	15.00	17.50
a.		Pair, one without overprint		
b.		Black overprint	250.00	—
		Nos. 113-121 (9)	56.00	45.15

The overprint reads: "Hukumat al Sharqi al Arabia, 1342." (Arab Government of the East, 1924).

Stamps of Hejaz, 1925, Overprinted in Black or Red

(Hejaz A9)

(Hejaz A10)

(Hejaz A11)

1925, Aug.

122	A9	1/8pi chocolate	1.25	3.50
a.		Inverted overprint	70.00	—
123	A9	1/4pi ultramarine	2.25	5.00
a.		Inverted overprint	70.00	—
124	A9	½pi carmine rose	1.75	1.50
a.		Inverted overprint	70.00	—
125	A10	1pi yellow green	1.75	4.00
126	A10	1½pi orange	4.00	6.50
a.		Inverted overprint	70.00	—
127	A10	2pi deep blue	5.00	9.00
128	A11	3pi dark green (R)	5.50	14.00
a.		Inverted overprint	90.00	—
129	A11	5pi orange brn	8.00	22.00
a.		Inverted overprint	85.00	—
		Nos. 122-129 (8)	29.50	65.50

The overprint reads: "Hukumat al Sharqi al Arabi. 1343 Sanat." (Arab Government of the East, 1925). Nos. 122-129 exist imperforate, and with overprint double.

Type of Palestine, 1918

1925, Nov. 1 **Wmk. 4** ***Perf. 14***

130	A1	1m dark brown	.60	3.50
131	A1	2m yellow	.85	.65
132	A1	3m Prussian bl	2.75	1.60
133	A1	4m rose	2.75	3.75
134	A1	5m orange	3.25	.60
135	A1	6m blue green	2.75	2.75
136	A1	7m yel brown	2.75	2.75
137	A1	8m red	2.75	1.60
138	A1	1pi gray	2.75	.75
139	A1	13m ultramarine	3.50	3.50
140	A1	2pi olive green	4.50	5.00
141	A1	5pi plum	9.50	10.00
142	A1	9pi bister	14.00	27.50
143	A1	10pi light blue	30.00	40.00
144	A1	20pi violet	50.00	90.00
		Nos. 130-144 (15)	132.70	193.95

This overprint reads: "Sharqi al-ardan" (East of Jordan).
For overprints see Nos. J12-J23.

Perf. 15x14

142a	A1	9pi	950.	1,500.
143a	A1	10pi	100.	110.
144a	A1	20pi	1,100.	1,100.
		Nos. 142a-144a (3)	2,150.	2,710.

Amir Abdullah ibn Hussein
A1 A2

1927-29 **Engr.** ***Perf. 14***

145	A1	2(m) Prus blue	2.50	1.25
146	A1	3(m) rose	3.75	3.00
147	A1	4(m) green	4.50	6.50
148	A1	5(m) orange	2.75	.35
149	A1	10(m) red	3.75	6.50
150	A1	15(m) ultra	3.50	.50
151	A1	20(m) olive grn	3.75	4.00
152	A2	50(m) claret	3.75	12.00
153	A2	90(m) bister	9.00	27.50
154	A2	100(m) lt blue	10.00	22.50
155	A2	200(m) violet	17.50	45.00
156	A2	500(m) dp brn ('29)	70.00	100.00
157	A2	1000(m) gray ('29)	165.00	190.00
		Nos. 145-157 (13)	299.75	419.10

For overprints see Nos. 158-168, B1-B12, J24-J29.

Stamps of 1927 Overprinted in Black

1928, Sept. 1

158	A1	2(m) Prus blue	3.00	3.50
159	A1	3(m) rose	3.50	4.50
160	A1	4(m) green	3.50	5.25
161	A1	5(m) orange	3.50	2.50
162	A1	10(m) red	3.75	5.75
163	A1	15(m) ultra	3.75	2.75
164	A1	20(m) olive grn	8.50	14.00
165	A2	50(m) claret	12.00	15.00
166	A2	90(m) bister	22.50	45.00
167	A2	100(m) lt blue	27.50	65.00
168	A2	200(m) violet	85.00	160.00
		Nos. 158-168 (11)	176.50	323.25

The overprint is the Arabic word "Dastour," meaning "Constitution." The stamps were in commemoration of the enactment of the law setting forth the Constitution.

A3

"MILS" or "L. P." at lower right and Arabic equivalents at upper left.

1930-36 **Engr.** ***Perf. 14***

Size: 17¼x21mm

169	A3	1m red brn ('34)	2.00	1.00
170	A3	2m Prus blue	1.00	.60
171	A3	3m rose	1.75	1.00
172	A3	3m green ('34)	2.50	1.25
173	A3	4m green	2.00	4.00
174	A3	4m rose ('34)	4.00	1.50
175	A3	5m orange	1.50	.45
a.		Perf. 13½x14 (coil) ('36)	35.00	20.00
176	A3	10m red	2.25	.25
177	A3	15m ultra	2.25	.30
a.		Perf. 13½x14 (coil) ('36)	32.50	17.50
178	A3	20m olive grn	3.25	.55

Size: 19¼x23½mm

179	A3	50m red violet	4.50	2.25
180	A3	90m bister	4.25	6.25
181	A3	100m light blue	5.00	6.00
182	A3	200m violet	17.50	18.00
183	A3	500m deep brown	32.50	57.50
184	A3	£1 gray	77.50	120.00
		Nos. 169-184 (16)	163.75	220.90

See Nos. 199-220, 230-235. For overprint see No. N15a.

1939 ***Perf. 13½x13***

Size: 17¼x21mm

169a	A3	1m red brown	6.50	4.50
170a	A3	2m Prussian blue	16.00	4.00
172a	A3	3m green	25.00	7.00
174a	A3	4m rose	90.00	29.00
175b	A3	5m orange	75.00	4.50
176a	A3	10m red	150.00	5.75
177b	A3	15m ultramarine	47.50	6.00
178a	A3	20m olive green	72.50	17.50
		Nos. 169a-178a (8)	482.50	78.25

For overprint see No. N3a.

Mushetta — A4

Nymphaeum, Jerash — A5

Kasr Kharana — A6

Kerak Castle — A7

Temple of Artemis, Jerash — A8

Aijalon Castle — A9

Khazneh, Rock-hewn Temple, Petra — A10

Allenby Bridge, River Jordan — A11

Ancient Threshing Floor A12

Amir Abdullah ibn Hussein A13

1933, Feb. 1 ***Perf. 12***

185	A4	1m dk brn & blk	1.75	1.40
186	A5	2m claret & blk	4.00	1.10
187	A6	3m blue green	4.25	1.50
188	A7	4m bister & blk	6.50	3.75
189	A8	5m orange & blk	4.50	3.75
190	A9	10m brown red	7.00	3.50
191	A10	15m dull blue	4.75	1.75
192	A11	20m ol grn & blk	6.75	5.50
193	A12	50m brn vio & blk	20.00	17.50
194	A6	90m yel & black	25.00	27.50
195	A8	100m blue & blk	27.50	35.00
196	A9	200m dk vio & blk	60.00	80.00

197	A10	500m brn & ver	190.00	*275.00*
198	A13	£1 green & blk	650.00	*950.00*
		Nos. 185-198 (14)	1,012.	*1,407.*

Nos. 194-197 are larger than the lower values in the same designs.

Amir Abdullah ibn Hussein — A14

Perf. 13x13½

1942, May 18 Litho. Unwmk.

199	A14	1m dull red brn	1.10	*4.00*
200	A14	2m dull green	2.00	*2.25*
201	A14	3m dp yel green	2.50	*4.50*
202	A14	4m rose pink	2.50	*4.50*
203	A14	5m orange yel	4.25	1.00
204	A14	10m dull ver	6.00	3.25
205	A14	15m deep blue	12.50	4.00
206	A14	20m dull ol grn	22.50	22.50
		Nos. 199-206 (8)	53.35	46.00

Type A14 differs from A3 in the redrawn inscription above the head and in the form of the "millieme" character at upper left.

For overprint see No. N1.

Abdullah Type of 1930-39

White Paper

1943-44 Engr. Wmk. 4 *Perf. 12*

Size: 17¾x21½mm

207	A3	1m red brown	.30	.70
208	A3	2m Prussian grn	1.50	1.25
209	A3	3m blue green	1.25	1.25
210	A3	4m deep rose	1.25	1.25
211	A3	5m orange	1.25	.30
212	A3	10m scarlet	2.25	1.25
213	A3	15m blue	2.25	1.50
214	A3	20m olive ('44)	2.25	1.00

Size: 20x24mm

215	A3	50m red lil ('44)	2.50	1.25
216	A3	90m ocher	5.00	6.00
217	A3	100m dp bl ('44)	6.50	3.00
218	A3	200m dk vio ('44)	8.00	10.00
219	A3	500m dk brn ('44)	11.00	12.50
220	A3	£1 black ('44)	20.00	27.50
		Nos. 207-220 (14)	65.30	68.75

See Nos. 230-235. For overprints see Nos. 255-256, 259, 264-269, RA23, N2-N4, N7, N12-N17.

Catalogue values for unused stamps in this section, from this point to the end of the section, are for Never Hinged items.

Independent Kingdom

Symbols of Peace and Liberty — A15

Perf. 11½

1946, May 25 Unwmk. Litho.

221	A15	1m sepia	.30	.25
222	A15	2m yel orange	.30	.25
223	A15	3m dl ol grn	.30	.25
224	A15	4m lt violet	.30	.25
225	A15	10m orange brn	.30	.25
226	A15	12m rose red	.30	.25
227	A15	20m dark blue	.35	.25
228	A15	50m ultra	.90	.75
229	A15	200m green	3.00	3.00
		Nos. 221-229 (9)	6.05	5.50

Independence of the Kingdom of Trans-Jordan.

Nos. 221-229 exist imperforate.

Abdullah Type of 1930-39

1947 Wmk. 4 Engr. *Perf. 12*

230	A3	3m rose carmine	.40	.30
231	A3	4m deep yel green	.40	.30
232	A3	10m violet	.60	.30
233	A3	12m deep rose	1.10	.80
234	A3	15m dull olive grn	1.25	.90
235	A3	20m deep blue	1.40	1.00
		Nos. 230-235 (6)	5.15	3.60

For overprints see Nos. 257-258, 260-263, RA24-RA25, N5-N6, N8-N11.

Parliament Building, Amman — A16

1947, Nov. 1 Engr. Unwmk.

236	A16	1m purple	.40	.25
237	A16	3m red orange	.40	.25
238	A16	4m yel green	.40	.25
239	A16	10m dk vio brn	.40	.25
240	A16	12m carmine	.40	.25
241	A16	20m deep blue	.50	.25
242	A16	50m red vio	.80	.35
243	A16	100m rose	1.00	.65
244	A16	200m dark green	1.60	1.50
		Nos. 236-244 (9)	5.90	4.00

Founding of the new Trans-Jordan parliament, 1947.

Nos. 236-244 exist imperforate.

Symbols of the UPU — A17

King Abdullah ibn Hussein — A18

1949, Aug. 1 Wmk. 4 *Perf. 13*

245	A17	1m brown	.40	.40
246	A17	4m green	.75	.75
247	A17	10m red	.95	.95
248	A17	20m ultramarine	1.60	1.60
249	A18	50m dull green	2.50	2.50
		Nos. 245-249 (5)	6.20	6.20

UPU, 75th anniv. For overprints see Nos. N18-N22.

Nos. 207-208, 211, 215-220, 230-235 Surcharged in Carmine, Black or Green

1952 Wmk. 4 *Perf. 12*

Size: 17¾x21½mm

255	A3	1f on 1m red brn (Bk)	.50	.50
256	A3	2f on 2m Prus grn	.50	.50
257	A3	3f on 3m rose car (Bk)	.50	.50
258	A3	4f on 4m dp yel grn	.50	.50
259	A3	5f on 5m org (G)	.75	.75
260	A3	10f on 10m vio	1.10	1.00
261	A3	12f on 12m dp rose (Bk)	1.10	1.00
262	A3	15f on 15m dl ol grn	1.40	.75
263	A3	20f on 20m dp bl	2.25	1.10

Size: 20x24mm

264	A3	50f on 50m red lil (G)	2.25	1.75
265	A3	90f on 90m ocher (G)	16.00	11.50
266	A3	100f on 100m dp bl	9.00	3.75
267	A3	200f on 200m dk vio	14.00	4.75
268	A3	500f on 500m dk brn	30.00	15.00
269	A3	1d on £1 black	75.00	20.00
		Nos. 255-269 (15)	154.85	63.35

This surcharge also exists on Nos. 199-203, 205, 209-210, 212-214. Numerous inverted, double and wrong color surcharges exist.

Relief Map — A19

Perf. 13½x13

1952, Apr. 1 Engr. Wmk. 4

270	A19	1f red brn & yel grn	.45	.45
271	A19	2f dk bl grn & red	.45	.45
272	A19	3f car & gray blk	.45	.45
273	A19	4f green & orange	.50	.50
274	A19	5f choc & rose vio	.55	.55
275	A19	10f violet & brown	.55	.55
276	A19	20f dark bl & blk	1.50	.80
277	A19	100f dp blue & brn	5.50	3.50
278	A19	200f purple & orange	13.00	6.75
		Nos. 270-278 (9)	22.95	14.00

Unity of Jordan, Apr. 24, 1950.

For overprints see Nos. 297-305.

Amir Abdullah ibn Hussein — A20

1952 Wmk. 4 *Perf. 11½*

279	A20	5f orange	.50	.50
280	A20	10f violet	.50	.50
281	A20	12f carmine	2.00	1.25
282	A20	15f olive	1.25	.50
283	A20	20f deep blue	1.25	.60

Size: 20x24½mm

Perf. 12x12½

284	A20	50f plum	2.75	1.00
285	A20	90f brn orange	7.50	3.75
286	A20	100f deep blue	8.00	2.50
		Nos. 279-286 (8)	23.75	10.60

Nos. RA5-RA7 Overprinted in Black or Carmine

Perf. 11½x12½

1953 Unwmk. Engr.

286A	PT1	10m carmine	57.50	47.50
286B	PT1	15m gray (C)	4.00	2.00
286C	PT1	20m dark brown	125.00	95.00

Same Overprint on Nos. NRA4-NRA7

286D	PT1	5m plum	80.00	47.50
286E	PT1	10m carmine	80.00	47.50
286F	PT1	15m gray (C)	80.00	47.50
286G	PT1	20m dk brn (C)	80.00	47.50
		Nos. 286A-286G (7)	506.50	334.50

In addition a few sheets of Nos. RA9, NRA1, NRA3, NRA8-NRA9 and RA37-RA41 have been reported with this overprint. It is doubtful whether they were regularly issued. See Nos. 344-347.

1953 Wmk. 4 *Perf. 11½x12½*

287	PT1	5f plum	.45	.25
288	PT1	10f carmine	.55	.25
289	PT1	15f gray (C)	1.25	1.00
290	PT1	20f dark brown (C)	2.75	1.50
		Nos. 287-290 (4)	5.00	3.00

King Hussein — A21

Unwmk.

1953, Oct. 1 Engr. *Perf. 12*

Portrait in Black

291	A21	1f dark green	.35	.25
292	A21	4f deep plum	.35	.25
293	A21	15f deep ultra	2.00	.40
294	A21	20f dark purple	3.25	.40
295	A21	50f dark blue grn	7.00	3.25
296	A21	100f dark blue	12.50	9.00
		Nos. 291-296 (6)	25.45	13.55

Accession of King Hussein, May 2, 1953.

Nos. 270-278 Overprinted in Black

1½mm Spacing

Nos. RA28-RA31 Overprinted in Black or Carmine ½mm Spacing

1953 Wmk. 4 *Perf. 13½x13*

297	A19	1f red brn & yel grn	.40	.40
298	A19	2f dk bl grn & red	.40	.40
299	A19	3f car & gray blk	.40	.40
300	A19	4f green & orange	.40	.40
301	A19	5f choc & rose vio	.40	.40
302	A19	10f violet & brown	1.25	.75
303	A19	20f dark bl & blk	1.25	.95
304	A19	100f dp blue & brn	7.25	1.75
305	A19	200f purple & org	10.00	6.50
		Nos. 297-305 (9)	21.75	11.95

Two main settings of the bars exist on Nos. 297-300 and 304 — the "normal" 1½mm spacing, and the "narrow" ½mm spacing. Values above are for normal spacing. Value of set with narrow spacing, $150.

El Deir Temple, Petra — A22

King Hussein — A22a

Dome of the Rock — A23

Al Aqsa Mosque — A23a

Designs: 4f, 500f, 1d, King Hussein. 3f, 5f, Treasury Bldg., Petra. 50f, 100f, 200f, Al Aqsa Mosque. 20f, Dome of the Rock.

1954 Unwmk. Engr. *Perf. 12½*

306	A22	1f dk bl grn & red brn	.35	.25
307	A22a	2f red & black	.35	.25
308	A22	3f dp redsh pur & vio bl	.35	.25
309	A22a	4f org brn & dk grn	.50	.30
310	A22	5f vio & dk grn	.50	.30
311	A23	10f pur & dk grn	.75	.75
312	A23a	12f car rose & sep	1.75	.70
313	A23	20f bl & gray grn	1.75	.35
314	A23a	50f dk bl & dp rose	3.75	1.25
315	A23a	100f dk grn & bl	3.25	.75
316	A23a	200f dp cl & pck bl	13.00	2.25
317	A22a	500f choc & purple	37.50	12.50
318	A22a	1d dk ol grn & rose brn	55.00	22.50
		Nos. 306-318 (13)	118.80	42.40

See Nos. 324-337. For overprint see No. 425.

Globe — A23b

Perf. 13½x13

1955, Jan. 1 Photo. Wmk. 195

319	A23b	15f green	.60	.45
320	A23b	20f violet	.60	.45
321	A23b	25f yellow brown	.75	.70
		Nos. 319-321 (3)	1.95	1.60

Founding of the APU, July 1, 1954.

Princess Dina Abdul Hamid and King Hussein A24

1955, Apr. 19 *Perf. 11x11½*

322	A24	15f ultramarine	2.25	.95
323	A24	100f rose brown	8.50	3.75

Marriage of King Hussein and Princess Dina Abdul Hamid.

Types of 1954

Design: 15f, Dome of the Rock.

Wmk. 305

1955-64 Engr. *Perf. 12½*

324	A22	1f dk bl grn & red brn ('57)	.40	.25
325	A22	2f red & blk ('57)	.40	.25
326	A22	3f dp plum & vio bl ('56)	.40	.25
327	A22	4f org brn & dk grn ('56)	.40	.25

328 A22 5f vio & dk grn ('56) .40 .25
329 A23 10f pur & grn ('57) 3.75 2.25
330 A23 12f car rose & sep 1.50 1.00
331 A23 15f dp brn & rose red .90 .25
332 A23 20f dp bl & dk grn ('57) .75 .25
333 A23 50f dk bl & dp rose 1.40 .35
334 A23 100f dk grn & dp bl ('62) 3.50 1.25
335 A23 200f dp cl & pck bl ('65) 9.50 2.25
336 A22 500f choc & pur ('65) 32.50 12.00
337 A22 1d dk ol grn & rose brn ('65) 57.50 20.00
Nos. 324-337 (14) 113.30 40.85

Envelope — A25

Wmk. 305

1956, Jan. 15 Engr. *Perf. 14*

"Postmarks" in Black

338 A25 1f light brown .35 .30
339 A25 4f dark car rose .35 .30
340 A25 15f blue .35 .30
341 A25 20f yellow olive .35 .30
342 A25 50f slate blue .75 .40
343 A25 100f vermilion 1.10 .70
Nos. 338-343 (6) 3.25 2.30

1st Arab Postal Congress in Amman.

Nos. RA1, RA3, RA8 and RA33 Overprinted in Carmine or Black

Perf. 11½x12½

1956, Jan. 5 Unwmk.

344 PT1 1m ultramarine .45 .45
345 PT1 3m emerald .45 .45
346 PT1 50m purple 1.10 1.00

Wmk. 4

347 PT1 100f orange (Bk) 6.75 3.50
Nos. 344-347 (4) 8.75 5.40

Numerous inverted, double and wrong color surcharges exist.

Torch of Liberty — A26

1958 Wmk. 305 Engr. *Perf. 12½*

348 A26 5f blue & red brown .35 .35
349 A26 15f bister brn & blk .45 .40
350 A26 35f blue grn & plum 1.00 .90
351 A26 45f car & olive grn 3.25 1.00
Nos. 348-351 (4) 5.05 2.65

10th anniv. of the Universal Declaration of Human Rights.

King Hussein — A27

Perf. 12x11½

1959 Wmk. 305 Engr.

Centers in Black

352 A27 1f deep green .35 .25
353 A27 2f violet .35 .25
354 A27 3f deep carmine .40 .25
355 A27 4f brown black .45 .25
356 A27 7f dark green .55 .25
357 A27 12f deep carmine .75 .25
358 A27 15f dark red .80 .25
359 A27 21f green .90 .25
360 A27 25f ocher 1.10 .25
361 A27 35f dark blue 1.75 .30
362 A27 40f olive green 2.50 .30
363 A27 50f red 3.00 .30
364 A27 100f blue green 4.00 .75
365 A27 200f rose lake 11.00 3.00
366 A27 500f gray blue 26.00 12.00
367 A27 1d dark purple 50.00 30.00
Nos. 352-367 (16) 103.90 48.90

For overprints see Nos. 423-424, 425a, 426-427.

Arab League Center, Cairo, and King Hussein — A28

Perf. 13x13½

1960, Mar. 22 Photo. Wmk. 328

368 A28 15f dull green & blk .35 .25

Opening of the Arab League Center and the Arab Postal Museum in Cairo.

World Refugee Year Emblem — A29

Wmk. 305

1960, Apr. 7 Litho. *Perf. 13½*

369 A29 15f pale blue & red .35 .25
370 A29 35f bister & blue .60 .45

World Refugee Year, 7/1/59-6/30/60. For overprints see Nos. 377-378.

Shah of Iran, King Hussein and Flags — A30

Perf. 13x13½

1960, May 15 Wmk. 305

Flags in Green, Red & Black

371 A30 15f yellow & black .55 .55
372 A30 35f blue & black .80 .80
373 A30 50f salmon & black 1.10 1.10
Nos. 371-373 (3) 2.45 2.45

Visit of Mohammed Riza Pahlavi, Shah of Iran, to Jordan, Nov. 2, 1959.

Oil Refinery, Zarka — A31

1961, May 1 Engr. *Perf. 14x13*

374 A31 15f dull vio & blue .35 .25
375 A31 35f dl vio & brick red .55 .40

Opening of oil refinery at Zarka.

Urban and Nomad Families and Chart — A32

Perf. 13x13½

1961, Oct. 15 Photo. Unwmk.

376 A32 15f orange brown .30 .25

First Jordanian census, 1961.

Nos. 369-370 Overprinted in English and Arabic, "In Memorial of Dag Hammarskjoeld 1904-1961," and Laurel Leaf Border

1961 Wmk. 305 Litho. *Perf. 13½*

377 A29 15f pale blue & red 4.00 3.75
378 A29 35f bister & blue 4.50 4.00

Dag Hammarskjold, Secretary General of the UN, 1953-1961.

Malaria Eradication Emblem — A33

Perf. 11x11½

1962, Apr. 15 Unwmk.

379 A33 15f bright pink .35 .25
380 A33 35f blue .45 .30

WHO drive to eradicate malaria. A souvenir sheet exists perf. and imperf. with one each of Nos. 379-380. Value, $5.50, perf. and imperf.

Dial and Exchange Building, Amman — A34

1962, Dec. 11 Engr. Wmk. 305

381 A34 15f blue & lilac .30 .25
382 A34 35f lilac & emer .35 .25

Telephone automation in Amman (in 1960).

Opening of the Port of 'Aqaba — A35

1962, Dec. 11

383 A35 15f lilac & blk .40 .25
384 A35 35f violet bl & blk .60 .30
a. Souvenir sheet of 2, #383-384 5.00 5.00

No. 384a imperf., same value.

Dag Hammarskjold and UN Headquarters, NY — A36

Perf. 14x14½

1963, Jan. 24 Photo. Unwmk.

385 A36 15f ultra, ol grn & brn red .45 .25
386 A36 35f ol, brn red & ultra .80 .45
387 A36 50f brn red, ol & ultra 1.25 .80
Nos. 385-387 (3) 2.50 1.50

17th anniv. of the UN and in memory of Dag Hammarskjold, Secretary General of the UN, 1953-61. An imperf. souvenir sheet contains one each of Nos. 385-387 with simulated perforations. Value $9.

Imperforates

Starting with No. 385, imperforates exist of many Jordanian stamps.

Church of St. Virgin's Tomb, Jerusalem — A37

Designs: No. 389, Basilica of the Agony, Gethsemane. No. 390, Church of the Holy Sepulcher, Jerusalem. No. 391, Church of the Nativity, Bethlehem. No. 392, Haram el-Khalil (tomb of Abraham), Hebron. No. 393, Dome of the Rock, Jerusalem. No. 394, Mosque of Omar el-Khatab, Jerusalem. No. 395, Al Aqsa Mosque, Jerusalem.

1963, Feb. 5 *Perf. 14½x14*

Center Multicolored

388 A37 50f blue 1.50 1.00
389 A37 50f dull red 1.50 1.00
390 A37 50f bright blue 1.50 1.00
391 A37 50f olive green 1.50 1.00
a. Vert. strip of 4, #388-391 15.00 —
392 A37 50f gray 1.50 1.00
a. Yellow (in center) omitted —
393 A37 50f purple 1.50 1.00
a. Yellow (in center) omitted —
394 A37 50f dull red 1.50 1.00
a. Yellow (in center) omitted —
395 A37 50f light purple 1.50 1.00
a. Vert. strip of 4, #392-395 15.00 —
b. Yellow (in center) omitted —
Nos. 388-395 (8) 12.00 8.00

Arab League Building, Cairo — A38

1963, July 16 Photo. *Perf. 13½x13*

396 A38 15f slate blue .45 .25
397 A38 35f orange red .65 .25

Arab League.

Wheat and UN Emblem — A39

Perf. 11½x12½

1963, Sept. 15 Litho. Wmk. 305

398 A39 15f lt bl, grn & black .30 .25
399 A39 35f lt grn, grn & blk .30 .25
a. Souvenir sheet of 2, #398-399 1.50 1.50

FAO "Freedom from Hunger" campaign. No. 399a imperf., same value.

East Ghor Canal, Pylon, Gear Wheel and Wheat — A40

1963, Sept. 20 *Perf. 14½x14*

400 A40 1f dull yel & black .35 .25
401 A40 4f blue & black .35 .25
402 A40 5f lilac & black .35 .25
403 A40 10f brt yel grn & blk .40 .25
404 A40 35f orange & black 1.25 .50
Nos. 400-404 (5) 2.70 1.50

East Ghor Canal Project.

UNESCO Emblem, Scales and Globe — A41

Perf. 13½x13

1963, Dec. 10 Unwmk.

405 A41 50f pale vio bl & red .70 .60
406 A41 50f rose red & blue .70 .60

15th anniv. of the Universal Declaration of Human Rights.

Red Crescent and King Hussein A42

1963, Dec. 24 Photo. *Perf. 14x14½*

407 A42 1f red & red lilac .30 .25
408 A42 2f red & bl green .30 .25
409 A42 3f red & dk blue .30 .25
410 A42 4f red & dk green .30 .25
411 A42 5f red & dk brown .30 .25
412 A42 85f red & dp green 1.10 .95

Design: Red Cross at right, no portrait

413 A42 1f red lilac & red .30 .25
414 A42 2f blue grn & red .30 .25
415 A42 3f dk blue & red .30 .25
416 A42 4f dk green & red .30 .25
417 A42 5f dk brown & red .30 .25
418 A42 85f dp green & red 4.00 1.50
Nos. 407-418 (12) 8.10 4.95

Centenary of the Intl. Red Cross. Two 100f imperf. souvenir sheets, red and red lilac, exist in the Red Crescent and Red Cross designs. Value, pair of sheets $50.

Hussein ibn Ali and King Hussein — A43

Perf. 11x11½

1963, Dec. 25 Litho. Unwmk.

419	A43 15f yellow & multi	.50	.25
420	A43 25f multicolored	.75	.35
421	A43 35f brt pink & multi	1.75	.85
422	A43 50f lt blue & multi	2.75	2.00
	Nos. 419-422 (4)	5.75	3.45

Arab Renaissance Day, June 10, 1916. Perf. and imperf. souvenir sheets exist containing one each of Nos. 419-422. Value: perf, $6.50; imperf, $9.

Nos. 359, 312, 357 and 361 Surcharged

Wmk. 305, Unwmk.

Perf. 12x11½, 12½

1963, Dec. 16 Engr.

423	A27 1f on 21f grn & blk	.40	.30
424	A27 2f on 21f grn & blk	.40	.30
425	A23 4f on 12f car rose & sepia	.45	.40
a.	4f on 12f dp car & blk (#357)	19.00	*22.50*
426	A27 5f on 21f grn & blk	.85	.50
427	A27 25f on 35f dk bl & blk	3.25	1.50
	Nos. 423-427 (5)	5.35	*3.00*

Pope Paul VI, King Hussein and Al Aqsa Mosque, Jerusalem — A44

Portraits and: 35f, Dome of the Rock. 50f, Church of the Holy Sepulcher. 80f, Church of the Nativity, Bethlehem.

1964, Jan. 4 Litho. *Perf. 13x13½*

428	A44 15f emerald & blk	.80	.30
429	A44 35f car rose & blk	1.00	.40
a.	Black omitted	—	
430	A44 50f brown & black	1.75	.90
431	A44 80f vio bl & blk	3.25	2.00
	Nos. 428-431 (4)	6.80	3.60

Visit of Pope Paul VI to the Holy Land, Jan. 4-6. An imperf. souvenir sheet contains 4 stamps similar to Nos. 428-431. Value $27.50

A45

Crown Prince Abdullah ben Al-Hussein A46

Design: 5f, Crown Prince standing, vert.

1964, Mar. 30 Photo. *Perf. 14*

432	A46 5f multicolored	.55	.25
433	A45 10f multicolored	.65	.50
434	A46 35f multicolored	1.50	1.00
	Nos. 432-434 (3)	2.70	1.75

2nd birthday of Crown Prince Abdullah ben Al-Hussein (b. Jan. 30, 1962).

Nos. 433 and 434 exist with gold color omitted.

A47

Mercury Astronauts, Spacecraft — A48

Designs: b, M. Scott Carpenter. c, Entering space. d, Alan Shepard. e, At launch pad. f, Virgil Grissom. g, After separation. h, Walter Schirra. i, Lift-off. j, John Glenn. Stamp has point down on b, d, f, h, j.

1964, Mar. 25 Photo. *Perf. 14*

435	A47 20f Block of 10, #a.-j.	12.00	6.50

Imperf

Size: 111x80mm

436	A48 100f multicolored	20.00	20.00

1964 Olympic Games, Tokyo — A49

Designs: 1f, 2f, 3f, 5f vertical.

Perf. 14½x14, 14x14½

1964, June 1 Litho. Unwmk.

446	A49 1f Basketball	.50	.25
447	A49 2f Volleyball	.50	.25
448	A49 3f Soccer	.50	.25
449	A49 4f Table Tennis	.50	.25
450	A49 5f Running	.50	.25
451	A49 35f Bicycling	1.75	1.10
452	A49 50f Fencing	2.50	1.50
453	A49 100f Pole vault	4.50	2.75
	Nos. 446-453 (8)	11.25	6.60

Oct. 10-25. An imperf. 200f greenish blue souvenir sheet in design of 100f exists. Value $35.

Mother and Child — A50

1964, June 1 Wmk. 305 *Perf. 14*

454	A50 5f multicolored	.30	.25
455	A50 10f multicolored	.30	.25
456	A50 25f multicolored	.30	.25
	Nos. 454-456 (3)	.90	.75

Social Studies Seminar, fourth session.

Pres. John F. Kennedy A51

1964, July 15 Unwmk.

457	A51 1f brt violet	.50	.40
458	A51 2f carmine rose	.50	.40
459	A51 3f ultramarine	.50	.40
460	A51 4f orange brown	.50	.40
461	A51 5f bright green	.50	.40
462	A51 85f rose red	18.50	11.00
	Nos. 457-462 (6)	21.00	13.00

President John F. Kennedy (1917-1963). An imperf. 100f brown souvenir sheet exists. Size of stamp: 58x83mm. Value $18.50.

Ramses II — A52

Perf. 14½x14

1964, July Litho. Wmk. 305

463	A52 4f lt blue & dark brn	.30	.25
464	A52 15f yellow & violet	.30	.25
465	A52 25f lt yel grn & dk red	.30	.25
	Nos. 463-465 (3)	.90	.75

UNESCO world campaign to save historic monuments in Nubia.

King Hussein and Map of Jordan and Israel — A53

1964, Sept. 5 Unwmk. *Perf. 12*

466	A53 10f multicolored	.40	.25
467	A53 15f multicolored	.40	.25
468	A53 25f multicolored	.40	.25
469	A53 50f multicolored	.70	.25
470	A53 80f multicolored	1.00	.45
	Nos. 466-470 (5)	2.90	1.45

Council of the Heads of State of the Arab League (Arab Summit Conference), Cairo, Jan. 13, 1964. An imperf. souvenir sheet contains Nos. 466-470 with simulated perforations. Value $4.

Pope Paul VI, King Hussein and Patriarch Athenagoras; Church of St. Savior, Church of the Holy Sepulcher and Dome of the Rock — A54

1964, Aug. 17 Litho.

471	A54 10f dk grn, sep & org	.50	.25
472	A54 15f claret, sep & org	.50	.25
473	A54 25f choc, sepia & org	.50	.25
474	A54 50f blue, sepia & org	1.00	.70
475	A54 80f brt grn, sep & org	2.25	.60
	Nos. 471-475 (5)	4.75	2.05

Meeting between Pope Paul VI and Patriarch Athenagoras of the Greek Orthodox Church in Jerusalem, Jan. 5, 1964. An imperf. souvenir sheet contains Nos. 471-475 with simulated perforations. Value $12.

A two-line bilingual overprint, "Papa Paulus VI World Peace Visit to United Nations 1965", was applied to Nos. 471-475 and the souvenir sheet. These overprints were issued Apr. 27, 1966. Value, unused: set, $6; souvenir sheet, $12.

Pagoda, Olympic Torch and Emblem A55

1964, Nov. 21 Litho. *Perf. 14*

476	A55 1f dark red	.45	.25
477	A55 2f bright violet	.55	.25
478	A55 3f blue green	.65	.25
479	A55 4f brown	.75	.30
480	A55 5f henna brown	.85	.35
481	A55 35f indigo	1.25	1.00
482	A55 50f olive	2.00	1.50
483	A55 100f violet blue	4.25	3.00
	Nos. 476-483 (8)	10.75	6.90

18th Olympic Games, Tokyo, Oct. 10-25. An imperf. 100f carmine rose souvenir sheet exists. Size of stamp: 82mm at the base. Value $20.

Scouts Crossing Stream on Log Bridge A56

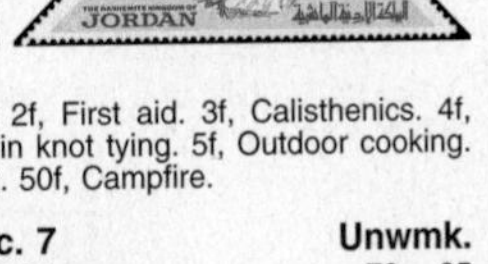

Designs: 2f, First aid. 3f, Calisthenics. 4f, Instruction in knot tying. 5f, Outdoor cooking. 35f, Sailing. 50f, Campfire.

1964, Dec. 7 Unwmk.

484	A56 1f brown	.70	.25
485	A56 2f bright violet	.70	.25
486	A56 3f ocher	.70	.25
487	A56 4f maroon	.70	.25
488	A56 5f yellow green	.70	.25
489	A56 35f bright blue	2.00	1.25
490	A56 50f dk slate green	3.50	1.75
	Nos. 484-490 (7)	9.00	4.25

Jordanian Boy Scouts. An imperf. 100f dark blue souvenir sheet in campfire design exists. Size of stamp: 104mm at the base. Value $22.50.

Russian Cosmonauts — A57

Designs: No. 491, Yuri Gagarin. No. 492, Gherman Titov. No. 493, Andrian G. Nikolayev. No. 494, Pavel R. Popovich. No. 495, Valeri Bykovski. No. 496, Valentina Tereshkova.

1965, Jan. 20 Litho. *Perf. 14*

491	A57 40f sepia & vio bl	1.25	.75
492	A57 40f pink & dk grn	1.25	.75
493	A57 40f lt bl & vio blk	1.25	.75
494	A57 40f olive & dk vio	1.25	.75
495	A57 40f lt grn & red brn	1.25	.75
496	A57 40f chlky bl & blk	1.25	.75
	Nos. 491-496 (6)	7.50	4.50

Russian cosmonauts. A blue 100f souvenir sheet exists showing portraits of the 6 astronauts and space-ship circling globe. This sheet received later an additional overprint honoring the space flight of Komarov, Feoktistov and Yegorov. Value $20, each.

For overprints see Nos. 527-527E.

UN Headquarters and Emblem A58

1965, Feb. 15 *Perf. 14x15*

497	A58 30f yel brn, pur & lt bl	.60	.25
498	A58 70f vio, lt bl & yel brn	1.00	.70

19th anniv. of the UN (in 1964). A souvenir sheet contains Nos. 497-498, imperf. Value $14.

Dagger in Map of Palestine — A59

1965, Apr. 9 Photo. *Perf. 11x11½*

499	A59 25f red & olive	4.50	1.25
a.	Red omitted	—	

Deir Yassin massacre, Apr. 9, 1948.

See Iraq Nos. 372-373 and Kuwait Nos. 281-282.

Volleyball Player and Cup — A60

1965, June Litho. *Perf. 14½x14*

500	A60 15f lemon	1.25	.25
501	A60 35f rose brown	1.50	.25
502	A60 50f greenish blue	2.25	.75
	Nos. 500-502 (3)	5.00	1.25

Arab Volleyball Championships. An imperf. 100f orange brown souvenir sheet exists. Size of stamp: 33x57mm. Value $22.50.

Cavalry Horsemanship — A61

Army Day: 10f, Tank. 35f, King Hussein and aides standing in army car.

1965, May 24

503	A61	5f green	.50	.25
504	A61	10f violet blue	.55	.25
505	A61	35f brown red	1.50	.55
		Nos. 503-505 (3)	2.55	1.05

John F. Kennedy A62

1965, June 1 Wmk. 305 *Perf. 14*

506	A62	10f black & brt green	.30	.25
507	A62	15f violet & orange	.50	.25
508	A62	25f brown & lt blue	.50	.30
509	A62	50f deep claret & emer	1.50	.60
		Nos. 506-509 (4)	2.80	1.40

John F. Kennedy (1917-63). An imperf. 50f salmon and dark blue souv. sheet exists. Value $17.50.

Pope Paul VI, King Hussein and Dome of the Rock — A63

Perf. 13½x14

1965, June 15 Litho. Wmk. 305

510	A63	5f brown & rose lil	.50	.25
511	A63	10f vio brn & lt yel grn	.90	.40
512	A63	15f ultra & salmon	1.10	.50
513	A63	50f black & rose	3.25	1.60
		Nos. 510-513 (4)	5.75	2.75

1st anniversary of the visit of Pope Paul VI to the Holy Land. An imperf. 50f violet and light blue souvenir sheet exists with simulated perforations. Value $25.

Jordan's Pavilion and Unisphere — A64

Perf. 14x13½

1965, Aug. Unwmk. Photo.

514	A64	15f silver & multi	.45	.25
515	A64	25f bronze & multi	.45	.25
516	A64	50f gold & multi	.85	.40
a.		Souvenir sheet of 1, 100f	3.25	3.00
		Nos. 514-516 (3)	1.75	.90

New York World's Fair, 1964-65.
No. 516a contains a 100f gold and multicolored stamp, type A64, imperf.

Library Aflame and Lamp — A64a

1965, Aug. Wmk. 305 *Perf. 11½x11*

517	A64a	25f black, grn & red	.50	.25

Burning of the Library of Algiers, 6/7/62.

ITU Emblem, Old and New Telecommunication Equipment — A65

1965, Aug. Litho. *Perf. 14x13½*

518	A65	25f lt blue & dk bl	.40	.25
519	A65	45f grnsh gray & blk	.60	.35

ITU, centenary. An imperf. 100f salmon and carmine rose souvenir sheet exists with carmine rose border. Size of stamp: 39x32mm. Value $3.

Syncom Satellite over Pagoda — A66

Designs: 10f, 20f, Rocket in space. 15f, Astronauts in cabin.

1965, Sept. *Perf. 14*

521	A66	5f multicolored	.30	.25
521A	A66	10f multicolored	.30	.25
521B	A66	15f multicolored	.50	.25
521C	A66	20f multicolored	.60	.30
521D	A66	50f multicolored	1.50	.75
		Nos. 521-521D (5)	3.20	1.80

Achievements in space research. A 50f multicolored imperf. souvenir sheet shows earth and Syncom satellite. Value $17.50.

Dead Sea — A66a

Designs: b, Qumran Caves. c, Dead Sea. d, Dead Sea Scrolls.

1965, Sept. 23 Photo. *Perf. 14*

522	A66a	35f Strip of 4, #a.-d.	6.00	6.00

Visit of King Hussein to France and U.S. — A66b

10f, With Charles DeGaulle. 20f, With Lyndon Johnson.

Wmk. 305

1965, Oct. 5 Litho. *Perf. 14*

523	A66b	5f shown	.30	.25
523A	A66b	10f multicolored	.30	.25
523B	A66b	20f multicolored	.65	.50
523C	A66b	50f like #523	1.50	1.10
		Nos. 523-523C (4)	2.75	2.10

No. 523C exists in a 50f imperf. souvenir sheet. Value $12.

Intl. Cooperation Year — A66c

1965, Oct. 24 *Perf. 14x13½*

524	A66c	5f brt org & dk org	.40	.25
524A	A66c	10f brt bl & dk bl	.75	.35
524B	A66c	45f brt grn & dk violet	2.10	1.40
		Nos. 524-524B (3)	3.25	2.00

Arab Postal Union, 10th Anniv. — A66d

1965, Nov. 5 *Perf. 15x14*

525	A66d	15f violet bl & blk	.30	.25
525A	A66d	25f brt yel grn & blk	.50	.35

Dome of the Rock — A66e

1965, Nov. 20 *Perf. 14x15*

526	A66e	15f multicolored	1.10	1.10
526A	A66e	25f multicolored	1.60	1.60

Nos. 491-496 with Spaceship & Bilingual Ovpt. in Blue

1966, Jan. 15 Litho. *Perf. 14*

527	A57	40f on No. 491	3.75	3.50
527A	A57	40f on No. 492	3.75	3.50
527B	A57	40f on No. 493	3.75	3.50
527C	A57	40f on No. 494	3.75	3.50
527D	A57	40f on No. 495	3.75	3.50
527E	A57	40f on No. 496	3.75	3.50
		Nos. 527-527E (6)	22.50	21.00

Both souvenir sheets mentioned after No. 496 exist overprinted in red violet. Value, $50 each.

King Hussein A67

Perf. 14½x14

1966, Jan. 15 Photo. Unwmk.

Portrait in Slate Blue

528	A67	1f orange	.40	.25
528A	A67	2f ultramarine	.40	.25
528B	A67	3f dk purple	.40	.25
528C	A67	4f plum	.40	.25
528D	A67	7f brn orange	.40	.25
528E	A67	12f cerise	.40	.25
528F	A67	15f olive brn	.40	.25

Portrait in Violet Brown

528G	A67	21f green	.55	.25
528H	A67	25f greenish bl	.55	.25
528I	A67	35f yel bister	.80	.35
528J	A67	40f orange yel	1.00	.35
528K	A67	50f olive grn	1.10	.25
528L	A67	100f lt yel grn	2.10	.40
528M	A67	150f violet	3.00	1.00
		Nos. 528-528M,C43-C45 (17)	46.90	27.10

Anti-tuberculosis Campaign — A67a

1966, May 17 Photo. *Perf. 14x15*

Blue Overprint

529	A67a	15f multicolored	.65	.50
529A	A67a	35f multicolored	1.10	.95
529B	A67a	50f multicolored	1.50	1.25
		Nos. 529-529B (3)	3.25	2.70

Unissued Freedom from Hunger stamps overprinted. Two imperf. souvenir sheets exist, one with simulated perforations. Value, each $10.

Nos. 529-529B with Added Surcharge Obliterated with Black Bars

1966, May 17 Photo. *Perf. 14x15*

530	A67a	15f on 15f + 15f	.75	.30
530A	A67a	35f on 35f + 35f	1.50	.75
530B	A67a	50f on 50f + 50f	2.75	1.25
		Nos. 530-530B (3)	5.00	2.30

A67b

Stations on Jesus' walk to Calvary along Via Dolorosa (Stations of the Cross): 1f, Condemned to death. 2f, Takes up cross. 3f, Falls the 1st time. 4f, Meets His mother. 5f, Simon helps carry cross. 6f, Woman wipes Jesus' brow. 7f, Falls 2nd time. 8f, Tells women not to weep. 9f, Falls 3rd time. 10f, Stripped of His garment. 11f, Nailed to cross. 12f, Death on cross. 13f, Removal from cross. 14f, Burial.
Denominations expressed in Roman numerals.

1966, Sept. 14 Photo. *Perf. 15x14*

531	A67b	1f multi	.40	.25
531A	A67b	2f multi	.40	.25
531B	A67b	3f multi	.40	.25
531C	A67b	4f multi	.50	.25
531D	A67b	5f multi	.60	.30
531E	A67b	6f multi	.60	.30
531F	A67b	7f multi	.80	.40
531G	A67b	8f multi	.90	.45
531H	A67b	9f multi	1.00	.50
531I	A67b	10f multi	1.10	.55
531J	A67b	11f multi	1.25	.60
531K	A67b	12f multi	1.40	.65
531L	A67b	13f multi	1.50	.70
531M	A67b	14f multi	1.60	.75
		Nos. 531-531M (14)	12.45	6.20

Souvenir Sheet

Imperf

531N	A67b	100f like #531	*30.00*	*27.50*

A67c

Astronauts and spacecraft from Gemini Missions 6-8: 1f, Walter M. Schirra. 2f, Thomas P. Stafford. 3f, Frank Borman. 4f, James A. Lovell. 30f, Neil Armstrong. 60f, David R. Scott.
100f, Gemini 6-8 astronauts.

1966, Nov. 15 Photo. *Perf. 15x14*

532	A67c	1f multi	.35	.25
532A	A67c	2f multi	.35	.25
532B	A67c	3f multi	.35	.25
532C	A67c	4f multi	.35	.25
532D	A67c	30f multi	1.50	.70
532E	A67c	60f multi	2.10	1.50
		Nos. 532-532E (6)	5.00	3.20

Imperf

Size: 119x89mm

532F	A67c	100f multi	*22.50*	*20.00*

Christmas — A67d

5f, Magi following star. 10f, Adoration of the Magi. 35f, Flight to Egypt, vert.

Perf. 14x15, 15x14

1966, Dec. 21 **Photo.**

533	A67d	5f multi	.35	.25
533A	A67d	10f multi	.35	.25
533B	A67d	35f multi	3.25	1.10
		Nos. 533-533B (3)	3.95	1.60

Souvenir Sheet

Imperf

533C	A67d	50f like #533A	*22.50*	*20.00*

King Hussein — A67e

Builders of World Peace: No. 534, Dag Hammarskjold. No. 534A, U Thant. No. 534B, Jawaharlal Nehru. No. 534C, Charles DeGaulle. No. 534D, John F. Kennedy. No. 534E, Lyndon B. Johnson. No. 534F, Pope John XXIII. No. 534G, Pope Paul VI. No. 534H, King Abdullah of Jordan.

1967, Jan. 5 **Photo.** ***Perf. 15x14***

Background Color

534	A67e	5f gray	.35	.25
534A	A67e	5f brt yel grn	.35	.25
534B	A67e	10f rose lilac	.35	.25
a.		"FILS" omitted	—	
534C	A67e	10f red brown	.35	.25
534D	A67e	35f olive green	.95	.70
534E	A67e	35f orange	.95	.70
a.		Gold (frame) omitted	—	
534F	A67e	50f rose claret	1.10	1.00
534G	A67e	50f yel bister	1.10	1.00
534H	A67e	100f brt blue	2.50	2.10
534I	A67e	100f dull blue	2.50	2.10
		Nos. 534-534I (10)	10.50	8.60

Imperf

Size: 99x64mm

534J	A67e	100f Kennedy, etc.	*22.50*	*22.50*
534K	A67e	100f DeGaulle, etc.	*22.50*	*22.50*

King Hussein — A67f

Photo. & Embossed

1967, Feb. 7 ***Imperf.***

Gold Portrait and Border

Diameter: 50f, 100f, 48mm; 200f, 54mm

Portrait of King Hussein

535	A67f	5f dk bl & sal	.75	.75
535A	A67f	10f pur & sal	.75	.75
535B	A67f	50f blk brn & vio	4.25	4.25
535C	A67f	100f dk ol grn & pink	5.00	5.00
535D	A67f	200f dp bl & bl	7.75	7.75

Portrait of Crown Prince Hassan

536	A67f	5f brt yel grn & blk	.75	.75
536A	A67f	10f vio & blk	.75	.75
536B	A67f	50f bl & blk	4.25	4.25
536C	A67f	100f bister & blk	5.00	5.00
536D	A67f	200f brt pink & blk	7.75	7.75

Portrait of John F. Kennedy

537	A67f	5f brt bl & lt grn	.75	.75
537A	A67f	10f dp grn & pink	.75	.75
537B	A67f	50f brt rose & org yel	3.25	3.25
537C	A67f	100f brn & app grn	4.25	4.25
537D	A67f	200f dk pur & pale grn	5.00	5.00
		Nos. 535-537D (15)	51.00	51.00

1968 Summer Olympic Games, Mexico A67g

Olympic torch and: 1f, Natl. University Library with O'Gormans mosaics, statue, Mexico City. 2f, Fishermen on Lake Patzcuaro. 3f, Natl. University buildings. 4f, Paseo de la Reforma, Mexico City. 30f, Guadalajara Cathedral. 60f, 100f, Palace of Fine Arts, Mexico City.

Perf. 14x15

1967, Mar. **Photo.** **Unwmk.**

538	A67g	1f lake, dk bl vio & blk	.30	.25
538A	A67g	2f blk, lake & dk bl vio	.30	.25
538B	A67g	3f dark bl vio, blk & lake	.30	.25
538C	A67g	4f bl, grn & brn	.30	.25
538D	A67g	30f grn, brn & bl	.60	.60
538E	A67g	60f brn, bl & grn	1.10	1.10
		Nos. 538-538E (6)	2.90	2.70

Souvenir Sheet

Imperf

538F	A67g	100f brn, dark bl & grn	22.50	22.50

Symbolic Water Cycle — A68

Perf. 14½x14

1967, Mar. 1 **Litho.** **Wmk. 305**

539	A68	10f dp org, blk & gray	.50	.25
540	A68	15f grnsh bl, blk & gray	.50	.35
541	A68	25f brt rose lil, blk & gray	.75	.50
		Nos. 539-541 (3)	1.75	1.10

Hydrological Decade (UNESCO), 1965-74.

UNESCO Emblem — A69

1967, Mar. 16

542	A69	100f multicolored	1.10	1.10

20th anniv. of UNESCO.

Dromedary A70

Animals: 2f, Karakul. 3f, Angora goat.

Perf. 14x15

1967, Feb. 11 **Photo.** **Unwmk.**

543	A70	1f dark brn & multi	1.10	.25
544	A70	2f yellow & multi	1.10	.25
545	A70	3f lt blue & multi	1.10	.25
		Nos. 543-545,C46-C48 (6)	12.30	3.15

A souvenir sheet exists with a 100f in design and colors of No. C47, simulated perforation and marginal animal design. Value $35.

Inauguration of WHO Headquarters, Geneva — A71

1967, Apr. 7 **Wmk. 305**

546	A71	5f emerald & blk	.40	.25
547	A71	45f dl orange & blk	.50	.30

Arab League Emblem and Hands Reaching for Knowledge — A72

1968, May 5 **Unwmk.** ***Perf. 11***

548	A72	20f org & slate grn	.45	.25
549	A72	20f brt pink & dk bl	.45	.25

Issued to publicize the literacy campaign.

"20" and WHO Emblem — A73

Perf. 14½x14

1968, Aug. 10 **Wmk. 305**

550	A73	30f multicolored	.60	.25
551	A73	100f multicolored	1.75	1.10

20th anniv. of the WHO.

European Goldfinch A74

Protected Game: 10f, Rock partridge, vert. 15f, Ostriches, vert. 20f, Sand partridge. 30f, Dorcas gazelle. 40f, Oryxes. 50f, Houbara bustard.

1968, Oct. 5 **Unwmk.** ***Perf. 13½***

552	A74	5f multicolored	3.25	1.25
553	A74	10f multicolored	6.50	1.25
554	A74	15f multicolored	8.50	1.50
555	A74	20f multicolored	8.50	1.75
556	A74	30f multicolored	5.25	1.25
557	A74	40f multicolored	8.00	1.50
558	A74	50f multicolored	12.50	3.00
		Nos. 552-558,C49-C50 (9)	77.00	25.50

Human Rights Flame — A75

1968, Dec. 10 **Litho.** ***Perf. 13***

559	A75	20f dp org, lt org & blk	.40	.25
560	A75	60f grn, lt blue & blk	.75	.45

International Human Rights Year.

Dome of the Rock, Jerusalem — A76

5f, 45f, Holy Kaaba, Mecca, & Dome of the Rock.

1969, Oct. 8 **Photo.** ***Perf. 12***

Size: 56x25mm

561	A76	5f dull vio & multi	.80	.25

Size: 36x25mm

562	A76	10f vio blue & multi	.80	.50
563	A76	20f Prus bl & multi	1.25	.60

Size: 56x25mm

564	A76	45f Prus bl & multi	2.10	.70
		Nos. 561-564 (4)	4.95	2.05

ILO Emblem — A77

1969, June 10 ***Perf. 13½x14***

565	A77	10f blue & black	.35	.25
566	A77	20f bister brn & blk	.35	.25
567	A77	25f lt olive & black	.35	.25
568	A77	45f lil rose & black	.50	.30
569	A77	60f orange & black	.75	.35
		Nos. 565-569 (5)	2.30	1.40

ILO, 50th anniversary.

Horses — A78

20f, White stallion. 45f, Mare and foal.

1969, July 6 **Unwmk.** ***Perf. 13½***

570	A78	10f dark bl & multi	1.50	.25
571	A78	20f dl green & multi	3.50	.60
572	A78	45f red & multi	6.50	1.75
		Nos. 570-572 (3)	11.50	2.60

Prince Hassan and Princess Tharwat — A79

Designs: 60f, 100f, Prince Hassan and bride in western bridal gown.

1969, Dec. 2 **Photo.** ***Perf. 12½***

573	A79	20f gold & multi	.50	.25
573A	A79	60f gold & multi	1.00	.65
573B	A79	100f gold & multi	1.50	1.25
c.		Strip of 3, #573-573B	3.25	3.25

Wedding of Crown Prince Hassan, 11/14/68.

The Tragedy and the Flight of the Refugees — A79a

Different design on each stamp. Each strip of 5 has five consecutive denominations.

Perf. 14½x13½

1969, Dec. 10 **Photo.**

574	A79a	1f-5f Strip of 5	11.00	11.00
f.-j.		1f-5f Any single		
574A	A79a	6f-10f Strip of 5	11.00	11.00
a.-e.		6f-10f Any single		
574B	A79a	11f-15f Strip of 5	11.00	11.00
a.-e.		11f-15f Any single		
574C	A79a	16f-20f Strip of 5	11.00	11.00
a.-e.		16f-20f Any single		
574D	A79a	21f-25f Strip of 5	11.00	11.00
a.-e.		21f-25f Any single		
574E	A79a	26f-30f Strip of 5	11.00	11.00
a.-e.		26f-30f Any single		

For surcharges see Nos. 870-875.

Inscribed: Tragedy in the Holy Lands

Different design on each stamp. Each strip of 5 has five consecutive denominations.

Perf. 14½x13½

1969, Dec. 10 **Photo.**

575	A79a	1f-5f Strip of 5	5.00	5.00
f.-j.		1f-5f Any single		
575A	A79a	6f-10f Strip of 5	5.00	5.00
a.-e.		6f-10f Any single		
575B	A79a	11f-15f Strip of 5	5.00	5.00
a.-e.		11f-15f Any single		
575C	A79a	16f-20f Strip of 5	5.00	5.00
a.-e.		16f-20f Any single		
575D	A79a	21f-25f Strip of 5	5.00	5.00
a.-e.		21f-25f Any single		
575E	A79a	26f-30f Strip of 5	5.00	5.00
a.-e.		26f-30f Any single		

For surcharges see Nos. 876-881.

Pomegranate Flower (inscribed "Desert Scabius") A80

Oranges A81

Black Bush Robin — A82

Designs: 15f, Wattle flower ("Caper"). 20f, Melon. 25f, Caper flower ("Pomegranate"). 30f, Lemons. 35f, Morning glory. 40f, Grapes. 45f, Desert scabius ("Wattle"). 50f, Olive-laden branch. 75f, Black iris. 100f, Apples. 180f, Masked shrike. 200f, Palestine sunbird. (Inscriptions incorrect on 5f, 15f, 25f and 45f.)

Perf. 14x13½ (flowers), 12 (fruit), 13½x14 (birds)

1969-70 Photo.

576	A80	5f yel & multi ('70)	.40	.25
577	A81	10f blue & multi	.40	.25
578	A80	15f tan & multi ('70)	.70	.25
579	A81	20f sepia & multi	.60	.25
580	A80	25f multi ('70)	1.00	.25
581	A81	30f vio bl & multi	1.00	.25
582	A80	35f multi ('70)	1.50	.25
583	A81	40f dull yel & multi	1.50	.25
584	A80	45f gray & multi ('70)	2.00	.25
585	A81	50f car rose & multi	2.00	.40
586	A80	75f multi ('70)	3.00	1.00
587	A81	100f dk gray & multi	3.25	1.25
588	A82	120f org & multi ('70)	10.00	2.00
589	A82	180f multi ('70)	17.50	4.75
590	A82	200f multi ('70)	20.00	7.00
		Nos. 576-590 (15)	64.85	18.65

Issued: Fruits, 11/22; flowers, 3/21; birds, 9/1.

Soccer — A83

Designs: 10f, Diver. 15f, Boxers. 50f, Runner. 100f, Bicyclist, vert. 150f, Basketball, vert.

1970, Aug. *Perf. 13½x14, 14x13½*

651	A83	5f green & multi	1.00	.25
652	A83	10f lt bl & multi	1.00	.25
653	A83	15f gray & multi	1.00	.25
654	A83	50f gray & multi	1.50	.65
655	A83	100f yellow & multi	2.25	1.25
656	A83	150f multicolored	3.25	2.25
		Nos. 651-656 (6)	10.00	4.90

Refugee Children — A84

Emblems and: 10F, Boy Fetching Water, UNICEF and Refugee Emblems. 15f, Girl and tents. 20f, Boy in front of tent.

1970, Aug.

657	A84	5f multicolored	.30	.25
658	A84	10f multicolored	.40	.25
659	A84	15f multicolored	.50	.25
660	A84	20f multicolored	.70	.25
		Nos. 657-660 (4)	1.90	1.00

Issued for Childhood Day.

Nativity Grotto, Bethlehem A85

Church of the Nativity, Bethlehem: 10f, Manger. 20f, Altar. 25f, Interior.

1970, Dec. 25 Photo. *Perf. 13½*

661	A85	5f blue & multi	.45	.25
662	A85	10f scarlet & multi	.45	.25
663	A85	20f rose lilac & multi	.80	.30
664	A85	25f green & multi	1.00	.35
		Nos. 661-664 (4)	2.70	1.15

Christmas.

Flag and Map of Arab League Countries A85a

1971, May 10 Photo. *Perf. 11½x11*

665	A85a	10f orange & multi	.40	.25
666	A85a	20f lt blue & multi	.40	.25
667	A85a	30f olive & multi	.40	.25
		Nos. 665-667 (3)	1.20	.75

25th anniversary of the Arab League.

Emblem and Doves — A86

Designs: 5f, Emblem and 4 races, vert. 10f, Emblem as flower, vert.

1971, July

668	A86	5f green & multi	.35	.30
669	A86	10f brick red & multi	.40	.30
670	A86	15f dk blue & multi	.50	.30
		Nos. 668-670 (3)	1.25	.90

Intl. Year Against Racial Discrimination.

Dead Sea — A87

Views of the Holy Land: 30f, Excavated building, Petra. 45f, Via Dolorosa, Jerusalem, vert. 60f, Jordan River. 100f, Christmas bell, Bethlehem, vert.

1971, Aug. *Perf. 14x13½, 13½x14*

671	A87	5f blue & multi	.90	.30
672	A87	30f pink & multi	1.75	.60
673	A87	45f blue & multi	2.25	.90
674	A87	60f gray & multi	3.75	1.50
675	A87	100f gray & multi	5.50	3.00
		Nos. 671-675 (5)	14.15	6.30

Tourist publicity.

Opening of UPU Headquarters, Bern in 1970 — A88

1971, Oct. *Perf. 11*

676	A88	10f brn, brn & yel grn	.40	.25
677	A88	20f dk vio, grn & yel grn	.70	.25

Averroes (1126-1198) — A89

Arab Scholars: 5f, Avicenna (980-1037). 20f, ibn-Khaldun (1332-1406). 25f, ibn-Tufail (?-1185). 30f, Alhazen (965?-1039?).

1971, Sept. *Perf. 12*

678	A89	5f gold & multi	.35	.25
679	A89	10f gold & multi	.35	.25
680	A89	20f gold & multi	.65	.25
681	A89	25f gold & multi	1.00	.35
682	A89	30f gold & multi	1.50	.75
		Nos. 678-682 (5)	3.85	1.85

Child Learning to Write — A90

1972, Feb. 9 Photo. *Perf. 11*

683	A90	5f ultra, brn & grn	.35	.25
684	A90	15f mag, brn & blue	.35	.25
685	A90	20f grn, brn & blue	.35	.25
686	A90	30f org, brn & blue	.75	.30
		Nos. 683-686 (4)	1.80	1.05

International Education Year.

Arab Mother and Child — A91

Mother's Day: 10f, Mothers and children, horiz. 20f, Mother and child.

1972, Mar. *Perf. 14x13½*

687	A91	10f lt grn & multi	.50	.25
688	A91	20f red brown & blk	.50	.25
689	A91	30f blue, brn & blk	.75	.25
		Nos. 687-689 (3)	1.75	.75

Pope Paul VI and Holy Sepulcher — A92

1972, Apr. Photo. *Perf. 14x13½*

690	A92	30f black & multi	1.00	.25

Easter. See Nos. C51-C52.

UNICEF Emblem, Children — A93

UNICEF Emblem and: 20f, Child playing with blocks spelling "UNICEF," vert. 30f, Mother and child.

1972, May *Perf. 11½x11, 11x11½*

691	A93	10f bl, vio bl & blk	.40	.25
692	A93	20f multicolored	.40	.25
693	A93	30f blue & multi	.50	.25
		Nos. 691-693 (3)	1.30	.75

25th anniv. (in 1971) of UNICEF.

UN Emblem, Dove and Grain — A94

1972, July *Perf. 11x11½*

694	A94	5f vio & multi	.50	.25
695	A94	10f multicolored	.50	.25
696	A94	15f black & multi	.50	.25
697	A94	20f green & multi	.50	.25
698	A94	30f multicolored	.85	.50
		Nos. 694-698 (5)	2.85	1.50

25th anniv. (in 1970) of the UN.

Al Aqsa Mosque, Jerusalem A95

Designs: 60f, Al Aqsa Mosque on fire. 100f, Al Aqsa Mosque, interior.

1972, Aug. 21 Litho. *Perf. 14½*

699	A95	30f green & multi	1.60	.25
700	A95	60f blue & multi	3.50	.85
701	A95	100f ocher & multi	5.50	1.50
		Nos. 699-701 (3)	10.60	2.60

3rd anniversary of the burning of Al Aqsa Mosque, Jerusalem.

House in Desert — A96

5f, Falconer, vert. 15f, Man on camel. 20f, Pipe line construction. 25f, Shepherd. 30f, Camels at water trough. 35f, Chicken farm. 45f, Irrigation canal.

1972, Nov. *Perf. 14x13½, 13½x14*

702	A96	5f multicolored	.55	.25
703	A96	10f shown	.55	.25
704	A96	15f multicolored	.55	.25
705	A96	20f multicolored	.95	.25
706	A96	25f multicolored	.95	.25
707	A96	30f multicolored	1.25	.45
708	A96	35f multicolored	1.50	.65
709	A96	45f multicolored	2.00	1.10
		Nos. 702-709 (8)	8.30	3.45

Life in the Arab desert.

Wasfi el Tell and Dome of the Rock — A97

Wasfi el Tell, Map of Palestine and Jordan — A98

Perf. 13x13½, 13½x13

1972, Dec. Photo.

710	A97	5f citron & multi	.45	.25
711	A98	10f red & multi	.50	.25
712	A97	20f dl blue & multi	1.00	.25
713	A98	30f green & multi	1.10	.85
		Nos. 710-713 (4)	3.05	1.60

In memory of Prime Minister Wasfi el Tell, who was assassinated in Cairo by Black September terrorists.

Trapshooting — A99

Designs: 75f, Trapshooter facing right, horiz. 120f, Trapshooter facing left, horiz.

1972, Dec. *Perf. 14x13½, 13½x14*

714	A99	25f multicolored	.80	.25
715	A99	75f multicolored	1.10	.80
716	A99	120f multicolored	2.10	1.00
		Nos. 714-716 (3)	4.00	2.05

World Trapshooting Championships.

Aero Club Emblem — A100

1973, Jan. Photo. *Perf. 13½x14*

717	A100	5f blue, blk & yel	.50	.25
718	A100	10f blue, blk & yel	.50	.25
		Nos. 717-718,C53-C55 (5)	4.10	2.05

Royal Jordanian Aero Club.

Peace Dove and Jordanian Flag — A101

10f, Emblem. 15f, King Hussein. 30f, Map of Jordan.

1973, Mar. *Perf. 11½*

719	A101	5f blue & multi	.45	.25
720	A101	10f pale grn & multi	.45	.25
721	A101	15f olive & multi	.45	.25
722	A101	30f yel grn & multi	.90	.45
		Nos. 719-722 (4)	2.25	1.20

Hashemite Kingdom of Jordan, 50th anniv.

Battle, Flag and Map of Palestine A102

10f, 2 soldiers in combat, map of Palestine. 15f, Map of Palestine, olive branch, soldier on tank.

1973, Apr. 10 Photo. *Perf. 11*

723	A102	5f crimson & multi	1.00	.40
724	A102	10f crimson & multi	1.50	.60
725	A102	15f grn, blue & brn	2.25	1.25
		Nos. 723-725 (3)	4.75	2.25

5th anniversary of Karama Battle.

Father and Child — A103

Father's Day: 20f, Father & infant. 30f, Family.

1973, Apr. 20 *Perf. 13½*

726	A103	10f citron & multi	.50	.25
727	A103	20f lt blue & multi	.75	.25
728	A103	30f multicolored	1.25	.55
		Nos. 726-728 (3)	2.50	1.05

Phosphate Mine — A104

10f, Cement factory. 15f, Sharmasil Dam. 20f, Kafrein Dam.

1973, June 25 Litho. *Perf. 13½x14*

729	A104	5f shown	.40	.25
730	A104	10f multicolored	.40	.25
731	A104	15f multicolored	.50	.25
732	A104	20f multicolored	.70	.25
		Nos. 729-732 (4)	2.00	1.00

Development projects.

Camel Racer — A105

Designs: Camel racing.

1973, July 21

733	A105	5f multicolored	.80	.25
734	A105	10f multicolored	.80	.25
735	A105	15f multicolored	.80	.25
736	A105	20f multicolored	.80	.25
		Nos. 733-736 (4)	3.20	1.00

Book Year Emblem A106

1973, Aug. 25 Photo. *Perf. 13x13½*

737	A106	30f dk grn & multi	.75	.25
738	A106	60f purple & multi	1.00	.35

Intl. Book Year. For overprints see Nos. 781-782.

Family — A107

Family Day: 30f, Family around fire. 60f, Large family outdoors.

1973, Sept. 18 Litho. *Perf. 13½*

739	A107	20f multicolored	.50	.25
740	A107	30f multicolored	.50	.25
741	A107	60f multicolored	1.00	.35
		Nos. 739-741 (3)	2.00	.85

Kings of Iran and Jordan, Tomb of Cyrus the Great and Mosque of Omar A108

1973, Oct. Litho. *Perf. 13*

742	A108	5f ver & multi	.50	.25
743	A108	10f brown & multi	.50	.25
744	A108	15f gray & multi	.75	.25
745	A108	30f blue & multi	1.00	.40
		Nos. 742-745 (4)	2.75	1.15

2500th anniversary of the founding of the Persian Empire by Cyrus the Great.

Palestine Week Emblem — A109

Palestine Week: 10f, Torch and laurel. 15f, Refugee family behind barbed wire, vert. 30f, Children, Map of Palestine, globe. Sizes: 5f, 10f, 30f; 38½x22mm. 15f, 25x46mm.

1973, Nov. 17 Photo. *Perf. 11*

746	A109	5f multicolored	.50	.25
747	A109	10f dl bl & multi	.65	.25
748	A109	15f yel grn & multi	.85	.25
749	A109	30f brt grn & multi	1.50	.40
		Nos. 746-749 (4)	3.50	1.15

Traditional Harvest — A110

Traditional and modern agricultural methods: 10f, Harvesting machine. 15f, Traditional seeding. 20f, Seeding machine. 30f, Ox plow. 35f, Plowing machine. 45f, Pest control. 60f, Horticulture.

1973, Dec. 25 *Perf. 13½*

750	A110	5f shown	.65	.25
751	A110	10f multicolored	.65	.25
752	A110	15f multicolored	.65	.25
753	A110	20f multicolored	.65	.25
754	A110	30f multicolored	1.00	.25
755	A110	35f multicolored	1.10	.25
756	A110	45f multicolored	1.25	.25
757	A110	60f multicolored	1.75	1.10
		Nos. 750-757,C56 (9)	10.20	4.60

Red Sea Fish — A111

Designs: Various Red Sea fishes.

1974, Feb. 15 Photo. *Perf. 14*

758	A111	5f multicolored	.50	.25
759	A111	10f multicolored	.60	.25
760	A111	15f multicolored	.75	.25
761	A111	20f multicolored	.90	.35
762	A111	25f multicolored	1.25	.40
763	A111	30f multicolored	2.00	.50
764	A111	35f multicolored	2.25	.80
765	A111	40f multicolored	2.75	1.00
766	A111	45f multicolored	3.00	1.10
767	A111	50f multicolored	5.00	1.25
768	A111	60f multicolored	6.25	1.75
		Nos. 758-768 (11)	25.25	7.90

Battle of Muta, 1250 — A112

20f, Yarmouk Battle, 636. 30f, Hitteen Battle, 1187.

1974, Mar. 15 Photo. *Perf. 13½*

769	A112	10f shown	.65	.25
770	A112	20f multicolored	1.25	.40
771	A112	30f multicolored	1.60	.65
		Nos. 769-771 (3)	3.50	1.30

Clubfooted Boy, by Murillo — A113

Paintings: 10f, Praying Hands, by Dürer. 15f, St. George and the Dragon, by Paolo Uccello. 20f, Mona Lisa, by Da Vinci. 30f, Hope, by Frederic Watts. 40f, Angelus, by Jean F. Millet, horiz. 50f, The Artist and her Daughter, by Angelica Kauffmann. 60f, Portrait of my Mother, by James Whistler, horiz. 100f, Master Hare, by Reynolds.

Perf. 14x13½, 13½x14

1974, Apr. 15 Litho.

772	A113	5f black & multi	1.50	.25
773	A113	10f black & gray	1.50	.25
774	A113	15f black & multi	1.50	.25
775	A113	20f black & multi	1.50	.25
776	A113	30f black & multi	1.50	.25
777	A113	40f black & multi	1.75	.25
778	A113	50f black & multi	2.00	.95
779	A113	60f black & multi	2.50	1.00
780	A113	100f black & multi	3.50	1.75
		Nos. 772-780 (9)	17.25	5.20

Nos. 737-738 Overprinted

1974, Apr. 20 Photo. *Perf. 13x13½*

781	A106	30f dk grn & multi	.70	.25
782	A106	60f purple & multi	1.00	.50

Intl. Conf. for Damascus History, Apr. 20-25.

UPU Emblem — A114

1974 *Perf. 13x12½*

783	A114	10f yel grn & multi	.40	.25
784	A114	30f blue & multi	.50	.25
785	A114	60f multicolored	.85	.30
		Nos. 783-785 (3)	1.75	.80

Centenary of Universal Postal Union.

Camel Caravan at Sunset — A115

3f, 30f, Palm at shore of Dead Sea. 4f, 40f, Hotel at shore. 5f, 50f, Jars from Qumran Caves. 6f, 60f, Copper scrolls, vert. 10f, 100f, Cracked cistern steps, vert. 20f, like 2f.

1974, June 25 Photo. *Perf. 14*

786	A115	2f multicolored	.50	.25
787	A115	3f multicolored	.50	.25
788	A115	4f multicolored	.50	.25
789	A115	5f multicolored	.75	.25
790	A115	6f multicolored	.75	.25
791	A115	10f multicolored	.75	.25
792	A115	20f multicolored	.50	.25
793	A115	30f multicolored	.65	.25
794	A115	40f multicolored	.75	.50
795	A115	50f multicolored	1.75	.40
796	A115	60f multicolored	2.25	.50
797	A115	100f multicolored	3.50	.85
		Nos. 786-797 (12)	13.15	4.25

WPY Emblem — A116

1974, Aug. 20 Photo. *Perf. 11*

798	A116	5f lt green, blk & pur	.30	.25
799	A116	10f lt green, blk & car	.30	.25
800	A116	20f lt green, blk & org	.40	.25
		Nos. 798-800 (3)	1.00	.75

World Population Year.

Water Skiing — A117

Water Skiing: 10f, 100f, Side view, horiz. 20f, 200f, Turning, horiz. 50f, like 5f.

Perf. 14x13½, 13½x14

1974, Sept. 20

801	A117	5f multicolored	.50	.25
802	A117	10f multicolored	.50	.25
803	A117	20f multicolored	.50	.25
804	A117	50f multicolored	.65	.25
805	A117	100f multicolored	1.25	.50
806	A117	200f multicolored	2.10	.95
		Nos. 801-806 (6)	5.50	2.45

Holy Kaaba, Mecca, and Pilgrims A118

1974, Nov. Photo. *Perf. 11*

807	A118	10f blue & multi	.75	.25
808	A118	20f yellow & multi	.80	.25

Pilgrimage season.

Amrah Palace — A119

Ruins: 20f, Hisham Palace. 30f, Kharraneh Castle.

1974, Nov. 25 Photo. *Perf. 14x13½*

809	A119	10f black & multi	.50	.25
810	A119	20f black & multi	.75	.30
811	A119	30f black & multi	1.25	.50
		Nos. 809-811 (3)	2.50	1.05

Jordanian Woman — A120

Designs: Various women's costumes.

1975, Feb. 1 Photo. *Perf. 12*

812	A120	5f lt green & multi	.45	.25
813	A120	10f yellow & multi	.50	.25
814	A120	15f lt blue & multi	.75	.30

815	A120	20f ultra & multi	1.10	.40
816	A120	25f green & multi	1.50	.85
		Nos. 812-816 (5)	4.30	2.05

Additional denominations of 30f, 35f, 40f, 50f, and 60f were produced but not issued.

Treasury, Petra — A121

Ommayyad Palace, Amman — A122

Designs: 30f, Dome of the Rock, Jerusalem. 40f, Columns, Forum of Jerash.

Perf. 14x13½, 13½x14

1975, Mar. 1 Photo.

824	A121	15f lt blue & multi	1.00	.25
825	A122	20f pink & multi	1.00	.25
826	A123	30f yellow & multi	1.25	.25
827	A122	40f lt blue & multi	1.60	.25
		Nos. 824-827,C59-C61 (7)	10.25	3.25

King Hussein — A123

1975, Apr. 8 Photo. *Perf. 14*

Size: 19x23mm

831	A123	5f green & ind	.50	.25
832	A123	10f vio & indigo	.50	.25
833	A123	15f car & indigo	.50	.25
834	A123	20f brn ol & ind	.50	.25
835	A123	25f vio bl & ind	.50	.25
836	A123	30f brown & ind	.50	.25
837	A123	35f vio & indigo	.50	.25
838	A123	40f orange & ind	.50	.25
839	A123	45f red lil & ind	.50	.25
840	A123	50f bl green & ind	.65	.25
		Nos. 831-840,C62-C68 (17)	21.00	13.00

Globe, "alia" and Plane — A125

Designs: 30f, Boeing 727 connecting Jordan with world, horiz. 60f, Globe and "alia."

1975, June 15 Photo. *Perf. 11*

853	A125	10f multicolored	.70	.25
854	A125	30f multicolored	.75	.25
855	A125	60f multicolored	1.40	.85
		Nos. 853-855 (3)	2.85	1.35

Royal Jordanian Airline, 30th anniversary.

Satellite Transmission System, Map of Mediterranean — A126

1975, Aug. 1 Photo. *Perf. 11*

856	A126	20f vio bl & multi	.90	.25
857	A126	30f green & multi	1.10	.75

Opening of satellite earth station.

Chamber of Commerce Emblem — A127

1975, Oct. 15 Photo. *Perf. 11*

858	A127	10f yellow & blue	.35	.25
859	A127	15f yel, red & blue	.35	.25
860	A127	20f yel, grn & blue	.35	.25
		Nos. 858-860 (3)	1.05	.75

Amman Chamber of Commerce, 50th anniv.

Hand Holding Wrench, Wall and Emblem A128

1975, Nov. Photo. *Perf. 11½*

861	A128	5f green, car & blk	.35	.25
862	A128	10f car, green & blk	.35	.25
863	A128	20f blk, green & car	.35	.25
		Nos. 861-863 (3)	1.05	.75

Three-year development plan.

Family and IWY Emblem — A129

IWY Emblem and: 25f, Woman scientist with microscope. 60f, Woman graduate.

1976, Apr. 27 Litho. *Perf. 14x13½*

864	A129	5f multicolored	.50	.25
865	A129	25f multicolored	.50	.25
866	A129	60f multicolored	1.00	.40
		Nos. 864-866 (3)	2.00	.90

International Women's Year.

Salt Industry — A130

Arab Labor Organization Emblem and: 30f, Welders. 60f, Ship at 'Aqaba.

1976, June 1 Litho. *Perf. 13½x14*

867	A130	10f gray & multi	.50	.25
868	A130	30f bister & multi	.50	.25
869	A130	60f brown & multi	.75	.40
		Nos. 867-869 (3)	1.75	.90

Arab Labor Organization.

Nos. 574-574E Srchd.

Perf. 14½x13½

1976, July 18 Strips of 5 Photo.

870	A79a	25f on 1f-5f	32.50	32.50
a.-e.		Any single, 1f-5f		
871	A79a	25f on 6f-10f	32.50	32.50
a.-e.		Any single, 6f-10f		
872	A79a	40f on 11f-15f	32.50	32.50
a.-e.		Any single, 11f-15f		
873	A79a	50f on 16f-20f	32.50	32.50
a.-e.		Any single, 16f-20f		
874	A79a	75f on 21f-25f	32.50	32.50
a.-e.		Any single, 21f-25f		
875	A79a	125f on 26f-30f	32.50	32.50
a.-e.		Any single, 26f-30f		

Nos. 575-575E Surcharged Same as Nos. 870-875

876	A79a	25f on 1f-5f	32.50	32.50
a.-e.		Any single, 1f-5f		
877	A79a	25f on 6f-10f	32.50	32.50
a.-e.		Any single, 6f-10f		
878	A79a	40f on 11f-15f	32.50	32.50
a.-e.		Any single, 11f-15f		
879	A79a	50f on 16f-20f	32.50	32.50
a.-e.		Any single, 16f-20f		
880	A79a	75f on 21f-25f	32.50	32.50
a.-e.		Any single, 21f-25f		
881	A79a	125f on 26f-30f	32.50	32.50
a.-e.		Any single, 26f-30f		

Tennis — A132

Designs: 10f, Athlete and wreath. 15f, Soccer. 20f, Equestrian and Jordanian flag. 30f, Weight lifting. 100f, Stadium, Amman.

1976, Nov. 1 Litho. *Perf. 14x13½*

990	A132	5f buff & multi	.75	.25
991	A132	10f lt bl & multi	.75	.25
992	A132	15f green & multi	.75	.25
993	A132	20f green & multi	.75	.25
994	A132	30f green & multi	1.00	.25
995	A132	100f multicolored	2.00	1.25
		Nos. 990-995 (6)	6.00	2.50

Sports and youth.

Dam — A133

Designs: Various dams.

1976, Dec. 7 Litho. *Perf. 14x13½*

996	A133	30f multicolored	1.00	.25
997	A133	60f multicolored	1.25	.70
998	A133	100f multicolored	2.25	1.10
		Nos. 996-998 (3)	4.50	2.05

Telephones, 1876 and 1976 — A134

125f, 1876 telephone and 1976 receiver.

1977, Feb. 17 Litho. *Perf. 11½x12*

999	A134	75f rose & multi	1.50	.95
1000	A134	125f blue & multi	2.00	1.25

Centenary of first telephone call by Alexander Graham Bell, Mar. 10, 1876.

Street Crossing, Traffic Light — A135

Designs: 75f, Traffic circle and light. 125f, Traffic light and signs, motorcycle policeman.

1977, May 4 Litho. *Perf. 11x12*

1001	A135	5f rose & multi	.55	.25
1002	A135	75f black & multi	1.50	.85
1003	A135	125f yellow & multi	2.25	1.40
		Nos. 1001-1003 (3)	4.30	2.50

International Traffic Day.

Plane over Ship — A136

Coat of Arms and: 25f, Factories and power lines. 40f, Fertilizer plant and trucks. 50f, Ground to air missile. 75f, Mosque and worshippers. 125f, Radar station and TV emblem.

1977, Aug. 11 Photo. *Perf. 11½x12*

1004	A136	10f sil & multi	.40	.25
1005	A136	25f sil & multi	.40	.25
1006	A136	40f sil & multi	.70	.35
1007	A136	50f sil & multi	.80	.40
1008	A136	75f sil & multi	.95	.60
1009	A136	125f sil & multi	1.75	1.00
		Nos. 1004-1009 (6)	5.00	2.85

Imperf

Size: 100x70mm

1009A	A136	100f multicolored	8.50	8.50

25th anniv. of the reign of King Hussein.

Child with Toy Bank — A137

Postal Savings Bank: 25f, Boy with piggy bank. 50f, Postal Savings Bank emblem. 75f, Boy talking to teller.

1977, Sept. 1 Litho. *Perf. 11½x12*

1010	A137	10f multicolored	.40	.25
1011	A137	25f multicolored	.60	.25
1012	A137	50f multicolored	.75	.40
1013	A137	75f multicolored	1.10	.65
		Nos. 1010-1013 (4)	2.85	1.55

King Hussein and Queen Alia — A138

1977, Nov. 1 Litho. *Perf. 11½x12*

1014	A138	10f lt grn & multi	.40	.25
1015	A138	25f rose & multi	.40	.25
1016	A138	40f yellow & multi	.50	.25
1017	A138	50f blue & multi	.70	.25
		Nos. 1014-1017 (4)	2.00	1.00

Queen Alia — A139

1977, Dec. 1 Litho. *Perf. 11½x12*

1018	A139	10f green & multi	.50	.25
1019	A139	25f brown & multi	.50	.25
1020	A139	40f blue & multi	.70	.25
1021	A139	50f yellow & multi	.95	.25
		Nos. 1018-1021 (4)	2.65	1.00

Queen Alia, died in 1977 air crash.

Jinnah, Flags of Pakistan and Jordan — A140

1977, Dec. 20 *Perf. 11½*

1022	A140	25f multicolored	.30	.25
1023	A140	75f multicolored	.70	.40

Mohammed Ali Jinnah (1876-1948), 1st Governor General of Pakistan.

APU Emblem, Members' Flags — A141

1978, Apr. 12 Litho. *Perf. 12x11½*

1024	A141	25f yellow & multi	.75	.50
1025	A141	40f buff & multi	1.25	.75

25th anniv. (in 1977), of Arab Postal Union.

Copper Coffee Set — A142

Handicraft: 40f, Porcelain plate and ashtray. 75f, Vase and jewelry. 125f, Pipe holder.

1978, May 30 Photo. *Perf. 11½x12*

1026	A142	25f olive & multi	.50	.25
1027	A142	40f lilac & multi	.65	.25
1028	A142	75f ultra & multi	1.10	.65
1029	A142	125f orange & multi	1.75	1.00
		Nos. 1026-1029 (4)	4.00	2.15

Roman Amphitheater, Jerash — A143

Tourist Views: 20f, Roman Columns, Jerash. 40f, Goat, grapes and man, Roman mosaic, Madaba. 75f, Rock formations, Rum, and camel rider.

1978, July 30 Litho. *Perf. 12*

1030 A143 5f multicolored .55 .25
1031 A143 20f multicolored .55 .25
1032 A143 40f multicolored 1.00 .25
1033 A143 75f multicolored 1.40 .75
Nos. 1030-1033 (4) 3.50 1.50

King Hussein and Pres. Sadat — A144

Designs: No. 1035, King Hussein and Pres. Assad, Jordanian and Syrian flags, horiz. No. 1036, King Hussein, King Khalid, Jordanian and Saudi Arabian flags, horiz.

1978, Aug. 20 *Perf. 11½x12*

1034 A144 40f multicolored .90 .50
1035 A144 40f multicolored .90 .50
1036 A144 40f multicolored .90 .50
Nos. 1034-1036 (3) 2.70 1.50

Visits of Arab leaders to Jordan.

Cement Factory — A145

Designs: 10f, Science laboratory. 25f, Printing press. 75f, Artificial fertilizer plant.

1978, Sept. 25 Litho. *Perf. 12*

1037 A145 5f multicolored .60 .25
1038 A145 10f multicolored .60 .25
1039 A145 25f multicolored .80 .25
1040 A145 75f multicolored 1.60 .90
Nos. 1037-1040 (4) 3.60 1.65

Industrial development.

"UNESCO" Scales and Globe — A146

1978, Dec. 5 Litho. *Perf. 12x11½*

1041 A146 40f multicolored .75 .35
1042 A146 75f multicolored 1.25 .70

30th anniversary of UNESCO.

1976-1980 Development Plan — A147

1979, Oct. 25 Litho. *Perf. 12½x12*

1043 A147 25f multicolored .30 .25
1044 A147 40f multicolored .70 .25
1045 A147 50f multicolored .95 .25
Nos. 1043-1045 (3) 1.95 .75

IYC Emblem, Flag of Jordan — A148

1979, Nov. 15 Litho. *Perf. 12x12½*

1046 A148 25f multicolored .50 .25
1047 A148 40f multicolored .75 .25
1048 A148 50f multicolored 1.25 .35
Nos. 1046-1048 (3) 2.50 .85

International Year of the Child.

1979 Population and Housing Census — A149

1979, Dec. 25 Litho. *Perf. 12½x12*

1049 A149 25f multicolored .50 .25
1050 A149 40f multicolored .70 .25
1051 A149 50f multicolored .80 .30
Nos. 1049-1051 (3) 2.00 .80

King Hussein — A150

1980 Litho. *Perf. 13½x13*

1052 A150 5f multicolored .30 .25
b. Inscribed 1981 .30 .25
1053 A150 10f multicolored .30 .25
b. Inscribed 1981 .30 .25
1055 A150 20f multicolored .30 .25
b. Inscribed 1981 .30 .25
1056 A150 25f multicolored .30 .25
a. Inscribed 1979 .30 .25
b. Inscribed 1981 .30 .25
1058 A150 40f multicolored .60 .25
a. Inscribed 1979 .50 .25
b. Inscribed 1981 .60 .25
1059 A150 50f multicolored .80 .25
1060 A150 75f multicolored 1.00 .30
1061 A150 125f multicolored 1.50 .35
a. Complete booklet, 4 each #1056, 1058-1061 17.50
Nos. 1052-1061 (8) 5.10 2.15

International Nursing Day — A151

1980, May 12 Litho. *Perf. 12x12½*

1062 A151 25f multicolored .50 .25
1063 A151 40f multicolored .70 .25
1064 A151 50f multicolored .85 .25
Nos. 1062-1064 (3) 2.05 .75

El Deir Temple, Petra — A152

1980 Litho. *Perf. 14½*

1065 A152 25f multicolored .60 .25
1066 A152 40f multicolored .90 .50
1067 A152 50f multicolored 1.25 .60
Nos. 1065-1067 (3) 2.75 1.35

World Tourism Conf., Manila, Sept. 27.

Hegira (Pilgrimage Year) — A153

1980, Nov. 11 Litho. *Perf. 14½*

1068 A153 25f multicolored .30 .25
1069 A153 40f multicolored .45 .25
1070 A153 50f multicolored .75 .30
1071 A153 75f multicolored 1.50 .40
1072 A153 100f multicolored 1.50 .70
Nos. 1068-1072 (5) 4.50 1.90

Souvenir Sheet

Imperf

1073 A153 290f multicolored 6.50 6.50

No. 1073 contains designs of Nos. 1068-1071.

11th Arab Summit Conference, Amman — A153a

1980, Nov. 25 Litho. *Perf. 14½*

1073A A153a 25f multi .40 .25
1073B A153a 40f multi .60 .25
1073C A153a 50f multi .80 .30
1073D A153a 75f multi 1.00 .45
1073E A153a 100f multi 1.10 .65
f. Souv. sheet of 5, #1073A-1073E, imperf. 6.50 6.50
Nos. 1073A-1073E (5) 3.90 1.90

A154

1981, May 8 Litho. *Perf. 14½*

1074 A154 25f multicolored .50 .25
1075 A154 40f multicolored .80 .60
1076 A154 50f multicolored .95 .70
Nos. 1074-1076 (3) 2.25 1.55

Red Crescent Society.

A155

1981, June 17 Litho. *Perf. 14x14½*

1077 A155 25f multicolored .75 .25
1078 A155 40f multicolored .90 .90
1079 A155 50f multicolored 1.25 .90
Nos. 1077-1079 (3) 2.90 2.05

13th World Telecommunications Day.

Nos. 174 and 832 — A156

40f, Nos. 313, 189, vert. 50f, Nos. 272, 222.

Perf. 13½x14½, 14½x13½

1981, July 1 Litho.

1080 A156 25f shown .55 .25
1081 A156 40f multicolored 1.00 .65
1082 A156 50f multicolored 1.10 .90
Nos. 1080-1082 (3) 2.65 1.80

Postal Museum opening.

A157

Arab Women: 25f, Khawla Bint El-Azwar, Ancient Warrior. 40f, El-Khansa (d.645), writer. 50f, Rabia El-Adawiyeh, religious leader.

1981, Aug. 25 Litho. *Perf. 14½x14*

1083 A157 25f multicolored .25 .25
1084 A157 40f multicolored 2.00 1.25
1085 A157 50f multicolored 3.00 1.50
Nos. 1083-1085 (3) 5.25 3.00

A158

1981, Oct. 16 Litho. *Perf. 14x14½*

1086 A158 25f multicolored .25 .25
1087 A158 40f multicolored .80 .55
1088 A158 50f multicolored 1.00 .65
Nos. 1086-1088 (3) 2.05 1.45

World Food Day.

Intl. Year of the Disabled — A159

1981, Nov. 14 Litho. *Perf. 14½x14*

1089 A159 25f multicolored .25 .25
1090 A159 40f multicolored 1.00 .70
1091 A159 50f multicolored 1.40 .90
Nos. 1089-1091 (3) 2.65 1.85

Hands Reading Braille — A160

1981, Nov. 14 *Perf. 14x14½*

1092 A160 25f multicolored .25 .25
1093 A160 40f multicolored 1.00 .70
1094 A160 50f multicolored 1.40 .90
Nos. 1092-1094 (3) 2.65 1.85

A161

Design: Hand holding jug and stone tablet.

1982, Mar. 10 Litho. *Perf. 14x14½*

1095 A161 25f multicolored .50 .25
1096 A161 40f multicolored 1.10 .60
1097 A161 50f multicolored 1.25 .80
Nos. 1095-1097 (3) 2.85 1.65

Nos. 1095-1097 inscribed 1981.

A162

1982, Apr. 12 Litho. *Perf. 14x14½*

1098 A162 10f multicolored .30 .25
1099 A162 25f multicolored .65 .25
1100 A162 40f multicolored .90 .65
1101 A162 50f multicolored 1.10 .80
1102 A162 100f multicolored 2.40 1.60
Nos. 1098-1102 (5) 5.35 3.55

30th anniv. of Arab Postal Union.

King Hussein and Rockets — A163

25f, Tanks crossing bridge. 40f, Jet. 50f, Tanks, diff. 100f, Raising flag.

1982, May 25 Litho. *Perf. 14½x14*

1103 A163 10f shown .30 .25
1104 A163 25f multicolored .65 .25
1105 A163 40f multicolored .90 .65
1106 A163 50f multicolored 1.25 .75
1107 A163 100f multicolored 2.25 1.50
Nos. 1103-1107 (5) 5.35 3.40

Independence and Army Day; 30th anniv. of King Hussein's accession to the throne.

Salt Secondary School — A164

1982, Sept. 12 Litho. *Perf. 14½x14*

1108 A164 10f multicolored .30 .25
1109 A164 25f multicolored .60 .25
1110 A164 40f multicolored .85 .60
1111 A164 50f multicolored 1.10 .65
1112 A164 100f multicolored 2.25 1.25
Nos. 1108-1112 (5) 5.10 3.00

International Heritage of Jerusalem — A165

10f, Gate to Old City. 25f, Minaret. 40f, Al Aqsa. 50f, Dome of the Rock. 100f, Dome of the Rock, diff.

1982, Nov. 14 Litho. *Perf. 14x14½*

1113 A165 10f multicolored .30 .25
1114 A165 25f multicolored 1.00 .45
1115 A165 40f multicolored 1.25 .80
1116 A165 50f multicolored 1.60 .90
1117 A165 100f multicolored 3.25 1.75
Nos. 1113-1117 (5) 7.40 4.15

Yarmouk Forces — A166

No. 1123, Armed Forces emblem.

1982, Nov. 14 *Perf. 14½x14*

1118 A166 10f pink & multi .30 .25
1119 A166 25f buff & multi .45 .25
1120 A166 40f yel & multi .80 .45
1121 A166 50f lt blue & multi .95 .60
1122 A166 100f pale grn & multi 2.10 1.40
Nos. 1118-1122 (5) 4.60 2.95

Size: 71x51mm

Imperf

1123 A166 100f tan & multi 15.00 15.00

2nd UN Conf. on Peaceful Uses of Outer Space, Vienna, Aug. 9-21 — A167

1982, Dec. 1 *Perf. 14½x14*

1124 A167 10f multicolored .30 .25
1125 A167 25f multicolored .50 .25
1126 A167 40f multicolored .75 .50
1127 A167 50f multicolored .95 .60
1128 A167 100f multicolored 2.00 1.25
Nos. 1124-1128 (5) 4.50 2.85

Birth Centenary of Amir Abdullah ibn Hussein — A168

1982, Dec. 13 Litho. *Perf. 14½*

1129 A168 10f multicolored .30 .25
1130 A168 25f multicolored .40 .25
1131 A168 40f multicolored .60 .45
1132 A168 50f multicolored .95 .80
1133 A168 100f multicolored 2.25 1.40
Nos. 1129-1133 (5) 4.50 3.15

Roman Ruins of Jerash — A169

10f, Temple colonnade. 25f, Arch. 40f, Columns. 50f, Ampitheater. 100f, Hippodrome.

1982, Dec. 29 Litho. *Perf. 15*

1134 A169 10f multicolored .30 .25
1135 A169 25f multicolored .90 .25
1136 A169 40f multicolored 1.40 .90
1137 A169 50f multicolored 1.75 1.00
1138 A169 100f multicolored 3.25 2.10
Nos. 1134-1138 (5) 7.60 4.50

King Hussein — A170

1983 Litho. *Perf. 14½x14*

1139 A170 10f multicolored .30 .25
1140 A170 25f multicolored .30 .25
1141 A170 40f multicolored .40 .30
1142 A170 60f multicolored .60 .40
1143 A170 100f multicolored 1.00 .65
1144 A170 125f multicolored 1.25 .70
Nos. 1139-1144 (6) 3.85 2.55

Issue dates: 10f, 60f, Feb. 1; 40f, Feb. 8; 25f, 100f, 125f, Mar. 3. Inscribed 1982.

Massacre at Shatilla and Sabra Palestinian Refugee Camps — A171

10f, 25f, 50f, No. 1149, Various victims. 40f, Children. No. 1150, Wounded child.

1983, Apr. 9 Litho. *Perf. 14½*

1145 A171 10f multicolored *.50 .25*
1146 A171 25f multicolored *1.00 .70*
1147 A171 40f multicolored *1.50 .90*
1148 A171 50f multicolored *2.00 1.25*
1149 A171 100f multicolored *3.00 2.00*
Nos. 1145-1149 (5) *8.00 5.10*

Souvenir Sheet

Imperf

1150 A171 100f multicolored *18.00*

Opening of Queen Alia Intl. Airport — A172

10f, Aerial view. 25f, Terminal buildings. 40f, Hangar. 50f, Terminal buildings, diff. 100f, Embarkation Bridge.

1983, May 25 Litho. *Perf. 12½*

1151 A172 10f multicolored .30 .25
1152 A172 25f multicolored .80 .25
1153 A172 40f multicolored 1.10 .80
1154 A172 50f multicolored 1.40 .90
1155 A172 100f multicolored 2.75 1.75
Nos. 1151-1155 (5) 6.35 3.95

Royal Jordanian Radio Amateurs' Society — A173

1983, Aug. 11 Litho. *Perf. 12*

1156 A173 10f multicolored .30 .25
1157 A173 25f multicolored .65 .25
1158 A173 40f multicolored .90 .65
1159 A173 50f multicolored 1.25 .75
1160 A173 100f multicolored 2.40 1.50
Nos. 1156-1160 (5) 5.50 3.40

Royal Academy for Islamic Cultural Research A174

10f, Academy Building. 25f, Silk carpet. 40f, Mosque, Amman. 50f, Dome of the Rock. 100f, Islamic city views.

1983, Sept. 16 Litho. *Perf. 12*

1161 A174 10f multicolored .30 .25
1162 A174 25f multicolored .70 .50
1163 A174 40f multicolored 1.10 .70
1164 A174 50f multicolored 1.50 .90
1165 A174 100f multicolored 2.75 1.75
Nos. 1161-1165 (5) 6.35 4.10

A 100f souvenir sheet shows letter from Mohammed. Value $15.

World Food Day — A175

10f, Irrigation canal. 25f, Greenhouses. 40f, Light-grown crops. 50f, Harvest. 100f, Sheep farm.

1983, Oct. 16 Litho. *Perf. 12*

1166 A175 10f multicolored .30 .25
1167 A175 25f multicolored .60 .25
1168 A175 40f multicolored 1.00 .60
1169 A175 50f multicolored 1.25 .70
1170 A175 100f multicolored 2.50 1.40
Nos. 1166-1170 (5) 5.65 3.20

World Communications Year — A176

10f, Radio switchboard operators. 25f, Earth satellite station. 40f, Symbols of communication. 50f, Emblems. 100f, Airmail letter.

1983, Nov. 14

1171 A176 10f multicolored .30 .25
1172 A176 25f multicolored 1.00 .25
1173 A176 40f multicolored 1.25 1.00
1174 A176 50f multicolored 1.50 1.00
1175 A176 100f multicolored 3.25 1.75
Nos. 1171-1175 (5) 7.30 4.25

Intl. Palestinian Solidarity Day — A177

Dome of the Rock, Jerusalem.

1983, Nov. 29 *Perf. 12*

1176 A177 5f multicolored .90 .45
1177 A177 10f multicolored 1.50 .70

35th Anniv. of UN Declaration of Human Rights — A178

1983, Dec. 10

1178 A178 10f multicolored .30 .25
1179 A178 25f multicolored .65 .25
1180 A178 40f multicolored .75 .65
1181 A178 50f multicolored 1.25 .75
1182 A178 100f multicolored 2.50 1.50
Nos. 1178-1182 (5) 5.45 3.40

Anti-Paralysis A179

1984, Apr. 7 *Perf. 13½x11½*

1183 A179 40f multicolored 1.10 .70
1184 A179 60f multicolored 1.60 .95
1185 A179 100f multicolored 2.75 1.60
Nos. 1183-1185 (3) 5.45 3.25

Anti-Polio Campaign.

Israeli Bombing of Iraq Nuclear Reactor A180

Various designs.

1984, June 7 Litho. *Perf. 13½x11½*

1186 A180 40f multicolored 1.60 .55
1187 A180 60f multicolored 2.00 .70
1188 A180 100f multicolored 3.25 1.25
Nos. 1186-1188 (3) 6.85 2.50

Independence and Army Day — A181

King Hussein and various armed forces.

1984, June 10

1189 A181 10f multicolored .30 .25
1190 A181 25f multicolored .65 .25
1191 A181 40f multicolored 1.00 .65
1192 A181 60f multicolored 1.60 .90
1193 A181 100f multicolored 2.75 1.60
Nos. 1189-1193 (5) 6.30 3.65

1984 Summer Olympics, Los Angeles A182

40f, Swimming. 60f, Shooting, archery. 100f, Gymnastics.

1984, July 28

1194 A182 25f shown .30 .25
1195 A182 40f multicolored .50 .30
1196 A182 60f multicolored 1.10 .45
1197 A182 100f multicolored 1.60 .75
Nos. 1194-1197 (4) 3.50 1.75

An imperf. 100f souvenir sheet exists picturing pole vaulting. Value $14.

Water and Electricity Year — A183

25f, Power lines, factory. 40f, Amman Power Station. 60f, Irrigation. 100f, Hydro-electric dam.

1984, Aug. 11

1198 A183 25f multicolored .45 .25
1199 A183 40f multicolored .70 .45
1200 A183 60f multicolored 1.10 .60
1201 A183 100f multicolored 1.75 1.10
Nos. 1198-1201 (4) 4.00 2.40

Coins — A184

40f, Omayyad gold dinar. 60f, Abbasid gold dinar. 125f, Hashemite silver dinar.

1984, Sept. 26 Photo. *Perf. 13*

1202 A184 40f multicolored 1.10 .60
1203 A184 60f multicolored 1.40 .80
1204 A184 125f multicolored 3.00 1.75
Nos. 1202-1204 (3) 5.50 3.15

Royal Society for the Conservation of Nature — A185

25f, Four antelopes. 40f, Grazing. 60f, Three antelopes. 100f, King Hussein, Queen Alia, Duke of Edinburgh.

1984, Oct. 18

1205 A185 25f multicolored .70 .25
1206 A185 40f multicolored 1.10 .70
1207 A185 60f multicolored 1.60 .95
1208 A185 100f multicolored 2.75 1.60
Nos. 1205-1208 (4) 6.15 3.50

Natl. Universities A186

Designs: 40f, Mu'ta Military University, Karak. 60f, Yarmouk University, Irbid. 125f, Jordan University, Amman.

1984, Nov. 14 *Perf. 13x13½*

1209 A186 40f multicolored .55 .40
1210 A186 60f multicolored .95 .55
1211 A186 125f multicolored 2.00 1.10
Nos. 1209-1211 (3) 3.50 2.05

Al Sahaba Tombs — A187

Designs: 10f, El Harath bin Omier el-Azdi and Derer bin El-Azwar. 25f, Sharhabil bin Hasna and Abu Obaidah Amer bin el-Jarrah. 40f, Muath bin Jabal. 50f, Zaid bin Haretha and Abdullah bin Rawaha. 60f, Amer bin Abi Waqqas. 100f, Jafar bin Abi Taleb.

1984, Dec. 5 Litho. *Perf. 13½x11½*

1212 A187 10f multicolored .30 .25
1213 A187 25f multicolored .50 .25
1214 A187 40f multicolored .75 .50
1215 A187 50f multicolored .95 .55
1216 A187 60f multicolored 1.25 .65
1217 A187 100f multicolored 2.00 1.25
Nos. 1212-1217 (6) 5.75 3.45

Independence and Army Day — A188

Designs: 25f, King Hussein, soldier descending mountain. 40f, King Hussein, Arab revolt flag, globe, Sharif Hussein. 60f, Flag, natl. arms, equestrian. 100f, Natl. flag, arms, Sharif Hussein.

1985, June 10 *Perf. 13x13½*

1218 A188 25f multicolored .45 .25
1219 A188 40f multicolored .90 .45
1220 A188 60f multicolored 1.40 .75
1221 A188 100f multicolored 2.25 1.40
Nos. 1218-1221 (4) 5.00 2.85

Men in Postal History — A189

40f, Sir Rowland Hill. 60f, Heinrich von Stephan. 125f, Yacoub al-Sukkar.

1985, July 1

1222 A189 40f multicolored .75 .45
1223 A189 60f multicolored 1.10 .65
1224 A189 125f multicolored 2.40 1.40
Nos. 1222-1224 (3) 4.25 2.50

1st Convention of Jordanian Expatriates A190

Various designs.

1985, July 20 Photo.

1225 A190 40f multicolored .75 .45
1226 A190 60f multicolored 1.10 .65
1227 A190 125f multicolored 2.40 1.40
Nos. 1225-1227 (3) 4.25 2.50

Intl. Youth Year — A191

Various designs.

1985, Aug. 11 Litho. *Perf. 13½x13*

1228 A191 10f multicolored .30 .25
1229 A191 25f multicolored .50 .25
1230 A191 40f multicolored .80 .50
1231 A191 60f multicolored 1.25 .70
1232 A191 125f multicolored 2.50 1.50
Nos. 1228-1232 (5) 5.35 3.20

World Tourism Organization, 10th Anniv. — A192

10f, Ruins of the Treasury, Petra. 25f, Jerash Temple. 40f, Roman baths. 50f, Jordanian valley town. 60f, Aqaba Bay. 125f, Roman amphitheater.

1985, Sept. 13 *Perf. 13½x13*

1233 A192 10f multicolored .30 .25
1234 A192 25f multicolored .50 .25
1235 A192 40f multicolored .80 .50
1236 A192 50f multicolored 1.00 .60
1237 A192 60f multicolored 1.25 .70
1238 A192 125f multicolored 2.50 1.40
Nos. 1233-1238 (6) 6.35 3.70

An imperf. 100f souvenir sheet exists picturing flower, 10 and natl. flag. Value $6.50.

UN Child Survival Campaign — A193

Various designs.

1985, Oct. 7

1239 A193 25f multicolored .50 .25
1240 A193 40f multicolored .75 .50
1241 A193 60f multicolored 1.25 .70
1242 A193 125f multicolored 2.50 1.50
Nos. 1239-1242 (4) 5.00 2.95

An imperf. 100f souvenir sheet exists picturing campaign emblem and the faces of healthy children. Value $12.

5th Jerash Festival A194

10f, Opening ceremony, 1980. 25f, Folk dancers. 40f, Dancers. 60f, Choir, Roman theater. 100f, King and Queen.

1985, Oct. 21

1243 A194 10f multicolored .30 .25
1244 A194 25f multicolored .45 .25
1245 A194 40f multicolored .90 .45
1246 A194 60f multicolored 1.50 .75
1247 A194 100f multicolored 2.40 1.50
Nos. 1243-1247 (5) 5.55 3.20

UN, 40th Anniv. — A195

1985, Oct. 25 Photo. *Perf. 13x13½*

1248 A195 60f multicolored 1.25 1.00
1249 A195 125f multicolored 2.50 2.00

King Hussein, 50th Birthday A196

Various photos of King.

1985, Nov. 14 Litho. *Perf. 14½*

1250 A196 10f multicolored .30 .25
1251 A196 25f multicolored .50 .25
1252 A196 40f multicolored .90 .50
1253 A196 60f multicolored 1.50 .75
1254 A196 100f multicolored 2.40 1.50
Nos. 1250-1254 (5) 5.60 3.25

An imperf. 200f souvenir sheet exists picturing flags, King Hussein and Dome of the Rock. Value $15.

Restoration of Al Aqsa Mosque, Jerusalem A196a

1985, Nov. 25 Litho. *Perf. 13x13½*

1254A A196a 5f multicolored *1.10 1.10*
1254B A196a 10f multicolored *2.40 2.25*

Police — A197

1985, Dec. 18

1255 A197 40f Patrol car 1.10 .25
1256 A197 60f Crossing guard 1.40 1.10
1257 A197 125f Police academy 3.00 2.00
Nos. 1255-1257 (3) 5.50 3.35

Launch of ARABSAT-1, 1st Anniv. — A198

60f, Satellite in orbit. 100f, Over map of Arab countries.

1986, Feb. 8 Litho. *Perf. 13½x13*

1258 A198 60f multicolored .85 .25
1259 A198 100f multicolored 1.40 .85

Arabization of the Army, 30th Anniv. — A199

40f, King Hussein presenting flag. 60f, Greeting army sergeant. 100f, Hussein addressing army.

1986, Mar. 1 *Perf. 11½x12½*

1260 A199 40f multicolored .75 .25
1261 A199 60f multicolored .90 .25
1262 A199 100f multicolored 1.60 .90
Nos. 1260-1262 (3) 3.25 1.40

An imperf. souvenir sheet exists with design of 100f. Value $10.

Natl. Independence, 40th Anniv. — A200

Design: King Abdullah decorating soldier.

1986, May 25 *Perf. 12½x11½*

1263 A200 160f multicolored 2.75 2.10

Arab Revolt against Turkey, 70th Anniv. A201

Unattributed paintings (details): 40f, The four sons of King Hussein, Prince of Mecca, vert. 60f, Sharif Hussein, retainers and bodyguard. 160f, Abdullah and followers on horseback.

Perf. 12½x11½, 11½x12½

1986, June 10

1264 A201 40f multicolored .65 .25
1265 A201 60f multicolored .85 .25
1266 A201 160f multicolored 2.50 1.25
Nos. 1264-1266 (3) 4.00 1.75

An imperf. 200f souvenir sheet exists picturing the Arab Revolt flag, Sharif Hussein and text from independence declaration. Value $9.

Intl. Peace Year — A202

1986, July 1 Litho. *Perf. 13½x13*

1267 A202 160f multicolored 2.25 1.25
1268 A202 240f multicolored 3.25 1.90

King Hussein Medical City Cardiac Center — A203

1986, Aug. 11

1269 A203 40f Cardiac Center .90 .25
1270 A203 60f Surgery 1.10 .90
1271 A203 100f Surgery, diff. 1.75 .95
Nos. 1269-1271 (3) 3.75 2.10

UN, 40th Anniv. A204

Excerpts from King Hussein's speech: 40f, In Arabic. 80f, Arabic, diff. 100f, English.

1986, Sept. 27 *Perf. 12½x11½*

1272 A204 40f multicolored .75 .25
1273 A204 80f multicolored 1.25 .85
1274 A204 100f multicolored 1.60 .85
Nos. 1272-1274 (3) 3.60 1.95

An imperf. 200f stamp 90x70mm exists picturing speech in Arabic and English, King Hussein at podium. Value $8.50.

Arab Postal Union, 35th Anniv. — A205

1987, Apr. 12 Litho. *Perf. 13½x13*

1275 A205 80f Old post office .85 .60
1276 A205 160f New post office 1.90 1.10

Chemical Soc. Emblem and Chemists A206

Designs: 60f, Jaber ibn Hayyan al-Azdi (720-813). 80f, Abu-al-Qasem al-Majreeti (950-1007). 240f, Abu-Bakr al-Razi (864-932).

1987, Apr. 24

1277 A206 60f multicolored .75 .50
1278 A206 80f multicolored 1.00 .60
1279 A206 240f multicolored 2.75 1.60
Nos. 1277-1279 (3) 4.50 2.70

SOS Children's Village — A207

80f, Village in Amman. 240f, Child, bird mural.

1987, May 7

1280 A207 80f multicolored 1.25 .70
1281 A207 240f multicolored 3.25 1.90

4th Brigade, 40th Anniv. — A208

80f, Soldiers in armored vehicle. 160f, Four veterans.

1987, June 10

1282 A208 60f shown 1.40 .95
1283 A208 80f multicolored 1.60 1.10

Size: 70x91mm

Imperf

1284 A208 160f multicolored 8.00 7.50
Nos. 1282-1284 (3) 11.00 9.55

Indigenous Birds — A209

10f, Hoopoe. 40f, Palestine sunbird. 50f, Black-headed bunting. 60f, Spur-winged plover. 80f, Greenfinch. 100f, Black-winged stilt.

1987, June 24

1285 A209 10f multicolored 1.60 .55
1286 A209 40f multicolored 1.60 .55
1287 A209 50f multicolored 2.00 .60
1288 A209 60f multicolored 2.50 .90
1289 A209 80f multicolored 3.00 1.25
1290 A209 100f multicolored 4.00 1.75
Nos. 1285-1290 (6) 14.70 5.60

King Hussein — A210

1987, June 24 Litho. *Perf. 13x13½*

1291 A210 60f multicolored .40 .30
1292 A210 80f multicolored .85 .40
1293 A210 160f multicolored 1.75 1.10
1294 A210 240f multicolored 2.50 1.75
Nos. 1291-1294 (4) 5.50 3.55

Battle of Hittin, 800th Anniv. — A211

Dome of the Rock and Saladin (1137-1193), Conqueror of Jerusalem — A212

60f, Battle, Jerusalem. 80f, Horseman, Jerusalem, Dome of the Rock. No. 1297, 100f, Saladin.

1987, July 4

1295 A211 60f multicolored .75 .70
1296 A211 80f multicolored 1.50 .85
1297 A211 100f multicolored 2.25 1.50
Nos. 1295-1297 (3) 4.50 3.05

Souvenir Sheet

Perf. 12x12½

1298 A212 100f shown 8.00 7.75

No. 1298 exists imperf.

Natl. Coat of Arms — A213

Perf. 11½x12½

1987, Aug. 11 Litho.

1299 A213 80f multicolored 1.00 .65
1300 A213 160f multicolored 2.00 1.25

Amman Industrial Park at Sahab — A214

1987, Aug. 11 *Perf. 13½x13*

1301 A214 80f multicolored 1.00 .80

University Crest — A215

University Entrance A216

Perf. 11½x11, 12½x11½

1987, Sept. 2

1302 A215 60f multicolored .80 .50
1303 A216 80f multicolored .95 .65

University of Jordan, 25th anniv.

UN Child Survival Campaign — A217

60f, Oral vaccine. 80f, Natl. flag, child. 160f, Growth monitoring.

1987, Oct. 5 Litho. *Perf. 13x13½*

1304 A217 60f multicolored .75 .60
1305 A217 80f multicolored 1.25 .80
1306 A217 160f multicolored 2.50 1.60
Nos. 1304-1306 (3) 4.50 3.00

Parliament, 40th Anniv. — A218

60f, Opening ceremony, 1947. 80f, In session, 1987.

1987, Oct. 20 *Perf. 13½x13*

1307 A218 60f dp mag & gold 1.00 .60
1308 A218 80f multi & gold 1.25 .80

A219

Special Arab Summit Conference, Amman — A220

1987, Nov. 8

1309 A219 60f multicolored .55 .50
1310 A219 80f multicolored .90 .55
1311 A219 160f multicolored 2.00 1.25
1312 A219 240f multicolored 2.75 2.00
Nos. 1309-1312 (4) 6.20 4.30

Size: 90x66mm

Imperf

1313 A220 100f multicolored 7.50 7.50

King Hussein, Dag Hammarskjold Peace Prize Winner for 1987 — A221

80f, Hussein, woman, vert.

1988, Feb. 6 Litho. *Perf. 12½*

1314 A221 80f multicolored .95 .75
1315 A221 160f shown 1.90 1.25

Natl. Victory at the 1987 Arab Military Basketball Championships A222

60f, Golden Sword Award. 80f, Hussein congratulating team. 160f, Jump ball.

1988, Mar. 1 *Perf. 13½x13*

1316 A222 60f multicolored .80 .50
1317 A222 80f multicolored 1.10 .65
1318 A222 160f multicolored 2.10 1.25
Nos. 1316-1318 (3) 4.00 2.40

WHO, 40th Anniv. — A223

1988, Apr. 7 Photo. *Perf. 13x13½*

1319 A223 60f multicolored 1.00 .70
1320 A223 80f multicolored 1.25 .90

Arab Scouts, 75th Anniv. — A224

1988, July 2 Litho. *Perf. 13x13½*

1321 A224 60f multicolored 1.00 .90
1322 A224 80f multicolored 1.25 1.10

Birds — A225

10f, Crested lark. 20f, Stone curlew. 30f, Redstart. 40f, Blackbird. 50f, Rock dove. 160f, Smyrna kingfisher.
310f, Six species.

1988, July 21 Litho. *Perf. 11½x12*

1323 A225 10f multi 2.25 .70
1324 A225 20f multi 2.25 .80
1325 A225 30f multi 2.25 .90
1326 A225 40f multi 3.25 1.00
1327 A225 50f multi 4.00 1.10
1328 A225 160f multi 11.00 1.75
Nos. 1323-1328 (6) 25.00 6.25

Size: 71x90mm

Imperf

1328A A225 310f multi 17.50 15.00

Restoration of San'a, Yemen Arab Republic — A226

1988, Aug. 11 Litho. *Perf. 12x11½*

1329 A226 80f multicolored .95 .70
1330 A226 160f multicolored 1.90 1.50

Historic Natl. Sites — A227

1988, Aug. 11 *Perf. 13½x13*

1331 A227 60f Umm Al-rasas .70 .50
1332 A227 80f Umm Qais .90 .70
1333 A227 160f Iraq Al-amir 1.90 1.50
Nos. 1331-1333 (3) 3.50 2.70

An imperf. souvenir sheet of 3 exists containing one each Nos. 1331-1333. Value $5.

1988 Summer Olympics, Seoul — A228

10f, Tennis. 60f, Character trademark. 80f, Running, swimming. 120f, Basketball. 160f, Soccer.
100f, Emblems.

1988, Sept. 17 Litho. *Perf. 13x13½*

1334 A228 10f multi .30 .25
1335 A228 60f multi .90 .70
1336 A228 80f multi 1.40 .90
1337 A228 120f multi 1.75 1.50
1338 A228 160f multi 2.50 1.75
Nos. 1334-1338 (5) 6.85 5.10

Size: 70x91mm

Imperf

1339 A228 100f multi 17.50 17.50

Royal Jordanian Airlines, 25th Anniv. — A229

60f, Ruins of Petra. 80f, Aircraft, world map.

1988, Dec. 15 Litho. *Perf. 11½x12*

1340 A229 60f multicolored 1.00 .75
1341 A229 80f multicolored 1.25 1.00

UN Declaration of Human Rights, 40th Anniv. — A230

1988, Dec. 10

1342 A230 80f multicolored .75 .60
1343 A230 160f multicolored 1.75 1.10

Arab Cooperation Council, Feb. 16 — A231

1989 Litho. *Perf. 13½x13*

1344 A231 10f shown .30 .25
1345 A231 30f multi, diff. .30 .25
1346 A231 40f multi, diff. .30 .25
1347 A231 60f multi, diff. 1.00 .95
Nos. 1344-1347 (4) 1.90 1.70

Martyrs of Palestine and Their Families A232

1989 *Perf. 14½*

1348 A232 5f multicolored .90 .30
1349 A232 10f multicolored .90 .30

Interparliamentary Union, Cent. — A233

1989 Litho. *Perf. 12*

1350 A233 40f multicolored .35 .25
1351 A233 60f multicolored .55 .35

Arab Housing Day and World Refuge Day — A234

Designs: 5f, Housing complex, emblems, vert. 60f, Housing complex, emblem.

1989

1352 A234 5f multicolored .30 .25
1353 A234 40f shown .55 .25
1354 A234 60f multicolored .75 .55
Nos. 1352-1354 (3) 1.60 1.05

Ministry of Agriculture, 50th Anniv. — A235

40f, Tree, anniv. emblem. 60f, Fruit tree, emblem, apiary.

1989 Litho. *Perf. 12*

1355 A235 5f shown .30 .25
1356 A235 40f multicolored .30 .25
1357 A235 60f multicolored 2.25 .25
Nos. 1355-1357 (3) 2.85 .75

Arabian Horse Festival A236

40f, Horse, building facade. 60f, Horse's head, vert. 100f, Mare and foal.

1989 *Perf. 12*

1358 A236 5f shown .40 .25
1359 A236 40f multicolored .85 .25
1360 A236 60f multicolored 2.40 .25
Nos. 1358-1360 (3) 3.65 .75

Size: 90x70mm

Imperf

1361 A236 100f multicolored *25.00 22.50*

Natl. Library Assoc. — A237

1989 *Perf. 12*

1362 A237 40f multicolored .30 .25
1363 A237 60f multicolored 1.00 .25

Mosque of the Martyr King Abdullah A238

1989 *Perf. 12*

1364 A238 40f multicolored .30 .25
1365 A238 60f multicolored 1.00 .25

Size: 90x70mm

Imperf

1366 A238 100f multicolored *6.75 6.75*

Mosaics — A239

5f, Man with Basket. 10f, Building. 40f, Deer. 60f, Man with stick. 80f, Town, horiz.

1989, Dec. 23 Litho. *Perf. 12*

1367 A239 5f multi .60 .30
1368 A239 10f multi .60 .30
1369 A239 40f multi 1.50 .50
1370 A239 60f multi 2.00 .65
1371 A239 80f multi 2.50 .90
Nos. 1367-1371 (5) 7.20 2.65

Size: 90x70mm

Imperf

1372 A239 100f like #1371, horiz. *17.50 17.50*

Arab Cooperation Council, 1st Anniv. A240

1990, Feb. 16 *Perf. 13*

1373 A240 5f multicolored .30 .25
1374 A240 20f multicolored .30 .25
1375 A240 60f multicolored .75 .45
1376 A240 80f multicolored 1.00 .65
Nos. 1373-1376 (4) 2.35 1.60

Nature Conservation A241

1990, Apr. 22

1377 A241 40f Horses .30 .25
1378 A241 60f Mountain .50 .25
1379 A241 80f Oasis .65 .35
Nos. 1377-1379 (3) 1.45 .85

Prince Abdullah's Arrival in Ma'an, 70th Anniv. A243

1990 Litho. *Perf. 13½x13*

1382 A243 40f org & multi .30 .25
1383 A243 60f grn & multi .40 .25

Size: 90x70mm

Imperf

1384 A243 200f multicolored *7.00 7.00*

UN Development Program, 40th Anniv. — A244

1990 *Perf. 13*

1385 A244 60f multicolored .30 .25
1386 A244 80f multicolored .55 .25

King Hussein — A245

1990-92 Litho. *Perf. 12x13½*

1387 A245 5f yel org & multi .30 .25
a. Slightly larger vignette, inscr. 1991 .30 .25
1390 A245 20f bl grn & multi .30 .25
1391 A245 40f orange & multi .30 .25
1393 A245 60f blue & multi .45 .45
1395 A245 80f pink & multi .70 .70
a. Slightly larger vignette, inscr. 1991 .70 .70
1397 A245 240f brown & multi 1.25 .90
1398 A245 320f red lilac & multi 1.75 1.25
1399 A245 1d yel green & multi 2.75 2.40
Nos. 1387-1399 (8) 7.80 6.45

No. 1390 dated 1991.
Issued: 20f, 1992; 5f, 60f, 80f 1990; others 1991.

Endangered Animals — A246

1991, Sept. 1 Litho. *Perf. 13x13½*

1401 A246 5f Nubian ibex .30 .25
1402 A246 40f Onager .50 .25
1403 A246 80f Arabian gazelle 2.25 .40
1404 A246 160f Arabian oryx 1.60 1.10
Nos. 1401-1404 (4) 4.65 2.00

Energy Rationalization Program A247

Designs: 5f, Light bulbs. 40f, Solar panels, sun, vert. 80f, Electric table lamp, vert.

Perf. 13½x13, 13x13½

1991, Oct. 3 Litho.

1405 A247 5f multicolored .30 .25
1406 A247 40f multicolored .30 .25
1407 A247 80f multicolored .70 .25
Nos. 1405-1407 (3) 1.30 .75

Grain Production for Food Security A248

5f, Different grains. 80f, Wheat stalk, kernels.

1991, Oct. 16 *Perf. 13½x13*

1408 A248 5f multicolored .30 .25
1409 A248 40f shown .30 .25
1410 A248 80f multicolored .70 .25
Nos. 1408-1410 (3) 1.30 .75

Palestinian Uprising A249

1991, Nov. 29 Litho. *Perf. 11*

1411 A249 20f multicolored 2.00 .75

Blood Donation Campaign A250

1991, Nov. 14 Litho. *Perf. 13½x13*

1412 A250 80f multicolored .75 .25
1413 A250 160f multicolored 1.50 .75

Expo '92, Seville — A251

1992, Feb. 20

1414 A251 80f multicolored .65 .25
1415 A251 320f multicolored 1.60 .95

Healthy Hearts — A252

80f, Man & woman, heart at center of scale, vert.

Perf. 13x13½, 13½x13

1992, Apr. 7 Litho.

1416 A252 80f multicolored .70 .25
1417 A252 125f multicolored .80 .50

SOS Children's Village, 'Aqaba — A253

1992, Apr. 30 Litho. *Perf. 13½x13*

1418 A253 80f shown .70 .25
1419 A253 125f Village .80 .50

1992 Summer Olympics, Barcelona A254

Stylized designs with Barcelona Olympic emblem: 5fr, Judo, 40f, Runner, vert. 80f, Diver. 125f, Flag, Cobi, map, vert. 160f, Table tennis.
100f, Incorporates all designs of set.

Perf. 13½x13, 13x13½

1992, July 25 Litho.

1420 A254 5f multicolored .30 .25
1421 A254 40f multicolored .30 .25
1422 A254 80f multicolored .50 .25
1423 A254 125f multicolored .75 .35
1424 A254 160f multicolored 1.10 .50
Nos. 1420-1424 (5) 2.95 1.60

Size: 70x90mm

Imperf

1425 A254 100f multicolored *15.00 12.00*

King Hussein, 40th Anniv. of Accession A255

Designs: 40f, Flags, King in full dress uniform, vert. 125f, King wearing headdress, flags. 160f, King in business suit, crown. 200f, Portrait.

1992, Aug. 11 *Perf. 13x13½*

1426 A255 40f multicolored .30 .25

Perf. 13½x13

1427 A255 80f shown .45 .25
1428 A255 125f multicolored .75 .35
1429 A255 160f multicolored 1.10 .50
Nos. 1426-1429 (4) 2.60 1.35

Size: 90x70mm

Imperf

1430 A255 200f multicolored *7.25 7.25*

Butterflies A256

5f, Danaus chrysippus. 40f, Aporia cartaegi. 80f, Papilio machaon. 160f, Pseudochazara telephassa. 200f, Same as Nos. 1431-1434.

1992, Dec. 20 **Litho.** *Perf. 13½x13*

1431 A256 5f multicolored .50 .25
1432 A256 40f multicolored 1.00 .25
1433 A256 80f multicolored 2.00 .50
1434 A256 160f multicolored 4.50 1.25
Nos. 1431-1434 (4) 8.00 2.25

Imperf

Size: 90x70mm

1435 A256 200f multicolored *17.50 17.50*

See Nos. 1448-1452.

Intl. Customs Day — A257

1993, Jan. 26 **Litho.** *Perf. 13½x13*

1436 A257 80f green & multi .60 .25
1437 A257 125f pale org & multi .90 .45

Royal Scientific Society — A258

1993, June 10 **Litho.** *Perf. 12½x13*

1438 A258 80f multicolored .50 .25

Es Salt Municipality, Cent. — A259

1993, Sept. 1 **Litho.** *Perf. 12*

1439 A259 80f pink & multi .60 .25
1440 A259 125f green & multi .90 .45
a. Souvenir sheet of 2, #1439-1440, imperf. *6.25 6.25*

No. 1440a sold for 200f.

Great Arab Revolt and Army Day — A260

Designs: 5f, Rockets, planes, tank, King Hussein, 40f, King Hussein, military activities. 80f, Amir Abdullah ibn Hussein, Dome of the Rock, map, flags. 125f, Amir Abdullah ibn Hussein, Dome of the Rock, riders. 100f, King Hussein, flags.

1993, June 10

1441 A260 5f multicolored .30 .25
1442 A260 40f multicolored .30 .25
1443 A260 80f multicolored .50 .25
1444 A260 125f multicolored .85 .35
Nos. 1441-1444 (4) 1.95 1.10

Size: 90x70mm

Imperf

1445 A260 100f multicolored *6.00 6.00*

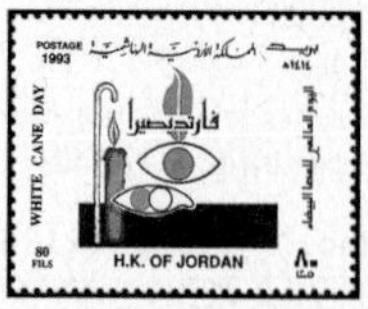

White Cane Day — A261

Design: 125f, Lighted world, cane, eye, vert.

1993, Oct. 23 **Litho.** *Perf. 12*

1446 A261 80f shown .60 .25
1447 A261 125f multicolored .90 .45

Butterfly Type of 1992

Designs: 5f, Lampides boeticus. 40f, Melanargria titea. 80f, Allancastria deyrollei. 160f, Gonepteryx cleopatra. 100f, Same designs as Nos. 1448-1451.

1993, Oct. 10 **Litho.** *Perf. 12*

1448 A256 5f multicolored .40 .25
1449 A256 40f multicolored .75 .30
1450 A256 80f multicolored 1.00 .40
1451 A256 160f multicolored 2.50 1.00
Nos. 1448-1451 (4) 4.65 1.95

Size: 83x65mm

Imperf

1452 A256 100f multicolored *25.00 25.00*

UN Declaration of Human Rights, 45th Anniv. — A262

1993, Dec. 10 *Perf. 12*

1453 A262 40f yellow & multi .30 .25
1454 A262 160f red & multi 1.10 .75

Recovery & Homecoming, 1st Anniv. — A263

King Hussein: 80f, Crowd. 125f, Waving to people. 160f, Embracing woman. 100f, Standing on airplane ramp.

1993, Nov. 25

1455 A263 80f multicolored .50 .25
1456 A263 125f multicolored .85 .40
1457 A263 160f multicolored 1.00 .50
Nos. 1455-1457 (3) 2.35 1.15

Size: 85x65

Imperf

1458 A263 100f multicolored *5.50 3.75*

World AIDS Day — A264

1993, Dec. 1 *Perf. 12*

1459 A264 80f red & multi .50 .25
1460 A264 125f green & multi .85 .45

Size: 83x70mm

Imperf

1461 A264 200f like #1459-1460 *6.25 4.50*

King Hussein — A265

King Hussein wearing: 40f, Military uniform. 80f, Traditional costume. 125f, Business suit. 160f, 100f, Dress uniform in portrait with Queen Noor.

1993, Nov. 14 *Perf. 12*

1462 A265 40f multicolored .30 .25
1463 A265 80f multicolored .50 .25
1464 A265 125f multicolored .80 .35
1465 A265 160f multi, horiz. 1.25 .50
Nos. 1462-1465 (4) 2.85 1.35

Size: 82x68mm

Imperf

1466 A265 100f multicolored *8.00 5.75*

Assumption of Constitutional Powers by King Hussein, 40th anniv.

Saladin (1138-1193), Dome of the Rock — A266

1993, Nov. 25 *Perf. 12*

1467 A266 40f blue & multi .30 .25
1468 A266 80f gray & multi .55 .25
1469 A266 125f yellow & multi .75 .40
Nos. 1467-1469 (3) 1.60 .90

Triumphal Arch, Jerash — A267

Perf. 12x13½ (5f, No. 80f, 1473A, 1475, 160f, 320f, 1d), 12 (25f, 40f, 50f, #1474C, 240f, No. 1478C, No. 1479), 14x13½ (75f, No. 1474, 150f, 200f, 300f, 400f), 13½x14 (#120f), 12¾x13¼ (#1479B)

1993-2003 **Litho.**

1470 A267 5f blue & multi .30 .25
1471 A267 25f pale vio & multi .30 .25
b. Perf 12¾x13¼, inscr. "2003" .30 .25
1471A A267 40f grn & multi .30 .25
1472 A267 50f yel & multi .30 .25
a. Perf 12, inscr. "1996" .30 .25
b. Perf 12¾x13¼ .30 .25
c. Perf 13½x14 .30 .25
d. As "b," inscr. "2003" .30 .25
1472E A267 75f buff & multi .40 .40
1473 A267 80f grn & multi .35 .25
1473A A267 100f red & multi .40 .25
b. Perf. 12 .40 .25
c. As "b," inscribed "1996" .40 .25
1474 A267 100f apple grn & multi .50 .50
a. Perf. 12 .50 .50
d. As "a," inscr. "1996" .50 .50
1474B A267 120f bl grn & multi .65 .65
1474C A267 125f lt bl & multi .60 .60
1475 A267 125f buff & multi .50 .25
a. Perf. 12 .50 .25
1475B A267 150f sal pink & multi .90 .90
1476 A267 160f yel & multi .65 .25
b. Perf. 12 .75 .25
c. As "b," inscribed "1994" .75 .25
1476A A267 200f gray & multi 1.10 1.10
d. Perf. 12 1.10 1.10
1477 A267 240f pink & multi 1.00 .25
b. Perf. 12x13½ .90 .25
c. perf 12, inscribed "1994" 1.25 1.25
1477A A267 300f pink & multi 1.75 1.75
d. Perf. 12 1.75 1.75
1478 A267 320f brn & multi 1.25 .35
1478A A267 320f sal & multi 1.25 .35
1478C A267 400f brt blue & multi 2.50 2.50
b. Perf. 13x13¼ 2.50 2.50
1479 A267 500f bister & multi 2.00 .85
a. Perf. 12x13½ 2.00 .85
1479B A267 500f yel & multi 2.50 2.50
1480 A267 1d olive & multi 4.00 1.25
a. Perf. 12¾x13¼ 5.00 1.25
Nos. 1470-1480 (22) 23.50 15.95

Nos. 1472E, 1473, 1473A , 1477b, 1479a are dated 1992; Nos. 1471A, 1473Ab, 1476b, 1993; No. 1474, 1994; No. 1477Ac, 1995; Nos. 1478Cb, 1479B, 1480a, 1997.

Issued: 5f, 320f, 1/13/93 (dated 1992); 25f, 1/18/96 (dated 1995); 40f, 1994; 80f, 125f, 160f, 1d, Nos. 1473A, 1477b, 1479a, 1/13/93; No. 1478C, 1993; Nos. 1473Ab, 1476b, 240f, 3/23/94; 50f, 1995; No. 1474C, 2/13/95; 75f, 100f, 120f, 150f, 200f, 300f, 400f, 5/15/96; Nos. 1476Ad, 1477Ad, 1/18/96; 500f, 10/25/96; No. 1478Cb, 5/10/98; Nos. 1479B, 1480a, 5/10/98.

For surcharges, see Nos. 2018, 2305-2314, 2384.

Hashemite Charity Organization A268

Designs: 80f, Loading supplies into plane. 125f, People gathering at plane.

1994, Mar. 20 **Litho.** *Perf. 12*

1481 A268 80f multicolored .55 .25
1482 A268 125f multicolored .80 .50

Third Hashemite Restoration of Al Aqsa Mosque, Dome of the Rock A269

King Hussein with various scenes of restoration.

1994, Apr. 18 **Litho.** *Perf. 12x12½*

1483 A269 80f yellow & multi .40 .25
1484 A269 125f lt orange & multi .70 .35
1485 A269 240f lilac & multi 1.25 .60
Nos. 1483-1485 (3) 2.35 1.20

Imperf

Size: 90x70mm

1486 A269 100f green & multi *8.00 5.50*

ILO, 75th Anniv. — A270

1994, June 13 **Litho.** *Perf. 12*

1487 A270 80f yellow & multi .45 .25
1488 A270 125f brt pink & multi .70 .35

Intl. Red Cross and Red Crescent Societies, 75th Anniv. — A271

160f, Doves, emblems, vert.

1994, May 8 *Perf. 12*

1489 A271 80f shown .45 .25
1490 A271 160f multicolored .80 .45

Size: 61x78mm

Imperf

1491 A271 200f #1489-1490 *11.00 8.25*

Intl. Year of the Family — A272

1994, Aug. 11 **Litho.** *Perf. 12*

1492 A272 80f green & multi .45 .25
1493 A272 125f pink & multi .80 .40
1494 A272 160f yellow & multi 1.00 .45
Nos. 1492-1494 (3) 2.25 1.10

Intl. Olympic Committee, Cent. — A273

Olympic rings and: 80f, Globe, venue symbols, vert. 100f, Jordanian colors. 125f, Venue symbols, diff., vert. 160f, shown. 240f, Torch.

1994, June 23

1495	A273	80f blue & multi		.40	.25
1496	A273	125f multicolored		.65	.30
1497	A273	160f multicolored		1.10	.40
1498	A273	240f multicolored		1.60	.65
		Nos. 1495-1498 (4)		3.75	1.60

Size: 90x70mm

Imperf

1499	A273	100f multicolored	*8.50*	*8.50*

Jordanian Participation in UN Peacekeeping Forces — A274

Designs: 80f, King Hussein greeting troops. 125f, King inspecting troops. 160f, Checkpoint.

1994, Aug. 11 **Litho.** ***Perf. 12***

1500	A274	80f multicolored	.45	.25
1501	A274	125f multicolored	.70	.35
1502	A274	160f multicolored	.85	.45
		Nos. 1500-1502 (3)	2.00	1.05

Water Conservation Day — A275

80f, Hands, water droplet. 125f, Water faucet, foods, factory. 160f, Child, rain drops.

1994, Nov. 14 **Litho.** ***Perf. 14***

1503	A275	80f multicolored	.60	.25
1504	A275	125f multicolored	1.00	.55
1505	A275	160f multicolored	1.25	.60
		Nos. 1503-1505 (3)	2.85	1.40

ICAO, 50th Anniv. — A276

1994, Oct. 25 ***Perf. 12***

1506	A276	80f green & multi	.45	.25
1507	A276	125f red & multi	.70	.35
1508	A276	160f blue & multi	.85	.45
		Nos. 1506-1508 (3)	2.00	1.05

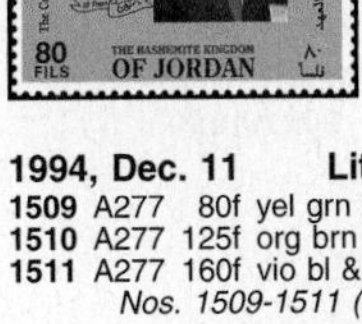

Crown Prince's Award, 10th Anniv. — A277

1994, Dec. 11 **Litho.** ***Perf. 12***

1509	A277	80f yel grn & multi	.70	.25
1510	A277	125f org brn & multi	.90	.55
1511	A277	160f vio bl & multi	1.25	.70
		Nos. 1509-1511 (3)	2.85	1.50

UN, 50th Anniv. — A278

1995, Apr. 1 **Litho.** ***Perf. 14***

1512	A278	80f green & multi	.65	.25
1513	A278	125f pink & multi	.95	.55

May Day — A279

80f, Emblem, workers, flag. 125f, Emblem, world map, worker. 160f, Hands holding wrench, torch, Jordanian map, emblem.

1995, May 1

1514	A279	80f multicolored	.45	.25
1515	A279	125f multicolored	.65	.40
1516	A279	160f multicolored	.90	.45
		Nos. 1514-1516 (3)	2.00	1.10

Jordan Week in Japan — A280

Globe in two hemishperes with olive branches and: 125f, Japanese, Jordanian flags. 160f, Flags above wall.

1995, May 22 **Litho.** ***Perf. 14***

1517	A280	80f green & multi	.45	.25
1518	A280	125f pink & multi	.70	.30
1519	A280	160f gray & multi	.85	.45
		Nos. 1517-1519 (3)	2.00	1.00

Opening of Al al-Bayt University — A281

1995, Feb. 8 **Litho.** ***Perf. 12***

1520	A281	80f aqua & multi	.50	.25
1521	A281	125f ol grn & multi	.75	.40
	a.	Souvenir sheet, #1520-1521, imperf.	3.75	3.25

No. 1521a sold for 200f. Nos. 1520-1521 are dated 1994.

Petra, the Rose City — A282

Archaeological discoveries: 50f, Amphitheater. 75f, Facial carvings, bowl, pitcher. 80f, Columns of building, vert. 160f, Front of building with columns, vert. 200f, Building in side of mountain.

1995, Aug. 11 **Litho.** ***Perf. 14***

1524	A282	50f multicolored	.30	.25
1525	A282	75f multicolored	.85	.25
1526	A282	80f multicolored	.95	.25
1527	A282	160f multicolored	1.75	.95
		Nos. 1524-1527 (4)	3.85	1.70

Size: 90x70mm

Imperf

1528	A282	200f multicolored	*20.00*	*20.00*

Arab League, 50th Anniv. — A283

1995, Sept. 20 **Litho.** ***Perf. 14***

1529	A283	80f green & multi	.45	.25
1530	A283	125f pink & multi	.70	.25
1531	A283	160f gray & multi	.85	.45
		Nos. 1529-1531 (3)	2.00	.95

FAO, 50th Anniv. — A284

Designs: 125f, "50," FAO emblem, shafts of grain. 160f, UN, FAO emblems, "50."

1995, Oct. 16 **Litho.** ***Perf. 14***

1532	A284	80f shown	.50	.25
1533	A284	125f multicolored	.85	.40
1534	A284	160f multicolored	1.00	.50
		Nos. 1532-1534 (3)	2.35	1.15

Middle East and North Africa Economic Summit, Amman — A285

1995, Oct. 29 ***Perf. 12***

1535	A285	80f brt pink & multi	.50	.25
1536	A285	125f org yel & multi	.75	.40

The Deaf — A286

125f, Emblems, hand sign.

1995, Nov. 30 ***Perf. 14***

1537	A286	80f shown	.50	.25
1538	A286	125f multicolored	.75	.35

King Hussein, 60th Birthday A287

Designs: 40f, Crown over King's picture in business suit. 80f, Crown, flag, dove, ruins of Petra, King in traditional head wear, military uniform. 100f, King dress uniform, crown, "60." 125f, King in traditional head wear, business suit, crown, flag, olive branch. 160f, Flag, King in business suit. 200f, "60," Dome of the Rock, King in dress uniform, olive branch.

1995, Nov. 14

1539	A287	25f multicolored	.30	.25
1540	A287	40f multicolored	.30	.25
1541	A287	80f multicolored	.45	.25
1542	A287	100f multicolored	.50	.25
1543	A287	125f multicolored	1.00	.35
1544	A287	160f multicolored	1.25	.45
		Nos. 1539-1544 (6)	3.80	1.80

Size: 83x63mm

Imperf

1545	A287	200f multicolored	*6.25*	*6.25*

Independence, 50th Anniv. — A288

King Hussein and: No. 1547, Outline map of Jordan, crown, dove of peace, Amir Abdullah ibn Hussein. 300f, Jordanian monuments, flag.

No. 1549, Map of Jordan surrounded by wreath, dove, national flags.

1996, May 25 **Litho.** ***Perf. 12***

1546	A288	100f multicolored	.55	.25
1547	A288	200f multicolored	1.10	.40
1548	A288	300f multicolored	1.75	.65
		Nos. 1546-1548 (3)	3.40	1.30

Size: 86x66mm

1549	A288	200f multicolored	*7.50*	*7.50*

1996 Summer Olympic Games, Atlanta — A289

1996 Olympic Games Emblem and: 50f, Natl. flag, Olympic rings, sports pictograms. 100f, Sports pictograms. 200f, Hands. 300f, Torch, Olympic rings, natl. flag.

1996, July 19 **Litho.** ***Perf. 12***

1550	A289	50f multicolored	.30	.25
1551	A289	100f multicolored	.70	.25
1552	A289	200f multicolored	1.60	.70
1553	A289	300f multicolored	2.50	1.10
		Nos. 1550-1553 (4)	5.10	2.30

Protection of the Ozone Layer — A290

1996, Sept. 16

1554	A290	100f multicolored	1.25	.25

UNICEF, 50th Anniv. — A291

1996, Dec. 11 **Litho.** ***Perf. 12***

1555	A291	100f green & multi	.60	.25
1556	A291	200f gray lilac & multi	1.00	.60

Crown Prince El-Hassan, 50th Birthday A292

Designs: 50f, On horseback. 100f, Wearing suit & tie, vert. No. 1559, Natl. flag, wearing traditional attire.

No. 1560, Wearing graduation cap.

1997, Mar. 20 **Litho.** ***Perf. 12***

1557	A292	50f multicolored	.30	.25
1558	A292	100f multicolored	.70	.25
1559	A292	200f multicolored	1.10	.70
		Nos. 1557-1559 (3)	2.10	1.20

Size: 84x64mm

Imperf

1560	A292	200f multicolored	*8.25*	*8.25*

Heinrich von Stephan (1831-97) — A293

1997, Apr. 8 **Litho.** ***Perf. 12***

1561	A293	100f multicolored	.90	.25
1562	A293	200f multicolored	1.60	.80

Discovery of the Madeba Mosaic Map, Cent. — A294

100f, Karak, vert. 200f, River Jordan. 300f, Jerusalem, vert.

No. 1566, Entire map.

1997, Apr. 7

1563	A294	100f multicolored	.75	.35
1564	A294	200f multicolored	1.50	.50
1565	A294	300f multicolored	2.50	.90
		Nos. 1563-1565 (3)	4.75	1.75

Size: 86x67mm

Imperf

1566 A294 100f multi *15.00 15.00*

Jordanian Rosefinch A295

1997, May 25 Litho. *Perf. 12*

1567	A295	50f multicolored	.30	.25
1568	A295	100f multi, diff.	.65	.25
1569	A295	150f multi, diff.	1.00	.45
1570	A295	200f multi, diff.	1.50	.65
		Nos. 1567-1570 (4)	3.45	1.60

Jerash Festival, 15th Anniv. — A296

Designs: 50f, Couples in traditional costumes, ruins. 100f, Symphony orchestra, silhouettes of buildings. 150f, Pillars, parade of dignitaries. 200f, Women in traditional costumes, crowd, ruins.

15d, Queen Noor lighting torch.

1997, July 23 Litho. *Perf. 12*

1571	A296	50f multicolored	.30	.25
1572	A296	100f multicolored	.60	.25
1573	A296	150f multicolored	.95	.45
1574	A296	200f multicolored	1.50	.65
		Nos. 1571-1574 (4)	3.35	1.60

Size: 90x70mm

Imperf

1575 A296 15d multicolored 8.50 8.50

Natl. Forum for Women — A297

Emblem and: 50f, Women in tradtional and modern dress, vert. 100f, Natl. flag, flame, book. 150fr, Natl. flag, women seated at conference table.

1997, Dec. 20 Litho. *Perf. 12*

1576	A297	50f multicolored	.30	.25
1577	A297	100f multicolored	.50	.25
1578	A297	150f multicolored	.80	.35
		Nos. 1576-1578 (3)	1.60	.85

Jordanian Team, 1997 Arab Soccer Champions A298

Designs: 50f, Team parading in stadium. 75f, Team in red uniforms. 100f, Team in white uniforms, ceremony.

200f, Formal presentation to King Hussein, motorcade.

1997, Dec. 15

1579	A298	50f multicolored	.30	.25
1580	A298	75f multicolored	.40	.25
1581	A298	100f multicolored	.55	.25
		Nos. 1579-1581 (3)	1.25	.75

Size: 91x70mm

Imperf

1582 A298 200f multicolored *9.00 7.50*

House of Parliament, 50th Anniv. — A299

100f, Outside view of building, drawing. 200f, Speaker, members assembled in chamber.

1997, Nov. 1 *Perf. 12½*

1583	A299	100f multicolored	.60	.25
1584	A299	200f multicolored	.90	.60

53rd General Meeting of Intl. Air Transport Association — A300

1997, Nov. 3 Litho. *Perf. 13x13½*

1585	A300	100f lt blue & multi	1.00	1.00
1586	A300	200f red & multi	1.00	1.00
1587	A300	300f gray & multi	1.00	1.00

Two additional stamps were issued in this set. The editors would like to examine them.

King Hussein II, 62nd Birthday — A301

1997, Nov. 14 Litho. *Perf. 13x13½*

Frame Color

1588	A301	100f red	1.00	1.00
1589	A301	200f gold	1.00	1.00
1590	A301	300f blue	1.00	1.00

Souvenir Sheet

Perf. 12

1590A A301 200f gold 8.50 8.50

No. 1590A contains one 44x60mm stamp.

Earth Day — A302

Children's drawings: 50f, Various ways of polluting air and water. 100f, Pollution from factory smoke, automobiles. 150f, Earth chained to various methods of pollution, vert.

1998, Apr. 29 Litho. *Perf. 14*

1591	A302	50f multicolored	.30	.25
1592	A302	100f multicolored	.50	.25
1593	A302	150f multicolored	.80	.50
		Nos. 1591-1593 (3)	1.60	1.00

Trans-Jordan Emirate, 75th Anniv. — A303

Designs: 100f, Camel rider holding flag, Amir Abdullah ibn Hussein. 200f, Camel rider holding flag, King Hussein. 300f, King Hussein, arms, #81, Amir Abdullah ibn Hussein.

1998, May 25 *Perf. 12*

1594	A303	100f multicolored	.50	.50
1595	A303	200f multicolored	1.00	1.00
1596	A303	300f multicolored	1.75	1.75
		Nos. 1594-1596 (3)	3.25	3.25

Size: 80x70mm

Imperf

1597 A303 300f like #1596 *8.50 8.50*

Mosaics, Um Ar-Rasas — A304

1998, July 22 Litho. *Perf. 14*

1598	A304	100f multicolored	.50	.50
1599	A304	200f multi, diff.	1.00	1.00
1600	A304	300f multi, diff.	1.75	1.75
		Nos. 1598-1600 (3)	3.25	3.25

Flowers — A305

50f, Purple & white, thorns. 100f, Poppies. 200f, Flower, map of Jordan.

1998, July 7

1601	A305	50f multicolored	.30	.25
1602	A305	100f multicolored	.60	.55
1603	A305	150f shown	1.00	.75
		Nos. 1601-1603 (3)	1.90	1.55

Size: 60x80mm

Imperf

1604 A305 200f multicolored *8.50 8.50*

2nd Arab Beekeepers Conference A306

Various pictures of bees, flowers, honeycomb.

1998, Aug. 3 Litho. *Perf. 14*

1605	A306	50f multicolored	.50	.40
1606	A306	100f multi, vert.	.85	.50
1607	A306	150f multicolored	1.25	.60
		Nos. 1605-1607 (3)	2.60	1.50

Size: 80x60mm

Imperf

1608 A306 200f Bees, flowers, emblem *9.00 9.00*

World Stamp Day — A307

100f, World map, emblems. 150f, Globe, stamps.

1998, Oct. 9 Litho. *Perf. 14*

1609	A307	50f shown	.30	.25
1610	A307	100f multicolored	.90	.90
1611	A307	150f multicolored	1.75	1.75
		Nos. 1609-1611 (3)	2.95	2.90

Universal Declaration of Human Rights, 50th Anniv. — A308

200f, Emblems, people.

1998, Dec. 10

1612	A308	100f shown	.60	.60
1613	A308	200f multicolored	1.00	1.00

King Hussein, 63rd Birthday A309

1998, Nov. 14 Litho. *Perf. 14x14½*

1614	A309	100f green & multi	.65	.45
1615	A309	200f violet & multi	1.25	1.00
1616	A309	300f vio blue & multi	2.25	1.50
		Nos. 1614-1616 (3)	4.15	2.95

Size: 90x70mm

Imperf

1617 A309 300f gold & multi *8.50 8.50*

Arab Police and Security Chiefs Meeting, 25th Anniv. (in 1997) — A310

Map of Arab world and: 100f, King Hussein, emblem. 200f, Flags of Arab countries, emblem, flame, vert. 300f, Beret.

1998, Nov. 18 *Perf. 14*

1618	A310	100f multicolored	.65	.65
1619	A310	200f multicolored	1.10	1.10
1620	A310	300f multicolored	2.00	1.75
		Nos. 1618-1620 (3)	3.75	3.50

Mustafa Wahbi (1899-1949), Poet — A311

1999, May 25 Litho. *Perf. 14¼*

1621 A311 100f multicolored .90 .90

Environmental Protection A312

Designs: 100f, Children, bandaged Earth. 200f, Earth as fruit in hands.

1999, Oct. 14 Litho. *Perf. 13¼x13¾*

1622	A312	100f multi	.50	.50
1623	A312	200f multi	1.00	1.00

Hijazi Railway Museum A313

Train and: 100f, 200f, Map of Jordan, museum building. 300f, Museum building.

1999, Sept. 7 Litho. *Perf. 13½x13¾*

1624-1626 A313 Set of 3 6.00 6.00

9th Arab Sports Tournament A314

Bird mascot, emblem and: 50f, Weight lifting, tennis, wrestling, soccer. 100f, Torch. No. 1629, Shooting, fencing, swimming, track & field, vert. 300f, Flag, map, discus thrower, tennis player.

No. 1631, Basketball, volleyball, boxing, swimming.

Perf. 13¼x13¾, 13¾x13¼

1999, Aug. 15 Litho.

1627	A314	50f multi	.30	.25
1628	A314	100f multi	.65	.65
1629	A314	200f multi	1.40	1.40
1630	A314	300f multi	2.25	2.25
		Nos. 1627-1630 (4)	4.60	4.55

Imperf

Size: 90x70mm

1631 A314 200f multi 3.25 3.25

UPU, 125th Anniv. — A315

Designs: 100f, "125," UPU emblems, stripes of airmail envelope. No. 1633, Airmail envelope with UPU emblem.

No. 1634, Like No. 1633, yellow background.

1999, Oct. 9 ***Perf. 13¼x13¾***
1632 A315 100f multi .65 .65
1633 A315 200f multi 1.10 1.10

Imperf

Size: 90x70mm

1634 A315 200f multi 2.50 2.50

Gulf of Aqaba Corals — A316

Designs: 50f, Pachyseris speciosa. 100f, Acropora digitifera. No. 1637, 200f, Oxypora lacera. 300f, Fungia echinata.
No. 1639, 200f, Gorgonia.

1999, Oct. 2 Litho. ***Perf. 13½x13¾***
1635-1638 A316 Set of 4 4.00 4.00

Imperf

Size: 90x70mm

1639 A316 200f multi *12.00 12.00*

Cradle of Civilizations A317

Archaeological sites — Petra: No. 1640, 100f, Al-Deir. No. 1641, 200f, Khazneh. No. 1642, 300f, Obelisk tomb.
Jerash: No. 1643, 100f, Cardo Maximus. No. 1644, 200f, Temple of Artemis. No. 1645, 300f, Nymphaeum.
Amman: No. 1646, 100f, Roman Theater. No. 1647, 200f, Citadel. No. 1648, 300f, Ain Ghazal statues.
Wadi Rum and Aqaba: No. 1649, 100f, Camel riders, Wadi Rum. No. 1650, 200f, House, Aqaba. No. 1651, Ruins, Aqaba.
Madaba: No. 1652, 100f, Mosaic. No. 1653, 200f, Church. No. 1654, 300f, Mosaic map of Jerusalem.
Baptism Site (Bethany): No. 1655, Plant life near water. No. 1656, 200f, Aerial view. No. 1657, 300f, Excavation site.
Aljoun: No. 1658, 100f, Ruins. No. 1659, 200f, Ruins diff. No. 1660, 300f, Ruins, diff.
Pella: No. 1661, 100f, Ruins of Byzantine cathedral. No. 1662, 200f, Three large pillars. No. 1663, 300f, Ruins.

1999-2000 Litho. ***Perf. 13½x14***
1640-1663 A317 Set of 24 23.00 23.00

Issued: Nos. 1640-1645, 10/24; Nos. 1646-1651, 10/31; Nos. 1652-1654, 12/22; Nos. 1655-1657, 12/23; Nos. 1658-1663, 3/7/00.
See Nos. 1688-1693. For surcharges, see Nos. 2317-2321, 2324-2325, 2378-2381.

Museum of Political History — A318

100f, Building interior. 200f, Museum entrance and plaza. 300f, Museum entrance.

1999, Nov. 14 Litho. ***Perf. 13½x14***
1664-1666 A318 Set of 3 3.75 3.75

Jordan Philatelic Club, 20th Anniv. A318a

Designs: 100f, #534H and other stamps. 200f, #284 and other stamps.

1999, Nov. 14 ***Perf. 14¼***
1666A-1666B A318a Set of 2 1.50 1.50

SOS Children's Village, Irbid — A318b

100f, SOS Children's Village 50th anniv. emblem, Jordanian flag. 200f, Woman, children.

1999, Nov. 23
1666C-1666D A318b Set of 2 1.50 1.50

Coronation of King Abdullah II — A319

1999, Dec. 27 Litho. ***Perf. 11¾***

Frame Color

1667 A319 100f red .90 .90
1668 A319 200f green .90 .90
1669 A319 300f blue .90 .90

Souvenir Sheet

1670 A319 200f gold 1.00 1.00

King Abdullah II and Queen Rania A319a

1999, Dec. 27 Litho. ***Perf. 11¾***
1670A A319a 100f red .95 .95
1670B A319a 200f green .95 .95
1670C A319a 300f blue .95 .95

Souvenir Sheet

1670D A319a 200f gold *5.25 5.25*

Issued: 1670D, 12/27/99.
Numbers have been reserved for three additional stamps in this set. The editors would like to examine any examples of them.

King Abdullah II, 38th Birthday — A320

King, crown and: 100f, Olive branches. 200f, Nos. #1672 #1674, Flag, "38," horiz. 300f, Flag, "38," eagle, olive branch, horiz.

Perf 12, Imperf (#1674)

2000, Jan. 30 Litho.
1671-1673 A320 Set of 3 3.00 3.00

Size: 90x74mm

1674 A320 200f multi *3.50 3.50*

Geneva Convention, 50th Anniv. — A321

Perf. 13½x13¾

2000, Feb. 15 Litho.
1675 Horiz. strip of 3 3.50 3.50
a. A321 100f lt bl & multi .50 .50
b. A321 200f ocher & multi 1.00 1.00
c. A321 300f gray & multi 1.50 1.50

Dated 1999.

Millennium — A322

No. 1678: a, Jordanian flag, "Jordan, The River & The Land of the Baptism" in English. b, Fish in river. c, As "a," with Arabic inscription.

Perf. 13¼x13¾

2000, Feb. 22 Litho.
1678 Strip of 3 3.25 3.25
a. A322 100f multi .45 .45
b. A322 200f multi .90 .90
c. A322 300f multi 1.25 1.25

King Abdullah II, Houses of Worship and Pope John Paul II — A323

Color of lower panel: 100f, Dull blue green. 200f, Lilac. 300f, Bright yellow green.

2000, Mar. 20 Litho. ***Perf. 12***
1679-1681 A323 Set of 3 3.25 3.25

Visit of Pope Paul VI to Jordan, 36th anniv.

Visit of Pope John Paul II to Jordan — A324

Pope John Paul II, King Abdullah II and: 100f, "2000." 200f, River. 300f, Vatican and Jordanian flags, map of Jordan. No. 1685, Pope, baptism of Christ, vert.

Perf 12, Imperf (#1685)

2000, Mar. 20
1682-1684 A324 Set of 3 3.25 3.25

Size: 70x90mm

1685 A324 200f multi *17.50 17.50*

World Meteorological Organization, 50th Anniv. — A325

Designs: 100f, Globe, emblem, anniversary emblem. 200f, Globe with arrows, emblem, anniversary emblem.

2000, Mar. 23 Litho. ***Perf. 12***
1686 A325 100f multi .75 .75
1687 A325 200f multi 1.25 1.25

Cradle of Civilizations Type of 1999

Archaeological sites — Palaces: No. 1688, 100f, Mushatta. No. 1689, 200f, Kharaneh. No. 1690, 300f, Amra.
Um Qais: No. 1691, 100f, Decumanus. No. 1692, 200f, Amphitheater. No. 1693, 300f, Ruins.

2000, Apr. 7 Litho. ***Perf. 13½x14***

Palaces

1688-1690 A317 Set of 3 4.00 4.00

Um Qais

1691-1693 A317 Set of 3 4.00 4.00
a. Sheet, #1640-1663, 1688-1693 40.00 —

For surcharges, see Nos. 2322-2323, 2382-2383.

Scouting in Jordan, 90th Anniv. — A326

"90" and: 100f, Emblem, Jordanian flag. 200f, Tents. 300f, Tents, Jordanian flag. No. 1697, Like No. 1694.

Perf 12, Imperf (#1697)

2000, May 11 Litho.
1694-1696 A326 Set of 3 5.00 5.00

Size: 90x70mm

1697 A326 200f multi *7.50 7.50*

Expo 2000, Hanover — A327

Designs: No. 1698, 200f, Inscribed clay tablet. 300f, Artifact with two heads.
No. 1700, 200f, King, Queen, Jordan pavilion interior.

2000, June 1 Litho. ***Perf. 11¾***

Granite Paper

1698-1699 A327 Set of 2 3.50 3.50

Imperf

Size: 90x70mm

1700 A327 200f multi 3.00 3.00

Palace of Justice — A328

Palace and: 100f, Scales of justice. 200f, Scales, Jordanian flag.

2000, June 25 Unwmk. ***Perf. 12***
1701 A328 100f multi .75 .75

Wmk. 388

1702 A328 200f multi 1.25 1.25

A number has been reserved for an additional stamp in this set. The editors would like to examine it.

Al-Amal Cancer Center — A329

Emblem and: 200f, Building. 300f, Family.

Perf. 11¾

2000, July 17 Litho. Unwmk.

Granite Paper

1704-1705 A329 Set of 2 3.75 3.75

Flora and Fauna — A330

Designs: 50f, Dove. 100f, Arabian oryx. 150f, Caracal. 200f, Red fox. 300f, Jal'ad iris. 400f, White broom.

2000, Sept. 28 ***Perf. 14¼***

Booklet Stamps

1706 A330 50f multi .35 .30
1707 A330 100f multi .75 .50
a. Booklet pane, 2 each #1706-1707 4.00 —

1708 A330 150f multi 1.25 .60
1709 A330 200f multi 1.50 .80
a. Booklet pane, 2 each #1708-1709 7.00 —
1710 A330 300f multi 2.50 1.75
1711 A330 400f multi 3.00 1.90
a. Booklet pane, 2 each #1710-1711 13.00 —
Booklet, #1707a, 1709a, 1711a 30.00

World Conservation Union — A331

Background color: 200f, Green. 300f, Blue.

2000, Oct. 4 ***Perf. 11¾***
Granite Paper
1712-1713 A331 Set of 2 3.50 3.50

Tourist Sites — A332

Designs: 50f, Petra. 100f, Jerash. 150f, Mount Nebo. 200f, Dead Sea. 300f, Aqaba. 400f, Wadi Rum.

2000, Oct. 9 ***Perf. 14¼***
Booklet Stamps
1714 A332 50f multi .35 .35
1715 A332 100f multi .75 .60
a. Booklet pane, 2 each #1714-1715 2.25 —
1716 A332 150f multi 1.25 .90
1717 A332 200f multi 1.75 1.10
a. Booklet pane, 2 each #1716-1717 6.00 —
1718 A332 300f multi 2.25 1.50
1719 A332 400f multi 2.75 2.25
a. Booklet pane, 2 each #1718-1719 10.00 —
Booklet, #1715a, 1717a, 1719a 22.50

King Hussein (1935-99) — A333

Designs: 50f, King, vert. No. 1721, 150f, No. 1723, 200f, King and wreath. No. 1722, 200f, King, symbols of industry and agriculture.

2000, Nov. 14 **Litho.** ***Perf. 11¾***
Granite Paper
1720-1722 A333 Set of 3 *2.75 2.75*
Size: 90x70mm
Imperf
1723 A333 200f multi *4.50 4.50*

UN High Commissioner for Refugees, 50th Anniv. — A334

Designs: 200f, Man, women, child. 300f, Emblem.

2000, Dec. 3 **Litho.** ***Perf. 11¾***
Granite Paper
1724-1725 A334 Set of 2 3.50 3.50

13th Arab Summit Conference A335

Emblem, map of Middle East and: 50f, Jordanian flag. 200f, Jordanian flags. 250f, King Abdullah II.

2001, Aug. 1 ***Perf. 14***
1726-1728 A335 Set of 3 3.00 3.00

Palestinian Intifada — A336

Dome of the Rock and: 200f, Rock throwers, man carrying flag. 300f, Rock throwers, Israeli troops.

2001, Aug. 5
1729-1730 A336 Set of 2 3.00 3.00

Mohammed Al-Dorra, Boy Killed in Intifada Crossfire — A337

Designs: 200f, Al-Dorra and father, Dome of the Rock. 300f, Close-up of Al-Dorra, Al-Dorra dead on father's lap.

2001, Aug. 5
1731-1732 A337 Set of 2 3.00 3.00

Healthy Non-smoking Students — A338

Designs: 200f, Students. 300f, Cartoon character, vert.

2001, Sept. 1
1733-1734 A338 Set of 2 3.00 3.00

Sports For People With Special Needs — A339

Stylized figures and: 200f, Man in wheelchair. 300f, Woman.

2001, Sept. 15
1735-1736 A339 Set of 2 3.00 3.00

Olive Trees — A340

Designs: 200f, Olives on branch, tree, map of Jordan. 300f, Woman picking olives, vert.

2001, Oct. 1
1737-1738 A340 Set of 2 3.00 3.00

Year of Dialogue Among Civilizations A341

Emblem and: 200f, Family, handshake, world map. 300f, Other stylized drawings.

2001, Oct. 21
1739-1740 A341 Set of 2 3.00 3.00

Cooperation Between Jordan and Japan — A342

Designs: 200f, Sheikh Hussein Bridge, flags. 300f, King Hussein Bridge, handshake.

2001, Nov. 12 **Litho.** ***Perf. 14¼***
1741-1742 A342 Set of 2 3.00 3.00

Jordan - People's Republic of China Diplomatic Relations, 25th Anniv. — A343

Designs: 200f, Dove with envelope. 300f, King Abdullah II and Chinese Pres. Jiang Zemin.

2002 ***Perf. 12***
1743-1744 A343 Set of 2 2.25 2.25

Amman, 2002 Arab Cultural Capital — A344

Designs: 100f, Arabic script, star. 200f, Pen, torch. 300f, Amphitheater.

2002 ***Perf. 14¼***
1745-1747 A344 Set of 3 3.00 3.00

Paintings — A345

Paintings by, 100f, Rafiq Laham. 150f, Mahmoud Taha, horiz. 200f, Mohanna Durra. 300f, Wijdan, horiz.

2002, July 2 ***Perf. 13¼***
1748-1751 A345 Set of 4 4.50 4.50

Vision 2020 — A346

Designs: 200f, Symbols of business and technology. 300f, Fingers, electronic device.

2002 **Litho.** ***Perf. 13¼***
1752-1753 A346 Set of 2 2.25 2.25

Migratory Birds — A347

Designs: 100f, Goldfinch. No. 1755, 200f, Rufous bush robin. 300f, White stork.
No. 1757, 200f, Golden oriole, goshawk, ortolan bunting, hoopoe.

2002 ***Perf. 13¼***
1754-1756 A347 Set of 3 4.00 4.00
Imperf
Size: 70x90mm
1757 A347 200f multi *8.50 8.50*

Hashemite Rulers — A348

No. 1758: a, Sherif Hussein bin Ali. b, King Abdullah. c, King Talal bin Abdullah. d, King Hussein bin Talal. e, King Abdullah II.

2003, July 2 **Litho.** ***Perf. 14***
1758 Miniature sheet of 5 4.50 4.50
a.-e. A348 200f Any single .75 .75

Salt Museum — A349

Views of building exterior: 150f, 250f.

2003, July 2
1759-1760 A349 Set of 2 1.75 1.75

Trees — A350

Designs: 50f, Cupressus sempervirens. 100f, Pistacia atlantica. 200f, Quercus aegilops.

2003, Aug. 7
1761-1763 A350 Set of 3 2.25 2.25

Flowers — A351

Designs: 50f, Cistanche tubulosa. 100f, Ophioglossum polyphyllum, vert. 150f, Narcissus tazetta. 200f, Gynandriris sisyrinchium, vert.

2003, Aug. 7
1764-1767 A351 Set of 4 3.00 3.00

Birds of Prey — A352

Designs: 100f, Ciraetus gallicus. No. 1769, 200f, Falco peregrinus. 300f, Accipiter nisus. No. 1771, 200f, Ciraetus gallicus, diff.

2003, Dec. 9 **Litho.** ***Perf. 14***
1768-1770 A352 Set of 3 3.50 3.50
Size: 70x90mm
Imperf
1771 A352 200f multi 6.00 6.00

Royal Cars Museum — A353

Designs: 100f, Red sports car. 150f, Black limousine. 300f, White limousine.
200f, Three automobiles.

2003, Dec. 23 **Litho.** ***Perf. 14***
1772-1774 A353 Set of 3 3.50 3.50
Size: 90x70mm
Imperf
1775 A353 200f multi 4.50 4.50

Jordan Post Company A354

Emblem and: 50f, Arch. 100f, Pillars, vert.

2003, Dec. 23 **Litho.** ***Perf. 14***
1776-1777 A354 Set of 2 1.00 1.00

Triumphal Arch Type of 1993-98

2003 Litho. ***Perf. 12¾x13¼***

Granite Paper

1777A A267 25f gray & multi — —

Arabian Horses — A355

Various horses: 5pi, 7.50pi, 12.50pi, 15pi, 25pi.
10pi, Two horses, horiz.

2004, Dec. 27 Litho. ***Perf. 14¼***

Granite Paper

1778-1782 A355 Set of 5 3.25 3.25

Imperf

Size: 90x70mm

1783 A355 10pi multi *8.50 8.50*

Ain Ghazal Statues — A356

Various statues: 5pi, 7.50pi, 12.50pi, 15pi, 25pi.
10pi, Two statues.

2004, Dec. 29 Granite Paper

1784-1788 A356 Set of 5 3.00 3.00

Imperf

Size: 70x90mm

1789 A356 10pi multi *5.00 5.00*

Children's Paintings A357

Various paintings: 5pi, 7.50pi, 12.50pi, 15pi, 25pi.
10pi, Parts of various paintings.

2004, Dec. 27 Granite Paper

1790-1794 A357 Set of 5 2.75 2.75

Imperf

Size: 90x70mm

1795 A357 10pi multi *5.50 5.50*

Miniature Sheet

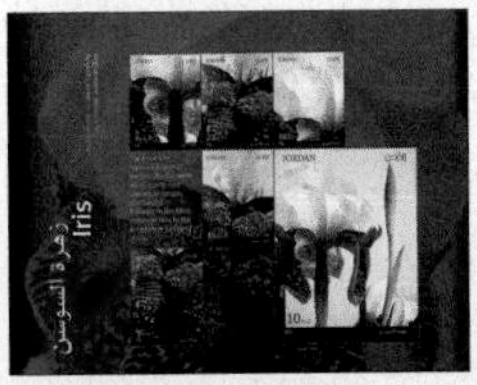

Nazareth Iris A358

No. 1796 — Various photographs of Nazareth Iris: a, 5pi. b, 7.50pi. c, 10pi (70x90mm). d, 12.50pi. e, 15pi. f, 25pi.

2004, Dec. 29 ***Perf. 14¼***

Granite Paper

1796 A358 Sheet of 6, #a-f *6.00 6.00*

Miniature Sheet

Details From Mosaic Floor of Church of the Holy Martyrs Lot and Procopius, Mount Nebo — A359

No. 1797: a, 10pi, Man with scythe (68x90mm). b, 10pi, Man with flute, grapes. c, 15pi, Building. d, 25pi, Man with Basket.

2004, Dec. 27 Litho.

Granite Paper

1797 A359 Sheet of 4, #a-d *6.00 6.00*

Expo 2005, Aichi, Japan — A360

No. 1798: a, Dead Sea salt crystal. b, Dead Sea salt crystal, diff. c, Dead Sea salt crystal, diff. d, Dead Sea (70x70mm).

2005, Aug. 7 Litho. ***Perf. 13¾***

1798	Sheet of 4	3.25	3.25
a.	A360 5pi multi	.30	.30
b.	A360 7.50pi multi	.45	.45
c.	A360 12.50pi multi	.75	.75
d.	A360 20pi multi	.90	.90

Fish — A361

Various Red Sea fish: 5f, 5pi, 7.50pi, 12.50pi.

Perf. 13½x13¾

2005, Dec. 27 Litho.

1799-1802 A361 Set of 4 2.50 2.50

Souvenir Sheet

1803 A361 20pi Lionfish *5.00 5.00*

Intl. Sports Year — A362

Children's drawings of: 1pi, Tennis player. 10pi, Medal winner. 15pi, Soccer game, horiz. No. 1807, 20pi, Swimmer, horiz.
No. 1808, Basketball player.

Perf. 13½x13¾, 13¾x13½

2005, Dec. 27

1804-1807 A362 Set of 4 3.50 3.50

Size: 71x90mm

Imperf

1808 A362 20pi multi *6.00 6.00*

Worldwide Fund for Nature — A363

Arabian oryx: 1.50pi, Grazing. 5pi, Three oryx. 7.50pi, Adults and juvenile. 12.50pi, Two adults.
20pi, Adult, three oryx in background.

2005, Dec. 27 ***Perf. 13¾x13½***

1809-1812 A363 Set of 4 *7.25 7.25*

Souvenir Sheet

1813 A363 20pi multi *22.50 22.50*

Child Protection A364

Designs: 7.50pi, Hands of adult and child. 10pi, Mother holding infant. 12.50pi, Adult hugging child.
20pi, Child.

2005, Dec. 27 ***Perf. 13¾***

1814-1816 A364 Set of 3 3.00 3.00

Size: 70x90mm

Imperf

1817 A364 20pi multi *6.50 6.50*

Friendship of Jordan and Japan — A365

Design: 7.50pi, Gallery of Japanese calligraphy. 12.50pi, Building. 15pi, Building at night.
20pi, Pottery in museum gallery.

2005, Dec. 27 ***Perf. 13¾x13½***

1818-1820 A365 Set of 3 2.75 2.75

Size: 70x90mm

Imperf

1821 A365 20pi multi *5.75 5.75*

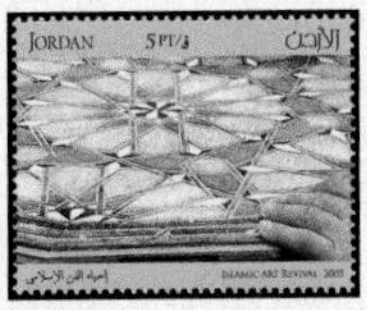

Islamic Art Revival — A366

Designs: 5pi, Woodworker. 7.50pi, Engraver. 10pi, Calligrapher. 15pi, Woodworker, diff.
20pi, Calligrapher, diff.

2005, Dec. 27 ***Perf. 13¾x13½***

1822-1825 A366 Set of 4 3.00 3.00

Size: 90x71mm

Imperf

1826 A366 20pi multi *6.00 6.00*

Modern Architecture — A367

Various buildings with panel color of: 7.50pi, Green. 10pi, Lemon, horiz. 12.50pi, Red brown.
20pi, Brown, horiz.

2006, Jan. 1 Litho. ***Perf. 14***

1827-1829 A367 Set of 3 3.50 3.50

Imperf

Size: 90x70mm

1830 A367 20pi multi *4.50 4.50*

Government Vehicles — A368

Designs: 10pi, Police car. 12.50pi, Fire truck. 17.50pi, Garbage truck. No. 1834, 20pi, Mail vans.
No. 1835, 20pi, Ambulance.

2006, Jan. 1 ***Perf. 14***

1831-1834 A368 Set of 4 3.75 3.75

Imperf

Size: 90x70mm

1835 A368 20pi multi *4.50 4.50*

Ancient Coins — A369

Various coins with background color of: 5pi, Purple. 7.50pi, Yellow brown. 10pi, Gray. 12.50pi, Blue. 15pi, Dark red.
30pi, Dark blue, horiz.

2006, Jan. 1 ***Perf. 13¾***

1836-1840 A369 Set of 5 4.50 4.50

Imperf

Size: 90x70mm

1841 A369 30pi multi *6.50 6.50*

2006 World Cup Soccer Championships, Germany — A370

Background color: 5pi, Light blue. 7.50pi, Yellow. 10pi, Tan. 12.50pi, Green. 15pi, Blue.
30pi, Yellow green, horiz.

2006, Jan. 1 ***Perf. 14***

1842-1846 A370 Set of 5 4.50 4.50

Imperf

Size: 90x70mm

1847 A370 30pi multi *5.50 5.50*

Art — A371

Various works of art by unnamed artists: 5pi, 10pi, 15pi. 20pi.
No. 1852, Four works of art, horiz.

2006, Oct. 21 Litho. ***Perf. 14¼***

Granite Paper

1848-1851 A371 Set of 4 3.50 3.50

Imperf

Size: 90x70mm

1852 A371 20pi multi *6.00 6.00*

Desert Reptiles — A372

Designs: 5pi, Lizard. 7.50pi, Snake. 10pi, Lizards. 12.50pi, Lizard, diff. 15pi, Lizard, horiz. 20pi, Snake, diff.
No. 1859, Lizard, diff., horiz.

2006, Oct. 21 ***Perf. 14¼***

Granite Paper

1853-1858 A372 Set of 6 3.25 3.25

Imperf

Size: 90x70mm

1859 A372 20pi multi *5.25 5.25*

Information and Communications Technology in Education — A373

Design: 7.50pi, Man at computer. 12.50pi, Woman punching keys on keypad. 15pi, Man and computer screen. 20pi, Man using cellular phone.
No. 1864, Circuit board, design of unissued 50f stamp showing finger punching keypad.

2006, Nov. 11 ***Perf. 14¼***

Granite Paper

1860-1863 A373 Set of 4 2.75 2.75

Imperf

Size: 70x90mm

1864 A373 20pi multi *5.50 5.50*

National Symbols — A374

Designs: 5pi, King Abdullah II in dress uniform. 7.50pi, King Abdullah II in suit and tie. 10pi, Jordanian soldiers, horiz. 12.50pi, King Abdullah II in camouflage uniform. 15pi, Flag, horiz. 20pi, Men in army uniforms and native garb, horiz. 25pi, Parade of tanks, horiz. 30pi, Flag and rose, horiz.

2006, Nov. 11 ***Perf. 14¼***

Granite Paper

1865-1872 A374 Set of 8 6.25 6.25

Pitchers and Spouted Pots — A375

Designs: 10pi, Spouted pot. 20pi, Spouted pot with legs. 30pi, Pitcher.
25pi, Spouted pot, horiz.

Perf. 13½x13¾

2007, Dec. 31 **Litho.**

1873-1875 A375 Set of 3 1.75 1.75

Imperf

Size: 90x70mm

1876 A375 25pi multi *2.25 2.25*

Culture and Identity — A376

Designs: 10pi, Books. No. 1878, 20pi, Lute. 25pi, Bottle. 30pi, Arabic text.
No. 1881, 20pi, Arabic text, paint brushes, bottle, lute, books.

2007, Dec. 31 ***Perf. 13½x13¾***

1877-1880 A376 Set of 4 2.40 2.40

Imperf

Size: 70x90mm

1881 A376 20pi multi *1.50 1.50*

Butterflies — A377

Various butterflies with denomination color of: 10pi, Orange. 15pi, Yellow green. 20pi, Gray. 25pi, Olive gray, horiz. 30pi, Orange, horiz.
40pi, Olive green, horiz.

Perf. 13½x13¾, 13¼x13½

2007, Dec. 31

1882-1886 A377 Set of 5 3.00 3.00

Imperf

Size: 90x70mm

1887 A377 40pi multi *4.50 4.50*

Aqaba — A378

Designs: 10pi, Arch and beach. 15pi, Scuba diver. 20pi, Motor boats. 30pi, Double-masted ship.

2008, July 16 **Litho.** ***Perf. 14¼***

Granite Paper

1888-1891 A378 Set of 4 2.10 2.10

Traditional Women's Clothing — A379

Designs: 10pi, Mafraq. 15pi, Ma'an. 20pi, Amman. 25pi, Jerash. 30pi, Salt.

2008, July 16 **Granite Paper**

1892-1896 A379 Set of 5 3.00 3.00

Fruit — A380

Designs: 10pi, Oranges. 15pi, Cherries. 20pi, Figs. 25pi, Pomegranates. 30pi, Grapes.

2008, July 16 **Granite Paper**

1897-1901 A380 Set of 5 3.00 3.00

Petra — A381

Designs: 10pi, Sculpture of face. 15pi, Ceramic plate. 20pi, Sculpture of grapevine. 25pi, Siq al Barid fresco. 30pi, Rock formations. 40pi, Treasury.

2008, July 16 **Litho.** ***Perf. 14¼***

Granite Paper

1902-1906 A381 Set of 5 3.00 3.00

Size: 66x86mm

1907 A381 40pi multi 1.25 1.25

Imperf

1908 A381 40pi multi 1.25 1.25

Bridge — A382

50th Anniversary Emblem of Engineer's Association — A383

2008, Sept. 22 **Litho.** ***Perf. 14¼***

Granite Paper

1909 A382 15pi shown .45 .45
1910 A383 20pi shown .60 .60
1911 A382 25pi Power station .70 .70
Nos. 1909-1911 (3) 1.75 1.75

2008 Summer Olympics, Beijing — A384

Desings: 20pi, Taekwondo. 30pi, Equestrian. 40pi, Table tennis. 50pi, Running.

2008, Sept. 22 **Litho.**

Granite Paper

1912-1915 A384 Set of 4 4.00 4.00

Musical Instruments A385

Designs: 20pi, Oud. 40pi, Rebab. 60pi, Zither. 80pi, Flutes. 100pi, Tambourine and drum.
50pi, Oud, rebab, zither, flutes, tambourine and drum, horiz.

2008, Sept. 22 ***Perf. 14¼***

Granite Paper

1916-1920 A385 Set of 5 8.50 8.50

Imperf

Size: 90x70mm

1921 A385 50pi multi 1.40 1.40

Flowers — A386

Designs: 5pi, Egyptian catchfly. 10pi, Lupine. 15pi, Judean viper's bugloss. 20pi, Pimpernel. 30pi, Asiatic crowfoot. 40pi, Grape hyacinth. No. 1928, 50pi, Large flowered sage. 60pi, Star of Bethlehem. 80pi, Pyramidalis. 100pi, Calotropis.
No. 1932, 50pi, Cyclamen, horiz.

2008, Nov. 25 **Litho.** ***Perf. 14¼***

Granite Paper

1922-1931 A386 Set of 10 12.00 12.00

Imperf

Size: 90x70mm

1932 A386 50pi multi 1.40 1.40

Art From Quseir Amra UNESCO World Heritage Site — A387

Designs: 40pi, Woman with arm raised. 60pi, Grapes. 80pi, Hunters on horseback, bath. 100pi, Face of woman.
50pi, Quseir Amra Palace.

2008, Nov. 25 ***Perf. 14¼x14***

Granite Paper

1933-1936 A387 Set of 4 8.00 8.00

Imperf

Size: 90x69mm

1937 A387 50pi multi 1.40 1.40

Hejaz Railway, Cent. — A388

Designs: 20pi, Train on bridge. 30pi, Locomotive and tender. 50pi, Station and road.

2009, Feb. 1 **Litho.** ***Perf. 14¼***

Granite Paper

1938-1940 A388 Set of 3 3.00 3.00

Dated 2008.

Birds — A389

Designs: 10pi, Mallard duck. 15pi, Saker. 20pi, Crouser cream. 30pi, Palestine sunbird. 40pi, Hoopoe. No. 1946, 50pi, Black francolin. 60pi, Little green bee-eater. 80pi, Sinai rosefinch.
No. 1949, 50pi, Kingfisher.

2009, Feb. 1 ***Perf. 14¼***

Granite Paper

1941-1948 A389 Set of 8 8.75 8.75

Imperf

Size: 90x70mm

1949 A389 50pi multi *4.75 4.75*

Dated 2008.

Arabian Coffee Tools — A390

Designs: 40pi, Mortar and pestle. 60pi, Coffee pots and roasting pan. 80pi, Coffee pot and cups. 100pi, Bowl, roasting pan and shovel.
50pi, Mortar, pestle, coffee pot, bowl, roasting pan and shovel.

2009, Mar. 1 ***Perf. 14¼***

Granite Paper

1950-1953 A390 Set of 4 8.00 8.00

Imperf

Size: 70x90mm

1954 A390 50pi multi *4.25 4.25*

Dated 2008.

Traditional Costumes — A391

Close-ups of costumes and: 40pi, Woman. 60pi, Woman, diff. 80pi, Woman, diff. 100pi, Man and woman.
50pi, Woman only.

2009, Mar. 1 ***Perf. 14¼***

Granite Paper

1955-1958 A391 Set of 4 8.00 8.00

Imperf

Size: 70x90mm

1959 A391 50pi multi *4.25 4.25*

Visit of Pope Benedict XVI to Jordan — A392

Designs: 20pi, Pope Benedict XVI, King Abdullah II, walkway to river. 30pi, Pope Benedict XVI. 40pi, Pope and King shaking hands.
50pi, Pope and King shaking hands, walkway to river, crucifix.

2009, May 8 ***Perf. 14¼***

Granite Paper

1960-1962 A392 Set of 3 2.60 2.60

Imperf

Size: 90x70mm

1963 A392 50pi multi *4.75 4.75*

King Abdullah II, 10th Anniv. of Accession to Throne — A393

2009, June 9 *Perf. 13¾*

Granite Paper

Background Color

1964 A393 10pi maroon	.30	.30
1965 A393 15pi dark blue	.45	.45
1966 A393 20pi bright blue	.60	.60
1967 A393 25pi tan	.70	.70
1968 A393 30pi dark green	.85	.85
1969 A393 35pi blue	1.00	1.00
1970 A393 40pi purple	1.10	1.10
1971 A393 45pi black	1.25	1.25
1972 A393 50pi brown	1.40	1.40
1973 A393 1d blue gray	3.00	3.00
Nos. 1964-1973 (10)	10.65	10.65

E-Government — A394

Designs: 20pi, Computer cables. 30pi, Spiral emblem. 40pi, Internet address of Jordanian government. 50pi, Letter, compass, Earth.

2009, Aug. 25 **Litho.** *Perf. 13¼*

Granite Paper

1974-1977 A394 Set of 4 4.00 4.00

A395

A396

A397

A398

A399

University emblems: No. 1983, Al-Hussein Bin Jalal University. No. 1984, Tafila Technical University. No. 1985, German-Jordanian University. No. 1986, Al-Balqa Applied University. No. 1987, Yarmouk University.

2009, Aug. 25 *Perf. 13¼*

Granite Paper

1978 A395 20pi multi	.60	.60
1979 A396 20pi multi	.60	.60
1980 A397 20pi multi	.60	.60
1981 A398 20pi multi	.60	.60
1982 A399 20pi multi	.60	.60
1983 A399 20pi multi	.60	.60
1984 A399 20pi multi	.60	.60
1985 A399 20pi multi	.60	.60
1986 A399 20pi multi	.60	.60
1987 A399 20pi multi	.60	.60
Nos. 1978-1987 (10)	6.00	6.00

Waterfalls, Ma'een — A400

Designs: 10pi, Waterfall, orange brown panel. 20pi, Building and mountain, fawn panel. 30pi, Waterfall, black panel. 40pi, Waterfall, gray green panel. 50pi, Waterfall, olive brown panel.
60pi, Waterfall, blue panel.

2009, Aug. 25 **Litho.**

Granite Paper

1988-1992 A400 Set of 5 4.25 4.25

Size: 70x91mm

Imperf

1993 A400 60pi multi 1.75 1.75

Animals — A401

Designs: 10pi, Horse. 20pi, Rabbits. 30pi, Fox. 40pi, Maha gazelle. 50pi, Gazelle.
60pi, Camel.

2009, Aug. 25 **Litho.**

Granite Paper

1994-1998 A401 Set of 5 4.25 4.25

Size: 70x91mm

Imperf

1999 A401 60pi multi 1.75 1.75

Vegetables — A402

No. 2000: a, Corn. b, Onions, garlic. c, Beans, peas, okra. d, Cabbages. e, Eggplants. f, Pumpkins. g, Bell peppers. h, Hot peppers. i, Radishes, turnips, beets. j, Tomatoes, zucchini.

2009, Aug. 25 *Perf. 13¼*

Granite Paper

2000 Sheet of 10 6.00 6.00
a.-j. A402 20pi Any single .60 .60

Environmental Protection — A403

Designs: 20pi, Tree, shrub, flower. 30pi, Man and fire. 40pi, Animals grazing. 50pi, Litter in stream.

2009 **Granite Paper** **Litho.**

2001-2004 A403 Set of 4 4.00 4.00

Insects — A404

Designs: 10pi, Beetle. 15pi, Butterfly. 20pi, Ladybug. 25pi, Bee. 30pi, Mantis. 40pi, Moth. 50pi, Dragonfly. 60pi, Fly. 80pi, Grasshopper. 100pi, Dragonflies.

2009, Dec. 13 **Litho.** *Perf. 13¼*

Granite Paper

2005-2014 A404 Set of 10 12.50 12.50

Nos. 588-590 Surcharged

Methods and Perfs As Before

2009, Dec. 20

2015 A82 80pi on 120f #588	2.25	2.25
2016 A82 80pi on 180f #589	2.25	2.25
2017 A82 80pi on 200f #590	2.25	2.25
Nos. 2015-2017 (3)	6.75	6.75

No. 1471b Surcharged

Perf. 12¾x13¼

2009, Dec. 20 **Litho.**

2018 A267 80pi on 25f multi 2.25 2.25

Tourism — A405

Sites in: 10pi, Ajlun. 20pi, Amman. 30pi, Karak. 40pi, Showbak.
50pi, Jerash.

2010, Oct. 3 *Perf. 14*

2019-2022 A405 Set of 4 3.00 3.00

Size: 90x70mm

Imperf

2023 A405 50pi multi 1.50 1.50

Miniature Sheet

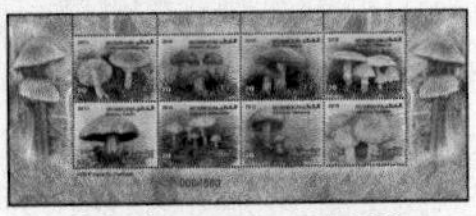

Mushrooms — A406

No. 2024: a, Cortinarius balteatus. b, Russula bicolor. c, Red fly agaric. d, Amanita muscaria. e, Boletus edulis. f, Amanita albocreata. g, Agaricus anderwij. h, Agaricus bisporus.

2010, Oct. 3 *Perf. 14*

2024 A406 20pi Sheet of 8, #a-h 4.50 4.50

Mosques in Jordan — A407

Designs: 10pi, Jordan University Mosque. 20pi, Abu-Darwiesh Mosque. 30pi, Al Hussainy Mosque. 40pi, King Abdullah Mosque. 50pi, King Hussein bin Talal Mosque.

2010, Nov. 30

2025-2029 A407 Set of 5 4.25 4.25

Sports — A408

Designs: 10pi, Skydiving. 20pi, Swimming. 30pi, Hot-air ballooning. 40pi, Racing boats.
50pi, Jordan Rally.

2010, Nov. 30 *Perf. 14*

2030-2033 A408 Set of 4 3.00 3.00

Size: 70x90mm

Imperf

2034 A408 50pi multi 1.50 1.50

Old Farming Tools — A409

Designs: 20pi, Millstone. 30pi, Flail. 40pi, Pitchfork. 50pi, Olive crushing wheel.

2011, Feb. 27 *Perf. 14*

2035-2038 A409 Set of 4 4.00 4.00

Dated 2010.

Development Zones — A410

Emblem of: No. 2039, 20pi, Dead Sea Development Zone. No. 2040, 20pi, Irbid Development Area. No. 2041, 20pi, Jabal Ajloun Development Area. No. 2042, 20pi, King Hussein Bin Talal Development Area. No. 2043, 20pi, Ma'an Development Area.

2011, Feb. 27

2039-2043 A410 Set of 5 3.00 3.00

Dated 2010.

Wild Herbs — A411

Designs: No. 2044, 20pi, Artemisia herba alba. No. 2045, 20pi, Capparis spinosa. No. 2046, 20pi, Lavandula vera. No. 2047, 20pi, Matricaria chamomilla. No. 2048, 20pi, Ocimum basilicum. No. 2049, 20pi, Salvia officinalis. No. 2050, 20pi, Thymus serpyllum. No. 2051, 20pi, Trigonella foenum-graecum.

2011, Feb. 27

2044-2051 A411 Set of 8 4.50 4.50

Dated 2010. Latin names of plants are misspelled on Nos. 2044, 2045, 2046, 2050 and 2051.

Junior and Cadet World Fencing Championships, Jordan — A412

Fencers and stylized fencer in panel in: 10pi, Red brown. 20pi, Blue violet. 30pi, Greenish blue. 40pi, Olive green. No. 2056, 50pi, Gray.
No. 2057, 50pi, Fencers, vert.

2011, Apr. 6 *Perf. 13x12¾*

2052-2056 A412 Set of 5 4.25 4.25

Size: 75x94mm

Imperf

2057 A412 50pi multi *6.00 6.00*

Jordan Rally A413

Various race cars: 10pu, 20pi, 30pi, 40pi, 50pi.
No. 2063, 50pi, Race car, ruins, helicopter.

2011, Apr. 14 *Perf. 13x12¾*

2058-2062 A413 Set of 5 4.25 4.25

Size: 95x74mm

Imperf

2063 A413 50pi multi *5.75 5.75*

Jewelry — A414

Designs: 20pi, Pendant on necklace. No. 2065, 30pi, Pendants, necklace and bracelet. 40pi, Ring. 50i, Necklace with pendants.
No. 2068, 30pi, Ring, diff.

2011, May 10 *Perf. 13¼x13*

Granite Paper

2064-2067 A414	Set of 4	4.00	4.00

Size: 77x77mm

Imperf

2068 A414 30pi multi		*5.00*	*5.00*

Dated 2010.

A415

A416

A417

A418

A419

A420

A421

A422

A423

Dams — A424

2011, May 10 *Perf. 13x13¼*

Granite Paper

2069 A415 20pi multi		.60	.60
2070 A416 20pi multi		.60	.60
2071 A417 20pi multi		.60	.60
2072 A418 20pi multi		.60	.60
2073 A419 20pi multi		.60	.60
2074 A420 20pi multi		.60	.60
2075 A421 20pi multi		.60	.60
2076 A422 20pi multi		.60	.60
2077 A423 20pi multi		.60	.60
2078 A424 20pi multi		.60	.60
Nos. 2069-2078 (10)		6.00	6.00

Size: 90x70mm

Imperf

2079 A424 30pi multi		*6.75*	*6.75*

Dated 2010.

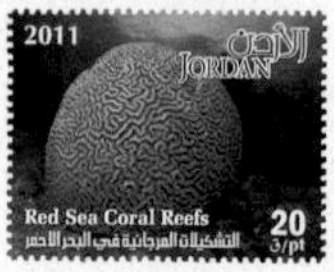
Red Sea Coral Reefs — A425

Designs: 20pi, Brain coral. 30pi, Coral, fish. No. 2082, 40pi, Coral. 50pi, Coral, diff. 60pi, Coral, diff. No. 2085, 40p, Coral, fish, diff.

2011, Sept. 28 **Litho.** *Perf. 14*

2080-2084 A425	Set of 5	5.75	5.75

Size: 90x70mm

Imperf

2085 A425 40pi multi		1.25	1.25

Ceramics — A426

Designs: 10pi, Jug with handle, head. 20pi, Item on pedestal. No. 2088, 30pi, Jug with handle. 40pi, Item with Arabic script. 50pi, Item with Arabic script and people. 60pi, Sphere on pedestal. No. 2092, 30p, Abstract tile designs.

2011, Sept. 28 *Perf. 14*

2086-2091 A426	Set of 5	6.00	6.00

Size: 70x90mm

Imperf

2092 A426 30pi multi		.85	.85

A427

A428

A429

A430

A431

A432

A433

A434

A435

Historical Path — A436

2011, Sept. 28 *Perf. 14*

2093 A427 20pi multi		.60	.60
2094 A428 20pi multi		.60	.60
2095 A429 20pi multi		.60	.60
2096 A430 20pi multi		.60	.60
2097 A431 20pi multi		.60	.60
2098 A432 20pi multi		.60	.60
2099 A433 20pi multi		.60	.60
2100 A434 20pi multi		.60	.60
2101 A435 20pi multi		.60	.60
2102 A436 20pi multi		.60	.60
Nos. 2093-2102 (10)		6.00	6.00

Crown Prince Hussein — A437

Denominations: 20pi, 30pi, 50pi.

2011 *Perf. 13½x13¼*

Granite Paper

2103-2105 A437	Set of 3	3.00	3.00

Old Astronomical Instruments — A438

Designs: 10pi, Astrolabe. 20pi, Telescope. 30pi, Sextant. 40pi, Sundial.

2011 *Perf. 13½x13¼*

Granite Paper

2106-2109 A438	Set of 4	3.00	3.00

Royal Jordanian Falcons Aerobatic Squad — A439

Designs: 10pi, Line of four airplanes. 20pi, Pilot in cockpit, three other airplanes. 30pi, Three airplanes. 40pi, Four airplanes in formation.

50pi, Four airplanes, Jordanian flag.

2011 *Perf. 13¼x13½*

Granite Paper

2110-2113 A439	Set of 4	3.00	3.00

Size: 90x70mm

Imperf

2114 A439 50pi multi		1.40	1.40

Souvenir Sheet

Preervation of Polar Regions and Glaciers — A440

No. 2115: a, 80pi, Penguins. b, 1d, Polar bear.

2012, Jan. 23 *Perf. 13½*

Granite Paper

2115 A440	Sheet of 2, #a-b	5.25	5.25

Dated 2011.

A441

A442

A443

A444

A445

King Abdullah II — A446

Design: 50pi, King Abdullah II and mosque, horiz.

2012, Jan. 30 *Perf. 13½x13¼*

Granite Paper

2116 A441 20pi multi		.60	.60
2117 A442 20pi multi		.60	.60
2118 A443 20pi multi		.60	.60
2119 A444 20pi multi		.60	.60
2120 A445 20pi multi		.60	.60
2121 A446 20pi multi		.60	.60
Nos. 2116-2121 (6)		3.60	3.60

Size: 90x70mm

Imperf

2122 A446 50pi multi		1.40	1.40

Labor Day — A447

Designs: 20pi, Raised fists. 30pi, Man with shovel. 40pi, Man with pick, woman and child. 50pi, Man with hard hat.

2012 *Perf. 13½x13¼*

Granite Paper

2123-2126 A447	Set of 4	4.00	4.00

World Telecommunications Day — A448

Designs: 30pi, Hands holding Earth. 40pi, Dish antennas. 50pi, Computer.

2012 Granite Paper Litho.
2127-2129 A448 Set of 3 3.50 3.50

2012 Summer Olympics, London — A449

Designs: 20pi, Equestrian. 30pi, Soccer. 40pi, Tennis. 50pi, Kayaking.

2012 Granite Paper
2130-2133 A449 Set of 4 4.00 4.00

Chess — A450

Various chess pieces: 30pi, 40pi, 50pi.

2012 Litho. *Perf. 11¾*
2134-2136 A450 Set of 3 3.50 3.50

Citrus Fruits — A451

Designs: 10pi, Kumquats. 20pi, Oranges. 30pi, Lemons. 40pi, Oranges, diff. 50pi, Pomelos.

2012 Litho. *Perf. 11¾*
2137-2141 A451 Set of 5 4.25 4.25

Miniature Sheets

A452

Prehistoric Animals — A453

No. 2142: a, Pteranodon in flight, back of Apatosaurus. b, Tyrannosaurus Rex and volcano. c, Triceratops and Stegosaurus. d, Horned dinosaur, legs of Tyrannosaurus Rex.

No. 2143: a, Head of Tyrannosaurus rex, waterfall. b, Apatosauruses. c, Raptors on shore. d, Three dinosaurs in water.

2012 Litho. *Perf. 11¾*
2142 A452 20pi Sheet of 4, #a-d 2.25 2.25
2143 A453 20pi Sheet of 4, #a-d 2.25 2.25

A454

A454a

A454b

A454c

A454d

A454e

A454f

Artists — A454g

2012 Litho. *Perf. 11¾*

2144	A454	20pi	multi	.60	.60
2145	A454a	20pi	multi	.60	.60
2146	A454b	20pi	multi	.60	.60
2147	A454c	20pi	multi	.60	.60
2148	A454d	20pi	multi	.60	.60
2149	A454e	20pi	multi	.60	.60
2150	A454f	20pi	multi	.60	.60
2151	A454g	20pi	multi	.60	.60
	Nos. 2144-2151 (8)			4.80	4.80

Jordan Library and Information Association, 50th Anniv. — A455

Designs: 40pi, Association emblem. 50pi, 50th anniversary emblem.

2013 Litho. *Perf. 14*
2152-2153 A455 Set of 2 2.60 2.60

Horses — A456

Designs: 10pi, Two horses. 20pi, One horse, horiz. 30pi, Two horses, horiz. 40pi, Head of horse, horiz. No. 2158, 50pi, Horse in water, horiz.

No. 2159, 50pi, Six horses, horiz.

2013, Dec. 2 Litho. *Perf. 11¾*
2154-2158 A456 Set of 5 4.25 4.25

Size: 90x70mm

Imperf

2159 A456 50pi multi 1.40 1.40

Dated 2012.

Ships — A457

Various ships, 20pi, 30pi, 40pi, 50pi. No. 2164, 50pi, Fleet of ships.

2013, Dec. 2 Litho. *Perf. 11¾*
2160-2163 A457 Set of 4 4.00 4.00

Size: 90x70mm

Imperf

2164 A457 50pi multi 1.40 1.40

Dated 2012.

Nature Reserves — A458

Designs: 10pi, Rocks. 20pi, Flowers, horiz. 30pi, Lake, horiz. 40pi, Plateaus, horiz. No. 2169, 50pi, Antelopes, horiz.

No. 2170, 50pi, Hillside village, horiz.

2014, Feb. 9 Litho. *Perf. 14*
2165-2169 A458 Set of 5 4.25 4.25

Size: 90x70mm

Imperf

2170 A458 50pi multi 1.40 1.40

Dated 2013.

Doors and Windows — A459

Designs: No. 2171, 20pi, Door, King Hussein's Mosque. No. 2172, 20pi, Door and window, Umayyad Palace. No. 2173, 20pi, Door, Royal Hashemite Court, vert. No. 2174, 20pi, Door and windows, Justice Palace, vert. No. 2175, 20pi, Window, Raghadan Palace, vert. No. 2176, 20pi, Door, Al-Salt School, vert. No. 2177, 20pi, Window, Al-Salt, vert.

2014, Feb. 9 Litho. *Perf. 14*
2171-2177 A459 Set of 7 4.00 4.00

Dated 2013.

A460

A461

A462

A463

A464

A465

A466

Birds — A467

2014, Feb. 9 Litho. *Perf. 14*

2178	A460	20pi	multi	.60	.60
2179	A461	20pi	multi	.60	.60
2180	A462	20pi	multi	.60	.60
2181	A463	20pi	multi	.60	.60
2182	A464	20pi	multi	.60	.60
2183	A465	20pi	multi	.60	.60
2184	A466	20pi	multi	.60	.60
2185	A467	20pi	multi	.60	.60
	Nos. 2178-2185 (8)			4.80	4.80

Dated 2013.

1933 Stamps and Map of Jordan — A468

Map of Jordan and stamp: No. 2186, 80pi, Jordan #191. No. 2187, 80pi, Jordan #197.

2014, Feb. 9 Litho. *Imperf.*
2186-2187 A468 Set of 2 4.50 4.50

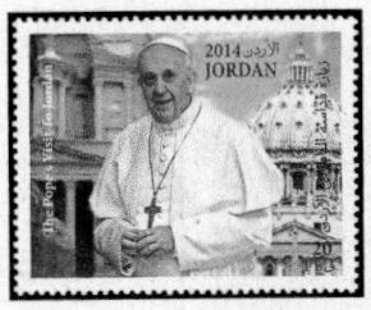

Visit of Pope Francis to Jordan — A469

Designs: 20pi, Pope Francis. 30pi, Pope Francis and King Abdullah II. 40pi, Pope Francis and dove, vert.

50pi, Flags of Vatican City and Jordan, Jordan #474, 1683, 1961, 2188.

2014, May 24 Litho. *Perf. 14¼*
2188-2190 A469 Set of 3 2.60 2.60

Imperf

Size: 90x70mm

2191 A469 50pi multi 1.40 1.40

First Papal visit to Jordan, 50th anniv. (No. 2191).

A470

A471

A472

A473

A474

Cartoons — A475

2014, July 1	Litho.	*Perf. 14*	
2192 A470 20pi multi		.60	.60
2193 A471 20pi multi		.60	.60
2194 A472 20pi multi		.60	.60
2195 A473 20pi multi		.60	.60
2196 A474 20pi multi		.60	.60
2197 A475 20pi multi		.60	.60
Nos. 2192-2197 (6)		3.60	3.60

Dated 2013.

Paintings A476

Paintings by: No. 2198, 20pi, Claude Monet. No. 2199, 20pi, Monet, diff. No. 2200, 20pi, J.M.W. Turner. No. 2201, 20pi, Joaquin Sorolla y Bastida. No. 2202, 20pi, Vincent van Gogh. No. 2203, 20pi, Peter Paul Rubens. No. 2204, 20pi, Monet, diff., vert. No. 2205, 20pi, Johannes Vermeer, vert.

2014	Litho.	*Perf. 11¾*
2198-2205 A476 Set of 8		4.50 4.50

Dated 2013.

Miniature Sheet

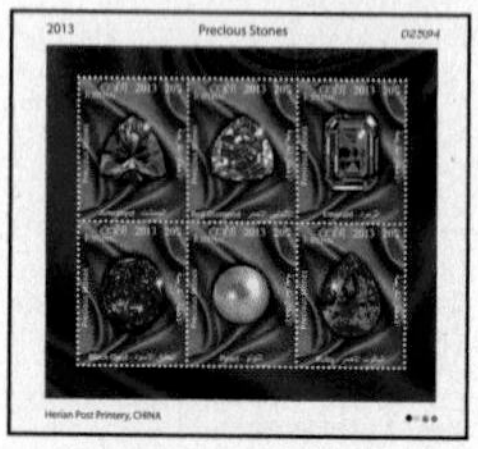

Gems A477

No. 2206: a, Amethyst. b, Red diamond. c, Emerald. d, Black opal. e, Pearl. f, Ruby.

2014	Litho.	*Perf. 11¾*
2206 A477 20pi Sheet of 6, #a-f		3.50 3.50

Dated 2013.

Euromed Postal Emblem and Mediterranean Sea — A478

2014, July 9	
2207 A478 80pi multi	2.25 2.25

Amman Chamber of Commerce, 90th Anniv. — A479

2014	Litho.	*Perf. 14¼*
2208 A479 40pi multi		1.25 1.25

Economic and Social Foundation for Military Retirees and Veterans A480

2014	Litho.	*Perf. 14¼*
2209 A480 40pi multi		1.25 1.25

Arab Lawyers Union — A481

2014	Litho.	*Perf. 14¼*
2210 A481 40pi multi		1.25 1.25

Jordanian Deaf Women's Association A482

2015	Litho.	*Perf. 14¼*
2211 A482 40pi multi		1.25 1.25

United Nations, 70th Anniv. — A483

Perf. 14¼x14½ Syncopated

2015, Dec. 13	Litho.
2212 A483 80pi multi	2.25 2.25

Jordanian Banknotes A484

Designs: 10pi, 1-dinar note. 20pi, 5-dinar note. 40pi, 10-dinar note. 60pi, 20-dinar note. 80pi, 50-dinar note.

Perf. 14¼x14½ Syncopated

2015, Dec. 13	Litho.
2213-2217 A484 Set of 5	6.00 6.00

Order of the Renaissance A485

Order of the Renaissance A486

Order of Independence A487

Al-Hussein Order of Military Merit — A488

Order of the Star of Jordan — A489

Al-Hussein Decoration for Distinguished Service — A490

Order of Hussein ibn Ali — A491

Medal of Honor — A492

Order of the Hashemite Star — A493

Royal Medal — A494

Perf. 14¼x14½ Syncopated

2015, Dec. 13		Litho.	
2218 A485 50pi multi		1.40	1.40
2219 A486 50pi multi		1.40	1.40
2220 A487 50pi multi		1.40	1.40
2221 A488 50pi multi		1.40	1.40
2222 A489 50pi multi		1.40	1.40
2223 A490 50pi multi		1.40	1.40
Perf. 14½x14¼ Syncopated			
2224 A491 50pi multi		1.40	1.40
2225 A492 50pi multi		1.40	1.40
2226 A493 50pi multi		1.40	1.40
2227 A494 50pi multi		1.40	1.40
Nos. 2218-2227 (10)		14.00	14.00

Decapolis A495

Designs: No. 2228, 50pi, Beit Ras. No. 2229, 50pi, Gerasa. No. 2230, 50pi, Quwayliba. No. 2231, 50pi, Umm Aljemal. No. 2232, 50pi, Umm Qais.

Perf. 14¼x14½ Syncopated

2015, Dec. 28	Litho.
2228-2232 A495 Set of 5	7.00 7.00

A496

A497

A498

Mosaics A499

Design: 60pi, Thalassa.

Perf. 14¼x14½ Syncopated

2015, Dec. 28	Litho.	
2233 A496 30pi multi	.85	.85
2234 A497 30pi multi	.85	.85
2235 A498 30pi multi	.85	.85
2236 A499 30pi multi	.85	.85
Nos. 2233-2236 (4)	3.40	3.40

Size: 90x70mm

Imperf

2237 A499 60pi multi	1.75 1.75

A500

A501

A502

A503

Handicrafts A504

Design: 60pi, Sand bottles.

Perf. 14¼x14½ Syncopated

2015, Dec. 28	Litho.	
2238 A500 30pi multi	.85	.85
2239 A501 30pi multi	.85	.85
2240 A502 30pi multi	.85	.85
2241 A503 30pi multi	.85	.85
2242 A504 30pi multi	.85	.85
Nos. 2238-2242 (5)	4.25	4.25

Size: 90x70mm

Imperf

2243 A504 60pi multi	1.75 1.75

Traditional Women's Clothing — A505

Woman from: No. 2244, 20pi, Ajloun. No. 2245, 20pi, Amman. No. 2246, 20pi, Badawi. No. 2247, 20pi, Jerash. No. 2248, 20pi, Karak. No. 2249, 20pi, Ma'an. No. 2250, 20pi, Madaba. No. 2251, 20pi, Mafraq. No. 2252, 20pi, Salt. No. 2253, 20pi, Tafilah. No. 2254, 20pi, Um Qais. No. 2255, 20pi, Wadi Rum.

Perf. 14½x14¼ Syncopated

2015, Dec. 28	Litho.
2244-2255 A505 Set of 12	6.75 6.75

Miniature Sheet

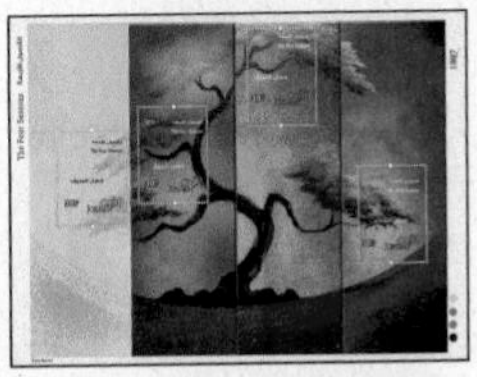

Four Seasons A506

No. 2256 — Tree leaves in: a, Spring (yellow background). b, Summer (green background). c, Autumn (orange brown background). d, Winter (blue background).

Perf. 14½x14¼ Syncopated

2015, Dec. 28 **Litho.**

2256 A506 30pi Sheet of 4, #a-d 3.50 3.50

Great Arab Revolt, Cent. — A507

Centenary emblem and: 10pi, Soldiers on camels. 20pi, Soldier on horse. 30pi, Jordanian kings. 50pi, Kingh Abdullah II. 100pi, Sharif Hussein.
40pi, Centenary emblem, vert.

Perf. 14¼x14½ Syncopated

2016, June 10 **Litho.**

2257-2261 A507 Set of 5 6.00 6.00

Size: 70x90mm

Imperf

2262 A507 40pi multi 1.25 1.25

Fish of the Mediterranean Sea — A508

Designs: No. 2263, 40pi, Axillary wrasse. No. 2264, 40pi, Blackback butterflyfish. No. 2265, 40pi, Butterfly blenny. No. 2266, 40pi, Lionfish. No. 2267, 40pi, Scorpionfish.

Perf. 14¼x14½ Syncopated

2016, June 30 **Litho.**

2263-2267 A508 Set of 5 5.75 5.75

First International Numismatic and Philatelic Fair, Amman A509

Background colors: 30pi, Yellow. 50pi, Dark red and red.

Perf. 14¼x14½ Syncopated

2016, July 28 **Litho.**

2268-2269 A509 Set of 2 2.25 2.25

Hiking Destinations A510

Designs: No. 2270, 40pi, Karak. No. 2271, 40pi, Ma'in. No. 2272, 40pi, Madaba. No. 2273, 40pi, Wadi Rum. No. 2274, 40pi, Ajlun, vert. No. 2275, 40pi, Madaba, vert. No. 2276, 40pi, Wadi Al Dab, vert.

Perf. 14¼x14½ Syncopated, 14½x14¼ Syncopated

2016, July 28 **Litho.**

2270-2276 A510 Set of 7 8.00 8.00

Arab Postal Day — A511

Background color: No. 2277, 40pi, Blue, denomination at LR. No. 2278, 40pi, Green, denomination at LL.

Perf. 14¼x14½ Syncopated

2016, Aug. 3 **Litho.**

2277-2278 A511 Set of 2 2.25 2.25

Women's Under-17 World Cup Soccer Tournament, Jordan — A512

Jordanian flag and silhouettes of players: 40pi, Dribbling ball (white silhouette). 50pi, Chasing ball (gray and white silhouettes). 60pi, Dribbling ball (black silhouette). 70pi, Kicking ball (black silhouette).

Perf. 14¼x14½ Syncopated

2016, Sept. 25 **Litho.**

2279-2282 A512 Set of 4 3.25 3.25

Ancient Castles and Palaces — A513

Designs: No. 2283, 30pi, Ajlun Castle. No. 2284, 30pi, Al-azraq Castle. No. 2285, 30pi, Umayyad Palace. No. 2286, 40pi, Aqaba Castle. No. 2287, 40pi, Karak Castle. No. 2288, 40pi, Shobak Castle.

Perf. 14¼x14½ Syncopated

2016, Oct. 20 **Litho.**

2283-2288 A513 Set of 6 6.00 6.00

Museum of Parliamentary Life, Amman — A514

Designs: 20pi, Emblem. 30pi, Museum gate and entrance. 40pi, Room. 50pi, Dais. 60pi, King Abdullah II.

Perf. 14¼x14½ Syncopated

2016, Nov. 7 **Litho.**

2289-2293 A514 Set of 5 5.75 5.75

28th Arab League Summit, Amman A515

Designs: 10pi, Map and flags of Arab League countries. 20pi, Summit venue. 30pi, Umayyad Palace, map and flag of Jordan. 40pi, "28th."
50pi, King Abdullah II.

2017, Mar. 29 **Litho.** ***Perf. 10***

Granite Paper

2294-2297 A515 Set of 4 3.00 3.00

Size: 96x80mm

Imperf

2298 A515 50pi multi 1.40 1.40

1996 Half-Piaster Coin — A516

1978 10-Fils Coin — A517

1949 100-Fils Coin — A518

2000 10-Piaster Coin — A519

1970 Quarter-Dinar Coin — A520

1977 Quarter-Dinar Coin — A521

2017, May 4 **Litho.** ***Perf. 10***

Granite Paper

2299	A516	40pi multi	1.10	1.10
2300	A517	40pi multi	1.10	1.10
2301	A518	40pi multi	1.10	1.10
2302	A519	40pi multi	1.10	1.10
2303	A520	40pi multi	1.10	1.10
2304	A521	40pi multi	1.10	1.10
		Nos. 2299-2304 (6)	6.60	6.60

No. 1472d Surcharged in Red Brown and Gray

Methods and Perfs. As Before

2017, July 20

Granite Paper

2305	A267	10pi on 50f #1472d	.30	.30
2306	A267	15pi on 50f #1472d	.45	.45
2307	A267	20pi on 50f #1472d	.60	.60
2308	A267	25pi on 50f #1472d	.70	.70
2309	A267	30pi on 50f #1472d	.85	.85
2310	A267	35pi on 50f #1472d	1.00	1.00
2311	A267	40pi on 50f #1472d	1.10	1.10
2312	A267	45pi on 50f #1472d	1.25	1.25
2313	A267	50pi on 50f #1472d	1.40	1.40
2314	A267	60pi on 50f #1472d	1.75	1.75
		Nos. 2305-2314 (10)	9.40	9.40

Trees — A522

Designs: 30pi, Spanish fir. 50pi, Turkey oak.

Perf. 14¾x14¼ Syncopated

2017, July 10 **Litho.**

2315-2316 A522 Set of 2 2.25 2.25

Nos. 1640, 1643, 1649, 1658, 1661, 1688, 1691 Surcharged in Black and Red and No. 1648 Surcharged in Black, Red and Green

c

d

Methods and Perfs. As Before

2017, Oct. 12

2317	A317(c)	20pi on 100f #1640	.60	.60
2318	A317(c)	20pi on 100f #1643	.60	.60
2319	A317(c)	20pi on 100f #1649	.60	.60
2320	A317(c)	20pi on 100f #1658	.60	.60
2321	A317(c)	20pi on 100f #1661	.60	.60
2322	A317(c)	20pi on 100f #1688	.60	.60
2323	A317(c)	20pi on 100f #1691	.60	.60
2324	A317(d)	30pi on 300f #1648	.85	.85
2325	A317(d)	50pi on 300f #1648	1.40	1.40
		Nos. 2317-2325 (9)	6.45	6.45

Fruit — A523

Designs: No. 2326, 20pi, Plums. No. 2327, 20pi, Pomegranate. No. 2328, 20pi, Peaches. No. 2329, 20pi, Figs. No. 2330, 20pi, Cactus fruit. No. 2331, 20pi, Grapes. No. 2332, 20pi, Blackberries. No. 2333, 20pi, Strawberries. No. 2334, 20pi, Cantaloupe. No. 2335, 20pi, Watermelon.

Perf. 14¼x14¾ Syncopated

2017, Oct. 12 **Litho.**

2326-2335 A523 Set of 10 5.75 5.75

Miniature Sheet

Birds A524

No. 2336: a, Carrier pigeon. b, Goldfinch. c, Buteo rufinus. d, Blackbird. e, Shunnarbird (rock partridge). f, Sinai rosefinch.

Perf. 14¼x14¾ Syncopated

2017, Oct. 12 **Litho.**

2336 A524 30pi Sheet of 6, #a-f 5.25 5.25

Medical Tourism Sites — A525

Designs: No. 2337, 40pi, Maeen Baths. No. 2338, 40pi, Afra Baths. No. 2339, 40pi, Dead Sea. No. 2340, 40pi, Jordan's Springs.

Perf. 14¼x14¾ Syncopated

2017, Nov. 21 **Litho.**

2337-2340 A525 Set of 4 4.50 4.50

UNESCO World Heritage Sites in Jordan — A526

Designs: No. 2341, 40pi, Baptism Site. No. 2342, 40pi, Petra. No. 2343, 40pi, Qusayr Amra. No. 2344, 40pi, Um er-Rasas. No. 2345, 40pi, Wadi Rum.

Perf. 14¼x14¾ Syncopated

2017, Nov. 21 **Litho.**

2341-2345 A526 Set of 5 5.75 5.75

A527

A528

A529

A530

A531

A532

Military Uniforms of Jordan — A533

Perf. 14¼x14¾ Syncopated

2017, Nov. 21 **Litho.**

2346 A527 30pi multi .85 .85
2347 A528 30pi multi .85 .85
2348 A529 30pi multi .85 .85
2349 A530 30pi multi .85 .85
2350 A531 30pi multi .85 .85
2351 A532 30pi multi .85 .85
2352 A533 30pi multi .85 .85
Nos. 2346-2352 (7) 5.95 5.95

A534

A535

A536

A537

Battle of Al-Karameh, 50th Anniv. — A538

2018, Mar. 21 **Litho.** ***Perf. 12***

2353 A534 30pi multi .85 .85
2354 A535 30pi multi .85 .85
2355 A536 30pi multi .85 .85
2356 A537 30pi multi .85 .85
Nos. 2353-2356 (4) 3.40 3.40

Souvenir Sheet

Imperf

2357 A538 50pi multi 1.40 1.40

Hashemite Restoration of Holy Places — A539

Designs: No. 2358, 40pi, Church of the Holy Sepulcher. No. 2359, 40pi, Saladin Pulpit. No. 2360, 40pi, Dome of the Rock.

2018, Apr. 23 **Litho.** ***Perf. 12***

2358-2360 A539 Set of 3 3.50 3.50

Miniature Sheet

Adventure Tourism — A540

No. 2361: a, Parachuting above Dead Sea. b, Rock climbing, Wadi Balua. c, Ultralight airplane flying, Wadi Rum. d, Tourists looking at waterfall, Wadi Mujib. e, Jet skiing, Aqaba. f, Rock climbing, Ajloun.

2018, May 24 **Litho.** ***Perf. 12***

2361 A540 20pi Sheet of 6, #a-f, + label 3.50 3.50

Miniature Sheet

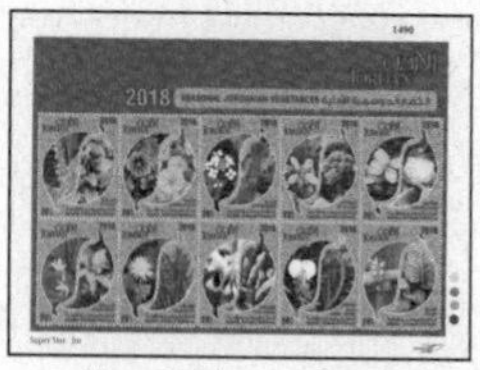

Vegetables — A541

No. 2362: a, Spinach. b, Common mallow. c, Watercress. d, Broccoli. e, Cauliflower. f, Corchorus. g, Dandelion. h, Fava beans. i, Green beans. j, Chard.

2018, June 28 **Litho.** ***Perf. 12***

2362 A541 20pi Sheet of 10, #a-j 5.75 5.75

Miniature Sheet

European and Mediterranean Style Houses — A542

No. 2363: a, House with telephone pole and light on pole at left. b, House with chimney and satellite dish on roof. c, House with large light on roof at left. d, House overlooking water. e, House with tile shingles. f, Stone house with green door and shutters.

2018, July 9 **Litho.** ***Perf. 12***

2363 A542 40pi Sheet of 6, #a-f 6.75 6.75

A543

A544

A545

A546

A547

Jerash Festival A548

2018, Aug. 2 **Litho.** ***Perf. 12***

2364 A543 30pi multi .85 .85
2365 A544 30pi multi .85 .85
2366 A545 30pi multi .85 .85
2367 A546 30pi multi .85 .85
2368 A547 30pi multi .85 .85
Nos. 2364-2368 (5) 4.25 4.25

Imperf

Size: 90x71mm

2369 A548 50pi multi 1.40 1.40

A549

A550

A551

A552

A553

A554

A555

Traditional Foods — A556

2018, Sept. 30 **Litho.** ***Perf. 12***

2370 Sheet of 8 4.80 4.80
a. A549 20pi multi .60 .60
b. A550 20pi multi .60 .60
c. A551 20pi multi .60 .60
d. A552 20pi multi .60 .60
e. A553 20pi multi .60 .60
f. A554 20pi multi .60 .60
g. A555 20pi multi .60 .60
h. A556 20pi multi .60 .60

Churches
A557

Designs: No. 2371, 30pi, Church of Christ, Khalda. No. 2372, 30pi, Church of the Latin, Kerak. No. 2373, 30pi, Church of Mount Nebo, Madaba. No. 2374, 30pi, Church of the Map, Madaba. No. 2375, 30pi, Coptic Church, Alabdali. No. 2376, 30pi, St. Ephrem Church, Sweifieh.

2018, Oct. 4 **Litho.** ***Perf. 12***
2371-2376 A557 Set of 6 5.25 5.25

Jordan Museum Artifacts
A558

No. 2377: a, Double-headed statue from Ayn Ghazal. b, Box from Pella. c, Statue of Ammonite king. d, Architectural relief depicting Melpomene. e, Rosette from Qaser Al-Mushatta.

2018, Nov. 15 **Litho.** ***Perf. 12***
2377 A558 30pi Sheet of 5, #a-e 4.25 4.25

Nos. 1644, 1653, 1659, 1662, 1689, 1692 Surcharged in Red and Black

Methods and Perfs. As Before

2018, Nov. 15
2378 A317 20pi on 200f #1644 .60 .60
2379 A317 20pi on 200f #1653 .60 .60
2380 A317 20pi on 200f #1659 .60 .60
2381 A317 20pi on 200f #1662 .60 .60
2382 A317 20pi on 200f #1689 .60 .60
2383 A317 20pi on 200f #1692 .60 .60
Nos. 2378-2383 (6) 3.60 3.60

No. 1472d Surcharged in Red and Black

Method and Perf. As Before

2018, Nov. 15
2384 A267 50pi on 50f #1472d 1.40 1.40

Miniature Sheet

Universal Declaration of Human Rights, 70th Anniv. — A559

No. 2385 — Emblem with: a, Violet background. b, White background, text in green. c, White background, text in violet. d, Green background.

2018, Dec. 10 **Litho.** ***Perf. 12***
2385 A559 50pi Sheet of 4, #a-d 5.75 5.75

A560

King Abdullah II's Accession to the Throne, 20th Anniv. — A561

Various photographs of King Abdullah II: 5pi, 10pi, 15pi, 20pi, 25pi, 30pi, 35pi, 40pi, 45pi, 50pi.
No. 2396, King Abdullah II in military uniform, coat of arms of Jordan.

Litho. With Foil Application

2019, Feb. 21 ***Perf. 14x12***
2386-2395 A560 Set of 10 7.75 7.75

Imperf

Size: 91x70mm

2396 A561 50pi multi 1.40 1.40

A562

A563

A564

A565

A566

Humanitarian Roles of the Army — A567

2019, Mar. 31 **Litho.** ***Perf. 12***
2397 A562 30pi multi .85 .85
2398 A563 30pi multi .85 .85
2399 A564 30pi multi .85 .85
2400 A565 30pi multi .85 .85
2401 A566 30pi multi .85 .85
2402 A567 30pi multi .85 .85
Nos. 2397-2402 (6) 5.10 5.10

Dead Sea Ultra Marathon, 25th Anniv. — A568

Various marathon runners: 30pi, 40pi, 50pi, 60pi.

2019, Apr. 1 **Litho.** ***Perf. 12***
2403-2406 A568 Set of 4 5.25 5.25

Souvenir Sheet

Dome of the Rock, Jerusalem — A569

2019, June 16 **Litho.** ***Perf. 12***
2407 A569 80pi multi 2.25 2.25

A570

A571

A572

A573

Traditional Clothing — A574

2019, July 8 **Litho.** ***Perf. 12***
2408 A570 40pi multi 1.10 1.10
2409 A571 40pi multi 1.10 1.10
2410 A572 40pi multi 1.10 1.10
2411 A573 40pi multi 1.10 1.10
Nos. 2408-2411 (4) 4.40 4.40

Imperf

2412 A574 50pi multi 1.40 1.40

Wonders of the World
A575

Designs: No. 2413, 40pi, Christ the Redeemer Statue, Brazil. No. 2414, 40pi, Great Wall of China, People's Republic of China. No. 2415, 40pi, Taj Mahal, India. No. 2416, 40pi, Colosseum, Italy. No. 2417, 40pi, Petra, Jordan. No. 2418, 40pi, Chichen Itza, Mexico. No. 2419, 40pi, Machu Picchu, Peru.

2019, July 8 **Litho.** ***Perf. 13¾x12***
2413-2419 A575 Set of 7 8.00 8.00

Miniature Sheet

Jordanian Heritage — A576

No. 2420: a, Earthenware urn in frame. b, Teapot. c, Tent, horiz. d, Weaver at loom, horiz. e, Dead birds hanging from branch, horiz. f, Images of rees carved in stone, horiz. g, Grain mill, horiz. h, Animal skin hanging from rope, horiz. i, Calligraphy brush and ink pot. j, Stringed instrument and bow.

2019, Aug. 8 **Litho.** ***Perf. 12***
2420 A576 20pi Sheet of 10, #a-j, + central label 5.75 5.75

Express Mail Service, 20th Anniv.
A577

2019, Oct. 9 **Litho.** ***Perf. 13¾x12***
2421 A577 80pi multi 2.25 2.25

Miniature Sheet

Y1SAT, First Jordanian Satellite — A578

No. 2422: a, Technicians wearing hair nets. b, Technician soldering. c, Technical team. d, Assembled Y1SAT. e, Finger and circuit board. f, Y1SAT in space.

2019, Oct. **Litho.** ***Perf. 12***
2422 A578 40pi Sheet of 6, #a-f 6.75 6.75

Miniature Sheet

Olive Picking
A579

No. 2423: a, 30pi, Man on ladder picking olives. b, 40pi, Two women picking olives. c, 50pi, Man using picking tool. d, 60pi, Three olive pickers.

2019, Nov. 28 **Litho.** ***Perf. 12***
2423 A579 Sheet of 4, #a-d 5.25 5.25

Flag of Palestinian Authority, Doves, and Dome of the Rock, Jerusalem
A580

Litho. & Embossed With Foil Application

2019, Dec. 24 ***Perf. 12***
2424 A580 120pi gold & multi 3.50 3.50

Jerusalem, capital of Palestinian Authority.

Arab League, 75th Anniv. — A581

2020, Mar. 21 **Litho.** ***Perf. 12***
2425 A581 120pi multi 3.50 3.50

Campaign Against COVID-19 Pandemic — A582

No. 2426: a, Police officer and police car. b, People participating in teleconference. c, People in meeting with leader at easel. d, People seated at table. e, Health care workers and ambulance. f, Delivery man with boxes. g, Soldier and military vehicle.

2021, Mar. 31 Litho. *Perf. 12*

2426		Sheet of 7	6.00	6.00
a.-g.	A582	30pi Any single	.85	.85

A583

A584

A585

A586

A587

A588

A589

A590

A591

A592

Establishment of the Emirate of Transjordan, Cent. — A603

Litho. & Embossed With Foil Application

2021, Apr. *Perf. 12*

2427	A583	100pi multi	—	—
2428	A584	100pi multi	—	—
2429	A585	100pi multi	—	—
2430	A586	100pi multi	—	—
2431	A587	100pi multi	—	—
2432	A588	100pi multi	—	—
2433	A589	100pi multi	—	—
2434	A590	100pi multi	—	—
2435	A591	100pi multi	—	—
2436	A592	100pi multi	—	—

Imperf

Litho. & Embossed With Foil Application

2438	A603	100pi multi	—	—

A608

The Martyr — A609

Litho. & Embossed With Foil Application

2021, June 23 *Perf. 12*

2443	A608	100pi gold & multi	3.00	3.00
2444	A609	100pi gold & multi	3.00	3.00

A610

A611

A612

A613

A614

A615

A616

Jordanian Nature Reserves — A617

2021, June 23 Litho. *Perf. 14*

2445		Sheet of 8	—	—
a.	A610	35pi multi	—	—
b.	A611	35pi multi	—	—
c.	A612	35pi multi	—	—
d.	A613	35pi multi	—	—
e.	A614	35pi multi	—	—
f.	A615	35pi multi	—	—
g.	A616	35pi multi	—	—
h.	A617	35pi multi	—	—

Miniature Sheet

Handicrafted Jewelry — A618

No. 2446: a, Beaded necklace. b, Necklace and pendant. c, Earrings. d, Pendant.

Litho. & Embossed With Foil Application

2021, July 12 *Perf. 12*

2446	A618	50pi Sheet of 4, #a-d	5.75	5.75

A619

A620

A621

A622

A623

A624

A625

Purebred Arabian Horses A626

2021, Aug. 31 Litho. *Perf. 12*

2447	A619	30pi multi	.85	.85
2448	A620	30pi multi	.85	.85
2449	A621	30pi multi	.85	.85
2450	A622	30pi multi	.85	.85
2451	A623	30pi multi	.85	.85
2452	A624	30pi multi	.85	.85
2453	A625	30pi multi	.85	.85
		Nos. 2447-2453 (7)	5.95	5.95

Size:120x70mm

Imperf

2454	A626	50pi multi	1.40	1.40

Musical Instruments — A627

Designs: No. 2455, 30pi, Zither. No. 2456, 30pi, Tambourine. No. 2457, 30pi, Piano. No. 2458, 30pi, Bouzouki. No. 2459, 30pi, Cello. No. 2460, 30pi, Clarinet. No. 2461, 30pi, Accordion. No. 2462, 30pi, Flute. No. 2463, 30pi, Violin. No. 2464, 30pi, Oud.

2021, Oct. 25 Litho. *Perf. 12*

2455-2464	A627	Set of 10	8.50	8.50

British Mandate Postage Stamps of Jordan, Cent. (in 2020) A628

2021, Oct. 26 Litho. *Imperf.*

2465	A628	100pi multi + label	3.00	3.00

A629

A630

A631

Inclusion of People with Disabilities in Society — A632

2021, Nov. 29 Litho. *Perf. 12*

2466	A629	50pi multi		1.40	1.40
2467	A630	50pi multi		1.40	1.40
2468	A631	50pi multi		1.40	1.40
2469	A632	50pi multi		1.40	1.40
	Nos. 2466-2469 (4)			5.60	5.60

A633

A634

A635

Return of Al Baqoura and Al Ghamr to Jordanian Control A636

Litho. & Embossed With Foil Application

2021, Nov. 29 *Perf. 12x14*

2470	A633	50pi sil & multi	1.40	1.40
2471	A634	50pi sil & multi	1.40	1.40
2472	A635	50pi sil & multi	1.40	1.40
2473	A636	50pi sil & multi	1.40	1.40
	Nos. 2470-2473 (4)		5.60	5.60

Miniature Sheet

Aerial Views of Cities A637

No. 2474: a, Al Shoubak. b, Ajlun. c, Amman. d, As Salt. e, Aqaba. f, Umm Qais.

Litho. & Embossed With Foil Application

2021, Nov. 29 *Perf. 12*

2474	A637	40pi Sheet of 6, #a-f	6.75	6.75

Madaba, 2022 Capital of Arab Tourism A638

Designs: No. 2475, 40pi, Fortress of Mukawir. No. 2476, 40pi, Ma'in Hot Springs. No. 2477, 40pi, Mount Nebo. No. 2478, 40pi, Tourist Street. No. 2479, 40pi, Wadi Al-Hidan. No. 2480, 40pi, St. George Church.
50pi, Mosaic map of Jerusalem.

2022, June 27 Litho. *Perf. 12*

2475-2480	A638	Set of 6	6.75	6.75

Size: 111x55mm

Imperf

2481	A638	50pi multi	1.40	1.40

A639

A640

A641

A642

A643

A644

A645

A646

Royal Tank Museum, Amman A647

Litho. & Embossed With Foil Application

2022, July 27 *Perf. 14*

2482	A639	40pi multi	—	—
2483	A640	40pi multi	—	—
2484	A641	40pi multi	—	—
2485	A642	40pi multi	—	—
2486	A643	40pi multi	—	—
2487	A644	40pi multi	—	—
2488	A645	40pi multi	—	—
2489	A646	40pi multi	—	—

Imperf

2490	A647	50pi multi	—	—

A648

A649

A650

A651

A652

A653

A654

A655

A656

Wildflowers A657

Perf. 13¼x13½

2022, Aug. 18 Litho.

2491	A648	30pi multi	.85	.85
2492	A649	30pi multi	.85	.85
2493	A650	30pi multi	.85	.85
2494	A651	30pi multi	.85	.85
2495	A652	30pi multi	.85	.85
2496	A653	30pi multi	.85	.85
2497	A654	30pi multi	.85	.85
2498	A655	30pi multi	.85	.85
2499	A656	30pi multi	.85	.85
2500	A657	30pi multi	.85	.85
	Nos. 2491-2500 (10)		8.50	8.50

SEMI-POSTAL STAMPS

Locust Campaign Issue

Nos. 145-156 Overprinted

1930, Apr. 1 Wmk. 4 *Perf. 14*

B1	A1	2(m) Prus blue		2.50	*4.00*
	a.	Inverted overprint		225.00	
B2	A1	3(m) rose		2.00	*4.00*
B3	A1	4(m) green		2.75	*5.00*
B4	A1	5(m) orange		22.50	17.50
	a.	Double overprint		400.00	
B5	A1	10(m) red		2.25	*3.75*
B6	A1	15(m) ultra		2.25	*3.50*
	a.	Inverted overprint		225.00	
B7	A1	20(m) olive grn		2.75	*4.50*
B8	A2	50(m) claret		5.50	*11.00*
B9	A2	90(m) bister		16.00	*47.50*
B10	A2	100(m) lt blue		17.50	*50.00*
B11	A2	200(m) violet		37.50	*100.00*
B12	A2	500(m) brown		100.00	*160.00*
	a.	"C" of "Locust" omitted		750.00	
	Nos. B1-B12 (12)			213.50	410.75

These stamps were issued to raise funds to help combat a plague of locusts.

Catalogue values for unused stamps in this section, from this point to the end of the section, are for Never Hinged items.

Jerusalem SP1

1997, Nov. 29 Litho. *Perf. 13½x13*

B13	SP1	100f +10f bl & multi	.90	.75
B14	SP1	200f +20f yel & multi	1.90	1.75
B15	SP1	300f +30f bl grn & multi	2.75	2.50
	Nos. B13-B15 (3)		5.55	5.00

Breast Cancer Prevention — SP2

2009, Aug. 25 Litho. *Perf. 13¼*
Granite Paper

B16	SP2	30pi +50pi multi	3.75	3.75

Jerusalem, Capital of Arab Culture — SP3

Panel color: 20pi+25pi, Orange. 30pi+25pi, Purple. 40pi+25pi, Red. 50pi+25pi, Gray green.

2009, Dec. 13 *Perf. 13¼*
Granite Paper

B17-B20	SP3	Set of 4	8.00	8.00

AIR POST STAMPS

Catalogue values for unused stamps in this section are for Never Hinged items.

Plane and Globe — AP1

Perf. 13½x13

1950, Sept. 16 Engr. Wmk. 4

C1	AP1	5f org & red vio	1.00	.80
C2	AP1	10f pur & brown	1.00	.80
C3	AP1	15f ol grn & rose car	1.00	.80
C4	AP1	20f deep blue & blk	1.25	1.25
C5	AP1	50f rose pink & dl grn	1.75	1.25
C6	AP1	100f blue & brown	3.00	3.00
C7	AP1	150f blk & red org	4.50	4.25
		Nos. C1-C7 (7)	13.50	12.15

Temple of Artemis, Jerash — AP2

1954 Unwmk. *Perf. 12*

C8	AP2	5f blue blk & org	.45	.25
C9	AP2	10f vio brn & ver	.80	.75
C10	AP2	25f bl grn & ultra	.90	.80
C11	AP2	35f dp plum & grnsh bl	1.00	.80
C12	AP2	40f car rose & blk	1.25	.80
C13	AP2	50f dp ultra & org yel	1.50	1.00
C14	AP2	100f dk bl & vio brn	1.75	1.75
C15	AP2	150f stl bl & red brn	3.00	2.25
		Nos. C8-C15 (8)	10.65	8.40

1958-59 Wmk. 305 *Perf. 12*

C16	AP2	5f blue blk & org	.45	.25
C17	AP2	10f vio brn & ver	.75	.25
C18	AP2	25f bl grn & ultra	.90	.40
C19	AP2	35f dp plum grnsh bl	.90	.60
C20	AP2	40f car rose & blk	1.10	.75
C21	AP2	50f dp ultra & org yel ('59)	2.00	1.00
		Nos. C16-C21 (6)	6.10	3.25

Stadium and Torch — AP3

Perf. 11x11½

1964, July 12 Litho. Wmk. 305

C22	AP3	1f yellow & multi	.40	.30
C23	AP3	4f red & multi	.40	.30
C24	AP3	10f blue & multi	.40	.30
C25	AP3	35f yel grn & multi	.80	.60
a.		Souvenir sheet of 4, #C22-C25	2.75	2.25
		Nos. C22-C25 (4)	2.00	1.50

Opening of Hussein Sports City. No. C25a also exists imperf.

Gorgeous Bush-Shrike AP4

Birds: 500f, Ornate hawk-eagle, vert. 1d, Gray-headed kingfisher, vert.

Perf. 14x14½

1964, Dec. 18 Photo. Unwmk.

Birds in Natural Colors

C26	AP4	150f lt grn, blk & car	30.00	13.00
C27	AP4	500f lt bl, blk & grn	70.00	35.00
C28	AP4	1d ol brn & blk	135.00	75.00
		Nos. C26-C28 (3)	235.00	123.00

Nos. C26-C28 exist imperf.

Pagoda, Olympic Torch and Emblem AP5

1965, Mar. 5 Litho. *Perf. 14*

C29	AP5	10f deep rose	.40	.40
C30	AP5	15f violet	.40	.40
C31	AP5	20f blue	.45	.45
C32	AP5	30f green	.45	.45
C33	AP5	40f brown	.60	.60
C34	AP5	60f carmine rose	.85	.85
		Nos. C29-C34 (6)	3.15	3.15

18th Olympic Games, Tokyo, Oct. 10-25, 1964. An imperf. 100f violet blue souvenir sheet exists. Size of stamp: 60x60mm. Value $12.50.

For overprints see Nos. C42A-C42F.

Forum, Jerash — AP6

Antiquities of Jerash: No. C36, South Theater. No. C37, Triumphal arch. No. C38, Temple of Artemis. No. C39, Cathedral steps. No. C40, Artemis Temple, gate. No. C41, Columns. No. C42, Columns and niche, South Theater. Nos. C39-C42 are vertical.

1965, June 22 Photo. *Perf. 14x15*

Center Multicolored

C35	AP6	55f bright pink	1.40	1.40
C36	AP6	55f light blue	1.40	1.40
C37	AP6	55f green	1.40	1.40
C38	AP6	55f black	1.40	1.40
C39	AP6	55f light green	1.40	1.40
C40	AP6	55f carmine rose	1.40	1.40
C41	AP6	55f gray	1.40	1.40
C42	AP6	55f blue	1.40	1.40
		Nos. C35-C42 (8)	11.20	11.20

Nos. C35-C38 are printed in horizontal rows of 4; Nos. C39-C42 in vertical rows of 4; sheets of 16.

Nos. C29-C34 with Bilingual Ovpt. and Rocket in Black

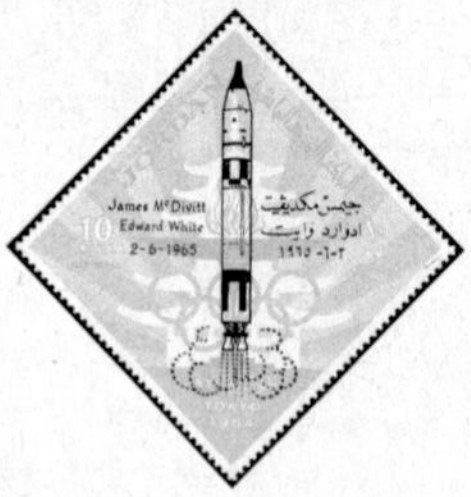

1965, Sept. 25 Litho. *Perf. 14*

C42A	AP5	10f deep rose	1.50	1.50
C42B	AP5	15f violet	2.00	2.00
C42C	AP5	20f blue	2.75	2.75
C42D	AP5	30f green	4.25	4.00
C42E	AP5	40f brown	5.50	5.50
C42F	AP5	60f carmine rose	7.50	7.50
		Nos. C42A-C42F (6)	23.50	23.25

The imperf. 100f blue souvenir sheet exists overprinted. Value $21.50.

King Hussein Type of Regular Issue

1966, Jan. 15 Photo. *Perf. 14½x14*

Portrait in Brown

C43	A67	200f brt blue grn	5.00	2.00
C44	A67	500f light green	11.00	8.00
C45	A67	1d light ultra	19.00	12.50
		Nos. C43-C45 (3)	35.00	22.50

Animal Type of Regular Issue, 1967

Animals: 4f, Striped hyena. 30f, Arabian stallion. 60f, Persian gazelle.

1967, Feb. 11 Photo. *Perf. 14x15*

C46	A70	4f dk brn & multi	2.00	.30
C47	A70	30f lt bl & multi	2.50	.60
C48	A70	60f yellow & multi	4.50	1.50
		Nos. C46-C48 (3)	9.00	2.40

Game Type of Regular Issue, 1968

Protected Game: 60f, Nubian ibex, vert. 100f, Wild ducks.

1968, Oct. 5 Litho. *Perf. 13½*

C49	A74	60f multicolored	9.50	5.00
C50	A74	100f multicolored	15.00	9.00

Easter Type of Regular Issue

Designs: 60f, Altar, Holy Sepulcher. 100f, Feet Washing, Holy Gate, Jerusalem.

1972, Apr. Photo. *Perf. 14x13½*

C51	A92	60f dk bl & multi	1.40	.70
C52	A92	100f multicolored	2.00	1.10

Aero Club Type of Regular Issue

15f, Two Piper 140s. 20f, R.J.A.C. Beechcraft. 40f, Aero Club emblem with winged horse.

1973, Jan. Photo. *Perf. 13½x14*

C53	A100	15f blue, blk & red	.70	.35
C54	A100	20f blue, blk & red	.80	.40
C55	A100	40f mag, blk & yel	1.60	.80
		Nos. C53-C55 (3)	3.10	1.55

Agriculture Type of Regular Issue

Design: 100f, Soil conservation.

1973, Dec. 25 *Perf. 13½*

C56	A110	100f multicolored	2.50	1.75

King Hussein Driving Car — AP7

1974, Dec. 20 *Perf. 12*

C57	AP7	30f multicolored	.60	.25
C58	AP7	60f multicolored	1.50	1.00

Royal Jordanian Automobile Club.

Building Type of Regular Issue

Designs: 50f, Palms, Aqaba. 60f, Obelisk tomb. 80f, Fort of Wadi Rum.

1975, Mar. 1 Photo. *Perf. 13½x14*

C59	A121	50f pink & multi	1.40	.65
C60	A121	60f lt bl & multi	1.75	.80
C61	A121	80f yellow & multi	2.25	.80
		Nos. C59-C61 (3)	5.40	2.25

Hussein Type of Regular Issue

1975, Apr. 8 Photo. *Perf. 14x13½*

Size: 22x27mm

C62	A123	60f dk grn & brn	1.25	.35
C63	A123	100f org brn & brn	2.00	.40
C64	A123	120f dp bl & brn	1.10	.65
C65	A123	180f brt mag & brn	1.75	1.10
C66	A123	200f grnsh bl & brn	2.25	1.50
C67	A123	400f pur & brown	3.25	2.50
C68	A123	500f orange & brn	4.25	4.00
		Nos. C62-C68 (7)	15.85	10.50

POSTAGE DUE STAMPS

Stamps of Regular Issue (Nos. 69, 66-68 Surcharged with New Value like No. 91) Overprinted

This overprint reads: "Mustahaq" (Tax or Due)

Typo. Ovpt. "Mustahaq" 10mm long

1923 Unwmk. *Perf. 11½*

J1	A7	½pi on 3pi ol brn	57.50	*60.00*
a.		Inverted overprint	200.00	200.00
b.		Double overprint	200.00	200.00

Handstamped Overprint 12mm long

J2	A7	½pi on 3pi ol brn	27.50	*35.00*
a.		Inverted overprint	55.00	—
b.		Double overprint	55.00	—
J3	A7	1pi dark blue	18.00	*21.00*
a.		Inverted overprint	50.00	—
b.		Double overprint	52.50	—
J4	A7	1½pi violet	21.00	*22.50*
a.		Inverted overprint	50.00	—
b.		Double overprint	52.50	—
J5	A7	2pi orange	25.00	*27.50*
a.		Inverted overprint	65.00	60.00
b.		Double overprint	70.00	—
		Nos. J1-J5 (5)	149.00	*166.00*

Stamps of Hejaz Handstamped

J6	A7	½pi red	2.50	*6.00*
J7	A7	1pi dark blue	6.00	*6.50*
J8	A7	1½pi violet	5.00	*7.50*
J9	A7	2pi orange	8.00	*8.00*
J10	A7	3pi olive brown	12.50	*17.50*
J11	A7	5pi olive green	15.00	*30.00*
		Nos. J6-J11 (6)	49.00	*75.50*

Type of Palestine, 1918, Overprinted

1925 Wmk. 4 *Perf. 14*

J12	A1	1m dark brown	2.50	*6.00*
J13	A1	2m yellow	4.25	*4.25*
J14	A1	4m rose	4.75	*6.75*
J15	A1	8m red	6.50	*12.00*
J16	A1	13m ultramarine	9.50	*12.00*
J17	A1	5pi plum	11.00	*19.00*
a.		Perf. 15x14	67.50	*85.00*
		Nos. J12-J17 (6)	38.50	*60.00*

The overprint reads: "Mustahaq. Sharqi al'Ardan." (Tax. Eastern Jordan).

Stamps of Palestine, 1918, Surcharged

1926

J18	A1	1m on 1m dk brn	10.00	*12.00*
J19	A1	2m on 1m dk brn	9.00	*12.00*
J20	A1	4m on 3m Prus bl	10.00	*15.00*
J21	A1	8m on 3m Prus bl	10.00	*15.00*
J22	A1	13m on 13m ultra	13.00	*17.00*
J23	A1	5pi on 13m ultra	16.00	*25.00*
		Nos. J18-J23 (6)	68.00	*96.00*

The surcharge reads "Tax — Eastern Jordan" and New Value.

Stamps of Regular Issue, 1927, Overprinted

1929

J24	A1	2m Prussian bl	2.50	*8.00*
J25	A1	10m red	2.50	*9.00*
J26	A2	50m claret	7.50	*22.50*
		Nos. J24-J26 (3)	12.50	*39.50*

With Additional Surcharge

J27	A1	1(m) on 3(m) rose	1.75	*9.00*
J28	A1	4(m) on 15(m) ultra	3.00	*11.00*
a.		Inverted surch. and ovpt.	200.00	350.00
J29	A2	20(m) on 100(m) lt bl	7.00	*20.00*
		Nos. J27-J29 (3)	11.75	*40.00*

D1

Size: 17¼x21mm

1929 Engr. *Perf. 14*

J30	D1	1m brown	1.40	*6.50*
a.		Perf. 13½x13	160.00	130.00
J31	D1	2m orange	2.75	*7.00*
J32	D1	4m green	4.00	*11.00*
J33	D1	10m carmine	7.00	*10.00*
J34	D1	20m olive green	13.00	*21.00*
J35	D1	50m blue	16.00	*32.50*
		Nos. J30-J35 (6)	44.15	*88.00*

See Nos. J39-J43 design with larger type. For surcharge see No. J52. For overprints see Nos. NJ1a, NJ3, NJ5a, NJ6-NJ7.

D2

1942 Unwmk. Litho. *Perf. 13x13½*

J36	D2	1m dull red brn	3.00	*24.00*
J37	D2	2m dl orange yel	9.00	*14.00*
J38	D2	10m dark carmine	12.00	*8.00*
		Nos. J36-J38 (3)	24.00	*46.00*

For overprints see Nos. NJ8-NJ10.

Type of 1929

1943-44 Engr. Wmk. 4 *Perf. 12*

Size: 17¾x21¼mm

J39	D1	1m orange brn	.70	*6.50*
J40	D1	2m yel orange	.90	*7.00*
J41	D1	4m yel green	.90	*9.00*

J42 D1 10m rose carmine 2.50 *12.00*
J43 D1 20m olive green 45.00 *90.00*
Nos. J39-J43 (5) 50.00 *124.50*

For overprints see Nos. J47-J51, NJ1-NJ2, NJ3a, NJ5, NJ6a.

Catalogue values for unused stamps in this section, from this point to the end of the section, are for Never Hinged items.

Nos. J39-J43, J35 Srchd. "FILS" & its Arabic Equivalent in Black, Green or Carmine

1952 **Wmk. 4** ***Perf. 12***
J47 D1 1f on 1m org brn (Bk) 2.00 2.00
J48 D1 2f on 2m yel org (G) 2.00 2.00
J49 D1 4f on 4m yel grn 2.50 2.50
J50 D1 10f on 10m rose car (Bk) 4.25 *4.75*
J51 D1 20f on 20m ol grn 10.00 *10.00*

Perf. 14
J52 D1 50f on 50m blue 9.50 *10.50*
Nos. J47-J52 (6) 30.25 *31.75*

This overprint exists on Nos. J34, J36-J38. Exists inverted, double and in wrong color.

D3

Inscribed: "The Hashemite Kingdom of the Jordan"

1952 **Engr.** ***Perf. 11½***
J53 D3 1f orange brown .65 *.85*
J54 D3 2f yel orange .65 *.85*
J55 D3 4f yel green .65 *.85*
J56 D3 10f rose carmine 1.25 *1.50*
J57 D3 20f yel brown 1.25 *1.75*
J58 D3 50f blue 3.50 *4.00*
Nos. J53-J58 (6) 7.95 *9.80*

Type of 1952 Redrawn

Inscribed: "The Hashemite Kingdom of Jordan"

1957 **Wmk. 305** ***Perf. 11½***
J59 D3 1f orange brown 1.00 *.40*
J60 D3 2f yel orange 1.00 *.40*
J61 D3 4f yel green 1.00 *.60*
J62 D3 10f rose carmine 1.25 *.55*
J63 D3 20f yel brown 1.75 *1.25*
Nos. J59-J63 (5) 6.00 *3.20*

OFFICIAL STAMP

Saudi Arabia No. L34 Overprinted

1924, Jan. **Typo.** ***Perf. 11½***
O1 A7 ½pi red 100.00

Overprint reads: "(Government) the Arabian East 1342."

No. O1 is not known genuine in used condition.

POSTAL TAX STAMPS

Catalogue values for unused stamps in this section are for Never Hinged items.

Mosque at Hebron — PT1

Designs: 10m, 15m, 20m, 50m, Dome of the Rock. 100m, 200m, 500m, £1, Acre.

Perf. 11½x12½
1947 **Unwmk.** **Engr.**
RA1 PT1 1m ultra .60 .40
RA2 PT1 2m carmine .70 .50
RA3 PT1 3m emerald .80 .75
RA4 PT1 5m plum 1.00 .85
RA5 PT1 10m carmine 1.10 1.00
RA6 PT1 15m gray 1.75 1.25
RA7 PT1 20m dk brown 3.00 1.50
RA8 PT1 50m purple 4.50 3.50
RA9 PT1 100m orange red 14.00 9.00
RA10 PT1 200m dp blue 37.50 22.50
RA11 PT1 500m green 80.00 60.00
RA12 PT1 £1 dk brown 140.00 130.00
Nos. RA1-RA12 (12) 284.95 231.25

Issued to help the Welfare Fund for Arabs in Palestine. Required on foreign-bound letters to the amount of half the regular postage.

For overprints and surcharges see Nos. 286A-286C, 344-346, RA37-RA46, NRA1-NRA12.

Nos. 211, 232 and 234 Overprinted in Black

1950 **Wmk. 4** ***Perf. 12***
RA23 A3 5m orange 20.00 *22.50*
RA24 A3 10m violet 30.00 *32.50*
RA25 A3 15m dull olive grn 35.00 *35.00*
Nos. RA23-RA25 (3) 85.00 *90.00*

Arch and Colonnade, Palmyra, Syria — PT2

Two types of 5m:
Type I — "A" with serifs. Arabic ovpt. 8mm wide.
Type II — "A" without serifs. Arabic ovpt. 5mm wide.

Black or Carmine Overprint

1950-51 **Engr.** ***Perf. 13½x13***
RA26 PT2 5m orange (I) 25.00 *20.00*
a. Type II ('51) 27.50 *2.75*
RA27 PT2 10m violet (C) 25.00 *22.50*

The overprint on No. RA27 is similar to that on RA23-RA25 but slightly bolder.

Type of 1947

Designs: 5f, Hebron Mosque. 10f, 15f, 20f, Dome of the Rock. 100f, Acre.

1951 **Wmk. 4** ***Perf. 11½x12½***
RA28 PT1 5f plum 1.00 1.00
RA29 PT1 10f carmine 1.00 1.00
RA30 PT1 15f gray 1.25 1.25
RA31 PT1 20f dk brown 1.50 1.50
RA33 PT1 100f orange 6.25 6.25
Nos. RA28-RA33 (5) 11.00 11.00

The tax on Nos. RA1-RA33 was for Arab aid in Palestine.

For overprints see Nos. 287-290, 347.

Postal Tax Stamps of 1947 Srchd. "FILS" or "J.D." & Their Arabic Equivalents & Bars in Carmine or Black

1952 **Unwmk.**
RA37 PT1 1f on 1m ultra .75 .45
RA38 PT1 3f on 3m emer 1.00 .45
RA39 PT1 10f on 10m car 1.50 .55
RA40 PT1 15f on 15m gray 2.00 1.25
RA41 PT1 20f on 20m dk brown 3.00 1.75
RA42 PT1 50f on 50m pur 6.00 3.75
RA43 PT1 100f on 100m org red 17.50 10.00
RA44 PT1 200f on 200m dp blue 45.00 27.50
RA45 PT1 500f on 500m grn 100.00 75.00
RA46 PT1 1d on £1 dk brn 150.00 140.00
Nos. RA37-RA46 (10) 326.75 260.70

"J.D." stands for Jordanian Dinar.

OCCUPATION STAMPS

Catalogue values for unused stamps in this section are for Never Hinged items.

For Use in Palestine

Stamps of Jordan Overprinted in Red, Black, Dark Green, Green or Orange Red

On No. 200

1948 **Unwmk.** ***Perf. 13x13½***
N1 A14 2m dull green (R) 8.00 8.00

On #207-209, 211, 230-235, 215-220

1948 **Wmk. 4** ***Perf. 12, 13½x13, 14***
N2 A3 1m red brown 1.00 .80
N3 A3 2m Prus grn (R) 1.00 .80
a. 2m Prussian blue, perf. 13½x13 (R) (#170a) 2.50 *2.50*
N4 A3 3m blue grn (R) 1.00 1.00
N5 A3 3m rose carmine .65 .65
N6 A3 4m dp yel grn (R) .65 .65
N7 A3 5m orange (G) .65 .65
N8 A3 10m violet (OR) 1.50 1.50
N9 A3 12m deep rose 1.50 .90
N10 A3 15m dl ol grn (R) 2.25 2.25
N11 A3 20m dp blue (R) 3.00 1.50
N12 A3 50m red lil (Dk G) 3.25 3.25
N13 A3 90m ocher (Dk G) 15.00 3.25
N14 A3 100m dp blue (R) 17.50 10.00
N15 A3 200m dk vio (R) 9.00 *15.00*
a. 200m vio, perf. 14 (R) (#182) 75.00 50.00
N16 A3 500m dk brn (R) 60.00 25.00
N17 A3 £1 black (R) 110.00 60.00
Nos. N2-N17 (16) 227.95 127.20

The first overprinting of these stamps include Nos. N1-N6, N9-N17. The second overprinting includes Nos. N1, N3, N5-N17, in inks differing in shade from the originals.

Many values exist with inverted or double overprint.

Jordan Nos. 245-249 Overprinted in Black or Red

1949, Aug. **Wmk. 4** ***Perf. 13***
N18 A17 1m brown (Bk) 1.75 1.75
N19 A17 4m green 1.75 1.75
a. "PLAESTINE" 80.00
N20 A17 10m red 1.75 1.75
N21 A17 20m ultra 1.75 1.75
N22 A18 50m dull green 3.50 3.50
a. "PLAESTINE" 75.00
Nos. N18-N22 (5) 10.50 10.50

The overprint is in one line on No. N22.
UPU, 75th anniversary.

OCCUPATION POSTAGE DUE STAMPS

Catalogue values for unused stamps in this section are for Never Hinged items.

Jordan Nos. J39, J30a, J40, J32, J41-J43, J34 and J35 Overprinted in Black, Red or Carmine

1948-49 **Wmk. 4** ***Perf. 12, 14***
NJ1 D1 1m org brn, perf. 12 3.50 *5.00*
a. Perf. 13½x13 (#J30a) 75.00 50.00
NJ2 D1 2m yel orange 4.00 *6.00*
NJ3 D1 4m grn (R) (#J32) 4.00 *6.00*
a. 4m yel grn (C) (#J41) 15.00 *18.00*
NJ5 D1 10m rose car (#J42) ('49) 4.00 *5.50*
a. Perf. 14 (#J33) 325.00
NJ6 D1 20m ol grn (R), perf. 14 3.75 *5.00*
a. Perf. 12 (R) (#J43) 95.00 95.00
NJ7 D1 50m blue (R) 4.25 *6.00*
Nos. NJ1-NJ3,NJ5-NJ7 (6) 23.50 *33.50*

The second overprinting of these stamps includes Nos. NJ1-NJ3, NJ3a and NJ5-NJ7, in inks differing in shade from the originals.

Double and inverted overprints exist.

Same Overprint in Black on Jordan Nos. J36-J38

1948-49 **Unwmk.** ***Perf. 13x13½***
NJ8 D2 1m dl red brn *175.00* *175.00*
NJ9 D2 2m dl org yel ('49) 20.00 *25.00*
NJ10 D2 10m dark car 17.50 *22.50*

OCCUPATION POSTAL TAX STAMPS

Catalogue values for unused stamps in this section are for Never Hinged items.

Postal Tax Stamps of 1947 Overprinted in Red or Black

1950
NRA1 PT1 1m ultra (R) .40 .75
NRA2 PT1 2m carmine .45 .75
NRA3 PT1 3m emer (R) .75 .85
NRA4 PT1 5m plum 1.00 .75
NRA5 PT1 10m carmine 1.25 .75
NRA6 PT1 15m gray (R) 2.75 .90
NRA7 PT1 20m dk brn (R) 4.50 1.50
NRA8 PT1 50m purple (R) 6.50 3.00
NRA9 PT1 100m org red 11.00 4.50
NRA10 PT1 200m dp blue (R) 27.50 14.50
NRA11 PT1 500m green (R) 75.00 42.50
NRA12 PT1 £1 dk brn (R) 140.00 75.00
Nos. NRA1-NRA12 (12) 271.10 145.75

For overprints see Nos. 286D-286G.

KARELIA

kə-'rē-lə-ə

LOCATION — In northwestern Soviet Russia
GOVT. — An autonomous republic of the Soviet Union
AREA — 55,198 sq. mi. (approx.)
POP. — 270,000 (approx.)
CAPITAL — Petrozavodsk (Kalininsk)

In 1921 the Karelians rebelled and for a short period a form of sovereignty independent of Russia was maintained.

100 Pennia = 1 Markka

Bear — A1

1922 Unwmk. Litho. *Perf. 11½, 12*

1 A1 5p dark gray 15.00 *55.00*
2 A1 10p light blue 15.00 *55.00*
3 A1 20p rose red 15.00 *55.00*
4 A1 25p yellow brown 15.00 *55.00*
5 A1 40p magenta 15.00 *55.00*
6 A1 50p gray green 15.00 *55.00*
7 A1 75p orange yellow 20.00 *55.00*
8 A1 1m pink & gray 20.00 *55.00*
9 A1 2m yel grn & gray 27.50 *110.00*
10 A1 3m lt blue & gray 27.50 *140.00*
11 A1 5m red lil & gray 27.50 *175.00*
12 A1 10m lt brn & gray 27.50 *275.00*
13 A1 15m green & car 27.50 *275.00*
14 A1 20m rose & green 27.50 *275.00*
15 A1 25m yellow & blue 30.00 *275.00*
Nos. 1-15 (15) 325.00 *1,965.*
Set, never hinged 450.00

Nos. 1-15 were valid Jan. 31-Feb. 16, 1922. Use probably ended Feb. 3, although cancellations of the 4th and 5th exist.

Nos. 7, 8, 10, 13, 14 and 15 exist imperf. Value, each pair $250 hinged; $500 never hinged. Other denominations may exist imperf.

Counterfeits abound.

OCCUPATION STAMPS

Issued under Finnish Occupation

Issued in the Russian territory of Eastern Karelia under Finnish military administration.

Types of Finland Stamps, 1930 Overprinted in Black

On A26

On A27-A28

1941 Unwmk. *Perf. 14*

N1 A26 50p brt yel grn .45 *1.00*
N2 A26 1.75m dk gray 1.25 *1.75*
N3 A26 2m dp org 1.75 *4.50*
N4 A26 2.75m yel org .85 *1.25*
N5 A26 3½m lt ultra 2.50 *4.50*
N6 A27 5m rose vio 6.00 *10.00*
N7 A28 10m pale brn 6.75 *12.00*
Nos. N1-N7 (7) 19.55 *35.00*
Set, never hinged 32.00

Types of Finland Stamps, 1930 Overprinted in Green

On A26

On A27-A29

N8 A26 50p brt yel grn .55 *.90*
N9 A26 1.75m dk gray .70 *1.00*
N10 A26 2m dp org 1.00 *2.40*
N11 A26 2.75m yel org .65 *1.25*
N12 A26 3½m lt ultra 1.25 *2.25*
N13 A27 5m rose vio 2.00 *5.00*
N14 A28 10m pale brown 4.25 *8.50*
N15 A29 25m green 4.50 *9.00*
Nos. N8-N15 (8) 14.90 *30.30*
Set, never hinged 35.00

Mannerheim Type of Finland Overprinted

1942

N16 A48 50p dk yel grn .95 *2.25*
N17 A48 1.75m slate bl .95 *2.25*
N18 A48 2m red org .95 *2.25*
N19 A48 2.75m brn org .80 *2.25*
N20 A48 3.50m brt ultra .80 *2.25*
N21 A48 5m brn vio .80 *2.25*
Nos. N16-N21 (6) 5.25 *13.50*
Set, never hinged 10.00

Same Overprint on Ryti Type of Finland

N22 A49 50p dk yel grn .80 *2.25*
N23 A49 1.75m slate bl .80 *2.25*
N24 A49 2m red org .80 *2.25*
N25 A49 2.75m brn org .95 *2.25*
N26 A49 3.50m brt ultra .95 *2.25*
N27 A49 5m brn vio .95 *2.25*
Nos. N22-N27 (6) 5.25 *13.50*
Set, never hinged 10.00

The overprint translates, "East Karelia Military Administration."

OCCUPATION SEMI-POSTAL STAMP

Arms of East Karelia — SP1

1943 Unwmk. Engr. *Perf. 14*

NB1 SP1 3.50m + 1.50m dk ol .90 *2.50*
Never hinged 2.50

This surtax aided war victims in East Karelia.

KATANGA

kə-'täŋ-gə

LOCATION — Central Africa
GOVT. — Republic
CAPITAL — Elisabethville

Katanga province seceded from the Congo (ex-Belgian) Republic in July, 1960, but established nations did not recognize it as an independent state. The UN declared the secession ended in Sept, 1961. The last troops surrendered Sept. 1963.

During the secession Katanga stamps were tolerated in the international mails, but the government authorizing them was not recognized.

100 Centimes = 1 Franc

Catalogue values for all unused stamps in this country are for Never Hinged items.

Belgian Congo Nos. 318-322 Overprinted "KATANGA"

Perf. 11½

1960, Sept. 12 Photo. Unwmk.

1 A94 50c golden brn, ocher & red brn
2 A94 1fr dk bl, pur & red brn
3 A94 2fr gray, brt bl & red brn
Nos. 1-3 (3) .65 .65

Inscription in French

4 A95 3fr gray & red 6.50 6.50

Inscription in Flemish

5 A95 3fr gray & red 6.50 6.50

Inverted overprints exist on No. 1-5. Values: 1-3 $9 each; 4-5 $15 each.

For surcharges see Nos. 50-51.

Animal Type of Belgian Congo, Nos. 306-317, Overprinted "KATANGA"

1960, Sept. 19 Granite Paper

6 A92 10c bl & brn
7 A93 20c red org & slate
8 A92 40c brn & bl
9 A93 50c brt ultra, red & sep
10 A92 1fr brn, grn & blk
11 A93 1.50fr blk & org yel
12 A92 2fr crim, blk & brn
13 A93 3fr blk, gray & lil rose
14 A92 5fr brn, dk brn & brt grn
15 A93 6.50fr bl, brn & org yel
16 A92 8fr org brn, ol bis & lil
17 A93 10fr multi
Nos. 6-17 (12) 52.50 27.50

Inverted overprints exist. Value $17.50 each.

Flower Type of Belgian Congo, Nos. 263-271, 274-281, Overprinted "KATANGA"

Flowers in Natural Colors

1960, Sept. 22 Granite Paper

18 A86 10c dp plum & ocher
19 A86 15c red & yel grn
20 A86 20c grn & gray
21 A86 25c dk grn & dl org
22 A86 40c grn & sal
23 A86 50c dk car & aqua
24 A86 60c bl grn & pink
25 A86 75c dp plum & gray
26 A86 1fr car & yel
27 A86 2fr ol grn & buff
28 A86 3fr ol grn & pink
29 A86 4fr choc & lil
30 A86 5fr dp plum & lt bl grn
31 A86 6.50fr dk car & lil
32 A86 7fr dk grn & fawn
33 A86 8fr grn & lt yel
34 A86 10fr dp plum & pale ol
Nos. 18-34 (17) 75.00 27.50

Inverted overprints exist. Value $24 each.

Carving and Mask Type of Belgian Congo, Nos. 241, 246, 254-256, Surcharged or Overprinted

1960, Sept. 22 *Perf. 12½*

35 A82 1.50fr on 1.25fr 1.75 .60
36 A82 3.50fr on 2.50fr 1.60 .75
37 A82 20fr red org & vio brn 5.75 4.00
38 A82 50fr dp org & blk 12.50 10.00
39 A82 100fr crim & blk brn 80.00 30.00
Nos. 35-39 (5) 101.60 45.35

Inverted surcharges and overprints exist. Values: No. 37, $60; No. 38, $70; No. 39, $110.

Map Type of Congo Democratic Republic, Nos. 356-365, Overprinted "11 / JUILLET / DE / L'ETAT DU KATANGA"

1960, Oct. 26 *Perf. 11½*

Granite Paper

40 A93a 20c brown .30 .25
41 A93a 50c rose red .30 .25
42 A93a 1fr green .30 .25
43 A93a 1.50fr red brn .30 .25
44 A93a 2fr rose car .30 .25
45 A93a 3.50fr lilac .30 .25
46 A93a 5fr brt bl .30 .25
47 A93a 6.50fr gray .30 .25
48 A93a 10fr orange .30 .25
49 A93a 20fr ultra .40 .25
Nos. 40-49 (10) 3.10 2.50

Inverted and double surcharges exist.

Belgian Congo Nos. 321-322 Surcharged

1961, Jan. 16

50 A95 3.50fr on 3fr #321 3.50 3.50
51 A95 3.50fr on 3fr #322 3.50 3.50

Inverted surcharges exist. Value $6.50 each.

A1

Preparing Meal — A1a

Family Group — A1b

Katangan Wood Carvings.

1961, Mar. 1 *Perf. 11½*

Granite Paper

52 A1 10c grn & lt grn .30 .25
53 A1 20c purple & lil .30 .25
54 A1 50c blue & lt bl .30 .25
55 A1 1.50fr ol grn & lt ol grn .30 .25
56 A1 2fr red brn & lt brn .30 .25
57 A1a 3.50fr dk blue & lt bl .30 .25
58 A1a 5fr bl grn & lt bl grn .30 .25
59 A1a 6fr org brn & tan .30 .25
60 A1a 6.50fr bl vio & gray vio .30 .25
61 A1a 8fr claret & pink .30 .25
62 A1b 10fr brnsh blk & dull mauve .30 .25
63 A1b 20fr dk ol & lt grn .30 .25
64 A1b 50fr brn & lt brn .60 .35
65 A1b 100fr Prus bl & lt bl 1.10 .75
Nos. 52-65 (14) 5.30 4.10

A2

1fr, 5fr, Abstract vehicle. 2.50fr, 6.50fr, Gear.

Granite Paper

1961, July 8 *Perf. 11½*

66 A2 50c blk, grn & red .30 .25
67 A2 1fr blk & blue .30 .25
68 A2 2.50fr blk & yellow .30 .25
69 A2 3.50fr blk, brn & scar .30 .25
70 A2 5fr blk & purple .40 .35
71 A2 6.50fr blk & orange .90 .60
Nos. 66-71 (6) 2.50 1.95

Katanga International Fair.
Imperfs exist. Value, set $45.

Air Katanga — A3

Design: 6.50fr, 10fr, Plane on ground.

1961, Aug. 1 *Perf. 11½*

Granite Paper

72 A3 3.50fr multicolored
73 A3 6.50fr multicolored
74 A3 8fr multicolored
75 A3 10fr multicolored
Nos. 72-75 (4) 6.00 6.00

Imperfs exist. Value, set $60.

Katanga Gendarmerie — A4

1962, Oct. 1 *Perf. 11½*

Granite Paper

76 A4 6fr multicolored
77 A4 8fr multicolored
78 A4 10fr multicolored
Nos. 76-78 (3) 4.25 4.25

Imperfs exist.Value, set $40.

SEMI-POSTAL STAMPS

Pres. Moise Tshombe SP1

1961, July 11 *Perf. 11½*

Granite Paper

B1	SP1	6.50fr + 5fr multi		
B2	SP1	8fr + 5fr multi		
B3	SP1	10fr + 5fr multi		
		Nos. B1-B3 (3)	7.00	5.00

Nos. B1-B3 exist imperf. Value, set $80.

POSTAGE DUE STAMPS

Belgian Congo Nos. J8a-J10a, J16-J19 Handstamped "KATANGA" in Blue

1960, Dec. 30 **Unwmk.** *Perf. 12½*

J1	D2	10c olive green		
J2	D2	20c dark ultra		
J3	D2	50c green		

Perf. 11½

J4	D3	1fr light blue		
J5	D3	2fr vermilion		
J6	D3	4fr purple		
J7	D3	6fr violet blue		
		Nos. J1-J7 (7)	30.00	30.00

This overprint also exists on Belgian Congo Nos. J11a-J12a, J13-J15. Value, set $180.

KAZAKHSTAN

ˌka-ˌzak-ˈstan

(Kazakstan)

LOCATION — Bounded by southern Russia, Uzbekistan, Kyrgyzstan, and China.
GOVT. — Independent republic, member of the Commonwealth of Independent States.
AREA — 1,049,155 sq. mi.
POP. — 16,824,825 (1999 est.)
CAPITAL — Astana

With the breakup of the Soviet Union on Dec. 26, 1991, Kazakhstan and ten former Soviet republics established the Commonwealth of Independent States.

100 Kopecks = 1 Ruble
100 Tijn = 1 Tenge (1993)

Catalogue values for all unused stamps in this country are for Never Hinged items.

Overprinted Stamps

The Philatelic Club of Alma Ata, Kazakhstan, has announced that various overprinted stamps of the USSR were not generally available nor were they in values reflecting actual postal rates.

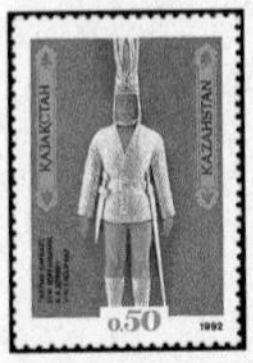

A1

Perf. 12x12½

1992, Mar. 23 **Litho.** **Unwmk.**

1	A1	50k multicolored	.40	.30

For surcharge, see No. 667.

Saiga Tatarica — A2

1992, Sept. 11 **Litho.** *Perf. 12*

2	A2	75k multicolored	.40	.30

Camels and Train, by K. Kasteev A3

1992, Sept. 11 **Litho.** *Perf. 12½x12*

3	A3	1r multicolored	.40	.30

Day of the Republic — A3a

1992, Dec. 16 **Litho.** *Perf. 12*

4	A3a	5r multicolored	.50	.50

Space Ship and Yurt — A4

Natl. Flag — A5

1993, Jan. 24 **Litho.** *Perf. 13x12½*

22	A4	1r green	.30	.25
23	A4	3r red	.30	.25
24	A4	10r golden brown	.30	.30
25	A4	25r purple	.70	.70

Perf. 14

26	A5	50r multicolored	1.25	1.25
		Nos. 22-26 (5)	2.85	2.75

See Nos. 64, 69, 108-115.

Space Mail — A6

1993, Mar. 5 **Litho.** *Perf. 13½*

35	A6	100r multicolored	1.50	1.50

New Year 1993 (Year of the Rooster) — A7

1993, Mar. 22 **Litho.** *Perf. 13x13½*

36	A7	60r yellow, black & red	1.60	1.60

See Nos. 54, 98, 141, 187A, 220, 268.

Cosmonauts' Day — A8

1993, Apr. 12 *Perf. 13½x13*

37	A8	90r multicolored	2.00	2.00

Pres. Nursultan Nazarbayev — A9

1993, Aug. 2 **Litho.** *Perf. 14*

38	A9	50r multicolored	1.00	1.00

Bukar Zhirav Kalkaman (1668-1781), Poet — A10

1993, Aug. 18 *Perf. 13½x13*

39	A10	15r multicolored	.50	.50

Map, Pres. Nursultan Nazarbayev A11

1993, Sept. 24 **Litho.** *Perf. 13*

40	A11	100r multicolored	1.60	1.25

Wildlife — A12

Designs: 5r, Selevinia betpakdalensis. 10r, Hystrix leucura. 15r, Vormela peregusna. 20r, Equis hemionus onager. 25r, Ovis orientalis. 30r, Acinonyx jubatus venaticus.

1993, Nov. 11 *Perf. 12x12½*

41	A12	5r multicolored	.30	.30
42	A12	10r multicolored	.35	.35
43	A12	15r multicolored	.40	.40
44	A12	20r multicolored	.45	.45
45	A12	25r multicolored	.50	.50
46	A12	30r multicolored	.55	.55
		Nos. 41-46 (6)	2.55	2.55

Nos. 1-46 were sold after the currency changeover as stamps denominated in one or both of the new currency units. Nos. 47-50, 54, 64 and 69 were sold as stamps denominated in tijn, and later as tenge.

1994 Winter Olympics, Lillehammer — A13

1994, Jan. 24 **Litho.** *Perf. 13½x13*

47	A13	15te Ice hockey	.30	.30
48	A13	25te Slalom skiing	.45	.45
49	A13	90te Ski jumping	1.25	1.25
50	A13	150te Speed skating	2.00	2.00
		Nos. 47-50 (4)	4.00	4.00

1994 Winter Olympics, Lillehammer — A14

No. 53 With 2 Line Cyrillic Inscription

Designs: 2te, Skiers Vladimir Smirnov, Kazakhstan; Bjorn Daehlie, Norway. 6.80te, 12te, Smirnov.

1994, Feb. 19 **Litho.** *Perf. 13x13½*

51		2te multicolored	.30	.30
52		6.80te multicolored	.70	.70
a.		A14 Pair, #51-52	1.50	1.50
53	A14	12te like No. 52	1.10	1.10
		Nos. 51-53 (3)	2.10	2.10

No. 53 has an additional two line Cyrillic inscription.

New Year Type of 1993
Size: 26x38mm

1994, Mar. 22 *Perf. 12*

54	A7	30te green, black & blue	.75	.50

New Year 1994 (Year of the Dog).

Space Program — A15

1994, Apr. 12 *Perf. 13½x13*

55	A15	2te multicolored	.50	.50

Souvenir Sheet

Russian Space Shuttle, Cosmonaut — A16

1994, July 12 *Perf. 13*

56	A16	6.80te Sheet of 4	3.50	3.50

Space Ship and Yurt Type of 1993

1994, July 12 **Litho.** *Perf. 11½*

64	A4	15ti blue	1.10	.95
69	A4	80ti lake	2.40	1.90

For surcharges see Nos. 70-76, 122.

Nos. 64, 69 Surcharged in Lake or Purple

1995-2004 **Litho.** *Perf. 11½*

70	A4	1te on 15ti #64	.30	.30
71	A4	2te on 15ti #64	.40	.40
72	A4	3te on 80ti #69 (P)	.40	.40
73	A4	4te on 80ti #69 (P)	.50	.50
74	A4	6te on 80ti #69 (P)	.60	.60
75	A4	8te on 80ti #69 (P)	1.10	1.10
76	A4	12te on 80ti #69 (P)	.90	.90
77	A4	20te on 80ti #69 (P)	1.10	1.10
78	A4	200te on 80ti #69 (P)	10.00	10.00
		Nos. 70-78 (9)	15.30	15.30

Issued: 1te, 2te, 12te, 2/2/95. 3te, 4te, 6te, 20te, 2/10/95. 8te, 9/25/95. 200te, 1/29/04.
Inverted surcharges exist.

Music Competition Festival — A18

Designs: 10te, Snow-covered mountain top. 15te, Aerial view of stadium at night.

1994, Aug. 1 *Perf. 13½*

81	A18	10te multicolored	.55	.55
82	A18	15te multicolored	.80	.80

For surcharges see Nos. 119A-119B.

Reptiles — A19

Designs: 1te, Agrionemys horsfieldi. 1.20te, Phrynocephalus mystaceus. 2te, Agkistrodon halys. 3te, Teratoscincus scincus. 5te, Trapelus sanguinolenta. 7te, Ophisaurus apodus. 10te, Varanus griseus.

1994, Oct. 10 *Perf. 12½x12*

83	A19	1te multicolored	.30	.25
84	A19	1.20te multicolored	.30	.25
85	A19	2te multicolored	.30	.30
86	A19	3te multicolored	.30	.30
87	A19	5te multicolored	.40	.40
88	A19	7te multicolored	.50	.50
		Nos. 83-88 (6)	2.10	2.00

Souvenir Sheet

89	A19	10te multicolored	1.25	1.25

Prehistoric Animals — A20

1te, Entelodon. 1.20te, Saurolophus. 2te, Plesiosaurus. 3te, Sordes pilosus. 5te, Mosasaurus. 7te, Megaloceros giganteum. 10te, Koelodonta antiquitatis.

1994, Nov. 24 Litho. *Perf. 12½x12*

90	A20	1te multicolored	.30	.25
91	A20	1.20te multicolored	.30	.25
92	A20	2te multicolored	.30	.25
93	A20	3te multicolored	.30	.30
94	A20	5te multicolored	.40	.40
95	A20	7te multicolored	.50	.50
		Nos. 90-95 (6)	2.10	1.95

Souvenir Sheet

96	A20	10te multicolored	1.40	1.40

Day of the Republic — A21

1994, Oct. 25 *Perf. 11½*

97	A21	2te multicolored	.60	.60

For surcharge see No. 160B.

New Year Type of 1993

1995, Mar. 22 Litho. *Perf. 14*

Size: 27x32mm

98	A7	10te blue, black & ultra	1.25	1.25

New Year 1995 (Year of the Boar).

Abai (Ibraghim) Kynanbaev (1845-1904), Poet — A22

1995, Mar. 31

99	A22	4te Portrait	.30	.30
100	A22	9te Portrait, diff.	.60	.60

Nos. 99-100 exist with "Kazakstan" spelled "Kazakstah." Value, set $9.

Space Day — A23

Designs: 10te, Cosmonauts Malenchenko, Musabaev and Merbold.

1995, Apr. 12 Litho. *Perf. 14*

101	A23	2te multicolored	3.50	3.50
102	A23	10te multicolored	13.50	13.50

Mahatma Gandhi (1869-1948) A24

1995, Oct. 2

103	A24	9te multicolored	2.50	2.50
104	A24	22te multicolored	6.00	6.00

End of World War II, 50th Anniv. — A25

Designs: 1te, Hero, battle scene. 3te, Heroine, tank. 5te, Dove, monument.

1995, May 9 Litho. *Perf. 14*

105	A25	1te multicolored	1.10	1.10
106	A25	3te multicolored	3.25	3.25
107	A25	5te multicolored	5.50	5.50
		Nos. 105-107 (3)	9.85	9.85

Spaceship and Yurt Type of 1993

1995, Mar. 24 Litho. *Perf. 14x14½*

108	A4	20ti orange	.30	.25
109	A4	25ti yellow brown	.35	.25
110	A4	50ti gray	.40	.25
111	A4	1te green	.50	.25
112	A4	2te blue	.65	.25
113	A4	4te bright pink	.85	.50
114	A4	6te gray green	1.00	.75
115	A4	12te lilac	2.10	1.50
		Nos. 108-115 (8)	6.15	4.00

Nos. 108-115 are inscribed "1995."

Paintings A26

Designs: 4te, "Springtime," by S. Mambeev. 9te, "Mountains," by Z. Shchardenov. 15te, "Kulash Baiseitova in role of Kyz Zhibek," by G. Ismailova, vert. 28te, "Kokpar," by K. Telzhanov.

1995, June 23 Litho. *Perf. 14*

116	A26	4te multicolored	.75	.75
117	A26	9te multicolored	1.25	1.25
118	A26	15te multicolored	2.50	2.50
119	A26	28te multicolored	4.50	4.50
		Nos. 116-119 (4)	9.00	9.00

Nos. 81-82 Ovptd.

1995, July 25 Litho. *Perf. 13½*

119A	A18	10te multicolored	1.10	1.10
119B	A18	15te multicolored	1.50	1.50

Dauletkerey (1820-87), Composer — A27

1995, Sept. 1 Litho. *Perf. 14*

120	A27	2te yellow & multi	.50	.50
121	A27	28te lake & multi	6.00	6.00

UN, 50th Anniv. — A28

1995, Nov. 24 Litho. *Perf. 14*

123	A28	10te multicolored	1.25	1.25
124	A28	36te gold & lt blue	4.75	4.75

Resurrection Cathedral A29

Circus A29a

Buildings in Alma-Ata: 2te, Culture Palace. 3te, Opera and Ballet House. 6te, Kazakh Science Academy. 48te, Dramatics Theatre.

Perf. 14, 13x12 (#126, 129)

1995-96 Litho.

125	A29	1te green	.50	.40
126	A29a	1te green	.25	.25
127	A29	2te blue	.75	.65
128	A29	3te red	.90	.80
129	A29a	6te olive	.60	.60
130	A29	48te brown	8.00	7.50
		Nos. 125-130 (6)	11.00	10.20

Issued: Nos. 125, 127-128, 130, 10/25/95; Nos. 126, 129, 7/5/96.

Raptors — A30

1te, Haliaeetus albicilla. 3te, Pandion haliaetus. 5te, Gypaetus barbatus. 6te, Gyps himalayensis. 30te, Falco cherrug. 50te, Aquila chrysaetus.

1995, Dec. 20 Litho. *Perf. 14*

131	A30	1te multicolored	.30	.25
132	A30	3te multicolored	.30	.30
133	A30	5te multicolored	.50	.50
134	A30	6te multicolored	.60	.60
135	A30	30te multicolored	2.00	2.00
136	A30	50te multicolored	3.50	3.50
		Nos. 131-136 (6)	7.20	7.15

New Year Type of 1993

Size: 27x32mm

1996, Mar. 21 Litho. *Perf. 14*

141	A7	25te lil, blk & red	2.25	2.25

New Year 1996 (Year of the Rat).

Space Day — A32

6te, Earth. 15te, Cosmonaut. 20te, Space station Mir.

1996, Apr. 12

142	A32	6te multicolored	1.75	1.75
143	A32	15te multicolored	2.75	2.75
144	A32	20te multicolored	4.50	4.50
		Nos. 142-144 (3)	9.00	9.00

Souvenir Sheet

Save the Aral Sea A33

Designs: a, Felis caracal. b, Salmo trutta aralensis. c, Hyaena hyaena. d, Pseudoscaphirhynchus kaufmanni. e, Aspiolucius esocinus.

1996, Apr. 20 Litho. *Perf. 14*

145	A33	20te Sheet of 5, #a.-e.	4.25	4.25

See Kyrgyzstan No. 107, Tadjikistan No. 91, Turkmenistan No. 52, Uzbekistan No. 113.

1996 Summer Olympic Games, Atlanta — A34

1996, June 19 Litho. *Perf. 14*

146	A34	4te Cycling	.60	.60
147	A34	6te Wrestling	1.50	1.50
148	A34	30te Boxing	5.75	5.75
		Nos. 146-148 (3)	7.85	7.85

Souvenir Sheet

149	A34	50te Hurdles	4.00	4.00

Issued: Nos. 146-148, 6/19/96; No. 149, 7/19/96.

Architectural Sites — A35

1te, Tomb, 8-9th cent. 3te, Mausoleum, 11-12th cent. 6te, Mausoleum, 13th cent.
30te, Hadji Ahmet Yassauy's Mausoleum, 14th cent.

1996, Sept. 27 Litho. *Perf. 14*

150	A35	1te multicolored	.50	.50
151	A35	3te multicolored	1.50	1.50
152	A35	6te multicolored	3.00	3.00
		Nos. 150-152 (3)	5.00	5.00

Souvenir Sheet

153	A35	30te multicolored	2.75	2.75

World Post Day — A37

1996, Oct. 9 Litho. *Perf. 14*

156	A37	9te shown	.85	.85
157	A37	40te UPU emblem	2.75	2.75

Zhambyl Zhabayev (1846-1945), Folksinger — A38

1996, Aug. 21

158	A38	12te multicolored	1.40	1.40

Space Station Mir — A39

1996, Oct. 2

159		46te multicolored	3.00	2.75
160		46te T. Aubakirov	3.00	2.75
a.		A39 Pair, #159-160	6.00	6.00

T. Aubakirov, 1st Kazak cosmonaut.

No. 97 Surcharged

1997, Oct. 25 Litho. *Perf. 11½*

160B	A21	21te on 2te multi	1.25	1.25

Surcharge adds numeral 1 to existing value to appear as 21, obliterates original date and adds new date.

Butterflies — A40

4te, Saturnia schenki. 6te, Parnassius patricius. 12te, Parnassius ariadne. 46te, Colias draconis.

1996, Nov. 21 Litho. *Perf. 14*

161	A40	4te multicolored	.30	.25
162	A40	6te multicolored	.35	.30
163	A40	12te multicolored	.50	.45
164	A40	46te multicolored	1.75	1.50
a.		Sheet of 10, 2 ea. #161-162, 3 ea. #163-164	9.00	9.00
		Nos. 161-164 (4)	2.90	2.50

Hunting Dogs — A41

1996, Nov. 29

165 A41 5te multicolored .55 .55

Souvenir Sheet

166 A41 100te like #165 4.00 4.00

No. 166 is a continuous design.

A42

Traditional Costumes, Furnishings: a, 10te, Woman outside tent. b, 16te, Man outside tent. c, 45te, Interior view of furnishings.

1996, Dec. 5

167 A42 Strip of 3, #a.-c. 6.00 6.00

Nos. 167a-167b have continuous design.

A43

Archives, Bicent.: 4te, Quill pen, candle, documents. 68te, Scroll, papers, book.

1996, Dec. 24

168 A43 4te brown .35 .35
169 A43 68te purple 2.40 2.40

Motion Pictures, Cent. — A44

Film scenes: a, Man in hat holding up fingers. b, Horse, woman, man. c, Two men, from "His Time Arrives." d, Woman holding paper, boy holding hat.

1996, Dec. 25 Litho. *Perf. 14*

170 A44 24te Sheet of 4, #a.-d. 9.50 9.50

Vormela Peregusna A45

1997, Feb. 12 Litho. *Perf. 14*

171 A45 6te shown .65 .65
172 A45 10te Adult .75 .75
173 A45 32te Two young 2.00 2.00
174 A45 46te Adult, tail up 2.50 2.50
a. Vert. strip of 4, #171-174, with horiz. gutters 10.00 10.00
b. Souv. sheet of 8, 2 ea. #171-174 12.00 12.00
Nos. 171-174 (4) 5.90 5.90

World Wildlife Fund.

Nos. 171-174 each printed in sheets of 10. No. 174b has no gutters between stamps.

Zodiac Constellations — A47

1997, Mar. 26 Litho. *Perf. 14*

176 A47 1te Aries .30 .25
177 A47 2te Taurus .30 .25
178 A47 3te Gemini .30 .25
179 A47 4te Cancer .30 .25
180 A47 5te Leo .30 .25
181 A47 6te Virgo .30 .25
182 A47 7te Libra .30 .25
183 A47 8te Scorpio .30 .25
184 A47 9te Sagittarius .30 .30
185 A47 10te Capricorn .30 .35
186 A47 12te Aquarius .40 .45
187 A47 20te Pisces .60 .70
b. Sheet of 12, #176-187 5.50 5.50

New Year Type of 1993 With Kazakhstan Inscribed in Both Cyrillic & Roman Letters

1997, Mar. 22 Litho. *Perf. 14*

187A A7 40te multicolored 1.75 1.75

New Year 1997 (Year of the Ox).

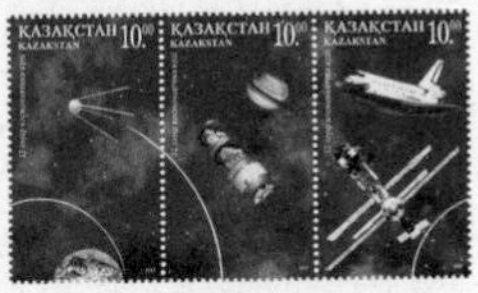

A48

Cosmonauts' Day: a, Earth, Sputnik. b, Space vehicle, Saturn. c, Space shuttle, space station.

1997, Apr. 12

188 A48 10te Strip of 3, #a.-c. 3.25 3.25

No. 188 has continuous design.

A49

1997, Apr. 23

189 A49 15te org yel & grn .50 .50
190 A49 60te org yel & grn 2.10 2.10

UNESCO World Book Day.

Mukhtar Auezov (1897-1961), Writer — A50

1997, May

191 A50 25te House 1.00 1.00
192 A50 40te Auezov at his desk 1.50 1.50

Orders and Medals — A51

Various medals.

1997, June 30 Litho. *Perf. 14*

193 A51 15te grn & yel ribbon .50 .50
194 A51 15te grn, red & pink ribbon .50 .50
195 A51 20te grn bl & multi .75 .75
196 A51 30te grn yel & multi 1.00 1.00
Nos. 193-196 (4) 2.75 2.75

Tulips — A52

15te, Tulipa regelii. No. 198, Tulipa greigii. No. 199, Tulipa alberti.

1997, Aug. 7 Litho. *Perf. 13½*

197 A52 15te multicolored .50 .50
198 A52 35te multicolored 1.40 1.40
199 A52 35te multicolored 1.40 1.40
Nos. 197-199 (3) 3.30 3.30

Paintings A53

Designs: No. 200, Roping of a Wild Horse, by Moldakhmet S. Kenbaev. No. 201, Shepherd, by Sh. T. Sariev, vert. No. 202, Fantastic Still Life, by Sergei I. Kalmykov, vert.

1997, Sept. 10 Litho. *Perf. 14*

200 A53 25te multicolored 1.10 1.10
201 A53 25te multicolored 1.10 1.10
202 A53 25te multicolored 1.10 1.10
Nos. 200-202 (3) 3.30 3.30

Agate A54

Azurite A55

1997, Oct. 15 Litho. *Perf. 14*

203 A54 15te shown .70 .70
204 A54 15te Chalcedony .70 .70
205 A55 20te shown 1.10 1.10
206 A55 20te Malachite 1.10 1.10
a. Souvenir sheet, #203-206 3.75 3.75
Nos. 203-206 (4) 3.60 3.60

Desert Fauna — A56

Designs: No. 207, Gylippus rickmersi. No. 208, Anemelobathus rickmersi. No. 209, Latrodectus pallidus. No. 210, Oculicosa supermirabilis.

1997, Nov. 26 Litho. *Perf. 14*

207 A56 30te multicolored 1.15 1.15
208 A56 30te multicolored 1.15 1.15
209 A56 30te multicolored 1.15 1.15
210 A56 30te multicolored 1.15 1.15
Nos. 207-210 (4) 4.60 4.60

Souvenir Sheet

Nature Park A57

Designs: a, Mountain goat. b, Trees on side of mountain. c, Rock formations, wildflowers.

1997, Dec. 22

211 A57 30te Sheet of 3, #a.-c. 3.00 3.00

See No. 257A.

A58

Sports — A59

Designs: No. 212, Woman, man riding horses. No. 213, Wrestling match. No. 214, Group of men on galloping horses.

1997, Dec. 30 Litho. *Perf. 14*

212 A58 20te multicolored 1.75 1.75
213 A58 20te multicolored 1.75 1.75
214 A58 20te multicolored 1.75 1.75
215 A59 20te multicolored 1.75 1.75
Nos. 212-215 (4) 7.00 7.00

1998 Winter Olympic Games, Nagano — A60

1998, Mar. 13 Litho. *Perf. 14*

216 A60 15te Figure skating .70 .50
217 A60 30te Biathlon 1.25 1.00

Children's Paintings — A61

1998, Mar. 20

218 A61 15te shown .55 .55
219 A61 15te Outdoor scene, horiz. .55 .55

New Year Type of 1993 with "Kazakhstan" inscribed in both Cyrillis and Roman letters

1998, Mar. 22 Litho. *Perf. 14*

220 A7 30te yel, blk & brn 1.75 1.75

New Year 1998 (Year of the Tiger).

Kurmangazy Sagyrbaev (1818-89), Composer — A62

No. 222, Ahmet Baitursynov (1873-1937), poet.

1998 Litho. *Perf. 14*

221 A62 30te multicolored 1.00 1.00
222 A62 30te multicolored 1.00 1.00

Issued: No. 221, 4/10/98. No. 222, 4/28/98.

Ancient Gold Folk Art — A63

15te, Ram's heads. 30te, Jeweled pendants, vert. 40te, Animal filigree diadem fragment.

1998, Apr. 30

223 A63 15te multicolored .55 .55
224 A63 30te multicolored .95 .95
225 A63 40te multicolored 2.00 2.00
Nos. 223-225 (3) 3.50 3.50

Cosmonaut's Day — A64

No. 226, Apollo 8, moon, sun. No.227, Apollo 8, moon, Earth. 50te, Vostok 6, Earth.

1998, May 4

226 A64 30te multi, vert. 1.10 1.10
227 A64 30te multi, vert. 1.10 1.10
a. Pair, #226-227, with tabs 4.25 4.25
228 A64 50te multi 1.75 1.75
Nos. 226-228 (3) 3.95 3.95

Astana, New Capital City — A64a

A65

Buildings: 10te, Mosque. 15te, Govt., vert. 20te, Parliament, vert. 25te, Office. 100te, Presidential office.

1998 Litho. *Perf. 13½*

229 A64a 10te brown .45 .45
230 A64a 15te dark blue .65 .65
231 A64a 15te blue .65 .65
232 A64a 20te green blue .80 .80
232A A64a 25te purple 1.50 1.50
Nos. 229-232A (5) 4.05 4.05

Souvenir Sheet

233 A65 100te multicolored 3.25 3.25

Issued: Nos. 229-232, 233, 6/10; 25te, 12/98. No. 230 is inscribed "AKMOLA" in Cyrillic. No. 231 is inscribed "ACTANA."

Souvenir Sheet

Climbing Mt. Everest — A67

1998, July 29 Litho. *Perf. 14*

239 A67 100te multicolored 4.25 4.25

Fauna — A68

Birds: No. 240, Ciconia nigra. No. 241, Phoenicopterus roseus. No. 242, Grus leucogeranus.
Wild cats: No. 243, Lynx lynx isabellinus. No. 244, Felis margarita. No. 245, Uncia uncia.

1998

240 A68 15te multicolored .70 .70
241 A68 30te multicolored 1.25 1.25
242 A68 50te multicolored 2.10 2.10
Nos. 240-242 (3) 4.05 4.05
243 A68 15te multicolored .70 .70
244 A68 30te multicolored 1.25 1.25
245 A68 50te multicolored 2.10 2.10
Nos. 243-245 (3) 4.05 4.05

Issued: Nos. 240-242, 7/31; Nos. 243-245, 8/8.

Souvenir Sheet

Admission of Kazakhstan to UPU — A69

1998, Oct. 9 Litho. *Perf. 14*

246 A69 50te multicolored 4.00 4.00

Natl. Arms A70

World Stamp Day A71

Republic, 5th Anniv. — A72

1998 Litho. *Perf. 13½*
Inscribed "1998"

247 A70 1te green .30 .25
a. Inscribed "1999" .30 .25
248 A70 2te blue .30 .25
a. Inscribed "1999" .30 .25
249 A70 3te red .30 .25
250 A70 4te bright pink .30 .30
251 A70 5te orange yellow .30 .30
a. Inscribed "1999" .30 .30
252 A70 8te orange .50 .50
253 A71 30te olive 1.40 1.40
254 A72 40te orange 1.60 1.60
Nos. 247-254 (8) 5.00 4.85

Issued; 1te-5te, 6/29; 8te-40te, 11/12. "1999" varieties issued: 1te, 1/28/00; 2te, 9/7/99; 5te, 11/12/99.
See Nos. 296, 299. Compare with Nos. 444-455.

Natl. Epic — A73

Horseman: 20te, Holding sword. 30te, Shooting bow and arrow. 40te, Charging with spear.

1998, Dec. *Perf. 14*

255 A73 20te multicolored 1.50 1.50
256 A73 30te multicolored 2.25 2.25
257 A73 40te multicolored 2.75 2.75
Nos. 255-257 (3) 6.50 6.50

Souvenir Sheet
Nature Park Type of 1997

Designs: a, Island in middle of lake, mountains. b, Lake, mountain peaks.

1998, Dec. Litho. *Perf. 14*

257A A57 30te Sheet of 2, #a.-b. 3.00 3.00

1999 Census A74

Space Communications A77

K. Satpayev (1899-1964)
A75 A76

1999 Litho. *Perf. 13½*

258 A74 1te green .30 .25
259 A75 15te rose lake .50 .50
260 A76 20te brown .65 .65
261 A77 30te olive 1.25 1.25
Nos. 258-261 (4) 2.70 2.65

Issued: 1te, 2/5/99; 30te, 3/19/99.
See Nos. 270, 272.

Trains — A78

Map showing Orenburg-Tashkent Rail Line, 1890-1906, and: 40te, Steam train. 50te, Diesel locomotive. 60te, Bullet train. 80te, Interurban train.

1999 *Perf. 14*

262 A78 40te yel & multi 1.50 1.50
263 A78 50te pink & multi 2.10 2.10
264 A78 60te grn & multi 2.50 2.50
265 A78 80te blue & multi 3.00 3.00
Nos. 262-265 (4) 9.10 9.10

Space Achievements — A79

50te, Soviet spacecraft, vert. 90te, Apollo 11 mission.

1999

266 A79 50te multicolored 7.00 7.00
267 A79 90te multicolored 14.00 14.00

Cosmonaut Day (No. 266), first manned lunar landing, 30th anniv. (No. 267).

New Year Type of 1993 with "Kazakhstan" inscribed in both Cyrillis and Roman letters

1999, Mar. 19 Litho. *Perf. 14*

268 A7 40te multicolored 3.50 3.50

New Year 1999 (Year of the Rabbit).

Space Communications Type of 1999 and

A79a

A79b

1999 Litho. *Perf. 13½*

270 A77 3te red .30 .30
271 A79a 4te bright pink .30 .30
272 A77 9te bright green .50 .50
273 A79b 10te purple .75 .75
274 A79a 30te olive green 1.10 1.10
Nos. 270-274 (5) 2.95 2.95

No. 273 is for the UPU, 125th Anniv.

Flowers — A80

Designs: 20te, Pseudoeremostachys severzowii. 30te, Rhaphidophyton regelii. 90te, Niedzwedkia semiretscenskia.

1999, June 28 Litho. *Perf. 14¼x14*

276 A80 20te multicolored 1.25 1.25
277 A80 30te multicolored 1.50 1.50
278 A80 90te multicolored 4.00 4.00
Nos. 276-278 (3) 6.75 6.75

Movies A81

No. 279: a, 15te, Film scene from 1929. b, 20te, Scenes from 1988, 1997, M. Berkovich. c, 30te, Scenes from 1935, 1938, 1957. d, 35te, Scenes from 1989, 1994, 1997. e, 50te, Alfred Hitchcock. f, 60te, Sergei Eisenstein.

1999 Litho. *Perf. 14*

279 A81 Sheet of 10, #e.-f., 2 each #a.-d. 9.00 9.00

Foxes — A82

Designs: 20te, Vulpes vulpes. 30te, Cuon alpinus. 90te, Vulpes corsac.

1999 Litho. *Perf. 14x 14¼*

280 A82 20te multicolored 1.50 1.10
281 A82 30te multicolored 2.25 1.90
282 A82 90te multicolored 6.00 5.25
Nos. 280-282 (3) 9.75 8.25

Souvenir Sheet

Environmental Protection — A83

Designs: a, 15te, Cessation of nuclear tests at Semipalatinsk, 10th anniv. b, 45te, Save the ozone layer. c, 60te, Save nature.

1999 Litho. *Perf. 14x13¾*

283 A83 Sheet of 3, #a.-c. 4.00 4.00

Kazakhstan Hockey Team — A84

1999 Litho. *Perf. 14*

284 A84 20te Face-off 1.40 1.40
285 A84 30te Team photo 1.75 1.75

10th Gusman Kosanov Memorial Track & Field Meet — A85

1999

286 A85 40te multi 2.00 2.00

Cosmonauts A86

40te, Talgat Musabayev. 50te, Toktar Aubakirov, vert.

1999 *Perf. 14*

287 A86 40te multicolored 1.60 1.60
288 A86 50te multicolored 1.90 1.90

Souvenir Sheet

UPU, 125th Anniv. A87

1999, Dec. 20 Litho. *Perf. 14x13¾*

289 A87 20te multi 1.75 1.75

Arms Type of 1998 and

Spireanthus Schrenhianus A88

Echo Satellite A89

Oil Rig A90

Mukhammed Khaidar Dulati (1499-1551), Historian A91

Sabit Mukanov (1900-73), Writer — A92

2000 **Litho.** ***Perf. 13½***

290	A88	1te green	.30	.25
291	A88	2te bright blue	.30	.25
291A	A89	5te orange yellow	.30	.25
292	A90	7te red	.40	.40
293	A91	8te dark blue	.30	.30
294	A92	10te olive green	.40	.40
295	A89	15te violet blue	.50	.50
296	A70	20te orange	.75	.75
297	A89	20te indigo	.80	.80
299	A70	50te blue	1.90	1.90
300	A88	50te blue	1.75	1.60
		Nos. 290-300 (11)	7.70	7.40

Issued: 7te, 20te, 50te, 1/18/00; 1te, 2te, No. 300, 11/24; 5te, 15te, No. 297, 9/28; 8te, 8/25; 10te, 6/30. 20te and 50te are dated 1999.

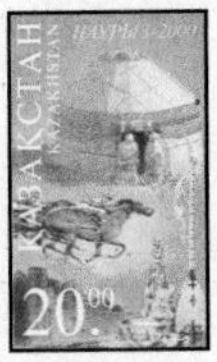

Navruz Bayram — A93

2000, Mar. 21 **Litho.** ***Imperf.***
301 A93 20te multi 4.00 4.00

Millennium — A94

2000, Mar. 24 **Litho.** ***Perf. 13½***
302 A94 30te org & blue green 2.50 2.50

Victory in World War II, 55th Anniv. — A95

2000, May 8 **Litho.** ***Perf. 13½***
303 A95 3te brown & red .30 .30

Souvenir Sheet

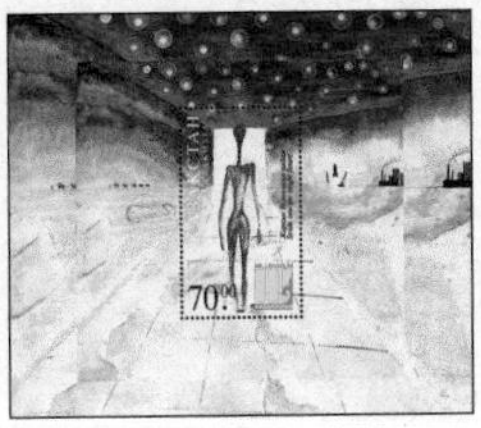
Millennium — A96

2000, June 1 ***Perf. 14x13¾***
304 A96 70te multi 3.00 3.00

Containers — A97

No. 305: a, 15te, Leather vessel for koumiss, Kazakhstan. b, 50te, Teapot, China.

2000, June 28 ***Perf. 12½x12***
305 A97 Horiz. pair, #a-b 3.00 3.00

See China (PRC) Nos. 3042-3043.

2000 Summer Olympics, Sydney — A98

Designs: 35te, Rowing. No. 307, 40te, Taekwondo. No. 308, 40te, Men's gymnastics. 50te, Triathlon.

2000, Sept. 15 ***Perf. 12***
306-309 A98 Set of 4 7.50 7.50

Souvenir Sheet

Turkistan, 1500th Anniv. — A99

Mausoleums of: a, 50te, Arystan Bab, 12th-20th cents. b, 50te, Karashash Ana, 12th-18th cents. c, 70te, Hadji Ahmet Yassauy, 14th cent.

2000, Oct. 19 ***Perf. 13½***
310 A99 Sheet of 3, #a-c 9.00 9.00
Complete booklet, #310 *16.00*

Bourzhan Momush-Uly (1910-82), Hero of the Soviet Union — A100

2000, Dec. 22 ***Perf. 13½***
311 A100 4te black & brown .60 .60

No. B1 Surcharged in Dark Blue

Method and Perf. as Before
2001, Jan. 26
Block of 3, #a-c, + Label
312 SP1 10te on 1te+30ti multi 1.00 1.00

No. 312 exists with double surcharge and inverted surcharge.

New Year Type of 1993 with "Kazakhstan" Inscribed in Both Cyrillic and Roman Letters

2001, Mar. 2 **Litho.** ***Perf. 13¾x14***
313 A7 40te org, blk & blue 1.60 1.60

Dated 2000. New Year 2000 (Year of the Snail).

Cosmonaut's Day — A101

Designs: 40te, Dogs Belka and Strelka. 70te, Rocket launch, vert.

2001, Mar. 6 ***Perf. 14***
314-315 A101 Set of 2 *5.00 5.00*

Dated 2000. Spaceflight of Belka and Strelka, 40th anniv., Baikonur Cosmodrome, 45th anniv.

New Year Type of 1993 with "Kazakhstan" Inscribed in Both Cyrillic and Roman Letters

2001, Mar. 21 **Litho.** ***Perf. 13¾x14***
316 A7 40te grn, blk & brn 1.40 1.40

New Year 2001 (Year of the Snake).

Souvenir Sheet

Ministry of Communications, 10th Anniv. — A102

2001, Apr. 4 ***Perf. 11½***
317 A102 100te multi *14.00 14.00*

Cosmonaut's Day — A103

Designs: 45te, Soyuz 11 and Salyut. 60te, Yuri Gagarin, Earth.

2001, Apr. 12 ***Perf. 14***
318-319 A103 Set of 2 4.00 4.00

Aquilegia Karatavica A104

School, Almaty A105

Phodopus Roborovskii — A106

Perf. 13½, 14 (#321, 326)
2001 **Litho.**

320	A104	3te olive green	.30	.30
321	A105	7te red violet	.30	.30
322	A106	8te orange	.35	.35
323	A104	10te yellow green	.40	.40
324	A106	15te dark blue	.55	.55
325	A106	20te deep blue	.65	.65
326	A105	30te greenish gray	.85	.85
327	A106	50te brown	1.40	1.40
		Nos. 320-327 (8)	4.80	4.80

See Nos. 399, 403-405.
Issued: 7te, 30te, 10/19/01.

Kazakh State Khans — A107

Designs: 50te, Abulkhair Khan (1693-1748). 60te, Abylai Khan (1711-81).

2001, May 24 **Litho.** ***Perf. 13¾x14***
328-329 A107 Set of 2 3.75 3.75

Dated 2000.

Owls — A108

Designs: 30te, Bubo bubo. 40te, Asio otus. 50te, Surnia ulula.

2001, June 7 ***Perf. 14***
330-332 A108 Set of 3 *7.75 7.75*

Dated 2000.

Communications Program 2030 — A109

2001, June 21 ***Perf. 14x13¾***
333 A109 40te multi 1.40 1.40

Dated 2000.

Souvenir Sheet

Lake Markakol A110

No. 334: a, Cervus elaphus. b, Ursus arctos. c, Brachymystax lenok.

2001, July 5 ***Perf. 13¾x14***
334 A110 30te Sheet of 3, #a-c *8.50 8.50*

Souvenir Sheet

Flora & Fauna A111

No. 335: a, 9te, Marmota bobac. b, 12te, Otis tarda. c, 25te, Larus relictus. d, 60te, Felis libyca. e, 90te, Nymphaea alba. f, 100te, Pelecanus crispus.

2001, July 19 ***Perf. 14x14¼***
335 A111 Sheet of 6, #a-f 6.00 6.00

Souvenir Sheet

Kazakh Railways, 10th Anniv. — A112

No. 336: a, 15te, Building. b, 20te, Turkestan-Siberia locomotive. c, 50te, Railroad workers.

2001, Aug. 4 ***Perf. 14x13¾***
336 A112 Sheet of 3, #a-c *22.50 22.50*

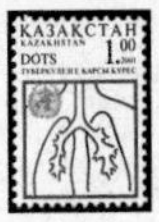
Medicine — A113

Designs: 1te, WHO emblem, lungs (tuberculosis prevention). 5te, Ribbon, book (AIDS prevention).

2001, Aug. 9 ***Perf. 13½***
337-338 A113 Set of 2 .60 .60

Intl. Year of Mountains (in 2002) — A114

Various mountains: 35te, 60te.

2001, Sept. 26 ***Perf. 14***
339-340 A114 Set of 2 3.50 3.50

Space Achievements — A115

Designs: 50te, Alexei Leonov's walk in space, 1965, vert. 70te, Apollo-Soyuz mission, 1975.

2001, Oct. 2
341-342 A115 Set of 2 *7.50 7.50*

Dated 2000.

Year of Dialogue Among Civilizations — A116

2001, Oct. 9 ***Perf. 13¾x14***
343 A116 45te multi 1.75 1.75

Worldwide Fund for Nature (WWF) — A117

Various views of Equus hemionus kulan: 9te, 12te, 25te, 50te.

2001, Nov. 1 *Perf. 14*
344-347 A117 Set of 4 3.25 3.25

Commonwealth of Independent States, 10th Anniv. — A118

2001, Dec. 12 Litho. *Perf. 14*
348 A118 40te multi 1.75 1.75

Visit of Pope John Paul II A119

No. 349: a, 20te, Pres. Nazarbayev, Pope. b, 50te, Pope, Pres. Nazarbayev.

2001, Dec. 14 *Perf. 11½*
349 A119 Horiz. pair, #a-b *5.50 5.50*

A120

Independence, 10th Anniv. — A121

No. 351: a, 9te, Monument of Independence, Almaty. b, 25te, Parliament, Astana. c, 35te, Pres. Nazarbayev.

2001 *Perf. 13½*
350 A120 40te multi 1.75 1.75

Souvenir Sheet

Perf. 13¾x14

351 A121 Sheet of 3, #a-c *5.50 5.50*

Issued: 40te, 12/18; No. 351, 12/16.

Native Attire A122

No. 352: a, 25te, Male attire. b, 35te, Female attire.

2001, Dec. 25 *Perf. 14x13¾*
352 A122 Horiz. pair, #a-b 2.75 2.75

2002 Winter Olympics, Salt Lake City — A123

Designs: 50te, Women's ice hockey. 150te, Freestyle skiing.

2002, Feb. 14 *Perf. 14*
353-354 A123 Set of 2 7.00 7.00

Most often collected with colored Olympic rings margin tab. Value, set $10.

New Year Type of 1993 With "Kazakhstan" Inscribed in Both Cyrillic and Roman Letters

2002, Mar. 21 *Perf. 11½*
355 A7 50te multi 2.00 2.00

New Year 2002 (Year of the Horse).

Horses — A124

Horses: 9te, English. 25te, Kustenai. 60te, Akhalteka.

2002, Mar. 28
356-358 A124 Set of 3 4.75 4.75

Pterygostemon Spathulatus A125

Gani Muratbaev (1902-25), Political Leader A126

Salpingotus Pallidus A127

Trade House, Petropavlovsk A128

Monument, Petropavlovsk A129

Gabiden Mustafin (1902-85), Writer A130

2002		**Litho.**	***Perf. 13½***	
359	A125	1te blue green	.30	.30
360	A125	2te blue	.35	.35
361	A125	3te green	.40	.40
362	A126	3te brown	.30	.25
363	A127	5te rose lilac	.30	.25
364	A128	6te red	.30	.25
365	A128	7te lilac	.30	.25
366	A129	8te orange	.30	.30
367	A125	10te violet	.60	.60
368	A130	10te blue	.30	.30
369	A125	12te pink	.70	.70
370	A127	15te dark blue	.40	.40
371	A129	23te gray blue	.70	.70
372	A125	25te purple	.90	.90
373	A125	35te olive green	1.10	1.10
374	A127	40te bister brown	1.25	1.25
375	A127	50te brown	1.60	1.60
		Nos. 359-375 (17)	10.10	9.90

Petropavlovsk, 250th anniv. (Nos. 364-366, 371). Issued: 1te, 2te, 5/7; Nos. 361, 367, 35te, 4/30; 5te, 15te, 40te, 50te, 4/4; 6te, 7te, 8te, 23te, 7/9; 12te, 25te, 5/14; No. 362, 12/19; No. 368, 12/18.

Cosmonauts Day — A131

Designs: 30te, Cosmonauts Yuri Baturin, Talgat Musabaev and first space tourist Dennis Tito. 70te, Globe, rocket, flags of US, Kazakhstan and Russia.

2002, Apr. 10 Litho. *Perf. 11¾*
376-377 A131 Set of 2 3.50 3.50

2002 World Cup Soccer Championships, Japan and Korea — A132

Two players, one with: No. 378, 10te, Jersey No. 8. No. 379, 10te, Jersey No. 7.

2002, May 31
378-379 A132 Set of 2 1.50 1.50

Transeurasia 2002 Conference — A133

2002, June 6 *Perf. 13½*
380 A133 30te multi 1.10 1.10

Souvenir Sheet

Flora and Fauna A134

No. 381: a, Leontopodium fedtschenkoanum. b, Mustela erminea. c, Aport Alexander apples.

2002, June 6 *Perf. 11¾x11½*
381 A134 30te Sheet of 3, #a-c 3.25 3.25

Art — A135

Designs: 8te, Kazakh Folk Epos, by E. Sidorkin, 1961. 9te, Makhambet, by M. Kisamedinov, 1973. 60te, Batyr, by Sidorkin, 1979.

2002, July 19 *Perf. 11¾*
382-384 A135 Set of 3 3.00 3.00

Birds A136

No. 385: a, 10te, Larus ichthyaetus pallas. b, 15te, Anthropoides virgo.

2002, Aug. 29 *Perf. 12*
385 A136 Horiz. pair, #a-b 2.00 2.00

See Russia No. 6709.

Marine Life A137

No. 386: a, 20te, Huso huso ponticus. b, 35te, Phoca caspica.

2002, Sept. 6
386 A137 Horiz. pair, #a-b 2.25 2.25

See Ukraine No. 483.

Souvenir Sheet

Taraz, 2000th Anniv. A138

2002, Sept. 25
387 A138 70te multi 2.25 2.25

Souvenir Sheet

International Year of Mountains — A139

2002, Oct. 4 *Perf. 11½x11¾*
388 A139 50te multi 1.60 1.60

Gabit Musrepov (1902-85) — A140

2002, Dec. 30 Litho. *Perf. 11½*
389 A140 20te multi .75 .75

Airplanes A141

Designs: 20te, Ilyushin-86. 40te, Tupolev-144 and map.

Perf. 11½x11¾

2002, Dec. 23 Litho.
390-391 A141 Set of 2 2.40 2.40

First Moscow to Alma Ata flight of Tupolev-144, 25th anniv. (No. 391).

Type of 1999, Types of 2000-01 Redrawn and

Monument to Victims of Political Reprisals A142

Selevinia Betpakdalensis A143

2003		**Litho.**	***Perf. 13½***	
392	A88	1te green	.30	.25
393	A142	1te red violet	.30	.25
394	A88	2te bright blue	.30	.25
394A	A77	3te red	.30	.25
395	A143	4te brown	.35	.35
396	A143	5te bister	.40	.40
397	A143	6te gray green	.40	.40
398	A143	7te dull green	.40	.40
399	A106	8te orange	.30	.25
400	A142	8te red brown	.30	.25
401	A77	9te dark blue	.35	.35
402	A143	10te blue	.30	.25
403	A106	15te deep blue	.45	.45
404	A106	20te gray blue	.55	.55
405	A106	35te dark green	1.40	1.40
406	A143	63te fawn	2.25	2.25
407	A77	84te purple	2.40	2.40
408	A77	100te orange	2.75	2.75
409	A143	150te claret	5.00	5.00
		Nos. 392-409 (19)	18.80	18.45

Issued: No. 392, 2te, 2/24; Nos. 393, 400, 4/17; 4te, 5te, 6te, 7te, 10te, 63te, 150te, 1/31; No. 399, 15te, 20te, 35te, 3/28; 84te, 100te, 5/30; 3te, 9te, 9/12.

Nos. 392 and 394 are dated "2003" and have smaller Cyrillic inscription of country name, and longer Roman inscription of country name than Nos. 290-291.

Nos. 394A is dated "2003" and has a smaller denomination with thinner zeroes than No. 270.

Nos. 399, 403 and 404 are dated "2003" and have taller Cyrillic inscription of country name than Nos. 322, 324-325.

Domestic and Wild Sheep — A144

Various rams, ewes and lambs: 20te, 40te, 50te.

2003, Feb. 26 ***Perf. 11½x11¾***
410-412 A144 Set of 3 3.50 3.50

New Year Type of 1993 With "Kazakhstan" Inscribed in Both Cyrillic and Roman Letters

2003, Mar. 21 ***Perf. 11½***
413 A7 40te lt bl, blk & dk bl 1.50 1.50

New Year 2003 (Year of the Ram).

Cosmonaut's Day — A145

Designs: 40te, Pioneer 10 and Jupiter. 70te, Mir Space Station, vert.

2003, Apr. 12 ***Perf. 11¾***
414-415 A145 Set of 2 3.50 3.50

Intl. Association of Academies of Science, 10th Anniv. — A146

2003, Apr. 23 **Litho.** ***Perf. 11½***
416 A146 50te multi 1.60 1.60

Souvenir Sheet

Ethnic Groups in Kazakhstan — A147

No. 417: a, Kazakhs (woman with red vest). b, Russians (woman with yellow blouse). c, Ukrainians (woman with blue vest).

2003, Apr. 29 **Litho.** ***Perf. 11¾x11½***
417 A147 35te Sheet of 3, #a-c 3.50 3.50

Musical Instruments — A148

Designs: 25te, Dombra. 50te, Kobyz.

2003, May 26
418-419 A148 Set of 2 2.25 2.25

Fairy Tales — A149

Designs: 30te, Aldar Kose and Alasha Khan. 40te, Aldar Kose and Karynbaj.

2003, June 27 ***Perf. 11½***
420-421 A149 Set of 2 2.00 2.00

Art — A150

Designs: 20te, Chess Match, by Arturo Ricci (1854-1919). 35te, Portrait of the Shepherd, sculpture by H. Nauryzbaev. 45te, Bowls of Koumiss, by Aisha Galimbaeva (1917-).

2003, July 7 ***Perf. 11¾***
422-424 A150 Set of 3 3.75 3.75

Famous Men — A151

Designs: No. 425, 60te, Tole Bey (1663-1756). No. 426, 60te, Kazybek Bey (1667-1763). No. 427, 60te, Aiteke Bey (1689-1766).

2003, Aug. 11 ***Perf. 11¾x11½***
425-427 A151 Set of 3 4.25 4.25

Halyk Bank, 80th Anniv. — A152

2003, Aug. 15 ***Perf. 11½x11¾***
428 A152 23te multi .70 .70

International Transit Conference, Almaty — A153

2003, Aug. 28
429 A153 40te multi 1.35 1.35

World Post Day — A154

2003, Oct. 9 ***Perf. 13½***
430 A154 23te pur & blue .65 .65

Houses of Worship, Almaty — A155

Designs: No. 431, 50te, Cathedral. No. 432, 50te, Mosque.

2003, Oct. 10 ***Perf. 11¾x11½***
431-432 A155 Set of 2 2.50 2.50

Tenge Currency, 10th Anniv. — A156

2003, Nov. 15 ***Perf. 13½***
433 A156 25te blue & yel org .65 .65

Paintings A157

No. 434: a, Baxt, by S. Ayitbaev, 1966. b, Tong. Onalik, by R. Ahmedov, 1962.

2003, Nov. 25 ***Perf. 12***
434 A157 100te Horiz. pair, #a-b *4.75 4.75*

See Uzbekistan No. 385.

Populus Diversifolia — A158

2003, Dec. 10 ***Perf. 11½***
435 A158 100te multi 2.10 2.10

Petroglyphs, Tamgaly A159

Designs. 25te, Cows. 30te, Man as sun on bull, vert.

Perf. 11½x11¾, 11¾x11½
2003, Dec. 19
436-437 A159 Set of 2 2.10 2.10

Abylkhan Kasteev (1904-73), Artist — A160

2004, Feb. 28 **Litho.** ***Perf. 11¾***
439 A160 115te multi 3.25 3.25

New Year Type of 1993 With "Kazakhstan" Inscribed in Both Cyrillic and Roman Letters

2004, Mar. 23 ***Perf. 11½***
440 A7 35te lt bl, dk bl & org 1.00 1.00

New Year 2004 (Year of the Monkey).

Cosmonaut's Day — A161

Designs: 40te, Mariner 10, vert. 50te, Luna 3.

Perf. 11¾x11½, 11½x11¾
2004, Apr. 12
441-442 A161 Set of 2 *2.00 2.00*

Kazakhstan Flag — A162

2004, Apr. 19 ***Perf. 13½***
443 A162 25te yel & brt blue .75 .75

Arms Type of 1998 Redrawn

2004		**Litho.**		***Perf. 13½***	
444	A70	1te	green	.30	.25
445	A70	2te	bright blue	.30	.25
446	A70	4te	bright pink	.30	.25
447	A70	5te	orange yellow	.30	.30
448	A70	10te	olive green	.40	.40
449	A70	16te	brt purple	.50	.50
450	A70	20te	purple	.60	.60
451	A70	35te	bright yellow	1.00	1.00
452	A70	50te	brt green	1.40	1.40
453	A70	72te	orange	1.90	1.90
454	A70	100te	greenish blue	2.75	2.75
455	A70	200te	vermilion	5.25	5.25
			Nos. 444-455 (12)	15.00	14.85

Issued: 1te, 2te, 4te, 4/19; 20te, 35te, 72te, 100te, 200te, 5/11; 5te, 10te, 16te, 50te, 6/10.

Nos. 444-455 are dated "2004," arms and "Kazakhstan" in Roman letters are larger and denominations are smaller than those features on Nos. 247-254.

No. 447 is dated "2004," arms and "Kazakhstan" in Roman letters are larger and denomination is smaller than those features on No. 251.

Souvenir Sheet

Kazakhstan Railways, Cent. — A163

2004, Apr. 22 **Litho.** ***Perf. 11¾x11½***
456 A163 150te multi 3.00 3.00

Souvenir Sheet

Ethnic Groups in Kazakhstan — A164

No. 457: a, Uzbeks (denomination at left). b, Germans (denomination at right).

2004, May 12
457 A164 65te Sheet of 2, #a-b 3.25 3.25

FIFA (Fédération Internationale de Football Association), Cent. — A165

FIFA emblem, soccer player and soccer ball at: No. 458, 100te, Left. No. 459, 100te, Center.

2004, May 21 **Litho. & Embossed**
458-459 A165 Set of 2 5.00 5.00

Children's Art — A166

Designs: No. 460, 45te, Yurts and sheep, by A. Sadykov. No. 461, 45te, Woman, by D. Iskhanova, vert.

2004, June 20 **Litho.** ***Perf. 11½***
460-461 A166 Set of 2 2.25 2.25

Souvenir Sheet

2004 Summer Olympics, Athens — A167

No. 462: a, 70te, Boxing. b, 115te, Shooting.

Litho., Margin Embossed

2004, June 28
462 A167 Sheet of 2, #a-b 3.75 3.75

Souvenir Sheet

Fauna in Altyn Emel Reserve A168

No. 463: a, Acgypius monacus. b, Capra sibirica. c, Gazella subgutturosa.

2004, Aug. 11 *Perf. 11½x11¾*
463 A168 50te Sheet of 3, #a-c 4.00 4.00

Souvenir Sheet

Kazaktelecom, 10th Anniv. — A169

Perf. 11½x11¾
2004, Aug. 18 **Litho.**
464 A169 70te multi 2.00 2.00

Alkei Khakan Margulan (1904-85), Archaeologist A170

2004, Sept. 23
465 A170 115te multi 2.25 2.25

Flowers A171

2004, Oct. 4 *Perf. 12¼x11½*
466 A171 25te multi + label .75 .75

Printed in sheets of 12 + 12 labels.

World Post Day Type of 2003

2004, Oct. 9 *Perf. 13½*
467 A154 3te red vio & blue .30 .30
468 A154 30te yel org & blue .80 .80

New Year 2005 — A172

2004, Nov. 23 *Perf. 13¼*
469 A172 65te multi 1.40 1.40

Musical Instruments — A173

No. 470: a, Adyma. b, Gizhak and bow.

2004, Nov. 29 *Perf. 11½x11¾*
470 A173 100te Horiz. pair, #a-b 4.50 4.50

See Tajikistan No. 248.

Saken Seifullin (1894-1939), Writer — A174

2004, Dec. 28
471 A174 35te multi .75 .75

Women's Headdresses — A175

No. 472: a, Kazakh headdress, denomination at left. b, Mongol headdress, denomination at right.

2004, Dec. 30
472 A175 72te Horiz. pair, #a-b 3.25 3.25

See Mongolia No. 2590.

Veterinary Research Institute, Cent. — A176

2005, Jan. 14 *Perf. 13½*
473 A176 7te multi .40 .40

Constitution, 10th Anniv. — A177

2005, Apr. 8 **Litho.** *Perf. 13½*

474	A177	1te blue & brn	.30	.25
475	A177	2te vio & brn	.30	.25
476	A177	3te brt grn & brn	.30	.25
477	A177	8te brt bl & brn	.30	.25
478	A177	10te red & brn	.30	.25
479	A177	(25te) red vio & brn	.60	.70
480	A177	50te olive & brn	1.00	1.10
481	A177	65te bl grn & brn	1.30	1.40
		Nos. 474-481 (8)	4.40	4.45

No. 479 is inscribed "A."

Europa — A178

2005, Apr. 14 **Litho.** *Perf. 11½x12¼*
482 A178 90te multi 5.00 5.00

End of World War II, 60th Anniv. — A179

2005, Apr. 28 **Litho.** *Perf. 13¼x13*
483 A179 72te multi 1.75 1.75

Souvenir Sheet

Baikonur Space Complex, 50th Anniv. A180

No. 484: a, Rocket. b, Buran space shuttle. c, Capsule and parachute.

2005, June 2 *Perf. 11½x11¾*
484 A180 72te Sheet of 3, #a-c 4.50 4.50

Peace and Harmony Palace A181

Litho. & Embossed

2005, July 6 *Perf. 13¼*
485 A181 65te multi 1.50 1.50

Minerals — A182

Designs: 50te, Azurite. 70te, Agate.

2005, July 12 **Litho.** *Perf. 11¾x11½*
486-487 A182 Set of 2 3.00 3.00

Fairy Tales Type of 2003

Designs: 35te, Aldar Kose and the Musician. 45te, Aldar Kose and the Raiser of Asses.

2005, Aug. 11
488-489 A149 Set of 2 1.90 1.90

Constitution, 10th Anniv. — A183

2005, Aug. 26
490 A183 72te multi 1.60 1.60

Souvenir Sheet

Olympic Gold Medalists — A184

No. 491: a, Zaksylik Ushkempirov, 1980, 48kg Greco-Roman wrestling. b, Vitaly Savin, 1988, 4x100m relay. c, Vasily Zhirov, 1996, light heavyweight boxing. d, Bekzat Sattarkhanov, 2000, featherweight boxing.

2005, Sept. 22 **Litho.** *Perf. 11¾*
491 A184 100te Sheet of 4, #a-d *9.00 9.00*

Akhmet Baitursynov (1873-1937), Writer — A185

Litho. with Foil Application

2005, Oct. 6 *Perf. 13¾x14*
492 A185 30te multi .80 .80

No. 492 not issued without gold overprint.

World Post Day — A186

2005, Oct. 8 **Litho.** *Perf. 13½*
493 A186 35te blue & pur .80 .80
494 A186 40te pur & red .95 .95

Dogs A187

No. 495: a, Kazakh hound (dog with curled tail). b, Estonian hound (white, black and brown dog).

2005, Oct. 19 *Perf. 11½x11¾*
495 A187 138te Horiz. pair, #a-b 4.75 4.75

See Estonia No. 523.

United Nations, 60th Anniv. — A188

2005, Oct. 31 *Perf. 13½*
496 A188 150te multi 3.00 3.00

New Year 2006 — A189

2005, Nov. 10 **Litho.** *Perf. 13¼*
497 A189 65te multi 1.50 1.50

Evgeny Brusilovsky (1905-81), Composer A190

2005, Nov. 18 *Perf. 11½x11¾*
498 A190 150te multi 2.75 2.75

Assembly of Peoples of Kazakhstan, 10th Anniv. — A191

2005, Nov. 24 *Perf. 13½*
499 A191 80te multi 1.75 1.75

Souvenir Sheet

National Symbols A192

No. 500: a, 70te, Flag and eagle. b, 70te, National anthem. c, 300te, Arms.

Litho. & Embossed

2005, Dec. 22 *Perf. 13¼*
500 A192 Sheet of 3, #a-c 7.00 7.00

Turgen Waterfall A193

Mountain Lake A194

2005, Dec. 23 **Litho.** *Perf. 13½*
501 A193 12te multi .50 .50
502 A194 100te multi 3.00 3.00

Hans Christian Andersen (1805-75), Author — A195

2005, Dec. 30 *Perf. 11¾x11½*
503 A195 200te multi 3.75 3.75

Parliament, 10th Anniv. — A196

2006, Jan. 17 Litho. ***Perf. 11½x11¾***
504 A196 50te multi 1.25 1.25

Abylai Khan, by Aubakir Ismailov — A197

Litho. With Foil Application

2006, Jan. 27 ***Perf. 13x13¼***
505 A197 94te multi 1.90 1.90

2006 Winter Olympics, Turin — A198

Perf. 11½x11¾
2006, Feb. 20 Litho.
506 A198 138te multi 2.50 2.50

Cosmonaut's Day — A199

Paintings of cosmonauts by: 100te, P. M. Popov. 120te, A. M. Stepanov.

2006, Apr. 12 ***Perf. 11¾x11½***
507-508 A199 Set of 2 4.50 4.50

Traditional Jewelry — A200

No. 509: a, Bracelet, Kazakhstan. b, Brooch, Latvia.

2006, Apr. 19 ***Perf. 11½x11¾***
509 A200 110te Horiz. pair, #a-b 4.50 4.50

See Latvia No. 650.

Saksaul Tree — A201

2006, Apr. 27 ***Perf. 11¾x11½***
510 A201 25te multi .60 .60

Europa — A202

2006, May 3
511 A202 210te multi 3.50 3.50
a. Tete-beche pair 10.00 10.00

Turkestan-Siberia Railway, 75th Anniv. — A203

2006, May 31 ***Perf. 13x13¼***
512 A203 200te multi 4.00 4.00

2006 World Cup Soccer Championships, Germany A204

2006, June 2 ***Perf. 11½x11¾***
513 A204 150te multi 2.75 2.75

Intl. Year of Deserts and Desertification A205

2006, July 7 ***Perf. 13¼***
514 A205 110te multi 2.10 2.10

Mosque, Astana — A206

2006		**Litho.**		***Perf. 13½x13¾***	
515	A206	5te	emerald	.30	.25
516	A206	8te	Prus blue	.40	.25
517	A206	10te	olive grn	.50	.25
518	A206	(25te)	purple	.90	.90
518A	A206	100te	dark blue	2.25	1.75
519	A206	110te	brown	2.50	2.00
520	A206	120te	green	2.75	2.25
521	A206	200te	red violet	4.50	3.50
			Nos. 515-521 (8)	14.10	11.15

Issued: 100te, 10/10/06; rest, 7/20/06.

Akzhan Mashani, Geologist, Cent. of Birth — A207

2006, July 21 Litho. ***Perf. 11½x11¾***
522 A207 85te multi 2.00 2.00

Houses of Worship in Almaty — A208

Designs: No. 523, 25te, Catholic Church (denomination in orange). No. 524, 25te, Synagogue (denomination in white).

2006, Aug. 17 ***Perf. 11¾x11½***
523-524 A208 Set of 2 1.10 1.10

Souvenir Sheet

Famous Men A209

No. 525: a, Chokan Valikhanov (1835-65), diplomat. b, Saken Sejfullin (1894-1938), poet. c, Nazir Tjurjakulov (1893-1937). d, Kanysh Satpaev (1899-1964), geologist.

2006, Aug. 20 ***Perf. 11½***
525 A209 90te Sheet of 4, #a-d 6.00 6.00

Third Meeting of Economic Cooperation Organization Postal Authorities, Turkey A210

2006, Sept. 15 ***Perf. 12***
526 A210 210te multi 3.50 3.50

See Iran No. 2917, Pakistan No. 1101 and Turkey No. 3041.

No. 526 Overprinted in Gold

2006, Sept. 22
527 A210 210te multi 3.50 3.50

Overprint corrects site of meeting from Istanbul to Ankara.

Ahmet Zhubanov (1906-68), Composer — A211

2006, Oct. 13 ***Perf. 11½***
528 A211 85te multi 1.75 1.75

Coats of Arms — A212

Arms of: 17te, Almaty. 80te, Astana.

2006, Oct. 20 Litho. ***Perf. 13½x13¾***
529-530 A212 Set of 2 2.00 2.00

New Year 2007 — A213

2006, Nov. 1 Litho. ***Perf. 13¼***
531 A213 25te multi .75 .75

Latif Khamidi (1906-83), Composer — A214

2006, Nov. 9 ***Perf. 11½x11¾***
532 A214 110te multi 2.00 2.00

Mukagali Makataev (1931-76), Writer — A215

2006, Nov. 29				***Perf. 13½x13¾***	
533	A215	1te	dark blue	.30	.25
534	A215	4te	olive grn	.30	.25
535	A215	7te	rose claret	.30	.25
536	A215	15te	red brown	.30	.30
			Nos. 533-536 (4)	1.20	1.05

Manash Kozybaev (1931-2002), Historian — A216

2006, Nov. 29					
537	A216	20te	brown	.45	.45
538	A216	30te	brn lake	.65	.65

Character From Opera *Silk Girl* — A217

2006, Dec. 15 ***Perf. 13¼***
539 A217 80te multi 1.25 1.25

Values are for stamps with surrounding selvage.

18th Century Helmet A218

2006, Dec. 15 ***Perf. 13x12¾***
540 A218 85te multi 1.75 1.75

Nikolai Repinsky (1906-69), Architect — A219

2006, Dec. 20				***Perf. 13½x13¾***	
541	A219	2te	brown	.30	.25
542	A219	3te	yel brn	.30	.25
543	A219	105te	gray grn	2.00	2.00
544	A219	150te	blue	3.00	3.00
545	A219	500te	rose claret	9.00	9.00
			Nos. 541-545 (5)	14.60	14.50

Miniature Sheet

Kurgalzhinsky Nature Reserve — A220

No. 546: a, 25te, Phoenicopterus roseus. b, 100te, Cygnus cygnus. c, 120te, Meles meles.

2006, Dec. 29 ***Perf. 11½x11¾***
546 A220 Sheet of 3, #a-c 5.50 5.50

KazTransOil, 10th Anniv. A221

2007, Apr. 12 Litho. ***Perf. 12¾***
547 A221 25te multi .60 .60

Cosmonaut's Day — A222

Designs: 80te, Konstantin E. Tsiolkovsky (1857-1935), rocket pioneer. 110te, Sergei P. Korolev (1906-66), aeronautical engineer.

2007, Apr. 12 ***Perf. 12¼x11¾***
548-549 A222 Set of 2 3.50 3.50

Europa
A223

No. 550 — Children's art: a, 25te, Scout bugler and tents. b, 65te, Scouts with backpacks, dog.

2007, May 8 ***Perf. 11½x11¾***
550 A223 Pair, #a-b 2.40 2.40

Scouting, cent.

63rd Session of UN Economic and Social Commission for Asia and the Pacific, Almaty
A224

2007, May 17 ***Perf. 12¾***
551 A224 25te multi .55 .55

Gali Ormanov (1907-78), Poet — A225

2007, Sept. 28 **Litho.** ***Perf. 11½***
552 A225 25te multi .55 .55

Conference on Interaction and Confidence-Building Measures in Asia, 15th Anniv. — A226

2007, Oct. 17 ***Perf. 13½***
553 A226 80te multi 1.75 1.75

Maulen Balakaev (1907-95), Philologist — A227

2007, Oct. 29 **Litho.** ***Perf. 13½***
554 A227 1te red brown .30 .25
555 A227 4te green .30 .25
556 A227 5te dk brown .30 .25
Nos. 554-556 (3) .90 .75

Almaty Zoo Animals
A228

No. 557: a, 25te, Zebras. b, 110te, Elephant.

2007, Oct. 31 **Litho.** ***Perf. 11½***
557 A228 Pair, #a-b 2.75 2.75

Printed in sheets containing 4 each of Nos. 557a and 557b, with a central label.

Hirundo Rustica — A229

2007, Nov. 15 ***Perf. 13½***
558 A229 20te multi .65 .40
559 A229 25te multi .75 .50
560 A229 50te multi 1.40 1.00
561 A229 100te multi 3.25 2.00
Nos. 558-561 (4) 6.05 3.90

Saddle — A230

2007, Nov. 27 ***Perf. 12***
562 A230 80te multi 1.75 1.75

Launch of Sputnik 1, 50th Anniv.
A231

2007, Nov. 27 ***Perf. 12½x12¾***
563 A231 500te multi 8.00 8.00

Karagand Arms
A232

Pavlodar Arms
A233

2007, Dec. 10 ***Perf. 13½x13¼***
564 A232 10te multi .55 .55
565 A233 10te multi .55 .55

Miniature Sheet

Olympic Gold Medalists — A234

No. 566: a, Vladimir Smirnov, 1994, 50-kilometer skiing. b, Yuri Melinichenko, 1996, Greco-Roman wrestling. c, Olga Shishigina, 2000, 100-meter hurdles. d, Ermahan Ibraimov, 2000, boxing.

2007, Dec. 28 ***Perf. 12x11½***
566 A234 150te Sheet of 4, #a-d 11.00 11.00

Souvenir Sheet

Peoples of Kazakhstan — A235

No. 567: a, Uighur man and woman (denomination at left). b, Tatar man and woman (denomination at right).

2007, Dec. 28 ***Perf. 11½***
567 A235 105te Sheet of 2, #a-b 4.25 4.25

New Year — A236

2008, Jan. 23 **Litho.** ***Perf. 13¼***
568 A236 25te multi .75 .75

Printed in sheets of 8 + central label.

Miniature Sheet

Women's Day
A237

No. 569 — Various flowers with: a, Denomination at LL. b, Denomination at LR. c, Denomination and country name at UL. d, Denomination and country name at UR, Kazakh text in lower panel justified at right. e, Denomination at L, country name at LL. f, Denomination and country name at UR, Kazakh text in lower panel justified at left.

2008, Mar. 14 ***Perf. 13¼***
569 A237 25te Sheet of 6, #a-f, + 3 labels 5.25 5.25

Navruz Bayram
A238

2008, Mar. 21 ***Perf. 12¾***
570 A238 25te multi .70 .70

2008 Summer Olympics, Beijing — A239

2008, Apr. 2 ***Perf. 14x14¼***
571 A239 25te multi .70 .70

Kazakhstan Postal Service, 15th Anniv.
A240

2008, Apr. 4 ***Perf. 12¾***
572 A240 25te multi .70 .70

Cosmonaut's Day — A241

Designs: 100te, Space Station Mir. 150te, International Space Station.

2008, Apr. 10 ***Perf. 14x14¼***
573-574 A241 Set of 2 5.50 5.50

Europa
A242

No. 575 — Color of dove: a, Blue. b, Red.

2008, May 6 ***Perf. 14x14¼***
575 A242 150te Horiz. pair, #a-b 5.25 5.25

2008 Summer Olympics, Beijing — A243

No. 576: a, Judo. b, Handball.

2008, Aug. 10 **Litho.** ***Perf. 14x14¼***
576 A243 100te Horiz. pair, #a-b 4.00 4.00

Deer
A244

No. 577: a, Cervus elaphus sibiricus. b, Cervus nippon.

2008, Sept. 18
577 A244 110te Horiz. pair, #a-b 4.00 4.00

See Moldova No. 596.

Ancient Jewelry From Iran and Kazakhstan
A245

No. 578: a, Buckle depicting snow leopard and mountains, 4th-5th cent. B.C., Kazakhstan. b, Gold medal depicting lions, 7th cent. B.C., Iran.

2008, Oct. 3 ***Perf. 14x14¼***
578 Horiz. pair + flanking label 4.50 4.50
a. A245 25te multi .55 .55
b. A245 150te multi 3.50 3.50

See Iran No. 2965.

Universal Declaration of Human Rights, 60th Anniv. — A246

Perf. 11¾x11½

2008, Dec. 10 **Litho.**
579 A246 25te multi .70 .70

Taiyr Zharakov (1908-65), Poet — A247

2008, Dec. 12 ***Perf. 11½***
580 A247 25te multi .70 .70

Shakarim Kudaiberdyuly (1859-1931), Poet — A248

2008, Dec. 12
581 A248 25te multi .70 .70

Alash Movement, 90th Anniv. — A249

2008, Dec. 18
582 A249 25te multi .70 .70

Musical Instruments — A250

No. 583: a, 25te, Zhelbuaz. b, 100te, Dauylpaz.

2008, Dec. 19
583 A250 Pair, #a-b 2.25 2.25

Paintings A251

No. 584: a, 25te, Portrait of Kenesary, by A. Kasteev. b, 100te, Guest, by S. Aitbayev.

2008, Dec. 19
584 A251 Pair, #a-b 2.50 2.50

Insects A252

No. 585: a, 25te, Callisthenes semenovi. b, 100te, Dorcadion acharlense.

2008, Dec. 22
585 A252 Pair, #a-b 2.50 2.50

Peter Aravin (1908-79), Musicologist — A253

Perf. 13¾x13½

2008, Dec. 25 **Litho.**
586 A253 10te multi .75 .75

Eagle — A254

2008, Dec. 25
587 A254 20te multi 1.00 1.00

Arms of Atyrau A255

Arms of Taraz A256

2008, Dec. 25 **Litho.** ***Perf. 14x13½***
588 A255 (25te) multi .80 .80
589 A256 (25te) multi .80 .80

Preservation of Polar Regions and Glaciers A257

2009, Mar. 12 **Litho.** ***Perf. 12¾***
590 A257 230te multi 3.75 3.75

Navruz Bayram A258

2009, Mar. 20
591 A258 25te multi .50 .50

Louis Braille (1809-52), Educator of the Blind — A259

2009, Mar. 26 ***Perf. 11½***
592 A259 230te multi 4.00 4.00

Europa — A260

Telescopes and: No. 593, 230te, Galileo Galilei, Moon. No. 594, 230te, Taurus constellation, Kazakhs looking at sky.

2009, Apr. 3
593-594 A260 Set of 2 8.00 8.00

Intl. Year of Astronomy.

Earrings — A261

No. 595 — Earring from: a, Korea, 5th-6th cent. b, Mongolia, 18th-19th cent. c, Kazakhstan, 2nd-1st cent, B.C.

2009, June 12 **Litho.** ***Perf. 13x12¾***
595 A261 Horiz. strip of 3 9.00 9.00
a.-c. 180te Any single 2.75 2.75

See South Korea No. 2313, Mongolia No. 2674.

Astronomy — A262

Designs: 180te, Telescope. 230te, Observatories.

2009, June 25 ***Perf. 13***
596-597 A262 Set of 2 6.25 6.25

Horsemen and Shield A263

2009, July 9 ***Perf. 12¾x12½***
598 A263 190te multi 3.50 3.50
a. Tête bêche pair 8.50 8.50

Maria Lizogub (1909-98), Painter — A264

2009, Aug. 25 ***Perf. 11½***
599 A264 180te multi 3.00 3.00

Kenen Azerbaev (1884-1976), Composer — A265

2009, Sept. 2
600 A265 180te multi 3.00 3.00

Garifolla Kurmangaliev (1909-93), Singer — A266

2009, Sept. 8
601 A266 180te multi 3.00 3.00

18th Session of World Tourism Organization, Astana — A267

2009, Oct. 5
602 A267 140te multi 2.10 2.10

Miniature Sheet

Ballet A268

No. 603: a, 180te, Dancers from Giselle (woman in white, man in black). b, 180te, Dancers from Don Quixote (woman in red, man in black and white). c, 180te, Dancers from Swan Lake (man and woman in white). d, 180te, Dancer from Tilep and Sarykyz. e, 230te, Dancer in red from Legend About Love. f, 230te, Dancer in blue from Bahchisarayski Fountain.

2009, Oct. 8 ***Perf. 13¼***
603 A268 Sheet of 6, #a-f 18.00 18.00

National Games A269

No. 604: a, 140te, Blindfolded man on horseback. b, 180te, Horsemen in competition.

2009, Nov. 16 ***Perf. 12***
604 A269 Pair, #a-b 5.00 5.00

Abdilda Tazhibaev (1909-98), Writer — A270

2009, Nov. 16 ***Perf. 11½***
605 A270 180te multi 3.00 3.00

Flora and Fauna — A271

Designs: No. 606, 180te, Crataegus ambigua. No. 607, 180te, Mellivora capensis.

2009, Dec. 3 **Litho.** ***Perf. 13***
606-607 A271 Set of 2 5.50 5.50

Iskander Tynyshpaev (1909-95), Cinematographer A272

2009, Dec. 9 ***Perf. 11½x11¾***
608 A272 25te multi .60 .60

Tuleu Basenov (1909-76), Architect — A273

2009, Dec. 30
609 A273 25te multi .60 .60

Birzhan Sal Kozhagululy (1834-97), Composer — A274

2009, Dec. 30
610 A274 25te multi .60 .60

Construction of Central Asian Gas Pipeline — A275

Perf. 12½x12¾

2009, Dec. 30 **Litho.**
611 A275 25te multi .60 .60

Kazakhstan Chairmanship of Organization for Security and Cooperation in Europe — A276

2010, Jan. 6 **Litho.** ***Perf. 12***
612 A276 230te multi 4.00 4.00

Navruz Bayram A277

2010, Apr. 15 ***Perf. 12¾***
613 A277 32te multi .75 .75

Victory in World War II, 65th Anniv. — A278

2010, Apr. 15 ***Perf. 12***
614 A278 32te multi .75 .75

2010 Winter Olympics, Vancouver A279

Designs: 32te, Ski jumper. 190te, Alpine skier.

2010, Apr. 29 **Litho.** ***Perf. 12***
615-616 A279 Set of 2 3.75 3.75

Europa A280

2010, May 5 ***Perf. 12¾***
617 A280 240te multi 3.75 3.75

Temirtau, 50th Anniv. — A281

2010, June 1 Litho. ***Perf. 14x14¼***
618 A281 32te multi .65 .65

Khan Shatyr Entertainment Center, Astana — A282

2010, July 1
619 A282 32te multi .65 .65

2010 World Cup Soccer Championships, South Africa — A283

2010, July 12
620 A283 240te multi 4.00 4.00

Arms of Chimkent A284

Arms of Aktyubinsk A285

2010 ***Perf. 14¼ Syncopated***
621 A284 5te multi .30 .25
622 A285 10te multi .30 .25

Issued: 5te, 8/17; 10te, 7/27.

Constitution, 15th Anniv. — A286

2010, Aug. 20 ***Perf. 14x14¼***
623 A286 32te multi .60 .60

Musa Baijanuly (1835-1929), Composer — A287

Perf. 13¾x13½ Syncopated
2010, Aug. 24
624 A287 (32te) multi .60 .60

Baikonur Cosmodrome, 55th Anniv. — A288

2010, Aug. 27 ***Perf. 13x13¼***
625 A288 190te multi 3.25 3.25

Mukhamedzhan Karataev (1910-95), Encyclopedia Editor — A289

Perf. 13¾x13½ Syncopated
2010, Sept. 22
626 A289 20te multi .45 .45

Souvenir Sheet

Baurjan Momasuhly (1910-82), World War II Hero — A290

2010, Sept. 24 ***Perf. 14x14¼***
627 A290 140te multi 2.50 2.50

Shokan Valikhanov (1835-65), Diplomat, Engineer — A291

2010, Oct. 21 ***Perf. 14¼x14***
628 A291 140te multi 2.50 2.50

See Russia No. 7246.

Frédéric Chopin (1810-49), Composer — A292

2010, Oct. 28 ***Perf. 14¼x14***
629 A292 240te multi 4.00 4.00

Water Agreement Between Kazakhstan and Kyrgyzstan, 10th Anniv. — A293

2010, Nov. 17 ***Perf. 14x14¼***
630 A293 32te multi .65 .65

Souvenir Sheet

Organization for Security and Cooperation in Europe Summit, Astana — A294

No. 631: a, 32te, Independence Monument and Kazakhstan flag. b, 140te, Pyramid of Peace. c, 190te, Ak Orda (Presidential Palace), Pyramid of Peace.

2010, Nov. 23 ***Perf. 14¼x14***
631 A294 Sheet of 3, #a-c 6.25 6.25

Birds of the Caspian Sea A295

No. 632: a, Phoenicopterus roseus. b, Ardeola ralloides.

2010, Nov. 24 **Litho.**
632 A295 140te Pair, #a-b 5.00 5.00

See Azerbaijan No. 938.

Seventh Asian Winter Games, Astana and Almaty A296

No. 633: a, 190te, Games emblem. b, 190te, Mascot freestyle skiing. c, 240te, Mascot ski jumping. d, 240te, Mascot ice skating.

2010, Dec. 21
633 A296 Block or horiz. strip of 4, #a-d 12.00 12.00

Mirzhakyp Dulatov (1885-1935), Poet — A297

Perf. 13½x13¾ Syncopated
2010, Dec. 28
634 A297 50te multi .80 .80

Fish in Astana Oceanarium — A298

No. 635: a, 32te, Rhinecanthus aculeatus. b, 190te, Zebrasoma veliferum.

2010, Dec. 30 ***Perf. 13½x13¾***
635 A298 Pair, #a-b 3.75 3.75

Souvenir Sheet

Fauna of Bayanaul Nature Reserve A299

No. 636: a, 32te, Tadorna ferruginea. b, 140te, Mustela nivalis. c, 190te, Capreolus pygargus.

2010, Dec. 30 ***Perf. 14x14¼***
636 A299 Sheet of 3, #a-c 8.00 8.00

On Nos. 636a-636c, country name is misspelled "Kazakhstah."

Souvenir Sheet

Peoples of Kazakhstan — A300

No. 637: a, 32te, Korean man and woman. b, 190te, Belarussian man and woman.

2010, Dec. 30 ***Perf. 14¼x14***
637 A300 Sheet of 2, #a-b 3.50 3.50

First Man in Space, 50th Anniv. — A301

2011, Feb. 28 ***Perf. 14x14¼***
638 A301 190te multi 3.00 3.00

Europa — A302

2011, Apr. 21 **Litho.**
639 A302 250te multi 4.00 4.00

Intl. Year of Forests.

Shanghai Cooperation Organization, 10th Anniv. — A303

2011, May 5 ***Perf. 14¼x14***
640 A303 210te multi 3.25 3.25

Campaign Against AIDS, 30th Anniv. — A304

2011, June 3 Litho. ***Perf. 14x13½***
641 A304 32te multi .70 .70

Eurasian Economic Community, 10th Anniv. — A305

2011, June 14 ***Perf. 14¼x14***
642 A305 32te multi .70 .70

Kasym Amanzholov (1911-55), Poet — A306

2011, July 14 ***Perf. 13½x14***
643 A306 32te multi .65 .65

Coins A307

No. 644 — Coin from: a, 7th cent. b, 13th cent. c, 14th cent. d, 16th cent.

2011, Sept. 7 ***Perf. 14x14¼***
644 A307 32te Block of 4, #a-d 2.00 2.00

Orymbek Zhautykov (1911-89), Mathematician A308

2011, Sept. 15
645 A308 32te multi .65 .65

Customs Union of Eurasian Economic Community — A309

2011, Sept. 22 *Perf. 14¼x14*
646 A309 32te multi .65 .65

Regional Communications Commonwealth, 20th Anniv. — A310

2011, Sept. 22 *Perf. 14x13½*
647 A310 150te multi 2.25 2.25

Gabdol Slanov (1911-69), Writer — A311

2011, Sept. 30 *Perf. 14x14¼*
648 A311 32te multi .65 .65

National Coat of Arms — A312

Perf. 14x14¼ Syncopated

2011, Oct. 5
649 A312 (32te) multi .50 .50
650 A312 50te multi .85 .85
651 A312 80te multi 1.25 1.25
652 A312 100te multi 1.50 1.50
653 A312 200te multi 3.00 3.00
654 A312 500te multi 8.00 8.00
Nos. 649-654 (6) 15.10 15.10

Umirzak Sultangazin (1936-2005), Director of Kazakhstan Space Reseach Institute — A313

2011, Oct. 20 *Perf. 14x14¼*
655 A313 32te multi .65 .65

Dina Nurpeisova (1861-1955), Musician — A314

2011, Oct. 25 *Perf. 14x14¼*
656 A314 32te multi .65 .65

Commonwealth of Independent States, 20th Anniv. — A315

2011, Nov. 10 *Perf. 14¼x14*
657 A315 150te multi 2.50 2.50

Independence, 20th Anniv. — A316

2011, Dec. 5
658 A316 32te multi .65 .65

Isatai Isabayev (1936-2007), Painter — A317

2011, Dec. 14 *Perf. 14x14¼*
659 A317 32te multi .65 .65

Miniature Sheet

Birds A318

No. 660: a, Turdus merula. b, Acridotheres tristis. c, Parus major. d, Corvus frugilegus. e, Pica pica. f, Columba livia. g, Corvus cornix. h, Passer domesticus.

2011, Dec. 14
660 A318 250te Sheet of 8, #a-h 30.00 30.00

Independence, 20th Anniv. — A319

2011, Dec. 15
661 A319 20te multi .45 .45

First Kazakh Antarctic Expedition A320

2011, Dec. 16
662 A320 190te multi 3.50 3.50

Petro Kazakhstan Kumkol Resources, 25th Anniv. — A321

2011, Dec. 22
663 A321 150te multi 2.25 2.25

Kazakhstan E-Government A322

2011, Dec. 31
664 A322 32te multi .65 .65

Dinmukhamed Konayev (1912-93), Politician — A323

2012, Jan. 27 *Perf. 14¼x14*
665 A323 100te multi 1.60 1.60

Katynkaragay National Park — A324

2012, Mar. 20 *Perf. 13½x13¾*
666 A324 110te multi 2.00 2.00

No. 1 Surcharged in Gold

Method and Perf. As Before

2012, Apr. 4
667 A1 50te on 50k #1 1.10 1.10

Europa — A325

2012, Apr. 11 **Litho.** *Perf. 14x14¼*
668 A325 250te multi 3.50 3.50

Hedgehogs — A326

No. 669: a, Erinaceus europaeus. b, Hemiechinus auritus.

2012, June 20
669 A326 190te Pair, #a-b 6.50 6.50

See Belarus Nos. 827-828.

Navruz Bayram — A327

2012, July 25
670 A327 190te multi 3.00 3.00

Space Vehicle — A328

2012, July 25
671 A328 250te multi 3.50 3.50

Ufa Ahmedsafin (1912-84), Hydrogeologist — A329

2012, Aug. 9 *Perf. 14¼x14*
672 A329 150te multi 2.25 2.25

Conference on a Nuclear Weapons-Free World, Astana — A330

2012, Aug. 27
673 A330 50te multi 1.00 1.00

Mezhit Begalin (1922-78), Film Director — A331

2012, Oct. 4 *Perf. 14x14¼*
674 A331 90te multi 1.40 1.40

Lev Gumilev (1912-92), Anthropologist — A332

2012, Oct. 11
675 A332 100te multi 1.50 1.50

Dmitri Snegin (1912-2001), Writer — A333

2012, Oct. 17 ***Perf. 13¾ Syncopated***
676 A333 80te multi 1.50 1.50

Shara Zhienkulova (1912-91), Dancer — A334

2012, Oct. 17
677 A334 100te multi 1.75 1.75

Paintings — A335

No. 678: a, Warriors, by P. Zaltsman, 1973. b, Milking a Red Camel, by A. Sadykhanov, 1986-87.

2012, Oct. 17 *Perf. 14¼x14*
678 A335 250te Vert. pair, #a-b 7.25 7.25

Mir Broadcasting Company, 20th Anniv. — A336

2012, Oct. 25
679 A336 10te multi .35 .35

Collective Security Treaty Organization, 10th Anniv. — A337

2012, Oct. 25
680 A337 80te multi 1.25 1.25

Zein Shashkin (1912-66), Writer — A338

Zhamal Omarova (1912-76), Singer — A339

Zhumagali Sain (1912-61), Poet — A340

Perf. 13¾ Syncopated

2012, Nov. 12

681	A338	5te multi	.30	.30
682	A339	10te multi	.30	.30
683	A340	20te multi	.45	.45
		Nos. 681-683 (3)	1.05	1.05

Kulyash Baiseitova (1912-57), Opera Singer — A341

Denominations: 2te, 50te, A.

Perf. 13¾ Syncopated

2012, Nov. 12

684-686 A341 Set of 3 2.00 2.00

No. 686 sold for 60te on day of issue.

Coat of Arms and Flag of Kazakhstan, 20th Anniv. — A342

2012, Nov. 20 ***Perf. 14¼x14***

687 A342 190te multi 2.75 2.75

Union of Designers, 25th Anniv. — A343

2012, Nov. 22

688 A343 80te multi 1.40 1.40

Diplomatic Relations Between Kazakhstan and Bulgaria, 20th Anniv. — A344

No. 689: a, Gold buckle depicting bird and deer, 8th-7th cent. B.C. b, Gold rhyton with design of deer's head, 4th cent. B.C.

2012, Dec. 14 ***Perf. 14¼x14***

689 A344 250te Horiz. pair, #a-b 7.25 7.25

Printed in sheets containing 4 pairs. See Bulgaria No. 4622.

Raoul Wallenberg (1912-47), Swedish Diplomat Who Saved Jews During World War II — A345

2012, Dec. 19 ***Perf. 14x14¼***

690 A345 250te multi 4.00 4.00

School, Astana A346

Lev N. Gumilev University, Astana A347

Mangylik El Triumphal Arch, Astana — A348

2012, Dec. 20

691	A346	100te multi	1.50	1.50
692	A347	100te multi	1.50	1.50
693	A348	100te multi	1.50	1.50
		Nos. 691-693 (3)	4.50	4.50

Traditional Costumes — A349

Designs: 150te, Man and woman, emblem of Regional Communications Commonwealth. 250te, Man and woman, no emblem.

2013, Jan. 23 ***Perf. 14¼x14***

694-695 A349 Set of 2 6.00 6.00

Miniature Sheet

2012 Summer Olympics Gold Medalists — A350

No. 696: a, Ilya Ilin, weight lifting (wearing blue and white uniform). b, Serik Sapiyev, boxing. c, Olga Rypakova, triple jump. d, Alexander Vinokourov, cycling. e, Svetlana Podobedova, weight lifting (wearing yellow uniform, with hand over heart). f, Zulfiya Chinshanlo, weight lifting (holding medal around neck, denomination at left). g, Maiya Maneza, weight lifting (holding medal around neck, denomination at right).

2013, Jan. 23

696 A350 150te Sheet of 7, #a-g, + label 17.50 17.50

Postman, by Nikolai Khludov — A351

2013, Apr. 25

697 A351 200te multi 3.00 3.00
a. Tête bêche pair 7.00 7.00

Miniature Sheet

Lunar Calendar Animals A352

No. 698: a, Mouse. b, Calf. c, Snow leopard. d, Rabbit. e, Snail. f, Snake. g, Horse. h, Sheep. i, Monkey. j, Chicks. k, Dog. l, Pig.

2013, Apr. 25 ***Perf. 14x14¼***

698 A352 100te Sheet of 12, #a-l 17.50 17.50

Rocket, Gull, Space Capsule and Parachute A353

Cosmonaut Valentina Tereshkova A354

Perf. 13½x13¾ Syncopated

2013, July 2 **Litho.**

699	A353	150te multi	2.00	2.00
700	A354	200te multi	3.00	3.00
a.		Pair, #699-700	6.00	6.00

Space flight of Tereshkova (first woman in space), 50th anniv. Nos. 699-700 each were printed in sheets of 6. No. 700a is from sheet containing three each of Nos. 699-700.

Souvenir Sheets

Pres. Nursultan Nazarbayev, Map of Kazakhstan — A355

Perf. 13½x13¾ Syncopated

2013, July 2 **Litho.**

701 A355 250te multi 4.00 4.00

Litho. With Foil Application

Perf. 14

Granite Paper

702 A355 900te multi 13.00 13.00

Establishment of diplomatic relations with various countries, 20th anniv. No. 701 contains one 55x33mm stamp. No. 702 contains one 50x30mm stamp.

Miniature Sheets

A356

Renaming of Akmola to Astana, 15th Anniv. — A357

No. 703: a, Presidential Palace. b, Palace of Independence and fountain. c, Bayterek Tower. d, Kazakh Eli Monument. No. 704: a, Pres. Nursultan Nazarbayev. b, Emblem of Astana with "1998." c, New cost of arms. d, Emblem of Expo 2017.

Perf. 13¾x13½ Syncopated

2013, July 4 **Litho.**

703 A356 100te Sheet of 4, #a-d 6.50 6.50
704 A357 100te Sheet of 4, #a-d 6.50 6.50

Miniature Sheet

Navruz Bayram A358

No. 705: a, Emblem of People's Assembly of Kazakhstan. b, Pres. Nursultan Nazarbayev waving at Navruz celebrations. c, Pres. Nazarbayev playing stringed instrument at Navruz celebrations. d, Emblem of Congress of Leaders of World and Traditional Religions, Astana.

Perf. 13¾x13½ Syncopated

2013, July 5 **Litho.**

705 A358 150te Sheet of 4, #a-d *8.00 8.00*

Miniature Sheet

Victory Day A359

No. 706: a, Pres. Nursultan Nazarbayev with hand over heart, floral bouquet. b, Flowers, Pres. Nazarbayev folding Kazakhstan flag. c, Eternal flame, flowers, parade. d, Pres. Nazarbayev shaking hands with veteran.

Perf. 13½ Syncopated

2013, July 5 **Litho.**

706 A359 90te Sheet of 4, #a-d, + 2 labels 5.25 5.25

Souvenir Sheet

Olympic Champions — A360

No. 707 — Kazakhstan flag and: a, Bakhtiyar Artayev, boxing, 2004 (denomination at UR). b, Alexander Parygin, pentathlon, 1996 (denomination at UL, Parygin not touching medal). c, Bakhyt Sarsekbayev, boxing, 2008 (denomination at UL, Sarsekbayev touching medal).

Perf. 13½x13¾ Syncopated

2013, July 16 **Litho.**

707 A360 150te Sheet of 3, #a-c, + label 6.75 6.75

Souvenir Sheet

Kazakhstan's Participation in 2010 and 2012 Nuclear Security Summits — A361

No. 708: a, Pres. Nursultan Nazarbayev at lectern at 2010 summit. b, U.S. Pres. Barack Obama, Pres. Nazarbayev, and Russian Pres. Dmitry Medvedev at 2012 summit.

Perf. 13¾x13½ Syncopated

2013, Aug. 28 **Litho.**

708 A361 150te Sheet of 2, #a-b 5.00 5.00

Miniature Sheet

Flowers A362

No. 709: a, 60te, Tulipa behmiana. b, 60te, Tulipa ostrowskiana. c, 100te, Papaver tianschanicum. d, 100te, Papaver pavoninum.

Perf. 13¼x13¾ Syncopated

2013, Oct. 4 **Litho.**

709 A362 Sheet of 4, #a-d 5.25 5.25

Souvenir Sheet

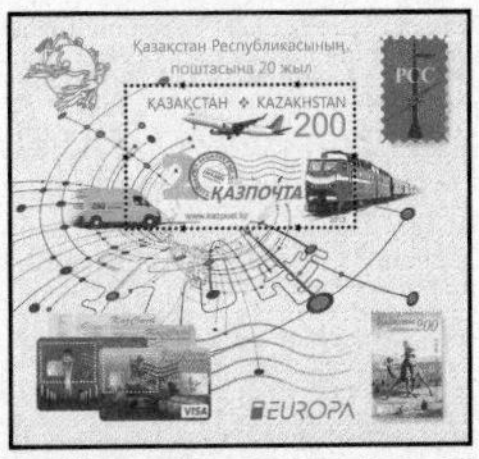

Kazakhstan Postal Service, 20th Anniv. — A363

Perf. 13½x13¾ Syncopated

2013, Oct. 9 **Litho.**

710 A363 200te multi 3.25 3.25

Miniature Sheet

Kazakhstan Coins — A364

No. 711: a, Obverse of 100,000-tenge gold coin. b, Reverse of 100,000-tenge gold coin of 2013. c, Obverse of 500-tenge silver coin. d, Reverse of 500-tenge silver coin of 2013.

Perf. 13¾x13¼ Syncopated

2013, Nov. 29 **Litho.**

711 A364 60te Sheet of 4, #a-d 4.25 4.25

Introduction of tenge currency, 20th anniv.

Miniature Sheet

Birds A365

No. 712: a, Chettusia gregaria. b, Tetrax tetrax. c, Aquila nipalensis. d, Numenius arquata. e, Oxyura leucocephala. f, Melanocorypha yeltoniensis.

Perf. 13½x14 Syncopated

2013, Dec. 25 **Litho.**

712 A365 150te Sheet of 6, #a-f 14.00 14.00

Souvenir Sheet

Wildlife of the Ustyurt Game Reserve A366

No. 713: a, 60te, Acinonyx jubatus. b, 150e, Saga pedo. c, 190te, Circaetus gallicus.

Perf. 13½x14 Syncopated

2013, Dec. 25 **Litho.**

713 A366 Sheet of 3, #a-c 6.00 6.00

Mukan Tolebayev (1913-60), Composer A367

Amre Kashaubayev (1888-1938), Singer A368

Valentina Tereshkova, First Woman in Space A369

Saiga A370

Perf. 13½x14½ Syncopated

2013, Dec. 27 **Litho.**

714 A367 1te pale yel & blk .35 .35
715 A368 3te lt grn & blk .35 .35
716 A369 5te lt bl & blk .35 .35

Perf. 14½x13½ Syncopated

717 A370 10te yel & blk .35 .35
Nos. 714-717 (4) 1.40 1.40

Tereshkova's space flight, 50th anniv. (No. 716).

Souvenir Sheet

Yurt Furnishings — A371

No. 718: a, Pillows and blankets on chest, edge of table. b, Trunks and chests, table with bowls and tureen. c, Curtains above bed with pillows.

Perf. 13½ Syncopated

2014, Jan. 15 **Litho.**

718 A371 200te Sheet of 3, #a-c 8.50 8.50

Souvenir Sheet

Communications History — A372

Perf. 13½x13¾ Syncopated

2014, Jan. 15 **Litho.**

719 A372 200te multi 3.25 3.25

Kulakhmet Khodzhikov (1914-86), Artist A373

Sabira Maykanovoy (1914-95), Actress A374

Ilyas Dzhansugurov (1894-1938), Poet — A375

2014 World Weight Lifting Championships, Almaty — A376

Perf. 14x14¼ Syncopated

2014 **Litho.**

720 A373 50te blk & lt bl .50 .50
721 A374 100te yel & blk 1.00 1.00
722 A375 100te yel & blk 1.00 1.00
723 A376 200te rose & blk 2.00 2.00
Nos. 720-723 (4) 4.50 4.50

Issued: 50te, 12/31; Nos. 721-722, 12/26; 200te, 12/29.

Souvenir Sheet

New Year 2014 (Year of the Horse) A377

2015, Jan. 12 **Litho.** ***Perf.***

724 A377 200te multi 3.00 3.00

Dated 2014.

Anna Akhmatova (1889-1966), Poet A378

Mikhail Lermontov (1814-41), Writer A379

2015, Jan. 12 **Litho.** ***Perf. 13x13½***

725 A378 60te multi .90 .90
726 A379 60te multi .90 .90

Dated 2014.

Employment Roadmap 2020 Emblem — A380

2015, Jan. 12 **Litho.** ***Perf. 12***

727 A380 150te multi 2.25 2.25

Dated 2014.

2013 Soyuz TMA-11M Flight A381

Voskhod Spacecraft, 50th Anniv. (in 2014) A382

Space Flight of Talgat Musabayev, 20th Anniv. (in 2014) — A383

Space Communications, 10th Anniv. — A384

2015, Jan. 12 **Litho.** ***Perf. 13x13½***

728 A381 150te multi 2.25 2.25
729 A382 150te multi 2.25 2.25
730 A383 150te multi 2.25 2.25
Nos. 728-730 (3) 6.75 6.75

Souvenir Sheet

731 A384 300te multi 4.25 4.25

Dated 2014.

Souvenir Sheet

Statue of Batyr Zhanibek Berdauletuly (1714-92) — A385

2015, Jan. 12 **Litho.** ***Perf. 13½x13***

732 A385 200te multi 3.00 3.00

Dated 2014.

Souvenir Sheet

Shaken Aimanov (1914-70), Actor — A386

2015, Jan. 12 **Litho.** ***Perf. 13½x13***

733 A386 200te multi 3.00 3.00

Dated 2014.

Miniature Sheet

Traditional Women's Headdresses — A387

No. 734 — Woman from: a, Shygys, 1955. b, Almaty, 1970. c, Karagandy, 19th cent. d, Pavlodar, 20th cent.

2015, Jan. 12 Litho. *Perf. 12*
734 A387 50te Sheet of 4, #a-d 3.00 3.00

Dated 2014.

Souvenir Sheet

Naurzum Nature Reserve A388

No. 735: a, Nymphaea candida. b, Haliaeetus albicilla. c, Alces alces.

2015, Jan. 12 Litho. *Perf. 13½x13*
735 A388 200te Sheet of 3, #a-c 8.75 8.75

Dated 2014.

Miniature Sheet

2014 Winter Olympics, Sochi, Russia — A389

No. 736: a, Short track speed skating. b, Figure skating. c, Snowboarding. d, Skeleton.

2015, Jan. 12 Litho. *Perf. 12*
736 A389 200te Sheet of 4, #a-d 11.50 11.50

Dated 2014.

Miniature Sheet

2014 Winter Paralympics, Sochi, Russia — A390

No. 737: a, Alpine skiing. b, Cross-country skiing. c, Sled hockey. d, Wheelchair curling.

2015, Jan. 12 Litho. *Perf. 13½x13*
737 A390 250te Sheet of 4, #a-d 14.00 14.00

Dated 2014.

Kazakhstan Chairmanship of Energy Charter Conference — A391

2015, Jan. 15 Litho. *Perf. 13½x13*
738 A391 100te multi 1.40 1.40

Dated 2014.

Ice Hockey — A392

2015, Jan. 15 Litho. *Perf. 12*
739 A392 100te multi 1.40 1.40

Dated 2014.

Nowruz A393

2015, Jan. 15 Litho. *Perf. 13*
740 A393 190te multi 3.00 3.00

No. 740 is printed in sheets of 7 + label and is dated 2014.

Europa A394

No. 741: a, Kobyz and bow, b, Dombra.

2015, Jan. 15 Litho. *Perf. 12*
741 A394 200te Pair, #a-b 5.25 5.25

No. 741 was printed in sheets containing 4 pairs + 2 labels, and is dated 2014.

Children's Art A395

No. 742 — Drawings depicting scenes from Kazakh fairy tales: a, Maktakyz and the Cat (yellow panels). b, Aldar-Koze (green panels). c, Beautiful Kunekey (blue panels). d, Alpamys Batyr (red panels).

2015, Jan. 15 Litho. *Perf. 12*
742 A395 50te Block or horiz. strip of 4, #a-d 3.00 3.00

Dated 2014.

Souvenir Sheet

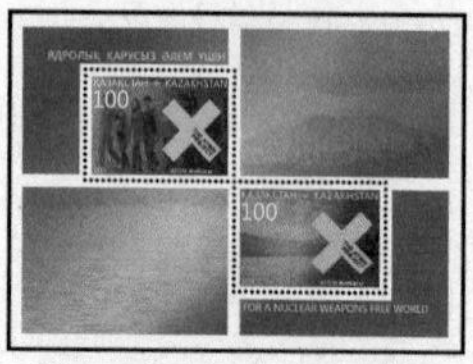

Campaign to End Nuclear Testing — A396

No. 743 — ATOM Project emblem and: a, People. b, Landscape.

2015, Jan. 15 Litho. *Perf. 13½x13*
743 A396 100te Sheet of 2, #a-b 3.00 3.00

Dated 2014.

Souvenir Sheet

Charlie Chaplin (1889-1977), Actor — A397

No. 744 — Chaplin with: a, 60te, Child actor (30x26mm). b, 100te, Dog (37x26mm). c, 200te, Camera (37x52mm).

2015, Jan. 15 Litho. *Perf. 13½x13*
744 A397 Sheet of 3, #a-c 5.25 5.25

Dated 2014.

Miniature Sheet

Zhoshy Khan Mausoleum — A398

No. 745: a, Interior of dome. b, Mausoleum, stone wall in foreground. c, Mausoleum, decorative fence in front of arch. d, Mausoleum, grass field in foreground.

2015, Jan. 15 Litho. *Perf. 13½x13*
745 A398 200te Sheet of 4, #a-d 11.00 11.00

Dated 2014.

Vaccines in Kazakhstan, Cent. — A399

2015, Jan. 15 Litho. *Perf. 13x13½*
746 A399 60te multi .80 .80

Souvenir Sheet

Victory in World War II, 70th Anniv. A400

No. 747: a, Rakhymzhan Koshkarbayev (1924-88), damaged Reichstag Building, medal at LL. b, Manshuk Mametova (1922-43), gun, medal at LR. c, Ivan Panfilov (1893-1941), Moscow buildings, medal at LL.

Perf. 14¼x14 Syncopated
2015, May 6 Litho.
747 A400 200te Sheet of 3, #a-c, + label 5.50 5.50

Eurasian Economic Union A401

Perf. 14¼x14 Syncopated
2015, May 22 Litho.
748 A401 100te multi 1.40 1.40

Ilyas Yesenberlin (1915-83), Writer A402

Malik Gabdullin (1915-73), Writer A403

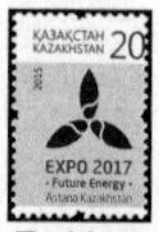

Emblem of Expo 2017, Astana A404

Space Walking, 50th Anniv. A405

Perf. 13½x14½ Syncopated
2015, June 18 Litho.

749	A402	5te	lt bl & blk	.60	.60
750	A403	10te	blk & stone	.60	.60
751	A404	20te	blk & pink	.60	.60
752	A405	(112te)	red & blue	1.25	1.25
			Nos. 749-752 (4)	3.05	3.05

See No. 780.

Souvenir Sheet

Assembly of the People of Kazakhstan, 20th Anniv. — A406

Perf. 14¼x14 Syncopated
2015, June 25 Litho.
753 A406 200te multi 2.00 2.00

Constitution, 20th Anniv. — A407

Perf. 14¼x14 Syncopated
2015, Aug. 25 Litho.
754 A407 (112te) multi 1.40 1.40

Kazakh Khanate, 550th Anniv. A408

Perf. 14¼x14 Syncopated
2015, Sept. 8 Litho.
755 A408 550te multi 7.00 7.00

Navruz Bayram — A409

Perf. 13¼ Syncopated

2015, Oct. 28 **Litho.**

756 A409 140te multi 1.75 1.75

Europa — A410

No. 757: a, 200te, Asyk Atu game pieces. b, 300te, Asyk Atu players and game pieces.

Perf. 13x13¼ Syncopated

2015, Oct. 28 **Litho.**

757 A410 Pair, #a-b 5.75 5.75

Diplomatic Relations Between Kazakhstan and United Arab Emirates — A411

No. 758: a, Sheikh Khalifa, flag of United Arab Emirates. b, Pres. Nursultan Nazarbayev, flag of Kazakhstan.

Perf. 13¼x13 Syncopated

2015, Oct. 28 **Litho.**

758 A411 200te Horiz. pair, #a-b 5.00 5.00

See United Arab Emirates No. 1137.

Postcrossing A412

Perf. 13x13¼ Syncopated

2015, Nov. 7 **Litho.**

759 A412 (140te) multi 1.75 1.75

Souvenir Sheet

Year of the Sheep A413

Perf. Syncopated

2015, Nov. 7 **Litho.**

760 A413 300te multi 3.25 3.25

Cosmonaut Aidyn Aimbetov — A414

Perf. 13¼ Syncopated

2015, Dec. 11 **Litho.**

761 A414 300te multi 2.50 2.50

First Spacewalk, 50th Anniv. — A415

No. 762: a, 200te, Alexei A. Leonov, first spacewalker. b, (200te), Leonov spacewalking, Voskhod 2.

Perf. 13½x13¼ Syncopated

2015, Dec. 11 **Litho.**

762 A415 Horiz. pair, #a-b 3.50 3.50

Expo 2017, Astana — A416

Perf. 13¼x13½ Syncopated

2015, Dec. 25 **Litho.**

763 A416 300te multi 2.50 2.50

Kenesary Street M. K. Kubrin Supermarket, Astana — A417

No. 764: a, (200te), Building in color. b, 200te, Building in Sepia.

Perf. 13¾x13 Syncopated

2015, Dec. 25 **Litho.**

764 A417 Pair, #a-b 3.25 3.25

Printed in sheets of 3 horizontal pairs of Nos. 764a-764b, + 3 flanking labels.

Souvenir Sheet

Aktobe Region A418

No. 765: a, 140te, Koblandy Batyr Memorial. b, 200te, Aliya Moldagulova Monument.

Perf. 13½x13¼ Syncopated

2015, Dec. 30 **Litho.**

765 A418 Sheet of 2, #a-b, + 2 labels 2.75 2.75

Kazhymukan Munaitpasov (1871-1948), Wrestler — A419

No. 766: a, 60te, Munaitpasov. b, 200te, Soviet warplane paid for by Munaitpasov, letter to Munaitpasov from Joseph Stalin.

Perf. 13¼x13 Syncopated

2016, Jan. 18 **Litho.**

766 A419 Pair. #a-b 2.00 2.00

Souvenir Sheet

Aksu-Zhabagly Nature Reserve — A420

No. 767: a, Tulipa greigii. b, Capra sibirica. c, Gypaetus barbatus.

Perf. 13¼x13 Syncopated

2016, Apr. 8 **Litho.**

767 A420 200te Sheet of 3, #a-c 5.25 5.25

Miniature Sheet

Tobet Dogs A421

No. 768: a, 60te, Two puppies (34x26mm). b, 140te, Dog, sheep, horses (37x26mm). c, 200te, Three dogs (37x26mm). d, 400te, Dog and sheep (37x52mm).

Perf. 13¼x13 Syncopated

2016, Apr. 27 **Litho.**

768 A421 Sheet of 4, #a-d 7.00 7.00

Regional Communications Commonwealth, 25th Anniv. — A422

Perf. 13¼x13 Syncopated

2016, Apr. 29 **Litho.**

769 A422 60te multi .60 .60

L. N. Gumilev Eurasian National University, 20th Anniv. — A423

Perf. 13¼x13 Syncopated

2016, May 23 **Litho.**

770 A423 60te multi .60 .60

Souvenir Sheet

Paintings by Yerbolat Tolepbay A424

No. 771: a, 250te, Kazakh Khans (country name at UL, 56x40mm). b, 250te, Seven Rules (country name at UR, 56x40mm). c, 500te, Pres. Nursultan Nazarbayev (28x40mm).

Perf. 13¼ Syncopated

2016, May 26 **Litho.**

771 A424 Sheet of 3, #a-c 8.75 8.75

Souvenir Sheet

Pres. Nursultan Nazarbayev — A425

Perf. 14x14¼ Syncopated

2016, June 13 **Litho.**

772 A425 (121te) multi 1.25 1.25

Miniature Sheet

Orders of Kazakhstan — A426

No. 773: a, Order of the Golden Eagle. b, Order of the Fatherland. c, Order of the First President of Kazakhstan Nursultan Nazarbayev. d, Order of the Leopard. e, Order of Glory. f, Order of Valor. g, Order of Nobility. h, Order of Friendship. i, Order of Honor.

Perf. 13½x13 Syncopated

2016, June 17 **Litho.**

773 A426 100te Sheet of 9, #a-i 7.75 7.75

Visit of French Pres. Charles de Gaulle to Baikonur Cosmodrome, 50th Anniv. — A427

No. 774: a, Rocket launch. b, De Gaulle, Soviet Union General Secretary Leonid Brezhnev and other dignitaries watching launch.

Perf. 13½x13¼ Syncopated

2016, June 24 **Litho.**

774 A427 (218te) Horiz. pair, #a-b — —

Souvenir Sheet

Akmola Region A428

No. 775: a, 140te, Mountain and lake. b, 200te, Mosque.

Perf. 13½ Syncopated

2016, June 24 **Litho.**

775 A428 Sheet of 2, #a-b, + 2 labels 2.75 2.75

Gennady Golovkin, Boxer A429

No. 776 — Golovkin with: a, (121te), Championship belts (52x37mm). b, (200te), Black boxing gloves and white trunks (37x21mm). c, 200te, Black robe, assistants holding belts (37x21mm). d, 200te, Blue and red boxing gloves (37x21mm) e, (218te), Ring ropes in background (37x21mm).

Perf. 12¾x13¼ Syncopated (#776a),
Perf. 13¼x12¾ Syncopated

2016, July 11 **Litho.**

776 A429 Sheet of 5, #a-e 8.25 8.25

Expo 2017 Emblem Type of 2015 and

Alikhan Bukeikhanov (1866-1937), Statesman A430

Morali Shamenov (1916-74), Union Leader A431

Ybyrai Altynsarin (1841-89), Educator — A432

Kayim Mukhmedzhanov (1916-2004), Poet — A433

Perf. 13½x14½ Syncopated

2016 **Litho.**

777 A430 5te pale bl & black .30 .25
778 A431 50te blk & lt blue .60 .60
779 A432 (121te) red & blue 1.25 1.25
780 A404 200te pink & blk 1.75 1.75
781 A433 (218te) blk & lilac 2.25 2.25
Nos. 777-781 (5) 6.15 6.10

Issued: Nos. 777, 779, 781, 7/12; Nos. 778, 780, 7/22.

100 Concrete Steps for Mangilik El National Goals — A434

Perf. 13¼ Syncopated

2016, Aug. 18 **Litho.**

782 A434 100te multi 1.00 1.00

A435

Perf. 12¾x13¼ Syncopated

2016, Aug. 18 **Litho.**

783 A435 60te multi .50 .50
a. Tete-beche pair 1.00 1.00

No. 783 was printed in sheets containing two tete-beche pairs.

Souvenir Sheet

Expo 2017, Astana A436

Perf. 13¼ Syncopated

2016, Aug. 19 **Litho.**

784 A436 300te multi 2.60 2.60

Traditional Foods — A437

Perf. 13¼ Syncopated

2016, Aug. 26 **Litho.**

785 A437 200te multi 1.75 1.75

Souvenir Sheet

Almaty Region A438

No. 786: a, 140te, Medeu skating rink. b, 200te, Tamgaly Gorge petroglyphs.

Perf. 13½ Syncopated

2016, Sept. 23 **Litho.**

786 A438 Sheet of 2, #a-b, + 2 labels 2.75 2.75

New Year — A439

Perf. Syncopated

2016, Oct. 21 **Litho.**

787 A439 100te multi .85 .85

No. 787 was printed in sheets of 4.

Souvenir Sheet

New Year 2016 (Year of the Monkey) A440

Perf. Syncopated

2016, Oct. 21 **Litho.**

788 A440 300te multi 2.60 2.60

Europa A441

No. 789: a, (218te), Expo 2017 emblem and buildings. b, 300te, Buildings, cyclist and wind generators.

Perf. 13½x13¼ Syncopated

2016, Oct. 21 **Litho.**

789 A441 (218te) Pair, #a-b — —

Kerey Khan (c.1428-70) and Zhanibek Khan (1428-80), Founders of Kazakh Khanate — A442

No. 790 — Khans: a, On scroll. b, On monument.

Perf. 13¼ Syncopated

2016, Nov. 2 **Litho.**

790 A442 200te Horiz. pair, #a-b 3.50 3.50

Printed in sheets of 8, containing 4 each Nos. 790a-790b.

2016 European Soccer Championships, France — A443

No. 791 — Soccer players, with player in red uniform at: a, Left. b, Right.

Perf. 13¼ Syncopated

2016, Nov. 2 **Litho.**

791 A443 (218te) Horiz. pair, #a-b 4.00 4.00

World Post Day — A444

Perf. 13¼ Syncopated

2016, Nov. 16 **Litho.**

792 A444 100te multi .85 .85

No. 792 was printed in sheets of 8 + central label.

Fourth National Sports Festival A445

No. 793: a, 100te, Kyz kuu. b, 200te, Kekpar.

Perf. 13¼ Syncopated

2016, Nov. 16 **Litho.**

793 A445 Horiz. pair, #a-b 2.60 2.60

Battle of Moscow, 75th Anniv. A446

No. 794: a, Soldiers at Battle of Moscow. b, World War II Monument, Almaty.

Perf. 13½x13¼ Syncopated

2016, Nov. 16 **Litho.**

794 A446 300te Horiz. pair, #a-b — —

Joint Issue between Kazakstan and Russia. See Russia No. 7785.

Souvenir Sheet

Atyrau Region A447

No. 795: a, 140te, Kurmangazy Palace of Culture. b, 200te, Biplane, medal and Hiuaz Dospanova Monument.

Perf. 13½ Syncopated

2016, Nov. 16 **Litho.**

795 A447 Sheet of 2, #a-b, + 2 labels 2.75 2.75

Miniature Sheet

Sharks in Astana Aquarium — A448

No. 796: a, Carcharhinus melanopterus. b, Triaenodon obesus. c, Chiloscyllium plagiosum. d, Negaprion brevirostris.

Perf. 13½ Syncopated

2016, Nov. 16 **Litho.**

796 A448 100te Sheet of 4, #a-d 3.50 3.50

Miniature Sheet

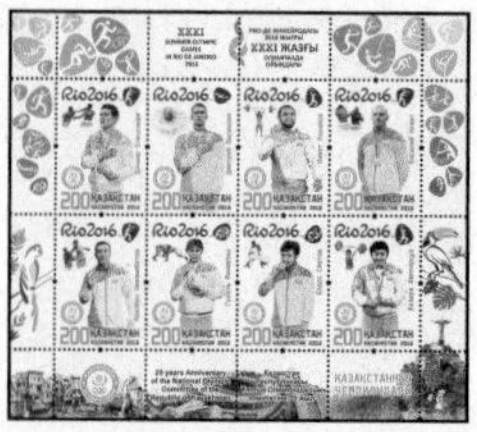

Gold and Silver Medalists at 2016 Summer Olympics — A449

No. 797: a, Gold medalist boxer Daniyar Yeleussinov. b, Gold medalist swimmer Dmitriy Balandin. c, Gold medalist weight lifter Nijat Rahimov. d, Silver medalist boxer Vasiliy Levit. e, Silver medalist boxer Adilbek Niyazymbetov. f, Silver medalist wrestler Guzel Manyurova. g, Silver medalist judo Yeldos Smetov. h, Silver medalist weight lifter Zhazira Zhapparkul.

Perf. 13¼ Syncopated

2016, Nov. 16 **Litho.**

797 A449 200te Sheet of 8, #a-h 13.50 13.50

Independence, 25th Anniv. — A450

Perf. 13¼x13½ Syncopated

2016, Dec. 5 **Litho.**

798 A450 100te multi — —

Endangered Mammals — A451

No. 799: a, Martes martes. b, Martes foina.

Perf. 13¼ Syncopated

2016, Dec. 5 **Litho.**

799 A451 200te Pair, #a-b 3.50 3.50

Printed in sheets of 8, 4 each of Nos. 799a-799b.

Souvenir Sheet

Alakol Nature Reserve A452

No. 800: a, Larus relictus. b, Pelecanus crispus. c, Perca schrenki.

Perf. 12¾x13¼ Syncopated

2016, Dec. 8 **Litho.**

800 A452 200te Sheet of 3, #a-c 5.00 5.00

Souvenir Sheet

28th Winter Universiade, Almaty — A453

Perf. 13¼ Syncopated

2016, Dec. 8 **Litho.**
801 A453 300te multi 2.60 2.60

Sauran Ruins — A454

Perf. 13¼ Syncopated

2016, Dec. 27 **Litho.**
802 A454 100te multi .95 .95

No. 802 was printed in sheets of 8 + label.

Astana Circus — A455

Perf. 13¼ Syncopated

2016, Dec. 27 **Litho.**
803 A455 150te multi 1.40 1.40

Souvenir Sheet

Endangered Flora — A456

No. 804: a, Iridodictyum kolpokowskianum. b, Malus sieversii. c, Crocus altavicus.

Perf. 13¼ Syncopated

2016, Dec. 27 **Litho.**
804 A456 200te Sheet of 3, #a-c 5.00 5.00

Fayzulla Galimzhanov (1891-1942) — A457

Perf. 13¼ Syncopated

2016, Dec. 30 **Litho.**
805 A457 100te multi .95 .95

Alash Orda Provisional Government, cent. (in 2017).

Gold and Silver Medalists at the 2016 Summer Paralympics — A458

No. 806: a, Gold medalist swimmer Zulfiya Gabidullina. b, Silver medalist power lifter Raushan Koyshibayeva.

Perf. 13½ Syncopated

2016, Dec. 30 **Litho.**
806 A458 200te Horiz. pair, #a-b 3.50 3.50

Souvenir Sheet

New Year A459

Perf. 13½ Syncopated

2016, Dec. 30 **Litho.**
807 A459 (218te) multi 1.90 1.90

28th Winter Universiade, Almaty — A460

Perf. 13½ Syncopated

2017, Jan. 30 **Litho.**
808 A460 200te multi 1.90 1.90

Kazakhstan Olympic Committee, 25th Anniv. — A461

Perf. 13½ Syncopated

2017, Mar. 2 **Litho.**
809 A461 100te multi 1.00 1.00

Expo 2017 Emblem Type of 2015 and

Expo 2017 Emblem
A462 A463

2017, Mar. 7 **Litho.** ***Perf. 13½x13***

810 A404	10te blk & orange	.30	.25
811 A404	50te blk & green	.30	.25
812 A462	(130te) red & blue	1.25	1.25
813 A463	(218te) blk & ultra	2.10	2.10
	Nos. 810-813 (4)	3.95	3.85

Nazir Tyuryakulov (1892-1937), Diplomat — A464

Kazybek (1667-1764), Bey
A465 A466

2017, Mar. 14 **Litho.** ***Perf. 13½x13***

814 A464	1te yel & blk	.30	.25
815 A465	5te lt bl & blk	.30	.25
816 A466	100te org yel & blk	1.00	1.00
	Nos. 814-816 (3)	1.60	1.50

Expo 2017, Astana — A467

2017, July 12 **Litho.** ***Perf. 13¼***
817 A467 300te multi 2.75 2.75

Souvenir Sheet

New Year 2017 (Year of the Rooster) A468

2017, Aug. 7 **Litho.** ***Perf.***
818 A468 300te multi 2.75 2.75

KazEOSat-1 A469

2017, Aug. 14 **Litho.** ***Perf. 12***
819 A469 (220te) multi 2.10 2.10

Kazakhstan No. 1 — A470

2017, Aug. 21 **Litho.** ***Perf. 12***
820 A470 (220te) multi 2.00 2.00

Kazakhstan postage stamps, 25th anniv.

Souvenir Sheet

Uncia Uncia A471

No. 821: a, Head of adult snow leopard. b, Snow leopard on rock ledge. c, Snow leopard kittens.

2017, Aug. 28 **Litho.** ***Perf. 12***
821 A471 300te Sheet of 3, #a-c 8.50 8.50

Novruz — A472

2017, Aug. 31 **Litho.** ***Perf.***
822 A472 300te multi 2.75 2.75

No. 822 was printed in sheets of 4.

Mausoleum of Khoja Ahmed Yasawi, Turkestan A473

2017, Aug. 31 **Litho.** ***Perf. 13x13¼***
823 A473 750te multi 7.00 7.00

Europa.

KazTransOil, 20th Anniv. — A474

2017, Sept. 8 **Litho.** ***Perf. 12***
824 A474 50te multi .50 .50

Diplomatic Relations Between Kazakhstan and Belarus, 25th Anniv. — A475

2017, Sept. 16 **Litho.** ***Perf. 12***
825 A475 (140te) multi 1.40 1.40

See Belarus No. 1061.

Souvenir Sheet

Flora A476

No. 826: a, Berberis iliensis. b, Juniperus sabina.

2017, Sept. 25 **Litho.** ***Perf. 12***
826 A476 200te Sheet of 2, #a-b 3.75 3.75

Miniature Sheet

2017 Automobiles — A477

No. 827: a, JAC S3. b, Hyundai Elantra. c, Peugeot 301. d, Skoda Superb. e, Lada Vesta. f, Kia Sportage.

2017, Oct. 2 **Litho.** ***Perf. 12***
827 A477 100te Sheet of 6, #a-f 5.75 5.75

Ministry of Foreign Affairs, 25th Anniv. — A478

2017, Oct. 10 **Litho.** ***Perf. 13x13½***
828 A478 100te pale blue & dk blue .95 .95

Bracelets, 20th Cent. — A479

Perf. 13¾x13½ Syncopated

2017, Oct. 15 **Litho.**
829 A479 300te multi 3.00 3.00

Mir Interstate Television and Radio Company, 25th Anniv. — A480

2017, Oct. 31 **Litho.** ***Perf. 13½x13***
830 A480 (130te) multi 1.25 1.25

See Belarus No. 1065, Russia No. 7870.

Souvenir Sheet

Attractions of East Kazakhstan Region — A481

No. 831: a, 140te, Khalifa Altai Mosque, Oskemen. b, 200te, Kozy Korpesh and Bayan Sulu Mausoleum, Tansyk.

2017, Nov. 3 **Litho.** ***Perf. 12***
831 A481 Sheet of 2, #a-b, + 2 labels 3.25 3.25

Souvenir Sheet

Karatau Nature Reserve A482

No. 832: a, Ovis ammon nigrimontana. b, Mustela erminea. c, Hedysarum mind-shelkense bajt.

2017, Nov. 6 **Litho.** ***Perf. 13x13½***
832 A482 200te Sheet of 2, #a-b 5.75 5.75

Souvenir Sheet

Attractions of Jambyl Region — A483

No. 833: a, 140te, Karakhan Mausoleum, Taraz. b, 200te, Aisha Bibi and Babaji Khatun Mausoleums, Taraz.

2017, Nov. 15 **Litho.** ***Perf. 12***
833 A483 Sheet of 2, #a-b, + 2 labels 3.25 3.25

Diplomatic Relations Between Kazakhstan and France, 25th Anniv. — A484

No. 834: a, (220te), Eagle and rooster. b, 500te, Bayterek Tower, Astana, and Eiffel Tower, Paris.

2017, Nov. 20 **Litho.** ***Perf. 13½x13***
834 A484 Horiz. pair, #a-b 6.75 6.75

Yurt and Decorated Chest — A485

2017, Nov. 23 **Litho.** ***Perf. 13¼***
835 A485 300te multi 2.75 2.75

New Year 2018 — A486

2017, Dec. 1 **Litho.** ***Perf. 13½x13***
836 A486 (220te) multi 2.10 2.10

No. 836 was printed in sheets of 5, of which there were four different types of sheet margins.

Alash Autonomy, Cent. — A487

2017, Dec. 25 **Litho.** ***Perf. 13½x13***
837 A487 100te multi 1.00 1.00

Kalaushi Begaliev (1927-2006), Prosecutor — A488

2017, Dec. 25 **Litho.** ***Perf. 13½x13***
838 A488 200te multi 2.00 2.00

Polish Gen. Wladyslaw Anders (1892-1970), and His Soldiers in Kazakhstan A489

2017, Dec. 25 **Litho.** ***Perf. 12***
839 A489 500te multi 4.50 4.50

Joint Issue between Kazakhstan & Poland. See Poland No. 4321.

Conference on Interaction and Confidence-Building Measures in Asia, 25th Anniv. — A490

2017, Dec. 26 **Litho.** ***Perf. 13½x13***
840 A490 100te multi 1.00 1.00

Admission to the United Nations, 25th Anniv. — A491

2017, Dec. 26 **Litho.** ***Perf. 13½x13***
841 A491 300te multi 3.00 3.00

Collective Securtiy Treaty, 25th Anniv. — A492

2017, Dec. 27 **Litho.** ***Perf. 13½x13***
842 A492 200te multi 1.90 1.90

Collective Securtiy Treaty Organization, 15th Anniv. — A493

2017, Dec. 27 **Litho.** ***Perf. 13½x13***
843 A493 200te multi 1.90 1.90

Miniature Sheet

Kazakhstan Animated Films, 50th Anniv. — A494

No. 844 — Scenes from *Why the Swallow Has a Tail With Horns*: a, Woman feeding birds. b, Dragon and fox. c, Animals with instruments, sleeping child. d, Bird, insect, fish, flowers. e, Dragons and birds. f, Woman, child and swallow.

2017, Dec. 27 **Litho.** ***Perf. 13½x13***
844 A494 100te Sheet of 6, #a-f 5.75 5.75

Souvenir Sheet

Ethnic Groups in Kazakhstan — A495

No. 845: a, Polish man and woman (denomination at UL). b, Turkish man and woman (denomination at UR).

2017, Dec. 27 **Litho.** ***Perf. 12***
845 A495 150te Sheet of 2, #a-b 3.00 3.00

Souvenir Sheet

New Year 2018 (Year of the Dog) A496

2018, Jan. 1 **Litho.** ***Perf.***
846 A496 300te multi 3.00 3.00

Bukhar Zhirau Kalkamanuli (1668-1771), Poet A497

Kurmangazy Sagyrbaey (1818-89), Composer A498

2018, Jan. 1 **Litho.** ***Perf. 13½x13***
847 A497 1te buff & black .30 .25
848 A498 5te lt blue & black .30 .25

Ursus Arctos Isabellinus — A499

2018, Jan. 1 **Litho.** ***Perf. 13x13½***
849 A499 10te blue vio & blk .30 .25
850 A499 20te green & black .30 .25
851 A499 100te brown & black 1.00 1.00
852 A499 200te brt blue & black 2.00 2.00
Nos. 849-852 (4) 3.60 3.50

Souvenir Sheet

Kazcosmos, 25th Anniv. — A500

No. 853: a, Rocket launch and satellite (40mm diameter). b, Kazakh cosmonauts (53x38mm).

Perf. (#853a), Perf. 13x13½ (#853b)
Litho. With Foil Application
2018, May 23
853 A500 900te Sheet of 2, #a-b 17.00 17.00

Astana as National Capital, 20th Anniv. — A501

2018, June 25 **Litho.** ***Perf. 12***
854 A501 (250te) multi 2.40 2.40

Magzhan Zhumabayev (1893-1938), Poet — A502

2018, June 25 **Litho.** ***Perf. 12***
855 A502 (250te) multi 2.40 2.40

Souvenir Sheet

2018 World Cup Soccer Championships, Russia — A503

2018, July 13 **Litho.** ***Perf.***
856 A503 900te multi 8.50 8.50

Ishim River Pedestrian Bridge, Astana A504

2018, July 30 **Litho.** ***Perf. 12***
857 A504 800te multi 7.50 7.50

Europa. No. 857 was printed in sheets of 3 + label.

ATOM Project for Abolition of Nuclear Testing — A505

2018, Aug. 28 **Litho.** ***Perf. 13x13½***
858 A505 300te multi 2.60 2.60

Souvenir Sheet

2018 Winter Olympics, Pyeongchang, South Korea — A506

No. 859 — Mogul skier with denomination and country name in: a, Dull rose. b, Gold.

Litho. & Embossed With Foil Application

2018, Sept. 3 ***Perf. 12¼x12***
859 A506 900te Sheet of 2, #a-b 16.00 16.00

Souvenir Sheet

West Kazakhstan Region — A507

No. 860: a, 140te, Academy Building, Oral. b, 250te, Kazakh Drama Theater, Oral.

2018, Sept. 7 Litho. *Perf. 12*
860 A507 Sheet of 2, #a-b, + 2 labels 3.50 3.50

Souvenir Sheet

Karaganda Region — A508

No. 861: a, 140te, Unity For The People Monument, Ulytau. b, 250te, Karaganda Region Central Mosque, Karaganda.

2018, Sept. 10 Litho. *Perf. 12*
861 A508 Sheet of 2, #a-b, + 2 labels 3.50 3.50

Souvenir Sheet

Aleksander Kolyadin, 2018 Paralympics Cross-country Skiing Gold Medalist — A509

No. 862 — Kolyadin: a, 800te, Standing. b, 900te, Racing.

Litho. & Embossed With Foil Application

2018, Sept. 14 *Perf. 12¾*
862 A509 Sheet of 2, #a-b 15.00 15.00

Souvenir Sheet

Ursus Arctos Isabellinus — A510

No. 863: a, 500te, Bear. b, 600te, Bear, horiz.

2018, Sept. 17 Litho. *Perf. 12*
863 A510 Sheet of 2, #a-b 9.75 9.75

Jewelry — A511

Litho. & Embossed With Foil Application

2018, Sept. 21 *Perf. 13x13½*
864 A511 300te sil & multi 2.60 2.60

Miniature Sheet

Items in National Museums — A512

No. 865: a, Square piece of jewelry with large stone at center. b, Saddle, 20th cent. c, Tie belt. d, Kobyz (string instrument). e, Bracelet, 19th cent.

Litho. & Embossed With Foil Application

2018, Sept. 24 *Perf. 13¼*
865 A512 600te Sheet of 5, #a-e 26.00 26.00

Miniature Sheet

Industries — A513

No. 866: a, Seamstresses in shop, sewing machine. b, Cotton production. c, Textiles, thread spools, flowers, pillow. d, Shoemakers, shoes and boot, vert. e, Workers at machinery, machined parts, vert. f, Seamstresses in shop, finished garments, vert.

Perf. 12x12¼, 12¼x12

2018, Sept. 28 Litho.
866 A513 300te Sheet of 6, #a-f 16.00 16.00

Nauryz (New Year) — A514

2018, Oct. 5 Litho. *Perf. 13*
867 A514 500te multi 4.50 4.50

Old Almaty Post and Telegraph Office A515

Kazakhstan No. 1 — A516

Children's Drawings A517

Drone, Robot and Modern Postal Equipment A518

Litho. & Embossed With Foil Application

2018 *Perf. 12*

868	A515	(250te) gold & multi		2.25	2.25
869	A516	(250te) gold & multi		2.25	2.25
870	A517	(250te) gold & multi		2.25	2.25
871	A518	(250te) gold & multi		2.25	2.25
		Nos. 868-871 (4)		9.00	9.00

Kazakh Postal Service, 25th anniv. Issued: No. 868, 10/9; No. 869, 10/16; No. 870, 10/23; No. 871, 10/30.

Sixth Congress of Leaders of World and Traditional Religions, Astana — A519

2018, Oct. 11 Litho. *Perf. 13½x13*
872 A519 (250te) multi 2.25 2.25

Utegen Seitov (1923-97), Prosecutor — A520

2018, Oct. 12 Litho. *Perf. 13½x13*
873 A520 (250te) multi 2.25 2.25

Souvenir Sheet

Animals in Almaty State Nature Reserve A521

No. 874: a, Capra sibirica. b, Parnassius apollo. c, Mustela erminea.

2018, Oct. 19 Litho. *Perf. 13½x13*
874 A521 500te Sheet of 3, #a-c 13.00 13.00

Souvenir Sheet

Endangered Trees — A522

No. 875: a, 250te, Armeniaca vulgaris. b, 300te, Louiseania ulmifolia.

2018, Oct. 26 Litho. *Perf. 12*
875 A522 Sheet of 2, #a-b 4.50 4.50

Kazakhstan's 2017-18 Seat on United Nations Security Council — A523

2018, Nov. 26 Litho. *Perf. 12*
876 A523 (250te) multi 2.25 2.25

Portrait of Latipa Hodzhikova, by Mariya Lizogub A524

2018, Nov. 27 Litho. *Perf. 13x13½*
877 A524 500te multi 4.50 4.50

Hodzikova (1892-1960), painter.

Miniature Sheet

New Year 2019 A525

No. 878: a, Christmas tree ornaments, denomination at UR (28x20mm). b, Christmas tree ornaments, denomination at UL (28x20mm). c, Snowman, Christmas tree and gifts (28x40mm). d, Christmas tree and gifts (28x40mm).

2018, Dec. 4 Litho. *Perf. 12*
878 A525 500te Sheet of 4, #a-d 17.50 17.50

Ermek Serkebayev (1926-2013), Singer — A526

2018, Dec. 11 Litho. *Perf. 13x13½*
879 A526 (250te) multi 2.25 2.25

Publication of Epic Poem "Kyz Zhibek," 125th Anniv. A527

Ayteke Bey Baybekuly (1644-1700), Poet A528

Saken Seifullin (1894-1939), Writer A529

Ilyas Zhansugurov (1894-1938), Poet A530

Turar Ryskulov (1894-1938), Communist Politician A531

Nurken Abdirov (1919-42), Military Aviator A532

Beimbet Mailin (1894-1938), Writer A533

Lutra Lutra Seistanica
A534

2019 Litho. *Perf. 13½x13*

880 A527 5te lt bl & blk .30 .25
881 A528 10te blk & yel .30 .25
882 A529 20te blk & pink .30 .25
883 A530 50te blk & lt bl .30 .25
884 A531 (130te) red & blue .70 .70
885 A532 200te pink & blk 1.10 1.10
886 A533 (250te) blk & lilac 1.40 1.40

Perf. 13x13½

887 A534 500te brt blue & blk 2.75 2.75
Nos. 880-887 (8) 7.15 6.95

Issued: 5te, 4/22; 10te, 4/1; 20te, 4/15; 50te, 4/4; (130te), 4/18; 200te, 4/11; (250te), 4/8; 500te, 4/25.

Egemen Kazakhstan Newspaper, Cent. — A535

2019, July 17 Litho. *Perf. 13*
888 A535 100te multi .95 .95

Souvenir Sheet

New Year 2019 (Year of the Pig) A536

2019, July 22 Litho. *Perf.*
889 A536 500te multi 4.25 4.25

Eurasian Economic Union, 5th Anniv. — A537

2019, Aug. 9 Litho. *Perf. 13*
890 A537 500te multi 4.25 4.25

Universal Postal Union, 145th Anniv. — A538

2019, Sept. 16 Litho. *Perf. 12*
891 A538 1000te multi 7.75 7.75

Souvenir Sheet

Space Communications, 15th Anniv. — A539

No. 892: a, Satellite dishes (40x28mm). b, Satellite in space (40mm diameter).

Perf. 12 (#892a), Perf. (#892b)
Litho. With Foil Application
2019, Sept. 16
892 A539 300te Sheet of 2, #a-b 5.00 5.00

Souvenir Sheet

Convention of the Rights of the Child, 25th Anniv. — A540

No. 893: a, Child drawing picture of astronaut holding Kazakhstan flag. b, Father, mother and daughter. c, Child in wheelchair.

Perf. 13¼x13½ Syncopated
2019, Nov. 4 Litho.
893 A540 (140te) Sheet of 3, #a-c 3.50 3.50

Mohandas K. Gandhi (1869-1948), Indian Nationalist Leader — A541

Perf. 13½x13¼ Syncopated
2019, Nov. 11 Litho.
894 A541 500te purple brn 4.25 4.25

Souvenir Sheet

Arrival in Petropavl of First Trans-Siberian Railway Train, 125th Anniv. — A542

Litho. With Foil Application
2019, Nov. 14 *Perf. 13¼*
895 A542 1000te multi 8.00 8.00

Souvenir Sheet

Children's Art — A543

No. 896 — Various works of children's art with large "A" at: a, UL. b, LL. c, UR.

2019, Nov. 25 Litho. *Perf. 12*
896 A543 (130te) Sheet of 3, #a-c 2.50 2.50

Souvenir Sheet

Flowers and "Congratulations" in Various Languages — A544

Litho. & Embossed
2019, Nov. 27 *Perf.*
897 A544 800te multi 5.25 5.25

Scene From Animated Film *Proud Girl* — A545

Scene From Animated Film *Sheep and Goat* — A546

Scene From Animated Film *Er Tostik and the Dragon* — A547

2019, Dec. 3 Litho. *Perf. 12*
898 Horiz. strip of 3 5.75 5.75
a. A545 300te multi 1.90 1.90
b. A546 300te multi 1.90 1.90
c. A547 300te multi 1.90 1.90

Printed in sheets containing two each Nos. 898a-898c.

Yuri Gagarin (1934-68), First Man in Space — A548

2019, Dec. 9 Litho. *Perf. 13x13½*
899 A548 1000te multi 6.25 6.25

Miniature Sheet

Mushrooms — A549

No. 900: a, Lactarius resimus. b, Morchella steppicola. c, Cantharellus cibarius. d, Leccinum vulpinum. e, Marasmius oreades. f, Boletus edulis.

Litho. & Embossed
2019, Dec. 10 *Perf. 13x13½*
900 A549 (280te) Sheet of 6, #a-f 10.50 10.50

Miniature Sheet

Butterflies — A550

No. 901: a, Papilio alexanor. b, Zerynthia polyxena. c, Iphiclides podalirius. d, Melanargia russiae. e, Vanessa atalanta. f, Pieris brassicae.

Litho. & Embossed
2019, Dec. 11 *Perf. 13x13½*
901 A550 (280te) Sheet of 6, #a-f 10.50 10.50

Lutra Lutra Seistanica — A551

No. 902: a, River otter on rock. b, River otter pups.

2019, Dec. 12 Litho. *Perf. 12x12¼*
902 A551 600te Pair, #a-b 7.50 7.50

Souvenir Sheet

Europa A552

No. 903 — Aquila chrysaetos: a, In flight. b, Head. c, Chick.

2019, Dec. 19 Litho. *Perf. 12x12¼*
903 A552 500te Sheet of 3, #a-c 9.50 9.50

Express Mail Services, 20th Anniv. A553

2019, Dec. 31 Litho. *Perf. 13x13½*
904 A553 310te multi 2.00 2.00

Souvenir Sheet

Aquatic Flowers A554

No. 905: a, Nymphaea alba. b, Nelumbo caspica.

2019, Dec. 31 Litho. *Perf. 12*
905 A554 310te Sheet of 2, #a-b 4.00 4.00

Miniature Sheet

Heavy Industry A555

No. 906: a, Mining. b, Iron factory. c, Nuclear power plant, smokestack, dam. d, Oil derricks. e, Train and truck factories. f, Chemical plant.

2019, Dec. 31 Litho. *Perf. 12*
906 A555 300te Sheet of 6, #a-f 11.50 11.50

Souvenir Sheet

Barsa-Kelmes Nature Reserve — A556

No. 907: a, Saiga tatarica. b, Equus hemionus onager. c, Tragopogon porrifolius.

2019, Dec. 31 Litho. *Perf. 13½x13*
907 A556 500te Sheet of 3, #a-c 9.75 9.75

Souvenir Sheet

Kostanay Region A557

No. 908: a, 140te, Yurt. b, 200te, Steam locomotive.

2019, Dec. 31 Litho. *Perf. 12*
908 A557 Sheet of 2, #a-b 2.25 2.25

Space Post, 50th Anniv. A558

2019, Dec. 31 Litho. ***Perf. 12¾***
909 A558 (310te) multi 2.50 2.50

No. 909 was printed in sheets of 4 + label.

Amina Umurazkova (1919-2006), Actress A559

Gulzkauhar Chumbalova (1919-58), Painter A560

Serali Lapin (1869-1919), Writer — A561

2019, Dec. 31 Litho. ***Perf. 13x13½***

910 A559 (310te) multi		2.00	2.00
911 A560 (310te) multi		2.00	2.00
912 A561 (310te) multi		2.00	2.00
	Nos. 910-912 (3)	6.00	6.00

National Museum, Nur-Sultan A562

No. 913 — Various photographs of National Museum with denomination at: a, UR. b, UL.

2019, Dec. 31 Litho. ***Perf. 12***
913 A562 300te Pair, #a-b 4.00 4.00

No. 913 was printed in sheets of 4 containing 2 each Nos. 913a-913b.

Souvenir Sheet

Kyzylorda Oblast — A563

No. 914: a, 140te, Baikonur Cosmodrome. b, 200te, Kyzylorda Railroad Station.

2019, Dec. 31 Litho. ***Perf. 12***
914 A563 Sheet of 2, #a-b 2.25 2.25

Miniature Sheet

Puppies A564

No. 915: a, Bulldog. b, Dalmatian. c, Beagle. d, German shepherd. e, Dachshund. f, Pembroke Welsh corgi. g, Siberian husky. h, Chow chow.

2019, Dec. 31 Litho. ***Perf. 13x13½***
915 A564 200te Sheet of 8, #a-h 10.50 10.50

Sapargali Begalin (1895-1983), Writer A565

Abai Kunanbayev (1845-1904), Poet A566

2020, May 4 Litho. ***Perf. 13½x13***

916 A565	50te	blk & lt blue	.40	.40
917 A566	(310te)	blk & dull blue	2.00	2.00

A567

A568

Fish — A569

Designs: 5te, Alosa kessleri volgensis. 10te, Salmo trutta caspius. 20te, Hucho taimen. 60te, Acipenser nudiventris. (130te), Stenodus leucichthys nelma. 200te, Salmo trutta araiensis.

2020, May 12 Litho. ***Perf. 13x13½***

918 A567	5te	pale blue green & blk	.30	.25
919 A568	10te	blk & yellow	.30	.25
920 A568	20te	blk & pink	.30	.25
921 A568	60te	blk & lt blue	.45	.45
922 A569	(130te)	red & blk	.95	.95
923 A568	200te	rose & blk	1.40	1.40
	Nos. 918-923 (6)		3.70	3.55

Kazakhstanskaya Pravda Newspaper, Cent. — A570

2020, June 22 Litho. ***Perf. 13x13½***
924 A570 100te lil & blk .80 .80

Campaign Against Corruption — A571

Perf. 13x13¼ Syncopated
2020, June 24 Litho.
925 A571 200te multi 1.60 1.60

United Nations, 75th Anniv. — A572

2020, June 27 Litho. ***Perf. 13x13½***
926 A572 (280te) lt blue & blk 2.25 2.25

Souvenir Sheet

New Year 2020 (Year of the Rat) A573

2020, Aug. 17 Litho. ***Perf.***
927 A573 500te multi 4.00 4.00

Constitution of Kazakhstan, 25th Anniv. — A574

Litho. With Foil Application
2020, Aug. 25 ***Perf. 13x13½***
928 A574 (130te) multi 1.10 1.10

Assembly of People of Kazakhstan, 25th Anniv. — A575

2020, Sept. 1 Litho. ***Perf. 12¼x12***
929 A575 (130te) multi 1.10 1.10

Zhuban Moldagaliev (1920-88), Poet — A576

2020, Sept. 24 Litho. ***Perf. 13x13½***
930 A576 200te multi 1.60 1.60

Ludwig van Beethoven (1770-1827), Composer — A577

2020, Oct. 15 Litho. ***Perf. 13¾x13***
931 A577 800te multi 6.00 6.00

No. 931 was printed in sheets of 5 + label.

Souvenir Sheet

Flora and Fauna of West Altai Nature Reserve A578

No. 932: a, Bubo bubo. b, Alces alces. c, Rubus idaeus.

2020, Oct. 21 Litho. ***Perf. 13x13½***
932 A578 500te Sheet of 3, #a-c 11.00 11.00

Batyrkhan Shukenov (1962-2015), Singer — A579

Perf. 13x13¼ Syncopated
2020, Oct. 28 Litho.
933 A579 (380te) black 2.40 2.40

Movie *Kyz Zhibek*, 50th Anniv. — A580

Perf. 13½x13 Syncopated
2020, Nov. 6 Litho.
934 A580 300te multi 2.25 2.25

No. 934 was printed in sheets of 4 + central label.

Movie *The End of Ataman*, 50th Anniv. — A581

Perf. 13½x13 Syncopated
2020, Nov. 13 Litho.
935 A581 300te multi 2.25 2.25

No. 935 was printed in sheets of 4 + central label.

Abu Nasr al-Farabi (c. 872-c. 950), Philosopher A582

Litho. With Foil Application
2020, Dec. 21 ***Perf. 13x13¼***
936 A582 500te red & multi 2.50 2.50

Dauletkerey Shygayuly (1820-87), Musician — A583

Perf. 13¼ Syncopated
2020, Dec. 22 Litho.
937 A583 300te multi 1.50 1.50

No. 937 was printed in sheets of 5 + label.

Emblems of UNESCO and Kazakhstan Man and Biosphere National Committee — A584

2020, Dec. 23 Litho. ***Perf. 13½x13***
938 A584 310te multi 1.50 1.50

Miniature Sheet

Minerals A585

No. 939: a, Gold. b, Nephrite. c, Silver. d, Iron. e, Manganese. f, Coal.

Perf. 13¼ Syncopated

2020, Dec. 24 Litho.
939 A585 300te Sheet of 6, #a-f 9.00 9.00

"Happy Postcrossing" A586

2020, Dec. 30 Litho. ***Perf. 13***
940 A586 (140te) multi .70 .70

Children's Drawings — A587

Litho. With Foil Application

2020, Dec. 30 ***Perf. 13½x13***
941 A587 310te red & multi 1.50 1.50

Victory in World War II, 75th anniv.

Baikonur Cosmodrome, 65th Anniv. — A588

Litho. With Foil Application

2020, Dec. 30 ***Perf. 13½x13***
942 A588 500te sil & multi 2.50 2.50

Golden Horde, 750th Anniv. — A589

Litho. With Foil Application

2020, Dec. 30 ***Perf. 12***
943 A589 750te gold & multi 3.75 3.75

Souvenir Sheet

Transport Workers Day A590

Litho. With Foil Application

2020, Dec. 30 ***Perf. 12x12¼***
944 A590 500te blue & multi 2.50 2.50

Souvenir Sheet

Kasym Khan (1445-1521), Uniter of Kazakh Tribes — A591

Litho. With Foil Application

2020, Dec. 30 ***Perf.***
945 A591 500te gold & multi 2.50 2.50

Souvenir Sheet

Post Riders on Horses Near Landmarks in Kazakhstan — A592

2020, Dec. 30 Litho. ***Perf. 13½***
946 A592 800te multi 4.75 4.75

Europa. Ancient Postal Routes.

Souvenir Sheet

Mangystau Region — A593

No. 947: a, 140te, Mt. Sherkala. b, 250te, Beket-Ata Underground Mosque.

2020, Dec. 30 Litho. ***Perf. 12***
947 A593 Sheet of 2, #a-b 1.90 1.90

Miniature Sheet

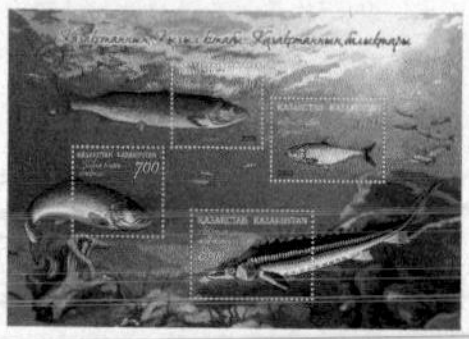

Fish A594

No. 948: a, 500te, Hucho taimen (30x26mm). b, 600te, Alosa kessleri volgensis (37x26mm). c, 700te, Salmo trutta aralensis (30x28mm). d, 8000te, Acipenser nudiventris (40x28mm).

Perf. 13½x13 (500te, 600te), 12 (700te, 800te)

2020, Dec. 30 Litho. & Embossed
948 A594 Sheet of 4, #a-d 13.00 13.00

Independence, 30th Anniv. — A595

Litho. With Foil Application

2021, Feb. 25 ***Perf. 13***
949 A595 (130te) gold & multi .65 .65

Zhambyl Zhabayev (1846-1945), Folksinger — A596

2021, Sept. 15 Litho. ***Perf. 13x13½***
950 A596 10te dark blue .30 .25

Kazhimukan Munaitpasov (1871-1948), Wrestler — A597

2021, Sept. 15 Litho. ***Perf. 13½x13***
951 A597 50te blk & lt blue .30 .25

L. N. Gumilyov Eurasian National University, 25th Anniv. — A598

2021, Sept. 21 Litho. ***Perf. 13x13½***
952 A598 (300te) brt blue 1.50 1.50

Gazella Subgutturosa A599

Ovis Ammon Karelini A600

Cervus Elaphus Bactrianus A601

Ovis Vignei Arcal A602

2021, Sept. 24 Litho. ***Perf. 13½x13***
953 A599 5te lt blue & blk .30 .25
954 A600 20te blk & pink .30 .25
955 A601 (130te) multi .65 .65
956 A602 200te cerise & blk 1.00 1.00
Nos. 953-956 (4) 2.25 2.15

Yuri Gagarin (1934-68), Cosmonaut — A603

2021, Oct. 5 Litho. ***Perf. 13¼***
957 A603 1000te multi 5.00 5.00

First manned spaceflight, 60th anniv.

Radio Broadcasting in Kazakhstan, Cent. — A604

2021, Oct. 7 Litho. ***Perf. 13x13½***
958 A604 100te black & lt blue .50 .50

Independence of Kazakhstan, 30th Anniv. and United Arab Emirates, 50th Anniv. — A605

No. 959: a, Flags of Kazakhstan and United Arab Emirates. b, Anniversary emblems.

Litho. With Foil Application

2021, Oct. 10 ***Perf. 12***
959 A605 550te Horiz. pair, #a-b 5.50 5.50

See United Arab Emirates No.

Souvenir Sheet

New Year 2021 (Year of the Ox) A606

2021, Oct. 18 Litho. ***Perf.***
960 A606 500te multi 2.50 2.50

Regional Communications Commonwealth, 30th Anniv. — A607

2021, Oct. 20 Litho. ***Perf. 13½x13***
961 A607 (380te) multi 1.90 1.90

Shymkent, 2200th Anniv. — A608

2021, Oct. 29 Litho. ***Perf. 13***
962 A608 (380te) multi 1.90 1.90

Souvenir Sheet

Ablai Khan (1711-81), Khan of the Middle Zhuz and Kazakh Khanate — A609

Litho. With Foil Application

2021, Nov. 22 ***Perf.***
963 A609 500te multi 2.50 2.50

Miniature Sheet

Kittens A610

No. 964: a, Maine coon. b, Abyssinian. c, British. d, Bambino. e, Oriental. f, American curl. g, Scottish fold. h, Bengal.

2021, Nov. 24 Litho. ***Perf. 13½x13***
964 A610 200te Sheet of 8, #a-h 8.00 8.00

Souvenir Sheet

Flora and Fauna of the Altyn-Emel Biosphere Reserve — A611

No. 965: a, Equus przewalskii. b, Mylabris quadripunctata. c, Paeonia tenuifolia.

2021, Nov. 26 Litho. *Perf. 12x12¼*
965 A611 600te Sheet of 3, #a-c 9.00 9.00

Souvenir Sheet

Endangered Animals — A612

No. 966: a, Capreolus pygargus. b, Sus scrofa.

Litho. & Embossed

2021, Nov. 29 *Perf. 13½*
966 A612 800te Sheet of 2, #a-b 8.00 8.00

Europa.

Souvenir Sheets

Attractions of Pavlodar Region — A613

Attractions of North Kazakhstan Region — A614

No. 967: a, 140te, Balanced rock, Bayanaul State National Park. b, 250te, Mashkhur-Jusup Mosque.

No. 968: a, 140te, Karasai and Agyntai Batyrs Memorial Complex. b, 250te, Syrymbet Manor.

2021, Dec. 14 Litho. *Perf. 12x12¼*
967 A613 Sheet of 2, #a-b 2.00 2.00
968 A614 Sheet of 2, #a-b 2.00 2.00

Miniature Sheet

Food Processing in Kazakhstan — A615

No. 969: a, Cows, milk bottling plant, containers of milk. b, Bakery and bread, vert. c, Butchers cutting meat, meat processing plant conveyor belt. d, Canned vegetables, vegetable canning production line. e, Combine in grain field, grain processing plant, bags of flour, vert. f, Sunflower, sunflower oil production line, bottles of oil.

Perf. 12x12¼ (horiz. stamps), 12¼x12 (vert. stamps)

2021, Dec. 15 Litho.
969 A615 300te Sheet of 6, #a-f 9.00 9.00

Sports of the 2020 Summer Olympics — A616

No. 970: a, Wrestling. b, Boxing.

2021, Dec. 22 Litho. *Perf. 12x12¼*
970 A616 800te Pair, #a-b 8.00 8.00

Printed in sheets containing two each of Nos. 970a-970b. The 2020 Summer Olympics was postponed until 2021 because of the COVID-19 pandemic.

Kazakhstan Gold Medalists at the 2020 Summer Paralympics — A617

No. 971: a, David Degtyarev, powerlifting (without cap). b, Daulet Temirzhan, judo (wearing cap).

2021, Dec. 22 Litho. *Perf. 12¼x12*
971 A617 200te Horiz. pair, #a-b 2.00 2.00

Printed in sheets containing two pairs. The 2020 Summer Paralympics was postponed until 2021 because of the COVID-19 pandemic.

Souvenir Sheet

Medical Workers' Day A618

Litho. With Foil Application

2021, Dec. 24 *Perf. 12x12¼*
972 A618 500te met blue & multi 2.50 2.50

Ungulates A619

No. 9730: a, Gazella subgutturosa. b, Cervus hanglu basctrianus.

2021, Dec. 27 Litho. *Perf. 13x13½*
973 A619 900te Pair, #a-b 9.00 9.00

Printed in sheets containing two each of Nos. 973a-973b.

Souvenir Sheet

Communication and Information Workers' Day — A620

Litho. With Foil Application

2021, Dec. 27 *Perf. 12x12¼*
974 A620 500te met blue & multi 2.50 2.50

Closure of Semipalatinsk Nuclear Weapons Test Site, 30th Anniv. — A621

2021, Dec. 28 Litho. *Perf. 13x13¼*
975 A621 300te multi 1.50 1.50

SEMI-POSTAL STAMPS

Cartoons SP1

a, Mother and child. b, Cow, rabbit. c, Horses.

1994, Nov. 3 Litho. *Perf. 12½x12*
B1 SP1 1te +30ti Block of 3 + label .75 .75

KENYA

'ke-nyə

LOCATION — East Africa, bordering on the Indian Ocean
GOVT. — Republic
AREA — 224,960 sq. mi.
POP. — 28,808,658 (1999 est.)
CAPITAL — Nairobi

Formerly a part of the British colony of Kenya, Uganda, Tanganyika, Kenya gained independence Dec. 12, 1963.

100 Cents = 1 Shilling

Catalogue values for all unused stamps in this country are for Never Hinged items.

Treetop Hotel and Elephants — A1

Designs: 5c, Cattle ranching. 10c, Wood carving. 15c, Riveter. 20c, Timber industry. 30c, Jomo Kenyatta facing Mt. Kenya. 40c, Fishing industry. 50c, Flag and emblem. 65c, Pyrethrum industry (daisies). 1sh, National Assembly bldg. 2sh, Harvesting coffee. 5sh, Harvesting tea. 10sh, Mombasa port. 20sh, Royal College, Nairobi.

Perf. 14x14½

1963, Dec. 12 Photo. Unwmk.

Size: 21x17½mm

1	A1	5c bl, buff & dk brn		.30	.40
2	A1	10c brown		.30	.25
	a.	Booklet pane of 4		.30	
3	A1	15c deep magenta		.80	.25
	a.	Booklet pane of 4		4.00	
4	A1	20c yel grn & dk brn		.30	.25
	a.	Booklet pane of 4		.40	
5	A1	30c yel & black		.30	.25
	a.	Booklet pane of 4		.55	
6	A1	40c blue & brown		.30	.25
7	A1	50c grn, blk & dp car		.50	.25
	a.	Booklet pane of 4		2.50	
8	A1	65c steel blue & yel		.45	.55

Perf. 14½

Size: 41½x25½mm

9	A1	1sh multicolored		.30	.25
10	A1	1.30sh grn, brn & blk		4.25	.25
11	A1	2sh multicolored		1.00	.30
12	A1	5sh ultra, yel grn & brn		1.00	.80
13	A1	10sh brn & dark brn		7.50	2.25
14	A1	20sh pink & grnsh blk		3.25	*8.00*
		Nos. 1-14 (14)		20.55	14.30

President Jomo Kenyatta and Flag of Kenya — A2

Flag and: 15c, Cockerel. 50c, African lion. 1.30sh, Hartlaub's touraco. 2.50sh, Nandi flame flower.

1964, Dec. 12 Photo. *Perf. 13x12½*

15	A2	15c lt violet & multi	.30	.25
16	A2	30c dk blue & multi	.30	.25
17	A2	50c dk brown & multi	.30	.25
18	A2	1.30sh multicolored	2.75	.50
19	A2	2.50sh multicolored	.40	*3.25*
		Nos. 15-19 (5)	4.05	*4.50*

Establishment of the Republic of Kenya, Dec. 12, 1964.

Greater Kudu — A3

Animals: 5c, Thomson's gazelle. 10c, Sable antelope. 15c, Aardvark. 20c, Senegal bush baby. 30c, Warthog. 40c, Zebra. 50c, Buffalo. 65c, Black rhinoceros. 70c, Ostrich. 1.30sh, Elephant. 1.50sh, Bat-eared fox. 2.50sh, Cheetah. 5sh, Vervet monkey. 10sh, Giant pangolin. 20sh, Lion.

1966-69 Unwmk. *Perf. 14x14½*

Size: 21x17mm

20	A3	5c gray, blk & org	.30	.25
21	A3	10c blk & yel grn	.30	.25
22	A3	15c dp org & blk	.30	.25
23	A3	20c ultra, lt brn & blk	.30	.25
24	A3	30c lt ultra & blk	.30	.25
25	A3	40c ocher & blk	.45	.25
26	A3	50c dp orange & blk	.45	.25
27	A3	65c dp yel grn & blk	.85	*2.00*
28	A3	70c rose lake & blk	3.25	1.75

Perf. 14½

Size: 41x25mm

29	A3	1sh gray bl, ol & blk	.85	.25
30	A3	1.30sh yel grn & blk	3.00	.35
31	A3	1.50sh brn org, brn & black	2.15	*3.00*
32	A3	2.50sh ol bis, yel & blk	3.00	1.25
33	A3	5sh brt grn, ultra & black	.65	.75
34	A3	10sh red brn, bis & black	2.40	*3.00*
35	A3	20sh ocher, bis, gold & black	6.85	*12.00*
		Nos. 20-35 (16)	25.40	26.10

Issued: No. 28, 31, 9/15/69; others, 12/12/66.

Branched Murex — A4

Sea shells: 5c, Morning pink. 10c, Episcopal miter. 15c, Strawberry-top shell. 20c, Humpback cowrie. 30c, variable abalone. 40c, Flame-top shell. 50c, Violet sailor. 60c, Bull's-mouth helmet. 70c, Pearly nautilus. 1.50sh, Neptune's trumpet. 2.50sh, Mediterranean tulip shell. 5sh, Fluctuating turban. 10sh, Textile cone. 20sh, Scorpion shell.

1971 Dec. 13 Photo. *Perf. 14½x14*
Size: 17x21mm

36 A4 5c bister & multi .30 *.55*
37 A4 10c dull grn & multi .30 .30
a. Booklet pane of 4 .60
38 A4 15c tan & multi .30 .30
a. Booklet pane of 4 .60
39 A4 20c tan & multi .30 .30
a. Booklet pane of 4 .75
40 A4 30c yellow & multi .30 .30
a. Booklet pane of 4 2.25
41 A4 40c gray & multi .30 .30
a. Booklet pane of 4 2.25
42 A4 50c buff & multi (*Janthina globosa*) .40 .35
a. Booklet pane of 4 3.50
43 A4 60c lilac & multi .40 *2.15*
44 A4 70c gray grn & multi (Nautilus pompileus) .55 *1.85*
a. Booklet pane of 4 5.00

Perf. 14½
Size: 25x41mm

45 A4 1sh ocher & multi .40 .45
46 A4 1.50sh pale grn & multi 1.25 .35
47 A4 2.50sh vio gray & multi 1.75 .35
48 A4 5sh lemon & multi 2.00 *.30*
49 A4 10sh multicolored 2.25 *.30*
50 A4 20sh gray & multi 3.25 *.30*
Nos. 36-50 (15) 14.05 *8.45*

Used values of Nos. 48-50 are for stamps with printed cancellations.
For surcharges see Nos. 53-55.

Nos. 42, 44 with Revised Inscription

1974, Jan. 20 *Perf. 14½x14*

51 A4 50c (Janthina janthina) 13.50 3.75
52 A4 70c (Nautilus pompilius) 11.75 7.00

Nos. 46-47, 50 Surcharged with New Value and 2 Bars

1975, Nov. 17 Photo. *Perf. 14½*

53 A4 2sh on 1.50sh multi 6.75 *5.00*
54 A4 3sh on 2.50sh multi 10.25 *19.25*
55 A4 40sh on 20sh multi 6.75 *12.00*
Nos. 53-55 (3) 23.75 *36.25*

Microwave Tower — A5

Designs: 1sh, Cordless switchboard and operators, horiz. 2sh, Telephones of 1880, 1930 and 1976. 3sh, Message switching center, horiz.

1976, Apr. 15 Litho. *Perf. 14½*

56 A5 50c blue & multi .30 .25
57 A5 1sh red & multi .30 .25
58 A5 2sh yellow & multi .30 .35
59 A5 3sh multicolored .45 .45
a. Souvenir sheet of 4 2.00 2.00
Nos. 56-59 (4) 1.35 1.30

Telecommunication development in East Africa. No. 59a contains 4 stamps similar to Nos. 56-59 with simulated perforations.

Akii Bua, Ugandan Hurdler — A6

Designs: 1sh, Filbert Bayi, Tanzanian runner. 2sh, Steve Muchoki, Kenyan boxer. 3sh, Olympic torch, flags of Kenya, Tanzania and Uganda.

1976, July 5 Litho. *Perf. 14½*

60 A6 50c blue & multi .30 .25
61 A6 1sh red & multi .30 .25
62 A6 2sh yellow & multi .40 .35
63 A6 3sh blue & multi .80 .55
a. Souv. sheet of 4, #60-63, perf. 13 6.50 6.50
Nos. 60-63 (4) 1.80 1.40

21st Olympic Games, Montreal, Canada, July 17-Aug. 1.

Tanzania-Zambia Railway — A7

Designs: 1sh, Nile Bridge, Uganda. 2sh, Nakuru Station, Kenya. 3sh, Class A locomotive, 1896.

1976, Oct. 4 Litho. *Perf. 14½*

64 A7 50c lilac & multi .40 .25
65 A7 1sh emerald & multi .70 .25
66 A7 2sh brt rose & multi 1.40 1.00
67 A7 3sh yellow & multi 1.50 1.40
a. Souv. sheet of 4, #64-67, perf. 13 9.00 9.00
Nos. 64-67 (4) 4.00 2.90

Rail transport in East Africa.
No. 67a exists imperf., value $22.50.

Nile Perch — A8

Game Fish: 1sh, Tilapia. 3sh, Sailfish. 5sh, Black marlin.

1977, Jan. 10 Litho. *Perf. 14½*

68 A8 50c multicolored .30 .25
69 A8 1sh multicolored .35 .25
70 A8 3sh multicolored 1.10 .60
71 A8 5sh multicolored 1.25 1.00
a. Souvenir sheet of 4, #68-71 11.00 11.00
Nos. 68-71 (4) 3.00 2.10

Festival Emblem and Masai Tribesmen Bleeding Cow — A9

Festival Emblem and: 1sh, Dancers from Uganda. 2sh, Makonde sculpture, Tanzania. 3sh, Tribesmen skinning hippopotamus.

1977, Jan. 15 *Perf. 13½x14*

72 A9 50c multicolored .30 .25
73 A9 1sh multicolored .30 .30
74 A9 2sh multicolored .65 .65
75 A9 3sh multicolored .80 .80
a. Souvenir sheet of 4, #72-75 5.00 5.00
Nos. 72-75 (4) 2.05 2.00

2nd World Black and African Festival, Lagos, Nigeria, Jan. 15-Feb. 12.

Automobile Passing through Village — A10

Safari Rally Emblem and: 1sh, Winner at finish line. 2sh, Car going through washout. 5sh, Car, elephants and Mt. Kenya.

1977, Apr. 5 Litho. *Perf. 14*

76 A10 50c multicolored .30 .25
77 A10 1sh multicolored .30 .35
78 A10 2sh multicolored .45 .55
79 A10 5sh multicolored 1.80 2.10
a. Souvenir sheet of 4, #76-79 5.00 5.00
Nos. 76-79 (4) 2.85 3.25

25th Safari Rally, Apr. 7-11.

Rev. Canon Apolo Kivebulaya A11

1sh, Uganda Cathedral. 2sh, Early grass-topped Cathedral. 5sh, Early tent congregation, Kigezi.

1977, June 20 Litho. *Perf. 14*

80 A11 50c multicolored .30 .25
81 A11 1sh multicolored .30 .25
82 A11 2sh multicolored .35 .40
83 A11 5sh multicolored 1.00 1.25
a. Souvenir sheet of 4, #80-83 1.75 1.75
Nos. 80-83 (4) 1.95 2.15

Church of Uganda, centenary.

Elizabeth II and Prince Philip at Sagana Lodge — A12

Designs: 5sh, "Treetops" observation hut, Aberdare Forest, and elephants, vert. 10sh, Pres. Jomo Kenyatta, Elizabeth II, crossed spears and shield. 15sh, Elizabeth II and Pres. Kenyatta in open automobile. 50sh, Elizabeth II and Prince Philip at window in Treetops.

1977, July 20 Litho. *Perf. 14*

84 A12 2sh multicolored .30 .25
85 A12 5sh multicolored .30 .25
86 A12 10sh multicolored .55 .55
87 A12 15sh multicolored .65 .65
a. Souvenir sheet of 1 1.25 1.25
Nos. 84-87 (4) 1.80 1.70

Souvenir Sheet

88 A12 50sh multicolored 3.50 3.50

Reign of Queen Elizabeth II, 25th anniv.

Pancake Tortoise A13

Wildlife Fund Emblem and; 1sh, Nile crocodile. 2sh, Hunter's hartebeest. 3sh, Red colobus monkey. 5sh, Dugong.

1977, Sept. 26 Litho. *Perf. 14x13½*

89 A13 50c multicolored .50 .25
90 A13 1sh multicolored .70 .30
91 A13 2sh multicolored 1.75 1.75
92 A13 3sh multicolored 2.50 2.50
93 A13 5sh multicolored 2.75 2.75
a. Souvenir sheet of 4, #90-93 9.00 9.00
Nos. 89-93 (5) 8.20 7.55

Endangered species.

Kenya-Ethiopia Border Point — A14

Designs: 1sh, Station wagon at Archer's Post. 2sh, Thika overpass. 5sh, Marsabit Game Lodge and elephant.

1977, Nov. 10 Litho. *Perf. 14*

94 A14 50c multicolored .30 .25
95 A14 1sh multicolored .30 .25
96 A14 2sh multicolored .40 .40
97 A14 5sh multicolored .80 .80
a. Souvenir sheet of 4, #94-97 2.25 2.25
Nos. 94-97 (4) 1.80 1.70

Opening of Nairobi-Addis Ababa highway.

Minerals Found in Kenya — A15

A16

10c, Gypsum. 20c, Trona. 30c, Kyanite. 40c, Amazonite. 50c, Galena. 70c, Silicified wood. 80c, Fluorite. 1sh, Amethyst. 1.50sh, Agate. 2sh, Tourmaline. 3sh, Aquamarine. 5sh, Rhodolite garnet. 10sh, Sapphire. 20sh, Ruby. 40sh, Green grossular garnet.

Perf. 14½x14, 14½ (A16)

1977, Dec. 13 Photo.

98 A15 10c multicolored 1.15 .25
99 A15 20c multicolored 1.85 .25
100 A15 30c multicolored 1.85 .25
101 A15 40c multicolored 1.40 .25
102 A15 50c multicolored 1.40 .25
103 A15 70c multicolored 7.00 .90
104 A15 80c multicolored 7.00 .75
105 A16 1sh multicolored 1.40 .25
106 A16 1.50sh multicolored 1.40 .40
107 A16 2sh multicolored 1.40 .35
108 A16 3sh multicolored 1.65 1.00
109 A16 5sh multicolored 1.65 1.25
110 A16 10sh multicolored 1.85 2.00
111 A16 20sh multicolored 4.25 3.00
112 A16 40sh multicolored 16.50 *20.00*
Nos. 98-112 (15) 51.75 31.15

The 10c, 20c, 40c, 50c and 80c were also issued in booklet panes of 4. The 50c was also issued in a booklet pane of 2.
For surcharge see No. 242.

Soccer, Joe Kadenge and World Cup — A17

World Cup and: 1sh, Mohammed Chuma receiving trophy, and his portrait. 2sh, Shot on goal and Omari S. Kidevu. 3sh, Backfield defense and Polly Ouma.

1978, Apr. 10 Litho. *Perf. 14x13½*

113 A17 50c green & multi .30 .25
114 A17 1sh lt brown & multi .30 .25
115 A17 2sh lilac & multi .30 *.70*
116 A17 3sh dk blue & multi .50 *1.00*
a. Souvenir sheet of 4, #113-116 3.75 3.75
Nos. 113-116 (4) 1.40 2.20

World Soccer Cup Championships, Argentina 78, June 1-25.

Boxing and Games' Emblem — A18

Games Emblem and: 1sh, Pres. Kenyatta welcoming 1968 Olympic team. 3sh, Javelin. 5sh, Pres. Kenyatta, boxing team and trophy.

1978, July 15 Photo. *Perf. 13x14*

117 A18 50c multicolored .30 .25
118 A18 1sh multicolored .30 .25
119 A18 3sh multicolored .70 .70
120 A18 5sh multicolored .85 .85
Nos. 117-120 (4) 2.15 2.05

Commonwealth Games, Edmonton, Canada, Aug. 3-12.

Overloaded Truck — A19

Road Safety: 1sh, Observe speed limit. 1.50sh, Observe traffic lights. 2sh, School crossing. 3sh, Passing. 5sh, Railroad crossing.

1978, Sept. 18 Litho. *Perf. 13½x14*

121 A19 50c multicolored .45 .25
122 A19 1sh multicolored .65 .25
123 A19 1.50sh multicolored 1.00 1.00
124 A19 2sh multicolored 1.55 1.50
125 A19 3sh multicolored 1.80 *2.25*
126 A19 5sh multicolored 2.00 *2.50*
Nos. 121-126 (6) 7.45 7.75

Pres. Kenyatta at Harambee Water Project Opening — A20

Kenyatta Day: 1sh, Prince Philip handing over symbol of independence, 1963. 2sh, Pres. Jomo Kenyatta addressing independence rally. 3sh, Stage at 15th independence anniversary celebration. 5sh, Handcuffed Kenyatta led by soldiers, 1952.

1978, Oct. 16 Litho. *Perf. 14*

127 A20 50c multicolored .35 .35
128 A20 1sh multicolored .35 .35
129 A20 2sh multicolored .45 .45
130 A20 3sh multicolored .70 .70
131 A20 5sh multicolored .95 .95
Nos. 127-131 (5) 2.80 2.80

Soldiers and Emblem — A21

Anti-Apartheid Emblem and: 1sh, Anti-Apartheid Conference. 2sh, Stephen Biko, South African Anti-Apartheid leader. 3sh, Nelson Mandela, jailed since 1961. 5sh, Bishop Lamont, expelled from Rhodesia in 1977.

1978, Dec. 11 Litho. *Perf. 14x14½*

132	A21 50c multicolored	.30	.30
133	A21 1sh multicolored	.30	.30
134	A21 2sh multicolored	.45	.45
135	A21 3sh multicolored	.65	.65
136	A21 5sh multicolored	.75	.75
	Nos. 132-136 (5)	2.45	2.45

Anti-Apartheid Year and Namibia's struggle for independence.

Children on School Playground A22

Children's Year Emblem and: 2sh, Boy catching fish. 3sh, Children dancing and singing. 5sh, Children and camel caravan.

1979, Feb. 5 Litho. *Perf. 14*

137	A22 50c multicolored	.35	.35
138	A22 2sh multicolored	.55	.55
139	A22 3sh multicolored	.70	.70
140	A22 5sh multicolored	1.00	1.00
	Nos. 137-140 (4)	2.60	2.60

International Year of the Child.

"The Lion and the Jewel" — A23

National Theater: 1sh, Dancers and drummers. 2sh, Programs of various productions. 3sh, View of National Theater. 5sh, "Genesis," performed by Nairobi City Players.

1979, Apr. 6 Litho. *Perf. 13½x14*

141	A23 50c multicolored	.30	.25
142	A23 1sh multicolored	.30	.30
143	A23 2sh multicolored	.35	.35
144	A23 3sh multicolored	.55	.55
145	A23 5sh multicolored	.75	.75
	Nos. 141-145 (5)	2.25	2.20

Village Workshop A24

Salvation Army Emblem and: 50c, Blind telephone operator, vert. 1sh, Care for the aged, vert. 5sh, Vocational training (nurse).

1979, June 4 *Perf. 13½x13, 13x13½*

146	A24 50c multicolored	.30	.30
147	A24 1sh multicolored	.30	.30
148	A24 3sh multicolored	.75	.75
149	A24 5sh multicolored	1.25	1.25
	Nos. 146-149 (4)	2.60	2.60

Salvation Army Social Services, 50th anniv.

Funeral Procession — A25

Kenyatta: 1sh, Taking oath of office. 3sh, Addressing crowd. 5sh, As young man with wooden trying plane.

1979, Aug. 22 Litho. *Perf. 13½x14*

150	A25 50c multicolored	.30	.25
151	A25 1sh multicolored	.30	.25
152	A25 3sh multicolored	.50	.50
153	A25 5sh multicolored	.75	.75
	Nos. 150-153 (4)	1.85	1.75

Jomo Kenyatta (1893-1978), first president of Kenya.

British East Africa No. 2, Hill, Signature — A26

Hill, Signature and: 1sh, Kenya, Uganda and Tanzania #54. 2sh, Penny Black. 5sh, Kenya #19.

1979, Nov. 27 Litho. *Perf. 14*

154	A26 50c multicolored	.30	.25
155	A26 1sh multicolored	.30	.25
156	A26 2sh multicolored	.30	.25
157	A26 5sh multicolored	.65	.65
	Nos. 154-157 (4)	1.55	1.40

Sir Rowland Hill (1795-1879), originator of penny postage.

Highways, Globe, Conference Emblem A27

Conference Emblem and: 1sh, Truck at Athi River, New Weighbridge. 3sh, New Nyali Bridge, Mombasa. 5sh, Jomo Kenyatta Airport Highway.

1980, Jan. 10 Litho. *Perf. 14*

158	A27 50c multicolored	.30	.25
159	A27 1sh multicolored	.30	.25
160	A27 3sh multicolored	.60	.60
161	A27 5sh multicolored	.85	.85
	Nos. 158-161 (4)	2.05	1.95

4th IRF African Highway Conference, Nairobi, Jan. 20-25.

Patient Airlift — A28

50c, Outdoor clinic. 1sh, Mule transport of patient, vert.. 3sh, Surgery, vert.

1980, Mar. 20 Litho. *Perf. 14½*

162	A28 50c multicolored	.30	.25
163	A28 1sh multicolored	.30	.25
164	A28 3sh multicolored	.65	.65
165	A28 5sh shown	1.00	1.00
a.	Souvenir sheet of 4, #162-165	2.75	2.75
	Nos. 162-165 (4)	2.25	2.15

Flying doctor service.

Hill Statue, Kidderminster and Mt. Kenya — A29

1980, May 6 Litho. *Perf. 14*

166	A29 25sh multicolored	1.25	1.25
a.	Souvenir sheet	1.50	*2.00*

London 1980 International Stamp Exhibition, May 6-14.

Pope John Paul II and Crowd — A30

Visit of Pope John Paul II to Kenya: 1sh, Pope, Nairobi Cathedral, papal flag and arms, vert. 5sh, Pope, papal and Kenya flags, dove, vert. 10sh, Pres. arap Moi of Kenya, Pope, flag of Kenya on map of Africa.

1980, May 8 *Perf. 13½*

167	A30 50c multicolored	.35	.25
168	A30 1sh multicolored	.45	.45
169	A30 5sh multicolored	1.00	1.00
170	A30 10sh multicolored	1.75	1.75
	Nos. 167-170 (4)	3.55	3.45

Sting Ray — A31

1980, June 27 Litho. *Perf. 14½*

171	A31 50c shown	.50	.25
172	A31 2sh Alkit snapper	1.25	.60
173	A31 3sh Sea slug	1.40	1.40
174	A31 5sh Hawksbill turtle	2.50	2.50
	Nos. 171-174 (4)	5.65	4.75

National Archives, 1904 — A32

1sh, Commissioner's Office, Nairobi, 1913. 1.50sh, Nairobi House, 1913. 2sh, Norfolk Hotel, 1904. 3sh, McMillan Library, 1929. 5sh, Kipande House, 1913.

1980, Oct. 9 Litho. *Perf. 14*

175	A32 50c shown	.30	.25
176	A32 1sh multicolored	.30	.25
177	A32 1.50sh multicolored	.30	.25
178	A32 2sh multicolored	.35	*.45*
179	A32 3sh multicolored	.50	*.95*
180	A32 5sh multicolored	.60	*1.50*
	Nos. 175-180 (6)	2.35	*3.65*

Woman in Wheelchair and Child — A33

1sh, Pres. arap Moi, team captain. 3sh, Blind mountain climbers, Mt. Kenya, 1965. 5sh, Disabled artist.

1981, Feb. 10 Litho. *Perf. 14x13½*

181	A33 50c shown	.30	.25
182	A33 1sh multicolored	.30	.25
183	A33 3sh multicolored	.55	.55
184	A33 5sh multicolored	1.00	1.00
	Nos. 181-184 (4)	2.15	2.05

International Year of the Disabled.

Longonot Earth Station Complex A34

1981, Apr. 4 Litho. *Perf. 14x14½*

185	A34 50c shown	.30	.30
186	A34 2sh Intelsat V	.40	.40
187	A34 3sh Longonot I	.50	.50
188	A34 5sh Longonot II	.85	.85
	Nos. 185-188 (4)	2.05	2.05

Conference Center, OAU Flag — A35

18th Organization for African Unity Conference, Nairobi: 1sh, Map of Africa showing Panaftel earth stations. 3sh, Parliament Building, Nairobi. 5sh, Jomo Kenyatta Intl. Airport. 10sh, OAU flag.

1981, June 24 Wmk. 373 *Perf. 13½*

189	A35 50c multicolored	.30	.25
190	A35 1sh multicolored	.30	.25
191	A35 3sh multicolored	.55	.55
192	A35 5sh multicolored	.70	.70
193	A35 10sh multicolored	1.40	1.40
a.	Souvenir sheet of 1, perf. 14½	2.00	2.00
	Nos. 189-193 (5)	3.25	3.15

St. Paul's Cathedral — A36

50c, Charles, Pres. arap Moi. 5sh, Britannia. 10sh, Charles. 25sh, Couple.

1981, July 29 Litho. *Perf. 14, 12*

194	A36 50c multicolored	.30	.25
195	A36 3sh shown	.30	.25
196	A36 5sh multicolored	.30	.30
197	A36 10sh multicolored	.30	*.60*
	Nos. 194-197 (4)	1.20	1.40

Souvenir Sheet

198	A36 25sh multicolored	1.50	1.50

Royal Wedding.

Perf. 12 comes from minisheets of 5 + label. Value, set of 4 sheets $7.50.

Reticulated Giraffe — A37

1981, Aug. 31 Litho. *Perf. 14½*

199	A37 50c shown	.30	.30
200	A37 2sh Bongo	.30	.30
201	A37 5sh Roan antelope	.65	.65
202	A37 10sh Mangabey	1.90	1.90
	Nos. 199-202 (4)	3.15	3.15

World Food Day — A38

1981, Oct. 16 Litho. *Perf. 14*

203	A38 50c Plowing	.25	.25
204	A38 1sh Rice field	.25	.25
205	A38 2sh Irrigation	.40	.40
206	A38 5sh Cattle	.90	.90
	Nos. 203-206 (4)	1.80	1.80

Ceremonial Tribal Costumes — A39

Perf. 14½x13½

1981, Dec. 18 Litho.

207	A39 50c Kamba	.45	.25
208	A39 1sh Turkana	.55	.25
209	A39 2sh Giriama	1.25	.80
210	A39 3sh Masai	1.75	*2.25*
211	A39 5sh Luo	2.00	*4.00*
	Nos. 207-211 (5)	6.00	7.55

Australopithecus Boisei — A40

2sh, Homo erectus. 3sh, Homo habilis. 5sh, Proconsul africanus.

1982, Jan. 16 Litho. *Perf. 14*

212	A40 50c shown	1.75	.40
213	A40 2sh multicolored	2.75	1.50
214	A40 3sh multicolored	3.00	*3.50*
215	A40 5sh multicolored	3.50	*5.00*
	Nos. 212-215 (4)	11.00	*10.40*

Scouting Year — A41

No. 216, Tree planting. No. 217, Paying homage. No. 218, Be Prepared. No. 219, Intl. friendship. No. 220, Helping disabled. No. 221, Community service. No. 222, Paxtu Cottage. No. 223, Lady Baden-Powell.

1982, June 2 Litho. *Perf. 14½*

216 A41 70c multicolored .50 .50
217 A41 70c multicolored .50 .50
a. Pair, #216-217 1.25 1.25
218 A41 3.50sh multicolored 1.25 1.25
219 A41 3.50sh multicolored 1.25 1.25
a. Pair, #218-219 3.00 3.00
220 A41 5sh multicolored 1.60 1.60
221 A41 5sh multicolored 1.60 1.60
a. Pair, #220-221 4.50 4.50
222 A41 6.50sh multicolored 2.25 2.25
223 A41 6.50sh multicolored 2.25 2.25
a. Pair, #222-223 6.25 6.25
Nos. 216-223 (8) 11.20 11.20

Souvenir Sheet

224 Sheet of 4 6.00 6.00
a. A41 70c like #216 .30 .25
b. A41 3.50sh like #218 1.00 1.00
c. A41 5sh like #220 1.50 1.50
d. A41 6.50sh like #222 2.00 2.00

1982 World Cup A42

Various soccer players on world map.

1982, July 5 Litho. *Perf. 12½*

225 A42 70c multicolored 1.25 .50
226 A42 3.50sh multicolored 2.75 2.50
227 A42 5sh multicolored 3.25 4.25
228 A42 10sh multicolored 4.75 *6.50*
Nos. 225-228 (4) 12.00 13.75

Souvenir Sheet

Perf. 13½x14

229 A42 20sh multicolored 6.00 6.00

A43

1982, Sept. 28 Litho. *Perf. 14½*

230 A43 70c Cattle judging .60 .25
231 A43 2.50sh Farm machinery 1.05 1.25
232 A43 3.50sh Musical ride 1.65 2.00
233 A43 6.50sh Emblem 2.50 *4.00*
Nos. 230-233 (4) 5.80 7.50

Agricultural Society, 80th anniv.

A44

70c, Microwave radio system. 3.50sh, Ship-to-shore communication. 5sh, Rural telecommunication. 6.50sh, Emblem.

1982, Oct. 27 Photo. *Perf. 11½*

Granite Paper

234 A44 70c multicolored .50 .25
235 A44 3.50sh multicolored 1.75 1.75
236 A44 5sh multicolored 2.25 2.25
237 A44 6.50sh multicolored 3.00 3.00
Nos. 234-237 (4) 7.50 7.25

ITU Plenipotentiaries Conf., Nairobi, Sept.

5th Anniv. of Kenya Ports Authority — A45

70c, Container cranes. 2sh, Cranes, diff. 3.50sh, Cranes, diff. 5sh, Mombasa Harbor map.

1983, Jan. 20 Litho. *Perf. 14*

238 A45 70c multicolored .70 .25
239 A45 2sh multicolored 1.60 1.60
240 A45 3.50sh multicolored 2.25 2.50
241 A45 5sh multicolored 2.95 2.95
a. Souvenir sheet of 4, #238-241 7.50 7.50
Nos. 238-241 (4) 7.50 7.30

No. 104 Surcharged

1983, Jan. Photo. *Perf. 14½x14*

242 A15 70c on 80c multicolored 1.50 1.50

A45a

70c, Coffee picking, vert. 2sh, Pres. arap Moi, vert. 5sh, Globe. 10sh, Masai dance.

1983, Mar. 14 Litho. *Perf. 14½*

243 A45a 70c multicolored .30 .25
244 A45a 2sh multicolored .30 .25
245 A45a 5sh multicolored .40 .40
246 A45a 10sh multicolored .85 .85
Nos. 243-246 (4) 1.85 1.75

Commonwealth Day.

Dichrostachys Cinerea A46

Dombeya Burgessiae A47

20c, Rhamphicarpa montana. 30c, Barleria eranthemoides. 40c, Commelina. 50c, Canarina abyssinica. 70c, Aspilia mossambicensis. 1sh, Dombeya burgessiae. 1.50sh, Lantana trifolia. 2sh, Adenium obesum. 2.50sh, Terminalia orbicularis. 3.50sh, Ceropegia ballyana. 5sh, Ruttya fruticosa. 10sh, Pentanisia ouranogyne. 20sh, Brillantaisia nyanzarum. 40sh, Crotalaria axillaris.

Perf. 14½x14, 14x14½

1983, Feb. 15 Photo.

247 A46 10c shown .50 .40
248 A46 20c multicolored .70 .40
249 A46 30c multicolored .70 .40
250 A46 40c multicolored .70 .40
251 A46 50c multicolored .70 .30
252 A46 70c multicolored .80 .25
253 A47 1sh multicolored .90 .25
254 A47 1.50sh multicolored 2.00 .65
255 A47 2sh multicolored 2.00 .65
256 A47 2.50sh multicolored 2.25 .65
257 A47 3.50sh multicolored 2.00 1.60
258 A47 5sh multicolored 1.60 1.50
259 A47 10sh multicolored 1.60 1.50
260 A47 20sh multicolored 1.75 *2.75*
261 A47 40sh multicolored 2.75 *8.00*
Nos. 247-261 (15) 20.95 *19.70*

See Nos. 350-354.

30th Anniv. of Customs Cooperation Council — A48

70c, Parcel check. 2.50sh, Headquarters, Mombasa. 3.50sh, Headquarters, Brussels. 10sh, Patrol boat.

1983, May 11 Litho. *Perf. 14½*

262 A48 70c multicolored .30 .25
263 A48 2.50sh multicolored .65 .30
264 A48 3.50sh multicolored .75 .40
265 A48 10sh multicolored 2.50 2.50
Nos. 262-265 (4) 4.20 3.45

World Communications Year — A49

70c, Satellite, dish antenna, vert. 2.50sh, Mailbox, birthday card, telephone, vert. 3.50sh, Jet, ship. 5sh, Railroad bridge, highway.

1983, July 4 Litho. *Perf. 14½*

266 A49 70c multicolored .65 .25
267 A49 2.50sh multicolored 1.50 1.50
268 A49 3.50sh multicolored 2.25 2.25
269 A49 5sh multicolored 2.50 2.50
Nos. 266-269 (4) 6.90 6.50

Intl. Maritime Organization, 25th Anniv. — A50

70c, Kilindini Harbor. 2.50sh, Life preserver. 3.50sh, Mombasa Container Terminal. 10sh, Marine Park.

1983, Sept. 22 Litho. *Perf. 14½*

270 A50 70c multicolored 1.00 .25
271 A50 2.50sh multicolored 2.00 1.50
272 A50 3.50sh multicolored 2.50 2.50
273 A50 10sh multicolored 3.00 *3.75*
Nos. 270-273 (4) 8.50 8.00

29th Commonwealth Parliamentary Conference A51

2.50sh, Parliament Bldg., vert. 5sh, State Opening, vert.

1983, Oct. 31 Litho. *Perf. 14*

274 A51 70c shown .35 .25
275 A51 2.50sh multicolored 1.25 1.25
276 A51 5sh multicolored 1.75 *2.25*
a. Souv. sheet of 3, #274-276 + label 3.50 3.50
Nos. 274-276 (3) 3.35 3.75

Royal Visit — A52

70c, Flags. 3.50sh, Sagana State Lodge. 5sh, Tree Tops Hotel. 10sh, Elizabeth II and Daniel arap Moi.

1983, Nov. 10 Litho. *Perf. 14*

277 A52 70c multicolored .50 .25
278 A52 3.50sh multicolored 1.70 1.50
279 A52 5sh multicolored 1.90 2.25
280 A52 10sh multicolored 2.95 4.50
Nos. 277-280 (4) 7.05 8.50

Souvenir Sheet

281 A52 25sh multicolored 5.50 5.50

No. 281 contains Nos. 277-280 without denominations showing simulated perforations.

President Daniel arap Moi, Monument A53

2sh, Tree planting. 3.50sh, Map, flag, emblem. 5sh, School, milk program. 10sh, People, flag, banner.

1983, Dec. 9 Litho. *Perf. 14½*

282 A53 70c shown .30 .25
283 A53 2sh multicolored .30 .25
284 A53 3.50sh multicolored .35 .35
285 A53 5sh multicolored .55 .55
286 A53 10sh multicolored .95 .95
Nos. 282-286 (5) 2.45 2.35

Souvenir Sheet

Imperf

287 A53 25sh multicolored *3.00 3.00*

Independence, 20th Anniv. No. 287 contains Nos. 282, 284-286 without denominations.

Rare Local Birds — A54

70c, White-backed night heron. 2.50sh, Quail plover. 3.50sh, Heller's ground thrush. 5sh, Papyrus gonolek. 10sh, White-winged Apalis.

1984, Feb. 6 Litho. *Perf. 14½x13½*

288 A54 70c multicolored 2.00 .40
289 A54 2.50sh multicolored 2.50 2.50
290 A54 3.50sh multicolored 3.75 3.75
291 A54 5sh multicolored 4.50 4.50
292 A54 10sh multicolored 5.75 *6.75*
Nos. 288-292 (5) 18.50 17.90

Intl. Civil Aviation Org., 40th Anniv. — A55

70c, Radar, vert. 2.50sh, Kenya School of Aviation. 3.50sh, Jet, Moi Intl. Airport. 5sh, Air traffic control center, vert.

1984, Apr. 2 Litho. *Perf. 14*

293 A55 70c multicolored .30 .25
294 A55 2.50sh multicolored .50 .50
295 A55 3.50sh multicolored .80 .80
296 A55 5sh multicolored 1.25 1.25
Nos. 293-296 (4) 2.85 2.80

1984 Summer Olympics A56

1984, May 21 *Perf. 14½*

297 A56 70c Running .40 .40
298 A56 2.50sh Hurdles .75 .75
299 A56 5sh Boxing 1.25 1.25
300 A56 10sh Field Hockey 4.00 4.00
Nos. 297-300 (4) 6.40 6.40

Souvenir Sheet

Imperf

301 A56 25sh Torch bearers 5.00 5.00

No. 301 contains designs of Nos. 297-300.

Bookmobile A57

70c, Emblem. 5sh, Adult library. 10sh, Children's library.

1984, Aug. 10 Litho. *Perf. 14½*

302 A57 70c multicolored .30 .25
303 A57 3.50sh shown .45 .45
304 A57 5sh multicolored .65 .65
305 A57 10sh multicolored .95 .95
Nos. 302-305 (4) 2.35 2.30

Intl. Fed. of Library Associations, 50th Conf.

Kenya Export Year (KEY) — A58

1984, Oct. 1 Litho. *Perf. 14*

306 A58 70c Emblem, vert. .30 .30
307 A58 3.50sh Airport 1.65 1.65
308 A58 5sh Harbor, vert. 2.50 2.50
309 A58 10sh Exports 3.50 3.50
Nos. 306-309 (4) 7.95 7.95

A59

70c, Doves, cross. 2.50sh, Doves, Hinduism symbol. 3.50sh, Doves, Sikhism symbol. 6.50sh, Doves, Islam symbol.

1984, Aug. 23 Litho. *Perf. 14x14½*

310 A59	70c multicolored	.30	.30
311 A59	2.50sh multicolored	1.00	1.00
312 A59	3.50sh multicolored	1.50	1.50
313 A59	6.50sh multicolored	2.75	2.75
	Nos. 310-313 (4)	5.55	5.55

World Conference on Religion and Peace, Nairobi, Aug. 23-31, 1984.

Tribal Costumes — A60

1984, Nov. 5 Litho. *Perf. 14½x13½*

314 A60	70c Luhya	.75	.30
315 A60	2sh Kikuyu	2.00	1.75
316 A60	3.50sh Pokomo	2.25	2.00
317 A60	5sh Nandi	2.75	2.75
318 A60	10sh Rendile	3.50	*4.25*
	Nos. 314-318 (5)	11.25	11.05

60th Anniv., World Chess Federation A61

70c, Nyayo Stadium, knight. 2.50sh, Fort Jesus, rook. 3.50sh, National Monument, bishop. 5sh, Parliament, queen. 10sh, Nyayo Fountain, king.

1984, Dec. 21 Litho. *Perf. 14½*

319 A61	70c multicolored	1.75	.50
320 A61	2.50sh multicolored	2.50	1.75
321 A61	3.50sh multicolored	3.00	2.00
322 A61	5sh multicolored	3.50	3.50
323 A61	10sh multicolored	5.50	*7.00*
	Nos. 319-323 (5)	16.25	14.75

Energy Conservation A62

70c, Stove, fire pit. 2sh, Solar panel. 3.50sh, Biogas tank. 10sh, Plowing field. 20sh, Energy conservation.

1985, Jan. 22 Litho. *Perf. 13½*

324 A62	70c multicolored	.30	.25
325 A62	2sh multicolored	.65	.65
326 A62	3.50sh multicolored	.80	.80
327 A62	10sh multicolored	2.40	2.40
328 A62	20sh multicolored	4.25	4.25
	Nos. 324-328 (5)	8.40	8.35

No. 328 contains Nos. 324-327 without denominations.

Girl Guides, 75th Anniv. — A63

1sh, Girl Guide, handicrafts. 3sh, Community service. 5sh, Lady Baden-Powell, Kenyan leader. 7sh, Food project.

1985, Mar. 27 Litho. *Perf. 13½*

329 A63	1sh multicolored	.85	.25
330 A63	3sh multicolored	1.65	1.00
331 A63	5sh multicolored	2.25	2.00
332 A63	7sh multicolored	3.25	*4.00*
	Nos. 329-332 (4)	8.00	7.25

Intl. Red Cross Day — A64

1985, May 8 *Perf. 14½*

333 A64	1sh Emblem	.75	.25
334 A64	4sh First Aid	2.25	2.25
335 A64	5sh Blood donation	2.75	2.75
336 A64	7sh Famine relief, cornucopia	3.75	*4.25*
	Nos. 333-336 (4)	9.50	9.50

A65

Diseases caused by microorganisms carried by insects.

1985, June 25

337 A65	1sh Malaria	1.65	.50
338 A65	3sh Leishmaniasis	3.25	3.25
339 A65	5sh Trypanosomiasis	3.50	3.50
340 A65	7sh Babesiosis	5.75	*9.00*
	Nos. 337-340 (4)	14.15	16.25

7th Intl. Congress on Protozoology, Nairobi, June 22-29.

UN Decade for Women — A66

1sh, Repairing water pipes. 3sh, Traditional food processing. 5sh, Basket weaving. 7sh, Dress making.

1985, July 15

341 A66	1sh multicolored	.35	.25
342 A66	3sh multicolored	.85	.70
343 A66	5sh multicolored	.95	.95
344 A66	7sh multicolored	1.50	1.50
	Nos. 341-344 (4)	3.65	3.40

43rd Intl. Eucharistic Congress, Nairobi, Aug. 11-18 — A67

1sh, The Last Supper. 3sh, Afro-Christian family. 5sh, Congress altar, Uhuru Park. 7sh, St. Peter Claver's Church.
25sh, Pope John Paul II.

1985, Aug. 15 *Perf. 13½*

345 A67	1sh multicolored	.70	.30
346 A67	3sh multicolored	2.00	1.50
347 A67	5sh multicolored	2.25	2.25
348 A67	7sh multicolored	2.50	*3.25*
	Nos. 345-348 (4)	7.45	7.30

Souvenir Sheet

349 A67	25sh multicolored	9.00	9.00

Flower Types of 1983

1sh, Dombeya burgessiae. 3sh, Calotropis procera. 4sh, Momordica foetida. 7sh, Oncoba spinosa.

1985 Photo. *Perf. 14½x14, 14½*

350 A46	80c like #250	3.00	*4.00*
351 A46	1sh multicolored	3.00	.80
352 A47	3sh multicolored	9.00	8.00
353 A47	4sh multicolored	3.00	*6.00*
354 A47	7sh multicolored	4.00	*7.50*
	Nos. 350-354 (5)	22.00	*26.30*

Endangered Wildlife — A68

1sh, Diceros bicornis. 3sh, Acinonyx jubatus. 5sh, Cercopithecus neglectus. 10sh, Equus greyvi. 25sh, Hunter pursuing game.

1985, Dec. 10 Litho. *Perf. 14½*

355 A68	1sh multicolored	2.15	.50
356 A68	3sh multicolored	2.45	2.00
357 A68	5sh multicolored	2.95	2.75
358 A68	10sh multicolored	5.75	*6.50*
	Nos. 355-358 (4)	13.30	11.75

Size: 130x122mm

Imperf

359 A68	25sh multicolored	9.50	9.50

Trees — A69

1sh, Borassus aethiopum. 3sh, Acacia xanthophloea. 5sh, Ficus natalensis. 7sh, Spathodea nilotica. 25sh, Glade.

1986, Jan. 24 *Perf. 14½*

360 A69	1sh multicolored	1.05	.25
361 A69	3sh multicolored	2.70	2.75
362 A69	5sh multicolored	3.60	4.75
363 A69	7sh multicolored	5.25	6.75
	Nos. 360-363 (4)	12.60	14.50

Size: 117x97mm

Imperf

364 A69	25sh multicolored	6.00	6.00

Intl. Peace Year — A70

1sh, Dove, UN emblem. 3sh, UN General Assembly, horiz. 7sh, Mushroom cloud. 10sh, Isaiah 2:4, horiz.

1986, Apr. 17 *Perf. 14½*

365 A70	1sh multicolored	.55	.55
366 A70	3sh multicolored	1.25	1.25
367 A70	7sh multicolored	2.40	2.40
368 A70	10sh multicolored	3.75	3.75
	Nos. 365-368 (4)	7.95	7.95

1986 World Cup Soccer Championships, Mexico — A71

1986, May 9

369 A71	1sh Dribbling	.85	.55
370 A71	3sh Penalty shot	1.70	1.10
371 A71	5sh Tackling	2.65	2.25
372 A71	7sh Champions	3.40	3.40
373 A71	10sh Heading the ball	4.35	4.35
	Nos. 369-373 (5)	12.95	11.65

Size: 110x86mm

Imperf

374 A71	30sh Harambee Stars	5.00	5.00

EXPO '86, Vancouver A72

1sh, Rural post office. 3sh, Container depot, Embakasi. 5sh, Plane landing. 7sh, Shipping exports. 10sh, Goods transport.

1986, June 11 *Perf. 13½x13*

375 A72	1sh multicolored	1.05	.60
376 A72	3sh multicolored	2.00	1.25
377 A72	5sh multicolored	3.10	2.40
378 A72	7sh multicolored	3.95	3.95
379 A72	10sh multicolored	5.25	5.25
	Nos. 375-379 (5)	15.35	13.45

TELECOM '86, Nairobi, Sept. 16-23 — A73

1sh, Telephone-computer links. 3sh, Telephones, 1876-1986. 5sh, Satellite communications. 7sh, Switchboards.

1986, Sept. 16 Litho. *Perf. 14½*

380 A73	1sh multicolored	.30	.30
381 A73	3sh multicolored	1.10	1.10
382 A73	5sh multicolored	1.85	1.85
383 A73	7sh multicolored	3.00	3.00
	Nos. 380-383 (4)	6.25	6.25

A74

Dhows (Ships) A75

1986, Oct. 30 Litho. *Perf. 14½*

384 A74	1sh Mashua	.70	.25
385 A74	3sh Mtepe	1.70	1.50
386 A74	5sh Dau La Mwao	2.50	3.00
387 A74	10sh Jahazi	5.00	5.00
	Nos. 384-387 (4)	9.90	9.75

Souvenir Sheet

388 A75	25sh Lamu, map	6.75	6.75

Christmas — A76

1986, Dec. 5 *Perf. 12*

389 A76	1sh Nativity, vert.	.30	.25
390 A76	3sh Shepherd boy, vert.	1.50	1.50
391 A76	5sh Angel, map	2.10	2.10
392 A76	7sh Magi	3.15	3.15
	Nos. 389-392 (4)	7.05	7.00

UNICEF, 40th Anniv. — A77

Child Survival Campaign: 1sh, Universal immunization by 1990. 3sh, Food and nutrition. 4sh, Oral rehydration. 5sh, Family planning. 10sh, Literacy of women.

1987, Jan. 6 Litho. *Perf. 14½*

393 A77	1sh multicolored	.50	.50
394 A77	3sh multicolored	1.00	1.00
395 A77	4sh multicolored	1.40	1.40
396 A77	5sh multicolored	1.80	1.80
397 A77	10sh multicolored	2.80	2.80
	Nos. 393-397 (5)	7.50	7.50

A78

Tourism A79

1987, Mar. 25 Litho. *Perf. 14½*

398	A78	1sh Akamba carvers	.60	.25
399	A78	3sh Beach	3.25	2.00
400	A78	5sh Escarpment	4.00	4.00
401	A78	7sh Pride of lions	6.00	6.00
		Nos. 398-401 (4)	13.85	12.25

Souvenir Sheet

402	A79	30sh Kenya geysers	12.50	12.50

Ceremonial Costumes — A80

1987, May 20 *Perf. 14½x13½*

403	A80	1sh Embu	1.00	.60
404	A80	3sh Kisii	2.15	1.40
405	A80	5sh Samburu	3.30	2.40
406	A80	7sh Taita	3.70	3.70
407	A80	10sh Boran	3.90	3.90
		Nos. 403-407 (5)	14.05	12.00

See Nos. 505-509.

Posts & Telecommunications Corp., 10th Anniv. — A81

1sh, Telecommunications satellite. 3sh, Rural post office, Kajiado. 4sh, Athletics. 5sh, Rural communication. 7sh, Speedpost.
25sh, Natl. Flag.

1987, July 1 Litho. *Perf. 13½*

408	A81	1sh multicolored	.75	.30
409	A81	3sh multicolored	1.75	1.75
410	A81	4sh multicolored	2.25	2.25
411	A81	5sh multicolored	2.40	2.40
412	A81	7sh multicolored	3.25	3.25
		Nos. 408-412 (5)	10.40	9.95

Souvenir Sheet

413	A81	25sh multicolored	4.00	4.00

A82

1sh, Volleyball. 3sh, Cycling. 4sh, Boxing. 5sh, Swimming. 7sh, Steeple chase.
30sh, Kasarani Sports Complex.

1987, Aug. 5 *Perf. 14½x14*

414	A82	1sh multicolored	.30	.25
415	A82	3sh multicolored	.55	.55
416	A82	4sh multicolored	.75	.75
417	A82	5sh multicolored	.90	.90
418	A82	7sh multicolored	1.25	1.25
		Nos. 414-418 (5)	3.75	3.70

Souvenir Sheet

Perf. 14x14½

419	A82	30sh multicolored	5.00	5.00

4th All Africa Games, Nairobi, Aug. 1-12. Nos. 414-418, vert.

A83

Medicinal herbs: 1sh, Aloe volkensii. 3sh, Cassia didymobotrya. 5sh, Erythrina abyssinica. 7sh, Adenium obesum. 10sh, Herbalist's clinic.

1987, Oct. 27 Litho. *Perf. 13½x14*

420	A83	1sh multicolored	.90	.65
421	A83	3sh multicolored	1.85	1.50
422	A83	5sh multicolored	2.50	2.40
423	A83	7sh multicolored	3.00	3.00
424	A83	10sh multicolored	4.15	4.15
		Nos. 420-424 (5)	12.40	11.70

Butterflies — A84

10c, Cyrestis camillus. 20c, Iolaus sidus. 40c, Vanessa cardui. 50c, Colotis euippe omphale. 70c, Precis westermanni. 80c, Colias electo. 1sh, Eronia leda. 1.50sh, Papilio dardanus planemoides. 2sh, Papilio rex. 2.50sh, Colotis phisadia. 3sh, Papilio desmondi teita. 3.50sh, Papilio demodocus. 4sh, Papilio phorcas. 5sh, Charaxes druceanus teita. 7sh, Cymothoe teita. 10sh, Charaxes zoolina. 20sh, Papilio dardanus. 40sh, Charaxes cithaeron kennethi.

1988-90 Photo. *Perf. 15x14*

424A	A84	10c multicolored	1.25	1.25
425	A84	20c multicolored	.35	.40
426	A84	40c multicolored	.50	.40
427	A84	50c multicolored	.50	.40
428	A84	70c multicolored	.50	.40
429	A84	80c multicolored	.50	.40
430	A84	1sh multicolored	.50	.30
430A	A84	1.50sh multicolored	5.00	1.25

Size: 25x41mm

Perf. 14½

431	A84	2sh multicolored	.75	.95
432	A84	2.50sh multicolored	.80	.95
433	A84	3sh multicolored	.80	.95
434	A84	3.50sh multicolored	.85	.95
435	A84	4sh multicolored	.90	*1.75*
436	A84	5sh multicolored	1.25	.70
437	A84	7sh multicolored	1.50	*2.50*
438	A84	10sh multicolored	2.50	1.75
439	A84	20sh multicolored	4.00	*3.50*
440	A84	40sh multicolored	7.25	*8.00*
		Nos. 424A-440 (18)	29.70	26.80

Issued: 10c, 9/1/89; 1.50sh, 5/18/90; others, 2/14/88.

Game Lodges — A85

1sh, Samburu. 3sh, Naro Moru River. 4sh, Mara Serena. 5sh, Voi Safari. 7sh, Kilimanjaro Buffalo Lodge. 10sh, Meru Mulika.

1988, May 31 Litho. *Perf. 14½*

441	A85	1sh multicolored	.75	.35
442	A85	3sh multicolored	1.10	1.10
443	A85	4sh multicolored	1.75	1.75
444	A85	5sh multicolored	1.90	1.90
445	A85	7sh multicolored	2.25	2.25
446	A85	10sh multicolored	2.75	2.75
		Nos. 441-446 (6)	10.50	10.10

World Expo '88, Brisbane — A86

EXPO '88 and Australia bicentennial emblems plus: 1sh, Stadium, site of the 1982 Commonwealth Games, and runners. 3sh, Flying Doctor Service aircraft. 4sh, HMS Sirius, a 19th cent. immigrant ship. 5sh, Ostrich and emu. 7sh, Pres. Daniel arap Moi, Queen Elizabeth II and Robert Hawke, prime minister of Australia. 30sh, Kenya Pavilion at EXPO '88.

1988, June 10

447	A86	1sh multicolored	.55	.55
448	A86	3sh multicolored	1.60	1.60
449	A86	4sh multicolored	2.75	2.75
450	A86	5sh multicolored	3.70	3.70
451	A86	7sh multicolored	4.60	4.60
		Nos. 447-451 (5)	13.20	13.20

Souvenir Sheet

452	A86	30sh multicolored	3.75	3.75

World Health Organization, 40th Anniv. — A87

1988, July 1 Litho. *Perf. 14½*

453	A87	1sh shown	.30	.25
454	A87	3sh Nutrition	1.05	1.05
455	A87	5sh Immunization	1.90	1.90
456	A87	7sh Water supply	2.75	2.75
		Nos. 453-456 (4)	6.00	5.95

1988 Summer Olympics, Seoul — A88

1988, Aug. 1 Litho. *Perf. 14½x14*

457	A88	1sh Handball	.40	.25
458	A88	3sh Judo	.85	.80
459	A88	5sh Weight lifting	1.25	1.25
460	A88	7sh Javelin	1.70	1.70
461	A88	10sh 400-meter relay	2.10	2.10
		Nos. 457-461 (5)	6.30	6.10

Souvenir Sheet

462	A88	30sh Tennis	4.50	4.50

Utensils — A89

1sh, Calabashes, vert. 3sh, Milk gourds, vert. 5sh, Cooking pots. 7sh, Winnowing trays. 10sh, Reed baskets.
25sh, Gourds, calabash, horn.

Perf. 14½x14, 14x14½

1988, Sept. 20 Litho.

463	A89	1sh multicolored	.45	.25
464	A89	3sh multicolored	.85	.65
465	A89	5sh multicolored	1.20	1.10
466	A89	7sh multicolored	1.50	1.50
467	A89	10sh multicolored	2.00	2.00
		Nos. 463-467 (5)	6.00	5.50

Souvenir Sheet

468	A89	25sh multicolored	3.00	3.00

10-Year Presidency of Daniel arap Moi — A90

Designs: 1sh, Swearing-in ceremony, 1978. 3sh, Promoting soil conservation. 3.50sh, Public transportation (bus), Nairobi. 4sh, Jua Kali artisans at market. 5sh, Moi University, Eldoret, established in 1985. 7sh, Hospital ward expansion. 10sh, British Prime Minister Margaret Thatcher and Pres. Moi inaugurating the Kapsabet Telephone Exchange, Jan. 6, 1988.

1988, Oct. 13 Litho. *Perf. 13½x14½*

469	A90	1sh multicolored	.60	.60
470	A90	3sh multicolored	1.50	1.50
471	A90	3.50sh multicolored	1.75	1.75
472	A90	4sh multicolored	1.95	1.95
473	A90	5sh multicolored	2.40	2.40
474	A90	7sh multicolored	3.00	3.00
475	A90	10sh multicolored	4.75	4.75
		Nos. 469-475 (7)	15.95	15.95

Independence, 25th Anniv. — A91

1sh, Natl. flag. 3sh, Coffee picking. 5sh, Model of postal headquarters. 7sh, Harambee Star Airbus A310-300. 10sh, Locomotive 9401.

1988, Dec. 9 Litho. *Perf. 11½*

476	A91	1sh multicolored	.30	.25
477	A91	3sh multicolored	1.60	1.60
478	A91	5sh multicolored	2.75	2.75
479	A91	7sh multicolored	4.00	4.00
480	A91	10sh multicolored	5.45	5.45
		Nos. 476-480 (5)	14.10	14.05

Natl. Monuments A92

1.20sh, Gedi Ruins, Malindi. 3.40sh, Vasco Da Gama Pillar, Malindi, vert. 4.40sh, Ishiakani Monument, Kiunga. 5.50sh, Ft. Jesus, Mombasa. 7.70sh, She Burnan Omwe, Lamu, vert.

1989, Mar. 15 Litho. *Perf. 14½*

481	A92	1.20sh multicolored	.40	.40
482	A92	3.40sh multicolored	1.00	1.00
483	A92	4.40sh multicolored	2.00	2.00
484	A92	5.50sh multicolored	2.50	2.50
485	A92	7.70sh multicolored	3.00	3.00
		Nos. 481-485 (5)	8.90	8.90

Red Cross, 125th Anniv. — A93

1.20sh, Anniv. and natl. soc. emblems. 3.40sh, First aid. 4.40sh, Disaster relief. 5.50sh, Jean-Henri Dunant. 7.70sh, Blood donation.

1989, May 8 Litho. *Perf. 14x13½*

486	A93	1.20sh multicolored	.30	.30
487	A93	3.40sh multicolored	1.10	1.10
488	A93	4.40sh multicolored	1.60	1.60
489	A93	5.50sh multicolored	2.15	2.15
490	A93	7.70sh multicolored	3.40	3.40
		Nos. 486-490 (5)	8.55	8.55

World Wildlife Fund — A94

Giraffes, Giraffa Camelopardalis Reticulata.

1989, July 12 Litho. *Perf. 14½*

491	A94	1.20sh multicolored	2.10	1.90
492	A94	3.40sh multicolored	4.40	4.25
493	A94	4.40sh multicolored	5.00	5.00
494	A94	5.50sh multicolored	6.00	*7.75*
		Nos. 491-494 (4)	17.50	18.90

Size: 80x110mm

Imperf

495	A94	30sh multicolored	10.00	10.00

No. 495 contains four labels like Nos. 491-494, perf. 14½, without denominations or WWF emblem.

Mushrooms — A95

1989, Sept. 6 Litho. *Perf. 14½*

496	A95	1.20sh Oyster	2.00	.65
497	A95	3.40sh Chestnut	2.90	2.40
498	A95	4.40sh White button	3.30	3.25
499	A95	5.50sh Termite	3.95	3.75
500	A95	7.70sh Shiitake	5.50	6.50
		Nos. 496-500 (5)	17.65	16.55

Jawaharlal Nehru, 1st Prime Minister of Independent India — A96

1.20sh, Independence struggle. 3.40sh, Education. 5.50sh, Portrait. 7.70sh, Industry.

1989, Nov. 9 Litho. *Perf. 13½x14*

501	A96	1.20sh multicolored	1.65	1.50
502	A96	3.40sh multicolored	2.10	2.00
503	A96	5.50sh multicolored	3.75	3.75
504	A96	7.70sh multicolored	6.25	6.25
		Nos. 501-504 (4)	13.75	13.50

Costume Type of 1980

1989, Dec. 8 Litho. *Perf. 14½x13½*

505	A80	1.20sh Kipsigis	1.05	.45
506	A80	3.40sh Rabai	2.15	2.50
507	A80	5.50sh Duruma	2.75	2.40
508	A80	7.70sh Kuria	3.85	3.75
509	A80	10sh Bajuni	4.75	4.75
		Nos. 505-509 (5)	14.55	13.85

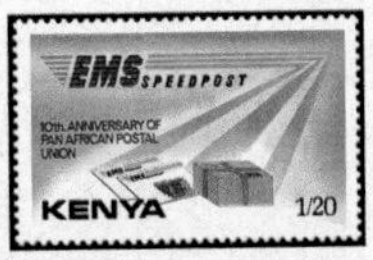

Pan-African Postal Union, 10th Anniv. — A97

1.20sh, EMS Speedpost. 3.40sh, Mail runner. 5.50sh, Mandera P.O.. 7.70sh, EMS, diff., vert. 10sh, PAPU emblem, vert.

Perf. 14x13½, 13½x14

1990, Jan. 31 Litho.

510	A97	1.20sh multicolored	.30	.30
511	A97	3.40sh multicolored	.90	.90
512	A97	5.50sh multicolored	1.10	1.10
513	A97	7.70sh multicolored	1.40	1.40
514	A97	10sh multicolored	1.75	1.75
		Nos. 510-514 (5)	5.45	5.45

Soccer Trophies — A98

Designs:1.50sh, Moi Golden Cup. 4.50sh, East & Central Africa Challenge Cup. 6.50sh, East & Central Africa Club Championship Cup. 9sh, World Cup.

1990, May 21 Litho. *Perf. 14½*

515	A98	1.50sh multicolored	.50	.50
516	A98	4.50sh multicolored	3.00	3.00
517	A98	6.50sh multicolored	4.00	4.00
518	A98	9sh multicolored	5.00	5.00
		Nos. 515-518 (4)	12.50	12.50

Penny Black 150th Anniv., Stamp World London '90 — A99

4.50sh, Great Britain No. 1. 6.50sh, Early British cancellations. 9sh, Main P.O.

1990, Apr. 27 Litho. *Perf. 11½*

519	A99	1.50sh shown	.35	.35
520	A99	4.50sh multicolored	1.30	1.30
521	A99	6.50sh multicolored	1.95	1.95
522	A99	9sh multicolored	2.85	2.85
a.		Souvenir sheet of 4, #519-522	7.50	7.50
		Nos. 519-522 (4)	6.45	6.45

No. 522a sold for 30 shillings.

ITU, 125th Anniv. — A100

Designs: 4.50sh, Telephone assembly. 6.50sh, ITU Anniv. emblem. 9sh, Telecommunications development.

1990, July 12

523	A100	1.50sh multicolored	.45	.25
524	A100	4.50sh multicolored	.90	.65
525	A100	6.50sh multicolored	1.25	1.10
526	A100	9sh multicolored	1.60	1.60
		Nos. 523-526 (4)	4.20	3.60

Common Design Types pictured following the introduction.

Queen Mother, 90th Birthday
Common Design Types

10sh, Queen Mother. 40sh, At garden party, 1947.

Perf. 14x15

1990, Aug. 4 Litho. Wmk. 384

527	CD343	10sh multicolored	1.30	1.30

Perf. 14½

528	CD344	40sh multicolored	4.75	4.75

Kenya African National Union (KANU), 50th Anniv. — A101

1.50sh, KANU flag. 2.50sh, Nyayo Monument. 4.50sh, KICC Party Headquarters. 5sh, Jomo Kenyatta. 6.50sh, Daniel T. arap Moi. 9sh, KANU mass meeting. 10sh, Voters.

1990, June 11

529	A101	1.50sh multicolored	.35	.25
530	A101	2.50sh multicolored	.40	.35
531	A101	4.50sh multicolored	.85	.85
532	A101	5sh multicolored	1.00	1.00
533	A101	6.50sh multicolored	1.10	1.10
534	A101	9sh multicolored	1.75	1.75
535	A101	10sh multicolored	1.75	1.75
		Nos. 529-535 (7)	7.20	7.05

Kenya Postage Stamps, Cent. — A102

Designs: 1.50sh, Kenya #431. 4.50sh, East Africa and Uganda Protectorates #2. 6.50sh, British East Africa #1. 9sh, Kenya and Uganda #25. 20sh, Kenya, Uganda, Tanzania #232.

1990, Sept. 5 Litho. *Perf. 14x14½*

536	A102	1.50sh multicolored	1.50	.45
537	A102	4.50sh multicolored	3.00	2.50
538	A102	6.50sh multicolored	4.00	3.75
539	A102	9sh multicolored	5.25	4.75
540	A102	20sh multicolored	8.50	8.50
		Nos. 536-540 (5)	22.25	19.95

Intl. Literacy Year — A103

1.50sh, Adult literacy class. 4.50sh, Radio teaching program. 6.50sh, Technical training. 9sh, Literacy year emblem.

1990, Nov. 30 Litho. *Perf. 13½x14*

541	A103	1.50sh multicolored	.55	.55
542	A103	4.50sh multicolored	1.35	1.35
543	A103	6.50sh multicolored	1.90	1.90
544	A103	9sh multicolored	2.95	2.95
		Nos. 541-544 (4)	6.75	6.75

1992 Summer Olympics, Barcelona A106

1991, Nov. 29 Litho. *Perf. 14x13½*

554	A106	2sh National flag	.45	.45
555	A106	6sh Basketball	1.90	1.90
556	A106	7sh Field hockey	2.50	2.50
557	A106	8.50sh Table tennis	3.00	3.00
558	A106	11sh Boxing	4.50	4.50
		Nos. 554-558 (5)	12.35	12.35

Fight AIDS — A107

2sh, You too can be infected. 6sh, Has no cure. 8.50sh, Casual sex is unsafe. 11sh, Sterilize syringe before use.

1991, Oct. 31 Litho. *Perf. 13½x14*

559	A107	2sh multicolored	1.25	.25
560	A107	6sh multicolored	2.50	2.25
561	A107	8.50sh multicolored	3.50	3.00
562	A107	11sh multicolored	4.75	4.75
		Nos. 559-562 (4)	12.00	10.25

Queen Elizabeth II's Accession to the Throne, 40th Anniv.
Common Design Type

1992, Feb. 6 Litho. *Perf. 14x13½*

563	CD349	3sh multicolored	.30	.25
564	CD349	8sh multicolored	.95	.95
565	CD349	11sh multicolored	1.20	1.20
566	CD349	14sh multicolored	1.35	1.35
567	CD349	40sh multicolored	4.00	4.00
		Nos. 563-567 (5)	7.80	7.75

Wildlife — A108

1992, May 8 *Perf. 14½*

568	A108	3sh Leopard	2.00	.35
569	A108	8sh Lion	2.75	2.00
570	A108	10sh Elephant	5.75	3.00
571	A108	11sh Buffalo	3.50	3.00
572	A108	14sh Rhinoceros	9.50	5.00
		Nos. 568-572 (5)	23.50	13.35

Vintage Cars — A109

Designs: 3sh, Intl. Harvester S.S. motor truck, 1926. 8sh, Fiat 509, 1924. 10sh, "R" Hupmobile, 1923. 11sh, Chevrolet Box Body, 1928. 14sh, Bentley Parkward, 1934.

1992, June 24 *Perf. 14½*

573	A109	3sh multicolored	1.95	.70
574	A109	8sh multicolored	2.65	1.90
575	A109	10sh multicolored	3.10	2.50
576	A109	11sh multicolored	3.50	3.50
577	A109	14sh multicolored	4.75	5.50
		Nos. 573-577 (5)	15.95	14.10

1992 Summer Olympics, Barcelona — A110

3sh, Runners. 8sh, Judo. 10sh, Women's volleyball. 11sh, 4x100-meter relay. 14sh, 10,000-meter run.

1992, July 24 Litho. *Perf. 14½*

578	A110	3sh multicolored	.45	.45
579	A110	8sh multicolored	1.55	1.55
580	A110	10sh multicolored	2.60	2.60
581	A110	11sh multicolored	2.60	2.60
582	A110	14sh multicolored	3.50	3.50
		Nos. 578-582 (5)	10.70	10.70

Christmas — A111

Designs: 3sh, Joseph, Jesus & animals in stable. 8sh, Mary holding Jesus in stable. 11sh, Map of Kenya, Christmas tree. 14sh, Adoration of the Magi.

1992, Dec. 14 Litho. *Perf. 13½x14*

583	A111	3sh multicolored	.45	.45
584	A111	8sh multicolored	1.10	1.10
585	A111	11sh multicolored	1.50	1.50
586	A111	14sh multicolored	1.75	1.75
		Nos. 583-586 (4)	4.80	4.80

Lighthouses — A112

Designs: 3sh, Asembo Bay, Lake Victoria. 8sh, Ras Serani, Mombasa. 11sh, Ras Serani, Mombasa, diff. 14sh, Gingira, Lake Victoria.

1993, Jan. 25 *Perf. 14½*

587	A112	3sh multicolored	2.75	1.10
588	A112	8sh multicolored	4.75	3.25
589	A112	11sh multicolored	6.00	5.25
590	A112	14sh multicolored	8.00	8.00
		Nos. 587-590 (4)	21.50	17.60

Birds — A113

Designs: 50c, Superb starling. 1sh, Red and yellow barbet. 1.50sh, Ross's turaco. 3sh, Greater honeyguide. 5sh, African fish eagle. 6sh, Vulturine guineafowl. 7sh, Malachite kingfisher. 8sh, Speckled pigeon. 10sh, Cinnamon-chested bee-eater. 11sh, Scarlet-chested sunbird. 14sh, Reichenow's weaver. 50sh, Yellow-billed hornbill. 80sh, Lesser flamingo. 100sh, Hadada ibis.

1993-99 Photo. *Perf. 15x14*

Granite Paper

594	A113	50c multi	.30	.25
597	A113	1sh multi	.30	.25
598	A113	1.50sh multi	.30	.25
600	A113	3sh multi	.30	.25
601	A113	5sh multi	.30	.25
601A	A113	6sh multi	*5.00*	1.00
602	A113	7sh multi	.45	.45
603	A113	8sh multi	.55	.55
604	A113	10sh multi	.65	.65
605	A113	11sh multi	.70	.70
606	A113	14sh multi	.90	.90

Size: 25x42mm

Perf. 14½

608	A113	50sh multi	3.25	3.25
609	A113	80sh multi	5.00	5.00
610	A113	100sh multi	6.50	6.50
		Nos. 594-610 (14)	24.50	20.25

Issued: 1.50sh, 5sh, 2/14/94; 6sh, 1999; others, 2/22/93.

17th World Congress of Rehabilatation Intl. — A114

3sh, Health care, vert. 8sh, Recreation. 10sh, Vocational training. 11sh, Recreation & sports. 14sh, Emblem, vert.

1993, July 1 Litho. *Perf. 14½*

611	A114	3sh multicolored	.90	.25
612	A114	8sh multicolored	1.40	.75
613	A114	10sh multicolored	1.75	1.75
614	A114	11sh multicolored	1.75	1.75
615	A114	14sh multicolored	2.10	2.10
		Nos. 611-615 (5)	7.90	6.60

Maendeleo ya Wanawake Organization, 42th Anniv. — A115

Designs: 3.50sh, Maendeleo House. 9sh, Planting trees. 11sh, Rural family planning services, vert. 12.50sh, Water nearer the people. 15.50sh, Maendeleo improved wood cookstove, vert.

Perf. 14x13½, 13½x14

1994, Mar. 17 Litho.

616	A115	3.50sh multicolored	1.10	.25
617	A115	9sh multicolored	1.60	.60
618	A115	11sh multicolored	1.25	1.25
619	A115	12.50sh multicolored	2.25	2.25
620	A115	15.50sh multicolored	2.50	2.50
		Nos. 616-620 (5)	8.70	6.85

Orchids — A116

Designs: 3.50sh, Ansellia africana. 9sh, Aerangis lutecalba. 12.50sh, Polystachya bella. 15.50sh, Brachycorythis kalbreyeri. 20sh, Eulophia guineensis.

1994, June 27 Litho. *Perf. 13½x14*

621	A116	3.50sh multicolored	1.85	.25
622	A116	9sh multicolored	2.50	1.00
623	A116	12.50sh multicolored	2.75	2.50
624	A116	15.50sh multicolored	3.35	3.35
625	A116	20sh multicolored	4.30	4.30
		Nos. 621-625 (5)	14.75	11.40

African Development Bank, 30th Anniv. — A117

1994, Nov. 21 Litho. *Perf. 14½*

626	A117	6sh KICC, Nairobi	1.25	.25
627	A117	25sh Isinya, Kajiado	4.50	4.50

Intl. Year of the Family — A118

6sh, Family planning. 14.50sh, Health. 20sh, Education, horiz. 25sh, Emblem, horiz.

1994, Dec. 22

628	A118	6sh multi	.85	.25
629	A118	14.50sh multi	3.10	1.50
630	A118	20sh multi	3.50	3.50
631	A118	25sh multi	3.50	3.50
		Nos. 628-631 (4)	10.95	8.75

Rotary, 50th Anniv. — A119

Designs: 6sh, Paul P. Harris, founder. 14.50sh, Rotary Club of Mombasa. 17.50sh, Polio plus vaccine. 20sh, Water projects. 25sh, Emblem, motto.

1994, Dec. 29 *Perf. 13½x14*

632	A119	6sh multicolored	.60	.25
633	A119	14.50sh multicolored	1.60	.75
634	A119	17.50sh multicolored	2.00	2.00
635	A119	20sh multicolored	2.25	2.25
636	A119	25sh multicolored	2.75	2.75
		Nos. 632-636 (5)	9.20	8.00

SPCA — A120

1995, Jan. 13 Litho. *Perf. 14½*

637	A120	6sh Donkey	.55	.25
638	A120	14.50sh Cattle	1.50	.55
639	A120	17.50sh Sheep	1.90	1.10
640	A120	20sh Dog	2.10	2.10
641	A120	25sh Cat	2.60	2.60
		Nos. 637-641 (5)	8.65	6.60

Kenya Society for Prevention of Cruelty to Animals.

Golf — A121

6sh, Man in vest. 17.50sh, Woman. 20sh, Man in red shirt. 25sh, Golf club.

1995, Feb. 28 Litho. *Perf. 14½*

642	A121	6sh multicolored	1.10	.25
643	A121	17.50sh multicolored	3.50	1.10
644	A121	20sh multicolored	3.75	1.80
645	A121	25sh multicolored	5.00	1.60
		Nos. 642-645 (4)	13.35	4.75

Traditional Crafts — A122

6sh, Perfume containers. 14.50sh, Basketry. 17.50sh, Preservation pots. 20sh, Gourds. 25sh, Wooden containers.

1995, Mar. 24 Litho. *Perf. 14x13½*

646	A122	6sh multicolored	.50	.25
647	A122	14.50sh multicolored	1.00	.95
648	A122	17.50sh multicolored	1.40	1.40
649	A122	20sh multicolored	1.75	1.75
650	A122	25sh multicolored	2.40	2.40
		Nos. 646-650 (5)	7.05	6.75

UN, 50th Anniv. — A123

Designs: 23sh, UN Headquarters, Nairobi. 26sh, People holding UN emblem. 32sh, UN Peacekeeper's helmet. 40sh, UN emblem.

1995, Oct. 24 Litho. *Perf. 13½*

651	A123	23sh multicolored	1.40	.70
652	A123	26sh multicolored	1.50	.90
653	A123	32sh multicolored	2.10	2.10
654	A123	40sh multicolored	2.25	2.25
		Nos. 651-654 (4)	7.25	5.95

ICIPE, 25th Anniv. — A124

1995, Sept. 29 Litho. *Perf. 13½*

655	A124	14sh Tse-tse fly	.75	.35
656	A124	26sh Tick	1.40	.90
657	A124	32sh Wild silk moth	1.75	1.25
658	A124	33sh Maize borer	1.90	1.90
659	A124	40sh Locust	2.25	2.25
		Nos. 655-659 (5)	8.05	6.65

FAO, 50th Anniv. — A125

14sh, Maize production. 28sh, Cattle rearing. 32sh, Poultry keeping. 33sh, Fishing. 40sh, Fruits.

1995, Oct. 16

660	A125	14sh multicolored	.90	.35
661	A125	28sh multicolored	2.00	1.00
662	A125	32sh multicolored	2.25	2.00
663	A125	33sh multicolored	2.25	2.25
664	A125	40sh multicolored	2.75	2.75
		Nos. 660-664 (5)	10.15	8.35

Miniature Sheets

1996 Summer Olympics, Atlanta — A126

No. 665: a, 14sh, Swimming. b, 20sh, Archery. c, 32sh, Javelin. d, 40sh, Fencing. e, 50sh, Discus. f, 20sh, Weight lifting.

No. 666: a, Pole vault. b, Equestrian. c, Diving. d, Track e, Torch bearer. f, Hurdles. g, Kayak. h, Boxing. i, Gymnastics.

No. 667 — Medal winners: a, Greg Louganis, diving. b, Muhammed Ali, boxing. c, Nadia Comaneci, gymnastics. d, Daley Thompson, decathlon. e, Kipchoge "Kip" Keino, track and field. f, Kornelia Enders, swimming. g, Jackie Joyner-Kersee, track and field. h, Michael Jordan, basketball. i, Shun Fujimoto, gymnastics.

No. 668, 100sh, Torch bearer. No. 669, 100sh, Gold medalist.

1996, Jan. 5 Litho. *Perf. 14*

665	A126	Sheet of 6, #a.-f.	10.50	10.50
666	A126 20sh	Sheet of 9, #a.-i.	11.25	11.25
667	A126 25sh	Sheet of 9, #a.-i.	*13.50*	*13.50*

Souvenir Sheets

668-669	A126	Set of 2	11.00	11.00

World Tourism Organization, 20th Anniv. — A127

1996, Jan. 31 Litho. *Perf. 13½*

670	A127	6sh Lions	.50	.25
671	A127	14sh Mount Kenya	1.00	.35
672	A127	20sh Water sports	1.50	.80
673	A127	25sh Hippopotomus	2.00	2.00
674	A127	40sh Culture	3.00	3.00
		Nos. 670-674 (5)	8.00	6.40

Perf. 13x13½

675	A127	50sh Giraffes, vert.	5.00	5.00

Wild Animals — A128

No. 676, Water buck. No. 677, Rhinoceros. No. 678, Cheetah. No. 679, Oryx. No. 680, Reticulated giraffe. No. 681, Bongo.

Booklet Stamps

1996 *Perf. 13x13½*

676	A128	20sh multicolored	1.40	.75
677	A128	20sh multicolored	1.40	.75
678	A128	20sh multicolored	1.40	.75
679	A128	20sh multicolored	1.40	.75
680	A128	20sh multicolored	1.40	.75
681	A128	20sh multicolored	1.40	.75
a.		Booklet pane of 6, #676-681	15.00	
		Complete booklet, 4 #681a	70.00	

Nos. 676-681 appear in No. 681a in two different orders. Complete booklet contains 2 of each type of pane.

1996 Summer Olympic Games, Atlanta — A129

1996, July 18 Litho. *Perf. 13½x14*

682	A129	6sh Woman running	.30	.30
683	A129	14sh Steeple chase	.60	.60
684	A129	20sh Victory lap	.90	.90
685	A129	25sh Boxing	1.10	1.10
686	A129	40sh Man running	1.90	1.90
		Nos. 682-686 (5)	4.80	4.80

Red Cross — A130

6sh, Emblem. 14sh, Blood donation. 20sh, Immunization. 25sh, Refugees. 40sh, Clean environment.

1996, Aug. 30 Litho. *Perf. 14*

687	A130	6sh multicolored	.40	.40
688	A130	14sh multicolored	.80	.80
689	A130	20sh multicolored	1.25	1.25
690	A130	25sh multicolored	1.50	1.50
691	A130	40sh multicolored	2.50	2.50
		Nos. 687-691 (5)	6.45	6.45

East African Wildlife Society — A131

1996, Sept. 10 Litho. *Perf. 14½*

693	A131	6sh Impala	.45	.45
694	A131	20sh Colobus monkey	1.60	1.60
695	A131	25sh Elephant	2.00	2.00
696	A131	40sh Black rhino	3.75	3.75
		Nos. 693-696 (4)	7.80	7.80

Lions Club Intl. — A132

1996, Oct. 31 Litho. *Perf. 13½*

697	A132	6sh Logo	.30	.30
698	A132	14sh Eye camps	.95	.95
699	A132	20sh Wheel chair	1.50	1.50
700	A132	25sh Ambulance	1.75	1.75
		Nos. 697-700 (4)	4.50	4.50

COMESA (Common Market for Eastern and Southern Africa — A133

1997, Jan. 15 Litho. *Perf. 13½x14*

701	A133	6sh COMESA logo	.30	.25
702	A133	20sh Natl. flag	1.40	1.40

Fish of Lake Victoria — A134

Haplochromis: No. 703, Orange rock hunter. No. 704, Chilotes. No. 705, Cinctus. No. 706, Nigricans.

1997, Jan. 31 *Perf. 14x13½*

703	A134	25sh multicolored	*1.50*	*.90*
704	A134	25sh multicolored	*1.50*	*.90*
705	A134	25sh multicolored	*1.50*	*.90*
706	A134	25sh multicolored	*1.50*	*.90*
		Nos. 703-706 (4)	*6.00*	*3.60*

World Wildlife Fund.

Locomotives A135

1997, Feb. 20 Litho. *Perf. 14x13½*

707	A135	6sh Class 94, 1981	.80	.25
708	A135	14sh Class 87, 1964	1.25	.45
709	A135	20sh Class 59, 1955	1.60	.70
710	A135	25sh Class 57, 1939	1.60	1.25
711	A135	30sh Class 23, 1923	2.25	2.00
712	A135	40sh Class 10, 1914	2.25	2.25
		Nos. 707-712 (6)	9.50	6.90

Dated 1996.

Fruits — A136

1997, Feb. 28 *Perf. 14½*

713	A136	6sh Orange	.30	.25
714	A136	14sh Pineapple	2.10	.50
715	A136	20sh Mango	3.00	2.00
716	A136	25sh Papaya	3.75	2.50
		Nos. 713-716 (4)	9.15	5.25

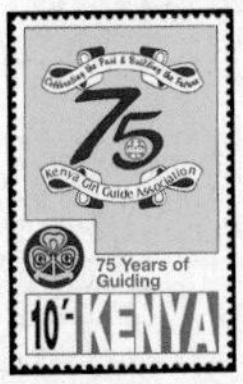

A137

Scouting Organizations: No. 717, Girl Guides, 75th anniv. No. 718, Lord Baden Powell. No. 719, Girl scouts hiking. No. 720, Rangers camping. No. 721, Girl Guides planting trees. No. 722, Boy Scouts first aid. No. 723, Boy Scouts camping. No. 724, Brownies.

1997, Sept. 1 **Litho.** *Perf. 14½*

717	A137	10sh multicolored	.35	.35
718	A137	10sh multicolored	.35	.35
a.		Pair, #717-718	.75	.75
719	A137	27sh multicolored	.90	.90
720	A137	27sh multicolored	.90	.90
a.		Pair, #719-720	2.25	2.25
721	A137	33sh multicolored	1.25	1.25
722	A137	33sh multicolored	1.25	1.25
a.		Pair, #721-722	3.00	3.00
723	A137	42sh multicolored	1.50	1.50
724	A137	42sh multicolored	1.50	1.50
a.		Pair, #723-724	3.50	3.50
		Nos. 717-724 (8)	8.00	8.00

Tourist Attractions A138

Designs: 10sh, Crocodile. 27sh, Hot Springs, Lake Bogoria. 30sh, Warthogs. 33sh, Wind surfing. 42sh, Traditional huts.

1997, Oct. 9 *Perf. 13½*

725	A138	10sh multicolored	1.25	.25
726	A138	27sh multicolored	2.00	1.60
727	A138	30sh multicolored	2.00	1.90
728	A138	33sh multicolored	2.25	2.25
729	A138	42sh multicolored	2.50	2.50
		Nos. 725-729 (5)	10.00	8.50

Vasco da Gama's Stop in Malindi, 500th Anniv. — A139

Designs: 10sh, Residents greeting ships as they arrive. 24sh, Three ships. 33sh, Map of voyage. 42sh, Ships in bay, monument.

1998, Apr. 4 **Litho.** *Perf. 13*

730	A139	10sh multicolored	.60	.30
731	A139	24sh multicolored	1.40	.75
732	A139	33sh multicolored	2.00	2.00
733	A139	42sh multicolored	2.50	2.50
		Nos. 730-733 (4)	6.50	5.55

Pan African Postal Union (PAPU) — A140

1998, June 10 **Litho.** *Perf. 14½*

734	A140	10sh Lion	1.75	.30
735	A140	24sh Buffalo	2.25	.85
736	A140	33sh Grant's gazelle	3.00	3.00
737	A140	42sh Cheetah	4.15	4.15
		Nos. 734-737 (4)	11.15	8.30

Souvenir Sheet

738	A140	50sh Hirola gazelle	4.00	4.00

Pres. Daniel arap Moi Taking Oath of Office, 1998 — A141

1998, Dec. 8 **Litho.** *Perf. 13½*

739	A141	14sh multicolored	1.50	.80

Turtles — A142

Designs: 17sh, Leatherback. 20sh, Green sea. 30sh, Hawksbill. 47sh, Olive Ridley. 59sh, Loggerhead.

2000, Apr. 13 **Litho.** *Perf. 13½x13¾*

740	A142	17sh multi	1.00	.35
741	A142	20sh multi	1.25	.40
742	A142	30sh multi	1.75	1.00
743	A142	47sh multi	2.50	2.50
744	A142	59sh multi	3.00	3.00
		Nos. 740-744 (5)	9.50	7.25

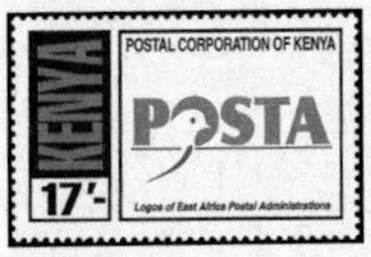

Emblems of East African Postal Administrations A143

Designs: 17sh, Postal Corporation of Kenya. 35sh, Uganda Posta Limited. 50sh, Tanzania Posts Corporation. 70sh, Postal Corporation of Kenya.

2000, May 31 *Perf. 13¾x13½*

745	A143	17sh multi	.85	.35
746	A143	35sh multi	1.60	1.25
747	A143	50sh multi	2.25	2.25
		Nos. 745-747 (3)	4.70	3.85

Souvenir Sheet

Perf. 13¼x13

748	A143	70sh multi	4.50	4.50

Crops — A144

2001, Feb. 28 **Photo.** *Perf. 14½x14*

749	A144	2sh Cotton	.30	.25
750	A144	4sh Bananas	.30	.25
751	A144	5sh Avocados	.30	.25
752	A144	6sh Cassava	.30	.25
753	A144	8sh Arrowroot	.30	.25
754	A144	10sh Papayas	.30	.25
755	A144	19sh Oranges	.50	.35
756	A144	20sh Pyrethrum	.50	.35
757	A144	30sh Peanuts	.75	.60
758	A144	35sh Coconuts	.90	.60
759	A144	40sh Sisal	1.00	.75
760	A144	50sh Cashews	1.25	.90

Size: 25x42mm

Perf. 14¼

761	A144	60sh Tea	1.50	1.00
762	A144	80sh Corn	2.00	1.50
763	A144	100sh Coffee	2.50	1.75
764	A144	200sh Finger millet	5.00	3.50
765	A144	400sh Sorghum	10.00	7.00
766	A144	500sh Sugar cane	12.50	8.50
		Nos. 749-766 (18)	40.20	28.30

2001 **Photo.** *Perf. 14¾ Horiz.*

Coil Stamps

766A	A144	5sh Avocados	*3.00*	*3.00*
766B	A144	10sh Papayas	*3.00*	*3.00*

Historic Sites of East Africa — A145

Designs: 19sh, Source of Nile River, Jinja, Uganda. 35sh, Lamu Fort, Kenya (28x28mm). 40sh, Olduvai Gorge, Tanzania. 50sh, Thimlich Ohinga, Kenya (28x28mm).

Perf. 14¼, 13½ (35sh, 50sh)

2002 **Litho.**

767-770	A145	Set of 4	7.50	7.50

Kenya - People's Republic of China Diplomatic Relations, 40th Anniv. A146

Flags of Kenya and People's Republic of China and: 21sh, Section of Mombasa Road. 66sh, Kasarani Stadium.

2003, Dec. 14 **Litho.** *Perf. 12*

771-772	A146	Set of 2	*7.50*	*7.50*

Mammals A147

Designs: 21sh, Lioness and baby oryx. 60sh, Leopard and cub. 66sh, Zebra and calf. 88sh, Bongo and calf.

2004, Nov. 19 **Litho.** *Perf. 14½*

773-776	A147	Set of 4	10.00	10.00

Easter — A148

Designs: 25sh, Jesus with hand raised. 65sh, Jesus condemned to death. 75sh, Crucifixion. 95sh, Jesus praying.

2005, Apr. 1 **Litho.** *Perf. 13½*

777-780	A148	Set of 4	10.50	10.50

Rotary International, Cent. — A149

Rotary emblem and: 25sh, Polio vaccination. 65sh, Donation of Jaipur feet. 75sh, Don Bosco Center, Nairobi. 95sh, Donation of sewing machine.

2005, May 26

781-784	A149	Set of 4	10.50	10.50

Native Costumes — A150

Designs: 21sh, Gabbra. 60sh, Pokot. 66sh, Meru. 88sh, Digo.

2005, Dec. 6 **Litho.** *Perf. 14½*

785-788	A150	Set of 4	8.00	8.00

Fish — A151

Designs: 25sh, Elephant snout fish. 55sh, Sudan catfish. 75sh, Nile perch. 95sh, Redbreast tilapia.

2006, May 4 **Litho.** *Perf. 13½x13*

789	A151	25sh multi	*100.00*	*25.00*
790	A151	55sh multi	*30.00*	—
791	A151	75sh multi	*30.00*	—
792	A151	95sh multi	*30.00*	—

24th Universal Postal Union Congress, Nairobi — A152

2006, Oct. 11 **Litho.** *Perf. 13½*

793	A152	25sh multi	1.25	1.25

Values are for stamps with surrounding selvage. Due to political unrest in Kenya, the UPU Congress was moved to Geneva, Switzerland.

Hippopotamus and Tortoise — A153

2006, Dec. 15 **Litho.** *Perf. 12½x13*

794	A153	25sh multi	2.00	2.00

Tourism — A155

2006, Dec. 15 *Perf. 13*

Booklet Stamps

795	A155	25sh Roan antelope	*8.00*	4.00
796	A155	25sh Weaver bird	*8.00*	4.00
797	A155	25sh Monkey	*8.00*	4.00
a.		Booklet pane of 3, #795-797	*25.00*	—
798	A155	25sh Turkana hut	*8.00*	4.00
799	A155	25sh Sports	*8.00*	4.00
800	A155	25sh Golf course	*8.00*	4.00
a.		Booklet pane of 3, #798-800	*25.00*	—
801	A155	25sh Abadares Waterfall	*8.00*	4.00
802	A155	25sh Balloon safari	*8.00*	4.00
803	A155	25sh Bull fighting	*8.00*	4.00
a.		Booklet pane of 3, #801-803	*25.00*	—
804	A155	25sh Chimpanzee	*8.00*	4.00
805	A155	25sh Maasai	*8.00*	4.00
806	A155	25sh Kit Mikaye	*8.00*	4.00
a.		Booklet pane of 3, #804-806	*25.00*	—
		Complete booklet, #797a, 800a, 803a, 806a	*100.00*	
		Nos. 795-806 (12)	*96.00*	48.00

Mountains A156

Designs: 25sh, Mt. Kenya, Kenya. 75sh, Mt. Ruwenzori, Uganda. 95sh, Mt. Kilimanjaro, Tanzania.

2007, Feb. 28 **Litho.** *Perf. 13½*

807-809	A156	Set of 3	10.00	10.00

Breast Cancer Awareness — A157

2007, Oct. 28 *Perf. 13¼*

810	A157	25sh multi	2.00	2.00

Ceremonial Costumes — A158

Men's and women's costumes: 25sh, Ogiek. 65sh, Sabaot. 75sh, Ribe. 95sh, Elmolo.

2007, Nov. 21 *Perf. 14½*
811-814 A158 Set of 4 8.25 8.25

National Arboretum, Cent. A159

Designs: 25sh, Cape chestnut tree and blossom. 65sh, Bhutan cypress tree, Tree Center. 75sh, Nandi flame tree and blossom. 95sh, Calabash nutmeg tree and blossom.

2007, Dec. 13 **Litho.** *Perf. 13¾*
815-818 A159 Set of 4 8.25 8.25

24th UPU Congress A160

Design: 25sh, Sitalunga gazelle in Saiwa Swamp. 65sh, Jackson's hartebeest at Ruma Park. 75sh, Steeplechase runner. 95sh, Kenyatta Intl. Conference Center, Nairobi.

2008, Feb. 7 **Litho.** *Perf. 14½*
819 A160 25sh multi *1.00* *.50*
820 A160 65sh multi *2.50* *1.50*
821 A160 75sh multi *3.00* *2.25*
822 A160 95sh multi *3.75* *3.75*
Nos. 819-822 (4) 10.25 8.00

Because of political turmoil in Kenya, the 24th UPU Congress was moved from Nairobi to Geneva, Switzerland.

2008 Summer Olympics, Beijing — A161

Designs: 25sh, Kenyan athletes holding Kenyan flag. 65sh, Women's volleyball, vert. 75sh, Women runners. 95sh, Boxing.

2008, Aug. 21 **Litho.** *Perf. 14½*
823-826 A161 Set of 4 7.50 7.50

Heroes of Kenya A162

Designs: 25sh, Vice-president Oginga Odinga (c. 1911-94), Pio Gama Pinto (1927-65), politician, Tom Mboya (1930-69), politician, Ronald Ngala (1923-72), politician. 65sh, The Kapenguria Six. 75sh, Dedan Kimathi (1920-57), rebel leader, Elijah Masinde (c. 1910-87), Bukusu tribal leader, Mekatilili Wa Menza, female leader of 1914 rebellion, Koitalel Samoei (1860-1905), Nandi chief. 95sh, Kenya Army Peacekeeping Force.

2008, Oct. 17 *Perf. 12¾x13¼*
827-830 A162 Set of 4 8.50 8.50

Theosophical Order of Service, Cent. — A163

2008, Nov. 17 **Litho.** *Perf. 14x13¾*
831 A163 25sh multi 1.25 1.25

Aga Khan, 50th Anniv.of Reign — A164

Designs: 25sh, Madrasa program (40x40mm). 65sh, Coastal rural support program (40x40mm). 75sh, Aga Khan Academy, Mombasa (44x30mm). 95sh, Aga Khan University Hospital, Nairobi (44x30mm).

Perf. 13, 14½ (75sh, 95sh)
2008, Dec. 13
832-835 A164 Set of 4 7.50 7.50

Blind Man — A165

2009, July 20 *Perf. 14½*
836 A165 25sh multi .65 .65

Louis Braille (1809-52), educator of the blind.

Postal Services A166

Designs: No. 837, 25sh, Man greeting woman, PostaPay emblem. No. 838, 25sh, Parcels, Posta Parcel emblem. No. 839, 25sh, Mailman and trucks, Posta Dispatch emblem. No. 840, 25sh, Stamp collector and stamps, Posta Philately emblem. No. 841, 25sh, Open post office box, Posta Direct Mail emblem. No. 842, 25sh, Agency services, Posta Kenya emblem. No. 843, 25sh, Woman reading letter, Posta Mail emblem. No. 844, 25sh, Man at open post office box, Posta Kenya emblem. No. 845, 25sh, Financial Services clerk and client, computer, Posta Money Order emblem. No. 846, 65sh, Postal worker with package at airport, EMS Kenya emblem. No. 847, 75sh, Narok Post Office, Posta Kenya emblem. No. 848, 95sh, People at water spigot, Posta Kenya emblem.

2009, Dec. 9 *Perf. 14x13¾*
837-848 A166 Set of 12 12.50 12.50
845a Sheet of 9, #837-845 *15.00* *15.00*

East Africa Natural History Society, Cent. — A167

Bird on branch and: 25sh, Taita African violet, Amegilla bee. 65sh, Reed frog. 75sh, Great blue turaco. 95sh, Golden-rumped sengi.

2010, Mar. 25 *Perf. 13*
Granite Paper
849-852 A167 Set of 4 6.75 6.75

Pan-African Postal Union, 30th Anniv. — A167a

2010, Nov. 30 **Litho.** *Perf. 14x13¾*
852A A167a 25sh multi .65 .65

Insects — A168

No. 853: a, Danaus chrysippus (African monarch). b, Pontia helice. c, Junonia hierta (Yellow pansy). d, Chiasmia subcurvaria. e, Catopsilia florella (African migrant). f, Belenois thysa (False dotted border). g, Leucinodes orbonalis sp. h, Gelechioidea sp. i, Eupithecia sp. cf. festiva. j, Nymphalidae. k, Paracrra mimesa. l, Hodebertia testalis. m, Alucitidae sp. n, Anthozela sp. n. o, Eucosmini gen. n. sp. n. p, Eucosmini sp. q, Zalaca snelleni. r, Yponomeuta strigillata. s, Tortrix dinota. t, Parotis sp. nr. prasinalis. u, Precis hierta. v, Colotis antevippe. w, Cryptophlebia semilunana. x, Hypolimnas misippus. y, Yponomeuta fumigatus.

No. 854: a, Oplostomus haroldi (Large hive beetle). b, Cartoblatta sp. (Cockroaches). c, Mormotomyia hirsuta. d, Cicindellidae. e, Nosognatha ruficollis. f, Hetrodinae sp. g, Helopeltis schoutedeni. h, Ceroctis sp. (Blister beetle). i, Bagrada cruciferarum. j, Popillia aeneipennis (Chafer). k, Lampetis sp. (Jewel beetle). l, Oryctes sp. (Rhinoceros beetle). m, Homoderus mellyi. n, Zonocerus variegatus. o, Leucospidae. p, Agnoscelis versicolor. q, Hispinae (Tortoise beetle). r, Curculionidae. s, Cypholoba perspicillaris. t, Lycidae. u, Milkweed bugs. v, Mylabris tristigma. w, Paederus sp. x, Pyrops turritus. y, Tenebrionidae.

No. 855: a, Fig wasp in flight. b, Ptyelus flavescens (Rain tree bug). c, Phlebotomus feeding. d, Fig wasp, head at bottom. e, Trithemis annulata (Dragonfly). f, Braconid wasp. g, Polistes sp. (Paper wasps). h, Helopeltis schoutedeni. i, Trithemis sp. (Dragonfly). j, Cicada. k, Silverfish. l, Stingless bee. m, Lipotriches sp. n, Bombyliidae. o, Bromophila caffra. p, Schistocerca gregaria. q, Plagiotryptus hippiscus. r, Reduviidae. s, Diopsidae (Stalk-eyed fly). t, Lamyra gulo and wasp prey. u, Dictyopharidae. v, Rhiniidae cf. Fainia sp. w, Locust. x, Megastigmus sp. m. y, Glossina morsitans feeding.

No. 856: a, Bactrocera invadens, head at top. b, Trirhithrum culcasiae. c, Trirhithrum coffeae. d, Bactrocera invadens, head at bottom. e, Bactrocera munroi. f, Caprophthoromyia dimidiata. g, Celidodacus obnubilus. h, Ceratitis caetrata. i, Ceratitis captiata. j, Ceratitis copelandi. k, Ceratitis cosyra. l, Ceratitis cuthbertsoni. m, Ceratitis rosa. n, Ceratitis stictica. o, Ceratitis whartoni. p, Conradtina acroleuca. q, Dacus apostata. r, Dacus frontalis. s, Dacus sphaeristicus. t, Dacus telfairae. u, Munromyia whartoni. v, Craspedoxantha sp. w, Taomyia marshalli. x, Themarictera laticeps. y, Trirhithrum albomaculatum.

2011, Nov. 16 *Perf. 13x13¼*
853 Sheet of 25 *150.00* *150.00*
a.-y. A168 25sh Any single *5.00* *5.00*
854 Sheet of 25 37.50 37.50
a.-y. A168 65sh Any single 1.50 1.50
855 Sheet of 25 44.00 44.00
a.-y. A168 75sh Any single 1.75 1.75
856 Sheet of 25 52.50 52.50
a.-y. A168 95sh Any single 2.10 2.10
Nos. 853-856 (4) 284.00 284.00

Intl. Center of Insect Physiology and Endocrinology, 40th anniv.

Promulgation of New Constitution — A169

2011 *Perf. 14½*
857 A169 25sh multi .60 .60

United Nations Environment Program, 40th Anniv. — A170

Designs: 30sh, Flags at UNEP regional office, Nairobi. 90sh, Buildings in Stockholm, Sweden. 110sh, Christ the Redeemer Statue, Rio de Janeiro.

2012 *Perf. 14*
858-860 A170 Set of 3 5.50 5.50

United Nations Environment Program, 40th Anniv. — A171

United Nations Environment Program emblem and emblem for: 30sh, Convention on International Trade in Endangered Species of Wild Fauna and Flora. 90sh, Montreal Protocol on Substances that Deplete the Ozone Layer. 110sh, Green Economy.

2012, June 22 **Litho.** *Perf. 14*
861-863 A171 Set of 3 5.50 5.50

Wangari Muta Maathai (1940-2011), 2004 Nobel Peace Laureate — A173

2012, Sept. 25 **Litho.** *Perf. 14*
867 A173 30sh multi .70 .70

Independence, 50th Anniv. — A174

No. 868: a, First airplane to land in Kenya, 1920. b, 1904 locomotive. c, East Africa Railway & Harbor train car. d, Jamhuri High School. e, Prince of Wales School. f, Machakos Girls School. g, Royal Technical College, University of Nairobi. h, Kenyatta University. i, Jomo Kenyatta University of Agriculture & Technology. j, Nairobi skyline. k, King George VI Hospital. l, Kenyatta National Hospital. m, Jomo Kenyatta International Airport. n, Mobile library. o, Kenya National Library, Nairobi. p, Horticulture. q, Poultry farming. r, Corn farming (maize). s, Beef farming. t, Dairy farming. u, Compulsory free primary education. v, Kenya National Adult Literacy Survey. w, Murang's Road Junction. x, Globe Cinema Complex. y, Oil prospecting.

No. 869: a, Pres. Uhuru Kenyatta and Deputy Pres. William Ruto. b, Queen Elizabeth II and Prince Philip, 1953. c, Lancaster House Conference, 1963. d, Dedan Kimathi. e, Mau Mau movement. f, Kapenguria Six. g, Kapenguria cells. h, Lowering of the Union Jack, 1963. i, Munyao Kisol hoisting Kenyan flag on Mt. Kenya, 1963. j, Promulgation of new constitution. k, First transition. l, Second transition. m, Third transition. n, Fourth transition. o, Parliament Building. p, First Cabinet, 1963. q, Colonial and current coats of arms. r, Colonial and current flags. s, Maps showing the eight provinces and 47 counties. t, Judiciary Building. u, Kenyatta Mausoleum. v, Old Provincial Commissioner's Office, 1913. w, Nyayo House. x, Baron Delamere, first governor of Nairobi. y, Kenya Defense Forces in Somalia.

No. 870: a, Fort Jesus, 1565. b, Kenya-Uganda railway line, 1896. c, Nyall Bridge, 1900. d, Gedi Ruins, 13th cent. e, First Post Office in Mombasa, 1902. f, First General Post Office in Mombasa, 1920. g, First General Post Office in Nairobi, 1944. h, Kenya National Archives, 1944. i, Macmillan Library, 1925. j, Nairobi National Museum, 1890. k, 1885 Mombasa coins. l, Maasai Morans. m, Luo traditional homestead. n, Karen Blixen Museum. o, Kipande House, 1913. p, Laikipia camel caravan. q, East Africa and Uganda Protectorates #53, Kenya #8. r, Chaka drummers. s, Obokano musical instrument. t, Vasco da Gama Pillar, Malindi. u, Naftali Temu, first Kenyan Olympic gold medalist. v, Pamela Jelimo, Janeth Jepkosgei, runners. w, Ezekiel Kemboi, 2004 Olympic steeplechase gold medalist. x, David Rudisha, 2012 Olympic 800-meter gold medalist. y, Kenya Rugby Union national team.

No. 871: a, Lion. b, Elephant. c, Leopard. d, Rhinoceros. e, Buffalo. f, Hippopotamus. g, Cheetah. h, Giraffe. i, Zebra. j, Warthog. k, Wildebeest migration. l, Bongo. m, Impala. n, Hyena. o, Jackal. p, Crocodiles on Tana River. q, Flamingos at Lake Nakuru. r, Ostriches. s, Colobus monkey. t, Falcon. u, Longonot Crater. v, Thompson Falls, Nyahururu. w, Mt. Kenya. x, Lake Turkana. y, Solar eclipse.

No. 872: a, Mail runner, 1880. b, Postman delivering letters in marketplace, 1902. c, Mail box, 1920, d, Modern postal delivery van. e, Letter boxes. f, Pillar box.

No. 873: a, East African coins, 1910-65. b, Kenyan coins, 1966-2010. c, East African bank notes, 1964. d, Kenyan banknotes, 1966.

150sh, Kenyan Presidents Jomo Kenyatta (c. 1897-1978), Daniel Arap Moi, Mwai Kibaki and Uhuru Kenyatta.

Perf. 13½x13¼ Syncopated
2013, Dec. 13 **Litho.**
868 Sheet of 25 17.50 17.50
a.-y. A174 30sh Any single .70 .70
869 Sheet of 25 44.00 44.00
a.-y. A174 75sh Any single 1.75 1.75
870 Sheet of 25 52.50 52.50
a.-y. A174 90sh Any single 2.10 2.10
871 Sheet of 25 75.00 75.00
a.-y. A174 110sh Any single 3.00 3.00
Nos. 868-871 (4) 189.00 189.00
872 A174 30sh Sheet of 6, #a-f — —
873 A174 30sh Sheet of 4, #a-d — —

Imperf

Size: 87x125mm

874 A174 150sh multi — —

No. 874 has simulated perfs.

Diplomatic Relations Between Kenya and People's Republic of China, 50th Anniv.
A175

Flags of Kenya and People's Republic of China and: 30sh, Ship, Kenyan and Chinese containers. 110sh, Cranes, Kenyan Pres. Uhuru Kenyatta, Chinese Pres. Xi Jinping.
150sh, Like 110sh.

2013, Dec. 20 Litho. *Perf. 12*

875-876 A175 Set of 2 3.25 3.25

Souvenir Sheet

877 A175 150sh multi 3.50 3.50

No. 877 contains one 76x50mm stamp.

Birds — A176

Designs: 30sh, Red and yellow barbet. 35sh, Scarlet-chested sunbird. 50sh, Yellow-billed hornbill. 55sh, Greater honeyguide. 65sh, Superb starling. 70sh, African fish eagle. 80sh, Lesser flamingo. 100sh, Hadada ibis. 110sh, Ross's turaco.

Perf. 13x13¼ Syncopated

2014 Litho.

878	A176	30sh multi	1.40	.70
879	A176	35sh multi	1.60	.80
880	A176	50sh multi	2.25	1.10
881	A176	55sh multi	2.50	1.25
882	A176	65sh multi	3.00	1.50
883	A176	70sh multi	3.25	1.60
884	A176	80sh multi	3.75	1.90
885	A176	100sh multi	4.50	2.25
886	A176	110sh multi	5.00	2.50
		Nos. 878-886 (9)	27.25	13.60

Nos. 878-886 have three punched holes at lower left.

St. John Bosco (1815-88) — A177

Design: 100sh, Bosco with children, horiz.

2015, Feb. 1 Litho. *Perf. 14¼x14½*

887 A177 35sh multi + label .80 .80

Souvenir Sheet

Perf. 13½ Syncopated

887A A177 100shmulti — —

No. 887 was printed in sheets of 20 + 20 labels. No. 887A contains one 70x30mm stamp.

United Nations, 70th Anniv. — A178

Perf. 13¾ Syncopated

2015, Oct. 2 Litho.

888 A178 35sh multi .70 .70

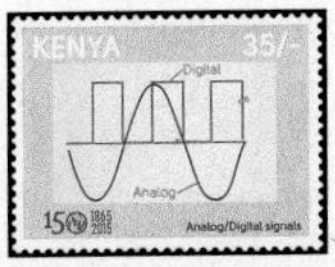

International Telecommunication Union, 150th Anniv. — A179

Designs: 35sh, Digital and analog signals. 90sh, Terrestrial services. 105sh, 150th anniv. emblem. 130sh, Space services.

2015 Litho. *Perf. 13x13¼*

889-892 A179 Set of 4 7.25 7.25

No. 892 the country name and denomination are smaller than on Nos. 889-891.

Big Game Animals — A180

Designs: 35sh, Elephant. 80sh, Lion, horiz. 90sh, Buffalo, horiz. 105sh, Leopard, horiz. 130sh, Rhinoceros.
175sh, Buffalo, lion, leopard, elephant and rhinoceros, horiz.

Perf. 13¼ Syncopated

2017, May 10 Litho.

893-897 A180 Set of 5 8.50 8.50

Size: 110x80mm

Imperf

898 A180 175sh multi 3.50 3.50

Mombasa-Nairobi Standard Gauge Railway — A181

Designs: 35sh, Mombasa Terminus. 50sh, Man standing on railroad track. 110sh, Train on bridge. 130sh, Locomotive. 150sh, Nairobi Terminus.
200sh, Like 50sh.

2017, May 31 Litho. *Perf. 14*

899-903 A181 Set of 5 9.25 9.25

Souvenir Sheet

Perf. 13¼x13

904 A181 200sh multi 4.00 4.00

No. 904 contains one 45x35mm stamp.

Kenya Pres. Uhuru Kenyatta and U.S. Pres. Barack Obama
A182

Perf. 13½x13¼

2017, Sept. 13 Litho.

905 A182 50sh multi + label 1.00 1.00

Visit of Pres. Obama to Kenya, 2nd anniv.

United Nations Sustainable Development Goals — A183

Designs: 50sh, Goal 7. 90sh, Goal 14. 105sh, Goal 13. 130sh, Goal 15.

Perf. 13½x13¼ Syncopated

2017, Oct. 9 Litho.

906-909 A183 Set of 4 7.25 7.25

Last Remaining Northern White Rhinoceroses
A184

Designs: 50sh, Female named Najin. 130sh, Male named Sudan, euthanized in March 2018. 160sh, Female named Fatu.
200sh, Two of the Northern white rhinoceroses, vert.

Perf. 13½ Syncopated

2018, May 11 Litho.

910-912 A184 Set of 3 6.75 6.75

Souvenir Sheet

913 A184 200sh multi 4.00 4.00

Souvenir Sheet

Nelson Mandela (1918-2013), President of South Africa — A185

2018, July 18 Litho. *Perf. 13½*

915 A185 100sh multi 2.00 2.00

Big Four Action Plan — A186

Designs: 30sh, Universal health coverage. 85sh, Affordable housing. 110sh, Enhancing manufacturing. 140sh, Food security and nutrition.

2019, May 29 Litho. *Perf. 14¼*

916-919 A186 Set of 4 7.25 7.25

World Sickle Cell Day, 10th Anniv. — A187

Designs: 10sh, Family. 50sh, Children. 110sh, Mother and infant. 140sh, Father and daughter.

2019, June 19 Litho. *Perf. 13*

920-923 A187 Set of 4 6.00 6.00

Posta House Headquarters, Nairobi — A188

2020, Jan. 31 Litho. *Perf. 14¼*

924 A188 30sh multi .60 .60

Postal Corporation of Kenya, 20th anniv.

Aga Khan University Hospital, Nairobi, 60th Anniv. — A189

Designs: 30sh, Hospital in 1963. 110sh, Hospital entrance. 140sh, Hospital campus.

2020, Feb. 15 Litho. *Perf. 14x14¼*

925-927 A189 Set of 3 5.50 5.50

POSTAGE DUE STAMPS

D1

Perf. 14x13½

1967-85 Litho. Unwmk.

"POSTAGE DUE" 12½mm long

J1	D1	5c dark red	.25	2.75
J2	D1	10c green	.35	2.75
J3	D1	20c dark blue	.70	3.25
J4	D1	30c reddish brown	1.00	4.00
J5	D1	40c brt red lilac	1.25	6.75

Perf. 14

J6	D1	80c brick red	1.00	6.25

Perf. 14x13½

J7	D1	1sh orange	1.75	*7.00*

"POSTAGE DUE" 11½mm long

Perf. 14¾x14

J8	D1	2sh pale violet	2.25	*4.00*
		Nos. J1-J8 (8)	8.55	*36.75*

Issued: 80c, 1978. 2sh, 1985; others, 1/3/67.
See Nos. J9-J14.

1969-70 *Perf. 14*

J1a	D1	5c	.25	5.25
J2a	D1	10c	.25	5.25
J3a	D1	20c	.45	5.75
J4a	D1	30c	.70	6.75
J5a	D1	40c	.80	*22.50*
J7a	D1	1sh	2.00	*13.50*
		Nos. J1a-J7a (6)	4.45	*59.00*

Issued: 1sh, 2/18/70; others, 12/16/69.

1971-73 *Perf. 14x15*

J1b	D1	5c	1.75	5.25
J2b	D1	10c	8.50	5.25
J3b	D1	20c	11.00	11.00
J4b	D1	30c	10.50	15.00
J5b	D1	40c	1.25	15.00
J7b	D1	1sh	17.00	*40.00*
		Nos. J1b-J7b (6)	50.00	91.50

Issued: 30c, 7/13/71; others, 2/20/73. The 10c, 20c, 1sh on chalky paper were issued 7/13/71.

1973, Dec. 12 *Perf. 15*

J1c	D1	5c	.45	4.00
J2c	D1	10c	.45	4.00
J3c	D1	20c	.45	5.00
J4c	D1	30c	.45	5.75
J5c	D1	40c	5.25	10.00
J7c	D1	1sh	1.75	*12.50*
		Nos. J1c-J7c (6)	8.80	41.25

1983 Wmk. 373 *Perf. 14x14¼*

J2d	D1	10c	.45	*2.00*
J3d	D1	20c	.45	*2.00*
J5d	D1	40c	8.50	*10.00*

Nos. J5, J7-J8 Redrawn

Perf. 14¾x14

1987-98 Litho. Unwmk.

J8A	D1	30c brown	.25	.25
J9	D1	40c bright red lilac	.25	.25
J10	D1	50c dark green	.25	.25
J10A	D1	80c red brown	.25	.25
J11	D1	1sh bright orange	.80	.80
	a.	light orange	.25	.25
J12	D1	2sh pale violet	.25	.25
J13	D1	3sh dark blue	.45	.45
J14	D1	5sh red brown	.45	.45
J15	D1	10sh brown	.45	.45
J16	D1	20sh red lilac	.80	.80
		Nos. J8A-J16 (10)	4.20	4.20

"KENYA" is 9mm wide on Nos. J9, J11. "CENTS" is 4½mm wide and "SHILLING" has cross bar on "G"; both are in a new font.
"KENYA" is 8½mm wide on No. J12. "POSTAGE DUE" is 11mm wide on Nos. J10, J11a, J15, J16.
Issued: 40c, 1sh, 1987; 10sh, 20sh, 1998; others, Dec. 6, 1993.

OFFICIAL STAMPS

Nos. 1-5 and 7 Overprinted

Perf. 14x14½

1964, Oct. 1 Photo. Unwmk.

Size: 21x17½mm

O1	A1	5c	blue, buff & dk brn	.25	.25
O2	A1	10c	brown	.25	.25
O3	A1	15c	dp magenta	1.25	.30
O4	A1	20c	yel green & dk brn	.30	.45
O5	A1	30c	yellow & black	.35	.65
O6	A1	50c	green, blk & dp car	2.75	1.10
			Nos. O1-O6 (6)	5.15	3.00

KENYA, UGANDA, & TANZANIA

'ke-nyə, ü-'gan-də, ˌtan-zə-'nē-ə

LOCATION — East Africa, bordering on the Indian Ocean
GOVT. — States in British Commonwealth
AREA — 679,802 sq. mi.
POP. — 42,760,000 (est. 1977)
CAPITAL — Nairobi (Kenya), Kampala (Uganda), Dar es Salaam (Tanzania)

Kenya became a crown colony in 1906, including the former East Africa Protectorate leased from the Sultan of Zanzibar and known as the Kenya Protectorate. In 1963 the colony became independent. Its stamps are listed under "Kenya."

The inland Uganda Protectorate, lying west of Kenya Colony, was declared a British Protectorate in 1894. Uganda became independent in 1962.

Tanganyika, a trust territory larger than Kenya or Uganda, was grouped with them postally from 1935 under the East African Posts & Telecommunications Administration. Tanganyika became independent in 1961. When it merged with Zanzibar in 1964, "Zanzibar" was added to the inscriptions on stamps issued under the E.A.P. & T. Administration. In 1965 the multiple inscription was changed to "Kenya, Uganda, Tanzania," variously arranged.

Zanzibar withdrew its own stamps in 1968, and K., U. & T. stamps became valid Jan. 1, 1968.

100 Cents = 1 Rupee
100 Cents = 1 Shilling (1922)
20 Shillings = 1 Pound

Catalogue values for unused stamps in this country are for Never Hinged items, beginning with Scott 90.

East Africa and Uganda Protectorates

King George V
A1 A2

1921 Typo. Wmk. 4 *Perf. 14*

Ordinary Paper

1	A1	1c	black	1.00	*1.90*
2	A1	3c	green	6.75	*16.50*
3	A1	6c	rose red	11.00	*22.50*
4	A1	10c	orange	10.00	1.40
5	A1	12c	gray	12.50	*150.00*
6	A1	15c	ultramarine	12.50	*22.50*

Chalky Paper

7	A1	50c	gray lilac & blk	16.50	*140.00*
8	A2	2r	blk & red, *blue*	95.00	*190.00*
9	A2	3r	green & violet	160.00	*450.00*
10	A2	5r	gray lil & ultra	190.00	*350.00*
11	A2	50r	gray grn & red	3,750.	*9,000.*
			Revenue cancel		425.00
			Nos. 1-10 (10)	515.25	*1,345.*

The name of the colony was changed to Kenya in August, 1920, but stamps of the East Africa and Uganda types were continued in use. Stamps of types A1 and A2 watermarked Multiple Crown and C A (3) are listed under East Africa and Uganda Protectorates. Used values for Nos. 8-11 are for postally used stamps. Examples with court cancels are worth considerably less.

For stamps of Kenya and Uganda overprinted "G. E. A." used in parts of former German East Africa occupied by British forces, see Tanganyika Nos. 1-9.

Kenya and Uganda

Nos. 18-85 were printed in various shades.

King George V
A3 A4

1922-27 Wmk. 4

18	A3	1c	brown	1.10	*4.75*
19	A3	5c	violet	7.50	1.00
20	A3	5c	grn ('27)	2.40	.55
21	A3	10c	green	1.75	.35
22	A3	10c	blk ('27)	4.50	.25
23	A3	12c	black	16.00	*29.00*
24	A3	15c	car rose	1.40	.25
25	A3	20c	orange	3.75	.25
26	A3	30c	ultra	4.50	.60
27	A3	50c	gray	2.75	.25
28	A3	75c	ol bister	11.00	*10.00*
29	A4	1sh	green	7.25	3.00
30	A4	2sh	gray lil	10.00	*21.00*
31	A4	2sh50c	brn ('25)	24.00	*125.00*
32	A4	3sh	gray blk	20.00	7.50
33	A4	4sh	gray ('25)	42.50	*135.00*
34	A4	5sh	carmine	27.50	27.50
35	A4	7sh50c	org ('25)	140.00	*350.00*
36	A4	10sh	ultra	82.50	*77.50*
37	A4	£1	org & blk	230.00	*340.00*
			Revenue cancel		30.00
38	A4	£2	brn vio & grn ('25)	1,200.	*2,100.*
			Revenue cancel		170.00
39	A4	£3	yel & dl vio ('25)	1,850.	—
			Revenue cancel		275.00
40	A4	£4	rose lil & blk ('25)	4,000.	—
			Revenue cancel		300.00
41	A4	£5	blue & blk	4,500.	—
			Revenue cancel		375.00
41A	A4	£10	grn & blk	*15,000.*	
			Revenue cancel		475.00
41B	A4	£20	grn & red ('25)	*34,500.*	
			Revenue cancel		850.00
41C	A4	£25	red & blk	*43,500.*	
			Revenue cancel		800.00
41D	A4	£50	brn & blk	*85,000.*	
			Revenue cancel		900.00
41E	A4	£75	gray & purple	*150,000.*	
			Revenue cancel		3,500.
41F	A4	£100	blk & red	*160,000.*	
			Revenue cancel		2,250.
			Nos. 18-37 (20)	640.40	*1,134.*

High face value stamps are known with revenue cancellations removed and forged postal cancellations added.

Common Design Types pictured following the introduction.

Kenya, Uganda, Tanganyika Silver Jubilee Issue

Common Design Type

1935, May Engr. *Perf. 13½x14*

42	CD301	20c ol grn & lt bl	2.50	.25
43	CD301	30c blue & brown	3.50	*3.00*
44	CD301	65c indigo & green	2.00	*3.00*
45	CD301	1sh brt vio & indigo	2.25	*5.50*
		Nos. 42-45 (4)	10.25	*11.75*
		Set, never hinged	27.00	
		Set, perf. "SPECIMEN"	175.00	

Kavirondo Cranes
A5

Dhow on Lake Victoria
A6

Lion
A7

Mount Kilimanjaro
A8

Jinja Bridge by Ripon Falls — A9

Mount Kenya — A10

Lake Naivasha — A11

Type I

Type II

FIVE CENTS
Type I — Left rope does not touch sail.
Type II — Left rope touches sail.

FIFTY CENTS:
Type I — Left rope does not touch sail.
Type II — Left rope touches sail.

Perf. 13, 14, 11½x13, 13x11½

Engr.; Typo. (10c, £1)

1935, May 1

46	A5	1c	red brn & blk	1.50	*3.50*
47	A6	5c	grn & blk (I)	4.00	.50
a.			Type II	*42.50*	10.00
b.			Perf. 13x11½ (I)	*9,750.*	*1,000.*
c.			Perf. 13x11½ (II)	*875.00*	*250.00*
48	A7	10c	black & yel	7.50	1.00
49	A8	15c	red & black	4.50	.25
50	A5	20c	red org & blk	4.00	.25
51	A9	30c	dk ultra & blk	5.25	1.25
52	A6	50c	blk & red vio (I)	7.00	.25
53	A10	65c	yel brn & blk	12.50	*3.50*
54	A11	1sh	grn & black	5.75	1.75
a.			Perf. 13x11½ ('36)	*1,600.*	150.00
55	A8	2sh	red vio & rose brn	14.00	4.75
56	A11	3sh	blk & ultra	22.50	*17.50*
a.			Perf. 13x11½	*2,600.*	
57	A9	5sh	car & black	27.50	*40.00*
58	A5	10sh	ultra & red vio	110.00	*135.00*
59	A7	£1	blk & scar	325.00	*425.00*
			Nos. 46-59 (14)	551.00	634.50
			Set, never hinged	900.00	
			Set, perf. "SPECIMEN"	525.00	

Coronation Issue

Common Design Type

1937, May 12 Engr. *Perf. 13½x14*

60	CD302	5c deep green	.25	.25
61	CD302	20c deep orange	.40	.35
62	CD302	30c brt ultra	.60	*1.75*
		Nos. 60-62 (3)	1.25	2.35
		Set, never hinged	1.90	
		Set, perf. "SPECIMEN"	150.00	

Kavirondo Cranes
A12

Dhow on Lake Victoria
A13

Lake Naivasha
A14

Jinja Bridge, Ripon Falls
A16

Mt. Kilimanjaro
A15

Lion
A17

1938-54 Engr. *Perf. 13x13½*

66	A12	1c	vio brn & blk ('42)	.25	*.50*
a.			1c red brown & gray black, perf. 13	3.00	.90
			Perf. 13x11½		
67	A13	5c	grn & blk	3.50	.55
68	A13	5c	red org & brn ('49)	8.00	*7.50*
a.			Perf. 13x12½ ('50)	3.00	*4.75*
69	A14	10c	org & brn	1.60	.25
a.			Perf. 14 ('41)	95.00	10.00
70	A14	10c	grn & blk ('49)	.35	*2.00*
a.			Perf. 13x12½ ('50)	2.75	.25
			Perf. 13x12½		
71	A14	10c	gray & red brn ('52)	1.00	.60
			Perf. 13½x13, 13x13½		
72	A15	15c	car & gray blk ('43)	4.25	4.00
a.			Booklet pane of 4	17.50	
b.			Perf. 13	24.00	.60
73	A15	15c	grn & blk ('52)	1.90	*7.00*
74	A12	20c	org & gray blk ('42)	5.75	.25
a.			Booklet pane of 4	24.00	
b.			Imperf., pair		
c.			Perf. 13	*35.00*	.30
d.			Perf. 14 ('41)	*45.00*	*5.00*
			Perf. 13x12½		
75	A13	25c	car & blk ('52)	1.50	*2.40*
			Perf. 13x13½		
76	A16	30c	dp bl & gray blk ('42)	2.00	.35
a.			Perf. 14 ('41)	*130.00*	12.50
b.			Perf. 13	*40.00*	.45
77	A16	30c	brn & pur ('52)	1.25	.45
78	A12	40c	brt bl & gray blk ('52)	1.75	*5.00*
			Perf. 13x12½		
79	A13	50c	gray blk & red vio (II) ('49)	7.25	.50
a.			Perf. 13x11½ (II)	14.00	1.10
b.			Perf. 13x11½ (I)	200.00	*250.00*
			Perf. 13x11½		
80	A14	1sh	yel brn & gray blk	20.00	.30
a.			Perf. 13x12½ ('49)	12.00	.65
			Perf. 13½x13		
81	A15	2sh	red vio & org brn ('44)	30.00	.40
a.			Perf. 13	*120.00*	9.00
b.			Perf. 14 ('41)	*62.50*	19.00
			Perf. 13x12½		
82	A14	3sh	gray blk & ultra ('50)	30.00	9.00
a.			Perf. 13x11½	30.00	9.00
			Perf. 13x13½		
83	A16	5sh	car rose & gray blk ('44)	30.00	2.00
a.			Perf. 13	*130.00*	21.00
b.			Perf. 14 ('41)	*35.00*	3.25
84	A12	10sh	ultra & red vio ('44)	42.50	11.00
a.			Perf. 13	120.00	37.50
b.			Perf. 14 ('41)	32.50	25.00
			Typo.		
			Perf. 14		
85	A17	£1	blk & scar ('41)	25.00	*27.50*
a.			Perf. 11½x13	300.00	170.00
b.			Perf. 12½ ('54)	12.00	*42.50*
			Nos. 66-85 (20)	217.85	*81.55*
			Set, never hinged	350.00	

Nos. 85-85b were printed on chalky paper. No. 85 also exists on ordinary paper, from a 1944 printing. Values are the same.

See Nos. 98-99.

South Africa Nos. 48, 57, 60 and 62 Surcharged

Basic stamps of Nos. 86-89 are inscribed alternately in English and Afrikaans.

1941-42 Wmk. 201 *Perf. 15x14, 14*

86	A6	5c on 1p car & gray, pair	1.10	*3.00*
a.		Single, English	.25	.25
b.		Single, Afrikaans	.25	.25
87	A17	10c on 3p ultra, pair	3.50	*10.00*
a.		Single, English	.30	.35
b.		Single, Afrikaans	.30	.35
88	A7	20c on 6p org & grn, pair	2.50	*3.75*
a.		Single, English	.25	.25
b.		Single, Afrikaans	.25	.25
89	A11	70c on 1sh lt bl & ol brn, pair	15.00	*5.50*
a.		Single, English	.50	.45
b.		Single, Afrikaans	.50	.45
		Nos. 86-89 (4)	22.10	22.25
		Set, never hinged	30.00	

Issued: Nos. 86-88, 7/1/41; No. 89, 4/20/42.

Values are for horizontal pairs. Vertical pairs are worth substantially less.

Catalogue values for unused stamps in this section, from this point to the end of the section, are for Never Hinged items.

Peace Issue
Common Design Type
Perf. 13½x14

1946, Nov. 11 Engr. Wmk. 4

90 CD303 20c red orange .25 .25
91 CD303 30c deep blue .40 .60

Silver Wedding Issue
Common Design Types

1948, Dec. 1 Photo. *Perf. 14x14½*

92 CD304 20c orange 1.00 .50

Engr.; Name Typo.
Perf. 11½x11

93 CD305 £1 red 50.00 *67.50*

UPU Issue
Common Design Types
Engr.; Typo. on Nos. 95 and 96

1949, Oct. 10 *Perf. 13, 11x11½*

94 CD306 20c red orange .25 .25
95 CD307 30c indigo 1.75 *2.25*
96 CD308 50c gray .40 1.00
97 CD309 1sh red brown .50 .50
Nos. 94-97 (4) 2.90 4.00

Type of 1949 with Added Inscription: "Royal Visit 1952"

1952, Feb. 1 Engr. *Perf. 13x12½*

98 A14 10c green & black .50 *2.00*
99 A14 1sh yel brn & gray blk 1.75 *3.25*

Visit of Princess Elizabeth, Duchess of Edinburgh, and the Duke of Edinburgh, 1952.

Coronation Issue
Common Design Type

1953, June 2 *Perf. 13½x13*

101 CD312 20c red orange & blk .40 .25

Owen Falls Dam — A18

Inscribed "ROYAL VISIT 1954"

1954, Apr. 28 *Perf. 12½x13*

102 A18 30c dp ultra & black .50 .25

Visit of Queen Elizabeth II and the Duke of Edinburgh, 1954.

Owen Falls Dam — A18a

Giraffe A19

Mt. Kilimanjaro A20

Elizabeth II — A21

5c, 30c, Owen Falls Dam (without "Royal Visit 1954"). 20c, 40c, 1sh, Lion. 15c, 1.30sh, 5sh, Elephants. 10sh, Royal Lodge, Sagana.

1954-59 *Perf. 12½x13, 13x12½*

103 A18a 5c choc & blk 1.75 .65
a. Booklet pane of 4 7.00
b. Vignette (dam) inverted *67,500.*
104 A19 10c carmine 1.75 .25
a. Booklet pane of 4 7.00
105 A20 15c lt blue & blk (no period below "c") ('58) 1.00 1.40
a. Booklet pane of 4 4.00
106 A20 15c lt blue & blk (period below "c") ('59) 1.00 1.40
a. Booklet pane of 4 4.00
107 A19 20c org & black 2.00 .25
a. Booklet pane of 4 8.00
b. Imperf., pair *1,300.* 1,500.
108 A18a 30c ultra & black 1.25 .25
a. Booklet pane of 4 6.00
b. Vignette (dam) inverted *32,500.*
109 A19 40c brown ('58) 1.50 .80
110 A19 50c dp red lilac 3.00 .25
a. Booklet pane of 4 14.00
111 A20 65c brn car & grn ('55) 3.00 1.50
112 A19 1sh dp mag & blk 3.00 .25
113 A20 1.30sh pur & red org ('55) 15.00 .25
114 A20 2sh dp grn & gray 14.00 1.25
115 A20 5sh black & org 20.00 3.25
116 A20 10sh ultra & black 35.00 5.75
117 A21 £1 black & ver 24.00 22.00
Nos. 103-117 (15) 127.25 39.50

No. 103b is unique.
For "Official" overprints see Tanganyika Nos. O1-O12.

Map Showing Lakes Victoria and Tanganyika — A22

Perf. 12½x13

1958, July 30 Engr. Wmk. 314

118 A22 40c green & blue .70 .40
119 A22 1.30sh violet & green .70 *1.00*

Cent. of the discovery of Lakes Victoria and Tanganyika by Sir Richard F. Burton and Capt. J. H. Speke.

Sisal — A23

A25

Mount Kenya and Giant Plants — A24

10c, Cotton. 15c, Coffee. 20c, Gnu. 25c, Ostriches. 30c, Thompson's gazelles. 40c, Manta ray. 50c, Zebras. 65c, Cheetah. 1.30sh, Murchison Falls & hippopotamuses. 2sh, Mt. Kilimanjaro & giraffes. 2.50sh, Candelabra tree & black rhinoceroses. 5sh, Crater Lake & Mountains of the Moon. 10sh, Ngorongoro Crater & buffaloes.

Perf. 14½x14

1960, Oct. 1 Photo. Wmk. 314

120 A23 5c dull blue .25 .25
121 A23 10c lt olive green .25 .25
a. Booklet pane of 4 .60
122 A23 15c dull purple .45 .25
a. Booklet pane of 4 1.75
123 A23 20c brt lilac rose .25 .25
a. Booklet pane of 4 1.20
124 A23 25c olive gray 3.25 1.25
125 A23 30c brt vermilion .25 .25
a. Booklet pane of 4 .90
126 A23 40c bright blue .25 .25
127 A23 50c dull violet .30 .25
a. Booklet pane of 4 1.90
128 A23 65c lemon .50 *1.75*

Engr.
Perf. 14

129 A24 1sh vio & red lilac 1.50 .25
130 A24 1.30sh choc & dk car 5.75 .25
131 A24 2sh dk bl & dull bl 7.50 .45
132 A24 2.50sh ol grn & dull bl 9.80 2.50
133 A24 5sh rose red & lil 4.25 .60
134 A24 10sh sl bl & ol grn 13.00 6.00

Perf. 13½x13

135 A25 20sh lake & bluish violet 25.00 *25.00*
Nos. 120-135 (16) 72.55 39.80

Booklets issued in 1961.
On Nos. 120-134, positions of "Kenya," "Uganda" and "Tanganyika" are rotated.
For "Official" overprints see Tanganyika Nos. O13-O20.

Agricultural Development A26

Design: 30c, 1.30sh, Farmer picking corn.

Unwmk.

1963, Mar. 21 Photo. *Perf. 14*

136 A26 15c lt ol grn & ultra .25 .25
137 A26 30c yel & red brown .30 .25
138 A26 50c dp org & ultra .40 .25
139 A26 1.30sh lt blue & red brn .80 *1.00*
Nos. 136-139 (4) 1.75 1.75

FAO "Freedom from Hunger" campaign.

Scholars and Open Book — A27

1963, June 28 Unwmk. *Perf. 14*

140 A27 30c multicolored .25 .25
141 A27 1.30sh multicolored .25 .25

Inauguration of University of East Africa.

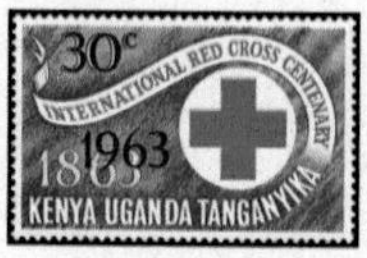
Red Cross — A28

1963, Sept. 2

142 A28 30c blue & red 1.25 .30
143 A28 50c bister brown & red 1.50 1.25

Centenary of International Red Cross.

Kenya, Uganda, Tanganyika and Zanzibar
Issued by the East African Common Services Organization. Not used in Zanzibar.

Japanese Crest and Olympic Rings — A29

Olympic Rings and Banners — A30

Unwmk.

1964, Oct. 25 Photo. *Perf. 14*

144 A29 30c org & dk purple .25 .25
145 A29 50c dk purple & org .25 .25
146 A30 1.30sh blue, grn & org .35 .25
147 A30 2.50sh blue, vio & lil rose .40 *.75*
Nos. 144-147 (4) 1.25 1.50

18th Olympic Games, Tokyo, Oct. 10-25.

Kenya, Uganda, Tanzania
Issued by the East African Common Services Organization.

Safari Rally Emblem and Leopard — A31

1.30sh, 2.50sh, Car on road through national park & emblem of the East African Safari Rally.

1965, Apr. 15 Unwmk. *Perf. 14*

148 A31 30c blue grn, yel & blk .25 .25
149 A31 50c brown, yel & blk .25 .25
150 A31 1.30sh lt ultra, ocher & green .25 .25
151 A31 2.50sh blue, dk grn & dull red .45 *1.10*
Nos. 148-151 (4) 1.20 1.85

13th East African Safari Rally, 4/15-19/65.

ITU Emblem, Old and Modern Communication Equipment A32

1965, May 17 Photo.

152 A32 30c lilac rose, gold & brn .25 .25
153 A32 50c gray, gold & brown .25 .25
154 A32 1.30sh lt vio bl, gold & brn .40 .25
155 A32 2.50sh brt bl grn, gold & brn 1.25 1.25
Nos. 152-155 (4) 2.15 2.00

Cent. of the ITU.

ICY Emblem A33

1965, Aug. 4 Unwmk. *Perf. 14*

156 A33 30c green & gold .25 .25
157 A33 50c slate blk & gold .25 .25
158 A33 1.30sh ultra & gold .40 .25
159 A33 2.50sh car & gold 1.00 1.00
Nos. 156-159 (4) 1.90 1.75

International Cooperation Year.

Game Park Lodge — A34

Tourist Publicity: 50c, Murchison Falls, Uganda. 1.30sh, Lake Nakuru, Kenya. 2.50sh, Deep-sea fishing, Tanzania.

1966, Apr. 4 Photo. *Perf. 14*

160 A34 30c ocher & multi .45 .25
161 A34 50c green & multi .55 .25
a. Blue omitted *425.00*
162 A34 1.30sh multicolored 2.75 .35
163 A34 2.50sh gray & multi 1.75 *2.25*
Nos. 160-163 (4) 5.50 3.10

Javelin Thrower and Games' Emblem — A35

1966, Aug. 2 Unwmk. *Perf. 14*

164 A35 30c multicolored .25 .25
165 A35 50c multicolored .25 .25
166 A35 1.30sh multicolored .25 .25
167 A35 2.50sh multicolored .30 *1.25*
Nos. 164-167 (4) 1.05 2.00

8th British Commonwealth and Empire Games, Jamaica, Aug. 4-13, 1966.

UNESCO Emblem — A36

1966, Oct. 3 Photo. *Perf. 14*

168 A36 30c rose red, brt grn & blk .45 .25
169 A36 50c lt brn, brt grn & blk .50 .25
170 A36 1.30sh gray, brt grn & blk 1.25 .25
171 A36 2.50sh yel, brt grn & blk 1.60 *4.25*
Nos. 168-171 (4) 3.80 5.00

20th anniv. of UNESCO.

Dragon Rapide — A37

Planes: 50c, Super VC10. 1.30sh, Comet 4. 2.50sh, F.27 Friendship.

1967, Jan. 23 **Unwmk.**

172	A37	30c multicolored	.30	.25
173	A37	50c multicolored	.40	.25
174	A37	1.30sh multicolored	.85	.30
175	A37	2.50sh multicolored	1.40	*3.00*
		Nos. 172-175 (4)	2.95	3.80

21st anniversary of East African Airways.

Pillar Tomb, East African Coast — A38

Designs: 50c, Man hunting elephant, petroglyph, Tanzania. 1.30sh, Clay head, Luzira, Uganda. 2.50sh, Proconsul skull, Rusinga Island, Kenya.

1967, May 2 **Photo.** ***Perf. 14***

176	A38	30c rose lake, blk & yel	.25	.25
177	A38	50c gray, black & ver	.60	.25
178	A38	1.30sh green, yel & blk	.85	.25
179	A38	2.50sh cop red, yel & blk	1.25	*2.50*
		Nos. 176-179 (4)	2.95	3.25

Archaeological relics of East Africa.

Emblems of Kenya, Tanzania and Tanganyika — A39

Photo.; Gold Impressed

1967, Dec. 1 ***Perf. 14½x14***

180	A39	5sh gray, black & gold	.50	*1.00*

Establishment of East African Community.

Mountain climber — A40

30c Mountain climber. 50c, Mount Kenya. 1.30sh, Mount Kilimanjaro. 2.50sh, Ruwenzori Mountains.

1968, Mar. 4 **Photo.** ***Perf. 14½***

181	A40	30c multicolored	.25	.25
182	A40	50c multicolored	.35	.25
183	A40	1.30sh multicolored	.60	.25
184	A40	2.50sh multicolored	1.10	*2.00*
		Nos. 181-184 (4)	2.30	2.75

Family and Rural Hospital — A41

Family and: 50c, Student nurse. 1.30sh, Microscope. 2.50sh, Mosquito and hand holding hypodermic.

1968, May 13 **Photo.** ***Perf. 13½***

185	A41	30c multicolored	.25	.25
186	A41	50c rose vio, blk & brt pink	.25	.25
187	A41	1.30sh brn org, blk & brt pink	.25	.25
188	A41	2.50sh gray, blk & brt pink	.30	*1.25*
		Nos. 185-188 (4)	1.05	2.00

20th anniv. of the WHO.

Stadium — A42

Designs: 50c, Diving tower. 1.30sh, Pylons and tracks. 2.50sh, Boxing ring, vert.

Perf. 14½x14, 14x14½

1968, Oct. 14 **Photo.**

189	A42	30c dull pur & gray grn	.25	.25
190	A42	50c brt grn, blk & gray	.25	.25
191	A42	1.30sh gray grn, blk & dk car	.25	.25
192	A42	2.50sh buff, brn org & brn blk	.30	*1.00*
		Nos. 189-192 (4)	1.05	1.75

19th Olympic Games, Mexico City, 10/12-27.

Railroad Ferry MV Umoja — A43

Water Transport: 50c, Transatlantic liner S.S. Harambee. 1.30sh, Lake motor vessel Victoria. 2.50sh, Ferry St. Michael.

1969, Jan. 20 **Photo.** ***Perf. 14***

193	A43	30c blue, gray & dk bl	.40	.25
194	A43	50c blue, gray & scar	.45	.25
195	A43	1.30sh bl, dk bl & dk green	.75	.25
196	A43	2.50sh bl, dk bl & org	1.40	*2.50*
		Nos. 193-196 (4)	3.00	3.25

Farm Workers and ILO Emblem — A44

ILO Emblem and: 50c, Construction. 1.30sh, Industry. 2.50sh, Shipping.

1969, Apr. 14 **Photo.** ***Perf. 14***

197	A44	30c green, blk & yel	.25	.25
198	A44	50c car rose, blk & car	.25	.25
199	A44	1.30sh dp org, blk & org	.25	.25
200	A44	2.50sh grnsh bl, blk & ultra	.25	*.75*
		Nos. 197-200 (4)	1.00	1.50

50th anniv. of the ILO.

Pope Paul VI, Mountains of the Moon, Papal Arms, Crested Crane — A45

1969, July 31 **Photo.** ***Perf. 14***

201	A45	30c dk blue, blk & gold	.25	.25
202	A45	70c plum, blk & gold	.25	.25
203	A45	1.50sh gray bl, blk & gold	.25	.25
204	A45	2.50sh dp vio, blk & gold	.30	*.90*
		Nos. 201-204 (4)	1.05	1.65

Visit of Pope Paul VI to Uganda, 7/31-8/2.

Euphorbia Tree in Shape of Africa, Development Bank Emblem — A46

Perf. 14x13½

1969, Dec. 8 **Litho.** **Unwmk.**

205	A46	30c brt grn, dk grn & gold	.25	.25
206	A46	70c plum, dk grn & gold	.25	.25
207	A46	1.50sh grnsh bl, dk grn & gold	.25	.25
208	A46	2.50sh brn org, dk grn & gold	.35	*.60*
		Nos. 205-208 (4)	1.10	1.35

African Development Bank, 5th anniv.

Amadinda, Uganda — A47

Musical Instruments: 30c, Marimba, Tanzania. 1.50sh, Nzomari (trumpet), Kenya. 2.50sh, Adeudeu, Kenya.

1970, Feb. 16 **Litho.** ***Perf. 11x12***

209	A47	30c multicolored	.25	.25
210	A47	70c multicolored	.30	.25
211	A47	1.50sh dk rose brn & org	.50	.25
212	A47	2.50sh multicolored	.90	*1.50*
		Nos. 209-212 (4)	1.95	2.25

Satellite Earth Station — A48

Designs: 70c, Radar station by day. 1.50sh, Radar station by night. 2.50sh, Satellite transmitting communications to and from earth.

1970, May 18 **Litho.** ***Perf. 14½***

213	A48	30c multicolored	.25	.25
214	A48	70c multicolored	.25	.25
215	A48	1.50sh org, blk & vio	.30	.25
216	A48	2.50sh dull bl & multi	.40	*2.00*
		Nos. 213-216 (4)	1.20	2.75

Opening of the East African Satellite Earth Station, Mt. Margaret, Kenya.

Runner — A49

1970, July 16 **Litho.** ***Perf. 14½***

217	A49	30c org brn, dk brn & blk	.25	.25
218	A49	70c grn, dk brn & blk	.25	.25
219	A49	1.50sh dull pur, dk brn & blk	.25	.25
220	A49	2.50sh grnsh bl, dk brn & blk	.25	*.80*
		Nos. 217-220 (4)	1.00	1.55

9th British Commonwealth Games, Edinburgh, July 16-25.

UN Emblem and People — A50

1970, Oct. 19 **Photo.** ***Perf. 14½***

221	A50	30c org brn, gold & black	.25	.25
222	A50	70c bl grn, gold & black	.25	.25
223	A50	1.50sh dull red brn, gold & blk	.25	.25
224	A50	2.50sh olive, gold & blk	.35	*1.50*
		Nos. 221-224 (4)	1.10	2.25

25th anniversary of the United Nations.

Conversion from Pounds to Kilograms A51

Designs: 70c, Conversion from Fahrenheit to centigrade. 1.50sh, Conversion from gallons to liters. 2.50sh, Conversion from miles to kilometers.

1971, Jan. 4 **Photo.** ***Perf. 14½***

225	A51	30c silver & multi	.25	.25
226	A51	70c silver & multi	.25	.25
227	A51	1.50sh silver & multi	.25	.25
228	A51	2.50sh silver & multi	.25	*.80*
		Nos. 225-228 (4)	1.00	1.55

Conversion to metric system of weights and measures.

Locomotive A52

Designs: Various locomotives.

1971, Apr. 19 **Photo.** ***Perf. 14½***

229	A52	30c gold & multi	.30	.25
230	A52	70c gold & multi	.35	.25
231	A52	1.50sh gold & multi	.80	.25
232	A52	2.50sh gold & multi	1.00	*2.00*
	a.	Souvenir sheet of 4, #229-232	8.50	*10.00*
		Nos. 229-232 (4)	2.45	2.75

70th anniversary of the completion of the Mombasa to Kisumu line.

Campaign Emblem and Cow — A53

Designs: 1.50sh, Like 30c. 70c, 2.50sh, Bull and Campaign Emblem.

1971, July 5 **Photo.** ***Perf. 14½***

233	A53	30c yel grn, blk & bis	.25	.25
234	A53	70c gray bl, blk & bis	.25	.25
235	A53	1.50sh mag, blk & bis	.25	.25
236	A53	2.50sh red org, blk & bis	.25	*.65*
		Nos. 233-236 (4)	1.00	1.40

Rinderpest campaign by the Organization for African Unity.

Meeting of Stanley and Livingstone — A54

1971, Oct. 28 **Litho.** ***Perf. 14***

237	A54	5sh multicolored	.40	.40

Centenary of the meeting at Ujiji of Dr. David Livingstone, missionary, and Henry M. Stanley, journalist, who had been sent to find Livingstone.

Modern Farming Village — A55

Designs: 30c, Pres. Julius K. Nyerere carried in triumph, 1961, vert. 1.50sh, University of Dar es Salaam. 2.50sh, Kilimanjaro International Airport.

1971, Dec. 9 ***Perf. 14***

238	A55	30c bister & multi	.25	.25
239	A55	70c lt blue & multi	.25	.25
240	A55	1.50sh lt green & multi	.25	.25
241	A55	2.50sh yel & multi	.50	*1.75*
		Nos. 238-241 (4)	1.25	2.50

10th anniv. of independence of Tanzania.

Flags of African Nations and Fair Emblem A56

1972, Feb. 23 ***Perf. 13½x14***

242	A56	30c lt bl & multi	.25	.25
243	A56	70c gray & multi	.25	.25
244	A56	1.50sh yel & multi	.25	.25
245	A56	2.50sh multicolored	.25	*.75*
		Nos. 242-245 (4)	1.00	1.50

First All-Africa Trade Fair, Nairobi, Kenya, Feb. 23-Mar. 5.

Child Drinking Milk, UNICEF Emblem — A57

25th Anniv. (in 1971) of UNICEF: 70c, Children playing ball. 1.50sh, Child writing on blackboard. 2.50sh, Boy playing with tractor.

1972, Apr. 24 Litho. *Perf. 14½x14*

246	A57	30c brn org & multi	.25	.25
247	A57	70c lt ultra & multi	.25	.25
248	A57	1.50sh yel & multi	.25	.25
249	A57	2.50sh green & multi	.25	*.75*
		Nos. 246-249 (4)	1.00	1.50

Hurdles, Olympic and Motion Emblems A58

1972, Aug. 28

250	A58	40c shown	.25	.25
251	A58	70c Running	.25	.25
252	A58	1.50sh Boxing	.25	.25
253	A58	2.50sh Hockey	.30	*1.50*
a.		Souvenir sheet of 4, #250-253	6.75	6.75
		Nos. 250-253 (4)	1.05	2.25

20th Olympic Games, Munich, 8/26-9/11.

Uganda Kob, Semliki Game Reserve A59

70c, Intl. Conf. Center. 1.50sh, Makerere Univ., Kampala. 2.50sh, Uganda arms.

1972, Oct. 9 Litho. *Perf. 14*

254	A59	40c shown	.25	.25
255	A59	70c multicolored	.30	.25
256	A59	1.50sh multicolored	.60	.30
257	A59	2.50sh multicolored	1.00	*2.00*
a.		Souvenir sheet of 4, #254-257, perf. 13x14	4.50	10.00
		Nos. 254-257 (4)	2.15	2.80

Uganda's independence, 10th anniv. No. 256 also for 50th anniv. of Makerere University, Kampala.

Flag of East Africa A60

1972, Dec. 1 Litho. *Perf. 14½x14*

258	A60	5sh multicolored	.85	.85

5th anniv. of the East African Community.

Anemometer, Lake Victoria Station — A61

WMO Emblem and: 70c, Release of weather balloon, vert. 1.50sh, Hail suppression by meteorological rocket. 2.50sh, Meteorological satellite receiving antenna.

1973, Mar. 5 Litho. *Perf. 14*

259	A61	40c multicolored	.25	.25
260	A61	70c ultra & multi	.25	.25
261	A61	1.50sh emer & multi	.25	.25
262	A61	2.50sh multicolored	.35	*1.00*
		Nos. 259-262 (4)	1.10	1.75

Cent. of intl. meteorological cooperation.

Scouts Laying Bricks — A62

Designs: 70c, Baden-Powell's gravestone, Nyeri, Kenya. 1.50sh, World Scout emblem. 2.50sh, Lord Baden-Powell.

1973, July 16 Litho. *Perf. 14*

263	A62	40c ocher & multi	.25	.25
264	A62	70c multicolored	.30	.25
265	A62	1.50sh multicolored	.50	.30
266	A62	2.50sh grn & ultra	1.25	*1.60*
		Nos. 263-266 (4)	2.30	2.40

24th Boy Scout World Conference (1st in Africa), Nairobi, Kenya, July 16-21.

International Bank for Reconstruction and Development and Affiliates' Emblems — A63

Designs: 40c, Arrows dividing 4 bank affiliate emblems. 70c, Vert. lines dividing 4 emblems. 1.50sh, Kenyatta Conference Center, Nairobi, vert.

1973, Sept. 24 Litho. *Perf. 14x13½*

267	A63	40c gray, blk & grn	.25	.25
268	A63	70c brn, gray & blk	.25	.25
269	A63	1.50sh lem, gray & blk	.25	*.30*
270	A63	2.50sh blk, org & gray	.25	*1.50*
a.		Souvenir sheet of 4	2.50	*10.00*
		Nos. 267-270 (4)	1.00	2.30

Intl. Bank for Reconstruction and Development and Affiliate Intl. Monetary Fund Meetings, Nairobi.

No. 270a contains stamps similar to Nos. 267-270 with simulated perforations.

INTERPOL Emblem, Policeman and Dog — A64

Designs: 70c, East African policemen and emblem. 1.50sh, INTERPOL emblem. 2.50sh, INTERPOL Headquarters, St. Cloud, France.

1973-74 Litho. *Perf. 14x14½*

271	A64	40c yellow & multi	.55	.25
272	A64	70c multicolored	.75	.25
273	A64	1.50sh violet & multi	1.25	.85
274	A64	2.50sh lemon & multi *(St. Clans)*	3.50	*4.75*
275	A64	2.50sh lemon & multi *(St. Cloud)* ('74)	5.25	*5.75*
		Nos. 271-275 (5)	11.30	11.85

50th anniv. of Intl. Criminal Police Org.

Issued: Nos. 271-274, Oct. 24, 1973.

Tea Factory, Nandi Hills — A65

1973, Dec. 12 Photo. *Perf. 13x14*

276	A65	40c shown	.25	.25
277	A65	70c Kenyatta Hospital	.25	.25
278	A65	1.50sh Nairobi Airport	.50	.25
279	A65	2.50sh Kindaruma hydroelectric plant	.75	*1.50*
		Nos. 276-279 (4)	1.75	2.25

10th anniversary of independence.

Afro-Shirazi Party Headquarters A66

Designs: 70c, Michenzani housing development. 1.50sh, Map of East Africa and television screen with flower. 2.50sh, Amaan Stadium.

1974, Jan. 12 Litho. *Perf. 13½x14*

280	A66	40c multicolored	.25	.25
281	A66	70c multicolored	.25	.25
282	A66	1.50sh black & multi	.35	.25
283	A66	2.50sh black & multi	.65	*2.25*
		Nos. 280-283 (4)	1.50	3.00

10th anniversary of Zanzibar revolution.

Symbol of Union — A67

Designs: 70c, Map of Tanganyika and Zanzibar, and handshake. 1.50sh, Map of Tanganyika and Zanzibar, and communications symbols. 2.50sh, Flags of Tanu, Tanzania and Afro-Shirazi Party.

1974, Apr. 24 Litho. *Perf. 14½*

284	A67	40c sepia & multi	.25	.25
285	A67	70c blue grn & multi	.25	.25
286	A67	1.50sh ultra & multi	.35	.25
287	A67	2.50sh multicolored	.65	*2.25*
		Nos. 284-287 (4)	1.50	3.00

Union of Tanganyika and Zanzibar, 10th anniv.

Family and Home — A68

Designs: 70c, Drummer at dawn. 1.50sh, Family hoeing, and livestock. 2.50sh, Telephonist, train, plane, telegraph lines.

1974, July 15 Litho. *Perf. 14½*

288	A68	40c multicolored	.25	.25
289	A68	70c multicolored	.25	.25
290	A68	1.50sh multicolored	.25	.25
291	A68	2.50sh multicolored	.70	*1.10*
		Nos. 288-291 (4)	1.45	1.85

17th Intl. Conf. on Social Welfare, 7/14-20.

Post and Telegraph Headquarters, Kampala — A69

Cent. of the UPU: 70c, Mail train and truck. 1.50sh, UPU Headquarters, Bern. 2.50sh, Loading mail on East African Airways VC-10.

1974, Oct. 9 Litho. *Perf. 14*

292	A69	40c lt green & multi	.25	.25
293	A69	70c gray & multi	.25	.25
294	A69	1.50sh yel & multi	.25	.25
295	A69	2.50sh lt blue & multi	.40	*1.10*
		Nos. 292-295 (4)	1.15	1.85

Family Planning Clinic — A70

World Population Year: 70c, "Tug of War." 1.50sh, Scales and world population figures. 2.50sh, World Population Year emblem.

1974, Dec. 16 Litho. *Perf. 14½*

296	A70	40c multicolored	.25	.25
297	A70	70c purple & multi	.25	.25
298	A70	1.50sh multicolored	.25	.25
299	A70	2.50sh blue blk & multi	.30	*1.25*
		Nos. 296-299 (4)	1.05	2.00

Seronera Wild Life Lodge, Tanzania — A71

Game lodges of East Africa: 70c, Mweya Safari Lodge, Uganda. 1.50sh, Ark-Aberdare Forest Lodge, Kenya. 2.50sh, Paraa Safari Lodge, Uganda.

1975, Feb. 24 Litho. *Perf. 14½*

300	A71	40c multicolored	.25	.25
301	A71	70c multicolored	.25	.25
302	A71	1.50sh multicolored	.25	.30
303	A71	2.50sh multicolored	.75	*1.75*
		Nos. 300-303 (4)	1.50	2.55

Wooden Comb, Bajun, Kenya — A72

African Artifacts: 1sh, Earring, Chaga, Tanzania. 2sh, Armlet, Acholi, Uganda. 3sh, Kamba gourd, Kenya.

1975, May 5 Litho. *Perf. 13½*

304	A72	50c gray & multi	.25	.25
305	A72	1sh gray & multi	.25	.25
306	A72	2sh multicolored	.30	.35
307	A72	3sh multicolored	.60	*1.25*
		Nos. 304-307 (4)	1.40	2.10

Map Showing OAU Members, Ugandan Flag — A73

OAU Emblem and: 50c, Entebbe Airport, horiz. 2sh, Nile Hotel, Kampala, horiz. 3sh, Ugandan Martyrs' Shrine, Namugongo.

Perf. 11½x11, 11x11½

1975, July 28 Litho.

308	A73	50c multicolored	.35	.25
309	A73	1sh multicolored	.35	.25
310	A73	2sh multicolored	.35	.50
311	A73	3sh multicolored	.55	*1.25*
		Nos. 308-311 (4)	1.60	2.25

Organization for African Unity (OAU), Summit Conf., Kampala, July 28 - Aug. 1.

Elephant, Kenya — A74

Protected animals: 1sh, Albino buffalo, Uganda. 2sh, Elephant, exhibit in National Museum, Kenya. 3sh, Abbott's duiker, Tanzania.

1975, Sept. 11 Litho. *Perf. 11x11½*

312	A74	50c multicolored	.60	.25
313	A74	1sh brown & multi	.65	.25
314	A74	2sh yel green & multi	1.60	1.50
315	A74	3sh blue grn & multi	2.25	2.25
		Nos. 312-315 (4)	5.10	4.25

Masai Villagers Bleeding Cow, Masai, Kenya — A75

Festival Emblem and: 1sh, Ugandan dancers. 2sh, Family, Makonde sculpture, Tanzania. 3sh, Skinning hippopotamus, East Africa.

1975, Nov. 3 Litho. *Perf. 13½x14*

316	A75	50c org brown & multi	.25	.25
317	A75	1sh brt green & multi	.25	.25
318	A75	2sh dk blue & multi	.55	*.80*
319	A75	3sh lilac & multi	.85	*1.25*
		Nos. 316-319 (4)	1.90	2.55

2nd World Black and African Festival of Arts and Culture, Lagos, Nigeria, Jan. 5 - Feb. 12.

Fokker Friendship, Nairobi Airport — A76

East African Airways, 30th anniv.: 1sh, DC-9 Kilimanjaro Airport. 2sh, Super VC10, Entebbe Airport. 3sh, East African Airways emblem.

1976, Jan. 2 Litho. Perf. 11½

320	A76	50c ultra & multi	1.10	.75
321	A76	1sh rose & multi	1.25	.75
322	A76	2sh orange & multi	3.25	3.25
323	A76	3sh black & multi	3.75	4.00
		Nos. 320-323 (4)	9.35	8.75

POSTAGE DUE STAMPS

Kenya and Uganda

D1

Perf. 14½x14

1928-33 Typo. Wmk. 4

J1	D1	5c deep violet	2.50	1.00
J2	D1	10c orange red	2.50	.60
J3	D1	20c yel green	4.00	4.25
J4	D1	30c ol brn ('31)	27.50	20.00
J5	D1	40c dull blue	6.50	*15.00*
J6	D1	1sh grnsh gray ('33)	72.50	*145.00*
		Nos. J1-J6 (6)	115.50	*185.85*
		Set, never hinged	190.00	

Kenya, Uganda, Tanganyika

D2

1935, May 1 Perf. 13½x14

J7	D2	5c violet	2.50	1.75
J8	D2	10c red	.35	.45
J9	D2	20c green	.50	.45
J10	D2	30c brown	1.50	.45
J11	D2	40c ultramarine	1.60	*3.50*
J12	D2	1sh gray	22.50	22.50
		Nos. J7-J12 (6)	28.95	*29.10*
		Set, never hinged	45.00	

OFFICIAL STAMPS

The 1959-60 "OFFICIAL" overprints on Nos. 103-104, 106-108, 110, 112-117, 120-123, 125, 127, 129, 133 are listed under Tanganyika, as they were used by the Tanganyika government.

KIAUCHAU

(Kiautschou)

LOCATION — A district of China on the south side of the Shantung peninsula.
GOVT. — German colony
AREA — 200 sq. mi.
POP. — 192,000 (approx. 1914).

The area was seized by Germany in 1897 and through negotiations that followed was leased to Germany by China.

100 Pfennig = 1 Mark
100 Cents = 1 Dollar (1905)

TSINGTAU ISSUES

Stamps of Germany, Offices in China 1898, with Additional Surcharge

a

b

c

On Nos. 1-9, a blue or violet line is drawn through "PF. 10 PF." All exist without this line. All examples of Nos. 1b, 2b and 3b lack the colored line.

The three surcharge types can most easily be distinguished by the differences in the lower loop of the "5."

"China" Overprint at 56 degree Angle

1900

1	A10(a)	5pfg on 10pf car	45.00	*52.50*
c.		Dbl. surch., one inverted	750.00	
2	A10(b)	5pfg on 10pf car	45.00	*52.50*
c.		Dbl. surch., one inverted	750.00	
3	A10(c)	5pfg on 10pf car	45.00	*52.50*
c.		Dbl. surch., one inverted	750.00	
		Nos. 1-3 (3)	135.00	157.50

"China" Overprint at 45 degree Angle

1a	A10(a)	5pfg on 10pf car	145.00	*130.00*
b.		Double surcharge	450.00	*575.00*
2a	A10(b)	5pfg on 10pf car	145.00	*130.00*
b.		Double surcharge	450.00	*575.00*
3a	A10(c)	5pfg on 10pf car	145.00	*130.00*
b.		Double surcharge	450.00	*575.00*
		Nos. 1a-3a (3)	435.00	390.00

Surcharged

d

e

5 Pf.

f

"China" Overprint at 48 degree Angle on Nos. 4-9

4	A10(d)	5pf on 10pf car	3,250.	4,000.
a.		Double surcharge	*8,250.*	*18,000.*
5	A10(e)	5pf on 10pf car	*3,250.*	*4,000.*
a.		Double surcharge	*8,250.*	*18,000.*
6	A10(f)	5pf on 10pf car	*3,250.*	*4,000.*
a.		Double surcharge	*8,250.*	*18,000.*
b.		5fP		*18,000.*
c.		As "b," double surcharge		—

With Add'l Handstamp **5**

7	A10(d)	5pf on 10pf car	*40,000.*	*50,000.*
8	A10(f)	5pf on 10pf car	*40,000.*	*50,000.*
a.		On No. 6b	—	—

With Additional Handstamp

9	A10(f)	5pf on 10pf car	*8,250.*	*12,500.*
a.		Double surcharge	*37,500.*	
b.		On No. 6a		
c.		On No. 6b		
d.		On No. 6c		

Kaiser's Yacht "Hohenzollern"
A1 A2

1901, Jan. Unwmk. Typo. Perf. 14

10	A1	3pf brown	1.75	1.75
11	A1	5pf green	1.75	1.50
12	A1	10pf carmine	2.25	1.90
13	A1	20pf ultra	7.00	7.50
14	A1	25pf org & blk, *yel*	12.00	*15.00*
15	A1	30pf org & blk, *sal*	12.00	*15.00*
16	A1	40pf lake & blk	14.00	*18.00*
17	A1	50pf pur & blk, *sal*	14.00	*21.00*
18	A1	80pf lake & blk, *rose*	26.00	*50.00*

Engr. Perf. 14½x14

19	A2	1m carmine	45.00	*82.50*
20	A2	2m blue	75.00	*100.00*
21	A2	3m blk vio	75.00	*180.00*
22	A2	5m slate & car	210.00	*600.00*
		Nos. 10-22 (13)	495.75	*1,094.*
		Set, never hinged	1,350.	

A3

A4

1905 Typo.

23	A3	1c brown	1.10	1.50
24	A3	2c green	1.75	1.50
25	A3	4c carmine	4.00	1.50
26	A3	10c ultra	7.50	5.00
27	A3	20c lake & blk	30.00	18.00
28	A3	40c lake & blk, *rose*	90.00	*90.00*

Engr.

29	A4	$½ carmine	65.00	*75.00*
30a	A4	$1 blue	135.00	120.00
31	A4	$1½ blk vio, 26x17 holes	1,050.	*1,400.*
a.		blk vio, 25x16 holes	*26,000.*	
32	A4	$2½ slate & car, 26x17 holes	1,350.	*4,500.*
a.		$2½ slate & car, 25x16 holes	2,000.	*3,250.*
		Nos. 23-32 (10)	2,734.	*6,213.*
		Set, never hinged	7,250.	

1905-16 Wmk. 125 Typo.

33	A3	1c brown ('06)	1.10	1.50
a.		1c yellow brown ('16)	.45	—
34	A3	2c green ('09)	1.10	*1.10*
a.		2c dark green ('14)	.45	*1.75*
35	A3	4c carmine ('09)	.90	*1.10*
36	A3	10c ultra ('09)	1.00	*3.25*
a.		10c blue	12.00	5.00
37	A3	20c lake & blk ('08)	2.60	*15.00*
38	A3	40c lake & blk, *rose*	3.00	*50.00*

Engr.

39	A4	$½ car, 26x17 holes ('07)	9.00	*65.00*
40	A4	$1 blue, 26x17 holes ('06)	11.50	*67.50*
41	A4	$1½ blk violet	11.00	*200.00*
42	A4	$2½ slate & car	45.00	*450.00*
		Nos. 33-42 (10)	86.20	854.45
		Set, never hinged	460.00	

Four values of the design A3 and A4 stamps in recognizably different shades were printed and released in 1918, but by then Germany had lost control of Kiauchau, and these stamps are not known used. The four stamps and their unused values are: 20c red & black, $1.75; $½ pale rose, $5.50; $1 bright blue, $6.75; $1½ gray violet, $20.

KIONGA

'kyoŋ-gə

LOCATION — Southeast Africa and northeast Mozambique, on Indian Ocean south of Rovuma River
GOVT. — Part of German East Africa
AREA — 400 sq. mi.

This territory, occupied by Portuguese troops during World War I, was allotted to Portugal by the Treaty of Versailles. Later it became part of Mozambique.

100 Centavos = 1 Escudo

Lourenco Marques No. 149 Surcharged in Red

1916, May 29 Unwmk. Perf. 11½

1	A2	½c on 100r bl, *bl*	22.00	17.50
2	A2	1c on 100r bl, *bl*	22.00	17.50
3	A2	2½c on 100r bl, *bl*	22.00	17.50
4	A2	5c on 100r bl, *bl*	22.00	17.50
		Nos. 1-4 (4)	88.00	70.00

Most of the stock of Lourenço Marques No. 149 used for these surcharges lacked gum. Unused examples with original gum are worth approximately 50% more than the values shown.

KIRIBATI

'kir-ə-ˌbas

LOCATION — A group of islands in the Pacific Ocean northeast of Australia
GOVT. — Republic
AREA — 277 sq. mi.
POP. — 85,501 (1999 est.)
CAPITAL — Tarawa

100 Cents = 1 Australian Dollar

Kiribati, former Gilbert Islands, consists of the Gilbert, Phoenix, Ocean and Line Islands.

Catalogue values for all unused stamps in this country are for Never Hinged items.

Watermark

Wmk. 380 — "POST OFFICE"

Kiribati Flag — A50

Parliament, London, Assembly, Tarawa — A51

Wmk. 373

1979, July 12 Litho. *Perf. 14*

325	A50	10c multicolored	.30	.30
326	A51	45c multicolored	.30	.50

Independence.

Training Ship Teraaka — A52

Designs: 3c, Passenger launch Tautunu. 5c, Hibiscus. 7c, Cathedral, Tarawa. 10c, House of Assembly, Bikenibeu Island. 12c, Betio harbor. 15c, Reef egret. 20c, Flamboyant tree. 25c, Moorish idol (fish). 30c, Frangipani blossoms. 35c, Chapel, Tangintebu Island. 50c, Hypolimnas bolina elliciana (butterfly). $1, Tarawa Lagoon ferry, Tabakea. $2, Sunset over lagoon. $5, Natl. flag.

1979-80 Wmk. 373

327	A52	1c multicolored	.30	.65
328	A52	3c multicolored	.30	.35
329	A52	5c multicolored	.30	.25
330	A52	7c multicolored	.30	.25
331	A52	10c multicolored	.30	.25
332	A52	12c multicolored	.30	*.25*
333	A52	15c multicolored	.30	.30
334	A52	20c multicolored	.30	*.30*
335	A52	25c multicolored	.30	*.30*
336	A52	30c multicolored	.30	.30
337	A52	35c multicolored	.30	.30
338	A52	50c multicolored	.70	.55
339	A52	$1 multicolored	.55	.60
340	A52	$2 multicolored	.55	.70
340A	A52	$5 multicolored	1.25	*3.00*
		Nos. 327-340A (15)	6.35	8.35

Issued: $5, 8/27/80; others, 7/12/79.

1980-81 Unwmk.

327a	A52	1c multi ('81)	.30	.35
328a	A52	3c multi ('81)	.30	.35
329a	A52	5c multi	.30	.35
330a	A52	7c multi	.30	.35
331a	A52	10c multi	.30	.35
332a	A52	12c multi	.30	.35
333a	A52	15c multi	.65	.35
334a	A52	20c multi ('81)	.30	.35
335a	A52	25c multi	.35	.35
336a	A52	30c multi ('81)	.30	.75
337a	A52	35c multi ('81)	.30	.75
338a	A52	50c multi ('81)	.90	1.10
339a	A52	$1 multi	.75	.75
340b	A52	$2 multi	1.40	1.05
340c	A52	$5 multi ('80)	2.25	3.75
		Nos. 327a-340c (15)	9.00	11.30

For overprints see Nos. O1-O15.

Gilbert and Ellice Islands No. 1 — A53

Simulated Cancel and: 20c, Gilbert and Ellice No. 70. 25c, Great Britain No. 139. 45c, Gilbert and Ellice No. 31.

Wmk. 373

1979, Oct. 4 Litho. *Perf. 14*

341	A53	10c multicolored	.30	.25
342	A53	20c multicolored	.30	.25
343	A53	25c multicolored	.30	.25
344	A53	45c multicolored	.30	.25
a.		Souvenir sheet of 4, #341-344	1.25	1.25
		Nos. 341-344 (4)	1.20	1.00

Sir Rowland Hill (1795-1879), originator of penny postage.

Boy Climbing Coconut Palm, IYC Emblem A54

IYC Emblem, Coat of Arms and: 10c, Boy and giant clam shell. 45c, Girl reading book. $1, Boy wearing garlands. All vert.

Perf. 14x13½, 13½x14

1979, Nov. 28 Litho.

345	A54	10c multicolored	.30	.25
346	A54	20c multicolored	.30	.25
347	A54	45c multicolored	.30	.25
348	A54	$1 multicolored	.30	.25
		Nos. 345-348 (4)	1.20	1.00

International Year of the Child.

Downrange Station — A55

National Space Development Agency of Japan (NASDA) Satellite Tracking: 45c, Experimental satellite trajectory (map). $1, Rocket launch, Tanegashima, Japan, vert.

1980, Feb. 20 Litho. *Perf. 14½*

349	A55	25c multicolored	.30	.25
350	A55	45c multicolored	.30	.25
351	A55	$1 multicolored	.30	.25
		Nos. 349-351 (3)	.90	.75

T.S. Teraaka, London 1980 Emblem — A56

25c, Air Tungaru plane, Bonriki Airport. 30c, Radio operator. $1, Bairiki post office.

1980, Apr. 30 Litho. Unwmk.

352	A56	12c shown	.30	.25
353	A56	25c multicolored	.30	.25
354	A56	30c multicolored	.30	.25
355	A56	$1 multicolored	.30	.35
a.		Souvenir sheet of 4, #352-355	.75	.85
		Nos. 352-355 (4)	1.20	1.10

London 1980 Intl. Stamp Exhib., May 6-14.

Achaea Janata — A57

25c, Ethmia nigroapicella. 30c, Utetheisa pulchelloides. 50c, Anua coronata.

1980, Aug. 27 Litho. *Perf. 14*

356	A57	12c shown	.30	.25
357	A57	25c multicolored	.30	.25
358	A57	30c multicolored	.30	.30
359	A57	50c multicolored	.45	.45
		Nos. 356-359 (4)	1.35	1.25

Capt. Cook Hotel — A58

1980, Nov. 19 Wmk. 373 *Perf. 13½*

360	A58	10c shown	.30	.25
361	A58	20c Stadium	.30	.25
362	A58	25c Intl. Airport, Bonriki	.30	.25
363	A58	35c National Library	.30	.25
364	A58	$1 Otintai Hotel	.30	.25
		Nos. 360-364 (5)	1.50	1.25

Acalypha Godseffiana — A59

30c, Hibiscus schizopetalus. 35c, Calotropis gigantea. 50c, Euphorbia pulcherrima.

Perf. 14x13½

1981, Feb. 18 Litho. Wmk. 373

365	A59	12c shown	.30	.25
366	A59	30c multicolored	.30	.25
367	A59	35c multicolored	.30	.25
368	A59	50c multicolored	.30	.25
		Nos. 365-368 (4)	1.20	1.00

Abaiang and Marakei Islands, String Figures A60

30c, Butaritari, Little Makin, house. 35c, Maiana, Coral Road. $1, Christmas Island, Resolution.

Wmk. 380

1981, May 6 Litho. *Perf. 14*

369	A60	12c shown	.30	.25
370	A60	30c multicolored	.30	.25
371	A60	35c multicolored	.30	.25
372	A60	$1 multicolored	.45	.45
		Nos. 369-372 (4)	1.35	1.20

Prince Charles, Lady Diana, Royal Yacht Charlotte A60a

Prince Charles and Lady Diana A60b

No. 373, Couple, The Katherine. No. 374, Couple. No. 375, The Osborne. No. 377, Britannia.

Wmk. 380

1981, July 29 Litho. *Perf. 14*

373	A60a	12c multi	.30	.25
a.		Bklt. pane of 4, perf. 12, unwmkd.	.75	
374	A60b	12c multi	.30	.25
375	A60a	50c multi	.35	.25
376	A60b	50c like #374	.40	.25
a.		Bklt. pane of 2, perf. 12, unwmkd.	2.25	
377	A60a	$2 multi	1.00	.75
378	A60b	$2 like #374	1.00	.75
		Nos. 373-378 (6)	3.35	2.50

Souvenir Sheet

Perf. 12

379	A60b	$1.20 like #374	2.00	2.00

Royal wedding.
Stamps of the same denomination issued in sheets of 7 (6 type A60a and 1 type A60b).

Bonriki Tuna Fish Bait Breeding Center — A61

1981, Nov. 19

380	A61	12c shown	.30	.25
381	A61	30c Fishing boat	.30	.25
382	A61	35c Cold storage, Betio	.30	.25
383	A61	50c Nei Manganibuka	.30	.25
a.		Souvenir sheet of 4, #380-383	1.50	1.50
		Nos. 380-383 (4)	1.20	1.00

Pomarine Jaegers — A62

2c, Mallards. 4c, Collared petrels. 5c, Blue-faced boobies. 7c, Friendly quail dove. 8c, Shovelers. 12c, Christmas Island warblers. 15c, Pacific plovers. 20c, Reef herons. 25c, Brown noddies. 30c, Brown boobies. 35c, Audubon's shearwaters. 40c, White-throated storm petrels, vert. 50c, Bristle-thighed curlews, vert. 55c, Fairy tern. $1, Scarlet-breasted lorikeets, vert. $2, Long-tailed cuckoo, vert. $5, Great frigate birds, vert.

1982-85 Litho. *Perf. 14*

384	A62	1c shown	.30	.25
385	A62	2c multicolored	.30	.25
386	A62	4c multicolored	.30	.25
387	A62	5c multicolored	.30	.25
388	A62	7c multicolored	.30	.25
389	A62	8c multicolored	.30	.25
390	A62	12c multicolored	.30	.25
391	A62	15c multicolored	.35	.35
392	A62	20c multicolored	.40	.50
392A	A62	25c multi ('83)	2.75	1.75
393	A62	30c multicolored	.55	.60
394	A62	35c multicolored	.75	.70
395	A62	40c multicolored	.70	.80
396	A62	50c multicolored	.75	.65
396A	A62	55c multi ('85)	12.50	*17.00*
397	A62	$1 multicolored	1.60	.85
398	A62	$2 multicolored	2.25	1.10
399	A62	$5 multicolored	4.50	4.00
		Nos. 384-399 (18)	29.20	30.05

Issued: 25c, 1/31/83; 55c, 11/19/85; others, 2/18/82.

For overprints see Nos. O16-O20.

Air Tungaru — A63

12c, De Havilland DH114 Heron. 30c, Britten-Norman Trislander. 35c, Casa 212 Aviocar. 50c, Boeing 727.

1982, Feb. 18 Wmk. 380

400	A63	12c multicolored	.30	.25
401	A63	30c multicolored	.30	.25
402	A63	35c multicolored	.30	.25
403	A63	50c multicolored	.40	.40
		Nos. 400-403 (4)	1.30	1.15

21st Birthday of Princess Diana, July 1 — A64

1982, May 19

404	A64	12c Mary of Teck, 1893	.30	.25
405	A64	50c Teck arms	.40	.40
406	A64	$1 Diana	.60	.60
		Nos. 404-406 (3)	1.30	1.25

Nos. 404-406 Overprinted: "ROYAL BABY"

1982, July 14

407	A64	12c multicolored	.30	.25
408	A64	50c multicolored	.40	.40
409	A64	$1 multicolored	.60	.60
		Nos. 407-409 (3)	1.30	1.25

Birth of Prince William of Wales, June 21.

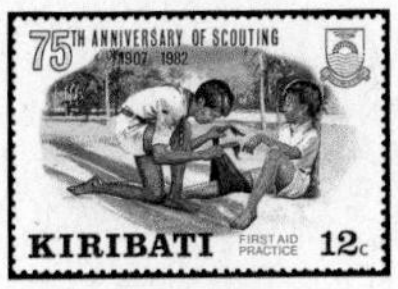

Scouting Year — A65

1982, Aug. 12

410 A65 12c First aid .30 .25
411 A65 25c Repairing boat .30 .25
412 A65 30c Saluting .30 .30
413 A65 50c Gilbert Islds. #304 .40 .40
Nos. 410-413 (4) 1.30 1.20

Visit of Queen Elizabeth II and Prince Philip — A66

Wmk. 380

1982, Oct. 23 Litho. *Perf. 14*

414 A66 12c Couple, dancer .30 .25
415 A66 25c Couple, boat .30 .25
416 A66 35c Philatelic Bureau .45 .45
Nos. 414-416 (3) 1.05 .95

Souvenir Sheet

417 A66 50c Queen Elizabeth II, vert. 1.30 1.30

Nos. 414-416 also issued in sheets of 6.

A67

12c, Obaia the Feathered legend. 30c, Robert Louis Stevenson Hotel, Abemama. 50c, Betio Harbor. $1, Map.

1983, Mar. 14 Wmk. 380 *Perf. 14*

418 A67 12c multicolored .30 .25
419 A67 30c multicolored .30 .25
420 A67 50c multicolored .30 .25
421 A67 $1 multicolored .30 .30
Nos. 418-421 (4) 1.20 1.05

Commonwealth day.

Map of Beru and Nikunau Islds., Canoe — A68

25c, Abemama, Kuria, Aranuka. 35c, Nonouti, vert. 50c, Tarawa, vert.

1983, May 19 Litho. *Perf. 14*

422 A68 12c shown .30 .25
423 A68 25c multicolored .30 .25
424 A68 35c multicolored .30 .25
425 A68 50c multicolored .30 .25
Nos. 422-425 (4) 1.20 1.00

See Nos. 436-439, 456-459, 475-479, 487-490.

Copra Industry — A69

Designs: 12c, Collecting fallen Coconuts. 25c, Selecting Coconuts for Copra. 30c, Removing Husk from Coconuts. 35c, Drying Copra in the Sun. 50c, Loading Copra, Betio Harbor.

1983, Aug. 8 Litho. *Perf. 14*

426 A69 12c multicolored .30 .25
427 A69 25c multicolored .35 .30
428 A69 30c multicolored .40 .35
429 A69 35c multicolored .45 .45
430 A69 50c multicolored .60 .60
Nos. 426-430 (5) 2.10 1.95

Battle of Tarawa, 40th Anniv. — A70

12c, War memorials. 30c, Battle map. 35c, Defense gun. 50c, Scenes, 1943, 1983. $1, Amphibious Assault Ship USS Tarawa.

1983, Nov. 17 Litho. Wmk. 380

431 A70 12c multicolored .30 .25
432 A70 30c multicolored .30 .25
433 A70 35c multicolored .30 .25
434 A70 50c multicolored .30 .30
435 A70 $1 multicolored .45 .45
Nos. 431-435 (5) 1.65 1.50

Map Type of 1983

1984, Feb. 14 Wmk. 380 *Perf. 14*

436 A68 12c Teraina .30 .25
437 A68 30c Nikumaroro .35 .35
438 A68 35c Kanton .40 .40
439 A68 50c Banaba .60 .60
Nos. 436-439 (4) 1.65 1.60

Local Ships — A71

12c, Tug boat. 35c, Ferry landing craft. 50c, Ferry. $1, Cargo and passanger boat.

1984, May 9 Litho. Wmk. 380

440 A71 12c multicolored .45 .25
441 A71 35c multicolored .65 .50
442 A71 50c multicolored 1.00 .75
443 A71 $1 multicolored 1.50 1.50
a. Souvenir sheet of 4, #440-443, perf. 13½ 4.00 4.00
Nos. 440-443 (4) 3.60 3.00

Ausipex '84 — A72

12c, South Tarawa sewer & water system. 30c, Fishing boat Nouamake. 35c, Overseas communications training. 50c, Intl. telecommunications link.

1984, Aug. 21 Litho. *Perf. 14*

444 A72 12c multicolored .30 .25
445 A72 30c multicolored .30 .25
446 A72 35c multicolored .30 .25
447 A72 50c multicolored .35 .35
Nos. 444-447 (4) 1.25 1.10

Legends — A73

Designs: 12c, Tabakea supporting Banaba on his back. 30c, Nakaa, Judge of the Dead. 35c, Naareau and Tiku-Tiku-Tamoamoa. 50c, Whistling Ghosts.

1984, Nov. 21 Wmk. 380 *Perf. 14*

448 A73 12c multicolored .30 .25
449 A73 30c multicolored .30 .25
450 A73 35c multicolored .30 .25
451 A73 50c multicolored .30 .25
Nos. 448-451 (4) 1.20 1.00

See Nos. 464-467.

Reef Fish — A74

12c, Tang. 25c, White-barred triggerfish. 35c, Surgeon fish. 80c, Squirrel fish.

1985, Feb. 19 Litho. *Perf. 14*

452 A74 12c multicolored .65 .30
453 A74 25c multicolored 1.10 .70
454 A74 35c multicolored 1.25 .90
455 A74 80c multicolored 2.00 2.00
a. Souvenir sheet of 4, #452-455 5.50 5.50
Nos. 452-455 (4) 5.00 3.90

See Nos. 540-554, 567.

Map Type of 1983

12c, Tabuaeran, frigate bird. 35c, Rawaki, coconuts. 50c, Arorae, xanthid crab. $1, Tamana, fish hook.

1985, May 9 Litho. *Perf. 13½*

456 A68 12c multicolored 1.00 .35
457 A68 35c multicolored 1.25 .50
458 A68 50c multicolored 1.50 .70
459 A68 $1 multicolored 2.00 1.50
Nos. 456-459 (4) 5.75 3.05

Intl. Youth Year — A76

15c, Boys playing soccer. 35c, Emblems. 40c, Girl processing fruit, vert. 55c, Intl. youth exchange.

1985, Aug. 5

460 A76 15c multicolored .75 .50
461 A76 35c multicolored 1.00 1.00
462 A76 40c multicolored 1.10 1.10
463 A76 55c multicolored 1.50 1.50
Nos. 460-463 (4) 4.35 4.10

Legends Type of 1984

15c, Nang Kineia & the Tickling Ghosts. 35c, Myth of Auriaria & Tituabine. 40c, First Coming of Babai at Arorae. 55c, Riiki & the Milky Way.

1985, Nov. 19 Wmk. 380 *Perf. 14*

464 A73 15c multicolored .50 .50
465 A73 35c multicolored .75 .75
466 A73 40c multicolored .90 .90
467 A73 55c multicolored 1.10 1.10
Nos. 464-467 (4) 3.25 3.25

Transport and Telecommunications Decade 1985-95 — A77

15c, Satellite network. 40c, Tarawa-Suva feeder service.

1985, Dec. 9 Litho. *Perf. 14*

468 A77 15c multicolored 2.25 2.00
469 A77 40c multicolored 3.25 3.00

Common Design Types pictured following the introduction.

Queen Elizabeth II 60th Birthday

Common Design Type

15c, Review of Girl Guides, Windsor Castle, 1938. 35c, Birthday parade, Buckingham Palace, 1980. 40c, With Prince Philip during royal tour, 1982. 55c, Banquet, Austrian embassy in London, 1966. $1, Visiting Crown Agents' offices, 1983.

1986, Apr. 21 *Perf. 14½x14*

470 CD337 15c scar, black & sil .30 .25
471 CD337 35c ultra & multi .30 .25
472 CD337 40c green & multi .30 .25
473 CD337 55c violet & multi .40 .40
474 CD337 $1 rose vio & multi .95 .95
Nos. 470-474 (5) 2.25 2.10

For overprints see Nos. 495-499.

Map Type of 1983

1986, June 17 Wmk. 380 *Perf. 14*

475 A68 15c Manra 2.75 1.75
476 A68 30c Birnie, McKean 3.50 1.90
477 A68 35c Orona 3.75 2.50
478 A68 40c Malden 4.50 3.00
479 A68 55c Vostok, Caroline, Flint 4.50 3.25
Nos. 475-479 (5) 19.00 12.40

Lizards — A79

15c, Lepidodactylus lugubris. 35c, Gehyra mutilata. 40c, Hemidactylus frenatus. 55c, Gehyra oceanica.

1986, Aug. 26 Unwmk. *Perf. 14*

480 A79 15c multicolored 1.50 .75
481 A79 35c multicolored 2.25 1.75
482 A79 40c multicolored 2.75 2.25
483 A79 55c multicolored 3.50 2.75
Nos. 480-483 (4) 10.00 7.50

See Nos. 491-494.

America's Cup — A80

Perf. 14x14½

1986, Dec. 29 Unwmk.

484 A80 Strip of 3 2.25 2.25
a. 15c Map of Australia .30 .25
b. 55c Course, trophy .55 .55
c. $1.50 Australia II 1.30 1.30

No. 484 has a continuous design.

Transport and Telecommunications Decade (1985-1995) — A81

Designs: 30c, Nei Moamoa, flagship of Kiribati overseas shipping line. 55c, Manual and electronic telephone switching systems.

1987, Mar. 31 Litho. *Perf. 14*

485 A81 30c multicolored 3.00 2.50
486 A81 55c multicolored 4.00 3.50

Map Type of 1983

15c, Starbuck, red-tailed tropicbird. 30c, Enderbury, white tern. 55c, Tabiteuea, pandanus. $1, Onotoa, Okai house.

1987, Sept. 22 Litho. Unwmk.

487 A68 15c multicolored .50 .45
488 A68 30c multicolored .60 .45
489 A68 55c multicolored .75 .50
490 A68 $1 multicolored 1.25 *1.75*
Nos. 487-490 (4) 3.10 3.15

Nos. 487-490 vert.

Lizard Type of 1986

1987, Oct. 27 *Perf. 15*

491 A79 15c Emoia nigra .30 .25
492 A79 35c Cryptoblepharus .30 .25
493 A79 40c Emoia cyanura .50 .50
494 A79 $1 Lipinia noctua .90 *1.50*
a. Souvenir sheet of 4, #491-494 2.00 2.00
Nos. 491-494 (4) 2.00 2.50

Nos. 470-474 Overprinted in Silver

Perf. 14½x14

1987, Nov. 30 Litho. Unwmk.

495 CD337 15c scar, black & sil .30 .25
496 CD337 35c ultra & multi .30 .30
497 CD337 40c green & multi .35 .35
498 CD337 55c violet & multi .45 .40
499 CD337 $1 rose vio & multi .90 *1.25*
Nos. 495-499 (5) 2.30 2.55

Intl. Red Cross and Red Crescent Organizations, 125th Annivs. — A83

15c, Jean Henri Dunant (1828-1910), founder. 35c, Red Cross volunteers on parade. 40c, Stretcher bearers. 55c, Gilbert and Ellice Islands #159.

Perf. 14½x14

1988, May 8 Litho. Unwmk.

500 A83 15c multicolored .75 .60
501 A83 35c multicolored 1.00 *1.25*
502 A83 40c multicolored 1.25 *1.40*
503 A83 55c multicolored 2.25 *3.25*
Nos. 500-503 (4) 5.25 *6.50*

A84

SYDPEX '88, Australia Bicentennial — A85

Emblem and: 15c, Australia-assisted causeway construction. 35c, Capt. Cook, map of Australia and Kiribati. No. 506, Australia bicentennial banknote obverse. No. 507, Bank note reverse. $2, "Logistic Ace."

1988, July 30 Litho. *Perf. 14½*
504 A84 15c multicolored .30 .30
505 A84 35c multicolored .60 .60
506 A84 $1 multicolored 1.50 1.50
507 A84 $1 multicolored 1.50 1.50
a. Pair, #506-507 5.00 5.00
Nos. 504-507 (4) 3.90 3.90

Souvenir Sheet
Perf. 13½x14
508 A85 $2 multicolored 6.00 6.00

Robert F. Stockton, 1st propeller-driven steamship, 150th anniv.

Transport and Telecommunications Decade (1985-1995) — A86

35c, Telephone operator, map. 45c, Betio-Bairiki Causeway.

Wmk. 373
1988, Dec. 28 Litho. *Perf. 14*
509 A86 35c multicolored 1.25 1.25
510 A86 45c multicolored 1.75 1.75

Ships — A87

15c, Brigantine Hound, 1835. 30c, Brig Phantom, 1854. 40c, HMS Alacrity, 1873. $1, Whaler Charles W. Morgan, 1851.

Wmk. 384
1989, May 26 Litho. *Perf. 14½*
511 A87 15c multicolored 1.15 .90
512 A87 30c multicolored 1.80 1.50
513 A87 40c multicolored 2.15 2.40
514 A87 $1 multicolored 3.40 3.75
Nos. 511-514 (4) 8.50 8.55

See Nos. 557-561, 687-690.

A88

Perf. 13½x14
1989, July 12 Litho. Wmk. 384
515 A88 15c House of Assembly .35 .35
516 A88 $1 Constitution 2.20 2.20

Natl. Independence, 10th anniv.

Moon Landing, 20th Anniv.
Common Design Type

Apollo 10: 20c, Service and command modules, launch escape system. 50c, Eugene A. Cernan, Thomas P. Stafford and John W. Young. 60c, Mission emblem. 75c, Splashdown, Honolulu. $2.50, Apollo 11 command module in space.

1989, July 20 *Perf. 14*
Size of Nos. 518-519: 29x29mm
517 CD342 20c multicolored .50 .50
518 CD342 50c multicolored .90 .90
519 CD342 60c multicolored 1.10 1.10
520 CD342 75c multicolored 1.25 1.25
Nos. 517-520 (4) 3.75 3.75

Souvenir Sheet
521 CD342 $2.50 multicolored 8.75 8.75

Birds — A89

No. 522, Eastern reef heron. No. 523, Brood in nest. No. 524, White-tailed tropicbird in flight. No. 525, Seated tropicbird.

Perf. 14½x14
1989, June 28 Litho. Wmk. 384
522 A89 15c multicolored 1.40 1.40
523 A89 15c multicolored 1.40 1.40
a. Pair, #522-523 3.25 3.25
524 A89 $1 multicolored 2.50 2.50
525 A89 $1 multicolored 2.50 2.50
a. Pair, #524-525 5.50 5.50
Nos. 522-525 (4) 7.80 7.80

Nos. 523a, 525a have continuous designs.
For overprints see Nos. 534-535.

Souvenir Sheets

A90

Perf. 14x13½
1989, Aug. 7 Litho. Wmk. 384
526 A90 $2 Gilbert & Ellice Isls. #58 6.00 6.00

A91

Workmen renovating the Statue of Liberty: a, Torch. b, Drilling copper sheeting. c, Glancing at a sketch of the statue.

Perf. 14x13½
1989, Sept. 25 Litho. Unwmk.
527 A91 Sheet of 3 5.50 5.50
a.-c. 35c any single 1.60 1.60

World Stamp Expo '89, Washington, DC, PHILEXFRANCE '89, Paris. No. 526 margin pictures #435, France #634 and US #2224.

Transport and Telecommunications Decade, 1985-95 — A92

1989, Oct. 16 Wmk. 384 *Perf. 14*
528 A92 30c shown 2.50 2.25
529 A92 75c MV *Mataburo* 3.75 3.25

Christmas — A93

Paintings: 10c, *Adoration of the Holy Child* (detail), by Denys Calvert. 15c, *Adoration of the Holy Child* (entire painting). 55c, *The Holy Family and St. Elizabeth*, by Rubens. $1, *Madonna with Child and Mary Magdalene*, School of Corregio.

1989, Dec. 1
530 A93 10c multicolored 1.00 .60
531 A93 15c multicolored 1.25 .75
532 A93 55c multicolored 2.50 1.25
533 A93 $1 multicolored 3.75 *6.50*
Nos. 530-533 (4) 8.50 9.10

Nos. 524-525 Ovptd.

1989, Oct. 21 Litho. *Perf. 14½x14*
534 A89 $1 on No. 524 4.00 4.00
535 A89 $1 on No. 525 4.00 4.00
a. Pair, #534-535 9.50 9.50

STAMPSHOW '89, Melbourne.

Penny Black 150th Anniv., Stamp World London '90 — A94

Stamps on stamps: 15c, Gilbert & Ellice #15, Great Britain #2. 50c, Gilbert & Ellice #8, Great Britain #1 canceled. 60c, Kiribati #384, Great Britain #58. $1, Gilbert Islands #269, Great Britain #3.

1990, May 1 Litho. *Perf. 14*
536 A94 15c multicolored 1.15 1.15
537 A94 50c multicolored 2.80 2.80
538 A94 60c multicolored 2.95 2.95
539 A94 $1 multicolored 3.10 3.10
Nos. 536-539 (4) 10.00 10.00

Fish Type of 1985

Fish: 1c, Blue-barred orange parrotfish. 5c, Honeycomb rock cod. 10c, Bluefin jack. 15c, Paddle tail snapper. 20c, Variegated emperor. 25c, Rainbow runner. 30c, Black saddled coral trout. 35c, Great barracuda. 40c, Convict surgeonfish. 50c, Violet squirrelfish. 60c, Freckled hawkfish. 75c, Pennant coral fish. $1, Yellow and blue sea perch. $2, Pacific sailfish. $5, Whitetip reef shark.

Wmk. 373
1990, July 12 Litho. *Perf. 14*
540 A74 1c multicolored .40 .40
541 A74 5c multicolored .50 .50
542 A74 10c multicolored .65 .65
543 A74 15c multicolored .75 .75
544 A74 20c multicolored .90 .90
545 A74 25c multicolored 1.00 .95
546 A74 30c multicolored 1.10 1.00
547 A74 35c multicolored 1.25 1.10
548 A74 40c multicolored 1.50 1.25
549 A74 50c multicolored 1.75 1.75
550 A74 60c multicolored 2.00 2.00
551 A74 75c multicolored 2.25 2.25
552 A74 $1 multicolored 3.00 2.50
553 A74 $2 multicolored 4.50 4.50
554 A74 $5 multicolored 7.75 *9.00*
Nos. 540-554 (15) 29.30 29.50

Dated 1990. See No. 567. For overprints see Nos. 587-590.

Queen Mother 90th Birthday
Common Design Types

75c, Queen Mother. $2, King, Queen & WWII bombing victim, 1940.

1990, Aug. 4 Wmk. 384 *Perf. 14x15*
555 CD343 75c multicolored 1.50 1.50
Perf. 14½
556 CD344 $2 multicolored 3.25 3.25

Ships Type of 1989

15c, Whaling ship Herald, 1851. 50c, Bark Belle, 1849. 60c, Schooner Supply, 1851. 75c, Whaling ship Triton, 1848.
$2, Convict transport Charlotte, 1789.

1990, Nov. 5 Litho. *Perf. 14½*
557 A87 15c multicolored 1.00 .75
558 A87 50c multicolored 1.60 1.50
559 A87 60c multicolored 1.75 1.75
560 A87 75c multicolored 2.25 2.25
Nos. 557-560 (4) 6.60 6.25

Souvenir Sheet
561 A87 $2 multicolored 8.00 8.00

Manta Ray — A95

1991, Jan. 17 Wmk. 373 *Perf. 14*
562 A95 15c shown 1.25 .60
563 A95 20c Manta ray, diff. 1.50 1.00
564 A95 30c Whale shark 1.75 1.75
565 A95 35c Whale shark, diff. 2.25 2.25
Nos. 562-565 (4) 6.75 5.60

World Wildlife Fund.

Fish Type of 1985

Design: 23c, Bennett's pufferfish.

1991, Apr. 30 Wmk. 384
567 A74 23c multicolored 1.75 1.75

For overprint see No. 587.

Elizabeth & Philip, Birthdays
Common Design Types

1991, June 17 *Perf. 14½*
571 CD345 65c multicolored 1.75 1.75
572 CD346 70c multicolored 1.75 1.75
a. Pair, #571-572 + label 4.00 4.00

Phila Nippon '91 — A96

Opening of new Tungaru Central Hospital: 23c, Aerial view. 50c, Traditional dancers. 60c, Main entrance. 75c, Foundation stone, plaque. $5, Ambulance, nursing staff.

1991, Nov. 16 *Perf. 13½x14*
573 A96 23c multicolored .50 .50
574 A96 50c multicolored 1.00 1.00
575 A96 60c multicolored 1.40 1.40
576 A96 75c multicolored 1.60 1.60
Nos. 573-576 (4) 4.50 4.50

Souvenir Sheet
577 A96 $5 multicolored 9.00 9.00

Christmas A97

Designs: 23c, Island mother and child. 50c, Family in island hut. 60c, Nativity Scene. 75c, Adoration of the Shepherds.

1991, Dec. 2 Wmk. 373
578 A97 23c multicolored .75 .60
579 A97 50c multicolored 1.25 1.25
580 A97 60c multicolored 1.75 1.75
581 A97 75c multicolored 2.25 2.25
Nos. 578-581 (4) 6.00 5.85

Queen Elizabeth II's Accession to the Throne, 40th Anniv.
Common Design Type

Wmk. 373
1992, Feb. 6 Litho. *Perf. 14*
582 CD349 23c multicolored .35 .35
583 CD349 30c multicolored .50 .50
584 CD349 50c multicolored .80 .80
585 CD349 60c multicolored 1.00 1.00
586 CD349 75c multicolored 1.20 1.20
Nos. 582-586 (5) 3.85 3.85

Nos. 550-551, 553, & 567 Ovptd.

Wmk. 384, 373
1992, June 1 Litho. *Perf. 14*
587 A74 23c on No. 567 .90 .80
588 A74 60c on No. 550 2.00 2.00
589 A74 75c on No. 551 2.45 2.45
590 A74 $2 on No. 553 2.70 3.00
Nos. 587-590 (4) 8.05 8.25

Marine Training Center, 25th Anniv. — A98

23c, Entrance. 50c, Cadets at morning parade. 60c, Fire school. 75c, Lifeboat training.

1992, Aug. 28 ***Perf. 14***

591	A98	23c multicolored	.65	.65
592	A98	50c multicolored	1.00	1.00
593	A98	60c multicolored	1.20	1.20
594	A98	75c multicolored	1.50	1.50
		Nos. 591-594 (4)	4.35	4.35

FAO, WHO — A99

23c, Children running. 50c, Night fishing. 60c, Fruit. 75c, Ship.

Wmk. 373

1992, Dec. 1 **Litho.** ***Perf. 14***

595	A99	23c multicolored	1.00	1.00
596	A99	50c multicolored	1.10	1.10
597	A99	60c multicolored	1.25	1.25
598	A99	75c multicolored	2.00	2.00
		Nos. 595-598 (4)	5.35	5.35

Water Birds — A100

No. 599, Phoenix petrel. No. 600, Cooks petrel. No. 601, Northern pintail. No. 602, Eurasian widgeon. No. 603, Spectacled tern. No. 604, Black naped tern. No. 605, Stilt wader. No. 606, Wandering tattler.

Wmk. 373

1993, May 28 **Litho.** ***Perf. 14½***

599	A100	23c multicolored	.60	.60
600	A100	23c multicolored	.60	.60
a.		Pair, #599-600	1.30	1.30
601	A100	60c multicolored	1.15	1.15
602	A100	60c multicolored	1.15	1.15
a.		Pair, #601-602	2.35	2.35
603	A100	75c multicolored	1.40	1.40
604	A100	75c multicolored	1.40	1.40
a.		Pair, #603-604	3.00	3.00
605	A100	$1 multicolored	1.60	1.60
606	A100	$1 multicolored	1.60	1.60
a.		Pair, #605-606	3.40	3.40
		Nos. 599-606 (8)	9.50	9.50

Insects — A101

23c, Chilocorus nigritus. 60c, Rodolia pumila. 75c, Rodolia cardinalis. $1, Cryptolaemus montrouzieri.

Perf. 14½x14

1993, Aug. 23 **Litho.** **Wmk. 373**

607	A101	23c multicolored	1.25	1.25
608	A101	60c multicolored	2.00	2.00
609	A101	75c multicolored	2.50	2.50
610	A101	$1 multicolored	3.00	*3.50*
		Nos. 607-610 (4)	8.75	9.25

Liberation of Kiribati, 50th Anniv. — A102

No. 611: a, Air reconnaissance of Tarawa Atoll. b, USS Nautilus surveys Tarawa. c, USS Indianapolis. d, USS Pursuit leads seaborne assault. e, Kingfisher spotter plane. f, Destroyers USS Ringgold and USS Dashiell. g, Sherman tank on seabed. h, Fighter plane in lagoon. i, Naval gun on seabed. j, First US aircraft to land on Betio Island.

No. 612: a, Transports disembark landing craft. b, Marines assault Betio Island. c, Sea and air assault of Betio. d, Marines pinned down in surf. e, USS Maryland firing broadside. f, Betio from the air. g, Memorial to US Navy dead. h, Memorial to expatriates. i, Memorial to Japanese dead. j, Battle map of Betio.

Wmk. 373

1993, Nov. 1 **Litho.** ***Perf. 14***

Sheets of 10

611	A102	23c #a.-j. + label	6.75	6.75
612	A102	75c #a.-j. + label	18.25	18.25

Christmas A103

23c, Shepherds. 40c, Three kings. 60c, Holy Family. 75c, Mother, children. $3, Madonna and Child.

Perf. 13½x14

1993, Dec. 1 **Litho.** **Wmk. 373**

613	A103	23c multicolored	.60	.40
614	A103	40c multicolored	.90	.90
615	A103	60c multicolored	1.25	*1.75*
616	A103	75c multicolored	1.55	*2.10*
		Nos. 613-616 (4)	4.30	5.15

Souvenir Sheet

617	A103	$3 multicolored	6.50	6.50

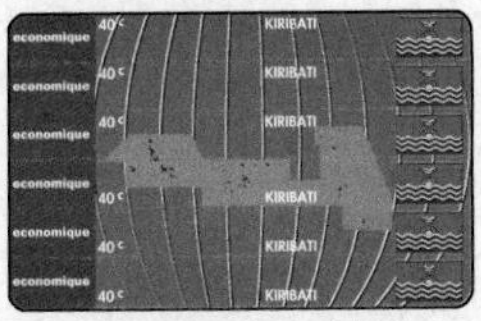

Stampcards — A104

Rouletted 6 on 2 or 3 Sides

1993, Nov. 1 **Litho.**

Self-Adhesive

Cards of 6 + 6 labels

618	A104	40c #a.-f.		*5.00*
619	A104	$1 #a.-f.		*12.00*
620	A104	$1.20 #a.-f.		*15.00*
621	A104	$1.60 #a.-f.		*22.50*
		Nos. 618-621 (4)		*54.50*

Nos. 619-621 are airmail. Individual stamps measure 70x9mm and have a card backing. Se-tenant labels on No. 618 inscribed "economique." Se-tenant labels on Nos. 619-621 inscribed "prioritaire AIR MAIL."

It has been stated that these stamps were available only from the Philatelic Bureau and were not accepted by local post offices as valid for postage, though this is contradicted by the Controller of Postal Services.

Souvenir Sheet

New Year 1994 (Year of the Dog) A105

Wmk. 373

1994, Feb. 18 **Litho.** ***Perf. 14***

622	A105	$3 multicolored	6.50	6.50

Hong Kong '94.

Whales — A106

Designs: 23c, Bryde's whale. 40c, Blue whale. 60c, Humpback whale. 75c, Killer whale.

1994, May 2

623	A106	23c multicolored	1.25	1.25
624	A106	23c multicolored	1.25	1.25
a.		Pair, #623-624	2.85	2.85
625	A106	40c multicolored	1.50	1.50
626	A106	40c multicolored	1.50	1.50
a.		Pair, #625-626	3.50	3.50
627	A106	60c multicolored	2.10	2.10
628	A106	60c multicolored	2.10	2.10
a.		Pair, #627-628	5.25	5.25
629	A106	75c multicolored	2.40	2.40
630	A106	75c multicolored	2.40	2.40
a.		Pair #629-630	5.75	5.75
		Nos. 623-630 (8)	14.50	14.50

Value at UL on Nos. 623, 625, 627, 629; at UR on others.

Nos. 624a-630a have continuous designs.

Environmental Protection — A107

Designs: 40c, Family on beach at sunset. 60c, Fish. 75c, Frigate birds.

1994, July 12

631	A107	40c multicolored	1.00	.90
632	A107	60c multicolored	1.10	1.10
633	A107	75c multicolored	1.60	1.60
		Nos. 631-633 (3)	3.70	3.60

Independence, 15th anniv.

Butterflies — A108

Designs: 1c, Diaphania indica. 5c, Herpetogamma licarsisalis. 10c, Parotis suralis. 12c, Sufetula sunidesalis. 20c, Aedia sericea. 23c, Anomis vitiensis. 30c, Anticarsia irrorata. 35c, Spodoptera litura. 40c, Mocis frugalis. 45c, Agrius convolvuli. 50c, Cephonodes picus. 55c, Gnathothlibus erotus. 60c, Macroglossum hirundo. 75c, Badamia exclamationis. $1, Precis villida. $2, Danaus plexippus. $3, Hypolimnas bolina (male). $5, Hypolimnas bolina (female).

1994, Aug. 19 ***Perf. 14½x14***

634	A108	1c multicolored	.30	.25
635	A108	5c multicolored	.30	.25
636	A108	10c multicolored	.30	.25
637	A108	12c multicolored	.30	.25
638	A108	20c multicolored	.30	.30
639	A108	23c multicolored	.40	.40
640	A108	30c multicolored	.55	.50
641	A108	35c multicolored	.60	.60
642	A108	40c multicolored	.70	.65
643	A108	45c multicolored	.75	.75
644	A108	50c multicolored	.80	.75
645	A108	55c multicolored	.95	.85
646	A108	60c multicolored	.95	.90
647	A108	75c multicolored	1.10	1.10
648	A108	$1 multicolored	1.55	1.55
a.		Souvenir sheet of 1	2.75	2.75
649	A108	$2 multicolored	2.90	*3.65*
650	A108	$3 multicolored	4.65	*5.50*
651	A108	$5 multicolored	8.00	*9.00*
		Nos. 634-651 (18)	25.40	27.50

No. 648a issued 2/12/97 for Hong Kong '97.

For overprints see Nos. 763-767.

Flowers — A109

23c, Nerium oleander. 60c, Catharanthus roseus. 75c, Ipomea pes-caprae. $1, Calophyllum mophyllum.

1994, Oct. 31

652	A109	23c multicolored	.65	.65
653	A109	60c multicolored	1.10	1.10
654	A109	75c multicolored	1.50	1.50
655	A109	$1 multicolored	2.00	2.00
		Nos. 652-655 (4)	5.25	5.25

A110

Constellations.

1995, Jan. 31

656	A110	50c Gemini	1.20	1.20
657	A110	60c Cancer	1.30	1.30
658	A110	75c Cassiopeia	1.50	1.50
659	A110	$1 Southern cross	2.00	2.00
		Nos. 656-659 (4)	6.00	6.00

A111

Scenes of Kiribati: No. 660: a, Architecture. b, Men, canoe, sailboat. c, Gun emplacement, Tarawa. d, Children, shells. e, Outdoor sports.

No. 661: a, Women traditionally attired. b, Windsurfing. c, Filleting fish. d, Snorkeling, scuba diving. e, Weaving.

Wmk. 384

1995, Apr. 3 **Litho.** ***Perf. 14½***

660	A111	30c Strip of 5, #a.-e.	4.00	4.00
661	A111	40c Strip of 5, #a.-e.	5.75	5.75
f.		Booklet pane, #660, #661 + 5 labels	12.00	*12.00*
		Complete booklet, #661f	13.00	

Visit South Pacific Year.

End of World War II, 50th Anniv.

Common Design Type

Designs: 23c, Grumman TBM-3E Avenger. 40c, Curtiss SOC. 3-1 seagull. 50c, Consolidated B-24J Liberator. 60c, Grumman Goose. 75c, Martin B-26 Marauder. $1, Northrop P-61B Black Widow. $2, Reverse of War Medal 1939-45.

Perf. 14x13½

1995, May 8 **Wmk. 373**

662	CD351	23c multicolored	.85	.85
663	CD351	40c multicolored	1.00	1.00
664	CD351	50c multicolored	1.15	1.15
665	CD351	60c multicolored	1.30	1.30
666	CD351	75c multicolored	1.80	1.80
667	CD351	$1 multicolored	2.45	2.45
		Nos. 662-667 (6)	8.55	8.55

Souvenir Sheet

Perf. 14

668	CD352	$2 multicolored	4.00	4.00

For overprints see Nos. 691-697.

Souvenir Sheet

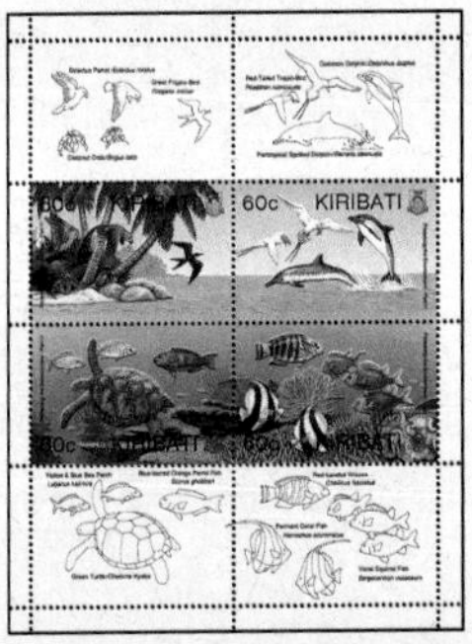

Environmental Protection — A112

Marine life: a, Electus parrot, great frigate bird, coconut crab. b, Red-tailed tropic bird, common dolphin, pantropical spotted dolphin. c, Yellow & blue sea perch, green turtle, blue-barred orange parrot fish. d, Pennant coral fish, red-banded wrasse, violet squirrel fish.

Wmk. 373

1995, July 12 **Litho.** ***Perf. 14***

669	A112	60c #a.-d. + 4 labels	5.00	5.00

For overprint see No. 672.

Souvenir Sheet

New Year 1995 (Year of the Boar) A113

$2, Sow, piglets.

1995, Sept. 1 Litho. *Perf. 13*
670 A113 $2 multicolored 4.25 4.25

Singapore '95.

Souvenir Sheet

Beijing '95 A114

Design: $2, like #670.

1995, Sept. 14
671 A114 $2 multicolored 4.25 4.25

No. 669 Overprinted for Jakarta '95

Wmk. 373
1995, Aug. 19 Litho. *Perf. 14*
672 A112 60c #a.-d. + 4 labels 10.00 10.00

Police Maritime Unit A115

Patrol boat RKS Teanoai: No. 673, In harbor. No. 674, Under way.

Wmk. 373
1995, Nov. 30 Litho. *Perf. 13*
673 75c multicolored 1.90 1.90
674 75c multicolored 1.90 1.90
a. A115 Pair, #673-674 4.00 4.00

Dolphins — A116

Designs: 23c, Pantropical spotted. 60c, Spinner. 75c, Fraser's. $1, Rough-toothed.

Wmk. 384
1996, Jan. 15 Litho. *Perf. 14*
675 A116 23c multicolored 1.25 .75
676 A116 60c multicolored 1.75 1.00
677 A116 75c multicolored 2.40 1.75
678 A116 $1 multicolored 2.75 *2.75*
Nos. 675-678 (4) 8.15 6.25

UNICEF, 50th Anniv. A117

Portion of UNICEF emblem and: a, Water faucet, clean water. b, Documents, chilren's rights. c, Hypodermic, health care. d, Open book, education.

Wmk. 373
1996, Apr. 22 Litho. *Perf. 13*
679 A117 30c Block of 4, #a.-d. 2.75 2.75

No. 679 is a continuous design.

Souvenir Sheet

CHINA '96, 9th Intl. Philatelic Exhibition — A118

1996, Apr. 30 Wmk. 384 *Perf. 13½*
680 A118 50c multicolored 2.00 2.00

New Year 1996, Year of the Rat.

Souvenir Sheet

No. 5609 Gilbert and Ellice Islands LMS Jubilee Class 4-6-0 Locomotive — A119

Wmk. 373
1996, June 8 Litho. *Perf. 12*
681 A119 $2 multicolored 3.75 3.75

CAPEX '96.

Sea Crabs — A120

23c, Rathbun red. 60c, Red & white painted. 75c, Red spotted. $1, Red spotted white.

Wmk. 373
1996, Aug. 6 Litho. *Perf. 14*
682 A120 23c multicolored .65 .50
683 A120 60c multicolored 1.50 1.10
684 A120 75c multicolored 1.75 1.75
685 A120 $1 multicolored 2.25 *2.75*
Nos. 682-685 (4) 6.15 6.10

Souvenir Sheet

Taipei '96 A121

Wmk. 384
1996, Oct. 21 Litho. *Perf. 14½*
686 A121 $1.50 Outrigger canoe 4.00 4.00

Ships Type of 1989

23c, Whaling ship, "Potomac," 1843. 50c, Barkentine "Southern Cross IV," 1891. 60c, Bark "John Williams III," 1890. $1, HMS Dolphin, 1765.

Wmk. 384
1996, Dec. 2 Litho. *Perf. 14½*
687 A87 23c multicolored .70 .55
688 A87 50c multicolored 1.10 1.10
689 A87 60c multicolored 1.30 1.30
690 A87 $1 multicolored 2.25 2.25
Nos. 687-690 (4) 5.35 5.20

Nos. 662-668 Ovptd.

Perf. 14x13½
1997, May 29 Litho. Wmk. 373
691 CD351 23c multicolored .60 .45
692 CD351 40c multicolored .85 .75
693 CD351 50c multicolored 1.10 1.00
694 CD351 60c multicolored 1.35 1.35
695 CD351 75c multicolored 1.55 1.55
696 CD351 $1 multicolored 2.00 2.00
Nos. 691-696 (6) 7.45 7.10

Souvenir Sheet
697 CD351 $2 multicolored 5.00 5.00

Queen Elizabeth II and Prince Philip, 50th Wedding Anniv. A122

No. 698, Queen Elizabeth II. No. 699, Horse team going down river bank. No. 700, Queen in open carriage. No. 701, Prince Philip. No. 702, Prince, Queen. No. 703, Riding horse.
$2, Queen, Prince in open carriage, horiz.

Perf. 14½x14
1997, July 10 Litho. Wmk. 373
698 50c multicolored 1.15 1.15
699 50c multicolored 1.15 1.15
a. A122 Pair, #698-699 2.50 2.50
700 60c multicolored 1.35 1.35
701 60c multicolored 1.35 1.35
a. A122 Pair, #700-701 2.90 2.90
702 75c multicolored 2.00 2.00
703 75c multicolored 2.00 2.00
a. A122 Pair, #702-703 4.40 4.40
Nos. 698-703 (6) 9.00 9.00

Souvenir Sheet
704 A122 $2 multicolored 6.50 6.50

Birds A123

Nos. 705-706, Rock dove. Nos. 707-708, Pacific pigeon. Nos. 709-710, Micronesian pigeon.

Wmk. 373
1997, Dec. 1 Litho. *Perf. 14*
705 50c Immature .90 .90
706 50c Adult .90 .90
a. A123 Pair, #705-706 1.90 1.90
707 60c Adult 1.20 1.20
708 60c Immature 1.20 1.20
a. A123 Pair, #707-708 2.60 2.60
709 75c Adult 1.40 1.40
710 75c Immature 1.40 1.40
a. A123 Pair, #709-710 3.00 3.00
Nos. 705-710 (6) 7.00 7.00

Nos. 705-706, 709-710 With Added Inscription

Wmk. 373
1997, Dec. 5 Litho. *Perf. 14*
711 50c on #705 1.10 1.10
712 50c on #706 1.10 1.10
a. A123 Pair, #711-712 2.50 2.50
713 75c on #709 1.80 1.80
714 75c on #710 1.80 1.80
a. A123 Pair, #713-714 3.80 3.80
Nos. 711-714 (4) 5.80 5.80

Asia '97.

Spiny Lobster — A124

No. 716, Crawling right. No. 717, Crawling left. No. 718, Looking upward.
No. 719, Looking straight forward.

Wmk. 373
1998, Feb. 2 Litho. *Perf. 14*
715 A124 25c shown .60 .60
716 A124 25c multicolored .60 .60
717 A124 25c multicolored .60 .60
718 A124 25c multicolored .60 .60
a. Strip of 4, #715-718 2.50 2.50

Souvenir Sheet
719 A124 $1.50 multicolored 3.00 3.00

World Wildlife Fund.

Diana, Princess of Wales (1961-97)
Common Design Type

Various portraits — No. 720: a, 50c. b, 60c. c, 75c.

Perf. 14½x14
1998, Mar. 31 Litho. Wmk. 373
719A CD355 25c multicolored .60 .60

Sheet of 4
720 CD355 #a.-c., 719A 4.00 4.00

No. 720 sold for $2.10 + 50c, with surtax from international sales being donated to the Princess Diana Memorial Fund, and surtax from national sales being donated to designated local charity.

Intl. Year of the Ocean — A125

Whales and dolphins: No. 721, Indo-Pacific humpbacked dolphin. No. 722, Bottlenose dolphin. No. 723, Short-snouted spinner dolphin. No. 724, Risso's dolphin. No. 725, Striped dolphin. No. 726, Sei whale. No. 727, Fin whale. No. 728, Minke whale.

Wmk. 373
1998, Oct. 1 Litho. *Perf. 14*
721 25c multicolored .55 .55
722 25c multicolored .55 .55
a. A125 Pair, #721-722 1.35 1.35
723 60c multicolored 1.15 1.15
724 60c multicolored 1.15 1.15
a. A125 Pair, #723-724 2.50 2.50
725 75c multicolored 1.60 1.60
726 75c multicolored 1.60 1.60
a. A125 Pair, #725-726 3.40 3.40
727 $1 multicolored 1.80 1.80
728 $1 multicolored 1.80 1.80
a. A125 Pair, #727-728 4.00 4.00
Nos. 721-728 (8) 10.20 10.20

Souvenir Sheet

Children of Kiribati — A125a

1998, Sept. 15
729 A125a $1 multicolored 2.00 2.00

Souvenir Sheet

Reuben K. Uatioa Stadium A126

Wmk. 373
1998, Oct. 23 Litho. *Perf. 14*
730 A126 $2 multicolored 3.25 3.25

Italia '98 World Philatelic Exhibition.

Greenhouse Effect — A127

Designs: 25c, Contributors to Greenhouse gases. 50c, Explanation of the Greenhouse Effect. 60c, Greenhouse Effect on Tarawa Atoll. 75c, Greenhouse Effect on Kiritimati Island.

$1.50, People in sailboat, "Kiribati way of life."

Wmk. 373

1998, Dec. 1 Litho. *Perf. 13½*

731	A127	25c multicolored	.45	.45
732	A127	50c multicolored	.70	.70
733	A127	60c multicolored	.95	.95
734	A127	75c multicolored	1.35	1.35
		Nos. 731-734 (4)	3.45	3.45

Souvenir Sheet

735	A127	$1.50 multicolored	4.75	4.75

Souvenir Sheet

HMS Resolution at Christmas Island — A128

Wmk. 373

1999, Mar. 19 Litho. *Perf. 14*

736	A128	$2 multicolored	3.75	3.75

Australia '99 World Stamp Expo.

IBRA '99, Philatelic Exhibition, Nuremberg A129

Ducks: 25c, Northern shoveller, male. 50c, Northern shoveller, female. 60c, Green-winged teal, male. 75c, Green-winged teal, female and ducklings.
$3, Green winged teal, male, duckling.

Wmk. 373

1999, Apr. 27 Litho. *Perf. 14*

737	A129	25c multicolored	.60	.50
738	A129	50c multicolored	1.10	.80
739	A129	60c multicolored	1.25	1.40
740	A129	75c multicolored	1.55	*2.00*
		Nos. 737-740 (4)	4.50	4.70

Souvenir Sheet

741	A129	$3 multicolored	5.50	5.50

Independence, 20th Anniv. — A130

Designs: 25c, Millennium Island. 60c, Map of Kiribati. 75c, Map of Nikumaroro. $1, Amelia Earhart, Lockheed 10E Electra airplane.

Wmk. 373

1999, July 12 Litho. *Perf. 13½*

742	A130	25c multicolored	.50	.50
743	A130	60c multicolored	.95	.95
744	A130	75c multicolored	1.25	1.25
745	A130	$1 multicolored	2.60	2.60
a.		Souvenir sheet, #744-745	3.50	3.50
		Nos. 742-745 (4)	5.30	5.30

1st Manned Moon Landing, 30th Anniv.

Common Design Type

Designs: 25c, Edwin Aldrin. 60c, Service module docks with lander. 75c, Apollo 11 on lunar surface. $1, Command module separates from service module.
$2, Earth as seen from moon.

Perf. 14x13¾

1999, July 20 Litho. Wmk. 384

746	CD357	25c multicolored	.60	.60
747	CD357	60c multicolored	1.10	1.10
748	CD357	75c multicolored	1.40	1.40
749	CD357	$1 multicolored	1.75	1.75
		Nos. 746-749 (4)	4.85	4.85

Souvenir Sheet

Perf. 14

750	CD357	$2 multicolored	3.75	3.75

No. 750 contains one 40mm circular stamp 40mm.

UPU, 125th Anniv., Christmas A131

Wmk. 373

1999, Oct. 9 Litho. *Perf. 13½*

751	A131	25c Santa in canoe	.50	.45
752	A131	60c Santa on dock	.85	.75
753	A131	75c Santa in sleigh	1.10	1.10
754	A131	$1 Santa at computer	1.30	1.30
		Nos. 751-754 (4)	3.75	3.60

Millennium — A132

Perf. 13¼x13

2000, Jan. 1 Litho. Wmk. 373

755	A132	25c Faith	.40	.35
756	A132	40c Harmony	.60	.55
757	A132	60c Hope	.80	.80
758	A132	75c Enlightenment	1.30	1.30
759	A132	$1 Peace	1.45	1.45
		Nos. 755-759 (5)	4.55	4.45

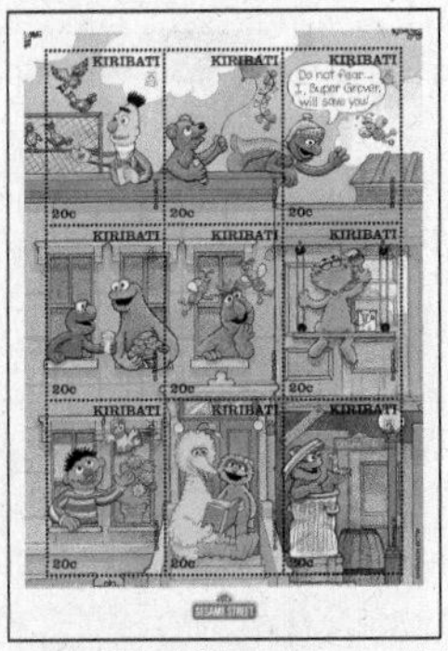

Sesame Street Characters — A133

No. 760: a, Bert. b, Baby Bear. c, Grover. d, Elmo, Cookie Monster. e, Telly Monster. f, Zoe. g, Ernie. h, Big Bird, Rosita. i, Oscar the Grouch.
No. 761, Grover as mailman.

Perf. 14½x14¾

2000, Mar. 22 Litho. Wmk. 373

760	A133	20c Sheet of 9, #a-i	3.75	3.75

Souvenir Sheet

761	A133	$1.50 multi	2.75	2.75

Souvenir Sheet

The Stamp Show 2000, London A134

2000, May 8 Wmk. 373 *Perf. 13¾*

762	A134	$5 Queen Elizabeth II	7.50	7.50

Nos. 635, 636, 638, 648 and 650 Ovptd.

Perf. 14½x14

2000, June 1 Wmk. 373

763	A108	5c multi	.35	.35
764	A108	10c multi	.35	.35
765	A108	20c multi	.40	.40
766	A108	$1 multi	1.30	1.30
767	A108	$3 multi	3.40	3.40
		Nos. 763-767 (5)	5.80	5.80

Prince William, 18th Birthday — A135

Various views of Prince William with Prince Charles.

Wmk. 373

2000, July 24 Litho. *Perf. 12¾*

768	A135	25c multi	.40	.40
769	A135	60c multi	.90	.90
770	A135	75c multi	1.25	1.25
771	A135	$1 multi	1.50	1.50
		Nos. 768-771 (4)	4.05	4.05

Ducks — A136

Designs: No. 772, 25c, Blue duck. No. 773, 25c, Green-winged teal. No. 774, 25c, Mallard. No. 775, 25c, Northern shoveler. No. 776, 25c, Pacific black duck. No. 777, 25c, Wandering whistling duck.

Wmk. 373

2001, Jan. 22 Litho. *Perf. 14*

772-777	A136	Set of 6	8.00	8.00

Souvenir Sheet

778	A136	$1 Gray teal	7.75	7.75

Water Conservation A137

Children's art by: 25c, Tiare Hongkai. 50c, Gilbert Z. Tluanga. 60c, Mantokataake Tebaiuea, vert. 75c, Tokaman Karanebo, vert. $2, Taom Simon.

2001, July 12 Litho. *Perf. 13¼*

779-783	A137	Set of 5	5.25	5.25

Phila Nippon '01 — A138

Development projects: 75c, Betio Port. $2, New Parliament House.

2001, Aug. 1

784-785	A138	Set of 2	5.00	5.00

Tourism A139

Designs: 75c, Norwegian Cruise Line ship, map of cruise to Fanning Island. $3, The Betsey, map of Fanning Island.

Perf. 13¼

2001, Nov. 14 Litho. Unwmk.

786-787	A139	Set of 2	5.75	5.75

Fish — A140

Designs: 5c, Paracanthurus hepatus. 10c, Centropyge flavissimus. 15c, Anthias squamipinnis. 20c, Centropyge loriculus. 25c, Acanthurus lineatus. 30c, Oxycirrhites typus. 40c, Dascyllus trimaculatus. 50c, Acanthurus achilles. 60c, Pomacentrus coeruleus. 75c, Acanthurus glaucopareus. 80c, Thalassoma lunare. 90c, Arothron meleagris. $1, Odonus niger. $2, Cephalopholis miniatus. $5, Pomacanthus imperator. $10, Balistoides conspicillum.

2002, Feb. 28 Unwmk. *Perf. 13*

788	A140	5c multi	.30	.25
789	A140	10c multi	.30	.30
790	A140	15c multi	.30	.30
791	A140	20c multi	.30	.30
792	A140	25c multi	.35	.35
793	A140	30c multi	.40	.40
794	A140	40c multi	.55	.55
795	A140	50c multi	.65	.65
796	A140	60c multi	.70	.70
797	A140	75c multi	.80	.80
798	A140	80c multi	1.00	1.00
799	A140	90c multi	1.30	1.30
800	A140	$1 multi	1.40	1.40
801	A140	$2 multi	2.80	2.80
802	A140	$5 multi	6.50	6.50
803	A140	$10 multi	11.50	11.50
		Nos. 788-803 (16)	29.15	29.10

For overprints, see Nos. 988-990.

Pacific Explorers — A141

Designs: 25c, Adm. Fabian von Bellingshausen and the Vostok, 1820. 40c, Capt. Charles Wilkes and the Vincennes, 1838-42. 60c, Capt. Edmund Fanning and the Betsey, 1798. 75c, Capt. Coffin and the Transit, 1823. $1, Commodore John Byron and the Dolphin, 1765. $2, Capt. Broughton and HMS Providence, 1795.
$5, Capt. James Cook, 1777, vert.

2002, Mar. 25 Wmk. 373 *Perf. 14*

804-809	A141	Set of 6	9.00	9.00

Souvenir Sheet

810	A141	$5 multi	8.50	8.50

In Remembrance of Sept. 11, 2001 Terrorist Attacks — A142

No. 811: a, 25c. b, $2.

2002, May 3 Wmk. 373 *Perf. 13¾*

811	A142	Vert. pair, #a-b	5.00	5.00

Issued in sheets of 2 pairs.

Reign of Queen Elizabeth II, 50th Anniv. — A143

Various photographs by Dorothy Wilding. Panel colors: 25c, Purple.
No. 812: a, Maroon. b, Purple.

2002, June 3 Wmk. 373 *Perf. 14*

812	A143	25c multi	1.25	1.25

Souvenir Sheet

813	A143	$2 Sheet of 2, #a-b	8.50	8.50

Christmas — A144

Ribbons and bow with various basketry weaves: 25c, 60c, 75c, $1, $2.50.

2002, Dec. 2 Litho. *Perf. 13x13¼*

814-818	A144	Set of 5	7.00	7.00

Cowrie Shells — A145

Designs: 25c, Cypraea mappa. 50c, Cypraea eglantina. 60c, Cypraea mauritiana.

75c, Cypraea cribaria. $1, Cypraea talpa. $2.50, Cypraea depressa.

Perf. 14½x14¼

2003, May 12 Litho. Unwmk.

819-824 A145 Set of 6 7.50 7.50
824a Souvenir sheet, #819-824 7.50 7.50

Coronation of Queen Elizabeth II, 50th Anniv.

Common Design Type

Designs: Nos. 825, 25c, 827a, $2, Queen and Prince Philip waving. Nos. 826, $3, 827b, $5, Prince Philip paying homage to Queen at coronation.

Perf. 14¼x14½

2003, June 2 Litho. Wmk. 373

Vignettes Framed, Red Background

825 CD363 $2 multicolored 1.75 1.75
826 CD363 $3 multicolored 2.50 2.50

Souvenir Sheet

Vignettes Without Frame, Purple Panel

827 CD363 Sheet of 2, #a-b 8.75 8.75

Powered Flight, Cent. A146

Designs: 25c, Sopwith Camel. 50c, Northrop Alpha. No. 830, 60c, DeHavilland Comet. 75c, Boeing 727. $1, English Electric Canberra. $2.50, Lockheed Martin F-22.
No. 834: a, 40c, Mitsubishi A6M-5 Zero. b, 60c, Grumman F6F Hellcat.

Wmk. 373

2003, Aug. 29 Litho. *Perf. 14*

Stamp + Label

828-833 A146 Set of 6 10.00 10.00

Souvenir Sheet

834 A146 Sheet of 2, #a-b 3.25 3.25

Christmas — A147

Christmas Island scenes: 25c, Teareba Taomeka, Tabwakea. 40c, Seventh Day Adventist Church, London. 50c, St. Teresa Catholic Church, Tabakea Village. 60c, Betaera Fou, London. 75c, Children, church bells, London. $1.50, Emanuira Church, London. $2.50, Church of Christ (60x24mm).

2003, Dec. 20 Unwmk. *Perf. 13¼*

835-841 A147 Set of 7 10.00 10.00
841a Souvenir sheet, #835-841 10.00 10.00

Road Safety — A148

No. 842: a, Accident. b, Automobile. c, Beverage can, drink, cigarette. d, Children.

2004, Apr. 7 Litho. *Perf. 13x13¼*

842 A148 Horiz. strip of 4 6.50 6.50
a. 30c multi .75 .75
b. 40c multi 1.10 1.10
c. 50c multi 1.30 1.10
d. 60c multi 1.60 1.40
e. Souvenir sheet, #842 6.50 6.50

World Health Day.

Bird Life International A149

Designs: 25c, Pacific golden plover. 40c, Whimbrel. 50c, Wandering tattler. 60c, Sanderling. 75c, Bar-tailed godwit. $2.50, Ruddy turnstone.
No. 849 — Bristle-thighed curlew: a, One in tree, one at water's edge. b, Head of bird. c, Front of bird, head facing right, vert. d, Back of bird, head facing left, vert. e, Two birds at water's edge.

Perf. 14¼x13¾

2004, Apr. 29 Litho. Unwmk.

843-848 A149 Set of 6 10.50 10.50

Souvenir Sheet

Perf. 14¼x14½

849 A149 $1 Sheet of 5, #a-e 13.00 13.00

2004 Summer Olympics, Athens — A150

Designs: 25c, Runners. 50c, Taekwondo. 60c, Weight lifting. 75c, Women's running.

2004, July 12 Wmk. 373 *Perf. 14*

850-853 A150 Set of 4 3.75 3.75

Souvenir Sheet

Celebration Games — A151

No. 854: a, Runners on track. b, Athletes, dancer, building.

2004, July 12

854 A151 $2.50 Sheet of 2, #a-b 9.00 9.00

Pacific Orchids — A152

No. 855: a, Dendrobium anosmum. b, Dendrobium chrysotoxum. c, Dendrobium laevifolium. d, Dendrobium mohlianum. e, Dendrobium pseudoglomeratum. f, Dendrobium purpureum. g, Grammatophyllum speciosum. h, Dendrobium williamsianum. i, Spathoglottis plicata. j, Vanda hindsii.

2004, Aug. 28 Unwmk. *Perf. 13½*

855 A152 Block of 10 16.50 16.50
a.-j. $1 Any single 1.60 1.50

Merchant Ships — A153

Designs: 50c, MV Montelucia. 75c, MS Pacific Princess. $2.50 MS Prinsendam. $5, MS Norwegian Wind.

2004, Oct. 25 Litho. *Perf. 13¼*

856-859 A153 Set of 4 14.50 14.50

Battle of Trafalgar, Bicent. A154

Designs: 25c, French 16-pounder cannon. 50c, San Ildefonso in action against HMS Defence. 75c, HMS Victory lashed to the Redoubtable. $1, Emperor Napoleon Bonaparte, vert. $1.50, HMS Victory. No. 865, $2.50, Vice-admiral Sir Horatio Nelson, vert.
No. 866: a, Admiral Federico Gravina. b, Santissima Trinidad.

2005, Mar. 29 Litho. *Perf. 13¼*

860-865 A154 Set of 6 12.00 12.00

Souvenir Sheet

866 A154 $2.50 Sheet of 2, #a-b 8.25 8.25

No. 864 has particles of wood from the HMS Victory embedded in the areas covered by a thermographic process that produces a raised, shiny effect.

End of World War II, 60th Anniv. A155

No. 867: a, Japanese Type 95 Ha-Go tank invading Gilbert Islands. b, Japanese A6M Zero fighter on Gilbert Islands. c, USS Argonaut and Nautilus land Marines at Butaritari in Carlson Raid. d, Pacific Fleet Admiral Chester W. Nimitz. e, USS Liscome Bay sunk by Japanese submarine. f, US Higgins landing craft approaching Tarawa Red Beach. g, F6F-3 Hellcats provide air cover over Tarawa Red Beach. h, LVTs hit the shore at Tarawa Red Beach. i, Sherman tank at Tarawa Red Beach. j, US Marines take cover on Tarawa Red Beach.
$5, Australian Prime Minister John Curtin, British Prime Minister Winston Churchill.

2005, Apr. 21 *Perf. 13¾*

867 A155 75c Sheet of 10, #a-j 14.50 14.50

Souvenir Sheet

868 A155 $5 multi 12.00 12.00

Pacific Explorer 2005 World Stamp Expo, Sydney (No. 868).

BirdLife International — A156

No. 869, 25c — Birds of Christmas Island: a, Lesser frigatebird. b, Red-tailed tropicbird. c, Blue noddy. d, Christmas shearwater. e, Sooty tern. f, Masked booby.
No. 870, $2 — Birds of Kiribati: a, White-tailed tropicbird. b, Black noddy. c, Red-footed booby. d, Wedge-tailed shearwater. e, White tern. f, Great frigatebird.

2005, Aug. 15 *Perf. 13¼x13*

Sheets of 6, #a-f

869-870 A156 Set of 2 25.00 25.00

Pope John Paul II (1920-2005) — A157

2005, Aug. 18 Litho. *Perf. 14*

871 A157 $1 multi 3.00 3.00

Battle of Trafalgar, Bicent. — A158

Designs: 25c, HMS Victory. 50c, Ships, horiz. $5, Admiral Horatio Nelson

2005, Oct. 18 Litho. *Perf. 13½*

872-874 A158 Set of 3 12.50 12.50

Worldwide Fund for Nature (WWF) — A159

Various depictions of harlequin shrimp: 50c, 60c, 75c, $5.

2005, Dec. 1 *Perf. 14*

875-878 A159 Set of 4 13.00 13.00
878a Miniature sheet, 2 each #875-878 22.50 22.50

Queen Elizabeth II, 80th Birthday — A160

Queen: 50c, As young woman. 75c, Wearing tiara, sepia photograph. $1, Wearing tiara, color photograph. $2, Wearing pink hat.
No. 883: a, $1.50, Like $1. b, $2.50, Like 75c.

2006, Apr. 21 Litho. *Perf. 14*

Stamps With White Frames

879-882 A160 Set of 4 9.50 9.50

Souvenir Sheet

Stamps Without White Frames

883 A160 Sheet of 2, #a-b 10.00 10.00

For surcharges, see Nos. 991-994.

Europa Stamps, 50th Anniv. — A161

Flags of European Union and Kiribati with gradiating background colors of: $2, Gray green. $2.50, Purple. $3, Yellowish brown. $5, Blue.

2006, May 4 *Perf. 13¼*

884-887 A161 Set of 4 20.00 20.00
887a Souvenir sheet, #884-887 20.00 20.00

Anniversaries — A162

No. 888, 25c: a, Charles Darwin and marine life. b, Fish and marine life.
No. 889, 50c: a, Isambard Kingdom Brunel. b, Glowing rivet.
No. 890, 75c: a, Christopher Columbus. b, Ship.
No. 891, $1: a, Thomas Alva Edison. b, Tin foil phonograph.
No. 892, $1.25: a, Wolfgang Amadeus Mozart. b, Violin and quill pen.
No. 893, $1.50: a, Concorde. b, Wing of Concorde, Concorde in flight.

2006, May 27 *Perf. 13x12½*

Horiz. Pairs, #a-b

888-893 A162 Set of 6 22.50 22.50

Darwin's voyage on the Beagle, 250th anniv., Birth of Brunel, bicent., Death of Columbus, 500th anniv., Death of Edison, 75th anniv., Birth of Mozart, 250th anniv., Inaugural Concorde flights, 30th anniv.

Dinosaurs A163

Designs: 25c, Ultrasaurus. 50c, Rhamphorhynchus. 60c, Dilophosaurus. 75c, Brachiosaurus. No. 898, $1, Minmi paravertebra. No. 899, $1, Eoraptor. $1.25, Stegosaurus. $1.50, Gigantosaurus.

2006, Sept. 15 *Perf. 13¼x13½*

894-901 A163 Set of 8 11.50 11.50

Miniature Sheet

Victoria Cross, 150th Anniv. A164

No. 902: a. Troop Sergeant Major John Berryman with Captain Webb at Balaclava. b, Private W. Norman bringing in two Russian prisoners. c, Sergeant Major John Greive saving officer's life at Balaclava. d, Private Thomas Beach rescuing Colonel Carpenter at Inkerman. e, Brevet Major C. H. Lumley engaged with Russian gunners in the Redan. f, Major F. C. Elton working in trenches.

2006, Oct. 20 Litho. *Perf. 13¼x12½*

902 A164 $1.50 Sheet of 6, #a-f, + 6 labels 17.50 17.50

60th Wedding Anniversary of Queen Elizabeth II and Prince Philip — A165

Designs: 50c, Portrait of Elizabeth and Philip. 75c, Wedding procession. $1, Bride and groom waving. $1.50, Queen reading.
$5, Wedding portrait.

2007, Jan. 31 Litho. *Perf. 13¾*

903-906 A165 Set of 4 6.00 6.00

Souvenir Sheet

Perf. 14

907 A165 $5 multi 7.75 7.75

No. 907 contains one 42x56mm stamp

Scouting, Cent. — A166

Designs: 25c, Scouts with Kiribati flag, hands tying neckerchief. 50c, Scouts learning about AIDS, Scout saluting. 75c, Scout leaders, hand with compass. $2, 1962 Scout shelter, hands lashing rope.

No. 912, vert.: a, $1, Emblem of Kiribati Scouts. b, $1.50, Lord Robert Baden-Powell.

Perf. 13x13¼

2007, Sept. 21 Litho. Wmk. 373

908-911 A166 Set of 4 7.50 7.50

Souvenir Sheet

Perf. 13¼x13

912 A166 Sheet of 2, #a-b 5.25 5.25

Princess Diana (1961-97) — A167

Designs: No. 913, 25c, Wearing white dress, facing right. No. 914, 25c, Wearing pink dress, facing left. 50c, Wearing pink dress, diff. No. 916, 75c, Wearing emerald necklace. No. 917, 75c, Wearing black and white dress. $1, Wearing red dress.

Perf. 13¼x12½

2007, Nov. 1 Litho. Unwmk.

913-918 A167 Set of 6 7.00 7.00

Military Uniforms — A168

Uniforms of: 25c, Royal Engineers. 40c, 95th Rifles. 50c, 24th Regiment of Foot. 60c, New Zealand soldiers. 75c, 93rd Sutherland Highlanders. 90c, Irish Guard. $1, Japanese soldiers. $1.50, United States Marine Corps.

2007, Nov. 20 Wmk. 373 *Perf. 14*

919-926 A168 Set of 8 12.00 12.00

Birds — A169

Designs: 5c, Great crested tern. 10c Eurasian teal. 15c, Laughing gull. 20c, Black-tailed godwit. 25c, Pectoral sandpiper. 50c, Band-rumped storm petrel. 60c, Sharp-tailed sandpiper. 75c, Gray-tailed tattler. 90c, Red phalarope. $1, Pink-footed shearwater. $2, Ring-billed gull. $5, Bonin petrel.

Wmk. 373

2008, Feb. 9 Litho. *Perf. 13¾*

927	A169 5c multi		.30	.25
928	A169 10c multi		.30	.25
929	A169 15c multi		.30	.30
930	A169 20c multi		.40	.40
931	A169 25c multi		.45	.45
932	A169 50c multi		.95	.95
933	A169 60c multi		1.10	1.10
934	A169 75c multi		1.40	1.40
935	A169 90c multi		1.75	1.75
936	A169 $1 multi		2.00	2.00
937	A169 $2 multi		4.25	4.25
a.	Souvenir sheet, #929, 933-937		10.00	10.00
938	A169 $5 multi		10.50	10.50
a.	Souvenir sheet, #927-928, 930-932, 938		12.50	12.50
	Nos. 927-938 (12)		23.70	23.60

For surcharges, see Nos. 984-987.

A170

Royal Air Force, 90th Anniv. A171

Designs: 25c, Avro Shackleton. 50c, Harrier GR3. 75c, Eurofighter Typhoon. $1, Vickers Valiant.
$2.50, Dambusters Raid.

Wmk. 373

2008, Apr. 1 Litho. *Perf. 14*

939-942 A170 Set of 4 5.50 5.50

Souvenir Sheet

943 A171 $2.50 multi 4.75 4.75

Phoenix Island Protected Area — A172

Designs: 40c, Huts. 75c, Map of Kanton Island. 80c, Map of various islands. 85c, Phoenix petrel. $1.25, Acropora nobilis and reef fish. $1.75, Blacktip reef shark.

2008, July 12 *Perf. 13¾*

944-949 A172 Set of 6 11.50 11.50

949a Souvenir sheet of 6, #944-949 11.50 11.50

2008 Summer Olympics, Beijing — A173

Designs: 25c, Bamboo, weight lifting. 50c, Dragon, running. 60c, Lanterns, cycling. 75c, Fish, javelin.

Wmk. 373

2008, Aug. 8 Litho. *Perf. 13½*

950-953 A173 Set of 4 3.75 3.75

Christmas — A174

No. 954, 25c: a, Lady Sacred Heart Church, Bairiki. b, Kiribati Protestant Church, Bikenibeu.

No. 955, 40c: a, Kaotitaeka Roman Catholic Church, Betio. b, Mormon Church, Iesu Kristo.

No. 956, 50c: a, Moaningaina Church, Eita. b, Sacred Heart Cathedral, Tarawa.

No. 957, 75c: a, St. Paul's Millennium Church, Betio. b, Kainkatikun Kristo Church, Naninimo.

Wmk. 406

2008, Dec. 8 Litho. *Perf. 13*

Pairs, #a-b

954-957 A174 Set of 4 5.00 5.00

957c Souvenir sheet, #954a-954b, 955a-955b, 956a-956b, 957a-957b 5.00 5.00

Explorers — A175

Designs: 25c, Sir Ernest Shackleton (1874-1922). 40c, Robert Falcon Scott (1868-1912). 50c, Captain James Cook (1728-79). 75c, Marco Polo (1254-1324). $1.50, Matthew Flinders (1774-1814). $1.75, John Cabot (c. 1450-99).

Wmk. 406

2009, Mar. 9 Litho. *Perf. 14*

958-963 A175 Set of 6 9.00 9.00

Naval Aviation, Cent. — A176

Aircraft: 40c, Grumman Avenger. 50c, Chance Vought Corsair. 75c, Westland Whirlwind helicopter. $1.25, McDonnell Douglas Phantom.
$3, Helicopter on deck of HMS Ark Royal.

Wmk. 406

2009, May 12 Litho. *Perf. 14*

964-967 A176 Set of 4 4.75 4.75

Souvenir Sheet

968 A176 $3 multi 5.00 5.00

Nos. 964-968 each were printed in sheets of 8 + central label.

Space Exploration — A177

Designs: 40c, Mars Science Laboratory. 50c, International Space Station. 75c, Space Shuttle Endeavour and Boeing transporter plane. $1.25, Launch of Apollo 12. No. 973, $3, Luna 16.

No. 974, $3, Astronaut on Moon, painting by Capt. Alan Bean, vert.

Wmk. 406

2009, July 20 Litho. *Perf. 13¼*

969-973 A177 Set of 5 9.25 9.25

Souvenir Sheet

Perf. 13x13½

974 A177 $3 multi 4.75 4.75

First man on the Moon, 40th anniv. No. 974 contains one 40x60mm stamp.

Battle of Britain, 70th Anniv. — A178

Stained-glass windows of Biggin Hill Memorial Chapel depicting: 25c, Aircraft servicing. 40c, Knight, English flag, airplanes. 50c, Parachute packing. 75c, Ground control. $1, Rescue services. $1.50, Royal Air Force emblem.
$3, Photograph of Sir Douglas Bader.

Wmk. 406

2010, Apr. 14 Litho. *Perf. 13*

975-980 A178 Set of 6 8.25 8.25

Souvenir Sheet

981 A178 $3 multi 5.75 5.75

Souvenir Sheet

Wedding of Prince William and Catherine Middleton — A179

Perf. 14¾x14¼

2011, Apr. 29 Litho. Wmk. 406

982 A179 $5 multi 11.00 11.00

No. 871 Overprinted

Unwmk.

2011, June 13 Litho. *Perf. 14*

983 A157 $1 multi 2.10 2.10

Nos. 927-930 Surcharged

Methods, Perfs and Watermarks As Before

2011, July

984	A169 25c on 5c #927	.50	.50
985	A169 30c on 10c #928	.60	.60
986	A169 50c on 20c #930	.95	.95
987	A169 75c on 15c #929	1.40	1.40
	Nos. 984-987 (4)	3.45	3.45

Nos. 794, 801 & 803 Ovptd.

Methods and Perfs As Before

2011, July

988 A140 40c on #794 .75 .75
989 A140 $2 on #801 3.75 3.75
990 A140 $10 on #803 19.00 19.00
Nos. 988-990 (3) 23.50 23.50

Nos. 879-882 Overprinted in Silver

Methods and Perfs. As Before

2012, June 4

991 A160 50c on #879 1.00 1.00
992 A160 75c on #880 1.50 1.50
993 A160 $1 on #881 2.00 2.00
994 A160 $2 on #882 4.00 4.00
Nos. 991-994 (4) 8.50 8.50

Worldwide Fund for Nature (WWF) — A180

Various views of Giant trevally.

2012, July 11 Litho. *Perf. 14¼x14*

995 Horiz. strip of 4 11.50 11.50
a. A180 80c multi 1.75 1.75
b. A180 $1 multi 2.10 2.10
c. A180 $1.50 multi 3.25 3.25
d. A180 $2 multi 4.25 4.25

Printed in sheets containing two each Nos. 995a-995d.

Miniature Sheet

Marine Life of Phoenix Islands Protected Area — A181

No. 996: a, 40c, Manta ray. b, 50c, Napoleon wrasse. c, 60c, Yellow and blueback fusiliers. d, 75c, Rainbow runners. e, $1, Green turtle. f, $1.50, Ornate butterflyfish. g, $2, Chrysiptera albata. h, $2.50, Small giant clam.

2012, Sept. 12 *Perf. 14¼x14*

996 A181 Sheet of 8, #a-h 19.00 19.00

Watercraft — A182

Designs: 5c, Christmas Island outrigger. 10c, Ferry to shore. 15c, Inter-island ferries. 20c, Fishing boats. 25c, Inter-island ferry. 30c, Te Tia Awaka and cargo boat. 35c, Bwaan Tetangira II. 40c, Passengers diving off outrigger Te Okarsi. 45c, Akenraoi in Abaiang Lagoon. 50c, Native house with outrigger. 55c, Moamoa. 60c, Container ship Kiribati Chief. 75c, Cruise liner Pride of Aloha. $1, Kiribati 36 yacht. $2, Pilot boat Teeitei. $5, Traditional outrigger.

Perf. 13¾

2013, Oct. 5 Litho. Unwmk.

997 A182 5c multi .30 .25
998 A182 10c multi .30 .25
999 A182 15c multi .30 .30
1000 A182 20c multi .40 .40
1001 A182 25c multi .50 .50
1002 A182 30c multi .60 .60
1003 A182 35c multi .65 .65
1004 A182 40c multi .75 .75
1005 A182 45c multi .85 .85
1006 A182 50c multi .95 .95
1007 A182 55c multi 1.00 1.00
1008 A182 60c multi 1.10 1.10
1009 A182 75c multi 1.40 1.40
1010 A182 $1 multi 1.90 1.90
1011 A182 $2 multi 3.75 3.75
1012 A182 $5 multi 9.50 9.50
a. Souvenir sheet of 16, #997-1012 24.50 24.50
Nos. 997-1012 (16) 24.25 24.15

Mangroves A183

Designs: 45c, Building and mangroves. 75c, Man and boys on beach near mangroves. $1, People near mangroves. $3, People planting mangroves.

2014, June 16 Litho. *Perf. 14x14½*

1013-1016 A183 Set of 4 10.00 10.00

2014 Commonwealth Games, Glasgow — A184

Designs: 25c, Weight lifter Davia Katoatau. 75c, Katoatau with medal.

No. 1019, horiz.: a, Kiribati team and flag-bearer. b, Scottish terrier wearing sweater with "Kiribati" sign.

2014, Sept. 8 Litho. *Perf. 14½*

1017-1018 A184 Set of 2 1.75 1.75

Souvenir Sheet

1019 A184 $2.50 Sheet of 2, #a-b 8.75 8.75

Souvenir Sheet

Butterflies — A185

No. 1020: a, $2, Meadow argus. b, $3, Blue moon.

Perf. 14¼x14

2015, May 27 Litho. Unwmk.

1020 A185 Sheet of 2, #a-b 7.75 7.75

Nos. 935, 938 Surcharged

Nos. 936-937 Overprinted

Methods, Perfs and Watermarks As Before

2015, July 17

1021 A169 40c on 90c #935 .60 .60
1022 A169 60c on $5 #938 .90 .90
1023 A169 $1 on #936 1.50 1.50
1024 A169 $2 on #937 3.00 3.00
Nos. 1021-1024 (4) 6.00 6.00

Queen Elizabeth II, 90th Birthday — A186

Queen Elizabeth II wearing: 25c, Blue green dress and hat. 75c, Beige jacket and hat. $1, Floral dress and white hat. $2.50, Tweed jacket and hat. $3.75, Blue jacket and hat. $5, Queen Elizabeth II and Prince Philip in Kiribati, 1982.

Perf. 13¼x13

2016, Apr. 21 Litho. Unwmk.

1025-1029 A186 Set of 5 13.00 13.00

Souvenir Sheet

1030 A186 $5 multi 7.75 7.75

2016 World Stamp Show, New York City — A187

Show emblem and: 25c, Participants in Independence celebrations. 75c, Participants in Independence celebrations, diff. $1.25, Boats on ground and in water. $3, Betio War Memorial.

Perf. 13x13¼

2016, May 28 Litho. Unwmk.

1031-1034 A187 Set of 4 7.75 7.75

Marine Training Center, 50th Anniv. — A188

Designs: 25c, Fisheries training. 75c, Cookery training. $1, Engine maintenance. $1.50, Transas bridge simulator.

No. 1039: a, $2, Marine Training Center. b, $3, Lifeboat training.

Unwmk.

2017, July 22 Litho. *Perf. 14*

1035-1038 A188 Set of 4 5.75 5.75

Souvenir Sheet

1039 A188 Sheet of 2, #a-b 8.00 8.00

Flowers — A189

Designs: 25c, Te Kanawa. 50c, Te Kaituru. 75c, Te Nikarairai. $1, Te Rooti. $2.50, Te Meeria. $4, Te Kiebu.

Perf. 13¼x13

2017, Oct. 14 Litho. Unwmk.

1040-1045 A189 Set of 6 14.00 14.00

Wedding of Prince Harry and Meghan Markle — A190

Designs: 25c, Prince Harry. 75c, Meghan Markle. $1.50, Couple. $2, Couple, diff. $5, Couple, diff.

2018, July 20 Litho. *Perf. 14*

1046-1049 A190 Set of 4 8.00 8.00

Souvenir Sheet

1050 A190 $5 multi 8.00 8.00

Military Anniversaries — A191

Designs: 25c, Map of Tarawa. 75c, Map of France.

No. 1053: a, $1, Map of Tarawa. b, $5, Map of France.

2018, Nov. 1 Litho. *Perf. 14*

1051-1052 A191 Set of 2 1.50 1.50

Souvenir Sheet

1053 A191 Sheet of 2, #a-b 8.75 8.75

Battle of Tarawa, 75th anniv. (Nos. 1051, 1053a); End of World War I (Nos. 1052, 1053b).

Birds — A192

Designs: 40c, Long-tailed jaeger. 50c, Leach's storm petrel. 75c, Juan Fernández petrel. $2.50, Sooty shearwater.

2019, July 1 Litho. *Perf. 14½*

1054-1057 A192 Set of 4 6.00 6.00
1057a Souvenir sheet of 4, #1054-1057 6.00 6.00

Independence, 40th anniv.

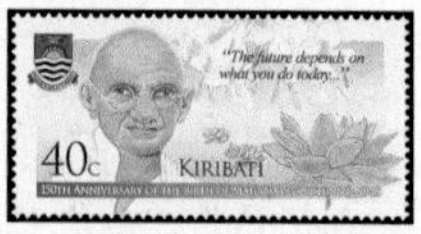

Mohandas K. Gandhi (1869-1948), Indian Nationalist Leader A193

Gandhi, flowers and quotation: 40c, "The future depends on what you do today. . ." 50c, "Where there is love there is light. . ." 75c, "Continue to grow and evolve. . ." $2.50, "My life is my message. . ."

No. 1062: a, $1.50, Spinning wheel, lotus flowers, "Life is but an endless series of experiments. . ." b, $5, Gandhi, flowers, "Speak only if it improves upon the silence. . ."

2019, Sept. 27 Litho. *Perf. 14½*

1058-1061 A193 Set of 4 5.75 5.75

Souvenir Sheet

1062 A193 Sheet of 2, #a-b 8.75 8.75

POSTAGE DUE STAMPS

Natl. Arms — D1

1981, Aug. 27 Litho. *Perf. 14*

J1 D1 1c brt pink & black .30 .25
J2 D1 2c greenish blue & blk .30 .25
J3 D1 5c brt yel grn & black .30 .25
J4 D1 10c lt red brown & blk .30 .25
J5 D1 20c ultra & black .30 .25
J6 D1 30c yel bister & black .30 .35
J7 D1 40c brt pur & black .30 .45
J8 D1 50c green & black .30 .50
J9 D1 $1 red orange & blk .30 .90
Nos. J1-J9 (9) 2.70 3.45

Imperfs exist from the liquidation of Format International. They are not errors.

OFFICIAL STAMPS

Nos. 327a-340c Overprinted "O.K.G.S."

1981, May Litho. Unwmk. *Perf. 14*

O1 A52 1c multicolored .30 .25
O2 A52 3c multicolored .30 .25
O3 A52 5c multicolored .30 .25
O4 A52 7c multicolored .30 .25
O5 A52 10c multicolored .30 .25
O6 A52 12c multicolored .30 .25
O7 A52 15c multicolored .30 .25
O8 A52 20c multicolored .30 .25
O9 A52 25c multicolored .30 .25
O10 A52 30c multicolored .30 .25
O11 A52 35c multicolored .30 .30
O12 A52 50c multicolored .40 .40
O13 A52 $1 multicolored .70 .70
O14 A52 $2 multicolored 1.20 1.20
O15 A52 $5 multicolored 3.00 3.00
Nos. O1-O15 (15) 8.60 8.10

Nos. O1-O15 have thick overprint.

1981			Wmk. 373	
O1a	A52	1c multi	4.00	4.25
O5a	A52	10c multi	20.00	21.00
O6a	A52	12c multi	6.00	6.00
O7a	A52	15c multi	20.00	20.00
O8a	A52	20c multi	13.00	13.00
O10a	A52	30c multi	8.00	9.00
O12a	A52	50c multi	7.50	7.50
O13a	A52	$1 multi	14.00	14.00
O14a	A52	$2 multi	16.00	17.00
O15a	A52	$5 multi	4.50	4.50
		Nos. O1a-O15a (10)	113.00	116.25

Nos. 390, 393-394, 396, 398 Overprinted "O.K.G.S."

1983, June 28		Litho.	*Perf. 14*	
O16	A62	12c multicolored	.45	.45
O17	A62	30c multicolored	.80	.80
O18	A62	35c multicolored	.90	.90
O19	A62	50c multicolored	1.25	1.25
O20	A62	$2 multicolored	3.75	3.75
		Nos. O16-O20 (5)	7.15	7.15

This overprint has shorter, thinner letters than the one used for Nos. O1-O15. It also exists on Nos. 327, 331-334, 336-340. These have been questioned.

KOREA

kə-'rē-ə

(Corea)

(Chosen, Tyosen, Tae Han)

LOCATION — Peninsula extending from Manchuria between the Yellow Sea and the Sea of Japan (East Sea)
GOVT. — Republic
AREA — 38,221 sq. mi.
POP. — 48,860,500 (2011 est.)
CAPITAL — Seoul

Korea (or Corea) an independent monarchy for centuries under Chinese influence, came under Japanese influence in 1876. Chinese and Japanese stamps were used there as early as 1877. Administrative control was assumed by Japan in 1905 and annexation followed in 1910. Postage stamps of Japan were used in Korea from 1905 to early 1946.

At the end of World War II, American forces occupied South Korea and Russian forces occupied North Korea, with the 38th parallel of latitude as the dividing line. A republic was established in 1948 following an election in South Korea. North Korea issues its own stamps.

100 Mon = 1 Poon
5 Poon = 1 Cheun
1000 Re = 100 Cheun = Weun
100 Weun = 1 Hwan (1953)
100 Chun = 1 Won (1962)

Catalogue values for unused stamps in this country are for Never Hinged items, beginning with Scott 283 in the regular postage section, Scott B5 in the semi-postal section, and Scott C23 in the airpost section.

Watermarks

Wmk. 257 — Curved Wavy Lines

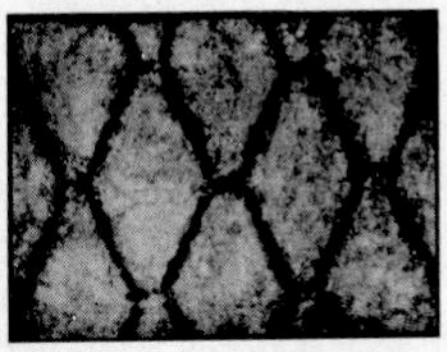

Wmk. 312 — Zigzag Lines

Wmk. 317 — Communications Department Emblem

Stylized Yin Yang
A1 A2

Perf. 8½ to 11½

1884		Typo.	Unwmk.	
1	A1	5m rose	52.50	*10,000.*
2	A2	10m blue	52.50	*10,000.*

Reprints and counterfeits of Nos. 1-2 exist.

These stamps were never placed in use. Values: 25 $5; 50 mon $6.50; 100 mon $9.

Counterfeits exist.

Yin Yang — A6

Perf. 10¾, 11½, 11¾ 12, 13, 13¼ and Compound

1895			Litho.	
6	A6	5p green (II)	30.00	16.00
b.		Vert. pair, imperf horiz.	425.00	—
c.		Horiz. pair, imperf. vert.	425.00	—
d.		Vertical pair, imperf. between	425.00	—
e.		Horiz. pair, imperf. btwn.	425.00	—
7	A6	10p blue (II)	110.00	37.50
a.		Horiz. pair, imperf. between	425.00	—
b.		Vert. pair, imperf. horiz.	425.00	—
8	A6	25p maroon (II)	70.00	30.00
a.		Horiz. pair, imperf. between	375.00	375.00
b.		Vert. pair, imperf. horiz.	375.00	375.00
9	A6	50p purple (II)	22.50	16.00
a.		Horiz. pair, imperf. between	400.00	400.00
b.		Vert, pair, imperf. horiz.	400.00	400.00
c.		Horiz. pair, imperf. vert.	400.00	400.00
		Nos. 6-9 (4)	232.50	99.50

No. 6a exists with sewing machine perforations vertically.

For overprints and surcharges see Nos. 10-17C, 35-38.

Counterfeits exist of Nos. 6-9 and all surcharges and overprints.

Overprinted "Tae Han" in Korean and Chinese Characters

1897			Red Overprint	
10	A6	5p green	87.50	35.00
a.		5p pale yellow green	200.00	150.00
b.		Inverted overprint	160.00	160.00
c.		Without ovpt. at bottom	150.00	130.00
d.		Without overprint at top	150.00	130.00
f.		Double overprint at top	140.00	140.00
g.		Overprint at bottom in blk	160.00	160.00
h.		Pair, one without overprint	450.00	450.00
i.		Double overprint at top, inverted at bottom	550.00	
11	A6	10p deep blue	115.00	65.00
a.		Without ovpt. at bottom	150.00	150.00
b.		Without overprint at top	150.00	150.00
c.		Double overprint at top	150.00	150.00
d.		Bottom overprint inverted	140.00	140.00
e.		Top ovpt. dbl., one in blk	210.00	210.00
f.		Top overprint omitted, bottom overprint inverted	450.00	
12	A6	25p maroon	130.00	65.00
a.		Overprint at bottom invtd.	150.00	150.00
b.		Overprint at bottom in blk	210.00	210.00
c.		Bottom overprint omitted	150.00	150.00
e.		Top ovpt. dbl., one in blk	225.00	225.00
f.		Top and bottom overprints double, one of each in blk	250.00	250.00
g.		Pair, one without overprint	425.00	425.00
13	A6	50p purple	82.50	50.00
a.		Without ovpt. at bottom	120.00	110.00
b.		Without overprint at top	120.00	110.00
c.		Bottom overprint double	120.00	110.00
e.		Pair, one without overprint	275.00	275.00
		Nos. 10-13 (4)	415.00	215.00

1897			Black Overprint	
13F	A6	5p green	500.00	160.00
13G	A6	10p deep blue	650.00	200.00
h.		Without ovpt. at bottom	450.00	
14	A6	25p maroon	825.00	200.00
a.		Without ovpt. at bottom	450.00	
b.		Without overprint at top	450.00	
c.		Double overprint at bottom	450.00	
15	A6	50p purple	650.00	160.00
a.		Without ovpt. at bottom	450.00	
		Nos. 13F-15 (4)	2,625.	

These stamps with black overprint, also No. 16A, are said not to have been officially authorized.

Nos. 6, 6a and 8 Surcharged in Red or Black

1900				
15B	A6	1p on 5p grn (R)	*7,000.*	*3,000.*
c.		Yellow green		
16	A6	1p on 25p mar	260.00	65.00

Same Surcharge in Red or Black on Nos. 10, 10a, 12, 12c and 14

16A	A6	1p on 5p grn (R)	975.00	550.00
b.		1p on 5p pale yellow green	1,050.	
17	A6	1p on 25p (#12)	65.00	40.00
a.		Figure "1" omitted	100.00	
b.		On #12c	90.00	70.00
17C	A6	1p on 25p (#14)	750.00	650.00

Counterfeit overprints and surcharges of Nos. 10-17C exist. See note after No. 15.

A8

A9

A10

A11

A12

A13

A14

A15

A16

A17

A18

A19

A20

A21

1900-01		Typo.	*Perf. 11*	
18	A8	2re gray	9.75	8.00
19	A9	1ch yellow grn	19.50	10.00
20B	A11	2ch pale blue	35.00	11.00
21	A12	3ch org red	19.50	16.00
a.		Vert. pair, imperf. horiz.	200.00	200.00
b.		Horiz. pair, imperf. btwn.		500.00
c.		3c brnsh org	21.00	17.50
d.		As "c," vert. pair, imperf. btwn.		500.00
22	A13	4ch carmine	34.00	16.00
23	A14	5ch pink	27.50	20.00
24	A15	6ch dp blue	34.00	20.00
25	A16	10ch pur ('01)	40.00	24.00
26	A17	15ch gray vio	62.50	40.00
27	A18	20ch red brown	110.00	52.50
31	A19	50ch ol grn & pink	500.00	190.00
a.		Pink omitted	—	—
32	A20	1wn rose, blk & bl	1,050.	325.00
33	A21	2wn pur & yel grn	1,300.	600.00
		Nos. 18-33 (13)	3,242.	1,333.

Nos. 22, 23, 25, 26, 33 exist imperf.

Some examples of Nos. 18-27 exist with forged Tae Han overprints in red. It is believed that Nos. 18 and 21 exist with genuine Tae Han overprints.

Reprints of No. 24 were made in light blue, perf. 12x13, in 1905 for a souvenir booklet. Value $135. See note after No. 54.

See Nos. 52-54.

Perf. 10

18a	A8	2re	17.00	5.25
19a	A9	1ch	17.00	5.50
20	A10	2ch blue	75.00	45.00
a.		Horiz. pair, imperf. btwn.	*725.00*	
20Ba	A11	2ch pale blue	—	—
21e	A12	3ch	15.50	9.00
22a	A13	4ch	45.00	20.00
23a	A14	5ch	40.00	10.00
24a	A15	6ch	47.50	12.00
26a	A17	15ch	*175.00*	*150.00*
27a	A18	20ch	*240.00*	*240.00*
		Nos. 18a-27a (10)	672.00	496.75

Emperor's Crown — A22

1902, Oct. 18			*Perf. 11½*	
34	A22	3ch orange	65.00	35.00

40th year of the reign of Emperor Kojong. An imperf. single was part of the 1905 souvenir booklet. Value $325. See note following No. 54.

Counterfeits exist.

Nos. 8 and 9 Handstamp Surcharged in Black

1ch

2ch

3ch

No. 37b

Perf. 11½, 12, 12½, 13 and Compound

1902				
35	A6	1ch on 25p rose car	26.00	20.00
b.		Horiz. pair, imperf. btwn.	275.00	
c.		Imperf.	90.00	
d.		Vert. pair, imperf. horiz.	275.00	
e.		On No. 12	—	—
36	A6	2ch on 25p maroon	32.50	30.00
b.		Imperf.	75.00	
d.		On No. 12	90.00	90.00
36E	A6	2ch on 50p purple	175.00	175.00
f.		Character "cheun" unabbreviated (in two rows instead of one)	250.00	175.00
37	A6	3ch on 50p plum	27.50	20.00
b.		With character "cheun" unabbreviated (in two rows instead of one)	2,400.	950.00

d. Horiz. pair, imperf. btwn. 200.00
e. Vert. pair, imperf. btwn. 200.00
g. On No. 13 240.00
38 A6 3ch on 25p maroon 65.00 62.50
Nos. 35-38 (5) 326.00 307.50

There are several sizes of these surcharges. Being handstamped, inverted and double surcharges exist.

Counterfeit surcharges exist.

Falcon — A23

1903 ***Perf. 13½x14***

39 A23 2re slate 10.00 10.00
40 A23 1ch violet brn 13.50 10.00
41 A23 2ch green 14.00 10.00
42 A23 3ch orange 12.50 10.00
43 A23 4ch rose 20.00 10.00
44 A23 5ch yellow brn 20.00 10.00
45 A23 6ch lilac 24.00 11.00
46 A23 10ch blue 29.00 13.50
47 A23 15ch red, *straw* 40.00 20.00
48 A23 20ch vio brn, *straw* 57.50 25.00
49 A23 50ch red, *grn* 170.00 100.00
50 A23 1wn vio, *lav* 425.00 210.00
51 A23 2wn vio, *org* 425.00 210.00
Nos. 39-51 (13) 1,261. 649.50

Values are for stamps with perfs touching the design.

Types of 1901

1903 ***Perf. 12½***

Thin, Semi-Transparent Paper

52 A19 50ch pale ol grn & pale pink *400.00 160.00*
53 A20 1wn rose, blk & bl *600.00 200.00*
54 A21 2wn lt vio & lt grn *875.00 250.00*
Nos. 52-54 (3) *1,875.* 610.00

No. 24, perf. 12x13, No. 34 imperf. and most examples of Nos. 52-54 unused are from souvenir booklets made up in 1905 when the Japanese withdrew all Korean stamps from circulation.

WARNING

In 1957 the Ministry of Communications issued 4000 presentation booklets containing Nos. 1-54 reproduced on watermark 312 paper.

Other presentation booklets included full-color reproductions of Nos. 1-54 and Japan No. 110 printed on the pages. Beware of wide-margined imperfs cut from these booklets.

Issued under US Military Rule

Stamps of Japan Nos. 331, 268, 342, 332, 339 and 337 Surcharged in Black

1946, Feb. 1 **Wmk. 257** ***Perf. 13***

55 A86 5ch on 5s brn lake 8.00 *17.50*
56 A93 5ch on 14s pur brn & pale rose 1.20 *3.00*
a. 5ch on 40s dark violet (error) 125.00
57 A154 10ch on 40s dk vio 1.20 *3.00*
58 A147 20ch on 6s lt ultra 1.20 *3.00*
a. 20ch on 27s rose brown (error) 125.00
b. Double surcharge 30.00
59 A151 30ch on 27s rose brn 1.20 *3.00*
a. 30ch on 6s light ultra (error) 125.00
b. Double surcharge 25.00
60 A151 5wn on 17s gray vio 7.25 *17.50*
Nos. 55-60 (6) 20.05 *47.00*
Set, never hinged 33.00

Five essays for this provisional issue exist both with and without additional overprint of two Chinese characters ("specimen") in vermilion. The essays are: 20ch on Japan No. 269; 50ch on No. 272; 1wn on No. 336; 1wn on No. 273; 10wn on No. 265. Values, each: $1,200 never hinged, $750 hinged. Other denominations have been reported.

Korean Family and Flag — A24

Arms of Korea — A25

Wmk. 257

1946, May 1 **Litho.** ***Perf. 10½***

61 A24 3ch orange yellow .75 1.60
62 A24 5ch green .75 1.60
63 A24 10ch carmine .75 1.60
64 A24 20ch dark blue .75 1.60
65 A25 50ch brown violet 3.00 *2.50*
66 A25 1wn lt brown 5.00 *3.25*
Nos. 61-66 (6) 11.00 *12.15*
Set, never hinged 18.50

Liberation from Japan.

Imperfs., Part Perfs.

Imperforate and part-perforate examples of a great many Korean stamps from No. 61 onward exist.

The imperfs. include Nos. 61-90, 93-97, 116-117, 119-126, 132-173, 182-186, 195, 197-199, 202A, 203, 204-205, 217, etc.

The part-perfs. include Nos. 62-65, 69, 72-73, 109, 111-113, 132, etc.

Printers waste includes printed on both sides, etc.

As the field is so extensive, the editors believe that they belong more properly in a specialized catalogue.

Dove — A26

1946, Aug. 15 **Unwmk.**

67 A26 50ch deep violet 7.50 *5.25*
Never hinged 12.50

First anniversary of liberation.

Perforations often are rough on stamps issued between Aug. 1946 and the end of 1954. This is not considered a defect.

Flags of US and Korea — A27

1946, Sept. 9 ***Perf. 11***

68 A27 10wn carmine 5.75 *4.50*
Never hinged 9.50

Resumption of postal communication with the US.

Astronomical Observatory, Kyongju — A28

Hibiscus with Rice A29

Map of Korea A30

Gold Crown of Silla Dynasty A31

Admiral Li Sun-sin A32

1946 ***Rouletted 12***

69 A28 50ch dark blue .95 *1.90*
70 A29 1wn buff .90 *2.00*
71 A30 2wn indigo 1.60 2.75
72 A31 5wn magenta 10.00 *20.00*
73 A32 10wn emerald 11.00 *18.50*
Nos. 69-73 (5) 24.45 *45.15*
Set, never hinged 37.50

Perf. 11

70a A29 1wn 1.75 *3.25*
71a A30 2wn 62.50 *120.00*
72a A31 5wn 62.50 *120.00*
Nos. 70a-72a (3) 126.75 *243.25*
Set, never hinged 240.00

Korean Phonetic Alphabet — A33

1946, Oct. 9 ***Perf. 11***

74 A33 50ch deep blue 4.50 4.50
Never hinged 8.50

500th anniv. of the introduction of the Korean phonetic alphabet (Hangul).

Li Jun A34

Admiral Li Sun-sin A35

Perf. 11½x11, 11½

1947, Aug. 1 **Litho.** **Wmk. 257**

75 A34 5wn lt blue green 6.75 *8.75*
76 A35 10wn light blue 7.25 *8.75*
Set, never hinged 25.00

Presentation Sheets

Starting in 1947 with No. 75, nearly 100 Korean stamps were printed in miniature or souvenir sheets and given to government officials and others. These sheets were released in quantities of 300 to 4,000. In 1957 the Ministry of Communications began to sell the souvenir sheets at post offices at face value to be used for postage. They are listed from No. 264a onward.

Letter-encircled Globe — A36

1947, Aug. 1 ***Perf. 11½x11***

77 A36 10wn light blue 10.50 *9.25*
Never hinged 18.00

Resumption of international mail service between Korea and all countries of the world.

Granite Paper

Starting with No. 77, most Korean stamps through No. 751, except those on Laid Paper, are on Granite Paper. Granite Paper is noted above listing if the issue was printed on both ordinary and Granite Paper, such as Nos. 360a-374A.

Arch of Independence, Seoul — A37

Tortoise Ship, First Ironclad War Vessel — A38

1948, Apr.

78 A37 20wn rose 5.00 *4.00*
79 A38 50wn dull red brown 80.00 40.00
Set, never hinged 150.00

Republic

Flag and Ballot A39

Woman and Man Casting Ballots A40

Perf. 11x11½

1948, May 10 **Litho.** **Wmk. 257**

80 A39 2wn orange 11.00 8.25
81 A39 5wn lilac rose 18.50 11.50
82 A39 10wn lt violet 29.00 20.00
83 A40 20wn carmine 65.00 30.00
84 A40 50wn blue 32.50 22.50
Nos. 80-84 (5) 156.00 92.25
Set, never hinged 220.00

South Korea election of May 10, 1948.

Korean Flag and Olive Branches — A41

Olympic Torchbearer and Map of Korea — A42

1948, June 1 ***Perf. 11x11½, 11½x11***

85 A41 5wn green 120.00 60.00
86 A42 10wn purple 37.50 22.50
Set, never hinged 270.00

Korea's participation in the 1948 Olympic Games.

National Assembly A43

1948, July 1 **Wmk. 257** ***Perf. 11½***

87 A43 4wn orange brown 22.50 *12.00*
Never hinged 37.50

Opening of the Assembly July 1, 1948. Exists without period between "5" and "31."

Korean Family and Capitol — A44

Flag of Korea — A45

1948, Aug. 1 **Litho.**

88 A44 4wn emerald 82.50 50.00
89 A45 10wn orange brown 32.50 *24.00*
Set, never hinged 200.00

Signing of the new constitution, 7/17/48.

Pres. Syngman Rhee — A46

1948, Aug. 5

90 A46 5wn deep blue 260.00 200.00
Never hinged 450.00

Inauguration of Korea's first president, Syngman Rhee.

Dove A47

Hibiscus A48

Two types of 5wn:
I — "1948" 3mm wide; top inscription 9mm wide; periods in "8.15." barely visible.
II — "1948" 4mm wide; top inscription 9½mm; periods in "8.15." bold and strong.

1948 ***Perf. 11, 11x11½***

91 A47 4wn blue 29.00 *30.00*
92 A48 5wn rose lilac (II) 65.00 50.00
a. Type I *120.00* 100.00
Set, never hinged 160.00

Issued to commemorate the establishment of Korea's republican government.

Li Jun A49

Observatory, Kyongju A50

Types of No. 94
Type I: The top inscription is 15¼-15½mm wide. The stars are small.
Type II: The top inscription is 15¾-16mm wide. The stars are larger than Type I.

1948, Oct. 1 ***Perf. 11½x11***

93 A49 4wn rose carmine .75 1.20
94 A50 14wn deep blue, I .75 1.20
a. light blue, I 140.00 100.00
Never hinged 320.00
b. dp bl, large die, I *350.00* *650.00*
Never hinged 600.00
c. Type II — —
Never hinged —
d. As a, Type II — —
Never hinged —
Set, never hinged 3.50

For surcharges see Nos. 127, 174, 176.
Issued: No. 94, 5/1949; No. 94b, 5/1949; No. 94c, 1949; No. 94d, 10/1949.
Two die sizes were used in printing No. 94: a small die, 19¾x24mm, and a large die, 20x24mm. Small dies were used on Nos. 94 and 94c.

Doves over UN Emblem — A51

1949, Feb. 12 **Wmk. 257** ***Perf. 11***

95 A51 10wn blue *30.00* *25.00*
Never hinged *52.50*

Arrival of the UN Commission on Korea, Feb. 12, 1949.

Korean Citizen and Census Date — A52

1949, Apr. 25

96 A52 15wn purple 40.00 30.00
Never hinged 72.50

Census of May 1, 1949.

Korean Boy and Girl — A53

1949, May 5

97 A53 15wn purple 22.50 20.00
Never hinged 40.00

20th anniv. of Children's Day, May 5, 1949.

Postman A54

Worker and Factory A55

Rice Harvesting A56

Japanese Cranes A57

Diamond Mountains A58

Ginseng Plant A59

South Gate, Seoul A60

Tabo Pagoda, Kyongju A61

1949 **Litho.** ***Perf. 11***

98 A54 1wn rose 3.25 3.25
99 A55 2wn dk blue gray 3.00 3.00
100 A56 5wn yellow green 14.00 9.50
101 A57 10wn blue green 1.20 1.20
102 A58 20wn orange brown .80 1.20
103 A59 30wn blue green .80 1.20
104 A60 50wn violet blue .80 1.20
105 A61 100wn dull yellow grn .80 1.20
Nos. 98-105 (8) 24.65 21.75
Set, never hinged 47.50

For surcharges see Nos. 129-131, 175, 177B-179, 181.

Phoenix and Yin Yang — A62

1949, Aug. 25

106 A62 15wn deep blue 27.50 22.50
Never hinged 52.50

1st anniv. of Korea's independence.

Express Train "Sam Chun Li" — A63

1949, Sept. 18 ***Perf. 11½x12***

107 A63 15wn violet blue 105.00 55.00
Never hinged 190.00

50th anniversary of Korean railroads.

Korean Flag — A64

Perf. 11½x11

1949, Oct. 15 **Wmk. 257**

108 A64 15wn red org, yel & dk bl 14.00 *15.00*
Never hinged 30.00

75th anniv. of the UPU.
No. 108 exists unwatermarked. These are counterfeit.

Hibiscus A65

Magpies and Map of Korea A66

Stylized Bird and Globe — A67

Diamond Mountains — A68

Admiral Li Sun-sin — A69

1949 **Wmk. 257** **Litho.** ***Perf. 11***

109 A65 15wn vermilion .60 *1.10*
110 A66 65wn deep blue 2.10 *2.10*
111 A67 200wn green .60 *1.10*
112 A68 400wn brown .60 *1.10*
113 A69 500wn deep blue .60 *1.10*
Nos. 109-113 (5) 4.50 *6.50*
Set, never hinged 7.50

For surcharges see Nos. 128, 177, 180.

Canceled to Order

More than 100 Korean stamps and souvenir sheets were canceled to order, the cancellation incorporating the date "67.9.20." These include 81 stamps between Nos. 111 and 327, 18 airmail stamps between Nos. C6 and C26, and 5 souvenir sheets between Nos. 313 and 332, etc.

Also exists with later dates and on other stamps.

These c-t-o stamps and souvenir sheets are sold for much less than the values shown below, which are for postally used examples.

A70

Ancient postal medal (Ma-Pae).

1950, Jan. 1

114 A70 15wn yellow green 22.50 *20.00*
115 A70 65wn red brown 11.50 *8.00*
Set, never hinged 65.00

50th anniv. of Korea's entrance into the UPU.

Revolutionists — A71

1950, Mar. 10 ***Perf. 11½***

116 A71 15wn olive 23.00 *20.00*
117 A71 65wn light violet 11.50 8.00
Set, never hinged 65.00

41st anniversary of Korea's declaration of Independence.

Korean Emblem and National Assembly — A72

1950, May 30

118 A72 30wn bl, red, brn & grn 15.00 10.00
Never hinged 26.00

2nd natl. election of the Korean Republic.

Syngman Rhee A73

Korean Flag and White Mountains A74

Flags of UN and Korea, Map of Korea — A75

1950, Nov. 20 **Wmk. 257** ***Perf. 11***

119 A73 100wn blue 4.50 *4.00*
120 A74 100wn green 4.50 *3.25*
121 A75 200wn dark green 3.25 *2.50*
Nos. 119-121 (3) 12.25 9.75
Set, never hinged 22.00

Crane — A76

Tiger Mural — A77

Dove and Flag A78

Postal Medal A79

Mural from Ancient Tomb — A80

1951 **Unwmk.** ***Perf. 11***

Ordinary Paper

122 A76 5wn org brn 1.60 *2.00*
123 A77 20wn purple 2.10 *2.75*
124 A78 50wn green 14.50 *13.50*
125 A79 100wn deep blue 27.00 13.50
126 A80 1000wn green 31.00 12.00
Nos. 122-126 (5) 76.20 43.75
Set, never hinged 125.00

Rouletted 12

122a A76 5wn orange brown 1.00 *1.50*
123a A77 20wn purple 1.00 *1.50*
124a A78 50wn green 2.75 *4.00*
125a A79 100wn blue 4.25 5.00
Nos. 122a-125a (4) 9.00 *12.00*
Set, never hinged 16.50

No. 126 also exists perforated 12½. See Nos. 187-189.

No. 93 Surcharged in Blue

1951 Wmk. 257 *Perf. 11½x11*

127 A49 100wn on 4wn rose car 3.25 5.00
a. Inverted surcharge 32.50 *65.00*
Never hinged 65.00

Nos. 109, 101, 102 and 104 Surcharged in Blue or Brown

Perf. 11

128 A65 200wn on 15wn 3.75 7.00
a. Inverted surcharge 32.50 *65.00*
Never hinged 65.00
129 A57 300wn on 10wn (Br) 5.25 6.00
a. Inverted surcharge 32.50
Never hinged 65.00
130 A58 300wn on 20wn 4.00 4.50
a. Inverted surcharge 35.00
Never hinged 75.00
131 A60 300wn on 50wn (Br) 45.00 4.00
Nos. 127-131 (5) 61.25 26.50
Set, never hinged 92.50

Size and details of surcharge varies. Numeral upright on Nos. 129 and 131; numeral slanted on Nos. 175 and 179. See Nos. 174-181.

On No. 130, the zeros in "300" are octagonal; on No. 177B they are oval.

Flags of US and Korea and Statue of Liberty A81

Design (blue stamps): Flag of same country as preceding green stamp, UN emblem and doves.

1951-52 Wmk. 257 *Perf. 11*
Flags in Natural Colors, Participating Country at Left

132 A81 500wn green 4.50 8.50
133 A81 500wn blue 4.50 8.50
134 A81 500wn grn *(Australia)* 5.00 10.00
135 A81 500wn blue 5.00 10.00
136 A81 500wn grn *(Belgium)* 5.00 10.00
137 A81 500wn blue 5.00 10.00
138 A81 500wn grn *(Britain)* 5.00 10.00
139 A81 500wn blue 5.00 10.00
140 A81 500wn grn *(Canada)* 5.00 10.00
141 A81 500wn blue 5.00 10.00
142 A81 500wn grn *(Colombia)* 5.00 10.00
143 A81 500wn blue 5.00 10.00
144 A81 500wn grn *(Denmark)* 25.00 *35.00*
145 A81 500wn blue 25.00 *35.00*
146 A81 500wn grn *(Ethiopia)* 5.00 10.00
147 A81 500wn blue 5.00 10.00
148 A81 500wn grn *(France)* 5.00 10.00
149 A81 500wn blue 5.00 10.00
150 A81 500wn grn *(Greece)* 5.00 10.00
151 A81 500wn blue 5.00 10.00
152 A81 500wn grn *(India)* 20.00 35.00
153 A81 500wn blue 20.00 35.00
154 A81 500wn grn *(Italy)* 5.50 20.00
a. Flag without crown ('52) 30.00 45.00
155 A81 500wn blue 5.50 20.00
a. Flag without crown ('52) 30.00 45.00
156 A81 500wn grn *(Luxembourg)* 20.00 35.00
157 A81 500wn blue 20.00 35.00
158 A81 500wn grn *(Netherlands)* 5.00 10.00
159 A81 500wn blue 5.00 10.00
160 A81 500wn grn *(New Zealand)* 5.00 10.00
161 A81 500wn blue 5.00 10.00
162 A81 500wn grn *(Norway)* 20.00 35.00
163 A81 500wn blue 20.00 35.00
164 A81 500wn grn *(Philippines)* 5.00 10.00
165 A81 500wn blue 5.00 10.00
166 A81 500wn grn *(Sweden)* 5.00 10.00
167 A81 500wn blue 5.00 10.00
168 A81 500wn grn *(Thailand)* 5.00 10.00
169 A81 500wn blue 5.00 10.00
170 A81 500wn grn*(Turkey)* 5.00 10.00
171 A81 500wn blue 5.00 10.00
172 A81 500wn grn *(Union of So. Africa)* 5.00 10.00
173 A81 500wn blue 5.00 10.00
Nos. 132-173 (42) 340.00 637.00
Set, never hinged 850.00

Twenty-two imperf. souvenir sheets of two, containing the green and the blue stamps for each participating country (including both types of Italy) were issued. Size: 140x90mm. Value, set hinged $875; never hinged $1,400.

Nos. 93-94, 101-105, 109-110 Surcharged Like Nos. 128-131 in Blue or Brown

1951 Wmk. 257 *Perf. 11½x11, 11*

174 A49 300wn on 4wn 3.00 *4.50*
a. Inverted surcharge 32.50 *65.00*
Never hinged 65.00
175 A57 300wn on 10wn (Br) 7.25 *5.50*
a. Inverted surcharge 32.50 *65.00*
Never hinged 65.00
176 A50 300wn on 14wn (Br) 5.50 *4.50*
a. 300wn on 14wn, #94a 2,250. 1,500.
Never hinged 4,000.
b. Inverted surcharge 32.50 *65.00*
Never hinged 65.00
c. 300wn on 14wn, #94b — —
Never hinged —
d. Inverted surcharge, #94b — —
Never hinged —
e. 300wn on 14wn, #94d — —
Never hinged —
177 A65 300wn on 15wn 3.00 *4.50*
a. Inverted surcharge 32.50 *65.00*
Never hinged 65.00
177B A58 300wn on 20wn 5.25 5.25
178 A59 300wn on 30wn (Br) 3.25 *4.50*
a. Inverted surcharge 32.50 *65.00*
Never hinged 65.00
179 A60 300wn on 50wn (Br) 2.75 4.00
180 A66 300wn on 65wn (Br) 3.25 *4.50*
a. Inverted monad 47.50 95.00
Never hinged 95.00
181 A61 300wn on 100wn 3.00 4.50
a. Inverted surcharge 45.00 *90.00*
Never hinged 90.00
Nos. 174-181 (9) 36.25 41.75
Set, never hinged 67.50

"300" slanted on Nos. 175, 177B and 179; "300" upright on Nos. 129 and 131. The surcharge exists double on several of these stamps.

No. 177B differs from No. 130 in detail noted after No. 131.

Syngman Rhee and "Happiness" A82

1952, Sept. 10 Litho. *Perf. 12½*

182 A82 1000wn dark green 7.50 *7.50*
Never hinged 14.00

Second inauguration of President Syngman Rhee, Aug. 15, 1952.

Sok Kul Am, Near Kyongju A83

Bool Gook Temple, Kyongju A84

Tombstone of Mu Yal Wang A85

Choong Yul Sa Shrine, Tongyung A86

1952 Wmk. 257 Typo. *Perf. 12½*

183 A83 200wn henna brown 1.60 *1.40*
184 A84 300wn green 1.35 1.00
185 A85 500wn carmine 2.10 *1.60*
186 A86 2000wn deep blue 1.60 1.00

Rough Perf. 10-11, 11½x11 and Compound
Litho.

186A A83 200wn henna brown 1.75 *1.35*
186B A84 300wn green 1.60 *1.00*
Nos. 183-186B (6) 10.00 7.35
Set, never hinged 19.50

Types of 1951
Designs slightly smaller

1952-53 *Rough Perf. 10-11*

187 A77 20wn purple 10.50 *5.00*
187A A78 50wn green 25.00 *23.00*
187B A79 100wn deep blue 2.10 1.50
187C A80 1000wn green 135.00 27.00
Nos. 187-187C (4) 172.60 56.50
Set, never hinged 340.00

Designs slightly larger
Perf. 12½

187D A78 50wn green 2.50 2.40
188 A79 100wn deep blue 1.75 *1.90*
189 A80 1000wn green ('53) 5.50 1.10
Nos. 187D-189 (3) 9.75 5.40
Set, never hinged 20.00

Type of 1952

1953

189A A85 500wn deep blue 24.00 *160.00*

All examples of No. 189A were affixed to postal cards before sale. Values are for stamps removed from the cards.

See Nos. 191-192, 203B, 248.

Types of 1952 and

Planting Trees — A87

Wmk. 257
1953, Apr. 5 Litho. *Perf. 12½*

190 A87 1h aqua .80 *.65*
191 A85 2h aqua .80 .50
192 A85 5h bright green 1.00 .50
193 A87 10h bright green 2.75 1.50
194 A86 20h brown 3.75 *2.00*
Nos. 190-194 (5) 9.10 5.15
Set, never hinged 17.00

See Nos. 203A, 247.

Map and YMCA Emblem — A88

1953, Oct. 25 *Perf. 13½*

195 A88 10h dk slate bl & red 4.75 *3.25*
Never hinged 9.00

50th anniv. of the Korean YMCA.

Tombstone of Mu Yal Wang — A88a

A89

Sika Deer — A90

1954, Apr. *Perf. 12½*

196 A88a 5h dark green 1.10 *1.20*
197 A89 100h brn car 7.50 2.60
198 A90 500h brn org 55.00 10.00
199 A90 1000h bister brown 100.00 20.00
Nos. 196-199 (4) 163.60 33.80
Set, never hinged 325.00

See Nos. 203C, 203D, 238-239, 248A, 250-251, 259, 261-262, 269-270, 279, 281-282.

Dok Do (Dok Island) — A91

Design: 10h, Dok Do, lateral view.

1954, Sept. 15

200 A91 2h claret 2.25 *2.40*
201 A91 5h blue 4.75 *2.40*
202 A91 10h blue green 8.50 *2.40*
Nos. 200-202 (3) 15.50 7.20
Set, never hinged 28.00

Moth and Flag — A92

Pagoda Park, Seoul — A92a

1954, Apr. 16 Wmk. 257 *Perf. 12½*

202A A92 10h brown 8.50 3.00
203 A92a 30h dark blue 1.00 1.40
Set, never hinged 18.50

See Nos. 203E, 260, 280.

Types of 1952-54

1955-56 Unwmk. *Perf. 12½*
Laid Paper

203A A87 1h aqua ('56) .30 *.50*
203B A85 2h aqua ('56) .30 *.50*
203C A88a 5h brt grn ('56) .40 *.50*
203D A89 100h brn car 42.50 7.00
203E A92a 200h violet 10.00 2.40
Nos. 203A-203E (5) 53.50 10.90
Set, never hinged 125.00

On No. 203C the right hand character is redrawn as in illustration above No. 212D.

Nos. 203A and 203C are found on horizontally and vertically laid paper.

Erosion Control on Mountainside — A93

1954, Dec. 12 Wmk. 257

204 A93 10h dk grn & yel grn 3.00 1.25
205 A93 19h dk grn & yel grn 3.50 *1.75*
Set, never hinged 11.00

Issued to publicize the 1954 forestation campaign.

Presidents Rhee and Eisenhower Shaking Hands — A94

1954, Dec. 25 *Perf. 13½*

206 A94 10h violet blue 1.90 *1.60*
207 A94 19h brown 2.10 *2.00*
208 A94 71h dull green 4.75 3.50
Nos. 206-208 (3) 8.75 7.10
Set, never hinged 15.50

Adoption of the US-Korea mutual defense treaty.

"Reconstruction" — A95

Wmk. 257
1955, Feb. 10 Litho. *Perf. 12½*

209 A95 10h brown 3.00 2.60
210 A95 15h violet 3.00 2.60
211 A95 20h blue 650.00 18.50
Never hinged 1,350.
212 A95 50h plum 7.00 3.00
Nos. 209-210,212 (3) 13.00
Nos. 209-212 (4) 26.70
Set, #209-210, 212, never hinged 25.00

Korea's industrial reconstruction.

1955, Oct. 19 Unwmk. *Perf. 12½*
Laid Paper

212A A95 15h violet 2.75 2.25
212B A95 20h blue 2.75 2.00
212C A95 50h plum 4.75 1.00
Nos. 212A-212C (3) 10.25 5.25
Set, never hinged 18.50

No. 212B is found on horizontally and vertically laid paper.

Same with Right Character at Top Redrawn

Original

Redrawn

1956, June 5 Unwmk. *Perf. 12½*
Laid Paper

212D A95 10h brown 2.75 *2.40*
212E A95 15h violet 2.75 *2.40*
212F A95 20h blue 2.75 1.10
a. Booklet pane of 6 175.00
Nos. 212D-212F (3) 8.25 5.90
Set, never hinged 16.00

Nos. 212D-212F are found on horizontally and vertically laid paper. See Nos. 248B, 256, 272, 276.

Rotary Emblem — A96

1955, Feb. 23 Wmk. 257 *Perf. 13½*

213 A96 20h violet 5.00 3.50
214 A96 25h dull green 1.75 1.50
215 A96 71h magenta 1.75 1.50
Nos. 213-215 (3) 8.50 6.50
Set, never hinged 15.00

Rotary International, 50th anniversary.

Syngman Rhee, 80th Birthday, Apr. 26 — A98

1955, Mar. 26

217 A98 20h deep blue 13.50 6.75
Never hinged 26.00

Flag and Arch of Independence — A99

1955, Aug. 15 Litho. *Perf. 13½*

218 A99 40h Turq green 6.00 1.60
219 A99 100h brn red 6.00 2.10
Set, never hinged 20.00

Tenth anniversary of independence.

UN Emblem in Circle of Clasped Hands — A100

1955, Oct. 24

221 A100 20h bluish green 2.50 2.00
222 A100 55h aqua 2.50 2.00
Set, never hinged 9.50

United Nations, 10th anniversary.

Olympic Torch and Runners — A101

1955, Oct. 23

223 A101 20h claret 3.50 2.00
224 A101 55h dark green 3.50 2.00
Set, never hinged 13.00

36th National Athletic Meet.

Adm. Li Sun-sin, Navy Flag and Tortoise Ship — A102

Perf. 13x13½
1955, Nov. 11 Unwmk.
Laid Paper

225 A102 20h violet blue 5.00 2.60
Never hinged 9.50

Korean Navy, 10th anniversary.

Rhee Monument near Seoul — A103

1956, Mar. 26 *Perf. 13½x13*

226 A103 20h dull green 3.25 2.60
Never hinged 7.00

81st birthday of Pres. Syngman Rhee.
No. 226 is found on horizontally and vertically laid paper.

Third Inauguration of Pres. Syngman Rhee — A104

1956, Aug. 15 *Perf. 13x13½*

227 A104 20h brown 72.50 30.00
228 A104 55h dark blue 27.00 12.00
Set, never hinged 170.00

Olympic Rings and Torch — A105

1956, Nov. 1 Litho. *Perf. 12½*
Laid Paper

229 A105 20h red orange 2.75 *2.40*
230 A105 55h brt green 2.75 *2.40*
Set, never hinged 10.50

16th Olympic Games in Melbourne, 11/22-12/8.

Central Post Office, Seoul A107

Stamp of 1884 A108

Mail Delivered by Donkey — A109

1956, Dec. 4 Laid Paper Unwmk.

232 A107 20h blue green 6.50 2.50
233 A108 50h rose carmine 11.50 6.00
234 A109 55h green 5.00 2.00
Nos. 232-234 (3) 23.00 10.50
Set, never hinged 42.50

Issued to commemorate Postal Day.

Types of 1954 Redrawn and

Hibiscus A110

King Sejong A111

Kyongju Observatory — A112

No Hwan Symbol; Redrawn Character

1956, Dec. 4 Unwmk. *Perf. 12½*
Laid Paper

235 A110 10h lilac rose 1.00 .75
236 A111 20h lilac 1.75 1.00
237 A112 50h violet 3.00 1.00
238 A89 100h brn car 12.50 4.00
239 A90 500h brn org 37.50 4.75
Nos. 235-239 (5) 55.75 11.50
Set, never hinged 100.00

On Nos. 238-239, the character after numeral has been omitted and the last character of the inscription has been redrawn as illustrated above No. 212D.

Nos. 235-236 are found on horizontally and vertically laid paper.

See Nos. 240-242, 253, 255, 258, 273, 275, 278, 291Bd, 291Bf, B3-B4.

Types of 1956

1957, Jan. 21 Wmk. 312 *Perf. 12½*

240 A110 10h lilac rose 1.00 .65
241 A111 20h red lilac 2.25 1.05
242 A112 50h violet 3.50 .65
Nos. 240-242 (3) 6.75 2.35
Set, never hinged 14.00

Telecommunication Symbols — A117

1957, Jan. 31 *Perf. 13½*

243 A117 40h lt ultra 1.50 1.20
244 A117 55h brt green 1.50 1.20
Set, never hinged 5.00

5th anniv. of Korea's joining the ITU.

Boy Scout and Emblem — A118

1957, Feb. 27 Wmk. 312

245 A118 40h pale purple 1.40 *1.35*
246 A118 55h lt magenta 1.40 *1.35*
Set, never hinged 5.25

50th anniversary of Boy Scout movement.

Types of 1953-56
Top Right Character Redrawn; Hwan Symbol Retained

1957 Wmk. 312 *Perf. 12½*

247 A87 1h aqua .65 *.55*
248 A85 2h aqua .65 *.55*
248A A88a 5h brt green .65 *.55*
248B A95 15h violet 3.25 2.00
Nos. 247-248B (4) 5.20 3.65
Set, never hinged 11.50

Redrawn Types of 1954, 1956 and

Planting Trees A119

South Gate, Seoul A120

Tiger A121

Diamond Mountains A122

No Hwan Symbol; Redrawn Character

1957 Wmk. 312 Litho. *Perf. 12½*

249 A119 2h aqua .30 *.40*
250 A88a 4h aqua .45 .40
251 A88a 5h emerald .45 .40
252 A120 10h green .50 .75
253 A110 20h lilac rose .65 .40
254 A121 30h pale lilac .65 .40
255 A111 40h red lilac .75 .35
a. Booklet pane of 6 80.00
256 A95 50h lake 4.00 2.00
257 A122 55h violet brn 1.50 1.50
258 A112 100h violet 1.75 1.00
259 A89 200h brown car 2.00 1.00
260 A92a 400h brt violet 32.50 4.75
261 A90 500h ocher 32.50 5.75
262 A90 1000h dk ol bis 80.00 10.50
Nos. 249-262 (14) 158.00 29.60
Set, never hinged 290.00

The "redrawn character" is illustrated above No. 212D.

See Nos. 268, 271, 274, 277, 291c, 291e.

Mercury and Flags of Korea and US — A123

1957, Nov. 7 Wmk. 312 *Perf. 13½*

263 A123 40h dp orange 1.00 *1.00*
264 A123 205h emerald 1.90 *2.00*
a. Souv. sheet of 2, #263-264, imperf. 850.00
Never hinged 1,500.
Set, never hinged 6.25

Treaty of friendship, commerce and navigation between Korea and the US.

Star of Bethlehem and Pine Cone — A124

Designs: 25h, Christmas tree and tassel. 30h, Christmas tree, window and dog.

1957, Dec. 11 Litho. *Perf. 12½*

265 A124 15h org, brn & grn 6.50 *2.00*
a. Souv. sheet of 1, imperf. 650.00
Never hinged 1,100.
266 A124 25h lt grn, yel & red 4.75 *2.00*
a. Souv. sheet of 1, imperf. 650.00
Never hinged 1,100.
267 A124 30h bl, lt grn & yel 14.50 3.00
a. Souv. sheet of 1, imperf. 650.00
Never hinged 1,100.
Nos. 265-267 (3) 25.75 7.00
Set, never hinged 40.00

Issued for Christmas and the New Year.

Redrawn Types of 1954-57
Wmk. 317

1957-59 Litho. *Perf. 12½*

268 A119 2h aqua .35 *.45*
269 A88a 4h aqua .45 .45
270 A88a 5h emerald ('58) .45 .45
271 A120 10h green .75 .45
272 A95 15h violet ('58) 2.50 2.25
273 A110 20h lilac rose .90 .35
274 A121 30h pale lil ('58) 1.00 .35
275 A111 40h red lilac 1.00 .35
276 A95 50h lake ('58) 5.00 .80
277 A122 55h vio brn ('59) 1.90 .85
278 A112 100h violet 1.75 .75

279 A89 200h brn car ('59) 2.25 .75
280 A92a 400h brt vio ('59) 57.50 6.00
281 A90 500h ocher ('58) 37.50 6.00
282 A90 1000h dk ol bis ('58) 80.00 10.00
Nos. 268-282 (15) 193.30 30.25
Set, never hinged 425.00

Nos. 268-282 have no hwan symbol, and final character of inscription is the redrawn one illustrated above No. 212D.
See No. 291B.

Catalogue values for unused stamps in this section, from this point to the end of the section, are for Never Hinged items.

Winged Envelope — A125

1958, May 20 **Wmk. 317**
283 A125 40h dk blue & red 2.10 .80
a. Souv. sheet of 1, imperf. *1,950.*

Issued for the Second Postal Week.

Children Looking at Industrial Growth — A126

Design: 40h, Hibiscus forming "10".

1958, Aug. 15 ***Perf. 13½***
284 A126 20h gray 1.90 .55
285 A126 40h dk carmine 2.25 .80
a. Souv. sheet of 2, # 284-285, imperf. 450.00

10th anniversary of Republic of Korea.

UNESCO Building, Paris — A127

1958, Nov. 3 **Wmk. 317**
286 A127 40h orange & green 1.45 .60
a. Souv. sheet of 1, imperf. 170.00

Opening of UNESCO. headquarters in Paris, Nov. 3.

Children Flying Kites A128

Christmas Tree and Fortune Screen A129

Children in Costume — A130

1958, Dec. 11 **Litho.** ***Perf. 12½***
287 A128 15h yellow green 2.10 .70
a. Souv. sheet of 1, imperf. 67.50
288 A129 25h blue, red & yel 2.10 .70
a. Souv. sheet of 1, imperf. 67.50
289 A130 30h yell, ultra & red 3.00 1.05
a. Souv. sheet of 1, imperf. 67.50
Nos. 287-289 (3) 7.20 2.45
Nos. 287a-289a (3) 202.50

Issued for Christmas and the New Year.

Flag and Pagoda Park — A131

1959, Mar. 1 ***Perf. 13½***
290 A131 40h rose lilac & brn 1.60 .60
a. Souv. sheet of 1, imperf. 115.00 115.00

40th anniv. of Independence Movement Day.

Korean Marines Landing — A132

1959, Apr. 15
291 A132 40h olive grn 1.60 .65
a. Souv. sheet of 1, imperf. 13.00 13.00

Korean Marine Corps, 10th anniversary.

Types of 1956-57
Souvenir Sheet
Wmk. 317

1959, May 20 **Litho.** ***Imperf.***
291B Sheet of 4 9.75 *9.25*
c. A120 10h green 1.40 .60
d. A110 20h lilac rose 1.40 .60
e. A121 30h pale lilac 1.40 .60
f. A111 40h red lilac 1.40 .60

3rd Postal Week, May 20-26.

WHO Emblem and Family — A133

1959, Aug. 17 **Wmk. 317** ***Perf. 13½***
292 A133 40h pink & rose vio 1.45 .65
a. Souv. sheet of 1, imperf. 10.50 10.50

10th anniv. of Korea's joining the WHO.

Diesel Train — A134

1959, Sept. 18 **Litho.**
293 A134 40h brown & bister 2.25 .65
a. Souv. sheet of 1, imperf. 23.00 23.00

60th anniversary of Korean railroads.

Relay Race and Emblem — A135

1959, Oct. 3
294 A135 40h lt bl & red brn 1.50 .70
a. Souv. sheet of 1, imperf. 16.50 16.50

40th National Athletic Meet.

Red Cross and Korea Map — A136

55h, Red Cross superimposed on globe.

1959, Oct. 27 ***Perf. 13½***
295 A136 40h red & bl grn 1.45 .60
296 A136 55h pale lilac & red 1.45 .60
a. Souv. sheet of 2, #295-296, imperf. 37.50 37.50

Centenary of the Red Cross idea.

Old Postal Flag and New Communications Flag — A137

1959, Dec. 4
297 A137 40h blue & red 1.45 .60
a. Souv. sheet of 1, imperf. 19.50 19.50

75th anniv. of the Korean postal system.

Mice and Chinese Happy New Year Character — A138

Designs: 25h, Children singing Christmas hymns. 30h, Red-crested crane.

1959, Dec. 15 ***Perf. 12½***
298 A138 15h gray, vio bl & pink 1.45 .40
a. Souv. sheet of 1, imperf. 27.00 27.00
299 A138 25h blue, red & emer 1.45 .40
a. Souv. sheet of 1, imperf. 27.00 27.00
300 A138 30h lt lilac, blk & red 2.75 .55
a. Souv. sheet of 1, imperf. 27.00 27.00
Nos. 298-300 (3) 5.65 1.35
Nos. 298a-300a (3) 81.00

Issued for Christmas and the New Year.

UPU Monument and Means of Transportation A139

Wmk. 317

1960, Jan. 1 **Litho.** ***Perf. 13½***
301 A139 40h grnsh bl & brn 1.60 .80
a. Souv. sheet of 1, imperf. 32.50 32.50

60th anniv. of Korean membership in the UPU.

Bee, Honeycomb and Clover A140

Snail and Money Bag A141

1960, Apr. 1 **Wmk. 317** ***Perf. 12½***
302 A140 10h emer, brn & org 1.45 1.00
303 A141 20h pink, bl & brn 1.60 1.00

Issued to encourage systematic saving by children. See No. 313, souvenir sheet.
See Nos. 377-380.

Uprooted Oak Emblem and Yin Yang — A142

1960, Apr. 7 **Wmk. 312** ***Perf. 13½***
304 A142 40h emer, car & ultra 1.45 .60
a. Souv. sheet of 1, imperf. 45.00 45.00

Issued to publicize World Refugee Year, July 1, 1959-June 30, 1960.

Dwight D. Eisenhower — A143

1960, June 19 **Litho.** **Wmk. 317**
305 A143 40h bl, red & bluish grn 4.00 1.60
a. Souv. sheet of 1, imperf. 30.00 30.00

Pres. Eisenhower's visit to Korea, June 19.

Children in School and Ancient Home Teaching — A144

1960, Aug. 3 **Wmk. 317** ***Perf. 13½***
306 A144 40h multicolored 1.45 .50
a. Souv. sheet of 1, imperf. 8.25 8.25

75th anniv. of the modern educational system.

Hibiscus and House of Councilors A145

1960, Aug. 8
307 A145 40h blue 1.45 .50
a. Souv. sheet of 1, imperf. 8.25 8.25

Inaugural session, House of Councilors.

Woman Holding Torch and Man with Flag — A146

1960, Aug. 15
308 A146 40h bis, lt bl & brn 1.75 .60
a. Souv. sheet of 1, imperf. 8.25 8.25

15th anniversary of liberation.

Weight Lifter — A147

40h, South Gate, Seoul, & Olympic emblem.

1960, Aug. 25 **Litho.**
309 A147 20h brn, lt bl & sal 1.50 .70
310 A147 40h brn, lt bl & dk bl 1.50 .70
a. Souv. sheet of 2, #309-310, imperf. 26.00 26.00

17th Olympic Games, Rome, 8/25-9/11.

Swallow and Telegraph Pole — A148

1960, Sept. 28 ***Perf. 13½***
311 A148 40h lt bl, lil & gray 1.60 .70
a. Souv. sheet of 1, imperf. 7.50 7.50

Establishment of telegraph service, 75th anniv.

Students and Sprout — A149

1960, Oct. 1 **Wmk. 317**
312 A149 40h bl, sal pink & emer 1.60 .60
a. Souv. sheet of 1, imperf. 7.00 7.00

Rebirth of the Republic.

Savings Types of 1960
Souvenir Sheet

1960, Oct. 7 ***Imperf.***
313 Sheet of two 5.00 5.00
a. A140 10h emer, brn & org 2.10 1.90
b. A141 20h pink, blue & brown 2.10 1.90

4th Postal Week, Oct. 7-13, and Intl. Letter Writing Week, Oct. 3-9.

Torch — A150

1960, Oct. 15 *Perf. 13½*

314 A150 40h dk bl, lt bl & yel 1.45 .50
a. Souv. sheet of 1, imperf. 6.75 6.75

Cultural Month (October).

UN Flag, Globe and Laurel — A151

1960, Oct. 24 **Litho.**

315 A151 40h rose lil, bl & grn 1.45 .50
a. Souv. sheet of 1, imperf. 6.50 6.50

15th anniversary of United Nations.

UN Emblem and Grave Markers — A152

1960, Nov. 1 **Wmk. 317**

316 A152 40h salmon & brn 1.45 .50
a. Souv. sheet of 1, imperf. 6.50 6.50

Establishment of the UN Memorial Cemetery, Tanggok, Pusan, Korea.

"Housing, Agriculture, Population" A153

1960, Nov. 15 *Perf. 13½*

317 A153 40h multicolored 1.45 .50
a. Souv. sheet of 1, imperf. 6.75 6.75

Issued to publicize the 1960 census.

Boy and Head of Ox — A154

Star of Bethlehem and Korean Sock — A155

Girl Giving New Year's Greeting — A156

1960, Dec. 15 **Litho.** *Perf. 12½*

318 A154 15h gray, brn & org yel 2.00 .40
a. Souv. sheet of 1, imperf. 9.00 9.00
319 A155 25h vio bl, red & grn 2.60 .40
a. Souv. sheet of 1, imperf. 9.00 9.00
320 A156 30h red, vio bl & yel 3.50 .60
a. Souv. sheet of 1, imperf. 9.75 9.75
Nos. 318-320 (3) 8.10 1.40
Nos. 318a-320a (3) 27.75

Issued for Christmas and the New Year.

UN Emblem, Windsock and Ancient Rain Gauge — A157

1961, Mar. 23 *Perf. 13½*

321 A157 40h lt blue & ultra 1.50 .50
a. Souv. sheet of 1, imperf. 4.00 4.00

1st World Meteorological Day.

Children, Globe and UN Emblem — A158

1961, Apr. 7 **Wmk. 317**

322 A158 40h salmon & brown 1.60 .50
a. Souv. sheet of 1, imperf. 4.00 4.00

10th World Health Day.

Students Demonstrating A159

1961, Apr. 19 **Litho.**

323 A159 40h red, grn & ultra 1.90 .75
a. Souv. sheet of 1, imperf. 10.00 10.00

1st anniv. of the Korean April revolution.

Workers — A160

1961, May 6

324 A160 40h brt green 1.45 .60
a. Souv. sheet of 1, imperf. 6.00 6.00

International Conference on Community Development, Seoul.

Girl Scout — A161

1961, May 10

325 A161 40h brt green 1.90 .60
a. Souv. sheet of 1, imperf. 13.00 13.00

15th anniversary of Korea's Girl Scouts.

Soldier's Grave — A162

Wmk. 317

1961, June 6 **Litho.** *Perf. 13½*

326 A162 40h blk & ol gray 2.75 1.20
a. Souv. sheet of 1, imperf. 10.00 10.00

6th National Mourning Day.

Soldier with Torch — A163

1961, June 16

327 A163 40h red brn & yellow 2.75 1.20
a. Souv. sheet of 1, imperf. 9.50 9.50

Military Revolution of May 16, 1961.

Map of Korea, Torch and Broken Chain — A164

1961, Aug. 15 **Wmk. 317** *Perf. 13½*

328 A164 40h dk bl, ver & aqua 2.75 1.20
a. Souv. sheet of 1, imperf. 5.75 5.75

16th anniv. of liberation.

Flag and Servicemen A165

1961, Oct. 1 **Litho.**

329 A165 40h vio bl, red & brn 3.00 1.25
a. Souv. sheet of 1, imperf. 5.25 5.25

Issued for Armed Forces Day.

Kyongbok Palace Art Museum — A166

1961, Nov. 1 **Wmk. 317** *Perf. 13½*

330 A166 40h beige & dk brn 1.90 .60
a. Souv. sheet of 1, imperf. 4.25 4.25

10th Natl. Exhibition of Fine Arts.

"UNESCO," Candle and Laurel — A167

1961, Nov. 4

331 A167 40h lt grn & dk bl 1.90 .60
a. Souv. sheet of 1, imperf. 4.00 4.00

15th anniv. of UNESCO.

Mobile X-Ray Unit — A168

1961, Nov. 16

332 A168 40h rose beige & red brn 1.50 .60
a. Souv. sheet of 1, imperf. 4.00 4.00

Tuberculosis Prevention Week.

Ginseng A169

King Sejong and Hangul Alphabet A170

Tristram's Woodpecker A171

Rice Farmer A172

Ancient Drums — A173

1961-62 **Unwmk.** **Litho.** *Perf. 12½*

338 A169 20h rose brn ('62) 2.00 1.20
339 A170 30h pale purple 5.25 1.00
340 A171 40h dk blue & red 5.00 1.00
341 A172 40h dk green ('62) 8.50 1.60
342 A173 100h red brown 11.00 2.00
Nos. 338-342 (5) 31.75 6.80

See Nos. 363-366, 368, 388-392, 517-519, B5-B7.

Globe with Map of Korea and ITU Emblem — A175

1962, Jan. 31 **Unwmk.** *Perf. 13½*

348 A175 40h ver & dk blue 1.90 .90
a. Souv. sheet of 1, imperf. 11.50 11.50

10th anniv. of Korea's joining the ITU.

Atomic Reactor and Atom Symbol — A176

1962, Mar. 30 **Litho.** *Perf. 13½*

349 A176 40h lt bl, sl grn & ol gray 2.10 .50

Inauguration of the Triga Mark II atomic reactor.

Malaria Eradication Emblem and Mosquito — A177

1962, Apr. 7 **Unwmk.**

350 A177 40h green & red org 1.50 .70
a. Souv. sheet of 1, imperf. 3.75 3.75

WHO drive to eradicate malaria.

YWCA Emblem and Girl — A178

1962, Apr. 20 *Perf. 13½*

351 A178 40h pink & dk blue 3.00 .60

40th anniv. of the Korean Young Women's Christian Association.

South Gate and FPA Emblem — A179

1962, May 12 **Wmk. 317**

352 A179 40h lt bl, dk vio & red 3.00 .75

Meeting of the Federation of Motion Picture Producers in Asia, May 12-16.

Men Pushing Cogwheel A180

Soldiers on Hang Kang Bridge A181

Yin Yang and Factory — A182

Wmk. 317

1962, May 16 Litho. *Perf. 13½*

353 A180	30h brn & pale olive	2.75	.85
a.	Souv. sheet of 1, Korean text	15.00	15.00
b.	Souv. sheet of 1, English text	25.00	20.00
354 A181	40h brn, lt bl & citron	2.75	.85
a.	Souv. sheet of 1, Korean text	15.00	15.00
b.	Souv. sheet of 1, English text	25.00	20.00
355 A182	200h ultra, yel & red	32.50	7.75
a.	Souv. sheet of 1, Korean text	50.00	50.00
b.	Souv. sheet of 1, English text	110.00	100.00
	Nos. 353-355 (3)	38.00	9.45

1st anniv. of the May 16th Revolution.

The souvenir sheets are imperf.

The sheets with English text also exist with "E" in "POSTAGE" omitted. The English-text sheets are not watermarked except those with "E" omitted. Value, $200 for set.

Tortoise Warship, 16th Century — A183

Design: 4w, Tortoise ship, heading right.

1962, Aug. 14 Unwmk. *Perf. 13½*

356 A183	2w dk bl & turq bl	15.00	1.50
357 A183	4w brnsh blk, turq grn & redsh pur	25.00	3.00

370th anniv. of Korea's victory in the naval battle with the Japanese off Hansan Island.

Flag, Scout Emblem and Tents — A184

Wmk. 312

1962, Oct. 5 Litho. *Perf. 13½*

358 A184	4w brown, bl & red	1.90	.75
a.	Souv. sheet of 1, imperf., unwmkd.	7.75	7.75

Wmk. 317

359 A184	4w green, bl & red	1.90	.75
a.	Souv. sheet of 1, imperf., unwmkd.	7.75	7.75

40th anniv. of Korean Boy Scouts.

Types of 1961-62 and

Hanabusaya Asiatica — A185

Folk Dancers — A185a

Miruk Bosal A186

Long-horned Beetle A186a

Symbols of Thrift and Development A186b

Meesun Blossoms and Fruit A186c

Library of Early Buddhist Scriptures A186d

Sika Deer A186e

King Songdok Bell, 8th Cent. A186f

Bodhisattva in Cavern Temple, Silla Dynasty A187

Tile of Silla Dynasty — A187a

Designs: 20ch, Jin-Do dog. 1.50w, Miruk Bosal. 2w, Ginseng. 3w, King Sejong. 4w, Rice farmer. 5w, Dragon waterpot. 10w, Ancient drums. 500w, Blue dragon fresco, Koguryo dynasty.

1962-63 Unwmk. Litho. *Perf. 12½*

Ordinary Paper

Size: 22x25mm, 25x22mm

360	A186	20ch gldn brown	1.40	.40
361	A185	40ch blue	1.40	.40
362	A186	50ch claret brn	1.40	.40
363	A185a	1w brt blue ('63)	3.25	.40
364	A169	2w red brown	4.75	.40
365	A170	3w violet brown	5.25	.40
366	A172	4w green	5.50	.40
367	A186	5w grnsh blue	6.25	1.00
368	A173	10w red brown	67.50	4.00
369	A186c	20w lil rose ('63)	14.00	1.60
370	A186d	40w dl pur ('63)	100.00	4.75
		Nos. 360-370 (11)	210.70	14.15

1964-66 Granite Paper

360a	A186	20ch org brn	.90	.25
361a	A185	40ch blue	.95	.25
362a	A186	50ch claret brn	.95	.25
362B	A186a	60ch blk ('66)	.95	.30
363a	A185a	1w bright blue	3.50	.25
363B	A186	1.50w dk sl grn ('66)	.70	.30
364a	A169	2w red brown	5.50	.40
365a	A170	3w vio brown	15.00	.30
366a	A172	4w green	6.75	.30
367a	A186	5w grnsh blue	32.50	1.50
367B	A186b	7w lil rose ('66)	3.25	.75
368a	A173	10w red brown	5.00	.40
369a	A186c	20w lilac rose	5.00	.40
370a	A186d	40w vio brown	50.00	2.25
371	A186e	50w red brn	62.50	1.50
372	A186f	100w slate grn	100.00	3.00
373	A187	200w dk & lt grn ('65)	27.50	3.00
374	A187a	300w sl grn & buff ('65)	55.00	4.00
374A	A187a	500w dk & lt bl ('65)	27.50	4.00
		Nos. 360a-374A (19)	403.45	23.40

The paper of Nos. 360a to 374A contains a few colored fibers; the paper of Nos. 385-396 contains many fibers.

Postal counterfeits exist of Nos. 369a, 370a, 371 and 372.

See Nos. 385-396, 516, 521-522, 582-584, 1076-1079, B8.

Map, Mackerel and Trawler — A188

1962, Oct. 10 *Perf. 13½*

375 A188	4w dk bl & grnsh bl	5.00	1.00

10th anniv. of the Pacific Fishery Council.

ICAO Emblem and Plane — A189

1962, Dec. 11 *Perf. 13½*

376 A189	4w blue & brown	2.40	.75
a.	Souv. sheet of 1, imperf.	9.25	9.25

10th anniv. of Korea's joining the ICAO.

Savings Types of 1960

1962-64 Unwmk. *Perf. 12½*

377 A140	1w emer, brn & org ('63)	7.25	1.25
a.	Granite paper	16.00	12.50
378 A141	2w pink, bl & brn	12.00	1.50
a.	Granite paper	14.00	2.50

Wmk. 317

379 A140	1w emer, brn & org ('64)	95.00	10.00
380 A141	2w pink, bl & brn ('64)	14.00	1.75
	Nos. 377-380 (4)	128.25	14.50

Wheat Emblem — A190

Wmk. 317

1963, Mar. 21 Litho. *Perf. 13½*

381 A190	4w emer, dk bl & ocher	1.50	.70
a.	Souv. sheet of 1, imperf.	4.50	4.50

FAO "Freedom from Hunger" campaign.

Globe and Letters — A191

1963, Apr. 1

382 A191	4w rose lil, ol & dk bl	2.25	.60
a.	Souv. sheet of 1, imperf.	4.50	4.50

1st anniv. of the formation of the Asian-Oceanic Postal Union, AOPU.

Centenary Emblem and World Map — A192

1963, May 8 Litho.

383 A192	4w org, red & gray	1.50	1.00
384 A192	4w lt bl, red & gray	1.50	1.00
a.	Souv. sheet of 2, #383-384, imperf.	12.50	12.50

Cent. of the Intl. Red Cross.

Types of 1961-63

Designs as before.

1963-64 Wmk. 317 *Perf. 12½*

Granite Paper

Size: 22x25mm, 25x22mm

385 A186	20ch gldn brn ('64)	1.25	.25
386 A185	40ch blue	1.25	.25
387 A186	50ch cl brn ('64)	1.25	.25
388 A185a	1w brt blue	3.25	.35
389 A169	2w red brown	6.25	.40
390 A170	3w vio brown	12.00	.35
391 A172	4w green	6.50	.60
392 A173	10w red brown	6.25	.60
393 A186c	20w lil rose ('64)	11.00	1.40
394 A186d	40w maroon	52.50	2.00
395 A186e	50w yel brown	70.00	2.00
396 A186f	100w slate grn	105.00	3.75
	Nos. 385-396 (12)	276.50	12.20

Hibiscus and "15" — A193

1963, Aug. 15 Wmk. 317 *Perf. 13½*

398 A193	4w vio bl, pale bl & red	3.00	1.20

15th anniversary of the Republic.

Army Nurse and Corps Emblem — A194

1963, Aug. 26 Litho.

399 A194	4w citron, grn & blk	2.25	.85

Army Nurses Corps, 15th anniversary.

First Five-Year Plan Issue

Transformer and Power Transmission Tower — A195

Irrigated Rice Fields — A196

No. 402, Cement factory. No. 403, Coal Miner. No. 404, Oil refinery. No. 405, Fishing industry (ships). No. 406, Cargo ship and cargo. No. 407, Fertilizer plant and grain. No. 408, Radar and telephone. No. 409, Transportation (plane, train, ship and map).

1962-66 Unwmk. *Perf. 12½*

400 A195	4w org & dk vio	27.50	3.00
401 A196	4w turq bl & blue	27.50	3.00

Wmk. 317

402 A195	4w dk bl & gray	13.00	1.60
403 A196	4w brnsh pink & choc	13.00	1.60
404 A195	4w yel ocher & bl	5.50	1.15
405 A196	4w turq grn & blk	5.50	1.15

Unwmk.

406 A195	4w pale pink & vio bl	1.90	.95
407 A196	4w gray brn & brn blk	1.90	.95
408 A195	7w ol bis & blk	3.25	1.00
409 A196	7w turq bl & blue	3.25	1.00
	Nos. 400-409 (10)	102.30	15.40

Economic Development Five-Year Plan.

Issued: Nos. 400-401, 12/28/62; Nos. 402-403, 9/1/63; Nos. 404-405, 6/15/64; Nos. 406-407, 6/1/65; Nos. 408-409, 6/1/66.

Ramses Temple, Abu Simbel A197

Wmk. 317

1963, Oct. 1 Litho. *Perf. 13½*

410	3w gray & ol gray	5.50	1.75
411	4w gray & ol gray	5.50	1.75
a.	Souv. sheet of 2, #410-411, imperf.	9.50	9.50
b.	A197 Pair, #410-411	11.50	4.25

UNESCO world campaign to save historic monuments in Nubia.

Rugby and Torch Bearer — A199

1963, Oct. 4 Wmk. 317 *Perf. 13½*

412 A199 4w gray, red brn & Pruss bl 3.75 1.30

44th National Athletic Games.

Nurse & Mobile X-Ray Unit — A200

1963, Nov. 6 *Perf. 13½*

413 A200 4w org & bluish blk 1.90 .75

10h anniv. of the Korean Natl. Tuberculosis Association.

Eleanor Roosevelt — A201

Design: 4w, Hands holding torch and globe.

1963, Dec. 10 Litho. Wmk. 317

414 A201 3w lt red brn & dk bl 1.60 1.00
415 A201 4w dl org, ol & dk bl 1.60 1.00
a. Souv. sheet of 2, 414-415, imperf. 5.75 5.75

Eleanor Roosevelt; 15th anniv. of the Universary Declaration of Human Rights.

Korean Flag and UN Headquarters — A202

1963, Dec. 12 Wmk. 317 *Perf. 13½*

416 A202 4w grnsh bl, ol & blk 1.60 .50
a. Souv. sheet of 1, imperf. 4.75 4.75

15th anniv. of Korea's recognition by the UN.

Tang-piri (Recorder) — A203

Musical Instruments: No. 418, Pyen-kyeng (chimes). No. 419, Chang-ko (drums). No. 420, Tai-keum (large flute). No. 421, Taipyeng-so (Chinese oboe). No. 422, Na-bal (brass trumpet). No. 423, Hyang-pipa (Chinese short lute). No. 424, Wul-keum (banjo). No. 425, Kaya-ko (zither), horiz. No. 426, Wa-kong-hu (harp), horiz.

1963, Dec. 17 Unwmk.

417 A203 4w pink, dk grn & mag 5.75 1.30
418 A203 4w lt bl, bl grn & dk bl 5.75 1.30
419 A203 4w pink, dk bl & brn 5.75 1.30
420 A203 4w tan, dk grn & dk brn 5.75 1.30
421 A203 4w yel, vio bl & brn 5.75 1.30
422 A203 4w grnsh gray, blksh brn & vio 5.75 1.30
423 A203 4w pink, dk bl & org brn 5.75 1.30
424 A203 4w turq grn, brnsh blk & bl 5.75 1.30
425 A203 4w rose pink, red brn & brnsh blk 5.75 1.30
426 A203 4w dl mauve, blk & grnsh bl 5.75 1.30
Nos. 417-426 (10) 57.50 13.00

Pres. Park and Capitol — A204

1963, Dec. 17 Wmk. 317

427 A204 4w black & brt grn 65.00 16.00

Inauguration of Pres. Park Chung Hee.

Symbols of Metric System — A205

1964, Jan. 1 Litho.

428 A205 4w multicolored 1.60 .75
a. Imperf., pair *75.00*

Introduction of the metric system.

UNESCO Emblem and Yin Yang — A206

1964, Jan. 30 Wmk. 317 *Perf. 13½*

429 A206 4w red, lt bl & ultra 1.90 .75

Korean Natl. Commission for UNESCO, 10th anniv.

Industrial Census — A207

1964, Mar. 23 Wmk. 317 *Perf. 13½*

430 A207 4w gray, blk & red brn 1.90 .75

National Mining and Industrial Census.

YMCA Emblem and Head — A208

1964, Apr. 12 Litho.

431 A208 4w app grn, dk bl & red 1.50 .60

50th anniv. of the Korean YMCA.

Unisphere, Ginseng and Cargo Ship — A209

Design: 100w, Korean pavilion and globe.

1964, Apr. 22 Wmk. 317 *Perf. 13½*

432 A209 40w buff, red brn & grn 5.00 1.30
433 A209 100w bl red brn & ultra 45.00 8.00
a. Souv. sheet of 2, imperf. 97.50 70.00

New York World's Fair, 1964-65.

Secret Garden, Changdok Palace, Seoul — A210

Views: 2w, Whahong Gate, Suwon. 3w, Uisang Pavilion, Yangyang-gun. 4w, Maitreya Buddha, Bopju Temple at Mt. Songni. 5w, Paekma River and Rock of Falling Flowers. 6w, Anab Pond, Kyongju. 7w, Choksok Pavilion, Chinju. 8w, Kwanghan Pavilion. 9w, Whaom Temple, Mt. Chiri. 10w, Chonjeyon Falls, Soguipo.

1964, May 25 Wmk. 317 *Perf. 13½*
Light Blue Background

434 A210 1w green 1.40 .50
435 A210 2w blksh gray 1.40 .50
436 A210 3w dk green 1.40 .50
437 A210 4w grn 2.60 .85
438 A210 5w violet 5.25 1.35
439 A210 6w vio blue 7.00 1.60
a. Souv. sheet of 2 (5w, 6w) 16.50 16.50
440 A210 7w choc 11.50 2.50
a. Souv. sheet of 2 (4w, 7w) 16.50 16.50
441 A210 8w red brown 11.50 2.25
a. Souv. sheet of 2 (3w, 8w) 16.50 16.50
442 A210 9w lt violet 13.50 2.40
a. Souv. sheet of 2 (2w, 9w) 16.50 16.50
443 A210 10w slate grn 17.50 3.25
a. Souv. sheet of 2 (1w, 10w) 16.50 16.50
Nos. 434-443 (10) 73.05 15.70
Nos. 439a-443a (5) 82.50 82.50

The five souvenir sheets are imperf.

Globe and Wheel — A211

1964, July 1 Litho. *Perf. 13½*

444 A211 4w lt ol grn, dl brn & ocher 1.50 .60
a. Souv. sheet of 1, imperf. 4.75 4.75

Colombo Plan for co-operative economic development of south and southeast Asia.

Hands and World Health Organization Emblem — A212

1964, Aug. 17 Wmk. 317 *Perf. 13½*

445 A212 4w brt yel grn, yel grn & blk 1.50 .60
a. Souv. sheet of 1, imperf. 4.75 4.75

15th anniv. of Korea's joining the UN.

Runner — A213

1964, Sept. 3

446 A213 4w red lil, grn & pink 3.75 1.20

45th Natl. Athletic Meet, Inchon, Sept. 3-8.

UPU Monument, Bern — A214

1964, Sept. 15

447 A214 4w pink, red brn & bl 1.60 .60
a. Souv. sheet of 1, imperf. 5.25 5.25

1st Intl. Cong. for establishing the UPU, 90th anniv.

Crane Hook and Emblem — A215

1964, Sept. 29 Wmk. 317 *Perf. 13½*

448 A215 4w red brn & dull grn 1.60 .60

5th Convention of the Intl. Federation of Asian and Western Pacific Contractors' Assoc. (IFAWPCA), Seoul, Sept. 29-Oct. 7.

Marathon Runners — A216

No. 453, "V," Olympic rings, laurel & track, vert.

1964, Oct. 10 Litho.

449 A216 4w shown 3.00 1.00
450 A216 4w Equestrian 3.00 1.00
451 A216 4w Gymnast 3.00 1.00
452 A216 4w Rowing 3.00 1.00
453 A216 4w multicolored 3.00 1.00
Nos. 449-453 (5) 15.00 5.00

18th Olympic Games, Tokyo, Oct. 10-25.

Souvenir Sheets of 1, Imperf., Unwmk.

449a A216 4w 4.25 4.25
450a A216 4w 4.25 4.25
451a A216 4w 4.25 4.25
452a A216 4w 4.25 4.25
453a A216 4w 4.25 4.25
Nos. 449a-453a (5) 21.25 21.25

Stamp of 1885 — A217

Yong Sik Hong — A218

1964, Dec. 4 Unwmk. *Perf. 13½*

454 A217 3w lilac, vio & dl bl grn 3.75 .95
455 A218 4w gray, vio bl & blk 5.25 1.20

80th anniv. of the Korean postal system. Hong Yong-Sik (1855-84) was Korea's 1st general postmaster.

Pine Branch and Cones — A219

No. 457, Plum Blossoms. No. 458, Forsythia. No. 459, Azalea. No. 460, Lilac. No. 461, Sweetbrier. No. 462, Garden balsam. No. 463, Hibiscus. No. 464, Crape myrtle. No. 465, Chrysanthemum lucidum. No. 466, Paulownia coreana. No. 467, Bamboo.

1965 Litho. *Perf. 13½*

456 A219 4w pale grn, dp grn & brn 2.25 .70
457 A219 4w gray, blk, rose & yel 2.25 .70
458 A219 4w lt bl, yel & brn 2.25 .70
459 A219 4w brt grn, lil rose & sal 2.25 .70
460 A219 4w red lil & brt grn 2.25 .70
461 A219 4w yel grn, grn, car & brn 2.25 .70
462 A219 4w bl, grn & red 2.25 .70
463 A219 4w bluish gray, rose red & grn 2.25 .70
464 A219 4w multicolored 2.25 .70
465 A219 4w pale grn, dk brn, grn & car rose 2.25 .70
466 A219 4w buff, ol grn & brn 2.25 .70
467 A219 4w ultra & emer 2.25 .70
Nos. 456-467 (12) 27.00 8.40

Souvenir Sheets of 1, Imperf.

456a A219 4w 3.00 3.00
457a A219 4w 3.00 3.00
458a A219 4w 3.00 3.00
459a A219 4w 3.00 3.00
460a A219 4w 3.00 3.00
461a A219 4w 3.00 3.00
462a A219 4w 3.00 3.00
463a A219 4w 3.00 3.00
464a A219 4w 3.00 3.00
465a A219 4w 3.00 3.00
466a A219 4w 3.00 3.00
467a A219 4w 3.00 3.00
Nos. 456a-467a (12) 36.00 36.00

Dancing Women, PATA Emblem and Tabo Tower — A220

1965, Mar. 26

468 A220 4w lt bl grn, dk brn & dk vio bl 1.35 .50
a. Souv. sheet of 1, imperf. 3.50 3.50

14th conf. of the Pacific Travel Association, Seoul, Mar. 26-Apr. 2.

Map of Viet Nam and Flag of Korean Assistance Group — A221

1965, Apr. 20 ***Perf. 13½***

469 A221 4w blk, lt yel grn & grnsh bl 1.25 .50
a. Souv. sheet of 1, imperf. 3.75 3.75

Issued to honor the Korean military assistance group in Viet Nam.

Symbols of 7-Year Plan — A222

1965, May 1 **Litho.**

470 A222 4w emer, dk grn & dk brn 1.25 .50

Issued to publicize the 7-year plan for increased food production.

Scales with Families and Homes — A223

1965, May 8

471 A223 4w lt & dk grn & gray 1.25 .50
a. Souv. sheet of 1, imperf. 3.25 3.25

May as Month of Family Planning.

ITU Emblem, Old and New Communication Equipment A224

1965, May 17

472 A224 4w lt bl, car & blk 1.25 .50
a. Souv. sheet of 1, imperf. 3.25 3.25

Cent. of the ITU.

UN Emblem and Flags of Australia, Belgium, Great Britain, Canada and Colombia A225

Gen. Douglas MacArthur and Flags of Korea, UN and US — A226

UN Emblem and Flags: No. 474, Denmark, Ethiopia, France, Greece and India. No. 475, Italy, Luxembourg, Netherlands, New Zealand and Norway. No. 476, Philippines, Sweden, Thailand, Turkey and South Africa.

1965, June 25

Flags in Original Colors

473 A225 4w gray & vio bl 1.50 .75
474 A225 4w grnsh bl & vio bl 1.50 .75
475 A225 4w grnsh bl & vio bl 1.50 .75
476 A225 4w grnsh bl & vio bl 1.50 .75
477 A226 10w lt bl, blk, vio bl & red 5.00 1.50
Nos. 473-477 (5) 11.00 4.50

15th anniv. of the participation of UN Forces in the Korean war.

Souvenir Sheets of 1, Imperf.

473a A225 4w 2.00 2.00
474a A225 4w 2.00 2.00
475a A225 4w 2.00 2.00
476a A225 4w 2.00 2.00
477a A226 10w 3.25 3.25
Nos. 473a-477a (5) 11.25 11.25

Flag, Factories and "20" — A227

South Gate, Seoul, Fireworks and Yin Yang — A228

1965, Aug. 15 **Litho.**

478 A227 4w lt bl, vio bl & red 2.75 .60
479 A228 10w vio bl, lt bl & red 3.75 .80

20th anniv. of liberation from the Japanese.

Factory, Leaf and Ants — A229

1965, Sept. 20 ***Perf. 13½***

480 A229 4w brt yel grn, brn & bister 1.25 .50

Issued to publicize the importance of saving.

Parabolic Antenna, Telephone Dial and Punched Tape — A230

Telegraph Operator, 1885 — A231

1965, Sept. 28

481 A230 3w lt bl, blk & ol 1.75 .65
482 A231 10w citron, Prus bl & blk 4.25 .85

80th anniv. of telegraph service between Seoul and Inchon.

Korean Flag and Capitol, Seoul — A232

1965, Sept. 28

483 A232 3w org, slate grn & bl grn 3.00 1.05

15th anniversary of recapture of Seoul.

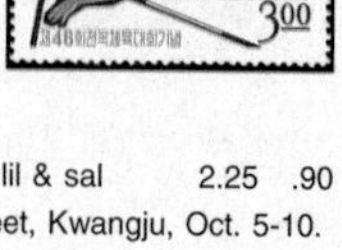

Pole Vault — A233

1965, Oct. 5

484 A233 3w black, lil & sal 2.25 .90

46th Natl. Athletic Meet, Kwangju, Oct. 5-10.

ICY Emblem — A234

UN Flag and Headquarters, NY — A235

1965, Oct. 24 **Litho.**

485 A234 3w lt & dk grn & org brn 1.20 .55
a. Souv. sheet of 1, imperf. 3.75 3.75
486 A235 10w lt bl, vio bl & grn 2.10 .75
a. Souv. sheet of 1, imperf. 3.75 3.75

ICY, 1965, and 20th anniv. of the UN.

Child Posting Letter — A236

Design: 10w, Airmail envelope, telephone.

1965, Dec. 4 ***Perf. 13½***

487 A236 3w bl grn, blk, grn & red 2.75 .95
488 A236 10w ol, dk bl & red 6.00 1.60

Tenth Communications Day.

Children with Sled — A237

Children and South Gate — A238

1965, Dec. 11 **Litho.** ***Perf. 12½***

489 A237 3w pale grn, vio bl & red 2.00 .65
490 A238 4w lt bl, grn, vio bl & red 3.50 1.10
a. Souv. sheet of 2, #489-490, imperf. 4.25 4.25

Issued for Christmas and the New Year.

Freedom House — A239

1966, Feb. 15 **Unwmk.** ***Perf. 12½***

491 A239 7w brt grn, blk & cit 2.00 .70
492 A239 39w lil, blk & pale grn 13.00 3.25
a. Souv. sheet of 2, #491-492, imperf. 22.50 17.50

Opening of "Freedom House" at Panmunjom.

Wildlife Issue

Mandarin Ducks — A240

Birds: 5w, Japanese cranes. 7w, Ring-necked pheasants.

1966, Mar. 15 **Litho.** ***Perf. 12½***

493 A240 3w multicolored 2.40 1.25
494 A240 5w multicolored 2.40 1.25
495 A240 7w multicolored 3.75 1.30

Alaska Pollack — A241

Fish: 5w, Manchurian trout. 7w, Yellow corvina.

1966, June 15

496 A241 3w bl, dk brn & yel 3.00 .90
497 A241 5w grnsh bl, blk & mag 3.50 .90
498 A241 7w brt grnsh bl, blk & yel 4.50 1.00

Firefly — A242

Insects: 5w, Grasshopper. 7w, Silk butterfly (sericinus telamon).

1966, Sept. 15

499 A242 3w multicolored 2.25 .90
500 A242 5w dp yellow & multi 2.75 .90
501 A242 7w lt blue & multi 3.00 1.00

Badger — A243

Animals: 5w, Asiatic black bear. 7w, Tiger.

1966, Dec. 15

502 A243 3w multicolored 3.00 .95
503 A243 5w multicolored 3.00 .95
504 A243 7w multicolored 3.50 .95
Nos. 493-504 (12) 37.05 12.25

Souvenir Sheets of 1, Imperf.

493a A240 3w 3.75 3.75
494a A240 5w 3.75 3.75
495a A240 7w 5.75 5.75
496a A241 3w 3.25 3.25
497a A241 5w 3.75 3.75
498a A241 7w 4.25 4.25
499a A242 3w 3.25 3.25
500a A242 5w 3.25 3.25
501a A242 7w 3.75 3.75
502a A243 3w 4.50 4.50
503a A243 5w 4.50 4.50
504a A243 7w 5.00 5.00
Nos. 493a-504a (12) 48.75 48.75

Hwansung-gun and Kwangnung Forests — A244

1966, Apr. 5 **Unwmk.** ***Perf. 12½***

505 A244 7w green & brown 1.50 .60

Forestation Movement.

Symbolic Newspaper Printing and Pen — A245

1966, Apr. 7 **Litho.**

506 A245 7w lt bl, vio brn & yel 1.35 .60

Tenth Newspaper Day.

Proper Guidance of Young People — A246

1966, May 1 **Unwmk.** ***Perf. 12½***

507 A246 7w Children & bell 1.35 .60

Opening of WHO Headquarters, Geneva — A247

1966, May 3 **Litho.**

508 A247 7w lt bl, blk & yel 1.50 .60
a. Souv. sheet of 1, imperf. 4.25 4.25
509 A247 39w bluish gray, yel & red 11.00 3.00

Girl Scout and Flag — A248

1966, May 10

510 A248 7w yel, emer & dk bl 2.10 .80

Girl Scouts of Korea, 20th anniversary.

Pres. Park and Flags of Korea, Malaysia, Thailand and Republic of China — A249

1966, May 10

511 A249 7w multicolored 7.50 2.10

State visits of President Chung Hee Park.

Women's Ewha University, Seoul, and Student — A250

1966, May 31

512 A250 7w lt bl, vio bl & dp org 1.35 .50

80th anniv. of modern education for women.

Types of 1961-66 Inscribed "Republic of Korea," and

Porcelain Incense Burner, 11th-12th Centuries A253

Celadon Vessel, 12th Century A254

Unjin Miruk Buddha, Kwanchok Temple — A255

60ch, Long-horned beetle. 1w, Folk dancers. 2w, Ginseng. 3w, King Sejong. 5w, Dragon waterpot. 7w, Symbols of thrift & development.

Perf. 12½

1966, Aug. 20 Unwmk. Litho.

Size: 22x19mm, 19x22mm

Granite Paper

516 A186a 60ch gray green .70 .25
517 A185a 1w green 3.75 .35
518 A169 2w blue green 1.00 .25
519 A170 3w dull red brn .50 .25
521 A186 5w gray green 5.00 .70
522 A186b 7w grnsh blue 4.75 .50

Size: 22x25mm

523 A253 13w vio blue 5.00 1.00
524 A254 60w green 27.50 1.35
525 A255 80w slate grn 7.25 1.35
Nos. 516-525 (9) 55.45 6.00

Souvenir Sheet

Carrier Pigeons A258

1966, July 13 Wmk. 317 *Imperf.*

Red Brown Surcharge

534 A258 7w on 40h emer & dk grn 3.50 3.50

6th Intl. Letter Writing Week, June 13-19. No. 534 was not issued without surcharge.

Children and World Map Projection — A259

1966, July 28 Unwmk. *Perf. 12½*

535 A259 7w pur, tan & bluish gray 2.00 .45
a. Souv. sheet of 1, imperf. 3.50 3.50

15th annual assembly of WCOTP (World Conf. of Teaching Profession), Seoul, July 28-Aug. 9.

Factory, Money Bag and Honeycomb A260

1966, Sept. 1 Unwmk. *Perf. 12½*

536 A260 7w multicolored 1.35 .50

Issued to publicize systematic saving.

Map of Korea, and People — A261

1966, Sept. 1 Litho.

537 A261 7w multicolored 1.35 .50

Ninth national census.

CISM Emblem and Round-Table Conference A262

1966, Sept. 29 Unwmk. *Perf. 12½*

538 A262 7w multicolored 1.35 .50
a. Souv. sheet of 1, imperf. 3.50 3.50

21st General Assembly of the Intl. Military Sports Council (CISM), Seoul, 9/29-10/9.

Flags of Korea and Viet Nam and Korean Soldiers — A263

1966, Oct. 1

539 A263 7w multicolored 9.00 2.10

1st anniv. of Korean combat troops in Viet Nam.

Wrestlers — A264

1966, Oct. 10

540 A264 7w red brn, buff & blk 2.40 1.00

47th Natl. Athletic Meet, Seoul, Oct. 10-15.

Lions Emblem and Map of Southeast Asia — A265

1966, Oct. 15

541 A265 7w multicolored 1.50 .90
a. Souv. sheet of 1, imperf. 3.75 3.75

5th East and Southeast Asia Lions Convention, Seoul, Oct. 15-17.

Seoul University Emblem — A266

1966, Oct. 15 Litho.

542 A266 7w multicolored 1.50 1.00

20th anniversary of Seoul University.

Anticommunist League Emblem — A267

1966, Oct. 31 Unwmk. *Perf. 12½*

543 A267 7w multicolored 1.50 .50
a. Souv. sheet of 1, imperf. 3.25 3.25

12th Conf. of the Asian Anticommunist League, Seoul, Oct. 31-Nov. 7.

Presidents Park and Johnson, Flags of US and Korea — A268

1966, Oct. 31 Litho. *Perf. 12½*

544 A268 7w multicolored 2.00 .75
545 A268 83w multicolored 13.00 3.50
a. Souv. sheet of 2, #544-545, imperf. 14.50 14.50

Visit of Pres. Lyndon B. Johnson to Korea.

UNESCO Emblem and Symbols of Learning — A269

1966, Nov. 4

546 A269 7w multicolored 1.50 .60
a. Souvenir sheets 3.50 3.50

20th anniv. of UNESCO.

Good Luck Bag and "Joy" A270

Ram and "Completion" A271

1966, Dec. 10 *Perf. 12½x13, 13x12½*

547 A270 5w multicolored 2.10 .60
a. Souv. sheet of 1, imperf. 3.75 3.75
548 A271 7w multicolored 3.75 .80
a. Souv. sheet of 1, imperf. 3.75 3.75

Issued for Christmas and the New Year.

Syncom Satellite over Globe — A272

1967, Jan. 31 Litho. *Perf. 12½*

549 A272 7w dk blue & multi 1.60 .60
a. Souv. sheet of 1, imperf. 4.00 4.00

15th anniv. of Korea's membership in the ITU.

Presidents Park and Lübke — A273

Perf. 12½

1967, Mar. 2 Litho. Unwmk.

550 A273 7w multicolored 2.40 1.15
a. Souv. sheet of 1, imperf. 4.25 4.25

Visit of Pres. Heinrich Lübke of Germany, Mar. 2-6.

Hand Holding Coin, Industrial and Private Buildings — A274

1967, Mar. 3

551 A274 7w lt green & blk brn 1.50 .60

1st anniv. of the Natl. Taxation Office.

Folklore Series

Okwangdae Clown — A275

5w, Sandi mask & dance, horiz. 7w, Hafoe mask.

1967, Mar. 15 Litho. *Perf. 12½*

552 A275 4w gray, blk & yel 2.10 .90
553 A275 5w multicolored 2.10 .90
554 A275 7w multicolored 3.00 1.00

Perfect Peace Dance — A276

Designs: 4w, Sword dance, horiz. 7w, Buddhist Monk dance.

1967, June 15

555 A276 4w multicolored 3.25 .90
556 A276 5w multicolored 3.75 .90
557 A276 7w multicolored 4.50 1.10

Girls on Seesaw — A277

Designs: 4w, Girls on swing, horiz. 7w, Girls dancing in the moonlight.

1967, Sept. 15

558 A277 4w multicolored 3.75 .90
559 A277 5w multicolored 3.75 1.00
560 A277 7w multicolored 6.00 1.20

Korean Shuttlecock — A278

Designs: 5w, Girls celebrating full moon, horiz. 7w, Archery.

1967, Dec. 15

561 A278 4w multicolored 3.00 .90
562 A278 5w multicolored 3.25 1.05
563 A278 7w multicolored 3.00 1.00
Nos. 552-563 (12) 41.45 11.75

Souvenir Sheets of 1, Imperf.

552a A275 4w 3.25 3.25
553a A275 5w 3.25 3.25
554a A275 7w 4.25 4.25
555a A276 4w 5.50 3.25
556a A276 5w 5.50 3.25
557a A276 7w 6.50 4.25
558a A277 4w 5.75 5.75
559a A277 5w 5.75 5.75
560a A277 7w 6.75 6.75
561a A278 4w 3.75 3.75
562a A278 5w 3.75 3.75
563a A278 7w 4.25 4.25
Nos. 552a-563a (12) 58.25 51.50

JCI Emblem and Kyunghoe Pavilion — A279

1967, Apr. 13 Litho. *Perf. 12½*

564 A279 7w dk brn, brt grn, bl & red 1.35 .60
a. Souv. sheet of 1, imperf. 3.50 3.50

Intl. Junior Chamber of Commerce Conf., Seoul, Apr. 13-16.

Emblem, Map of Far East — A280

1967, Apr. 24 Unwmk. *Perf. 12½*

565 A280 7w vio bl & multi 1.35 .60
a. Souv. sheet of 1, imperf. 3.50 3.50

Issued to publicize the 5th Asian Pacific Dental Congress, Seoul, Apr. 24-28.

EXPO '67 Korean Pavilion — A281

1967, Apr. 28

566 A281 7w yel, blk & red 3.25 .75
567 A281 83w lt bl, blk & red 22.50 4.50
a. Souv. sheet of 2, #566-567, imperf. 18.00 18.00

EXPO '67, Intl. Exhibition, Montreal, Apr. 28-Oct. 27, 1967.

Worker, Soldier, Emblem and Buildings — A282

1967, May 1

568 A282 7w multicolored 1.50 .60

Veterans' Day, May 1.

Second Five-Year Plan Issue

Nut and Arrows — A283

No. 570, Iron wheel and rail. No. 571, Express highway. No. 572, Cloverleaf intersection. No. 573, Rising income for fishermen and farmers (oysters, silk worm, mushrooms and bull's head). No. 574, Machine industry (cogwheels, automobile, wrench and motor). No. 575, Harbor. No. 576, Housing projects plans. No. 577, Atomic power plant. No. 578, Four Great River Valley development.

1967-71 Litho. *Perf. 12½*

569 A283 7w blk, red brn & dl org 6.50 1.20
570 A283 7w dl org, yel & blk 6.50 1.20
571 A283 7w grn, bl & ol 12.00 2.00
572 A283 7w dk brn, yel & grn 7.00 2.00

Perf. 13x12½

573 A283 7w brn, grn, yel & org 1.50 .40
574 A283 7w dk bl, lil rose & buff 1.50 .40
575 A283 10w dk bl, bl, yel & grn 1.50 .40
576 A283 10w lt bl, bl, grn & red 1.50 .40

Photo. *Perf. 13*

577 A283 10w blk, car & bl 1.50 .40
578 A283 10w blk, grn & brn 1.50 .40
Nos. 569-578 (10) 41.00 8.80

Second Economic Development Five-Year Plan.

Issued: Nos. 569-570, 6/1/67; Nos. 571-572, 12/5/68; Nos. 573-574, 12/5/69; Nos. 575-576, 12/5/70; Nos. 577-578, 12/5/71.

President Park and Phoenix — A284

1967, July 1 Unwmk. *Perf. 12½*

579 A284 7w multicolored 23.00 6.00
a. Souv. sheet of 1, imperf. 62.50 62.50

Inauguration of President Park Chung Hee for a 2nd term, July 1, 1967.

Korean Boy Scout, Emblem and Tents — A285

20w, Korean Boy Scout emblem, bridge & tents.

1967, Aug. 10 Litho. *Perf. 12½*

580 A285 7w multicolored 1.50 .60
a. Souv. sheet of 1, imperf. 4.75 4.75
581 A285 20w multicolored 5.00 2.25
a. Souv. sheet of 1, imperf. 4.75 4.75

3rd Korean Boy Scout Jamboree, Hwarangdae, Seoul, Aug. 10-15.

Types of 1962-66 Redrawn (Inscribed "Republic of Korea")

Designs: 20w, Meesun blossoms and fruit. 40w, Library of early Buddhist scriptures. 50w, Deer.

1967, Aug. 25 Granite Paper

582 A186c 20w green & lt bl grn 77.50 2.00
583 A186d 40w dk grn & lt ol 45.00 2.00
584 A186e 50w dk brn & bister 8.50 1.50
Nos. 582-584 (3) 131.00 5.50

The printing of redrawn designs of the regular issue of 1962-66 became necessary upon discovery of large quantities of counterfeits, made to defraud the post. The position of the denominations was changed and elaborate fine background tracings were added.

Freedom Center and Emblem A286

Hand Breaking Chain A287

1967, Sept. 25 Litho. *Perf. 12½*

586 A286 5w multicolored 1.45 .65
a. Souv. sheet of 1, imperf. 4.75 4.75
587 A287 7w multicolored 1.60 .65
a. Souv. sheet of 1, imperf. 4.75 4.75

1st Conf. of the World Anti-Communist League, WACL, Taipei, China, Sept. 25-29.

Boxing — A288

Design: 7w, Women's basketball.

1967, Oct. 5

588 A288 5w tan & multi 2.25 .70
589 A288 7w pale rose & multi 3.25 .70

48th Natl. Athletic Meet, Seoul, Oct. 5-10.

Students' Memorial, Kwangjoo — A289

1967, Nov. 3 Litho. *Perf. 12½*

590 A289 7w lt green & multi 1.50 .50

Issued for Student Day commemorating 1929 students' uprising against Japan.

Symbolic Water Cycle — A290

1967, Nov. 20

591 A290 7w multicolored 1.50 .60

Hydrological Decade (UNESCO), 1965-74.

Children Spinning Top A291

Monkey and Oriental Zodiac A292

1967, Dec. 10

592 A291 5w sal, org & vio bl 3.00 .75
a. Souv. sheet of 1, imperf. 3.75 3.75
593 A292 7w yel bis, brn & vio bl 3.75 .75
a. Souv. sheet of 1, imperf. 3.75 3.75

Issued for Christmas and New Year.

Parabolic Antenna and Electric Waves — A293

1967, Dec. 21

594 A293 7w lt bl, blk & yel 1.50 .70
a. Souv. sheet of 1, imperf. 3.75 3.75

Opening of the natl. microwave communications network, Dec. 21.

Carving from King Songdok Bell — A294

Earrings, 6th Cent. A295

Flag A296

Perf. 13x12½

1968, Feb. 1 Litho. Unwmk.

Granite Paper

595 A294 1w yellow & brown .80 .25
596 A295 5w dk green & yellow 3.25 .55
597 A296 7w dark blue & red 1.50 .55
Nos. 595-597 (3) 5.55 1.35

WHO, 20th Anniv. — A297

1968, Apr. 7 Unwmk. *Perf. 12½*

598 A297 7w multicolored 1.50 .60
a. Souv. sheet of 1, imperf. 3.75 3.75

EATA Emblem and Korean Buildings — A298

1968, Apr. 9 Litho.

599 A298 7w multicolored 1.50 .60
a. Souv. sheet of 1, imperf. 4.25 4.25

2nd General Meeting of the East Asia Travel Association (EATA), Seoul, Apr. 9-13.

Door Knocker, Factories and Emblem — A299

1968, May 6 Unwmk. *Perf. 12½*

600 A299 7w multicolored 1.50 .60
a. Souv. sheet of 1, imperf. 4.00 4.00

2nd Conf. of the Confederation of Asian Chambers of Commerce and Industry, Seoul.

Pres. Park and Emperor Haile Selassie — A300

1968, May 18 Litho.

601 A300 7w multicolored 3.75 1.40
a. Souv. sheet of 1, imperf. 7.25 7.25

Visit of Haile Selassie I, May 18-20.

Mailman's Pouch — A301

Mailman — A302

1968, May 31 Unwmk. *Perf. 12½*

602 A301 5w multicolored 1.50 .70
603 A302 7w multicolored 1.50 .70

First Postman's Day, May 31, 1968.

Atom Diagram and Symbols of Development A303

1968, June 1 Litho.

604 A303 7w dk bl, citron & ver 1.50 .60

Issued to promote science and technology.

Kyung Hee University and Conference Emblem — A304

1968, June 18 Unwmk.

605 A304 7w bl, pink & blk 1.50 .50
a. Souv. sheet of 1, imperf. 5.00 5.00

2nd Conf. of the Intl. Association of University Presidents.

Liberated People — A305

1968, July 1 Litho. *Perf. 12½*

606 A305 7w multicolored 1.50 .60

Issued to publicize the movement to liberate people under communist rule.

Peacock and Industrial Plant — A306

1968, Aug. 15 Unwmk. *Perf. 12½*

607 A306 7w multicolored 1.50 .60

Republic of Korea, 20th anniversary.

Fair Entrance — A307

1968, Sept. 9 Unwmk. ***Perf. 12½***

608 A307 7w lilac & multi 1.50 .60

Issued to publicize the first Korean Trade Fair, Seoul, Sept. 9-Oct. 18.

Assembly Emblem and Pills — A308

1968, Sept. 16 Litho.

609 A308 7w multicolored 1.50 .60

3rd General Assembly of the Federation of Asian Pharmaceutical Associations, Seoul, Sept. 16-21.

Soldier, Insigne and Battle Scene — A309

No. 611, Sailor, insigne & ship's guns. No. 612, Servicemen & flags. No. 613, Aviator, insigne & planes. No. 614, Marine, insigne & landing group.

1968, Oct. 1

610	A309 7w green & org	7.50	2.00
611	A309 7w lt & dk blue	7.50	2.00
612	A309 7w dk blue & org	7.50	2.00
613	A309 7w dk & lt blue	7.50	2.00
614	A309 7w orange & grn	7.50	2.00
a.	Vert. strip of 5, #610-614	42.50	14.00

20th anniv. of the Korean armed forces.

Colombo Plan Emblem and Globe — A310

1968, Oct. 8 Litho. ***Perf. 12½***

615 A310 7w dk brn, pale sal & grn 1.50 .60

19th meeting of the Consultative Committee of the Colombo Plan, Seoul, Oct. 8-28.

Bicycling (Type I) — A311

Type II — (2nd line flush left)

No. 617, Bicycling, Type II. No. 618-619, Wrestling. No. 620-621, Boxing. No. 622-623, Olympic flame, "68" & symbols of various sports events.

1968, Oct. 12 Unwmk. ***Perf. 12½***

616	A311 7w pink & multi (I)	14.00	4.25
617	A311 7w pink & multi (II)	14.00	4.25
a.	Souv. sheet of 2, #616-617, imperf.	10.50	10.50
b.	Pair, #616-617	35.00	35.00
618	A311 7w olive & multi (I)	14.00	12.00
619	A311 7w olive & multi (II)	14.00	12.00
a.	Souv. sheet of 2, #618-619, imperf.	10.50	10.50
b.	Pair, #618-619	35.00	35.00
620	A311 7w orange & multi (I)	14.00	12.00
621	A311 7w orange & multi (II)	14.00	12.00
a.	Souv. sheet of 2, #620-621, imperf.	10.50	10.50
b.	Pair, #620-621	35.00	35.00
622	A311 7w bluish grn & multi (I)	14.00	12.00
623	A311 7w bluish grn & multi (II)	14.00	12.00
a.	Souv. sheet of 2, #622-623, imperf.	10.50	10.50
b.	Pair, #622-623	35.00	35.00
	Nos. 616-623 (8)	112.00	80.50

19th Olympic Games, Mexico City, 10/12-27.

The position of the "7" is reversed on Nos. 619, 621, 623 as are the designs of Nos. 619, 621.

"Search for Knowledge" and School Girls — A312

1968, Oct. 15

624 A312 7w multicolored 1.50 .60

60th anniv. of public secondary education for women.

Coin and Statistics — A313

1968, Nov. 1

625 A313 7w multicolored 1.50 .50

National Wealth Survey.

Memorial to Students' Uprising — A314

1968, Nov. 23

626 A314 7w gray & multi 1.90 .65

Issued to commemorate the anti-communist students' uprising, Nov. 23, 1945.

Men With Banners Declaring Human Rights — A315

1968, Dec. 10

627 A315 7w multicolored 1.50 .60

Declaration of Human Rights, 20th anniv.

Christmas Decorations A316

Cock and Good Luck Characters A317

1968, Dec. 11

628	A316 5w salmon & multi	8.75	1.00
a.	Souv. sheet of 1, imperf.	7.25	7.25
629	A317 7w multicolored	9.50	1.00
a.	Souv. sheet of 1, imperf.	7.25	7.25

Issued for Christmas and the New Year.

UN Emblems and Korean House — A318

1968, Dec. 12

630 A318 7w lt blue & multi 1.50 .60

20th anniv. of the recognition of the Republic of Korea by the UN.

Regional Boy Scout Conf. — A319

Design: Boy Scout Emblem.

1968, Sept. 30 Litho. ***Perf. 12½***

631 A319 7w black & multi 2.10 .75

Sam-il Movement, 50th Anniv. — A320

Design: Torch, map and students Demonstrating against Japan, 1919.

1969, Mar. 1 Unwmk. ***Perf. 12½***

632 A320 7w multicolored 1.50 .60

Hyun Choong Sa Shrine and Tortoise Ships — A321

1969, Apr. 28 Unwmk. ***Perf. 12½***

633 A321 7w deep bl, grn & brn 1.50 .60

Completion of the Hyun Choong Sa Shrine at Onyang, dedicated to the memory of Adm. Li Sun-sin.

Pres. Park and Tuanku Nasiruddin of Malaysia — A322

1969, Apr. 29 Litho.

634	A322 7w yellow & multi	3.50	1.20
a.	Souv. sheet of 1, imperf.	*57.50*	*57.50*

Visit of Tuanku Ismail Nasiruddin, ruler of Malaysia, Apr. 29, 1969.

Hanabusaya Asiatica — A323

Old Man's Mask — A323a

Stone Lamp, 8th Cent. — A323b

Chipmunk — A323c

Flag of Korea — A324

Flag of Korea — A324a

Ancient Drums — A325

Flag of Korea — A325a

Red-crested Cranes — A326

Tiger Lily — A326a

Highway and Farm A327

Pitcher (12-13th Centuries) A328

Ceramic Duck (Water Jar) — A329

Bee — A329a

Library of Early Buddhist Scriptures A330

Vase, Yi dynasty (17th-18th Centuries) A331

Miruk Bosal A332

Gold Crown, Silla Dynasty A333

Granite Paper (Lithographed); Ordinary Paper (Photogravure)

Perf. 13x12, 12x13 (Litho.); 13½x12½, 12½x13½ (Photo.)

Litho. (40ch, Nos. 641, 650); Photo.

1969-74 Unwmk.

635	A323	40ch green	1.20	.35
636	A323a	1w dk rose brn ('74)	.40	.25
637	A323b	5w brt plum	2.00	.25
638	A323c	5w brn red ('74)	.35	.25
639	A324	7w blue ("7.00")	3.50	.50
640	A324a	7w brt blue ("7")	2.00	.30
641	A325	10w ultra	30.00	1.00
642	A325a	10w dk blue ("10") ('70)	2.00	.25
643	A326	10w bl & dk bl ('73)	1.15	.35
644	A326a	10w grn & multi ('73)	.90	.25
645	A327	10w grn, red & gray ('73)	.70	.25
647	A328	20w green	1.75	.50
648	A329	30w dull grn ('70)	6.75	.70
649	A329a	30w yel & dk brn ('74)	.65	.25
650	A330	40w vio bl & pink	42.50	1.90
651	A331	40w ultra & lilac	1.75	.70
652	A332	100w dp claret & yel	75.00	1.90
653	A333	100w brn & yel ('74)	37.50	2.40
		Nos. 635-653 (18)	210.10	12.35

See No. 1090. For surcharge see No. B18. Counterfeits exist of No. 653.

Red Cross, Faces and Doves — A336

1969, May 5 Litho. *Perf. 12½*

654	A336	7w multicolored	1.75	.45
a.		Souv. sheet of 1, imperf.	5.00	5.00

50th anniv. of the League of Red Cross Societies.

Savings Bank, Factories and Highway — A337

1969, May 20 Unwmk. *Perf. 12½*

655	A337	7w yellow grn & multi	1.50	.60

Second Economy Drive.

Pres. Park, Pres. Thieu and Flags of Korea and Viet Nam — A338

1969, May 27 Litho.

656	A338	7w pink & multi	3.00	1.15
a.		Souv. sheet of 1, imperf.	7.75	7.75

Visit of Pres. Nguyen Van Thieu of Viet Nam, May 27.

"Reforestation and Parched Fields" A339

Growing and Withering Plants A340

1969, June 10

657	A339	7w multicolored	1.50	.50
658	A340	7w multicolored	1.50	.50

Issued to publicize the need for prevention of damages from floods and droughts.

Apollo 11, Separation of Second Stage — A341

No. 660, Apollo 11, separation of 3rd Stage. No. 661, Orbits of command & landing modules around moon. No. 662, Astronauts gathering rock samples on moon. 40w, Spacecraft splashdown.

1969, Aug. 15 Unwmk. *Perf. 12½*

659	A341	10w indigo, bl & red	3.50	1.30
660	A341	10w indigo, bl & red	3.50	1.30
661	A341	20w indigo, bl, red & lem	3.50	1.30
662	A341	20w indigo, bl, red & lem	3.50	1.30
663	A341	40w indigo, bl & red	3.50	1.30
a.		Souv. sheet of 5, #659-663, imperf.	33.00	33.00
b.		Strip of 5, #659-663	20.00	13.50

Man's 1st landing on the moon, July 20, 1969. US astronauts Neil A. Armstrong and Col. Edwin E. Aldrin, Jr., with Lieut. Col. Michael Collins piloting Apollo 11.

Fable Issue

Girl and Stepmother A342

Kongji and Patji (Cinderella): 7w, Sparrows help Kongji separate rice. 10w, Ox helps Kongji to weed a field. 20w, Kongji in a sedan chair on the way to the palace.

1969, Sept. 1 Litho. *Perf. 12½*

664	A342	5w apple grn & multi	3.75	1.10
665	A342	7w yellow & multi	3.75	1.10
666	A342	10w lt violet & multi	6.25	1.20
667	A342	20w lt green & multi	6.25	1.20

The Sick Princess — A343

"The Hare's Liver": 7w, Hare riding to the palace on back of turtle. 10w, Hare telling a lie to the King to save his life. 20w, Hare mocking the turtle.

1969, Nov. 1 *Perf. 13x12½*

668	A343	5w yellow & multi	2.00	.85
669	A343	7w lt vio & multi	2.00	.85
670	A343	10w lt grnsh bl & multi	2.00	.95
671	A343	20w lt yel grn & multi	3.75	.95

Mother Meeting Tiger — A344

"The Sun and the Moon": 7w, Tiger disguised as mother at children's house. 10w, Tiger, and children on tree. 20w, Children safe on cloud, and tiger falling to his death.

1970, Jan. 5

672	A344	5w orange & multi	2.00	.65
673	A344	7w gray grn & multi	2.00	.65
674	A344	10w lt green & multi	2.00	.80
675	A344	20w gray & multi	4.00	.80

Woodcutter Stealing Fairy's Clothes — A345

Designs: No. 677, Woodcutter with wife and children. No. 678, Wife taking children to heaven. No. 679, Husband joining family in heaven.

1970, Mar. 5

676	A345	10w dull bl grn & multi	2.40	.95
677	A345	10w buff & multi	2.40	.95
678	A345	10w lt grnsh bl & multi	2.40	.95
679	A345	10w pink & multi	2.40	1.10

Heungbu and Wife Release Healed Swallow — A346

Designs: No. 681, Heungbu and wife finding gold treasure in gourd. No. 682, Nolbu and wife with large gourd. No. 683, Demon emerging from gourd punishing evil Nolbu and wife.

1970, May 5 *Perf. 12½*

680	A346	10w lt grnsh bl & multi	6.50	1.20
681	A346	10w org & multi	6.50	1.20
682	A346	10w app grn & multi	6.50	1.20
683	A346	10w tan & multi	6.50	1.20
		Nos. 664-683 (20)	75.35	19.85

Souvenir Sheets of 1, Imperf.

664a	A342	5w	14.50	14.50
665a	A342	7w	14.50	14.50
666a	A342	10w	14.50	14.50
667a	A342	20w	14.50	14.50
668a	A343	5w	4.50	4.50
669a	A343	7w	4.50	4.50
670a	A343	10w	4.50	4.50
671a	A343	20w	4.50	4.50
672a	A344	5w	4.25	4.25
673a	A344	7w	4.25	4.25
674a	A344	10w	4.25	4.25
675a	A344	20w	4.25	4.25
676a	A345	10w	4.25	4.25
677a	A345	10w	4.25	4.25
678a	A345	10w	4.25	4.25
679a	A345	10w	4.25	4.25
680a	A346	10w	13.50	13.50
681a	A346	10w	13.50	13.50
682a	A346	10w	13.50	13.50
683a	A346	10w	13.50	13.50
		Nos. 664a-683a (20)	164.00	164.00

1869 Locomotive and Diesel Train — A347

Early Locomotive — A347a

Perf. 12½

1969, Sept. 18 Litho. Unwmk.

684	A347	7w yellow & multi	1.90	.65
685	A347a	7w green & multi	1.90	.65

70th anniversary of Korean Railroads.

Formation of F-5A Planes — A348

Design: No. 687, F-4D Phantom.

1969, Oct. 1 Photo. *Perf. 13½x13*

686	A348	10w blue, blk & car	4.75	.70

Litho. *Perf. 13x12½*

687	A348	10w multicolored	6.75	.70

20th anniversary of Korean Air Force.

Cha-jun Game — A349

1969, Oct. 3

688	A349	7w ap grn, dk bl & blk	1.20	.40

10th National Festival of Traditional Skills.

Institute of Science and Technology — A350

1969, Oct. 23

689	A350	7w bister, grn & choc	1.20	.40

Completion of the Korean Institute of Science and Technology, Hongnung, Seoul.

Pres. Park and Diori Hamani — A351

1969, Oct. 27

690	A351	7w yel grn & multi	2.10	.90
a.		Souv. sheet of 1, imperf.	12.00	12.00

Visit of Diori Hamani, Pres. of Niger, Oct. 27.

Korean Wrestling — A352

No. 692, Fencing. No. 693, Korean karate (taekwondo). No. 694, Volleyball, vert. No. 695, Soccer, vert.

1969, Oct. 28 *Perf. 13x12½, 12½x13*

691	A352	10w yel grn & multi	2.75	.85
692	A352	10w blue & multi	2.75	.85
693	A352	10w green & multi	2.75	.85
694	A352	10w olive & multi	2.75	.85
695	A352	10w ultra & multi	2.75	.85
		Nos. 691-695 (5)	13.75	4.25

50th Natl. Athletic Meet, Seoul, Oct. 28-Nov. 2.

Allegory of National Education Charter — A353

1969, Dec. 5 Litho. *Perf. 12½x13*

696	A353	7w dull yel & multi	1.20	.35

1st anniv. of the proclamation of the Natl. Education Charter.

Toy Dogs and Lattice Pattern — A354

Candle, Lattice Door and Fence — A355

1969, Dec. 11 Photo. *Perf. 13½*

697	A354	5w green & multi	1.40	.50
698	A355	7w blue & multi	1.40	.75

Issued for New Year 1970.

UPU Monument, Bern, and Korean Woman — A356

1970, Jan. 1 Photo. *Perf. 13x13½*

699	A356	10w multicolored	10.50	3.50

70th anniv. of Korea's admission to the UPU.

Education Year Emblem and Book — A357

1970, Mar. 10 Litho. *Perf. 12½x13*

700	A357	10w pink & multi	6.00	2.25

International Education Year 1970.

EXPO '70 Emblem, Seated Buddha, Korean Pavilion — A358

1970, Mar. 15 *Perf. 13x12½*

701	A358	10w multicolored	6.00	1.45

Issued to publicize EXPO '70 International Exhibition, Osaka, Japan, March 15-Sept. 13.

Korean Youths and 4-H Club Emblem — A359

1970, Mar. 28 *Perf. 12½x13*

702	A359	10w yellow & multi	2.75	.75

Issued to publicize the 15th Korean 4-H Club Central Contest, Suwon, March 28.

Money and Bank Emblem — A360

1970, Apr. 9 Litho. *Perf. 13x12½*

703	A360	10w yellow & multi	1.90	.75

3rd annual Board of Governors' meeting of the Asian Development Bank, Seoul, 4/9-11.

Royal Palanquin A361

1899 Streetcar A362

Historic Means of Transportation: No. 706, Emperor Sunjong's Cadillac, 1903. No. 707, Nieuport biplane, 1922.

Perf. 13x13½, 13½x13

1970, May 20 **Photo.**

704 A361 10w citron & multi 2.50 .85
705 A362 10w yellow & multi 2.50 .85
706 A362 10w ocher & multi 2.50 .85
707 A362 10w aqua & multi 2.50 .85
Nos. 704-707 (4) 10.00 3.40

UPU Headquarters A363

1970, May 30 ***Perf. 13½x13***

708 A363 10w multicolored 1.25 .35

New UPU Headquarters in Bern, Switzerland.

Map, Radar and Satellite A364

1970, June 2 ***Perf. 13x13½***

709 A364 10w sky bl, vio bl & blk 1.90 .75

Issued to commemorate the completion of the Kum San Earth Station of the International Satellite Consortium (INTELSAT).

"PEN" and Manuscript Paper — A365

1970, June 28 **Photo.** ***Perf. 13x13½***

710 A365 10w bl grn, bl & car 1.25 .35

37th Intl. P.E.N. Cong. (Poets, Playwrights, Editors, Essayists and Novelists), Seoul, June 28-July 4.

Seoul-Pusan Expressway — A366

1970, June 30

711 A366 10w multicolored 1.90 .75

Opening of Seoul-Pusan Expressway.

Postal Code Symbol and Number — A367

1970, July 1

712 A367 10w multicolored 1.25 .40

Issued to publicize the introduction of postal zone numbers, July 1, 1970.

Mail Sorting Machine — A368

1970, July 2

713 A368 10w lt vio & multi 1.25 .40
a. Souv. sheet, 2 each #712-713 92.50 92.50

Mechanization of Korean postal system.

Boy and Children's Hall — A369

1970, July 25

714 A369 10w pink & multi 1.25 .40

Paintings Issue

Jongyangsa Temple and Mt. Kumgang, by Chong Son (1676-1759) A370

The Fierce Tiger, by Shim Sa-yung (1707-1769) A371

Paintings: No. 716, Mountains and Rivers, by Yi In-moon (1745-1821). No. 717, Mountains and Rivers in Moonlight, by Kim Doo-ryang (1696-1763).

Perf. 13x13½, 13½x13

1970, Aug. 31 **Photo.**

715 A370 10w blue & multi 2.25 .75
716 A370 10w buff & multi 2.25 .75
717 A371 10w multicolored 2.25 .75

1970, Oct. 30

Paintings: No. 719, Cats and Sparrows, by Pyun Sang-byuk (18th century). No. 720, Dog with puppies, by Yi Am (1499-?).

718 A371 30w multicolored 8.75 1.60
719 A371 30w multicolored 8.75 1.60
720 A371 30w multicolored 8.75 1.60

Nos. 718-720 exist imperf. Value, set $50.

1970, Dec. 30

Paintings: No. 721, Cliff and Boat, by Kim Hong-do (1745-?). No. 722, Cock, Hens and Chick, by Pyun Sang-byuk (early 18th century). No. 723, Woman Playing Flute, by Shin Yun-bok (late 18th century).

721 A371 10w yel brn, blk & red 2.25 .75
722 A371 10w pale rose, blk & grn 2.25 .75
723 A371 10w multicolored 2.25 .75
Nos. 715-723 (9) 39.75 9.30

Souvenir Sheets of 2

715a	A370	10w		5.00	5.00
716a	A370	10w		5.00	5.00
717a	A371	10w		5.00	5.00
718a	A371	30w	Imperf	31.00	31.00
719a	A371	30w	Imperf	31.00	31.00
720a	A371	30w	Imperf	31.00	31.00
721a	A371	10w		8.00	8.00
722a	A371	10w		8.00	8.00
723a	A371	10w		8.00	8.00
Nos. 715a-723a (9)				132.00	132.00

Nos. 715a-717a have simulated perforations. Background color of stamps on No. 717a is yellow instead of greenish gray as on No. 717.

Nos. 718a-720a exist perf, twice the imperf values.

Nos. 721a-723a exist imperf. Value, each $3.50.

P.T.T.I. Emblem and Map of Far East — A372

1970, Sept. 6 **Litho.** ***Perf. 13x12½***

724 A372 10w lt yel grn, bl & dk bl 1.60 .50

Opening of the Councillors' Meeting of the Asian Chapter of the Postal, Telegraph and Telephone Intl. Org., Sept. 6-12.

Korean WAC and Emblem — A373

1970, Sept. 6 **Photo.** ***Perf. 13x13½***

725 A373 10w blue & multi 1.60 .50

20th anniv. of the founding of the Korean Women's Army Corps.

Pres. Park, Korean Flag and Means of Transportation — A374

Pres. Park, Highways, Factories — A375

1970 ***Perf. 13x13½, 13½x13***

726 A374 10w vio bl, blk & car 8.25 3.00
727 A375 10w dk bl, grnsh bl & blk 13.50 3.00

Presidents Park and Hernandez, Flags of Korea, Salvador — A376

1970, Sept. 28 **Litho.** ***Perf. 13x12½***

728 A376 10w dk bl, red & blk 3.00 1.45
a. Souv. sheet of 1, imperf. 82.50 82.50

Visit of Gen. Fidel Sanchez Hernandez, President of El Salvador.

The first printing of 30,000 of No. 728a spelled "Salvadol." Second printing, also 30,000, corrected the error. Value is for first printing. Value, 2nd printing $7.50, unused or used.

People and Houses — A377

1970, Oct. 1 **Litho.** ***Perf. 13x12½***

729 A377 10w lilac & multi 1.35 1.15

Natl. census of population & housing, Oct. 1.

Diver — A378

1970, Oct. 6 **Photo.** ***Perf. 12½x13½***

730 A378 10w shown 4.25 .95
a. Souv. sheet of 2, imperf. 9.25 9.25
731 A378 10w Field hockey 4.25 .95
a. Souv. sheet of 2, imperf. 9.25 9.25
732 A378 10w Baseball 4.25 .95
a. Souv. sheet of 2, imperf. 9.25 9.25
Nos. 730-732 (3) 12.75 2.85
Nos. 730a-732a (3) 27.75

51st Natl. Athletic Games, Seoul, Oct. 6-11.

Police Emblem and Activities — A379

1970, Oct. 21 **Litho.** ***Perf. 12½***

733 A379 10w ultra & multi 1.50 .55

The 25th Policemen's Day.

Freedom Bell, UN Emblem over Globe — A380

1970, Oct. 24 **Photo.** ***Perf. 13x13½***

734 A380 10w blue & multi 1.60 .55

25th anniversary of United Nations.

Kite and Holly A380a

Boar A381

1970, Dec. 1 **Litho.** ***Perf. 13***

735 A380a 10w lt blue & multi 1.45 .60
a. Souvenir sheet of 3 7.00 7.00
736 A381 10w green & multi 1.45 .60
a. Souvenir sheet of 3 7.00 7.00

New Year 1971.

Pres. Park Quotation, Globe and Telecommunications Emblems — A382

1970, Dec. 4 **Photo.**

737 A382 10w multicolored 1.60 .55

For the 15th Communications Day.

Power Dam A383

Crate Wrapped in World Map, & Ships — A383a

Irrigation Project & Farm — A383b

Coal Mining — A384

Cement Factory — A384a

Fertilizer Factory — A384b

Increased National Income (Scales) — A384c

Increased Savings (factories, bee & coins) — A384d

Highway Intersection — A385

1971 ***Perf. 13x13½, 13½x13***

738 A383 10w blue & multi 2.25 .55
739 A383a 10w pale lil & multi 2.25 .55
740 A383b 10w green & multi 2.25 .55
741 A384 10w bl grn, lt bl & blk 1.25 .45
742 A384a 10w lt bl, vio & brt mag 1.25 .45
743 A384b 10w vio, grn & bis 1.25 .45
744 A384c 10w pink & multi 1.40 .65
745 A384d 10w lt bl grn & multi 1.40 .65
746 A385 10w violet & multi 1.40 .65
Nos. 738-746 (9) 14.70 4.95

Economic Development.

Souvenir Sheets of 1, Imperf.

738a A383 10w 6.50 6.50
739a A383a 10w 6.50 6.50
740a A383b 10w 6.50 6.50

Souvenir Sheets of 2, Imperf.

741a A384 10w 6.50 6.50
742a A384a 10w 6.50 6.50
743a A384b 10w 6.50 6.50
744a A384c 10w 4.75 4.75
745a A384d 10w 4.75 4.75
746a A385 10w 4.75 4.75
Nos. 738a-746a (9) 53.25 53.25

No. 739a exists without date. Value $40.

Torch, Globe and Spider — A386

1971, Mar. 1 **Litho.** ***Perf. 12½x13***

747 A386 10w gray & multi 1.60 .45

March, the month for anti-espionage and victory over communism.

Reservist, Reserve Forces Emblem — A387

1971, Apr. 3 **Photo.** ***Perf. 13½x13***

748 A387 10w lt ultra & multi 1.60 .45

Home Reserve Forces Day, Apr. 3.

WHO Emblem, Stethoscope, Microscope — A388

1971, Apr. 7

749 A388 10w lt bl, pur & yel 1.60 .50

20th World Health Day, Apr. 7.

Subway Tunnel and Train — A389

1971, Apr. 12 **Litho.** ***Perf. 12½x13***

750 A389 10w multicolored 1.60 .45

Seoul subway construction start.

First Asian Soccer Games, Seoul, May 2-13 — A390

1971, May 2

751 A390 10w grn, dk brn & blk 1.90 .60

Veterans Flag and Veterans — A391

1971, May 8 **Photo.** ***Perf. 13x13½***

752 A391 10w ultra & multi 1.45 .45

20th Korean Veterans Day.

Girl Scouts and Emblem — A392

1971, May 10

753 A392 10w lilac & multi 1.50 .45

25th anniversary of the Korean Federation of Girl Scouts.

Torch and Development — A393

1971, May 16

754 A393 10w lt blue & multi 1.45 .45

10th anniversary of May 16th revolution.

"Telecommunication" A394

1971, May 17

755 A394 10w blue & multi 1.45 .45

3rd World Telecommunications Day.

UN Organizations A395

Korean Flag A396

No. 756, ILO. No. 757, FAO. No. 758, General Assembly (UN Headquarters). No. 759, UNESCO. No. 760, WHO. No. 761, World Bank. No. 762, Intl. Development Association (IDA). No. 763, Security Council. No. 764, Intl. Finance Corp. (IFC). No. 765, Intl. Monetary Fund. No. 766, ICAO. No. 767, Economic and Social Council. No. 768, Korean Flag. No. 769, Trusteeship Council. No. 770, UPU. No. 771, ITU. No. 772, World Meteorological Org. (WMO). No. 773, Intl. Court of Justice. No. 774, Intl. Maritime Consultative Org. No. 775, UNICEF. No. 776, Intl. Atomic Energy Agency. No. 777, UN Industrial Development Org. No. 778, UN Commission for the Unification and Rehabilitation of Korea. No. 779, UN Development Program. No. 780, UN Conf. on Trade and Development.

1971, May 30 ***Perf. 13½x13***

756 A395 10w grn, blk & pink 3.75 1.15
757 A395 10w pink, blk & bl 3.75 1.15
758 A395 10w bl, blk, grn & pink 3.75 1.15
759 A395 10w pink, blk & bl 3.75 1.15
760 A395 10w grn, blk & pink 3.75 1.15
761 A395 10w pink, blk & bl 3.75 1.15
762 A395 10w blue, blk & pink 3.75 1.15
763 A395 10w grn, blk & pink 3.75 1.15
764 A395 10w blue, blk & pink 3.75 1.15
765 A395 10w pink, blk & bl 3.75 1.15
766 A395 10w blue, blk & pink 3.75 1.15
767 A395 10w grn, blk & pink 3.75 1.15
768 A396 10w blue, blk & pink 3.75 1.15
769 A395 10w grn, blk & pink 3.75 1.15
770 A395 10w blue, blk & pink 3.75 1.15
771 A395 10w pink, blk & bl 3.75 1.15
772 A395 10w blue, blk & pink 3.75 1.15
773 A395 10w grn, blk & pink 3.75 1.15
774 A395 10w blue, blk & pink 3.75 1.15
775 A395 10w pink, blk & bl 3.75 1.15
776 A395 10w grn, blk & pink 3.75 1.15
777 A395 10w pink, blk & bl 3.75 1.15
778 A395 10w blue, blk & pink 3.75 1.15
779 A395 10w pink, blk & bl 3.75 1.15
780 A395 10w grn, blk & pink 3.75 1.15
Nos. 756-780 (25) 93.75 28.75

Sheet of 50 incorporates 2 each of Nos. 756-780.

Boat Ride, by Shin Yun-bok A397

Man and Boy under Pine Tree — A398

Paintings by Shin Yun-bok: No. 782, Greeting travelers. No. 783, Sword dance. No. 784, Lady traveling with servants. No. 785, Man and woman on the road.

Perf. 13x13½, 13½x13

1971, June 20 **Photo.**

781 A397 10w multicolored 6.25 1.90
782 A397 10w multicolored 6.25 1.90
783 A397 10w multicolored 6.25 1.90
784 A397 10w multicolored 6.25 1.90
785 A397 10w multicolored 6.25 1.90
b. Vert. strip of 5, #781-785 40.00 40.00
786 A398 10w multicolored 6.00 1.90
Nos. 781-786 (6) 37.25 11.40

Souvenir Sheets of 2

781a A397 10w 11.50 11.50
782a A397 10w 11.50 11.50
783a A397 10w 11.50 11.50
784a A397 10w 11.50 11.50
785a A397 10w 11.50 11.50
786a A398 10w 11.50 11.50
Nos. 781a-786a (6) 69.00 69.00

Types A397-A398 with Inscription at Left

Paintings: No. 787, Farmyard scene, by Kim Deuk-shin. No. 788, Family living in valley, by Lee Chae-kwan. No. 789, Man reading book under pine tree, by Lee Chae-kwan.

1971, July 20

787 A397 10w pale grn & multi 3.25 1.60
788 A398 10w pale grn & multi 3.25 1.60
789 A398 10w lt yel grn & multi 3.25 1.60
Nos. 787-789 (3) 9.75 4.80

Souvenir Sheets of 2

787a A397 10w 8.75 8.75
788a A398 10w 8.75 8.75
789a A398 10w 8.75 8.75
Nos. 787a-789a (3) 26.25 26.25

Teacher and Students, by Kim Hong-do — A399

Paintings by Kim Hong-do (Yi Dynasty): No. 791, Wrestlers. No. 792, Dancer and musicians. No. 793, Weavers. No. 794, At the Well.

1971, Aug. 20 ***Perf. 13½x13***

790 A399 10w blk, lt grn & rose 5.50 2.75
791 A399 10w blk, lt grn & rose 5.50 2.75
792 A399 10w blk, lt grn & rose 5.50 2.75
793 A399 10w blk, lt grn & rose 5.50 2.75
794 A399 10w blk, lt grn & rose 5.50 2.75
b. Horiz. strip of 5, #790-794 33.00 33.00

Souvenir Sheets of 2

790a A399 10w 11.50 11.50
791a A399 10w 11.50 11.50
792a A399 10w 11.50 11.50
793a A399 10w 11.50 11.50
794a A399 10w 11.50 11.50
Nos. 790a-794a (5) 57.50 57.50

Pres. Park, Highway and Phoenix — A400

1971, July 1 ***Perf. 13½x13***

795 A400 10w grn, blk & org 20.00 3.00
a. Souvenir sheet of 2 70.00 70.00

Inauguration of President Park Chung Hee for a third term, July 1.

Campfire and Tents — A401

1971, Aug. 2 **Photo.** ***Perf. 13x13½***

796 A401 10w blue grn & multi 1.60 .35

13th Boy Scout World Jamboree, Asagiri Plain, Japan, Aug. 2-10.

Symbol of Conference — A402

1971, Sept. 27 ***Perf. 13***

797 A402 10w multicolored 1.25 .45
a. Souvenir sheet of 2 45.00 45.00

Asian Labor Ministers' Conference, Seoul, Sept. 27-30.

Archers A403

1971, Oct. 8 **Photo.** ***Perf. 13x13½***

798 A403 10w shown 2.00 .70
a. Souvenir sheet of 3 *32.00* 32.00
799 A403 10w Judo 2.00 .70
a. Souvenir sheet of 3 *32.00* 32.00

52nd National Athletic Meet.

Taeguk on Palette — A404

1971, Oct. 11 ***Perf. 13½x13***

800 A404 10w yellow & multi 1.25 .50

20th National Fine Arts Exhibition.

Physician, Globe and Emblem — A405

1971, Oct. 13

801 A405 10w multicolored 1.25 .50

7th Congress of the Confederation of Medical Associations in Asia and Oceania.

Symbols of Contest Events — A406

1971, Oct. 20 Photo. ***Perf. 13x13½***

802 A406 10w multicolored 1.25 .50
a. Souvenir sheet of 2 37.50 37.50

2nd National Skill Contest for High School Students.

Slide Caliper and KS Emblem — A407

1971, Nov. 11 ***Perf. 13x13½***

803 A407 10w multicolored 1.25 .50

10th anniversary of industrial standardization in Korea.

Rats A408

Japanese Crane A409

1971, Dec. 1

804 A408 10w multicolored 1.60 .35
a. Souvenir sheet of 3 23.00 23.00
805 A409 10w multicolored 1.60 .35
a. Souvenir sheet of 3 23.00 23.00

New Year 1972.

Emblem of Hangul Hakhoe and Hangul Letters — A410

1971, Dec. 3 **Photo.**

806 A410 10w dk blue & multi 1.25 .30

50th anniversary of Korean Language Research Society (Hangul Hakhoe).

Red Cross Headquarters and Map of Korea — A411

1971, Dec. 31 ***Perf. 13½x13***

807 A411 10w multicolored 1.75 .55
a. Souvenir sheet of 2 11.50 11.50

First South and North Korean Red Cross Conference, Panmunjom, Aug. 20, 1971.

Globe and Book — A412

1972, Jan. 5 ***Perf. 13x13½***

808 A412 10w multicolored 1.10 .35
a. Souvenir sheet of 2 11.50 11.50

International Book Year 1972.

Intelsat 4 Sending Signals to Korea — A413

1972, Jan. 31 ***Perf. 13½x13***

809 A413 10w dk blue & multi 1.10 .35

Korea's entry into ITU, 20th anniv.

Figure Skating, Sapporo '72 Emblem — A414

Design: No. 811, Speed skating.

1972, Feb. 3 ***Perf. 13x13½***

810 A414 10w lt & dk bl & car 1.60 .55
811 A414 10w lt & dk bl & car 1.60 .55
a. Souvenir sheet of 2, #810-811 11.50 11.50

11th Winter Olympic Games, Sapporo, Japan, Feb. 3-13.

Map of Korea with Forest Sites — A415

1972, Mar. 10 Photo. ***Perf. 13x13***

812 A415 10w buff, bl grn & red 1.20 .35

Publicity for forests planted to mark hope for re-unification of Korea.

Junior Chamber of Commerce Emblem and Beetles — A416

1972, Mar. 19 ***Perf. 13½x13***

813 A416 10w pink & multi 1.20 .35

Junior Chamber of Commerce, 20th anniversary.

UN Emblem, Agriculture and Industry — A417

1972, Mar. 28 ***Perf. 13x13½***

814 A417 10w violet, grn & car 1.20 .35

Economic Commission for Asia and the Far East (ECAFE), 25th anniversary.

Flags — A418

1972, Apr. 1 ***Perf. 13½x13***

815 A418 10w blue & multi 1.20 .35

Asian-Oceanic Postal Union, 10th anniv.

Homeland Reserve Forces Flag — A419

1972, Apr. 1 Photo. ***Perf. 13x13½***

816 A419 10w yellow & multi 1.45 .40

Homeland Reserve Forces Day, Apr. 1.

YWCA Emblem, Butterflies — A420

1972, Apr. 20

817 A420 10w violet & multi 1.50 .40

50th anniv. of the YWCA of Korea.

Community Projects — A421

1972, May 1 ***Perf. 13x13½***

818 A421 10w pink & multi 1.20 .40

Rural rehabilitation and construction movement.

Korean Flag & Inscription — A422

1972, May 1

819 A422 10w green & multi 1.20 .40

Anti-espionage and victory over communism month.

Children with Balloons — A423

1972, May 5 ***Perf. 13½x13***

820 A423 10w yellow & multi 1.20 .40

Children's Day, May 5.

King Munyong's Gold Earrings — A424

Design: No. 822, Gold ornament from King's crown, vert.

1972, May 10 ***Perf. 13½x13, 13x13½***

821 A424 10w green & multi 1.30 .40
822 A424 10w green & multi 1.30 .40

National treasures from tomb of King Munyong of Paekche, who reigned 501-523.

Kojo Island — A425

National parks: No. 823, Crater Lake.

1972, May 30 ***Perf. 13½x13***

823 A425 10w blue grn & multi 3.25 .40
824 A425 10w green & multi 3.25 .40

UN Conference on Human Environment, Stockholm, June 5-16 — A426

10w, Daisy, environment emblem.

1972, May 30 Litho. ***Perf. 13x13½***

825 A426 10w multicolored 1.20 .35
a. Souvenir sheet of 2 7.75 7.75

7th Meeting of Asian-Pacific Council (ASPAC) — A427

10w, Gwanghwa Gate, flags of participants.

1972, June 14

826 A427 10w multicolored 1.20 .35

Third Five-Year Plan Issue

Farm and Fish Hatchery — A428

No. 828, Steel industry and products. No. 829, Globe and cargo.

1972, July 1 Photo. ***Perf. 13½x13***

827 A428 10w shown 1.90 .50
828 A428 10w multicolored 1.90 .50
829 A428 10w multicolored 1.90 .50
Nos. 827-829 (3) 5.70 1.50

3rd Economic Development Five-Year Plan.

Weight Lifting — A429

1972, Aug. 26 Photo. ***Perf. 13x13½***

830 A429 20w shown 1.20 .45
831 A429 20w Judo 1.20 .45
a. Souvenir sheet of 2, #830-831 5.75 5.75
b. Pair, #830-831 5.00 2.50
832 A429 20w Boxing 1.20 .45
833 A429 20w Wrestling 1.20 .45
a. Souvenir sheet of 2, #832-833 6.00 6.00
b. Pair, #832-833 5.00 2.50
Nos. 830-833 (4) 4.80 1.80

20th Olympic Games, Munich, Aug. 26-Sept. 11. Nos. 831b, 833b each printed checkerwise.

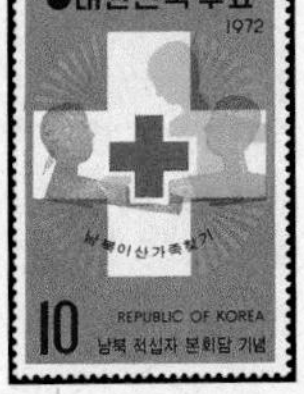

Families Reunited by Red Cross — A430

1972, Aug. 30 Photo. ***Perf. 13½x13***

834 A430 10w lt blue & multi 1.90 .60
a. Souvenir sheet of 2 24.00 24.00

Plenary meeting of the South-North Red Cross Conference, Pyongyang, Aug. 30, 1972.

Bulkuk-sa Temple, Kyongju Park — A431

Bopju-sa Temple, Mt. Sokri Park — A432

1972, Sept. 20 Photo. ***Perf. 13½x13***

835 A431 10w brown & multi 1.35 .45
836 A432 10w blue & multi 1.35 .45

National parks.

"5" and Conference Emblem — A433

1972, Sept. 25 ***Perf. 13x13½***

837 A433 10w vio blue & multi 1.15 .35

Fifth Asian Judicial Conf., Seoul, 9/25-29.

Lions Emblem, Taeguk Fan — A434

1972, Sept. 28 ***Perf. 13½x13***

838 A434 10w multicolored 1.30 .35

11th Orient and Southeast Asian Lions Convention, Seoul, Sept. 28-30.

Scout Taking Oath, Korean Flag and Scout Emblem — A435

1972, Oct. 5

839 A435 10w yellow & multi 1.90 .45

Boy Scouts of Korea, 50th anniversary.

Children and Ox A436

Children in Balloon A437

1972, Dec. 1 Photo. ***Perf. 13x13½***

840 A436 10w green & multi 1.30 .40
a. Souvenir sheet of 2 4.50 4.50
841 A437 10w blue & multi 1.30 .40
a. Souvenir sheet of 2 4.50 4.50

New Year 1973.

Mt. Naejang Park and Temple — A438

Mt. Sorang and Madeungryong Pass — A439

1972, Dec. 10 ***Perf. 13x13½, 13½x13***

842 A438 10w multicolored 1.35 .40
843 A439 10w multicolored 1.35 .40

National parks.

Pres. Park, Korean Flag and Modern Landscape A440

1972, Dec. 27 ***Perf. 13x13½***

844 A440 10w multicolored 8.50 2.00
a. Souvenir sheet of 2 65.00 65.00

Inauguration of Park Chung Hee for a 4th term as president of Korea.

Tourism Issue

Kyongbok Palace (National Museum) — A441

Mt. Sorak and Kejo-am Temple — A442

1973, Feb. 20 Photo. ***Perf. 13½x13***

845 A441 10w multicolored 1.25 .40
846 A442 10w multicolored 1.25 .40

Palmi Island and Beach A443

Sain-am Rock, Mt. Dokjol A444

1973, Apr. 20 ***Perf. 13x13½***

847 A443 10w multicolored 1.45 .40
848 A444 10w multicolored 1.50 .40

Shrine for Adm. Li Sun-sin A445

Limestone Cavern, Kusan-ni A446

1973, June 20

849 A445 10w multicolored 1.50 .40
850 A446 10w multicolored 1.45 .40

Namhae Bridge — A447

Hongdo Island — A448

1973, Aug. 20 ***Perf. 13½x13***

851 A447 10w multicolored 1.45 .35
852 A448 10w multicolored 1.45 .35

Mt. Mai — A449

Tangerine Orchard, Cheju Island — A450

1973, Oct. 20

853 A449 10w multicolored .90 .25
854 A450 10w multicolored .90 .25
Nos. 845-854 (10) 13.10 3.60

Praying Family — A451

1973, Mar. 1 ***Perf. 13x13½***

855 A451 10w yellow & multi 1.20 .50

Prayer for national unification.

Flags of Korea and South Viet Nam, Victory Sign — A452

1973, Mar. 1

856 A452 10w violet & multi 1.20 .30

Return of Korean Expeditionary Force from South Viet Nam.

Workers, Factory, Cogwheel — A453

1973, Mar. 10 **Unwmk.**

857 A453 10w blue & multi 1.00 .30

10th Labor Day.

Satellite, WMO Emblem — A454

1973, Mar. 23

858 A454 10w blue & multi 1.00 .30
a. Souvenir sheet of 2 5.00 5.00

Cent. of Intl. Meteorological Cooperation.

King's Ceremonial Robe — A455

Traditional Korean Costumes (Yi dynasty): No. 860, Queen's ceremonial dress. No. 861, King's robe. No. 862, Queen's robe. No. 863, Crown Prince. No. 864, Princess. No. 865, Courtier. No. 866, Royal bridal gown. No. 867, Official's wife. No. 868, Military official.

1973 Photo. ***Perf. 13½x13***

859 A455 10w ocher & multi 3.25 .70
860 A455 10w salmon & multi 3.25 .70
861 A455 10w rose lil & multi 3.00 .90
862 A455 10w apple grn & multi 3.00 .90
863 A455 10w lt blue & multi 2.75 .90
864 A455 10w lil rose & multi 2.75 .90
865 A455 10w yellow & multi 1.35 .50
866 A455 10w lt blue & multi 1.50 .90
867 A455 10w ocher & multi 1.50 .90
868 A455 10w lil rose & multi 1.50 .90
Nos. 859-868 (10) 23.85 8.20

Issued: Nos. 859-860, 3/30; Nos. 861-862, 5/30; Nos. 863-864, 7/30; Nos. 865-866, 9/30; Nos. 867-868, 11/30.

Souvenir Sheets of 2

859a A455 10w (#1) 7.00 7.00
860a A455 10w (#2) 7.00 7.00
861a A455 10w (#3) 7.50 7.50
862a A455 10w (#4) 7.50 7.50
863a A455 10w (#5) 7.00 7.00
864a A455 10w (#6) 7.00 7.00
865a A455 10w (#7) 4.25 4.25
866a A455 10w (#8) 4.25 4.25
867a A455 10w (#9) 4.25 4.25
868a A455 10w (#10) 4.25 4.25
Nos. 859a-868a (10) 60.00 60.00

Parenthetical numbers after souvenir sheet listings appear in top marginal inscriptions.

Nurse Holding Lamp — A456

1973, Apr. 1 ***Perf. 13½x13***

869 A456 10w rose & multi 1.15 .30

50th anniv. of Korean Nurses Association.

Homeland Reservists and Flag — A457

1973, Apr. 7 ***Perf. 13x13½***

870 A457 10w yellow & multi 1.35 .30

Homeland Reserve Forces Day on 5th anniversary of their establishment.

Table Tennis Player, and Globe A458

1973, May 23 ***Perf. 13x13½***

871 A458 10w pink & multi 2.25 .65

Victory of Korean women's table tennis team, 32nd Intl. Table Tennis Championships, Sarajevo, Yugoslavia, Apr. 5-15.

World Vision Children's Choir A459

1973, June 25 ***Perf. 13x13½***

872 A459 10w multicolored 1.30 .30

20th anniversary of World Vision International, a Christian service organization.

Converter, Pohang Steel Works — A460

1973, July 3 ***Perf. 13x13½***

873 A460 10w blue & multi .95 .45

Inauguration of Pohang iron and steel plant.

INTERPOL Emblem — A461

1973, Sept. 3 ***Perf. 13½x13***

874 A461 10w lt violet & multi 1.10 .25

50th anniversary of the International Criminal Police Organization (INTERPOL).

Children with Stamp Albums — A462

1973, Oct. 12 *Perf. 13½x13*

875 A462 10w dp grn & multi .85 .30
a. Souvenir sheet of 2 14.50 14.50

Philatelic Week, Oct. 12-18.

Woman Hurdler A463

1973, Oct. 12 *Perf. 12½x13½*

876 A463 10w shown 1.10 .30
877 A463 10w Tennis player 1.10 .30

54th Natl. Athletic Meet, Pusan, Oct. 12-17.

Soyang River Dam, Map Showing Location — A464

1973, Oct. 15 *Perf. 13½x13*

878 A464 10w blue & multi .50 .25

Inauguration of Soyang River Dam and hydroelectric plant.

Fire from Match and Cigarette — A465

1973, Nov. 1 *Perf. 13x13½*

879 A465 10w multicolored .65 .25

10th Fire Prevention Day.

Tiger and Candles A466

Toys A467

1973, Dec. 1 Photo. *Perf. 13x13½*

880 A466 10w emerald & multi .95 .30
a. Souvenir sheet of 2 4.50 4.50
881 A467 10w blue & multi .95 .30
a. Souvenir sheet of 2 4.50 4.50

New Year 1974.

Human Rights Flame, and Head — A468

1973, Dec. 10 *Perf. 13½x13*

882 A468 10w orange & multi .70 .25

25th anniversary of Universal Declaration of Human Rights.

Musical Instruments Issue

Komunko, Six-stringed Zither A469

Design: 30w, Nagak, shell trumpet.

1974, Feb. 20 Photo. *Perf. 13x13½*

883 A469 10w lt bl, blk & brn 1.00 .30
884 A469 30w orange & multi 2.75 .50

1974, Apr. 20

Designs: 10w, Tchouk; wooden hammer in slanted box, used to start orchestra. 30w, Eu; crouching tiger, used to stop orchestra.

885 A469 10w brt blue & multi 1.10 .25
886 A469 30w lt green & multi 2.25 .35

1974, June 20

Designs: 10w, A-chaing, 7-stringed instrument. 30w, Kyobang-ko, drum.

887 A469 10w dull yel & multi 1.30 .25
888 A469 30w salmon pink & multi 2.25 .35

1974, Aug. 20

Designs: 10w, So, 16-pipe ritual instrument. 30w, Kaikeum, 2-stringed fiddle.

889 A469 10w lt blue & multi .80 .30
890 A469 30w brt pink & multi 1.60 .40

1974, Oct. 20

10w, Pak (clappers). 30w, Pyenchong (bell chimes).

891 A469 10w lt lilac & multi .95 .30
892 A469 30w lemon & multi 1.90 .40
Nos. 883-892 (10) 15.90 3.40

Souvenir Sheets of 2

883a	A469	10w	(#1)	4.25	4.25
884a	A469	30w	(#2)	7.25	7.25
885a	A469	10w	(#3)	3.50	3.50
886a	A469	30w	(#4)	5.50	5.50
887a	A469	10w	(#5)	3.50	3.50
888a	A469	30w	(#6)	5.50	5.50
889a	A469	10w	(#7)	2.25	2.25
890a	A469	30w	(#8)	3.75	3.75
891a	A469	10w	(#9)	2.75	2.75
892a	A469	30w	(#10)	5.00	5.00
	Nos. 883a-892a (10)			43.25	43.25

Fruit Issue

Apricots — A470

1974, Mar. 30 Photo. *Perf. 13x13½*

893 A470 10w shown .90 .30
894 A470 30w Strawberries 2.10 .40

1974, May 30

895 A470 10w Peaches .90 .30
896 A470 30w Grapes 2.10 .45

1974, July 30

897 A470 10w Pears .60 .30
898 A470 30w Apples 2.00 .45

1974, Sept. 30

899 A470 10w Cherries .75 .30
900 A470 30w Persimmons 1.90 .45

1974, Nov. 30

901 A470 10w Tangerines .60 .30
902 A470 30w Chestnuts 1.25 .35
Nos. 893-902 (10) 13.10 3.60

Souvenir Sheets of 2

893a	A470	10w	(#1)	3.25	3.25
894a	A470	30w	(#2)	6.75	6.75
895a	A470	10w	(#3)	3.25	3.25
896a	A470	30w	(#4)	6.00	6.00
897a	A470	10w	(#5)	2.75	2.75
898a	A470	30w	(#6)	6.50	6.50
899a	A470	10w	(#7)	2.10	2.10
900a	A470	30w	(#8)	4.25	4.25
901a	A470	10w	(#9)	2.40	2.40
902a	A470	30w	(#10)	3.00	3.00
	Nos. 893a-902a (10)			40.25	40.25

Reservist and Factory — A471

1974, Apr. 6 Photo. *Perf. 13½x13*

903 A471 10w yellow & multi .70 .25

Homeland Reserve Forces Day.

WPY Emblem and Scales — A472

1974, Apr. 10 *Perf. 13x13½*

904 A472 10w salmon & multi .55 .25
a. Souvenir sheet of 2 4.25 4.25

World Population Year 1974.

Train and Communications Emblem — A473

1974, Apr. 22 *Perf. 13½x13*

905 A473 10w multicolored .65 .25

19th Communications Day.

Emblem and Stylized Globe — A474

1974, May 6 Photo. *Perf. 13*

906 A474 10w red lilac & multi .55 .25

22nd Session of Intl. Chamber of Commerce (Eastern Division), Seoul, May 6-8.

New Dock at Inchon — A475

1974, May 10

907 A475 10w yellow & multi .65 .25

Dedication of dock, Inchon.

UNESCO Emblem, "20" and Yin Yang — A476

1974, June 14 Photo. *Perf. 13*

908 A476 10w org yel & multi .55 .25

20th anniversary of the Korean National Commission for UNESCO.

EXPLO '74 Emblems — A477

Design: No. 910, EXPLO emblem rising from map of Korea.

1974, Aug. 13 Photo. *Perf. 13*

909 A477 10w orange & multi .50 .25
910 A477 10w blue & multi .50 .25

EXPLO '74, International Christian Congress, Yoido Islet, Seoul, Aug. 13-18.

Subway, Bus and Plane — A478

1974, Aug. 15

911 A478 10w green & multi .80 .25

Inauguration of Seoul subway (first in Korea), Aug. 15, 1974.

Target Shooting A479

1974, Oct. 8 Photo. *Perf. 13x13½*

912 A479 10w shown .55 .25
913 A479 30w Rowing 1.75 .40

55th National Athletic Meet.

UPU Emblem — A480

1974, Oct. 9 *Perf. 13*

914 A480 10w yellow & multi .45 .25
a. Souvenir sheet of 2 4.50 4.50

Cent. of UPU. See No. C43.

International Landmarks — A481

1974, Oct. 11

915 A481 10w multicolored .55 .25

Intl. People to People Conf., Seoul, 10/11-14.

Korea Nos. 1-2 — A482

1974, Oct. 17

916 A482 10w lilac & multi .70 .25
a. Souvenir sheet of 2 7.25 7.25

Philatelic Week, Oct. 17-23 and 90th anniversary of first Korean postage stamps.

Taekwondo and Kukkiwon Center — A483

1974, Oct. 18

917 A483 10w yellow grn & multi .55 .25

First Asian Taekwondo (self-defense) Games, Seoul, Oct. 18-20.

Presidents Park and Ford, Flags and Globe — A484

1974, Nov. 22 Photo. *Perf. 13*

918 A484 10y multicolored .95 .30
a. Souvenir sheet of 2 7.50 7.50

Visit of Pres. Gerald R. Ford to South Korea.

Yook Young Soo — A485

1974, Nov. 29

919 A485 10w green .95 .30
920 A485 10w orange .95 .30
921 A485 10w lilac .95 .30
922 A485 10w blue .95 .30
a. Souvenir sheet of 4, #919-922 32.00 32.00
b. Block of 4, #919-922 3.75 3.00

Yook Young Soo (1925-1974), wife of Pres. Park.

Rabbits A486

Good-luck Purse A487

1974, Dec. 1 Litho. ***Perf. 12½x13***

923 A486 10w multicolored .70 .25
a. Souvenir sheet of 2 4.00 4.00
924 A487 10w multicolored .70 .25
a. Souvenir sheet of 2 4.00 4.00

New Year 1975.

Good-luck Key and Pigeon — A488

1975, Jan. 1 Photo. ***Perf. 13***

925 A488 10w lt blue & multi .55 .25

Introduction of Natl. Welfare Insurance System.

UPU Emblem and "75" A489

UPU Emblem and Paper Plane A490

1975, Jan. 1

926 A489 10w yellow & multi .55 .25
927 A490 10w lt blue & multi .55 .25

75th anniv. of Korea's membership in UPU.

Dr. Albert Schweitzer, Map of Africa, Hypodermic Needle — A491

1975, Jan. 14

928 A491 10w olive .95 .35
929 A491 10w brt rose .95 .35
930 A491 10w orange .95 .35
931 A491 10w brt green .95 .35
a. Block of 4, #928-931 4.75 3.00

Folk Dance Issue

Dancer — A492

No. 933, Dancer with fan.

1975, Feb. 20 Photo. ***Perf. 13***

932 A492 10w emerald & multi .70 .25
933 A492 10w brt blue & multi .70 .25

No. 934, Woman with butterfly sleeves. No. 935, Group of Women.

1975, Apr. 20

934 A492 10w yel grn & multi .70 .25
935 A492 10w yellow & multi .70 .25

No. 936, Pongsan mask dance. No. 937, Pusan mask dance.

1975, June 20

936 A492 10w pink & multi .70 .25
937 A492 10w blue & multi .70 .25

No. 938, Buddhist drum dance. No. 939, Bara (cymbals) dance.

1975, Aug. 20

938 A492 20w yellow & multi 1.25 .40
939 A492 20w salmon & multi 1.25 .40

Bupo Nori — A492a

No. 940, Sogo dance.

1975, Oct. 20

940 A492 20w blue & multi 1.35 .40
941 A492a 20w yellow & multi 1.35 .40
Nos. 932-941 (10) 9.40 3.10

Souvenir Sheets of 2

932a A492 10w (#1) 1.75 1.75
933a A492 10w (#2) 1.75 1.75
934a A492 10w (#3) 1.60 1.60
935a A492 10w (#4) 1.60 1.60
936a A492 10w (#5) 1.60 1.60
937a A492 10w (#6) 1.60 1.60
938a A492 20w (#7) 2.50 2.50
939a A492 20w (#8) 2.50 2.50
940a A492 20w (#9) 2.50 2.50
941a A492 20w (#10) 2.50 2.50
Nos. 932a-941a (10) 19.90 19.90

Globe and Rotary Emblem — A493

1975, Feb. 23

942 A493 10w multicolored .60 .25

Rotary International, 70th anniversary.

Women and IWY Emblem — A494

1975, Mar. 8

943 A494 10w multicolored .60 .25

International Women's Year 1975.

Flower Issue

Violets A495

Anemones A496

1975, Mar. 15

944 A495 10w orange & multi .65 .25
945 A496 10w yellow & multi .65 .25

Clematis Patens — A496a

No. 946, Rhododendron.

1975, May 15

946 A495 10w dk grn & multi .75 .25
947 A496a 10w yel grn & multi .75 .25

No. 948, Thistle. No. 949, Iris.

1975, July 15

948 A495 10w emerald & multi .75 .25
949 A495 10w blue & multi .75 .25

Broad-bell Flowers — A496b

No. 951, Bush clover.

1975, Sept. 15

950 A496b 20w yellow & multi 1.30 .30
951 A495 20w blue grn & multi 1.25 .30

No. 952, Camellia. No. 953, Gentian.

1975, Nov. 15

952 A495 20w yellow & multi 1.90 1.45
953 A496 20w salmon & multi 1.75 .45
Nos. 944-953 (10) 10.50 4.00

Forest and Water Resources — A497

1975, Mar. 20

954 A497 Strip of 4 4.50 3.00
a. 10w Saemaeul forest .70 .30
b. 10w Dam and reservoir .70 .30
c. 10w Green forest .70 .30
d. 10w Timber industry .70 .30

Natl. Tree Planting Month, Mar. 21-Apr. 20.

Map of Korea, HRF Emblem — A498

1975, Apr. 12 Photo. ***Perf. 13***

955 A498 10w blue & multi .65 .25

Homeland Reserve Forces Day.

Lily A499

Ceramic Jar A500

Ceramic Vase A501

Adm. Li Sun-sin A502

1975 Photo. ***Perf. 13½x13***

963 A499 6w green & bl grn .55 .25
964 A500 50w gray grn & brn .75 .25
965 A501 60w brown & yellow .95 .25
966 A502 100w carmine 2.25 .50
Nos. 963-966 (4) 4.50 1.25

Issued: Nos. 964-965, 3/15/75; Nos. 963, 966, 10/10/75.

Metric System Symbols — A507

1975, May 20 ***Perf. 13***

975 A507 10w salmon & multi .60 .25

Centenary of International Meter Convention, Paris, 1875.

Praying Soldier, Incense Burner — A508

1975, June 6 Photo. ***Perf. 13***

976 A508 10w multicolored .55 .25

20th Memorial Day.

Flags of Korea, UN and US — A509

Designs (Flags of): No. 978, Ethiopia, France, Greece, Canada, South Africa. No. 979, Luxembourg, Australia, Great Britain, Colombia, Turkey. No. 980, Netherlands, Belgium, Philippines, New Zealand, Thailand.

1975, June 25 Photo. ***Perf. 13***

977 A509 10w dk blue & multi .70 .30
978 A509 10w dk blue & multi .70 .30
979 A509 10w dk blue & multi .70 .30
980 A509 10w dk blue & multi .70 .30
a. Strip of 4, #977-980 4.00 2.75

25th anniv. of beginning of Korean War.

Presidents Park and Bongo, Flags of Korea and Gabon — A510

1975, July 5

981 A510 10w blue & multi .60 .25
a. Souvenir sheet of 2 2.75 2.75

Visit of Pres. Albert Bongo of Gabon, 7/5-8.

Scout Emblem, Tents and Neckerchief — A511

1975, July 29 Photo. ***Perf. 13***

982 A511 10w shown .80 .30
983 A511 10w Pick and oath .80 .30
984 A511 10w Tents .80 .30
985 A511 10w Ax, rope and tree .80 .30
986 A511 10w Campfire .80 .30
a. Strip of 5, #982-986 4.75 3.50

Nordjamb 75, 14th Boy Scout Jamboree, Lillehammer, Norway, July 29-Aug. 7.

Flame and Broken Chain — A512

Balloons with Symbols of Development over Map — A513

1975, Aug. 15 ***Perf. 13½x13***

987 A512 20w gold & multi .75 .25
988 A513 20w silver & multi .75 .25

30th anniversary of liberation.

Taekwondo — A514

1975, Aug. 26 ***Perf. 13***

989 A514 20w multicolored .60 .25

2nd World Taekwondo Championships, Seoul, Aug. 25-Sept. 1.

National Assembly and Emblem — A515

1975, Sept. 1 Photo. ***Perf. 13½x13***

990 A515 20w multicolored .60 .25

Completion of National Assembly Building.

Convention Emblem and Dump Truck — A516

1975, Sept. 7 Photo. *Perf. 13½x13*
991 A516 20w ultra & multi .60 .25

14th Convention of the Intl. Fed. of Asian and Western Pacific Contractors.

Cassegrainian Telescope and Morse Key — A517

1975, Sept. 28
992 A517 20w red lil, org & blk .60 .25

90th anniversary of Korean telecommunications system.

Stalactite Cave, Yeongweol A518

View of Mt. Sorak A519

1975, Sept. 28
993 A518 20w multicolored .65 .25
994 A519 20w multicolored .65 .25

International Tourism Day.

Armed Forces Flag and Missiles — A519a

1975, Oct. 1 Photo. *Perf. 13*
994A A519a 20w multicolored .60 .25

Armed Forces Day.

Gymnastics A520

Handball A521

1975, Oct. 7 Photo. *Perf. 13*
995 A520 20w yellow & multi .50 .25
996 A521 20w multicolored .50 .25

56th Natl. Athletic Meet, Taegu, Oct. 7-12.

Stamp Collecting Kangaroo — A522

1975, Oct. 8
997 A522 20w multicolored .60 .25

Philatelic Week, Oct. 8-14.

Hands and UN Emblem — A523

1975, Oct. 24
998 A523 20w multicolored .60 .25

United Nations, 30th anniversary.

Red Cross and Activities — A524

1975, Oct. 30
999 A524 20w orange, red & brn .60 .25

Korean Red Cross, 70th anniversary.

Emblem and Dove — A525

1975, Nov. 30 Photo. *Perf. 13*
1000 A525 20w multicolored .60 .25

Asian Parliamentary Union, 10th anniv.

Children Playing A526

Dragon A527

1975, Dec. 1
1001 A526 20w multicolored .65 .25
a. Souvenir sheet of 2 1.90 1.90
1002 A527 20w multicolored .65 .25
a. Souvenir sheet of 2 1.90 1.90

New Year 1976.

Inchong-Bukpyong Railroad — A528

1975, Dec. 5 Photo. *Perf. 13*
1003 A528 20w multicolored .60 .25

Opening of electric cross-country railroad.

Butterfly Issue

Dilipa Fenestra — A529

Butterflies: No. 1005, Luehdorfia puziloi.

1976, Jan. 20 Photo. *Perf. 13*
1004 A529 20w dp rose & multi 1.60 .30
1005 A529 20w dp blue & multi 1.60 .30

Butterflies: No. 1006, Papilio xuthus linne. No. 1007, Parnassius bremeri.

1976, Mar. 20
1006 A529 20w yellow & multi 1.60 .30
1007 A529 20w yel grn & multi 1.60 .30

Byasa Alcinous Klug — A529a

Butterflies: No. 1008, Colias erate esper.

1976, June 20
1008 A529 20w lt violet & multi 1.50 .30
1009 A529a 20w citron & multi 1.50 .30

Graphium Sarpedon — A529b

Butterflies: No. 1010, Hestina assimilis.

1976, Aug. 20
1010 A529 20w tan & multi 2.00 .70
1011 A529b 20w lt gray & multi 1.90 .70

Fabriciana Nerippe A529c

Nymphalis Xanthomelas A529d

1976, Oct. 20
1012 A529c 20w lt grn & multi 2.60 .80
1013 A529d 20w lilac & multi 2.60 .80
Nos. 1004-1013 (10) 18.50 4.80

Emblems of Science, Industry and KIST — A530

1976, Feb. 10 Photo. *Perf. 13*
1014 A530 20w multicolored .60 .25

Korean Institute of Science and Technology (KIST), 10th anniversary.

Birds Issue

A531

A532

No. 1015, Siberian Bustard. No. 1016, White-naped Crane.

1976, Feb. 20 Photo. *Perf. 13x13½*
1015 A531 20w multicolored 1.25 .35
1016 A532 20w multicolored 1.25 .35

A532a

A532b

No. 1017, Blue-winged pitta. No. 1018, Tristam's woodpecker.

1976, May 20
1017 A532a 20w multicolored 1.25 .35
1018 A532b 20w multicolored 1.25 .35

A532c

A532d

No. 1019, Wood pigeon. No. 1020, Oyster catcher.

1976, July 20
1019 A532c 20w multicolored 1.25 .35
1020 A532d 20w multicolored 1.25 .35

A532e

A532f

No. 1021, Black-faced spoonbill. No. 1022, Black stork.

1976, Sept. 20
1021 A532e 20w multicolored 1.25 .35
1022 A532f 20w multicolored 1.25 .35

A532g

A532h

No. 1023, Whooper swan. No. 1024, Black vulture.

1976, Nov. 20
1023 A532g 20w multicolored 3.25 1.15
1024 A532h 20w multicolored 3.25 1.15
Nos. 1015-1024 (10) 16.50 5.10

1876 and 1976 Telephones, Globe — A533

1976, Mar. 10
1025 A533 20w multicolored .60 .25

Centenary of first telephone call by Alexander Graham Bell, Mar. 10, 1876.

Homeland Reserves — A534

1976, Apr. 3 Photo. *Perf. 13½x13*
1026 A534 20w multicolored .60 .25

8th Homeland Reserve Forces Day.

"People and Eye" — A535

1976, Apr. 7 *Perf. 13x13½*
1027 A535 20w multicolored .60 .25

World Health Day; "Foresight prevents blindness."

Pres. Park, New Village Movement Flag A536

Intellectual Pursuits A537

No. 1030, Village improvement. No. 1031, Agriculture. No. 1032, Income from production.

1976, Apr. 22
1028 A536 20w shown 1.45 .45
1029 A537 20w shown 1.45 .45
1030 A537 20w multicolored 1.45 .45
1031 A537 20w multicolored 1.45 .45
1032 A537 20w multicolored 1.45 .45
a. Strip of 5, #1028-1032 10.00 6.00

6th anniv. of Pres. Park's New Village Movement for National Prosperity.

Mohenjo-Daro A538

1976, May 1 *Perf. 13½x13*
1033 A538 20w multicolored .60 .25

UNESCO campaign to save the Mohenjo-Daro excavations in Pakistan.

13-Star and 50-Star Flags — A539

American Bicentennial (Bicentennial Emblem and): No. 1035, Statue of Liberty. No. 1036, Map of US and Mt. Rushmore monument. No. 1037, Liberty Bell. No. 1038, First astronaut on moon.

1976, May 8 ***Perf. 13x13½***

1034	A539	100w blk, dp bl & red	2.60	.85
a.		Souvenir sheet of 1	5.50	5.50
1035	A539	100w blk, dp bl & red	2.60	.85
1036	A539	100w blk, dp bl & red	2.60	.85
1037	A539	100w blk, dp bl & red	2.60	.85
1038	A539	100w blk, dp bl & red	2.60	.85
		Nos. 1034-1038 (5)	13.00	4.25

Girl Scouts, Campfire and Emblem — A540

1976, May 10
1039 A540 20w orange & multi 1.00 .25

Korean Federation of Girl Scouts, 30th anniv.

Stupas, Buddha of Borobudur — A541

1976, June 10
1040 A541 20w multicolored .60 .25

UNESCO campaign to save the Borobudur Temple, Java.

"Life Insurance" — A542

1976, July 1 **Photo.** ***Perf. 13x13½***
1041 A542 20w multicolored .60 .25

National Life Insurance policies: "Over 100 billion-won," Apr. 30, 1976.

Volleyball — A543

1976, July 17
1042 A543 20w shown .50 .25
1043 A543 20w Boxing .50 .25

21st Olympic Games, Montreal, Canada, July 17-Aug. 1.

Children and Books — A544

1976, Aug. 10 ***Perf. 13½x13***
1044 A544 20w brown & multi .60 .25

Books for children.

Civil Defense Corps, Flag and Members — A545

1976, Sept. 15 ***Perf. 13x13½***
1045 A545 20w multicolored .60 .25

Civil Defense Corps, first anniversary.

Chamsungdan, Mani Mountain — A546

Front Gate, Tongdosa Temple — A547

1976, Sept. 28 ***Perf. 13½x13***
1046 A546 20w multicolored .70 .25
1047 A547 20w multicolored .70 .25

International Tourism Day.

Cadets and Academy — A548

1976, Oct. 1
1048 A548 20w multicolored .60 .25

Korean Military Academy, 30th anniversary.

Leaves and Stones, by Cheong Ju — A549

1976, Oct. 5 ***Perf. 13x13½***
1049 A549 20w blk, gray & red .60 .25
a. Souvenir sheet of 2 4.25 4.25

Philatelic Week, Oct. 5-11.

Snake-headed Figure, Bas-relief A550

Door-pull and Cranes A551

1976, Dec. 1 **Photo.** ***Perf. 13x13½***

1050	A550	20w multicolored	.60	.25
a.		Souvenir sheet of 2	2.25	2.25
1051	A551	20w multicolored	.60	.25
a.		Souvenir sheet of 2	2.25	2.25

New Year 1977.

Arrows, Cogwheels, Worker at Lathe — A552

No. 1053, Arrows, Cogwheels, ship in dock.

1977, Jan. 20 **Photo.** ***Perf. 13½x13***
1052 A552 20w multicolored .60 .25
1053 A552 20w multicolored .60 .25

4th Economic Development Five-Year Plan.

Satellite Antenna and Microwaves — A553

1977, Jan. 31 ***Perf. 13x13½***
1054 A553 20w multicolored .60 .25

Membership in ITU, 25th anniv.

Korean Broadcasting Center — A554

1977, Feb. 16 ***Perf. 13½x13***
1055 A554 20w multicolored .60 .25

50th anniversary of broadcasting in Korea.

Parents and Two Children — A555

1977, Apr. 1 **Photo.** ***Perf. 13½x13***
1056 A555 20w brt grn & orange 2.10 .25

Family planning.

Reservist on Duty — A556

1977, Apr. 2 ***Perf. 13x13½***
1057 A556 20w multicolored .60 .25

9th Homeland Reserve Forces Day.

Head with Symbols — A557

1977, Apr. 21 **Photo.** ***Perf. 13x13½***
1058 A557 20w dp lilac & multi .60 .25

10th anniversary of Science Day.

Book, Map, Syringe — A558

1977, Apr. 25
1059 A558 20w blue & multi .60 .25

35th Intl. Meeting on Military Medicine.

Boy with Flowers and Dog — A559

1977, May 5
1060 A559 20w multicolored .60 .25

Proclamation of Children's Charter, 20th anniversary.

Veteran's Emblem and Flag — A560

1977, May 8
1061 A560 20w multicolored .60 .25

25th anniversary of Korean Veterans' Day.

Buddha, 8th Century, Sokkulam Grotto — A561

1977, May 25 **Photo.** ***Perf. 13x13½***
1062 A561 20w sepia & olive .55 .25
a. Souvenir sheet of 2 4.50 4.50

"2600th" anniversary of birth of Buddha.

Ceramic Issues

Jar with Grape Design, 17th Century A562

Celadon Vase, Bamboo Design, 12th Century A563

1977, Mar. 15 **Photo.** ***Perf. 13x13½***
1063 A562 20w vio brn & multi 1.75 .30
1064 A563 20w gray, grn & bis 1.75 .30

Celadon Jar with Peonies A564

Vase with Willow Reed Peony Pattern A565

Perf. 13x13½, 13½x13
1977, June 15 **Photo.**
1065 A564 20w multicolored .95 .30
1066 A565 20w multicolored .95 .30

Celadon Manshaped Wine Jug — A566

Celadon Melon-shaped Vase — A567

1977, July 15
1067 A566 20w multicolored .90 .25
1068 A567 20w multicolored .90 .25

1977, Aug. 15

Designs: No. 1069, White porcelain bowl with inlaid lotus vine design. No. 1070, Black Koryo ware vase with plum blossom vine.

1069 A564 20w multicolored .90 .25
1070 A565 20w multicolored .90 .25

Punch'ong Jar A568

Celadon Cylindrical Vase A569

1977, Nov. 15

1071	A568	20w multicolored	.85	.25
1072	A569	20w multicolored	.85	.25
		Nos. 1063-1072 (10)	10.70	2.70

Types of 1962-66
Designs as Before

1976-77 Litho. *Perf. 12½*
Granite Paper

1076	A187	200w brn & lt grn	*25.00*	*7.00*
1077	A187a	300w sl grn & sal ('76)	*50.00*	*8.00*
1078	A187a	300w brn & sal	*50.00*	*8.00*
1079	A187a	500w pur & lt grn	*100.00*	*10.00*

Magpie A570

Nature Protection A571

"Family Planning" A572

Children on Swing A573

Ceramic Horseman A574

Muryangsu Hall, Busok Temple A575

Pagoda, Pobjusa Temple A576

Gold Crown, from Chonmachong Mound A577

Monster Mask Tile, 6th or 7th Century — A578

Flying Angels from Bronze Bell from Sangwon-sa, 725 A.D. — A579

Perf. 12½x13½, 13½x12½

1977-79 Photo.

1088	A570	3w lt blue & blk	.60	.25
1090	A326	10w emer & blk	.55	.25
1091	A571	20w multicolored	.65	.25
1092	A572	20w emer & blk ('78)	1.00	.25
1093	A573	20w grn & org ('79)	.45	.25
1097	A574	80w lt brn & sep	1.60	.35
1099	A575	200w salmon & brn	1.75	.50
1100	A576	300w brn purple	2.25	.60
1101	A577	500w multicolored	25.00	1.35

Perf. 13½x13

1102	A578	500w brown & pur	13.50	1.00

Perf. 13

1103	A579	1000w slate grn ('78)	7.75	1.20
		Nos. 1088-1103 (11)	55.10	6.25

Ulleung Island — A580

Design: No. 1105, Haeundae Beach.

1977, Sept. 28 Photo. *Perf. 13*

1104	A580	20w multicolored	.60	.25
1105	A580	20w multicolored	.60	.25

World Tourism Day.

Armed Forces Day — A581

1977, Oct. 1 Photo. *Perf. 13*

1106	A581	20w green & multi	.60	.25

Mt. Inwang after the Rain, by Chung Seon (1676-1759) A582

1977, Oct. 4

1107	20w mountain, clouds	.85	.25
1108	20w mountain, house	.85	.25
a.	Souvenir sheet of 2	7.50	7.50
b.	A582 Pair, #1107-1108	2.00	1.50

Philatelic Week, Oct. 4-10.

Rotary Emblem on Bronze Bell, Koryo Dynasty — A584

1977, Nov. 10 Photo. *Perf. 13*

1109	A584	20w multicolored	.55	.25

Korean Rotary Club, 50th anniversary.

Korean Flag on Mt. Everest — A585

1977, Nov. 11

1110	A585	20w multicolored	.85	.25

Korean Mt. Everest Expedition, reached peak, Sept. 15, 1977.

Children and Kites A586

Horse-headed Figure, Bas-relief A587

1977, Dec. 1 Photo. *Perf. 13*

1111	A586	20w multicolored	.40	.25
a.		Souvenir sheet of 2	2.00	2.00
1112	A587	20w multicolored	.40	.25
a.		Souvenir sheet of 2	2.00	2.00

New Year 1978.

Clay Pigeon Shooting — A588

Designs: No. 1114, Air pistol shooting. No. 1115, Air rifle shooting and target.

1977, Dec. 3

1113	A588	20w multicolored	.50	.25
a.		Souvenir sheet of 2 ('78)	4.00	4.00
1114	A588	20w multicolored	.50	.25
a.		Souvenir sheet of 2 ('78)	4.00	4.00
1115	A588	20w multicolored	.50	.25
a.		Souvenir sheet of 2 ('78)	4.00	4.00
		Nos. 1113-1115 (3)	1.50	.75
		Nos. 1113a-1115a (3)	12.00	

42nd World Shooting Championships, Seoul, 1978.

Boeing 727 over Globe, ICAO Emblem — A589

1977, Dec. 11

1116	A589	20w multicolored	.55	.25

25th anniv. of Korea's membership in the ICAO.

Plane, Cargo, Freighter and Globe — A590

1977, Dec. 22 Photo. *Perf. 13*

1117	A590	20w multicolored	.55	.25

Korean exports.

Ships and World Map — A591

1978, Mar. 13 Photo. *Perf. 13*

1118	A591	20w multicolored	.55	.25

Maritime Day.

Stone Pagoda Issue

Four Lions Pagoda, Hwaom-sa — A592

Seven-storied Pagoda, T'appyongri — A592a

1978, Mar. 20 Photo. *Perf. 13*

1119	A592	20w lt green & multi	1.25	.30
1120	A592a	20w ocher & multi	1.25	.30

Punhwang-sa Temple — A593

Miruk-sa Temple — A593a

1978, May 20

1121	A593	20w lt green & blk	1.25	.30
1122	A593a	20w grn, brn & yel	1.25	.30

Tabo Pagoda, Pulguk-sa — A592b

Three-storied pagoda, Pulguk-sa — A592c

1978, June 20

1123	A592b	20w gray, lt grn & blk	.95	.25
1124	A592c	20w lilac & black	.95	.25

Kyongch'on sa Temple — A594

Octagonal Pagoda, Wolchong-sa Temple — A594a

1978, July 20 *Perf. 13½x12½*

1125	A594	20w gray & brn	1.60	.30
1126	A594a	20w lt green & blk	1.60	.30

13-storied Pagoda, Jeonghye-sa — A592d

Three-storied Pagoda, Jinjeon-sa — A592e

1978, Nov. 20 *Perf. 13x13½*

1127	A592d	20w pale grn & multi	.55	.25
1128	A592e	20w lilac & multi	.55	.25
		Nos. 1119-1128 (10)	11.20	2.80

Ants and Coins — A595

1978, Apr. 1

1129	A595	20w multicolored	.55	.25

Importance of saving.

Reservist with Flag — A596

1978, Apr. 1

1130	A596	20w multicolored	.55	.25

10th Homeland Reserve Forces Day.

Seoul Cultural Center — A597

1978, Apr. 1

1131 A597 20w multicolored .75 .25

Opening of Seoul Cultural Center.

National Assembly in Plenary Session — A598

1978, May 31

1132 A598 20w multicolored .55 .25

30th anniversary of National Assembly.

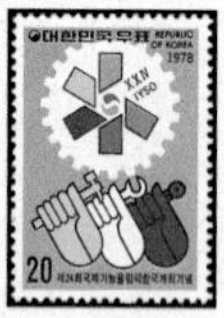

Hands Holding Tools, Competition Emblem — A599

1978, Aug. 5 Photo. *Perf. 13*

1133 A599 20w multicolored .55 .25
a. Souvenir sheet of 2 3.25 3.25

24th World Youth Skill Olympics, Busan, Aug. 30-Sept. 15.

Bell of Joy and Crater Lake, Mt. Baegdu — A600

1978, Aug. 15

1134 A600 20w multicolored .55 .25

Founding of republic, 30th anniversary.

Nurse, Badge and Flowers — A601

1978, Aug. 26

1135 A601 20w multicolored .55 .25

Army Nurse Corps, 30th anniversary.

Sobaeksan Observatory — A602

1978, Sept. 13 Photo. *Perf. 13*

1136 A602 20w multicolored .55 .25

Opening of Sobaeksan Natl. Observatory.

Kyunghoeru Pavilion, Kyongbok Palace, Seoul — A603

Design: No. 1138, Baeg Do (island).

1978, Sept. 28

1137 A603 20w multicolored .45 .25
1138 A603 20w multicolored .45 .25

Tourist publicity.

Customs Flag and Officers — A604

1978, Sept. 28

1139 A604 20w multicolored .45 .25

Cent. of 1st Korean Custom House, Busan.

Armed Forces — A605

1978, Oct. 1 Photo. *Perf. 13*

1140 A605 20w multicolored .45 .25

Armed Forces, 30th anniversary.

Clay Figurines, Silla Dynasty — A606

1978, Oct. 1

1141 A606 20w lt green & blk .45 .25

Culture Month, October 1978.

Portrait of a Lady, by Shin Yoon-bok — A607

1978, Oct. 24

1142 A607 20w multicolored .50 .25
a. Souvenir sheet of 2 3.50 3.50

Philatelic Week, Oct. 24-29.

Young Men, YMCA Emblem — A608

1978, Oct. 28

1143 A608 20w multicolored .45 .25

75th anniv. of founding of Korean YMCA.

Hand Protecting Against Fire — A609

1978, Nov. 1 Photo. *Perf. 13*

1144 A609 20w multicolored .45 .25

Fire Prevention Day, Nov. 1.

Winter Landscape A610

Ram-headed Figure, Bas-relief A611

1978, Dec. 1 Photo. *Perf. 13x13½*

1145 A610 20w multicolored .55 .25
a. Souvenir sheet of 2 1.75 1.75
1146 A611 20w multicolored .55 .25
a. Souvenir sheet of 2 1.75 1.75

New Year 1979.

Hibiscus, Students, Globe — A612

1978, Dec. 5

1147 A612 20w multicolored .45 .25

Proclamation of National Education Charter, 10th anniversary.

President Park — A613

1978, Dec. 27

1148 A613 20w multicolored 1.00 .25
a. Souvenir sheet of 2 11.00 11.00

Inauguration of Park Chung Hee for fifth term as president.

Nature Conservation Issue

Golden Mandarinfish A614

Lace-bark Pines A615

1979, Feb. 20 Photo. *Perf. 13x13½*

1149 A614 20w multicolored 1.60 .25
1150 A615 20w multicolored 1.60 .25

Mandarin Ducks A616

Neofinettia Orchid A617

1979, May 20

1151 A616 20w multicolored 1.60 .25
1152 A617 20w multicolored 1.60 .25

Goral A618

Lilies of the Valley A619

1979, June 20

1153 A618 20w multicolored 1.60 .25
1154 A619 20w multicolored 1.60 .25

Rain Frog A620

Asian Polypody A621

1979, Nov. 25

1155 A620 20w multicolored 1.60 .25
1156 A621 20w multicolored 1.60 .25

Firefly A622

Meesun Tree A623

1980, Jan. 20

1157 A622 30w multicolored 1.60 .25
1158 A623 30w multicolored 1.60 .25
Nos. 1149-1158 (10) 16.00 2.50

Samil Monument — A624

1979, Mar. 1 Photo. *Perf. 13x13½*

1159 A624 20w multicolored .45 .25

Samil independence movement, 60th anniv.

Worker and Bulldozer — A625

1979, Mar. 10 *Perf. 13½x13*

1160 A625 20w multicolored .45 .25

Labor Day.

Hand Holding Tools, Gun and Grain — A626

1979, Apr. 1 *Perf. 13x13½*

1161 A626 20w multicolored .45 .25

Strengthening national security.

Tabo Pagoda, Pulguk-sa Temple — A627

Women, Silk Screen A628

Art Treasures: No. 1163, Statue. No. 1164, Crown. No. 1165, Celadon Vase.

1979, Apr. 1

1162 A627 20w gray bl & multi .55 .25
1163 A627 20w bister & multi .55 .25
1164 A627 20w violet & multi .55 .25
1165 A627 20w brt grn & multi .55 .25
1166 A628 60w multicolored .90 .30
a. Souvenir sheet of 2 3.75 3.75
Nos. 1162-1166 (5) 3.10 1.30

5000 years of Korean art.
See Nos. 1175-1179, 1190.

Pulguk-sa Temple and PATA Emblem — A629

1979, Apr. 16 *Perf. 13½x13*

1167 A629 20w multicolored .45 .25

28th Pacific Area Travel Association (PATA) Conf., Seoul, Apr. 16-18, and Gyeongju, Apr. 20-21.

Presidents Park and Senghor — A630

1979, Apr. 22 *Perf. 13½x13*
1168 A630 20w multicolored .45 .25
a. Souvenir sheet of 2 1.75 1.75

Visit of Pres. Leopold Sedar Senghor of Senegal.

Basketball — A631

1979, Apr. 29 *Perf. 13x13½*
1169 A631 20w multicolored .45 .25

8th World Women's Basketball Championship, Seoul, Apr. 29-May 13.

Children and IYC Emblem — A632

1979, May 5 Photo. *Perf. 13½x13*
1170 A632 20w multicolored .45 .25
a. Souvenir sheet of 2 1.75 1.75

International Year of the Child.

Traffic Pollution — A633

1979, June 5 Photo. *Perf. 13x13½*
1171 A633 20w green & dk brn .75 .25

Pollution control.

Flags, Presidents Park and Carter — A634

1979, June 29 *Perf. 13½x13*
1172 A634 20w multicolored .45 .25
a. Souvenir sheet of 2 1.75 1.75

Visit of Pres. Jimmy Carter.

Korean Exhibition Center — A635

1979, July 3
1173 A635 20w multicolored .45 .25

Opening of Korean Exhibition Center.

Jet, Globe, South Gate — A636

1979, Aug. 1 Photo. *Perf. 13½x13*
1174 A636 20w multicolored .45 .25

10th anniversary of Korean airlines.

Art Treasure Types

Designs: No. 1175, Porcelain jar, 17th century. No. 1176, Man on horseback, ceremonial pitcher, horiz. No. 1177, Sword Dance, by Shin Yun-bok. No. 1178, Golden Amitabha with halo, 8th century. No. 1179, Hahoe ritual mask.

1979 Photo. *Perf. 13x13½, 13½x13*
1175 A627 20w lilac & multi .60 .25
1176 A627 20w multicolored .60 .25
1177 A628 60w multicolored 1.00 .30
a. Souvenir sheet of 2 4.75 4.75
Nos. 1175-1177 (3) 2.20 .80

Issued: No. 1177, 9/1; Nos. 1175-1176, 10/15.

1979, Nov. 15
1178 A627 20w dp green & multi .50 .25
1179 A627 20w multicolored .50 .25

Yongdu Rock — A637

1979, Sept. 28
1180 A637 20w shown .50 .25
1181 A637 20w Mt. Mai, vert. .50 .25

World Tourism Day.

People, Blood and Heart — A637a

1979, Oct. 1 *Perf. 13½x13*
1182 A637a 20w multicolored .70 .25

Blood Banks, 4th anniversary.

"My Life in the Year 2000" — A638

1979, Oct. 30 *Perf. 13½x13*
1183 A638 20w multicolored .45 .25
a. Souvenir sheet of 2 1.60 1.60

Philatelic Week, Oct. 30-Nov. 4.

Monkey-headed Figure, Bas-relief A639

Children Playing Yut A640

1979, Dec. 1
1184 A639 20w multicolored .45 .25
a. Souvenir sheet of 2 1.35 1.35
1185 A640 20w multicolored .45 .25
a. Souvenir sheet of 2 1.35 1.35

New Year 1980.

Inauguration of Pres. Choi Kyu-hah — A641

1979, Dec. 21
1186 A641 20w multicolored .50 .25
a. Souvenir sheet of 2 4.75 4.75

President Park — A642

1980, Feb. 2 Photo. *Perf. 13x13½*
1187 A642 30w orange brn .80 .25
1188 A642 30w dull purple .80 .25
a. Souvenir sheet of 2 3.50 3.50
b. Pair, #1187-1188 2.00 2.00

President Park Chung Hee (1917-1979) memorial.

Art Treasure Type of 1979 and

Dragon-shaped Kettle — A643

Design: 60w, Landscape, by Kim Hong-do.

Perf. 13½x13, 13x13½
1980, Feb. 20 Photo.
1189 A643 30w multicolored .80 .25
1190 A628 60w multicolored .90 .30
a. Souvenir sheet of 2 3.75 3.75

Art Treasure Issue

Heavenly Horse, Saddle A644

Dragon Head, Banner Staff A645

Tiger, Granite Sculpture A647

Mounted Nobleman Mural A646

Human Face, Roof Tile A648

Deva King Sculpture A650

White Tiger Mural — A649

Earthenware Ducks — A651

Tiger, Folk Painting — A653

Perf. 13½x13, 13x13½
1980-83 Photo.
1191 A644 30w multicolored .70 .25
1192 A645 30w multicolored .70 .25
1193 A646 30w multicolored .70 .25
1194 A647 30w multicolored .70 .25
1195 A648 30w multicolored .70 .25
1196 A649 30w multicolored .70 .25
Engr. *Perf. 12½x13*
1197 A650 30w black .90 .25
1198 A650 30w red .90 .25
1983 Litho. *Perf. 13*
1199 1000w bis brn & red brn 5.25 .80
1200 1000w bis brn & red brn 5.25 .80
a. A651 Pair, #1199-1200 10.50 5.00
1201 A653 5000w multicolored 23.00 5.00
a. Souvenir sheet, perf. 13½x13 30.00
Nos. 1191-1201 (11) 39.50 8.60

Issued: Nos. 1191-1192, 4/20; Nos. 1193-1194, 5/20; Nos. 1195-1196, 8/20; Nos. 1197-1198, 11/20. Nos. 1199-1200, 11/25/83. No. 1201, 12/1/83.

No. 1201a for PHILAKOREA '84. No. 1201a exists imperf. Value $150.

Lotus Blossoms and Ducks A656

Tiger and Magpie A657

1980, Mar. 10 *Perf. 13x13½, 13½x13*
1203 A656 30w multicolored .60 .25
1204 A657 60w multicolored 1.40 .45

Red Phoenix (in Form of Rooster) — A658

Moon Over Mt. Konryun A659

No. 1207, Sun over Mt. Konryun. No. 1207a has continuous design.

1980, May 10 *Perf. 13x13½*
1205 A658 30w multicolored .55 .25
1206 A659 60w multicolored 1.60 .45
1207 A659 60w multicolored 1.60 .45
a. Souvenir sheet of 2, #1206-1207 4.75 4.75
b. Pair, #1206-1207 4.25 3.50
Nos. 1205-1207 (3) 3.75 1.15

Rabbits Pounding Grain in a Mortar A660

Dragon in the Clouds A661

1980, July 10 Photo. *Perf. 13x13½*
1208 A660 30w multicolored .65 .25
1209 A661 30w multicolored .65 .25

Pine Tree, Pavilion, Mountain A662

Flowers and Birds, Bridal Room Screen A663

1980, Aug. 9 Photo. *Perf. 13x13½*
1210 A662 30w multicolored .60 .25
1211 A663 30w multicolored .95 .30

Tortoises and Cranes — A664

Symbols of longevity: a, cranes, tortoises. b, buck. c, doe. d, waterfall.

1980, Nov. 10 Photo. ***Perf. 13½x13***
1212 A664 Strip of 4 6.75 4.50
a.-d. 30w any single 1.35 .25

New Community Movement, 10th Anniv. — A668

1980, Apr. 22 ***Perf. 13x13½***
1216 A668 30w multicolored .45 .25

Freighters at Sea — A669

1980, Mar. 13
1217 A669 30w multicolored .45 .25

Increase of Korea's shipping tonnage to 5 million tons.

Soccer — A670

1980, Aug. 23 ***Perf. 13x13½***
1218 A670 30w multicolored .45 .25

10th President's Cup Soccer Tournament, Aug. 23-Sept. 5.

Mt. Sorak A671

Paikryung Island A672

Perf. 12½x13½
1980, Apr. 10 Photo.
1219 A671 15w multicolored .35 .25
1220 A672 90w multicolored 1.00 .25

Flag — A673

1980, Sept. 10 ***Perf. 13½x13***
1221 A673 30w multicolored .40 .25

Coil Stamp
Perf. Vert.
1221A A673 30w multicolored 1.10 .25

No. 1221A issued 2/1/87.

UN Intervention, 30th Anniv. — A674

1980, June 25 ***Perf. 13x13½***
1222 A674 30w multicolored .50 .25

Election of Miss World in Seoul — A675

1980, July 8
1223 A675 30w multicolored .50 .25

Women's Army Corps, 30th Anniversary A676

1980, Sept. 6 ***Perf. 13½x13***
1224 A676 30w multicolored .50 .25

Baegma River — A677

Three Peaks of Dodam — A678

1980, Sept. 28
1225 A677 30w multicolored .35 .25
1226 A678 30w multicolored .35 .25

Inauguration of Pres. Chun Doo-hwan — A679

1980, Sept. 1
1227 A679 30w multicolored .60 .25
a. Souvenir sheet of 2 3.25 3.25

Ear of Corn — A680

1980, Oct. 20 ***Perf. 13x13½***
1228 A680 30w multicolored .50 .25

12th population and housing census.

Symbolic Tree — A681

1980, Oct. 27
1229 A681 30w multicolored .50 .25

National Red Cross, 75th anniversary.

"Mail-Delivering Angels" — A682

1980, Nov. 6 ***Perf. 13½x13***
1230 A682 30w multicolored .50 .25
a. Souvenir sheet of 2 1.60 1.60

Philatelic Week, Nov. 6-11.

Korea-Japan Submarine Cable System Inauguration — A683

1980, Nov. 28 ***Perf. 13x13½***
1231 A683 30w multicolored .50 .25

Rooster A684

Cranes A685

1980, Dec. 1
1232 A684 30w multicolored .50 .25
a. Souvenir sheet of 2 1.60 1.60
1233 A685 30w multicolored .50 .25
a. Souvenir sheet of 2 1.60 1.60

New Year 1981.

Second Inauguration of Pres. Chun Doo-hwan — A686

1981, Mar. 3 Photo. ***Perf. 13½x13***
1234 A686 30w multicolored .55 .25
a. Souvenir sheet of 2 1.60 1.60

Ship Issue

Oil Tanker A687

Cargo Ship A688

1981, Mar. 13 ***Perf. 13½x13, 13x13½***
1235 A687 30w multicolored .45 .25
1236 A688 90w multicolored .80 .25

5th Maritime Day.

Oil Tanker — A689

Cargo Ship — A690

1981, May 10 Photo. ***Perf. 13½x13***
1237 A689 30w multicolored .45 .25
1238 A690 90w multicolored .85 .30

Tug Boat — A691

Stern Trawler — A692

1981, July 10 ***Perf. 13½x13***
1239 A691 40w multicolored .65 .25
1240 A692 100w multicolored 1.05 .30

Log Carrier — A693

Auto Carrier — A694

1981, Aug. 10
1241 A693 40w multicolored .65 .25
1242 A694 100w multicolored 1.05 .30

Chemical Carrier — A695

Passenger Boat — A696

1981, Nov. 10 Engr. ***Perf. 13x12½***
1243 A695 40w black .65 .25
1244 A696 100w dk blue 1.10 .30
Nos. 1235-1244 (10) 7.70 2.70

11th Natl. Assembly Opening Session — A697

1981, Apr. 17 Photo. ***Perf. 13½x13***
1245 A697 30w gold & dk brn .45 .25

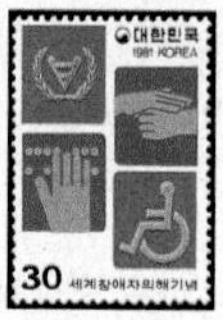
Hand Reading Braille, Helping Hands — A698

90w, Man in wheelchair.

1981, Apr. 20 Photo. ***Perf. 13x13½***
1246 A698 30w shown .35 .25
1247 A698 90w multicolored .70 .25

International Year of the Disabled.

Ribbon and Council Emblem — A699

1981, June 5 Photo. ***Perf. 13x13½***
1248 A699 40w multicolored .45 .25

Advisory Council on Peaceful Unification Policy (North and South Korea) anniv.

Clena River and Mountains — A700

1981, June 5
1249 A700 30w shown .35 .25
1250 A700 90w Seagulls .75 .25

10th World Environment Day.

Pres. Chun and Pres. Suharto of Indonesia — A701

Pres. Chun Visit to Asia: b, King of Malaysia. c, Korean, Singapore flags. d, King Bhumibol Adulyadej of Thailand. e, Pres. Marcos of Philippines.

1981, June 25 ***Perf. 13½x13***
1251 Strip of 5 4.00 3.00
a.-e. A701 40w, any single .55 .25
f. Souvenir sheet of 5, imperf. 2.50 2.50

Size: 49x33mm
Perf. 13x13½
1252 A701 40w multicolored .55 .25
a. Souvenir sheet of 2, imperf. 2.40 2.40

36th Anniv. of Liberation — A702

1981, Aug. 15 Photo. ***Perf. 13x13½***
1253 A702 40w multicolored .45 .25

Tolharubang, "Stone Grandfather" A704

Rose of Sharon A705

Porcelain Jar, 17th Cent. — A706

Chomsongdae Observatory, 7th Cent. — A707

Mounted Warrior, Earthenware Jug, 5th Cent. A708

Family Planning A709

Walking Stick A710

Ryu Kwan-soon (1904-20), Martyr A711

"Tasan" Chung Yak-yong, Lee Dynasty Scholar A712

Ahn Joong-geun (1879-1910), Martyr A713

Ahn Chang-ho (1878-1938), Independence Fighter A714

Koryo Celadon Incense Burner A715

Kim Ku (1876-1949), Statesman A716

Mountain Landscape Brick Bas-relief A717

Mandarin Duck, Celadon Incense Burner — A718

Perf. 13½x12½ (Nos. 1256, 1257, 1266), 13, 13½x13, 13x13½

1981-89 Photo., Engr.

1255	A704	20w multi ('86)	.45	.25
1256	A705	40w multi	.55	.25
1257	A706	60w multi	.55	.25
1258	A707	70w multi	.65	.25
1259	A708	80w multi ('83)	.70	.25
1260	A709	80w multi ('86)	.90	.25
1261	A710	80w multi ('89)	2.25	.25
1262	A711	100w mauve	.95	.25
1263	A712	100w gray blk ('86)	3.00	.25
1264	A713	200w lt ol grn & ol	1.30	.25
1265	A714	300w dl lil ('83)	1.90	.25
1266	A715	400w multi	5.75	.45
1267	A715	400w pale grn & multi ('83)	3.50	.35
1268	A716	450w dk vio brn ('86)	2.40	.35
1269	A717	500w multi	3.50	.60
1270	A718	700w multi ('83)	4.25	.65
		Nos. 1255-1270 (16)	32.60	5.15

Inscription and denomination of No. 1266, colorless, No. 1267, dark brown.

See Nos. 1449, 1449C, 1594F.

Coil Stamp

Photo. ***Perf. 13 Horiz.***

1271 A707 70w multicolored 2.00 .50

Girl Flying Model Plane — A721

Air Force Chief of Staff Cup, 3rd Aeronautic Competition: Various model planes.

1981, Sept. 20 ***Perf. 13½x13***

1272	Strip of 5	4.00	3.50
a.	A721 10w multi	.50	.25
b.	A721 20w multi	.50	.25
c.	A721 40w multi	.50	.25
d.	A721 50w multi	.65	.30
e.	A721 80w multi	.80	.35

WHO Emblem, Citizens — A722

1981, Sept. 22 ***Perf. 13x13½***

1273 A722 40w multicolored .45 .25

WHO, 32nd Western Pacific Regional Committee Meeting, Seoul, Sept. 22-28.

World Tourism Day — A723

1981, Sept. 28

1274 A723 40w Seoul Tower .45 .25

1275 A723 40w Ulreung Isld. .45 .25

Bicycle Racing — A724

1981, Oct. 10 ***Perf. 13½x13***

1276 A724 40w shown .40 .25

1277 A724 40w Swimming .40 .25

62nd Natl. Sports Festival, Seoul, 10/10-15.

Flags, Presidents Chun and Carazo — A725

1981, Oct. 12 ***Perf. 13½x13***

1278 A725 40w multicolored .45 .25

Visit of Pres. Rodrigo Carazo Odio of Costa Rica, Oct. 12-14.

World Food Day — A726

1981, Oct. 16 ***Perf. 13x13½***

1279 A726 40w multicolored .45 .25

First Natl. Aviation Day — A727

1981, Oct. 30 ***Perf. 13½x13***

1280 A727 40w multicolored .45 .25

1988 Olympic Games, Seoul — A728

1981, Oct. 30 ***Perf. 13x13½***

1281 A728 40w multicolored .55 .25

9th Philatelic Week, Nov. 18-24 — A729

1981, Nov. 18 ***Perf. 13½x13***

1282 A729 40w multicolored .45 .25

a. Souvenir sheet of 2 1.75 1.75

Camellia and Dog — A730

Children Flying Kite — A731

1981, Dec. 1 ***Perf. 13x13½***

1283	A730 40w multicolored	.55	.25
a.	Souvenir sheet of 2	1.75	1.75
1284	A731 40w multicolored	.55	.25
a.	Souvenir sheet of 2	1.75	1.75

New Year 1982 (Year of the Dog).

Hangul Hakhoe Language Society, 60th Anniv. — A732

1981, Dec. 3 ***Perf. 13½x13***

1285 A732 40w multicolored .45 .25

Telecommunications Authority Inauguration — A733

1982, Jan. 4 Photo. ***Perf. 13x13½***

1286 A733 60w multicolored .45 .25

Scouting Year — A734

1982, Feb. 22

1287 A734 60w multicolored .45 .25

60th Anniv. of YWCA in Korea — A735

1982, Apr. 20 Photo. ***Perf. 13x13½***

1288 A735 60w multicolored .45 .25

Intl. Polar Year Centenary — A736

1982, Apr. 21 ***Perf. 13½x13***

1289 A736 60w multicolored .55 .25

60th Children's Day — A737

1982, May 5 ***Perf. 13½x13***

1290 A737 60w multicolored .45 .25

Visit of Liberian Pres. Samuel K. Doe, May 9-13 — A738

1982, May 9 Litho. ***Perf. 13x12½***

1291 A738 60w multicolored .55 .25

a. Souvenir sheet of 2, imperf. 1.75 1.75

Centenary of US-Korea Treaty of Amity — A739

No. 1292, Statue of Liberty, pagoda. No. 1293, Emblem.

1982, May 18 Photo. ***Perf. 13½x13***

1292	A739 60w multicolored	.70	.25
1293	A739 60w multicolored	.70	.25
a.	Souvenir sheet of 2	3.00	3.00
b.	Pair, #1292-1293	1.50	1.50

Visit of Zaire Pres. Mobutu Sese Seko, June 7-10 — A740

1982, June 7 Litho. ***Perf. 13x12½***

1294 A740 60w multicolored .45 .25

a. Souvenir sheet of 2, imperf. 1.75 1.75

Historical Painting Issue

Gen. Kwon Yul's Victory at Haengju, by Oh Seung-woo A747

Designs: No. 1295, Territorial Expansion by Kwanggaeto the Great, by Lee Chong-sang, 1975. No. 1296, Gen. Euljimunduck's Victory at Salsoo, by Park Kak-soon, 1975. No. 1297, Shilla's Repulse of Tang's Army, by Oh Seung-woo. No. 1298, Gen. Kang Kam-chan's Victory at Kyiju, by Lee Yong-hwan. No. 1299, Admiral Yi Sun-sin's Victory at Hansan, 1592, by Kim Hyung-ku. No. 1300, Gen. Kim Chwa-jin's Battle at Chungsanri, by Sohn Soo-kwang. No. 1302, Kim Chong-suh's Exploitation of Yukjin, 1434, by Kim Tae.

1982 Photo. ***Perf. 13x13½***

1295	A747 60w multicolored	.75	.35
1296	A747 60w multicolored	1.25	.50
1297	A747 60w multicolored	.90	.30
1298	A747 60w multicolored	.90	.30
1299	A747 60w multicolored	1.00	.40
1300	A747 60w multicolored	1.00	.40
1301	A747 60w shown	1.30	.40
1302	A747 60w multicolored	1.30	.40
	Nos. 1295-1302 (8)	8.40	3.05

Issued: Nos. 1295-1296, 6/15; Nos. 1297-1298, 7/15; Nos. 1299-1300, 10/15; Nos. 1301-1302, 12/15.

55th Intl. YMCA Convention, Seoul, July 20-23 — A749

1982, July 20

1303	A749 60w multicolored		.45	.25

Flags, Presidents Chun and Arap Moi — A750

Pres. Chun's Visit to Africa & Canada: No. 1304, Kenya (Pres. Daniel T. Arap Moi), Aug. 17-19. No. 1305, Nigeria (Pres. Alhaji Shehe Shagari), Aug. 19-22. No. 1306, Gabon (Pres. El Hadj Omar Bongo), Aug. 22-24. No. 1307, Senegal (Pres. Abdou Diouf), Aug. 24-26. No. 1308, Canada, Aug. 28-31.

1982, Aug. 17 ***Perf. 13½x13***

1304	A750	60w multicolored	.45	.25
1305	A750	60w multicolored	.45	.25
1306	A750	60w multicolored	.45	.25
1307	A750	60w multicolored	.45	.25
1308	A750	60w multicolored	.45	.25
	Nos. 1304-1308 (5)		2.25	1.25

Souvenir Sheets of 2

1304a	A750	60w	2.10	2.10
1305a	A750	60w	2.10	2.10
1306a	A750	60w	2.10	2.10
1307a	A750	60w	2.10	2.10
1308a	A750	60w	2.10	2.10
	Nos. 1304a-1308a (5)		10.50	10.50

Natl. Flag Centenary — A751

1982, Aug. 22

1309	A751 60w multicolored	.45	.25
a.	Souvenir sheet of 2	2.40	2.40

2nd Seoul Open Intl. Table Tennis Championship, Aug. 25-31 — A752

1982, Aug. 25

1310	A752 60w multicolored	.50	.25

27th World Amateur Baseball Championship Series, Seoul, Sept. 4-18 — A753

1982, Sept. 4 **Engr.** ***Perf. 13***

1311	A753 60w red brown	.75	.25

Seoul Intl. Trade Fair (SITRA '82), Sept. 24-Oct. 18 — A754

1982, Sept. 17 **Photo.** ***Perf. 13½x13***

1312	A754 60w multicolored	.45	.25

Philatelic Week, Oct. 15-21 — A755

Design: Miners reading consolatory letters.

1982, Oct. 15

1313	A755 60w multicolored	.45	.25
a.	Souvenir sheet of 2	1.60	1.60

Visit of Indonesian Pres. Suharto, Oct. 16-19 — A756

1982, Oct. 16 **Litho.** ***Perf. 13x12½***

1314	A756 60w multicolored	.45	.25
a.	Souvenir sheet of 2, imperf.	1.50	1.50

A757

1982, Nov. 3 ***Perf. 13½x13***

1315	A757 60w multicolored	.45	.25

37th Jaycee (Intl. Junior Chamber of Commerce) World Congress, Seoul, Nov. 3-18.

2nd UN Conference on Peaceful Uses of Outer Space, Vienna, Aug. 9-21 — A758

1982, Nov. 20 ***Perf. 13x13½***

1316	A758 60w multicolored	.40	.25

New Year 1983 (Year of the Boar) — A759

No. 1317, Magpies, money bag. No. 1318, Boar, bas-relief.

1982, Dec. 1

1317	A759 60w multicolored	.45	.25
a.	Souvenir sheet of 2	2.10	2.10
1318	A759 60w multicolored	.45	.25
a.	Souvenir sheet of 2	2.10	2.10

Flags of Korea and Turkey — A760

1982, Dec. 20 ***Perf. 13***

1319	A760 60w multicolored	.45	.25
a.	Souvenir sheet of 2, imperf.	1.75	1.75

Visit of Pres. Kenan Evren of Turkey, Dec. 20-23.

Letter Writing Campaign — A761

1982, Dec. 31 **Photo.** ***Perf. 13x13½***

1320	A761 60w multicolored	.45	.25

First Intl. Customs Day — A762

1983, Jan. 26 ***Perf. 13½x13***

1321	A762 60w multicolored	.50	.25

Korean-made Vehicle Issue

Hyundai Pony-2 — A764

Daewoo Maepsy — A765

Super Titan Truck — A768

Flat-bed Truck — A770

1983 **Photo.** ***Perf. 13½x13***

1322	A764	60w Keohwa Jeep	.80	.25
1323	A764	60w shown	.80	.25
a.		Pair, #1322-1323	2.10	2.10
1324	A765	60w shown	.75	.25
1325	A764	60w Kia minibus	.75	.25
a.		Pair, #1324-1325	2.00	2.00
1326	A764	60w Highway bus	.85	.25
1327	A768	60w shown	.85	.25
1328	A764	70w Dump truck	1.15	.25
1329	A770	70w shown	1.15	.25
1330	A764	70w Cement mixer	1.10	.25
1331	A764	70w Oil truck	1.05	.25
		Nos. 1322-1331 (10)	9.25	2.50

Issued: Nos. 1322-1323, 2/25; Nos. 1324-1325, 3/25; Nos. 1326-1327, 5/25; Nos. 1328-1329, 7/25; Nos. 1330-1331, 8/25.

Visit of Malaysian Seri Paduka Baginda, Mar. 22-26 — A773

1983, Mar. 22

1332	A773 60w multicolored	.45	.25
a.	Souvenir sheet of 2	1.25	1.25

Postal Service Issue

General Bureau of Postal Administration Building — A774

Mailman, 1884 — A776

Ancient Mail Carrier — A778

Nos. 1-2 — A780

Pre-modern Period Postal Symbol, Mailbox — A782

Designs: No. 1334, Seoul Central PO. No. 1336, Mailman on motorcycle, 1983. No. 1338, Modern mail transport. No. 1340, No. 1201. No. 1342, Current postal symbol, mailbox.

1983-84 **Photo.** ***Perf. 13½x13***

1333	A774	60w multicolored	.65	.25
1334	A774	60w multicolored	.65	.25
1335	A776	70w multicolored	.80	.25
1336	A776	70w multicolored	.80	.25
1337	A778	70w multicolored	.80	.25
1338	A778	70w multicolored	.80	.25
1339	A780	70w multicolored	.65	.25
1340	A780	70w multicolored	.65	.25
1341	A782	70w multicolored	.65	.25
1342	A782	70w multicolored	.65	.25
		Nos. 1333-1342 (10)	7.10	2.50

PHILAKOREA '84, Seoul, Oct. 22-31, 1984.

Issued: Nos. 1333-1334, 4/22; Nos. 1335-1336, 6/10; Nos. 1337-1338, 8/10; Nos. 1339-1340, 2/10/84; Nos. 1341-1342, 3/10/84.

Teachers' Day — A784

60w, Village schoolhouse, score.

1983, May 15 **Photo.** ***Perf. 13x13½***

1343	A784 60w multicolored	.50	.25
a.	Souvenir sheet of 2	1.75	2.00

World Communications Year — A785

1983, June 20

1344	A785 70w multicolored	.55	.25
a.	Souvenir sheet of 2	1.50	1.50

Communications Life Insurance Inauguration A786

1983, July 1 **Photo.** ***Perf. 13½x13***

1345	A786 70w multicolored	.60	.25

Science and Technology Symposium, Seoul, July 4-8 — A787

1983, July 4

1346	A787 70w multicolored	.50	.25

Visit of Jordan's King Hussein, Sept. 10-13 — A788

70w, Pres. Hwan, King Hussein, flags.

1983, Sept. 10 **Litho.** ***Perf. 13x12½***

1347	A788 70w multicolored	.50	.25
a.	Souvenir sheet of 2, imperf.	1.60	1.60

ASTA, 53rd World Travel Congress, Seoul — A789

1983, Sept. 25 **Photo.** ***Perf. 13***

1348	A789 70w multicolored	.55	.25

A790

1983, Oct. 4 **Photo.** ***Perf. 13***

1349	A790 70w multicolored	.55	.25
a.	Souvenir sheet of 2	1.60	1.60

70th Inter-Parliamentary Union Conference.

A791

1983, Oct. 6 Photo. *Perf. 13*

1350 A791 70w Gymnastics .55 .25
1351 A791 70w Soccer .55 .25

64th National Sports Festival.

Pres. Chun and Pres. U San Yu of Burma — A791a

Pres. Chun's Curtailed Visit to Southwest Asia: No. 1351B, India. No. 1351C, Pres. Junius R. Jayawardene, Sri Lanka. No. 1351D, Australia, flag. No. 1351E, New Zealand, flag. Withdrawn after one day due to political assassination.

1983, Oct. 8 Photo. *Perf. 13½x13*

1351A A791a 70w multicolored 1.30 .60
1351B A791a 70w multicolored 1.30 .60
1351C A791a 70w multicolored 1.30 .60
1351D A791a 70w multicolored 1.30 .60
1351E A791a 70w multicolored 1.30 .60
Nos. 1351A-1351E (5) 6.50 3.00

Souvenir Sheets of 2

1351f A791a 70w 4.25 4.25
1351g A791a 70w 4.25 4.25
1351h A791a 70w 4.25 4.25
1351i A791a 70w 4.25 4.25
1351j A791a 70w 4.25 4.25
Nos. 1351f-1351j (5) 21.25 21.25

Water Resource Development — A792

1983, Oct. 15 Litho. *Perf. 13*

1352 A792 70w multicolored .55 .25

Newspaper Publication Cent. — A793

1983, Oct. 31 Litho. *Perf. 13*

1353 A793 70w multicolored .55 .25

Natl. Tuberculosis Assoc., 30th Anniv. — A794

1983, Nov. 6 Photo. *Perf. 13*

1354 A794 70w multicolored .55 .25

Presidents Chun and Reagan, Natl. Flags — A795

1983, Nov. 12 Photo. *Perf. 13*

1355 A795 70w multicolored .65 .25
a. Souvenir sheet of 2 2.50 2.50

Visit of Pres. Ronald Reagan, Nov. 12-14.

11th Philatelic Week — A796

1983, Nov. 18 Photo. *Perf. 13*

1356 A796 70w multicolored .55 .25
a. Souvenir sheet of 2 2.40 2.40

New Year 1984
A797 A798

No. 1357, Mouse, stone wall relief. No. 1358, Cranes, pine tree.

1983, Dec. 1 Photo. *Perf. 13*

1357 A797 70w multicolored .70 .25
a. Souvenir sheet of 2 2.50 2.50
1358 A798 70w multicolored .70 .25
a. Souvenir sheet of 2 2.50 2.50

Bicentenary of Catholic Church in Korea — A799

1984, Jan. 4 Photo. *Perf. 13x13½*

1359 A799 70w Cross .60 .25
a. Souvenir sheet of 2 3.00 3.00

Visit of Brunei's Sultan Bolkiah- Apr. 7-9 — A800

1984, Apr. 7 Litho. *Perf. 13x12½*

1360 A800 70w multicolored .55 .25
a. Souvenir sheet of 2, imperf. 1.75 1.75

Visit of Qatar's Sheik Khalifa, Apr. 20-22 — A801

1984, Apr. 20

1361 A801 70w multicolored .55 .25
a. Souvenir sheet of 2, imperf. 1.60 1.60

Girl Mailing Letter — A802

Mailman in City — A803

1984, Apr. 22 Photo. *Perf. 13½x13*

1362 A802 70w multicolored .55 .25
a. Souvenir sheet of 2 1.60 1.60
1363 A803 70w multicolored .55 .25
a. Souvenir sheet of 2 1.60 1.60

Korean postal service.

Visit of Pope John Paul II, May 3-7 — A808

1984, May 3 Engr. *Perf. 12½*

1368 A808 70w dk brn .65 .25

Photogravure & Engraved

1369 A808 70w multicolored .65 .25
a. Souvenir sheet of 2, #1368-1369, perf. 13½ 2.40 2.40

Tools, Brushes, Flower — A809

1984, May 11 Photo. *Perf. 13x13½*

1370 A809 70w multicolored .55 .25

Workers' Cultural Festival.

Jet, Ship, Asia Map — A810

1984, May 21 Photo. *Perf. 13x13½*

1371 A810 70w multicolored .55 .25

Customs Cooperation Council 63rd-64th Sessions, Seoul, May 21-25.

Visit of Sri Lanka's Pres. Jayewardene, May 27-30 — A811

70w, Asia map, flags, flowers.

1984, May 27 *Perf. 13½x13*

1372 A811 70w multicolored .55 .25
a. Souvenir sheet of 2 1.50 1.50

Advertising Congress Emblem — A812

1984, June 18 Photo. *Perf. 13x13½*

1373 A812 70w multicolored .55 .25

14th Asian Advertising Cong., Seoul, June 18-21.

'88 Olympic Expressway Opening — A813

1984, June 22

1374 A813 70w multicolored .60 .25

Intl. Olympic Committee, 90th Anniv. — A814

1984, June 23

1375 A814 70w multicolored .55 .25

Asia-Pacific Broadcasting Union, 20th Anniv. — A815

70w, Emblem, microphone.

1984, June 30 *Perf. 13½x13*

1376 A815 70w multicolored .55 .25

Visit of Senegal's Pres. Diouf, July 9-12 — A816

70w, Flags of Korea & Senegal.

1984, July 9 Litho. *Perf. 13x12½*

1377 A816 70w multicolored .55 .25
a. Souvenir sheet of 2, imperf. 1.75 1.75

1984 Summer Olympics A817

Lithographed and Engraved

1984, July 28 *Perf. 12½*

1378 A817 70w Archery .70 .25
1379 A817 440w Fencing 2.60 .65

Korean Protestant Church Cent. — A818

Stained glass windows.

1984, Aug. 16 *Perf. 13*

1380 A818 70w Crucifixion .70 .25
1381 A818 70w Cross, dove .70 .25
a. Souvenir sheet of 2 5.25 5.25
b. Pair, #1380-1381 1.75 1.75

Groom on Horseback — A819

Wedding Procession: a, Lantern carrier. b, Groom. c, Musician. d, Bride in sedan chair (52x33mm).

1984, Sept. 1 Photo. *Perf. 13x13½*

1382 Strip of 4 3.75 1.50
a.-d. A819 70w any single .70 .25
e. Souvenir sheet 2.10 2.10

No. 1382e contains No. 1382d.

Pres. Chun's Visit to Japan, Sept. 6-8 — A820

70w, Chun, flag, Mt. Fuji.

1984, Sept. 6 Litho. *Perf. 13x12½*

1383 A820 70w multicolored .55 .25
a. Souvenir sheet of 2, imperf. 1.75 1.75

Visit of Gambia's Pres. Jawara, Sept. 12-17 — A821

70w, Flags of Korea & Gambia.

1984, Sept. 12

1384 A821 70w multicolored .55 .25
a. Souvenir sheet of 2, imperf. 1.75 1.75

Visit of Gabon's Pres. Bongo, Sept. 21-23 — A822

70w, Flags of Korea & Gabon.

1984, Sept. 21 *Perf. 13*

1385 A822 70w multicolored .55 .25
a. Souvenir sheet of 2, imperf. 1.75 1.75

Seoul Intl. Trade Fair — A823

1984, Sept. 18 Photo. ***Perf. 13x13½***

1386	A823 70w Products	.55	.25

65th Natl. Sports Festival, Taegu, Oct. 11-16 — A824

1984, Oct. 11 Photo. ***Perf. 13½x13***

1387	A824 70w Badminton	.60	.25
1388	A824 70w Wrestling	.60	.25

Philakorea '84 Stamp Show, Seoul, Oct. 22-31 — A825

No. 1389, South Gate, stamps. No. 1390, Emblem under magnifier, vert.

1984, Oct. 22 ***Perf. 13½x13, 13x13½***

1389	A825 70w multicolored	.55	.25
a.	Souvenir sheet of 4	3.25	3.25
1390	A825 70w multicolored	.55	.25
a.	Souvenir sheet of 4	3.25	3.25

Visit of Maldives Pres. Maumoon Abdul Gayoom, Oct. 29-Nov. 1 A826

1984, Oct. 29 Litho. ***Perf. 13x12½***

1392	A826 70w multicolored	.55	.25
a.	Souvenir sheet of 2, imperf.	1.90	1.90

Chamber of Commerce and Industry Cent. — A827

1984, Oct. 31 Photo. ***Perf. 13x13½***

1393	A827 70w "100"	.55	.25

Children Playing Jaegi-chagi — A828

New Year 1985 (Year of the ox).

1984, Dec. 1 Photo. ***Perf. 13x13½***

1394	A828 70w Ox, bas-relief	.55	.25
a.	Souvenir sheet of 2	1.60	1.60
1395	A828 70w shown	.55	.25
a.	Souvenir sheet of 2	1.60	1.60

Intl. Youth Year — A829

1985, Jan. 25 Photo. ***Perf. 13½x13***

1396	A829 70w IYY emblem	.55	.25

Korean Folkways Series

A830

No. 1397, Pounding rice. No. 1398, Welcoming full moon. No. 1399, Wrestling. No. 1400, Janggi, Korean chess.

1985 Photo. ***Perf. 13x13½***

1397	A830 70w multicolored	.70	.25
1398	A830 70w multicolored	.70	.25
1399	A830 70w multicolored	.85	.25
1400	A830 70w multicolored	.85	.25

Issued: Nos. 1397-1398, 2/19; Nos. 1399-1400, 8/20.

Modern Art Series

Rocky Mountain in the Early Spring, 1915, by Shimjoen, (Ahn Jung-shik) A831

Still-life with a Doll, 1927, by Suhlcho, (Lee Chong-woo) A832

Spring Day on a Farm, 1961, by Eijai, (Huh Paik-ryun, 1903-1977) — A833

The Exorcist, 1941, by Chulma, (Kim Chung-hyun, 1901-1953) — A834

Chunhyang-do, by Kim Un-ho — A835

Flowers, by Lee Sang-bum A836

Image of A Friend, by Ku Bon-wung A837

Woman in a Ski Suit, by Son Ung-seng A838

Valley of the Peach Blossoms, 1964, by Pyen Kwan-Sik (1899-1976) A839

Rural Landscape, 1940, by Lee Yong-Wu (1904-1952) A840

Male, 1932, by Lee Ma-Dong A841

Woman with a Water Jar on Her Head, 1944, by Yun Hyo-Chung (1917-1967) A842

Photo.; Litho. & Engr. (#1411-1412)

1985-87 ***Perf. 13½x13, 13x13½***

1401	A831 70w multicolored	.75	.25
1402	A832 70w multicolored	.75	.25
1403	A833 70w multicolored	.75	.25
1404	A834 70w multicolored	.75	.25
1405	A835 80w multi ('86)	1.15	.40
1406	A836 80w multi ('86)	1.15	.40
1407	A837 80w multi ('86)	1.15	.40
1408	A838 80w multi ('86)	1.15	.40
1409	A839 80w multi ('87)	*3.00*	.85
1410	A840 80w multi ('87)	*3.00*	.85
1411	A841 80w multi ('87)	*3.00*	.85
1412	A842 80w multi ('87)	*3.00*	.85
	Nos. 1401-1412 (12)	*19.60*	6.00

Issued: Nos. 1401-1402, 4/10; Nos. 1403-1404, 7/5; Nos. 1405-1408, 12/1; Nos. 1409-1412, 6/12.

State Visit of Pres. Chun to the US — A843

Photo. & Engr.

1985, Apr. 24 ***Perf. 13***

1413	A843 70w multicolored	.60	.25
a.	Souvenir sheet of 2	1.75	1.75

Coastal and Inland Fish Series

Gak-si- Bung-eo (silver carp) — A844

Dot-sac-chi (sword fish) — A845

Eoreumchi A846

Sweetfish A847

Sardine — A848

Hammerhead Shark — A849

Cham-jung- go-ji — A850

Swi-ri — A851

Oar Fish — A852

Devil-ray — A853

1985-87 Photo. ***Perf. 13½x13***

1414	A844 70w multicolored	.70	.25
1415	A845 70w multicolored	.70	.25
1416	A846 70w multi ('86)	1.60	.55
1417	A847 70w multi ('86)	1.60	.55
1418	A848 70w multi ('86)	1.60	.55
1419	A849 70w multi ('86)	1.60	.55
1420	A850 80w multi ('87)	2.50	1.00
1421	A851 80w multi ('87)	2.50	1.00
1422	A852 80w multi ('87)	2.50	1.00
1423	A853 80w multi ('87)	2.50	1.00
	Nos. 1414-1423 (10)	17.80	6.70

Issued: Nos. 1414-1415, 5/30; Nos. 1416-1423, 7/25.

Yonsei University and Medical School, Cent. — A854

Photogravure and Engraved

1985, May 6 ***Perf. 13***

1424	A854 70w Underwood Hall	.55	.25

State Visit of Pres. Mohammad Zia-Ul-Haq of Pakistan, May 6-10 — A855

1985, May 6 Photo. *Perf. 13x13½*

1425 A855 70w multicolored .55 .25
a. Souvenir sheet of 2 1.60 1.60

State Visit of Pres. Luis Alberto Monge of Costa Rica, May 19-23 — A856

1985, May 18 *Perf. 13½x13*

1426 A856 70w multicolored .55 .25
a. Souvenir sheet of 2 1.60 1.60

State Visit of Pres. Hussain Muhammad Ershad of Bangladesh, June 15-19 — A857

1985, June 15

1427 A857 70w multicolored .55 .25
a. Souvenir sheet of 2, imperf. 1.60 1.60

State Visit of Pres. Joao Bernardo Vieira of Guinea-Bissau, June 25-28 — A858

1985, June 25

1428 A858 70w multicolored .55 .25
a. Souvenir sheet of 2, imperf. 1.60 1.60

Liberation from Japanese Occupation Forces, 40th Anniv. — A859

Heavenly Lake, Mt. Paektu, natl. flower.

1985, Aug. 14 Litho. *Perf. 13x12½*

1429 A859 70w multicolored .55 .25

Music Series

The Spring of My Home, Music by Hong Nan-pa and Lyrics by Lee Won-su A860

A Leaf Boat, Music by Yun Yong-ha and Lyrics by Park Hong-Keun A861

Half Moon, 1924, by Yun Keuk-Young A862

Let's Go and Pick the Moon, by Yun Seok-Jung and Park Tae Hyun A863

1985-86 Photo. *Perf. 13x13½*

1430 A860 70w multicolored .80 .25
1431 A861 70w multicolored .80 .25
1432 A862 70w multicolored 1.00 .30
1433 A863 70w multicolored 1.60 .50

Issued: Nos. 1430-1431, 9/10; Nos. 1432-1433, 6/25/86.

Korean Folkways Series

Korean Farm Music — A864

No. 1434 — Musicians with: a, Flag, hand gong. b, Drum flute. c, Drum, hand gong. d, Taborets, ribbons. e, Taboret, sun, woman, child. Has continuous design.

1986, Aug. 26 Photo. *Perf. 13½x13*

1434 Strip of 5 6.75 6.75
a.-e. A864 70w, any single 1.10 .25

Music Series

Barley Field, by Park Wha-mok and Yun Yong-ha A865

Magnolia, by Cho Young-Shik and Kim Dong-jin A866

1987, Mar. 25 Photo. *Perf. 13x13½*

1435 A865 80w multicolored 2.50 1.00
1436 A866 80w multicolored 2.50 1.00

Korean Folkways Series

Chusok, Harvest Moon Festival A867

No. 1437 — Harvest moon dance: a, Eight dancers, harvest moon. b, Four dancers, festival wheels, balloons. c, Three dancers, children on see-saw. d, Four dancers, women preparing meal.

1987, Sept. 10 Photo. *Perf. 13x13½*

1437 A867 Strip of 4 16.00 16.00
a.-d. 80w any single 3.25 .85

Folkways and Music Series

Tano, Spring Harvest Festival A868

No. 1438: a, Woman on shore, riding a swing. b, Sweet flag coiffures. c, Boy picking flowers, girl on swing. d, Boys wrestling.

1988, Aug. 25 Photo. *Perf. 13x13½*

1438 A868 Strip of 4 5.50 5.50
a.-d. 80w multicolored 1.10 .40

Sick for Home, by Lee Eun-sang and Kim Kong-jin A869

Pioneer, by Yoon Hae-young and Cho Doo-nam A870

1988, Nov. 15

1439 A869 80w multicolored .70 .25
1440 A870 80w multicolored .70 .25

Mask Dance (Talchum) — A871

No. 1441: a, Two mask dancers with scarves. b, Dancers with fans. c, Dancers with scarf and laurel or fan. d, Three dancers, first as an animal and two more carrying fan and bells or torch.

1989, Feb. 25

1441 A871 Strip of 4 5.00 5.00
a.-d. 80w any single 1.10 .40

Korean Telecommunications, Cent. — A872

70w, Satellite, emblem, dish receiver.

1985, Sept. 28 *Perf. 13½x13*

1442 A872 70w multicolored .55 .25

World Bank Conference, Seoul, Oct. 8-11 — A873

1985, Oct. 8 *Perf. 13x13½*

1443 A873 70w Emblem .55 .25

Intl. Bank for Reconstruction & Development, 40th Anniv.

UN, 40th Anniv. — A874

1985, Oct. 24 *Perf. 13½x13*

1444 A874 70w Emblem, doves .55 .25

Natl. Red Cross, 80th Anniv. — A875

1985, Oct. 26

1445 A875 70w red, blk & bl .55 .25

Segment of Canceled Cover — A876

1985, Nov. 18 Photo. *Perf. 13½x13*

1446 A876 70w multicolored .55 .25

12th Philatelic Week, Nov. 18-23.

New Year 1986 — A877

Lithographed and Engraved

1985, Dec. 2 *Perf. 13x13½*

1447 A877 70w multicolored .55 .25

Mt. Fuji, Korean Airlines Jet — A878

1985, Dec. 18 Photo.

1448 A878 70w brt bl, blk & red .65 .30

Normalization of diplomatic relations between Korea and Japan, 20th anniv.
See No. C44.

Statesman Type of 1986 and Types of 1981-86

Engr., Photo. (40w)

1986-87 *Perf. 13*

1449 A716 550w indigo 2.75 .40

Coil Stamps

Perf. 13 Vert.

1449A A704 20w multicolored .65 .35
1449B A705 40w multicolored .75 .30
1449C A708 80w multicolored 1.25 .55
Nos. 1449A-1449C (3) 2.65 1.20

Issue dates: 550w, Dec. 10; others, 1987.

Intl. Peace Year — A879

1986, Jan. 15 Photo. *Perf. 13x13½*

1450 A879 70w multicolored .60 .25

See No. C45.

State Visits of Pres. Chun — A880

Portrait, natl. flags and: No. 1452, Parliament, Brussels. No. 1453, Eiffel Tower, Paris. No. 1454, Cathedral, Cologne. No. 1455, Big Ben, London.

1986, Apr. 4 Litho. *Perf. 12½x13*

1452 A880 70w multicolored .65 .30
1453 A880 70w multicolored .65 .30
1454 A880 70w multicolored .65 .30
1455 A880 70w multicolored .65 .30
Nos. 1452-1455 (4) 2.60 1.20

Souvenir Sheets of 2

Perf. 13½

1452a A880 70w 3.00 3.00
1453a A880 70w 3.00 3.00
1454a A880 70w 3.00 3.00
1455a A880 70w 3.00 3.00
Nos. 1452a-1455a (4) 12.00 12.00

Science Series

Observatories A881

Designs: No. 1456, Chomsongdae Observatory, Satellites. No. 1457, Kwanchondae Observatory, Halley's Comet.

1986, Apr. 21 *Perf. 13½x13*

1456 70w multicolored 2.60 .80
1457 70w multicolored 2.60 .80
a. A881 Pair, #1456-1457 6.50 2.40

Weather — A883

Designs: No. 1458, Wind observatory stone foundation, Chosun Dynasty. No. 1459, Rain gauge, Sejong Period to Chosun Dynasty.

1987, Apr. 21 Photo. *Perf. 13½*

1458 80w multicolored 2.75 .90
1459 80w multicolored 2.75 .90
a. A883 Pair, #1458-1459 7.00 3.25

Clocks — A885

Designs: No. 1460, *Chagyokru*, water clock invented by Chang Yongshil and Kim Bin in 1434. No. 1461, *Angbuilgu*, sundial completed during King Sejong's reign (1418-1450).

1988, Apr. 21 Photo. *Perf. 13½x13*

1460	80w multicolored	.70	.30
1461	80w multicolored	.70	.30
a.	A885 Pair, #1460-1461	1.90	1.90

Early Printing Methods — A887

Designs: No. 1462, Sutra manuscript (detail) printed from wood type, Shila Dynasty, c.704-751. No. 1463, Two characters from a manuscript printed from metal type, Koryo, c.1237.

1989, Apr. 21

1462	80w buff & sepia	1.45	.35
1463	80w buff & sepia	1.45	.35
a.	A887 Pair, #1462-1463	3.00	2.25

A889

Designs: No. 1464, 7th century gilt bronze Buddha. No. 1465, Bronze Age dagger, spear molds.

1990, Apr. 21

1464	100w multicolored	.55	.25
1465	100w multicolored	.55	.25
a.	A889 Pair, #1464-1465	1.35	1.35
	Complete bklt., 2 each #1464-1465	2.50	
	Nos. 1456-1465 (10)	16.10	5.20

Pairs have continuous designs.

Souvenir Booklets

Booklets containing the stamps listed below have a stamp, pair or strip of stamps, tied to the booklet cover with a first day cancel.

1464-1465, 1523-1524, 1529-1532, 1535-1536, 1539-1540, 1553, 1559-1566, 1572-1576, 1583-1584, 1595-1608, 1613-1621, 1622-1623B, 1624, 1635-1650, 1655-1656, 1657-1668, 1669-1676, 1678-1690, 1693-1699, 1700-1702, 1713-1714, 1745-1748, 1751-1758, 1763-1764, 1767-1768, 1770-1773, 1776-1787, 1797, 1799-1802, 1803-1806, 1810-1811.

Assoc. of Natl. Olympic Committees, 5th General Assembly, Seoul, Apr. 21-25 — A891

1986, Apr. 21 *Perf. 13x13½*

1466	A891 70w multicolored	.55	.25

Souvenir Sheet

Butterflies — A892

1986, May 22 Litho. *Perf. 13½*

1467	A892 Sheet of 6	24.00	24.00
a.	70w multicolored	2.75	1.35
b.	370w multicolored	2.75	1.35
c.	400w multicolored	2.75	1.35
d.	440w multicolored	2.75	1.35
e.	450w multicolored	2.75	1.35
f.	470w multicolored	2.75	1.35

AMERIPEX '86, Chicago, May 22-June 1. No. 1467 contains stamps of different sizes (370w, 42x41mm; 400w, 42x33mm; 440w, 39x45mm; 450w, 32x42mm; 470w, 33x44mm); margin continues the designs.

Women's Education, Cent. — A893

1986, May 31 *Perf. 13x12½*

1468	A893 70w multicolored	.55	.25

State Visit of Pres. Andre Kolingba, Central Africa — A894

1986, June 10 *Perf. 13*

1469	A894 70w multicolored	.55	.25
a.	Souvenir sheet of 2, imperf.	1.50	1.50

Completion of Han River Development Project — A895

1986, Sept. 10 Litho. *Perf. 13*

1470	Strip of 3	4.00	4.00
a.	A895 30w Bridge	1.05	.30
b.	A895 60w Buildings	1.05	.30
c.	A895 80w Seoul Tower, buildings	1.05	.30

Printed in a continuous design.

Fireworks, Seoul Tower A896

Games Emblem A897

1986, Sept. 20 Photo. *Perf. 13x13½*

1471	A896 80w multicolored	.65	.30
a.	Souvenir sheet of 2	6.25	6.25
1472	A897 80w multicolored	.65	.30
a.	Souvenir sheet of 2	6.25	6.25

Souvenir Sheet

10th Asian Games, Seoul, Sept. 20-Oct. 5 A898

1986, Oct. 31

1473	A898 550w multicolored	19.00	19.00

Juan Antonio Samaranch, Korean IOC Delegation, 1981 — A899

1986, Sept. 30

1474	A899 80w multicolored	.95	.40

Intl. Olympic Committee decision to hold 24th Olympic Games in Seoul, 5th anniv.

Philatelic Week — A900

1986, Nov. 18 Photo. *Perf. 13½x13*

1475	A900 80w Boy fishing for stamp	.65	.25

New Year 1987 (Year of the Hare) — A901

1986, Dec. 1 Photo. *Perf. 13x13½*

1476	A901 80w multicolored	.85	.30

Birds — A902

1986, Dec. 20 *Perf. 13x14*

1477	A902 80w Waxwing	1.25	.35
1478	A902 80w Oriole	1.25	.35
1479	A902 80w Kingfisher	1.25	.35
1480	A902 80w Hoopoe	1.25	.35
1481	A902 80w Roller	1.25	.35
a.	Strip of 5, #1477-1481	6.75	6.75

Coil Stamps
Perf. 14 Horiz.

1481B	A902 80w like No. 1479	2.40	.60
1481C	A902 80w like No. 1480	2.40	.60
1481D	A902 80w like No. 1481	2.40	.60
1481E	A902 80w like No. 1477	2.40	.60
1481F	A902 80w like No. 1478	2.40	.60
g.	Strip of 5, #1481B-1481F	21.00	21.00

Wildlife Conservation A903

Endangered species: No. 1482, Panthera tigris altaica. No. 1483, Felis bengalensis. No. 1484, Vulpes vulpes. No. 1485, Sus scrofa.

1987, Feb. 25 Photo. *Perf. 13½x13*

1482	A903 80w multicolored	2.00	.60
1483	A903 80w multicolored	2.00	.60
1484	A903 80w multicolored	2.00	.60
1485	A903 80w multicolored	2.00	.60
a.	Strip of 4, #1482-1485	9.50	9.50

Flowers — A904

No. 1486, Dicentra spectabilis. No. 1487, Hanabusaya asiatica. No. 1488, Erythronium japonicum. No. 1489, Dianthus chinensis. No. 1490, Chrysanthemum zawadskii coreanum.

1987, Mar. 20 Photo. *Perf. 14x13*

1486	A904 550w multicolored	2.25	.50
1487	A904 550w multicolored	2.25	.50
1488	A904 550w multicolored	2.25	.50
1489	A904 550w multicolored	2.25	.50
1490	A904 550w multicolored	2.25	.50
a.	Strip of 5, #1486-1490	13.50	13.50

Coil Stamps
Perf. 13 Vert.

1490B	A904 550w like No. 1486	2.40	.75
1490C	A904 550w like No. 1487	2.40	.75
1490D	A904 550w like No. 1488	2.40	.75
1490E	A904 550w like No. 1489	2.40	.75
1490F	A904 550w like No. 1490	2.40	.75
g.	Strip of 5, #1490B-1490F	16.00	16.00

State Visit of Pres. Ahmed Abdallah Abderemane of the Comoro Isls., Apr. 6-9 — A905

1987, Apr. 6 Litho. *Perf. 13½x13*

1491	A905 80w multicolored	.55	.25
a.	Souvenir sheet of 2	2.10	2.10

Electrification of Korea, Cent. — A906

1987, Apr. 10 Photo.

1492	A906 80w multicolored	.55	.25

Int'l. Assoc. of Ports and Harbors, 15th General Session, Seoul — A907

1987, Apr. 25 Photo. *Perf. 13½x13*

1493	A907 80w multicolored	.55	.25

State Visit of Pres. U San Yu of Burma — A908

1987, June 8 Litho. *Perf. 13½x13*

1494	A908 80w multicolored	.55	.25
a.	Souvenir sheet of 2	1.90	1.90

Year of The Communications for Information Society — A909

No. 1495, Map, digital telephone. No. 1496, Emblem.

1987, June 30 *Perf. 13x13½*

1495	A909 80w multicolored	.60	.25
1496	A909 80w multicolored	.60	.25

Introduction of automatic switching telephone system.

Independence Hall, Monument to the Nation A910

Statue of Indomitable Koreans, Nat'l. Flag A911

1987, Aug. 14 Photo. ***Perf. 13½x13***
1497 A910 80w multicolored .95 .30
a. Souvenir sheet of 2 11.00 11.00
1498 A911 80w multicolored .95 .30
a. Souvenir sheet of 2 11.00 11.00

Opening of Independence Hall, Aug. 15.

16th Pacific Science Congress, Seoul, Aug. 20-30 — A912

1987, Aug. 20 ***Perf. 13x13½***
1499 A912 80w multicolored .65 .25
a. Souvenir sheet of 2 3.00 3.00

State Visit of Pres. Virgilio Barco of Colombia — A913

1987, Sept. 8 Litho. ***Perf. 13½x13***
1500 A913 80w multicolored .55 .25
a. Souvenir sheet of 2 2.10 2.10

Installation of 10-millionth Telephone — A914

1987, Sept. 28 ***Perf. 13½x13***
1501 A914 80w multicolored .55 .25

Armed Forces, 39th Anniv. — A915

Armed Forces Day: Servicemen, flags of three military services.

1987, Sept. 30 Litho. ***Perf. 13***
1502 A915 80w multicolored .75 .25

14th Philatelic Week, Nov. 18-24 — A916

80w, Boy playing the nalrali.

1987, Nov. 18 Photo. ***Perf. 13½***
1503 A916 80w multicolored .65 .25

A917

1987, Nov. 28 Litho.
1504 A917 80w multicolored .90 .35

Signing of the Antarctic Treaty by Korea, 1st anniv.

A918

1987, Dec. 1 Photo.
1505 A918 80w multicolored 1.15 .30

New Year 1988 (Year of the Dragon).

Natl. Social Security Program — A919

1988, Jan. 4 Litho. ***Perf. 13½x13***
1506 A919 80w multicolored .65 .25

Completion of the Korean Antarctic Base — A919a

1988, Feb. 16 Photo. ***Perf. 13x13½***
1506A A919a 80w multicolored 1.00 .30

Inauguration of Roh Tae-Woo, 13th President — A920

1988, Feb. 24 Photo. ***Perf. 13½x13***
1507 A920 80w multicolored 2.50 .40
a. Souvenir sheet of 2 20.00 20.00

World Wildlife Fund — A921

White-naped crane *(Grus vipio)* displaying various behaviors: a, Calling (1). b, Running (2). c, Spreading wings (3). d, Flying (4).

1988, Apr. 1 ***Perf. 13x13½***
1508 Strip of 4 7.00 7.00
a.-d. A921 80w any single 1.20 .65

Intl. Red Cross & Red Crescent Organizations, 125th Annivs. — A922

1988, May 7 Photo. ***Perf. 13x13½***
1509 A922 80w multicolored .65 .25

Telepress Medium, 1st Anniv. — A923

1988, June 1 Litho.
1510 A923 80w multicolored .55 .25

Pierre de Coubertin, Olympic Flag — A924

Olympic Temple — A925

View of Seoul A926

Folk Dancers A927

Litho. & Engr.

1988, Sept. 16 ***Perf. 13½x13***
1511 A924 80w multicolored .85 .30
1512 A925 80w multicolored .85 .30

Photo.

Perf. 13x13½
1513 A926 80w multicolored .85 .30
1514 A927 80w multicolored .85 .30
Nos. 1511-1514 (4) 3.40 1.20

1988 Summer Olympics, Seoul.

Souvenir Sheets of 2

1511a A924 80w 1.75 1.75
1512a A925 80w 1.75 1.75
1513a A926 80w 1.75 1.75
1514a A927 80w 1.75 1.75
Nos. 1511a-1514a (4) 7.00 7.00

Margin inscriptions on Nos. 1511a-1512a are photo.

OLYMPHILEX '88, Sept. 19-28, Seoul — A928

1988, Sept. 19 Photo. ***Perf. 13x13½***
1515 A928 80w multicolored .55 .25
a. Souvenir sheet of 2 1.75 1.75

22nd Congress of the Intl. Iron and Steel Institute, Seoul — A929

1988, Oct. 8 ***Perf. 13½x13***
1516 A929 80w multicolored .55 .25

A930

No. 1518, Archer seated in wheelchair.

1988, Oct. 15 ***Perf. 13x13½***
1517 A930 80w shown .90 .55
1518 A930 80w multicolored .65 .30

1988 Natl. Special Olympics (Paralympics), Seoul.

A931

1988, Dec. 1 Photo. ***Perf. 13x13½***
1519 A931 80w multicolored .95 .25

New Year 1989 (Year of the Snake).

Souvenir Sheet

Successful Completion of the 1988 Summer Olympics, Seoul — A932

1988, Dec. 20 Litho. ***Perf. 13x12½***
1520 A932 550w Opening ceremony 13.50 13.50

Music Series

Arirang A933

Doraji A934

Pakyon Falls A935

Chonan-Samkori A936

Natl. ballads.

1989-90 Photo. ***Perf. 13x13½***
1521 A933 80w multicolored .65 .25
1522 A934 80w multicolored .65 .25

Litho.

1523 A935 80w multicolored .65 .25
Complete booklet, 4 #1523 5.50
1524 A936 80w multicolored .65 .25
Complete booklet, 4 #1524 5.50

Issued: Nos. 1521-1522, 3/27; Nos. 1523-1524, 2/26/90.

Korean Folkways Series

Willowing Bow — A937

Spinning Wheel — A938

Treating Threads — A939

Weaving Fabric — A940

Litho. & Engr.

1990, Sept. 25 ***Perf. 13½x13***
1525 A937 100w multicolored .95 .30
1526 A938 100w multicolored .95 .30
1527 A939 100w multicolored .95 .30
1528 A940 100w multicolored .95 .30
a. Strip of 4, #1525-1528 4.25 4.25

Music Series

Orchard Avenue A941

In Flower Garden A942

A Swing A943

Longing for Mt. Keumkang A944

1991-92 Litho. ***Perf. 13x13½***
1529 A941 100w multicolored .80 .30
Complete booklet, 4 #1529 7.00
1530 A942 100w multicolored .80 .30
Complete booklet, 4 #1530 7.00
1531 A943 100w multicolored .65 .25
Complete booklet, 4 #1531 7.00
1532 A944 100w multicolored .65 .25
Complete booklet, 4 #1532 7.00

Issued: Nos. 1529-1530, 3/27; Nos. 1531-1532, 7/13/92.

14th Asian-Pacific Dental Congress — A945

1989, Apr. 26 Photo. ***Perf. 13x13½***
1533 A945 80w multicolored .55 .25

Rotary Intl. Convention, Seoul, May 21-25 — A946

1989, May 20 Photo. *Perf. 13x13½*
1534 A946 80w multicolored .65 .25

19th Cong. of the Intl. Council of Nurses, Seoul, May 28-June 2 — A947

1989, May 27
1535 A947 80w multicolored .65 .25
Complete booklet, 4 #1535 4.50

Information Industry Month — A948

1989, June 1
1536 A948 80w multicolored .65 .25
Complete booklet, 4 #1536 4.50

World Environment Day — A949

1989, June 5
1537 A949 80w multicolored .65 .25

Asia-Pacific Telecommunity, 10th Anniv. — A950

1989, July 1 Photo. *Perf. 13x13½*
1538 A950 80w multicolored .65 .25

French Revolution, Bicent. — A951

1989, July 14 Litho. *Perf. 13½x13*
1539 A951 80w multicolored .55 .25
Complete booklet, 4 #1539 4.50

Federation of Asian and Oceanian Biochemists 5th Congress — A952

1989, Aug. 12 Photo.
1540 A952 80w multicolored .55 .25
Complete booklet, 4 #1540 4.50

Modern Art Series

A White Ox, by Lee Joong-Sub A953

A Street Stall, by Park Lae-hyun A954

A Little Girl, by Lee Bong-Sang A955

An Autumn Scene, by Oh Ji-ho A956

Litho. & Engr.; Photo. (#1542, 1544)
1989, Sept. 4 *Perf. 13x13½, 13½x13*
1541 A953 80w multicolored .70 .30
1542 A954 80w multicolored .70 .30
1543 A955 80w multicolored .70 .30
1544 A956 80w multicolored .70 .30
Nos. 1541-1544 (4) 2.80 1.20

Allegory: The Valiant Spirit of Koreans — A965

1989, Sept. 12 Litho. *Perf. 13½x13*
1553 A965 80w multicolored .55 .25
Complete booklet, 4 #1553 4.50

1988 Seoul Olympics and the World Korean Sports Festival.

Personification of Justice and Ancient Codex — A966

1989, Sept. 18
1554 A966 80w multicolored .65 .25

Constitutional Court, 1st anniv.

Fish

A967 A968

A969 A970

No. 1555, Oplegnathus fasciatus. No. 1556, Cobitis multifasciata. No. 1557, Liobagrus mediadiposalis. No. 1558, Monocentris japonicus.

1989, Sept. 30 Photo. *Perf. 13½x13*
1555 A967 80w multicolored .75 .30
1556 A968 80w multicolored .75 .30
1557 A969 80w multicolored .75 .30
1558 A970 80w multicolored .75 .30

A971 A972

A973 A974

No. 1559, Hapalogenys mucronatus. No. 1560, Fugu niphobles. No. 1561, Oncorhynchus masou. No. 1562, Rhodeus ocellatus.

1990, July 2
1559 A971 100w multicolored .80 .30
Complete booklet, 4 #1559 8.75
1560 A972 100w multicolored .80 .30
Complete booklet, 4 #1560 8.75
1561 A973 100w multicolored .80 .30
Complete booklet, 4 #1561 8.75
1562 A974 100w multicolored .80 .30
Complete booklet, 4 #1562 8.75

A975

A976

A977

A978

No. 1563, Microphyso- gobio longidorsalis. No. 1564, Gnathopogon majimae. No. 1565, Therapon oxyrhnchus. No. 1566, Psettina ijimae.

1991, June 8
1563 A975 100w multicolored .85 .25
Complete booklet, 4 #1563 8.75
1564 A976 100w multicolored .85 .25
Complete booklet, 4 #1564 8.75
1565 A977 100w multicolored .85 .25
Complete booklet, 4 #1565 8.75
1566 A978 100w multicolored .85 .25
Complete booklet, 4 #1566 8.75
Nos. 1555-1566 (12) 9.60 3.40

Light of Peace Illuminating the World — A979

1989, Oct. 4
1567 A979 80w multicolored .55 .25

44th Intl. Eucharistic Cong., Seoul, Oct. 4-8.

29th World Congress of the Intl. Civil Airports Assoc., Seoul, Oct. 17-19 — A980

1989, Oct. 17
1568 A980 80w multicolored .55 .25

Philatelic Week — A981

1989, Nov. 18 Photo. *Perf. 13x13½*
1569 A981 80w Lantern .55 .25
a. Souvenir sheet of 2 1.90 1.90

Two Cranes A982

Folk Festival Customs A983

1989, Dec. 1 *Perf. 13x13½, 13½x13*
1570 A982 80w multicolored .70 .25
a. Souvenir sheet of 2 1.75 1.75
1571 A983 80w multicolored .70 .25
a. Souvenir sheet of 2 1.75 1.75

New Year 1990.

World Meteorological Day — A984

1990, Mar. 23 *Perf. 13½x13*
1572 A984 80w multicolored .55 .25
Complete booklet, 4 #1572 6.25

UNICEF in Korea, 40th Anniv. — A985

1990, Mar. 24 *Perf. 13x13½*
1573 A985 80w multicolored .55 .25
Complete booklet, 4 #1573 6.25

Cheju-Kohung Fiber Optic Submarine Cable — A986

1990, Apr. 21 *Perf. 13½x13*
1574 A986 80w multicolored .55 .25
Complete booklet, 4 #1574 6.25

Saemaul Movement, 20th Anniv. — A987

1990, Apr. 21
1575 A987 100w multicolored .55 .25
Complete booklet, 4 #1575 6.25

Youth Month — A988

1990, May 1
1576 A988 100w multicolored .65 .25
Complete booklet, 4 #1576 6.25

Type of 1981 and

Korean Flag A989

Korean Stork A990

White Magnolia A991

Korean White Pine A991a

Cart-shaped Earthenware A992

Fire Safety A993

Environmental Protection A994

Traffic Safety A995

Waiting One's Turn A996

Saving Energy A997

Child Protection A997a

Purification of Language Movement A997b

Rose of Sharon A997c

Give Life to Water A997d

Ginger Jar — A998

Chong-IP'um-Song, Pine Tree Natl. Monument — A999

Drum, Drum Dance A1001

Mask, Wrestlers A1002

Hong Yong-Sik A1003

King Sejong, Korean Alphabet A1004

Dragon Head, Banner Staff A1005

Gilt-bronze Buddha Triad with Inscription of Keymi A1006

Photo., Litho. (#1582), Litho. & Engr. (#1594)

1990-96 ***Perf. 13½x13, 13x13½***

1577 A989 10w multi .40 .25
1578 A990 20w multi .40 .25
1579 A991 30w multi .45 .25
1580 A991a 40w multi .40 .25
1581 A992 50w multi .55 .25
1582 A993 80w multi 3.00 .30
1583 A994 100w multi 8.00 .35
Complete booklet, 10 #1583 85.00
1584 A995 100w multi 2.00 .35
Complete booklet, 10 #1584 20.00
1585 A996 100w multi 1.90 .25
1586 A997 100w multi 1.10 .25
1587 A997a 100w multi 1.10 .25
1588 A997b 100w multi 1.25 .25
1589 A997c 110w multi .90 .25
1590 A997d 110w multi 1.00 .25
1591 A998 150w multi 1.30 .25
a. Booklet pane, 20 #1591 16.50
Complete booklet, #1591a 19.00
1592 A999 160w multi 1.30 .25
1593 A1001 370w multi 2.50 .45
1594 A1002 440w multi 3.25 .50
1594A A1003 600w multi 4.00 .65
1594B A1004 710w multi 4.75 .80
1594C A1005 800w multi 5.00 .80
1594D A1006 900w multi 5.75 .70
Nos. 1577-1594D (22) 50.30 8.15

Issued: No. 1583, 6/5; 600w, 6/25; 150w, 7/2; 800w, 7/10; No. 1584, 7/25; 50w, 9/28; 80w, 11/1; No. 1585, 6/26/91; No. 1586, 11/1/91; No. 1587, 4/5/92; No. 1588, 11/2/92; 370w, 440w, 3/22/93; 10w, No. 1589, 3/30/93; 160w, 710w, 4/30/93; 20w, 30w, 40w, 5/24/93; No. 1590, 7/1/93; 900w, 9/20/93; #1591a, 3/20/96.

See Nos. 1715-1738, 1846, 1851-1852, 1860, 1862.

Coil Stamps

1990 **Litho.** ***Perf. 13 Horiz.***
1594E A992 50w multicolored .90 .30

Perf. 13 Vert.
1594F A706 60w multicolored .70 .25
1594G A994 100w multicolored 1.50 .60
1594H A997c 110w multicolored 1.10 .25
Nos. 1594E-1594H (4) 4.20 1.40

Seoul Mail Center — A1007

1990, July 4 **Litho.** ***Perf. 13½x13***
1595 A1007 100w multicolored .65 .25
a. Souvenir sheet of 2 2.00 2.00
Complete booklet, 4 #1595 4.50

8th Korean Boy Scout Jamboree — A1008

1990, Aug. 8 ***Perf. 13x13½***
1596 A1008 100w multicolored .65 .25
Complete booklet, 4 #1596 5.00

Wild Flowers

Lilium A1009

Aster A1010

Adonis A1011

Scabiosa A1012

1990, Aug. 25 **Photo.**
1597 A1009 370w multicolored 1.60 .70
Complete booklet, 4 #1597 15.00
1598 A1010 400w multicolored 2.00 .90
Complete booklet, 4 #1598 19.50
1599 A1011 440w multicolored 1.90 .80
Complete booklet, 4 #1599 18.00
1600 A1012 470w multicolored 2.25 .80
Complete booklet, 4 #1600 21.00

A1013

No. 1601, Aerides japonicum. No. 1602, Heloniopsis orientalis. No. 1603, Aquilegia buergeriana. No. 1604, Gentiana zollingeri.

1991, July 26
1601 A1013 100w multicolored .60 .25
Complete booklet, 4 #1601 4.75
1602 A1013 100w multicolored .60 .25
Complete booklet, 4 #1602 4.75
1603 A1013 370w multicolored 1.75 .55
Complete booklet, 4 #1603 13.50
1604 A1013 440w multicolored 2.00 .60
Complete booklet, 4 #1604 16.00

1992, June 22 **Photo.** ***Perf. 13x13½***

No. 1605, Lychnis wilfordii. No. 1606, Lycoris radiata. No. 1607, Commelina communis. No. 1608, Calanthe striata.

1605 A1013 100w multicolored .60 .30
Complete booklet, 4 #1605 5.00
1606 A1013 100w multicolored .60 .30
Complete booklet, 4 #1606 5.00
1607 A1013 370w multicolored 1.60 .55
Complete booklet, 4 #1607 13.00
1608 A1013 440w multicolored 1.90 .60
Complete booklet, 4 #1608 15.00
Nos. 1597-1608 (12) 17.40 6.60

See Nos. 1751-1762, 1869-1872, 1907-1910.

Anglican Church of Korea, Cent. — A1021

1990, Sept. 29 **Litho.** ***Perf. 13x13½***
1609 A1021 100w .65 .25

Opening of Seoul Tower, 10th Anniv. — A1022

1990, Oct. 15
1610 A1022 100w blk, red & bl .65 .25

National Census — A1023

1990, Oct. 20 ***Perf. 13x13½***
1611 A1023 100w multicolored .55 .25

UN Development Program, 40th Anniv. — A1024

1990, Oct. 24
1612 A1024 100w multicolored .55 .25

Philatelic Week — A1025

Litho. & Engr.

1990, Nov. 16 ***Perf. 13x13½***
1613 A1025 100w multicolored .65 .25
a. Souvenir sheet of 2 4.00 4.00
Complete booklet, 4 #1613 5.00

New Year 1991 (Year of the Sheep) A1026

Two Cranes A1027

1990, Dec. 1 **Litho.** ***Perf. 13x13½***
1614 A1026 100w multicolored .60 .25
Complete booklet, 4 #1614 4.50
1615 A1027 100w multicolored .60 .25
Complete booklet, 4 #1615 4.50
a. Souv. sheet of 2, #1614-1615 5.25 5.25

Taejon Expo '93

A1028

A1029

1990, Dec. 12
1616 A1028 100w multicolored .75 .30
a. Souvenir sheet of 2 1.60 1.60
Complete booklet, 4 #1616 6.25
1617 A1029 440w multicolored 1.90 .75
a. Souvenir sheet of 2 5.25 5.25
Complete booklet, 4 #1617 22.50

A1030

A1031

1991, Mar. 23
1618 A1030 100w multicolored .70 .30
a. Souvenir sheet of 2 1.60 1.60
Complete booklet, 4 #1618 5.75
1619 A1031 100w multicolored .70 .30
a. Souvenir sheet of 2 1.60 1.60
Complete booklet, 4 #1619 5.75

A1032

A1033

1992, Aug. 7 **Photo.** ***Perf. 13½x13***
1620 A1032 100w multicolored .65 .25
a. Souvenir sheet of 2 1.35 1.35
Complete booklet, 4 #1620 3.75
1621 A1033 100w multicolored .65 .25
a. Souvenir sheet of 2 1.35 1.35
Complete booklet, 4 #1621 3.75

Government Pavilion — A1034

Intl. Pavilion — A1035

Recycling Art Pavilion A1035a

Telcom Pavilion A1035b

1993, Aug. 7
1622 A1034 110w multi .70 .25
a. Souvenir sheet of 2 1.25 1.25
Complete booklet, 4 #1622 5.00
1623 A1035 110w multi .70 .25
c. Souvenir sheet of 2 1.25 1.25
Complete booklet, 4 #1623 5.00
1623A A1035a 110w multi .70 .25
d. Souvenir sheet of 2 1.25 1.25
Complete booklet, 4 #1623A 5.00
1623B A1035b 110w multi .70 .25
e. Souvenir sheet of 2 1.25 1.25
Complete booklet, 4 #1623B 5.00
Nos. 1616-1623B (10) 8.15 3.15

Saemaul Minilibrary, 30th Anniv. — A1036

1991, Feb. 1 **Litho.** ***Perf. 13½x13***
1624 A1036 100w multicolored .60 .25
Complete booklet, 4 #1624 4.25

Moth
A1037

Beetle
A1038

Butterfly
A1039

Beetle
A1040

Cicada — A1041

1991, Apr. 8 Photo. *Perf. 13½x13*

1625 A1037 100w shown .85 .25
1626 A1038 100w shown .85 .25
1627 A1039 100w shown .85 .25
1628 A1040 100w shown .85 .25
1629 A1041 100w shown .85 .25
1630 A1040 100w Water beetle .85 .25
1631 A1040 100w Bee .85 .25
1632 A1040 100w Lady bug .85 .25
1633 A1037 100w Dragonfly .85 .25
1634 A1037 100w Grasshopper .85 .25
a. Strip of 10, #1625-1634 11.00 12.00

Printed in sheets of 100 with each row shifted one design.

Traditional Performing Arts Center, 40th Anniv. — A1042

1991, Apr. 10 *Perf. 13x13½*

1635 A1042 100w multicolored .65 .25
Complete booklet, 4 #1635 4.50

Korean Provisional Government in Shanghai, 72nd Anniv. — A1043

1991, Apr. 13 *Perf. 13½x13*

1636 A1043 100w multicolored .65 .25
Complete booklet, 4 #1636 4.50

Hire the Handicapped A1044

1991, Apr. 20

1637 A1044 100w multicolored .65 .25
Complete booklet, 4 #1637 5.00

Teachers' Day, 10th Anniv. — A1045

1991, May 15 Litho. *Perf. 13½x13*

1638 A1045 100w multicolored .65 .25
Complete booklet, 4 #1638 4.50

A1046

1991, Aug. 8 Litho. *Perf. 13x13½*

1639 A1046 100w multicolored .65 .25
a. Souvenir sheet of 2 1.60 1.60
Complete booklet, 4 #1639 7.25

17th World Scouting Jamboree.

YMCA World Assembly — A1047

1991, Aug. 22 Litho. *Perf. 13x13½*

1640 A1047 100w multicolored .65 .25
Complete booklet, 4 #1640 7.25

Natl. Desire for Reunification — A1048

1991, Sept. 11 Litho. *Perf. 13x13½*

1641 A1048 100w multicolored .65 .25
Complete booklet, 4 #1641 6.50

Admission to UN — A1049

1991, Sept. 18 *Perf. 13½x13*

1642 A1049 100w multicolored .65 .25
Complete booklet, 4 #1642 5.25

Musical Instruments

Deerskin Drum (Galgo) A1050

Mouth Organ (Saenghwang) A1051

Seated Drum A1052

Small Gong A1053

Designs: No. 1645, Brass chimes (Unra). No. 1646, Large gong (Jing). No. 1649, Dragon drum. No. 1650, Single bell chime.

1991-92 Photo. *Perf. 13x13½*
Background color

1643 A1050 100w gray .75 .30
Complete booklet, 4 #1643 5.00
1644 A1051 100w tan .75 .30
Complete booklet, 4 #1644 5.00
1645 A1050 100w lt violet .75 .30
Complete booklet, 4 #1645 5.00
1646 A1050 100w pale green .75 .30
Complete booklet, 4 #1646 5.00
1647 A1052 100w gray .80 .30
Complete booklet, 4 #1647 5.00
1648 A1053 100w tan .80 .30
Complete booklet, 4 #1648 5.00
1649 A1052 100w pale violet .80 .30
Complete booklet, 4 #1649 5.00
1650 A1053 100w pale green .80 .30
Complete booklet, 4 #1650 5.00
Nos. 1643-1650 (8) 6.20 2.40

Issued: Nos. 1643-1646, 9/26; others, 2/24/92.

Month of Culture — A1056

1991, Oct. 1 Litho. *Perf. 13x13½*

1655 A1056 100w multicolored .65 .25
Complete booklet, 4 #1655 4.50

Telecom '91 — A1057

1991, Oct. 7 Photo.

1656 A1057 100w multicolored .65 .25
Complete booklet, 4 #1656 5.00

Sixth World Telecommunication Exhibition & Forum, Geneva, Switzerland.

Beauty Series

A1058

A1059

Kottam Architectural Patterns
A1060 A1061

1991, Oct. 26

1657 A1058 100w multicolored .85 .30
1658 A1059 100w multicolored .85 .30
1659 A1060 100w multicolored .85 .30
1660 A1061 100w multicolored .85 .30
a. Block or strip of 4, #1657-1660 4.25 4.25
Complete booklet, 2 #1660a —

A1062

A1063

Norigae
A1064 A1065

1992, Sept. 21 Photo. & Engr.

1661 A1062 100w multicolored .70 .30
1662 A1063 100w multicolored .70 .30
1663 A1064 100w multicolored .70 .30
1664 A1065 100w multicolored .70 .30
a. Block or strip of 4, #1661-1664 3.75 3.75
Complete booklet, 2 #1664a —

A1066

A1067

Tapestries
A1068 A1069

1993, Oct. 11 Photo. *Perf. 13x13½*

1665 A1066 110w multicolored .60 .30
1666 A1067 110w multicolored .60 .30
1667 A1068 110w multicolored .60 .30
1668 A1069 110w multicolored .60 .30
a. Block or strip of 4, #1665-1668 3.00 3.00
Complete booklet, 2 #1668a —

Philatelic Week — A1070

1991, Dec. 5 Photo. *Perf. 13x13½*

1669 A1070 100w multicolored .65 .25
a. Souvenir sheet of 2 1.50 1.50
Complete booklet, 4 #1669 4.50

New Year 1992, Year of the Monkey
A1071 A1072

1991, Dec. 2 Photo. & Engr.

1670 A1071 100w multicolored .70 .25
a. Souvenir sheet of 2 1.90 1.90
Complete booklet, 4 #1670 5.00
1671 A1072 100w multicolored .70 .25
a. Souvenir sheet of 2 1.90 1.90
Complete booklet, 4 #1671 5.00

Hibiscus Syriacus, Natl. Flower — A1073

1992, Mar. 9 Photo. *Perf. 13x13½*
Background color

1672 A1073 100w lt green 1.10 .40
1673 A1073 100w lt blue 1.10 .40

Im-Jin War, 400th Anniv. — A1074

1992, May 23 Photo. *Perf. 13½x13*

1674 A1074 100w multicolored .55 .25
Complete booklet, 4 #1674 4.50

Science Day, 25th Anniv. — A1075

1992, Apr. 21 Photo. *Perf. 13½x13*

1675 A1075 100w multicolored .55 .25
Complete booklet, 4 #1675 4.50

Pong-Gil Yoon, Assassin of Japanese Occupation Leaders, 60th Anniv. of Execution — A1076

Photo. & Engr.
1992, Apr. 29 *Perf. 13x13½*

1676 A1076 100w multicolored .55 .25
Complete booklet, 4 #1676 4.50

60th Intl. Fertilizer Assoc. Conf. — A1077

Photo & Engr.

1992, May 25 ***Perf. 13x13½***

1678 A1077 100w multicolored .55 .25
Complete booklet, 4 #1678 4.50

1992 Summer Olympics, Barcelona — A1078

No. 1679, Pole vault. No. 1680, Rhythmic gymnastics.

1992, July 25 Photo. ***Perf. 13x13½***

1679 A1078 100w multi .65 .25
Complete booklet, 4 #1679 4.50
1680 A1078 100w multi .65 .25
Complete booklet, 4 #1680 4.50

21st Universal Postal Congress, Seoul, 1994 — A1079

Designs: No. 1681, Korean Exhibition Center, Namdae-mun Gate. No. 1682, Stone statue of Tolharubang, Songsan Ilchulbong Peak.

1992, Aug. 22 Photo. ***Perf. 13½x13***

1681 A1079 100w red vio & multi .60 .25
a. Souvenir sheet of 2 1.50 1.50
Complete booklet, 4 #1681 4.50
1682 A1079 100w brown & multi .60 .25
a. Souvenir sheet of 2 1.50 1.50
Complete booklet, 4 #1682 4.50

A1086

Litho. & Engr.

1992, Oct. 10 ***Perf. 13x13½***

1683 A1086 100w sal & red brn .55 .25
Complete booklet, 4 #1683 4.50

Pong-Chang Yi (1900-1932), would-be assassin of Japanese Emperor Hirohito.

A1087

Design: No. 1684, Hwang Young-Jo, 1992 Olympic marathon winner. No. 1685, Shon Kee-Chung, 1936 Olympic Marathon Winner.

1992, Oct. 10 **Litho.**

1684 A1087 100w multicolored .70 .25
1685 A1087 100w grn & multi .70 .25
a. Pair, #1684-1685 1.90 1.90
b. Souv. sheet of 2, #1684-1685 4.00 4.00
Complete booklet, 2 #1685a 9.00

Discovery of America, 500th Anniv. — A1088

1992, Oct. 12 **Photo.**

1686 A1088 100w multicolored .70 .25
Complete booklet, 4 #1686 8.00

Philatelic Week — A1089

1992, Nov. 14 Photo. ***Perf. 13½x13***

1687 A1089 100w multicolored .55 .25
a. Souvenir sheet of 2 1.60 1.60
Complete booklet, 4 #1687 4.50

New Year 1993 (Year of the Rooster)
A1090 A1091

1992, Dec. 1 Photo. ***Perf. 13x13½***

1688 A1090 100w multicolored .70 .25
a. Souvenir sheet of 2 1.90 1.90
Complete booklet, 4 #1688 5.00
1689 A1091 100w multicolored .70 .25
a. Souvenir sheet of 2 1.90 1.90
Complete booklet, 4 #1689 5.00

Intl. Conference on Nutrition, Rome — A1092

1992, Dec. 5 ***Perf. 13½x13***

1690 A1092 100w multicolored .55 .25
Complete booklet, 4 #1690 4.50

Seoul Art Center, Grand Opening — A1093

1993, Feb. 15 Photo. ***Perf. 13½x13***

1691 A1093 110w multicolored .55 .25
Complete booklet, 4 #1691 4.50

Inauguration of Kim Young Sam, 14th President — A1094

1993, Feb. 24

1692 A1094 110w multicolored 1.00 .30
a. Souvenir sheet of 2 5.75 5.75

Student Inventions Exhibition — A1095

1993, May 27 Photo. ***Perf. 13x13½***

1693 A1095 110w lilac & silver .55 .25
Complete booklet, 4 #1693 5.25

A1096

1993, June 14 Photo. ***Perf. 13x13½***

1694 A1096 110w multicolored .55 .25
Complete booklet, 4 #1694 5.25

UN Conference on Human Rights, Vienna.

Mushrooms — A1098

No. 1696, Ganoderma lucidum. No. 1697, Pleurotus ostreatus. No. 1698, Lentinula edodes. No. 1699, Tricholoma matsutake.

1993, July 26 Photo. ***Perf. 13x13½***

1696 A1098 110w multicolored .50 .25
Complete booklet, 4 #1696 5.00
1697 A1098 110w multicolored .50 .25
Complete booklet, 4 #1697 5.00
1698 A1098 110w multicolored .50 .25
Complete booklet, 4 #1698 5.00
1699 A1098 110w multicolored .50 .25
Complete booklet, 4 #1699 5.00
Nos. 1696-1699 (4) 2.00 1.00

See Nos. 1770-1773, 1803-1806, 1883-1886, 1912-1915, 1935.

A1099

1993, Aug. 28 Photo. ***Perf. 13x13½***

1700 A1099 110w multicolored .65 .25
Complete booklet, 4 #1700 3.75

19th World Congress of Intl. Society of Orthopedic Surgery and Trauma Study.

O-Dol-Odo-Gi
A1100

Ong-He-Ya
A1101

1993, Sept. 13

1701 A1100 110w multicolored .65 .25
Complete booklet, 4 #1701 3.75
1702 A1101 110w multicolored .65 .25
Complete booklet, 4 #1702 3.75

Visit Korea Year '94
A1112 A1113

1993, Sept. 27 Photo. ***Perf. 13x13½***

1713 A1112 110w multicolored .55 .25
Complete booklet, 4 #1713 3.75
1714 A1113 110w multicolored .55 .25
Complete booklet, 4 #1714 3.75

Type of 1993 and

Squirrel
A1114

Physalis Alkekengi
A1115

Scops Owl
A1116

Reduce Garbage
A1117

Narcissus
A1118

Little Tern
A1119

Sea Turtle
A1120

Airplane
A1122

Passenger Airplane
A1123

Porcelain Chicken Water Dropper
A1124

Celadon Water Dropper
A1125

Gilt Bronze Bongnae-san Incense Burner
A1127

Celadon Pitcher — A1128

Designs: 300w, Van. 540w, Train. 1190w, Passenger ship.

Perf. 13½x13, 13x13½ (210w, 1050w, #1728, 1732, 1734), 13½x12½ (60w, 90w), 12½x13½ (180w, 200w)

Photo., Litho. (#1726), Photo. & Engr. (#1734)

1993-95

1715 A1114 60w multi .50 .30
1716 A1115 70w multi .45 .25
1717 A1116 90w multi .65 .30
1718 A1117 110w multi .85 .25
1719 A997c 120w multi .85 .25
1720 A1118 130w multi .85 .30
a. Booklet pane of 20 16.50
Complete booklet, #1720a 16.50
1721 A1119 180w multi 1.25 .30
1722 A1120 200w multi 1.60 .30
1723 A1119 210w multi 1.40 .25
1724 A1123 300w multi 1.90 .40
1725 A1122 330w multi 2.75 .25
1726 A1123 390w multi 2.50 .45
a. Booklet pane of 10 29.00
Complete booklet, #1726a 29.00
1727 A1122 400w multi 2.00 .35
a. Booklet pane, 10 #1727 23.00
Complete booklet, #1727a 23.00
1728 A1124 400w multi 2.00 .35
1729 A1125 500w multi 2.25 .55
1730 A1123 540w multi 3.00 .65
1731 A1122 560w multi 3.25 .50
1732 A1127 700w multi 3.50 .75
1733 A1004 910w like #1594B 5.25 1.00
1734 A1128 930w blue & multi 5.25 .85
1735 A1128 930w tan & multi 5.25 1.00
a. Booklet pane of 10 67.50
Complete booklet, #1735a 67.50
1736 A1128 1050w multi 5.50 .80
1737 A1123 1190w multi 6.00 1.10
1738 A1122 1300w multi 7.25 .95
Nos. 1715-1738 (24) 66.05 12.45

Issued: No. 1718, 11/1/93; 910w, 2/15/94; 90w, 4/22/94; 130w, 8/20/94; 80w, 9/12/94; 390w, No. 1734, 1190w, 10/1/94; 540w, 11/1/94; 300w, 11/18/94; 60w, 200w, 12/19/94;
No. 1720a, 2/28/95; 70w, 3/15/95; No. 1737, 3/11/95; No. 1735a, 3/20/95; 700w, 6/15/95; No. 1728, 8/28/95; No. 1727, 10/16/95; 1050w, 1300w, 10/25/95; 210w, 560w, 11/1/95; 500w, 11/6/95;
120w, 330w, 11/11/95; No. 1727a, 3/27/96.

Five versions of booklets with No. 1720a exist with blocks of different colors at the top of the booklet cover. The blocks of color match color bars printed in the selvage of the attached booklet pane.

See Nos. 1847-1848, 1857.

Coil Stamp

1990 **Litho.** ***Perf. 13 Vert.***

1739 A1118 130w multicolored 4.50 .40

Philatelic Week — A1144

1993, Nov. 13 Photo. *Perf. 13x13½*

1745	A1144 110w multicolored	.65	.25
a.	Souvenir sheet of 2	1.35	1.35
	Complete booklet, 4 #1745	8.00	

21st UPU Congress, Seoul — A1145

No. 1746, Dancer, muscians. No. 1747, Weavers, horiz.

Perf. 13x13½, 13½x13

1993, Nov. 18

1746	A1145 110w multicolored	.55	.25
a.	Souvenir sheet of 2	1.40	1.40
	Complete booklet, 4 #1746	4.75	
1747	A1145 110w multicolored	.55	.25
a.	Souvenir sheet of 2	1.40	1.40
	Complete booklet, 4 #1747	4.75	

Trade Day, 30th Anniv. — A1146

1993, Nov. 30 *Perf. 13½x13*

1748	A1146 110w multicolored	.55	.25
	Complete booklet, 4 #1748	4.50	

New Year 1994 (Year of the Dog) — A1147

1993, Dec. 1 *Perf. 13½x13, 13x13½*

1749	A1147 110w shown	.90	.25
a.	Souvenir sheet of 2	1.60	1.60
1750	A1147 110w Stuffed toy dog, vert.	.90	.25
a.	Souvenir sheet of 2	1.60	1.60

Flower Type of 1991

No. 1751, Weigela bortensis. No. 1752, Caltha palustris. No. 1753, Iris ruthenica. No. 1754, Aceriphyllum rosii. No. 1755, Leontopodium japonicum. No. 1756, Geranium eriostemon. No. 1757, Lycoris aurea. No. 1758, Gentiana jamesii. No. 1759, Halenia corniculata. No. 1760, Erthyronium japonicum. No. 1761, Iris odaesanensis. No. 1762, Leontice microrrhyncha.

1993-95 Photo. *Perf. 13x13½*

1751	A1013 110w multicolored	.70	.25
	Complete booklet, 4 #1751	3.50	
1752	A1013 110w multicolored	.70	.25
	Complete booklet, 4 #1752	3.50	
1753	A1013 110w multicolored	.70	.25
	Complete booklet, 4 #1753	3.50	
1754	A1013 110w multicolored	.70	.25
	Complete booklet, 4 #1754	3.50	
1755	A1013 130w multicolored	.95	.25
	Complete booklet, 4 #1755	5.00	
1756	A1013 130w multicolored	.95	.25
	Complete booklet, 4 #1756	5.00	
1757	A1013 130w multicolored	.95	.25
	Complete booklet, 4 #1757	5.00	
1758	A1013 130w multicolored	.95	.25
	Complete booklet, 4 #1758	5.00	
1759	A1013 130w multicolored	.95	.25
	Complete booklet, 6 #1759	5.00	
1760	A1013 130w multicolored	.95	.25
	Complete booklet, 6 #1760	5.00	
1761	A1013 130w multicolored	.95	.25
	Complete booklet, 6 #1761	5.00	
1762	A1013 130w multicolored	.95	.25
	Complete booklet, 6 #1762	5.00	
	Nos. 1751-1762 (12)	10.40	3.00

Issued: Nos. 1751-1754, 12/20/93; Nos. 1755-1758, 10/4/94; Nos. 1759-1762, 7/24/95.

Visit Korea Year
A1148 A1149

No. 1763, Masked dancer. No. 1764, Piper, clouds.

1994, Jan. 11 Photo. *Perf. 13x13½*

1763	A1148 110w multicolored	.60	.25
	Complete booklet, 4 #1763	2.75	
1764	A1149 110w multicolored	.60	.25
	Complete booklet, 4 #1764	2.75	

21st UPU Congress, Seoul — A1150

1994, Jan. 24 *Perf. 13½x13*

1765	A1150 300w multicolored	1.30	.45
a.	Souvenir sheet of 2	3.25	3.25
b.	Booklet pane of 10	27.00	
	Complete booklet, #1765b	27.00	

Samil Independence Movement, 75th Anniv. — A1151

1994, Feb. 28 Photo. *Perf. 13x13½*

1766	A1151 110w multicolored	.50	.25

Wildlife Protection — A1152

No. 1767, Sasakia charonda. No. 1768, Allomyrina dichotoma.

1994, Mar. 7 Photo. *Perf. 13½x13*

1767	A1152 110w multicolored	.70	.25
a.	Souvenir sheet of 2	1.75	1.75
	Complete booklet, 4 #1767	3.75	
1768	A1152 110w multicolored	.70	.25
a.	Souvenir sheet of 2	1.75	1.75
	Complete booklet, 4 #1768	3.75	

Intl. Year of the Family — A1153

1994, May 14 Photo. *Perf. 13*

1769	A1153 110w multicolored	.55	.25

Mushroom Type of 1993

No. 1770, Oudemansiella platyphylla. No. 1771, Morchella esculenta. No. 1772, Cortinarius purpurascens. No. 1773, Gomphus floccosus.

1994, May 30 Photo. *Perf. 13x13½*

1770	A1098 110w multicolored	.50	.25
a.	Souvenir sheet of 2	1.35	1.35
	Complete booklet, 4 #1770	2.50	
1771	A1098 110w multicolored	.50	.25
a.	Souvenir sheet of 2	1.35	1.35
	Complete booklet, 4 #1771	2.50	
1772	A1098 110w multicolored	.50	.25
a.	Souvenir sheet of 2	1.35	1.35
	Complete booklet, 4 #1772	2.50	
1773	A1098 110w multicolored	.50	.25
a.	Souvenir sheet of 2	1.35	1.35
	Complete booklet, 4 #1773	2.50	
	Nos. 1770-1773 (4)	2.00	1.00
	Nos. 1770a-1773a (4)	5.40	5.40

Opening of War Memorial Center — A1154

1994, June 10 Photo. *Perf. 13*

1774	A1154 110w multicolored	.55	.25

PHILAKOREA '94, Seoul — A1155

1994, June 13 *Perf. 13*

1775	A1155 910w multicolored	3.75	1.25
a.	Souvenir sheet of 1	4.00	4.00
b.	Booklet pane of 10	37.50	
	Complete booklet, #1775b	37.50	

Stamps from No. 1775b have a straight edge at either top or bottom.

Beauty Series

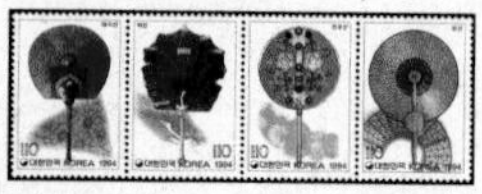

Fans A1156

1994, July 18 Photo. *Perf. 13x13½*

1776	110w Taeguk	.60	.25
1777	110w Crane	.60	.25
1778	110w Pearl	.60	.25
1779	110w Wheel	.60	.25
a.	A1156 Strip of 4, #1776-1779	3.00	3.00
	Complete booklet, 2 #1779a	13.50	

Gates A1160

No. 1780, Lofty Gate, traditional Yungban residence. No. 1781, Pomosa Temple. No. 1782, Osumun (Fish Water) Gate, Changdukkung Palace. No. 1783, Pullomun Gate, Changdukkung Palace.

1995, May 22 Photo. *Perf. 13x13½*

1780	130w multicolored	.60	.25
1781	130w multicolored	.60	.25
1782	130w multicolored	.60	.25
1783	130w multicolored	.60	.25
a.	A1160 Strip of 4, #1780-1783	3.00	3.00
	Complete booklet, 2 #1783a	*13.50*	

Pouches A1164

1996, Nov. 1 Photo. *Perf. 13x13½*

1784	150w multicolored	.60	.25
1785	150w multicolored	.60	.25
1786	150w multicolored	.60	.25
1787	150w multicolored	.60	.25
a.	A1164 Strip of 4, #1784-1787	3.00	3.00
	Complete booklet, 2 #1787a	*13.50*	
	Nos. 1776-1787 (12)	7.20	3.00

A1168

PHILAKOREA '94 — A1169

No. 1788, Winter scene. No. 1789, Grape vines. No. 1790, Cranes.

1994, Aug. 16 Photo. *Perf. 13*

1788	A1168 130w multi	1.00	.25
a.	Souvenir sheet of 2	1.40	1.40
b.	Booklet pane of 10	10.50	
	Complete booklet, #1788b	10.50	
1789	A1168 130w multi	1.00	.25
a.	Souvenir sheet of 2	1.40	1.40
b.	Booklet pane of 10	10.50	
	Complete booklet, #1789b	12.50	
1790	A1168 130w multi	1.00	.25
a.	Souvenir sheet of 2	1.40	1.40
b.	Booklet pane of 10	10.50	
	Complete booklet, #1790b	10.50	
	Nos. 1788-1790 (3)	3.00	.75

Souvenir Sheet

Litho. & Engr.

1791	Sheet of 7	9.75	9.00
a.	A1169 130w Crane, mountains	.40	.25
b.	A1169 300w Two cranes, sun	.95	.40
c.	A1169 370w Two cranes in trees	1.20	.50
d.	A1169 400w Two deer	1.30	.55
e.	A1169 440w Turtle, rapids	1.50	.60
f.	A1169 470w River	1.50	.60
g.	A1169 930w Trees	3.00	1.10

21st UPU Congress, Seoul — A1170

No. 1792, Pens, glasses, stamps. No. 1793, Sword dance. No. 1794, Dove holding envelope. No. 1795, Hong Yong-sik, Heinrich Von Stephan, horiz.

1994, Aug. 22 Photo. *Perf. 13*

1792	A1170 130w multicolored	.55	.25
a.	Souvenir sheet of 2	1.50	1.50
b.	Booklet pane of 10	6.50	
	Complete booklet, #1792b	6.50	
1793	A1170 130w multicolored	.55	.25
a.	Souvenir sheet of 2	1.50	1.50
b.	Booklet pane of 10	6.50	
	Complete booklet, #1793b	6.50	
1794	A1170 130w multicolored	.55	.25
a.	Souvenir sheet of 2	1.50	1.50
b.	Booklet pane of 10	6.50	
	Complete booklet, #1794b	6.50	
1795	A1170 370w multicolored	1.50	.60
a.	Souvenir sheet of 2	3.25	3.25
b.	Souvenir sheet of 4, #1792-1795	7.00	7.00
c.	Booklet pane of 10	45.00	
	Complete booklet, #1795b	45.00	
	Nos. 1792-1795 (4)	3.15	1.35

A1171

1994, Sept. 27

1796	A1171 130w multicolored	.60	.25

Seoul, Capital of Korea, 600th anniv.

A1172

1994, Nov. 19 Photo. *Perf. 13x13½*

1797	A1172 130w multicolored	.60	.25
a.	Souvenir sheet of 2	1.50	1.50
	Complete booklet, 4 #1797	5.25	

Philatelic Week. Complete booklet has one No. 1797 tied to cover with first day cancel.

A1173

1994, Nov. 29

1798	A1173 130w multicolored	.60	.25

Seoul becomes Korea's capital, 600th anniv.

New Year 1995 (Year of the Boar) — A1174

1994, Dec. 1 *Perf. 13½x13*

1799	A1174 130w shown	.60	.25
a.	Souvenir sheet of 2	1.50	1.50
	Complete booklet, 4 #1799	6.00	
1800	A1174 130w Family outing	.60	.25
a.	Souvenir sheet of 2	1.50	1.50
	Complete booklet, 4 #1800	6.00	

Wildlife Protection — A1175

1995, Jan. 23 Photo. *Perf. 13½x13*

1801	A1175 130w Rana plancyi	.70	.30
a.	Souv. sheet of 2, imperf.	1.75	1.75
	Complete booklet, 4 #1801	5.50	
1802	A1175 130w Bufo bufo	.70	.30
a.	Souv. sheet of 2, imperf.	1.75	1.75
	Complete booklet, 4 #1802	5.50	

Mushroom Type of 1993

Designs: No. 1803, Russula virescens. No. 1804, Lentinus lepideus. No. 1805, Coprinus comalus. No. 1806, Laetiporus sulphureus.

1995, Mar. 31 Photo. ***Perf. 13x13½***

1803 A1098 130w multicolored .70 .30
a. Souvenir sheet of 2 1.40 1.40
Complete booklet, 4 #1803 5.50
1804 A1098 130w multicolored .70 .30
a. Souvenir sheet of 2 1.40 1.40
Complete booklet, 4 #1804 5.50
1805 A1098 130w multicolored .70 .30
a. Souvenir sheet of 2 1.40 1.40
Complete booklet, 4 #1805 5.50
1806 A1098 130w multicolored .70 .30
a. Souvenir sheet of 2 1.40 1.40
Complete booklet, 4 #1806 5.50
Nos. 1803-1806 (4) 2.80 1.20

Completion of HANARO Research Reactor — A1176

1995, Apr. 7 ***Perf. 13½x13***

1807 A1176 130w multicolored .70 .35
Complete booklet, 4 #1807 5.00

Modern Judicial System, Cent. — A1177

1995, Apr. 25 Litho. ***Perf. 13x13½***

1808 A1177 130w multicolored .60 .25

Modern Legal Education, Cent. — A1178

1995, Apr. 25 ***Perf. 13½x13***

1809 A1178 130w multicolored .60 .25

Cartoons — A1179

130w, "Dooly, the Little Dinosaur," baby, porpoise. 440w, "Kochuboo," riding in airplane.

1995, May 4

1810 A1179 130w multicolored .65 .35
a. Souvenir sheet of 1 1.45 1.45
Complete booklet, 4 #1810 5.00
1811 A1179 440w multicolored 1.60 .55
a. Souvenir sheet of 1 3.00 3.00
Complete booklet, 4 #1811 11.00

78th Lions Clubs Intl. Convention A1180

1995, July 4 Photo. ***Perf. 13½x13***

1812 A1180 130w multicolored .70 .25

Liberation Day, 50th Anniv. — A1181

Design: 440w, Mountain, yin/yang symbol.

1995, Aug. 14 Photo. ***Perf. 13½x13***

1813 A1181 130w multicolored .60 .25
a. Booklet pane of 10 11.50
Complete booklet, #1813a 11.50
b. Souvenir sheet of 2 1.45 1.45

Size: 97x19mm

Perf. 13x13½

1814 A1181 440w multicolored 1.60 .55
a. Souvenir sheet of 1 2.40 2.40

Opening of Bohyunsan Optical Astronomical Observatory — A1183

1995, Sept. 13 Litho. ***Perf. 13x13½***

1816 A1183 130w multicolored .70 .25
Complete booklet, 6 #1816 7.00

Literature Series

Kuji-ga Song (The Turtle's Back Song) A1184

Chongeop-sa Song A1185

A1186

A1187

Record of Travel to Five Indian Kingdoms A1188

A Poem to the Sui General Yu Zhong Wen A1189

A1190

A1191

A1192

A1193

A1194

A1195

Perf. 13x13½, 13½x13

1995-99 **Photo.**

1817 A1184 130w multi .65 .25
a. Souvenir sheet of 2 1.40 1.40
Complete booklet, 6 #1817 5.75
1818 A1185 130w multi .65 .25
a. Souvenir sheet of 2 1.40 1.40
Complete booklet, 6 #1818 5.75
1819 A1186 150w multi .60 .25
a. Souvenir sheet of 2 1.45 1.45
Complete booklet, 10 #1819 *11.50*
1820 A1187 150w multi .60 .25
a. Souvenir sheet of 2 1.45 1.45
Complete booklet, 10 #1820 *11.50*
1821 A1188 170w multi .65 .25
a. Souvenir sheet of 2 1.35 1.35
Complete booklet, 10 #1821 9.00
1822 A1189 170w multi .65 .25
a. Sheet of 2 1.35 1.35
Complete booklet, 10 #1822 9.00

Photo. & Engr.

1823 A1190 170w multi .60 .25
Complete booklet, 10 #1823 9.00
a. Souvenir sheet of 1 1.10 1.10
1824 A1191 170w multi .60 .25
Complete booklet, 10 #1824 9.00
a. Souvenir sheet of 1 1.10 1.10
1825 A1192 170w multi .60 .30
Complete booklet, 10 #1825 9.00
1826 A1193 170w multi .60 .30
Complete booklet, 10 #1826 9.00
1827 A1194 170w multi .60 .30
Complete booklet, 10 #1827 9.00
1828 A1195 170w multi .60 .30
Complete booklet, 10 #1828 9.00
Nos. 1817-1828 (12) 7.40 3.20

Souvenir Sheets

1828A A1192 340w multi 1.60 1.60
1828B A1193 340w multi 1.60 1.60
1828C A1194 340w multi 1.60 1.60
1828D A1195 340w multi 1.60 1.60

Issued: Nos. 1817-1818, 9/25/95; Nos. 1819-1820, 9/16/96; Nos. 1821-1822, 12/12/97; Nos. 1823-1824, 9/14/98; Nos. 1825-1828D, 10/20/99

FAO, 50th Anniv. — A1196

Litho. & Engr.

1995, Oct. 16 ***Perf. 13***

1829 A1196 150w dp vio & blk .70 .25
Complete booklet, 10 #1829 *8.75*

Korean Bible Society, Cent. — A1197

1995, Oct. 18 **Litho.**

1830 A1197 150w multicolored .60 .25
Complete booklet, 10 #1830 *8.75*

Population and Housing Census — A1198

1995, Oct. 20

1831 A1198 150w multicolored .60 .25
Complete booklet, 10 #1831 *8.75*

UN, 50th Anniv. — A1199

1995, Oct. 24 **Photo.**

1832 A1199 150w multicolored .70 .25
Complete booklet, 10 #1832 *8.75*

Wilhelm Röntgen (1845-1923), Discovery of the X-Ray, Cent. — A1200

1995, Nov. 8 ***Perf. 13½x13***

1833 A1200 150w multicolored 1.20 .25
Complete booklet, 10 #1833 16.00

Philatelic Week — A1201

1995, Nov. 18 Photo. ***Perf. 13x13½***

1834 A1201 150w multicolored .70 .25
a. Souvenir sheet of 2 1.45 1.45
Complete booklet, 10 #1834 *8.75*

A1202

New Year 1996 (Year of the Rat) — A1203

1995, Dec. 1 ***Perf. 13x13½, 13½x13***

1835 A1202 150w multicolored .75 .25
a. Souvenir sheet of 2 1.90 1.90
Complete booklet, 10 #1835 *10.00*
1836 A1203 150w multicolored .75 .25
a. Souvenir sheet of 2 1.90 1.90
Complete booklet, 10 #1836 *10.00*

Normalization of Korea-Japan Relations, 30th Anniv. — A1204

1995, Dec. 18 Litho. ***Perf. 13x13½***

1837 A1204 420w multicolored 1.75 .60
Complete booklet, 4 #1837 *8.75*

Types of 1993-97 and

Gallicrex Cinerea A1206

Zosterops Japonica A1208

Luffa Cylindrica A1209

Numenius Madagascariensis A1210

Cambaroides Similis A1211

747 Airplane A1215

Mare and Colt — A1221

Soksu Stone Carving — A1223

Bronze Incense Burner in Shape of Lotus Flowers — A1224

Photo., Photo. & Embossed (#1844)

1996-98 ***Perf. 13x13½, 13½x13***

1839 A1206 50w multi .60 .25
1840 A1208 80w multi .65 .25
1841 A1209 100w multi 1.00 .25
1842 A1118 140w multi 1.20 .25

Perf. 13

1843 A1210 170w multi 2.00 .25
1844 A1210 170w like #1843, braille inscription 1.90 .40

Perf. 13x13½, 13½x13

1845 A1211 170w multi 1.60 .30
1846 A997c 190w multi 1.60 .30
1847 A1119 260w multi 2.00 .35

Perf. 13x14

1848 A1119 300w Alauda arvensis 1.75 .35

Perf. 13½x13, 13x13½, 13 (#1855)

1849 A1215 340w grn bl & multi 2.10 .40
1850 A1215 380w lt lilac & multi 2.50 .45

1851 A1001 420w like #1593 3.00 .40
1852 A1002 480w like #1594 3.25 .45
1854 A1221 800w multi 3.50 .50
1855 A1223 1000w multi 5.00 .95
1856 A1224 1170w multi 5.75 1.45
1857 A1128 1190w multi 6.75 1.45
1858 A1215 1340w brt grn & multi 8.00 1.20
1859 A1215 1380w pink & multi 8.00 1.40
Nos. 1839-1859 (20) 62.15 11.60

Coil Stamps

Perf. 13 Horiz., 13 Vert. (#1860, 1862)

1996-97 Photo.
1860 A998 150w like #1591 1.20 .60
1861 A1211 170w like No. 1845 1.30 .30
1862 A997c 190w like No. 1846 1.35 .30
Nos. 1860-1862 (3) 3.85 1.20

Issued: 300w, 1/22/96; No. 1860, 2/1/96; 420w, 480w, 3/20/96; 1000w, 12/16/96; 100w, 3/5/97; 80w, 7/1/97; Nos. 1845-1846, 9/1/97; 340w, 380w, 1340w, 1380w, 9/12/97; Nos. 1842, 1847, 1856, 1857, 11/1/97; Nos. 1861, 1862, 11/18/97; No. 1843, 12/15/97; 50w, 2/19/98; 800w, 4/4/98; No. 1844, 10/15/98.

Opening of China-Korea Submarine Fiber Optic Cable System — A1229

1996, Feb. 8 Litho. *Perf. 13½x13*
1863 A1229 420w multicolored 1.75 .45
Complete booklet, 4 #1863 *9.25*

See People's Republic of China No. 2647.

Korea Institute of Science and Technology, 30th Anniv. — A1230

1996, Feb. 10 Photo. *Perf. 13½x13*
1864 A1230 150w multicolored .70 .25
Complete booklet, 10 #1864 *8.75*

Protection of Nature — A1231

No. 1865, Geoclemys reevesii. No. 1866, Scincella laterale.

1996, Mar. 5 Photo. *Perf. 13½x13*
1865 A1231 150w multicolored .70 .25
a. Souvenir sheet of 2 1.75 1.75
Complete booklet, 10 #1865 *17.50*
1866 A1231 150w multicolored .70 .25
a. Souvenir sheet of 2 1.75 1.75
Complete booklet, 10 #1866 *17.50*

Successful Launches of Mugunghwa Satellites — A1232

1996, Mar. 18 Photo. *Perf. 13*
1867 A1232 150w multicolored .70 .25
Complete booklet, 10 #1867 *8.75*

Tongnip Shinmum, First Privately Published Newspaper, Cent. — A1233

So Chae-p'il, lead article of first issue.

Litho. & Engr.

1996, Apr. 6 *Perf. 13*
1868 A1233 150w multicolored .70 .25
Complete booklet, 10 #1868 *10.00*

Wildflower Type of 1992

No. 1869, Cypripedium macranthum. No. 1870, Trillium tschonoskii. No. 1871, Viola variegata. No. 1872, Hypericum ascyron.

1996, Apr. 22 Photo. *Perf. 13*
1869 A1013 150w multicolored .95 .25
Complete booklet, 10 #1869 *11.50*
1870 A1013 150w multicolored .95 .25
Complete booklet, 10 #1870 *11.50*
1871 A1013 150w multicolored .95 .25
Complete booklet, 10 #1871 *11.50*
1872 A1013 150w multicolored .95 .25
Complete booklet, 10 #1872 *11.50*
Nos. 1869-1872 (4) 3.80 1.00

Korea Military Academy, 50th Anniv. — A1234

1996, May 1 Litho. *Perf. 13½x13*
1873 A1234 150w multicolored .70 .25
Complete booklet, 10 #1873 *9.00*

Cartoons — A1235

No. 1874, Gobau running. No. 1875, Kkach'i in swordfight.

1996, May 4 Photo.
1874 A1235 150w multicolored .70 .25
a. Souvenir sheet of 1 1.45 1.45
Complete booklet, 10 #1874 *9.00*
1875 A1235 150w multicolored .70 .25
a. Souvenir sheet of 1 1.45 1.45
Complete booklet, 10 #1875 *9.00*

Girl Scouts of Korea, 50th Anniv. — A1236

1996, May 10 Litho.
1876 A1236 150w multicolored .70 .25
Complete booklet, 10 #1876 *10.00*

35th IAA World Advertising Congress — A1237

1996, June 8 Litho. *Perf. 13*
1877 A1237 150w multicolored .70 .25
Complete booklet, 10 #1877 *8.25*

Campaign Against Illegal Drugs — A1238

1996, June 26 Photo. *Perf. 13½x13*
1878 A1238 150w multicolored .70 .25
Complete booklet, 10 #1878 *10.00*

Winter Universiade '97, Muju-Chonju A1239

No. 1880, Emblem, vert.

1996, July 1 *Perf. 13½x13, 13x13½*
1879 A1239 150w shown .70 .25
Complete booklet, 10 #1879 *8.75*
1880 A1239 150w multicolored .70 .25
Complete booklet, 10 #1880 *8.75*

1996 Summer Olympic Games, Atlanta
A1240 A1241

1996, July 20 *Perf. 13x13½*
1881 A1240 150w multicolored .70 .25
Complete booklet, 10 #1881 *12.50*
1882 A1241 150w multicolored .70 .25
Complete booklet, 10 #1882 *12.50*

Mushroom Type of 1993

Designs: No. 1883, Paxillus atrotomentosus. No. 1884, Sarcodon imbricatum. No. 1885, Rhodophyllus crassipes. No. 1886, Amanita inaurata.

1996, Aug. 19 Photo. *Perf. 13x13½*
1883 A1098 150w multicolored .70 .25
a. Souvenir sheet of 2 1.40 1.40
Complete booklet, 10 #1883 *12.50*
1884 A1098 150w multicolored .70 .25
a. Souvenir sheet of 2 1.40 1.40
Complete booklet, 10 #1884 *12.50*
1885 A1098 150w multicolored .70 .25
a. Souvenir sheet o 2 1.40 1.40
Complete booklet, 10 #1885 *12.50*
1886 A1098 150w multicolored .70 .25
a. Souvenir sheet of 2 1.40 1.40
Complete booklet, 10 #1886 *12.50*
Nos. 1883-1886 (4) 2.80 1.00

Souvenir Sheets

2002 World Cup Soccer Championships, Korea — A1242

No. 1887, Players, Korean flag. No. 1888, 2 players.

1996, Aug. 1 Photo. *Perf. 13½*
1887 A1242 400w Sheet of 4 6.75 6.75
1888 A1242 400w Sheet of 4 6.75 6.75

Korean Alphabet, 550th Anniv. — A1243

Litho. & Engr.

1996, Oct. 9 *Perf. 13x13½*
1889 A1243 150w multicolored .70 .25
a. Souvenir sheet of 2 1.35 1.35
Complete booklet, 10 #1889 *10.50*

Suwon Castle, Bicent. — A1244

Photo. & Engr.

1996, Oct. 10 *Perf. 13½x13*
1890 A1244 400w multicolored 1.90 .55

Seoul Natl. University, 50th Anniv. — A1245

1996, Oct. 15 Photo. *Perf. 13½x13*
1891 A1245 150w multicolored .70 .25
Complete booklet, 10 #1891 *9.50*

Philatelic Week — A1246

Painting: Poppy and a Lizard, by Shin Saimdang.

1996, Nov. 18 Photo. *Perf. 13x13½*
1892 A1246 150w multicolored .70 .25
a. Souvenir sheet of 2 1.40 1.40
Complete booklet, 10 #1892 *11.00*

A1247

New Year 1997 (Year of the Ox) — A1248

1996, Dec. 2 *Perf. 13*
1893 A1247 150w multicolored .85 .25
a. Souvenir sheet of 2 1.50 1.50
Complete booklet, 10 #1893 *13.00*
1894 A1248 150w multicolored .85 .25
a. Souvenir sheet of 2 1.50 1.50
Complete booklet, 10 #1894 *13.00*

Winter Universiade '97, Muju-Chonju — A1249

1997, Jan. 24 Photo. *Perf. 13*
1895 A1249 150w Skier .65 .25
Complete booklet, 10 #1895 *11.50*
a. Souvenir sheet of 2 1.25 1.25
1896 A1249 150w Ice skater .65 .25
Complete booklet, 10 #1896 *11.50*
a. Souvenir sheet of 2 1.25 1.25

Modern Banking System in Korea, Cent. — A1250

1997, Feb. 19 Litho. *Perf. 13½x13*
1897 A1250 150w multicolored .70 .25
Complete booklet, 10 #1897 *11.50*

A1251

1997, Apr. 10 *Perf. 13x13½*
1898 A1251 150w multicolored .60 .25
Complete booklet, 10 #1898 *10.00*

97th Inter-Parliamentary Conference, 160th Inter-Parliamentary Council.

World Book & Copyright Day — A1252

1997, Apr. 23 Litho.
1899 A1252 150w multicolored .70 .25
Complete booklet, 10 #1899 *10.00*

Cartoons — A1253

No. 1900, Mother holding child from "A Long, Long Journey in Search of Mommy." No. 1901, Girl in air holding medal from "Run, Run, Hannie."

1997, May 3 Photo. *Perf. 13½x13*
1900 A1253 150w multicolored .60 .25
a. Souvenir sheet of 1 1.05 1.05
Complete booklet, 10 #1900 *13.50*
1901 A1253 150w multicolored .60 .25
a. Souvenir sheet of 1 1.05 1.05
Complete booklet, 10 #1901 *13.50*

Nos. 1900a, 1901a are continuous designs.

2nd Pusan East Asian Games — A1254

1997, May 10 Litho. *Perf. 13x13½*
1902 A1254 150w multicolored .70 .25
Complete booklet, 10 #1900 *10.00*

2002 World Cup Soccer, Korea/Japan
A1255 A1256

No. 1903, Jules Rimet, founder of World Cup. No. 1904, Painting of Ch'ukkuk match.

1997, May 31 Photo. *Perf. 13x13½*
1903 A1255 150w multicolored .75 .25
a. Souvenir sheet of 2 1.90 1.90
Complete booklet, 10 #1903 11.50
1904 A1256 150w multicolored .75 .25
a. Souvenir sheet of 3 2.00 2.00
Complete booklet, 10 #1904 11.50

Wildlife Protection — A1257

Fish: No. 1905, Pungitius sinensis. No. 1906, Coreoperca kawamebari.

1997, June 5 *Perf. 13*
1905 A1257 150w multicolored .70 .25
a. Souvenir sheet of 2 1.25 1.25
Complete booklet, 10 #1905 11.50
1906 A1257 150w multicolored .70 .25
a. Souvenir sheet of 2 1.25 1.25
Complete booklet, 10 #1906 11.50

Wildflower Type of 1992

No. 1907, Belamcanda chinensis. No. 1908, Hylomecon ernale. No. 1909, Campanula takesimana. No. 1910, Magnolia sieboldii.

1997, June 19 Photo. *Perf. 13*
1907 A1013 150w multicolored .70 .25
Complete booklet, 10 #1907 12.50
1908 A1013 150w multicolored .70 .25
Complete booklet, 10 #1908 12.50
1909 A1013 150w multicolored .70 .25
Complete booklet, 10 #1909 12.50
1910 A1013 150w multicolored .70 .25
Complete booklet, 10 #1910 12.50
Nos. 1907-1910 (4) 2.80 1.00

1997 Kwangju Biennale — A1258

1997, July 1
1911 A1258 150w multicolored .60 .25
Complete booklet, 10 #1911 9.50

Mushroom Type of 1993

Designs: No. 1912, Inocybe fastigiata. No. 1913, Panaeolus papilionaceus. No. 1914, Ramaria flava. No. 1915, Amanita muscaria.

1997, July 21 Photo. *Perf. 13x13½*
1912 A1098 150w multicolored .70 .25
a. Souvenir sheet of 2 1.30 1.30
1913 A1098 150w multicolored .70 .25
a. Souvenir sheet of 2 1.30 1.30
1914 A1098 150w multicolored .70 .25
a. Souvenir sheet of 2 1.30 1.30
1915 A1098 150w multicolored .70 .25
a. Souvenir sheet of 2 1.30 1.30
Nos. 1912-1915 (4) 2.80 1.00

85th World Dental Congress, Seoul — A1259

1997, Sept. 5 Photo. *Perf. 13½x13*
1916 A1259 170w multicolored .65 .25

Opening of Port of Mokpo, Cent. — A1260

Litho. & Engr.

1997, Oct. 1 *Perf. 13½x13*
1917 A1260 170w multicolored .65 .25

Soongsil Academy, Cent. — A1261

1997, Oct. 10 Photo. & Engr.
1918 A1261 170w multicolored .65 .25

Beauty Series

Wrapping Cloths — A1262

1997, Nov. 3 Photo. *Perf. 13x13½*
1919 170w multicolored .85 .25
1920 170w multicolored .85 .25
1921 170w multicolored .85 .25
1922 170w multicolored .85 .25
a. A1262 Strip of 4, #1919-1922 4.00 4.00

Philatelic Week — A1266

1997, Nov. 18
1923 A1266 170w multicolored .75 .25
a. Souvenir sheet of 2 1.25 1.25

New Year 1998 (Year of the Tiger)
A1267 A1268

1997, Dec. 1 Photo. *Perf. 13x13½*
1924 A1267 170w multicolored .90 .25
a. Souvenir sheet of 2 1.60 1.60
1925 A1268 170w multicolored .90 .25
a. Souvenir sheet of 2 1.60 1.60

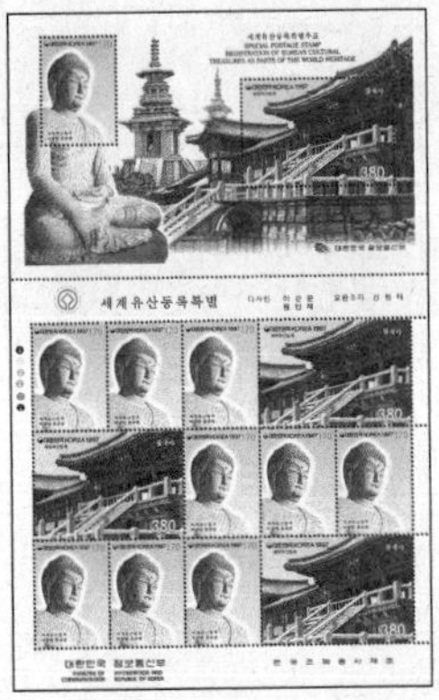

Pulguksa Temple A1269

Litho. & Engr.

1997, Dec. 9 *Perf. 13x13½*
1926 A1269 Sheet of 14 35.00 35.00
a. 170w Buddha, Sokkuram Grotto 1.00 1.00
b. 380w Temple 4.00 4.00

Top part of No. 1926 contains one each Nos. 1926a-1926b and is separated from the bottom portion of the sheet by a row of perforations. The lower part of No. 1926 contains 9 No. 1926a and 3 No, 1926b.

Electric Power in Korea, Cent. — A1271

1998, Jan. 26 Photo. *Perf. 13½x13*
1927 A1271 170w multicolored .70 .25

Inauguration of the 15th President, Kim Dae-jung — A1272

1998, Feb. 25 Litho. *Perf. 13½x13*
1928 A1272 170w multicolored .90 .35
a. Souvenir sheet of 1 5.75 5.75

Protection of Wild Animals and Plants — A1273

Designs: a, Panthera pardus orientalis. b, Selenarctos thibetanus ussuricus. c, Lutra lutra. d, Moschus moschiferus.

1998, Mar. 21 *Perf. 13x13½*
1929 Sheet of 12 24.00 24.00
a.-d. A1273 340w Any single 1.50 .30

Top part of No. 1929 contains one each No. 1929a-1929d and is separated from the bottom portion of the sheet by a row of perforations. The lower part of No. 1929 contains 2 each Nos. 1929a-1929d.

Cartoons — A1274

Designs: 170w, Boy daydreaming while holding flower, from "Aktong-i," by Lee Hi-jae. 340w, Mother on motorcycle, son making fists from "Challenger," by Park Ki-jong.

1998, May 4 Photo. *Perf. 13½x13*
1930 A1274 170w multicolored .75 .25
a. Souvenir sheet of 1 .75 .75
b. Booklet pane of 10 19.00
Complete booklet, #1930b 19.00

Photo. & Engr.
1931 A1274 340w multicolored 1.45 1.25
a. Souvenir sheet of 1 1.50 1.50
b. Booklet pane of 10 24.00
Complete booklet, #1931b 24.00

Natl. Assembly, 50th Anniv. — A1275

1998, May 30 Litho. *Perf. 13½x13*
1932 A1275 170w multicolored .70 .25

2002 World Cup Soccer Championships, Korea/Japan — A1276

Designs: a, Player. b, Two players. c, Player heading ball. d, Player performing bicycle kick.

1998, May 30 *Perf. 13x13½*
1933 A1276 Strip of 4, #a.-d. 4.00 4.00
a.-d. 170w any single .70 .25
e. Souvenir sheet, #1933 3.25 3.25

Information Culture Special — A1277

Communication through the ages: a, Rock drawings. b, Horseback messenger, beacon fire. c, Telephone, mailbox. d, Computers.

1998, June 1 Litho. *Perf. 13½x13*
1934 Strip of 4 4.00 4.00
a.-c. A1277 170w any single .60 .25
d. A1277 340w multicolored 1.25 .45

No. 1934d is 68x70mm.

Mushroom Type of 1993

Designs: a, Pseudocolus schellenbergiae. b, Cyptotrama asprata. c, Laccaria vinaceoavellanea. d, Phallus rugulosus.

1998, July 4
1935 Sheet of 16 17.00 17.00
a.-d. A1098 170w Any single .75 .30

Left part of No. 1935 contains 3 each Nos. 1935a-1935d, with each strip in a different order. This is separated from the right portion of the sheet by a row of perforations. The right part of No. 1935 contains 1 each Nos. 1935a-1935d.

Republic of Korea, 50th Anniv. — A1278

1998, Aug. 14 Photo. *Perf. 13½x13*
1937 A1278 170w multicolored .70 .25

Philatelic Week — A1279

1998, Aug. 19 *Perf. 13x13½*
1938 A1279 170w multicolored .70 .25
a. Souvenir sheet of 2 1.20 1.20

A1280

1998, Sept. 24 Photo. *Perf. 13x13½*
1939 A1280 170w multicolored .70 .25
Complete booklet, 10 #1939 10.00

1998 Pusan Intl. Film Festival.

Founding of Songkyunkwan, 600th Anniv. — A1281

Photo. & Engr.

1998, Sept. 25 *Perf. 13*
1940 A1281 170w multicolored .70 .25
Complete booklet, 5 #1940 4.50

A1282

1998, Oct. 1
1941 A1282 170w multicolored .70 .25
Complete booklet, 10 #1941 7.25

Korean Armed Forces, 50th anniv.

World Stamp Day — A1283

1998, Oct. 9
1942 A1283 170w multicolored .75 .25
Complete booklet, 10 #1942 6.50

Beauty Series

Ceramics — A1284

No. 1944, Box with cranes on lid. No. 1945, Fish. No. 1946, Red, white blossom with blue leaf. No. 1947, Frog. No. 1948, Dragon. No. 1949, Monkeys. No. 1950, Pagoda.

1998, Nov. 20 Photo. *Perf. 13*

1943	A1284 170w multicolored		.80	.35
1944	A1284 170w multicolored		.80	.35
1945	A1284 170w multicolored		.80	.35
1946	A1284 170w multicolored		.80	.35
1947	A1284 170w multicolored		.80	.35
1948	A1284 170w multicolored		.80	.35
1949	A1284 170w multicolored		.80	.35
1950	A1284 170w multicolored		.80	.35
a.	Block of 8, #1243-1250		8.50	7.50

New Year 1999 (Year of the Rabbit) — A1286

1998, Dec. 1 *Perf. 13x13½*

1952	A1286 170w multicolored	.75	.25
	Complete booklet, 10 #1952	8.75	

Woodblock of Buddhist Tripitaka Koreana, Haeinsa Temple — A1287

Haeinsa Temple Changgyong P'anjon Complex — A1288

Litho. & Engr.

1998, Dec. 9 *Perf. 13½*

1953	Sheet of 12	28.00	28.00
a.	A1287 170w multicolored	.95	.50
b.	A1288 380w multicolored	2.75	1.60

Top part of No. 1953 contains one each Nos. 1953a-1953b and is separated from the bottom portion of the sheet by a row of perforations. The lower part of No. 1953 contains 6 No. 1953a and 4 No. 1953b.

Opening of Kunsan Port, Cent. — A1289

1999, May 1 Litho. *Perf. 13¼*

1954	A1289 170w multicolored	.65	.25

Opening of Masan Port, Cent. A1290

1999, May 1

1955	A1290 170w multicolored	.85	.25

Cartoons — A1291

No. 1956, Boy and dog, "Tokgo T'ak," by Lee Sang-mu. No. 1957, Choson Dynasty robber, "Im Kkuk-jung," by Lee Du-ho. No. 1958, Fighter against alien invaders, "Rai-Fi," by Kim San-ho, vert.

1999, May 3 Photo. *Perf. 13½*

1956	A1291 170w multicolored	.65	.30
1957	A1291 170w multicolored	.65	.30
1958	A1291 170w multicolored	.65	.30
	Nos. 1956-1958 (3)	1.95	.90

Souvenir Sheets

1959	A1291 340w like #1956	1.45	1.25
1960	A1291 340w like #1957	1.45	1.25
1961	A1291 340w like #1958	1.45	1.25
	Nos. 1959-1961 (3)	4.35	3.75

Nos. 1959-1961 are continuous designs.

A1292

Raptors: a, Falco peregrinus. b, Accipiter soloensis. c, Bubo bubo. d, Haliaeetus pelagicus.

1999, June 5 Litho. *Perf. 13x13¼*

1962	Sheet of 12	27.00	27.00
a.-b.	A1292 170w each	1.00	.30
c.-d.	A1292 340w each	1.90	.50

Top part of No. 1962 contains one each Nos. 1962a-1962d and is separated from the bottom portion of the sheet by a row of perforations. The lower part of No. 1962 contains 2 blocks of Nos. 1962a-1962d.

A1293

1999, June 12 Photo. *Perf. 13x13¼*

1963	A1293 170w multicolored	.65	.25
	Complete booklet, 10 #1963	12.50	

1999 Intl. Olympic Committee Congress, Seoul.

Johann Wolfgang von Goethe, German Poet (1749-1832) — A1294

Litho. & Engr.

1999, Aug. 12 *Perf. 13x13½*

1964	A1294 170w multicolored	.85	.30

Souvenir Sheet

1965	A1294 480w multicolored	2.40	2.40

See Germany No. 2052.

Kumgang Mountain by Kyomjae (1676-1759) A1295

1999, Aug. 13 Litho.

1966	A1295 170w multicolored	.75	.30

Souvenir Sheet

1967	A1295 340w multicolored	1.25	1.25

Korean National Railroad, Cent. — A1296

Litho. & Engr.

1999, Sept. 18 *Perf. 13x13¼*

1968	A1296 170w multicolored	.75	.30
	Complete booklet, 10 #1968	10.00	

Millennium — A1297

A1297a

A1297b

A1297c

A1297d

A1297e

A1297f

A1297g

A1297h

A1297i

A1297j

Prehistoric sites and artifacts — No. 1969: a, Paleolithic ruins, Chungok-ri (black denomination at LL). b, Neolithic sites, Amsa-dong (white denomination at UR). c, Neolithic shell mound ruins, Tongsam-dong (black denomination at LR). d, Dolmen, Pukon-ri (black denomination at UR). e, Bronze Age artifacts and ruins, Songguk-ri. f, Rock carvings, Ulsan.

Three Countries Era artifacts — No. 1970: a, Tiger-shpaed belt buckle from tomb of Sarari, duck-shaped earthenware container, Kyongsang. b, Gold crown, silver cup from Hwangnamdae tomb. c, Wall painting of hunting scene from Tomb of the Dancers, Chibanri. d, Gold diadem ornaments, curved jade pieces from tomb of King Muryong. e, Gold crown from Koryong, armor from Kimhae. f, Decorative tiles, Anapji Pond.

Ancient Choson to Unified Shilla periods — No. 1971: a, Writing, site of Asadal, ancient capital of Choson. b, Korean wrestlers. c, King Kwanggaet'o, stone stele, and circular artifact with writing. d, Archers on horseback. e, Admiral Chang Po-go, ship.

Koryo dynasty — No. 1972: a, Writing and buildings (civil service examinations). b, Monk and Tripitaka Koreana wood blocks. c, Jade and movable metal type. d, Scholar An-hyang, writing and buildings. e, Mun Ik-jom, cotton plants and spinning wheel.

Early Choson dynasty — No. 1973: a, King Sejong and Korean alphabet. b, Korean script and Lady Shin Saimdang, calligrapher and painter. c, Yi Hwang and Yi I and Confucian academy building. d, Admiral Yi Sun-shin and turtle boat. e, Sandae-nori mask dance dramas.

Late Choson Dynasty — No. 1974: a, Tongui Pogam, medical treatises by Huh Joon (anatomic diagram, mortar and pestle) b, Dancer and Musicians, by Kim Hong-do. c, Plum Blossoms and Bird, by Chong Yak-yong and building. d, Map of Korea, by Kim Chong-ho and compass. e, Carved stone monument at Tongchak Peasant Uprsing Memorial Hall.

Historic relics of Koryo and Choson Dynasties — No. 1975: a, Container, pitcher, Kangjin kiln site. b, Fenced-off monument and Nirvana Hall, Pongjungsa Temple (yellow building). c, Hahoe and Pyongsan wooden masks. d, Kunjong Hall, Kyongbok Palace. e, Dream Journey to the Peach Blossom land, by An Kyon. f, Water clock of King Sejong.

Joseon Dynasty — No. 1976: a, Spring Outing, by Sin Yun-bok. b, Chusa-style calligraphy, birthplace of Kim Jeong-hui. c, Beacon Lighthouse, book of technical drawings. d, Myeongdong Cathedral. e, Wongaksa Theater, performers. f, KITSAT-1 satellite.

Vision of the Future — No. 1977: a, Bicycle with wheels represening the two Koreas. b, Rainbow (environmental protection). c, Human genome project. d, IMT 2000 and satellites. e, Children's drawing of space travel. f, Solar-powered vehicle, windmills.

Pre-independence historic events and personalities — No. 1978: a, Kim Ku. b, March 1 Independence Movement, Declaration of Independence. c, Establishment of Korean interim government. d, Ahn Ik-tae, composer of national anthem. e, Yun Dong-ju, poet.

Historic events since independence — No. 1979: a, Liberation after World War II (People with flag). b, Korean War (soldiers, barbed wire). c, Construction of Seoul-Busan Expressway. d, Saemaul Undong movement (workers and flag). e, 1988 Summer Olympics, Seoul.

1999-2001 Litho. *Perf. 13x13½*

1969	A1297	Sheet of 6	5.50	5.50
a.-f.		170w any single	.70	.30
1970	A1297a	Sheet of 6	5.50	5.50
a.-f.		170w any single	.70	.30

Perf. 13½

1971	A1297b	Sheet of 5 + label	5.75	5.75
a.-e.		170w any single	.70	.30

Photo.

1972	A1297c	Sheet of 5 + label	5.75	5.75
a.-e.		170w any single	.70	.30
1973	A1297d	Sheet of 5 + label	5.75	5.75
a.-e.		170w any single	.70	.30
1974	A1297e	Sheet of 5 + label	7.25	7.25
a.-e.		170w Any single	.70	.30

Perf. 13

1975	A1297f	Sheet of 6	7.50	7.50
a.-f.		170w Any single	.90	.30
1976	A1297g	Sheet of 6	6.25	6.25
a.-f.		170w Any single	.70	.30
1977	A1297h	Sheet of 6	5.75	5.75
a.-f.		170w Any single	.70	.30

Perf. 13½

1978	A1297i	Sheet of 5 + label	7.50	7.50
a.-e.		170w Any single	.90	.30
1979	A1297j	Sheet of 5 + label	5.50	5.50
a.-e.		170w Any single	.70	.30
		Nos. 1969-1979 (11)	68.00	68.00

Issued: No. 1969, 10/2; No. 1970, 11/16; No. 1971, 1/3/00; No. 1972, 3/2/00; No. 1973, 5/1/00; No. 1974, 7/1/00; No. 1975, 9/1/00; No. 1976, 11/1/00; No. 1977, 1/2/01; No. 1978, 4/2/01; No. 1979, 7/2/01.

UPU, 125th Anniv. — A1298

1999, Oct. 9 Litho. *Perf. 13x13½*

1980	A1298	170w multi	.75	.25

Beauty Series

A1299

a, Purple panel, 4 orange flowers in purple and blue vase, rabbit, duck. b, Blue green panel, red jar, rooster. c, Orange panel, 4 orange flowers in yellow vase. d, Purple panel, fish, purple vase with flower decoration. e, Blue green panel, fish in net. f, Red panel, crab. g, Purple panel, birds, red flowers. h, Orange panel, deer, 3 orange flowers.

1999, Nov. 3 Litho. *Perf. 13x13¼*

1981	A1299	Sheet of 8, #a.-h.	13.50	13.50
a.-h.		340w any single	1.60	.50

New Year 2000 (Year of the Dragon) — A1300

1999, Dec. 1 Photo.

1982	A1300	170w multi	.75	.30
a.		Souvenir sheet of 2	1.50	1.50

A1301

Registration of Korean Sites on World Heritage List — A1302

Litho. & Engr.

1999, Dec. 9 *Perf. 13x13¼*

1983		Sheet of 10	17.50	17.50
a.	A1301	170w multicolored	1.00	.30
b.	A1302	340w multicolored	2.60	.55

Top part of No. 1983 contains one each Nos. 1983a-1983b. The lower part of No. 1983 contains 4 each Nos. 1983a-1983b.

Flag A1303

Nycticorax Nycticorax A1304

Vitis Amurensis A1305

Purpuricenus Lituratus A1306

Eophona Migratoria A1307

Limenitis Populi A1310

Plow A1311

Sseore A1311a

Sowing Basket, Namtae A1311b

Hoes A1311c

Namu-janngun, Jaetbak A1311d

Yongdurei A1311e

Winnower, Thresher A1311f

Meongseok, Wicker Tray A1311g

Mortar, Pestle, Grindstone A1311h

Carrier, Rice Chest A1311i

Hibiscus Syriacus A1312

Chionectes Opilio A1313

Falco Tinnunculus — A1314

Hibiscus Syriacus A1314a

Hibiscus Syriacus A1314b

Ficedula Zanthopygia — A1315

Hibiscus Syriacus A1315a

Celadon Pitcher A1316

Porcelain Container A1316a

Hong Yong-Sik, 1st General Postmaster A1317

Koryo Jade Ornament A1319

Kylin Roof-End Tile A1320

Ridge-End Tile A1321

Porcelain Vase With Bamboo Design A1322

Crown From Tombs of Shinch'on-ni A1323

Malus Asiatica A1326

Aquilegia Flabeliata — A1327

Perf. 13¼x13 (#2000, 2002, 2004, 2005), 13x13¼ (#2001, 2003, 2006, 2007), 12¾x13¾ (#1984-1990, 1996), 13¾x12¾ (#1986, 1991, 1993, 1994, 1995, 1997, 1998)

1999-2003 Photo.

1984	A1303	10w multi	.35	.25
1985	A1304	20w multi	.45	.30
1986	A1305	30w multi	.45	.35
1987	A1306	40w multi	.45	.30
1988	A1307	60w multi	.45	.35
1989	A1310	160w multi	.65	.30
1990		Horiz. strip of 10	15.50	10.00
a.	A1311	170w multi	1.00	.30
b.	A1311a	170w multi	1.00	.30
c.	A1311b	170w multi	1.00	.30
d.	A1311c	170w multi	1.00	.30
e.	A1311d	170w multi	1.00	.30
f.	A1311e	170w multi	1.00	.30
g.	A1311f	170w multi	1.00	.30
h.	A1311g	170w multi	1.00	.30
i.	A1311h	170w multi	1.00	.30
j.	A1311i	170w multi	1.00	.30

1991	A1312	190w	multi	1.00	.30
1992	A1313	200w	multi	1.05	.35
1993	A1314	210w	multi	.90	.30
1994	A1314a	220w	multi	1.00	.30
1995	A1314b	240w	multi	1.45	.40
1996	A1315	280w	multi	1.10	.40
1997	A1315a	310w	multi	1.30	.60
1998	A1316	400w	multi	1.45	.80
1999	A1316a	500w	multi	1.90	.85
2000	A1317	600w	multi	2.60	.85
2001	A1319	700w	multi	3.25	.85
2002	A1320	1290w	multi	5.75	1.90
2003	A1321	1310w	multi	6.00	1.90
2004	A1320	1490w	buff & multi	6.25	2.60
2005	A1321	1510w	brn & multi	6.25	2.60
2006	A1322	1520w	multi	5.50	2.50
2007	A1323	2000w	multi	7.25	1.20

Booklet Stamps
Self-Adhesive
Serpentine Die Cut 11¼x11½, 11½x11¼

2008	A1326	190w	multi	1.45	.75
a.	Booklet pane of 20			25.00	
2008A	A1327	190w	multi	1.45	.75
a.	Booklet pane of 20			25.00	
	Nos. 1984-2008A (26)			75.20	32.05

Issued: 600w, 11/15; 2000w, 11/1; 20w, 700w, 1/17/00; 40w, 6/10/00; No. 1990, 1/20/01; 200w, 3/5/01. 160w, 210w, 280w, 1290w, 1310w, 1/15/02; 10w, 3/6/03; 30w, 9/10/01; 60w, 3/15/02; 400w, 4/11/03; 1490w, 1510w, 1/1/03; Nos. 2008-2008A, 7/1/03; 500w, 7/11/03; No. 1991, 220w, 240w, 310w, 1520w, 11/1/04.

2002 World Cup Soccer Championships, Korea & Japan — A1328

Various players in action.

1999, Dec. 31 Photo. ***Perf. 13x13½***
Denomination Color

2009	170w orange		.70	.35
2010	170w green		.70	.35
2011	170w red		.70	.35
2012	170w blue		.70	.35
a.	A1328 Strip of 4, #2009-2012		3.25	3.25
b.	Souvenir sheet, #2009-2012		3.50	3.50

Korea's Entry into UPU, Cent. — A1329

2000, Jan. 3 Photo. ***Perf. 13¼x13***
2013 A1329 170w multi .75 .30
Booklet, 10 #2013 12.50

Steam Locomotives A1330

Designs: No. 2014, Pashi. No. 2015, Teho. No. 2016, Mika. No. 2017, Hyouki.

2000, Feb. 1 Photo. ***Perf. 13¾x12¾***

2014	A1330 170w tan, blk & vio		.70	.30
2015	A1330 170w pink, blk & vio		.70	.30
2016	A1330 170w gray, blk & vio		.70	.30
2017	A1330 170w cit, blk & vio		.70	.30
a.	Block of 4, #2014-2017		3.75	3.75
	Booklet, 2 #2017a		—	

Endangered Flowers — A1331

a, Lilium cernuum. b, Hibiscus hamabo. c, Sedirea japonica. d, Cypripedium japonicum.

2000, Feb. 25 ***Perf. 13x13¼***
2018 Sheet of 12 17.50 17.50
a.-d. A1331 170w any single 1.10 .30

Top part of No. 2018 contains one each of Nos. 2018a-2018d and the lower part contains two each. No. 2018 is impregnated with floral scent.

World Water Day — A1332

2000, Mar. 22 Photo. ***Perf. 13¼x13***
2019 A1332 170w multi .65 .30
Booklet, 10 #2019 10.00

World Meteorological Organization, 50th Anniv. — A1333

2000, Mar. 23 ***Perf. 13x13¼***
2020 A1333 170w multi .75 .30
Booklet, 10 #2020 10.00

Love — A1334

2000, Apr. 20 Photo. ***Perf. 13¼***
2021 A1334 170w multi 1.10 .30

No. 2021 has floral scent.
Value is for stamp with surrounding selvage.

Cyber Korea 21 Technology Plan — A1335

2000, Apr. 22 Litho. ***Perf. 13¼x13***
2022 A1335 170w multi .80 .30
Booklet, 10 #2022 10.50

Cartoons — A1336

Designs: No. 2023: Goindol, by Park Soo-dong (cavemen). No. 2024, Youngsim-i, by Bae Gum-taek (girl with lipstick).

2000, May 4 Photo. ***Perf. 13x13¼***

2023	A1336 170w multi	.70	.35
a.	Souvenir sheet of 1	.95	.95
	Booklet, 10 #2023	10.50	
2024	A1336 170w multi	.70	.35
a.	Souvenir sheet of 1	.95	.95
	Booklet, 10 #2024	10.50	

Summit Meeting Between North and South Korea — A1337

2000, June 12 Photo. ***Perf. 13¼x13***
2025 A1337 170w multi .65 .45

41st Intl. Mathematical Olympiad — A1338

2000, July 13 Photo. ***Perf. 13x13¼***
2026 A1338 170w multi .85 .35
Booklet, 10 #2026 10.50

Literature Series

The Nine Cloud Dream, by Kim Man-jung A1339

From the Sea to a Child, by Chun Nam-seon A1340

Tears of Blood, by Yi In-jik A1341

Yolha Diary, by Park Ji-won A1342

The Fisherman's Calendar, by Yun Seon-do — A1343

2000, Aug. 1 ***Perf. 13¼x13, 13x13¼***

2027	A1339 170w multi	.85	.35
a.	Souvenir sheet of 1	1.00	1.00
2028	A1340 170w multi	.85	.35
a.	Souvenir sheet of 1	1.00	1.00
2029	A1341 170w multi	.85	.35
a.	Souvenir sheet of 1	1.00	1.00
2030	A1342 170w multi	.85	.35
a.	Souvenir sheet of 1	1.00	1.00
2031	A1343 170w multi	.85	.35
a.	Souvenir sheet of 1	1.00	1.00
	Nos. 2027-2031 (5)	4.25	1.75

The Puljongdae Cliff of Mt. Kumgang, by Chong Son — A1344

2000, Aug. 2 Litho. ***Perf. 13¼x13***
2032 A1344 340w multi 1.45 .65
a. Souvenir sheet of 1 1.60 1.45

Philately Week.

2000 Summer Olympics, Sydney — A1345

2000, Sept. 15 Photo. ***Perf. 13x13¼***
2033 A1345 170w multi .75 .40

Public Secondary Schools, Cent. A1346

2000, Oct. 2 Litho. & Engr. ***Perf. 13***
2034 A1346 170w multi .70 .40

Third Asia-Europe Summit Meeting, Seoul — A1347

2000, Oct. 20 Photo. ***Perf. 13¼x13***
2035 A1347 170w multi .70 .35

Intl. Council of Graphic Design Associations Millennium Congress — A1348

2000, Oct. 25 ***Perf. 13x13¼***
2036 A1348 170w org & blk .70 .35

Cartoon Character Gobau. 50th Anniv. A1349

2000, Nov. 1 Litho. ***Perf. 13¼***
2037 A1349 170w multi .70 .35

Beauty Series

Tortoise-shell Comb A1350

Woman's Ceremonial Headdress A1351

Butterfly-shaped Hair Pin — A1352

Dragon and Phoenix Hair Pins — A1353

2000, Nov. 16 Photo. ***Perf. 13¼x13***

2038	Horiz. strip of 4	4.25	4.25
a.	A1350 170w multi	.70	.40
b.	A1351 170w multi	.70	.40
c.	A1352 170w multi	.70	.40
d.	A1353 170w multi	.70	.40

Seoul World Cup Stadium A1354

Busan Sports Complex Main Stadium A1355

Daegu Sports Complex Stadium A1356

Incheon Munhak Stadium A1357

Gwangju World Cup Stadium A1358

Daejeon World Cup Stadium A1359

Ulsan Munsu Soccer Stadium A1360

Suwon World Cup Stadium A1361

Jeonju World Cup Stadium A1362

Jeju World Cup Stadium A1363

2000, Nov. 24 Photo. *Perf. 13¼x13*

2039	Block of 10	13.50	10.00
a.	A1354 170w multi	1.15	.35
b.	A1355 170w multi	1.15	.35
c.	A1356 170w multi	1.15	.35
d.	A1357 170w multi	1.15	.35
e.	A1358 170w multi	1.15	.35
f.	A1359 170w multi	1.15	.35
g.	A1360 170w multi	1.15	.35
h.	A1361 170w multi	1.15	.35
i.	A1362 170w multi	1.15	.35
j.	A1363 170w multi	1.15	.35
k.	Souvenir sheet, #2039a-2039b	2.75	2.75
l.	Souvenir sheet, #2039c-2039d	2.75	2.75
m.	Souvenir sheet, #2039e-2039f	2.75	2.75
n.	Souvenir sheet, #2039g-2039h	2.75	2.75
o.	Souvenir sheet, #2039i-2039j	2.75	2.75

New Year 2001 (Year of the Snake) — A1364

2000 Photo. *Perf. 13¼*

2040	A1364 170w multi	.95	.35
a.	Souvenir sheet of 2	1.75	1.75

Self-Adhesive

Serpentine Die Cut 10¼

2041	A1364 170w multi	1.25	.35

Issued: No. 2040, 12/1; No. 241, 12/22. No. 2041 issued in sheets of 10.

King Sejong and Hunmin Chongun Manuscript A1365

Annals of the Choson Dynasty and Repository A1365a

Litho. & Engr.

2000, Dec. 9 *Perf. 13x13¼*

2042	Sheet of 8	15.50	15.50
a.	A1365 340w multi	1.50	.90
b.	A1365a 340w multi	1.50	.90

Addition of Hunmin Chongun manuscript and Annals of the Choson Dynasty to UNESCO Memory of the World Register. Top part of No. 2042 contains one each Nos. 2042a-2042b the lower part contains three each Nos. 2042a-2042b.

Awarding of Nobel Peace Prize to Pres. Kim Dae-jung A1366

2000, Dec. 9 Photo.

2043	A1366 170w multi	.85	.35
a.	Souvenir sheet of 1	2.25	2.25

Oksun Peaks, by Kim Hong-do — A1367

2001, Jan. 10 Photo. *Perf. 13¼*

2044	A1367 170w multi	.80	.35

Visit Korea Year.

A1368

A1369

A1370

Diesel and Electric Trains — A1371

2001, Feb. 1 Photo. *Perf. 13¾x12¾*

2045	Block of 4	3.75	3.75
a.	A1368 170w multi	.85	.40
b.	A1369 170w multi	.85	.40
c.	A1370 170w multi	.85	.40
d.	A1371 170w multi	.85	.40

Endangered Flowers — A1372

Designs: a, Diapensia lapponica. b, Rhododendron aureum. c, Jeffersonia dubia. d, Sedum orbiculatum.

2001, Feb. 26 *Perf. 13x13¼*

2046	Sheet of 12	14.50	14.50
a.-d.	A1372 170w Any single	.80	.45

Top part of No. 2046 contains one each Nos. 2046a-2046d, the lower part contains two each Nos. 2046a-2046d.

Opening of Inchon Intl. Airport — A1373

2001, Mar. 29

2047	A1373 170w multi	.75	.40

Intl. Olympic Fair, Seoul — A1374

2001, Apr. 27 *Perf. 13¼x13*

2048	A1374 170w multi	.75	.40
a.	Souvenir sheet of 2	1.90	1.90

Personalized Greetings — A1375

Designs: No. 2049, 170w, Hugging bears. No. 2050, 170w, Carnation. No. 2051, 170w, Congratulations. No. 2052, 170w, Birthday cake.

2001 Photo. *Perf. 13¼*

Stamps + Labels

2049-2052	A1375 Set of 4	7.25	3.75

Issued: Nos. 2049-2050, 4/30; No. 2051, 6/1; No. 2052, 7/2. Each stamp was issued in sheets of 20+20 labels that could be personalized. Each sheet sold for 700w.

Cartoons — A1376

Designs: No. 2053, Iljimae, by Ko Woo-young (shown). No. 2054, Kkeobeongi, by Kil Chang-duk (student at desk).

2001, May 4 Photo. *Perf. 13x13¼*

2053	A1376 170w multi	.70	.35
a.	Souvenir sheet of 1	1.60	1.60
2054	A1376 170w multi	.70	.35
a.	Souvenir sheet of 1	1.60	1.60

2002 World Cup Soccer Championships, Japan and Korea — A1377

Years of previous championships, soccer players, flags and scenes from host countries: a, 1954, Switzerland, mountains. b, 1986, Mexico, Chichen Itza. c, 1990, Italy, Colosseum. d, 1994, US, World Trade Center and Statue of Liberty. e, 1998, France, Eiffel Tower.

2001, May 31 *Perf. 13¼x13*

2055	A1377 Horiz. strip of 5	4.75	4.25
a.-e.	170w Any single	.80	.35
f.	Souvenir sheet, 2 #2055a	1.60	1.60
g.	Souvenir sheet, 2 #2055b	1.60	1.60
h.	Souvenir sheet, 2 #2055c	1.60	1.60
i.	Souvenir sheet, 2 #2055d	1.60	1.60
j.	Souvenir sheet, 2 #2055e	1.60	1.60

Kkakdugi A1378

Bossam Kimchi — A1379

Dongchimi A1380

Baechu Kimchi — A1381

2001, June 15 *Perf. 13x13¼*

2056	Vert. strip of 4	3.50	3.50
a.	A1378 170w multi	.65	.35
b.	A1379 170w multi	.65	.35
c.	A1380 170w multi	.65	.35
d.	A1381 170w multi	.65	.35

Roses — A1382

2001, July 18 Photo. *Perf. 13¼*

2057	A1382 170w Red Queen	.75	.35
a.	Souvenir sheet of 2	1.90	1.90
2058	A1382 170w Pink Lady	.75	.35
a.	Souvenir sheet of 2	1.90	1.90

Phila Korea 2002, (Nos. 2057a, 2058a).

Love — A1383

2001, Aug. 2

2059	A1383 170w multi	.70	.40
a.	Souvenir sheet of 2	1.75	1.75

World Ceramics Exhibition — A1384

2001, Aug. 10 *Perf. 13x13¼*

2060	A1384 170w multi	.70	.35

53rd Session of the Intl. Statistical Institute — A1385

2001, Aug. 22 Litho. *Perf. 13¼x13*

2061	A1385 170w multi	.70	.35

Korea Minting and Security Printing Corp., 50th Anniv. — A1386

Litho. & Engr.

2001, Sept. 28 *Perf. 13¼*

2062	A1386 170w multi	.70	.40

Intl. Council of Industrial Design Societies Congress, Seoul — A1387

2001, Oct. 8 Photo. *Perf. 13x13¼*

2063	A1387 170w multi	.70	.35

Year of Dialogue Among Civilizations — A1388

2001, Oct. 9 Litho.

2064	A1388 170w multi	.70	.35

Intl. Organization of Supreme Audit Institutions, 17th Congress — A1389

2001, Oct. 19 *Perf. 13¼x13*

2065	A1389 170w blue & red	.70	.35

Orchids — A1390

No. 2066: a, Habenaria radiata. b, Orchis cyclochila. c, Dendrobium moniliforme. d, Gymnadenia camschatica.

2001, Nov. 12 Photo. *Perf. 13¼x13*

2066	A1390 Horiz. strip of 4	4.50	4.50
a.-d.	170w Any single	.75	.40

No. 2066 is impregnated with orchid scent.

New Year 2002 (Year of the Horse) — A1391

2001, Dec. 3 ***Perf. 13x13¼***

2067 A1391 170w multi		.75	.40
a.	Souvenir sheet of 2	1.90	1.90

Seonjeongjeon Hall, Changdeok Palace — A1392

Injeongjeon Hall, Changdeok Palace A1393

Litho. & Engr.

2001, Dec. 10 ***Perf. 13x13¼***

2068	Sheet of 10	17.50	14.00
a.	A1392 170w multi	.85	.35
b.	A1393 340w multi	1.60	.70

Top part of No. 2068 contains one each Nos. 2068a-2068b. The lower part of No. 2068 contains 4 each Nos. 2068a-2068b.

Priority Mail — A1394

2002, Jan. 15 Photo. ***Perf. 13¼x13***

Background Color

2069 A1394 280w orange	1.45	.45
2070 A1394 310w blue	1.60	.50
2071 A1394 1380w green	4.50	2.40
2072 A1394 1410w red	4.50	2.40
Nos. 2069-2072 (4)	12.05	5.75

See Nos. 2113-2114, 2127.

Lily A1395

Roses — A1395a

Fish A1396

Chick — A1396a

2002, Jan. 15 Photo. ***Perf. 13¼***

Stamp + Label

2073 A1395 190w multi	2.00	1.00
2073A A1395a 190w multi	2.00	1.00
2074 A1396 190w multi	2.00	1.00
2074A A1396a 190w multi	2.00	1.00
Nos. 2073-2074A (4)	8.00	4.00

Nos. 2073, 2073A and 2074 are impregnated with scents of items depicted. Labels could be personalized.

Korea's Entrance in Intl. Telecommunications Union, 50th Anniv. — A1397

2002, Jan. 31 Photo. ***Perf. 13x13¼***

2075 A1397 190w multi	.70	.35

Trains A1398

No. 2076: a, Blue and white locomotive. b, Green, yellow and white locomotive. c, Green, yellow and white locomotive pulling cars. d, Red, yellow and white locomotive pulling cars.

2002, Feb. 4 Photo. ***Perf. 13¾x12¾***

2076 A1398 190w Block of 4, #a-d	4.25	4.25

Dye Plants A1399

No. 2077: a, Carthamus tinctorius. b, Lithospermum erythrorhizon. c, Fraxinus rhynchophylla. d, Persicaria tinctoria.

2002, Feb. 25 Photo. ***Perf. 13¼x13***

2077 A1399 190w Block of 4, #a-d	4.25	3.50

See No. 2117, 2140, 2170.

Intl. Flower Exhibition, Anmyeon Island — A1400

2002, Apr. 26 ***Perf. 13¼***

2078 A1400 190w multi	.85	.35

Cartoons — A1401

Designs: No. 2079, Girl from "Wogdoggle Dugdoggle," by Mi-Na Hwang. No. 2080, Schoolmaster and children from "Mengkkong-i Seodang Village School," by Seung-woon Yoon.

2002, May 4 ***Perf. 13¼x13***

2079 A1401 190w multi		.85	.35
a.	Souvenir sheet of 1	1.05	1.05
2080 A1401 190w multi		.85	.35
a.	Souvenir sheet of 1	1.05	1.05

64th Rally of Intl. Federation of Camping and Caravanning, Donghae — A1402

2002, May 16

2081 A1402 190w multi	*1.60*	.40

2002 World Cup Soccer Championships, Japan and Korea — A1403

No. 2082: a, Player with pink feet, part of map of Europe. b, Player with blue green feet, part of map of North and Central America. c, Player with blue violet feet, part of map of southeast Asia. d, Player with purple feet, part of map of southern Africa. e, Player with brown orange feet, part of map of South America.

2002, May 31 ***Perf.***

2082 A1403 190w Sheet, 2 each #a-e, + label		10.00	10.00
f.	Souvenir sheet, 2 #2082a	1.00	.40
g.	Souvenir sheet, 2 #2082b	1.00	.40
h.	Souvenir sheet, 2 #2082c	1.00	.40
i.	Souvenir sheet, 2 #2082d	1.00	.40
j.	Souvenir sheet, 2 #2082e	1.00	.40

Korean Cuisine A1404

No. 2083: a, Jeolpyeon (blue background). b, Shirutteok (red background). c, Injeolmi (tan background). d, Songpyeon (green background).

2002, June 15 ***Perf. 13x13¼***

2083 A1404 190w Block of 4, #a-d	3.75	3.75

Women's Week — A1405

2002, July 1 Litho. ***Perf. 13x13¼***

2084 A1405 190w multi	.70	.35

Philakorea 2002 World Stamp Exhibition, Seoul — A1406

Designs: No. 2085, Children, globe. No. 2086, Child, stamps showing flags of the world.

2002, July 1 Photo. ***Perf. 13¼***

2085 A1406 190w multi		.75	.35
a.	Souvenir sheet of 2	1.75	1.75
2086 A1406 190w multi		.75	.35
a.	Souvenir sheet of 2	1.75	1.75

Regions of Korea

Busan A1407

Chungbuk — A1408

Chungnam — A1409

Daegu A1410

Daejeon A1411

Gangwon — A1412

Gwangju A1413

Gyeongbuk — A1414

Gyeonggi — A1415

Gyeongnam — A1416

Incheon A1417

Jeju A1418

Jeonbuk A1419

Jeonnam A1420

Seoul A1421

Ulsan A1422

No. 2087: a, Dongnaeyaryu Festival. b, Cliffs.

No. 2088: a, Martial arts. b, Beopju Temple.

No. 2089: a, Weaver. b, Men in sailboat.

No. 2090: a, Forest and river. b, Gwanbong Seokjoyeorae statue.

No. 2091: a, Daeok Science Town, scientist at work. b, Expo Science Park.

No. 2092: a, Gangneung mask drama. b, Ulsanbawi Rock.

No. 2093: a, Men playing tug-of-war game. b, Statues and tower at May 18th Cemetery.

No. 2094: a, Men playing game with tied logs. b, Dokdo Island.

No. 2095: a, Yangjubyeol Sandaenori mask dance. b, Panmunjom Freedom House.

No. 2096: a, Goseong Ogwangdae clowns performing. b, Rock formations in Hallyeo Haesang Natl. Maritime Park.
No. 2097: a, Chamseongdam dancers. b, Cliffs.
No. 2098: a, Traditional house and gate. b, Mt. Halla.
No. 2099: a, Iri folk band. b, Mt. Mai.
No. 2100: a, Ganggang Sullae circle dance. b, Odong Island.
No. 2101: a, Songpa Sandaenori mask dance. b, Heung-injimun Fortress.
No. 2102: a, Cheoyongmu mask dance. b, Cheonjeonnigakseok prehistoric inscriptions.

2002, Aug. 1 ***Perf. 13x13¼***

2087 A1407 190w	Horiz. pair, #a-b	1.60	.70
2088 A1408 190w	Horiz. pair, #a-b	1.60	.70
2089 A1409 190w	Horiz. pair, #a-b	1.60	.70
2090 A1410 190w	Horiz. pair, #a-b	1.60	.70
2091 A1411 190w	Horiz. pair, #a-b	1.60	.70
2092 A1412 190w	Horiz. pair, #a-b	1.60	.70
2093 A1413 190w	Horiz. pair, #a-b	1.60	.70
2094 A1414 190w	Horiz. pair, #a-b	1.60	.70
2095 A1415 190w	Horiz. pair, #a-b	1.60	.70
2096 A1416 190w	Horiz. pair, #a-b	1.60	.70
2097 A1417 190w	Horiz. pair, #a-b	1.60	.70
2098 A1418 190w	Horiz. pair, #a-b	1.60	.70
2099 A1419 190w	Horiz. pair, #a-b	1.60	.70
2100 A1420 190w	Horiz. pair, #a-b	1.60	.70
2101 A1421 190w	Horiz. pair, #a-b	1.60	.70
2102 A1422 190w	Horiz. pair, #a-b	1.60	.70
Nos. 2087-2102 (16)		25.60	11.20

Philakorea 2002 World Stamp Exhibition, Seoul — A1423

2002, Aug. 2 ***Perf. 13¼x13***

2103 A1423 190w multi .70 .35
a. Sheet of 2, imperf. 2.00 2.00

Philately Week — A1424

2002, Aug. 2 ***Perf. 13¼***

2104 A1424 190w multi .70 .35
a. Souvenir sheet of 2 1.90 1.90

South Korean Soccer Team's Fourth Place Finish at World Cup Championships — A1425

No. 2105: a, Coach Guus Hiddink. b, Goalie (jersey #1). c, Player with red shirt with white accents. d, Player with red shirt with white accents, with white sock. e, Player with white shirt with red accents, ball near shoulder. f, Player (jersey #5). g, Player (jersey #6). h, Player (jersey #7). i, Player (jersey #8.) j, Player (jersey #9). k, Player (jersey #10). l, Player with ball hiding part of head. m, Goalie with red hair, white gloves with dark trim. n, Player (jersey #13). o, Player (jersey #14). p, Player (jersey #15). q, Player with white shirt with red accents, with white sock. r, Player (jersey #17). s, Player (jersey #18). t, Player (jersey #19). u, Player (jersey #20). v, Player (jersey #21). w, Player (jersey #22). x, Goalie with brown hair, black gloves with red trim.

2002, Aug. 7 ***Perf. 13¼x13***

2105 A1425 190w Sheet of 24, #a-x 18.50 18.50

14th Asian Games, Busan A1426

2002, Sept. 28 **Litho.** ***Perf. 13***

2106 A1426 190w multi .80 .40
a. Souvenir sheet of 2 2.00 2.00

8th Far East and South Pacific Games for the Disabled, Busan — A1427

2002, Oct. 26 **Photo.** ***Perf. 13x13¼***

2107 A1427 190w multi .75 .35

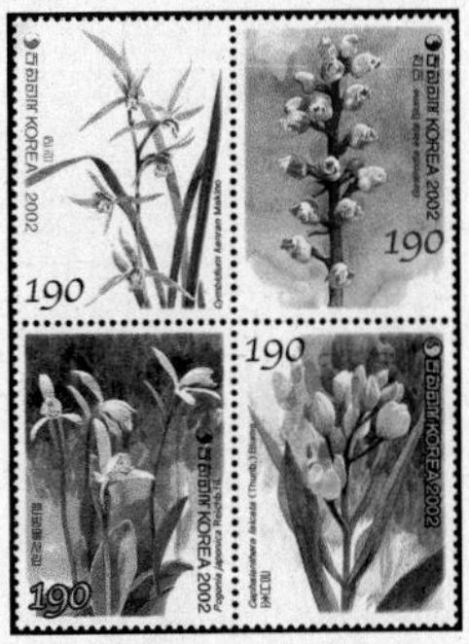

Orchids — A1428

No. 2108: a, Cymbidium kanran. b, Gastrodia elata. c, Pogonia japonica. d, Cephalanthera falcata.

2002, Nov. 12 ***Perf. 13¼x13***

2108 A1428 190w Block of 4, #a-d 4.00 4.00

No. 2108 is impregnated with orchid scent.

Martial Arts A1429

No. 2109: a, Taekwondo (white clothes). b, Kung Fu (red clothes).

2002, Nov. 20 ***Perf. 13x13¼***

2109 A1429 190w Horiz. pair, #a-b 1.75 1.75

See People's Republic of China No. 3248.

New Year 2003 (Year of the Ram) — A1430

2002, Dec. 2

2110 A1430 190w multi .85 .40
a. Souvenir sheet of 2 1.90 1.90

Gongsimdon Observation Tower, Hwaseong Fortress A1431

Banghwasuryu Pavilion, Hwaseong Fortress — A1432

2002, Dec. 9 **Litho. & Engr.**

2111 Sheet of 10 15.00 15.00
a. A1431 190w multi .80 .40
b. A1432 280w multi 1.25 .65

Top part of No. 2111 contains one each of Nos. 2111a-2111b. The lower part contains 4 each Nos. 2111a-2111b.

South Korea — Viet Nam Diplomatic Relations, 10th Anniv. — A1433

No. 2112: a, Dabo Pagoda, Gyeongju (denomination at right). b, Mot Cot Pagoda, Hanoi, Viet Nam (denomination at left).

2002, Dec. 21 **Photo.** ***Perf. 13¼x13***

2112 A1433 190w Horiz. pair, #a-b 2.00 1.50

See Viet Nam Nos. 3167-3168.

Priority Mail Type of 2002

2003, Jan. 1 **Photo.** ***Perf. 13¼x13***

Background Color

2113 A1394 1580w lilac 5.25 4.75
2114 A1394 1610w brown 5.25 4.75

Korean Immigration to the US, Cent. — A1434

2003, Jan. 13 **Photo.** ***Perf. 13¼x13***

2115 A1434 190w multi .80 .40

Gondola Car — A1435

Box Car — A1436

Tanker Car — A1437

Hopper Car — A1438

2003, Feb. 4 ***Perf. 13¾x13***

2116 Block of 4 4.00 3.25
a. A1435 190w multi .70 .35
b. A1436 190w multi .70 .35
c. A1437 190w multi .70 .35
d. A1438 190w multi .70 .35

Dye Plants Type of 2002

No. 2117: a, Rubia akane. b, Rhus javanica. c, Sophora japonica. d, Isatis tinctoria.

2003, Feb. 22 **Photo.** ***Perf. 13¼x13***

2117 A1399 190w Horiz. strip of 4, #a-d 3.50 2.50

Inauguration of Pres. Roh Moo-hyun A1439

2003, Feb. 25 ***Perf. 13x13¼***

2118 A1439 190w multi 1.35 .65
a. Souvenir sheet of 1 2.00 2.00

Traditional Culture

Footwear A1440

Sedan Chairs A1441

Lighting Implements — A1442

Tables A1443

No. 2119: a, Unhye (denomination at LL, date at LR). b, Mokhwa (denomination at UR, date at L). c, Jipsin (denomination at UL, date at LR). d, Namaksin (denomination at LR, date at LL).
No. 2120: a, Eoyeon (no handles). b, Choheon (wheeled). c, Saingyo (with handles and roof). d, Nanyeo (with handles only).
No. 2121: a, Jojokdeung (round lantern). b, Deungjan (lamp oil container). c, Juchilmokje Yukgakjedeung (hexagonal lantern). d, Brass candlestick holder with butterfly design.
No. 2122: a, Gujok-ban (round table with legs connected at base. b, Punghyeol-ban (12-sided table, denomination at top). c, Ilju-ban (12-sided table, denomination at top). d, Haeju-ban (octagonal table).

2003 **Engr.** ***Perf. 12½***

2119 A1440 190w Horiz. strip of 4, #a-d 4.00 2.50
2120 A1441 190w Horiz. strip of 4, #a-d 4.00 2.50
2121 A1442 190w Horiz. strip of 4, #a-d 4.00 2.50
2122 A1443 190w Horiz. strip of 4, #a-d 4.00 2.50
Nos. 2119-2122 (4) 16.00 10.00

Issued: No. 2119, 3/19; No. 2120, 5/19; No. 2121, 7/25; No. 2122, 9/25.

Cartoons — A1444

Designs: No. 2123, The Goblin's Cap, by Shin Moon-soo (shown). No. 2124, The Sword of Fire, by Kim Hye-rin (woman with sword).

2003, May 2 **Photo.** ***Perf. 13x13¼***

2123 A1444 190w multi .75 .35
a. Souvenir sheet of 1 1.05 1.05
2124 A1444 190w multi .75 .35
a. Souvenir sheet of 1 1.05 1.05

Lighthouse Construction in Korea, Cent. — A1445

2003, May 30 ***Perf. 13¼x13***

2125 A1445 190w multi .75 .35

Dasik — A1446

Yeot Gangjeong A1447

Yakgwa — A1448

Yugwa — A1449

2003, June 13 ***Perf. 13x13¼***

2126	Block or strip of 4	2.60	2.10
a.	A1446 190w multi	.55	.35
b.	A1447 190w multi	.55	.35
c.	A1448 190w multi	.55	.35
d.	A1449 190w multi	.55	.35

Nos. 2126a-2126d were printed in sheets of 20 that yield four No. 2126 and one vertical strip of four of Nos. 2126a-2126d.

Priority Mail Type of 2002

2003, July 1 Photo. ***Perf. 13¼x13***

Background Color

2127 A1394 420w blue green 4.50 1.00

Philately Week — A1450

2003, Aug. 1 ***Perf. 13¼***

2128	A1450 190w multi	.75	.35
a.	Souvenir sheet of 2, imperf.	1.90	1.90

2003 Summer Universiade, Daegu — A1451

2003, Aug. 21 ***Perf. 13x13¼***

2129	A1451 190w multi	.75	.35
a.	Souvenir sheet of 2	1.90	1.90

YMCA in Korea, Cent. — A1452

2003, Oct. 28 Photo. ***Perf. 13¼x13***

2130 A1452 190w multi .75 .35

Soong Eui School, Cent. — A1453

2003, Oct. 31 ***Perf. 13x13¼***

2131 A1453 190w multi .75 .35

Natl. Tuberculosis Association, 50th Anniv. — A1454

2003, Nov. 6 **Litho.**

2132 A1454 190w black & red .75 .35

Orchids A1455

No. 2133: a, Cremastra appendiculata. b, Cymbidium lancifolium. c, Orchis graminifolia. d, Bulbophyllum drymoglossum.

2003, Nov. 12 Photo. ***Perf. 13¼x13***

2133 A1455 190w Block of 4, #a-d 3.75 3.75

No. 2133 is impregnated with a floral scent.

New Year 2004 (Year of the Monkey) — A1456

2003, Dec. 1 ***Perf. 13x13¼***

2134	A1456 190w multi	.75	.35
a.	Souvenir sheet of 2	1.90	1.90

A1457

Dolmens A1458

Litho. & Engr.

2003, Dec. 9 ***Perf. 13x13¼***

2135	Sheet of 10	13.50	13.50
a.	A1457 190w multi	.90	.40
b.	A1458 280w multi	1.25	.65

Top part of No. 2135 contains one each of Nos. 2135a-2135b. The lower part contains 4 each Nos. 2135a-2135b.

South Korea — India Diplomatic Relations, 30th Anniv. — A1459

No. 2136: a, Cheomsongdae Astronomical Observatory, Gyeongju, South Korea. b, Jantar Mantar, Jaipur, India.

2003, Dec. 10 Photo. ***Perf. 13¼x13***

2136 A1459 190w Horiz. pair, #a-b 2.25 2.00

Dokdo Island Flora and Fauna — A1460

No. 2137: a, Calystegia soldanella. b, Aster spathulifolius, butterfly. c, Calonectris laucomelas. d, Larus crassirostris.

2004, Jan. 16 ***Perf. 13x13¼***

2137	A1460 Horiz. strip of 4	*15.50*	—
a.-d.	190w Any single	*3.75*	*3.75*

Korean National Commission for UNESCO, 50th Anniv. — A1461

2004, Jan. 30

2138 A1461 190w multi .75 .30

Multiple Tie Tamper A1462

Ballast Regulator A1463

Track Inspection Car — A1464

Ballast Cleaner A1465

2004, Feb. 4 ***Perf. 13¾x12¾***

2139	Block of 4	3.50	3.50
a.	A1462 190w brown & multi	.70	.40
b.	A1463 190w lilac & multi	.70	.40
c.	A1464 190w blue green & multi	.70	.40
d.	A1465 190w blue & multi	.70	.40

Dye Plants Type of 2002

No. 2140: a, Juglans regia. b, Acer ginnala. c, Pinus densiflora. d, Punica granatum.

2004, Feb. 25 ***Perf. 13¼x13***

2140 A1399 190w Block of 4, #a-d 3.00 3.00

12th World Water Day — A1466

2004, Mar. 22 Litho. ***Perf. 13x13¼***

2141 A1466 190w multi .75 .40

A1467

2004, Mar. 25 **Photo.**

2142 A1467 190w multi .80 .40

Korean Meteorological Service, cent.

Inauguration of High Speed Railroads — A1468

2004, Apr. 1 ***Perf. 13¼x13***

2143 A1468 190w multi .80 .40

A1469

Winners of Future of Science Stamp Design Contest — A1470

Perf. 13¼x13, 13x13¼

2004, Apr. 21 **Photo.**

2144	A1469 190w multi	.80	.40
2145	A1470 190w multi	.80	.40

A1471

Cartoons: No. 2146, Wicked Boy Simsultong, by Lee Jeong-moon (shown). No. 2147, Nation of Winds, by Kim Jin.

2004, May 4 Photo. ***Perf. 13x13¼***

2146	A1471 190w multi	.80	.40
a.	Souvenir sheet of 1	1.10	1.10
2147	A1471 190w multi	.80	.40
a.	Souvenir sheet of 1	1.10	1.10

A1472

2004, May 21

2148 A1472 190w multi .55 .35

FIFA (Fédération Internationale de Football Association), cent.

Korean Cuisine A1473

No. 2149: a, Sinseollo (blue background). b, Hwayangjeok (green background). c, Bibimbap (pink background). d, Gujeolpan (orange background).

2004, June 15

2149 A1473 190w Block of 4, #a-d 3.25 3.25

Traditional Culture

Needlework Equipment — A1474

Head Coverings — A1475

No. 2150: a, Octagonal storage basket. b, Thimbles with flower decorations. c, Cylindrical bobbin, bobbin and thread. d, Needle cases.

No. 2151: a, Gold crown with tassels. b, Bamboo hat with untied neck band. c, Gauze hat. d, Horsehair hat with tied neck band.

2004 **Engr.** ***Perf. 12½***

2150	A1474 190w Horiz. strip of 4, #a-d	3.50	3.50
2151	A1475 190w Horiz. strip of 4, #a-d	3.50	3.50

Issued: No. 2150, 6/24; No. 2151, 8/20.

National Academies, 50th Anniv. A1476

No. 2152: a, National Academy of Science. b, National Academy of Arts.

2004, July 16 Litho. ***Perf. 13x13¼***

2152 A1476 190w Horiz. pair, #a-b 1.60 1.60

Congratulations A1477

2004, July 22 Photo. ***Perf. 13¼***

2153 A1477 190w multi .80 .40
a. Souvenir sheet of 2 1.75 1.75

2004 Summer Olympics, Athens — A1478

2004, Aug. 13 ***Perf. 13x13¼***

2154 A1478 190w multi .80 .40

Bridges A1479

No. 2155: a, Geumcheongyo Bridge (two arches). b, Jeongotgyo Bridge (pillars and flat slabs). c, Jincheon Nongdari Bridge (loose rocks). d, Seungseongyo Bridge (single arch).

Perf. 13¼ Syncopated

2004, Sept. 24

2155 A1479 190w Block of 4, #a-d 3.50 3.50

Intl. Council of Museums, 20th General Conference, Seoul — A1480

2004, Oct. 1 ***Perf. 13x13¼***

2156 A1480 190w multi .80 .40

Obaegnahan A1481

Seonjakjiwat A1482

Baengnokdam A1483

Oreum — A1484

2004, Oct. 18

2157 Block of 4 3.50 3.50
a. A1481 190w multi .70 .35
b. A1482 190w multi .70 .35
c. A1483 190w multi .70 .35
d. A1484 190w multi .70 .35

Flag A1485

Flowers A1486

Flower and Bee A1487

Lamb, Church and Bible A1488

Children and Lotus Flower A1489

Stylized Animals A1490

Teddy Bear A1491

Dinosaur A1492

Flower and Envelope A1493

2004, Nov. 1 Photo. ***Perf. 13¼***

2158 A1485 220w multi + label 2.10 1.35
2159 A1486 220w multi + label 2.10 1.35
2160 A1487 220w multi + label 2.10 1.35
2161 A1488 220w multi + label 2.10 1.35
2162 A1489 220w multi + label 2.10 1.35
2163 Strip of 4 + 4 alternating labels 8.75 8.75
a. A1490 220w multi + label 2.10 2.00
b. A1491 220w multi + label 2.10 2.00
c. A1492 220w multi + label 2.10 2.00
d. A1493 220w multi + label 2.10 2.00
Nos. 2158-2163 (6) 19.25 15.50

Labels attached to Nos. 2158-2163 could be personalized.

Orchids — A1494

No. 2164: a, Goodyera maximowicziana. b, Sarcanthus scolopendrifolius. c, Calanthe sieboldii. d, Bletilla striata.

2004, Nov. 12 ***Perf. 13¼x13***

2164 A1494 220w Block of 4, #a-d 3.50 3.50

No. 2164 is impregnated with orchid scent.

New Year 2005 (Year of the Chicken) — A1495

2004, Dec. 1 ***Perf. 13x13¼***

2165 A1495 220w multi .90 .45
a. Souvenir sheet of 2 1.90 1.90

Daenungwon Tumuli Park, Seosuhyeong Ceramics, Royal Crown of Geumgwanchong — A1496

Anapji Pond, Scissors, Buddha, Lion Incense Burner A1497

2004, Dec. 9 Litho. & Engr.

2166 Sheet of 10 14.00 14.00
a. A1496 310w multi 1.00 .55
b. A1497 310w multi 1.00 .55

Top part of No. 2166 contains one each of Nos. 2166a-2166b. The lower part contains 4 each of Nos. 2166a-2166b.

Fish of Marado Island — A1498

No. 2167: a, Girella punctata. b, Epinephelus septemfasciatus. c, Chromis notata. d, Sebastiscus marmoratus.

2005, Jan. 18 Photo.

2167 Horiz. strip of 4 5.75 5.75
a.-d. A1498 220w Any single 1.20 .50

Cloning of Human Embryonic Stem Cells, 1st Anniv. A1499

2005, Feb. 12 ***Perf. 12¾x13½***

2168 A1499 220w multi 2.75 1.00

Rotary International, Cent. — A1500

2005, Feb. 23 ***Perf. 13¼x13***

2169 A1500 220w multi .80 .40

Dye Plants Type of 2002

No. 2170: a, Taxus cuspidata. b, Smilax china. c, Clerodendron trichotomum. d, Gardenia jasminoides.

2005, Feb. 25

2170 A1399 220w Block of 4, #a-d 3.75 3.75

Gyeonggi Province Tourism — A1501

2005, Mar. 10 Litho. ***Perf. 13x13¼***

2171 A1501 220w multi .75 .40

A1502

Information and Communication of the Future — A1503

2005, Apr. 22 Photo. ***Perf. 13¼x13***

2172 A1502 220w multi .75 .40

Perf. 13x13¼

2173 A1503 220w multi .75 .40

Korea University, Cent. — A1504

2005, May 4 Litho. ***Perf. 13x13¼***

2174 A1504 220w multi .85 .40

57th Intl. Whaling Commission Meeting, Ulsan — A1505

2005, May 27 Photo. ***Perf. 13¼x13***

2175 A1505 220w multi .95 .40

Neobani (Broiled Beef) — A1506

Bindaetteok (Fried Ground Mung Beans) — A1507

Jeongol (Stew) — A1508

Hwajeon (Fried Rice Cakes and Flower Petals) — A1509

2005, June 15 ***Perf. 13x13¼***

2176 Block of 4 3.75 3.75
- *a.* A1506 220w multi .85 .40
- *b.* A1507 220w multi .85 .40
- *c.* A1508 220w multi .85 .40
- *d.* A1509 220w multi .85 .40

Goguryeo Kingdom — A1510

No. 2177: a, Sword, armored soldier on horse. b, Armored soldiers on horses, Onyeo Fortress, Baek-am Castle.

Perf. 13x13¼ Syncopated

2005, July 1

2177 A1510 310w Vert. pair, #a-b 3.00 3.00

Strix Aluco A1513

Arctous Ruber A1514

Parus Major A1516

Crinum Asiaticum A1517

Planned City A1521

Brown Hawk Owl A1522

Rose of Sharon A1523

Sungnyemun Gate — A1524

Suwon Hwaseong Fortress — A1524a

Haeundae Dongbaek Island — A1524b

Dodamsambong Peaks — A1524c

Hongdo Island — A1524d

Cheomseongdae Observatory — A1524e

Gwanghallu Pavilion — A1524f

Gyeongpodae Pavilion — A1524g

Baengnokdam Lake — A1524h

Whistling Swans A1525

Charonia Sauliae A1526

Charonia Sauliae — A1526a

Pitta Nympha — A1526b

Celadon Incense Burner A1527

Buncheong Jar A1529

Buncheong Jar — A1530

Jar With Clay Figurines — A1530a

Jar With Clay Figurines — A1530b

Gold Earrings — A1530c

Gilt Bronze Pagoda — A1531

Vessel With Dragon's Head — A1531a

Lofty Scholar Contemplating Water, Painting by Kang Hui An — A1531b

National Seal — A1531c

Euryale Ferox A1532

Flag A1533

2005-14 **Photo.** ***Perf. 13¾x12¾***

2178 A1513 50w multi .75 .25
2179 A1514 70w multi .45 .25

Perf. 12¾x13¾

2180 A1516 90w multi .65 .25

Perf. 13¾x12¾

2181 A1517 100w multi .65 .25

Perf. 13x13¼

2182 A1521 220w multi .95 .25
2183 A1522 250w multi 1.05 .35

Perf. 13½

2184 A1523 250w multi + label 2.00 .35

Perf. 13x13¾

2185 Horiz. strip of 9 8.75 8.75
- *a.* A1524 300w multi .55 .25
- *b.* A1524a 300w multi .55 .25
- *c.* A1524b 300w multi .55 .25
- *d.* A1524c 300w multi .55 .25
- *e.* A1524d 300w multi .55 .25
- *f.* A1524e 300w multi .55 .25
- *g.* A1524f 300w multi .55 .25
- *h.* A1524g 300w multi .55 .25
- *i.* A1524h 300w multi .55 .25

Perf. 13¾x13

2186 A1525 340w multi 1.00 .40

Perf. 12¾x13¾

2187 A1526 360w multi .65 .30

Perf. 13x13¾

2188 A1526a 390w multi 1.00 .25

Perf. 13x13¼

2189 A1526b 400w multi .90 .35
2190 A1527 1000w multi 3.00 1.00
2191 A1529 1720w multi 4.50 1.75

Perf. 13x13½

2192 A1530 1750w multi 5.50 1.90

Perf. 13x13¼

2193 A1530a 1770w multi 4.00 1.50

Perf. 13x13½

2194 A1530b 1930w multi 4.00 .90

Perf. 13¾x13½

2195 A1530c 1930w multi 4.00 2.00

Perf. 13x13½

2196 A1531 2000w multi 6.00 1.60

Perf. 13¾x13½

2197 A1531a 2000w multi 4.00 1.90
2198 A1531b 3000w multi 5.75 2.75
2199 A1531c 3550w multi 7.00 3.25
Nos. 2180-2199 (20) 65.35 30.05

Self-Adhesive

Serpentine Die Cut 11¾x11½

2200 A1532 250w multi 1.30 .25

Serpentine Die Cut 11½x11¼

2201 A1533 270w multi .60 .25

Issued: 50w, 9/1; 1720w, 8/1; 90w, 6/5/06; 100w, 3/2/06; 220w, 12/27/05. Nos. 2183, 2184, 2186, 2192, 11/1/06. 70w, 7/10/07. No. 2200, 6/30/08. No. 2190, 11/17/09; No. 2196, 5/25/09. Nos. 2187, 2193, 2201, 10/1/11. Nos. 2185, 2188, 2194, 11/11/13. Nos. 2189, 2197, 11/20/14. Nos. 2195, 2198, 8/7/14; No. 2199, 10/28/14.

No. 2190 was printed in sheets of 20 stamps and 20 labels that could be personalized.

Nos. 2197C, 2198A, 2198B and 2198C each have a die cut hole in the shape of the Korean Peninsula in the lower right corner of the stamp.

Happy Birthday — A1536

2005, Aug. 3 **Photo.** ***Perf. 13¼***

2203 A1536 220w multi .85 .35
- *a.* Souvenir sheet of 2 1.90 1.90

Philately Week. Portions of the design were printed with a thermochromic ink that changes color when warmed.

Liberation of Korea, 60th Anniv. — A1537

No. 2204: a, Charter and headquarters of provisional government. b, Proclamation of Korean Independence. c, Soldiers taking oath. d, Emblem of 60th anniv. of Korean liberation.

2005, Aug. 12 ***Perf. 13¼x13***

2204 Horiz. strip of 4 7.75 7.75
- *a.* A1537 480w multi 1.25 .75
- *b.* A1537 520w multi 1.25 1.00
- *c.* A1537 580w multi 1.50 1.10
- *d.* A1537 600w multi 1.50 1.25

Fusion of Eastern and Western Cultures — A1538

2005, Aug. 18 **Litho.** ***Perf. 13x13¼***

2205 A1538 220w multi .85 .45

Hangang Bridge A1539

Expogyo A1540

Banghwa Bridge A1541

Tongyeong Bridge A1542

Perf. 13¼ Syncopated

2005, Sept. 23 **Photo.**

2206 Block of 4 3.75 3.75
- *a.* A1539 220w multi .70 .40
- *b.* A1540 220w multi .70 .40
- *c.* A1541 220w multi .70 .40
- *d.* A1542 220w multi .70 .40

Ikki Falls — A1543

Piagol Valley — A1544

Cheonwangbong Peak — A1545

Baraebong Peak — A1546

2005, Oct. 18 *Perf. 13x13¼*

2207 Horiz. strip of 4 5.00 5.00
a. A1543 220w multi .90 .40
b. A1544 220w multi .90 .40
c. A1545 220w multi .90 .40
d. A1546 220w multi .90 .40

Korean Red Cross, Cent. — A1547

2005, Oct. 27

2208 A1547 220w multi .85 .50

Relocation and Reopening of National Museum — A1548

2005, Oct. 28 *Perf. 13¼x13*

2209 A1548 220w multi .85 .50

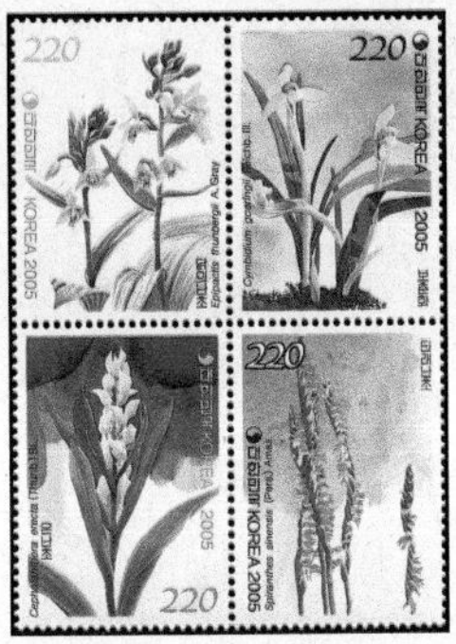
Orchids — A1549

No. 2210: a, Epipactis thunbergii. b, Cymbidium goeringii. c, Cephalanthera erecta. d, Spiranthes sinensis.

2005, Nov. 11

2210 A1549 220w Block of 4, #a-d 3.75 3.75

2005 Asian-Pacific Economic Cooperation Economic Leaders' Meeting, Busan — A1550

No. 2211: a, The Sun, the Moon and Five Peaks. b, Murimaru APEC House, Dongbaek Island.

2005, Nov. 18 Photo. *Perf. 13x13¼*

2211 A1550 220w Horiz. pair, #a-b 1.60 1.60

New Year 2006 (Year of the Dog) — A1551

2005, Dec. 1

2212 A1551 220w multi .85 .50
a. Souvenir sheet of 2 1.90 1.90

Jikjisimcheyojeol, Book Produced in 1377 by Movable Type — A1552

Seungjeongwon Ilgi, Diaries of the Joseon Dynasty — A1553

2005, Dec. 9 **Litho. & Engr.**

2213 Sheet of 10 15.00 15.00
a. A1552 310w multi 1.25 .60
b. A1553 310w multi 1.25 .60

Top part of No. 2213 contains one each of Nos. 2213a-2213b. The lower part contains 4 each of Nos, 2213a-2213b.

Wildlife of Baengnyeongdo A1554

Designs: No. 2214, Phoca vitulina largha. No. 2215, Phalacrocorax pelagicus. No. 2216, Orithyia sinica. No. 2217, Ammodytes personatus.

2006, Jan. 18 **Photo.**

2214 A1554 220w multi .95 .50
2215 A1554 220w multi .95 .50
2216 A1554 220w multi .95 .50
2217 A1554 220w multi .95 .50
a. Horiz. strip of 4, #2214-2217 4.00 4.00
b. Sheet, 1 each #2214-2217, 3 #2217a + 2 labels 18.50
Nos. 2214-2217 (4) 3.80 2.00

Designation of Cheju Island as Island of World Peace — A1555

2006, Jan. 27 *Perf. 13¾x12¾*

2218 A1555 220w multi .85 .50

Exports

Automobiles A1556

Semiconductors A1557

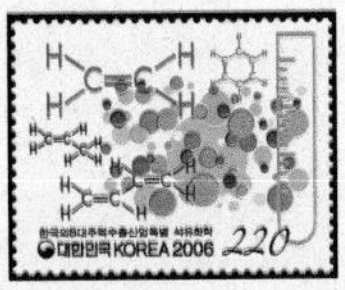
Petrochemicals A1558

Electronics A1559

Machinery A1560

Ships — A1561

Steel — A1562

Textiles — A1563

2006, Mar. 15 *Perf. 13x13¼*

2219 Block of 8 6.50 6.50
a. A1556 220w multi .75 .50
b. A1557 220w multi .75 .50
c. A1558 220w multi .75 .50
d. A1559 220w multi .75 .50
e. A1560 220w multi .75 .50
f. A1561 220w multi .75 .50
g. A1562 220w black .75 .50
h. A1563 220w multi .75 .50

Gyeongnam Goseong Dinosaur World Expo — A1564

Serpentine Die Cut 11¼x11

2006, Apr. 14

2220 A1564 Horiz. pair 1.90 1.35
a. 220w Iguanodon .80 .50
b. 220w Megaraptor .80 .50

A1565

Children's Drawings on Automated World — A1566

2006, Apr. 21 *Perf. 13x13¼, 13¼x13*

2221 A1565 220w multi .85 .50
2222 A1566 220w multi .85 .50

Dongguk University, Cent. — A1567

2006, May 8 Litho. *Perf. 13x13¼*

2223 A1567 220w multi, *cream* .85 .40

Sookmyung Women's University, Cent. A1568

Perf. 12¾x13¾

2006, May 22 **Photo.**

2224 A1568 220w multi .85 .40

2006 World Cup Soccer Championships, Germany — A1569

2006, June 2 Photo. *Perf. 13¼*

2225 A1569 220w multi + label 4.00 —

No. 2225 was printed in sheets of 14 stamps + 14 labels picturing members of South Korean World Cup soccer team + one large label picturing entire team. Sheets sold for 6000w.

A1570

2006 World Cup Soccer Championships, Germany — A1571

Perf. 12¾x13¾

2006, June 9 **Photo.**

2226 Pair 1.75 1.35
a. A1570 220w multi .75 .45
b. A1571 220w multi .75 .45

Goguryeo Kingdom A1572

No. 2227: a, Janggun Tomb and Sanseongha Tombs. b, Sun and Moon Gods from Ohoebun Tomb No. 4.

Perf. 13x13¼ Syncopated

2006, July 3 **Photo.**

2227 A1572 480w Vert. pair, #a-b 3.75 3.75

No. 2227 was printed in sheets containing seven of each stamp.

Philately Week — A1573

No. 2228: a, Denomination below heart. b, Denomination above heart.

2006, Aug. 3 Photo. *Perf. 13¼*

2228 A1573 220w Pair, #a-b 1.45 1.45
c. Souvenir sheet, #2228a-2228b 1.90 1.90

Skateboarding — A1574

No. 2229: a, Tail stole. b, Drop in. c, Backside spin. d, Backside grab.

Serpentine Die Cut 11¾x11¼

2006, Sept. 5 **Self-Adhesive**

2229 A1574 220w Block of 4, #a-d		3.50	3.50

World Ginseng Expo, Geumsan — A1575

2006, Sept. 22 ***Perf. 13x13¼***

2230 A1575 220w multi	.85	.40

Jindo Bridge A1576

Changseon-Samcheonpo Bridge — A1577

Olympic Bridge A1578

Seohae Bridge A1579

Perf. 13¼ Syncopated

2006, Sept. 26

2231	Block of 4	3.50	3.50
a.	A1576 220w multi	.70	.40
b.	A1577 220w multi	.70	.40
c.	A1578 220w multi	.70	.40
d.	A1579 220w multi	.70	.40

Hangeul Day — A1580

2006, Oct. 9 ***Perf. 13x13¼***

2232 A1580 (220w) multi	.85	.40

Use of Hangeul as official Korean writing system, 560th anniv.

Sahmyook University, Cent. — A1581

2006, Oct. 10

2233 A1581 220w multi	.85	.40

Lineage A1582

Maple Story A1583

Ragnarok A1584

Gersang A1585

Legend of Mir III A1586

Kartrider A1587

Mu A1588

Pangya A1589

Fortress 2 Forever Blue A1590

Mabinogi A1591

Serpentine Die Cut 11¾

2006, Nov. 9

2234	Block of 10	10.00	10.00
a.	A1582 250w multi	.90	.60
b.	A1583 250w multi	.90	.60
c.	A1584 250w multi	.90	.60
d.	A1585 250w multi	.90	.60
e.	A1586 250w multi	.90	.60
f.	A1587 250w multi	.90	.60
g.	A1588 250w multi	.90	.60
h.	A1589 250w multi	.90	.60
i.	A1590 250w multi	.90	.60
j.	A1591 250w multi	.90	.60

Internet games.

Janggunbong Peak — A1592

Ulsanbawi Rock — A1593

Daecheongbong Peak — A1594

Sibiseonnyeotang Valley — A1595

2006, Nov. 16 ***Perf. 13x13¼***

2235	Block of 4	3.75	3.25
a.	A1592 250w multi	.80	.55
b.	A1593 250w multi	.80	.55
c.	A1594 250w multi	.80	.55
d.	A1595 250w multi	.80	.55

New Year 2007 (Year of the Pig) — A1596

2006, Dec. 1 **Photo.** ***Perf. 13x13¼***

2236	A1596 250w multi	.85	.40
a.	Souvenir sheet of 2	1.75	1.75

Text of Heungboga and Pansori Singer A1597

Mo Heung-gap, Pansori Singer A1598

Litho. & Engr.

2006, Dec. 8 ***Perf. 13x13¼***

2237	Sheet of 10	22.00	22.00
a.	A1597 480w multi	2.10	1.75
b.	A1598 480w multi	2.10	1.75

Top part of No. 2237 contains one each of Nos. 2237a-2237b. The lower part contains 4 each of Nos. 2237a-2237b.

A1599

Sharing and Caring — A1600

2006, Dec. 14 **Photo.** ***Perf. 13x13¼***

2238 A1599 250w multi	.85	.25

Perf. 13¼x13

2239 A1600 250w multi	.85	.25

No. 2238 is impregnated with a pine scent; No. 2239 with a chocolate scent.

Nakdong River in Autumn A1601

Nakdong River in Winter A1602

Nakdong River in Spring A1603

Nakdong River in Summer A1604

Perf. 13¼ Syncopated

2007, Jan. 18 **Photo.**

2240	Block of 4	3.25	3.00
a.	A1601 250w multi	.70	.25
b.	A1602 250w multi	.70	.25
c.	A1603 250w multi	.70	.25
d.	A1604 250w multi	.70	.25

Megatron/Matrix A1605

TV Buddha — A1606

The More the Better — A1607

Oh-Mah (Mother) A1608

2007, Jan. 29 ***Perf. 13¼***

2241	Sheet of 12, 3 each #a-d	12.00	12.00
a.	A1605 250w multi	.75	.25
b.	A1606 250w multi	.75	.25
c.	A1607 250w multi	.75	.25
d.	A1608 250w multi	.75	.25

Art by Nam June Paik (1932-2006).

National Debt Repayment Movement, Cent. — A1609

2007, Feb. 21 **Photo.** ***Perf. 13x13¼***

2242 A1609 250w multi	.85	.25

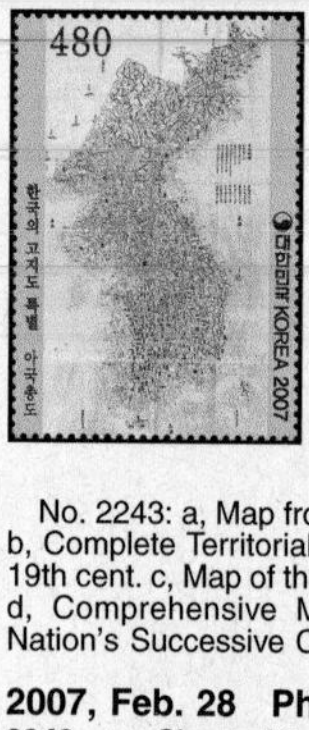

Maps of Korea — A1610

No. 2243: a, Map from Atlas of Korea, 1780. b, Complete Territorial Map of the Great East, 19th cent. c, Map of the Eight Provinces, 1531. d, Comprehensive Map of the World and Nation's Successive Capitals, 1402.

2007, Feb. 28 **Photo.** ***Perf. 13½x13***

2243	Sheet of 8, 2 each #a-d	17.50	17.50
a.	A1610 480w multi	1.20	1.20
b.	A1610 520w multi	1.50	1.50
c.	A1610 580w multi	1.75	1.75
d.	A1610 600w multi	1.75	1.75

Daehan Hospital, Seoul, Cent. — A1611

2007, Mar. 15 Litho. *Perf. 13x13¼*

2244 A1611 250w multi .85 .25

Ninth Asia Pacific Orchid Conference, Goyang — A1612

2007, Mar. 16 Photo.

2245 A1612 250w multi .85 .25

Biology Year — A1613

2007, Mar. 19 *Perf. 13¼x13*

2246 A1613 250w multi .85 .25

a. Souvenir sheet of 2 2.25 2.25

Sunflower A1614

2007, Mar. 21 Litho. *Perf. 13¼*

2247 A1614 250w multi + label 2.50 2.50

Printed in sheets of 20 stamps + 20 labels and 14 stamps + 14 labels that sold for 7500w. Labels could be personalized.

Clover A1615

Pig A1616

2007, Mar. 21 Photo. *Perf. 13¼*

2248 A1615 250w multi + label 2.75 2.75

2249 A1616 250w multi + label 2.75 2.75

Nos. 2248-2249 were each printed in sheets of 9 stamps + 9 labels. Each sheet sold for 4300w. Labels could be personalized.

Chinese Bride and Groom A1617

Indian Bride and Groom A1618

Malaysian Bride and Groom A1619

Eurasian Bride and Groom A1620

No. 2250 — Korean brides and grooms with: e, Mountains in background. f, Flowers on orange background. g, Flowers and foliage in background. h, Ducks in background.

2007, Mar. 30 *Perf. 13¼x13*

2250 Block of 8 9.00 9.00

a. A1617 250w multi .60 .40

b. A1618 250w multi .60 .40

c. A1619 250w multi .60 .40

d. A1620 250w multi .60 .40

e. A1620 480w multi 1.25 1.00

f. A1620 520w multi 1.40 1.25

g. A1620 580w multi 1.75 1.50

h. A1620 600w multi 1.90 1.50

See Singapore No. 1241.

Opening of Fortress Wall in Mt. Bugaksan A1621

2007, Apr. 5 Photo. *Perf. 13¾x12¾*

2251 A1621 250w multi .85 .30

A1622

Internet Culture — A1623

2007, Apr. 20 Litho. *Perf. 13¼x13*

2252 A1622 250w multi .85 .30

Photo.

2253 A1623 250w multi .85 .30

Children's Charter, 50th Anniv. — A1624

Serpentine Die Cut

2007, May 4 Photo.

Self-Adhesive

2254 A1624 250w multi .85 .30

No. 2254 is impregnated with a strawberry scent.

Dispatch of Special Envoys to Second Hague Peace Conference, Cent. — A1625

Litho. & Engr.

2007, June 27 *Perf. 13x13¼*

2255 A1625 250w multi .85 .30

A1626

Goguryeo Kingdom A1627

No. 2256: a, Cooks preparing food. b, Host welcoming guest.

Perf. 13 Syncopated

2007, July 2 Photo.

2256 Sheet of 14, 7 each #a-b 20.00 20.00

a. A1626 480w multi 1.25 .60

b. A1627 480w multi 1.25 .60

Philately Week A1628

No. 2257: a, Korea #1. b, Korea #2.

2007, Aug. 1 Photo. *Perf. 13x13¼*

2257 Horiz. pair 2.00 2.00

a.-b. A1628 250w Either single .75 .30

c. Souvenir sheet, #2257 2.25 2.25

Rollerblading — A1629

No. 2258: a, Drop-in. b, Flip. c, Spin. d, Grind.

Serpentine Die Cut 11¾x11¼

2007, Sept. 5 Photo.

Self-Adhesive

2258 A1629 250w Block of 4, #a-d 4.00 4.00

Korean Bar Association, Cent. — A1630

2007, Sept. 21 Litho. *Perf. 13x13¼*

2259 A1630 250w multi .85 .30

Gwangan Bridge A1631

Seongsu Bridge A1632

Seongsan Bridge A1633

Yeongjong Bridge A1634

Perf. 13¼x13½ Syncopated

2007, Sept. 28 Photo.

2260 Block of 4 3.50 3.50

a. A1631 250w multi .75 .30

b. A1632 250w multi .75 .30

c. A1633 250w multi .75 .30

d. A1634 250w multi .75 .30

Inter-Korean Summit, Pyongyang, North Korea — A1635

2007, Oct. 2 *Perf. 13¼x13*

2261 A1635 250w multi .85 .30

Hyeongje Falls — A1636

Rimyeongsu Falls — A1637

Lake Samjiyeon A1638

Lake Chonji — A1639

2007, Oct. 18 Photo. *Perf. 13x13½*

2262 Block of 4 3.50 3.50

a. A1636 250w multi .75 .30

b. A1637 250w multi .75 .30

c. A1638 250w multi .75 .30

d. A1639 250w multi .75 .30

A1640

A1641

A1642

Korean Films — A1643

No. 2263: a, Arirang, 1926. b, The Ownerless Ferryboat, 1932. c, Looking for Love, 1928. d, Chunhyangjeon, 1935.

2007, Oct. 26 *Perf. 13x13¼*

2263 Sheet of 16, 4 each #a-d 16.00 16.00

a. A1640 250w multi .75 .30

b. A1641 250w multi .75 .30

c. A1642 250w multi .75 .30

d. A1643 250w multi .75 .30

A1644

Protection of Children's Rights — A1645

2007, Nov. 20 Photo. ***Perf. 13x13¼***
2264 A1644 250w multi .85 .30

Litho.

Perf. 13¼x13
2265 A1645 250w multi .85 .30

Opening of New Central Post Office, Seoul A1646

No. 2266: a, Hanseong Post Office, 1915, and new building. b, New building.

2007, Nov. 22 Photo. ***Perf. 13x13¼***
2266 A1646 250w Horiz. pair, #a-b 2.00 2.00

No. 2266 printed in sheet containing 7 pairs.

New Year 2008 (Year of the Rat) — A1647

2007, Nov. 30
2267 A1647 250w multi .85 .30
a. Souvenir sheet of 2 1.50 1.50

Tapdeunggut Exorcism, Dano Festival, Gangneung — A1648

Gwanno Mask Drama, Dano Festival A1649

2007, Dec. 7 Litho. & Engr.
2268 Sheet of 10, 5 each #a-b 18.00 18.00
a. A1648 480w multi 1.50 .75
b. A1649 480w multi 1.50 .75

Top part of No. 2268 contains one each of Nos. 2268a-2268b. The lower part contains 4 each of Nos. 2268a-2268b.

Seomjin River in Autumn A1650

Seomjin River in Winter A1651

Seomjin River in Spring A1652

Seomjin River in Summer A1653

Perf. 13½x13¼ Syncopated

2008, Jan. 18 Photo.
2269 Block of 4 3.25 3.25
a. A1650 250w multi .75 .30
b. A1651 250w multi .75 .30
c. A1652 250w multi .75 .30
d. A1653 250w multi .75 .30

Miniature Sheet

King Sejong Antarctic Station A1654

No. 2270 — Penguins and: a, Scientists on snowmobiles. b, Station.

2008, Feb. 15 Photo. ***Perf. 13¼***
2270 A1654 250w Sheet of 10, 5 each #a-b 12.50 12.50

Inauguration of Pres. Lee Myung-Bak — A1655

2008, Feb. 25 Photo. ***Perf. 13x13¼***
2271 A1655 250w multi .85 .30
a. Souvenir sheet of 1 2.00 2.00

African Savanna A1656

No. 2272: a, African child and mask. b, Leopard. c, Elephant. d, Zebra.

Die Cut Perf. (outer edge) x Serpentine Die Cut 11 (radial sides) x Die Cut (inner edge)

2008, Mar. 26 Self-Adhesive
2272 A1656 250w Block of 4, #a-d, + central label 4.00 4.00

Philakorea 2009 Intl. Stamp Exhibition, Seoul — A1657

No. 2273 — Dancers: a, Buchaechum (orange background). b, Salpurichum (pink background). c, Seungmu (blue background). d, Taepyeongmu (green background).

2008, Apr. 10 ***Perf. 13¼x13***
2273 Horiz. strip or block of 4 3.25 3.25
a.-d. A1657 250w Any single .75 .30
e. Souvenir sheet, #2273a-2273d, + label 3.00 3.00

A1658

Winning Designs in "Mailboxes of the Future" Children's Stamp Design Contest — A1659

2008, Apr. 22 Photo. ***Perf. 13¼x13***
2274 A1658 250w multi .85 .30

Litho.

Perf. 13x13¼
2275 A1659 250w multi .85 .30

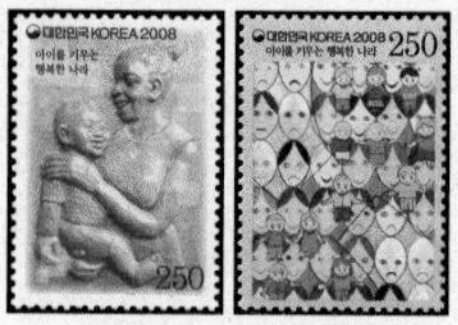

Nurturing of Children
A1660 A1661

Litho., Engr. & Embossed

2008, May 8 ***Perf. 13x13¼***
2276 A1660 250w multi .85 .30

Litho.
2277 A1661 250w multi .85 .30

Sun and Moon A1662

Hands Making Heart A1663

Tree-lined Path A1664

Roses A1665

2008, May 19 Photo. ***Perf. 13¼***
2278 A1662 250w multi + label 1.50 1.50
2279 A1663 250w multi + label 1.50 1.50
2280 A1664 250w multi + label 1.50 1.50
2281 A1665 250w multi + label 1.50 1.50
Nos. 2278-2281 (4) 6.00 6.00

Nos. 2278-2279 each were printed in sheets of 3 stamps + 3 labels, No. 2280 was printed in sheets of 14 stamps + 15 labels, and No. 2281 was printed in sheets of 20 stamps + 20 labels. Labels could be personalized.

Organization for Economic Cooperation and Development Ministerial Meeting, Seoul A1666

2008, June 17 ***Perf. 13¼***
2282 A1666 250w multi .85 .30

Yun Bong-Gil (1908-32), Assassin of Japanese Colonial Generals — A1667

2008, June 20
2283 A1667 250w multi .85 .30

Miniature Sheet

Dangun Wanggeom — A1668

No. 2284: a, Hwanung descending from heavens at Taebaek Mountain. b, Bear and tiger who prayed to become human. c, Birth of Dangun Wanggeom. d, Dangun Wanggeom as adult.

2008, July 10 Photo. ***Perf. 13¼x13***
2284 A1668 250w Sheet of 12, 3 each #a-d 6.00 6.00

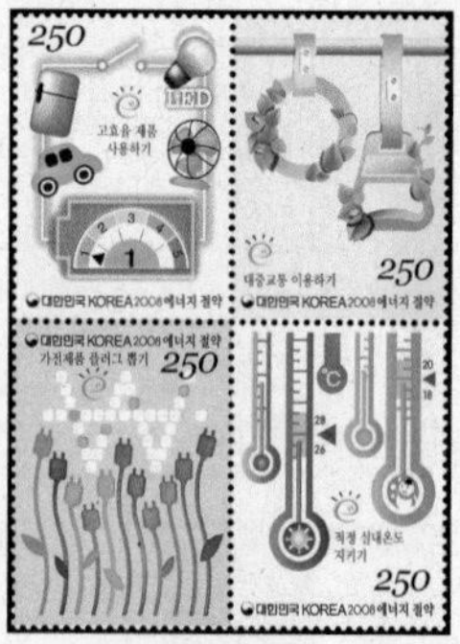

Energy Conservation — A1669

No. 2285: a, Open electrical circuit, car, refrigerator, light bulb, fan, meter. b, Hand-straps for public transportation. c, Electrical plugs on flower stems. d, Thermometers.

2008, Aug. 1 Photo. ***Perf. 13¼x13***
2285 A1669 250w Block or horiz. strip of 4, #a-d 3.00 3.00

Philately Week A1670

No. 2286: a, South Korea #34. b, South Korea #176.

2008, Aug. 7 Photo. ***Perf. 13¼x13***
2286 A1670 250w Pair, #a-b 1.50 1.50
c. Souvenir sheet, #2286a-2286b 2.00 2.00

2008 Summer Olympics, Beijing — A1671

2008, Aug. 8 Photo. ***Perf. 13¼x13***
2287 A1671 250w multi .85 .30

Republic of Korea, 60th Anniv. — A1672

2008, Aug. 14
2288 A1672 250w multi .85 .30

Korean Language Society, Cent. A1673

2008, Aug. 29 ***Perf. 12¾x13½***
2289 A1673 250w multi .85 .30

Seoul Water Works, Cent. — A1674

2008, Sept. 1 Litho. ***Perf. 13x13¼***
2290 A1674 250w multi .85 .30

Amateur Radio Direction Finding Championships, Hwaseong — A1675

2008, Sept. 2
2291 A1675 250w multi .85 .30

Snowboarding — A1676

No. 2292: a, Carving turn. b, Indy grab. c, Nose grab. d, Air.

Serpentine Die Cut 11¾x11¼
2008, Sept. 5 Photo.
Self-Adhesive
2292 A1676 250w Block of 4, #a-d 3.50 3.50

Salvation Army in Korea, Cent. — A1677

2008, Oct. 1 Photo. ***Perf. 13x13¼***
2293 A1677 250w multi .85 .30

Republic of Korea Armed Forces, 60th Anniv. — A1678

2008, Oct. 1
2294 A1678 250w multi .85 .30

Diplomatic Relations Between South Korea and Thailand, 50th Anniv. — A1679

No. 2295: a, Chakri Mahaprasat Hall, Thailand (denomination at left). b, Juhamnu Pavilion, South Korea (denomination at right).

2008, Oct. 1 Litho. ***Perf. 13¼***
2295 A1679 250w Pair, #a-b 2.50 2.50

See Thailand No. 2383.

Manmulsang A1680

Gwimyeonam Rock — A1681

Outer Geumgangsan A1682

Sangpaldam Pools — A1683

2008, Oct. 17 Photo. ***Perf. 13x13½***
2296 Block of 4 3.25 3.25
a. A1680 250w multi .75 .30
b. A1681 250w multi .75 .30
c. A1682 250w multi .75 .30
d. A1683 250w multi .75 .30

Korean Films A1684

No. 2297: a, A Coachman, 1961 (blue background). b, Wedding Day, 1956 (dull lilac background). c, The Seashore Village, 1965 (dull green background). d, Mother and a Guest, 1961 (gray olive background).

2008, Oct. 27 Litho. ***Perf. 13x13½***
2297 A1684 250w Block of 4, #a-d 3.25 3.25

Upo Wetlands A1685

2008, Oct. 28 Photo. ***Perf. 13¼***
2298 A1685 250w multi .85 .30

Tenth Ramsar Convention Meeting, Changwon.

Masks A1686

No. 2299: a, Chwibari Mask, Korea (denomination at LL). b, Big head Buddha mask, Hong Kong (denomination at LR).

2008, Nov. 6 ***Perf. 13¼x13***
2299 A1686 250w Horiz. pair, #a-b 2.00 2.00

See Hong Kong Nos. 1337-1338.

New Year 2009 (Year of the Ox) — A1687

2008, Dec. 1 ***Perf. 13x13¼***
2300 A1687 250w multi 1.00 .30
a. Souvenir sheet of 2 2.00 2.00

Louis Braille (1809-52), Educator of the Blind A1688

2009, Jan. 2 ***Perf. 12¾x13½***
2301 A1688 250w multi .85 .30

Intl. Year of Astronomy — A1689

No. 2302: a, Whirlpool Galaxy M51. b, Planetary Nebula NGC 3132.

2009, Jan. 15 Photo. ***Perf. 13x13¼***
2302 A1689 250w Horiz. pair, #a-b 1.50 1.50

Geum River in Autumn A1690

Geum River in Winter A1691

Geum River in Spring A1692

Geum River in Summer A1693

Perf. 13¼ Syncopated
2009, Feb. 10
2303 Block or horiz. strip of 4 3.25 3.25
a. A1690 250w multi .70 .30
b. A1691 250w multi .70 .30
c. A1692 250w multi .70 .30
d. A1693 250w multi .70 .30

A1694

Designs: No. 2304, 250w, Panagbenga Flower Festival, Baguio, Philippines. No. 2305, 250w, Cow Play, Hangawi, South Korea.

2009, Mar. 3 Photo. ***Perf. 13x13¼***
2304-2305 A1694 Set of 2 1.50 1.50

Diplomatic relations between South Korea and the Philippines, 60th anniv.

Historic Trees A1695

No. 2306: a, Fir tree (Natural Monument No. 495) (22x50mm). b, Zelkova tree (Natural Monument No. 478), horiz. (44x25mm). c, Ginkgo tree (Natural Monument No. 30) (22x50mm). d, Seosongnyeong tree (Natural Monument No. 294), horiz. (44x25mm).

2009, Apr. 3 Litho. ***Perf. 12¾***
2306 A1695 250w Block of 4, #a-d 3.25 3.25

Republic of Korea Marine Corps, 60th Anniv. — A1696

2009, Apr. 15 ***Perf. 12½***
2307 A1696 250w multi .85 .30

A1697

Asia Becoming One — A1698

2009, Apr. 22 Photo. ***Perf. 13¼x13***
2308 A1697 250w multi .85 .30

Litho.
Perf. 13x13¼
2309 A1698 250w multi .85 .30

A1699

Love For the Earth — A1700

2009, Apr. 22 Litho. ***Perf. 13¼x13***
2310 A1699 250w multi .85 .30

Photo.
Perf. 13x13¼
2311 A1700 250w multi .85 .30

Cartooning in Korea, Cent. — A1701

2009, June 2 Litho. ***Perf. 13x13¼***
2312 A1701 250w multi .85 .30

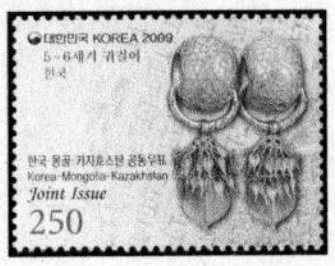

Earrings From Korea, 5th-6th Cent. — A1702

Earrings From Mongolia, 18th-19th Cent. — A1703

Earrings From Kazakhstan, 2nd-1st Cent. B.C. — A1704

2009, June 12 Photo. *Perf. 13x13¼*

2313	Strip of 3	2.50	2.50
a.	A1702 250w multi	.65	.30
b.	A1703 250w multi	.65	.30
c.	A1704 250w multi	.65	.30

See Kazakhstan No. 595, Mongolia No. 2674.

Cave Lake and Lava Tubes A1705

Lava Tubes, Stalactites and Stalagmite A1706

Litho. & Engr.

2009, June 26 *Perf. 13x13¼*

2314	Sheet of 10, 5 each #a-b	7.00	7.00
a.	A1705 250w multi	.75	.30
b.	A1706 250w multi	.75	.30

Jeju Volcanic Island and Lava Tubes UNESCO World Heritage Site.

Philately Week A1707

No. 2315: a, Korea #19. b, South Korea #639.

2009, July 30 Photo. *Perf. 13¼x13*

2315	Pair	1.50	1.50
a.-b.	A1707 250w Either single	.70	.30
c.	Souvenir sheet, #2315	.70	.30

A1708

A1709

A1710

A1711

A1712

A1713

A1714

Bird Drawings — A1715

2009, July 30 Litho. *Perf. 13¼x13*

2316	Block of 8	4.50	4.50
a.	A1708 250w multi	.50	.30
b.	A1709 250w multi	.50	.30
c.	A1710 250w multi	.50	.30
d.	A1711 250w multi	.50	.30
e.	A1712 250w multi	.50	.30
f.	A1713 250w multi	.50	.30
g.	A1714 250w multi	.50	.30
h.	A1715 250w multi	.50	.30
i.	Souvenir sheet of 2, #2316a, 2316e	2.00	2.00
j.	Souvenir sheet of 2, #2316b, 2316f	2.00	2.00
k.	Souvenir sheet of 2, #2316c, 2316g	2.00	2.00
l.	Souvenir sheet of 2, #2316d, 2316h	2.00	2.00

Philakorea 2009, Seoul.

Command From God To Move Country's Capital — A1716

Establishment of East Buyeo — A1717

Birth of King Geumwawang A1718

King Geumwawang on Throne — A1719

2009, Aug. 18 Photo. *Perf. 13x13¼*

2317	Sheet of 12, 3 each #a-d	7.00	7.00
a.	A1716 250w multi	.50	.30
b.	A1717 250w multi	.50	.30
c.	A1718 250w multi	.50	.30
d.	A1719 250w multi	.50	.30

Legend of King Geumwawang of the Buyeo Kingdom.

Green Energy A1720

No. 2318: a, House with solar panels, bicycle. b, Automobile with solar panels. c, Wind turbines. d, Dam.

2009, Aug. 21 Photo. *Perf. 13¼*

2318	A1720 250w Block of 4, #a-d	2.00	2.00

Groundbreaking for Taekwondo Park, Muju-gun A1721

2009, Sept. 4 *Perf. 13¾x12¾*

2319	A1721 250w multi	.85	.30

BMX Bicycling — A1722

No. 2320: a, X-up. b, No hand jump. c, One foot can can. d, Superman seat grab.

Serpentine Die Cut 11¾x11¼

2009, Sept. 8 Photo.

2320	A1722 250w Block of 4, #a-d	2.00	2.00

Rice A1723

No. 2321: a, Rice flowers and plants. b, Red, black and white rice grains.

2009, Sept. 25 Litho. *Perf. 13¼*

2321	Pair	1.00	1.00
a.-b.	A1723 250w Either single	.50	.30

Third Organization for Economic Cooperation and Development World Forum, Busan A1724

2009, Oct. 27 Litho. *Perf. 13¼*

2322	A1724 250w multi	.75	.30

A1725

A1726

A1727

Korean Films — A1728

No. 2323: a, Chilsu and Mansu, 1988. b, Never, Never Forget Me, 1976. c, A Road to Sampo, 1975. d, Yalkae, A Joker in High School, 1976.

2009, Oct. 27 *Perf. 13x13¼*

2323	Block or strip of 4	2.50	2.50
a.	A1725 250w multi	.50	.30
b.	A1726 250w multi	.50	.30
c.	A1727 250w multi	.50	.30
d.	A1728 250w multi	.50	.30

Diplomatic Relations Between South Korea and Brazil, 50th Anniv. — A1729

No. 2324: a, Octavio Frias de Oliveira Bridge, Brazil (denomination at UL). b, Incheon Bridge, South Korea (denomination at UR).

2009, Oct. 30 *Perf. 13¼*

2324	A1729 250w Pair, #a-b	1.25	1.25

See Brazil No. 3113.

New Year 2010 (Year of the Tiger) — A1730

2009, Dec. 1 Photo. *Perf. 13x13¼*

2325	A1730 250w multi	.75	.30
a.	Souvenir sheet of 2	1.25	1.25

Visit Korea Year — A1731

No. 2326: a, Stylized face, denomination in blue. b, People as Korean flag, denomination in white.

2010, Jan. 4 Photo. *Perf. 13¼x13*

2326	A1731 250w Pair, #a-b	1.00	1.00

2010 Winter Olympics, Vancouver A1732

No. 2327: a, Figure skater. b, Speed skater.

2010, Feb. 12 *Perf. 12¾x13½*

2327	A1732 250w Pair, #a-b	1.00	1.00

Diplomatic Relations Between South Korea and Malaysia, 50th Anniv. — A1733

No. 2328: a, Panthera tigris altaica. b, Panthera tigris jacksoni.

2010, Feb. 23 Litho. *Perf. 13¼*

2328	A1733 250w Pair, #a-b	1.00	1.00

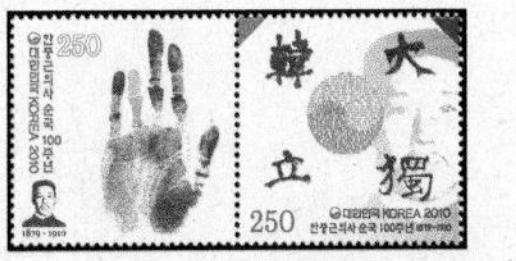

Ahn Jung-geun (1879-1910), Assassin of Ito Hirobumi, Japanese Resident-General of Korea — A1734

No. 2329 — Ahn Jung-geun and: a, Hand-print. b, Characters written on Korean flag with blood from his severed finger.

Litho. & Engr.

2010, Mar. 26 ***Perf. 13¼***

2329 A1734 250w Pair, #a-b 1.00 1.00

Seoul National University of Technology, Cent. A1735

Jinju National University, Cent. A1736

2010, Apr. 1 Photo. ***Perf. 12¾x13½***

2330 A1735 250w multi .50 .30
2331 A1736 250w multi .50 .30

Historic Trees A1737

No. 2332: a, Old Buddha's plum tree (Natural Monument No. 486) (22x50mm). b, Pine tree (Natural Monument No. 290), horiz (44x25mm). c, Entwined Chinese junipers (Natural Monument No. 88) (22x50mm). d, Three Thunbergii camphor trees (Natural Monument No. 481), horiz. (44x25mm).

2010, Apr. 5 Litho. ***Perf. 12¾***

2332 A1737 250w Block of 4, #a-d 2.00 2.00

Mo Tae Bum — A1738

Le Sang Hwa — A1739

Lee Seung Hoon — A1740

Kim Yu Na — A1741

Kwak Yoon Gy — A1742

Kim Seoung Il — A1743

Park Seung Hi — A1744

Sung Si Bak — A1745

Lee Eun Byul — A1746

Lee Jung Su — A1747

Lee Ho Suk — A1748

2010, May 6 Photo. ***Perf. 13½x12¾***

2333	Sheet of 11 + label	7.00	7.00
a.	A1738 250w multi	.60	.30
b.	A1739 250w multi	.60	.30
c.	A1740 250w multi	.60	.30
d.	A1741 250w multi	.60	.30
e.	A1742 250w multi	.60	.30
f.	A1743 250w multi	.60	.30
g.	A1744 250w multi	.60	.30
h.	A1745 250w multi	.60	.30
i.	A1746 250w multi	.60	.30
j.	A1747 250w multi	.60	.30
k.	A1748 250w multi	.60	.30

Medalists at 2010 Winter Olympics, Vancouver.

Han River in Spring A1749

Han River in Summer A1750

Han River in Autumn A1751

Han River in Winter A1752

2010, May 11 ***Perf. 13½ Syncopated***

2334	Block or strip of 4	2.00	2.00
a.	A1749 250w multi	.50	.30
b.	A1750 250w multi	.50	.30
c.	A1751 250w multi	.50	.30
d.	A1752 250w multi	.50	.30

2010 World Cup Soccer Championships, South Africa — A1753

Perf. 13¼x13½

2010, June 11 Photo.

2335 A1753 250w multi .75 .30

World Refugee Day, 10th Anniv. A1754

2010, June 18 ***Perf. 13¼***

2336 A1754 250w multi .60 .30

Diplomatic Relations Between South Korea and United Arab Emirates, 30th Anniv. — A1755

No. 2337: a, Flag of United Arab Emirates and air-conditioning tower. b, Flag of South Korea and Mt. Amisan Chimney, Gyeongbokgung Palace.

2010, June 18 Photo. ***Perf. 13x13¼***

2337 A1755 250w Pair, #a-b 1.00 1.00

See United Arab Emirates No. 990.

Start of Korean War, 60th Anniv. — A1756

2010, June 25 ***Perf. 13½x13***

2338 A1756 250w multi .60 .30

Philately Week A1757

No. 2339: a, South Korea #1197. b, South Korea #1198.

2010, July 29 ***Perf. 13¼x13¼x13***

2339	Pair, #a-b	1.00	1.00
a.-b.	A1757 250w Either single	.50	.30
c.	Souvenir sheet, #2339a-2339b	1.25	1.25

Dinosaurs A1758

No. 2340: a, Herrerasaurus. b, Coelophysis. c, Plateosaurus. d, Riojasaurus.

Perf. 13¼ Syncopated

2010, Aug. 5 Litho. & Engr.

2340	Sheet of 12, 3 each #2340a-2340d	7.50	7.50
a.-b.	A1758 250w Either single	.50	.30
c.-d.	A1758 340w Either single	.50	.30

23rd Intl. Union of Forest Research Organizations World Congress, Seoul — A1759

Litho. & Embossed

2010, Aug. 23 ***Perf. 12½***

2341 A1759 340w multi .75 .30

Legend of Goguryeo Jumong — A1760

No. 2342: a, King Geumwa and soldiers meet woman. b, Baby Jumong, birds and animals. c, Jumong and others fleeing King Geumwa on horseback. d, Jumong on horse and followers at Jolboncheon.

2010, Sept. 14 Photo. ***Perf. 13x13½***

2342 A1760 250w Block of 4, #a-d 2.00 2.00

A1761

A1762

A1763

Korean Films — A1764

No. 2343: a, Seopyeonje, 1993. b, Shiri, 1999. c, Tae Guk Gi: The Brotherhood of War, 2004. d, Take Off, 2009.

2010, Oct. 27 Litho. ***Perf. 13x13¼***

2343	Block of 4	2.00	2.00
a.	A1761 250w multi	.50	.30
b.	A1762 250w multi	.50	.30
c.	A1763 250w multi	.50	.30
d.	A1764 250w multi	.50	.30

Recycling — A1765

No. 2344: a, Flowers in pot. b, Recycling robot.

2010, Nov. 11 Photo. ***Perf. 13¼x13***

2344 A1765 250w Pair, #a-b 1.00 1.00

Miniature Sheet

G20 Summit, Seoul A1766

No. 2345 — Summit emblem and: a, World map. b, Gate.

2010, Nov. 11 ***Perf. 13x13¼***

2345 A1766	Sheet of 14, 7 each #a-b	10.00	10.00
a.-b.	250w Either single	.60	.35

New Year 2011 (Year of the Rabbit) — A1767

2010, Dec. 1 ***Perf. 13x13¼***

2346	A1767 250w multi	.50	.30
a.	Souvenir sheet of 2	1.00	1.00

A1768

Personalized Stamps — A1769

2010, Dec. 1 Photo. *Perf. 13x13¼*

Denomination Color

2347 A1768 250w green *2.00 2.00*
2348 A1768 250w blue *2.00 2.00*
2349 A1768 250w red brown *2.00 2.00*

Perf. 13¼x13½

2350 A1769 250w green *2.25 2.25*
2351 A1769 250w blue *2.25 2.25*
2352 A1769 250w red brown *2.25 2.25*
Nos. 2347-2352 (6) 12.75 12.75

Nos. 2347-2349 each were available in sheets of 6 that sold for 5500w and sheets of 20 that sold for 9500w. Nos. 2350-2352 each were sold in sheets of 14 that sold for 8000y. images could be personalized.

Miniature Sheet

Characters in Pororo, the Little Penguin — A1770

No. 2353: a, Eddy, the Fox. b, Crong, the Baby Dinosaur on balloon. c, Pororo wearing helmet. d, Petty, the girl Penguin. e, Pipi and Popo, the Aliens. f, Poby, the Polar Bear. g, Harry, the Hummingbird on ball. h, Loopy, the Beaver with basket. i, Tong Tong, the Dragon. j, Rody, the Robot.

2011, Feb. 22 Photo. *Die Cut*

Self-Adhesive

2353 A1770 Sheet of 10 5.50 5.50
a.-j. 250w Any single .50 .30

Historic Trees A1771

No. 2354: a, Japanese black pine trees at Sancheondan (Natural Monument No. 160) (22x50mm). b, Ginkgo tree at Yogwang-ri (Natural Monument No. 84), horiz. (44x25mm). c, Pine tree at Chukji-ri (Natural Monument No. 491) (22x50mm). d, Zelkova tree at Haksaru (Natural Monument No. 407), horiz. (44x25mm).

2011, Apr. 5 Litho. *Perf. 12¾*

2354 A1771 250w Block of 4, #a-d 2.25 2.25

Diplomatic Relations Between South Korea and Portugal, 50th Anniv. — A1772

No. 2355: a, Korean turtle ship, denomination at UL. b, Portuguese nau, denomination at UR.

2011, Apr. 15 Photo. *Perf. 13x13¼*

2355 Sheet of 14, 7 each #2355a-2355b 12.00 12.00
a.-b. A1772 250w Either single .75 .30

See Portugal Nos. 3305-3306.

Family A1773

No. 2356: a, Stick-figure family and house. b, Heads in bunch of grapes.

2011, May 13 Photo. *Perf. 13x13¼*

2356 A1773 250w Pair, #a-b 1.25 1.25

Bamboo Grove, Damyang A1774

Tea Field, Boesong A1775

Upo Swamp, Changnyeong — A1776

Jusanji Pond, Cheongsong A1777

2011, May 27 *Perf. 13¼*

2357 Block of 4 2.50 2.50
a. A1774 250w multi .55 .30
b. A1775 250w multi .55 .30
c. A1776 250w multi .55 .30
d. A1777 250w multi .55 .30

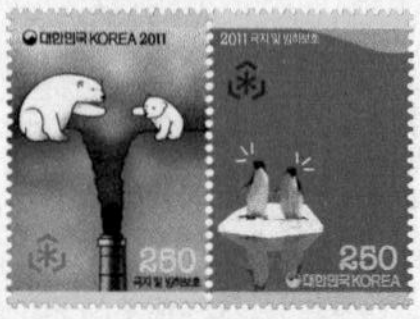

Preservation of Polar Regions and Glaciers — A1778

No. 2358: a, Polar bears. b, Penguins.

2011, June 3 Litho. *Perf. 13x13¼*

2358 A1778 250w Pair, #a-b 1.25 1.25

Shinheung Military Academy, Chugaga, Cent. — A1779

2011, June 10 Photo.

2359 A1779 250w multi .75 .30

Tomb of King Taejo A1780

Tomb of King Sejong A1781

Litho. & Engr.

2011, June 30 *Perf. 13x13¼*

2360 Sheet of 10, 5 each #2360a-2360b 6.50 6.50
a. A1780 250w multi .60 .30
b. A1781 250w multi .60 .30

Royal Tombs of the Joeson Dynasty UNESCO World Heritage Site.

Korea Disaster Relief Association, 50th Anniv. — A1782

2011, July 13 Photo. *Perf. 13x13¼*

2361 A1782 250w multi .75 .30

Philately Week A1783

No. 2362 — Paintings: a, Sansu (mountain and houses), by Jo Seok-jin (denomination in green). b, Jangsongnakil (rider on horse), by Ji Woon-young (denomination in bister brown). c, Unnangjasang (portrait), by Chae Yong-sin (denomination in red brown). d, Gunmado (horses), by Kim Ki-chang (denomination in gold).

2011, July 28 *Perf. 13*

2362 A1783 250w Block of 4, #a-d 2.50 2.50
e. Souvenir sheet of 4, #2362a-2362d 3.00 3.00

Selection of Pyeongchang as Host of 2018 Winter Olympics A1784

2011, Aug. 3 *Perf. 13x13¼*

2363 A1784 250w multi .75 .30

Dinosaurs A1785

No. 2364: a, Scelidosaurus. b, Stegosaurus. c, Allosaurus. d, Dilophosaurus.

Perf. 13¼ Syncopated

2011, Aug. 11 Litho. & Engr.

2364 Sheet of 12, 3 each #2364a-2364d *12.00 12.00*
a.-d. A1785 340w Any single .65 .30

Intl. Association of Athletics Federations World Championships, Daegu — A1786

No. 2365: a, Runners. b, Pole vault.

2011, Aug. 26 Litho. *Perf. 13¼*

2365 A1786 250w Pair, #a-b 1.50 1.50

Tripitaka Koreana, 1000th Anniv. — A1787

2011, Sept. 23 Photo. *Perf. 13x13¼*

2366 A1787 250w multi .75 .30

Personalized Stamp — A1788

2011, Oct. 1 Photo. *Perf. 13x13¼*

2367 A1788 270w multi — —

Vignette portion could be personalized. Three additional stamps were issued in this set. The editors would like to examine any examples.

Tenth Session of the Conference of the Parties to the United Nations Convention to Combat Desertification, Changwon A1792

2011, Oct. 10 Photo. *Perf. 13¼x13*

2371 A1792 270w multi .75 .30

Ipo Weir, Han River A1793

Gongju Weir, Geum River A1794

Seungchon Weir, Yeongsan River A1795

Gangjeong-Goryeong Weir, Nakdong River — A1796

2011, Oct. 21 *Perf. 13¼*

2372 Block of 4 2.25 2.25
a. A1793 270w multi .55 .30
b. A1794 270w multi .55 .30
c. A1795 270w multi .55 .30
d. A1796 270w multi .55 .30

Diplomatic Relations Between South Korea and Australia, 50th Anniv. — A1797

No. 2373: a, Korean woman playing haegeum. b, Australian aborigine playing didgeridoo.

2011, Oct. 28 Photo. *Perf. 13¼x13*

2373 A1797 270w Horiz. pair, #a-b 1.25 1.25

See Australia Nos. 3587-3588.

A1798

A1799

A1800

Daejoyong of the Balhae Kingdom — A1801

2011, Nov. 17 *Perf. 13x13¼*

2374 Sheet of 12, 3 each #a-d, + label 6.00 6.00
a. A1798 270w multi .50 .25
b. A1799 270w multi .50 .25
c. A1800 270w multi .50 .25
d. A1801 270w multi .50 .25

New Year 2012 (Year of the Dragon) — A1802

2011, Dec. 1

2375 A1802 270w multi .75 .30
a. Souvenir sheet of 2 1.25 1.25

South Korean Achievement of One Trillion Dollars in Trade — A1803

No. 2376: a, Automobile, computer chip, smart phone, container ship. b, Flag of South Korea, skyscraper.

2011, Dec. 7

2376 A1803 270w Horiz. pair, #a-b 1.25 1.25

Diplomatic Relations Between South Korea and Mexico, 50th Anniv. A1804

No. 2377: a, Juvenile gray whale, denomination at right. b, Adult gray whale, denomination at left.

2012, Jan. 26 **Litho.** *Perf. 13¼*

2377 A1804 270w Vert. pair, #a-b 1.25 1.25

See Mexico Nos. 2771-2772.

Miniature Sheet

Characters in Pucca Animated Television Series — A1805

No. 2378: a, Ssoso, with stick and birds (blue green, light blue and gray background). b, Abyo, with frog (green andd light green background). c, Pucca, with heart (yellow and orange background). d, Garu, with cat (orange and light orange background. e, Ching, with mirror (pink and light pink background). f, Bruce, with guns (purple and gray background). g, Ho-Oh, with flame (purple and pink background). h, Santa (bright blue and light blue background). i, Nini, with earrings (gray blue background). j, Woo-Wuh, with rolling pins and dishes (dark blue and purple background).

Serpentine Die Cut 10¼ Vert.

2012, Feb. 22 **Photo.**

Self-Adhesive

2378 A1805 Sheet of 10 6.00 6.00
a.-j. 270w Any single .55 .30

Diplomatic Relations Between South Korea and Colombia, 50th Anniv. — A1806

No. 2379: a, Coffee beans and bush. b, Ginseng flowers and root.

2012, Mar. 9 *Perf. 13x13¼*

2379 A1806 270w Pair, #a-b 1.25 1.25

See Colombia No. 1374.

2012 Nuclear Security Summit, Seoul A1807

No. 2380 — Ribbon and: a, World map. b, Dove, flag of South Korea.

2012, Mar. 26 *Perf. 13¼x13*

2380 A1807 270w Horiz. pair, #a-b 1.25 1.25

Historic Trees A1808

No. 2381: a, Zelkova tree at Segan-ri (Natural Monument No. 493) (22x50mm). b, Trifoliate orange tree at Gapgot-ri (Natural Monument No. 78), horiz. (44x25mm). c, Spring cherry tree at Hwaeomsa Temple (Natural Monument No. 38) (22x50mm). d, Asian fringe trees at Gwangyang-eup (Natural Monument No. 235), horiz. (44x25mm).

2012, Apr. 5 **Litho.** *Perf. 12¾*

2381 A1808 270w Block of 4, #a-d 1.90 .95

Winning Art in Stamp Design Contest A1809

No. 2382: a, Hearts in ski cap, by Yeonju Chung. b, Children carrying rainbow, by Glen M. Isaac.

2012, Apr. 25 **Photo.** *Perf. 13¼x13*

2382 A1809 270w Horiz. pair, #a-b .95 .50

Expo 2012, Yeosu — A1810

Nos. 2383 and 2384 — Expo 2012 emblem and mascot, fish and: a, Korea Pavilion. b, Theme Pavilion. c, Big-O. d, Sky Tower.

2012, May 11

2383 Horiz. strip of 4 1.90 .95
a.-d. A1810 270w Any single .45 .25

Perf. 13x13¼

2384 Horiz. strip of 4 1.90 .95
a.-d. A1810 270w Any single, 26x36mm .45 .25

No. 2383 was printed in sheets containing five strips. No. 2384 was printed in sheets of 10 containing two strips and two additional examples of No. 2384d.

Korea Trade Investment Promotion Agency (KOTRA), 50th Anniv. — A1811

No. 2385: a, 50th anniversary emblem, world map. b, Agency headquarters.

2012, June 14 *Perf. 13¼x13*

2385 A1811 270w Horiz. pair, #a-b .95 .50

Gungnamji Pond, Buyeo A1812

Daegwallyeong Sheep Ranch — A1813

Cheonjiyeon Waterfalls, Jeju Island A1814

Dinosaur Ridge, Mt. Seoraksan A1815

2012, June 20 *Perf. 13¼*

2386 Block of 4 1.90 .95
a. A1812 270w multi .45 .25
b. A1813 270w multi .45 .25
c. A1814 270w multi .45 .25
d. A1815 270w multi .45 .25

2012 Summer Olympics, London — A1816

No. 2387: a, Swimming, Tower Bridge. b, Archery, Big Ben.

2012, July 27 *Perf. 13x13¼*

2387 A1816 270w Vert. pair, #a-b .95 .50

Mask and Ogyeon Hall, Hahoe Village A1817

Hyangdan, Yangdong Village A1818

2012, July 12 **Litho.** *Perf. 13x13¼*

2388 Sheet of 10, 5 each #2388a-2388b 4.75 4.75
a. A1817 270w multi .45 .45
b. A1818 270w multi .45 .45

Historic Villages of Korea UNESCO World Heritage Site.

Dinosaurs A1819

No. 2384: a, Pachycephalosaurus. b, Tyrannosaurus. c, Oviraptor. d, Protoceratops.

Perf. 13¼ Syncopated

2012, Aug. 8 **Litho.**

2389 Sheet of 12, 3 each # 2389a-2389d *12.00 12.00*
a.-d. A1819 360w Any single *1.00 1.00*

Philately Week A1820

No. 2390 — Paintings: a, The Back Alley, by Dong Jin Seo (yellow green panel). b, Namhyangjip (A House Facing South), by Ji Ho Oh (blue panel). c, Tugye (Cockfighting), by Joong Seop Lee (pink panel). d, Chodong (Early Winter), by Sang Beom Lee (dull orange panel).

2012, Aug. 9 **Photo.** *Perf. 13*

2390 A1820 270w Block of 4, #a-d 1.90 .95
e. Souvenir sheet of 4, #2390a-2390d 1.90 .95

World Conservation Congress, Jeju Island — A1821

2012, Sept. 6 *Perf. 13¼*

2391 A1821 270w multi .50 .25

A1822

A1823

A1824

A1825

Park Hyeokgeose (69 B.C.-4 A.D.), Silla Kingdom Monarch
A1826

2012, Nov. 21 ***Perf. 13x13¼***

2392 Horiz. strip of 5 2.50 1.25
a. A1822 270w multi .50 .25
b. A1823 270w multi .50 .25
c. A1824 270w multi .50 .25
d. A1825 270w multi .50 .25
e. A1826 270w multi .50 .25

New Year 2013 (Year of the Snake)
A1827 A1828

2012, Dec. 3 ***Perf. 13x13¼***

2393 A1827 270w multi .50 .25
2394 A1828 270w multi .50 .25
a. Souvenir sheet of 2, #2393-2394 1.00 .50

Inauguration of 18th President, Park Geun-hye — A1830

2013, Feb. 25 **Photo.** ***Perf. 13¼***

2396 A1830 270w multi .50 .25
a. Souvenir sheet of 2 — —

Miniature Sheet

Characters in Robocar Poli — A1831

No. 2397: a, Roy the Fire Truck. b, Amber the Ambulance. c, Poli the Police Car. d, Helly the Helicopter. e, Dumpoo the Dump Truck. f, Cap the Taxi. g, Posty the Postal Van. h, Spooky the Tow Truck. i, School B the School Bus. j, Cleany the Street Sweeper.

Serpentine Die Cut 11½x9

2013, Mar. 12 **Self-Adhesive**

2397 A1831 Sheet of 10 5.00
a.-j. 270w Any single .50 .25

Korean Baseball Players
A1832

No. 2398: a, Jang Hyo-Jo (1956-2011) at bat. b, Choi Dong-Won (1958-2011) pitching.

2013, Mar. 29 **Photo.** ***Perf. 13¼x13***

2398 A1832 (270w) Pair, #a-b — —

Diplomatic Relations Between Peru and South Korea, 50th Anniv. — A1833

No. 2399: a, Seongsan Ilchulbong, South Korea, South Korean and Peruvian flags at LR. b, Machu Picchu, Peru, South Korean and Peruvian flags at LL.

2013, Apr. 1 **Photo.** ***Perf. 13x13¼***

2399 A1833 270w Horiz. pair, #a-b .95 .50

See Peru No. 1810.

Suncheon Bay Garden Expo 2013 — A1834

2013, Apr. 19 **Photo.** ***Perf. 13¾x13***

2400 A1834 270w multi .50 .25

Information and Communication Day — A1835

No. 2401: a, Boy and girl holding envelope with heart, satellite, smartphone (blue background). b, Mailbox with letter in slot, robot, girl with parcels (orange yellow background). c, Boy on satellite dish, girl on television with legs (yellow background). d, Girl and robot in rocket circling Earth (purple background).

2013, Apr. 22 **Photo.** ***Perf. 13¼x13***

2401 Horiz. strip of 4 2.00 1.00
a.-d. A1835 270w Any single .50 .25

Law Day — A1836

2013, Apr. 25 **Photo.** ***Perf. 13x13¼***

2402 A1836 270w multi .50 .25

Restoration of Sungnyemun Gate — A1837

2013, May 10 **Litho.** ***Perf. 13¼x13***

2403 A1837 270w multi .50 .25

Ahn Chang-ho (1878-1938), Founder of Young Korean Academy
A1838

2013, May 13 **Photo.** ***Perf. 13x13¼***

2404 A1838 270w multi .50 .25

Diplomatic Relations Between Slovakia and South Korea, 20th Anniv. — A1839

No. 2405: a, Pansori performers, South Korea (woman and drummer). b, Lúcnica Art Ensemble dancers, Slovakia.

2013, May 31 **Photo.** ***Perf. 13x13¼***

2405 A1839 270w Pair, #a-b 1.00 .50

See Slovakia Nos. 663-664.

Diplomatic Relations Between Germany and Korea, 130th Anniv. — A1840

No. 2406: a, Gyeongbokgung Palace, Seoul. b, Temple of the Sun, Bayreuth, Germany.

2013, June 5 **Litho.** ***Perf. 12¾x13***

2406 A1840 270w Horiz. pair, #a-b 1.00 .50

See Germany Nos. 2739-2740.

Energy Conservation — A1841

No. 2407: a, Leaves and smokestacks. b, Coin entering slot in piggy bank with electric cord as tail. c, Air conditioner and fans on balance with melting iceberg. d, Boy on stylized bicycle.

2013, June 26 **Photo.** ***Perf. 13¼***

2407 A1841 270w Block or horiz. strip of 4, #a-d 2.00 1.00

Philately Week — A1846

No. 2412: a, Girl writing letter. b, Girl placing letter in mailbox. c, Boy with magnifying glass examining stamp. d, Boy looking at stamp album.

600w, Combined design elements of Nos. 2412a-2412d (108x26mm).

2013, Aug. 8 **Photo.** ***Perf. 13¼x13***

2412 Block or horiz. strip of 4 2.25 1.25
a.-d. A1846 300w Any single .55 .30

Souvenir Sheet

2413 Sheet of 2 #2413a 2.25 1.25
a. A1846 600w Single stamp 1.10 .60

Philakorea 2014 World Stamp Exhibition, Seoul.

Korean Coast Guard, 60th Anniv. — A1847

2013, Sept. 10 **Photo.** ***Perf. 13x13¼***

2414 A1847 300w multi .55 .30

Diplomatic Relations Between Indonesia and South Korea, 40th Anniv. — A1848

No. 2415: a, Small lion figure from Korean folk play, large bull figure from Indonesian folk play (denomination at left). b, Large lion figure, small bull figure (denomination at UR).

2013, Sept. 17 **Photo.** ***Perf. 13x13¼***

2415 A1848 300w Pair, #a-b 1.10 .55

See Indonesia No. 2363.

Conference on Cyberspace, Seoul — A1849

2013, Oct. 17 **Litho.** ***Perf. 13x13¼***

2416 A1849 300w multi .55 .30

A1850

A1851

A1852

A1853

Onjo of the Baekje Kingdom — A1854

2413, Nov. 20 **Photo.** ***Perf. 13x13¼***

2417 Horiz. strip of 5 3.00 1.50
a. A1850 300w multi .60 .30
b. A1851 300w multi .60 .30
c. A1852 300w multi .60 .30
d. A1853 300w multi .60 .30
e. A1854 300w multi .60 .30

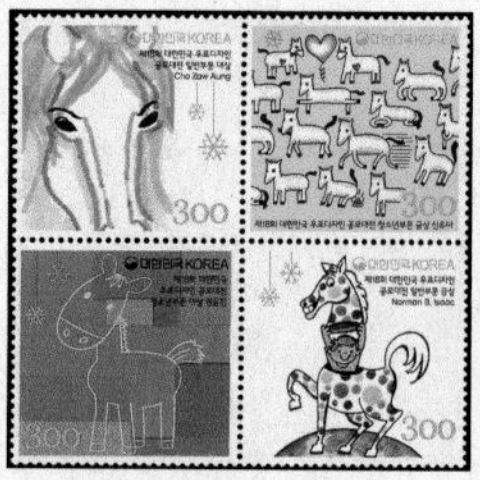

New Year 2014 (Year of the Horse) A1855

No. 2418 — Snowflakes and: a, Close-up of horse's head. b, Horses and heart (yellow background). c, Line drawing of horse with multicolored squares and rectangles in background. d, Boy inside of horse raising horse's head.

No. 2419 — Combined designs of No. 2418 with cropped design of: a, No. 2418a at left. b, No. 2418b at left. c, No. 2418c at left. d, No. 2418d at left.

2013, Dec. 2 **Photo.** ***Perf. 13¼***

2418 A1855 300w Block of 4, #a-d 2.40 1.25

Souvenir Sheet

2419 A1855 630w Sheet of 4, #a-d 5.00 2.50

No. 2419 contains four 108x36mm stamps.

Miniature Sheet

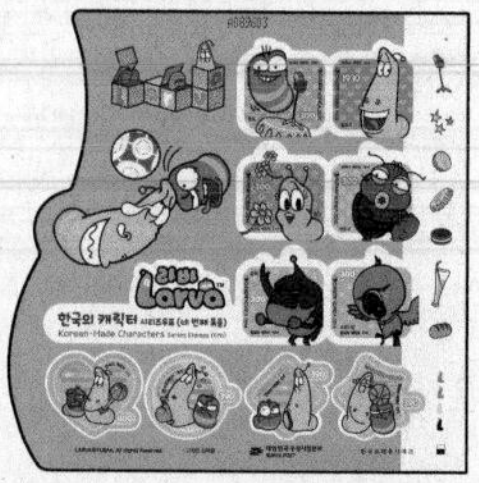

Characters from *Larva* Animated Television Series — A1856

No. 2420: a, Red at microphone. b, Pink and flowers. c, Brown and dung ball. d, Black with boxing gloves. e, Prussian (bird). f, Yellow eating roll and sweating, Red. g, Red, Yellow with open mouth. h, Yellow and Red with basketball. i, Red, Yellow holding lollipop. j, Yellow with open mouth.

Serpentine Die Cut 10

2014, Feb. 28 **Photo.**

2420 A1856 Sheet of 10 9.50
a.-e. 300w Any single .55 .25
f.-h. 390w Any single .75 .35
i. 400w multi .75 .40
j. 1930w multi 3.75 1.90

Cadastral Resurveying A1857

No. 2421: a, 300w, Map of South Korea, surveying equipment. b, 390w, Smart phone.

2014, Mar. 20 Photo. *Perf. 13¼x13*
2421 A1857 Pair, #a-b 1.40 .70

Poets A1858

No. 2422: a, Han Yongun (1879-1944), pink background. b, Lee Yuksa (1904-44), green background. c, Yun Dongju (1917-45), blue background.

2014, Apr. 9 Photo. *Perf. 13x13¼*
2422 A1858 (300w) Horiz. strip of 3, #a-c 1.75 .85

Philakorea 2014 World Stamp Exhibition, Seoul — A1859

No. 2423: a, 300w, Minhwa painting of birds and flowers. b, 300w, Hahoe wooden mask. c, 300w, Four Onggi pots. d, 300w, Neck of gayageum (stringed instrument). e, 300w, Baekja porcelain moon jar. f, 300w, Building roofs. g, 540w, Hanbok (traditional clothing). h, 540w, Hangeul (Korean text).

2014, May 16 Litho. *Perf. 13¼x13*
2423 A1859 Block of 8, #a-h 5.75 3.00

2014 World Cup Soccer Championships, Brazil — A1860

No. 2424 — Emblem and: a, 300w, Player and ball running toward goal. b, 540w, Players and ball.

2014, June 3 Photo. *Perf. 13x13¼*
2424 A1860 Pair, #a-b 1.75 .85

2014 Intl. Congress of Mathematics, Seoul — A1861

No. 2425 — Person and: a, Pythagorean theorem. b, Leonhard Euler's trail (Seven Bridges of Königsburg problem). c, Blaise Pascal's triangle of binomial coefficients.

2014, July 15 Photo. *Perf. 13¼*
2425 Vert. strip of 3 2.25 1.10
a.-b. A1861 300w Either single .60 .30
c. A1861 540w multi 1.00 .50

Printed in sheets containing 5 strips + 3 labels.

17th Asian Games, Incheon — A1862

No. 2426: a, Cricket. b, Wrestling. c, Squash. d, Bowling. e, Gymnastics. f, Mascots.

2014, July 31 Photo. *Perf. 13¼x13*
2426 Horiz. strip of 6 4.50 2.25
a.-d. A1862 300w Any single .60 .30
e.-f. A1862 540w Either single 1.00 .50

Printed in sheet containing 3 strips + 6 labels.

Arirang Dancer A1863

No. 2427: a, Feet of Arirang dancer. b, Head and arms of Arirang dancer.

2014, Aug. 7 Litho. *Perf. 12¾*
Thick Paper
2427 A1863 Vert. pair 4.50 2.25
a. 300w multi .60 .30
b. 1930w multi 3.75 1.90

Philately Week A1864

No. 2428: a, 300w, Bird with letter in tree. b, 300w, Family holding large stamps. c, 540w, Children making person out of stamps. d, 540w, Stamp train.

2014, Aug. 8 Photo. *Perf. 13¼*
2428 A1864 Block or horiz. strip of 4, #a-d 3.50 1.75

Visit of Pope Francis to South Korea A1865

No. 2429 — Pope Francis and: a, 300w, Coat of arms. b, 540w, Dove.

2014, Aug. 8 Photo. *Perf. 13¼x13*
2429 A1865 Pair, #a-b 1.75 .85

60th Baekje Cultural Festival — A1866

No. 2430: a, 300w, Gold earrings, top of incense burner. b, 540w, Base of incense burner and pagoda.

2014, Aug. 21 Photo. *Perf. 13x13¼*
2430 A1866 Vert. pair, #a-b 1.75 .85

A1867

Conference of the parties to the Convention on biological diversity, Pyeongchang.

2014, Sept. 16 Photo. *Perf. 13¼x13*
2431 A1867 300w multi .60 .30

Gwanggan Bridge — A1868

Log Fence Near House, Jeju Island — A1869

Beacon Towers — A1870

Emblem of 2014 International Telecommunication Union Plenipotentiary Conference, Busan — A1871

2014, Oct. 1 Photo. *Perf. 13x13¼*
2432 Horiz. strip of 4 3.00 1.50
a. A1868 300w multi .60 .30
b. A1869 300w multi .60 .30
c. A1870 300w multi .60 .30
d. A1871 540w multi 1.10 .55

Diplomatic Relations Between South Korea and Uruguay, 50th Anniv. — A1872

Designs: No. 2433, Korean Nong-ak dancers and musicians. No. 2434, Uruguayan Candombe dancers and musicians.

2014, Oct. 7 Photo. *Perf. 13x13¼*
2433 A1872 300w multi .55 .30
2434 A1872 540w multi 1.00 .50
a. Horiz. pair, #2433-2434 1.60 .80

Nos. 2433-2434 were printed in sheets of 18 containing nine of each stamp. See Uruguay No. 2484.

Korean Day — A1873

2014, Oct. 7 Litho. *Perf. 13¼x13*
2435 A1873 300w multi .55 .30

Period of Nine Leaders — A1874

Turtle Song — A1875

Six Golden Eggs — A1876

Birth of King Suro — A1877

Wedding of King Suro — A1878

2014, Nov. 20 Photo. *Perf. 13x13¼*
2436 Horiz. strip of 5 3.75 1.75
a. A1874 300w multi .55 .25
b. A1875 300w multi .55 .25
c. A1876 300w multi .55 .25
d. A1877 540w multi 1.00 .50
e. A1878 540w multi 1.00 .50

Legend of King Suro of the Gaya Kingdom.

A1879

A1880

A1881

New Year 2015 (Year of the Sheep) — A1882

2014, Dec. 1 Litho. *Perf. 14¼*
2437 Block or horiz. strip of 4 2.25 1.00
a. A1879 300w multi .55 .25
b. A1880 300w multi .55 .25
c. A1881 300w multi .55 .25
d. A1882 300w multi .55 .25
e. Souvenir sheet of 4, #2437a-2437d 2.25 1.00

Miniature Sheet

Constellations — A1883

No. 2438: a, Gemini (twins). b, Taurus (bull). c, Aries (ram). d, Pisces (fish). e, Aquarius (watere bearer). f, Capricorn (goat). g, Sagittarius (archer). h, Scorpio (scorpion). i, Libra (scales). j, Virgo (virgin). k, Leo (lion). l, Cancer (crab). m, Canis Major (dog). n, Cassiopeia (queen). o, Cygnus (swan). p, Boötes (herdsman with club).

Nos. 2438a-2438l (outer ring) are 31mm radially; Nos. 2438m-2438p are 26mm radially.

Serpentine Die Cut 6¼ on 2 Sides
2015, Feb. 27 Litho.
Self-Adhesive
2438 A1883 Sheet of 16 + 5 labels 9.00
a.-p. 300w Any single .55 .25

Happy School Life A1884

No. 2439 — Winning designs in stamp design contest: a, Children at desks. b, School roof, clock, faces of children. c, Children holding letter. d, Faces of children as puzzle pieces.

2015, Mar. 3 Litho. *Perf. 13¼*

2439 A1884 300w Block of 4, #a-d 2.25 1.10

Seventh World Water Forum, Daegu and Gyeongbuk — A1885

2015, Mar. 12 Litho. *Die Cut*

Self-Adhesive

2440 A1885 300w multi .55 .30

Endangered Wildlife — A1886

No. 2441: a, Female wolf and pups. b, Male wolf.

Litho. With Foil Application

2015, Mar. 26 *Perf. 14¼*

2441 A1886 300w Horiz. pair, #a-b 1.10 .55

c. Souvenir sheet of 2, #2441a-2441b 1.10 .55

Scientists — A1887

No. 2442: a, Benjamin W. Lee (1935-77), theoretical physicist (purple panel). b, Seok Ju Myeong (1908-50), entomologist (pink panel). c, Han Man Choon (1921-84), electrical engineer (green panel).

Litho. With Foil Application

2015, Apr. 10 *Perf. 14*

2442 Horiz. strip of 3 1.75 .90

a.-c. A1887 (300w) Any single .55 .30

Diplomatic Relations Between South Korea and Bolivia, 50th Anniv. — A1888

No. 2443: a, Phibalura flavirostris. b, Mergus squamatus.

2015, Apr. 24 Litho. *Perf. 14x13½*

2443 A1888 (300w) Pair, #a-b 1.10 .55

See Bolivia No. 1616.

Mangiyeoga Seal A1889

Ssangri Seal A1890

Ucheonhasa Seal — A1891

Hyangcheonsimjeongseohwajigi Seal — A1892

2015, May 15 Litho. *Perf. 14¼*

2444	Horiz. strip of 4	2.25	1.10
a.	A1889 (300w) pur & multi	.55	.25
b.	A1890 (300w) yel grn & multi	.55	.25
c.	A1891 (300w) pink & multi	.55	.25
d.	A1892 (300w) turq grn & multi	.55	.25
e.	Souvenir sheet of 4, #2444a-2444d	2.25	1.10

Seals of the Joseon Dynasty.

Major Sim Il A1893

Captain Kim Gyo-su A1894

Vice Admiral Son Won-il (1909-80) A1895

Brigadier General Lee Geun-seok A1896

Police Inspector General Cha Il-hyeok A1897

General James Alward Van Fleet (1892-1992) A1898

Lieutenant Colonel James Power Carne (1906-86) A1899

First Lieutenant Jin Du-tae A1900

Lieutenant Colonel Ralph Monclar (1892-1964) A1901

Captain William Hamilton Shaw (1922-50) A1902

Serpentine Die Cut 6½ Vert.

2015, June 1 Photo.

Self-Adhesive

2445	Block of 10	5.50	
a.	A1893 (300w) multi	.55	.25
b.	A1894 (300w) multi	.55	.25
c.	A1895 (300w) multi	.55	.25
d.	A1896 (300w) multi	.55	.25
e.	A1897 (300w) multi	.55	.25
f.	A1898 (300w) multi	.55	.25
g.	A1899 (300w) multi	.55	.25
h.	A1900 (300w) multi	.55	.25
i.	A1901 (300w) multi	.55	.25
j.	A1902 (300w) multi	.55	.25

Heroes of the Korean War.

Tourist Destinations — A1903

No. 2446: a, Aerial view of Yeongwol Donggang River. b, Aerial view of Chungju Chungjuho Lake. c, Confluence of Namhangang and Bukhangang Rivers. d, Rocks of Goesan Hwayang Gugok.

2015, June 3 Litho. *Perf. 14x13½*

2446 A1903 (300w) Block or horiz. strip of 4, #a-d 2.25 1.10

2015 Universiade, Gwangju — A1904

No. 2447: a, Mascot. b, Soccer and stadium. c, Rhythmic gymnastics, Asian Culture Complex. c, Taekwondo, Ipseokdae Rock.

2015, June 23 Litho. *Perf. 13½x14*

2447	Horiz. strip of 4	2.25	1.00
a.-d.	A1904 (300w) Any single	.55	.25
e.	Souvenir sheet of 4, #2447a-2447d	2.25	1.00

Silk Road Cultural Festival, Gyeongju A1905

2015, July 10 Litho. *Perf. 14x13½*

2448 A1905 (300w) multi .55 .25

Emblem A1906

President Kim Koo (1876-1949) A1907

Serpentine Die Cut 10½ on 2 Sides

2015, Aug. 4 Litho.

Self-Adhesive

2449	A1906 (300w) multi	.50	.25
2450	A1907 (300w) multi	.50	.25
a.	Horiz. pair, #2449-2450	1.00	
b.	Souvenir sheet of 2, #2449-2450	1.00	

Bamboo Forest in Snow — A1908

Bamboo Stem — A1909

Bamboo Forest — A1910

Bamboo Shoots — A1911

2015, Aug. 13 Litho. *Perf. 14*

2451	Block of 4	2.00	1.00
a.	A1908 (300w) multi	.50	.25
b.	A1909 (300w) multi	.50	.25
c.	A1910 (300w) multi	.50	.25
d.	A1911 (300w) multi	.50	.25

Nos. 2451a-2451d are impregnated with a bamboo scent.

Lee Byung-chul (1910-87), Founder of Samsung Group — A1912

Chung Ju-yung (1915-2001), Founder of Hyundai Groups — A1913

Litho. & Embossed

2015, Aug. 26 *Perf. 14x13½*

2452	Horiz. pair	1.00	.50
a.	A1912 (300w) multi	.50	.25
b.	A1913 (300w) multi	.50	.25

World Military Games, Mungyeong — A1914

No. 2453: a, Skydivers. b, Shooting. c, Mascots. d, Pentathlon competitors scaling wall.

2015, Sept. 16 Litho. *Perf. 13x13¼*

2453 A1914 (300w) Block or horiz. strip of 4, #a-d 2.10 1.10

A1915

Personalized Stamps — A1916

2015, Sept. 21 Photo. *Perf. 13¼*

2454 A1915 (300w) gray & black — —

Perf. 13¼x13½

2455 A1916 (300w) gray & black — —

No. 2454 was printed in sheets of 14 + central label. No. 2455 was printed in sheets of 6 + label and sheets of 20. Vignette area of stamp could be personalized. The images shown above are some of many stamps produced and sold by Korea Post on their personalized stamp creation apparatus.

Namhansanseong UNESCO World Heritage Site — A1917

No. 2456 — Aerial view of buildings and: a, Courtyard (49x33mm). b, Gate (49x21mm).

Perf. 13¾x13¼

2015, Oct. 29 Litho. & Engr.

2456 A1917 (300w) Vert. pair, #a-b 1.10 .55

Post Culture Week A1918

No. 2457 — Winning art in stamp design contest: a, Open envelope, musical notes, posthorn. b, People and envelope on snail. c, Children following mailman on bicycle. d, Children and large mailbox.

2015, Nov. 18 Litho. *Perf. 13x13¼*

2457 A1918 (300w) Block of 4, #a-d 2.10 1.10

Souvenir Sheet

New Year 2016 (Year of the Monkey) A1919

Designs: Nos. 2458a, 2459a, Monkey in tree. Nos. 2458b, 2459b, Six monkeys, gifts and flowers.

2015, Dec. 1 Litho. *Perf. 14½x14¾*

2458 A1919 (300w) Sheet of 2, #a-b 1.10 .55

Self-Adhesive

Serpentine Die Cut 9x9¼

2459 A1919 Horiz. pair 1.10
a.-b. (300w) Either single .55 .25

Korea Institute of Science and Technology, 50th Anniv. — A1920

No. 2460: a, Technician and machinery. b, Building and monument.

2016, Feb. 4 Litho. *Perf. 13x13¼*

2460 A1920 300w Pair, #a-b 1.00 .50

Lutra Lutra A1921

No. 2461: a, Adult and juveniles. b, Head of animal.

Litho. With Foil Application

2016, Mar. 15 *Perf. 14¼x14*

2461 A1921 390w Horiz. pair, #a-b 1.40 .70
c. Souvenir sheet of 2, #2461a-2461b 1.40 .70

A1922

Winning Art in International Stamp Design Contest — A1923

No. 2462: a, People painting peace dove on wall. b, Peace dove over rainbow. c, Children, trees, peace sign. d, Peace dove as balloon.

No. 2463: a, Man wearing seat belt. b, Woman and child in rain. c, Earth as person's head. d, People in floating hard hat.

2016, Mar. 24 Litho. *Perf. 13x13¼*

2462 A1922 300w Block of 4, #a-d 2.10 1.10
2463 A1923 300w Block of 4, #a-d 2.10 1.10

Scientists — A1924

No. 2464: a, Jang Yeong-sil (1390-1443), mechanical engineer. b, Heo Jun (1538-1615), physician. c, Ree Taikyue (1902-92), chemist.

Litho. With Foil Application

2016, Apr. 21 *Perf. 14¼x14*

2464 A1924 300w Horiz. strip of 3, #a-c 1.60 .80

Won Buddhism, Cent. — A1925

Litho. & Embossed With Foil Application

2016, Apr. 28 *Perf. 13x13¼*

2465 A1925 300w multi .55 .30

2016 Rotary International Convention, Goyang — A1926

2016, May 2 Litho. *Perf. 13¼x13*

2466 A1926 300w multi .55 .30

Sorokdo National Hospital, Cent. A1927

No. 2467 — Building and: a, Statue. b, Joined hands.

2016, May 17 Litho. *Perf. 13¾*

2467 A1927 300w Pair, #a-b 1.00 .50

Nam Ja-hyeon (1872-1933), Female Military Leader — A1928

Ju Si-gyeong (1876-1914), Independence Activist — A1929

Serpentine Die Cut 12 Vert.

2016, June 1 Litho.

Self-Adhesive

2468 Horiz. pair 1.00
a. A1928 300w multi .50 .25
b. A1929 300w multi .50 .25

Diplomatic Relations Betwen France and Korea, 130th Anniv. — A1930

No. 2469: a, Korean Celadon incense burner, 12th cent. b, French reliquary.

2016, June 3 Litho. *Perf. 13¼x14*

2469 A1930 300w Horiz. pair, #a-b 1.10 .55

See France Nos. 5043-5044.

Stephen Kim Su-hwan (1922-2009), Cardinal A1931

Master Seongcheol (1912-93), Buddhist Monk A1932

Perf. 13½x12¾

2016, June 27 Litho.

2470 A1931 300w multi .55 .30
2471 A1932 300w multi .55 .30

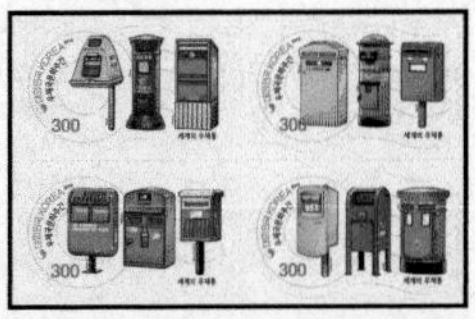

Mailboxes of the World — A1933

No. 2472 — Mailboxes from: a, Brazil, People's Republic of China, and Canada. b, France, India, and Japan. c, Mexico, Malaysia, and New Zealand. d, Switzerland, United States, and United Kingdom.

Serpentine Die Cut 8¾ at Right

2016, July 19 Litho.

Self-Adhesive

2472 A1933 Block of 4, #a-d 2.25
a.-d. 300w Any single .55 .30

Tourism A1934

No. 2473: a, Hadong Simri Cherry Blossom Road. b, Yeongdeok Blue Road. c, Jeju Olle Trail. d, Woljeongsan Jeonnamu Forest Trail.

2016, Aug. 12 Litho. *Perf. 13¼*

2473 A1934 300w Block or horiz. strip of 4, #a-d 2.25 1.10

Lighthouses — A1935

No. 2474: a, Oryukdo Lighthouse. b, Ulgi Lighthouse. c, Somaemuldo Lighthouse. d, Eocheongdo Lighthouse.

Litho. With Foil Application

2016, Aug. 25 *Perf. 13½*

2474 A1935 300w Block or horiz. strip of 4, #a-d 2.25 1.10

Painting by Lee Jung-Seop (1916-56) A1936

Litho. With Foil Application

2016, Sept. 1 *Perf. 14x13¼*

2475 A1936 300w multi .55 .30

Gold Crowns A1937

No. 2476 — Background color: a, Purple. b, Green. c, Red. d, Blue.

Litho. & Embossed With Foil Application

2016, Sept. 21 *Perf. 14x13¼*

2476 A1937 300w Block or horiz. strip of 4, #a-d 2.25 1.10

Kia Tigers Cap and Mascot — A1938

Nexen Heroes Cap and Mascot — A1939

Doosan Bears Cap and Mascot — A1940

Lotte Giants Cap and Mascot — A1941

Samsung Lions Cap and Mascot — A1942

NC Dinos Cap and Mascot — A1943

SK Wyverns Cap and Mascot — A1944

LG Twins Cap and Mascot — A1945

KT Wiz Cap and Mascot — A1946

Hanhwa Eagles Cap and Mascot — A1947

Litho. & Embossed With Foil Application

Serpentine Die Cut 12 At Bottom

2016, Oct. 7 Self-Adhesive

2477 Sheet of 10 5.50
a. A1938 300w multi .55 .30
b. A1939 300w multi .55 .30
c. A1940 300w multi .55 .30
d. A1941 300w multi .55 .30
e. A1942 300w multi .55 .30
f. A1943 300w multi .55 .30
g. A1944 300w multi .55 .30
h. A1945 300w multi .55 .30
i. A1946 300w multi .55 .30
j. A1947 300w multi .55 .30

Korean Baseball Organization League teams.

A1948

Baekje Historic Areas UNESCO World Heritage Site
A1949

Perf. 13¾x13½

2016, Oct. 28 — Litho. & Engr.

2478 Sheet of 10, 5 each #2478a-2478b — 17.50 8.50
a. A1948 1000w multi — 1.75 .85
b. A1949 1000w multi — 1.75 .85

A1950

A1951

A1952

Joseon Dynasty Seals — A1953

2016, Nov. 10 — Litho. — *Perf. 14¼*

2479 Horiz. strip of 4 — 2.20 1.20
a. A1950 300w multi — .55 .30
b. A1951 300w multi — .55 .30
c. A1952 300w multi — .55 .30
d. A1953 300w multi — .55 .30
e. Souvenir sheet of 4, #2479a-2479d — 2.20 1.20

Animals in the Demilitarized Zone — A1954

No. 2480: a, Great tit on barbed wire. b, Black-faced spoonbills.

2016, Nov. 22 — Litho. — *Perf. 14x13½*

2480 A1954 300w Pair, #a-b — 1.10 .55

New Year 2017 (Year of the Rooster)
A1955

No. 2481 — Rooster and: a, Snowflakes. b, Sun.

Litho. & Embossed With Foil Application

2016, Dec. 1 — *Perf. 13¾*

2481 A1955 300w Pair, #a-b — 1.10 .55
c. Souvenir sheet of 4, 2 each #2481a-2481b — 2.20 1.10

Kim Bong-ryong (1902-94), Inlayer of Mother-of-Pearl
A1956

Kim Jeom-sun (1918-2008), Hemp Weaver
A1957

Lee Chi-ho (1910-2006), Ornament Painter
A1958

Cheong Sang-won (1926-2003), Furniture Maker
A1959

Litho. With Foil Application

2017, Jan. 25 — *Perf. 14¼*

2482 Block or horiz. strip of 4 — 2.20 1.20
a. A1956 300w multi — .55 .30
b. A1957 300w multi — .55 .30
c. A1958 300w multi — .55 .30
d. A1959 300w multi — .55 .30

Miniature Sheet

Webtoons — A1960

No. 2483: a, I Love You, by Kang Full (elderly couple on motorcycle, 39x36mm). b, With God, by Ju Homin (three people in traditional costumes, 35x40mm). c, Incomplete Life, by Yoon Taeho (man with briefcase, 36x37mm). d, The Sound of Your Heart, by Cho Seok (man, woman and dogs, 40x40mm).

Serpentine Die Cut 9

2017, Feb. 10 — Litho.

Self-Adhesive

2483 A1960 Sheet of 4 — 2.20
a.-d. 300w Any single — .55 .30

Nemorhaedus Caudatus — A1961

No. 2484: a, Adult and juvenile gorals. b, Head of goral.

Litho. With Foil Application

2017, Feb. 20 — *Perf. 14¼*

2484 A1961 300w Horiz. pair, #a-b — 1.10 .55
c. Souvenir sheet of 2, #2484a-2484b — 1.10 .55

Miniature Sheet

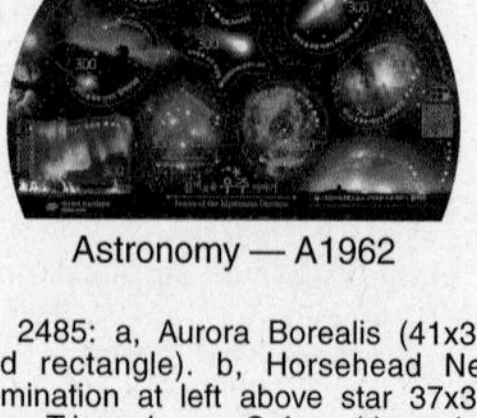

Astronomy — A1962

No. 2485: a, Aurora Borealis (41x31mm curved rectangle). b, Horsehead Nebula (denomination at left above star 37x35mm oval). c, Triangulanum Galaxy (denomination just above left end of inscription, 37x35mm oval). d, Messier 81 (spiral galaxy, denomination above middle of lower inscription, 37x37mm oval). e, Messier 82 (denomination above right end of inscription, 37x35mm oval). f, Orion Nebula (denomination above middle of lower inscription, 37x35mm oval). g, Observatory (51x25mm semicircle). h, Pleiades (36x36mm pentagon). i, Comet Lovejoy (36x36mm star). j, Rosette Nebula (37mm diameter).

Serpentine Die Cut, Serpentine Die Cut 11½ Vert. (#2485a), Serpentine Die Cut 11 (#2485g), Serpentine Die Cut 11½ (#2485h, 2485i)

Litho. With Foil Application

2017, Mar. 21 — Self-Adhesive

2485 A1962 Sheet of 10 — 5.50
a.-j. 300w Any single — .55 .30

Flag
A1963

Hibiscus
A1964

Buncheong Jar — A1965

2017, Apr. 3 — Photo. — *Perf. 12¾x13½*

2486 A1963 330w multi — .60 .30
2487 A1964 420w multi — .75 .40

Perf. 13½

2488 A1965 1960w multi — 3.50 1.75
Nos. 2486-2488 (3) — 4.85 2.45

Self-Adhesive

Serpentine Die Cut 11½

2489 A1963 330w multi — .60 .30
2490 A1964 420w multi — .75 .40

A map of the Korean Peninsula is laser cut in the lower right corner of No. 2488.

Woodang (Lee Hoe-yeong, 1862-1932), Nationalist Leader — A1966

2017, Apr. 21 — Litho. — *Perf. 13x12¾*

2491 A1966 330w multi — .60 .30

King Sejong (1397-1450)
A1967

Choi Mu-seon (1325-95), Inventor and Military Commander
A1968

Woo Jang-chan (1898-1959), Botanist — A1969

2017, Apr. 27 — Litho. — *Perf. 14*

2492 Strip of 3 — 1.80 .90
a. A1967 330w multi — .60 .30
b. A1968 330w multi — .60 .30
c. A1969 330w multi — .60 .30

Members of Korean Science and Technology Hall of Fame.

Winning Art in Postage Stamp Design Contest
A1970

No. 2493: a, Love of Hedgehogs, by Lee Su-jeong. b, My Home Filled With Love, by Jeong-Seo-han. c, A Family's Laughter, by Jang-Suk-yeong. d, The Happiness a Letter Brings, by Im Yu-ra.

2017, May 2 — Litho. — *Perf. 13*

2493 A1970 330w Block of 4, #a-d — 2.40 1.25

Hearts are laser cut on Nos. 2493a-2493d.

Soswaewon Garden
A1971

Mungyeongsaejae Pass — A1972

Ullimsanbang Villa and Gardens
A1973

Jinjuseong Fortress
A1974

2017, May 15 — Litho. — *Perf. 13¼*

2494 Block of 4 — 2.40 1.20
a. A1971 330w multi — .60 .30
b. A1972 330w multi — .60 .30
c. A1973 330w multi — .60 .30
d. A1974 330w multi — .60 .30

Korean National Parks, 50th Anniv., and National Parks Service, 30th Anniv.
A1975

No. 2495 — Park ranger with: a, Magnifying glass and flowers. b, Binoculars, flowers and wildlife.

Litho. With Foil Application

2017, May 29 — *Perf. 13x13¼*

2495 A1975 330w Horiz. pair, #a-b — 1.20 .60

Wildlife in the Demilitarized Zone — A1976

No. 2496: a, Squirrel and army helmet. b, Kingfisher on barbed wire.

2017, June 5 — Litho. — *Perf. 14x13½*

2496 A1976 330w Pair, #a-b — 1.20 .60

Iron powder particles are affixed to No. 2496a.

2017 World Taekwondo Championships, Muju — A1977

2017, June 16 — Litho. — *Perf. 13x13½*

2497 A1977 330w multi — .60 .30

Kim Tong-ni (1913-95), Writer — A1978

Pak Kyongni (1926-2008), Writer — A1979

2017, June 27 Litho. *Perf. 13¼*

2498 A1978 330w multi .60 .30
2499 A1979 330w multi .60 .30

Korean Independence Hall, 30th Anniv. — A1980

No. 2500: a, Independence Hall and "30." b, Statue of Indomitable Koreans.

Litho. & Embossed

2017, Aug. 1 *Perf. 14*

2500 A1980 330w Pair, #a-b 1.20 .60

A1981

Inauguration of Pres. Moon Jae-in — A1982

2017, Aug. 17 Photo. *Perf. 13¼x13*

2501 A1981 330w multi .60 .30

Souvenir Sheet

2502 A1982 420w multi .75 .40

A1983

A1984

A1985

Joseon Dynasty Seals — A1986

2017, Sept. 1 Litho. *Perf. 14x14¼*

2503 Horiz. strip of 4 2.40 1.25
a. A1983 330y multi .60 .30
b. A1984 330y multi .60 .30
c. A1985 330y multi .60 .30
d. A1986 330y multi .60 .30
e. Souvenir sheet of 4, #2503a-2503d 2.40 1.25

A1987

A1988

A1989

Highways A1990

Litho. With Foil Application

2017, Sept. 28 *Perf. 13½*

2504 Block or horiz. strip of 4 2.40 1.20
a. A1987 330w multi .60 .30
b. A1988 330w multi .60 .30
c. A1989 330w multi .60 .30
d. A1990 330w multi .60 .30

A1991

Namsadang Nori UNESCO Intangible Cultural Heritage A1992

Litho. & Engr. With Foil Application

2017, Oct. 27 *Perf. 13¾x13½*

2505 Sheet of 10, 5 each #2505a-2505b 6.00 3.00
a. A1991 330w gold & multi .60 .30
b. A1992 330w gold & multi .60 .30

Miniature Sheets

A1993

2018 Winter Olympics, Pyeongchang — A1994

No. 2506: a, Alpensia Ski Jumping Center. b, Mascot marching. c, Emblem of 2018 Winter Olympics. d, Mascot alpine skiing. e, Mascot in biathlon. f, Mascots in two-man bobsled. g, Mascot cross-country skiing. h, Mascot curling. i, Mascot figure skating. j, Mascot freestyle skiing.

No. 2507: a, PyeongChang Olympic Stadium. b, Mascot with arms extended. c, Mascot playing ice hockey. d, Mascot on luge. e, Mascots in Nordic combined skiing event. f, Mascot in short track speed skating event. g, Mascot on skeleton. h, Mascot ski jumping. i, Mascot snowboarding. j, Mascot speed skating.

2017, Nov. 1 Litho. *Perf. 13x13¼*

2506 A1993 Sheet of 10 6.00 3.00
a.-j. 330w Any single .60 .30
2507 A1994 Sheet of 10 6.00 3.00
a.-j. 330w Any single .60 .30

Diplomatic Relations Between South Korea and Sri Lanka, 40th Anniv. — A1995

No. 2508: a, Korean dancer (green background). b, Sri Lankan dancer (blue background).

2017, Nov. 14 Litho. *Perf. 13¼x13*

2508 A1995 330w Pair, #a-b 1.20 .60

See Sri Lanka Nos. 2121-2122.

Snail Mailing Letter A1996

Chrysalis on Mailbox A1997

Chrysalis Under Mailbox A1998

Mailbox, Butterfly and Snail A1999

2017, Nov. 21 Litho. *Perf. 13¾*

2509 Horiz. strip of 4 2.40 1.20
a. A1996 330w multi .60 .30
b. A1997 330w multi .60 .30
c. A1998 330w multi .60 .30
d. A1999 330w multi .60 .30

New Year 2018 (Year of the Dog) A2000

No. 2510: a, Five dogs. b, Dog and snowflakes.

Litho. With Holographic Foil

2017, Dec. 1 *Perf. 13x13¼*

2510 A2000 330w Pair, #a-b 1.20 .60
c. Souvenir sheet of 4, 2 each #2510a-2510b 2.40 1.20

Miniature Sheet

2018 Winter Paralympics, Pyeongchang — A2001

No. 2511: a, Emblem of the 2018 Winter Paralympics. b, Torch. c, Mascot with Paralympics Alpine ski. d, Mascot in Paralympics arabiathlon. e, Mascot Paralympics cross-country skiing. f, Mascot carrying torch. g, Mascot with arm extended. h, Mascot playing Paralympics ice hockey. i, Mascot on Paralympics snowboard. j, Mascot in wheelchair curling event.

2018, Jan. 18 Litho. *Perf. 13*

2511 A2001 Sheet of 10 6.00 3.00
a.-j. 330w Any single .60 .30

Opening of 2018 Winter Olympics, Pyeongchang — A2002

No. 2512: a, Olympic torch. b, Gold, silver and bronze medals.

2018, Feb. 9 Litho. *Perf. 13x13¼*

2512 A2002 330w Horiz. pair, #a-b 1.25 .60

Join Our Hands, by Chan Wing Chi A2003

From Person to Person, by Hong Seo-jeong A2004

One Flame, by Moon Seo-hyun A2005

Create the World Together, by Kim Si-hyun A2006

A Bicycle Through Which We Become One, by Park Kyeong-jin — A2007

2018, Feb. 22 Litho. *Perf. 13¼*

2513 Horiz. strip of 5 3.00 1.50
a. A2003 330w multi .60 .30
b. A2004 330w silver & multi .60 .30
c. A2005 330w silver & multi .60 .30
d. A2006 330w multi .60 .30
e. A2007 330w multi .60 .30

Winning art in public stamp design contest.

Members of Korea Science and Technology Hall of Fame — A2008

No. 2514: a, Gim Jeong-ho (1804-66), cartographer (orange panel). b, Yi Cheon (1376-1451), engineer (violet panel). c, Choi Hyeong-sup (1920-2004), president of Korea Institute of Science and Technology (green blue panel).

Litho. With Foil Application

2018, Mar. 21 *Perf. 14*

2514 A2008 330w Vert. strip of 3, #a-c 2.00 1.00

University of Seoul, Cent. — A2009

2018, Apr. 2 Litho. *Perf. 14x13¼*

2515 A2009 330w multi .65 .30

Musicians — A2010

No. 2516: a, Kim Chun-heung (1909-2007), yanggeum player (brown background). b, Shin Kwae-dong (1910-77), geomungo player (dull violet blue background). c, Kim Yun-deok (1918-78), gaygeum player (reddish purple background).

Litho. With Foil Application

2018, Apr. 30 ***Perf. 13¼x14***

2516 A2010 330w Vert. strip of 3, #a-c 2.00 1.00

Miniature Sheets

A2011

South Korean 2018 Winter Olympics Medalists — A2012

No. 2517: a, Olympic cauldron. b, Kyeong-ae Kim, curling silver medalist. c, Dong-hyun Kim, bobsledding silver medalist. d, Min-seok Kim, speed skating silver amd bronze medalist. e, Bo-reum Kim, speed skating silver medalist. f, Seon-yeong Kim, curling silver medalist. g, A-lang Kim, speed skating gold medalist. h, Yeong-mi Kim, curling silver medalist. i, Ye-jin Kim, speed skating gold medalist. j, Eun-jung Kim, curling gold medalist. k, Cho-hi Kim, curling silver medalist. l, Tae-yun Kim, speed skating bronze medalist. m, Young-woo Seo, bobsledding silver medalist. n, Yi-ra Seo, speed skating bronze medalist.

No. 2518: a, Suk-hee Shim, speed skating gold medalist. b, Yun-jong Won, bobsledding silver medalist. c, Sung-bin Yun, skeleton gold medalist. d, Sang-ho Lee, snowboarding silver medalist. e, Sang-hwa Lee, speed skating silver medalist. f, Seung-hoon Lee, speed skating gold and silver medalist. g, Yu-bin Lee, speed skating gold medalist. h, Hyo-jun Lim, speed skating gold and bronze medalist. i, Jung-lin Jun, bobsledding silver medalist. j, Jae-won chung, speed skating silver medalist. k, Min-kyu Cha, speed skating silver medalist. l, Min-jeong Choi, speed skating gold medalist. m, Dae-heon Hwang, speed skating silver medalist. n, Closing ceremony.

2018, May 4 **Photo.** ***Perf. 13x13¼***

2517	A2011 Sheet of 14	8.50	4.25
a.-n.	330y Any single	.60	.30
2518	A2012 Sheet of 14	8.50	4.25
a.-n.	330y Any single	.60	.30

Democratic Elections in South Korea, 70th Anniv. — A2013

No. 2519: a, People going to polling places. b, Building.

Litho. With Foil Application

2018, May 10 ***Perf. 14x13¾***

2519 A2013 330w Pair, #a-b 1.25 .60

Mudeungsan Mountain A2014

Bukhansan Mountain A2015

Juwangsan Mountain A2016

Taebaeksan Mountain A2017

Litho. With Stone Grit Affixed

2018, May 24 ***Perf. 14x13½***

2520	Block or horiz. strip of 4	2.60	1.25
a.	A2014 330w multi	.65	.30
b.	A2015 330w multi	.65	.30
c.	A2016 330w multi	.65	.30
d.	A2017 330w multi	.65	.30

Miniature Sheet

South Korean Paralympians at 2018 Winter Paralympics — A2018

No. 2521: a, Paralympian holding medal, Paralympic skiiers. b, Paralympic ice hockey players wearing white uniforms, red area at left. c, Paralympic ice hockey players, two players with helmets touching at left. d, Paralympic ice hockey players in action, puck on goal line near goal. e, Paralympic ice hockey players wearing blue uniforms, gathered near net at right. f, One Paralympic ice hockey player wearing blue uniform, six with white uniforms.

2018, May 31 **Litho.** ***Perf. 13x13¼***

2521	A2018 Sheet of 6	3.75	1.90
a.-f.	330y Any single	.60	.30

Crafts A2019

No. 2522: a, Three Chaesang bamboo boxes. b, Embroidered flowers. c, Braided string tassels. d, Traditional clothing.

Litho. & Embossed With Foil Application

2018, June 1 ***Perf. 14x14¼***

2522 A2019 330w Block of 4, #a-d 2.60 1.25

Nature in the Demilitarized Zone — A2020

No. 2523: a, Flowers sprouting through crack in army helmet. b, Deer near fence.

2018, June 25 **Litho.** ***Perf. 14x13¼***

2523 A2020 330w Pair, #a-b 1.25 .60

Protected Wildlife — A2021

No. 2524: a, Tursiops aduncus. b, Neophocaena asiaeorientalis. c, Phoca largha. d, Callorhinus ursinus.

Litho. With Foil Application

2018, July 10 ***Perf. 13¼***

2524 A2021 330w Block of 4, #a-d 2.40 1.25

Painters A2022

No. 2525: a, Park Sookeun (1914-65), painting of woman. b, Chang Ucchin (1917-90), painting of bird.

Litho. With Foil Application

2018, July 25 ***Perf. 14x14¼***

2525 A2022 330w Pair, #a-b 1.25 .60

Porcelain Jar — A2023

2018, Aug. 1 **Photo.** ***Perf. 13¾x13½***

2526 A2023 2130w multi 4.00 2.00

A map of the Korean Peninsula is laser cut in the lower right corner of No. 2526.

Yun Bong-gil (1908-32), Hongkew Park, Shanghai Bomber, and Yun Bong-gil Memorial Hall, Shanghai A2024

Ahn Chang-ho (1876-1938), Korean Independence Activist, and Korean National Association Memorial Hall, Los Angeles — A2025

Yi Jun (1859-1907), Diplomat, and Yi Jun Peace Museum, The Hague, Netherlands A2026

Ahn Jung-geun (1879-1910), Assassin of Hirobumi Ito, and Ahn Jung-geun Memorial Hall, Harbin, People's Republic of China — A2027

Litho. With Foil Application

2018, Aug. 6 ***Perf. 13x13¼***

2527	Block or strip of 4	2.40	1.25
a.	A2024 330w multi	.60	.30
b.	A2025 330w multi	.60	.30
c.	A2026 330w multi	.60	.30
d.	A2027 330w multi	.60	.30

19th World Amateur Radio Direction Finding Championships, Sokcho-si A2028

Perf. 13¼x13½

2018, Aug. 31 **Litho.**

2528 A2028 330w multi .60 .30

Portions of the design were printed with thermochromic ink which changes color when warmed.

Chung-Ang University, Seoul, Cent. — A2029

Litho. With Foil Application

2018, Sept. 3 ***Perf. 13¼x13½***

2529 A2029 330w multi .60 .30

13th World Firefighters Games, Chungju — A2030

2018, Sept. 10 **Litho.** ***Perf. 13x13¼***

2530 A2030 330w multi .60 .30

Summit Meeting of North Korean Chairman Kim Jong Un and South Korean Pres. Moon Jae-in — A2031

2018, Sept. 12 **Photo.** ***Perf. 13¼***

2531 A2031 330w multi .60 .30

Publication of *Mokminsimseo,* and Return of Its Author, Dasan (1762-1836) From Exile, 200th Anniv. — A2032

2018, Sept. 14 **Litho.** ***Perf. 14¼***

2532 A2032 330w multi .60 .30

Universal Declaration of Human Rights, 70th Anniv. — A2033

2018, Oct. 1 Litho. *Perf. 13x13¼*
2533 A2033 330w multi .60 .30

Postal Culture Week A2034

No. 2534 — Calligraphy with denomination at: a, LL. b, UR.

Litho. With Foil Application
2018, Oct. 2 *Perf. 13¾x13¼*
2534 A2034 330w Horiz. pair, #a-b 1.25 .60

Hong Beom-do (1868-1943), General — A2035

2018, Oct. 12 Litho. *Perf. 14x13¼*
2535 A2035 330w multi .60 .30

Lions A2036

No. 2536: a, Korean incense burner cover, c. 8th-9th cent. (reddish purple panel). b, Persian gold rhyton, c. 5th cent. B.C., (red violet panel)

Litho. With Foil Application
2018, Oct. 23 *Perf. 13¾x13¼*
2536 A2036 330w Horiz. pair, #a-b 1.25 .60

See Iran No. 3195.

Women Divers of Jeju UNESCO Intangible Heritage A2037

No. 2537: a, Three divers (52x24mm). b, Two divers harvesting shells (52x36mm).

Litho. With Foil Application
2018, Nov. 21 *Perf. 14x13¼*
2537 A2037 330w Vert. pair, #a-b 1.25 .60

New Year 2019 (Year of the Pig) A2038

No. 2538: a, Pig in costume. b, Pig facing left.

Litho. With Foil Application (#2538a), Litho. With Hologram (#2438b)
2018, Dec. 3 *Perf. 13¾*
2538 A2038 330w Pair, #a-b 1.25 .60
c. Souvenir sheet of 4, 2 each #2538a-2538b 2.50 1.25

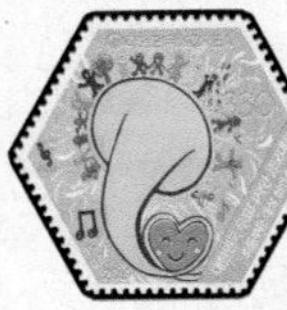

A2039

A2040

A2041

A2042

Winning Art in Postage Stamp Design Contest — A2043

Litho. With Foil Application
2019, Jan. 22 *Perf. 13*
2539 Staggered horiz. strip of 5 3.00 1.50
a. A2039 330w sil & multi .60 .30
b. A2040 330w sil & multi .60 .30
c. A2041 330w sil & multi .60 .30
d. A2042 330w sil & multi .60 .30
e. A2043 330w sil & multi .60 .30

Photograph of Magnified Knee Tissues — A2044

Photograph of Magnified Pimple on Rabbit's Ear — A2045

Photograph of Magnified Intestinal Cells — A2046

Photograph of Magnified Rat Retina — A2047

Litho. With Foil Application
2019, Feb. 19 *Perf. 13x13¼*
2540 Block or horiz. strip of 4 2.40 1.25
a. A2044 330w sil & multi .60 .30
b. A2045 330w sil & multi .60 .30
c. A2046 330w sil & multi .60 .30
d. A2047 330w sil & multi .60 .30

March 1st Independence Movement, Cent. — A2048

Litho. With Foil Application
2019, Feb. 28 *Perf. 14*
2541 A2048 330w gold & multi .60 .30

Ki-ok Kwon (1901-88), First Female Korean Aviator A2049

Cha-jeong Park (1909-44), Independence Activist A2050

Gyeong-shin Ahn (1888-?), Independence Activist A2051

Maria Kim (1892-1944), Independence Activist A2052

Litho. With Foil Application
2019, Mar. 15 *Perf. 13¾x13¼*
2542 Block or horiz. strip of 4 2.40 1.25
a. A2049 330w sil & multi .60 .30
b. A2050 330w sil & multi .60 .30
c. A2051 330w sil & multi .60 .30
d. A2052 330w sil & multi .60 .30

KAI KT-1 Woongbi A2053

KAI T-50 Golden Eagle — A2054

KAI FA-50 Fighting Eagle — A2055

Litho. & Embossed With Foil Application
2019, Mar. 20 *Perf. 13¼x13½*
2543 Horiz. strip of 3 1.80 .90
a. A2053 330w sil & multi .60 .30
b. A2054 330w sil & multi .60 .30
c. A2055 330w sil & multi .60 .30

Korean Provisional Government, Cent. A2056

Litho. With Foil Application
2019, Apr. 11 *Perf. 14¼x13¾*
2544 A2056 330w gold & multi .60 .30

Soon-ji Yi (1406-65), Astronomer A2057

Seok-jeong Choi (1646-1715), Mathematician A2058

Dong-hyuk Ahn (1907-2004), Chemical Engineer — A2059

Litho. With Foil Application
2019, Apr. 19 *Perf. 14*
2545 Horiz. strip of 3 1.80 .90
a. A2057 330w multi .60 .30
b. A2058 330w multi .60 .30
c. A2059 330w multi .60 .30

Redefinition of International System of Units — A2060

2019, May 20 Litho. *Perf. 14x13¼*
2546 A2060 330w multi .55 .30

Miniature Sheet

Kakao Friends A2061

No. 2547 — Inscriptions: a, Muzi & Con. b, Apeach. c, Ryan. d, Frodo. e, Neo. f, Tube. g, Love. h, Friendship. i, Happiness. j, Jay-G.

Litho. With Foil Application
2019, May 30 *Perf. 13¼x13*
2547 A2061 Sheet of 10 6.50 3.25
a.-j. 380w Any single .65 .30

Corals A2062

No. 2548: a, Dendronephthya suensoni. b, Dendronephthya mollis. c, Dendronephthya putteri. d, Dendronephthya alba.

Litho. With Foil Application
2019, June 5 *Perf. 13*
2548 A2062 Block of 4 2.60 1.25
a.-d. 380w Any single .65 .30

Seol-hee Baek (1924-2010), Singer A2063

Hye-on In (1919-2002), Singer A2064

Perf. 13¾x13½
2019, June 21 Litho.
2549 A2063 380y gold & multi .65 .30
2550 A2064 380y gold & multi .65 .30

Flag A2065

Rose of Sharon A2066

Cat and Chrysanthemums, by Sang-byeok Byeon (1730-75) — A2067

2019, July 1 Photo. ***Perf. 12¾x13½***

2551	A2065	380w multi	.65	.35
2552	A2066	470w multi	.80	.40

Perf. 13½

2553	A2067	2180w gold & multi	3.75	1.90
		Nos. 2551-2553 (3)	5.20	2.65

A map of the Korean Peninsula is laser cut in the lower right corner of No. 2553.

18th World Swimming Championships, Gwangju — A2068

2019, July 12 Litho. ***Perf. 14¼x14***

2554	A2068	380w multi	.65	.30

Hwang-ok Heo, Legendary Queen of Korea — A2069

Princess Suriratra (Later Queen Heo) — A2070

2019, July 30 Litho. ***Perf. 14x14¼***

2555	Pair	1.30	.60
a.	A2069 380w multi	.65	.30
b.	A2070 380w multi	.65	.30

See India Nos. 3123-3124.

Songho Beach, Haenam A2071

Chaeseokgang, Buan — A2072

Jeongdongjin Beach, Gangneung A2073

Kkotji Beach, Taean A2074

2019, Aug. 6 Litho. ***Perf. 14x13¼***

2556	Block or horiz. strip of 4	2.60	1.25
a.	A2071 380w multi	.65	.30
b.	A2072 380w multi	.65	.30
c.	A2073 380w multi	.65	.30
d.	A2074 380w multi	.65	.30

A2075

A2076

A2077 A2078

A2079 A2080

A2081 A2082

A2083 A2084

A2085 A2086

A2087 A2088

A2089

Evolution of the South Korean Flag — A2090

2019, Aug. 14 Litho. ***Perf. 14½***

2557	Sheet of 16	10.50	5.00
a.	A2075 380w multi	.65	.30
b.	A2076 380w multi	.65	.30
c.	A2077 380w multi	.65	.30
d.	A2078 380w multi	.65	.30
e.	A2079 380w multi	.65	.30
f.	A2080 380w multi	.65	.30
g.	A2081 380w multi	.65	.30
h.	A2082 380w multi	.65	.30
i.	A2083 380w multi	.65	.30
j.	A2084 380w multi	.65	.30
k.	A2085 380w multi	.65	.30
l.	A2086 380w multi	.65	.30
m.	A2087 380w multi	.65	.30
n.	A2088 380w multi	.65	.30
o.	A2089 380w multi	.65	.30
p.	A2090 380w multi	.65	.30

National Parks and Flora — A2091

No. 2558: a, Seoraksan National Park, South Korea and Pinus pumila (orange panel). b, Northern Velebit National Park and Fianthus velebiticus, Croatia (green panel).

2019, Aug. 29 Litho. ***Perf. 13x13¼***

2558	A2091	380w Pair #a-b	1.30	.60

South Korea and Croatia joint issue. See Croatia Nos. 1138-1139.

Evolution of the Woman's Hanbok A2092

No. 2559 — Woman in hanbok from: a, 1800s. b, 1900s. c, 1500s. d, 1600s-1700s.

2019, Sept. 9 Litho. ***Perf. 14***

2559	A2092	380w Block or horiz. strip of 4, #a-d	2.60	1.25

Republic of Korea Air Force, 70th Anniv. A2093

Litho. With Foil Application

2019, Sept. 20 ***Perf. 14***

2560	A2093	380w sil & multi	.65	.30

100th National Sports Festival, Seoul — A2094

2019, Sept. 26 Litho. ***Perf. 14½***

2561	A2094	380w multi	.65	.30

Korean Motion Pictures, Cent. — A2095

2019, Oct. 25 Litho. ***Perf. 13¼***

2562	A2095	380w multi	.65	.30

Falconry, UNESCO Intangible Cultural Heritage A2096

No. 2563: a, Falcon and handler (53x24mm). b, Falcon and pheasant (53x36mm).

Perf. 13¾x13¼

2019, Nov. 27 Litho.

2563	A2096	380w Vert. pair #a-b	1.30	.60

New Year 2020 (Year of the Rat) A2097

No. 2564: a, Rat in heart of flowers. b, Two rats.

Litho. With Hologram Affixed

2019, Dec. 2 ***Perf. 13***

2564	A2097 380w Pair #a-b	1.30	.60
c.	Souvenir sheet of 4, 2 each #2564a-2564b	2.60	1.25

Rice Growing Technology A2098

Integrated Steel Technology A2099

Ship Design and Construction Technology A2100

Dynamic Random Access Memory Semiconductor Technology A2101

Hantaan Virus Vaccine A2102

Satellite Technology A2103

Nuclear Power Plant Design Technology A2104

Lithium Ion Battery Technology A2105

2019, Dec. 27 Litho. ***Perf. 14¼x14***

2565	Block of 8	5.25	2.40
a.	A2098 380w multi	.65	.30
b.	A2099 380w multi	.65	.30
c.	A2100 380w multi	.65	.30
d.	A2101 380w multi	.65	.30
e.	A2102 380w multi	.65	.30
f.	A2103 380w multi	.65	.30
g.	A2104 380w multi	.65	.30
h.	A2105 380w multi	.65	.30

KUH-1EM Fire Fighting Helicopter A2106

KUH-1P Police Helicopter A2107

KUH-1FS Forest Service Helicopter A2108

Litho. With Foil Application

2020, Mar. 20 ***Perf. 14x14¼***

2566	Horiz. strip of 3	2.00	.90
a.	A2106 380w sil & multi	.65	.30
b.	A2107 380w sil & multi	.65	.30
c.	A2108 380w sil & multi	.65	.30

Deoksugung Seokjojeon, Seoul — A2109

Jagyeongjeon Hall, Gyeongbokgung Palace, Seoul — A2110

Buyongjeong Pavilion, Changdeokgung Palace, Seoul — A2111

Main Hall, Changyeonggung Palace, Seoul — A2112

Royal Palaces A2113

No. 2568: a, Deoksugung Seokjojeon, Seoul. b, Main Hall, Changyeonggung Palace, Seoul. c, Buyongjeong Pavilion, Changdeokgung Palace, Seoul. d, Jagyeongjeon Hall, Gyeongbokgung Palace, Seoul.

2020, Mar. 26 Litho. *Perf. 13*

2567 Block or strip of 4 2.60 1.25
a. A2109 380w multi .65 .30
b. A2110 380w multi .65 .30
c. A2111 380w multi .65 .30
d. A2112 380w multi .65 .30

Souvenir Sheet
Litho. & Embossed With Foil Application
Perf. 14

2568 A2113 Sheet of 4 6.00 3.00
a. 690w multi 1.10 .55
b. 840w multi 1.40 .70
c. 1010w multi 1.60 .80
d. 1090w multi 1.75 .90

Duksung Women's University, Cent. — A2114

Litho. With Foil Application
2020, Apr. 18 *Perf. 14*
2569 A2114 380w gold & multi .65 .30

International Year of Plant Health — A2115

2020, May 29 Litho. *Perf. 14¼x14*
2570 A2115 380w multi .65 .30

Battle of Bongodong, Cent. — A2116

2020, June 5 Litho. *Perf. 14x13¼*
2571 A2116 380w multi .65 .30

Korean Sport and Olympic Committee, Cent. — A2117

2020, June 30 Litho. *Perf. 14*
2572 A2117 380w multi .65 .30

Agency for Defense Development, 50th Anniv. — A2118

2020, July 16 Litho. *Perf. 13*
2573 A2118 380w multi .65 .30

Protected Marine Life — A2119

No. 2574: a, Zostera marina. b, Hippocampus kuda. c, Hippocampus trimaculata. d, Phyllospadix japonicus.

Litho. With Foil Application
2020, Aug. 7 *Perf. 14¼*
2574 A2119 380w Block of 4, #a-d 2.60 1.25

Evolution of the Men's Hanbok A2120

No. 2575 — Men's traditional clothing from: a, 1700s-1800s. b, 1900s. c, 1500s. d, 1600s.

2020, Sept. 4 Litho. *Perf. 14*
2575 A2120 380w Block or horiz. strip of 4, #a-d 2.60 1.30

Warrior on Horseback Earthenware Cup — A2121

2020, Sept. 23 Litho. *Perf. 13½*
2576 A2121 2480w multi 4.25 2.10

A map of the Korean Peninsula is laser cut in the lower right corner of No. 2576.

A2122

Yu Gwansun (1902-20), Independence Activist Killed by Japanese Colonial Authorities — A2123

Perf. 13¼x13½
2020, Sept. 28 Litho.
2577 A2122 380w multi .65 .35

Souvenir Sheet
On Silk-Faced Paper
Perf. 13¼x13
2578 A2123 2480w multi 4.25 2.10

Ssireum (Korean Wrestling), UNESCO Intangible Cultural Heritage A2124

No. 2579 — Various wrestlers with denomination in: a, Blue panel (52x25mm). b, Red panel (52x36mm).

2020, Oct. 8 Litho. *Perf. 14½*
2579 A2124 380w Vert. pair, #a-b 1.40 .70

Battle of Qingshanli (Cheongsanri), Cent. — A2125

2020, Oct. 21 Litho. *Perf. 13¾x14¼*
2580 A2125 380w multi .70 .35

Children's Book Illustrations — A2126

No. 2581 — Illustration from: a, Magic Candles (red orange denomination). b, Dokkaebi and the Rice Cake Peddler (gray blue denomination). c, When Spring Comes to the DMZ (orange yellow denomination). d, Wave (blue denomination).

Litho. With Foil Application
2020, Nov. 20 *Perf. 13½x13¼*
2581 A2126 380w Block or horiz. strip of 4, #a-d 2.75 1.40

Philately Week.

New Year 2021 (Year of the Ox) A2127

No. 2582: a, Cow and calf. b, Cow wearing bells.

Litho. and Embossed With Foil Application
2020, Dec. 1 *Perf. 13¾*
2582 A2127 380w Pair #a-b 1.40 .70
c. Souvenir sheet of 4, 2 each #2582a-2582b 2.80 1.40

Bears A2128

No. 2583: a, Ursus thibetanus ussuricus. b, Ursus arctos arctos.

2020, Dec. 15 Litho. *Perf. 14¼*
2583 A2128 380w Pair #a-b 1.40 .70

Diplomatic relations between South Korea and Russia, 30th anniv. See Russia No. 8222.

Geostationary Satellites — A2129

No. 2584: a, Cheonrian 1 satellite (blue denomination at UR). b, Cheonrian 2A satellite (red denomination at UR). c, Cheonrian 2B satellite (blue denomination at UL).

Litho. With Foil Application
2021, Jan. 26 *Perf. 13¾x13¼*
2584 A2129 380w Horiz. strip of 3, #a-c 2.10 1.10

Korea Advanced Institute of Science and Technology, 50th Anniv. A2130

2021, Feb. 16 Litho. *Perf. 13¼*
2585 A2130 380w multi .70 .35

Korean Heritage Items Recently Repatriated — A2131

No. 2586: a, Empress Myeongseong Okbo (lilac background). b, Celadon monkey (orange brown background). c, Gyeonju face pattern (blue background). d, Ten-story pagoda (green background).

Litho. & Embossed With Foil Application
2021, Feb. 16 *Perf. 13¼*
2586 A2131 Block or horiz. strip of 4 2.80 1.40
a.-d. 380w Any single .70 .35

Neo-Confucian Academy, Dalseong A2132

Neo-Confucian Academy, Nonsan — A2133

Neo-Confucian Academy, Andong — A2134

Neo-Confucian Academy, Jangseong A2135

Neo-Confucian Academies — A2136

No. 2588 — Academy in: a, Nonsan. b, Dalseong. c, Jangseong. d, Andong.

2021, Mar. 11 Litho. *Perf. 13*

2587	Block or horiz. strip of 4	2.80	1.40
a.	A2132 380w multi	.70	.35
b.	A2133 380w multi	.70	.35
c.	A2134 380w multi	.70	.35
d.	A2135 380w multi	.70	.35

Souvenir Sheet

Perf. 14

2588	A2136 Sheet of 4	6.50	3.25
a.	690w sil & multi	1.25	.60
b.	840w sil & multi	1.50	.75
c.	1010w sil & multi	1.75	.90
d.	1090w sil & multi	2.00	1.00

T-50B Jet — A2137

KUH-1 Helicopter A2138

RQ-101 Unmanned Aerial Vehicle A2139

Litho. With Foil Application

2021, Mar. 25 *Perf. 13¼x13½*

2589	Horiz. strip of 3	2.10	1.10
a.	A2137 380w multi	.70	.35
b.	A2138 380w multi	.70	.35
c.	A2139 380w multi	.70	.35

A2140 A2141

A2142 A2143

A2144 A2145

A2146 A2147

Painted Folding Screen Panels, by Jang Seung-up (1843-97)
A2148 A2149

2021, Apr. 6 Litho. *Perf. 14¼*

2590	Sheet of 10 + 20 labels	7.00	3.50
a.	A2140 380w multi	.70	.35
b.	A2141 380w multi	.70	.35
c.	A2142 380w multi	.70	.35
d.	A2143 380w multi	.70	.35
e.	A2144 380w multi	.70	.35
f.	A2145 380w multi	.70	.35
g.	A2146 380w multi	.70	.35
h.	A2147 380w multi	.70	.35
i.	A2148 380w multi	.70	.35
j.	A2149 380w multi	.70	.35

Astronomical Clock A2150

Rain Gauge A2151

Water Clock A2152

Sundial A2153

2021, Apr. 21 Litho. *Perf. 13¼x13½*

2591	Block or horiz. strip of 4	2.80	1.40
a.	A2150 380w multi	.75	.35
b.	A2151 380w multi	.75	.35
c.	A2152 380w multi	.75	.35
d.	A2153 380w multi	.75	.35

Astronomy and earth science of the Joseon Dynasty.

Geumgangsan Mountain, Fan Painting by Jeong Seon — A2154

Precious Vessels and Flowering Plants, Fan Painting by Lee Doyeong and Go Huidong A2155

Plum Blossoms, Fan Painting by Shin Myeongyeon A2156

Chatting Under Pine Trees by the Stream, Fan Painting by Yi Inmun A2157

Elegant Gathering in the Western Garden, Fan Painting by Kim Hongdo A2158

Gazing at a Waterfall Under a Pine Tree, Fan Painting by Yi Insang A2159

Litho. With Foil Application

2021, May 17 *Perf. 14¼x13¾*

2592	Block or vert. strip of 6	4.25	2.10
a.	A2154 380w gold & multi	.70	.35
b.	A2155 380w gold & multi	.70	.35
c.	A2156 380w gold & multi	.70	.35
d.	A2157 380w gold & multi	.70	.35
e.	A2158 380w gold & multi	.70	.35
f.	A2159 380w gold & multi	.70	.35

Protected Turtles — A2160

No. 2593: a, Eretmochelys imbricata. b, Caretta caretta. c, Dermochelys coriacea. d, Chelonia mydas.

Litho. With Foil Application

2021, May 31 *Perf. 14¼*

2593	A2160 Block of 4	2.80	1.40
a.-d.	380w Any single	.70	.35

A2161

A2162

A2163

Sculptures of Mythological Beasts at Gyeongbokgung Palace — A2164

Litho. & Engr.

2021, June 22 *Perf. 13¼*

2594	Block or horiz. strip of 4	3.50	1.60
a.	A2161 470w multi	.85	.40
b.	A2162 470w multi	.85	.40
c.	A2163 470w multi	.85	.40
d.	A2164 470w multi	.85	.40

Daecheong Lake — A2165

Hoengseong Lake — A2166

Yongdam Lake — A2167

Soyang Lake — A2168

2021, July 1 Litho. *Perf. 14x13¼*

2595	Block or horiz. strip of 4	2.80	1.40
a.	A2165 380w multi	.70	.35
b.	A2166 380w multi	.70	.35
c.	A2167 380w multi	.70	.35
d.	A2168 380w multi	.70	.35

Baeksu Coastal Road — A2169

Heonhwa Road — A2170

Sinchang Windmill Coastal Road — A2171

Mulmi Coastal Road — A2172

Litho. With Foil Application

2021, July 15 *Perf. 14*

2596	Block or horiz. strip of 4	2.80	1.40
a.	A2169 380w sil & multi	.70	.35
b.	A2170 380w sil & multi	.70	.35
c.	A2171 380w sil & multi	.70	.35
d.	A2172 380w sil & multi	.70	.35

Walled Town, Gochang A2173

Walled Town, Nagan A2174

Walled town, Haemi A2175

Litho. With Foil Application

2021, Aug. 4 *Perf. 13¼*

2597	Horiz. strip of 3	2.00	1.10
a.	A2173 380w cop & multi	.65	.35
b.	A2174 380w cop & multi	.65	.35
c.	A2175 380w cop & multi	.65	.35

St. Andrew Kim Taegon (1821-46), Martyred Priest — A2176

Litho. With Foil Application

2021, Aug. 20 *Perf. 13*

2598	A2176 380w gold & multi	.65	.35

Lycaena Dispar A2177

Yugwa (Rice Cakes) A2178

Terpsiphone Atrocaudata — A2179

Flag and Hunminjeongeum Script — A2180

Crataegus Pinnatifida A2181

Rose of Sharon A2182

Hangeul Alphabet A2183

Celadon Ewer A2184

2021 Litho. *Perf. 12¾*

2599	A2177	10w multi	.30	.30
2600	A2178	50w multi	.30	.30
2601	A2179	100w multi	.30	.30
2602	A2180	430w multi	.75	.35
2603	A2181	500w multi	.85	.40
2604	A2182	520w multi	.90	.45

Perf. 13½

2605	A2183	1000w multi	1.75	.85

Litho. With Foil Application

2606	A2184	2530w multi	4.50	2.25
		Nos. 2599-2606 (8)	9.65	5.20

Issued: Nos. 2599-2601, 10/29; Nos. 2602, 2604, 2606, 9/1; Nos. 2603, 2605, 12/17.

A map of the Korean Peninsula is laser cut in the lower right corner of Nos. 2605 and 2606.

Oil Tanker A2185

Container Ship — A2186

Bulk Cargo Ship — A2187

Liquid Natural Gas Ship — A2188

Litho. With Foil Application

2021, Sept. 15 *Perf. 13¼x13½*

2607	Block or horiz. strip of 4	3.00	1.40
a.	A2185 430w sil & multi	.75	.35
b.	A2186 430w sil & multi	.75	.35
c.	A2187 430w sil & multi	.75	.35
d.	A2188 430w sil & multi	.75	.35

Jultagi (Korean Tightrope Walking) UNESCO Intangible Cultural Property A2189

No. 2608: a, Tightrope walker above wire (52x24mm). b, Tightrope walker on rope (52x36mm).

Litho. With Foil Application

2021, Sept. 30 *Perf. 14x13½*

2608	A2189	430w Vert. pair. #a-b	1.50	.70

The Story of Baekdu Mountain, Children's Book by Ryu Jae-su — A2190

Half Past Four, Children's Book by Yun Seok-jung A2191

Manhee's Home, Children's Book by Kwon Yoon-duck A2192

Children of the Dong River, Children's Book by Kim Jae-hong A2193

Litho. With Foil Application

2021, Oct. 25 *Perf. 14x14¼*

2609	Block or horiz. strip of 4	3.00	1.40
a.	A2190 430w gold & multi	.75	.35
b.	A2191 430w gold & multi	.75	.35
c.	A2192 430w gold & multi	.75	.35
d.	A2193 430w gold & multi	.75	.35

Philately Week.

Korean Jindo A2194

Sapsali A2195

Donggyeongi A2196

Litho. With Foil Application

2021, Oct. 29 *Perf. 14*

2610	Horiz. strip of 3	2.25	1.10
a.	A2194 430w gold & multi	.75	.35
b.	A2195 430w gold & multi	.75	.35
c.	A2196 430w gold & multi	.75	.35

Medicinal Plants — A2197

No. 2611: a, Lonicera japonica. b, Angelica gigas. c, Epimedium koreanum. d, Leonurus japonicus.

Litho. With Foil Application

Perf. 13½x13¼ Syncopated

2021, Nov. 10

2611	A2197	Block or horiz. strip of 4	3.00	1.40
a.-d.		430w Any single	.75	.35

A2198

A2199

A2200

Children's Hanboks — A2201

2021, Nov. 18 Litho. *Perf. 13¼x13*

2612	Block or horiz. strip of 4	3.00	1.40
a.	A2198 430w multi	.75	.35
b.	A2199 430w multi	.75	.35
c.	A2200 430w multi	.75	.35
d.	A2201 430w multi	.75	.35

New Year 2022 (Year of the Tiger) A2202

No. 2613: a, Head of tiger and snowflakes. b, Tiger, paw prints and hearts.

Litho. & Embossed With Foil Application

2021, Dec. 1 *Perf. 14¼*

2613	A2202	430w Pair, #a-b	1.50	.70
c.		Souvenir sheet of 4, 2 each #2613a-2613b	3.00	1.40

Portraits of Joseon Kings A2203

No. 2614: a, King Yeongjo wearing red robe (1694-1776). b, King Taejo wearing blue robe (1335-1408).

Litho. With Foil Application

2022, Feb. 7 *Perf. 13¼x13*

2614	A2203	430w Pair, #a-b	1.50	.75

Bamboo Investiture Book A2204

Robe of Prince Yeong A2205

Seal of Princess Deokon (1822-44) A2206

White Jade Butterfly Pendants A2207

Litho. With Foil Application

2022, Feb. 14 *Perf. 13¼x13½*

2615	Block or horiz. strip of 4	3.00	1.40
a.	A2204 430w multi	.75	.35
b.	A2205 430w multi	.75	.35
c.	A2206 430w multi	.75	.35
d.	A2207 430w multi	.75	.35

Yun Yong-ha (1922-65), Composer A2208

Perf. 13½x13¾

2022, Mar. 16 Litho.

2616	A2208	430w multi	.70	.35

SEMI-POSTAL STAMPS

Catalogue values for unused stamps in this section are for Never Hinged items.

Field Hospital — SP1

Nurses Supporting Patient — SP2

Perf. 13½x14, 14x13½

1953, Aug. 1 Litho. Wmk. 257

Crosses in Red

B1	SP1	10h + 5h bl grn	14.00	2.25
B2	SP2	10h + 5h blue	14.00	2.25

The surtax was for the Red Cross. Nos. B1-B2 exist imperf.

Type of Regular Issue, 1956, with Added inscription at Upper Left

1957, Sept. 1 Wmk. 312 *Perf. 12½*

Granite Paper

B3	A111	40h + 10h lt bl grn	8.25	2.75

Wmk. 317

B4	A111	40h + 10h lt bl grn	8.25	2.75

The surtax was for flood relief.

Rice Farmer Type of Regular Issue, 1961-62

1963, July 10 Wmk. 317 *Perf. 12½*

B5	A172	4w + 1w dk bl	6.50	1.25

The surtax was for flood victims in southern Korea.

1965, Oct. 1 Unwmk. *Perf. 12½*

B6	A172	4w + 2w indigo	3.00	.75

The surtax was for flood relief.

1965, Oct. 11

B7	A172	4w + 2w magenta	3.00	.75

The surtax was for a scholarship fund.

Type of Regular Issue 1964-66

1966, Nov. 10 Litho. *Perf. 12½*

Granite Paper

B8	A186b	7w + 2w car rose	4.50	1.25

The surtax was to help the needy.

Soldier with Wife and Child — SP3

1967, June 20 *Perf. 12½x13*

B9 SP3 7w + 3w rose lil & blk 4.50 .75

The surtax was for veterans of the war in Viet Nam and their families.

Reservist — SP4

1968, Aug. 1 Litho. *Perf. 13x12½*

B10 SP4 7w + 3w grn & blk 7.00 1.25

Issued for the fund-raising drive to arm reservists.

Flag — SP5

1968, Nov. 1 Litho. Unwmk.

B11 SP5 7w + 3w dk bl & red 27.50 4.00

The surtax was for disaster relief.

1969, Feb. 15

B12 SP5 7w + 3w lt grn, dk bl & red 7.50 1.00

Surtax for military helicopter fund.

Flag Type of 1968 Redrawn Zeros Omitted

1969, Nov. 1 Litho. *Perf. 13x12½*

B13 SP5 7w + 3w dk bl & red 27.50 1.00

The surtax was for the searchlight fund.

"Pin of Love" — SP6

1972, Aug. 1 Photo. *Perf. 13½x12½*

B14 SP6 10w + 5w blue & car 1.25 .75

Disaster relief.

"Pin of Love" — SP7

1973, July 1 Photo. *Perf. 12½x13½*

B15 SP7 10w + 5w multicolored .65 .50

Disaster relief.

Paddle and Ball — SP8

1973, Aug. 1 Photo. *Perf. 13½x12½*

B16 SP8 10w + 5w multicolored .65 .50

Surtax was for gymnasium to be built to commemorate the victory of the Korean women's table tennis team at the 32nd World Table Tennis Championships.

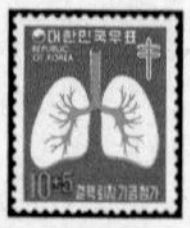

Lungs — SP9

1974, Nov. 1 *Perf. 13½x12½*

B17 SP9 10w + 5w green & red .75 .25

Surtax was for tuberculosis control.

No. 647 Surcharged

Perf. 13½x12½

1977, July 25 Photo.

B18 A328 20w + 10w green *12.50 12.50*

Surtax was for flood relief.

Seoul 1988 Olympic Games Series

'88 Seoul Games Emblem SP10

Korean Tiger, Mascot SP11

1985, Mar. 20 Photo. *Perf. 13x13½*

B19 SP10 70w + 30w blk & multi .45 .25
B20 SP11 70w + 30w blk & multi .45 .25
a. Souvenir sheet of 2, #B19-20 1.10 1.10

Track and Field — SP12

1985, June 10

B21 SP12 70w + 30w shown .45 .25
B22 SP12 70w + 30w Rowing .45 .25
a. Souvenir sheet of 2, #B21-B22 1.10 1.10

1985, Sept. 16

B23 SP12 70w + 30w Boxing .45 .25
B24 SP12 70w + 30w Women's basketball .45 .25
a. Souvenir sheet of 2, #B23-B24 1.10 1.10

1985, Nov. 1

B25 SP12 70w + 30w Canoeing .45 .30
B26 SP12 70w + 30w Cycling .45 .30
a. Souvenir sheet of 2, #B25-B26 1.10 1.10

Surtax for the 24th Summer Olympic Games, Sept. 17-Oct. 2, 1988.

Equestrian — SP18

Designs: No. B28, Fencing. No. B29, Soccer. No. B30, Gymnastic rings.

1986, Mar. 25 Photo. *Perf. 13x13½*

B27 SP18 70w + 30w multi .45 .25
B28 SP18 70w + 30w multi .45 .25
B29 SP18 70w + 30w multi .45 .25
B30 SP18 70w + 30w multi .45 .25

Souvenir Sheets

B31 Sheet of 4 9.50 9.50
a. SP18 370w + 100w like #B27 2.25 2.25
B32 Sheet of 4 9.50 9.50
a. SP18 400w + 100w like #B28 2.25 2.25
B33 Sheet of 4 9.50 9.50
a. SP18 440w + 100w like #B29 2.25 2.25
B34 Sheet of 4 9.50 9.50
a. SP18 470w + 100w like #B30 2.25 2.25

1986 Photo. *Perf. 13x13½*

No. B35, Weight lifting. No. B36, Team handball. No. B37, Judo. No. B38, Field hockey.

B35 SP18 80w +50w multi .55 .25
B36 SP18 80w +50w multi .55 .25
B37 SP18 80w +50w multi .55 .25
B38 SP18 80w +50w multi .55 .25

Souvenir Sheets

B39 Sheet of 4 8.25 8.25
a. SP18 370w + 100w like #B35 1.90 1.90
B40 Sheet of 4 8.25 8.25
a. SP18 400w + 100w like #B36 1.90 1.90
B41 Sheet of 4 9.00 9.00
a. SP18 440w + 100w like #B37 2.10 2.10
B42 Sheet of 4 9.00 9.00
a. SP18 470w + 100w like #B38 2.10 2.10

Issue dates: Nos. B35-B36, B39-B40, Oct. 10; others, Nov. 1.

1987, May 25 Photo. *Perf. 13x13½*

No. B43, Women's tennis. No. B44, Wrestling. No. B45, Show jumping. No. B46, Diving.

B43 SP18 80w +50w multi .65 .40
B44 SP18 80w +50w multi .65 .40
B45 SP18 80w +50w multi .65 .40
B46 SP18 80w +50w multi .65 .40

1987, Oct. 10

No. B47, Table Tennis. No. B48, Men's shooting. No. B49, Women's archery. No. B50, Women's volleyball.

B47 SP18 80w +50w multi .65 .40
B48 SP18 80w +50w multi .65 .40
B49 SP18 80w +50w multi .65 .40
B50 SP18 80w +50w multi .65 .40

1988, Mar. 5 Photo. *Perf. 13x13½*

B51 SP18 80w +20w Sailing .45 .25
B52 SP18 80w +20w Taekwondo .45 .25

1988, May 6 Photo. *Perf. 13½x13*

No. B53, Torch relay, horiz. No. B54, Olympic Stadium, horiz.

B53 SP18 80w +20w multi .45 .25

Litho. & Engr.

B54 SP18 80w +20w multi .45 .25

See Greece No. 1627.

Souvenir Sheets of 2

B43a	SP18	80w +50w	3.00	3.00
B44a	SP18	80w +50w	3.00	3.00
B45a	SP18	80w +50w	3.00	3.00
B46a	SP18	80w +50w	3.00	3.00
B47a	SP18	80w +50w	3.00	3.00
B48a	SP18	80w +50w	3.00	3.00
B49a	SP18	80w +50w	3.00	3.00
B50a	SP18	80w +50w	3.00	3.00
B51a	SP18	80w +20w	3.00	3.00
B52a	SP18	80w +20w	3.00	3.00
B53a	SP18	80w +20w	3.00	3.00
B54a	SP18	80w +20w	3.00	3.00

AIR POST STAMPS

Four-motor Plane and Globe — AP1

Perf. 11½x11

1947-50 Litho. Wmk. 257

C1 AP1 50wn carmine rose 8.25 2.25
a. Horiz. pair, imperf. btwn. *165.00*

Perf. 11

C2 AP1 150wn blue ('49) 1.25 1.25
a. "KORFA" 12.50 *.30*
C3 AP1 150wn green ('50) 7.50 4.00
Nos. C1-C3 (3) 17.00
Set, never hinged 30.00

Nos. C2-C3 are redrawn and designs differ slightly from type AP1.
Issued: 50wn, 10/1.
For surcharge see No. C5.

Plane and Korea Map — AP2

1950, Jan. 1

C4 AP2 60wn light blue 16.00 15.00
Never hinged 27.50

No. C2 Surcharged with New Value and Wavy Lines in Black

1951, Oct. 10

C5 AP1 500wn on 150wn bl 3.75 2.25
Never hinged 6.25
a. "KORFA" 20.00 *50.00*
Never hinged 30.00
b. Surcharge inverted 125.00

Douglas C-47 and Ship — AP3

Perf. 13x12½

1952, Oct. 15 Litho. Wmk. 257

C6 AP3 1200wn red brown .90 .60
C7 AP3 1800wn lt blue 1.50 .60
C8 AP3 4200wn purple 1.90 1.25
Nos. C6-C8 (3) 4.30 2.45
Set, never hinged 7.25

Nos. C6-C8 exist imperf.

1953, Apr. 5

C9 AP3 12h dp blue 1.00 .60
C10 AP3 18h purple 1.50 .60
C11 AP3 42h Prus green 2.10 1.25
Nos. C9-C11 (3) 4.60 2.45
Set, never hinged 7.75

Douglas DC-7 over East Gate, Seoul — AP4

1954, June 15 *Perf. 12½*

C12 AP4 25h brown 2.00 1.25
C13 AP4 35h deep pink 2.75 1.00
C14 AP4 38h dark green 2.75 1.50
C15 AP4 58h ultra 2.75 1.75
C16 AP4 71h deep blue 6.50 2.00
Nos. C12-C16 (5) 16.75 7.50
Set, never hinged 27.50

Nos. C12-C16 exist imperf.
Counterfeits exist of Nos. C12-C16.

Type of 1954 Redrawn

1956, July 20 Unwmk.

Laid Paper

C17 AP4 70h brt bluish grn 5.00 3.00
C18 AP4 110h brown 3.25 3.00
C19 AP4 205h magenta 9.75 5.00
Nos. C17-C19 (3) 18.00 11.00
Set, never hinged 30.00

Nos. C18-C19 are found on horizontally and vertically laid paper.

1957, July Wmk. 312 *Perf. 12½*

Granite Paper

C20 AP4 70h brt bluish grn 4.75 3.00
C21 AP4 110h brown 4.75 3.00
C22 AP4 205h magenta 9.50 5.00
Nos. C20-C22 (3) 19.00 11.00
Set, never hinged 32.50

On the redrawn stamps, Nos. C17-C22, the lines of the entire design are lighter, and the colorless character at right end of bottom row has been redrawn as in illustration above No. 212D.

Catalogue values for unused stamps in this section, from this point to the end of the section, are for Never Hinged items.

Girl on Palace Balcony — AP5

Designs: 100h, Suwon Castle. 200h, Songnyu Gate, Tuksu Palace. 400h, Kyunghoeru Pavilion.

Perf. 12½

1961, Dec. 1 Unwmk. Litho.

C23 AP5 50h lt blue & violet 12.50 5.00
C24 AP5 100h pale grn & sepia 22.50 8.00
C25 AP5 200h pale grn & brn 32.50 8.00
C26 AP5 400h grn & pale bl 42.50 10.00
Nos. C23-C26 (4) 110.00 31.00

Values in Won; Same Designs; Underlined Zeros Added

1962-63

C27 AP5 5w lt bl & vio ('63) 67.50 20.00
C28 AP5 10w pale grn & sepia 45.00 15.00

C29	AP5	20w pale grn & brn ('63)		225.00	50.00
C30	AP5	40w grn & pale bl ('63)		60.00	25.00
		Nos. C27-C30 (4)		397.50	110.00

1964, May 10 Wmk. 317 *Perf. 12½*

Granite Paper

C32	AP5	10w pale grn & sepia	12.50	4.00
C33	AP5	20w pale grn & brn	42.50	12.00
C34	AP5	40w pale bl & grn	25.00	8.00
		Nos. C32-C34 (3)	80.00	24.00

Granite Paper

1964, Oct. Unwmk. *Perf. 12½*

Designs: 39w, Girl on palace balcony. 64w, Suwon Castle. 78w, Songnyu Gate, Tuksu Palace. 112w, Kyunghoeru Pavilion.

C35	AP5	39w vio bl & gray olive	7.50	2.50
C36	AP5	64w bl & grnsh gray	10.50	2.50
C37	AP5	78w grnsh bl & ultra	19.00	5.00
C38	AP5	112w blue & green	8.00	2.50
		Nos. C35-C38 (4)	45.00	12.50

World Map and Plane — AP6

Designs: 135w, Plane over eastern hemisphere. 145w, Plane over world map. 180w, Plane over world map.

1973, Dec. 30 Photo. *Perf. 13x12½*

C39	AP6	110w pink & multi	6.75	4.00
C40	AP6	135w yel grn & red	7.75	4.00
C41	AP6	145w lt bl & rose	9.00	4.00
C42	AP6	180w lilac & yellow	27.00	8.00
		Nos. C39-C42 (4)	50.50	20.00

UPU Type of 1974

1974, Oct. 9 Photo. *Perf. 13*

C43	A480	110w blue & multi	2.25	.75
a.		Souvenir sheet of 2	11.50	11.50

Mt. Fuji, Korean Airlines Jet Type

1985, Dec. 18 Photo. *Perf. 13x13½*

C44	A878	370w brt bl, blk & red	1.25	.75

Int'l Year of Peace Type

1986, Jan. 15 Photo. *Perf. 13x13½*

C45	A879	400w multicolored	1.25	.75

Issued in sheets with two blocks of four.

KOREA, DEMOCRATIC PEOPLE'S REPUBLIC

kə-'rē-ə

LOCATION — Peninsula extending from Manchuria between the Yellow Sea and the Sea of Japan (East Sea)
GOVT. — Republic
AREA — 47,398 sq. mi.
POP. — 24,589,122 (2011 est.)
CAPITAL — Pyongyang

At the end of World War II, American forces occupied South Korea and Russian forces occupied North Korea, with the 38th parallel of latitude as the dividing line. North Korea was administered by a Provisional People's Committee after Feb. 9, 1946. Unoverprinted Japanese stamps continued to be used until the first North Korean issue of March 12, 1946. On Sept. 9, 1948, the Democratic People's Republic of Korea was established, and the last Soviet troops left Korea by the end of the year.

100 Chon = 1 Won (1962)

Catalogue values for unused stamps in this country are for Never Hinged items.

North Korean stamps were issued without gum, unless otherwise noted.
Early issues typically exist in a variety of color shades.
Used values are for cancelled-to-order stamps from 1957-on. Postally used stamps are worth more. Examples on non-philatelic covers are scarce, especially for 1946-1960 issues.

REPRINTS

During 1955-57 the North Korean Postal Administration created "reprints," actually imitations, of most 1946-56 issues for sale to collectors. These reprints were postally valid, and in some cases may have served real postal needs, but most were created for and sold to overseas collectors.
The reprints are more finely printed than the original stamps and are normally printed on a higher quality white wove paper. They often differ from the original printings in both size and design details. Specific distinguishing characteristics are provided below, with the descriptions of each issue.

SOVIET OCCUPATION

Rose of Sharon A1

Diamond Mountains (small "50") A2

Diamond Mountains (large "50") — A3

Perf 11, Rouletted 12(#3), 11x Imperf or Imperf x11 (#4,5)

1946, Mar. 12-1955 Litho.

1 A1 20ch red 85.00 *300.00*
2 A2 50ch apple grn ('46) 55.00 *82.50*
 a. 50ch yel green, *buff* 55.00 *82.50*
3 A2 50ch car rose *2,000.* *1,650.*
4 A3 50ch rose red 165.00 125.00
 a. Perf 12 ('48) 165.00 125.00
 c. Perf 10 ('55) — —
5 A3 50ch violet 18.00 —
 a. Perf 11 ('50) 300.00 —
 b. Imperf ('50) 55.00 —
 c. Perf 10 ('55) — —
 d. ImperfxPerf 11, soft paper, vert. lines 20.00
 e. Vert. pair, *tete-beche* 1,250.
 f. 10¾xImperf. — —
 Nos. 1-5 (5) 2,323. 2,158.

No. 4 has lines of colored dots along the horizontal rouletting.
Design sizes: No. 1, 18x21.5-22mm; No. 4, 17.5-18x22-23mm.
Reprints of No. 1 are in yellow green, perf 8½, 8½x9½, 10 or imperf, and measure 18-18.5x23mm. Denomination panel is 4mm high, rather than 3mm. Value $10.
Reprints of No. 4 are perf 10, 10x10½, 11 or imperf, on gummed paper, and measure 17.5-18x22-22.5mm. The double frame lines are clearly separated, and the figures of value are thin and well-formed. Value $10.

Gen. Kim Il Sung (1912-1994) — A4

1946, Aug. 15 Litho. *Pin-Perf*

6 A4 50ch brown 700.00 550.00

First anniversary of liberation from Japan.
No. 6 has lines of colored dots along the horizontal pin perforations.
No. 6 is inscribed in Korean, Chinese and Russian.
No. 6 in deep violet brown and a 50ch red, similar in design, were printed for presentation to officials and privileged people. Value, $1,900 and $2,250, respectively.

#21c Control overprint

Several varieties of overprints were used to validate various stamps during the chaotic months following the landing of United Nations' forces at Inchon in mid-September 1950, the retreat of North Korean forces to the far north by October, and their renewed advance, after the entry of the Chinese Volunteer Army into the war. Validation overprints are known on Nos. 10, 14, 16, 21, 22, 26, 27, 28, 29, and 31. Other stamps with validation overprints are of dubious origin.

Peasants — A5

Pin-Perf 12, Imperf (#10)

1947, Apr. 22-1955 Litho.

7 A5 1w turquoise 450.00 55.00
8 A5 1w violet ('49) 800.00 175.00
9 A5 1w dk bl, *buff* ('50) 110.00 55.00
10 A5 1w dark blue ('50) 60.00 60.00
 a. Perf 11ximperf ('50) 6.00 *60.00*
 b. Perf 10 ('55) — —

1st anniversary of agrarian reform.
Nos. 7-9 have lines of colored dots along the horizontal pin perforations.
Reprints of type A5 measure 21x24mm, versus the originals' 21-21.5x24-25mm, are finely printed in light blue and are perf 9, 10½, 11 or imperf. Value $10.

Worker and Factory — A6

1948, June 5 Litho. *Perf. 11*

11 A6 50ch dark blue 3,200. 1,250.

Second anniversary of the Labor Law.
Design size: 20-20.5x31mm.
Reprints measure 20x30-30.5mm and are perf 9, 10½, 11 or imperf. Value, $10 perf, $10 imperf.

Workers and Flag — A7

1948, Aug. 15

12 A7 50ch red brown *4,000.* 1,500.

Third anniversary of liberation from Japan.

Flag and Map — A8

1948, Aug. 20

13 A8 50ch indigo & red 2,500. 800.00

Adoption of the Constitution of the Democratic People's Republic of Korea, July 10, 1948.

DEMOCRATIC PEOPLE'S REPUBLIC

North Korean Flag — A9

1948, Sept. 19 *Rouletted 12*

14 A9 25ch reddish violet 15.00 *100.00*
 a. Perf. 10¼xroulette — —
15 A9 50ch gray blue 20.00 *50.00*
 a. Perf 10½ 40.00 *75.00*
 b. Perf. 10½xroulette — —

Establishment of the People's Republic, 9/9/48.
Design size: 23x30mm.
Reprints of No. 14 are in blue, on gummed paper, perf 9, 10½ or imperf. Size 20.5x28mm. Value, $10.
No. 15a is perforated over rouletting.

North Korean Flag — A10

1949, Feb. 9

16 A10 6w red & blue 4.00 *12.00*
 a. Perf 10¼ 35.00 *35.00*

No. 16 exists on both brownish wove and white wove papers.
Design size: 24x32.5-33mm.
Reprints are perf 10¼, 11 or imperf. Size 19x26.5mm. On the originals, the top and bottom panels are blue, with the center field red. On the reprints, these colors are reversed. Value, $10.
For surcharge see No. 42. For overprint see No. 76.

A11

Kim Il Sung University, Pyongyang — A12

1949

17 A11 1w violet 400.00 200.00
 a. Perf. 11 — —
18 A12 1w blue 1,200. 125.00

Issue dates: No. 17, 8/9; No. 18, Sept.
Design size: 34x21mm.
Reprints of No. 17 are in slate lilac to reddish lilac, perf 8½, 9, 9x9½, 10 or imperf, on gummed paper. Size 31.5-32x20-20.5mm. Value, $10 perf, $10 imperf.

North Korean Flags
A13 A14

Perf 11 or Rouletted 12 (#19)

1949, Aug. 15

With or Without Gum

19 A13 1w red, grn & blue 700.00 200.00
 a. Imperfx11 700.00 200.00
20 A14 1w red, grn & turq 1,200. *200.00*

4th anniversary of Liberation from Japan.
Design sizes: No. 19, 20.5x31mm; No. 20, 20x29.5mm.

Order of the National Flag — A15

Rouletted 12, Imperf (#23)

1950, Apr. 4-1956 Litho.

21 A15 1w pale sage green 7.00 *12.00*
 a. 1w olive green 7.00 *12.00*
 b. 1w yellow green 7.00 *12.00*
 c. With control overprint ('51) — —
 d. 1w emerald green 7.00 12.00
22 A15 1w red orange 20.00 *125.00*

Typographed

23 A15 1w brown orange *6,000.* *1,250.*
24 A15 1w dark green ('51) 60.00 *25.00*
 a. Perf 10¼ ('56) 90.00 —

11xImperf.

25 A15 1w light green 150.00 60.00

Design sizes: No. 21, 23-23.5x37mm; No. 22, 20x32mm; No. 23, 22.5-23x36-37mm; No. 24, 22x35.5mm; No. 25, 22.5x36mm.
Reprints of type A15 are in dull blue green on white paper, perf 10¼ or imperf, size 22x35mm, or in red orange on white paper, perf 8½, 9, 10½, 10ximperf or imperf, size 20-20.5x32.5mm. Value (orange), $10 perf.

Flags, Liberation Monument A16

Flags, Soldier A17

Peasant and Worker A18

Tractor A19

1950, June 20-1956

Lithographed, Thin Paper

Roul. 12xImperf, Roul. 12 (#28, 29)

26 A16 1w indigo, lt blue & red 3.50 *17.50*
 a. Perf 10¼ ('55) 12.00 *24.50*
27 A16 2w brown orange 9.00 *60.00*
28 A17 2w red, stl bl & blk 5.00 *17.50*
 a. Perf 10¼ ('55) 12.00 *24.00*
29 A18 6w green 6.50 —
30 A19 10w brown 9.50 —

Typographed, Thin Paper, Roul. 12

31 A18 6w red 3.50 *17.50*
 a. Perf 10¼ ('55) 29.00 *24.00*
 b. Thick brownish paper, imperf x roul. 12 29.00 *24.00*

32 A19 10w brown 3.50 —
a. Thick brownish paper, imperf x roul. 12 36.00 *32.50*
Nos. 26-32 (7) 40.50 112.50

Fifth anniversary of liberation from Japan.

Design sizes: No. 30, 20x27.5mm; No. 31, 22x33mm; No. 32, 22x30mm.

Reprints of No. 26 are on medium white paper, distinguishable by numerous design differences, among which are: characters in top inscription are 1½mm high, rather than 1mm, with 3 short lines at either side, rather than 2; top corner ornaments have a dark center, rather than white; 4 ray beams at left of monument, rather than 3; no dots on right face of spire, while originals have 3 small dots; value numerals within well-formed circles.

Reprints of Nos. 28 and 29 are on medium white paper, perf 10¼, 11 or imperf. No. 28 reprints are in light green, No. 29 in rose red, dull blue and black. Value, $10 each.

Reprints of type A19 are 22x31mm in size, on medium white paper and are perf 10¼ or imperf.

Capitol, Seoul — A20

1950, July 10 Litho. *Roul. 12*

33 A20 1w bl grn, red & blue 40.00 *300.00*

Capture of Seoul.

Order of Ri Sun Sin — A21

1951, Apr. 5 Typo. *Imperf*

34 A21 6w orange 15.00 15.00
a. Perf 10¼ 30.00 —

No. 34 also exists perf 9x10½.

No. 34 is on brownish laid paper. Design size: 21.5-22x29.5-30mm.

Reprints are on white paper, perf 10¼ or imperf. Size 21.5x30mm. On the reprints, the center of the lower left point of the star is open; on the originals, it is hatched. Value, $10 each.

For surcharge see No. 43.

Hero Kim Ki Ok — A22

1951, Apr. 17

35 A22 1w blue 19.50 19.50
a. Perf 10¼ *180.00* —

No. 35 was printed on unbleached and off-white wood-pulp laid papers, with wood chips visible. The laid lines are often difficult or impossible to detect.

Design size: 23-23.5x35.5-36mm.

Reprints are on white wove paper, perf 10¼, 10½ or imperf. Size 22.5x33.5mm. Value, $10 each.

Soviet and North Korean Flags A23

Hero Kim Ki U A24

N. Korean, Chinese & Russian Soldiers — A25

1951, Aug. 15-1955 Litho. *Roul. 12*

36	A23	1w dark blue	75.00	*75.00*
37	A23	1w red	200.00	*200.00*
38	A24	1w dark blue	125.00	*125.00*
39	A24	1w red	125.00	*125.00*
40	A25	2w dark blue	50.00	*50.00*
41	A25	2w red	50.00	*50.00*
		Nos. 36-41 (11)	1,720.	*1,720.*

Perf 10¼ Over Roulette (1955)

36a	A23	1w dark blue	55.00	*55.00*
37a	A23	1w red	200.00	*200.00*
38a	A24	1w dark blue	200.00	*200.00*
39a	A24	1w red	125.00	*125.00*
40a	A25	2w dark blue	55.00	*55.00*
41a	A25	2w red	30.00	*30.00*
		Nos. 36a-41a (11)	1,655.	*1,655.*

Nos. 36-41 and 36a-41a exist on both coarse buff and white wove papers. Values are the same. Various perfs and roulettes and roulettes exists; not all combinations are known.

Design sizes: Nos. 36 and 37, 17x23.5mm; Nos. 38 and 39, 16x23mm; Nos. 40 and 41, 23x16.5mm.

Reprints of No. 36 are perf 9, 10½x10 or imperf. Size 15.5-16x22.5mm.

Reprints of No. 38 are perf 9, 10 or imperf. They have no lines of shading between the characters in the top inscription.

Reprints of No. 40 are perf 9, 10 or imperf. Size 22-22.5x16.5mm. The Korean "Won" character at lower right is in 4 parts, rather than 3.

Reprints are all light ultramarine. Value, $10 each.

Nos. 16, 34 Surcharged

On No. 16

On No. 34

1951, Nov. 1 *Imperf*

42 A10 5w on 6w red & blue (#16) 150.00 60.00
43 A21 5w on 6w org (#34) 1,000. 725.00

Order of Soldier's Honor — A26

1951, Nov. 15-1956

44 A26 40w scarlet (16.5x25mm) 22.50 4.50
a. Perf 10¼ ('56) 22.50 7.75
45 A26 40w scarlet (17x24mm) 12.00 4.50
a. Perf 10¼ ('56) 12.00 7.75

Victory Propaganda — A27

1951, Nov. 15-1956

46 A27 10w dark blue 15.00 7.75
47 A27 10w dark blue 15.00 7.75
a. Perf 10¼ ('56) 22.50 22.50

No. 47 also exists perf 8½.

Design sizes: No. 46, 17x25.5mm; No. 47, 16.5-17x25mm.

Reprints are in light blue, perf 10¼, 11 or imperf. Size 16.5-17x25mm. Value and inscription at bottom are outlined and clear against cross-hatched background. Value, $10 each.

Ri Su Dok, Guerilla Hero — A28

1952, Jan. 10-1955

48 A28 70w brown 15.00 3.50
a. Perf 10¼ ('55) 25.00 12.00
b. 70w black brown 120.00
c. As "b," perf 10¼ 60.00

Dove, Flag & Globe — A29

1952, Jan. 20-1957

49 A29 20w scar, dp bl & lt bl 24.00 6.00
a. Perf 10¼ ('55) 24.00 12.00

Peace Propaganda.

No. 49 also exists perf 8½, 11 and rouletted 11½.

No. 49 was printed on off-white or buff paper, with broken lines between stamps. Design size: 22x31-31.5mm.

Reprints are perf 10¼ or imperf, in red, slate blue and pale turquoise blue on white paper. Size 22x31mm. They lack the broken lines between stamps. Value, each $50.

Gen. Pang Ho-san — A30

1952, Apr.

50 A30 10w dull purple 60.00 24.00

Honoring North Korean General Bang Ho San.

No. 50 is also known with locally-applied rough perforation.

Labor Day — A31

1952, Apr. 20-1955 *Imperf*

51 A31 10w rose red 300.00 *300.00*
a. Perf 10¼ ('55) 300.00 *300.00*

Enforcement of the Labor Law, 6th Anniv. — A32

1952, June 1-1955

52 A32 10w light blue 350.00 *350.00*
a. Perf 10¼ ('55) — —

Design size: 18x26mm. Broken lines between stamps.

Reprints are in dull or slate blue, on thick, gummed paper, with no broken lines between stamps. Size 17.5x25.5-26mm. Value, $10 each.

Day of Anti-U.S. Imperialist Struggle — A33

1952, June 4-1956

53 A33 10w rose red 180.00 150.00
a. Perf 10¼ ('56) 180.00 —

Design size: 17.5x25.5-26mm. Broken lines between stamps.

Reprints are in bright rose red, perf 10, 10¼, 11 or imperf. on thick, gummed paper, with no broken lines between stamps. Size 17.5x26mm. Value, $10 each.

North Korean-Chinese Friendship — A34

1952, July 25-1956

54 A34 20w deep blue 50.00 24.00
a. Perf 10¼ ('56) 50.00 —

Design size: 18x21.5mm. Printed on thin white wove paper, with clearly discernible mesh pattern.

Reprints are perf 10¼, 11 or imperf, on thick white wove paper, with no pattern visible. Size 18.5-19x21.5-22mm. Value, $10 each.

Flags & Monument A35

Soldier & Monument A36

1952-55

55 A35 10w carmine 150.00 150.00
a. Perf 10¼ ('55) 200.00 —
56 A36 10w scarlet 275.00 275.00
a. Perf 10¼ ('55) 350.00 350.00

Seventh Anniversary of Liberation from Japan.

Issue dates: No. 55, 7/25/52; No. 56, 8/1/52.

Design sizes: No. 55, 20.5-21x27.5-28mm; No. 56, 29.5-30x18.5mm.

Reprints of No. 55 are in vermilion, on thick paper, perf 10½, 11 or imperf. Size 20.5x27-27.5mm. Value, $10 each.

Reprints of No. 56 are in rose red, perf 10, 10¼, 11 or imperf. Size 30.5-31x18.5-19mm. Value, $10 each.

Note: Original are typographed; reprints are lithographed on thin white paper.

International Youth Day — A37

1952, Oct. 20-1955

57 A37 10w deep green 72.50 80.00
a. Perf 10¼ ('55) 72.50 —

No. 57 is on thick paper, with very thin gum. Design size: 20.5-21x28mm.

Reprints are on thin to medium paper, without gum, perf 10¼, 11 or imperf. Size 20x27mm. Value, $10 each.

Soldiers in Battle A38

Soldier and Flag A39

1953, Jan. 20-1955

58 A38 10w rose carmine 130.00 130.00
a. Perf 10¼ ('55) 130.00 —
59 A39 40w red brown 60.00 60.00
a. Perf 10¼ ('55) 75.00 —

Fifth Anniversary of the Founding of the Korean People's Army.

Design sizes: No. 58, 21.5-22x26-26.5mm; No. 59, 21.5x27mm.

Reprints of No. 58 are on thick, gummed paper, perf 10¼, 11 or imperf. Size: 21.5-22x26.5mm. Value, $10 each.

Reprints of No. 59 are on thick, gummed paper, perf 10, 10½, 11 or imperf. Size: 21.5x26.5mm. Value, $10 each.

Woman with Flag A40

Women and Globe A41

1953, Mar. 1-1955

60 A40 10w carmine 60.00 60.00
a. Perf 10¼ ('55) 60.00 —
61 A41 40w yellow green 72.50 72.50
a. Perf 10¼ ('55) 72.50 —

International Women's Day.

Design sizes: No. 60, 20x29.5mm; No. 61, 21x29mm.

Reprints of No. 60 are in rose carmine, on thin paper, perf 10¼, 11 or imperf. Size 20.5x30mm.

Reprints of No. 61 may be distinguished from the originals by design differences: the dove's wing consists of many small feathers (3 large feathers on original), the women's mouths are all open (closed on original), and 3 thin connected lines on center woman's shirt (3 thick separate lines on original). Value, $10 each.

Worker
A42

Workers
Marching
A43

1953, Apr. 15-1955

62 A42 10w yellow green 60.00 60.00
a. Perf 10¼ ('55) 72.50 —
63 A43 40w orange brown 60.00 60.00
a. Perf 10¼ ('55) 72.50 —

May Day

Reprints of No. 62 are in green or emerald green, perf 9½x8½, 10¼, 11 or imperf. Among many design differences, they have 4 horizontal lines between flag and frame line at upper left, many short hatching lines between frame line and top inscription, many horizontal lines between flag and flag pole at upper right, and won letter clear. On originals, there are one or no lines at upper left, no lines between frame line and top inscription, no lines between flag and flag pole, and the won character is not clearly defined. Value, $10 each.

Reprints of No. 63 are perf 10, 10¼ or imperf. On the reprints, the right flag pole touches the frame line, and the left center element of the won character resembles a "T." On the originals, the right flag pole does not touch the frame line, and the center element of the won character resembles an inverted "L." Value, $10 each.

Soldier
A44

Battle
A45

1953, June 1-1955

64 A44 10w greenish blue 110.00 110.00
a. Perf 10¼ ('55) 110.00 —
65 A45 40w scarlet 110.00 130.00
a. Perf 10¼ ('55) 110.00 —

Day of Anti-U.S. Imperialist Struggle.

Nos. 64 and 65 were issued with gum. Design sizes: 10w, 24x33mm; 40w, 24-24.5x33mm.

Reprints of No. 64 and 65 are on thick paper, perf 10¼, 11 or imperf. Design sizes: 10w, 23.5-24x32mm; 40w, 24x32-32.5mm. No. 64 is in turquoise blue, No. 65 in vermilion or orange vermilion. Value, $10 each.

4th World Festival of
Youth & Students
A46 A47

1953, June 10-1955 With Gum

66 A46 10w dp dl bl & pale turq bl 72.50 72.50
a. Perf 10¼ ('55) 85.00 —
67 A47 20w gray grn &pink 60.00 36.00
a. Perf 10¼ ('55) 72.50 —

Two types of reprints of No. 66 exist. On the reprints, the forelocks of the center and right heads have detailed hairlines, and the right head shows eye and eyebrow. On the originals, both features are solid. Value, $10 each.

Victory Issue — A48

1953, June 1-1955 With Gum

68 A48 10w brn & yel 360.00 400.00
a. Perf 10¼ ('55) 325.00 500.00

8th Anniversary of
Liberation from
Japan — A49

1953, Aug. 5-1955

69 A49 10w red orange *4,000.* *4,000.*

Design size: 25x35.5mm.

Reprints are perf 10¼ or imperf. Size: 24.5-25x34.5-35mm. Left side of monument is shaded, and windows are fully drawn and shaded. On the originals, the monument is unshaded, and the windows are only partially drawn and half shaded. Value, $10 each.

5th Anniv. Founding of
D.P.R.K. — A50

1953, Aug. 25-1955

70 A50 10w dp blue & red 72.50 72.50
a. Perf 10¼ ('55) 95.00 —

Design size: 21.5-22x29.5-30mm. Inscribed "1948-1953."

Reprints are in blue and vermilion, perf 9x9½ or imperf and are inscribed "1948-1955." Size: 22.5x30mm. Value, each $100.

Liberation
Monument — A51

1953, Dec. 25-1955 With Gum

71 A51 10w deep slate 72.50 47.50
a. Perf 10¼ ('55) 72.50 —

Design size: 20x31mm.

Reprints are in deep gray. Size: 19-19.5x30.5-31mm. Value, $10 each.

Worker & Crane — A52

1954, Jan. 25-1955 With Gum

72 A52 10w light blue 85.00 55.00
a. Perf 10¼ ('55) 110.00 —

Reconstruction and Economic Development.

Design size: 22x31.5mm.

Reprints are in greenish blue or dull blue, without gum. Size: 21.5x31mm. The horizontal lines defining the sky and clouds are clear and even, and the details of the crane are distinct. Value, $10 each.

Korean People's Army,
6th Anniv. — A53

1954, Jan. 25-1955 With Gum

73 A53 10w dp car red 350.00 —
a. Perf 10¼ ('55) 350.00 —
b. Rouletted 350.00

Design size: 23.5-24x38mm.

Reprints are in vermilion or orange vermilion. Size: 23-23.5x37.5-38mm. The design is much clearer than in the originals, with thin distinct characters in top inscription and complete unbroken frame line at right. Value, $10 each.

International Women's
Day — A54

1954, Feb. 25-1955 With Gum

74 A54 10w carmine 250.00 250.00
a. Perf 10¼ ('55) 300.00 —

Design size: 19.5-20x29-29.5mm.

Reprints are in vermilion. Size: 20-20.5x29.5-30mm. The USSR and PRC flags at top right are legible, and the shading under the center and right women's chins is represented by several fine lines (solid on originals). Value, $10 each.

Labor Day — A55

1954, Apr. 15-1955 With Gum

75 A55 10w vermilion 72.50 72.50
a. Perf 10¼ ('55) 72.50 —

Design size: 20x27-27.5mm.

Reprints are in orange vermilion, perf 8½x9, 9, 10¼ or imperf. Size: 19-19.5x26-26.5. Value, $10 each.

No. 16 overprinted "Fee Collected" in Korean 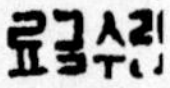

1954, May (?)

76 A10 6w red & blue 1,750. 1,750.

Day of Anti-U.S.
Imperialist
Struggle — A56

1954, June 10-1955 With Gum

77 A56 10w red brown 210.00 *210.00*
a. Perf 10¼ ('55) 210.00 *210.00*

National Congress of
Young Activists — A57

1954, July 20-1955 With Gum

78 A57 10w blue, red & slate 600.00 300.00
a. Perf 10¼ ('55) — —

Design size: 20x30mm.

Reprints are in blue, scarlet vermilion & deep slate. Size: 19.5-20x29-29.5mm. On the originals, the worker's hand is beneath the tassel of the flag and is less than 1mm from the frame line. On the reprints, hand is to the right of the tassel and 2mm from frame line. Value, $10 each.

Liberation from Japan,
9th Anniv. — A58

1954, Aug. 1-1955 With Gum

79 A58 10w chestnut 50.00 50.00
a. Perf 10¼ ('55) 50.00 —

Design size: 20-20.5x30mm.

Reprints of No. 79 are perf 10¼, 11 or imperf. Size: 20x29-29.5mm. Soldier's nose line straight and strong, 3 lines of cooling holes in gun barrel (2 on originals). Value, $10 each.

North Korean
Flag — A59

1954, Aug. 25-1955 With Gum

80 A59 10w blue & dp red 100.00 *100.00*
a. Perf 10¼ ('55) 120.00 —

Design size: 24x31.5-32mm.

Reprints are in dull blue and bright rose red. Size: 25-25.5x30.5-31mm. Value, $10 each.

Taedong Gate,
Pyongyang — A60

1954, Sept. 1-1956 With Gum

81 A60 5w reddish brown 15.00 3.75
a. Perf 10¼ ('56) 22.50 —
82 A60 5w lilac brown 15.00 3.75
a. Perf 10¼ ('56) 22.50 —

Hwanghae Iron
Works — A61

Hwanghae Iron
Works & Workers —
A61a

No. 84, Hwanghae Iron Works & workers, horiz.

1954, Nov. 1-1956

83 A61 10w light blue 22.50 3.00
a. Perf 10¼ ('55) 45.00 —
84 A61a 10w chocolate 22.50 3.00
a. Perf 10¼ ('55) 45.00 —
b. Roul. 9x8½ ('56) 50.00 50.00

Korean People's Army,
7th Anniversary — A62

1955, Jan. 25 With Gum

85 A62 10w rose red 36.00 36.00
a. Perf 10¼ 36.00 —

International Women's
Day — A63

1955, Feb. 25 With Gum

86 A63 10w deep blue 36.00 36.00
a. Perf 10¼ 45.00 —

Reprints are in blue, perf 10¼, imperf and imperf x 10¼. Corners of design are clearly and uniformly indented. Value, $10 each.

A63a

A63b

Labor Day

1955, Apr. 16 With Gum

86A A63a 10w green 60.00 30.00
a. Perf 10¼ — —
86B A63b 10w violet brown 60.00 30.00
a. Perf 10¼ 60.00 —

Design sizes: No. 86A, 19.5-20x30mm. No. 86B, 19x30mm.

Reprints of No. 86A measure 19.5x29mm. Reprints of 86B measure 19x29.5mm and are without gum. Value, $10 each.

Admiral Ri Sun-Sin — A64

1955, May 14-1956

87 A64 1w blue, *pale green* 15.00 15.00
 a. Perf 10¼ ('56) 18.00 —
88 A64 2w rose, *buff* 15.00 1.50
 a. Perf 10¼ ('56) 22.00 —
89 A64 2w rose red ('56) 30.00 2.75
 a. Perf 10¼ ('56) 30.00 —
 Nos. 87-89 (3) 60.00 19.25

No. 89 is redrawn, with a larger "2."

Design sizes: Nos. 87, 88, 20x29-30mm.

Reprints of No. 87 are in dull blue, on pale apple green, perf 10¼, 11½x10½, imperf, or roul. 8½. Size 19x28-28.5mm. Reprints of No. 88 are 19-19.5x28.-28.5mm in size. Value, $10 each.

Labor Law, 9th Anniv. — A65

1955, May 30

90 A65 10w rose 90.00 90.00
 a. Perf 10¼ — —

No. 90 was issued with a very thin yellow gum. Design size: 18.5-19x27.5-28mm.

Reprints exist perf 10¼, 11 or imperf. Size 18-18.5x27-27.5mm. Value unused, $10 each.

Korea-U.S.S.R. Friendship Month
A66 A67

1955, July ***Perf. 10***

91 A66 10w rose red 30.00 —
 a. Imperf 30.00 21.00
92 A66 10w org red & vio blue 30.00 —
 a. Imperf 30.00 21.00
93 A67 20w red & lt blue 30.00 —
 a. Imperf 30.00 24.00
 b. Inscription below flag in two colors — —
 c. As "b," imperf — —
94 A67 20w ver & lt blue 24.00 —
 a. Imperf 24.00 21.00
 Nos. 91-94 (4) 114.00

Issue dates: Nos. 91, 93, 7/16; Nos. 92, 94, 7/20.

Design sizes: No. 91, 22x32.5mm; No. 92, 29.5x43mm; No. 93, 18.5x32mm; No. 94, 24.5-25x42.5x43mm.

Reprints of No. 94 are in light vermilion and light blue, perf 10¼, 11 or imperf, with a very thin gum. Size: 24-24.5x42-43mm. The two blue bands of the flag are solidly colored, with many white spots. On the originals, this area consists of fine lines with few or no white areas. Value, $10 each.

Liberation from Japan, 10th Anniv. — A68

1955, July 20 ***Perf. 10¼***

95 A68 10w dull green 24.00 —
 a. Imperf 24.00 18.00
96 A68 10w ver, dull blue & chestnut 24.00 —
 a. Imperf 24.00 18.00

Design sizes: No. 95, 21.5-22x31.5-32mm; No. 96, 29-29.5-42-43mm.

Reprints of No. 95 are in dull blue green, perf 10¼, 11 or imperf, on gummed paper. Size: 21-21.5x31mm. Reprints of No. 96 are in rose red, dull to greenish blue and yellow brown, perf 10¼ or imperf. Size: 28-28.5x42.5-43mm. Value, $10 each.

Standing Rock in Sea-Kumgang Maritime Park — A69

1956, Jan. 20

97 A69 10w blue, *bluish* 20.00 —
 a. Imperf 25.00 25.00

People's Army, 8th Anniv. — A70

1956, Jan. 20

98 A70 10w lt brn, *pale yel grn* 100.00 *100.00*
 a. Imperf *90.00* *90.00*

Design size: 20x27-27.5mm.

Reprints are in chestnut on pale sage green paper, perf 10¼, 11 or imperf. Size: 19.5-20x27mm. Creases in the soldier's shirt are distinct, and nose and eyes are strongly shaded. Value, $10 each.

May Day — A71

1956, Apr. 29

99 A71 10w blue *100.00* *100.00*
 a. Imperf *100.00* *100.00*

Design size: 23.5-24x35-35.5mm.

Reprints are perf 10¼, 11 or imperf, on gummed paper. Size: 23.5x35mm. Clear hatching lines at right of top inscription; many feathers in dove's wing. Value, $10 each.

Ryongwang Pavilion and Taedong Gate, Pyongyang — A72

1956, May 8

100 A72 2w light blue *55.00* *55.00*
 a. Imperf *55.00* *55.00*
 b. Rouletted 85.00 —

Reprints of No. 100 are on thicker, gummed paper. The tail of the central left element in the "won" inscription at lower right extends beyond the left edge of the L-shaped character beneath it. Value, $6.

Moranbong Theater, Pyongyang — A73

1956, May 8

101 A73 40w light green 30.00 12.00
 a. Imperf 85.00 72.50

Labor Law, 10th Anniv. — A74

1956, June 7

102 A74 10w dark brown 8.00 2.50
 a. Perf 9 *80.00* *60.00*
 b. Imperf 180.00 120.00

Korean Children's Union, 10th Anniv. — A75

1956, June 7

103 A75 10w dk brown 15.00 6.50
 a. Imperf *160.00* *35.00*

Law on Equality of the Sexes, 10th Anniv. — A76

1956, July 10

104 A76 10w dark brown 10.00 3.75
 a. Perf 9 *25.00* *15.00*
 b. Imperf 35.00 17.50

Nationalization of Major Industries, 10th Anniv. — A77

1956, July 10

105 A77 10w dark brown 90.00 —
 a. Imperf *210.00* —

Liberation from Japan, 11th Anniv. — A78

1956, July 24

106 A78 10w rose red 14.00 3.25
 a. Imperf *160.00* *30.00*

Machinist — A79

1956, July 28

107 A79 1w dark brown 3.75 2.00
 a. Perf 9 *12.50* *8.00*
 b. Imperf 32.50 14.00

Kim Il Sung University, 10th Anniv. — A80

1956, Sept. 30

108 A80 10w dark brown 10.00 9.00
 a. Imperf *32.50* *14.00*

4th Congress, Korean Democratic Youth League — A81

1956, Nov. 3

109 A81 10w dark brown 14.00 3.25
 a. Imperf 32.50 18.00

Model Peasant — A82

1956, Nov. 14

110 A82 10w rose 7.50 2.25
 a. Imperf 21.00 11.00
 b. Rouletted — —

220th Anniv. Birth of Pak Ji Won (1737-1805) — A83

1957, Mar. 4

111 A83 10w blue 5.00 1.25
 a. Imperf 19.00 10.00

Tabo Pagoda in Pulguk Temple
A84

Ulmil Pavilion, Pyongyang
A85

1957, Mar. 20

112 A84 5w light blue 6.00 2.50
 a. Rouletted — —
 b. Perf 11 (with gum) — —
 c. Imperf 87.50 21.00
113 A85 40w gray green 7.50 3.25
 a. Perf 11 — —
 b. Imperf 22.50 11.00

No. 113b was issued both with and without gum.

Productivity Campaign — A86

1957, July 4 **With or Without Gum**

114 A86 10w ultramarine 6.75 4.50
 a. Perf 11 — —
 b. Imperf 32.50 15.00

Steelworker
A87

Voters Marching
A88

1957, Aug.

115 A87 1w orange 3.50 .75
 a. Imperf 9.50 4.25
116 A87 2w brown 3.50 .75
 a. Imperf 9.50 4.25
117 A88 10w vermilion 17.50 3.25
 a. Imperf 65.00 35.00
 Nos. 115-117 (3) 24.50 4.75

Second General Election.

There are two types of the 1w. On type 1, the won character is approx. 2½mm in diameter and is distinct. On type 2, the character is approx. 1½mm in diameter and is virtually illegible.

Issued: 10w, 8/10; 1w, 2w, 8/13.

Founding of Pyongyang, 1530th Anniv. — A89

1957, Sept. 28 ***Perf. 10***

118 A89 10w blue green 3.00 .65
 a. Imperf 30.00 9.00

Lenin
A90

Lenin & Flags
A91

Kim Il Sung at Pochonbo
A92

Pouring Steel
A93

1957

119 A90 10w gray blue 2.00 .95
a. Imperf 30.00 9.00
120 A91 10w blue green 2.00 .95
a. Imperf 30.00 9.00
b. Rouletted 13 — —
121 A92 10w red 2.00 .95
a. Imperf 30.00 9.00
b. Rouletted 13 — —
122 A93 10w red orange 4.50 .95
a. Imperf 120.00 13.00
b. Rouletted 13 — —
Nos. 119-122 (4) 10.50 3.80

40th Anniversary of the Russian October Revolution.

Issued: Nos. 119, 120, 9/30; No. 121, 10/3; 122, 10/16.

No. 120 exists with gum.

4th Congress World Federation of Trade Unions — A94

1957, Oct. 3

123 A94 10w ultra & lt grn 2.50 1.10
a. Imperf 30.00 11.00

No. 123a exists with or without gum.

Russian Friendship Month — A95

1957, Oct. 16

124 A95 10w green 4.50 1.10
a. Imperf *210.00 140.00*

Doctor Weighing Baby — A96

Bandaging Hand — A97

1957, Nov. 1

125 A96 1w red 9.00 1.25
a. Imperf 65.00 12.00
126 A96 2w red 9.00 1.25
a. Imperf 65.00 12.00
b. Rouletted — —
127 A97 10w red 35.00 3.75
a. Imperf 130.00 35.00
Nos. 125-127 (3) 53.00 6.25

Red Cross.

No. 126 exists without or without gum. No. 126a was issued with gum.

Flying Dragon Kettle
A98

Flying Dragon Incense Burner
A99

1958, Jan. 14

128 A98 10w blue 11.00 1.40
a. Imperf 87.50 18.00
129 A99 10w gray green 11.00 1.40
a. Imperf 87.50 18.00

Nos. 128a and 129a exist with or without gum.

Woljong Temple Pagoda — A100

1958, Feb. 21 ***Perf. 10***

130 A100 5w lt green 1.75 .65
a. Imperf 24.50 11.50
b. Rouletted — —

Perf. 10½

131 A100 10w lt blue 5.00 2.25
a. Imperf 30.00 16.00
b. Rouletted — —

No. 130 was issued with gum.

Soldier
A101

Soldier, Flag & Hwanghae Iron Works
A102

1958, Feb. **Photo** ***Perf. 10***

132 A101 10w blue 7.25 1.00
a. Imperf 52.50 19.00
b. Rouletted — —
c. Perf 11 — —

Litho

133 A102 10w rose 10.00 1.10
a. Imperf 52.50 19.00

10th Anniversary of the Korean People's Army.

No. 133 was issued with or without gum.

Rocket Launch, Sputnik
A103

Sputnik in Orbit
A104

Designs: 40w, Sputnik over observatory.

1958, Mar. 26 **Photo.**

134 A103 10w dull blue green 7.75 4.50
a. Imperf 65.00 19.00
135 A104 20w dull blue green 7.75 4.50
a. Imperf 65.00 19.00
b. Rouletted — —
136 A104 40w dull blue green 7.75 4.50
a. Imperf 65.00 19.00
137 A103 70w dull blue green 9.00 8.00
a. Imperf 100.00 30.00
Nos. 134-137 (4) 32.25 21.50

International Geophysical Year.

Nos. 134-137 exist with or without gum.

Young Socialist Constructors Congress — A105

1958, May 12 **Litho.**

138 A105 10w blue 4.00 1.10
a. Imperf 27.00 10.00

Opening of Hwanghae Iron Works — A106

1958, May 22

139 A106 10w lt blue 8.50 1.25
a. Imperf 37.50 12.50

Commemorative Badge — A107

1958, May 27

140 A107 10w multicolored 6.25 1.35
a. Imperf 25.00 6.00
b. Perf 11 — —
c. Rouletted — —

Departure of Chinese People's Volunteers. See No. 150.

4th International Democratic Women's Congress — A108

1958, June 5

141 A108 10w blue 2.50 .95
a. Imperf 40.00 11.00

Congress Emblem — A109

1958, July 4

142 A109 10w grn & red brn 3.50 2.40
a. Imperf 27.50 6.25
b. Perf 11 11.00 —

First Congress of the Young Workers of the World Federation of Trade Unions.

Apartment House, East Pyongyang — A110

1958, July 24

143 A110 10w lt blue 5.00 1.25
a. Imperf 25.00 8.75
b. Perf 11 — —

Workers' Apartment House, Pyongyang — A111

1958, Aug. 21

144 A111 10w blue green 5.00 1.25
a. Imperf 25.00 8.75

Hungnam Fertilizer Plant — A112

Pyongyang Railway Station — A113

DPRK Arms
A114

Weaver
A115

Dam, Pyongyang — A116

1958 **Litho**

145 A112 10w blue green 6.00 .95
a. Imperf *145.00 18.00*
b. Perf 11 — —
146 A113 10w dp blue green *22.00* 3.50
a. Imperf *165.00 42.50*
b. Perf 11 — —
147 A114 10w red brn & yel grn 4.50 1.00
a. Imperf *350.00 120.00*

Photo

148 A115 10w sepia 17.50 3.75
a. Imperf *225.00 62.50*
149 A116 10w sepia 29.00 12.00
a. Imperf *165.00 35.00*
Nos. 145-149 (5) 79.00 21.20

10th Anniversary Korean People's Republic.

Issued: Nos. 145, 146, 8/21; No. 147, 9/7; Nos. 148, 149, 9/10.

Soldier and Troop Train — A117

1958, Sept. 10 **Photo.** ***Perf. 10***

150 A117 10w sepia 45.00 11.50
a. Imperf *360.00 77.50*

Departure of Chinese People's Volunteers.

Transplanting Rice Seedlings — A118

1958, Sept. 10 **Litho.**
With or Without Gum

151 A118 10w sepia 2.00 .65
a. Imperf 15.00 6.75

Winged Horse of Chollima — A119

1958, Sept. 16

152 A119 10w brick red 3.50 .65
a. Imperf 29.00 4.00

National Congress of the Innovators in Production.

North Korea-China Friendship Month — A120

1958, Oct. 8 **With or Without Gum**

153 A120 10w multicolored 2.25 .60
a. Imperf 17.50 4.25
b. Rouletted — —

National Congress of Agricultural Cooperatives
A121

1959, Jan. 5 **With or Without Gum**

154 A121 10w dk grnish blue 3.25 .80
a. Imperf 17.50 4.00

Gen. Ulchi Mundok — A122

1959, Feb. 11 **With Gum**

155 A122 10w lilac brn & yel 8.00 1.60
a. Imperf *30.00 14.00*

See Nos. 157-159 and 209-212.

National Women's Workers Congress — A123

1959, Mar. 29
With or Without Gum

156 A123 10ch brown & red 4.25 1.45
a. Imperf *57.50* —

Jeon Bong-jun A124

Kang Kam Chan A125

Ulchi Mundok — A126

1959, Apr. 1

157 A124 2ch blue, *lt green* 2.25 .40
a. Imperf *100.00* —
158 A125 5ch lilac brn, *buff* 2.50 .45
a. Imperf *100.00* —
159 A126 10ch red brn, *cream* 5.00 .60
a. Imperf *100.00* —
Nos. 157-159 (3) 9.75 1.45

Nos. 157-159 were issued with gum. Nos. 157a-159a were issued with or without gum.

Soviet Luna 1 Moon Rocket Launch — A127

1959, May 4 ***Perf. 10, 10½***

160 A127 2ch dk vio, *pale buff* 15.00 8.00
a. Imperf 260.00 57.50
161 A127 10ch bl, *pale grn* 30.00 11.50
a. Imperf 260.00 57.50

Issued with gum (perf 10) or without gum (perf 10½). Nos. 160a and 161a were issued with gum.

Land Irrigation Program — A128

1959, May 27 ***Perf. 10***

162 A128 10ch multicolored 11.00 3.25
a. Imperf 40.00 11.00

Slogan-inscribed Tree, Chongbong Bivouac — A129

Statue of Kim Il Sung — A130

Mt. Paektu — A131

1959, June 4 ***10, 10¾ (#164)***

163 A129 5ch multicolored 3.50 1.30
a. Imperf *95.00* 17.50
b. Perf 10¾ — —
c. Rouletted — —
164 A130 10ch blue & grnsh bl 3.50 1.30
a. Imperf *70.00* 17.50
165 A131 10ch violet blue 5.50 —
a. Imperf *70.00* —
Nos. 163-165 (3) 12.50 2.60

22nd Anniversary of the Battle of Pochondo. No. 164 was issued with gum.

Chollima Tractor — A132

Jongihwa-58 Electric Locomotive A133

Red Star-58 Bulldozer A134

Chollima Excavator A135

SU-50 Universal Lathe — A136

Sungri-58 Truck — A137

With or Without gum

1959, June 12 ***Perf. 10¾***

166 A132 1ch multicolored 1.50 .50
a. Imperf *72.50* 33.00
b. Rouletted — —
167 A133 2ch multicolored 11.00 3.50
a. Imperf *145.00* 62.50
b. Rouletted — —
168 A134 2ch multicolored 2.50 .70
a. Imperf *97.50* 18.00
b. Rouletted — —
169 A135 5ch multicolored 2.50 1.25
a. Imperf *230.00* —
b. Rouletted — —
170 A136 10ch multicolored 2.50 .95
a. Imperf *230.00* —
b. Rouletted — —
171 A137 10ch multicolored 4.50 .70
a. Imperf *230.00* —
Nos. 166-171 (6) 24.50 7.60

Machine-building Industry.

Armistice Building, Panmunjom A138

Anti-U.S. Protester A139

Anti-South Korean Emigration Campaign A140

Peaceful Reunification of Korea A141

1959, June 25 **With Gum**

172 A138 10ch dk blue & blue 3.50 .25
a. Imperf *175.00* —
b. Perf 10¼ — —
173 A139 20ch dk blue & lt blue 1.35 .45
174 A140 20ch sepia & brn 9.00 2.50
175 A141 70ch dk brn & lt brn 40.00 11.00
a. Imperf *125.00* —
b. Perf 10¼xRoul — —
Nos. 172-175 (4) 53.85 14.20

Day of Struggle for the withdrawal of U.S. troops from South Korea.

Metal Type — A142

Samil Wolgan Monthly Breaking Chains — A143

Flag with Symbols of Peace and Literature A144

Korean Alphabet of 1443 — A145

1959, Aug. 1

176 A142 5ch sepia 25.00 9.50
177 A143 5ch green & red 7.50 3.00
178 A144 10ch bright blue 7.50 3.00
179 A145 10ch dp bl & pale bl 11.00 4.75
a. Souvenir sheet of 4, #176-179 imperf 105.00 52.50
Nos. 176-179 (4) 51.00 20.25

International Book and Fine Arts Exhibition, Leipzig.

Nos. 176 and 178 were issued with gum. Nos. 177, 179 and 179a were issued without gum.

Milk Cow Farm — A146

Pig Farm — A147

1959, Sept. 20

180 A146 2ch multicolored 4.00 1.00
181 A147 5ch multicolored 5.75 1.30

No. 180 was issued without gum, No. 181 with gum.

Economic Development

Cement Making — A148

Hydroelectrical Dam — A149

Salt Making — A150

Construction — A151

Grain — A152

Sugar — A153

Steel-Making A154

Fishing — A155

Iron-Making — A156

Coal Mining — A157

Textile Production — A158

Fruit — A159

Perf. 10½ (#182), 11

1959, Sept. 20-1960

182 A148 1ch multicolored .70 .55
a. Imperf *175.00* —
183 A149 2ch multicolored 1.90 .55
a. Imperf *175.00* —
184 A150 5ch multicolored 3.00 .70
a. Imperf *175.00* —
185 A151 10ch multicolored 3.25 1.00
a. Imperf *175.00* —
186 A152 10ch multicolored 1.50 .60
a. Imperf *175.00* —
187 A153 10ch multicolored 2.75 .55
a. Imperf *175.00* —
188 A154 10ch multicolored 2.50 .60
a. Imperf *175.00* —
189 A155 10ch multicolored 2.25 .60
a. Imperf *175.00* —

190 A156 10ch multicolored			1.50	.60
191 A157 10ch multicolored			2.50	.60
192 A158 10ch multicolored			1.50	.60
a. Imperf			*175.00*	—
193 A159 10ch multicolored ('60)			3.75	.55
Nos. 182-193 (12)			27.10	7.50

No. 193 issued August 1960.

Nos. 183 and 185 were issued with gum, the other values without gum.

Musk Deer — A160

Sable — A161

Marten — A162

Otter — A163

Sika Deer — A164

Pheasant — A165

1959-62 ***Perf. 11***

194 A160 5ch multicolored	6.00	.70
195 A161 5ch multicolored	6.00	.70
196 A162 5ch multicolored	6.00	.70
197 A163 5ch multicolored	6.00	.70
198 A164 10ch multicolored	6.00	.70
199 A165 10ch multicolored	27.50	2.25
Nos. 194-199 (6)	57.50	5.75

Game Preservation.

Issued: No. 198, 10/24/59; No. 199, 3/25/60; No. 194, 11/11/60; Nos. 195-197, 1/24/62.

Nos. 198 and 199 were issued with gum, Nos. 194-197 without gum.

3rd Korean Trade Unions Congress — A166

1959, Nov. 4 **With Gum**

200 A166 5ch multicolored	1.30	.30

Electric Locomotive A167

Freighter — A168

1959, Nov. 5 **With Gum**

201 A167 5ch brnsh purple	20.00	3.00
202 A168 10ch slate green	8.25	2.50

Korean People's Army, 12th Anniv. — A169

1960, Feb. 8 **With Gum**

203 A169 5ch blue	250.00	140.00

Sword Dance A170

Janggo Dance A171

Peasant Dance — A172

1960, Feb. 25

204 A170 5ch multicolored	4.50	.40
205 A171 5ch multicolored	4.50	.40
206 A172 10ch multicolored	4.50	.40
Nos. 204-206 (3)	13.50	1.20

Women of 3 Races, Dove A173

Woman Worker A174

1960, Mar. 8 **With Gum**

207 A173 5ch grnish blue & red vio	3.00	.25
208 A174 10ch grn & org	3.00	.50

50th Anniv. of International Women's Day.

Kim Jong Ho, Geographer A175

Kim Hong Do, Painter A176

Pak Yon, Musician A177

Jong Ta San, Scholar A178

1960 **With Gum**

209 A175 1ch gray & pale grn	2.75	.25
210 A176 2ch dp blue & yel buff	3.25	.25
211 A177 5ch grnish blue & grnish yel	12.00	.25
212 A178 10ch brn & yel	3.25	.25
Nos. 209-212 (4)	21.25	1.00

Issued: 1ch-5ch, 3/16/60; 10ch 6/60.

Grapes — A179

Wild fruits: No. 214, Fruit of Actinidia arguta planch. No. 215, Pine-cone. No. 216, Hawthorn berries. No. 217, Chestnuts.

1960, Apr. 8 **With Gum**

213 A179 5ch multicolored	2.75	.90
214 A179 5ch multicolored	2.75	.90
215 A179 5ch multicolored	2.75	.90
216 A179 10ch multicolored	3.00	1.10
217 A179 10ch multicolored	3.00	1.10
Nos. 213-217 (5)	14.25	4.90

Nos. 214-215 also exist imperf.

Lenin, 90th Birthday — A180

1960, Apr. 22 **With Gum**

218 A180 10ch violet brown	1.60	.25

Koreans and Caricature of U.S. Soldier — A181

1960, June 20 **With Gum**

219 A181 10ch dark blue	7.00	.65

Day of Struggle for Withdrawal of U.S. Troops from South Korea.

Mao Tse-Tung Plaza A182

Taedong River Promenade A183

Youth Street — A184

People's Army Street — A185

Stalin Street — A186

1960, June 29 **With Gum**

220 A182 10ch gray green	1.50	.35
221 A183 20ch dk bl green	2.75	.40
222 A184 40ch blackish green	4.00	.75
223 A185 70ch emerald	7.25	1.75
224 A186 1w blue	10.00	3.00
Nos. 220-224 (5)	25.50	6.25

Views of rebuilt Pyongyang.

Luna 3 — A187

Luna 2 — A188

1960, July 15

225 A187 5ch multicolored	8.00	7.50
226 A188 10ch multicolored	11.50	3.25

Soviet space flights.

The 5ch was issued with gum, the 10ch without gum.

Mirror Rock — A189

Devil-faced Rock — A190

Dancing Dragon Bridge — A191

Nine Dragon Falls — A192

Mt. Diamond on the Sea — A193

1960, July 15-1961

227 A189 5ch multicolored	1.75	.25
228 A190 5ch multicolored	1.75	.30
229 A191 10ch multi ('61)	6.25	.30
230 A192 10ch multicolored	5.50	.35
231 A193 10ch multicolored	2.00	.25
Nos. 227-231 (5)	17.25	1.45

Diamond Mountains scenery.
No. 229 issued 2/8/61.
See Nos. 761-764.

Lily A194

Rhododendron A195

Hibiscus A196

Blue Campanula A197

Mauve Campanula — A198

1960, July 15-1961 **With Gum**

232	A194	5ch multicolored		1.75	.25
233	A195	5ch multicolored		1.75	.25
234	A196	10ch multicolored		2.50	.45
235	A197	10ch multicolored		2.50	.45
236	A198	10ch multi ('61)		2.50	.45
		Nos. 232-236 (5)		11.00	1.85

No. 236 issued 6/1/61.

Nos. 232-234 and 236 also exist without gum.

"The Arduous March" — A199

Crossing the Amnok River — A200

Young Communist League Meeting — A201

Showing the Way at Pochonbo A202

Return to Pyongyang A203

1960, July 26

237	A199	5ch carmine red	.65	.25
238	A200	10ch deep blue	1.50	.25
239	A201	10ch deep blue	1.50	.25
240	A202	10ch carmine red	1.50	.25
241	A203	10ch carmine red	1.50	.25
		Nos. 237-242 (5)	6.65	1.25

Revolutionary activities of Kim Il Sung.

15th Anniv. Liberation from Japan — A204

1960, Aug. 6

242 A204 10ch multicolored 6.00 .25

North Korean-Soviet Friendship Month — A205

1960, Aug. 6

243 A205 10ch lake, *cream* *19.00* 4.00

Okryu Bridge — A206

Grand Theater — A207

Okryu Restaurant A208

1960, Aug. 11

244	A206	10ch gray blue	4.00	.35
245	A207	10ch dull violet	3.50	.25
246	A208	10ch turquoise	1.50	.25
		Nos. 244-246 (3)	9.00	.85

Pyongyang buildings.

Tokro River Dam — A209

1960, Sept. 9 **With Gum**

247 A209 5ch slate blue 2.75 .25

Inauguration of Tokro River Hydroelectric Power Station.

World Federation of Trade Unions, 15th Anniv. — A210

1960, Sept. 16

248 A210 10ch blue & lt blue 2.10 .25

Repatriation of Korean Nationals from Japan — A211

1960, Sept. 26

249 A211 10ch brnish violet 6.50 .30

Korean-Soviet Friendship — A212

1960, Oct. 5 **With Gum**

250 A212 10ch brn & org 1.90 .25

Liberation Day Sports Festival, Pyongyang — A213

Designs: 5ch (No. 251), Runner. 5ch (No. 252), Weight-lifter. 5ch (No. 253), Cyclist. 5ch (No. 254), Gymnast. 5ch (No. 255), Soccer players, horiz. 10ch (No. 256), Swimmer, horiz. 10ch (No. 257), Moranbong Stadium, horiz.

1960, Oct. 5

251-257 A213 Set of 7 13.50 2.50

Chinese & North Korean Soldiers A214

Friendship Monument A215

1960, Oct. 20 **With Gum**

258	A214	5ch rose	1.60	.25
259	A215	10ch dp blue	1.60	.25

10th Anniversary of Chinese People's Volunteers' Entry into Korean War.

World Federation of Democratic Youth, 15th Anniv. — A216

1960, Nov. 11

260 A216 10ch multicolored 2.00 .25

Woodpecker A217

Mandarin Ducks A218

Scops Owl — A219

Oriole — A220

1960-61

261	A217	2ch yel grn & multi	7.25	.40
262	A218	5ch blue & multi	7.75	.50
263	A219	5ch lt blue & multi	12.50	1.00
264	A220	10ch lt bl grn & multi	7.75	1.00
		Nos. 261-264 (4)	35.25	2.90

Issued: No. 262, 12/15/60; No. 264, 3/15/61; No. 261, 4/22/61; No. 263, 6/1/61.

Wrestling A221

Swinging A222

Archery A223

Seesaw A224

1960-61

265	A221	5ch dull grn & multi	1.75	.25
266	A222	5ch yel & multi ('61)	1.75	.25
267	A223	5ch yel gold & multi	8.50	.75
268	A224	10ch lt bl grn & multi	1.75	.25
		Nos. 265-268 (4)	13.75	1.50

Issued: Nos. 265, 267-268, 12/15/60; No. 266 issued 1/6/61.

Agriculture A225

Light Industry A226

Korean Workers' Party Flag — A227

Power Station — A228

Steel-Making A229

1961, Jan. 1

269	A225	5ch multicolored	1.75	.25
270	A226	5ch multicolored	3.00	.25
271	A227	10ch multicolored	.85	.25
272	A228	10ch multicolored	1.75	.25
273	A229	10ch multicolored	1.25	.25
		Nos. 269-273 (5)	8.60	1.25

Wild Ginseng — A230

Design: 10ch, cultivated ginseng

1961

274	A230	5ch multicolored	4.50	.25
275	A230	10ch multicolored	4.50	.25

Issued: 10ch, 1/5; 5ch, 3/15.

A231

A232

A233

Factories — A234

1961, Feb. 8 **With Gum**

276	A231	5ch red & pale yel	1.25	.25
277	A232	10ch bl grn & pale yel	2.75	.25
278	A233	10ch dp vio blue & pale yel	2.75	.25
279	A234	20ch vio & pale yel	3.25	.50
		Nos. 276-279 (4)	10.00	1.25

Construction of Vinalon Factory.

See Nos. 350-353.

Pyongyang Students' and Children's Palace — A235

1961, Feb. 8 **With Gum**

280 A235 2ch red, *yellow* .90 .25

Korean Revolution Museum — A236

1961, Feb. 8 **With Gum**

281 A236 10ch red .75 .25

Soviet Venus Rocket — A237

1961, Feb. 8

282	A237	10ch turq bl & multi	5.00	.25

Tractor-Plow A238 — Disk-Harrow A239

Wheat Harvester A240 — Corn Harvester A241

Tractors — A242

1961, Feb. 21 **With Gum**

283	A238	5ch violet	.85	.25
284	A239	5ch blue green	.85	.25
285	A240	5ch dp gray green	.85	.25
286	A241	10ch violet blue	1.25	.25
287	A242	10ch purple	1.25	.25
		Nos. 283-287 (5)	5.05	1.25

Opening of Industrial College — A243

1961, Mar. 1 **With Gum**

288	A243	10ch red brn, *buff*	3.00	.25

Agrarian Reform Law, 15th Anniv. — A244

1961, Mar. 1 **With Gum**

289	A244	10ch dull green, *yel*	3.00	.25

20-Point Political Program, 20th Anniv. — A245

1961, Mar. 15 **With Gum**

290	A245	10ch dull vio, *pale yel*	2.00	.25

Mackerel — A246 Dolphin — A247

Whale — A248 Tunny — A249

Walleye Pollack — A250

1961, Apr. 3

291	A246	5ch yel grn & multi	3.50	.45
292	A247	5ch lt blue & multi	8.00	1.30
293	A248	10ch lt grnish blue & multi	8.50	.45
294	A249	10ch gray & multi	8.50	.45
295	A250	10ch dk grn & multi	8.50	.45
		Nos. 291-295 (5)	37.00	3.10

Crane-Mounted Tractor — A251

"Sungri-1010" Truck A252

Vertical Milling Machine A253

Victory April-15 Automobile A254

8-Meter Turning Lathe A255

Radial Boring Lathe A256

Hydraulic Press A257

750-Kg Air Hammer A258

200mm Boring Lathe A259

3,000-Ton Press A260

3-Ton Air Hammer A261

Ssangma-15 Excavator A262

Jangbaek Excavator A263

400-HP Diesel Engine A264

Honing Lathe A265

Trolley A266

8-Meter Planer A267

Boring Lathe A268 — Hobbing Lathe A269

Tunnel Drill — A270

1961-65

296	A251	1ch red brown	2.50	.25
297	A252	2ch dk brown	2.50	.25
298	A253	2ch dk green	.90	.25
299	A253	2ch grayish brn	50.00	11.00
300	A254	4ch dk blue	6.25	.25
301	A255	5ch dk green	3.50	.25
302	A256	5ch dk bl gray	1.90	.25
a.		5ch dark gray green	50.00	11.00
303	A257	5ch bl green	1.90	.25
304	A258	5ch red brown	1.60	.25
305	A259	5ch sl violet	2.25	.25
306	A260	10ch gray violet	3.25	.25
a.		10ch dark blue	50.00	.25
307	A261	10ch blue	3.00	.25
308	A261	10ch brown	*200.00*	*50.00*
309	A262	10ch dk vio gray	1.60	.25
310	A263	10ch dk green	3.25	.25
311	A264	10ch dk sl blue	3.25	.25
312	A265	10ch dk green	3.00	.25
313	A266	40ch dk blue	12.00	.25
314	A267	90ch dk bl green	5.25	.30
315	A268	1w dk vio brown	16.00	.45
316	A269	5w dk brown	32.50	3.25
317	A270	10w vio brown	50.00	6.75
		Nos. 296-317 (22)	406.40	75.75

Issued: 1ch, 4/22/61; 2ch, 4/27/61; Nos. 301, 306, 5/20/61; Nos. 307, 308, 3/13/62; Nos. 302, 317, 7/30/62; 5w, 9/5/62; No. 302a, 9/15/62; No. 308, 12/26/62; Nos. 297, 298, 2/11/63; No. 303, 4/9/63; 90ch, 5/15/63; 4ch, 6/15/63; 40ch, 9/13/63; 1w, 10/16/63; No. 310, 3/20/64; No. 305, 4/28/64; No. 311, 6/25/64; No. 312, 1/1/65.

Nos. 296, 297, 301, 303, 306 and 316 are perf 10¾. Other values are perf 12½.

Nos. 296-302, 304-307 and 309-315 were issued with gum. Nos. 303, 308, 316 and 317 were issued without gum.

Nos. 296-297, 301, 303, 306-308 and 316 are lithographed. Other values are engraved.

Reforestation Campaign — A271

1961, Apr. 27 **With Gum**

318	A271	10ch green	2.25	.30

Peaceful Reunification of Korea — A272

1961, May 9

319	A272	10ch multicolored	27.00	2.25

Young Pioneers (Children's Union) of Korea, 15th Anniv. — A273

Designs: 5ch, Pioneers swimming. 10ch (No. 321), Pioneer bugler. 10ch (No. 322) Pioneer visiting battlefield.

1961, June 1

320-322	A273	Set of 3	6.00	.90

Labor Law, 15th Anniv. — A274

1961, June 21 **With Gum**

323	A274	10ch dp blue, *pale yel*	1.60	.25

Plums — A275 Peaches — A276

Apples A277 — Persimmons A278

Pears — A279

1961, July 11

324	A275	5ch multicolored	1.40	.25
325	A276	5ch multicolored	1.40	.25
326	A277	5ch multicolored	1.40	.25
327	A278	10ch multicolored	1.40	.25
328	A279	10ch multicolored	1.40	.25
		Nos. 324-328 (5)	7.00	1.25

Yuri Gagarin & Vostok I — A280

1961, July 11

329	A280	10ch dp bl & pale bl	3.00	.70
330	A280	10ch red vio & pale bl	3.00	.70

First manned space flight, April 12.

Nationalization of Industry, 15th Anniv. — A281

1961, July 11 **With Gum**

331	A281	10ch lt red brown	18.00	.80

Sex Equality Law, 15th Anniv. — A282

1961, July 27 **With Gum**

332	A282	10ch brn red & rose	1.10	.25

Children Planting Tree — A283

Children: 5ch (No. 334), Reading book. 10ch (No. 335), Playing with ball. 10ch (No. 336), Building a toy house. 10ch (No. 337), Waving banner.

1961, Aug. 29

333-337	A283	Set of 5	5.75	.80

Livestock Breeding
A284

Fishing Industry
A285

Farming
A286

Textile Industry
A287

1961, Aug. 29

338	A284 5ch multicolored		2.00	.25
339	A285 10ch multicolored		1.75	.25
340	A286 10ch multicolored		3.00	.25
341	A287 10ch multicolored		2.75	.30
	Nos. 338-341 (4)		9.50	1.05

Improvement of living standards.

Kim Il Sung Writing Under Tree — A288

Kim Il Sung at Desk — A289

Soldiers Studying — A290

1961, Sept. 8 **With Gum**

342	A288 10ch violet	1.35	.50
343	A289 10ch dull violet	1.35	.50
344	A290 10ch dp blue & yel	2.50	.50
	Nos. 342-344 (3)	5.20	1.50

15th Anniv. of Kim Il Sung's "Ten-Point Program of the Association for the Restoration of the Fatherland."

Kim Il Sung & Party Banner
A291

Party Emblem, Workers
A292

Chollima Statue — A293

1961, Sept. 8 **With Gum**

345	A291 10ch brown red	.85	.45
346	A292 10ch green	.85	.45
347	A293 10ch violet	.85	.45
	Nos. 345-347 (3)	2.55	1.35

4th Korean Workers' Party Congress.

Miners' Day — A294

1961, Sept. 12 **With Gum**

348 A294 10ch brown 11.50 .65

Pak In Ro (1561-1642), Poet — A295

1961, Sept. 12

349 A295 10ch dk blue & gray blue 3.25 .25

Aldehyde Shop — A296

Polymerization & Saponification Shops — A297

Glacial Acetic Acid Shops — A298

Spinning Shop — A299

1961, Oct. 17 **With Gum**

350	A296 5ch red & pale yel	1.25	.25
351	A297 10ch dp blue & pale yel	1.90	.25
352	A298 10ch dk brn & pale yel	1.90	.25
353	A299 20ch purple & pale yel	3.00	.35
	Nos. 350-353 (4)	8.05	1.10

Completion of Vinalon Factory.

Korean & Soviet Flags — A300

Korean & Chinese Flags — A301

1961, Oct. 26

354	A300 10ch multicolored	2.00	.50
355	A301 10ch multicolored	2.00	.50

North Korean Friendship Treaties with the Soviet Union and China.

Day of Sports and Physical Culture — A302

Sports: 2ch, Table tennis. 5ch, Flying model glider. 10ch (No. 358), Basketball. 10ch (No. 359), Rowing. 10ch (No. 360), High jump. 20ch, Emblem.

1961, Nov. 4 **With Gum**

356-361 A302 Set of 6 9.00 1.60

No. 209 Surcharged in Violet

1961, Nov. 5

362 5ch on 1ch gray & pale grn 200.00 150.00

Centenary of publication of "Taedongyojido," map.

Janggun Rock — A303

Chonbul Peak — A304

Mansa Peak — A305

Kiwajip Rock — A306

Mujigae Rock — A307

1961, Nov. 29 **With Gum**

363	A303 5ch slate	1.35	.25
364	A304 5ch brown	1.35	.25
365	A305 10ch br lilac	2.50	.25
366	A306 10ch sl blue	2.50	.25
367	A307 10ch dk blue	2.50	.25
	Nos. 363-367 (5)	10.20	1.25

Mt. Chilbo scenes.

Protection of State Property — A308

1961, Nov. 29 **With Gum**

368 A308 10ch gray green 1.25 .25

WFTU Emblem — A309

1961, Nov. 29 **With Gum**

369 A309 10ch multicolored 1.50 .30

5th Congress of World Federation of Trade Unions.

"Red Banner" Electric Locomotive
A310

1961, Nov. 29 **With Gum**

370 A310 10ch vio & buff 17.00 1.60

Railway Electrification.

Winter Sports — A311

Designs (all 10ch): No. 371, Figure skater. No. 372, Speed skater. No. 373, Ice hockey. No. 374, Skiier.

Figures in Sepia

1961, Dec. 12 **With Gum**

371-374 A311 Set of 4 9.00 .75

Six Objectives of Production

Steel — A312

Coal — A313

Grain — A314

Textiles — A315

Sea-Foods
A316

Apartments
A317

1962, Jan. 1 **With Gum**

375	A312 5ch multicolored	1.25	.25
376	A313 5ch multicolored	8.50	.40
377	A314 10ch multicolored	1.25	.25
378	A315 10ch multicolored	3.75	.25
379	A316 10ch multicolored	3.50	.25
380	A317 10ch multicolored	1.25	.25
	Nos. 375-380 (6)	19.50	1.65

See Nos. 442-447.

Animals

Korean Tiger
A318

Racoon Dog
A319

Badger — A320

Bear — A321

1962, Jan. 24

381	A318 2ch multicolored	5.00	.25
382	A319 2ch lt grn & brn	3.50	.25
383	A320 5ch lt bl grn & lt red brn	2.40	.25
384	A321 10ch grn & brn	3.50	.25
	Nos. 381-384 (4)	14.40	1.00

Traditional Musical Instruments

Kayagum A322

Jotae (Flute) A323

Wolgum A324

Haegum A325

Wagonghu — A326

1962, Feb. 2

385	A322	10ch	multicolored	3.25	.25
386	A323	10ch	multicolored	3.25	.25
387	A324	10ch	multicolored	3.25	.25
388	A325	10ch	multicolored	3.25	.25
389	A326	10ch	multicolored	3.25	.25
	Nos. 385-389 (5)			16.25	1.25

See Nos. 472-476.

Butterflies

Luehdorfia puziloi A327

Sericinus telamon A328

Parnassius nomion A329

Inachusio A330

1962, Mar. 13

390	A327	5ch	multicolored	4.00	.25
391	A328	10ch	multicolored	4.00	.25
392	A329	10ch	multicolored	4.00	.25
393	A330	10ch	multicolored	4.00	.25
	Nos. 390-393 (4)			16.00	1.00

G. Titov & Vostok 2 — A331

1962, Mar. 13

394	A331	10ch	multicolored	3.50	.25

Second Soviet Manned Space Flight.

Kim Il Sung Commanding Troops — A332

Kim Il Sung Adressing Workers A333

Perf. 10¾ (#397), 12½

1962, Apr. 14 Engr. With Gum

395	A332	10ch	blue	1.20	.25
396	A333	10ch	green	1.20	.25
397	A333	10ch	rose red	1.20	.25
	Nos. 395-397 (3)			3.60	.75

Marshall Kim Il Sung's 50th Birthday.

Kim Chaek A334

Kang Kon A335

An Kil — A336

Ryu Kyong Su — A337

Kim Jong Suk — A338

Choe Chun Guk — A339

1962, Apr. 23 ***Perf. 12½***

With Gum

398	A334	10ch	dark brown	6.25	.25
399	A335	10ch	dark blue	6.25	.25
400	A336	10ch	rose	6.25	.25
401	A337	10ch	dark brown	6.25	.25
402	A338	10ch	dark blue gray	6.25	.25
403	A338	10ch	dark blue green	6.25	.25
404	A339	10ch	violet brown	6.25	.25
	Nos. 398-404 (7)			43.75	1.75

Anti-Japanese Revolutionary Fighters.
See Nos. 480-484.

National Mothers' Meeting, Pyongyang A340

1962, May 23 Litho. ***Perf. 10¾***

405	A340	10ch	multicolored	2.00	.50

Black-faced Spoonbill A341

Brown Hawk Owl A342

Eastern Broad-billed Roller A343

Black Paradise Flycatcher A344

Whistling Swan — A345

1962, May 23 ***Perf. 10¾***

406	A341	5ch	multicolored	3.00	.35
407	A342	5ch	multicolored	11.00	.45
408	A343	10ch	multicolored	6.25	.45
409	A344	10ch	multicolored	6.25	.45
410	A345	20ch	multicolored	7.75	.50
	Nos. 406-410 (5)			34.25	2.20

Beneficial birds.

Battle of Pochonbo, 25th Anniv. — A346

1962, May 23

411	A346	10ch	multicolored	2.00	.25

Croaker — A347

Hairtail — A348

Japanese Croaker — A349

Japanese Sea Bass — A350

Gizzard Shad — A351

1962, June 28

412	A347	5ch	dp grn & multi	1.75	.25
413	A348	5ch	dp blue & multi	1.75	.25
414	A349	10ch	apple grn & multi	3.00	.25
415	A350	10ch	vio blue & multi	3.00	.25
416	A351	10ch	grn & multi	3.00	.25
	Nos. 412-416 (5)			12.50	1.25

Sea Fish.

Brush Case A352

Ink Container A353

Ink Slab Case — A354

Writing Brush Stand — A355

Paperweight A356

Ink Slab — A357

Filing Cabinet — A358

Kettle — A359

1962, July 30 Centers in Black

417	A352	4ch	pale blue	1.40	.25
418	A353	5ch	ochre	1.40	.25
419	A354	10ch	pale green	1.90	.25
420	A355	10ch	salmon	1.90	.25
421	A356	10ch	violet	1.90	.25
422	A357	10ch	orange brown	1.90	.25
423	A358	10ch	pale yellow	1.90	.25
424	A359	40ch	gray	4.25	.50
	Nos. 417-424 (8)			16.55	2.25

Antiques of the Koryo and Yi Dynasties.
Nos. 418 and 420 were issued with gum, the other values without gum.

Jong Ta San — A360

1962, July 30 Engr. ***Perf. 12½***

425	A360	10ch	dp brnish violet	1.50	.25

200th Anniv. birth of Jong Ta San, philosopher.

National Assembly Elections
A361 A362

1962, Oct. 3 **Litho.** ***Perf. 10¾***
426 A361 10ch multicolored 2.50 .45
427 A362 10ch multicolored 2.50 .45

Pyongyang, 1535th Anniv. — A363

1962, Oct. 15 **With Gum**
428 A363 10ch pale blue & blk 1.10 .25

Launch of Soviet Manned Rockets Vostok 3 & 4 — A364

1962, Nov. 12
429 A364 10ch multicolored 3.50 .70

Spiraea
A365

Echinosophoora koreensis
A366

Codonopsis sylvestris
A367

Ginseng
A368

1962, Nov. 30
430 A365 5ch multicolored 1.90 .25
431 A366 10ch multicolored 1.90 .25
432 A367 10ch multicolored 1.90 .25
433 A368 10ch multicolored 1.90 .25
Nos. 430-433 (4) 7.60 1.00

Korean plants.

Uibangryuchui — A369

1962, Dec. 26
434 A369 10ch multicolored 5.00 .35

485th anniversary of publication of the medical encyclopedia *Uibangryuchui*, printed with moveable type.

Korean Academy of Sciences, 10th Anniv. — A370

1962, Dec. 26
435 A370 10ch dull ultra & pale turq grn 2.00 .25

Fishing — A371

1962, Dec. 30
436 A371 10ch ultra 5.00 .25

European Mink — A372

Korean Hare
A373

Eurasian Red Squirrel
A374

Goral
A375

Siberian Chipmunk
A376

1962, Dec. 30-1963
437 A372 4ch app grn & red brn 1.50 .40
438 A373 5ch lt grn & gray ('63) 1.50 .40
439 A374 10ch yel & gray 2.50 .40
440 A375 10ch pale grn & dk brn 2.50 .40
441 A376 20ch lt gray blue & red brn 5.00 .40
Nos. 437-441 (5) 13.00 2.00

Fur-bearing animals.
No. 438 issued 12/30/63.

Coal — A377

Grain — A378

Textiles
A379

Apartment Construction
A380

Steel — A381

Seafood
A382

1963, Jan. 1
442 A377 5ch multicolored 1.50 .25
443 A378 10ch multicolored 1.25 .25
444 A379 10ch multicolored 1.50 .25
445 A380 10ch multicolored 1.25 .25
446 A381 10ch multicolored 1.25 .25
447 A382 40ch multicolored 3.75 .50
Nos. 442-447 (6) 10.50 1.75

Consolidation of the Achievement of the 6 Objectives. For surcharge, see No. 4539.

Korean People's Army, 15th Anniv. — A383

Designs: 5ch, Airman. 10ch (No. 449), Soldier. 10ch (No. 450), Sailor.

1963, Feb. 1 **Engr.** ***Perf. 12½***
With Gum
448-450 A383 Set of 3 6.00 .65

Peony — A384

Rugosa Rose — A385

Rhododendron
A386

Campion
A387

Orchid — A388

1963, Mar. 21 **Litho.** ***Perf. 10¾***
451 A384 5ch gray & multi 1.10 .25
452 A385 10ch grnsh yel & multi 1.50 .25
453 A386 10ch lemon & multi 1.50 .25
454 A387 10ch br yel & multi 1.50 .25
455 A388 40ch green & multi 5.00 .45
Nos. 451-455 (5) 10.60 1.45

Korean flowers.

Sword Dance
A389

Fan Dance
A390

1963, Apr. 15
456 A389 10ch multicolored 7.50 .25
457 A390 10ch multicolored 7.50 .25

International Music and Dance Competition, Pyongyang, April 16-May 17.

South Korea Uprising of April 19, 3rd Anniv. — A391

1963, Apr. 19
458 A391 10ch multicolored 1.50 .25

Karl Marx — A392

1963, Apr. 23 **Engr.** ***Perf. 12½***
With Gum
459 A392 10ch ultra 2.75 .25

Youth Day — A393

Designs: 2ch, Children in chemistry class. 5ch, Children running. 10ch (No. 462), Girl chasing butterfly. 10ch (No. 463), Boy leading chorus.

1963, June 15 **Litho.** ***Perf. 10¾***
460-463 A393 Set of 4 12.00 1.00

Armed Koreans & Caricature of American Soldier
A394

1963, June 25
464 A394 10ch multicolored 1.90 .25

Month of Struggle for the Withdrawal of U.S. Troops from South Korea.

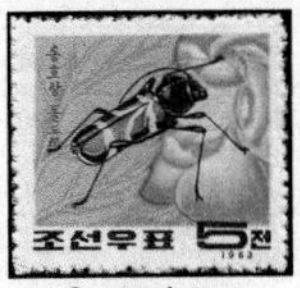

Cyrtoclytus caproides
A395

Cicindela chinensis
A396

Purpuricenus lituratus — A397

Agapanthia pilicornus — A398

1963, July 24
465 A395 5ch multicolored 3.00 .25
466 A396 10ch multicolored 4.00 .25
467 A397 10ch multicolored 4.00 .25
468 A398 10ch multicolored 4.00 .25
Nos. 465-468 (4) 15.00 1.00

Korean beetles.

Victory in Korean War, 10th Anniv. — A399

1963, July 27
469 A399 10ch multicolored 1.75 .25

National Emblem A400

North Korean Flag A401

1963, Aug. 15

470	A400	10ch	multicolored	*20.00*	—
471	A401	10ch	multicolored	*20.00*	—

No. 471 exists with background in blue. Not issued. Value $750.

Ajaeng (Zither) A402

Phyongyong (Jade Chimes) A403

Saenap (Flute) A404

Rogo (Drums) A405

Phiri (Pipe) — A406

1963, Sept. 13

472	A402	5ch	multicolored	1.50	.25
473	A403	5ch	multicolored	1.50	.25
474	A404	10ch	multicolored	2.50	.25
475	A405	10ch	multicolored	2.50	.25
476	A406	10ch	multicolored	2.50	.25
			Nos. 472-476 (5)	10.50	1.25

Korean traditional musical instruments.

Nos. 472 and 475 were issued with gum, the other values without gum.

South Gate, Kaesong A407

Taedong Gate, Pyongyang A408

Pothong Gate, Pyongyang — A409

1963, Sept. 13 Engr. *Perf. 12½*
With Gum

477	A407	5ch	black	.50	.25
478	A408	10ch	brown	1.25	.25
479	A409	10ch	blue	1.25	.25
			Nos. 477-479 (3)	3.00	.75

Korean historic buildings.

See Nos. 537-538.

Kwon Yong Byok A410

Ma Tong Hui A411

Pak Tal — A412

Ri Je Sun — A413

Kim Yong Bom — A414

1963, Oct. 10 With Gum

480	A410	5ch	brown	6.00	—
481	A411	5ch	brown purple	6.00	—
482	A412	10ch	grnsh slate	6.00	—
483	A413	10ch	carmine rose	6.00	—
484	A414	10ch	black brown	70.00	50.00

Anti-Japanese revolutionary fighters.

Nurse & Children at Playground A415

Teacher & Children at Fairground A416

1963, Nov. 30 Litho. *Perf. 10¾*

485	A415	10ch	multicolored	.80	.25
486	A416	10ch	multicolored	.80	.25

Child welfare.

Hwajang Temple A417

Hyangsan Stream A418

Kwanum Pavilion & Pagoda — A419

Sangwon Temple — A420

1963, Nov. 30

487	A417	5ch	multicolored	1.00	.25
488	A418	10ch	multicolored	5.25	.25
489	A419	10ch	multicolored	2.50	.25
490	A420	10ch	multicolored	2.50	.25
			Nos. 487-490 (4)	11.25	1.00

Mount Myohyang.

Arming the People A421

Technical Innovation A422

Mining Industry A423

Building Homes A424

1963, Dec. 5 Engr. *Perf. 12½*
With Gum

491	A421	5ch	dp rose red	.50	.25
492	A422	10ch	red brown	3.25	.25
493	A423	10ch	gray violet	1.90	.25
494	A424	10ch	gray black	3.50	.25
			Nos. 491-494 (4)	9.15	1.00

Seven-Year Plan.

Sowing Gourd Seeds — A425

Saving a Swallow A426

Swallow Carrying Gourd Seed — A427

Sawing Gourd — A428

Treasure Pouring from Gourd — A429

1963, Dec. 5 Litho. *Perf. 10¾*

495	A425	5ch	multicolored	1.25	.25
496	A426	10ch	multicolored	2.50	.25
497	A427	10ch	multicolored	2.50	.25
498	A428	10ch	multicolored	2.00	.25
499	A429	10ch	multicolored	2.00	.25
			Nos. 495-499 (5)	10.25	1.25

Tale of Hung Bu.

Pistol Shooting A430

Small-Caliber Rifle Shooting A431

Rifle Shooting A432

1963, Dec. 15

500	A430	5ch	multicolored	.90	.25
501	A431	10ch	multicolored	1.60	.25
502	A432	10ch	multicolored	1.60	.25
			Nos. 500-502 (3)	4.10	.75

Marksmanship Competition.

Chongjin Mill — A433

Sinuiju Mill — A434

1964, Jan. 10 Engr. *Perf. 12½*
With Gum

503	A433	10ch	brn violet	1.10	.25
504	A434	10ch	gray	1.10	.25

Chemical fiber industry.

Wonsan General Strike, 35th Anniv. — A435

1964, Jan. 14 With Gum

505	A435	10ch	brown	1.50	.25

Korean Alphabet, 520th Anniv. — A436

1964, Jan. 15 Litho. *Perf. 10¾*

506	A436	10ch	multicolored	1.25	.25

Lenin's Death, 40th Anniv. — A437

1964, Jan. 22 Engr. *Perf. 12½*
With Gum

507	A437	10ch	rose red	1.50	.25

Whaler — A438

Trawler — A439

Purse-Seine Boat — A440

Dragnet Boat — A441

1964, Feb. 10 Litho. *Perf. 10¾*

508	A438	5ch	multicolored	1.75	.25
509	A439	5ch	multicolored	1.75	.25
510	A440	10ch	multicolored	3.50	.25
511	A441	10ch	multicolored	3.50	.25
			Nos. 508-511 (4)	10.50	1.00

Korean fishing industry.

March 1 Popular Uprising, 45th Anniv. — A442

1964, Feb. 10 Engr. *Perf. 12½*
With Gum

512 A442 10ch dark violet 1.00 .25

Kabo Peasant War, 70th Anniv. — A443

1964, Feb. 15 With Gum

513 A443 10ch violet black 1.00 .25

Students' and Children's Palace, Pyongyang A444

1964, Mar. 3 With Gum

514 A444 10ch grnsh black .75 .25

5th Congress, Democratic Youth League of Korea — A445

1964, May 12 Litho. *Perf. 10¾*

515 A445 10ch multicolored 1.00 .25

Electric Train — A446

1964, May 21

516 A446 10ch multicolored 10.50 .45

Electrification of Railway between Pyongyang and Sinuiju.

Popular Movement in Chongsan-ri A447

1964, June 4 Engr. *Perf. 12½*
With Gum

517 A447 5ch chestnut 275.00 125.00

Drum Dance A448

Dance of Ecstasy A449

Small Drum Dance — A450

1964, June 15 Litho. *Perf. 10¾*

518 A448 2ch multicolored 1.50 .50
519 A449 5ch multicolored 2.50 .50
520 A450 10ch multicolored 4.25 .55
Nos. 518-520 (3) 8.25 1.55

Korean folk dances.

For the Sake of the Fatherland A451

1964, June 15 Engr. *Perf. 12½*
With Gum

521 A451 5ch carmine red 2.60 .25

Li Su Bok, soldier.

Nampho Smelter — A452

Hwanghae Iron Works — A453

1964 With Gum

522 A452 5ch bronze green 6.00 .25
523 A453 10ch gray 4.00 .25

Issued: 5ch, 6/15. 10ch, 10/15.

Asian Economic Seminar, Pyongyang A454

Design: 10ch, Flags, industrial skyline and cogwheel.

1964, June 15 Litho. *Perf. 10¾*

524 A454 5ch multicolored .80 .25
525 A454 10ch multicolored 1.25 .25

Koreans and Statue of Kang Ho Yong, War Hero — A455

1964, June 25

526 A455 10ch multicolored 1.40 .25

Korean Reunification

Domestic Poultry A456

Designs: 2ch, Chickens. 4ch, White chickens. 5ch (No. 529), Black chickens. 5ch (No. 530), Varicolored chickens. 40ch, Helmet guineafowl.

1964, Aug. 5

527-531 A456 Set of 5 7.25 2.00

9th Winter Olympic Games, Innsbruck A457

Designs: 5ch, Skier. 10ch (No. 533), Slalom skier. 10ch (No. 534), Speed skater.

1964, Aug. 5

532-534 A457 Set of 3 4.00 .50

Flags & "Tobolsk," Repatriation Ship A458

Welcoming Repatriates A459

1964, Aug. 13

535 A458 10ch multicolored 2.25 .25
536 A459 30ch multicolored 2.25 .25

5th anniversary of agreement for the repatriation of Korean nationals in Japan.

Thonggun Pavilion, Uiju — A460

Inphung Pavilion, Kanggye City — A461

1964, Aug. 22 Engr. *Perf. 12½*
With Gum

537 A460 5ch black violet .60 .25
538 A461 10ch emerald .75 .25

Korean historic sites.

18th Olympic Games, Tokyo — A462

Designs: 2ch, Rifleman. 5ch, Cyclists, vert. 10ch (No. 541), Runner. 10ch (No. 542), Wrestlers, vert.. 40ch, Volleyball, vert.

Photo, Centers Litho

1964, Sept. 5 *Perf. 10¾*

539-543 A462 Set of 5 5.00 1.00

Nos. 539-543 exist imperf. Value, $18 unused, $5 canceled.

Sinking of the *General Sherman,* 1866 — A463

1964, Sept. 28 Engr. *Perf. 12½*
With Gum

544 A463 30ch red brown 5.50 .50

Kim Il Sung & Guerrilla Fighters — A464

Kim Il Sung Speaking to Peasants — A465

Battle of Xiaowangqing A466

1964, Sept. 28 Engr. *Perf. 12½*
With Gum

545 A464 2ch brt violet .60 .25
546 A465 5ch blue 1.15 .25
547 A466 10ch grnsh black 1.25 .25
Nos. 545-547 (3) 3.00 .75

Revolutionary paintings.

Kwangju Students' Uprising, 35th Anniv. — A467

1964, Oct. 15 With Gum

548 A467 10ch blue violet 2.40 .25

Weight Lifter A468

Runner A469

Boxers — A470

Soccer Goalie — A471

GANEFO Emblem — A472

1964, Oct. 15 Litho. *Perf. 10¾*

549 A468 2ch multicolored .60 .25
550 A469 5ch multicolored .60 .25
551 A470 5ch multicolored .60 .25
552 A471 10ch multicolored 1.25 .25
553 A472 10ch multicolored 1.00 .25
Nos. 549-553 (5) 4.05 1.25

1st Games of New Emerging Forces (GANEFO), Djakarta, Indonesia, 1963.

Nos. 549-553 exist imperf. Value, $12 unused, $5 canceled.

Wild Animals — A473

Animals: 2ch, Lynx. 5ch, Leopard cat. 10ch (No. 556), Yellow-throated marten. 10ch (No. 559), Leopard.

1964, Nov. 20 Engr. *Perf. 12½*
With Gum

554-557 A473 Set of 4 13.00 .90

Fighting South Vietnam — A474

1964, Dec. 20 Litho. *Perf. 10¾*

558 A474 10ch multicolored 1.25 .25

Support for North Vietnam.

Prof. Kim Bong Han — A475

"Bonghan" Duct — A476

"Bonghan" Corpuscle — A477

1964, Dec. 20 Photo. *Perf. 10¾*

559 A475 2ch ol grn & brown 1.30 .25
560 A476 5ch multicolored 1.60 .25
561 A477 10ch multicolored 2.10 .25
Nos. 559-561 (3) 5.00 .75

Kyongrak Biological System.

Technical Revolution A478

Ideological Revolution A479

Cultural Revolution A480

1964, Dec. 30 **Litho.**

562 A478 5ch multicolored .30 .25
563 A479 10ch multicolored .55 .25
564 A480 10ch multicolored .55 .25
Nos. 562-564 (3) 1.40 .75

Ideological, Technical and Cultural Revolutions in the Countryside.

"For Arms" — A481

1964, Dec. 30 **Engr.** ***Perf. 12½***
With Gum

565 A481 4ch brown 1.40 .25

Revolutionary painting.

Consumer Goods A482

Livestock Breeding A483

"All for the Grand Chollima March" — A484

1964, Dec. 30 **Litho.** ***Perf. 10¾***

566 A482 5ch multicolored 1.50 .25
567 A483 10ch multicolored 1.50 .25
568 A484 10ch multicolored 1.10 .25
Nos. 566-568 (3) 4.10 .75

Seven-Year Plan.

No. 566 was issued with gum, Nos. 567 and 568 without gum.

Nos. 566-568 also exist imperf. Value, unused $100.

Battle of Luozigou — A485

Battle of Fusong County Seat — A486

Battle of Hongqihe A487

1965, Jan. 20 **Engr.** ***Perf. 12½***
With Gum

569 A485 10ch dp slate green 1.00 .25
570 A486 10ch deep violet 1.00 .25
571 A487 10ch slate violet 1.00 .25
Nos. 569-571 (3) 3.00 .75

Guerrilla warfare against Japan 1934-1940.

Tuman River — A488

Taedong River — A489

Amnok River — A490

1965, Feb. 27 **Litho.** ***Perf. 10¾***

572 A488 2ch multicolored .90 .25
573 A489 5ch multicolored 3.50 .25
574 A490 10ch multicolored 1.60 .25
Nos. 572-574 (3) 6.00 .75

Korean rivers.

1st Congress of the Union of Agricultural Working People of Korea — A491

1965, Mar. 25 **With Gum**

575 A491 10ch multicolored 1.50 .25

Furnacemen, Workers A492

1965, Mar. 25 **With Gum**

576 A492 10ch multicolored 1.00 .25

Ten Major Tasks of Seven-Year Plan.

Sinhung Colliery — A493

Tanchou — A494

1965, Mar. 31 **Engr.** ***Perf. 12½***
With Gum

577 A493 10ch olive black 1.50 .25
578 A494 40ch violet 4.50 .25

35th anniversary of workers' uprisings.

Sunhwa River Works — A495

1965, Mar. 31 **Litho.** ***Perf. 10¾***
With Gum

579 A495 10ch multicolored .75 .25

A496

South Korean Uprising of April 19, 5th Anniv. — A497

1965, Apr. 10 **With Gum**

580 A496 10ch multicolored .75 .25
581 A497 40ch multicolored 1.25 .25

Nos. 580-581 exist imperf. Value, $5 unused.

Construction of Pyongyang Thermal Power Station — A498

1965, Apr. 10 **With Gum**

582 A498 5ch dp brn & lt blue 1.90 .25

No. 582 exists imperf. Value, $5 unused.

1st Afro-Asian Conf., Bandung, 10th Anniv. — A499

1965, Apr. 18 **With Gum**

583 A499 10ch multicolored .85 .25

Crowd Rejoicing A500

Japanese Koreans Demonstrating for Reunification A501

1965, Apr. 27 **Photo.** **With Gum**

584 A500 10ch blue & red 1.00 .25
585 A501 40ch multicolored 1.25 .25

10th Anniv. of the General Association of Koreans in Japan.

Nos. 584-585 exist imperf. Value, $25 unused.

Workers Demonstrating A502

1965, May 10 **Engr.** ***Perf. 12½***
With Gum

586 A502 10ch brown 2.75 .25

35th Anniv. of General Strike at Pyongyang Rubber Goods Factory.

Workers in Battle — A503

Korean & African Soldiers — A504

1965, June 20 **Photo.** ***Perf. 10¾***
With Gum

587 A503 10ch multicolored 1.60 .25
588 A504 40ch multicolored 3.00 .25

2nd Asian-African Conference, Algiers (subsequently canceled).

Nos. 587-588 exist imperf. Value, $18 unused.

Victory-64 10-Ton Truck — A505

1965, June 20 **Engr.** ***Perf. 12½***
With Gum

589 A505 10ch grnsh blue 2.25 .25

Kim Chang Gol — A506

Jo Kun Sil — A507

An Hak Ryong — A508

1965, June 20 **With Gum**

590 A506 10ch slate .75 .25
591 A507 10ch red brown .75 .25
592 A508 40ch violet 2.50 .25
Nos. 590-592 (3) 4.00 .75

War heroes.

See Nos. 775-777 and 827-830.

Postal Ministers' Conference, Peking — A509

1965, June 20 **Photo.** ***Perf. 10¾***
With Gum

593 A509 10ch red, yel & blk 2.00 .25

Lake Samil — A510

Jipson Peak — A511

Kwanum Waterfalls A512

1965, June 20 **Litho.** **With Gum**

594 A510 2ch multicolored .85 .25
595 A511 5ch multicolored 1.40 .25
596 A512 10ch multicolored 4.00 .25
Nos. 594-596 (3) 6.25 .75

Diamond Mountain Scenery.

Nos. 594-596 exist imperf. Value, unused $100.

Kusimuldong A513

Lake Samji — A514

1965, June 20 **Photo.** **With Gum**

597 A513 5ch slate blue .75 .25
598 A514 10ch grnsh blue 1.00 .25

Revolutionary battle sites.

Soccer Player
A515

Emblem & Stadium
A516

1965, Aug. 1 Litho. With Gum

599 A515 10ch multicolored 1.40 .25
600 A516 10ch multicolored 1.40 .25

GANEFO Games, Pyongyang.

Nos. 599-600 exist imperf, with gum. Value, $15 unused.

Liberation from Japan, 20th Anniv. — A517

1965, Aug. 15 With Gum

601 A517 10ch multicolored 1.00 .25

Friedrich Engels, 145th Anniv. Birth — A518

1965, Sept. 10 Engr. *Perf. 12½*
With Gum

602 A518 10ch brown .50 .25

Sports — A519

Designs: 2ch, Pole vault. 4ch, Javelin. 10ch (No. 605), Discus. 10ch (No. 606), High jump. 10ch (No. 607), Shot put.

1965, Sept. 24 Litho. *Perf. 11*
With Gum

603-607 A519 Set of 5 4.00 .90

Nos. 603-607 exist imperf, without gum. Value. $18 unused.

Korean Workers' Party, 20th Anniv.
A520

Designs: No. 608a, 10ch, Korean fighters. No. 608b, 10ch, Party emblem. No. 608c, 10ch, Lenin & Marx. No. 608d, 10ch, Workers marching. No. 608e, 10ch, Soldiers & armed workers. No. 608f, 40ch, Workers.

1965, Oct. 10 Photo. *Perf. 13X13½*
With Gum

608 A520 Block of 6, #a.-f. 55.00 22.50
608g Souvenir sheet of 6, #608-613 600.00 *400.00*

Chongjin Steel Mill — A521

Kim Chaek Iron Works — A522

1965, Nov. 25 Engr. *Perf. 12½*
With Gum

614 A521 10ch deep violet 5.00 .25
615 A522 10ch sepia 5.00 .25

Rainbow Trout — A523

Dolly Trout — A524

Grass Carp — A525

Carp — A526

Manchurian Trout — A527

Crucian Carp — A528

1965, Dec. 10 Photo. *Perf. 13½*
With Gum

616 A523 2ch multicolored .75 .25
617 A524 4ch multicolored 1.00 .25
618 A525 10ch multicolored 2.25 .25
619 A526 10ch multicolored 2.25 .25
620 A527 10ch multicolored 2.25 .25
621 A528 40ch multicolored 3.50 .50
Nos. 616-621 (6) 12.00 1.75

Freshwater fishes.

Nos. 616-621 exist imperf, without gum. Value $20 unused.

House Building
A529

Hemp Weaving
A530

Blacksmith
A531

Wrestling
A532

School
A533

Dance
A534

1965, Dec. 15 Engr. *Perf. 12½*
With Gum

622 A529 2ch green .70 .25
623 A530 4ch maroon 1.35 .25
624 A531 10ch violet 1.75 .25
625 A532 10ch carmine red 1.90 .25
626 A533 10ch blue 1.20 .25
627 A534 10ch brown 1.10 .25
Nos. 622-627 (6) 8.00 1.50

Paintings by Kim Hong Do, 18th century Korean artist.

Students' Extracurricular Activities — A535

Designs: 2ch, Children in workshop. 4ch, Boxing. 10ch (No. 630), Playing violin. 10ch (No. 631), Chemistry lab.

1965, Dec. 15 Litho. *Perf. 13¼*
With Gum

628-631 A535 Set of 4 2.75 .50

Nos. 628-631 exist imperf. Value, unused $75.

Whaler — A536

Service Vessel — A537

1965, Dec. 15 Engr. *Perf. 12½*
With Gum

632 A536 10ch deep blue 1.75 .25
633 A537 10ch slate green 1.75 .25

Korean fishing boats.

Black-capped Kingfisher
A538

Korean Great Tit
A539

Blue Magpie — A540

White-faced Wagtail — A541

Migratory Korean Grosbeak — A542

Perf. 11, 13½ (#640)
1965, Dec. 30 Litho. With Gum

634 A538 4ch pale yel & multi 2.25 .25
635 A539 10ch pale sal & multi 3.00 .25
636 A540 10ch pale grnsh blue & multi 3.00 .25
637 A541 10ch yel & multi 3.00 .25
638 A542 40ch pale yel grn & multi 8.50 .75
Nos. 634-638 (5) 19.75 1.75

Korean birds.

Nos. 634-638 exist imperf, without gum. Value $29 unused.

Korean sericulture — A543

Designs: 2ch, Silkworm moth & cocoon. No. 640, 10ch, Ailanthus silk moth. No. 641, 10ch, Chinese Oak silk moth.

1965, Dec. 30 Engr. *Perf. 12½*
With Gum

639-641 A543 Set of 3 100.00 2.75

Hooded Crane
A544

Japanese White-necked Crane
A545

Manchurian Crane
A546

Gray Heron
A547

1965, Dec. 30 With Gum

642 A544 2ch olive brown 3.75 .25
643 A545 10ch dp vio blue 4.00 .45
644 A546 10ch slate purple 4.00 .45
645 A547 40ch slate green 7.00 .80
Nos. 642-645 (4) 18.75 1.95

Wading birds. For surcharge, see No. 4540.

Mollusks — A548

Designs: 5ch, Japanese common squid. 10ch, Giant Pacific octopus.

1965, Dec. 31 Litho. *Perf. 11*
With Gum

646-647 A548 Set of 2 4.00 3.00

Nos. 646-647 exist imperf, without gum. Value $8 unused.

Korean Ducks — A549

Designs: 2ch, Spotbill. 4ch, Ruddy shelduck. 10ch, Mallard. 40ch, Baikal teal.

1965, Dec. 31 Litho. *Perf. 11*
With Gum

648-651 A549 Set of 4 15.00 1.75

Nos. 648-651 exist imperf. Value $30 unused.

Circus, Pyongyang
A550

Trapeze Performers
A551

Balancing Act
A552

Seesawing
A553

Tightrope Walker — A554

1965, Dec. 31 **Photo.**

652	A550	2ch	multicolored	.75	.25
653	A551	10ch	multicolored	2.00	.25
654	A552	10ch	multicolored	2.00	.25
655	A553	10ch	multicolored	2.00	.25
656	A554	10ch	multicolored	2.00	.25
			Nos. 652-656 (5)	8.75	1.25

Korean acrobatics.

Nos. 652-655 were issued with gum, No. 656 without gum.

Korean Flowers — A555

Designs: No. 657, 4ch, Marvel-of-Peru. No. 658, 10ch, Peony (violet background). No. 659, 10ch, Moss rose (yellow background). No. 660, 10ch, Magnolia (light blue background).

1965, Dec. 31 **Litho.**

657-660 A555 Set of 4 12.00 .95

No. 657 was issued without gum, Nos. 658-60 with gum.

Nos. 657-660 exist imperf, without gum. Value $20 unused.

Yachts — A556

Designs: No. 661, 2ch, Finn Class. No. 662, 10ch, Dragon Class (blue background). No. 663, 10ch, 5.5 Class (violet background). No. 664, 40ch, Star Class.

1965, Dec. 31 **With Gum** ***Perf. 13½***

661-664 A556 Set of 4 6.00 1.75

Nos. 661-664 exist imperf, without gum. Value $10 unused.

10ch depicting Netherlands class yacht, with blue background, not issued. Value $750.

1st Congress of the Org. of Solidarity of Peoples of Asia, Africa and Latin America — A557

1966, Jan. 3 **With Gum** ***Perf. 11***

665 A557 10ch multicolored .50 .25

Hosta A558

Dandelion A559

Lily of the Valley A560

Pink Convolvulus A561

Catalpa Blossom — A562

1966, Jan. 15 **With Gum**

666	A558	2ch	multicolored	1.25	.25
667	A559	4ch	multicolored	1.25	.25
668	A560	10ch	multicolored	1.75	.25
669	A561	10ch	multicolored	1.75	.25
670	A562	40ch	multicolored	5.25	.70
			Nos. 666-670 (5)	11.25	1.70

Korean wildflowers.

Imperfs exist, without gum. Value, $25 unused.

Primrose A563

Brillian Campion A564

Amur Pheasant's Eye — A565

Orange Lily — A566

Rhododendron — A567

1966, Feb. 10 **With Gum**

671	A563	2ch	multicolored	1.00	.25
672	A564	4ch	multicolored	1.00	.25
673	A565	10ch	multicolored	1.40	.25
674	A566	10ch	multicolored	1.40	.25
675	A567	90ch	multicolored	7.25	.95
			Nos. 671-675 (5)	12.05	1.95

Korean wildflowers.

Land Reform Law, 20th Anniv. — A568

1966, Mar. 5 **With Gum**

676 A568 10ch multicolored 1.75 .50

Battle of Jiansanfen A569

Battle of Taehongdan A570

Battle of Dashahe — A571

1966, Mar. 25 **Engr.** ***Perf. 12½***

677	A569	10ch	violet brown	.60	.25
678	A570	10ch	dp blue green	.60	.25
679	A571	10ch	brown carmine	.60	.25
			Nos. 677-679 (3)	1.80	.75

Battles of the anti-Japanese revolution.

No. 678 was issued without gum, the other values with gum.

Art Treasures of the Silla Dynasty — A572

Designs: 2ch, Covered bowl. 5ch, Jar. 10ch, Censer.

1966, Apr. 30 **With Gum**

680-682 A572 Set of 3 4.50 .55

Labor Day, 80th Anniv. — A573

1966, May 1 **Litho.** ***Perf. 11***
With Gum

683 A573 10ch multicolored .75 .25

Assoc. for the Restoration of the Fatherland, 30th Anniv. — A574

1966, May 5 **Photo.** **With Gum**

684 A574 10ch brn red & yel .75 .25

Farmer A575

Worker A576

1966, May 30 **Litho.** **With Gum**

685	A575	5ch	multicolored	.50	.25
686	A576	10ch	multicolored	.75	.25

Young Pioneers, 20th Anniv. — A577

1966, June 6 **With Gum**

687 A577 10ch multicolored 1.00 .25

Kangson Steel Works — A578

Pongung Chemical Works — A579

1966, June 10 **Engr.** ***Perf. 12½***
With Gum

688	A578	10ch	gray	5.00	.25
689	A579	10ch	deep red	5.00	.25

Korean Factories.

Fish — A580

Designs: 2ch, Saury. 5ch, Pacific cod. No. 692, Chum salmon. No. 693, Mackerel. 40ch, Pink salmon.

1966, June 10 **Photo.** ***Perf. 11***

690-694 A580 Set of 5 15.00 4.50

Nos. 690-692 were issued with gum, Nos. 693-694 without gum.

Nos. 690-694 exist imperf, without gum. Value, $22, either unused or cancelled.

Prof. Kim Bong Han & Kyongrak Biological System — A581

1966, June 30 **Photo.** **With Gum**

695	A581	Block of 8, #a.-h.	11.00	8.00
695i		Souvenir sheet of 8, #695-702	125.00	100.00

Voshkod 2 — A582

Luna 9 — A583

Luna 10 — A584

1966, June 30

703	A582	5ch	multicolored	.30	.25
704	A583	10ch	multicolored	1.00	.25
705	A584	40ch	multicolored	1.75	.35
			Nos. 703-705 (3)	3.05	.85

Space Flight Day.

Nos. 703-705 exist imperf. Value, $8 unused.

Jules Rimet Cup — A585

Dribbling A586

Goal-keeper A587

1966, July 11 **Litho.**

706	A585	10ch	multicolored	1.90	.25
707	A586	10ch	multicolored	1.90	.25
708	A587	10ch	multicolored	1.90	.25
			Nos. 706-708 (3)	5.70	.75

World Cup Championship.

Nos. 706-708 exist imperf. Value, $20 unused.

Battle of Naphalsan A588

Battle of Seoul A589

Battle of Height 1211 — A590

1966, July 27 **Engr.** ***Perf. 12½***
With Gum

709	A588	10ch	red violet	1.10	.25
710	A589	10ch	deep green	1.10	.25
711	A590	10ch	violet	1.10	.25
	Nos. 709-711 (3)			3.30	.75

Korean War of 1950-53.

Sex Equality Law, 20th Anniv. — A591

1966, July 30 **Litho.** ***Perf. 11***
With Gum

712	A591	10ch	multicolored	1.50	.30

Nationalization of Industry, 20th Anniv. — A592

1966, Aug. 10 **With Gum**

713	A592	10ch	multicolored	1.10	.25

Water Jar Dance A593

Bell Dance A594

Dancer in Mural Painting A595

Sword Dance A596

Golden Cymbal Dance — A597

1966, Aug. 10

714	A593	5ch	multicolored	1.40	.25
715	A594	10ch	multicolored	2.50	.25
716	A595	10ch	multicolored	2.50	.25
717	A596	15ch	multicolored	2.50	.25
718	A597	40ch	multicolored	4.50	.30
	Nos. 714-718 (5)			13.40	1.30

Korean Folk Dances.

5ch and 10ch issued with or without gum. Other values issued without gum.

Nos. 714-718 exist imperf, without gum. Value, $20 unused.

Attacking U.S. Soldier A598

Worker with Child A599

Industrialization — A600

1966, Aug. 15 **Engr.** ***Perf. 12½***
With Gum

719	A598	10ch	deep green	1.25	.25
720	A599	10ch	red violet	1.25	.25
721	A600	10ch	violet	5.75	.40
	Nos. 719-721 (3)			8.25	.90

Korean Reunification Campaign.

Crop-spraying A601

Observing Forest Fire — A602

Geological Survey — A603

Fish Shoal Detection A604

1966, Sept. 30 **Photo.** ***Perf. 11***

722	A601	2ch	multicolored	.50	.25
723	A602	5ch	multicolored	7.00	.25
724	A603	10ch	multicolored	1.75	.25
725	A604	40ch	multicolored	1.75	.25
	Nos. 722-725 (4)			11.00	1.00

Industrial uses of aircraft.

2ch, 5ch issued without gum. 10ch, 40ch issued with gum.

Nos. 722-725 exist imperf, without gum. Value, $20 unused.

A three-value set honoring revolutionary fighters, with designs similar to types A334-A339, was prepared but not issued. Value $3,500.

Kim Il Sung University, 20th Anniv. — A605

1966, Oct. 1 **Engr.** ***Perf. 12½***
With Gum

726	A605	10ch	slate violet	1.75	.30

Imperforate Stamps

Imperforate varieties are without gum, unless otherwise noted.

1st Asian GANEFO Games — A606

Designs: a, 5ch, Judo. b, 10ch, Basketball. c, 10ch, Table tennis.

1966, Oct. 30 **Litho.** ***Perf. 11***

727	A606	Strip of 3, #a-c	2.00	.55
		Strip of 3, #a-c imperf	50.00	—

Scarlet Finch A607

Hoopoe A608

Korean Crested Lark — A609

Brown Thrush — A610

White-bellied Black Woodpecker — A611

1966, Oct. 30

730	A607	2ch	multicolored	2.25	.25
731	A608	5ch	multicolored	2.50	.25
732	A609	10ch	multicolored	2.75	.30
733	A610	10ch	multicolored	2.75	.30
734	A611	40ch	multicolored	5.75	.80
	Nos. 730-734 (5)			16.00	1.90
	Set of 5, imperf			32.00	—

Korean birds. For surcharge, see No. 4513.

Construction A612

Machine-Tool Production A613

Worker & Graph — A614

Miners A615

1966, Nov. 20

735	A612	5ch	multicolored	.40	.25
736	A613	10ch	multicolored	.75	.25
737	A614	10ch	multicolored	.75	.25
738	A615	40ch	multicolored	2.10	.45
	Nos. 735-738 (4)			4.00	1.20

Propaganda for increased production.

Nos. 735-737 issued with gum. No. 738 issued without gum.

Parachuting A616

Show Jumping — A617

Motorcycling A618

Telegraphists' Competition A619

1966, Nov. 30 **Engr.** ***Perf. 12½***
With Gum

739	A616	2ch	dark brown	.90	.25
740	A617	5ch	org vermilion	.65	.25
741	A618	10ch	dp violet blue	3.25	.30
742	A619	40ch	deep green	2.10	.25
	Nos. 739-742 (4)			6.90	1.05

National Defense sports.

Samil Wolgan Magazine, 30th Anniv. — A620

1966, Dec. 1 **Photo.** ***Perf. 11***

743	A620	10ch	multicolored	—	—

Korean Deer — A621

Designs: 2ch, Red deer. 5ch, Sika deer. No. 746, 10ch, Reindeer (grazing). No. 747, 10ch, Japanese sambar (erect). 70ch, Fallow deer.

1966, Dec. 20 **Litho.**

744-748	A621	Set of 5	18.00	4.50
		Imperf, #744-748	—	—

No. 747 was issued with gum. Other values issued without gum. For surcharge, see No. 4560.

Wild Fruit — A622

Designs: 2ch, Blueberries. 5ch, Pears. 10ch (No. 751), Plums. 10ch (No. 752), Schizandra. 10ch (No. 753), Raspberries. 40ch, Jujube.

1966, Dec. 30

749-754	A622	Set of 6	6.00	.65
		Imperf, #749-754	12.50	—

Samson Rocks A623

Ryonju Pond A624

Jinju Pond A625

The Ten Thousand Rocks, Manmulsang A626

1966, Dec. 30 Litho. *Perf. 11*

755	A623	2ch multicolored	1.00	.25
756	A624	4ch multicolored	4.00	.25
757	A625	10ch multicolored	1.00	.25
758	A626	10ch multicolored	4.00	.25
		Nos. 755-758 (4)	10.00	1.00

Diamond Mountains scenery.

Nos. 755-758 are inscribed "1964" but were actually issued in 1966.

2ch and 4ch issued without gum. 10ch values issued with gum.

Onpo — A627

Myohyang A628

Songdowon A629

Hongwon A630

1966, Dec. 30 Engr. *Perf. 12½*
With Gum

759	A627	2ch blue violet	1.00	.30
760	A628	4ch turquoise green	1.15	.30
761	A629	10ch dp blue green	1.75	.30
762	A630	40ch black	3.25	.40
		Nos. 759-762 (4)	7.15	1.30

Korean rest homes.

Korean People's Army, 19th Anniv. — A631

1967, Feb. 8 Photo. *Perf. 11*

763 A631 10ch multicolored .75 .25

Livestock Farming — A632

Designs: 5ch, Sow. 10ch, Goat. 40ch, Bull.

1967, Feb. 28 Litho.

764-766	A632	Set of 3	7.50	1.60
		Imperf, #764-766	60.00	—

5ch, 10ch issued without gum. 40ch issued both with and without gum.

Battle of Pochonbo, 30th Anniv. — A633

1967, Feb. 28 Photo. With Gum

767 A633 10ch multicolored .75 .25

Universal Compulsory Technical Education — A634

1967, Apr. 1

768 A634 10ch multicolored .75 .25

29th World Table Tennis Championships, Pyongyang — A635

10ch, 40ch designs similar to 5ch.

1967, Apr. 11 Litho.

769-771	A635	Set of 3	3.25	.60
		Imperf, #769-771	110.00	—

5ch issued with or without gum. 10ch, 40ch issued without gum. For surcharge, see No. 4514.

People Helping Guerrillas, Wangyugou A636

Blowing Up Railway Bridge — A637

Shooting Down Japanese Plane — A638

1967, Apr. 25 Engr. With Gum

772	A636	10ch deep violet	.50	.25
773	A637	10ch dk vio brown	4.25	.25
774	A638	10ch slate	.50	.25
		Nos. 772-774 (3)	5.25	.75

Paintings of the guerrilla war against Japan.

Ri Tae Hun — A639

Choe Jong Un — A640

Kim Hwa Ryong — A641

1967, Apr. 25 With Gum

775	A639	10ch slate	1.00	.25
776	A640	10ch reddish violet	3.00	.25
777	A641	10ch ultramarine	1.00	.25
		Nos. 775-777 (3)	5.00	.75

Heroes of the Republic.

Labor Day — A642

1967, May 1 Litho.

778 A642 10ch multicolored .75 .25

Pre-School Education A643

Designs of children: 5ch, Learning to count. 10ch, Making model tractor. 40ch, Playing with ball.

1967, June 1

779-781 A643 Set of 3 4.50 .75

Victory Monument, Battle of Pochonbo A644

1967, June 4

782 A644 10ch multicolored 1.00 .25

Military Sculpture — A645

Designs: 2ch, Soldier attacking tank. 5ch, Soldiers with musical instruments. 10ch, Soldier in heroic pose. 40ch, Soldier and child.

1967, June 25 Photo.

783-786 A645 Set of 4 3.00 .75

2ch issued with or without gum. Other values issued without gum.

Medicinal Plants — A646

Designs: 2ch, Polygonatum japonicum. 5ch, Abelmoschus manihat. 10ch (No. 789), Rehmannia glutinosa (olive yellow). 10ch (No. 790), Scutellaria baicalensis (turquoise blue background). 10ch (No. 791), Pulsatilla koreana (violet blue). 40ch, Tanacetum boreale.

1967, July 20 Photo.

787-792 A646 Set of 6 11.00 1.00

Nos. 787-789, 791 issued with or without gum. Nos. 790, 792 issued without gum.

Korean People's Army — A647

Designs: 5ch, Aviator, sailor, soldier. 10ch (No. 794), Officer decorating soldier. 10ch (No. 795), Soldier and farmer.

1967, July 25

793-795 A647 Set of 3 2.50 .85

5ch issued with or without gum. 10ch values issued without gum.

Freighter "Chollima" A648

1967, July 30 Engr. With Gum

796 A648 10ch deep green 2.00 .25

Drilling Rock — A649

Felling Trees — A650

Reclaiming Tideland — A651

1967, Aug. 5

797	A649	5ch black brown	.60	.25
798	A650	10ch blue green	.80	.25
799	A651	10ch slate	1.10	.25
		Nos. 797-799 (3)	2.50	.75

Revolutionary paintings.

5ch issued without gum. 10ch values issued with gum.

Crabs — A652

Designs: 2ch, Erimaculus isenbeckii. 5ch, Neptunus trituberculatus. 10ch, Paralithodes camtschatica. 40ch, Chionoecetes opilio.

1967, Aug. 10 Photo.

800-803 A652 Set of 4 8.00 .90

Reunification of Korea Propaganda A653

1967, Aug. 15 Litho.

804 A653 10ch multicolored 4.00 .35

A five-value set, featuring details from famous Korean paintings of the 15th-16th centuries, was prepared for release in August, 1967, but was not issued. Value $2,500.

A 10ch stamp celebrating the 10th anniversary of the launch of the first USSR space satellite was prepared for release on Sept. 10 but was not issued. Value $1,500.

Waterfalls — A654

Designs: 2ch, Tongrim waterfalls 10ch, Sanju waterfall, Mt. Myohyang. 40ch, Sambang waterfall, Mt. Chonak.

1967, Oct. 10
805-807 A654 Set of 3 12.00 .80

2ch issued with or without gum. 10ch, 40ch issued without gum.

"For Fresh Great Revolutionary Upsurge" A655

Designs: 5ch, Ship, train and truck. 10ch (No. 809), Machine industry. 10ch (No. 810), Truck, bulldozer, tractor and farmers. 10ch (No. 811), Construction machinery, buildings. 10ch (No. 812), Chollima flying horse and banners.

1967, Nov. 1 **Engr.**
808-812 A655 Set of 5 11.00 1.00

Russian Revolution, 50th Anniv. — A656

1967, Nov. 7 **Photo.**
813 A656 10ch multicolored 1.50 .25

Korean Elections A657

Designs: 10ch (No. 814), Voters and flags. 10ch (No. 815), Woman casting ballot (vert.)

1967, Nov. 23 **Litho.**
814-815 A657 Set of 2 3.50 1.00

Raptors — A658

Designs: 2ch, Black vulture. 10ch, Rough-legged buzzard. 40ch, White-tailed eagle.

1967, Dec. 1 **Photo.**
816-818 A658 Set of 3 14.00 1.75

2ch issued with or without gum. 10ch, 40ch issued without gum. For surcharge, see No. 4512.

Chongjin A659

Hamhung A660

Sinuiju — A661

1967, Dec. 20 **Engr.** **With Gum**
819 A659 5ch bronze green 1.10 .25
820 A660 10ch violet 1.10 .25
821 A661 10ch red violet 1.10 .25
Nos. 819-821 (3) 3.30 .75

Korean cities.

Whaler Firing Harpoon — A662

With or Without Gum

1967, Dec. 30
822 A662 10ch ultramarine 2.50 .25

Soldier with Red Book — A663

Soldier Mounting Bayonet A664

Worker and Bayoneted Rifle — A665

Litho or Photo (#829)

1967, Dec. 30
823 A663 10ch multicolored .40 .25
824 A664 10ch multicolored .40 .25
825 A665 10ch multicolored .40 .25
Nos. 823-825 (3) 1.20 .75

Korean People's Army, 20th Anniv. A666

Designs: a, Airman, soldier and sailor. b, Soldier, battle in background. c, Soldier & KDPR arms. d, Soldier & flag. e, Soldier with Red Book. f, Three soldiers, North Korean flag. g, Soldier & worker. h, Soldier saluting. i, Soldier attacking. j, Soldier, sailor & airman beneath flag.

1968, Feb. 3 **Litho.**
826 A666 Sheet of 10 80.00 *30.00*
a.-j. 10ch, any single .45 .25

Ri Su Bok (1934-51) A667

Han Kye Ryol (1926-51) A668

1968, Feb. 10 **Engr.** **With Gum**
827 A667 10ch dark rose *550.00*
828 A667 10ch light violet 1.00 .25
829 A668 10ch dark green 550.00
830 A668 10ch lt blue violet 1.00 .25
Nos. 827-830 (4) 1,102. .50

War heroes.

Nos. 827 and 829 were prepared but not issued.

Apartment Building, Pyongyang — A669

1968, Mar. 5 **Litho.** **With Gum**
831 A669 10ch bright blue 1.00 .25

Kim Il Sung, 56th Birthday — A670

1968, Apr. 15 **With Gum**
832 A670 40ch multicolored 1.10 .35

Printed in sheets of four stamps.

Exists in a miniature sheet of one, which is rare (2 examples reported),

Kim Il Sung's Family Home in Mangyongdae — A671

Leaving Home at Age 13 — A672

Mangyong Hill — A673

Kim Il Sung with Father A674

Kim Il Sung with Mother A675

1968, Apr. 15
833 A671 10ch multicolored 1.50 .25
834 A672 10ch multicolored 1.50 .25
835 A673 10ch multicolored 1.50 .25
836 A674 10ch multicolored 1.50 .25
837 A675 10ch multicolored 1.50 .25
Nos. 833-837 (5) 7.50 1.25

Childhood of Kim Il Sung.

See Nos. 883-887, 927-930.

Dredger *2 September* — A676

1968, June 5
838 A676 5ch green 1.40 .25
839 A676 5ch blue *850.00 600.00*

Matsutake Mushroom A677

Shiitake Mushroom A678

Meadow Mushroom — A679

1968, Aug. 10 **Photo.** **With Gum**
840 A677 5ch multicolored 20.00 .55
841 A678 10ch multicolored 40.00 .90
842 A679 10ch multicolored 40.00 .90
Nos. 840-842 (3) 100.00 2.35

Founding of the Korean Democratic People's Republic, 20th Anniv. — A680

Designs: a, Statue of national arms. b, North Korean flag. c, Worker, peasant & flag. d, Soldier & flag. e, Flying Horse of Chollima. f, Soldiers & tanks. g, Battle scene. h, Workers, banner & monument.

1968, Sept. 2 **Litho.** **With Gum**
843 A680 Block of 8, #a.-h. 40.00 *35.00*
a.-h. 10ch, any single 1.50 .25

Kaesong Students' and Children's Palace — A681

1968, Oct. 5 **With Gum**
844 A681 10ch greenish blue .50 .25

Domestic Goods — A682

Designs: 2ch, Shopper with domestic items. 5ch, Textile manufacturing. 10ch, Cannery.

1968, Nov. 5 **Photo.** **With Gum**
845-847 A682 Set of 3 2.75 .65

Kim Il Sung's 10-Point Program — A683

Design: 10ch, Two soldiers, Red Book, horiz.

1968, Dec. 5 **Litho.**
848-849 A683 Set of 2 1.10 .25

Increasing Agricultural Production A684

Designs: 5ch, Woman carrying eggs. 10ch (No. 851), Woman harvesting wheat. 10ch (No. 852), Woman holding basket of fruit.

1968, Dec. 10 **Photo.** **With Gum**
850-852 A684 Set of 3 1.40 .55

Shellfish
A685

Designs: 5ch (No. 853), Scallop. 5ch (No. 854), Clam. 10ch, Mussel.

1968, Dec. 20 **With Gum**
853-855 A685 Set of 3 6.00 .50

Details of Battle of Pochonbo Victory Monument
A686

Designs (all 10ch): No. 856, Kim Il Sung at head of columns, vert. No. 857, shown. No. 858, Figures marching to right, green sky at right (42.75x28mm). No. 859, Figures marching to left (55.5x28mm). No. 860, Figures marching to right (55.5x28mm). No. 861, Figures marching to left, sky at right (42.75x28mm). No. 862, Figures marching to left, sky at left (42.75x28mm).

1968, Dec. 30
856-862 A686 Set of 7 3.50 1.35

Grand Theater, Pyongyang
A687

1968, Dec. 30
863 A687 10ch dark brown 1.10 .25

Revolutionary Museum, Pochonbo
A688

1968, Dec. 30
864 A688 2ch dark green .55 .25

Rural Technical Development
A689

Designs: 2ch, Irrigation. 5ch, Mechanization of agriculture. 10ch, Electrification. 40ch, Mechanical fertilization and spraying.

1969, Feb. 25
865-868 A689 Set of 4 2.50 .80

Rabbits
A690

Designs: 2ch, Gray rabbits. 10ch (No. 870), White rabbits. 10ch (No. 871), Black rabbits. 10ch (No. 872), Brown rabbits. 40ch, White rabbits.

1969, Mar. 10
869-873 A690 Set of 5 10.00 1.10

Nos. 869-873 were issued both with and without gum.

Public Health — A691

Designs: 2ch, Old man & girl. 10ch, Nurse with syringe. 40ch, Doctor with woman & child.

1969, Apr. 1
874-876 A691 Set of 3 4.25 .60

Farm Machines
A692

Designs: 10ch (No. 877), Rice sower. 10ch (No. 878), Rice harvester. 10ch (No. 879), Herbicide sprayer. 10ch (No. 880), Wheat & barley thresher.

1969, Apr. 10 **Engr.**
877-880 A692 Set of 4 3.25 .80

Mangyongdae — A693

Ponghwa
A694

1969, Apr. 15 **Litho.**
881 A693 10ch multicolored 1.75 .25
882 A694 10ch multicolored 1.75 .25

Revolutionary historical sites.

Early Revolutionary Years of Kim Il Sung — A695

Designs (all 10ch): No. 883, Kim crossing into Manchuria 1926, aged 13. No. 884, Kim talking to four students around table (blue green frame). No. 885, Kim speaking outdoors to Young Communist League meeting (apple green frame). No. 886, Kim speaking to Young Communist League meeting indoors (lilac frame). No. 887, Kim leading demonstration against teachers (peach frame).

1969, Apr. 15
883-887 A695 Set of 5 3.25 1.00

No. 884 was issued with gum. The other values were issued without gum.

Kang Pan Sok (1892-1932), Mother of Kim Il Sung — A696

Designs (all 10ch): No. 888, Birthplace at Chilgol. No. 889, Resisting Japanese police in home. No. 890, Meeting with women's revolutionary association.

1969, Apr. 21 **Photo.**
888-890 A696 Set of 3 4.50 .60

Bivouac Sites in War against Japan — A697

Designs: 5ch, Pegaebong. 10ch (No. 892), Mupho, horiz. 10ch (No. 893), Chongbong. 40ch, Konchang, horiz.

1969, Apr. 21
891-894 A697 Set of 4 3.00 .80

Chollima Statue — A698

1969, May 1
895 A698 10ch blue .85 .25

Poultry — A699

Designs: 10ch (No. 896), Mangyong chickens. 10ch (No. 897), Kwangpho ducks.

1969, June 1 **Engr.**
896-897 A699 Set of 2 5.75 .50

Socialist Education System — A700

Designs: 2ch, Kim Il Sung & children. 10ch, Student & worker with books. 40ch, Male & female students, figure "9."

1969, June 1 **Photo.**
898-900 A700 Set of 3 2.25 .60

Pochonbo Battlefield Memorials
A701

Designs: 5ch, Machine gun platform on mountainside. 10ch (No. 902), Statue of Kim Il Sung, vert. 10ch (No. 903), Aspen Tree monument (stele & enclosed tree trunk). 10ch (No. 904), Konjang Hill monument (within forest).

1969, June 4
901-904 A701 Set of 4 2.25 .80

Kim Hyong Jik (1894-1926), Father of Kim Il Sung — A702

Designs: 10ch (No. 905), Teaching at Myongsin School. 10ch (No. 906), Outdoor meeting with five other members of Korean National Association.

1969, July 10
905-906 A702 Set of 2 1.90 .40

A 10ch stamp honoring the Juvenile Chess Game of Socialist Countries was prepared for release Aug. 5, 1969, but was not issued. Value $1,000.

Sports Day, 20th Anniv. — A703

1969, Sept. 10
907 A703 10ch multicolored 1.10 .25

Korean Revolution Museum, Pyongyang — A704

1969, Sept. 10 **Litho.**
908 A704 10ch dk blue green .85 .25

Pres. Nixon Attacked by Pens — A705

1969, Sept. 18 **Litho.**
909 A705 10ch multi 3.25 .25

Anti-U.S. Imperialism Journalists' Conference, Pyongyang.

Implementation of the 10-Point Program
A706

Designs: 5ch, Soldiers, battle. 10ch (No. 911), Globe, bayonets attacking dismembered U.S. soldier. 10ch (No. 912), Workers holding Red Books & slogan, vert.

1969, Oct. 1 **Photo.**
910-912 A706 Set of 3 10.00 .75

Reunification of Korea — A707

Designs: 10ch (No. 913), Kim Il Sung, marching workers. 10ch (No. 914), Worker & soldier bayoneting U.S. soldier. 50ch, Armed workers in battle, horiz.

1969, Oct. 1 **Litho.**
913-915 A707 Set of 3 1.75 .70

Refrigerator-Transport Ship "Taesongsan" — A708

1969, Dec. 20 **Engr.**
916 A708 10ch slate purple 1.50 .30

Korean Fish — A709

Designs: 5ch, Yellowtail. 10ch, Dace. 40ch, Mullet.

1969, Dec. 20 **Photo.**
917-919 A709 Set of 3 6.50 .65

Guerrilla Conference Sites — A710

Designs: 2ch, Dahuangwai, 1935. 5ch, Yaoyinggou, 1935 (log cabin). 10ch, Xiaohaerbaling, 1940 (tent).

1970, Feb. 10
920-922 A710 Set of 3 1.50 .50

Mt. Paektu, Birthplace of the Revolution A711

Views of Mt. Paektu (all 10ch): No. 923, Lake Chon (dull green, tan, black). No. 924, Janggun Peak (pale peach, dull blue, black). No. 925, Piryu Peak (dull yellow, blue green, black). No. 926, Pyongsa Peak (brown orange, blue, red violet).

1970, Mar. 10
923-926 A711 Set of 4 3.00 .70

See Nos. 959-961.

Support for North Vietnam — A712

1970, Mar. 10
927 A712 10ch multicolored .75 .25

Revolutionary Activities of Kim Il Sung — A713

Designs (all 10ch): No. 928, Receiving his father's pistols from his mother. No. 929, Receiving smuggled pistols from his mother (other young revolutionaries present). No. 930, Kim speaking with four farmers in field. No. 931, Kim speaking at Kalun meeting.

1970, Apr. 15 **Litho.**
928-931 A713 Set of 4 6.00 1.00

Lenin Birth Centenary — A714

Design: 10ch (No. 933), Lenin with cap, in three-quarter profile.

1970, Apr. 22 **Photo.**
932-933 A714 Set of 2 1.75 .45

Assoc. of Koreans in Japan, 15th Anniv. — A715

Designs (both 10ch): No. 934, Red. No. 935, Maroon.

1970, Apr. 27 **Engr.**
934-935 A715 Set of 2 3.00 .90

Worker-Peasant Red Guard — A716

Design: 10ch (No. 936), Factory worker in uniform, vert.

1970, May 5 **Photo.**
936-937 A716 Set of 2 1.25 .50

Peasant Education A717

Designs: 2ch, Students & newspapers. 5ch, Peasant reading book. 10ch, Students in class.

1970, June 25
938-940 A717 Set of 3 1.75 .50

Army Electrical Engineer — A718

1970, June 25
941 A718 10ch purple brown 1.00 .25

Month of the Campaign for Withdrawal of U.S. Troops from South Korea — A719

Design: 10ch, Soldier & partisan.

1970, June 25
942-943 A719 Set of 2 1.75 .25

Anti-U.S., South Korea Propaganda A720

1970, June 25 **Engr.**
944 A720 10ch deep violet .75 .25

Campaign for Increased Productivity A721

Designs (all 10ch): No. 945, Quarryman. No. 946, Steelworker. No. 947, Machinist. No. 948, Worker with bag. No. 949, Construction worker. No. 950, Railway flagman.

1970, Sept. 10 **Photo.**
945-950 A721 Set of 6 5.50 1.50

Workers' Party Program — A722

Designs: 5ch, Peasant, farm scene. 10ch, Steelworker. 40ch, Soldiers.

1970, Oct. 5 **Engr.**
951-953 A722 Set of 3 5.50 .70

Korean Workers' Party, 25th Anniv. — A723

1970, Oct. 10 **Photo.**
954 A723 10ch multicolored 1.00 .25

5th Korean Workers' Party Congress A724

Issued in miniature sheet of 10, with one 40ch value (No. 955j) and nine 10ch values. Designs: a, Kim Il Sung, marchers. b, Family & apartment buildings. c, Soldier with Red Book. d, Soldier with binoculars, various weapons. e, Steelworker. f, Workers killing U.S. soldier. g, Farmers. h, Students. i, Schoolgirl with Red Book, atomic energy symbol. j, Cooperation with South Korean guerillas.

1970, Nov. 2 **Litho.**
955 Sheet of 10, #a.-j. 900.00
a.-i. A724 10ch Any single 1.40 .50
j. A724 40ch multi 600.00

Soon after release, a design error was discovered on No. 955j, and this stamp was removed from souvenir sheets remaining in stock, usually with the bottom selvage. This is the form in which this set is commonly offered. Value, $25. The full sheet of 10 is scarce.

League of Socialist Working Youth of Korea, 25th Anniv. — A725

1971, Jan. 17 **Photo.**
956 A725 10ch multicolored .55 .25

Nanhutou Conference, 35th Anniv. — A726

1971, Feb. 28
957 A726 10ch multicolored .55 .25

Land Reform Law, 25th Anniv. — A727

1971, Mar. 5
958 A727 2ch multicolored .55 .25

Mt. Paektu, Second Issue — A728

Designs: 2ch, Mountainscape. 5ch, Paektu Waterfalls, vert. 10ch, Western Peak.

1971, Mar. 10
959-961 A728 Set of 3 5.00 .60

Revolutionary Museums A729

Designs (all 10ch): No. 962, Mangyongdae (red orange & ultramarine). No. 963, Phophyong (yellow & brown). No. 964, Junggang (salmon & green).

1971, Apr. 1
962-964 A729 Set of 3 2.00 .75

Coal Production 6-Year Plan — A730

1971, Apr. 1
965 A730 10ch multicolored 1.50 .25

Revolutionary Activities of Kim Il Sung — A731

Designs (all 10ch): No. 966, Portrait, vert. No. 967, Kim addressing crowd at guerrilla base camp. No. 968, Kim speaking with children on hillside. No. 969, Kim reviewing Anti-Japanese Guerrilla Army 1932.

1971, Apr. 15 **Litho.**
966-969 A731 Set of 4 3.50 .90

May Day — A732

1971, May 1 **Photo.**
970 A732 1w multicolored 4.00 .45

Association for the Restoration of the Fatherland, 35th Anniv. — A733

1971, May 5
971 A733 10ch multicolored 1.50 .25

Battles in the Musan Area Command (1939) — A734

Designs: 5ch, Sinsadong Monument. 10ch, Taehongdan Monument, with encased machine guns, horiz. 40ch, Musan headquarters (log cabins in forest), horiz.

1971, May 23
972-974 A734 Set of 3 2.50 .70

Koreans in Japan — A735

1971, May 25
975 A735 10ch chocolate .75 .25

A 10ch stamp commemorating the Asia-Africa Invitational Table Tennis Game for Friendship was prepared for release on May 27, 1971, but was not issued. Value $750.

Korean Children's Union, 25th Anniv. — A736

1971, June 6
976 A736 10ch multicolored .75 .25

6th Congress, League of Socialist Working Youth of Korea — A737

Designs: 5ch, Marchers & banners. 10ch, Marchers, banners & globe with map of Korea.

1971, June 21
977-978 A737 Set of 2 1.75 .25

Labor Law, 25th Anniv. — A738

1971, June 24

979 A738 5ch multicolored 1.00 .25

Sex Equality Law, 25th Anniv. — A739

1971, July 30

980 A739 5ch multicolored .75 .25

Universal Compulsory Primary Education, 15th Anniv. — A740

1971, Aug. 1

981 A740 10ch multicolored .80 .25

South Korean Revolutionaries A741

Designs: 5ch, Choe Yong Do (1923-69). 10ch (No. 983), Kim Jong Thae (1926-69), portrait with rioters killing U.S. soldier. 10ch (No. 984), Guerrilla fighter with machine gun & Red Book, battle scene.

1971, Aug. 1

982-984 A741 Set of 3 3.50 1.15

Nationalization of Industry, 25th Anniv. — A742

1971, Aug. 10

985 A742 5ch multicolored 2.75 .25

Anti-Imperialist, Anti-U.S. Struggle A743

Designs: 10ch (No. 986), N. Korean soldier, U.S. prisoners. 10ch (No. 987), S. Korean guerrilla fighter. 10ch (No. 988), N. Vietnamese soldiers, map. 10ch (No. 989), Cuban soldier, map. 10ch (No. 990), African guerrilla fighters, map. 40ch, six soldiers of various nationalities bayoneting dismembered U.S. soldier.

1971, Aug. 12

986-991 A743 Set of 6 *15.00* 3.00

Kim Il Sung University, 25th Anniv. — A744

1971, Oct. 1

992 A744 10ch multicolored 1.00 .25

Large Machines — A745

Designs: 2ch, 6,000-ton press. 5ch, Refrigerated cargo ship "Ponghwasan." 10ch (No. 995), Sungrisan heavy truck. 10ch (No. 996), Bulldozer.

1971, Nov. 2 **Litho.**

993-996 A745 Set of 4 6.50 .50

Tasks of the 6-Year Plan — A746

Designs (all 10ch): No. 997, Workers & text on red field. No. 998, Mining. No. 999, Consumer goods. No. 1000, Lathe. No. 1001, Construction equipment. No. 1002, Consumer electronic products. No. 1003, Grains, farming. No. 1004, Railway track, transportation. No. 1005, Freighter. No. 1006, Hand with wrench, manufacturing scenes. No. 1007, Crate & export goods on dock.

1971, Nov. 2 **Photo.**

997-1007 A746 Set of 11 30.00 3.75

Cultural Revolution A747

Designs: 2ch, Technical students, university. 5ch, Mechanic. 10ch (No. 1010), Chemist. 10ch (No. 1011), Composer at piano. 10ch (No. 1012), Schoolchildren.

1971, Nov. 2

1008-1012 A747 Set of 5 *10.00* .90

Ideological Revolution A748

Designs (all 10ch): No. 1013, Workers with Red Books, banners. No. 1014, Worker with hydraulic drill. No. 1015, Two workers reading Red Book. No. 1016, Workers' lecture.

1971, Nov. 2

1013-1016 A748 Set of 4 *6.00* .50

Improvement in Living Standards A749

1971, Nov. 2

1017 A749 10ch multicolored *2.50* .25

Solidarity with International Revolutionary Forces — A750

Designs (all 10ch): No. 1018, Revolutionary placards being driven into U.S. soldier. No. 1019, Japanese militarists being hammered by mallet. No. 1020, Bayoneted rifles held aloft. No. 1021, Armed international revolutionaries advancing, horiz.

1971, Nov. 2

1018-1021 A750 Set of 4 *5.00* .80

6-Year Plan — A751

1971, Nov. 2

1022 A751 10ch multicolored 3.50 .25

Three sets were prepared for release on Nov. 2, 1971, but were not issued: Butterflies (3 stamps), value $2,500; Korean Reunification (2 10ch stamps), value $750; Cultural Revolution/Improvement of the People's Living Standards (7 10ch stamps), value $5,000.

Samil Wolgan Monthly, 35th Anniv. — A752

1971, Dec. 1

1023 A752 10ch multicolored 3.50 .25

Domestic Printings

Sometime in the early 1970s, the DPRK post office begin to produce separate printings of some issues for domestic use. These stamps were generally printed on poorer quality white or brownish unsurfaced papers and demonstrated poorer overall production values. Serious students of the period are now working to identify just which stamps exist in this form and how to easily distinguish them from the higher-quality printings intended for sale to foreign collectors. At this time, these domestic-use printings are generally sold for $5-$20 per stamp.

Poultry Breeding A753

Designs: 5ch, Chicks. 10ch, Chickens & automated henhouse. 40ch, Eggs, canned chicken, dead chickens hanging on hooks.

1972, Feb. 1

1024-1026 A753 Set of 3 3.50 .95

War Films A754

Designs (all 10ch): No. 1027, Man & woman, from *Vintage Shrine.* No. 1028, Guerrilla bayoneting soldier in back, from *The Fate of a Self-Defense Corps Member.* No. 1029, Young woman with a pistol, from *Sea of Blood.*

1972, Apr. 1

1027-1029 A754 Set of 3 *6.00* .30

A 10ch value picturing *The Flower Girl* was prepared but not issued. Value $2,000.

Kim Il Sung — A755

Kim at Military Conference — A756

Kim by Lake Chon A757

Various portraits of Kim Il Sung: No. 1030, shown. No. 1031, In heroic pose. No. 1032, shown. No. 1033, In wheatfield. No. 1034, In factory. No. 1035, With foundry workers. No. 1036, Aboard whaling ship. No. 1037, Visiting hospital. No. 1038, Visiting fruit farm. No. 1039, With railroad surveyors. No. 1040, With women workers. No. 1041, Sitting with villagers. No. 1042, Touring chicken plant. No. 1043, On park bench with children. No. 1044, Portrait with marchers.

1972, Apr. 15 **Litho.**

1030 A755 5ch multicolored .25 .25
a. Strip of 3, #1030-1031, 1044 2.40
1031 A755 5ch multicolored .25 .25
1032 A756 5ch multicolored .25 .25
a. Pair, #1032, 1043 1.20
1033 A756 10ch multicolored .55 .25
a. Block of 10, #1033-1042 10.50
1034 A756 10ch multicolored 2.40 .40
1035 A756 10ch multicolored .25 .25
1036 A756 10ch multicolored .70 .25
1037 A756 10ch multicolored 1.05 .25
1038 A756 10ch multicolored .25 .25
1039 A756 10ch multicolored 2.40 .25
1040 A756 10ch multicolored 1.50 .25
1041 A756 10ch multicolored .25 .25
1042 A756 10ch multicolored .50 .25
1043 A755 40ch multicolored .65 .25
1044 A756 1wn multicolored 1.00 .40
Nos. 1030-1044 (15) 12.25 4.05

Souvenir Sheet

1045 A757 3wn multicolored 10.00 6.00

60th birthday of Kim Il Sung.

Nos. 1030-1031 and 1044, 1032 and 1043, and 1033-1042, respectively, were printed setenant within their sheets.

A 4-stamp set (2ch, 5ch, 10ch and 15ch values) honoring the 20th Olympic Games were prepared but not issued. Value $3,000.

Guerrilla Army, 40th Anniv. — A758

1972, Apr. 25 **Photo.**

1046 A758 10ch multicolored 4.00 1.00

Revolutionary Sites — A759

Designs: 2ch, Ryongpho. 5ch, Onjong. 10ch, Kosanjin. 40ch, Jonsung.

1972, July 27 **Litho.**
1047-1050 A759 Set of 4 2.25 .50

Olympic Games, Munich — A760

Designs: 2ch, Volleyball. 5ch, Boxing, horiz. 10ch (No. 1053), Judo. 10ch (No. 1054), Wrestling, horiz. 40ch, Rifle-shooting.

1972, Oct. 1
1051-1055 A760 Set of 5 4.00 1.00

Chollima Street, Pyongyang — A761

Designs (street scenes): 5ch, salmon & black. 10ch (No. 1057), dull yellow & black. 10ch (No. 1058), green & black.

1972, Nov. 1
1056-1058 A761 Set of 3 5.50 .85

Resource Management A762

Designs: 5ch, Dredging river. 10ch, Forest conservation. 40ch, Tideland reclamation.

1972, Nov. 1 **Photo.**
1059-1061 A762 Set of 3 2.75 .35

6-Year Plan - Metallurgical A763

Designs (all 10ch): No. 1062, Sheet metal, ingots, smelters. No. 1063, Pipes, foundry.

1972, Nov. 1
1062-1063 A763 Set of 2 3.75 .35

6-Year Plan — Mining Industry A764

Designs (all 10ch): No. 1064, Iron ore. No. 1065, Coal.

1972, Nov. 1 **Litho.**
1064-1065 A764 Set of 2 4.50 .45

Three Major Goals of the Technical Revolution A765

Designs (all 10ch): No. 1066, Agricultural mechanization. No. 1067, Industrial automation. No. 1068, Lightening of women's household chores.

1972, Nov. 2 **Photo.**
1066-1068 A765 Set of 3 6.00 .60

6-Year Plan - Machine-Building — A766

Designs (all 10ch): No. 1069, Machine tools. No. 1070, Electronics & automation tools. No. 1071, Single-purpose machines.

1972, Nov. 2 **Photo.**
1069-1071 A766 Set of 3 3.50 .60

6-Year Plan — Chemical Industry A767

Designs (all 10ch): No. 1072, Chemical fertilizers, herbicides, insecticides. No. 1073, Tire, tubing, various chemical products.

1972, Nov. 2
1072-1073 A767 Set of 2 2.50 .40

6-Year Plan — Light Industry A768

Designs (all 10ch): No. 1074, Clothing, textiles. No. 1075, Clothing, kitchenware. No. 1076, Household Goods.

1972, Nov. 2
1074-1076 A768 Set of 3 3.50 .60

6-Year Plan - Rural Economy A769

Designs (all 10ch): No. 1077, Irrigating field. No. 1078, Bulldozers levelling field. No. 1079, Applying chemical fertilizer.

1972, Nov. 2 **Litho.**
1077-1079 A769 Set of 3 3.50 .65

6-Year Plan - Transportation A770

Designs (all 10ch): No. 1080, Electric train. No. 1081, New railway construction. No. 1082, Coastal & river transport.

1972, Nov. 2
1080-1082 A770 Set of 3 8.00 .60

6-Year Plan - Military A771

Designs (all 10ch): No. 1083, Soldier with artillery shell. No. 1084, Navy gunner. No. 1085, Air Force pilot in cockpit.

1972, Nov. 2
1083-1085 A771 Set of 3 6.00 .60

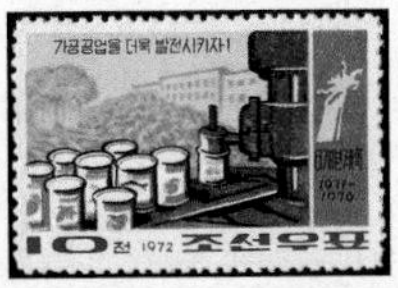

6-Year Plan - Food Storage A772

Designs (all 10ch): No. 1086, Food Processing. No. 1087, Packing foodstuffs. No. 1088, Food storage (radishes, fruit, fish).

1972, Nov. 2 **Photo.**
1086-1088 A772 Set of 3 10.00 .55

Struggle for Reunification of Korea — A773

Designs (all 10ch): No. 1089, South Koreans with banners praising Kim Il Sung. No. 1090, S. Korean guerrillas killing U.S. & S. Korean soldiers. No. 1091, March of armed S. Korean workers. No. 1092, S. Koreans rioting, rioters on top of U.S. tank. No. 1093, N. Koreans demonstrating in support of S. Korean revolutionaries. No. 1094, International revolutionaries condemning U.S. soldier. No. 1095, S. Korean marchers carrying banner & Red Book.

1972, Nov. 2
1089-1095 A773 Set of 7 13.00 1.20

A 10ch anti-United States propaganda stamp was prepared for release Nov. 2, 1972, but not issued. Value $750.

Machine Tools — A774

Designs: 5ch, Single-axis automatic lathe. 10ch, *Kusong-3* lathe. 40ch, 2,000-ton crank press.

1972, Dec. 1 **Litho.**
1096-1098 A774 Set of 3 6.00 1.00

National Elections — A775

Designs (both 10ch): No. 1099, Voter with registration card. No. 1100, Voter casting ballot.

1972, Dec. 12 **Photo.**
1099-1100 A775 Set of 2 3.00 .50

Korean People's Army, 25th Anniv. A776

Designs: 5ch, Soldier. 10ch, Sailor. 40ch, Pilot.

1973, Feb. 8
1101-1103 A776 Set of 3 8.00 1.60

Mangyongdae Historic Sites — A777

Scenes from Kim Il Sung's childhood: 2ch, Wrestling site. 5ch, "Warship" rock. 10ch (No. 1106), Swinging tree, vert. 10ch (No. 1107), Sliding rock. 40ch, Fishing spot on riverside.

1973, Apr. 15
1104-1108 A777 Set of 5 4.50 1.00

Mansu Hill Monument — A778

Designs: 10ch (No. 1109), Anti-Japanese revolutionary monument. 10ch (No. 1110), Socialist Revolution & Construction monument. 40ch, Statue of Kim Il Sung. 3w, Korean Revolution Museum, hrz.

1973, Apr. 15 **Litho.**
1109-1112 A778 Set of 4 14.50 2.50

Secret Revolutionary Camps in the 1932 Guerrilla War — A780

Designs: 10ch (No. 1113), Karajibong Camp. 10ch (No. 1114), Soksaegoi Camp.

1973, Apr. 26
1113-1114 A780 Set of 2 1.50 .25

Anti-Japanese Propaganda — A781

1973, June 1
1115 A781 10ch multicolored .60 .25

Reunification of Korea — A782

Designs: 2ch, Finger pointing down at destroyed U.S. tanks. 5ch, Electric train, crane lifting tractor. 10ch (No. 1118), Hand holding declaration, map of Korea. 10ch (No. 1119), Leaflets falling on happy crowd. 40ch, Flag & globe.

1973, June 23
1116-1120 A782 Set of 5 6.50 .75

Trucks & Tractors — A783

Designs: 10ch (No. 1121), Trucks. 10ch (No. 1122), Bulldozer, tractors.

1973, July 1 **Photo.**
1121-1122 A783 Set of 2 1.60 .30

Socialist Countries' Junior Women's Volleyball Games — A784

1973, July 27 **Litho.**
1123 A784 10ch multicolored 1.10 .25

North Korean Victory in the Korean War — A785

Designs: 10ch (No. 1124), Triumphant N. Koreans & battlefield scene. 10ch (No. 1125), N. Koreans & symbols of military & industrial power.

1973, July 27 **Photo.**
1124-1125 A785 Set of 2 3.25 .30

Mansudae Art Troupe A786

Dances: 10ch, *Snow Falls,* dancers with red streamers. 25ch, *Bumper Harvest of Apples.* 40ch, *Azalea of the Fatherland.*

1973, Aug. 1 **Litho.**
1126-1128 A786 Set of 3 4.50 .75

Compulsory Secondary Education, 10th Anniv. — A787

1973, Sept. 1
1129 A787 10ch multicolored .85 .25

Writings of Kim Il Sung — A788

Designs (all 10ch): No. 1130, *On Juche in Our Revolution* (claret scene). No. 1131, *Kim Il Sung Selected Works,* crowd holding glowing book aloft. No. 1132, *Let Us Further Strengthen Our Socialist System,* four figures holding open book aloft.

1973, Sept. 1
1130-1132 A788 Set of 3 2.50 .40

See Nos. 1180-1181.

DPRK, 25th Anniv. — A789

Designs: 5ch, Foundation of the republic ("1948-1973"). 10ch, Korean War ("1950-1953"). 40ch, Farmer, worker & soldier with scenes of economic development in background ("1948-1973").

1973, Sept. 9
1133-1135 A789 Set of 3 3.50 .80

Mt. Myohyang Scenes — A790

Designs: 2ch, Popwang Peak. 5ch, Inhodae Rock. 10ch, Taeha Falls, vert. 40ch, Ryongyon Falls, vert.

1973, Oct. 1 **Photo.**
1136-1139 A790 Set of 4 8.25 .75

Party Founding Museum A791

1973, Oct. 10
1140 A791 1w multicolored 3.50 .70

People's Athletic Meeting — A792

Designs: 2ch, Soccer player, basketball players. 5ch, High jumper, women sprinters. 10ch (No. 1143), Wrestlers, skier. 10ch (No. 1144), Speed skaters, skier. 40ch, Parachutist, motorcyclists.

1973, Nov. 1 **Litho.**
1141-1145 A792 Set of 5 6.50 .75

Socialist Countries' Junior Weightlifting Competition — A793

1973, Nov. 21
1146 A793 10ch multicolored 1.40 .25

Moran Hill Scenery — A794

Designs: 2ch, Chongryu Cliff. 5ch, Moran Waterfalls. 10ch, Pubyok Pavilion. 40ch, Ulmil Pavilion.

1973, Nov. 1
1147-1150 A794 Set of 4 9.25 1.00

Mt. Kumgang Scenery — A795

Designs: 2ch, Mujigae (Rainbow) Bridge. 5ch, Suspension bridge, Okryu Valley, horiz. 10ch (No. 1153), Chonnyo Peak. 10ch (No. 1154), Chilchung Rock & Sonji Peak, horiz. 40ch, Sujong & Pari Peaks, horiz.

1973, Nov. 1
1151-1155 A795 Set of 5 8.25 1.00

Magnolia — A796

1973, Nov. 1
1156 A796 10ch multicolored 2.25 .40

South Korean Revolutionary Struggle — A797

Designs (both 10ch): No. 1157, Mob beating U.S. soldier. No. 1158, Armed demonstrators killing U.S. soldier.

1973, Nov. 2 **Photo.**
1157-1158 A797 Set of 2 5.25 .30

Scenes from *Butterflies and Cock* Fairy Tale — A798

Designs: 2ch, Cock appearing in the village of butterflies. 5ch, Butterflies discussing how to repel cock. No. 1161, 10ch, Cock chasing butterflies with basket. No. 1162, 10ch, Butterflies luring cock up cliff. 40ch, Cock chasing butterflies off cliff edge. 90ch, Cock drowning.

1973, Dec. 1 **Litho.**
1159-1164 A798 Set of 6 17.50 1.20

For surcharge, see No. 4556.

Revolutionary Sites — A799

Designs: 2ch, Buildings, Yonphung. 5ch, Buildings, iron-rail fence, Hyangha. 10ch, Three buildings surrounding courtyard, Changgol. 40ch, Monuments in park-like setting, Paeksong.

1973, Dec. 1
1165-1168 A799 Set of 4 3.25 .60

Modern Buildings in Pyongyang A800

Designs: 2ch, Science Library, Kim Il Sung University. 5ch, Building No. 2, Kim Il Sung University, vert. 10ch, War Museum. 40ch, People's Palace of Culture. 90ch, Pyongyang Indoor Stadium.

1973, Dec. 1 **Photo.**
1169-1173 A800 Set of 5 4.00 1.00

Nos. 1171-1172 are 60x24mm.

Socialist Constitution of North Korea — A801

Designs (all 10ch): No. 1174, Socialist Constitution, national scenes. No. 1175, Marchers with Red Book & national arms. No. 1176, Marchers with Red Books, national flag, banners.

1973, Dec. 27 **Litho.**
1174-1176 A801 Set of 3 2.75 1.00

Korean Songbirds — A802

Designs: 5ch, Great reed warbler. 10ch (No. 1178), Gray starling (green background). 10ch (No. 1179), Daurian starling (pink background).

1973, Dec. 28 **Photo.**
1177-1179 A802 Set of 3 13.00 1.75

Writings of Kim Il Sung — A803

Designs: No. 1180, 10ch, *Let Us Intensify the Anti-Imperialist, Anti-U.S. Struggle,* bayonets threatening U.S. soldier. No. 1181, 10ch, *On the Chollima Movement and the Great Upsurge of Socialist Construction,* Chollima statue.

1974, Jan. 10 **Litho.**
1180-1181 A803 Set of 2 1.75 .35

Opening of Pyongyang Metro A804

Designs (all 10ch): No. 1182, Train at platform. No. 1183, Escalators. No. 1184, Underground station hall.

1974, Jan. 20
1182-1184 A804 Set of 3 3.00 .50

Socialist Construction A805

Designs (all 10ch): No. 1185, Capital construction. No. 1186, Industry (foundry), vert. No. 1187, Agriculture. No. 1188, Transport. No. 1189, Fishing industry.

1974, Feb. 20
1185-1189 A805 Set of 5 10.00 1.15

Theses on the Socialist Rural Question in Our Country, 10th Anniv. of Publication — A806

1974, Feb. 25
1190 A806 10ch Strip of 3, #a-c 4.00 .75

Farm Machines A807

Designs: 2ch, Compost sprayer. 5ch, *Jonjin* tractor. 10ch, *Taedoksan* tractor (with flat bed).

1974, Feb. 25 **Photo.**
1193-1195 A807 Set of 3 3.50 .50

N. Korean Victories at 1973 Sports Contests — A808

Designs: 2ch, Archery (Grenoble). 5ch, Gymnastics (Varna). 10ch, Boxing (Bucharest). 20ch, Volleyball (Pyongyang). 30ch, Rifle-shooting (Sofia). 40ch, Judo (Tbilisi). 60ch, Model aircraft flying (Vienna), horiz. 1.50w, Table tennis (Beijing), horiz.

Perf. 11, 12 (#1196, 1202-1203)

1974, Mar. 10 **Litho.**
1196-1203 A808 Set of 8 11.00 2.00

For surcharges, see Nos. 4562, 4564, 4600.

D.P.R.K.: World's First Tax-Free Country A809

1974, Apr. 1 ***Perf. 11***
1204 A809 10ch multicolored 1.25 .25

Revolutionary Activities of Kim Il Sung — A810

Designs (all 10ch): No. 1205, Kim at Nanhutou Meeting (in log room). No. 1206, Kim writing the 10-Point Program in forest. No. 1207, Kim instructing revolutionary (sitting on bench, outdoor winter scene). No. 1208, Kim at Battle of Laoheishan.

1974, Apr. 15 ***Perf. 12***
1205-1208 A810 Set of 4 3.50 .70

Scenes from the Revolutionary Opera *The Flower Girl* — A811

Designs: 2ch, Kkot Pun's blind younger sister. 5ch, Death of Kkot Pun's mother. 10ch, Kkot Pun resists landlord. 40ch, Kkot Pun setting out on the road of revolution.

1974, Apr. 30
1209-1212 A811 Set of 4 12.00 .60

Souvenir Sheet

1213 A811 50ch multicolored 16.50 1.50

No. 1213 contains one larger 50ch value, depicting Kroi Pun (The Flower Girl) and the flowers of Revolution, imperf.

Pyongyang Zoo, 15th Anniv. — A812

A813

Designs: 2ch, Wildcat. 5ch, Lynx. No. 1216, 10ch, Fox. No. 1217, 10ch. Wild boar. 20ch, Wolf. 40ch, Bear. 60ch, Leopard. 70ch, Korean tiger. 90ch, Lion.

No. 1223: a, 10ch, Wildcat. b, 30ch, Lynx. c, 50ch, Leopard. d, 60ch, Tiger.

1974, May 10 ***Perf. 11***
1214-1222 A812 Set of 9 14.50 2.50

Souvenir Sheet

1223 A813 Sheet of 4, imperf 60.00 —

For surcharges, see Nos. 4541, 4579.

Wild Roses — A814

Designs: 2ch, Prickly wild rose. 5ch, Yellow sweet briar. 10ch (No. 1226), Pink aromatic rose. 10ch (No. 1227), Aronia sweet briar (yellow centers). 40ch, Rosa rugosa.

1974, May 20
1224-1228 A814 Set of 5 8.25 1.00

Souvenir Sheet

Kim Il Sung with Children A815

1974, June 1 ***Imperf***
1229 A815 1.20w multicolored 8.25 7.50

Wild Flowering Plants — A816

Designs: 2ch, Chinese trumpet vine. 5ch, Day lily. 10ch, Shooting star lily. 20ch, Tiger lily. 40ch, Azalea. 60ch, Yellow day lily.

1974, May 20 ***Perf. 11***
1230-1235 A816 Set of 6 7.50 1.00

Universal Postal Union, Cent. — A817

U.P.U. emblem and: 10ch, Letter carrier and construction site. 25ch, Chollima statue. 40ch, World map & airplanes.

1974, June 30 ***Perf. 12***
1236-1238 A817 Set of 3 6.00 .50

A 60ch souvenir sheet was prepared but not issued. Value $750. For surcharge, see No. 4567.

Amphibians A818

Designs: 2ch, Black spotted frog. 5ch, Oriental fire belly toad. 10ch, North American bull frog. 40ch, Common toad.

1974, July 10 ***Perf. 11***
1239-1242 A818 Set of 4 14.50 1.50

For surcharge, see No. 4542.

Soviet Space Flights A819

Designs: 10ch, Electron 1 & 2. 20ch, Proton 1. 30ch, Venera 3. 40ch, Venera 5 & 6. 50ch, Launch of Chinese satellite Chicomsat 1. 1w, Space flight of dogs "Bjelka" and "Strjelka."

1974, July 10
1243-1246 A819 Set of 4 3.00 .50

Souvenir Sheets

Imperf

1247 A819 50ch multicolored 8.25 1.00
1248 A819 1w multicolored 16.00 2.60

Nos. 1247-1248 each contain one 47x72mm stamp.

Korean Paintings A820

Designs: 2ch, Woman in Namgang Village. 5ch, Old Man on the Raktong River (60x49mm). 10ch, Inner Kumgang in the Morning. 20ch, Mt. Kumgang (60x49mm). 1.50w, Evening Glow Over Kangson.

1974, July 10
1249-1252 A820 Set of 4 6.00 .80

Souvenir Sheet

Imperf

1253 A820 1.50w multicolored 11.00 10.00

For surcharge, see No. 4592.

Korean Civil Aviation A821

Designs: 2ch, Antonov AN-2. 5ch, Lisunov LI-2. 10ch, Ilyushin IL-14P. 40ch, Antonov AN-24. 60ch, Ilyushin IL-18. 90ch, Antonov AN-24.

1974, Aug. 1
1254-1258 A821 Set of 5 9.25 1.75

Souvenir Sheet

Imperf

1259 A821 90ch multicolored 13.00 6.50

No. 1264 contains one 49x30mm stamp.

Alpine Plants — A822

Designs: 2ch, Rhododendron. 5ch, White mountain-avens. 10ch, Shrubby cinquefoil. 20ch, Poppies. 40ch, Purple mountain heather. 60ch, Oxytropis anertii.

1974, Aug. 10 ***Perf. 12***
1260-1265 A822 Set of 6 8.00 1.50

Korean Paintings A823

Designs: 10ch, Sobaek Stream in the Morning. 20ch, Combatants of Mt. Laohei (60x40mm).. 30ch, Spring on the Terraced Field. 40ch, Night of Tideland. 60ch, Daughter.

1974, Aug. 15 ***Perf. 11***
1266-1270 A823 Set of 5 12.00 2.00

For surcharge, see No. 4563.

Italian Communist Newspaper L'Unita, 50th Anniv. — A824

1974, Sept. 1 ***Imperf***
1271 A824 1.50w multicolored 24.50 5.00

Revolutionary Sites — A825

Designs: 5ch, Munmyong. 10ch, Unha (log cabin).

1974, Sept. 9 ***Perf. 11***
1272-1273 A825 Set of 2 1.40 .25

Oil-producing Crops — A826

Designs: 2ch, Sesame. 5ch, Perilla-oil plant. 10ch, Sunflower. 40ch, Castor bean.

1974, Sept. 30
1274-1277 A826 Set of 4 7.00 1.30

For surcharge, see No. 4543.

Revolutionary Activities of Kim Il Sung — A827

Designs (all 10ch): No. 1278, Portrait in guerrilla uniform, vert. No. 1279, On horseback. No. 1280, Helping a farm family. No. 1281, Negotiating anti-Japanese united front with Chinese commander.

1974, Oct. 10 ***Perf. 12***
1278-1281 A827 Set of 4 6.00 .75

No. 1278 is 42x65mm. Nos. 1279-1281 are 52x34.5mm.

Grand Monument on Mansu Hill — A828

Designs (all 10ch): No. 1282, Soldiers marching right, lead figure holding rifle aloft. No. 1283, Soldiers marching left, lead figure holding rifle aloft. No. 1284, Workers marching right, lead figure holding torch aloft. No. 1285, Workers marching left, lead figure holding torch aloft.

1974, Oct. 10 ***Perf. 11***
1282-1285 A828 Set of 4 3.00 .70

Deep-Sea Fishing — A829

Designs: a, 2ch, Factory ship *Chilbosan*. b, 5ch, Factory ship *Paektusan*. c, 10ch, Cargo ship *Moranbong*. d, 20ch, All-purpose ship. e, 30ch, Trawler. f, 40ch, Stern trawler.

1974, Nov. 20

1286 A829 Block of 6 7.00 1.75
a.-f. Any single 1.10 .30

A830

Kim Il Sung's Crossing of the Amnok River, 50th Anniv.

1975, Feb. 3 ***Perf. 12***

1287 A830 10ch multicolored .65 .25

Pak Yong Sun A831

33rd World Table Tennis Championships — A832

1975, Feb. 16 ***Perf. 11x12***

1288 A831 10ch multicolored 3.00 .25

Souvenir Sheet

Imperf

1289 A832 80ch multicolored 3.25 1.50

Honoring Pak Yong Sun, winner of the 33rd World Table Tennis Championship, Calcutta.

Pyongyang Zoo — A833

Designs: 10ch (No. 1290), Zebra. 10ch (No. 1291), African buffalo. 20ch, Giant panda, horiz. 25ch, Bactrian camel. 30ch, Indian elephant, horiz.

Perf. 12¼, 10¾ (#1291, 1294)

1975, Feb. 20

1290-1294 A833 Set of 5 7.00 1.15

Koguryo Period Tomb Paintings, 7th Century — A834

Designs: 10ch, Blue dragon. 15ch, White tiger. 25ch, Red phoenix, vert. 40ch, Turtle and snake.

1975, Mar. 20 ***Perf. 12***

1295-1298 A834 Set of 4 6.00 1.00

The Guerrilla Base in Spring (1968) A835

Guerrilla Army Landing at Unggi (1969) A836

The Sewing Team Members (1961) A837

North Manchuria of China in Spring (1969) — A838

Comrade Kim Jong Suk Giving Guidance to the Children's Corps Members (1970) — A839

1975, Mar. 30

1299 A835 10ch multicolored .55 .25
1300 A836 10ch multicolored .55 .25
1301 A837 15ch multicolored .85 .25
1302 A838 20ch multicolored 1.75 .25
1303 A839 30ch multicolored 1.40 .25
Nos. 1299-1303 (5) 5.10 1.25

Korean Paintings, Anti-Japanese Struggle. Compare with Nos. 1325-1329, 1330-1335.

Cosmonauts' Day — A840

Designs: 10ch, Cosmonaut. 30ch, Lunokhod-2 on Moon, horiz. 40ch, Soyuz and Saiyut coupling, horiz.

1975, Apr. 12 ***Perf. 11¾***

1304-1306 A840 Set of 3 3.00 .50

Revolutionary Activities of Kim Il Sung — A841

Multicolor portraits of Kim Il Sung: 10ch (No. 1307), Speaking with troops in tent (aqua frame). 10ch (No. 1308), Greeting peasants bringing supplies (tan frame). 10ch (No. 1309), Speaking to crowd, arm upraised (light blue frame). 10ch (No. 1310), With soldiers around winter campfire (pale tan frame). 10ch (No. 1311), Lecturing to troops (pink frame). 15ch, At head of troop column in forest. 25ch, Standing by lake. 30ch, Speaking with peasants, child in lap. 40ch, Presiding over staff meeting, in tent.

1975, Apr. 15 ***Perf. 12***

1307-1315 A841 Set of 9 8.25 2.00

Souvenir Sheet

Victory Monument — A842

1975, Apr. 15 ***Imperf***

1316 A842 1w multicolored 16.50 4.00

Battle of Pochonbo, 38th Anniversary.

Flower Basket & Kim Il Sung's Birthplace A843

Kim Il Sung's Birthplace, Mangyongdae — A844

1975, Apr. 15 ***Perf. 12***

1317 A843 10ch multicolored .35 .25
1318 A844 40ch multicolored 1.60 .25

63rd Birthday of Kim Il Sung.

April 19 South Korean Popular Uprising, 15th Anniv. — A845

1975, Apr. 19 ***Perf. 11***

1319 A845 10ch multicolored .65 .25

Ri Dynasty Paintings — A846

Designs: 5ch, *Kingfisher at Lotus Pond.* 10ch, *Crabs.* 15ch, *Rose of Sharon.* 25ch, *Lotus and Water Bird.* 30ch, *Tree Peony and Cock and Hen.*

1975, May 10

1320-1324 A846 Set of 5 13.00 1.25

On the Road of Advance Southward (1966) — A847

The Assigned Post (1968) — A848

For the Sake of the Fatherland (1965) — A849

Retaliation (1970) — A850

The Awaited Ranks (1970) A851

1975, May 10

1325 A847 5ch multicolored 2.25 .25
1326 A848 10ch multicolored 1.25 .25
1327 A849 15ch multicolored 1.90 .25
1328 A850 25ch multicolored 2.75 .25
1329 A851 30ch multicolored 4.50 .25
Nos. 1325-1329 (5) 12.65 1.25

Korean Paintings, Anti-Japanese Struggle. For surcharge, see No. 4606.

Blue Signal Lamp (1960) — A852

Pine Tree (1966) — A853

Night with Snowfall (1963) A854

Smelters (1968) A855

Reclamation of Tideland (1961) — A856

Mt. Paekgum (1966) A857

1975, May 20

1330	A852	10ch multicolored	1.10	.25
1331	A853	10ch multicolored	3.75	.25
1332	A854	15ch multicolored	1.10	.25
1333	A855	20ch multicolored	1.25	.25
1334	A856	25ch multicolored	1.25	.25
1335	A857	30ch multicolored	1.25	.25
		Nos. 1330-1335 (6)	9.70	1.50

Korean Paintings. For surcharge, see No. 4596.

Chongryon Assoc. of Koreans in Japan, 20th Anniv. — A858

1975, May 25 ***Perf. 11¾***

1336	A858	10ch multicolored	1.10	—
1337	A858	3w multicolored	40.00	—

Marathon Race of Socialist Countries — A859

1975, June 8 ***Imperf***

1338 A859 1w multicolored 22.50 4.00

Diving — A860

Divers: 10ch, Man entering water feet-first. 25ch, Man performing somersault pike. 40ch, Woman entering water head-first.

1975, June 20 ***Perf. 10¾***

1339-1341 A860 Set of 3 3.25 .75

Month of Anti-U.S. Joint Struggle — A861

1975, June 25 ***Perf. 12¼***

1342 A861 10ch multicolored 1.40 .25

Fresh-Water Fish A862

Fish: 10ch (No. 1343), Memorial fish, swimming to left. 10ch (No. 1344), White fish, swimming to right. 15ch, Notch-jowl. 25ch, Amur catfish. 30ch (No. 1347), Catfish, swimming to right. 30ch (No. 1348), Snakehead, swimming to left.

1975, June 25 ***Perf. 10¾***

1343-1348 A862 Set of 6 8.00 1.10

A863

10th International Socialist Countries' Junior Friendship Soccer Tournament — A864

Soccer players, with diff. stadiums in background: 5ch, Green border. 10ch, Tan border. 15ch, Lilac border. 20ch, Pale violet border. 50ch, Dull gold border.

Perf. 10¾, Imperf (#1354)

1975, July 10

1349-1353 A863 Set of 5 4.50 1.00

Souvenir Sheet

1354 A864 1w multicolored 8.25 3.25

Parrots — A865

Parrots: 10ch, Blue & yellow macaw. 15ch, Sulphur-crested cockatoo. 20ch, Blyth's parakeet. 25ch, Rainbow lory. 30ch, Budgerigar.

1975, July 10 ***Perf. 12***

1355-1359 A865 Set of 5 17.50 1.50

For surcharge, see No. 4581.

Saesallim Street A866

Apartment House A867

Pothonggang Hotel — A868

1975, July 20 ***Perf. 11, 12 (#1360)***

1360	A866	90ch multicolored	20.00	20.00
1361	A867	1w multicolored	25.00	25.00
1362	A868	2w multicolored	35.00	35.00
		Nos. 1360-1362 (3)	80.00	80.00

New street, buildings in Pyongyang.

Blossoms — A869

Blossoms of Flowering Trees: 10ch, White peach. 15ch, Red peach. 20ch, Red plum. 25ch, Apricot. 30ch, Cherry.

1975, Aug. 20 ***Perf. 10¾***

1363-1367 A869 Set of 5 7.50 1.50

Diamond Mts. Landscapes — A870

Designs: 5ch, Sejon Peak. 10ch, Chonson Rock. 15ch, Pisa Gate. 25ch, Manmulsang. 30ch, Chaeha Peak.

1975, Aug. 20 ***Perf. 11¾***

1368-1372 A870 Set of 5 7.50 1.00

Flowers — A871

Designs: 5ch, Azalea. 10ch, White azalea. 15ch, Mountain rhododendron. 20ch, White rhododendron. 25ch, Rhododendron. 30ch, Yellow rhododendron.

1975, Aug. 30 ***Perf. 10¾***

1373-1378 A871 Set of 6 6.50 1.50

A872

Aerial Sports for National Defence — A873

Designs: 5ch (No. 1379), Gliders. 5ch (No. 1380), Remote-controlled model airplane. 10ch (No. 1381), Parachutist in free fall, vert. 10ch (No. 1382), Parachutists landing, vert. 20ch, Parachutist with bouquet of flowers. 50ch, Formation skydiving.

Perf. 12x11¾, Imperf (#1384)

1975, Sept. 9

1379-1383 A872 Set of 5 5.00 .75

Souvenir Sheet

1384 A873 50ch multicolored 6.00 .50

Flowers — A874

Fruit tree blossoms: 10ch, Wild apple. 15ch, Wild pear. 20ch, Hawthorn. 25ch, Chinese quince. 30ch, Flowering quince.

1975, Sept. 30 ***Perf. 12¼x12***

1385-1389 A874 Set of 5 5.00 1.25

Korean Workers' Party, 30th Anniv. — A875

Designs: 2ch (No. 1390), Symbolic creation of the Juche Idea. 2ch (No. 1391), Korean soldiers above American graves. 5ch (No. 1392), Hand holding torch with Juche inscription. 5ch (No. 1393), Monument of Chollima, idealized city. 10ch (No. 1394), Chollima winged horse and rider with banner. 10ch (No. 1395), Worker with Red Book. 25ch, South Koreans rioting. 70ch, Map of Korea, Red Book, flowers.

90ch (No. 1398), Kim Il Sung addressing workers, horiz. stamp, vert. souvenir sheet. 90ch (No. 1399), Kim with crowd of workers, city skyline in background, horiz. stamp, horiz. souvenir sheet.

Perf. 12, Imperf (#1398-1399)

1975, Oct. 10

1390-1397	A875	Set of 8	7.00	2.00
1398-1399	A875	Set of 2 sheets	8.25	4.00

Return of Kim Il Sung to Pyongyang, 30th Anniv. — A876

1975, Oct. 14 ***Perf. 12***

1400 A876 20ch multicolored 1.00 .25

Redong Sinmun, 30th Anniv. — A877

1975, Nov. 1 ***Perf. 11***

1401	A877	10ch multicolored	.85	.25
a.		1w, souvenir sheet, imperf.	5.50	5.00

Hyonmu Gate — A878

Taedong Gate — A879

Pothong Gate — A880

Jongum Gate — A881

Chilsong Gate — A882

Perf. 12x12¼, 12¼x12 (#1406)

1975, Nov. 20

1402 A878 10ch multicolored 1.40 .25
1403 A879 10ch multicolored 1.40 .25
1404 A880 15ch multicolored 1.90 .25
1405 A881 20ch multicolored 3.50 .25
1406 A882 30ch multicolored 5.00 .40
Nos. 1402-1406 (5) 13.20 1.40

Ancient gates of Pyongyang.

Mt. Chilbo Views A883

Designs: No. 1407, 10ch, Mae Rock (pale green border). No. 1408, 10ch, Jangsu Peak (pale yellow border). 15ch, Suri Peak. 20ch, Jangsu Peak, diff. 30ch, Rojok Peak.

1975, Nov. 30 ***Perf. 12x11¾***

1407-1411 A883 Set of 5 10.00 1.25

Wangjaesan Monument — A884

Designs: 10ch, Workers marching. 15ch, Soldiers marching. 25ch, Monument beacon tower, vert. 30ch, Base of tower, statues of Kim Il Sung, workers and soldiers.

Perf. 11¾, 10¾ (#1413)

1975, Dec. 20

1412-1415 A884 Set of 4 2.75 .75

Banners, Slogan — A885

Banners, Workers A886

1976, Jan. 17 ***Perf. 12***

1416 A885 2ch multicolored .35 .25
1417 A886 70ch multicolored .80 .50

League of Socialist Working Youth, 30th Anniv.

Ducks & Geese — A887

Designs: 10ch, Geese. 20ch, Domesticated ducks. 40ch, Kwangpo ducks.

Perf. 12, 12x12¼ (#1418)

1976, Feb. 5

1418-1420 A887 Set of 3 7.25 .50

Perf. 11

1418a 10ch multi — —
1419a 10ch multi — —

For surcharge, see No. 4519.

Korean People's Army, Sculpture — A888

Designs: 5ch, *Oath.* 10ch (No. 1422), *Unity Between Men and Officers,* horiz. 10ch (No. 1423), *This Flag to the Height.*

Perf. 12, 12¼x12 (#1421)

1976, Feb. 8

1421-1423 A888 Set of 3 2.75 .50

Rural Road at Evening (1965) — A889

Passing-on Technique (1970) — A890

Mother (1965) — A891

Medical Examination in Kindergarten (1970) — A892

Doctress of the Village (1970) A893

1976, Feb. 10 ***Perf. 12***

1424 A889 10ch multicolored .50 .25
1425 A890 15ch multicolored .55 .25
1426 A891 25ch multicolored .85 .25
1427 A892 30ch multicolored 1.50 .25
1428 A893 40ch multicolored 1.75 .25
Nos. 1424-1428 (5) 5.15 1.25

Modern Korean paintings.

Agrarian Reform Law, 30th Anniv. A894

1976, Mar. 5 ***Perf. 12***

1429 A894 10ch multicolored .65 .25

Telephone Communication Centenary — A895

Designs: 2ch, Telephones and communication satellite. 5ch, Satellite and antenna. 10ch, Satellite and telecommunications systems. 15ch, Telephone and lineman. 25ch, Satellite and map of receiving stations. 40ch, Satellite and cable-laying barge.
50ch, Satellite and antique telephone.

Surface Coated Paper

1976, Mar. 12 ***Perf. 13¼***

1430-1435 A895 Set of 6 8.75 1.00
1435a Sheet of 8, as #1430-1436 + label, ordinary paper 10.00 —

Souvenir Sheet

Imperf, Without Gum

1436 A895 50ch multicolored 3.25 .50

Flowers A896

Designs: 5ch, Cosmos. 10ch, Dahlia. 20ch, Zinnia. 40ch, China aster.

1976, Mar. 20 ***Perf. 12***

1437-1440 A896 Set of 4 3.00 1.00

Pukchong Conference, 15th Anniv. — A897

Designs: 5ch, Fruit processing industry. 10ch, Fruit and orchards.

1976, Apr. 7 ***Perf. 11½x12***

1441-1442 A897 Set of 2 2.10 .25

Locomotives A898

Designs: 5ch, Pulgungi electric train. 10ch, Jaju underground electric train. 15ch, Saeppyol diesel locomotive.

1976, Apr. 10 ***Perf. 11¾***

1443-1445 A898 Set of 3 3.25 .50

For surcharges, see Nos. 4594, 4603.

Many North Korean issues from 1976 on were also issued imperforate. These imperfs were issued for sale for hard currency, mostly to overseas collectors, and were not valid for postage.

Limited quantities of many sets from Scott No. 1446 on were issued without gum.

Day of Space Flight — A899

Designs: 2ch, Satellite. 5ch, Space station. 10ch, Communications satellite. 15ch, Future space station. 25ch, Satellite. 40ch, Communications satellite.
50ch, Lunar surface vehicle.

1976, Apr. 12 ***Perf. 13¼***

1446-1451 A899 Set of 6 3.25 1.00

Souvenir Sheet

Imperf

1452 A899 50ch multicolored 1.60 .50

A900

Kim Il Sung, 64th Birthday A901

1976, Apr. 15 ***Perf. 12***

1453 A900 10ch multicolored .85 .25

Souvenir Sheet

Imperf

1454 A901 40ch multicolored 5.00 .75

A902

3rd Asian Table Tennis Championships — A903

Designs: 5ch, Paddle and ribbon. 10ch, Three female players with bouquet. 20ch, Female player. 25ch, Male player.

Without Gum

1976, Apr. 25 — ***Perf. 12***
1455-1458 A902 Set of 4 — 3.00 1.00

Souvenir Sheet
Imperf

1459 A903 50ch multicolored — 3.50 1.00

For surcharges, see Nos. 4582, 4593, 4607.

Association for the Restoration of the Fatherland, 40th Anniv. — A904

1976, May 5 — ***Perf. 12***
1460 A904 10ch multicolored — .75 .25

Pheasants A905

Designs: 2ch, Golden pheasant. 5ch, Lady Amherst's pheasant. 10ch, Silver pheasant. 15ch, Reeves' pheasant. 25ch, Copper pheasant. 40ch, Albino ring-necked pheasant. 50ch, Ring-necked pheasant.

Surface Coated Paper

1976, May 5 — ***Perf. 11¾***
1461-1466 A905 Set of 6 — 5.00 1.50
1466a Sheet of 8, as #1461-1467 + label, perf 12, ordinary paper — 12.00 12.00

Souvenir Sheet
Imperf

1467 A905 50ch multicolored — 3.50 1.50

Potong River Monument — A906

1976, May 21 — ***Perf. 11½***
1468 A906 10ch multicolored — 75.00 —
a. Perf. 10¾ — — —

21st Olympic Games, Montreal A907

Stadium, Olympic rings, and: 2ch, Runners. 5ch, Diver. 10ch, Judo. 15ch, Gymnast. 25ch, Gymnast. 40ch, Fencers.
50ch, Runner with Olympic Torch.

Surface Coated Paper

1976, July 17 — ***Perf. 13¾***
1469-1474 A907 Set of 6 — 6.75 1.25
1474a Sheet of 8, as #1469-1475 + label, perf 12, ordinary paper — 9.00 —

Souvenir Sheet
Imperf

1475 A907 50ch multicolored — 3.50 1.50

For overprints and surcharges, see Nos. 1632-1638, 4568.

Winners, 21st Olympic Games, Montreal — A908

Designs: 2ch, Bronze Medal, Hockey — Pakistan. 5ch, Bronze Medal, Free Pistol — Rudolf Dollinger (Austria). 10ch, Silver Medal, Boxing — Li Byong Uk (DPRK). 15ch, Silver Medal, Cycling — Daniel Morelon (France). 25ch, Gold Medal, Marathon — Waldemar Cierpinski (DDR). 40ch, Gold Medal, Boxing — Ku Yong Jo (DPRK).
50ch, Gold, Silver, Bronze Medals.

Multicolored, with Winners' Inscriptions in Silver
Surface Coated Paper

1976, Aug. 2 — ***Perf. 13¼***
1476-1481 A908 Set of 6 — 6.00 1.00
1481a Sheet of 8, as #1476-1482 + label — 9.00 —

Souvenir Sheet
Imperf

1482 A908 50ch multicolored — 4.00 2.00

Same, with Different Winners' Names

Designs: 2ch, Swimming — David Wilkie (UK). 5ch, Running — Lass Viren (Finland). 10ch, Weight Lifting — Vasili Alexeev (USSR). 15ch Swimming — Kornelia Ender (DDR). 25ch, Platform Diving — Klaus Dibiasi (Italy). 40ch, Boxing — Ku Yong Jo (DPRK). No. 1489, 50ch, Gymnastics — Nadia Comaneci (Romania).
No. 1490, 50ch, Kornelia Ender.

Ordinary Paper

1976, Aug. 2 — ***Perf. 13¼***
1483-1489 A908 Sheet of 7 + label — 10.00 4.00

Souvenir Sheet
Imperf

1490 A908 50ch multi — 4.00 2.00

For overprints, see Nos. 1639-1645.

Winners, 21st Olympic Games, Montreal — A909

Designs: 2ch, Boxing — Ku Yong Jo (DPRK). 5ch, Gymnastics — Nadie Comaneci (Romania). 10ch, Pole Vault — Tadeusz Slusarski (Poland). 15ch, Hurdling — Guy Drut (France). 25ch, Cycling — Bernt Johansson (Sweden). 40ch, Soccer (DDR).
50ch, Boxing — Ko Yong Do (DPRK).

Surface Coated Paper

1976, Aug. 2 — ***Perf. 13¼***
1491-1496 A909 Set of 6 — 6.00 1.25
1496a Sheet of 12, as #1491-1497, + 5 labels, ordinary paper — 8.00 —

Souvenir Sheet
Imperf

1497 A909 50ch multicolored — 3.00 .50

International Activities A910

Designs: 2ch, UPU Headquarters, Bern. 5ch, World Cup. 10ch, Montreal Olympics Stadium. 15ch, Runner with Olympic Torch. 25ch, Satellite, junk. 40ch, Satellites.
50ch, World map.

Surface Coated Paper

1976, Aug. 5 — ***Perf. 13¼***
1506-1511 A910 Set of 6 — 5.00 1.50
1511a Sheet of 7, #1506-1512 + label, ordinary paper — 7.00 —

Souvenir Sheet
Imperf

1512 A910 50ch multicolored — 2.50 2.50

For overprints, see Nos. 1646-1652.

Embroidery A911

Designs: 2ch, Marsh Magpies. 5ch, Golden Bird. 10ch, Deer. 15ch, Golden Bird. 25ch, Fairy. 40ch, Tiger.
50ch, Tiger.

Surface Coated Paper

1976, Aug. 8 — ***Perf. 12***
1513-1518 A911 Set of 6 — 7.50 1.50
1518a Sheet of 8, as #1513-1519 + label, perf 13¾, ordinary paper — 18.00 —

Souvenir Sheet
Imperf

1519 A911 50ch multicolored — 4.00 .50

For surcharges, see Nos. 4598, 4599, 4604.

Model Airplane Championships (1975) — A912

Designs: 5ch, Trophy, certificate and medal. 10ch, Trophy and medals. 20ch, Model airplane and emblem. 40ch, Model glider and medals.

Without Gum

1976, Aug. 15 — ***Perf. 12***
1520-1523 A912 Set of 4 — 4.75 1.00

5th Summit Conference of Non-Aligned States — A913

1976, Aug. 16 — **Without Gum**
1524 A913 10ch multicolored — .50 .25

Locomotives A914

Designs: 2ch, "Pulgungi" diesel locomotive. 5ch, "Saeppyol" diesel locomotive. 10ch, "Saeppyol" diesel locomotive (diff.). 15ch, Electric train. 25ch, "Kumsong" diesel locomotive. 40ch, "Pulgungi" electric locomotive.
50ch, "Kumsong" diesel locomotive.

Surface Coated Paper

1976, Sept. 14 — ***Perf. 12x11¾***
1525-1530 A914 Set of 6 — 5.50 1.00
1530a Sheet of 8, as #1525-1531 + label, perf 10½ — 15.00 —

Souvenir Sheet
Imperf

1531 A914 50ch multicolored — 6.00 3.50

House of Culture — A915

Without Gum

1976, Oct. 7 — ***Perf. 12***
1532 A915 10ch black & brown — 75.00 —
a. Perf. 10¾ — — —

Revolutionary Activities of Kim Il Sung — A916

Kim Il Sung: 2ch, Visiting the Tosongrang. 5ch, With peasants on hillside. 10ch, With boy and man at seashore. 15ch, Giving house to farm-hand. 25ch, On muddy road at front, with driver and girl. 40ch, Walking in rain with umbrella.
50ch, Watching boy draw picture by roadside.

1976, Oct. 10 — ***Perf. 13¼***
1533-1538 A916 Set of 6 — 3.00 .75

Souvenir Sheet
Imperf

1539 A916 50ch multicolored — 2.00 1.50

Down-With-Imperialism Union, 50th Anniv. — A917

Without Gum

1976, Oct. 17 — ***Perf. 12***
1540 A917 20ch multicolored — 1.00 .25

21st Olympic Games, Montreal — A918

Olympic Rings, stadium and: 5ch, Fencer. 10ch, Weightlifter. 15ch, Horse racer. 20ch, Runner. 25ch, Shot putter. 40ch, Basketball player.
60ch, Yacht race.

Simulated 3-D Printing Using Plastic Overlays

1976, Dec. 21 — ***Imperf.***
1541-1546 A918 Set of 6 — 25.00 25.00

Souvenir Sheet

1547 A918 60ch multicolored — 45.00 45.00

No. 1547 Overprinted with Gold Medal Winners' Names, Events

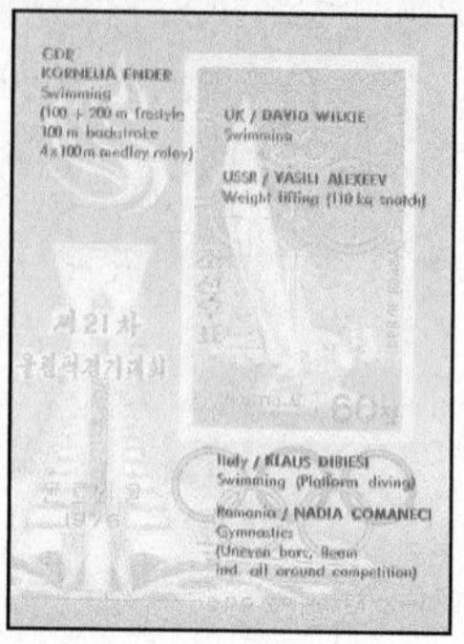

1548 A918 60ch multicolored — —

New Year — A919

Without Gum

1977, Jan. 1 *Perf. 12¼x12*
1549 A919 20ch multicolored .50 .25

21st Olympic Games, Montreal (1976) A920

Designs: 5ch, Reverse of Bronze Medal, Montreal skyline. 10ch, Obverse of Bronze Medal, diff. Montreal skyline. 15ch, Obverse of Silver Medal, stadium. 20ch, Reverse of Silver Medal, stadium. 25ch, Reverse of Gold Medal, Olympic Flame. 40ch, Obverse of Gold Medal, Olympic Flame.
60ch, Gold, Silver and Bronze Medals.

Simulated 3-D Printing Using Plastic Overlays

1977, Jan. 23 *Imperf.*
1550-1555 A920 Set of 6 25.00 25.00

Souvenir Sheet

1556 A920 60ch multicolored 55.00 55.00

No. 1556 Overprinted with Gold Medal Winners' Names, Events

1557 A920 60ch multicolored — —

National Costumes of Li Dynasty — A921

Seasonal costumes: 10ch, Spring. 15ch, Summer. 20ch, Autumn. 40ch, Winter.

1977, Feb. 10 *Perf. 11¾x12*
1558-1561 A921 Set of 4 4.00 1.00
1561a Sheet of 4, #1558-1561 5.00 —

No. 1561 is airmail.

Korean Cultural Relics (5th-12th Centuries) — A922

Designs: 2ch, Two Deva kings, Koguryo Dynasty. 5ch, Gold-copper ornament, Koguryo Dynasty. 10ch, Bronze Buddha, Koguryo Dynasty. 15ch, Gold-copper Buddha, Paekje Dynasty. 25ch, Gold crown, Koguryo Dynasty, horiz. 40ch, Gold-copper ornament, Koguryo Dynasty, horiz. 50ch, Gold crown, Silla Dynasty.

1977, Feb. 26 *Perf. 13¼*
1562-1568 A922 Set of 7 5.75 1.60
1568a Sheet of 8, #1562-1568 + label 6.00 —

No. 1568 is airmail.

Five-Point Program for Land Development A923

Without Gum

1977, Mar. 5 *Perf. 12*
1569 A923 10ch multicolored .50 .25

21st Olympic Games, Montreal (1976) — A924

Events, winner's name, nationality, and: 5ch, Cycling. 10ch, Weightlifting. 15ch, Judo. 20ch, Wrestling. 25ch, Football (soccer). 40ch, Boxing.
60ch, Boxing.

Simulated 3-D Printing Using Plastic Overlays

1977, Mar.8 *Imperf.*
1570-1575 A924 Set of 6 45.00 45.00

Souvenir Sheet

1576 A924 60ch multicolored — —

Korean National Association, 60th Anniv. A925

Without Gum

1977, Mar. 23 *Perf. 11¾*
1577 A925 10ch multicolored .65 .25

34th World Table-Tennis Championships A926

Designs: 10ch, Emblem and trophy. 15ch, Pak Yong Sun. 20ch, Pak Yong Sun with trophy. 40ch, Pak Yong Ok and Yang Ying with trophy.

1977, Apr. 5 *Perf. 12*
1578-1581 A926 Set of 4 4.00 .90

No. 1581 is airmail. For surcharge, see No. 4518.

Kim Il Sung, 65th Birthday A927

Painting of Kim Il Sung: 2ch, Leading Mingyuehkou Meeting. 5ch, Commanding encirclement operation. 10ch, Visiting workers in Kangson. 15ch, Before battle. 25ch, Visiting school. 40ch, Looking over grain fields.
50ch, Kim Il Sung among the artists.

1977, Apr. 15 *Perf. 12*
1582-1587 A927 Set of 6 2.25 .50

Souvenir Sheet

1588 A927 50ch multicolored 1.50 .90

Trolley Buses — A928

Designs: 5ch, "Chollima 72." 10ch, "Chollima 74."

Without Gum

1977, Apr. 20 *Perf. 12*
1589-1590 A928 Set of 2 3.00 .25

Korean People's Revolutionary Army, 45th Anniv. — A929

Without Gum

1977, Apr. 25 *Perf. 12*
1591 A929 40ch multicolored 1.50 .25

Battle of Pochonbo, 40th Anniv. — A930

Without Gum

1977, June 4 *Perf. 13¼*
1592 A930 10ch multicolored .50 .25

Porcelain — A931

Designs: 10ch, White ceramic teapot, Koryo dynasty. 15ch, White ceramic vase, Ri dynasty. 20ch, Celadon vase, Koryo dynasty. 40ch, Celadon vase, Koryo dynasty, diff.

1977, June 10 *Perf. 13¼*
1593-1596 A931 Set of 4 3.50 .75
1596a Sheet of 4, #1593-1596 7.00 .95

No. 1596 is airmail.

Postal Service — A932

Designs: 2ch, Railway, ship and trucks. 10ch, Postwoman delivering mail. 30ch, Mil Mi-8 helicopter. 40ch, Airliner and world map.

Without Gum

1977, June 28 *Perf. 13¼*
1597-1600 A932 Set of 4 5.00 1.25

For surcharges, see Nos. 4515, 4561.

A 3-stamp set and souvenir sheet commemorating the Second Conference of Third World Youth was prepared for release July 1, 1977, but was not issued. Value $3,500.

Butterflies A933

Designs: 2ch, Rapala arata. 5ch, Colias aurora. 10ch, Limenitis populi. 15ch, Anax partherope julius. 25ch, Sympetrum pademontanum elatum.
50ch, Papilio maackii.

1977, July 25 *Perf. 12x12¼*
1601-1606 A933 Set of 6 7.00 1.00
1606a Sheet of 6, #1601-1606 15.00 —

No. 1606 is airmail.

Cats and Dogs

A934 A935

Cats: 2ch, Gray cat. 10ch, Black and white cat. 25ch, Ginger cat.
Dogs: 5ch, Brindled dog. 15ch, Chow. 50ch, Pungsang.

1977, Aug. 10 *Perf. 11¾x12*
1607-1609 A934 Set of 3 6.00 .50
1609a Sheet of 3, #1607-1609 8.00 —
1610-1612 A935 Set of 3 4.00 .50
1612a Sheet of 3, #1610-1612 6.00 —

No. 1612 is airmail.

Visit of Pres. Tito of Yugoslavia A936

Color of Frame: 10ch, blue green; 15ch, dk gray; 20ch, pale orange; 40ch, light gray.

1977, Aug. 25 *Perf. 12*
1613-1616 A936 Set of 4 40.00 8.00

11-Year Compulsory Education, 5th Anniv. A937

Without Gum

1977, Sept. 1 ***Perf. 13¼x13½***
1617 A937 10ch multicolored .50 .25

Shell-Fish and Fish — A938

Designs: 2ch, Mactra sulcataria. 5ch, Natica fortunei. 10ch, Arca inflata. 25ch, Rapana thomasiana. 50ch, Sphoeroides porphyreus.

1977, Sept. 5 ***Perf. 11¾x12***
1618-1622 A938 Set of 5 6.00 1.25
1622a Sheet of 6, #1618-1622 + label 8.00 —

No. 1622 is airmail. For surcharges, see Nos. 4565, 4578.

Publication of Kim Il Sung's *Theses on Socialist Education* — A939

Designs: 10ch, Students, banners and *Theses*. 20ch, Students, crowd and *Theses*.

1977, Sept. 5
1623-1624 A939 Set of 2 1.25 .25

Int'l Seminar on the Juche Idea — A940

Designs: 2ch, Juche Torch. 5ch, Interracial crowd holding copies of Kim's Red Book. 10ch, Chollima statue, flags. 15ch, Joined hands of different races, banner and globe. 25ch, Map of Korea. 40ch, Crowd and slogan. 50ch, Seminar emblem.

1977, Sept. 14 ***Perf. 11¾x12***
1625-1630 A940 Set of 6 3.50 .60

Souvenir Sheet

Imperf

1631 A940 50ch multicolored 3.00 1.00

Stamps of 1976 Overprinted

On Montreal Olympics, #1469-1474

Methods & Perfs as Before

1977, Nov. 8
1632-1637 A907 Set of 6 9.00 —
1637a On #1474a, sheet of 8 10.00 —

Souvenir Sheet

Imperf

1638 A907 50ch multicolored 5.00 —

On Montreal Olympics Medal Winners, #1476-1482

1639-1644 A908 Set of 6 13.00 —
1644a On #1481a, sheet of 8 15.00 —

Souvenir Sheet

Imperf

1645 A908 50ch multicolored 5.00 —

On International Activities, #1506-1512

1646-1651 A910 Set of 6 10.00 —
1651a On #1511a, sheet of 8 15.00 —

Souvenir Sheet

Imperf

1652 A910 50ch multicolored 5.00 —

Amphilex '77 International Stamp Exhibition, Amsterdam.

Election of Deputies, Supreme People's Assembly — A941

1977, Nov. 11 ***Perf. 12¼x12***
1653 A941 10ch multicolored .50 .25

Argentina '78, World Soccer Championship — A942

Designs: 10ch, Defense. 15ch, Attack. 40ch, Tackle.
50ch, Shot.

1977, Dec. 10 ***Perf. 13½***
1654-1656 A942 Set of 3 3.50 .75
1656a Sheet of 4, as #1654-1657 10.00 —

Souvenir Sheet

Imperf

1657 A942 50ch multicolored 2.50 —

Reelection of Kim Il Sung — A943

1977, Dec. 15 ***Perf. 12***
1658 A943 10ch multicolored .60 .25

Org. for Communication Cooperation of Socialist Countries, 20th Anniv. — A944

Without Gum

1977, Dec. 16 ***Perf. 11¾x12***
1659 A944 10ch multicolored .50 .25

New Year — A945

1978, Jan. 1 ***Perf. 13¼***
1660 A945 10ch multicolored .60 .25

Winter Olympic Games, Sapporo-Innsbruck A946

Designs: 2ch, 19th century skater. 5ch, Skier. 10ch, Ice ballet. 15ch, Hunter on skis. 20ch, 18th century woman skiier. 25ch, Medieval Scandinavian hunter. 40ch, Skiier.
50ch, Landscape. 60ch, Speed skater.

1978, Feb. 18 ***Perf. 13¼***
1661-1667 A946 Set of 7 6.00 1.00
1667a Sheet of 10, as #1661-1669 + label 9.00 —

Souvenir Sheets

1668 A946 50ch multicolored 5.00 .50
1669 A946 60ch multicolored 4.00 .50

No. 1667 is airmail.
For overprints, see Nos. 1821-1829.

Postal History — A947

Designs: 2ch, Post rider and horse token. 5ch, Postman on motorcycle. 10ch, Electric train and postal van. 15ch, Mail steamer and Mi-8 helicopter. 25ch, Tupolev Tu-154 jetliner and satellite. 40ch, Dove and UPU headquarters.
50ch, Dove and UPU emblem. 60ch, Dove and UPU headquarters.

1978, Mar. 2 ***Perf. 13¼***
1670-1675 A947 Set of 6 6.00 1.00
1675a Sheet of 8, as #1670-1677 8.00 —

Souvenir Sheets

1676-1677 A947 Set of 2 6.00 —

No. 1675 is airmail.

Rubens, 400th Anniv. Birth — A948

2ch, 5ch, 40ch, 50ch, Self-portrait, same design.

1978, Mar. 20
1678-1680 A948 Set of 3 3.50 .75
1680a Sheet of 4, as #1678-1681 6.00 —

Souvenir Sheet

1681 A948 50ch multicolored 3.00 1.50

Farm Machines A949

Designs: 10ch (No. 1682), *Chungsong* tractor. 10ch (No. 1683), Sprayer.

1978, Apr. 1 ***Perf. 11¾x12***
1682-1683 A949 Set of 2 2.50 .25

Pre-Olympics, Moscow 1980 — A950

Equestrian events: 2ch, Show jumping. 5ch, Jumping bar. 10ch, Cross Country. 15ch, Dressage. 25ch, Water splash. 40ch, Dressage (diff.).
50ch, 3-Step bar jump.

1978, Apr. 1 ***Perf. 13¼***
1684-1689 A950 Set of 6 3.50 1.50
1689a Sheet of 8, as #1684-1690 + label 7.00 —

Souvenir Sheet

1690 A950 50ch multicolored 2.50 —

Korean People's Army Day — A951

Designs: 5ch, Soldier, battle scene. 10ch, Pilot, soldier, sailor saluting.

1978, Apr. 1 ***Perf. 11¾x12***
1691-1692 A951 Set of 2 4.00 1.00

Meeting of Kim Il Sung and Hua Guo Feng of the People's Republic of China — A951a

Denominations: 15ch, 20ch.

1978, May ***Perf. 12***
1692B-1692C A951a Set of 2

This set includes a third stamp and a souvenir sheet, which the editors would like to examine.
Released prior to the meeting between Kim Il Sung and Hua Guo Feng and withdrawn when the meeting was canceled.

Ships A952

Korean ships: 2ch, Cargo ship *Mangyongbong*. 5ch, Freighter *Hyoksin*. 10ch, Freighter *Chongchongang*. 30ch, Tanker *Sonbang*. 50ch, Freighter *Taedonggang*.

1978, May 5 ***Perf. 13¼***
1693-1697 A952 Set of 5 6.00 1.25
1697a Sheet of 6, as #1693-1697+ label 8.00 —

No. 1697 is airmail.

History of the World Cup — A953

World Cup Winners (all 20ch, except Nos. 1709, 1710): No. 1698, Uruguay 1930. No. 1699, Italy 1934. No. 1700, France 1938. No. 1701, Brazil 1950. No. 1702, Switzerland 1954. No. 1703, Sweden 1958. No. 1704, Chile 1962. No. 1705, England 1966. No. 1706, Mexico 1970. No. 1707, West Germany 1974. No. 1708, Argentina 1978. 50ch (No. 1709), Soccer players and emblem, horiz.
50ch (No. 1710), World Cup and championship emblem.

1978, June 1

1698-1709 A953 Set of 12 10.00 3.00
1709a Sheet of 12, as #1698-1708, 1710 12.00 —

Souvenir Sheet

1710 A953 50ch multicolored 6.00 .60

No. 1709 is airmail.
For overprints, see Nos. 2051-2063.

World Cup Winners A954

Designs: 5ch, Uruguay, 1930, 1950. 10ch, Italy, 1934, 1938. 15ch, West Germany, 1954, 1974. 25ch, Brazil, 1958, 1962, 1970. 40ch, England, 1966. 50ch, World Cup, vert.
50ch, World Cup.

1978, June 1

1711-1716 A954 Set of 6 5.00 1.25
1716a Sheet of 6, as #1711-15, 1717 6.00 —

Souvenir Sheet

1717 A954 50ch multicolored 4.00 .75

No. 1716 is airmail.

Art of the Revolution A955

Designs: 10ch, Opera, *Sea of Love.* 15ch, Embroidered kerchief with floral design in the form of map of Korea. 20ch, *Tansimjul* dance.
40ch, *Song of Korea.*

1978, June 2

1718-1720 A955 Set of 3 4.50 .90

Souvenir Sheet

1721 A955 40ch multicolored 2.50 .50

Domestic Printings

Beginning in the 1970s, a number of North Korean stamps have been reprinted for sale and use within the country. Typically, these printings were on unsurfaced paper, with poorer production qualities, and without gum.

Second Seven-Year Plan — A956

Designs: 5ch, Electricity and Coal. 10ch, Steel and nonferrous metals. 15ch, Machine products and chemical fertilizers. 30ch, Cement and fishing. 50ch, Grain and tideland reclamation.

1978, June 15 ***Perf. 11½x12***

1722-1726 A956 Set of 5 3.25 .90
1722a 5ch Unsurfaced white paper, without gum 8.00 —
1723a 10ch Unsurfaced white paper, without gum 8.00 —
1724a 15ch Unsurfaced white paper, without gum 8.00 —
1725a 30ch Unsurfaced white paper, without gum 5.00 —

History of Olympic Games & Winners A957

Games emblems / medal winners (all 20ch): No. 1727, Athens 1896 / Alfred Flatow. No. 1728, Paris 1900 / Michel Theato. No. 1729, London 1908 / Wyndham Halswelle. No. 1730, Stockholm 1912 / William Kinnear. No. 1731, Antwerp 1920 / Paul Anspach. No. 1732, Paris 1924 / Ugo Frigerio. No. 1733, Amsterdam 1928 / Ahmed El Quafi. No. 1734, Berlin 1936 / Robert Charpentier. No. 1735, London 1948 / Josef Stalder. No. 1736, Helsinki 1952 / Laszlo Papp. No. 1737, Melbourne 1956 / Ronald Delany. No. 1738, Rome 1960 / Jolanda Balas. No. 1739, Tokyo 1964 / Valery Brumel. No. 1740, Mexico 1968 / Vera Caslavska. No. 1741, Munich 1972 / Li Ho Jun.
50ch, Montreal 1976 / Ku Yong Jo.

1978, June 16 ***Perf. 13¼***

1727-1741 A957 Set of 15 12.00 4.50
1741a Sheet of 16, as #1727-1741 14.00 —

Souvenir Sheet

1742 A957 50ch multicolored 2.00 .75

Passenger Aircraft — A958

Designs: 2ch, Douglas DC-8-63 jetliner and Comte AC-4 Gentleman. 10ch, Ilyushin Il-62M jetliner and Avia BH-25. 15ch, Douglas DC-8-63 jetliner and Savola Marchetti S-71. 20ch, Tupolev Tu-144 jetliner and Kalinin K-5. 25ch, Tupolev Tu-154 jetliner and Antonov An-2 biplane. 30ch, Ilyushin Il-18 airliner and '30s-era airplane. 40ch, Concorde supersonic jetliner and Wibault 283 trimotor.
50ch, Airbus.

1978, July 25

1743-1749 A958 Set of 7 6.00 1.00
1749a Sheet of 8, as #1743-1750 10.00 —

Souvenir Sheet

1750 A958 50ch multicolored 2.50 .50

For surcharge, see No. 4586.

White-Bellied Black Woodpecker Preservation — A959

Designs: 5ch, Dryocopus richardsi, map of habitat, inset map of Korea. 10ch, Woodpecker and eggs. 15ch, Woodpecker feeding young. 25ch, Woodpecker feeding young, diff. 50ch, Woodpecker on tree trunk.

1978, Aug. 5 ***Perf. 11¾x12***

1751-1755 A959 Set of 5 9.00 2.50
1755a Sheet of 6, #1751-1755 + label 11.00 —

For surcharge, see No. 4583.

Democratic People's Republic of Korea, 30th Anniv. — A960

Designs (all 10ch): No. 1756, Building and flag. No. 1757, Flag with silhouetttes of workers and peasants. No. 1758, Flag with aviator and two soldiers. No. 1759, Chollima statue and city. No. 1760, Workers demonstrating, map of Korea in background. No. 1761, Asian, European and African clasping hands, with torch and "Solidarity" in background.

Without Gum

1978, Sep. 9 ***Perf. 13½x13¼***

1756-1761 A960 Set of 6 4.00 .75
1758a 10ch Unsurfaced toned paper 10.00 —
1759a 10ch Unsurfaced toned paper 15.00 —
1760a 10ch Unsurfaced toned paper 15.00 —

Paintings by Ri Am (16th Century) — A961

Designs: 10ch, *Cat and Pup.* 15ch, *Cat on a Tree.* 40ch, *A Pair of Wild Geese.*

1978, Oct. 16 ***Perf. 13¼***

1762-1764 A961 Set of 3 8.00 1.25
1764a Sheet of 4, #1762-1764 + label 11.00 —

World Cup Winners, Argentina '78 A962

Soccer players: 10ch, Argentina, Champion. 15ch, Holland, Sub-Champion. 25ch, Brazil, Third Place.
50ch, Argentina, Champion.

1978, Dec. 15

1765-1767 A962 Set of 3 3.00 .50
1767a Sheet of 4, as #1765-1768 12.00 —

Souvenir Sheet

1768 A962 50ch multicolored 2.50 1.50

New Year — A963

Without Gum

1979, Jan. 1 ***Perf. 12***

1769 A963 10ch multicolored .50 .25

A964

International Year of the Child — A965

Kim Il Sung and children: 5ch, With Children's Corps members in Maanshan. 10ch, Children's Corps members in classroom. 15ch, "The New Year Gathering." 20ch, by roadside, with snowman, kite. 30ch, Looking at children's school work.
Children: 10ch, Tug of war. 15ch, Ballerinas. 20ch, Children of different races holding hands in circle around globe. 25ch, Singing at piano. 30ch, Playing on toy airplane ride.
No. 1780, Kim visiting a kindergarten. No. 1781, as No. 1777.

1979, Jan. 1 ***Perf. 13¼x13½***

1770-1774 A964 Set of 5 4.00 1.00
1775-1779 A965 Set of 5 3.00 1.00

Souvenir Sheets

Imperf

1780 A964 50ch multicolored 2.50 1.75
1781 A965 50ch multicolored 2.50 1.75

Nos. 1770-1779 were issued with setenant labels. Nos. 1780-1781 exist perf. 13¼x13½.

A set of four stamps depicting roses, similar to Type A970, was prepared for release on Jan. 5, 1979, but was not issued.

Story of Two Generals — A966

Designs: 5ch, Two warriors on horseback. 10ch (No. 1783), Man blowing feather. 10ch (No. 1784), Two generals fighting Japanese invaders. 10ch (No. 1785), Two generals on horseback.

Without Gum

1979, Jan. 10 ***Perf. 11¾x12***

1782-1785 A966 Set of 4 3.00 .50

Worker-Peasant Red Guards, 20th Anniv. — A967

Without Gum

1979, Jan. 14 ***Perf. 12x11¾***

1786 A967 10ch multicolored .50 .25

Airships A968

Designs: 10ch, Clement-Bayard Airship *Fleurus.* 20ch, NI *Norge.*
50ch, *Graf Zeppelin.*

1979, Feb. 27 ***Perf. 13¼***

1787-1788 A968 Set of 2 2.00 .40
1788a Sheet of 3, as #1787-1789 8.00 —

Souvenir Sheet

1789 A968 50ch multicolored 3.00 1.75

March 1 Popular Uprising, 60th Anniv. — A969

Without Gum

1979, Mar. 1 ***Perf. 11¾x12***

1790 A969 10ch multicolored .60 .25

Roses — A970

Designs: 5ch, Rose. 10ch, Red star rose. 15ch, Flamerose. 20ch, Yellow rose. 30ch, White rose. 50ch, Deep pink rose.

1979, Apr. 18 ***Perf. 13¼***
1791-1796 A970 Set of 6 4.00 1.10
1796a Sheet of 6, #1791-1796 5.50 —

No. 1796 is airmail.

35th World Table Tennis Championships, Pyongyang — A971

Designs: 5ch, Championship Cup. 10ch, Female doubles. 15ch, Female singles. 20ch, Male doubles. 30ch, Male singles.
50ch, Chollima statue. "Welcome."

1979, Apr. 25
1797-1801 A971 Set of 5 3.00 .75
1801a Sheet of 6, as #1797-1802 7.50 —

Souvenir Sheet

1802 A971 50ch multicolored 3.00 .45

For surcharges, see Nos. 4516, 4531.

"Let Us Step Up Socialist Construction Under the Banner of the Juche Idea" — A972

Designs: 5ch, Marchers, banner. 10ch (No. 1804), Map of Korea. 10ch (No. 1805), Hand holding torch.

Without Gum

1979, Apr. 28 ***Perf. 12***
1803-1805 A972 Set of 3 3.00 .25
1803a 5ch Unsurfaced dull white paper 15.00 —
1804a 10ch Unsurfaced dull white paper 15.00 —
1805a 10ch Unsurfaced dull white paper 15.00 —

Order of Honor of the Three Revolutions — A973

1979, May 2 **Without Gum**
1806 A973 10ch dp blue & lt blue 1.50 .25
a. Unsurfaced dull white paper 15.00 —

World Telecommunications Day — A974

1979, May 17 **Without Gum**
1807 A974 10ch multicolored 1.00 .25

Battle in Musan Area, 40th Anniv. — A975

1979, May 23 **Without Gum**
1808 A975 10ch multicolored .60 .25

Int'l Friendship Exhibition A976

1979, May 29 **Without Gum**
1809 A976 10ch multicolored .60 .25

Albrecht Dürer, 450th Anniv. Death — A977

Details from Dürer paintings: 15ch, Peonies. 20ch, Akeley. 25ch, A Big Tuft of Grass. 30ch, Wing of a Bird.
50ch, Like 30ch.

1979, June 8 ***Perf. 13¼***
1810-1813 A977 Set of 4 5.50 .75
1813a Souvenir sheet of 4, #1810-1813 9.00 —

Souvenir Sheet

1814 A977 50ch multicolored 3.50 .60

For surcharge, see No. 4584.

Olympic Games, Moscow 1980 A978

Olympic Torch, Moscow 1980 emblem and: 5ch, Fencers. 10ch, Gymnast. 20ch, Yacht race. 30ch, Runner. 40ch, Weightlifter.
50ch, Horse jump.

1979, July 1
1815-1819 A978 Set of 5 3.50 1.25
1819a Sheet of 6, as #1815-1820 5.00 —

Souvenir Sheet

1820 A978 50ch multicolored 3.00 1.50

Nos. 1661-1669 Overprinted

1979, July 17
1821-1827 A946 Set of 7 10.00 3.50
1827a Sheet of 10, as #1821-1829 + label 18.00 —

Souvenir Sheets

1828 A946 50ch multicolored 4.25 1.50
1829 A946 60ch multicolored 8.50 —

No. 1827 is airmail.

Koguryo Dynasty Horsemen A979

Designs: 5ch, Hunting. 10ch, Archery contest. 15ch, Drummer. 20ch, Rider blowing horn. 30ch, Horse and rider in chain mail. 50ch, Hawk hunting.

1979, Aug. 1
1830-1835 A979 Set of 6 5.25 .75
1835a Sheet of 6, as #1830-1835 9.00 —

No. 1835 s airmail.

Olympic Games, Moscow 1980 — A980

Designs: 5ch, Judo. 10ch, Volleyball. 15ch, Cycling. 20ch, Basketball. 25ch, One-oared boat. 30ch, Boxing. 40ch, Shooting. 50ch, Gymnastics.

1979, Aug. 5 ***Perf. 11¾x12***
1836-1842 A980 Set of 7 5.00 1.25
1842a Sheet of 8, as #1836-1843 + label 9.00 —

Souvenir Sheet

1843 A980 50ch multicolored 3.00 1.00

Ri Dynasty Knights' Costumes — A981

Designs: 5ch, Knight in armor. 10ch, Knight in ceremonial dress. 15ch, Knight in armor (diff.) 20ch, Soldier in uniform. 30ch, Knight in armor (diff.) 50ch, Knight in armor (diff.)

1979, Aug. 6 ***Perf. 11¾***
1844-1849 A981 Set of 6 4.25 .75
1849a Sheet of 6, #1844-1849 6.50 —

No. 1849 is airmail.

1980 Summer Olympics, Moscow — A982

Designs: 10ch, Judo. 15ch, Handball. 20ch, Archery. 25ch, Field hockey. 30ch, Boat race. 40ch, Soccer.
50ch, Horse race.

1979, Sept. 5 ***Perf. 11¾x11½***
1850-1855 A982 Set of 6 5.25 1.25
1855a Sheet of 8, #1850-1856 + label 8.00 —

Souvenir Sheet

1856 A982 50ch multi 3.00 1.25

For surcharges, see Nos. 4585, 4595.

Chongbong Monument — A983

Without Gum

1979, Sep. 10 ***Perf. 12***
1857 A983 10ch multicolored .60 .25

Sika Deer — A984

Designs: 5ch, Breeder feeding fawn from bottle. 10ch, Doe and suckling fawn. 15ch, Deer drinking from stream. 20ch, Buck walking. 30ch, Deer running.
50ch, Antlers.

1979, Oct. 5 ***Perf. 13½***
1858-1863 A984 Set of 6 4.00 1.25
1863a Sheet of 6, #1858-1863 6.00 —

Central Zoo, Pyongyang — A985

Designs: 5ch, Moscovy ducks. 10ch, Ostrich. 15ch, Turkey. 20ch, Pelican. 30ch, Guinea fowl. 50ch, Mandarin ducks.

1979, Oct. 9 ***Perf. 12***
1864-1869 A985 Set of 6 6.00 1.75
1869a Sheet of 6, #1864-1869 8.00 —

No. 1869 is airmail. For surcharge, see No. 4569.

Int'l Year of the Child — A986

Designs: 20ch (No. 1870), Girl with toy sail boat. 20ch (No. 1871), Boy with toy train. 20ch (No. 1872), Boy with model biplane. 20ch (No. 1873), Boy with model spaceman. 30ch (No. 1874), Boy with toy motor boat. 30ch (No. 1875), Boy sitting on toy train. 30ch (No. 1876), Boy with model airplane. 30ch (No. 1877), Boy with model spaceman.
Souvenir Sheets (all 80ch): No. 1878, Boy and model ocean liner. No. 1879, Boy and girl with model train. No. 1880, Boy and Concorde. No. 1881, Girl and satellite.
Miniature sheets of 4: No. 1882, Nos. 1870, 1874, 1878 + label. No. 1883, Nos. 1871, 1875, 1879 + label. No. 1884, Nos. 1872, 1876, 1880 + label. No. 1885, Nos. 1873, 1877, 1881 + label.

1979, Oct. 13 ***Perf. 12x11¾***
1870-1877 A986 Set of 8 13.50 2.75

Souvenir Sheets

1878-1881 A986 Set of 4 27.50 2.75

Miniature Sheets

1882-1885 A986 Set of 4 27.50 2.75

For surcharges, see Nos. 4520, 4532.

Int'l Year of the Child A987

Children playing soccer: 20ch, Kicking. 30ch, Dribbling.
80ch, Tackling.

1979, Nov. 15 ***Perf. 12x11¾***
1886-1887 A987 Set of 2 5.50 .75
1887a Sheet of 3, as #1886-1888 11.00 —

Souvenir Sheet

1888 A987 80ch multicolored 5.50 .75

Marine Life — A988

Designs: 20ch, Devil stinger fish (*Inimicas japonicus*). 30ch, Black rockfish (*Sebastes schlegeli*). 50ch, Northern sea lion (*Eumetopias jubatus*).

1979, Dec. 4

1889-1891 A988 Set of 3 3.75 .75
1891a Sheet of 3, #1889-1891 5.50 —

Winter Olympics Games, Lake Placid A989

Designs: 10ch, Figure skating (Irina Rodnina and Aleksandr Zaitsev). 20ch, Ice hockey (Soviet team). 30ch, Ladies' ski relay team. 40ch, Cross-country skiing (Sergei Saveliev, USSR), vert. 50ch, Ladies' speed skating (Tatiana Averina), vert.
60ch, Ice dancing (Ludmila Pakhomova and Aleksandr Gorshkov), stamp vert.

1979, Dec. 9

1892-1896 A989 Set of 5 6.00 1.50
1892a Sheet of 3, #1892-1894 5.00 —
1895a Sheet of 3, as #1895-1897 10.00 —

Souvenir Sheet

1897 A989 60ch multicolored 5.50 4.50

Honey Bees — A990

Designs: 20ch, Bee gathering nectar. 30ch, Bee and blossoms. 50ch, Bee over flower.

1979, Dec. 22

1898-1900 A990 Set of 3 6.00 .60
1900a Sheet of 3, #1898-1900 8.00 —

Kim Il Sung's Birthplace, Hoeryang A991

Sinpha Revolutionary Museum — A992

1979, Dec. 24

1901 A991 10ch multicolored .75 .25
1902 A992 10ch multicolored .75 .25

Revolutionary historical sites.

New Year — A993

1980, Jan. 1

1903 A993 10ch multicolored 1.00 .25

Studying — A994

1980, Jan. 10 ***Perf. 12x11¾***

1904 A994 10ch multicolored .50 .25

Unryul Mine Conveyor Belt — A995

1980, Jan. 20 ***Perf. 11¾x12***

1905 A995 10ch multicolored 1.00 .25

Kim Il Sung, Soldiers and Children A996

Children Playing A997

Kim Visiting Kindergarten — A998

International Day of the Child

Type A997 (all 10ch): No. 1907, Black, Asian and White children with "6" and "1." No. 1908, Children playing accordion. No. 1909, Children on airplane ride. No. 1910, Children on rocket ride. No. 1911, Children riding tricycles. No. 1912, Children playing with model train.

1980, Jan. 28 ***Perf. 12x11¾***

1906 A996 10ch multicolored .35 .25
1907 A997 10ch multicolored 1.60 .35
1908 A997 10ch multicolored .35 .25
1909 A997 10ch multicolored .60 .25
1910 A997 10ch multicolored 2.25 .50
1911 A997 10ch multicolored .50 .25
1912 A997 10ch multicolored .35 .25
Nos. 1906-1912 (7) 6.00 2.10

Souvenir Sheet

Perf. 13¼

1913 A998 50ch multicolored 3.00 1.25

Chongsan-ri Monument A999

Chongsan-ri Party Headquarters A1000

1980, Feb. 5 ***Perf. 11¾x12***

1914 A999 10ch multicolored .50 .25
1915 A1000 10ch multicolored .50 .25

Monument in Honor of Kim Jong Suk's Return — A1001

1980, Feb. 16

1916 A1001 10ch multicolored .50 .25

Explorers A1002

Designs: 10ch, Vasco Nunez be Balboa (Spain). 20ch, Francisco de Orellana (Spain). 30ch, Haroun Tazieff (France). 40ch, Sir Edmund Hillary (New Zealand) and Shri Tenzing (Nepal).
70ch, Ibn Battuta (Morocco).

1980, Feb. 18 ***Perf. 13¼***

1917-1920 A1002 Set of 4 5.00 1.10
1920a Sheet of 6, as #1917-1921 + label 10.00 —

Souvenir Sheet

1921 A1002 70ch multicolored 4.50 1.50

Ryongpo Revolutionary Museum A1003

1980, Feb. 23 ***Perf. 11¾***

1922 A1003 10ch lt blue & black .50 .25

Rowland Hill (1795-1879), Centenary of Death — A1004

Rowland Hill and stamps of: 30ch, Germany, Great Britain (#1), Russia, Switzerland, DPRK and Wurttemberg. 50ch, Great Britain (#1, pair), France, Roman States, Canada, Two Sicilies and India.

1980, Mar. 1

1923-1924 A1004 Set of 2 8.50 1.40
1924a Sheet of 2, #1923-1924 10.00 —

World Red Cross Day — A1005

Designs: No. 1925, 10ch, Emblem of DPRK Red Cross. No. 1926, 10ch, Jean-Henri Dunant. No. 1927, 10ch, Nurse and infant. No. 1928, 10ch, Red Cross ship. No. 1929, 10ch, Red Cross helicopter. No. 1930, 10ch, Nurse with child and doll. No. 1931, 10ch, Map, Red Cross, transports.
50ch, Nurse with syringe.

1980, Apr. 17 ***Perf. 11¾x11½***

1925-1931 A1005 Set of 7 8.00 1.50
1931a Sheet of 8, as #1925-1932 15.00 —

Souvenir Sheet

1932 A1005 50ch multicolored 5.50 1.75

For overprints and surcharges, see Nos. 2043-2050, 4517, 4570.

Conquerors of the Sea — A1006

Designs: 10ch, Fernando Magellan (Portugal). 20ch, Fridtjof Nansen (Norway). 30ch, Auguste and Jacques Piccard (Sweden). 40ch, Jacques Cousteau (France).
70ch, Capt. James Cook (UK).

1980, Apr. 30 ***Perf. 13¼***

1933-1936 A1006 Set of 4 10.00 1.90
1936a Sheet of 6, as #1933-1937 + label 16.00 —

Souvenir Sheet

1937 A1006 70ch multicolored 6.50 1.50

London 1980 Int'l Philatelic Exhibition A1007

Designs: 10ch, Great Britain #1 and Korean stamps. No. 1939, 20ch, British Guiana One-Cent Magenta and Korean cover. No. 1940, 30ch, Korea #1 (in blue) and modern Korean First Day Cover. 40ch, DPRK Nos. 1 (in green) and 1494. No. 1942, 50ch, DPRK Nos. 470-471.
No. 1943: a, 20ch, Like 10ch. b, 30ch, Like No. 1939. c, 50ch, Like 40ch.

1980, May 6

1938-1942 A1007 Set of 5 10.00 1.50

Souvenir Sheet

1943 A1007 Sheet of 3, #a-c 15.00 1.50

Nos. 1941, 1943c are airmail.

Conquerors of Sky and Space — A1008

Designs: 10ch, Wright Brothers (USA). 20ch, Louis Bleriot (France). 30ch, Anthony Fokker (USA). 40ch, Secondo Campini (Italy) and Sir Frank Whittle (UK).
70ch, Count Ferdinand von Zeppelin (Germany).

1980, May 10

1944-1947 A1008 Set of 4 6.00 1.25
1947a Sheet of 6, as #1944-1948 + label 13.00 —

Souvenir Sheet

1948 A1008 70ch multicolored 5.00 1.25

Conquerors of the Universe — A1009

Designs: 10ch, Spaceships. 20ch, Spaceship landing on another planet. 30ch, Spaceships landing on another planet, greeted by dinosaurs. 40ch, Spaceship, dinosaurs.
70ch, Spaceman and dragons.

1980, May 20 ***Perf. 11¾x12***

1949-1952 A1009 Set of 4 3.50 1.25
1952a Sheet of 6, as #1949-1953 + label 12.00 —

Souvenir Sheet

1953 A1009 70ch multicolored 3.50 1.25

Chongryon, 25th Anniv. — A1010

1980, May 25 *Perf. 12¼x12*

1954 A1010 10ch multicolored .50 .25

Chongryon is the General Association of Korean Residents in Japan.

Pyongyang Maternity Hospital — A1011

1980, May 30 *Perf. 12*

1955 A1011 10ch multicolored 1.10 .25

Changgwang Health Complex A1012

1980, June 2 *Perf. 11¾x12*

1956 A1012 2ch black & lt blue .60 .25

Korean Revolutionary Army, 50th Anniv. — A1013

1980, July 6 *Perf. 12*

1957 A1013 10ch multicolored .60 .25

Regular Issue — A1014

Designs (all 10ch): No. 1958, Workers' hostel, Samjiyon. No. 1959, *Chongsanri* rice harvester. No. 1960, *Taedonggang* rice transplanter. No. 1961, Corn harvester. No. 1962, Samhwa Democratic Propaganda Hall. No. 1963, Songmun-ri revolutionary historic building (with trees). No. 1964, Sundial. No. 1965, Turtle ship. No. 1966, Phungsan dog. No. 1967, Quail.

Perf. 11¾, 11½ (#1960, 1965), 12x11¾ (#1964)

1980

1958-1967 A1014 Set of 10 25.00 3.00

Issued: Nos. 1958-1961, 7/25. Nos. 1962-1967, 8/1.

6th Congress, Workers' Party of Korea — A1015

"Leading the van in the Arduous March" A1016

"The great leader inspires and encourages colliers on the spot." — A1017

Designs (all 10ch): No. 1968, Party emblem, fireworks. No. 1969, Students, Red Book. No. 1970, Workers, banner, Red Book. No. 1971, Young workers, one with accordion. No. 1972, Worker holding wrench aloft. No. 1973, Four young workers, one with streamer, building in background. No. 1974, Map, propaganda slogans. No. 1975, Workers marching with three banners, smoke stacks in background.

1980, July 30 *Perf. 12¼x12*

1968-1975 A1015 Set of 8 6.00 1.25

Souvenir Sheets

1976 A1016 50ch multicolored 3.00 .75
1977 A1017 50ch multicolored 2.00 .75

World Cup Soccer Championship 1978-1982 — A1018

Designs: 20ch, Two soccer players dribbling ball. 30ch, Tackling.
40ch, Tackling (diff.). 60ch, Moving in to tackle.

1980, Aug. 5 *Perf. 12*

1978-1979 A1018 Set of 2 7.50 2.00
1979a Sheet of 4, as #1978-1980 18.00 —

Souvenir Sheet

1980 A1018 Sheet of 2 + label 16.00 2.00
a. 40ch multicolored 3.00 1.00
b. 60ch multicolored 4.00 1.00

Winter Olympic Games 1980, Gold Medal Winners A1019

Designs: 20ch, Irina Rodnina and Aleksandr Zaitsev.
1w, Natalia Linitschnuk and Gennadi Karponosov.

1980, Aug. 10 *Perf. 13¼*

1981 A1019 20ch multicolored 6.50 1.60
a. Sheet of 2, as #1981-1982 15.00 —

Souvenir Sheet

1982 A1019 1w multicolored 6.50 2.00

Albrecht Dürer, 450th Anniv. Death — A1020

Designs: 20ch, *Soldier with Horse.*
1w, *Horse and Rider.*

1980, Aug. 18 *Perf. 11¾x12*

1983 A1020 20ch multicolored 6.50 1.60
a. Sheet of 2 as #1983-1984 20.00 —

Souvenir Sheet

1984 A1020 1w multicolored 10.00 2.75

Johannes Kepler, 350th Anniv. Death — A1021

Designs: 20ch, Kepler, astrolabe and satellites.
1w, Kepler, astrolabe and satellites (diff.).

1980, Aug. 25

1985 A1021 20ch multicolored 2.75 1.25
a. Sheet of 2, as #1985-1986 12.00 —

Souvenir Sheet

1986 A1021 1w multicolored 6.50 2.25

3rd Int'l Stamp Fair Essen 1980 A1022

Designs, Stamps from German and Russian Zeppelin sets, respectively: 10ch, 1m and 30k. 20ch, 2m and 35k. 30ch, 4m and 1r.
50ch, Russian 2r Polar Flight stamp and DPRK No. 1780 stamp.

1980, Sep. 25 *Perf. 13¼*

1987-1989 A1022 Set of 3 6.50 1.25
1989a Sheet of 4, as #1987-1990 30.00 —

Souvenir Sheet

1990 A1022 50ch multicolored 9.00 2.50

A1023

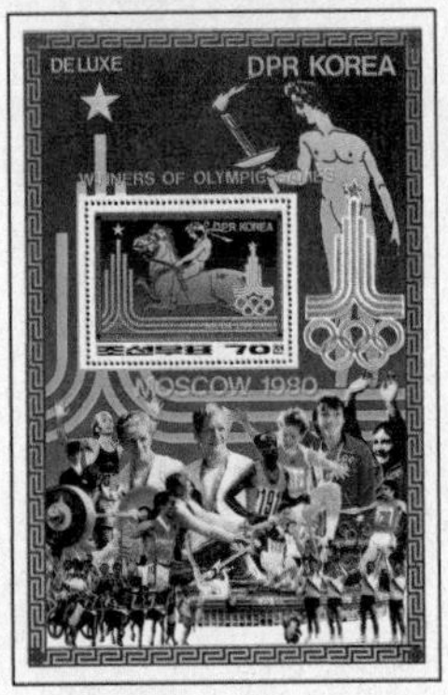

Moscow Olympic Games Winners A1024

Designs: 10ch, Free pistol shooting — Aleksandr Melentiev (USSR). 20ch, 4000m Individual pursuit bicycle race — Robert Dill-Bundi (Switzerland). 25ch, Gymnastics — Stoyan Deltchev (Bulgaria). 30ch, Free style wrestling — K). 35ch, Weight-lifting — Ho Bong Choi (DPRK). 40ch, Running — Marita Koch (DDR). 50ch, Modern pentathlon — Anatoly Starostin (USSR).
No. 1998, Boxing — Teofilo Stevenson (Cuba). No. 1999, Ancient Greek rider on horse.

1980, Oct. 20 *Perf. 12x11¾*

1991-1997 A1023 Set of 7 7.00 2.25
1997a Sheet of 8, as #1991-1998 12.00 —

Souvenir Sheet

1998 A1023 70ch multicolored 2.75 2.00
1999 A1024 70ch multicolored 4.50 2.00

Josip Broz Tito (1892-1980) A1025

1980, Dec. 4 *Perf. 12¼x12*

2000 A1025 20ch multicolored 1.00 .25

First Post-WWII Lufthansa Flight, 25th Anniv. — A1026

Designs: 20ch, Convair CV 340 airliner.
1w, Airbus A 300.

1980, Dec. 10 *Perf. 13¼*

2001 A1026 20ch multicolored 6.00 2.25
a. Sheet of 2, as #2001-2002 15.00 —

Souvenir Sheet

2002 A1026 1w multicolored 8.00 3.25

Liverpool-Manchester Railway, 150th Anniv. — A1027

Designs: 20ch, *The Rocket.*
1w, Locomotive pulling passenger car and horse car.

1980, Dec. 16 *Perf. 11¾*

2003 A1027 20ch multicolored 6.75 3.00
a. Sheet of 2, as #2003-2004 20.00 —

Souvenir Sheet

2004 A1027 1w multicolored 8.00 3.00

Electric Train Centenary A1028

Designs: 20ch, First E-type electric and steam locomotives.
1w, Electric locomotive exhibited in Berlin, 1879.

1980, Dec. 24 *Perf. 13¼*

2005 A1028 20ch multicolored 6.75 2.50
a. Sheet of 2, as #2005-2006 22.00 —

Souvenir Sheet

2006 A1028 1w multicolored 13.00 2.75

Dag Hammarskjold (1905-61), 75th Anniv. of Birth — A1029

Designs: 20ch, Hammarskjold and UN Building.
1w, Hammarskjold (diff.).

1980, Dec. 26 *Perf. 11¾*

2007 A1029 20ch multicolored 4.00 2.75
a. Sheet of 2, as #2007-2008 10.00 —

Souvenir Sheet

2008 A1029 1w multicolored 5.00 2.75

World Chess Championship, Merano — A1030

Designs: 20ch, Bobby Fischer-Boris Spassky chess match.

1w, Viktor Korchnoi-Anatoly Karpov chess match.

1980, Dec. 28 ***Perf. 13¼***

2009 A1030 20ch multicolored 7.50 2.25
a. Sheet of 2, as #2009-2010 18.00 —

Souvenir Sheet

2010 A1030 1w multicolored 10.00 2.25

Robert Stolz (1880-1975), Composer, Birth Cent. — A1031

Designs: 20ch, Stoltz with music from *At the Flower Bed.*

1w, Stoltz working with stamp collection.

1980, Dec. 30

2011 A1031 20ch multicolored 4.00 1.25
a. Sheet of 2, as #2011-2012 12.00 —

Souvenir Sheet

2012 A1031 1w multicolored 6.00 1.40

New Year — A1032

1981, Jan. 1 ***Perf. 12***

2013 A1032 10ch multicolored 1.00 .25

Fairy Tales — A1033

Designs (all 10ch): No. 2014 Russian fairy tale. No. 2015 Icelandic. No. 2016, Swedish. No. 2017, Irish. No. 2018, Italian. No. 2019, Japanese. No. 2020, German.

70ch (No. 2021): Korean fairy tale, *A Gold Nugget and Maize Cake.*

1981, Jan. 30 ***Perf. 13¼***

2014-2020 A1033 Set of 7 12.00 4.00
2020a Sheet of 8, as #2014-2021 18.00 —

Souvenir Sheet

2021 A1033 70ch multicolored 5.75 3.00

International Year of the Child, 1979.

Changgwang Street, Pyongyang A1034

1981, Feb. 16 ***Perf. 11¾x12***

2022 A1034 10ch multicolored .75 .25

World Soccer Cup Championship ESPAÑA '82 — A1035

Designs: 10ch, Tackling. 20ch, Kicking. 30ch, Feinting.

70ch, Three players.

1981, Feb. 20 ***Perf. 13¼***

2023-2025 A1035 Set of 3 10.00 3.00
2025a Sheet of 4, as #2023-2026 17.00 —

Souvenir Sheet

2026 A1035 70ch multicolored 9.00 3.50

For overprints, see Nos. 2216.

World Soccer Cup Championship ESPAÑA '82 (2nd issue) — A1036

Designs: 10ch, Emblem, map and cup. 15ch, Dribbling. 20ch, Heading ball. 25ch, Tackling. 30ch, Pass.

70ch, Sliding tackle.

1981, Feb. 28

2027-2031 A1036 Set of 5 10.00 4.00
2031a Sheet of 6, as #2027-2032 18.00 —

Souvenir Sheet

2032 A1036 70ch multicolored 9.00 3.00

Implementations of Decisions of 6th Korean Workers' Party Congress — A1037

Designs: 2ch, Marchers with book, banners. 10ch (No. 2034), Worker with book. 10ch (No. 2035), Workers and factory. 10ch (No. 2036), Electricity generation (horiz.). 10ch (No. 2037), Factory, construction scene (horiz.). 10ch (No. 2038), Cement factory, fertilizer (horiz.). 30ch, Fishing, fabrics (horiz.). 40ch, Grain, port facilities (horiz.). 70ch, Clasped hands, map of Korea. 1w, Hand holding torch, "peace" and "solidarity" slogans.

1981, Mar. 15 ***Perf. 12¼***

2033-2042 A1037 Set of 10 6.00 2.50
2033a 2ch Unsurfaced white paper, without gum 10.00 —
2034a 10ch Unsurfaced white paper, without gum 10.00 —
2035a 10ch Unsurfaced white paper, without gum 10.00 —
2039a 30ch Unsurfaced white paper, without gum 10.00 —
2040a 40ch Unsurfaced white paper, without gum 10.00 —
2041a 70ch Unsurfaced white paper, without gum 10.00 —
2042a 1w Unsurfaced white paper, without gum 10.00 —

Nos. 1925-1932 Overprinted For Nobel Prize Winners in Medicine

1981, Mar. 20 ***Perf. 11¾x11½***

2043-2049 A1005 Set of 7 9.00 3.00
2049a Sheet of 8, as #2043-2050 12.00 —

Souvenir Sheet

2050 A1005 50ch multicolored 9.00 —

Nos. 1698-1710 Overprinted History of the World Cup

1981, Mar. 20 ***Perf. 13¼***

2051-2062 A953 Set of 12 24.00 —
2062a Sheet of 12, #2051-2062 25.00 —

Souvenir Sheet

2063 A953 50ch multicolored 12.00 —

Copa de Oro Mini-World Cup Championships — A1038

Designs: 20ch, Uruguayan and Brazilian soccer players.

1w, Goalkeeper blocking ball.

1981, Mar. 27

2064 A1038 20ch multicolored 4.00 1.25

Souvenir Sheet

2065 A1038 1w multicolored 8.00 1.00

España '82 A1039

Nos. 2066-2068 depict different designs incorporating bleachers and crowds, with images of soccer players and trophy that appear or disappear, depending upon the angle from which the stamps are viewed. This effect is created by printing on multiple layers of thin plastic, with gummed paper backing.

1981, Apr. 10 ***Imperf.***

2066-2067 A1039 Set of 2, 20ch, 30ch 25.00 9.00

Souvenir Sheet

2068 A1039 1w multicolored 25.00 25.00

Nos. 2066-2068 are airmail.

Naposta '81 Int'l Stamp Exhibition, Stuttgart A1040

Designs: 10ch, Dornier Do-X flying boat. 20ch, Count von Zeppelin and airship LZ-120. 30ch, Goetz von Berlichingen (1480-1562), German knight and subject of poem by Johann von Goethe (1749-1832), also pictured.

70ch, Mercedes-Benz W 196, 1954 automobile.

1981, Apr. 28 ***Perf. 12x11¾***

2069-2071 A1040 Set of 3 9.00 1.75

Souvenir Sheet

Perf. 11½x11¾

2072 A1040 70ch multicolored 6.00 3.00

World Telecommunications Day — A1041

1981, May 17 ***Perf. 11¾x11½***

2073 A1041 10ch multicolored 2.75 .25

Flowers A1042

Designs: 10ch, Iris pseudodacorus. 20ch, Iris pallasii. 30ch, Gladiolus gandavensis.

1981, May 20 ***Perf. 12x11¾***

2074-2076 A1042 Set of 3 3.50 1.60
2076a Sheet of 3, #2074-2076 4.00 —

WIPA 1981 Stamp Exhibition, Vienna A1043

Designs: 20ch, Austrian WIPA 1981 and Rudolf Kirchschlager stamps. 30ch, Austrian Maria Theresa and Franz Josef stamps.

50ch, Kim Il Sung and Korean Children's Union choir, vert.

1981, May 22 ***Perf. 13¼***

2077-2078 A1043 Set of 2 6.00 1.60

Souvenir Sheet

Perf. 11½

2079 A1043 50ch multicolored 6.00 2.75

International Gymnastc Federation, Centen. — A1044

Gymnastic events: 10ch, Rings. 15ch, Pommel horse. 20ch, Long horse. 25ch, Floor. 30ch, Hoop.

70ch, Ribbon, horiz.

1981, May 25 ***Perf. 11¾x12***

2080-2084 A1044 Set of 5 4.00 1.40
2084a Sheet of 6, as #2080-2085 15.00 —

Souvenir Sheet

Perf. 11½x11¾

2085 A1044 70ch multicolored 3.00 1.00

For overprints, see Nos. 2270-2275.

Mingyuehgou Meeting, 50th Anniv. — A1045

1981, June 15 ***Perf. 12¼x12***

2086 A1045 10ch multicolored .50 .25

Taen Work System, 20th Anniv. — A1046

1981, June 25 ***Perf. 12x12¼***

2087 A1046 10ch multicolored .50 .25

New System of Agricultural Guidance, 20th Anniv. — A1047

1981, June 25

2088 A1047 10ch multicolored .50 .25

Anti-Japanese Women's Assoc., 55th Anniv. — A1048

1981, July 5 ***Perf. 12¼***

2089 A1048 5w multicolored 12.00 1.00

Opera *Sea of Blood*, 10th Anniv. — A1049

1981, July 17 *Perf. 12*
2090 A1049 10w multicolored 30.00 10.00

Joan of Arc, 550th Anniv. Death — A1050

Designs: 10ch (No. 2091), Joan of Arc. 10ch (No. 2092a), Archangel Michael. 70ch, Joan of Arc in armor.
No. 2094, as No. 2092b.

1981, July 20
2091 A1050 multicolored 3.50 .75
2092 Sheet of 2, #2092a-2092b 9.00 —
a. 10ch multicolored — —
b. 70ch multicolored — —

Souvenir Sheet
Perf. 11½
2094 A1050 70ch multicolored 7.00 1.90

Down-with-Imperialism Union, 55th Anniv. — A1051

1981, July 25 *Perf. 12¼*
2095 A1051 1w multicolored 6.00 2.00

Rembrandt, 375th Birth Anniv. — A1052

Designs: 10ch, *Young Girl by the Window.* 20ch, *Rembrandt's Mother.* 30ch, *Saskia van Uylenburgh.* 40ch, *Pallas Athenae.*
70ch, *Self-portrait.*

1981, July 25 *Perf. 13¼*
2096-2099 A1052 Set of 4 7.50 3.00

Souvenir Sheet
2100 A1052 70ch multicolored 6.00 3.25

Symposium of the Non-Aligned Countries on Increasing Agricultural Production — A1053

Designs: 10ch, Emblem, banners over Pyongyang. 50ch, Harvesting grain. 90ch, Marchers with banners, tractors, fields, factories.

1981, Aug. 26 *Perf. 12*
2101-2103 A1053 Set of 3 2.25 1.10

Royal Wedding — A1054

Designs: 10ch, St. Paul's Cathedral. 20ch, Prince Charles on Great Britain #599. 30ch, Princess Diana. 40ch, Prince Charles in military uniform.
70ch, Prince Charles and Princess Diana.

1981, Sept. 18 *Perf. 13¼*
2104-2107 A1054 Set of 4 11.00 3.25

Souvenir Sheet
2108 A1054 70ch multicolored 16.50 5.50

For overprints, see Nos. 2205-2209.

Reubens Paintings — A1055

Designs: 10ch, *The Four Philosophers.* 15ch, *Portrait of Helena Fourment.* 20ch, *Portrait of Isabella Brandt.* 25ch, *The Education of Maria de Medici.* 30ch, *Helena Fourment and Her Child.* 40ch, *Helena Fourment in Her Wedding Dress.*
70ch, *Portrait of Nikolaas Rubens.*

1981, Sept. 20 *Perf. 11¾x12*
2109-2114 A1055 Set of 6 10.00 3.00

Souvenir Sheet
Perf 11½
2115 A1055 70ch multicolored 6.00 3.00

Royal Wedding — A1056

Designs: a, 10ch, Prince Charles and Princess Diana wedding portrait. b, 20ch, Charles and Diana with Flower Girl. c, 30ch, Charles and Diana leaving St. Paul's Cathedral. d, 40ch, Wedding portrait (diff.)
70ch, Charles and Diana with Queen Elizabeth on balcony.

1981, Sept. 29 *Perf. 13¼*
2116 A1056 Sheet of 4, #a.-d. 17.50 4.50

Souvenir Sheet
2120 A1056 70ch multicolored 25.00 6.00

No. 2120 exist imperf.

Philatokyo '81 International Stamp Exhibition, Tokyo — A1057

Design: 10ch, Rowland Hill and first stamps of Great Britain, Japan and DPRK. 20ch, DPRK World Fairy Tale stamps. 30ch, Three Japanese stamps.
70ch, Exhibition Hall.

1981, Oct. 9 *Perf. 11¾x11x½*
2121-2123 A1057 Set of 3 9.00 2.50
2123a Sheet of 4, as #2121-2124, perf 12x11½ 27.50 —

Souvenir Sheet
2124 A1057 70ch multicolored 7.50 2.10

Philatokyo '81 — A1058

Designs (both 10ch): No. 2125, Two DPRK stamps. No. 2126, DPRK stamp featuring Juche torch.

1981, Oct. 9 *Perf. 12x12¼*
2125-2126 A1058 Set of 2 4.00 1.40

League of Socialist Working Youth of Korea, 7th Congress A1059

1981, Oct. 20 *Perf. 12x11¾*
2127 A1059 10ch multicolored .25 .25
2128 A1059 80ch multicolored 1.00 .35

Bulgarian State, 1300th Anniv. — A1060

1981, Oct. 20 *Perf. 12x12¼*
2129 A1060 10ch multicolored .50 .25

Georgi Dimitrov (1882-1949), Birth Centenary — A1061

1981, Nov. 5 *Perf. 12*
2130 A1061 10ch multicolored .50 .25

Philatelia '81 Int'l Stamp Fair, Frankfurt-am-Main — A1062

1981, Nov. 14 *Perf. 13¼*
2131 A1062 20ch multicolored 3.00 .45

A1063

Philexfrance '82 International Stamp Exhibition, Paris — A1064

Designs: 10ch, Count Ferdinand von Zeppelin, *Graf Zeppelin*, Concorde. 20ch, Aircraft — Santos-Dumont 1905, Brequet 1930, Brequet Provence 1950, Concorde 1970. 30ch, Mona Lisa, six French stamps.

No. 2135: 10ch, Hotel des Invalides, Paris. 20ch, Pres. Mitterand of France. 30ch, International Friendship Building. 70ch, Kim Il Sung.
No. 2136: 60ch, Two French stamps picturing Rembrandt portrait and Picasso painting.

1981, Dec. 1 *Perf. 13¼*
2132-2134 A1063 Set of 3 10.00 2.00
2135 Sheet of 4, #a.-d. 7.50 2.50
a. A1064 10ch multicolored 1.25 .50
b. A1064 20ch multicolored 1.25 .50
c. A1064 30ch multicolored 1.25 .50
d. A1064 70ch multicolored 1.25 .50

Souvenir Sheet
2136 A1063 60ch multicolored 7.50 2.25

New Year — A1065

1982, Jan. 1 *Perf. 12*
2137 A1065 10ch multicolored .90 .25

"Korea Prospering Under the Wise Leadership of the Party" — A1066

Party emblem and: 2ch, banners. 10ch (No. 2139), Iron industry. 10ch (No. 2140), Produce, city, countryside. 10ch (No. 2141), Film industry. 10ch (No. 2142), Mining. 10ch (No. 2143), Lighthouse, helicopter. 40ch, Idealized cityscape.

1982, Feb. 1
2138-2144 A1066 Set of 7 7.00 1.50

A1067

Pablo Picasso (1881-1973), Painter, Birth Centenary — A1068

Designs (Nos. 2145-2148): 10ch, *La Coiffure.* 20ch, *Woman Leaning on Arm.* 25ch, *Child with Pigeon.* 35ch, *Portrait of Gertrude Stein.*
No. 2149: 10ch, *Paulo on a Donkey.* 20ch, *Harlequin.* 25ch, *Reading a Letter.* 35ch, *Harlequin* (diff.) 80ch, *Minotaur.* 90ch, *Mother and Child.*
Nos. 2150-2151: 80ch, *Minotaur.* 90ch, *Mother and Child.*

1982, Mar. 30 *Perf. 11¾*
2145-2148 A1067 Set of 4 6.50 1.50
2149 Sheet of 6, #a.-f. 14.00 2.75
a. A1067 10ch multicolored 2.25 .45
b. A1067 20ch multicolored 2.25 .45
c. A1067 25ch multicolored 2.25 .45
d. A1067 35ch multicolored 2.25 .45
e. A1067 80ch multicolored 2.25 .45

f. A1067 90ch multicolored 2.25 .45

Souvenir Sheets

2150-2151 A1068 Set of 2 8.00 4.00

A1069

A1070

Kim Il Sung, 70th Birthday A1071

Type A1069 (both 10ch): No. 2152, Kim Il Sung's Birthplace. No. 2153, Fireworks over Pyongyang.

Type A1070 (10ch), paintings of Kim Il Sung: No. 2154, "The Day Will Dawn." No. 2155, Signaling the start of the Pochonbo battle. No. 2156, Groundbreaking of Potong River Project. No. 2157, Embracing bereaved children. No. 2158, Directing operations at front. No. 2159, "On the Road of Advance." No. 2160, Speaking with workers at Kangson Steel Plant. No. 2161, Talking with peasants. No. 2162, Choosing site for reservoir.

Type A1070 (20ch): No. 2163, Visiting Komdok Valley. No. 2164, With Red Flag Company. No. 2165, With farmers. No. 2166, Opening metallurgical plant. No. 2167, Talking with smelters. No. 2168, At chemical plant. No. 2169, With fishermen.

No. 2170, Kim surrounded by adoring Koreans. No. 2171, Kim as a boy.

Perf. 11¾x12 (#2151-2152), 12x11¾

1982, Apr. 15

2152-2169 Set of 18 8.00 2.25

Souvenir Sheets

Perf. 13¼

2170-2171 A1071 60ch Set of 2 5.00 1.75

All type A1070 stamps were issued with setenant labels bearing inscriptions relating to theme of stamp. Values are for stamps with labels attached.

Korean People's Army, 50th Anniv. — A1072

1982, Apr. 25 ***Perf. 12***

2172 A1072 10ch multicolored .50 .25

ESSEN '82 Int'l Stamp Fair — A1073

1982, Apr. 28 ***Perf. 11¾x12***

2173 A1073 30ch multicolored 5.00 .50

Four Nature-Remaking Tasks — A1074

1982, Apr. 30 ***Perf. 12***

2174 A1074 10ch multicolored .60 .25

Issued to publicize the program for nature transformation contained in the Second Seven-Year Plan, which included irrigation, land reclamation, terracing, afforestation and water conservation, and reclamation of tidal lands.

Princess Diana, 21st Birthday — A1075

Princess Diana (Nos. 2175-2177): 10ch, As a baby. 20ch, As little girl on swing. 30ch, As little girl wearing red parka.

No. 2178: 50ch, As girl, wearing blue turtleneck sweater. 60ch, With long hair, wearing gray hat. 70ch, Wearing white hat. 80ch, Wearing white blouse and sweater.

Nos. 2179-2180: 40ch, Diana pushing her brother on swing. 80ch, As No. 2178d.

1982, May 1 ***Perf. 13¼***

2175-2177 A1075 Set of 3 4.00 1.00
2178 Sheet of 4, #a.-d. 18.00 5.50
a. A1075 50ch multicolored 3.50 1.25
b. A1075 60ch multicolored 3.50 1.25
c. A1075 70ch multicolored 3.50 1.25
d. A1075 80ch multicolored 3.50 1.25

Souvenir Sheets

2179-2180 A1075 Set of 2 10.00 5.00

For overprints, see Nos. 2210-2215.

Tower of the Juche Idea — A1076

1982, May 21 ***Perf. 12***

2182 A1076 2w multicolored 7.50 2.00

Arch of Triumph — A1077

1982, May 22

2183 A1077 3w multicolored 8.50 2.00

Tigers — A1078

Nos. 2184-2185: 20ch, Tiger cubs. 30ch, Tiger cubs (diff.)

No. 2186 (designs horizontal): 30ch, Tiger cub with mother. 40ch, Two cubs playing. 80ch, Two cubs playing, diff.

Nos. 2187: 80ch, Two cubs, horiz.

Perf. 11¾x12 (#2185-2186), 12x11¾

1982, May 30

2184-2185 A1078 Set of 2 7.00 1.00
2186 Sheet of 3, #a.-c. 16.00 3.00
a. A1078 30ch multicolored 3.00 .50
b. A1078 40ch multicolored 3.00 .50
c. A1078 80ch multicolored 3.00 .50

Souvenir Sheet

2187 A1078 80ch Multicolored 6.00 1.50

ESPANA '82 World Cup Championship — A1079

Flags and players of: 10ch, Group 1 countries — Italy, Peru, Poland, Cameroun. 20ch, Group 2 countries — Germany, Chile, Algeria, Austria. 30ch, Group 3 countries — Argentina, Hungary, Belgium, El Salvador. 40ch, Group 4 countries — Great Britain, Czechoslovakia, France, Kuwait. 50ch, Group 5 countries — Spain, Yugoslavia, Honduras, Northern Ireland. 60ch, Group 6 countries — Brazil, Scotland, USSR, New Zealand.

1w, Soccer players, flags, trophy and ESPANA '82 emblem.

1982, June 12 ***Perf. 13¼***

2188-2193 A1079 Set of 6 13.00 4.00

Souvenir Sheet

2194 A1079 1w multicolored 11.00 4.00

For overprints, see Nos. 2217-2223.

Space Exploration — A1080

Designs: 10ch, Rocket launch. 20ch, Spaceship over planet.

No. 2197a, Spaceship between planets.

No. 2198, Spaceship exploring desert area of other planet.

1982, June 20 ***Perf. 11¾x11½***

2195-2196 A1080 Set of 2 4.00 1.75
2197 Sheet of 3, #2195-2196, 2197a + label 6.50 2.75
a. A1080 80ch multicolored 2.25 .75

Souvenir Sheet

2198 A1080 80ch multicolored 4.00 1.60

Johann von Goethe (1749-1832), Writer, 150th Death Anniv. — A1081

Silhouettes: 10ch, Charlotte von Stein, 20ch, Goethe's sister. 25ch, Charlotte Buff. 35ch, Lili Schönemann.

No. 2203: 10ch, Goethe's mother. 20ch, Angelika Kauffman. 25ch, Anna Amalia. 35ch, Charlotte von Lengefeld. 80ch, Goethe.

No. 2204: 80ch, Goethe.

1982, July 25 ***Perf. 11¾x12***

2199-2202 A1081 Set of 4 4.00 1.60
2203 Sheet of 5, #a.-e. + label 9.00 2.00
a. A1081 10ch multicolored 1.75 .50
b. A1081 20ch multicolored 1.75 .50
c. A1081 25ch multicolored 1.75 .50
d. A1081 35ch multicolored 1.75 .50
e. A1081 80ch multicolored 1.75 .50

Souvenir Sheet

2204 A1081 80ch multicolored 4.00 1.75

Nos. 2104-2108 Overprinted in Blue

1982, Aug. 20

2205-2208 A1054 Set of 4 15.00 —

Souvenir Sheet

2209 A1054 70ch multicolored 15.00 —

Nos. 2175-2180 Overprinted in Blue

1982, Aug. 20

2210-2212 A1075 Set of 3 15.00 —
2213 Sheet of 4, #a-d 30.00 —

Souvenir Sheets

2214-2215 A1075 Set of 2 25.00 —

Nos. 2025a, 2188-2194 Overprinted in Blue

1982, Aug. 25

2216 A1035 Sheet of 4, #a.-d. 14.00 —
a. 10ch multicolored 1.00 —
b. 20ch multicolored 2.00 —
c. 30ch multicolored 3.00 —
d. 70ch multicolored 6.00 —
2217-2222 A1079 Set of 6 15.00 —

Souvenir Sheet

2223 A1079 1w multicolored 12.50 —

ESPANA '82 World Soccer Cup Winners — A1082

Designs: 20ch, Player holding World Cup aloft. 30ch, Three players with World Cup.

No. 2226: 30ch, as No. 2222. 40ch, As No. 2223. 80ch, King Juan Carlos of Spain and two players with World Cup.

No. 2227: 80ch, as No. 2226c.

1982, Aug. 30 ***Perf. 13¼***

2224-2225 A1082 Set of 2 4.00 1.00
2226 Sheet of 3, #a.-c. + label 10.00 —
a. A1082 30ch multicolored — —
b. A1082 40ch multicolored — —
c. A1082 80ch multicolored — —

Souvenir Sheet

2227 A1082 80ch multicolored 9.00 2.00

A1083

1st Wedding Anniv. of Prince and Princess of Wales A1084

1982, Sept. 21

2228 A1083 30ch multicolored 10.00 4.00

Souvenir Sheet

2229 A1084 80ch multicolored 15.00 5.00

No. 2228 was issued in sheets of four stamps and two labels.

Birth of Prince William of Wales — A1085

Designs: 10ch, Charles and Diana with Prince William (Charles in suit, Diana in pink hat and dress). 20ch, Couple with William. 30ch, Couple with William (diff.). 40ch, Diana with William. 50ch, Diana with William (diff.).

No. 2235: 10ch, Diana holding bouquet. 20ch, Charles carrying William, with Diana. 30ch, Charles carrying William, with Diana (diff.). 80ch, Couple with William (diff.).

No. 2236 (horiz.): 40ch, Charles and Diana. 50ch, Charles and Diana in evening dress. 80ch, Charles holding William, with Diana.

Nos. 2237-2238 (both 80ch): Diana holding William, with Royal Family; Diana holding William, with godparents.

1982, Sept. 29

2230-2234 A1085 Set of 5 16.00 5.00
2235 Sheet of 4, #a.-d. 16.00 6.25
a. A1085 10ch multicolored 3.25 1.25
b. A1085 20ch multicolored 3.25 1.25
c. A1085 30ch multicolored 3.25 1.25
d. A1085 80ch multicolored 3.25 1.25
2236 Sheet of 3, #a.-c. 16.00 6.25
a. A1085 40ch multicolored 4.25 1.75
b. A1085 50ch multicolored 4.25 1.75
c. A1085 80ch multicolored 4.25 1.75

Souvenir Sheets

2237-2238 A1085 Set of 2 24.00 10.00

A1086

Birth of Prince William of Wales — A1087

Nos. 2239-2244 are composed of layered plastic, on gummed paper, which creates two different images on each stamp, depending on the angle at which it is viewed.

30ch: No. 2239, Charles, Diana and William/Diana holding William. No. 2240, Charles, Diana and William (diff.)/Couple with William (Charles in suit, Diana in pink hat and dress).

No. 2241, Diana and William/Charles and Diana with William (Charles in suit, Diana in blue dress).

80ch: No. 2242, Diana and William, Portrait of Diana/Charles. No. 2243, Diana and William, St. Paul's Church/Wedding portrait of Royal Couple. No. 2244, Charles and Diana with William/Diana holding bouquet.

1982, Oct. 1 ***Imperf.***

2239-2241 A1086 Set of 3 35.00 —

Souvenir Sheets

2242-2244 A1087 Set of 3 60.00 —

Nos. 2242-2244 have simulated rouletting.

Bicentenary of Manned Flight A1088

Designs: 10ch, Baldwin's airship *Nulli Secundus II*, 1908. 20ch, Tissandier Brothers' airship, 1883. 30ch, Parseval *PL VIII*, 1912. 40ch, Count Lennox's balloon *Eagle*, 1834.

No. 2249: 10ch, Pauley and Durs Egg's airship, *The Dolphin*, 1818. 20ch, Guyton de Morveau's balloon, 1784. 30ch, Sir George Cayley's airship, 1837. 40ch, Camille Vert's balloon *Poisson Volant*, 1859. 80ch, Dupuy de Lôme's airship, 1872.

No. 2250: Masse's oar-powered balloon, 1784, vert.

1982, Nov. 21 ***Perf. 13¼***

2245-2248 A1088 Set of 4 7.00 2.00
2249 Sheet of 5, #a.-e. + label 13.00 6.00
a. A1088 10ch multicolored 2.25 1.00
b. A1088 20ch multicolored 2.25 1.00
c. A1088 30ch multicolored 2.25 1.00
d. A1088 40ch multicolored 2.25 1.00
e. A1088 80ch multicolored 2.25 1.00

Souvenir Sheet

2250 A1088 80ch multicolored 4.50 2.00

Bicentenary of Manned Flight — A1089

Designs: 10ch, Balthasar Antoine Dunker's *Utopic Balloon Post*, 1784-90. 20ch, "and they fly into heaven and have no wings." 30ch, Pierre Testu-Brissy's balloon flight with horse, 1796. 40ch, Test flight of Gaston Tissandier's balloon *Zenith*, 1875.

No. 2255: 10ch, Montgolfier balloon at Versailles, 1783. 20ch, Montgolfier Brothers' balloon, 1783. 30ch, Charles' hydrogen balloon landing at Nesle. 40ch, Blanchard and Jeffries' flight over the English Channel, 1785. 80ch, Henri Giffard's balloon *Le Grand Ballon Captif* at World's Fair, 1878.

No. 2256: "Ballons Monte" balloon mail service from besieged Paris, 1870-1871.

1982, Dec. 10

2251-2254 A1089 Set of 4 12.00 4.00
2255 Sheet of 5, #a.-e. + label 25.00 6.50
a. A1089 10ch multicolored 4.50 1.25
b. A1089 20ch multicolored 4.50 1.25
c. A1089 30ch multicolored 4.50 1.25
d. A1089 40ch multicolored 4.50 1.25
e. A1089 80ch multicolored 4.50 1.25

Souvenir Sheet

2256 A1089 80ch multicolored 5.00 2.00

Tale of the Hare A1090

Designs: 10ch, Turtle searching for hare. 20ch, Turtle and hare going to Dragon King Palace. 30ch, Hare swindling Dragon King, demanding her liver. 40ch, Hare cheating turtle.

1982, Dec. 25 ***Perf. 12***

2257-2260 A1090 Set of 4 8.00 1.25

Socialist Constitution, 10th Anniv. — A1091

1982, Dec. 27

2261 A1091 10ch multicolored .50 .25

New Year — A1092

1983, Jan. 1 ***Perf. 12¼x12***

2262 A1092 10ch multicolored .50 .25

Saenal Newspaper, 55th Anniv. A1093

1983, Jan. 15 ***Perf. 11½x11¾***

2263 A1093 10ch multicolored .90 .25

Rembrandt Paintings — A1094

Designs: 10ch, *Man in Oriental Costume.* 20ch, *The Noble Slav.* 30ch, *Dr. Tulp's Anatomy Lesson* (detail). 40ch, *Two Scholars Disputing.*

No. 2268: 10ch, *Child with Dead Peacocks.* 20ch, *Old Man in Fur Hat.* 30ch, *Portrait of a Fashionable Couple.* 40ch, *Woman with Child.* 80ch, *Woman Holding an Ostrich Feather Fan.*

No. 2269: 80ch, *Self-Portrait.*

1983, Jan. 25 ***Perf. 11¾x11½***

2264-2267 A1094 Set of 4 8.00 1.50
2268 Sheet of 5, #a.-e. + label 15.00 7.50
a. A1094 10ch multicolored 2.00 1.00
b. A1094 20ch multicolored 2.00 1.00
c. A1094 30ch multicolored 2.00 1.00
d. A1094 40ch multicolored 2.00 1.00
e. A1094 80ch multicolored 2.00 1.00

Souvenir Sheet

Perf. 11¾x12

2269 A1094 80ch multicolored 4.00 1.25

Nos. 2080-2085 Overprinted "XXIII Summer Olympic Games 1984" and Olympic Rings

1983, Feb. 10

2270-2274 A1044 Set of 5 *20.00* —
2274a Sheet of 6, as #2270-2275 *75.00* —

Souvenir Sheet

2275 A1044 70ch multicolored *25.00* —

Luposta Int'l Air Mail Exhib., Köln A1095

Virgin and Child, by Stephan Lochner A1096

1983, Jan. 25 ***Perf. 11¾x11½***

2276 30ch multicolored 3.00 1.00
2277 40ch multicolored 3.00 1.00
a. A1095 Pair, #2276-2277 7.00 3.00

Souvenir Sheet

Perf. 13¼

2278 A1096 80ch multicolored 3.50 1.75

Wangjaesen Meeting, 50th Anniv. — A1097

1983, Mar. 11 ***Perf. 11½x11¾***

2279 A1097 10ch multicolored .50 .25

Karl Marx, Centenary of Death — A1098

1983, Mar. 14 ***Perf. 11¾x12***

2280 A1098 10ch multicolored 2.25 .25

Thousand-ri Journey for Learning, 60th Anniv. — A1099

1983, Mar. 16 ***Perf. 12***

2281 A1099 10ch multicolored 1.00 .25

A1100

Raphael (1483-1520), 500th Birth Anniv. — A1101

Designs: 10ch, *Madonna of the Goldfinch.* 30ch, *Madonna of the Grand Duke.* 50ch (No. 2284), *Madonna of the Chair.*

No. 2285: 20ch, *The School of Athens* (detail). 50ch (No. 2285b), *Madonna of the Lamb.* 80ch, *The Beautiful Gardener.*

No. 2286: 80ch, *Madonna of St. Sixte.*

1983, Mar. 20 ***Perf. 13½***

2282-2284 A1100 Set of 3 6.00 1.00
2285 Sheet of 3, #a.-c. + label 15.00 3.50
a. A1100 20ch multicolored 4.00 .75
b. A1100 50ch multicolored 4.00 .75
c. A1100 80ch multicolored 4.00 .75

Souvenir Sheet

2286 A1101 80ch multicolored 4.50 1.25

Pyongyang Buildings A1102

Designs: 2ch, Chongryu Restaurant. 10ch (No. 2288), Munsu Street. 10ch (No. 2289), Ice Rink. 40ch, Department Store No. 1. 70ch, Grand People's Study House.

1983, Apr. 7 ***Perf. 12¼***

2287-2291 A1102 Set of 5 6.00 .75
2287a 2ch Unsurfaced white paper, without gum 10.00 —
2288a 10ch Unsurfaced white paper, without gum 10.00 —
2289a 10ch Unsurfaced white paper, without gum 10.00 —
2290a 40ch Unsurfaced white paper, without gum 10.00 —
2291a 40ch Unsurfaced white paper, without gum 10.00 —

Int'l Institute of the Juche Idea, 5th Anniv. — A1103

1983, Apr. 9 ***Perf. 12¼x12***

2292 A1103 10ch multicolored .50 .25

Pre-Olympic Games, Los Angeles '84 — A1104

Designs (values in gold): 20ch (No. 2293), Judo. 30ch (No. 2294), Judo (diff.). 40ch (No. 2295), Boxing. 50ch (No. 2296), Weightlifting.

No. 2297 (values in black): 20ch, Wrestling. 30ch, Judo (diff.). 40ch, Shooting. 50ch, Wrestling. (diff.) 80ch, Boxing (diff.).

No. 2298: 80ch, Judo (diff.)

1983, Apr. 20 ***Perf. 11¼***

2293-2296 A1104 Set of 4 13.00 1.50
2297 Sheet of 5, #a.-e. + label 25.00 1.00
a. A1104 20ch multicolored 4.00 .25
b. A1104 30ch multicolored 4.00 .25
c. A1104 40ch multicolored 4.00 .25
d. A1104 50ch multicolored 4.00 .25
e. A1104 80ch multicolored 4.00 .25

Souvenir Sheet

Perf. 13½

2298 A1104 80ch multicolored 10.00 1.00

World Communications Year — A1105

1983, Apr. 30 ***Perf. 11¾x12***

2299 A1105 10ch multicolored 2.00 .25

TEMBAL '83 Int'l Topical Stamp Exhib., Basel — A1106

Designs: 20ch, Emblem, giant panda and stamp. 30ch, Emblem, DPRK flag and "Basel Dove" stamp (Switzerland No. 3L1).

1983, May 21 ***Perf. 12***

2300-2301 A1106 Set of 2 7.50 .75

Old Ships — A1107

Designs: 20ch, *Colourful Cow* (Hamburg, 1402). 35ch, *Great Harry* (England, 1555). 50ch, *Eagle of Lübeck* (Lübeck, 1567).

No. 2305: 20ch, Turtle Boat (Korea, 1592). 35ch, Admiral Li Sun Sin (1545-98), inventor of the Turtle Boat. 50ch, *Merkur* (Prussia, 1847). 80ch, *Duchess Elisabeth* (West Germany).

No. 2306: 80ch, *Christoforo Colombo* (Italy).

1983, May 30 ***Perf. 11x11¼***

2302-2304 A1107 Set of 3 5.00 1.50
2305 Sheet of 4, #a.-d. + 2 labels 12.00 2.50
a. A1107 20ch multicolored 3.00 .50
b. A1107 35ch multicolored 3.00 .50
c. A1107 50ch multicolored 3.00 .50
d. A1107 80ch multicolored 3.00 .50

Souvenir Sheet

Perf. 13½x13¼

2306 A1107 80ch multicolored 6.00 3.00

Steam Locomotives — A1108

Designs: 20ch, *Locomotion* (Great Britain, 1825). 35ch, *De Adler* (Germany, 1835). 50ch, *Austria* (1837).

No. 2310: 20ch, *Drache* (Germany, 1848. 35ch, Korean Train. 50ch, Bristal and Exeter Railway locomotive (Great Britain, 1853). 80ch, Caledonian Railway locomotive (Great Britain, 1859).

No. 2311: 80ch, *Ilmarinen* (Finland, 1860).

1983, June 20 ***Perf. 12x11¾***

2307-2309 A1108 Set of 3 13.00 2.50
2310 Sheet of 4, #a.-d. + 2 labels 40.00 3.50
a. A1108 20ch multicolored 3.00 .75
b. A1108 35ch multicolored 3.00 .75
c. A1108 50ch multicolored 3.00 .75
d. A1108 80ch multicolored 3.00 .75

Souvenir Sheet

Perf. 12

2311 A1108 80ch multicolored 30.00 1.50

Publication of the Five-Point Policy for Korean Reunification, 10th Anniv. — A1109

1983, June 23 ***Perf. 12¼***

2312 A1109 10ch multicolored 1.40 .25

World Conference of Journalists Against Imperialism and for Friendship and Peace — A1110

Designs: 10ch, Emblem, Tower of Juche Idea, fireworks, "Welcome." 40ch, Emblem, clasped hands, rainbow, "Friendship." Emblem, map, hand with raised forefinger, "Korea Is One."

1983, July 2 ***Perf. 12x11¾***

2313-2315 A1110 Set of 3 1.75 .30

"Let's Create the Speed of the 80s" — A1111

1983, July 10 ***Perf. 12x12¼***

2316 A1111 10ch multicolored .50 .25

Korean War, 30th Anniv. — A1112

1983, July 27

2317 A1112 10ch multicolored .50 .25

Bangkok 1983 Int'l Stamp Exhib. — A1113

Designs: 40ch, *Gorch Foch* and DPRK #1693. 80ch, Bangkok temple, Great Britain #1 and DPRK IYC stamp.

1983, Aug. 4 ***Perf. 12x11¾***

2318 A1113 40ch multicolored 3.50 1.00

Souvenir Sheet

Perf. 11½x11¾

2319 A1113 80ch multicolored 7.00 3.50

A1114

Winter Olympic Games, Sarajevo 1984 A1115

Designs: 10ch, Skiier. 30ch, Figure skaters. 50ch, Ski jumper.

No. 2323 (all vert.): 20ch, Woman figure skater. 50ch, Hockey player. 80ch, Speed skater.

No. 2324, 80ch, Skier shooting rifle (biathlon).

1983, Aug. 20

2320-2322 A1114 Set of 3 8.00 1.50
2323 Sheet of 3, #a.-c., perf 11¾x12 17.00 2.75
a. A1114 20ch multicolored 4.00 .75
b. A1114 50ch multicolored 4.00 .75
c. A1114 80ch multicolored 4.00 .75

Souvenir Sheet

2324 A1115 80ch multicolored 7.50 1.25

Democratic People's Republic of Korea, 35th Anniv. — A1116

1983, Sept. 9 ***Perf. 13¼x13½***

2325 A1116 10ch multicolored .65 .25

Folk Games — A1117

Designs: 10ch (No. 2326), Archery. 40ch (No. 2327), Seesaw. No. 2328: 10ch, Flying kites. 40ch, Swinging.

1983, Sept. 20 ***Perf. 11¾x12***

2326-2327 A1117 Set of 2 5.00 .50
2328 Sheet of 2, #a.-b. 2.50 .40
a. A1117 10ch multicolored .75 .25
b. A1117 40ch multicolored .75 .25

Korean-Chinese Friendship — A1118

1983, Oct. 25 ***Perf. 12***

2329 A1118 10ch multicolored .75 .25

A1119

World Communications Year — A1120

Designs: 30ch (No. 2330), *Redong Sinmun* and magazine. 40ch (No. 2331), Letters and forms of postal transport.

No. 2332: 30ch, Communications satellite, satellite dish. 40ch, TV camera and relay tower. 80ch, Telephone and satellite dishes.

No. 2333, 80ch, Emblem, communications satellite.

1983, Oct. 30 ***Perf. 13½***

2330-2331 A1119 Set of 2 9.00 1.75
2332 Sheet of 3, #a.-c. 5.50 1.00
a. A1119 30ch multicolored 1.00 .25
b. A1119 40ch multicolored 1.00 .25
c. A1119 80ch multicolored 1.00 .25

Souvenir Sheet

2333 A1120 80ch multicolored 6.00 1.25

A1121

Paintings by Peter Paul Rubens — A1122

No. 2334, *Portrait of Helene Fourmet.*
No. 2335 (both horiz.): a, Detail from *Portrait of a Young Lady.* b, *Diana Returning from Hunt.*
No. 2336: *The Bear Hunt.*

1983, Nov. 10

2334 A1121 40ch multicolored 2.00 .50
2335 Sheet of 2, #a.-b. 4.50 1.25
a. A1121 40ch multicolored 1.75 .45
b. A1121 80ch multicolored 1.75 .45

Souvenir Sheet

2336 A1122 80ch multicolored 3.25 .75

Olympic Games, Los Angeles 1984 — A1123

Designs: 10ch, Sprinter. 30ch, Cyclists. 50ch, Volleyball.
No. 2340: 20ch, Show jumping. 50ch, Fencing. 80ch, Gymnastics.
No. 2341: 80ch, Judo.

1983, Nov. 30 ***Perf. 11½***

2337-2339 A1123 Set of 3 10.50 1.25
2340 Sheet of 3, #a.-c. 30.00 2.00
a. A1123 20ch multicolored 7.00 .50
b. A1123 50ch multicolored 7.00 .50
c. A1123 80ch multicolored 7.00 .50

Souvenir Sheet

2341 A1123 80ch multicolored 3.50 1.00

Six deluxe souvenir sheets of one, each denominated 1w, exist. Value, set of 6 sheets, $100.

A1124

Antonio Correggio (1489-1534), 450th Death Anniv. — A1125

Designs: 20ch, *St. Catherine.* 35ch, *Madonna.* 50ch, *Madonna with St. John.*
No. 2345: a, *Morning* (detail). b, *Morning* (diff. detail). c, *St. Catherine* (diff.). d, *Madonna and Child.*
No. 2346: *Madonna and Child with Music-Making Angels.*

1983, Dec. 12 ***Perf. 13¼***

2342-2344 A1124 Set of 3 5.00 1.25
2345 Sheet of 4, #a.-d. 12.00 3.50
a. A1124 20ch multicolored 2.50 .75
b. A1124 35ch multicolored 2.50 .75
c. A1124 50ch multicolored 2.50 .75
d. A1124 80ch multicolored 2.50 .75

Souvenir Sheet

2346 A1125 80ch multicolored 4.50 1.25

Cats — A1126

Domestic cats, each different, denominated 10ch. Frame color: No. 2347, green. No. 2348, gray. No. 2349, gold. No. 2350, red. No. 2351, blue.

1983, Dec. 20

2347-2351 A1126 Set of 5 12.00 .50

Six souvenir sheets inscribed Sarajevo '84, each containing one 1w stamp, were issued on Dec. 31, 1983. Value $80.

New Year — A1127

1984, Jan. 1 ***Perf. 12***

2352 A1127 10ch multicolored 1.00 .25

Korean Workers Party — A1128

Designs (both 10ch): No. 2353, Komdok General Mining Enterprise, Ore-dressing Plant No. 3, and Party flag. No. 2354, Worker holding books, and Party flag.

1984, Feb. 16

2353-2354 A1128 Set of 2 1.00 .25
2353a 10ch Unsurfaced white paper, without gum 20.00 —
2354a 10ch Unsurfaced white paper, without gum 20.00 —

Farm Worker, Grain — A1129

1984, Feb. 25

2355 A1129 10ch multicolored .60 .25

Publication of the *Theses on the Socialist Rural Question in Our Country,* 20th anniv.

Changdok School, Chilgol — A1130

Kim's Birthplace, Rejoicing Crowd — A1131

1984, Apr. 15

2356 A1130 5ch multicolored .50 .25
a. Unsurfaced white paper, without gum 15.00 —
2357 A1131 10ch multicolored .50 .25
a. Unsurfaced white paper, without gum 20.00 —

Kim Il Sung, 72nd birthday.

A1132

España '84 Int'l Stamp Exhib. — A1133

Designs: 10ch, *Spanish Riding School of Vienna,* by Julius von Blaas. 20ch, *Ferdinand of Austria,* by Rubens.
No. 2360: 80ch, *Spanish Riding School,* by von Blaas.

1984, Apr. 27 ***Perf. 13½***

2358-2359 A1132 Set of 2 3.50 .75

Souvenir Sheet

2360 A1133 80ch multicolored 6.50 1.25

Kiyang Irrigation System, 25th Anniv. A1134

1984, Apr. 30

2361 A1134 10ch multicolored .75 .25

Raphael, 500th Anniv. of Birth (in 1983) — A1135

Designs: 10ch, *Portrait of Angolo Doni.* 20ch, *Portrait of La Donna Velata.* 30ch, *Portrait of Jeanne d'Aragon.*
80ch, *St. Sebastian.*

1984, Apr. 30 ***Perf. 11¾x12***

2362-2364 A1135 Set of 3 4.00 1.00

Souvenir Sheet

Perf. 11¾x11½

2365 A1135 80ch multicolored 3.50 1.25

Socialist Construction — A1136

1984, May 20 ***Perf. 12***

2366 A1136 10ch multicolored .75 .25

1984 Winter Olympics Games Medal Winners — A1137

Designs: 20ch (No. 2367), Speed skating (Karin Enke, DDR). 30ch (No. 2368), Bobsledding (DDR).
No. 2369: 10ch, Ski jumping (Matti Nykaenen, Finland). 20ch (No. 2369b), Slalom (Max Julen, Switzerland). 30ch (No. 2369c), Downhill skiing (Maria Walliser, Switzerland).
No. 2370 (both vert.): 40ch, Cross-country skiing (Thomas Wassberg, Sweden). 80ch, Cross-country skiing (Maria Liisa Hamalainen).
No. 2371 (vert.): 80ch, Biathlon (Peter Angerer, West Germany).

1984, May 20 ***Perf. 13½***

2367-2368 A1137 Set of 2 3.50 .85
2369 Sheet of 3, #a.-c. 25.00 1.25
a. A1137 10ch multicolored 6.00 .35
b. A1137 20ch multicolored 6.00 .35
c. A1137 30ch multicolored 6.00 .35
2370 Sheet of 2, #a.-b. 5.00 1.00
a. A1137 40ch multicolored 2.00 .40
b. A1137 80ch multicolored 2.00 .40

Souvenir Sheet

2371 A1137 80ch multicolored 3.50 1.00

Essen '84 Int'l Stamp Exhib. A1138

Designs: 20ch, Type "202" express locomotive (1939). 30ch, Type "E" freight locomotive (1919).
No. 2374: 80ch, Type "D" locomotive in Germany.

1984, May 26 ***Perf. 12x11¾***

2372-2373 A1138 Set of 2 10.00 1.00

Souvenir Sheet

2374 A1138 80ch multicolored 9.00 1.25

Edgar Degas, 150th Birth Anniv. — A1139

Designs: 10ch, *Mlle. Fiocre in the Ballet 'La Source.'* 20ch, *The Dance Foyer at the Rue le Peletier Opera.* 30ch, *Race Meeting.*
No. 2378: 80ch, *Dancers at the Bars.*

1984, June 10 ***Perf. 12***

2375-2377 A1139 Set of 3 8.00 1.25

Souvenir Sheet

Perf. 11½

2378 A1139 80ch multicolored 4.50 1.25

Irrigation Experts Meeting A1140

1984, June 16 ***Perf. 11¾x12***

2379 A1140 2ch multicolored .80 .25

UPU Congress/Hamburg 1984 Stamp Exhib. — A1141

No. 2381: 80ch, *Gorch Fock,* DPRK stamp depicting Turtle Boat.

1984, June 19
2380 A1141 20ch multicolored 3.50 .35

Souvenir Sheet
Perf. 11¾x11½

2381 A1141 80ch multicolored 6.00 2.00

Tripartite Talks Proposal — A1142

1984, June 25 ***Perf. 12¼***
2382 A1142 10ch multicolored .75 .25

Alfred Bernhard Nobel, 150th Birth Anniv. (in 1983) — A1143

Designs: 20ch, Nobel in laboratory. 30ch, Nobel portrait.
No. 2385: 80ch, Nobel portrait, diff.

1984, June 30 ***Perf. 13½***
2383-2384 A1143 Set of 2 8.00 .75

Souvenir Sheet

2385 A1143 80ch multicolored 7.00 2.00

Nos. 2383 and 2384 were issued se-tenant with labels depicting Nobel's laboratory and home, respectively.

Improvement of Korean Living Standards A1144

1984, July 10 ***Perf. 11¾x12***
2386 A1144 10ch multicolored .70 .25

Kuandian Conf., 65th Anniv. — A1145

1984, Aug. 17 ***Perf. 12x12¼***
2387 A1145 10ch multicolored 1.25 .25

Sunhwa School, Mangyongdae A1146

1984, Aug. 17 ***Perf. 12***
2388 A1146 10ch multicolored 1.10 .25

School of Kim Il Sung's father, Kim Hyong Jik.

A1147

A1148

Flowers: 10ch, *Cattleya loddigesii.* 20ch, *Thunia bracteata.* 30ch, *Phalaenopsis amabilis.*
No. 2392: 80ch, *Kimilsungia.*

1984, Aug. 20
2389-2391 A1147 Set of 3 4.00 .60

Souvenir Sheet

2392 A1148 80ch multicolored 5.00 1.00

Fishing Industry A1149

Designs: 5ch, Swordfish and trawler. 10ch, Marlin and trawler. 40ch, *Histiophorus orientalis.*

1984, Aug. 25
2393-2395 A1149 Set of 3 4.50 1.00

Revolutionary Museum, Chilgol — A1150

1984, Aug. 29
2396 A1150 10ch multicolored .90 .25

"Let's All Become the Kim Hyoks and Cha Gwang Sus of the '80s!" — A1151

1984, Aug. 31
2397 A1151 10ch multicolored .90 .25

Orient Express, Centenary A1152

Designs: 10ch, Inauguration of a French railway line in 1860. 20ch, Opening of a British railway line in 1821. 30ch, Inauguration of Paris-Rouen line, 1843.
No. 2401: 80ch, Interior views of passenger cars, 1905.

1984, Sept. 7 ***Perf. 13½x13¼***
2398-2400 A1152 Set of 3 8.00 1.25

Souvenir Sheet

2401 A1152 80ch multicolored 7.00 1.75

Greenwich Meridian Time, Centenary — A1153

Designs: 10ch, Clockface, astronomical observatory.
No. 2403: 80ch, Clock face, buildings, Chollima statue.

1984, Sept. 15 ***Perf. 12***
2402 A1153 10ch multicolored 4.00 —

Souvenir Sheet
Perf. 11¾x11½

2403 A1153 80ch multicolored 6.00 1.25

Hamhung Grand Theater A1154

1984, Sept. 21
2404 A1154 10ch multicolored .90 .25

Automation of Industry — A1155

1984, Sept. 25 ***Perf. 12¼***
2405 A1155 10ch multicolored .90 .25
a. Unsurfaced white paper, without gum 8.00 —

A1156

18th Century Korean Paintings — A1157

Designs: 10ch, *Dragon Angler.* 20ch, *Ox Driver,* horiz. 30ch, *Bamboo,* horiz.
80ch, *Autumn Night.*

1984, Sept. 30 ***Perf. 12 (#2406), 13¼***
2406-2408 A1156 Set of 3 4.00 .60

Souvenir Sheet
Perf. 13¼

2409 A1157 80ch multicolored 3.50 1.25

K.E. Tsiolkovski (1857-1935), Russian Space Scientist — A1158

Designs: 20ch, Portrait. 30ch, Earth, sputnik.
No. 2412: 80ch, Rocket launch.

1984, Oct. 5 ***Perf. 11¾***
2410-2411 A1158 Set of 2 2.00 .45

Souvenir Sheet
Perf. 11¾x11½

2412 A1158 80ch multicolored 4.00 .75

Container Ships A1159

Designs: 10ch, *Pongdaesan.* 20ch, *Ryongnamsan.* 30ch, *Rungrado.*
No. 2416: 80ch, *Kumgangsan*

1984, Oct. 6 ***Perf. 12x11¾***
2413-2415 A1158 Set of 3 4.00 .85

Souvenir Sheet
Perf. 12

2416 A1159 80ch multicolored 5.00 1.25

A1160

A1161

Wild Animals: 10ch, Spotted hyenas. 20ch, Caracal. 30ch, Black-backed jackals. 40ch, Foxes.
80ch, Falcon.

1984, Oct. 13 ***Perf. 13¼***
2417-2420 A1160 Set of 4 4.50 1.00

Souvenir Sheet

2421 A1161 80ch multicolored 6.50 1.25

Marie Curie (1867-1934), Physicist, 50th Death Anniv. — A1162

No. 2423: 80ch, Portrait of Mme. Curie.

1984, Oct. 21 ***Perf. 12***
2422 A1162 10ch multicolored 4.00 .25

Souvenir Sheet
Perf. 11¾x11½

2423 A1162 80ch multicolored 6.00 1.25

A1163

Birds: 10ch, Hoopoe. 20ch, South African crowned cranes. 30ch, Saddle-bill stork. 40ch, Chestnut-eared Aracari.
No. 2428: 80ch, Black kite.

1984, Nov. 5 *Perf. 11½*
2424-2427 A1163 Set of 4 8.50 1.25

Souvenir Sheet

2428 A1163 80ch multicolored 8.50 1.25

Space Exploration — A1164

Designs: 10ch, Cosmonaut. 20ch, Cosmonaut on space-walk. 30ch, Cosmonaut (diff.)
No. 2432: 80ch, Moon vehicle.

1984, Nov. 15 *Perf. 12*
2429-2431 A1164 Set of 3 3.00 .60

Souvenir Sheet

2432 A1164 80ch multicolored 4.00 1.00

Russian Icebreakers A1165

Designs: 20ch, *Arktika*. 30ch, *Ermak*.
No. 2435: 80ch, *Lenin*.

1984, Nov. 26 *Perf. 13¼*
2433-2434 A1165 Set of 2 3.25 .60

Souvenir Sheet

2435 A1165 80ch multicolored 5.00 1.25

A1166

Dmitri Mendeleev (1834-1907), Chemist, 150th Birth Anniv. — A1167

1984, Dec. 1 *Perf. 13¼*
2436 A1166 10ch multicolored 1.75 .25

Souvenir Sheet

2437 A1167 80ch multicolored 4.00 1.25

Historic European Royalty, Scenes — A1168

British Monarchs — A1169

Queen Elizabeth II — A1170

Type A1168: No. 2438 (all 10ch): a, Konrad III, 1149 (Germany). b, Henry VIII (England). c, Henry VI (England). d, King John (England). e, Fleet of Elizabeth I (England). f, Philip II Augustus (France). g, Thames and London Bridge, 1616. h, Elizabeth I (England). i, Charles VII, parade (England).

No. 2439 (all 10ch): a, Prince Eugene, 1706 (Savoy). b, Kaiser Wilhelm II (Germany). c, Philip V (Spain). d, Ludwig II (Bavaria). e, Alfonso XIII (Spain). f, Mary Stuart (Scotland). g, Charles Edward Stuart, 1745 (Scotland). h, Marie-Louise (Austria). i, Charles V, 1547 (Spain).

No. 2440 (Horiz., all 10ch): a, Maria Theresa (Austria). b, Francis I, 1814 (Austria). c, Leopold II, 1844 (Austria). d, Louis XVIII (France). e, Versailles, 1688. f, Louis XIV (France). g, Prince Wilhelm (Germany). h, Franz Joseph I (Austria). i, Ludwig II (Bavaria).

No. 2441 (Horiz., all 10ch): a, Napoleon III (France. b, Rudolph of Habsburg, Basel 1273. c, Henry IV (France). d, Louis XII (France). e, Maximilian I (Holy Roman Empire). f, Peter the Great, Amsterdam Harbor (Russia). g, Louis VIII (France). h, Don Juan/Battle of Lepanto, 1571. i, Neuschwaustein Castle.

Type A1169: No. 2442 (all 10ch): a, William I. b, Richard II. c, Henry V. d, Henry VI. e, Richard III. f, Edward IV. g, Henry VII. h, Henry VIII, full length portrait. i, Henry VIII, ¾-face portrait, as young man.

No. 2443 (all 10ch): a, Henry VIII, ¾-face portrait, as middle-aged man. b, Mary I. c, Elizabeth I, facing left. d, Edward VI. e, Elizabeth I, facing right. f, Lady Jane Grey. g, Mary, Queen of Scots. h, James I. i, Charles I.

No. 2444 (all 10ch): a, Charles I. b, Henrietta Marie. c, Charles II. d, James II. e, George I, seated. f, William IV. g, Queen Anne, full-length portrait. h, George I, in profile. i. Queen Mary II.

No. 2445 (all 10ch): a, Queen Anne, with her son, William, Duke of Gloucester. b, George II, facing forward. c, George II, in profile. d, George IV. e, George III. f, William III. g, William IV. h, Queen Victoria. i, Prince Albert.

No. 2446 (all 10ch): a, Edward VII. b, Queen Alexandra. c, George V and Royal Family. d, George VI. e, George VI and Royal Family. f, Queen Elizabeth II. g, Prince Charles. h, Prince William of Wales, with Prince Charles and Princess Diana. i, Princess Diana.

Sheets of 9, #a.-i.

1984, Dec. 20 *Perf. 12¼x12*

Types A1168-A1169

2438-2446 Set of 9 125.00 —

Souvenir Sheet

Perf. 11½

2447 A1170 80ch multicolored 20.00 12.00

Kim Il Sung's Visits to Eastern Europe — A1171

No. 2448 (all 10ch): a, USSR. b, Poland. c, DDR. d, Czechoslovakia.
No. 2249 (all 10ch): a, Hungary. b, Bulgaria. c, Romania.
No. 2450: 10ch, China.

1984, Dec. 30 *Perf. 12*
2448 A1171 Sheet of 4, #a.-d. 4.50 1.25
2449 A1171 Sheet of 3, #a.-c. 3.50 1.00

Souvenir Sheet

Perf. 11½

2450 A1171 10ch multicolored *50.00* 1.00

New Year — A1172

1985, Jan. 1 *Perf. 12*
2451 A1172 10ch multicolored 1.90 .25

Kim Il Sung's 1,000-ri Journey, 60th Anniv. A1173

1985, Jan. 22 *Perf. 12¼*
2452 A1173 Pair, #a.-b. 2.25 .25
a. 5ch multicolored .75 .25
b. 10ch multicolored .75 .25

A1174

History of the Motorcar — A1175

Designs: 10ch, Gugnot's Steam Car, 1769. 15ch, Goldsworthy Steam Omnibus, 1825. 20ch, Gottlieb Daimler diesel car, 1885. 25ch, Benx three-wheeled diesel car, 1886. 30ch, Peugot diesel car, 1891.
80ch, Wind-power car.

1985, Jan. 25 *Perf. 11½*
2453-2457 A1174 Set of 5 7.00 .85

Souvenir Sheet

2458 A1175 80ch multicolored 4.50 1.25

Secret Camp, Mt. Paektu — A1176

1985, Feb. 16 *Perf. 12*
2459 A1176 10ch multicolored .65 .25

Korean Revolution Headquarters

Lighthouses — A1177

10ch, Taechodo. 20ch, Sodo. 30ch, Pido. 40ch, Suundo.

1985, Feb. 23 *Perf. 12¼x11¾*
2460-2463 A1177 Set of 4 9.00 1.25

For surcharges, see Nos. 4533-4534.

The Hedgehog Defeats the Tiger, Fairy Tale — A1178

Designs: 10ch, Tiger bragging about his strength. 20ch, Tiger going to stamp on rolled-up hedgehog. 30ch, Hedgehog clinging to tiger's nose. 35ch, Fleeing tiger. 40ch, Tiger crawling before hedgehog.

1985, Mar. 6 *Perf. 11½*
2464-2468 A1178 Set of 5 6.50 1.25

A1179

Mushrooms: 10ch, Pieurotus cornucopiae. 20ch, Pluerotus ostreatus. 30ch, Catathelasma ventricosum.

1985, Mar. 16
2469-2471 A1179 Set of 3 6.00 .65

For surcharge, see No. 4521.

A1180

World Cup Soccer 1954-1966 — A1181

Designs: 10ch, W. Germany vs. Hungary, 1954. 20ch, Brazil vs. Sweden, 1958. 30ch, Brazil vs. Czechoslovakia, 1962. 40ch, England vs. W. Germany, 1966.
80ch, DPRK team in quarter final, 1966.

1985, Mar. 20 *Perf. 13¼*
2472-2475 A1180 Set of 4 4.50 1.00

Souvenir Sheet

2476 A1181 80ch multicolored 4.00 1.25

A1182

World Cup Soccer 1970-1986 — A1183

Designs: 10ch, Brazil vs. Italy, 1970. 20ch, W. Germany vs. Netherlands, 1974. 30ch, Argentina vs. Netherlands, 1978. 40ch, Italy vs. W. Germany, 1982.
80ch, Aztec Stadium, Mexico City.

1985, Mar. 20 *Perf. 13¼*
2477-2480 A1182 Set of 4 4.50 1.00

Souvenir Sheet

2481 A1183 80ch multicolored 4.00 1.25

Kim Il Sung, 73rd Birthday A1184

1985, April 15 *Perf. 12*
2482 A1184 10ch multicolored .65 .25

4th Century Musical Instruments — A1185

Designs: 10ch, Horn player. 20ch So (pan-pipes) player.

1985, May 7 *Perf. 11½*
2483-2484 A1185 Set of 2 3.50 .25

Chongryon Hall, Tokyo — A1186

1985, May 25
2485 A1186 10ch deep brown .65 .25

30th anniv. of Chongryon, the General Association of Korean Residents in Japan.

A1187

Mammals: 5ch, Common marmoset (callithrix jacchus). 10ch, Ring-tailed lemur (Lemur catta).

1985, June 7
2486-2487 A1187 Set of 2 2.50 .25

National Emblem — A1188

1985, June 20
2488 A1188 80ch multicolored 3.00 .70

A1189

Argentina '85 Int'l Stamp Exhib. — A1190

Designs: 10ch, Buenos Aires and Argentina stamp. 20ch, Iguaçu Falls and Argentine, DPRK stamps, horiz.
80ch, Gaucho.

1985, July 5 *Perf. 11¾*
2489-2490 A1189 Set of 2 3.50 .25

Souvenir Sheet

2491 A1190 80ch multicolored 4.00 4.00

12th World Youth and Students' Festival, Moscow — A1191

Designs: 10ch, Korean dancer with streamer, gymnast. 20ch, Spassky Tower, Festival emblem. 30ch, Youths of different races.

1985, July 27 *Perf. 12¼*
2492-2494 A1191 Set of 3 3.50 .75

Pyongyang Buildings — A1192

Designs: 2ch, Phyonghwa Pavilion. 40ch, Skyscraper apartments, Chollima Street.

1985, Aug. 1 *Perf. 12*
2495-2496 A1192 Set of 2 1.00 .25
2495a 2ch Thick toned unsurfaced paper, without gum 10.00 —
2496a 40ch Thick toned unsurfaced paper, without gum 5.00 —

A1193

Liberation, 40th Anniv. — A1194

Designs: 5ch, Soldiers, battle scene. 10ch (No. 2498), Korean and Russian soldier with raised arms. 10ch (No. 2499), Japanese soldiers surrendering. 10ch (No. 2500), Crowd with banners, Flame of Juche. 10ch (No. 2501), Student marchers with banners. 10ch (No. 2502), Liberation monument, vert. 40ch, Students bearing banners.
80ch, Monument.

1985, Aug. 15 *Perf. 11½*
2497-2503 A1193 Set of 7 3.50 1.25
2497a 5ch Toned unsurfaced paper, without gum 8.00 —
2498a 10ch Toned unsurfaced paper, without gum 8.00 —
2499a 10ch Toned unsurfaced paper, without gum 8.00 —
2500a 10ch Toned unsurfaced paper, without gum 8.00 —
2501a 10ch Toned unsurfaced paper, without gum 8.00 —
2502a 10ch Toned unsurfaced paper, without gum 8.00 —
2503a 40ch Toned unsurfaced paper, without gum 8.00 —

Souvenir Sheet

2504 A1194 80ch multicolored 2.00 2.00

A1195

Halley's Comet — A1196

Designs: 10ch, Halley and Comet. 20ch, Comet, diagram of course, space probe.
80ch, Comet's trajectory.

1985, Aug. 25 *Perf. 13½*
2505-2506 A1195 Set of 2 2.25 .25

Souvenir Sheet

2507 A1196 80ch multicolored 4.00 1.25

Flowers — A1197

Designs: 10ch, Hippeastrum hybridum. 20ch, Camellia japonica. 30ch, Cyclamen persicum.

1985, Sept. 10 *Perf. 12*
2508-2510 A1197 Set of 3 7.00 .65

A1198

Koguryo Culture, 4th-6th Centuries A.D. — A1199

Designs: 10ch, Hero. 15ch, Heroine. 20ch, Flying fairy. 25ch, Hunting.
50ch, Pine tree.

1985, Sep. 30 *Perf. 13¼*
2511-2514 A1198 Set of 4 4.00 .65
2514a Sheet of 4, #2511-2514 4.00 1.00

Souvenir Sheet

Perf. 12

2515 A1199 50ch multicolored 3.00 .75

Nos. 2511-2514 were issued both in separate sheets and in setenant sheets of four stamps (No. 2514a).

Korean Worker's Party, 40th Anniv. — A1200

Designs: 5ch, Party Founding Museum. 10ch (No. 2517), Soldier, workers. 10ch (No. 2518), Miner, workers. 40ch, Worker, peasant, professional worker holding up Party emblem.
No. 2520: 90ch, People holding bouquets of flowers.

1985, Oct. 10 *Perf. 11½*
2516-2519 A1200 Set of 4 1.75 .75
2516a 5ch Thick toned unsurfaced paper, without gum 5.00 —
2517a 10ch Thick toned unsurfaced paper, without gum 10.00 —
2518a 10ch Thick toned unsurfaced paper, without gum 5.00 —
2519a 40ch Thick toned unsurfaced paper, without gum 10.00 —

Souvenir Sheet

2520 A1200 90ch multicolored 1.75 .50

Kim Il Sung's Return, 40th Anniv. — A1201

1985, Oct. 14 *Perf. 12*
2521 A1201 10ch red brn & lt grn 1.00 .25
a. Dull white unsurfaced paper, without gum 8.00 —

Italia '85, Int'l Stamp Exhib., Rome — A1202

Designs: 10ch, Colosseum, Rome, and DPRK stamp. 20ch, *The Holy Family*, by Raphael. 30ch. Head of Michelangelo's *David*, vert.
No. 2525: 80ch, Pantheon, Rome.

1985, Oct. 25 *Perf. 11½*
2522-2524 A1202 Set of 3 2.75 .65

Souvenir Sheet

2525 A1202 80ch multicolored 4.00 1.25

South-West German Stamp Bourse, Sindelfingen A1203

Designs, Mercedes Benz: 10ch, Type 300, 1960. 15ch, Type 770. 20ch, Type W150, 1937. 30ch, Type 600, 1966.
No. 2530: 80ch, Mercedes Benz, Type W31, 1938.

1985, Oct. 25
2526-2529 A1203 Set of 4 6.50 .65

Souvenir Sheet

Perf. 11¾

2530 A1203 80ch multicolored 5.25 .75

A1204

13th World Cup Championship, Mexico City — A1205

Designs: 20ch, Dribbling and sliding tackle. 30ch, Jumping kick.
80ch, Goalkeeper and Mexican monuments.

1985, Nov. 1 ***Perf. 13¼***
2531-2532 A1204 Set of 2 3.25 .50

Souvenir Sheet

2533 A1205 80ch multicolored 4.50 1.10

Int'l Youth Year — A1206

Designs: 10ch, Traditional dance. 20ch, Sculpture depicting gymnasts. 30ch, Scientific research.
No. 2537: 80ch, Young people of different races.

1985, Nov. 9 ***Perf. 11½***
2534-2536 A1206 Set of 3 3.25 .50

Souvenir Sheet

2537 A1206 80ch multicolored 4.25 1.00

A1207

13th World Cup Championship, Mexico City — A1208

Designs: 20ch, Dribbling. 30ch, Tackling. 80ch, Goalkeeper, bullfighter.

1985, Nov. 20 ***Perf. 12***
2538-2539 A1207 Set of 2 3.25 .50

Souvenir Sheet

2540 A1208 80ch multicolored 4.50 1.00

Juche Torch — A1209

New Year

1986, Jan. 1 ***Perf. 12x12¼***
2541 A1209 10ch multicolored 1.15 .25

History of the Motor Car — A1210

Designs: 10ch, Amédée Bollée and Limousine, 1901. 20ch, Stewart Rolls, Henry Royce and Silver Ghost, 1906. 25ch, Giovanni Agnelli and Fiat car, 1912. 30ch, Ettore Bugatti and Royal coupe, 1928. 40ch, Louis Renault and fiacre, 1906.
No. 2547: 80ch, Gottlieb Daimler, Karl Benz and Mercedes S, 1927.

1986, Jan. 20 ***Perf. 11½***
2542-2546 A1210 Set of 5 8.75 1.15

Souvenir Sheet

2547 A1210 80ch multicolored 6.75 .75

World Chess Championship, Moscow — A1211

Designs: 20ch, Gary Kasparov.
No. 2549: 80ch, Kasparov-Karpov chess match.

1986, Feb. 5 ***Perf. 11¾x12***
2548 A1211 20ch multicolored 2.00 .25

Souvenir Sheet

Perf. 12

2549 A1211 80ch multicolored 4.50 1.15

For surcharges, see Nos. 4522-4523.

Revolutionary Martyrs' Cemetery, Pyongyang A1212

Designs: 5ch, Cemetery Gate. 10ch, Bronze sculpture of draped flag, soldier, workers (detail).

1986, Feb. 10 ***Perf. 12***
2550-2551 A1212 Set of 2 1.35 .25

Songgan Revolutionary Site, 37th Anniv. of Kim Il Sung's Visit — A1213

1986, Feb. 16
2552 A1213 10ch multicolored .85 .25

Mt. Myohyang Historic Buildings A1214

Designs: 10ch, Buddhist Scriptures Museum. 20ch, Taeung Hall of the Pohyon Temple.

1986, Feb. 20 ***Perf. 12¼***
2553-2554 A1214 Set of 2 1.75 .25

Tropical Fish — A1215

Designs: 10ch, Heniochus acuminatus. 20ch, Amphiprion frenatus.

1986, Mar. 12 ***Perf. 11½***
2555-2556 A1215 Set of 2 2.25 .30

World Cup Championship, Mexico City — A1216

Designs, soccer players and flags of: 10ch, Italy, Bulgaria, Argentina. 20ch, Mexico, Belgium, Paraguay, Iraq. 25ch, France, Canada, USSR, Hungary. 30ch, Brazil, Spain, Algeria, Northern Ireland. 35ch, W. Germany, Uruguay, Scotland, Denmark. 40ch, Poland, Portugal, Morocco, England.
No. 2563: 80ch, Soccer players, World Cup, gold soccer ball, boots.

1986, Mar. 21 ***Perf. 12***
2557-2562 A1216 Set of 6 9.00 1.45

Souvenir Sheet

2563 A1216 80ch multicolored 6.00 .60

For overprints see Nos. 2599-2605.

4th Spring Friendship Art Festival, Pyongyang A1217

1986, Apr. 5
2564 A1217 1w multicolored 2.75 .60

Mercedes-Benz, 60th Anniv. — A1218

Designs: 10ch (No. 2565), Daimler No. 1 ("Motorwagen"), 1886. 10ch (No. 2566), Benz-Velo, 1894. 20ch (No. 2567), Mercedes, 1901. 20ch (No. 2568), Benz limousine, 1909. 30ch (No. 2569), Mercedes Tourenwagen, 1914. 30ch (No. 2570), Mercedes Benz 170/6 cylinder, 1931. 40ch (No. 2571), Mercedes Benz 380, 1933. 40ch (No. 2572), Mercedes Benz 540K, 1936.
No. 2573: 80ch, Mercedes-Simplex Phaeton, 1904.

1986, Apr. 8 ***Perf. 11½***
2565-2572 A1218 Set of 8 8.25 1.75

Souvenir Sheet

2573 A1218 80ch multicolored 4.50 1.15

Kim Il Sung, 74th Birthday — A1219

1986, Apr. 15 ***Perf. 12***
2574 A1219 10ch multicolored .60 .25

Association for the Restoration of the Fatherland, 50th Anniv. — A1220

1986, May 5 ***Perf. 11¾x12***
2575 A1220 10ch multicolored .60 .25

Intl. Year of Peace — A1221

Designs: 10ch, Dove carrying letter. 20ch, Dove, UN Headquarters. 30ch, Dove, globe, broken missiles.
No. 2579: 80ch, Sculpture of children and dove.

1986, June 18 ***Perf. 11¾x12***
2576-2578 A1221 Set of 3 3.75 1.15

Souvenir Sheet

Perf. 11¾x11½

2579 A1221 80ch multicolored 4.50 .75

Mona Lisa, by da Vinci — A1222

1986, July 9 ***Perf. 13½x13¼***
2580 A1222 20ch multicolored 2.75 .25

Irises — A1223

Designs: 20ch, Pink iris. 30ch, Violet iris.
No. 2583: 80ch, Magenta iris.

1986, July 20 ***Perf. 11½***
2581-2582 A1223 Set of 2 4.50 .50

Souvenir Sheet

2583 A1223 80ch multicolored 6.00 1.00

Tennis Players — A1224

Designs: 10ch, Kim Un Suk. 20ch, Ivan Lendl. 30ch, Steffi Craf. 50ch, Boris Becker.

1986, July 30 ***Perf. 13½***
2584 A1224 Block of 4, #a.-d. 6.50 .90
a. 10ch multicolored 1.35 .25
b. 20ch multicolored 1.35 .25
c. 30ch multicolored 1.35 .25
d. 50ch multicolored 1.35 .25
e. 10ch Toned unsurfaced paper, without gum 10.00 —

No. 2584 was printed in sheets containing two setenant blocks.
No. 2584d is airmail.

Stampex '86 Stamp Exhib., Adelaide — A1225

Designs: 10ch, Cockatoo; 80ch, Kangaroo, map of Australia, emblems.

1986, Aug. 4 *Perf. 11½*
2585 A1225 10ch multicolored 5.00 .25

Souvenir Sheet

2586 A1225 80ch multicolored 5.00 1.00

L'Unita Festival, Milan — A1227

Designs: 10ch, First issue of *L'Unita*. 20ch, Milan Cathedral. 30ch, Michelangelo's *Pieta*, vert.
No. 2590: 80ch, Enrico Berlinguer, Italian Communist Party leader.

1986, Aug. 26
2587-2589 A1227 Set of 3 5.00 2.25

Souvenir Sheet

2590 A1227 80ch multicolored 4.25 .75

National Festival of *L'Unita*, the Italian Communist Party newspaper.

A1228

Stockholmia '86 Int'l Stamp Exhib., Stockholm — A1229

Design: 10ch, Icebreaker *Express II* and Swedish stamp.
80ch, UPU emblem, mail coach and Swedish stamps.

1986, Aug. 28
2591 A1228 10ch multicolored 1.75 .25

Souvenir Sheet

2592 A1229 80ch multicolored 6.50 1.35

DPRK Postage Stamps, 40th Anniv. — A1230

Designs: 10ch, Perf green reprint of Scott No. 1. 15ch, Imperf green reprint of Scott No. 1. 50ch, Scott No. 5.

1986, Sep. 12 *Perf. 12¼x12*
2593-2595 A1230 Set of 3 5.50 1.35

No. 2595 is airmail.

DPRK Postage Stamps, 40th Anniv. — A1231

Designs: 10ch, Postal emblems, DPRK #387, 2505. 15ch, Postal emblems, General Post Office, Pyongyang, DPRK #1529, 1749. 50ch, Postal emblems, Kim Il Jung. DPRK #1, #1 reprint in green, vert.

1986, Oct. 5 *Perf. 12*
2596-2598 A1231 Set of 3 7.25 .90

No. 2598 is airmail. For surcharge, see No. 4580.

Nos. 2557-2563 Overprinted with World Cup Soccer Championship Results

1986, Oct. 14
2599-2604 A1216 Set of 6 14.50 2.25

Souvenir Sheet

2605 A1216 80ch multicolored 9.00 1.30

Down-with-Imperialism Union, 60th Anniv. — A1232

1986, Oct. 17 *Perf. 11½*
2606 A1232 10ch multicolored .65 .25

Gift Animals House, 1st Anniv. A1233

1986, Oct. 18 *Perf. 12x11¾*
2607 A1233 2w multicolored 7.75 .85
a. Toned unsurfaced paper, without gum 10.00 —

United Nations Educational, Scientific and Cultural Organization (UNESCO), 40th anniv. — A1234

Designs: 10ch, Schoolchildren. 50ch, UNESCO emblem, Grand People's Study House, televion, communications satellite and dish, horiz.

1986, Nov. 4 *Perf. 12*
2608-2609 A1234 Set of 2 4.25 1.15

Inter-Sputnik, 15th Anniv. — A1235

1986, Nov. 15
2610 A1235 5w multicolored 9.00 2.00
a. Toned unsurfaced paper, without gum 10.00 —

West Sea Barrage A1236

Designs: 10ch, Oil tanker, lock. 40ch, Aerial view of dam. 1.20w, Aerial view of dam (diff.)

1986, Nov. 20 *Perf. 12x11¾*
2611-2613 A1236 Set of 3 7.75 .90
2611a 10ch Toned unsurfaced paper, without gum 5.00 —
2612a 40ch Toned unsurfaced paper, without gum 8.00 —
2613a 1.20w Toned unsurfaced paper, without gum 8.00 —

Mushrooms and Minerals — A1237

Designs: a, 10ch Lengenbachite. b, 10ch Clitocybe infundibuliformis. c, 15ch Rhodocrosite. d, 15ch Morchella esculenta. e, 50ch Annabergite. f, 50ch Russula.

1986, Nov. 23 *Perf. 13¼*
2614 A1237 Block of 6, #a.-f. 15.00 1.15
a. 10ch multicolored 2.25 .25
b. 10ch multicolored 2.25 .25
c. 15ch multicolored 2.25 .25
d. 15ch multicolored 2.25 .25
e. 50ch multicolored 2.25 .25
f. 50ch multicolored 2.25 .25

Printed in setenant blocks within the sheet. Nos. 2614e and 2614f are airmail.

A1238

Exhib. of North Korean 3-D Photos and Stamps, Lima — A1239

Design: 10ch, Machu Picchu and DPRK #1402.
80ch, Korean and Peruvian children.

1986, Nov. 25 *Perf. 13¼x13½*
2615 A1238 10ch multicolored 1.75 .25

Souvenir Sheet

2616 A1239 80ch multicolored 8.25 1.75

New Year — A1240

Designs: 10ch, Sun, pine tree. 40ch, Hare.

1987, Jan. 1 *Perf. 12*
2617-2618 A1240 Set of 2 3.25 .50
2617a Perf. 13½ — —

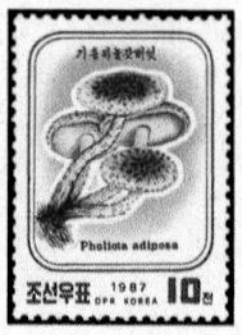
A1241

Fungi — A1242

Designs: 10ch, *Pholiota adiposa*. 20ch, *Cantharellus cibarius*. 30ch, *Boletus impolitus*. 80ch, *Gomphidius rutilus*.

1987, Jan. 5 *Perf. 11½*
2619-2621 A1241 Set of 3 5.25 .75

Souvenir Sheet

2622 A1242 80ch multicolored 6.50 1.35

For surcharge, see No. 4535.

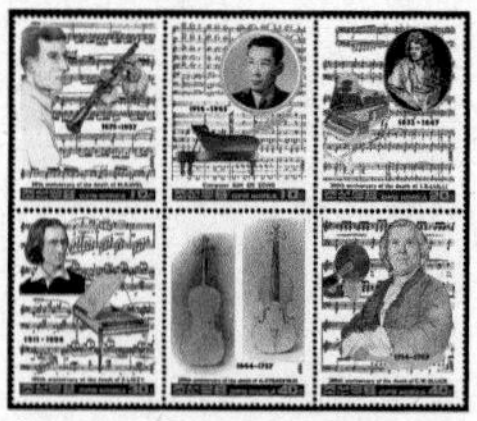
Famous Composers, Death Anniv. — A1243

Designs: 10ch (No. 2623a), Maurice Ravel (1875-1937). 10ch (No. 2623b), Kim Ok Song (1916-65). 20ch, Giovanni Lully (1632-67). 30ch, Franz Liszt (1811-86). 40ch (No.2623e), Stradivarius violins (Antonio Stradivari, 1644-1737). 40ch (No. 2623f), Christoph Gluck (1714-87).

1987, Jan. 29 *Perf. 13¼*
2623 A1243 Block of 6, #a.-f. 11.00 1.00
a. 10ch multicolored 1.35 .25
b. 10ch multicolored 1.35 .25
c. 20ch multicolored 1.35 .25
d. 30ch multicolored 1.35 .25
e. 40ch multicolored 1.35 .25
f. 40ch multicolored 1.35 .25

No. 2623 was printed in se-tenant blocks of six within the sheet.

Kim Jong Il, 45th Birthday A1244

1987, Feb. 16
2624 A1244 80ch multicolored 2.25 .40

Buildings — A1245

Designs: 5ch, East Pyongyang Grand Theater. 10ch, Pyongyang Koryo Hotel (vert.). 3w, Rungnado Stadium.

1987, Feb. 23 *Perf. 12*
2625-2627 A1245 Set of 3 6.75 1.10
2625a 5ch Stiff brown paper, without gum 9.00 —
2626a 10ch Stiff brown paper, without gum 4.50 —
2627a 3w Stiff brown paper, without gum 4.50 —

Sailing Ships — A1246

Designs: 20ch, *Gorch Fock.* 30ch, *Tovarisch*, vert.. 50ch (No. 2630), *Belle Poule*, vert. 50ch (No. 2631), *Sagres II*, vert. 1w (No. 2632), Merchantman, Koryo Period (918-1392). 1w (No. 2633), *Dar Mlodziezy*, vert..

1987, Feb. 25 ***Perf. 13¼***

2628-2633 A1246 Set of 6 10.50 2.50

Nos. 2630-2633 are airmail.

Fire Engines — A1247

Designs: 10ch, German fire engine. 20ch, Benz fire engine. 30ch, Chemical fire engine. 50ch, Soviet fire engine.

1987, Feb. 27 ***Perf. 12***

2634-2637 A1247 Set of 4 9.00 1.10

No. 2637 is airmail.

Road Safety — A1248

Designs (multiple traffic signs): 10ch (No. 2638), Blue sign lower center. 10ch (No. 2639), Red sign lower center. 20ch, Various signs. 50ch, Various signs (diff.)

1987, Feb. 27

2638-2641 A1248 Set of 4 6.75 .85

Nos. 2641 is airmail.

Butterflies and Flowers — A1249

Designs: No. 2642, Apatura ilia and spiraea. No. 2643, Ypthinia argus and fuchsia. No. 2644, Neptis philyra and aguilegia. No. 2645, Papilio protenor and chrysanthemum. No. 2646, Parantica sita and celosia. No. 2847, Vanessa indica and hibiscus.

1987, Mar. 12

2642-2647 A1249 Set of 6 10.00 1.35

For surcharge, see No. 4524.

Korean National Assoc., 70th Anniv. — A1250

Design: 10ch, Association Monument, Pyongyang.

1987, Mar. 23 ***Perf. 11½***

2648 A1250 10ch multicolored .60 .25

5th Spring Friendship Art Festival — A1251

1987, Apr. 6

2649 A1251 10ch multicolored .65 .25

A1252

Kim Il Sung, 75th Birthday — A1253

Designs: No. 2650, Mangyong Hill. No. 2651, Kim Il Sung's birthplace, Mangyongdae, horiz. No 2652, Painting, *Profound Affection for the Working Class.* No. 2653, Painting, *A Bumper Crop of Pumpkins.*

1987, Apr. 15 ***Perf. 12***

2650	A1252	10ch multicolored	.50	.25
2651	A1252	10ch multicolored	.50	.25
2652	A1253	10ch multicolored	.50	.25
2653	A1253	10ch multicolored	.50	.25
		Nos. 2650-2653 (4)	2.00	1.00

Horses — A1254

Designs: No. 2654a, Bay. No. 2654b, Bay, diff. No. 2654c, Gray, rearing. No. 2654d, White horse on beach.

1987, Apr. 20 ***Perf. 13¼***

2654	A1254	Block of 4, #a.-d.	6.50	1.90
a.		10ch multicolored	.50	.25
b.		10ch multicolored	.50	.25
c.		40ch multicolored	2.25	.65
d.		40ch multicolored	2.25	.65

No. 2654 was printed in se-tenant blocks of four within the sheet.

Transport — A1255

Designs: No. 2655, Electric train *Juche.* No. 2656, Electric train *Mangyongdae.* No. 2657, *Sputnik I*, vert. No. 2658, Laika, first animal in space, vert. No. 2659, Tupolev Tu-144 jetliner. No. 2660, Concorde jetliner. No. 2661, Count Ferdinand von Zeppelin and LZ-4. No. 2662, Zeppelin and diagrams of airships.

1987, Apr. 30

2655	A1255	10ch multicolored	.60	.25
2656	A1255	10ch multicolored	.60	.25
a.		Pair, #2655-2656	.75	.40
2657	A1255	10ch multicolored	.60	.25
2658	A1255	20ch multicolored	1.00	.25
a.		Pair, #2657-2658	1.75	.40
2659	A1255	20ch multicolored	1.00	.25
2660	A1255	20ch multicolored	1.00	.25
a.		Pair, #2659-2660	2.25	.40
2661	A1255	30ch multicolored	1.35	.25
2662	A1255	80ch multicolored	4.25	.90
a.		Pair, #2661-2662	6.50	1.15
		Nos. 2655-2662 (8)	10.40	2.65

Nos. 2655/2656, 2657/2658, 2659/2660, 2661/2662 were printed se-tenant within their sheets.

No. 2662 is airmail.

CAPEX '87 Int'l Stamp Exhibition, Toronto — A1256

Designs: 10ch, Musk ox. 40ch, Jacques Cartier, *Grand Hermine* and modern ice-breaker, horiz. 60ch, Ice hockey, Calgary '88, horiz.

1987, May 30 ***Perf. 11***

2663-2665 A1256 Set of 3 5.50 1.15

Int'l Circus Festival, Monaco — A1257

Designs: No. 2666, Trapeze artists. No. 2667, "Brave Sailors" (N. Korean acrobatic troupe), vert. No. 2668, Korean performers receiving prize. No. 2669, Clown and elephant, vert. 40ch, Performing cat, horses. 50ch, Prince Rainier and family applauding.

1987, May 31 ***Perf. 12***

2666-2671 A1257 Set of 6 8.75 1.35

No. 2871 is airmail.

Battle of Pochonbo, 50th Anniv. — A1258

1987, June 4 ***Perf. 11½***

2672 A1258 10ch multicolored .75 .25

Chongchun Street Sports Complex — A1259

Designs: 5ch, Various sports. 10ch, Indoor swimming pool. 40ch, Weightlifting gymnasium. 70ch, Table-tennis gymnasium. 1w, Angol football stadium. 1.20w, Handball gymnasium.

1987, June 18 ***Perf. 12***

2673-2678	A1259	Set of 6	9.00	2.00
2675a	40ch	Toned unsurfaced paper, without gum	8.00	—
2676a	70ch	Toned unsurfaced paper, without gum	8.00	—
2677a	1w	Toned unsurfaced paper, without gum	8.00	—
2678a	1.20w	Toned unsurfaced paper, without gum	8.00	—

For surcharge, see No. 4259D.

Worldwide Fund for Nature (WWF) — A1260

Aix galericulata: No. 2679, On branch. No. 2680, On shore. No. 2681, In water and on shore. No. 2682, In water.

1987, Aug. 4 ***Perf. 13¼***

2679-2682 A1260 Set of 4 10.50 1.75

For surcharge, see No. 4605.

A1261

OLYMPHILEX '87 Stamp Exhibition, Rome — A1262

1987, Aug. 29 ***Perf. 13¼***

2683 A1261 10ch multicolored 1.35 .25

Souvenir Sheet

2684 A1262 80ch multicolored 6.50 1.15

Railway Uniforms — A1263

No. 2685, Electric train and Metro dispatcher. No. 2686, Underground station and conductress. No. 2687, Train and conductress. No. 2688, Train and railway dispatcher. No. 2689, Orient Express and conductor. No. 2690, Express train and ticket inspector.

1987, Sep. 23

2685-2690 A1263 Set of 6 6.75 1.15

HAFNIA '87 Int'l Stamp Exhibition, Copenhagen — A1264

Designs: 40ch, White stork. 60ch, The Little Mermaid and sailing ship *Danmark.*

1987, Sep. 26

2691-2692 A1264 Set of 2 4.75 .65

A1265

Winter Olympic Games, Calgary — A1266

40ch: No. 2693, Figure skating. No. 2694, Ski jump. No. 2695, Downhill skiing. No. 2696, Cross-country skiing.

1987, Oct. 16
2693-2696 A1265 Set of 4 7.25 .90

Souvenir Sheet

2697 A1266 80ch multicolored 4.75 .90

PHILATELIA '87 (Koln) and 750th Anniv. Berlin — A1267

Designs: 10ch, Victory Column. 20ch, Reichstag, horiz. 30ch, Pfaueninsel Castle. 40ch, Charlottenburg Castle, horiz.
80ch, Olympic Stadium.

1987, Nov. 5 ***Perf. 12***
2698-2701 A1267 Set of 4 135.00

Souvenir Sheet
Perf. 11½x12

2702 A1267 80ch multicolored 90.00

Roland Garros Birth Centenary and Tennis as an Olympic Sport — A1268

Designs: 20ch (No. 2703), Roland Garros (1888-1918), aviator; 20ch (No. 2704), Ivan Lendl and trophy; 40ch, Steffi Graf.
No. 2706: 80ch, Steffi Graf and trophy.

1987, Nov. 10 ***Perf. 13¼***
2703-2705 A1268 Set of 3 6.75 .75

Souvenir Sheet
Perf. 11½x12

2706 A1268 80ch multicolored 9.00 2.75

Kim Jong Suk (1917-49), Revolutionary Hero — A1269

1987, Dec. 24
2707 A1269 80ch multicolored 2.25 .50

Pyongyang Buildings — A1270

Dragon — A1271

1988, Jan. 1 ***Perf. 12***
2708 A1270 10ch multicolored .60 .25
2709 A1271 40ch multicolored 1.35 .25

New Year.

Saenal Newspaper, 60th Anniv. — A1272

1988, Jan. 15 ***Perf. 11½***
2710 A1272 10ch multicolored .85 .25

A1273

Kim Jong Il, 46th Birthday — A1274

Designs: 10ch, Kim Jong Il's birthplace, Mt. Paektu. 80ch, Kim Jong Il.

1988, Feb. 16 ***Perf. 12x11¾***
2711 A1273 10ch multicolored .50 .25

Souvenir Sheet

2712 A1274 80ch multicolored 2.25 .50

Int'l Red Cross, 125th Anniv. — A1275

Designs: a, Henry Dunant. b, N. Korean Red Cross emblem, map. c, International Committee Headquarters, Geneva; d, Doctor examining child, Pyongyang Maternity Hospital.
80ch, Red Cross and Red Crescent, flags, globe.

1988, Feb. 17 ***Perf. 12***
2713 A1275 Sheet of 4 6.50 .85
a. 10ch multicolored 1.60 .25
b. 20ch multicolored 1.60 .25
c. 20ch multicolored 1.60 .25
d. 40ch multicolored 1.60 .25

Souvenir Sheet

2714 A1275 80ch multicolored 4.25 .75

A1276

Columbus' Discovery of America, 500th Anniv. — A1277

10ch, *Santa Maria*. 20ch, *Pinta*. 30ch, *Nina*.
80ch, Columbus.

1988, Mar. 10 ***Perf. 13¼***
2718 A1276 Strip of 3 4.75 .75
a. 10ch multicolored 1.15 .25
b. 20ch multicolored 1.15 .25
c. 30ch multicolored 1.15 .25

Souvenir Sheet

2719 A1277 80ch multicolored 4.75 .75

Nos. 2718a-2718c were printed together in the sheet in se-tenant strips of three.

JUVALUX '88 — A1278

Designs: 40ch, Hot air balloons. 60ch, Steam engine, railroad map of Luxembourg 1900.

1988, Mar. 29
2720-2721 A1278 Set of 2 4.75 .75

JUVALUX '88 International Youth Stamp Exhibition, Luxembourg.

6th Spring Friendship Art Festival — A1279

Designs: 10ch, Singer. 1.20w, Dancers.

1988, Apr. 7 ***Perf. 12***
2722-2723 A1279 Set of 2 4.00 1.15
2722a 10ch, on toned unsurfaced paper, without gum 8.00 —

Int'l Institute of the Juche Idea, 10th Anniv. — A1280

1988, Apr. 9
2724 A1280 10ch multicolored .50 .25

A1281

Kim Il Sung, 76th Birthday — A1282

Designs: 10ch, Kim Il Sung's Birthplace, Mangyongdae.
80ch, Kim Il Sung and schoolchildren.

1988, Apr. 15
2725 A1281 10ch multicolored .50 .25

Souvenir Sheet

2726 A1282 80ch multicolored 2.25 .40

FINLANDIA '88 Int'l Stamp Exhibition, Helsinki — A1283

Designs: 40ch, *Urho* ice-breaker. 60ch, Matti Nykänen, Finnish Olympic ski-jumping gold and silver medallist.

1988, May 2 ***Perf. 13¼***
2727-2728 A1283 Set of 2 4.50 .60

ITALIA '90, 14th World Soccer Championships — A1284

Designs: 10ch, Soccer match. 20ch, Postcard for 1934 Championship. 30ch, Player tackling, horiz.
80ch, Italian team, 1982 winners, horiz.

1988, May 19
2729-2731 A1284 Set of 3 4.75 .50

Souvenir Sheet

2732 A1284 80ch multicolored 4.25 .60

13th World Festival of Youth and Students — A1285

Designs: No. 2734, Festival emblem. No. 2735, Woman dancer. No. 2736, Woman, gymnast, Angol Sports Village. No. 2737, Map of Korea, globe and doves. No. 2738, Finger pointing at broken rockets ("Let's build a new world without nuclear weapons"). No. 2739, Three hands of different races releasing dove.

1988, May 27 ***Perf. 12***

2734-2739 A1285 Set of 6 6.75 1.15

2734a 10ch Thick toned unsurfaced paper, without gum 8.00 —

2735a 10ch Thick toned unsurfaced paper, without gum 8.00 —

2736a 10ch Thick toned unsurfaced paper, without gum 8.00 —

2739a 1.20w Thick toned unsurfaced paper, without gum 8.00 —

Eight Fairies of Mt. Kumgang, Folk-Tale — A1286

Designs: 10ch, Fairy playing the *haegum.* 15ch, Fairies with rainbow. 20ch, Fairy and herdsman husband. 25ch, Couple with infant. 30ch, Couple with son and daughter. 35ch, Family on rainbow, returning to Mt. Kumgang.

1988, June 20

2740-2745 A1286 Set of 6 4.50 1.00

PRAGA '88 Int'l Stamp Exhibition, Prague — A1287

Designs: 20ch, Mallard ducks. 40ch, Vladimir Remek, Czechoslovak cosmonaut.

1988, June 26 ***Perf. 13¼***

2746-2747 A1287 Set of 2 3.75 .45

Birds — A1288

Designs: 10ch, Red crossbill (*Loxia curvirostra japonica*). 15ch, Stonechat (*Saxicola torquata stejnegeri*). 20ch, European nuthatch (*Sitta eoropaea hondoensis*). 25ch, Great spotted woodpecker (*Dendrocopos major japonicus*). 30ch, Common kingfisher (*Alcedo atthis bengalensis*). 35ch, Bohemian waxwing (*Bombycilla garrula centralasiae*).

1988, July 9 ***Perf. 12***

2748-2753 A1288 Set of 6 9.00 1.60

For surcharge, see No. 4530.

A1289

RICCIONE '88 Int'l Stamp Fair — A1290

1988, July 25

2754 A1289 20ch multicolored .85 .25

Souvenir Sheet

2755 A1290 80ch multicolored 3.50 .50

A1291

Australia Bicentenary — A1292

Designs: 10ch, Emu. 15ch, Statin bower birds. 25ch, Kookaberra, vert.
80ch, H.M.S. *Resolution.*

1988, July 30 ***Perf. 13¼***

2756-2758 A1291 Set of 3 3.75 .60

Souvenir Sheet

2759 A1292 80ch multicolored 4.50 .60

Ships — A1293

Designs: 10ch, Floating crane *5-28.* 20ch, Cargo ship *Hwanggumsan.* 30ch, Cargo ship *Jangjasan Chongnyon-ho.* 40ch, Passenger ship *Samjiyon.*

1988, Aug. 12 ***Perf. 12***

2760-2763 A1293 Set of 4 5.00 .80

A1294

Count Ferdinand von Zeppelin, 150th Birth Anniv. — A1295

Designs: 10ch, LZ 13 *Hansa.* 20ch, LZ 10 *Schwaben.* 30ch, LZ 11 *Viktoria Luise.* 40ch, LZ 3.
1w, Count von Zeppelin.

1988, Aug. 21 ***Perf. 11¼***

2764-2767 A1294 Set of 4 5.00 .80

Souvenir Sheet

Perf. 13¼

2768 A1295 1w multicolored 4.50 .90

Kim Il Sung and Jambyn Batmunkh — A1296

1988, Aug. 30 ***Perf. 12***

2769 A1296 10ch multicolored .75 .25

Kim Il Sung's visit to Mongolia.

National Heroes Congress — A1297

1988, Sep. 1 ***Perf. 11¾***

2770 A1297 10ch multicolored 4.25 .25

A1298

Independence, 40th Anniversary — A1299

Designs: 5ch, Tower of Juche Idea. 10ch (No. 2772), Worker, factory. 10ch (No. 2773), Soldier and Mt. Paektu. 10ch (No. 2774), Map, broken U.S. missile. 10ch (No. 2775), Hand holding sign, peace march, globe, doves.
1.20w, Kim Il Sung presiding over design of DPRK flag and emblem.

1988, Sept. 9 ***Perf. 12***

2771-2775 A1298 Set of 5 1.60 .50

2771a 5ch Toned unsurfaced paper, without gum 20.00 —

Souvenir Sheet

Perf. 11½

2776 A1299 1.20w multicolored 2.25 .75

FILACEPT '88 Philatelic Exhib., The Hague — A1300

Designs: 40ch, *Sunflowers,* by Vincent Van Gogh. 60ch, *The Chess Game,* by Lucas van Leyden.

1988, Sept. 18 ***Perf. 13½***

2777-2778 A1300 Set of 2 6.75 1.30

Emblem — A1301

1988, Sep. 23 ***Perf. 11½***

2779 A1301 10ch multicolored .60 .25

16th Conference of the Ministers of Communications of Socialist Countries.

Dump Trucks A1302

Designs: 20ch, *Jaju 82* 10-ton truck. 40ch, *Kumsusan* 40-ton truck.

1988, Sept. 18 ***Perf. 13½***

2780-2781 A1302 Set of 2 1.75 .75

Paintings by O Un Byol — A1303

Designs: 10ch, *Owl.* 15ch, *Dawn.* 20ch, *The Beautiful Rose Received by the Respected Marshall.* 25ch, *The Sun and Bamboo.* 30ch, *Autumn.*

1988, Oct. 5 ***Perf. 11½***

2782-2786 A1303 Set of 5 5.50 .85

Historic Locomotives — A1304

Designs: 10ch, *Junggi No. 35.* 20ch, *Junggi No. 22.* 30ch, *Jongihwa No. 3.* 40ch, *Junggi No. 307.*

1988, Oct. 28 ***Perf. 12***

2787-2790 A1304 Set of 4 4.50 .75

A1305

Calgary '88 Winter Olympic Games Winners — A1306

Designs: 10ch, Pirmin Zurbriggen (Switzerland). 20ch, Yvonne Van Gennip (Netherlands). 30ch, Marjo Matikainen (Finland). 40ch, USSR hockey team.
80ch, Katarina Witt (DDR).

1988, Nov. 1 ***Perf. 13¼***
2791-2794 A1305 Set of 4 3.25 1.15

Souvenir Sheet

2795 A1306 80ch multicolored 2.25 .50
a. Overprinted with names of winners in selvage 2.25 .50

First Man and Woman in Space — A1307

Designs: 20ch, Yuri Gagarin. 40ch, Valentina Tereshkova.

1988, Nov. 12 ***Perf. 13¼***
2796 A1307 Pair, #a.-b. 1.60 .60
a. 20ch multicolored .40 .25
b. 40ch multicolored 1.00 .45

A1308

INDIA '89 Int'l Philatelic Exhib., New Delhi — A1309

Design: 20ch, Jawaharlal Nehru (1889-1964), 100th anniversary of birth.
60ch, *Fan Dance*, Korean Folk Dance.

1988, Dec. 15 ***Perf. 11¾x12***
2797 A1308 20ch multicolored 1.10 .25

Souvenir Sheet

Perf. 11¾x11½

2798 A1309 60ch multicolored 3.25 .40

New Year — A1310

Designs: 10ch, Chollima Statue. 20ch, Painting, *Dragon Angler.* 40ch, *Tortoise Serpent,* Kangso tomb mural painting, horiz.

1989, Jan. 1 ***Perf. 13¼***
2799-2801 A1310 Set of 3 3.25 .50

Archery — A1311

Designs: 10ch, Archery. 15ch, Rifle shooting. 20ch, Pistol shooting. 25ch, Parachuting. 30ch, Launching model glider.

1989, Jan. 10 ***Perf. 12***
2802-2806 A1311 Set of 5 4.25 .75

National defense training.

A1312

Pets Presented to Kim Il Sung — A1313

Designs: 10ch, Dobermann pinscher. 20ch, Labrador. 25ch, German shepherd. 30ch, Border collies, horiz. 35ch, Serval, horiz.
80ch, *Felix libica.*

1989, Jan. 23 ***Perf. 13½***
2807-2811 A1312 Set of 5 4.50 .85

Souvenir Sheet

2812 A1313 80ch multicolored 3.75 .60

Kim Jong Il, 47th Birthday — A1314

1989, Feb. 16 ***Perf. 11¾x12***
2813 A1314 80ch multicolored 1.75 .45

Agriculture — A1315

1989, Feb. 25 ***Perf. 12***
2814 A1315 10ch multicolored .65 .25
a. Toned unsurfaced paper, without gun 5.00 —

25th anniversary of publication of Kim Il Sung's *Theses on the Socialist Rural Question in Our Country.*

Mushrooms and Wild Fruits — A1316

Designs: 10ch, Rozites caperata and Vitisamurensis. 20ch, Amanita caesarea and Schizandra chinensis. 25ch, Lactarius hygrophoides and Eleagnus crispa. 30ch, Agaricus placomyces and Actinidia arguta. 35ch, Agaricus arvensis and Lycium chinense. 40ch, Suillus grevillei and Juglans cordiformis.
1w, Gomphidius roseus and Diospyros lotus.

1989, Feb. 27 ***Perf. 12***
2815-2820 A1316 Set of 6 7.25 1.15

Souvenir Sheet

Perf. 11½x11¾

2821 A1316 1w multicolored 4.25 .85

13th World Youth and Students' Festival — A1317

Designs: 10ch, Girl. 20ch, Children of different races. 30ch, Fairy, rainbow. 40ch, Young people and Tower of Juche Idea.

1989, Mar. 18 ***Perf. 12¼***
2822-2825 A1317 Set of 4 2.50 .90
2822a 10ch Soft toned unsurfaced paper, without gum 15.00 —
2823a 20ch Soft toned unsurfaced paper, without gum 8.00 —
2824a 30ch Soft toned unsurfaced paper, without gum 8.00 —
2825a 40ch Soft toned unsurfaced paper, without gum 8.00 —
2825b 40ch Stiff dull white unsurfaced paper, without gum 8.00 —

A1318

Butterflies and Insects — A1319

Designs: 10ch, Parnassius eversmanni. 15ch, Colias heos. 20ch, Dilipa fenestra. 25ch, Buthus martensis. 30ch, Trichogramma ostriniae. 40ch, Damaster constricticollis.
80ch, Parnassius nomion.

1989, Mar. 23 ***Perf. 12***
2826 A1318 Sheet of 6, #a.-f. 5.50 .90

Souvenir Sheet

2827 A1319 80ch multicolored 3.50 .75

Spring Friendship Art Festival — A1320

1989, Apr. 6
2828 A1320 10ch multicolored .75 .25

Kim Il Sung, 77th Birthday — A1321

1989, Apr. 15 ***Perf. 11½***
2829 A1321 10ch multicolored .50 .25
a. Toned unsurfaced paper, without gum 10.00 —

Battle of the Musan Area, 50th Anniv. — A1322

1989, May 19 ***Perf. 12***
2830 A1322 10ch multicolored 1.00 .25

Jamo System of Dance Notation — A1323

Designs: 10ch, Mexican dance. 20ch, Ballet duet in *Don Quixote.* 25ch, Dance of Guinea. 30ch, Cambodian folk dance.
80ch, Korean folk dance.

1989, May 30
2831-2834 A1323 Set of 4 3.50 .60

Souvenir Sheet

2835 A1323 80ch multicolored 3.00 .50

A1324

A1325

1989, June 8 ***Perf. 11½***
2836 A1324 5ch deep blue .25 .25
a. Soft toned unsurfaced paper, without gum 15.00 —
2837 A1325 10ch red brown .30 .25

13th World Festival of Youth and Students.

Cartoon, *Badger Measures the Height* — A1326

Designs: 10ch, Badger racing cat and bear to flag pole. 40ch, Cat and bear climbing pole, while badger measures shadow. 50ch, Badger winning the prize.

1989, June 21
2838-2840 A1326 Set of 3 3.75 .60

Astronomy — A1327

20ch, Chomosongdae Observatory.
80ch, Saturn (horiz.)

1989, June 29 ***Perf. 12***
2841 A1327 20ch multicolored 1.30 .25

Souvenir Sheet

2842 A1327 80ch multicolored 2.75 .50

Eugène Delacroix's *Liberty Guiding the People* — A1328

1989, July 7 ***Perf. 12x11½***
2843 A1328 70ch multicolored 2.75 1.75

PHILEXFRANCE '89, Int'l Philatelic Exhib., Paris.

BRASILIANA '89, Int'l Philatelic Exhib., Rio de Janeiro — A1329

1989, July 28 ***Perf. 12***
2844 A1329 40ch Pele, #1714 1.30 .30

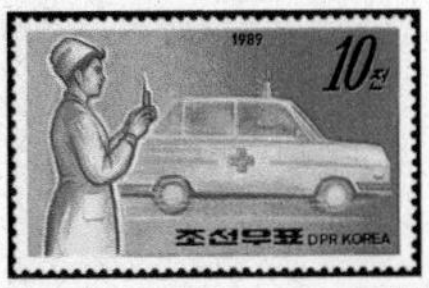

Fire Brigade and Emergency Medical Services — A1330

Designs: 10ch, Nurse and ambulance. 20ch, Surgeon and ambulance. 30ch, Fireman and fire engine. 40ch, Fireman and fire engine (diff.)

1989, Aug. 12
2845-2848 A1330 Set of 4 5.50 .60

Plants Presented as Gifts to Kim Il Sung — A1331

Designs: 10ch, Kafir lily (Clivia miniata). 15ch, Tulips (Tulipa gesneriana). 20ch, Flamingo lily (Anthurium andreanum). 25ch, Rhododendron obtusum. 30ch, Daffodils (Narcissus pseudonarcissus).
80ch, (Gerbera hybrida).

1989, Aug. 19
2849-2853 A1331 Set of 5 5.00 .90

Souvenir Sheet

2854 A1331 80ch multicolored 4.25 .50

150th Anniv. of Postage Stamps / STAMP WORLD LONDON '90 Int'l Philatelic Exhib. — A1332

Designs: 5ch, Letter, ship, plane, map. 10ch, Letters and mail box. 20ch, Stamps, magnifying glass, tongs. 30ch, Fiirst stamps pf DPRK. 40ch, UPU emblem, headquarters, Berne. 50ch, Sir Rowland Hill and Penny Black.

1989, Aug. 27
2855-2860 A1332 Set of 6 6.75 1.15

A1333

Alpine Flowers — A1334

Designs: 10ch, Iris setosa. 15ch, Aquilegia japonica. 20ch, Bistorta incana. 25ch, Rhodiola elongata. 30ch, Sanguisorba sitchensis. 80ch, Trollius japonicus.

1989, Sept. 8 ***Perf. 11½***
2861-2865 A1333 Set of 5 4.75 .90

Souvenir Sheet

2866 A1334 80ch multicolored 3.25 .50

Trees bearing Anti-Japanese Patriotic Slogans — A1335

Designs: 10ch, "20 million compatriots, an anti-Japanese heroine of Korea rose on Mt. Paektu," inscribed on tree, Mt. Paektu. 3w, "The future of Korea is bright with the Luminous Star of Mt. Paektu," inscribed on tree, Qun-dong, Pyongyang. 5w, "The General Star of Mt. Paektu shines three thousand-ri expanse of land," inscribed on tree, Mt. Kanbaek.

1989, Sept. 21 ***Perf. 12¼***
2867-2869 A1335 Set of 3 16.50 10.00

Compare with No. 2885.

Children's Games — A1336

Designs: 10ch, Girl skipping rope. 20ch, Boy with whirligig. 30ch, Boy flying kite. 40ch, Girl spinning top.

1989, Sept. 30 ***Perf. 12***
2870 A1336 Block of 4, #a.-d. 3.75 .75
a. 10ch multicolored .25 .25
b. 20ch multicolored 1.60 .25
c. 30ch multicolored .50 .25
d. 40ch multicolored .60 .25

Int'l March for Peace and Reunification of Korea — A1337

1989, Oct. 1 ***Perf. 11½x12***
2871 A1337 80ch multicolored 2.75 1.60

Locomotives — A1338

Designs: 10ch, Electric train entering station yard. 20ch, Electric train crossing bridge. 25ch, Diesel locomotive. 30ch, Diesel locomotive (diff.). 40ch, Steam locomotive. 50ch, Steam locomotive (diff.).

1989, Oct. 19 ***Perf. 11¾x12¼***
2872-2877 A1338 Set of 6 5.50 1.15

14th World Soccer Championship, *Italia '90* — A1339

Designs: 10ch, Players and map of Italy. 20ch, Free kick. 30ch, Goal scrimmage. 40ch, Goalkeeper blocking ball.

1989, Oct. 28 ***Perf. 12x11¾***
2878-2881 A1339 Set of 4 3.75 .60

Magellan A1340

1989, Nov. 25 ***Perf. 12***
2882 A1340 30ch multicolored 1.15 .25

Descobrex '89 International Philatelic Exhibition, Portugal.

A1341

A1342

10ch, Mangyong Hill and snow-covered pine branches. 20ch, Koguryo warriors.

Perf. 11½ (#2883), 12 (#2884)

1990, Jan. 1
2883 A1341 10ch multicolored .25 .25
a. Toned unsurfaced paper, without gum 15.00 —
2884 A1342 20ch multicolored 1.10 .25
a. Toned unsurfaced paper, without gum 5.00 —

New Year.

Tree, Mt. Paektu, Bearing Anti-Japanese Patriotic Slogan — A1343

1990, Jan. 12 ***Perf. 11½***
2885 A1343 5ch multicolored .50 .25
a. Toned unsurfaced paper, without gum 5.00 —

Dogs — A1344

Designs: 20ch, Ryukwoli. 30ch, Phalryuki. 40ch, Komdungi. 50ch, Olruki.

1990, Jan. 17
2886 A1344 Sheet of 4 5.00 1.35
a. 20ch multicolored .85 .25
b. 30ch multicolored .85 .25
c. 40ch multicolored .85 .25
d. 50ch multicolored .85 .25

Birthplace, Mt. Paektu — A1345

1990, Feb. 16
2887 A1345 10ch dp red brn .50 .25
a. Brown unsurfaced paper, without gum 5.00 —

Kim Jong Il's 48th birthday.

Stone Age Man — A1346

Designs: 10ch, Primitive man, stone tools. 20ch, Paleolithic and Neolithic men, camp scene.

1990, Feb. 21
2888-2889 A1346 Set of 2 2.75 .30

Bridges — A1347

Designs: 10ch, Rungra Bridge, Pyongyang. 20ch, Pothong Bridge, Pyongyang. 30ch, Suspension bridge between Sinuiju-Ryucho Island. 40ch, Chungsongui Bridge, Pyongyang.

1990, Feb. 27 ***Perf. 11½***
2890-2893 A1347 Set of 4 4.25 .60
2890a 10ch Thin, coarse brownish paper, without gum 5.00 —

Traditional Warriors' Costumes — A1348

Designs: 20ch, Infantryman (3rd century BC-7th century AD). 30ch, Archer. 50ch, Commander in armor (3rd century BC-7th century AD). 70ch, Koguryo Period officer (10th-14th centuries).

1990, Mar. 18
2894-2897 A1348 Set of 4 5.75 1.75
2897a 70ch Dull white unsurfaced paper, without gum 5.00 —

Crabs — A1349

Designs: 20ch, Atergatis subdentatus. 30ch, Platylambrus validus. 50ch, Uca arcuata.

1990, Mar. 25
2898-2900 A1349 Set of 3 2.75 .60

Dancers — A1350

1990, Apr. 7
2901 A1350 10ch multicolored .50 .25

Spring Friendship Art Festival, Pyongyang.

A1351

Kim Il Sung's 78th Birthday A1352

Designs: 10ch, 'Fork in the Road' Monument, Mangyongdae Revolutionary Site. 80ch, Kim Il Sung.

1990, Apr. 15 ***Perf. 11½x11¾***

2902 A1351 10ch multicolored .50 .25

Souvenir Sheet

2903 A1352 80ch multicolored 2.25 .50

Cacti — A1353

Designs: 10ch, Gynmocalycium sp. 30ch, Phyllocactus hybridus. 50ch, Epiphyllum truncatum.

1990, Apr. 21 ***Perf. 12¼***

2904-2906 A1353 Set of 3 3.75 .60

A1354

Stamp World London '90 — A1355

Designs: 20ch, Exhibition emblem. 70ch, Sir Rowland Hill.

1990, May 3 ***Perf. 11½***

2907 A1354 20ch multicolored .85 .25

Souvenir Sheet

2908 A1355 70ch multicolored 2.50 1.10

A1356

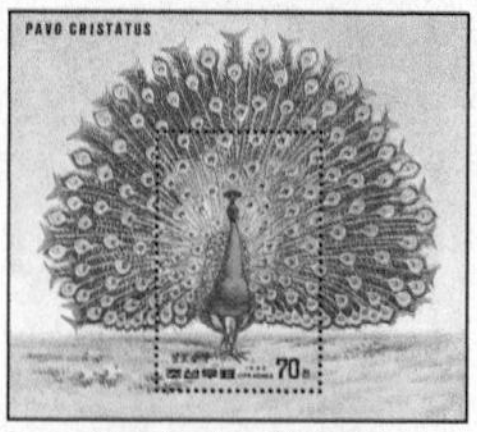

Peafowl — A1357

Designs: 10ch, Congo peafowl (Afropavo congensis). 20ch, Common peafowl (Pavo cristatus). 70ch, Common peafowl with tail displayed.

1990, May 10 ***Perf. 11¾x12***

2909-2910 A1356 Set of 2 2.75 .60

Souvenir Sheet

2911 A1357 70ch multicolored 2.75 .60

Bio-engineering — A1358

Designs: 10ch, Dolphin and submarine. 20ch, Bat and sonar dish, satellite. 30ch, Eagle and airplanes. 40ch, Squid and jets.

1990, May 24

2912 A1358 Sheet of 4, #a.-d. 6.50 1.15
a. 10ch multicolored 1.15 .25
b. 20ch multicolored 1.15 .25
c. 30ch multicolored 1.15 .25
d. 40ch multicolored 1.15 .25

BELGICA '90 Int'l Philatelic Exhib., Brussels — A1359

Designs: 10ch, Rembrandt, *Self Portrait.* 20ch, Raphael, *Self Portrait.* 30ch, Rubens, *Self Portrait.*

1990, June 2 ***Perf. 12¼x12***

2913-2915 A1359 Set of 3 2.00 .40

Düsseldorf '90, 10th Int'l Youth Philatelic Exhib. — A1360

Designs: 20ch, Steffi Graf, tennis player, with bouquet. 30ch, Exhibition emblem. 70ch, K.H. Rummenigge, German soccer player.

1990, June 20

2916-2918 A1360 Set of 3 6.50 .75

A1361

Designs: 10ch, Games mascot, Workers' Stadium, Beijing. 30ch, Chollina Statue and Korean athletes. 40ch, Games emblem, athletes.

1990, July 14

2919-2921 A1361 Set of 3 1.75 .60

11th Asian Games, Beijing (Nos. 2919-2920). Third Asian Winter Games, Samjiyon (No. 2921).

14th World Cup Soccer Championship A1362

Designs: 15ch, Emblem of F.I.F.A. (Federation of Football Associations). 20ch, Jules Rimet. 25ch, Soccer ball. 30ch, Olympic Stadium, Rome. 35ch, Goalkeeper. 40ch, Emblem of the German Football Association. 80ch, Emblem of German Football Association and trophy.

1990, Aug. 8 ***Perf. 13½***

2922-2927 A1362 Set of 6 5.50 .90

Souvenir Sheet

2928 A1362 80ch multicolored 2.75 1.35

New Zealand '90 Int'l Philatelic Exhib., Auckland A1363

1990, Aug. 24 ***Perf. 12***

2929 A1363 30ch multicolored 1.60 .40

Summer at Chipson Peak — A1364

1990, Aug. 24 ***Perf. 11½***

2930 A1364 80ch multicolored 2.75 .50

Europa '90 International Stamp Fair, Riccione.

Koguryo Wedding Procession A1365

Designs: 10ch, Man on horse blowing bugle. 30ch, Bridegroom on horse. 50ch, Bride in carriage. 1w, Man on horse beating drum.

1990, Sept. 3 ***Perf. 12***

2931 Strip of 4, #a.-d. 5.50 .75
a. A1365 10ch multicolored 1.15 .25
b. A1365 30ch multicolored 1.15 .25
c. A1365 50ch multicolored 1.15 .25
d. A1365 1w multicolored 1.15 .25

Printed in setenant strips of four within the sheet.

A1366

Pan-National Rally for Peace and Reunification of Korea — A1367

Designs: 10ch, Rally emblem, crowd descending Mt. Paektu. 1w, Crowd watching dancers.

1990, Sept. 15

2932 A1366 10ch multicolored .50 .25

Souvenir Sheet

2933 A1367 1w multicolored 2.50 .50

Insects — A1368

Designs: 20ch, Praying mantis (Mantis religiosa). 30ch, Lady bug (Coccinella septempunctata). 40ch, Pheropsophus jussoensis. 70ch, Phyllium siccifolium.

1990, Sept. 20

2934-2936A A1368 Set of 4 5.50 1.00

Soccer Players — A1369

No. 2938, North and South Korean players entering May Day Stadium.

1990, Oct. 11

2937 A1369 Pair, #a.-b. 2.50 .40
a. 10ch multicolored 1.15 .25
b. 20ch multicolored 1.15 .25

Souvenir Sheet

2938 A1369 1w multicolored 4.25 .75

North-South Reunification Soccer Games, Pyongyang.

National Reunification Concert — A1370

1990, Oct. 17

2939 A1370 10ch multicolored .50 .25

Farm Animals — A1371

Designs: 10ch, Ox. 20ch, Pig. 30ch, Goat. 40ch, Sheep. 50ch, Horse.

1990, Oct. 18

2940-2944 A1371 Set of 5 5.25 .80
2944a Sheet of 10, 2 ea #2940-2944 12.00 1.60

A1372

A1373

Chinese Entry Into Korean War, 40th Anniv. — A1374

Designs: 10ch, N. Korean and Communist Chinese soldiers. 20ch, Korean civilians welcoming Chinese soldiers. 30ch, Battle scene, victorious soldiers. 40ch, Postwar reconstruction.
80ch, Friendship Monument.

1990, Oct. 23

2945 A1372 10ch multicolored	.25	.25
2946 A1373 20ch multicolored	.75	.25
2947 A1373 30ch multicolored	.90	.25
2948 A1373 40ch multicolored	1.35	.25
Nos. 2945-2948 (4)	3.25	1.00

Souvenir Sheet

Perf. 11¾x11½

2949 A1374 80ch multicolored	2.75	.50

For overprint see No. 3282.

UN Development Program, 40th Anniv. — A1375

1990, Oct. 24 ***Perf. 13¼***

2950 A1375 1w multicolored	3.75	1.10

Fish — A1376

Designs: 10ch, Sturgeon (Acipenser mikadoi). 20ch, Sea bream (Sparus macrocephalus). 30ch, Flying fish (Cypsilurus agoö). 40ch, Fat greenling (Heragrammos otakii). 50ch, Ray (Myliobatus tobeijei).

1990, Nov. 20 ***Perf. 12***

2951-2955 A1376 Set of 5	5.25	1.75
2955a Sheet of 10, 2 ea #2951-2955	11.00	3.75

New Year — A1377

1990, Dec. 1

2956 A1377 40ch multicolored	1.60	.25

Birds — A1378

Designs: 10ch, Moorhen (Gallinula chloropus). 20ch, Jay (Garrulus glandarius). 30ch, Three-toed woodpecker (Picodes tridactylus). 40ch, Whimbrel (Numenius phaeopus). 50ch, Water rail (Rallus aquaticus)

1990, Dec. 18 ***Perf. 12***

2957-2961 A1378 Set of 5	6.00	1.75
2961a Sheet of 10, 2 ea #2957-2961	12.00	4.50

A1379

Pandas — A1380

Designs: 10ch, Giant panda. 20ch, Two giant pandas feeding. 30ch, Giant panda on limb. 40ch, Giant panda on rock. 50ch, Pair of giant pandas. 60ch, Giant panda in tree.

1991, Jan. 10 ***Perf. 11¾x12***

2962-2967 A1379 Set of 6	6.50	1.60
2967a Sheet of 6, #2962-2967	6.50	1.60

Souvenir Sheet

Perf. 11½

2968 A1380 1w multicolored	3.00	.60

For surcharges, see No. 4536-4537.

A1381

Revolutionary Sites — A1382

1991, Jan. 10 ***Perf. 12***

2969 A1381 5ch Changsan	.25	.25
2970 A1382 10ch Oun	.30	.25

Endangered Birds — A1383

Designs: 10ch, Black-faced spoonbills (Platalea minor). 20ch, Gray herons (Ardea cinerea). 30ch, Great egrets (Egretta alba). 40ch, Manchurian cranes (Grus japonensis). 50ch, Japanese white-necked cranes (Grus vipio). 70ch, White storks (Ciconia boyciana).

1991, Feb. 5

2971-2976 A1383 Set of 6	5.50	1.30
2976a Sheet of 6, #2971-2976	6.75	1.60

Alpine Butterflies A1384

Designs: 10ch, Clossiana angarensis. 20ch, Erebia embla. 30ch, Nymphalis antiopa. 40ch, Polygonia c-album). 50ch, Colias erate. 60ch, Thecla betulae.

1991, Feb. 20 ***Perf. 13¼***

2977-2982 A1384 Set of 6	6.75	2.25
2982a Sheet of 6, #2977-2982	6.75	2.25

Fungi — A1385

Designs: 10ch, Hydnum repandum. 20ch, Phylloporus rhodoxanthus. 30ch, Calvatia craniformis. 40ch, Ramaria botrytis. 50ch, Russula integra.

1991, Feb. 26 ***Perf. 12x12¼***

2983-2987 A1385 Set of 5	4.50	1.15
2987a Sheet of 10, 2 ea #2983-2987	9.00	2.25

For surcharge, see No. 4546.

A1386

Revolutionary Sites — A1387

1991, Mar. 15 ***Perf. 12***

2988 A1386 10ch Kumchon	.30	.25
2989 A1387 40ch Samdung	1.10	.30

A1388

Silkworm Research — A1389

Designs: 10ch, Dr. Kye Ung (1893-1967), silkworm researcher. 20ch, Chinese oak silk moth, Antheraea pernyi. 30ch, Attacus ricini. 40ch, Antheraea yamamai. 50ch, Bombyx mori. 60ch, Aetias artemis.

1991, Mar. 27

2990 A1388 10ch multicolored	.25	.25
2991 A1389 20ch multicolored	.60	.30
2992 A1389 30ch multicolored	.75	.40
2993 A1389 40ch multicolored	1.10	.50
2994 A1389 50ch multicolored	1.45	.75
2995 A1389 60ch multicolored	1.75	.75
a. Sheet of 6, #2990-2995	6.00	3.25
Nos. 2990-2995 (6)	5.90	2.95

9th Spring Friendship Art Festival, Pyongyang — A1390

1991, Apr. 3

2996 A1390 10ch multicolored	.50	.25

Antarctic Exploration — A1391

Designs: 10ch, Penguins. 20ch, Research station. 30ch, Elephant seals. 40ch, Research ship. 50ch, Black-backed gulls.
80ch, DPRK flag and map of Antarctica.

1991, Apr. 20 ***Perf. 11¾x12***

2997-3001 A1391 Set of 5	5.50	1.15
3001a Sheet of 6, #2997-3002	8.25	1.60

Souvenir Sheet

Perf. 11¾

3002 A1391 80ch multicolored	2.75	.50

A single stamp like that in No. 3002 is included in No. 3001a.

85th Interparliamentary Union Conference, Pyongyang — A1392

Designs: 10ch, Peoples Palace of Culture. 1.50w, Conference emblem and azalea.

1991, Apr. 29 ***Perf. 12***

3003-3004 A1392 Set of 2	4.50	1.30

Map and Kim Jong Ho — A1393

1991, May 8 ***Perf. 11¾x12***

3005 A1393 90ch multicolored	2.25	.75

Dinosaurs A1394

Designs: a, 10ch, Cynognathus. b, 20ch, Brontosaurus. c, 30ch, Stegosaurus and allosaurus. d, 40ch, Pterosauria. e, 50ch, Ichthyosaurus.

1991, May 21 ***Perf. 12x11¾***

3006 A1394 Strip of 5 + label	6.75	1.60
3006f Sheet of 5 + label	15.50	1.75

Barcelona '92 Olympic Games A1395

Designs: No. 3011, 10ch, 100-Meter dash. No. 3012, 10ch, Hurdle race. No. 3013 20ch, Broad jump. No. 3014, 20ch, Throwing discus. No. 3015, 30ch, Shot-put. No. 3016, 30ch, Pole vault. No. 3017, 40ch, High jump. No. 3018, 40ch, Javelin throw.
No. 3019, 80ch, 400-meter race. No. 3020, 80ch, 1500-meter race.

1991, June 18

3011-3018 A1395 Set of 8	3.75	1.30
3018a Sheet of 10, #3011-3020	11.50	2.50

Souvenir Sheets

Perf. 11½x11¾

3019-3020 A1395 Set of 2	3.25	1.15

No. 3018a contains single stamps from Nos. 3019-3020 in addition to Nos. 3011-3018.

Cats A1396

Designs: 10ch, Cats and birds. 20ch, Cat and rat. 30ch, Cat and butterfly. 40ch, Cats and ball. 50ch, Cat and frog.

1991, July 21 *Perf. 13¼*
3021-3025 A1396 Set of 5 4.75 2.00

For surcharges, see Nos. 4538, 4547.

Riccione '91 Int'l Stamp Fair — A1397

1991, Aug. 27 *Perf. 11¾x12*
3026 A1397 80ch multicolored 2.50 .60

Horses — A1398

Designs: 10ch, Equus caballus. 20ch, Equus asinus and Equus caballus. 30ch, Equus przewalskii. 40ch, Equus asinus. 50ch, Equus caballus, diff.

1991, Sept. 2 *Perf. 13½*
3027-3031 A1398 Set of 5 4.50 1.15
3031a Sheet of 5, #3027-3031 4.50 1.30

A1399

Phila Nippon '91 International Stamp Exhibition — A1400

Fish: 10ch, Pennant coral fish (Heniochus acuminatus). 20ch, Big-spotted trigger fish (Balistoides conspicillum). 30ch, Anemone fish (Amphiprion frenatus). 40ch, Blue surgeon fish (Paracanthurus hepatus). 50ch, Angel fish (Pterophyllum eimekei).
80ch, Tetras (Hyphessobrycon innesi).

1991, Sept. 20 *Perf. 12x12¼*
3032-3036 A1399 Set of 5 4.50 1.15
3036a Sheet of 5, #3032-3036 4.50 1.15

Souvenir Sheet
Perf. 11¾

3037 A1400 80ch multicolored 4.50 .60

No. 3036 is airmail.

Flowers — A1401

Designs: 10ch, Begonia. 20ch, Gerbera. 30ch, Rhododendrons. 40ch, Phalaenopsis. 50ch, Impatiens sultani. 60ch, Streptocarpus.

1991, Oct. 16 *Perf. 12¼x12*
3038-3043 A1401 Set of 6 6.00 1.60
3043a Sheet of 6, #3038-3043 6.00 1.75

Nos. 3041-3043 commemorate Canada '92 International Youth Stamp Exhibition, Montreal, and include the exhibition emblem.

Panmunjon A1402

1991, Oct. 12 *Perf. 12*
3044 A1402 10ch multicolored .60 .25

Magnolia — A1403

1991, Nov. 1 *Perf. 11½*
3045 A1403 10ch multicolored .60 .25

DPRK National Flower.

Women's World Soccer Championship, China — A1404

Designs: 10ch, Dribbling. 20ch, Dribbling, diff. 30ch, Heading the ball. 40ch, Overhead kick. 50ch, Tackling. 60ch, Goalkeeper.

1991, Nov. 3 *Perf. 12*
3046-3051 A1404 Set of 6 6.00 1.60
3051a Sheet of 6, #3046-3051 6.00 1.75

A1405

Monkeys — A1406

Designs: 10ch, Squirrel monkeys (Samiri sciureus). 20ch, Pygmy marmosets (Cebuella pygmaea). 30ch, Red-handed tamarins (Saquinas midas).
80ch, Monkey leaping.

1992, Jan. 1
3052-3054 A1405 Set of 3 2.00 .65
3054a Sheet of 3, #3052-3054 2.25 .75

Souvenir Sheet
Perf. 11¾x11½

3055 A1406 80ch multicolored 2.25 .90

A1407

Birds of Prey — A1408

Designs: 10ch, Bubo bubo. 20ch, Buteo buteo. 30ch, Haliaeetus vocifer. 40ch, Haliaeetus pelagicus. 50ch, Aquila chrysaetos.
80ch, Falco tinnunculus.

1992, Jan. 5 *Perf. 13¼*
3056-3060 A1407 Set of 5 4.50 1.60
3060a Sheet of 12, 2 #3056-3060 + 2 labels 9.00 3.25

Souvenir Sheet
Perf. 11½

3061 A1408 80ch multicolored 2.25 .60

No. 3060a, Granada '92 International Stamp Exhibition. For surcharge, see No. 4609.

A1409

50th Birthday of Kim Jong Il — A1410

Designs: 10ch, Birthplace, Mt. Paektu. 20ch, Mt. Paektu. 30ch, Lake Chon on top of Mt. Paektu. 40ch, Lake Samji.
80ch, *Snowstorm in Mt. Paektu.*

1992, Feb. 16 *Perf. 12x11¾*
3062-3065 A1409 Set of 4 3.00 .75

Souvenir Sheet
Perf. 11¾x11½

3066 A1410 80ch multicolored 2.75 .60

Transport A1411

Designs: 10ch, Bus, "Jipsam 88." 20ch, Bus, "Pyongyang 86." 30ch, Trolley bus, "Chollima 84." 40ch, Bus, "Kwangbok Sonyon." 50ch, Tram. 60ch, July 17 Tram.

1992, Feb. 20 *Perf. 12¼*
3067-3072 A1411 Set of 6 6.00 1.60
3072a Sheet of 6, #3067-3072 6.00 1.75

No. 3072a, Essen '92 International Stamp Fair.

Spring Fellowship Art Festival, Pyongyang — A1412

1992, Apr. 7
3073 A1412 10ch multicolored .50 .25

A1413

80th Birthday of Kim Il Sung — A1414

Revolutionary Sites: 10ch (No. 3074), Birthplace, Mangyongdao. 10ch (No. 3075), Party emblem, Turubong. 10ch (No. 3076), Map, Ssuksom. 10ch (No. 3077), Statue of soldier, Tongchang. 40ch (No. 3078), Chollima Statue, Kangson. 40ch (No. 3079), Cogwheels, Taean. 1.20w, Monument, West Sea Barrage.
80ch, Kim Il Sung among participants in the April Spring Friendship Art Festival.

1992, Apr. 15
3074-3080 A1413 Set of 7 6.75 2.00

Souvenir Sheet
Perf. 11½

3081 A1414 80ch multicolored 2.75 .60

No. 2080 is airmail.

Kang Ban Sok, Mother of Kim Il Sung, Birth Centenary — A1415

1992, Apr. 21 *Perf. 13¼*
3082 A1415 80ch multicolored 2.00 .60

Korean People's Army, 60th Anniv. — A1416

Designs (all 10ch): No. 3083, Soldier, troops on parade. No. 3084, Pilot, soldiers. No. 3085, Soldier with two civilian women.

1992, Apr. 25 *Perf. 12¼*
3083-3085 A1416 Set of 3 1.00 .25
3085a Sheet of 9, 4 #3085, 2 ea. #3083-3084 + label 2.75 .90

25th Olympic Games, Barcelona '92 A1417

Women's events: 10ch, Hurdle race. 20ch, High jump. 30ch, Shot-put. 40ch, 200-meter race. 50ch, Broad jump. 60ch, Javelin throw.
80ch, 800-meter race.

1992, May 10 *Perf. 12x11¾*
3086-3091 A1417 Set of 6 6.00 1.60
3091a Sheet of 8, #3086-3092 + label 8.75 2.25

Souvenir Sheet

3092 A1417 80ch multicolored 2.50 .60

Prehistoric Man — A1418

Designs: 10ch, Planting crops. 20ch, Family in shelter, with cooking pot. 30ch, Plowing. 40ch, Indoor life. 50ch, Laying a dolmen.

1992, June 1 *Perf. 12x11¾*
3093-3097 A1418 Set of 5 4.50 1.15
3097a Sheet of 5, #3093-3097 + label 5.50 1.30

Birds — A1419

Designs: 10ch, Dryocopus javensis. 20ch, Phasianis colchicus. 30ch, Ciconia boyciana. 40ch, Pitta brachyura. 50ch, Syrrhaptes paradoxus. 60ch, Lyrurus tetrix.
80ch, Sturnus sturnus.

1992, June 28 *Perf. 11½*
3098-3103 A1419 Set of 6 6.50 1.60
3103a Sheet of 7, #3098-3104 + label 13.50 —

Souvenir Sheet

3104 A1419 80ch multicolored 3.25 1.30

No. 3103a contains a single stamp from No. 3104 in addtion to Nos. 3098-3103.

North-South Joint Statement, 20th Anniv. — A1420

1992, July 4
3105 A1420 1.50w multicolored 4.25 1.30

Souvenir Sheet

3106 A1420 3w multicolored 8.25 2.50

No. 3106 contains two copies of No. 3105 and label.

Flowers — A1421

Designs: 10ch, Bougainvillea spectabilis. 20ch, Ixora chinensis. 30ch, Dendrobium taysuwie. 40ch, Columnea gloriosa. 50ch, Crinum. 60ch, Ranunculus asiaticus.

1992, July 15 *Perf. 12¼*
3107-3112 A1421 Set of 6 6.00 1.60
3112a Sheet of 8, #3107-3112 + 2 labels 6.50 1.75

No. 3112a, Genova '92 International Stamp Exhibition.

The Solar System — A1422

No. 3113: a, Satellite, Venus, Earth, Mars. b, Jupiter. c, Saturn. d, Uranus. e, Neptune, Pluto.
80ch, Earth.

1992, Aug. 10 *Perf. 11½*
3113 A1422 50ch Strip of 5, #a-e 7.25 2.25
3113f Sheet of 5, #3113, + 5 labels 8.25 2.50

Souvenir Sheet

3114 A1422 80ch multicolored 2.25 1.35

Riccione '92 Int'l Stamp Fair — A1423

Designs: 10ch, C-class yacht. 20ch, Sailboard. 30ch, Rager-class yacht. 40ch, Pin-class yacht. 50ch, 470-class yacht. 60ch, Fair emblem.

1992, Aug. 27 *Perf. 12¼*
3119-3124 A1423 Set of 6 6.00 2.00
3119a Sheet of 6 stamps, 2 ea. #3119, 3121, 3123 6.00 2.25
3120a Sheet of 6 stamps, 2 ea. #3120, 3122, 3124 6.00 2.25

A1424

U.C. Sampdoria, Italian Soccer Champion 1991 — A1425

Designs: a, 20ch, Moreno Mannini, defender. b, 30ch, Gianluca Vialli, forward. c, 40ch, Pietro Vierchowod, back. d, 50ch, Fausto Pari, center-half. e, 60ch, Roberto Mancini, forward. f, 1w, club president.
1w, Vialli and Riccardo Garrone, president of club sponsor, ERG.

1992, Aug. 31 *Perf. 12*
3125 A1424 Sheet of 6, #a.-f. 8.25 2.75

Souvenir Sheet

Perf. 11½x12

3131 A1425 1w multicolored 2.75 1.35

A1426

8th World Taekwondo Championship, Pyongyang — A1427

Designs: 10ch, Team pattern. 30ch, Side kick. 50ch, Flying high kick. 70ch, Flying twisting kick. 90ch, Black-belt breaking tiles with fist.
1.20w, Flying twin foot side kick; Choe Hong Hin, president of International Taekwon-Do Federation, in margin.

1992, Sept. 1 *Perf. 12*
3132-3136 A1426 Set of 5 7.25 2.25
3136a Sheet of 5, #3132-3136 + label 7.25 2.25

Souvenir Sheet

3137 A1427 1.20w multicolored 3.75 1.60

No. 3137 is airmail.

Frogs and Toads — A1428

Designs: No. 3138, 40ch, Rana chosenica. No. 3139, 40ch, Rana arvalis. No. 3140, 40ch, Bufo bufo. No. 3141, 70ch, Rana nigromaculata. No. 3142, 70ch , Hyla japonica. No. 3143, 70ch Rana coreana.

1992, Sept. 10 *Perf. 12¼*
3138-3143 A1428 Set of 6 9.00 2.75
3139a Sheet of 8, 4 #3139, 2 ea. #3138, #3140 + label 13.50 4.50
3142a Sheet of 8, 4 #3142, 2 ea. #3141, #3143 + label 13.50 4.50

No. 3143 is airmail.

World Environment Day — A1429

Designs: 10ch, Rhododendron mucronulatum. 30ch, Hirundo rustica. 40ch, Stewartia koreana. 50ch, Dictoptera aurora. 70ch, Metasequoia glyptostroboides. 90ch, Hynobius leechi. 1.20w, Gingko biloba. 1.40w, Cottus poecilopus.

1992, Oct. 20 *Perf. 12*
3144-3151 A1429 Set of 8 17.50 4.50
3151a Sheet of 8 stamps, #3144-3151 18.00 4.75

Nos. 3150 and 3151 are airmail.

Whales and Dolphins A1430

Designs: No. 3152, 50ch, Balaenoptera physalus. No. 3153, 50ch, Delphinus delphis. No. 3154, 50ch, Orcinus orca. No. 3155, 50ch, Megaptera nodosa. No. 3156, 50ch, Berardius bairdii. No. 3157, 50ch, Physeter catadon.

1992, Oct. 20
3152-3157 A1430 Set of 6 11.00 2.50
3152a Sheet of 3, #3152-3154 5.00 1.15
3155a Sheet of 3, #3155-3157 5.00 1.15

No. 3157 is airmail. For surcharges, see No. 4548, 4588.

New Year (Year of the Rooster) — A1431

Chickens in various cartoon forms: 10ch, Hen and chicks. 20ch, Young hen. 30ch, Strong cock. 40ch, Prince cock. 50ch, Princess hen. 60ch, King cock.
1.20w, Cock.

1992, Dec. 7 *Perf. 11½*
3158-3163 A1431 Set of 6 6.00 1.60
3163a Sheet of 4, #3158-3160, 3163c 3.75 1.35
3163b Sheet of 4, #3161-3163, 3163c 4.50 1.75

Souvenir Sheet

3163C A1431 1.20w multicolored 4.50 .90

A single stamp like that in No. 3163C is included in Nos. 3163a and 3163b. For surcharges, see Nos. 4525-4526.

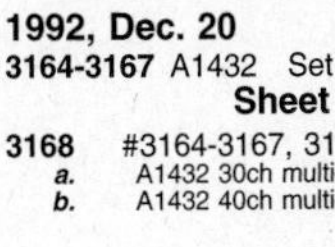
N. Korean Gold Medal Winners at Barcelona Olympics A1432

Designs: 10ch, Choe Chol Su (boxing). 20ch, Pae Kil Su (gymnastics). 50ch, Ri Hak Son (Wrestling). 60ch, Kim Il (wrestling).
No. 3168: a, 30ch, Archer, flame, gold medal, flags of DPRK and Spain. b, 40ch, Emblem, game mascot and Church of the Holy Family, Barcelona.

1992, Dec. 20 *Perf. 12*
3164-3167 A1432 Set of 4 4.25 1.10

Sheet of 6

3168 #3164-3167, 3168a-3168b 6.50 .60
a. A1432 30ch multicolored .35 .25
b. A1432 40ch multicolored .50 .30

Fungi — A1433

Designs: 10ch, Golden mushroom (Flammulina velutipes). 20ch, Shaggy caps (Coprinus comatus). 30ch, Ganoderma lucidum. 40ch, Brown mushroom (Lentinus edodes). 50ch, (Volvaria bombycina). 60ch, (Sarcodon aspratus).
1w, Scarlet caterpillar (Cordyceps militaris).

1993, Jan. 10 *Perf. 11½*
3169-3174 A1433 Set of 6 6.75 2.25
3169a Sheet of 4, #3169, 3172, 3174, 3175 6.50 2.00
3170a Sheet of 4, #3170, 3171, 3173, 3175 6.50 2.00

Souvenir Sheet

3175 A1433 1w multicolored 4.25 .75

A single stamp like that in No. 3175 is included in Nos. 3169a and 3170a.

A1434

Korean Plants — A1435

Designs: 10ch, Keumkangsania asiatica. 20ch, Echinosophora koreensis. 30ch, Abies koreana. 40ch, Benzoin angustifolium. 50ch, Abeliophyllum distichum. 60ch, (Abelia mosanensis).
1w, Pentactina rupicola.

1993, Jan. 20 *Perf. 12¼*
3176-3181 A1434 Set of 6 6.50 1.75
3181a Sheet of 6, #3176-3181 6.50 2.00

Souvenir Sheet

Perf. 11½

3182 A1435 1w multicolored 3.25 1.75

8th Congress of the League of Socialist Working Youth of Korea — A1436

Designs: 10ch, Youths, banner. 20ch, Flame, emblem, motto.

1993, Jan. 25 *Perf. 12¼*
3183-3184 A1436 Set of 2 1.35 .40

Phophyong Revolutionary Site Tower & March Corps Emblem — A1437

1993, Jan. 29 *Perf. 12x12¼*
3185 A1437 10ch multicolored .50 .25

70th anniv. of the 250-mile Journey for Learning.

Tower of the Juche Idea, Grand Monument, Mt. Wangjae — A1438

1993, Feb. 11
3186 A1438 60ch multicolored .50 .25

60th anniv. of the Wangjaesan Meeting.

A1439

Kim Jong Il, 51st Birthday — A1440

Designs: 10ch, Kimjongilia (Begonia).
1w, Kim Il Sung writing poem praising Kim Jong Il. Illustration of stamp only. Sheet measures 170mmx95mm, with marginal inscriptions that include reproductions of Kim Il Sung's poem.

1993, Feb. 16 ***Perf. 12***
3187 A1439 10ch multicolored .90 .25

Souvenir Sheet
Perf. 13¼
3188 A1440 1w multicolored 3.25 .75

Sea Fish — A1441

Designs: 10ch, Pilot fish (Naucrates ductor). 20ch, Japanese stingray (Dasyatis akajei). 30ch, Moonfish (Lampris guttatus). 40ch, Coelacanth (Latimeria chalumnae). 50ch, Grouper (Epinephelus moara).
1.20w, Mako shark (Isurus oxyrhynchus).

1993, Feb. 25 ***Perf. 11½***
3189-3193 A1441 Set of 5 4.50 1.15
3189a Sheet of 2, #3189, #3194 3.00 .45
3190a Sheet of 2, #3190, #3193 3.00 .45
3191a Sheet of 2, #3191, #3192 3.00 .45

Souvenir Sheet
3194 A1441 1.20w multicolored 4.25 .75

A single stamp like that in No. 3194 is included in No. 3189a.
No. 3194, Naposta '93.

Spring on the Hill, 18th century Korean Painting — A1442

1993, Mar. 20 ***Perf. 12x11½***
3195 A1442 Sheet of 5 6.00 1.60
a.-e. 40ch, any single .90 .30

Spring Friendship Art Festival A1443

1993, Apr. 5 ***Perf. 12x12¼***
3196 A1443 10ch multicolored .75 .25

For surcharge, see No. 4602.

A1444

Kim Il Sung, 80th Birthday, and Publication of *With the Century* — A1445

Designs: 10ch, *With the Century*, Kim Il Sung's Memoir.
1w, Kim Il Sung writing *With the Century.*

1993, Apr. 15
3197 A1444 10ch multicolored .50 .25

Souvenir Sheet
Perf. 11½
3198 A1445 1w multicolored 3.25 .75

A1446

Pyongyang Scenes — A1447

Designs: 10ch, Kwangbok Street. 20ch, Chollima Street. 30ch, Munsu Street. 40ch, Moranbong Street. 50ch, Thongil Street.
1w, Changgwang Street.

1993, Apr. 20 ***Perf. 12x11¾***
3199-3203 A1446 Set of 5 4.25 1.15

Souvenir Sheet
Perf. 11½
3204 A1447 1w multicolored 3.25 .75

Insects — A1448

Designs: 10ch, Fly (Trichogramma dendrolimi). 20ch, Fly (Brachymeria obscurata). 30ch, Cricket (Metrioptera brachyptera). 50ch, Cricket (Gryllus campestris). 70ch, Beetle (Geocoris pallidipennis). 90ch, Wasp (Cyphononyx dorsalis).

1993, May 10 ***Perf. 12x12¼***
3205-3210 A1448 Set of 6 9.00 2.00
3205a Sheet of 3, #3205, 3207, 3210 4.50 1.15
3206a Sheet of 3, #3206, 3208, 3209 4.50 1.15

Nos. 3205-3210 were issued both in separate sheets and in sheets of 3.

A1449

A1450

1993, May 19 ***Perf. 11½***
3211 A1449 10ch multicolored .50 .25

Souvenir Sheet
Perf. 13¼
3212 A1450 1.20w multicolored 3.75 .75

Release of Ri In Mo, North Korean war correspondent, from South Korean prison.

World Cup Soccer Championship, U.S.A. — A1451

World Cup and soccer players: 10ch, Tackling. 20ch, Kicking. 30ch, Kicking (diff.). 50ch, Tackling (diff.). 70ch, Blocking. 90ch, Feinting.

1993, May 25 ***Perf. 11½***
3213-3218 A1451 Set of 6 7.75 2.00
3213a Sheet of 3, #3213, 3215, 3218 4.00 1.15
3214a Sheet of 3, #3214, 3216, 3217 4.00 1.15

Birds — A1452

Designs: 10ch, Gray-headed green woodpecker (Picus canus). 20ch, King of paradise (Cicinnurus regius. 30ch, Lesser bird of paradise (Paradisea minor). 40ch, Paradise whydah (Steganura paradisea). 50ch, Magnificent bird of paradise (Diphyllodes magnificus). 60ch, Greater bird of paradise (Paradisea apoda).

1993, May 29 ***Perf. 12***
3219-3224 A1452 Set of 6 6.50 1.60
3219a Sheet of 4, 2 ea. #3219, 3224 3.75 1.00
3220a Sheet of 4, 2 ea. #3220, 3223 3.75 1.00
3221a Sheet of 2, #3221, #3222 3.75 1.00

Nos. 3221, 3221a, 3222, Indopex '93 International Stamp Exhibition, Surabaya, Indonesia.

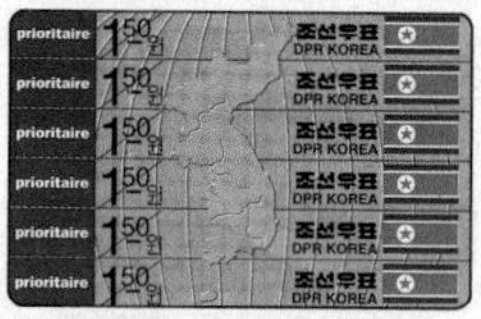
Stampcard — A1453

Design: Map of Korean peninsula.

1993, May 29 ***Rouletted***
Self-adhesive
3225 A1453 Card of 6 stamps 20.00 20.00
a.-f. 1.50w, any single 3.00 3.00

For surcharges, see No. 3441.

Korean World Champions — A1454

Designs: 10ch, Kim Myong Nam (weight-lifting, 1990). 20ch, Kim Kwang Suk (gymnastics, 1991). 30ch, Pak Yong Sun (table tennis, 1975, 1977). 50ch, Kim Yong Ok (radio direction-finding, 1990). 70ch, Han Yun Ok (taekwondo, 1987, 1988, 1990). 90ch, Kim Yong Sik (free-style wrestling, 1986, 1989).

1993, June 15 ***Perf. 12x11¾***
3226-3231 A1454 Set of 6 8.25 2.00
3226a Sheet of 6, 2 ea. #3226, 3228, 3231 8.25 2.25
3227a Sheet of 6, 2 ea. #3227, 3229, 3230 8.25 2.25

For surcharge, see No. 4573.

Fruits and Vegetables — A1455

Designs: 10ch, Cabbage and chili peppers. 20ch, Squirrel and horse chestnuts. 30ch, Peach and grapes. 40ch, Birds and persimmons. 50ch, Tomatoes, eggplant and cherries. 60ch, Onion, radishes, garlic bulbs.

1993, June 25 ***Perf. 11¾x12***
3232-3237 A1455 Set of 6 6.00 1.60
3232a Sheet of 3, #3232, 3235, 3237 2.25 .85
3232b As "a.," ovptd. "Polska '93" 4.50 1.15
3233c Sheet of 3, #3233, 3234, 3236 2.25 .85

National Emblem — A1456

1993, July 5 ***Perf. 12***
3238 A1456 10ch vermilion .60 .25

For surcharge, see No. 4259A.

Korean War, 40th Anniv. — A1457

A1458

A1459

A1460

Kim Leading Soldiers on the Front — A1461

Kim Surveying Battlefield — A1462

Kim Making 1953 Victory Speech — A1463

Designs: No. 3239, 10ch, Soldiers and civilian women. No. 3240, 10ch, Officer and enlisted man. No. 3241, 10ch, Anti-aircraft missiles on military trucks. No. 3242, 10ch, Guided missiles on carriers. No. 3243, 10ch, Self-propelled missile launchers.
No. 3244, 1w, Kim Il Jong taking salute of paraders.
No. 3245, 10ch, Victory statue (soldier with flag). No. 3246, 10ch, Machine-gunners and refugees. 40ch, Soldiers and flag.
No. 3248a, 10ch, Kim Il Sung conducting planning meeting. b, 20ch, Kim inspecting artillery unit. No. 3249a, 10ch, Kim directing battle for Height 1211. b, 20ch, Kim encouraging machine gun crew. No. 3250a, 10ch, Kim at munitions factory. b, 20ch, Kim directing units of the Second Front. No. 3251a, 10ch, Kim with tank commanders. b, 20ch, Kim directing airmen. No. 3252a, 10ch, Kim with victorious soldiers. b, 20ch, Musicians.

1993, July 27
3239-3243 A1457 Set of 5 2.25 .75

Souvenir Sheet
Perf. 13¼
3244 A1458 1w multicolored 3.75 .50

Perf. 11¾x12
3245-3247 A1459 Set of 3 2.00 .50
3247a Sheet of 3, #3245-3247 2.25 .60

Souvenir Sheets of 2, #a-b
Perf. 11½
3248-3252 A1460 Set of 5 4.50 1.30

Souvenir Sheets
Perf. 13¼
3253 A1461 80ch multicolored 4.25 .60
3254 A1462 80ch multicolored 4.25 .60
3255 A1463 1w multicolored 5.50 .60

National Reunification Prize Winners — A1464

Designs: 10ch, Choe Yong Do (1923-69). 20ch, Kim Gu (1875-1949). 30ch, Hong Myong Hui (1888-1968). 40ch, Ryo Un Hyong (1886-1947). 50ch, Kim Jong Thae (1926-69). 60ch, Kim Chaek (1903-51).

1993, Aug. 1 ***Perf. 12***
3256-3261 A1464 Set of 6 6.00 1.60

A1465

Taipei '93 Int'l Philatelic Exhib. — A1466

Designs: 20ch, *Robina sp.* 30ch, *Hippeastrum cv.* 1w, Deer.

1993, Aug. 14
3262-3263 A1465 Set of 2 1.35 .45

Souvenir Sheet
3264 A1466 1w multicolored 3.25 1.35

350th Anniv. Birth of Sir Isaac Newton, Mathematician and Scientist — A1467

Designs: 10ch, Portrait of Newton. 20ch, Apple tree and formula for Law of Gravitation. 30ch, Reflecting telescope invented by Newton. 50ch, Formula of Binomial Theorem. 70ch, Newton's works, statue.

1993, Sept. 1 ***Perf. 12¼x12***
3265-3269 A1467 Set of 5 6.75 1.35
3265a Sheet of 3, #3265, 3266, 3269 3.50 3.50
3265b Sheet of 3, #3265, 3267, 3268 3.50 3.50

For surcharge, see No. 4597.

A1468

Restoration of the Tomb of King Tongmyong, Founder of Koguryo — A1469

Designs: 10ch, King Tongmyong shooting arrow. 20ch, King Tongmyong. 30ch, Restoration monument. 40ch, Jongrung Temple of the Tomb of King Tongmyong. 50ch, Tomb.
80ch, Kim Il Sung visiting restored tomb.

1993, Sept. 10
3270-3274 A1468 Set of 5 4.25 1.15

Souvenir Sheet
Perf. 11½
3275 A1469 80ch multicolored 2.25 1.35

Bangkok '93 Int'l Philatelic Exhib. — A1470

First stamps of North Korea and Thailand.

1993, Oct. 1
3276 A1470 1.20w multicolored 4.50 1.75

Orchids — A1471

Designs: 10ch, Cyrtopodium andresoni. 20ch, Cattleya. 30ch, Cattleya intermedia "Oculata." 40ch, Potinaria "Maysedo godonsia." 50ch, "Kimilsungia."

1993, Oct. 15 ***Perf. 12***
3277-3281 A1471 Set of 5 5.50 1.15
3281a Strip of 5, #3277-3281 5.50 5.50
3277b-3281b Set of 5 complete booklets, each containing 5 stamps 27.00

Nos. 3277b-3281b each contain horizontal strips of 5 of one value, taken from sheets. For surcharge, see No. 4549.

No. 2949 Overprinted

1993, Nov. 16
3282 A1373 80ch multicolored 2.25 1.35

Mao Zedong, Birth Centennial.

A1472

A1473

Mao Zedong, Birth Centennial — A1474

Designs: 10ch, Mao in Yannan (1940). 20ch, Mao in Beijing (1960). 30ch, Mao voting (1953). 40ch, Mao with middle-school students (1959).
No. 3287: Nos. 3283-3286 and: a, Mao proclaiming People's Republic of China (1949). b, Mao and his son, Mao Anying, in Xiangshan, Beijing (1949). c, Mao and Kim Il Sung (1975).
No. 3288: As No. 3287c.

1993, Dec. 26 ***Perf. 11½***
3283-3286 A1472 Set of 4 3.00 .85

Souvenir Sheets
3287 A1473 Sheet of 7 5.50 5.50
a. 25ch multicolored .50 .30
b. 25ch multicolored .50 .30
c. 1w multicolored 1.75 .85
3288 A1474 1w multicolored 1.75 1.75

A1475

A1476

New Year, Year of the Dog — A1477

Designs: 10ch, Phungsan. 20ch, Yorkshire terriers. 30ch, Gordon setter. 40ch, Pomeranian. 50ch, Spaniel with pups.
No. 3294, Pointer.
No. 3295, 2 #3289, 1 #3294a; No. 3296, 2 #3290, 1 #3294a; No. 3297, 2 #3291, 1 #3294a; No. 3298, 2 #3292, 1 #3294a; No. 3299, 2 #3293, 1 #3294a.

1994, Jan. 1 ***Perf. 12***
3289-3293 A1475 Set of 5 4.50 .90
3289a-3293a Set of 5 complete booklets, each containing 5 stamps 22.50

Souvenir Sheet
3294 A1476 1w multicolored 4.25 1.15

Sheets of 3, #a.-c.
Perf. 12
3295-3299 A1477 Set of 5 27.00 27.00

Nos. 3289a-3293a each contain horizontal strips of 5 of one value, taken from sheets.

A1478

Kim Jong Il, 52nd Birthday — A1479

Designs: 10ch, Purple hyosong flower (Prinula polyantha). 40ch, Yellow hyosong flower (Prinula polyantha).
No. 3302, Kim Il Sung and Kim Jong Il, from embroidery *The Sun of Juche.*

1994, Feb. 16 ***Perf. 13¼***
3300-3301 A1478 Set of 2 1.35 .45
a. Pair, #3300-3301 1.60 1.60

Souvenir Sheet
3302 A1479 1w multicolored 3.25 1.15

Nos. 3300-3301 exist in a miniature sheet containing 4 of each value, with central label depicting Jong Il Peak and *Kimjongilia.*

Goldfish — A1480

Designs: 10ch, Red and black dragon-eye. 30ch, Red and white bubble-eye. 50ch, Red and white long-finned wenyu. 70ch, Red and white fringetail.

1994, Feb. 18 ***Perf. 12***

3303 A1480 Sheet of 4		6.00	1.15
a.	10ch multicolored	1.45	.25
b.	30ch multicolored	1.45	.25
c.	50ch multicolored	1.45	.25
d.	70ch multicolored	1.45	.25

A1481

Publication of the *Program of Modeling the Whole Society on the Juche Idea*, 20th Anniv. — A1482

Kim Il Sung proclaiming the *Program*, 1974.

1994, Feb. 19

3307 A1481 20ch multicolored .50 .25

Souvenir Sheet

Perf. 11½

3308 A1482 1.20w multicolored 4.00 1.15

A1483

A1484

Publication of Kim Il Sung's *Theses on the Socialist Rural Question in Our Country*, 30th Anniv. — A1485

Designs: 10ch (No. 3309), Woman propagandist, sound truck. 10ch (No. 3310), Electrical generator, pylon. 10ch (No. 3311), Farm, farm equipment, piles of grain. 40ch (No. 3312), Lab technician with microscope. 40ch (No. 3313), Dancers celebrating bounty harvest.

No. 3314, Kim Il Sung in field. No. 3315, Kim Jong Il walking through field with peasants.

1994, Feb. 25 ***Perf. 12***

3309-3313 A1483 Set of 5 3.25 .85

Souvenir Sheets

Perf. 11½

3314 A1484 1w multicolored 2.25 1.15
3315 A1485 1w multicolored 2.25 1.15

Ships — A1486

Designs: 20ch, Passenger ship, *Mangyongbong-92*. 30ch, Cargo ship, *Osandok*. 40ch, Processing stern trawler, *Ryongaksan*. 50ch, Stern trawler.

80ch, Passenger ship, *Maekjon No. 1*.

1994, Mar. 25 ***Perf. 12***

3316-3319 A1486 Set of 4		4.25	1.15
3320 Sheet of 6, #3316-3319 + 2 #3320a		9.00	2.25
a.	A1486 80ch multicolored	2.25	.75

DPRK Flag — A1487

1994, Mar. 30 ***Perf. 13¼***

3321 A1487 10ch car & dp blue		.50	.25
a.	Perf. 12	—	—

For surcharges, see Nos. 4259B and 4571.

A1488

Kim Il Sung, 82nd Birthday — A1489

Designs: 10ch, Magnolia and Kim's home. 40ch, Kimilsungia and Kim's home.

No. 3324, Five 40ch stamps, together forming design of Lake Chon (crater lake of Mt. Paektu), with *Song of General Kim Il Sung* music within design, lyrics in sheet margin.

1994, Apr. 15 ***Perf. 12***

3322-3323 A1488 Set of 2		1.35	.50
3323a	10ch Sheet of 8	6.50	2.00
3323b	40ch Sheet of 8	6.50	2.00

Souvenir Sheet

3324 A1489 2w Sheet of 5		6.50	6.50
a.-e.	40ch any single	1.15	1.15

Alpine Plants of the Mt. Paektu Area — A1490

Designs: 10ch, Chrysoplenium sphaerospermum. 20ch, Campanula cephalotes. 40ch, Trollius macropetafus. 50ch, Sedum kamtschaticum.

1w, Dianthus repens.

1994, Apr. 25 ***Perf. 13¼***

3325-3329 A1490 Set of 5		4.25	1.15
3325a	Sheet of 3, #3325, 3327, #3330	4.00	1.60
3326a	Sheet of 3, #3326, 3328, 3329	4.00	1.60

Souvenir Sheet

3330 A1490 1w multicolored 3.25 1.35

A single stamp like that in No. 3330 is included in No. 3325a.

A1491

Int'l Olympic Committee Centenary — A1492

Designs: 10ch, Olympic rings, DPRK flag. 20ch, Pierre de Coubertin, founder. 30ch, Olympic flag, flame. 50ch, IOC Centenary Congress emblem.

No. 3335, Runner with Olympic Torch. No. 3336, Juan Antonio Samaranch, IOC President and new IOC headquarters.

1994, May 2 ***Perf. 12***

3331-3334 A1491 Set of 4 3.75 .90

Souvenir Sheets

Perf. 13¼

3335-3336 A1492 Set of 2 6.00 1.75

International Federation of Red Cross and Red Crescent Societies, 75th Anniv. — A1493

Designs: a, 10ch, Train, pedestrians crossing on overpass ("Prevention of traffic accident"). b, 20ch, Medical personnel in Red Cross boat ("Relief on the Sea"). c, 30ch, Man and girl planting tree ("Protection of the environment"). d, 40ch, Dam, sailboat on lake ("Protection of drought damage").

1994, May 5

3337 A1493 Strip of 4, #a.-d. 3.25 2.25

No. 3225 Surcharged

1994, May 29 Self-adhesive ***Imperf***

3341 A1452 1.60w on 1.50w Card of 6		28.00	28.00
a.-f.	1.60w on 1.50w, any single	7.00	7.00

A1494

Seals — A1495

Designs: 10ch, Northern fur seal (Callorhinus ursinus). 40ch, Southern elephant seal (Mirounga leonina). 60ch, Southern sea lion (Otaria byronia).

No. 3345: 20ch, California sea lion (Zalophus californianus). 30ch, Ringed seal (Phoca hispida). 50ch, Walrus (Odobenus rosmarus).

No. 3346, Harp seal (Pagophilus groenlandicus).

1994, June 10 ***Perf. 11½***

3342-3344 A1494 Set of 3		3.75	.85
3345 A1494 Sheet of 3		4.25	.90
a.	20ch multicolored	.75	.25
b.	30ch multicolored	1.15	.25
c.	50ch multicolored	2.00	.50

Souvenir Sheet

3346 A1495 1w multicolored 3.25 .90

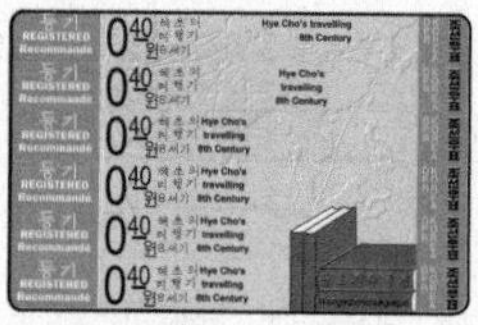

Stampcard — A1496

Map of Asia, books.

1994, June 17 ***Rouletted***

Self-adhesive

3347 A1496 Card of 6 stamps		10.00	10.00
a.-f.	40ch, any single	1.65	1.65

Hye Cho's 8th century travels in Central Asia and India.

Stampcard — A1497

Korean Tigers.

1994, June 18 ***Rouletted***

Self-adhesive

3348 A1497 Card of 6 stamps		30.00	30.00
a.-f.	1.40w, any single	5.00	5.00

A1498

Kim Il Sung's Leadership of the Korean Workers' Party, 30th Anniv. — A1499

Designs (all 40ch): a, Kim and supporters on cliff ledge, overlooking lake. b, Kim on mountain top, pointing across lake to Mt. Paektu. c, Kim on film set. d, Kim visiting restaurant. e, Kim reviewing tank corps. f, Kim at conference, shaking hands onstage as audience applauds.

1994, June 19 ***Perf. 12***

3349 A1498 Sheet of 6		8.00	2.50
3349g	Booklet pane of 6, 3 ea. #3349a-3349b	8.00	—
	Complete booklet, #3349g	8.50	
3349h	Booklet pane of 6, 3 ea. #3349c, 3349e	8.00	—
	Complete booklet, #3349h	8.50	
3349i	Booklet pane of 6, 3 ea. #3349d, 3349f	8.00	—
	Complete booklet, #3349i	8.50	

Souvenir Sheet

Perf. 11½

3350 A1499 1w multicolored 2.75 .90

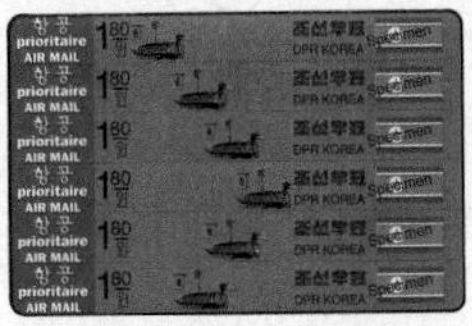
Stampcard — A1500

Turtle ship.

1994, June 20 *Rouletted*

Self-adhesive

3356 A1500 Card of 6 stamps 33.00 33.00
a.-f. 1.80w, any single 5.50 5.50

A1501

A1502

Mollusks — A1503

Designs: 30ch, Phalium strigatum. 40ch, Gomphina veneriformis.

No. 3359: a, 10ch, Cardium muticum, No. 3358 and the stamp found in No. 3361.

No. 3360: a, 20ch, Buccinum bayani, No. 3357 and the stamp found in No. 3361.

No. 3361: Neverita didyma

1994, June 25 *Perf. 12*

3357-3358 A1501 Set of 2 2.25 .60

Sheets of 3, #a.-c.

Perf. 13¼

3359-3360 A1502 Set of 2 13.00 9.00

Souvenir Sheet

3361 A1503 1.20w multicolored 4.50 1.30

For surcharge, see No. 4608.

Circus Acrobats — A1504

Designs: a, 10ch, Flying trapeze. b, 20ch, Rope dance. c, 30ch, Seesaw. d, 40ch, Unicycle show.

1994, July 7 *Perf. 11½*

3362 A1504 Sheet of 4, #a.-d. 3.75 1.15

A1505

Centenary of Birth of Kim Hyong Jik (1894-1926), Father of Kim Il Sung — A1506

1994, July 10 *Perf. 13¼*

3363 A1505 10ch multicolored .50 .25

Souvenir Sheet

Perf. 11¾x11½

3364 A1506 1w multicolored 3.25 1.15

Jeon Bong-jun & Battle Scene — A1507

1994, July 15 *Perf. 12*

3365 A1507 10ch multicolored .60 .25

Centenary of Kabo Peasant War.

Inoue Shuhachi — A1508

1994, July 30 *Perf. 13¼*

3366 A1508 1.20w multicolored 3.75 1.15

Award of the First International Kim Il Sung Prize to Inoue Shuhachi, Director General of the International Institute of the Juche Idea (Japan).

Workers Marching — A1509

1994, Aug. 1 *Perf. 11½*

3367 A1509 10ch multicolored .50 .25

Workers' Party Economic Strategy.

Fossils — A1510

Designs: 40ch (No. 3368), Onsong fish. 40ch (No. 3369), Metasequoia. 40ch (No. 3370), Mammoth teeth. 80ch, Archaeopteryx.

No. 3372 contains 2 each Nos. 3368, 3371. No. 3373 contains 2 each Nos.3369, 3371. No. 3374 contains 2 each Nos. 3370-3371.

1994, Aug. 10 *Perf. 12*

3368-3371 A1510 Set of 4 12.00 1.60
Complete booklet, 7 #3368 14.50
Complete booklet, 7 #3369 14.50
Complete booklet, 7 #3370 14.50
Complete booklet, 7 #3371 29.00

Souvenir Sheets

3372-3374 A1510 Set of 3 sheets 23.00 18.00

Medicinal Plants — A1511

Designs: 20ch, Acorus calamus. 30ch, Arctium lappa.

No. 3377 (133x86mm): a, 80ch, Lilium lancifolium. b, 80ch, Codonopsis lanceolata.

No. 3378 (56x83mm): 1w, Ginseng (Panax schinseng), vert.

1994, Aug. 25

3375-3376 A1511 Set of 2 1.60 .50
Complete booklet, 10 #3375 6.50
Complete booklet, 10 #3376 9.50

Souvenir Sheets

Perf. 13¼

3377-3378 A1511 Set of 2 sheets 7.25 1.75

Calisthenics — A1512

Gymnastic routines: a, 10ch, Ribbon twirling. b, 20ch, Ball. c, 30ch, Hoop. d, 40ch, Ribbon twirling (diff.). e, 50ch, Clubs.

1994, Sept. 7 *Perf. 12*

3379 A1512 Strip of 5 + label 5.00 1.35

No. 3379 was printed in sheets of 18, containing three No. 3379 in horizontal rows, with a different label in each row.

A1513

A1514

Zhou Enlai (1898-1976), Birth Centenary — A1515

Portraits of Zhou Enlai: 10ch, As student revolutionary (1919). 20ch, Arrival in Northern Shansi after Long March (1936). 30ch, At Conference of Asian and African Countries, Bandung, Indonesia (1955). 40ch, Speaking with children.

No. 3384: 80ch, Zhou Enlai and Kim Il Sung (1970).

No. 3385: 10ch, as #3380. a, 20ch, Zhou leading Nanchang Uprising (1927). 40ch, as #3383. 80ch, as #3384.

No. 3386: 20ch, as #3381. a, 20ch, Zhou and Mao Tzedong at airport, horiz. 30ch, as #3383. 80ch, as #3385b.

1994, Oct. 1 *Perf. 11½*

3380-3383 A1513 Set of 4 3.00 .90

Souvenir Sheets

Perf. 13¼

3384 A1514 80ch multicolored 2.50 .90

Perf 11½ (Vert. stamps), 11¾x12¼ (Horiz. stamps)

3385-3386 A1515 Set of 2 8.75 3.75

Nos. 3380-3383 were issued in sheets of 30 (6x5), with a label beneath each stamp.

World Environment Day — A1516

Each sheetlet contains two 50ch stamps with designs reflecting environmental issues. Themes: No. 3387, Prevention of air pollution. No. 3388, Preventation of water pollution. No. 3389, Protection of animal resources. No. 3390, Protection of forest resources.

1994, Oct. 5 *Perf. 12*

Sheets of 2

3387-3390 A1516 Set of 4 11.50 11.50

A1517

A1518

Kim Il Sung (1912-94) — A1519

Photos of Kim Il Sung (all 40ch).

No. 3391: a, As young man (1927). b, With Kim Jong Suk, his first wife and mother of Kim Jong Il. c, As captain in Soviet army (1944).

No. 3392: Speaking at lectern upon return to Pyongyang (1945). b, Sitting at desk in office of People's Committee of North Korea. c, Speaking at microphone.

1994, Oct. 8

3391 A1517 Sheet of 3, #a.-c. 3.75 1.75
3392 A1518 Sheet of 3, #a.-c. 3.75 1.75

Souvenir Sheet

Perf. 12¼x11¾

3393 A1519 1w multicolored 3.50 1.15

Compare with Nos. 3401-3403.

A1520

World Cup '94, 15th World Soccer Championship — A1521

Soccer Players Dribbling: 10ch, Player No. 4. 20ch, Player No. 5. 30ch, Player No. 6. 40ch, Player No. 7. 1w, Player No. 8. 1.50w, Player No. 9.

1994, Oct. 13 ***Perf. 13½***

3394-3399 A1520 Set of 6 11.00 5.50
3399a Sheet of 6, #3394-3399 16.50 9.00

Souvenir Sheet

3400 A1521 2.50w multicolored 6.75 3.75

Nos. 3394-3400 were also issued imperf. Value: set, $24; souvenir sheet, $15.

Nos. 3394-3399 exist in sheetlets on one, perf and imperf. Value: perf, $24; imperf, $47.50.

A1522

Kim Il Sung (1912-94) — A1523

Photos of Kim Il Sung (all 40ch).

No. 3401: a, Making radio broadcast (1950). b, With soldiers (1951). c, Clapping hands, crowd of soldiers in background (1953).

No. 3402: a, Talking with workers at Chongjin Steel Plant (1959). b, Standing in field, Onchon Plain. c, Talking on telephone.

No. 3403, Kim Il Sung and Kim Jong Il.

1994, Oct. 15 ***Perf. 12***

Sheets of 3

3401-3402 A1522 Set of 2 7.25 3.75

Perf. 12¼x11¾

3403 A1523 1w multicolored 3.25 1.35

Compare with Nos. 3391-3393.

A1524

North Korean-Chinese Friendship — A1525

1w, Kim Il Sung with Mao Zedong.

1994, Oct. 25 ***Perf. 11½***

3404 A1524 40ch multicolored 1.35 .50

Souvenir Sheet

Perf. 13¼

3405 A1525 1.20w multicolored 4.00 1.75

Composers — A1526

Designs: No. 3406, Ri Myon Sang (1908-89), score from *It Snows.* No. 3407, Pak Han Gyu (1919-92), score from *Nobody Knows.* No. 3408, Ludwig van Beethoven (1770-1827), score of *Piano Sonata No. 14.* No. 3409, Wolfgang Mozart (1756-91), score of *Symphony No. 39.*

1994, Nov. 25 ***Perf. 11½***

3406-3409 A1526 50ch Set of 4 6.00 2.00

For surcharge, see No. 4550.

National Emblem — A1527

1994, Dec. 10 ***Perf. 12***

3410 A1527 1w dp bl green 3.75 .90
3411 A1527 3w deep brown 7.25 2.25

For surcharge, see No. 4575.

A1528

A1529

Gold Medal Winners, Winter Olympic Games, Lillehammer — A1530

Designs: 10ch, Pernilla Wiberg (Sweden), Alpine combined skiing. 20ch, Deborah Compagnoni (Italy), Slalom. 30ch, Oksana Baiul (Ukraine), Figure skating. 40ch, Dan Jansen (USA), Speed skating. 1w (No. 3416), Yubow Jegorowa (Russia), Cross-country skiing. 1w (No. 3417), Bonnie Blair (USA), Speed skating.

No. 3418, Bjorn Dāehlie and Norwegian skiing team, Alpine combined skiing. No. 3419, Jekaterina Gordejewa and Serge Grinkow (Russia), Pairs figure skating. No. 3420, Vreni Schneider (Switzerland), Alpine combined skiing. No. 3421, Georg Hackl (Germany), Luge. No. 3422, Jens Weissflog (Germany), Ski jumping. No. 3423, Masashi Abe, Takanori Kono, Kenji Ogiwara (Japan), Cross-country skiing.

No. 3424, Tommy Moe (USA), Downhill skiing.

1994, Dec. 20 ***Perf. 13¼***

3412-3417 A1528 Set of 6 10.00 2.75
3417a Sheet of 6, #3412-3417 11.00 4.50

Souvenir Sheets

3418-3423 A1529 1w Set of 6 16.50 5.50
3424 A1530 2.50w multicolored 7.25 1.35

New Year — Year of the Pig — A1531

Designs: 20ch, Pigs relaxing. 40ch, Pigs going to work.

Each 1w: No. 3427, Pigs carrying pumpkin. No. 3428, Piglets bowing to adult pig.

1995, Jan. 1 ***Perf. 11½***

3425-3426 A1531 Set of 2 1.40 .65
3426a Sheet of 4, 2 ea #3425-3426 3.00 3.00

Souvenir Sheets

3427-3428 A1531 Set of 2 5.00 4.00

No. 3426a inscribed in margins for Singapore '95 Intl. Stamp Exhibition. Issued, 9/1.

World Tourism Org., 20th Anniv. — A1532

Designs, each 30ch: a, Tower of the Juche Idea, Pyongyang. b, Pison Falls on Mt. Myohyang. c, Myogilsang (relief carving of Buddha), Mt. Kumgang.

1995, Jan. 2 ***Perf. 12¼***

3429 A1532 Sheet of 3, #a.-c. + label 3.00 .90

Mangyondae, Badasgou, Emblem — A1533

1995, Jan. 22 ***Perf. 11½***

3430 A1533 40ch multicolored 1.10 .90

70th anniversary of 250-Mile Journey for the Restoration of the Fatherland.

A1534

A1535

A1536

Kim Jong Il, 53rd Birthday — A1537

Designs: 10ch, Jong Il Peak (Mt. Paekdu) and 50th Birthday Ode Monument.

No. 3432 (horiz.): a, 20ch Kim Il Sung and Kim Jong Il; b, 80ch Kim Jong Il inspecting the West Sea Barrage. No. 3433 (vert.): a, 40ch Kim Jong Il in business suit; b, Kim Jong Il in uniform in Taesongsan Martyrs' Cemetary. No. 3434: 1w, Kim Jong Il inspecting the Ryongsong Machine Complex.

1995, Feb. 16 ***Perf. 12¼***

3431 A1534 10ch multicolored .25 .25

Souvenir Sheets

3432 A1535 Sheet of 2, #a.-b. 2.10 1.50
3433 A1536 Sheet of 2, #a.-b. 1.90 1.25
3434 A1537 1w multicolored 2.10 2.10

Mausoleum of King Tangun — A1537a

King Tangun and Mausoleum — A1537b

Designs: 10ch, Monument. 30ch, Straight bronze dagger tower. 50ch, Monument inscribed with King Tangun's exploits. 70ch, Gate of mausoleum.

50ch, King Tangun and Mausoleum.

1995, Feb. 25 ***Perf. 12¼***

3434A-3434D A1537a Set of 4 3.25 3.25

Souvenir Sheet

Perf. 11½

3434E A1537b 1.40w multi 3.00 3.00

Lighthouses — A1538

Designs: 20ch, Tamaedo Lighthouse. 1.20w, Phido Lighthouse, West Sea Barrage.

1995, Mar. 10 *Perf. 13½*
3435-3436 A1538 Set of 2 4.00 1.75

Mushrooms — A1539

Designs: 20ch, Russula virescens. 30ch, Russula atropurpurea.
1w, Caesar's Mushroom (Amanita caesarea.

1995, Mar. 25
3437-3438 A1539 Set of 2 1.75 .60
3437a Booklet pane of 10 #3437 3.50 —
Complete booklet, #3437a 4.00
3438a Booklet pane of 10 #3438 17.00 —
Complete booklet, #3438a 17.50 —

Souvenir Sheet

3439 A1539 1w multicolored 4.50 2.50

For surcharges, see Nos. 4527-4528.

Tree Planting Day — A1540

1995, Apr. 6 *Perf. 11½*
3440 A1540 10ch multicolored .50 .25
a. Sheet of 6 3.00 3.00

No. 3225 Surcharged with New Values

1995, Apr. 8 *Rouletted*
3441 Card of 6 stamps 6.00 6.00
a.-f. 30ch on 1.50w, any single 1.00 1.00

Finlandia '95.

Mangyongdae, Birthplace of Kim Il Sung A1541

Tower of Juche Idea and Kimilsungia A1542

Kim Il Sung and Children A1543

1995, Apr. 15 *Perf. 11½*
3442 A1541 10ch multicolored .25 .25
a. Sheet of 6 1.35 1.35
b. Booklet pane of 5 — —
Complete booklet, #3442b —
3443 A1542 40ch multicolored 1.15 .90
a. Sheet of 6 6.75 6.75
b. Booklet pane of 5 — —
Complete booklet, #3443b —

Souvenir Sheet

Perf. 13½

3444 A1543 1w multicolored 3.25 3.25

Kim Il Sung, 82nd birthday. For surcharge, see No. 4610.

A1544

Kim Il Sung's Visit to China, 20th Anniv. A1545

Designs: 10ch, Deng Xiaoping waving. 20ch, Deng sitting in armchair, vert.
50ch, Kim and Deng sitting in armchairs.

1995, Apr. 17 *Perf. 13½*
3445-3446 A1544 Set of 2 1.15 1.15

Souvenir Sheet

Perf. 11½

3447 A1545 50ch multicolored 1.75 1.75

A1546

A1547

Asian-African Conf., Bandung, 40th Anniv. — A1548

Designs: 10ch, Site of Bendung Conference. 50ch, Kim Il Sung receiving honorary doctorate from Indonesia University.
1w, Kim Il Sung and Kim Jong Il at Conference 40th Anniversary ceremony.

1995, Apr. 18 *Perf. 11½*
3448 A1546 10ch multicolored .25 .25
3449 A1547 50ch multicolored 1.60 .65

Souvenir Sheet

3450 A1548 1w multicolored 3.25 3.25

A1549

Int'l Sports and Cultural Festival for Peace, Pyongyang — A1550

Designs: 20ch, Emblem. 40ch (No. 3452), Dancer. 40ch (No. 3453), Inoki Kanji, leader of Sports Peace Party of Japan.
1w, Nikidozan, wrestling champion.

1995, Apr. 28
3451-3453 A1549 Set of 3 2.75 1.75
3451a Sheet of 3, 1 #3451 + 2 #3452 2.75 1.75
3453a Sheet of 3, 2 #3453 + 1 as #3454 6.50 3.75

Souvenir Sheet

3454 A1550 1w multicolored 3.25 3.25

Amethyst — A1551

1995, May 2
3455 A1551 20ch multicolored .90 .40
a. Sheet of 6 6.75 6.75
b. Booklet pane of 10 9.00 —
Complete booklet, #3455b 10.00

Finlandia '95. No. 3455a marginal selvage contains a mountain valley scene and is inscribed "Finlandia 95." No. 3455b has selvage around the block of 10 stamps.

White Animals — A1552

Each 40ch: No. 3456, Tree sparrow (*Passer montanus*). No. 3457, Sea slug (*Stichopus japonicus*).

1995, May 12 *Perf. 13½*
3456-3457 A1552 Set of 2 2.25 1.35
3457a Sheet of 6, 3 #3456 + 3 #3457 8.25

Fossils — A1553

Designs: a, 50ch, Ostrea. b, 1w, Cladophiebis (fern).

1995, May 15 *Perf. 12*
3458 A1553 Pair, #a.-b. 3.75 1.60
c. Booklet pane of 7, 4 #3458a, 3 #3458b — —
Complete booklet, #3458c —

Traditional Games — A1554

Designs: 30ch, Chess. 60ch, Taekwondo. 70ch, Yut.

1995, May 20 *Perf. 11½*
3459-3461 A1554 Set of 3 4.75 1.75
3459a Sheet of 2 #3459 + label 1.60 1.60
3460a Sheet of 2 #3460 + label 3.75 3.75
3461a Sheet of 2 #3461 + label 5.50 5.50
3461b Booklet pane of 6, 2 ea. #3459-3461 9.50 —
Complete booklet. #3461b 10.00

General Assoc. of Koreans in Japan, 40th Anniv. — A1555

1995, May 25
3462 A1555 1w multicolored 3.25 .85

Atlanta '96 — A1556

Designs, each 50ch: No. 3463, Weight lifter. No. 3464, Boxing.
1w, Marksman shooting clay pigeon.

1995, June 2
3463-3464 A1556 Set of 2 3.00 1.15
3464a Sheet of 2 #3463 + 2 #3464 6.75 6.75

Souvenir Sheet

3465 A1556 1w multicolored 4.50 4.50

Fungi — A1557

Designs: 40ch, Russula citrina. 60ch, Craterellus cornucopioides. 80ch, Coprinus comatus.

1995, July 1 *Perf. 13¼*
3466-3468 A1557 Set of 3 6.00 1.75
3466a Booklet pane of 10 #3466 13.00 —
Complete booklet, #3466a 13.50
3467a Booklet pane of 10 #3467 19.00 —
Complete booklet, #3467a 20.00
3468a Booklet pane of 10 #3468 26.00 —
Complete booklet, #3468a 27.00

For surcharge, see No. 4553.

A1558

A1559

A1560

Kim Il Sung, 1st Death Anniv. — A1561

No. 3469, 1w, Kim addressing conference for development of agriculture in African countries, 1981.
No. 3470: a, 10ch, Kim greeting Robert Mugabe, President of Zimbabwe. b, 70ch, Kim with King Norodom Sihanouk of Cambodia.
No. 3471: a, 20ch, Kim receiving honorary doctorate, Algeria University, 1975. b, 50ch, Kim with Fidel Castro, 1986.
No. 3472: a, 30ch, Kim talking with Ho Chi Minh, 1958. b, 40ch, Kim greeting Che Guevara, 1960.

1995, July 8

3469 A1558 1w multicolored 2.50 2.50
3470 A1559 Sheet of 2, #a.-b. 2.00 2.00
3471 A1560 Sheet of 2, #a.-b. 2.25 2.25
3472 A1561 Sheet of 2, #a.-b. 1.75 1.75

Liberation, 50th Anniv. — A1562

Designs: 10ch, Korean army officer. 30ch, Map of Korea, family. 60ch, Hero of the DPRK medal.

No. 3476, a, 20ch revolutionary soldier, #3414, 2 each.

No. 3477, a, 40ch demonstrators, #3474, 2 each.

1995, Aug. 15 ***Perf. 11½***

3473-3475 A1562 Set of 3 2.50 1.15
3475a Booklet pane of 5, #3473-3475, 3476a, 3477a 4.25 —
Complete booklet, #3475a 4.50

Souvenir Sheets

3476 Sheet of 4 2.25 2.25
a. A1562 20ch multicolored .50 .25
3477 Sheet of 4 4.25 4.25
a. A1562 40ch multicolored .90 .45

1st Military World Games — A1564

1995, Sept. 4

3479 A1564 40ch multicolored .90 .45

A1565

A1566

Korea-China Friendship — A1567

Designs: No. 3480, 80ch, Kim Il Sung and Mao Zedong. No. 3481, 80ch, Kim and Zhou Enlai.

No. 3482: a, 50ch, Kim and Zhou Enlai. b, 50ch, Kim receiving gift from Deng Ying-Chao, Premier of the State Council of the People's Republic of China.

1995, Oct. 1 ***Perf. 12¼***

3480 A1565 80ch multicolored 1.35 1.35
3481 A1566 80ch multicolored 1.35 1.35
3482 A1567 Sheet of 2, #a.-b. 2.00 2.00

A1568

Korean Workers' Party, 50th Anniv. — A1569

Designs: 10ch, Korean Workers' Party Emblem and Banner. 20ch, Statue of three workers holding party symbols. 40ch, Monument to founding of Party.

No. 3486, Kim Il Sung.

1995, Oct. 10 ***Perf. 11½***

3483-3485 A1568 Set of 3 1.45 .75

Souvenir Sheet

Perf. 13½

3486 A1569 1w multicolored 2.50 2.50

Kim Il Sung's Return to Korea, 50th Anniv. — A1570

Design: 50ch, Arch of Triumph, Pyongyang.

1995, Oct. 14 ***Perf. 11½***

3487 A1570 10ch multicolored .55 .25

Great Tunny — A1571

Fish

No. 3488, Great tunny. No. 3489, Pennant coralfish. No. 3490, Needlefish. No. 3491, Bullrout. No. 3492, Imperial butterfly fish.

1995 ***Perf. 13¼***

3488 A1571 40ch choc & blk 1.25 .35
3489 A1571 50ch choc & blk 1.50 .40
3490 A1571 50ch choc & blk 1.50 .40
3491 A1571 60ch choc & blk 1.75 .45
3492 A1571 5w choc & blk 15.00 3.50
a. Horiz. strip of 5, #3488-3492 22.50 5.00

Machines

10ch, 40-ton truck *Kumsusan.* 20ch, Large bulldozer. 30ch, Hydraulic excavator. 40ch, Wheel loader, vert. 10w, Tractor *Chollima-80,* vert.

3493 A1571 10ch choc & blk .35 .25
a. Perf. 11¼ — —
3494 A1571 20ch choc & blk .75 .25
3495 A1571 30ch choc & blk 1.00 .25
3496 A1571 40ch choc & blk 1.60 .30
3497 A1571 10w choc & blk 27.50 7.50
a. Horiz. strip of 5, #3493-3497 32.50 10.00

Animals

30ch, Giraffe, vert. 40ch, Ostrich, vert. 60ch, Bluebuck, vert. 70ch, Bactrian camel. 3w, Indian rhinoceros.

3498 A1571 30ch choc & blk .85 .25
3499 A1571 40ch choc & blk 1.10 .35
3500 A1571 60ch choc & blk 1.60 .50
3501 A1571 70ch choc & blk 2.00 .55
3502 A1571 3w choc & blk 8.00 2.25
a. Horiz. strip of 5, #3498-3502 16.00 4.00

Sculptures of Children

30ch, Boy and pigeon, vert. 40ch, Boy and goose, vert. 60ch, Girl and geese vert. 70ch, Boy and girl comparing heights, vert. 2w, Boy and girl with soccer ball, vert.

3503 A1571 30ch choc & blk .85 .25
3504 A1571 40ch choc & blk 1.10 .35
3505 A1571 60ch choc & blk 1.60 .50
3506 A1571 70ch choc & blk 2.00 .50
3507 A1571 2w choc & blk 5.75 1.60
a. Vert. strip of 5, #3503-3507 13.00 4.00

Buildings

60ch, Pyongyang Circus. 70ch, Country apartment building. 80ch, Pyongyang Hotel. 90ch, Urban apt. towers. 1w, Sosan Hotel.

3508 A1571 60ch choc & blk 1.75 .50
3509 A1571 70ch choc & blk 2.00 .55
3510 A1571 80ch choc & blk 2.25 .65
3511 A1571 90ch choc & blk 2.50 .75
3512 A1571 1w choc & blk 2.75 .85
a. Horiz. strip of 5, #3508-3512 13.00 4.00

Issued: Nos. 3488-3492, 10/20; Nos. 3493-3497, 11/2; Nos. 3498-3502, 11/20; Nos. 3503-3507, 12/5; Nos. 3508-3512, 12/15.

Nos. 3488-3492, 3493-3497, 3498-3502, 3503-3507, and 3508-3512 were printed in vertical (Nos. 3503-3507) or horizontal se-tenant strips within their sheets.

For surcharge, see No. 4259C.

No. 3512B

No. 3512D

1995, Oct. 20 ***Rouletted x Imperf***

Stampcards

Self-Adhesive

3512B black, *gold,* card of 8 6.00 6.00
a. 20ch single stamp .75 .75
3512D card of 2 50.00 50.00
e. 20ch red, *gold* — —
f. 17.80w On 20ch, red, *gold* — —

50th anniversary of the first North Korean stamps.

Kim Hyong Gwon, Kim Il Sung's Uncle, 90th Birth Anniv. — A1572

1995, Nov. 4 ***Perf. 12½x12***

3513 A1572 1w multicolored 2.50 1.35

New Year — A1573

Rodents: a, 20ch, Guinea pig. b, 20ch, Squirrel. 30ch, White mouse.

1996, Jan. 1 ***Perf. 11½***

3514 A1573 Strip of 3, #a.-c. 2.75 .75

No. 3514 was issued in sheetlets of eight stamps, two each Nos. 3514a-3514b and four No. 3514c, plus one center label picturing an idyllic landscape, inscribed "1996."

League of Socialist Working Youth, 50th Anniv. — A1574

1996, Jan. 17

3517 A1574 10ch multicolored .50 .25

Reconstruction of Tomb of King Wanggon of Koryo — A1575

Designs: 30ch, Restoration monument, horiz. 40ch, Entrance gate to royal cemetery. 50ch, King Wanggon's tomb, horiz.

1996, Jan. 30

3518-3520 A1575 Set of 3 3.25 .90

Teng Li-Chuang (Chinese Singer) — A1576

1996, Feb. 1 ***Perf. 13¼***

3521 A1576 40ch multicolored 1.35 .50

3rd Asian Winter Games, Harbin, China — A1577

Designs, each 30ch: a, Kim Song Sun, Korean speed skater. b, Ye Qiaobo, Chinese sprint skater.

1996, Feb 4 ***Perf. 11½***

3522 A1577 Sheet of 2, #a.-b. 3.25 .50

See No. 3556.

A1578

Kim Jong Il, 54th Birthday — A1579

10ch, Jong Il Peak and *Kimjongilia.* 80ch, Kim Jong Il and soldiers.

1996, Feb. 16

3523 A1578 10ch multicolored .50 .25

Souvenir Sheet

Perf. 13¼

3524 A1579 80ch multicolored 2.50 .75

5th Paektusan Prize International Figure Skating Championship. A1580

Various pairs figure skaters: 10ch, 20ch, 30ch.
50ch, Women's individual skating.

1996, Feb. 17 *Perf. 11½*

3525-3527	A1580 Set of 3	1.75	.55
3527a	Booklet pane of 4, #3525-3527, 3528a	5.00	—
	Complete booklet, #3527a	5.50	

Souvenir Sheet

3528	Sheet of 4	3.25	.90
a.	A1580 50ch multi	3.00	

Folk Tales — A1581

Screen painting by Ryu Suk: 8 stamps in continuous design, within 206mmx84mm skeetlet.

1996, Mar. 2

3529	Sheet of 8	4.50	2.00
a.-h.	A1581 any single	.55	.25

Agrarian Reform Law, 50th Anniv. — A1582

1996, Mar. 5

3530 A1582 10ch multicolored .50 .25

No. 3530 was issued in sheetlets of six, containing 5 No. 3530 and a label depicting a music score, *Song of Plowing.*

First North Korean Stamps, 50th Anniv. — A1583

1996, Mar. 12

3531 A1583 1w multicolored 3.00 .80

Yangzhou, China — A1584

Taihou Lake, China — A1585

1996, Mar. 20

3532	A1584 50ch multicolored	1.60	.50
3533	A1585 50ch multicolored	1.60	.50

Chinese Imperial Post, Centennial.

A1586

Kim Il Sung, 83rd Birthday — A1587

Designs: 10ch, Birthplace, Mangyondae.
1w, Portrait of Kim Il Sung.

1996, Apr. 15

3534 A1586 10ch multicolored .50 .25

Souvenir Sheet

3535 A1587 1w multicolored 3.00 .80

China '96 Int'l Stamp Exhib., Beijing — A1588

Designs: No. 3536, Seacoast gateway. No. 3537, Haiyin Pool.
60ch. Pantuo Stone.

1996, Apr. 22 *Perf. 13½*

3536-3537 A1588 10ch Set of 2 .50 .25

Souvenir Sheet

Perf. 11½

3538 A1588 60ch multicolored 1.45 .55

Folk Games — A1589

Designs: 20ch, Kicking stone handmill. 40ch, Shuttlecock. 50ch, Sledding.

1996, May 2

3539-3541	A1589 Set of 3	3.25	.90
3539a-3541a	Set of 3 sheets of 2 + label	6.50	6.50

Assoc. for the Restoration of the Fatherland, 60th Anniv. — A1590

1996, May 5

3542	A1590 10ch multicolored	.50	.25
a.	Sheet of 5 #3542 + label	2.25	1.35

Ri Po Ik — A1591

1996, May 31 *Perf. 13½*

3543 A1591 1w multicolored 2.75 5.00

Ri Po Ik, Kim Il Sung's grandmother, 125th birth anniv.

Polar Animals — A1592

Designs, 50ch: No. 3544a, Arctic fox. No. 3544b, Polar bear. No. 3545a, Emperor penguins. No. 3546b, Leopard seals.

1996, June 2 *Perf. 11½*

3544-3545 A1592 Set of 2 sheets 6.00 3.75

A1593

Korea Children's Union, 50th Anniv. — A1594

Designs: 10ch, Boy saluting.
1w, Painting of Kim Il Sung with Children's Union members, *There's Nothing to Envy in the World.*

1996, June 6

3546 A1593 10ch multicolored .50 .25

Souvenir Sheet

Perf. 11½x12

3547 A1594 1w multicolored 2.75 .80

Locomotives A1595

Designs, all 50ch: No. 3548, Steam locomotive, facing left. No. 3549, Electric locomotive, facing right. No. 3550, Steam locomotive, facing right. No. 3551, Electric locomotive, facing left.

1996, June 6 *Perf. 11½*

3548-3551 A1595 Set of 4 3.25 1.15

Capex '96 World Philatelic Exhibition. For surcharge, see No. 4551.

Kim Chol Ju, Kim Il Sung's Brother, 80th Birth Anniv. — A1596

1996, June 12 *Perf. 13¼*

3552 A1596 1.50w multicolored 4.00 1.75

Open Book — A1597

1996, June 15 *Perf. 13½*

3553 A1597 40ch multicolored 1.00 .50

760th anniversary of publication of the *Complete Collection of Buddhist Scriptures Printed from 80,000 Wooden Blocks.*

Labor Law, 50th Anniv. — A1598

1996, June 24 *Perf. 11½*

3554 A1598 50ch multicolored .50 .40

Seasonal Birds — A1599

Designs: 10ch, Broad-billed roller. 40ch, Tricolor flycatcher. 50ch, Cuckoo.

1996, July 5

3555 A1599 Sheet of 3, #a.-c. 3.75 1.75

See No. 3569.

3rd Asian Winter Games, Harbin, China (2nd issue) — A1600

Design same as No. 3522, but with a new 30ch value picturing Ye Qiaobo replacing No, 3522b

1996, July 5

3556	A1600 Sheet of 2	1.60	.90
a.	30ch multi	.80	.40

Kumsusan Memorial Palace — A1601

Outdoor Crowd, Statue of Kim Il Sung — A1602

Hymn, *The Leader will be with us forever* — A1603

Statue of Kim Il Sung in hall of the Kumsusan Memorial Palace — A1604

1996, July 8 ***Perf. 12***
3557 A1601 10ch multicolored .25 .25

Souvenir Sheets

Perf. 13¼, 12 (#3558)

3558 A1602 1w multicolored 2.75 .90
3559 A1603 1w multicolored 2.75 .90
3560 A1604 1w multicolored 2.75 .90

Kim Il Sung, 2nd Death Anniv.

A1605

Designs, both 10ch: No. 3561, Kim Il Sung meeting Mao Zedong of China, 1954. No. 3562, Kim Il Sung meeting Jiang Zemin of China, 1991.
80ch, Kim shaking hands with Deng Xiaoping of China, horiz.

1996, July 11 ***Perf. 11½***
3561-3562 A1605 Set of 2 .50 .25

Souvenir Sheet

3563 A1605 80ch multicolored 2.00 .90

26th Olympic Games, Atlanta — A1606

Designs, each 50ch: No. 3564, Soccer. No. 3565, Tennis. No. 3566, Hammer throw. No. 3567, Baseball.

1996, July 19 ***Perf. 12¼***
3564-3567 A1606 Set of 4 5.00 1.75

Sexual Equality Law, 50th Anniv. — A1607

1996, July 30 ***Perf. 11½***
3568 A1607 10ch multicolored .25 .25

Seasonal Bird Type

Designs: 10ch, Crested shelduck. 40ch, Demoiselle crane. 50ch, White swan.

1996, Aug. 5
3569 A1600 Sheet of 3, #a.-c. 2.50 1.15

Industrial Nationalization, 50th Anniv. — A1608

1996, Aug. 10 ***Perf. 11½***
3570 A1608 50ch multicolored .85 .40

UNICEF, 50th Anniv. — A1609

Designs: 10ch, Boy with ball, net. 20ch, Boy playing with building blocks. 50ch, Boy eating meal, holding watermelon slice. 60ch, Girl playing accordion.

1996, Aug. 20
3571-3574 A1609 Set of 4 2.50 1.00

Nos. 3571-3574 were issued in sheets of four, one containing 2 No. 3571, 1 No. 3574 and a label, the other containing 2 No. 3572, 1 No. 3573 and a different label.

1st Asian Gymnastics Championship, Changsha, China — A1610

No. 3575: a, Pae Kil Su (N. Korea), men's pommel. b, Chen Cui Ting (China), rings. c, Li Jing (China). d, Kim Kwang Suk (N. Korea), asymmetrical bars.

1996, Sept. 24
3575 A1610 15ch Sheet of 4, #a-d, + 2 labels 1.35 .55

Kim Il Sung University, 50th Anniv. — A1611

1996, Oct. 1
3579 A1611 10ch multicolored .50 .25

Tiger — A1612

Designs, 50ch: No. 3580, Tiger. No. 3581, Royal spoonbill.
80ch: Stylized dove/hand nurturing sapling, growing out of planet Earth.

1996, Oct. 13
3580-3581 A1612 Set of 2 2.75 .65

Souvenir Sheet

3582 A1612 80ch multicolored 6.00 1.35

Nos. 3580-3581 were each printed in sheets of four, containing three stamps and a label.

Down-with-Imperialism Union, 70th Anniv. — A1613

1996, Oct. 17
3583 A1613 10ch multicolored .25 .25

A1614

Designs: a, 30ch Huang Ji Gwang. b, 10ch, Score of theme song of film *Red Mountain Ridge*. c, 30ch Huang Ji Gwang heroically dying in battle.

1996, Oct. 25
3584 A1614 Sheet of 3, #a.-c. 1.75 .90

Hwang Ji Gwang, Chinese Volunteer, hero of Korean War, 44th death anniiv.

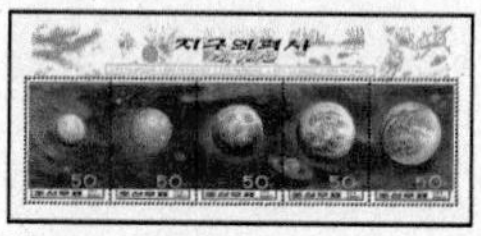

History of the Earth — A1615

Each 50ch: a, Earth 7.5 billion years ago. b, 4.5-5 billion years ago. c, 450 million-4.5 billion years ago. d, 100-450 million years ago. e, 100 million years ago to the present.

1996, Nov. 1 ***Perf. 13½***
3585 A1615 Sheet of 5, #a.-e. 7.25 3.75

Freshwater Fish — A1616

Designs, 20ch: No. 3586, Japanese eel. No. 3587, Menada gray mullet.
80ch, Silver carp.

1996, Nov. 20 ***Perf. 11½***
3586-3587 A1616 Set of 2 1.35 .35

Souvenir Sheet

3588 A1616 80ch multicolored 2.75 .75

Kim Jong Il' Appointment as Supreme Commander of the People's Army, 5th Anniv. — A1617

1996, Dec. 24 ***Perf. 12***
3589 A1617 20ch multicolored .55 .25

New Year — Year of the Ox — A1618

Designs, 70ch: No. 3590, *Ox Driver*, by Kim Tu Ryang. No. 3591, Bronze ritual plate decorated with a tiger and two bulls. No. 3592, Cowboy and bull. No. 3593, Cowboy playing flute, sitting on bull.
80ch, *Kosong People's Support to the Front.*

1997, Jan. 1 ***Perf. 11¾***
3590-3593 A1618 Set of 4 7.25 1.75
3591a, 3593a Set of 2 sheets 7.25 1.75

Souvenir Sheet

3594 A1618 80ch multicolored 2.75 .75

No. 3591a contains Nos. 3590 and 3591, with a central label depicting a bull's head surrounded by zodiacal signs. No. 3593a contains Nos. 3592 and 3593, with the same label.

Flowers and Butterflies, by Nam Kye-u (1811-88) — A1619

Designs, each 50ch: a, Three butterflies, flower. b, One small butterfly, flower. c, Large butterfly, leaves.

1997, Jan. 5 ***Perf. 12¼x11¾***
3595 A1619 Sheetlet of 3, #a.-c. 4.25 .90
d. Booklet pane of 6, 2 each #3595a-3595b 8.25 —
Complete booklet, #3595d 8.25

Paintings of Cats and Dogs — A1620

Designs, 50ch: No. 3598, Puppy in basket, touching noses with kitten. No. 3599, Two dogs in basket, kitten.
No. 3600: a, Cat in basket, with dog and skein of yarn alongside. b, Kitten in basket with fruit and flowers, puppy alongside.

1997, Jan. 25 ***Perf. 11¾x12¼***
3598-3599 A1620 Set of 2 3.00 .90

Sheets of 4

3600 Sheet of 4, #3598, 3600b, 2 #3600a 3.25 1.35
a. A1620 50ch multicolored 1.35
b. A1620 50ch multicolored 1.35
3601 Sheet of 4, #3599, #3600a, 2 #3600b 3.25 1.35

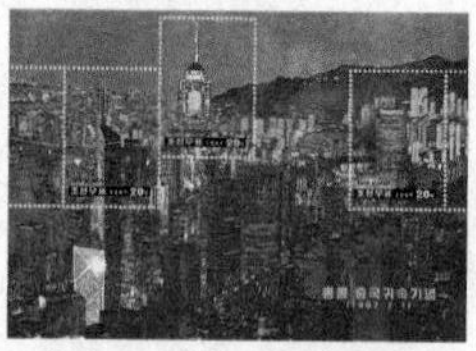

Return of Hong Kong to China — A1621

Hong Kong nightscape, each 20ch: a, Skyscraper with double antennae. b, Skyscraper with single spire. c, Round skyscraper, high-rise apartment buildings.

1997, Feb. 1 ***Perf. 13½***
3602 A1621 Sheet of 3, #a.-c. 2.25 .60

A1622

Kim Jong Il, 55th Birthday — A1623

Designs: 10ch, Birthplace, Mt. Paekdu.

No. 3604, Kim Il Sung and Kim Jong Il with farm machine. No. 3605, Kim Jong Il inspecting a Korean People's Army unit.

1997, Feb. 16 *Perf. 12*
3603 A1622 10ch multicolored .50 .25

Souvenir Sheets

3604-3605 A1623 1w Set of 2 5.00 1.60

6th Paektusan Prize Int'l Figure Skating Championships, Pyongyang A1624

Pairs skating, different routines, 50ch: No. 3606, pale reddish brown. No. 3607, blue. No. 3608, green.

1997, Feb. 17 *Perf. 11½*
3606-3608 A1624 Set of 3 3.75 .90
3607a Sheet of 4, 2 ea #3606, 3607 5.00 1.35
3608a Booklet pane of 6, 2 ea. #3606-3608 7.25 —
Complete booklet, #3608a 7.75
3608b Sheet of 4, 2 ea #3607, 3608 5.00 1.35

Kye Sun Hui, Women's Judo Gold Medalist, 1996 Summer Olympic Games, Atlanta — A1625

1997, Feb. 20
3611 A1625 80ch multicolored 2.25 .55
3611a Booklet pane of 5 #3611 — —
Complete booklet, #3611a —

Choe Un A — A1626

1997, Feb. 25
3612 A1626 80ch multicolored 2.75 .55
a. Booklet pane of 5
Complete booklet, #3612a

Issued to honor Choe Un A, a seven-year-old entrant in the World Go Championships.

Apricots — A1627

Various types of apricots, 50ch: No. 3613, Prunus ansu. No. 3614, Prunus mandshurica. No. 3615, Prunus armeniaca. No. 3616, Prunus sibirica.

1997, Mar. 4 *Perf. 11¼*
3613-3616 A1627 Set of 4 5.50 1.35
3616a Sheet of 8, 2 ea#3613-3616 11.00 2.75

Foundation of Korean National Assoc., 80th Anniv. — A1628

1997, Mar. 23 *Perf. 12¼*
3617 A1628 10ch lt brn & dk grn .50 .25
a. Sheet of 8 3.75 .90

A1629

Reforestation Day, 50th Anniv. — A1630

Designs: 10ch, Pine sapling.
No. 3619, Kim Il Sung planting sapling on Munsu Hill.

1997, Apr. 6 *Perf. 11½*
3618 A1629 10ch multicolored .50 .25
Complete booklet, 8 #3618

Souvenir Sheet
Perf. 13¼

3619 A1630 1w multicolored 2.75 .85

A1631

A1632

Kim Il Sung, 85th Birth Anniv. — A1633

Designs: 10ch, Kim's birthplace, Mangyongdae. 20ch, Sliding rock, horiz. 40ch, Warship Rock, horiz.
Each 1w: No. 3623, Painting of Kim among crowd symbolic of the Korean people. No. 3624, Kim in business suit, surrounded by flowers.

1997, Apr. 15 *Perf. 12¼*
3620-3622 A1631 Set of 3 1.75 .50

Souvenir Sheets
Perf. 13¼ (#3623), 11¾x12¼ (#3624)

3623 A1632 1w multicolored 2.50 .85
3624 A1633 1w multicolored 2.50 .85

A1634

Korean People's Army, 65th Anniv. — A1635

Designs: 10ch, KPA cap badge, rockets and jet fighters.
1w, Kim Il Sung and Kim Jong Il at military review.

1997, Apr. 25 *Perf. 11½*
3625 A1634 10ch multicolored .50 .25

Souvenir Sheet
Perf. 12¼x11¾

3626 A1635 1w multicolored 2.75 .85

A1636

North-South Agreement, 25th Anniv. — A1637

Designs: 10ch, Map of Korea.
1w, Monument to Kim Il Sung's Autograph, Phanmunjom.

1997, May 4 *Perf. 11½*
3627 A1636 10ch multicolored .90 .25

Souvenir Sheet
Perf. 12x11½

3628 A1637 1w multicolored 3.75 .85

A1638

Each 10ch: No. 3629, Tower of Juche Idea, flag. No. 3630, Man with flag. No. 3631, Soldier, miner, farmer, scientist.

1997, May 25 *Perf. 12¼x12*
3629-3631 A1638 Set of 3 .85 .40

Int'l Friendship Exhib., Myohyang Mountains — A1639

Each 70ch: No. 3632, Exhibition Center. No. 3633, Statue of Kim Il Sung in exhibition entrance hall. No. 3634, Ivory sculpture *Native House in Mangyongdae*. No. 3635, Stuffed crocodile holding wooden cups, with ashtray.

1997, May 30 *Perf. 11¾*
3632-3635 A1639 Set of 4 sheets 6.75 4.50

Battle of Poconbo, 60th Anniv. — A1640

1997, June 4 *Perf. 11½*
3636 A1640 40ch multicolored 1.15 .35
a. Sheet of 6 6.75 6.75
b. Booklet pane of 6 #3636 6.75 —
Complete booklet, #3636b 7.25

No. 3636b contains six stamps in a horizontal strip, within decorative selvage.

Rice Transplantation, Mirin Plain, 50th Anniv. — A1641

Each 1w: No. 3637, Kim Il Sung transplanting rice. No. 3638, Kim Il Sung inspecting a rice-transplanting machine.

1997, June 7 *Perf. 13¼*
3637-3638 A1641 Set of 2 sheets 5.25 1.60

A1642

Return of Hong Kong to China — A1643

No. 3639, each 20ch: a, Signing the Nanjing Treaty, 1842. b, Signing the China-Britain Joint Statement, 1984. c, Deng Xiaoping and Margaret Thatcher. d, Jiang Zenin and Tong Jianhua.
97ch, Deng Xiaoping.

1997, July 1 ***Perf. 11¾***
3639 A1642 Sheet of 4, #a.-d. 2.75 .75

Souvenir Sheet
Perf. 13¼

3640 A1643 97ch multicolored 2.75 .90

Fossils — A1644

Designs: 50ch, Redlichia chinensis. 1w, Ptychoparia coreanica.

1997, July 5 ***Perf. 11½***
3641 A1644 Pair, #a.-b. 4.50 1.15
c. Booklet pane, 5 #3641a 8.00 —
Complete booklet #3641c 8.25
d. Booklet pane, 5 #3641b 16.00 —
Complete booklet #3641d 16.50

Nos. 3641c-3641d each contain horizontal strips of five stamps.

Kim Il Sung, 3rd Death Anniv. — A1645

Each 50ch, Portrait of Kim Il Sung and: No. 3643, Kim speaking at party conference, 1985. No. 3644, Kim inspecting Kim Chaek Ironworks, 1985. No. 3645, Kim at Songsin Cooperative Farm, Sadong District, 1993. No. 3646, Kim being cheered by performing artists, 1986. No. 3647, Kim visiting Jonchon Factory, Jagang Province, 1991. No. 3648, Kim receiving bouquet from soldiers.

1997, July 8 ***Perf. 11¾x12***
3643-3648 A1645 Set of 6 8.25 2.00
3645a Sheet of 3, #3643-3645 4.25 1.75
3648a Sheet of 3, #3646-3648 4.25 1.75

Folk Games — A1646

Designs: 30ch, Blindman's Bluff. 60ch, Jackstones. 70ch, Arm wrestling.

1997, July 26 ***Perf. 11½***
3649-3651 A1646 Set of 3 4.25 1.15
3649a-3651a Set of 3 sheets 8.25 3.75
3651b Booklet pane of 6, 2 ea. #3649-3651 8.25 —
Complete booklet, #3651b 8.75

Nos. 3649a-3651a each contain 2 stamps + a central label.
No. 3281b contains two each of Nos. 3649-3651, printed in a se-tenant block (3x2), with decorative selvage.

Traditional Korean Women's Clothing — A1647

Designs: 10ch, Spring costume. 40ch, Summer. 50ch, Autumn. 60ch, Winter.

1997, Aug. 10
3652-3655 A1647 Set of 4 4.25 1.75
3652a-3654a Set of 3 sheets 16.50 11.00

No. 3652a contains 2 each Nos. 3652-3653; No. 3653a contains 2 each Nos. 3653-3654; No. 3654a contains 2 each Nos. 3654-3655.

Chongryu Bridge — A1648

Both 50ch: No. 3656, Night view of Chongryu Bridge. No. 3657, Panoramic view.

1997, Aug. 25
3656-3657 A1648 Set of 2 2.75 .90
3657a Sheet of 2, #3656-3657 3.25 1.35
3657b Booklet pane of 6, 3 ea. #3656-3657 8.25 —
Complete booklet, #3657b 8.75

A1649

Juche Era and Sun Day, 85th Anniv. — A1650

10ch, Sun, magnolias, banner, balloons.
Each 1w: No. 3659, Kim Il Sung, slogan, doves. No. 3660, Kim, birthplace Mongyangdae. No. 3661, Kim, Lake Chon, Mt. Paekdu. No. 3662, Kim, Kumsusan Memorial Palace.

1997, Sept. 3 ***Perf. 13¼***
3658 A1649 10ch multicolored .50 .25

Souvenir Sheets

3659-3662 A1650 Set of 4 sheets 10.00 5.50

Theses on Socialist Education, 20th Anniv. of Publication A1651

1997, Sept. 5 ***Perf. 11½***
3663 A1651 10ch multicolored .50 .25

No. 3663 was issued in sheetlets of 6.

Air Koryo — A1652

Sheets of 2 stamps and central label: 20ch, TU-134. 30ch, TU-154. 50ch, IL-62.

1997, Sept. 14 ***Perf. 13¼***
3664-3666 A1652 Set of 3 sheets 4.50 1.35
3665a Complete booklet, pane of 8, 4 ea. #3664, 3666 6.50
3666a Complete booklet, pane of 8, 4 ea. #3665, 3666 7.25

Korean Membership in World Tourism Org., 10th Anniv. — A1653

Views of Mt. Chilbo, each 50ch: No. 3667, Kim Chol Ung. No. 3668, Rojok Beach. No. 3669, Chonbul Peak.

1997, Sept. 22 ***Perf. 12***
3667-3669 A1653 Set of 3 4.25 1.15
3669a Sheet, #3667-3669 + label 4.50 1.30

Kumgang Mountains — A1654

Each 50ch: No. 3670, Kumgang Gate. No. 3671, Podok Hermitage.

1997, Oct. 2
3670-3671 A1654 Set of 2 2.75 .75
3670a Booklet pane of 5 #3670 6.75 —
Complete booklet, #3670a 7.25
3671a Sheet of 6, 3 each #3670-3671 9.00 3.75
3671b Booklet pane of 5 #3671 6.75 —
Complete booklet, #3671b 7.25

Mangyongdae Revolutionary School, 50th Anniv. — A1655

1997, Oct. 12 ***Perf. 11½***
3672 A1655 40ch multicolored 1.15 .30
a. Booklet pane of 6 6.75 —
Complete booklet, #3672a 7.25

Gift Animals — A1656

Animals presented to Kim Il Sung as gifts from foreign governments: 20ch, Lion (from Ethiopia, 1987). 30ch, Jaguar (Japan, 1992). 50ch, Barbary sheep (Czechoslovakia, 1992). 80ch, Scarlet macaw (Austria, 1979).

1997, Oct. 15
3673-3676 A1656 Set of 4 5.00 1.15
3673a Sheet of 8, 2 each #3673-3676 10.00 4.50
3673b Booklet pane of 8, 2ea. #3673-3676 10.00 —
Complete booklet, #3673b 11.00

For surcharges, see No. 4554-4555.

Qu Shao Yun, Chinese Volunteer Hero — A1657

Designs: a, 30ch, Bust of Qu Shao Yun. b, 10ch, Monument to Qu Shao Yun. c, 30ch, Qu Shao Yun burning to death in battle.

1997, Oct. 18
3677 A1657 Sheet of 3, #a.-c. 2.00 .75

Sports — A1658

Designs: No. 3678, 50ch, Bowling. No. 3679, 50ch, Fencing. No. 3680, 50chGolf.

1997, Nov. 10 ***Perf. 13¼***
3678-3680 A1658 Set of 3 4.75 1.15
3680a Sheet, 2 each #3678-3680 + 2 labels 10.00 4.50

For surcharge, see No. 4574.

Snails — A1659

Each 50ch: a, Two snails copulating. b, Snail laying eggs. c, Snail.

1997, Nov. 15 ***Perf. 12¼***
3681 A1659 Strip of 3, #a.-c. 4.50 1.75
d. Sheet of 6, 2 each #3681a-3681c 8.75 3.75
e. Booklet pane of 6, 2 ea. #3681a-3681c 8.75 —
Complete booklet, #3681e 9.00

Shanghai Int'l Stamp & Coin Exhib. — A1660

1997, Nov. 19 ***Perf. 11½***
3684 A1660 Sheet of 2, #a.-b. 2.25 .90
a. 30ch multicolored .90 .30
b. 50ch multicolored 1.35 .55

New Year — Year of the Tiger
A1661 A1662

Designs: 10ch, "Juche 87," pine boughs, temple. 50ch (No. 3686), Tiger in rocket. 50ch (No. 3687), Tiger in ship.
80ch, Tiger in train.

Perf. 13¼, 11½ (#3686-3687)

1997, Dec. 15
3685 A1661 10ch multicolored .25 .25
3686 A1662 50ch multicolored .85 .25
3687 A1662 50ch multicolored .85 .25
a. Sheet of 4, 1 ea #3686-#3687, 2 #3688a 4.25 1.75
Nos. 3685-3687 (3) 1.95 .75

Souvenir Sheet

3688 A1662 80ch multicolored 1.75 .75
a. Perf. 11½ — —
b. Booklet pane of 8, 2 each #3686-3687, 4 #3688a — —
Complete booklet, #3688b —

Complete booklet sold for 5.40w.

Birthplace, Hoeryong A1663

Kim Jong Suk, 80th Birth Anniv. — A1664

1997, Dec. 24 ***Perf. 13¼***
3689 A1663 10ch multicolored .50 .25

Souvenir Sheet

3690 A1664 1w multicolored 2.75 .75

Winter Olympic Games, Nagano, Japan — A1665

Designs: 20ch, Skiing. 40ch, Speed skating.

1998, Feb. 7 *Perf. 11½*

3691-3692 A1665 Set of 2 1.15 .60
3692a Sheet of 4, 2 ea #3691-#3692 2.25 1.15
3692b Booklet pane of 8, 4 ea. #3691-3692 4.50 —
Complete booklet, #3692b 5.00

A1666

Kim Jong Il, 56th Birthday — A1667

Designs: 10ch, Birth date ("2.16"). 3w, Birthplace, log cabin on Mt. Paekdu.

1998, Feb. 16

3693 A1666 10ch multicolored .50 .25

Souvenir Sheet

3694 A1667 3w multicolored 4.25 1.75

A1668

Paintings of Mt. Paekdu Wildlife — A1669

Designs, 50ch: No. 3695, Korean tigers. No. 3696, White crane.
No. 3697, 50ch: a, Bears. b, Racoons.

1998, Mar. 6 *Perf. 11¾x12*

3695-3696 A1668 Set of 2 1.75 .90
3696a Booklet pane of 8, 2 ea. #3695-3696, 3697a-3697b 7.25 —
Complete booklet, #3696a 7.75

Souvenir Sheet

3697 A1669 Sheet of 4, #3695-3696, 3697a-3697b 3.75 1.75
a. A1668 50ch multicolored .90 .50
b. A1668 50ch multicolored .90 .50

Kim Il Sung's 1000-ri Journey, 75th Anniv. — A1670

1998, Mar. 16 *Perf. 11½*

3698 A1670 10ch multicolored .50 .25
a. Sheet of 10 4.50 1.35

Appt. of Kim Jong Il as Chairman of the Nat'l Defense Commission, 5th Anniv. — A1671

1998, Apr. 9

3699 A1671 10ch multicolored .50 .25

A1672

Kim Il Sung, 86th Birth Anniv. — A1673

Designs: 10ch, Birthplace, flags, flowers.
Circular stamps, each 80ch, within 84x155mm sheetlets, depicting portraits of Kim Il Sung at different stages in his life: #3701, As child. #3702, As middle school student. #3703, As young revolutionary. #3704, In suit and tie, ca. 1946. #3705, In military uniform during Korean War. #3706, As middle-aged man, in uniform. #3707, As middle-aged man, in suit and tie. #3708, As old man in suit and tie.

1998, Apr. 15

3700 A1672 10ch multicolored .50 .25

Souvenir Sheets

3701-3708 A1673 Set of 8 8.25 3.75

North-South Joint Conference, 50th Anniv. — A1674

1998, Apr. 21 *Perf. 13¼*

3709 A1674 10ch multicolored .50 .25

16th World Cup Soccer Championship, France — A1675

Designs: 30ch, Dribbling. 50ch, Kicking.

1998, May 5 *Perf. 11½*

3710-3711 A1675 Set of 2 1.45 5.00
3711a Sheet of 6, 2 ea #3710-#3711, #3712 5.50 2.75
3711b Booklet pane of 10, 5 ea. #3710-3711 7.25 —
Complete booklet, #3711b 7.75

Souvenir Sheet

3712 A1675 80ch multicolored 1.45 5.00

A single stamp like that in No. 3712 is included in No. 3711a.

A1676

Int'l Friendship Art Exhib., Mt. Myohyang — A1677

Designs, 1w: No. 3713, *Diagram of Automatic Space Station* (USSR). No. 3714, Ceramic flower vase (Egypt). No. 3715, *Crane* (USA).
1w, Kim Il Sung receiving a gift from Deng Xiaoping.

1998, May 20 *Perf. 11¾*

3713-3715 A1676 Set of 3 4.25 2.00
3714a Sheet of 2, #3713 & #3714 2.50 1.30
3715a Sheet of 2, #3713 & #3715 2.50 1.30

Souvenir Sheet

Perf. 13¼

3716 A1677 1w multicolored 1.75 .90

A1678

Korean Art Gallery — A1679

Designs: 60ch, *A Countryside in May.* 1.40w, *Dance.*
3w, *Heart-to-heart Talk with a Peasant.*

1998, May 20

3717-3718 A1678 Set of 2 2.75 1.35

Souvenir Sheet

3719 A1679 3w multicolored 4.25 2.00

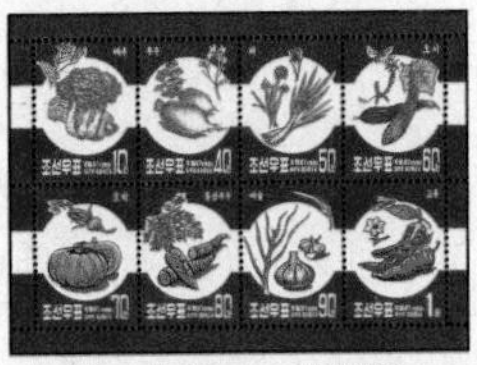

Vegetables — A1680

Designs: 10ch, Cabbage. 40ch, Radish. 50ch, Green onion. 60ch, Cucumber. 70ch, Pumpkin. 80ch, Carrot. 90ch, Garlic. 1w, Red pepper.

1998, May 20 *Perf. 13¼*

3720 A1680 Sheet of 8, #a.-h. 8.25 4.25

A1681

Int'l Year of the Ocean — A1682

Designs: 10ch, Hydro-Meteorological Headquarters building, ship, oceanographic floating balloons, dolphins, emblem. 80ch, Woman holding child, yachts, emblem.
5w, Vasco da Gama (1460-1524), Portuguese explorer.

1998, May 22

3730-3731 A1681 Set of 2 1.75 .85
3731a Sheet of 4, 2 ea. #3730-3731 1.75 .85

Souvenir Sheet

3732 A1682 5w multicolored 6.75 3.50

A1683

Korean Central History Museum, Pyongyang — A1684

Designs: 10ch, Stone Age tool. 2.50w, Fossil monkey skull.
4w, Kim Il Sung visiting the museum.

1998, June 15

3733-3734 A1683 Set of 2 3.75 1.75

Souvenir Sheet

3735 A1684 4w multicolored 5.50 2.75

A1685

Dr. Ri Sung Gi (1905-96), Inventor of Vinalon — A1686

Designs: 40ch, Dr. Ri Sung Gi and diagram of vinalon nuclear structure.
80ch, Gi working in laboratory.

1998, June 15 *Perf. 11½*

3736 A1685 40ch multicolored .60 .25
a. Booklet pane of 10
Complete booklet, #3736a

Souvenir Sheet

3737 A1686 80ch multicolored 1.25 .85

Squirrels and Hedgehogs Cartoon — A1687

Designs: 20ch, Squirrel and Commander of Hedgehog Unit. 30ch, Commander of Hedgehog Unit receiving invitation to banquet celebrating bumper crop. 60ch, Weasel Commander and mouse. 1.20w, Bear falling dead-drunk. 2w, Weasel Commander and mice invading the flower village. 2.50w, Hedgehog scout saving the squirrel.

1998, June 15

3738-3743 A1687 Set of 6 11.00 5.50
3743a Sheet of 6, #3737-3743 11.00 5.50

A1688

Return of Hong Kong to China, 1st Anniv. — A1689

Designs, 10w: No. 3744, Deng Xiaoping (1904-97), Chinese Prime Minister. No. 3745, Mao Zedong. No. 3746, Kim Il Sung.

No. 3747, Deng Xiaoping, Mao Zedong and Kim Il Sung, horiz.

1998, July 1

Embossed with gold foil application

3744-3746 A1688 Set of 3 30.00 10.00

Souvenir Sheet

3747 A1689 10w Gold & multi 10.00 10.00

Young Wild Mammals A1690

Designs: 10ch, Tiger cub. 50ch, Donkey foal. 1.60w, Elephant. 2w, Lion cubs.

1998, July 10 ***Perf. 11½***

3748-3751 A1690 Set of 4 4.50 2.25
3751a Booklet pane of 8, 2 each #3748-3751 — —
Complete booklet, #3751a —

Complete booklet sold for 8.60w.

A1691

A1692

Korean War "Victory," 45th Anniv. — A1693

Designs: 45ch, War monument, flag.

No. 3753, Kim Il Sung inspecting the front. No. 3754, Gaz-67 jeep and map of Korea, showing Kim's inspection route.

1998, July 27 ***Perf. 13¼***

3752 A1691 45ch multicolored .25 .25

Souvenir Sheets

3753 A1692 2w multicolored 2.00 1.00
3754 A1693 2w multicolored 2.00 1.00

Embroidery — A1694

Designs: 10ch, *White Herons in Forest.* 40ch, *Carp.* 1.20w, *Hollyhock.* 1.50w, *Cockscomb.*

4w, *Pine and Cranes.*

1998, Aug. 10 ***Perf. 11¾x12***

3755-3758 A1694 Set of 4 2.50 1.25
3758a Booklet pane of 6, #3757, 3758, 2 each #3755-3756 — —
Complete booklet, #3758a —

Complete booklet sold for 3.90w.

Perf. 12x12¼

3759	Sheet of 5, #a.-e. + label	5.75	3.00
a.	A1694 10ch multicolored	.25	.25
b.	A1694 40ch multicolored	.40	.25
c.	A1694 1.20w multicolored	1.00	.50
d.	A1694 1.50w multicolored	1.00	.50
e.	A1694 4w multicolored	2.50	1.25

Souvenir Sheet

Perf. 11¾x12

3760 A1694 4w multicolored 3.00 1.50

Traditional Costumes — A1695

Designs: 10ch, Pouch. 50ch, Playthings (dress ornaments). 1.50w, Hairpin. 1.90w, Ornamental silver sword.

1998, Aug. 20 ***Perf. 11½***

3761-3764 A1695 Set of 4 3.00 1.50
3763a Sheet of 20, 10 se-tenant pairs #3761 and #3763 15.00 7.50
3764a Sheet of 20, 10 se-tenant pairs #3762 and #3764 15.00 7.50
3764b Booklet pane of 8, 2 each #3761-3764 — —
Complete booklet, #3764b —

Complete booklet sold for 8.20w.

Launch of *Kwangmyongsong I*, DPRK's First Earth Satellite — A1696

Designs: 40ch, Rocket, satellite, world map and flag.

1.50w, Rocket, earth and satellite orbit.

1998, Aug. 31 ***Perf. 13¼***

3765 A1696 40ch multicolored .35 .25

Souvenir Sheet

3766 A1696 1.50w multicolored 1.25 .65

A1697

Acclamation of Kim Jong Il as Chairman of the DPRK National Defense Commission — A1698

Designs: 10ch, Proclamation, *Kimjongilia.* 1w, Kim Jong Il.

1998, Sept. 5 ***Perf. 11½***

3767 A1697 10ch multicolored .25 .25

Souvenir Sheet

Perf. 13¼

3768 A1698 1w multicolored .75 .40

A1699

Korean DPR, 50th Anniversary — A1700

Designs: 10ch, State Arms, Flag, Tower of Juche Idea.

No. 3770: a, Kim Il Sung saluting crowd from balcony. b, Kim raising cap to crowd in street. c, Kim in suit and white hat, with fruit, stylized and idealized Korean peninsula in background.

1998, Sept. 9 ***Perf. 13¼***

3769 A1699 10ch multicolored .25 .25
3770 A1700 1w Sheet of 6, 2 each a-c 4.50 2.25

Poster: "Let Us Push Ahead with the Forced March for Final Victory" — A1701

1998, Sept. 15 ***Perf. 11½***

3773 A1701 10ch multicolored .25 .25

A1702

Korean DPR, 50th Anniversary (2nd Issue) — A1703

1998, Sept. 20 ***Perf. 13¼***

3774 A1702 40ch multicolored .35 .25

Perf. 11½

3775 A1703 1w multicolored 1.00 .50

Summer Olympic Games, Sydney — A1704

Designs: 20ch, Cyclist. 50ch, Soccer. 80ch, Show jumping. 1.50w, Javelin throwing. 2.50w, Basketball.

1998, Sept. 25

3776-3779 A1704 Set of 4 2.50 1.25
3778a Sheet of 3, #3777, 3778, as #3780 3.00 1.50
3779a Sheet of 3, #3776, 3779, as #3780 3.00 1.50

Souvenir Sheet

3780 A1704 2.50w multi 2.00 1.00

For surcharge, see No. 4529.

Plants Presented as Gifts to Kim Jong Il — A1705

Designs: 20ch, Cyclamen persicum. 2w, Dianthus chinensis.

1998, Sept. 28 ***Perf. 11½***

3781-3782 A1705 Set of 2 1.60 .80

Nat'l Vaccination Day — A1706

1998, Oct. 20 ***Perf. 13¼***

3783 A1706 40ch multicolored .35 .25
a. Sheet of 6 2.10 1.00

Worldwide Fund for Nature (WWF) — A1707

Panthera pardus orientalis: No. 3784, 1w, Climbing branch. No. 3785, 1w, Walking in snow. No. 3786, 1w, Looking to left. No. 3787, 1w, Head, full-face.

1998, Oct. 21

3784-3787 A1707 Set of 4 4.00 2.00
3787a Sheet of 16, 4 se-tenant blocks of #3784-3787 16.00 8.00

For surcharges, see Nos. 4589-4590.

A1708

Land and Environment Conservation Day — A1709

Designs: 10ch, Canal, countryside. 40ch, Modern highway exchange, apartment towers.
1w, Kim Il Sung breaking ground for construction of Pothong River project.

1998, Oct. 23 ***Perf. 11½***

3788-3789 A1708 Set of 2 .45 .25

Souvenir Sheet

Perf. 12x12¼

3790 A1709 1w multicolored .75 .40

Italia '98 Int'l stamp Exhib., Milan — A1710

1998, Oct. 23 ***Perf. 12¼x12***

3791 A1710 2w multicolored 1.50 .75

A1711

Designs: a, 20ch, Peng Dehuai and Kim Il Sung. b, 20ch, Peng Dehuai, Zhou Enlai, Mao Zedong. c, 30ch, Marshal Peng Dehuai. d, 30ch, Painting, *On the Front.*

1998, Oct. 24 ***Perf. 11½***

3792 A1711 Sheet of 4, #a-d .75 .40

Birth centenary of Peng Dehuai, Commander of the Chinese People's Volunterrs in the Korean War.

Liu Shaoqi — A1712

Designs: 10ch, Liu Shaoqi. 20ch, Liu sitting with Mao Zedong (1965). 30ch, Liu and his daughter, Xiao Xiao (1964). 40ch, Liu sitting with his wife, Wang Guangmei (1961).

1998, Nov 24 ***Perf. 13¼***

3796-3799 A1712 Set of 4 .75 .40

Souvenir Sheet

Perf. 11¾x12¼

3800 A1712 1w multicolored .75 .40

A1713

Victory in Korean-Japanese War, 400th Anniv. — A1714

Designs: 10ch, Victory monument, Yonsang area, Yonan fortress, banners. 30ch, Naval victory monument, Myongryang area, Gen. Ri Sun Sin, turtleship. 1.60w, Monument to Buddhist priest Hyujong, Sosan-Chonghodang, Hyujong, sword, helmet.
No. 3804, *Sea Battle Off Hansan Islet in 1592.*

1998, Nov 24 ***Perf. 11½***

3801-3803 A1713 Set of 3 1.50 .75
3803a Sheet of 15, 5 se-tenant strips of #3801-3803 7.50 3.75

Souvenir Sheet

3804 A1714 10w multicolored 7.50 3.00

DPRK Entry into INTERSPUTNIK, 15th Anniv. — A1715

1998, Nov. 25 ***Perf. 13¼***

3805 A1715 1w dp grn & lt grn .75 .40

Korean Goats — A1716

Goat with background color of: 10c, Green. 1w, Purple.

1998, Nov. 26

3806-3807 A1716 Set of 2 .80 .40

For surcharge, see No. 4576.

Sculpture, *A Floral Carriage of Happiness* A1717

Quotation from Kim Il Sung — A1718

Designs: 10ch, Sculpture, panoramic view of Mangyongdae Schoolchildren's Palace.
1w, Kim Il Sung quotation, "Children are the treasure of our country. Korea of the future is theirs."

1998, Nov. 26 ***Perf. 11½***

3808 A1717 40ch multicolored .35 .25
a. Sheet of 4 2.00 1.00

Souvenir Sheet

3809 A1718 1w multicolored .75 .40

Univeral Declaration of Human Rights, 50th Anniv. — A1719

1998, Dec. 10

3810 A1719 20ch multicolored .25 .25

Reptiles — A1720

Designs: a, 10ch, Reeves turtle. b, 40ch, Skink. c, 60ch, Loggerhead turtle. d, 1.20w, Leatherback turtle.

1998, Dec. 15 ***Perf. 13¼***

3811 A1720 Block of 4, #a-d 1.75 .90
e. Sheet of 16, 4 #3811 17.00 3.50
f. Complete booklet, 3 ea. #3811 13.00

Mt. Chilbo — A1721

Designs: 30ch, Thajong Rock. 50ch, Peasant Rock. 1.70w, Couple Rock.

1998, Dec. 15 ***Perf. 11½***

3815-3817 A1721 Set of 3 1.75 .90

Tale of Chung Hyang — A1722

Designs: 40ch, Marriage of Ri Mong Ryong and Song Chun Hyang. 1.60w, Pyon Hak Do watching Chun Hyang. 2.50w, Ri Mong Ryong and Chun Hyang.
50ch, Chun Hyang in wedding veil.

1998, Dec. 20

3818-3820 A1722 Set of 3 3.50 1.75
3821 Sheet of 4, #3818-3820, 3821a 5.00 2.50
a. A1722 multicolored 1.00 .50

Chollima Statue A1723

Arch of Triumph A1724

Tower of Juche Idea — A1725

1998, Dec. 22 ***Perf. 13¼***

3822	A1723	10ch	red	.25	.25
3823	A1724	10ch	red	.25	.25
3824	A1725	10ch	red	.25	.25
3825	A1725	20ch	red org	.25	.25
3826	A1723	30ch	red org	.35	.25
3827	A1724	40ch	yel brown	.40	.25
3828	A1725	40ch	yel brown	.40	.25
3829	A1723	70ch	yel grn	.65	.35
3830	A1724	70ch	yel grn	.65	.35
3831	A1724	1.20w	green	1.10	.55
3832	A1723	1.50w	blue green	1.50	.75
3833	A1725	2w	blue	2.00	1.00
3834	A1724	3w	blue	2.75	1.40
3835	A1723	5w	dk blue	5.00	2.50
3836	A1725	10w	violet	9.75	5.00
	Nos. 3822-3836 (15)			25.55	13.65

For surcharges, see Nos. 4577, 4591, 4611.

New Year — Year of the Rabbit — A1726

Designs: 10ch, Rabbit meeting Lion on the road. 1w, Rabbit using mirror to lure lion into pit. 1.50w, Rabbit laughing at Lion in trap.
2.50w, Rabbit.

1999, Jan. 1 ***Perf. 11½***

3837-3839 A1726 Set of 3 2.00 1.00
3840 Sheet of 4, #3837-3839, 3840a 4.00 2.00
a. A1726 2.50w multicolored 2.00 1.00
b. Booklet pane of 8, 2 each #3837-3839, 3840a — —
Complete booklet, #3840b —

Complete booklet sold for 10.40w.

Worker-Peasant Red Guards, 40th Anniv. — A1727

1999, Jan. 14 ***Perf. 13¼***

3841 A1727 10ch multicolored .25 .25

Kim Jong Il, 57th Birthday — A1728

40ch, Log cabin (birthplace) on Mt. Paekdu.

1999, Feb. 16 ***Perf. 11½***

3842 A1728 40ch multicolored .35 .25

Publication of Kim Il Sung's *Theses on the Socialist Rural Question in Our Country* — A1729

1999, Feb. 25 ***Perf. 13¼***

3843 A1729 10ch multicolored .25 .25

March 1 Popular Uprising, 80th Anniv. — A1730

1999, Feb. 25

3844 A1730 10ch olive brn & black .25 .25

Turtle Ship — A1731

1999, Mar. 19

3845 A1731 2w multicolored 1.60 .80
a. Booklet pane of 5 #3845 — —
Complete booklet, #3845a —

Australia '99 World Stamp Expo, Melbourne. Complete booklet sold for 10.20w.

A1732

Kim Il Sung, 87th Birth Anniv. — A1733

Designs: 10ch, Childhood Home, Mangyongdae. No. 3847, Kim Il Sung.

1999, Apr. 15 ***Perf. 11½***

3846 A1732 10ch multicolored .25 .25

Souvenir Sheet

Perf. 11½x12

3847 A1733 2w multicolored 1.60 .80

45th World Table Tennis Championships, Belgrade — A1734

1999, Apr. 26 ***Perf. 11½***

3848 A1734 1.50w multicolored 1.20 .60

For surcharge, see No. 4559.

Ibra '99 Int'l Stamp Exhib., Nuremberg A1735

1999, Apr. 27

3849 A1735 1w multicolored .85 .40

For surcharge, see No. 4557.

Central Zoo, Pyongyang, 40th Anniv. — A1736

Designs: 50ch, Chimpanzee, rhinoceros. 60ch, Manchurian crane, deer. 70ch, Zebra, kangaroo.
2w, Tiger.

1999, Apr. 30 ***Perf. 13¼***

3850-3852 A1736 Set of 3 1.60 .80
3852a Booklet pane of 6, 2 each #3850-3852 — —
Complete booklet, #3852a —

Souvenir Sheet

3853 A1736 2w multicolored 1.75 .90

For surcharge, see No. 4552.
Complete bookletof No. 3852a sold for 3.80w.

Central Botanical Garden, Pyongyang, 40th Anniv. — A1737

Designs: 10ch, *Benzoin obtusilobum.* 30ch, *Styrax obassia.* 70ch, *Petunia hybrida.* 90ch, *Impatiens hybrida.*
2w, *Kimsungilia* and *Kimjongilia.*

1999, Apr. 30 ***Perf. 11½***

3854-3857 A1737 Set of 4 1.60 .80
3857a Sheet of 4, #3854-3857 1.75 .90
3857b Booklet pane of 12, 3 each #3854-3857 — —
Complete booklet, #3857b —

Complete booklet sold for 6.20w.

Souvenir Sheet

3858 A1737 2w multicolored 1.75 .90

Three Revolution Exhibit — A1738

Designs: 60ch, Light Industry Hall. 80ch, Heavy Industry Hall

1999, May 2

3859-3860 A1738 Set of 2 1.20 .60

Three Revolution (ideological, technical, cultural) Exhibition, Ryonmotdong, Sosong District, Pyongyang.

Asia-Pacific Telecommunications Union, 20th Anniv. — A1739

1999, May 8 ***Perf. 13¼***

3861 A1739 1w multicolored .80 .40

Battle of Musan Area, 60th Anniv. — A1740

1999, May 19 ***Perf. 11½***

3862 A1740 10ch multicolored .25 .25

A1741

Charles Darwin, 190th Birth Anniv. A1742

No. 3863: a, 30ch, Seagulls. b, 50ch, Bats. c, 1w, Dolphins. d, 1.20w, Rider on horseback. e, 1.50w, Korean dancer in traditional dress.

1999, May 20 **Sheet of 5 + labels**

3863 A1741 #a-e 3.00 1.50

Souvenir Sheet

Perf. 13¼x12

3864 A1742 2w multicolored 4.00 2.00

Diego Velazquez (1599-1660), Artist, 400th Birth Anniv. — A1743

Designs: No. 3869, 50ch, *Princess Margarita in a White Dress.* No. 3866, 50ch, *Men Drawing Water from a Well.*
3.50w, *Self-portrait.*

1999, May 30 ***Perf. 11¾***

3869-3870 A1743 Set of 2 1.00 .50

Souvenir Sheet

3871 A1743 3.50w multicolored 3.00 1.50
a. Sheet of 3, #3869-3871 4.00 2.00
b. Booklet pane of 6, 2 each #3869-3871 — —
Complete booklet, #3871b —

Complete booklet sold for 9.20w.

Medium and Small Hydroelectric Power Stations — A1744

Designs: 50ch, Rimyongsu Power Station. 1w, Janggasan Power Station.

1999, May 30 ***Perf. 11½***

3872-3873 A1744 Set of 2 1.20 .60

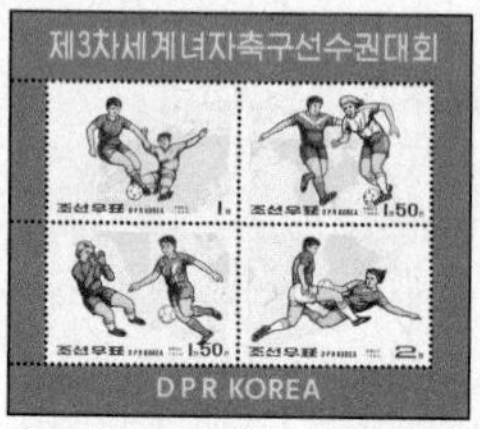

3rd Women's World Soccer Championship, USA — A1745

Designs: a, 1w, Dribbling. b, 1.50w, Tackling. c, 1.50w, Goal shot. d, 2w, Knee kick.

1999, June 8 ***Perf. 13¼***

3874 A1745 Sheet of 4, #a-d 5.00 2.50
e. Booklet pane of 4, #3874a-3874d — —
Complete booklet, #3874e —

Complete booklet sold for 6.20w.

Mars Exploration — A1746

Designs, each 2w: a, Vostock Rocket. b, Satellite over Martian crater. c, Mars probe landing, Martian moons.

1999, June 10 ***Perf. 11½***

3878 A1746 Sheet of 3, #a.-c. 4.75 2.50

Movie, *The Nation and Destiny* — A1747

Scenes from film: a, Man holding candlestick. b, Man in white coat, woman with pistol. c, Old man in prison cell. d, Man in protective suit, with goggles on hat.

1999, June 10

3879 A1747 1w Sheet of 4, #a-d 3.20 1.60
e. Booklet pane of 8, 2 each #3879a-3879d — —
Complete booklet, #3879e —

Complete booklet sold for 8.20w.

Tourism — Mt. Kumgang A1748

Designs: 20ch, Samil Lagoon. 40ch, Samson Rocks, vert. 60ch, Standing Rock. 80ch, Kuryong Waterfall. 1w, Kwimyon Rock.

1999, June 15 ***Perf. 12***

3883-3887 A1748 Set of 5 2.50 1.25

UPU, 125th Anniv. A1749

1999, June 20 ***Perf. 11½***

3888 A1749 2w multicolored 1.40 .70

PHILEXFANCE '99 — A1750

2.50w, First stamps of France (1870) and DPRK (1946).

1999, July 2 ***Perf. 12***

3889 A1750 2.50w multicolored 2.00 1.00

Kim Il Sung, 5th Death Anniv. A1751

Designs: a, Kim Il Sung's Mercedes. b, Kim's railway car.

1999, July 8 ***Perf. 11½***

3890 A1751 1w Sheet of 2, #a-b 1.60 .80

Kim Hyong Jik (1894-1926), Revolutionary, 105th Anniv. Birth — A1752

10ch, Chinese characters for "Jiwon" ("Aim High"), Kim Hyong Jik's motto, and Mangyong Hill.

1999, July 10

3892 A1752 10ch multicolored .25 .25

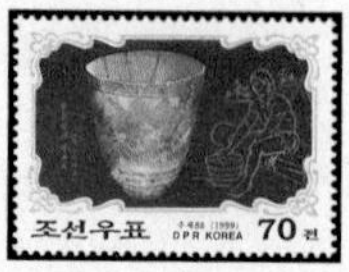

History of Ceramics A1753

Designs: 70ch, Engraved-patterned vessel (5000 B.C.). 80ch, Wit and beauty jar (3rd-4th Centuries). 1w, Flowered jar. 1.50w, Lotus decoration celadon kettle (10th-14th Centuries). 2.50w, White china pot with blue flower (15th Century).

1999, July 15 *Perf. 13¼*
3893-3897 A1753 Set of 5 5.00 2.50

Fish Breeding A1754

Designs: 50ch, Silver carp. 1w, Common carp. 1.50w, Spotted silver carp.

1999, July 20
3898-3900 A1754 Set of 3 2.40 1.20
3900a Booklet pane of 6, 2 each #3898-3900 — —
Complete booklet, #3900a —

Complete booklet sold for 6.20w.

Year of Nat'l Independence and Great Solidarity — A1755

1999, Aug. 5
3901 A1755 40ch multicolored .35 .25

Repatriation of Korean Nationals in Japan, 40th Anniv. — A1756

1999, Aug. 16 *Perf. 11½*
3902 A1756 1.50w multicolored 1.25 .60

Year For a Turning Point in Building a Powerful Nation — A1757

1999, Aug. 17
3903 A1757 40ch multicolored .35 .25

7th World Athletic Championships, Seville — A1758

Designs: 30ch, 100-Meter Race. 40ch, Hurdles. 80ch, Discus.

1999, Aug. 18
3904-3906 A1758 Set of 3 1.20 .60

Gift Plants — A1759

No. 3907: a, Acalypha hispida Burm f. b, Allamanda neriifolia Hook. c, Begonia x hiemalis Fotsch. d, Fatsia japonica Decne. e, Streptocarpus hydrida hort. f, Streptocarpus rexii Lindl.

1999, Aug. 20
3907 A1759 40ch Sheet of 6, #a-f 2.00 1.00

22nd UPU Congress & China '99 World Philatelic Exhib. — A1760

Paintings by Qiu Ying: a, *Play a Flute to Call Phoenix*. b, *Six Friends in a Pine Forest*. c, *Relics Kept in the Bamboo Field*. d, *Ladies Morning Dressing*.

1999, Aug. 21
3913 A1760 40ch Sheet of 4, #a-d 1.50 .75

Mushrooms A1761

Designs: 40ch, Grifola frondosa. 60ch Lactarius volemus. 1w, Cariolus versicolor.

1999, Aug. 25
3917-3919 A1761 Set of 3 2.00 1.00

For surcharge, see No. 4558.

Cacti — A1762

Designs: 40ch, *Aporocactus flagelliformis*. 50ch *Astrophytum ornatum*. 60ch, *Gymnocalycium michanorichii*.

1999, Sept. 1
3920-3922 A1762 Set of 3 1.25 .60

Animals of the Zodiac — A1763

No. 3923: a, Rat. b, Ox. c, Tiger. d, Rabbit. e, Dragon. f, Snake.
No. 3924: a, Horse. b, Sheep. c, Monkey. d, Rooster. e, Dog. f, Pig.

1999, Sept. 10 *Perf. 12½*
Sheets of 6, #a-f
3923-3924 A1763 10ch Set of 2 2.00 1.00

Crustaceans — A1764

Designs: 50ch, Pendalus hypsinotus 70ch, Penaeus orientalis. 80ch, Homarus vulgarus.

1999, Sept. 10 *Perf. 11½*
3935-3937 A1764 Set of 3 2.00 1.00
3937a Booklet pane of 6, 2 each #3935-3937 — —
Complete booklet, #3937a —

Complete booklet sold for 4.20w.

A1765

Jong Song Ok, Marathon Runner — A1766

1999, Sept. 20 *Perf. 13¼*
3938 A1765 40ch multicolored .35 .25
a. Booklet pane of 6 #3938 — —
Complete booklet, #3938a —

Complete booklet sold for 2.60w.

Souvenir Sheet

3939 A1766 2w multicolored 1.60 .80

Victory of Jong Song Ok, Women's Marathon winner at 7th IAAF World Championships, Seville.

DPRK-China Diplomatic Relations, 50th Anniv. — A1767

Designs: 40ch, Mt. Kumgang, Korea. 60ch, Mt. Lushan, China.

1999, Oct. 5 *Perf. 12¼x11¼*
3940-3941 A1767 Set of 2 1.00 .50
3941a Sheet of 4, #3940-3941 + 2 labels 3.00 1.50

Nos. 3940-3941 were printed both in sheetlets of 6, containing three vertical se-tenant pairs of the two stamps, and in sheetlets of 4, containing a horizontal se-tenant pair and two labels.

A1768

Return of Macao to China — A1769

Type A1768, 1w, Portrait of Pres. Jiang Zemin of China: No. 3942, Gold frame. No. 3943, Green frame.
Type A1769: 20ch (a), Deng Xiaoping sharing toast with Portuguese Prime Minister. 20ch (b), Jiang Zemin shaking hands with He Houhua, newly-appointed mayor of Macao special administrative region. 80ch (c), Mao Zedong at National Day Celebration, Tiananmen Square, 1951. Nos. 3944a-3944c, gold background. Nos. 3945a-3945c, green background.

1999, Nov. 10 *Perf. 13¼*
3942-3943 A1768 Set of 2 sheets 2.00 1.00
3944-3945 A1769 Set of 2 sheets, #a-c 2.50 1.25

New Year — April 19 Uprising, 40th Anniv. — A1770

2000, Jan. 1 *Perf. 11½*
3946 A1770 10ch multicolored .25 .25

A1771

Koguryo Era (2nd Century B.C.-7th Century A.D.) — A1772

Designs: 70ch, Yellow dragon. 1.60w, Blue dragon.

2000, Jan. 1
3947 A1771 70ch multicolored .70 .35
Complete booklet, 8 #3947 —

Souvenir Sheet
Perf. 11½x11¾

3948 A1772 1.60w multicolored 1.60 .80

Complete booklet sold for 5.80w.

Painting, *Rural Life* (18th Century) — A1773

No. 3949: a, Peasants weeding. b, Weaving hemp cloth. c, Peasants threshing grain. d, Riverside market.

2000, Jan. 25 *Perf. 13¼*
3949 A1773 40ch Sheet of 4, #a-d 1.60 .80

Mt. Paekdu Rock Formations A1774

Designs, 20ch: No. 3953, Dinosaur-shaped rock. No. 3954, Eagle-shaped rock. No. 3955, Owl-shaped rock.

2000, Jan. 30
3953-3955 A1774 Set of 3 .70 .35

Pongsan Mask Dance — A1775

Folk dances: a, 50ch, Chuibari mask dance. b, 80ch, Ryangban mask dance. c, 1w, Malttugi mask dance.

2000, Feb. 3 ***Perf. 11½***
3956 A1775 Sheet of 3, #a-c 2.25 1.10

Cats — A1776

Designs: No. 3959, 50ch, Cat on windowsill. No. 3960, 50ch, Kittens playing. No. 3961, 50ch, Mother cat and kittens in basket.

2000, Feb. 3 ***Perf. 13¼***
3959-3961 A1776 Set of 3 1.75 .85
3961a Booklet pane of 8, 2 #3959, 3 each #3960-3961 — —
Complete booklet, #3961a —

Complete booklet sold for 4.20w.

Fauna — A1777

No. 3962: Cats: a, Singapura. b, Blue Abyssinian. c, Oriental. d, Scottish fold tabby.
No. 3963: Dogs: a, Shiba inu. b, Yorkshire terrier. c, Japanese chin. d, Afghan hound.
No. 3964: Horses: a, Przewalski's horse. b, Gray cob. c, White horse. d, Donkeys.
No. 3965: Pandas: a, In tree. b, Eating. c, Leaning against tree. d, Mother and cub.
No. 3966: Bears: a, Two polar bears. b, Mother and cub. c, Bear standing. d, Bear reclining.
No. 3967: Snakes: a, Mexican lance-headed rattlesnake (Crotalus polystictus). b, Scarlet king snake (Lampropeltis triangulum elapsoides). c, Green tree python (Chondropython viridis). d, Blood python (Python curtus).
No. 3968: Dinosaurs: a, Corythosaurus. b, Psittacosaurus. c, Megalosaurus. d, Muttaburrasaurus.
No. 3969: Marine Mammals: a, Burmeister's porpoise (Phocoena spinipinnis). b, Finless porpoise (Neophocaena phocaenoides). c, Bottle-nosed dolphin (Tursiops truncatus).d, Curvier's beaked whale (Ziphius cavirostris).
No. 3970: Sharks: a, Port Jackson shark (Heterodontus portusjacksoni). b, Great hammerhead shark (Sphyrna mokarran). c, Zebra shark (Stegostoma fasciatum). d, Ornate Wobbegong carpet shark (Orectolobus cavirostris).
No. 3971: Ducks: a, Ruddy shelduck (Tadorna ferruginea). b, European widgeon (Anas penelope). c, Mandarin drake (Aix galericulata). d, Hottentot teal (Anas hottentota).
No. 3972: Owls: a, Little owl (Athene noctua). b, Ural owl (Strix uralensis). c, Great horned owl (Bubo virginianus). d, Snowy owl (Nyctea scandiaca).
No. 3973: Parrots: a, Slaty-headed parakeet (Psittacula himalayana). b, Male eclectus parrot (Eclectus roratus). c, Major Mitchell's cockatoo (Cacatua leadbeateri). d, Female eclectus parrot (Eclectus roratus).
No. 3974: Butterflies: a, Indian leaf butterfly (Kallima paralekta). b, Spanish festoon (Zerynthia rumina). c, Male and female emerald swallowtails (Papillo palinurus). d, Bhutanitis lidderdalii.
No. 3975: Bees: a, Bumble bee. b, Bumble bee on flower. c, Honey bee (Apis mellifera). d, Honey bee fighting spider.
No. 3976: Spiders: a, Micrommata virescens. b, Araneus quadratus. c, Dolomedes fimbriatus. d, Aculepeira ceropegia.

2000, Feb. 10 **Sheets of 4, #a-d**
3962-3976 A1777 2w Set of 15 150.00 150.00

Kim Jong Il, 59th Birthday — A1778

Design: Birthplace, Mt. Paekdu.

2000, Feb. 16 ***Perf. 11½***
4022 A1778 40ch multicolored .40 .25

Dinosaurs — A1779

Designs: a, Triceratops. b, Saltasaurus. c, Tyrannosaurus.

2000, Mar. 5 ***Perf. 13¼***
4023 A1779 1w Sheet of 3, #a-c 3.50 1.75
d. Sheet of 3, ovptd. with show emblem in margin 3.50 1.75

No. 4023d, Espana 2000 International Stamp Exhibition, Madrid. Issued, 10/6/06.

A1780

Monkeys — A1781

Designs: No. 4026, 50ch, Western tarsier (Tarsius spectrum). No. 4027, 50ch, Patas monkey (Erythrocebus patas).
2w, Mona monkey (Cercopithecus mona).

2000, Mar. 25 ***Perf. 11½***
4026-4027 A1780 Set of 2 1.00 .50
4027a Sheet of 4, 2 each #4026-4027 2.25 1.10
4027b Booklet pane of 8, 4 each #4026-4027 — —
Complete booklet, #4027b —

Complete booklet sold for 4.20w.

Souvenir Sheet

4028 A1781 2w multicolored 1.80 .90

Nos. 4026-4027 were issued both separately in panes of 10 and together in sheets of 4.

Butterflies — A1782

No. 4029: a, 40ch Peacock (Inachus io). b, 60ch, Swallowtail (Papilio machaon). c, 80ch, Mimic (Hypolimnas misippus Linnaeus). d, 1.20w, (Papilio bianor cramer).

2000, Mar. 25
4029 A1782 Sheet of 4, #a-d 3.50 1.75
e. Booklet pane of 8, 2 each #4029a-4029d — —
Complete booklet, #4029e —

Complete booklet sold for 6.20w.

Grand Chollima March — A1783

2000, Mar. 28
4033 A1783 10ch multicolored .25 .25

55th anniversary of the Korean Workers' Party.

April 19 Popular Uprising, 40th Anniv. — A1784

2000, April 1
4034 A1784 10ch multicolored .25 .25

Sun's Day — A1785

2000, April 15
4035 A1785 40ch multicolored .40 .25

88th anniversary of birth of Kim Il Sung. For surcharge, see No. 4587.

Mun Ik Hwan — A1786

2000, April 25 ***Perf. 13¼***
4036 A1786 50ch multicolored .60 .25

Issued in honor of Mun Ik Hwan (1918-94), South Korean political activist, winner of 1990 National Reunification Prize.

Millennium; Korean Workers' Party, 55th Anniv. — A1787

Designs: 40ch, Chollima statue, flag, symbols of national power. 1.20w, Dove with letter, map, "2000."

2000, May 5
4037-4038 A1787 Set of 2 1.75 .85

A1788

Orchids — A1789

Designs: 20ch, Cattleya intermedia. 50ch, Dendrobium moschatum. 70ch, Brassolaeliocattleya.
2w, Laeliocattleya.

2000, May 15
4039-4041 A1788 Set of 3 1.60 .80
4041a Booklet pane of 8, 2 each #4039-4040, 4 #4041 — —
Complete booklet, #4041a —

Complete booklet sold for 4.40w, and exists imperforate.

Souvenir Sheet

4042 A1789 2w multicolored 2.00 1.00

Bridges — A1790

Designs: 20ch, Okryn Bridge. 30ch, Ansan Bridge. 1w, Rungna Bridge.

2000, May 21
4043-4045 A1790 Set of 3 2.25 1.10
4045a Booklet pane of 8, 2 #4043, 3 each #4044-4045 — —
Complete booklet, #4045a —

Complete booklet sold for 4.50w.

WIPA 2000 Int'l Stamp Exhib., Vienna — A1791

Traditional Korean musical instruments and folk dances: a, 1w, Okryugum and Jaenggang dance. b, 1.50w, Bungum and Full Moon Viewing dance. c, 1.50w, Janggo drum and "Trio" dance.

2000, May 30
4046 A1791 Sheet of 3, #a-c 4.00 2.00

Nos. 4046b-4046c are airmail stamps.

Children's Songs — A1792

Designs: 40ch, Song "Halfmoon," two children in boat. 60ch, Song "Kangram Nostalgia," boy and girl.
1.50w, Song "Spring in Home Village," boy and girl with flowers.

2000, June 1 ***Perf. 11¾x12¼***
4049-4050 A1792 Set of 2 1.00 .50

Souvenir Sheet

4051 A1792 1.50w multicolored 1.75 .85

Cephalopods — A1793

Designs: 40ch, Nautilus pompilius. 60ch, Octopus vularis.
1.50w, Ommastrephes sloanei pacificus.

2000, June 15 ***Perf. 11½***
4052-4053 A1793 Set of 2 1.25 .60

Souvenir Sheet

4054 A1793 1.50w multicolored 1.75 .85
a. Booklet pane of 8, 4#4052, 2 each #4053-4054 — —
Complete booklet, #4054a —

No. 4054a exists imperforate. Complete booklet sold for 6w.
For surcharges, see Nos. 4544-4545.

Mandarin Ducks — A1794

Designs: No. 4055, 50ch, Pair of ducks, couple on bridge. No. 4056, 50ch, Pair of ducks, couple in row boat.
1w, Pair of ducks, ducklings.

2000, June 16 ***Perf. 11¾x12¼***

4055-4056 A1794 Set of 2	1.00	.50
4056a Booklet pane of 7, 3 #4055, 4 #4056	3.75	1.75
Complete booklet, #4056a	3.75	

Souvenir Sheet

4057 A1794 1w multicolored	1.00	.50

Nos. 4055-4056 were issued both in separate sheets of 9 (3x3) and in booklet panes of 7, containing 3 No. 4055 and 4 No. 4056, in an alternating arrangement. Complete booklet sold for 3.70w.
For overprints, see Nos. 4071-4073.

Sports A1795

Designs: 80ch, Table tennis. 1w, Basketball. 1.20w, Baseball.

2000, July 7 ***Perf. 13¼***

4058-4060 A1795 Set of 3	3.50	1.75
4060a Booklet pane of 7, 2 each #4058-4059, 3 #4060	—	—
Complete booklet, #4060a	—	

Issed in sheets of 6, 2 each of Nos. 4058-4060. Complete booklet sold for 7.40w.

Trucks — A1796

Designs: 40ch, *Sungri-61 NA*. 70ch, Flat-bed truck. 1.50w, *Konsol* 25-50n dump truck.

2000, July 24 ***Perf. 12***

4061-4063 A1796 Set of 3	2.75	1.50

Korean People's Army — A1797

Portraits of KPA commanders and weapons: 60ch, Ri Tae Hun and 76mm field gun, 80ch, Ko hyon Bink and T-34 tank. 1w, Paek Ki Rah and Yak-9P pursuit plane.

2000, July 27

4064-4066 A1797 Set of 3	2.25	1.10

Issed in sheets of 6, 2 each of Nos. 4064-4066.

Minerals A1798

Designs: 30ch, Fluorite. 60ch, Graphite. 1.60w, Magnesite.

2000, Aug. 15 ***Perf. 13¼***

4067-4069 A1798 Set of 3	1.10	.60
4069a Booklet pane of 8, 3 each #4067-4068, 2 #4069	—	—
Complete booklet, #4069a	—	

Complete booklet sold for 6.10w.

Souvenir Sheet

4070 A1798 1.60w multicolored	1.60	.80

Nos. 4055-4057 Overprinted

2000, Aug. 15 ***Perf. 13¼***

4071 A1794 50ch On #4055	.50	.25
4072 A1794 50ch On #4056	.50	.25
a. Booklet pane of 7, 3 #4071, 4 #4072	—	—
Complete booklet, #4072a	—	

Complete booklet sold for 7.20w.

Souvenir Sheet

4073 1w On #4057	1.00	.50

International Stamp Exhibition, Jakarta.

Sydney 2000, Summer Olympic Games — A1799

Designs: a, 80ch, Swimmer. b, 1.20, Cyclist. c, 2w, Runner.

2000, Sept. 15 ***Perf. 13½***

4074 A1799 Sheet of 3, #a-c	4.25	2.25

Myohyang Mountain A1800

Designs: 40ch (No. 4077), Sanju Falls, wild pig and piglet. 40ch (No. 4078), Inho Rock, Fallow deer, pair. 1.20w, Stag and fawn.

2000, Sept. 27 ***Perf. 13¼***

4077-4079 A1800 Set of 3	2.00	1.00

A1801

Korean Workers' Party, 55th Anniv. A1802

Designs: 40ch, Party emblem, Party Museum.
No. 4082: a, Kim Il Sung. b, Kim Jong Il. c, Kim Jong Suk.

2000, Oct. 10 ***Perf. 13¼***

4081 A1801 40ch multicolored	.25	.25

Souvenir Sheet

4082 A1802 50ch Sheet of 3, #a-c	1.50	.70

Land Rezoning Project — A1803

10ch, Flags, bulldozer and trucks, urban scene and rice fields.

2000, Oct. 15

4083 A1803 10ch multicolored	.25	.25

A1804

Tae Hongdae Potato Farms — A1805

Designs: 40ch, Potatoes, pigs, scientist, collective farm.
2w, painting, *The Great Leader President Kim Il Sung Brought a Bumper Crop of Potato in the Paektu Pleateau.*

2000, Oct. 20 ***Perf. 11½***

4084 A1804 40ch multicolored	.40	.25

Souvenir Sheet

4085 A1805 2w multicolored	1.75	.90

Kim Jong Il & Pres. Jiang Zemin — A1806

2000, Oct. 21 ***Perf. 11¾x12¼***

4086 A1806 1.20w multicolored	1.75	.85

Visit of Kim Jong Il to China.

Kim Jong Il & Pres. Kim Dae Jung — A1807

2000, Oct. 23 ***Perf. 11½x12***

4087 A1807 2w multicolored	2.75	1.50

North-South Korean Summit Talks, Pyongyang.

Kim Jong Il & Pres. Putin — A1808

2000, Oct. 24 ***Perf. 11¾x11½***

4088 A1808 1.50w multicolored	2.25	1.10

Visit of Kim Jong Il to Russia.

Chinese & Korean Soldiers — A1809

Chinese People's Volunteers' Entry Into Korean War, 50th Anniv. — A1810

No. 4090: a, 10ch, Soldiers crossing the Amnok River. b, 10ch, Battle scene. c, 50ch, Kim Il Sung and Chinese officers. d, 50ch, Mao Zedong presiding over meeting to decide upon entry into Korean War. e, 80ch, Chinese soldiers observing battle.

2000, Oct. 25 ***Perf. 13¼***

4089 A1809 30ch multicolored	.65	.35
4090 A1810 Sheet of 5, #a-e	2.25	1.10

Alpine Flowers — A1811

Designs: 30ch, Aquilegia oxysepala. 50ch, Brilliant campion (Lychnis fulgens). 70ch, Self-heal (Prunela vulgaris).

2000, Nov. 5 ***Perf. 13½***

4095-4097 A1811 Set of 3	1.50	.60

Nos. 4095-4097 were printed in sheets containing a decorative label.

A1812

Repatriation of Long-Term Prisoners of War — A1813

Designs: 80ch, Returning prisoners receiving bouquets of flowers from women in Pyongyang. 1.20w, Prisoners welcomed by crowd, in front of statue of Kim Il Sung.

2000, Dec. 20

4098 A1812 80ch multi	1.00	.50
4099 A1813 1.20w sil & multi	1.25	.60

New Year — A1814

10ch, Flag, trees, factory, missiles, ship, jet planes.

2001, Jan. 1 ***Perf. 11½***
4100 A1814 10ch multicolored .25 .25

New Year (2nd Issue) A1815

Tale of the White Snake: 10ch, White Snake meeting Xu Xian. 40ch, Stealing the Immortal Greass. 50ch, White and Green Snakes and Xu Xian. 80ch, Flooding of Jinshan Hill.
1.20w, White Snake and Green Snake.

2001, Jan. 1 ***Perf. 12½x12***
4101-4104 A1815 Set of 4 3.75 1.75
4104a Sheet of 4, #4101-4104 3.75 1.75

Souvenir Sheet

4105 A1815 1.20w multicolored 2.50 1.10

Nos. 4101-4104 were each issued singly in larger sheets and in combination in sheets of 4 (No. 4104a).

A1816

World Chess Champions — A1817

Designs: 10ch, E. Lasker (1868-1941) and J.R. Capablanca (1888-1942). 20ch, A. Alekhine (1892-1946) and E. Euwe (1901-80). 30ch, M. Botvinnik (1911-95) and V. Smylov (b. 1921). 40ch, T. Petrosian (1929-84) and M. Tal (1936-93). 50ch, B. Spassky (b. 1937) and R. Fisher (b. 1943). 1w, A. Karpov (b. 1954) and G. Kasparov (b. 1963).
2.50w, Wilhelm Steinmetz (1836-1900).

2001, Jan. 5 ***Perf. 13½***
4106-4111 A1816 Set of 6 5.00 2.50
4111a Sheet of 6, #4106-4111 5.00 2.50
4111b Booklet pane of 6, #4106-4111 5.25 —
Complete booklet, #4111b 5.75 —

Souvenir Sheet

4112 A1817 2.50w multicolored 5.00 2.50

No. 4111b contains Nos. 4106-4111 in a se-tenant vertical strip of six, with narrow decorative selvage.
For overprints, see Nos. 4129-4135.

Ri-Dynasty Men's Costumes — A1818

Designs: 10ch, Trousers and jacket. 40ch, Vest. 50ch, Magoja. 70ch, Turumagi
1.50w, Wedding attire.

2001, Jan. 19 ***Perf. 12x12½***
4113-4116 A1818 Set of 4 3.50 1.75
4116a Sheet of 5, #4113-4116, 4117a 7.00 3.50
4116b Booklet pane of 6, #4113-4114, 4116, 4117a, 2 #4115 7.75 —
Complete booklet, #4116b 8.00

Souvenir Sheet

4117 A1818 1.50w multicolored 3.50 1.75

Nos. 4113-4116 were each issued both in large sheets and within sheets of 5, in combination with the 1.50w (No. 4117a) value contained in the souvenir sheet, No. 4117.
No. 4116b contains the six stamps in a se-tenant horizontal strip with narrow distinctive selvage.

Fire Engines A1819

Fire-fighting vehicles and logos warning against specific fire hazards: 20ch, Small 2-door vehicle (small appliances). 30ch, Large ladder truck (oil can). 40ch, 2-door truck with closed back (match). 60ch, Small truck with ladder and external hose port (gas can).
2w, Old-fashioned fire truck with ladder (cigarette).

2001, Jan. 20 ***Perf. 12½x12***
4118-4121 A1819 Set of 4 3.50 1.75
4121a Booklet pane of 12, 3 ea. #4118-4121 10.00 —
Complete booklet, #4121a 10.50
4121b Sheet of 5, #4118-4121, type of #4122 + label 11.00

Souvenir Sheet

4122 A1819 2w multicolored 4.50 2.25

No. 4121a contains three attached se-tenant blocks of Nos. 4118-4121, arranged horizontally, with inscribed selvage on left and right sides.

Hong Kong 2001 Stamp Exhibition — A1820

1.40w, Black-naped oriole (Oriolus chinensis).

2001, Feb. 1 ***Perf. 11½***
4123 A1820 1.40w multicolored 2.75 1.50

Kim Jong Il, 59th Birthday — A1821

10ch, Jong Il Peak in Paekdu Range, *Kimjongilia*.

2001, Feb. 10 ***Perf. 13½***
4124 A1821 10ch multicolored .35 .25

New Millenium, Joint Editorial *Rodong Sinmun, Josoninmingun* and *Chongnyonjonwi* Newspapers — A1822

10ch, Flag, symbols of Industry, Agriculture, Transportation

2001, Mar. 5
4125 A1822 10ch multicolored .35 .25

Log Cabin at Revolutionary Headquarters on Mt. Paekdu — A1823

2001, Mar. 7 ***Perf. 11½***
4126 A1823 40ch multicolored .70 .30

Kim Il Sung's Birthplace at Mangyongdae A1824

Portraits of Kim Il Sung — A1825

No. 1428 (each 80ch): a, As child. b, As Jilin-Yuwen Middle School student. c, As anti-Japanese revolutionary. d, As leader in early DPRK period. e, As supreme commander of the Korean People's Army. f, As leader during post-Korean War period. g, Portrait in middle age. h, Portrait in old age.

2001, Apr. 10 ***Perf. 13½***
4127 A1824 10ch multicolored .45 .25

Sheet of 8

4128 A1825 Sheet of 8, #a.-#g 11.00 5.75

Day of the Sun.

Nos. 4106-4112 Overprinted in Gold with Biographical Information

2001, Apr. 20
4129-4134 A1816 Set of 6 5.75 3.00

Souvenir Sheet

4135 A1817 2.50w multicolored 5.75 3.00

Kim Jong Il — A1826

2001, Apr. 25 ***Perf. 12***
4136 A1826 1w multicolored 1.75 .85

Propaganda issue, with the theme "Long Live the Great Victory of Songun Politics!"

Highways A1827

Designs: 40ch, Pyongyang-Kaesong motorway. 70ch, Pyongyang-Hyangsan tourist expressway. 1.20w, Youth Hero motorway. 1.50w, Pyongyang-Wonsan tourist expressway.

2001, May 7 ***Perf. 12½x12***
4137-4140 A1827 Set of 4 6.25 3.00

Historical Pavilions A1828

Designs: 40ch, Ryongwang Pavilion in Pyongyang. 80ch, Inphung Pavilion in Kanggye. 1.50w, Paeksang Pavilion in Anju. 2w, Thonggun Pavilion in Uiju.

2001, May 15 ***Perf. 13¼***
4141-4144 A1828 Set of 4 8.00 4.00
4144a Booklet pane of 4, #4141-4144 8.00 —
Complete booklet, #4144a 8.50

No. 4144a contains Nos. 4141-4144 in a se-tenant block of four, within decorative selvage.

Education in Class Consciousness A1829

2001, June 5
4145 A1829 10ch multicolored .35 .25

Korean Birds — A1830

Designs: 10ch, Luscinia svecica. 40ch, Anser anser. 80ch, Diomedea albatrus. 1w, Charadrius dubius. 1.20w, Uria aalge. 1.50w, Delichon urbica.

2001, June 9 ***Perf. 11½***
4146 A1830 Sheet of 6, #a.-f. 10.00 5.00
g. Booklet pane of 8, #4146c-4146f, 2 ea. #4146a-4146b 11.50 —
Complete booklet, #4146g 12.50

BELGICA 2001 Philatelic Exhibition.
No. 4146g contains the eight stamps in a se-tenant horizontal (4x2) block with inscribed selvage on left and right sides.

Chinese Communist Party, 80th Anniv. — A1831

Designs, each 80ch: No. 4147, Mao Zedong. No. 4148, Deng Xiaoping. No. 4149, Jiang Zemin.

2001, June 15
4147-4149 A1831 Set of 3 4.25 2.00

Compare with Nos. 4226-4228.

Mt. Kumol — A1832

Designs: 10ch, Woljong Temple. 40ch, Revolutionary site. 70ch, Potnamu Pavilion. 1.30w, Rock of Tak Peak. 1.50w, Ryongyon Falls.

2001, July 9 ***Perf. 12x12¼***
4150 A1832 Sheet of 5, #a.-e. + label 6.75 3.50
f. Booklet pane of 5, #4150a-4150e + label 7.00 —
Complete booklet, #4150f 7.50

No. 4150f contains the stamps and labels of No. 4150 in the same format, but top and bottom marginal selvage is blank, with side selvage containing maple leaf on left and inscriptions on left and right.

Protected Plants — A1833

Designs: 10ch, Rheum Coreanum. 40ch, Forsythia densiflora. 1w, Rhododendron yedoense. 2w, Iris setosa.

2001, July 20 *Perf. 13½*

4151-4154 A1833 Set of 4 6.25 3.00
4154a Booklet pane of 6, #4152, 4154, 2 ea. #4151, 4153 8.00 —
Complete booklet, #4154a 9.00

No. 4154a contains the six stamps in a se-tenant vertical strip of 6, with inscribed selvage on top and bottom margins.

Orchids — A1834

Designs: 10ch, Eria pannea. 40ch, Cymbidium. 90ch, Sophrolaeliocattleya. 1.60w, Cattleya trianae.
No. 4159: 2w, Cypripedium macranthum.

2001, Aug. 1

4155-4158 A1834 Set of 4 6.75 3.50
4158a Booklet pane of 6, #4155-4156, 4158, #4159a, 2 #4157 13.00 —
Complete booklet, #4158a 14.00

Souvenir Sheet

4159 A1834 2w multicolored 4.50 2.25

No. 4158a contains the six stamps in a se-tenant horizontal strip of 6, with decorative selvage on left and right sides.

Lighthouses — A1835

Designs: 40ch, Pibaldo Lighthouse. 70ch, Soho Lighthouse. 90ch, Komalsan Lighthouse.
No. 4163: 1.50w, Alsom Lighthouse.

2001, Aug. 18

4160-4162 A1835 Set of 3 4.50 2.25
4162a Booklet pane of 6, #4160-4161, 2 #4162, 2 #4163a 14.00 —
Complete booklet, #4162a 14.50
4162b Sheet of 4, #4160-4162, 4163a 8.00 4.00

Souvenir Sheet

4163 A1835 1.50w multicolored 3.50 1.75

Nos. 4160-4162 were issued both separately in large sheets and together, with the 1.50w value from No. 4163, in a sheet of 5 (No.4162b). No. 4162a contains the six stamps in a horizontal strip of 6, with thin plain selvage.

Kim Po Hyon (1871-1955), Grandfather of Kim Il Sung — A1836

2001, Aug. 19

4164 A1836 1w multicolored 1.75 .85

Protected Animals A1837

Designs: 10ch, Ciconia nigra. 40ch, Aegypius monachus. 70ch, Hydropotes inermis. 90ch, Nemorhaedus goral.
1.30w, Bubo bubo.

2001, Sept. 2

4165-4168 A1837 Set of 4 4.50 2.25
4168a Sheet of 5, #4165-4168, 4169a + label 8.00 —
4168b Booklet pane of 6, #4165-1467, 1469a, 2 x 1468 9.00 —
Complete booklet, #4168b 9.50

Souvenir Sheet

4169 A1837 1.30w multicolored 2.75 1.50

Nos. 4165-4168 were issued both separately in large sheets and together, with the 1.30w value from No. No. 4169, in a sheet of 5 (No. 4168a).
No. 4168b contains the six stamps in a se-tenant vertical strip, within narrow decorated selvage.
For surcharge, see No. 4572.

Olympic Games 2008, Beijing — A1838

Designs, each 56ch: a, Deng Ya Ping, Gold medalist ('96), Women's Singles, Table Tennis. b, Jiang Zemin, PRC president. c, Wang Jun Xia, Chinese athlete. d, Li Ning, Chinese gymnast. e, Fu Ming Xia, Chinese diver.

2001, Sept. 10 *Perf. 12½*

4170 A1838 Sheet of 5, #a.-e. 5.75 2.75

Cycle Sports — A1839

Designs: 10ch, Cycle soccer. 40ch, Road racing. 1.50w, Mountainbike racing. 2w, Indoor race.

2001, Sept. 20 *Perf. 12*

4171 A1839 Sheet of 4, #a.-d. 8.00 4.00

Space Exploration — A1840

Designs: 10ch, Yuri Gagarin (1934-68), Soviet Cosmonaut. 40ch, Apollo 11 Moon Landing. 1.50w, *Kwangmyongsong*, North Korean satellite (1998). 2w, Edmund Hailey (1656-1742), Halley's Comet and *Giotto* satellite.

2001, Sept. 25

4172 A1840 Sheet of 4, #a.-d. 7.50 3.50
e. Booklet pane of 5, #4172a-4172c, 2 #1472d 12.00 —
Complete booklet, #4172e 13.00

No. 4172e contains five stamps in a se-tenant horizontal strip.

Vladimir Putin and Kim Jong Il — A1841

2001, Oct. 12 *Perf. 12½x12*

4173 A1841 1.50w multicolored 2.50 1.25

Visit of Kim Jong Il to Russia.

Kim Jong Il and Jiang Zemin — A1842

2001, Oct. 25 *Perf. 11½x12*

4174 A1842 1.50w multicolored 2.50 1.25

Meeting between Kim Jong Il and Jiang Zemin, president of the People's Republic of China.

Kim Jong Suk in Battle — A1843

2001, Nov. 24 *Perf. 12½x12*

4175 A1843 1.60w multicolored 3.50 1.75

Kim Jong Suk, anti-Japanese revolutionary hero, 84th birth anniv.

Kim Jong Il Inspecting Troops — A1844

2001, Dec. 1 *Perf. 13½*

4176 A1844 1w multicolored 1.75 .85

10th anniv. of appointment of Kim Jong Il as Supreme Commander of the Korean People's Army.

Chollima Statue — A1845

2002, Jan. 1

4177 A1845 10ch multicolored .35 .25

New Year.

A1846

A1847

Horses from painting *Ten Horses*, by Wang Zhi Cheng (1702-68): 10ch, White horse. 40ch, Bay. 60ch, Pinto. 1.30w, Piebald.
1.60w, Black stallion, from painting *Horse Master Jiu Fang Gao*, by Xu Bei Hong (1895-1953).

2002, Jan. 1

4178-4181 A1846 Set of 4 4.25 2.00
4181a Sheet of 5, #4178-4181, 4182a 7.25 3.50
4181b Booklet pane of 6, #4178, 4181, 2 each #4179-4180 10.00 —
Complete booklet, #4181b 10.00

Souvenir Sheet

4182 A1847 1.60w multicolored 2.75 1.50

Traditional New Year — Year of the Horse.
Nos. 4178-4181 were issued both separately in large sheets and together, with the 1.60w value from No. 4182, in a sheet of 5 (No. 4181a).
Complete booklet sold for 3.60w.

Flower Basket — A1848

Kim Jong Il with Soldiers — A1849

Kim Jong Il — A1850

Kim Il Sung, Kim Jong Il, Kim Jong Suk — A1851

2002, Feb. 1 ***Perf. 13½***

4183 A1848 10ch multicolored .35 .25

Souvenir Sheets

4184 A1849 1.50w multicolored 2.75 1.50

Perf. 11½x12

4185 A1850 2w multicolored 3.50 1.75

Perf. 12x12½

4186 A1851 Sheet of 3, #a.-c. 6.75 3.50

Kim Jong Il, 60th Birthday.
No. 4185 bears a metallic gold application.

Centenary of First Zeppelin Flight A1852

Designs: 40ch, LZ-1. 80ch, LZ-120. 1.20w, Zeppelin NT.
2.40w, Zeppelin NT (different view).

2002, Feb. 5 ***Perf. 12***

4187-4189 A1852 Set of 3 4.25 2.00
4189a Sheet of 4, #4187-4189, 4190a 8.50 4.25

Souvenir Sheet

4190 A1852 2.40w multicolored 4.25 2.00
a. Booklet pane of 4, #4187-4190 *16.00* —
Complete booklet, #4190a *16.00*

Nos. 4187-4187 were issued both separately in large sheets and together, with the 2.40w value from No. 4190, in a sheet of 4 (No. 4189a). Complete booklet sold for 4.90w.

Banner, Torch, Soldiers — A1853

2002, Feb. 25 ***Perf. 13½***

4191 A1853 10ch multicolored .35 .25

Annual joint editorial of the three state newspapers, *Rodong Sinmun, Josoninmingum* and *Chongnyonjonwi.*

Mushrooms — A1854

Designs: a, 10ch, Collybia confluons. b, 40ch, Sparassis laminosa. c, 80ch, Amanita vaginata. d, 1.20w, Russia integra. e, 1.50w, Pholiota squarrosa.

2002, Feb. 25 ***Perf. 13½***

4192 A1854 Block of 5, #a-e + label 7.50 3.75
f. Booklet pane of 5, #4192a-4192e, + label *19.00* —
Complete booklet, #4192f *19.00*

Complete booklet sold for 4.20w.

A1855

A1856

Kim Il Sung (1912-1994) — A1857

Designs: 10ch, Kim Il Sung's birthplace, *Kimsungilia.*
Nos. 4198-4200 (each 1.50w): No, 4198, Kim Il Sung with Kim Jong Suk (1941). No. 4199, Kim Il Sung as student, with black cap (1927). No. 4200, Kim Il Sung and Kim Chaek, political commissar.
No. 4201: 2w, Portrait of Kim Il Sung.

2002, Mar. 15 ***Perf. 13½***

4197 A1855 10ch multicolored .35 .25

Souvenir Sheets

4198-4200 A1856 1.50w Set of 3 6.75 3.50

With Gold Metallic Application

Perf. 11½x12

4201 A1857 2w multicolored 3.50 1.75

Kang Pan Suk — A1858

2002, Mar. 21 ***Perf. 11½x11¾***

4202 A1858 1w multicolored 1.75 .85

Kang Pan Sok, mother of Kim Il Sung, 110th birth anniv.

20th April Spring Friendship Art Festival — A1859

2002, Mar. 25 ***Perf. 13¼***

4203 A1859 10ch multicolored .60 .25

Locomotives A1860

Designs: 10ch, Kanghaenggun 1.5-01 electric train. 40ch, Samjiyon 1001 electric train. 1.50w, Steam locomotive. 2w, Steam locomotive, diff.
No. 4208, 2w, Pulgungi 5112 diesel locomotive.

2002, Apr. 10 ***Perf. 11½***

4204-4207 A1860 Set of 4 6.75 3.50

Souvenir Sheet

4208 A1860 2w multicolored 3.50 1.75
a. Booklet pane of 5, #4204-4208 27.50 —
Complete booklet, #4208a *27.50*

For surcharge, see No. 4566. Complete booklet sold for 6.20w.

He Baozhen, 100th Anniv. Birth — A1861

Designs: a, 1w, He Baozhen and Liu Shaoqi in 1923. b, 40ch, He Baozhen's family. c, 30ch, Family home in Dao xian County, Henan Province. d, 10ch, Letter in Chinese, from Liu Ying, a wife of Zhang Wentian, Chinese Communist Party official. e, 20ch, Monument at He Baozhen's birthplace.

2002, Apr. 20 ***Perf. 13¼***

4209 A1861 Sheet of 5, #a.-e. 3.50 1.75

He Baozhen, first wife of Liu Shaoqi, Chairman of the People's Republic of China 1959-68.

Shells — A1862

Designs: 10ch, Cristaria plicata. 40ch, Lanceolaria cospidata kuroda. 1w, Schistodesmus lampreyanus. 1.50w, Lamprotula coreana.

2002, Apr. 21

4210-4213 A1862 Set of 4 5.75 2.75
4213a Booklet pane of 6, #4212-4213. 2 each #4210-4211 *15.00* —
Complete booklet, #4213a *15.00*

For surcharge, see No. 4601. Complete booklet sold for 3.70w.

A1863

Korean People's Army, 70th Anniv. — A1864

Designs: 10ch, Soldier, sailor, pilot, symbolizing the three branches of the armed forces.
1.60w, Kim Il Sung and Kim Jong Il walking with army officers and political functionaries.

2002, Apr. 25 ***Perf. 12¼x11¾***

4214 A1863 10ch multicolored .35 .25

Souvenir Sheet

4215 A1864 1.60w multicolored 2.75 1.50

Legend 'Arirang' — A1865

Designs: a, 10ch, Ri Rang and Song Bu as children. b, 40ch, As young adults. c, 50ch, Ri Rang killing the landlord. d, 1.50w, Song Bu.

2002, Apr. 28 ***Perf. 13¼***

4216 A1865 Sheet of 4, #a.-d. 4.25 2.00

A1866

Mass Gymnastics and Artistic Performance of 'Arirang' — A1867

Designs: 10ch, Actors. 20ch, Cartoon characters. 30ch, Dancer holding fan. 40ch, Dancer, gymnasts with hoops.
1w, Dancer with tambourine.

2002, Apr. 28 ***Perf. 12¼***

4217-4220 A1866 Set of 4 1.75 .85

Souvenir Sheet

4221 A1867 1w multicolored 2.00 1.00

Nos. 4217-4220 were each issued in sheets of 6, with pictorial margins and Arirang logo.

Symbols of Modern Science & Industry
A1868

2002, May 2 *Perf. 13¼*

4222 A1868 10ch multicolored .35 .25

Science and Technology promotion: "Science and Technology are the Driving Force of Building a Great Prosperous Powerful Nation."

Ryongmun Cavern — A1869

Designs: a, 10ch, Pink stalactite. b, 20ch, Green stalactite. c, 30ch, Golden stalagmite. d, 40ch, Rough-surfaced orange stalagmite.

2002, May 25 *Perf. 11½*

4223 A1869 Sheet of 4, #a.-d. 2.75 1.50

Monument — A1870

2002, May 2 *Perf. 13¼*

4224 A1870 10ch multicolored .35 .25

30th Anniv. of the Elucidation of the Three Principles for National Reunification.

Butterflies — A1871

Designs: a, 10ch, Stauropus fagi. b, 40ch, Agrias claudina. c, 1.50w, Catocala nupta. d, 2w, Morpho rhetenor.

2002, June 30 *Perf. 11¾*

4225 A1871 Block of 4, #a.-d. 8.50 4.25

e. Booklet pane of 5, #4225a, 4225c-4225d, 2 #4225b *17.50* —

Complete booklet, #4225e *17.50*

Complete booklet sold for 4.60w.

Nos. 4147-4149 with Added Flags in Margins

A1872

2002, June 30 *Perf. 11½*

4226-4228 A1872 Set of 3 sheets 4.75 2.25

16th National Congress of the Communist Party of China, Beijing, Nov. 8-14.

Compare with Nos. 4147-4149.

Elderly Man, Child, Hospital
A1873

2002, July 5 *Perf. 12¼*

4229 A1873 10ch multicolored .35 .25

50th Anniv. of Universal Free Medical System.

Kim Jong Suk (1917-49) — A1874

Designs: a, 10ch, As child. b, 40ch, As young woman in Children's Corps. c, 1w, In army uniform. d, 1.50w, With long hair, in civilian clothing.

2002, July 20 *Perf. 13¼*

4230 A1874 Sheet of 4, #a.-d. 2.50 1.25

Kim Jong Suk, first wife of Kim Il Sung and mother of Kim Jong Il.

Soldier, Worker, Farmer — A1875

2002, July 29 *Perf. 11½*

4231 A1875 10ch multicolored .35 .25

30th anniv. of the DPRK Constitution.

A1876

World Red Cross & Red Crescent Day — A1877

No. 4232: a, 3w, Korean returnees. b, 12w, Red Cross medics administering first aid. c, 150w, North Korean truck delivering aid to South Korean flood victims.

No. 4233: 80w, AIDS victim, family.

2002, Sept. 20 *Perf. 13¼*

Sheet of 6

4232 A1876 Sheet, 2 each #a.-c. 5.75 2.50

Souvenir Sheet

4233 A1877 80w multicolored 1.75 .85

a. Booklet pane of 5, #4232c, 4233, 2 each #4232a, 4232b *11.00* —

Complete booklet, #4233a *11.00*

Complete booklet sold for 2.75w.

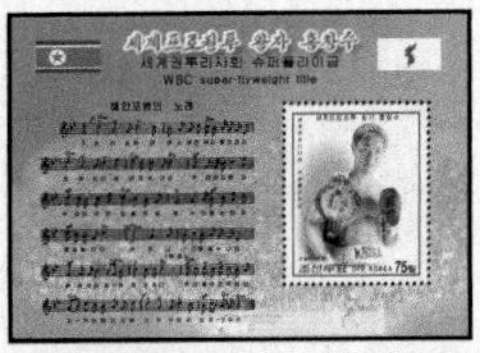

Hong Chang Su, 2000 World Super-Flyweight Boxing Champion — A1878

2002, Sept. 25 *Perf. 11½*

4234 A1878 75w multicolored 1.75 .85

Souvenir Sheets

Kim Jong Il with Pres. Putin — A1879

Kim Jong Il Shaking Hands with Pres. Putin — A1880

No. 4235 measures 85x70mm, No. 4236 120x100mm.

2002, Oct. 15 *Perf. 13¼*

4235 A1879 70w multicolored 1.75 .85

4236 A1880 120w multicolored 2.25 1.10

Kim Jong Il's Visit to Russia

Siamese Cat — A1881

Cavalier King Charles Spaniel — A1882

Designs: 12w, Phungsan dog. 100w, White shorthair cat. 150w, Black and white shorthair cat.

2002, Oct. 20 *Perf. 12*

4237-4240 A1881 Set of 4 5.75 2.75

4240a Booklet pane of 6, #4239-4240, 2 each #4237-4238 *16.00* —

Complete booklet, #4240a *16.00*

Souvenir Sheet

4241 A1882 150w multicolored 3.50 1.75

a. Inscr. "World Philatelic Exhibition Bangkok 2003" and emblem in margin 3.50 1.75

No. 4241a issued 10/4/2003. Complete booklet sold for 295w. No. 4240a exists imperforate.

Minerals — A1883

Designs: a, 3w, Pyrite. b, 12w, Magnetite. c, 130w, Calcite. d, 150w, Galena.

2002, Oct. 25 *Perf. 13¼*

4242 A1883 Block of 4, #a-d 6.25 3.50

e. Booklet pane of 5, #4242am 4242cm 4242d, 2 each #4242b *15.00* —

Complete booklet, #4242e *15.00* —

Complete booklet sold for 322w.

Kim Jong Il and PM Junichiro Signing Declaration — A1884

Kim Jong Il with Japanese Prime Minister Koizumi Junichiro — A1885

Japan-Korea Bilateral Declaration

No. 4246 measures 90x80mm, No. 4247 75x65mm.

2002, Oct. 25 **Souvenir Sheets**

4246 A1884 120w multicolored 2.25 1.10

4247 A1885 150w multicolored 3.50 1.75

Kim Il Sung's Birthplace, Mangyongdae
A1886

Kim Jong Il's Birthplace, Mt. Paektu
A1887

Kim Jong Suk's Birthplace, Hoeryong
A1888

Kimilsungia
A1889

Torch, Tower of Juche Idea
A1890

DPRK Flag
A1891

Kimjongilia
A1892

Magnolia Blossom
A1893

DPRK Coat of Arms
A1894

Chollima Statue
A1895

Victory Monument
A1896

Party Founding Monument
A1897

Perf. 11½, 13¼x13½ (#4252-4253, 4256-4259)

2002, Nov. 20

4248	A1886	1w violet brn	.25	.25
4249	A1887	3w blue green	.25	.25
4250	A1888	5w olive brn	.25	.25
4251	A1889	10w dk lilac rose	.25	.25
4252	A1890	12w dk reddish brn	.25	.25
4253	A1891	20w dp blue & red	.40	.25
4254	A1892	30w brnsh red	.60	.25
4255	A1893	40w dp grnsh blue	.75	.40
4256	A1894	50w dk brown	.85	.50
4257	A1895	70w dk olive grn	1.10	.60
4258	A1896	100w brown	1.75	.85
4259	A1897	200w dk lilac rose	3.50	1.75
		Nos. 4248-4259 (12)	10.20	5.85

See No. 4877. For surcharges, see Nos. 4877A, 4877F.

Nos. 2675a, 3238, 3321, 3493a Surcharged

Surcharge without period (a)

Surcharge with period (b)

2002 ***Method and Perfs as Before***

4259A	A1456(a)	3w on 10ch	—
4259B	A1487(a)	3w on 10ch	—
4259C	A1571(b)	3w on 10ch	—
4259D	A1259(b)	3w on 40ch	—

New Year — A1898

2003, Jan. 1 ***Perf. 13¼***

4260 A1898 3w multicolored .35 .25

A1899

Animated Film, *Antelopes Defeat Bald Eagles* — A1900

Designs: 3w, Mother antelope pleading with bald eagle stealing her baby. 50w, Antelopes uniting to defeat bald eagle. 70w, Bald eagle eating fish poisoned by antelopes. 100w, Mother antelope reunited with her child.

150w, Antelopes carrying litter full of fruit.

2003, Jan. 1

4261-4264	A1899	Set of 4	3.00	1.50
4264a		Booklet pane of 8, 2 each #4261-4264	*25.00*	—
		Complete booklet, #4264a	*25.00*	

Souvenir Sheet

4265 A1900 150w multicolored 1.75 .85

Complete booklet sold for 461w.

Folk Festivals — A1901

Designs: 3w, Mother and children greeting Full Moon (Lunar New Year, Jan. 15). 12w, Dancers with Full Moon (Lunar New Year). 40w, Two girls on swing (Spring Festival). 70w, Mother and daughter laying flowers on anti-Japanese martyrs' monument (Hangawi - Harvest Moon Festival). 140w, Peasant dance (Hangawi - Harvest Moon Festival).

112w, Wresting (Spring Festival).

2003, Jan. 20 ***Perf. 11¾***

4266-4270 A1901 Set of 5 3.25 1.50

Souvenir Sheet

4271 A1901 112w multicolored 1.75 .75

Soldier — A1902

2003, Feb. 14 ***Perf. 13¼***

4272 A1902 12w multicolored .50 .25

Annual joint editorial of the three state newspapers, *Rodong Sinmun, Josoninmingum* and *Chongnyonjonwi.*

Weapons, Proclamation
A1903

2003, Feb. 15

4273 A1903 30w multicolored .60 .25

North Korean withdrawal from the Nuclear Non-Proliferation Treaty.

Ode Monument — A1904

Sunrise at Mt. Paektu — A1905

2003, Feb. 16 ***Perf. 12¼x11¼***

4274 A1904 3w multicolored .35 .25

Souvenir Sheet

4275 A1905 75w multicolored 1.10 .60

Kim Jong Il, 61st Birthday.

A1906

Ships — A1907

Designs: 15w, Cargo ship *Paekmagang.* 50w, Dredger *Konsol.* 70w, Passenger ship *Undok No. 2.* 112w, Cargo ship *Piryugang.*

150w, Excursion ship *Pyongyang No. 1.*

2003, Feb. 18 ***Perf. 13½***

4276-4279	A1906	Set of 4	3.50	1.75
4279a		Booklet pane of 6, #4276-4277, 2 each #4278-4279	*20.00*	—
		Complete booklet, #4279a	*20.00*	

Souvenir Sheet

4280 A1907 150w multicolored 2.00 1.00

Complete booklet sold for 444w.

A1908

Cars Used by Kim Il Sung — A1909

Designs: 3w, *Zis.* 14w, *Gaz.* 70w, *Pobeda.* 90w, *Mercedes Benz.*

150w, Painting by Kim San Gon *Delaying His Urgent Journey.*

2003, Feb. 20 ***Perf. 11¾***

4281-4284	A1908	Set of 4	2.50	1.25
4284a		Booklet pane of 6, #4281-4282, 2 each #4283-4284	*18.50*	—
		Complete booklet, #4284a	*18.50*	

Souvenir Sheet

4285 A1909 150w multicolored 2.25 1.10

Complete booklet sold for 352w.

Book — A1910

2003, Mar. 15 **Souvenir Sheet**

4286 A1910 120w multicolored 2.00 .90

On the Art of Cinema, by Kim Jong Il, 30th anniv. of publication.

Army Trumpeter, Map, Soldiers Marching — A1911

2003, Mar. 16

4287 A1911 15w multicolored .35 .25

80th anniv. of Kim Il Sung's "250-mile Journey for Learning."

Soldier & Workers — A1912

2003, Mar. 29

4288 A1912 3w multicolored .25 .25

Propaganda issue: "Let us meet the requirements of Songun in ideological viewpoint, fighting spirit and way of life!"

A1913

Election of Kim Jong Il as Chairman of the DPRK National Defense Commission, 10th Anniv. — A1914

Designs: 3w, Flags, "10."

No. 4290: a, 12w, Kim Jong Il with computer. b, 70w, Kim with military officers, pointing. c, 112w, Kim, with military officers, hand raised.

2003, Apr. 9

4289 A1913 3w multicolored .25 .25

Souvenir Sheet

4290 A1914 Sheet of 3, #a.-c. 4.00 2.00

Kim Il Sung's Birthplace, Mangyongdae, *Kimsungilia* — A1915

2003, Apr. 15

4291 A1915 3w multicolored .25 .25

Day of the Sun—Kim Il Sung, 91st birth anniv.

A1916

Medals and Orders Presented to Kim Il Sung — A1917

Designs: 12w, Order of Suhbaatar (Mongolia, 1953). 35w, National Order of Grand Cross (Madagascar, 1985). 70w, Order of Lenin (USSR, 1987). 140w, Order of Playa Giron (Cuba, 1987).

120w, Kim Il Sung being presented with medal by Fidel Castro (1986).

2003, Apr. 15 ***Perf. 13¼***

4292-4295 A1916 Set of 4 4.00 2.00

Souvenir Sheet

Perf. 13¼

4296 A1917 120w multicolored 1.75 .75

Insects — A1918

Designs: a, 15w, *Pantala flavescens*. b, 70w, *Tibicen japonicus*. c, 220w, Xylotrupes dichotomus. d, 300w, *Lycaena dispar*.

2003, Apr. 20 ***Perf. 13¼***

4297 A1918 Sheet of 4, #a.-d. 10.00

e. Booklet pane of 6, #4297c, 4297d, 2 each #4297a-4297b *20.00* —

Complete booklet, #4297e *20.00*

Complete booklet sold for 705w.

Korean National Dishes A1919

Designs: 3w, Glutinous rice cake. 30w, Thongkimchi. 70w, Sinsollo.

120w, Pyongyang cold noodles.

2003, May 1 ***Perf. 11¾***

4298-4300 A1919 Set of 3 1.75 .85

Souvenir Sheet

4301 A1919 120w multicolored 1.75 .85

Victory Monument, Battle in Musan Area — A1920

2003, May 19 ***Perf. 12¾***

4302 A1920 90w multicolored 1.50 .75

Ryangchon Temple A1921

Designs: 3w, Manse Pavilion. 12w, Buddhist statues. 40w, Painting of Buddha with two saints. 50w, Painting of Buddha with four saints.

120w, Taeung Hall, main shrine of temple.

2003, May 30 ***Perf. 13¼***

4303-4306 A1921 Set of 4 2.00 1.00

Souvenir Sheet

4307 A1921 120w multicolored 2.00 1.00

Map, Song "We Are One" — A1922

2003, June 1

4308 A1922 60w multicolored 1.10 .50

Wild Animals — A1923

Designs: a, 3w, Tigers. b, 70w, Bears. c, 150w, Wild boars. d, 230w, Roe deer.

2003, June 10

4309 A1923 Sheet of 4, #a.-d. 2.50

e. Booklet pane of 4, #4309a-4309d 30.00 —

Complete booklet, #4309e 30.00

Complete booklet sold for 460w.

Public Bonds of 1950, 2003 — A1924

2003, July 25 ***Perf. 13½***

4310 A1924 140w multicolored 2.50 1.25

Campaign to promote purchase of public bonds.

A1925

A1926

DPRK "Victory" in Korean War, 50th Anniv. — A1927

Designs: 3w, Distinguished Service Medal. No. 4312: Kim Il Sung in commander's uniform.

No. 4313: a, 12w, Kim delivering radio address. 35w, Kim talking to soldiers. c, 70w, Kim ratifying armistace agreement. d, 140w, Kim in uniform.

No. 4314: a, 12w, Kim smiling, surrounded by soldiers. 35w, Kim inspecting soldier. c, 70w, Kim Il Sung, Kim Jong Il inspecting army training. d, 140w, Middle-aged Kim Il Sung in suit and tie.

No. 4315: a, 12w, Kim Jong Il receiving bouquet from female soldier. 35w, Kim Jong Il being applauded by soldiers. c, 70w, Kim Jong Il on military inspection. d, 140w, Smiling Kim Jong Il.

2003, July 27 ***Perf. 13¼***

4311 A1925 3w multicolored .25 .25

Souvenir Sheet

4312 A1926 120w multicolored 2.00 1.00

Sheets of 4

Perf. 11½

4313-4315 A1927 Set of 3 13.50 6.50

Orchids — A1928

Designs: a, 3w, Minicattleya coerulea. b, 100w, Phalanopsis aphrodite. c, 150w, Calanthe discolor. d, 200w, Dendrobium snowflake.

2003, July 29 ***Perf. 13¼***

4316 A1928 Sheet of 4, #a.-d. 8.25 4.00

e. Booklet pane of 4, #4316a-4316d 8.25 —

Complete booklet, #4316e 8.75

No. 4316e contains Nos. 4316a-4316d in a horizontal strip of four, with selvage similar to that of No. 4316.

A1929

Birds — A1930

Designs: 12w, Grus vipio. 70w, Nycticorax nycticorax. 100w, Columba livia var domestricus. 120w, Nymphicus hollandicus. 150w, Strix aluco.

225w, Pseudogyps africanus.

2003, Aug. 4 ***Perf. 13¼***

4317-4321 A1929 Set of 5 7.00 3.50

4321a Booklet pane of 6, #4317-4318, 4320-4321, 2 #4319 *19.50* —

Complete booklet, #4321a *19.50*

Souvenir Sheet

Perf. 11¾

4322 A1930 225w multicolored 3.50 2.10

Complete booklet sold for 567w.

Arctic & Antarctic Animals — A1931

Designs: a, 15w, Adelie penguins (Pygoscelis adeliae). b, 70w, Walrus (Odobenus rosmarus). c, 140w, Polar bear and cubs (Thalarctos maritimus). d, 150w, Bowhead whale (Balaena mysticetus). e, 220w, Spotted seals (Phoca largha).

2003, Aug. 20 ***Perf. 11½***

4323 A1931 Sheet of 5, #a.-e. + label 11.00 5.25

a. Booklet pane of 5 + label —

Complete booklet 15.00

No. 4323a contains one pane, with stamps and label in same arrangement as in No. 4323, surrounded by selvage containing a distinctive arrangement of Polar animals on a primarily yellowish background.

Mushrooms — A1932

Designs: a, 3w, Pholiota flammans. b, 12w, Geastrum fimbriatum. c, 70w, Coprinus atramentarius. d, 130w, Pleuotus cornucopiae.

250w, Elfvingia applanata.

2003, Sept. 5 ***Perf. 13¼***

4324 A1932 Block of 4, #a-d 4.00 2.10

Souvenir Sheet

4328 A1932 250w multicolored 4.75 2.40

a. Booklet pane of 5, #4324a-4324d, 4328 *23.00* —

Complete booklet, #4328a *23.00*

Complete booklet sold for 480w. No. 4328a exists imperforate.

Korean Stamp Exhibition Hall — A1933

Korean Stamps, Interior of Hall — A1934

2003, Sept. 5

4329 A1933 3w multicolored .30 .30
4330 A1934 60w multicolored 1.25 .50

Korean Stamp Exhibition celebrating the 55th anniversary of the DPRK and the inauguration of the Korean Stamp Exhibition Hall.

A1935

A1936

55th Anniv. Founding of DPRK — A1937

Designs: 3w, DPRK Arms, Flag.

No. 4332: Kim Il Sung.

Sheets of 2 with central label: No. 4333: a, 60w, "The Birth of a New Korea" (Kim saluting marchers carrying DPRK flag). b, 60w, "In the Period of Building a New Korea" (Kim Jong Suk and factory workers). No. 4334: a, 60w, "Braving Through a Rain of Bullets Personally" (Kim in jeep in war zone). b, 60w, "Comrade Kim Il Sung, Ever-Victorious Iron-Willed Commander, Personally Commanding the Battle at Height 1211" (Kim on bluff, pointing to battlefield.) No. 4335: a, 60w, "We Trust and Follow Only You, the Leader" (Kim being greeted by villagers). b, 60w, "The Great Leader Kim Il Sung Giving On-the-Spot Guidance to the Pukchang Thermal Power Station" (Kim and factory workers). No. 4336: a, 60w, "The Victory of Korean Revolution Will Be Ensured by the Arms in Our Hand" (Kim speaking to soldiers, Kim Jong Il standing behind). b, 60w, "Keeping Up Songun Politics as All-Powerful Means" (Smiling Kim walking with soldiers symbolizing modern arms).

2003, Sept. 9 ***Perf. 11½***

4331 A1935 3w multicolored .30 .30

Souvenir Sheet

Perf. 13¼

4332 A1936 120w multicolored 2.40 1.25

Sheets of 2, #a.-b. + label

Perf. 12¼x12

4333-4336 A1937 Set of 4 7.00 3.50

Mao Zedong, 110th Birth Anniv. — A1938

No. 4337: a, 20w, Young Mao speaking at political meeting; b, 30w, Mao walking on shore with woman carrying manuscript. No. 4338: a, 30w, Mao addressing Red partisans; b, 30w, Mao (wearing trenchcoat) leading partisans in field. No. 4339: a, 20w, Mao talking with workers, soldiers; b, 30w, Mao in casual setting, leading discussion with soldiers. No. 4340: a, 30w, Mao addressing crowd in Beijing; b, 30w, Mao with people of various races and nationalities.

No. 4341: Sheet containing Nos. 4337-4338, with attached large label depicting 110 stamps picturing Mao and denominated 140w, the price for which the sheet was sold. No. 4342: Same, but containing Nos. 4339-4340.

2003, Dec. 26 ***Perf. 13¼***

Se-Tenant Pairs with Label Between

4337-4340 A1938 Set of 4 4.00 2.10

Souvenir Sheets

4341-4342 A1938 Set of 2 4.75 2.40

New Year — A1939

Design: 2w, Soldier, workers, tower.

2004, Jan. 1 ***Perf. 11½***

4343 A1939 3w multicolored .30 .30

For surcharge, see No. 4877B.

A1940

Monkeys — A1941

Designs: 3w, *Cebus apella*. 60w, *Papio doguera*. 70w, *Cercopithecus aethiops*. 100w, *Saguinus oedipus*.
155w, *Macaca mulatta*.

2004, Jan. 1

4344-4347 A1940 Set of 4 4.75 2.40

Souvenir Sheet

4348 A1941 155w multicolored 3.00 2.40
a. Booklet pane of 5, #4344-4348 23.00 —
Complete booklet, #4348a 23.00

Complete booklet sold for 403w. See Nos. 4351-4355.

Lunar New Year's Day — A1942

2004, Jan. 1

4349 A1942 3w multicolored .30 .30

Souvenir Sheet

First Chinese Manned Space Flight — A1943

Designs: a, 91w, Yang Liwei, first Chinese cosmonaut (46mm diameter). b, 98w, Landing capsule, parachute, helicopter (54x45mm).

Perf. 13¼, Perf. (#4350a)

2004, Jan. 30

4350 A1943 Sheet of 2, #a.-b. 3.00 1.50
c. Booklet pane, 2 each #4350a-4350b — —
Complete booklet, #4350c —
d. #4350 with Hong Kong 2004 emblem opvt. in sheet margin 3.00 1.50

Booklets containing No. 4350c were issued with and without the Hong Kong 2004 emblem on the cover.

Nos. 4344-4348 with Hong Kong 2004 Emblem

2004, Jan. 30

4351-4354 A1940 Set of 4 4.75 2.40

Souvenir Sheet

4355 A1941 155w multicolored 3.00 1.50

Joint Editorial *Rodong Sinmun*, *Josoninmingun* and *Chongnyonjonwi* Newspapers A1944

2004, Feb. 15 ***Perf. 13¼***

4357 A1944 3w multicolored .30 .30

A1945

Kim Jong Il, 62nd Birthday — A1946

No. 4358: 3w, Kim Jong Il's birthplace, Mt. Paektu.

No. 4359 (each 30w): a, "The Thaw of Sobaek Stream" (Spring). b, "The Thunderclap of Jong Il Peak" (Summer). c, "The Secret Camp in Autumn" (Autumn). d, "Hoarfrost in February" (Winter).

2004, Feb. 16 ***Perf. 11½***

4358 A1945 3w multicolored .30 .30

Souvenir Sheet

Perf. 13¼

4359 A1946 Sheet of 4, #a.-d. 2.40 1.25

Kim Jong Il — A1947

2004, Feb. 19 ***Perf. 13¼***

4360 A1947 120w multicolored 2.40 1.25

30th anniv, of publication of the *Program of Modelling the Whole Society on the Juche Idea.*

Rural Village — A1948

Kim Il Sung and Farmers — A1949

2004, Feb. 25 ***Perf. 11½***

4361 A1948 3w multicolored .30 .30

Souvenir Sheet

Perf. 12½ x11¾

4362 A1949 120w multicolored 2.10 2.10

40th anniv. of publication of the "Theses on the Socialist Rural Question in Our Country."

Lighthouses — A1950

Designs: a, 3w, Sokgundo Lighthouse. b, 12w, Yubundo Lighthouse. c, 100w, Jangdokdo Lighthouse. d, 195w, Amryongdan Lighthouse.

2004, Mar. 20 ***Perf. 11¾x12½***

4363 A1950 Sheet of 4, #a.-d. 6.00 3.00
e. Booklet pane of 4, #4363a-4363d 6.00 —
Complete booklet, #4363e 6.50

No. 4363e contains Nos. 4363a-4363d in a horizontal strip of 4, surrounded by a seashore selvage.

A1951

Board Games — A1952

Designs: a, 3w, Korean Chess. b, 12w, Goe. c, 90w, Yut. d, 120w, Kknoni (Chinese Checkers).
98w, Playing Korean Chess.

2004, Mar. 20 *Perf. 13¼*

4364 A1951 Sheet of 4, #a.-d. 4.75 2.40
e. Booklet pane of 5, #4364a-4364b. 4364d, 2 x 4364c 6.00 —
Complete booklet, #4363e 6.50

Souvenir Sheet

4365 A1952 98w multicolored 2.40 1.25

No. 4364e contains Nos. 4364a-4364d in a horizontal strip of 5, which includes a second copy of the 90w value, with a distinctive printed selvage.

Kim Il Sung's Birthplace, Mangyongdae A1953

Kim Il Sung — A1954

2004, Apr. 15 *Perf. 13¼*

4366 A1953 3w multicolored .30 .30

Souvenir Sheet

Perf. 11¾

4367 A1954 120w multicolored 2.10 1.10

Kim Il Sung, 92nd birth anniv.

A1955

Tok Islands — A1956

No. 4368: a, 3w, 19th century map of Korea. b, 12w, Western island. c, 106w, Eastern island.
No. 4369: 116w, Both islands, sea gulls.

2004, Apr. 20 *Perf. 11½*

4368 A1955 Sheet, #a.-c. + label 3.00 1.50

Souvenir Sheet

Perf.

4369 A1956 116w multicolored 2.40 1.25
a. Booklet pane of 4, #4368a-4368c, 4369 — —
Complete booklet, #4369a —

Fossils — A1957

No. 4370: a, 3w, Calcinoplax antiqua. b, 12w, Podozamites lanceolatus. c, 70w, Comptonia naumannii. d, 140w, Clinocardium asagaiense.
No. 4371: 120w, Tingia carbonica.

2004, May 20 *Perf. 13¼*

4370 A1957 Sheet of 4, #a.-d. 4.75 2.40
e. Booklet pane of 5, #4370a-4370d, #4371a 6.00 —
Complete booklet, #4370e 6.50 —

Souvenir Sheet

Perf. 12½

4371 A1957 120w multicolored 2.40 1.25
a. single stamp 2.40 1.25

Cacti — A1958

No. 4372: a, 70w, *Notocactus leninghausii.* b, 90w, *Echinocactus grusonii.* c, 100w, *Gymnocalycium baldianum.* d, 140w, *Mammillaria insularis.*

2004, June 2 *Perf. 11¾x12¼*

4372 A1958 Sheet of 4, #a.-d. 6.00 3.00
e. Ovptd. "World Stamp Championship 2004" and Singapore 2004 emblem in margin 6.00 3.00
f. Booklet pane of 4, #4372a-4372d *16.00* —
Complete booklet, #4372f *16.00*

Complete booklet sold for 416w. No. 4372e was issued 8/28.

A1959

Unofficial Visit of Kim Jong Il to China — A1960

No. 4373: a, 74w, Kim Jong Il with Hu Jintao, President of the People's Republic of China.
No. 4374: a, 3w, Kim shaking hands with Hu Jintao. b, 12w, Kim with Jiang Zemin, President of China 1997-2003. c, 40w, Kim with Wu Bangguo, Chinese Communist Party leader. d, 60w, Kim clapping hands at outdoor reception.
No. 4375: a, 3w, Kim with Wen Jiabao, Premier of the State Council of the PRC. b, 12w, Kim with Jia Qinglin, Chinese Communist Party leader. c, 40w, Kim with Zeng Qinghong, Vice-President of the PRC. d, 60w, Kim visiting Tianjin.

2004, June 18 *Perf. 13¼*

Souvenir Sheet

4373 A1959 74w multicolored 1.50 .70
a. As No. 4373, diff. (horiz.) selvage 1.50 .70

Sheets of 4, #a-d

4374-4375 A1960 Set of 2 4.00 2.10
4375e Booklet pane of 9, #4373a, 4374a-d, 4375a-d 6.00 —
Complete booklet, #4375e 6.50

No. 4373a is from the booklet No. 4375e.

WPK Flag — A1961

A1962

Kim Jong Il's Appointment to the Central Committee of the Workers' Party of Korea, 40th Anniv. — A1963

No. 4377: a, 12w, Kim reading at desk. b, 100w, Kim standing in front of renderings of proposed Samjiyon Battle Site memorial.
No. 4378: a, 12w, Kim inspecting power station in Jagang Province. b, 100w, Kim with army officers.
No. 4379: a, 12w, Kim visiting the Komdok mine. b, 100w, Kim, outdoor photo portrait.
No. 4380: 130w, Kim Jong Il and Kim Il Sung.

2004, June 19

4376 A1961 3w multicolored .30 .30

Sheets of 2

4377-4379 A1962 Set of 3 6.00 3.00

Souvenir Sheet

4380 A1963 130w multicolored 1.50 .70

A1964

A1965

Kim Il Sung, 10th Death Anniv. — A1966

No. 4381: 3w, *Kimilsungia,* monument to Kim Il Sung.
No. 4382: a, 12w, Kim Il Sung and Kim Jong Il visiting State Academy of Sciences. b, 116w, Kim Il Sung and Kim Jong Il on Mt. Paektu.
No. 4383: a, 12w, Kim Il Sung with workers b, 116w, Kim directing farmers at Chongan co-operative farm.
No. 4384: a, 12w, Kim with soldiers. b, 116w, Kim with children.
No. 4385: a, 12w, Kim embracing Rev. Mun Ik Hwan. 116w, Kim talking on telephone.
No. 4386: 112w, Kim waving.

2004, July 8 *Perf. 11¾*

4381 A1964 3w multicolored .30 .30

Sheets of 4, #a-d

4382-4385 A1965 Set of 4 8.25 4.00

Souvenir Sheet

4386 A1966 112w multicolored 1.90 .85

Monument — A1967

2004, July 10 *Perf. 11¾*

4387 A1967 112w multicolored 1.90 .85

Kim Hyong Jik, father of Kim Il Sung, 110th birth anniv.

A1968

A1969

Deng Xiaoping, Birth Centennial — A1970

No. 4388: a, 3w, Deng Xiaoping as a student in France. b, 12w, Deng hiking on the Huangshan. c, 35w, Deng saluting at military review. d. 50w, Deng addressing rally celebrating the 35th anniversary of the People's Republic of China.
No. 4389a: Kim Il Sung being greeted by Deng, Chinese crowd during visit to China.
No. 4390: 80w, Deng at seashore.

2004, July 15 *Perf. 13¼*

4388 A1968 Strip of 4, #4a-d + label 1.90 .85

Sheet of 5

4389 A1969 Sheet, #4388, 4389a, label 3.00 1.50
a. 70w multicolored .85 .50

Souvenir Sheet

4390 A1970 80w multicolored 1.50 .70

Fresh Water Fish — A1971

Designs: a, 3w, Carassius auratus. b, 12w, Tlilapia nilotica. c, 140w, Ophiocephalus argus. d, 165w, Clarias gariepinus.

2004, Aug. 10

4391 A1971 Sheet of 4, #a.-d. 5.50 2.75

28th Olympic Games, Athens — A1972

Designs: a, 3w, Boxing. b, 12w, Soccer. c, 85w, Track and field events. d, 140w, Gymnastics.

2004, Aug. 10

4392 A1972 Block or strip of 4, #a.-d. 4.00 2.25
e. Booklet pane of 4, #a.-d. 4.00 —
Complete booklet, #4392e 4.75

No. 4392 was printed in panes of 8 stamps, 2 sets of Nos. 4392a-4392d, with decorative margin depicting athletes, Olympic emblems and Korean inscription. No. 4392e contains Nos. 4392a-4392d in a horizontal strip, with plain marginal selvage.

For overprints, see No. 4409.

Fire Engines — A1973

Designs: a, 3w, Mercedes Benz ladder truck. b, 12w, Fire truck. c, 40w, Jelcz pumper truck. d, 105w, Mercedes Benz fire truck.
97w, ladder truck, diff.

2004, Aug. 15

4393 A1973 Sheet of 4, #a.-d. 3.00 1.50
e. Booklet pane of 4, #a.-d. 3.00 —
Complete booklet, #4393e 3.50
f. A1973 97w Souvenir sheet 1.90 .85

No. 4393e contains Nos. 4393a-4393d in a vertical strip, with marginal selvage similar to that of the sheet.

Airplanes — A1974

Designs: a, 3w, Airbus A340-600. b, 97w, Concorde. c, 104w, Graf Zeppelin DO-X. d, 116w, Junkers JU 52/3m.

2004, Aug. 20 ***Perf. 12***

4394 A1974 Sheet of 4, #a.-d. 6.25 3.25
e. Booklet pane of 4, #a.-d. 6.25 —
Complete booklet, #4394e 6.75

No. 4394e contains Nos. 4394a-4394d in a horizontal strip, with pale yellow marginal selvage, with simple ruled lines and inscription.

Visit of Japanese Prime Minister Koizumi Zunichiro — A1975

2004, Aug. 25 ***Perf. 11¾***

4395 A1975 220w multicolored 3.75 1.90

A1976

2004, Sept. 21

4396 A1976 112w multicolored 1.90 .85

An Jung Gun (1879-1910), assassin of Japanese Prime Minister Ito Hirdoumi in 1909, 125th birth anniv.

A1977

Kim Jong Suk (1917-49), Mother of Kim Jong Il — A1978

Designs: 3w, Kim Jong Suk's pistol.
97w, Kim Jong Suk.

2004, Sept. 22 ***Perf. 13¼***

4397 A1977 3w multicolored .30 .30

Souvenir Sheet

Perf. 12

4398 A1978 97w multicolored 1.90 .85

World Wildlife Fund — A1979

Swans: 3w, Swan in profile, looking left. 97w, Swan, ¾ profile, head turned to left. 104w, Two swans, one with outstretched wings. 120w, Two swans in water.

2004, Sept. 30 ***Perf. 11½***

4399-4402 A1979 Set of 4 5.75 3.00
4402a Booklet pane of 4, #4399-4102 5.75 —
Complete booklet, #4402a 6.25

Nos. 4399-4402 were each printed in sheets of 4, with decorative selvage. No. 4402a contains the four stamps in a horizontal se-tenant strip, surrounded by plain selvage.

A1980

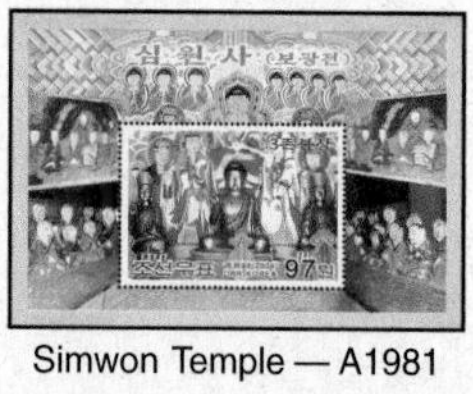

Simwon Temple — A1981

Designs: 3w, View of Powkang Hall.
97w, Interior of Powkang Hall, with three golden Buddha statues.

2004, Oct. 5 ***Perf. 11¾***

4403 A1980 3w multicolored .30 .30

Souvenir Sheet

Perf. 13¼

4404 A1981 97w multicolored 2.10 1.10

Sidelfingen International Stamp Fair — A1982

Electric trains: a, 3w, Red and blue train. b, 40w, Yellow train. c, 75w, Green and white train. d, 150w, Red and green train.
120w, Vintage electric train.

2004, Nov. 5 ***Perf. 11½***

4405 A1982 Sheet of 4, #a.-d. 4.50 2.25

Souvenir Sheet

4406 A1982 120w multicolored 2.40 1.25
a. 120w stamp from souvenir sheet 2.40 1.25
b. Booklet pane of 5, #4405a-4405d, #4606a 7.50 —
Complete booklet, #4406b 8.25

A1983

Repatriation of Korean Nationals in Japan, 45th Anniv. — A1984

Designs: 3w, Repatriation ship *Mangyongbong.*
80w, Kim Il Sung with repatriated Korean children.

2004, Dec. 16 ***Perf. 11½***

4407 A1983 3w multicolored .30 .30

Souvenir Sheet

Perf. 11¾

4408 A1984 80w multicolored 1.50 .70

No. 4392 Overprinted in Silver

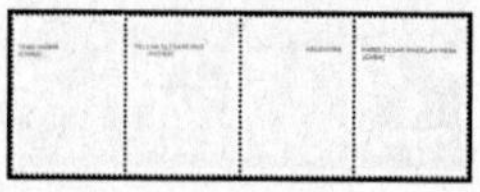

Overprints: a, 3w, Mario Cesar Kindelan Mesa (Boxing, Cuba). b, 12w, Argentine Soccer Team. c, 85w, Yelena Slesarenko (Women's High Jump, Russia). d, 140w, Teng Haibin (Women's Gymnastics, China).

2004, Dec. 20 ***Perf. 13¼***

4409 A1972 Block or strip of 4, #a.-d. 4.25 2.25

New Year 2005 — A1985

2005, Jan. 1

4410 A1985 3w multicolored .30 .30

A1986

New Year 2005 — Year of the Rooster — A1987

Domestic fowl, millet stalk figures: 3w, Rooster. 12w, Hen.
No. 4413: a, 3w, Chick. b, 70w, Rooster, chick. c, 100w, Rooster. d, 140w, Basket of eggs.

2005, Jan. 1

4411 A1986 3w multicolored .30 .30
4412 A1986 12w multicolored .70 .35
4413 A1987 Sheet of 4, #a.-d. 4.75 .30
e. Booklet pane of 6, #4411-4412, #4413a-d 5.50 —
Complete booklet, #4413e 5.70

No. 4413e contains all six values of the set, printed in a se-tenant strip of six, within a plain yellow and green border.

Hen, Classic Chinese Painting — A1988

Souvenir Sheet

2005, Jan. 10 ***Perf. 11½***

4414 A1988 97w multicolored 1.90 .85

Kim Il Sung's 250-Mile Journey, 80th Anniv. — A1989

Souvenir Sheet

2005, Jan. 22 ***Perf. 11¾***

4415 A1989 120w multicolored 1.90 .85

Statue of Kim Il Sung, Chongsan-ri — A1990

Souvenir Sheet

2005, Feb. 8 ***Perf. 13¼***
4416 A1990 120w multicolored 1.80 .85

Creation of the Chongsan-ri Spirit and Chongsan-ri Method.

Songun Scenes — A1991

Designs: a, 3w, Sunrise at Mt. Paektu. b, 12w, Snowscape. c, 40w, Royal azaleas on Chol Pass. d, 50w, Jangja River. e, 60w, Ullim Falls. f, 70w, Handure Plain. g, 70w, Potato blossoms at Taehongdan. h, 100w, Poman-ri.

2005, Feb. 10 ***Perf. 12¼***
4417 A1991 Sheet of 8, #a.-h. 6.00 3.00

A1992

A1993

Kim Jong Il, 63rd Birthday — A1994

Design: 3w, *Kimjongilia*, mountains.
No. 4419, *216 Peaks Around Lake Chon on Mt. Paektu*, summer scenes, each 50w: a, Mountains, lake on lower right. b, Mountains, lake across foreground. c, Mountains, lake in foreground, shore at lower right.
No. 4420, *216 Peaks Around Lake Chon on Mt. Paektu*, winter scenes, each 50w: a, Mountains, frozen lake in foreground. b, Mountains. lake in foreground, sun showing over peaks. c, Mountains, lake in left foreground.

2005, Feb. 16 ***Perf. 13¼***
4418 A1992 3w multicolored .30 .30

Sheets of 3, #a.-c.

Perf. 12
4419 A1993 multicolored 2.40 1.25
4420 A1994 multicolored 2.40 1.25

Joint Editorial *Rodong Sinmun, Josoninmingun* and *Chongnyonjonwi* Newspapers A1995

2005, Feb. 16 ***Perf. 13¼***
4421 A1995 3w multicolored .30 .30

A1996

Naming of the *Kimilsungia*, 40th Anniv. — A1997

Designs: 3w, *Kimilsungia* and Kimilsungia-Kimjongilia Exhibition Hall.
120w: Kim Il Sung receiving a *Kimilsungia* plant from Pres. Sukarno of Indonesia.

2005, Apr. 13
4422 A1996 3w multicolored .30 .30

Souvenir Sheet

4423 A1997 120w multicolored 1.90 .85

A1998

Kim Il Sung, 93rd Birth Anniv. — A1999

Designs: 3w, *Kimilsungia* and Mangyong Hill.
112w: Kim Il Sung standing in front of straw-thatched house at Mangyongdae.

2005, Apr. 15
4424 A1998 3w multicolored .30 .30

Souvenir Sheet

Perf. 11¾
4425 A1999 112w multicolored 1.90 .85

48th World Table Tennis Championships, Shanghai — A2000

Designs: 3w, Pak Young Sun, Korea. b, 5w, Mao Zedong playing table tennis at the Communist base in Yanan. c, 12w, Wang Liqin, China. d, 20w, J.O. Waldner, Sweden. e, Zhang Yining, China. f, 102w, Werner Schlager, Austria.

2005, Apr. 23 ***Perf. 11½***
4426 A2000 Sheet of 6, #a.-f. 3.75 1.90
g. Booklet pane of 6, #4426a-4426f 3.75 —
Complete booklet, #4426g 4.25

No. 4426g contains Nos. 4426a-4426f in a se-tenant horizontal strip of six, surrounded by blue selvage depicting the Shanghai 2005 emblem, stylized athletes and Korean inscription.

Pandas — A2001

Designs: 15w, Panda on tree limb. 45w, Panda walking. 70w, Two pandas. 140w, Panda standing
120w, Panda with cub.

2005, May 3 ***Perf. 13¼***
4427-4430 A2001 Set of 4 4.75 .30
4430a Booklet pane of 5, #4427-4430, 4432a 4.75 —
Complete booklet, #4430a 5.25

Sheet of 5

4431 A2001 Sheet, #4427-4430, 4432a 7.00 3.00

Souvenir Sheet

4432 A2001 120w multicolored 3.50 —
a. Single stamp

Nos. 4427-4430 were each issued in separate large panes. No. 4430a contains Nos. 4427-30, 4432a in a se-tenant horizontal strip of 5, with plain white marginal selvage.
For overprints, see Nos. 4451-4455.

Ecosystem of Tok Island — A2002

Designs: a, 3w, *Dianthus superbus*. b, 3w, *Eumetopia jubata*. c, 12w, Seagull. d, 50w, *Lysimachia mauritania Lam.*
e, 97w: Eastern and Western islands, Tok Island.

Perf. 11¼, Perf. (#4433e)

2005, May 5
4433 A2002 Sheet of 9, #4433e, 2 each #4433a-4433d + 2 labels 14.00 7.00
f. Booklet pane, #4433e — —
g. Booklet pane of 8, 2 each #4433a-4433d, perf. 11¼ on 3 sides — —
Complete booklet, # 4433f, 4433g —

A2003

General Association of Korean Residents in Japan, 50th Anniv. — A2004

Designs: 3w, Korean family waving flag.
130w: Kim Il Sung shaking hands with man in suit.

2005, May 25 ***Perf. 13¼***
4434 A2003 3w multicolored .30 .30

Souvenir Sheet

4435 A2004 130w multicolored 1.60 .85

Fauna — A2005

Designs, each 40w: No. 4436, Korean Tiger. No. 4437, Sable.

2005, June 1
4436 40w multicolored .85 .50
4437 40w multicolored .85 .50
a. A2005 Pair, #4436-4437 with label between 2.40 1.25
b. Booklet pane, 2 #4437a 2.40 —
Complete booklet, #4437b 3.00

See Russia No. 6911.

A2006

Koguryo Historic Site — A2007

Designs: a, Tomb of a general of Koguryo. b, 70w, Tomb mural depicting hunting scene. c, 100w, Mt. Songsan fortress. d, 130w, Gilded arrowheads.
97w: Monument at Mausoleum of King Kwanggaetho.

2005, June 14
4438 A2006 Sheet of 4, #a.-d. 4.75 2.40
e. Booklet pane, #4438a-4438d, 4439a 7.00 —
Complete booklet, #4438e 6.50

Souvenir Sheet

4439 A2007 97w multicolored 2.40 1.25
a. 97w Single from souvenir sheet 2.40 1.25

No. 4438a contains Nos. 4438a-4438d in a horizontal strip of 4, with No. 4439a placed separately, within a 69mmx279mm sheetlet with selvage depicting hunting scene, artifacts and inscription.

Kim Chol Ju (1919-35), Brother of Kim Il Sung. — A2008

Souvenir Sheet

2005, June 14 ***Perf. 11½***
4440 A2008 170w multicolored 1.90 .85

A2009

North-South Joint Declaration, 5th Anniv. — A2010

Designs, all 112w: a, Kim Jong Il and S. Korean President Kim Dae Jung shaking hands. b, Kim Jong Il and Kim Dae Jung standing side-by-side. c, Kim Il Jong and Kim Dae Jung sitting together at table with large flower arrangement. d, Kim Dae Jong and Kim Il Jong at conference table.

167w, Kim Dae Jung and Kim Jong Il smiling, shaking hands, with representatives in background.

2005, June 15

4441 A2009 Sheet of 4, #a.-d. 7.00 3.50

Souvenir Sheet

4442 A2010 167w multicolored 2.50 1.50

A2011

Amur Tiger — A2012

Designs: a, 3w, Tiger looking left. b, 12w, Tiger growling. c, 130w, Tiger looking forward. d, 200w, Tiger growling, turned to right.

150w: Tiger with cubs.

2005, July 10 ***Perf. 11¾***

4443 A2011 Sheet of 4, #a.-d. 4.75 2.40

e. Booklet pane, #4443a-4443d 4.75 —

Complete booklet, #4443e 5.25

Souvenir Sheet

Perf. 11½

4444 A2012 150w multicolored 2.40 1.25

No. 4443e contains Nos. 4443a-4443d in a horizontal strip of 4, within selvage depicting forest skyline and inscription "Panthera tigris altaika."

Map of Korea — A2013

Souvenir Sheet

2005, July 25 ***Perf. 11½***

4445 A2013 130w multicolored 1.90 .90

"June 25-July 27 - Period of Joint Anti-US Struggle" — A2014

Design: 3w, Korean soldier, U.S. POWs, military cemetary, military vehicles.

2005, July 27 ***Perf. 12***

4446 A2014 3w multicolored .30 .30

A2015

A2016

A2017

National Liberation, 60th Anniv. — A2018

Design: 3w, Arch of Triumph, magnolia.

No. 4448: a, 60w, Kim Il Sung receiving his father's pistol from his mother. b, 60w, Kim Il Sung founding the Juche-oriented revolutionary armed force. c, 60w, Kim Il Sung commanding the battle at Taehongdan. 60w, Kim Il Sung addressing staff on eve of final offensive against the Japanese. 102w, Kim Il Sung, WWII-era photo.

No. 4449: a, Kim Il Sung on ship en route to Wonsan Port landing. b, 60w, Kim Il Sung visiting Kangson Steel Works. c, 60w, Kim Il Sung delivering speech. d, 60w, Kim Il Sung meeting his grandparents, upon his return to Korea. e, 102w, Kim Il Sung with microphone.

No. 4450: 128w, Kim Il Sung.

2005, Aug. 15 ***Perf. 13¼***

4447 A2015 3w multicolored .30 .30

Sheets of 5

4448 A2016 Sheet, #a.-e. 4.75 2.40

4449 A2017 Sheet, #a.-e. 4.75 2.40

Souvenir Sheet

4450 A2018 128w multicolored 1.90 .90

Nos. 4427-4430, 4432 Overprinted "Taipei 2000" and Emblem in Red and Blue

2005, Aug. 19 ***Perf. 13¼***

4451-4454 A2001 Set of 4 4.75 2.50

Souvenir Sheet

4455 A2001 120w multicolored 2.50 1.25

18th Asian International Stamp Exhibition, Taipei.

A2019

National Costumes — A2020

Designs: a, 3w, Woman in red dress. b, 80w, Woman in blue dress. c, 100w, Woman in green dress. d, 120w, Woman in white dress with fur collar.

140w, Children.

2005, Aug. 30 ***Perf. 11½***

4456 A2019 Sheet of 4, #a.-d. 4.00 2.10

4456e Booklet pane of 4, #4456a-d 4.00 —

Complete booklet, #4456e 4.50

Souvenir Sheet

Perf. 11¾

4457 A2020 140w multicolored 2.10 1.10

No. 4456e contains Nos. 4456a-d in a horizontal strip of 4, without the small decorative labels that are printed below the stamps in No. 4456. The stamps are surrounded by a narrow selvage similar to that of the sheet of 4.

Korean Workers' Party, 60th Anniv. — A2021

Design: 3w, Korean soldier and workers, banners, proclamation of Joint Slogan.

2005, Sept. 8 ***Perf. 13¼***

4458 A2021 3w multicolored .30 .30

A2022

A2023

A2024

A2025

Korean Workers' Party, 60th Anniv. — A2026

Design: 3w, Monument to founding of Party.

No. 4460: a, 12w, Kim Il Sung organizing Down-with-Imperialism Union. b, 30w, Kim Il Sung forming the first Juche-oriented Party organization. c, 60w, Kim Il Sung discussing a draft resolution to Communist Party leaders. d, 90w, Kim Il Sung addressing Central Committee of the Communist Party.

No. 4461: a, 12w, Kim Il Sung at bank of microphones, addressing 6th Congress of the WPK. b, 30w, Kim Il Sung and Kim Jong Il with military officers. c, 60w, Kim Jong Il inspecting Tabaksol Company, a camouflaged army unit. d, 90w, Kim Jong Il addressing crowd in stadium.

No. 4462: 120w, Kim Il Sung. No. 4463: 120w, Kim Jong Il.

2005, Oct. 10 ***Perf. 13¼***

4459 A2022 3w multicolored .25 .25

Sheets of 4

Perf. 11¾

4460 A2023 Sheet, #a.-d. 2.40 1.25

4461 A2024 Sheet, #a.-d. 2.40 1.25

Souvenir Sheets

Perf. 13¼

4462 A2025 120w multicolored 1.50 .70

4463 A2026 120w multicolored 1.50 .70

Bees — A2027

Designs: a, 3w, Four bees surrounding queen. 12w, Two bees attending to larva. 128w, Bee filling comb cell with honey. 200w, Bee flying.

2005, Oct. 20 ***Perf. 11½***
4464 A2027 Sheet of 4, #a.-d. 4.75 2.40
e. Booklet pane, as #4464a-4464d 4.75 —
Complete booklet, #4443e 5.25

No. 4464e contains four stamps like Nos. 4464a-4464d, but with slightly less yellow in the comb background and a slightly paler blue on the blue design elements. It bears a marginal selvage, with Korean inscription at left and three bees at right.

United Nations, 60th Anniv. — A2028

2005, Oct. 24 ***Perf. 13¼***
4465 A2028 15w multicolored .35 .30

A2029

Kaesong Historic Site — A2030

No 4466: a, 35w, Pogwang Hall. b, 35w, Monument to Taegakguksa. c, 35w, Pojo Hall. d, 75w, Ryongthong Temple.
No. 4467: a, 35w, Taesong Shrine. b, 35w, Myongryun Hall. c, 35w, Metal type (round). d, 75w, Sam Gate.

2005, Oct. 31 ***Perf. 12***
Sheets of 4, #a.-d.
4466 A2029 multicolored 2.40 1.25
4467 A2030 multicolored 2.40 1.25

Nos. 4466-4467 each contain three non-denominated labels.

Kim Hyong Gwon Monument — A2031

Souvenir Sheet

2005, Nov. 4 ***Perf. 11½***
4468 A2031 120w multicolored 1.90 .90

Kim Hyong Gwon (1905-36), uncle of Kim Il Sung.

Ulsa Treaty, Centennial A2032

2005, Nov. 17 ***Perf. 11¾***
4469 A2032 12w multicolored .35 .30

Ulsa Treaty, under which Korea became a Japanese protectorate.

A2033

A2034

Kaesong Historic Site — A2035

No 4470: a, 35w, Kaesong Namdaemun. b, 35w, Mausoleum of King Kongmin. c, 35w, Sonjuk Bridge. d, 35w, Sungyang Private School. e, 35w, Anhwa Temple (Five Hundred Rahan). f, 35w, Tomb of Pak Ji Won (Yonam).
No. 4471: a, 35w, King Wanggon, founder of Kingdom of Koryo, 935 A.D., round. b, 35w, Front Gate at Mausoleum of King Wanggon. c, 75w, Mausoleum of King Wanggon.
No. 4472: a, 35w, Fortress on Mt. Taehung (North Gate). b, 35w, Marble statue of Kwanumbosal, Kwanum Temple. c, 75w, Pakyon Falls.

Sheet of 6, #a.-f. + 6 labels

2005, Nov. 18 ***Perf. 11½***
4470 A2033 multicolored 1.90 .90

Sheet of 3, #a.-c. + 2 labels
Perf. 13¼
4471 A2034 multicolored 1.90 .90

Sheet of 3, #a.-c. + 4 labels
Perf. 12¼ (a, b); 11½ (c)
4472 A2035 multicolored 1.90 .90

Visit to DPRK by Hu Jintao, President of the People's Republic of China — A2036

Design: a, 35w, Kim Jong Il meeting with Hu Jintao. b, 35w, Kim Jong Il and Hu Jintao visiting the Taean Friendship Glass Factory. c, 35w, Kim Jong Il and Hu Jintao at state banquet. d, 102w, Kim Jong Il shaking hands with Hu Jintao.

Perf. 11½, 13¼ (#4473d)
2005, Dec. 15 **Sheet of 4, #a.-d.**
4473 A2036 multicolored 3.00 1.50

New Year 2006 — A2037

2006, Jan. 1 **Litho.** ***Perf. 11½***
4474 A2037 3w multi .30 .30

New Year 2006 (Year of the Dog) — A2038

Various dogs: 3w, 70w.
No. 4477 — Various dogs: a, 15w. b, 100w. c, 130w.

2006, Jan. 1 ***Perf. 13¼***
4475-4476 A2038 Set of 2 1.90 .65
4477 A2038 Sheet of 5, #4475-4476, 4477a-4477c 5.25 2.75
d. Souvenir sheet of 1 #4477c 3.00 1.50
Complete booklet, #4475-4476, 4477a-4477c 7.00

Complete booklet sold for 335w.

A2039

League of Socialist Working Youth, 60th Anniv. A2040

No. 4478: a, 3w, Kim Il Sung and microphone. b, 111w, Kim Il Sung and crowd. c, 150w, Kim Jong Il receiving torch.

2006, Jan. 17 ***Perf. 13¼***
4478 A2039 Sheet of 3, #a-c 6.00 2.40

Souvenir Sheet
Perf. 11½x12
4479 A2040 128w multi 3.00 1.50

A2041

New Year 2006 (Year of the Dog) A2042

Photo. & Engr.
2006, Jan. 29 ***Perf. 11x11¼***
4480 A2041 12w multi .30 .30

Souvenir Sheet
Perf. 11½x11¼
4481 A2042 70w multi 1.25 .60

Down With Imperialism Union, 80th Anniv. — A2043

2006, Feb. 9 **Litho.** ***Perf. 13½***
4482 A2043 3w multi .30 .30

Miniature Sheet

2006 Winter Olymics, Turin A2044

No. 4483: a, 15w, Ice dancing. b, 85w, Ice hockey. c, 110w, Ski jumping. d, 135w, Speed skating.

2006, Feb. 10 ***Perf. 13¼***
4483 A2044 Sheet of 4, #a-d 5.75 3.00
4483e Booklet pane of 4, #4483a-4483d 6.00 —
Complete booklet, #4483e 6.00

Complete booklet sold for 362w.

A2045

Kim Jong Il, 64th Birthday A2046

No. 4485: a, 12w, Polemonium racemosum. b, 45w, Day lily. c, 100w, Dandelion. d, 140w, Parnassia palustris.

2006, Feb. 16 ***Perf. 13½***
4484 A2045 3w multi .30 .30

Souvenir Sheet
4485 A2046 Sheet of 4, #a-d 4.75 2.50

A2047

Visit of Kim Jong Il to People's Republic of China A2048

No. 4486 — Kim Jong Il: a, 3w, At Crop Research Institute. b, 12w, At optical fiber factory. c, 35w, At Three Gorges Dam. d, 70w, At Guangzhou Intl. Conference and Exhibition Center. e, 100w, At air conditioner factory. f, 120w, At port of Yandian.
102w, Kim Jong Il and Hu Jintao.

2006, Mar. 4 ***Perf. 12x12¼***
4486 A2047 Sheet of 6, #a-f 5.50 3.00

Souvenir Sheet
Perf. 11¾
4487 A2048 102w multi 1.90 .85

A2049

Agrarian Reform Law, 60th Anniv. A2050

2006, Mar. 5 ***Perf. 11½***
4488 A2049 12w multi + label .30 .30

Souvenir Sheet
4489 A2050 150w multi 1.40 1.25

Souvenir Sheet

First North Korean Postage Stamps, 60th Anniv. A2051

2006, Mar. 12 ***Perf. 11¾***
4490 A2051 158w multi 2.60 1.40

Mt. Kumgang Scenery — A2052

Designs: 3w, Pibong Falls. 12w, Podok Hermitage. 35w, Sokka Peak. 50w, Jipson Peak. 70w, Chongsok Rocks, horiz. 100w, Sejon Peak, horiz. 120w, Chonhwa Rock, horiz. 140w, Piro Peak, horiz.

2006, Mar. 15 ***Perf. 11¾x12¼***
4491-4498 A2052 Set of 8 8.75 4.50

Belgica 2006 World Youth Philatelic Exhibition, Brussels — A2053

Designs: No. 4499, 140w, Jules Verne (1828-1905), writer. No. 4500, 140w, Tyto alba, Volvariella speciosa, Scouting emblem. No. 4501, 140w, Disa grandiflora, Nymphalidae. No. 4502, 140w, Australopithecus afarensis, rocks. No. 4503, 140w, Alaskan malamute, Birman cat, Scouting emblem. No. 4504, 140w, Sunflowers, by Vincent Van Gogh. No. 4505, 140w, Soccer ball, chess knight, table tennis paddle and ball. No. 4506, 140w, Tursiops truncatus, Scouting emblem. No. 4507, 140w, Maglev train, horiz. No. 4508, 140w, 1962 Ernst Grube Type S 4000-1 fire truck, horiz.

2006, Apr. 13 ***Perf. 11¾***
4499-4508 A2053 Set of 10 23.00 11.50

Kim Il Sung, 94th Anniv. of Birth A2054

2006, Apr. 15 ***Perf. 11½***
4509 A2054 3w multi + label .30 .30

Association for the Restoration of the Fatherland, 70th Anniv. — A2055

2006, May 5 ***Perf. 13½***
4510 A2055 3w multi .30 .30

Pothong River Improvement Project, 60th Anniv. — A2056

2006, May 21 ***Perf. 12***
4511 A2056 12w multi .30 .30

Various Stamps of 1963-2002 Surcharged in Black and Red

No. 4563

No. 4565

No. 4590

No. 4606

Methods and Perfs. As Before

2006

4512	A658	3w on 2ch #816 (R)	—	—
4513	A608	3w on 5ch #731	—	—
4514	A635	3w on 10ch #770	—	—
4515	A932	3w on 10ch #1598	—	—
4516	A971	3w on 10ch #1798	—	—
4517	A1005	3w on 10ch #1929	—	—
4518	A926	3w on 15ch #1579	—	—
4519	A887	3w on 20ch #1419	—	—
4520	A986	3w on 20ch #1873 (R)	—	—
4521	A1179	3w on 20ch #2470	—	—
4522	A1211	3w on 20ch #2548	—	—
4523	A1211	3w on 20ch #2548 (R)	—	—
4524	A1249	3w on 20ch #2645	—	—
4525	A1431	3w on 20ch #3159	—	—
4526	A1431	3w on 20ch #3159 (R)	—	—
4527	A1539	3w on 20ch #3437	—	—
4528	A1539	3w on 20ch #3437 (R)	—	—
4529	A1704	3w on 20ch #3776	—	—
4530	A1288	3w on 25ch #2751	—	—
4531	A971	3w on 30ch #1801	—	—
4532	A986	3w on 30ch #1875	—	—
4533	A1177	3w on 30ch #2462	—	—
4534	A1177	3w on 30ch #2462 (R)	—	—
4535	A1241	3w on 30ch #2621	—	—
4536	A1379	3w on 30ch #2964	—	—
4537	A1379	3w on 30ch #2964 (R)	—	—
4538	A1396	3w on 30ch #3023	—	—
4539	A382	3w on 40ch #447	—	—
4540	A547	3w on 40ch #645 (R)	—	—
4541	A812	3w on 40ch #1219	—	—
4542	A818	3w on 40ch #1242	—	—
4543	A826	3w on 40ch #1277	—	—
4544	A1793	3w on 40ch #4052	—	—
4545	A1793	3w on 40ch #4052 (R)	—	—
4546	A1385	3w on 50ch #2987	—	—
4547	A1396	3w on 50ch #3025	—	—
4548	A1430	3w on 50ch #3154	—	—
a.		Double surcharge		
4549	A1471	3w on 50ch #3281	—	—
4550	A1526	3w on 50ch #3408 (R)	—	—
4551	A1595	3w on 50ch #3548 (R)	—	—
4552	A1736	3w on 60ch #3851	—	—
4553	A1557	3w on 80ch #3468	—	—
4554	A1656	3w on 80ch #3676	—	—
4555	A1651	3w on 80ch #3676 (R)	—	—
4556	A798	3w on 90ch #1164	—	—
4557	A1735	3w on 1w #3849	—	—
4558	A1761	3w on 1w #3919	—	—
4559	A1734	3w on 1.50w #3848	—	—
4560	A621	12w on 2ch #744	—	—
4561	A932	12w on 2ch #1597	—	—
4562	A808	12w on 20ch #1199	—	—
4563	A823	12w on 30ch #1268 (R)	—	—
4564	A808	12w on 40ch #1201	—	—
4565	A938	12w on 50ch #1622	—	—
4566	A1860	12w on 2w #4207	—	—
4567	A817	101w on 10ch #1236	—	—
4568	A907	101w on 10ch #1471	—	—
4569	A985	101w on 10ch #1865	—	—
4570	A1005	101w on 10ch #1926	—	—
4571	A1487	101w on 10ch #3321	—	—
4572	A1837	101w on 10ch #4165	—	—
4573	A1454	101w on 30ch #3228	—	—
4574	A1658	101w on 50ch #3680	—	—
4575	A1527	101w on 1w #3410	—	—
4576	A1716	101w on 1w #3807	—	—
4577	A1724	101w on 1.20w #3831	—	—
4578	A938	128w on 5ch #1619	—	—
4579	A812	128w on 10ch #1216	—	—
4580	A1231	128w on 15ch #2597	—	—
4581	A865	128w on 20ch #1357	—	—
4582	A903	128w on 20ch #1457	—	—
4583	A959	128w on 25ch #1754	—	—
4584	A977	128w on 25ch #1812	—	—
4585	A982	128w on 25ch #1853	—	—
4586	A958	128w on 40ch #1749	—	—
4587	A1785	128w on 40ch #4035	—	—
4588	A1430	128w on 50ch #3157	—	—
4589	A1707	128w on 1w #3785	—	—
4590	A1707	128w on 1w #3785 (R)	—	—
4591	A1725	128w on 2w #3833	—	—
4592	A820	134w on 5ch #1250	—	—
4593	A903	134w on 5ch #1455	—	—
4594	A898	134w on 10ch #1444	—	—
4595	A982	134w on 10ch #1850	—	—
4596	A855	134w on 20ch #1333	—	—
4597	A1467	134w on 30ch #3267	—	—
4598	A911	134w on 40ch #1518	—	—
4599	A911	134w on 40ch #1518 (R)	—	—
4600	A806	134w on 1.50w #1203	—	—
4601	A1862	134w on 1.50w #4213	—	—
4602	A1443	158w on 10ch #3196	—	—
4603	A898	158w on 15ch #1445	—	—
4604	A911	158w on 15ch #1516	—	—
4605	A1260	158w on 20ch #2680	—	—
4606	A850	158w on 25ch #1328	—	—
4607	A902	158w on 25ch #1458	—	—
4608	A1501	158w on 30ch #3357	—	—
4609	A1407	158w on 40ch #3059	—	—
4610	A1542	158w on 40ch #3443	—	—
4611	A1723	158w on 5w #3835	—	—

Nos. 4562-4564, 4581, 4588, 4598-4599, 4604-4605 are airmail.

Korean Children's Union, 60th Anniv. — A2057

2006, June 6 **Litho.** ***Perf. 13½***
4612 A2057 3w multi .30 .30

2006 World Cup Soccer Championships, Germany — A2058

Various soccer players in action: 3w, 130w, 160w, 210w.

2006, June 9 ***Perf. 13½***
4613-4616 A2058 Set of 4 8.25 4.00
4616a Souvenir sheet, #4616 + label 3.50 1.75
4616b Booklet pane of 4, #4613-4616 8.50 —
Complete booklet, #4616b 8.50

Issued: No. 4616a, 10/21/09. Italia 2009 Intl. Philatelic Exhibition (No. 4616a).
Complete booklet sold for 520w.

Souvenir Sheet

Kim Chol Ju (1919-35) — A2059

2006, June 12 ***Perf. 11½x12***
4617 A2059 170w multi 2.75 1.50

Souvenir Sheet

Ri Su Bok (1933-51), War Hero and Poet — A2060

2006, July 27 ***Perf. 11¾***
4618 A2060 120w multi 2.10 1.00

Miniature Sheet

Circus Performers — A2061

Designs: a, 3w, Trapeze artists (42x35mm). b, 12w, Aerial acrobatic troupe (42x35mm). c, 130w, Seesaw jumper (42x35mm). d, 200w, Juggler (42x64mm).

Perf. 11½, 11½x12 (200w)

2006, Aug. 10 Litho.

4619 A2061 Sheet of 4, #a-d 6.00 3.00

Korean Cuisine A2062

Designs: 3w, Kimchi. 12w, Umegi. 130w, Rice cake dumplings with bean paste. 200w, Sweet rice.

2006, Aug. 12 ***Perf. 13½***

4620-4623 A2062 Set of 4 6.00 3.00

4623a Booklet pane of 4, #4620-4623 6.00 —

Complete booklet, #4623a 6.00

Sea Mammals A2063

Designs: 3w, Megaptera nodosa. 70w, Balaenoptera musculus. 160w, Physeter catodon. 240w, Inia geoffrensis.

2006, Aug. 20 ***Perf. 11¾***

4624-4627 A2063 Set of 4 7.75 3.75

4627a Booklet pane of 4, #4624-4627 7.75 —

Complete booklet, #4627a 7.75

Motorcycles A2064

Various motorcycles.

2006, Sept. 1 ***Perf. 11½***

4628 Horiz. strip of 4 8.25 4.25

a. A2064 3w multi .25 .25

b. A2064 102w multi 1.60 .85

c. A2064 150w multi 2.40 1.25

d. A2064 240w multi 3.75 1.90

e. Booklet pane of 4, #4628a-4628d 8.25 —

Complete booklet, #4628e 8.25

Sinking of the General Sherman, 140th Anniv. — A2065

2006, Sept. 2 Litho. ***Perf. 13¼***

4629 A2065 130w multi 2.25 1.10

Owls — A2066

Designs: 12w, Tyto alba. 111w, Strix uralensis. 130w, Strix aluco. 160w, Nyctea scandiaca.

2006, Sept. 10 ***Perf. 11¾***

4630-4633 A2066 Set of 4 6.75 3.50

4633a Booklet pane of 4, #4630-4633 6.75 —

Complete booklet, #4633a 6.75

For overprints see Nos. 4648-4651.

Souvenir Sheet

Kim Il Sung University, 60th Anniv. — A2067

2006, Oct. 1 ***Perf. 11½x12***

4634 A2067 70w multi 1.25 .60

Famous Koreans — A2068

Designs: 3w, Ulgi Mundok, general. 12w, So Hui (942-998), diplomat and general. 35w, Kim Ung So (1564-1624), general. 70w, Kang Kam Chan (948-1031), general. 102w, Yongae Somun, general. 130w, Ri Kyu Bo (1168-1241), poet. 160w, Mun Ik Jom (1329-98), civil official.

2006, Oct. 2 ***Perf. 13½***

4635-4641 A2068 Set of 7 8.25 4.50

A2069

Down With Imperialism Union, 80th Anniv. — A2070

No. 4643: a, 70w, Kim Il Sung and followers (50x38mm). b, 102w, Kim Il Sung (46mm diameter). c, 120w, Kim Il Sung and followers on railroad track (50x38mm).

2006, Oct. 17 Litho. ***Perf. 13¼***

4642 A2069 3w multi —

Souvenir Sheet

Perf. 11¾ (#4643a, 4643c), Perf.

4643 A2070 Sheet of 3, #a-c 5.00 2.50

Red Cross Society of North Korea, 60th Anniv. — A2071

2006, Oct. 18 Litho. ***Perf. 13½***

4644 A2071 30w multi .55 .30

Souvenir Sheet

Secondary Education for Koreans in Japan, 60th Anniv. — A2072

2006, Oct. 21 ***Perf. 13¼***

4645 A2072 110w multi 1.90 .95

Miniature Sheet

Koguryo Tombs UNESCO World Heritage Site — A2073

No. 4646 — Murals: a, 3w, King (30x42mm). b, 70w, Queen (30x42mm). c, 130w, Subak (52x34mm). d, 135w, Procession (52x34mm). e, 160w, Kitchen (52x34mm).

Perf. 13¼ (3w, 70w), 12¼x11¾

2006, Nov. 4 Litho.

4646 A2073 Sheet of 5, #a-e —

Souvenir Sheet

Joson University, 50th Anniv. — A2074

2006, Nov. 4 ***Perf. 11½***

4647 A2074 110w multi + label 1.90 .95

Nos. 4630-4633 Overprinted in Gold

Methods and Perfs As Before

2006, Nov. 16

4648 A2066 12w on #4630 .30 .30

4649 A2066 111w on #4631 1.75 .90

4650 A2066 130w on #4632 2.10 1.25

4651 A2066 160w on #4633 2.60 1.40

Nos. 4648-4651 (4) 6.75 3.85

Belgica 2006 World Youth Stamp Exhibition. Location of the overprint varies.

Souvenir Sheet

Wooden Sculpture Presented by People's Army Soldiers to Kim Jong Il — A2075

2006, Dec. 24 Litho. ***Perf. 11½x12***

4652 A2075 130w multi 2.25 1.10

New Year 2007 — A2076

2007, Jan. 1 Litho. ***Perf. 13½***

4653 A2076 3w multi .30 .30

New Year 2007 (Year of the Pig) — A2077

Various pigs: 3w, 45w.

No. 4656 — Various pigs: a, 70w. b, 130w.

2007, Jan. 1 ***Perf. 11½***

4654-4655 A2077 Set of 2 .85 .40

4656 A2077 Sheet, #4654-4655, 4656a, 4656b 4.00 2.10

c. Booklet pane, #4654-4655, 4656a, 4656b 4.00 —

Complete booklet, #4656c 4.00

d. Souvenir sheet of 1 #4656a 1.20 .60

A2078

Kim Jong Il, 65th Birthday A2079

Designs: 3w, Kimiljonghwa begonia and butterfly.

No. 4658 — Mountain, lake and musical score: a, 12w. b, 70w. c, 100w. d, 140w.

2007, Feb. 16 ***Perf. 13¼***

4657 A2078 3w multi .30 .30

4658 A2079 Sheet of 4, #a-d 5.25 2.60

Symbols of Progress — A2080

2007, Feb. 28 ***Perf. 13¼***

4659 A2080 3w multi .30 .30

Annual joint editorial of state newspapers.

Butterflies A2081

Designs: 15w, Callicore selima. 85w, Morpho rhetenor. 110w, Atrophaneura alcinous. 160w, Parnassius bremeri.

2007, Mar. 5

4660-4663 A2081 Set of 4 6.25 3.00
4663a Booklet pane of 4, #4660-4663 6.25 —
Complete booklet, #4663a 6.25

Miniature Sheet

Koguryo Tombs UNESCO World Heritage Site — A2082

No. 4664 — Anak Tomb No. 3 paintings: a, 3w, Stable (60x42mm). b, 70w, Well (60x42mm). c, 130w, Milling area (30x42mm). d, 160w, Man blowing horn (30x42mm).

2007, Mar. 10

4664 A2082 Sheet of 4, #a-d 6.25 3.00
e. Booklet pane of 4, #4664a-4664d 6.25 —
Complete booklet, #4664e 6.25

Korean National Association, 90th Anniv. A2083

2007, Mar. 23

4665 A2083 12w multi .30 .30

Ludwig van Beethoven (1770-1827), Composer A2084

2007, Mar. 26

4666 A2084 80w multi 1.40 .65

Mangyongdae, Birthplace of Kim Il Sung — A2085

Paintings of Kim Il Sung A2086

Kim Il Sung and Family A2087

No. 4668: a, 45w, The Great Leader Kim Il Sung on the 250-Mile Journey for Learning. b, 70w, The Great Leader Kim Il Sung Who Braved Through the Arduous Road of the Anti-Japanese War. c, 100w, Ever Victorious Road. d, 160w, At the Field Predicting the Rich Harvest.

2007, Apr. 15 ***Perf. 13¼***

4667 A2085 3w multi .30 .30

Perf. 11¾

4668 A2086 Sheet of 4, #a-d 6.25 3.00

Souvenir Sheet

Perf. 11¾x11½

4669 A2087 130w multi 2.25 1.10

Kim Il Sung (1912-94).

Miniature Sheet

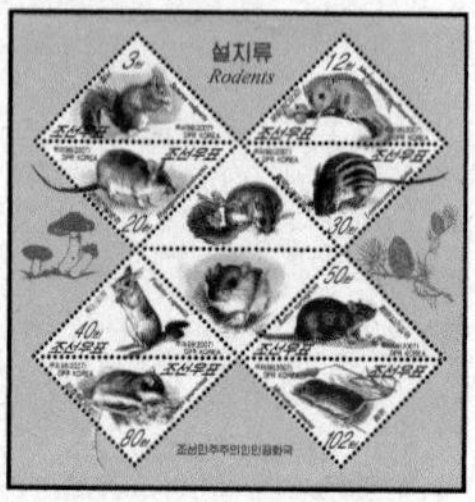

Rodents A2088

No. 2088: a, 3w, Sciururs vulgaris. b, 12w, Muscardinus avellanarius. c, 20w, Hypogeomys antimena. d, 30w, Lemniscomys striatus. e, 40w, Pedetes capensis. f, 50w, Rattus norvegicus. g, 80w, Eliomys quercinus. h, 102w, Micromys minutus.

2007, Apr. 20 ***Perf. 13x13x12¼***

4670 A2088 Sheet of 8, #a-h, + 2 labels 5.50 3.75

Korean People's Army Soldiers and Mt. Paektu — A2089

Leaders Reviewing Troops — A2090

Kim Il Sung and Kim Jong Il Reviewing Troops — A2091

No. 4672: a, 80w, Kim Il Sung and Kim Jong Il reviewing troops. b, 100w, Kim Jong Il and soldiers.

2007, Apr. 25 ***Perf. 13¼***

4671 A2089 12w multi .30 .30

Perf. 11¾

4672 A2090 Sheet of 2, #a-b 3.00 1.50

Souvenir Sheet

Perf. 12x11½

4673 A2091 120w multi 2.00 1.00

Korean People's Army, 75th anniv.

Prevention of Bird Flu — A2092

2007, May 10 ***Perf. 13¼***

4674 A2092 85w multi 1.60 .70

Miniature Sheet

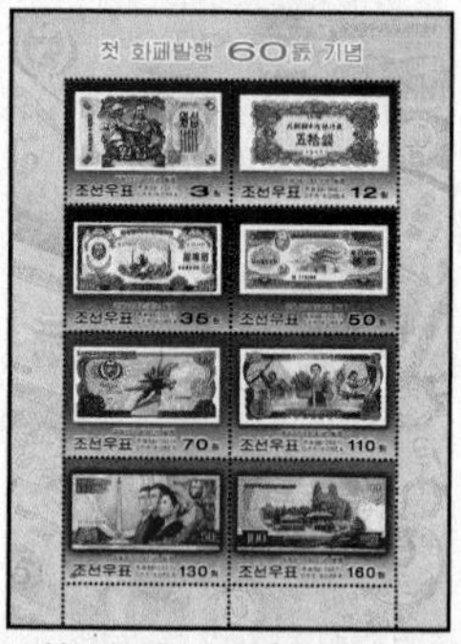

First North Korean Currency, 60th Anniv. — A2093

No. 4675 — Banknotes: a, 3w, 10-won note of 1947. b, 12w, 50-chon note of 1947. c, 35w, 100-won note of 1959. d, 50w, 10-won note of 1959. e, 70w, 10-won note of 1978. f, 110w, 1-won note of 1978. g, 130w, 50-won note of 1992. h, 160w, 100-won note of 1992.

2007, May 20 **Litho.**

4675 A2093 Sheet of 8, #a-h 9.25 4.75

Souvenir Sheet

Battle of Pochonbo, 70th Anniv. — A2094

2007, June 4 ***Perf. 11½x12***

4676 A2094 120w multi 2.00 1.00

Fish — A2095

Designs: 15w, Naso lituratus. 50w, Carassius auratus. 110w, A. citrinellus. 200w, Symphysodon discus.

2007, July 1 ***Perf. 13¼***

4677-4680 A2095 Set of 4 6.25 3.00
4680a Booklet pane of 4, #4677-4680 6.25 —
Complete booklet, #4680a 6.25

Self-disembowelment of Ri Jun at Hague Intl. Peace Conference, Cent. — A2096

2007, July 14

4681 A2096 110w brn & grn 1.90 .95

Fossils A2097

Designs: 15w, Tetracorallia. 70w, Neuropteridium. 130w, Yoldia. 200w, Rhinoceros mandible.

2007, July 20

4682-4685 A2097 Set of 4 7.00 3.75
4685a Booklet pane of 4, #4682-4685 7.00 —
Complete booklet, #4685a 7.00

Miniature Sheet

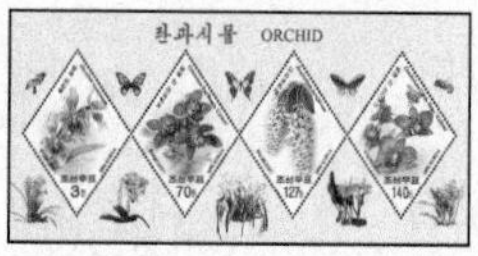

Orchids A2098

No. 4686: a, 3w, Oncidium wyattianum. b, 70w, Cymbidium Red Beauty "Carmen." c, 127w, Dendrobium thyrsifolium. d, 140w, Dendrobium Candy Stripe "Kodama."

2007, Aug. 3 ***Perf. 12¾***

4686 A2098 Sheet of 4, #a-d 5.50 2.75
e. Booklet pane of 4, #4686a-4686d 5.50 —
Complete booklet, #4686e 5.50

Women's Soccer A2099

No. 4687 — Various women soccer players making plays: a, 12w. b, 40w. c, 70w. d, 110w. e, 140w.

2007, Sept. 10 ***Perf.***

4687 A2099 Sheet of 5, #a-e 6.00 3.00

Souvenir Sheet

4688 A2099 130w shown 2.25 1.10

Miniature Sheet

Flowers A2100

No. 4689: a, Gladiolus gandavensis. b, Iris ensata. c, Rosa hybrida. d, Nelumbo nucifera.

2007, Sept. 26 ***Perf. 13¼***

4689 A2100 30w Sheet of 4, #a-d 2.10 1.00
e. Booklet pane of 4, #4689a-4689d 2.10 —
Complete booklet, #4689e 2.10

See Russia No. 7045.

Miniature Sheets

A2101

2008 Summer Olympics, Beijing — A2102

Nos. 4690 and 4691 — Mascots: a, 3w, Beibei. b, 12w, Jingjing. c, 30w, Huanhuan. d, 70w, Yingying. e, 140w, Nini.
2008 Olympics emblem and: 300w, Hurdler, shooter, group of athletes. 500w, Athletes holding flower bouquets.

2007, Oct. 15 Litho. *Perf.*
4690 A2101 Sheet of 5, #a-e — —

Litho. With Three-Dimensional Plastic Affixed

4691 A2101 Sheet of 5, #a-e — —

Printed on Plastic DVD Without Gum

4692 A2102 300w multi *12.50 12.50*
4693 A2102 500w multi *20.00 20.00*

No. 4691 sold for 500w, and stamps have other three-dimensional images.

Furniture and Household Furnishings A2103

Designs: 3w, Seal box. 12w, Ornamental chest. 40w, Collapsible dressing table. 70w, Wardrobe. 110w, Chest of drawers. 130w, Chest of drawers, diff.

2007, Nov. 1 Litho. *Perf. 13¼*
4694-4699 A2103 Set of 6 8.00 6.00
4699a Booklet pane of 6, #4694-4699 8.00 —
Complete booklet, #4699a 8.00

Food — A2104

Designs: 12w, Potato and rice cakes. 50w, Yongchae kimchi. 70w, Fermented flatfish. 110w, Potato cakes.

2007, Nov. 5
4700-4703 A2104 Set of 4 5.25 3.75
4703a Booklet pane of 4, #4700-4703 5.25 —
Complete booklet, #4703a 5.25

Souvenir Sheet

Summit Meeting of Pres. Kim Jong Il and South Korean Pres. Roh Moo Hyun A2105

2007, Nov. 10 *Perf. 11½x12*
4704 A2105 170w multi 3.75 3.00

Miniature Sheets

Scenes From Arirang Gymnastics Performance — A2106

No. 4705 — Various scenes: a, 12w. b, 50w.
No. 4706 — Various scenes: a, 120w. b, 155w.

2007, Nov. 15 *Perf. 11½*
Sheets of 2, #a-b, + Label
4705-4706 A2106 Set of 2 6.00 4.00

Paintings of Kim Dong Ho — A2107

Designs: 3w, Plowing. 12w, Weaving a Straw Mat. 70w, Thrashing. 130w, Archery.

2007, Nov. 18 *Perf. 13¼*
4707-4710 A2107 Set of 4 4.75 3.00
4710a Booklet pane of 4, #4707-4710 4.75 —
Complete booklet, #4710a 4.75

Souvenir Sheet

Visit of Viet Nam Communist Party Secretary General Nong Duc Manh — A2108

2007, Dec. 16 *Perf. 12x11½*
4711 A2108 120w multi 2.60 1.75

Home of Kim Jong Suk A2109

Paintings Depicting Kim Jong Suk A2110

No. 4713: a, 30w, Kim Jong Suk and Kim Il Sung (54x45mm). b, 70w, Kim Jong Suk (45mm diameter). c, 110w, Kim Jong Suk in battle (54x45mm).

2007, Dec. 24 *Perf. 12x11½*
4712 A2109 3w multi .35 .30

Souvenir Sheet
Perf. 13¼, Perf. (#4713b)

4713 A2110 Sheet of 3, #a-c 4.75 3.50

New Year 2008 — A2111

2008, Jan. 1 Litho. *Perf. 13¼*
4714 A2111 3w multi .30 .30

Publication of Saenal Sinmun, 80th Anniv. — A2112

2008, Jan. 15
4715 A2112 85w multi 1.50 .75

Joint Editorials of State Newspapers A2113

Red flag in upper left corner and: No. 4716, 3w, Arms and flag of North Korea, tower. No. 4717, 3w, Soldiers. No. 4718, 12w, Soldier and flag. No. 4719, 12w, Soldiers, factories and electrical tower, horiz. 30w, Woman and food, horiz. 120w, Musicians, children playing soccer, building. 130w, Men and woman, doves, map of Korea.

2008, Jan. 30 *Perf. 11¾*
4716-4722 A2113 Set of 7 6.75 4.75

Parrots — A2114

Designs: 15w, Melopsittacus undulatus. 85w, Agapornis roseicollis. 155w, Agapornis personata, horiz. 170w, Two Melopsittacus undulatus, horiz.

2008, Feb. 5 *Perf. 13¼*
4723-4726 A2114 Set of 4 9.50 7.00
4726a Booklet pane of 4, #4723-4726 9.50 —
Complete booklet, #4726a 9.50

Souvenir Sheet

Naming of Kimjongilhwa Begonia, 20th Anniv. — A2115

2008, Feb. 13 *Perf. 11½x12*
4727 A2115 85w multi 2.10 1.50

A2116

Flowers A2117

Designs: 3w, Pyrethrum hybridum.
No. 4729: a, 12w, Tulipa gesneriana (30x42mm). b, 70w, Adonis amurensis (30x42mm). c, 120w, Mathiola incana (30x42mm). d, 155w, Kimjongilhwa begonia (44mm diameter).

2008, Feb. 16 *Perf. 13¼*
4728 A2116 3w multi .50 .30
4729 A2117 Sheet of 4, #a-d 7.50 5.25

Kim Jong Il, 66th birthday.

Kim Il Sung Birthplace Type of 2002

2008, Mar. 15 Litho. *Perf. 11½*
4730 A1886 3w red .50 .30

For surcharge, see No. 4877C.

Miniature Sheet

Publication of "On the Art of Cinema," by Kim Jong Il, 35th Anniv. — A2118

No. 4731 — Various actors and actresses: a, 3w, Musician. b, 85w, Man holding gun. c, 135w, Martial artist. d, 170w, Man, woman and children.

2008, Mar. 15 *Perf. 13¼*
4731 A2118 Sheet of 4, #a-d 6.50 3.25

250-Mile Journey for Learning, 85th Anniv. — A2119

2008, Mar. 16 *Perf. 12*
4732 A2119 15w multi .50 .30

2008 Summer Olympics, Beijing — A2120

No. 4733: a, 3w, Soccer. b, 12w, Basketball. c, 30w, Tennis. d, 70w, Table tennis.

2008, Mar. 28 ***Perf. 13¼***
4733 A2120 Block or horiz. strip of 4, #a-d 2.60 1.25

Famous Men — A2121

Designs: 85w, Choe Yong (1316-88), military leader. 160w, Ho Jun (1546-1615), doctor.

2008, Mar. 29 ***Perf. 12***
4734-4735 A2121 Set of 2 4.00 2.10

Election of Kim Jong Il as Chairman of National Defense Commission, 15th Anniv. — A2122

2008, Apr. 9 ***Perf. 13¼***
4736 A2122 12w multi .50 .30

Souvenir Sheet

Election of Kim Jong Il as Chairman of National Defense Commission, 15th Anniv. — A2123

2008, Apr. 9 ***Perf. 11½x12***
4737 A2123 120w multi — —

International Friendship Exhibition — A2124

Gifts to Kim Il Sung: 3w, Pitcher and oil lamp. 85w, Painting of rooster. 155w, Throne. 135w, Vase with two handles.

2008, Apr. 15 ***Perf. 11½***
4738-4740 A2124 Set of 3 4.00 2.10

Souvenir Sheet

4741 A2124 135w multi 3.50 1.50

North-South Joint Conference, 60th Anniv. — A2125

2008, Apr. 21 ***Perf. 12***
4742 A2125 12w gray green .50 .30

Mushrooms — A2126

Designs: 12w, Amanita muscaria. 50w, Armillariella mellea. 135w, Macrolepota procera. 155w, Tricholoma terreum.

2008, May 8 ***Perf. 11½***
4743-4746 A2126 Set of 4 6.50 3.75
4746a Booklet pane of 4, #4743-4746 6.50 —
Complete booklet, #4746a 6.50

Buildings on Mt. Ryongak — A2127

Designs: 35w, Two buildings. 155w, Building and wall.

2008, May 25 ***Perf. 13¼***
4747-4748 A2127 Set of 2 3.75 2.10

Musical Instruments — A2128

Designs: 15w, Hyangbipha (stringed instrument). 50w, Phiri (contrabassoon). 120w, Jangsaenap (oboe). 160w, Kayagum (zither), horiz.

2008, June 1 ***Perf. 13¼***
4749-4752 A2128 Set of 4 6.50 3.75
4752a Booklet pane of 4, #4749-4752 6.50 —
Complete booklet, #4752a 6.50

Opera Scenes and Scores A2129

Designs: 3w, Sea of Blood. 12w, The Flower Girl. 85w, The True Daughter of the Party. 120w, Tell Oh Forest. 155w, The Song of Mt. Kumgang.

2008, June 5 ***Perf. 12x11½***
4753-4757 A2129 Set of 5 6.75 4.75

North Korea No. 1 and Romania No. 1 — A2130

2008, June 20 ***Perf. 12¼x11¾***
4758 A2130 85w multi 1.90 .95

EFIRO 2008 Intl. Stamp Exhibition, Bucharest, Romania.

Capture of the USS Pueblo, 40th Anniv. A2131

2008, June 25 ***Perf. 12¼x11¾***
4759 A2131 12w multi .50 .30

Souvenir Sheet

Olympic Torch Relay in Pyongyang — A2132

2008, June 26 ***Perf. 11¾x12¼***
4760 A2132 120w multi 2.60 1.40

Minerals A2133

Designs: 12w, Serpentine. 75w, Copper pyrite. 135w, Sphalerite. 155w, Molybdenite.

2008, July 5 ***Perf. 12¼x11¾***
4761-4764 A2133 Set of 4 7.00 4.00
4764a Booklet pane of 4, #4761-4764 7.00 —
Complete booklet, #4764a 7.00

Souvenir Sheets

A2134

A2135

Korean War Ceasefire, 55th Anniv. — A2136

No. 4765: a, 3w, Kim Il Sung leading troop crossing of Han River. b, 120w, Kim Il Sung with troops.

No. 4766: a, 35w, Kim Il Sung and seated troops. b, 155w, Celebration.

85w, Kim Il Sung at battleground.

2008, July 27 ***Perf. 12x11½***
4765 A2134 Sheet of 2, #a-b 2.40 1.40
4766 A2135 Sheet of 2, #a-b 3.50 2.10

Perf. 11½

4767 A2136 85w multi 1.90 1.00

Souvenir Sheet

Jong Il Peak, 20th Anniv. of Renaming — A2137

2008, Aug. 9 ***Perf. 13¼***
4768 A2137 120w multi 2.60 1.50

Food — A2138

Designs: 3w, Rice and wormwood cakes. 70w, Rice cakes. 135w, Pancakes. 155w, Garlic in soy sauce.

2008, Aug. 20 **Litho.** ***Perf. 13¼***
4769-4772 A2138 Set of 4 6.25 3.75
4772a Booklet pane of 4, #4769-4772 6.25 —
Complete booklet, #4772a 6.25

A2139

Songun Revolutionary Leadership — A2140

2008, Aug. 25
4773 A2139 12w multi .30 .30

Souvenir Sheet

4774 A2140 135w multi 2.75 1.50

Miniature Sheet

Koguryo Tombs UNESCO World Heritage Site — A2141

No. 4775 — Anak Tomb No. 3 paintings: a, 3w, Mask dance (60x42mm). b, 90w, Janghaedok, aide to King Kogukwon (30x42mm). c, 120w, Garage (60x42mm). d, 155w, Stable (60x42mm).

2008, Sept. 2 **Litho.** ***Perf. 13¼***
4775 A2141 Sheet of 4, #a-d, + label 6.25 3.75
e. Booklet pane of 4, #4775a-4775d 6.25 —
Complete booklet, #4775e 6.25

A2142

Flag — A2143

2008, Sept. 9 ***Perf. 11½***
4776 A2142 3w multi .50 .30
4777 A2143 155w multi 3.00 1.75

See No. 4876.

A2144

Creation of North Korea, 60th Anniv. A2145

Designs: 3w, Chollima Statue, flag of North Korea, city and flowers. 12w, Torch, flag of the Supreme Commander, people. 70w, Soldiers. 120w, People on horses. 160w, Handshake. 155w, Creation of National Flag and Arms.

2008, Sept. 9 ***Perf. 13¼***
4778-4782 A2144 Set of 5 6.25 4.00

Souvenir Sheet

4783 A2145 155w multi 3.00 1.50

Transportation A2146

Designs: No. 4784, 680w, Niña, ship of Christopher Columbus. No. 4785, 680w, 1910 Russian steam engine. No. 4786, 680w, Hindenburg over Lake Constance. No. 4787, 680w, Siberian husky dog sled team. No. 4788, 680w, Ivan Basso, cyclist. No. 4789, 680w, Mercedes-Benz-Mets LF 16 fire truck. No. 4790, 680w, Two Ferrari Enzos. No. 4791, 680w, Eurostar train. No. 4792, 680w, Concorde. No. 4793, 680w, Laika the dog and Sputnik 2.

2008, Sept. 15 ***Perf.***
4784-4793 A2146 Set of 10 180.00 150.00

Nos. 4784-4793 each were printed in sheets of 2.

Souvenir Sheet

Salvelinus Malma — A2147

2008, Oct. 2 **Litho.** ***Perf. 13¼***
4794 A2147 135w multi 2.40 1.10

Miniature Sheet

Moran Hill, Pyongyang — A2148

No. 4795: a, 3w, Small shelter and bridge. b, 45w, Large shelter and walkway. c, 100w, Flora with small shelter, bridges and Pyongyang in distance. d, 135w, Building with steps.

2008, Oct. 20
4795 A2148 Sheet of 4, #a-d 5.00 3.00

Introduction of Compulsory Secondary Education, 50th Anniv. — A2149

2008, Nov. 1
4796 A2149 12w multi .50 .30

Soldier and Flag — A2150

Woman in Bean Field — A2151

2008, Nov. 17
4797 A2150 12w multi .35 .30
4798 A2151 85w multi 1.50 .70

Furniture A2152

Designs: 50w, Haeju table. 70w, Inkstone table. 120w, Dressing table with drawer. 170w, Jewel box.

2008, Dec. 3
4799-4802 A2152 Set of 4 6.50 3.50
4802a Booklet pane of 4, #4799-4802 6.50 —
Complete booklet, #4802a 6.50

Souvenir Sheet

Ulmil Pavilion, Moran Hill, Pyongyang — A2153

Litho. With Three-Dimensional Plastic Affixed

2008, Dec. 15 ***Perf. 13¼***

Without Gum

4803 A2153 85w multi 2.40 1.25

New Year 2009 — A2154

2009, Jan. 1 **Litho.** ***Perf. 11½***
4804 A2154 3w multi .50 .30

For surcharge, see No. 4877D.

A2155

Red Guards, 50th Anniv. A2156

2009, Jan. 14 ***Perf. 11¾***
4805 A2155 12w multi .50 .30

Souvenir Sheet

4806 A2156 160w multi 3.00 2.00

Traditional Games A2157

Designs: 3w, Tug-of-war. 120w, Knee fighting.

2009, Jan. 25 ***Perf. 13¼***
4807-4808 A2157 Set of 2 2.40 1.50

Kim Jong Il, 67th Birthday — A2158

Unnamed butterfly and flowers: 3w, Crinum bracteatum. 12w, Begonia. 120w, Callistemon phoeniceus. 160w, Plumeria rubra.

2009, Feb. 16 ***Perf. 11¾***
4809-4812 A2158 Set of 4 5.25 3.00

Souvenir Sheet

Proclamation of Juche Model for Society, 50th Anniv. — A2159

2009, Feb. 19 ***Perf. 11½x12***
4813 A2159 170w multi 3.25 1.90

Souvenir Sheets

A2160

A2161

A2162

Joint Editorials of State Newspapers — A2163

No. 4814: a, 3w, Torch, Chollima statue. b, 170w, Symbols of industry and transportation.
No. 4815: a, 12w, Food crops, canned foods, city. b, 150w, Musical instruments, sheet music, orchestra, soccer players.
No. 4816: a, 30w, Soldiers, flag, ships, airplanes and missiles. b, 120w, Soldiers, flags, city.
No. 4817: a, 80w, Map of Korea, text. b, 100w, Hands crushing bomb.

2009, Feb. 22 ***Perf. 11½***
4814 A2160 Sheet of 2, #a-b, + 2 labels 3.25 2.10
4815 A2161 Sheet of 2, #a-b, + 2 labels 3.00 1.90
4816 A2162 Sheet of 2, #a-b, + 2 labels 2.75 1.90
4817 A2163 Sheet of 2, #a-b, + 2 labels 3.25 2.10
Nos. 4814-4817 (4) 12.25 8.00

For surcharge, see No. 4877E.

Souvenir Sheets

China 2009 World Stamp Exhibition, Luoyang — A2164

No. 4818: a, 3w, Flowers. b, 100w, Flowers, diff.
No. 4819: a, 12w, Statue of horse. b, 90w, Building, steps, sculpture.

2009, Feb. 25 ***Perf. 11¾***

Sheets of 2, #a-b

4818-4819 A2164 Set of 2 5.25 2.40
4819c Booklet pane of 4, #4818a-4818b, 4819a-4819b 5.25 —
Complete booklet, #4819c 5.25

March 1 Uprising Against Japan, 90th Anniv. A2165

2009, Mar. 1 ***Perf. 12¼x11¾***
4820 A2165 90w multi 1.90 1.25

Intl. Women's Day, Cent. — A2166

2009, Mar. 8 ***Perf. 13¼***

4821 A2166 35w multi .60 .35

Gifts to Kim Il Sung A2167

Designs: 3w, Painting of horses. 12w, Fossil fish. 140w, Rifle. 150w, Bear skin.

2009, Apr. 15 ***Perf. 13¼***

4822-4825 A2167 Set of 4 5.50 3.50
4825a Booklet pane of 4, #4822-4825 5.50 —
Complete booklet, #4825a 5.50

Complete booklet sold for 322w.

Central Zoo, Pyongyang, 50th Anniv. — A2168

Birds: 12w, Anthropoides paradisea. 70w, Accipiter gentilis. 120w, Larus argentatus. 140w, Balearica pavonina.

2009, Apr. 30 ***Perf. 11¾x12¼***

4826-4829 A2168 Set of 4 6.25 3.75
4829a Booklet pane of 4, #4826-4829 6.25 —
Complete booklet, #4829a 6.25

Central Botanical Garden, Pyongyang, 50th Anniv. — A2169

Trees: 3w, Catalpa ovata. 50w, Betula platyphylla. 120w, Juglans cordiformis. 160w, Metasequoia glyptostroboides.

2009, Apr. 30 ***Perf. 13¼***

4830-4833 A2169 Set of 4 6.25 3.75
4833a Booklet pane of 4, #4830-4833 6.25 —
Complete booklet, #4833a 6.25

Complete booklet sold for 350w.

Sports A2170

Designs: 12w, Baseball. 90w, Bowling. 160w, Fencing. 200w, Golf.

2009, May 2

4834-4837 A2170 Set of 4 7.75 3.75
4837a Booklet pane of 4, #4834-4837 7.75 —
Complete booklet, #4837a 7.75

No. 4189a Surcharged in Gold

No. 4838: a, 20w on 40ch, LZ1. b, 40w on 80ch, LZ120. c, 1w+109w on 1.20w, Zeppelin NT. d, 2w+168w on 2.40w, Zeppelin NT, diff.

Method and Perf As Before

2009, May 5

4838 A1852 Sheet of 4, #a-d 6.25 4.00

Naposta '09 and IBRA '09, Essen, Germany. On Nos. 4838c and 4838d, the obliterator covers the part of the original denomination expressed in chon.

Children's Union Camp — A2171

Children: 3w, Mountaineering. 80w, Collecting butterflies. 120w, At campfire. 170w, At beach.

2009 **Litho.** ***Perf. 11½***

4839-4842 A2171 Set of 4 6.25 3.75
4842a Booklet pane of 4, #4839-4842 6.25 —
Complete booklet, #4842a 6.25
4842b Souvenir sheet of 4, #4839-4842 6.25 3.75

Issued: Nos. 4839-4842, 4842a, 5/6; No. 4842b, 5/14. Hong Kong 2009 Intl. Stamp Exhibition (No. 4842b).

Souvenir Sheet

Battle of Musan, 70th Anniv. A2172

2009, May 22 ***Perf. 13¼***

4843 A2172 120w multi 2.90 1.50

Miniature Sheet

Kim Jong Il as Member of Central Committee of Workers' Party, 45th Anniv. — A2173

No. 4844 — Kim Jong Il: a, 3w, At desk. b, 12w, At machine shop. c, 120w, Wearing white lab jacket. d, 170w, Looking inside cooking pot.

2009, June 19 ***Perf. 11¾***

4844 A2173 Sheet of 4, #a-d 5.75 3.50

Universal Postal Union, 135th Anniv. — A2174

2009, June 20 ***Perf. 13¼***

4845 A2174 50w multi 1.10 .60

Insects — A2175

Designs: 50w, Vespa mandarinia, rose. 90w, Cicindela japonica, dandelion. 120w, Locusta migratoria, plant. 140w, Aphaenogaster famelica, mushroom.

2009, July 1 ***Perf. 11½***

4846-4849 A2175 Set of 4 7.00 4.75
4849a Booklet pane of 4, #4846-4849 7.00 —
Complete booklet, #4849a 7.00

Okryu Restaurant, Pyongyang A2176

Renovated Pyongyang Buildings — A2177

No. 4851: a, 3w, Kim Chaek University Library (35x28mm). b, 70w, Taedongmun Theater (35x28mm). c, 90w, Chongryu Restaurant (70x28mm). d, 150w, Pyongyang Grand Theater (70x28mm).

2009, July 2 ***Perf. 13¼***

4850 A2176 12w multi .40 .35

Perf. 11½

4851 A2177 Sheet of 4, #a-d 5.25 3.25

Miniature Sheet

Eternal Sun of Juche A2178

No. 4852 — Paintings: a, 12w, The Great Leader Kim Il Sung Drawing the Brush Into Our Party's Emblem. b, 50w, First Military Flag. c, 70w, Birth. d, 140w, Every Field With Bumper Harvest.

2009, July 8 ***Perf. 13¼***

4852 A2178 Sheet of 4, #a-d 5.25 3.25

Nurse and Child — A2179

Ambulance and Hospital A2180

2009, July 25

4853 A2179 12w multi .40 .30
4854 A2180 150w multi 2.60 1.75

Souvenir Sheet

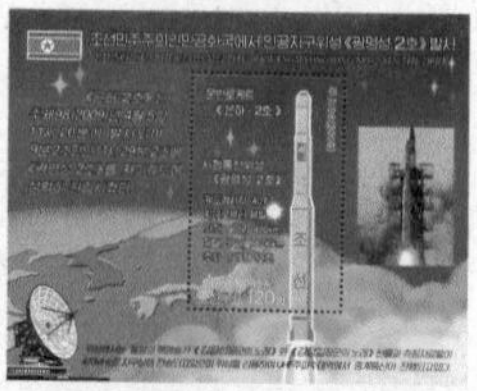

Launch of Kwangmyongsong 2 Rocket — A2181

2009, July 27 ***Perf. 11½x12***

4855 A2181 120w multi 2.75 1.50

Souvenir Sheet

Northern Area Victory Monument, Hamgyong Province — A2182

2009, Aug. 3 ***Perf. 13¼***

4856 A2182 120w multi 2.75 1.50

Musical Instruments — A2183

Designs: 12w, Saenap. 80w, Drum. 140w, Sogoghu. 170w, Flute.

2009, Aug. 5 **Litho.**

4857-4860 A2183 Set of 4 6.50 3.50

150-Day Innovation Campaign A2184

2009, Aug. 10

4861 A2184 12w multi .40 .30

Fish — A2185

Ships and: 15w, Theragra chalcogramma. 60w, Cyprinus carpio. 140w, Euthynnus pelamis. 160w, Mugil cephalus.

2009, Sept. 1

4862-4865 A2185 Set of 4 6.25 3.75
4865a Booklet pane of 4, #4862-4865 6.25 —
Complete booklet, #4865a 6.25

Miniature Sheets

Intl. Year of Astronomy — A2186

No. 4866, 95w: a, Chollima Statue, solar eclipse. b, Galileo Galilei, telescope, planets, satellite.

No. 4867, 95w: a, Rabbits, solar eclipse. b, Planets, galaxy.

No. 4868, 95w: a, Dogs, total solar eclipse. b, Chomsongdae Observatory.

2009, Aug. 29 **Litho.** ***Perf. 13½***

Sheets of 2, #a-b, + 2 Labels

4866-4868 A2186 Set of 3 9.50 7.00
4868c Souvenir sheet of 1, #4868a 1.40 .95
4868d Booklet pane of 6, #4866a-4866b, 4867a-4867b, 4868a-4868b 9.50 —
Complete booklet, #4868d 9.50

Souvenir Sheets

A2187

Year of Friendship With People's Republic of China — A2188

No. 4869: a, #3287c, 3384, 3716. b, #3563, 4374b, 4473c.
No. 4870: a, Five stamps. b, Six stamps.

2009, Sept. 2 ***Perf. 13½***

4869 A2187 60w Sheet of 2, #a-b 2.40 1.25
4870 A2188 60w Sheet of 2, #a-b 2.40 1.25

Miniature Sheet

Birdpex 2010, Antwerp, Belgium A2189

No. 4871: a, 12w, Coturnicops exquisitus. b, 90w, Porzana pusilla. c, 170w, Porzana fusca.

2009, Sept. 12 ***Perf. 11½***

4871 A2189 Sheet of 5, #4871c, 2 each #4871a-4871b, + label 6.00 3.25
d. Booklet pane of 3, #4871a-4871c 4.50 —
Complete booklet, #4871d 4.50

Souvenir Sheet

Intl. Red Cross and Red Crescent Year A2190

No. 4872 — Flags of Red Cross, North Korea and: a, 75w, Jean-Henri Dunant, founder of Red Cross. b, 95w, Disaster risk reduction. c, 95w, First aid.

2009, Sept. 21 ***Perf. 13½***

4872 A2190 Sheet of 3, #a-c 4.25 2.25

Souvenir Sheet

Kim Jong Suk (1917-49), Mother of Kim Jong Il — A2191

No. 4873: a, 90w, Portrait (33x45mm). b, 100w, Kim Jong Suk with troops, horiz. (57x36mm).

2009, Sept. 22

4873 A2191 Sheet of 2, #a-b 3.25 1.60

Miniature Sheet

People's Republic of China, 60th Anniv. A2192

No. 4874: a, 10w, Chinese President Hu Jintao. b, 67w, Chinese astronauts. c, 67w, National Stadium, Beijing. d, 84w, National Grand Theater, Beijing.

2009, Oct. 1

4874 A2192 Sheet of 4, #a-d 4.00 2.40

Worldwide Fund for Nature (WWF) — A2193

No. 4875 — Platalea minor and: a, Snail. b, Fish. c, Crab. d, Shrimp.

2009, Oct. 5 ***Perf. 13½***

4875 Horiz. strip of 4 6.25 3.25
a. A2193 3w multi .25 .25
b. A2193 12w multi .25 .25
c. A2193 99w multi 1.75 .80
d. A2193 266w multi 4.25 2.25
e. Sheet of 8, 2 each #4875a-4875d, + label 13.00 6.25

Flag and Torch Types of 2002-08

2009, Oct. 15 **Litho.** ***Perf. 11½***

4876 A2142 10w multi .30 .30

Perf. 13¼

4877 A1890 30w multi .50 .30

Nos. 4249, 4252, 4343, 4730, 4804 and 4814a Surcharged

Methods and Perfs As Before

2009, Oct.

4877A A1887 10w on 3w #4249 *1.10 1.10*
4877B A1939 10w on 3w #4343 *1.10 1.10*
4877C A1886 10w on 3w #4730 *1.10 1.10*
4877D A2154 10w on 3w #4804 *1.10 1.10*
4877E A2160 10w on 3w #4814a *1.10 1.10*
4877F A1890 30w on 12w #4252 *3.50 3.50*
Nos. 4877A-4877F (6) 9.00 9.00

Reptiles — A2194

Designs: 15w, Chamaeleo jacksonii. 50w, Naja naja. 110w, Caretta caretta, horiz. 160w, Crocodylus niloticus, horiz.

2009, Oct. 20

4878-4881 A2194 Set of 4 5.50 2.75
4881a Booklet pane of 4, #4878-4881 5.75 —
Complete booklet, #4881a 5.75

Miniature Sheets

Lighthouses — A2195

No. 4882: a, Cape Palliser Lighthouse, New Zealand, and Sousa chinensis. b, Tater Du Lighthouse, United Kingdom, and Mary Rose. c, Hornby Lighthouse, Australia, and Passat, Germany. d, Rubjerg Knude Lighthouse, Denmark, and Wappen von Hamburg.
No. 4883: a, Bengtskär Lighthouse, Finland, and Phoebastria albatrus. b, Fanad Lighthouse, Ireland, and Bolma rugosa. c, Cordouan Lighthouse, France, and Sterna fuscata. d, Brandaris Lighthouse, Netherlands, and Pleurotomaria africana.
No. 4884: a, Cape St. Vincent Lighthouse, Portugal, and Sula bassana. b, Europa Point Lighthouse, Gibraltar, and Lambis scorpio. c, Vorontsov Lighthouse, Ukraine, and Grampus griseus. d, Gelendzhik Lighthouse, Russia, and Gibbula magus.
No. 4885: a, Hoy High Lighthouse, Scotland, and Delphinus delphis. b, Lindesnes Lighthouse, Norway, and Stenella coeruleoalba. c, Reykjanesviti Lighthouse, Iceland, and Chlamys varia. d, Seal Point Lighthouse, South Africa, and Chroicocephalus ridibundus.

2009, Oct. 24 **Litho.** ***Perf. 13x13½***

4882 A2195 760w Sheet of 4, #a-d 50.00 50.00
e. Souvenir sheet of 2 #4882a 24.00 24.00
f. Souvenir sheet of 2 #4882b 24.00 24.00
g. Souvenir sheet of 2 #4882c 24.00 24.00
h. Souvenir sheet of 2 #4882d 24.00 24.00
4883 A2195 760w Sheet of 4, #a-d 50.00 50.00
e. Souvenir sheet of 2 #4883a 24.00 24.00
f. Souvenir sheet of 2 #4883b 24.00 24.00
g. Souvenir sheet of 2 #4883c 24.00 24.00
h. Souvenir sheet of 2 #4883d 24.00 24.00
4884 A2195 760w Sheet of 4, #a-d 50.00 50.00
e. Souvenir sheet of 2 #4884a 24.00 24.00
f. Souvenir sheet of 2 #4884b 24.00 24.00
g. Souvenir sheet of 2 #4884c 24.00 24.00
h. Souvenir sheet of 2 #4884d 24.00 24.00
4885 A2195 760w Sheet of 4, #a-d 50.00 50.00
e. Souvenir sheet of 2 #4885a 24.00 24.00
f. Souvenir sheet of 2 #4885b 24.00 24.00
g. Souvenir sheet of 2 #4885c 24.00 24.00
h. Souvenir sheet of 2 #4885d 24.00 24.00

Souvenir Sheet

Repatriation of Korean Nationals in Japan, 50th Anniv. — A2196

2009, Dec. 16 **Litho.** ***Perf. 11½x12***

4887 A2196 160w multi 2.60 1.25

Miniature Sheet

End of Juche 98 A2197

No. 4888: a, 10w, Launch of Kwangmyongsong No. 2 satellite. b, 20w, CNC machine tool industry. c, 20w, Oxygen separator, finished steel products, train and vehicles. d, 30w, Construction vehicles. e, 50w, Namhung Gasification Project, crane with pipe. f, 50w, Apartment buildings on Mansudae Street, Pyongyang. g, 57w, Sturgeons, ostriches, chicken, pig. h, 70w, Apples, farm, Migok-ri model village.i, 80w, Audience, soccer players, singer.

2009, Dec. 31 **Litho.** ***Perf. 13½***

4888 A2197 Sheet of 9, #a-i 6.25 3.25

Souvenir Sheet

Kim Jong Il and Workers A2198

2009, Dec. 31 **Litho.** ***Perf. 13¼***

4889 A2198 100w multi 1.60 .80

End of Juche 98.

New Year 2010 — A2199

2010, Jan. 1 ***Perf. 13¼***

4890 A2199 10w multi .30 .30

Tigers — A2200

Tiger and: 30w, Sun. 67w, Tree. 171w, Tiger and cubs, horiz.

2010, Jan. 5 **Litho.** ***Perf. 11¾x12¼***

4891-4892 A2200 Set of 2 1.60 .80
4892a Booklet pane of 4, 2 each #4891-4892 3.50 —
Complete booklet, #4892a 3.50

Souvenir Sheet

Litho. with Three-Dimensional Plastic Affixed

Perf. 13¼

Without Gum

4893 A2200 171w multi 2.75 1.50

Complete booklet sold for 213w. No. 4893 contains one 60x42mm stamp.

Wildlife A2201

Designs: 35w, Ailuropoda melanoleuca. 60w, Aix galericulata. 80w, Lagenorhynchus obliquidens. 110w, Panthera pardus.

2010, Jan. 30 **Litho.** ***Perf. 13¼***

4894-4897 A2201 Set of 4 4.75 2.40
4897a Booklet pane of 4, #4894-4897 *11.00* —
Complete booklet, #4897a *11.00*

Complete booklet sold for 304w. No. 4897a exists imperforate.

Miniature Sheet

2010 Winter Olympics, Vancouver — A2202

No. 4898: a, 10w, Ice hockey. b, 40w, Figure skating. c, 50w, Speed skating. d, 70w, Skiing.

2010, Feb. 1 ***Perf. 13***

4898 A2202 Sheet of 8, 2 each #a-d 5.50 5.50

See No. 4919.

Kim Jong Il, 68th Birthday A2203

No. 4899: a, 10w, Impatiens sultanii Royal Rose. b, 50w, Gazania hybrida. c, 70w, Paeonia suffructicosa. d, 110w, Bougainvillea glabra Sanderiana.

2010, Feb. 16 ***Perf. 11½***

4899 A2203 Vert. strip or block of 4, #a-d, + 8 labels 4.25 2.10
e. Booklet pane of 4, #4899a-4899d, + 8 labels 4.50 —
Complete booklet, #4899e 4.50

Complete booklet sold for 259w.

Miniature Sheet

Joint Editorials of State Newspapers — A2204

No. 4900: a, 10w, People, soldier, Party Founding Monument, flowers. b, 20w, Woman, city, manufactured items. c, 30w, Woman carrying crops, vegetables. d, 57w, Worker, factory, train, dam. e, 67w, Soldiers. f, 95w, People holding flag showing mpa of unified Korea. g, 125w, Doves, map showing unified Korea.

2010, Feb. 20 ***Perf. 13¼***

4900 A2204 Sheet of 7, #a-g, + 2 labels 6.50 3.50

A2205

Anti-Imperialism Posters — A2206

2010, Mar. 5

4901 A2205 76w multi 1.40 .65
4902 A2206 95w multi 1.60 .75

Cats — A2207

Designs: 10w, Cat, chicks. 70w, Cats, flower, butterfly. 133w, Cat, mouse. 170w, Cat, kittens, ball of yarn.

2010, Mar. 25 ***Perf. 11½***

4903-4906 A2207 Set of 4 6.25 3.25
4906a Booklet pane of 4, #4903-4906 6.50 —
Complete booklet, #4906a 6.50

Complete booklet sold for 402w.

Souvenir Sheet

Birds A2208

No. 4907: a, 30w, Brachyramphus perdix. b, 125w, Gallinago solitaria. c, 133w, Porzana paykullii.

2010, Apr. 9

4907 A2208 Sheet of 3, #a-c, + 3 labels 4.75 2.40
d. Booklet pane of 3, #4907a-4907c 5.00 —
Complete booklet, #4907d 5.00

Antverpia 2010 International Philatelic Exhibition, Antwerp. Complete booklet sold for 307w.

Gifts to Kim Il Sung — A2209

Designs: 10w, Eagle figurine. 30w, Crane figurine. 95w, Tiger painting. 152w, Sea turtle figurine, horiz.

2010, Apr. 15 ***Perf. 13¼***

4908-4911 A2209 Set of 4 4.75 2.40

Orchids and Insects — A2210

Designs: 30w, Sophronitella brevipenduncu-lata, bee. 80w, Epidendrum radiatum, dragonfly. 120w, Cymbidium Lillian Stewart "Red Carpet," bee. 152w Dendrobium hybrid, butterfly.

2010, Apr. 20 ***Perf. 11½***

4912-4915 A2210 Set of 4 6.25 3.25
4915a Booklet pane of 4, #4912-4915 6.75 —
Complete booklet, #4915a 6.75

Nos. 4912-4915 each were printed in sheets of 5 + label. Complete booklet sold for 401w.

Souvenir Sheet

Expo 2010, Shanghai — A2211

No. 4916: a, 10w, Chollima statue, city, flowers. b, 80w, Children watering plant, wind turbines, wildlife.

2010, May 1 **Litho.**

4916 A2211 Sheet of 2, #a-b, + 2 labels 1.50 .75

Miniature Sheet

Table Tennis A2212

No. 4917: a, 10w, Man with green shirt. b, 30w, Woman with red shirt. c, 95w, Woman with blue shirt. d, 152w, Man with pink shirt.

2010, May 10 ***Perf.***

4917 A2212 Sheet of 4, #a-d 4.75 2.50
e. Booklet pane of 4, #4917a-4917d 5.00 —
Complete booklet, #4917e 5.00

Complete booklet sold for 306w.

Joint Slogans — A2213

2010, May 12 ***Perf. 11½***

4918 A2213 10w multi .30 .30

No. 4898 With Flags of Countries Winning Depicted Events Added at Left of Athlete

Miniature Sheet

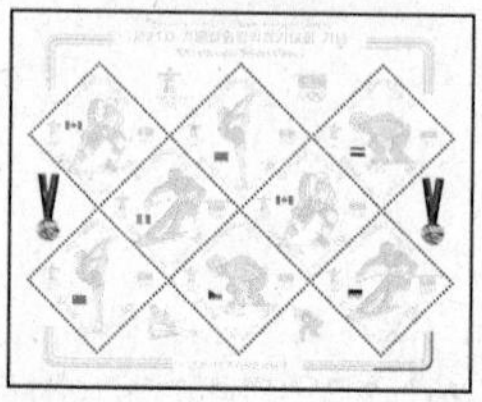

No. 4919: a, 10w, Ice hockey, flag of Canada. b, 40w, Figure skating, flag of People's Republic of China. c, 50w, Speed skating, flag of Netherlands. d, 50w, Speed skating, flag of Czech Republic. e, 70w, Skiing, flag of Italy. f, 70w, Skiing, flag of Germany.

2010, May 25 ***Perf. 13***

4919 A2202 Sheet of 8, #4919c-4919f, 2 each #4919a-4919b 5.25 5.25

Souvenir Sheet

Dinosaurs — A2214

No. 4920: a, 10w, Brontosaurus. b, 125w, Allosaurus. c, 152w, Pterodactylus.

2010, June 16 ***Perf. 12¾***

4920 A2214 Sheet of 3, #a-c, + label 4.75 2.40
d. Booklet pane of 3, #4920a-4920c 5.00 —
Complete booklet, #4920d 5.00
e. As #4920, with Euro-phila 2010 emblem in sheet margin 5.25 2.60

Complete booklet sold for 306w.
Issued: No. 4920e, 10/2.

2010 World Cup Soccer Championships, South Africa — A2215

No. 4921 — Shirt colors of soccer players: a, 20w, Green, yellow. b, 57w, Yellow, blue. c, 190w, Red, white.
114w, Yellow, white.

2010, May 31 ***Perf. 13¼***

4921 A2215 Sheet of 3, #a-c, + 3 labels 4.25 2.25

Souvenir Sheet

4922 A2215 114w multi 1.90 .95
a. Booklet pane of 4, #4921a-4921c, 4922 6.75 —
Complete booklet, #4922a 6.75

Complete booklet sold for 400w.

Souvenir Sheet

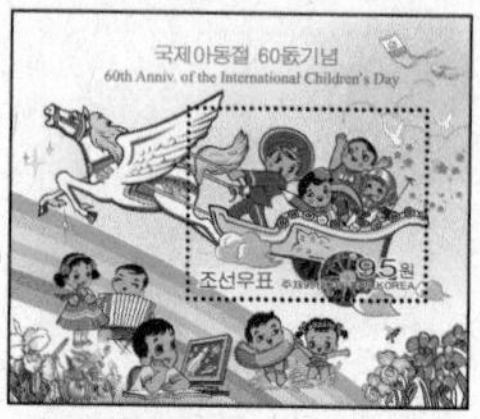

Intl. Children's Day, 60th Anniv. — A2216

2010, June 1 ***Perf. 11¾***

4923 A2216 95w multi 1.60 .85
a. As #4923, with Bangkok 2010 emblem in sheet margin 1.60 .85

Issued: No. 4923a, 8/4.

Joint Declaration of June 15, 2000 on Reunification of Korea — A2217

2010, June 15 ***Perf. 13¼***

4924 A2217 190w multi 3.25 1.60

A2218

A2219

A2220

Visit of Kim Jong Il to People's Republic of China A2221

No. 4925 — Kim Jong Il: a, 20w, And Chinese man pointing. b, 40w Pointing. c, 67w, Walking.

No. 4926 — Kim Jong Il: a, 20w, Standing next to woman. b, 35w, With leg raised. c, 80w, Looking through window.

No. 4927 — Kim Jong Il: a, 30w, Standing next to Chinese Pres. Hu Jintao. b, 40w, Seated at table with Pres. Hu. c, 70w, Shaking hands with Pres. Hu.

60w, Kim Jong Il and Pres. Hu.

2010, June 20 ***Perf. 13¼***

4925 A2218 Sheet of 3, #a-c, + 6 labels 2.10 1.10
4926 A2219 Sheet of 3, #a-c, + 6 labels 2.25 1.15
4927 A2220 Sheet of 3, #a-c, + 3 labels 2.40 1.25
Nos. 4925-4927 (3) 6.75 3.50

Souvenir Sheet

Perf. 11½x12

4928 A2221 60w multi 1.00 .45

Miniature Sheet

Children's Animated Films — A2222

No. 4929 — Scenes from children's animated films: a, 10w, Butterfly and Cock. b, 30w, A Clever Raccoon Dog. c, 95w, A Hedgehog Defeats a Tiger. d, 133w, Regret of Rabbit.

2010, June 30 ***Perf. 13¼***
4929 A2222 Sheet of 4, #a-d 4.50 2.25

Souvenir Sheet

Azaleas A2223

2010, July 1 **Litho.**
4930 A2223 85w multi 1.50 .70

Souvenir Sheet

National Anthem A2224

2010, July 5 ***Perf. 13½***
4931 A2224 50w black .80 .40

A2225

Liberation of Korea, 65th Anniv. — A2226

No. 4932 — Paintings: a, 10w, The Great Leader Forming the Korean Revolutionary Army. b, 15w, Bloody and Long Anti-Japanese War. c, 20w, The Azalea in the Fatherland. d, 40w, Pyongyang in New Spring. e, 100w, Historical That Night.
60w, February Festival on the Eve of Korea's Liberation.

2010, Aug. 15 ***Perf. 13¼***
4932 A2225 Sheet of 5, #a-e, + label 3.00 1.60

Souvenir Sheet

4933 A2226 60w multi 1.00 .45

A2227

A2228

Start of Songun Revolutionary Leadership, 50th Anniv. — A2229

No. 4935 — Paintings: a, 15w, General Kim Jong Il Instilling the Traditions of Mt. Paektu in the Soldiers (63x41mm). b, 30w, Military Song of Victory (50x38mm). c, 55w, General to the Frontline, Children to the Camp (50x38mm). d, 80w, Saying He Feels Happiest Among the Soldiers (50x38mm).
70w, Blizzard on Mt. Paektu.

2010, Aug. 25 ***Perf. 11½***
4934 A2227 10w multi .30 .30

Perf. 12x11½ (#4935a), 11¾

4935 A2228 Sheet of 4, #a-d 3.00 1.50

Souvenir Sheet

Perf. 11¾

4936 A2229 70w multi 1.25 .60

Souvenir Sheet

Diplomatic Relations Between North Korea and Cuba, 50th Anniv. — A2230

2010, Aug. 29 **Litho.** ***Perf. 11¾***
4937 A2230 85w multi 1.75 .80

Paintings — A2231

Designs: 15w, Pine Tree and Hawk, by Sin Yun Bok. 35w, Waves of Ongchon, by Jong Son. 70w, Reeds and Wild Geese, by Jo Sok Jin. 100w, After Picking Medicinal Herbs, by Kim Hong Do.

2010, Sept. 1 **Litho.** ***Perf. 13¼***
4938-4941 A2231 Set of 4 3.75 1.90
4941a Booklet pane of 4, #4938-4941 3.75 —
Complete booklet, #4941a 3.75

A2232

A2233

A2234

A2235

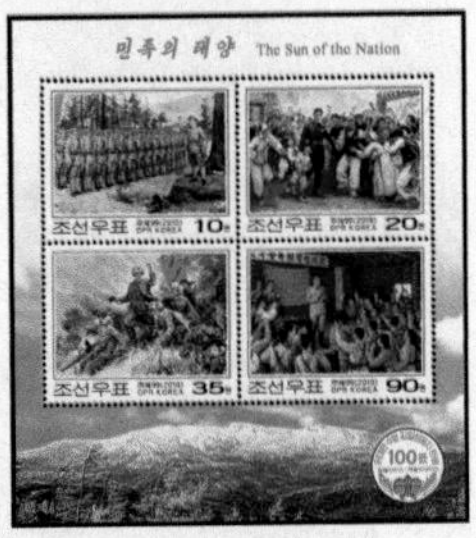

A2236

A2237

Pres. Kim Il Sung (1912-94) — A2238

No. 4942: a, 20w, Kim Il Sung being educated by father. b, 55w, Kim Il Sung being educated by mother.
No. 4943: a, 25w, Kim Jong Suk defending Kim Il Sung (64x42mm). b, 30w, Kim Il Sung at secret camp on Mt. Paektu in spring (45x35mm). c, 45w, Kim Il Sung on horseback leading other riders (454x35mm).
No. 4944: a, 10w, Kim Il Sung crossing Amnok River in winter. b, 30w, Kim Il Sung leading protest against Jilin-Hoeryong railway. c, 40w, Kim Il Sung reporting at Youth League meeting. d, 55w, Kang Pan Sok handing over pistols to Kim Il Sung.
No. 4945: a, 20w, Gunshot of Pochonbo. b, 30w, Kim Il Sung burning Minsaengdan documents. c, 40w, Kim Il Sung with members of children's corps. d, 45w, Kim Il Sung leading soldiers.
No. 4946: a, 10w, Kim Il Sung speaking to Anti-Japanese People's Guerilla Army. b, 20w, Kim Il Sung with people after establishing People's Revolutionary Government. c, 35w, Kim Il Sung leading soldiers, diff. d, 90w, Kim Il Sung founding Association for the Restoration of the Fatherland.
50w, Kim Il Sung at podium giving speech. 60w, Kim Il Sung leading solders, diff.

Perf. 13¼, 12x11½ (#4943a)

2010, Sept. 5 **Litho.**
4942 A2232 Sheet of 2, #a-b, + label 1.25 .60
4943 A2233 Sheet of 3, #a-c, + label 1.60 .80
4944 A2234 Sheet of 4, #a-d 2.10 1.10
4945 A2235 Sheet of 4, #a-d 2.10 1.10
4946 A2236 Sheet of 4, #a-d 2.40 1.25
Nos. 4942-4946 (5) 9.45 4.85

Souvenir Sheets

Perf. 11¾

4947 A2237 50w multi .95 .45
4948 A2238 60w multi 1.10 .50

Expo 2010, Shanghai — A2239

2010, Sept. 6 **Litho.** ***Perf. 11½***
4949 A2239 25w multi .40 .30

No. 4949 was printed in sheets of 6 + 9 labels.

A2240

Entry of Chinese People's Volunteer Army Into Korean War, 60th Anniv. A2241

Designs: 25w, Chinese soldier and Korean woman.
No. 4951: a, 10w, Meeting to decide on the entry of Chinese Volunteer Army into the Korean War, by Gao Quan. (60x42mm). b, 15w, North Korean and Chinese soldiers fighting together (30x42mm). c, For the Peace sculpture (60x42mm). d, Korean children with doves (30x42mm).

2010, Sept. 10 **Litho.** ***Perf. 13¼***
4950 A2240 25w multi .50 .30
4951 A2241 Sheet of 4, #a-d, + 2 labels 1.25 .65

A2242

A2243

Worker's Party of Korea, 65th Anniv. A2244

Designs: 10w, Flag of Worker's Party.
No. 4953 — Kim Il Sung: a, 20w, On naval vessel. b, 25w, At rail yard. c, 50w, With farmers. d, 50w, At technology display. e, 60w, With fabric vendor.
70w, Kim Il Sung with party flag.

2010, Oct. 10 **Litho.** ***Perf. 11¾***
4952 A2242 10w multi .30 .30
4953 A2243 Sheet of 6, #4952, 4953a-4953e 3.75 1.75

Souvenir Sheet

Perf. 13½

4954 A2244 70w multi 1.25 .60

A2245

Visit of Kim Jong Il to People's Republic of China A2246

Designs: No. 4955, Kim Jong Il shaking hands with Chinese Pres. Hu Jintao.
No. 4956 — Kim Jong Il: a, 30w, Signing guestbook at Julin Middle School. b, 42w, Inspecting railway coach. c, 70w, Holding bottle at food processing plant.

2010, Oct. 28 Litho. *Perf. 11½x12*
4955 A2245 70w multi 1.25 .65
Perf. 11½
4956 A2246 Sheet of 3, #a-c, + 5 labels 2.75 1.25

Conference of Worker's Party of Korea, Pyongyang — A2247

2010, Oct. 30 *Perf. 13¼*
4957 A2247 30w multi .60 .30

New Year 2011 (Juche 100) — A2248

2011, Jan. 1 Litho.
4958 A2248 10w multi .30 .30

Souvenir Sheet

Year of the Rabbit A2249

Rabbits — No. 4959: a, 70w, Two rabbits. b, 140w, Two rabbits, diff.

2011, Jan. 5 *Perf. 11½*
4959 A2249 Sheet of 2, #a-b 4.75 1.90
c. Booklet pane of 2, #4959a-4959b, + 2 labels 5.00 —
Complete booklet, #4959c 5.00
d. Like #4959, with inscriptions and emblems added in sheet margin 5.25 1.90

Complete booklet sold for 224w.
Issued: No. 4959d, 3/3/12. Added inscriptions on No. 4959d are for Frimung 2012 and Huddex 2012 Stamp Shows, Huddinge, Sweden.

Souvenir Sheet

Indipex 2011 World Philatelic Exhibition, New Delhi — A2250

2011, Feb. 12 *Perf. 13¼*
4960 A2250 70w multi 1.75 .65

Zoo Animals Given to Kim Jong Il as Gifts — A2251

Designs: 30w, Capra hircus. 42w, Cercopithecus aethiops. 112w, Cebuella pygmaea. 125w, Hystrix indica, horiz.

2011, Feb. 16 *Perf. 11½*
4961-4964 A2251 Set of 4 7.00 2.75
4964a Horiz. strip of 4, #4961-4964 7.25 2.75
4964b Booklet pane of 4, #4961-4964 7.25 —
Complete booklet, #4964b 7.50

Kim Jong Il, 69th birthday. Nos. 4961-4964 were printed in sheets of 8, containing 2 of each stamp, + 3 labels. Complete booklet sold for 323w.

Fourth International Martial Arts Games, Tallinn, Estonia — A2252

No. 4965: a, 42w, Emblem. b, 56w, Karate. c, 70w, Pankration. d, 112w, Muaythai.
No. 4966, 70w, Taekwondo.

2011, Feb. 23 Litho.
4965 A2252 Sheet of 4, #a-d, + 4 labels 5.25 2.60
Souvenir Sheet
4966 A2252 70w multi + label 1.25 .65

Joint Editorials of State Newspapers A2253

Red flag at upper left and: No. 4967, 10w, Two women, three men and pink ribbon. No. 4968, 10w, Man with arm extended, symbols of progress. 30w, Farmer holding sheaf of wheat, train, truck, tractor and food. 70w, Soldiers and flags. 112w, Two men and woman punching missile, map of Korea, vert.

2011, Feb. 25 *Perf. 13¼*
4967-4971 A2253 Set of 5 5.75 2.10

Birds — A2254

Designs: 30w, Paradisaea raggiana. 42w, Cygnus olor. 75w, Pulsatrix perspicillata. 133w, Goura victoria.

2011, Mar. 2 *Perf. 11½*
4972-4975 A2254 Set of 4 2.00 2.75
4975a Booklet pane of 4, #4972-4975 7.25 —
Complete booklet, #4975a 7.25

Nos. 4972-4975 were printed in sheets of 8 containing 2 of each stamp + 4 labels. Complete booklet sold for 294w.

Flag of North Korea, Magnolia Flowers, North Korea No. 4 — A2255

2011, Mar. 12 *Perf. 13¼*
4976 A2255 30w multi .70 .30

First North Korean postage stamps, 65th anniv.

Miniature Sheets

A2256

Treaty on Friendship Between North Korea and People's Republic of China, 50th Anniv. — A2257

No. 4977: a, Mao Zedong at microphones proclaiming foundation of People's Republic of China, fireworks (30x42mm). b, Mao Zedong and Pres. Kim Il Sung shaking hands, 1975 (54x45mm). c, Mao Zedong at microphone holding Chinese coat of arms (30x42mm). d, Mao Zedong at microphone in front of crowd (56x38mm). e, Mao Zedong in front of Chinese flag (28x38mm). f, Mao Zedong and Deng Xiaoping shaking hands (56x38mm).
No. 4978: a, Mao Zedong and Pend Dehuai, wearing cap (45x33mm). b, Mao Zedong and Pres. Kim Il Sung shaking hands (36x45mm). c, Mao Zedong and Chen Yi at table with cup and saucer (45x33mm). d, Mao Zedong and Liu Shaoqi, pointing (56x38mm). e, Mao Zedong and Zhou Enlai, teapot and glasses on table (28x38mm). f, Mao Zedong and Zhu De clapping (56x38mm).

Perf. 13¼ (#4977a-4977c, 4978a-4978c), 11½
2011, Mar. 15
4977 A2256 10w Sheet of 6, #a-f 1.50 .50
4978 A2257 10w Sheet of 6, #a-f 1.50 .45

Souvenir Sheet

Intl. Year of Volunteers — A2258

No. 4979 — Red Cross and: a, 30w, Disaster risk reduction. b, 42w, Promotion activities. c, Emergency relief activities.

2011, Mar. 31 Litho. *Perf. 13¼*
4979 A2258 Sheet of 3, #a-c, + 2 labels 3.50 1.25

Apples on Branch A2259

Kim Il Sung at Fruit Orchard A2260

2011, Apr. 7 *Perf. 12*
4980 A2259 30w multi .60 .30
Souvenir Sheet
Perf. 11¾
4981 A2260 70w multi 1.90 .65

Pukchong Enlarged Meeting of the Presidium of the Central Committee of the Workers' Party of Korea, 50th anniv.

Flowers A2261

No. 4982: a, 30w, Kimilsungia. b, 42w, Callistephus chinensis. c, 70w, Iris ensata var. hortensis. d, 98w, Rosa hybrida. e, 112w, Lilium hybridum cv. Enchantment.

2011, Apr. 15 *Perf. 13*
4982 A2261 Sheet of 5, #a-e 7.00 3.25
f. Booklet pane of 5, #4982a-4982e 7.25 —
Complete booklet, #4982f 7.25

Birthday of Pres. Kim Il Sung. No. 4982f sold for 366w.

Sites in Pyongyang A2262

Designs: 30w, Yonggwang Metro Station. 42w, Mangyongdae School Children's Palace. 56w, May Day Stadium. 70w, People's Palace of Culture. 84w, Arch of Triumph. 98w, State Theater. 112w, Party Founding Museum. 140w, Birthpace of Pres. Kim Il Sung.

2011, Apr. 20 *Perf. 12¼x11¾*
4983-4990 A2262 Set of 8 12.50 5.50
4990a Booklet pane of 8, #4983-4990 12.50 —
Complete booklet, #4990a 12.50

No. 4990a sold for 646w.

Magnolia Seiboldii — A2263

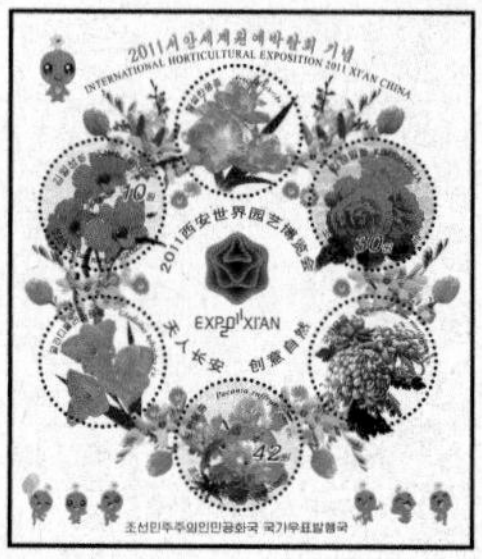

Flowers A2264

No. 4992: a, 10w, Kimilsungia. b, 30w, Kimjongilia. c, 42w, Paeonia suffructicosa.

2011, Apr. 28 *Perf. 13¼*

4991	A2263	30w multi	.60	.30

Souvenir Sheet

Perf.

4992	A2264	Sheet of 3, #a-c, + 3 labels	1.40	.75
d.		Booklet pane of 4, #4991, 4992a-4992c	*2.40*	—
		Complete booklet, #4992d	*2.40*	

2011 Intl. Horticultural Exposition, Xi'an, People's Republic of China. Complete booklet sold for 126w.

Miniature Sheet

Circus Performers — A2265

No. 4993: a, 42w, Woman suspended by neck. b, 70w, Woman juggling while hanging from trapeze. c, 98w, Unicyclist, members of rope skipping act. d, 140w, Rope skipping act.

2011, May 5 ***Perf.***

4993	A2265	Sheet of 4, #a-d	8.50	3.25

Souvenir Sheet

Chollima Statue, Pyongyang — A2266

2011, May 20 *Perf. 11¾x12¼*

4994	A2266	98w multi	2.40	.85

Souvenir Sheet

Apples, Taedonggang Combined Fruit Farm — A2267

2011, June 5 *Perf. 12¼x11¾*

4995	A2267	70w multi	1.75	.65

Orchids A2268

No. 4996: a, 10w, Vanda hybrida. b, 30w, Laeliocattleya. c, 70w, Laelia gouldiana. d, 142w, Phalaenopsis.

2011, June 20 *Perf. 13¼*

4996	A2268	Block or horiz. strip of 4, #a-d	4.75	2.40
e.		Booklet pane of 4, #4996a-4996d	5.25	—
		Complete booklet, #4996e	5.50	

No. 4996e sold for 266w.

A2269

A2270

A2271

A2272

A2273

A2274

A2275

A2276

A2277

A2278

A2279

A2280

A2281

A2282

A2283

A2284

A2285

A2286

A2287

A2288

A2289

A2290

A2291

A2292

A2293

A2294

Pres. Kim Il Sung (1912-94) — A2295

Various paintings depicting scenes in the life of Kim Il Sung.

No. 5020: a, 25w, October Morning (64x42mm). b, 30w, Kim Il Sung Drawing the Brush Into the Party's Emblem (45x36mm). c, 45w, Kim Il Sung Making Report at Inaugural Conference of the Central Organizational Committee of the Communist Party of North Korea (45x36mm).

2011, July 5 **Litho.** *Perf. 13½*

4997	A2269	10w multi + label	.30	.30
4998	A2270	10w multi + label	.30	.30
4999	A2271	10w multi + label	.30	.30
5000	A2272	30w multi + label	.70	.30
5001	A2273	30w multi + label	.70	.30
5002	A2274	30w multi + label	.70	.30
5003	A2275	30w multi + label	.70	.30
5004	A2276	30w multi + label	.70	.30
5005	A2277	30w multi + label	.70	.30
5006	A2278	30w multi + label	.70	.30
5007	A2279	30w multi + label	.70	.30
5008	A2280	30w multi + label	.70	.30
5009	A2281	30w multi + label	.70	.30
5010	A2282	42w multi + label	1.00	.35
5011	A2283	42w multi + label	1.00	.35
5012	A2284	42w multi + label	1.00	.35
5013	A2285	42w multi + label	1.00	.35
5014	A2286	42w multi + label	1.00	.35
5015	A2287	42w multi + label	1.00	.35
5016	A2288	42w multi + label	1.00	.35
5017	A2289	42w multi + label	1.00	.35
5018	A2290	42w multi + label	1.00	.35
5019	A2291	42w multi + label	1.00	.35
		Nos. 4997-5019 (23)	17.90	7.40

Miniature Sheet

Perf. 12x11½ (#5020a), 13½

5020	A2292	Sheet of 3, #a-c, + label	1.75	.85

Souvenir Sheets

Perf. 13½

5021	A2293	40w multi	.85	.35

Perf. 11¾

5022	A2294	50w multi	1.10	.45
5023	A2295	60w multi	1.25	.55
		Nos. 5021-5023 (3)	3.20	1.35

Souvenir Sheets

A2296

A2297

Visit of Kim Jong Il to People's Republic of China A2298

2011, July 15 **Litho.** ***Perf. 12¼x11¾***

5024	A2296	90w multi	2.50	.80

5025 A2297 90w multi 2.50 .80

Perf. 11¾

5026 A2298 90w multi + label 2.00 .80
Nos. 5024-5026 (3) 7.00 2.40

Intl. Year of Chemistry — A2299

2011, July 29 ***Perf. 13½x13¼***
5027 A2299 50w multi 1.25 .55

Camellias and Birds A2300

No. 5028: a, Denomination at LL. b, Denomination at UR.

2011, July 30 ***Perf. 11½***
5028 A2300 20w Horiz. pair, #a-b 2.00 .35

Souvenir Sheet

Intl. Year of Forests A2301

2011, July 30 ***Perf. 13¼***
5029 A2301 100w multi 2.40 .90

Souvenir Sheet

Diplomatic Relations Between North Korea and the European Union, 10th Anniv. — A2302

2011, Aug. 1 ***Perf. 12x11½***
5030 A2302 140w multi 3.50 1.75

Miniature Sheet

Cacti and Insects A2303

No. 5031: a, 30w, Gymnocalycium schuetzianum and bee. b, 70w, Rebutia euanthema and butterfly. c, 98w, Rebutia xanthocarpa and grasshopper. d, 112w, Notocactus herteri and beetle.

2011, Aug. 5 ***Perf. 11½***
5031 A2303 Sheet of 4, #a-d 7.25 2.75
e. Booklet pane of 4, #5031a-5031d 7.50 —
Complete booklet, #5031e 7.75

Complete booklet sold for 324w.

2018 World Cup Soccer Championships, Russia — A2304

Various soccer players with city names inscribed at side: No. 5032, 200w, Nizhniy Novgorod. No. 5033, 200w, Krasnodar. No. 5034, 200w, Kaliningrad. No. 5035, 200w, Moscow. No. 5036, 200w, Sochi. No. 5037, 200w, Rostov-na-Donu. No. 5038, 200w, St. Petersburg.

2011, Aug. 31 **Stamps + Labels**
5032-5038 A2304 Set of 7 35.00 11.50
5038a Sheet of 7, #5032-5038, + 2 labels 35.00 11.50
5038b Booklet pane of 7, #5032-5038, without labels 35.00 —
Complete booklet, #5038b 35.00

Complete booklet sold for 1414w.

Dinosaurs A2305

No. 5039: a, Megalosaurus bucklandi. b, Staurikosaurus pricei. c, Chasmosaurus belli.

2011, Sept. 5 ***Perf. 12¼x11¾***
5039 Horiz. strip of 3 5.25 2.60
a. A2305 42w multi .75 .35
b. A2305 98w multi 1.75 .85
c. A2305 140w multi 2.50 1.25
d. Booklet pane of 3, #5039a-5039c 5.50 —
Complete booklet, #5039d 5.50

Complete booklet sold for 294w.

World Leisure Expo 2011, Hangzhou, People's Republic of China — A2306

Emblems and: 10w, Samil Lagoon. 30w, Xihu.

2011, Sept. 17 ***Perf. 13¼***
5040-5041 A2306 Set of 2 .90 .35

Fire Engines A2307

No. 5042: a, 70w, Mercedes-Benz fire engine. b, 98w, ZIL ladder truck.
No. 5043: a, 30w, ZIL fire engine. b, 140w, Mercedes-Benz ladder truck.

2011, Oct. 5 ***Perf. 13¼***
5042 A2307 Sheet of 2, #a-b, + 2 labels 4.00 1.40
5043 A2307 Sheet of 2, #a-b, + 2 labels 4.00 1.40
c. Booklet pane of 4, #5042a-5042b, 5043a-5043b, + 2 labels 8.75 —
Complete booklet, #5043c 8.75

Complete booklet sold for 352w.

Famous People — A2308

Designs: 10w, Pak Yon (1378-1458). musician. 30w, Sinsa Im Dang (1504-51), painter. 50w, Jong Yak Yong (1762-1836), philosopher. 70w, Ryu Rin Sok (1842-1915), military leader.

2011, Oct. 15
5044-5047 A2308 Set of 4 3.50 1.40

Souvenir Sheet

Kim Jong Il and Chinese State Councilor Dai Bingguo — A2309

2011, Oct. 18
5048 A2309 70w multi 1.75 1.25

Souvenir Sheets

A2310

A2311

Visit of Kim Jong Il to Russia A2312

2011, Oct. 18 **Litho.** ***Perf. 11½x12***
5049 A2310 70w multi — —

Perf. 13¼

5050 A2311 70w multi — —
5051 A2312 70w multi — —

A2313

A2314

A2315

A2316

Friendship Between North Korea and People's Republic of China — A2317

Design: No. 5052, 10w, Mao Zedong Going to Anyuan. No. 5053: a, 10w, Mao Zedong. b, 10w, Mao Zedong in army vehicle reviewing troops. c, 10w, Mao Zedong writing. d, 30w, Kim Il Sung in suit and tie. e, 30w, Kim Il Sung and Mao Zedong shaking hands. f, 30w, Kim Il Sung and Mao Zedong standing at military parade.

No. 5054: a, 10w, Deng Xiaoping. b, 10w, Deng Xiaoping in automobile reviewing troops. c, 10w, Deng Xiaoping saluting. d, 30w, Kim Il Sung in black shirt. e, 30w, Deng Xiaoping and Kim Il Sung embracing. f, Deng Xiaoping and Kim Il Sung standing.

No. 5055: a, 10w, Jiang Zemin. b, 10w, Jiang Zemin in automobile reviewing troops. c, 10w, Jiang Zemin at ceremony returning Hong Kong to China. d, 30w, Kim Jong Il wearing glasses. e, 30w, Kim Jong Il and Jiang Zemin shaking hands. f, 30w, Jiang Zemin and Kim Jong Il shaking hands, cameramen.

No. 5056: a, 10w, Hu Jintao. b, 10w, Hu Jintao in automobile reviewing troops. c, 10w, Hu Jintaou holding Olympic torch. d, 30w, Kim Jong Il without glasses. e, 30w, Hu Jintao walking with Kim Jong Il. f, 30w, Kim Jong Il and Hu Jintao shaking hands.

Perf. 13¼ (#5052), 11¾x12¼

2011, Oct. 28 **Litho.**
5052 A2313 10w multi .30 .30

Miniature Sheets

5053 A2314 Sheet of 6, #a-f 3.00 2.25
5054 A2315 Sheet of 6, #a-f 3.00 2.25
5055 A2316 Sheet of 6, #a-f 3.00 2.25
5056 A2317 Sheet of 6, #a-f 3.00 2.25
Nos. 5052-5056 (5) 12.30 9.30

Publication of Taedongyojido Map of Korea by Kim Jong Ho, 150th Anniv. — A2318

2011, Nov. 5 ***Perf. 13¼***
5057 A2318 98w multi 2.40 .90

Minerals
A2319

Designs: 30w, Limonite, crucible with molten metal. 42w, Kotoite, rocket. 58w, Wollastonite, ceramic vases. 98w, Stibnite, tractor and parts.

2011, Dec. 5

5058-5061 A2319 Set of 4 5.75 2.10
5061a Booklet pane of 4, #5057-5060 6.00 —
Complete booklet, #5060a 6.00

Complete booklet sold for 242w.

A2320

Appointment of Kim Jong Il as Supreme Commander of Army, 20th Anniv. — A2321

No. 5062 — Kim Jong Il and: a, 10w, Pilots. b, 30w, Tank soldiers. c, 70w, Sailors. d, 98w, Soldiers carrying packs.

No. 5063, Kim Jong Il and military officer reviewing troops in military vehicle.

2011, Dec. 24

5062 A2320 Sheet of 4, #a-d, + central label 3.75 1.90

Souvenir Sheet

Perf. 11¾

5063 A2321 98w multi 2.40 1.90

Souvenir Sheets

Kim Jong Il (1942-2011) — A2322

Kim Jong Il and Son, Kim Jong Un
A2323

2011, Dec. 29 ***Perf. 12¼x11¾***

5064 A2322 70w multi 1.50 .70
5065 A2323 70w multi 1.50 .70

New Year 2012 — A2324

2012, Jan. 1 ***Perf. 13¼***

5066 A2324 10w multi .30 .30

Dragons
A2325

No. 5067 — Various dragons: a, 10w. b, 30w. c, 60w.

2012, Jan. 5 ***Perf. 11½***

5067 A2325 Horiz. strip of 3, #a-c 2.40 1.00

No. 5067 was printed in sheets containing two strips of 3.

Mt. Paektu
A2326

Designs: 20w, Lake Samji and Mt. Paektu. 30w, Lake Chon on Mt. Paektu.

2012, Jan. 17 ***Perf. 12¼x11¾***

5068-5069 A2326 Set of 2 1.20 .50

Butterflies — A2327

No. 5070: a, 30w, Pachliopta coon. b, 70w, Agrias pericles. c, 90w, Buthanitis lidderdalei. d, 120w, Cethosia biblis.

2012, Jan. 25 ***Perf. 11½***

5070 A2327 Block of 4, #a-d 7.00 3.00
e. Booklet pane of 4, #5070a-5070d, + 2 labels 7.25 —
Complete booklet, #5070e 7.25

Complete booklet sold for 324w.

Joint Editorials of State Newspapers
A2328

Red flag at upper left and: No. 5071, 10w, Birthplace of Kim Il Sung, torch, soldier, workers. No. 5072, 10w, City buildings, packaged foods, crops and farm animals, horiz. No. 5073, 30w, Torch, symbols of industry, train and truck. No. 5074, 30w, Soldier holding rifle with bayonet, flags, missiles. 40w, Fist squashing people, U.S. Capitol. 50w, Dove, North Korea highlighted on map, rainbow.

2012, Jan. 27 ***Perf. 13¼***

5071-5076 A2328 Set of 6 3.50 1.40

Calls for Victory by Central Committee and Central Military Commission
A2329

2012, Jan. 30 **Litho.**

5077 A2329 10w multi .30 .30

Architecture — A2330

Designs: 60w, Kopernik House, Moscow, Mansudae Street Apartment Buildings, Pyongyang. 100w, Patriarch House, Moscow, East Pyongyang Grand Theater. No. 5080, 140w, Grand People's Study House, Pyongyang, Gnezdikovskiy Palace, Moscow. 190w, Apartement house, Pyongyang, Egg House, Moscow. 210w, Hyangsan Hotel, Pyongyang, Weber Villa, Moscow.

No. 5083, 140w, Patriarch House, Moscow and National Theater, Pyongyang at night.

2012, Jan. 30 ***Perf. 12***

5078-5082 A2330 Set of 5 16.00 6.25

Souvenir Sheet

Perf. 12x11½

5083 A2330 140w multi 3.25 1.40
a. Souvenir sheet of 6, #5078-5083, perf. 12x11½, + 3 labels 16.50 6.75
b. Booklet pane of 6, #5078-5083, perf. 12x11½ 16.50 —
Complete booklet, #5083b 16.50

Nos. 5078-5082 were each printed in sheets of 5 + label. Complete booklet sold for 854w.

A2331

A2332

Birthday of Kim Jong Il (1942-2011) — A2333

Designs: 10w, Kimjongilia flower.

No. 5085: a, 40w, Kim Jong Il, soldiers and artillery. 70w, Kim Jong Il, people with flags and sled.

No. 5085, 70w, Kimg Jong Il.

2012, Feb. 16 ***Perf. 13¼***

5084 A2331 10w multi .30 .30
5085 A2332 Sheet of 2, #a-b, + 3 labels 2.75 1.00

Souvenir Sheet

Perf. 11½x12

5086 A2333 70w multi 1.75 .70

Ceramics — A2334

Designs: 30w, Container with lotus flower pattern. 40w, Container with dragon and cloud design.

70w, Pitcher and bowl.

2012, Mar. 10 ***Perf. 11½***

Stamps + Labels

5087-5088 A2334 Set of 2 1.75 .70

Souvenir Sheet

5089 A2334 70w multi + label 1.75 .70
a. Booklet pane of 3, #5087-5089, + 7 labels 5.25 —
Complete booklet, #5089a 5.25

Complete booklet sold for 154w.

Posthumous Granting of Title of Generalissimo to Kim Jong Il — A2335

2012, Mar. 20 ***Perf. 13¼***

5090 A2335 10w multi .30 .30

Birthplace of Kim Jong Il — A2336

2012, Mar. 20

5091 A2336 10w multi .30 .30

Designation of Feb. 16 (birthday of Kim Jong Il) as Day of the Shining Star.

Floriade 2012 World Horticultural Expo, Venlo, Netherlands — A2337

2012, Mar. 22 **Litho.**

5092 A2337 30w multi .50 .30

Korean National Association, 95th Anniv.
A2338

2012, Mar. 23 ***Perf. 13¼***

5093 A2338 30w citron .85 .30

Opening of Korean Stamp Museum, Pyongyang
A2339

2012, Apr. 15 ***Perf. 11½***

5094 A2339 10w multi .30 .30

A2340

A2341

A2342

A2343

A2344

A2345

A2346

A2347

A2348

A2349

Pres. Kim Il Sung (1912-94) — A2350

No. 5102 — Kim Il Sung: a, With adults and children. b, Wearing hat, addressing men. c, Seated behind microphone. d, With workers at plant.

No. 5103 — Kim Il Sung: a, At trainyard. b, With workers at textile factory. c, Holding ear of corn, with farmers in field. d, Holding ear of corn, with agricultural scientists.

No. 5104 — Kim Il Sung: a, With pilots. b, Seated, talking to soldiers. c, With soldiers inspecting artillery. d, Wearing white jacket, walking with military.

2012, Apr. 15 ***Perf. 11½***

5095 A2340 30w multi + label .90 .30
5096 A2341 30w multi + label .90 .30
5097 A2342 30w multi + label .90 .30
5098 A2343 30w multi + label .90 .30
5099 A2344 30w multi + label .90 .30
5100 A2345 30w multi + label .90 .30
5101 A2346 30w multi + label .90 .30
Nos. 5095-5101 (7) 6.30 2.10

Miniature Sheets

Perf. 13¼

5102 A2347 20w Sheet of 4, #a-d 2.10 .70
5103 A2348 30w Sheet of 4, #a-d 3.00 1.10
5104 A2349 40w Sheet of 4, #a-d 3.75 1.40
Nos. 5102-5104 (3) 8.85 3.20

Souvenir Sheet

Perf. 11¾

5105 A2350 70w multi 1.75 1.00

A2351

A2352

Pres. Kim Il Sung (1912-94) — A2353

Designs: 10w, Birthplace of Kim Il Sung, flowers.

No. 5107: a, 70w, Kim Il Sung in field with children. b, 100w, Kim Il Sung seated, holding hand of girl.

No. 5108, 100w, Kim Il Sung at birthplace.

2012, Apr. 15 ***Perf. 13¼***

5106 A2351 10w multi .40 .30

Miniature Sheet

Perf. 11¾

5107 A2352 Sheet of 2, #a-b 3.75 1.40

Souvenir Sheet

Perf. 11½x12

5108 A2353 100w multi 2.40 1.00

Souvenir Sheet

Kang Pan Sok (1892-1932), Mother of Kim Il Sung — A2354

2012, Apr. 21 ***Perf. 11¾***

5109 A2354 70w multi 1.75 .70

Flags of Guerilla Army, North Korea and Supreme Commander A2355

Kim Il Sung in Military Uniform A2356

2012, Apr. 25 ***Perf. 13¼***

5110 A2355 30w multi .90 .30

Souvenir Sheet

Perf. 11½x12

5111 A2356 70w multi 1.75 .70

Korean People's Army, 80th anniv.

Roses — A2357

Color of roses: 30w, Pink and white. 50w, Yellow. 70w, Red.

2012, Apr. 30 ***Perf. 12½***

5112-5114 A2357 Set of 3 3.50 1.50
5114a Booklet pane of 3, #5112-5114, + label 3.75 —
Complete booklet, #5114a 4.00

Values are for stamps with surrounding selvage. Complete booklet sold for 164w.

Principles for National Reunification, 40th Anniv. — A2358

2012, May 3 ***Perf. 11½***

5115 A2358 50w red & blue 1.10 .50

2012 Summer Olympics, London — A2359

Designs: 10w, Track and field. 30w, Judo. 70w, Rhythmic gymnastics. 110w, Swimming and diving.

2012, May 3 ***Perf. 13¼***

5116-5119 A2359 Set of 4 5.00 2.10
5119a Booklet pane of 4, #5116-5119 5.25 —
Complete booklet, #5119a 5.50

Complete booklet sold for 234w.

Souvenir Sheet

Erection of Statues to Kim Il Sung and Kim Jong Il in Pyongyang — A2360

2012, May 30

5120 A2360 50w multi 1.25 .50

Locomotives A2361

Designs: 50w, Songun Pulgungi 1. 70w, Velaro D407. 90w, Renfe 112.

2012, May 31

5121-5123 A2361 Set of 3 5.00 1.90
5123a Booklet pane of 3, #5121-5123 5.25 —
Complete booklet, #5123a 5.25

Complete booklet sold for 224w.

Battle of Pochonbo, 75th Anniv. — A2362

2012, June 4

5124 A2362 30w multi .85 .30

Souvenir Sheet

2012 Planete Timbres Stamp Exhibition, Paris — A2363

2012, June 9 ***Perf. 12¼x11¾***

5125 A2363 70w multi 1.75 .70

2012 World Stamp Championships, Jakarta, Indonesia — A2364

2012, June 18 ***Perf. 11½***

5126 A2364 30w multi .75 .30

Birds — A2365

Designs: 50w, Fringilla montifringilla. 70w, Zosterops erythropleura. 90w, Uragus sibiricus.

2012, June 30 **Litho.**

5127-5129 A2365 Set of 3 4.75 1.75

5129a Booklet pane of 3, #5127-5129, + label 5.00 —

Complete booklet, #5129a 5.00

Complete booklet sold for 224w.

Free Universal Medical System, 60th Anniv. — A2366

2012, July 5 ***Perf. 13¼***

5130 A2366 30w multi .90 .30

Souvenir Sheets

Mao Zedong (1893-1976) and Poetry — A2367

Kim Il Sung (1912-94) and Quotes — A2368

No. 5131: a, The Yellow Crane Pavilion, poem by Mao Zedong (character at UL a diagonal line) (34x52mm). b, Mao Zedong writing (54x42mm). c, Huichang, poem by Mao Zedong (complex character with vertical line at UL).

No. 5132: a, 7½ lines of text from reminiscences of Kim Il Sung, and signature (34x52mm). b, Kim Il Sung writing (54x42mm). c, 8 lines of text from reminiscences of Kim Il Sung, and signature (34x52mm).

Perf. 11¾x12¼, 13¼ (#5131b, 5132b)

2012, July 15

5131 A2367 10w Sheet of 3, #a-c .60 .30

5132 A2368 30w Sheet of 3, #a-c 1.60 .80

Souvenir Sheet

Fourth Conference of the Korean Workers' Party — A2369

No. 5133: a, Kim Jong Il wearing glasses (1941-2011). b, Kim Jong Un.

2012, July 20 ***Perf. 11¾x12¼***

5133 A2369 30w Sheet of 2, #a-b 1.50 .60

A2370

Korean Children's Union, 66th Anniv. — A2371

2012, Aug. 10 ***Perf. 13¼***

5134 A2370 10w multi .30 .30

Souvenir Sheet

5135 A2371 70w multi 1.60 .65

Mother's Day — A2372

2012, Sept. 20 ***Perf. 11½***

5136 A2372 10w multi .30 .30

Miniature Sheets

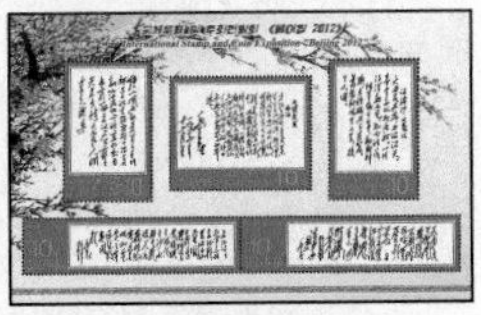

A2373

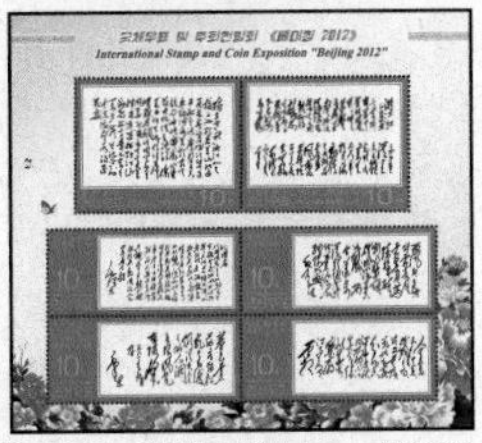

Poetry of Mao Zedong (1893-1976) — A2374

No. 5137: a, The People's Liberation Army Captures Nanjing (5½ lines) (34x52mm). b, Swimming (large white areas at UL and LR) (54x42mm). c, Beidaihe (6 full long lines of characters, 2 shorter lines at sides) (34x52mm). d, The Long March (3mm from line at right to frame) (84x21mm). e, Mt. Liupan (6mm from line at right to frame) (84x21mm).

No. 5138: a, Changsha (line at left with 2 characters) (54x42mm). b, Reply to Comrade Guo Moruo (white area in middle of poem (54x42mm). c, Snow (line at right three characters) (63x27mm). d, Loushan Pass (12 lines) (63x27mm). e, In Praise of the Photo Taken by Comrade Lijin of the Fairy Cave at Mt. Lushan (second line from left is single character) (63x27mm). f, The Double Ninth (13 lines with large whtie areas at top and bottom) (63x27mm).

Perf. 11¾x12¼ (#5137a, 5137c), 13¼

2012, Sept. 25

5137 A2373 10w Sheet of 5, #a-e 1.10 .50

5138 A2374 10w Sheet of 6, #a-f 2.00 .60

Beijing 2012 Intl. Stamp and Coin Exposition.

Giant Pandas — A2375

Designs: 70w, Panda on branch. 90w, Adult and juvenile panda.

120w, Two adult pandas, horiz.

2012, Dec. 14 **Litho.** ***Perf. 11½***

5139-5140 A2375 Set of 2 2.75 1.50

Souvenir Sheet

Perf. 13½

5141 A2375 120w multi 2.25 1.10

No. 5141 contains one 90x42mm stamp.

Compulsory Education A2376

2012, Dec. 15 **Litho.** ***Perf. 13¼***

5142 A2376 10w multi .30 .30

Souvenir Sheets

A2377

Kim Jong Il (1942-2011) — A2378

2012, Dec. 17 **Litho.** ***Perf. 11½x12***

5143 A2377 50w multi 1.10 .50

Perf. 13¼

5144 A2378 50w multi 1.10 .50

Souvenir Sheet

Kim Jong Suk (1917-49) — A2379

2012, Dec. 24 ***Perf.***

5145 A2379 70w multi 1.75 .65

Constitution, 40th Anniv. — A2380

2012, Dec. 27 ***Perf. 13¼***

5146 A2380 30w multi .70 .30

Souvenir Sheet

Launch of Kwangmyongsong 3-2 Satellite — A2381

2012, Dec. 30 **Litho.** ***Perf. 13¼***

5147 A2381 50w multi 1.00 .45

New Year 2013 A2382

2013, Jan. 1 **Litho.** ***Perf. 11¾***

5148 A2382 10w multi .25 .25

Stylized Snake — A2383

2013, Jan. 5 **Litho.** ***Perf. 11½***

5149 A2383 10w multi .25 .25

No. 5149 was printed in sheets of 16 + 4 labels.

Sports — A2384

Designs: 30w, Tennis. 50w, Cricket. 70w, Cycling. 90w, Rugby.

2013, Jan. 20 **Litho.** ***Perf. 13¼***

5150-5153 A2384 Set of 4 3.75 1.90

5153a Booklet pane of 4, #5150-5153 4.00 —

Complete booklet, #5153a 4.00

Complete booklet sold of 254w.

A2386

A2387

Kim Jong Il (1942-2011) — A2388

Desings: 5154, Kim Jong Il as child, in oval frame. 5155, shown.

2013, Feb. 16 Litho. *Perf. 11¾*
5154 A2386 10w multi .25 .25
5155 A2386 10w multi .25 .25

Souvenir Sheets

5156 A2387 50w multi .80 .40
5157 A2388 50w multi .80 .40

New Year's Speech — A2389

Emblem and: No. 5158, 10w, Man with arm extended, rocket, sheaf of wheat, tower for electric lines, train, steel products. No. 5159, 10w, Woman, soldiers, flag, sculptures. No. 5160, 30w, Soccer player, city skyline, silhouettes of musicians and soldiers. No. 5161, 30w, Map of Korean Peninsula, doves.

2013, Feb. 19 Litho. *Perf. 11½*
5158-5161 A2389 Set of 4 1.25 .60
5161a Souvenir sheet of 4, #5158-5161 1.25 .60

Souvenir Sheet

Kim Jong Un Making New Year's Speech A2390

2013, Feb. 19 Litho. *Perf. 11¾*
5162 A2390 50w multi .80 .40

A2391

A2392

A2393

Military Posters in Korean Art Gallery, Pyongyang A2394

2013, Feb. 25 Litho. *Perf. 11½*
5163 A2391 10w multi .25 .25
5164 A2392 10w multi .25 .25
5165 A2393 30w multi .45 .25
5166 A2394 30w multi .45 .25
Nos. 5163-5166 (4) 1.40 1.00

International Red Cross, 150th Anniv. — A2395

2013, Mar. 6 Litho. *Perf. 13¼*
5167 A2395 30w multi .45 .25

Miniature Sheet

Marine Life A2396

No. 5168: a, 30w, Carcharodon carcharias (44mm diameter). b, 50w, Caretta caretta (38x28mm). c, 90w, Peprilus simillina (28x38mm). d, 110w, Hippocampus histrix (28x38mm).

2013, Mar. 21 Litho. *Perf. 11½*
5168 A2396 Sheet of 4, #a-d 4.25 2.10
e. Booklet pane of 4, #5168a-5168d 4.50 —
Complete booklet, #5168e 4.50

Complete booklet sold for 294w.

Election of Kim Jong Il as Chairman of National Defense Commission, 20th Anniv. — A2397

2013, Apr. 9 Litho. *Perf. 13¼*
5169 A2397 30w multi .45 .25

Souvenir Sheet

Monkeys A2398

No. 5170: a, 10w, Monkey. b, 20w, Adult and juvenile monkey.

Litho. & Engr.

2013, Apr. 10 *Perf. 12*
5170 A2398 Sheet of 2, #a-b .45 .25

Flowers — A2399

Designs: 30w, Zinnia elegans cv. Scarlet Flame. 50w, Celosia cristata. 70w, Dahlia x cultorum. 90w, Tropaeolum majus.

2013, Apr. 15 Litho. *Perf. 13¼*
5171-5174 A2399 Set of 4 3.75 1.90
5174a Booklet pane of 4, #5171-5174 4.00 —
Complete booklet, #5174a 4.00

Birthday of Kim Il Sung. Nos. 5171-5174 were printed in sheets of 4 + 2 labels. Complete booklet sold for 254w.

Passage of Kumsusan Palace of the Sun Preservation Law — A2401

2013, Apr. 25 Litho. *Perf. 13¼*
5176 A2401 30w multi .45 .25

Values are for stamps with surrounding selvage.

Australia 2013 World Stamp Exhibition, Melbourne — A2402

2013, May 10 Litho. *Perf. 11½*
5177 A2402 30w multi .45 .25

Miniature Sheet

Owls A2404

No. 5179: a, 40w, Surnia ulula. b, 60w, Nyctea scandiaca. c, 80w, Athene noctua. d, 100w, Tyto alba.

2013, May 22 Litho. *Perf. 13¼*
5179 A2404 Sheet of 8, 2 each #5179a-5179d, + 4 labels 8.50 4.25
e. Booklet pane of 4, #5179a-5179d, + 2 labels 4.50 —
Complete booklet, #5179e 4.50

Complete booklet sold for 294w.

Souvenir Sheet

Meeting of Kim Jong Il and Chinese Leaders A2405

No. 5180 — Meeting with Kim Jong Il at: a, Left. b, Right.

2013, June 10 Litho. *Perf. 12x11½*
5180 A2405 30w Sheet of 2, #a-b, + 4 labels .95 .45

Souvenir Sheet

Mt. Paektu A2406

No. 5181: a, Sun over Hyangdo Peak. b, Mountains surrounding Lake Chon. c, Shore of Lake Chon. d, Mt. Paektu, trees in foreground.

2013, June 10 Litho. *Perf. 12x11½*
5181 A2406 10w Sheet of 4, #a-d, + 2 labels .60 .30

Bees — A2407

Various bees and orchids: 30w, 70w, 110w.

2013, June 12 Litho. *Perf. 13¼*
5182-5184 A2407 Set of 3 3.25 1.60
5184a Booklet pane of 3, #5182-5184, + label 3.50 —
Complete booklet, #5184a 3.50

Complete booklet sold for 224w.

A2408

Soldiers — A2409

2013, June 25 Litho. *Perf. 13¼*
5185 A2408 10w multi .25 .25
5186 A2409 150w multi 2.25 1.10

Arctic and Antarctic Animals A2410

Designs: 30w, Aptenodytes excelsior. 50w, Rangifer tarandus.

2013, July 7 Litho. *Perf.*
5187-5188 A2410 Set of 2 — —
5188a Booklet pane of 2, #5187-5188, + 2 labels — —
Complete booklet, #5188a

Nos. 5187-5188 were each printed in sheets of 3 + label.

Souvenir Sheet

Pyongyang Folk Park — A2411

No. 5189: a, Tower of the Juche Idea, Arch of Triumph. b, Pagoda at Kumgang Temple, vert.

2013, July 20 Litho. *Perf. 11½*
5189 A2411 30w Sheet of 2, #a-b .95 .45

Victory Sculpture — A2413

Ceasefire in Korean War, 60th Anniv. — A2514

Kim Il Sung Delivering Radio Address — A2415

Kim Il Sung at Rally A2416

No. 5195: a, 50w, Kim Il Sung. b, 70w, Kim Il Sung and soldiers.

Perf. 13¼, 11½x11¾ (#5195)

2013, July 27 **Litho.**

5194	A2413	10w multi	.25	.25

Souvenir Sheets

5195	A2514	Sheet of 2, #a-b, + 3 labels	1.90	.95
5196	A2415	70w multi	1.10	.55
5197	A2416	70w multi	1.10	.55

Thailand 2013 World Stamp Exhibition, Bangkok — A2417

2013, Aug. 2 **Litho.** ***Perf. 13¼***

5198	A2417	10w multi	.25	.25

Souvenir Sheet

7th Congress of Korean Children's Union — A2419

2013, Aug. 10 **Litho.** ***Perf. 13¼***

5200	A2419	70w multi	1.10	.55

Horses — A2420

Designs: 30w, Shire horses. 50w, Orlov trotter.
70w, Thoroughbred horses, horiz.

2013, Aug. 28 **Litho.** ***Perf. 13¼***

5201-5202	A2420	Set of 2	1.25	.60

Souvenir Sheet

5203	A2420	70w multi	1.10	.55
a.		Booklet pane of 3, #5301-5303	2.60	—
		Complete booklet, #5203a	2.60	

Complete booklet sold for 164w.

A2421

Founding of the Democratic People's Republic of Korea, 65th Anniv. — A2422

No. 5205: a, Kim Il Sung and flags. b, Kim Jong Il and mountain.

2013, Sept. 9 **Litho.** ***Perf. 11½***

5204	A2421	30w multi	.50	.25

Souvenir Sheet

Perf. 13¼

5205	A2422	50w Sheet of 2, #a-b	1.60	.80

Mangyongdae in Spring — A2423

Rungna Island in Summer A2424

Moran Hill in Autumn — A2425

Ryongwang Pavilion in Winter — A2426

2013, Sept. 25 **Litho.** ***Perf. 13¼***

5206	A2423	30w multi	.50	.25
5207	A2424	50w multi	.80	.40
5208	A2425	70w multi	1.10	.55
5209	A2426	110w multi	1.75	.85
		Nos. 5206-5209 (4)	4.15	2.05

Ships — A2427

Designs: 30w, Restaurant ship Taedonggang. 50w, Cargo ship Kumrung No. 5. 90w, Refrigerator cargo ship Rimyongsu No. 7. 110w, Refrigerator cargo ship Turubong No. 3.

2013, Oct. 15 **Litho.** ***Perf. 11½***

5210-5213	A2427	Set of 4	4.25	2.10
5213a		Booklet pane of 4, #5210-5213	4.50	—
		Complete booklet, #5213a	4.50	

Complete booklet sold for 294w.

Soldier Commanding Speedier Construction, Skiers at Masik Pass Resort — A2428

2013, Oct. 20 **Litho.** ***Perf. 13¼x13½***

5214	A2428	30w multi	.45	.25

Fossils A2430

Designs: 30w, Ditomopharangia. 70w, Dumangia. 110w, Hormotoma.

2013, Nov. 10 **Litho.** ***Perf. 13***

5219-5221	A2430	Set of 3	3.25	1.60
5221a		Booklet pane of 3, #5219-5221 + label	3.50	—
		Complete booklet, #5221a	3.50	

Complete booklet sold for 224w.

Souvenir Sheets

Kim Jong Il (1942-2011) and Soldiers — A2435

Kim Jong Il Inspecting Cotton — A2436

Perf. 13½x13¼

2013, Dec. 17 **Litho.**

5226	A2435	50w multi	.80	.40
5227	A2436	70w multi	1.10	.55

Paintings — A2437

Designs: No. 5228, 30w, Hawk, by Kim Tuk Sin. No. 5229, 30w, Tiger, by Kim Tuk Sin. No. 5230, 50w, Eagle, by Jang Sung Up. No. 5231, 50w, Carp, by Jo Sok Jin. 70w, Cats, by Pyon Sang Byok.

Perf. 11¾x12¼

2013, Dec. 21 **Litho.**

5228-5232	A2437	Set of 5	3.50	1.75

Intl. Year of Water Cooperation A2438

2013, Dec. 26 **Litho.** ***Perf. 11½***

5233	A2438	30w multi	.45	.25

Worker-Peasant Red Guards, 55th Anniv. — A2440

2014, Jan. 14 **Litho.** ***Perf. 11½***

5235	A2440	30w multi + label	.50	.25

Foods A2441

Designs: 10w, Peaches and melons. 30w, Eggplants and grapes. 50w, Pumpkins and kiwis. 70w, Chestnuts and mushrooms. 90w, Chinese mustard and persimmons. 110w, Radish, Chinese cabbage, peppers, garlic and pears.

2014, Jan. 20 **Litho.** ***Perf. 12¼x11½***

5236-5241	A2441	Set of 6	5.50	2.25
5241a		Booklet pane of 6, #5236-5241	5.75	—
		Complete booklet, #5241a	5.75	

Complete booklet sold for 374w.

Ceramics — A2442

Designs: 30w, 12th century Celadon vase. 40w, 19th century porcelain jar.

2014, Jan. 25 **Litho.** ***Perf. 11½***

Stamp + label

5242-5243	A2442	Set of 2	1.10	.55
5243a		Booklet pane of 2, #5242-5243, + 6 labels	1.40	—
		Complete booklet, #5243a	1.40	

Complete booklet sold for 84w.

A2443

A2444

A2445

A2446

A2447

New Year's Address of Kim Jong Un — A2448

Perf. 13¼x13½, 13½x13¼

2014, Feb. 1			**Litho.**		
5244	A2443	10w multi		.25	.25
5245	A2444	10w multi		.25	.25
5246	A2445	10w multi		.25	.25
5247	A2446	30w multi		.45	.25
5248	A2447	30w multi		.45	.25
5249	A2448	30w multi		.45	.25
	Nos. 5244-5249 (6)			2.10	1.50

2014 Winter Olympics, Sochi, Russia A2449

Designs: 30w, Skiing. 50w, Speed skating. 70w, Ice hockey. 90w, Bobsledding.

2014, Feb. 7 Litho. ***Perf. 13¼x13½***

5250-5253	A2449	Set of 4	3.75	1.90
5253a		Booklet pane of 4, #5250-5253	4.00	—
		Complete booklet, #5253a	4.00	

Complete booklet sold for 254w.

Souvenir Sheet

Kim Jong Il (1942-2011), 72nd Birthday — A2453

2014, Feb. 16 Litho. ***Perf. 11½x12***

5257 A2453 50w multi .80 .40

Traditional Sports A2458

Designs: 10w, Wrestling. 30w, Archery. 50w, Horse racing.

Perf. 13½x13¼

2014, Mar. 10 **Litho.**

5262-5264 A2458 Set of 3 1.40 .70

Souvenir Sheet

International Years — A2459

No. 5265: a, Intl. Year of Family Farming. b, Intl. Year of Crystallography.

2014, Mar. 21 Litho. ***Perf. 11½***

5265 A2459 50w Sheet of 2, #a-b, + 2 labels 1.60 .80

Souvenir Sheet

Munsu Water Park, Pyongyang — A2461

No. 5267: a, Water slide (32mm diameter). b, Swimming pools (64x30mm).

Perf. 11¾x11½ (#5267b)

2014, Apr. 3 **Litho.**

5267 A2461 30w Sheet of 2, #a-b .95 .45

Korean Alphabet, 570th Anniv. — A2462

2014, Apr. 10 Litho. ***Perf. 13¼***

5268 A2462 30w multi .50 .25

No. 5268 was printed in sheets of 8 + central label.

Plants Presented to Kim Il Sung — A2463

Designs: 30w, Zygopetalum mackayi. 60w, Oncidium splendidum. 90w, Paphiopedilum insigne. 120w, Bletilla striata.

2014, Apr. 15 Litho. ***Perf. 13¼***

5269-5272	A2463	Set of 4	4.75	2.40
5272a		Booklet pane of 4, #4269-5272	5.00	—
		Complete booklet, #5272a	5.00	

Nos. 5269-5272 were each printed in sheets of 3 + label. Complete booklet sold for 314w.

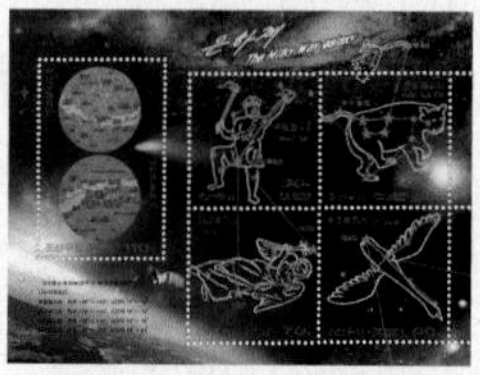
Astronomy — A2464

No. 5273: a, 30w, Boötes (35x35mm). b, 50w, Ursa Major (35x35mm). c, 70w, Virgo (35x35mm). d, 90w, Cygnus (35x35mm). e, Milky Way and maps of constellations (35x53mm).

Perf. 11½, 11¾x12¼ (110w)

2014, Apr. 20 **Litho.**

5273	A2464	Sheet of 5, #a-e	5.50	2.75
f.		Booklet pane of 5, #5273a-5273e	5.75	—
		Complete booklet, #5273f	5.75	

Complete booklet sold for 364w.

2014 Intl. Horticultural Exposition, Qingdao, People's Republic of China — A2465

2014, Apr. 25 Litho. ***Perf. 13¼***

5274 A2465 30w multi .50 .25

Fish and Shellfish — A2467

Designs: 50w, Rhodeus ocellatus ocellatus, Anodonta calypigos. 70w, Apogon semilineatus, Glycymeris albolineata. 90w, Diodon halacanthus, Atrina pectinata japonica. 110w, Cyclopterus lumpus, Pinctata margarittfera.

2014, May 11 Litho. ***Perf. 13¼***

5276-5279	A2467	Set of 4	5.00	2.50
5279a		Booklet pane of 4, #5276-5279	5.25	—
		Complete booklet, #5279a	5.25	

Complete booklet sold for 334w.

On No. 5278 the scientific name is mispelled "Diodon halacanthus." It should read "Diodon holocanthus." On No. 5279 the sientific name is mispelled "Pinctata..." It should read "Pinctada..."

Universal Postal Union, 140th Anniv. — A2468

2014, May 29 Litho. ***Perf. 11½***

5280 A2468 30w multi .50 .25

Admission of North Korea into UPU, 40th anniv. Printed in sheets of 5 + label.

2014 World Cup Soccer Championships, Brazil — A2469

Player in red shirt: 40w, #12 Dribbling ball. 60w, Tackling opponent, horiz. 80w, #11 Dribbling ball.

100w, Player in yellow shirt.

2014, June 12 Litho. ***Perf. 13¼***

5281-5283 A2469 Set of 3 2.75 1.40

Souvenir Sheet

5284	A2469	110w multi	1.75	.85
a.		Booklet pane of 4, #5281-5284	4.75	—
		Complete booklet, #5284a	4.75	

Complete booklet sold for 304w.

International Olympic Committee, 120th Anniv. — A2470

2014, June 16 Litho. ***Perf. 13¼***

5285 A2470 30w multi .50 .25

A2471

Kim Jong Il's Leadership of Central Committee of Workers' Party, 50th Anniv. — A2472

No. 5286 — Paintings of Kim Jong Il: a, Visiting Mt. Taedok military post. b, With arms around office workers. c, In barley field. d, Surrounded by people.

50w, Kim Jong Il.

2014, June 19 Litho. ***Perf. 11¾***

5286 A2471 30w Sheet of 4, #a-d 1.90 .95

Souvenir Sheet

Perf. 11¾x12¼

5287 A2472 50w multi .80 .40

Medicinal Plants — A2476

Designs: 30w, Aronia melanocarpa. 50w, Lycium chinense. 70w, Ginkgo biloba. 110w, Crataegus pinnatifida var. major.

2014, July 17 Litho. ***Perf. 13¼***

5291-5294	A2476	Set of 4	4.00	2.00
5294a		Booklet pane of 4, #5291-5294	4.25	—
		Complete booklet, #5294a	4.25	

Complete booklet sold for 275w.

Sports A2477

Designs: 30w, Table tennis. 50w, Running. 90w, Weight lifting. 110w, Judo.

2014, July 25 Litho. *Perf. 13*

5295-5298 A2477	Set of 4	4.25	2.10
5298a	Booklet pane of 4, #5295-5298	4.50	—
	Complete booklet, #5298a	4.50	

Complete booklet sold for 295w.

Worldwide Fund for Nature (WWF) — A2478

No. 5299 — Grus japonensis: a, In flight. b, Adult and chick. c, Adults in water. d, Adults and chicks.

2014, Aug. 5 Litho. *Perf. 13¼*

5299	Horiz. strip of 4	3.25	1.75
a.	A2478 10w multi	.25	.25
b.	A2478 30w multi	.45	.25
c.	A2478 50w multi	.75	.40
d.	A2478 110w multi	1.75	.85
e.	Booklet pane of 4, #5299a-5299d	3.50	—
	Complete booklet, #5299e	3.50	

Complete booklet sold for 215w.

AIR POST STAMPS

Lisunov Li-2 Airliner over Pyongyang — AP1

1958, Feb. 4 Photo. *Perf. 10*

C1	AP1 20w blue	11.00	2.00
a.	Imperf	22.50	10.00
b.	Perf 11	12.00	2.50
c.	Rouletted	15.00	10.00

Korean Civil Aviation.

REPUBLIC OF KOSOVO

ˈko-sə̦-ˌvō

LOCATION — North of Albania and Macedonia
GOVT. — REPUBLIC
AREA — 4,212 sq. mi.
POP. — 2,100,000 (2007 est.)
CAPITAL — Pristina

From 1974 to 1990, Kosovo was an autonomous province of Serbia, a republic within Yugoslavia. In 1990, the autonomy of Kosovo was revoked. A Separatist faction declared Kosovo independence that year, but only Albania recognized it. In 1999, the United Nations Security Council placed Kosovo under a transitional United Nations Administration, and the institutions created by the independent Kosovo were replaced with the United Nations Interim Administration. Starting in 2000, postage stamps were issued by the United Nations Interim Administration, and these can be found as part of the listings for United Nations. The Kosovo Assembly declared independence on Feb. 17, 2008. Kosovo was recognized as independent by numerous countries soon thereafter, and the United Nations Interim Administration ceased issuing stamps. Serbia maintains its claim to the territory.

100 pfennigs = 1 mark
100 cents = (€)1 (2002)

Catalogue values for all unused stamps in this country are for Never Hinged items.

Peace in Kosovo — A1

Designs: 20pf, Mosaic depicting Orpheus, c. 5th-6th cent., Podujeve. 30pf, Dardinian idol, Museum of Kosovo. 50pf, Silver coin of Damastion from 4th cent. B.C. 1m, Statue of Mother Teresa, Prizren. 2m, Map of Kosovo.

Perf. 13½x13, 13½x13¼ (30pf)

2000, Mar. 14 Litho. Unwmk.

1	A1	20pf multicolored	.65	.65
2	A1	30pf multicolored	1.25	1.25
3	A1	50pf multicolored	1.60	1.60
4	A1	1m multicolored	2.00	1.80
5	A1	2m multicolored	3.75	3.50
		Nos. 1-5 (5)	9.25	8.80

Nos. 1-5 were demonetized July 1, 2002.

> Beginning with No. 6, Kosovan stamps were not available to collectors through the United Nations Postal Administration.

Peace in Kosovo — A2

Designs: 20pf, Bird. 30pf, Street musician. 50pf, Butterfly and pear. 1m, Children and stars. 2m, Globe and handprints.

2001, Nov. 12 Litho. *Perf. 14*

6	A2	20pf multicolored	1.00	1.00
7	A2	30pf multicolored	1.25	1.25
8	A2	50pf multicolored	2.00	2.00
9	A2	1m multicolored	4.00	4.00
10	A2	2m multicolored	7.50	7.50
		Nos. 6-10 (5)	15.75	15.75

Peace in Kosovo Type of 2001 With Denominations in Euros Only

2002, May 2 Litho. *Perf. 14*

11	A2	10c Like #6	.75	.75
12	A2	15c Like #7	1.00	1.00
13	A2	26c Like #8	1.50	1.50
14	A2	51c Like #9	4.50	4.50
15	A2	€1.02 Like #10	8.00	8.00
		Nos. 11-15 (5)	15.75	15.75

Christmas — A3

Designs: 50c, Candles and garland. €1, Stylized men.

2003, Dec. 20 Litho. *Perf. 14*

16	A3	50c multicolored *(30,000)*	7.50	7.50
17	A3	€1 multicolored *(30,000)*	14.50	14.50

Return of Refugees A4

Five Years of Peace A5

2004, June 29 Litho. *Perf. 13¼x13*

18	A4	€1 multicolored *(40,000)*	7.00	7.00
19	A5	€2 multicolored *(40,000)*	16.00	16.00

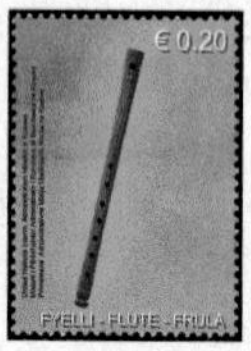

Musical Instruments — A6

2004, Aug. 31 Litho. *Perf. 13¼x13*

20	A6	20c Flute *(30,000)*	5.00	5.00
21	A6	30c Ocarina *(30,000)*	10.00	10.00

Aprons — A7

Vests — A8

Designs: 20c, Apron from Prizren. 30c, Apron from Rugova. 50c, Three vests. €1, Two vests.

2004, Oct. 28 Litho. *Perf. 13x13¼*

22	A7	20c multicolored *(30,000)*	5.50	5.50
23	A7	30c multicolored *(30,000)*	8.50	8.50
24	A8	50c multicolored *(30,000)*	12.00	12.00
25	A8	€1 multicolored *(30,000)*	26.00	26.00
		Nos. 22-25 (4)	52.00	52.00

Mirusha Waterfall — A9

2004, Nov. 26 Litho. *Perf. 13x13¼*

26	A9	€2 multicolored *(40,000)*	7.50	7.50

House — A10

2004, Dec. 14 Litho. *Perf. 13x13¼*

27	A10	50c multicolored *(40,000)*	4.50	4.50

Flowers — A11

2005, June 29 Litho. *Perf. 13½*

28	A11	15c Peony *(50,000)*	2.25	2.25
29	A11	20c Poppies *(50,000)*	3.25	3.25
30	A11	30c Gentian *(50,000)*	5.00	5.00
		Nos. 28-30 (3)	10.50	10.50

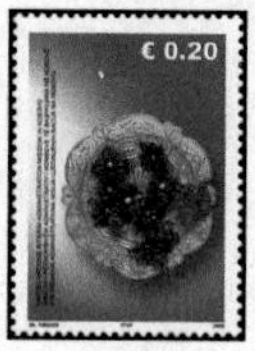

A12

Handicrafts — A13

2005, July 20 *Perf. 13¼x13*

31	A12	20c shown *(40,000)*	2.50	2.50
32	A12	30c Cradle *(40,000)*	3.00	3.00
33	A13	50c shown *(40,000)*	3.25	3.25
34	A12	€1 Necklace *(40,000)*	4.25	4.25
		Nos. 31-34 (4)	13.00	13.00

Village — A14

Town — A15

City — A16

2005, Sept. 15 *Perf. 13x13½*

35	A14	20c multicolored *(50,000)*	2.00	2.00
36	A15	50c multicolored *(110,000)*	3.00	3.00
37	A16	€1 multicolored *(110,000)*	6.00	6.00
		Nos. 35-37 (3)	11.00	11.00

Archaeological Artifacts — A17

2005, Nov. 2 *Perf. 13½x13*

38	A17	20c shown *(25,000)*	1.25	1.25
39	A17	30c Statue *(25,000)*	1.75	1.75
40	A17	50c Sculpture *(25,000)*	2.50	2.50
41	A17	€1 Helmet *(25,000)*	7.50	7.50
		Nos. 38-41 (4)	13.00	13.00

Minerals — A18

2005, Dec. 10 *Perf. 13x13½*

42	A18	€2 multicolored *(45,000)*	10.00	10.00

A19

Europa — A20

2006, July 20 *Perf. 13¼x13*

43	A19	50c multicolored *(60,000)*	2.25	2.25
44	A20	€1 multicolored *(60,000)*	4.25	4.25

Exists Imperf. Value set of two, $75.

Fauna — A21

2006, May 23 Litho. *Perf. 13*

45	A21	15c Wolf *(190,000)*	1.00	1.00
46	A21	20c Cow *(190,000)*	1.25	1.25
47	A21	30c Pigeon *(190,000)*	1.40	1.40
48	A21	50c Swan *(190,000)*	1.60	1.60
49	A21	€1 Dog *(190,000)*	2.75	2.75
a.		Souvenir sheet, #45-49, + label *(15,000)*	8.75	8.75
		Nos. 45-49 (5)	8.00	8.00

Nos. 45-49 are inscribed CPU. Stamps with "Leoprint" imprint are from No. 63a.

No. 49a exists in two shades of green selvage.

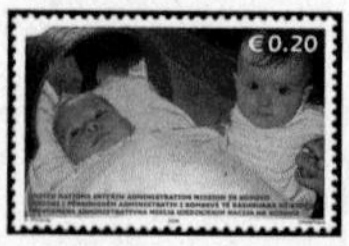

Children — A22

Designs: 20c, Children in cradle. 30c, Children reading. 50c, Girls dancing. €1, Child in water.

2006, June 30 Litho. *Perf. 13*

50	A22	20c multicolored *(40,000)*	1.00	1.00
51	A22	30c multicolored *(40,000)*	1.25	1.25
52	A22	50c multicolored *(40,000)*	1.75	1.75
53	A22	€1 multicolored *(40,000)*	3.50	3.50
a.		Souvenir sheet, #50-53 *(12,500)*	7.75	7.75
		Nos. 50-53 (4)	7.50	7.50

Nos. 50-53 were printed by CPU & Moare. No. 53a was printed by two printers: 7,500 inscribed "CPU&Moare," and 5,000 inscribed "Leoprint."

Nos. 50-53 from CPO & Moare exists imperforate. Value, set, $75.

No. 53a by CPU & Moare exists imperforate. Value $75.

A23

A24

A25

Tourist Attractions A26

2006, Sept. 1 Litho. *Perf. 13*

54 A23 20c multicolored *(40,000)* 1.00 1.00
55 A24 30c multicolored *(40,000)* 1.25 1.25
56 A25 50c multicolored *(40,000)* 1.75 1.75
57 A26 €1 multicolored *(40,000)* 3.25 3.25
a. Souvenir sheet, #54-57 *(12,500)* *9.50 9.50*
Nos. 54-57 (4) 7.25 7.25

Nos. 54-57 were printed by CPU & Moare. No. 57a was printed by two printers: 7,500 inscribed "CPU&Moare," and 5,000 inscribed "Leoprint."

Intl. Peace Day — A27

2006, Sept. 21 Litho. *Perf. 13*

58 A27 €2 multicolored *(40,000)* 7.00 7.00

Ancient Coins — A28

Various coins.

2006, Nov. 1 Litho. *Perf. 13*

59 A28 20c multicolored *(30,000)* 1.00 1.00
60 A28 30c multicolored *(30,000)* 1.50 1.50
61 A28 50c multicolored *(30,000)* 1.75 1.75
62 A28 €1 multicolored *(30,000)* 3.25 3.25
a. Souvenir sheet, #59-62 *(15,000)* *9.50 9.50*
Nos. 59-62 (4) 7.50 7.50

Nos. 59-62 are inscribed CPU. Stamps with "Leoprint" imprint are from No. 63a.

No. 62a exists imperforate. Value, $75.

Sculpture — A29

2006, Dec. 1 Litho. *Perf. 13*

63 A29 €2 multicolored *(45,000)* 8.00 8.00
a. Miniature sheet, #45-57, 59-63, + 2 labels *(5,000)* *80.00 80.00*

Convention on the Rights of Persons With Disabilities — A30

Emblems of handicaps and: 20c, Children and butterfly. 50c, Handicapped women. 70c, Map of Kosovo. €1, Stylized flower.

2007, Apr. 23 Litho. *Perf. 14x14¼*

64 A30 20c multicolored *(15,000)* 1.25 1.25
65 A30 50c multicolored *(15,000)* 2.50 2.50
66 A30 70c multicolored *(15,000)* 3.00 3.00
67 A30 €1 multicolored *(15,000)* 3.75 3.75
a. Souvenir sheet, #64-67 *(20,000)* *12.50 12.50*
Nos. 64-67 (4) 10.50 10.50

Color shades vary widely. Printer's waste of this issue exists in the marketplace, including partial prints, missing design elements, and missing colors.

Two varieties of No. 67a, exist differing in text surrounding the stamps. It has not been established if both varieties were officially issued.

Scouting, Cent. — A31

Europa — A32

2007, May 12 Litho. *Perf. 13¼*

68 A31 70c multicolored *(35,000)* 4.25 4.25
69 A32 €1 multicolored *(35,000)* 6.25 6.25
a. Souvenir sheet, #68-69 *(15,000)* *90.00 90.00*

A33

A34

A35

International Children's Day — A36

2007, June 1 Litho. *Perf. 13¼*

70 A33 20c multicolored *(38,000)* 1.25 1.25
71 A34 30c multicolored *(38,000)* 1.50 1.50
72 A35 70c multicolored *(38,000)* 2.50 2.50
73 A36 €1 multicolored *(38,000)* 4.00 4.00
Nos. 70-73 (4) 9.25 9.25

Nos. 70-73 exist imperf. Value, set $45

Native Costumes — A37

Designs: 20c, Serbian woman. 30c, Prizren Region woman. 50c, Sword dancer. 70c, Drenica Region woman. €1, Shepherd, Rugova.

2007, July 6 Litho. *Perf. 13½x13¼*

74 A37 20c multicolored *(35,000)* 1.25 1.25
75 A37 30c multicolored *(35,000)* 1.75 1.75
76 A37 50c multicolored *(35,000)* 2.00 2.00
77 A37 70c multicolored *(35,000)* 2.50 2.50
78 A37 €1 multicolored *(35,000)* 3.25 3.25
a. Souvenir sheet, #74-78, + label *(15,000)* *12.50 12.50*
Nos. 74-78 (5) 10.75 10.75

Masks — A38

Various masks.

Perf. 13½x13¼

2007, Sept. 11 Litho.

79 A38 15c multicolored *(38,000)* .75 .75
80 A38 30c multicolored *(38,000)* 1.00 1.00
81 A38 50c multicolored *(38,000)* 2.00 2.00
82 A38 €1 multicolored *(38,000)* 3.00 3.00
Nos. 79-82 (4) 6.75 6.75

Sports — A39

Designs: 20c, Soccer ball, basketball, two people standing, person in wheelchair. 50c, Wrestlers. €1, Symbols of 24 sports.

2007, Oct. 2 Litho. *Perf. 13¼x13½*

83 A39 20c multicolored *(38,000)* 1.00 1.00
84 A39 50c multicolored *(38,000)* 2.25 2.25
85 A39 €1 multicolored *(38,000)* 4.00 4.00
Nos. 83-85 (3) 7.25 7.25

Nos. 83-85 exist imperf. Value, set $65.

Architecture — A40

Designs: 30c, Stone bridge, Vushtrri. 50c, Hamam, Prizren. 70c, Tower. €1, Tower, diff.

2007, Nov. 6 Litho. *Perf. 13¼*

86 A40 30c multicolored *(38,000)* 1.50 1.50
87 A40 50c multicolored *(38,000)* 2.00 2.00
88 A40 70c multicolored *(38,000)* 2.50 2.50
89 A40 €1 multicolored *(38,000)* 3.50 3.50
Nos. 86-89 (4) 9.50 9.50

Nos. 86-89 exist imperf. Value, set $85.

Locomotives — A41

Designs: €1, Diesel locomotive. €2, Steam locomotive

2007, Dec. 7 Litho. *Perf. 13¼*

90 A41 €1 multicolored *(50,000)* 4.00 4.00
91 A41 €2 multicolored *(50,000)* 8.00 8.00

Nos. 90-91 exist imperf. Value, set $125.

Skanderbeg (1405-68), Albanian National Hero — A42

2008, Jan. 17 Litho. *Perf. 13¼*

92 A42 €2 multicolored *(140,000)* 7.50 7.50

No. 92 exists imperf. Value, $35.

Kosovo declared its independence from Serbia on Feb. 17, 2008, ending the United Nations Interim Administration. Stamps issued after Feb. 17, 2008, by the Republic of Kosovo will be listed under Kosovo in the *Scott Standard Postage Stamp Catalogue.*

Republic of Kosovo

A42

Teacher's Day — A43

2008, Mar. 7 Litho. *Perf. 13x13¼*

93 A42 70c multi 2.25 2.25
94 A43 €1 multi 3.25 3.25

Independence — A44

2008, Mar. 19 *Perf. 13¼x13*

Stamps With White Frames

95 Vert. pair 5.50 5.50
a. A44 20c vio blue & multi .75 .50
b. A44 70c red & multi 3.00 2.00

Souvenir Sheet

Stamp With Colored Border

96 A44 70c red & multi *7.00 7.00*

Earth Day — A45

Designs: 30c, Globe, olive branch. 50c, Trees. 70c, Tree, parched land. €1, Man holding tree.

2008, Apr. 22 *Perf. 13x13¼*

97-100 A45 Set of 4 8.00 8.00

Europa — A46

Designs: Nos. 101, 103a, 70c, Handwritten letter, pen. Nos. 102, 103b, €1, Letter folded into paper airplane.

2008, May 9 Litho.

Stamps With White Frames

101-102 A46 Set of 2 *7.50 7.50*

Souvenir Sheet

Stamps With Colored Frames

103 A46 Sheet of 2, #a-b *20.00 20.00*

Filigree — A47

Designs: 10c, Chest. 15c, Earring. 20c, Figurine of woman. 50c, Necklace. €1, Necklace, diff.

2008, June 12 *Perf. 13¼x13*

104-108 A47 Set of 5 6.75 6.75

A48 A49

Medicinal Herbs
A50 A51

2008, Sept. 9 Litho. *Perf. 13¼x13*

109 Horiz. strip of 4 8.00 8.00
a. A48 30c multi .75 .75
b. A49 50c multi 1.00 1.00
c. A50 70c multi 2.00 2.00
d. A51 €1 multi 2.75 2.75

Exists Imperf. Value, strip $135.

Breast Cancer Prevention — A52

2008, Oct. 15 Litho. *Perf. 13¼x13*

110 A52 €1 multi 7.00 7.00

Albanian Alphabet, Cent. — A53

No. 111: a, 70c, Alphabet. b, €1, Notebook page for handwriting practice.

2008, Nov. 14 *Perf. 13x13¼*

111 A53 Vert. pair, #a-b 4.50 4.50

Adem Jashari (1955-98), Independence Leader — A54

2008, Nov. 28 *Perf. 13¼x13*

112 A54 €2 multi 6.00 6.00

A55 A56

A57 Visual Arts — A58

2008, Dec. 2 Litho. *Perf. 13¼*

113 Horiz. strip of 4 8.00 8.00
a. A55 20c multi .55 .55
b. A56 50c multi 1.10 1.10
c. A57 70c multi 1.75 1.75
d. A58 €1 multi 2.50 2.50

William G. Walker, Head of Kosovo Verification Mission — A59

Torn Page — A60

2009, Jan. 15

114 A59 50c multi 1.25 1.25
115 A60 70c multi 2.25 2.25

Reçak Massacre, 10th anniv.

Independence, 1st Anniv. — A61

No. 116: a, €1, Hand with pen, independence declaration. b, €2, Flag of Kosovo, date of independence.
Illustration reduced.

2009, Feb. 16 Litho. *Perf. 13¼*

116 A61 Horiz. pair, #a-b 8.00 8.00

Edith Durham (1863-1944), Writer — A62

2009, Mar. 21

117 A62 €1 multi 3.25 3.25

A63

Decan Monastery — A64

Designs: No. 118, €1, Monastery. No. 119, €2, Monastery, diff.
No. 120: a, €1, Window. b, €2, Painting of Jesus.

2009, Apr. 22

118-119 A63 Set of 2 7.00 7.00

Souvenir Sheet

120 A64 Sheet of 2, #a-b 7.50 7.50

Europa — A65

Designs: €1, Map of Europe, ring of stars, man and girl at telescope. No. 122, €2, Boy and rocket on map of Europe (with white frame around stamp).
No. 123, Like #122, without white frame around stamp.

2009, May 9

121-122 A65 Set of 2 9.50 9.50

Souvenir Sheet

123 A65 €2 multi 10.00 10.00

Intl. Year of Astronomy.

A66 A67

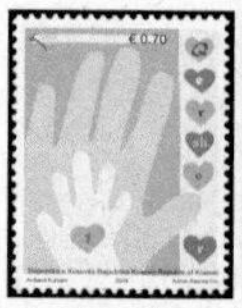

Declaration of the Rights of the Child, 20th Anniv.
A68 A69

2009, June 1

124 A66 20c multi .75 .75
125 A67 50c multi 1.75 1.75
126 A68 70c multi 2.50 2.50
127 A69 €1 multi 3.50 3.50
Nos. 124-127 (4) 8.50 8.50

Kosovo's Friendship With United States — A70

2009, Sept. 4

128 A70 €2 multi 7.00 7.00

Lorenc Antoni (1909-91), Composer — A71

2009, Sept. 23

129 A71 €1 multi 4.50 4.50

Germany Weeks in Kosovo — A72

2009, Oct. 3 Litho. *Perf. 13¼*

130 A72 €1 multi 3.50 3.50

Pjeter Bogdani (c. 1630-89), Writer — A73

2009, Nov. 22

131 A73 €1 multi 3.25 3.25

Art — A74

Works by: 30c, M. Mulliqi. 50c, I. Kodra. 70c, G. Gjokaj. €1, M. Mulliqi, diff.

2009, Dec. 4

132-135 A74 Set of 4 7.00 7.00

A75

Film Personalities — A76

Designs: No. 136, 30c, Faruk Begolli (1944-2007), actor and director. No. 137, 70c, Melihate Qena (1939-2005), actress. €1, Abdurrahman Shala (1922-94), actor and producer.
No. 139: a, 30c, Unnamed person in yellow. b, 70c, Unnamed person in brown, diff.

2010, Jan. 26

136-138 A75 Set of 3 5.50 5.50

Souvenir Sheet

139 A76 Sheet of 2, #a-b 3.25 3.25

Emblems of Kosovo Police, Defense Forces and Security Forces
A77

Police and Emblem
A78

Security Forces — A79

2010, Feb. 16 Litho.

140 A77 30c multi .85 .85
141 A78 50c multi 1.40 1.40
142 A79 70c multi 1.90 1.90
Nos. 140-142 (3) 4.15 4.15

A80

Europa
A81

Designs: €1, Child reading book under tree. No. 144, €2, Child leaving open book.
No. 145, €2, Boy sitting on book.

2010, May 5 *Perf. 13¼*

143-144 A80 Set of 2 8.00 8.00

Souvenir Sheet

Perf. 14x14¼

145 A81 €2 multi 5.25 5.25
a. Perf. 13¼ — —

2010 World Cup Soccer Championships, South Africa — A82

Designs: €1, Map of Kosovo and emblem of Kosovo Soccer Federation, map of Africa with soccer field. €2, Map of Kosovo and emblem of Kosovo Soccer Federation, map of Africa on soccer ball.

No. 148: a, Soccer ball as pendant on multicolored ribbon. b, Flag of South Africa on soccer ball.

2010, June 29 ***Perf. 13¼***
146-147 A82 Set of 2 8.00 8.00

Souvenir Sheet
Perf. 14¼x14

148 A82 50c Sheet of 2, #a-b 3.50 3.50

Azem (1889-1924) and Shota (1895-1927) Galica, Fighters for Albanian Independence — A83

2010, July 14 ***Perf. 13¼***
149 A83 €2 multi 5.25 5.25

National Parks — A84

Scenery from: 20c, Mirusha National Park. 50c, Rugova National Park. 70c, Gjeravica National Park. €1, Sharri National Park.

2010, Aug. 2 **Litho.**
150-153 A84 Set of 4 6.25 6.25

Mother Teresa (1910-97), Humanitarian — A85

2010, Aug. 26 ***Perf. 13***
154 A85 €1 multi 2.75 2.75

See Albania No. 2889, Macedonia No. 529.

A86

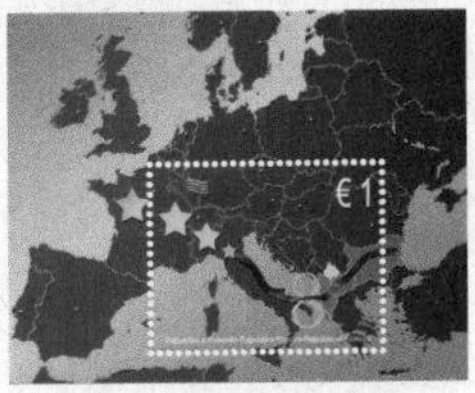

Traffic in the Pathways of Integration — A87

2010, Sept. 9 **Litho.** ***Perf. 13¼***
155 A86 70c multi 2.25 2.25

Souvenir Sheet
Perf. 14¼x14

156 A87 €1 multi 3.50 3.50

A88

A89

A90

A91

Birds A92

No. 161: a, 30c, Brown bird on branch. b, 30c, Blue and red bird on wire. c, 70c, Bird in flight. d, 70c, Blue and red bird on wire, bird in flight.

2010, Sept. 23 ***Perf. 14x14¼***

157	A88	30c multi	.85	.85
158	A89	50c multi	1.50	1.50
159	A90	70c multi	2.00	2.00
160	A91	€1 multi	3.00	3.00
		Nos. 157-160 (4)	7.35	7.35

Souvenir Sheet

161 A92 Sheet of 4, #a-d 7.50 7.50

Local Foods — A93

Designs: 70c, Beehive, honeycombs, jar of honey. €1, Plates of food.

2010, Nov. 8 ***Perf. 14¼x14***
162-163 A93 Set of 2 4.75 4.75

Campaign Against Violence Towards Women — A94

2010, Nov. 25
164 A94 €1 multi 3.00 3.00

Historical Photographs of Basare — A95

Various street scenes: 50c, 70c, €1.

2010, Dec. 6
165-167 A95 Set of 3 6.50 6.50

A96

Independence, 3rd Anniv. — A97

2011, Feb. 27 ***Perf. 14¼x14***

168	A96	€1 multi	2.50	2.50
169	A97	€2 multi	5.50	5.50

Elena Gjika (Dore D'Istria, 1828-88), Writer — A98

2011, Mar. 8 ***Perf. 14x14¼***
170 A98 €1 multi 2.75 2.75

Prizren — A99

Designs: 20c, Houses on hillside. 50c, House and benches. 70c, View of city.

2011, Mar. 15
171-173 A99 Set of 3 4.00 4.00

A100

A101

Intl. Year of Forests A102

2011, May 9 ***Perf. 14¼x14***

174	A100	€1 multi	3.00	3.00
175	A101	€2 multi	5.75	5.75

Souvenir Sheet

176 A102 €2 multi 6.00 6.00

Archaeology — A103

Designs: 10c, Building ruins. 15c, Building ruins, diff. €1, Bas-relief head.

2011, June 7 ***Perf. 14x14¼***
177-179 A103 Set of 3 3.75 3.75

Compare No. 178 with Nos. 243A and 329.

A104

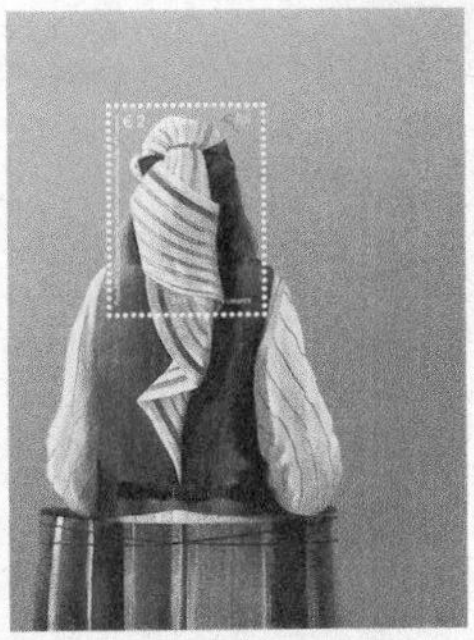

Traditional Costumes of Hasit Region — A105

Designs: 30c, Shoes. 50c, Women's dress. 70c, Pouch. €1, Vest. €2, Kerchief.

2011, Oct. 19
180-183 A104 Set of 4 6.75 6.75

Souvenir Sheet

184 A105 €2 multi 5.50 5.50

A106

A107

A108

Mills A109

2011, Nov. 2

185	A106	50c multi	1.40	1.40
186	A107	70c multi	2.00	2.00
187	A108	€1 multi	2.75	2.75
		Nos. 185-187 (3)	6.15	6.15

Souvenir Sheet
Perf. 14¼x14

188 A109 €2 multi 5.50 5.50

A110

Caves — A111

2011, Nov. 15 ***Perf. 14x14¼***

189	A110	70c multi	1.90	1.90
190	A111	€1 multi	2.75	2.75

Rooster — A112

Rooster facing: 70c, Right. €1, Left.

2011, Nov. 21
191-192 A112 Set of 2 4.75 4.75

Esat Mekuli (1916-93), Poet — A113

2011, Dec. 17 ***Perf. 14¼x14***
193 A113 €1 multi 2.60 2.60

Enver Zymeri (1979-2011), Police Officer — A114

2011, Dec. 26
194 A114 €1 multi 2.60 2.60

Mitrovica — A115

Designs: €1, Monument, workers, street, aerial view of city. €2, Old and new street scenes.

2012, Jan. 20 ***Perf. 14¼x14***
195-196 A115 Set of 2 8.00 8.00

A116

Freedom Fighters — A117

2012, Jan. 27
197 A116 €1 multi 2.60 2.60
198 A117 €1 multi 2.60 2.60

Rexho Mulliqi (1923-82), Composer — A118

2012, Feb. 23
199 A118 €1 multi 2.75 2.75

Butterflies A119

Various butterflies: 10c, 70c, €1. €2, Butterflies and orchids.

2012, Mar. 9 ***Perf. 14x14¼***
200-202 A119 Set of 3 4.75 4.75

Souvenir Sheet

203 A119 €2 multi 6.00 6.00

A120

Europa — A121

Designs: €1, Cliff and valley. No. 205, €2, House.
No. 206, €2, Buildings and bridge.

2012, Apr. 12 ***Perf. 14¼x14***
204-205 A120 Set of 2 8.00 8.00

Souvenir Sheet

206 A121 €2 multi 5.75 5.75

Lakes — A122

Designs: 20c, Badovac Lake. 50c, Gazivoda Lake. 70c, Lake Licenat.

2012, May 3 ***Perf. 14x14¼***
207-209 A122 Set of 3 3.75 3.75

Compare Nos. 208 and 331.

Isa Boletini (1864-1916), Kosovar Freedom Fighter A123

Hasan Prishtina (1873-1933), Prime Minister of Albania A124

2012, May 21 ***Perf. 14¼x14***
210 A123 70c multi 1.75 1.75
211 A124 €1 multi 2.50 2.50

Bride in Archway — A125

2012, June 18
212 A125 €1 multi 2.50 2.50

Mejlinda Kelmendi, Kosovar Judoka Competing for Albania at 2012 Summer Olympics — A126

No. 213: a, 70c, Three images of Kelmendi. b, €1, Two images of Kelmendi.

2012, July 25 ***Perf. 14x14¼***
213 A126 Pair, #a-b 4.25 4.25

Printed in sheets containing two pairs.

A127

A128

Myths and Legends — A129

2012, Sept. 5 ***Perf. 14¼x14***
214 A127 70c multi 1.90 1.90
215 A128 €1 multi 2.60 2.60

Souvenir Sheet

Perf. 14x14¼

216 A129 €2 multi 5.25 5.25

Traditional Dances — A130

Various dancers: 50c, 70c, €1.

2012, Oct. 25 ***Perf. 14¼x14***
217-219 A130 Set of 3 5.75 5.75

Albanian Independence, Cent. — A131

2012, Nov. 27
220 A131 €1 multi 2.60 2.60

Marin Barleti (c.1450-c. 1512), Historian — A132

2012, Dec. 26
221 A132 €1 multi 2.75 2.75

Independence, 5th Anniv. — A133

2013, Feb. 17 ***Perf. 14x14¼***
222 A133 €2 multi 5.25 5.25

Pristina — A134

Designs: 50c, Old and modern photographs of Pristina. 70c, Drawing of Pristina buildings. €1, People near building, Pristina skyline.

2013, Mar. 20 ***Perf. 14¼x14***
223-225 A134 Set of 3 5.75 5.75

A135

A136

Museum Exhibits A137

No. 228 — Table with window and small wall niche at: a, Left. b, Right.

2013, Apr. 5 ***Perf. 14x14¼***
226 A135 70c multi 1.90 1.90
227 A136 €1 multi 2.60 2.60

Souvenir Sheet

Perf. 14¼x14

228 A137 €1 Sheet of 2, #a-b 5.25 5.25

A138

A139

Postal Transportation — A140

No. 231: a, Horse-drawn wagon. b, Postman on scooter.

2013, May 2 **Litho.** ***Perf. 14x14¼***
229 A138 €1 multi 2.60 2.60
230 A139 €2 multi 5.25 5.25

Souvenir Sheet

Perf. 14¼x14

231 A140 €1 Sheet of 2, #a-b 5.25 5.25

Mountain Scenery — A141

Designs: 50c, Mt. Gjeravica. 70c Rugova Canyon (Gryka e Rugoves). €1, Mt. Gjeravica, diff.

2013, June 14 Litho. *Perf. 14¼x14*

232-234 A141 Set of 3 6.00 6.00

Villages — A142

Designs: 50c, Stublla e Eperme. 70c, Opoja. €1, Lluka e Eperme.

2013, July 18 Litho. *Perf. 14x14¼*

235-237 A142 Set of 3 6.00 6.00

235a Dated "2016" 1.10 1.10

Famous Women A143

No. 238: a, 50c, Hyrije Hana (1929-2004), radio broadcaster. b, 70c, Xheve Lladrovici (1955-98), freedom fighter. c, €1, Katarina Josipi (1923-69), actress.

2013, Aug. 15 Litho. *Perf. 14¼x14*

238 A143 Horiz. strip of 3, #a-c 5.50 5.50

Bajram Curri (1862-1925), Albanian Politician A144

2013, Sept. 9 Litho. *Perf. 14x14¼*

239 A144 €1 multi 2.75 2.75

Paintings by Adem Kastrati (1930-2000) A145

Various paintings depicting: a, 70c, Buildings on hill. b, €1, Sheep and shepherds. c, €2, Musicians.

2013, Sept. 26 Litho. *Perf. 14x14¼*

240 A145 Vert. strip of 3, #a-c 10.00 10.00

Pristina University A146

2014, Oct. 28 Litho. *Perf. 14x14¼*

241 A146 €1 multi 2.75 2.75

Singers — A147

No. 242: a, 20c, Qamili i Vogel (1923-91). b, 30c, Sali Krasniqi (1919-87). c, 50c, Dervish Shaqa (1912-85).

2013, Nov. 15 Litho. *Perf. 14x14¼*

242 A147 Vert. strip of 3, #a-c 2.75 2.75

d. As #242a, dated "2015" — —

Bekim Fehmiu (1936-2010), Actor — A148

2013, Dec. 5 Litho. *Perf. 14¼x14*

243 A148 €1 multi 2.75 2.75

Building Ruins — A148a

2013 Litho. *Perf. 14¼x14*

243A A148a 15c multi — —

b. Dated "2014" — —

Compare No. 243A with Nos. 178 and 329.

Paintings by Muslim Mulliqi (1934-98) — A149

Various paintings.

2014, Jan. 13 Litho. *Perf. 14¼x14*

244 Horiz. strip of 4 7.75 7.75

a. A149 30c multi .80 .80

b. A149 60c multi 1.60 1.60

c. A149 90c multi 2.50 2.50

d. A149 €1 multi 2.75 2.75

Mountain Climbers — A150

Mountaineering — A151

2014, Feb. 7 Litho. *Perf. 14¼x14*

245 A150 €1 multi 2.75 2.75

Souvenir Sheet

246 A151 €2 multi 5.50 5.50

Pec — A152

Buildings in Pec: €1, Color photograph. €2, Sepia-toned photograph.

2014, Mar. 10 Litho. *Perf. 14x14¼*

247-248 A152 Set of 2 8.25 8.25

World Shotokan Karate Championships, Pristina — A153

No. 249 — Two karateka and: a, 80c, Colored belts and "5." b, 90c, Map of Kosovo and world.

€2, Karateka and map of Kosovo and world.

2014, Apr. 3 Litho. *Perf. 14x14¼*

249 A153 Pair, #a-b 4.75 4.75

Souvenir Sheet

250 A153 €2 multi 5.50 5.50

No. 249 was printed in sheets containing two pairs + label.

Ibrahim Rugova Highway A154

No. 251: a, €1, Bridge and interchange. b, €2, Entrance and exit ramps.

2014, Apr. 25 Litho. *Perf. 14x14¼*

251 A154 Pair, #a-b 8.25 8.25

Europa — A155

Musical instruments: €1, Two instruments. No. 253, €2, Lakuta.

No. 254, €2, Four instruments, horiz.

2014, May 8 Litho. *Perf. 14¼x14*

252-253 A155 Set of 2 8.25 8.25

Souvenir Sheet

Perf. 14x14¼

254 A155 €2 multi 5.50 5.50

Flowers — A156

Designs: 80c, Liliaceae. 90c, Gladiolus illyricus. €1, Tulipa kosovarica.

€2, Red flowers.

2014, June 12 Litho. *Perf. 14¼x14*

255-257 A156 Set of 3 7.50 7.50

Souvenir Sheet

258 A156 €2 multi 5.50 5.50

Jeronim de Rada (1814-1903), Writer — A157

2014, July 3 Litho. *Perf. 14¼x14*

259 A157 €1 multi 2.75 2.75

Woven Items — A158

Various woven items.

2014, Aug. 8 Litho. *Perf. 14¼x14*

260 Horiz. strip or block of 4, #a-d 8.75 8.75

a. A158 60c multi 1.60 1.60

b. A158 80c multi 2.10 2.10

c. A158 90c multi 2.40 2.40

d. A158 €1 multi 2.60 2.60

Fehmi (1950-98) and Xheve (1955-98) Lladrovci, Freedom Fighters — A159

2014, Sept. 22 Litho. *Perf. 14x14¼*

261 A159 €2 multi 5.00 5.00

Adrian Krasniqi (1972-97), Freedom Fighter — A160

2014, Oct. 16 Litho. *Perf. 14¼x14*

262 A160 €1 multi 2.50 2.50

Tringe Smajli (1880-1917), Freedom Fighter — A161

2014, Nov. 2 Litho. *Perf. 14¼x14*

263 A161 €1 multi 2.50 2.50

Intl. Year of Crystallography A162

Various mineral crystals: €1, €2.

2014, Nov. 20 Litho. *Perf. 14x14¼*

264-265 A162 Set of 2 7.50 7.50

Granting of Intl. Olympic Committee Membership to Kosovo Olympic Committee — A163

2014, Dec. 5 Litho. *Perf. 14¼x14*

266 A163 €2 multi 5.00 5.00

No. 266 was printed in sheets of 6 + 3 labels.

Gjakova — A164

Various street scenes: €1,€2.

2015, Jan. 23 Litho. ***Perf. 14¼x14***
267-268 A164 Set of 2 7.00 7.00

Circular Labyrinth, Smira — A165

2015, Feb. 12 Litho. ***Perf. 14¼x14***
269 A165 €1 multi 2.50 2.50

Lynx — A166

Designs: 80c, Lynx in tree. 90c, Head of lynx. €1, Head of lynx, flag and map of Kosovo.

2015, Mar. 19 Litho. ***Perf. 14x14¼***
270-272 A166 Set of 3 *6.00 6.00*

Hashim Hajdini (1949-99), Patriot — A167

2015, Mar. 27 Litho. ***Perf. 14¼x14***
273 A167 €1 multi 2.50 2.50

Waterfall — A168

Designs: 60c, Bridge and rapids. 80c, Rock-strewn river. 90c, Tree near small waterfall.

2015, Apr. 15 Litho. ***Perf. 14¼x14***
274 A168 30c multi .70 .70
275 A168 60c multi 1.40 1.40
276 A168 80c multi 1.90 1.90
277 A168 90c multi 2.00 2.00

Compare Nos. 274 and 330.

Ilaz Kodra (1966-99), Military Leader — A169

2015, Apr. 30 Litho. ***Perf. 14¼x14***
278 A169 €2 multi 4.75 4.75

A170

A171

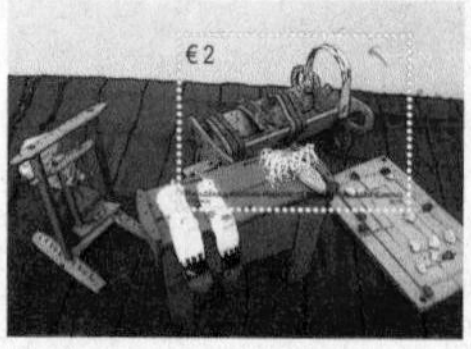

Europa A172

2015, May 4 Litho. ***Perf. 14x14¼***
279 A170 €1 multi 2.50 2.50
280 A171 €2 multi 4.75 4.75

Souvenir Sheet

281 A172 €2 multi 4.75 4.75

Ukshin Hoti (1943-99), Philosopher A173

2015, June 17
282 A173 €1 multi 2.50 2.50

Traditional Clothing — A174

Designs: 80c, Men's clothing. 90c, Women's clothing. €1, Decorated bag.
€2, Vest.

2015, July 1 ***Perf. 14¼x14***
283-285 A174 Set of 3 6.00 6.00

Souvenir Sheet

286 A174 €2 multi 4.75 4.75

Diaspora A175

2015, Aug. 2 Litho. ***Perf. 14x14¼***
287 A175 €2 multi 4.75 4.75

Mark (1926-98), Pren (1964-99), Kole (1967-99), and Meme (1973-99) Lleshi, Patriots — A176

2015, Aug. 7 Litho. ***Perf. 14¼x14***
288 A176 €1 multi 4.75 4.75

Grapes and Wine Making — A177

Designs: 60c, Embroidered grape design. 80c, Grapes, wine bottle and glass. 90c, Vineyard.
€2, Woman harvesting grapes.

2015, Sept. 18 Litho. ***Perf. 14¼x14***
289-291 A177 Set of 3 5.25 5.25

Souvenir Sheet

292 A177 €2 multi 4.75 4.75

Anton Ceta (1920-95), Folklorist, Founder of Reconciliation Committee A178

2015, Nov. 3 Litho. ***Perf. 14x14¼***
293 A178 €1 multi 2.50 2.50

Archaeological Artifacts — A179

2015, Dec. 15 Litho. ***Perf. 14¼x14***
294 A179 €2 multi 4.75 4.75

Street in Vucitrrn — A180

Vojinovic Tower, Vucitrn — A181

2016, Jan. 18 Litho. ***Perf. 14x14¼***
295 A180 €1 multi 2.50 2.50
296 A181 €2.10 multi 4.75 4.75

Skender Rexhepi (1965-99), Kosovo Liberation Army Hero — A182

Luan Haradinaj (1973-97), Kosovo Liberation Army Hero — A183

2016, Feb. 17 Litho. ***Perf. 14¼x14***
297 A182 €1 multi 2.50 2.50
298 A183 €1 multi 2.50 2.50

Art of Rexhep Ferri — A184

Various paintings.

2016, Feb. 29 Litho. ***Perf. 14¼x14***
299 Horiz. strip of 3 4.75 4.75
a. A184 40c multi .90 .90
b. A184 80c multi 1.75 1.75
c. A184 90c multi 2.00 2.00

Souvenir Sheet

Mountain Tourism A185

2016, Mar. 28 Litho. ***Perf. 14x14¼***
300 A185 €2.10 multi + label 4.75 4.75

See Macedonia No. 704.

Agim Ramadani (1963-99), Kosovo Liberation Army Commander A186

Sali Cekaj (1956-99), Kosovo Liberation Army Commander A187

2016, Apr. 9 Litho. ***Perf. 14¼x14***
301 A186 €1 multi 2.25 2.25
302 A187 €1 multi 2.25 2.25

A188

A189

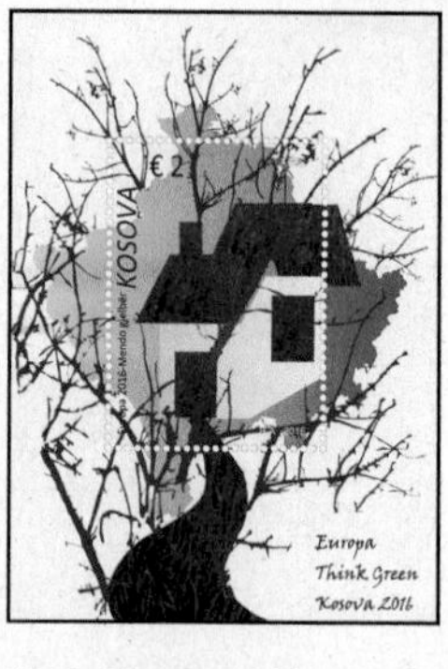

Europa A190

2016, May 9 Litho. ***Perf. 14x14¼***
303 A188 €1 multi 2.50 2.50
304 A189 €2.10 multi 4.75 4.75

Souvenir Sheet

Perf. 14¼x14

305 A190 €2 multi 4.75 4.75

Think Green Issue.

2016 European Individual Chess Championships, Gjakova — A191

2016, May 23 Litho. ***Perf. 14x14¼***
306 A191 €1.80 multi 4.00 4.00

No. 306 was printed in sheets of 2.

Mushrooms — A192

Designs: 60c, Boletus edulis. 80c, Morchella vulgaris. €1.30, Leccinum scabrum. 90c, Amanita muscaria.

2016, July 4 Litho. *Perf. 14¼x14*

306A-306C A192	Set of 3	6.00	6.00
307 A192	Sheet of 4, #306A, 306B, 306C, 307a	8.00	8.00
a.	90c multi	2.00	2.00

Nos. 306A, 306B and 306C have misspelled Latin names.

2016 Summer Olympics, Rio de Janeiro — A193

Emblem of the Kosovo Olympic Committee and: €1, Flag of Kosovo. €2.10, Judoka. €2, Stylized sprinter.

2016, July 29 Litho. *Perf. 14x14¼*

308-309 A193	Set of 2	7.00	7.00

Souvenir Sheet

310 A193	€2 multi	4.50	4.50

Canonization of St. Teresa of Calcutta — A194

2016, Aug. 15 Litho. *Perf. 14x14¼*

311 A194	€2.10 multi	4.75	4.75

Dervish Rozhaja (1934-96), Biologist — A195

2016, Aug. 23 Litho. *Perf. 14x14¼*

312 A195	€1.30 multi	3.00	3.00

Kosovo's Affiliation With Soccer Organizations A196

Inscriptions: €1.30, Kosovo in UEFA. €2.10, Kosovo in FIFA.

2016, Sept. 2 Litho. *Perf. 14x14¼*

313-314 A196	Set of 2	7.75	7.75

Fruits — A197

Designs: 40c, Apples and apple pie. 60c, Pears, juice and cookie. 80c, Blackberries and blackberry jam.

2016, Sept. 20 Litho. *Perf. 14x14¼*

315-317 A197	Set of 3	4.00	4.00

Traditional Costumes — A198

Designs: 80c, Women's blouse and vest. 90c, Woman wearing costume. €2, Man and woman in costumes.

2016, Oct. 15 Litho. *Perf. 14¼x14*

318-319 A198	Set of 2	3.75	3.75

Souvenir Sheet

320 A198	€2 multi	4.50	4.50

Tetrau Urogallus A199

Bird facing: 90c, Left. €1.30, Right.

2016, Oct. 28 Litho. *Perf. 14x14¼*

321-322 A199	Set of 2	5.00	5.00

Dodona Puppet Theater — A200

Designs: 80c, Puppet of girl with basket. 90c, Puppets of men on horseback.

2016, Nov. 12 Litho. *Perf. 14x14¼*

323-324 A200	Set of 2	3.75	3.75

Mountain Tourism — A201

Various photographs of Boge Ski Resort: 60c, 80c, 90c.

2016, Dec. 19 Litho. *Perf. 14*

325-327 A201	Set of 3	4.75	4.75

80th Birthday of Ismail Kadare, Writer — A202

2016, Dec. 20 Litho. *Perf. 14x14¼*

328 A202	€1 multi	2.10	2.10

Building Ruins A203

Waterfall A204

Gazivoda Lake — A205

2016 Litho. *Perf. 14¼x14*

329 A203	15c multi	.35	.35
330 A204	30c multi	—	—

Perf. 14x14¼

331 A205	50c multi	—	—

Compare Nos. 329 with Nos. 178 and 243A. Compare Nos. 330-331 with Nos. 274 and 208.

Buildings in Ferizaj — A206

Designs: €1.30, Buildings at night. €2, Mosque and buildings in daylight.

2017, Jan. 20 Litho. *Perf. 14¼x14*

332-333 A206	Set of 2	7.25	7.25

Farm Animals — A207

Designs: 20c, Bardoka ewes.
No. 335: a, Red goat. b, Syke ewe and lamb. c, Bardoka ram.

2017, Feb. 4 Litho. *Perf. 14x14¼*

334 A207	20c multi	.45	.45
335	Horiz. strip of 3	4.00	4.00
a. A207	40c multi	.85	.85
b. A207	50c multi	1.10	1.10
c. A207	90c multi	1.90	1.90

Malush Ahmeti (1951-99), Kosovo Liberation Army Commander A208

Nesimi Dervishdana (1964-81), Independence Demonstrator Shot by Yugoslavian Army — A209

2017, Feb. 17 Litho. *Perf. 14x14¼*

336 A208	€1.30 multi	2.75	2.75
337 A209	€1.30 multi	2.75	2.75

Flowers — A210

Designs: 80c, Solenanthus krasniqi. 90c, Aster albanicus. €1, Tulipa luanica.

2017, Mar. 3 Litho. *Perf. 14¼x14*

338-340 A210	Set of 3	5.75	5.75

Xheladin Gashi (1946-2005), General — A211

2017, Mar. 21 Litho. *Perf. 14x14¼*

341 A211	€1.30 multi	2.75	2.75

Enver Hadri (1941-90), Assassinated Human Rights Activist — A212

2017, Apr. 2 Litho. *Perf. 14x14¼*

342 A212	€1.30 multi	3.00	3.00

Ulpiana Baptistry — A213

2017, Apr. 18 Litho. *Perf. 14x14¼*

343 A213	€2 multi	4.50	4.50

Ulpiana Castle — A214

Prizren Fortress — A215

Novo Brdo Fortress A216

2017, May 9 Litho. *Perf. 14x14¼*

344 A214	€1 multi	2.25	2.25
345 A215	€2 multi	4.50	4.50

Souvenir Sheet

346 A216	€2 multi	4.50	4.50

Europa.

A217

A218

A219

Paintings by Engjell Berisha (1926-2010) — A220

2017, June 6 Litho. *Perf. 14¼x14*

347	Horiz. strip of 4	7.75	7.75
a. A217	60c multi	1.40	1.40
b. A218	80c multi	1.90	1.90
c. A219	90c multi	2.10	2.10
d. A220	€1 multi	2.25	2.25

Esat Stavileci (1942-2015), Law Professor A221

2017, July 11 Litho. *Perf. 14x14¼*

348 A221	€1.30 multi	3.25	3.25

Diving From the Fshetje Bridge — A222

Design: €1.80, Drawing of diver. €2, Photograph of diver, vert.

2017, July 21 Litho. *Perf. 14x14¼*

349 A222	€1.80 multi	4.25	4.25

Souvenir Sheet

Perf. 14¼x14

350 A222	€2 multi	4.75	4.75

Tekke of Sheikh Bani, Gjakova — A223

Architecture — A224

No. 352: a, 60c, Tekke of Sheikh Bani (inscription at LR, date at LL). b, 80c, Cathedral of Perpetual Succor, Prizren. c, 90c, Patriarchal Monastery, Pec. d, €1, Hadum Mosque, Gjakova.

2017, Aug. 4 Litho. *Perf. 14x14¼*

351 A223 60c multi 1.50 1.50

Miniature Sheet

352 A224 Sheet of 4, #a-d 8.00 8.00

Traditional Clothing of Medvegja — A225

Designs: €1, Women's kerchief. No. 354, €2, Beaded vest.
No. 355, €2, Women's shoes.

2017, Sept. 6 Litho. *Perf. 14¼x14*

353-354 A225 Set of 2 7.00 7.00

Souvenir Sheet

355 A225 €2 multi 4.75 4.75

Woman Breastfeeding Child — A226

2017, Oct. 6 Litho. *Perf. 14¼x14*

356 A226 €2 multi 4.75 4.75

Protestant Reformation, 500th Anniv. — A227

2017, Oct. 21 Litho. *Perf. 14¼x14*

357 A227 €1.80 multi 4.25 4.25

Eliot Engel, U.S. Congressman — A228

2017, Nov. 20 Litho. *Perf. 14¼x14*

358 A228 €2 multi 4.75 4.75

Kosovo Ballet, 45th Anniv. — A229

Designs: €1, Female dancer. €2, Male and female dancers.

2017, Dec. 1 Litho. *Perf. 14x14¼*

359-360 A229 Set of 2 7.25 7.25

Famous Men — A230

Designs: No. 361, €1.30, Pajazit Nushi (1933-2015), psychologist. No. 362, €1.30, Mark Krasniqi (1920-2015), writer.

2017, Dec. 3 Litho. *Perf. 14x14¼*

361-362 A230 Set of 2 6.25 6.25

Skanderbeg (1405-68), Albanian National Hero — A231

2018, Jan. 17 Litho. *Perf. 14¼x14*

363 A231 €2 multi 5.00 5.00

Birds — A232

Designs: 50c, Falco tinnunculus. €1, Oriolus oriolus.
No. 366: a, Upupa epops. b, Podiceps cristatus. c, Sturnus vulgaris.

2018, Jan. 31 Litho. *Perf. 14x14¼*

364-365 A232 Set of 2 3.50 3.50

Miniature Sheet

366 A232 Sheet of 5, #364, 365, 366a-366c, + label 8.50 8.50

a.	40c multi	1.00	1.00
b.	60c multi	1.50	1.50
c.	80c multi	2.00	2.00

Republic of Kosovo, 10th Anniv. — A233

2018, Feb. 17 Litho. *Perf. 14x14¼*

367 A233 €2.10 multi 5.25 5.25

Adem Jashari (1955-98), Kosovo Liberation Army Leader — A234

No. 368: a, €1.80, Adem Jashari Memorial, Prekaz. b, €2, Dove and burning house.

2018, Mar. 5 Litho. *Perf. 14¼x14*

368 A234 Pair, #a-b 9.50 9.50

Aerial View of Gjilan — A235

Gjilan in 1925 — A236

2018, Apr. 12 Litho. *Perf. 14x14¼*

369 A235 €1 multi 2.40 2.40

370 A236 €2 multi 4.75 4.75

A237

A238

Bridges A239

2018, May 9 Litho. *Perf. 14¼x14*

371 A237 €1 multi 2.40 2.40

372 A238 €2 multi 4.75 4.75

Souvenir Sheet

Perf. 14x14¼

373 A239 €2 multi 4.75 4.75

Europa.

Nazim Gaffuri and Stak Mark Mirdita, Martyrs — A240

2018, May 25 Litho. *Perf. 14x14¼*

374 A240 €1.30 multi 3.00 3.00

2018 World Cup Soccer Championships, Russia — A241

Designs: €1, Player dribbling ball. €2.10, Goalkeeper and ball.
2, Players and World Cup trophy.

2018, June 14 Litho. *Perf. 14x14¼*

375-376 A241 Set of 2 7.25 7.25

Souvenir Sheet

377 A241 €2 multi 4.75 4.75

Writers — A242

Designs: No. 378, €1.30, Azem Shkreli (1938-97). No. 379, €1.30, Anton Pashku (1937-95).

2018, June 30 Litho. *Perf. 14¼x14*

378-379 A242 Set of 2 6.00 6.00

A243

A244

Pottery — A245

2018, July 17 Litho. *Perf. 14x14¼*

380 A243 60c multi 1.40 1.40

381 A244 80c multi 1.90 1.90

382 A245 90c multi 2.10 2.10

Nos. 380-382 (3) 5.40 5.40

Generals — A246

Designs: No. 383, €1.30, Brigadier General Bekim Berisha (1966-98). No. 384, €1.30, General Bedri Shala (1969-98).

2018, Aug. 10 Litho. *Perf. 14¼x14*

383-384 A246 Set of 2 6.00 6.00

Flowers — A247

Designs: 30c, Achillea clypeolata. 40c, Viola dukadjivica. 60c, Crocus flavus. 80c, Adonis microcarpa. 90c, Leontopodium alpinum.

2018, Aug. 24 Litho. *Perf. 14¼x14*

385-389 A247 Set of 5 7.00 7.00

A248

Coins and Mosaics From Dresnik Archaeological Site — A249

2018, Sept. 20 Litho. *Perf. 14x14¼*

390 A248 €2.10 multi 5.00 5.00

Souvenir Sheet

391 A249 €2 multi 4.75 4.75

Fehmi Agani (1932-99), Politician A250

Ejup Statovci (1940-97), Law Professor A251

2018, Oct. 1 Litho. *Perf. 14¼x14*

392 A250 €1.30 multi 3.00 3.00

393 A251 €1.30 multi 3.00 3.00

Fadil Vokrri (1960-2018), Soccer Player — A252

2018, Oct. 9 Litho. *Perf. 14x14¼*

394 A252 €2.10 multi 4.75 4.75

A253

Shota Ensemble, 70th Anniv. — A254

2018, Nov. 2 Litho. *Perf. 14x14¼*

395 A253 €1.30 multi 3.00 3.00
396 A254 €1.80 multi 4.25 4.25

Afrim Zhitia (1965-89) and Fahri Fazliu (1963-89), Freedom Fighters — A255

2018, Nov. 2 Litho. *Perf. 14x14¼*

397 A255 €1.30 multi 3.00 3.00

Xhelal Hajda (1967-98) and Selajdin Mullaabazi (1970-98), Freedom Fighters — A256

2018, Nov. 16 Litho. *Perf. 14¼x14*

398 A256 €1.30 multi 3.00 3.00

Adem Demaçi (1936-2018), Politician and Writer — A257

2018, Nov. 28 Litho. *Perf. 14¼x14*

399 A257 €2 multi 4.50 4.50

Martyrs of Gjakova — A258

2018, Dec. 21 Litho. *Perf. 14¼x14*

400 A258 €1.30 multi 3.00 3.00

No. 400 was printed in sheets of 5 + label.

League of Prizren, 140th Anniv. — A259

2018, Dec. 28 Litho. *Perf. 14¼x14*

401 A259 €2.10 multi 4.75 4.75

No. 401 was printed in sheets of 5 + label.

A260

Kaçanik — A261

2019, Jan. 17 Litho. *Perf. 14x14¼*

402 A260 €1 multi 2.40 2.40
403 A261 €2 multi 4.75 4.75

Blinaja National Park — A262

Designs: 40c, Buck. 50c, Deer. 60c, Wildlife near stream.

No. 407: a, Wildlife, hut at left. b, Wildlife, hut at upper right.

2019, Feb. 20 Litho. *Perf. 14¼x14*

404-406 A262 Set of 3 3.50 3.50

Souvenir Sheet

407 A262 €1 Sheet of 2, #a-b 4.50 4.50

Binaja National Park Type of 2019

2019 Litho. *Perf. 14¼x14*

Stamps With White Frames

407C A262 40c Like #404 — —
407D A262 50c Like #405 — —

Idriz Seferi (1847-1927), Commander in Uprisings of 1910 and 1912 A263

Shaban Polluzha (1871-1945), Military Leader A264

Marie Shllaku (1922-46), Politician A265

Ismail Imer Thaçi, Teacher and Military Hero A266

2019, Mar. 25 Litho. *Perf. 14¼x14*

408 Horiz. strip of 4 12.00 12.00
a. A263 €1.30 multi 3.00 3.00
b. A264 €1.30 multi 3.00 3.00
c. A265 €1.30 multi 3.00 3.00
d. A266 €1.30 multi 3.00 3.00

Paintings by Esat Valla A267

No. 409 — Various unnamed paintings: a, 80c. b, 90c. c, €1.

2019, Apr. 22 Litho. *Perf. 14¼x14*

409 A267 Horiz. strip of 3, #a-c 6.25 6.25

Paintings by Esat Valla Type of 2019

2019 Litho. *Perf. 14¼x14*

Stamp With White Frames

409D A267 €1 Like #409c — —

Europa — A268

Designs: €1, Buzzard. No. 411, €2, Turtle dove.

No. 412, €2, Great tit, Red-backed shrike, Rock thrush, horiz.

2019, May 9 Litho. *Perf. 14¼x14*

410-411 A268 Set of 2 6.75 6.75

Souvenir Sheet

Perf. 14x14¼

412 A268 €2 multi 4.50 4.50

U.S. Pres. Woodrow Wilson (1856-1924) A269

2019, May 29 Litho. *Perf. 14x14¼*

413 A269 €2 multi *10.00 10.00*

Hillary Rodham Clinton, United States Secretary of State From 2009-13 — A270

2019, June 12 Litho. *Perf. 14x14¼*

414 A270 €2 multi 4.50 4.50

Miniature Sheet

Placement of Kosovo Under Transitional United Nations Administration and NATO-led Peacekeeping Force, 20th Anniv. — A271

No. 415: a, U.S. President Bill Clinton. b, Prime Minister of Great Britain Tony Blair. c, U.S. Secretary of State Madeleine Albright. d, U.S. General Wesley Clark.

2019, June 12 Litho. *Perf. 14¼x14*

415 A271 €2 Sheet of 4, #a-d 18.00 18.00

A272

A273

A274

Modern Art — A275

2019, July 10 Litho. *Perf. 14¼x14*

416 A272 30c multi .70 .70
417 A273 40c multi .90 .90
418 A274 60c multi 1.40 1.40
419 A275 80c multi 1.75 1.75
Nos. 416-419 (4) 4.75 4.75

Nexhmije Pagarusha (1933-2020), Singer — A276

2019, Aug. 8 Litho. *Perf. 14¼x14*

420 A276 €2.10 multi 4.75 4.75

Nexhmije Pagarusha Type of 2019

2019 Litho. *Perf. 14¼x14*

Stamp With White Frames

420A A276 €2.40 Like #420 — —

A277

A278

2019 Basketball World Championships, People's Republic of China — A279

2019, Aug. 30 Litho. *Perf. 14x14¼*

421 A277 €1.80 multi 4.00 4.00
422 A278 €2 multi 4.50 4.50

Souvenir Sheet

423 A279 €2 multi 4.50 4.50

Basketball Type of 2019

2019 Litho. *Perf. 14x14¼*

Stamp With White Frames

423A A277 €1.80 Like #421 — —

Ahmet Gashi (1888-1977), Educator A280

Shtjefen Gjeçovi (1874-1929), Folklorist A281

Mehmet Gjevori (1910-2007), Educator — A282

2019, Sept. 26 Litho. *Perf. 14¼x14*

424	A280	€1.30 multi		3.00	3.00
425	A281	€1.30 multi		3.00	3.00
426	A282	€1.30 multi		3.00	3.00
		Nos. 424-426 (3)		9.00	9.00

Trepca Miners' Strike, 30th Anniv. — A283

2019, Oct. 16 Litho. *Perf. 14x14¼*

427 A283 €1.80 multi 4.00 4.00

A284

A285

A286

Children's Day — A287

2019, Nov. 20 Litho. *Perf. 14x14¼*

428	A284	50c multi	1.10	1.10
429	A285	60c multi	1.40	1.40
430	A286	80c multi	1.75	1.75
431	A287	90c multi	2.00	2.00
		Nos. 428-431 (4)	6.25	6.25

A288

Agimi Cultural and Artistic Society, 75th Anniv. — A289

2019, Nov. 22 Litho. *Perf. 14x14¼*

432	A288	€1 multi	2.25	2.25
433	A289	€2 multi	4.50	4.50

A290

Christmas and New Year's — A291

2019, Dec. 10 Litho. *Perf. 14¼x14*

434	A290	90c multi	2.00	2.00
435	A291	€1 multi	2.25	2.25

Podujeva A292

No. 436: a, €1, Buildings along Llap River. b, €2, Aerial view of buildings and river.

2020, Jan. 31 Litho. *Perf. 13*

436 A292 Vert. pair, #a-b 6.75 6.75

University of Pristina, 50th Anniv. — A293

2020, Feb. 11 Litho. *Perf. 13*

437 A293 €2 multi 4.50 4.50

Miniature Sheet

Flora A294

No. 438: a, 30c, Sanguisorba albanica. b, 40c, Taxus baccata. c, 50c, Sempervivum kosanini. d, 60c, Halacsya sendtneri. e, 90c, Primula halleri.

2020, Mar. 10 Litho. *Perf. 14¼x14*

438 A294 Sheet of 10, 2 each #438a-438e, + central label — —

Pristina Half-Marathon, 20th Anniv. — A295

2020, May 20 Litho. *Perf. 14x14¼*

439 A295 €1.80 multi 4.00 4.00

Postman Delivering Mail — A296

Horse-drawn Mail Cart — A297

Ship, Train, Carrier Pigeon, Map of Europe A298

2020, June 1 Litho. *Perf. 14x14¼*

440	A296	€1 multi	2.25	2.25
441	A297	€2 multi	4.50	4.50

Souvenir Sheet

442 A298 €2 multi 4.50 4.50

Europa.

Proclamation of the Republic of Kosovo, 30th Anniv. — A299

2020, July 2 Litho. *Perf. 14x14¼*

443 A299 €2 multi 4.75 4.75

Campaign Against Spread of COVID-19 A300

No. 444 — Stylized COVID-19 viruses and: a, Globe, protective face masks on hearts. b, Protective face mask on dove. c, Protective face mask on map of Kosovo, hands and water droplets.

2020, Aug. 14 Litho. *Perf. 14x14¼*

444		Horiz. strip of 3	5.50	5.50
a.	A300	30c multi	.75	.75
b.	A300	90c multi	2.25	2.25
c.	A300	€1 multi	2.40	2.40

Printed in sheets of 6 containing two each of Nos. 444a-444c.

First Albanian School, Stubell — A301

2020, Sept. 1 Litho. *Perf. 14x14¼*

445 A301 €2.10 multi 5.00 5.00

Paintings by Tahir Emra — A302

Various unnamed paintings.

2020, Sept. 22 Litho. *Perf. 14x14¼*

446		Horiz. strip of 3	6.50	6.50
a.	A302	80c multi	1.90	1.90
b.	A302	90c multi	2.10	2.10
c.	A302	€1 multi	2.40	2.40

Heroine of Kosovo — A303

2020, Oct. 22 Litho. *Perf. 14¼x14*

447 A303 €2.10 multi — —

Lakes A304

No. 448 — Various lakes: a, €1.30. b, €2.10

2020, Nov. 5 Litho. *Perf. 14x14¼*

448 A304 Horiz. pair, #a-b 8.25 8.25

Children's Day — A305

No. 449 — Children: a, €1, With kites and balloons. b, €1.80, Playing with balls.

2020, Nov. 24 Litho. *Perf. 14x14¼*

449 A305 Vert. pair, #a-b 6.75 6.75

Holy Archangels Monastery, Prizren — A306

2020. Dec. 10 Litho. *Perf. 14x14¼*

450 A306 €1.80 multi 4.50 4.50

Pansy — A307

Roses — A308

Flowers — A309

2020, Dec. 10 Litho. *Perf. 14¼x14*

451	A307	10c multi	.25	.25
452	A308	15c multi	.40	.40
453	A309	20c multi	.50	.50
		Nos. 451-453 (3)	1.15	1.15

Tribute to Medical Personnel Working During the COVID-19 Pandemic A310

2021, Jan. 28 Litho. *Perf. 14*

454 A310 €2.10 multi 5.25 5.25

A311

Skenderaj A312

2021, Feb. 8 Litho. *Perf. 14x14¼*

455	A311	€1 multi	2.40	2.40
456	A312	€2 multi	5.00	5.00

Protests for Republic Status in Yugoslavia and Human Rights, 40th Anniv. — A313

2021, Mar. 11 Litho. *Perf. 14x14¼*

457 A313 €1.80 multi 4.25 4.25

Theater Personalities — A314

No. 458: a, Besim Sahatçiu (1935-2005), director. b, Leze Qena (1935-2020), actress.

2021, Mar. 25 Litho. *Perf. 14¼x14*
458 A314 €1.30 Pair, #a-b 6.25 6.25

Siqeva Spring — A315

Gorozhupi Spring — A316

King's Spring — A317

2021, Apr. 7 Litho. *Perf. 14x14¼*
459 Horiz. strip of 3 5.75 5.75
a. A315 60c multi 1.50 1.50
b. A316 80c multi 2.00 2.00
c. A317 90c multi 2.25 2.25

Roe Deer — A317a

2021, May 7 Litho. *Perf. 14x14¼*
459D A317a €1 multi 2.50 2.50

Europa.

Endangered Animals — A318

Designs: €1, Roe deer. No. 461, Brown bear.
No. 462, Roe deer, diff.

2021, May 7 Litho. *Perf. 14x14¼*
460 A318 €1 multi 2.50 2.50
461 A318 €2 multi 5.00 5.00

Souvenir Sheet

462 A318 €2 multi 5.00 5.00

Europa.

Fruits — A319

No. 463: a, Miedra (raspberries). b, Dredheza (wild strawberries). c, Qershiza (wild blueberries).

€2, Wild strawberries, wild blueberries, and raspberries, horiz.

2021, June 4 Litho. *Perf. 14¼x14*
463 Strip of 3 6.50 6.50
a. A319 80c multi 1.90 1.90
b. A319 90c multi 2.10 2.10
c. A319 €1 multi 2.40 2.40

Souvenir Sheet

Perf. 14x14¼

464 A319 €2 multi 4.75 4.75

Traditional Games — A320

No. 465: a, €1.30, Stick throwing. b, €1.80, Rock throwing.

2021, July 2 Litho. *Perf. 14x14¼*
465 A320 Pair, #a-b 7.50 7.50

2020 Summer Olympics, Tokyo — A321

No. 466: a, €1, Judokas, Olympic rings. b, €2.10, Judokas, flag of Kosovo.
€2, Wrestling.

2021, July 20 Litho. *Perf. 14x14¼*
466 A321 Pair, #a-b 7.50 7.50

Souvenir Sheet

467 A321 €2 multi 4.75 4.75

The 2020 Summer Olympics were postponed until 2021 because of the COVID-19 pandemic.

Columba Illyrica — A322

2021, Aug. 17 Litho. *Perf. 14*
468 A322 €2.10 multi 5.00 5.00

Independence Referendum, 30th Anniv. — A323

2021, Sept. 26 Litho. *Perf. 14*
469 A323 €2.10 multi 5.00 5.00

COVID-19 Vaccination Campaign A324

No. 470 — Hypodermic needle and: a, Man and woman. b, Teacher with books. c, Mother and infant. d, Pregnant woman.

2021, Oct. 8 Litho. *Perf. 14*
470 Horiz. strip or block of 4 4.25 4.25
a. A324 30c multi .70 .70
b. A324 40c multi .90 .90
c. A324 50c multi 1.25 1.25
d. A324 60c multi 1.40 1.40

Stamps With White Frames

471 A324 30c Like #470a — —
472 A324 40c Like #470b — —
473 A324 50c Like #470c — —
474 A324 60c Like #470d — —

A325

Handcrafted Items — A326

No. 475: a, €1, Hats. b, €2, Horse collars.
No. 476, €2, Hands sewing fabric.

2021, Dec. 10 Litho. *Perf. 14*
475 A325 Pair, #a-b 7.00 7.00

Souvenir Sheet

476 A326 €2 multi 4.50 4.50

No. 475 was printed in sheets of 6 containing 3 each of Nos. 475a-475b.

Art By Simon Shiroka (1927-94) — A327

No. 477 — Various unnamed works of art with denominations of: a, 60c. b, €1. c, €1.30.

2021, Nov. 4 Litho. *Perf. 14*
477 A327 Horiz. strip of 3, #a-c 6.75 6.75

Carvings by Luan Mulliqi A328

No. 478 — Various unnamed works of art with denominations of: a, 50c. b, 80c. c, €1. d, €1.30.

2022, Jan. 31 Litho. *Perf. 14*
478 A328 Block of 4, #a-d 8.25 8.25

2022 Winter Olympics, Beijing — A329

Designs: €1, Skier. €2.10, Ski jumper, snowboarder, figure skaters, speed skaters.
€2, Skiers.

2022, Feb. 17 Litho. *Perf. 14*
479-480 A329 Set of 2 7.00 7.00

Souvenir Sheet

481 A329 €2 multi 4.50 4.50

Lipjan A330

No. 482: a, €1, Aerial view of Lipjan. b, €2, Church of the Presentation, Lipjan.

2022, Mar. 9 Litho. *Perf. 14*
482 A330 Pair, #a-b 6.75 6.75

Legend of Rozafa A332

Gogomeli the Scarecrow A333

Legend of the Old Woman's Tears A334

2022, May 9 Litho. *Perf. 14¼x14*
484 A332 €1 multi 2.25 2.25
485 A333 €2 multi 4.25 4.25

Souvenir Sheet

Perf. 14x14¼

486 A334 €2 multi 4.25 4.25

Europa.

Presidential and Parliamentary Elections, 30th Anniv. — A335

2022, May 24 Litho. *Perf. 14x14¼*
487 A335 €2.10 multi 4.50 4.50

Tahir Zemaj (1952-2003), Commander-in-Chief of Armed Forces of Republic of Kosovo — A336

Mehe Uka (1962-96), Teacher and Hero of Kosovo A337

Tahir Meha (1943-81), Liberation Activist A338

Ismet Rrahmani (1962-98), Teacher and Liberation Activist — A339

2022, June 12 Litho. *Perf. 14¼x14*
488 A336 €1.30 multi 2.75 2.75
489 A337 €1.30 multi 2.75 2.75
490 A338 €1.30 multi 2.75 2.75
491 A339 €1.30 multi 2.75 2.75
Nos. 488-491 (4) 11.00 11.00

Global Peace — A340

2022, June 20 Litho. *Perf. 14x14¼*
492 A340 €2.10 multi 4.50 4.50

A341

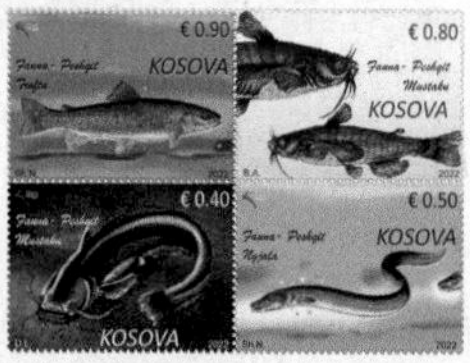

Fish A342

Designs: Nos. 493, 494a, 40c, Mustaku (one catfish). No. 494b, 50c, Ngjala (eels). No. 494c, 80c, Mustaku (two catfish). No. 494d, 90c, Trofta (trout).

2022, July 29 Litho. *Perf. 14x14¼*
493 A341 40c multi .85 .85
494 A342 Block or horiz. strip of 4, #a-d 5.50 5.50

Dua Lipa, Singer, Model and Philanthropist — A343

2022, Aug. 7 Litho. *Perf. 14¼x14*
495 A343 €1.80 multi 3.75 3.75

Kosovo Ballet, 50th Anniv. — A344

No. 496 — "50" and: a, €1.30, Photograph of ballerina. b, €1.80, Drawing of ballerina.

2022, Sept. 1 Litho. *Perf. 14x14¼*
496 A344 Pair, #a-b 6.25 6.25

School Classroom A345

2022, Sept. 20 Litho. *Perf. 14x14¼*
497 A345 €2 multi 4.00 4.00

Naim Frasheri Association of Albanian Teachers, 30th anniv.

Doors of Prizren A346

No. 498: a, 90c, Door with metal knocker. b, €1, Doors.

2022, Oct. 10 Litho. *Perf. 14¼x14*
498 A346 Pair, #a-b 3.75 3.75

A347

A348

Mountain Log Cabins A349

2022, Nov. 15 Litho. *Perf. 14x14¼*
499 A347 90c multi 1.90 1.90
500 A348 €2 multi 4.25 4.25

Souvenir Sheet

501 A349 €2 multi 4.25 4.25

KUWAIT

ku-'wāt

LOCATION — Northwestern coast of the Persian Gulf
GOVT. — Sheikdom
AREA — 7,000 sq. mi.
POP. — 1,991,115 (1999 est.)
CAPITAL — Kuwait

Kuwait was under British protection until June 19, 1961, when it became a fully independent state.

16 Annas = 1 Rupee
100 Naye Paise = 1 Rupee (1957)
1000 Fils = 1 Kuwaiti Dinar (1961)

Catalogue values for unused stamps in this country are for Never Hinged items, beginning with Scott 72 in the regular postage section, Scott C5 in the air post section, and Scott J1 in the postage due section.

There was a first or trial setting of the overprint with the word "Koweit." Twenty-four sets of regular and official stamps were printed with this spelling. Value for set, *$55,000.*

Catalogue values for Nos. 1-71 used, are for postally used examples. Stamps with telegraph cancellations are worth less.

Iraqi Postal Administration

Stamps of India, 1911-23, Overprinted

a

b

1923-24 Wmk. 39 *Perf. 14*
1 A47(a) ½a green 4.75 *15.00*
a. Double overprint 400.00
b. Vertical pair, one without overprint *2,200.*
2 A48(a) 1a dk brn 8.00 *5.50*
a. Double overprint 550.00
b. Vertical pair, one without overprint *2,750.*
3 A58(a) 1½a choc 6.75 *13.50*
4 A49(a) 2a violet 5.75 *9.50*
a. 2a reddish purple 15.50
5 A57(a) 2a6p ultra 4.25 *8.75*
6 A51(a) 3a brn org 5.00 *26.50*
7 A51(a) 3a ultra ('24) 12.50 *4.50*
8 A52(a) 4a ol green 11.50 *27.00*
9 A53(a) 6a bister 13.00 *16.00*
10 A54(a) 8a red vio 12.00 *57.50*
11 A55(a) 12a claret 16.00 *62.50*
12 A56(b) 1r grn & red brn 50.00 *55.00*
a. 1r dp turq grn & org brown 62.00 80.00
13 A56(b) 2r brn & car rose 67.50 *120.00*
14 A56(b) 5r vio & ultra 140.00 *275.00*
15 A56(b) 10r car & grn 275.00 *600.00*
Nos. 1-15 (15) 632.00 *1,296.*

Overprint "a" on India No. 102 is generally considered unofficial.

Nos. 1-4, 6-7 exist with inverted overprint. None of these are believed to have been sold at the Kuwait post office.

For overprints see Nos. O1-O13.

1926-35 India Stamps Overprinted — c

1929-37 Wmk. 196
17 A47 ½a green 6.50 3.00
18 A71 ½a green ('34) 11.00 2.00
19 A48 1a dark brown 7.75 4.00
20 A72 1a dk brown ('34) 16.50 1.25
21 A60 2a dk violet 9.50 2.00
22 A60 2a vermilion 27.50 *95.00*
23 A49 2a ver ('34) 17.50 6.75
a. Small die 8.75 3.00
24 A51 3a ultramarine 6.00 3.50
25 A51 3a car rose ('34) 9.00 4.50
26 A61 4a olive green 40.00 *100.00*
27 A52 4a ol green ('34) 17.50 *14.50*
28 A53 6a bister ('37) 27.50 *70.00*
29 A54 8a red violet 10.00 15.00
30 A55 12a claret 35.00 *50.00*

Overprinted — d

31 A56 1r grn & brn 27.50 *50.00*
32 A56 2r orange & carmine 25.00 *75.00*
33 A56 5r dk vio & ultra ('37) 145.00 *325.00*
34 A56 10r car & grn ('34) 325.00 *550.00*
35 A56 15r ol grn & ultra ('37) 1,000. *1,300.*
Nos. 17-35 (19) 1,764. *2,672.*

For overprints see Nos. O15-O25.

Stamps of India, 1937, Overprinted Type "c" or "d"

1939 Wmk. 196 *Perf. 13½x14*
45 A80(c) ½a brown 4.25 *3.50*
46 A80(c) 1a carmine 4.25 *3.50*
47 A81(c) 2a scarlet 4.50 *5.00*
48 A81(c) 3a yel green 6.00 3.25
49 A81(c) 4a dark brown 25.00 *30.00*
50 A81(c) 6a peacock blue 16.00 *20.00*
51 A81(c) 8a blue violet 17.50 *35.00*
52 A81(c) 12a car lake 12.00 *85.00*
53 A82(d) 1r brown & slate 16.00 *8.75*
a. Elongated "T" 675.00 725.00
54 A82(d) 2r dk brn & dk vio 5.00 *27.50*
a. Elongated "T" 700.00 1,200.
55 A82(d) 5r dp ultra & dk green 12.00 *30.00*
a. Elongated "T" 1,100. 2,100.
56 A82(d) 10r rose car & dk violet 50.00 *100.00*
a. Double overprint 650.00 —
b. Elongated "T" 1,600.
57 A82(d) 15r dk grn & dk brn 75.00 *225.00*
a. Elongated "T" 3,750.
Nos. 45-57 (13) 247.50 *576.50*
Set, never hinged 400.00

The elongated "T" variety was corrected in later printings.

Indian Postal Administration

From May 24, 1941, until August 1947, the Kuwaiti postal service was administered by India, and during 1941-45 unoverprinted Indian stamps were used in Kuwait.

Kuwait postal services were administered by Pakistan from August 1947 through March 1948. Control was transferred to Great Britain on April 1, 1948.

Stamps of India 1940-43, Overprinted in Black

1945 Wmk. 196 *Perf. 13½x14*
59 A83 3p slate 2.75 *10.00*
60 A83 ½a rose violet 1.75 *5.50*
61 A83 9p lt green 2.75 *18.50*
62 A83 1a car rose 2.00 *2.50*
63 A84 1½a dark purple 2.75 *11.00*
64 A84 2a scarlet 3.00 *8.50*
65 A84 3a violet 4.00 *16.00*
66 A84 3½a ultramarine 3.75 *17.50*
67 A85 4a chocolate 4.00 *4.75*
68 A85 6a peacock blue 11.00 22.50
69 A85 8a blue violet 5.75 15.00
70 A85 12a car lake 6.00 9.00
71 A81 14a rose violet 11.00 *24.00*
Nos. 59-71 (13) 60.50 *164.75*
Set, never hinged 110.00

Catalogue values for unused stamps in this section, from this point to the end of the section, are for Never Hinged items.

British Postal Administration

See Oman (Muscat) for similar stamps with surcharge of new value only.

Great Britain Nos. 258 to 263, 243 and 248 Surcharged in Black

1948-49 Wmk. 251 *Perf. 14½x14*
72 A101 ½a on ½p grn 6.00 *4.25*
73 A101 1a on 1p ver 6.00 2.50
74 A101 1½a on 1½p lt red brown 6.75 2.50
75 A101 2a on 2p lt org 6.00 2.50
76 A101 2½a on 2½p ultra 6.25 1.25
77 A101 3a on 3p violet 6.25 1.10
a. Pair, one without surcharge *20,000.* —
78 A102 6a on 6p rose lil 6.25 1.00
79 A103 1r on 1sh brn 13.50 2.50

Great Britain Nos. 249A, 250 and 251A Surcharged in Black

Wmk. 259 *Perf. 14*
80 A104 2r on 2sh6p yel grn 14.50 9.00
81 A104 5r on 5sh dull red 19.00 9.00
81A A105 10r on 10sh ultra 95.00 11.50
Nos. 72-81A (11) 185.50 47.10
Set, hinged 123.00

Issued: Nos. 72-81, 4/48; 10r, 7/4/49.

Bars of surcharge at bottom on No. 81A.

Silver Wedding Issue

Great Britain Nos. 267 and 268 Surcharged in Black

Perf. 14½x14, 14x14½

1948 Wmk. 251
82 A109 2½a on 2½p brt ultra 4.50 3.00
83 A110 15r on £1 deep chalky blue 65.00 42.50

Three bars obliterate the original denomination on No. 83.

Olympic Games Issue

Great Britain Nos. 271 to 274 Surcharged "KUWAIT" and New Value in Black

1948 *Perf. 14½x14*
84 A113 2½a on 2½p brt ultra 1.90 4.50
85 A114 3a on 3p dp violet 2.10 4.50
86 A115 6a on 6p red violet 2.25 4.50
87 A116 1r on 1sh dk brown 2.75 4.50
Nos. 84-87 (4) 9.00 18.00

A square of dots obliterates the original denomination on No. 87.

UPU Issue

Great Britain Nos. 276 to 279 Surcharged "KUWAIT", New Value and Square of Dots in Black

1949, Oct. 10
89 A117 2½a on 2½p brt ultra 1.25 *2.50*
90 A118 3a on 3p brt vio 1.50 *3.00*
91 A119 6a on 6p red vio 1.60 *3.00*
92 A120 1r on 1sh brown 1.75 1.75
Nos. 89-92 (4) 6.10 10.25

Great Britain Nos. 280-285 Surcharged Like Nos. 72-79 in Black

1950-51 **Wmk. 251** *Perf. 14½x14*
93 A101 ½a on ½p lt org 2.75 1.50
94 A101 1a on 1p ultra 2.75 1.60
95 A101 1½a on 1½p green 2.75 2.25
96 A101 2a on 2p lt red brown 2.75 1.50
97 A101 2½a on 2½p ver 2.75 2.75
98 A102 4a on 4p ultra ('50) 2.75 1.50

Great Britain Nos. 286-288 Surcharged in Black

Perf. 11x12
Wmk. 259
99 A121 2r on 2sh6p green 24.00 8.75
100 A121 5r on 5sh dl red 30.00 10.00
101 A122 10r on 10sh ultra 50.00 11.00
Nos. 93-101 (9) 120.50 40.85

Longer bars, at lower right, on No. 101.
Issued: 4a, 10/2/50; others, 5/3/51.

Stamps of Great Britain, 1952-54 Surcharged "KUWAIT" and New Value in Black or Dark Blue

1952-54 **Wmk. 298** *Perf. 14½x14*
102 A126 ½a on ½p red org ('53) .30 *3.00*
103 A126 1a on 1p ultra ('53) .30 .25
104 A126 1½a on 1½p green .25 *1.75*
105 A126 2a on 2p red brn ('53) .35 .25
106 A127 2½a on 2½p scarlet .40 *1.75*
107 A127 3a on 3p dk pur (Dk Bl) ('54) .55 .25
108 A128 4a on 4p ultra ('53) 1.60 1.00
109 A129 6a on 6p lilac rose ('54) 2.25 .25
111 A132 12a on 1sh3p dk green ('53) 6.00 2.50
112 A131 1r on 1sh6p dk blue ('53) 4.75 .25
Nos. 102-112 (10) 16.75 11.25

Coronation Issue

Great Britain Nos. 313-316 Surcharged "KUWAIT" and New Value in Black

1953, June 3
113 A134 2½a on 2½p scarlet 3.75 2.00
114 A135 4a on 4p brt ultra 3.25 2.00
115 A136 12a on 1sh3p dk grn 5.00 3.50
116 A137 1r on 1sh6p dk blue 4.00 1.00
Nos. 113-116 (4) 16.00 8.50

Squares of dots obliterate the original denominations on Nos. 115 and 116.

Great Britain Stamps of 1955-56 Surcharged "KUWAIT" and New Value in Black

1955 **Wmk. 308** *Perf. 11x12*
117 A133 2r on 2sh6p dk brown 9.00 3.25
118 A133 5r on 5sh crimson 10.00 8.00
119 A133 10r on 10sh dp ultra 11.00 6.00
Nos. 117-119 (3) 30.00 17.25

The surcharge on Nos. 117-119 exists in two types.

1956 *Perf. 14½x14*
120 A126 ½a on ½p red org .35 *1.75*
121 A126 1a on 1p ultra .50 *3.25*
122 A126 1½a on 1½p green .40 *.85*
123 A126 2a on 2p red brn .40 *.50*
124 A127 2½a on 2½p scar .85 *4.00*
125 A128 4a on 4p ultra 4.75 3.50
126 A129 6a on 6p lil rose 2.25 .40
127 A132 12a on 1sh3p dk grn 10.00 8.00
128 A131 1r on 1sh6p dk bl 12.00 .35
Nos. 120-128 (9) 31.50 *22.60*

Great Britain Nos. 317-325, 328 and 332 Surcharged "KUWAIT" and New Value in Black

1957-58 **Wmk. 308** *Perf. 14½x14*
129 A129 1np on 5p lt brown .35 *.70*
130 A126 3np on ½p red org .75 *4.00*
131 A126 6np on 1p ultra .75 *1.25*
132 A126 9np on 1½p green .75 *3.25*
133 A126 12np on 2p red brn .75 *4.25*
134 A127 15np on 2½p scar, type I .75 *5.50*
a. Type II ('58) 55.00 *115.00*
135 A127 20np on 3p dk pur .80 .45
136 A128 25np on 4p ultra 2.75 3.25
137 A129 40np on 6p lilac rose 1.00 .30
138 A130 50np on 9p dp ol grn 5.75 4.00
139 A132 75np on 1sh3p dk grn 6.50 6.00
Nos. 129-139 (11) 20.90 *32.95*

The arrangement of the surcharge varies on different values; there are three bars through value on No. 138.

Sheik Abdullah
A1

Dhow
A2

Oil Derrick — A3

Designs: 50np, Pipe lines. 75np, Main square, Kuwait. 2r, Dhow, derrick and Sheik. 5r, Mosque and Sheik. 10r, Oil plant at Burgan and Sheik.

Perf. 12½
1959, Feb. 1 **Unwmk.** **Engr.**
140 A1 5np green 1.00 .25
141 A1 10np rose brown .70 .25
142 A1 15np yellow brown .60 .25
143 A1 20np gray violet .60 .25
144 A1 25np vermilion 1.00 .25
145 A1 40np rose claret 4.50 1.25

Perf. 13½x13
146 A2 40np dark blue 1.00 .25
147 A2 50np carmine 1.00 .25
148 A2 75np olive green 1.00 .45

Perf. 14x13½
149 A3 1r claret 1.50 .55
150 A3 2r red brn & dp bl 4.75 1.00
151 A3 5r green 9.00 2.75
152 A3 10r purple 27.50 6.75
Nos. 140-152 (13) 54.15 14.50

No. 140-141 and 145 were issued in 1958 for local use. They became valid for international mail on Feb. 1, 1959, but No. 145 was withdrawn after two weeks.

Sheik Abdullah and Flag — A4

1960, Feb. 25 **Engr.** *Perf. 14*
153 A4 40np olive grn & red .65 .25
154 A4 60np blue & red .95 .30

10th anniv. of the accession of Sheik Sir Abdullah As-Salim As-Sabah.

Types of 1959, Redrawn

Designs: 20f, 3d, Mosque and Sheik. 25f, 100f, Vickers Viscount. 30f, 75f, Dhow, derrick and Sheik. 35f, 90f, Shuwaikh secondary school. 45f, 1d, Wara Hill, Burgan oil field.

1961 *Perf. 12½*
155 A1 1f green .45 .25
156 A1 2f rose brown .45 .25
157 A1 4f yellow brown .45 .25
158 A1 5f gray violet .50 .25
159 A1 8f yellowish orange .50 .25
160 A1 15f rose claret .50 .25

Perf. 14x13½, 13½ (40f, 250f)
161 A3 20f green .55 .25
162 A3 25f blue .75 .25
163 A3 30f red brn & dp bl .80 .25
164 A3 35f ver & black .90 .30
165 A2 40f dark blue 1.00 .30
166 A3 45f violet brown 1.20 .30
167 A3 75f green & sepia 1.75 .75
168 A3 90f ultra & brown 1.60 .65
169 A3 100f rose red 2.60 .30
170 A2 250f olive green 10.00 1.50
171 A3 1d orange 17.50 4.00
172 A3 3d brick red 47.50 25.00
Nos. 155-172 (18) 89.00 35.35

Nos. 165 and 170 are 32x22mm.
Issued: 75f, 90f, 4/27; 35f, 5/8; others, 4/1.

Symbols of Telecommunications
A5

Perf. 11½
1962, Jan. 11 **Unwmk.** **Photo.**
Granite Paper
173 A5 8f blue & black .60 .25
174 A5 20f rose & black 1.40 .60

4th Arab Telecommunications Union Conference.

Mubarakiya School and Sheiks Abdullah and Mubarak
A6

1962, Apr. 15 **Unwmk.** *Perf. 11½*
175 A6 8f gldn brn, blk, org & gold 1.00 .25
176 A6 20f lt blue, blk, org & gold 2.00 .45

50th anniversary of Mubarakiya School.

Arab League Building, Cairo, and Emblem — A7

1962, Apr. 23 *Perf. 13½x13*
177 A7 20f purple .50 .25
178 A7 45f brown 1.50 .65

Arab Publicity Week, Mar. 22-28.

Flag of Kuwait — A8

1962, June 19 *Perf. 11½*
Flag in Green, Black & Red
179 A8 8f black & tan .60 .25
180 A8 20f black & yellow .90 .30
181 A8 45f black & lt blue 1.75 .45
182 A8 90f black & lilac 2.75 1.25
Nos. 179-182 (4) 6.00 2.25

Issued for National Day, June 19.

Malaria Eradication Emblem — A9

1962, Aug. 1 *Perf. 13½x13*
183 A9 4f slate green & yel grn .50 .25
184 A9 25f green & gray 1.50 .75

WHO drive to eradicate malaria.
No. 184 has laurel leaves added and inscription rearranged.

Cogwheel, Oil Wells, Camels and Modern Building
A10

Perf. 11x13
1962, Dec. 8 **Unwmk.** **Litho.**
185 A10 8f multicolored .55 .25
186 A10 20f multicolored .90 .35
187 A10 45f multicolored 1.50 .70
188 A10 75f multicolored 2.75 1.25
Nos. 185-188 (4) 5.70 2.55

Bicentenary of the Sabah dynasty.

Mother and Child — A11

1963, Mar. 21 Photo. *Perf. 14½x14*

189 A11	8f yel, red, blk & green	.40	.25
190 A11	20f blue, red, blk & grn	.50	.40
191 A11	45f lt ol, red, blk & grn	1.15	.70
192 A11	75f gray, red, blk & grn	1.40	.80
	Nos. 189-192 (4)	3.45	2.15

Issued for Mother's Day, Mar. 21, 1963.

Wheat Emblem, Date Palm, Cow and Sheep — A12

1963, Mar. 21 *Perf. 14x14½*

193 A12	4f red brn, lt blue & grn	.60	.25
194 A12	8f brown, yel & green	.75	.40
195 A12	20f red brn, pale vio & green	1.15	.75
196 A12	45f red brn, rose & green	2.00	1.75
	Nos. 193-196 (4)	4.50	3.15

FAO "Freedom from Hunger" campaign.

Test Tube, Oil Drops and Ship — A13

1963, Apr. 15 Photo. *Perf. 14½x14*

197 A13	4f brown, yel & blue	.50	.25
198 A13	20f green, yel & blue	.75	.30
199 A13	45f brt mag, yel & blue	1.75	.65
	Nos. 197-199 (3)	3.00	1.20

Issued for Education Day.

Sheik Abdullah, Flags and Map of Kuwait — A14

1963, June 19 *Perf. 14x13*

Flags in Black, Bright Green & Red; Denominations in Black

200 A14	4f ultramarine	1.40	.65
201 A14	5f ocher	1.75	1.10
202 A14	20f bright purple	6.25	4.75
203 A14	50f olive brn	13.00	6.00
	Nos. 200-203 (4)	22.40	12.50

Second anniversary of National Day.

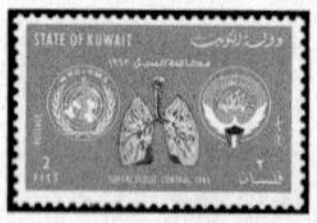

Lungs and Emblems of World Health Organization and Kuwait Tuberculosis Society — A15

1963, July 27 *Perf. 13x13½*

Design in Yellow, Black, Emerald & Red

204 A15	2f ocher	.55	.25
205 A15	4f dark green	.70	.25
206 A15	8f lt violet blue	1.00	.30
207 A15	20f rose brown	2.25	.80
	Nos. 204-207 (4)	4.50	1.60

Issued to publicize tuberculosis control.

Sheik Abdullah, Scroll and Scales of Justice — A16

1963, Oct. 29 Photo. *Perf. 11x13*

Center in Gray

208 A16	4f dp red & red brn	.35	.25
209 A16	8f dk green & red brn	.50	.25
210 A16	20f vio brn & red brn	.75	.30
211 A16	45f brn org & red brn	1.25	.65
212 A16	75f purple & red brown	1.90	1.25
213 A16	90f ultra & red brown	3.00	3.00
	Nos. 208-213 (6)	7.75	5.70

Promulgation of the constitution.

Soccer — A17

Sports: 4f, Basketball. 5f, Swimming, horiz. 8f, Track. 15f, Javelin, horiz. 20f, Pole vault, horiz. 35f, Gymnast on rings, horiz. 45f, Gymnast on parallel bars.

1963, Nov. 8 Unwmk. *Perf. 14½x14*

214 A17	1f multicolored	.35	.25
215 A17	4f multicolored	.35	.25
216 A17	5f multicolored	.35	.25
217 A17	8f multicolored	.60	.25
218 A17	15f multicolored	.80	.35
219 A17	20f multicolored	1.10	.40
220 A17	35f multicolored	2.00	.80
221 A17	45f multicolored	3.50	1.75
	Nos. 214-221 (8)	9.05	4.30

Arab School Games of 1963.

UNESCO Emblem, Scales and Globe — A18

1963, Dec. 10 Litho. *Perf. 13x12½*

222 A18	8f violet, blk & pale grn	.50	.30
223 A18	20f gray, black & yel	1.00	.60
224 A18	25f blue, black & tan	2.25	.90
	Nos. 222-224 (3)	3.75	1.80

15th anniv. of the Universal Declaration of Human Rights.

Sheik Abdullah — A19

Perf. 12½x13

1964, Feb. 1 Unwmk. Photo.

Portrait in Natural Colors

225 A19	1f gray & silver	.25	.25
a.	Booklet pane of 6 ('66)	2.25	
226 A19	2f brt blue & silver	.25	.25
227 A19	4f ocher & silver	.30	.25
a.	Booklet pane of 6 ('66)	2.25	
228 A19	5f fawn & silver	.30	.25
229 A19	8f dk brown & sil	.30	.25
230 A19	10f citron & sil	.40	.25
a.	Booklet pane of 6 ('66)	2.25	
b.	Silver (country name and denomination) omitted	*4,600.*	
231 A19	15f brt green & sil	.75	.25
a.	Booklet pane of 6 ('66)	6.00	
232 A19	20f blue gray & sil	.55	.25
a.	Booklet pane of 6 ('66)	3.75	
b.	Silver (country name and denomination) omitted	*4,900.*	
233 A19	25f green & silver	.65	.30
234 A19	30f gray grn & sil	.75	.30
235 A19	40f brt vio & sil	1.10	.45
236 A19	45f violet & silver	1.20	.55
237 A19	50f olive & silver	1.25	.55
238 A19	70f red lilac & sil	1.50	.65
239 A19	75f rose red & sil	2.00	.80
240 A19	90f ultra & silver	3.00	.80
241 A19	100f pale lilac & sil	3.50	.65

Perf. 14x14½

Size: 25x30mm

242 A19	250f brown & sil	10.00	2.50
243 A19	1d brown vio & sil	35.00	7.00
	Nos. 225-243 (19)	63.05	16.55

Ramses II Battling the Hittites (from Abu Simbel) — A20

Engr. & Litho.

1964, Mar. 8 *Perf. 13x12½*

244 A20	8f buff, ind & maroon	.40	.25
245 A20	20f lt blue, indigo & vio	1.00	.60
246 A20	30f bluish grn, ind & vio	1.60	.70
	Nos. 244-246 (3)	3.00	1.55

UNESCO world campaign to save historic monuments in Nubia.

Mother and Child — A21

1964, Mar. 21 Litho. *Perf. 14x13*

247 A21	8f green, gray & vio blk	.30	.25
248 A21	20f green, red & vio blk	.80	.25
249 A21	30f grn, ol bis & vio blk	1.10	.40
250 A21	45f grn, saph & vio blk	1.40	.70
	Nos. 247-250 (4)	3.60	1.60

Issued for Mother's Day, Mar. 21.

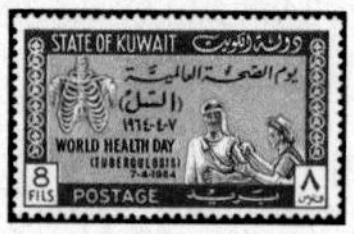

Nurse Giving TB Test, and Thorax — A22

Perf. 13x13½

1964, Apr. 7 Photo. Unwmk.

251 A22	8f brown & green	.60	.25
252 A22	20f green & rose red	1.90	.60

Issued for World Health Day (fight against tuberculosis), Apr. 7, 1964.

Microscope and Dhow — A23

1964, Apr. 15 *Perf. 12½x13*

253 A23	8f multicolored	.55	.25
254 A23	15f multicolored	.65	.25
255 A23	20f multicolored	1.10	.30
256 A23	30f multicolored	1.75	.70
	Nos. 253-256 (4)	4.05	1.50

Issued for Education Day.

Doves and State Seal A24

1964, June 19 Litho. *Perf. 13½*

Seal in Blue, Brown, Black, Red & Green

257 A24	8f black & bister brn	.50	.25
258 A24	20f black & green	.80	.30
259 A24	30f black & gray	1.60	.60
260 A24	45f black & blue	1.75	.85
	Nos. 257-260 (4)	4.65	2.00

Third anniversary of National Day.

Arab Postal Union Emblem — A25

1964, Nov. 21 Photo. *Perf. 11x11½*

261 A25	8f lt blue & brown	.50	.25
262 A25	20f yellow & ultra	.90	.30
263 A25	45f olive & brown	1.60	.90
	Nos. 261-263 (3)	3.00	1.45

Permanent Office of the APU, 10th anniv.

Conference Emblem — A26

1965, Feb. 8 Litho. *Perf. 14*

264 A26	8f black, org brn & yel	1.00	.25
265 A26	20f multicolored	1.50	.30

First Arab Journalists' Conference.

Oil Derrick, Dhow, Sun and Doves — A27

1965, Feb. 25 *Perf. 13½*

266 A27	10f lt green & multi	.40	.25
267 A27	15f pink & multi	.85	.25
268 A27	20f gray & multi	1.50	.50
	Nos. 266-268 (3)	2.75	1.00

Fourth anniversary of National Day.

Mother and Children — A28

1965, Mar. 21 Unwmk. *Perf. 13½*

269 A28	8f multicolored	.50	.25
270 A28	15f multicolored	.80	.45
271 A28	20f multicolored	1.25	.70
	Nos. 269-271 (3)	2.55	1.40

Mother's Day, Mar. 21.

Weather Balloon — A29

1965, Mar. 23 Photo. *Perf. 11½x11*

272 A29	4f deep ultra & yellow	.70	.25
273 A29	5f blue & dp orange	.80	.25
274 A29	20f dk blue & emerald	1.50	1.25
	Nos. 272-274 (3)	3.00	1.75

Fifth World Meteorological Day.

Census Chart, Map and Family — A30

1965, Mar. 28 Litho. *Perf. 13½*

275 A30	8f multicolored	.35	.25
276 A30	20f multicolored	.80	.30
277 A30	50f multicolored	2.10	1.00
	Nos. 275-277 (3)	3.25	1.55

Issued to publicize the 1965 census.

ICY Emblem — A31

1965, Mar. 7 Engr.

278 A31	8f red & black	.60	.25
279 A31	20f lt ultra & black	1.25	.30
280 A31	30f emerald & black	2.50	.60
	Nos. 278-280 (3)	4.35	1.15

International Cooperation Year.

Dagger in Map of Palestine — A31a

Perf. 11x11½

1965, Apr. 9 Photo. Unwmk.

281	A31a	4f red & ultra	2.25	.35
282	A31a	45f red & emerald	4.75	1.40

Deir Yassin massacre, Apr. 9, 1948. See Iraq Nos. 372-373 and Jordan No. 499.

Tower of Shuwaikh School and Atom Symbol — A32

1965, Apr. 15 Litho. *Perf. 14x13*

283	A32	4f multicolored	.40	.25
284	A32	20f multicolored	.90	.45
285	A32	45f multicolored	1.75	1.10
		Nos. 283-285 (3)	3.05	1.80

Issued for Education Day.

ITU Emblem, Old and New Communication Equipment — A33

1965, May 17 *Perf. 13½x14*

286	A33	8f dk blue, lt bl & red	.40	.30
287	A33	20f green, lt grn & red	1.50	.40
288	A33	45f red, pink & blue	3.00	1.50
		Nos. 286-288 (3)	4.90	2.20

ITU, centenary.

Library Aflame and Lamp — A33a

1965, June 7 Photo. *Perf. 11*

289	A33a	8f black, green & red	1.00	.25
290	A33a	15f black, red & green	2.25	.45

Burning of Library of Algiers, June 7, 1962.

Falcon — A34

1965, Dec. 1 Engr. *Perf. 13*
Center in Sepia

291	A34	8f red lilac	2.75	.30
292	A34	15f olive green	2.40	.30
293	A34	20f dark blue	3.50	.60
294	A34	25f orange	3.75	.80
295	A34	30f emerald	4.75	.90
296	A34	45f blue	9.50	1.50
297	A34	50f claret	11.00	1.60
298	A34	90f carmine	19.00	2.75
		Nos. 291-298 (8)	56.65	8.75

Book and Wreath Emblem — A35

1966, Jan. 10 Photo. *Perf. 14x15*

299	A35	8f lt violet & multi	.50	.25
300	A35	20f brown red & multi	.90	.45
301	A35	30f blue & multi	1.60	.75
		Nos. 299-301 (3)	3.00	1.45

Issued for Education Day.

Sheik Sabah al-Salim al-Sabah — A36

1966, Feb. 1 Photo. *Perf. 14x13*

302	A36	4f lt blue & multi	.30	.25
303	A36	5f pale rose & multi	.45	.25
304	A36	20f multicolored	.75	.25
305	A36	30f lt violet & multi	1.10	.35
306	A36	40f salmon & multi	1.40	.50
307	A36	45f lt gray & multi	1.50	.60
308	A36	70f yellow & multi	3.00	1.25
309	A36	90f pale green & multi	4.50	1.75
		Nos. 302-309 (8)	13.00	5.20

Wheat and Fish — A37

1966, Feb. 15 *Perf. 11x11½*

310	A37	20f multicolored	2.75	1.00
311	A37	45f multicolored	4.00	1.75

"Freedom from Hunger" campaign.

Eagle, Banner, Scales and Emblems A38

1966, Feb. 25 Litho. *Perf. 12½x13*

312	A38	20f tan & multi	1.40	.40
313	A38	25f lt green & multi	1.40	.60
314	A38	45f gray & multi	3.25	1.40
		Nos. 312-314 (3)	6.05	2.40

Fifth anniversary of National Day.

Wheel of Industry and Map of Arab Countries — A39

1966, Mar. 1 *Perf. 14x13½*

315	A39	20f brt blue, brt grn & blk	1.00	.30
316	A39	50f lt red brn, brt grn & black	1.75	.80

Issued to publicize the conference on industrial development in Arab countries.

Mother and Children — A40

1966, Mar. 21 *Perf. 11½x11*

317	A40	20f pink & multi	1.00	.30
318	A40	45f multicolored	2.25	.80

Mother's Day, Mar. 21.

Medical Conference Emblem — A41

1966, Apr. 1 Photo. *Perf. 14½x14*

319	A41	15f blue & red	.90	.90
320	A41	30f red & blue	1.60	.90

Fifth Arab Medical Conference, Kuwait.

Composite View of a City — A42

1966, Apr. 7 Litho. *Perf. 12½x13*

321	A42	8f multicolored	1.00	.25
322	A42	10f multicolored	1.75	.30

Issued for World Health Day, Apr. 7.

Inauguration of WHO Headquarters, Geneva — A43

1966, May 3 Litho. *Perf. 11x11½*

323	A43	5f dull sal, ol grn & vio bl	.80	.25
324	A43	10f lt grn, ol grn & vio blue	1.60	.25

Traffic Signal at Night — A44

1966, May 4

325	A44	10f green, red & black	1.00	.25
326	A44	20f green, red & black	1.25	.45

Issued for Traffic Day.

"Blood Transfusion" — A45

1966, May 5 *Perf. 13½*

327	A45	4f multicolored	.90	.25
328	A45	8f multicolored	1.50	.70

Blood Bank Day, May 5.

Sheik Ahmad and Ship Carrying First Crude Oil Shipment — A46

1966, June 30 *Perf. 13½*

329	A46	20f multicolored	1.00	.55
330	A46	45f multicolored	2.25	1.10

20th anniv. of the first crude oil shipment, June 30, 1946.

Ministry of Guidance and Information A47

1966, July 25 Photo. *Perf. 11½x11*

331	A47	4f rose & brown	.40	.25
332	A47	5f yel brn & brt grn	.50	.25
333	A47	8f brt green & purple	.70	.25
334	A47	20f salmon & ultra	1.40	.30
		Nos. 331-334 (4)	3.00	1.05

Opening of Ministry of Guidance and Information Building.

Fishing Boat, Lobster, Fish, Crab and FAO Emblem — A48

1966, Oct. 10 Litho. *Perf. 13½*

335	A48	4f buff & multi	1.25	.25
336	A48	20f lt lilac & multi	3.00	1.10

Fisheries' Conference of Near East Countries under the sponsorship of the FAO, Oct. 1966.

United Nations Flag — A49

1966, Oct. 24 *Perf. 13x14*

337	A49	20f blue, dk blue & pink	1.50	.30
338	A49	45f blue, dk bl & pale grn	2.75	1.40

Issued for United Nations Day.

UNESCO Emblem — A50

1966, Nov. 4 Litho. *Perf. 12½x13*

339	A50	20f multicolored	1.40	.30
340	A50	45f multicolored	2.75	1.25

20th anniversary of UNESCO.

Kuwait University Emblem — A51

1966, Nov. 27 Photo. *Perf. 14½*
Emblem in Yellow, Bright Blue, Green and Gold

341	A51	8f lt ultra, vio & gold	.70	.25
342	A51	10f red, brown & gold	.90	.25
343	A51	20f lt yel grn, slate & gold	2.00	.30
344	A51	45f buff, green & gold	4.00	1.50
		Nos. 341-344 (4)	7.60	2.30

Opening of Kuwait University.

Jabir al-Ahmad al-Jabir and Sheik Sabah — A52

1966, Dec. 11 *Perf. 14x13*

345	A52	8f yel green & multi	.75	.25
346	A52	20f yellow & multi	1.50	.30
347	A52	45f pink & multi	3.75	1.25
		Nos. 345-347 (3)	6.00	1.80

Appointment of the heir apparent, Jabir al-Ahmad al-Jabir.

Scout Badge and Square Knot — A52a

1966, Dec. 21 Litho. *Perf. 14x13*

347A	A52a	4f lt ol green & fawn	1.75	.45
347B	A52a	20f yel brn & blue grn	5.00	1.50

Kuwait Boy Scouts, 30th anniversary.

"Symbols of Science and Peace" — A53

1967, Jan. 15 Litho. *Perf. 13x14*

348	A53	10f multicolored	1.25	.25
349	A53	45f multicolored	4.75	.65

Issued for Education Day.

Fertilizer Plant — A54

1967, Feb. 19 Unwmk. *Perf. 13*

350 A54 8f lt blue & multi 1.00 .25
351 A54 20f cream & multi 2.50 .45

Opening of Chemical Fertilizer Plant.

Sun, Dove and Olive Branch — A55

1967, Feb. 25 Litho. *Perf. 13*

352 A55 8f salmon & multi 1.25 .25
353 A55 20f yellow & multi 3.00 .45

Sixth anniversary of National Day.

Map of Arab States and Municipal Building — A56

1967, Mar. 11 *Perf. 14½x13*

354 A56 20f gray & multi 1.50 .60
355 A56 30f lt brown & multi 2.75 1.50

1st conf. of the Arab Cities Org., Kuwait.

Family — A57

1967, Mar. 21 Litho. *Perf. 13x13½*

356 A57 20f pale rose & multi 1.50 .60
357 A57 45f pale green & multi 3.00 1.50

Issued for Family Day, Mar. 21.

Arab League Emblem — A58

1967, Mar. 27 *Perf. 13x14*

358 A58 8f gray & dk blue 1.00 .25
359 A58 10f bister & green 2.00 .25

Issued for Arab Publicity Week.

Sabah Hospital and Physicians at Work — A59

1967, Apr. 7 *Perf. 14x13*

360 A59 8f dull rose & multi 1.50 .25
361 A59 20f gray & multi 2.50 .65

Issued for World Health Day.

Two Heads of Ramses II — A60

1967, Apr. 17 *Perf. 13½*

362 A60 15f citron, green & brn 1.50 .30
363 A60 20f chalky blue, grn & pur 2.50 .65

Arab Week to Save the Nubian Monuments.

Traffic Policeman A61

1967, May 4 Litho. *Perf. 14x13*

364 A61 8f lt green & multi 2.00 .35
365 A61 20f rose lilac & multi 4.25 .85

Issued for Traffic Day.

ITY Emblem — A62

1967, June 4 Photo. *Perf. 13*

366 A62 20f Prus blue, lt bl & blk 1.25 .30
367 A62 45f rose lilac, lt bl & blk 2.75 1.25

International Tourist Year.

Arab League Emblem and Hands Reaching for Knowledge — A63

1967, Sept. 8 Litho. *Perf. 13x14*

368 A63 8f blue & multi 1.75 .25
369 A63 20f dull rose & multi 3.25 .75

Issued to publicize the literacy campaign.

Map of Palestine and UN Emblem — A64

1967, Oct. 24 Litho. *Perf. 13*

370 A64 20f blue & pink 2.25 .30
371 A64 45f orange & pink 5.00 1.00

Issued for United Nations Day.

Factory and Cogwheels A65

1967, Nov. 25 Photo. *Perf. 13*

372 A65 20f crimson & yellow 1.50 .30
373 A65 45f gray & yellow 2.75 1.50

3rd Conf. of Arab Labor Ministers, Kuwait.

Flag and Open Book — A66

1968, Jan. 15 Litho. *Perf. 14*

374 A66 20f brt blue & multi 1.25 .30
375 A66 45f yel orange & multi 3.50 1.25

Issued for Education Day.

Map of Kuwait and Oil Derrick — A67

1968, Feb. 23 Litho. *Perf. 12*

376 A67 10f multicolored 1.25 .35
377 A67 20f multicolored 3.50 1.25

30th anniv. of the discovery of oil in the Greater Burgan Field.

Sheik Sabah and Sun — A68

1968, Feb. 25 Litho. *Perf. 14x15*

378 A68 8f red lilac & multi .90 .25
379 A68 10f lt blue & multi 1.00 .25
380 A68 15f violet & multi 1.25 .25
381 A68 20f vermilion & multi 1.60 .35
Nos. 378-381 (4) 4.75 1.10

Seventh anniversary of National Day.

Open Book and Emblem — A69

1968, Mar. 2 *Perf. 14*

382 A69 8f yellow & multi .50 .25
383 A69 20f lilac rose & multi 1.25 .25
384 A69 45f orange & multi 2.25 1.25
Nos. 382-384 (3) 4.00 1.75

Issued for Teachers' Day.

Family Picnic — A70

1968, Mar. 21 *Perf. 13½x13*

385 A70 8f blue & multi .60 .25
386 A70 10f red & multi .90 .25
387 A70 15f lilac & multi 1.00 .25
388 A70 20f dk brown & multi 1.75 .25
Nos. 385-388 (4) 4.25 1.00

Issued for Family Day.

Sheik Sabah, Arms of WHO and Kuwait A71

1968, Apr. 7 Photo. *Perf. 12*

389 A71 20f brt lilac & multi 1.75 .65
390 A71 45f multicolored 4.25 1.50

20th anniv. of WHO.

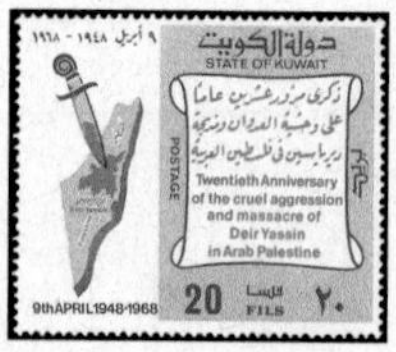

Dagger in Map of Palestine A72

1968, Apr. 9 Litho. *Perf. 14*

391 A72 20f lt blue & vermilion 3.00 .70
392 A72 45f lilac & vermilion 5.25 1.25

Deir Yassin massacre, 20th anniv.

Street Crossing — A74

1968, May 4 Photo. *Perf. 14x14½*

395 A74 10f dk brown & multi 1.10 .50
396 A74 15f brt violet & multi 1.60 .75
397 A74 20f green & multi 2.75 1.00
Nos. 395-397 (3) 5.45 2.25

Issued for Traffic Day.

Map of Palestine and Torch — A75

1968, May 15 Litho. *Perf. 13½x12½*

398 A75 10f lt ultra & multi 1.25 .50
399 A75 20f yellow & multi 3.00 .65
400 A75 45f aqua & multi 5.25 2.10
Nos. 398-400 (3) 9.50 3.25

Issued for Palestine Day.

Palestinian Refugees A76

1968, June 5 Litho. *Perf. 13x13½*

401 A76 20f pink & multi .75 .25
402 A76 30f ultra & multi 1.25 .50
403 A76 45f green & multi 2.00 .65
404 A76 90f lilac & multi 4.25 2.00
Nos. 401-404 (4) 8.25 3.40

International Human Rights Year.

Museum of Kuwait — A77

Perf. 12½

1968, Aug. 25 Unwmk. Engr.

405 A77 1f dk brown & brt grn .60 .25
406 A77 2f dp claret & grn .60 .25
407 A77 5f black & orange .60 .25
408 A77 8f dk brown & grn .60 .25
409 A77 10f Prus blue & cl .90 .25
410 A77 20f org brown & blue 1.50 .25
411 A77 25f dk blue & orange 1.75 .25
412 A77 30f Prus blue & yel grn 2.25 .30
413 A77 45f plum & vio black 3.50 .70
414 A77 50f green & carmine 4.00 1.25
Nos. 405-414 (10) 16.30 4.00

Man Reading Book, Arab League, UN and UNESCO Emblems — A78

1968, Sept. 8 Litho. *Perf. 12½x13*

415 A78 15f blue gray & multi .75 .25
416 A78 20f pink & multi 2.00 .30

Issued for International Literacy Day.

Map of Palestine on UN Building and Children with Tent — A79

1968, Oct. 25 Litho. *Perf. 13*

417 A79 20f multicolored .65 .25
418 A79 30f gray & multi .95 .50
419 A79 45f salmon pink & multi 1.40 .60
Nos. 417-419 (3) 3.00 1.35

Issued for United Nations Day.

Kuwait Chamber of Commerce — A80

1968, Nov. 6 Litho. *Perf. 13½x12½*

420 A80 10f dp orange & dk brn .80 .25
421 A80 15f rose claret & vio bl .90 .25
422 A80 20f brown org & dk green 1.25 .50
Nos. 420-422 (3) 2.95 1.00

Opening of the Kuwait Chamber of Commerce Building.

Conference Emblem — A81

1968, Nov. 10 Litho. *Perf. 13*

Emblem in Ocher, Blue, Red and Black

423 A81 10f dk brown & blue .60 .25
424 A81 15f dk brown & orange .75 .25
425 A81 20f dk brown & vio blue .90 .50
426 A81 30f dk brown & org brn 1.25 .60
Nos. 423-426 (4) 3.50 1.60

14th Conference of the Arab Chambers of Commerce, Industry and Agriculture.

Shuaiba Refinery — A82

1968, Nov. 18 *Perf. 13½*

Emblem in Red, Black and Blue

427 A82 10f black & lt blue grn .65 .25
428 A82 20f black & gray 1.20 .40
429 A82 30f black & salmon 1.40 .65
430 A82 45f black & emerald 2.50 1.20
Nos. 427-430 (4) 5.75 2.50

Opening of Shuaiba Refinery.

Koran, Scales and People — A83

1968, Dec. 19 Photo. *Perf. 14x14½*

431 A83 8f multicolored .55 .25
432 A83 20f multicolored 1.25 .60
433 A83 30f multicolored 1.90 .85
434 A83 45f multicolored 2.25 1.25
Nos. 431-434 (4) 5.95 2.95

The 1400th anniversary of the Koran.

Boeing 707 — A84

1969, Jan. 1 Litho. *Perf. 13½x14*

435 A84 10f brt yellow & multi .80 .25
436 A84 20f green & multi 1.10 .55
437 A84 25f multicolored 1.60 .85
438 A84 45f lilac & multi 3.00 1.10
Nos. 435-438 (4) 6.50 2.75

Introduction of Boeing 707 service by Kuwait Airways.

Globe, Retort and Triangle A85

1969, Jan. 15 *Perf. 13*

439 A85 15f gray & multi 1.25 .30
440 A85 20f multicolored 1.25 .70

Issued for Education Day.

Kuwait Hilton Hotel — A86

1969, Feb. 15 Litho. *Perf. 14x12½*

441 A86 10f brt blue & multi .90 .25
442 A86 20f pink & multi 1.50 .35

Opening of the Kuwait Hilton Hotel.

Teachers' Society Emblem, Father and Children — A87

1969, Feb. 15 *Perf. 13*

443 A87 10f violet & multi .75 .25
444 A87 20f rose & multi 1.50 .40

Issued for Education week.

Wreath, Flags and Dove — A88

1969, Feb. 25 Photo. *Perf. 14½x14*

445 A88 15f lilac & multi .60 .25
446 A88 20f blue & multi 1.00 .35
447 A88 30f ocher & multi 1.40 .60
Nos. 445-447 (3) 3.00 1.20

Eighth anniversary of National Day.

Emblem, Teacher and Students — A89

1969, Mar. 8 Litho. *Perf. 13x12½*

448 A89 10f multicolored .90 .25
449 A89 20f deep red & multi 1.50 .60

Issued for Teachers' Day.

Family — A90

1969, Mar. 21 *Perf. 13½*

450 A90 10f dark blue & multi .80 .25
451 A90 20f deep car & multi 1.60 .35

Issued for Family Day.

Avicenna, WHO Emblem, Patient and Microscope — A91

1969, Apr. 7 Litho. *Perf. 13½*

452 A91 15f red brown & multi 1.50 .25
453 A91 20f lt green & multi 3.50 .35

Issued for World Health Day, Apr. 7.

Motorized Traffic Police — A92

1969, May 4 Litho. *Perf. 12½x13*

454 A92 10f multicolored 2.00 .25
455 A92 20f multicolored 4.00 .65

Issued for Traffic Day.

ILO Emblem — A93

1969, June 1 *Perf. 11½*

456 A93 10f red, black & gold .60 .25
457 A93 20f lt blue grn, blk & gold 1.40 .35

50th anniv. of the ILO.

S.S. Al Sabahiah — A94

1969, June 10 Litho. *Perf. 13½*

458 A94 20f multicolored 1.50 .60
459 A94 45f multicolored 3.50 1.60

4th anniversary of Kuwait Shipping Co.

UNESCO Emblem, Woman, Globe and Book — A95

1969, Sept. 8 Litho. *Perf. 13½*

460 A95 10f blue & multi .60 .25
461 A95 20f rose red & multi 1.40 .50

International Literacy Day, Sept. 8.

Sheik Sabah — A96

1969-74 Litho. *Perf. 14*

462 A96 8f lt blue & multi .40 .25
463 A96 10f pink & multi .45 .25
464 A96 15f gray & multi .50 .25
465 A96 20f yellow & multi .55 .25
466 A96 25f violet & multi .75 .30
467 A96 30f sal & multi 1.00 .35
468 A96 45f tan & multi 1.50 .50
469 A96 50f yel grn & multi 1.60 .50
470 A96 70f multicolored 1.90 .75
471 A96 75f ultra & multi 2.50 .90
472 A96 90f pale rose & multi 2.50 1.00
a. 90f brownish rose & multi 2.50 1.00
473 A96 250f lilac & multi 8.00 2.75
473A A96 500f gray green & multi 19.00 7.00
473B A96 1d lilac rose & multi 32.50 11.00
Nos. 462-473B (14) 73.15 26.05

Issued: Nos. 473A-473B, 1/12/74; others 10/5/69.

UN Emblem and Scroll — A97

1969, Oct. 24 Litho. *Perf. 13*

474 A97 10f emer & multi .70 .25
475 A97 20f bister & multi 1.35 .30
476 A97 45f rose red & multi 3.50 1.10
Nos. 474-476 (3) 5.55 1.65

Issued for United Nations Day.

Radar, Satellite Earth Station, Kuwait — A98

Design: 45f, Globe and radar, vert.

1969, Dec. 15 Photo. *Perf. 14½*

477 A98 20f silver & multi 1.75 .30
478 A98 45f silver & multi 3.75 1.10

Inauguration of the Kuwait Earth Station for Satellite Communications.

Globe with Science Symbols, and Education Year Emblem — A99

1970, Jan. 15 Photo. *Perf. 13½x13*

479 A99 20f brt lilac & multi 1.00 .30
480 A99 45f blue & multi 2.00 1.00

International Education Year.

Shoue — A100

Old Kuwaiti Vessels: 10f, Sambook. 15f, Baghla. 20f, Batteel. 25f, Boom. 45f, Bakkara. 50f, Shipbuilding.

1970, Feb. 1 *Perf. 14½x14*

481 A100 8f multicolored .60 .30
482 A100 10f multicolored .65 .40
483 A100 15f multicolored 1.10 .50
484 A100 20f multicolored 1.60 .65
485 A100 25f multicolored 2.00 .75
486 A100 45f multicolored 3.00 1.40
487 A100 50f multicolored 3.75 1.60
Nos. 481-487 (7) 12.70 5.60

Refugee Father and Children — A101

1970 Photo. *Perf. 14x12½*

488 A101 20f red brown & multi 2.50 .65
489 A101 45f olive & multi 5.00 2.00

Issued for Universal Palestinian Refugees Week, Dec. 16-22, 1969.

Kuwait Flag, Emblem and Sheik Sabah — A102

1970, Feb. 25 *Perf. 13½x13*

490 A102 15f silver & multi 1.00 .30
491 A102 20f gold & multi 1.40 .30

Ninth anniversary of National Day.

Dome of the Rock, Jerusalem, and Boy Commando A103

Designs: 20f, Dome and man commando. 45f, Dome and woman commando.

1970, Mar. 4 Litho. *Perf. 13*

492 A103 10f pale violet & multi 1.75 .85
493 A103 20f lt blue & multi 3.50 1.75
494 A103 45f multicolored 7.25 3.75
Nos. 492-494 (3) 12.50 6.35

Honoring Palestinian commandos.

Parents and Children A104

1970, Mar. 21 *Perf. 14*

495 A104 20f multicolored .75 .25
496 A104 30f pink & multi 1.50 .35

Issued for Family Day.

Map of Arab League Countries, Flag and Emblem
A104a

1970, Mar. 22 ***Perf. 11½x11***

497 A104a 20f lt blue, grn & lt brn .90 .25
498 A104a 45f sal, grn & dk pur 1.60 .60

25th anniversary of the Arab League.

Census Graph and Kuwait Arms — A105

1970, Apr. 1 **Litho.** ***Perf. 13½x13***

499 A105 15f dull orange & multi .60 .25
500 A105 20f yellow & multi .80 .45
501 A105 30f pink & multi 1.10 .55
Nos. 499-501 (3) 2.50 1.25

Issued to publicize the 1970 census.

"Fight Cancer," Kuwait Arms, WHO Emblem — A106

1970, Apr. 7 ***Perf. 13½x13***

502 A106 20f blue, vio bl & rose lil 1.50 .50
503 A106 30f dl yel, vio bl & lil rose 1.75 .70

World Health Organization Day, Apr. 7, and to publicize the fight against cancer.

Traffic Signs — A107

1970, May 4 **Photo.** ***Perf. 13½***

504 A107 20f multicolored 2.00 .65
505 A107 30f multicolored 2.75 1.10

Issued for Traffic Day.

Red Crescent — A108

1970, May 8 **Litho.** ***Perf. 12½x13½***

506 A108 10f yellow & multi .60 .25
507 A108 15f emerald & multi 1.40 .45
508 A108 30f tan & multi 3.00 .80
Nos. 506-508 (3) 5.00 1.50

Intl. Red Crescent and Red Cross Day.

Opening of UPU Headquarters, Bern — A109

1970, May 25 **Photo.** ***Perf. 12x11½***

509 A109 20f multicolored 1.25 .30
510 A109 30f multicolored 1.75 .75

Sheik Sabah — A110

1970, June 15 **Photo.** ***Perf. 14***

511 A110 20f silver & multi 1.60 .50
512 A110 45f gold & multi 3.25 1.00
a. Miniature sheet of 2 8.50 5.00

Nos. 511-512 have circular perforation around vignette set within a white square of paper, perforated on 4 sides. No. 512a contains 2 imperf. stamps similar to Nos. 511-512.

UN Emblem, Symbols of Peace, Progress, Justice — A111

1970, July 1 **Litho.** ***Perf. 13½x12½***

513 A111 20f lt green & multi .75 .25
514 A111 45f multicolored 1.50 .55

25th anniversary of the United Nations.

Tanker Loading Crude Oil from Sea Island — A112

1970, Aug. 1 ***Perf. 13½x13***

515 A112 20f multicolored 1.75 .50
516 A112 45f multicolored 3.25 1.10

Issued to publicize the artificial "Sea Island" loading facilities in Kuwait.

"Writing," Kuwait and UN Emblems — A113

1970, Sept. 8 **Photo.** ***Perf. 13½***

517 A113 10f brt blue & multi 1.25 .25
518 A113 15f brt green & multi 1.50 .55

International Literacy Day, Sept. 8.

National Guard and Emblem — A114

1970, Oct. 20 **Photo.** ***Perf. 13x13½***

519 A114 10f gold & multi 1.25 .25
520 A114 20f silver & multi 2.25 .55

First National Guard graduation.

Flag of Kuwait, Symbols of Development
A115

1971, Feb. 25 **Litho.** ***Perf. 12***

521 A115 20f gray & multi 1.75 .40
522 A115 30f multicolored 2.50 .55

Tenth anniversary of National Day.

Charles H. Best, Frederick G. Banting — A116

1971, Apr. 7 **Litho.** ***Perf. 14***

523 A116 20f multicolored 2.00 .40
524 A116 45f multicolored 4.25 .80

World Health Day; discoverers of insulin.

Globe with Map of Palestine — A117

1971, May 3 **Litho.** ***Perf. 12½x13***

525 A117 20f yel green & multi 2.00 1.10
526 A117 45f lilac & multi 3.75 2.25

International Palestine Week.

ITU Emblem and Waves — A118

1971, May 17 **Photo.** ***Perf. 13x13½***

527 A118 20f silver, dk red & blk 1.25 .30
528 A118 45f gold, dk red & blk 2.75 .85

3rd World Telecommunications Day.

Men of 3 Races — A119

1971, June 5 **Litho.** ***Perf. 11½x11***

529 A119 15f red brown & multi .85 .30
530 A119 30f ultra & multi 1.40 .65

Intl. Year against Racial Discrimination.

Arab Postal Union Emblem — A120

1971, Aug. 30 ***Perf. 13x12½***

531 A120 20f brown & multi 1.10 .30
532 A120 45f blue & multi 1.90 .80

25th anniv. of the Conf. of Sofar, Lebanon, establishing the Arab Postal Union.

Symbols of Learning, UNESCO and Kuwait Emblems — A121

1971, Sept. 8 ***Perf. 12***

533 A121 25f dull yellow & multi 1.00 .25
534 A121 60f lt blue & multi 2.25 1.10

International Literacy Day, Sept. 8.

Soccer — A122

Design: 30f, Soccer, different.

1971, Dec. 10 ***Perf. 13***

535 A122 20f green & multi 2.25 .55
536 A122 30f ultra & multi 3.25 1.00

Regional Sports Tournament, Kuwait, Dec.

UNICEF Emblem and Arms of Kuwait
A123

Litho. & Engr.

1971, Dec. 11 ***Perf. 11x11½***

537 A123 25f gold & multi .90 .35
538 A123 60f silver & multi 2.10 .80

25th anniv. of UNICEF.

Book Year Emblem — A124

1972, Jan. 2 **Litho.** ***Perf. 14x13***

539 A124 20f black & buff 1.00 .45
540 A124 45f black & lt blue grn 2.25 1.00

International Book Year.

Kuwait Emblem with 11 Rays, Olive Branch — A125

1972, Feb. 25 **Litho.** ***Perf. 13x13½***

541 A125 20f pink, gold & multi 1.25 .30
542 A125 45f lt blue, gold & multi 2.25 1.00

11th anniversary of National Day.

Telecommunications Center — A126

1972, Feb. 28 ***Perf. 13½***

543 A126 20f lt blue & multi 1.75 .50
544 A126 45f multicolored 4.50 1.50

Opening of Kuwait Telecommunications Center.

"Your Heart is your Health" — A127

1972, Apr. 7 **Photo.** ***Perf. 14½x14***

545 A127 20f red & multi 2.25 .60
546 A127 45f red & multi 5.25 1.60

World Health Day.

Nurse and Child — A128

1972, May 8 **Litho.** ***Perf. 12½x13***

547 A128 8f vio bl, red & emer 1.25 .30
548 A128 40f pink & multi 5.25 1.40

Red Cross and Red Crescent Day.

Soccer, Olympic Emblems
A129

1972, Sept. 2 **Litho.** ***Perf. 14½***

549 A129 2f shown .45 .25
550 A129 4f Running .45 .25
551 A129 5f Swimming .55 .25
552 A129 8f Gymnastics .60 .25
553 A129 10f Discus .95 .30
554 A129 15f Equestrian 1.35 .35
555 A129 20f Basketball 1.50 .40
556 A129 25f Volleyball 1.60 .55
Nos. 549-556 (8) 7.45 2.60

20th Olympic Games, Munich, 8/26-9/11.

FAO Emblem, Vegetables, Fish and Ship — A130

1972, Sept. 9 Litho. *Perf. 14x13½*

557 A130 5f blue & multi .60 .40
558 A130 10f emerald & multi 1.90 1.10
559 A130 20f orange & multi 3.50 2.25
Nos. 557-559 (3) 6.00 3.75

11th FAO Regional Conference in the Near East, Kuwait, Sept.

National Bank Emblem A131

1972, Nov. 15 Photo. *Perf. 13x14*

560 A131 10f green & multi .60 .25
561 A131 35f dull red & multi 2.00 .90

20th anniversary of Kuwait National Bank.

Capitals — A132

Relics of Failaka: 5f, View of excavations. 10f, Acanthus leaf capital. 15f, Excavations.

1972, Dec. 4 Litho. *Perf. 12*

562 A132 2f lilac rose & multi .40 .25
563 A132 5f bister & multi .55 .25
564 A132 10f lt blue & multi 1.75 .30
565 A132 15f green & multi 2.40 .40
Nos. 562-565 (4) 5.10 1.20

Flower and Kuwait Emblem — A133

1973, Feb. 25 Litho. *Perf. 13½x13*

566 A133 10f lt olive & multi .70 .25
567 A133 20f multicolored 1.35 .40
568 A133 30f yellow & multi 2.10 .90
Nos. 566-568 (3) 4.15 1.55

12th anniversary of National Day.

INTERPOL Emblem — A134

1973, June 3 Litho. *Perf. 12*

569 A134 10f emerald & multi 1.25 .75
570 A134 15f red orange & multi 2.00 1.00
571 A134 20f blue & multi 3.00 1.25
Nos. 569-571 (3) 6.25 3.00

50th anniv. of Intl. Criminal Police Org. (INTERPOL).

I.C.M.S. Emblem and Flag of Kuwait — A135

1973, June 24 *Perf. 13*

572 A135 30f gray & multi 1.50 .55
573 A135 40f brown & multi 2.50 .80

Intl. Council of Military Sports, 25th anniv.

Kuwait Airways Building — A136

1973, July 1 Litho. *Perf. 12½x14*

574 A136 10f lt green & multi .75 .25
575 A136 15f lilac & multi 1.00 .30
576 A136 20f lt ultra & multi 1.25 .50
Nos. 574-576 (3) 3.00 1.05

Opening of Kuwait Airways Corporation Building.

Weather Map of Suez Canal and Persian Gulf Region A137

1973, Sept. 4 Photo. *Perf. 14*

577 A137 5f red & multi 1.00 .25
578 A137 10f green & multi 1.35 .30
579 A137 15f multicolored 1.90 .60
Nos. 577-579 (3) 4.25 1.15

Intl. meteorological cooperation, cent.

Sheiks Ahmad and Sabah A138

1973, Nov. 12 Photo. *Perf. 14*

580 A138 10f lt green & multi .75 .25
581 A138 20f yel orange & multi 1.75 .40
582 A138 70f lt blue & multi 5.00 1.50
Nos. 580-582 (3) 7.50 2.15

Stamps overprinted "Kuwait," 50th anniv.

Mourning Dove, Eurasian Hoopoe, Rock Dove, Stone Curlew A139

Designs: Birds and traps.

1973, Dec. 1 Litho. *Perf. 14*

Size (single stamp): 32x32mm

583 A139 Block of 4 5.50 5.50
a. 5f Mourning dove .70 .25
b. 5f Eurasian hoopoe .70 .25
c. 5f Rock dove .70 .25
d. 5f Stone curlew .70 .25
584 A139 Block of 4 7.25 7.25
a. 8f Great gray shrike .90 .35
b. 8f Red-backed shrike .90 .35
c. 8f Rufous-backed shrike .90 .35
d. 8f Black-naped oriole .90 .35
585 A139 Block of 4 8.00 8.00
a. 10f Willow warbler 1.00 .45
b. 10f Great reed warbler 1.00 .45
c. 10f Blackcap 1.00 .45
d. 10f Common (barn) swallow 1.00 .45
586 A139 Block of 4 11.50 11.50
a. 15f Common rock thrush 1.50 1.50
b. 15f European redstart 1.50 1.50
c. 15f Wheatear 1.50 1.50
d. 15f Bluethroat 1.50 1.50
587 A139 Block of 4 13.50 13.50
a. 20f Houbara bustard 1.60 1.60
b. 20f Pin-tailed sandgrouse 1.60 1.60
c. 20f Ypecaha wood rail 1.60 1.60
d. 20f Spotted crake 1.60 1.60

Size (single stamp): 35x35mm

588 A139 Block of 4 17.50 17.50
a. 25f American sparrow hawk 2.00 2.00
b. 25f Great black-backed gull 2.00 2.00
c. 25f Purple heron 2.00 2.00
d. 25f Wryneck 2.00 2.00
589 A139 Block of 4 25.00 25.00
a. 30f European bee-eater 3.00 3.00
b. 30f Goshawk 3.00 3.00
c. 30f Gray wagtail 3.00 3.00
d. 30f Pied wagtail 3.00 3.00
590 A139 Block of 4 32.50 32.50
a. 45f Crossbows 4.25 4.25
b. 45f Tent-shaped net 4.25 4.25
c. 45f Hand net 4.25 4.25
d. 45f Rooftop trap 4.25 4.25
Nos. 583-590 (8) 120.75 120.75

Human Rights Flame — A141

1973, Dec. 10 Litho. *Perf. 12*

594 A141 10f red & multi .75 .25
595 A141 40f lt green & multi 2.00 .55
596 A141 75f lilac & multi 3.50 1.50
Nos. 594-596 (3) 6.25 2.30

25th anniv. of the Universal Declaration of Human Rights.

Promoting Animal Resources — A142

1974, Feb. 16 Litho. *Perf. 12½*

597 A142 30f violet blue & multi 1.50 .40
598 A142 40f rose & multi 1.75 1.00

4th Congress of the Arab Veterinary Union, Kuwait.

Stylized Wheat and Kuwaiti Flag — A143

1974, Feb. 25 *Perf. 13½x13*

599 A143 20f lemon & multi .60 .25
600 A143 30f bister brn & multi 1.40 .40
601 A143 70f silver & multi 3.00 1.25
Nos. 599-601 (3) 5.00 1.90

13th anniversary of National Day.

Conference Emblem and Sheik Sabah — A144

1974, Mar. 8 *Perf. 12½*

602 A144 30f multicolored 2.50 .55
603 A144 40f yellow & multi 4.00 1.10

12th Conf. of the Arab Medical Union and 1st Conf. of the Kuwait Medical Soc.

Tournament Emblem — A145

1974, Mar. 15

604 A145 25f multicolored 1.50 .50
605 A145 45f multicolored 2.75 1.10

Third Soccer Tournament for the Arabian Gulf Trophy, Kuwait, Mar. 1974.

Scientific Research Institute A146

1974, Apr. 3 Photo. *Perf. 12½*

606 A146 15f magenta & multi 2.00 .45
607 A146 20f green & multi 2.50 .65

Opening of Kuwait Scientific Research Institute.

Arab Postal Union, Kuwait and UPU Emblems A147

1974, May 1 *Perf. 13x14*

608 A147 20f gold & multi .75 .25
609 A147 30f gold & multi 1.00 .45
610 A147 60f gold & multi 1.75 .80
Nos. 608-610 (3) 3.50 1.50

Centenary of Universal Postal Union.

Telephone Dial with Communications Symbols and Globe — A148

1974, May 17 *Perf. 14x13½*

611 A148 10f blue & multi 1.00 .25
612 A148 30f multicolored 2.00 .60
613 A148 40f black & multi 3.00 .80
Nos. 611-613 (3) 6.00 1.65

World Telecommunications Day, May 17.

Emblem of Unity Council and Flags of Member States — A149

1974, June 25 Litho. *Perf. 13½*

614 A149 20f red, black & green 1.50 .45
615 A149 30f green, black & red 1.50 .65

17th anniversary of the signing of the Arab Economic Unity Agreement.

WPY Emblem, Embryo, "Growth" A150

1974, Aug. 19 Litho. *Perf. 14x14½*

616 A150 30f black & multi 1.50 .40
617 A150 70f violet blue & multi 3.00 1.50

World Population Year.

Development Building and Emblem — A151

1974, Oct. 30 Litho. *Perf. 13x13½*

618 A151 10f pink & multi .90 .25
619 A151 20f ultra & multi 1.50 .45

Kuwait Fund for Arab Economic Development.

Emblem of Shuaiba Industrial Area A152

1974, Dec. 17 Litho. *Perf. 12½x12*

620 A152 10f lt blue & multi 1.00 .25
621 A152 20f salmon & multi 2.50 .45
622 A152 30f lt green & multi 3.00 1.00
Nos. 620-622 (3) 6.50 1.70

Shuaiba Industrial Area, 10th anniversary.

Arms of Kuwait and "14" — A153

1975, Feb. 25 Litho. *Perf. 13x13½*

623 A153 20f multicolored .75 .30
624 A153 70f yel green & multi 2.00 .85
625 A153 75f rose & multi 3.25 1.00
Nos. 623-625 (3) 6.00 2.15

14th anniversary of National Day.

Male and Female Symbols A154

1975, Apr. 14 Photo. *Perf. 11½x12*

626 A154 8f lt green & multi .45 .25
627 A154 20f rose & multi .50 .25
628 A154 30f blue & multi .85 .45
629 A154 70f yellow & multi 2.25 1.10
630 A154 100f black & multi 4.00 1.40
Nos. 626-630 (5) 8.05 3.45

Kuwaiti census 1975.

IWY and Kuwaiti Women's Union Emblems A155

1975, June 10 Litho. *Perf. 14½*

631 A155 15f brown org & multi 1.10 .25
632 A155 20f olive & multi 1.40 .40
633 A155 30f violet & multi 2.00 .65
Nos. 631-633 (3) 4.50 1.30

International Women's Year.

Classroom and UNESCO Emblem — A156

1975, Sept. 8 Litho. *Perf. 12½x12*

634 A156 20f green & multi 1.10 .25
635 A156 30f multicolored 1.90 .65

International Literacy Day.

Symbols of Measurements — A157

1975, Oct. 14 Photo. *Perf. 14x13*

636 A157 10f green & multi 1.00 .25
637 A157 20f purple & multi 1.50 .45

World Standards Day.

UN Flag, Rifle and Olive Branch — A158

1975, Oct. 24 Litho. *Perf. 12x12½*

638 A158 20f multicolored .90 .25
639 A158 45f orange & multi 2.10 .80

United Nations, 30th anniversary.

Sheik Sabah — A159

1975, Dec. 22 Litho. *Perf. 12½x12*

640 A159 8f yellow & multi 1.20 .25
641 A159 20f lilac & multi 1.60 .40
642 A159 30f buff & multi 1.90 .50
643 A159 50f salmon & multi 2.75 .75
644 A159 90f lt blue & multi 5.00 1.25
645 A159 100f multicolored 6.25 1.50
Nos. 640-645 (6) 18.70 4.65

"Progress" A160

1976, Feb. 25 Litho. *Perf. 12*

646 A160 10f multicolored .75 .25
647 A160 20f multicolored 1.50 .35

15th anniversary of National Day.

Medical Equipment, Emblem and Surgery — A161

1976, Mar. 1 Litho. *Perf. 14½*

648 A161 5f dull green & multi .50 .25
649 A161 10f blue & multi 1.50 .45
650 A161 30f gray & multi 4.00 1.50
Nos. 648-650 (3) 6.00 2.20

Kuwait Medical Assoc., 2nd annual conference.

Telephones, 1876 and 1976 — A162

1976, Mar. 10 Litho. *Perf. 12*

651 A162 5f orange & black .80 .25
652 A162 15f lt blue & black 1.90 .35

Centenary of first telephone call by Alexander Graham Bell, Mar. 10, 1876.

Human Eye — A163

Photo. & Engr.

1976, Apr. 7 *Perf. 11½*

653 A163 10f multicolored 1.00 .25
654 A163 20f black & multi 1.60 .30
655 A163 30f multicolored 2.00 .85
Nos. 653-655 (3) 4.60 1.40

World Health Day: "Foresight prevents blindness."

Red Crescent Emblem — A164

1976, May 8 Litho. *Perf. 12x11½*

656 A164 20f brt green, blk & red .65 .30
657 A164 30f vio blue, blk & red 1.15 .55
658 A164 45f yellow, blk & red 2.00 .90
659 A164 75f lilac rose, blk & red 4.25 2.25
Nos. 656-659 (4) 8.05 4.00

Kuwait Red Crescent Society, 10th anniv.

Modern Suburb of Kuwait — A165

1976, June 1 Photo. *Perf. 13x13½*

660 A165 10f light green & multi 1.00 .25
661 A165 20f salmon & multi 1.75 .35

Habitat, UN Conference on Human Settlements, Vancouver, Canada, May 31-June 11.

Basketball, Kuwait Olympic Emblem — A166

Designs: 8f, Running. 10f, Judo. 15f, Fieldball. 20f, Gymnastics. 30f, Water polo. 45f, Soccer. 70f, Swimmers at start.

1976, July 17 Litho. *Perf. 14½*

662 A166 4f black & multi .40 .25
663 A166 8f red & multi .40 .25
664 A166 10f green & multi .45 .25
665 A166 15f lemon & multi .60 .25
666 A166 20f blue & multi .70 .30
667 A166 30f lilac & multi 1.15 .55
668 A166 45f multicolored 1.60 .75
669 A166 70f brown & multi 2.25 1.10
Nos. 662-669 (8) 7.55 3.70

21st Olympic Games, Montreal, Canada, July 17-Aug. 1.

Various Races, Map of Sri Lanka — A167

1976, Aug. 16 Photo. *Perf. 14*

670 A167 20f dk blue & multi .65 .25
671 A167 30f purple & multi .90 .55
672 A167 45f green & multi 1.40 .75
Nos. 670-672 (3) 2.95 1.55

5th Summit Conf. of Non-aligned Countries, Colombo, Sri Lanka, Aug. 9-19.

"UNESCO," Torch and Kuwait Arms — A168

1976, Nov. 4 Litho. *Perf. 12x11½*

673 A168 20f yel green & multi .75 .25
674 A168 45f scarlet & multi 2.00 .60

30th anniversary of UNESCO.

Blindman's Buff — A169

Popular games. 5f, 15f, 30f, vertical.

Perf. 14½x14, 14x14½

1977, Jan. 10 Litho.

675 A169 5f Pot throwing .35 .25
676 A169 5f Kite flying .35 .25
677 A169 5f Balancing sticks .35 .25
678 A169 5f Spinning tops .35 .25
a. Block of 4, #675-678 2.25 2.25
679 A169 10f shown .65 .30
680 A169 10f Rowing .65 .30
681 A169 10f Hoops .65 .30
682 A169 10f Ropes .65 .30
a. Block of 4, #679-682 3.25 3.25
683 A169 15f Rope skipping 1.10 .45
684 A169 15f Marbles 1.10 .45
685 A169 15f Cart steering 1.10 .45
686 A169 15f Teetotum 1.10 .45
a. Block of 4, #683-686 5.50 5.50
687 A169 20f Halma 1.25 .60
688 A169 20f Model boats 1.25 .60
689 A169 20f Pot and candle 1.25 .60
690 A169 20f Hide and seek 1.25 .60
a. Block of 4, #687-690 6.50 6.50
691 A169 30f Throwing bones 1.50 .80
692 A169 30f Mystery gifts 1.50 .80
693 A169 30f Hopscotch 1.50 .80
694 A169 30f Catch as catch can 1.50 .80
a. Block of 4, #691-694 7.50 7.50
695 A169 40f Bowls 2.75 1.10
696 A169 40f Sword fighting 2.75 1.10
697 A169 40f Mother and child 2.75 1.10
698 A169 40f Fivestones 2.75 1.10
a. Block of 4, #695-698 13.00 13.00
699 A169 60f Hiding a cake 3.50 1.75
700 A169 60f Chess 3.50 1.75
701 A169 60f Dancing 3.50 1.75
702 A169 60f Treasure hunt 3.50 1.75
a. Block of 4, #699-702 17.00 17.00
703 A169 70f Hobby-horses 4.25 2.00
704 A169 70f Hide and seek 4.25 2.00
705 A169 70f Catch 4.25 2.00
706 A169 70f Storytelling 4.25 2.00
a. Block of 4, #703-706 20.00 20.00
Nos. 675-706 (32) 61.40 29.00

Diseased Knee — A170

1977, Feb. 15 *Perf. 13x13½*

707 A170 20f yellow & multi .75 .25
708 A170 30f multicolored 1.25 .45
709 A170 45f red & multi 1.50 .70
710 A170 75f black & multi 2.50 1.25
Nos. 707-710 (4) 6.00 2.65

World Rheumatism Year.

Sheik Sabah — A171

1977, Feb. 25 Photo. *Perf. 13½x13*

711 A171 10f multicolored .55 .25
712 A171 15f multicolored .70 .30
713 A171 30f multicolored 1.40 .55
714 A171 80f multicolored 1.75 1.10
Nos. 711-714 (4) 4.40 2.20

16th National Day.

Kuwait Tower — A172

1977, Feb. 26 *Perf. 14x13½*

715 A172 30f multicolored 1.00 .25
716 A172 80f multicolored 3.00 1.10

Inauguration of Kuwait Tower.

APU Emblem — A173

1977, Apr. 12 Litho. *Perf. 13½x14*

717 A173	5f yellow & multi	.45	.25
718 A173	15f pink & multi	.55	.25
719 A173	30f lt blue & multi	1.10	.30
720 A173	80f lilac & multi	2.60	1.10
	Nos. 717-720 (4)	4.70	1.90

Arab Postal Union, 25th anniversary.

Electronic Tree — A174

1977, May 17 Litho. *Perf. 12x12½*

721 A174	30f brown & red	1.75	.40
722 A174	80f green & red	3.75	1.50

World Telecommunications Day.

Sheik Sabah — A175

1977, June 1 Photo. *Perf. 11½x12*

723 A175	15f blue & multi	1.25	1.10
724 A175	25f yellow & multi	2.00	1.10
725 A175	30f red & multi	2.50	1.60
726 A175	80f violet & multi	6.75	2.75
727 A175	100f dp org & multi	8.00	3.50
728 A175	150f ultra & multi	12.00	4.00
729 A175	200f olive & multi	16.00	6.00
	Nos. 723-729 (7)	48.50	20.05

Games Emblem — A176

1977, Oct. 1 Litho. *Perf. 12*

730 A176	30f multicolored	1.10	.50
731 A176	80f multicolored	2.40	1.10

4th Asian Basketball Youth Championship, Oct. 1-15.

Dome of the Rock, Bishop Capucci, Fatima Bernawi, Sheik Abu Tair — A177

1977, Nov. 1 *Perf. 14*

732 A177	30f multicolored	3.00	1.25
733 A177	80f multicolored	7.00	3.00

Struggle for the liberation of Palestine.

Children and Houses — A178

Children's Paintings: No. 735, Women musicians. No. 736, Boats. No. 737, Women preparing food, vert. No. 738, Women and children, vert. No. 739, Seated woman, vert.

1977, Nov. Photo. *Perf. 13½x13*

734 A178	15f lt green & multi	.50	.30
735 A178	15f yellow & multi	.50	.30
736 A178	30f brt yellow & multi	1.00	.60
737 A178	30f lt violet & multi	1.00	.60
738 A178	80f black & multi	2.50	1.60
739 A178	80f rose & multi	2.50	1.60
	Nos. 734-739 (6)	8.00	5.00

Dentist Treating Patient — A179

1977, Dec. 3

740 A179	30f green & multi	1.75	.50
741 A179	80f violet & multi	3.25	1.40

10th Arab Dental Union Congress, Kuwait, Dec. 3-6.

Ships Unloading Water — A180

Kuwait water resources. 30f, 80f, 100f, vert.

Perf. 14x13½, 13½x14

1978, Jan. 25 Litho.

742	Block of 4	1.75	1.75
a.	5f shown	.30	.25
b.	5f Home delivery by camel	.30	.25
c.	5f Man with water bags	.30	.25
d.	5f Man with wheelbarrow	.30	.25
743	Block of 4	2.75	2.75
a.	10f Well	.50	.25
b.	10f Trough	.50	.25
c.	10f Water hole	.50	.25
d.	10f Irrigation	.50	.25
744	Block of 4	3.50	3.50
a.	15f Sheep drinking	.65	.25
b.	15f Laundresses	.65	.25
c.	15f Sheep and camels drinking	.65	.25
d.	15f Water stored in skins	.65	.25
745	Block of 4	4.00	4.00
a.	20f Animals at well	.80	.25
b.	20f Water in home	.80	.25
c.	20f Water pot	.80	.25
d.	20f Communal fountain	.80	.25
746	Block of 4	5.00	5.00
a.	25f Distillation plant	.95	.30
b.	25f Motorized delivery	.95	.30
c.	25f Water trucks	.95	.30
d.	25f Water towers	.95	.30
747	Block of 4	7.00	7.00
a.	30f Shower bath	1.40	.40
b.	30f Water tower	1.40	.40
c.	30f Gathering rain water	1.40	.40
d.	30f 2 water towers	1.40	.40
748	Block of 4	15.50	15.50
a.	80f Donkey with water bags	3.00	1.10
b.	80f Woman with water can	3.00	1.10
c.	80f Woman with water skin	3.00	1.10
d.	80f Loading tank car	3.00	1.10
749	Block of 4	20.00	20.00
a.	100f Truck delivering water	4.00	1.25
b.	100f Barnyard water supply	4.00	1.25
c.	100f Children at water basin	4.00	1.25
d.	100f Well in courtyard	4.00	1.25
	Nos. 742-749 (8)	59.50	59.50

Radar, Torch, Minarets — A181

1978, Feb. 25 Litho. *Perf. 14x14½*

750 A181	30f multicolored	.75	.25
751 A181	80f multicolored	1.75	.80

17th National Day.

Man with Smallpox, Target — A182

1978, Apr. 17 Litho. *Perf. 12½*

752 A182	30f violet & multi	1.25	.40
753 A182	80f green & multi	3.00	1.10

Global eradication of smallpox.

Antenna and ITU Emblem — A183

1978, May 17 *Perf. 14*

754 A183	30f silver & multi	.75	.30
755 A183	80f silver & multi	2.00	.85

10th World Telecommunications Day.

Sheik Sabah — A184

1978, June 28 Litho. *Perf. 13x14*

Portrait in Brown

Size: 21½x27mm

756 A184	15f green & gold	.40	.25
757 A184	30f orange & gold	.65	.45
758 A184	80f rose lilac & gold	1.50	1.10
759 A184	100f lt green & gold	1.75	1.25
760 A184	130f lt brown & gold	2.00	1.75
761 A184	180f violet & gold	3.50	2.75

Size: 23½x29mm

762 A184	1d red & gold	*15.00*	*9.00*
763 A184	4d blue & gold	*67.50*	*40.00*
	Nos. 756-763 (8)	92.30	56.55

Mt. Arafat, Pilgrims, Holy Kaaba — A185

1978, Nov. 9 Photo. *Perf. 11½*

764 A185	30f multicolored	1.25	.40
765 A185	80f multicolored	3.25	1.25

Pilgrimage to Mecca.

UN and Anti-Apartheid Emblems — A186

1978, Nov. 27 Litho. *Perf. 12*

766 A186	30f multicolored	.75	.30
767 A186	80f multicolored	1.75	1.00
768 A186	180f multicolored	4.00	2.00
	Nos. 766-768 (3)	6.50	3.30

Anti-Apartheid Year.

Refugees, Human Rights Emblems — A187

1978, Dec. 10 Photo. *Perf. 13x13½*

769 A187	30f multicolored	1.00	.35
770 A187	80f multicolored	2.25	.80
771 A187	100f multicolored	3.25	1.75
	Nos. 769-771 (3)	6.50	2.90

Declaration of Human Rights, 30th anniv.

Information Center — A188

1978, Dec. 26 Photo. *Perf. 13*

772 A188	5f multicolored	.40	.25
773 A188	15f multicolored	.55	.25
774 A188	30f multicolored	.95	.35
775 A188	80f multicolored	2.10	1.00
	Nos. 772-775 (4)	4.00	1.85

New Kuwait Information Center.

Kindergarten A189

1979, Jan. 24 Photo. *Perf. 13½x14*

776 A189	30f multicolored	.90	.50
777 A189	80f multicolored	2.10	1.10

International Year of the Child.

Flag and Peace Doves — A190

1979, Feb. 25 *Perf. 14½x14*

778 A190	30f multicolored	1.00	.45
779 A190	80f multicolored	2.00	1.10

18th National Day.

Modern Agriculture in Kuwait — A191

1979, Mar. 13 Photo. *Perf. 14*

780 A191	30f multicolored	.75	.45
781 A191	80f multicolored	2.25	1.10

4th Congress of Arab Agriculture Ministers of the Gulf and Arabian Peninsula.

World Map, Book, Symbols of Learning — A192

1979, Mar. 22

782 A192	30f multicolored	1.00	.45
783 A192	80f multicolored	2.25	1.10

Cultural achievements of the Arabs.

Children with Balloons — A193

Children's Paintings: No. 785, Boys flying kites. No. 786, Girl and doves. No. 787, Children and houses, horiz. No. 788, Four children, horiz. No. 789, Children sitting in circle, horiz.

1979, Apr. 18 Photo. *Perf. 14*

784 A193	30f yellow & multi	1.15	.55
785 A193	30f buff & multi	1.15	.55
786 A193	30f pale yel & multi	1.15	.55
787 A193	80f lt blue & multi	2.60	1.25
788 A193	80f yel green & multi	2.60	1.25
789 A193	80f lilac & multi	2.60	1.25
	Nos. 784-789 (6)	11.25	5.40

Cables, ITU Emblem, People — A194

1979, May 17

790 A194	30f multicolored	.85	.40
791 A194	80f multicolored	2.40	1.10

World Telecommunications Day.

Military Sports Council Emblem — A195

1979, June 1 Photo. *Perf. 14*

792 A195	30f multicolored	1.00	.40
793 A195	80f multicolored	2.50	1.25

29th Intl. Military Soccer Championship.

Child, Industrial Landscape, Environmental Emblems — A196

1979, June 5 *Perf. 12x11½*
794 A196 30f multicolored 1.50 .60
795 A196 80f multicolored 3.50 1.60

World Environment Day, June 5.

Children Holding Globe, UNESCO Emblem — A197

1979, July 25 Litho. *Perf. 11½x12*
796 A197 30f multicolored .75 .40
797 A197 80f multicolored 1.75 1.00
798 A197 130f multicolored 3.50 1.50
Nos. 796-798 (3) 6.00 2.90

Intl. Bureau of Education, Geneva, 50th anniv.

Kuwait Kindergartens, 25th Anniversary — A198

Children's Drawings: 80f, Children waving flags.

1979, Sept. 15 Litho. *Perf. 12½*
799 A198 30f multicolored .85 .40
800 A198 80f multicolored 2.40 1.00

Pilgrims at Holy Ka'aba, Mecca Mosque — A199

1979, Oct. 29 *Perf. 14x14½*
801 A199 30f multicolored 1.25 .50
802 A199 80f multicolored 3.25 1.00

Hegira (Pilgrimage Year).

International Palestinian Solidarity Day — A200

1979, Nov. 29 Photo. *Perf. 11½x12*
803 A200 30f multicolored 2.75 .95
804 A200 80f multicolored 6.75 2.00

Kuwait Airways 25th Anniversary A201

1979, Dec. 24 Photo. *Perf. 13x13½*
805 A201 30f multicolored 1.50 .60
806 A201 80f multicolored 3.50 1.75

19th National Day — A202

1980, Feb. 25 Litho. *Perf. 14x14½*
807 A202 30f multicolored 1.00 .40
808 A202 80f multicolored 2.50 1.00

1980 Population Census — A203

1980, Mar. 18 *Perf. 13½x14*
809 A203 30f multicolored 1.10 .35
810 A203 80f multicolored 2.40 1.00

World Health Day — A204

1980, Apr. 7
811 A204 30f multicolored 2.25 .35
812 A204 80f multicolored 4.75 1.25

Kuwait Municipality, 50th Anniversary — A205

1980, May 1 Photo. *Perf. 14*
813 A205 15f multicolored .75 .25
814 A205 30f multicolored 1.50 .50
815 A205 80f multicolored 3.75 1.25
Nos. 813-815 (3) 6.00 2.00

Citizens of Kuwait — A206

Future Kuwait (Children's Drawings): 80f, Super highway.

1980, May 14 Litho. *Perf. 14x14½*
816 A206 30f multicolored 1.50 .50
817 A206 80f multicolored 4.50 1.50

World Environment Day — A207

1980, June 5 Litho. *Perf. 12x11½*
818 A207 30f multicolored 1.50 .45
819 A207 80f multicolored 4.50 1.10

Swimming, Moscow '80 and Kuwait Olympic Committee Emblems — A208

1980, July 19 Litho. *Perf. 12x12½*
820 A208 15f Volleyball .55 .25
821 A208 15f Tennis .55 .25
a. Vert. pair, #820-821 1.35 1.35
822 A208 30f shown .80 .35
823 A208 30f Weight lifting .80 .35
824 A208 30f Basketball .80 .35
825 A208 30f Judo .80 .35
a. Block of 4, #822-825 5.50 5.50
826 A208 80f Gymnast 2.00 1.00
827 A208 80f Badminton 2.00 1.00
828 A208 80f Fencing 2.00 1.00
829 A208 80f Soccer 2.00 1.00
a. Block of 4, #826-829 11.50 11.50
Nos. 820-829 (10) 12.30 5.90

22nd Summer Olympic Games, Moscow, July 19-Aug. 3.

20th Anniversary of OPEC — A209

1980, Sept. 16 Litho. *Perf. 14x14½*
830 A209 30f multicolored 1.75 .50
831 A209 80f multicolored 3.25 1.10

Hegira (Pilgrimage Year) — A210

1980, Nov. 9 Photo. *Perf. 12x11½*
832 A210 15f multicolored .85 .25
833 A210 30f multicolored 1.40 .45
834 A210 80f multicolored 3.25 1.25
Nos. 832-834 (3) 5.50 1.95

Dome of the Rock, Jerusalem A211

1980, Nov. 29 *Perf. 12x11½*
835 A211 30f multicolored 3.00 .90
836 A211 80f multicolored 8.00 2.50

International Palestinian Solidarity Day.

Avicenna (980-1037), Philosopher and Physician — A212

1980, Dec. 7 *Perf. 12x12½*
837 A212 30f multicolored 2.25 .35
838 A212 80f multicolored 4.25 1.20

Conference Emblem — A213

1981, Jan. 12 Photo. *Perf. 13½x13*
839 A213 30f multicolored 1.00 .65
840 A213 80f multicolored 3.25 1.60

First Islamic Medical Conference.

Girl in Wheelchair A214

International Year of the Disabled: 30f, Man in wheelchair playing billiards, vert.

Perf. 13½x13, 13x13½
1981, Jan. 26 Photo.
841 A214 30f multicolored 1.00 .40
842 A214 80f multicolored 3.00 1.40

20th National Day — A215

1981, Feb. 25 Litho. *Perf. 13x13½*
843 A215 30f multicolored 1.25 .40
844 A215 80f multicolored 3.00 1.40

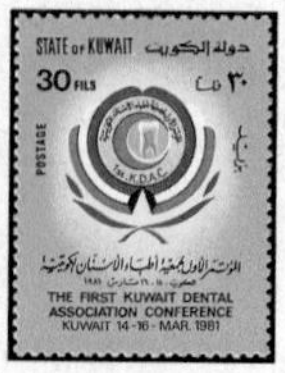
First Kuwait Dental Association Conference — A216

1981, Mar. 14 *Perf. 11½x12*
845 A216 30f multicolored 2.25 1.00
846 A216 80f multicolored 6.25 2.25

A217

1981, May 8 Photo. *Perf. 14*
847 A217 30f multicolored 1.75 1.00
848 A217 80f multicolored 4.75 2.25

Intl. Red Cross day.

A218

1981, May 17 Litho. *Perf. 14½x14*
849 A218 30f multicolored 1.50 .50
850 A218 80f multicolored 3.25 2.25

13th World Telecommunications day.

World Environment Day — A219

1981, June 5 Photo. *Perf. 12*
851 A219 30f multicolored 1.75 .60
852 A219 80f multicolored 4.75 1.75

Sief Palace — A220

A221

1981, Sept. 16 Litho. *Perf. 12*
853 A220 5f multicolored .25 .25
854 A220 10f multicolored .25 .25
855 A220 15f multicolored .25 .25
856 A220 25f multicolored .25 .25
857 A220 30f multicolored .25 .25
858 A220 40f multicolored .40 .25
859 A220 60f multicolored .65 .25
860 A220 80f multicolored .85 .45
861 A220 100f multicolored 1.10 .65
862 A220 115f multicolored 1.25 .80
863 A220 130f multicolored 1.40 1.00
864 A220 150f multicolored 1.75 1.00
865 A220 180f multicolored 2.10 1.10
866 A220 250f multicolored 3.00 1.25
867 A220 500f multicolored 6.00 2.25
868 A221 1d multicolored 12.50 3.75
869 A221 2d multicolored 27.50 6.00
870 A221 3d multicolored 40.00 11.00
871 A221 4d multicolored 50.00 15.00
Nos. 853-871 (19) 149.75 46.00

Islamic Pilgrimage A222

1981, Oct. 7 Photo. *Perf. 13x13½*
872 A222 30f multicolored 1.00 .60
873 A222 80f multicolored 3.75 1.50

World Food Day — A223

1981, Oct. 16 **Litho.** ***Perf. 13***
874 A223 30f multicolored 1.25 .60
875 A223 80f multicolored 4.00 1.50

A224

1981, Dec. 30 **Photo.** ***Perf. 14***
876 A224 30f multicolored 1.25 .50
877 A224 80f multicolored 3.50 1.50

20th anniv. of national television.

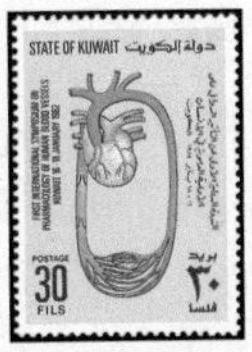

A225

1982, Jan. 16 **Photo.** ***Perf. 14***
878 A225 30f multicolored 1.25 1.10
879 A225 80f multicolored 4.50 1.75

First Intl. Pharmacology of Human Blood Vessels Symposium, Jan. 16-18.

21st Natl. Day — A226

1982, Feb. 25 ***Perf. 13½x13***
880 A226 30f multicolored 1.00 .45
881 A226 80f multicolored 3.00 1.25

Scouting Year — A227

1982, Mar. 22 **Photo.** ***Perf. 12x11½***
882 A227 30f multicolored 1.25 .60
883 A227 80f multicolored 3.75 1.50

Arab Pharmacists' Day — A228

1982, Apr. 2 **Litho.** ***Perf. 12x11½***
884 A228 30f lt green & multi 1.75 .60
885 A228 80f pink & multi 4.75 1.60

World Health Day — A229

1982, Apr. 7 **Litho.** ***Perf. 13½x13***
886 A229 30f multicolored 1.50 .90
887 A229 80f multicolored 4.50 2.75

Arab Postal Union, 30th Anniv. — A230

1982, Apr. 12 **Photo.** ***Perf. 13½x13***
888 A230 30f multicolored 1.50 .50
889 A230 80f multicolored 5.00 1.50

TB Bacillus Centenary — A231

1982, May 24 **Litho.** ***Perf. 11½x12***
890 A231 30f multicolored 2.00 .90
891 A231 80f multicolored 5.50 2.75

1982 World Cup — A232

1982, June 17 **Photo.** ***Perf. 14***
892 A232 30f multicolored 1.50 .50
893 A232 80f multicolored 4.50 1.50

10th Anniv. of Science and Natural History Museum — A233

1982, July 14 ***Perf. 14***
894 A233 30f multicolored 4.50 2.00
895 A233 80f multicolored 11.00 5.00

6th Anniv. of United Arab Shipping Co. — A234

Designs: Freighters.

1982, Sept. 1 ***Perf. 13***
896 A234 30f multicolored 1.50 .45
897 A234 80f multicolored 3.75 1.25

Arab Day of the Palm Tree — A235

1982, Sept. 15 ***Perf. 14***
898 A235 30f multicolored 1.00 .45
899 A235 80f multicolored 2.50 1.25

Islamic Pilgrimage A236

1982, Sept. 26 **Litho.**
900 A236 15f multicolored .75 .30
901 A236 30f multicolored 1.50 .50
902 A236 80f multicolored 4.00 1.50
Nos. 900-902 (3) 6.25 2.30

Desert Flowers & Plants — A237

Frame colors: No. 903a, green. b, violet. c, deep salmon. d, rose red. e, pale brown. f, deep green. g, pale orange. h, brown red. i, tan. j, violet blue.

No. 904: a, yellow green. b, pink. c, pale blue. d, dark blue. e, pale gray green. f, lake. g, pale orange. h, blue. i, red lilac. j, red orange.

No. 905: a, brown. b, pink. c, blue. d, olive green. e, orange red. f, dark blue. g, green. h, rose. i, bister. j, pale orange.

No. 906: a, yellow green. b, dark blue. c, pale orange. d, rose red. e, green. f, gray violet. g, gray blue. h, violet. i, yellow brown. j, orange red.

No. 907: a, lilac. b, blue green. c, pale orange. d, pale brown. e, violet blue. f, yellow. g, green blue. h, purple. i, pale brown. j, pale orange.

1983, Jan. 25 **Litho.** ***Perf. 12***
903 Strip of 10 4.75 4.75
a.-j. A237 10f any single .40 .30
904 Strip of 10 6.00 6.00
a.-j. A237 15f any single .45 .30
905 Strip of 10 10.00 10.00
a.-j. A237 30f any single .75 .60
906 Strip of 10 12.00 12.00
a.-j A237 40f any single, horiz. .90 .75
907 Strip of 10 27.00 27.00
a.-j. A237 80f any single, horiz. 2.00 1.10
Nos. 903-907 (5) 59.75 59.75

22nd Natl. Day — A238

1983, Feb. 25 **Litho.** ***Perf. 12½***
908 A238 30f multicolored 1.00 .35
909 A238 80f multicolored 2.75 1.25

25th Anniv. of Intl. Maritime Org. — A239

1983, Mar. 17 **Photo.** ***Perf. 14***
910 A239 30f multicolored .75 .30
911 A239 80f multicolored 2.25 .90

Map of Middle East and Africa, Conference Emblem — A240

1983, Mar. 19 ***Perf. 13***
912 A240 15f multicolored .50 .25
913 A240 30f multicolored 1.00 .50
914 A240 80f multicolored 2.75 1.50
Nos. 912-914 (3) 4.25 2.25

3rd Intl. Conference on the Impact of Viral Diseases on the Development of the Middle East and Africa, Mar. 19-27.

World Health Day — A241

1983, Apr. 7 ***Perf. 12x11½***
915 A241 15f multicolored .75 .30
916 A241 30f multicolored 1.25 .70
917 A241 80f multicolored 3.50 1.90
Nos. 915-917 (3) 5.50 2.90

World Communications Year — A242

1983, May 17 **Photo.** ***Perf. 13x13½***
918 A242 15f multicolored .75 .30
919 A242 30f multicolored 1.25 .70
920 A242 80f multicolored 3.25 2.00
Nos. 918-920 (3) 5.25 3.00

World Environment Day — A243

1983, June 5 **Litho.** ***Perf. 12½***
921 A243 15f multicolored .60 .30
922 A243 30f multicolored 1.40 .70
923 A243 80f multicolored 4.50 2.00
Nos. 921-923 (3) 6.50 3.00

Wall of Old Jerusalem A244

1983, July 25 **Litho.** ***Perf. 12***
924 A244 15f multicolored 1.00 .25
925 A244 30f multicolored 2.00 .55
926 A244 80f multicolored 4.50 1.75
Nos. 924-926 (3) 7.50 2.55

World Heritage Year.

Islamic Pilgrimage A245

1983, Sept. 15 **Photo.** ***Perf. 11½***
927 A245 15f multicolored .60 .25
928 A245 30f multicolored 1.40 .55
929 A245 80f multicolored 3.50 1.75
Nos. 927-929 (3) 5.50 2.55

Intl. Palestinian Solidarity Day — A246

1983, Nov. 29 **Photo.** ***Perf. 14***
930 A246 15f multicolored .65 .25
931 A246 30f multicolored 1.60 .65
932 A246 80f multicolored 4.25 1.75
Nos. 930-932 (3) 6.50 2.65

21st Pan Arab Medical Congress, Jan. 30-Feb. 2 — A247

1984, Jan. 30 **Litho.** ***Perf. 14½x14***
933 A247 15f purple & multi .65 .25
934 A247 30f blue grn & multi 1.60 .65
935 A247 80f pink & multi 3.75 1.75
Nos. 933-935 (3) 6.00 2.65

Key, Natl. Emblem, and Health Establishments Emblem — A248

1984, Feb. 20 **Photo.** ***Perf. 13x13½***
936 A248 15f multicolored .55 .25
937 A248 30f multicolored .95 .45
938 A248 80f multicolored 3.00 1.50
Nos. 936-938 (3) 4.50 2.20

Inauguration of Amiri and Al-Razi Hospitals, Allergy Center and Medical Stores Center.

23rd National Day — A249

1984, Feb. 25 Litho. *Perf. 13½*

939	A249 15f multicolored		.75	.25
940	A249 30f multicolored		1.25	.45
941	A249 80f multicolored		3.50	1.50
	Nos. 939-941 (3)		5.50	2.20

2nd Kuwait Intl. Medical Science Conf., Mar. 4-8 — A250

1984, Mar. 4 Photo. *Perf. 12*
Granite Paper

942	A250 15f multicolored	.75	.25
943	A250 30f multicolored	1.50	.65
944	A250 80f multicolored	3.75	1.70
	Nos. 942-944 (3)	6.00	2.60

30th Anniv. of Kuwait Airways Corp. — A251

1984, Mar. 15 *Perf. 13½*

946	A251 30f multicolored	1.25	1.00
947	A251 80f multicolored	3.75	2.00

Al-Arabi Magazine, 25th Anniv. — A252

1984, Mar. 20 *Perf. 14½x14*

948	A252 15f multicolored	.60	.25
949	A252 30f multicolored	1.15	.50
950	A252 80f multicolored	3.25	1.40
	Nos. 948-950 (3)	5.00	2.15

World Health Day — A253

1984, Apr. 7 *Perf. 12*

951	A253 15f multicolored	.75	.25
952	A253 30f multicolored	1.25	.45
953	A253 80f multicolored	3.50	1.50
	Nos. 951-953 (3)	5.50	2.20

Hanan Kuwaiti Orphan Village, Sudan — A254

1984, May 15 Litho. *Perf. 12*

954	A254 15f multicolored	.75	.25
955	A254 30f multicolored	1.25	.45
956	A254 80f multicolored	3.50	1.50
	Nos. 954-956 (3)	5.50	2.20

Intl. Civil Aviation Org., 40th Anniv. — A255

1984, June 12

957	A255 15f multicolored	.75	.35
958	A255 30f multicolored	1.25	.80
959	A255 80f multicolored	3.50	2.00
	Nos. 957-959 (3)	5.50	3.15

Arab Youth Day — A256

1984, July 5 *Perf. 13½*

960	A256 30f multicolored	1.25	.65
961	A256 80f multicolored	4.00	1.75

1984 Summer Olympics — A257

1984, July 28 *Perf. 15x14*

962	A257 30f Swimming	.65	.65
963	A257 30f Hurdles	.65	.65
a.	Pair, #962-963	1.75	1.75
964	A257 80f Judo	1.90	1.90
965	A257 80f Equestrian	1.90	1.90
a.	Pair, #964-965	4.75	4.75
	Nos. 962-965 (4)	5.10	5.10

10th Anniv. of the Science Club — A258

1984, Aug. 11 Photo. *Perf. 13½x13*

966	A258 15f multicolored	.50	.35
967	A258 30f multicolored	1.25	.75
968	A258 80f multicolored	2.75	2.00
	Nos. 966-968 (3)	4.50	3.10

Islamic Pilgrimage A259

1984, Sept. 4 Photo. *Perf. 12x11½*

969	A259 30f multicolored	1.50	.75
970	A259 80f multicolored	3.50	2.00

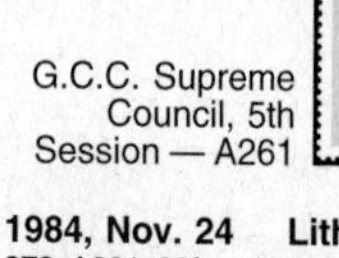

INTELSAT '84, 20th Anniv. — A260

1984, Oct. 1 Litho. *Perf. 13½x14*

971	A260 30f multicolored	1.75	.80
972	A260 80f multicolored	4.25	1.90

G.C.C. Supreme Council, 5th Session — A261

1984, Nov. 24 Litho. *Perf. 15x14*

973	A261 30f multicolored	1.25	.65
974	A261 80f multicolored	3.75	1.75

Map of Israel, Fists, Shattered Star of David — A262

1984, Nov. 29 Photo. *Perf. 12*

975	A262 30f multicolored	1.75	.75
976	A262 80f multicolored	4.50	2.00

Intl. Palestinian Solidarity Day.

Globe, Emblem — A263

1984, Dec. 24 *Perf. 12x11½*
Granite Paper

977	A263 30f multicolored	1.25	.75
978	A263 80f multicolored	3.50	2.00

Kuwait Oil Co., 50th anniv.

Intl. Youth Year — A264

1985, Jan. 15 *Perf. 13½*

979	A264 30f multicolored	1.00	.30
980	A264 80f multicolored	2.75	1.25

24th Natl. Day — A265

1985, Feb. 25 Litho. *Perf. 14x15*

981	A265 30f multicolored	1.00	.40
982	A265 80f multicolored	4.00	1.25

Intl. Program for the Development of Communications A266

1985, Mar. 4 Photo. *Perf. 11½*
Granite Paper

983	A266 30f multicolored	1.25	.50
984	A266 80f multicolored	3.50	1.60

1st Arab Gulf Week for Social Work — A267

1985, Mar. 13 Photo. *Perf. 13½x13*

985	A267 30f multicolored	1.25	.50
986	A267 80f multicolored	3.00	1.60

Kuwait Dental Assoc. 3rd Conference A268

1985, Mar. 23 Litho. *Perf. 13½*

987	A268 30f multicolored	1.50	.80
988	A268 80f multicolored	3.50	2.00

1985 Census — A269

1985, Apr. 1 *Perf. 14x13½*

989	A269 30f multicolored	1.50	.50
990	A269 80f multicolored	3.50	1.60

World Health Day — A270

1985, Apr. 7 Photo. *Perf. 13½x13*

991	A270 30f multicolored	1.50	.55
992	A270 80f multicolored	3.25	1.60

Names of Books, Authors and Poets in Arabic A271

1985, May 20 *Perf. 12*
Granite Paper

993	A271 Block of 4	6.75	4.00
a.-d.	30f any single	1.40	.75
994	A271 Block of 4	16.50	10.00
a.-d.	80f any single	3.50	1.40

Central Library, 50th anniv.

World Environment Day — A272

1985, June 5 *Perf. 11½*

995	A272 30f multicolored	2.00	.75
996	A272 80f multicolored	4.50	2.00

Org. of Petroleum Exporting Countries, 25th Anniv. — A273

1985, Sept. 1 *Perf. 13x13½*

997	A273 30f multicolored	1.75	.55
998	A273 80f multicolored	4.25	1.60

Inauguration of Civil Information System — A274

1985, Oct. 1 Photo. *Perf. 12x11½*

999	A274 30f multicolored	1.50	.55
1000	A274 80f multicolored	3.75	1.60

Intl. Day of Solidarity with Palestinian People — A275

1985, Nov. 29 Photo. *Perf. 12*

1001	A275 15f multicolored	1.10	.55
1002	A275 30f multicolored	1.90	1.00
1003	A275 80f multicolored	4.25	2.75
	Nos. 1001-1003 (3)	7.25	4.30

25th Natl. Day — A276

1986, Feb. 25 Litho. *Perf. 15x14*

1004	A276 15f multicolored	.75	.30
1005	A276 30f multicolored	1.50	.70
1006	A276 80f multicolored	3.75	2.00
	Nos. 1004-1006 (3)	6.00	3.00

Natl. Red Crescent Soc., 20th Anniv. — A277

1986, Mar. 26 Photo. *Perf. 13½*

1007	A277 20f multicolored	1.10	.40
1008	A277 25f multicolored	1.40	.60
1009	A277 70f multicolored	4.00	1.75
	Nos. 1007-1009 (3)	6.50	2.75

World Health Day — A278

1986, Apr. 7 *Perf. 13½x13*

1010	A278 20f multicolored	1.00	.65
1011	A278 25f multicolored	1.50	.80
1012	A278 70f multicolored	3.75	2.25
	Nos. 1010-1012 (3)	6.25	3.70

Intl. Peace Year — A279

1986, June 5 Litho. *Perf. 13½*

1013	A279 20f multicolored	1.00	.45
1014	A279 25f multicolored	1.75	.70
1015	A279 70f multicolored	3.75	1.75
	Nos. 1013-1015 (3)	6.50	2.90

United Arab Shipping Co., 10th Anniv. — A280

1986, July 1 Photo. *Perf. 12x11½*

1016	A280 20f Al Mirqab	1.25	.50
1017	A280 70f Al Mubarakiah	5.25	2.00

Gulf Bank, 25th Anniv. — A281

1986, Oct. 1 Photo. *Perf. 12½*

1018	A281 20f multicolored	1.00	.55
1019	A281 25f multicolored	1.50	.65
1020	A281 70f multicolored	4.50	1.90
	Nos. 1018-1020 (3)	7.00	3.10

Sadu Art — A282

Various tapestry weavings.

1986, Nov. 5 Photo. *Perf. 12x11½*
Granite Paper

1021	A282 20f multicolored	.85	.40
1022	A282 70f multicolored	2.75	1.50
1023	A282 200f multicolored	6.50	3.75
	Nos. 1021-1023 (3)	10.10	5.65

Intl. Day of Solidarity with the Palestinian People — A283

1986, Nov. 29 *Perf. 14*

1024	A283 20f multicolored	1.75	.85
1025	A283 25f multicolored	2.50	1.10
1026	A283 70f multicolored	6.25	3.25
	Nos. 1024-1026 (3)	10.50	5.20

5th Islamic Summit Conference A284

1987, Jan. 26 Litho. *Perf. 14½*

1027	A284 25f multicolored	1.00	.45
1028	A284 50f multicolored	2.00	.80
1029	A284 150f multicolored	6.00	2.25
	Nos. 1027-1029 (3)	9.00	3.50

26th Natl. Day — A285

1987, Feb. 25 *Perf. 13½x14*

1030	A285 50f multicolored	1.75	.60
1031	A285 150f multicolored	5.25	2.00

Natl. Health Sciences Center — A286

1987, Mar. 15 Photo. *Perf. 12x11½*
Granite Paper

1032	A286 25f multicolored	1.00	.35
1033	A286 150f multicolored	5.00	2.00

3rd Kuwait Intl. Medical Sciences Conference on Infectious Diseases in Developing Countries.

World Health Day — A287

1987, Apr. 7 Photo. *Perf. 13x13½*

1034	A287 25f multicolored	.75	.40
1035	A287 50f multicolored	1.40	.70
1036	A287 150f multicolored	4.75	2.00
	Nos. 1034-1036 (3)	6.90	3.10

Day of Ghods (Jerusalem) A288

1987, June 7 Photo. *Perf. 12x11½*

1037	A288 25f multicolored	.90	.35
1038	A288 50f multicolored	1.90	.75
1039	A288 150f multicolored	5.25	2.50
	Nos. 1037-1039 (3)	8.05	3.60

Islamic Pilgrimage to Miqat Wadi Mihrim — A289

1987, Aug. Photo. *Perf. 13½x14½*

1040	A289 25f multicolored	1.10	.35
1041	A289 50f multicolored	1.90	.80
1042	A289 150f multicolored	5.00	2.50
	Nos. 1040-1042 (3)	8.00	3.65

Arab Telecommunications Day — A290

1987, Sept. 9 Litho. *Perf. 14x13½*

1043	A290 25f multicolored	.75	.35
1044	A290 50f multicolored	1.75	.80
1045	A290 150f multicolored	5.00	2.50
	Nos. 1043-1045 (3)	7.50	3.65

World Maritime Day — A291

1987, Sept. 24 *Perf. 12x11½*
Granite Paper

1046	A291 25f multicolored	1.00	.35
1047	A291 50f multicolored	2.00	.75
1048	A291 150f multicolored	5.75	2.00
	Nos. 1046-1048 (3)	8.75	3.10

Al Qurain Housing Project — A292

1987, Oct. 5 *Perf. 13x13½*

1049	A292 25f multicolored	.70	.35
1050	A292 50f multicolored	1.50	.60
1051	A292 150f multicolored	4.25	1.75
	Nos. 1049-1051 (3)	6.45	2.70

Port Authority, 10th Anniv. — A293

1987, Nov. 16 Litho. *Perf. 14½*

1052	A293 25f multicolored	1.00	.35
1053	A293 50f multicolored	1.75	.80
1054	A293 150f multicolored	5.75	2.25
	Nos. 1052-1054 (3)	8.50	3.40

A294

1987, Nov. 29 *Perf. 14x13½*

1055	A294 25f multicolored	.90	.35
1056	A294 50f multicolored	1.60	.70
1057	A294 150f multicolored	5.00	2.25
	Nos. 1055-1057 (3)	7.50	3.30

Intl. Day of Solidarity with the Palestinian People.

A295

1988, Feb. 3 Photo. *Perf. 14*

1058	A295 25f multicolored	.75	.30
1059	A295 50f multicolored	1.25	.50
1060	A295 150f multicolored	3.50	1.25
	Nos. 1058-1060 (3)	5.50	2.05

Women's Cultural and Social Soc., 25th anniv.

A296

1988, Feb. 25

1061	A296 25f multicolored	.75	.30
1062	A296 50f multicolored	1.25	.50
1063	A296 150f multicolored	3.50	1.25
	Nos. 1061-1063 (3)	5.50	2.05

National Day, 27th anniv.

A297

1988, Apr. 7 Litho. *Perf. 14x15*

1064	A297 25f multicolored	.80	.30
1065	A297 50f multicolored	1.50	.75
1066	A297 150f multicolored	4.00	1.75
	Nos. 1064-1066 (3)	6.30	2.80

World Health Day, WHO 40th anniv.

A298

1988, Apr. 24 Photo. *Perf. 12*
Granite Paper

1067	A298 35f multicolored	1.00	.35
1068	A298 50f multicolored	1.50	.65
1069	A298 150f multicolored	5.00	2.00
	Nos. 1067-1069 (3)	7.50	3.00

Regional Marine Environment Day. Kuwait Regional Convention on the Marine Environment, 10th anniv. See Iraq Nos. 1333-1336.

A299

1988, July 10 Photo. *Perf. 14*

1070	A299 25f multicolored	1.00	.25
1071	A299 50f multicolored	1.50	.60
1072	A299 150f multicolored	5.00	1.75
	Nos. 1070-1072 (3)	7.50	2.60

Kuwait Teachers Soc., 25th anniv.

Pilgrimage to Mecca — A300

1988, Sept. 12 Litho. *Perf. 13½x14*

1073	A300 25f multicolored	1.10	.25
1074	A300 50f multicolored	2.00	.55
1075	A300 150f multicolored	6.00	1.75
	Nos. 1073-1075 (3)	9.10	2.55

Palestinian "Children of Stone" Fighting Israelis — A301

1988, Sept. 15 Photo. *Perf. 13x13½*

1076	A301 50f multicolored	1.75	.70
1077	A301 150f multicolored	6.50	2.50

Palestinian Uprising. Dated 1987.

Arab Housing Day — A302

1988, Oct. 3

1078	A302	50f multicolored	1.25	.60
1079	A302	100f multicolored	2.50	1.25
1080	A302	150f multicolored	4.25	1.75
		Nos. 1078-1080 (3)	8.00	3.60

Intl. Day for Solidarity with the Palestinian People — A303

1988, Nov. 29 Litho. *Perf. 14x13*

1081	A303	50f multicolored	1.50	.60
1082	A303	100f multicolored	3.25	1.25
1083	A303	150f multicolored	5.75	1.75
		Nos. 1081-1083 (3)	10.50	3.60

A304

1988, Dec. 5 *Perf. 13x14*

1084	A304	50f multicolored	1.20	.50
1085	A304	100f multicolored	2.60	1.00
1086	A304	150f multicolored	4.25	1.50
		Nos. 1084-1086 (3)	8.05	3.00

Intl. Volunteers Day.

A305

1989, Feb. 18 Litho. *Perf. 14x13½*

1087	A305	50f multicolored	1.00	.50
1088	A305	100f multicolored	2.00	1.00
1089	A305	150f multicolored	3.50	1.50
		Nos. 1087-1089 (3)	6.50	3.00

18th Arab Engineering Conference.

28th Natl. Day — A306

1989, Feb. 25 *Perf. 13x13½*

1090	A306	50f multicolored	1.25	.50
1091	A306	100f multicolored	2.25	1.00
1092	A306	150f multicolored	4.00	1.50
		Nos. 1090-1092 (3)	7.50	3.00

5th Natl. Dental Assoc. Conference — A307

1989, Mar. 30 Litho. *Perf. 13½x13*

1093	A307	50f multicolored	1.00	.50
1094	A307	150f multicolored	3.00	1.25
1095	A307	250f multicolored	4.50	2.00
		Nos. 1093-1095 (3)	8.50	3.75

World Health Day — A308

1989, Apr. 7 *Perf. 13x13½*

1096	A308	50f multicolored	.70	.40
1097	A308	150f multicolored	2.25	1.25
1098	A308	250f multicolored	3.75	2.00
		Nos. 1096-1098 (3)	6.70	3.65

A309

1989, May 10 *Perf. 13x14*

1099	A309	50f multicolored	.80	.40
1100	A309	150f multicolored	2.50	1.25
1101	A309	250f multicolored	4.25	2.00
		Nos. 1099-1101 (3)	7.55	3.65

Arab Board for Medical Specializations, 10th anniv.

A310

1989, June 10 Litho. *Perf. 14x15*

1102	A310	50f multicolored	.90	.50
1103	A310	200f multicolored	3.50	2.25
1104	A310	250f multicolored	4.50	2.75
		Nos. 1102-1104 (3)	8.90	5.50

Natl. Journalists Assoc., 25th anniv.

Al-Taneem Mosque — A311

1989, July 9 Litho. *Perf. 13½x14½*

1105	A311	50f multicolored	1.00	.50
1106	A311	150f multicolored	3.00	1.50
1107	A311	200f multicolored	4.00	2.00
		Nos. 1105-1107 (3)	8.00	4.00

Pilgrimage to Mecca.

Arab Housing Day — A312

1989, Oct. 2 *Perf. 13½*

1108	A312	25f multicolored	.80	.25
1109	A312	50f multicolored	1.75	.50
1110	A312	150f multicolored	5.75	1.75
		Nos. 1108-1110 (3)	8.30	2.50

Annual Greenery Week Celebration — A313

1989, Oct. 15 *Perf. 13½x13*

1111	A313	25f multicolored	.75	.25
1112	A313	50f multicolored	1.75	.50
1113	A313	150f multicolored	5.00	1.50
		Nos. 1111-1113 (3)	7.50	2.25

Dhow — A314

Numbers in Black, Moon and Dhow in Gold

1989, Nov. 1 *Perf. 14x15*

Coil Stamps

1114	A314	50f brt apple grn	*3.00*	*3.00*
1115	A314	100f brt blue	*5.50*	*5.50*
1116	A314	200f vermilion	*10.00*	*10.00*
		Nos. 1114-1116 (3)	*18.50*	*18.50*

Nos. 1114-1116 available only at two post office locations, where they were dispensed from machines. Printed in rolls of 3000 consecutively numbered stamps. Stamps with overprinted asterisks but lacking printed numbers are from the ends of coil rolls.

Gulf Investment Corp., 5th Anniv. — A315

1989, Nov. 4 *Perf. 15x14*

1117	A315	25f multicolored	.80	.25
1118	A315	50f multicolored	1.50	.60
1119	A315	150f multicolored	4.50	1.60
		Nos. 1117-1119 (3)	6.80	2.45

Declaration of Palestinian State, 1st Anniv. — A316

1989, Nov. 15 Litho. *Perf. 14x15*

1120	A316	50f multicolored	1.25	.50
1121	A316	150f multicolored	4.00	1.75
1122	A316	200f multicolored	5.50	2.25
		Nos. 1120-1122 (3)	10.75	4.50

Zakat House, Orphan Sponsorship Program — A317

1989, Dec. 10 *Perf. 13½x13*

1123	A317	25f multicolored	.55	.35
1124	A317	50f multicolored	1.25	.85
1125	A317	150f multicolored	3.75	2.00
		Nos. 1123-1125 (3)	5.55	3.20

Kuwait Police, 50th Anniv. — A318

1989, Dec. 30 Litho. *Perf. 15x14*

1126	A318	25f gray & multi	1.00	.35
1127	A318	50f lt ultra & multi	2.25	.85
1128	A318	150f lt violet & multi	7.00	2.00
		Nos. 1126-1128 (3)	10.25	3.20

National Day, 29th Anniv. — A319

1990, Feb. 25 *Perf. 14x13½*

1129	A319	25f multicolored	1.25	.35
1130	A319	50f multicolored	2.00	.85
1131	A319	150f multicolored	6.50	2.00
		Nos. 1129-1131 (3)	9.75	3.20

World Meteorological Day — A320

1990, Mar. 23 Litho. *Perf. 13½x14*

1132	A320	50f multicolored	2.50	.60
1133	A320	100f multicolored	5.75	1.40
1134	A320	150f multicolored	8.25	2.00
		Nos. 1132-1134 (3)	16.50	4.00

World Health Day — A321

1990, Apr. 7 *Perf. 14x15*

1135	A321	50f multicolored	2.75	.60
1136	A321	100f multicolored	5.75	1.40
1137	A321	150f multicolored	7.50	2.00
		Nos. 1135-1137 (3)	16.00	4.00

Hawk — A322

1990, July 7 Litho. *Perf. 14½*

1138	A322	50f blue & gold	6.00	*10.00*
1139	A322	100f maroon & gold	8.00	*11.50*
1140	A322	150f green & gold	11.00	*13.50*
		Nos. 1138-1140 (3)	25.00	*35.00*

Liberation of Kuwait — A323

1991 Litho. *Perf. 14½*

1141	A323	25f multicolored	1.25	.40
1142	A323	50f multicolored	2.50	.80
1143	A323	150f multicolored	6.50	2.50
		Nos. 1141-1143 (3)	10.25	3.70

Peace — A324

1991, May *Perf. 13½x14*

1144	A324	50f multicolored	1.25	.85
1145	A324	100f multicolored	2.50	1.60
1146	A324	150f multicolored	4.00	2.50
		Nos. 1144-1146 (3)	7.75	4.95

Reconstruction — A325

1991, May

1147	A325	50f multicolored	1.25	.85
1148	A325	150f multicolored	3.25	2.00
1149	A325	200f multicolored	4.00	2.75
		Nos. 1147-1149 (3)	8.50	5.60

Liberation of Kuwait — A326

Flags of forces joining international coalition for liberation of Kuwait: a, Sweden. b, USSR. c, U.S. d, Kuwait. e, Saudi Arabia. f, UN. g, Singapore. h, France. i, Italy. j, Egypt. k, Morocco. l, UK. m, Philippines. n, UAE. o, Syria. p, Poland. q, Australia. r, Japan. s, Hungary. t, Netherlands. u, Denmark. v, New Zealand. w, Czechoslovakia. x, Bahrain. y, Honduras. z, Turkey. aa, Greece. ab, Oman. ac, Qatar. ad, Belgium. ae, Sierra Leone. af, Argentina. ag, Norway. ah, Canada. ai, Germany. aj, South Korea. ak, Bangladesh. al, Bulgaria. am, Senegal. an, Spain. ao, Niger. ap, Pakistan.

No. 1151, Flags of all forces of coalition.

1991, July 25 Litho. *Perf. 14½*

1150		50f Sheet of 42	*85.00*	*85.00*
a.-ap.	A326	Any single	*1.75*	*1.75*

Size: 87x134mm

Imperf

1151	A326	1d multicolored	*37.50*	*37.50*

Invasion of Kuwait, 1st Anniv. — A327

50f, Human terror. 100f, Invasion of Kuwait. 150f, Environmental terrorism, horiz. 250f, Desert Storm.

1991, Aug. 2 *Perf. 14½*
1152 A327 50f multi *2.25* 1.00
1153 A327 100f multi *4.25* 1.50
1154 A327 150f multi *6.50* 2.50

Size: 90x65mm

Imperf

1155 A327 250f multi *12.50 12.50*
Nos. 1152-1155 (4) *25.50* 17.50

12th Gulf Cooperation Council Summit — A328

Design: 150f, Tree of flags.

1991, Dec. 23 Litho. *Perf. 14½*
1156 A328 25f multicolored .75 .55
a. see footnote .80 .55
1157 A328 150f multicolored 4.25 3.25
a. Sheet, 2 ea #1156-1157 *11.00 11.00*
b. Sheet, 2 ea #1156a, 1157 *11.00 11.00*

No. 1156a has tree with inscriptions (country names in Arabic) in colors of flags shown on No. 1157.

Intl. Literacy Year — A329

1992, Feb. 12 Litho. *Perf. 13½x13*
1158 A329 50f dark blue & buff 1.25 .75
1159 A329 100f dark blue & cit 2.50 1.50
1160 A329 150f dk blue & pale lil 3.50 2.00
Nos. 1158-1160 (3) 7.25 4.25

Dated 1990.

OPEC, 30th Anniv. (in 1990) — A330

1992, Oct. 29 *Perf. 14½x13½*
1161 A330 25f red & multi 1.00 .50
1162 A330 50f yellow & multi 2.00 1.00
1163 A330 150f green & multi 5.50 3.00
Nos. 1161-1163 (3) 8.50 4.50

31st Natl. Day — A331

1992 *Perf. 14½*
1164 A331 50f Flag, doves 1.25 .50
1165 A331 150f Flags 3.75 1.50
a. Min. sheet, 2 ea #1164-1165 10.00 10.00

Liberation Day (No. 1165). Issue dates, 50f, Feb. 25; 150f, Feb. 26.

Don't Forget Our P.O.W.'s — A332

50f, Flag, chains. 150f, Cell bars, chains.

1991, Nov. 16
1166 A332 50f multicolored 1.25 .75
1167 A332 150f multicolored 4.00 2.25
a. Min. sheet, 2 each #1166-1167 *15.00 15.00*

Dated 1991. Issued: 50f, 2/25; 150f, 2/26.

Camels — A333

1991, Nov. 16 *Perf. 12½*
1168 A333 25f pink & multi .90 .90
1169 A333 50f beige & multi 1.50 1.50
1170 A333 150f lt violet & multi 3.75 3.75
1171 A333 200f blue & multi 4.50 4.50
1172 A333 350f orange & multi 9.00 9.00
Nos. 1168-1172 (5) 19.65 19.65

Environmental Terrorism, by Jafar Islah — A334

Designs: No. 1174, Snake, flag, map. No. 1175, Skull, dead fish. No. 1176, Dying camel.

1992, June *Perf. 14½*
1173 A334 150f multicolored 3.25 1.50
1174 A334 150f multicolored 3.25 1.50
1175 A334 150f multicolored 3.25 1.50
1176 A334 150f multicolored 3.25 1.50
a. Block of 4, #1173-1176 15.00 15.00
b. Minature sheet of 4, #1173-1176 22.50 22.50
Nos. 1173-1176 (4) 13.00 6.00

Earth Summit, Rio De Janeiro. No. 1176a printed in continuous design.

EXPO '92, Seville — A335

Designs: No. 1177, Kuwaiti Pavilion, La Giralda Tower, Seville. No. 1178, Dhows. No. 1179, Dhow. No. 1180, Pavilion, dhow.

Flags of Spain or Kuwait and: No. 1181, Pavilion. No. 1182, La Giralda Tower. No. 1183, La Giralda Tower, dhow. No. 1184, Pavilion, dhow.

1992, June 19
1177 A335 50f multicolored .90 .90
1178 A335 50f multicolored .90 .90
1179 A335 50f multicolored .90 .90
1180 A335 50f multicolored .90 .90
a. Block of 4, #1177-1180 4.00 4.00
1181 A335 150f multicolored 2.75 2.75
1182 A335 150f multicolored 2.75 2.75
1183 A335 150f multicolored 2.75 2.75
1184 A335 150f multicolored 2.75 2.75
a. Block of 4, #1181-1184 13.50 13.50
b. Miniature sheet of 8, #1177-1184 25.00 25.00
Nos. 1177-1184 (8) 14.60 14.60

Nos. 1180a, 1184a have continuous designs.

Palace of Justice — A336

1992, July 4 *Perf. 12½*
1185 A336 25f lilac & multi .60 .30
1186 A336 50f lil rose & multi 1.25 .50
1187 A336 100f yel grn & multi 2.00 1.00
1188 A336 150f yel org & multi 3.00 1.40
1189 A336 250f blue grn & multi 4.50 2.25
Nos. 1185-1189 (5) 11.35 5.45

1992 Summer Olympics, Barcelona — A337

Olympic flag, Fahed Al Ahmed Al Sabah, member of the Intl. Olympic committee and: 50f, Swimmer, soccer player. 100f, Runner, basketball player. 150f, Judo, equestrian.

1992, July 25 *Perf. 14½*
1190 A337 50f multicolored 1.50 .65
1191 A337 100f multicolored 3.50 1.25
1192 A337 150f multicolored 5.00 2.00
Nos. 1190-1192 (3) 10.00 3.90

Invasion by Iraq, 2nd Anniv. — A338

Children's paintings: No. 1193, Tanks, people holding signs, two people being tortured. No. 1194, Truck, Iraqi soldiers looting. No. 1195, Iraqi soldiers killing civilians, tanks. No. 1196, Houses ablaze. No. 1197, Tanks, civilians, soldiers. No. 1198, Planes bombing in attack on fort. No. 1199, Tank, civilians holding flags, signs. No. 1200, Battlefield.

1992, Aug. 2 Litho. *Perf. 14x14½*
1193 A338 50f multicolored .90 .90
1194 A338 50f multicolored .90 .90
1195 A338 50f multicolored .90 .90
1196 A338 50f multicolored .90 .90
a. Block of 4, #1193-1196 4.00 4.00
1197 A338 150f multicolored 2.75 2.75
1198 A338 150f multicolored 2.75 2.75
1199 A338 150f multicolored 2.75 2.75
1200 A338 150f multicolored 2.75 2.75
a. Block of 4, #1197-1200 13.50 13.50
b. Min. sheet of 8, #1193-1200 25.00 25.00
Nos. 1193-1200 (8) 14.60 14.60

Extinguishing of Oil Well Fires, 1st Anniv. — A339

Various scenes showing oil well fire being extinguished.

1992 Litho. *Perf. 14½*
1201 A339 25f multi, vert. .50 .35
1202 A339 50f multi, vert. 1.00 .70
1203 A339 150f multi, vert. 3.00 2.00
1204 A339 250f multicolored 5.25 3.50
Nos. 1201-1204 (4) 9.75 6.55

Kuwait Tower — A340

1993, Jan. 16 Litho. *Perf. 14x15*

Background Color

1205 A340 25f lilac .40 .35
1206 A340 100f blue 1.40 1.25
1207 A340 150f salmon 2.25 1.75
Nos. 1205-1207 (3) 4.05 3.35

A341

1993, Feb. 25 Litho. *Perf. 13½x14*
1208 A341 25f green & multi .40 .35
1209 A341 50f blue & multi .85 .70
1210 A341 150f pink & multi 2.25 1.75
Nos. 1208-1210 (3) 3.50 2.80

National Day, 32nd anniv.

Liberation Day, 2nd Anniv. — A342

1993, Feb. 26 *Perf. 15x14*
1211 A342 25f org yel & multi .50 .35
1212 A342 50f green & multi 1.25 .75
1213 A342 150f red lilac & multi 3.25 1.75
Nos. 1211-1213 (3) 5.00 2.85

Remembering Prisoners of War — A343

Designs: 50f, Prisoner shackled in cell, vert. 150f, Shackled hand pointing to cell window, bird. 200f, Cell, prisoner's face, vert.

Perf. 13½x14, 14x13½

1993, May 15 Litho.
1214 A343 50f multicolored .85 .85
1215 A343 150f multicolored 2.25 2.25
1216 A343 200f multicolored 2.75 2.75
Nos. 1214-1216 (3) 5.85 5.85

18th Deaf Child Week — A344

1993, Apr. 20 Litho. *Perf. 11½x12*

Granite Paper

1217 A344 25f gray & multi .40 .40
1218 A344 50f green & multi .85 .85
1219 A344 150f yellow & multi 3.00 2.50
1220 A344 350f blue & multi 5.25 4.75
Nos. 1217-1220 (4) 9.50 8.50

A345

1993, Aug. 2 Litho. *Perf. 13½x14*
1221 A345 50f green & multi .75 .60
1222 A345 150f orange & multi 2.75 1.75

Invasion by Iraq, 3rd anniv.

Kuwait Airforce, 40th Anniv. — A346

1993, Dec. 9 Litho. *Perf. 13x13½*
1223 A346 50f blue & multi .75 .60
1224 A346 150f green & multi 2.75 1.75

Natl. Day, 33rd Anniv. — A347

1994, Feb. 25 Litho. *Perf. 13½x14*
1225 A347 25f salmon & multi .65 .40
1226 A347 50f yellow & multi 1.25 .75
1227 A347 150f green & multi 3.25 1.75
Nos. 1225-1227 (3) 5.15 2.90

Liberation Day, 3rd Anniv. — A348

1994, Feb. 26

1228	A348	25f yellow & multi	.65	.40
1229	A348	50f blue & multi	1.25	.75
1230	A348	150f gray green & multi	3.50	1.90
		Nos. 1228-1230 (3)	5.40	3.05

Central Bank of Kuwait, 25th Anniv. — A349

1994, Apr. 20 Litho. *Perf. 13½x13*

1231	A349	25f salmon & multi	.65	.40
1232	A349	50f green & multi	1.20	.75
1233	A349	150f blue violet & multi	3.50	2.00
		Nos. 1231-1233 (3)	5.35	3.15

A350

A351

Intl. Year of the Family — A352

1994, May 15 Litho. *Perf. 13*

1234	A350	50f multicolored	.75	.75
1235	A351	150f multicolored	2.25	2.25
1236	A352	200f multicolored	3.25	3.00
		Nos. 1234-1236 (3)	6.25	6.00

A353

1994, June 5 Litho. *Perf. 14*

1237	A353	50f yellow & multi	.80	.80
1238	A353	100f blue & multi	1.60	1.60
1239	A353	150f green & multi	2.50	2.50
		Nos. 1237-1239 (3)	4.90	4.90

Industrial Bank of Kuwait, 20th anniv.

Martyr's Day — A354

1994, June 15 Litho. *Perf. 13*

1240	A354	50f Whirlpool	1.00	.50
1241	A354	100f Shifting sands	2.00	1.00
1242	A354	150f Finger print	3.00	2.25
1243	A354	250f Clouds	3.50	2.50
a.		Min. sheet of 4, #1240-1243	10.00	10.00
		Nos. 1240-1243 (4)	9.50	6.25

ILO, 75th Anniv. — A355

1994, June 25 Litho. *Perf. 14*

1244	A355	50f vio & multi	.75	.75
1245	A355	150f pink & multi	2.50	2.50
1246	A355	350f blue & multi	5.75	5.00
		Nos. 1244-1246 (3)	9.00	8.25

A356

1994, Aug. 2 Litho. *Perf. 12½x13½*

1247	A356	50f green blue & multi	1.10	.75
1248	A356	150f blue & multi	3.00	2.00
1249	A356	350f lilac & multi	7.00	5.00
		Nos. 1247-1249 (3)	11.10	7.75

Invasion by Iraq, 4th anniv.

Port Authority — A357

1994, Aug. 31 Litho. *Perf. 12½x14*

1250	A357	50f pink & multi	1.50	.75
1251	A357	150f blue & multi	4.00	2.00
1252	A357	350f green & multi	9.50	5.00
		Nos. 1250-1252 (3)	15.00	7.75

Science Club, 20th Anniv. — A358

1994, Sept. 11 *Perf. 14*

1253	A358	50f blue & multi	1.00	.75
1254	A358	100f green & multi	2.10	1.50
1255	A358	150f red & multi	2.75	2.00
		Nos. 1253-1255 (3)	5.85	4.25

A359

Designs showing emblem and: 50f, Map of Arab countries, building. 100f, Windows, building. 150f, Doors below portico.

1994, Nov. 12 *Perf. 11½*

1256	A359	50f multicolored	1.00	.75
1257	A359	100f multicolored	1.60	1.25
1258	A359	150f multicolored	3.50	2.25
		Nos. 1256-1258 (3)	6.10	4.25

Arab Towns Organization, opening of headquarters.

ICAO, 50th Anniv. — A360

Designs: 100f, Emblems, sailing ship. 150f, Emblems, co-operation, co-ordination. 350f, Emblem, airplane in flight.

1994, Dec. 7 *Perf. 14½*

1259	A360	100f silver, gold & multi	2.25	2.25
1260	A360	150f silver, gold & multi	3.50	3.50
1261	A360	350f gold & multi	7.50	5.75
		Nos. 1259-1261 (3)	13.25	11.50

Kuwait Airways, 40th Anniv. — A361

1994, Dec. 20 *Perf. 13x14*

1262	A361	50f lake & multi	1.00	.75
1263	A361	100f green & multi	1.75	1.25
1264	A361	150f slate & multi	3.25	2.25
		Nos. 1262-1264 (3)	6.00	4.25

1995 Census — A362

1995, Feb. 6 Litho. *Perf. 14*

1265	A362	50f yellow & multi	1.00	.75
1266	A362	100f green & multi	1.75	1.25
1267	A362	150f brown & multi	3.25	2.25
		Nos. 1265-1267 (3)	6.00	4.25

National Day, 34th Anniv. — A363

1995, Feb. 25 *Perf. 13*

1268	A363	25f blue & multi	.75	.40
1269	A363	50f yellow & multi	1.25	.75
1270	A363	150f lilac & multi	3.50	1.75
		Nos. 1268-1270 (3)	5.50	2.90

Liberation Day, 4th Anniv. — A364

1995, Feb. 26

1271	A364	25f blue & multi	.85	.40
1272	A364	50f green & multi	1.60	.75
1273	A364	150f rose lilac & multi	4.75	1.75
		Nos. 1271-1273 (3)	7.20	2.90

Medical Research A365

50f, Medical building. 100f, Classroom instruction. 150f, Map of Kuwait.

1995, Mar. 20 *Perf. 14*

1274	A365	50f multi	1.00	.75
1275	A365	100f multi	1.50	1.25
1276	A365	150f multi	3.00	2.00
		Nos. 1274-1276 (3)	5.50	4.00

Arab League, 50th Anniv. — A366

Designs: 50f, Kuwaiti, league flags over emblems, map, vert. 100f, Flags over "50," emblem. 150f, Flags as clasping hands, vert.

1995, Mar. 22 *Perf. 13*

1277	A366	50f multicolored	1.00	.75
1278	A366	100f multicolored	1.50	1.25
1279	A366	150f multicolored	3.00	2.00
		Nos. 1277-1279 (3)	5.50	4.00

World Health Day — A367

1995, Apr. 7 Litho. *Perf. 13½x13*

1280	A367	50f blue & multi	1.00	.75
1281	A367	150f pink & multi	3.75	2.00
1282	A367	200f yellow & multi	4.25	2.75
		Nos. 1280-1282 (3)	9.00	5.50

Volleyball, Cent. — A368

Designs: 50f, One gold ball. 100f, Gold "1," one gold ball. 150f, "1," both balls in gold.

1995, June 5 Litho. *Perf. 14*

1283	A368	50f shown	1.00	1.00
1284	A368	100f multicolored	2.00	2.00
1285	A368	150f multicolored	3.50	3.00
		Nos. 1283-1285 (3)	6.50	6.00

Invasion by Iraq, 5th Anniv. — A369

1995, Aug. 2 Litho. *Perf. 13*

1286	A369	50f purple & multi	1.50	.75
1287	A369	100f red & multi	2.50	1.25
1288	A369	150f green & multi	4.50	2.00
		Nos. 1286-1288 (3)	8.50	4.00

UN, 50th Anniv. — A370

1995, Aug. 12 *Perf. 13x13½*

1289	A370	25f multi	.75	.50
1290	A370	50f orange & multi	1.50	1.00
1291	A370	150f bl grn & multi	2.75	1.75
		Nos. 1289-1291 (3)	5.00	3.25

FAO, 50th Anniv. — A371

People in traditional dress with: 50f, Cattle, camels, sheep. 100f, Fish, boat. 150f, Poultry, fruits, vegetables.

1995, Sept. 21 *Perf. 13½x13*

1292	A371	50f multicolored	1.00	1.00
1293	A371	100f multicolored	1.50	1.50
1294	A371	150f multicolored	3.00	3.00
a.		Min. sheet of 3, #1292-1294	6.00	6.00
		Nos. 1292-1294 (3)	5.50	5.50

A372

World Standards Day — A373

1995, Oct. 14 *Perf. 13*

1295	A372	50f multicolored	1.00	.75
1296	A373	100f green & multi	1.50	1.25
1297	A373	150f violet & multi	3.00	2.00
		Nos. 1295-1297 (3)	5.50	4.00

Flowers — A374

Designs: 5f, Onobrychis ptolemaica. 15f, Convolvulus oxyphyllus. 25f, Papaver rhoeas.

50f, Moltkiopsis ciliata. 150f, Senecio desfontainei.

1995, Nov. 15 Litho. *Perf. 14½*

1298 A374 5f multicolored .55 .30
1299 A374 15f multicolored .75 .40
1300 A374 25f multicolored 1.40 .75
1301 A374 50f multicolored 2.40 1.25
1302 A374 150f multicolored 4.75 2.00
Nos. 1298-1302 (5) 9.85 4.70

Natl. Day, 35th Anniv. — A375

1996, Feb. 25 *Perf. 14*

1303 A375 25f lil rose & multi .75 .40
1304 A375 50f blue green & multi 1.40 .75
1305 A375 150f salmon & multi 4.50 2.00
Nos. 1303-1305 (3) 6.65 3.15

Liberation Day, 5th Anniv. — A376

1996, Feb. 26

1306 A376 25f violet & multi .75 .40
1307 A376 50f brown & multi 1.40 .75
1308 A376 150f blue green & multi 4.50 2.00
Nos. 1306-1308 (3) 6.65 3.15

Arab City Day — A377

1996, Mar. 1 *Perf. 13½*

1309 A377 50f yel grn & multi 1.00 1.00
1310 A377 100f pink & multi 2.00 2.00
1311 A377 150f blue green & multi 3.00 3.00
Nos. 1309-1311 (3) 6.00 6.00

A378

1996, Jan. 27 *Perf. 14*

1312 A378 50f blue & multi 1.00 1.00
1313 A378 100f gray & multi 2.00 2.00
1314 A378 150f rose lilac & multi 3.00 3.00
Nos. 1312-1314 (3) 6.00 6.00

Scouting in Kuwait, 60th Anniv. — A379

50f, On top of watchtower. 100f, Drawing water from well. 150f, Planting seedling.

1996, Jan. 14 *Perf. 13½*

1315 A379 50f yellow & multi 1.25 1.25
1316 A379 100f lilac & multi 3.00 3.00
1317 A379 150f blue green & multi 4.75 4.75
Nos. 1315-1317 (3) 9.00 9.00

Kuwait Money Show — A380

1996, Jan. 2 *Perf. 14*

1318 A380 25f gold & multi .75 .75
1319 A380 100f blue & multi 2.50 2.50
1320 A380 150f dk gray & multi 3.75 3.75
Nos. 1318-1320 (3) 7.00 7.00

7th Kuwait Dental Assoc. Conference — A381

1996, Mar. 27 Litho. *Perf. 14x13½*

1321 A381 25f orange & multi .65 .65
1322 A381 50f violet & multi 1.10 1.10
1323 A381 150f blue & multi 3.25 3.25
Nos. 1321-1323 (3) 5.00 5.00

UNESCO, 50th Anniv. — A382

1996, Apr. 10 *Perf. 13½x14*

1324 A382 25f violet & multi .60 .60
1325 A382 100f green & multi 1.90 1.90
1326 A382 150f orange & multi 3.50 3.50
Nos. 1324-1326 (3) 6.00 6.00

1st Oil Exports, 50th Anniv. — A383

1996, June 30 Litho. *Perf. 13*

1327 A383 25f multicolored .75 .75
1328 A383 100f gray & multi 2.50 2.50
1329 A383 150f bister & multi 3.75 3.75
Nos. 1327-1329 (3) 7.00 7.00

Rule of Al-Sabah Family, Cent. — A384

1996, Aug. 12

1330 A384 25f shown .65 .65
1331 A384 50f Shiek, flags 1.10 1.10
1332 A384 150f like #1330 3.25 3.25
Nos. 1330-1332 (3) 5.00 5.00

1996 Summer Olympic Games, Atlanta — A385

1996, Oct. 5 *Perf. 13½*

1333 A385 25f Shooting .60 .60
1334 A385 50f Running 1.20 1.20
1335 A385 100f Weight lifting 2.40 2.40
1336 A385 150f Fencing 4.00 4.00
Nos. 1333-1336 (4) 8.20 8.20

A 750f souvenir sheet exists. Value $150.

Kuwait University, 30th Anniv. — A386

1996, Nov. 27 Litho. *Perf. 13½x14*

1337 A386 25f green & multi .65 .65
1338 A386 100f blue & multi 2.10 2.10
1339 A386 150f yellow & multi 3.25 3.25
Nos. 1337-1339 (3) 6.00 6.00

1st Children's Cultural Festival — A387

1996, Nov. 20 *Perf. 14x13½*

1340 A387 25f brn gray & multi .65 .65
1341 A387 100f multicolored 2.10 2.10
1342 A387 150f yel grn & multi 3.25 3.25
Nos. 1340-1342 (3) 6.00 6.00

3rd Al-Qurain Cultrual Festival — A388

1996, Nov. 20 *Perf. 14*

1343 A388 50f orange & multi 1.25 1.25
1344 A388 100f blue & multi 2.25 2.25
1345 A388 150f green & multi 3.50 3.50
Nos. 1343-1345 (3) 7.00 7.00

Liberation Tower — A389

1996, Dec. 10 *Perf. 13x13½*

1346 A389 5f red & multi .25 .25
1347 A389 10f yel bis & multi .25 .25
1348 A389 15f brt rose & multi .40 .30
1349 A389 25f pale pink & multi .50 .45
a. Booklet pane of 4 —
Complete booklet, #1349a —
1350 A389 50f violet & multi 1.25 1.00
a. Booklet pane of 4 —
Complete booklet, #1350a —
1351 A389 100f brt yel & multi 2.25 1.50
1352 A389 150f blue & multi 3.75 2.50
a. Booklet pane of 4 —
Complete booklet, #1352a —
1353 A389 200f pink & multi 3.00 3.75
1354 A389 250f dp bl & multi 6.00 4.50
1355 A389 350f blue & multi 8.50 6.00
Nos. 1346-1355 (10) 26.15 20.50
Set of 3 booklets, Nos. 1349a-1350a, 1352a *35.00*

National Day, 36th Anniv. — A390

1997, Feb. 25 Litho. *Perf. 14½*

1356 A390 25f blue & multi .80 .30
1357 A390 50f lilac & multi 1.50 1.50
1358 A390 150f orange & multi 4.50 4.50
Nos. 1356-1358 (3) 6.80 6.30

Liberation Day, 6th Anniv. — A391

1997, Feb. 26 *Perf. 13x13½*

1359 A391 25f tan & multi .80 .80
1360 A391 50f lilac & multi 1.50 1.50
1361 A391 150f blue & multi 4.50 4.50
Nos. 1359-1361 (3) 6.80 6.80

Marine Life — A392

No. 1368: Various views of a school of shrimp: a, b, c, d, 25f. e, f, g, h, 50f. i, j, k, l, 100f. m, n, o, p, 150f.

1997, Jan. 15 *Perf. 14½*

1362 A392 25f Maid .40 .40
1363 A392 50f Sheim .75 .75
1364 A392 100f Hamoor 1.50 1.50
1365 A392 150f Sobaity 2.25 2.25
1366 A392 200f Nagroor 3.25 3.25
1367 A392 350f Zobaidy 5.50 5.50
Nos. 1362-1367 (6) 13.65 13.65

Sheet of 16

1368 A392 Sheet of 16, #a.-p. 24.00 24.00

Montreal Protocol on Substances that Deplete Ozone Layer, 10th Anniv. — A393

1997, Sept. 16 Litho. *Perf. 13½x13*

1369 A393 25f blue & multi .60 .60
1370 A393 50f violet & multi 1.10 1.10
1371 A393 150f bl grn & multi 3.50 3.50
Nos. 1369-1371 (3) 5.20 5.20

Industries Exhibition — A394

1997, Oct. 1

1372 A394 25f brt pink & multi .60 .60
1373 A394 50f green & multi 1.10 1.10
1374 A394 150f blue & multi 3.50 3.50
Nos. 1372-1374 (3) 5.20 5.20

22nd Kuwait Arabic Book Exhibition — A395

1997, Nov. 19 Litho. *Perf. 13½x13*

Border Color

1375 A395 25f pink .60 .60
1376 A395 50f blue 1.10 1.10
1377 A395 150f blue green 3.50 3.50
Nos. 1375-1377 (3) 5.20 5.20

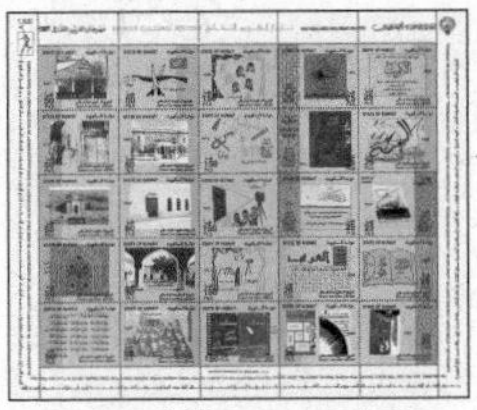

Cultural History — A396

a, 50f, Qibliya Girls School, 1937. b, 50f, Scissors cutting ribbon, Fine Arts Exhibition, 1959. c, 150f, Folk Theatre Group, 1956. d, 25f, 1st Book Fair, 1975. e, 25f, Kuwait Magazine, 1928. f, 50f, Mubarakiya School, 1912. g, 50f, Kuwait Natl. Museum, 1958. h, 150f, Academy of Music, 1972. i, 25f, A'lam Al-Fikr (periodical), 1970. j, 25f, Al'Bitha Magazine, 1946. k, 50f, Building complex, 1953 (Al-Arabi Magazine). l, 50f, Building, 1959. m, 150f, Al-Sharqiya Cinema, 1955. n, 25f, Al'Lam Al Ma'rifa (periodical), 1978. o, 25f, Dalil Almohtar Fi Alaam al-Bihar (boat), 1923. p, 50f, Alma'had Aldini (arabesques), 1947. q, 50f, Folklore Center, 1956. r, 150f, Theatrical Academy, 1967. s, 25f, Al-Arabi Magazine, 1958. t, 25f, Public Library (book), 1923. u, 50f, Al Ma'Arif Printing Press (Arabic writing), 1947. v, 50f, Literary Club, 1924. w, 150f, Bas Ya Bahar (1st Kuwaitii feature film), 1970. x, 25f, Al Thaqafa Al-Alamiya (periodical), 1981. y, 25f, The World Theatre (periodical), 1969.

1997, Nov. 30

1378 A396 Sheet of 25, #a.-y. 30.00 30.00

Nos. 1378a-1378y each contain year date of event depicted.

Educational Science Museum, 25th Anniv. — A397

Designs: 25f, Whale, quadrant, vert. 50f, Space exploration, whale, dinosaur. No. 1381, Astronaut, dinosaur, satellite dish, airplane, globe, skeleton encircling whale, vert. No. 1382, Coelacanth.

Perf. 13½x13, 13x13½

1997, Nov. 1 Litho.

1379 A397 25f multicolored 1.00 .65
1380 A397 50f multicolored 2.00 1.00
1381 A397 150f multicolored 6.75 3.25
Nos. 1379-1381 (3) 9.75 4.90

Souvenir Sheet

1382 A397 150f multicolored 17.00 17.00

No. 1382 is a continuous design and sold for 1d.

18th Summit of Gulf Cooperation Countries A398

Designs: 25f, Flags of member countries, doves, vert. 50f, Map, birds with flag colors. 150f, Doves perched atop flags, vert.

1997, Dec. 20 ***Perf. 13½x14***

1383 A398 25f multicolored	.75	.75
1384 A398 50f multicolored	1.50	1.50
1385 A398 150f multicolored	4.75	4.75
a. Bklt. pane of 3, #1383-1385	*22.50*	
Complete booklet, #1385a	*22.50*	
Nos. 1383-1385 (3)	7.00	7.00

National Day, 37th Anniv. — A399

1998, Feb. 25 Litho. ***Perf. 13x13½***

1386 A399 25f yellow & multi	.80	.80
1387 A399 50f pink & multi	1.40	1.40
1388 A399 150f blue & multi	4.25	4.25
Nos. 1386-1388 (3)	6.45	6.45

Liberation Day, 7th Anniv. — A400

1998, Feb. 26

1389 A400 25f yellow & multi	.80	.80
1390 A400 50f orange & multi	1.40	1.40
1391 A400 150f green & multi	4.25	4.25
Nos. 1389-1391 (3)	6.45	6.45

Say No to Drugs — A401

1998, Mar. 16 Litho. ***Perf. 13½x13***

1392 A401 25f tan & multi	.80	.80
1393 A401 50f blue & multi	1.40	1.40
1394 A401 150f white & multi	4.25	4.25
Nos. 1392-1394 (3)	6.45	6.45

Chernobyl disaster, 10th Anniv. — A402

1997, May 2 Litho. ***Perf. 13½x13***

1395 A402 25f orange & multi	.80	.80
1396 A402 50f blue & multi	1.40	1.40
1397 A402 150f red & multi	4.25	4.25
Nos. 1395-1397 (3)	6.45	6.45

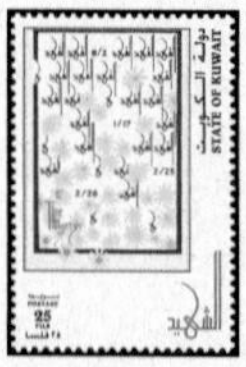

Martyrs — A403

25f, Dates, 1/17, 2/25, 2/26, flowers. 50f, Stylized tree. 150f, Lines, inscriptions.

No. 1401: a, Man with hands in dirt. b, Three boys emptying basket of dirt.

1998, Mar. 31 Litho. ***Perf. 14***

1398 A403 25f multicolored	.75	.75
1399 A403 50f multicolored	1.25	1.25
1400 A403 150f multicolored	4.00	4.00
a. Bklt. pane, 2 ea #1398-1400	22.50	
Complete booklet, #1400a	22.50	

Perf. 14½ Between

Size: 31x54mm

1401 A403 500f Pair, a.-b.	24.00	24.00
Nos. 1398-1401 (4)	30.00	30.00

Ban Land Mines — A405

Stylized amputees using crutches for support: 25f, Two people. 50f, One person. 150f, Two people, nurse.

500f, Three people, nurse.

1998, Aug. 2 ***Perf. 14½***

1402 A405 25f multicolored	1.00	1.00
1403 A405 50f multicolored	2.00	2.00
1404 A405 150f multicolored	5.00	5.00

Size: 89x82mm

Imperf

1405 A405 500f multicolored	13.00	13.00
Nos. 1402-1405 (4)	21.00	21.00

Life in Pre-Oil Kuwait — A406

Designs: 25f, Seated at ceremonial meal. 50f, Building boat. 100f, Weaving. 150f, Loading boat. 250f, Pouring water from water skin into bowl. 350f, Man with pigeons.

1998, Apr. 14 Litho. ***Perf. 14***

Booklet Stamps

1406 A406 25f multicolored	.50	.50
1407 A406 50d multicolored	1.00	1.00
1408 A406 100f multicolored	2.00	2.00
1409 A406 150f multicolored	3.00	3.00
1410 A406 250f multicolored	5.00	5.00
1411 A406 350f multicolored	7.00	7.00
a. Booklet pane, #1406-1411	27.50	
Complete booklet, #1411a	27.50	

1998, Sept. 1 Litho. ***Perf. 14***

25f, Man shaving another man's head. 50f, Woman using grindstone. 100f, Man pulling thread through cloth. 150f, Man gluing artifacts together. 250f, Potter. 350f, Veiled woman holding rope.

Booklet Stamps

1412 A406 25f multicolored	.50	.50
1413 A406 50f multicolored	1.00	1.00
1414 A406 100f multicolored	2.00	2.00
1415 A406 150f multicolored	3.00	3.00
1416 A406 250f multicolored	5.00	5.00
1417 A406 350f multicolored	7.00	7.00
a. Booklet pane, #1412-1417	27.50	
Complete booklet, #1417a	27.50	

Emblem of Kuwait Post — A407

1998, Oct. 3 Litho. ***Perf. 13x13½***

1418 A407 25f green & multi	.50	.50
1419 A407 50f blue & multi	1.00	1.00
1420 A407 100f brt pink & multi	1.50	1.50
1421 A407 150f orange & multi	2.75	2.75
1422 A407 250f brick red & multi	4.25	4.25
Nos. 1418-1422 (5)	10.00	10.00

Intl. Year of the Ocean A408

1998, June 1 Litho. ***Perf. 13½***

1423 A408 25f green & multi	1.00	1.00
1424 A408 50f blue & multi	2.00	2.00
1425 A408 150f lilac & multi	6.00	6.00
Nos. 1423-1425 (3)	9.00	9.00

No. 1424 is 27x37mm.

Union of Consumer Co-operative Societies, 25th Anniv. — A409

1998, July 1 Litho. ***Perf. 13½x13***

1426 A409 25f buff & multi	1.00	1.00
1427 A409 50f blue & multi	2.00	2.00
1428 A409 150f multicolored	6.00	6.00
Nos. 1426-1428 (3)	9.00	9.00

Children's Cultural House — A410

1998, Nov. 28 Litho. ***Perf. 13½x13***

1429 A410 25f yellow & multi	.80	.80
1430 A410 50f grn, yel & multi	1.75	1.75
1431 A410 150f green & multi	4.50	4.50
Nos. 1429-1431 (3)	7.05	7.05

A411

1998, Dec. 10 ***Perf. 14x14½***

1432 A411 25f multicolored	.80	.80
1433 A411 50f multicolored	1.75	1.75
1434 A411 150f multicolored	4.50	4.50
Nos. 1432-1434 (3)	7.05	7.05

Universal Declaration of Human Rights, 50th anniv.

A412

1998 Litho. ***Perf. 14x14½***

1435 A412 25f orange & multi	.75	.75
1436 A412 50f violet & multi	1.25	1.25
1437 A412 150f green & multi	4.00	4.00
Nos. 1435-1437 (3)	6.00	6.00

The Public Authority for Applied Education and Training, 25th anniv.

Organ Transplantation in Kuwait, 20th Anniv. — A413

1999 Litho. ***Perf. 13x13½***

1438 A413 50f Liver	1.50	1.50
1439 A413 150f Heart	4.50	4.50

Liberation Day, 8th Anniv. — A414

1999, Feb. 26

1440 A414 50f Building	1.50	1.50
1441 A414 150f Building, diff.	4.50	4.50

Sief Palace Complex A415

Various buildings in complex.

1999 ***Perf. 15x14***

1442 A415 25f multicolored	.40	.40
1443 A415 50f multicolored	.70	.70
1444 A415 100f multicolored	1.75	1.75
1445 A415 150f multicolored	2.75	2.75
1446 A415 250f multicolored	5.25	5.25
1447 A415 350f multicolored	7.00	7.00
a. Booklet pane, #1442-1447	22.50	
Complete booklet, #1447a	22.50	
Nos. 1442-1447 (6)	17.85	17.85

Al Arabi Magazine — A416

1999 ***Perf. 13½x13***

1448 A416 50f violet & multi	1.75	1.75
1449 A416 150f green & multi	4.75	4.75

Natl. Day, 38th Anniv. — A417

1999 ***Perf. 13x13½***

1450 A417 50f brown & multi	1.50	1.50
1451 A417 150f blue & multi	4.50	4.50

Hawk A418

Sailing Ship A419

50f, Camel. 100f, Traditional Boat.

1999(?)-2003 Litho. ***Perf. 14½x14***

1452 A418 25f multicolored	.90	.90
1453 A418 50f multicolored	1.75	1.75

Coil Stamp

1453A A419 100f multicolored	2.50	2.50
1454 A419 150f multicolored	5.50	5.50
Nos. 1452-1454 (4)	10.65	10.65

Issued: 100f, Jan. 2003.

Science Club, 25th Anniv. — A420

Background color: 50f, Blue. 150f, Green. 350f, Red.

1999, Oct. 20 Litho. ***Perf. 13x13¼***

1455-1457 A420 Set of 3	17.00	17.00

Intl. Civil Aviation Day — A421

1999, Dec. 7 Litho. ***Perf. 13x13¼***

1458 A421 50f multi	1.25	1.25
1459 A421 150f multi	3.25	3.25
1460 A421 250f multi	5.50	5.50
Nos. 1458-1460 (3)	10.00	10.00

UPU, 125th Anniv. — A421a

Panel colors: 50f, Orange. 150f, Purple. 350f, Green.

1d, Two hemispheres.

1999 Litho. *Perf. 13¼x13*
1460A-1460C A421a Set of 3 11.00 11.00
1460Ce Booklet pane, #1460A-1460C + label 11.00
Booklet, #1460Ce 11.00

Size: 100x75mm

Imperf

1460D A421a 1d multi 16.00 16.00

Kuwait Intl. Airport — A422

2000, Jan. 2 *Perf. 13¼x13*
1461 A422 50f multi .85 .85
1462 A422 150f multi 2.00 2.00
1463 A422 250f multi 4.50 4.50
Nos. 1461-1463 (3) 7.35 7.35

National Day, 39th Anniv. — A423

2000
1464 A423 25f multi .65 .65
1465 A423 50f multi 1.25 1.25
1466 A423 150f multi 4.25 4.25
Nos. 1464-1466 (3) 6.15 6.15

Liberation Day, 9th Anniv. — A424

2000
1467 A424 25f multi 1.25 1.25
1468 A424 50f multi 3.75 3.75
1469 A424 150f multi 5.00 5.00
Nos. 1467-1469 (3) 10.00 10.00

Kuwait Conference for Autism and Communication Deficits — A425

Designs: 25f, Puzzle pieces, three children, Kuwait Tower. 50f, Puzzle pieces, children. 150f, Children, Kuwait Tower, flowers.

2000 *Perf. 13x13¼*
1470 A425 25f multi .65 .65
1471 A425 50f multi 1.25 1.25
1472 A425 150f multi 4.25 4.25
Nos. 1470-1472 (3) 6.15 6.15

Kuwait City — A425a

Background colors: 50f, Blue. 150f, Green. 350f, Red violet.

2000, Apr. 24 Litho. *Perf. 14x14½*
1472A-1472C A425a Set of 3 8.50 8.50

Third Special Education Week — A425b

Background color: 50f, Yellow. 150f, Salmon. 350f, Blue.

2000, May 10 *Perf. 13¼x13*
1472D-1472F A425b Set of 3 8.50 8.50

2000 Summer Olympics, Sydney — A425c

Emblems of 2002 Olympics, Kuwait Olympic Committee and: 25f, Judo. 50f, Shooting. 150f, Swimming. 200f, Weight lifting. 250f, Hurdles. 350f, Soccer.

No. 1472M, Emblems of 2002 Olympics, Kuwait Olympic Committee and judo, swimming, shooting, weight lifting, hurdles and soccer.

2000 Litho. *Perf. 13x13¼*
1472G-1472L A425c Set of 6 20.00 20.00

Souvenir Sheet

Size: 98x69mm

1472M A425c 1d multi *55.00 55.00*

Sixth Gulf Cooperation Council Countries Joint Stamp Exhibition, Kuwait — A425d

Denomination color: 25f, Blue. 50f, Red. 150f, Green.
1d, Emblems of previous exhibitions.

2000 Litho. *Perf. 14¼*
1472N-1472P A425d Set of 3 4.50 4.50

Size: 146x112mm

Imperf

1472Q A425d 1d multi 17.00 17.00

Intl. Investment Forum — A426

Background colors: 25f, Gray. 50f, White. 150f, Black.

2000, Mar. 4 Litho. *Perf. 13x13¼*
1473-1475 A426 Set of 3 8.00 8.00

National Committee for Missing and Prisoner of War Affairs — A426a

Designs: 25f, Emblem. 50f, Emblem and chains. 150f, Emblem and years.

2000, Aug. 2 Litho. *Perf. 13x13¼*
1475A-1475C A426a Set of 3 3.25 3.25

Kuwaiti Dental Association, 25th Anniv. — A426b

Frame color: 50f, Pink. 150f, Light blue. 350f, Lilac.

2000, Oct. 15 *Perf. 13¼x13*
1475D-1475F A426b Set of 3 6.50 6.50

World Environment Day — A427

Denominations, 50f, 150f, 350f.

2000 Litho. *Perf. 13x13¼*
1476-1478 A427 Set of 3 9.00 9.00

Gulf Investment Corporation, 15th Anniv. — A428

New Gulf Investment Corporation headquarters, emblem, "15" and frame color of: 25f, Green. 50f, Blue. 150f, Red.

2000, Oct. 31 Litho. *Perf. 13x13¼*
1479-1481 A428 Set of 3 8.00 8.00

General Administration of Customs, Cent. — A429

Denominations: 50f, 150f, 350f.

2000 Litho. *Perf. 13¼x14*
1482-1484 A429 Set of 3 6.75 6.75
a. Booklet pane, #1482-1484 15.00
Complete booklet, #1484a 15.00

Imperf

Size: 100x75mm

1485 A429 1d multi 13.50 13.50

No. 1485 contains one 47x28mm perf. 13¼x14 non-denominated label.

Hala Fibrayar — A430

Panel colors: 25f, Purple. 50f, Red violet. 150f, Blue.

2001 Litho. *Perf. 13¼x13*
1486-1488 A430 Set of 3 4.75 4.75

Prisoners of War — A431

Background colors: 25f, White. 50f, Blue & blue green. 150f, Multicolored.

2001 *Perf. 13x13¼*
1489-1491 A431 Set of 3 5.50 5.50

UN High Commissioner for Refugees, 50th Anniv. — A432

Various depictions of anniversary emblem: 25f, 50f, 150f.

2001
1492-1494 A432 Set of 3 4.75 4.75

Kuwait, 2001 Arab Cultural Capital — A433

Background colors: 25f, Yellow. 50f, Green. 150f, Blue.

2001
1495-1497 A433 Set of 3 4.75 4.75

Liberation Day, 10th Anniv. — A434

Frame color: 25f, Lilac. 50f, Blue. 150f, Yellow.

2001 *Perf. 13¼x13*
1498-1500 A434 Set of 3 4.75 4.75

National Day, 40th Anniv. — A435

Frame color: 25f, Orange. 50f, Yellow. 150f, Blue green.

2001
1501-1503 A435 Set of 3 4.75 4.75

Kuwait Diving Team, 10th Anniv. — A436

"10" and: 25f, Fish. 50f, Divers. 150f, Shark, turtle, vert.

2001 *Perf. 13x13¼, 13¼x13*
1504-1506 A436 Set of 3 4.75 4.75

Radio Kuwait, 50th Anniv. — A437

Frame color: 25f, Yellow brown. 50f, Blue, vert. 150f, Red, vert.

2001 *Perf. 13x13¼, 13¼x13*
1507-1509 A437 Set of 3 4.75 4.75

Intifada — A438

Dome of the Rock, Jerusalem: 25f, 50f, 150f.

2001 *Perf. 13x13¼*
1510-1512 A438 Set of 3 5.00 5.00

Year of Dialogue Among Civilizations — A439

Background colors: 25f, Orange & yellow. 50f, Dark & light green. 150f, Rose & pink.

2001 *Perf. 13¼x13*
1513-1515 A439 Set of 3 4.75 4.75

Human Rights — A440

Designs: 25f, Hands covering man's face, vert. 50f, Barbed wire, clock, man's face. 150f, Chains, globe, child, woman.

2001 *Perf. 13¼x13, 13x13¼*
1516-1518 A440 Set of 3 4.75 4.75

A441

A442

AWQAF Foundation — A443

2001 ***Perf. 14x13***
1519 A441 25f multi .50 .50
1520 A442 50f multi 1.00 1.00
1521 A443 150f multi 3.25 3.25
Nos. 1519-1521 (3) 4.75 4.75

Kuwait Fund for Arab Economic Development, 40th Anniv. — A444

Background colors: 25f, Yellow. 50f, Green & gray.

2001 ***Perf. 13¼x13***
1522-1523 A444 Set of 2 1.75 1.75

Touristic Enterprises Company, 25th Anniv. — A445

Stylistic flora: 25f, 50f, 100f, 150f.
250f, Combined designs of four stamps.

2001 ***Perf. 13¼x13***
1524-1527 A445 Set of 4 7.50 7.50

Size: 60x80mm

Imperf

1528 A445 250f multi 6.00 6.00

National Bank of Kuwait, 50th Anniv. — A447

Emblem and: 25f, Facade of old building. 50f, Modern building. 150f, Camels.

2002, Jan. 16 **Litho.** ***Perf. 13x13¼***
1532-1534 A447 Set of 3 5.50 5.50

Liberation Day, 11th Anniv. — A448

Background color: 25f, Light blue. 50f, Light yellow. 150f, White.

2002, Feb. 26 ***Perf. 13¼x13***
1535-1537 A448 Set of 3 5.50 5.50

Social Development Office, 10th Anniv. — A449

Background color: 25f, Light yellow. 50f, Light blue.

2002, Apr. 21
1538-1539 A449 Set of 2 1.75 1.75

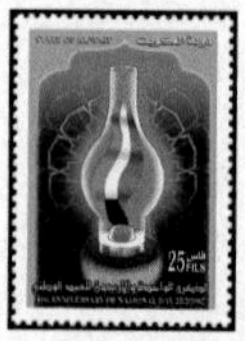

41st National Day — A450

Frame color: 25f, Orange. 50f, Green. 150f, Purple.

2002, Feb. 25 **Litho.** ***Perf. 13¼x13***
1540-1542 A450 Set of 3 4.50 4.50

Nomadism From the Hejaz to Africa — A451

Top panel color: 25f, Pale orange. 50f, Blue. 150f, Purple.

2002, Mar. 11
1543-1545 A451 Set of 3 5.00 5.00

Rehabilitation of Al-Qurain Landfill Site — A452

Panel color: 25f, Blue. 50f, Purple. 150f, Green.

2002, Apr. 1
1546-1548 A452 Set of 3 4.50 4.50

Kuwait Scientific Center A453

Designs; Nos. 1549a, 1550e, Lapwing. Nos. 1549b, 1550d, Spur-winged plover. Nos. 1549c, 1550c, Eurasian river otter. Nos. 1549d, 1550b, Saltwater crocodile. Nos. 1549e, 1550i, Fennec fox. Nos. 1549f, 1550h, Caracal. Nos. 1549g, 1550g, Cushion sister starfish. Nos. 1549h, 1550f, Cuttlefish. Nos. 1549i, 1550m, Sand tiger shark. Nos. 1549j, 1550l, Lionfish. Nos. 1549k, 1550k, Kestrel. Nos. 1549l, 1550j, Egyptian fruit bat. Nos. 1549m, 1550a, Science center.

Perf. 13¼x13¾, 14x13¼ (#1550k)

2002, Apr. 17
1549 Sheet of 13 24.00 24.00
a.-l. A453 25f Any single .25 .25
m. A453 50f multi .30 .30
1550 Booklet of 13 panes 40.00
a.-m. A453 50f Any single pane .30 .30

Imperf

Size: 80x60mm

1551 A453 250f shown 12.00 12.00

Stamp sizes: Nos. 1549a-1549l, 30x25mm; No. 1549m, 45x27mm. Nos. 1550a-1550j, 1550l-1550m, 50x36mm; No. 1550k, 32x48mm.

Kuwait Foundation for the Advancement of Sciences, 25th Anniv. (in 2001) — A454

Foundation emblem and: 25f, 25th anniversary emblem. 50f, 25th anniversary emblem and building. 150f, Map of Kuwait, vert.

Perf. 13x13¼, 13¼x13

2002 ? **Litho.**
1552-1554 A454 Set of 3 4.75 4.75

Intl. Volunteers Year (in 2001) — A455

Background colors: 25f, White. 50f, Lilac. 150f, Yellow.

2002 ? ***Perf. 13¼x13***
1555-1557 A455 Set of 3 4.50 4.50

National Council for Culture, Arts and Letters, 25th Anniv. — A456

Panel color: 25f, Lilac. 50f, Olive green. 150f, Bright blue.
500f, Lilac.

2002 ? ***Perf. 13¼x13***
1558-1560 A456 Set of 3 4.50 4.50

Souvenir Sheet

Imperf

1561 A456 500f multi 10.00 10.00

No. 1561 contains one 42x58mm stamp.

Kuwait Society of Engineers, 40th Anniv. — A457

Panel color at LR: 25f, Brown. 50f, Bright green. 150f, Yellow green.

2002 ***Perf. 13x13¼***
1562-1564 A457 Set of 3 4.50 4.50

Public Authority for Applied Education and Training, 20th Anniv. — A458

"20," "1982-2002" and: 25f, Men at work. 50f, Surgeon. 100f, Man with machine. 150f, Building and Kuwait flag. 250f, Ironworkers.

2002 ***Perf. 13¼x13***
1565-1569 A458 Set of 5 10.00 10.00

42nd National Day — A459

Frame color: 25f, Green. 50f, Red. 150f, Blue.

2003, Feb. 25 **Litho.** ***Perf. 13x13¼***
1570-1572 A459 Set of 3 6.75 6.75

Martyr's Bureau — A460

Emblem and: 25f, Ship. 50f, Flag on Qarow Island. 150f, Fingerprint. 350f, Map of Kuwait.

2003
1573-1576 A460 Set of 4 14.00 14.00
1576a Booklet pane, #1573-1576 14.00 —
Complete booklet, #1576a 14.00

Intl. Day Against Desertification — A461

Designs: 25f, Dead tree. 50f, Log. 150f, Palm trees.

2003 **Litho.** ***Perf. 13¼x13***
1577-1579 A461 Set of 3 5.50 5.50

Commercial Bank of Kuwait, 43rd Anniv. — A462

"43" and: 25f, Geometric design. 50f, Old bank building. 150f, New bank building.

2003 ***Perf. 13***
1580-1582 A462 Set of 3 5.00 5.00

Kuwait Awqaf Public Foundation, 10th Anniv. — A463

Emblem, "10," and: 50f, Building, family. 100f, Fingers. 150f, Man, minaret.

2004, Jan. 19
1583-1585 A463 Set of 3 6.00 6.00

A464

A465

Ministry of Information, 50th Anniv. — A466

2003
1586 A464 25f multi .65 .65
1587 A465 100f multi 2.25 2.25
1588 A466 150f multi 3.50 3.50
Nos. 1586-1588 (3) 6.40 6.40

43rd National Day — A467

Designs: 25f, Palm tree. 50f, Pearl in shell. 150f, Fortress, flags. 350f, Buildings, dhow.

2004, Feb. 25 ***Perf. 13¼x13***
1589-1592 A467 Set of 4 12.00 12.00

Kuwait Airways, 50th Anniv. — A468

Various airplanes: 25f, 50f, 75f, 100f, 125f, 150f.

2004, Dec. 18 Litho. *Perf. 13x13¼*

1593-1598	A468	Set of 6	12.00	12.00

Kuwait Petroleum Corporation, 25th Anniv. — A469

Headquarters: 50f, In daytime. 75f, With sun on horizon. 125f, At night.

2005, Jan. 1 *Perf. 14½*

1599-1601	A469	Set of 3	8.00	8.00

44th National Day — A470

Sheikhs, dhow, eagle and: 75f, Towers. 125f, Truck at port.

2005, Feb. 25 *Perf. 14*

1602-1603	A470	Set of 2	4.00	4.00

Liberation Day, 14th Anniv. — A471

Sheikhs, flag and: 50f, Airplane, satellite dish. 150f, Tower.

2005, Feb. 26

1604-1605	A471	Set of 2	6.00	6.00

Technical Education, 50th Anniv. — A472

Background color: 25f, Purple. 50f, Red. 75f, Orange. 125f, Green.

2005, Mar. 15

1606-1609	A472	Set of 4	6.25	6.25

Flags and Emblems — A473

Designs: No. 1610, Triangular 1961 ship and harbor flag. No. 1611, 1940 official flag. No. 1612, 1903 special event flag. No. 1613, 1940-50 ruling family flag. No. 1614, Two 1914 right triangle flags. No. 1615, 1921-40, 1956-62 and 1962 emblems.

No. 1616, 1962-56 emblem. No. 1617, 1921-40 emblem.

No. 1618, Right triangle flag of 1914 with Arabic script and emblem in center and script along short side like that on No. 1613. No. 1619, Right triangle flag of 1914 with Arabic script in center. No. 1620, Right triangle flag of 1914 with Arabic script in center and script along short side.

No. 1621, Triangular 1921 ship and harbor flag. No. 1622, Like No. 1610. No. 1623, Rectangular 1961 ship and harbor flag. No. 1624, Rectangular 1921 ship and harbor flag.

No. 1625, 1914-61 official flag. No. 1626, 1871-1914 official flag. No. 1627, 1746-1871 official flag. No. 1628, Like No. 1611. No. 1629, 1921-61 official flag.

No. 1630, 1903 special event flag. No. 1631, 1866 special event flag. No. 1632, 1921 special event flag.

No. 1633, 1921-40 ruling family flag with two white stripes. No. 1634, Like No. 1613, with colored background. No. 1635, 1921-40 ruling family flag with one white stripe.

2005, Oct. 15 Litho. *Perf. 14x13¾*

1610	A473	200f multi	3.00	3.00
1611	A473	250f multi	4.25	4.25

Perf. 14

Size: 40x30mm

1612	A473	350f multi	5.25	5.25
1613	A473	500f multi	8.50	8.50

Perf. 14x13¾

Size: 60x30mm

1614	A473	1d multi	14.50	14.50
1615	A473	1d multi	14.50	14.50
	Nos. 1610-1615 (6)		50.00	50.00

Booklet Stamps

Self-Adhesive

Die Cut Perf. 13

Size:40x34mm

1616	A473	100f multi	2.50	2.50
1617	A473	100f multi	2.50	2.50
a.	Booklet pane, #1616-1617		5.00	

Die Cut Perf. 13x13¼

Size: 40x30mm

1618	A473	175f multi	4.75	4.75
1619	A473	175f multi	4.75	4.75
1620	A473	175f multi	4.75	4.75
a.	Booklet pane, #1618-1620		14.50	

Die Cut Perf. 10x10¾

Size: 30x20mm

1621	A473	200f multi	4.75	4.75
1622	A473	200f multi	4.75	4.75
1623	A473	200f multi	4.75	4.75
1624	A473	200f multi	4.75	4.75
a.	Booklet pane, #1621-1624		19.00	
1625	A473	250f multi	4.75	4.75
1626	A473	250f multi	4.75	4.75
1627	A473	250f multi	4.75	4.75
1628	A473	250f multi	4.75	4.75
1629	A473	250f multi	4.75	4.75
a.	Booklet pane #1625-1629		24.00	

Die Cut Perf. 13x13¼

Size: 40x30mm

1630	A473	350f multi	7.50	7.50
1631	A473	350f multi	7.50	7.50
1632	A473	350f multi	7.50	7.50
a.	Booklet pane, #1630-1632		22.50	
1633	A473	500f multi	12.00	12.00
1634	A473	500f multi	12.00	12.00
1635	A473	500f multi	12.00	12.00
a.	Booklet pane, #1633-1635		36.00	
	Complete booklet, #1617a, 1620a, 1624a, 1629a, 1632a, 1635a		125.00	
	Nos. 1616-1635 (20)		120.50	120.50

Civil Defense — A474

Designs: 50f, Civil defense workers and emergency vehicles. 75f, Civil defense workers and children. 125f, Civil defene workers.

2005, Nov. 15 Litho. *Perf. 14½*

1636-1638	A474	Set of 3	5.75	5.75

Al-Arabi Al-Saghir Children's Magazine, 20th Anniv. — A475

Background colors: 100f, Blue. 200f, Yellow. 350f, Red.

2006, Feb. 1 Litho. *Perf. 14¼x13¾*

1639-1641	A475	Set of 3	13.00	13.00

45th National Day — A476

Frame color: 75f, Purple. 200f, Green. 250f, Black. 350f, Red.

2006, Feb. 25 *Perf. 13¼*

1642-1645	A476	Set of 4	15.00	15.00

A477

Gulf Cooperation Council, 25th Anniv. — A478

Litho. With Foil Application

2006, May 25 *Perf. 14*

1646	A477	50f multi	5.00	5.00

Imperf

Size: 165x105mm

1647	A478	500f multi	17.50	17.50

See Bahrain Nos. 628-629, Oman Nos. 477-478, Qatar Nos. 1007-1008, Saudi Arabia No. 1378, and United Arab Emirates Nos. 831-832.

Emblem — A479

A480

A481

A482

A483

A484

A485

A486

A487

A488

A489

A490

A491

A492

A493

A494

A495

A496

A497

A498

A499

A500

A501

A502

A503

A504

A505

A506

A507

A508

A509

A510

A511

A512

A513

A514

A515

A516

A517

A518

A519

A520

Coins A521

2006, May 30 Litho. *Perf. 13¼*

1648	Sheet of 28, #1648b-1648v, 7#1648a	25.00	25.00
a.	A479 50f lt blue & multi	.75	.75
b.	A480 50f multi	.75	.75
c.	A481 50f multi	.75	.75
d.	A482 50f multi	.75	.75
e.	A483 50f multi	.75	.75
f.	A484 50f multi	.75	.75
g.	A485 50f multi	.75	.75
h.	A486 50f multi	.75	.75
i.	A487 50f multi	.75	.75
j.	A488 50f multi	.75	.75
k.	A489 50f multi	.75	.75
l.	A490 50f multi	.75	.75
m.	A491 50f multi	.75	.75
n.	A492 50f multi	.75	.75
o.	A493 50f multi	.75	.75
p.	A494 50f multi	.75	.75
q.	A495 50f multi	.75	.75
r.	A496 50f multi	.75	.75
s.	A497 50f multi	.75	.75
t.	A498 50f multi	.75	.75
u.	A499 50f multi	.75	.75
v.	A500 50f multi	.75	.75
1649	Sheet of 28, #1649b-1649v, 7#1649a	70.00	70.00
a.	A479 150f pink & multi	2.25	2.25
b.	A501 150f multi	2.25	2.25
c.	A502 150f multi	2.25	2.25
d.	A503 150f multi	2.25	2.25
e.	A504 150f multi	2.25	2.25
f.	A505 150f multi	2.25	2.25
g.	A506 150f multi	2.25	2.25
h.	A507 150f multi	2.25	2.25
i.	A508 150f multi	2.25	2.25
j.	A509 150f multi	2.25	2.25
k.	A510 150f multi	2.25	2.25
l.	A511 150f multi	2.25	2.25
m.	A512 150f multi	2.25	2.25
n.	A513 150f multi	2.25	2.25
o.	A514 150f multi	2.25	2.25
p.	A515 150f multi	2.25	2.25
q.	A516 150f multi	2.25	2.25
r.	A517 150f multi	2.25	2.25
s.	A518 150f multi	2.25	2.25
t.	A519 150f multi	2.25	2.25
u.	A520 150f multi	2.25	2.25
v.	A521 150f multi	2.25	2.25

Islamic Development Bank Group annual meeting.

15th Asian Games, Doha, Qatar — A522

Designs: 25f, Tennis. 50f, Bowling. 150f, Shooting. 250f, Equestrian. 350f, Fencing.

2006 Litho. *Perf. 14½*
1650-1654 A522 Set of 5 16.00 16.00

Campaign Against Hypertension — A523

Frame colors: 50f, Green. 150f, Red. 350f, Brown.

2007, Jan. 15 *Perf. 13¼x13*
1655-1657 A523 Set of 3 9.75 9.75

46th National Day — A524

Sky color: 25f, Dark blue. 50f, Blue. 150f, Orange brown.

2007, Feb. 25
1658-1660 A524 Set of 3 6.50 6.50

Liberation Day, 16th Anniv. — A525

Frame color: 25f, Red. 50f, Dark blue. 150f, Purple.

2007, Feb. 26 Litho. *Perf. 13x13¼*
1661-1663 A525 Set of 3 6.75 6.75

Kuwait University, 40th Anniv. (in 2006) — A526

Color behind emblem: 25f, Blue. 50f, Yellow. 150f, Green. 350f, Red.

2007, Mar. 20
1664-1667 A526 Set of 4 12.00 12.00

Kuwait Oil Tanker Company, 50th Anniv. — A527

Background colors: 25f, Pale blue. 50f, Pale green. 150f, Gray.

Litho. & Embossed With Foil Application

2007, Nov. 25 *Perf. 13*
1668-1670 A527 Set of 3 7.50 7.50

Kuwait Philatelic & Numismatic Society, 1st Anniv. — A528

2007, Dec. 5 Litho. *Perf. 13¼*

1671	A528 Horiz. strip of 3	7.50	7.50
a.	25f Coin	1.00	1.00
b.	50f Kuwait #146	1.60	1.60
c.	150f Society emblem	4.25	4.25

No. 1671c is 60x35mm.

47th National Day — A529

Designs: 25f, Women voting. 150f, Stylized people, dhows, fish, towers, horiz.

Perf. 13¼x13, 13x13¼

2008, Feb. 25 Litho.
1672-1673 A529 Set of 2 5.00 5.00

Liberation Day, 17th Anniv. — A530

Hand holding map of Kuwait with background color of: 25f, Dull rose. 50f, Purple.

2008, Feb. 26 Litho. *Perf. 13x13¼*
1674-1675 A530 Set of 2 3.75 3.75

First Gulf Cooperation Council Women's Sports Tournament — A531

No. 1676 — Emblem and: a, Gymnastics. b, Running. c, Shooting. d, Basketball. e, Tennis.

No. 1677, horiz. — Emblem, five sports with background color of: a, Orange. b, Red. c, Purple. d, Olive green. e, Red violet.

2008, Mar. 5 Litho. *Perf. 13¼x13*

1676	Vert. strip of 5	5.00	5.00
a.-e.	A531 25f Any single	.80	.80

Perf. 13x13¼

1677	Horiz strip of 5	15.00	15.00
a.-e.	A531 150f Any single	2.40	2.40

Diplomatic Relations Between Kuwait and Romania, 45th Anniv. — A532

No. 1678: a, Kuwaiti man building ship model. b, Romanian woman weaving.

500f, Flags of Romania and Kuwait, handshake, vert.

2008, June 21 *Perf. 13¼x13*

1678	Horiz. pair + 2 labels	*13.00*	*13.00*
a.-b.	A532 150f Either single + label	*6.25*	*6.25*
c.	Miniature sheet, 4 #1678	*52.50*	—

Souvenir Sheet

Perf. 13x13¼

1679 A532 500f multi *26.00 26.00*

Labels of Nos. 1678a and 1678b are separated from stamps by a partial row of perforations. The labels, which have different designs, are to the left of No. 1678a and to the right of No. 1678b. The labels are adjacent to each other on half of the pairs on No. 1678c. No. 1678 was also printed in sheets containing 6 pairs, two of which have the labels adjacent. Value, $60.

See Romania Nos. 5053-5054.

Old Kuwait — A533

Designs: 25f, Drummer and swordsmen. 50f, Drummers and boat painter. 100f, Street with thatched roof. 150f, Fair. 200f, Man and minarets. 250f, Donkey riders at town gate. 350f, Boats in harbor. 500f, People at town gate.

2008, Aug. 1 *Perf. 13*

1680	A533 25f multi	.40	.40
1681	A533 50f multi	.65	.65
1682	A533 100f multi	1.20	1.20
1683	A533 150f multi	1.75	1.75
1684	A533 200f multi	2.40	2.40
1685	A533 250f multi	3.00	3.00
1686	A533 350f multi	4.50	4.50
1687	A533 500f multi	6.00	6.00
	Nos. 1680-1687 (8)	19.90	19.90

48th National Day A534

Frame color: 25f, Black. 50f, Green. 150f, Red.

250f, No frame.

2009, Feb. 25 Litho. *Perf. 13¼*
1688-1690 A534 Set of 3 5.00 5.00

Size: 100x66mm

Imperf

1691 A534 250f multi 6.00 6.00

Liberation Day, 18th Anniv. — A535

Denomination color: 25f, Green. 50f, Red. 150f, Black.

2009, Feb. 26 *Perf. 13¾*
1692-1694 A535 Set of 3 4.00 4.00

Kuwait Finance House — A536

Denomination color: 25f, White. 50f, Silver. 150f, Gold.

Litho. & Embossed

2009, June 21 *Perf. 13¾*

1695-1697 A536 Set of 3 4.00 4.00

Kuwait Chamber of Commerce and Industry, 50th Anniv. — A537

Designs: 25f, Building. 50f, Dhow. 150f, Cogwheels.

2009 Granite Paper Litho.

1698-1700 A537 Set of 3 4.00 4.00

49th National Day — A538

Designs: 25f, Buildings and falcon. 50f, Sheikhs and falcon. 150f, Sheikhs and buildings.

2010, Feb. 25 Litho. *Perf. 13¼x13*

1701-1703 A538 Set of 3 5.75 5.75

Liberation Day, 19th Anniv. — A539

Designs: 25f, Children's drawing of people waving flags in car and on side of road. 50f, Child waving flags. 150f, Fabric art of girls wearing dresses in colors of Kuwait flag.

2010, Feb. 26 *Perf. 13x13¼*

1704-1706 A539 Set of 3 4.50 4.50

Jerusalem, Capital of Arab Culture — A540

Denomination color: 25f, Green. 50f, Red.

2010, Mar. 26 *Perf. 13¼x13*

1707-1708 A540 Set of 2 6.50 6.50

Kuwait E-Gate — A541

Frame color: 25f, Pink. 50f, Yellow. 150f, Light green.

2010, Apr. 20 *Perf. 14x13¼*

1709-1711 A541 Set of 3 5.50 5.50

Organization of the Petroleum Exporting Countries, 50th Anniv. — A542

Background color: 25f, Gray. 50f, Light blue. 150f, White.

Litho. & Embossed With Foil Application

2010, May 23 *Perf. 13¾*

1712-1714 A542 Set of 3 6.50 6.50

A543

Liberation Day, 20th Anniv. and National Day, 50th Anniv. — A544

No. 1715: a, Flag, shiekh, "20." b, Dove, sheikhs, flag, "20." c, Flag, sheikh, "50." d, Flag, sheikh, "50," diff.

Litho. & Embossed With Foil Application

2011, Feb. 25 *Perf. 13¼*

1715	Horiz. strip of 4	4.00	4.00
a.	A543 25f silver & multi	1.00	1.00
b.	A544 25f silver & multi	1.00	1.00
c.	A543 25f gold & multi	1.00	1.00
d.	A544 25f gold & multi	1.00	1.00

A souvenir sheet with a lithographed 250f stamp was produced in limited quantities. Value, *$50.*

A545

A546

A547

A548

Commercial Bank of Kuwait, 50th Anniv. (in 2010) — A549

2011, Sept. Litho. *Perf. 13¼*

1716	Horiz. strip of 5	5.00	5.00
a.	A545 50f multi	1.00	1.00
b.	A546 50f multi	1.00	1.00
c.	A547 50f multi	1.00	1.00
d.	A548 50f multi	1.00	1.00
e.	A549 50f multi	1.00	1.00

15th General Assembly of Arab Towns Organization, Kuwait (in 2010) A550

No. 1717 — Stylized tree and man emblem, Arab Towns Organization emblem, and background color of: a, Rose brown. b, Yellow. c, Chocolate. d, Yellow green. e, Blue. f, Gray green. g, Gray. h, Tan. i, Orange brown. j, Brown.

2011, Nov. 5 *Perf. 13½*

1717	Block of 10	10.00	10.00
a.-j.	A550 50f Any single	1.00	1.00

Miniature Sheet

Kuwait Fund for Arab Economic Development, 50th Anniv. — A551

No. 1718: a, 50th anniversary emblem, red background. b, Airport terminal with overhanging roof. c, Airport runway. d, Airplane at Banjul Intl. Airport, Gambia. e, Pipeline. f, Offshore oil rig. g, Workers examining produce. h, Farm. i, Well. j, Water works. k, Dump truck on hill. l, Culvert, hill in background. m, Electrical station. n, Ships in harbor. o, Highway bridge in populated area. p, Highway interchange. q, Elevated highway near hill. r, Culvert with three round holes. s, Elevated highway, diff.

Sheet of 20

2011, Dec. *Perf. 14¼*

1718 A551 150f 2 #1718a, 1 each #1718b-1718s 32.50 32.50

Emir Abdullah III (1895-1965) A552

Emir Sabah III (1913-77) A553

Emir Jaber III (1926-2006) A554

Emir Saad (1930-2008) A555

Crown Prince Nawaf A556

Emir Sabah IV A557

Sheikh Ahmad (1885-1950) A558

Sheikh Salim (1864-1921) A559

Sheikh Jaber II (1860-1917) A560

Sheikh Mubarak (1840-1915) A561

Independence, 51st Anniv. — A562

No. 1720 — Flags and scenes of Kuwait and: a, Sheikh Mubarak (40x30mm). b, Sheikh Jaber II (40x30mm). c, Emir Abdullah III (80x30mm). d, Emir Sabah III (40x30mm). e, Emir Jaber III (40x30mm). f, Sheikh Salim (40x30mm). g, Sheikh Ahmad (40x30mm). h, Nine ruling sheikhs and emirs (80x30mm). i, Emir Saad (40x30mm). j, Emir Sabah IV (40x30mm).

2012, Feb. 25 *Perf. 13*

1719	Sheet of 10	*25.00*	*25.00*
a.	A552 100f multi	*2.50*	*2.50*
b.	A553 100f multi	*2.50*	*2.50*
c.	A554 100f multi	*2.50*	*2.50*
d.	A555 100f multi	*2.50*	*2.50*
e.	A556 100f multi	*2.50*	*2.50*
f.	A557 100f multi	*2.50*	*2.50*
g.	A558 100f multi	*2.50*	*2.50*
h.	A559 100f multi	*2.50*	*2.50*
i.	A560 100f multi	*2.50*	*2.50*
j.	A561 100f multi	*2.50*	*2.50*

Perf. 13x13¼

1720	A562 Sheet of 10	*25.00*	*25.00*
a.-j.	150f Any single	*2.50*	*2.50*

A563

A564

A565

A566

A567

A568

A569

A570

A571

Liberation Day, 21st Anniv. — A572

2012, Feb. 26 *Perf. 13¼x13*

1721	Sheet of 10	*12.50*	*12.50*
a.	A563 50f multi	*1.25*	*1.25*
b.	A564 50f multi	*1.25*	*1.25*
c.	A565 50f multi	*1.25*	*1.25*
d.	A566 50f multi	*1.25*	*1.25*
e.	A567 50f multi	*1.25*	*1.25*
f.	A568 50f multi	*1.25*	*1.25*
g.	A569 50f multi	*1.25*	*1.25*

h.	A570 50f multi	1.25	1.25
i.	A571 50f multi	1.25	1.25
j.	A572 50f multi	1.25	1.25

Miniature Sheet

Membership in UNESCO, 50th Anniv. (in 2010) — A573

No. 1722 — UNESCO membership 50th anniv. emblem and: a, Kuwaiti flag, emblems of Intangible Cultural Heritage, Intl. Festival of Cultural Diversity, Italian National UNESCO Commission, and UNESCO Associated Schools, white background. b, Emblem of Italian National UNESCO Commission, bister and olive background, denomination 3mm tall at UR. c, Intl. Festival of Cultural Diversity emblem, lilac background. d, Stylized "U" and "O", green and red stripes at bottom. e, Stylized figure of man with arms raised, dull orange background. f, Intl. Astronomical Union emblem, orange and green background. g, Man and Biosphere (MaB) emblem, blue and white background. h, Intangible Cultural Heritage emblem, gray and white background. i, Global Geoparks Network emblem, orange background with blue and white concentric circles. j, Multicolored squares below UNESCO emblem, blue and lilac background. k, UNESCO Associated Schools emblem, blue background with brown stripe at bottom. l, Kuwaiti flag, emblems of Global Geoparks Network, Intl. Festival of Cultural Diversity (with French inscription) and Intl. Bureau of Education, white background. m, UNESCO Institute for Lifelong Learning emblem, red, white and blue background. n, Intl. Bureau of Education (IBE) emblem, white background in blue frame. o, World Heritage emblem, orange background with yellow circle. p, Stylized dove, olive and bister background, denomination 2½mm tall at UR. q, Circle and blue stripes, light blue background. r, UNESCO Chair in Sustainable Mountain Development emblem, UHI Millennium Institute emblem, pink and white background with brown stripes at top and bottom. s, Intl. Festival of Cultural Diversity emblem with French inscription, gray background. t, UNESCO spiral emblem, blue and dull orange background.

2012, June 6 *Perf. 14*

1722 A573 150f Sheet of 20, #a-t 45.00 45.00

A574

A575

A576

A577

A578

A579

A580

A581

A582

A583

A584

A585

A586

A587

A588

A589

A590

A591

A592

Children's Art — A593

2012, Nov.

1723	Sheet of 20	20.00	20.00
a.	A574 50f multi	1.00	1.00
b.	A575 50f multi	1.00	1.00
c.	A576 50f multi	1.00	1.00
d.	A577 50f multi	1.00	1.00
e.	A578 50f multi	1.00	1.00
f.	A579 50f multi	1.00	1.00
g.	A580 50f multi	1.00	1.00
h.	A581 50f multi	1.00	1.00
i.	A582 50f multi	1.00	1.00
j.	A583 50f multi	1.00	1.00
k.	A584 50f multi	1.00	1.00
l.	A585 50f multi	1.00	1.00
m.	A586 50f multi	1.00	1.00
n.	A587 50f multi	1.00	1.00
o.	A588 50f multi	1.00	1.00
p.	A589 50f multi	1.00	1.00
q.	A590 50f multi	1.00	1.00
r.	A591 50f multi	1.00	1.00
s.	A592 50f multi	1.00	1.00
t.	A593 50f multi	1.00	1.00

Kuwait Society for the Handicapped.

Miniature Sheet

Partnership Between Kuwait and United Nations, 50th Anniv. — A594

No. 1724 — 50th anniversary emblem and: a, United Nations Headquarters, flags of United Nations and member nations, emblem of Kuwait (60x30mm). b, United Nations House, Kuwait, emblems of various United Nations ororganizations (60x30mm). c, United Nations Secretary General Ban Ki-moon and Sheikh Sabah (30x40mm). d, Emblems of Kuwait and United Nations, national flags (30x40mm). e, Hoisting of Kuwaiti flag at United Nations Headquarters (30x40mm). f, Sheikh Sabah at podium at United Nations (30x40mm). g, United Nations House, and United Nations flag (30x40mm). h, Dhow (30x40mm). i, Kuwait Towers (30x40mm). j, Emblem at United Nations House (30x40mm).

Perf. 13¼x13¼x14x13¼ (#1724a-1724b), 14

2013, Dec. 1 **Litho.**

1724 A594 50f Sheet of 10, #a-j 7.50 7.50

A595 A596

A597 A598

A599

A600

A601

A602

A603

53rd National Day — A604

Perf. 13¾x13½

2014, Feb. 25 **Litho.**

1725	Sheet of 10	40.00	40.00
a.	A595 350f multi	4.00	4.00
b.	A596 350f multi	4.00	4.00
c.	A597 350f multi	4.00	4.00
d.	A598 350f multi	4.00	4.00
e.	A599 350f multi	4.00	4.00
f.	A600 350f multi	4.00	4.00
g.	A601 350f multi	4.00	4.00
h.	A602 350f multi	4.00	4.00
i.	A603 350f multi	4.00	4.00
j.	A604 350f multi	4.00	4.00

A605

A606

A607

A608

A609

A610

A611

A612

A613

Liberation Day, 23rd Anniv. — A614

Perf. 13¾x13½

2014, Feb. 26 **Litho.**

1726	Sheet of 10	40.00	40.00
a.	A605 350f multi	4.00	4.00
b.	A606 350f multi	4.00	4.00
c.	A607 350f multi	4.00	4.00
d.	A608 350f multi	4.00	4.00
e.	A609 350f multi	4.00	4.00
f.	A610 350f multi	4.00	4.00
g.	A611 350f multi	4.00	4.00
h.	A612 350f multi	4.00	4.00
i.	A613 350f multi	4.00	4.00
j.	A614 350f multi	4.00	4.00

19th Gulf Cooperation Council Stamp Exhibition, Kuwait — A615

2014, May 4 Litho. *Perf. 13*

1727 A615 25f multi *1.10 1.10*

No. 1727 was printed in sheets of 10 with each stamp in sheet having a different background.

Modern Schools A616

Opening Schools Abroad A617

Female Education A618

Nutrition and Health Care A619

Sheikh Abdullah Al Jabir Al Sabah (1895-1965) A620

Student Activities A621

Girl Scouts — A622

Heritage Arts — A623

Boy Scouts — A624

Sheikh Abdullah Al Jabir Al Sabah A625

Perf. 14, 13¼ (#1728j)

2014, Nov. 5 Litho.

1728	Sheet of 10	*8.50*	*8.50*
a.	A616 50f multi	*.85*	*.85*
b.	A617 50f multi	*.85*	*.85*
c.	A618 50f multi	*.85*	*.85*
d.	A619 50f multi	*.85*	*.85*
e.	A620 50f multi	*.85*	*.85*
f.	A621 50f multi	*.85*	*.85*
g.	A622 50f multi	*.85*	*.85*
h.	A623 50f multi	*.85*	*.85*
i.	A624 50f multi	*.85*	*.85*
j.	A625 50f multi	*.85*	*.85*

Souvenir Sheets

Perf. 13x13½

1729 A625 250f multi *5.00 5.00*

Litho. With Foil Application

1730 A625 250f gold & multi *5.00 5.00*

Nos. 1729-1730 each contain one 40x60mm stamp.

A626

A627

A628

A629

A630

A631

A632

A633

A634

Kuwait Awqaf Public Foundation, 20th Anniv. — A635

2014, Nov. 10 Litho. *Perf. 13x13¼*

1731	Sheet of 10	*11.00*	*11.00*
a.	A626 25f multi	*1.10*	*1.10*
b.	A627 25f multi	*1.10*	*1.10*
c.	A628 25f multi	*1.10*	*1.10*
d.	A629 25f multi	*1.10*	*1.10*
e.	A630 25f multi	*1.10*	*1.10*
f.	A631 25f multi	*1.10*	*1.10*
g.	A632 25f multi	*1.10*	*1.10*
h.	A633 25f multi	*1.10*	*1.10*
i.	A634 25f multi	*1.10*	*1.10*
j.	A635 25f multi	*1.10*	*1.10*

A636

A637

A638

A639

A640

A641

A642

A643

A644

International Autism Conference, Kuwait — A645

2014, Nov. 11 Litho. *Perf. 13¾x14*

1732	Sheet of 10	*10.00*	*10.00*
a.	A636 50f multi	*1.00*	*1.00*
b.	A637 50f multi	*1.00*	*1.00*
c.	A638 50f multi	*1.00*	*1.00*
d.	A639 50f multi	*1.00*	*1.00*
e.	A640 50f multi	*1.00*	*1.00*
f.	A641 50f multi	*1.00*	*1.00*
g.	A642 50f multi	*1.00*	*1.00*
h.	A643 50f multi	*1.00*	*1.00*
i.	A644 50f multi	*1.00*	*1.00*
j.	A645 50f multi	*1.00*	*1.00*

Towers A646

No. 1733: a, Post Tower. b, Liberation Tower.

2014, Nov. 23 Litho. *Perf. 14¼*

1733 A646 1d Horiz. pair, #a-b *22.50 22.50*

Miniature Sheet

52nd National Day (in 2013) A647

No. 1734: a, Musician and dancers (60x30mm). b, Children surrounding sheikh (60x30mm). c, Male dancers wearing waist sashes (30x45mm). d, Female dancers wearing yellow and black costume (30x45mm). e, Male dancers wearing black vests (30x45mm). f, Female dancers wearing purple and yellow costumes (30x45mm). g, Musician and male dancers (30x45mm). h, Girls wearing turquoise green dresses (30x45mm). i, Boys wearing violet and blue costumes, girls in background (30x45mm). j, Female dancers with striped skirts (30x45mm).

2014, Dec. 21 Litho. *Perf. 13x13¼*

1734 A647 150f Sheet of 10, #a-j *17.50 17.50*

Miniature Sheet

Liberation Day, 22nd Anniv. (in 2013) — A648

No. 1735: a, Soldiers and black vehicles with flags (90x30mm). b, Ships (90x30mm). c, Sheikh meeting troops (45x30mm). d, Soldiers in personnel carriers in parade (45x30mm). e, Soldiers carrying guns (45x30mm). f, Helicopter and flag (45x30mm). g, Soldiers with white boots marching in parade (45x30m). h, Airplanes in flight with colored contrails (45x30mm). i, Police on motorcycles in parade (45x30mm). j, Soldiers on small boat (45x30mm).

2014, Dec. 21 Litho. *Perf. 14¼*

1735 A648 50f Sheet of 10, #a-j *6.00 6.00*

Miniature Sheet

Diplomatic Relations Between Kuwait and European Countries, 50th Anniv. — A649

No. 1736: a, Netherlands. b, Spain. c, Coat of arms of Kuwait. d, Germany. e, Hungary. f, Denmark. g, Greece. h, Turkey. i, Belgium. j, Italy.

2014, Dec. 21 Litho. *Perf. 13¼*

1736 A649 150f Sheet of 10, #a-j *18.00 18.00*

A650

A651

A652

A653

A654

A655

A656

A657

A658

Constitution, 50th Anniv. — A659

Perf. 13¾x14, 14x13¾ (#1737j)

2014, Dec. 21 Litho.

1737	Sheet of 10	*55.00*	*55.00*
a.	A650 500f multi	*5.50*	*5.50*
b.	A651 500f multi	*5.50*	*5.50*
c.	A652 500f multi	*5.50*	*5.50*
d.	A653 500f multi	*5.50*	*5.50*
e.	A654 500f multi	*5.50*	*5.50*
f.	A655 500f multi	*5.50*	*5.50*
g.	A656 500f multi	*5.50*	*5.50*
h.	A657 500f multi	*5.50*	*5.50*
i.	A658 500f multi	*5.50*	*5.50*
j.	A659 500f multi	*5.50*	*5.50*

Miniature Sheet

Kuwaiti Graduate Society, 50th Anniv. A660

No. 1738 — Emblem and: a, Five men at circular dais (60x40mm). b, Pictures of Kuwaiti prisoners of war (60x40mm). c, Man in army uniform, woman with hands over mouth (30x40mm). d, Men at Kuwaiti Graduate Society Symposium (30x40mm). e, Kuwaitis for Jerusalem emblem (30x40mm). f, Book cover with Arabic text and "2007" (30x40mm). g, Book cover with Arabic text, broken pencil and "1995-2007" (30x40mm). h, Book cover depicting stylized head and neck (30x40mm). i, Page of Arabic text (30x40mm). j, Jigsaw puzzle with missing pieces (30x40mm).

2014, Dec. 27 Litho. *Perf. 13¼x13*

1738 A660 50f Sheet of 10, #a-j *7.00 7.00*

Emir Sabah IV — A661

Background color: 350f, Blue. 500f, Olive green. 750f, Light blue. 1d, Light gray. 250f, Brown.

Litho. With Foil Application

2014, Dec. 30 *Perf. 13¾x13½*

1739-1742 A661 Set of 4 *30.00 30.00*

Souvenir Sheet

Perf. 13x14x14x14

1743 A661 250f multi *5.00 5.00*

No. 1743 contains one 120x90mm stamp.

Miniature Sheet

54th National Day A662

No. 1744: a, Towers, children wearing red, white and green caps. b, Male dancers. c, Female dancers. d, Child with flag of Kuwait painted on face.

2015, Feb. 25 Litho. *Perf. 13¼*

1744 A662 150f Sheet of 4, #a-d 7.50 7.50

Martyrs — A663

No. 1745: a, Ahmad S. Alenezi. b, Ahmad K. Alenezi. c, Edris B. Alshammari. d, Ebrahim A. Alsubaie. e, Ebrahim J. Naif. f, Hamed K. Alshammari. g, Jamal S. Alsalem. h, Jshai'aan A. Almutairi. i, Jasem N. Alfadhli. j, Ahmad N. Alenezi. k, Khalaf A. Alenezi. l, Humoud S. Rashdan. m, Hamad Y. Alsultan. n, Hasan T. Alfadegh. o, Hasan R. Alshammari. p, Zakariya A. Bohamad. q, Refa'ie A. Almutairi. r, Rajaan W. Alazmi. s, Ra'ed M. Sabri. t, Daham H. Alshammari. u, Diaa A. Alsayegh. v, Safnan M. Althaferi. w, Sulaiman A. Sulaiman. x, Salman N. Alazmi. y, Salem M. Alenezi.

No. 1746: a, Abdulrahman N. Abdulrahman. b, Abduljaleel E. Khaleel. c, Abbas A. Muhammad. d, Ayed K. Albraikan. e, Tareq M. Alfadhli. f, Faleh S. Althaferi. g, Ghazwan H. Hawas. h, Obaid S. Alshammari. i, Abdullah E. Saleh. j, Abdulkareem T. Ali. k, Kulaib S. Farhan. l, Kamil R. Jabr. m, Fahad A. Alsabah. n, Fraih B. Alshammari. o, Fayez A. Arashidi. p, Muhammad Q. Alenezi. q, Muhammad O. Muhammad. r, Muhammad J. Alaibany. s, Mohsen A. Alenezi. t, Mut'eb S. Alshammari. u, Mutlaq M. Almutairi. v, Mus'heb M. Mutlaq. w, Meshael N. Aladwani. x, Mur'ie N. Alenezi. y, Muhammad H. Althaydi.

No. 1747: a, Khalid A. Alb'aijan. b, Hamdan M. Alenezi. c, Jamal S. Allengawi. d, Anwar A. Alrefai. e, Warid M. Jadran. f, Muhammad M. Alobaid. g, Majed R. Alkhseli. h, Fahad R. Althaferi. i, Farhan S. Alruwaili. j, Sahmi M. Alsubaie. k, Adel A. Alhaie. l, Abdulaziz S. Kashaan. m, Mufreh K. Alenezi. n, Mansour G. Alkhseli. o, Matar G. Almajdi. p, Sana A. Alfudari. q, Rashid K. Althaferi. r, Mussayer F. Alshammari. s, Abdulrahman M. Abdullah. t, Muhammad S. Alenezi. u, Ali E. Alraihan. v, Ibrahim E. Abdullah. w, Ali A. Alsa'baa. x, Wahid M. Safri, y, Musaed A. Alaskari.

No. 1748: a, Abdullatif A. Alhamdan. b, Bassam M. Sadeq. c, Nawaf M. Alhashan. d, Abdulhusain A. Albughbish. e, Muhammad J. Jaber. f, Jafar A. Taqi. g, Habib M. Alsheikh. h, Abdulrasoul H. Husain. i, Mansour H. Mansour. j, Faisal B. Albahar. k, Salem A. Alkanderi. l, Baqer A. Almousawi. m, Khalid A. Alsamhan. n, Nasser G. Aladwani, o, Mahmoud K. Aljasem. p, Mubarak F. Alnout. q, Bader R. Abdulwahab. r, Ghazi F. Aloutaibi. s, Sabbar A. Alenezi. t, Saleh H. Saleh. u, Ahmad A. Kherallah. v, Ibrahim A. Meshael. w, Muhammad H. Altawash. x, Saad S. Alshammari. y, Hammad S. Alshammari.

2015, Feb. 26 Litho. *Perf. 14*

1745	Sheet of 25	7.50	7.50
a.-y.	A663 25f Any single	.30	.30
1746	Sheet of 25	7.50	7.50
a.-y.	A663 25f Any single	.30	.30
1747	Sheet of 25	7.50	7.50
a.-y.	A663 25f Any single	.30	.30
1748	Sheet of 25	7.50	7.50
a.-y.	A663 25f Any single	.30	.30
	Nos. 1745-1748 (4)	30.00	30.00

Liberation Day, 24th anniv.

Kuwait Institute for Scientific Research — A664

No. 1749: a, Brid. b, Technician adjusting scientific equipment. c, Scientists in laboratory. d, Three test tubes. e, Fish. f, Satellite dishes. g, Building, cars parked at left. h, Bottles. i, Headquarters and reflecting pond. j, Headquarters, diff.

2015, Mar. Litho. *Perf. 13x13½*

1749 A664 50f Sheet of 10, #a-j 7.00 7.00

A666

A667

A668

A669

A670

A671

A672

A673

A674

Independence, 55th Anniv. — A675

Die Cut Perf. 16

2016, Feb. 25 Litho.

Self-Adhesive

1751	Sheet of 10	—	—
a.	A666 50f multi	—	—
b.	A667 50f multi	—	—
c.	A668 50f multi	—	—
d.	A669 50f multi	—	—
e.	A670 50f multi	—	—
f.	A671 50f multi	—	—
g.	A672 50f multi	—	—
h.	A673 50f multi	—	—
i.	A674 50f multi	—	—
j.	A675 50f multi	—	—

Souvenir Sheet

First Post Office in Kuwait, Cent. (in 2015) A678

Design: 500f, British Residency House, Safa Post Office, Kishk Shaikh Mubarak, Umm Mohammed Alsabah House, and General Post Office.

2017, Dec. Litho. *Perf. 13¾x13½*

1761 A678 500f multi — —

Five additional stamps were issued in this set. The editors would like to examine any examples.

Miniature Sheet

Abdul Hussain Abdul Rida (1939-2017), Actor — A679

No. 1762 — Stamp size: a, 86x103mm. b, 40x52mm.

Perf. 13¾x14 (#1762a), 13 (#1762b)

2018, Dec. 16 Litho.

1762 A679 150f Sheet of 10, #1762a, 9 #1762b — —

AIR POST STAMPS

Air Post Stamps of India, 1929-30, Overprinted type "d"

1933-34 **Wmk. 196** ***Perf. 14***

C1	AP1	2a dull green	24.00	*27.50*
C2	AP1	3a deep blue	5.00	*3.50*
C3	AP1	4a gray olive	160.00	*225.00*
C4	AP1	6a bister ('34)	8.00	*4.50*
		Nos. C1-C4 (4)	197.00	*260.50*

Counterfeits of Nos. C1-C4 exist.

Catalogue values for unused stamps in this section, from this point to the end of the section, are for Never Hinged items.

Dakota and Comet Planes — AP1

Perf. 11x11½

1964, Nov. 29 **Litho.** **Unwmk.**

C5	AP1	20f multicolored	2.00	.30
C6	AP1	25f multicolored	2.25	.40
C7	AP1	30f multicolored	2.50	.65
C8	AP1	45f multicolored	4.00	.90
		Nos. C5-C8 (4)	10.75	2.25

10th anniversary of Kuwait Airways.

POSTAGE DUE STAMPS

Catalogue values for unused stamps in this section are for Never Hinged items.

D1

Perf. 14x15

1963, Oct. 19 **Unwmk.** **Litho.**

Inscriptions in Black

J1	D1	1f ocher	.60	.30
J2	D1	2f lilac	.70	.45
J3	D1	5f blue	1.00	.30
J4	D1	8f pale green	1.60	.55
J5	D1	10f yellow	2.00	1.00
J6	D1	25f brick red	3.25	3.25
		Nos. J1-J6 (6)	9.15	5.85

D2

1965, Apr. 1 ***Perf. 13***

J7	D2	4f rose & yellow	.50	.30
J8	D2	15f dp rose & blue	1.75	.55
J9	D2	40f blue & brt yel grn	3.00	1.25
J10	D2	50f green & pink	3.75	1.75
J11	D2	100f dk blue & yel	5.50	3.25
		Nos. J7-J11 (5)	14.50	7.10

OFFICIAL STAMPS

Stamps of India, 1911-23, Overprinted

Nos. O1-O9

Nos. O10-O14

1923-24 **Wmk. 39** ***Perf. 14***

O1	A47	½a green	6.50	*50.00*
O2	A48	1a brown	5.50	*27.50*
O3	A58	1½a chocolate	5.00	*65.00*
O4	A49	2a violet	11.00	*50.00*
O5	A57	2a6p ultra	7.00	*80.00*
O6	A51	3a brown org	7.50	*75.00*
O7	A51	3a ultra ('24)	7.75	*75.00*
O8	A52	4a olive grn	6.25	*75.00*
O9	A54	8a red violet	9.50	*110.00*
O10	A56	1r grn & brn	35.00	*190.00*
O11	A56	2r brn & car rose	37.50	*275.00*
O12	A56	5r vio & ultra	125.00	*475.00*
O13	A56	10r car & grn	250.00	*440.00*
O14	A56	15r ol grn & ultra	425.00	*675.00*
		Nos. O1-O14 (14)	938.50	*2,663.*

Stamps of India, 1926-30, Overprinted

Nos. O15-O20

Nos. O21-O25

1929-33 **Wmk. 196**

O15	A48	1a dk brown	6.50	*42.50*
O16	A60	2a violet	70.00	*250.00*
O17	A51	3a blue	6.00	*55.00*
O18	A61	4a ol green	6.75	*90.00*
O19	A54	8a red violet	9.00	*130.00*
O20	A55	12a claret	45.00	*225.00*
O21	A56	1r green & brn	14.00	*275.00*
O22	A56	2r buff & car rose	18.00	*400.00*
O23	A56	5r dk vio & ultra	50.00	*500.00*
O24	A56	10r car & green	85.00	*850.00*
O25	A56	15r olive grn & ultra	300.00	*1,450.*
		Nos. O15-O25 (11)	610.25	*4,268.*

KYRGYZSTAN

ˌkir-gi-ˈstan

(Kirghizia)

LOCATION — Bounded by Kazakhstan, Uzbekistan, Tadjikistan and China.
GOVT. — Independent republic, member of the Commonwealth of Independent States.
AREA — 77,180 sq. mi.
POP. — 4,546,055 (1999 est.)
CAPITAL — Bishkek

With the breakup of the Soviet Union on Dec. 26, 1991, Kyrgyzstan and ten former Soviet republics established the Commonwealth of Independent States.

In 2013, the Universal Postal Union announced that a second postal organization, Kyrgyz Express Post, was granted permission to provide unrestricted postal services throughout the country. This allowed for competition between the state corporation, Kyrgyz Pochtasy, the original UPU-designated postal operator in Kyrgyzstan having post offices nationwide, and Kyrgyz Express Post for postal business. Listings for stamps issued by Kyrgyz Express Post follow those of the listings for stamps from Kyrgyz Pochtasy.

100 Kopecks = 1 Ruble
100 Tyiyn = 1 Som

Catalogue values for all unused stamps in this country are for Never Hinged items.

ISSUES OF KYRGYZ POCHTASY

Sary-Chelek Nature Preserve — A1

Unwmk.

1992, Feb. 4 **Litho.** ***Perf. 12***

1	A1	15k multicolored	.55	.55

Hawk — A2

1992, Aug. 31 **Litho.** ***Perf. 12½x12***

2	A2	50k multicolored	.65	.65

Man with Cattle, by G.A. Aytiev — A3

1992, Aug. 31

3	A3	1r multicolored	.40	.40

Handicrafts — A4

1992, Dec. 1 **Litho.** ***Perf. 12x11½***

4	A4	1.50r multicolored	.55	.55

Sites and Landmarks — A5

Designs: 10k, Petroglyphs. 50k, 11th Cent. tower, vert. 1r + 25k, Mausoleum, vert. 2r + 50k, 12th Cent. mausoleum. 3r, Yurt. 5r + 50k, Statue of epic hero Manas, Pishpek. 9r, Commercial complex, Pishpek. 10r, Native jewelry.

1993, Mar. 21 **Litho.** ***Perf. 12***

5	A5	10k multicolored	.25	.25
6	A5	50k multicolored	.25	.25
7	A5	1r +25k multi	.25	.25
8	A5	2r +50k multi	.25	.25
9	A5	3r multicolored	.25	.25
10	A5	5r +50k multi	.30	.30
11	A5	9r multi	.50	.50
		Nos. 5-11 (7)	2.05	2.05

Souvenir Sheet

12	A5	10r multicolored	1.00	1.00

Nos. 5-11 exist imperf. Value, set *$22.50.*

Independence and Admission to UN, 2nd Anniv. — A6

50t, Map. 60t, UN emblem, flag, building, vert.
No. 15a, 120t, like #13. No. 15b, 130t, like #14.

Perf. 13x12½, 12½x13

1993, Aug. 31 **Litho.**

13	A6	50t multicolored	1.00	1.00
14	A6	60t multicolored	1.25	1.25

Souvenir Sheet

Imperf

15	A6	Sheet of 2, #a.-b.	5.25	5.25

Nos. 15a-15b have simulated perforations.

Russia Nos. 4598, 5838, 5984 Surcharged in Violet Blue, Prussian Blue or Black

Methods and Perfs as Before

1993, Apr. 6

16	A2765	10r on 1k #5838 (VB)	.30	.25
17	A2765	20r on 2k #5984 (PB)	.35	*.50*
18	A2139	30r on 3k #4598 (Blk)	.45	*.70*
		Nos. 16-18 (3)	1.10	*1.45*

Russia Nos. 4599-4600 Surcharged in Blue or Red

Methods and Perfs as Before

1993, June 29

19	A2138	20t on 4k #4599 (Bl)	.70	.70
20	A2139	30t on 6k #4600 (R)	1.00	1.00

New Year 1994 (Year of the Dog) — A7

1994, Feb. 10 **Litho.** ***Perf. 12x12½***

26	A7	60t multicolored	.80	.80

No. 26 exists imperf. Value, $1.75.

Musical Instrument A8

1993, Dec. 30 **Litho.** ***Perf. 13x12½***

27	A8	30t Komuz	.40	.40

Souvenir Sheet

Perf. 13

28	A8	140t multi	16.00	16.00

No. 28 exists imperf. Value $45.
Issued: No. 27, 12/30; No. 28, 4/4/94.

Panthera Uncia — A9

1994, Mar. 21 **Litho.** ***Perf. 12½x12***

29	A9	10t shown	.35	.35
30	A9	20t Lying down	.40	.40
31	A9	30t Seated	.65	.65
32	A9	40t Up close	.85	.85
		Nos. 29-32 (4)	2.25	2.25

World Wildlife Fund.

Flowers — A10

Perf. 12x12½, 12½x12

1994, Aug. 31 **Litho.**

Color of Flower

33	A10	1t violet & white	.25	.25
34	A10	3t white & yellow, horiz.	.25	.25
a.		Miniature sheet of 6	1.60	1.60
35	A10	10t red & yellow	.40	.40
36	A10	16t white & yellow	.40	.40
37	A10	20t pink & yellow	.50	.50
38	A10	30t white & yellow	.55	.55
39	A10	40t yellow & brown	.65	.65
a.		Miniature sheet of 6, #33, #35-39	6.50	6.50
b.		Strip of 7, #33-39	4.00	4.00
		Nos. 33-39 (7)	3.00	3.00

Souvenir Sheet

40	A10	50t yellow & orange	1.60	1.60

Nos. 33-39 exist imperf. Value, set $4.75.
For surcharge see No. 141.

Minerals — A11

1994, Dec. 1 Litho. *Perf. 13½x13*

41 A11 80t Fluorite-Cinnabar .65 .65
42 A11 90t Calcite .70 .70
43 A11 100t Getchellite .80 .80
44 A11 110t Barite .85 .85
45 A11 120t Orpiment .90 .90
46 A11 140t Stibnite 1.25 1.25
Nos. 41-46 (6) 5.15 5.15

Souvenir Sheet

47 A11 200t Cinnabar 3.50 3.50
a. Miniature sheet of 6 10.00 10.00

No. 47a contains Nos. 42-46 and single from No. 47.

Fish — A12

Designs: 110t, Glyptosternum reticulatum. 120t, Leuciscus schmidti. 130t, Piptychus dybowskii. 140t, Nemachilus strauchi. 200t, Cyprinus carpio.

1994, Dec. 1 *Perf. 13x13½*

48 A12 110t multicolored .55 .55
49 A12 120t multicolored .60 .60
50 A12 130t multicolored .65 .65
51 A12 140t multicolored .80 .80
a. Miniature sheet, #48-51 2.75 2.75
Nos. 48-51 (4) 2.60 2.60

Souvenir Sheet

52 A12 200t multicolored 2.25 2.25

Wild Animals — A13

No. 60: a, 130t, Raptor, diff. b, 170t, Bighorn sheep.

Perf. 12x12½, 12½x12

1995, Apr. 21 Litho.

53 A13 110t Bear .30 .30
54 A13 120t Snow leopard, horiz. .30 .30
55 A13 130t Raptor .35 .35
56 A13 140t Woodchuck, horiz. .40 .40
57 A13 150t Raptor, horiz. .45 .45
58 A13 160t Vulture .50 .50
59 A13 190t Fox, horiz. .65 .65
Nos. 53-59 (7) 2.95 2.95

Souvenir Sheet

60 A13 Sheet of 2, #a.-b. 1.50 1.50

Nos. 53-60 exist imperf. Value, set $6.50.

Natl. Costumes — A14

1995, Mar. 24 *Perf. 12x12½*

61 A14 50t shown .30 .30
62 A14 50t Man with mandolin .30 .30
63 A14 100t Man with falcon .45 .45
64 A14 100t Woman seated .45 .45
Nos. 61-64 (4) 1.50 1.50

Nos. 61-64 exist imperf. Value, set $2.50.

Traffic Safety — A15

1995, Mar. 24 *Perf. 12*

65 A15 200t multicolored .85 .85

Souvenir Sheet

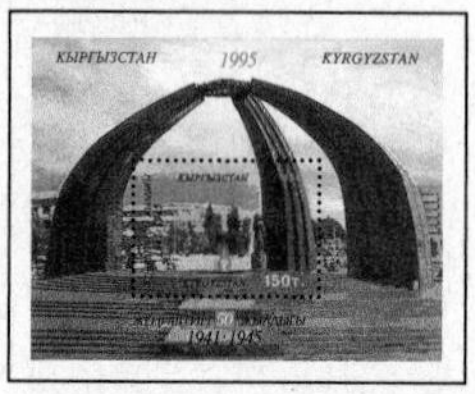
End of World War II, 50th Anniv. A16

1995, May 4 Litho. *Perf. 12x12½*

66 A16 150t multicolored 1.40 1.40

UPU Intl. Letter Week — A17

1995, Oct. 3 Litho. *Perf. 12x12½*

67 A17 200t multicolored 1.10 1.10

Natl. Arms — A18

1995, Oct. 13 *Perf. 12*

68 A18 20t purple .35 .35
69 A18 50t blue .35 .35
70 A18 100t brown .45 .45
71 A18 500t green 1.50 1.50
Nos. 68-71 (4) 2.65 2.65

Compare with design A37.

Horses — A19

Various adult, juvenile horses.

1995, Oct. 16 *Perf. 12½x12, 12x12½*

Background Color

72 A19 10t ocher .25 .25
73 A19 50t light brown, vert. .25 .25
74 A19 100t org brn, vert. .25 .25
75 A19 140t brn ocher, vert. .40 .40
76 A19 150t pink .60 .60
77 A19 200t gray .60 .60
78 A19 300t grnsh yel .65 .65
Nos. 72-78 (7) 3.00 3.00

Souvenir Sheet

79 A19 600t Herd of horses, vert. 2.50 2.50

Raptors — A20

1995, Sept. 12 *Perf. 12x12½*

80 A20 10t Pandion haliaetus .25 .25
81 A20 50t Aquila rapax .30 .30
82 A20 100t Gyps himalayensis .35 .35
83 A20 140t Falco cherrug .40 .40
84 A20 150t Circaetus gallicus .45 .45
85 A20 200t Gypaetus barbatus .50 .50
86 A20 300t Aquila chrysaetos .70 .70
Nos. 80-86 (7) 2.95 2.95

Souvenir Sheet

87 A20 600t Halliaeetus albicilla 2.75 2.75

"Aquila" spelled wrong on No. 86.

Nos. 80-87 exist imperf. Value: Nos. 80-86, $4.25; No. 87, $3.

Souvenir Sheet

UN, 50th Anniv. A21

Designs: a, UN headquarters, NYC. b, Mountains, rainbow.

1995, Oct. 24 Litho. *Perf. 12½x12*

88 A21 100t Sheet of 2, #a.-b. 1.10 1.10

Natural Wonders of the World A22

10t, Nile River. 50t, Kilimanjaro. 100t, Sahara Desert. 140t, Amazon River, vert. 150t, Grand Canyon, vert. 200t, Victoria Falls, vert. 350t, Mount Everest. 400t, Niagara Falls.

Issyk-Kul Lake, Kyrgyzstan: No. 97, Raptor, row boat, sail boats. No. 98, Water bird, motor boat, row boat.

1995, Dec. 29 *Perf. 11½*

89 A22 10t multicolored .30 .30
90 A22 50t multicolored .35 .35
91 A22 100t multicolored .45 .45
92 A22 140t multicolored .50 .50
93 A22 150t multicolored .55 .55
94 A22 200t multicolored .70 .70
95 A22 350t multicolored .90 .90
96 A22 400t multicolored 1.25 1.25
Nos. 89-96 (8) 5.00 5.00

Souvenir Sheets

97 A22 600t multicolored 2.00 2.00
98 A22 600t multicolored 2.00 2.00

Reptiles — A23

Designs: 20t, Psammophis lineolatum. No. 100, Natrix tessellata. No. 101, Eublepharis macularius. 100t, Agkistrodon halys. 150t, Eremias arguta. 200t, Elaphe dione. 250t, Asymblepharus. 500t, Lacerta agilis.

1996, Feb. 2 *Perf. 12½x12*

99 A23 20t multicolored .25 .25
100 A23 50t multicolored .30 .30
101 A23 50t multicolored .30 .30
102 A23 100t multicolored .30 .30
103 A23 150t multicolored .50 .50
104 A23 200t multicolored .60 .60
105 A23 250t multicolored .65 .65
Nos. 99-105 (7) 2.90 2.90

Souvenir Sheet

106 A23 500t multicolored 2.25 2.25

Souvenir Sheet

Save the Aral Sea A24

Designs: a, Felis caracal. b, Salmo trutta aralensis. c, Hyaena hyaena. d, Pseudoscaphirhynchus kaufmanni. e, Aspiolucius esocinus.

1996, Apr. 29 Litho. *Perf. 14*

107 A24 100t Sheet of 5, #a.-e. 4.00 4.00

See Kazakhstan No. 145. Tadjikistan No. 91, Turkmenistan No. 52, Uzbekistan No. 113.

Fauna A27

a, Aquila chrysaetos. b, Capra falconeri. c, Ovis ammon. d, Gyps himalayensis. e, Equus hemionus. f, Canis lupus. g, Ursus arctor. h, Saiga tatarica.

1997, Aug. 29 Litho. *Perf. 12x12½*

114 A27 600t Sheet of 8, #a.-h. 7.00 7.00

See No. 117.

New Year 1998 (Year of the Tiger) — A28

1998, June 5 Litho. *Perf. 13½x14*

115 A28 600t multicolored 1.40 1.40

Butterflies — A29

Designs: a, Parnasius actius. b, Colias christophi. c, Papilio machaon. d, Colias thisoa. e, Parnassius delphius. f, Panassius tianschanicus.

1998, June 5

116 A29 600t Sheet of 6, #a.-f. 4.50 4.50

Fauna Type of 1997

a, 600t, Capreolus capreolus. b, 1000t, Oriolus oriolus. c, 600t, Pandion haliaetus. d, 1000t, Uncia uncia. e, 600t, Upupa epops. f, 600t, Ciconia ciconia. g, 1000t, Alcedo atthis. h, 1000t, Falco tinnunculus.

1998, June 5 Litho. *Perf. 12x12½*

117 A27 Sheet of 8, #a-h *10.00 10.00*

Dinosaurs — A31

Designs: a, Saurolophus, vert. b, Euoplocephalus. c, Velociraptor. d, Tyrannosaurus, vert. e, Gallimimus. f, Protoceratops.

Perf. 14x13½, 13½x14

1998, Dec. 4 Litho.

118 A31 10s Sheet of 6, #a.-f. 6.00 6.00

Universal Declaration of Human Rights, 50th Anniv. — A32

a, Andrei Sakharov (1921-89). b, Crowd of people raising their arms. c, Martin Luther King, Jr. d, Mahatma Gandhi. e, Eleanor Roosevelt.

1998, Dec. 4 *Perf. 14x13½*

119 A32 10s Sheet of 5, #a.-e. + label 4.75 4.75

No. 119 exists with 2 different inscriptions on label.

Constitution, 5th Anniv. — A33

1998, Dec. ***Perf. 12***
120 A33 1000t multi 1.60 1.60

Imperf

Size: 120x90mm

120A A33 10,000t multi *50.00 50.00*

No. 120A, issued 2/5/99.

Fauna A34

Designs: a, 600t, Fish, denomination UR. b, 1000t, Duck standing beside rocks. c, 1000t, Two birds. d, 1000t, Duck standing beside water. e, 1000t, Duck swimming. f, 1000t, Rodent. g, 1000t, Bird. h, 600t, Fish, denomination UL.

1998, Dec. Litho. ***Perf. 12***
121 A34 Sheet of 8, #a.-h. 7.50 7.50

No. 121 exists imperf. Value, $9.50.

Corsac Fox (Vulpes Corsac) — A35

World Wildlife Fund: Nos. 122a, 123a, 10s, Adult sitting. Nos. 122b, 123b, 10s, Adult sleeping. Nos. 122c, 123c, 30s, Two standing. Nos. 122d, 123d, 50s, Adult with young.

1999, Apr. 27 Litho. ***Perf. 12½x12***
122 A35 Block of 4, #a.-d. 5.50 5.50

Size: 48x34mm

Perf. 13½

123 A35 Block of 4, #a.-d. 7.50 7.50

Nos. 123a-123d each contain a holographic image. Soaking in water may affect the hologram. IBRA '99, World Philatelic Exhibition, Nuremberg (No. 123). No. 123 was issued in sheets of 8 stamps.

For overprints and surcharges, see Nos. 175, 384.

Aleksandr Pushkin (1799-1837), Poet — A36

No. 124: a, 36t, Knight, giant. b, 6s, Man, woman, fish. c, 10s, Archer, angel. d, 10s, King in carriage.

20s, Portrait of Pushkin.

1999, June Litho. ***Perf. 12x12½***
124 A36 Strip of 4, #a.-d. 3.75 3.75

Souvenir Sheet

125 A36 20s multicolored 3.75 3.75

No. 124 printed in sheets of 8 stamps. Nos. 124-125 exist imperf. Value, set $10.

Natl. Arms — A37

1999, July Litho. ***Perf. 11¼x11½***
126 A37 20t dark blue .80 .80

Souvenir Sheet

China 1999 World Philatelic Exhibition — A38

No. 131: a, 10s, Ailuropoda melanoleuca. b, 15s, Strix leptogrammica.

1999, Aug. 21 Litho. ***Perf. 13x12½***
131 A38 Sheet of 2, #a.-b. 2.50 2.50

Exists imperf. Value $3.25.

12th World Kickboxing Championships, Bishkek — A39

Emblem, globe and: No. 132, White background. No. 133, Blue panel. c, No. 134, Green, red, and black panels.

No. 135: a, Black background. b, Yellow and brown panels.

1999, Oct. 7 Litho. ***Perf. 13¼***
132 A39 3s multi .70 .70
133 A39 3s multi .70 .70
134 A39 3s multi .70 .70
Nos. 132-134 (3) 2.10 2.10

Souvenir Sheet

Perf. 12½

135 A39 6s Sheet of 2, #a.-b., + label *2.00 2.00*

No. 135 contains 37x26mm stamps.

UPU, 125th Anniv. — A40

6s, Airplane, man on horse.

1999, Oct. ***Perf. 14x14¼***
136 A40 3s shown .55 .55
137 A40 6s multicolored 1.10 1.10

Dogs A41

No. 138: a, 3s, Taigan. b, 6s, Tasy. c, 6s, Afghan hound. d, 10s, Saluki. e, 15s, Mid-Asian shepherd. f, 15s, Akbash dog. g, 20s, Chow chow. h, 25s, Akita.

2000, Mar. 18 Litho. ***Perf. 12¼x12***
138 A41 Sheet of 8, #a-h 7.50 7.50

Exists imperf. Value $12.

Kyrgyzstan postal officials have declared as "not authentic and not valid" stamps with a face value of 20s depicting the Beatles, Madonna, Pop music stars, Tiger Woods, 2000 French Olympic gold medal winners, Mushrooms, American Political Cartoons concerning the 2000 Presidential election, The Simpsons, Superman, and Warner Brothers cartoon characters.

Bulat Minzhilkiev(1940-98), Opera Singer — A42

2000, Apr. 20 Litho. ***Perf. 14x14¼***
139 A42 5s multi *1.25 1.25*

Victory in World War II, 55th Anniv. — A43

Heroes: a, Cholponbay Tuleberdiev (1922-42). b, I. V. Panfilov (1893-1941), vert. c, Duyshenkul Shopokov (1915-41).

Perf. 14x14¼ (#140a, 140c), 14¼x14 (#140b)

2000, May 20 Litho.
140 A43 6s Vert. strip of 3, #a-c *2.75 2.75*

Issued in sheets of 2 each Nos. 140a-140c.

No. 33 Surcharged

2000, Sept. 22 Litho. ***Perf. 12x12½***
141 A10 36t on 1t multi .50 *.90*

No. 141 exists with bar obliterators with smaller numerals and with thinner numerals and rosette obliterators in magenta. Value: each, $13.

2000 Summer Olympics, Sydney — A44

Designs: 1s, Wrestling. 3s, Hurdles, vert. 6s, Boxing. 10s, Weight lifting, vert.

Perf. 14x14¼, 14¼x14

2000, Sept. 23
142-145 A44 Set of 4 *3.75 3.75*

Kyrgyzstan postal officials have declared as "not authentic and not valid" a sheet of nine 20s stamps depicting the History of Golf.

Atay Ogunbaev, Composer — A45

2000, Oct. 28 Litho. ***Perf. 14x14¼***
146 A45 6s multi .85 .85

Butterflies A46

Designs: No. 147, 3s, Aglais urticae. No. 148, 3s, Argynnis aglaja. No. 149, 3s, Colias thisoa. No. 150, 3s, Inachis io. No. 151, 3s, Papilio machaon. No. 152, 3s, Parnassius apollo.

2000, Nov. 18 ***Perf. 13½***
147-152 A46 Set of 6 *4.50 4.50*

Kyrgyzstan postal officials have declared as "not authentic and not valid" stamps with a face value of 20s in sheets of 6 depicting Jennifer Aniston and Tennis, and sheets of 9 depicting Backstreet Boys, Beverly Hills 90210, Minerals, Penguins, Tom and Jerry, Prince William, Babylon 5 and the End of Mir.

Intl. Year of Mountains (in 2002) — A47

Designs: No. 153, 10s, Khan-Tengri Mountain, 7,010 meters. No. 154, 10s, Victory Peak, 7,439 meters. No. 155, 10s, Lenin Peak, 7,134 meters.

2000, Dec. 23 Litho. ***Perf. 13½***
153-155 A47 Set of 3 *3.25 3.25*
a. Souvenir sheet, #153-155 + label *3.25 3.25*

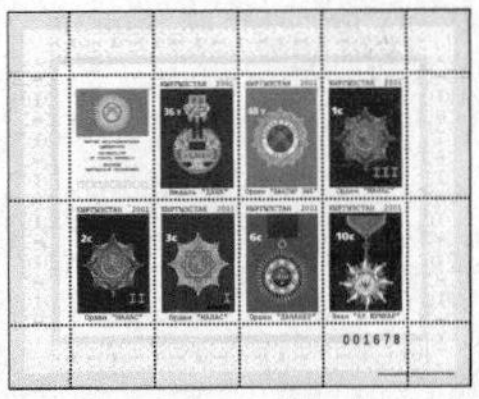

Medals A48

No. 156: a, 36t, Dank. b, 48t, Baatyr Jene. c, 1s, Manas (third class). d, 2s, Manas (second class). e, 3s, Manas (first class). f, 6s, Danaker. g, 10s, Ak Shumkar.

2001, Jan. 20 Litho. ***Perf. 14¼x14***
156 A48 Sheet of 7, #a-g, + label *3.25 3.25*

UN High Commissioner for Refugees — A49

2001, Mar. 10 Litho. ***Perf. 14x14¼***
157 A49 10s multi .95 .95

New Year 2001 (Year of the Snake) — A50

2001, Mar. 17
158 A50 6s multi .80 .80

Exists imperf. Value $2.25.

Year of Dialogue Among Civilizations — A51

2001, Apr. 14 ***Perf. 13½***
159 A51 10s multi *1.25 1.25*

Intl. Year of Mountains — A52

Mountains and: Nos. 160, 163a, 10s, Horses crossing stream. Nos. 161, 163b, 10s, Grazing animals, yurt. Nos. 162, 163c, 10s, Valley.

2001, July 7 ***Perf. 14x14¼***

With White Frame

160-162 A52 Set of 3 *3.50 3.50*

Souvenir Sheet

Without White Frame

163 A52 10s Sheet of 3, #a-c, + label *4.00 4.00*

Bishkek Buildings — A53

Designs: 48t, Communications Building. 1s, Town Hall. 3s, Opera House.

2001, July 7 ***Perf. 14x13¼***

164 A53 48t slate gray *.30 .25*
165 A53 1s olive gray *.30 .30*
166 A53 3s violet brown *.40 .40*
a. Horiz. strip, #164-166 *1.00 1.00*

Intl. Year of Ecotourism (in 2002) — A54

Designs: No. 167, 10s, Mountains, lake. No. 168, 10s, Mountains, field of flowers. No. 169, 10s, Sailboat on lake.
No. 170, Mosque, vert.

2001, July 21 ***Perf. 14x14¼***

167-169 A54 Set of 3 *4.00 4.00*

Souvenir Sheet

Imperf (Simulated Perfs)

170 A54 10s multi *2.40 2.40*

Independence, 10th Anniv. — A55

Designs: 1.50s, Eagle, mountain. 7s, Pres. Askar Akaev, flag.
11.50s, Governmental building.

2001, Aug. 29 ***Perf. 14x14¼***

171-172 A55 Set of 2 *4.50 4.50*

Souvenir Sheet

173 A55 11.50s Sheet of 1 + 8 labels *4.75 4.75*

Kurmanbek Baatyr, 500th Anniv. of Birth — A56

2001, Sept. 8 ***Perf. 14¼x14***

174 A56 1.50s multi *.90 .90*

Nos. 123a-123b Surcharged and Nos. 123c-123d Overprinted With Text Only

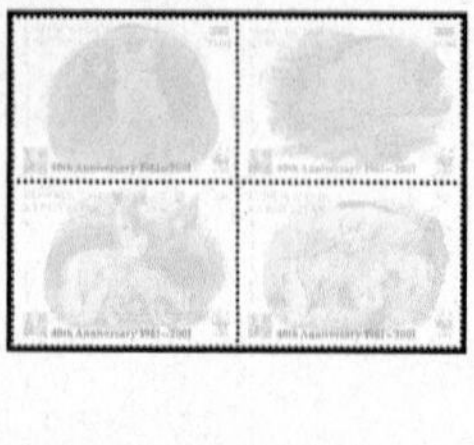

No. 175: a, 25s on 10s #123a. b, 25s on 10s, #123b. c, 30s #123c. d, 50s #123d.

Litho. With Hologram

2001 ***Perf. 13½***

175 A35 Block of 4, #a-d *7.75 7.75*

Regional Communications Accord, 10th Anniv. — A57

2001, Oct. 20 Litho. ***Perf. 14¼x14***

176 A57 7s multi 1.20 1.20

Commonwealth of Independent States, 10th Anniv. — A58

2001, Dec. 8

177 A58 6s Prus bl & yel *1.00 1.00*

Kyrgyzstan postal officials have declared as "illegal":

Stamps with a face value of 20s in sheets of nine depicting Shrek, Harry Potter, Concorde, Dogs, Tigers, Formula 1 racing, Mother Teresa, and The Beatles;

Stamps with various face values in sheets of nine depicting Defenders of Peace and Freedom, Superman, Green Lantern, Flash, Ironman, Legends of Baseball;

Stamps with various values in sheets of three depicting Princess Diana and Elvis Presley;

Stamps with a face value of 20s in sheets of six depicting Harley Davidson motorcycles;

Souvenir sheets of one 100s stamp depicting Harry Potter and Penguins.

2002 Winter Olympics, Salt Lake City — A59

Designs: 50t, Speed skating. 1.50s, Biathlon. 7s, Ice hockey. 10s, Ski jumping.
50s, Downhill skiing.

2002, Feb. 23 Litho. ***Perf. 14x14¼***

178-181 A59 Set of 4 *2.25 2.25*

Souvenir Sheet

182 A59 50s multi + label *5.50 5.50*

New Year 2002 (Year of the Horse) — A60

2002, Mar. 23 ***Perf. 14x14¼***

183 A60 1s multi *1.10 1.10*

2002 World Cup Soccer Championships, Japan and Korea — A61

No. 184: a, 1.50s. b, 3s. c, 7.20s. d, 12s. e, 24s. f, 60s.

2002, Apr. 13 ***Perf. 14¼x14***

184 A61 Sheet of 6, #a-f *11.00 11.00*

No. 184 exists with an overprint in silver or gold with scores of the final and third place matches of the tournament. Value: each, $25.

Kyrgyzstan/Pakistan Diplomatic Relations, 10th Anniv. — A62

2002, Apr. 18 ***Perf. 14¼x14***

185 A62 12s multi *1.25 1.25*

Kyrgyzstan postal officials have declared as "illegal":

Stamps with a face value of 20s in sheets of nine depicting Pandas, Dinosaurs, Marine Life, Cats and Scouting Emblem, and the Beatles.

Stamps with various face values in sheets of nine depicting Caricatures of World Cup Soccer Players (3 sheets).

Summer Olympics A63

No. 186: a, 1s, Discus, Greece #125 (Athens, 1896). b, 2s, Boxing, France #113 (Paris, 1900). c, 3s, Diving, US #324 (St. Louis, 1904). d, 5s, Weight lifting, Great Britain #127 (London, 1908). e, 7s, Rowing, Sweden #97 (Stockholm, 1912). f, 7s, Hurdles, Belgium #B48 (Antwerp, 1920).

No. 187: a, 1s, Rhythmic gymnastics, France #201 (Paris, 1924). b, 2s, Diving, Netherlands #B25 (Amsterdam, 1928). c, 3s, Table tennis, US #718 (Los Angeles, 1932). d, 5s, Running, Germany #B86 (Berlin, 1936). e, 7s, Fencing, Great Britain #274 (London, 1948). f, 7s, Men's gymnastics (pommel horse), Finland #B112 (Helsinki, 1952).

No. 188: a, 1.50s, Volleyball, Australia #277 (Melbourne, 1956). b, 3s, Tennis, Italy #799 (Rome, 1960). c, 5s, Swimming, Japan #B12 (Tokyo, 1964). d, 5s, Judo, Mexico #990 (Mexico City, 1968). e, 7.20s, Kayaking, Germany #B490e (Munich, 1972). f, 12s, Yachting, Canada #B11 (Montreal, 1976).

No. 189: a, 1.50s, Men's gymnastics (rings), Russia #B99 (Moscow, 1980). b, 3s, Synchronized swimming, US #2085a (Los Angeles, 1984). c, 5s, Cycling, South Korea #B54 (Seoul, 1988). d, 5s, High jump, Spain #B197 (Barcelona, 1992). e, 7.20s, Sailboarding, US #3068a (Atlanta, 1996). f, 12s, Women's gymnastics, Australia #1779 (Sydney, 2000).

2002, Aug. 28 Litho. ***Perf. 13x13¼***

Sheets of 6, #a-f, + 3 labels

186-189 A63 Set of 4 *12.00 12.00*

Jalal-Abad A64

Talas A65

Osh — A66

2002, Dec. 7 ***Perf. 13½***

190	A64	20t claret	*.30*	*.30*
191	A65	50t claret	*.30*	*.30*
192	A66	60t claret	*.30*	*.30*
193	A64	1s Prussian bl	*.30*	*.30*
194	A65	1.50s Prussian bl	*.30*	*.30*
195	A66	2s blue gray	*.30*	*.30*
196	A64	3s blue gray	*.45*	*.45*
197	A65	7s blue gray	*.90*	*.90*
198	A66	10s Prussian bl	*1.25*	*1.25*
		Nos. 190-198 (9)	*4.40*	*4.40*

Kyrgyzstan postal officials have declared as "illegal":

Sheets of 9 with various denominations depicting Looney Tunes Characters (Merry Cristmas! (sic)) (2 different), Harry Potter, 71st Academy Awards, MTV Video Awards.

Sheets of 9 with 20s denominations depicting 20th Century Dreams (5 different), Chess, Teddy bears, MTV Video Awards.

Sheet of 6 with various denominations depicting Dinosaurs.

Sheet of 3 with various denominations depicting Pope John Paul II.

Nos. 33, 35 Surcharged in Red or Black

No. 34 Surcharged

Methods and Perfs As Before

2002, Dec. 28

199	A10	1.50s on 1t multi (R)	*.30*	*.30*
200	A10	3.60s on 3t multi	*.40*	*.40*
201	A10	7s on 10t multi	*.80*	*.80*
		Nos. 199-201 (3)	1.50	1.50

New denomination is at left on No. 201.
Nos. 199-201 exist imperf. Value, set $3.

Olmoskhan Atabekova (1922-87) — A67

2003, Jan. 11 Litho. ***Perf. 14¼x14***

202 A67 7.20s multi .75 .75

Intl. Association of Academies of Science, 10th Anniv. — A68

Emblem and: 1.50s, Atom model. 7.20s, Circles.

2003, Mar. 8 ***Perf. 14x14¼***

203-204 A68 Set of 2 1.00 1.00

Gold and Bronze Artifacts From Sakov A69

No. 205: a, 1.50s, Two figurines of people. b, 3s, Coin. c, 3.60s, Lion. d, 5s, Idol with horns. e, 7s, Rooster. f, 10s, Goats. g, 20s, Bird on coin. h, 42s, Animal's head.
No. 206, Mask.

2003, May 10 ***Perf. 14x14¼***

205 A69 Sheet of 8, #a-h *9.75 9.75*

Souvenir Sheet

Imperf. (With Simulated Perforations)

206 A69 42s multi *6.00 6.00*

No. 205 exists imperf. with simulated perforations. Value $15.

Bishkek Post Office, 125th Anniv. — A70

Bishkek Post Office, emblem, dove and: 1s, Airplane. 3s, Covered wagon and Jeep. 7s, Covered wagon.
50s, "1878-2003."

2003, May 31 ***Perf. 14x14¼***
207-209 A70 Set of 3 1.50 1.50

Souvenir Sheet
Imperf. (With Simulated Perforations)

210 A70 50s multi 5.50 5.50

Famous Men A71

Various men: a, 1.50s. b, 3s. c, 3.60s. d, 5s. e, 7.20s. f, 10s. g, 18s. h, 20s. i, 25s. j, 30s.

2003, June 20 ***Perf. 14x14¼***
211 A71 Sheet of 10, #a-j 13.00 13.00

Issyk Kul A72

No. 212: a, 1s, Rahat. b, 1.50s, Raduga. c, 2s, Teltoru. d, 3s, Kyrgyzskoe Vzmorije. e, 3.60s, Tamga. f, 5s, Solnyshko. g, 7s, Vityaz. h, 8s, Ak Bermet. i, 12s, Royal Beach. j, 20s, Luchezarnoe Poberejie.

2003, Aug. 15 ***Perf. 13½x13¾***
212 A72 Sheet of 10, #a-j, + 10 labels 6.50 6.50

Lunar New Year Animals A73

No. 213: a, 1.50s, Rat. b, 3s, Ox. c, 5s, Tiger. d, 7s, Hare. e, 12s, Dragon. f, 12s, Snake. g, 15s, Horse. h, 15s, Sheep. i, 20s, Monkey. j, 20s, Cock. k, 25s, Dog. l, 25s, Pig.

2003, Aug. 25 ***Perf. 13x13¼***
213 A73 Sheet of 12, #a-l, +4 labels 14.00 14.00

National Symbols — A74

History of Syma Chan A75

Designs: No. 214, 3s, Flag. No. 215, 3s, National anthem. 5s, Coat of arms.

2003, Oct. 4 **Litho.** ***Perf. 13½***
214-216 A74 Set of 3 *1.75 1.75*
216a Souvenir sheet, #214-216 *1.75 1.75*

Souvenir Sheet

217 A75 12s multi *2.00 2.00*

New Year 2003 (Year of the Sheep) — A76

2003, Dec. 30 **Litho.** ***Perf. 14x14¼***
218 A76 1.50s multi .70 .70

Meerim Fund, 10th Anniv. — A77

Designs: 1.50s, Fund emblem, buildings. 7s, Fund emblem, buildings, diff.
20s, Fund emblem.

2004, Feb. 17 **Litho.** ***Perf. 14x14¼***
219-220 A77 Set of 2 *1.50 1.50*

Souvenir Sheet
Perf. 13½

221 A77 20s multi *3.00 3.00*

No. 221 contains one 37x51mm stamp.

New Year 2004 (Year of the Monkey) — A78

2004, Apr. 3 **Litho.** ***Perf. 14x14¼***
222 A78 3s multi .80 .80

Automobiles — A79

No. 223: a, 3.60s, 1913 Peugeot. b, 3.60s, 1999 Mercedes-Benz. c, 10s, 1996 Volvo S40. d, 10s, 1908 Ford. e, 15s, 1932 Alfa-Romeo. f, 15s, 1972 VAZ 2101. g, 25s, 1998 Nissan. h, 25s, 1950 ZIS-110.

2004, May 1 **Litho.** ***Perf. 14x13½***
223 A79 Sheet of 8, #a-h *9.00 9.00*

No. 223 exists imperf. Value $16.

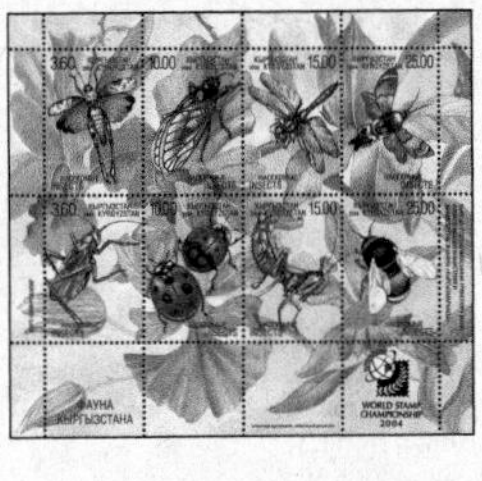

Insects A80

No. 224: a, 3.60s, Insect with red wings. b, 3.60s, Grasshopper. c, 10s, Cricket. d, 10s, Ladybugs. e, 15s, Dragonfly. f, 15s, Praying mantis. g, 25s, Moth with red wings. h, 25s, Bee.

2004, May 15
224 A80 Sheet of 8, #a-h *8.50 8.50*

2004 Singapore World Stamp Championship.
No. 224 exists imperf. Value $15.

FIFA (Fédération Internationale de Football Association), Cent. — A81

No. 225: a, 5s, Soccer ball. b, 6s, FIFA emblem, soccer ball, athletic shoes. c, 7s, Soccer player with red shirt. d, 10s, Soccer player with white shirt.

2004, May 21 **Litho.** ***Perf. 14x14¼***
225 A81 Block of 4, #a-d *2.75 2.75*

No. 12 Surcharged

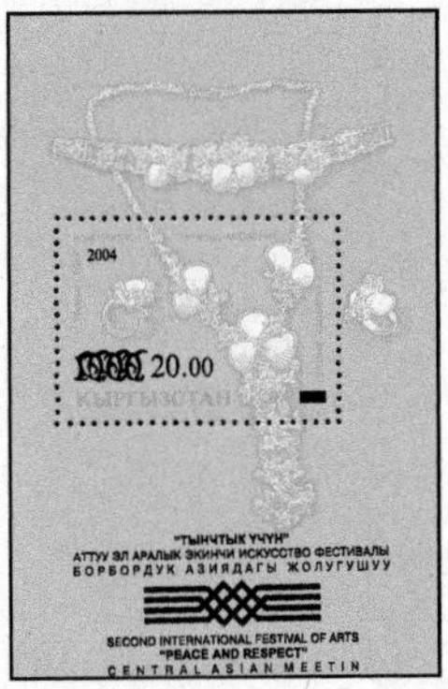

2004, June 19 **Litho.** ***Perf. 12***
226 A5 20s on 10r #12 *2.50 2.50*

Peace and Respect Intl. Festival of Arts.

Karakol Region A82

Naryn Region A83

Tokmok Region — A84

2004, July 6 **Litho.** ***Perf. 13½x13¾***

227	A82	10t	indigo	.25	.25
228	A83	20t	dark green	.25	.25
229	A84	50t	dark brown	.25	.25
230	A82	60t	blue	.25	.25
231	A83	1s	blue green	.25	.25
232	A84	2s	brown	.25	.25
233	A82	3s	violet	.50	.50
234	A83	5s	green	.75	.75
235	A84	7s	light brown	1.00	1.00
			Nos. 227-235 (9)	3.75	3.75

Chynykei Biy (1788-1874) A85

2004, Sept. 18 **Litho.** ***Perf. 14x14¼***
236 A85 3s multi .65 .65

National Academy of Sciences, 50th Anniv. — A86

Emblem and: 1.50s, Old building. 3.60s, New building.

2004, Nov. 6
237-238 A86 Set of 2 .95 .95

Basketball — A87

Basketball player and: 1.50s, Coach Nikolay Zvenchukov. 3.60s, Coach Kubat Karabekov.

2004, Dec. 4
239-240 A87 Set of 2 2.00 2.00

Falcon — A88

2004-05 **Litho.** ***Perf. 13¼x14***

241	A88	10t	green	.40	.40
242	A88	50t	blue	.40	.40
243	A88	1s	brown	.75	.75
			Nos. 241-243 (3)	1.55	1.55

Issued: 1s, 12/28/04. 50t, 2/12/05. 10t, 6/16/05.
Nos. 241-243 exist imperf. Value, set $20.

New Year 2005 (Year of the Rooster) — A89

2005, Mar. 21 **Litho.** ***Perf. 14***
244 A89 3s multi 1.10 1.10

No. 244 exists imperf. Value, $10.

Souvenir Sheet

Salizhan Sharipov, Astronaut — A90

2005, Apr. 20 **Litho.** ***Perf. 13¾***
245 A90 100s multi *13.50 13.50*

Folk Art — A91

Various folk art objects.

2005, Apr. 23 ***Perf. 14¼x14***

246	Strip of 6	*4.50*	*4.50*
a.	A91 2s orange panel	*.25*	*.25*
b.	A91 3.60s light blue panel	*.25*	*.25*
c.	A91 7s green panel	*.55*	*.55*
d.	A91 12s green panel	*.85*	*.85*
e.	A91 15s bright pink panel	*1.10*	*1.10*
f.	A91 20s orange panel	*1.50*	*1.50*

Souvenir Sheet

247 A91 40s multi *4.50 4.50*

End of World War II, 60th Anniv. — A92

2005, May 6 ***Perf. 14x14¼***
248 A92 5s multi *.85 .85*

End of World War II, 60th Anniv. — A93

World War II personalities: No. 249, 5s, Gen. Tito. No. 250, 5s, Cervi Brothers. No. 251, 5s, Ferruccio Parri. No. 252, 10s, Air Marshal Sir Hugh Dowding. No. 253, 10s, Gen. George S. Patton. No. 254, 10s, Gen. Konstantin Rokossovsky. No. 255, 10s, Gen. Harold Alexander. No. 256, 10s, Gen. Omar N. Bradley. No. 257, 10s, Gen. Charles de Gaulle. No. 258, 10s, Gen. Jean Leclerc. No. 259, 10s, Field Marshal Bernard Montgomery. No. 260, 10s, Gen. Ivan Konev. No. 261, 10s, Marshal Georgy Zhukov. No. 262, 10s, Gen. Dwight D. Eisenhower. No. 263, 10s, Marshal Semyon Timoshenko. No. 264, 10s, Gen. Vasily Chuikov. No. 265, 15s, Pres. Franklin D. Roosevelt. No. 266, 15s, Prime Minister Winston Churchill. No. 267, 15s, King George VI. No. 268, 15s, Joseph Stalin.

Embossed on Metal

2005, June 18 ***Die Cut Perf 12½***

Self-Adhesive

249-268 A93 Set of 20 *60.00 60.00*

National Games — A94

2005, Aug. 6 Litho. ***Perf. 14¼x14***

269 A94 3s multi .60 .60

World Summit on the Information Society, Tunis — A95

2005, Sept. 10 ***Perf. 14x14¼***

270 A95 3.60s multi .75 .75

Falcon — A96

2005, Sept. 14 Litho. ***Perf. 13¼x14***

271 A96 60t violet .60 .60

No. 271 exists imperf. Value $5.75.

Souvenir Sheet

Lakes A97

No. 272: a, 7s, Lake Chatyrkul. b, 20s, Lake Sonkul. c, 25s, Lake Sarychelek. d, 30s, Lake Issyk-Kul.

2005, Dec. 10 ***Perf. 14x14¼***

272 A97 Sheet of 4, #a-d 6.25 6.25

Europa Stamps, 50th Anniv. (in 2006) — A98

Designs: 15s, Uzgen Minaret, Kyrgyzstan. 20s, Acropolis, Athens, Greece. 25s, Buran Tower, Kyrgyzstan. 45s, Kolossi Castle, Limassol, Cyprus. 60s, Tash Rabat, Kyrgyzstan. 85s, St. Mark's Basilica, Venice, Italy.

2005, Dec. 29 ***Perf. 13¼x13***

273-278 A98 Set of 6 17.50 17.50

278a Souvenir sheet, #273-278 17.50 17.50

Nos. 273-278 and 278a exist imperf. Values: set, $20; sheet, $20.

Tugolbai Sydykbekov (1912-97), Writer — A99

2006, Jan. 7 ***Perf. 14x14¼***

279 A99 10s multi 1.00 1.00

New Year 2006 (Year of the Dog) — A100

2006, Feb. 4

280 A100 3s multi .70 .70

No. 280 exists imperf. Value, $10.

2006 Winter Olympics, Turin — A101

2006, Mar. 11

281 A101 5s multi .80 .80

No. 281 exists imperf. Value, $7.50.

Falcon — A102

2006 Litho. ***Perf. 13¼x14***

282 A102 50t Prus blue .30 .30

283 A102 1s car lake .40 .40

284 A102 3s black .50 .50

Nos. 282-284 (3) 1.20 1.20

Issued: 50t, 4/15; 1s, 5/6; 3s, 8/5.

Nos. 282-284 exist imperf. Value, each $6.50.

2006 World Cup Soccer Championships, Germany — A103

2006, June 9 Litho. ***Perf. 14x14¼***

285 A103 15s multi 1.25 1.25

Miniature Sheet

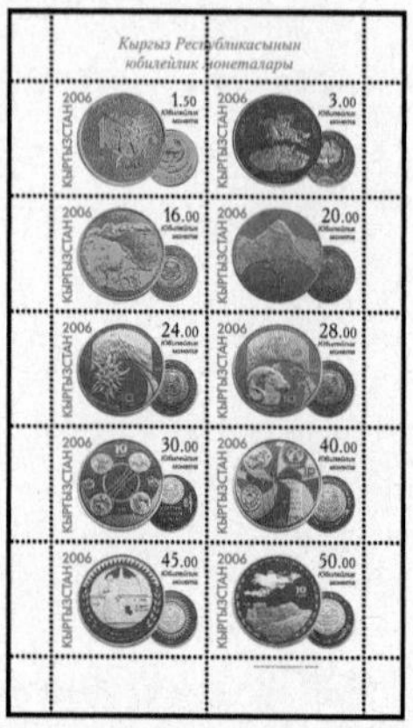

Commemorative Coins — A104

No. 286: a, 1.50s, 1995 100-som gold coin. b, 3s, 1995 10-som silver coin. c, 16s, 2000 100-som gold coin. d, 20s, 2001 10-som silver coin. e, 24s, 2002 10-som silver coin depicting flower. f, 28s, 2002 10-som silver coin depicting ram. g, 30s, 2003 10-som silver and gold coin depicting other coins. h, 40s, 2003 10-som silver and gold coin depicting national symbols. i, 45s, 2005 10-som silver coin. j, 50s, 2005 10-som silver and gold coin.

2006, June 24

286 A104 Sheet of 10, #a-j *17.50 17.50*

Regional Communications Commonwealth, 15th Anniv. — A105

2006, Sept. 23 Litho. ***Perf. 14x14¼***

287 A105 12s multi 1.25 1.25

Souvenir Sheet

Public Buildings in Bishkek A106

No. 288: a, Sports arena (two word inscription, large tree at left). b, Theater (three word inscription). c, Philharmonic hall (one word inscription). d, Museum (two word inscription, no tree).

2006, Sept. 30 ***Perf. 12¾x13¼***

288 A106 12s Sheet of 4, #a-d 4.00 4.00

Intl. Telecommunications Union Plenipotentiary Conference, Antalya, Turkey — A107

2006, Oct. 7 Litho. ***Perf. 13x13½***

289 A107 25s multi 2.25 2.25

Defense of Moscow in World War II, 65th Anniv. — A108

2006, Nov. 11 ***Perf. 14x14¼***

290 A108 7s multi .70 .70

No. 290 exists imperf. Value, $8.

Miniature Sheet

Kyrgyz Cinema, 65th Anniv. A109

No. 291: a, S. Chokmorov (on horse). b, B. Bejshenaliev (man wearing hat). c, T. Tursunbaeva (woman wearing headdress). d, B. Kydykeeva (two women).

2006, Dec. 9

291 A109 12s Sheet of 4, #a-d 4.25 4.25

New Year 2007 (Year of the Pig) — A110

2007, Jan. 27 Litho. ***Perf. 14x14¼***

292 A110 3s multi .50 .50

No. 292 exists imperf. Value, $8.50.

Miniature Sheet

Paintings A111

No. 293: a, Chingiz Aitmatov (seated man with striped shirt). b, Syimenkul Chokmorov (seated man with clasped hands). c, Kurmangazy Azykbaev (man playing flute). d, Omor Sultanov (seated man wearing light gray suit). e, Zhylkychy Zhakypov (man with dark blue shirt).

2007, Mar. 3 Litho. ***Perf. 14x14¼***

293 A111 12s Sheet of 5, #a-e, + label 5.50 5.50

No. 293 exists imperf. Value, $30.

Kyrgyz National Games — A112

2007, May 5 Litho. ***Perf. 14x14¼***

294 A112 7s multi .65 .65

No. 294 exists imperf. Value, $8.50.

Miniature Sheet

Bishkek-Osh Highway, 50th Anniv. — A113

No. 295: a, Tunnel. b, Road turning to left. c, Road turning to right. d, Straight road.

2007, May 19 ***Perf. 13x13¼***

295 A113 25s Sheet of 4, #a-d 6.75 6.75

Aigul — A114

Flower and: 1s, Solid blue background. 100s, Mountains in background.

2007, June 23 ***Perf. 13¼x14***

296 A114 1s multi .50 .50

Souvenir Sheet

Perf. 13¼x13

297 A114 100s multi 8.00 8.00

No. 296 exists imperf. Value, $7.

No. 297 contains one 30x40mm stamp.

Miniature Sheet

Seventh Conference of Shanghai Cooperation Organization — A115

No. 298 — Flags of: a, Kazakhstan. b, Kyrgyzstan. c, People's Republic of China. d, Russia. e, Tajikistan. f, Uzbekistan.

2007, Aug. 16 ***Perf. 13¾x14½***
298 A115 12s Sheet of 6, #a-f 5.75 5.75

Miniature Sheet

Birds of Prey A116

No. 299: a, Haliaeetus albicilla. b, Falco rusticolus. c, Aquila chrysaetus. d, Accipiter gentilis. e, Milvus migrans. f, Falco peregrinus.

2007, Nov. 30 **Litho.** ***Perf. 14¼***
299 A116 25s Sheet of 6, #a-f 12.00 12.00

Santa Claus — A117

2007, Dec. 1 ***Perf. 14x14¼***
300 A117 3s multi .55 .55

No. 300 exists imperf. Value, $7.75.

New Year 2008 (Year of the Rat) — A118

2008, Jan. 19 ***Perf. 14¼x14***
301 A118 7s multi .95 .95

No. 301 exists imperf. Value, $8.

Mammals — A119

Designs: Nos. 302, 310a, 7s, Uncia uncia. Nos. 303, 310b, 7s, Ailuropoda melanoleuca. Nos. 304, 310c, 12s, Panthera tigris. Nos. 305, 310d, 12s, Ailurus fulgens. Nos. 306, 310e, 16s, Hystrix cristata. Nos. 307, 310f, 16s, Pygathrix roxellana. Nos. 308, 310g, 25s, Otocolobus manul. Nos. 309, 310h, 25s, Ovis ammon.

2008, Jan. 19 ***Perf. 14x13½***
Stamps With White Frames
302-309 A119 Set of 8 9.50 9.50

Souvenir Sheet
Stamps With Colored Frames
310 A119 Sheet of 8, #a-h 9.25 9.25

Nos. 302-309 exist imperf. Value, set $17.

Kyrgyz National Games — A120

2008, Mar. 1 ***Perf. 14¼x14***
311 A120 5s multi .70 .70

No. 311 exists imperf. Value, $6.50.

2008 Summer Olympics, Beijing — A121

No. 312: a, Soccer. b, Wrestling. c, Javelin. d, Basketball.

2008, Mar. 1 ***Perf. 12½x13***
312 A121 20s Block of 4, #a-d 6.25 6.25

Souvenir Sheet

Mountains — A122

No. 313: a, Khan-Tengri, Kyrgyzstan. b, Sabalan Peak, Iran.

2008, Mar. 8 ***Perf. 13x13¼***
313 A122 16s Sheet of 2, #a-b, + central label *4.00 4.00*

See Iran No. 2964.

Outlines of Stamps, Mountain, Kyrgyz Post Emblem — A123

2008 **Litho.** ***Perf. 14x13¼***
314 A123 50t multi .25 .25
315 A123 1s multi .25 .25
316 A123 3s multi .25 .25
317 A123 7s multi .65 .65
Nos. 314-317 (4) 1.40 1.40

Issued: 1s, 3s, 4/2. 50t, 7s, 5/10.
Nos. 314-317 exist imperf. Value, set $20.

Heroes of the Kyrgyz Republic and Medals — A124

Designs: 10s, Sabira Kumushalieva (1917-2007), actress. 15s, Absamat Masaliev (1933-2004), politician.

2008, Apr. 5 **Litho.** ***Perf. 14x14¼***
318-319 A124 Set of 2 2.50 2.50

Nos. 318-319 exist imperf. Value, set $12.50.

Miniature Sheets

Civil Aircraft A125

No. 320: a, JAK-12. b, MI-2. c, AN-2. d, TU-154. e, IL-14. f, IL-18. g, AN-24. h, MI-4.

No. 321: a, AN-28. b, JAK-40. c, AN-26. d, TU-134. e, IL-76. f, A-320. g, MI-8.

No. 322: a, Sopwith. b, Air-6. c, P5. d, Po-2. e, Ju-52/3. f, ANT-9. g, Mi-1. h, Li-2.

2008 ***Perf. 14x13¼***
320 A125 20s Sheet of 8, #a-h, + central label 11.00 11.00

Perf. 13x13½
321 A125 20s Sheet of 7, #a-g, + label 10.50 10.50
322 A125 20s Sheet of 8, #a-h, + label 10.50 10.50

Issued: No. 320, 5/24; No. 321, 9/20; No. 322, 11/1.

Hats — A126

Various hats: 6s, 7s, 12s, 50s.

2008, June 28 **Litho.** ***Perf. 14¼x14***
323-326 A126 Set of 4 5.50 5.50

Nos. 323-326 exist imperf. Value, set $22.50.

Yaks A127

No. 325: a, Buka yak (denomination on cloud). b, Mamalak yak (denomination on light blue sky and mountain). c, Inek yak facing right (denomination on purple mountain). d, Inek yak facing left (denomination on dark blue sky and mountain).

2008, July 26 ***Perf. 13x13¼***
327 A127 25s Block of 4, #a-d 6.50 6.50

Isa Akhunbaev (1908-75), Surgeon — A128

2008, Aug. 30 ***Perf. 14¼x14***
328 A128 12s multi .90 .90

No. 328 exists imperf. Value, $7.

No. 312 Overprinted in Red

No. 329: a, #312a (Soccer) with overprint at bottom. b, #312b (Wrestling) with overprint at bottom. c, #312c (Javelin) with overprint at top. d, #312d (Basketball) with overprint at top. e, #312d with overprint at bottom. f, #312c with overprint at bottom. g, #312b with overprint at top. h, #312a with overprint at top.

2008, Nov. 22 **Litho.** ***Perf. 12½x13***
329 A121 20s Sheet of 8, #a-h 21.00 21.00

Campaign Against Drug Abuse — A129

2008, Dec. 6 ***Perf. 14¼x14***
330 A129 12s multi 1.25 1.25

No. 330 exists imperf. Value, $6.50.

New Year 2009 (Year of the Ox) — A130

2009, Feb. 1 ***Perf. 14x14¼***
331 A130 25s multi 1.60 1.60

No. 331 exists imperf. Value, $6.

Ishembai Abdraimov (1914-2001), Soviet Pilot — A131

2009, Feb. 26 ***Perf. 14¼x14***
332 A131 10s multi .85 .85

No. 332 exists imperf. Value, $6.25.

Kok-boru (Buzkashi) A132

2009, Apr. 25 ***Perf. 14x14¼***
333 A132 25s multi 1.60 1.60

No. 333 exists imperf. Value, $6.

Miniature Sheet

Horses A133

No. 334 — Various horses: a, 16s. b, 42s. c, 50s. d, 60s.

2009, May 30 ***Perf. 13x13½***
334 A133 Sheet of 4, #a-d 9.00 9.00

Worldwide Fund for Nature (WWF) — A134

Saker falcon: 10s, Head. 15s, On nest. 25s, In flight. 50s, On nest, with chicks.

2009, June 20 ***Perf. 13½x14***
335-338 A134 Set of 4 5.50 5.50
338a Sheet, 4 each #335-338 22.00 22.00

Nos. 335-338 and 338a exist imperf. Values: set of four, $13; sheet of 16, $42.50.

Miniature Sheet

Scenes From Writings of Chynghyz Aitmatov (1928-2008) — A135

No. 339: a, 7s, Woman, horse, cart and farmer in field. b, 12s, Man and horse. c, 16s, Woman and truck. d, 21s, Women near train. e, 28s, Man carrying boy. f, 30s, Boy with binoculars, buck. g, 45s, Birds flying above horse and rider. h, 60s, Men in canoe.

2009, Aug. 13 **Litho.** ***Perf. 13x13¼***
339 A135 Sheet of 8, #a-h, + label 11.00 11.00

Barpy Alykulov (1884-1949), Poet — A136

2009, Aug. 22 Litho. *Perf. 14x13½*
340 A136 16s multi .95 .95

No. 340 exists imperf. Value, $6.

Horses Type of 2009

Designs: 16s, Like #334a. 42s, Like #334b. 50s, Like #334c. 60s, Like #334d.

2009, Sept. 19 Litho. *Perf. 14x14¼*
341-344 A133 Set of 4 9.00 9.00

Nos. 341-344 were each printed in sheets of 6.

Nos. 341-344 exist imperf. Value, set $30.

National Library, 75th Anniv. — A137

2009, Sept. 30 *Perf. 13½x14*
345 A137 12s multi .90 .90

No. 345 exists imperf. Value, $5.75.

Miniature Sheet

Glaciers A138

No. 346: a, 12s, Ak-Sai Glacier. b, 16s, Kotur Glacier. c, 21s, Semenovsky Glacier. d, 28s, Zvezdochka Glacier. e, 45s, North Inylchek Glacier. f, 60s, South Inylchek Glacier.

2009, Dec. 12 *Perf. 13x13¼*
346 A138 Sheet of 6, #a-f 10.50 10.50

No. 346 exists imperf. Value, $32.50.

Railways of Kyrgyzstan A139

Designs: 16s, Station. 42s, Train on bridge. 50s, Train leaving tunnel. 60s, Train on bridge over highway.

2009, Dec. 19 *Perf. 14x14¼*
347-350 A139 Set of 4 10.00 10.00

Nos. 347-350 exist imperf. Value, set $32.50.

United Nations Declaration of the Rights of the Child, 50th Anniv. (in 2009) — A140

2010, Feb. 6
351 A140 21s multi 1.50 1.50

New Year 2010 (Year of the Tiger) — A141

2010, Feb. 6
352 A141 25s multi 1.60 1.60

2010 Winter Olympics, Vancouver — A142

Designs: 21s, Cross-country skiing. 28s, Biathlon. 45s, Giant slalom. 60s, Snowboarding.

2010, Feb. 12 *Perf. 14¼x14*
353-356 A142 Set of 4 10.50 10.50

Peonies A143

No. 357: a, 25s, Flowers. b, 30s, Flower.

2010, Mar. 30 *Perf. 12½*
357 A143 Horiz. pair, #a-b 3.75 3.75
c. Souvenir sheet, #357b 2.40 2.40

Victory in World War II, 65th Anniv. — A144

2010, Apr. 10 *Perf. 14x14¼*
358 A144 12s multi .75 .75

Miniature Sheet

Kyrgyz National Museum of Fine Arts, 75th Anniv. A145

No. 359 — Paintings: a, 12s, Portrait of Y. M. Vengerov, by Ilya E. Repin, 1916. b, 16s, Cabbage Field, by Robert R. Falk, 1910. c, 21s, Dishes on a Red Cloth, by Pyotr P. Konchalovsky, 1916. d, 24s, Seascape in the Crimea, by Ivan K. Ayvazovsky, 1866. e, 28s, Autumn Djailoo, by Semen A. Chuykov, 1945. f, 30s, Evening in the South of Kyrgyzstan, by Gapar A. Aitiev, 1967. g, 42s, Autumn Garden, by A. Ignatev, 1989. h, 45s, By Night, by D. N. Deymant, 1971.

2010, Apr. 24 *Perf. 13x13¼*
359 A145 Sheet of 8, #a-h, + central label 13.00 13.00

2010 World Cup Soccer Championships, South Africa — A146

Players and: 24s, Emblem. 30s, World Cup. 42s, Emblem, diff. 60s, World Cup, diff.

2010, June 26 Litho. *Perf. 14x14¼*
360-363 A146 Set of 4 9.50 9.50

Ancient Silver Jewelry — A147

Designs: 16s, Earrings. 24s, Buttons. 58s, Bangles. 66s, Hair ornaments.

2010, July 31 *Perf. 13½*
364-367 A147 Set of 4 10.00 10.00

Souvenir Sheet

Kambar-Ata 2 Hydroelectric Station — A148

No. 368: a, 28s, Explosion. b, 42s, Station under construction. c, 60s, Station under construction, diff.

2010, Aug. 31 *Perf. 13x13¼*
368 A148 Sheet of 3, #a-c 7.50 7.50

Souvenir Sheet

Intl. Telecommunications Union Plenipotentiary Conference, Guadalajara, Mexico — A149

2010, Sept. 25 *Perf. 13*
369 A149 100s multi 6.00 6.00

Famous Men — A150

Designs: 12s, Togolok Moldo (1860-1942), poet. 16s, Murataly Kurenkeev (1860-1949), composer. 21s, Zhenizhok Coco Uulu (1860-1918), poet. 28s, Itzhak Razzakov (1910-79), statesman.

2010 *Perf. 14¼x14*
370-373 A150 Set of 4 4.00 4.00

Issued: 28s, 10/25; others, 10/23.

Turtles — A151

Designs: 16s, Agrionemys horstieldi. 24s, Pseudemys scripta. 48s, Geochelone elegans. 72s, Testudo kleinmanni.

2010, Dec. 11 *Perf. 14x14¼*
374-377 A151 Set of 4 9.00 9.00

New Year 2011 (Year of the Rabbit) — A152

2011, Jan. 29
378 A152 24s multi 1.40 1.40

Miniature Sheet

Animals and National Reserves — A153

No. 379: a, 7s, Eagle, Ala-Archa Reserve. b, 12s, Bear, Chon-Kemin Reserve. c, 16s, Buck, Naryn Reserve. d, 21s, Ram, Sary-Chelek Reserve. e, 24s, Fish, Issyk-Kul Reserve. f, 28s, Duck, Karatal-Zhapryk Reserve. g, 42s, Falcon, Besh-Tash Reserve. h, 45s, Cat, Sarychat-Ertash Reserve. i, 60s, Pheasant, Padysha-Ata Reserve.

2011, Feb. 25 *Perf. 13x13¼*
379 A153 Sheet of 9, #a-i 13.50 13.50

Souvenir Sheet

First Man in Space, 50th Anniv. A154

No. 380: a, 60s, Vostok 1. b, 90s, Yuri Gagarin (1934-68), first cosmonaut.

2011, Apr. 2 *Perf. 13¼x13*
380 A154 Sheet of 2, #a-b 8.00 8.00

2011 Intl. Ice Hockey Federation Championships, Slovakia — A155

Intl. Ice Hockey Federation emblem and: 28s, Player approaching goalie with puck. 42s, Two players and puck.

2011, May 14 *Perf. 14x14¼*
381-382 A155 Set of 2 4.00 4.00
382a Miniature sheet of 6, 3 each #381-382 12.50 12.50

Miniature Sheet

Bishkek Bus Station, 30th Anniv. A156

No. 383 — Vehicles: a, 12s, PAZ-672 bus, RAF-22038 van. b, 16s, Ikarus-256 bus, GAZ-M24 Volga taxi. c, 21s, LAZ 697R Tourist bus, UAZ-2206 van. d, 24s, Ford E series van, Volvo B12B bus. e, 30s, Volkswagen Transporter T4 van, Setra S 431 dt bus. f, 42s, Mercedes Sprinter 313 van, Mitsubishi Fuso Aero Queen bus.

2011, July 21 *Perf. 13x13¼*
383 A156 Sheet of 6, #a-f + central label 8.50 8.50

No. 123 Overprinted in Gold with Nos. 123c and 123d Surcharged in Metallic Red

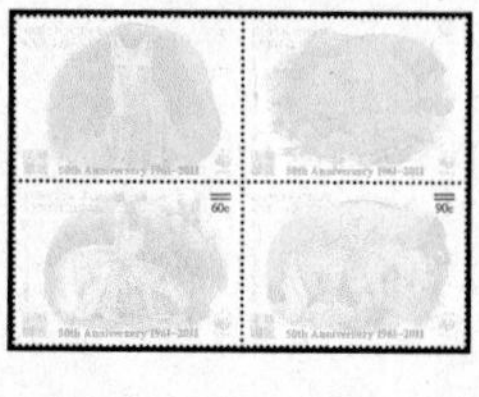

No. 384: a, Overprint on #123a. b, Overprint on #123b. c, 60s on 20s #123c. d, 90s on 50s #123d.

Litho. With Hologram

2011, Aug. 5 *Perf. 13½*
384 A35 Block of 4, #a-d *20.00 20.00*

Plum Blossoms A157

No. 385: a, 16s, Denomination at UL. b, 60s, Denomination at UR.

2011, Aug. 15 **Litho.** *Perf. 13*
385 A157 Horiz. pair, #a-b 4.50 4.50

Regional Communications Commonwealth, 20th Anniv. — A158

2011, Oct. 1 *Perf. 14x14¼*
386 A158 28s multi 1.75 1.75

Souvenir Sheet

Independence, 20th Anniv. — A159

2011, Oct. 1 *Perf. 14*
387 A159 100s multi 6.00 6.00

Commonwealth of Independent States, 20th Anniv. — A160

2011, Oct. 8 *Perf. 14x14¼*
388 A160 42s multi 2.75 2.75

Mushrooms — A161

Designs: 16s, Agaricus. 28s, Pleurotus. 42s, Marasmius oreades. 72s, Lycoperdon.

2011, Nov. 12 **Litho.** *Perf. 14¼x14*
389-392 A161 Set of 4 9.00 9.00

Musical Instruments — A162

Designs: 16s, Surnai (wind instrument). 24s, Dobulbas (drum). 48s, Kyl kayak (stringed instrument with bow). 60s, Ooz komuz (mouth harp).

2011, Nov. 26
393-396 A162 Set of 4 8.25 8.25

Airships — A163

Designs: 12s, Dirigible of Henri Giffard. 28s, LZ-127 Graf Zeppelin. 45s, AU-30 Argus dirigible. 48s, Dirigible of the future.

2011, Dec. 17 *Perf. 14x14¼*
397-400 A163 Set of 4 7.75 7.75

New Year 2012 (Year of the Dragon) — A164

2012, Jan. 14 *Perf. 13¼*
401 A164 36s multi 2.10 2.10

Printed in sheets of 4.

Miniature Sheet

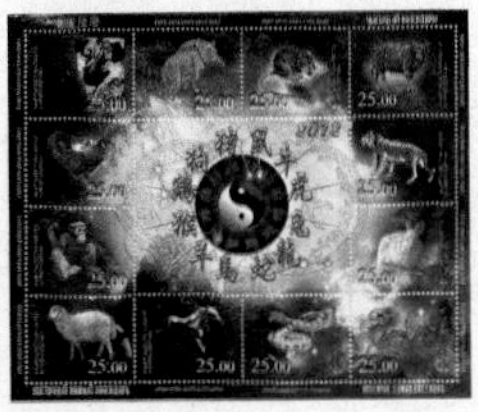

Oriental Lunar Calendar Animals A165

No. 402: a, Dog. b, Boar. c, Rat. d, Ox. e, Rooster. f, Tiger. g, Monkey. h, Rabbit. i, Sheep. j, Horse. k, Snake. l, Dragon.

2012, Jan. 14 *Perf. 13¾x13½*
402 A165 25s Sheet of 12, #a-l, + central label 18.00 18.00

Women's Headdresses A166

Various headdresses: 16s, 28s, 45s, 60s.

2012, Feb. 25 *Perf. 13*
403-406 A166 Set of 4 8.50 8.50

Helianthus — A167

2012, Mar. 29 *Perf. 14¼x14*
407 A167 42s multi 2.50 2.50

Bolot Beishenaliev (1937-2002), Actor — A168

Gapar Aitiev (1912-84), Artist — A169

2012, Apr. 28 **Litho.**
408 A168 23s multi 1.25 1.25
409 A169 49s multi 2.75 2.75

Miniature Sheet

Inventions — A170

No. 410: a, 21s, Writing. b, 23s, Bread. c, 45s, Wheel. d, 49s, Money.

2012, June 2 *Perf. 14*
410 A170 Sheet of 4, #a-d 8.25 8.25

2012 World Stamp Championship, Jakarta, Indonesia.

United Nations Environment Program, 40th Anniv. — A171

2012, June 5 *Perf. 14x14¼*
411 A171 45s multi 2.75 2.75

National Games — A172

2012, Aug. 4 **Litho.** *Perf. 14x14¼*
412 A172 28s multi 1.75 1.75

Battle of Borodino, Bicent. A173

No. 413: a, 12s, Battlefield Monument, Borodino. b, 45s, Triumphal Arch, Moscow.

2012, Aug. 25 *Perf. 14¼x14*
413 A173 Pair, #a-b 3.50 3.50

Snow Leopard — A174

Designs: 17s, Leopard. 20s, Leopard, diff. 23s, Head of leopard. 30s, Three leopards.

2012, Sept. 15 *Perf. 14x14¼*
414-417 A174 Set of 4 5.75 5.75

Man and Woman in Traditional Costumes and Emblem of Regional Communications Commonwealth — A175

2012, Oct. 20 *Perf. 14¼x14*
418 A175 30s multi 1.75 1.75

Inscribed Tablets A176

No. 419 — Tablet from: a, 35s, 8th cent. b, 40s, 9th cent.

2012, Nov. 3
419 A176 Horiz. pair, #a-b 4.50 4.50

Gen. Ysakbek Monuev (1902-49) A177

Ormon Khan (1792-1854), Kyrgyz Tribal Leader A178

2012, Nov. 24
420 A177 35s multi 2.25 2.25
421 A178 40s multi 2.50 2.50

Prehistoric Animals — A179

Designs: 23s, Kyrgyzsaurus. 30s, Xenacanthidae. 40s, Longisquama. 52s, Mammoth.

2012, Dec. 8 *Perf. 14x14¼*
422-425 A179 Set of 4 9.50 9.50

Souvenir Sheet

Mayan Calendar A180

No. 426: a, 29s, Mayan calendar. b, 52s, Mayan pyramid.

2012, Dec. 21 *Perf. 14*
426 A180 Sheet of 2, #a-b 5.25 5.25

New Year 2013 (Year of the Snake) — A181

2013, Feb. 16 *Perf. 14x14¼*
427 A181 30s multi 2.00 2.00

2012 Universal Postal Congress International Stamp Exhibition, Doha, Qatar — A182

No. 428: a, 28s, Gold medal diploma awarded to Kyrgyzstan. b, 43s, Exhibition emblem.

2013, Feb. 23
428 A182 Pair, #a-b 4.25 4.25

No. 428 was printed in sheets containing three pairs.

Miniature Sheet

Walnuts A183

No. 429: a, 17s, Cluster of walnuts on tree branch. b, 20s, Walnuts with opened husks. c, 23s, Walnut in husk, walnuts in shell, opened walnut, jar of product containing walnuts. d,

29s, Walnut in shell, kernels. e, 35s, Basket of walnuts. f, 40s, Walnut grove, mountains.

2013, Mar. 9
429 A183 Sheet of 6, #a-f 9.50 9.50

National Horse Games — A184

2013, Mar. 23
430 A184 35s multi 2.25 2.25

Spaceflight of Valentina Tereshkova, First Woman in Space, 50th Anniv. — A185

2013, Apr. 13
431 A185 50s multi 3.25 3.25

Introduction of Som Currency, 20th Anniv. — A186

2013, Apr. 27
432 A186 28s multi 1.75 1.75

Marco Polo Argali (Mountain Sheep) — A187

Design: 29s, Head of ram. 35s, Adult and juveniles grazing. 40s, Ram on mountain ledge. 52s, Ram in winter.

2013, May 18
433-436 A187 Set of 4 11.00 11.00
436a Souvenir sheet of 4, #433-436 11.00 11.00

Kozhomkul (1888-1955), Wrestler — A188

2013, June 8
437 A188 30s multi 1.75 1.75

Sulayman Mountain — A189

2013, June 22
438 A189 45s multi 3.00 3.00

Miniature Sheet

Worldwide Fund for Nature (WWF) — A190

No. 439 — Snow leopard: a, 29s, Resting on rock. b, 35s, Leaping. c, 43s, Standing on rock. d, 52s, Kittens.

2013, July 13
439 A190 Sheet of 4, #a-d 10.50 10.50

Intl. Forum on Snow Leopard Conservation, Bishkek.

Regional Communications Commonwealth Emblem, Train, Airplane, Satellite Dish, Cover and Tablet — A191

2013, Aug. 17 Litho. ***Perf. 14x14¼***
440 A191 36s multi 1.90 1.90

Miniature Sheet

13th Shanghai Cooperation Organization Council of Heads of State Session, Bishkek — A192

No. 441 — Emblems or coat of arms of: a, 12s, Kazakhstan. b, 17s, Kyrgyzstan. c, 20s, People's Republic of China. d, 23s, Russia. e, 30s, Tajikistan. f, 35s, Uzbekistan.

Litho. With Foil Application

2013, Sept. 13 ***Perf. 13½x13¼***
441 A192 Sheet of 6, #a-f 6.50 6.50

Nasirdin Isanov (1943-91), First Prime Minister of Kyrgyzstan — A193

2013, Oct. 1 Litho. ***Perf. 14x14¼***
442 A193 17s multi 1.25 1.25

Kyrgyz Khaganate, 1170th Anniv. — A194

No. 443: a, 20s, Kyrgyz soldier wearing helmet, map of Khaganate. b, 23s, Mounted soldiers. c, 30s, Mounted soildier and petroglyphs.

2013, Nov. 16 Litho. ***Perf. 14¼x14***
443 A194 Horiz. strip of 3, #a-c 4.25 4.25

Printed in sheets of 6 containing two of each stamp.

Medicinal Plants — A195

Designs: 20s, Capparis spinosa. 30s, Aconitum leucostomum. 35s, Hippophae rhamnoides. 52s, Glycyrrhiza glabra.

2013, Dec. 14 Litho. ***Perf. 14¼x14***
444-447 A195 Set of 4 9.25 9.25

New Year 2014 (Year of the Horse) — A196

2014, Feb. 16 Litho. ***Perf. 14x14¼***
448 A196 35s multi 2.25 2.25

2014 Winter Olympics, Sochi, Russia — A197

Designs: 12s, Speed skating. 21s, Cross-country skiing. 52s, Freestyle skiing. 74s, Bobsledding.

2014, Feb. 22 Litho. ***Perf. 14x14¼***
449-452 A197 Set of 4 8.25 8.25

Jousting Horsemen A198

2014, Mar. 22 Litho. ***Perf. 14x14¼***
453 A198 30s multi 1.90 1.90

Aykol Manas Monument, Bishkek — A199

2014, Apr. 15 Litho. ***Perf. 13¼x14***

Background Color

454	A199	20s	green gray	.95	.95
455	A199	23s	blue gray	1.10	1.10
456	A199	30s	lilac	1.40	1.40
457	A199	93s	lt green	4.50	4.50
458	A199	100s	lt orange	4.75	4.75
		Nos. 454-458 (5)		12.70	12.70

Children on Sleds — A200

2014, May 10 Litho. ***Perf. 14x14¼***
459 A200 40s multi 2.25 2.25

Medicinal Plants — A201

Designs: 20s, Tussilago farfara. 23s, Ferula foetida. 35s, Ziziphora clinopodioides. 40s, Helichrysum maracandicum.

2014, May 31 Litho. ***Perf. 12¼x12***
460-463 A201 Set of 4 6.00 6.00

Worldwide Fund for Nature (WWF) — A202

Aegypius monachus: 29s, Head. 35s, In flight. 62s, Adult and chick in nest. 74s, On ground.

2014, June 21 Litho. ***Perf. 14x14¼***
464-467 A202 Set of 4 11.00 11.00
467a Block of 4, #464-467 11.00 11.00

Miniature Sheet

Soccer Players A203

No. 468: a, 29s, Five players. b, 35s, Three players. c, 40s, Two players. d, 52s, Four players.

2014, July 1 Litho. ***Perf. 12x12¼***
468 A203 Sheet of 4, #a-d 8.00 8.00

Dooronbek Sadyrbaev (1939-2008), Film Director, and Medal — A204

2014, July 26 Litho. ***Perf. 14x14¼***
469 A204 35s multi 1.90 1.90

Carpets — A205

UNESCO emblem and: 35s, Ala-kiyiz. 45s, Shyrdak.

2014, Aug. 16 Litho. ***Perf. 12x12¼***
470-471 A205 Set of 2 4.50 4.50

Nos. 470-471 each were printed in sheets of 5 + label.

Communist Leaders — A206

Designs: 20s, Imanaly Aidarbekov (1884-1938). 29s, Abdykerim Sydykov (1889-1938). 35s, Abdykadyr Orozbekov (1889-1938).

2014, Aug. 31 Litho. ***Perf. 14¼x14***
472-474 A206 Set of 3 4.00 4.00

Souvenir Sheet

Kyrgyz State Technical University, 60th Anniv. — A207

No. 475: a, 52s, University building and statue. b, 62s, University building, no statue.

2014, Sept. 18 Litho. ***Perf. 12x12¼***
475 A207 Sheet of 2, #a-b 6.00 6.00

Souvenir Sheet

International Telecommunication Union Plenipotentiary Conference, Busan, South Korea — A208

2014, Oct. 11 Litho. ***Perf. 12x12¼***
476 A208 30s multi 1.90 1.90

Toktogul Satylganov (1864-1933), Poet A209

Suimenkul Chokmorov (1939-92), Film Actor A210

2014, Nov. 1 Litho. *Perf. 12¼x12*
477 A209 35s multi 2.00 2.00
478 A210 40s multi 2.25 2.25

Kyrgyz Flag and People A211

2014, Dec. 6 Litho. *Perf. 13x13½*
479 A211 30s multi 1.90 1.90

Souvenir Sheet

Cotton A212

No. 480: a, 35s, Cotton bolls and leaves. b, 52s, Cotton bolls.

2014, Dec. 13 Litho. *Perf. 12x12¼*
480 A212 Sheet of 2, #a-b 4.50 4.50

Endangered Animals — A213

Designs: 23s, Ursus arctos. 30s, Otocolobus manul. 40s, Cuon alpinus. 52s, Lynx lynx linnaeus.

2014, Dec. 20 Litho. *Perf. 14x14¼*
481-484 A213 Set of 4 7.75 7.75

New Year 2015 (Year of the Sheep) — A214

2015, Feb. 7 Litho. *Perf. 12x12¼*
485 A214 40s multi 2.25 2.25

Sheep Breeds A215

No. 486: a, 35s, Aykol. b, 52s, Mountain merino.

2015, Feb. 21 Litho. *Perf. 12x12¼*
486 A215 Pair, #a-b 4.50 4.50

Famous People A216

No. 487: a, 29s, Korgool Dosuev (1890-1962), singer. b, 35s, Zhumamudin Sheraliev (1915-94), musician. c, 40s, Myskal Omurkanova (1915-76), singer. d, 52s, Alykul Osmonov (1915-50), poet.

2015, Mar. 21 Litho. *Perf. 14¼x14*
487 A216 Horiz. strip of 4, #a-d 7.75 7.75

Dogs and Cats — A217

Designs: 29s, Ainu. 35s, Persian cat. 62s, Siamese cat. 74s, Taigan.

2015, Apr. 4 Litho. *Perf. 12x12¼*
488-491 A217 Set of 4 9.50 9.50
491a Souvenir sheet of 4, #488-491 9.50 9.50

Victory in World War II, 70th Anniv. — A218

70th anniv. emblem and: 30s, Taranchiev Ismailbek (1923-44), fighter pilot. 40s, War memorial, soldiers, tanks, map, vert. 52s, Otorbayev Asanbek (1925-45), soldier.

Perf. 12x12¼, 12¼x12
2015, May 2 Litho.
492-494 A218 Set of 3 6.50 6.50

No. 493 was printed in sheets of 2.

Souvenir Sheet

Eurasian Economic Union — A219

2015, May 16 Litho. *Perf. 13*
495 A219 202s multi 10.50 10.50

Miniature Sheet

Paintings A220

No. 496: a, 15s, Poet, by G. Aytiev and D. Kozhakhmetov. b, 18s, Labyrinth, by D. Nurgaziev. c, 20s, Old Street of Osh City, by U. Akynov. d, 30s, Poppies, by Erbol Dogdurbek. e, 35s, Mystic Night, by D. Umetov. f, 40s, Touching Eternity, by S. A. Chuykov. g, 52s, Holiday, by S. Chokmorov. h, 59s, South Beach, by S. Torobekov.

2015, July 18 Litho. *Perf. 12x12¼*
496 A220 Sheet of 8, #a-h, + central label 13.50 13.50

Scenes From the Epic of Manas — A221

No. 497 — Various scenes: a, 20s. b, 35s. c, 74s.

2015, Aug. 1 Litho. *Perf. 12x12¼*
497 A221 Vert. strip of 3, #a-c 6.75 6.75

Zhusup Balasagun, 10th Cent. Poet, and Kyrgyzstan National University — A222

2015, Aug. 22 Litho. *Perf. 14x14¼*
498 A222 52s multi 2.75 2.75

Cars of the 21st Century — A223

Designs: 33s, Terrafugia TF-X concept flying car. 36s, Mercedes-Benz F015 concept car. 39s, Tesla Model S. 83s, Toyota Mirai.

2015, Oct. 10 Litho. *Perf. 12x12¼*
499-502 A223 Set of 4 8.50 8.50
502a Sheet of 8, 2 each #499-502, + label 17.00 17.00

Nos. 499-502 were each printed in sheets of 5 + label.

Worldwide Fund for Nature (WWF) — A224

Whooper swans: 36s, Three in flight. 39s, Adult and chicks in water. 48s, Adult in water. 117s, Adult extending wings.

2015, Nov. 28 Litho. *Perf. 12*
503-506 A224 Set of 4 10.00 10.00
506a Souvenir sheet of 8, 2 each #503-506 20.00 20.00

Souvenir Sheet

2015 Asian Juniors Chess Championship, Kyrgyzstan — A225

No. 507 — Various chess pieces on board with background colors of: a, 48s, Light green and light blue. b, 55s, Pink and light orange.

2015, Nov. 28 Litho. *Perf. 12*
507 A225 Sheet of 2, #a-b 4.25 4.25

New Year 2016 (Year of the Monkey) — A226

2016, Feb. 6 Litho. *Perf. 12x12¼*
508 A226 76s multi 3.25 3.25

Flowers — A227

Designs: 36s, Tulipa kolpakovskiana. 39s, Tulip Porto. 48s, Orchid Rio Bamba. 55s, Cattleya Queen Sirikhit Diamond Crown orchid.

2016, Feb. 13 Litho. *Perf. 12¼x12*
509-512 A227 Set of 4 7.75 7.75
512a Souvenir sheet of 4, #509-512 7.75 7.75

Regional Communications Commonwealth, 25th Anniv. — A228

2016, Mar. 12 Litho. *Perf. 14¼x14*
513 A228 55s multi 2.25 2.25

Writers — A229

Designs: 48s, Zhakypbek Boogachy (1866-1935). 83s, Nasirdin Baytemirov (1916-96).

2016, Mar. 26 Litho. *Perf. 14¼x14*
514-515 A229 Set of 2 5.75 5.75

Commonwealth of Independent States, 25th Anniv. — A230

2016, Apr. 30 Litho. *Perf. 14¼x14*
516 A230 83s multi 4.00 4.00

Souvenir Sheet

Manned Space Flights, 55th Anniv. A231

No. 517: a, 22s, Rocket launch. b, 117s, Docked spacecraft, spacewalker.

2016, May 14 Litho. *Perf. 12*
517 A231 Sheet of 2, #a-b 6.25 6.25

Souvenir Sheet

Bishkek Trolleybus Management, 65th Anniv. — A232

No. 518 — Trolleybuses: a, 39s, BMZ-5298.01 (56x20mm). b, 55s, MTB-82 (40x29mm). c, 83s, MTB-82D (30x27mm).

Perf. 13 At Bottom (39s), 12 (55s), 13½x13 (83s)
2016, June 25 Litho.
518 A232 Sheet of 3, #a-c 8.00 8.00

Souvenir Sheet

Independence, 25th Anniv. — A233

2016, July 23 Litho. *Perf. 12¼x12*
519 A233 100s multi 4.75 4.75

Taylak (1796-1838), Warrior — A234

2016, July 30 Litho. *Perf. 12¼x12*
520 A234 55s multi 2.60 2.60

2016 Summer Olympics, Rio de Janeiro — A235

Designs: 22s, Taekwondo. 31s, Soccer. 55s, Golf. 117s, Wrestling.

2016, Aug. 4 Litho. *Perf. 12x12¼*
521-524 A235 Set of 4 10.50 10.50

Souvenir Sheet

2016 World Nomad Games, Cholpon-Ata — A236

2016, Sept. 3 Litho. *Perf. 13*
525 A236 117s multi 5.25 5.25

Traditional Cuisine — A237

2016, Sept. 17 Litho. *Perf. 12x12¼*
526 A237 76s multi 3.50 3.50

Arachnids — A238

Designs: 20s, Lycosa singoriensis. 22s, Eresus collari. 31s, Solifugae. 117s, Mesobuthus eupeus.

2016, Oct. 5 Litho. *Perf. 12x12¼*
527-530 A238 Set of 4 8.50 8.50
530a Souvenir sheet of 4, #527-530 8.50 8.50

Paintings by Vladimir V. Obraztsov (1891-1934) A239

No. 531: a, Return from the Red Army, 1930. b, Conspiracy, 1932.
No. 532: a, Near Globe, 1930. b, On the Way to China, 1932.
39s, The Guerrillas, 1932.

2016, Nov. 11 Litho. *Perf. 13x13½*
531 A239 Vert. pair 2.25 2.25
a. 20s multi .85 .85
b. 31s multi 1.40 1.40
532 A239 Vert. pair 6.25 6.25
a. 22s multi 1.00 1.00
b. 117s multi 5.25 5.25
533 A239 39s multi 1.75 1.75
Nos. 531-533 (3) 10.25 10.25

Yurts — A240

Designs: 22s, Guest yurt. 117s, Yurt, family and horse.

2016, Nov. 26 Litho. *Perf. 12x12¼*
534-535 A240 Set of 2 6.00 6.00

Heroism of Panfilov Division's 28 Guardsmen, 75th Anniv. — A241

2016, Dec. 10 Litho. *Perf. 12x12¼*
536 A241 83s multi 4.00 4.00

No. 536 was printed in sheets of 6 + 2 labels.

New Year 2017 (Year of the Rooster) — A242

2017, Jan. 25 Litho. *Perf. 12x12¼*
537 A242 76s multi 3.50 3.50

Worldwide Fund for Nature (WWF) — A243

Pelecanus crispus: 22s, One bird in flight. 31s, Two birds in flight. 39s, One bird on water. 117s, Three birds on water.

2017, Feb. 25 Litho. *Perf. 12x12¼*
538-541 A243 Set of 4 9.75 9.75
541a Souvenir sheet of 8, 2 each #538-541 19.50 19.50

Tulipa Greigii — A244

Ciconia Nigra — A245

2017, Mar. 25 Litho. *Perf. 12x12¼*
542 A244 39s multi 1.90 1.90
543 A245 48s multi 2.25 2.25
a. Souvenir sheet of 4, 2 each #542-543 8.50 8.50

National Horse Games — A246

2017, Apr. 15 Litho. *Perf. 12x12¼*
544 A246 83s multi 4.00 4.00

Protected Natural Areas — A247

No. 545 — UNESCO emblem and: a, Sary-Chelek State Natural Park. b, Besh-Aral State Natural Park. c, Padysha-Ata State Natural Park.

2017, May 6 Litho. *Perf. 12x12¼*
545 Vert. strip of 3 7.25 7.25
a. A247 39s multi 2.00 2.00
b. A247 48s multi 2.40 2.40
c. A247 55s multi 2.75 2.75

Printed in sheets containing two each Nos. 545a-545c.

Famous People — A248

Designs: 39s, Saira Kiyizbaeva (1917-88), opera singer. 55s, Sagymbai Orozbakov (1867-1930), narrator of epic poem, "Manas."

2017, May 20 Litho. *Perf. 12¼x12*
546-547 A248 Set of 2 4.50 4.50

Souvenir Sheet

Abdylas Maldybaev National Opera and Ballet Theater, 75th Anniv. — A249

No. 548: a, 39s, Bulat Minzhikiev (1940-97), opera singer. b, 48s, Painting of dancers on theater ceiling. c, 55s, Dmitri Shostakovich (1906-75), composer.

2017, June 24 Litho. *Perf. 12¼x12*
548 A249 Sheet of 3, #a-c 7.00 7.00

Baitik Kanaev (1820-86), Leader of Solto People — A250

2017, July 8 Litho. *Perf. 12¼x12*
549 A250 76s multi 4.00 4.00

Year of Morality, Education and Culture — A251

2017, Aug. 12 Litho. *Perf. 12x12¼*
550 A251 76s multi 4.00 4.00

Souvenir Sheet

International Snow Leopard and Ecosystem Forum, Bishkek — A252

No. 551: a, 39s, Snow leopard in grass. b, 117s, Snow leopard on rocks.

2017, Aug. 15 Litho. *Perf. 12x12¼*
551 A252 Sheet of 2, #a-b 6.50 6.50

Heroes of the Kyrgyz Republic — A253

Medal and: 35s, Ishak Razzakov (1910-79), politician. 55s, Turdakun Usubaliev (1919-2015), politician.

2017, Oct. 14 Litho. *Perf. 12x12¼*
552-553 A253 Set of 2 4.75 4.75

Souvenir Sheet

Emblem of Collective Security Treaty Organization and Flags of Member Countries — A254

2017, Oct. 21 Litho. *Perf. 12x12¼*
554 A254 193s multi 9.75 9.75

Collective Security Treaty, 125th anniv., Collective Security Treaty Organization, 15th anniv.

Endangered Animals — A255

Designs: 36s, Lynx lynx. 39s, Marmota menzbieri. 48s, Cervus elaphus asiaticus. 55s, Martes foina.

2017, Nov. 4 Litho. *Perf. 12¼x12*
555-558 A255 Set of 4 9.00 9.00
558a Souvenir sheet of 4, #555-558 9.00 9.00

October Revolution, Cent. — A256

2017, Nov. 18 Litho. *Perf. 12x12¼*
559 A256 83s multi 4.50 4.50

Miniature Sheet

Kyrgyz Epic, *Er Toshtuk* A257

No. 560: a, 22s, Toshtuk. b, 39s, Toshtuk on horse. c, 48s, Multi-headed monster and horse's head. d, 55s, Toshtuk, woman and camel.

2017, Dec. 2 Litho. *Perf. 12*
560 A257 Sheet of 4, #a-d 8.25 8.25

Rice Varieties — A258

Designs: 22s, Ak Turpak. 83s, Devzira.

2017, Dec. 29 Litho. *Perf. 12*
561-562 A258 Set of 2 5.50 5.50
562a Souvenir sheet of 2, #561-562 5.50 5.50

Containers and RCC Emblem — A259

2017, Dec. 30 Litho. *Perf. 12*
563 A259 76s multi 3.75 3.75

Miniature Sheet

New Year 2018 (Year of the Dog) A260

No. 564: a, 55s, One dog. b, 76s, Two dogs.

2018, Jan. 22 Litho. *Perf.*
564 A260 Sheet of 4, 2 each #a-b 13.00 13.00

2018 Winter Olympics, Pyeongchang, South Korea — A261

Designs: 22s, Ski jumping. 31s, Figure skating. 48s, Ice hockey. 117s, Snowboarding.

2018, Feb. 22 Litho. *Perf. 12*
565-568 A261 Set of 4 11.00 11.00
568a Souvenir sheet of 4, #565-568 11.00 11.00

Belt Wrestling — A262

2018, Mar. 17 Litho. *Perf. 12*
569 A262 76s multi 4.00 4.00

Souvenir Sheet

Som and Tyiyn Currencies, 25th Anniv. — A263

2018, Apr. 5 Litho. *Perf. 13½x13¼*
570 A263 117s multi 6.25 6.25

2018 World Cup Soccer Championships, Russia — A264

Designs: 20s, Two soccer players. 27s, Two soccer players, diff. 48s, Two soccer players, diff. 102s, Three soccer players.

2018, May 3 Litho. *Perf. 12*
571-574 A264 Set of 4 10.00 10.00
574a Souvenir sheet of 4, #571-574 10.00 10.00

Jusup Mamay (1918-2014), Narrator of Epic "Manas" — A265

2018, June 14 Litho. *Perf. 12*
575 A265 76s multi 3.75 3.75

Beetles — A266

Designs: 22s, Scarabaeidae sensu lato. 31s, Lucanus cervus. 83s, Oryctes nasicornis. 117s, Cetonia aurata.

2018, July 28 Litho. *Perf. 14x14¼*
576-579 A266 Set of 4 13.00 13.00
579a Souvenir sheet of 4, #576-579 13.00 13.00

Souvenir Sheet

2018 International Telecommunications Union Plenipotentiary Conference, Dubai — A267

2018, Aug. 25 Litho. *Perf. 13x13¼*
580 A267 117s multi 6.00 6.00

Surma-Tash State Nature Reserve — A268

2018, Sept. 15 Litho. *Perf. 14x14¼*
581 A268 76s multi 4.25 4.25

Roses — A269

Designs: 20s, Indigoletta climbing hybrid tea roses. 48s, Nicole roses. 55s, Floribunda roses. 83s, Damask roses.

2018, Oct. 13 Litho. *Perf. 14¼x14*
582-585 A269 Set of 4 10.00 10.00
585a Souvenir sheet of 4, #582-585 10.00 10.00

Earth Features — A270

Designs: 20s, Arslanbob Waterfall. 26s, Kokomeren River. 76s, Lake Merzbacher. 98s, Ala-Archa Pass.

2018, Nov. 17 Litho. *Perf. 14x14¼*
586-589 A270 Set of 4 11.00 11.00
589a Souvenir sheet of 4, #586-589 11.00 11.00

Souvenir Sheet

Kumtor Gold Mine A271

2018, Dec. 8 Litho. *Perf. 13*
590 A271 259s multi 11.50 11.50

Souvenir Sheet

Rukh Ordo Cultural Center, Cholpon Ata, 90th Anniv. A272

2018, Dec. 10 Litho. *Perf. 12*
591 A272 130s multi 7.00 7.00

Miniature Sheet

New Year 2019 (Year of the Pig) A273

No. 592: a, 46s, Pig and piglets. b, 98s, Pig.

2019, Jan. 22 Litho. *Perf.*
592 A273 Sheet of 4, 2 each #a-b 11.00 11.00

2019 Asian Cup Soccer Tournament, United Arab Emirates — A274

Various soccer players: 20s, 26s, 176s.

2019, Feb. 18 Litho. *Perf. 14¼x14*
593-595 A274 Set of 3 7.25 7.25
595a Sheet of 3, #593-595, + 3 labels 7.25 7.25

Dragonflies — A275

Designs: 20s, Libellula quadrimaculata. 36s, Sympycna fusca. 130s, Sonjagaster coronatus.

2019, Apr. 4 Litho. *Perf. 14¼x14*
596-598 A275 Set of 3 6.00 6.00
598a Sheet of 3, #596-598 6.00 6.00

Souvenir Sheet

Yuri Gagarin (1934-68), First Man in Space — A276

2019, May 4 Litho. *Perf. 13x13½*
599 A276 130s multi 4.25 4.25

Royal Philatelic Society, 150th Anniv. A277

Designs: 76s, Agroprom Building, Bishkek. 98s, Tower Bridge, London.

2019, May 25 Litho. *Perf. 13x12¾*
600-601 A277 Set of 2 5.75 5.75

Nos. 600-601 were each printed in sheets of 5 + label.

China 2019 World Stamp Exhibition, Wuhan, People's Republic of China — A278

No. 602: a, One tiger. b, Two tigers.

2019, June 11 Litho. *Perf. 14xx14¼*
602 Horiz. pair + central label 5.75 5.75
a. A278 20s multi .75 .75
b. A278 130s multi 5.00 5.00

Shanghai Cooperation Organization Summit, Bishkek — A279

2019, July 6 Litho. *Perf. 13*
603 A279 76s multi 2.60 2.60

No. 603 was printed in sheets of 5 + label.

Eurasian Economic Union, 5th Anniv. — A280

2019, Aug. 9 Litho. *Perf. 13*
604 A280 76s multi 2.60 2.60

No. 604 was printed in sheets of 5 + label.

Famous People — A281

Designs: 26s, Darkul Kuyukova (1919-97), actress. 46s, Tattybübü Tursunbayeva (1944-81), actress. 76s, Alymkul Usenbaev (1894-1963), musician.

2019, Aug. 20 Litho. *Perf. 14¼x14*
605-607 A281 Set of 3 5.25 5.25

Nos. 605-607 were each printed in sheets of 5 + label.

Kurmanjan Datka History and Ethnographic Museum, Gulcha — A282

2019, Sept. 28 Litho. *Perf. 14x14¼*
608 A282 98s multi 3.50 3.50

Poppies — A283

Designs: 46s, Papaver orientale. 76s, Papaver rhoeas. 98s, Papaver refracta.

2019, Oct. 12 Litho. *Perf. 12*
609-611 A283 Set of 3 7.25 7.25
611a Sheet of 3, #609-611 7.25 7.25

Toguz Korgul Game — A284

2019, Oct. 18 Litho. *Perf. 14x14¼*
612 A284 76s multi 2.75 2.75

No. 612 was printed in sheets of 5 + label.

Portrait of Aleksey I. Shevtsov, by Ilya E. Repin (1844-1930) — A285

2019, Oct. 26 Litho. *Perf. 14¼x14*

613 A285 98s multi 3.50 3.50

No. 613 was printed in sheets of 5 + label.

Flora — A286

Designs: 36s, Abies semenovii. 76s, Snow lotus. 98s, Tulipa zenaidae.

2019, Nov. 23 Litho. *Perf. 14¼x14*

614-616 A286 Set of 3 7.25 7.25

Ducks — A287

Various ducks: 26s, 98s, 130s.

2019, Nov. 30 Litho. *Perf. 12*

617-619 A287 Set of 3 8.75 8.75

619a Sheet of 3, #617-619 8.75 8.75

Miniature Sheet

International Civil Aviation Organization, 75th Anniv. — A288

No. 620 — Various airplanes at: a, 20s, Manas Airport. b, 26s, Osh Airport. c, 36s, Issyl-Kul Airport. d, 46s, Karakol Airport. e, 98s, Batken Airport.

2019, Dec. 13 Litho. *Perf. 14x14¼*

620 A288 Sheet of 5, #a-e, + label 7.75 7.75

Mohandas K. Gandhi (1869-1948), Indian Nationalist Leader — A289

2019, Dec. 14 Litho. *Perf. 14¼x14*

621 A289 98s multi 3.75 3.75

No. 621 was printed in sheets of 5 + label.

Minerals — A290

Designs: 36s, Amethyst. 46s, Zircon. 98s, Tourmaline.

2019, Dec. 21 Litho. *Perf. 14¼x14*

622-624 A290 Set of 3 6.50 6.50

Miniature Sheet

New Year 2020 (Year of the Rat) A291

No. 625: a, 46s, Two rats. b, 98s, One rat.

2020, Feb. 20 Litho. *Perf.*

625 A291 Sheet of 4, 2 each #625a-625b 8.25 8.25

Miniature Sheet

Pomegranates — A292

No. 626: a, 20s, Pomegranate flowers. b, 26s, Pomegranates on tree. c, 36s, Pomegranate juice. d, 46s, Two unopened and one split pomegranates. e, 76s, Split pomegranates. f, 98s, Pomegranate shrub.

2020, Mar. 23 Litho. *Perf. 14x14¼*

626 A292 Sheet of 6, #a-f 7.00 7.00

Melis Ubukeev (1935-96), Film Director — A293

2020, Mar. 28 Litho. *Perf. 14x14¼*

627 A293 98s multi 2.25 2.25

International Year of Plant Health — A294

2020, Apr. 4 Litho. *Perf. 14x14¼*

628 A294 98s multi 2.50 2.50

United Nations, 75th Anniv. — A295

2020, Apr. 11 Litho. *Perf. 14x14¼*

629 A295 98s multi 2.25 2.25

Miniature Sheet

Victory in World War II, 75th Anniv. A296

No. 630 — War heroes: a, 20s, Talgat Yakubekovich Begeldinov (1922-2014). b, 26s, Evdokia Borisovna Pasko (1919-2017). c, 36s, Kalyynur Usenbekovich Usenbekov (1921-2003). d, 46s, Nasyr Baitursynov (1918-95). e, 76s, Kirill Ivanovich Bukhantsev (1919-84).

2020, July 4 Litho. *Perf. 14x14¼*

630 A296 Sheet of 5, #a-e, + label 4.75 4.75

Dogs — A297

Designs: 75s, Taigan. 98s, Dobot.

2020, July 11 Litho. *Perf. 14x14¼*

631-632 A297 Set of 2 4.00 4.00

632a Souvenir sheet of 2, #631-632 4.00 4.00

Plercotus Austriacus A298

Designs. 36s, Bat in flight. 76s, Close-up of head. 98s, Bat in cave.

2020, Aug. 14 Litho. *Perf. 14x14¼*

633-635 A298 Set of 3 4.75 4.75

Kuliypa Konduchalova (1920-2013), Politician, and Hero of Kyrgyzstan Medal — A299

2020, Aug. 21 Litho. *Perf. 14x14¼*

636 A299 76s multi 1.75 1.75

Rescue Services — A300

Designs. 31s, Fire fighters. 37s, Police. 143s, Emergency medical service.

2020, Oct. 2 Litho. *Perf. 14x14¼*

637-639 A300 Set of 3 4.75 4.75

639a Souvenir sheet of 3, #637-639, + 3 labels 4.75 4.75

Nos. 637-639 were each printed in sheets of 5 + label.

Man Playing Ordo — A301

2020, Oct. 9 Litho. *Perf. 14x14¼*

640 A301 79s multi 1.90 1.90

Medicinal Plants — A302

Designs. 33s, Rosa. 39s, Crataegus. 143s, Berberis.

2020, Nov. 27 Litho. *Perf. 14¼x14*

641-643 A302 Set of 3 5.00 5.00

Fish — A303

Designs. 56s, Gymnodiptychus dybowskii. 66s, Leuciscus bergi Kaschkarov. 118s, Salmo ischshan.

2020, Dec. 11 Litho. *Perf. 14x14¼*

644-646 A303 Set of 3 5.50 5.50

646a Souvenir sheet of 3, #644-646 5.50 5.50

Spiders — A304

Designs. 56s, Dictynomorpha strandi. 66s, Zygiella kirgisica bakhvalov. 118s, Clubiona rybini.

2020, Dec. 18 Litho. *Perf. 14x14¼*

647-649 A304 Set of 3 5.50 5.50

649a Souvenir sheet of 3, #647-649 5.50 5.50

Miniature Sheet

New Year 2021 (Year of the Ox) A305

No. 650: a, 55s, Brown ox and calf. b, 66s, Black-and-white cow and calf.

2021, Feb. 5 Litho. *Perf.*

650 A305 Sheet of 4, 2 each #650a-650b 5.50 5.50

Meles Leucurus — A306

Various depictions of badger on log. 55s, 66s, 118s.

2021, Apr. 2 Litho. *Perf. 14x14¼*

651-653 A306 Set of 3 5.50 5.50

653a Souvenir sheet of 3, #651-653 5.50 5.50

Souvenir Sheet

Mantis Religiosa A307

2021, Apr. 9 Litho. *Perf. 13x13½*

654 A307 140s multi 3.25 3.25

Miniature Sheet

Quinces A308

No. 655: a, 18s, Bee pollinating quince blosssom. b, 22s, Quinces on tree. c, 31s, Whole and cut quinces. d, 37s, Quinces and jar of quince preserves. e, 55s, Quince tree. f, 66s, Quinces in basket.

2021, Apr. 16 Litho. *Perf. 12x12¼*

655 A308 Sheet of 6, #a-f 5.75 5.75

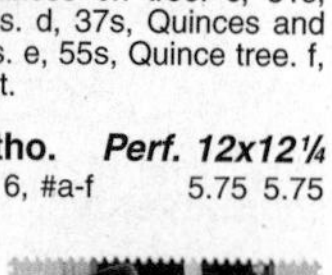

First Manned Space Flight, 60th Anniv. — A309

Designs: 31s, Yuri Gagarin (1934-68), first man in space, and Sergei Korolev (1907-66), rocket engineer. 118s, Vostok rocket launch, Valentina Tereshkova, first woman in space.

2021, May 7 Litho. *Perf. 14*
656-657 A309 Set of 2 3.75 3.75
657a Souvenir sheet of 2, #656-657 3.75 3.75

Regional Communications Commonwealth, 30th Anniv. — A310

2021, June 11 Litho. *Perf. 14x14¼*
658 A310 79s multi 1.90 1.90

No. 658 was printed in sheets of 5 + label.

Commonwealth of Independent States, 30th Anniv. — A311

2021, June 25 Litho. *Perf. 14¼x14*
659 A311 79s multi 1.90 1.90

2020 Summer Olympics, Tokyo — A312

Designs: 37s, Swimming. 66s, Fencing. 140s, Pole vault.

2021, July 16 Litho. *Perf. 14¼x14*
660-662 A312 Set of 3 5.50 5.50
662a Souvenir sheet of 3, #660-662 5.50 5.50

The 2020 Summer Olympics were postponed until 2021 because of the COVID-19 pandemic.

Independence, 30th Anniv. — A313

2021, Aug. 30 Litho. *Perf. 14¼x14*
663 A313 66s multi 1.50 1.50

Souvenir Sheet

Kyrgyz With a Golden Eagle, Sculpture by Evgeny Lanceray (1848-86) — A314

2021, Sept. 10 Litho. *Perf. 13*
664 A314 140s multi 3.25 3.25

Tulipa Sylvestris Var. Turkestanica Regel — A315

Various depictions of tulip with denominations of 31s, 37s, and 140s.

2021, Sept. 17 Litho. *Perf. 14¼x14*
665-667 A315 Set of 3 4.75 4.75
667a Souvenir sheet of 3, #665-667 4.75 4.75

Suyunbay Eraliev (1921-2016), Poet — A316

2021, Oct. 15 Litho. *Perf. 12x12¼*
668 A316 79s multi 1.90 1.90

Merops Apiaster — A317

Various depictions of European bee-eater with denominations of 55s, 66s, and 118s.

2021, Oct. 22 Litho. *Perf. 14¼x14*
669-671 A317 Set of 3 5.50 5.50
671a Souvenir sheet of 3, #669-671 5.50 5.50

Souvenir Sheet

Horse With Traditional Harness and Saddle — A318

2021, Oct. 29 Litho. *Perf. 13*
672 A318 140s multi 3.25 3.25

Eremias Nikolskii — A319

Various depictions of Kyrgyz racerunner with denominations of 37s, 55s, and 140s.

2021, Dec. 3 Litho. *Perf. 12*
673-675 A319 Set of 3 5.25 5.25
675a Souvenir sheet of 3, #673-675 5.25 5.25

Trollius Lilacinus — A320

Various depictions of Trollius lilacinus with denominations of 31s, 66s, and 118s.

2021, Dec. 10 Litho. *Perf. 12*
676-678 A320 Set of 3 5.00 5.00
678a Souvenir sheet of 3, #676-678 5.00 5.00

Souvenir Sheet

Satymkul Dzhumanazarov (1951-2007), Bronze Medalist in Marathon at 1980 Summer Olympics — A321

2021, Dec. 17 Litho. *Perf. 13x13½*
679 A321 140s multi 3.25 3.25

Diplomatic Relations Between Kyrgyzstan and Poland, 30th Anniv. — A322

Diplomatic Relations Between Kyrgyzstan and Denmark, 30th Anniv. — A323

Diplomatic Relations Between Kyrgyzstan and Sweden, 30th Anniv. — A324

Diplomatic Relations Between Kyrgyzstan and Norway, 30th Anniv. — A325

Diplomatic Relations Between Kyrgyzstan and Vatican City, 30th Anniv. — A326

2022, Apr. 22 Litho. *Perf. 12*
680 A322 66s multi 1.50 1.50
681 A323 66s multi 1.50 1.50
682 A324 66s multi 1.50 1.50
683 A325 66s multi 1.50 1.50
684 A326 66s multi 1.50 1.50
Nos. 680-684 (5) 7.50 7.50

Kyrgyzstan's Admittance Into United Nations, 30th Anniv. — A327

2022, Apr. 29 Litho. *Perf. 12*
685 A327 76s multi 1.75 1.75

New Year 2022 (Year of the Tiger) — A328

2022, May 17 Litho. *Perf. 12*
686 A328 79s multi 1.90 1.90

2022 Winter Olympics, Beijing — A329

Designs: 58s, Ski jumping. 69s, Figure skating. 118s, Luge.

2022, May 17 Litho. *Perf. 12*
687-689 A329 Set of 3 5.75 5.75

Pistachio Nuts — A330

Designs: 58s, Pistachio tree and nuts. 69s, Nuts on tree branch, harvested nut. 118s, Shelled and unshelled nuts.

2022, May 31 Litho. *Perf. 12*
690-692 A330 Set of 3 5.75 5.75

Diplomatic Relations Between Kyrgyzstan and Germany, 30th Anniv. — A331

2022, June 10 Litho. *Perf. 12*
693 A331 66s multi 1.50 1.50

Abdulmanap Magomedovich Nurmagomedov (1962-2020), Judoka and Combat Sports Coach — A332

2022, Aug. 10 Litho. *Perf. 12*
694 A332 65s multi 1.50 1.50

Miniature Sheet

2022 MonacoPhil Philatelic Exhibition — A333

No. 695 — Silhouette of: a, 65s, Napoleon Bonaparte (1769-1821), Emperor of France. b, 75s, Elephants. c, 105s, Soldiers on horseback. d, 159s, Red Fort, Delhi, India.

2022, Aug. 19 Litho. *Perf. 12*
695 A333 Sheet of 4, #a-d 10.00 10.00

Eurasian Economic Commission, 10th Anniv. — A334

2022, Aug. 26 Litho. *Perf. 12*
696 A334 65s multi 1.60 1.60

Dair A. Asanov (1922-2009), Major General in Army of the Soviet Union — A335

2022, Oct. 21 Litho. *Perf. 12*
697 A335 65s multi 1.50 1.50

Goldfish — A336

Inscriptions: 65s, Carassius auratus. 75s, Comet Carassius auratus. 106s, Carassius gibelio forma auratus.

2022, Oct. 28 Litho. *Perf. 12*
698-700 A336 Set of 3 5.75 5.75

Traditional Kyrgyz Costumes — A337

Designs: 65s, Woman. 75s, Woman and child. 159s, Man and woman.

2022, Nov. 4 Litho. *Perf. 12*
701-703 A337 Set of 3 7.00 7.00

Bayali Isakeev (1897-1938), Chairman of the Council of People's Commissars of the Kyrgyz Soviet Socialist Republic — A338

2022, Nov. 16 Litho. *Perf. 12*

704 A338 65s multi 1.50 1.50

SEMI-POSTAL STAMPS

Natl. Epic Poem, Manas, Millennium — SP1

SP2

Designs: 10t+5t, Woman with bird in hand. 20t+10t, Bird on man's wrist. No. B3, Women watching as baby held up. No. B4, Woman with spear, leading horse. 40t+15t, Warrior looking at dead dragon. No. B6, Warrior on horse holding axe. No. B7, Man wearing tall hat on horseback. No. B8, Warrior with sword on horseback.

No. B9, Man in red cradling fallen warrior. No. B10, Man in black seated in desert, tornado.

Perf. 12, Imperf

1995, June 16 Litho.

B1	SP1	10t +5t grnsh bl & ol brn	.40	.40
B2	SP1	20t +10t grnsh bl & ol brn	.40	.40
B3	SP1	30t +10t grnsh bl & ol brn	.40	.40
B4	SP1	30t +10t grnsh bl & ol brn	.40	.40
B5	SP1	40t +15t grnsh bl & ol brn	.40	.40
B6	SP1	50t +15t grnsh bl & ol brn	.40	.40
B7	SP1	50t +15t grnsh bl & ol brn	.40	.40
B8	SP1	50t +15t grnsh bl & ol brn	.40	.40
a.		Sheet of 8, #B1-B8 + label	4.00	4.00

Souvenir Sheets

B9	SP2	2s +50t multi	2.00	2.00
B10	SP2	2s +50t multi	2.00	2.00

1996 Summer Olympic Games, Atlanta — SP3

Designs: 100t+20t, Equestrian events. 140t+30t, Boxing. 150t+30t, Archery. 300t+50t, Judo, hot air balloon, sailing, water skiing.

1996, July 10 Litho. *Perf. 12½x12*

B11	SP3	100t +20t multi	.30	.30
B12	SP3	140t +30t multi	.60	.60
B13	SP3	150t +30t multi	.80	.80
B14	SP3	300t +50t multi	1.25	1.25
		Nos. B11-B14 (4)	2.95	2.95

Town of Osh, 3000th Anniv. SP4

No. B15: a, Globe, mountains, mosque, "Osh" and "3000." b, Mosque with three arches, mountains (green panel at UR). c, Solomon's Throne (mosque on mountain). d, Mausoleum of Asaf ibn Burkiya (denomination at LL).

Illustration reduced.

2000, Feb. 19 Litho. *Perf. 13½*

B15 SP4 6s +25t Sheet of 4, #a-d *3.50 3.50*

Exists imperf. Value $5.

Kurmanzhan Datka, 190th Anniv. of Birth — SP5

2001, Oct. 13 Litho. *Perf. 14x14¼*

B16 SP5 10s +70t ind & gray 1.60 1.60

KYRGYZ EXPRESS POST

On May 21, 2013, Kyrgyz Express Post was declared a designated postal operator by the Universal Postal Union, marking the first time the UPU has had two designated postal operators in one country. Kyrgyz Express Post company was created in March 2012 and granted a license from the Kyrgyzstan Ministry of Transport and Communications on Dec. 7, 2012 to offer all types of postal services to customers and to compete with the state corporation Kyrgyz Pochtasy, which has post offices across the country. At the time Kyrgyz Express Post issued its first stamps, it had two post offices and a philatelic bureau in Bishkek.

A1

Methods of Postal Conveyance — A2

Designs: 500s, Jet airplane.

No. 2: a, 25s, Post rider. b, 50s, Locomotive. c, 250s, Mail van.

700s, Dove carrying letter, Universal Postal Union emblem.

2014, Nov. 18 Litho. *Perf. 14x14½*

1	A1	500s multi	15.00	15.00
2	A1	Sheet of 4, #1, 2a-2c	24.00	24.00

Souvenir Sheet of 1 + 8 Labels

Perf. 13 Syncopated

3 A2 700s multi 20.00 20.00

No. 1 was printed in panes of 4.

Wild Animals — A3

Designs: 250s, Panthera uncia.

No. 5: a, 15s, Falco cherrug. b, 25s, Bos grunniens. c, 125s, Capra sibirica alaiana.

2014, Nov. 19 Litho. *Perf. 14x14¾*

4	A3	250s multi	7.50	7.50
5	A3	Sheet of 4, #4 & 5a-5c	15.00	15.00

No. 4 was printed in sheets of 4.

Falconry A4

Designs: No. 6, 75s, Falcon in flight, denomination at LR. No. 7, 75s, Falcon in flight, denomination at LL. No. 8, 75s, Falcon approaching rabbit.

Perf. 13 Syncopated

2015, May 14 Litho.

6-8	A4	Set of 3	8.00	8.00
8a		Souvenir sheet of 3, #6-8	8.00	8.00

Souvenir Sheet

First Walks in Space, 50th Anniv. A5

Spacewalker: a, 50s, Alexei Leonov. b, 150s, Edward White.

2015, July 2 Litho. *Perf.*

9 A5 Sheet of 2, #a-b 6.75 6.75

Souvenir Sheet

Penny Black, 175th Anniv. A6

2015, July 2 Litho. *Perf. 13¼x13*

10 A6 250s multi 8.25 8.25

Famous Men A7

Designs: 50s, Dante Alighieri (1265-1321), writer. 100s, Pyotr Ilyich Tchaikovsky (1840-93), composer.

Perf. 13 Syncopated

2015, Sept. 2 Litho.

11-12 A7 Set of 2 5.00 5.00

International Years — A8

Designs: 50s, Intl. Year of Soils. 75s, Intl. Year of Light.

Perf. 13 Syncopated

2015, Sept. 2 Litho.

13-14	A8	Set of 2	4.25	4.25
14a		Vert. pair, #13-14	4.25	4.25

Nos. 13-14 were each printed in sheets of 8. No. 14a was printed in sheets containing 4 pairs.

Souvenir Sheet

Horses A9

No. 15: a, Chestnut horse. b, Chestnut horse with white blaze.

2015, Dec. 21 Litho. *Perf. 14¾x14*

15 A9 100s Sheet of 2, #a-b 5.50 5.50

Minerals — A10

Designs: No. 16, 50s, Aragonite. No. 17, 50s, Realgar. 75s, Stibnite. 100s, Kyanite.

2016, Jan. 6 Litho. *Perf. 14x14¾*

16-19	A10	Set of 4	8.00	8.00
19a		Souvenir sheet of 4, #16-19	8.00	8.00

A11

Yeti — A12

Litho. With Foil Application

Serpentine Die Cut 12¾

2016, May 19 Self-Adhesive

Coil Stamps

20	A11	(150s) multi	4.50	4.50
21	A12	(250s) multi	7.50	7.50
a.		Booklet pane of 4, 2 each #20-21	24.00	—
		Complete booklet, #21a	24.00	

Souvenir Sheets

Philataipei 2016 World Stamp Exhibition, Taipei — A13

2016 World Stamp Show, New York A14

2016, June 3 Litho. *Perf. 14x14½*

22	A13	150s multi	4.50	4.50
23	A14	250s multi	7.50	7.50

Taigan Hunting Dogs A15

Designs: 50s, Black dog. 100s, Mottled dog. 150s, Dog chasing wolf.

Perf. 13 Syncopated

2016, July 28 Litho.

24-26	A15	Set of 3	9.00	9.00
26a		Souvenir sheet of 3, #24-26	9.00	9.00

Flowers — A16

Designs: No. 27, 50s, Iris orchioides. No. 28, 50s, Leontopodium ochroleucum. No. 29, 100s, Primula turkestanica. No. 30, 100s, Tulipa greigii.
200s, Papaver rhoeas.

2016, July 29 Litho. *Perf. 14x14½*
27-30 A16 Set of 4 9.00 9.00
30a Souvenir sheet of 4, #27-30 9.00 9.00

Souvenir Sheet

31 A16 200s multi 6.00 6.00

2016 Summer Olympics, Rio de Janeiro — A17

Designs: 50s, Cycling. 150s, Tennis.

2016, Aug. 5 Litho. *Perf. 14x14½*
32-33 A17 Set of 2 6.00 6.00

Nos. 32-33 each were printed in sheets of 4+2 labels.

2016 World Nomad Games, Cholpon-Ata A18

No. 34: a, Mounted archery. b, Equestrian wrestling. c, Burning horseman.

2016, Aug. 8 Litho. *Perf. 14x14½*
34 Horiz. strip of 3 9.00 9.00
a. A18 50s multi 1.50 1.50
b. A18 100s multi 3.00 3.00
c. A18 150s multi 4.50 4.50

Souvenir Sheet

Independence of Kyrgyzstan, 25th Anniv. — A19

Perf. 13 Syncopated

2016, Aug. 30 Litho.
35 A19 150s multi 4.50 4.50

42nd Chess Olympiad, Baku, Azerbaijan A20

2016, Sept. 1 Litho. *Perf. 14x14½*
36 A20 100s multi 3.00 3.00

No. 36 was printed in sheets of 4 + 2 labels.

Composers and Musicians A21

Designs: No. 37, 50s, Sergei Prokofiev (1891-1953), composer. No. 38, 50s, Yehudi Menuhin (1916-99), violinist. No. 39, 100s, Antonin Dvorák (1841-1904), composer. No. 40, 100s, Wolfgang Amadeus Mozart (1756-1791), composer.

2016, Sept. 8 Litho. *Perf. 14x14½*
37-40 A21 Set of 4 9.00 9.00
40a Souvenir sheet of 4, #37-40 9.00 9.00

Nos. 37-40 each were printed in sheets of 4 + 2 labels.

Schooner Issyk-Kul A22

Ship Progress of Kyrgyzstan A23

President of Kyrgyzstan's Cruiser Moscow — A24

Torpedo Boat — A25

2016, Nov. 25 Litho. *Perf. 14x14½*
41 A22 50s multi 1.50 1.50
42 A23 50s multi 1.50 1.50
43 A24 100s multi 3.00 3.00
44 A25 100s multi 3.00 3.00
a. Souvenir sheet of 4, #41-44 9.00 9.00
Nos. 41-44 (4) 9.00 9.00

New Year 2017 — A26

Designs: 50s, Christmas tree and sleigh. 100s, Rooster.

Perf. 13 Syncopated

2017, Feb. 3 Litho.
45-46 A26 Set of 2 4.50 4.50

Nos. 45-46 each were printed in sheets of 5 + label.

Mushrooms — A27

Designs: No. 47, 50s, Pleurotus ostreatus. No. 48, 50s, Leccinum scabrum. No. 49, 100s, Morchella conica. No. 50, 100s, Pleurotus eryngii.

2017, Apr. 6 Litho. *Perf. 14½x14*
47-50 A27 Set of 4 9.00 9.00
50a Souvenir sheet of 4, #47-50 9.00 9.00

Fourth Islamic Solidarity Games, Baku, Azerbaijan A28

Designs: No. 51, 50s, Wrestling. No. 52, 50s, Weight lifting. 75s, Table tennis. 100s, Soccer.

2017, May 26 Litho. *Perf. 14x14½*
51-54 A28 Set of 4 8.00 8.00
54a Souvenir sheet of 4, #51-54, + 2 labels 8.00 8.00

Souvenir Sheet

Historic and Cultural Ties With China A29

No. 55: a, 50s, Li Bai (701-62), poet. b, 100s, Illustration for poem "The Ching-Ting Mountain."

Perf. 13 Syncopated

2017, June 29 Litho.
55 A29 Sheet of 2, #a-b 4.50 4.50

Horses — A30

No. 56: a, 50s, Trakehner horse. b, 100s, New Kirgiz horse.

2017, June 30 Litho. *Perf. 14x14½*
56 A30 Pair, #a-b 4.50 4.50

See Belarus No. 1052.

Flowers — A31

Designs: 50s, Peony. 100s, Chrysanthemum.

Perf. 13 Syncopated

2017, July 7 Litho.
57-58 A31 Set of 2 4.50 4.50

19th International Botanical Congress, Shenzen, People's Republic of China.

Traditional Hunting — A32

Designs: 50s, Archer on horseback. 75s, Hunter on horseback releasing falcon. 100s, Taigan hunting dog chasing fox.

Perf. 13 Syncopated

2017, July 14 Litho.
59-61 A32 Set of 3 6.50 6.50
61a Souvenir sheet of 3, #59-61 6.50 6.50

Space Exploration, 60th Anniv. — A33

Designs: 50s, Sputnik. 1. 75s, Apollo Lunar Rover. 100s, Tiangong-2 Space Laboratory.

2017, Nov. 15 Litho. *Perf. 14x14½*
62-64 A33 Set of 3 6.50 6.50
64a Souvenir sheet of 3, #62-64 6.50 6.50

Souvenir Sheet

National Bank of the Kyrgyz Republic, 25th Anniv. A34

No. 65: a, 50s, 2013 10-som coin depicting Gazella subgutturosa (34x34mm). b, 100s, 2016 500-som banknote and 1-som, 3-som and 10-som coins (34x68mm). c, 100s, 2015 10-som coin depicting Otis tarda (34x34mm).

Perf. 13 Syncopated

2017, Nov. 17 Litho. & Embossed
65 A34 Sheet of 3, #a-c, + label 7.25 7.25

Souvenir Sheet

International Year of Sustainable Tourism for Development — A35

No. 65: a, 50s, Manas Peak. b, 100s, Kel-Suu Lake.

2017, Nov. 20 Litho. *Perf. 14x14½*
66 A35 Sheet of 2, #a-b 5.75 5.75

Armed Forces of Kyrgyzstan, 25th Anniv. — A36

Designs: No. 67, 50s, Truck-mounted missile launchers. No. 68, 50s, Soldier and armored troop carrier. 75s, Soldiers searching for land mines. 100s, Helicopter and tank.

2017, Nov. 22 Litho. *Perf. 14x14½*
67-70 A36 Set of 4 8.00 8.00
70a Sheet of 4, #67-70, + 2 labels 8.00 8.00

Souvenir Sheet

Great Silk Road A37

Perf. 13 Syncopated

2017, Nov. 24 Litho. & Embossed
71 A37 150s multi 4.50 4.50

Famous People — A38

Designs: No. 72, 50s, Jonathan Swift (1667-1745), writer. No. 73, 50s, Sir Arthur C. Clarke (1917-2008), science fiction writer. 75s, Marie Sklodowska-Curie (1867-1934), chemist and physicist. No. 75, 100s, Gioachino Rossini (1792-1868), composer. No. 76, 100s, J. R. R. Tolkien (1892-1973), writer.

2017, Dec. 31 Litho. *Perf. 14x14½*
72-76 A38 Set of 5 11.00 11.00
76a Sheet of 5, #72-76, + label 11.00 11.00

Nos. 72-76 were each printed in sheets of 4 + 2 labels.

New Year 2018 (Year of the Dog) — A39

Litho. With Foil Application

2018, Jan. 30 *Perf. 13 Syncopated*
77 A39 100s gold & multi 3.00 3.00

No. 77 was printed in sheets of 5 + label.

Souvenir Sheet

2018 Winter Olympics, PyeongChang, South Korea — A40

No. 78: a, 50s, Alpine skiing. b, 50s, Biathlon.

2018, Feb. 23 Litho. *Perf. 14x14½*
78 A40 Sheet of 2, #a-b 6.00 6.00

Karl Marx (1818-83), Political Theorist — A41

2018, May 5 Litho. *Perf. 14x14½*
79 A41 100s multi 3.00 3.00

No. 79 was printed in sheets of 5 + label.

Birds — A42

Designs: 50s, Ibidorhyncha struthersii. 75s, Sitta tephronota. 100s, Anthropoides virgo. 150s, Bubo bubo.

2018, May 22 Litho. *Perf. 14x14½*
80-83 A42 Set of 4 11.00 11.00
83a Souvenir sheet of 4, #80-83 11.00 11.00

Bridges — A43

Designs: 50s, Highway bridge, Kara-Kul. 150s, Railroad bridge, Kuduk.

2018, June 22 Litho. *Perf. 14x14½*
84-85 A43 Set of 2 6.00 6.00
85a Souvenir sheet of 2, #84-85 6.00 6.00

18th Asian Games, Jakarta, Indonesia — A44

Designs: 100s, Swimming, canoeing, yacht racing. 150s, Taekwondo, volleyball, golf, cycling.

2018, July 6 Litho. *Perf. 14x14½*
86-87 A44 Set of 2 7.50 7.50
87a Souvenir sheet of 2, #86-87 7.50 7.50

43rd Chess Olympiad, Batumi, Georgia — A45

2018, Aug. 20 Litho. *Perf. 14x14½*
88 A45 100s multi 3.00 3.00

Butterflies A46

Designs: 50s, Parnassius loxias tashkorensis. 100s, Colias regia. 150s, Colias christophi.

2018, Sept. 7 Litho. *Perf. 14x14½*
89-91 A46 Set of 3 8.75 8.75
91a Souvenir sheet of 3, #89-91 8.75 8.75

Nos. 89-91 were each printed in sheets of 5 + label.

Souvenir Sheet

Diplomatic Relations Between Kyrgyzstan and Latvia, 25th Anniv. — A47

No. 92: a, 50s, Monument to Manas the Great, Bishkek. b, 150s, Lacplesis on Freedom Monument, Riga, Latvia.

2018, Oct. 5 Litho. *Perf. 14½x14*
92 A47 Sheet of 2, #a-b, + central label 5.75 5.75

See Latvia No. 1003.

Diplomatic Relations Between Kyrgyzstan and Belarus, 25th Anniv. — A48

2018, Oct. 18 Litho. *Perf. 14x14½*
93 A48 75s multi 2.25 2.25

No. 93 was printed in sheets of 6 + 3 central labels. See Belarus No. 1116.

Ivan Turgenev (1818-83), Writer — A49

2018, Nov. 9 Litho. *Perf. 14x14½*
94 A49 50s multi 1.50 1.50

No. 94 was printed in sheets of 5 + label.

Issyk-Kul Lighthouses A50

Ships and: 100s, Lighthouse at left. 150s, Two lighthouses at right.

2018, Nov. 16 Litho. *Perf. 14x14½*
95-96 A50 Set of 2 7.25 7.25
96a Souvenir sheet of 2, #95-96, + 2 labels 7.25 7.25

Diplomatic Relations Between Kyrgyzstan and Malta, 25th Anniv. — A51

UNESCO World Heritage Sites: 100s, Burana Tower, Kyrgyzstan. 150s, City of Valletta, Malta.

2018, Nov. 23 Litho. *Perf. 14x14½*
97-98 A51 Set of 2 7.25 7.25
98a Souvenir sheet of 2, #97-98, + 2 labels 7.25 7.25

See Malta No. 1644.

Endangered Species — A52

Designs: 50s, Vormela peregusna. 75s, Otocolobus manul. 100s, Lynx lynx isabellinus. 150s, Ursus arctos isabellinus.

2018, Dec. 7 Litho. *Perf. 14x14½*
99-102 A52 Set of 4 11.00 11.00
102a Souvenir sheet of 4, #99-102 11.00 11.00

Nos. 99-102 were each printed in sheets of 5 + label.

Chinghiz Aitmatov (1928-2008), Writer — A53

2018, Dec. 10 Litho. *Perf. 14x14½*
103 A53 75s multi 2.25 2.25

No. 103 was printed in sheets of 5 + label.

Aleksandr Solzhenitsyn (1918-2008), Writer — A54

2018, Dec. 11 Litho. *Perf. 14x14½*
104 A54 100s multi 3.00 3.00

No. 104 was printed in sheets of 5 + label.

New Year 2019 (Year of the Pig) — A55

Litho. With Foil Application
2019, Jan. 31 *Perf. 13 Syncopated*
105 A55 100s gold & multi 3.00 3.00

No. 105 was printed in sheet of 5 + label.

Poisonous Mushrooms — A56

Designs: 50s, Clitocybe dealbata. 75s, Agaricus xanthodermus. 100s, Hypholoma fasciculare. 150s, Lepiota brunneoincarnata.

2019, Mar. 14 Litho. *Perf. 14¾x14*
106-109 A56 Set of 4 11.00 11.00
109a Souvenir sheet of 4, #106-109 11.00 11.00

Nos. 106-109 were each printed in sheets of 5 + label.

Cats — A57

Designs: 50s, Scottish Fold cat. 100s, Siberian cat. 150s, Maine Coon cat.

2019, Mar. 22 Litho. *Perf. 14x14¾*
110-112 A57 Set of 3 8.75 8.75
112a Souvenir sheet of 3, #110-112 8.75 8.75

Dmitri I. Mendeleev (1834-1907), Creator of Periodic Table of Elements — A58

2019, Apr. 12 Litho. *Perf. 14x14¾*
113 A58 100s multi 3.00 3.00

International Year of the Periodic Table.

Tetrax Tetrax — A59

Perf. 13 Syncopated
2019, May 9 Litho.
114 A59 150s multi 4.25 4.25

Souvenir Sheet

Karakol, 150th Anniv. A60

2019, July 9 Litho. *Perf. 14x14¾*
115 A60 250s multi 7.25 7.25

First Man on the Moon, 50th Anniv. A61

2019, July 20 Litho. *Perf. 14x14¾*
116 A61 150s multi 4.50 4.50

Endangered Reptiles and Amphibians — A62

Designs: 50s, Varanus griseus. 75s, Agrionemys horsfieldii. 100s, Rana asiatica Bedriaga. 150s, Vipera renardi.

2019, Sept. 6 Litho. *Perf. 14x14¾*
117-120 A62 Set of 4 11.00 11.00
120a Souvenir sheet of 4, #117-120 11.00 11.00

Nos. 117-120 were each printed in sheets of 5 + label.

Motorcycles A63

Designs: 50s, Chopper based on 1982 Ural M-67-36. 75s, 2001 Yamaha XV1600. 100s, Custom motorcycle based on 1983 Ural M-67-36. 150s, Café Racer based on 1990 IZH Planeta-5.

2019, Oct. 16 Litho. *Perf. 14x14¾*
121-124 A63 Set of 4 11.00 11.00
124a Souvenir sheet of 4, #121-124 11.00 11.00

Nos. 121-124 were printed in sheets of 4.

Beekeeping — A64

Designs: 50s, Honeybees at hive entrance. 100s, Honeybees on honeycomb. 150s, Beekeeper tending hive.

Perf. 13 Syncopated
2019, Oct. 28 Litho.
125-127 A64 Set of 3 8.75 8.75
127a Souvenir sheet of 3, #125-127 8.75 8.75

Nos. 125-127 were printed in sheets of 4.

Turdakun Usubaliev (1919-2015), Politician A65

2019, Nov. 5 Litho. *Perf. 14x14¾*
128 A65 100s multi 3.00 3.00

No. 128 was printed in sheets of 5 + label.

Nikolai Rimsky-Korsakov (1844-1908), Composer — A66

Rembrandt van Rijn (1606-69), Painter — A67

Leonardo da Vinci (1452-1519), Sculptor and Painter — A68

2019, Nov. 18 Litho. *Perf. 14x14¾*

129 A66	75s multi	2.25	2.25
130 A67	100s multi	3.00	3.00

Souvenir Sheet

Perf. 14¾x14

131 A68	250s multi + label	7.25	7.25

Nos. 129-130 were printed in sheets of 4.

New Year 2020 (Year of the Rat) — A69

Perf. 13 Syncopated

2019, Dec. 2 Litho.

132 A69	100s multi	3.00	3.00

No. 132 was printed in sheet of 5 + label.

Highest Mountain Peaks in Kyrgyzstan — A70

Designs: 50s, Jengish Chokusu. 100s, Lenin Peak. 150s, Khan Tengri.

2020, Feb. 21 Litho. *Perf. 14x14½*

133-135 A70	Set of 3	8.75	8.75
135a	Souvenir sheet of 3, #133-135	8.75	8.75

Nos. 133-135 were each printed in sheets of 4 + 2 labels.

Jewelry and Women A71

No. 136: a, 100s, Kyrghiz woman and jewelry. b, 150s, Ukrainian woman and jewelry.

2020, Dec. 9 Litho. *Perf. 14x14½*

136 A71	Horiz. pair, #a-b	6.00	6.00

No. 136 was printed in sheets of 4 pairs with 2 central labels. See Ukraine No. 1280.

A72

Famous Men A73

Designs: 75s, Ivan Bunin (1870-1953), 1933 Nobel laureate in literature. 100s, Federico Fellini (1920-93), film director. 150s, Ludwig van Beethoven (1770-1827), composer. 250s, Raphael (1483-1520), painter.

2020, Dec. 14 Litho. *Perf. 14x14½*

137-139 A72	Set of 3	8.00	8.00

Souvenir Sheet

Perf. 13½x13 Syncopated

140 A73	250s multi + label	6.00	6.00

Nos. 137-139 were each printed in sheets of 4 + 2 labels.

Bicyclist — A74

2020, Dec. 15 Litho. *Perf. 14x14½*

141 A74	150s multi + 3 labels	3.75	3.75

Act Now Climate Action Campaign. No. 141 was printed in sheets of 3 + 9 labels.

Online Chess Olympiad — A75

2020, Dec. 16 Litho. *Perf. 14½x14*

142 A75	100s multi	2.50	2.50
a.	Tete-beche pair	5.00	5.00

Leptopoecile Sophiae — A76

2020, Dec. 17 Litho. *Perf. 14x14½*

143 A76	150s multi	3.75	3.75

No. 143 was printed in sheets of 5 + label.

Souvenir Sheet

Opening of Central Mosque of Imam Al-Sarakhsi, Bishkek — A77

Perf. 13x13¼ Syncopated

2020, Dec. 21 Litho.

144 A77	250s multi	6.00	6.00

See Turkey No. 3737.

Dogs — A78

Designs: 50s, Dalmatian. 100s, Alaskan malamute. 150s, Akita-inu.

Perf. 13 Syncopated

2020, Dec. 22 Litho.

145-147 A78	Set of 3	7.25	7.25
147a	Souvenir sheet of 3, #145-147	7.25	7.25

Nos. 145-147 were each printed in sheets of 5 + label.

New Year 2021 (Year of the Ox) — A79

Litho. With Foil Application

2020, Dec. 31 *Perf. 13 Syncopated*

148 A79	100s gold & redsh vio	2.50	2.50

No. 148 was printed in sheets of 5 + label.

Endangered Fish — A80

Designs: 50s, Scizothorax issykkuli. 75s, Capoetobrama kuschakewitschi. 100s, Glyptosternon reticulatum. 150s, Aspiolucius esocinus.

2021, Mar. 18 Litho. *Perf. 14x14½*

149-152 A80	Set of 4	9.00	9.00
152a	Souvenir sheet of 4, #149-152	9.00	9.00

Nos. 149-152 were each printed in sheets of 5 + label.

Gypaetus Barbatus A81

2021, Mar. 31 Litho. *Perf. 14x14½*

153 A81	175s multi	4.25	4.25

No. 153 was printed in sheets of 5 + label.

Yuri Nikulin (1921-97), Circus Clown — A82

2021, Apr. 17 Litho. *Perf. 14x14½*

154 A82	150s multi	3.50	3.50

No. 154 was printed in sheets of 5 + label.

Saimaluu Tash Petroglyphs A83

Designs: 50s, Animals. 150s, Person with rays around head. 175s, Person and animals.

2021, May 18 Litho. *Perf. 14x14½*

155-157 A83	Set of 3	9.00	9.00
157a	Souvenir sheet of 3, #155-157 + 3 labels	9.00	9.00

Nos. 155-157 were each printed in sheets of 5 + label.

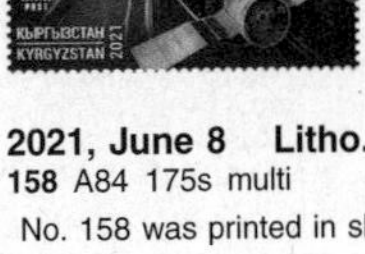

Salyut Space Station, 50th Anniv. — A84

2021, June 8 Litho. *Perf. 14x14½*

158 A84	175s multi	4.25	4.25

No. 158 was printed in sheets of 5 + label.

International Year of Fruits and Vegetables A85

2021, June 29 Litho. *Perf. 14x14½*

159 A85	150s multi	3.50	3.50

No. 159 was printed in sheets of 5 + label.

Woodpeckers — A86

Designs: 150s, Dendrocoptes medius. 175s, Dendrocopos leucopterus.

2021, Dec. 31 Litho. *Perf. 14½x14*

160-161 A86	Set of 2	7.75	7.75
161a	Souvenir sheet of 2, #160-161	7.75	7.75

Nos. 160-161 were each printed in sheets of 5 + label. See Croatia No. 1244.

COVID-19 Pandemic A87

Designs: 150s, Girl with protective mask blowing at dandelions. 175s, Boy with protective mask eating lollipop.

2021, Dec. 31 Litho. *Perf. 14x14½*

162-163 A87	Set of 2	7.75	7.75
163a	Souvenir sheet of 2, #162-163, + 2 labels	7.75	7.75

Nos. 162-163 were each printed in sheets of 5 + label.

Pamir Highway — A88

Designs: 150s, Vehicles on mountainside highway. 175s, Automobile on highway near valley.

2021, Dec. 31 Litho. *Perf. 14x14½*

164-165 A88	Set of 2	7.75	7.75
165a	Souvenir sheet of 2, #164-165, + 2 labels	7.75	7.75

Nos. 164-165 were each printed in sheets of 4 + 2 labels.

Famous Men — A89

Designs: 75s, Walter Scott (1771-1832), writer. 100s, Johannes Kepler (1571-1630), astronomer and mathematician. 150s, Fyodor Dostoevsky (1821-81), writer. 175s, Albrecht Dürer (1471-1528), painter.

2021, Dec. 31 Litho. *Perf. 14x14½*

166-169 A89	Set of 4	12.00	12.00

Nos. 166-169 were each printed in sheets of 5 + label.

New Year 2022 (Year of the Tiger) — A90

Perf. 13 Syncopated

2021, Dec. 31 Litho.

170 A90	150s multi	3.50	3.50

No. 170 was printed in sheets of 5 + label.

KYRGYZ EXPRESS POST SEMI-POSTALS

Campaign Against COVID-19 Pandemic SP1

2020, Dec. 30 Litho. ***Perf. 14x14½***

B1	SP1	150s+50s multi	5.00	5.00

No. B1 was printed in sheets of 5 + label. Surtax for Help the Children Charitable Foundation.

LABUAN

lə-'bü-ən

LOCATION — An island in the East Indies, about six miles off the northwest coast of Borneo
GOVT. — A British possession, administered as a part of the North Borneo Colony
AREA — 35 sq. mi.
POP. — 8,963 (estimated)
CAPITAL — Victoria

The stamps of Labuan were replaced by those of Straits Settlements in 1906.

100 Cents = 1 Dollar

Queen Victoria — A1

On Nos. 1, 2, 3, 4 and 11 the watermark is 32mm high. It is always placed sideways and extends over two stamps.

1879, May Engr. Wmk. 46 ***Perf. 14***

1	A1	2c green	1,625.	975.00
2	A1	6c orange	240.00	225.00
3	A1	12c carmine	1,925.	850.00
4	A1	16c blue	77.50	*200.00*
		Nos. 1-4 (4)	3,868.	2,250.

See Nos. 5-10, 16-24, 33-39, 42-48. For surcharges see Nos. 12-15, 25, 31, 40-41.

1880-82 Wmk. 1

5	A1	2c green	34.00	*57.50*
6	A1	6c orange	145.00	*160.00*
7	A1	8c carmine ('82)	135.00	*135.00*
8	A1	10c yel brown	210.00	*100.00*
9	A1	12c carmine	330.00	*400.00*
10	A1	16c blue ('81)	100.00	130.00
		Nos. 5-10 (6)	954.00	*982.50*

A2

A3

A3a

A4

1880-83 Wmk. 46

11	A2	6c on 16c blue (with additional "6" across original value) R)	4,200.	1,325.

Wmk. 1

12	A2	8c on 12c car	1,825.	1,000.
a.		Original value not obliterated	3,600.	2,000.
b.		Additional surcharge "8" across original value	2,300.	1,450.
c.		"8" inverted	2,100.	1,200.
d.		As "a," "8" inverted	*4,200.*	—
13	A3	8c on 12c car ('81)	475.	525.
14	A3a	8c on 12c car ('81)	160.	170.
a.		"Eighr"	*22,500.*	
b.		Inverted surcharge	*16,000.*	
c.		Double surcharge	2,900.	2,400.
15	A4	$1 on 16c blue (R) ('83)	*4,800.*	

On No. 12 the original value is obliterated by a pen mark in either black or red.

Types of 1879 Issue

1883-86 Wmk. 2

16	A1	2c green	30.00	*55.00*
a.		Horiz. pair, imperf. btwn.	18,500.	
17	A1	2c rose red ('85)	4.25	*20.00*
18	A1	8c carmine	325.00	120.00
19	A1	8c dk violet ('85)	50.00	9.25
20	A1	10c yellow brn	62.50	*57.50*
21	A1	10c black brn ('86)	40.00	*72.50*
22	A1	16c blue	115.00	*215.00*
23	A1	16c gray blue ('86)	125.00	*180.00*
24	A1	40c ocher	37.50	*145.00*
		Nos. 16-24 (9)	789.25	*874.25*

Nos. 1-10, 16-24 are in sheets of 10.
For surcharges see Nos. 26-30, 32.

A5

A6

A7

1885 Wmk. 1

25	A5	2c on 16c blue	1,150.	*1,100.*

Wmk. 2

26	A5	2c on 8c car	275.00	*550.00*
a.		Double surcharge		—
27	A6	2c on 16c blue	135.00	*200.00*
a.		Double surcharge		*7,500.*
28	A7	2c on 8c car	80.00	*145.00*

A8

1891 Black or Red Surcharge

29	A8	6c on 8c violet	16.50	17.00
a.		6c on 8c dark violet	625.00	210.00
b.		Double surcharge	390.00	—
c.		As "a," "Cents" omitted	550.00	550.00
d.		Inverted surcharge	90.00	*85.00*
e.		Dbl. surch., one inverted	1,100.	—
f.		Dbl. surch., both inverted	1,100.	—
g.		"6" omitted	625.00	
h.		Pair, one without surcharge	2,000.	2,000.
30	A8	6c on 8c dk vio (R)	1,550.	825.00
a.		Inverted surcharge	1,850.	925.00

Wmk. 46

31	A8	6c on 16c blue	2,800.	2,300.
a.		Inverted surcharge	15,500.	8,250.

Wmk. 2

32	A8	6c on 40c ocher	14,000.	5,750.
a.		Inverted surcharge	12,000.	9,000.

Types of 1879 Issue

1892 Engr. Unwmk.

33	A1	2c rose	7.25	4.25
34	A1	6c yellow green	14.50	5.75
35	A1	8c violet	13.50	*19.50*
36	A1	10c brown	30.00	9.50
37	A1	12c deep ultra	16.00	8.00
38	A1	16c gray	30.00	*45.00*
39	A1	40c ocher	27.50	*45.00*
		Nos. 33-39 (7)	138.75	137.00

The 2c, 8c and 10c are in sheets of 30; others in sheets of 10.

Nos. 39 and 38 Surcharged

1893

40	A1	2c on 40c ocher	200.00	110.00
a.		Inverted surcharge	500.00	*675.00*
41	A1	6c on 16c gray	450.00	180.00
a.		Inverted surcharge	675.00	350.00
b.		Surcharge sideways	675.00	375.00
c.		"Six" omitted	—	—
d.		"Cents" omitted	—	—
e.		Handstamped "Six Cents"	*2,275.*	

Surcharges on Nos. 40-41 each exist in 10 types. Counterfeits exist.

No. 41e was handstamped on examples of No. 41 on which the surcharge failed to print or was printed partially or completely albino.

From Jan. 1, 1890, to Jan. 1, 1906, Labuan was administered by the British North Borneo Co. Late in that period, unused remainders of Nos. 42-83, 53a, 63a, 64a, 65a, 66a, 68a, 85-86, 96-118, 103a, 107a, J1-J9, J3a and J6a were canceled to order by bars forming an oval. Values for these stamps used are for those with this form of cancellation, unless described as postally used, which are for stamps with dated town cancellations. Nos. 63b, 64b, 65b, 104a, J6a, and possibly others, only exist c.t.o.

For detailed listings of Labuan, see the *Scott Classic Specialized Catalogue.*

Types of 1879 Issue

1894, Apr. Litho.

42	A1	2c bright rose	2.00	.65
43	A1	6c yellow green	27.50	.65
a.		Horiz. pair, imperf. btwn.	*11,250.*	
44	A1	8c bright violet	29.00	.65
45	A1	10c brown	60.00	.65
46	A1	12c light ultra	37.50	.80
47	A1	16c gray	40.00	.65
48	A1	40c orange	60.00	.65
		Nos. 42-48 (7)	256.00	4.70

Counterfeits exist.

Dyak Chieftain A9

Malayan Sambar A10

Sago Palm A11

Argus Pheasant A12

Arms of North Borneo A13

Dhow A14

Saltwater Crocodile A15

Mt. Kinabalu A16

Arms of North Borneo — A17

Perf. 12 to 16 and Compound

1894 Engr.

49	A9	1c lilac & black	2.00	.65
a.		Vert. pair, imperf. between	1,300.	575.00
50	A10	2c blue & black	3.00	.65
a.		Imperf., pair	725.00	
51	A11	3c bister & black	4.50	.65
52	A12	5c green & black	38.50	1.10
a.		Horiz. pair, imperf. between	*1,800.*	
53	A13	6c brn red & blk	3.00	.65
a.		Imperf., pair	725.00	350.00
54	A14	8c rose & black	13.00	.65
a.		8c red & black	32.50	2.40
55	A15	12c orange & black	27.50	.65
56	A16	18c ol brn & blk	29.00	.65
b.		Vert. pair, imperf. between		*2,500.*
57	A17	24c lilac & blue	22.50	1.30
		Nos. 49-57 (9)	143.00	6.95

Perf. 13½-14

49b	A9	1c lilac & black	16.50	
50b	A10	2c blue & black	7.00	
51a	A11	3c bister & black	17.50	—
52b	A12	5c green & black	50.00	—
53b	A13	6c brn red & blk		3.00
54b	A14	8c rose & black	45.00	1.00
54c	A14	8c red & black	45.00	
55a	A15	12c orange & black	77.50	2.75
56c	A16	18c ol brn & blk	85.00	
56d	A16	18c ol bister & blk	32.50	
57b	A17	24c lilac & blue	20.00	1.25
57c	A17	24c mauve & blue	40.00	

Perf. 13½-14, compound 14½-15

49c	A9	1c lilac & black	40.00	
50c	A10	2c blue & black	42.50	
51b	A11	3c bister & black	—	
53c	A13	6c brn red & blk		—

Perf. 13½-14, compound 12-13

49d	A9	1c lilac & black	40.00	1.10
50d	A10	2c blue & black	—	
51c	A11	3c bister & black	55.00	
52c	A12	5c green & black	65.00	
53d	A13	6c brn red & blk	—	
55b	A15	12c orange & black	—	
56e	A16	18c ol bister & blk	—	

Perf. 12-13

49e	A9	1c lilac & black	—	
50e	A10	2c blue & black	190.00	
51d	A11	3c bister & black	—	
52d	A12	5c green & black	210.00	
53e	A13	6c brn red & blk	260.00	
55c	A15	12c orange & black	—	

For overprints see Nos. 66-71.

A18

1895, June Litho. ***Perf. 14***

58	A18	4c on $1 red	4.25	.50
59	A18	10c on $1 red	11.50	.50
60	A18	20c on $1 red	52.50	.50
61	A18	30c on $1 red	57.50	1.50
62	A18	40c on $1 red	57.50	1.50
		Nos. 58-62 (5)	183.25	4.50

A19

A20

A21

1896

63	A19	25c blue green	45.00	.80
a.		Imperf, pair		72.50
b.		Without overprint	35.00	2.00
c.		As "b," imperf, pair	60.00	
64	A20	50c claret	42.50	.80
a.		Imperf, pair		72.50
b.		Without overprint	32.50	2.00
c.		As "b," imperf, pair	52.50	
65	A21	$1 dark blue	82.50	1.25
a.		Imperf, pair		72.50
b.		Without overprint	50.00	3.00
c.		As "b," imperf, pair	60.00	
		Nos. 63-65 (3)	170.00	2.85

For surcharges and overprint see Nos. 93-95, 116-118, 120.

Nos. 49-54 Overprinted

1896 ***Perf. 12 to 15 and Compound***

66	A9	1c lilac & black	26.00	1.75
a.		"JEBILEE"	1,450.	360.00
b.		"JUBILE"	*3,000.*	
c.		Orange overprint	325.00	24.00
67	A10	2c blue & black	52.50	1.75
a.		Vert. pair, imperf. btwn.	1,525.	—
b.		"JEBILEE"	1,850.	—
c.		"JUBILE"	*3,500.*	—
d.		Vert. strip of 3, imperf between	*8,000.*	
68	A11	3c bister & black	50.00	1.50
a.		"JEBILEE"	2,250.	850.00
b.		"JUBILE"	—	—
69	A12	5c green & black	72.50	1.50
a.		Double overprint	975.00	
70	A13	6c brown red & blk	47.50	1.00
a.		Double overprint	975.00	—
b.		"JUBILE"	*3,600.*	—
71	A14	8c rose & black	57.50	1.00
a.		Double overprint	—	*3,000.*
		Nos. 66-71 (6)	306.00	8.50

Cession of Labuan to Great Britain, 50th anniv.

Perf. 13½-14

66d A9 1c lilac & black 35.00
e. Double overprint 450.00 —
f. Orange overprint 350.00
67e A10 2c blue & black 52.50
68c A11 3c bister & black 57.50 1.50
d. Triple overprint 1,150.
69b A12 5c green & black 72.50 1.50
70c A13 6c brown red & blk —
71b A14 8c rose & black 52.50 1.00

Perf. 13½-14, compound 14½-15

67f A10 2c blue & black — 50.00
68e A11 3c bister & black —
70d A13 6c brown red & blk —
71c A14 8c rose & black 60.00 22.50

Perf. 13½-14, compound 12-13

66g A9 1c lilac & black 47.50
h. Orange overprint —
67g A10 2c blue & black 57.50
68f A11 3c bister & black 450.00 200.00
g. Double overprint 425.00 195.00
h. Triple overprint 775.00 —
69c A12 5c green & black —

Perf. 12-13

69i A9 1c lilac & black —

Cession of Labuan to Great Britain, 50th anniv.

Dyak Chieftain A22

Malayan Sambar A23

Sago Palm A24

Argus Pheasant A25

A26

Dhow — A27

Saltwater Crocodile A28

Mt. Kinabalu "Postal Revenue" A29

Coat of Arms — A30

Perf. 13½ to 16 and Compound

1897-1900 **Engr.**

72 A22 1c lilac & black 8.00 .60
72A A22 1c red brn & blk 3.75 .80
73 A23 2c blue & black 32.50 .90
a. Vert. pair, imperf between 1,125.
b. Horiz. pair, imperf between 1,550.
75 A24 3c bister & blk 10.00 .60
a. Vert. pair, imperf between 1,325. 675.00
76 A25 5c green & blk 67.50 .85
78 A26 6c brn red & blk 16.00 .60
a. Vert. pair, imperf between 850.00
79 A27 8c red & black 25.00
80 A28 12c red & black 40.00 2.50
82 A30 24c gry lil & bl 14.50 .60
Nos. 72-82 (9) 217.25 7.45

Perf. 13½-14

72Ab A22 1c red brn & blk 25.00 .80
73c A23 2c blue & black 26.00 .80
74 A23 2c grn & blk ('00) 4.50 .35
a. Horiz. pair, imperf between 3,100. 1,550.
75b A24 3c bister & blk 10.00 .60
76b A25 5c green & blk 67.50 .90
77 A25 5c lt bl & blk ('00) 27.50 .80
78b A26 6c brn red & blk 8.00 .60
79a A27 8c red & black 60.00 1.00
79b A27 8c vermilion & black 14.50 .80
80a A28 12c red & black 140.00 3.00
81 A29 18c ol bis & blk 125.00 2.40
82a A30 24c gry lil & bl 57.50 2.40

Perf. 13½-14, compound 14½-15

72c A22 1c lilac & black —

Perf. 13½-14, compound 12-13

73d A23 2c blue & black 62.50
74b A23 2c grn & blk ('00) —
75c A24 3c bister & blk 25.00 2.00
76c A25 5c green & blk —
77a A25 5c lt bl & blk ('00) —
78c A26 6c brn red & blk 8.25
79c A27 8c red & black 52.50 3.25

Perf. 16

72Ad A22 1c red brn & blk 25.00
73e A23 2c blue & black 8.50
79d A27 8c red & black 7.50
81a A29 18c ol bis & blk 15.00 .60
a. Vert. pair, imperf between 3,750.

No. 72A used exists only perf. 13½x14.
For surcharges see Nos. 87-89, 110-112.

"Postage & Revenue" A31

"Postage & Revenue" A32

Perf. 13½ to 16 and Compound

1897

83 A31 18c bister & black 95.00 2.40
84 A32 24c brn lil & bl 50.00
a. ocher & blue — 4.75

Perf. 13½-14

83a A31 18c bister & black —
84b A32 24c brn lilac & blue 52.50 2.40

Perf. 13½-14, compound 12-13

83c A31 18c bister & black 145.00
84c A32 24c brn lilac & blue
83b A31 18c bister & black 10.00
84d A32 24c brn lilac & blue 57.50

For surcharges see Nos. 92, 115.

"Postage & Revenue" A33

"Postage & Revenue" A34

1898 ***Perf. 14½-15***

85 A33 12c red & black — 4.00
86 A34 18c bister & black 72.50

Perf. 13½-14

85a A33 12c red & black 50.00
86a A34 18c bister & black 42.50 3.75

Perf. 13½-14, compound 14½-15

85b A33 12c red & black —

Perf. 13½-14, compound 12-13

86b A34 18c bister & black 52.50

Perf. 12-13

86c A34 18c bister & black —

Perf. 16

85c A33 12c red & black 77.50
86d A34 18c bister & black 57.50

No. 85a cto is always perf. 13½x14.
For surcharges see Nos. 90-91, 113-114.

Regular Issue Surcharged in Black

1899 ***Perf. 14½-15***

87 A25 4c on 5c grn & blk 62.50 30.00
88 A26 4c on 6c brn red & blk 34.00 22.50
89 A27 4c on 8c red & blk 72.50 52.50
90 A33 4c on 12c red & blk 67.50 42.50
91 A34 4c on 18c bis & blk 40.00 21.50
a. Double surcharge 575.00 675.00
92 A32 4c on 24c lil & bl 40.00 36.00

Perf. 14

93 A19 4c on 25c blue grn 7.25 8.00
94 A20 4c on 50c claret 8.75 8.00
95 A21 4c on $1 dk blue 8.75 8.00
Nos. 87-95 (9) 341.25 229.00

Perf. 13½-14

88a A26 4c on 6c brn red & blk 45.00 45.00
89a A27 4c on 8c red & blk 52.50 37.50
90a A33 4c on 12c red & blk 62.50 50.00
92a A32 4c on 24c lil & bl 50.00 36.00

Perf. 13½-14, compound 12-13

88b A26 4c on 6c brn red & blk 60.00 72.50
89b A27 4c on 8c red & blk 35.00 45.00
90b A33 4c on 12c red & blk 72.50 77.50
92b A32 4c on 24c lil & bl 50.00 35.00

Perf. 12-13

89c A27 4c on 8c red & blk —

Perf. 16

90c A33 4c on 12c red & blk 62.50 47.50
92c A32 4c on 24c lil & bl 55.00 57.50

Orangutan A35

Sun Bear A36

Railroad Train — A37

Perf. 12 to 16 and Compound

1899-1901

96 A35 4c yel brn & blk 10.00 .75
a. Vert. pair, imperf. btwn. 1,450.
b. Perf 13½-14, compound 12-13 57.50
97 A35 4c car & blk ('00) 22.50 .90
97a A35 4c car & blk ('00) 6.00 .60
b. Perf 13½-14, compound 12-13 52.50 1.50
c. Perf 16 —
98 A36 10c gray vio & dk brn, perf. 14½-15 ('02) 60.00 .75
99 A37 16c org brn & grn (G) ('01) 60.00 3.00
a. Perf 14½-15 190.00
b. Perf 13½-14, compound 12-13 100.00
c. Perf 12-13 440.00
Nos. 96-99 (4) 152.50 5.40

Crown — A38

Perf. 12½ to 16 and Compound

1902-03 **Engr.**

99A A38 1c vio & black 6.75 .60
100 A38 2c grn & blk 5.00 .35
100A A38 3c sepia & blk 4.00 .35
101 A38 4c car & blk 4.00 .35
102 A38 8c org & blk 15.00 .80
103 A38 10c sl blue & brn 4.00 .35
a. Vert. pair, imperf. between 925.00
104 A38 12c yel & black 16.00 .35
a. Vert. strip of 3, imperf. horiz. 4,000.
105 A38 16c org brn & grn 5.75 .35
a. Vert. pair, imperf. between — 2,300.
106 A38 18c bis brn & blk 4.00 .35
107 A38 25c grnsh bl & grn 12.00 .60
a. 25c greenish blue & black 625.00
108 A38 50c gray lil & vio 12.00 2.75
109 A38 $1 org & red brn 10.00 2.75
Nos. 99A-109 (12) 98.50 9.95

Perf. 14½-15

99Ab A38 1c vio & black 105.00
100b A38 2c green & blk 125.00
101a A38 4c car & black 10.00
102a A38 8c org & black 9.50
103b A38 10c sl blue & brn 9.25 .60
107b A38 25c grnsh bl & grn 18.00 .75
109a A38 $1 org & red brn 12.00 2.40

Perf. 13½-14, compound 12-13

99Ac A38 1c vio & black 92.50
101b A38 4c car & black 82.50
108a A38 50c gray lil & vio 19.50

Perf. 16

104b A38 12c yel & black 14.50

Line Through "B" of "LABUAN"

Perf. 13½-14

99Ad A38 1c vio & black 95.00 11.50
100c A38 2c green & blk 85.00 11.50
100Ac A38 3c sepia & blk 82.50 11.25
101c A38 4c car & black 87.50 11.50
102b A38 8c org & black 140.00 12.50
103c A38 10c sl blue & brn 87.50 11.50
104c A38 12c yel & black 160.00 11.50
105b A38 16c org brn & grn 100.00 11.50
106a A38 18c bis brn & blk 95.00 11.25
107c A38 25c grnsh bl & grn 140.00 12.50
108b A38 50c gray lil & vio 210.00 27.50
109b A38 $1 org & red brn 195.00 27.50
Nos. 99Ad-109b (#) * *

There are 3 known examples of No. 104a, all cto. A 16c vertical pair, imperf between has been reported. The editors would like to receive evidence of the existence of this item.

Regular Issue of 1896-97 Surcharged in Black

1904 ***Perf. 14½x15***

110 A25 4c on 5c grn & blk 57.50 17.00
111 A26 4c on 6c brn red & blk 14.50 17.00
112 A27 4c on 8c red & blk 30.00 17.00
113 A33 4c on 12c red & blk 50.00 17.00
a. Perf 16 52.50 —
114 A34 4c on 18c bis & blkm perf. 13½-14 30.00 17.00
a. Perf 13½-14, comp. 12-13 42.50
b. Perf 12-13 —
115 A32 4c on 24c brn lil & bl 19.25 17.00
a. Perf 13½-14 42.50
b. Perf 13½-14, comp. 12-13 52.50
c. Perf 16 35.00 17.00
116 A19 4c on 25c blue grn 10.00 17.00
117 A20 4c on 50c clar 10.00 17.00
a. Double surcharge 400.00
118 A21 4c on $1 dark blue 14.00 17.00
Nos. 110-118 (9) 235.25 153.00

Stamps of North Borneo, 1893, and Labuan No. 65a Overprinted in Black

a

b

c

1905

119 A30(a) 25c slate bl 1,325. 1,100.
120 A21(c) $1 blue 1,050.
121 A33(b) $2 gray grn 4,000.
122 A34(c) $5 red vio 7,250. 1,850.
a. $5 dull purple 7,000. 1,800.
123 A35(c) $10 brown 55,000. 14,500.

Nos. 119, 120 and 123 do not exist postally used. No. 120 exists only cto.

POSTAGE DUE STAMPS

Regular Issues Overprinted

1901 **Unwmk.** ***Perf. 14***

J1 A23 2c grn & blk 27.50 1.10
a. Double overprint 425.00
J2 A24 3c bis & blk 37.50 1.00
J3b A35 4c car & black 60.00 .60
a. Double overprint 875.00
J4 A25 5c lt blue & blk 57.50 1.50
J5 A26 6c brn red & blk 50.00 1.10
J6 A27 8c red & black 110.00 3.00
a. Center inverted, ovpt. reading down 12,000.
J7 A33 12c red & black 170.00 6.75
a. Overprint reading down 1,125.

J8	A34	18c ol bis & blk	40.00	1.75
J9	A32	24c brn lil & bl	77.50	7.75
		Nos. J1-J9 (9)	630.00	24.55

See note after No. 41.

The stamps of Labuan were superseded by those of Straits Settlements in 1906.

LAGOS

'lā-,gäs

LOCATION — West Africa, bordering on the former Southern Nigeria Colony
GOVT. — British Crown Colony and Protectorate
AREA — 3,460 sq. mi. (approx.)
POP. — 1,500,000 (1901)
CAPITAL — Lagos

This territory was purchased by the British in 1861 and placed under the Governor of Sierra Leone. In 1874 it was detached and formed part of the Gold Coast Colony until 1886 when the Protectorate of Lagos was established. In 1899 Lagos and the territories of the Royal Niger Company were surrendered to the Crown of Great Britain and formed into the Northern and Southern Nigeria Protectorates. In 1906 Lagos and Southern Nigeria were united to form the Colony and Protectorate of Southern Nigeria.

12 Pence = 1 Shilling

Queen Victoria — A1

1874-75 Typo. Wmk. 1 *Perf. 12½*

1	A1	1p lilac	80.00	50.00
2	A1	2p blue	80.00	45.00
3	A1	3p red brown ('75)	130.00	45.00
4	A1	4p rose	150.00	50.00
5	A1	6p blue green	150.00	20.00
6	A1	1sh orange ('75)	425.00	70.00
a.		Value 15½mm instead of 16½mm long	700.00	160.00
		Nos. 1-6 (6)	1,015.	280.00

1876 *Perf. 14*

7	A1	1p lilac	50.00	21.00
8	A1	2p blue	80.00	15.00
9	A1	3p red brown	120.00	30.00
10	A1	4p rose	225.00	12.50
11	A1	6p green	130.00	7.00
12	A1	1sh orange	950.00	95.00
		Nos. 7-12 (6)	1,555.	180.50

The 4p exists with watermark sideways.

1882-1902 Wmk. 2

13	A1	½p green ('86)	2.25	.95
14	A1	1p lilac	42.50	27.50
15	A1	1p car rose	2.25	.95
16	A1	2p blue	200.00	8.50
17	A1	2p gray	100.00	9.50
18	A1	2p lil & bl ('87)	8.50	3.25
19	A1	2½p ultra ('91)	8.00	2.00
a.		2½p blue	90.00	57.50
20	A1	3p orange brn	30.00	8.75
21	A1	3p lil & brn org ('91)	3.00	*3.75*
22	A1	4p rose	225.00	14.00
23	A1	4p violet	160.00	12.50
24	A1	4p lil & blk ('87)	2.50	2.00
25	A1	5p lil & grn ('94)	3.00	*12.50*
26	A1	6p olive green	9.00	*55.00*
27	A1	6p lil & red vio ('87)	5.50	3.50
28	A1	6p lilac & car rose ('02)	5.75	*13.50*
29	A1	7½p lilac & car rose ('94)	4.50	*40.00*
30	A1	10p lil & yel ('94)	4.50	*15.00*
31	A1	1sh org ('85)	21.00	*25.00*
32	A1	1sh yel grn & blk ('87)	6.50	*32.50*
33	A1	2sh6p ol brn ('86)	375.00	325.00
34	A1	2sh6p green & car rose ('87)	27.50	*92.50*
35	A1	5sh blue ('86)	750.00	550.00
36	A1	5sh grn & ultra ('87)	50.00	*175.00*
37	A1	10sh brn vio ('86)	2,750.	2,000.
38	A1	10sh grn & brn ('87)	120.00	*275.00*

Excellent forgeries exist of Nos. 33, 35 and 37 on paper with genuine watermark.

No. 24 Surcharged in Black

1893

39	A1	½p on 4p lilac & blk	11.50	4.00
a.		Double surcharge	70.00	62.50
b.		Triple surcharge	175.00	
c.		½p on 2p lilac & blue (#18)	—	27,500.

Four settings of surcharge.

Only one used example is known of No. 39c. The two unused examples are in museums.

King Edward VII — A3

1904, Jan. 22

40	A3	½p grn & bl grn	3.00	*6.25*
41	A3	1p vio & blk, *red*	1.25	.25
42	A3	2p violet & ultra	6.75	7.00
43	A3	2½p vio & ultra, *bl*	1.50	*1.75*
44	A3	3p vio & org brn	3.25	2.00
45	A3	6p vio & red vio	40.00	11.50
46	A3	1sh green & blk	40.00	*47.50*
47	A3	2sh6p grn & car rose	160.00	*325.00*
48	A3	5sh grn & ultra	150.00	*350.00*
49	A3	10sh green & brn	350.00	*975.00*
		Nos. 40-49 (10)	755.75	*1,726.*

1904-05 Wmk. 3

Ordinary or Chalky Paper

50	A3	½p grn & bl grn	14.50	3.00
51a	A3	1p vio & blk, *red*	1.75	.25
52	A3	2p violet & ultra	5.50	3.50
53a	A3	2½p vio & ultra, *bl*	2.00	*18.50*
54	A3	3p vio & org brn	4.00	1.50
55a	A3	6p vio & red vio	5.00	1.75
56	A3	1sh green & blk	22.50	*30.00*
57	A3	2sh6p grn & car rose	27.50	*75.00*
58	A3	5sh grn & ultra	27.50	*110.00*
59	A3	10sh green & brn	100.00	*275.00*
		Nos. 50-59 (10)	210.25	*518.50*

See *Scott Classic Specialized Catalogue of Stamps & Covers* for detailed listings of ordinary and chalky paper varieties.

The stamps of Lagos were superseded by those of Southern Nigeria.

LAOS

'laus

LOCATION — In northwestern Indo-China
GOVT. — Republic
AREA — 91,400 sq. mi.
POP. — 5,407,453 (1999 est.)
CAPITAL — Vientiane

Before 1949, Laos was part of the French colony of Indo-China and used its stamps until 1951. The kingdom was replaced by the Lao Peoples Democratic Republic Dec. 2, 1975.

100 Cents = 1 Piaster
100 Cents = 1 Kip (1955)

Imperforates

Most Laos stamps issued during 1951-75 exist as imperforate proofs in issued and trial colors, and also as proofs in small presentation sheets in issued colors. Many post-1975 issues exist imperforate.

Paper

Most Laos stamps issued before 1976 exist on both white and yellowish papers in approximately equal quantities. Souvenir sheets from this period were printed primarily on yellowish paper. Souvenir sheets printed on white paper are scarce.

Catalogue values for all unused stamps in this country are for Never Hinged items.

Boat on Mekong River A1

King Sisavang-Vong A2

Laotian Woman — A3

Designs: 50c, 60c, 70c, Luang Prabang. 1pi, 2pi, 3pi, 5pi, 10pi, Temple at Vientiane.

1951-52 Unwmk. Engr. *Perf. 13*

1	A1	10c dk grn & emer	.60	.25
2	A1	20c dk car & car	.60	.25
3	A1	30c ind & dp ultra	2.00	1.25
4	A3	30c ind & pur ('52)	1.00	.30
5	A1	50c dark brown	.50	.50
6	A1	60c red & red org	.50	.50
7	A1	70c ultra & bl grn	1.25	.50
8	A3	80c brt grn & dk bl green ('52)	1.25	.60
9	A1	1pi dk pur & pur	1.25	.50
10	A3	1.10pi dark plum & carmine ('52)	1.25	1.25
11	A2	1.50pi blk brn & vio brown	1.60	1.25
12	A3	1.90pi indigo & dp blue ('52)	1.50	1.25
13	A1	2pi dk grn & gray green	20.00	9.00
14	A1	3pi dk car & red	2.50	1.50
15	A3	3pi choc & black brown ('52)	1.75	1.50
16	A1	5pi ind & dp ultra	3.25	1.75
17	A1	10pi blk brn & vio brown	4.25	2.00
		Nos. 1-17 (17)	45.05	24.15
		Set, hinged	25.00	

A booklet containing 26 souvenir sheets was issued in 1952 on the anniversary of the first issue of Laos stamps. Each sheet contains a single stamp in the center (Nos. 1-17, C2-C4, J1-J6). Value $300.

See No. 223.

UPU Monument and King Sisavang-Vong — A4

1952, Dec. 7

18	A4	80c ind, blue & pur	.90	.80
19	A4	1pi dk car, car & org brown	.90	.80
20	A4	1.20pi dk pur, pur & ultra	1.00	.90
21	A4	1.50pi dk grn, bl grn & dk brn	1.25	1.00
22	A4	1.90pi blk brn, vio brn & dk Prus grn	1.50	1.25
		Nos. 18-22,C5-C6 (7)	16.55	14.75

Laos' admission to the UPU, May 13, 1952.

Court of Love — A5

1953, July 14

23	A5	4.50pi indigo & bl grn	.85	.55
24	A5	6pi gray & dark brn	1.25	.55

Composite of Laotian Temples A6

1954, Mar. 4

25	A6	2pi indigo & redsh vio	27.50	20.00
26	A6	3pi blk brn & scar	27.50	20.00
		Nos. 25-26,C13 (3)	175.00	135.00

Accession of King Sisavang-Vong, 50th anniv.

See No. C13.

Buddha Statue and Monks — A7

1956, May 24 Engr. *Perf. 13*

27	A7	2k reddish brown	2.50	1.75
28	A7	3k black	3.00	2.00
29	A7	5k chocolate	4.50	3.00
		Nos. 27-29,C20-C21 (5)	64.00	51.75

2500th anniversary of birth of Buddha.

See Nos. C20-C21.

UN Emblem — A8

1956, Dec. 14 *Perf. 13½x13*

30	A8	1k black	.65	.45
31	A8	2k blue	.90	.70
32	A8	4k bright red	1.25	.95
33	A8	6k purple	1.40	1.10
		Nos. 30-33,C22-C23 (6)	13.95	12.95

Admission of Laos to the UN, 1st anniv.

Khouy Player — A9

Khene Player — A10

Musical Instrument: 8k, Ranat.

1957, Mar. 25 Unwmk. *Perf. 13*

34	A9	2k multicolored	1.75	1.10
35	A10	4k multicolored	2.00	1.25
36	A9	8k org, bl & red brn	2.50	2.00
		Nos. 34-36,C24-C26 (6)	14.75	10.45

See Nos. 224, C24-C26.

Harvesting Rice — A11

Drying Rice — A12

1957, July 22 Engr. *Perf. 13*

37	A11	3k shown	.90	.60
38	A12	5k shown	1.25	.75
39	A12	16k Winnowing rice	2.00	1.50
40	A11	26k Polishing rice	4.00	2.00
		Nos. 37-40 (4)	8.15	4.85

Elephants A13

Various Elephants: 30c, 5k, 10k, 13k, vert.

1958, Mar. 17

41	A13	10c multi	1.00	.50
42	A13	20c multi	1.00	.50
43	A13	30c multi	1.00	.50
44	A13	2k multi	1.50	.90
45	A13	5k multi	2.75	1.50
46	A13	10k multi	3.00	2.00
47	A13	13k multi	5.00	2.50
		Nos. 41-47 (7)	15.25	8.40

For surcharge see No. B5.

Globe and Goddess A14

UNESCO Building and Mother with Children — A15

Designs: 70c, UNESCO building, globe and mother with children. 1k, UNESCO building and Eiffel tower.

1958, Nov. 3 Engr. *Perf. 13*

48	A14	50c multicolored	.50	.25
49	A15	60c emer, vio & maroon	.65	.25
50	A15	70c ultra, rose red & brn	.65	.25
51	A14	1k ol bis, cl & grnsh bl	1.00	.60
		Nos. 48-51 (4)	2.80	1.35

UNESCO Headquarters in Paris opening, Nov. 3.

King Sisavang-Vong A16

1959, Sept. 16 Unwmk.

52	A16	4k rose claret	.35	.35
53	A16	6.50k orange red	.35	.35
54	A16	9k bright pink	.35	.35
55	A16	13k green	.75	.60
		Nos. 52-55 (4)	1.80	1.65

For surcharges see Nos. 112-113, B4.

Dancers A17

Student and Torch of Learning A18

Education and Fine Arts: 3k, Globe, key of knowledge and girl student. 5k, Dancers and temple.

1959, Oct. 1 Engr. *Perf. 13*

56	A17	1k vio blk, ol & bl	.50	.30
57	A18	2k maroon & black	.55	.30
58	A17	3k slate grn & vio	.85	.30
59	A18	5k rose vio, yel & brt grn	1.10	.60
		Nos. 56-59 (4)	3.00	1.50

Portal of Wat Phou, Pakse — A19

Historic Monuments: 1.50k, That Inghang, Savannakhet, horiz. 2.50k, Phou Temple, Pakse, horiz. 7k, That Luang, Vientiane. 11k, That Luang, Vientiane, horiz. 12.50k, Phousi, Luang Prabang.

1959, Nov. 2 Unwmk. *Perf. 13*

60	A19	50c sepia, grn & org	.30	.25
61	A19	1.50k multi	.35	.25
62	A19	2.50k pur, vio bl & ol	.50	.40
63	A19	7k vio, olive & claret	.75	.50
64	A19	11k brn, car & grn	.90	.75
65	A19	12.50k bl, vio & bister	1.25	.80
		Nos. 60-65 (6)	4.05	2.95

Due to poor quality control, numerous color varieties exist.

Funeral Urn and Monks A20

King Sisavang-Vong A21

Designs: 6.50k, Urn under canopy. 9k, Catafalque on 7-headed dragon carriage.

1961, Apr. 29 Engr. *Perf. 13*

66	A20	4k black, bis & org	.85	.75
67	A20	6.50k black & bister	1.00	.75
68	A20	9k black & bister	1.10	.85
69	A21	25k black	3.00	2.25
		Nos. 66-69 (4)	5.95	4.60

King Sisavang-Vong's (1885-1959) funeral, Apr. 23-29, 1961.

King Savang Vatthana — A22

1962, Apr. 16 *Perf. 13*

Portrait in Brown and Carmine

70	A22	1k ultramarine	.50	.25
71	A22	2k lilac rose	.60	.25
72	A22	5k greenish blue	.70	.30
73	A22	10k olive	.85	.40
		Nos. 70-73 (4)	2.65	1.20

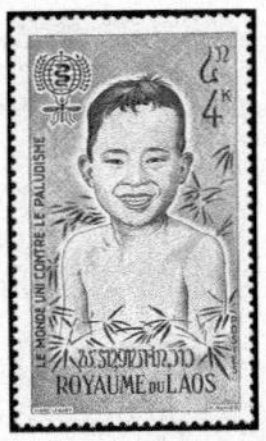

Boy and Malaria Eradication Emblem — A23

9k, Girl. 10k, Malaria eradication emblem.

1962, July 19 Engr.

74	A23	4k bluish grn, blk & buff	.60	.25
75	A23	9k lt bl, blk & lt brn	.80	.40
76	A23	10k ol, bis & rose red	1.25	.45
		Nos. 74-76 (3)	2.65	1.10

WHO drive to eradicate malaria.

Nos. 74-76 exist imperf.

An imperf. souvenir sheet on white paper with light blue inscription exists. Value, $350. Three other varieties of this sheet also exist: off white paper with light blue inscription, value, $500; white paper with dark blue inscription, value, $350; and off white paper with dark blue inscription, value, $650.

A24

A25

Designs: 50c, Modern mail service (truck, train, plane). 70c, Globe, stamps, dancer. 1k, Ancient mail service (messenger on elephant). 1.50k, Royal Messenger

1962, Nov. 15 Unwmk. *Perf. 13*

77	A24	50c multicolored	.60	.60
78	A24	70c multicolored	.60	.60
79	A25	1k dp clar, grn & blk	1.25	1.25
80	A25	1.50k multicolored	1.00	1.00
		Nos. 77-80 (4)	3.45	3.45

Souvenir sheets exist. One contains the 50c and 70c; the other, the 1k and 1.50k. The sheets exist both perf and imperf in a souvenir booklet of four sheets. Value intact booklet, $350.

Fishermen with Nets — A26

Threshing Rice — A27

Designs: 5k, Plowing and planting in rice paddy. 9k, Woman with infant harvesting rice.

1963, Mar. 21 *Perf. 13*

81	A26	1k grn, bister & pur	.35	.30
82	A27	4k bister, bl & grn	.45	.35
83	A26	5k grn, bis & indigo	.65	.45
84	A27	9k grn, vio bl & ocher	1.00	.50
a.		Min. sheet of 4, #81-84, imperf.	5.00	5.00
b.		As "a," left panel of No. 83 green instead of brown	*100.00*	*100.00*
		Nos. 81-84 (4)	2.45	1.60

FAO "Freedom from Hunger" campaign.

No. 84a exists on yellowish and white papers; No. 84b exists only on yellowish paper.

No. 84b exists with gold inscriptions. Value $450.

Queen Khamphouy Handing out Gifts — A28

1963, Oct. 10 Engr.

85	A28	4k brn, dp car & blue	.50	.40
86	A28	6k grn, red, yel & bl	.60	.50
87	A28	10k bl, dp car & dk brn	.90	.65
a.		Miniature sheet of 3, #85-87	4.00	4.00
		Nos. 85-87 (3)	2.00	1.55

Centenary of the International Red Cross.

Man Holding UN Emblem — A29

1963, Dec. 10 Unwmk. *Perf. 13*

88	A29	4k dk bl, dp org & vio brn	1.50	.80

15th anniv. of the Universal Declaration of Human Rights.

No. 88 also was issued imperf. Value, $15.

Temple of That Luang, Map of Nubia and Ramses II — A30

1964, Mar. 8 Engr.

89	A30	4k multicolored	.40	.40
90	A30	6k multicolored	.60	.60
91	A30	10k multicolored	.75	.75
a.		Miniature sheet of 3, #89-91	3.00	3.00
		Nos. 89-91 (3)	1.75	1.75

UNESCO world campaign to save historic monuments in Nubia. No. 91a sold for 25k.

Ceremonial Chalice — A31

Designs: 15k, Buddha. 20k, Soldier leading people through Mekong River Valley. 40k, Royal Palace, Luang Prabang.

1964, July 30 Unwmk. *Perf. 13*

92	A31	10k multicolored	.40	.30
93	A31	15k multicolored	.60	.40
94	A31	20k multicolored	.80	.60
95	A31	40k multicolored	1.25	.75
a.		Miniature sheet of 4, #92-95	3.50	3.50
		Nos. 92-95 (4)	3.05	2.05

"Neutral and Constitutional Laos." When the stamps are arranged in a block of four with 40k and 15k in first row and 10k and 20k in second row, the map of Laos appears.

A souvenir booklet containing No. 95a exists. Value, $45.

Prince Vet and Wife Mathie — A32

Scenes from Buddhist Legend of Phra Vet Sandone: 32k, God of the Skies sending his son to earth. 45k, Phaune's daughter with beggar husband. 55k, Beggar cornered by guard and dogs.

1964, Nov. 17 Photo. ***Perf. 13x12½***

96 A32 10k multicolored .50 .50
97 A32 32k multicolored .75 .75
98 A32 45k multicolored 1.00 1.00
99 A32 55k multicolored 1.25 1.25
a. Miniature sheet of 4 5.00 3.75
Nos. 96-99 (4) 3.50 3.50

No. 99a contains 4 imperf. stamps similar to Nos. 96-99.

A souvenir booklet containing No. 99a without the sheet number exists. Value, $100.

Lao Women — A33

1964, Dec. 15 Engr. ***Perf. 13***

100 A33 25k blk, org brn & pale ol .75 .75
Nos. 100,C43-C45 (4) 3.45 2.35

Butterflies — A34

10k, Cethosia biblis. 25k, Precis cebrene. 40k, Dysphania militaris.

1965, Mar. 13 Unwmk. ***Perf. 13***

Size: 36x36mm

101 A34 10k multi 2.25 1.25
102 A34 25k multi 4.25 1.75

Size: 48x27mm

103 A34 40k multi 10.50 2.50
Nos. 101-103,C46 (4) 22.50 8.00

See. No. C46.

Teacher and School, American Aid — A35

Designs: 25k, Woman at Wattay Airport, French aid, horiz. 45k, Woman bathing child and food basket, Japanese aid. 55k, Musicians broadcasting, British aid, horiz.

1965, Mar. 30 Engr. ***Perf. 13***

104 A35 25k bl grn, brn & car rose .45 .30
105 A35 45k ol grn & brn .95 .50
106 A35 55k brt bl & bister 1.25 .65
107 A35 75k multicolored 1.75 .80
Nos. 104-107 (4) 4.40 2.25

Issued to publicize foreign aid to Laos.

Hophabang Temple — A36

1965, Apr. 23 Unwmk. ***Perf. 13***

108 A36 10k multicolored .75 .35

Telewriter, Map of Laos and Globe — A37

30k, Communication by satellite & map of Laos. 50k, Globe, map of Laos & radio.

1965, June 15 Engr. ***Perf. 13***

109 A37 5k vio bl, brn & red lil .30 .25
110 A37 30k bl, org brn & sl grn .65 .50
111 A37 50k crim, lt bl & bis 1.25 .90
a. Miniature sheet of 3, #109-111 4.75 4.75
Nos. 109-111 (3) 2.20 1.65

ITU, centenary.

A souvenir booklet containing No. 111a exists. Value, $35.

Nos. 52-53 Surcharged in Dark Blue with New Value and Bars

1965, July 5 Unwmk. ***Perf. 13***

112 A16 1k on 4k rose claret .70 .25
113 A16 5k on 6.50k org red .70 .25

Mother and Child, UNICEF and WHO Emblems — A38

1965, Sept. 1 Engr. ***Perf. 13***

114 A38 35k lt ultra & dk red .85 .70
a. Miniature sheet 4.75 4.75

Mother and Child Protection movement, 6th anniv.

Map of Laos and UN Emblem — A39

1965, Nov. 3 ***Perf. 12½x13***

115 A39 5k emer, gray & vio bl .30 .25
116 A39 25k lil rose, gray & vio bl .45 .35
117 A39 40k bl, gray & vio bl .70 .50
Nos. 115-117 (3) 1.45 1.10

UN, 20th anniv. Although first day covers were canceled "Oct. 24," the actual day of issue is reported to have been Nov. 3.

Tikhy (Hockey) — A40

Pastimes: 10k, Two bulls fighting. 25k, Canoe race. 50k, Rocket festival.

1965, Dec. 23 Engr. ***Perf. 13***

118 A40 10k org, brn & gray .30 .25
119 A40 20k grn, ver & dk bl .40 .30
120 A40 25k brt blue & multi .40 .35
121 A40 50k orange & multi .90 .50
Nos. 118-121 (4) 2.00 1.40

Slaty-headed Parakeet — A41

Birds: 15k, White-crested laughing thrush. 20k, Osprey. 45k, Bengal roller.

1966, Feb. 10 Engr. ***Perf. 13***

122 A41 5k car rose, ol & brn .85 .50
123 A41 15k bluish grn, brn & blk 1.25 .60
124 A41 20k dl bl, sep & bister 2.10 1.00
125 A41 45k vio, Prus bl & sepia 4.25 2.40
Nos. 122-125 (4) 8.45 4.50

WHO Headquarters, Geneva — A42

1966, May 3 Engr. ***Perf. 13***

126 A42 10k bl grn & indigo .30 .25
127 A42 25k car & dk green .40 .30
128 A42 50k ultra & black .85 .70
a. Miniature sheet of 3, #126-128 19.00 19.00
Nos. 126-128 (3) 1.55 1.25

Inauguration of the WHO Headquarters, Geneva. No. 128a sold for 150k.

Ordination of Buddhist Monk — A43

Folklore: 25k, Women building ceremonial sand hills. 30k, Procession of the Wax Pagoda, vert. 40k, Wrist-tying ceremony (3 men, 3 women), vert.

1966, May 20 ***Perf. 13***

129 A43 10k multicolored .30 .25
130 A43 25k multicolored .45 .30
131 A43 30k multicolored .75 .50
132 A43 40k multicolored 1.00 .70
Nos. 129-132 (4) 2.50 1.75

UNESCO Emblem — A44

1966, July 7 Engr. ***Perf. 13***

133 A44 20k ocher & gray .30 .25
134 A44 30k brt blue & gray .40 .30
135 A44 40k brt green & gray .55 .30
136 A44 60k crimson & gray .80 .45
a. Miniature sheet, #133-136 6.00 6.00
Nos. 133-136 (4) 2.05 1.30

UNESCO, 20th anniv. No. 136a sold for 250k.

Addressed Envelope Carrier Pigeon, Globe and Hand with Quill Pen — A45

1966, Sept. 7 Engr. ***Perf. 13***

137 A45 5k red, brn & bl .30 .25
138 A45 20k bl grn, blk & lil .45 .30
139 A45 40k bl, red brn & dk ol bister .55 .35
140 A45 45k brt rose lil, bl grn & black .75 .50
a. Min. sheet of 4, #137-140 6.00 6.00
Nos. 137-140 (4) 2.05 1.40

Intl. Letter Writing Week, Oct. 6-12. No. 140a sold for 250k.

Sculpture from Siprapouthbat Temple — A46

Sculptures: 20k, from Visoun Temple. 50k, from Xiengthong Temple. 70k, from Visoun Temple.

1967, Feb. 21 Engr. ***Perf. 12½x13***

141 A46 5k olive grn & grn .30 .25
142 A46 20k brn ol & gray bl .70 .40
143 A46 50k dk brn & dp claret 1.25 .50
144 A46 70k dk brn & dk magenta 1.50 .80
Nos. 141-144 (4) 3.75 1.95

General Post Office — A47

1967, Apr. 6 Engr. ***Perf. 13***

145 A47 25k brn, grn & vio brn .35 .25
146 A47 50k ind, brt blue & grn .55 .40
147 A47 70k dk red, grn & brn 1.25 .75
Nos. 145-147 (3) 2.15 1.40

Inauguration of the new Post and Telegraph Headquarters.

Snakehead A48

Fish: 35k, Giant catfish. 45k, Spiny eel. 60k, Knifefish.

1967, June 8 Engr. ***Perf. 13x12½***

148 A48 20k dl bl, bis & blk 1.25 .50
149 A48 35k aqua, bis & gray 1.50 .60
150 A48 45k pale grn, bis & ol brn 2.50 .70
151 A48 60k sl grn, bis & blk 3.75 .80
Nos. 148-151 (4) 9.00 2.60

Drumstick Tree Flower — A49

Blossoms: 55k, Turmeric. 75k, Peacock flower. 80k, Pagoda tree.

1967, Aug. 10 Engr. ***Perf. 12½x13***

152 A49 30k red lil, yel & grn .60 .35
153 A49 55k org, mag & lt grn .90 .45
154 A49 75k bl, red & lt grn 1.25 .65
155 A49 80k brt grn, mag & yel 1.50 .75
Nos. 152-155 (4) 4.25 2.20

Banded Krait — A50

Reptiles: 40k, Marsh crocodile. 100k, Malayan moccasin. 200k, Water monitor.

1967, Dec. 7 Engr. ***Perf. 13***

156 A50 5k emer, ind & yel .85 .40
157 A50 40k sep, lt grn & yel 1.75 .60
158 A50 100k lt grn, brn & ocher 3.50 1.75
159 A50 200k grn, blk & bister 8.50 5.00
Nos. 156-159 (4) 14.60 7.75

Human Rights Flame A51

1968, Feb. 8 Engr. ***Perf. 13***

160 A51 20k brt grn, red & grn .30 .25
161 A51 30k brn, red & grn .40 .30
162 A51 50k brt bl, red & grn .80 .60
a. Souv. sheet of 3, #160-162 5.00 5.00
Nos. 160-162 (3) 1.50 1.15

Intl. Human Rights Year. No. 162a sold for 250k.

WHO Emblem — A52

1968, July 5 Engr. ***Perf. 12½x13***

163 A52 15k rose vio, ver & ocher .30 .25
164 A52 30k brt bl, brt grn & ocher .30 .25
165 A52 70k ver, plum & ocher .55 .40
166 A52 110k brn, brt rose lil & ocher .90 .55

167 A52 250k brt grn, brt bl & ocher 2.40 1.50
a. Souv. sheet of 5, #163-167 6.50 6.50
Nos. 163-167 (5) 4.45 2.95

WHO, 20th anniv. No. 167a sold for 500k.

Parade and Memorial Arch — A53

Designs: 20k, Armored Corps with tanks. 60k, Three soldiers with Laotian flag.

1968, July 15 *Perf. 13*

168 A53 15k multicolored .35 .25
169 A53 20k multicolored .45 .35
170 A53 60k multicolored .90 .45
Nos. 168-170,C52-C53 (5) 5.95 3.15

Laotian Army. For souvenir sheet see No. C53a.

Chrysochroa Mnizechi — A54

Insects: 50k, Aristobia approximator. 90k, Eutaenia corbetti.

1968, Aug. 28 **Engr.** *Perf. 13*

171 A54 30k vio bl, grn & yel .90 .35
172 A54 50k lil, blk & ocher 1.50 .50
173 A54 90k bis, blk & org 2.25 1.25
Nos. 171-173,C54-C55 (5) 8.40 4.20

See. Nos. C54-C55.

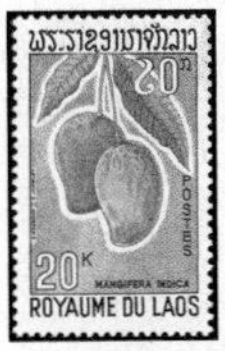

Mangoes — A55

Fruits: 50k, Tamarind. 180k, Jackfruit, horiz. 250k, Watermelon, horiz.

1968, Oct. 3 **Engr.** *Perf. 13*

174 A55 20k ind, lt bl & emer .40 .25
175 A55 50k lt bl, emer & brn .70 .40
176 A55 180k sep, org & yel grn 2.00 1.10
177 A55 250k sep, bis & emer 2.75 1.60
Nos. 174-177 (4) 5.85 3.35

Hurdling A56

1968, Nov. 15 **Engr.** *Perf. 13*

178 A56 15k shown .50 .50
179 A56 80k Tennis 1.00 .50
180 A56 100k Soccer 1.00 .50
181 A56 110k High jump 1.50 1.00
Nos. 178-181 (4) 4.00 2.50

19th Olympic Games, Mexico City, 10/12-27.

Wedding of Kathanam and Nang Sida — A57

Design: 200k, Thao Khathanam battling the serpent Ngou Xouang and the giant bird Phanga Houng. Design from panels of the central gate of Ongtu Temple, Vientiane. Design of 150k is from east gate.

1969, Feb. 28 **Photo.** *Perf. 12x13*

182 A57 150k blk, gold & red 2.00 1.25
183 A57 200k blk, gold & red 2.75 1.75

Soukhib Ordered to Attack — A58

Scenes from Royal Ballet: 15k, Pharak pleading for Nang Sita. 20k, Thotsakan reviewing his troops. 30k, Nang Sita awaiting punishment. 40k, Pharam inspecting troops. 60k, Hanuman preparing to rescue Nang Sita.

1969 **Photo.** *Perf. 14*

184 A58 10k multicolored .50 .25
185 A58 15k blue & multi .70 .40
186 A58 20k lt bl & multi .70 .50
187 A58 30k salmon & multi 1.00 .55
188 A58 40k salmon & multi 1.60 .70
189 A58 60k pink & multi 2.00 1.10
Nos. 184-189,C56-C57 (8) 17.00 8.50

See Nos. C56-C57. For surcharges see Nos. B12-B17, CB1-CB2.

ILO Emblem and Basket Weavers at Vientiane Vocational Center — A59

1969, May 7 **Engr.** *Perf. 13*

190 A59 30k claret & violet .50 .40
191 A59 60k slate grn & vio brn 1.00 .75
Nos. 190-191,C58 (3) 7.00 4.40

ILO, 50th anniv.

Chinese Pangolin A60

1969, Nov. 6 **Photo.** *Perf. 13x12*

192 A60 15k multicolored .60 .25
193 A60 30k multicolored 1.00 .50
Nos. 192-193,C59-C61 (5) 7.85 3.85

See Nos. C59-C61.

That Luang, Luang Prabang — A61

King Sisavang-Vong A62

1969, Nov. 19 **Engr.** *Perf. 13*

194 A61 50k dk brn, bl & bister .80 .60
195 A62 70k maroon & buff 1.40 1.00
a. Pair, #194-195 + label 3.50 3.50

Death of King Sisavang-Vong, 10th anniv.

Carved Capital from Wat Xiengthong A63

1970, Jan. 10 **Photo.** *Perf. 12x13*

196 A63 70k multicolored 1.75 1.25
Nos. 196,C65-C66 (3) 5.15 2.90

Kongphene (Midday) Drum A64

Designs: 55k, Kongthong (bronze) drum.

1970, Mar. 30 **Engr.** *Perf. 13*

197 A64 30k bl gray, ol & org 1.00 .60
198 A64 55k ocher, blk & yel grn 1.75 1.35
Nos. 197-198,C67 (3) 5.75 3.45

See No. C67.

Lenin Explaining Electrification Plan, by L. Shmatko — A65

1970, Apr. 22 **Litho.** *Perf. 12½x12*

199 A65 30k blue & multi 1.10 .55
200 A65 70k rose red & multi 1.40 .75

Lenin (1870-1924), Russian communist leader.

Silk Weaver and EXPO Emblem — A66

1970, July 7 **Engr.** *Perf. 13*

201 A66 30k shown .70 .30
202 A66 70k Woman winding thread 1.00 .80
Nos. 201-202,C69 (3) 3.45 2.35

Laotian silk industry; EXPO '70 Intl. Exposition, Osaka, Japan, Mar. 15-Sept. 13.
See No. C69.

Wild Boar — A67

1970, Sept. 7 **Engr.** *Perf. 13*

203 A67 20k green & dp brn .55 .25
204 A67 60k dp brn & ol bis 1.00 .45
Nos. 203-204,C70-C71 (4) 9.30 4.45

See Nos. C70-C71.

Buddha, UN Headquarters and Emblem — A68

1970, Oct. 24 **Size: 22x36mm**

205 A68 30k ultra, brn & rose red .70 .40
206 A68 70k brt grn, sep & vio 1.40 .60
Nos. 205-206,C75 (3) 4.50 2.10

UN, 25th anniv.
See No. C75.

Nakhanet, Symbol of Arts and Culture A69

85k, Rahu swallowing the moon.

1971, Feb. 5

207 A69 70k shown 1.00 .60
208 A69 85k multicolored 1.40 .85
Nos. 207-208,C76 (3) 4.80 2.45

Silversmithing A70

1971, Apr. 12 **Engr.** *Perf. 13*

Size: 36x36mm

209 A70 30k shown .35 .25
210 A70 50k Pottery .55 .35

Size: 47x36mm

211 A70 70k Boat building 1.10 .40
Nos. 209-211 (3) 2.00 1.00

Laotian and African Children, UN Emblem A71

60k, Women musicians, elephants, UN emblem.

1971, May 1 **Engr.** *Perf. 13*

212 A71 30k lt grn, brn & blk .50 .30
213 A71 60k yel, pur & dull red 1.10 .50

Intl. year against racial discrimination.

Miss Rotary, Wat Ho Phrakeo — A72

Design: 30k, Monk on roof of That Luang and Rotary emblem, horiz.

1971, June 28 **Engr.** *Perf. 13*

214 A72 30k purple & ocher .60 .40
215 A72 70k gray ol, dk bl & rose 1.25 .55

Rotary International, 50th anniversary.

Dendrobium Aggregatum — A73

50k, Asocentrum ampullaceum, horiz. 70k, Trichoglottis fasciata, horiz.

Perf. 12½x13, 13x12½

1971, July 7 **Photo.**

Size: 26x36, 36x26mm

216 A73 30k shown 1.00 .50
217 A73 50k multicolored 1.40 .95
218 A73 70k multicolored 2.00 1.25
Nos. 216-218,C79 (4) 8.90 4.20

See Nos. 230-232, C79, C89.

Palm Civet — A74

Animals: 40k, like 25k. 50k, Lesser mouse deer. 85k, Sika deer.

1971, Sept. 16 **Engr.** ***Perf. 13***

219 A74 25k pur, dk bl & blk .80 .45
220 A74 40k grn, ol bis & blk 1.00 .60
221 A74 50k brt grn & ocher 1.50 .70
222 A74 85k sl grn, grn & brn orange 2.50 1.25
Nos. 219-222,C83 (5) 10.05 5.75

See No. C83.

Types of 1952-57 with Ornamental Panels and Inscriptions

Designs: 30k, Laotian woman. 40k, So player (like #C25). 50k, Rama (like #C19).

1971, Oct. 31

223 A3 30k brn vio & brn .50 .30
224 A10 40k sepia, blk & ver .70 .50
225 AP7 50k ultra, blk & salmon 1.00 .70
Nos. 223-225,C84 (4) 4.20 2.90

Souvenir Sheet

225A A3 Sheet of 3 6.00 6.00
b. 60k 2.00 2.00
c. 85k 2.00 2.00

20th anniv. of Laotian independent postal service. All stamps inscribed: "Vingtième Anniversaire de la Philatélie Lao," "Postes" and "1971." No. 225A contains No. 223 and 60k and 85k in design of 30k, sold for 250k.

Children Learning to Read — A75

70k, Scribe writing on palm leaves.

1972, Jan. 30 **Engr.** ***Perf. 13***

Size: 36x22mm

226 A75 30k shown .35 .30
227 A75 70k multicolored .70 .50
Nos. 226-227,C87 (3) 2.80 1.80

Intl. Book Year.
See No. C87.

Nam Ngum Hydroelectric Dam, Monument and ECAFE Emblem — A76

1972, Mar. 28 **Engr.** ***Perf. 13***

228 A76 40k grn, ultra & lt brn .35 .25
229 A76 80k grn, brn ol & dk bl .70 .40
Nos. 228-229,C88 (3) 2.45 1.45

25th anniv. of the Economic Commission for Asia and the Far East (ECAFE), which helped build the Nam Ngum Hydroelectric Dam.
See No. C88.

Orchid Type of 1971

Orchids: 40k, Hynchostylis giganterum. 60k, Paphiopedilum exul. 80k, Cattleya, horiz.

1972, May 5 **Photo.** ***Perf. 13***

Size: 26x36mm, 36x26mm

230 A73 40k lt bl & multi .95 .35
231 A73 60k multicolored 1.60 .45
232 A73 80k lt bl & multi 2.00 .50
Nos. 230-232,C89 (4) 8.55 2.80

Woman Carrying Water, UNICEF Emblem A77

Children's drawings: 80k, Child learning bamboo-weaving, UNICEF emblem.

1972, July 20 **Engr.** ***Perf. 13***

233 A77 50k blue & multi .70 .50
234 A77 80k brown & multi 1.00 .65
Nos. 233-234,C90 (3) 3.10 2.15

25th anniv. (in 1971) of UNICEF.
See No. C90.

Attopeu Costume, Religious Ceremony — A78

Design: 90k, Phongsaly festival costume.

1973, Feb. 16 **Engr.** ***Perf. 13***

235 A78 40k maroon & multi .50 .30
236 A78 90k multicolored 1.10 .50
Nos. 235-236,C101-C102 (4) 4.90 2.60

See Nos. C101-C102.

Lion from Wat That Luang and Lions Emblem — A79

1973, Mar. 30 **Engr.** ***Perf. 13***

237 A79 40k vio bl, rose cl & lil .70 .25
238 A79 80k pur, org brn & yel 1.10 .40
Nos. 237-238,C103 (3) 3.70 1.40

Lions International of Laos.

Dr. Hansen, Map of Laos, "Dok Hak" Flowers A80

1973, June 28 **Engr.** ***Perf. 13***

239 A80 40k multicolored .60 .30
240 A80 80k multicolored 1.25 .45

Centenary of the discovery by Dr. Armauer G. Hansen of the Hansen bacillus, the cause of leprosy.

Wat Vixun, Monk Blessing Girl Scouts — A81

1973, Sept. 1 **Engr.** ***Perf. 13***

241 A81 70k ocher & brown .90 .40
Nos. 241,C106-C107 (3) 3.25 1.10

25th anniv. of Laotian Scout Movement.

INTERPOL Headquarters A82

1973, Dec. 22 **Engr.** ***Perf. 13x12½***

242 A82 40k greenish bl .45 .25
243 A82 80k brown .75 .60
Nos. 242-243,C110 (3) 2.60 1.45

Intl. Criminal Police Org., 50th anniv.

Boy Mailing Letter — A83

1974, Apr. 30 **Engr.** ***Perf. 13***

244 A83 70k bl, lt grn & ocher 1.00 .25
245 A83 80k lt grn, bl & ocher 1.20 .40
Nos. 244-245,C114-C115 (4) 11.95 3.65

UPU, cent.

Blue Sage — A84

50k, Water lilies, horiz. 80k, Scheffler's kapokier, horiz.

1974, May 17

Size: 26x36mm, 36x26mm

246 A84 30k grn & vio .55 .40
247 A84 50k multicolored .90 .50
248 A84 80k multicolored 1.25 .75
Nos. 246-248,C116 (4) 8.20 4.65

See No. C116.

Mekong River Ferry — A85

90k, Samlo (passenger tricycle), vert.

1974, July 31 **Engr.** ***Perf. 13***

249 A85 25k red brn & choc .40 .40
250 A85 90k brown ol & lt ol 1.25 1.25
Nos. 249-250,C117 (3) 4.15 3.15

See No. C117.

Marconi, Indigenous Transmission Methods, Transistor Radio — A86

1974, Aug. 28 **Engr.** ***Perf. 13***

251 A86 60k multicolored .50 .50
252 A86 90k multicolored .75 .75
Nos. 251-252,C118 (3) 3.50 2.35

Guglielmo Marconi (1874-1937), Italian electrical engineer and inventor.
See No. C118.

Diastocera Wallichi Tonkinensis A87

90k, Macrochenus isabellunus. 100k, Purpuricenus malaccensis.

1974, Oct. 23 **Engr.** ***Perf. 13***

253 A87 50k shown .90 .60
254 A87 90k multicolored 1.40 .85
255 A87 100k multicolored 1.75 .90
Nos. 253-255,C119 (4) 5.80 3.35

See No. C119.

Temple, Houeisai, and Sapphire — A88

110k, Sapphire panning at Attopeu.

1975, Feb. 12 **Engr.** ***Perf. 13x12½***

256 A88 100k bl, brn & grn 1.50 .50
257 A88 110k multicolored 1.75 .75

King Sisavang-Vong, Princes Souvanna Phouma and Souphanou-Vong — A89

1975, Feb. 21 **Engr.** ***Perf. 13***

258 A89 80k olive & multi 1.00 .40
259 A89 300k multicolored 1.75 .90
260 A89 420k multicolored 2.00 1.25
Nos. 258-260 (3) 4.75 2.55

1st anniv. of Peace Treaty of Vientiane.
A souvenir sheet exists, embossed on paper with a foil application. Value, $10.

Fortuneteller Working on Forecast for New Year (Size of pair: 100x27mm) — A90

New Year Riding Rabbit, and Tiger (Old Year) — A92

Designs: 40k, Chart of New Year symbols. 200k, Fortune teller. 350k, As shown.

1975, Apr. 14 **Engr.** ***Perf. 13***

261 40k bister & red brn .50 .25
262 200k bis, red brn & sl 1.40 .80
a. A90 Pair, #261-262 2.25 1.75
263 A92 350k blue & multi 2.50 1.60
Nos. 261-263 (3) 4.40 2.65

New Year 1975, Year of the Rabbit.

UN Emblem, "Equality" — A93

200k, IWY emblem, man and woman.

1975, June 19 **Engr.**

264 A93 100k dl bl & vio bl .55 .40
265 A93 200k multi 1.20 .85
a. Miniature sheet of 2, #264-265 5.50 5.50

International Women's Year.

UPU, Cent. A93a

Designs: 15k, Runner, rocket reaching orbit, vert. 30k, Docked Soyuz capsules, chariot, vert. 40k, Biplane, Concorde. 1000k, Apollo spacecraft. 1500k, Apollo spacecraft, astronaut, vert. No. 266F, Wagon train, Lunar Rover. No. 266G, Mail truck, Concorde. No. 266H, stagecoach. No. 266I, Zeppelin, locomotive.

Perf. 13x14, 14x13

1975, July 7 **Litho.**

266 A93a 10k multi .30 .25
b. Souvenir sheet of 1 *12.50 12.50*
266A A93a 15k multi .50 .25
b. Souvenir sheet of 1 *12.50 12.50*

266B	A93a	30k multi	.70	.35
a.		Souvenir sheet of 1	*12.50*	*12.50*
266C	A93a	40k multi	.90	.60
a.		Souvenir sheet of 1	*12.50*	*12.50*
266D	A93a	1000k multi	2.75	2.00
a.		Souvenir sheet of 1	*12.50*	*12.50*
266E	A93a	1500k multi	4.75	3.00
a.		Souvenir sheet of 1	*12.50*	*12.50*
		Nos. 266-266E (6)	9.90	6.45

Litho. & Embossed

Perf. 13½

266F	A93a	2500k gold & multi	11.00	11.00
a.		Souvenir sheet of 1	*95.00*	*95.00*
266G	A93a	3000k gold & multi	11.00	11.00
a.		Souvenir sheet of 1	*90.00*	*90.00*

Souvenir Sheets

266H	A93a	2500k gold & multi	*35.00*	*35.00*
266I	A93a	3000k gold & multi	*30.00*	*30.00*

Nos. 266D-266E, 266G-266I are airmail.

Nos. 266-266E also exist imperf. Value, set of six pairs $150. Nos. 266b, 266Ab and 266Ba-266Ea also exist imperf. Value, set of six sheets $375. Nos. 266Fa, 266Ga and 266H-266I also exist imperf. Value, set of four sheets $550.

Both perforated and imperforate souvenir sheets with blue space images in the selvage exist for 266D and 266E. Value for set of four $35.

No. 266F exists perf and imperf. in sheets of 4.

Apollo-Soyuz Mission — A93b

Designs: 125k, Astronauts, Thomas Stafford, Vance D. Brand, Donald Slayton. 150k, Cosmonauts Alexei Leonov, Valery Koubasov. 200k, Apollo-Soyuz link-up. 300k, Handshake in space. 450k, Preparation for re-entry. 700k, Apollo splashdown.

1975, July 7 Litho. *Perf. 14x13*

267	A93b	125k multicolored	.80	.75
267A	A93b	150k multicolored	.95	.75
267B	A93b	200k multicolored	1.50	1.00
267C	A93b	300k multicolored	2.00	1.50
267D	A93b	450k multicolored	3.25	1.75
267E	A93b	700k multicolored	3.75	1.50
		Nos. 267-267E (6)	12.25	7.25

Nos. 267D-267E are airmail.

Nos. 267-267E exist imperf. Value, set $55.00

Nos. 267-267E exist in souvenir sheets of 1. Value, set perf. $75., set imperf. $150.

Scene from Vet Sandone Legend — A94

Designs: Scenes from Buddhist legend of Prince Vet Sandone.

1975, July 22 Photo. *Perf. 13*

268	A94	80k multicolored	.65	.30
268A	A94	110k multicolored	.70	.40
268B	A94	120k multicolored	.90	.50
268C	A94	130k multicolored	1.50	.60
		Nos. 268-268C (4)	3.75	1.80

American Revolution, Bicent. — A94a

Presidents: 10k, Washington, J. Adams, Jefferson, Madison. 15k, Monroe, J.Q. Adams, Jackson, Van Buren. 40k, Harrison, Tyler, Polk, Taylor. 50k, Filmore, Pierce, Buchanon, Lincoln. 100k, Johnson, Grant, Hayes, Garfield. 123k, Arthur, Cleveland, Harrison. 150k, McKinley, Roosevelt, Taft, Wilson. 200k, Harding, Coolidge, Hoover, Roosevelt. 1000k, Truman, Eisenhower, Kennedy. 1500k, L. Johnson, Nixon, Ford.

1975, June Litho. *Perf. 13½*

269	A94a	10k multicolored	*5.00*	—
269A	A94a	15k multicolored	*5.00*	—
269B	A94a	40k multicolored	*5.00*	—
269C	A94a	50k multicolored	*5.00*	—
269D	A94a	100k multicolored	*5.00*	—
269E	A94a	123k multicolored	*5.00*	—
269F	A94a	150k multicolored	*5.00*	—
269G	A94a	200k multicolored	*5.00*	—
269H	A94a	1000k multicolored	*5.00*	—
269I	A94a	1500k multicolored	*5.00*	—
		Nos. 269-269I (10)	*50.00*	

Nos. 269H-269I are airmail. These stamps were not approved by the Laotian government, however they were offered for sale at the Laotian post offices and used as valid postage for a brief period before being withdrawn. There is some question as to whether 269C-269G were sold in the Laotian post offices, however in period covers indicate that they probably were. Also exists imperf., set of 10, $200. Souvenir sheets of one exist both perforated, value $235, and imperforate, value $2,650.

Buddha, Stupas of Borobudur A95

Design: 200k, Borobudur sculptures and UNESCO emblem.

1975, Aug. 20 Engr. *Perf. 13*

270	A95	100k indigo & multi	.85	.40
271	A95	200k multicolored	1.60	.85
a.		Miniature sheet of 2, #270-271	2.50	2.50

UNESCO campaign to save Borobudur Temple, Java.

Coat of Arms of Republic — A96

1976, Dec. 2 Litho. *Perf. 14*

272	A96	1k blue & multi	.30	.25
273	A96	2k rose & multi	.30	.25
274	A96	5k brt grn & multi	.30	.25
275	A96	10k lilac & multi	.50	.40
276	A96	200k orange & multi	3.50	2.25
a.		Min. sheet of 5, #272-276	10.00	10.00
		Nos. 272-276 (5)	4.90	3.40

Nos. 272-276 exist imperforate. Value, set $70.

Imperforate miniature sheets of 1 of Nos. 272-276 exist. Value, set $100. In 2021, this set of imperforate miniature sheets of 1 were handstamp overprinted in red to commemorate the 60th anniversary of diplomatic relations between Laos and People's Republic of China.

For overprints and surcharges, see Nos. 426A, 426V, 508C, 676H, 1903.

Thathiang Pagoda, Vientiane — A97

Designs: 2k, 80k, 100k, Phonsi Pagoda, Luang Prabang. 30k, 300k, like 1k.

1976, Dec. 18 *Perf. 13½*

277	A97	1k multicolored	.30	.25
278	A97	2k multicolored	.40	.25
279	A97	30k multicolored	.85	.50
280	A97	80k multicolored	1.75	1.00
281	A97	100k multicolored	2.50	1.40
a.		Souv. sheet of 3, #278, 280-281	5.25	
b.		As a, imperf.	12.00	
282	A97	300k multicolored	4.00	2.50
a.		Souv. sheet of 3, #277, 279, 282	5.25	
b.		As a, imperf.	12.00	
		Nos. 277-282 (6)	9.80	5.90

Nos. 277-282 exist imperf. Value, set $45.

Silversmith A98

Perf. 13x12½, 12½x13

1977, Apr. 1 Litho.

283	A98	1k shown	.30	.25
284	A98	2k Weaver	.30	.25
285	A98	20k Potter	.65	.25
286	A98	50k Basket weaver, vert.	1.25	.40
		Nos. 283-286 (4)	2.50	1.15

Miniature sheets of 2 exist, perf. and imperf. Values: perf, $13; imperf. $16.

For overprints, see Nos. 426B, 426C, 426D, 426E, 426R, 676B.

Cosmonauts A.A. Gubarev, G.M. Grechko — A99

Government Palace, Vientiane, Kremlin, Moscow A100

20k, 50k, Lenin speaking on Red Square.

Perf. 12x12½, 12½x12

1977, Oct. 25 Litho.

287	A99	5k multicolored	.30	.25
288	A99	20k multicolored	.40	.25
289	A99	50k multicolored	.70	.30
290	A99	60k multicolored	.90	.40
291	A100	100k multicolored	1.40	.65
a.		Souv. sheet of 3, #288, 290-291	6.00	6.00
292	A100	250k multicolored	2.25	1.50
a.		Souv. sheet of 3, #287, 289, 292	6.00	6.00
		Nos. 287-292 (6)	5.95	3.35

60th anniv. of Russian October Revolution.

Nos. 287-292 exist imperf. Value, set $15.

For overprints, see Nos. 426F, 426N, 676C, 676F, 676I.

Natl. Arms — A101

1978, May 26 Litho. *Perf. 12½*

293	A101	5k dull org & blk	.30	.25
294	A101	10k tan & black	.35	.25
295	A101	50k brt pink & blk	.50	.25
296	A101	100k yel grn & blk	1.25	.45
297	A101	250k violet & blk	2.00	.85
		Nos. 293-297 (5)	4.40	2.05

For overprints, see Nos. 426G, 676J.

A102

Army Day: 20k, Soldiers with flag. 40k, Fighters and burning house, horiz. 300k, Anti-aircraft battery.

Perf. 12½x12¼, 12½x12¾

1978, Sept. 15 Litho.

298	A102	20k multicolored	.30	.25
299	A102	40k multicolored	.55	.25
300	A102	300k multicolored	2.10	1.00
		Nos. 298-300 (3)	2.95	1.50

Nos. 298-300 exist imperf. Value, set $55.

For overprints see No. 426O, 426Q, 676A, 676L.

Marchers with Banner — A103

1978, Dec. 2 Litho. *Perf. 11½*

301	A103	20k shown	.50	.25
302	A103	50k Women with flag	.70	.25
303	A103	400k Dancer	2.25	1.40
a.		Sheet of 3, #301-303, imperf.	4.25	
		Nos. 301-303 (3)	3.45	1.90

National Day. A second printing in slightly different colors and with rough perforation exists; values the same. Stamps in souvenir sheet are in reverse order.

Electronic Tree, Map of Laos, ITU Emblem — A104

Design: 250k, Electronic tree, map of Laos and broadcast tower.

1979, Jan. 18 Litho. *Perf. 12½*

304	A104	30k multicolored	.30	.25
305	A104	250k multicolored	2.50	1.00

World Telecommunications Day, 1978.

Nos. 304-305 exist imperf. Value, set $10.

For overprints, see Nos. 426P, 426W, 676K.

Woman Mailing Letter — A105

10k, 80k, Processing mail. 100k, like 5k.

1979, Jan. 18

306	A105	5k multicolored	.30	.25
307	A105	10k multicolored	.30	.25
308	A105	80k multicolored	1.00	.30
309	A105	100k multicolored	1.40	.40
		Nos. 306-309 (4)	3.00	1.20

Asian-Oceanic Postal Union, 15th anniv.

Nos. 306-309 exist imperf. Value, set $12.50.

For overprints, see Nos. 426H, 426J, 426K, 426T, 426U, 676E, 676G.

Intl. Year of the Child — A106

No. 310, Playing with ball, vert. No. 311, Studying. No. 312, Playing musical instruments. No. 313, Breast-feeding, vert. No. 314, Map, globe, vert. No. 315, Immunization, vert. No. 316, Girl dancing, vert.

1979 Litho. *Perf. 11*

Without Gum

310	A106	20k multicolored	.30	.25
311	A106	50k multicolored	.40	.25
312	A106	100k multicolored	1.00	.35
313	A106	200k multicolored	2.00	.65
314	A106	200k multicolored	1.75	.65
315	A106	500k multicolored	6.00	1.50
316	A106	600k multicolored	4.00	1.50
		Nos. 310-316 (7)	15.45	5.15

Issued: Nos. 310-311, 313, 315, 8/1; others, 12/25.

Imperf sheets of 4 containing Nos. 310-311, 313, 315 and of 3 containing Nos. 312, 314, 316 exist. Value for both sheets $25.

Two varieties of imperf sheet of 3 exist: inscribed "1979" or "1975" on No. 314 vignette. Sheet with "1975" imprint is very scarce.

Nos. 310-316 exist with double perfs, part perfs, and imperf between. Value $35 each.

Traditional Modes of Transportation A107

1979, Oct. 9 *Perf. 12½x13*

No.	Type	Description	Unused	Used
317	A107	5k Elephants, buffalo, pirogues	.30	.25
318	A107	10k Buffalo, carts	.30	*.35*
319	A107	70k like 10k	.65	*1.50*
320	A107	500k like 5k	2.50	2.00
		Nos. 317-320 (4)	3.75	*4.10*

Nos. 317-320 exist imperf. Value, set $15.

For overprints, see Nos. 426I, 426L, 426M, 426S, 676D.

5th Anniv. of the Republic A108

30c, Agriculture, vert. 50c, Education, health services. 1k, Three women, vert. 2k, Hydroelectric energy.

1980, May 30 *Perf. 11*

No.	Type	Description	Unused	Used
321	A108	30c multicolored	.35	.25
322	A108	50c multicolored	.60	.25
323	A108	1k multicolored	.75	.40
324	A108	2k multicolored	1.75	1.10
		Nos. 321-324 (4)	3.45	2.00

Imperf. souvenir sheet of 4 exists in three types. Values: vowel missing above first Lao word at top of sheet, $20; vowel 9mm above first Lao word, $10; vowel 7.5mm above first Lao word, $10.

Lenin, 110th Birth Anniv. — A109

1980, July 5 *Perf. 12x12½, 12½x12*

No.	Type	Description	Unused	Used
325	A109	1k Lenin reading	.30	.25
326	A109	2k Writing	.45	.25
327	A109	3k Lenin, red flag, vert.	.65	.40
328	A109	4k Orating, vert.	1.25	.55
		Nos. 325-328 (4)	2.65	1.45

Nos. 325-328 exist imperf. Value, set $12.50.

Imperf. souvenir sheet of 4 exists. Value $5.

From this point to No. 1365, used values are for CTO stamps. For Nos. 426A-426W, 676A-676L, 1318A-1318C, 1359, used values are for postally used stamps.

5th Anniv. of the Republic A110

50c, Threshing rice. 1.60k, Logging. 4.60k, Veterinary medicine. 5.40k, Rice paddy.

1980, Dec. 2 *Perf. 11*

Without Gum

No.	Type	Description	Unused	Used
329	A110	50c multicolored	.30	.25
330	A110	1.60k multicolored	.70	.30
331	A110	4.60k multicolored	1.40	.50
332	A110	5.40k multicolored	1.75	.80
		Nos. 329-332 (4)	4.15	1.85

Imperf. souvenir sheet of 4 exists. Value $10. Without inscription, value $100.

A111

Globe, Broken Chains — A111a

Grain, Cracked Bomb — A111b

1981, June 26 *Perf. 12x12½*

Without Gum

No.	Type	Description	Unused	Used
333	A111	60c shown	.30	.25
334	A111a	4.60k multicolored	1.75	.80
335	A111b	5.40k multicolored	2.00	.85
a.		Souv. sheet of 3, #333-335, imperf.	7.00	7.00
		Nos. 333-335 (3)	4.05	1.90

26th Communist Party (PCUS) Congress. No. 335a sold for 15k.

Souvenir Sheet

PHILATOKYO '81 — A112

1981, Sept. 20 *Perf. 13*

Without Gum

No.	Type	Description	Unused	Used
336	A112	10k Pandas	6.00	4.00

1982 World Cup Soccer Championships, Spain — A113

1981, Oct. 15 *Perf. 12½*

Without Gum

No.	Type	Description	Unused	Used
337	A113	1k Heading ball	.30	.25
338	A113	2k Dribble	.40	.25
339	A113	3k Kick	.55	.25
340	A113	4k Goal, horiz.	.75	.25
341	A113	5k Dribble, diff.	1.00	1.00
342	A113	6k Kick, diff.	1.40	.80
		Nos. 337-342 (6)	4.40	2.80

Intl. Year of the Disabled — A114

3k, Office worker. 5k, Teacher. 12k, Weaver, fishing net.

1981 **Without Gum** *Perf. 13*

No.	Type	Description	Unused	Used
343	A114	3k multicolored	1.60	.40
344	A114	5k multicolored	2.00	.80
345	A114	12k multicolored	4.00	2.00
		Nos. 343-345 (3)	7.60	3.20

Wildcats A115

10c, Felis silvestris ornata. 20c, Felis viverrinus. 30c, Felis caracal. 40c, Neofelis nebulosa. 50c, Felis planiceps. 9k, Felis chaus.

1981 **Without Gum** *Perf. 12½*

No.	Type	Description	Unused	Used
346	A115	10c multicolored	.30	.25
347	A115	20c multicolored	.30	.25
348	A115	30c multicolored	.35	.25
349	A115	40c multicolored	.40	.25
350	A115	50c multicolored	.45	.25
351	A115	9k multicolored	3.50	1.25
		Nos. 346-351 (6)	5.30	2.50

6th Anniv. of the Republic A116

3k, Satellite dish, flag. 4k, Soldier, flag. 5k, Map, flag, women, soldier.

1981, Dec. **Without Gum** *Perf. 13*

No.	Type	Description	Unused	Used
352	A116	3k multicolored	*65.00*	.30
353	A116	4k multicolored	*80.00*	.40
354	A116	5k multicolored	*110.00*	.50
		Nos. 352-354 (3)	*255.00*	1.20

Indian Elephants A117

1k, Head. 2k, Carrying log in trunk. 3k, Transporting people. 4k, In trap. 5k, Adult and young. 5.50k, Herd.

1982, Jan. 23 *Perf. 12½x13*

Without Gum

No.	Type	Description	Unused	Used
355	A117	1k multicolored	.30	.25
356	A117	2k multicolored	.60	.25
357	A117	3k multicolored	.80	.30
358	A117	4k multicolored	1.10	.30
359	A117	5k multicolored	1.50	.55
360	A117	5.50k multicolored	2.25	.70
		Nos. 355-360 (6)	6.55	2.35

Laotian Wrestling — A118

Various moves.

1982, Jan. 30 *Perf. 13*

Without Gum

No.	Type	Description	Unused	Used
361	A118	50c multicolored	.30	.25
362	A118	1.20k multi, diff.	.30	.25
363	A118	2k multi, diff.	.30	.25
364	A118	2.50k multi, diff.	.35	.25
365	A118	4k multi, diff.	.60	.35
366	A118	5k multi, diff.	1.00	.55
		Nos. 361-366 (6)	2.85	1.90

Water Lilies — A119

30c, Nymphaea zanzibariensis. 40c, Nelumbo nucifera gaertn rose. 60c, Nymphaea rosea. 3k, Nymphaea nouchali. 4k, Nymphaea white. 7k, Nelumbo nucifera gaertn white.

1982, Feb. 10 *Perf. 12½x13*

Without Gum

No.	Type	Description	Unused	Used
367	A119	30c multicolored	.30	.25
368	A119	40c multicolored	.30	.25
369	A119	60c multicolored	.30	.25
370	A119	3k multicolored	.65	.25
371	A119	4k multicolored	1.00	.25
372	A119	7k multicolored	1.75	.30
		Nos. 367-372 (6)	4.30	1.55

Birds — A120

50c, Hirundo rustica, vert. 1k, Upupa epops, vert. 2k, Alcedo atthis, vert. 3k, Hypothymis azurea. 4k, Motacilla cinerea. 10k, Orthotomus sutorius.

1982, Mar. 9 *Perf. 13*

Without Gum

No.	Type	Description	Unused	Used
373	A120	50c multicolored	.30	.25
374	A120	1k multicolored	.30	.25
375	A120	2k multicolored	.50	.25
376	A120	3k multicolored	.65	.25
377	A120	4k multicolored	1.25	.25
378	A120	10k multicolored	2.75	.80
		Nos. 373-378 (6)	5.75	2.05

A121

1982 World Cup Soccer Championships, Spain — A122

Various match scenes.

1982, Apr. 7 **Without Gum**

No.	Type	Description	Unused	Used
379	A121	1k multicolored	.30	.25
380	A121	2k multicolored	.40	.25
381	A121	3k multicolored	.55	.30
382	A121	4k multicolored	.70	.40
383	A121	5k multicolored	1.00	.45
384	A121	6k multicolored	1.25	.55
		Nos. 379-384 (6)	4.20	2.20

Souvenir Sheet

No.	Type	Description	Unused	Used
385	A122	15k multicolored	4.00	4.00

Nos. 379-384 exist imperf.

Butterflies A123

1k, Herona marathus. 2k, Neptis paraka. 3k, Euripus halitherses. 4k, Lebadea martha. 5k, Iton semamora. 6k, Elymnias hypermnestra.

1982, May 5 *Perf. 12½x13*

Without Gum

No.	Type	Description	Unused	Used
386	A123	1k multicolored	.30	.25
387	A123	2k multicolored	.60	.25
388	A123	3k multicolored	.75	.30
389	A123	4k multicolored	1.25	.30

Size: 42x26mm

Perf. 12½

No.	Type	Description	Unused	Used
390	A123	5k multicolored	2.00	.70

Size: 54x36½mm

Perf. 13x12½

No.	Type	Description	Unused	Used
391	A123	6k multicolored	2.50	.70
		Nos. 386-391 (6)	7.40	2.50

Souvenir Sheet

PHILEXFRANCE '82 — A124

10k, Temple, Vientiane.

1982, June 9 *Perf. 13*

Without Gum

392 A124 10k multicolored 2.75 2.75

River Vessels A125

50c, Raft. 60c, River punt. 1k, Houseboat. 2k, Passenger steamer. 3k, Ferry. 8k, Self-propelled barge.

1982, June 24 **Without Gum**

393 A125 50c multicolored .30 .25
394 A125 60c multicolored .30 .25
395 A125 1k multicolored .30 .25
396 A125 2k multicolored .35 .25
397 A125 3k multicolored .55 .40
398 A125 8k multicolored 1.50 .70
Nos. 393-398 (6) 3.30 2.10

Pagodas A126

1982, Aug. 2 **Without Gum**

399 A126 50c Chanh .30 .25
400 A126 60c Inpeng .30 .25
401 A126 1k Dong Mieng .30 .25
402 A126 2k Ho Tay .35 .25
403 A126 3k Ho Pha Keo .60 .30
404 A126 8k Sisaket 1.60 .65
Nos. 399-404 (6) 3.45 1.95

Dogs — A127

1982, Oct. 13 **Without Gum**

405 A127 50c Poodle .30 .25
406 A127 60c Samoyed .30 .25
407 A127 1k Boston terrier .30 .25
408 A127 2k Cairn terrier .40 .25
409 A127 3k Chihuahua .75 .40
410 A127 8k Bulldog 2.50 .65
Nos. 405-410 (6) 4.55 2.05

World Food Day — A128

1982, Oct. 16 **Without Gum**

411 A128 7k Watering seedlings 1.75 .65
412 A128 8k Planting rice 2.00 .80

Classic Automobiles A129

1982, Nov. 7 **Without Gum**

413 A129 50c 1925 Fiat .30 .25
414 A129 60c 1925 Peugeot .30 .25
415 A129 1k 1925 Berliet .30 .25
416 A129 2k 1925 Ballot .40 .25
417 A129 3k 1926 Renault .75 .40
418 A129 8k 1925 Ford 2.00 .65
Nos. 413-418 (6) 4.05 2.05

7th Anniv. of the Republic A130

50c, Kaysone Phomvihan, vert. 1k, Tractors, field, industry. 2k, Cows, farm. 3k, Truck, microwave dish. 4k, Nurse, child, vert. 5k, Education. 6k, Folk dancer, vert.

1982, Dec. 2 **Without Gum**

419 A130 50c multicolored .30 .25
420 A130 1k multicolored .30 .25
421 A130 2k multicolored .45 .25
422 A130 3k multicolored .65 .25
423 A130 4k multicolored .90 .40
424 A130 5k multicolored 1.10 .40
425 A130 6k multicolored 1.40 .50
Nos. 419-425 (7) 5.10 2.30

Nos. 419-425 exist imperf.

Bulgarian Flag, Coat of Arms and George Dimitrov (1882-1949), Bulgarian Statesman A131

1982, Dec. 15 *Perf. 12½*

Without Gum

426 A131 10k multicolored 1.90 1.10

Nos. 272, 276, 283, 284, 286-288, 293, 298, 299, 304-309, 317-319 Ovptd. in Red or Black

Methods and Perfs as before

1982

426A	A96	1k	multi	*70.00*	*70.00*
426B	A98	1k	multi (Bk)	*75.00*	*75.00*
426C	A98	1k	multi	*55.00*	*55.00*
426D	A98	2k	multi	*50.00*	*50.00*
426E	A98	2k	multi (Bk)	*65.00*	*65.00*
426F	A99	5k	multi	*85.00*	*85.00*
426G	A101	5k	dull org & blk	*75.00*	*75.00*
426H	A105	5k	multi	*55.00*	*55.00*
426I	A107	5k	multi	*35.00*	*35.00*
426J	A105	10k	multi (Bk)	*70.00*	*70.00*
426K	A105	10k	multi	*70.00*	*70.00*
426L	A107	10k	multi (Bk)	*65.00*	*65.00*
426M	A107	10k	multi	*175.00*	*175.00*
426N	A99	20k	multi	—	—
426O	A102	20k	multi	*175.00*	*175.00*
426P	A104	30k	multi	*75.00*	*75.00*
426Q	A102	40k	multi	*85.00*	*85.00*
426R	A98	50k	multi	*85.00*	*85.00*
426S	A107	70k	multi	*115.00*	*115.00*
426T	A105	80k	multi (Bk)	*125.00*	*125.00*
426U	A105	100k	multi	*175.00*	*175.00*
426V	A96	200k	org & multi (Bk)	*275.00*	*275.00*
426W	A104	250k	multi (Bk)	*450.00*	*450.00*
	Nos. 426A-426W (23)			*2,505.*	*2,505.*

Many overprint varieties exist.

Nos. 426A, 426B, 426E, 426H, 426J, 426L, 426Q, 426R, 426S, 426T, 426U, and 426V exist with inverted "8".

Nos. 426C and 426D exist with "I" instead of "1".

No. exists 426C with "a" instead of "2".

No. 426F exists with double overprint. Nos. 426J, 426N, and 426V exist with double overprint, one inverted. No. 426J exists with double overprint, one inverted, with the "1" in the upright overprint inverted.

No. 426N exists with inverted overprint.

No. 426H exists with "1" inverted.

Nos. 426O and 426P exist with small "2".

Both the "9" and the "2" wore out to the point where these numbers are almost invisible in some overprints. These seeming omission errors appear most prominently with the missing "9" in No. 426E, and the missing "2" in No. 426H.

Constitution of the USSR, 60th Anniv. — A132

1982, Dec. 30 **Without Gum**

427 A132 3k Kremlin .65 .40
428 A132 4k Maps .90 .55

Souvenir Sheet

Perf. 13½x13

428A Sheet of 2 3.75 2.00
b. A132 5k like 3k 1.25 .65
c. A132 10k like 4k 2.50 1.75

Nos. 428Ab-428Ac not inscribed in Laotian at top; buff and gold decorative margin contains the inscription.

1984 Summer Olympics, Los Angeles — A133

1983, Jan. 25 *Perf. 13*

Without Gum

429 A133 50c Hurdling .30 .25
430 A133 1k Women's javelin .30 .25
431 A133 2k Basketball .35 .25
432 A133 3k Diving .55 .25
433 A133 4k Gymnastics .75 .40
434 A133 10k Weight lifting 2.10 .80
Nos. 429-434 (6) 4.35 2.20

Souvenir Sheet

435 A133 15k Soccer 3.25 2.00

No. 435 contains one stamp 32x40mm. Nos. 429-434 exist imperf.

Horses — A134

Various breeds.

1983, Feb. 1 **Without Gum**

436 A134 50c multicolored .30 .25
437 A134 1k multi, diff. .30 .25
438 A134 2k multi, diff. .40 .25
439 A134 3k multi, diff. .65 .25
440 A134 4k multi, diff. .80 .30
441 A134 10k multi, diff. 2.75 .80
Nos. 436-441 (6) 5.20 2.10

Nos. 436-441 exist imperf.

A135

Raphael, 500th Birth Anniv. — A136

Paintings (details) by Raphael: 50c, St. Catherine of Alexandra, Natl. Gallery, London. 1k, Adoration of the Kings (spectators), Vatican. 2k, Granduca Madonna, Pitti Gallery, Florence. 3k, St. George and the Dragon, The Louvre, Paris. 4k, Vision of Ezekiel, Pitti Gallery. No. 447, Adoration of the Kings (Holy Family), Vatican. No. 448, Coronation of the Virgin, Vatican.

1983, Mar. 9 *Perf. 12½x13*

Without Gum

442 A135 50c multicolored .30 .25
443 A135 1k multicolored .30 .25
444 A135 2k multicolored .35 .25
445 A135 3k multicolored .60 .25
446 A135 4k multicolored .75 .30
447 A135 10k multicolored 2.50 .80
Nos. 442-447 (6) 4.80 2.10

Souvenir Sheet

Perf. 13x13½

448 A136 10k multicolored 2.50 1.50

INTERCOSMOS Space Cooperation Program — A137

Cosmonaut and flags of USSR and participating nations.

1983, Apr. 12 *Perf. 12½*

449 A137 50c Czechoslovakia .30 .25
450 A137 50c Poland .30 .25
451 A137 1k East Germany .30 .25
452 A137 1k Bulgaria .30 .25
453 A137 2k Hungary .40 .25
454 A137 3k Mongolia .65 .25
455 A137 4k Romania .80 .25
456 A137 6k Cuba 1.25 .40
457 A137 10k France 2.25 .80
Nos. 449-457 (9) 6.55 2.95

Souvenir Sheet

Perf. 13½x13

458 A137 10k Vietnam 2.75 1.50

No. 458 contains one stamp 32x40mm. Date of issue: 7/24/83.

A138

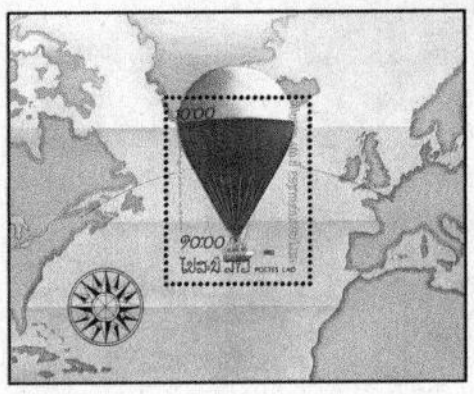

First Manned Balloon Flight, Bicent. A139

Various balloons.

1983, May 4 *Perf. 12½x13*

459 A138 50c shown .30 .25
460 A138 1k multi, diff. .30 .25
461 A138 2k multi, diff. .35 .25
462 A138 3k multi, diff. .50 .25
463 A138 4k multi, diff. .65 .40
464 A138 10k multi, diff. 2.25 .80
Nos. 459-464 (6) 4.35 2.20

Souvenir Sheet

Perf. 13½x13

465 A139 10k shown 2.40 1.50

Nos. 459-464 exist imperf.

Souvenir Sheet

TEMBAL '83, Basel A140

10k, German Maybach.

1983, May 21 *Perf. 13x13½*

Without Gum

466 A140 10k multi 3.00 1.60

No. 466 exists imperf.

Flora — A141

1k, Dendrobium sp. 2k, Aerides odoratum. 3k, Dendrobium aggregatum. 4k, Dendrobium. 5k, Moschatum. 6k, Dendrobium sp., diff.

1983, June 10 *Perf. 13*

Without Gum

467 A141 1k multicolored .30 .25
468 A141 2k multicolored .40 .25
469 A141 3k multicolored .60 .25
470 A141 4k multicolored .75 .25
471 A141 5k multicolored 1.10 .30
472 A141 6k multicolored 1.40 .50
Nos. 467-472 (6) 4.55 1.80

Nos. 467-472 exist imperf.

1984 Winter Olympics, Sarajevo A142

1983, July 2 **Without Gum**

473 A142 50c Downhill skiing .30 .25
474 A142 1k Slalom .30 .25
475 A142 2k Ice hockey .40 .25
476 A142 3k Speed skating .70 .25
477 A142 4k Ski jumping .85 .30
478 A142 10k Luge 2.25 .80
Nos. 473-478 (6) 4.80 2.10

Souvenir Sheet

Perf. 13x13½

479 A142 15k 2-Man bobsled 3.50 1.50

No. 479 contains one 40x32mm stamp. Nos. 473-478 exist imperf.

Souvenir Sheet

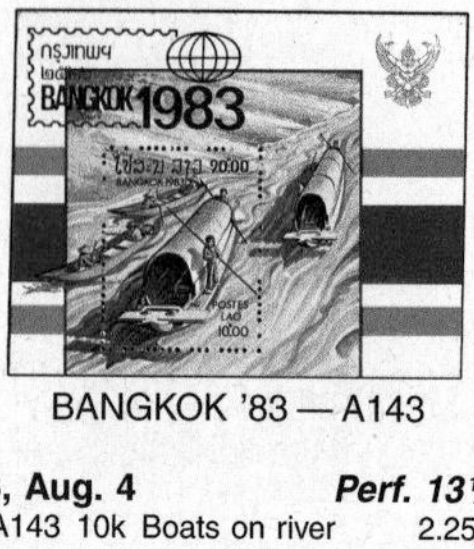

BANGKOK '83 — A143

1983, Aug. 4 *Perf. 13½x13*

480 A143 10k Boats on river 2.25 1.50

No. 480 exists imperf. Value, $60.

Mekong River Fish — A144

1k, Notopterus chitala. 2k, Cyprinus carpio. 3k, Pangasius sp. 4k, Catlocarpio siamensis. 5k, Morulius sp. 6k, Tilapia nilotica.

1983, Sept. 5 *Perf. 12½*

Without Gum

481 A144 1k multicolored .30 .25
482 A144 2k multicolored .40 .25
483 A144 3k multicolored .65 .25
484 A144 4k multicolored .75 .25
485 A144 5k multicolored 1.10 .30
486 A144 6k multicolored 1.50 .50
Nos. 481-486 (6) 4.70 1.80

Nos. 481-486 exist imperf.

Explorers and Their Ships A145

1k, Victoria, Magellan. 2k, Grand Hermine, Cartier. 3k, Santa Maria, Columbus. 4k, Cabral and caravel. 5k, Endeavor, Capt. Cook. 6k, Pourquoi-Pas, Charcot.

1983, Oct. 8 *Perf. 13x12½*

Without Gum

487 A145 1k multicolored .30 .25
488 A145 2k multicolored .40 .25
489 A145 3k multicolored .65 .25
490 A145 4k multicolored .75 .25
491 A145 5k multicolored 1.10 .30
492 A145 6k multicolored 1.50 .50
Nos. 487-492 (6) 4.70 1.80

No. 492 incorrectly inscribed "CABOT."

Domestic Cats — A146

1983, Nov. 9 *Perf. 12½x13*

Without Gum

493 A146 1k Tabby .30 .25
494 A146 2k Long-haired Persian .60 .25
495 A146 3k Siamese .75 .25
496 A146 4k Burmese .85 .25
497 A146 5k Persian 1.25 .30
498 A146 6k Tortoiseshell 1.75 .50
Nos. 493-498 (6) 5.50 1.80

Nos. 493-498 exist imperf.

Karl Marx (1818-1883) A147

4k, Marx, 3 flags, diff., vert. 6k, Marx, flag of Laos.

1983, Nov. 30 *Perf. 13*

Without Gum

499 A147 1k shown .30 .25
500 A147 4k multi 1.00 .25
501 A147 6k multi 1.60 .55
Nos. 499-501 (3) 2.90 1.05

8th Anniv. of the Republic A148

1k, Elephant dragging log, vert. 4k, Oxen, pig. 6k, Produce, vert.

1983, Dec. 2 *Perf. 12½x13, 13x12½*

Without Gum

502 A148 1k multicolored .30 .25
503 A148 4k multicolored 1.00 .25
504 A148 6k multicolored 1.60 .55
Nos. 502-504 (3) 2.90 1.05

Nos. 502-504 exist imperf.

World Communications Year — A149

50c, Teletype. 1k, Telephone. 4k, Television. 6k, Satellite, dish receiver.

1983, Dec. 15 *Perf. 13*

505 A149 50c multicolored .30 .25
506 A149 1k multicolored .30 .25
507 A149 4k multicolored .65 .30
508 A149 6k multicolored 1.00 .55
Nos. 505-508 (4) 2.25 1.35

Nos. 275, 306 Overprinted in Red

1983 Method and Perf. As Before

508B A105 5k multi *450.00* —
508C A96 10k lilac & multi *575.00* —

1984 Winter Olympics, Sarajevo A150

50c, Women's figure skating. 1k, Speed skating. 2k, Biathlon. 4k, Luge. 5k, Downhill skiing. 6k, Ski jumping. 7k, Slalom.
10k, Ice hockey.

1984, Jan. 16

509 A150 50c multicolored .30 .25
510 A150 1k multicolored .30 .25
511 A150 2k multicolored .40 .25
512 A150 4k multicolored .80 .30
513 A150 5k multicolored 1.00 .30
514 A150 6k multicolored 1.25 .50
515 A150 7k multicolored 1.50 .55
Nos. 509-515 (7) 5.55 2.40

Souvenir Sheet

Perf. 13½x13

516 A150 10k multicolored 2.25 1.50

Nos. 509-511, 514-515 vert. No. 516 contains one stamp 32x40mm.

World Wildlife Fund — A151

Panthera tigris.

1984, Feb. 1 *Perf. 13*

517 A151 25c Adult, vert. *.50* .25
518 A151 25c shown *.50* .25
519 A151 3k Nursing cubs *5.00* 1.25
520 A151 4k Two cubs, vert. *8.00* 1.75
Nos. 517-520 (4) *14.00* 3.50

1984 Summer Olympics, Los Angeles — A152

Gold medals awarded during previous games, and athletes. 50c, Athens 1896, women's diving. 1k, Paris 1900, women's volleyball. 2k, St. Louis 1904, running. 4k, London 1908, basketball. 5k, Stockholm 1912, judo. 6k, Antwerp 1920, soccer. 7k, Paris 1924, gymnastics. 10k, Moscow 1980, wrestling.

1984, Mar 26

521 A152 50c multicolored .30 .25
522 A152 1k multicolored .30 .25
523 A152 2k multicolored .60 .25
524 A152 4k multicolored 1.10 .25
525 A152 5k multicolored 1.25 .30
526 A152 6k multicolored 1.60 .40
527 A152 7k multicolored 1.90 .50
Nos. 521-527 (7) 7.05 2.20

Souvenir Sheet

Perf. 12½

528 A152 10k multicolored 2.75 1.50

No. 528 contains one stamp 32x40mm.

Musical Instruments A153

1984, Mar. 27 *Perf. 13*

529 A153 1k Tuned drums .30 .25
530 A153 2k Xylophone .40 .25
531 A153 3k Pair of drums .65 .25
532 A153 4k Hand drum .90 .30
533 A153 5k Barrel drum 1.10 .30
534 A153 6k Pipes, string instrument 1.25 .50
Nos. 529-534 (6) 4.60 1.85

Natl. Day — A154

1984, Mar. 30 *Perf. 12½*

535 A154 60c Natl. flag .35 .25
536 A154 1k Natl. arms .50 .25
537 A154 2k like 1k .75 .25
Nos. 535-537 (3) 1.60 .75

For surcharges, see Nos. 1884-1886, 1899-1901.

Chess — A155

Illustrations of various medieval and Renaissance chess games.
10k, Royal game, human chessmen.

1984, Apr. 14 *Perf. 12½x13*

538 A155 50c multi .30 .25
539 A155 1k multi, diff. .30 .25
540 A155 2k multi, red brn board, diff. .50 .25
541 A155 2k multi, blk board, diff. .50 .25
542 A155 3k multi, diff. .70 .30
543 A155 4k multi, diff. 1.25 .30
544 A155 8k multi, diff. 2.25 .50
a. Souv. sheet of 6, #538-540, 542-544, with gutter between — —
Nos. 538-544 (7) 5.80 2.10

Souvenir Sheet

Perf. 13½x13

545 A155 10k multi 3.25 2.50

World Chess Federation, 60th anniv. No. 545 contains one stamp 32x40mm.

ESPANA '84, Madrid — A156

Paintings: 50c, Cardinal Nino de Guevara, by El Greco. 1k, Gaspar de Guzman, Duke of

Olivares, on Horseback, byVelazquez. No. 548, The Annunciation, by Murillo. No. 549, Portrait of a Lady, by Francisco de Zurburan (1598-1664). 3k, The Family of Charles IV, by Goya. 4k, Two Harlequins, by Picasso. 8k, Abstract, by Miro. 10k, Burial of the Count of Orgaz, by El Greco.

1984, Apr. 27 *Perf. 12½*

546	A156	50c multicolored	.30	.25
547	A156	1k multicolored	.30	.25
548	A156	2k multicolored	.45	.25
549	A156	2k multicolored	.45	.25
550	A156	3k multicolored	.65	.30
551	A156	4k multicolored	.90	.30
552	A156	8k multicolored	1.75	.50
		Nos. 546-552 (7)	4.80	2.10

Souvenir Sheet

Perf. 13½x13

553	A156	10k multicolored	4.75	2.50

No. 553 contains one stamp 32x40mm and also exists imperf.

Woodland Flowers — A157

50c, Adonis aestivalis. 1k, Alpinia speciosa. No. 556, 2k, Aeschynanthus speciosus. No. 557, 2k, Cassia lechenaultiana. 3k, Datura meteloides. 4k, Quamoclit pennata. 8k, Commelina benghalensis.

1984, May 11 *Perf. 13*

554	A157	50c multicolored	.30	.25
555	A157	1k multicolored	.30	.25
556	A157	2k multicolored	.45	.25
557	A157	2k multicolored	.45	.25
558	A157	3k multicolored	.65	.30
559	A157	4k multicolored	.90	.30
560	A157	8k multicolored	1.75	.50
		Nos. 554-560 (7)	4.80	2.10

Nos. 554-560 exist imperf.

A158

19th UPU Congress, Hamburg — A159

Classic sport and race cars.

1984, June 19

561	A158	50c Nazzaro	.30	.25
562	A158	1k Daimler	.30	.25
563	A158	2k Delage	.35	.25
564	A158	2k Fiat S 57/14B	.35	.25
565	A158	3k Bugatti	.50	.30
566	A158	4k Itala	.65	.30
567	A158	8k Blitzen Benz	1.40	.50
		Nos. 561-567 (7)	3.85	2.10

Souvenir Sheet

Perf. 12½

568	A159	10k Winton Bullet	1.90	1.25

Paintings by Correggio (1494-1534) — A160

Designs: 50c, Madonna and Child (Holy Family). 1k, Madonna and Child (spectators). No. 571, Madonna and Child (Holy Family, diff.). No. 572, Mystical Marriage of St. Catherine (Catherine, child, two women). 3k, The Four Saints. 4k, Noli Me Tangere. 8k, Christ Bids Farewell to the Virgin Mary. 10k, Madonna and Child, diff.

1984, June 26 *Perf. 13*

569	A160	50c multicolored	.30	.25
570	A160	1k multicolored	.30	.25
571	A160	2k multicolored	.45	.25
572	A160	2k multicolored	.45	.25
573	A160	3k multicolored	.65	.30
574	A160	4k multicolored	.75	.30
575	A160	8k multicolored	1.40	.50
		Nos. 569-575 (7)	4.30	2.10

Souvenir Sheet

Perf. 13½x13

576	A160	10k multicolored	3.25	1.75

No. 576 contains one stamp 32x40mm, and exists imperforate.

Space Exploration — A161

No. 577, Luna 1. No. 578, Luna 2. No. 579, Luna 3. No. 580, Sputnik 2, Kepler, horiz. No. 581, Lunokhod 2, Newton, horiz. No. 582, Luna 13, Jules Verne, horiz. No. 583, Space station, Copernicus, horiz.

1984, July 12 *Perf. 13*

577	A161	50c multicolored	.30	.25
578	A161	1k multicolored	.30	.25
579	A161	2k multicolored	.35	.25
580	A161	2k multicolored	.35	.25
581	A161	3k multicolored	.75	.25
582	A161	4k multicolored	1.00	.40
583	A161	8k multicolored	1.75	.65
		Nos. 577-583 (7)	4.80	2.30

Reptiles A162

No. 584, Malaclemys terrapin. No. 585, Bungarus fasciatus. No. 586, Python reticulatus. No. 587, Python molurus, vert. No. 588, Gekko gecko. No. 589, Natrix subminiata. No. 590, Eublepharis macularius.

1984, Aug. 20

584	A162	50c multicolored	.30	.25
585	A162	1k multicolored	.30	.25
586	A162	2k multicolored	.40	.25
587	A162	2k multicolored	.40	.25
588	A162	3k multicolored	.75	.25
589	A162	4k multicolored	1.00	.40
590	A162	8k multicolored	1.90	.65
		Nos. 584-590 (7)	5.05	2.30

Marsupials A163

No. 591, Schoinobates volans. No. 592, Ornithorhynchus anatinus. No. 593, Sarcophilus harrisii. No. 594, Lasiorhinus latifrons. No. 595, Thylacinus cynocephalus. No. 596, Dasyurops maculatus. No. 597, Wallabia isabelinus.

10k, Macropus rufus.

1984, Sept. 21

591	A163	50c multicolored	.30	.25
592	A163	1k multicolored	.30	.25
593	A163	2k multicolored	.40	.25
594	A163	2k multicolored	.40	.25
595	A163	3k multicolored	.75	.25
596	A163	4k multicolored	1.00	.40
597	A163	8k multicolored	1.90	.65
		Nos. 591-597 (7)	5.05	2.30

Souvenir Sheet

Perf. 12½

598	A163	10k multicolored	2.75	1.50

AUSIPEX '84, Melbourne. No. 598 contains one stamp 32x40mm and also exists imperf.

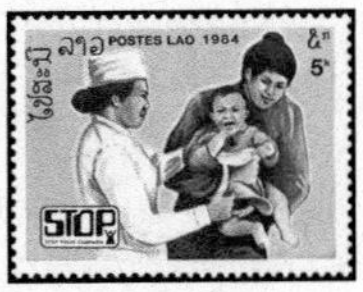

Stop Polio Campaign A164

1984, Sept. 29 *Perf. 13*

599	A164	5k shown	1.10	.55
600	A164	6k Vaccinating child	1.20	.55

Art — A165

No. 601, Dragon (hand rail). No. 602, Capital. No. 603, Oval panel. No. 604, Deity. No. 605, Leaves. No. 606, Floral pattern. No. 607, Lotus flower (round panel).

1984, Oct. 26

601	A165	50c multicolored	.30	.25
602	A165	1k multicolored	.30	.25
603	A165	2k multicolored	.40	.25
604	A165	2k multicolored	.40	.25
605	A165	3k multicolored	.80	.25
606	A165	4k multicolored	1.25	.40
607	A165	8k multicolored	2.50	.65
		Nos. 601-607 (7)	5.95	2.30

Nos. 601-604 and 607 vert.

9th Anniv. of the Republic A166

1k, River boats. 2k, Aircraft. 4k, Bridge building. 10k, Surveying, construction.

1984, Dec. 17

608	A166	1k multicolored	.50	.25
609	A166	2k multicolored	.70	.25
610	A166	4k multicolored	1.20	.65
611	A166	10k multicolored	2.50	.95
		Nos. 608-611 (4)	4.90	2.10

1986 World Cup Soccer Championships, Mexico — A167

Various match scenes and flag of Mexico.

1985, Jan. 18

612	A167	50c multicolored	.30	.25
613	A167	1k multi, diff.	.30	.25
614	A167	2k multi, diff.	.50	.25
615	A167	3k multi, diff.	.65	.25
616	A167	4k multi, diff.	.85	.30
617	A167	5k multi, diff.	1.10	.40
618	A167	6k multi, diff.	1.40	.65
		Nos. 612-618 (7)	5.10	2.35

Souvenir Sheet

Perf. 12½

619	A167	10k multi, diff.	2.25	1.50

No. 619 contains one stamp 32x40mm. Nos. 612-618 exist imperf.

Motorcycle, Cent. — A168

1k, 1920 Gnome Rhone. 2k, 1928 F.N. M67C. 3k, 1930 Indian Chief. 4k, 1914 Rudge Multi. 5k, 1953 Honda Benly J. 6k, 1938 CZ.

1985, Feb. 25 *Perf. 12½*

620	A168	50c shown	.30	.25
621	A168	1k multicolored	.30	.25
622	A168	2k multicolored	.40	.25
623	A168	3k multicolored	.60	.25
624	A168	4k multicolored	.80	.30
625	A168	5k multicolored	1.10	.40
626	A168	6k multicolored	1.25	.65
		Nos. 620-626 (7)	4.75	2.35

Nos. 620-626 exist imperf.

Mushrooms — A169

No. 627, Amanita muscaria. No. 628, Boletus edulis. No. 629, Coprinus comatus. No. 630, Amanita rubescens. No. 631, Xerocomus subtomentosus. No. 632, Lepiota procera. No. 633, Paxillus involutus.

1985, Apr. 8 *Perf. 13*

627	A169	50c multicolored	.30	.25
628	A169	1k multicolored	.30	.25
629	A169	2k multicolored	.50	.25
630	A169	2k multicolored	.50	.25
631	A169	3k multicolored	.75	.30
632	A169	4k multicolored	1.00	.40
633	A169	8k multicolored	2.00	.60
		Nos. 627-633 (7)	5.35	2.30

Nos. 627-633 exist imperf.

End of World War II, 40th Anniv. — A169a

1k, Battle of Kursk. 2k, Red Army parade, Moscow. 4k, Battle of Stalingrad. 5k, Battle for Berlin. 6k, Victory parade through Brandenburg Gate.

1985, May **Litho.** *Perf. 12½x12*

633A	A169a	1k multicolored	1.40	.25
633B	A169a	2k multicolored	2.50	.25
633C	A169a	4k multicolored	4.00	.40
633D	A169a	5k multicolored	5.00	.50
633E	A169a	6k multicolored	5.50	.55
		Nos. 633A-633E (5)	18.40	1.95

Lenin, 115th Birth Anniv. — A170

1k, Reading Pravda, horiz. 10k, Addressing revolutionaries.

1985, June 28 *Perf. 12½*

634	A170	1k multicolored	.35	.25
635	A170	2k shown	2.00	.30
636	A170	10k multicolored	2.00	.30
		Nos. 634-636 (3)	4.35	.85

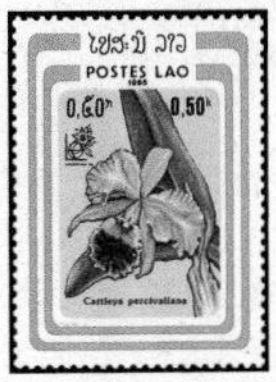

Orchids — A171

50c, Cattleya percivaliana. 1k, Odontoglossum luteo-purpureum. No. 639, Cattleya luedemanniana. No. 640, Maxillaria sanderiana. 3k, Miltonia vexillaria. 4k, Oncidium varicosum. 8k, Cattleya dowiana aurea.

10k, Catasetum fimbriatum.

1985, July 5 *Perf. 13*

637	A171	50c multicolored	.30	.25
638	A171	1k multicolored	.30	.25
639	A171	2k multicolored	.45	.25
640	A171	2k multicolored	.45	.25
641	A171	3k multicolored	.70	.25
642	A171	4k multicolored	1.00	.30
643	A171	8k multicolored	2.25	.65
		Nos. 637-643 (7)	5.45	2.20

Souvenir Sheet

Perf. 13½x13

644	A171	10k multicolored	2.75	1.50

ARGENTINA '85, Buenos Aires. No. 644 contains one stamp 32x40mm.

Fauna — A172

2k, Macaca mulatta. 3k, Bos sauveli. 4k, Hystrix leucura, horiz. 5k, Selenarctos thibotanus, horiz. 10k, Manis pentadactyla.

1985, Aug. 15 *Perf. 13*

645	A172	2k multicolored	.35	.25
646	A172	3k multicolored	.55	.25
647	A172	4k multicolored	.80	.30
648	A172	5k multicolored	1.00	.30
649	A172	10k multicolored	2.00	.65
		Nos. 645-649 (5)	4.70	1.75

Nos. 645-49 exist imperf.

Apollo-Soyuz Flight, 10th Anniv. — A173

50c, Apollo launch pad, vert. 1k, Soyuz launch pad, vert. No. 652, Apollo approaching Soyuz. No. 653, Soyuz approaching Apollo. 3k, Apollo, astronauts. 4k, Soyuz, cosmonauts. 8k, Docked spacecrafts.

1985, Sept. 6

650	A173	50c multicolored	.30	.25
651	A173	1k multicolored	.30	.25
652	A173	2k multicolored	.40	.25
653	A173	2k multicolored	.65	.25
654	A173	3k multicolored	.80	.25
655	A173	4k multicolored	1.00	.30
656	A173	8k multicolored	1.60	.65
		Nos. 650-656 (7)	5.05	2.20

Nos. 650-656 exist imperf.

Aircraft — A174

1985, Oct. 25

657	A174	50c Fiat	.30	.25
658	A174	1k Cant z.501	.30	.25
659	A174	2k MF-5	.40	.25
660	A174	3k Macchi Castoldi	.65	.25
661	A174	4k Anzani	.80	.25
662	A174	5k Ambrosini	1.00	.30
663	A174	6k Piaggio	1.10	.35
		Nos. 657-663 (7)	4.55	1.90

Souvenir Sheet

Perf. 13x13½

664	A174	10k MF-4	4.50	2.40

ITALIA '85, Rome. No. 664 contains one stamp 40x32mm and also exists imperf.
Nos. 657-663 exist imperf.

Miniature Sheet

Columbus's Fleet — A175

1985, Oct. 25 *Perf. 13*

665	A175	Sheet of 5 + 4 labels	15.00	7.50
a.		1k Pinta	.50	.25
b.		2k Nina	.75	.25
c.		3k Santa Maria	1.25	.30
d.		4k Columbus	1.50	.40
e.		5k Map of 1st voyage	2.00	1.50

ITALIA '85.

UN, 40th Anniv. — A176

1985, Oct.

666	A176	2k UN and natl. flag	.55	.25
667	A176	3k Coats of arms	.80	.30
668	A176	10k Map, globe	2.50	1.00
		Nos. 666-668 (3)	3.85	1.55

Health — A177

1k, Mother feeding child. 3k, Immunization, horiz. 4k, Hospital care, horiz. 10k, Breast-feeding.

1985, Nov. 15

669	A177	1k multicolored	.40	.25
670	A177	3k multicolored	.80	.25
671	A177	4k multicolored	.95	.30
672	A177	10k multicolored	2.00	.80
		Nos. 669-672 (4)	4.15	1.60

10th Anniv. of the Republic A178

1985, Dec. 2

673	A178	3k shown	.65	.25
674	A178	10k multi, diff.	2.50	1.00

People's Revolutionary Party, 30th Anniv. — A179

1985, Dec. 30

675	A179	2k shown	.95	.25
676	A179	8k multi, diff.	2.50	.65

Nos. 276, 286, 289, 291-292, 297, 299-300, 305, 308-309, 319 Overprinted in Red

Methods and Perfs As Before

1985

676A	A102	40k multi	40.00	40.00
676B	A98	50k multi	40.00	40.00
676C	A99	50k multi	100.00	100.00
676D	A107	70k multi	40.00	40.00
676E	A105	80k multi	50.00	50.00
676F	A100	100k multi	120.00	120.00
676G	A105	100k multi	50.00	50.00
676H	A96	200k org & multi	110.00	110.00
676I	A100	250k multi	150.00	150.00
676J	A101	250k vio & blk	170.00	170.00
676K	A104	250k multi	120.00	120.00
676L	A102	300k multi	120.00	120.00
		Nos. 676A-676L (12)	1,110.	1,110.

Overprint varieties exist. An inverted "8" exists in 676A. Inverted overprints exist on 676B and 676K. An overprint reading "1895" instead of "1985" exists both upright and inverted on 676B.

1986 World Cup Soccer Championships, Mexico — A180

Various match scenes.

1986, Jan. 20

677	A180	50c multicolored	.30	.25
678	A180	1k multi, diff.	.30	.25
679	A180	2k multi, diff.	.40	.25
680	A180	3k multi, diff.	.50	.25
681	A180	4k multi, diff.	.70	.25
682	A180	5k multi, diff.	.80	.30
683	A180	6k multi, diff.	1.10	.40
		Nos. 677-683 (7)	4.10	1.95

Souvenir Sheet

Perf. 13x13½

684	A180	10k multi, diff.	2.00	.90

No. 684 contains one stamp 40x32mm.

27th Congress of the Communist Party of the Soviet Union — A180a

4k, Cosmonaut, spacecraft. 20k, Lenin.

1986, Jan. Litho. *Perf. 12x12½*

684A	A180a	4k multicolored	2.50	.30
684B	A180a	20k multicolored	7.50	1.00

Flowering Plants — A181

50c, Pelargonium grandiflorum. 1k, Aquilegia vulgaris. 2k, Fuchsia globosa. 3k, Crocus aureus. 4k, Althaea rosea. 5k, Gladiolus purpureo. 6k, Hyacinthus orientalis.

1986, Feb. 28 *Perf. 13*

685	A181	50c multicolored	.30	.25
686	A181	1k multicolored	.30	.25
687	A181	2k multicolored	.45	.25
688	A181	3k multicolored	.65	.25
689	A181	4k multicolored	.80	.30
690	A181	5k multicolored	1.00	.40
691	A181	6k multicolored	1.25	.55
		Nos. 685-691 (7)	4.75	2.25

Butterflies — A182

50c, Aporia hippia. 1k, Euthalia irrubescens. 2k, Japonica lutea. 3k, Pratapa ctesia. 4k, Kallina inachus. 5k, Ixias pyrene. 6k, Parantica sita.

1986, Mar. 30

692	A182	50c multicolored	.30	.25
693	A182	1k multicolored	.30	.25
694	A182	2k multicolored	.45	.25
695	A182	3k multicolored	.65	.25
696	A182	4k multicolored	.80	.30
697	A182	5k multicolored	1.00	.40
698	A182	6k multicolored	1.25	.55
		Nos. 692-698 (7)	4.75	2.25

A183

First Man in Space, 25th Anniv. A184

Designs: 50c, Launch, Baikonur Space Center, vert. 1k, Interkosmos communications satellite, vert. 2k, Salyut space station. 3k, Yuri Gagarin, Sputnik 1 disengaging stage. 4k, Luna 3, the Moon, vert. 5k, Leonov on first space walk, vert. 6k, Luna 16 lifting off Moon, vert. 10k, Spacecrafts docking.

1986, Apr. 12

699	A183	50c multicolored	.30	.25
700	A183	1k multicolored	.30	.25
701	A183	2k multicolored	.40	.25
702	A183	3k multicolored	.65	.25
703	A183	4k multicolored	.80	.25
704	A183	5k multicolored	1.00	.40
705	A183	6k multicolored	1.10	.50
		Nos. 699-705 (7)	4.55	2.15

Souvenir Sheet

Perf. 13x13½

706	A184	10k multicolored	2.50	1.00

No. 706 exists imperf.

Fauna A185

50c, Giraffa camelopardalis. 1k, Panthera leo. 2k, Loxodonta africana africana. 3k, Macropus rufus. 4k, Gymnobelideus leadbeateri. 5k, Phoenicopterus ruber. 6k, Ailuropoda melanoleucus.
10k, Bison, vert.

1986, May 22 *Perf. 12½x13, 13x12½*

707	A185	50c multicolored	.30	.25
708	A185	1k multicolored	.30	.25
709	A185	2k multicolored	.40	.25
710	A185	3k multicolored	.70	.25
711	A185	4k multicolored	1.00	.25
712	A185	5k multicolored	1.25	.30
713	A185	6k multicolored	1.50	.55
		Nos. 707-713 (7)	5.45	2.10

Souvenir Sheet

Perf. 13½x13

714	A185	10k multicolored	3.00	1.50

Nos. 707-712 vert.
No. 714 has the Ameripex '86 stamp exhibition logo in the margin.

Pheasants — A187

50c, Argusianus argus. 1k, Cennaeus nycthemerus. 2k, Phasianus colchicus. 3k, Chrysolophus amherstiae. 4k, Symaticus reevesii. 5k, Chrysolophus pictus. 6k, Syrmaticus soemmerringii.

1986, June 29 *Perf. 12½x13*

715	A187	50c multicolored	.30	.25
716	A187	1k multicolored	.30	.25
717	A187	2k multicolored	.45	.25
718	A187	3k multicolored	.60	.25
719	A187	4k multicolored	.80	.25
720	A187	5k multicolored	1.00	.30
721	A187	6k multicolored	1.25	.40
		Nos. 715-721 (7)	4.70	1.95

Snakes A188

No. 722, Elaphe guttata. No. 723, Thalerophis richardi. No. 724, Lampropeltis doliata annulata. No. 725, Diadophis amabilis. No. 726, Boiga dendrophila. No. 727, Python molurus. No. 728, Naja naja.

1986, July 21 ***Perf. 12½x13, 13x12½***

722	A188	50c	multicolored	.30	.25
723	A188	1k	multicolored	.30	.25
724	A188	1k	multicolored	.35	.25
725	A188	2k	multicolored	.40	.25
726	A188	4k	multicolored	.70	.25
727	A188	5k	multicolored	1.00	.30
728	A188	8k	multicolored	1.25	.40
			Nos. 722-728 (7)	4.30	1.95

Nos. 722-723 and 728 vert.

Halley's Comet A189

50c, Acropolis, Athens. #730a, 1k, Bayeux Tapestry. #730b, 2k, Edmond Halley. #731a, 3k, Vega space probe. #731b, 4k, Galileo. #732a, 5k, Comet. #732b, 6k, Giotto probe.

1986, Aug. 22 ***Perf. 12½x13***

729	A189	50c	multi	.30	.25
730	A189		Pair, #a.-b.	.75	.40
731	A189		Pair, #a.-b.	1.25	.50
732	A189		Pair, #a.-b.	2.25	.70
			Nos. 729-732 (4)	4.55	1.85

Souvenir Sheet

Perf. 13x13½

733	A189	10k	Comet, diff.	2.50	1.25

Nos. 730-732 printed in continuous designs. Sizes of Nos. 730a, 731a, 732a: 46x25mm; Nos. 730b, 731b, 732b; 23x25mm. No. 733 contains one 40x32mm stamp.

Dogs — A190

50c, Keeshond. 1k, Elkhound. 2k, Bernese. 3k, Pointing griffon. 4k, Sheep dog (border collie). 5k, Irish water spaniel. 6k, Briard. 10k, Brittany spaniels.

1986, Aug. 28 ***Perf. 13***

737	A190	50c	multicolored	.30	.25
738	A190	1k	multicolored	.30	.25
739	A190	2k	multicolored	.45	.25
740	A190	3k	multicolored	.65	.25
741	A190	4k	multicolored	.85	.25
742	A190	5k	multicolored	1.00	.30
743	A190	6k	multicolored	1.25	.55
			Nos. 737-743 (7)	4.80	2.10

Souvenir Sheet

Perf. 13x13½

744	A190	10k	multicolored	2.10	1.10

STOCKHOLMIA '86. Nos. 738-743 horiz. No. 744 contains one 40x32mm stamp. Nos. 737-743 exist imprf.

Cacti — A191

Designs: 50c, Mammillaria matudae. 1k, Mammillaria theresae. 2k, Ariocarpus trigonus. 3k, Notocactus crassigibbus. 4k, Astrophytum asterias hybridum. 5k, Melocactus manzanus. 6k, Astrophytum ornatum hybridum.

1986, Sept. 28 ***Perf. 13***

745	A191	50c	multicolored	.30	.25
746	A191	1k	multicolored	.30	.25
747	A191	2k	multicolored	.40	.25
748	A191	3k	multicolored	.65	.25
749	A191	4k	multicolored	.80	.25
750	A191	5k	multicolored	1.00	.30
751	A191	6k	multicolored	1.10	.40
			Nos. 745-751 (7)	4.55	1.95

Nos. 745-751 exist imperf.

Intl. Peace Year — A192

3k, Natl, arms, dove, globe. 5k, Dove, shattered bomb. 10k, Emblem held aloft.

1986, Oct. 24

752	A192	3k	multicolored	.75	.25
753	A192	5k	multicolored	1.10	.40
754	A192	10k	multicolored	2.25	1.00
			Nos. 752-754 (3)	4.10	1.65

UNESCO Programs in Laos — A193

3k, Vat Phu Champasak ruins. 4k, Satellite dish, map, globe. 9k, Laotians learning to read, horiz.

1986, Nov. 4

755	A193	3k	multicolored	.70	.25
756	A193	4k	multicolored	1.00	.30
757	A193	9k	multicolored	1.75	.65
			Nos. 755-757 (3)	3.45	1.20

1988 Winter Olympics, Calgary A194

1987, Jan. 14

758	A194	50c	Speed skating	.30	.25
759	A194	1k	Biathlon	.30	.25
760	A194	2k	Pairs figure skating	.40	.25
761	A194	3k	Luge	.60	.25
762	A194	4k	4-Man bobsled	.75	.25
763	A194	5k	Ice hockey	1.00	.30
764	A194	6k	Ski jumping	1.10	.40
			Nos. 758-764 (7)	4.45	1.95

Souvenir Sheet

Perf. 13½x13

765	A194	10k	Slalom	2.25	1.10

Nos. 758-760 vert. No. 765 contains one stamp 32x40mm.

1988 Summer Olympics, Seoul A195

50c, Women's gymnastics. 1k, Women's discus. 2k, Running. 3k, Equestrian. 4k, Women's javelin. 5k, High jump. 6k, Wrestling. 10k, Runners leaving start.

1987, Feb. 2 ***Perf. 12½x13, 13x13½***

766	A195	50c	multicolored	.30	.25
767	A195	1k	multicolored	.30	.25
768	A195	2k	multicolored	.40	.25
769	A195	3k	multicolored	.65	.25
770	A195	4k	multicolored	.75	.25
771	A195	5k	multicolored	1.00	.30
772	A195	6k	multicolored	1.10	.40
			Nos. 766-772 (7)	4.50	1.95

Souvenir Sheet

Perf. 12½

773	A195	10k	multicolored	2.00	1.00

Nos. 766, 768, 770 and 772 vert. No. 773 contains one 40x32mm stamp.
Nos. 766-772 exist imperf.

Dogs — A196

50c, Great Dane. 1k, Labrador retriever. 2k, St. Bernard. 3k, Schippercke. 4k, Alsatian (German shepherd). 5k, Beagle. 6k, Spaniel.

1987, Mar. 5 ***Perf. 12½x13***

774	A196	50c	multicolored	.30	.25
775	A196	1k	multicolored	.30	.25
776	A196	2k	multicolored	.40	.25
777	A196	3k	multicolored	.65	.25
778	A196	4k	multicolored	.75	.25
779	A196	5k	multicolored	1.00	.30
780	A196	6k	multicolored	1.25	.55
			Nos. 774-780 (7)	4.65	2.10

Space Flight, 30th Anniv. — A197

1987, Apr. 12 ***Perf. 13***

781	A197	50c	Sputnik 1	.30	.25
782	A197	1k	Sputnik 2	.30	.25
783	A197	2k	Cosmos 87	.40	.25
784	A197	3k	Cosmos	.50	.25
785	A197	4k	Mars	.65	.25
786	A197	5k	Luna 1	.80	.30
787	A197	9k	Luna 3, vert.	1.25	.50
			Nos. 781-787 (7)	4.20	2.05

Packet Ships and Stampless Packet Letters — A198

Canada No. 282 A199

50c, "Montreal". 1k, "Paid Montreal". 2k, "Paid" and "Montreal Nov 24". 3k, "Williamsbvrg" and "Forwarded". 4k, "Montreal Fe 18 1844". 5k, "Paid" and "Montreal Jy 10 1848". 6k, "Paid" and "Montreal Paid Ap 16 1861 Canada".

1987, May 12

788	A198	50c	multicolored	.30	.25
789	A198	1k	multicolored	.30	.25
790	A198	2k	multicolored	.35	.25
791	A198	3k	multicolored	.55	.25
792	A198	4k	multicolored	.75	.25
793	A198	5k	multicolored	.85	.30
794	A198	6k	multicolored	1.10	.40
			Nos. 788-794 (7)	4.20	1.95

Souvenir Sheet

Perf. 12½

795	A199	10k	multicolored	2.50	1.25

CAPEX '87.

Orchids — A200

3k, Vanda teres. 7k, Laeliocattleya. 10k, Paphiopedilum hibrido. 39k, Sobralia. 44k, Paphiopedilum hibrido, diff. 47k, Paphiopedilum hibrido, diff. 50k, Cattleya trianaei. 95k, Vanda tricolor.

1987, Aug. 10 **Litho.** ***Perf. 13***

796	A200	3k	multicolored	.30	.25
796A	A200	7k	multicolored	.30	.25
796B	A200	10k	multicolored	.40	.25
796C	A200	39k	multicolored	.75	.25
796D	A200	44k	multicolored	.80	.30
796E	A200	47k	multicolored	1.00	.40
796F	A200	50k	multicolored	1.10	.40
			Nos. 796-796F (7)	4.65	2.10

Souvenir Sheet

Perf. 12½

796G	A200	95k	multicolored	2.25	1.10

No. 796G contains one 32x40mm stamp.
Nos. 796, 796A-796G exist imperf.

Automobiles A201

1987, July 2 **Litho.** ***Perf. 12½***

797	A201	50c	Toyota 480	.30	.25
798	A201	1k	Alfa 33	.30	.25
799	A201	2k	Ford Fiesta	.40	.25
800	A201	3k	Datsun	.65	.25
801	A201	4k	Vauxhall Cavalier	.80	.25
802	A201	5k	Renault 5	1.00	.30
803	A201	6k	Rover-800	1.25	.55
			Nos. 797-803 (7)	4.70	2.10

Miniature Sheet

Perf. 13

804	A201	10k	Talbot	2.10	1.00

HAFNIA '87, Denmark A202

Various Indian elephants.

1987, Sept. 2 ***Perf. 13***

805	A202	50c	Adult, calf	.30	.25
806	A202	1k	Two adults, calf	.30	.25
807	A202	2k	Adult eating grass	.40	.25
808	A202	3k	Adult, diff.	.60	.25
809	A202	4k	Adult, calf drinking	.75	.25
810	A202	5k	Adult, diff.	.90	.30
811	A202	6k	Adult, vert.	1.10	.40
			Nos. 805-811 (7)	4.35	1.95

Souvenir Sheet

812	A202	10k	Herd, diff.	2.25	1.10

No. 812 contains one stamp 40x32mm.

Horses A203

Perf. 13x12½, 12½x13

1987, June 3 **Litho.**

813	A203	50c	multicolored	.30	.25
814	A203	1k	multi, diff.	.30	.25
815	A203	2k	multi, diff.	.40	.25
816	A203	3k	multi, diff.	.60	.25
817	A203	4k	multi, diff.	.75	.25
818	A203	5k	multi, diff.	1.00	.30
819	A203	6k	multi, diff.	1.10	.40
			Nos. 813-819 (7)	4.45	1.95

Nos. 814-819 vert.

Fish — A204

Designs: 3k, Botia macracantha. 7k, Oxymocanthus longirostris. 10k, Adioryx caudimaculatus. 39k, Synchiropus splendidus. 44k, Cephalopolis miniatus. 47k, Dendrochirus zebra. 50k, Pomacantus semicirculatus.

1987, Oct. 14 **Litho.** ***Perf. 13x12½***

820	A204	3k	multicolored	.30	.25
821	A204	7k	multicolored	.30	.25
822	A204	10k	multicolored	.40	.25
823	A204	39k	multicolored	.70	.25
824	A204	44k	multicolored	.80	.30

825 A204 47k multicolored 1.00 .40
826 A204 50k multicolored 1.10 .40
Nos. 820-826 (7) 4.60 2.10

World Food Day — A205

1k, Tending crops. 3k, Harvesting corn, vert. 5k, Harvesting wheat. 63k, Youths, fish, vert. 142k, Tending pigs, chickens.

1987, Oct. 16 ***Perf. 13***
827 A205 1k multicolored .30 .25
828 A205 3k multicolored .30 .25
829 A205 5k multicolored .30 .25
830 A205 63k multicolored 1.25 .50
831 A205 142k multicolored 2.40 1.00
Nos. 827-831 (5) 4.55 2.25

Cultivation of Rice in Mountainous Regions A206

1987, Nov. 9 ***Perf. 13***
832 A206 64k Tilling soil 1.25 .30
833 A206 100k Rice paddy 1.90 .80

October Revolution, Russia, 70th Anniv. — A207

Paintings: 1k, Wounded soldier on battlefield. 2k, Mother and child. 4k, Storming the Winter Palace. 8k, Lenin and revolutionaries. 10k, Rebuilding Red Square.

1987, Nov. ***Perf. 12x12½***
834 A207 1k multicolored .30 .25
835 A207 2k multicolored .40 .25
836 A207 4k multicolored .70 .25
837 A207 8k multicolored 1.25 .50
838 A207 10k multicolored 1.75 .65
Nos. 834-838 (5) 4.40 1.90

For surcharges, see Nos. 1882-1883.

Women Wearing Regional Costumes — A208

1987, Dec. 2
839 A208 7k Mountain .30 .25
840 A208 38k Urban .80 .25
841 A208 144k Mountain, diff. 2.75 1.10
Nos. 839-841 (3) 3.85 1.60

Nos. 839-841 exist imperf.

A209

1988 Winter Olympics, Calgary — A210

1988, Jan.10 ***Perf. 13x12½***
842 A209 1k Bobsled .30 .25
843 A209 4k Biathlon .30 .25
844 A209 20k Skiing .45 .25
845 A209 42k Ice hockey .75 .30
846 A209 63k Speed skating 1.10 .50
847 A209 70k Slalom 1.25 .55
Nos. 842-847 (6) 4.15 2.10

Souvenir Sheet
Perf. 13

848 A210 95k Slalom, diff. 2.25 1.10

No. 848 contains one stamp 40x32mm.

ESSEN '88 — A211

Locomotives: 6k, Sans Pareil, vert. 15k, Rocket, vert. 20k, Royal George. 25k, Trevithick. 30k, Novelty. 100k, Tom Thumb. 95k, Locomotion.

1988 ***Perf. 12½x13, 13x12½***
849 A211 6k multicolored .30 .25
850 A211 15k multicolored .30 .25
851 A211 20k multicolored .45 .25
852 A211 25k multicolored .55 .25
853 A211 30k multicolored .65 .25
854 A211 100k multicolored 1.90 .80
Nos. 849-854 (6) 4.15 2.05

Souvenir Sheet
Perf. 13

855 A211 95k multicolored 2.25 1.10

No. 855 contains one stamp 40x32mm. Nos. 849-854 exist imperf.

Intl. Year of Shelter for the Homeless A212

1k, Building frame of house. 27k, Cutting lumber. 46k, Completed house. 70k, Community.

1988 **Litho.** ***Perf. 13***
856 A212 1k multicolored .30 .25
857 A212 27k multicolored .55 .25
858 A212 46k multicolored 1.00 .30
859 A212 70k multicolored 1.60 .65
Nos. 856-859 (4) 3.45 1.45

Dinosaurs A213

3k, Tyrannosaurus. 7k, Ceratosaurus nasicornis, vert. 39k, Iguanodon bernissartensis, vert. 44k, Scolosaurus, vert. 47k, Phororhacus, vert. 50k, Trachodon.
95k, Pteranodon.

Perf. 13x12½, 12½x13
1988, Mar. 3 **Litho.**
860 A213 3k multicolored .30 .25
861 A213 7k multicolored .30 .25
862 A213 39k multicolored .75 .25
863 A213 44k multicolored .80 .40
864 A213 47k multicolored 1.00 .40
865 A213 50k multicolored 1.10 .40
Nos. 860-865 (6) 4.25 1.95

Souvenir Sheet
Perf. 12½

866 A213 95k multicolored 2.25 1.10

JUVALUX '88. Nos. 861-864 vert.
Identifications on Nos. 860 and No. 865 are switched.
No. 866 contains one 40x32mm stamp.

WHO, 40th Anniv. — A214

5k, Students, teacher. 27k, Pest control. 164k, Public water supply, vert.

1988, Apr. 8 ***Perf. 12½***
867 A214 5k multicolored .30 .25
868 A214 27k multicolored .50 .25
869 A214 164k multicolored 3.00 1.25
Nos. 867-869 (3) 3.80 1.75

Flowers — A215

8k, Plumieria rubra. 9k, Althaea rosea. 15k, Ixora coccinea. 33k, Cassia fistula. 64k, Dahlia coccinea (pink). 69k, Dahlia coccinea (yellow).
95k, Plumieria, Althaea, Ixora.

1988 ***Perf. 13x12½***
870 A215 8k multicolored .30 .25
871 A215 9k multicolored .30 .25
872 A215 15k multicolored .40 .25
873 A215 33k multicolored .75 .25
874 A215 64k multicolored 1.25 .50
875 A215 69k multicolored 1.50 .55
Nos. 870-875 (6) 4.50 2.05

Souvenir Sheet
Perf. 13

876 A215 95k multicolored 2.50 1.25

FINLANDIA '88. No. 876 contains one 32x40mm stamp.

Birds — A216

6k, Pelargopsis capensis. 10k, Coturnix japonica. 13k, Psittacula roseata. 44k, Treron bicincta. 63k, Pycnonotus melanicterus. 64k, Ducula badia.

1988 ***Perf. 13***
877 A216 6k multicolored .30 .25
878 A216 10k multicolored .30 .25
879 A216 13k multicolored .40 .25
880 A216 44k multicolored .85 .25
881 A216 63k multicolored 1.10 .50
882 A216 64k multicolored 1.10 .55
Nos. 877-882 (6) 4.05 2.05

1988 Summer Olympics, Seoul — A217

2k, Javelin. 5k, Long jump. 10k, Horizontal bar. 12k, Canoeing. 38k, Balance beam. 46k, Fencing. 100k, Wrestling.
95k, Horizontal bar, diff.

1988 ***Perf. 12½x12***
883 A217 2k multicolored .30 .25
884 A217 5k multicolored .30 .25
885 A217 10k multicolored .40 .25
886 A217 12k multicolored .50 .25
887 A217 38k multicolored .80 .25
888 A217 46k multicolored 1.00 .30
889 A217 100k multicolored 2.00 .70
Nos. 883-889 (7) 5.30 2.25

Souvenir Sheet
Perf. 13

889A A217 95k multicolored 2.10 1.00

No. 889A contains one 40x32mm stamp.
Nos. 883-889 exist imperf.

Decorative Stencils — A218

1k, Scarf. 2k, Pagoda entrance, vert. 3k, Pagoda wall, vert. 25k, Pagoda pillar. 163k, Skirt.

1988 ***Perf. 13***
890 A218 1k multicolored .30 .25
891 A218 2k multicolored .30 .25
892 A218 3k multicolored .35 .25
893 A218 25k multicolored .50 .25
894 A218 163k multicolored 3.00 1.50
Nos. 890-894 (5) 4.45 2.50

Completion of the 5-Year Plan (1981-85) A219

20k, Health care. 40k, Literacy. 50k, Irrigation. 100k, Communication, transport.

1988 **Litho.** ***Perf. 13***
895 A219 20k multicolored .40 .25
896 A219 40k multicolored .80 .40
897 A219 50k multicolored 1.00 .55
898 A219 100k multicolored 1.75 1.00
Nos. 895-898 (4) 3.95 2.20

Intl. Red Cross and Red Crescent Organizations, 125th Annivs. — A220

Designs: 4k, Dove, 3 stylized figures representing mankind, vert. 52k, Giving aid to the handicapped, vert. 144k, Child immunization.

1988
899 A220 4k multi .30 .25
900 A220 52k multi 1.10 .55
901 A220 144k multi 2.75 1.50
Nos. 899-901 (3) 4.15 2.30

Chess Champions A220a

1k, R. Segura. 2k, Adolph Anderssen. 3k, P. Morphy. 6k, W. Steinitz. 7k, E. Lasker. 12k, J.R. Capablanca. 172k, A. Alekhine.

1988 **Litho.** ***Perf. 13***
901A A220a 1k multicolored .30 .25
901B A220a 2k multicolored .30 .25
901C A220a 3k multicolored .30 .25
901D A220a 6k multicolored .30 .25
901E A220a 7k multicolored .30 .25
901F A220a 12k multicolored .40 .25
901G A220a 172k multicolored 3.00 1.10
Nos. 901A-901G (7) 4.90 2.60

Nos. 901C is incorrectly inscribed "Murphy."

1990 World Cup Soccer Championships, Italy — A221

Various plays.

1989 ***Perf. 13x12½***
902 A221 10k multi .30 .25
903 A221 15k multi, diff. .30 .25
904 A221 20k multi, diff. .40 .25
905 A221 25k multi, diff. .55 .25
906 A221 45k multi, diff. .80 .30
907 A221 105k multi, diff. 2.00 .80
Nos. 902-907 (6) 4.35 2.10

Souvenir Sheet
Perf. 13

907A	A221	95k multi, diff.	2.10	1.10

No. 907A contains one 40x32mm stamp.

INDIA '89 — A222

Cats.

1989, Jan. 7 *Perf. 12½*

908	A222	5k multi	.30	.25
909	A222	6k multi, diff.	.30	.25
910	A222	10k multi, diff.	.40	.25
911	A222	20k multi, diff.	.60	.25
912	A222	50k multi, diff.	1.10	.40
913	A222	172k multi, diff.	3.25	1.00
		Nos. 908-913 (6)	5.95	2.40

Souvenir Sheet
Perf. 13

914	A222	95k multi, diff.	2.10	1.00

No. 914 contains one 32x40mm stamp.

1992 Winter Olympics, Albertville A223

Various figure skaters.

1989, May 1 *Perf. 13*

915	A223	9k multi, vert.	.30	.25
916	A223	10k shown	.30	.25
917	A223	15k multi, diff., vert.	.35	.25
918	A223	24k multi, diff., vert.	.50	.25
919	A223	29k multi, diff., vert.	.65	.25
920	A223	114k multi, diff., vert.	2.00	1.00
		Nos. 915-920 (6)	4.10	2.25

Souvenir Sheet
Perf. 12½

921	A223	95k Pairs figure skating	2.10	1.10

No. 921 contains one 32x40mm stamp.

People's Army, 40th Anniv. — A224

2k, Military school, vert. 3k, Health care. 250k, Ready for combat.

1989, Jan. 20 *Perf. 13*

922	A224	1k shown	.30	.25
923	A224	2k multicolored	.30	.25
924	A224	3k multicolored	.30	.25
925	A224	250k multicolored	6.00	1.00
		Nos. 922-925 (4)	6.90	1.75

1992 Summer Olympics, Barcelona A225

5k, Pole vault, vert. 15k, Gymnastic rings, vert. 20k, Cycling. 25k, Boxing. 70k, Archery, vert. 120k, Swimming, vert.
95k, Baseball.

Perf. 12x12½, 12½x12

1989, June 1 **Litho.**

926	A225	5k multicolored	.30	.25
927	A225	15k multicolored	.30	.25
928	A225	20k multicolored	.30	.25
929	A225	25k multicolored	.40	.30
930	A225	70k multicolored	1.10	.55
931	A225	120k multicolored	1.75	.65
		Nos. 926-931 (6)	4.15	2.25

Souvenir Sheet
Perf. 13

932	A225	95k multicolored	2.10	1.10

No. 932 contains one 32x40mm stamp.

PHILEXFRANCE '89 — A226

Paintings by Picasso: 5k, *Beggars by the Edge of the Sea.* 7k, *Maternity.* 8k, *Portrait of Jaime S. Le Bock.* 9k, *Harlequins.* 105k, *Dog with Boy.* 114k, *Girl Balancing on Ball.*
95k *Woman in Hat.*

1989, July 17 *Perf. 12½x13*

933	A226	5k multi	.30	.25
934	A226	7k multi	.30	.25
935	A226	8k multi	.30	.25
936	A226	9k multi	.35	.25
937	A226	105k multi	1.75	.65
938	A226	114k multi	2.00	.80
		Nos. 933-938 (6)	5.00	2.45

Souvenir Sheet
Perf. 12½

939	A226	95k multicolored	2.10	1.10

No. 939 contains one 32x40mm stamp.

Cuban Revolution, 30th Anniv. — A227

1989, Apr. 20 **Litho.** *Perf. 13*

940	A227	45k shown	1.10	.40
941	A227	50k Flags	1.25	.40

Fight the Destruction of Forests — A228

4k, Planting saplings. 10k, Fight forest fires. 12k, Do not chop down trees. 200k, Map of woodland.

1989, Mar. 30 **Litho.** *Perf. 13*

942	A228	4k multicolored	.30	.25
943	A228	10k multicolored	.30	.25
944	A228	12k multicolored	.30	.25
945	A228	200k multicolored	3.25	1.00
		Nos. 942-945 (4)	4.15	1.75

Nos. 944-945 are vert.

Jawaharlal Nehru (1889-1964), Indian Statesman — A229

1989, Nov. 9 **Litho.** *Perf. 12½*

946	A229	1k multicolored	.30	.25
947	A229	60k multi, horiz.	1.10	.50
948	A229	200k multi, diff.	3.50	1.10
		Nos. 946-948 (3)	4.90	1.85

Mani Ikara Zapota — A230

No. 950, Psidium guajava. No. 951, Annona sguamosa. No. 952, Durio zibethinus. No. 953, Punica granatum. No. 954, Moridica charautia.

1989, Sept. 18 *Perf. 12½x13*

949	A230	5k shown	.30	.25
950	A230	20k multicolored	.40	.25
951	A230	20k multicolored	.40	.25
952	A230	30k multicolored	.55	.25
953	A230	50k multicolored	.90	.50
954	A230	172k multicolored	3.00	1.00
		Nos. 949-954 (6)	5.55	2.50

A231

Historic Monuments: No. 955, That Sikhotabong, Khammouane. No. 956, That Dam, Vientiane. No. 957, That Ing Hang, Savannakhet. No. 958, Ho Vay Phra Thatluang, Vientiane.

1989, Oct. 19 **Litho.** *Perf. 12½*

955	A231	5k multicolored	.30	.25
956	A231	15k multicolored	.30	.25
957	A231	61k multicolored	1.10	.55
958	A231	161k multicolored	2.75	1.25
		Nos. 955-958 (4)	4.45	2.30

1992 Summer Olympics, Barcelona A232

1990, Mar. 5 **Litho.** *Perf. 12½x13*

959	A232	10k Basketball	.30	.25
960	A232	30k Hurdles	.45	.25
961	A232	45k High jump	.65	.25
962	A232	50k Cycling	.75	.30
963	A232	60k Javelin	.90	.50
964	A232	90k Tennis	1.40	.80
		Nos. 959-964 (6)	4.45	2.35

Souvenir Sheet

965	A232	95k Rhythmic gymnastics	2.00	1.00

Nos. 959-964 exist imperf.

1992 Winter Olympics, Albertville A233

10k, Speed skating. 25k, Cross country skiing, vert. 30k, Slalom skiing. 35k, Luge. 80k, Ice dancing, vert. 90k, Biathlon.
95k, Hockey, vert.

1990, June 20 *Perf. 13*

966	A233	10k multicolored	.30	.25
967	A233	25k multicolored	.40	.25
968	A233	30k multicolored	.45	.25
969	A233	35k multicolored	.55	.25
970	A233	80k multicolored	1.25	.55
971	A233	90k multicolored	1.40	.65
		Nos. 966-971 (6)	4.35	2.20

Souvenir Sheet

972	A233	95k multicolored	2.00	1.00

New Zealand Birds — A234

Designs: 10k, Prosthemadera novaeseelandie. 15k, Alauda arvensis. 20k, Haemotopus unicolor. 50k, Phalacrocorax carbo. 60k, Demigretta sacra. 100k Apteryx australis mantelli. 95k, Phalacrocorax corunculatus.

1990, Aug. 24 *Perf. 12½*

973	A234	10k multicolored	.30	.25
974	A234	15k multicolored	.35	.25
975	A234	20k multicolored	.45	.25
976	A234	50k multicolored	.90	.30
977	A234	60k multicolored	1.10	.50
978	A234	100k multicolored	1.90	.80
		Nos. 973-978 (6)	5.00	2.35

Souvenir Sheet

979	A234	95k multicolored	2.25	1.10

World Stamp Expo, New Zealand '90. No. 979 contains one 32x40mm stamp and also exists imperf.

That Luang Temple, 430th Anniv. — A235

1990, July 25 *Perf. 13x12½, 12½x13*

980	A235	60k 1867	1.50	.50
981	A235	70k 1930	1.75	.65
982	A235	130k 1990, vert.	3.25	1.25
		Nos. 980-982 (3)	6.50	2.40

Ho Chi Minh (1890-1969), Vietnamese Leader — A236

40k, Addressing people. 60k, With Laotian President. 160k, Waving, vert.

1990, May 11 *Perf. 13*

983	A236	40k multicolored	.90	.30
984	A236	60k multicolored	1.40	.45
985	A236	160k multicolored	3.75	1.25
		Nos. 983-985 (3)	6.05	2.00

UN Development Program, 40th Anniv. — A237

30k, Surgeons. 45k, Fishermen. 80k, Flight controller, vert. 90k, Power plant.

1990, Oct. 24 **Litho.** *Perf. 13*

986	A237	30k multicolored	.75	.25
987	A237	45k multicolored	1.25	.30
988	A237	80k multicolored	2.00	.75
989	A237	90k multicolored	2.25	.90
		Nos. 986-989 (4)	6.25	2.20

15th Anniv. of the Republic A238

Designs: 15k, Placing flowers at monument. 20k, Celebratory parade. 80k, Visiting sick. 120k, Women marching with banner.

1990, Dec. 2 **Litho.** *Perf. 13*

990	A238	15k multicolored	.40	.25
991	A238	20k multicolored	.60	.25
992	A238	80k multicolored	2.00	.90
993	A238	120k multicolored	3.00	1.25
		Nos. 990-993 (4)	6.00	2.65

New Year's Day — A239

1990, Nov. 20

994	A239	5k shown	.30	.25
995	A239	10k Parade	.30	.25
996	A239	50k Ceremony	.90	.40

Size: 40x29mm

997	A239	150k Ceremony, diff.	2.50	1.25
		Nos. 994-997 (4)	4.00	2.15

World Cup Soccer Championships, Italy — A240

Designs: Various soccer players in action.

1990 **Litho.** ***Perf. 13***

998	A240	10k multicolored	.30	.25
999	A240	15k multicolored	.30	.25
1000	A240	20k multicolored	.45	.25
1001	A240	25k multicolored	.55	.25
1002	A240	45k multicolored	.85	.30
1003	A240	105k multicolored	1.90	.80
		Nos. 998-1003 (6)	4.35	2.10

Souvenir Sheets

Perf. 12½

1004	A240	95k multi, horiz.	2.00	1.00

Perf. 13

1004A	A240	95k multi	2.00	1.00

No. 1004 contains one 39x31mm stamp; No. 1004A one 32x40mm stamp.

Intl. Literacy Year — A241

50k, Woman with child, vert. 60k, Monk teaching class. 150k, Two women, man reading.

1990, Feb. 27 **Litho.** ***Perf. 12½***

1005	A241	10k shown	.30	.25
1006	A241	50k multicolored	1.00	.75
1007	A241	60k multicolored	1.25	.90
1008	A241	150k multicolored	3.00	1.25
		Nos. 1005-1008 (4)	5.55	3.15

Stamp World London '90 — A242

Stamps, modes of mail transport: 15k, Great Britain #1, stagecoach. 20k, US #1, train. 40k, France #3, balloons. 50k, Sardinia #1, post rider. 60k, Indo-China #3, elephant. 95k, Laos #272, jet. 100k, Spain #1, sailing ship.

1990, Apr. 26 **Litho.** ***Perf. 13x12½***

1009	A242	15k multicolored	.30	.25
1010	A242	20k multicolored	.40	.25
1011	A242	40k multicolored	.70	.25
1012	A242	50k multicolored	1.00	.30
1013	A242	60k multicolored	1.10	.50
1014	A242	100k multicolored	1.90	.75
		Nos. 1009-1014 (6)	5.40	2.30

Souvenir Sheet

Perf. 13

1015	A242	95k multicolored	2.00	1.00

No. 1015 contains one 40x32mm stamp.
Nos. 1009-1014 exist imperf.

Endangered Animals A242a

10k, Brow-antlered deer. 20k, Gaur. 40k, Wild water buffalo. 45k, Kouprey. 120k, Javan rhinoceros.

1990, Sept. 15 **Litho.** ***Perf. 12½***

1015A	A242a	10k multicolored	.30	.25
1015B	A242a	20k multicolored	.40	.25
1015C	A242a	40k multicolored	.70	.25
1015D	A242a	45k multicolored	.75	.30
1015E	A242a	120k multicolored	1.75	1.00
		Nos. 1015A-1015E (5)	3.90	2.05

A243

1992 Olympics, Barcelona and Albertville A244

No. 1016, 2-man canoe. No. 1017, 1-man kayak. No. 1018, Bobsled, vert. No. 1019, Cross country skiing. No. 1020, Ski jumping. No. 1021, Biathlon. No. 1022, Diving, vert. No. 1023, Sailing, vert. No. 1024, Speed skating. No. 1025, Swimming.

No. 1026, 2-man kayak. No. 1027, Slalom skiing, vert.

Perf. 12½x12, 12x12½, 13 (A244)

1991, Jan. 25

1016	A243	22k multi	.30	.25
1017	A243	32k multi	.30	.25
1018	A244	32k multi	.30	.25
1019	A244	135k multi	.50	.25
1020	A244	250k multi	.85	.25
1021	A244	275k multi	1.00	.30
1022	A243	285k multi	1.00	.30
1023	A243	330k multi	1.20	.35
1024	A244	900k multi	2.75	1.00
1025	A243	1000k multi	2.50	1.00
		Nos. 1016-1025 (10)	10.70	4.20

Souvenir Sheets

Perf. 12½, 13½x13

1026	A243	700k multi	2.75	1.00
1027	A244	700k multi	2.75	1.00

No. 1026 contains one 40x32mm stamp. No. 1027 contains one 32x40mm stamp.

Tourism A245

Designs: 155k, Rapids, Champassak. 220k, Vangvieng. 235k, Waterfalls, Saravane, vert. 1000k Plain of Jars, Xieng Khouang, vert.

1991 ***Perf. 13x12½, 12½x13***

1028	A245	155k multicolored	.55	.25
1029	A245	220k multicolored	.80	.30
1030	A245	235k multicolored	1.00	.35
1031	A245	1000k multicolored	3.25	1.10
		Nos. 1028-1031 (4)	5.60	2.00

1994 World Cup Soccer Championships A246

Designs: Various players in action.

1991 **Litho.** ***Perf. 13***

1032	A246	32k multicolored	.30	.25
1033	A246	330k multicolored	.75	.35
1034	A246	340k multi, vert.	.85	.40
1035	A246	400k multicolored	1.00	.45
1036	A246	500k multicolored	1.25	.65
		Nos. 1032-1036 (5)	4.15	2.10

Souvenir Sheet

Perf. 13½x13

1037	A246	700k multi, vert.	2.00	1.00

No. 1037 contains one 32x40mm stamp.

Espamer '91, Buenos Aires — A247

25k, Mallard 4-4-2. 32k, Pacific 231 4-6-2. 285k, American style 4-8-4. 650k, Canadian Pacific 4-6-2. 750k, Beyer-Garrant 4-8-2 2-8-4.
700k, Inter-city diesel.

1991, June 30 **Litho.** ***Perf. 12½x12***

1038	A247	25k multicolored	.30	.25
1039	A247	32k multicolored	.30	.25
1040	A247	285k multicolored	.90	.35
1041	A247	650k multicolored	2.00	.75
1042	A247	750k multicolored	2.25	1.10
		Nos. 1038-1042 (5)	5.75	2.70

Souvenir Sheet

Perf. 12½

1043	A247	700k multicolored	2.00	1.00

Espamer '91, Buenos Aires. No. 1039 does not show denomination or country in Latin characters. Size of Nos. 1038, 1040-1042: 44x28mm.

Musical Celebrations A248

Designs: 220k, Man playing mong, vert. 275k, Man, woman singing Siphandone, vert. 545k, Man, woman singing Khapngum. 690k, People dancing.

1991, July 10 **Litho.** ***Perf. 13***

1044	A248	20k multicolored	.30	.25
1045	A248	220k multicolored	.55	.25
1046	A248	275k multicolored	.75	.30
1047	A248	545k multicolored	1.25	.65
1048	A248	690k multicolored	1.75	1.00
		Nos. 1044-1048 (5)	4.60	2.45

Butterflies A248a

55k, Sasakia charonda. 90k, Luendorfia puziloi. 255k, Papilio bianor. 285k, Papilio machaon. 900k, Graphium doson.
700k, Cyrestis thyodamas.

1991, Oct. 15 **Litho.** ***Perf. 12½x12***

1048A	A248a	55k multicolored	.30	.25
1048B	A248a	90k multicolored	.30	.25
1048C	A248a	255k multicolored	.90	.25
1048D	A248a	285k multicolored	1.00	.30
1048E	A248a	900k multicolored	2.50	1.10
		Nos. 1048A-1048E (5)	5.00	2.15

Souvenir Sheet

Perf. 13

1048F	A248a	700k multicolored	3.25	1.25

No. 1048F contains one 40x32mm stamp. Phila Nippon '91.

Arbor Day — A249

700k, 6 people planting trees. 800k, Nursery.

1991, June 1 ***Perf. 12½***

1049	A249	250k multicolored	.70	.35
1050	A249	700k multicolored	1.60	.80
1051	A249	800k multicolored	2.00	1.10
		Nos. 1049-1051 (3)	4.30	2.25

1992 Winter Olympics, Albertville — A250

Perf. 12½x12, 12x12½

1992, Jan. 12 **Litho.**

1052	A250	200k Bobsled	.50	.25
1053	A250	220k Skiing	.60	.25
1054	A250	250k Skiing, horiz.	.70	.25
1055	A250	500k Luge	1.25	.30
1056	A250	600k Figure skater	1.50	.80
		Nos. 1052-1056 (5)	4.55	1.85

Souvenir Sheet

Perf. 12½

1057	A250	700k Speed skater	2.00	1.00

No. 1057 contains one 32x40mm stamp.

1992 Summer Olympics, Barcelona — A251

1992, Feb. 21 **Litho.** ***Perf. 12½***

1058	A251	32k Women's running	.30	.25
1059	A251	245k Baseball	.70	.25
1060	A251	275k Tennis	.80	.25
1061	A251	285k Basketball	.90	.30
1062	A251	900k Boxing, horiz.	2.25	1.00
		Nos. 1058-1062 (5)	4.95	2.05

Souvenir Sheet

1062A	A251	700k Diving	2.00	1.00

No. 1062A contains one 40x32mm stamp.

World Health Day — A252

Designs: 200k, Spraying for mosquitoes. 255k, Campaign against smoking. 330k, Receiving blood donation. 1000k, Immunizing child, vert.

1992, Apr. 7

1063	A252	200k multicolored	.50	.25
1064	A252	255k multicolored	.70	.30
1065	A252	330k multicolored	.90	.65
1066	A252	1000k multicolored	2.25	1.25
		Nos. 1063-1066 (4)	4.35	2.45

A253

Flags, ball and players: 260k, Argentina, Italy. 305k, Germany, Great Britain. 310k, US, World Cup trophy (no players). 350k, Italy, Great Britain. 800k, Germany, Argentina.
700k, Goalie.

1992, May 1 **Litho.** ***Perf. 13***

1067	A253	260k multicolored	.60	.25
1068	A253	305k multicolored	.65	.25
1069	A253	310k multicolored	.70	.30
1070	A253	350k multicolored	.80	.50
1071	A253	800k multicolored	1.90	1.00
		Nos. 1067-1071 (5)	4.65	2.30

Souvenir Sheet

Perf. 12½

1072	A253	700k multicolored	3.25	1.65

1994 World Cup Soccer Championships, US.

A254

Children playing: 220k, Playing drum. 285k, Jumping rope, horiz. 330k, Walking on stilts. 400k, Escape from line, horiz.

1992, Nov. 8 **Litho.** ***Perf. 13***

1073	A254	220k multi	.85	.25
1074	A254	285k multi	1.10	.25
1075	A254	330k multi	1.25	.30
1076	A254	400k multi	1.60	.65
		Nos. 1073-1076 (4)	4.80	1.45

For surcharge, see No. 1902.

Poisonous Snakes — A255

280k, Naja naja kaouthia. 295k, Naja naja atra. 420k, Trimeresurus wagleri. 700k, Ophiophagus hannah, vert.

Perf. 12½x13, 13x12½

1992, July 10 **Litho.**

1078 A255 280k multicolored .85 .25
1079 A255 295k multicolored .85 .25
1080 A255 420k multicolored 1.25 .35
1081 A255 700k multicolored 2.25 1.00
Nos. 1078-1081 (4) 5.20 1.85

Restoration of Wat Phou — A256

Different views of Wat Phou.

Perf. 13x12½, 12½x13

1992, Aug. 22 **Litho.**

1082 A256 185k multicolored .50 .30
1083 A256 220k multicolored .60 .30
1084 A256 1200k multi, horiz. 3.75 1.40
Nos. 1082-1084 (3) 4.85 2.00

Genoa '92 — A257

Sailing ships and maps by: 100k, Juan Martinez. 300k, Piri Reis, vert. 350k, Paolo del Pozo Toscanelli. 400k, Gabriel de Vallseca. 455k, Juan Martinez, diff. 700k, Juan de la Cosa.

Perf. 13x12½, 12½x13

1992, Sept. 12

1085 A257 100k multicolored .30 .25
1086 A257 300k multicolored .85 .25
1087 A257 350k multicolored 1.10 .25
1088 A257 400k multicolored 1.20 .50
1089 A257 455k multicolored 1.60 .65
Nos. 1085-1089 (5) 5.05 1.90

Souvenir Sheet

Perf. 13

1090 A257 700k multicolored 2.75 1.00

Traditional Costumes of the Montagnards — A258

Various costumes.

1992, Oct. 2 **Litho.** ***Perf. 13***

1091 A258 25k multicolored .30 .25
1092 A258 55k multicolored .30 .25
1093 A258 400k multicolored 1.25 .50
1094 A258 1200k multicolored 4.00 1.25
Nos. 1091-1094 (4) 5.85 2.25

A259

UN, UNESCO emblems, stylized faces and: 330k, Drum. 1000k, Traditional flute.

1991, Nov. 1 **Litho.** ***Perf. 13***

1095 A259 285k shown .85 .35
1096 A259 330k multicolored 1.00 .35
1097 A259 1000k multicolored 3.00 1.25
Nos. 1095-1097 (3) 4.85 1.95

Cultural Development Decade, 1988-1997.

Apes — A260

1992, Dec. 22

1098 A260 10k Black gibbon .30 .25
1099 A260 100k Douc langur .30 .25
1100 A260 250k Pileated gibbon .75 .35
1101 A260 430k Francois langur 1.10 .50
1102 A260 800k Pygmy loris 2.00 .80
Nos. 1098-1102 (5) 4.45 2.15

Natl. Customs — A261

Designs: 100k, Woman praying before Buddha, vert. 160k, Procession. 1500k, People giving food to monks.

1992, Dec. 2 ***Perf. 12½***

1103 A261 100k multicolored .30 .25
1104 A261 140k multicolored .40 .25
1105 A261 160k multicolored .45 .25
1106 A261 1500k multicolored 4.50 2.25
Nos. 1103-1106 (4) 5.65 3.00

First Subway System, 130th Anniv. — A262

1993, Jan. 9 **Litho.** ***Perf. 13***

1107 A262 15k New York .30 .25
1108 A262 50k Berlin .30 .25
1109 A262 100k Paris .30 .25
1110 A262 200k London .75 .35
1111 A262 900k Moscow 2.75 1.40
Nos. 1107-1111 (5) 4.40 2.50

Souvenir Sheet

Perf. 13x13½

1112 A262 700k Antique engine, vert. 3.00 1.25

No. 1112 contains one 32x40mm stamp.

Frogs — A263

55k, Kaloula pulchra. 90k, Xenopus muelleri. 100k, Centrolenella vireovittata, vert. 185k, Bufo marinus. 1200k, Hyla arborea, vert.

1993, Feb. 1 **Litho.** ***Perf. 12½***

1113 A263 55k multicolored .30 .25
1114 A263 90k multicolored .30 .25
1115 A263 100k multicolored .35 .25
1116 A263 185k multicolored .70 .35
1117 A263 1200k multicolored 3.50 1.25
Nos. 1113-1117 (5) 5.15 2.35

Animals — A264

45k, Tupaia glis. 60k, Cynocephalus volans. 120k, Loris grasilis. 500k, Tarsium spectrum. 600k, Symphalangus syndactylus.

1993, Mar. 13 **Litho.** ***Perf. 13***

1118 A264 45k multicolored .30 .25
1119 A264 60k multicolored .30 .25
1120 A264 120k multicolored .45 .25
1121 A264 500k multicolored 1.60 .75
1122 A264 600k multicolored 1.90 1.25
Nos. 1118-1122 (5) 4.55 2.75

Native Houses A265

Various houses.

1993, July 12 **Litho.** ***Perf. 13***

1123 A265 32k multi, vert. .50 .40
1124 A265 200k multicolored 1.50 .60
1125 A265 650k multicolored 5.00 1.00
1126 A265 750k multicolored 6.75 1.75
Nos. 1123-1126 (4) 13.75 3.75

Campaign Against Illegal Drugs — A266

Designs: 200k, Drugs, skull smoking cigarette. 430k, Burning confiscated drugs. 900k, Instructor showing danger of drugs to audience.

1993, June 26 ***Perf. 12½***

1127 A266 200k multicolored .65 .35
1128 A266 430k multicolored 1.50 .75
1129 A266 900k multicolored 3.25 1.40
Nos. 1127-1129 (3) 5.40 2.50

Shells — A267

20k, Chlamys senatorius nobilis. 30k, Epitonium prestiosum. 70k, Lambis rugosa. 500k, Conus aulicus. 1000k, Lambis millepeda.

1993, May 29 **Litho.** ***Perf. 12x12½***

1130 A267 20k multicolored .30 .25
1131 A267 30k multicolored .30 .25
1132 A267 70k multicolored .30 .25
1133 A267 500k multicolored 1.60 .75
1134 A267 1000k multicolored 3.00 1.40
Nos. 1130-1134 (5) 5.50 2.90

Birds of Prey — A268

10k, Aquila clanga. 100k, Athene brama. 330k, Circus melanoleucos. 1000k, Circaetus gallicus.

1993, Aug. 10 **Litho.** ***Perf. 13***

1135 A268 10k multicolored .30 .25
1136 A268 100k multicolored .50 .25
1137 A268 330k multicolored 1.50 .50
1138 A268 1000k multicolored 4.00 1.40
Nos. 1135-1138 (4) 6.30 2.40

No. 1137 is horiz.

Environmental Protection A269

Designs: 32k, Fighting forest fire. 40k, Animals around clean river. 260k, Rice paddies. 1100k, Water buffalo, people in water.

1993, Sept. 25 **Litho.** ***Perf. 13***

1139 A269 32k multicolored .30 .25
1140 A269 40k multicolored .30 .25
1141 A269 260k multicolored 1.00 .35
1142 A269 1100k multicolored 4.25 1.40
Nos. 1139-1142 (4) 5.85 2.25

Bangkok '93 — A270

Butterflies: 35k, Narathura atosia. 80k, Parides philoxenus. 150k, Euploea harrisi. 220k, Ixias pyrene. 500k, Elymnias hypermnestra. 700k, Stichopthalma louisa.

1993, Oct. 1 **Litho.** ***Perf. 13***

1143 A270 35k multicolored .30 .25
1144 A270 80k multicolored .30 .25
1145 A270 150k multicolored .45 .25
1146 A270 220k multicolored .75 .35
1147 A270 500k multicolored 2.00 .85
Nos. 1143-1147 (5) 3.80 1.95

Souvenir Sheet

1148 A270 700k multicolored 3.00 1.50

No. 1148 contains one 40x32mm stamp.

1994 World Cup Soccer Championships, US — A271

Various soccer players.

1993, Nov. 3 ***Perf. 13***

1149 A271 10k multicolored .30 .25
1150 A271 20k multicolored .30 .25
1151 A271 285k multicolored 1.10 .25
1152 A271 400k multicolored 1.60 .50
1153 A271 800k multicolored 3.25 1.25
Nos. 1149-1153 (5) 6.55 2.50

Souvenir Sheet

Perf. 12½

1154 A271 700k multicolored 2.75 1.40

Nos. 1154 contains one 32x40mm stamp.

Prehistoric Birds — A272

10k, Hesperornis. 20k, Dronte. 150k, Archaeopterix. 600k, Phororhachos. No. 1159, 700k, Dinornis maximus.
No. 1160, 700k, Teratornis, horiz.

1994, Jan. 20 **Litho.** ***Perf. 13***

1155 A272 10k multi .30 .25
1156 A272 20k multi .30 .25
1157 A272 150k multi .60 .25
1158 A272 600k multi 2.00 .50
1159 A272 700k multi 2.25 1.00
Nos. 1155-1159 (5) 5.45 2.25

Souvenir Sheet

1160 A272 700k multi 2.50 1.25

Intl. Olympic Committee, Cent. — A273

100k, Flag, flame. 250k, Ancient Olympians. 1000k, Baron de Coubertin, Olympic runner.

Perf. 12x12½, 12½x12

1994, Mar. 15 **Litho.**

1161 A273 100k multi, vert. .30 .25
1162 A273 250k multi .75 .25
1163 A273 1000k multi, vert. 3.25 1.50
Nos. 1161-1163 (3) 4.30 2.00

1994 World Cup Soccer Championships, U.S. — A274

Various soccer plays.

1994, June 15 Litho. *Perf. 12½*

1164	A274	40k multicolored		.30	.25
1165	A274	50k multicolored		.30	.25
1166	A274	60k multicolored		.30	.25
1167	A274	320k multicolored		1.10	.35
1168	A274	900k multicolored		3.25	1.00
		Nos. 1164-1168 (5)		5.25	2.10

Souvenir Sheet

Perf. 13

1169	A274	700k multicolored	3.75	1.65

No. 1169 contains one 32x40mm stamp and is also known imperf.

Pagodas — A275

Various ornate gables.

1994, July 1 Litho. *Perf. 12½*

1170	A275	30k multicolored	.30	.25
1171	A275	150k multicolored	.55	.25
1172	A275	380k multicolored	1.25	.40
1173	A275	1100k multicolored	3.75	1.65
		Nos. 1170-1173 (4)	5.85	2.55

Nos. 1170-1173 exist imperf.

World Wildlife Fund — A276

50k, Ursus Malayanus. 90k, Adult. 200k, Cub, adult. 220k, Adult standing.

1994, July 23

1174	A276	50k multi	.75	.25
1175	A276	90k multi	1.00	.40
1176	A276	200k multi	2.25	1.00
1177	A276	220k multi	3.25	1.25
		Nos. 1174-1177 (4)	7.25	2.90

Reptiles — A277

70k, Natrix natrix. 80k, Natrix tessellata. 90k, Salamandra salamandra. 600k, Triturus alpestris. 700k, Triturus cristatus. 800k, Lacerta viridis.

1994, Aug. 1 Litho. *Perf. 12½*

1178	A277	70k multi, horiz.	.30	.25
1179	A277	80k multi, horiz.	.35	.25
1180	A277	90k multi, horiz.	.40	.25
1181	A277	600k multi, horiz.	2.50	.50
1182	A277	800k multicolored	3.25	1.25
		Nos. 1178-1182 (5)	6.80	2.50

Souvenir Sheet

1183	A277	700k multi, horiz.	3.25	1.25

No. 1183 contains one 40x32mm stamp.

Intl. Year of the Family — A278

Designs: 500k, Mother taking child to school, horiz. No. 1186, Mother walking with children. No. 1187, Family.

1994, Sept. 24

1184	A278	200k multicolored	.85	.35
1185	A278	500k multicolored	2.10	.75
1186	A278	700k multicolored	3.25	1.25
		Nos. 1184-1186 (3)	6.20	2.35

Souvenir Sheet

1187	A278	700k multicolored	3.25	1.25

No. 1187 contains one 32x40mm stamp.

Drums — A279

Designs: 440k, Two people with hanging drum. 450k, Barrel shaped drum. 600k, Hanging drum.

Perf. 12½, 13x12½ (#1189)

1994, Oct. 20 Litho.

1188	A279	370k multicolored	1.60	.40
1189	A279	440k multicolored	1.75	.50
1190	A279	450k multicolored	1.75	.50
1191	A279	600k multicolored	2.40	.75
		Nos. 1188-1191 (4)	7.50	2.15

No. 1189 is 40x29mm.

Elephants — A280

400k, Beside railing. 890k, Being ridden, vert.

1994, Nov. 25

1192	A280	140k shown	.55	.25
1193	A280	400k multi	1.60	.80
1194	A280	890k multi	3.25	1.40
		Nos. 1192-1194 (3)	5.40	2.45

Peace Bridge Between Laos and Thailand — A281

1994, Apr. 8 Litho. *Perf. 14x14½*

1195	A281	500k multicolored	2.50	1.25

Buddha — A282

15k, Phra Xayavoraman 7. 280k, Phra Thong Souk. 390k, Phra Monolom. 800k, Phra Ongtu.

1994, Aug. 25 Litho. *Perf. 13*

1196	A282	15k multicolored	.30	.25
1197	A282	280k multicolored	1.25	.35
1198	A282	390k multicolored	1.60	.50
1199	A282	800k multicolored	3.50	1.40
		Nos. 1196-1199 (4)	6.65	2.50

Dinosaurs — A283

1994, Dec. 8

1200	A283	50k Theropod	.30	.25
1201	A283	380k Iguanodon	1.75	.65
1202	A283	420k Sauropod	2.00	.75
		Nos. 1200-1202 (3)	4.05	1.65

World Tourism Organization, 20th Anniv. — A284

60k, Traditional music. 250k, Traditional dance. 400k, Traditional food. 650k, Waterfalls, vert.

1995, Jan. 2 Litho. *Perf. 12½*

1203	A284	60k multi	.30	.25
1204	A284	250k multi	1.00	.25
1205	A284	400k multi	1.75	.50
1206	A284	650k multi	2.75	.90
		Nos. 1203-1206 (4)	5.80	1.90

Souvenir Sheet

Perf. 13

1207	A284	700k like #1206, vert.	4.00	2.40

No. 1207 contains one 32x44mm stamp.

Dinosaurs — A285

1995, Feb. 20 *Perf. 12½*

1208	A285	50k Tracodon	.30	.25
1209	A285	70k Protoceratops	.30	.25
1210	A285	300k Brontosaurus	1.25	.35
1211	A285	400k Stegosaurus	1.75	.50
1212	A285	600k Tyranosaurus	2.50	.75
		Nos. 1208-1212 (5)	6.10	2.10

Birds — A286

50k, Acridotheres javanicus. 150k, Starnus burmannicus. 300k, Acridotheres tristis. 700k, Gracula religiosa.

1995, Mar. 10

1213	A286	50k multicolored	.30	.25
1214	A286	150k multicolored	.65	.25
1215	A286	300k multicolored	1.25	.40
1216	A286	700k multicolored	3.00	.90
		Nos. 1213-1216 (4)	5.20	1.80

Nos. 1213-1216 exist imperf.

Francophonie, 25th Anniv. — 1216A

Designs: 50k, People with arms linked. 380k, Temple. 420k, Map of Laos.

1995, Mar. 20 Litho. *Perf. 13*

1216A	A286a	50k multi	.30	.25
1216B	A286a	380k multi	1.50	.65
1216C	A286a	420k multi	1.75	.75
		Nos. 1216A-1216C (3)	3.55	1.65

Antique Containers A287

70k, "Hanche" cup, vert. 200k, Resin bowl. 450k, Button design bowl. 600k, Loving cup.

1995, May 1 Litho. *Perf. 12½*

1217	A287	70k multi	.30	.25
1218	A287	200k multi	.85	.25
1219	A287	450k multi	1.90	.55
1220	A287	600k multi	2.50	.75
		Nos. 1217-1220 (4)	5.55	1.80

1996 Atlanta Pre-Olympics A288

1995, Apr. 5

1221	A288	60k Pole vault	.30	.25
1222	A288	80k Javelin	.35	.25
1223	A288	200k Hammer throw	.85	.25
1224	A288	350k Long jump	1.60	.40
1225	A288	700k High jump	3.25	.90
		Nos. 1221-1225 (5)	6.35	2.05

Souvenir Sheet

1226	A288	700k Baseball	3.25	1.90

No. 1226 contains one 40x32mm stamp.

Rocket Festival — A289

Designs: 80k, Launching rocket from scaffolding, vert. 160k, Carrying rocket in procession led by monk. 500k, Man carrying rocket on shoulder. 700k, People looking at rockets on tripods.

1995, June 1 Litho. *Perf. 13*

1227	A289	80k multicolored	.30	.25
1228	A289	160k multicolored	.65	.25
1229	A289	500k multicolored	1.90	.55
1230	A289	700k multicolored	2.50	.90
		Nos. 1227-1230 (4)	5.35	1.95

Domestic Cats — A290

Designs: 40k, Red tabby longhair. 50k, Siamese seal point. 250k, Red tabby longhair. 400k, Tortoise-shell shorthair. 650k, Tortoise-shell shorthair, vert. 700k, Tortoise-shell shorthair.

1995, July 25 Litho. *Perf. 12½*

1231	A290	40k multicolored	.30	.25
1232	A290	50k multicolored	.30	.25
1233	A290	250k multicolored	.80	.25
1234	A290	400k multicolored	1.20	.30
1235	A290	650k multicolored	1.40	.75
		Nos. 1231-1235 (5)	4.00	1.80

Souvenir Sheet

1236	A290	700k multicolored	2.50	1.90

No. 1236 contains one 40x32mm stamp.

Insect-Eating Plants — A291

Designs: 90k, Nepenthes villosa. 100k, Dionaea muscipula. 350k, Sarracenia flava. 450k, Sarracenia purpurea. 500k, Nepenthes ampullaria.
1000k, Nepenthes gracilis.

1995, Aug. 24

1237	A291	90k multicolored	.30	.25
1238	A291	100k multicolored	.40	.25
1239	A291	350k multicolored	1.20	.35
1240	A291	450k multicolored	1.60	.35
1241	A291	500k multicolored	2.00	.75
		Nos. 1237-1241 (5)	5.50	1.95

Souvenir Sheet

1242	A291	1000k multicolored	4.50	2.00

No. 1242 contains one 40x32mm stamp.

Insects — A292

Designs: 40k, Lucanus cervus. 50k, Melolontha melolontha. 500k, Xylocopa violacea. 800k, Tettigonia viridissima.

1995, Sept. 20

1243 A292 40k multicolored .30 .25
1244 A292 50k multicolored .30 .25
1245 A292 500k multicolored 2.00 .50
1246 A292 800k multicolored 2.75 .90
Nos. 1243-1246 (4) 5.35 1.90

FAO, 50th Anniv. — A293

Designs: 80k, Cattle grazing. 300k, Farmer tilling rice paddy. 1000k, Planting, irrigating rice paddies, stocking pond with fish.

1995, Oct. 16 Litho. *Perf. 12½*

1247 A293 80k multicolored .30 .25
1248 A293 300k multicolored 1.00 .50
1249 A293 1000k multicolored 3.50 1.70
Nos. 1247-1249 (3) 4.80 2.45

Traditional Culture — A294

Designs: 50k, Man with musical instrument, two women. 280k, Dance. 380k, Playing game with bamboo poles. 420k, Woman, man with musical instruments.

1996, Jan. 10

1250 A294 50k multicolored .30 .25
1251 A294 280k multicolored 1.40 .35
1252 A294 380k multicolored 2.00 .50
1253 A294 420k multicolored 2.25 .50
Nos. 1250-1253 (4) 5.95 1.60

1996 Summer Olympics, Atlanta — A295

30k, Cycling. 150k, Soccer. 200k, Basketball, vert. 300k, Running, vert. 500k, Shooting. 1000k, Pole vault.

1996, Feb. 20

1254 A295 30k multi .30 .25
1255 A295 150k multi .75 .25
1256 A295 200k multi 1.00 .25
1257 A295 300k multi 1.50 .30
1258 A295 500k multi 2.50 .65
Nos. 1254-1258 (5) 6.05 1.70

Souvenir Sheet

1259 A295 1000k multi 3.50 1.70

No. 1259 contains one 38x30mm stamp.

Fauna — A296

Designs: 40k, Helarctos malayanus. 60k, Pelecanus philippensis. 200k, Panthera pardus. 250k, Papilio machaon. 700k, Python molurus.

1996, Feb. 26 Litho. *Perf. 13*

1260 A296 40k multicolored .30 .25
1261 A296 60k multicolored .35 .25
1262 A296 200k multicolored 1.10 .25
1263 A296 250k multicolored 1.25 .30
1264 A296 700k multicolored 3.00 .90
Nos. 1260-1264 (5) 6.00 1.95

Intl. Women's Day — A297

20k, Weaving textile. 290k, Instructing calisthenics. 1000k, Feeding infant, vert.

1996, Mar. 8

1265 A297 20k multicolored .30 .25
1266 A297 290k multicolored 1.10 .30
1267 A297 1000k multicolored 3.50 1.70
Nos. 1265-1267 (3) 4.90 2.25

A298

Various soccer plays.

1996, May 3 Litho. *Perf. 13*

1268 A298 20k multicolored .30 .25
1269 A298 50k multicolored .30 .25
1270 A298 300k multicolored .60 .30
1271 A298 400k multicolored .75 .50
1272 A298 500k multicolored 1.00 .60
Nos. 1268-1272 (5) 2.95 1.90

Souvenir Sheet

1273 A298 1000k multicolored 2.50 1.50

1998 World Soccer Cup Championships, France.
No. 1273 contains one 32x40mm stamp.

Rats — A299

1996, Apr. 15 Litho. *Perf. 13½x13*

1274 A299 50k purple & multi .30 .25
1275 A299 340k blue & multi 1.40 .65
1276 A299 350k green & multi 1.40 .65
1277 A299 370k red & multi 1.50 .75
Nos. 1274-1277 (4) 4.60 2.30

New Year 1996 (Year of the Rat).

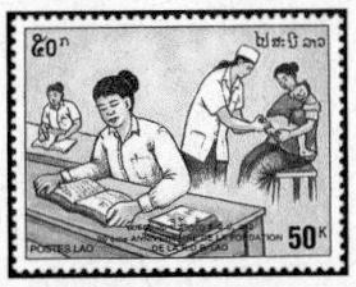

Laos Rural Development Program, 20th Anniv. — A300

50k, Instruction for giving medical care. 280k, Irrigation system. 600k, Bridge over waterway.

1995, Dec. 2 *Perf. 13*

1278 A300 50k multicolored .30 .25
1279 A300 280k multicolored .55 .50
1280 A300 600k multicolored 1.50 1.00
Nos. 1278-1280 (3) 2.35 1.75

UN, 50th Anniv. — A301

Designs: 290k, Men seated at round table. 310k, Men playing game, checkers. 440k, Boys in swing, playing ball.

1995, Oct. 24

1281 A301 290k multicolored 1.00 .40
1282 A301 310k multicolored 1.10 .50
1283 A301 440k multicolored 1.50 .75
Nos. 1281-1283 (3) 3.60 1.65

Antique Aircraft — A302

25k, Morane. 60k, Sopwith Camel. 150k, De Haviland DH-4. 250k, Albatros. 800k, Caudron.

1996, July 5 Litho. *Perf. 13*

1284 A302 25k multicolored .30 .25
1285 A302 60k multicolored .30 .25
1286 A302 150k multicolored .65 .25
1287 A302 250k multicolored 1.10 .35
1288 A302 800k multicolored 2.50 1.00
Nos. 1284-1288 (5) 4.85 2.10

Capex '96.

Carts — A303

1996, Aug. 21

1289 A303 50k shown .30 .25
1290 A303 100k Cart, diff. .40 .25
1291 A303 440k Pulled by oxen 1.50 .65
Nos. 1289-1291 (3) 2.20 1.15

Flowers — A304

Designs: 50k, Dendrobium secundum. 200k, Ascocentrum miniatum. 500k, Aerides multiflorum. 520k, Dendrobium aggregatum.

1996, Oct. 25 Litho. *Perf. 13*

1292 A304 50k multicolored .30 .25
1293 A304 200k multicolored .75 .25
1294 A304 500k multicolored 1.90 .65
1295 A304 520k multicolored 2.00 .65
Nos. 1292-1295 (4) 4.95 1.80

Draft Horses — A305

Various breeds.

1996, Nov. 5 Litho. *Perf. 13*

1296 A305 50k yellow & multi .30 .25
1297 A305 80k green & multi .30 .25
1298 A305 200k pink & multi .55 .25
1299 A305 400k blue & multi 1.25 .50
1300 A305 600k yellow & multi 1.75 .75
Nos. 1296-1300 (5) 4.15 2.00

Souvenir Sheet

1301 A305 1000k pink & multi 3.00 1.50

No. 1301 contains one 32x40mm stamp.

UNICEF, 50th Anniv. — A306

200k, Children in school. 500k, Child breastfeeding, vert. 600k, Woman pumping water.

1996, Dec. 11 Litho.

1302 A306 200k multicolored .80 .30
1303 A306 500k multicolored 2.00 .90
1304 A306 600k multicolored 2.40 1.25
Nos. 1302-1304 (3) 5.20 2.45

Greenpeace, 25th Anniv. A306a

Turtles: 150k, Dermochelys coriacea on sand. 250k, Dermochelys coriacea in surf. 400k, Erethochelys imbricata. 450k, Chelonia agassizi.

1996, Dec. 27 Litho. *Perf. 13*

1304A A306a 150k multicolored .80 .25
1304B A306a 250k multicolored 1.25 .50
1304C A306a 400k multicolored 2.00 .80
1304D A306a 450k multicolored 2.25 .90
e. Souvenir sheet, #1304A-1304D 6.50 4.75
Nos. 1304A-1304D (4) 6.30 2.45

Steam Locomotives A307

Designs: 100k, Kinnaird, 1846. 200k, Pioneer, 1836, portrait of George Stephenson. 300k, Portrait of Robert Stephenson, Long Boiler Express, 1848. 400k, Adler, 1835. 500k, Lord of the Isles, 1851-84. 600k, The Columbine, 1845.

2000k, Best friend of Charleston, 1830.

Perf. 12½x12, 12x13 (#1306-1309)

1997 Litho.

1305 A307 100k multicolored .30 .25
1306 A307 200k multicolored .40 .25
1307 A307 300k multicolored .60 .35
1308 A307 400k multicolored .75 .50
1309 A307 500k multicolored 1.00 .65
1310 A307 600k multicolored 1.25 .75
Nos. 1305-1310 (6) 4.30 2.75

Souvenir Sheet

Perf. 12½

1311 A307 2000k multicolored 3.25 3.00

Nos. 1305 and 1310 are 43.5x27mm. Nos. 1306-1309 are 42x21mm.
No. 1311 contains one 40x32mm stamp.

Parrots — A308

Designs: 50k, Agapornis personata. 150k, Agapornis cana. 200k, Agapornis lilianae. 400k, Agapornis fischeri. 500k, Agapornis nigregenis. 800k, Agapornis roseicollis.

2000k, Agapornis taranta.

1997 *Perf. 12½*

1312 A308 50k multicolored .30 .25
1313 A308 150k multicolored .45 .25
1314 A308 200k multicolored .60 .25
1315 A308 400k multicolored 1.00 .50
1316 A308 500k multicolored 1.10 .65
1317 A308 800k multicolored 1.75 1.00
Nos. 1312-1317 (6) 5.20 2.90

Souvenir Sheet

1318 A308 2000k multicolored 5.00 4.00

No. 1318 contains one 32x40mm stamp.

Year of the Ox — A308a

Designs: 300k, Ox, rider with flag, vert. 440k, Ox, rider with umbrella.

1997 Litho. *Perf. 13x13½, 13½x13*

1318A A308a 50k multi .30 .25
1318B A308a 300k multi 1.60 1.40
1318C A308a 440k multi 2.25 1.75
Nos. 1318A-1318C (3) 4.15 3.40

Cooking Utensils — A309

50k, Cooking over open fire, vert. 340k, Traditional food containers. 370k, Traditional meal setting.

1997

1319	A309	50k multicolored	.30	.25
1320	A309	340k multicolored	1.00	.55
1321	A309	370k multicolored	1.00	.60
		Nos. 1319-1321 (3)	2.30	1.40

Orchids — A310

Designs: 50k, Roeblingiana. 100k, Findlayanum. 150k, Crepidatum. 250k, Sarcanthus birmanicus. 400k, Cymbidium lowianum. 1000k, Dendrobium gratiossissimum. 2000k, Chamberlainianum.

1997 Litho. *Perf. 12½*

1322	A310	50k multicolored	.30	.25
1323	A310	100k multicolored	.35	.25
1324	A310	150k multicolored	.45	.25
1325	A310	250k multicolored	.60	.35
1326	A310	400k multicolored	.90	.50
1327	A310	1000k multicolored	1.75	1.25
		Nos. 1322-1327 (6)	4.35	2.85

Souvenir Sheet

1328	A310	2000k multicolored	4.25	3.50

No. 1328 contains one 32x40mm stamp.

Elephants A311

Elephas maximus: 100k, Adult, vert. 250k, Adult holding log. 300k, Adult, calf.

Loxodonta africana: 350k, Adult. 450k, Adult in water. 550k, Adult, vert. 2000k, Head of adult.

1997 Litho. *Perf. 12½*

1329	A311	100k multicolored	.30	.25
1330	A311	250k multicolored	.60	.35
1331	A311	300k multicolored	.65	.35
1332	A311	350k multicolored	.70	.40
1333	A311	450k multicolored	.85	.55
1334	A311	550k multicolored	1.20	.65
		Nos. 1329-1334 (6)	4.30	2.55

Souvenir Sheet

1335	A311	2000k multicolored	4.25	3.00

No. 1335 contains one 32x40mm stamp.

Head Pieces and Masks — A312

Various designs.

1997 Litho. *Perf. 12½*

1336	A312	50k multi, vert.	.30	.25
1337	A312	100k multi, vert	.30	.25
1338	A312	150k multi	.40	.25
1339	A312	200k multi, vert.	.55	.25
1340	A312	350k multi, vert.	1.25	.40
		Nos. 1336-1340 (5)	2.80	1.40

1998 World Cup Soccer Championships, France — A313

Various soccer plays.

1997 Litho. *Perf. 12½*

1341	A313	100k multicolored	.30	.25
1342	A313	200k multicolored	.50	.25
1343	A313	250k multicolored	.55	.30
1344	A313	300k multicolored	.55	.30
1345	A313	350k multicolored	.65	.40
1346	A313	700k multicolored	.95	.80
		Nos. 1341-1346 (6)	3.50	2.30

Souvenir Sheet

1347	A313	2000k multicolored	3.50	2.50

Sailing Ships — A314

50k, Phoenician. 100k, 13th cent. ship. 150k, 15th cent. vessel. 200k, Portuguese caravel, 16th cent. 400k, Dutch, 17th cent. 900k, HMS Victory.

2000k, Grand Henry, 1514.

1997 *Perf. 13*

1348	A314	50k multicolored	.30	.25
1349	A314	100k multicolored	.30	.25
1350	A314	150k multicolored	.35	.25
1351	A314	200k multicolored	.40	.25
1352	A314	400k multicolored	.80	.40
1353	A314	900k multicolored	1.40	.80
		Nos. 1348-1353 (6)	3.55	2.20

Souvenir Sheet

1354	A314	2000k multicolored	3.50	2.50

No. 1354 contains one 40x28mm stamp.

Canoe Races — A315

Designs: 50k, Team in red shirts, team in yellow shirts rowing upward. 100k, Crowd cheering on teams. 300k, Teams rowing left. 500k, People standing in canoe cheering on teams.

1997 Litho. *Perf. 12½*

1355	A315	50k multicolored	.30	.25
1356	A315	100k multicolored	.30	.25
1357	A315	300k multicolored	.75	.30
1358	A315	500k multicolored	1.25	.55
		Nos. 1355-1358 (4)	2.60	1.35

Admission of Laos to ASEAN — A316

Central flag: a, Brunei. b, Indonesia. c, Laos. d, Malaysia. e, Taiwan. f, Philippines. g, Singapore. h, Thailand. i, Viet Nam.

1997, July 23 Litho. *Perf. 14x14½*

1359	A316	550k Strip of 9, #a.-i.	9.50	9.50
j.		Sheet of 9, #1359a-1359i + label	15.00	15.00

Nos. 1359a-1359i also exist in souvenir sheets of 1. No. 1359 was not available in the philatelic market until 8/98.

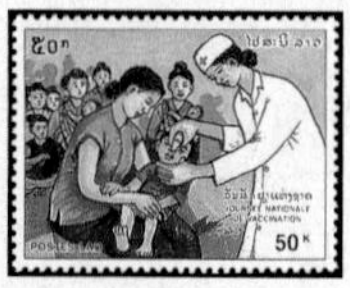

Vaccination Day — A317

Design: 50k, Child receiving oral vaccination. 340k, Child receiving shot. 370k, Child in wheelchair.

1997, Jan. 3 Litho. *Perf. 13x13¼*

1363	A317	50k multi	*.30*	.25
1364	A317	340k multi	*1.50*	.65
1365	A317	370k multi	*1.60*	.75
		Nos. 1363-1365 (3)	*3.40*	1.65

For surcharges, see Nos. 1949-1950.

Beginning with No. 1366, used values are for postally used stamps.

Pseudoryx Saola — A319

Various views of Pseudoryx saola.

1997, Feb. 10 *Perf. 13x13¼, 13¼x13*

1366	A319	350k multi	*1.60*	*1.60*
1367	A319	380k multi, vert.	*1.75*	*1.75*
1368	A319	420k multi	*2.00*	*2.00*
		Nos. 1366-1368 (3)	*5.35*	*5.35*

For surcharges, see Nos. 1951-1952.

ASEAN (Assoc. of South East Asian Nations), 30th Anniv. A321

1997, Aug. 8 Litho. *Perf. 13*

1373	A321	150k Headquarters	.90	.65
1374	A321	600k Map of Laos	3.50	2.75

Fishing — A322

Designs: 50k, Holding large net with a pole, vert. 100k, Casting net. 450k, Woman using small net, vert. 600k, Placing fish traps in water.

1997

1375	A322	50k multicolored	.30	.25
1376	A322	100k multicolored	.60	.30
1377	A322	450k multicolored	2.00	1.60
1378	A322	600k multicolored	2.75	2.00
		Nos. 1375-1378 (4)	5.65	4.15

New Year 1998 (Year of the Tiger) — A323

1998

1379	A323	150k green & multi	.90	.70
1380	A323	350k gray & multi	1.75	1.60
1381	A323	400k pale lilac & multi	1.90	1.75
		Nos. 1379-1381 (3)	4.55	4.05

Canoes A325

Designs: 1100k, Barque. 1200k, Covered pirogue. 2500k, Motorized pirogue.

1998 Litho. *Perf. 14½x14*

1387	A325	1100k multicolored	2.50	2.50
1388	A325	1200k multicolored	2.75	2.75
1389	A325	2500k multicolored	6.25	6.25
		Nos. 1387-1389 (3)	11.50	11.50

A326

Various wind musical instruments.

1998 *Perf. 14x14½*

1390	A326	900k multicolored	2.25	2.25
1391	A326	1200k multicolored	3.25	3.25
1392	A326	1500k multicolored	4.00	4.00
		Nos. 1390-1392 (3)	9.50	9.50

A327

Buddha Luang, Phabang.

1998

1393	A327	3000k multicolored	7.50	7.50

Orchids A328

Designs: 900k, Paphiopedilum callosum. 950k, Paphiopedilum concolor. 1000k, Dendrobium thyrsiflorum, vert. 1050k, Dendrobium lindleyi, vert.

1998 *Perf. 14½x14, 14x14½*

1394	A328	900k multicolored	2.75	2.75
1395	A328	950k multicolored	3.00	3.00
1396	A328	1000k multicolored	3.00	3.00
1397	A328	1050k multicolored	3.25	3.25
		Nos. 1394-1397 (4)	12.00	12.00

Universal Declaration of Human Rights, 50th Anniv. A329

Designs: 170k, Women voting. 300k, Children in classroom.

1998 *Perf. 14½x14*

1398	A329	170k multicolored	2.25	2.25
1399	A329	300k multicolored	3.75	3.75

Historic Sites — A330

Designs: 10,000k, Hotay Vat Sisaket, vert. 25,000k, Vat Phou. 45,000k, That Luong.

Perf. 14x14¼, 14¼x14

1998, Sept. 1 Litho.

1400-1402	A330	Set of 3	*120.00*	*120.00*

People's Army, 50th Anniv. A331

Designs: 1300k, Soldiers, flag, flowers. 1500k, Soldiers, cave, jungle, vert.

1999, Jan. 20 Litho. *Perf. 13¼*

1403	A331	1300k multi	*4.00*	*1.40*
1404	A331	1500k multi	*5.00*	*1.50*

Souvenir Sheet

Visit Laos Year (in 2000) A331a

Various temples: b, 2500k. c, 4000k, d, 5500k, e, 8000k.

1999, Aug. 1 Typo. *Perf. 13¼*
Gold Stamps

1404A A331a Sheet of 4, #b-e	25.00	25.00
f. As 1404A, with larger margins with Thaipex 99 and China Stamp Exhibition 99 emblems	30.00	30.00
g. As 1404A, with larger margins with China 1999 Philatelic Exhibition emblem	30.00	30.00

No. 1404Af issued 8/2; No. 1404Ag issued 8/4.

Luang Prabang World Heritage Site A332

Designs: 400k, Commemorative marker, vert. 1150k, Building. 1250k, Vat Xiengthong (building with curved roof).

1999, Feb. 2

1405 A332 400k multi	*2.50*	*.80*
1406 A332 1150k multi	*5.50*	*1.50*
1407 A332 1250k multi	*6.50*	*2.00*
Nos. 1405-1407 (3)	*14.50*	*4.30*

Tourism A333

Designs: 200k, Yaos, Muong Sing. 500k, Phadeang, Vangvieng District. 1050k, That Makmo, Luang Prabang. 1300k, Patuxay, Vientiane, vert.

Perf. 14¾x14, 14x14¾
1999, Mar. 2 Litho.

1408 A333 200k multi	*1.00*
1409 A333 500k multi	*1.50*
1410 A333 1050k multi	*2.50*
1411 A333 1300k multi	*3.50*
Nos. 1408-1411 (4)	*8.50*

Nocturnal Creatures — A334

Designs: 900k, Glaucidium brodiei. 1600k, Otus lempiji. 2100k, Tyto alba. 2800k, Chironax melanocephalus.

1999, July 2 Litho. *Perf. 14x14½*

1412 A334 900k multi	*1.50*	*1.00*
1413 A334 1600k multi	*3.00*	*2.00*
1414 A334 2100k multi	*3.50*	*3.00*
1415 A334 2800k multi	*5.00*	*4.00*
Nos. 1412-1415 (4)	*13.00*	*10.00*

New Year 1999 (Year of the Rabbit) — A335

1500k, Rabbit, other animals of calendar cycle. 1600k, Rabbit.

1999, Apr. 15 Litho. *Perf. 14x14¼*

1416 A335 1500k multi, vert.	*7.00*	*5.00*

Perf. 14¾x14

1417 A335 1600k multi, horiz.	*8.00*	*6.00*

Farming Implements A336

1999, May 1 Litho. *Perf. 14¾x14*

1418 A336 1500k Plow	*2.50*	*1.50*
1419 A336 2000k Yoke	*3.00*	*2.00*
1420 A336 3200k Plow, diff.	*4.00*	*3.00*
Nos. 1418-1420 (3)	*9.50*	*6.50*

UPU, 125th Anniv. A337

1999, Oct. 9

1421 A337 2600k shown	*5.00*	*3.00*
1422 A337 3400k Postman	*7.00*	*4.00*

Wildlife A338

700k, Rhinoceros sondaicus. 900k, Bubalus bubalis. 1700k, Prionodon pardicolor. 1800k, Cervus unicolor. 1900k, Panthera leo.

Perf. 14¾x14, 14x14¾
1999, Nov. 10

1423 A338 700k multi	*1.50*	*.60*
1424 A338 900k multi, vert.	*1.75*	*.80*
1425 A338 1700k multi	*3.00*	*1.50*
1426 A338 1800k multi	*3.25*	*1.75*
1427 A338 1900k multi, vert.	*3.50*	*1.90*
Nos. 1423-1427 (5)	*13.00*	*6.55*

Expo '99, Kunming, China — A339

Designs: 300k, Carved tree stump. 900k, China Hall. 2300k, Science and Technology Hall. 2500k, Laos traditional wooden house.

1999, Oct. 15 *Perf. 14¾x14*

1428 A339 300k multi	*.70*	*.25*
1429 A339 900k multi	*1.50*	*.75*
1430 A339 2300k multi	*3.25*	*1.90*
1431 A339 2500k multi	*4.50*	*2.00*
Nos. 1428-1431 (4)	*9.95*	*4.90*

Millennium — A340

No. 1432, 2000k: a, Airport, bus, hospital. b, Temple, tractor, elephant. c, Building, truck. d, River, waterfalls.

2000, Jan. 1 Litho. *Perf. 13½*

1432 A340 Block of 4, #a-d	*10.00*	*5.50*
e. Souvenir sheet, #1432	*12.00*	*6.75*

No. 1432e sold for 10,000k. No. 1432e exists imperf. Value, $30.

New Year 2000 (Year of the Dragon) A341

Dragons: 1800k, And other zodiac animals. 2300k, In water.

2000, Apr. 1 *Perf. 14½x14*

1433-1434 A341 Set of 2	5.50	1.25

Wedding Costumes — A342

Designs: 800k, Lao Theung. 2300k, Lao Lum. 3400k, Lao Sung.

2000, Oct. 30 *Perf. 14x14½*

1435-1437 A342 Set of 3	4.50	3.00

Children's Drawings A343

Designs: 300k, Waterfall. 400k, Forest fire. 2300k, Animals at river. 3200k, Animals at river, vert.

2000, June 1 *Perf. 14½x14, 14x14½*

1438-1441 A343 Set of 4	7.50	3.00

Bangkok 2000 Stamp Exhibition — A344

Orchids: 500k, Dendrobium draconis. 900k, Paphiopedilum hirsutissimum. 3000k, Dendrobium sulcatum. 3400k, Rhynchostylis gigantea.

2000, Mar. 25 *Perf. 14x14½*

1442-1445 A344 Set of 4	10.00	3.00
1445a Souv. sheet, #1442-1445, perf. 13½	15.00	15.00

No. 1445a sold for 10,000k. No. 1445a exists imperf. Value, $80.

Peacocks — A345

700k, Male with feathers down, vert., 1000k, Male with feathers up, vert., 1800k, Female. 3500k, Male and female.
10,000k, Male with feathers up, vert.

2000, July 10 *Perf. 14x14½, 14½x14*

1446-1449 A345 Set of 4	4.50	2.50

Souvenir Sheet
Perf. 13½
Litho. With Foil Application

1450 A345 10,000k multi	7.50	7.50

2000 Summer Olympics, Sydney A346

Designs: 500k, Cycling. 900k, Boxing. 2600k, Judo. 3600k, Kayaking.

2000, Sept. 15 Litho. *Perf. 14½x14*

1451-1454 A346 Set of 4	6.00	3.00
1454a Souvenir sheet, #1451-1454, perf. 13½	10.00	10.00

No. 1454a sold for 10,000k. No. 1454a exists imperf. Value, $40.

Laotian postal officials have declared as "illegal" a sheet of stamps for Great People of the 20th Century (Elvis Presley, Roberto Clemente, Marilyn Monroe, Dr. Martin Luther King, Jr., Pope John Paul II, Frank Sinatra, Albert Einstein, Princess Diana and Walt Disney) and stamps depicting Tiger Woods, Payne Stewart, Arnold Palmer, Elvis Presley, Marilyn Monroe, John Lennon and the Beatles.

Women's Costumes — A347

2000, Mar. 8 Litho. *Perf. 14¼x14½*

1455 A347 100k Kor Loma	.30	.25
1456 A347 200k Kor Pchor	.40	.25
1457 A347 500k Nhuan Krom	.50	.25
1458 A347 900k Taidam	2.00	.40
1459 A347 2300k Yao	3.00	1.00
1460 A347 2500k Meuy	3.00	1.10
1461 A347 2600k Sila	1.50	1.10
1462 A347 2700k Hmong	3.50	1.25
1463 A347 2800k Yao, diff.	3.50	1.25
1464 A347 3100k Kor Nukkuy	3.50	1.40
1465 A347 3200k Kor Pouxang	3.50	1.40
1466 A347 3300k Yao Lanten	2.00	1.40
1467 A347 3400k Khir	2.25	1.50
1468 A347 3500k Kor	4.00	1.50
1469 A347 3900k Hmong, diff.	4.00	1.75
Nos. 1455-1469 (15)	36.95	15.80

Laotian-Japanese Bridge Project — A348

Flags, various views of bridge: 900k, 2700k, 3200k.

2000, Aug. 2 *Perf. 14½x14*

1470-1472 A348 Set of 3	5.00	2.75

Souvenir Sheet

No. 1472A: b, 4000k, Similar to #1470. c, 7500k, Similar to #1471. d, 8500k, Similar to #1472.

2000 Typo. *Perf. 13¼x13½*

1472A A348 Sheet of 3, #b-d	15.00	15.00

No. 1472A contains three 48x33mm stamps in gold. No. 1472A exists imperf. Value, $40.

Tourism — A349

Designs: 300k, Phousy Stupa, Luang Prabang. 600k, Than Chang Cave. 2800k, Inhang Stupa. 3300k, Buddha, Phiawat Temple.

2000, Nov. 23 *Perf. 14x14½*

1473-1476 A349 Set of 4	6.00	3.00

Lao People's Democratic Republic, 25th Anniv. A350

2000, Dec. 2 *Perf. 13¼*

1477 A350 4000k multi	2.75	1.50

Mekong River at Twilight A351

Various views: 900k, 2700k, 3400k.

2000, June 20 *Perf. 14½x14*
1478-1480 A351 Set of 3 5.00 2.50

Anti-Drug Campaign A352

Designs: 100k, Poppy field. 4000k, Burning of seized drugs.

2000, June 26 **Litho.**
1481-1482 A352 Set of 2 3.50 1.50

Souvenir Sheet

Route 13 Bridge Reconstruction Project — A353

Bridge in: a, Savannakhet. b, Saravane. c, Pakse.

2000, Feb. 14 *Perf. 13¼*
1483 A353 4000k Sheet of 3, #a-c 9.00 9.00

Souvenir Sheet

Anti-Polio Campaign — A354

No. 1484: a, 900k, People receiving vaccine. b, 2500k, Family, map of Laos.

2000, June 1
1484 A354 Sheet of 2, #a-b 3.50 3.50

Millennium — A355

Designs: 3200k, Satellite, telecommunication dishes, map of Laos, student. 4000k, High tension lines, dam.

2001, Jan. 1 *Perf. 14x14½*
1485-1486 A355 Set of 2 4.00 2.50

New Year 2001 (Year of the Snake) A356

Designs: 900k, Snake coiled around branch. 3500k, Snake, other zodiac animals.

2001, Apr. 15 *Perf. 14½x14*
1487-1488 A356 Set of 2 4.00 2.00

Cockfighting A357

Pair of cocks fighting: 500k, 900k, 3300k, 3500k.
10,000k, Single cock, vert.

2001, Mar. 10 *Perf. 14½x14*
1489-1492 A357 Set of 4 5.50 3.25

Souvenir Sheet
Perf. 13¼

1493 A357 10,000k multi 7.50 7.50

No. 1493 contains one 36x50mm stamp. No. 1493 exists imperf. Value, $40.

Laos-People's Republic of China Diplomatic Relations, 40th Anniv. — A358

2001, Apr. 25 *Perf. 14¼x14½*
1494 A358 1000k multi 1.25 .40

Phila Nippon '01 — A359

Birds: Nos. 1495, 1499a, 700k, Egretta intermedia. Nos. 1496, 1499b, 800k, Bubulcus ibis (36x50mm). Nos. 1497, 1499c, 3100k, Ardea cinera (36x50mm). Nos. 1498, 1499d, 3400k, Egretta alba.

Perf. 14½x14, 13¼ (#1496-1497)
2001, Aug. 1 **With White Frames**
1495-1498 A359 Set of 4 6.00 3.00

Souvenir Sheet
Without White Frames
Perf. 13¼

1499 A359 Sheet of 4, #a-d 7.50 7.50

No. 1499 sold for 10,000k. No. 1499 exists imperf. Value, $50.

Mortars and Pestles A360

Designs: 900k, Two women using large hand-held pestle, vert. 2600k, Water-driven mortar and pestle. 3500k, Woman operating mechanical mortar and pestle, vert.

Perf. 14x14½, 14½x14
2001, Nov. 15
1500-1502 A360 Set of 3 4.50 2.25

Ceremonies A361

Designs: 300k, Pou Nyer and Nya Nyer, vert. 600k, Hae Nang Sangkhan, vert. 1000k, Sand Stupa. 2300k, Hae Prabang, vert. 4000k, Takbat, vert.

2001, Apr. 13 *Perf. 14x14½, 14½x14*
1503-1507 A361 Set of 5 7.50 3.50

Buddhist Art — A362

Designs: 200k, Himavanta. 900k, Vanapavesa. 3200k, Kumarakanda. 3600k, Sakkapabba.

2001, Dec. 5 *Perf. 13¼*
1508-1511 A362 Set of 4 6.00 3.25
1511a Souvenir sheet, #1508-1511 7.00 7.00

No. 1511a exists imperf. Value, $50.

Men's Costumes — A363

Designs: 100k, Yao Mane. 200k, Gnaheun. 500k, Katou. 2300k, Hmong Dam. 2500k, Harlak. 2600k, Kui. 2700k, Krieng. 3100k, Khmu Nhuan. 3200k, Ta Oy. 3300k, Tai Theng. 3400k, Hmong Khao. 3500k, Gnor. 3600k, Phouthai Na Gnom. 4000k, Yao. 5000k, Hmong.

2001, Feb. 20 *Perf. 14¼x14½*

1512	A363	100k	multi	.30	.25
1513	A363	200k	multi	.30	.25
1514	A363	500k	multi	.30	.25
1515	A363	2300k	multi	1.25	.80
1516	A363	2500k	multi	1.40	.85
1517	A363	2600k	multi	1.40	.85
1518	A363	2700k	multi	1.50	.90
1519	A363	3100k	multi	1.60	1.00
1520	A363	3200k	multi	1.75	1.10
1521	A363	3300k	multi	1.75	1.10
1522	A363	3400k	multi	1.75	1.25
1523	A363	3500k	multi	2.00	1.25
1524	A363	3600k	multi	2.00	1.25
1525	A363	4000k	multi	2.25	1.50
1526	A363	5000k	multi	2.75	1.90
	Nos. 1512-1526 (15)			22.30	14.50

Buddhist Temple Doors — A364

Various doors: 600k, 2300k, 2500k, 2600k.

2001, Sept. 17 **Litho.** *Perf. 14x14½*
1527-1530 A364 Set of 4 6.00 3.00

Frangipani Flowers A365

Designs: 1000k, White flowers. 2500k, Pink flowers, vert. 3500k, Red flowers.

2001, Oct. 2 *Perf. 14½x14, 14x14½*
1531-1533 A365 Set of 3 4.50 2.50
a. Souvenir sheet, #1531-1533, perf. 13¼ 6.00 4.00

Intl. Volunteers Year — A366

2001, Dec. 29 *Perf. 13¼*
1534 A366 1000k multi 2.50 .40

Women's Costumes — A367

Designs: 200k, Meuy. 300k, Leu. 500k, Tai Kouane. 700k, Tai Dam. 1000k, Tai Men. 1500k, Lanten. 2500k, Hmong. 3000k, Phouxang. 3500k, Taitheng. 4000k, Tai O. 5000k, Tai Dam, diff.

2002, Jan. 10 *Perf. 14x14½*

1535	A367	200k	multi	.30	.25
1536	A367	300k	multi	.30	.25
1537	A367	500k	multi	.30	.25
1538	A367	700k	multi	.30	.25
1539	A367	1000k	multi	.50	.30
1540	A367	1500k	multi	.70	.45
1541	A367	2500k	multi	1.25	.75
1542	A367	3000k	multi	1.50	.95
1543	A367	3500k	multi	1.75	1.10
1544	A367	4000k	multi	2.00	1.25
1545	A367	5000k	multi	2.25	1.60
	Nos. 1535-1545 (11)			11.15	7.40

Intl. Year of Mountains A368

Designs: No. 1546, 1500k, Pha Tang. No. 1547, 1500k, Phou Phamane.

2002, Mar. 30 *Perf. 14½x14*
1546-1547 A368 Set of 2 2.50 1.10

Nos. 1546-1547 are a corrected printing. The first printing, which was erroneously inscribed "LAO PRD" instead of "LAO PDR," was removed from sale after a few panes had been sold. Value, set of 2 $100.

New Year 2002 (Year of the Horse) A369

Designs: 1500k, Horse, zodiac animals. 3500k, Galloping horse.

2002, Apr. 14
1548-1549 A369 Set of 2 3.00 1.60

Laos - Viet Nam Cooperation — A370

Designs: 2500k, Musical instruments. 3500k, Laotian leader with Ho Chi Minh, horiz.

2002, July 18 *Perf. 13*
1550-1551 A370 Set of 2 3.25 1.90

Phila Korea 2002 World Stamp Exhibition, Seoul — A371

Insects: Nos. 1552a, 1553a, Sagra femorata. Nos. 1552b, 1552b, Cerambycidae. Nos. 1552c, 1553c, Chrysochroa mniszechii. Nos. 1552d, 1553d, Anoplophora sp. Nos. 1552e, 1553e, Chrysochroa sandersi. Nos. 1552f, 1553f, Mouhotia batesi. Nos. 1552g, 1553g, Megaloxantha assamensis. Nos. 1552h, 1553h, Eupatorus gracillicornis.

2002, Aug. 1 *Perf. 14½x14*
Insects and Colored Backgrounds

1552 Vert. strip of 8 5.00 5.00
a.-h. A371 1000k Any single .50 .30

Souvenir Sheet
Insects On Vegetation

1553 A371 1000k Sheet of 8, #a-h 5.00 5.00

No. 1553 exists imperf. Value, $45.

Admission to UPU, 50th Anniv. — A372

2002, May 20 **Litho.** *Perf. 13x13¼*
1554 A372 3000k black 2.00 2.00

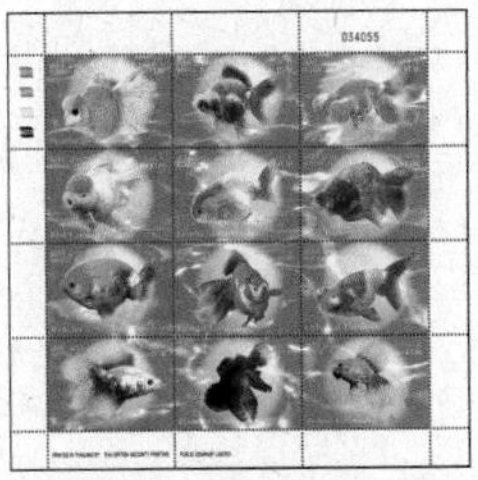

Goldfish A373

No. 1555: a, Pearlscale goldfish. b, Moor. c, Bubble eyes goldfish. d, Red-capped oranda. e, Lionhead goldfish. f, Pom pom. g, Ranchu. h, Fantail goldfish. i, Celestial goldfish. j, Ryukin. k, Brown oranda. l, Veiltail goldfish.

2002, Oct. 2 ***Perf. 13¼***
1555 A373 1000k Sheet of 12, #a-l 6.00 6.00

No. 1555 exists imperf. Value, $25.

Buffalo Fighting — A374

Various buffalo: 200k, 300k, 3000k, 4000k.

2002, Dec. 15 ***Perf. 13x13¼***
1556-1559 A374 Set of 4 4.50 3.00

Souvenir Sheet

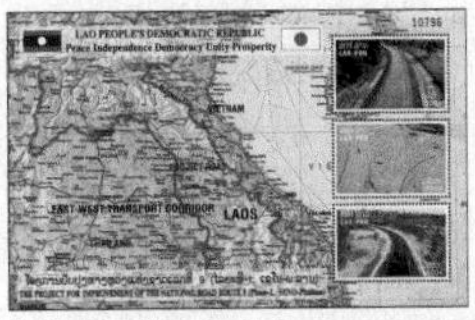

National Route 9 Improvement Project — A375

No. 1560: a, Curve. b, Interchange. c, Curve and building.

2002, Dec. 18 **Litho.** ***Perf. 13¼***
1560 A375 1500k Sheet of 3, #a-c 6.00 6.00

Vat Phou World Heritage Site — A376

Designs: 1500k, Temple, vert. 3000k, Temple, diff. 4000k, Statue of Buddha, vert.
10,000k, Stone carving.

2003, Feb. 14 ***Perf. 14x14½, 14½x14***
1561-1563 A376 Set of 3 4.50 2.60

Souvenir Sheet

Perf. 13¼

1564 A376 10,000k multi 6.00 6.00

No. 1564 contains one 93x27mm stamp.

Butterflies — A377

No. 1565: a, Hasora schoenherr. b, Spindasis lohita. c, Graphium sarpedon. d, Polyura schreiber. e, Castalius rosimon. f, Dalias pasithoe. g, Pachliopta aristolochiae. h, Papilio memnon.
10,000k, Danaus genutia.

2003, Mar. 8 ***Perf. 14½x14***
1565 A377 Block of 8 6.00 6.00
a.-h. 1000k Any single .60 .35

Souvenir Sheet

Perf. 13¼

1566 A377 10,000k multi *6.00 6.00*

No. 1566 exists imperf. Value, $30.

New Year 2003 (Year of the Goat) — A378

Designs: 2500k, Two goats. 5000k, Goat, zodiac animals.

2003, Apr. 15 ***Perf. 14½x14***
1567-1568 A378 Set of 2 5.00 2.25

Orchids — A379

Designs: 200k, Phalaenopsis Paifang's Golden Lion. 300k, Coelogyne lentiginosa. 500k, Phalaenopsis sumatrana. 1000k, Phalaenopsis bellina. 1500k, Paphiopedilum appletonianum. 2000k, Vanda bensonii. 2500k, Dendrobium harveyanum. 3000k, Paphiopedilum glaucophyllum. 3500k, Paphiopedilum gratrixianum. 4000k, Vanda roeblingiana. 5000k, Phalaenopsis Lady Sakhara.

2003, Apr. 25 ***Perf. 14½x14¼***

1569	A379	200k	multi	.30	.25
1570	A379	300k	multi	.40	.25
1571	A379	500k	multi	.60	.25
1572	A379	1000k	multi	.70	.30
1573	A379	1500k	multi	.80	.45
1574	A379	2000k	multi	1.00	.60
1575	A379	2500k	multi	1.25	.75
1576	A379	3000k	multi	1.40	.90
1577	A379	3500k	multi	1.75	1.00
1578	A379	4000k	multi	1.75	1.25
1579	A379	5000k	multi	2.25	1.50
	Nos. 1569-1579 (11)			12.20	7.50

Wood Handicrafts A380

Designs: 500k, Bowl. 1500k, Pitcher and goblets. 2500k, Fluted bowl. 3500k, Bowl, vert.

2003, May 10 ***Perf. 13***
1580-1583 A380 Set of 4 4.75 2.40

Traditional Games — A381

Designs: 1000k, Walking on stringed coconut shells. 3000k, Top spinning. 4000k, Field hockey.

2003, June 1
1584-1586 A381 Set of 3 3.50 2.40

Stop Hunting Campaign A382

Designs: 1500k, Deer. 2000k, Gun. 4500k, Wild animals.

2003, July 25 **Litho.** ***Perf. 13***
1587-1589 A382 Set of 3 3.75 2.50

Fruit — A383

Designs: 500k, Mango. 1500k, Watermelon. 2500k, Custard apple. 4000k, Pineapple.

2003, Aug. 8 ***Perf. 14½x14***
1590-1593 A383 Set of 4 4.50 2.60

Palm Leaf Manuscripts — A384

Designs: 500k, Monk writing palm leaf manuscript. 1500k, Palm leaf manuscript. 2500k, Manuscript casket. 3000k, Ho Tai.

2003, Sept. 12 ***Perf. 14x14½***
1594-1597 A384 Set of 4 4.00 3.00

Bangkok 2003 Intl. Philatelic Exhibition — A385

Buddhas of Luang Prabang: 500k, Pha Sene Souk. 1500k, Pha Gnai. 3000k, Pha Ong Luang. 3500k, Pha Ong Sene.
10,000k, Pha Attharatsa.

2003, Oct. 4 ***Perf. 14x14½***
1598-1601 A385 Set of 4 5.00 3.25

Souvenir Sheet

Perf. 13½

1602 A385 10,000k multi 6.00 6.00

No. 1602 contains one 30x95mm stamp. No. 1602 exists imperf. Value, $30.

Textiles — A386

Various textiles with panel colors of: 500k, Blue. 1000k, Red brown. 3000k, Green. 4000k, Yellow brown.

2003, Dec. 1 ***Perf. 14x14½***
1603-1606 A386 Set of 4 5.00 3.00

Installed Emerald Buddha A387

2004, Feb. 5 **Litho.** ***Perf. 14½x14***
1607 A387 5500k multi 3.00 1.90

Birds — A388

Designs: 2000k, Buceros bicornis. 2500k, Pycnonotus jocosus. 3000k, Ploceus hypoxanthus. 3500k, Alcedo atthis. 4000k, Magalaima incognita. 4500k, Serilophus lunatus. 5000k, Lacedo pulchella. 5500k, Eurylaimus ochromalus.

2004, Feb. 20 ***Perf. 14¼x14½***
1608-1615 A388 Set of 8 13.50 11.00

Dolphins A389

Two dolphins: 1500k With heads above water. 2500k, Leaping out of water. 3500k, Underwater.

2004, Mar. 29 ***Perf. 14½x14***
1616-1618 A389 Set of 3 3.50 2.50

New Year 2004 (Year of the Monkey) A390

Designs: 500k, Two monkeys. 4500k, Monkey, zodiac animals.

2004, Apr. 15
1619-1620 A390 Set of 2 2.75 1.75

FIFA (Fédération Internationale de Football Association), Cent. — A391

No. 1621 — FIFA emblem and: a, Flags of various countries. b, Soccer players.

2004, May 21 ***Perf. 13½***
1621 A391 12,000k Pair, #a-b 12.00 10.00

Values are for stamps with surrounding selvage.

Children's Day — A392

Designs: 3500k, Four children. 4500k, Children, globe, school.

2004, June 1 ***Perf. 14½x14***
1622-1623 A392 Set of 2 3.50 2.60

11th ASEAN Postal Business Meeting — A393

2004, July 5 **Litho.** ***Perf. 14x14½***
1624 A393 5000k multi 3.00 1.75

Worldwide Fund for Nature (WWF) — A394

No. 1625 — Cuora amboinensis: a, 5000k, In water. b, 5500k, On rock near water. c, 6000k, Pair. d, 7000k, Head, feet and shell.

2004, Aug. 16 **Litho.** ***Perf. 13½x14***
1625 A394 Block of 4, #a-d 6.00 5.00

Dances — A395

Designs: 1000k, Tangwai. 1500k, Khabthoume Luangprabang. 2000k, Lao Lamvong. 2500k, Salavan.

2004, Aug. 23 ***Perf. 14x14¾***
1626-1629 A395 Set of 4 3.25 2.10
1629a Souvenir sheet, #1626-1629, perf. 13¼ 5.00 5.00

No. 1629a sold for 10,000k. No. 1629a exists imperf. Value, $40.

Marigolds — A396

Designs: 3500k, Yellow, orange marigolds. 5000k, Red and orange marigolds. 5500k, Decorations made with marigolds.

2004, Sept. 28 ***Perf. 13¼x13***
1630-1632 A396 Set of 3 4.75 4.75

Scenes From Ramakian A397

Various scenes: 3500k, 4500k, 5500k, 6500k.

2004, Oct. 10 ***Perf. 13¼***
1633-1636 A397 Set of 4 9.00 6.75

Naga Fireball — A398

Designs: 2000k, Figure above river, serpent in river. 3000k, Buildings, serpent, horiz. 3500k, Fireball in serpent's mouth, horiz. 4000k, Fireballs above serpent.

2004, Oct. 28 ***Perf. 13 Syncopated***
1637-1640 A398 Set of 4 4.25 4.25

Betel Tray — A399

Designs: 2000k, Betel nuts, bowls and containers. 4000k, Betel nut and leaf. 6000k, Betel tray.

2004, Nov. 11 **Litho.** ***Perf. 13***
1641-1643 A399 Set of 3 4.00 4.00

Laos — Sweden Diplomatic Relations, 40th Anniv. — A400

2004, Dec. 12 **Litho.** ***Perf. 13x13½***
1644 A400 8500k multi 4.00 2.75

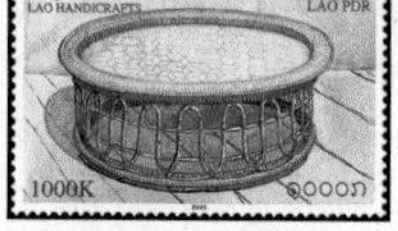
Handicrafts A401

Designs: 1000k, Short, round basket. 2000k, Paddle. 2500k, Basket with handle, vert. 5500k, Basket with handle and lid, vert.

Perf. 14½x14, 14x14½
2005, Mar. 10 **Litho.**
1645-1648 A401 Set of 4 5.25 3.25

New Year 2005 (Year of the Rooster) A402

Rooster and: 2000k, Hen. 7500k, Zodiac animals.

2005, Apr. 13 ***Perf. 14½x14***
1649-1650 A402 Set of 2 5.00 3.50

Daily Buddhas — A403

Buddha for: 500k, Sunday. 1000k, Monday. 1500k, Tuesday, horiz. 2000k, Wednesday. 2500k, Thursday. 3000k, Friday. 3500k, Saturday.

Perf. 14x14½, 14½x14
2005, May 15 **Litho.**
1651-1657 A403 Set of 7 6.50 4.50

Rice — A404

Designs: 1500k, Rice plants. 3000k, Cooked rice on plate, horiz. 6500k, Bundles of rice plants, horiz.

Perf. 13 Syncopated
2005, June 1 **Litho.**
1658-1660 A404 Set of 3 5.25 3.25

Mekong River Giant Catfish A405

Designs: 3500k, Shown. 6500k, Catfish, diff.

2005, July 13 **Litho.** ***Perf. 14½x14***
1661-1662 A405 Set of 2 4.75 3.25

Gold Panning — A406

Designs: 2000k, Pan. 7500k, Woman panning for gold, vert.

Perf. 13 Syncopated
2005, Aug. 1 **Litho.**
1663-1664 A406 Set of 2 4.00 3.00

Folk Songs — A407

Designs: 1000k, Two musicians standing. 3500k, Two musicians seated. 5500k, Four musicians, horiz.

2005, Sept. 2
1665-1667 A407 Set of 3 4.50 3.00

Europa Stamps, 50th Anniv. (in 2006) — A408

Designs: 6000k, Stonehenge, England, and Plain of Jars, Laos. No. 1669, 7000k, Knossos Palace, Greece, and Patuxay, Laos. No. 1670, 7000k, Colosseum, Rome, and Wat Phu, Laos. No. 1671, 7500k, Stave Church, Lom, Norway, and Wat Xieng Thong, Laos. No. 1672, 7500k, Notre Dame Cathedral, Paris, and That Luang, Laos. 8000k, Trier Cathedral, Germany, and Wat Phra Keo, Laos.

2005, Oct. 24 **Litho.** ***Perf. 14¾x14***
1668-1673 A408 Set of 6 15.00 12.50
1673a Souvenir sheet, #1668-1673 30.00 30.00

No. 1673a exists imperf. Value, $60.

People's Democratic Republic, 30th Anniv. — A409

Designs: 500k, Flag and building. 1000k, Map, people and flag. 2000k, Flag and coat of arms. 5000k, "30," Coat of arms and people.

2005, Dec. 2 ***Perf. 13***
1674-1677 A409 Set of 4 4.50 2.50

Diplomatic Relations with Thailand, 55th Anniv. — A410

2005, Dec. 19
1678 A410 7500k multi 4.50 2.25

Laos-United Nations Cooperation, 50th Anniv. — A411

Designs: No. 1679, 3000k, Rice harvesters. No. 1679A, 3000k, Children at school gate. No. 1679B, 3000k, Infant health care.

2005, Oct. 24 **Litho.** ***Perf. 13x13¼***
1679-1679B A411 Set of 3 4.50 3.50
1679Bc Souvenir sheet, #1679-1679B 15.00 15.00

No. 1679Bc sold for 15,000k.

Lao People's Democratic Republic, 30th Anniv. — A411b

2005, Dec. 16 **Litho.** ***Perf. 13¼x13***
1679H A411b 15,500k multi 9.00 5.50

Souvenir Sheet

1679I A411b 20,000k multi 10.00 7.00

Diplomatic Relations Between Laos and Japan, 50th Anniv. — A411c

Designs: 7000k, Flowers. 20,000k, Temples.

2005, Dec. 30 ***Perf. 13***
1679J A411c 7000k multi 4.50 2.60

Size: 170x130mm

Imperf

1679K A411c 20,000k multi 15.00 15.00

Statue of King Phangum Lenglathorany — A412

2006, Mar. 9 **Litho.** ***Perf. 14x14½***
1680 A412 8500k multi 3.50 2.60

A souvenir sheet containing one perf. 13½ example of No. 1680 sold for 20,000k.

New Year 2006 (Year of the Dog) — A413

Designs: 2000k, Dog. 6500k, Dog, zodiac animals.

2006, Apr. 14 ***Perf. 14½x14***
1681-1682 A413 Set of 2 6.50 3.50

AGL Insurance in Laos, 15th Anniv. — A414

AGL Insurance emblem and: 8000k, Car, minivan and motorcycle. 8500k, Map of Laos. 9500k, Family.

2006, May 1 ***Perf. 13***
1683-1685 A414 Set of 3 11.00 7.75

Friendship Between Vientiane and Moscow — A415

Laotian and Russian: 7500k, Women. 8500k, Sculptures and houses of worship.

2006, May 1
1686-1687 A415 Set of 2 8.00 4.75
1687a Souvenir sheet, #1686-1687 10.00 10.00

No. 1687a sold for 20,000k.

Diplomatic Relations Between Laos and People's Republic of China, 45th Anniv. — A416

2006, July 7 ***Perf. 13x12¾***
1688 A416 8500k multi 5.00 5.00

No. 1688 exists imperf. Value, $20.

Shrimp — A417

Various depictions of shrimp: 1000k, 2000k, 4000k, 6000k.

2006, July 10 ***Perf. 13***
1689-1692 A417 Set of 4 7.00 4.00
1692a Souvenir sheet, #1689-1692 8.50 8.50

No. 1692a sold for 15,000k.

Léopold Sédar Senghor (1906-2001), First President of Senegal A418

2006, Sept. 4
1693 A418 8500k multi 5.00 3.00

Bronze Drums — A419

Various drums with background colors of: 2000k, Red brown. 3500k, Blue. 7500k, Olive green.

2006, Oct. 9
1694-1696 A419 Set of 3 7.00 4.00
1696a Souvenir sheet, #1694-1696 9.00 9.00

No. 1696a sold for 15,000k.

Xieng Khouane Temple — A420

Various views of temple and sculptures: 1000k, 2500k, 3000k, 5000k.

2006, June 10 Litho. *Perf. 13*
1697-1700 A420 Set of 4 6.50 4.00

Bananas — A421

Designs: 1000k, Pisang Masak Hijau. 2000k, Pisang Mas. 4000k, Pisang Ambon. 8000k, Pisang Awak.

2006, Nov. 1
1701-1704 A421 Set of 4 7.50 5.00

Opening of Second Thai-Lao Friendship Bridge — A422

Designs: No. 1705, 7500k, Bridge in daylight. No. 1706, 7500k, Bridge at night.

2006, Dec. 20
1705-1706 A422 Set of 2 8.00 5.00

Jewelry — A423

Designs: 2000k, Pins. 5000k, Bracelet. 7000k, Earrings. 7500k, Necklace and pendant.

2007, Jan. 15 Litho. *Perf. 13¼x13*
1707-1710 A423 Set of 4 11.00 8.00
1710a Souvenir sheet, #1707-1710 14.00 12.00

No. 1710a sold for 25,000k.

Crabs — A424

Various crabs: 1000k, 2000k, 7000k, 7500k.

2007, Feb. 20 *Perf. 13x13¼*
1711-1714 A424 Set of 4 9.00 6.50
1714a Souvenir sheet, #1711-1714, perf. 13½x13¾ 10.00 9.00

No. 1714a sold for 20,000k.

New Year 2007 (Year of the Pig) — A425

Designs: No. 1715, 7500k, Pig and piglets. No. 1716, 7500k, Pig, zodiac animals.

2007, Apr. 15 *Perf. 13x13¼*
1715-1716 A425 Set of 2 8.00 5.75

Takbat Festival — A425a

Designs: 2000k, Monks standing, women placing items on ground. 5000k, Woman reaching into monk's bowl. 7500k, Women holding bowls.

2007, July 10 Litho. *Perf. 13*
1716A-1716C A425a Set of 3 7.00 5.50

Association of South East Asian Nations (ASEAN), 40th Anniv. — A426

Designs: 7000k, Typical house, Laos.

No. 1718: a, Like 7000k. b, Secretariat Building, Bandar Seri Begawan, Brunei. c, National Museum of Cambodia. d, Fatahillah Museum, Jakarta, Indonesia. e, Malayan Railway Headquarters Building, Kuala Lumpur, Malaysia. f, Yangon Post Office, Myanmar. g, Malacañang Palace, Philippines. h, National Museum of Singapore. i, Vimanmek Mansion, Bangkok, Thailand. j, Presidential Palace, Hanoi, Viet Nam.

2007, Aug. 8 Litho. *Perf. 13*
1717 A426 7000k multi 3.00 3.00
1718 Sheet of 10 7.00 7.00
a.-j. A426 700k Any single .50 .40

See Brunei No. 607, Burma No. 370, Cambodia No. 2339, Indonesia Nos. 2120-2121, Malaysia No. 1170, Philippines Nos. 3103-3105, Singapore No. 1265, Thailand No. 2315, and Viet Nam Nos. 3302-3311.

Transportation — A426a

Designs: 2000k, Airplanes. 5000k, Ferry. 7500k, Trucks.

2007, Sept. 1 Litho. *Perf. 13*
1718K-1718M A426a Set of 3 7.00 6.00

That Luang Festival — A426b

Designs: 2000k, Monks leading procession. 5000k, Procession with temple in background. 8000k, Temple at night.

2007, Nov. 13
1718N-1718P A426b Set of 3 7.50 5.75

Traditional Foods — A426c

Designs: 2000k, Sticky rice cooked in bamboo tubes. 5500k, Green papaya salad. 7500k, Grilled chicken.

2007, Dec. 30
1718Q-1718S A426c Set of 3 7.50 5.75

Worldwide Fund for Nature (WWF) — A427

Hylobates lar: 6000k, Head. 7000k, Adult and juvenile. 8000k, With open mouth. 9000k, Two adults.

2008 Litho. *Perf. 13½x14*
1719-1722 A427 Set of 4 12.00 7.25
1722a Miniature sheet, 4 each #1719-1722 120.00 120.00

Nos. 1719-1722, 1722a exist imperf. Value, Nos. 1719-1722 imperf. block of 4 $40.

2008 Summer Olympics, Beijing — A428

Designs: No. 1723, 5000k, Taekwondo. No. 1724, 5000k, High jump. No. 1725, 5000k, Cycling. No. 1726, 5000k, Soccer.

2008, Apr. 17 *Perf. 12½x13*
1723-1726 A428 Set of 4 8.00 4.75

Nos. 1723-1726 each were printed in sheets of 16. Two sheet varieties exist: English inscriptions in the top and bottom selvage, and a combination of English (right and bottom selvage) and Ukrainian (top and left selvage) inscriptions. Sheets with the English and Ukrainian inscriptions are scarce. Value, set of four singles of Nos. 1723-1726 each with attached Ukrainian selvage $20.

Elephant Festival A429

Designs: 1000k, Tuskless elephant and rider. 2000k, Two elephants and riders. 3000k, Man in crowd holding rope. 5000k, Tusked elephant with rider. 7500k, Woman decorating elephant. 8500k, Elephants moving logs. 20,000k, Elephants, riders and guides.

2008, Jan. 14 Litho. *Perf. 13*
1727-1732 A429 Set of 6 12.00 11.00

Size: 146x110mm
Imperf
1733 A429 20,000k multi + label 12.50 8.50

Coffee — A430

Designs: Nos. 1734, 1737a, 3000k, Mug and roasted coffee beans. Nos. 1735, 1737b, 5000k, Coffee berries. Nos. 1736, 1737c, 6000k, Roasted coffee beans.

2008, Feb. 11 Litho. *Perf. 13*
Size: 30x45mm
1734-1736 A430 Set of 3 8.00 6.25

Souvenir Sheet
Perf. 13¼x13
1737 A430 Sheet of 3, #a-c 10.00 8.00

No. 1737 contains three 32x43mm stamps and sold for 18,000k.

Cotton — A432

Designs: Nos. 1739, 1742a, 1000k, Woman at cotton gin. Nos. 1740, 1742b, 5000k, Cotton plant. Nos. 1741, 1742c, 5500k, Cotton plant, diff.

2008, Apr. 10 *Perf. 13*
Size: 45x30mm
1739-1741 A432 Set of 3 7.50 5.25

Souvenir Sheet
Perf. 13½x13¾
1742 A432 Sheet of 3, #a-c 8.50 6.75

No. 1742 contains three 42x32mm stamps and sold for 15,000k.

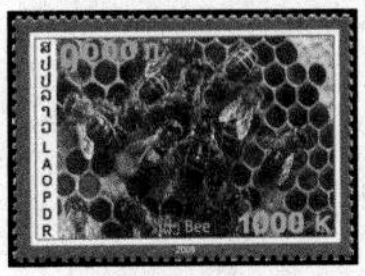
Bees — A434

Designs: 1000k, Bees and honeycomb. 4000k, Bees on flower. 6000k, Beehive. 8500k, Bee in flight.

2008, June 13 *Perf. 13*
1747-1750 A434 Set of 4 11.00 8.75

Waterfalls — A435

Designs: Nos. 1751, 1755a, 500k, Taat Fan Waterfall. Nos. 1752, 1755b, 2000k, Tad Sae Waterfall, horiz. Nos. 1753, 1755c, 5000k, Kuang Si Waterfall. Nos. 1754, 1755d, 6500k, Khonphapheng Waterfall, horiz.

2008, July 28 *Perf. 13*
Sizes: 30x45mm, 45x30mm (Horiz. Stamps)
1751-1754 A435 Set of 4 9.00 6.25

Souvenir Sheet
Perf. 13¾x13½, 13½x13¾
1755 A435 Sheet of 4, #a-d 9.50 7.25

No. 1755 contains two 32x42mm stamps and two 42x32mm stamps and sold for 16,000k.

Eggplants A436

Designs: Nos. 1756, 1760a, 1000k, White eggplants. Nos. 1757, 1760b, 2000k, Green eggplants. Nos. 1758, 1760c, 4000k, Green, striped eggplants. Nos. 1759, 1760d, 5500k, Purple eggplants.

2008, Oct. 1 *Perf. 13*
Size: 45x30mm
1756-1759 A436 Set of 4 8.00 5.75

Souvenir Sheet
1760 A436 Sheet of 4, #a-d 9.00 6.75

No. 1760 contains four 42x32mm stamps and sold for 15,000k.

Hmong New Year — A437

Designs: Nos. 1761, 1765a, 1000k, Woman. Nos. 1762, 1765b, 5500k, Two oxen, horiz. Nos. 1763, 1765c, 6000k, Musician. Nos. 1764, 1765d, 7500k, Two women holding umbrellas, horiz.

2008, Dec. 1 ***Perf. 13***

Size: 30x45mm, 45x30mm (Horiz. Stamps)

1761-1764 A437 Set of 4 12.00 9.00

Souvenir Sheet

Perf. 13¾x13½, 13½x13¾

1765 A437 Sheet of 4, #a-d 12.50 9.00

No. 1765 contains two 32x42mm stamps and two 42x32mm stamps.

Antiquities of Laos — A438

Designs: Nos. 1766, 1770a, 1000k, Haw Phra Kaew. Nos. 1767, 1770b, 2000k, Plain of Jars. Nos. 1768, 1770c, 4000k, Phat That Luang. Nos. 1769, 1770d, 7500k, Temple.

2009, Jan. 3 ***Perf. 13***

Stamps With White Frames

1766-1769 A438 Set of 4 8.50 5.00

Souvenir Sheet

Stamps With Colored Frames

1770 A438 Sheet of 4, #a-d 8.50 5.25

No. 1770 sold for 15,000k.

A439

A440

A441

Army, 60th Anniv. — A442

2009, Jan. 20

1771 A439 2000k multi 2.00 1.25
1772 A440 2000k multi 2.00 1.25
1773 A441 2000k multi 2.00 1.25
1774 A442 2000k multi 2.00 1.25
a. Souvenir sheet of 4, #1771-1774 6.00 6.00
Nos. 1771-1774 (4) 8.00 5.00

No, 1774a sold for 10,000k.

A443

A444

Opening of Laos-Thailand Rail Link — A445

2009, Mar. 5

1775 A443 3000k multi 2.00 1.50
1776 A444 3000k multi 2.00 1.50
1777 A445 3000k multi 2.00 1.50
a. Souvenir sheet of 3, #1775-1777 12.00 12.00
Nos. 1775-1777 (3) 6.00 4.50

No. 1777a sold for 15,000k.

China 2009 World Stamp Exhibition — A446

Color of flower: No. 1778, 7500k, White. No. 1779, 7500k, Red.

2009, Mar. 20

1778-1779 A446 Set of 2 8.00 6.50
1779a Souvenir sheet of 2, #1778-1779 12.00 12.00

No. 1779a sold for 20,000k, and exists imperf.

Flowers A447

Designs: 500k, Mari flower. 2000k, Ixora. 4000k, White Vuddish flowers (Calotropis gigantea). 7500k, Lilac Vuddish flowers (Calotropis gigantea).

2009, May 15

1780-1783 A447 Set of 4 6.00 5.00
1783a Souvenir sheet of 4, #1780-1783 8.00 6.00

No. 1783a sold for 15,000k.

Rice Alcohol — A448

Designs: 1000k, Pots with sticks. 2000k, Horn and pot. 5500k, Man and pot.

2009, Aug. 11

1784-1786 A448 Set of 3 5.00 5.00

A souvenir sheet containing Nos. 1784-1786 sold for 18,000k.

Postmarks — A449

No. 1787 — Postmark of: a, R. P. Vientiane. b, Centre de Tri. c, Phongsaly. d, Luangnamtha. e, Oudomxay. f, Bokeo. g, Luangpabang. h, Huaphan. i, Sayaboury. j, Xiengkhouang. k, Vientiane. l, Bolikhamxay. m, Khammouane. n, Savannakhet. o, Saravan. p, Sekong. q, Champasack. r, Attapeu.

2009, Oct. 9 ***Perf. 13½***

1787 Sheet of 18 17.50 17.50
a.-r. A449 2000r Any single .75 .50

25th South East Asian Games, Vientiane A450

Mascots and: 5000k, Red background. 7000k, Flag, blue background.

2009, Dec. 9 ***Perf. 14½x14***

1788-1789 A450 Set of 2 6.50 6.50
1789a Souvenir sheet of 2, #1788-1789 9.00 9.00

No. 1789a sold for 15,000k.

Nos. 1788-1789 exist in a souvenir sheet of 4 containing 2 each, along with 4 labels that could be personalized.

Wat Simuong — A451

Designs: 4000k, Statue. 5000k, Stone temple. 6000k, Temple.

2009, Dec. 7 ***Perf. 13***

1790-1792 A451 Set of 3 9.00 9.00
1792a Souvenir sheet of 3, #1790-1792 11.00 11.00

No. 1792a sold for 18,000k.

Flora — A452

Designs: 1000k, Litsea cubeba. 3000k, Orthosiphon stamineus, vert. 4000k, Strychnos nux-vomica, vert. 5000k, Zingiber sp. 8000k, Styrax tonkinensis, vert. 9000k, Aquilaria crassna, vert.

2010, Jun. 30 **Litho.**

1793-1798 A452 Set of 6 25.00 25.00
1797a Souvenir sheet of 3 — —
1798a Souvenir sheet of 3 — —

No. 1797a contains Nos. 1794, 1795, and 1797. No. 1798a contains Nos. 1793, 1796, and 1798.

Rural Life — A453

Designs: 1000k, Huts and people near stream. 6000k, Weavers. 12,000k, Woman and children winnowing rice.

2010, Feb. 5

1799-1801 A453 Set of 3 10.00 10.00
1801a Souvenir sheet of 3, #1799-1801 12.00 12.00

No. 1801a sold for 20,000k.

Laotian Landscapes A454

Designs: 1000k, Cave entrance. 3000k, Lake. 4000k, Boat on river. 10,000k, Canyon.

2010, Apr. 1

1802-1805 A454 Set of 4 10.00 10.00
1805a Souvenir sheet of 4, #1802-1805 12.00 12.00

No. 1805a sold for 20,000k.

Rice Blessing Festival — A455

Designs: 4000k, Boy placing stick in clay pot. 5000k, Offering. 11,000k, People looking at burning candles.

2010, July 26

1806-1808 A455 Set of 3 12.00 12.00
1808a Souvenir sheet of 3, #1806-1808 11.00 11.00
1808b Souvenir sheet of 1 #1808 11.00 11.00

No. 1808b sold for 15,000k.

Wild Fruit — A456

Color of fruit: 500k, Brown. 1500k, Red. 8000k, Yellow orange. 9000k, Green.

2010. Sept. 1

1809-1812 A456 Set of 4 12.00 12.00
1812a Souvenir sheet of 4, #1809-1812 12.50 12.50

No. 1812a sold for 20,000k.

Vientiane, 450th Anniv. A457

Emblem and Pha That Luang Stupa, Vientiane, in: 1000k, 1889. 3000k, 1910. 5000k, 1935. 6000k, 2010.

20,000k, Golden Stupa and statue, vert.

2010, Nov. 15 **Litho.** ***Perf. 14½x14***

1813-1816 A457 Set of 4 8.50 8.50

Souvenir Sheet

Litho. & Embossed With Foil Application

1817 A457 20,000k gold & multi 12.00 12.00

No. 1817 contains one 48x60mm stamp.

People's Democratic Republic of Laos, 35th Anniv. A458

Designs: 5000k, Army officer pointing. 6000k, Soldiers and large gun, vert. 10,000k, Laotian leaders and soldiers. No. 1821a, Like 10,000k.

2010, Dec. 2 **Litho.** ***Perf. 13***

1818-1820 A458 Set of 3 11.00 11.00
1821 A458 Souvenir sheet of 3, #1818, 1819, 1821a 18.00 18.00
a. 9000k multi 5.00 5.00

Selection of Luang Prabang as UNESCO World Heritage Site, 15th Anniv. — A459

Various views of Luang Prabang festivals: 2000k, 3000k, 5000k, 10,000k.

2010, Dec. 12

1822-1825 A459 Set of 4 12.00 12.00
1825a Souvenir sheet of 4, #1822-1825 12.00 12.00

Traditional Women's Costumes — A460

Various women in traditional costumes: 1000k, 3000k, 4000k, 5000k, 8000k.

2011, Jan. 31
1826-1830 A460 Set of 5 12.00 12.00

Potters and Pottery — A461

Designs: 1000k, Potter. 3000k, Clay pot. 5000k, Decorated clay pot. 6000k, Potter, diff.

2011, Mar. 14
1831-1834 A461 Set of 4 10.00 10.00

Peonies A462

No. 1835: a, 7000k, Pink peonies. b, 8000k, White peonies.

2011, Mar. 20 ***Perf. 12½***
1835 A462 Pair, #a-b 10.00 10.00
c. Souvenir sheet of 1 #1835b 7.00 7.00

Nos. 1835 and 1835a exist imperforate.

Diplomatic Relations Between Laos and Thailand, 60th Anniv. — A463

Designs: No. 1836, 8000k, Laotian woman with black skirt. No. 1837, 8000k, Thai woman with yellow dress. No. 1838, 8000k, White frangipani flowers. No. 1839, 8000k, Yellow Cassia fistula flowers.

2011, Apr. 22 ***Perf. 13***
1836-1839 A463 Set of 4 20.00 20.00
1839a Souvenir sheet of 4, #1836-1839 25.00 25.00

No. 1839a sold for 35,000k. See Thailand No. 2602.

Dipmomatic Relations Beween Laos and People's Republic of China, 50th Anniv. — A464

2011, Apr. 25
1840 A464 9000k multi 5.00 5.00

A souvenir sheet containing one No. 1840 sold for 20,000k.

Orchids A465

Paphiopedilum barbigerum var. sulivongii: 1000k, One flower. 9000k, Three flowers. 11,000k, One flower, with leaves.

2011, May 22
1841-1843 A465 Set of 3 20.00 20.00
1843a Souvenir sheet of 3, #1841-1843 30.00 30.00

No. 1843a sold for 25,000k. Imperforate examples of No. 1843a sold for 35,000k.

Forest Products — A466

Products harvested from trees: 3000k, Lac resin. 4000k, Cinnamon. 5000k, Malva nuts. 6000k, Gurjum balsam. 11,000k, Dammar gum. 12,000k, Beeswax, horiz.

2011, June 15 ***Perf. 13***
1844-1849 A466 Set of 6 25.00 25.00
1848a Souvenir sheet of 3, #1844, 1847, 1848, imperf., on card, without gum — —
1849a Souvenir sheet of 3, #1845, 1846, 1849, imperf., on card, without gum — —

Nos. 1848a and 1849a each sold for 22,000k.

Wildlife Conservation A467

Designs: 1000k, Asian elephant. 3000k, Tiger. 5000k, Saola. 8000k, Red-shanked douc langur.

2011, July 13
1850-1853 A467 Set of 4 12.00 12.00
1853a Souvenir sheet of 4, #1850-1853 15.00 15.00

No. 1853a sold for 20,000k.

Lotus Flowers A468

No. 1854: a, 7000k, Lotus flower. b, 8000k, Lotus flower, diff.

2011, Aug. 12
1854 A468 Horiz. pair, #a-b 9.00 9.00

No. 1854 exists as a souvenir sheet of 3 pairs.

A469

A470

City Pillar, Vientiane A471

2011, Nov. 10
1855 A469 9000k multi 6.00 6.00
1856 A470 9000k multi 6.00 6.00
1857 A471 9000k multi 6.00 6.00
a. Souvenir sheet of 3, #1855-1857 20.00 20.00
Nos. 1855-1857 (3) 18.00 18.00

No. 1857a sold for 30,000k.

Miniature Sheet

Architecture in Vientiane and Moscow — A472

No. 1858: a, 6000k, Pha That Luang, Vientiane. b, 7000k, St. Basil's Cathedral, Moscow. c, 8000k, Temple, Vientiane. d, 9000k, Egg House, Moscow.

2011, Dec. 3 ***Perf. 14¼x14***
1858 A472 Sheet of 4, #a-d 25.00 25.00

No. 1858 exists imperforate. For overprint, see No. 1873.

New Year 2012 (Year of the Dragon) — A473

2012, Jan. 10 Litho. ***Perf. 13¼***
1859 A473 8000k multi 4.50 4.50

No. 1859 was printed in sheets of 4.

Laos Pres. Kaysone Phomvihane (1920-92), North Viet Nam Pres. Ho Chi Minh (1890-1969), Flags of Laos and Viet Nam — A474

Buildings in Laos and Viet Nam — A475

2012, July 18 Litho. ***Perf. 13x12¾***
1860 A474 4000k multi 2.50 2.50
1861 A475 12,000k multi 6.50 6.50

See Viet Nam Nos. 3458-3459.

Asia-Europe Summit Meeting, Vientiane A476

Emblems for summit and: 9000k, Laotian temple. 11,000k, Map with Europe and Southeast Asis highlighted.

2012, Nov. 5 Litho. ***Perf. 13x12¾***
1862-1863 A476 Set of 2 9.00 9.00

An imperforate souvenir sheets containing No. 1862 sold for 20,000k. A souvenir sheet containing No. 1863 sold for 20,000k.

Silk Processing A477

Designs: 2000k, Boiling of silk cocoons. 3000k, Spinning of silk. 4000k, Collection of cocoons. 5000k, Mulberries on tree.

2013, Apr. 22 Litho. ***Perf. 13***
1864-1867 A477 Set of 4 7.25 7.25
1867a Souvenir sheet of 4, #1864-1867 13.00 13.00

No. 1867a sold for 25,000k and exists imperforate.

Miniature Sheet

Cultural Cooperation Between Laos and Russia — A478

No. 1868: a, 6000k, Patuxai Gate, Vientiane. b, 7000k, Triumphal Arch, Moscow. c, 8000k, Pagoda, Laos. d, 9000k, Tower, Russia.

2013, July 5 Litho. ***Perf. 14¼x14***
1868 A478 Sheet of 4, #a-d 22.00 22.00

No. 1868 exists imperforate.

Fish — A479

Designs: 2000k, Clupisoma sinense. 4000k, Hemibarus filamentus. 6000k, Great white catfish. 9000k, Bagarius yarrelli.

2013, July 6 Litho. ***Perf. 13***
1869-1872 A479 Set of 4 11.00 11.00
1872a Souvenir sheet of 4, #1869-1872 13.00 13.00

No. 1872a sold for 25,000k and exists imperforate.

No. 1858 Overprinted in Red and Blue

Methods and Perfs. As Before

2013, July 10
1873 A472 Sheet of 4, #a-d *57.50 57.50*

Nos. 1873a-1873d are Nos. 1858a-1858d with a different part of the overprint covering the sheet. No. 1873 exixts imperforate.

Stupas — A480

Designs: 1000k, Xiengkhoeng Stupa, Huaphanh. 2000k, Wat That Noi Stupa, Luang Prabang. 3000k, Makmo Stupa, Luang Prabang. 4000k, Phonphao Stupa, Luang Prabang. 10,000k, Phousi Stupa, Luang Prabang.

2013, Nov. 11 Litho. *Perf. 13*
1874-1878 A480 Set of 5 9.75 9.75

Perforate and imperforate souvenir sheets containing one example of No. 1874 exist. Each sheet sold for 25,000k.

Fourth International Mekong Bridge — A481

Designs: No. 1879, 8000k, Border check-point and parking lot. No. 1880, 8000k, Bridge.

2013, Dec. 11 Litho. *Perf. 13*
1879-1880 A481 Set of 2 7.50 7.50
1880a Souvenir sheet of 2, #1879-1880 12.50 12.50

No. 1880a sold for 25,000k and exists imperforate.

First Laos-Thailand Friendship Bridge, 20th Anniv. — A482

No. 1881 — Bridge and: a, Sai Buddha Image Procession Festival, Nong Khai, Thailand, and Wax Candle Procession Festival, Vientiane. b, Pho Chai Temple, Nong Khai, and On Teu Temple, Vientiane.

2014, Apr. 8 Litho. *Perf. 14½x14*
1881 A482 9000k Horiz. pair, #a-b 8.00 8.00
c. Souvenir sheet of 2, #1881a-1881b 9.00 9.00

No. 1881c sold for 20,00k and exists imperforate. See Thailand No. 2807.

Nos. 535-537, 834-835 Handstamp Srchd.

Methods and Perfs. As Before
2014, July 22
1882 A207 5000k on 1k #834 3.00 3.00
1883 A207 8000k on 2k #835 4.75 4.75
1884 A154 10,000k on 60c #535 6.00 6.00
1885 A154 11,000k on 1k #536 6.50 6.50
1886 A154 12,000k on 2k #537 7.00 7.00
Nos. 1882-1886 (5) 27.25 27.25

A483

A484

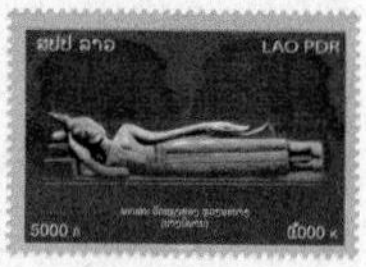
A485

Buddhas — A486

2014, Oct. 8 Litho. *Perf. 13*
1887 A483 5000k multi 2.40 2.40
1888 A484 5000k multi 2.40 2.40
1889 A485 5000k multi 2.40 2.40
1890 A486 5000k multi 2.40 2.40
a. Souvenir sheet of 4, #1887-1890 12.50 12.50

No. 1890a sold for 25,000k and exists imperf.

Tourist Attractions A487

Designs: No. 1891, 5000k, Wat Nonglamchanh, Savannakhet Province. No. 1892, 5000k, Tham Ting Cave, Luang Prabang Province. No. 1893, 5000k. Wat Sisaket Tripitaka Hall, Vientiane. No. 1894, 5000k, Sikhottabong Stupa, Khammuan Province. 9000k, Wat Phiawat, Xiengkhuang Province.

2014, Nov. 11 Litho. *Perf. 13*
1891-1895 A487 Set of 5 14.00 14.00
1895a Souvenir sheet of 4, #1892-1895 16.00 16.00

No. 1895a sold for 25,000k and exists imperf. A souvenir sheet containing No. 1891 sold for 25,000k and exists imperf.

Monuments — A488

Designs: No. 1896, 5000k, King Saya Setthathirath. No. 1897, 5000k, King Chao Anouvong. 11,000k, King Fangoum Maharath.

2014, Dec. 1 Litho. *Perf. 13*
1896-1898 A488 Set of 3 9.75 9.75
1898a Souvenir sheet of 3, #1896-1898 12.50 12.50

No. 1898a sold for 25,000k and exists imperf.

Nos. 276a, 535-537 and 1073 Surcharged

Methods and Perfs. As Before
2015
1899 A154 10,000k on 60c #535 4.50 4.50
1900 A154 11,000k on 1k #536 5.00 5.00
1901 A154 12,000k on 2k #537 5.50 5.50
1902 A254 13,000k on 220k #1073 6.00 6.00
Nos. 1899-1902 (4) 21.00 21.00

Souvenir Sheet
1903 Sheet of 5, #1903a-1903e (#276a) 32.50 32.50
a. A96 14,000k on 1k #272 6.50 6.50
b. A96 14,000k on 2k #273 6.50 6.50
c. A96 14,000k on 5k #274 6.50 6.50
d. A96 14,000k on 10k #275 6.50 6.50
e. A96 14,000k on 200k #276 6.50 6.50

Issued: 11,000k, 2/19; 10,000k, 12,000k, 13,000k, 2/26; No. 1903, 3/13.

National Posts and Telecommunications Day, 50th Anniv. — A489

Designs: No. 1904, 10,000k, Satellite dish, telegraph key, telephone, people carrying sacks, airplane, letters, mailbox. No. 1905, 10,000k, Communications workers.

2015, Mar. 13 Litho. *Perf. 13*
1904-1905 A489 Set of 2 9.50 9.50
1905a Souvenir sheet of 2, #1904-1905 12.00 12.00

No. 1905a sold for 25,000k and exists imperf.

Flags and Emblem of Association of Southeast Asian Nations — A490

2015, Aug. 8 Litho. *Perf. 13½*
1906 A490 13,000k multi — —
a. Souvenir sheet of 1 — —

No. 1906 sold for 25,000k and exists imperforate.
See Brunei No. 656, Burma Nos. 417-418, Cambodia No. 2428, Indonesia No. 2428, Malaysia No. 1562, Philippines No. 3619, Singapore No. 1742, Thailand No. 2875, Viet Nam No. 3529.

Houses of Worship — A491

Designs: No. 1907, 9000k, Pha That Luang, Vientiane. No. 1908, 9000k, Cathedral of the Intercession of the Holy Virgin, Bogolyubovo, Russia.

2015, Oct. 7 Litho. *Perf. 13½*
1907-1908 A491 Set of 2 8.75 8.75
1908a Souvenir sheet of 2, #1907-1908 — —

No. 1908a sold for 25,000k and exists imperforate. See Russia No. 7697.

National Day, 40th Anniv. — A492

Designs: No. 1909, 5000k, Flag of Laos. No. 1910, 5000k, People in parade carrying flags, emblem of Laos and photograph of Kaysone Phomvihane. No. 1911, 5000k, Four Laotians. No. 1912, 5000k, Cooling towers and high-speed train.

2015, Dec. 2 Litho. *Perf. 13*
1909-1912 A492 Set of 4 9.75 9.75
1912a Souvenir sheet of 4, #1909-1912 — —

No. 1912a sold for 25,000k and exists imperforate.

Selection of Luang Prabang as UNESCO World Heritage Site, 20th Anniv. — A493

Designs: No. 1913, 5000k, Laotian people, spinning wheel. No. 1914, 5000k, Bridge and boats. No. 1915, 5000k, Buddhist monks. No. 1916, 5000k, Building on stilts.

2015, Dec. 7 Litho. *Perf. 13*
1913-1916 A493 Set of 4 9.75 9.75
1916a Souvenir sheet of 4, #1913-1916 — —

No. 1916a sold for 22,000k and exists imperforate.

Laotian International Women's Group, 26th Anniv. — A494

2016, Mar. 8 Litho. *Perf. 13*
1917 A494 13,000k multi 6.00 6.00
a. Souvenir sheet of 1 — —

No. 1917a sold for 25,000k and exists imperforate.

Dhamma Assembly Hall, Wat That Luang — A495

2016, Nov. 14 Litho. *Perf. 13*
1918 A495 15,000k multi 7.00 7.00
a. Souvenir sheet of 1 7.00 7.00
b. As "a," imperf. 7.00 7.00

That Luang Stupa Foundation, 450th Anniv. — A496

Designs: No. 1919, 9000k, Shown, gray sky. No. 1920, 9000k, Stupa, blue sky.
No. 1921, 9000k: a, Like No. 1919, orange background. b, Like No. 1920, orange background.

2016, Nov. 16 Litho. *Perf. 13*
1919-1920 A496 Set of 2 9.00 9.00

Souvenir Sheet
1921 A496 9000k Sheet of 2, #a-b 9.00 9.00
c. As No. 1921, imperf. 9.00 9.00

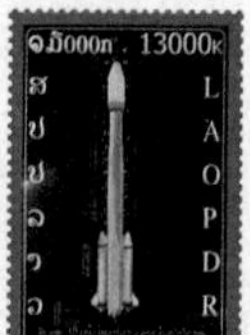
Launch of Lao Sat-1, 1st Anniv. — A497

Designs: 13,000k, Rocket launch. 15,000k, Lao Sat-1 in space.

2016, Nov. 21 Litho. *Perf. 13*
1922 A497 13,000k multi — —
a. Souvenir sheet of 1 — —
1923 A497 15,000k multi — —

No. 1922a sold fro 18,000k and exists imperforate.

A498

A499

A500

Laotian Traditional Wedding — A501

2016, Dec. 19 Litho. *Perf. 13*

1924 A498 8000k multi	4.00	4.00
a. Souvenir sheet of 1	—	—
1925 A499 8000k multi	4.00	4.00
1926 A500 8000k multi	4.00	4.00
1927 A501 8000k multi	4.00	4.00
Nos. 1924-1927 (4)	16.00	16.00

No. 1924a sold for 10,000k and exists imperforate.

Flags and National Flowers Association of Southeast Asian Nations — A502

National flower, flag of: No. 1928, 1000k, Sphaerocoryne affinis, Cambodia. No. 1929, 1000k, Dillenia suffruticosa, Brunei. No. 1930, 1000k, Jasminum sambac, Philippines. No. 1931, 1000k, Vanda Miss Joaquim, Singapore. No. 1932, 1000k, Phalaenopsis amabilis, Indonesia. No. 1933, 1000k, Plumeria, Laos. No. 1934, 1000k, Pterocarpus macrocarpus, Myanmar. No. 1935, 1000k, Hibiscus rosa-sinensis, Malaysia. No. 1936, 1000k, Cassia fistula, Thailand. No. 1937, 1000k, Lotus, Viet Nam.

2016, Dec. 26 Litho. *Perf. 13*

1928-1937 A502 Set of 10	—	—
1937a Souvenir sheet of 10, #1928-1937	—	—

No. 1937a sold for 18,000k and exists imperforate.

Traditional Women's Clothing — A503

Women wearing various garments: 1000k, 2000k, 3000k, 9000k.
15,000k, Three women in traditional clothing.

2017, Mar. 8 Litho. *Perf. 13*

1938-1941 A503 Set of 4	8.00	8.00

Size: 140x140mm

Imperf

1942 A503 15,000k multi + perforated label	—	—

Label on No. 1942 lacks a denomination. No. 1942 exists with the label lacking perforations.

Flower and Emblem of Association of Southeast Asian Nations — A504

2017, Aug. 8 Litho. *Perf. 13*

1943 A504 9000k multi	—	—

Tree House, Bokeo Province — A505

2017, Dec. 25 Litho. *Perf. 13*

1944 A505 10,000k multi	—	—
a. Souvenir sheet of 1	—	—

No. 1944a sold for 15,000k, and exists imperforate.

Ethnic Groups of Laos — A506

Designs: 1000k, Phong woman. 2000k, Thaineua woman. 3000k, Ngouan woman. 8000k, Katu woman.

2017, Dec. 28 Litho. *Perf. 13*

1945-1948 A506 Set of 4	—	—

A souvenir sheet containing No. 1948 sold for 18,000k and exists imperforate.

Nos. 1364-1365, 1367-1368 Handstamp Surcharged

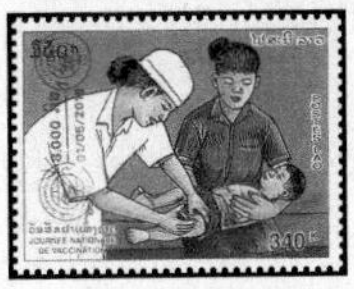

Methods and Perfs. As Before

2018, May 1

1949 A317 8000k on 340k #1364	—	—
1950 A317 8000k on 370k #1365	—	—
1951 A319 17,000k on 380k #1367	—	—
1952 A319 20,000k on 420k #1368	—	—

Zodiac Animals — A507

Designs: No. 1953, 2000k, Rat. No. 1954, 2000k, Ox. No. 1955, 2000k, Tiger. No. 1956, 2000k, Rabbit. No. 1957, 2000k, Dragon. No. 1958, 2000k, Snake. No. 1959, 2000k, Horse. No. 1960, 2000k, Goat. No. 1961, 2000k, Monkey. No. 1962, 2000k, Rooster. No. 1963, 2000k, Dog. No. 1964, 2000k, Pig.

2018, Sept. 18 Litho. *Perf. 13½*

1953-1964 A507 Set of 12	—	—
1964a Souvenir sheet of 12, #1953-1964	—	—

No. 1964a sold for 25,000k and exists imperforate

Laotian Man and Woman and Emblem of Association of Southeast Asian Nations — A508

2019 Litho. *Perf. 13*

1965 A508 8000k multi	—	—

A souvenir sheet of 1 sold for 20,000k and exists imperf..

A509

Victory Gate Monument — A510

2019 Litho. *Perf. 13*

1966 A509 8000k multi	—	—
1967 A510 8000k multi	—	—
a. Souvenir sheet of 2, #1966-1967	—	—

No. 1967a sold for 20,000k and exists imperforate.

A511

A512

Antique Mortars A513

2019 Litho. *Perf. 13*

1968 A511 8000k multi	—	—
1969 A512 8000k multi	—	—
1970 A513 8000k multi	—	—
a. Souvenir sheet of 3, #1968-1970	—	—

No. 1970a sold for 25,000k and exists imperforate.

SEMI-POSTAL STAMPS

Laotian Children — SP1

Unwmk.

1953, July 14 Engr. *Perf. 13*

B1 SP1 1.50pi + 1pi multi	2.40	2.25
B2 SP1 3pi + 1.50pi multi	2.75	2.25
B3 SP1 3.90pi + 2.50pi multi	3.00	2.50
Nos. B1-B3 (3)	8.15	7.00

The surtax was for the Red Cross.

Nos. 52 and 46 Surcharged: "1k ANNEE MONDIALE DU REFUGIE 1959-1960"

1960, Apr. 7

B4 A16 4k + 1k car red	3.50	3.50
B5 A13 10k + 1k multicolored	5.00	5.00

World Refugee Year, July 1, 1959-June 30, 1960. The surcharge was for aid to refugees.

Flooded Village — SP2

40k+10k, Flooded market place and truck. 60k+15k, Flooded airport and plane.

1967, Jan. 18 Engr. *Perf. 13*

B6 SP2 20k + 5k multi	.45	.25
B7 SP2 40k + 10k multi	.85	.55
B8 SP2 60k + 15k multi	1.40	1.25
a. Miniature sheet of 3	6.00	6.00
Nos. B6-B8 (3)	2.70	2.05

The surtax was for victims of the Mekong Delta flood. No. B8a contains one each of Nos. B6-B8. Size: 148x99mm. Sold for 250k.

Women Working in Tobacco Field — SP3

1967, Oct. 5 Engr. *Perf. 13*

B9 SP3 20k + 5k multi	.75	.40
B10 SP3 50k + 10k multi	1.25	.75
B11 SP3 60k + 15k multi	2.00	1.10
a. Souv. sheet of 3, #B9-B11	4.50	4.50
Nos. B9-B11 (3)	4.00	2.25

Laotian Red Cross, 10th anniv. No. B11a sold for 250k+30k.

Nos. 184-189 Surcharged: "Soutien aux Victimes / de la Guerre / + 5k"

1970, May 1 Photo. *Perf. 14*

B12 A58 10k + 5k multi	.50	.30
B13 A58 15k + 5k multi	.60	.30
B14 A58 20k + 5k multi	.65	.30
B15 A58 30k + 5k multi	.85	.30
B16 A58 40k + 5k multi	1.25	.50
B17 A58 60k + 5k multi	1.30	.60
Nos. B12-B17,CB1-CB2 (8)	11.65	6.05

AIR POST STAMPS

Weaving AP1

Design: 3.30pi, Wat Pra Keo.

Unwmk.

1952, Apr. 13 Engr. *Perf. 13*

C1 AP1 3.30pi dk pur & pur	2.25	1.00
C2 AP1 10pi ultra & bl grn	2.00	1.25
C3 AP1 20pi deep cl & red	3.50	2.75
C4 AP1 30pi blk brn & dk brn violet	4.50	4.25
Nos. C1-C4 (4)	12.25	9.25

See note following No. 17.

UPU Monument and King Sisavang-Vong — AP2

1952, Dec. 7

C5 AP2 25pi vio bl & indigo	5.00	4.50
C6 AP2 50pi dk brn & vio brn	6.00	5.50

Laos' admission to the UPU, May 13, 1952.

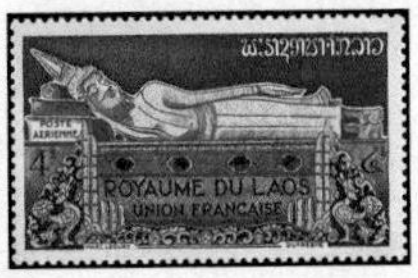
AP3

AP4

Designs: Various Buddha statues.

1953, Nov. 18

C7 AP3 4pi dark green 1.25 .60
C8 AP4 6.50pi dk bl green 1.25 .60
C9 AP4 9pi blue green 1.75 .90
C10 AP3 11.50pi red, yel & dk vio brn 2.75 1.25
C11 AP4 40pi purple 4.50 1.75
C12 AP4 100pi olive 8.00 4.50
Nos. C7-C12 (6) 19.50 9.60

Great Oath of Laos ceremony.

Accession Type of Regular Issue

1954, Mar. 4 **Unwmk.**

C13 A6 50pi indigo & bl grn 120.00 95.00
Hinged 75.00

Ravana AP6

Sita and Rama — AP7

Scenes from the Ramayana: 4k, Hanuman, the white monkey. 5k, Ninh Laphath, the black monkey. 20k, Lucy with a friend of Ravana. 30k, Rama.

1955, Oct. 28 **Engr.** ***Perf. 13***

C14 AP6 2k bl grn, emer & ind .75 .45
C15 AP6 4k red brn, dk red brn & ver 1.20 .90
C16 AP6 5k scar, sep & olive 1.90 1.40
C17 AP7 10k blk, org & brn 3.75 1.60
C18 AP7 20k vio, dk grn & olive 5.25 2.75
C19 AP7 30k ultra, blk & salmon 6.75 4.00
Nos. C14-C19 (6) 19.60 11.10

See No. 225.

Buddha Type of Regular Issue, 1956

1956, May 24

C20 A7 20k carmine rose 27.00 20.00
C21 A7 30k ol sepia & brn 27.00 25.00

2500th anniversary of birth of Buddha.

UN Emblem — AP8

1956, Dec. 14

C22 AP8 15k light blue 4.25 4.25
C23 AP8 30k deep claret 5.50 5.50

Admission of Laos to the UN, 1st anniv.

Types of Regular Issue, 1957

Musical Instruments: 12k, Khong vong. 14k, So. 20k, Kong.

1957, Mar. 25 **Unwmk.** ***Perf. 13***

C24 A9 12k multicolored 2.50 1.60
C25 A10 14k multicolored 2.75 1.90
C26 A10 20k bl grn, yel grn & pur 3.25 2.60
Nos. C24-C26 (3) 8.50 6.10

Monk Receiving Alms — AP9

Monks Meditating in Boat AP10

18k, Smiling Buddha. 24k, Ancient temple painting (horse and mythological figures.)

1957, Nov. 5

C27 AP9 10k dk pur, pale brn & dk grn 1.25 1.25
C28 AP10 15k dk vio brn, brn org & yel 1.25 1.25
C29 AP9 18k slate grn & ol 1.50 1.50
C30 AP10 24k claret, org yel & blk 3.25 3.25
Nos. C27-C30 (4) 7.25 7.25

No. C28 measures 48x27mm. No. C30, 48x36mm. See No. C84.

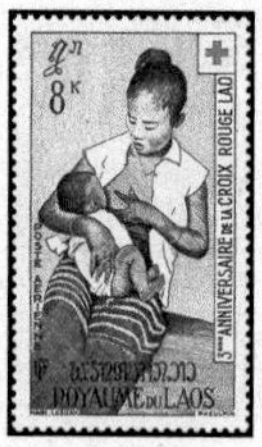

Mother Nursing Infant — AP11

1958, May 2 **Cross in Red**

C31 AP11 8k lil gray & dk gray 1.30 .75
C32 AP11 12k red brn & brn 1.50 1.00
C33 AP11 15k sl grn & bluish green 1.60 1.00
C34 AP11 20k bister & vio 2.10 1.50
Nos. C31-C34 (4) 6.50 4.25

3rd anniversary of Laotian Red Cross.

Plain of Stones, Xieng Khouang — AP12

Papheng Falls, Champassak — AP13

Natl. Tourism Industry: 15k, Buffalo cart. 19k, Buddhist monk and village.

1960, July 1 **Engr.** ***Perf. 13***

C35 AP12 9.50k bl, ol & claret .50 .50
C36 AP13 12k vio bl, red brn & gray .50 .50
C37 AP13 15k yel grn, ol gray & cl .75 .75
C38 AP12 19k multicolored 1.00 1.00
Nos. C35-C38 (4) 2.75 2.75

Pou Gneu Nha Gneu Legend AP14

Garuda AP15

Hanuman, the White Monkey AP16

Nang Teng One Legend AP17

1962, Feb. 19 **Unwmk.** ***Perf. 13***

C39 AP14 11k grn, car & ocher .60 .60
C40 AP15 14k ultra & org .60 .60
C41 AP16 20k multicolored .80 .80
C42 AP17 25k multicolored .90 .90
Nos. C39-C42 (4) 2.90 2.90

Makha Bousa festival.

Yao Hunter — AP18

1964, Dec. 15 **Engr.** ***Perf. 13***

C43 AP18 5k shown .55 .25
C44 AP18 10k Kha hunter .55 .35
C45 AP18 50k Meo woman 1.60 1.00
a. Min. sheet of 4, #100, C43-C45 7.50 6.50
Nos. C43-C45 (3) 2.70 1.60

No. C45a exists imperf in a booklet. Value, intact booklet $75.

Butterfly Type of 1965

1965, Mar. 13 **Size: 48x27mm**

C46 A34 20k Attacus atlas 5.50 2.50

Phayre's Flying Squirrel — AP19

Designs: 25k, Leopard cat. 75k, Javan mongoose. 100k, Crestless porcupine. 200k, Binturong.

1965, Oct. 7 **Engr.** ***Perf. 13***

C47 AP19 25k dk brn, yel grn & ocher .50 .25
C48 AP19 55k brown & blue .75 .35
C49 AP19 75k brt grn & brn 1.00 .50
C50 AP19 100k ocher, brn & blk 1.75 1.10
C51 AP19 200k red & black 3.50 2.50
Nos. C47-C51 (5) 7.50 4.70

Army Type of Regular Issue

Design: 200k, 300k, Parading service flags before National Assembly Hall.

1968, July 15 **Engr.** ***Perf. 13***

C52 A53 200k multicolored 1.75 .85
C53 A53 300k multicolored 2.50 1.25
a. Souv. sheet of 5, #168-170, C52-C53 6.00 6.00

No. C53a sold for 600k.

Insect Type of Regular Issue

Insects: 120k, Dorysthenes walkeri, horiz. 160k, Megaloxantha bicolor, horiz.

1968, Aug. 28 **Engr.** ***Perf. 13***

C54 A54 120k brn, org & blk 1.50 .85
C55 A54 160k rose car, Prus bl & yel 2.25 1.25

Ballet Type of Regular Issue

Designs: 110k, Sudagnu battling Thotsakan. 300k, Pharam dancing with Thotsakan.

1969 **Photo.** ***Perf. 14***

C56 A58 110k multicolored 3.50 1.75
a. Souv. sheet of 4, #187-189, C56, imperf. 24.00 24.00
C57 A58 300k multicolored 7.00 3.25
a. Souv. sheet of 4, #184-186, C57, imperf. 24.00 24.00

No. C56a sold for 480k; No. C57a for 650k.

For surcharges see Nos. CB1-CB2.

Timber Industry, Paksane — AP20

1969, May 7 **Engr.** ***Perf. 13***

C58 AP20 300k olive bister & blk 5.50 3.25

ILO, 50th anniversary.

Animal Type of Regular Issue

Animals: 70k, Malaysian black bear. 120k, White-handed gibbon, vert. 150k, Indochinese tiger.

1969, Nov. 6 **Photo.** ***Perf. 12x13***

C59 A60 70k multicolored 1.10 .60
C60 A60 120k multicolored 2.40 1.10
C61 A60 150k multicolored 2.75 1.40
Nos. C59-C61 (3) 5.85 3.10

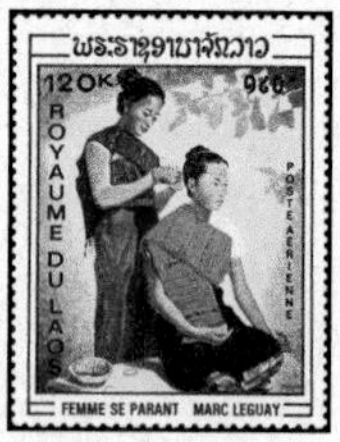

Hairdressing, by Marc Leguay — AP21

Paintings: No. C63, Village Market, by Marc Leguay, horiz. No. C64, Tree on the Bank of the Mekong, by Marc Leguay, horiz.

1969-70 **Photo.** ***Perf. 12x13, 13x12***

C62 AP21 120k multicolored 1.00 .40
C63 AP21 150k multicolored 2.00 .65
C64 AP21 150k multi ('70) 2.00 .65
Nos. C62-C64 (3) 5.00 1.70

See Nos. C72-C74.

Wat Xiengthong, Luang Prabang AP22

1970, Jan. 10 ***Perf. 12x13, 13x12***

C65 AP22 100k Library, Wat Sisaket, vert. 1.40 .65
C66 AP22 120k shown 2.00 1.00

Drum Type of 1970

1970, Mar. 30 **Engr.** ***Perf. 13***

C67 A64 125k Pong wooden drum, vert. 3.00 1.50

Franklin D. Roosevelt (1882-1945) AP23

1970, Apr. 12

C68 AP23 120k olive & slate 1.60 1.10

EXPO '70 Type of Regular Issue

Design: 125k, Woman boiling cocoons in kettle, and spinning silk thread.

1970, July 7 **Engr.** ***Perf. 13***

C69 A66 125k olive & multi 1.75 1.25

See note after No. 202.

Animal Type of Regular Issue

1970, Sept. 7 **Engr.** ***Perf. 13***

C70 A67 210k Leopard 2.75 1.25
C71 A67 500k Gaur 5.00 2.50

Painting Type of 1969-70

Paintings by Marc Leguay: 100k, Village Foot Path. 120k, Rice Field in Rainy Season, horiz. 150k, Village Elder.

Perf. 11½x13, 13x11½

1970, Dec. 21 **Photo.**

C72	AP21	100k multicolored	1.10	1.10
C73	AP21	120k multicolored	1.40	1.40
C74	AP21	150k multicolored	1.60	1.60
		Nos. C72-C74 (3)	4.10	4.10

UN Type of Regular Issue

125k, Earth Goddess Nang Thorani wringing her hair; UN Headquarters and emblem.

1970, Oct. 24 ***Perf. 13***
Size: 26x36mm

C75	A68	125k brt bl, pink & dk grn	2.40	1.10

Hanuman and Nang Matsa AP24

1971, Feb. 5 ***Perf. 13***

C76	AP24	125k multicolored	2.40	1.00

Orchid Type of Regular Issue

Design: 125k, Brasilian cattleya.

1971, July **Photo.** ***Perf. 13x12½***
Size: 48x27mm

C79	A73	125k multi	4.50	1.50

Laotian and French Women, That Luang Pagoda and Arms — AP25

1971, Aug. 6 **Engr.** ***Perf. 13***

C80	AP25	30k brn & dull red	.25	.25
C81	AP25	70k vio & lilac	.50	.40
C82	AP25	100k slate grn & grn	.70	.55
		Nos. C80-C82 (3)	1.45	1.20

Kinship between the cities Keng Kok, Laos, and Saint Astier, France.

Animal Type of Regular Issue

1971, Sept. 16

C83	A74	300k Javan rhinoceros	4.25	2.75

Type of 1957 with Ornamental Panel and Inscription

Design: Monk receiving alms (like No. C27).

1971, Oct. 31 **Engr.** ***Perf. 13***

C84	AP9	125k dk pur, pale brn & dk grn	2.00	1.40

20th anniv. of Laotian independent postal service. No. C84 inscribed: "Vingtième Anniversaire de la Philatélie Lao," "Poste Aerienne" and "1971."

Sunset Over the Mekong, by Chamnane Prisayane AP26

Design: 150k, "Quiet Morning" (village scene), by Chamnane Prisayane.

1971, Dec. 20 **Photo.** ***Perf. 13x12***

C85	AP26	125k black & multi	1.00	1.00
C86	AP26	150k black & multi	1.25	1.25

Book Year Type of Regular Issue

Design: 125k, Father teaching children to read palm leaf book.

1972, Jan. 30 **Engr.** ***Perf. 13***
Size: 48x27mm

C87	A75	125k bright purple	1.75	1.00

Dam Type of Regular Issue

Design: 145k, Nam Ngum Hydroelectric Dam and ECAFE emblem.

1972, Mar. 28 **Engr.** ***Perf. 13***

C88	A76	145k brown, bl & grn	1.40	.80

Orchid Type of Regular Issue

1972, May 5 **Photo.** ***Perf. 13x12½***
Size: 48x27mm

C89	A73	150k Vanda teres, horiz.	4.00	1.50

UNICEF Type of Regular Issue

Design: 120k, Boy riding buffalo to water hole (child's drawing).

1972, July **Engr.** ***Perf. 13***

C90	A77	120k multicolored	1.40	1.00

Nakharath, Daughter of the Dragon King — AP27

Wood carvings from Wat Sikhounvieng Dongmieng, Vientiane: 120k, Nang Kinnali, Goddess from Mt. Kailath. 150k, Norasing, Lion King from Himalayas.

1972, Sept. 15 **Engr.** ***Perf. 13***

C91	AP27	100k blue green	.70	.70
C92	AP27	120k violet	.80	.80
C93	AP27	150k brn orange	1.10	1.10
		Nos. C91-C93 (3)	2.60	2.60

That Luang Religious Festival AP28

1972, Nov. 18 **Engr.** ***Perf. 13***

C94	AP28	110k Presentation of wax castles	.90	.90
C95	AP28	125k Procession	1.10	1.10

Workers in Rice Field, by Leguay — AP29

Paintings by Mark Leguay: No. C97, Women and water buffalo in rice field. Nos. C98, Rainy Season in Village (Water buffalo in water). No. C99, Rainy Season in Village (Water buffalo on land). 120k, Mother and Child.

1972, Dec. 23 **Photo.** ***Perf. 13***

C96	AP29	50k multicolored	.45	.45
C97	AP29	50k multicolored	.45	.45
C98	AP29	70k multicolored	.65	.65
C99	AP29	70k multicolored	.65	.65
C100	AP29	120k yel & multi	1.25	1.25
		Nos. C96-C100 (5)	3.45	3.45

Nos. C97, C99 have denomination and frame at right.

Costume Type of Regular Issue

Women's Costumes: 120k, Luang Prabang marriage costume. 150k, Vientiane evening costume.

1973, Feb. 16 **Engr.** ***Perf. 13***

C101	A78	120k multicolored	1.40	.80
C102	A78	150k brown & multi	1.90	1.00

Lions Club Emblems, King Sayasettha-Thirath — AP30

1973, Mar. 30 **Engr.** ***Perf. 13***

C103	AP30	150k rose & multi	1.90	.75

Lions Club of Vientiane.

Rahu with Rockets and Sputnik AP31

Space achievements: 150k, Laotian festival rocket and US lunar excursion module.

1973, May 11 **Engr.** ***Perf. 13***

C104	AP31	80k ultra & multi	.55	.35
C105	AP31	150k buff & ultra	1.00	.45

Dancing Around Campfire AP32

Design: 125k, Boy Scouts helping during Vientiane Flood, 1966.

1973, Sept. 1 **Engr.** ***Perf. 13***

C106	AP32	110k vio & orange	1.10	.30
C107	AP32	125k Prus grn & bis	1.25	.40

Laotian Scout Movement, 25th anniv.

Sun Chariot and WMO Emblem AP33

Design: 90k, Nang Mékhala, the weather goddess, and WMO emblem, vert.

1973, Oct. 24 **Engr.** ***Perf. 13***

C108	AP33	90k vio, red & ocher	.75	.35
C109	AP33	150k ocher, red & brn ol	.85	.50

Intl. meteorological cooperation, cent.

Woman in Poppy Field, INTERPOL Emblem AP34

1973, Dec. 22 **Engr.** ***Perf. 13***

C110	AP34	150k vio, yel grn & red	1.40	.60

Intl. Criminal Police Org., 50th anniv.

Phra Sratsvady, Wife of Phra Phrom — AP35

Designs: 110k, Phra Indra on 3-headed elephant Erawan. 150k, Phra Phrom, the Creator, on phoenix. Designs show giant sculptures in park at Thadeua.

1974, Mar. 23 **Engr.** ***Perf. 13***

C111	AP35	100k lilac, red & blk	.80	.40
C112	AP35	110k car, vio & brn	1.00	.50
C113	AP35	150k ocher, vio & sepia	1.25	.70
		Nos. C111-C113 (3)	3.05	1.60

UPU Emblem, Women Reading Letter AP36

1974 **Engr.** ***Perf. 13***

C114	AP36	200k lt brn & car	3.75	1.00
C115	AP36	500k lilac & red	6.00	2.00
a.		Souvenir sheet	5.50	5.50

Centenary of Universal Postal Union. Issue dates: 200k, Apr. 30; 500k, Oct. 9.

Flower Type of 1974

1974, May 17 **Size: 36x36mm**

C116	A84	500k Pitcher plant	5.50	3.00

Transportation Type of Regular Issue

1974, July 31 **Engr.** ***Perf. 13***

C117	A85	250k Sampan	2.50	1.50

Marconi Type of 1974

Old & new means of communications.

1974, Aug. 28 **Engr.** ***Perf. 13***

C118	A86	200k vio bl & brn	2.25	1.10

Insect Type of 1974

110k, Sternocera multipunctata.

1974, Oct. 23 **Engr.** ***Perf. 13***

C119	A87	110k grn, blue & red	1.75	1.00

Boeing 747 — AP37

1986, June 2 **Litho.** ***Perf. 12½***

C120	AP37	20k shown	3.50
C121	AP37	50k IL86	8.00

AIR POST SEMI-POSTAL STAMPS

Nos. C56-C57 Surcharged: "Soutien aux Victimes / de la Guerre / + 5k"

1970, May 1 **Photo.** ***Perf. 13***

CB1	A58	110k + 5k multi	3.00	1.50
CB2	A58	300k + 5k multi	3.50	2.25

The surtax was for war victims.

POSTAGE DUE STAMPS

Vat-Sisaket Monument D1

Boat and Raft D2

Perf. 13½x13

1952-53 **Unwmk.** **Engr.**

J1	D1	10c dark brown	.40	.25
J2	D1	20c purple	.40	.25
J3	D1	50c carmine	.50	.25
J4	D1	1pi dark green	.60	.25
J5	D1	2pi deep ultra	.70	.25
J6	D1	5pi rose violet	1.25	1.00
J7	D2	10pi indigo ('53)	2.00	.80
		Nos. J1-J7 (7)	5.85	3.05

Serpent — D3

1973, Oct. 31 Photo. *Perf. 13*

J8	D3	10k yellow & multi	.40	.25
J9	D3	15k emerald & multi	.45	.25
J10	D3	20k blue & multi	.60	.25
J11	D3	50k scarlet & multi	.75	.40
		Nos. J8-J11 (4)	2.20	1.15

PARCEL POST STAMPS

Wat Ong Theu — PP1

2000, June 7 Litho. *Die Cut*
Self-Adhesive
Serial Number in Black

Q1	PP1	5000k orange	*5.00*	*5.00*
Q2	PP1	40,000k milky blue	*30.00*	*30.00*
Q3	PP1	60,000k gray blue	*32.50*	*32.50*
Q4	PP1	80,000k cerise	*55.00*	*55.00*
Q5	PP1	100,000k carmine	*65.00*	*65.00*
Q6	PP1	250,000k ultra	*160.00*	*160.00*
		Nos. Q1-Q6 (6)	347.50	347.50

Phra That Luang PP2

2003, Aug. 14 *Die Cut*
Self-Adhesive
Serial Number in Black

Q7	PP2	5000k vio bl & bl	5.00	5.00
Q8	PP2	40,000k claret & red	30.00	30.00
Q9	PP2	60,000k grn & claret	45.00	45.00
Q10	PP2	90,000k red & blue	70.00	70.00
		Nos. Q7-Q10 (4)	150.00	150.00

Pha That Luang, Vientiane PP7

2013, July 3 Litho. *Imperf.*
Self-Adhesive
Frame Color

Q17	PP7	50,000k blue	25.00	20.00
Q18	PP7	100,000k red	45.00	37.50
Q19	PP7	200,000k green	85.00	67.50
		Nos. Q17-Q19 (3)	155.00	125.00

LATAKIA

ˌla-tə-ˈkē-ə

LOCATION — A division of Syria in Western Asia
GOVT. — French Mandate
AREA — 2,500 sq. mi.
POP. — 278,000 (approx. 1930)
CAPITAL — Latakia

This territory, included in the Syrian Mandate to France under the Versailles Treaty, was formerly known as Alaouites. The name Latakia was adopted in 1930. See Alaouites and Syria.

100 Centimes = 1 Piaster

Stamps of Syria Overprinted in Black or Red

Perf. 12x12½, 13½

1931-33 Unwmk.

1	A6	10c red violet	1.25	1.25
2	A6	10c vio brn ('33)	1.60	1.60
3	A6	20c dk blue (R)	1.25	1.25
4	A6	20c brn org ('33)	1.60	1.60
5	A6	25c gray grn (R)	1.25	1.25
6	A6	25c dk bl gray (R) ('33)	1.60	1.60
7	A9	50c violet	2.00	2.00
8	A15	75c org red ('32)	3.25	3.25
9	A10	1p green (R)	2.40	2.40
10	A11	1.50p bis brn (R)	3.25	3.25
11	A11	1.50p dp grn ('33)	4.00	4.00
12	A12	2p dk vio (R)	4.00	4.00
13	A13	3p yel grn (R)	6.00	6.00
14	A14	4p orange	5.50	5.50
15	A15	4.50p rose car	5.75	5.75
16	A16	6p grnsh blk (R)	5.75	5.75
17	A17	7.50p dl blue (R)	5.50	5.50
a.		Inverted overprint	650.00	
18	A18	10p dp brown (R)	9.50	9.50
a.		Inverted overprint	650.00	
19	A19	15p dp green (R)	11.00	11.00
20	A20	25p violet brn	24.00	24.00
21	A21	50p dk brown (R)	22.50	22.50
a.		Inverted overprint	650.00	
22	A22	100p red orange	55.00	55.00
		Nos. 1-22 (22)	177.95	177.95

AIR POST STAMPS

Air Post Stamps of Syria, 1931, Overprinted in Black or Red

1931-33 Unwmk. *Perf. 13½*

C1	AP2	50c ocher	1.25	1.25
a.		Inverted overprint	1,200.	1,200.
C2	AP2	50c blk brn (R) ('33)	2.50	2.50
C3	AP2	1p ches brn	2.50	2.50
C4	AP2	2p Prus blue (R)	4.00	4.00
C5	AP2	3p blue grn (R)	5.50	5.50
C6	AP2	5p red violet	7.00	7.00
C7	AP2	10p sl grn (R)	8.75	8.75
C8	AP2	15p orange red	12.50	12.50
C9	AP2	25p orange brn	24.00	24.00
C10	AP2	50p black (R)	40.00	40.00
C11	AP2	100p magenta	42.50	42.50
		Nos. C1-C11 (11)	150.50	150.50

POSTAGE DUE STAMPS

Postage Due Stamps of Syria, 1931, Overprinted

1931 Unwmk. *Perf. 13½*

J1	D7	8p blk, *gray bl* (R)	26.00	26.00
J2	D8	15p blk, *dl rose* (R)	26.00	26.00

Stamps of Latakia were superseded in 1937 by those of Syria.

LATVIA

ˈlat-vē-ə

(Lettonia, Lettland)

LOCATION — Northern Europe, bordering on the Baltic Sea and the Gulf of Riga
GOVT. — Independent Republic
AREA — 25,395 sq. mi.
POP. — 2,353,874 (1999 est.)
CAPITAL — Riga

Latvia was created a sovereign state following World War I and was admitted to the League of Nations in 1922. In 1940 it became a republic in the Union of Soviet Socialist Republics. Latvian independence was recognized by the Soviet Union on Sept. 6, 1991.

100 Kapeikas = 1 Rublis
100 Santims = 1 Lat (1923, 1993)
100 Kopecks = 1 Ruble (1991)
100 Cents = 1 Euro (2014)

Catalogue values for unused stamps in this country are for Never Hinged items, beginning with Scott 300 in the regular postage section, Scott B150 in the semi-postal section, and Scott 2N45 in the Russian Occupation section.

Watermarks

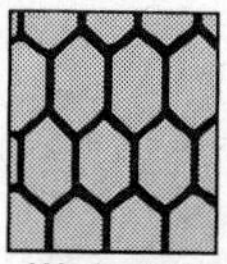

Wmk. 108 Honeycomb

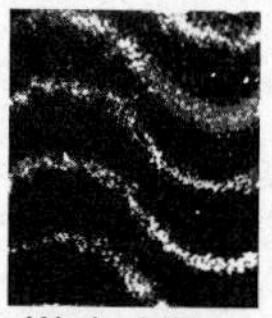

Wmk. 145 — Wavy Lines

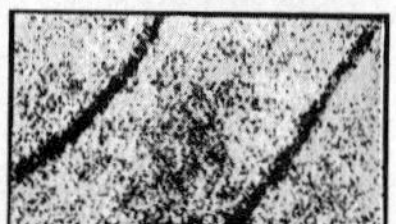

Wmk. 181 Wavy Lines

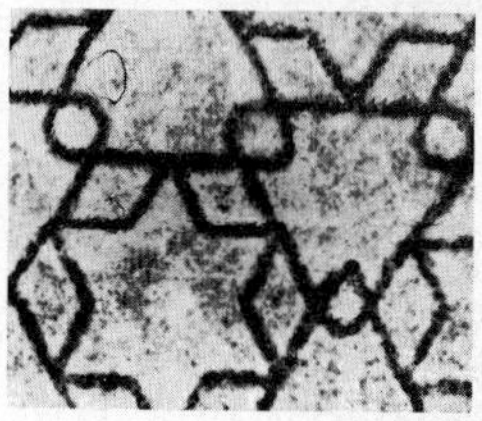

Wmk. 197 — Star and Triangles

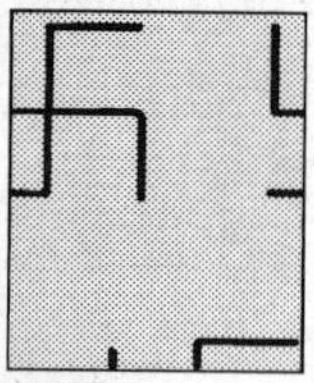

Wmk. 212 Multiple Swastikas

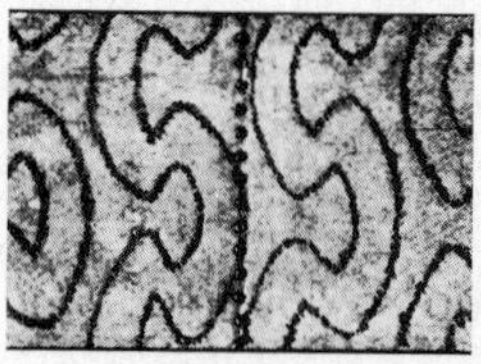

Wmk. 265 — Multiple Waves

Wmk. 387 — Squares and Rectangles

Arms — A1

Printed on the Backs of German Military Maps
Unwmk.

1918, Dec. 18 Litho. *Imperf.*

1	A1	5k carmine	.75	1.50

Perf. 11½

2	A1	5k car ver	.75	1.50

Values given are for stamps where the map on the back is printed in brown and black. Maps printed only in black are valued at: No. 1 unused $2.00; used $5.75; No. 2 unused $1.20, used $2.50. Stamps with no map at all valued: No. 1 unused $1.50, used $3.25; No. 2 unused $1.20, used $2.25. Stamps with no printing on the back are from the outer rows of some sheets.

See No. 1007.

Redrawn
Paper with Ruled Lines

1919 *Imperf.*

3	A1	5k carmine	.25	.25
4	A1	10k dark blue	.25	.25
5	A1	15k green	.50	.50

Perf. 11½

6	A1	5k carmine	2.40	*4.00*
7	A1	10k dark blue	2.40	*4.00*
8	A1	15k deep green	7.25	*9.50*
		Nos. 3-8 (6)	13.05	18.50

In the redrawn design the wheat heads are thicker, the ornament at lower left has five points instead of four, and there are minor changes in other parts of the design.

The sheets of this and subsequent issues were usually divided in half by a single line of perforation gauging 10. Thus stamps are found with this perforation on one side.

1919 Pelure Paper *Imperf.*

9	A1	3k lilac	4.75	4.50
10	A1	5k carmine	.25	.25
11	A1	10k deep blue	.25	.25
12	A1	15k dark green	.25	.25
13	A1	20k orange	.25	.25
13A	A1	25k gray	40.00	*47.50*
14	A1	35k dark brown	.25	.25
15	A1	50k purple	.25	.25
16	A1	75k emerald	2.50	*2.75*
		Nos. 9-16 (9)	48.75	56.25

Perf. 11½, 9½

17	A1	3k lilac	35.00	30.00
18	A1	5k carmine	.80	.80
19	A1	10k deep blue	4.00	3.50
20	A1	15k dark green	2.75	*4.00*
21	A1	20k orange	3.75	*4.50*
22	A1	35k dark brown	4.50	*6.50*
23	A1	50k purple	5.50	*8.00*
24	A1	75k emerald	8.00	*11.00*
		Nos. 17-24 (8)	64.30	*68.30*

Values are for perf 11½. Examples Perf 9½ sell for more.

Nos. 17-24 are said to be unofficially perforated varieties of Nos. 9-16.

1919 Wmk. 108 *Imperf.*

25	A1	3k lilac	.30	.25
26	A1	5k carmine	.30	.25
27	A1	10k deep blue	.30	.25
28	A1	15k deep green	.30	.25
29	A1	20k orange	.35	.25
30	A1	25k gray	.40	.35
31	A1	35k dark brown	.35	.25
32	A1	50k purple	.35	.25
33	A1	75k emerald	.35	.25
		Nos. 25-33 (9)	3.00	2.35

The variety "printed on both sides" exists for 3k, 10k, 15k, 20k and 35k. Value, $20 each.

See Nos. 57-58, 76-82. For surcharges and overprints see Nos. 86, 132-133, 2N1-2N8, 2N12-2N19.

Liberation of Riga — A2

1919 Wmk. 108

43	A2	5k carmine	.25	.25
44	A2	15k deep green	.25	.25
45	A2	35k brown	.35	*.80*
		Nos. 43-45 (3)	.85	1.30

Unwmk.
Pelure Paper

49	A2	5k carmine	9.50	*16.00*
50	A2	15k deep green	9.50	*16.00*
51	A2	35k brown	21.00	16.00
		Nos. 49-51 (3)	40.00	48.00

For surcharge and overprints see Nos. 87, 2N9-2N11, 2N20-2N22.

Rising Sun — A4

1919 *Imperf.*

55	A4	10k gray blue	.80	.50

Perf. 11½

56	A4	10k gray blue	.80	*1.50*

Type of 1918

1919 Laid Paper *Perf. 11½*

57	A1	3r slate & org	1.00	1.00
58	A1	5r gray brn & org	1.00	1.00

See No. 82.

Independence Issue

Allegory of One Year of Independence — A5

Wove Paper
Size: 33x45mm

1919, Nov. 18 **Unwmk.**

59	A5	10k brown & rose	1.25	*2.00*

Laid Paper

60	A5	10k brown & rose	1.25	*2.00*

Size: 28x38mm

61	A5	10k brown & rose	.30	*.40*
a.		Imperf.	50.00	
62	A5	35k indigo & grn	.30	*.40*
a.		Vert. pair, imperf. btwn.	50.00	45.00

Back of No. 63 Block

Wmk. 197
Thick Wove Paper
Blue Design on Back

63	A5	1r green & red	.45	.45
		Nos. 59-63 (5)	3.55	5.25

There are two types of Nos. 59 and 60. In type I the trunk of the tree is not outlined. In type II it has a distinct white outline.

No. 63 was printed on the backs of unfinished 5r bank notes of the Workers and Soldiers Council, Riga.

For surcharges see Nos. 83-85, 88, 94.

Warrior Slaying Dragon — A6

1919-20 **Unwmk.** *Perf. 11½*
Wove Paper

64	A6	10k brown & car	.50	.50
a.		Horiz. pair, imperf. btwn.	55.00	45.00
65	A6	25k ind & yel grn	.50	.50
a.		Pair, imperf. btwn.	55.00	45.00
66	A6	35k black & bl ('20)	.50	.50
a.		Horiz. pair, imperf. btwn.	55.00	45.00
67	A6	1r dp gray grn & brn ('20)	.50	.50
a.		Horiz. pair, imperf. vert.	50.00	40.00
b.		Horiz. pair, imperf. btwn.	50.00	40.00
		Nos. 64-67 (4)	2.00	2.00
		Set, never hinged	5.75	

Issued in honor of the liberation of Kurzeme (Kurland). The paper sometimes shows impressed quadrille lines.

For surcharges see Nos. 91-93.

Latgale Relief Issue

Latvia Welcoming Home Latgale Province — A7

Partial Design of No. 68 Back

Brown and Green Design on Back

1920, Mar.

68	A7	50k dk green & rose	.50	.50
a.		Horiz. pair, imperf. vert.	50.00	
69	A7	1r slate grn & brn	.50	.50
a.		Horiz. pair, imperf. vert.	50.00	
		Set, never hinged	10.00	

No. 68-69 were printed on the backs of unfinished bank notes of the government of Colonel Bermondt-Avalov and on the so-called German "Ober-Ost" money.

For surcharges see Nos. 95-99.

First National Assembly Issue

Latvia Hears Call to Assemble — A8

1920

70	A8	50k rose	.50	.30
a.		Imperf., pair	9.00	*11.00*
71	A8	1r blue	.50	.30
a.		Vert. pair, imperf. btwn.	45.00	45.00
b.		Imperf., pair	20.00	15.00
72	A8	3r dk brn & grn	.50	*.80*
73	A8	5r slate & vio brn	1.00	.80
		Nos. 70-73 (4)	2.50	2.20
		Set, never hinged	10.00	

For surcharges see Nos. 90, 134.

Type of 1918 Issue
Wove Paper

1920-21 **Unwmk.** *Perf. 11½*

76	A1	5k carmine	.25	.25
78	A1	20k orange	.25	.25
79	A1	40k lilac ('21)	.30	.25
80	A1	50k violet	.35	.25
81	A1	75k emerald	.35	.25
82	A1	5r gray brn & org ('21)	1.50	1.00
		Nos. 76-82 (6)	3.00	2.25
		Set, never hinged	6.00	

No. 63 Surcharged in Black, Brown or Blue

1920, Sept. 1

83	A5	10r on 1r grn & red (Bk)	1.00	*1.60*
84	A5	20r on 1r grn & red (Br)	2.50	*3.25*
85	A5	30r on 1r grn & red (Bl)	3.50	*4.00*
		Nos. 83-85 (3)	7.00	*8.85*
		Set, never hinged	17.50	

Types of 1919 Surcharged

1920-21 **Wmk. 108** *Perf. 11½*

86	A1	2r on 10k dp blue	1.75	*7.25*
87	A2	2r on 35k brown	.50	*5.50*
		Set, never hinged	5.00	

No. 62 Surcharged in Red

Unwmk.

88	A5	2r on 35k ind & grn	.40	*.50*
		Never hinged	.80	

No. 70 Surcharged in Blue

1921

90	A8	2r on 50k rose	.50	.60
		Never hinged	1.00	

Nos. 64-66 Surcharged in Red or Blue

1920-21

91	A6	1r on 35k blk & bl (R)	.35	.40
92	A6	2r on 10k brn & rose (Bl)	.60	.80
93	A6	2r on 25k ind & grn (R)	.35	.40
a.		Imperf.	—	
		Nos. 91-93 (3)	1.30	1.60
		Set, never hinged	3.25	

On Nos. 92 and 93 the surcharge reads "DIVI 2 RUBLI."

No. 83 with Added Surcharge

1921 **Wmk. 197**

94	A5	10r on 10r on 1r	1.50	1.00
		Never hinged	5.00	

Latgale Relief Issue of 1920 Surcharged in Black or Blue

1921, May 31 **Unwmk.**

95	A7	10r on 50k	1.25	.80
a.		Imperf.	—	
96	A7	20r on 50k	3.75	4.00
97	A7	30r on 50k	5.00	4.00
98	A7	50r on 50k	7.50	5.00
99	A7	100r on 50k (Bl)	17.50	16.00
		Nos. 95-99 (5)	35.00	29.80
		Set, never hinged	62.50	

Excellent counterfeits exist.

Arms and Stars for Vidzeme, Kurzeme & Latgale — A10

Type I, slanting cipher in value.
Type II, upright cipher in value.

Perf. 10, 11½ and Compound
Wmk. Similar to 181

1921-22 **Typo.**

101	A10	50k violet (II)	.50	.30
102	A10	1r orange yel	.50	.50
103	A10	2r deep green	.25	.25
104	A10	3r brt green	.65	.45
105	A10	5r rose	1.40	.40
106	A10	6r dp claret	2.00	.80
107	A10	9r orange	1.25	.55
108	A10	10r blue (I)	1.25	.25
109	A10	15r ultra	3.25	.50
a.		Printed on both sides	*50.00*	
110	A10	20r dull lilac (II)	20.00	2.00

Coat of Arms — A11

1922, Aug. 21 *Perf. 11½*

111	A11	50r dk brn & pale brn (I)	30.00	4.50
112	A11	100r dk bl & pale bl (I)	35.00	4.50
		Nos. 101-112 (12)	96.05	15.00
		Set, never hinged	200.00	

Nos. 101-131 sometimes show letters and numerals of the paper maker's watermark "PACTIEN LIGAT MILLS 1858." Stamps showing part of the inscription command a 100 percent premium. Pairs with the complete year "1858" command a 300 percent premium.

See Nos. 126-131, 152-154.

A12

2 SANTIMS
Type A, tail of "2" ends in an upstroke.
Type B, tail of "2" is nearly horizontal.

1923-25 *Perf. 10, 11, 11½*

113	A12	1s redsh pur	.40	.25
114	A12	2s yel org (A)	.60	.35
115	A12	4s dark green	.60	.25
a.		Horiz. pair, imperf. btwn.	55.00	50.00
116	A12	5s lt green ('25)	2.50	.65
117	A12	6s grn, *yel* ('25)	3.50	.25
118	A12	10s rose red (I)	1.50	.25
a.		Horiz. pair, imperf. btwn.	55.00	50.00
119	A12	12s claret	.25	.40
120	A12	15s brn, *sal*	3.50	.25
a.		Horiz. pair, imperf. btwn.	55.00	50.00
121	A12	20s dp blue (II)	1.50	.25
122	A12	25s ultra ('25)	.50	.25
123	A12	30s pink (I) ('25)	5.00	.25
124	A12	40s lilac (I)	2.00	.25
125	A12	50s lil gray (II)	3.75	.35
126	A11	1 l dk brn & pale brn	12.50	1.00
127	A11	2 l dk blue & blue	20.00	1.60
130	A11	5 l dp grn & pale grn	60.00	5.00
131	A11	10 l car rose & pale rose (I)	3.00	6.00
		Nos. 113-131 (17)	121.10	17.60
		Set, never hinged	250.00	

Value in "Santims" (1s); "Santimi" (2s-6s) or "Santimu" (others).

See note after No. 112.
See Nos. 135-151, 155-157. For overprints and surcharges see Nos. 164-167, B21-B23.

Nos. 79-80 Surcharged

No. 72 Surcharged

1927 **Unwmk.** *Perf. 11½*

132	A1	15s on 40k lilac	.40	.40
133	A1	15s on 50k violet	1.15	*1.50*
134	A8	1 l on 3r brn & grn	9.00	7.00
		Nos. 132-134 (3)	10.55	8.90
		Set, never hinged	24.00	

Types of 1923-25 Issue

1927-33 **Wmk. 212** *Perf. 10, 11½*

135	A12	1s dull violet	.25	.25
136	A12	2s org yel (A)	.35	.25
137	A12	2s org yel (B) ('33)	.30	.25
138	A12	3s org red ('31)	.25	.25
139	A12	4s dk green ('29)	3.50	2.25
140	A12	5s lt green ('31)	.50	.25
141	A12	6s grn, *yel*	.25	.25
142	A12	7s dk green ('31)	.50	.25
143	A12	10s red (I)	2.50	.70
144	A12	10s grn, *yel* (I) ('32)	10.00	.25
145	A12	15s brn, *sal*	3.50	.45

146 A12 20s pink (I) 5.00 .25
147 A12 20s pink (II) 6.00 .25
148 A12 30s lt blue (I) 1.25 .40
149 A12 35s dk blue ('31) 1.50 .25
150 A12 40s dl lil (I) ('29) 2.25 .25
151 A12 50s gray (II) 2.50 .45
152 A11 1 l dk brn & pale brn 8.00 .30
153 A11 2 l dk bl & bl ('31) 30.00 2.25
154 A11 5 l grn & pale grn ('33) 140.00 30.00
Nos. 135-154 (20) 218.40 39.80
Set, never hinged 400.00

The paper of Nos. 141, 144 and 145 is colored on the surface only.

See note above No. 113 for types A and B, and note above No. 101 for types I and II.

Type of 1927-33 Issue Paper Colored Through

1931-33 ***Perf. 10***
155 A12 6s grn, *yel* .25 .25
156 A12 10s grn, *yel* (I) ('33) 15.00 .25
157 A12 15s brn, *salmon* 3.00 .25
Nos. 155-157 (3) 18.25 .75
Set, never hinged 37.50

View of Rezekne — A13

Designs (Views of Cities): 15s, Jelgava. 20s, Cesis (Wenden). 30s, Liepaja (Libau). 50s, Riga. 1 l, Riga Theater.

1928, Nov. 18 Litho. ***Perf. 10, 11½***
158 A13 6s dp grn & vio 1.00 .40
159 A13 15s dk brn & ol grn 1.00 .40
160 A13 20s cerise & bl grn 1.25 .45
161 A13 30s ultra & vio brn 1.50 .40
162 A13 50s dk gray & plum 1.50 1.00
163 A13 1 l blk brn & brn 3.75 1.75
Nos. 158-163 (6) 10.00 4.40
Set, never hinged 20.00

10th anniv. of Latvian Independence.

Riga Exhibition Issue

Stamps of 1927-33 Overprinted

1932, Aug. 30 ***Perf. 10, 11***
164 A12 3s orange 1.00 .50
165 A12 10s green, *yel* 1.00 .50
166 A12 20s pink (I) 2.10 1.00
167 A12 35s dark blue 4.75 2.00
Nos. 164-167 (4) 8.85 4.00
Set, never hinged 30.00

Riga Castle A19

Arms and Shield A20

Allegory of Latvia A21

Ministry of Foreign Affairs A22

1934, Dec. 15 Litho. ***Perf. 10½, 10***
174 A19 3s red orange .25 .25
175 A20 5s yellow grn .25 .25
176 A20 10s gray grn 1.00 .25
177 A21 20s deep rose 1.00 .25
178 A22 35s dark blue .35 .25
179 A19 40s brown .35 .25
Nos. 174-179 (6) 3.20 1.50
Set, never hinged 6.00

Atis Kronvalds A23

A. Pumpurs A24

Juris Maters A25

Mikus Krogzemis (Auseklis) A26

1936, Jan. 4 Wmk. 212 ***Perf. 11½***
180 A23 3s vermilion 3.50 *4.75*
181 A24 10s green 3.50 *4.75*
182 A25 20s rose pink 3.50 *6.00*
183 A26 35s dark blue 3.50 *6.00*
Nos. 180-183 (4) 14.00 21.50
Set, never hinged 35.00

President Karlis Ulmanis — A27

1937, Sept. 4 Litho. ***Perf. 10, 11½***
184 A27 3s org red & brn org .25 .25
185 A27 5s yellow grn .25 .25
186 A27 10s dk sl grn .75 .60
187 A27 20s rose lake & brn lake 1.50 .60
188 A27 25s black vio 2.25 1.25
189 A27 30s dark blue 2.25 1.25
190 A27 35s indigo 1.00 1.00
191 A27 40s lt brown 2.00 1.25
192 A27 50s olive blk 2.25 1.50
Nos. 184-192 (9) 12.50 7.95
Set, never hinged 25.00

60th birthday of President Ulmanis.

Independence Monument, Rauna (Ronneburg) A28

Monument Entrance to Cemetery at Riga A29

Independence Monument, Jelgava A30

War Memorial, Valka A31

Independence Monument, Iecava — A32

Independence Monument, Riga — A33

Tomb of Col. Kalpaks — A34

Thick Paper

Unwmk.

1937, July 12 Litho. ***Perf. 10***
193 A28 3s vermilion .65 *.90*
194 A29 5s yellow grn .65 *.90*
195 A30 10s deep grn .65 *.50*
196 A31 20s carmine 1.60 *1.00*
197 A32 30s lt blue 2.25 2.00

Wmk. 212

Engr. ***Perf. 11½***

Thin Paper

198 A33 35s dark blue 2.25 2.00
199 A34 40s brown 3.50 3.00
Nos. 193-199 (7) 11.55 10.30
Set, never hinged 25.00

View of Vidzeme A35

General J. Balodis A37

President Karlis Ulmanis — A38

Views: 5s, Latgale. 30s, Riga waterfront. 35s, Kurzeme. 40s, Zemgale.

1938, Nov. 17 ***Perf. 10, 10½x10***
200 A35 3s brown org .25 .25
a. Booklet pane of 4 *45.00*
201 A35 5s yellow grn .25 .25
a. Booklet pane of 4 *45.00*
202 A37 10s dk green .25 .25
a. Booklet pane of 2 *45.00*
203 A38 20s red lilac .25 .25
a. Booklet pane of 2 *45.00*
204 A35 30s deep blue .90 .25
205 A35 35s indigo .90 .25
a. Booklet pane of 2 *45.00*
206 A35 40s rose violet 1.25 .25
Nos. 200-206 (7) 4.05 1.75
Set, never hinged 12.00

The 20th anniversary of the Republic.

School, Riga — A42

Independence Monument, Riga — A45

President Karlis Ulmanis — A49

Designs: 5s, Castle of Jelgava. 10s, Riga Castle. 30s, Symbol of Freedom. 35s, Community House Daugavpils. 40s, Powder Tower and War Museum, Riga.

1939, May 13 Photo. ***Perf. 10***
207 A42 3s brown orange .25 .80
208 A42 5s deep green .50 .80
209 A42 10s dk slate grn .75 .80
210 A45 20s dk car rose 1.50 1.60
211 A42 30s brt ultra 1.00 .80
212 A42 35s dark blue 1.50 1.60
213 A45 40s brown violet 2.00 1.00
214 A49 50s grnsh black 3.00 1.00
Nos. 207-214 (8) 10.50 8.40
Set, never hinged 20.00

5th anniv. of National Unity Day.

Harvesting Wheat A50

Apple A51

1939, Oct. 8
215 A50 10s slate green .90 .60
216 A51 20s rose lake .90 .65
Set, never hinged 3.00

8th Agricultural Exposition held near Riga.

Arms and Stars for Vidzeme, Kurzeme and Latgale — A52

1940
217 A52 1s dk vio brn .30 .30
218 A52 2s ocher .40 .30
219 A52 3s red orange .25 .25
220 A52 5s dk olive brn .25 .25
221 A52 7s dk green .30 .30
222 A52 10s dk blue grn .75 .25
224 A52 20s dp car red .75 .25
225 A52 30s dp red brn 1.25 .30
226 A52 35s brt ultra .25 *.80*
228 A52 50s dk slate grn 1.75 .80
229 A52 1 l olive green 3.50 2.40
Nos. 217-229 (11) 9.75 6.20
Set, never hinged 25.00

Catalogue values for unused stamps in this section, from this point to the end of the section, are for Never Hinged items.

Natl. Arms — A70

1991, Oct. 19 Litho. ***Perf. 13x12½***
300 A70 5k multicolored *5.00* *5.00*
301 A70 10k multicolored .40 .40
302 A70 15k multicolored .50 .50
303 A70 20k multicolored .65 .65
304 A70 40k multicolored 1.25 1.25
305 A70 50k multicolored 1.75 1.75

Size: 28x32mm

Perf. 13½x14

306 A70 100k silver & multi 2.75 2.75
307 A70 200k gold & multi 5.00 5.00
Nos. 300-307 (8) 17.30 17.30

Most issues, Nos. 300-342, have one blocked value that was not freely available at Latvian post offices.

Russia Nos. 5984, 5985a Ovptd. "LATVIJA" and Srchd. in Red Lilac, Orange, Green, Violet

1991, Dec. 23 Photo. ***Perf. 12x11½***
308 A2765 100k on 7k (RL) *.50* .50
a. Vert. pair, one without ovpt. 8.00
b. Litho., perf. 12x12½ *.50* .50

Perf. 12x12½

Litho.

309 A2765 300k on 2k (O) *.85* .85
a. Vert. pair, one without ovpt. 8.00
310 A2765 500k on 2k (G) *1.25* 1.25
a. Vert. pair, one without ovpt. 8.00
311 A2765 1000k on 2k (V) *2.40* 2.40
a. Vert. pair, one without ovpt. 8.00
Nos. 308-311 (4) *5.00* 5.00

On Nos. 308-311 the sixth row of the sheet was not surcharged.

Forgeries exist.

Liberty Monument, Riga — A71

1991, Dec. 28 *Perf. 12½x13*

312 A71 10k ol brn & multi .25 .25
313 A71 15k violet & multi *1.00 1.00*
314 A71 20k bl grn & multi .80 .80
315 A71 30k ol grn & multi .90 .90
316 A71 50k choc & multi 1.25 1.25
317 A71 100k dp blue & multi 1.25 1.25
Nos. 312-317 (6) 5.45 5.45

A72

A73

Monuments — A74

1992, Feb. 29 *Perf. 14*

318 A72 10k black .25 .25
319 A73 20k violet black .40 .25
320 A73 30k brown .55 .25
321 A72 30k purple .55 .25
322 A74 40k violet blue .75 .25
323 A74 50k green .90 .25
324 A73 50k olive green .90 .25
325 A74 100k red brown 1.75 .60
326 A72 200k blue 2.75 1.10
Nos. 318-326 (9) 8.80 3.45

Russia Nos. 4599, 5984, 5985a Ovptd. "LATVIJA" and Srchd. in Red, Brown, Emerald and Violet

1992, Apr. 4 Photo. *Perf. 12x11½*

327 A2765 1r on 7k (R) .25 .25

Perf. 12x12½

Litho.

328 A2765 3r on 2k (Br) .40 .25
329 A2765 5r on 2k (E) .65 .35
330 A2765 10r on 2k (V) 1.10 .75
331 A2138 25r on 4k 2.25 1.75
Nos. 327-331 (5) 4.65 3.35

Surcharged denominations expressed in rubles (large numerals) and kopecks (small zeros).

Birds of the Baltic Shores — A75

Litho. & Engr.

1992, Oct. 3 *Perf. 12½x13*

Booklet Stamps

332 A75 5r Pandion haliaetus .35 .35
333 A75 5r Limosa limosa .35 .35
334 A75 5r Mergus merganser .35 .35
335 A75 5r Tadorna tadorna .35 .35
a. Booklet pane of 4, #332-335 2.25

See Estonia Nos. 231-234a, Lithuania Nos. 427-430a, and Sweden Nos. 1975-1978a.

Christmas — A76

2r, 10r Angels with children around Christmas tree. 3r, Angels with musical instruments, Christmas tree. 15r, Nativity scene.

1992, Nov. 21 Litho. *Perf. 13½x13*

336 A76 2r silver & multi *1.00 1.00*
337 A76 3r multicolored *.30 .25*
338 A76 10r gold & multi *1.00 .60*
339 A76 15r multicolored *1.50 1.00*
Nos. 336-339 (4) 3.80 2.85

Russia Nos. 4728, 5107, 5109 Surcharged in Brown or Blue

Perfs. & Printing Methods as Before

1993, Feb. 26

340 A2229 50r on 6k #4728 (Br) *.75 .55*
341 A2435 100r on 6k #5109 *1.60 1.00*
342 A2435 300r on 6k #5107 *4.25 3.00*
Nos. 340-342 (3) 6.60 4.55

Traditional Costumes — A77

1993, Apr. 29 Litho. *Perf. 13x13½*

343 A77 5s Kuldiga *.25 .25*
344 A77 10s Alsunga *.30 .25*
345 A77 20s Lielvarde *.55 .30*
346 A77 50s Rucava *1.50 .80*
347 A77 100s Zemgale *3.00 1.50*
348 A77 500s Ziemellatgale *15.00 12.00*
a. Miniature sheet of 6, #343-348 *25.00 25.00*
Nos. 343-348 (6) 20.60 15.10

See Nos. 400-401, 415-416, 440-441, 466-467.

21st Natl. Song Festival
A78 A79

1993, July 3 Litho. *Perf. 12½x13*

349 A78 3s rose brn, gold & black *1.00 .50*
350 A78 5s purple, gold & black *1.50 .80*
351 A79 15s multicolored *2.00 1.25*
Nos. 349-351 (3) 4.50 2.55

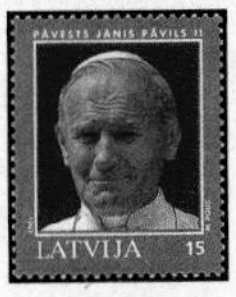

A80

1993, Aug. 28 Litho. *Perf. 14*

352 A80 15s Pope John Paul II *1.10 .90*

A81

1993, Nov. 11 Litho. *Perf. 12½x13*

353 A81 5s silver, black & red *.70 .30*
354 A81 15s gold, black & red *1.30 .45*

Independence, 75th anniv.

A82

1994, Apr. 2 Litho. *Perf. 14*

355 A82 15s multicolored *1.00 .60*

Evalds Valters, actor, 100th birthday.

A83

1994, Apr. 20 Litho. *Perf. 12½x13*

356 A83 5s Biathlon *.40 .40*
357 A83 10s 2-man bobsled *.85 .40*
358 A83 15s Luge *1.00 .65*
359 A83 100s Men's figure skating *5.75 3.25*
Nos. 356-359 (4) 8.00 4.70

Souvenir Sheet

360 A83 200s like #357 *8.00 7.00*

1994 Winter Olympics, Lillehammer.

Ethnographical Open Air Museum — A84

1994, Apr. 30 Litho. *Perf. 13x12½*

361 A84 5s multicolored *.80 .35*

1994 Basketball Festival, Riga — A85

1994, June 4 Litho. *Perf. 12½x13*

362 A85 15s multicolored *1.10 .55*

Provincial Municipal Arms — A86

Nos. 363-377A are inscribed with the year date of issue below the design. The year noted in each description is the date that appears on the stamp.

Perf. 13x12½, 14x14¼ (#373)

1994-2007

363 A86 1s Kurzeme, "1994" .25 .25
a. "1996" .25 .25
b. "1997" .75 .25
c. "1998" .25 .25
d. Perf 14x14¼, "1999" 1.25 .50
e. As "d," "2002" .25 .25
f. Perf. 13¼x13¾, "2006" .25 .25
g. As "f," "2007" .25 .25
h. As "d," "2011" .25 .25
i. As "d," "2012" .25 .25
364 A86 2s Auce, "1996" .40 .25
a. "1997" .40 .25
b. "1998" .30 .25
c. Perf 14x14¼, "1999" 1.25 1.25
d. As "c," "2000" .40 .25
e. As "c," "2002" .25 .25
f. Perf 13¼x13¾, "2005" .25 .25
g. As "f," "2006" .25 .25
h. As "f," "2007" .25 .25
i. As "c," "2011" .25 .25
j. As "c," "2012" .25 .25
k. As "c," "2013" .25 .25
365 A86 3s Zemgale, 1994 .55 .35
a. Perf 14x14¼, "1999" .55 .35
b. As "a," "2000" .55 .35
c. As "a," "2002" .25 .25
d. Perf 13¼x13¾, "2005" .25 .25
e. As "d," "2006" .25 .25
f. As "d," "2007" .25 .25
g. Perf. 14x14¼, "2010" .25 .25
h. As "g," "2011" .25 .25
i. As "g," "2012" .25 .25
j. As "g," "2013" .25 .25
366 A86 5s Vidzeme, "1994" .55 .25
a. "1996" .50 .50
b. Perf 14x14¼, "1999" .50 .50
c. As "b," "2000" .50 .50
367 A86 8s Livani, "1995" .50 .40
a. "1996" .50 .40
368 A86 10s Latgale, "1994" .50 .50
a. "1997" 1.60 1.00
b. "1998" .50 .50
369 A86 13s Preili, "1996" .70 .70
a. Perf. 14x14¼, "2010" .50 .50
370 A86 16s Ainazi, "1995" .80 .80
a. "1996" 1.00 1.00
371 A86 20s Grobina, "1995" 1.00 1.00
a. "1996" 1.00 1.00
372 A86 24s Tukums, "1995" 1.10 1.10
a. "1996" 1.10 1.10
373 A86 28s Madona, "1996" 1.75 1.50
374 A86 30s Riga, "1994" 1.50 1.50
375 A86 36s Priekule, "1996" 2.25 1.50
376 A86 50s Natl. arms, "1994" 2.25 2.25

Size: 29x24mm

Perf. 14

377 A86 100s Riga *4.25 2.50*
377A A86 200s Natl. arms *8.75 4.75*
Nos. 363-377A (16) 27.10 19.60

Issued: No. 363, 6/21/94; No. 363a, 1/30/96; No. 363b, 2/5/97; No. 363c, 1/12/98; No. 363d, 1/20/99; No. 363e, 2/6/02; No. 363f, 9/9/06; No. 363g, 6/8/07; No. 363h, 6/8/11; No. 363i, 3/15/12. No. 364, 4/12/96; No. 364a, 2/5/97; No. 364b, 2/11/98; No. 364c, 1/20/99; No. 364d, 4/26/00; No. 364e, 2/6/02; No. 364f, 9/10/05; No. 364g, 9/9/06; No. 364h, 6/8/07. No. 364i, 6/8/11; No. 364j, 3/15/12. No. 364k, 3/3/13. No. 365, 6/21/94; No. 365a, 3/16/99; No. 365b, 4/26/00; No. 365c, 2/6/02; No. 365d, 9/10/05; No. 365e, 9/9/06; No. 365f, 6/8/07; No. 365g, 2/15/10; No. 365h, 6/8/11; No. 365i, 3/15/12. No. 365j, 3/3/13. No. 366, 6/21/94; No. 366a, 1/30/96; No. 366b, 1/20/99; No. 366c, 4/26/00. No. 367, 6/1/95; No. 367a, 1/30/96. No. 368, 6/21/94; No. 368a, 8/28/97; No. 368b, 8/4/98. No. 369, 4/12/96; No. 369a, 3/12/10 No. 370, 6/1/95; No. 370a, 4/8/96. No. 371, 6/1/95; No. 371a, 9/6/96. No. 372, 6/1/95; No. 372a, 4/8/96. No. 373, 11/5/96. No. 374, 12/21/94. No. 375, 11/5/96. Nos. 376, 377, 378, 12/21/94.

See Nos. 450-451, 472-473, 482-483, 506-507, 525-526.

A87

1994, Sept. 24 Litho. *Perf. 14*

378 A87 5s multicolored *.80 .30*

University of Latvia, 75th anniv.

A88

Items balanced on scales (Europa): 10s, Latvian coins. 50s, Locked chest, money card.

1994, Oct. 29 Litho. *Perf. 14x13½*

379 A88 10s multicolored *.65 .25*
a. Tete-beche pair *1.75 1.75*
380 A88 50s multicolored *2.75 1.50*
a. Tete-beche pair *7.00 6.00*

Dormouse — A89

1994, Nov. 19 Litho. *Perf. 13½x13*

381 A89 5s shown *.45 .35*
382 A89 10s Among leaves *.75 .35*
383 A89 10s Eating berries *.75 .35*
384 A89 15s Berry, large mouse *1.50 .50*
Nos. 381-384 (4) 3.45 1.55

World Wildlife Fund.

A90

Christmas: 3s, Angel. 8s, Angels playing flute & violin. 13c, Angels singing. 100s, Candles.

1994, Dec. 3 *Perf. 14*

385 A90 3s multicolored *.30 .25*
386 A90 8s multicolored *.55 .25*
387 A90 13s multicolored *1.00 .30*
388 A90 100s multicolored *5.00 2.10*
Nos. 385-388 (4) 6.85 2.90

A91

Children's Fairy Tales, by Margarita Staraste: 5s, Elf with candle. No. 390, Small bear in snow. No. 391, Boy on sled.

Perf. 13x12½ on 3 Sides

1994, Dec. 17 Booklet Stamps

389 A91 5s multicolored *.50 .50*
390 A91 10s multicolored *.50 .50*
391 A91 10s multicolored *.50 .50*
a. Booklet pane, 2 each #389-391 *3.00*
Complete booklet, #391a + label *3.25*
Nos. 389-391 (3) 1.50 1.50

A92

1995, Feb. 18 **Perf. 14**
392 A92 10s multicolored .80 .50

European safe driving week.

A93

1995, Mar. 4 **Litho.** **Perf. 14**
393 A93 15s silver, blue & red .75 .60

UN, 50th anniv.

A94

Via Baltica Highway Project: Nos. 394, 395b, Castle, Bauska, Latvia. No. 395a, Beach Hotel, Parnu, Estonia. No. 395c, Kaunas, Lithuania.

1995, Apr. 20 **Litho.** **Perf. 14**
394 A94 8s multicolored .50 .50

Souvenir Sheet

395 A94 18s Sheet of 3, #a.-c. 2.75 2.75

See Estonia Nos. 288-289, Lithuania Nos. 508-509.

A95

8s, Dendrocopos leucotos. 20s, Crex crex. 24s, Chlidonias leucopterus.

1995, July 8 **Litho.** **Perf. 12½**
396 A95 8s multicolored .50 .50
397 A95 20s multicolored 1.20 1.20
398 A95 24s multicolored 1.60 1.60
Nos. 396-398 (3) 3.30 3.30

European nature conservation year.

Julian Cardinal Vaivods, Birth Cent. — A96

1995, Aug. 18 **Litho.** **Perf. 14**
399 A96 8s multicolored .65 .50

Traditional Costume Type of 1993

1995, Sept. 8 **Litho.** **Perf. 13x13½**
400 A77 8s Nica .40 .40

Souvenir Sheet

401 A77 100s Like #400 4.50 4.50

Friendly Appeal, by Karlis Ulmanis, 60th Anniv. — A97

1995, Sept. 8 **Perf. 14**
402 A97 8s multicolored .50 .50

Riga, 800th Anniv. — A98

1995, Sept. 23 **Perf. 13½**
403 A98 8s Natl. Opera .40 .40
404 A98 16s Natl. Theatre .80 .80

Size: 45x27mm

405 A98 24s Academy of Arts 1.00 1.00
406 A98 36s State Art Museum 1.50 1.50
Nos. 403-406 (4) 3.70 3.70

See Nos. 508-511, 529-531, 529-531.

Peace and Freedom — A99

Heroes from national epic, Lacplesis, dates of independence: 16s, Spidola with sword and shield, 1918. 50s, Lacplesis with leaves and banner, 1991.

1995, Nov. 15 **Litho.** **Perf. 13½**
407 A99 16s multicolored .75 .75
a. Tete beche pair 2.50 2.50
408 A99 50s multicolored 2.25 2.25
a. Tete beche pair 5.00 5.00

Europa.

Christmas — A100

Designs: No. 409, Characters surrounding Christmas tree at night. No. 410, Santa gliding through sky holding candle. 15s, Characters outside snow-covered house. 24s, Santa standing between dog and cat.

1995, Dec. 2
409 A100 6s multicolored .55 .25
410 A100 6s multicolored .55 .25
411 A100 15s multicolored .30 .60
412 A100 24s multicolored 2.25 1.00
Nos. 409-412 (4) 3.65 2.10

Pauls Stradins (1896-1958), Physician — A101

1996, Jan. 17 **Litho.** **Perf. 14**
413 A101 8s multicolored .40 .25

Zenta Maurina (1897-1978) — A102

1996, May 10 **Litho.** **Perf. 13½x14**
414 A102 36s multicolored 1.60 .95
a. Tete beche pair 3.25 3.25

Europa.

Traditional Costume Type of 1993

1996, May 18 **Litho.** **Perf. 13x13½**
415 A77 8s Barta .50 .25

Souvenir Sheet

416 A77 100s like No. 415 4.00 3.00

Souvenir Sheet

Children's Games — A103

1996, June 8 **Litho.** **Perf. 14x13½**
417 A103 48s Sheet of 1 2.75 2.25

1996 Summer Olympic Games, Atlanta — A104

Perf. 14x13½, 13½x14

1996, June 19
418 A104 8s Cycling,vert. .40 .25
419 A104 16s Basketball, vert .70 .40
420 A104 24s Walking, vert. .80 .50
421 A104 36s Canoeing 1.50 .80
Nos. 418-421 (4) 3.40 1.95

Souvenir Sheet

422 A104 100s Javelin 4.50 3.50

Nature Museum, 150th Anniv. — A105

Butterflies: 8s, Papilio machaon. 24s, Catocala fraxini. 80s, Pericallia matronula.

1996, Aug. 30 **Perf. 13**
423 A105 8s multicolored .35 .25
424 A105 24s multicolored .90 .45
425 A105 80s multicolored 3.75 1.90
Nos. 423-425 (3) 5.00 2.60

Car Production in Latvia — A106

Designs: 8s, 1912 Russo-Balt fire truck. 24s, 1899 Leutner-Russia. 36s, 1939 Ford-Vairogs.

1996, Oct. 25 **Litho.** **Perf. 13x12½**
426 A106 8s multicolored .35 .25
427 A106 24s multicolored 1.20 .55
428 A106 36s multicolored 1.50 .85
Nos. 426-428 (3) 3.05 1.65

City of Riga, 800th Anniv. — A107

1996, Dec. 5 **Litho.** **Perf. 13½**
429 A107 8s Building front .40 .25

Size: 30x26mm

430 A107 16s Stained glass window .75 .40

Size: 37x26mm

431 A107 24s Buildings 1.25 .55
432 A107 30s Art figures 1.25 .70
Nos. 429-432 (4) 3.65 1.90

Christmas — A108

Designs: 6s, Santa's elves, presents. 14s, Santa on skis, dog, children in animal costumes. 20s, Child in front of Christmas tree, santa in chair, pets.

1996, Dec. 7 **Perf. 14**
433 A108 6s multicolored .30 .25
434 A108 14s multicolored .70 .35
435 A108 20s multicolored 1.00 .50
Nos. 433-435 (3) 2.00 1.10

See Nos. 458-460.

Birds — A109

Designs: 10s, Caprimulgus eurpaeus. 20s, Aquila clanga. 30s, Acrocephalus paludicola.

1997, Feb. 8 **Perf. 13x12½**
436 A109 10s multicolored .50 .25
437 A109 20s multicolored .90 .45
438 A109 30s multicolored 1.40 .70
Nos. 436-438 (3) 2.80 1.40

Turn of the Epochs — A110

1997, Mar. 25 **Litho.** **Perf. 14**
439 A110 10s multicolored .70 .35

Traditional Costume Type of 1993

1997, Apr. 3 **Perf. 13x13½**
440 A77 10s Rietumvidzeme 1.25 .80

Souvenir Sheet

441 A77 100s like #440 4.25 3.50

Stamp Day.

Legend of Rozi Turaidas — A111

1997, Apr. 26 **Litho.** **Perf. 12½x13**
442 A111 32s multicolored 1.50 .70
a. Tete beche pair 3.50 3.50

Europa.

Old Baltic Ships — A112

Designs: 10s, Linijkugis, 17th cent.
No. 444: a, Linijkugis, 17th cent., diff. b, Kurenas 16th cent. c, Maasilinn ship, 16th cent.

1997, May 10 **Perf. 14x14½**
443 A112 10s multicolored .50 .40

Souvenir Sheet

444 A112 20s Sheet of 3, #a.-c. 3.00 2.75

See Estonia Nos. 322-323, Lithuania Nos. 571-572.

Port of Ventspils, Cent. — A113

1997, May 21 **Litho.** **Perf. 13½x14**
445 A113 20s Hermes, Poseidon .90 .50

Children's Activities — A114

Designs: 10s, Stamp collecting. 12s, Riding dirt bike, vert. 20s, Boy in hockey uniform, girl in skiwear, vert. 30s, Tennis, soccer, basketball.

1997, June 7 **Perf. 13½x13**
446 A114 10s multicolored .45 .25
447 A114 12s multicolored .60 .30
448 A114 20s multicolored .90 .45
449 A114 30s multicolored 1.25 .75
Nos. 446-449 (4) 3.20 1.75

Municipal Arms Type of 1994

1997-2005 **Litho.** **Perf. 13x12½**

Date imprint below design

450 A86 10s Valmiera, "1997" 1.00 .50
a. "1998" 1.00 .50
b. Perf 14x14¼, "1999" 1.00 .50
c. "2000" 1.00 .50

d.	Perf. 13¼x13¾, "2001"	1.00	.50
e.	"2005"	1.00	.40
451	A86 20s Rezekne, "1997"	2.25	1.00

Issued: No. 450, 9/6/97; No. 450a, 1/12/98; No. 450b, 1/20/99; No. 450c, 4/26/00; No. 450d, 9/12/01; No. 450e, 9/10/05. No. 451, 9/6/97.

Nature Preserves — A115

1997, Oct. 18 Litho. *Perf. 13x12½*

452	A115 10s Moricsala, 1912	*.50*	*.25*
453	A115 30s Slitere, 1921	*1.50*	*.80*

See Nos. 464-465.

City of Riga, 800th Anniv. — A116

10s, Woman, house, 12th cent. 20s, Monument to Bishop Albert, seal of the bishop, rosary, writing tool, 13th-16th cent. 30s, Riga castle, weapons used during Middle Ages. 32s, Houses, arms of Riga, statue of St. John.

1997, Nov. 27 Litho. *Perf. 13x14*

454	A116 10s multicolored	.50	.30
455	A116 20s multicolored	.85	.45
456	A116 30s multicolored	1.25	.70

Size: 27x26mm

457	A116 32s multicolored	1.40	.80
	Nos. 454-457 (4)	4.00	2.25

See Nos. 468-471, 488-491, 508-511, 529-531.

Christmas Type of 1996

People dressed in masks, costumes for mummery: 8s, Santa, bear. 18s, Two goats. 28s, Horse.

1997, Nov. 29 *Perf. 14*

458	A108 8s multicolored	.40	.25
459	A108 18s multicolored	.90	.40
460	A108 28s multicolored	1.40	.60
	Nos. 458-460 (3)	2.70	1.25

A117

1998, Jan. 31 Litho. *Perf. 14x13½*

461	A117 20s multicolored	1.00	*.75*

1998 Winter Olympic Games, Nagano.

A118

Statue at Spridisi, museum home of Anna Brigadere(1861-1933), writer.

1998, Feb. 21 Litho. *Perf. 13½*

462	A118 10s multicolored	.65	.35

National Song Festival — A119

1998, Mar. 28 Litho. *Perf. 13x14*

463	A119 30s multicolored	2.50	1.25
a.	Tete beche pair	5.50	5.50

Europa.

Nature Preserves Type of 1997

1998, Apr. 30 *Perf. 13x12½*

464	A115 10s Grini, 1936	.45	.25
465	A115 30s Teici, 1982	1.25	1.00

Traditional Costume Type of 1993

No. 467, Krustpils, man wearing crown of leaves.

1998, May 9 *Perf. 13x13½*

466	A77 10s Krustpils region	.75	.30

Souvenir Sheet

467	A77 100s multicolored	5.00	5.00

City of Riga, 800th Anniv., Type of 1997

10s, Dannenstern House, 16th and 17th cent. coins issued by kings of Poland and Sweden, 17th cent. wooden sculpture. 20s, City Library, monument to G. Herder, poet, philosopher, teacher. 30s, 18th cent. arsenal, column celebrating defeat of Napoleon's troops, octant, compass. 40s, Sculpture of Mother Latvia at Warriors' Cemetery, entrance to Cemetery, obv. & rev. of 5 lat coin, 1930.

1998, May 29 Litho. *Perf. 13x14*

468	A116 10s multicolored	.45	.25
469	A116 20s multicolored	1.00	.45
470	A116 30s multicolored	1.30	.60
471	A116 40s multicolored	1.75	.85
	Nos. 468-471 (4)	4.50	2.15

No. 468 is 30x26mm.

Municipal Arms Type of 1994

1998-2004 Litho. *Perf. 13¼x13¾*

Date imprint below design

472	A86 15s Bauska, "1998"	.55	.40
473	A86 30s Liepaja, "1998"	1.25	1.00
a.	Perf 13½x14, "2004"	1.35	1.10

Issued: No. 472, 473, 9/26/98; No. 473a, 9/7/04.

World Stamp Day — A120

1998, Oct. 20 Litho. *Perf. 14*

474	A120 30s #2, various stamps	1.25	.75

Dome Church, Riga, 1211 — A121

1998, Oct. 23

475	A121 10s multicolored	.70	.40

Pres. Janis Cakste (1859-1927) — A122

1998, Nov. 11 *Perf. 14x13½*

476	A122 10s multicolored	.50	.35

See No. 497, 515, 524.

Independence, 80th Anniv. — A123

1998, Nov. 14 *Perf. 13x12½*

477	A123 10s shown	.45	.30
478	A123 30s Arms, flags	1.40	.90

Christmas — A124

Christmas elves: 10s, Rolling snow balls. 20s, Decorating tree, preparing presents. 30s, Pulling sled over snow.

1998, Nov. 28 *Perf. 13½x14*

479	A124 10s multicolored	.55	.35
480	A124 20s multicolored	1.20	.75
481	A124 30s multicolored	1.50	.95
	Nos. 479-481 (3)	3.25	2.05

Municipal Arms Type of 1994

1999-2004 Litho. *Perf. 13¼x13¾*

Date imprint below design

482	A86 15s Ogre, "1999"	.80	.45
a.	"2000"	.90	.55
483	A86 40s Jelgava, "1999"	2.00	1.10
a.	"2004"	1.50	.85

Issued: No. 482, 2/12/99; No. 482a, 2/25/00. No. 483, 4/10/99; No. 483a, 9/7/04.

Nature Parks and Reserves — A125

Europa: 30s, Krustkalnu Nature Reserve. 60s, Gauja Natl. Nature Park.

1999, Mar. 20 *Perf. 13x12½*

484	A125 30s multicolored	1.75	1.00
485	A125 60s multicolored	4.00	2.00

Council of Europe, 50th Anniv. — A126

1999, Apr. 24

486	A126 30s multicolored	1.50	1.00

Rudolfs Blaumanis (1863-1908), Writer — A127

1999, Apr. 24 *Perf. 14x13*

487	A127 110s multicolored	*4.25*	2.00

City of Riga, 800th Anniv. Type

10s, Streetcar. 30s, Schooner "Widwud." 40s, Airplane. 70s, TK-type locomotive.

Perf. 13¼x13¾

1999, June 26 Litho.

488	A116 10s multicolored	.40	.30
489	A116 30s multicolored	1.20	.80
490	A116 40s multicolored	1.60	1.10
491	A116 70s multicolored	2.50	1.75
	Nos. 488-491 (4)	5.70	3.95

No. 488 is 30x27mm.

Aglona Basilica — A129

1999, July 10 Litho. *Perf. 14x14½*

492	A129 15s multicolored	.80	.40
	Complete booklet, 6 #492	12.00	

"Baltic Chain," 10th Anniv. — A130

Families and flags: 15s, No. 494a, Latvian. No. 494: b, Lithuanian. c, Estonian.

1999, Aug. 23 Litho. *Perf. 12½x13*

493	A130 15s multicolored	1.25	.50

Souvenir Sheet

494	A130 30s Sheet of 3, #a.-c.	4.25	4.00

See Estonia Nos. 366-367, Lithuania Nos. 639-640.

Rundāle Palace — A131

1999, Sept. 25 Litho. *Perf. 14*

495	A131 20s multicolored	.90	.65

See Nos. 512, 536, 578.

Landscape, by Julijs Feders (1838-1909) A132

1999, Oct. 13 Litho. *Perf. 13½*

496	A132 15s multi	.85	.55

Presidents Type of 1998

15s, Pres. Gustavs Zemgals (1871-1939).

1999, Nov. 16 Litho. *Perf. 14x13½*

497	A122 15s multicolored	.75	.55

A134

1999, Nov. 25 *Perf. 14x14½*

498	A134 40s multi	2.00	1.00

UPU, 125th anniv.

A135

Christmas and Millennium: 12s, Santa, tree, candle. 15s, Santa, tree, children. 40s, Santa, tree with ornaments.

1999, Nov. 27 *Perf. 14¼*

499	A135 12s multi	.65	.30
500	A135 15s multi	.80	.40
501	A135 40s multi	2.00	1.00
	Nos. 499-501 (3)	3.45	1.70

Nude, by J. Rozentals — A136

Perf. 14½x14¼

2000, Feb. 26 Litho.

502	A136 40s multi	2.00	1.50

Aleksandrs Caks (1901-50), Poet — A137

2000, Apr. 8 Litho. *Perf. 14x13½*

503	A137 40s multi	2.00	.90
	Booklet, 6 #503	12.50	

Europa, 2000

Common Design Type

2000, May 9

504	CD17 60s multi	5.00	2.40
a.	Tete beche pair	10.00	10.00

Ice Hockey A138

Wmk. 387

2000, June 21 **Litho.** ***Perf. 14***

505 A138 70s multi + label 3.25 1.75

Issued in sheets of 8 + 8 labels. Vertical columns of four labels, which depict players Helmut Balderis, Vitalijs Samoilovs, Sandis Ozolinsh and Arturs Irbe, flank a central block of eight stamps. Color photos of the players appear at left or right of the labels.

Municipal Arms Type of 1994

2000-05 **Unwmk.** ***Perf. 13¼x13¾***

Date imprint below design

506	A86 15s Daugavpils, "2000"	.75	.50
a.	"2005"	.65	.45
507	A86 15s Jūrmala, "2000"	.75	.50
a.	"2001"	.75	.50
b.	"2002"	.75	.50
c.	"2005"	.65	.45

Issued: No. 506, 7/6/00; No. 506a, 8/5/05. No. 507, 7/6/00; No. 507a, 9/12/01; No. 507b, 1/12/02; No. 507c, 8/5/05.

City of Riga, 800th Anniv. Type of 1995

Designs: 20s, Central Market. No. 509, Riga Zoo. No. 510, Riga Dome Organ. 70s, Powder Tower.

2000, July 22 ***Perf. 13¼x14***

Size: 40x28mm

508 A98 20s multi 1.00 .50

Size: 47x28mm

509 A98 40s multi 1.75 1.00
Complete booklet, 6 #509 10.50

Perf. 14x13¼

Size: 28x32mm

510	A98 40s multi	1.75	1.00
511	A98 70s multi	3.00	1.25
	Nos. 508-511 (4)	7.50	3.75

Palace Type of 1999

2000, Aug. 12 ***Perf. 13¼x14***

512 A131 40s Jelgava Palace 1.75 1.00
Booklet, 6 #512 11.50

2000 Summer Olympics, Sydney A139

2000, Sept. 15 ***Perf. 14¼x14***

513 A139 70s multi + label 3.00 2.00

See No. 518.

Millennium — A140

No. 514: a, 15s, Freedom Monument, Riga. b, House of Blackheads, Riga.

Perf. 14x13¼

2000, Sept. 28 **Litho.** **Wmk. 387**

514	A140 Pair + label	3.00	2.75
a.	15s multi	.80	.40
b.	50s multi	2.00	1.10

President Type of 1998

Perf. 13¾x13¼

2000, Nov. 11 **Unwmk.**

515 A122 15s Alberts Kveisis (1881-1936) .80 .50

Orthodox Cathedral — A141

2000, Nov. 17 ***Perf. 14***

516 A141 40s multi 1.75 1.00

See Nos. 537, 559, 573.

Red Cross — A142

2000, Nov. 22

517 A142 15s multi .75 .45

Olympics Type of 2000

2000, Nov. 22

518 A139 40s multi 1.75 1.00

Issued in sheets of 4 + 2 different labels depicting gold medal winner Igors Vihrovs.

Christmas — A143

Designs: 12s, Watch. No. 520, 15s, Angels. No. 521, 15s, Madonna and child.

2000, Nov. 25

519-521 A143 Set of 3 1.90 1.00

International Recognition of Latvia, 80th Anniv. — A144

2001, Jan. 13 **Litho.** ***Perf. 14***

522 A144 40s multi 1.75 1.25

Kad Silavas Mostas, by Vilhelmis Purvitis — A145

Perf. 14¼x14½

2001, Feb. 1 **Litho.** **Unwmk.**

523 A145 40s multi 2.75 1.50
Booklet, 6 #523 16.50

President Type of 1998

2001, Feb. 17 ***Perf. 13¾x13¼***

524 A122 15s Karlis Ulmanis (1877-1942) .75 .40

Municipal Arms Type of 1994

2001-06 ***Perf. 13¼x13¾***

Date imprint below design

525	A86 5s Smiltene, "2001"	.60	.30
a.	"2002"	.60	.30
b.	"2005"	.30	.30
c.	"2006"	.30	.30
d.	Perf. 14x14¼, "2011"	.30	.30
e.	As "d," "2012"	.30	.30
f.	As "d," "2013"	.30	.30
526	A86 15s Kuldiga, "2001"	.70	.40
a.	"2002"	.70	.40

Issued: No. 525, 3/5/01; No. 525a, 9/16/02; No. 525b, 9/10/05; No. 525c, 9/9/06. No. 525d, 6/8/11; No. 525e, 3/15/12; No. 525f, 3/3/13. No. 526, 3/5/01; No. 526a, 9/16/02.

Narrow Gauge Locomotive — A146

2001, Mar. 24 ***Perf. 14***

527 A146 40s multi 1.75 1.25

Europa — A147

2001, Apr. 14

528	A147 60s multi	3.50	1.75
a.	Tete beche pair	4.50	4.50

Riga, 800th Anniv. Type of 1995

Riga in: No. 529a, 20th cent. No. 529b, 21st cent. 60s, 16th cent. 70s, 17th cent.

2001, May 24 **Litho.** ***Perf. 13¾x13½***

Size: 29x33mm (each stamp)

529 A98 15s Horiz. pair, #a-b 1.50 .75

Size: 47x28mm

Perf. 13½x13¾

530	A98 60s multi	2.50	1.25
531	A98 70s multi	2.75	1.40
	Nos. 529-531 (3)	6.75	3.40

Kakisa Dzirnavas, by Karlis Skalbe — A148

2001, June 9 ***Perf. 13¾***

532 A148 40s multi 1.75 1.00
Booklet, 6 #532 10.50

Souvenir Sheet

Mikhail Tal (1936-92), Chess Champion — A149

2001, Aug. 18 **Litho.** ***Perf. 14***

533 A149 100s multi 4.50 3.50

Baltic Coast Landscapes — A150

Designs: 15s, No. 535a, Vidzeme. No. 535b, Palanga. No. 535c, Lahemaa.

2001, Sept. 15 ***Perf. 13½***

534 A150 15s multi 2.00 1.00
Booklet, 6 #534 13.00

Souvenir Sheet

535	Sheet of 3	4.25	3.50
a.-c.	A150 30s Any single	1.25	.75

See Estonia Nos. 423-424, Lithuania Nos. 698-699.

Palace Type of 1999

2001, Oct. 24 ***Perf. 14½x14***

536	A131 40s Cesvaines Palace	2.00	1.25
a.	Perf. 13¼x14	2.00	1.25
b.	Booklet pane, 6 #536a	12.00	—
	Booklet, #536b	12.00	

House of Worship Type of 2000

2001, Nov. 3 ***Perf. 13¾x14***

537 A141 70s Riga Synagogue 3.00 1.50
Booklet, 6 #537 24.00

Latvian Seamen A151

Designs: 15s, Krisjanis Valdemars (1825-91), founder of Naval College. 70s, Duke Jekabs Ketlers (1610-82), shipbuilder.

2001, Nov. 14 ***Perf. 13¼x14***

538-539 A151 Set of 2 3.50 2.25

Christmas — A152

Designs: 12s, Rabbits. No. 541, 15s, Dog, rabbit. No. 542, 15s, Lambs.

2001, Nov. 22 ***Perf. 13¼***

540-542 A152 Set of 3 2.00 1.25

Town Arms — A153

2002, Jan. 29 **Litho.** ***Perf. 13¼x13¾***

543	A153 5s Ludza	.40	.35
544	A153 10s Dobele	.60	.50
a.	Perf. 14x14¼, dated "2012"	.50	.50
b.	As "a," "2013"	.40	.50
545	A153 15s Sigulda	.80	.60
	Nos. 543-545 (3)	1.80	1.45

See Nos. 565-567, 585-587, 609-611, 638-640, 670-672, 696-698, 726-728, 753-755, 776-777, 798-800, 824-826.

Issued: No. 544a, 3/15/12; No. 544b, 3/3/13.

2002 Winter Olympics, Salt Lake City — A154

2002, Feb. 8 ***Perf. 13¼x13¾***

546	A154 40s multi	2.00	1.25
a.	Booklet pane of 6, perf. 13¼x13¾ on 3 sides	17.00	—
	Booklet, #546a	17.00	

2002 Winter Paralympics, Salt Lake City — A155

2002, Mar. 5 ***Perf. 14¼x13¾***

547 A155 15s multi *1.00* .70

Refugees, by Jekabs Kazaks — A156

2002, Apr. 20 **Litho.** ***Perf. 14½x14¼***

548 A156 40s multi *2.00* 1.25

Europa — A157

2002, May 4 ***Perf. 14***

549	A157 60s multi	2.50	1.75
a.	Tete-beche pair	6.00	6.00

Endangered Plants — A158

Designs: 15s, Cypripedium calceolus. 40s, Trapa natans.

2002, May 25 ***Perf. 13¾***

550-551 A158 Set of 2 2.50 1.50

See Nos. 568-569, 589-590, 612-613.

Latvian Armed Forces — A159

2002, June 15 ***Perf. 13¾x13¼***

552 A159 40s multi 1.60 1.10

Janis Jaunsudrabins (1877-1962), Writer — A160

2002, July 6 *Perf. 13¾x13½*
553 A160 40s multi 1.75 1.10
a. Booklet pane of 6, perf. 13¾x13½ on 3 sides 12.00
Booklet, #553a 12.00

Kristians Johans Dals (1839-1904) and Ship — A161

2002, July 20 *Perf. 13¼x13¾*
554 A161 70s multi 2.75 1.75

Fish — A162

Designs: 15s, Gadus morhua callarias. 40s, Siluris glanis.

2002, Aug. 10 Litho. *Perf. 14*
555-556 A162 Set of 2 2.50 1.75
a. Booklet pane, perf. 14 on 3 sides 15.00
Booklet, #556a 15.00

Souvenir Sheet

Venta River Bridge A163

2002, Aug. 24 *Perf. 12¾x12½*
557 A163 100s multi 4.25 3.50

Jaunmoku Palace — A164

2002, Sept. 14 *Perf. 14¼x13¾*
558 A164 40s multi 1.75 1.25

House of Worship Type of 2000

70s, Grebenschikov Old Belief Praying House.

2002, Oct. 12 *Perf. 13¾x14*
559 A141 70s multicolored 3.00 1.75
a. Booklet pane of 6, perf. 13¾x14 on 3 sides 20.00
Booklet, #559a 20.00

Mittens — A165

2002, Nov. 2 *Perf. 13¼x13¾*
560 A165 15s multi .85 .50

See Nos. 579, 604, 629.

Christmas — A166

Designs: 12s, Elf on sack, Christmas tree. No. 562, 15s, Angel, Christmas tree. No. 563, 15s, Elves on gift.

2002, Nov. 23 *Perf. 13¾x13¼*
561-563 A166 Set of 3 2.00 1.25

A Man Entering a Room, by Niklavs Strunke (1894-1966) — A167

2003, Jan. 25 Litho. *Perf. 13¼x14*
564 A167 40s multi 1.75 1.25

Town Arms Type of 2002

2003, Feb. 15 *Perf. 13¼x13¾*
565 A153 10s Balvi .50 .25
566 A153 15s Gulbene .65 .40
567 A153 20s Ventspils .90 .60
Nos. 565-567 (3) 2.05 1.25

Endangered Plants Type of 2002

Designs: 15s, Ophrys insectifera. 30s, Taxus baccata.

2003, Mar. 21 *Perf. 13¾*
568 A158 15s multi .75 .50
569 A158 30s multi 1.75 1.00
a. Perf. 14½x14¼ on 3 sides 2.00 1.00
b. Booklet pane, 6 #569a 12.00 —
Complete booklet, #569b 12.00

Straumeni, by Edvarts Virza (1883-1940) — A168

2003, Apr. 12 *Perf. 13¾x13¼*
570 A168 40s multi 1.75 1.25

Europa — A169

2003, May 3 Litho. *Perf. 13¼x13¾*
571 A169 60s multi 2.75 1.75
a. Tete beche pair 6.00 6.00

Kolka Lighthouse — A170

2003, May 17 *Perf. 13¾x13¼*
572 A170 60s multi 2.50 1.75

See Nos. 602, 626, 662, 676, 709, 746.

House of Worship Type of 2000

2003, June 6 *Perf. 13¼x13¾*
573 A141 70s Salvation Temple, horiz. 3.00 1.75

Souvenir Sheet

Gauja River Bridge, Sigulda A171

2003, July 19
574 A171 100s multi 4.75 3.75

Fish — A172

Designs: 15s, Thymallus thymallus. 30s, Salmo salar.

2003, Aug. 2 *Perf. 14x13¾*
575 A172 15s multi .75 .50
576 A172 30s multi 1.75 1.25
a. Booklet pane of 6, perf. 14x13¾ on 3 sides 13.00 —
Complete booklet, #576a 13.00

Motacilla Alba — A173

2003, Aug. 30 *Perf. 14¾x14*
577 A173 15s multi 1.00 .50

Palace Type of 1999

2003, Sept. 27 *Perf. 14¼x13¾*
578 A131 40s Birini Palace 1.75 1.25
a. Booklet pane of 6 11.00
Complete booklet, #578a 11.00

Mittens Type of 2002

2003, Oct. 11 *Perf. 14x13¾*
579 A165 15s Libiesi mittens .80 .45

Motorcycle Racing — A174

2003, Oct. 31 *Perf. 13¼x13¾*
580 A174 70s multi 3.00 1.75
a. Booklet pane of 6 20.00 —
Complete booklet, #580a 20.00

Christmas — A175

Designs: 12s, Madonna and Child with two angels. No. 582, 15s, The Annunciation (golden brown frame). No. 583, 15s, Nativity (gray frame).

2003, Nov. 22 *Perf. 13¾x14¼*
581-583 A175 Set of 3 2.25 1.25

Still Life with Triangle, by Romans Suta — A176

2004, Jan. 25 Litho. *Perf. 13¼x14*
584 A176 40s multi 1.75 1.00

Town Arms Type of 2002

2004, Feb. 14 *Perf. 13¼x13¾*
585 A153 5s Valka .30 .30
586 A153 15s Cesis .60 .60
587 A153 20s Saldus .80 .80
Nos. 585-587 (3) 1.70 1.70

Reinis (1839-1920) and Matiss (1848-1926) Kaudzites, Writers — A177

2004, Mar. 20 *Perf. 13¾*
588 A177 40s multi 1.60 1.00

Endangered Plants Type of 2002

Designs: 15s, Gentiana cruciata. 30s, Onobrychis arenaria.

2004, Apr. 3
589-590 A158 Set of 2 2.00 1.25

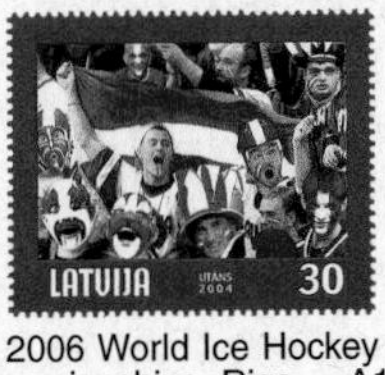

2006 World Ice Hockey Championships, Riga — A178

2004, Apr. 17 Litho. *Perf. 13¼x13¾*
591 A178 30s multi 1.50 .80
a. Booklet pane of 4, perf. 13¼x13¾ on 3 sides 15.00 —
Complete booklet, #591a 15.00

Admission to European Union — A179

Designs: No. 592, 30s, Stars, map of Europe, flags of newly-added countries. No. 593, 30s, Seven stars.

2004, May 1 *Perf. 13x13¼*
592-593 A179 Set of 2 2.50 1.75

Europa — A180

2004, May 8 Litho. *Perf. 13¼x13¾*
594 A180 60s multi 2.50 1.75
a. Tete beche pair 5.50 5.50

European Soccer Championships, Portugal — A181

2004, June 3 *Perf. 14x13½*
595 A181 30s multi 1.40 1.25

Fish — A182

Designs: 15s, Oncorhynchus mykiss. 30s, Psetta maxima.

2004, June 26 *Perf. 13¼x14*
596 A182 15s multi .60 .40
597 A182 30s multi 1.50 .90
a. Booklet pane of 6, perf. 13¼x14 on 3 sides 11.00 —
Complete booklet, #597a 11.00

See Nos. 620-621.

Visit of Pres. Bill Clinton to Latvia, 10th Anniv. — A183

2004, July 6 *Perf. 13¾x13¼*
598 A183 40s multi 1.75 1.25

Souvenir Sheet

Dzelzcela Bridge, Riga — A184

2004, July 24 *Perf. 13¼x13¾*
599 A184 100s multi 4.25 4.25

2004 Summer Olympics, Athens — A185

2004, Aug. 14 Litho. *Perf. 14*
600 A185 30s multi 1.25 .90

St. Jacob's Cathedral — A186

Perf. 13¾x13¼

2004, Aug. 28 **Litho.**
601 A186 40s multi 1.75 1.25

Lighthouse Type of 2003

2004, Sept. 18
602 A170 60s Mikelbaka 2.75 1.50
a. Booklet pane of 4, perf. 13¾x13¼ on 3 sides 12.00 —
Complete booklet, #602a 12.00

Jaunpils Palace — A187

2004, Oct. 15 ***Perf. 14¼x13¾***
603 A187 40s multi 1.75 1.25
a. Booklet pane of 6, perf. 14¼x13¾ on 3 sides 11.00 —
Complete booklet, #603a 11.00

See Nos. 628, 678.

Mittens Type of 2002

2004, Nov. 6 ***Perf. 13¼x13¾***
604 A165 15s Piebalga mittens .80 .50

Christmas — A188

Designs: 12s, Children, rabbit, bird, heart. No. 606, 15s, Snowman, birds. No. 607, 15s, Angel.

2004, Dec. 4 ***Perf. 13¾x13¼***
605-607 A188 Set of 3 1.75 1.25

1905 Revolution, Cent. — A189

2005, Jan. 13 **Litho.** ***Perf. 13¾x13¼***
608 A189 15s multi 1.10 .65

Town Arms Type of 2002

2005, Feb. 11 ***Perf. 13¼x13¾***
609 A153 15s Aluksne .60 .40
610 A153 15s Talsi .60 .40
611 A153 40s Jekabpils 1.50 1.25
Nos. 609-611 (3) 2.70 2.05

Endangered Plants Type of 2002

Designs: 20s, Pulsatilla patens. 30s, Allium ursinum.

2005, Mar. 5 ***Perf. 13¼***
612-613 A158 Set of 2 2.00 1.25
613a Booklet pane of 6 #613, perf. 13¼ on 3 sides 12.00 —
Complete booklet, #613a 12.00

Krimuldas Church, 800th Anniv. — A190

2005, Mar. 19 ***Perf. 13¼x13¾***
614 A190 40s multi 1.60 1.00

The Adventures of Baron Munchausen, by Rudolph Erich Raspe — A191

2005, Apr. 1 **Litho.** ***Perf. 13¼x13¾***
615 A191 30s multi 1.25 .90

Europa — A192

2005, Apr. 23
616 A192 60s multi 2.50 1.50
a. Tete beche pair 6.00 6.00

Mother and Child, by Janis Rozentals A193

2005, May 8 ***Perf. 14x13¼***
617 A193 40s multi 1.60 1.00
a. Booklet pane of 4, perf. 14x13¼ on 3 sides 7.25 —
Complete booklet, #617a 7.25

Baumanu Karlis (1835-1905), Composer of National Anthem — A194

2005, May 21 ***Perf. 13¾x13¼***
618 A194 20s multi .80 .50

Kaive Oak — A195

Serpentine Die Cut 14

2005, June 11 **Self-Adhesive**
619 A195 15s multi 1.00 .75

Printed in sheets of 8.

Fish Type of 2004

Designs: 15s, Lampetra fluviatilis. 40s, Clupea harengus membras.

2005, Aug. 13 **Litho.** ***Perf. 13¼x14***
620-621 A182 Set of 2 2.25 1.50

Pope John Paul II (1920-2005) — A196

2005, Aug. 14 ***Perf. 14¼x13½***
622 A196 15s multi .80 .50

Souvenir Sheet

Latvian National Library A197

2005, Aug. 27 ***Perf. 13¼x12¾***
623 A197 100s multi 4.00 3.75

Janis Plieksans (Rainis), (1865-1929), Writer — A198

2005, Sept. 10 ***Perf. 14¼***
624 A198 40s multi 1.60 1.00
a. Booklet pane of 6, perf. 14¼ on 3 sides 11.00 —
Complete booklet, #624a 11.00

Souvenir Sheet

Bridge Over Railroad Tracks, Riga A199

2005, Sept. 24 ***Perf. 13¼x13¾***
625 A199 100s multi 5.50 4.00

Lighthouse Type of 2003

2005, Oct. 8 **Litho.** ***Perf. 14x13¼***
626 A170 40s Daugavgrivas 1.75 1.00
a. Booklet pane of 4, perf. 14x13¼ on 3 sides 8.50 —
Complete booklet, #626a 8.50

Gunars Astra (1931-88), Human Rights Activist in Soviet Union — A200

2005, Oct. 22 ***Perf. 13½x14¼***
627 A200 15s multi .60 .40

Palace Type of 2004

2005, Nov. 5 ***Perf. 13¼x14***
628 A187 40s Durbes Palace, horiz. 1.60 1.00

Mittens Type of 2002

2005, Nov. 26 ***Perf. 13¼x13¾***
629 A165 20s Dienvidlatgale mittens .80 .50

Christmas — A201

Designs: 12s, Goat riding on wolf's back. No. 631, 15s, Woman, dog near tree, vert. No. 632, 15s, Cat, woman carrying rooster, vert.

2005, Dec. 3 ***Serpentine Die Cut 15***

Self-Adhesive
630-632 A201 Set of 3 1.75 1.25

Europa Stamps, 50th Anniv. — A202

Latvian Europa stamps: Nos. 633, 637a, 10s, #414. Nos. 634, 637b, 15s, #463. Nos. 635, 637c, 15s, #442. Nos. 636, 637d, 20s, #484-485.

2006, Jan. 7 **Litho.** ***Perf. 13¾x13¼***
633-636 A202 Set of 4 2.50 1.50

Souvenir Sheet

Perf. 13½ Syncopated
637 A202 Sheet of 4, #a-d 2.25 2.25

No. 637 contains four 45x28mm stamps.

Town Arms Type of 2002

2006, Jan. 11 ***Perf. 13¼x13¾***
638 A153 7s Aizkraukle .30 .25
639 A153 22s Kraslava .80 .60
640 A153 31s Limbazi 1.25 .90
Nos. 638-640 (3) 2.35 1.75

2006 Winter Olympics, Turin — A203

2006, Feb. 4 ***Perf. 14***
641 A203 45s multi 1.75 1.25

Stamerienas Palace — A204

2006, Feb. 25 ***Perf. 14¼x13¾***
642 A204 95s multi 3.50 2.25

Zvartes Iezis — A205

Serpentine Die Cut 14

2006, Mar. 11 **Self-Adhesive**
643 A205 22s multi .80 .55

Printed in sheets of 8.

Souvenir Sheet

Raunu Railroad Bridge A206

2006, Mar. 25 ***Perf. 13½x14***
644 A206 100s multi 3.75 3.25

2006 World Ice Hockey Championships, Riga — A207

Perf. 13½x14¼

2006, Mar. 31 **Litho.**
645 A207 55s multi + label 2.00 1.25
a. Booklet pane of 4, perf. 13½x14¼ on 3 sides, without labels 10.00 —
Complete booklet, #645a 10.00

Cesis, 800th Anniv. — A208

Various sites in Cesis: 22s, 31s, 45s, 55s. 45s and 55s are horiz.

Perf. 13¼x13¾, 13¾x13¼

2006, Apr. 7
646-649 A208 Set of 4 6.00 4.00

Traditional Jewelry — A209

No. 650: a, Brooch, Latvia. b, Bracelet, Kazakhstan.

2006, Apr. 19 ***Perf. 14x13¾***
650 A209 22s Horiz. pair, #a-b 1.75 1.00

See Kazakhstan No. 509.

Europa — A210

2006, May 3 ***Perf. 13½x14¼***
651 A210 85s multi 3.25 2.50
a. Tete beche pair 7.00 7.00

Ciganiete ar Tamburinu, by Karlis Huns — A211

2006, May 13 ***Perf. 13¼x14***
652 A211 40s multi 1.50 1.00
a. Booklet pane of 4, perf. 13¼x14 on 3 sides 7.00 —
Complete booklet, #652a 7.00

A212

Personalizable Stamps — A213

2006, June 9 ***Perf. 13¾***
653 A212 31s yel bister 1.25 1.00
654 A213 31s yel bister 1.25 1.00

Stamp vignettes could be personalized by customers, presumably for an extra fee.

"Big Christopher" Statue — A214

2006, June 16 ***Perf. 14x13½***
655 A214 36s multi 1.40 1.00

Art by Anna Koshkina — A215

Booklet Stamp

Die Cut Perf. 14½x13 on 3 Sides

2006, Aug. 11 **Self-Adhesive**
656 A215 22s multi .90 .60
a. Booklet pane of 8 7.25

Volunteer Army, 15th Anniv. — A216

2006, Aug. 23 ***Perf. 13½x14***
657 A216 22s multi .90 .60

Staburags — A217

2006, Sept. 9 **Litho.** ***Perf. 14¼x13¾***
658 A217 58s multi 2.25 1.50
a. Tete beche pair 5.00 5.00

Wild Animals and Their Tracks — A218

Designs: 45s, Lynx lynx. 55s, Cervus elaphus.

2006, Sept. 23 ***Perf. 14¼x13½***
659-660 A218 Set of 2 3.75 2.50
659a Booklet pane of 4 #659, perf. 14¼x13½ on 3 sides 7.50 —
Complete booklet, #659a 7.50
659b Tete beche pair 4.00 4.00
660a Tete beche pair 4.50 4.50

See Nos. 691-692, 719-720, 744-745.

Pansija Pili, Novel by Anslavs Eglitis (1906-93) — A219

2006, Oct. 14 **Litho.** ***Perf. 13¼x13½***
661 A219 67s multi 2.50 1.50

Lighthouse Type of 2003

2006, Oct. 27 ***Perf. 14¼x13½***
662 A170 40s Mersraga Lighthouse 1.50 1.00
a. Booklet pane of 4, perf. 14¼x13½ on 3 sides 7.00 —
Complete booklet, #662a 7.00

NATO Summit, Riga — A220

2006, Nov. 17 ***Perf. 13¾x13¼***
663 A220 55s multi 2.25 1.25

Christmas — A221

Cookies in shape of: 18s, Christmas tree. 22s, Star. 31s, Crescent moon. 45s, Bell.

Serpentine Die Cut 14

2006, Nov. 17 **Self-Adhesive**
664-667 A221 Set of 4 4.50 3.25

Oskars Kalpaks (1882-1919), First Commander-in-chief of Latvian Army — A222

2007, Jan. 6 ***Perf. 14¼x14***
668 A222 22s multi .85 .60

Mobile Telecommunications in Latvia, 15th Anniv. — A223

2007, Jan. 19
669 A223 22s multi .85 .60
a. Tete beche pair 2.00 2.00

Town Arms Type of 2002

2007, Feb. 3 ***Perf. 13¼x13¾***
670 A153 5s Staicele .25 .25
a. Perf. 14x14¼, "2010" .25 .25
671 A153 10s Sabile .35 .25
672 A153 22s Vecumnieki .80 .65
Nos. 670-672 (3) 1.40 1.15

Issued: No. 670a, 3/12/10.

Tilts Tornkalna, Painting by Ludolfs Liberts (1895-1959) — A224

2007, Feb. 17 ***Perf. 14¼x14***
673 A224 58s multi 2.25 1.50

Pauls Stradins Museum of the History of Medicine, Riga, 50th Anniv. — A225

2007, Mar. 9 ***Perf. 14x14¼***
674 A225 22s multi .85 .60

Baltic Coast — A226

Serpentine Die Cut 14

2007, Mar. 24 **Self-Adhesive**
675 A226 22s multi .85 .60

Lighthouse Type of 2003

2007, Apr. 14 ***Perf. 13¾x13½***
676 A170 67s Papes Lighthouse 2.50 1.75
a. Booklet pane of 4, perf. 13¾x13½ on 3 sides 12.00 —
Complete booklet, #676a 12.00

Europa — A227

2007, Apr. 28 **Litho.** ***Perf. 13½x14¼***
677 A227 85s multi 3.25 2.50
a. Tete beche pair 7.50 7.50

Scouting, cent.

Palace Type of 2004

2007, June 8 **Litho.** ***Perf. 13½x14¼***
678 A187 22s Krustpils, horiz. .85 .60

UNESCO World Heritage Sites — A228

Designs: 36s, Historic Center of Riga. 45s, Historic Centers of Straslund and Wismar, Germany.

2007, July 12 **Litho.** ***Perf. 14x13¾***
679-680 A228 Set of 2 3.50 2.50

See Germany Nos. 2449-2450.

Sigulda, 800th Anniv. — A229

Designs: 22s, New Sigulda Castle. 31s, Bobsled course. 40s, Sigulda Castle ruins.

Serpentine Die Cut 15¼

2007, Aug. 10 **Self-Adhesive**
681-683 A229 Set of 3 3.75 2.50

Berries and Mushrooms — A230

Designs: 22s, Vaccinium vitis-idaea. 58s, Cantharellus cibarius.

2007, Aug. 25 ***Perf. 14x13½***
684 A230 22s multi .80 .55
a. Tete beche pair 2.00 2.00
685 A230 58s multi 2.25 1.50
a. Booklet pane of 4, perf. 14x13½ on 3 sides 10.00 —
Complete booklet, #685a 10.00
b. Tete beche pair 5.00 5.00

See Nos. 715-716, 742-743, 767-768.

Organized Soccer in Latvia, Cent. — A231

2007, Sept. 8 ***Perf. 13¾***
686 A231 45s multi 1.75 1.75

Values are for stamps with surrounding selvage.

Souvenir Sheet

Aiviekstі Railroad Bridge A232

2007, Oct. 13 ***Perf. 14***
687 A232 100s multi 3.75 3.75

Latvia Post, 375th Anniv. — A233

Designs: 22s, Postrider. 31s, Postal worker and van.

Serpentine Die Cut 15

2007, Oct. 20 **Litho.**

Self-Adhesive

688-689 A233 Set of 2 2.10 1.60

13th Century Decorations A234

2007, Nov. 3 ***Perf. 13¼x14***
690 A234 60s multi 2.50 1.75

Wild Animals and Their Tracks Type of 2006

Designs: 45s, Vulpes vulpes. 55s, Alces alces.

2007, Nov. 16 ***Perf. 14¼x13½***
691 A218 45s multi 1.75 1.25
a. Tete beche pair 3.50 3.50
692 A218 55s multi 2.25 1.50
a. Tete beche pair 5.00 5.00

Christmas — A235

Christmas tree and children with: 22s, Musical instruments. 31s, Cookies. 45s, Skis and sled.

Serpentine Die Cut 15

2007, Nov. 24 **Self-Adhesive**

693-695 A235 Set of 3 3.75 3.00

Town Arms Type of 2002 With Country Name at Top

2008, Feb. 9 ***Perf. 13¼x13¾***

696 A153 22s Salaspils .75 .60
697 A153 28s Plavinas .95 .75
698 A153 45s Saulkrasti 1.60 1.25
Nos. 696-698 (3) 3.30 2.60

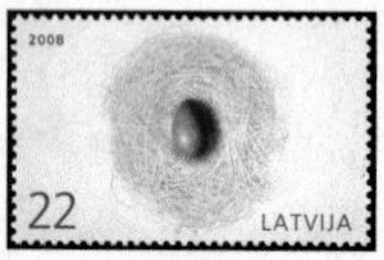

Easter — A236

2008, Feb. 23 ***Perf. 13¼x13***

699 A236 22s multi .80 .80

Augli, by Leo Svemps — A237

2008, Mar. 8 **Litho.** ***Perf. 13x13¼***

700 A237 63s multi 2.40 2.40

State Awards of the Baltic Countries — A238

Designs: Nos. 701, 702a, Order of Three Stars, Latvia. No. 702b, Order of Vytautas the Great, Lithuania. No. 702c, Order of the National Coat of Arms, Estonia.

2008, Mar. 15 ***Perf. 13½x13¾***

701 A238 31s multi 1.25 1.25

Souvenir Sheet

702 A238 31s Sheet of 3, #a-c 3.50 3.50

On No. 701, the second line of type above the medal is 18mm wide, while it is 15mm wide on No. 702a.

See Estonia Nos. 592-593, Lithuania Nos. 862-863.

Worldwide Fund for Nature (WWF) — A239

Bats: 22s, Barbastella barbastellus. 31s, Myotis dasycneme. 45s, Barbastella barbastellus, vert. 55s, Myotis dasycneme, vert.

Perf. 13½x14¼, 14¼x13½

2008, Apr. 12

703 A239 22s multi .80 .80
a. Tete beche pair 1.75 1.75
704 A239 31s multi 1.15 1.15
a. Tete beche pair 2.75 2.75
705 A239 45s multi 1.60 1.60
a. Tete beche pair 3.50 3.50
706 A239 55s multi 1.75 1.75
a. Tete beche pair 4.50 4.50
Nos. 703-706 (4) 5.30 5.30

Europa — A240

Designs: 45s, Letters and postcards. 85s, Person writing letter.

2008, Apr. 22 ***Perf. 13½***

707 A240 45s multi 1.75 1.75
a. Tete beche pair 4.00 4.00
708 A240 multi 3.25 3.25
a. Tete beche pair 7.50 7.50

Lighthouse Type of 2003

2008, May 5 ***Perf. 14¼x13½***

709 A170 63s Akmenraga Lighthouse 2.25 2.25
a. Booklet pane of 4, perf. 14¼x13½ on 3 sides 12.00 —
Complete booklet, #709a 12.00

European Orienteering Championships, Ventspils — A241

2008, May 23 **Litho.** ***Perf. 13x13¼***

710 A241 45s multi 1.60 1.60
a. Tete beche pair 4.00 4.00

Nature Protection — A242

Serpentine Die Cut 12½

2008, June 7 **Self-Adhesive**

711 A242 22s multi .85 .85

Riga Museum Foundations A243

2008, June 26 ***Perf. 13x13½***

712 A243 22s multi .85 .85

2008 Summer Olympics, Beijing — A244

2008, Aug. 8 ***Perf. 13½x13***

713 A244 63s multi 2.25 2.25

Sudraba Fairy Tale — A245

Perf. 14¼x13½

2008, Aug. 23 **Litho.**

714 A245 22s multi .85 .85
a. Tete beche pair 1.90 1.90

Berries and Mushrooms Type of 2007

Designs: 22s, Vaccinium myrtillus. 58s, Leccinum aurantiacum.

2008, Sept. 6 ***Perf. 14x13½***

715 A230 22s multi .80 .80
a. Tete beche pair 2.00 2.00
716 A230 58s multi 2.00 2.00
a. Perf. 13½x14 on 3 sides 2.25 2.25
b. Booklet pane of 4 #716a 9.00 —
Complete booklet, #716b 9.00
c. Tete beche pair 4.50 4.50

Souvenir Sheet

Kandavas Bridge — A246

2008, Sept. 27 ***Perf. 14***

717 A246 100s multi 3.75 3.75

Tautas Fronte Newspaper, 20th Anniv. — A247

2008, Oct. 8 ***Perf. 13½***

718 A247 22s multi .85 .85
a. Tete beche pair 1.75 1.75

Wild Animals and Their Tracks Type of 2006

Designs: 45s, Martes martes. 55s, Castor fiber.

2008, Oct. 10 ***Perf. 14¼x13½***

719 A218 45s multi 1.75 1.75
a. Tete beche pair 3.50 3.50
720 A218 55s multi 2.25 2.25
a. Tete beche pair 5.00 5.00

Maris Strombergs, 2008 BMX Cycling Olympic Gold Medalist A248

2008, Oct. 24 ***Perf. 13½***

721 A248 22s multi .85 .85

Plate, Bow and Tablecloth — A249

2008, Oct. 25 ***Perf. 13½x13¾***

722 A249 28s multi 1.00 1.00

Latvian Republic, 90th Anniv. — A250

2008, Nov. 7 ***Perf. 13¼x13***

723 A250 31s multi 1.25 1.25

Mezotnes Palace — A251

2008, Nov. 8 ***Perf. 13½x14¼***

724 A251 63s multi 2.40 2.40

Christmas — A252

2008, Nov. 28 ***Perf. 14¼x13¾***

725 A252 25s multi .90 .90

Town Arms Type of 2002 With Country Name at Top

2009, Jan. 10 **Litho.** ***Perf. 14x14¼***

726 A153 33s Dagda 1.25 1.25
727 A153 35s Balozi 1.40 1.40
728 A153 60s Stende 2.00 2.00
Nos. 726-728 (3) 4.65 4.65

Brooch, 8th Cent. A. D. — A253

2009, Jan. 24 ***Perf. 14***

729 A253 98s multi 3.50 3.50
a. Tete beche pair 7.50 7.50

Dancing Boy and Animals Folktale — A254

2009, Feb. 21 ***Perf. 13¼***

730 A254 40s multi 1.50 1.50

Souvenir Sheet

Preservation of Polar Regions and Glaciers — A255

No. 731: a, 35s, Polar bear. b, 55s, Penguins.

2009, Mar. 18 **Litho.** ***Perf. 13¼***

731 A255 Sheet of 2, #a-b 3.75 3.75

Europa — A256

Designs: 50s, Janis Ikaunieks, astronomer, and Baldone Observatory telescope. 55s, Map of solar system, asteroid, University of Latvia Institute of Astronomy, radio telescope, five astronomers.

2009, Apr. 2 ***Perf. 14x13¾***

732 A256 50s multi 2.25 2.25
a. Tete beche pair 4.75 4.75
733 A256 55s multi 2.50 2.50
a. Tete beche pair 5.25 5.25

Intl. Year of Astronomy.

Natl. Museum of History — A257

2009, May 14 ***Perf. 13½***

734 A257 35s multi 1.40 1.40

Basketball — A258

Player from opposing team and: 35s, Male Latvian team player, 1935. 40s, Female TTT Riga player. 60s, Male ASK Riga player.

120s, Latvian player in 2009 Women's European Basketball Championships.

2009, June 6

735-737 A258 Set of 3 5.25 5.25

Souvenir Sheet

738 A258 120s multi 4.50 4.50

Nos. 735-737 each were printed in sheets of 9 + label.

Bauska, 400th Anniv. — A259

2009, July 10 Litho. ***Perf. 13½x14***
739 A259 38s multi 1.35 1.35

Steam Locomotive A260

2009, Aug. 5 Litho. ***Perf. 13½***
740 A260 35s multi 1.40 1.40

Souvenir Sheet

Dienvidu Bridge, Riga A261

2009, Aug. 22
741 A261 100s multi 4.00 4.00

Berries and Mushrooms Type of 2007

Designs: 55s, Fragaria vesca. 60s, Russula paludosa.

2009, Sept. 12
742 A230 55s multi 2.25 2.25
a. Tete beche pair 5.00 5.00
743 A230 60s multi 2.50 2.50
a. Tete beche pair 5.50 5.50
b. Perf. 13½ on 3 sides 2.50 2.50
c. Booklet pane of 4 #743b 11.00 —
Complete booklet, #743c 11.00

Wild Animals and Their Tracks Type of 2006

Designs: 35s, Canis lupus. 98s, Lepus europaeus.

2009, Oct. 21 ***Perf. 13½x14¼***
744 A218 35s multi 1.25 1.25
a. Tete beche pair 2.75 2.75
745 A218 98s multi 4.00 4.00
a. Tete beche pair 8.25 8.25

Lighthouse Type of 2003

2009, Nov. 5 Litho. ***Perf. 13¼***
746 A170 63s Liepaja Lighthouse 2.60 2.60

Republic of Latvia, 91st Anniv. — A262

Designs: 35s, Formation of Latvian People's Council, Nov. 17, 1918. 40s, Proclamation of Latvian Republic, Nov. 18, 1918. 100s, First meeting of Constitutional Assembly, May 1, 1920.

2009, Nov. 14 Litho. ***Perf. 14***
747-749 A262 Set of 3 6.75 6.75

Christmas — A263

Designs: 35s, Horse Christmas ornament, building. 55s, Fish Christmas ornament, building. 60s, Snowflake Christmas ornament.

2009, Nov. 27 ***Perf. 13¼***
750-752 A263 Set of 3 5.75 5.75

Town Arms Type of 2002 With Country Name at Top

2010, Jan. 16 Litho. ***Perf. 14x14¼***
753 A153 35s Viesite 1.25 1.25
754 A153 40s Ligatne 1.40 1.40
755 A153 55s Iecava 2.00 2.00
Nos. 753-755 (3) 4.65 4.65

2010 Winter Olympics, Vancouver A264

2010, Feb. 5 ***Perf. 13¼x13¾***
756 A264 55s multi 2.10 2.10

Peonies — A265

2010, Mar. 26 ***Perf. 13¼***
757 A265 35s multi 1.25 1.25
a. Tete beche pair 2.75 2.75

Europa — A266

Designs: 55s, Girl holding books, characters from children's books. 120s, Boy reading book, ship, castle, mountain.

2010, Apr. 9 Litho. ***Perf. 13½x13¼***
758 A266 55s multi 2.00 2.00
a. Tete beche pair 4.25 4.25
759 A266 120s multi 4.00 4.00
a. Tete beche pair 8.75 8.75

Expo 2010, Shanghai — A267

2010, Apr. 23 ***Perf. 13¼***
760 A267 150s multi 5.25 5.25

Declaration of May 4, 1990, 20th Anniv. — A268

2010, May 4
761 A268 35s multi 1.40 1.40
a. Tete beche pair 3.00 3.00

Fire Fighting Museum — A269

2010, May 21
762 A269 98s multi 3.75 3.75
a. Tete beche pair 7.75 7.75

Birds — A270

Designs: 35s, Coracias garrulus. 98s, Bubo bubo, vert.

Perf. 14x13¾, 13¾x14
2010, June 18
763-764 A270 Set of 2 5.00 5.00
See Nos. 790-791.

Talsos Sports Hall — A271

2010, July 16 ***Perf. 13¼***
765 A271 150s multi 5.75 5.75

RP Series Locomotive A272

2010, Aug. 5 ***Perf. 13¼x13½***
766 A272 40s multi 1.50 1.50

Berries and Mushrooms Type of 2007

Designs: 55s, Rubus ideus. 120s, Leccinum scabrum.

2010, Sept. 10 ***Perf. 13½x13¼***
767 A230 55s multi 2.00 2.00
a. Tete beche pair 4.50 4.50
768 A230 120s multi 4.75 4.75
a. Tete beche pair 9.75 9.75

Lighthouse Type of 2003

2010, Oct. 15 Litho. ***Perf. 13½x13¼***
769 A170 98s Uzavas Lighthouse 3.75 3.75
a. Booklet pane of 4, perf. 13½x13¼ on 3 sides 16.00 —
Complete booklet, #769a 16.00

Republic of Latvia, 92nd Anniv. — A273

National symbols: 35s, Flag. 38s, Arms. 98s, Anthem.

2010, Nov. 12 Litho. ***Perf. 14***
770-772 A273 Set of 3 6.50 6.50

Christmas — A274

Designs: 35s, Girl, cat, Christmas tree. 60s, Boy with gift, bird in tree.

2010, Dec. 3 ***Perf. 13½x13¼***
773 A274 35s multi 1.35 1.35
a. Tete beche pair 3.00 3.00
774 A274 60s multi 2.40 2.40
a. Tete beche pair 5.00 5.00

New Year 2011 (Year of the Rabbit) — A275

2011, Jan. 14 Litho. ***Perf. 13½x13¼***
775 A275 35s multi 1.40 1.40

Town Arms Type of 2002 With Country Name at Top

2011, Feb. 25 Litho. ***Perf. 14x14¼***
776 A153 35s Ikskiles 1.10 1.10
777 A153 98s Carnikavas 4.25 4.25

Rose — A276

2011, Mar. 25 ***Perf. 13½x13¼***
778 A276 35s multi 1.35 1.35
a. Tete beche pair 3.00 3.00

Europa — A277

Animals in forest: 55s, Deer. 120s, Wolf.

2011, Apr. 8 ***Perf. 14x13¾***
779 A277 55s multi 1.90 1.90
a. Tete beche pair 4.00 4.00
780 A277 120s multi 4.00 4.00
a. Tete beche pair 8.50 8.50

Intl. Year of Forests.

Souvenir Sheet

Struve Geodetic Arc A278

No. 781: a, 35s, Map of arc and stone. b, 55s, Map and Friedrich Georg Wilhelm von Struve (1793-1864), astronomer.

2011, May 5 ***Perf. 13¼x13½***
781 A278 Sheet of 2, #a-b 3.25 3.25

First Coin of Riga, 800th Anniv. — A279

2011, May 23 ***Perf. 13½x13¼***
782 A279 98s multi 3.75 3.75
a. Tete beche pair 8.00 8.00

Johanna (1904-90) and Zanis Lipke (1900-87), Rescuers of Jews During World War II — A280

2011, July 4 ***Perf. 14x13¾***
783 A280 60s multi 2.25 2.25
a. Tete beche pair 5.00 5.00

Phoenix III Passenger Coach — A281

2011, Aug. 5 ***Perf. 13¼x13½***
784 A281 33s multi 1.25 1.25

A282

A283

Personalized Stamps — A284

2011, Aug. 22 *Perf. 13¾*

785 A282 35s yel bis & blk	1.30	1.30
786 A283 55s yel bis & blk	2.10	2.10
787 A284 60s yel bis & blk	2.25	2.25
Nos. 785-787 (3)	5.65	5.65

The generic vignettes shown for Nos. 785-787 could be personalized by customers for an extra fee.

Latvian Cycling Federation, 125th Anniv. — A285

2011, Aug. 25 *Perf. 14x13¾*

788 A285 35s multi	1.40	1.40

Port of Riga — A286

2011, Sept. 2 Litho. *Perf. 13¼x13½*

789 A286 60s multi	2.25	2.25

Birds Type of 2010

Designs: 35s, Hippolais icterina. 98s, Circaetus gallicus, vert.

2011, Sept. 23 Litho. *Perf. 14x13¾*

790 A270 35s multi	1.25	1.25
a. Perf. 13¾x14 on 3 sides, granite paper	1.25	1.25
b. Booklet pane of 4 #790a	8.50	—
Complete booklet, #790b	8.50	

Perf. 13¾x14

791 A270 98s multi	3.75	3.75
a. Perf. 13¾x14 on 3 sides, granite paper	3.75	3.75
b. Booklet pane of 4 #791a	15.00	—
Complete booklet, #791b	15.00	

Parventa Library, Ventspils — A287

2011, Oct. 14 *Perf. 13½x13¼*

792 A287 100s multi	4.00	4.00

Republic of Latvia, 93rd Anniv. — A288

Designs: 35s, Merchant fleet ships and their captains. 60s, Krisjanis Valdemars, founder of Latvian Naval School, Ainazi. 100s, Admiral Teodors Spade, Navy emblem, ships and sailors.

2011, Nov. 11 *Perf. 14*

Granite Paper

793-795 A288 Set of 3	7.50	7.50

Christmas — A289

Designs: 35s, Reindeer with clothesline between antlers, Santa Claus with ripped bag. 60s, Santa Claus pushing reindeer and bag on dragon's back.

2011, Dec. 2 *Perf. 13¼*

Granite Paper

796-797 A289 Set of 2	3.75	1.90

Town Arms Type of 2002 With Country Name At Top

2012, Jan. 7 *Perf. 13¼x13¾*

798 A153 33s Piltene	1.25	.90
799 A153 35s Riga	1.40	1.00
800 A153 38s Lielvardes Novads	1.50	1.10
Nos. 798-800 (3)	4.15	3.00

Nos. 798-800 are dated "2011."

Library No. 1 Restaurant, Riga — A290

2012, Jan. 27 *Perf. 13¼*

801 A290 35s multi	1.40	1.40

Lilies — A291

2012, Feb. 11

802 A291 35s multi	1.40	1.40
a. Tete beche pair	3.00	3.00

Europa — A292

Designs: 55s, Dancers. 120s, National Opera House.

2012, Mar. 17 *Perf. 14*

803 A292 55s multi	2.10	2.10
a. Tete beche pair	4.50	4.50
804 A292 120s multi	4.50	4.50
a. Tete beche pair	9.50	9.50

Riga Zoo, Cent. A293

2012, Apr. 14 *Perf. 13¼*

805 A293 Block or horiz. strip of 3 + label	6.00	6.00
a. 35s Lion	1.40	1.40
b. 55s Horse	2.10	2.10
c. 60s Frog	2.25	2.25
d. Booklet pane of 4 #805c, perf. 13¼ on 3 sides	9.50	—
Complete booklet, #805d	9.50	

Janis Misins (1862-1945), Librarian — A294

2012, Apr. 25 *Perf. 13¼*

806 A294 98s multi	3.75	3.75
a. Tete beche pair	8.00	8.00

Port of Ventspils A295

2012, May 11 *Perf. 13¼x13½*

807 A295 35s multi	1.25	1.25

Birds — A296

Designs: 35s, Hirundo rustica. 98s, Carduelis carduelis.

2012, June 16 Litho. *Perf. 13¾x14*

808-809 A296 Set of 2	5.00	5.00

2012 Summer Olympics, London — A297

2012, July 14 *Perf. 13¼x13½*

810 A297 60s multi	2.25	2.25
a. Tete beche pair	5.00	5.00

Ungurmuiza Manor — A298

2012, Aug. 18

811 A298 98s multi	3.75	3.75

Friedrich Zander (1887-1933), Rocketry Pioneer — A299

2012, Aug. 23 *Perf. 13¼*

812 A299 60s multi	2.25	2.25
a. Tete beche pair	5.00	5.00

Souvenir Sheet

Duchy of Courland and Semigallia, 450th Anniv. — A300

No. 813: a, 35s, Duke Ernsts Johans Birons (1690-1772). b, 55s, Duke Jekabs Kettlers (1610-82).

Granite Paper

2012, Sept. 21 *Perf. 13¼x13½*

813 A300 Sheet of 2, #a-b	3.50	3.50

Riga Technical University, 150th Anniv. — A301

2012, Oct. 8 *Perf. 13¼*

814 A301 98s multi	3.75	3.75

Railway Bridges — A302

Train and: Nos. 815, 816a, Carnikava Bridge, Latvia. No. 816b, Lyduvenai Bridge, Lithuania. No. 816c, Narva Bridge, Estonia.

2012 *Perf. 13¼*

815 A302 35s multi	1.40	1.40

Souvenir Sheet

816 A302 55s Sheet of 3, #a-c	6.00	6.00

Issued: No. 815, 10/8; No. 816, 10/25. See Estonia Nos. 713-714, Lithuania Nos. 985-986.

Republic of Latvia, 94th Anniv. — A303

Composers: 35s, Emils Darzins (1875-1910). 60s, Jazeps Vitols (1863-1948). 100s, Talivaldis Kenins (1919-2008).

2012, Nov. 10 Litho. *Perf. 14*

817-819 A303 Set of 3	7.25	7.25

Latvian Medalists at 2012 Summer Olympics, London — A304

Designs: No. 820, 35s, Martins Plavins and Janis Smedins, beach volleyball bronze medalists. No. 821, 35s, Maris Strombergs, BMX cycling gold medalist.

2012, Nov. 23 *Perf. 13¼*

820 A304 35s multi	1.30	1.30
a. Tete beche pair	2.75	2.75
821 A304 35s multi	1.30	1.30
a. Tete beche pair	2.75	2.75

Christmas — A305

Designs: 35s, Girl, gifts, Christmas tree. 60s, Snow-covered house.

2012, Nov. 30 *Perf. 14x13¾*

822 A305 35s multi	1.25	1.25
a. Tete beche pair	2.75	2.75
823 A305 60s multi	2.50	2.50
a. Tete beche pair	5.25	5.25

Town Arms Type of 2002 With Country Name at Top

2013, Jan. 13 *Perf. 14*

824 A153 35s Varaklani	1.40	1.40
825 A153 60s Strencu Novads	2.40	2.40
826 A153 98s Varkavas Novads	3.75	3.75
Nos. 824-826 (3)	7.55	7.55

Janis Uzraugs, Cyclist — A306

2013, Jan. 30 *Perf. 13¾x13½*

827 A306 35s multi	1.40	1.40

Starting with No. 827, 2013 stamps also have euro denominations, in anticipation of a change to the euro currency in 2014.

Dailes Theater, Riga — A307

2013, Feb. 15 *Perf. 13¼x13½*

828 A307 100s multi	3.75	3.75

Irises — A308

2013, Mar. 8 *Perf. 13¼*

829 A308 35s multi	1.40	1.40
a. Tete beche pair	3.00	3.00

Europa — A309

Postal vehicles: 55s, Horse-drawn carriage, rail car. 120s, Airplane, truck, van, bicycle.

2013, Apr. 19 ***Perf. 14x13¾***
Granite Paper

830 A309 55s multi 2.10 2.10
a. Tete beche pair 4.50 4.50
b. Booklet pane of 4, perf. 14x13¼ on 3 sides 8.50 —
Complete booklet, #830b 8.50
831 A309 120s multi 4.50 4.50
a. Tete beche pair 9.50 9.50

Souvenir Sheet

Paul Walden (1863-1957), Chemist — A310

2013, May 14 ***Perf. 13¼***
Granite Paper

832 A310 100s multi 4.00 4.00

Birds — A311

Designs: 35s, Clangula hyemalis. 98s, Merops apiaster, vert.

Perf. 14x13¾, 13¾x14
2013, June 7 **Litho.**

833-834 A311 Set of 2 5.25 5.25

Souvenir Sheet

25th Latvian Song and Dance Festival A312

No. 835: a, Singers. b, Dancers.

2013, June 28 **Litho.** ***Perf. 13¼***

835 A312 35s Sheet of 2, #a-b 2.60 2.60

Cover With Russia (Wenden) No. L2 — A313

2013, July 12 **Litho.** ***Perf. 13¼***
Granite Paper

836 A313 100s multi 3.75 3.75

First postage stamp issued in Latvia, 150th anniv.

Cats — A314

Designs: 35s, Kittins in basket. 98s, Cats in doorway,vert.

Perf. 14x13¾, 13¾x14
2013, July 29 **Litho.**

837-838 A314 Set of 2 5.00 5.00

Port of Liepaja — A315

2013, Aug. 23 **Litho.** ***Perf. 13½***

839 A315 98s multi 3.75 3.75

Latvia University of Agriculture, 150th Anniv. — A316

2013, Sept. 16 **Litho.** ***Perf. 13¼***

840 A316 40s multi 1.60 1.60

Mark Rothko (1903-70), Painter — A317

2013, Sept. 25 **Litho.** ***Perf. 13¾x14***

841 A317 60s multi 2.40 2.40

Latvian Popular Front, 25th Anniv. — A318

2013, Oct. 5 **Litho.** ***Perf. 13¾x14***

842 A318 35s multi 1.40 1.40

Printing in Latvia, 425th Anniv. — A319

2013, Oct. 22 **Litho.** ***Perf. 13¼***
Granite Paper

843 A319 60s multi 2.40 2.40

No. 843 was printed in sheets of 8 + 4 labels.

Pink Ribbon and Flower — A320

2013, Oct. 30 **Litho.** ***Perf. 14***

844 A320 4s multi .40 .40

Breast cancer awareness.

Republic of Latvia, 95th Anniv. — A321

Writers: 35s, Rainis (1865-1929). 60s, Rudolfs Blaumanis (1863-1908). 98s, Zenta Maurina (1897-1978).

2013, Nov. 8 **Litho.** ***Perf. 13¾***

845-847 A321 Set of 3 7.50 7.50

Christmas — A322

Falling snow and: 35s, Girl on rocking horse, Christmas gifts. 60s, Girl and cats on building's roof.

2013, Nov. 22 **Litho.** ***Perf. 14x13¾***
Granite Paper

848-849 A322 Set of 2 3.75 3.75

100 Cents = 1 Euro

Flowers — A323

Designs: 3c, Narcissi. 47c, Crocuses. 57c, Pansies. 78c, Cornflowers. 85c, Poppies. €1.39, Asters.

2014, Jan. 2 **Litho.** ***Perf. 14***

850 A323 3c multi .30 .25
a. Dated "2016" .30 .25
b. Dated "2022" .30 .30
851 A323 47c multi 1.40 .30
852 A323 57c multi 1.75 .90
853 A323 78c multi 2.25 1.25
854 A323 85c multi 2.75 1.40
855 A323 €1.39 multi 4.00 2.10
a. Souvenir sheet of 6, #850-855 13.00 13.00
Nos. 850-855 (6) 12.45 6.20

See Nos. 867-870, 895-899.

Issued: No. 850a, 1/29/16; No. 850b, 6/2/22.

Imants Ziedonis (1933-2013), Poet — A324

2014, Jan. 6 **Litho.** ***Perf. 13¼x13¾***

856 A324 50c multi 1.40 1.10

Bildmuseet, Umea, Sweden — A325

National Library, Riga, Latvia — A326

2014, Jan. 16 **Litho.** ***Perf. 13¼***
Granite Paper

857 A325 50c multi 1.30 1.30
858 A326 78c multi 2.00 2.00

Selection of Umea and Riga as European Capitals of Culture. See Sweden Nos. 2720-2721.

2014 Winter Olympics, Sochi, Russia — A327

2014, Feb. 7 **Litho.** ***Perf. 13¼x13½***
Granite Paper

859 A327 85c multi 2.00 1.75

Personalized Stamp With Horizontal Orientation A328

Personalized Stamp With Vertical Orientation — A329

Perf. 13¼x13½, 13½x13¼
2014, Feb. 28 **Litho.**

860 A328 50c multi 1.40 .70
861 A329 50c multi 1.40 .70
862 A328 78c multi 2.25 1.10
863 A329 78c multi 2.25 1.10
864 A328 85c multi 2.40 1.25
865 A329 85c multi 2.40 1.25
Nos. 860-865 (6) 12.10 6.10

Stamps with generic images of museums and their displays were made available on Nos. 860, 863 and 865. Stamps with generic images of airplanes were made available on Nos. 861, 862 and 864.

Tulips — A330

2014, Mar. 7 **Litho.** ***Perf. 13¼***

866 A330 50c multi 1.60 1.10

Flowers Type of 2014

Designs: 1c, Daisies. 4c, Hepatica. 7c, Marigolds. 50c, Lily of the valley.

2014, Mar. 22 **Litho.** ***Perf. 14***

867 A323 1c multi .30 .30
a. Dated "2015" .30 .30
b. Dated "2016" .30 .30
c. Dated "2017" .30 .30
d. Dated "2019" .25 .25
f. Dated "2022" .30 .30
868 A323 4c multi .30 .30
a. Dated "2015" .30 .30
b. Dated "2016" .30 .30
c. Dated "2017" .30 .30
d. Dated "2019" .25 .25
e. Dated "2021" .25 .25
f. Dated "2022" .30 .30
869 A323 7c multi .30 .30
a. Dated "2015" .30 .30
c. Dated "2017" .30 .30
d. Dated "2019" .25 .25
e. Dated "2021" .25 .25
f. Dated "2022" .30 .30

Granite Paper

870 A323 50c multi 1.40 1.40
b. Dated "2016," plain paper 1.10 1.10
Nos. 867-870 (4) 2.30 2.30

Issued: Nos. 867a, 868a, 869a, 5/5/15; Nos. 867b, 870a, 1/29/16; No. 868b, 7/12/16; Nos. 867c, 868c, 869b, 1/13/17; Nos. 867d, 868d, 869d, 1/15/19; Nos. 868e, 869e, 1/15/21; Nos. 867f, 868f, 1/10/22; No. 869f, 6/2/22.

Diplomatic Relations With Georgia, 20th Anniv. — A331

Perf. 13¼x13½
2014, Mar. 28 **Litho.**
Granite Paper

871 A331 85c multi 2.00 1.25

See Georgia No. 491.

Europa — A332

Musical instruments: 78c, Kokle (zither). €1.71, Dudas (bagpipe).

2014, Apr. 11 **Litho.** ***Perf. 14x13¾***
Granite Paper

872-873 A332 Set of 2 7.00 3.50
872a Booklet pane of 4 #872, perf. 14x13¾ on 3 sides 10.00 —
Complete booklet, #872a 10.00

Emblem of *Te!* Television Show — A333

2014, Apr. 17 **Litho.** ***Perf. 13¼x13¾***
Granite Paper

874 A333 50c deep lilac 1.50 1.10

Birds — A334

Designs: 50c, Lymnocryptes minimus. €1.39, Upupa epops, vert.

Perf. 13¾x14, 14x13¾

2014, May 16 **Litho.**
875-876 A334 Set of 2 5.25 2.60

Latvian Medalists at 2014 Winter Olympics — A335

Designs: No. 877, 50c, Martin Dukurs, silver medalist in skeleton. No. 878, 50c, Daumants Dreiskens, Oskars Melbardis, Janis Strenga, Arvis Vilkaste, silver medalists in four-man bobsled. No. 879, 50c, Juris Sics, Andris Sics, bronze medalists in men's doubles luge. No. 880, 50c, Juris Sics, Andris Sics, Martins Rubenis, Eliza Tiruma, bronze medalists in Mixed team relay luge.

2014, May 27 **Litho.** ***Perf. 13¼***
Granite Paper
877-880 A335 Set of 4 5.50 2.75

Nos. 877-880 each were printed in sheets of 4.

Janis Cimze (1814-81), Collector and Publisher of Folk Songs — A336

2014, July 3 **Litho.** ***Perf. 13¼x13½***
Granite Paper
881 A336 57c multi 1.60 .80

Turaida Castle, 800th Anniv. — A337

2014, July 11 **Litho.** ***Perf. 13¼x13½***
882 A337 50c multi 1.40 .70

Baltic Chain Demonstration, 25th Anniv. — A338

Designs: 50c, Three women.
No. 884: a, Five adults and one child. b, Like #883. c, Man and child.

2014, Aug. 23 **Litho.** ***Perf. 13¼***
883 A338 50c multi 1.40 .70

Souvenir Sheet

884 A338 78c Sheet of 3, #a-c 6.25 3.25

See Estonia Nos. 764-765; Lithuania No. 1031.

Gothards Fridrihs Stenders (1714-96), Lexicographer — A339

2014, Aug. 24 **Litho.** ***Perf. 13¼***
885 A339 €1.39 multi 3.75 1.90

No. 885 was printed in sheets of 8 + 4 labels.

Ainazu Lighthouse — A340

2014, Sept. 12 **Litho.** ***Perf. 13¼***
886 A340 71c multi 1.90 .95

Latvian Academy of Arts — A341

2014, Oct. 17 **Litho.** ***Perf. 13¼***
887 A341 €1.42 multi 3.50 1.75

Republic of Latvia, 96th Anniv. — A342

Designs: 57c, Painter. 64c, Graphic artist. 78c, Sculptor.

2014, Nov. 7 **Litho.** ***Perf. 14***
888-890 A342 Set of 3 5.00 2.50

Christmas — A343

Designs: 50c, Forest in winter. 85c, City in winter, horiz.

2014, Nov. 27 **Litho.** ***Perf. 13½***
891-892 A343 Set of 2 3.50 1.75

Singing Trees — A344

2014, Dec. 4 **Litho.** ***Perf. 14x13¾***
893 A344 50c multi 1.25 .60

Latvian Presidency of Council of the European Union — A345

2015, Jan. 6 **Litho.** ***Perf. 13¾x14***
894 A345 64c multi 1.50 .75

Flowers Type of 2014

Designs: 10c, Crocuses. 25c, Asters. 70c, Lilies. 78c, Gerbera daisies. €2.13, Pansies.

2015, Jan. 9 **Litho.** ***Perf. 14***
Dated "2015"

895	A323	10c multi	.30	.25
a.		Dated "2017"	.30	.25
c.		Dated "2022"	.30	.30
896	A323	25c multi	.65	.30
a.		Dated "2018"	.60	.30
b.		Dated "2021"	.60	.30
c.		Dated "2022"	.60	.30
897	A323	70c multi	1.75	.80
898	A323	78c multi	2.00	.90
899	A323	€2.13 multi	5.00	2.50
a.		Dated "2018"	5.00	2.50
		Nos. 895-899 (5)	9.70	4.75

Issued: No. 895a, 1/13/17. Nos. 896a, 899a, 6/8/18; No. 896b, 1/15/21; Nos. 895c, 896c, 1/10/22.

Green Week — A346

2015, Jan. 15 **Litho.** ***Perf. 13¼x13¾***
900 A346 50c multi 1.25 .60

Arms of Riga — A347

National Arms — A348

2015, Jan. 30 **Litho.** ***Perf. 14x13¾***

901	A347	€1 sil & multi	2.25	1.10
a.		Dated "2019"	2.25	1.10
902	A348	€2 sil & multi	4.50	2.25
a.		Dated "2019"	4.50	2.25
903	A348	€5 gold & multi	11.50	5.75
		Nos. 901-903 (3)	18.25	9.10

Issued: Nos. 901a, 902a, 3/22/19.

Jelgava, 750th Anniv. — A349

2015, Feb. 5 **Litho.** ***Perf. 13½***
904 A349 €1.71 multi 3.75 1.90

Asterolepis Ornata and Fossils — A350

2015, Feb. 20 **Litho.** ***Perf. 13¼***
905 A350 71c multi 1.60 .80

Helianthus — A351

2015, Mar. 6 **Litho.** ***Perf. 13¼***
906 A351 50c multi 1.10 .55

Europa — A352

Designs: 78c, Dolls. €1.71, Teddy bears.

2015, Apr. 10 **Litho.** ***Perf. 14x13¾***

907	A352	78c multi	1.75	.90
a.		Tete-beche pair	3.50	3.50
b.		Booklet pane of 4, perf. 14x13¾ on 3 sides	7.00	—
		Complete booklet, #907b	7.00	
908	A352	€1.71 multi	4.00	2.00

Kurzemes Literary Society, 200th Anniv. — A353

2015, Apr. 21 **Litho.** ***Perf. 13¼***
909 A353 85c multi 1.90 .95

No. 909 was printed in sheets of 10 + 2 central labels.

Independence, 25th Anniv. — A354

2015, Apr. 29 **Litho.** ***Perf. 13¼x13½***
910 A354 50c multi 1.25 .60

World Press Freedom Day — A355

2015, May 3 **Litho.** ***Perf. 13¼x13¾***
911 A355 57c multi 1.40 .70

Latvian Fire Services, 150th Anniv. — A356

2015, May 15 **Litho.** ***Perf. 13¼***
912 A356 €1.42 multi 3.25 1.60

Birds — A357

Designs: 71c, Oriolus oriolus. €1.42, Pluvialis apricaria, vert.

Perf. 14x13¾, 13¾x14

2015, June 26 **Litho.**
913-914 A357 Set of 2 5.25 2.75

Rundales Palace — A358

2015, July 24 **Litho.** ***Perf. 13¼***
915 A358 €1.57 multi 3.50 1.75

Miniature Sheet

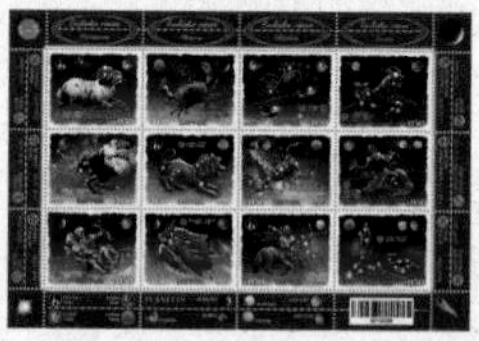

Signs of the Zodiac A359

No. 916: a, Aries. b, Cancer. c, Libra. d, Capricorn. e, Taurus. f, Leo. g, Scorpio. h, Aquarius. i, Gemini. j, Virgo. k, Sagittarius. l, Pisces.

2015, Aug. 7 **Litho.** ***Perf. 13¼***
916 A359 50c Sheet of 12, #a-l 13.50 6.75

Salacgrivas Lighthouse — A360

Perf. 13¼x13½

2015, Aug. 21 **Litho.**
917 A360 78c multi 1.75 .85

Poets A361

No. 918: a, Rainis (1865-1929). b, Aspazija (1865-1943).

Perf. 13¼x13½

2015, Sept. 11 **Litho.**
918 A361 50c Sheet of 2, #a-b 2.25 1.10

Latvian Riflemen, Cent. — A362

2015, Oct. 25 Litho. ***Perf. 13¼x13½***
919 A362 €1.71 multi 3.75 1.90

Republic of Latvia, 97th Anniv. — A363

Architects: 50c, Janis Fridrihs Baumanis (1834-91). 64c, Eizens Laube (1880-1967), Janis Alksnis (1869-1939), Konstantins Peksens (1859-1928). €1.39, Marta Stana (1913-72).

2015, Nov. 13 Litho. ***Perf. 14***
920-922 A363 Set of 3 5.50 2.75

Nos. 920-922 were each printed in sheets of 8 + central label.

Christmas — A364

Designs: 50c, Gift box, pine cones and Christmas ornaments. 85c, Christmas ornaments and pine cones.

Serpentine Die Cut 14¼x15 Syncopated

2015, Dec. 3 Litho.

Self-Adhesive

923-924 A364 Set of 2 3.00 1.50

Attack of Soviet Forces Against Latvian Barricades, 25th Anniv. — A365

2016, Jan. 13 Litho. ***Perf. 13¼***
925 A365 54c multi 1.25 .60

Coats of Arms of Municipalities — A366

Designs: 50c, Alsunga. 57c, Beverina. €1.39, Smiltene.

Serpentine Die Cut 20x18 Syncopated

2016, Jan. 29 Litho.

Self-Adhesive

926 A366 50c red & multi 1.10 .55
927 A366 57c blue & multi 1.25 .60
928 A366 €1.39 tan & multi 3.00 1.50
Nos. 926-928 (3) 5.35 2.65

See Nos. 956-958, 984-986, 1011-1013, 1040-1044, 1063-1065.

Stuffed Male and Female Tetrao Tetrix from Latvian Natural History Museum — A367

2016, Feb. 19 Litho. ***Perf. 13¼***
929 A367 €1.71 multi 3.75 1.90

Nymphaea — A368

2016, Mar. 4 Litho. ***Perf. 13¼***
930 A368 50c multi 1.25 .60

Souvenir Sheet

Janis Rozentals (1866-1916), Painter — A369

No. 931: a, Kardinasana (Temptation), painting by Rozentals. b, Rozentals.

2016, Mar. 18 Litho. ***Perf. 13¼***
931 A369 50c Sheet of 2, #a-b 2.25 1.10

2016 Floorball World Championships, Riga — A370

2016, Apr. 9 Litho. ***Perf. 13¼x13½***
932 A370 64c multi 1.50 .75

A371 Europa — A372

2016, May 9 Litho. ***Perf. 13¼***
933 A371 78c multi 1.75 .85
934 A372 78c multi 1.75 .85
a. Tete-beche pair 3.50 3.50
b. Booklet pane of 4, perf. 13¼ on 3 sides 7.00 —
Complete booklet, #934b 7.00

Think Green Issue.

Birds — A373

Designs: 71c, Glaucidium passerinum. €1.71, Dendrocopos major.

2016, May 20 Litho. ***Perf. 13¾x14***
935-936 A373 Set of 2 5.50 2.75

Souvenir Sheet

1941 Deportation of Latvians to Siberia, 75th Anniv. — A374

No. 937 — Photographs of deportees and inscription: a, "14.06.1941." b, "Litene."

2016, June 14 Litho. ***Perf. 13¼***
937 A374 50c Sheet of 2, #a-b 2.25 1.10

Cesis Concert Hall — A375

2016, July 15 Litho. ***Perf. 13¼x13½***
938 A375 €1.57 multi 3.50 1.75

Gustavs Erenpreiss (1891-1956), Bicycle Manufacturer — A376

2016, July 23 Litho. ***Perf. 13¼***
939 A376 50c multi 1.10 .55

Restoration of Latvian Independence, 25th Anniv. — A377

2016, Aug. 21 Litho. ***Perf. 13¼***
940 A377 50c multi 1.10 .55

Bikernieki Race Track, 50th Anniv. — A378

2016, Sept. 9 Litho. ***Perf. 13¼x13¾***
941 A378 57c multi 1.25 .65

Krustpils Railroad Station — A379

2016, Sept. 12 Litho. ***Perf. 13¾***
942 A379 €1.49 multi 3.50 1.75

Latvian Admission to the United Nations, 25th Anniv. — A380

2016, Sept. 18 Litho. ***Perf. 14x13¾***
943 A380 54c multi 1.25 .60

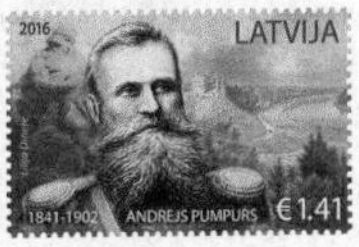

Andrejs Pumpurs (1841-1902), Poet and Army Officer — A381

Perf. 13¼x13½

2016, Sept. 22 Litho.
944 A381 €1.41 multi 3.25 1.60

Ovisi Lighthouse — A382

2016, Oct. 7 Litho. ***Perf. 13¼***
945 A382 90c multi 2.00 2.00
a. Booklet pane of 4, perf. 13¼ on 3 sides 8.00 —
Complete booklet, #945a 8.00

Archbishop Janis Pommers (1876-1934) — A383

2016, Oct. 12 Litho. ***Perf. 13¼***
946 A383 50c multi 1.10 1.10

Barquentine Andreas Weide — A384

2016, Oct. 28 Litho. ***Perf. 13¼***
947 A384 61c multi 1.40 1.40

Baltic Assembly, 25th Anniv. — A385

2016, Nov. 8 Litho. ***Perf. 13½x13¼***

Stamp With White Frame

948 A385 50c multi 1.10 1.10

Souvenir Sheet

Stamp With Multicolored Frame

949 A385 €1.39 multi 3.00 3.00

See Estonia Nos. 827-828, Lithuania Nos. 1088-1089.

Souvenir Sheet

Medalists at 2016 Paralympics, Rio de Janeiro — A386

No. 950: a, Diana Dadzite, javelin gold medalist. b, Aigars Apinis, discus gold medalist. c, Edgars Bergs, shot put bronze medalist.

2016, Nov. 15 Litho. ***Perf. 13¼***
950 A386 50c Sheet of 3, #a-c, + label 3.25 3.25

Republic of Latvia, 98th Anniv. — A387

Designs: 50c, Janis Lusis, Dainis Kula and Inese Jaunzeme, Olympic gold medalists in javelin. 57c, Uljana Semjonova and Janis Krumins, Olympic medalists in basketball. €1.42, Sandis Ozolinsh, Sergejs Zoltoks, Arturs Irbe, Helmuts Balderis, Karlis Skrastins, past Latvian National Team and National Hockey League players.

2016, Nov. 17 Litho. ***Perf. 14***
951-953 A387 Set of 3 5.50 5.50

A388

Christmas — A389

Serpentine Die Cut 14¼x15 Syncopated

2016, Nov. 25 **Litho.**

Self-Adhesive

954 A388 50c multi 1.10 1.10
955 A389 78c multi 1.75 1.75

Coats of Arms of Municipalities Type of 2016

Designs: 50c, Olaine. 57c, Rojas. €1.39, Malpils.

Serpentine Die Cut 20x18 Syncopated

2017, Jan. 13 **Litho.**

Self-Adhesive

956 A366 50c green & multi 1.10 .55
957 A366 57c blue & multi 1.25 .60
958 A366 €1.39 red & multi 3.00 1.50
Nos. 956-958 (3) 5.35 2.65

Rosa Canina — A390

2017, Feb. 17 **Litho.** ***Perf. 13¼***
959 A390 €1.42 multi 3.00 1.50

Freesia — A391

2017, Mar. 3 **Litho.** ***Perf. 13¼***
960 A391 64c multi 1.40 .70

Europa — A392

Designs: 78c, Cesvaine Palace. €1.71, Bauska Castle.

2017, Apr. 21 **Litho.** ***Perf. 14x13¾***
961 A392 78c multi 1.75 .85
a. Tete-beche pair 3.50 1.75
b. Booklet pane of 4, perf. 14x13¾ on 3 sides 7.00 —
Complete booklet, #961b 7.00
962 A392 €1.71 multi 3.75 1.90

Schooner Abraham — A393

2017, May 9 **Litho.** ***Perf. 13¼***
963 A393 61c multi 1.40 .70

Family Day — A394

2017, May 15 **Litho.** ***Perf. 13¼***
964 A394 50c multi 1.10 .55

Souvenir Sheet

Janis Tidemanis (1897-1964), Painter — A395

No. 965: a, Masks, by Tidemanis. b, Tidemanis.

2017, May 26 **Litho.** ***Perf. 13¼***
965 A395 50c Sheet of 2, #a-b 2.25 1.10

1903 Krastin Automobile A396

2017, June 2 **Litho.** ***Perf. 13¼x13½***
966 A396 €1.39 multi 3.25 1.60

Meles Meles — A397

2017, June 16 **Litho.** ***Perf. 14x13¾***
967 A397 85c multi 2.00 1.00

Birds — A398

Designs: 50c, Motacilla flava. €1.41, Porzana parva.

2017, July 14 **Litho.** ***Perf. 14x13¾***
968-969 A398 Set of 2 5.00 2.50

Ceramic Sculpture by Dainis Pundurs — A399

2017, Aug. 18 **Litho.** ***Perf. 13¼***
970 A399 €1.49 multi 3.75 1.90

Rojas Lighthouse — A400

2017, Sept. 8 **Litho.** ***Perf. 13¼***
971 A400 90c multi 2.10 1.10
a. Booklet pane of 4, perf. 13¼ on 3 sides 8.50 —
Complete booklet, #971a 8.50

University of Latvia Natural Sciences Academic Center — A401

2017, Sept. 28 **Litho.** ***Perf. 13¼***
972 A401 €1.39 multi 3.25 1.60

Eduards Veidenbaums (1867-92), Poet — A402

2017, Oct. 3 **Litho.** ***Perf. 13¼***
973 A402 57c multi 1.40 .70

Venta-1, First Latvian Satellite A403

2017, Oct. 6 **Litho.** ***Perf. 13¼x13½***
974 A403 85c multi 2.00 1.00

Anti-Corruption Campaign — A404

2017, Oct. 10 **Litho.** ***Perf. 13¼***
975 A404 50c multi 1.25 .60

Andreas Knopken (c. 1468-1539) and Martin Luther (1483-1546), Religious Reformers — A405

2017, Oct. 27 **Litho.** ***Perf. 13¼***
976 A405 85c multi 2.00 1.00

Protestant Reformation, 500th anniv.

Republic of Latvia, 99th Anniv. — A406

Designs: 50s, Friedrich Zander (1887-1933), rocket designer, Karlis Steins (1911-83), astronomer, Janis Ikaunieks (1912-69), astronomer, and Arturs Balklavs (1933-2005), astronomer. 57s, Surgeons Romans Lacis, Pauls Stradins (1896-1958) and Viktors Kalnberzs. €1.42, Chemists Pauls Valdens (1863-1957), Janis Stradins and Wilhelm Ostwald (1853-1932).

2017, Nov. 3 **Litho.** ***Perf. 14***
977-979 A406 Set of 3 6.00 6.00

Souvenir Sheet

Alona Ostapenko, 2017 French Open Tennis Champion — A407

2017, Nov. 10 **Litho.** ***Perf. 13¼***
980 A407 €1.42 multi 3.50 3.50

A408

A409

Christmas — A410

Serpentine Die Cut 14¼x14½ Syncopated

2017, Nov. 24 **Litho.**

Self-Adhesive

981 A408 50c multi 1.25 1.25
982 A409 78c multi 1.90 1.90
983 A410 85c multi 2.10 2.10
Nos. 981-983 (3) 5.25 5.25

Coats of Arms of Municipalities Type of 2016

Designs: 50c, Kegums. 57c, Rundale. €1.39, Seja.

Serpentine Die Cut 20x18 Syncopated

2018, Jan. 19 **Litho.**

Self-Adhesive

984 A366 50c citron & multi 1.25 .60
985 A366 57c car lake & multi 1.40 .70
986 A366 €1.39 dk grn & multi 3.50 1.75
Nos. 984-986 (3) 6.15 3.05

2018 Winter Olympics, PyeongChang, South Korea — A411

2018, Feb. 2 **Litho.** ***Perf. 14x13¾***
987 A411 61c multi 1.50 .75

Gypsum Rock in Latvia Museum of Natural History — A412

2018, Feb. 16 **Litho.** ***Perf. 13¼***
988 A412 €1.42 multi 3.50 1.75

Souvenir Sheet

Ansis Cirulis (1883-1942), Painter — A413

No. 989: a, *Shipping,* stained-glass panels by Cirulis. b, Cirulis and stained-glass window.

2018, Feb. 23 **Litho.** ***Perf. 13¼***
989 A413 50c Sheet of 2, #a-b 2.50 1.25

Flag and Map of Latvia — A414

Serpentine Die Cut 14 on 3 Sides

2018, Mar. 9 **Litho.**

Self-Adhesive

990 A414 50c multi 1.25 .60

Independence, cent.

Europa — A415

Designs: 78c, Jugla Railway Bridge. €1.49, Gauja River Bridge.

2018, Apr. 20 **Litho.** ***Perf. 14x13¾***
991 A415 78c multi 1.90 .95
a. Booklet pane of 4, perf. 13¾ on 3 sides 7.75 —
Complete booklet, #991a 7.75
992 A415 €1.49 multi 3.75 1.90

No. 991a contains two vertical tete-beche pairs.

Amphitheater, Garden of Destiny — A416

2018, May 18 **Litho.** ***Perf. 13¼***
993 A416 61c multi 1.50 .75

Birds — A417

Designs: 50c, Tringa totanus. €1.41, Aegithalos caudatus.

2018, June 8 Litho. *Perf. 14x13¼*
994-995 A417 Set of 2 4.50 2.25

Republic of Latvia, Cent. — A418

Designs: 54c, Haralds Mednis (1906-2000), conductor. 57c, Dancers. €1.42, People and Ligo Festival banner.

2018, June 29 Litho. *Perf. 14*
996-998 A418 Set of 3 6.00 3.00

1939 Ford-Vairogs V8 Automobile A419

2018, July 13 Litho. *Perf. 13¼x13½*
999 A419 €1.39 multi 3.25 1.60

Najas Tenuissima — A420

2018, Aug. 10 Litho. *Perf. 13¼*
1000 A420 85c multi 2.00 1.00

Curonian Kings — A421

2018, Sept. 7 Litho. *Perf. 13¼x13½*
1001 A421 €5 multi 11.50 5.75

Visit of Pope Francis to Latvia — A422

2018, Sept. 24 Litho. *Perf. 13¼*
1002 A422 61c multi 1.40 .70

Souvenir Sheet

Diplomatic Relations Between Latvia and Kyrgyzstan, 25th Anniv. — A423

No. 1003: a, Lacplesis on Freedom Monument, Riga. b, Monument to Manas the Great, Bishkek, Kyrgyzstan.

2018, Oct. 5 Litho. *Perf. 13½*
1003 A423 €1.10 Sheet of 2, #a-b, + central label 5.00 2.50

See Kyrgyz Express Post No. 92.

Riga Latvian Society, 150th Anniv. — A424

2018, Oct. 12 Litho. *Perf. 13¼x13½*
1004 A424 54c multi 1.25 .60

Ragaciema Lighthouse — A425

2018, Oct. 19 Litho. *Perf. 13¼*
1005 A425 64c multi 1.50 .75

Souvenir Sheet

Oskars Melbardis and Janis Strenga, Bronze Medalists in Bobsledding at 2018 Winter Olympics — A426

2018, Nov. 1 Litho. *Perf. 13¼*
1006 A426 €3.06 multi 7.00 3.50

Arms Type of 1918 Redrawn With Euro Denominations

2018, Nov. 16 Litho. *Perf. 14*
1007 A1 54c carmine 1.25 .60

First Latvian postage stamps, cent.

Christmas — A427

Designs: 50c, Man, woman, dog and cat, holiday feast. 78c, Person in bear costume dancing. 85c, Family welcoming Santa Claus.

Serpentine Die Cut 14½x15 Syncopated

2018, Nov. 23 Litho.

Self-Adhesive

1008-1010 A427 Set of 3 5.00 2.50

Coats of Arms of Municipalities Type of 2016

Designs: 50c, Tukums. 54c, Aizpute. 57c, Rucava.

Serpentine Die Cut 20x18 Syncopated

2019, Jan. 18 Litho.

Self-Adhesive

1011 A366 50c green & multi 1.25 .60
1012 A366 54c red & multi 1.25 .60
1013 A366 57c blue & multi 1.40 .70
Nos. 1011-1013 (3) 3.90 1.90

Souvenir Sheet

Johans Valters (1869-1932), Painter — A428

No. 1014: a, Farm Girl, by Valters. b, Valters.

2019, Feb. 8 Litho. *Perf. 13¼*
1014 A428 50c Sheet of 2, #a-b 2.25 1.10

Gnorimus Nobilis — A429

2019, Feb. 15 Litho. *Perf. 13¼*
1015 A429 €1.57 multi 3.75 1.90

Sliteres Lighthouse — A430

2019, Mar. 15 Litho. *Perf. 13¼*
1016 A430 90c multi 2.00 1.00

Matisa Street Water Tower, Riga — A431

2019, Mar. 29 Litho. *Perf. 13¼*
1017 A431 61c multi 1.40 .70

Europa — A432

Motacilla alba: 78c, Entire bird. €1.71, Head of bird.

2019, Apr. 26 Litho. *Perf. 14x13¾*
1018 A432 78c multi 1.75 .90
a. Booklet pane of 4, perf. 14x13¾ on 3 sides 7.00 —
Complete booklet, #1018a 7.00
1019 A432 €1.71 multi 4.00 2.00

Mother's Day — A433

2019, May 10 Litho. *Perf. 13¼*
1020 A433 50c multi 1.10 .55

1938 Ford-Vairogs V8 Fire Truck — A434

2019, May 24 Litho. *Perf. 13¼x13½*
1021 A434 €1.39 multi 3.25 1.60

Ligo Day Floral Crown — A435

Serpentine Die Cut 14¾x14¼ Syncopated

2019, June 13 Litho.

Self-Adhesive

1022 A435 50c multi 1.10 .55

Rihards Zarins (1869-1939), Graphic Artist and Stamp Designer — A436

2019, June 27 Litho. *Perf. 13¼*
1023 A436 57c multi 1.40 .70

No. 1023 was printed in sheets of 8 + 4 central labels.

Latvian Army, Cent. — A437

Designs: No. 1024, 50c, Helicopters and crew members. No. 1025, 50c, Tank. No. 1026, 50c, Ships.

2019, July 10 Litho. *Perf. 13¼x13½*
1024-1026 A437 Set of 3 3.50 1.75

Passerby, Painting by Blind Child Attending Strazsumuiza Boarding School — A438

2019, July 26 Litho. *Perf. 13¼*
1027 A438 90c multi 2.00 1.00

Clanga Pomarina — A439

2019, Aug. 16 Litho. *Perf. 14x13¾*
1028 A439 78c multi 1.75 .85

Latvian Academy of Art, Cent. — A440

2019, Aug. 20 Litho. *Perf. 13½*
1029 A440 85c multi 1.90 .95

Father's Day — A441

2019, Sept. 8 Litho. *Perf. 13¼*
1030 A441 50c multi 1.10 .55

University of Latvia, Cent. — A442

Designs: 57c, Old building. 85c, Modern building.

2019, Sept. 27 Litho. *Perf. 14*
1031-1032 A442 Set of 2 3.25 1.60

Nos. 1031-1032 were each printed in sheets of 8 + 4 labels.

Ivan Zavoloko (1897-1984), Educator and Clergyman — A443

2019, Oct. 3 Litho. *Perf. 14*
1033 A443 90c multi 2.00 1.00

Garlieb Merkelis (1769-1850), Writer — A444

2019, Nov. 1 Litho. ***Perf. 13¼x13½***

1034 A444 €1.42 multi 3.25 1.60

Defeat of the Bermontian Army (West Russian Volunteer Army), Cent. — A445

2019, Nov. 7 Litho. ***Perf. 13¼x13½***

1035 A445 50c multi 1.10 .55

Christmas — A446

Designs: 50c, Mouse on ice skates. 78c, Two snowmen. 85c, Girl wearing stocking cap.

Serpentine Die Cut 14¾x14¼ Syncopated

2019, Nov. 22 Litho.

Self-Adhesive

1036-1038 A446 Set of 3 4.75 2.40

National Armed Forces Staff Battalion, Cent. — A447

Perf. 13¼x13½

2019, Dec. 10 Litho.

1039 A447 50c multi 1.10 .55

Coats of Arms of Municipalities Type of 2016

Designs: €1, Durbe. €1.29, Krimulda. €1.35, Koknese. €1.42, Babite. €1.54, Vilani.

Serpentine Die Cut 20x18 Syncopated

2020, Jan. 3 Litho.

Self-Adhesive

1040 A366	€1	sil & dp blue	2.25	1.10
1041 A366	€1.29	gold & red	3.00	1.50
1042 A366	€1.35	sil, gold & brn pur	3.00	1.50
1043 A366	€1.42	sil & multi	3.25	1.60
1044 A366	€1.54	sil, gold & emer	3.50	1.75
Nos. 1040-1044 (5)			15.00	7.45

Riga State Technical School, Cent. — A448

2020, Jan. 10 Litho. ***Perf. 13½***

1045 A448 €1 multi 2.25 1.10

Four-masted Ship Eurasia — A449

2020, Jan. 31 Litho. ***Perf. 13¼***

1046 A449 €1.27 multi 1.75 .85

Baltic Amber — A450

2020, Feb. 14 Litho. ***Perf. 13¼***

1047 A450 €2.69 multi 6.00 3.00

Europa — A451

Designs: €1.35, Mail deliverer on bicycle. €1.42, Post rider and coach.

2020, May 8 Litho. ***Perf. 13¼***

1048-1049 A451 Set of 2 6.25 3.25

Ancient Postal Routes.

Alises Street Water Tower, Riga — A452

2020, May 15 Litho. ***Perf. 13¼***

1050 A452 €1.71 multi 3.75 1.90

International Year of Plant Health — A453

2020, May 29 Litho. ***Perf. 13¾***

1051 A453 €2.25 multi 5.00 2.50

Birds — A454

Designs: €1.27, Tetrastes bonasia. €2.14, Alcedo atthis.

2020, June 19 Litho. ***Perf. 13¾***

1052-1053 A454 Set of 2 7.75 4.00

Banuta, Opera by Alfreds Kalnins (1879-1951), Cent. — A455

2020, July 3 Litho. ***Perf. 13¼x13½***

1054 A455 €1 multi 2.40 1.25

Souvenir Sheet

Gustavs Klucis (1895-1938), Photographer and Poster Designer — A456

No. 1055: a, *Construction,* 1921 poster design. b, Klucis.

2020, July 10 Litho. ***Perf. 13¼***

1055 A456 €1 Sheet of 2, #a-b 4.75 2.40

Gospel of Jersika, 750th Anniv. — A457

2020, Aug. 21 Litho. ***Perf. 13¼***

1056 A457 €1 multi 2.40 1.25

No. 1056 was printed in sheets of 8 + 4 labels.

Emilija Gudriniece (1920-2004), Organic Chemist A458

Perf. 13¼x13½

2020, Sept. 18 Litho.

1057 A458 €1 multi 2.40 1.25

Janis Dalins (1904-78), Race Walker — A459

2020, Oct. 23 Litho. ***Perf. 13¼***

1058 A459 €1 multi 2.40 1.25

Eduard Smilgis (1886-1966), Founder of Dailes Theater and Director — A460

2020, Nov. 19 Litho. ***Perf. 13¼***

1059 A460 €1 multi 2.40 1.25

Dailes Theater, Riga, cent.

Christmas — A461

Designs: €1, Santa Claus holding lantern. €1.42, Santa Claus and reindeer with gift. €1.54, Santa Claus carrying Christmas tree, boy on sled.

Serpentine Die Cut 14¾x14¼ Syncopated

2020, Nov. 27 Litho.

Self-Adhesive

1060-1062 A461 Set of 3 9.50 4.75

Coats of Arms of Municipalities Type of 2016

Designs: 62c, Grobina. 89c, Engure. €1, Ropazi.

Serpentine Die Cut 20x18 Syncopated

2021, Jan. 8 Litho.

Self-Adhesive

1063 A366	62c	red & multi	1.50	.75
1064 A366	89c	brt blue & multi	2.25	1.10
1065 A366	€1	blue grn & multi	2.40	1.25
Nos. 1063-1065 (3)			6.15	3.10

Ministry of Foreign Affairs Building, Riga — A462

2021, Jan. 26 Litho. ***Perf. 13¼***

1066 A462 €1 multi 2.40 1.25

International Recognition of Latvian Sovereignty, cent.

Barquentine Mercator — A463

2021, Feb. 19 Litho. ***Perf. 13¼***

1067 A463 €1.27 multi 3.00 1.50

Ernests Birznieks-Upitis (1871-1960), Writer — A464

2021, Mar. 26 Litho. ***Perf. 13¼***

1068 A464 €1.27 multi 3.00 1.50

Endangered Animals — A465

Designs: €1, Margaritifera margaritifera. €1.27, Ciconia nigra.

2021, Apr. 23 Litho. ***Perf. 14***

1069-1070 A465 Set of 2 5.50 2.75

Europa.

Ciekurkains Water Tower, Riga — A466

2021, May 14 Litho. ***Perf. 13¼***

1071 A466 €1 multi 2.50 1.25

2021 Ice Hockey World Championships, Latvia — A467

2021, May 21 Litho. ***Perf. 13¼x13½***

1072 A467 €1.71 multi 4.25 2.10

Latvian Soccer Federation, Cent. — A468

2021, May 27 Litho. ***Perf. 13¼***

1073 A468 €1 multi 2.50 1.25

Souvenir Sheet

National Symbols A469

No. 1074 — Latvian: a, Flag. b, Coat of arms.

2021, June 15 Litho. ***Perf. 13¼***

1074 A469 €1 Sheet of 2, #a-b 4.75 2.40

Gladiolus Imbricatus — A470

2021, July 2 Litho. ***Perf. 13¼***

1075 A470 €1.27 multi 3.00 1.50

Birds — A471

Designs: €1, Perdix perdix. €1.27, Pyrrhula pyrrhula.

2021, July 16 Litho. *Perf. 14x13¾*
1076-1077 A471 Set of 2 5.50 2.75

Items in Porcelain Museum, Riga — A472

2021, Aug. 6 Litho. *Perf. 13¼*
1078 A472 €1 multi 2.40 1.25

Latvian National Guard, 30th Anniv. — A473

Perf. 13¼x13½
2021, Aug. 11 Litho.
1079 A473 €1 multi 2.40 1.25

Riga State Gymnasium No. 1 — A474

Perf. 13¼x13½
2021, Aug. 27 Litho.
1080 A474 €1 multi 2.40 1.25

Souvenir Sheet

Janis Pauluks (1906-84), Painter — A475

No. 1081: a, Felicita in a Colored Dress, by Janis Pauluks. b, Pauluks.

2021, Sept. 2 Litho. *Perf. 13¼*
1081 A475 €1 Sheet of 2, #a-b 4.75 2.40

Irbe Lighthouse — A476

2021, Sept. 17 Litho. *Perf. 13¼*
1082 A476 €1.27 multi 3.00 1.50

Souvenir Sheet

Janis Lusis (1939-2020), Gold Medalist Javelin Thrower at 1968 Summer Olympics — A477

2021, Sept. 24 Litho. *Perf. 13¼*
1083 A477 €2.69 multi 6.25 3.25

Illustration by Anita Paegle From *The Ghost of Roses* — A478

2021, Oct. 1 Litho. *Perf. 13¼x13½*
1084 A478 €1 multi 2.40 1.25

Janis Poruks (1871-1911), Writer — A479

2021, Oct. 13 Litho. *Perf. 13¼*
1085 A479 €1 multi 2.40 1.25

Christmas — A480

Designs: €1, Cat, Christmas tree and ornaments. €1.42, Dog and Christmas gifts. €1.54, Mouse and pine cones.

Serpentine Die Cut 14¼x14¾ Syncopated
2021, Nov. 15 Litho.
Self-Adhesive
1086-1088 A480 Set of 3 9.00 4.50

Latvian 3-on-3 Basketball Team, Gold Medalists at 2020 Summer Olympics — A481

2021, Nov. 29 Litho. *Perf. 13¼*
1089 A481 €1 multi 2.25 1.10

The 2020 Summer Olympics were postponed until 2021 because of the COVID-19 pandemic.

Domesticated Animals — A482

Designs: €1.20, Cat. €1.47, Dog. €1.56, Rooster and hen. €1.75, Goose.

Serpentine Die Cut 20x18 Syncopated
2022, Jan. 14 Litho.
Self-Adhesive
1090 A482 €1.20 multi 2.75 1.40
1091 A482 €1.47 multi 3.25 1.60
1092 A482 €1.56 multi 3.50 1.75
1093 A482 €1.75 multi 4.00 2.00
Nos. 1090-1093 (4) 13.50 6.75

Gaff Schooner Eufrosine, 120th Anniv. — A483

2022, Jan. 21 Litho. *Perf. 13¼*
1094 A483 €1.44 multi 3.25 1.60

Items in Latvian Sports Museum, Riga — A484

2022, Jan. 25 Litho. *Perf. 13¼*
1095 A484 €1.44 multi 3.25 1.60

Vilhelms Purvitis (1872-1945), Painter — A485

2022, Mar. 4 Litho. *Perf. 13¼*
1096 A485 €1.20 multi 2.75 1.40

Svarcmuiza Manor, Riga — A486

2022, Mar. 11 Litho. *Perf. 13¼*
1097 A486 €2.34 multi 5.25 2.60

Gunars Astra (1931-88), Anti-Soviet Dissident — A487

2022, Mar. 25 Litho. *Perf. 13¼*
1098 A487 €1.20 multi 2.75 1.40

Heavenly Father Feeding Grass Snakes — A488

Heavenly Father On White Horse — A489

2022, Apr. 8 Litho. *Perf. 14x13¾*
1099 A488 €1.77 multi 3.75 1.90
1100 A489 €1.98 multi 4.25 2.10

Europa.

Alice's Adventures in Wonderland, by Lewis Carroll — A490

2022, Apr. 29 Litho. *Perf. 13¼x13½*
1101 A490 €1.20 multi 2.60 1.30

Latvian Constitution, Cent. — A491

2022, May 6 Litho. *Perf. 13¼*
1102 A491 €1.20 multi 2.60 1.30

Latvian Olympic Committee, Cent. — A492

2022, May 11 Litho. *Perf. 13¼*
1103 A492 €1.20 multi 2.60 1.30

Renovation of Museum of the Occupation of Latvia, Riga — A493

2022, May 18 Litho. *Perf. 13¼x13½*
1104 A493 €1.20 multi 2.60 1.30

University of Latvia Botanical Garden, Cent. — A494

2022, June 2 Litho. *Perf. 13¼*
1105 A494 €1.20 multi 2.60 1.30

Lobelia Dortmanna — A495

2022, June 17 Litho. *Perf. 13¼*
1106 A495 €1.20 multi 2.50 1.25

Birds — A496

Designs: €1.20, Apus apus. €1.47, Pica pica.

2022, July 8 Litho. *Perf. 13¾*
1107-1108 A496 Set of 2 5.50 2.75

Diplomatic Relations Between Latvia and the United States, Cent. — A497

2022, July 28 Litho. *Perf. 13½x13¼*
1109 A497 €1.98 multi 4.00 2.00

Water Tower, Riga — A498

2022, Aug. 12 Litho. *Perf. 13¼*
1110 A498 €1.20 multi 2.40 1.25

Concordat Between Latvia and Vatican City, Cent. — A500

2022, Sept. 1 Litho. *Perf. 13¼x13½*
1112 A500 €2.46 multi 4.50 2.25

See Vatican City No. 1803.

Souvenir Sheet

Hilda Vika (1897-1963), Painter — A501

No. 1113: a, In Autumn, by Hilda Vika. b, Vika.

2022, Sept. 23 Litho. *Perf. 13¼*
1113 A501 €1.20 Sheet of 2, #a-b 4.75 2.40

Janis Stradins (1933-2019), President of Latvian Academy of Sciences — A502

2022, Oct. 7 **Litho.** ***Perf. 13¼***
1114 A502 €1.20 multi 2.40 1.25

Latvian Parliament, Cent. — A503

2022, Oct. 20 **Litho.** ***Perf. 14***
1115 A503 €1.20 multi 2.40 1.25

Zenta Maurina (1897-1978), Writer — A504

2022, Oct. 28 **Litho.** ***Perf. 13¼***
1116 A504 €1.20 multi 2.40 1.25

Christmas — A505

Designs: €1.20, Four gnomes. €1.50, Two gnomes. €1.98, Three gnomes.

Serpentine Die Cut 14¼x14¾ Syncopated

2022, Nov. 11 **Litho.**

Self-Adhesive

1117-1119 A505 Set of 3 9.75 5.00

SEMI-POSTAL STAMPS

"Mercy" Assisting Wounded Soldier — SP1

Brown and Green Design on Back

1920 **Unwmk.** **Typo.** ***Perf. 11½***
B1 SP1 20(30)k dk brn & red .50 *1.20*
B2 SP1 40(55)k dk bl & red .50 *1.20*
B3 SP1 50(70)k dk grn & red .50 *1.60*
B4 SP1 1(1.30)r dl sl & red .50 *1.60*

Wmk. 197

Blue Design on Back

B5 SP1 20(30)k dk brn & red .70 *1.20*
B6 SP1 40(55)k dk bl & red .70 *1.20*
a. Vert. pair, imperf. btwn. 40.00
B7 SP1 50(70)k dk grn & red .70 *1.60*
B8 SP1 1(1.30)r dk sl & red .70 *2.40*

Wmk. Similar to 145

Pink Paper ***Imperf.***

Brown, Green and Red Design on Back

B9 SP1 20(30)k dk brn & red 1.00 *2.50*
B10 SP1 40(55)k dk bl & red 1.00 *2.50*
B11 SP1 50(70)k dk grn & red 1.00 *2.50*
B12 SP1 1(1.30)r dk sl & red 2.00 *4.25*
Nos. B1-B12 (12) 9.80 *23.75*
Set, never hinged 22.50

These semi-postal stamps were printed on the backs of unfinished bank notes of the Workers and Soldiers Council, Riga, and the Bermondt-Avalov Army. Blocks of stamps showing complete banknotes on reverse are worth approximately three times the catalogue value of the stamps.

Nos. B1-B8 Surcharged

Brown and Green Design on Back

1921 **Unwmk.** ***Perf. 11½***
B13 SP1 20k + 2r dk brn & red 2.50 *4.00*
B14 SP1 40k + 2r dk bl & red 2.50 *4.00*
B15 SP1 50k + 2r dk grn & red 2.50 *4.00*
B16 SP1 1r + 2r dk sl & red 2.50 *4.00*

Wmk. 197

Blue Design on Back

B17 SP1 20k + 2r dk brn & red 10.00 *40.00*
B18 SP1 40k + 2r dk bl & red 10.00 *40.00*
B19 SP1 50k + 2r dk grn & red 10.00 *40.00*
B20 SP1 1r + 2r dk sl & red 10.00 *40.00*
Nos. B13-B20 (8) 50.00 *176.00*
Set, never hinged 150.00

Regular Issue of 1923-25 Surcharged in Dark Blue and Light Blue

1923 **Wmk. Similar to 181** ***Perf. 10***
B21 A12 1s + 10s redsh pur .70 *1.75*
B22 A12 2s + 10s yel org .70 *1.75*
B23 A12 4s + 10s dk green .70 *1.75*
Nos. B21-B23 (3) 2.10 *5.25*
Set, never hinged 5.00

The surtax benefited the Latvian War Invalids Society.

Lighthouse and Harbor, Liepaja (Libau) SP2

Church at Liepaja SP5

Coat of Arms of Liepaja — SP6

Designs: 15s (25s), City Hall, Liepaja. 25s (35s), Public Bathing Pavilion, Liepaja.

1925, July 23 ***Perf. 11½***
B24 SP2 6s (12s) red brn & dp blue 3.75 *5.50*
B25 SP2 15s (25s) dk bl & brn 2.25 *4.00*
B26 SP2 25s (35s) vio & dk grn 3.75 *4.00*
B27 SP5 30s (40s) dk blue & lake 6.75 *12.00*
B28 SP6 50s (60s) dk grn & vio 9.75 *16.00*
Nos. B24-B28 (5) 26.25 *41.50*
Set, never hinged 55.00

Tercentenary of Liepaja (Libau). The surtax benefited that city. Exist imperf. Value, unused set $500.

President Janis Cakste — SP7

1928, Apr. 18 **Engr.**
B29 SP7 2s (12s) red orange 2.25 *3.25*
B30 SP7 6s (16s) deep green 2.25 *3.25*
B31 SP7 15s (25s) red brown 2.25 *3.25*
B32 SP7 25s (35s) deep blue 2.25 *3.25*
B33 SP7 30s (40s) claret 2.25 *3.25*
Nos. B29-B33 (5) 11.25 *16.25*
Set, never hinged 35.00

The surtax helped erect a monument to Janis Cakste, 1st pres. of the Latvian Republic.

Venta River — SP8

Allegory, "Latvia" — SP9

View of Jelgava — SP10

National Theater, Riga — SP11

View of Cesis (Wenden) SP12

Riga Bridge and Trenches SP13

Perf. 11½, Imperf.

1928, Nov. 18 **Wmk. 212** **Litho.**
B34 SP8 6s (16s) green 2.50 *2.75*
B35 SP9 10s (20s) scarlet 2.50 *2.75*
B36 SP10 15s (25s) maroon 2.50 *2.75*
B37 SP11 30s (40s) ultra 2.50 *2.75*
B38 SP12 50s (60s) dk gray 2.50 *2.75*
B39 SP13 1 l (1.10 l) choc 2.50 *2.75*
Nos. B34-B39 (6) 15.00 *16.50*
Set, never hinged 35.00

The surtax was given to a committee for the erection of a Liberty Memorial.

Z. A. Meierovics — SP14

1929, Aug. 22 ***Perf. 11½, Imperf.***
B46 SP14 2s (4s) orange 3.00 3.00
B47 SP14 6s (12s) dp grn 3.00 3.00
B48 SP14 15s (25s) red brown 3.00 3.00
B49 SP14 25s (35s) deep blue 3.00 3.00
B50 SP14 30s (40s) ultra 3.00 3.00
Nos. B46-B50 (5) 15.00 15.00
Set, never hinged 42.50

The surtax was used to erect a monument to Z. A. Meierovics, Latvian statesman.

Tuberculosis Cross SP15

Allegory of Hope for the Sick SP16

Gustavs Zemgals SP17

Riga Castle SP18

Daisies and Double-barred Cross SP20

Tuberculosis Sanatorium, near Riga SP22

Cakste, Kviesis and Zemgals SP23

Designs: No. B61, Janis Cakste, 1st pres. of Latvia. No. B63, Pres. Alberts Kviesis.

1930, Dec. 4 **Typo.** ***Perf. 10, 11½***
B56 SP15 1s (2s) dk vio & red org .75 *.85*
B57 SP15 2s (4s) org & red org .75 *.85*
B58 SP16 4s (8s) dk grn & red .75 *.85*
B59 SP17 5s (10s) brt grn & dk brn 1.50 *1.75*
B60 SP18 6s (12s) ol grn & bister 1.50 *1.75*
B61 SP17 10s (20s) dp red & blk 2.20 *2.25*
B62 SP20 15s (30s) mar & dl green 2.25 *2.25*
B63 SP17 20s (40s) rose lake & ind 2.25 *2.25*
B64 SP22 25s (50s) multi 3.00 *3.50*
B65 SP23 30s (60s) multi 3.50 *4.00*
Nos. B56-B65 (10) 18.45 *20.30*
Set, never hinged 55.00

Surtax for the Latvian Anti-Tuberculosis Soc. For surcharges see Nos. B72-B81.

J. Rainis and New Buildings, Riga — SP24

Character from Play and Rainis — SP25

Characters from Plays — SP26

Rainis and Lyre — SP27

Flames, Flag and Rainis — SP28

1930, May 23 **Wmk. 212** ***Perf. 11½***
B66 SP24 1s (2s) dull violet .75 *3.25*
B67 SP25 2s (4s) yellow org .75 *3.25*
B68 SP26 4s (8s) dp green .75 *3.25*
B69 SP27 6s (12s) yel grn & red brown .75 *3.25*
B70 SP28 10s (20s) dark red 22.50 *47.50*
B71 SP27 15s (30s) red brn & yel grn 22.50 *47.50*
Nos. B66-B71 (6) 48.00 *108.00*
Set, never hinged 95.00

Sold at double face value, surtax going to memorial fund for J. Rainis (Jan Plieksans, 1865-1929), writer and politician.
Exist imperf. Value twice that of perf. stamps.

Nos. B56 to B65 Surcharged in Black With Bars

Nos. B56 to B65 Surcharged in Black Without Bars

1931, Aug. 19 *Perf. 10, 11½*

B72	SP18 9s on 6s (12s)	1.00	*2.00*
B73	SP15 16s on 1s (2s)	12.50	24.00
B74	SP15 17s on 2s (4s)	1.25	*2.00*
B75	SP16 19s on 4s (8s)	3.75	*8.50*
B76	SP17 20s on 5s (10s)	2.50	*8.50*
B77	SP20 23s on 15s (30s)	1.00	*1.50*
B78	SP17 25s on 10s (20s)	2.50	*4.50*
B79	SP17 35s on 20s (40s)	3.75	*7.00*
B80	SP22 45s on 25s (50s)	10.00	*20.00*
B81	SP23 55s on 30s (60s)	12.50	*32.50*
	Nos. B72-B81 (10)	50.75	*110.50*
	Set, never hinged	110.00	

The surcharge replaces the original total price, including surtax.

Nos. B73-B81 have no bars in the surcharge. The surtax aided the Latvian Anti-Tuberculosis Society.

Lacplesis, the Deliverer — SP29

Designs: 1s, Kriva telling stories under Holy Oak. 2s, Enslaved Latvians building Riga under knight's supervision. 4s, Death of Black Knight. 5s, Spirit of Lacplesis over freed Riga.

Inscribed: "AIZSARGI" (Army Reserve)

1932, Feb. 10 *Perf. 10½, Imperf.*

B82	SP29 1s (11s) vio brn & bluish	2.50	2.50
B83	SP29 2s (17s) ocher & ol green	2.50	2.50
B84	SP29 3s (23s) red brn & org brown	2.50	2.50
B85	SP29 4s (34s) dk grn & green	2.50	2.50
B86	SP29 5s (45s) grn & emerald	2.50	2.50
	Nos. B82-B86 (5)	12.50	12.50
	Set, never hinged	22.00	

Surtax aided the Militia Maintenance Fund.

Marching Troops — SP30

Infantry in Action — SP31

Nurse Binding Soldier's Wound SP32

Army Soup Kitchen SP33

Gen. J. Balodis — SP34

1932, May *Perf. 10½, Imperf.*

B87	SP30 6s (25s) ol brn & red violet	4.00	*6.50*
B88	SP31 7s (35s) dk bl grn & dark blue	4.00	*6.50*
B89	SP32 10s (45s) ol grn & blk brn	4.00	*6.50*
B90	SP33 12s (55s) lake & ol green	4.00	*6.50*
B91	SP34 15s (75s) red org & brn vio	4.00	*6.50*
	Nos. B87-B91 (5)	20.00	*32.50*
	Set, never hinged	45.00	

The surtax aided the Latvian Home Guards.

Symbolical of Unified Latvia SP35

Symbolical of the Strength of the Latvian Union SP36

Aid to the Sick SP37

"Charity" SP38

Wmk. 212

1936, Dec. 28 **Litho.** *Perf. 11½*

B92	SP35 3s orange red	1.50	*2.50*
B93	SP36 10s green	1.50	*2.50*
B94	SP37 20s rose pink	1.50	*3.00*
B95	SP38 35s blue	1.50	*3.00*
	Nos. B92-B95 (4)	6.00	*11.00*
	Set, never hinged	12.00	

Souvenir Sheets

SP39

1938, May 12 **Wmk. 212** *Perf. 11*

B96	SP39 Sheet of 2	12.00	*50.00*
	Never hinged	22.50	
a.	35s Justice Palace, Riga	2.00	*5.00*
b.	40s Power Station, Kegums	2.00	*5.00*

Sold for 2 l. The surtax of 1.25 l was for the National Reconstruction Fund.

No. B96 exists imperf.

Overprinted in Blue with Dates 1934 1939 and "15" over "V"

1939

B97	SP39 Sheet of 2	15.00	*75.00*
	Never hinged	40.00	

5th anniv. of Natl. Unity Day. Sold for 2 lats. Surtax for the Natl. Reconstruction Fund.

Natl. Olympic Committee — SP50

1992, Feb. 8 **Litho.** *Perf. 13½x13*

Background Color

B150	SP50 50k +25k gray	.60	.60
B151	SP50 50k +25k buff	1.25	1.25
B152	SP50 100k +50k bister	.80	.80
	Nos. B150-B152 (3)	2.65	2.65

No. B150 inscribed "Berlin 18.09.91."

Flags of Latvia and Ukraine — SP51

2022, Mar. 10 **Litho.** *Perf. 13¼*

B153	SP51 €1.44 + (€1.50) multi	6.75	6.75

No. B153 was printed in sheets of 3 + 1 label. The sheet sold for €9 with half of the proceeds of the sale of the stamps going to the Ziedot.lv charity fund for Ukrainian assistance after its invasion by Russia.

AIR POST STAMPS

Blériot XI — AP1

Wmk. Wavy Lines Similar to 181

1921, July 30 **Litho.** *Perf. 11½*

C1	AP1 10r emerald	3.00	4.50
a.	Imperf.	6.00	*35.00*
C2	AP1 20r dark blue	3.00	4.50
a.	Imperf.	6.00	*35.00*
	Set, perf, never hinged	12.00	
	Set, imperf, never hinged	25.00	

1928, May 1

C3	AP1 10s deep green	4.50	1.60
C4	AP1 15s red	2.00	1.60
C5	AP1 25s ultra	3.75	2.50
a.	Pair, imperf. btwn.	35.00	
	Nos. C3-C5 (3)	10.25	5.70
	Set, never hinged	16.00	

Nos. C1-C5 sometimes show letters of a paper maker's watermark "PACTIEN LIGAT MILLS."

1931-32 **Wmk. 212** *Perf. 11½*

C6	AP1 10s deep green	1.00	.90
a.	Perf. 11	12.00	*14.50*
C7	AP1 15s red	1.50	1.00
a.	Perf. 11	120.00	32.50
C8	AP1 25s deep blue ('32)	8.50	1.25
a.	Perf. 11	28.00	14.50
	Nos. C6-C8 (3)	11.00	3.15
	Set, never hinged	22.50	

Type of 1921 Overprinted or Surcharged in Black

1933, May 26 **Wmk. 212** *Imperf.*

C9	AP1 10s deep green	40.00	*80.00*
C10	AP1 15s red	40.00	*80.00*
C11	AP1 25s deep blue	40.00	*80.00*
C12	AP1 50s on 15s red	200.00	*525.00*
C13	AP1 100s on 25s dp blue	200.00	*525.00*
	Nos. C9-C13 (5)	520.00	*1,290.*
	Set, never hinged	825.00	

Honoring and financing a flight from Riga to Bathurst, Gambia. The plane crashed at Neustettin, Germany.

Counterfeits exist of Nos. C1-C13.

AIR POST SEMI-POSTAL STAMPS

Durbes Castle, Rainis Birthplace SPAP1

Wmk. 212

1930, May 26 **Litho.** *Perf. 11½*

CB1	SPAP1 10s (20s) red & olive green	6.50	*14.50*
CB2	SPAP1 15s (30s) dk yel grn & cop red	6.50	*14.50*
	Set, never hinged	25.00	

Surtax for the Rainis Memorial Fund.

Imperf.

CB1a	SPAP1 10s (20s)	10.00	*27.50*
CB2a	SPAP1 15s (30s)	10.00	*27.50*
	Set, never hinged	40.00	

Nos. C6-C8 Surcharged in Magenta, Blue or Red

1931, Dec. 5

CB3	AP1 10s + 50s dp grn (M)	6.50	*7.50*
CB4	AP1 15s + 1 l red (Bl)	6.50	*7.50*
CB5	AP1 25s + 1.50 l dp blue	6.50	*7.50*
	Nos. CB3-CB5 (3)	19.50	*22.50*
	Set, never hinged	40.00	

Surtax for the Latvian Home Guards.

Imperf.

CB3a	AP1 10s + 50s	10.00	*11.00*
CB4a	AP1 15s + 1 l	10.00	*11.00*
CB5a	AP1 25s + 1.50 l	10.00	*11.00*
	Nos. CB3a-CB5a (3)	30.00	*33.00*
	Set, never hinged	55.00	

SPAP2

1932, June 17 *Perf. 10½*

CB6	SPAP2 10s (20s) dk sl grn & grn	12.50	*25.00*
CB7	SPAP2 15s (30s) brt red & buff	12.50	*25.00*
CB8	SPAP2 25s (50s) dp bl & gray	12.50	*25.00*
	Nos. CB6-CB8 (3)	37.50	*75.00*
	Set, never hinged	75.00	

Surtax for the Latvian Home Guards.

Imperf.

CB6a	SPAP2 10s (20s)	12.50	*25.00*
CB7a	SPAP2 15s (30s)	12.50	*25.00*
CB8a	SPAP2 25s (50s)	12.50	*25.00*
	Nos. CB6a-CB8a (3)	37.50	*75.00*
	Set, never hinged	75.00	

Icarus SPAP3

Leonardo da Vinci SPAP4

Charles Balloon SPAP5

Wright Brothers Biplane SPAP6

Bleriot Monoplane SPAP7

1932, Dec. *Perf. 10, 11½*

CB9	SPAP3 5s (25s) ol bis & grn	17.50	*20.00*
CB10	SPAP4 10s (50s) ol brn & gray grn	17.50	*20.00*
CB11	SPAP5 15s (75s) red brn & gray grn	17.50	*20.00*
CB12	SPAP6 20s (1 l) gray grn & lil rose	17.50	*20.00*
CB13	SPAP7 25s (1.25 l) brn & bl	17.50	*20.00*
	Nos. CB9-CB13 (5)	87.50	100.00
	Set, never hinged	150.00	

Issued to honor pioneers of aviation. The surtax of four times the face value was for wounded Latvian aviators.

Imperf.

CB9a	SPAP3	5s (25s)	17.50	*20.00*
CB10a	SPAP4	10s (50s)	17.50	*20.00*
CB11a	SPAP5	15s (75s)	17.50	*20.00*
CB12a	SPAP6	20s (1 l)	17.50	*20.00*
CB13a	SPAP7	25s (1.25 l)	17.50	*20.00*
		Nos. CB9a-CB13a (5)	87.50	100.00
		Set, never hinged	175.00	

Icarus Falling SPAP8

Monument to Aviators SPAP9

Proposed Tombs for Aviators
SPAP10 SPAP11

1933, Mar. 15 ***Perf. 11½***

CB14	SPAP8	2s (52s) blk & ocher	14.00	*20.00*
CB15	SPAP9	3s (53s) blk & red org	14.00	*20.00*
CB16	SPAP10	10s (60s) blk & dk yel green	14.00	*20.00*
CB17	SPAP11	20s (70s) blk & cerise	14.00	*20.00*
		Nos. CB14-CB17 (4)	56.00	*80.00*
		Set, never hinged	125.00	

50s surtax for wounded Latvian aviators.

Imperf.

CB14a	SPAP8	2s (52s)	15.00	*21.00*
CB15a	SPAP9	3s (53s)	15.00	*21.00*
CB16a	SPAP10	10s (60s)	15.00	*21.00*
CB17a	SPAP11	20s (70s)	15.00	*21.00*
		Nos. CB14a-CB17a (4)	60.00	84.00
		Set, never hinged	135.00	

Biplane Taking Off — SPAP12

Designs: 7s (57s), Biplane under fire at Riga. 35s (1.35 l), Map and planes.

1933, June 15 **Wmk. 212** ***Perf. 11½***

CB18	SPAP12	3s (53s) org & sl blue	19.00	*40.00*
CB19	SPAP12	7s (57s) sl bl & dk red brn	19.00	*40.00*
CB20	SPAP12	35s (1.35 l) dp ultra & ol blk	19.00	*40.00*
		Nos. CB18-CB20 (3)	57.00	*120.00*
		Set, never hinged	135.00	

Surtax for wounded Latvian aviators. Counterfeits exist.

Imperf.

CB18a	SPAP12	3s (53s)	22.50	*42.50*
CB19a	SPAP12	7s (57s)	22.50	*42.50*
CB20a	SPAP12	35s (1.35 l)	22.50	*42.50*
		Nos. CB18a-CB20a (3)	67.50	*127.50*
		Set, never hinged	140.00	

American Gee-Bee SPAP13

English Seaplane S6B — SPAP14

Graf Zeppelin over Riga — SPAP15

DO-X — SPAP16

1933, Sept. 5 ***Perf. 11½***

CB21	SPAP13	8s (68s) brn & gray blk	40.00	*85.00*
CB22	SPAP14	12s (1.12 l) brn car & ol grn	40.00	*85.00*
CB23	SPAP15	30s (1.30 l) bl & gray blk	50.00	*90.00*
CB24	SPAP16	40s (1.90 l) brn vio & indigo	40.00	*85.00*
		Nos. CB21-CB24 (4)	170.00	345.00
		Set, never hinged	275.00	

Surtax for wounded Latvian aviators.

Imperf.

CB21a	SPAP13	8s (68s)	40.00	*85.00*
CB22a	SPAP14	12s (1.12 l)	40.00	*85.00*
CB23a	SPAP15	30s (1.30 l)	50.00	*95.00*
CB24a	SPAP16	40s (1.90 l)	40.00	*90.00*
		Nos. CB21a-CB24a (4)	170.00	*355.00*
		Set, never hinged	275.00	

OCCUPATION STAMPS

Issued under German Occupation

German Stamps of 1905-18 Handstamped

Red Overprint

1919 **Wmk. 125** ***Perf. 14, 14½***

1N1	A22	2½pf gray	275.00	*325.00*
1N2	A16	5pf green	225.00	100.00
1N3	A22	15pf dk vio	375.00	100.00
1N4	A16	20pf blue vio	135.00	65.00
1N5	A16	25pf org & blk, *yel*	475.00	325.00
1N6	A16	50pf pur & blk, *buff*	475.00	325.00

Violet Blue Overprint

1N7	A22	2½pf gray	275.00	*325.00*
1N8	A16	5pf green	225.00	120.00
1N9	A16	10pf carmine	190.00	47.50
1N10	A22	15pf dk vio	325.00	325.00
1N11	A16	20pf bl vio	135.00	65.00
1N12	A16	25pf org & blk, *yel*	675.00	525.00
1N13	A16	50pf pur & blk, *buff*	675.00	525.00
		Nos. 1N1-1N13 (13)	4,460.	3,173.

Inverted and double overprints exist, as well as counterfeit overprints.

Some experts believe that Nos. 1N1-1N7 were not officially issued. All used examples are canceled to order.

Russian Stamps Overprinted

1941, July

1N14	A331	5k red (#734)	1.00	*4.25*
1N15	A109	10k blue (#616)	1.00	*4.25*
1N16	A332	15k dk grn (#735)	32.50	*72.50*
1N17	A97	20k dull grn (#617)	1.00	*4.25*
1N18	A333	30k dp blue (#736)	1.00	*4.25*
1N19	A111	50k dp brn (#619A)	3.50	*10.00*
		Nos. 1N14-1N19 (6)	40.00	*99.50*
		Set, never hinged	77.50	

Issued: 20k, 30k, 7/17; 5k, 10k, 7/18; 15k, 7/19; 50k, 7/23.

Nos. 1N14-1N19 were replaced by German stamps in mid-October. On Nov. 4, 1941, German stamps overprinted "Ostland" (Russia Nos. N9-N28) were placed into use.

The overprint exists on imperf examples of the 10k and 50k stamps. Value, each $800.

Counterfeit overprints exist.

KURLAND

German Stamps Surcharged

1945, Apr. 20

1N20	A115	6pf on 5pf dp yel grn (#509)	37.50	*72.50*
		Never hinged	72.50	
1N21	A115	6 pf 10pf dk brn (#511A)	15.00	*30.00*
		Never hinged	27.50	
a.		Inverted surcharge	100.00	*175.00*
		Never hinged	175.00	
b.		Double surcharge	85.00	*150.00*
		Never hinged	150.00	
1N22	A115	6 pf on 20pf blue	8.50	*14.50*
		Never hinged	16.00	
a.		Inverted surcharge	100.00	*175.00*
		Never hinged	175.00	
b.		Double surcharge	85.00	*150.00*
		Never hinged	150.00	

Germany Nos. MQ1 & MQ1a Surcharged

Perf 13½

1N23	MPP1	12pf on (-) red brn, (#MQ1)	42.50	*72.50*
		Never hinged	82.50	
a.		Inverted surcharge	150.00	*275.00*
		Never hinged	275.00	
b.		Double surcharge	150.00	*275.00*
		Never hinged	275.00	

Rouletted

1N24	MPP1	12pf on (-) red brn, (#MQ1a)	6.50	*16.00*
		Never hinged	16.00	
a.		Inverted surcharge	75.00	*135.00*
		Never hinged	135.00	
b.		Double surcharge	67.50	*120.00*
		Never hinged	120.00	
		Nos. 1N20-1N24 (5)	110.00	*205.50*
		Set, never hinged	200.00	

Nos. 1N20-1N24 were used in the German-held enclave of Kurland (Courland) from April 20-May 8, 1945.

Counterfeit surcharges are plentiful.

ISSUED UNDER RUSSIAN OCCUPATION

Fake overprints/surcharges exist on Nos. 2N1-2N36.

The following stamps were issued at Mitau during the occupation of Kurland by the West Russian Army under Colonel Bermondt-Avalov.

Stamps of Latvia Handstamped

On Stamps of 1919

1919 **Wmk. 108** ***Imperf.***

2N1	A1	3k lilac	40.00	*52.50*
2N2	A1	5k carmine	40.00	*52.50*
2N3	A1	10k dp blue	140.00	*240.00*
2N4	A1	20k orange	40.00	*52.50*
2N5	A1	25k gray	40.00	*52.50*
2N6	A1	35k dk brown	40.00	*52.50*
2N7	A1	50k purple	40.00	*52.50*
2N8	A1	75k emerald	40.00	*80.00*

On Riga Liberation Stamps

2N9	A2	5k carmine	40.00	*52.50*
2N10	A2	15k dp green	20.00	*40.00*
2N11	A2	35k brown	20.00	*40.00*

Stamps of Latvia Overprinted

On Stamps of 1919

2N12	A1	3k lilac	6.00	*9.50*
2N13	A1	5k carmine	6.00	*9.50*
2N14	A1	10k dp blue	120.00	*200.00*
2N15	A1	20k orange	12.00	*20.00*
2N16	A1	25k gray	27.50	*60.00*
2N17	A1	35k dk brown	20.00	*27.50*
2N18	A1	50k purple	20.00	*27.50*
2N19	A1	75k emerald	20.00	*27.50*

On Riga Liberation Stamps

2N20	A2	5k carmine	4.00	*8.00*
2N21	A2	15k dp green	4.00	*8.00*
2N22	A2	35k brown	4.00	*8.00*
a.		Inverted overprint	*200.00*	
		Nos. 2N1-2N22 (22)	743.50	*1,173.*

The letters "Z. A." are the initials of "Zapadnaya Armiya"-i.e. Western Army.

Russian Stamps of 1909-17 Surcharged

On Stamps of 1909-12

Perf. 14, 14½x15

Unwmk.

2N23	A14	10k on 2k grn	6.00	*8.00*
a.		Inverted surcharge	*30.00*	
2N24	A15	30k on 4k car	8.00	*8.00*
2N25	A14	40k on 5k cl	8.00	*9.50*
2N26	A15	50k pn 10k dk bl	6.00	*8.00*
2N27	A11	70k on 15k red brn & bl	6.00	*8.00*
a.		Inverted surcharge	*200.00*	
2N28	A8	90k on 20k bl & car	12.00	*16.00*
2N29	A11	1r on 25k grn & vio	6.00	8.00
2N30	A11	1½r on 35k red brn & grn	47.50	65.00
2N31	A8	2r on 50k vio & grn	12.00	16.00
a.		Inverted surcharge	*120.00*	
2N32	A11	4r on 70k brn & org	20.00	27.50

Perf. 13½

2N33	A9	6r on 1r pale brn, brn & org	27.50	40.00

On Stamps of 1917

Imperf

2N34	A14	20k on 3k red	6.00	*8.00*
2N35	A14	40k on 5k claret	95.00	*100.00*
2N36	A12	10r on 3.50r mar & lt grn	80.00	*80.00*
a.		Inverted surcharge	*300.00*	
		Nos. 2N23-2N36 (14)	340.00	*402.00*

Eight typographed stamps of this design were prepared in 1919, but never placed in use. They exist both perforated and imperforate. Value, set, imperf. $1, perf. $2.

Reprints and counterfeits exist.

Catalogue values for unused stamps in this section, from this point to the end of the section, are for Never Hinged items.

Arms of Soviet Latvia — OS1

1940 **Typo.** **Wmk. 265** ***Perf. 10***

2N45	OS1	1s dk violet	.25	.25
2N46	OS1	2s orange yel	.25	.25
2N47	OS1	3s orange ver	.25	.25
2N48	OS1	5s dk olive grn	.25	.25
2N49	OS1	7s turq green	.25	.80
2N50	OS1	10s slate green	2.00	.40
2N51	OS1	20s brown lake	1.20	.25
2N52	OS1	30s light blue	2.40	.40
2N53	OS1	35s brt ultra	.25	.40
2N54	OS1	40s chocolate	2.00	1.20
2N55	OS1	50s lt gray	2.50	1.20
2N56	OS1	1 l lt brown	3.25	1.50
2N57	OS1	5 l brt green	24.00	13.50
		Nos. 2N45-2N57 (13)	38.85	20.65

Used values of Nos. 2N45-2N57 are for CTOs. Commercially used examples are worth three times as much.

LEBANON

'le-bə-nən

(Grand Liban)

LOCATION — Asia Minor, bordering on the Mediterranean Sea
GOVT. — Republic
AREA — 4,036 sq. mi.
POP. — 3,562,699 (1999 est.)
CAPITAL — Beirut

Formerly a part of the Syrian province of Turkey, Lebanon was occupied by French forces after World War I. It was mandated to France after it had been declared a separate state. Limited autonomy was granted in 1927 and full independence achieved in 1941. The French issued two sets of occupation stamps (with T.E.O. overprint) for Lebanon in late 1919. The use of these and later occupation issues (of 1920-24, with overprints "O.M.F." and "Syrie-Grand Liban") was extended to Syria, Cilicia, Alaouites and Alexandretta. By custom, these are all listed under Syria.

100 Centimes = 1 Piaster
100 Piasters = 1 Pound

Watermark

Wmk. 400

Catalogue values for unused stamps in this country are for Never Hinged items, beginning with Scott 177 in the regular postage section, Scott B13 in the semi-postal section, Scott C97 in the airpost section, Scott CB5 in the airpost semi-postal section, Scott J37 in the postage due section, and Scott RA11 in the postal tax section.

Issued under French Mandate

Stamps of France 1900-21 Surcharged

1924 Unwmk. *Perf. 14x13½*

1	A16	10c on 2c vio brn	1.60	1.60
a.		Inverted surcharge	45.00	45.00
2	A22	25c on 5c orange	1.60	1.60
3	A22	50c on 10c green	1.60	1.60
4	A20	75c on 15c sl grn	2.75	2.40
5	A22	1p on 20c red brn	1.60	1.60
a.		Double surcharge	45.00	45.00
b.		Inverted surcharge	45.00	45.00
6	A22	1.25p on 25c blue	4.50	2.40
a.		Double surcharge	42.50	42.50
7	A22	1.50p on 30c org	2.75	2.00
8	A22	1.50p on 30c red	2.75	2.40
9	A20	2.50p on 50c dl bl	2.40	2.00
a.		Inverted surcharge	37.50	37.50

Surcharged

10	A18	2p on 40c red & pale bl	5.50	3.75
a.		Inverted surcharge	27.50	27.50
11	A18	3p on 60c vio & ultra	8.00	6.75
12	A18	5p on 1fr cl & ol grn	10.00	7.50
13	A18	10p on 2fr org & pale bl	15.00	12.00
a.		Inverted surcharge	50.00	50.00
14	A18	25p on 5fr dk bl & buff	22.50	19.00
a.		Inverted surcharge	85.00	85.00
		Nos. 1-14 (14)	82.55	66.60

Broken and missing letters and varieties of spacing are numerous in these surcharges.
For overprints see Nos. C1-C4.

Stamps of France, 1923, (Pasteur) Surcharged "GRAND LIBAN" and New Values

15	A23	50c on 10c green	3.50	1.10
a.		Inverted surcharge	37.50	27.50
16	A23	1.50p on 30c red	4.50	2.25
17	A23	2.50p on 50c blue	3.75	1.10
a.		Inverted surcharge	32.50	30.00
		Nos. 15-17 (3)	11.75	4.45

Commemorative Stamps of France, 1924, (Olympic Games) Surcharged "GRAND LIBAN" and New Values

18	A24	50c on 10c gray grn & yel grn	25.00	*25.00*
a.		Inverted surcharge	350.00	
19	A25	1.25p on 25c rose & dk rose	25.00	*25.00*
a.		Inverted surcharge	350.00	
20	A26	1.50p on 30c brn red & blk	25.00	*25.00*
a.		Inverted surcharge	350.00	
21	A27	2.50p on 50c ultra & dk bl	25.00	*25.00*
a.		Inverted surcharge	350.00	
		Nos. 18-21 (4)	100.00	100.00

Stamps of France, 1900-24, Surcharged

1924-25

22	A16	0.10p on 2c vio brn	1.00	.50
23	A22	0.25p on 5c orange	1.25	.75
24	A22	0.50p on 10c green	2.00	1.40
25	A20	0.75p on 15c gray grn	1.75	1.10
26	A22	1p on 20c red brn	1.50	.95
27	A22	1.25p on 25c blue	2.25	1.60
28	A22	1.50p on 30c red	2.00	1.25
29	A22	1.50p on 30c orange	62.50	57.50
30	A22	2p on 35c vio ('25)	2.25	1.60
31	A20	3p on 60c lt vio ('25)	3.00	2.10
32	A20	4p on 85c ver	3.50	2.50

Surcharged

33	A18	2p on 40c red & pale bl	2.25	1.60
a.		2nd line of Arabic reads "2 Piastre" (singular)	2.50	.50
34	A18	2p on 45c grn & bl ('25)	27.50	22.50
35	A18	3p on 60c vio & ultra	3.50	2.50
36	A18	5p on 1fr cl & ol grn	4.25	3.25
37	A18	10p on 2fr org & pale bl	9.75	8.50
38	A18	25p on 5fr dk bl & buff	15.00	13.50
		Nos. 22-38 (17)	145.25	123.10

Last line of surcharge on No. 33 has four characters, with a 9-like character between the third and fourth in illustration. Last line on No. 33a is as illustrated.
The surcharge may be found inverted on most of Nos. 22-38, and double on some values.
For overprints see Nos. C5-C8.

Stamps of France 1923-24 (Pasteur) Surcharged as Nos. 22-32

39	A23	0.50p on 10c green	2.00	.85
a.		Inverted surcharge	35.00	25.00
b.		Double surcharge	40.00	21.00
40	A23	0.75p on 15c green	2.25	1.40
41	A23	1.50p on 30c red	2.75	1.40
a.		Inverted surcharge	35.00	25.00
42	A23	2p on 45c red	5.00	3.50
a.		Inverted surcharge	35.00	21.00
43	A23	2.50p on 50c blue	2.00	.95
a.		Inverted surcharge	35.00	21.00
b.		Double surcharge	40.00	21.00
44	A23	4p on 75c blue	5.00	3.50
		Nos. 39-44 (6)	19.00	11.60

France Nos. 198 to 201 (Olympics) Surcharged as Nos. 22-32

45	A24	0.50p on 10c	32.50	*32.50*
46	A25	1.25p on 25c	32.50	*32.50*
47	A26	1.50p on 30c	32.50	*32.50*
48	A27	2.50p on 50c	32.50	*32.50*
		Nos. 45-48 (4)	130.00	130.00

France No. 219 (Ronsard) Surcharged

49	A28	4p on 75c bl, *bluish*	3.50	3.50
a.		Inverted surcharge	67.50	52.50

Cedar of Lebanon
A1

Crusader Castle, Tripoli
A3

View of Beirut — A2

Designs: 50c, Crusader Castle, Tripoli. 75c, Beit-ed-Din Palace. 1p, Temple of Jupiter, Baalbek. 1.25p, Mouktara Palace. 1.50p, Harbor of Tyre. 2p, View of Zahle. 2.50p, Ruins at Baalbek. 3p, Square at Deir-el-Kamar. 5p, Castle at Sidon. 25p, Square at Beirut.

1925 Litho. *Perf. 12½, 13½*

50	A1	0.10p dark violet	.50	.25

Photo.

51	A2	0.25p olive black	.95	.25
52	A2	0.50p yellow grn	.75	.25
53	A2	0.75p brn orange	.75	.25
54	A2	1p magenta	2.00	.80
55	A2	1.25p deep green	2.25	1.40
56	A2	1.50p rose red	2.00	.25
57	A2	2p dark brown	1.25	.25
58	A2	2.50p peacock bl	2.00	.80
59	A2	3p orange brn	2.75	1.10
60	A2	5p violet	3.00	1.40
61	A3	10p violet brn	7.50	2.10
62	A2	25p ultramarine	20.00	12.00
		Nos. 50-62 (13)	45.70	21.10

For surcharges and overprints see Nos. 63-107, B1-B12, C9-C38, CB1-CB4.

Stamps of 1925 with Bars and Surcharged

1926

63	A2	3.50p on 0.75p brn org	1.50	1.50
64	A2	4p on 0.25p ol blk	2.50	2.50
65	A2	6p on 2.50p pck bl	2.00	2.00
66	A2	12p on 1.25p dp grn	1.40	1.40
67	A2	20p on 1.25p dp grn	6.75	6.75

Stamps of 1925 with Bars and Surcharged

68	A2	4.50p on 0.75p brn org	2.75	2.75
69	A2	7.50p on 2.50p pck bl	2.75	2.75
70	A2	15p on 25p ultra	2.75	2.75
		Nos. 63-70 (8)	22.40	22.40

No. 51 with Bars and Surcharged

1927

71	A2	4p on 0.25p ol blk	2.50	2.50

Issues of Republic under French Mandate

Stamps of 1925 Issue Overprinted in Black or Red

1927

72	A1	0.10p dark vio (R)	.55	.25
a.		Black overprint	37.50	
73	A2	0.50p yellow grn	.55	.25
74	A2	1p magenta	.55	.25
75	A2	1.50p rose red	.80	.60
76	A2	2p dark brown	1.10	.90
77	A2	3p orange brn	.90	.25
78	A2	5p violet	1.75	1.00
79	A3	10p violet brn	2.25	1.10
80	A2	25p ultramarine	19.00	8.00
		Nos. 72-80 (9)	27.45	12.60

On Nos. 72 and 79 the overprint is set in two lines. On all stamps the double bar obliterates GRAND LIBAN.

Same Overprint on Provisional Issues of 1926-27

15 PIASTERS ON 25 PIASTERS
TYPE I — "République Libanaise" at foot of stamp.
TYPE II — "République Libanaise" near top of stamp.

81	A2	4p on 0.25p ol blk	.75	.25
82	A2	4.50p on 0.75p brn org	.85	.25
83	A2	7.50p on 2.50p pck bl	1.10	.25
84	A2	15p on 25p ultra (I)	7.50	5.25
a.		Type II	11.50	8.00
		Nos. 81-84 (4)	10.20	6.00

Most of Nos. 72-84 are known with overprint double, inverted or on back as well as face.

Stamps of 1927 Overprinted in Black or Red

1928

86	A1	0.10p dark vio (R)	.80	.60
a.		French overprint omitted, on #50		
87	A2	0.50p yel grn (Bk)	2.00	1.50
a.		Arabic overprint inverted	35.00	25.00
88	A2	1p magenta (Bk)	1.00	.70
a.		Inverted overprint	35.00	25.00
89	A2	1.50p rose red (Bk)	2.00	1.50
90	A2	2p dk brn (R)	2.75	2.10
90A	A2	2p dk brn (Bk+R)	110.00	110.00
91	A2	3p org brn (Bk)	1.90	1.40
92	A2	5p violet (Bk+R)	3.50	2.75
93	A2	5p violet (R)	3.00	2.40
a.		French ovpt. below Arabic	30.00	14.00
94	A3	10p vio brn (Bk)	5.00	4.25
a.		Double overprint	100.00	90.00
b.		Double overprint inverted		
c.		Inverted overprint	100.00	70.00
95	A2	25p ultra (Bk+R)	11.50	10.50
95A	A2	25p ultra (R)	13.00	13.00
		Nos. 86-95A (12)	156.45	150.70

On all stamps the double bar with Arabic overprint obliterates Arabic inscription.

Same Overprint on Nos. 81-84

96	A2	4p on 0.25p (Bk+R)	2.00	1.50
97	A2	4.50p on 0.75p (Bk)	2.00	1.50
98	A2	7.50p on 2.50p (Bk+R)	4.50	3.50
99	A2	7.50p on 2.50p (R)	7.00	6.00
100	A2	15p on 25p (II) (Bk+R)	11.00	9.50
a.		Arabic overprint inverted		
101	A2	15p on 25p (I) (R)	14.00	12.00
		Nos. 96-101 (6)	40.50	34.00

The new values are surcharged in black. The initials in ( ) refer to the colors of the overprints.

Stamps of 1925 Srchd. in Red or Black

1928-29 ***Perf. 13½***

102	A2	50c on 0.75p brn org (Bk) ('29)	1.50	1.90
103	A2	2p on 1.25p dp grn	1.50	1.90
104	A2	4p on 0.25p ol blk	1.50	1.90
a.		Double surcharge	35.00	25.00
105	A2	7.50p on 2.50p pck bl	2.50	2.75
a.		Double surcharge	40.00	25.00
b.		Inverted surcharge	55.00	25.00
106	A2	15p on 25p ultra	22.50	10.00
		Nos. 102-106 (5)	29.50	18.45

On Nos. 103, 104 and 105 the surcharged numerals are 3¼mm high, and have thick strokes.

No. 86 Surcharged in Red

1928

107	A1	5c on 0.10p dk vio	1.75	.30

Silkworm, Cocoon and Moth — A4

1930, Feb. 11 **Typo.** ***Perf. 11***

108	A4	4p black brown	15.00	15.00
109	A4	4½p vermilion	15.00	15.00
110	A4	7½p dark blue	15.00	15.00
111	A4	10p dk violet	15.00	15.00
112	A4	15p dark green	15.00	15.00
113	A4	25p claret	15.00	15.00
		Nos. 108-113 (6)	90.00	90.00

Sericultural Congress, Beirut. Presentation imperfs exist.

Pigeon Rocks, Ras Beirut — A5

View of Bickfaya — A8

Beit-ed-Din Palace — A10

Crusader Castle, Tripoli — A11

Ruins of Venus Temple, Baalbek — A12

Ancient Bridge, Dog River — A13

Belfort Castle — A14

Afka Falls — A19

20c, Cedars of Lebanon. 25c, Ruins of Bacchus Temple, Baalbek. 1p, Crusader Castle, Sidon Harbor. 5p, Arcade of Beit-ed-Din Palace. 6p, Tyre Harbor. 7.50p, Ruins of Sun Temple, Baalbek. 10p, View of Hasbeya. 25p, Government House, Beirut. 50p, View of Deir-el-Kamar. 75c, 100p, Ruins at Baalbek.

1930-35 **Litho.** ***Perf. 12½, 13½***

114	A5	0.10p brn org	.60	.25
115	A5	0.20p yellow brn	.60	.25
116	A5	0.25p deep blue	.75	.45

Photo.

117	A8	0.50p orange brn	3.00	1.50
118	A11	0.75p ol brn ('32)	1.50	1.00
119	A8	1p deep green	1.75	1.25
120	A8	1p brn vio ('35)	3.00	1.00
121	A10	1.50p violet brn	3.25	1.90
122	A10	1.50p dp grn ('32)	3.50	1.50
123	A11	2p Prussian bl	4.50	1.60
124	A12	3p black brown	4.50	1.60
125	A13	4p orange brn	4.75	1.60
126	A14	4.50p carmine	5.00	1.60
127	A13	5p greenish blk	3.00	1.50
128	A13	6p brn violet	5.25	2.75
129	A10	7.50p deep blue	5.00	1.60
130	A10	10p dk ol grn	9.00	1.60
131	A19	15p blk violet	11.50	3.50
132	A19	25p blue green	20.00	6.00
133	A8	50p apple grn	60.00	15.00
134	A11	100p black	70.00	19.00
		Nos. 114-134 (21)	220.45	66.45

See Nos. 135, 144, 152-155. For surcharges see Nos. 147-149, 161, 173-174.

Pigeon Rocks Type of 1930-35 Redrawn

1934 **Litho.** ***Perf. 12½x12***

135	A5	0.10p dull orange	6.75	4.00

Lines in rocks and water more distinct. Printer's name "Hélio Vaugirard, Paris," in larger letters.

Cedar of Lebanon A23

President Emile Eddé A24

Dog River Panorama — A25

1937-40 **Typo.** ***Perf. 14x13½***

137	A23	0.10p rose car	.50	.25
137A	A23	0.20p aqua ('40)	.50	.25
137B	A23	0.25p pale rose lilac ('40)	.50	.25
138	A23	0.50p magenta	.50	.25
138A	A23	0.75p brown ('40)	.50	.25

Engr.

Perf. 13

139	A24	3p dk violet	4.00	.75
140	A24	4p black brown	.75	.25
141	A24	4.50p carmine	1.00	.25
142	A25	10p brn carmine	2.25	.25
142A	A25	12½p dp ultra ('40)	1.00	.25
143	A25	15p dk grn ('38)	4.00	.75
143A	A25	20p chestnut ('40)	1.00	.25
143B	A25	25p crimson ('40)	1.50	.60
143C	A25	50p dk vio ('40)	5.00	1.60
143D	A25	100p sepia ('40)	3.50	2.25
		Nos. 137-143D (15)	26.50	8.45

Nos. 137A, 137B, 138A, 142A, 143A, 143B, 143C, and 143D exist imperforate.

For surcharges see Nos. 145-146A, 150-151, 160, 162, 175-176.

View of Bickfaya — A26

Type A8 Redrawn

1935 (?) **Photo.** ***Perf. 13½***

144	A26	0.50p orange brown	17.50	9.75

Arabic inscriptions more condensed.

Stamps of 1930-37 Surcharged in Black or Red

1937-42 ***Perf. 13, 13½***

145	A24	2p on 3p dk vio	1.50	1.50
146	A24	2½p on 4p blk brn	1.50	1.50
146A	A24	2½p on 4p black brown (R) ('42)	1.50	1.50
147	A10	6p on 7.50p dp bl (R)	4.00	4.00

Stamps of 1930-35 and Type of 1937-40 Surcharged in Black or Red

Perf. 13½, 13

148	A8	7.50p on 50p ap grn	2.50	2.50
149	A11	7.50p on 100p blk (R)	2.50	2.50
150	A25	12.50p on 7.50p dk bl (R)	5.00	5.00

Type of 1937-40 Srchd. in Red

1939 **Engr.** ***Perf. 13***

151	A25	12½p on 7.50p dk bl	2.00	2.00
		Nos. 145-151 (8)	20.50	20.50

Type of 1930-35 Redrawn Imprint: "Beiteddine-Imp.-Catholique-Beyrouth-Liban."

1939 **Litho.** ***Perf. 11½***

152	A10	1p dk slate grn	2.25	.25
153	A10	1.50p brn violet	2.25	.75
154	A10	7.50p carmine lake	2.25	1.10
		Nos. 152-154 (3)	6.75	2.10

Bridge Type of 1930-35 Imprint: "Degorce" instead of "Hélio Vaugirard"

1940 **Engr.** ***Perf. 13***

155	A13	5p grnsh blue	1.50	.25

Exists imperforate.

Independent Republic

Amir Beshir Shehab — A27

1942, Sept. 18 **Litho.** ***Perf. 11½***

156	A27	0.50p emerald	3.00	3.00
157	A27	1.50p sepia	3.00	3.00
158	A27	6p rose pink	3.00	3.00
159	A27	15p dull blue	3.00	3.00
		Nos. 156-159 (4)	12.00	12.00

1st anniv. of the Proclamation of Independence, Nov. 26, 1941. See Nos. C80-C81.

Nos. 156-159 exist imperforate.

Nos. 140, 154 and 142A Surcharged in Blue, Green or Black

1943 ***Perf. 13, 11½***

160	A24	2p on 4p (Bl)	6.00	*6.25*
161	A10	6p on 7.50p (G)	2.60	.85
162	A25	10p on 12½p (Bk)	2.60	.85
		Nos. 160-162 (3)	11.20	7.95

The surcharge is arranged differently on each value.

Parliament Building — A28

Government House, Beirut — A29

1943 **Litho.** ***Perf. 11½***

163	A28	25p salmon rose	12.00	5.00
164	A29	50p bluish green	12.00	5.00
165	A28	150p light ultra	12.00	5.00
166	A29	200p dull vio brn	12.00	5.00
		Nos. 163-166 (4)	48.00	20.00
		Nos. 163-166,C82-C87 (10)	137.25	93.00

2nd anniv. of Proclamation of Independence. Nos. 163-166 exist imperforate. For overprints see Nos. 169-172.

Quarantine Station, Beirut — A30

Black Overprint

1943, July 8 **Photo.**

167	A30	10p cerise	5.50	3.50
168	A30	20p light blue	5.50	3.50
		Nos. 167-168,C88-C90 (5)	25.00	17.75

Arab Medical Congress, Beirut.

Nos. 163 to 166 Overprinted in Blue, Violet, Red or Black

1944

169	A28	25p sal rose (Bl)	15.00	15.00
170	A29	50p bluish grn (V)	15.00	15.00
171	A28	150p lt ultra (R)	15.00	15.00
172	A29	200p dull vio brn (Bk)	17.50	15.00
		Nos. 169-172,C91-C96 (10)	218.25	208.25

Return to office of the president and his ministers, Nov. 22, 1943.

Type of 1930 and No. 142A Surcharged in Violet, Black or Carmine

1945 Unwmk. Engr. *Perf. 13*

173	A13	2p on 5p dk bl grn (V)		1.25	.25
174	A13	3p on 5p dk bl grn (Bk)		1.25	.25
175	A25	6p on 12½p deep ultra (Bk)		1.50	.35
176	A25	7½p on 12½p deep ultra (C)		2.50	.95
		Nos. 173-176 (4)		6.50	1.80

Trees at bottom on Nos. 175 and 176.

Catalogue values for unused stamps in this section, from this point to the end of the section, are for Never Hinged items.

Citadel of Jubayl (Byblos) — A31

Crusader Castle, Tripoli — A32

1945 Litho. *Perf. 11½*

177	A31	15p	violet brown	4.50	3.50
178	A31	20p	deep green	4.50	3.50
179	A32	25p	deep blue	4.50	3.50
180	A32	50p	dp carmine	7.50	4.00
			Nos. 177-180,C97-C100 (8)	71.00	34.60

See Nos. 229-233.

Soldiers and Flag of Lebanon — A33

1946 Litho.

Stripes of Flag in Red Orange

181	A33	7.50p	red & pale lil	1.40	.25
182	A33	10p	lil & pale lilac	2.40	.25
183	A33	12.50p	choc & yel grn	3.25	.25
184	A33	15p	sepia & pink	4.00	.25
185	A33	20p	ultra & pink	3.50	.30
186	A33	25p	dk grn & yel grn	5.50	.35
187	A33	50p	dk bl & pale bl	12.00	1.25
188	A33	100p	gray blk & pale bl	16.00	2.50
			Nos. 181-188 (8)	48.05	5.40

Type of 1946 Ovptd. in Red

1946, May 8

Stripes of Flag in Red

189	A33	7.50p	choc & pink	1.50	.25
190	A33	10p	dk vio & pink	1.75	.25
191	A33	12.50p	lake & vio gray	2.00	.45
192	A33	15p	lt grn & yel grn	3.25	.65
193	A33	20p	sl grn & yel grn	3.00	.70
194	A33	25p	sl bl & pale bl	5.00	.95
195	A33	50p	ultra & vio gray	7.50	.90
196	A33	100p	blk & pale bl	11.00	2.25
			Nos. 189-196 (8)	35.00	6.40

See Nos. C101-C106, note after No. C106.

Cedar of Lebanon A34

Night Herons over Mt. Sanin A35

1946-47 Unwmk. *Perf. 10½*

197	A34	0.50p	red brn ('47)	.80	.25
198	A34	1p	purple ('47)	1.20	.25
199	A34	2.50p	violet	2.75	.25
200	A34	5p	red	3.25	.25
201	A34	6p	gray ('47)	4.00	.25

Perf. 11½

202	A35	12.50p	deep car	24.00	.25
			Nos. 197-202,C107-C110 (10)	98.25	9.10

For surcharge see No. 246.

A36

Crusader Castle, Tripoli — A37

1947 Litho. *Perf. 14x13½*

203	A36	0.50p	dark brown	1.25	.25
204	A36	2.50p	bright green	1.60	.25
205	A36	5p	car rose	3.50	.25

Perf. 11½

206	A37	12.50p	rose pink	9.00	.45
207	A37	25p	ultramarine	9.00	.50
208	A37	50p	turq green	25.00	1.00
209	A37	100p	violet	34.00	5.25
			Nos. 203-209 (7)	83.35	7.95

A38

Zubaida Aqueduct — A39

1948 *Perf. 14x13½*

210	A38	0.50p	blue	.65	.25
211	A38	1p	yel brown	.75	.25
212	A38	2.50p	rose violet	.95	.25
213	A38	3p	emerald	2.40	.25
214	A38	5p	crimson	2.75	.25

Perf. 11½

215	A39	7.50p	rose red	6.00	.25
216	A39	10p	dl violet	4.25	.25
217	A39	12.50p	blue	9.00	.40
218	A39	25p	blue vio	15.00	.90
219	A39	50p	green	27.50	4.75
			Nos. 210-219 (10)	69.25	7.80

See Nos. 227A-228A, 234-237. For surcharge see No. 245.

Europa A40

Avicenna A41

1948 Litho.

220	A40	10p	dk red & org red	4.75	1.40
221	A40	12.50p	pur & rose	5.50	1.90
222	A40	25p	ol grn & pale green	6.50	1.50
223	A41	30p	org brn & buff	7.25	1.50
224	A41	40p	Prus grn & buff	10.50	1.50
			Nos. 220-224 (5)	34.50	7.80

UNESCO. Nos. 220 to 224 exist imperforate (see note after No. C145).

Camel Post Rider — A42

1949, Aug. 16 Unwmk. *Perf. 11½*

225	A42	5p	violet	1.60	.40
226	A42	7.50p	red	2.40	.60
227	A42	12.50p	blue	3.25	1.00
			Nos. 225-227,C148-C149 (5)	24.00	9.50

UPU, 75th anniv. See note after No. C149.

Cedar Type of 1948 Redrawn and Jubayl Type of 1945

Original

Redrawn

1949 Litho. *Perf. 14x13½*

227A	A38	0.50p	blue	2.75	.25
228	A38	1p	red orange	2.75	.25
228A	A38	2.50p	rose lilac	13.00	.35

Perf. 11½

229	A31	7.50p	rose red	4.00	.25
230	A31	10p	violet brn	7.00	.25
231	A31	12.50p	deep blue	14.00	.25
232	A31	25p	violet	25.00	.40
233	A31	50p	green	47.50	1.90
			Nos. 227A-233 (8)	116.00	3.90

On No. 227A in left numeral tablet, top of "P" stands higher than flag of the 1¼mm high "5." On No. 210, tops of "P" and the 2mm "5" are on same line.

On No. 228, "1 P." is smaller than on No. 211, and has no line below "P."

On No. 228A, the "O" does not touch tablet frame; on No. 212, it does. No. 228A exists on gray paper.

Cedar Type of 1948 Redrawn and

Ancient Bridge across Dog River — A43

1950 Litho. *Perf. 14x13½*

234	A38	0.50p	rose red	.40	.25
235	A38	1p	salmon	1.00	.25
236	A38	2.50p	violet	1.50	.25
237	A38	5p	claret	3.50	.25

Cedar slightly altered and mountains eliminated.

Perf. 11½

238	A43	7.50p	rose red	3.50	.25
239	A43	10p	rose vio	5.00	.25
240	A43	12.50p	light blue	11.00	.25
241	A43	25p	deep blue	15.00	1.25
242	A43	50p	emerald	35.00	5.00
			Nos. 234-242 (9)	75.90	8.00

See Nos. 251-255, 310-312.

Flags and Building — A44

1950, Aug. 8 *Perf. 11½*

243	A44	7.50p	gray	2.00	.25
244	A44	12.50p	lilac rose	2.00	.25
			Nos. 243-244,C150-C153 (6)	15.25	4.20

Conf. of Emigrants, 1950. See note after No. C153.

Nos. 213 and 201 Surcharged with New Value and Bars in Carmine

1950 Unwmk. *Perf. 14x13½, 10½*

245	A38	1p on 3p	emerald	1.25	.25
246	A34	2.50p on 6p	gray	1.25	.25

Cedar — A45

1951 Litho. *Perf. 14x13½*

247	A45	0.50p	rose red	.40	.25
248	A45	1p	light brown	.80	.25
249	A45	2.50p	slate gray	3.75	.25
250	A45	5p	rose lake	4.50	.25

Bridge Type of 1950, Redrawn

Typo. *Perf. 11½*

251	A43	7.50p	red	4.50	.25
252	A43	10p	dl rose vio	6.00	.25
253	A43	12.50p	blue	11.00	.25
254	A43	25p	dull blue	20.00	.50
255	A43	50p	green	40.00	3.75
			Nos. 247-255 (9)	90.95	6.00

Nos. 238-242 are lithographed from a fine-screen halftone; "P" in the denomination has serifs. Nos. 251-255 are typographed and much coarser; "P" without serifs.

Cedar A46

Ruins at Baalbek A47

Design: 50p, 100p, Beaufort Castle.

1952 Litho. *Perf. 14x13½*

256	A46	0.50p	emerald	1.00	.25
257	A46	1p	orange brn	1.10	.25
258	A46	2.50p	grnsh blue	2.50	.25
259	A46	5p	car rose	3.75	.25

Perf. 11½

260	A47	7.50p	red	4.50	.25
261	A47	10p	brt violet	6.25	.70
262	A47	12.50p	blue	7.00	.70
263	A47	25p	violet bl	7.75	1.40
264	A47	50p	dk blue grn	21.00	2.75
265	A47	100p	chocolate	42.50	7.50
			Nos. 256-265 (10)	97.35	14.30

Cedar of Lebanon A48

Postal Administration Building A49

1953 *Perf. 14x13½*

266	A48	0.50p	blue	.85	.25
267	A48	1p	rose lake	1.10	.25
268	A48	2.50p	lilac	1.25	.25
269	A48	5p	emerald	2.25	.25

Perf. 11½

270	A49	7.50p	car rose	3.25	.25
271	A49	10p	dp yel grn	4.50	.65
272	A49	12.50p	aquamarine	6.25	.75
273	A49	25p	ultra	8.25	1.40
274	A49	50p	violet brn	16.50	3.00
			Nos. 266-274 (9)	44.20	7.05

See No. 306.

A50

Gallery, Beit-ed-Din Palace — A51

1954 *Perf. 14x13½*

275	A50	0.50p	blue	.30	.25
276	A50	1p	dp orange	.50	.25
277	A50	2.50p	purple	.80	.25
278	A50	5p	blue green	1.75	.25

Perf. 11½

279	A51	7.50p	dp carmine	2.75	.25
280	A51	10p	dl ol grn	4.00	.35
281	A51	12.50p	blue	7.00	1.00
282	A51	25p	vio blue	9.00	2.75
283	A51	50p	aqua	17.00	5.00
284	A51	100p	black brn	37.50	9.00
			Nos. 275-284 (10)	80.60	19.35

Arab Postal Union Issue

Globe — A52

1955, Jan. 1 Litho. *Perf. 13½x13*

285	A52	12.50p	blue green	1.25	.25
286	A52	25p	violet	1.75	.25
			Nos. 285-286,C197 (3)	4.25	.75

Founding of the APU, July 1, 1954.

Cedar A53

Jeita Cave A54

1955 *Perf. 14x13½*

287	A53	0.50p	violet blue	.50	.25
288	A53	1p	vermilion	.60	.25
289	A53	2.50p	purple	.90	.25
290	A53	5p	emerald	1.10	.25

Perf. 11½

291	A54	7.50p	deep orange	1.75	.25
292	A54	10p	yellow grn	2.00	.25
293	A54	12.50p	blue	2.50	.25
294	A54	25p	dp vio blue	4.50	.25
295	A54	50p	dk gray grn	8.50	.45
			Nos. 287-295 (9)	22.35	2.45

See Nos. 308-309, 315-318, 341-343A. For overprint see No. 351.

Cedar of Lebanon A55

Globe and Columns A56

1955 Unwmk. *Perf. 13x13½*

296	A55	0.50p	dark blue	.25	.25
297	A55	1p	deep orange	.50	.25
298	A55	2.50p	deep violet	.65	.25
299	A55	5p	green	1.25	.25
300	A56	7.50p	yel org & cop red	1.50	.25
301	A56	10p	emer & sal	1.75	.25
302	A56	12.50p	ultra & bl grn	2.00	.25
303	A56	25p	dp ultra & brt pink	3.50	.25
304	A56	50p	dk grn & lt bl	4.50	.25
305	A56	100p	dk brn & sal	7.00	.50
			Nos. 296-305 (10)	22.90	2.75

For surcharge see No. 333.

Cedar Type of 1953 Redrawn

1956 Litho. *Perf. 13x13½*

306	A48	2.50p	violet	10.00	1.75

No. 306 measures 17x20½mm. The "2p.50" is in Roman (upright) type face.

Cedar Type of 1955 Redrawn & Bridge Type of 1950, Second Redrawing

1957 Litho. *Perf. 13x13½*

308	A53	0.50p	light ultra	.45	.25
309	A53	2.50p	claret	.90	.25

Perf. 11½

310	A43	7.50p	vermilion	2.00	.40
311	A43	10p	brn orange	2.40	.50
312	A43	12.50p	blue	3.25	.75
			Nos. 308-312 (5)	9.00	2.15

On Nos. 308 and 309 numerals are slanted and clouds slightly changed.

Nos. 310-312 inscribed "Liban" instead of "Republique Libanaise," and different Arabic characters.

Runners — A57

1957, Sept. 12 Litho. *Perf. 13*

313	A57	2.50p	shown	1.20	.25
314	A57	12.50p	Soccer players	1.75	.30
			Nos. 313-314,C243-C244 (4)	9.20	3.55

Second Pan-Arab Games, Beirut.

A souvenir sheet of 4 contains Nos. 313-314, C243-C244. Value, $130.

Cedar Type of 1955 Redrawn and

Workers A58

Ancient Potter A59

1957 Unwmk. *Perf. 13x13½*

315	A53	0.50p	light blue	.25	.25
316	A53	1p	light brown	.40	.25
317	A53	2.50p	bright vio	.40	.25
318	A53	5p	light green	.65	.25

Perf. 11½, 13½x13 (A59)

319	A58	7.50p	crim rose	1.00	.25
320	A58	10p	dull red brn	1.00	.25
321	A58	12.50p	bright blue	1.20	.25
322	A59	25p	dull blue	4.00	.25
323	A59	50p	yellow grn	5.00	.25
324	A59	100p	sepia	5.75	.60
			Nos. 315-324 (10)	19.65	2.85

The word "piaster" is omitted on No. 315; on Nos. 316 and 318 there is a line below "P"; on No. 317 there is a period between "2" and "50."

Nos. 315-318 are 16mm wide and have three shading lines above tip of cedar. See No. 343A and footnote.

For surcharges see Nos. 334-335, 339.

Cedar of Lebanon A60

Soldier and Flag A61

1958 Litho. *Perf. 13*

325	A60	0.50p	blue	.40	.25
326	A60	1p	dull orange	.60	.25
327	A60	2.50p	violet	.80	.25
328	A60	5p	yellow grn	1.20	.25
329	A61	12.50p	bright blue	1.75	.25
330	A61	25p	dark blue	2.00	.25
331	A61	50p	orange brn	2.25	.25
332	A61	100p	black brn	3.25	.35
			Nos. 325-332 (8)	12.25	2.10

For surcharges see Nos. 336-338.

No. 304 Surcharged

1959, Sept. 1

333	A56	30p	on 50p dk grn & lt bl	1.60	.25

Arab Lawyers Congress. See No. C265.

No. 323 Surcharged

1959 *Perf. 13½x13*

334	A59	30p	on 50p yel grn	1.40	.25
335	A59	40p	on 50p yel grn	2.00	.30

Convention of the Assoc. of Arab Emigrants in the United States.

Nos. 329-330 and 323 Surcharged with New Value and Bars

1959 *Perf. 13, 13½x13*

336	A61	7.50p	on 12.50p brt bl	1.00	.25
337	A61	10p	on 12.50p brt bl	1.20	.25
338	A61	15p	on 25p dark blue	1.30	.25
339	A59	40p	on 50p yel grn	1.75	.25
			Nos. 336-339,C271 (5)	7.85	1.30

Arab League Center, Cairo — A62

Perf. 13x13½

1960, May 23 Unwmk. Litho.

340	A62	15p	lt blue green	.75	.25

Opening of the Arab League Center and the Arab Postal Museum in Cairo.

For overprint see No. 352.

Cedar Type of 1955, Second Redrawing

1960 Litho. *Perf. 13x13½*

341	A53	0.50p	light violet	1.00	.25
342	A53	1p	rose claret	1.00	.25
343	A53	2.50p	ultramarine	1.20	.25
343A	A53	5p	light green	1.40	.25
			Nos. 341-343A (4)	4.60	1.00

Nos. 341-343A are 16½-17mm wide and have two shading lines above cedar. In other details they resemble the redrawn A53 type of 1957 (Nos. 315-318).

President Fuad Chehab — A63

1960 Photo. *Perf. 13½*

344	A63	0.50p	bl grn & dp bluish grn	.25	.25
345	A63	2.50p	olive	.25	.25
346	A63	5p	green	.25	.25
347	A63	7.50p	rose brown	.35	.25
348	A63	15p	bright blue	.75	.25
349	A63	50p	lilac	1.60	.25
350	A63	100p	brown	3.75	.25
			Nos. 344-350 (7)	7.20	1.75

Nos. 343A and 340 Overprinted in Red

1960, Nov. Litho. *Perf. 13x13½*

351	A53	5p	light green	.70	.25
352	A62	15p	lt blue green	1.40	.25

Arabian Oil Conference, Beirut.

President Fuad Chehab — A64

1961, Feb. Litho. *Perf. 13½x13*

353	A64	2.50p	blue & light bl	.50	.25
354	A64	7.50p	dark vio & pink	1.00	.25
355	A64	10p	red brn & yel	1.50	.25
			Nos. 353-355 (3)	3.00	.75

Cedar A65

Post Office, Beirut A66

1961 Unwmk. Litho. *Perf. 13*

356	A65	2.50p	green	.75	.25

Redrawn

357	A65	2.50p	orange	1.25	.25
358	A65	5p	maroon	1.25	.25
359	A65	10p	black	1.50	.25

Nos. 357-359 have no clouds.

Perf. 11½

361	A66	2.50p	rose carmine	.75	.25
362	A66	5p	bright green	1.40	.25
363	A66	15p	dark blue	2.10	.25
			Nos. 356-363 (7)	9.00	1.75

Cedars — A67

10p, 15p, 50p, 100p, View of Zahle.

1961 Litho. *Perf. 13*

365	A67	0.50p	green	.45	.25
366	A67	1p	brown	.45	.25
367	A67	2.50p	ultramarine	.45	.25
368	A67	5p	carmine	.65	.25
369	A67	7.50p	violet	.85	.25
370	A67	10p	dark brown	2.25	.25
371	A67	15p	dark blue	2.50	.25
372	A67	50p	dark green	2.75	.25
373	A67	100p	black	3.25	.35
			Nos. 365-373 (9)	13.60	2.35

See Nos. 381-384.

Unknown Soldier Monument — A68

1961, Dec. 30 Unwmk. *Perf. 12*

374	A68	10p	shown	3.00	.25
375	A68	15p	Soldier & flag	3.75	.25

Anniv. of Lebanon's independence; evacuation of foreign troops, Dec. 31, 1946.

See Nos. C329-C330.

Bugler — A69

Scout Carrying Flag and Scout Emblem — A70

Designs: 2.50p, First aid. 6p, Lord Baden-Powell. 10p, Scouts building campfire.

1962, Mar. 1 Litho. *Perf. 12*

376	A69	0.50p	yel grn, blk & yel	1.20	.25
377	A70	1p	multicolored	1.20	.25
378	A70	2.50p	dk red, blk & grn	1.20	.25
379	A69	6p	multicolored	1.20	.25
380	A70	10p	dp bl, blk & yel	1.20	.25
			Nos. 376-380,C331-C333 (8)	8.65	2.10

50th anniversary of Lebanese Boy Scouts.

Type of 1961 Redrawn

Designs as before.

1962 Unwmk. *Perf. 13*

381	A67	0.50p	yellow green	1.20	.25
382	A67	1p	brown	1.20	.25
383	A67	2.50p	ultramarine	1.30	.25
384	A67	15p	dark blue	3.25	.25
			Nos. 381-384,C341-C342 (6)	14.30	1.65

Temple of Nefertari, Abu Simbel — A71

1962, Aug. 1 **Unwmk.** ***Perf. 13***

390 A71 5p light ultra 1.00 .25
391 A71 15p brn lake & mar 1.40 .25

Campaign to save the historic monuments in Nubia. See Nos. C351-C352.

Cherries — A72

Designs: 50c, 2.50p, 7.50p, Cherries. 1p, 5p, Figs. 10p, 17.50p, 30p, Grapes. 50p, Oranges. 100p, Pomegranates.

1962 **Vignette Multicolored** **Litho.**

392 A72 0.50p violet blue 1.50 .25
393 A72 1p gray blue 1.50 .25
394 A72 2.50p brown 1.50 .25
395 A72 5p bright blue 1.50 .25
396 A72 7.50p lilac rose 1.50 .25
397 A72 10p chocolate 1.75 .25
398 A72 17.50p slate 2.50 .25
399 A72 30p slate grn 2.75 .25
400 A72 50p green 3.00 .25
401 A72 100p brown blk 5.00 .50
Nos. 392-401,C359-C366 (18) 31.65 5.05

Elementary Schoolboy — A73

1962, Oct. 1 **Litho.** ***Perf. 12***

404 A73 30p multicolored 1.20 .25

Students' Day, Oct. 1. See No. C355.

Cedar of Lebanon
A74 A75

1963-64 **Unwmk.** ***Perf. 13x13½***

405 A74 0.50p green 5.75 .25
406 A75 0.50p gray grn ('64) 1.20 .25
407 A75 2.50p ultra ('64) 1.20 .25
408 A75 5p brt pink ('64) 1.30 .25
409 A75 7.50p orange ('64) 1.40 .25
410 A75 17.50p rose lil ('64) 1.75 .25
Nos. 405-410 (6) 12.60 1.50

Bicyclist — A76

1964, Feb. 11 **Litho.** ***Perf. 13***

415 A76 2.50p shown 1.20 .25
416 A76 5p Basketball 1.20 .25
417 A76 10p Track 1.20 .25
Nos. 415-417,C385-C387 (6) 5.40 1.50

4th Mediterranean Games, Naples, Sept. 21-29, 1963.

Hyacinth — A77

1964 **Unwmk.** ***Perf. 13x13½***
Size: 26x27mm

418 A77 0.50p shown 1.20 .25
419 A77 1p Hyacinth 1.20 .25
420 A77 2.50p Hyacinth 1.20 .25
421 A77 5p Cyclamen 1.20 .25
422 A77 7.50p Cyclamen 1.20 .25

Perf. 13
Size: 26x37mm

423 A77 10p Poinsettia 1.20 .25
424 A77 17.50p Anemone 2.00 .25
425 A77 30p Iris 3.00 .25
426 A77 50p Poppy 5.75 .40
Nos. 418-426,C391-C397 (16) 23.75 4.15

See Nos. C391-C397.

Temple of the Sun, Baalbek — A78

1965, Jan. 11 **Litho.** ***Perf. 13x13½***

429 A78 2.50p blk & red org 1.60 .25
430 A78 7.50p black & blue 2.25 .25
Nos. 429-430,C420-C423 (6) 7.40 1.70

International Festival at Baalbek.

Swimmer — A79

1965, Jan. 23 **Engr.** ***Perf. 13***

431 A79 2.50p shown 2.00 .25
432 A79 7.50p Fencer 2.25 .25
433 A79 10p Basketball, vert. 3.25 .25
Nos. 431-433,C424-C426 (6) 9.00 1.50

18th Olympic Games, Tokyo, Oct. 10-25, 1964.

Birds — A80

5p, Bullfinch. 10p, European goldfinch. 15p, Hoopoe. 17.50p, Rock partridge. 20p, Golden Oriole. 32.50p, European bee-eater.

1965 **Engr.** ***Perf. 13***

434 A80 5p multicolored 6.50 .25
435 A80 10p multicolored 10.50 .25
436 A80 15p multicolored 8.00 .25
437 A80 17.50p multicolored 9.75 .25
438 A80 20p shown 12.00 .25
439 A80 32.50p multicolored 16.00 .25
Nos. 434-439 (6) 62.75 1.50

For surcharge see No. 459.

Cow and Calf — A81

1965 **Photo.** ***Perf. 11x12***

440 A81 0.50p shown 1.60 .25
441 A81 1p Rabbit 1.75 .25
442 A81 2.50p Ewe & lamb 2.00 .25
Nos. 440-442 (3) 5.35 .75

Hippodrome, Beirut — A82

1p, Pigeon Rocks. 2.50p, Tabarja. 5p, Ruins, Beit-Méry. 7.50p, Statue and ruins, Anjar.

1966 **Unwmk.** ***Perf. 12x11½***

443 A82 0.50p gold & multi 1.40 .25
444 A82 1p gold & multi 1.60 .25
445 A82 2.50p gold & multi 1.75 .25
446 A82 5p gold & multi 2.00 .25
447 A82 7.50p gold & multi 2.25 .25
Nos. 443-447 (5) 9.00 1.25

See Nos. C486-C492. For surcharge see No. 460.

ITY Emblem and Cedars — A83

1967 **Photo.** ***Perf. 11x12***

448 A83 0.50p lem, blk & brt bl 1.00 .25
449 A83 1p sal, blk & brt bl 1.00 .25
450 A83 2.50p gray, blk & brt bl 1.25 .25
451 A83 5p lt rose lil, blk & brt bl 1.25 .25
452 A83 7.50p yel, blk & brt bl 1.75 .25
Nos. 448-452 (5) 6.25 1.25

Intl. Tourist Year; used as a regular issue. See Nos. C515-C522. For surcharge see No. 461.

Goat and Kid — A84

1968, Feb. **Photo.** ***Perf. 12x11½***

453 A84 0.50p shown 2.40 .25
454 A84 1p Cattle 3.25 .25
455 A84 2.50p Sheep 4.00 .25
456 A84 5p Camels 5.00 .25
457 A84 10p Donkey 5.75 .25
458 A84 15p Horses 7.50 .25
Nos. 453-458 (6) 27.90 1.50

See Nos. C534-C539.

No. 439 Surcharged in Black

1972, Apr. **Engr.** ***Perf. 13***

459 A80 25p on 32.50p multi 18.00 .25

Nos. 447 and 452 Surcharged with New Value and Bars

Perf. 12x11½, 11x12

1972, May **Photo.**

460 A82 5p on 7.50p multi *3.75* .25
461 A83 5p on 7.50p multi *3.75* .25

Cedar — A85

1974 **Litho.** ***Perf. 11***

462 A85 0.50p orange & olive *.25* .25

Army Badge — A86

1980, Dec. 28 **Litho.** ***Perf. 11½***

463 A86 25p multicolored 2.00 .25

Army Day. See Nos. C792-C793.

Pres. Elias Sarkis — A87

1981, Sept. 23 **Photo.** ***Perf. 14x13½***

464 A87 125p multicolored 2.75 .80
465 A87 300p multicolored 2.75 1.60
466 A87 500p multicolored 7.50 2.40
Nos. 464-466 (3) 13.00 4.80

World Food Day, Oct. 16, 1981 — A88

1982, Nov. 23 **Photo.** ***Perf. 12x11½***

467 A88 50p Stork carrying food packages 1.75 .30
468 A88 75p Wheat, globe 2.00 .50
469 A88 100p Produce 2.25 .65
Nos. 467-469 (3) 6.00 1.45

World Communications Year — A89

1983, Dec. 19 **Photo.** ***Perf. 14***

470 A89 300p multicolored 6.00 1.75

Illustrations from Khalil Gibran's The Prophet — A90

1983, Dec. 19 ***Perf. 13½x14***

471 A90 200p The Soul Is Back 2.75 1.00
472 A90 300p The Family 4.25 1.75
473 A90 500p Self-portrait 7.50 2.40
474 A90 1000p The Prophet 15.00 4.75
a. Souvenir sheet, #471-474 32.50 32.50
Nos. 471-474 (4) 29.50 9.90

No. 474a sold for £25.

Scouting Year — A91

1983, Dec. 19 ***Perf. 14***

475 A91 200p Rowing 2.60 .50
476 A91 300p Signaling 3.00 .60
477 A91 500p Camp 5.50 1.00
Nos. 475-477 (3) 11.10 2.10

Cedar of Lebanon — A93

1984, Dec. **Photo.** ***Perf. 14½x13½***

481 A93 5p multicolored 1.60 .25

Flowers — A94

1984, Dec. **Photo.** ***Perf. 14½x13½***

482 A94 10p Iris of Sofar 1.40 .25
483 A94 25p Periwinkle 2.00 .30
484 A94 50p Flowering thorn 2.60 .40
Nos. 482-484 (3) 6.00 .95

For surcharges see Nos. 531-532.

Defense — A95

1984, Dec. Photo. *Perf. 14½x13½*

485 A95 75p Dove over city 3.50 .90
486 A95 150p Soldier, cedar 4.75 1.90
487 A95 300p Olive wreath, cedar 6.25 3.50
Nos. 485-487 (3) 14.50 6.30

Temple Ruins — A96

1985 Photo. *Perf. 13½x14½*

488 A96 100p Fakra 3.00 .55
489 A96 200p Bziza 3.50 1.10
490 A96 500p Tyre 6.50 2.75
Nos. 488-490 (3) 13.00 4.40

Pres. Gemayel, Map of Lebanon, Dove, Text — A97

1988, Feb. 1 Litho. *Perf. 14*

491 A97 £50 multicolored 4.00 1.60

Pres. Gemayel, Military Academy Graduate — A98

1988, Mar. 9

492 A98 £25 multicolored 4.50 1.35

Booklets containing Nos. 491-492, were given to dignitaries. Value for booklet, $110.

Arab Scouts, 75th Anniv. — A99

1988, Mar. 9 *Perf. 13½x14½*

493 A99 £20 multicolored 4.50 1.10

UN Child Survival Campaign — A100

1988, Mar. 9 *Perf. 14½x13½*

494 A100 £15 multicolored 2.75 .60

Prime Minister Rashid Karame (1921-1987), Satellite, Flags, Earth — A101

1988, Mar. 9 *Perf. 13½x14½*

495 A101 £10 multicolored 2.00 .50

1st World Festival for Youths of Lebanese Descent in Uruguay — A102

1988, Mar. 9

496 A102 £5 multicolored 2.00 .50

Cedar — A103

1989 Photo. *Perf. 13x13½*

497 A103 £50 dk grn & vio 2.40 .30
498 A103 £70 dk grn & brn 2.75 .40
499 A103 £100 dk grn & brt yel 3.25 .40
500 A103 £200 dk grn & bluish grn 4.75 1.00
501 A103 £500 dk grn & brt yel grn 8.75 2.40
Nos. 497-501 (5) 21.90 4.50

Independence, 50th Anniv. — A104

Designs: £200, Al Muntazah Restaurant, Zahle, 1883. £300, Sea Castle, Sidon, vert. £500, Presidential Palace, Baabda. £1000, Army graduation ceremony, vert. £3000, Beirut 2000, architectural plan. £5000, Pres. Elias Harawi, Lebanese flag, vert.

1993 Litho. *Perf. 14*

502 A104 £200 multi 1.60 .25
503 A104 £300 multi 2.10 .50
504 A104 £500 multi 3.25 .75
505 A104 £1000 multi 4.75 1.60
506 A104 £3000 multi 8.50 2.75
507 A104 £5000 multi 16.50 7.50
Nos. 502-507 (6) 36.70 13.35

For overprints, see Nos. 533B, 533C, 533G.

Size: 126x150mm

Imperf

508 A104 £10,000 multi 52.50 52.50

A105

Environmental Protection: £100, Stop polluting atmosphere. £200, Stop fires. £500, Trees, building. £1000, Birds, trees in city. £2000, Mosaic of trees. £5000, Green tree in middle of polluted city.

1994, May 7 Litho. *Perf. 13½x13*

509 A105 £100 multicolored 1.90 .25
510 A105 £200 multicolored 2.25 .50
511 A105 £500 multicolored 3.75 1.00
512 A105 £1000 multicolored 6.00 1.75
513 A105 £2000 multicolored 9.75 3.00
514 A105 £5000 multicolored 22.00 7.00
Nos. 509-514 (6) 45.65 13.50

For overprints see Nos. 533D, 533H, 537.

A106

1995, May 6 Litho. *Perf. 13½x13*

515 A106 £1500 Martyr's Day 7.00 3.00

For overprint see No. 534.

Anniversaries and Events — A107

£500, UNICEF, 50th anniv., horiz. £1000, Intl. Year of the Family (1994), horiz. £2000, ILO, 75th anniv. (in 1994), horiz. £3000, Bar Association (Berytus Nutrix Legum), 75th anniv.

1996, Feb. 21 Litho. *Perf. 14*

516 A107 £500 multi, horiz. 3.50 .90
517 A107 £1000 multi, horiz. 5.50 1.90
518 A107 £2000 multi, horiz. 9.50 3.50
519 A107 £3000 multicolored 14.00 5.50
Nos. 516-519 (4) 32.50 11.80

For overprints, see Nos. 533E, 534A, 535A.

Anniversaries and Events of 1995 — A108

£100, Opening of Museum of Arab Postage Stamps. £500, FAO, 50th anniv. £1000, UN, 50th anniv. £2000, Arab League, 50th anniv. £3000, Former Pres. René Moawad (1925-89).

1996, Feb. 21 *Perf. 13½x13*

520 A108 £100 multicolored 2.10 .25
521 A108 £500 multicolored 3.50 .90
522 A108 £1000 multicolored 5.50 1.75
523 A108 £2000 multicolored 9.00 3.25
524 A108 £3000 multicolored 14.00 5.25
Nos. 520-524 (5) 34.10 11.40

For overprints see Nos. 533A, 533F, 533I, 535-536.

Massacre at Cana — A109

1997, Oct. 13 Litho. *Perf. 14*

525 A109 £1100 multicolored *20.00 10.00*

For overprint, see No. 533J.

1997 Visit of Pope John Paul II to Lebanon — A110

1998, May 11 Litho. *Perf. 13½x13*

526 A110 £10,000 multi *120.00 100.00*

For overprint see Nos. 533O, 538.

Fakhr al-Din Palace, Deir-el-Kamar A111

£100, Chehab Palace, Hasbaya, vert. £300, ESCWA Building, Beirut, vert. £1100, Grand Seraglio, Beirut.

1999 Litho. *Perf. 12*

527 A111 £100 multicolored 1.50 .25
528 A111 £300 multicolored 2.50 .45
529 A111 £500 shown 3.00 .80
530 A111 £1100 multicolored 6.00 1.75
Nos. 527-530 (4) 13.00 3.25

Nos. 484, 485 and C775 Surcharged in Silver and Black

Methods and Perfs. as before

1999

531 A94 £100 on 50p (#484) 1.75 .25
532 A95 £300 on 75p (#485) 2.50 .45
533 AP154 £1100 on 70p (#C775) 6.00 1.75
Nos. 531-533 (3) 10.25 2.45

Nos. 502, 504-505, 511-512, 516, 518-522, 525 Overprinted in Gold

Similar to Nos. 534-538 but with Symbol Oriented as a Cross

Methods and Perfs As Before

1999

533A A108 £100 multi *20.00*
533B A104 £200 multi *20.00*
533C A104 £500 multi (#504) *32.50* —
533D A105 £500 multi (#501) *35.00* —
533E A107 £500 multi *35.00*
533F A108 £500 multi (#521) *35.00* —
533G A104 £1000 multi (#505) *70.00* —
533H A105 £1000 multi *60.00*
533I A108 £1000 multi (#522) *40.00* —
533J A109 £1100 multi (#525) *425.00* —
533K A106 £1500 multi *50.00*
533L A107 £2000 multi *95.00*
533M A107 £3000 multi (#519) *140.00* —
533N A105 £5000 multi *275.00*
533O A110 £10,000 multi (#526) *550.00* —
Nos. 533A-533O (15) *1,883.*

Nos. 514, 515, 523, 524 and 526 Overprinted in Gold or Silver

Methods and Perfs As Before

1999

534 A106 £1500 multi 16.00 5.00
535 A108 £2000 multi 24.00 9.00
536 A108 £3000 multi (S) 31.00 12.50
537 A105 £5000 multi 42.50 17.50
538 A110 £10,000 multi 85.00 40.00
Nos. 534-538 (5) 198.50 84.00

Cedar of Lebanon — A112

Perf. 13x13¼, 11x11¼ (£500, £1000, £1100)

1999-2000 Litho. Unwmk.

539 A112 £100 dark red .50 .25
540 A112 £300 Prus blue 1.00 .35

Wmk. 400

541 A112 £500 green 1.50 .65
a. Perf. 13x13¼ 1.50 .65
b. Booklet pane, 10 #541a 15.00
Booklet, #541b 15.00
542 A112 £1000 blue 3.50 1.25
543 A112 £1100 olive brn 3.75 1.40
a. Perf. 13x13¼ 3.75 1.40
b. Booklet pane, 10 #543a 37.50
Booklet, #543b 37.50
544 A112 £1500 vio blue 4.50 1.90
a. Booklet pane, 10 #544 45.00
Booklet, #544a 45.00
b. Perf. 11x11¼ 4.50 1.90
Nos. 539-544 (6) 14.75 5.80

Cedar of Lebanon Type of 2000 Redrawn

Perf. 11x11¼, 13x13¼ (£1000)

2001-02 Litho. Unwmk.

Numerals 1½mm Tall

544C A112 £500 olive grn ('02) *1.60 1.25*
544D A112 £1000 blue *3.25 2.50*
544E A112 £1100 brown *3.75 2.75*
544F A112 £1500 purple *5.25 3.75*
g. Perf. 13x13¼ *27.50 27.50*
Nos. 544C-544F (4) *13.85 10.25*

On Nos. 539-544, numerals are 2mm tall.

A113

2001 Litho. ***Perf. 11¼x11***
545 A113 £1100 multi 4.50 2.00

Geneva Conventions, 50th Anniv. (in 1999) — A114

Red Cross/Red Crescent — A115

2001 Litho. ***Perf. 11x11½***
546 A114 £500 shown 2.50 1.00
547 A114 £1100 "50," fist 5.00 2.00
548 A115 £1500 shown 6.25 3.00
Nos. 546-548 (3) 13.75 6.00

SOS Children's Villages — A116

2001
549 A116 £300 multi 2.25 1.00

Prisoners in Israel — A117

2001
550 A117 £500 multi 4.00 2.00

Ibrahim Abd el Al (1908-59), Hydrologist A118

2001
551 A118 £1000 multi 4.25 2.00

Abdallah Zakher (1680-1748), Printer — A119

2001
552 A119 £1000 multi 6.50 3.00

Elias Abu Chabke (1904-49), Poet — A120

2001 ***Perf. 11½x11***
553 A120 £1500 multi 13.50 6.50

Saint Joseph University, 125th Anniv. (in 2000) — A121

2001 ***Perf. 11x11½***
554 A121 £5000 multi 17.50 8.50

Economic & Social Commission for Western Asia, 25th Anniv. (in 1999) — A122

2001 ***Perf. 11½x11***
555 A122 £10,000 multi 32.50 20.00

Arab Woman's Day — A123

2002, Feb. 1 Litho. ***Perf. 13¼x13½***
556 A123 £1000 multi 3.50 2.75

Arab League Summit Conference, Beirut — A124

Arab League member flags and: £2000, Emblem. £3000, Cedar tree, Lebanese Pres. Emile Lahoud.

2002, Mar. 27
557-558 A124 Set of 2 18.50 11.00

Souvenir Sheet

Israeli Withdrawal From Southern Lebanon, 2nd Anniv. — A125

No. 559: a, Pres. Emile Lahoud, flag. b, Pres. Lahoud holding book. c, Pres. Lahoud and map. d, Pres. Lahoud receiving sword.

2002, Mar. 27 ***Perf. 13¼***
559 A125 £1100 Sheet of 4, #a-d 11.00 9.50

Souvenir Sheet

Martyrs of Justice A126

2002, June 14 ***Perf. 13¼x13½***
560 A126 £3000 multi 7.00 5.75

UPU, 125th Anniv. (in 1999) — A127

2002, Oct. 11 Litho. ***Perf. 13½x13¼***
561 A127 £2000 multi 7.00 3.25

City Views A128

Ruins A129

Paleontonlogy A130

Designs: £100 Old souk, Zouk Mikael. £300, Old souk, Sidon. £500, Byblos. £1000, Souk, Tripoli. £1100, Bziza. £1500, Arqa. £2000, Niha. £3000, Mousailaha Citadel. £5000, Libanobythus milkii in amber. £10,000, Nematonotus longispinus fossil.

Perf. 13¼x13½, 13½x13¼

2002-03 Litho.

562 A128 £100 multi .50 .25
563 A128 £300 multi .90 .50
564 A128 £500 multi 1.75 .90
565 A128 £1000 multi 2.50 1.75
566 A129 £1100 multi 3.00 2.00
567 A129 £1500 multi 3.50 2.75
568 A129 £2000 multi 4.50 3.75
569 A129 £3000 multi 7.25 5.75
570 A130 £5000 multi 24.00 9.25
571 A130 £10,000 multi 37.50 18.00
Nos. 562-571 (10) 85.40 44.90

Issued: £100, £300, 10/11; £1000, £1500, £2000, £3000, £10,000, 11/20; £500, £1100, 12/20; £5000, 1/8/03.

Ninth Francophone Summit, Beirut A131

Summit emblem and: No. 572, £1500, Mountains. No. 573, £1500, Pres. Emile Lahoud.

2002, Oct. 23 ***Perf. 13¼x13½***
572-573 A131 Set of 2 7.00 5.50

Beirut, 1999 Arab Cultural Capital — A132

2002, Nov. 13
574 A132 £2000 multi 5.00 4.00

Independence, 60th Anniv. (in 2001) — A133

Stylized flag and: No. 575, £1250, Crowd viewing horse and rider. No. 576, £1250, Men and flag on staff. No. 577, £1750, Arabic text. No. 578, £1750, Soldier saluting group of men. £6000, Vignettes of Nos. 575-578.

2003, Dec. 5 Litho. ***Perf. 12¾x13***
575-578 A133 Set of 4 20.00 20.00

Imperf

Size: 160x110mm

579 A133 £6000 multi 22.50 22.50

Faqra Ski Resort — A134

2004 Litho. ***Perf. 11x11¼***
580 A134 £500 multi *2.50 2.50*

General Post Office, Beirut — A135

Post office in: £100, 1953. £300, 2002.

2004 ***Perf. 11¼x11***
581-582 A135 Set of 2 *2.50 2.50*

Al Bustan Festival — A136

2004 Litho. ***Perf. 11x11¼***
583 A136 £1000 multi 4.00 4.00

St. George's Hospital, Beirut, 125th Anniv. (in 2003) A137

2004, Oct. 28 Litho. ***Perf. 11x11¼***
584 A137 £3000 multi 5.50 5.50

Ski Resorts — A138

2004 Litho. ***Perf. 11x11¼, 11¼x11***
585 A138 £100 Kamouaa .70 .70
586 A138 £100 Aayoun Siman .70 .70
587 A138 £250 Laklouk, vert. 1.35 1.35
588 A138 £300 Zaarour 1.75 1.75
589 A138 £300 Kanat Bakish 1.75 1.75
590 A138 £1000 Cedres 3.75 3.75
Nos. 585-590 (5) 8.25 8.25

Issued: No. 585, 10/28; £250, 11/26; No. 588, 10/28; Nos. 586, 589, £1000, 12/10.

Baalbeck Intl. Festival
A139

Tyre Festival
A140

Beiteddine Festival
A141

Byblos Intl. Festival
A142

Perf. 11x11¼, 11¼x11

2004, Nov. 26 **Litho.**

591	A139	£500 multi	.80	.80
592	A140	£1250 multi	2.00	2.00
593	A141	£1400 multi	2.25	2.25
594	A142	£1750 multi	2.75	2.75
		Nos. 591-594 (4)	7.80	7.80

Rotary International, Cent. — A143

2005, Feb. 23 ***Perf. 11¼x11***
595 A143 £3000 multi 6.25 6.25

Beirut Buildings — A144

Designs: £100, Rafiq Hariri Intl. Airport. £250, Parliament. £300, Camille Chamoun Sports Center. £500, National Museum. £1000, Governmental Palace. £1250, Bank of Lebanon. £1400, St. Paul's Cathedral. £1750, Bahaeddine Hariri Mosque. £2000, Presidential Palace.

2005 **Litho.** ***Perf. 13x13½***
596-604 A144 Set of 9 25.00 25.00

Issued: £100, £300, £500, £1000, 10/11; others, 11/11.

Pres. Rafiq Hariri (1944-2005)
A145

Designs: No. 605, £1250, Pres. Hariri, flag. No. 606, £1250, Pres. Hariri, mosque, church and statues. No. 607, £1750, Pres. Hariri, mosque. No. 608, £1750, Child kissing picture of Pres. Hariri.

2006, Feb. 13 ***Perf. 13¼x13***
605-608 A145 Set of 4 15.00 15.00
608a Souvenir sheet, #605-608, imperf. 10.50 10.50

No. 608a has embossed margin and simulated perforations between stamps.

Arabic Book Exhibition — A146

2007, Apr. 18 **Litho.** ***Perf. 13x13¼***
609 A146 £1000 multi 2.25 2.25

Basil Fuleihan (1963-2005), Economy Minister
A147

Fuleihan: £500, Wearing cap and gown, suit and tie. £1500, With flags of Lebanon and European Union. £2000, With flag of Lebanon.
£4000, Vignettes of Nos. 610-612, map and flag of Lebanon.

2007, Apr. 18 ***Perf. 13¼x13***
610-612 A147 Set of 3 10.00 10.00

Size: 160x100mm

Imperf

613 A147 £4000 multi 6.00 6.00

Pres. Fouad Chehab (1902-73)
A148

2007, June 4 ***Perf. 13¼x13***
614 A148 £1400 multi 2.40 2.40

World Summit on the Information Society, Tunis (in 2005) — A149

2007, July 2 ***Perf. 13x13¼***
615 A149 £100 multi .50 .50

Léopold Sédar Senghor (1906-2001), First President of Senegal
A150

2007, July 2 ***Perf. 13¼x13***
616 A150 £300 multi .75 .75

Intl. Year of Sports and Physical Education (in 2005) — A151

2007, July 2 ***Perf. 13x13¼***
617 A151 £500 multi 1.25 1.25

OPEC Development Fund, 30th Anniv. — A152

2007, July 2
618 A152 £1400 multi 2.25 2.25

Baalbeck Intl. Festival, 50th Anniv.
A153

50th anniv. emblem and: £1000, Names of performers. £5000, Female performers.

2007, July 2 ***Perf. 13¼x13***
619-620 A153 Set of 2 12.00 12.00

Islamic Makassed Association of Sidon, 125th Anniv. (in 2004)
A154

Emblem and: £1400, Pres. Rafiq Hariri. £1750, Prime Minister Riad El Solh.

2007, July 2
621-622 A154 Set of 2 9.00 9.00

Islamic Makassed Association of Beirut, 125th Anniv. (in 2003)
A155

Emblem and: £250, "125" in Arabian script. £500, Prime Minister Saeb Salam. £1400, Pres. Rafiq Hariri. £1750, Omar El Daouk.

2007, July 2
623-626 A155 Set of 4 9.00 9.00

Souvenir Sheet

2006 Ascent of Mt. Everest by Maxime Chaya
A156

2007, July 2
627 A156 £3000 multi 9.00 9.00

2004 Return of Freed Prisoners — A157

2007, July 2 ***Imperf.***
628 A157 £5000 multi 10.00 10.00

Souvenir Sheet

Hills, by Nizar Daher
A158

2007, July 2 **Litho.** ***Perf. 13¼x13***
629 A158 £5000 multi 10.00 10.00

Rotary International District 2450 Conference, Beirut
A159

2008, Apr. 30 **Litho.** ***Perf. 13¼x13***
630 A159 £2000 multi 3.00 3.00

Kahlil Gibran (1883-1931), Writer and Artist — A160

Designs: £100, Mother and Her Child. £500, Sultana. £1400, Gibran Museum, Bsharri. £2000, Gibran.
£4000, Gibran and vignettes of Nos. 631-634, horiz.

2008, Apr. 30 ***Perf. 13x13¼***
631-634 A160 Set of 4 11.00 11.00

Imperf

Size: 160x110mm

635 A160 £4000 multi 5.75 5.75

Army Day — A161

Emblem and: £500, Soldier and flag of Lebanon. £1000, Stylized flag of Lebanon. £1250, Soldier holding wheat stalks. £1750, Eye.
£4500, Soldiers and vignettes of Nos. 636-639.

2008 **Litho.** ***Perf. 13¼x13***
636-639 A161 Set of 4 8.00 8.00

Size: 160x110mm

Imperf

640 A161 £4500 multi 8.00 8.00

Souvenir Sheet

Arab Postal Day
A162

No. 641 — Emblem and: a, World map and pigeon. b, Camel caravan.

Perf. 13¼ Vert. Through Center

2008
641 A162 £5000 Sheet of 2, #a-b 20.00 20.00

Stamps have simulated perforations on three sides.

Lebanon Post, 10th Anniv.
A163

Simulated postmarks, Lebanon Post emblem, streamers, airplane and: £1250, "10" in Arabian script. £1750, Open envelope and "10th anniversary."

£3000, Simulated postmarks, Lebanon Post emblem, streamers, airplane and vignettes of Nos. 642-643.

2008 ***Perf. 13¼x13***

642-643 A163 Set of 2 5.50 5.50

Size: 160x110mm

Imperf

644 A163 £3000 multi 6.75 6.75

Trees and Map of Mediterranean Area — A164

2008, Nov. 20 ***Perf. 13***

645 A164 £1750 multi 2.40 2.40

See France No. 3569.

Gen. François El Hajj (1953-2007) A165

2009, Jan. 8 ***Perf. 13x13¼***

646 A165 £1750 multi 2.60 2.60

Universal Declaration of Human Rights, 60th Anniv. A166

2009, Jan. 8 ***Perf. 13¼x13***

647 A166 £2000 multi 4.00 4.00

Dated 2008.

Beirut, World Book Capital — A167

2009, Sept. 17 Litho. ***Perf. 13x13¼***

648 A167 £750 multi *2.50 2.50*

Jerusalem, Capital of Arab Culture A168

2009, Sept. 17 ***Perf. 13¼x13***

649 A168 £1000 multi 3.00 3.00

Pierre Deschamps (1873-1958), Founder of French Lay Mission A169

2009, Sept. 17

650 A169 £500 blue & black .85 .85

Sixth Francophone Games, Beirut A170

2009, Sept. 28

651 A170 £1000 multi 2.40 2.40

Fire Fighters — A171

Fire fighters with panel color of: £100, Green. £250, Red.

2010, Aug. 2 Litho. ***Perf. 13x13¼***

652-653 A171 Set of 2 .50 .50

Nature Reserves — A172

2010, Aug. 2

654 A172 £300 multi .45 .45

Architecture — A173

Various buildings with frame color of: £500, Red. £1000, Blue. £1200, Red.

2010, Aug. 2 ***Perf. 13¼x13***

655-657 A173 Set of 3 3.75 3.75

Soap Production A174

2010, Aug. 2 ***Perf. 13x13¼***

658 A174 £1400 multi 1.90 1.90

Soldier, Map of Lebanon — A175

2010, Aug. 2

659 A175 £1750 multi 2.40 2.40

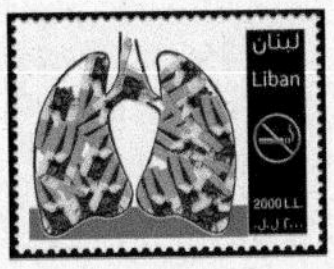

Lungs and Cigarette Butts — A176

2010, Aug. 2

660 A176 £2000 multi 2.75 2.75

Syringe and Arrows — A177

2010, Aug. 2 ***Perf. 13¼x13***

661 A177 £5000 black & red 7.00 7.00

Imam Al Ouzaai (707-74) A178

2010, Oct. 9

662 A178 £1000 multi 1.40 1.40

Grand Mufti Hassan Khaled (1921-89) A179

Musa as-Sadr (1929-78), Religious Leader — A180

2010, Oct. 9 ***Perf. 13¼x13***

663 A179 £1400 multi 2.00 2.00

Perf. 13x13¼

664 A180 £1400 multi 2.00 2.00

Assassinated Political Leaders — A181

Designs: No. 665, £1400, Kamal Jumblatt (1917-77). No. 666, £1400, Prime Minister Rashid Karami (1921-87). No. 667, £1400, President René Moawad (1925-89). No. 668, £1400, President Bachir Gemayel (1947-82), horiz.

2010, Oct. 9 ***Perf. 13x13¼, 13¼x13***

665-668 A181 Set of 4 8.00 8.00

World Tourism Day — A182

2010, Oct. 9 ***Perf. 13x13¼***

669 A182 £2000 multi 3.00 3.00

Dove and Flowers — A183

2010, Oct. 9

670 A183 £3000 multi 6.00 6.00

Source of the Alphabet — A184

Arab Permanent Postal Commission A185

Famous People — A186

Designs: £1750, Sabah, singer and actress. £2250, Nabih Abou El-Hossn, actor. £2750, Hassan Alaa Eddine (1939-75), comedian. £3000, Caracalla Dance Ensemble. £5000, Alfred (1924-2006), Michel (1921-1981) and Youssef (1926-2001) Basbous, sculptors. £10,000, Said Akl, poet.

2011, May 23 Litho. ***Perf. 13x13¼***

671 A184 £250 multi .35 .35
672 A185 £500 multi .70 .70
673 A186 £1750 multi 2.50 2.50
674 A186 £2250 multi 3.25 3.25
675 A186 £2750 multi 4.00 4.00
676 A186 £3000 multi 4.25 4.25
677 A186 £5000 multi 7.50 7.50
678 A186 £10,000 multi 15.00 15.00
Nos. 671-678 (8) 37.55 37.55

Famous People Type of 2011 and

Ehden Reserve A187

Pres. Suleiman Franjieh (1910-92) A188

Designs: £1500, Fayrouz, singer. £2000, Wadih El-Safi, singer.

Perf. 13x13¼, 13¼x13 (£1000)

2011, June 27

679 A187 £750 multi 1.10 1.10
680 A188 £1000 multi 1.40 1.40
681 A186 £1500 multi 2.10 2.10
682 A186 £2000 multi 3.00 3.00
Nos. 679-682 (4) 7.60 7.60

Pres. Michel Suleiman A189

Pres. Suleiman and: £750, Cedar trees. £1750, People at President's Summer Residence, Beiteddine. £2500, Dove with flags of Syria and Lebanon on wings. £2750, United Nations emblem.

2011, Nov. 5 ***Perf. 13¼x13***

683-686 A189 Set of 4 12.00 12.00

Mother's Day — A190

2012, Mar. 12 ***Perf. 13x13¼***

687 A190 £2000 multi *72.50 72.50*

Lions International in Lebanon, 60th Anniv. — A191

2012, Apr. 2
688 A191 £750 multi 1.60 1.60

Pope Benedict XVI and Pres. Michel Suleiman A192

2012, Sept. 15 ***Perf. 13¼x13***
689 A192 £1250 multi 2.10 2.10

Visit of Pope Benedict XVI to Lebanon.

Beirut Marathon, 10th Anniv. — A193

2012, Nov. 12
690 A193 £750 multi 1.25 1.25

Christmas A194

2012, Nov. 13 ***Perf. 13x13¼***
691 A194 £2000 multi 3.25 3.25

World Map and Statue of Lebanese Man — A195

2012, Nov. 21 Litho. ***Perf. 13x13¼***
692 A195 £500 multi *5.00 5.00*

Adel Osseiran (1905-98), Politician A196

2012, Nov. 21 Litho. ***Perf. 13¼x13***
693 A196 £1000 multi 1.60 1.60

National Scientific Research Council, 50th Anniv. A197

2012, Dec. 10
694 A197 £250 multi .45 .45

Pres. Michel Suleiman — A198

2012, Dec. 13 ***Perf. 13x13¼***
695 A198 £250 multi *10.00 10.00*

Ghassan Tueni (1926-2012), Journalist and Politician — A199

2012, Dec. 14
696 A199 £750 multi 1.25 1.25

100th Birthday (in 2011) of Said Akl, Poet — A200

2012, Dec. 26 ***Perf. 13¼x13***
697 A200 £500 multi .80 .80

Mother's Day — A201

2013, Mar. 20 ***Perf. 13x13¼***
698 A201 £2000 multi *3.00 3.00*

Lebanon Post, 15th Anniv. — A202

2013, Nov. 11 Litho. ***Perf. 13x13¼***
699 A202 £3000 multi 3.00 3.00

Amin Maalouf, Member of French Academy A203

2013, Nov. 19 Litho. ***Perf. 13¼x13***
700 A203 £100 multi 1.00 1.00

Independence, 70th Anniv. — A204

2013, Nov. 27 Litho. ***Perf. 13x13¼***
701 A204 £1000 multi 1.75 1.75

Christmas — A205

2013, Dec. 16 Litho. ***Perf. 13¼x13***
702 A205 £2000 multi 3.00 3.00

Armenian Genocide Monument, Bikfaya — A206

2014, Apr. 15 Litho. ***Perf. 13¼x13***
703 A206 £2000 multi 2.50 2.50

Medicine, Law and Engineering Faculties of St. Joseph University, Cent. — A207

2014, Apr. 29 Litho. ***Perf. 13x13¼***
704 A207 £500 multi .85 .85

Famous Women — A208

Designs: No. 705, £2000, Laure Moughhaizel (1929-97), women's rights advocate. No. 706, £2000, Mounira el Solh (1911-2010), advocate for women's rights and the disabled. No. 707, £2000, Alexandra Issa el Khoury, President of Lebanese Red Cross. No. 708, £2000, Anissa Najjar, founder of Al Ahlia Magazine.

2014, May 22 Litho. ***Perf. 13¼x13***
705-708 A208 Set of 4 14.00 14.00

Bank of Lebanon, 50th Anniv. — A209

2014, June 2 Litho. ***Perf. 13x13¼***
709 A209 £1750 multi 1.50 1.50

Father's Day — A210

2014, June 17 Litho. ***Perf. 13¼x13***
710 A210 £1750 multi 1.50 1.50

Euromed Postal Emblem and Mediterranean Sea — A211

2014, July 9 Litho. ***Perf. 13x13¼***
711 A211 £1000 multi 1.00 1.00

2014 World Cup Soccer Championships, Brazil — A212

Designs: £1750, Mascot. £2000, Emblem.

2014, July 12 Litho. ***Perf. 13¼x13***
712-713 A212 Set of 2 7.25 7.25

Monsignor Germanos Mouakkad (1853-1912), Missionary — A213

2014, Sept. 5 Litho. ***Perf. 13¼x13***
714 A213 £250 multi .60 .60

Youssef Bey Karam (1823-89), Leader of 1866-67 Rebellion Against Ottoman Rule — A214

2014, Nov. 10 Litho. ***Perf. 13¼x13***
715 A214 £1750 multi 1.50 1.50

Writers — A215

Designs: No. 716, £1750, Kamal Youssef El-Hage (1917-76). No. 717, £1750, Ounsi El-Hage (1937-2014). No. 718, £1750, Joseph Harb (1941-2014).

2014, Nov. 10 Litho. ***Perf. 13¼x13***
716-718 A215 Set of 3 8.75 8.75

Independence, 71st Anniv. — A216

2014, Nov. 22 Litho. ***Perf. 13¼x13***
719 A216 £2750 multi 2.75 2.75

Christmas and New Year's Day — A217

2014, Dec. 16 Litho. ***Perf. 13¼x13***
720 A217 £5000 multi 6.00 6.00

Monastery of Saints Cyprian and Justina, Kfifane — A218

Monastery of Saint Saviour, Joun — A219

Monastery of St. John Castle, Beit Mery — A220

2015, Jan. 15 Litho. ***Perf. 13x13¼***
721 A218 £250 multi 1.75 1.75
722 A219 £250 multi .50 .50

Perf. 13¼x13

723 A220 £250 multi .50 .50
Nos. 721-723 (3) 2.75 2.75

Said Freiha (1912-78), Founder and Publisher of Dar Assayad News Magazine — A221

2015, Jan. 20 Litho. ***Perf. 13x13¼***
724 A221 £1750 multi 3.25 3.25

Emblem of General Security Forces A222

Emblem of Internal Security Forces A223

2015, Mar. 17 Litho. ***Perf. 13¼x13***
725 A222 £1750 multi 1.75 1.75
726 A223 £1750 multi 1.75 1.75

Mother's Day — A224

2015, Mar. 20 Litho. ***Perf. 13¼x13***
727 A224 £2000 multi 2.00 2.00

Pierre Sadek (1938-2013), Political Cartoonist A225

2015, May 26 Litho. ***Perf. 13x13¼***
728 A225 £2250 multi 2.25 2.25

Famous People — A226

Designs: No. 729, £1750, Amin al-Hafez (1926-2009), prime minister. No. 730, £1750, Leila Osseiran (1934-2007), writer and wife of Amin al-Hafez.

2015, July 7 Litho. ***Perf. 13¼x13***
729-730 A226 Set of 2 6.50 6.50

Euromed Postal Emblem, Boats of the Mediterranean Sea — A227

2015, July 9 Litho. ***Perf. 13x13¼***
731 A227 £5000 multi 5.00 5.00

Politicians A228

Designs: No. 732, £1750, Riad El Solh (1894-1951), first prime minister. No. 733, £1750, Bechara El Khoury (1890-1964), prime minister and president.

2015, July 14 Litho. ***Perf. 13x13¼***
732-733 A228 Set of 2 6.50 6.50

The Red Sunset, by Saliba Douaihy (1915-94) A229

2015, Aug. 11 Litho. ***Perf. 13¼x13***
734 A229 £2000 multi 2.00 2.00

Flag Day — A230

2015, Nov. 21 Litho. ***Perf. 13x13¼***
735 A230 £2000 multi 2.00 2.00

End of 2015 — A231

2015, Dec. 30 Litho. ***Perf. 13¼x13***
736 A231 £2000 multi 2.00 2.00

Jawad Boulos (1900-82), Historian A232

Hani Fahs (1946-2014), Shiite Cleric A233

2016, Feb. 17 Litho. ***Perf. 13¼x13***
737 A232 £2000 multi 2.00 2.00
738 A233 £2000 multi 2.00 2.00

Flags and Church of Saidet et Tallé, Deir al-Qamar — A234

2016, Apr. 2 Litho. ***Perf. 13¼x13***
739 A234 £250 multi .50 .50

Labor Day — A235

2016, Apr. 30 Litho. ***Perf. 13x13¼***
740 A235 £2000 multi 2.00 2.00

Martyr's Day — A236

2016, May 5 Litho. ***Perf. 13x13¼***
741 A236 £2000 multi 2.00 2.00

Fish of the Mediterranean Sea — A237

2016, July 9 Litho. ***Perf. 13x13¼***
742 A237 £2250 multi 2.25 2.25

Baalbek International Festival, 60th Anniv. — A238

2016, July 26 Litho. ***Perf. 13x13¼***
743 A238 £2000 multi 2.00 2.00

Lebanese Olympic Committee — A239

2016, Aug. 5 Litho. ***Perf. 13¼x13***
744 A239 £250 multi .50 .50

Elie Snaifer (1935-2005), Comedian — A240

2016, Sept. 6 Litho. ***Perf. 13¼x13***
745 A240 £250 multi .50 .50

Admittance to Universal Postal Union, 70th Anniv. — A241

2016, Oct. 8 Litho. ***Perf. 13x13¼***
746 A241 £2000 multi 2.00 2.00

Université la Sagesse, 140th Anniv. (in 2015) A242

2016, Oct. 22 Litho. ***Perf. 13¼x13***
747 A242 £2000 multi 2.00 2.00

Arab Postal Day — A243

Globe at: No. 748, £10,000, Right (blue background). No. 749, £10,000, Left (blue green background).

2016, Nov. 4 Litho. ***Perf. 13¼x13***
748-749 A243 Set of 2 37.50 37.50

Famous Men — A244

Contributors to Lebanese independence: No. 750, £250, Habib Abou Chahla, Speaker of Parliament. No. 751, £250, Adnan Al Hakim, member of Parliament. No. 752, £250, Saadi Al Mounla (1890-1975), Prime minister. No. 753, £250, Majid Arslan (1908-83), governmental minister. No. 754, £250, Rashid Baydoun (1889-1971), governmental minister. No. 755, £250, Camille Chamoun (1900-87), President. No. 756, £250, Mohamad El Fadi, member of Parliament. No. 757, £250, Hamid Frangieh (1907-81), member of Parliament. No. 758, £250, Pierre Gemayel (1905-84), member of Parliament. No. 759, £250, Sabri Hamadeh (1902-76), Speaker of Parliament. No. 760, £250, Maroun Kanaan (1890-1981), deputy of Jezzine. No. 761, £250, Abdul Hamid Karami (1890-1950), Prime minister. No. 762, £250, Henri Pharaon (1901-93), foreign minister. No. 763, £250, Saeb Salam (1905-2000), Prime minister. No. 764, £250, Selim Takla (1895-1945), foreign minister.

2016, Nov. 18 Litho. ***Perf. 13x13¼***
750-764 A244 Set of 15 7.25 7.25

Independence Day.

American University of Beirut, 150th Anniv. — A245

2016, Dec. 3 Litho. ***Perf. 13x13¼***
765 A245 £2000 multi 2.00 2.00

Zaki Nassif (1918-2004), Composer — A246

2016, Dec. 15 Litho. ***Perf. 13¼x13***
766 A246 £2000 multi 2.00 2.00

New Year 2017 — A247

2016, Dec. 29 Litho. ***Perf. 13¼x13***
767 A247 £5000 multi 5.00 5.00

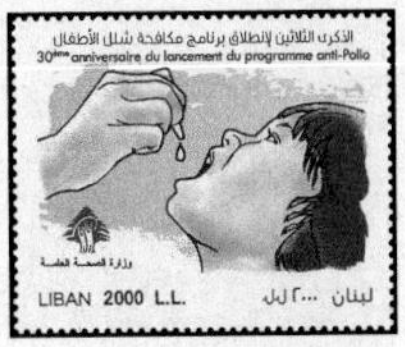

Anti-Polio Campaign, 30th Anniv. A248

2017, Jan. 20 Litho. ***Perf. 13¼x13***
768 A248 £2000 multi 2.00 2.00

International Women's Day — A249

2017, Mar. 29 Litho. ***Perf. 13¼x13***
769 A249 £10,000 multi 10.00 10.00

Museums — A250

Designs: No. 770, £2000, Sursock Museum. No. 771, £2000, Minerals from Mineral Museum, Beirut. No. 772, £2000, Sculptures from National Museum, Beirut.

2017, May 16 Litho. ***Perf. 13x13¼***
770-772 A250 Set of 3 12.00 12.00

National Museum, 75th anniv. (No. 772).

Dar Al Aytam Al Islamiya Orphanage A251

2017, June 13 Litho. ***Perf. 13x13¼***
773 A251 £2000 multi 2.00 2.00

World Music Day — A252

2017, June 21 Litho. ***Perf. 13¼x13***
774 A252 £250 multi .65 .65

Cedar of Lebanon — A253

2017, July 8 Litho. ***Perf. 13¼x13***
775 A253 £2250 multi 2.25 2.25

Mikhail Naimy (1889-1998), Writer — A254

2017, July 22 Litho. ***Perf. 13x13¼***
776 A254 £250 multi .65 .65

Army Day — A255

2017, July 31 Litho. ***Perf. 13¼x13***
777 A255 £2000 multi 2.00 2.00

Carlos Ghosn, Automobile Industry Executive — A256

2017, Aug. 28 Litho. ***Perf. 13¼x13***
778 A256 £2000 multi 2.00 2.00

Zalfa Chamoun (1910-71), Wife of Pres. Camille Chamoun — A257

2017, Oct. 6 Litho. ***Perf. 13x13¼***
779 A257 £2000 multi 2.00 2.00

Nasri Chamessedine (1927-83), Singer — A258

2017, Oct. 19 Litho. ***Perf. 13x13¼***
780 A258 £250 multi .65 .65

Caritas Lebanon Charity — A259

2017, Nov. 3 Litho. ***Perf. 13¼x13***
781 A259 £2000 multi 2.00 2.00

Mohamad Baalbaki (1921-2017), Journalist A260

2017, Nov. 9 Litho. ***Perf. 13¼x13***
782 A260 £2000 multi 2.00 2.00

Pres. Michel Aoun — A261

Pres. Aoun and Crowd A262

People Carrying Large Flag of Lebanon A263

2017, Dec. 6 Litho. ***Perf. 13x13¼***
783 A261 £5000 multi 5.00 5.00

Perf. 13¼x13
784 A262 £5000 multi 5.00 5.00
785 A263 £5000 multi 5.00 5.00
Nos. 783-785 (3) 15.00 15.00

St. Valentine's Day — A264

2018, Feb. 7 Litho. ***Perf. 13x13¼***
786 A264 £2000 multi 2.00 2.00

No. 786 has a heart-shaped hole.

Mohamad Chatah (1951-2013), Assassinated Diplomat — A265

2018, Feb. 22 Litho. ***Perf. 13x13¼***
787 A265 £250 multi .50 .50

Mahmoud Kahil (1936-2013), Editorial Cartoonist — A266

2018, Mar. 7 Litho. ***Perf. 13¼x13***
788 A266 £2000 multi 2.00 2.00

Rachid Solh (1926-2014), Prime Minister — A267

2018, Mar. 16 Litho. ***Perf. 13¼x13***
789 A267 £250 multi .50 .50

Elie Saab, Fashion Designer — A268

Litho. With Foil Application

2018, Mar. 29 ***Perf. 13¼x13***
790 A268 £2000 gold & multi 2.00 2.00

Sunset, Painting by Nizar Daher — A269

2018, Apr. 19 Litho. ***Perf. 13x13¼***
791 A269 £2000 multi 2.00 2.00

Our Lady of Mantara Shrine, Maghdouché A270

2018, Apr. 30 Litho. ***Perf. 13x13¼***
792 A270 £1750 multi 1.75 1.75

Traffic Safety Campaign A271

2018, May 2 Litho. ***Perf. 13x13¼***
793 A271 £2000 multi 2.00 2.00

2018 World Cup Soccer Championships, Russia — A272

2018 World Cup emblem and: £1250, Mascot Zabivaka. £2250, Soccer ball and Russian buildings.

2018, June 13 Litho. ***Perf. 13¼x13***
794-795 A272 Set of 2 6.75 6.75

A273

Litho. With Foil Application

2018, June 25 ***Perf. 13x13¼***
796 A273 £5000 multi 5.00 5.00

Riad Salamé, 25th Anniv. as Governor of the Central Bank of Lebanon.

Nasrallah Sfeir, Cardinal Patriarch Emeritus of Antioch and the Levant — A274

2018, July 3 Litho. ***Perf. 13x13¼***
797 A274 £2000 multi 2.00 2.00

Beiteddine Palace, Beiteddine A275

2018, July 9 Litho. ***Perf. 13x13¼***
798 A275 £2250 multi 2.25 2.25

Dr. Ghaleb Chahine, Politician, 50th Anniv. of Death — A276

2018, Aug. 8 Litho. ***Perf. 13¼x13***
799 A276 £500 multi 1.00 1.00

Emily Nasrallah (1931-2018), Writer — A277

2018, Sept. 5 Litho. ***Perf. 13x13¼***
800 A277 £1250 multi 1.25 1.25

Independence, 75th Anniv. — A278

2018, Nov. 19 Litho. ***Perf. 13¼x13***
801 A278 £10,000 multi 10.00 10.00

Sami Solh (1887-1968), Prime Minister — A279

2018, Dec. 27 Litho. ***Perf. 13x13¼***
802 A279 £1250 multi 1.25 1.25

Miniature Sheet

Mother's Day A280

No. 803 — Flower with petals in: a, Dark blue. b, Blue. c, Bright blue. d, Light blue. e, Pale blue. f, Dark purple. g, Red violet. h, Purple. i, Lilac. j, Pale lilac. k, Dark magenta. l, Magenta. m, Lilac rose. n, Pink. o, Pale pink. p, Bright vermilion. q, Orange red. r, Orange. s, Yellow. t, White.

2019, Mar. 20 Litho. ***Perf. 13¼x13***
803 A280 Sheet of 20 *150.00 150.00*
a.-t. £1250 Any single *7.50 7.50*

Waste Sorting — A281

Recycling emblem and: No. 804, £500, Organic waste (green background). No. 805, £500, Recyclable material (red background). No. 806, £500, Non-recyclable material (gray background).

2019, Apr. 9 Litho. ***Perf. 13¼x13***
804-806 A281 Set of 3 3.00 3.00

International Migratory Bird Day — A282

Designs: No. 807, £2250, Carduelis carduelis. No. 808, £2250, Cyanistes caeruleus. No. 809, £2250, Ciconia ciconia.

2019, May 13 Litho. ***Perf. 13x13¼***
807-809 A282 Set of 3 13.50 13.50

Court of Cassation, Cent. A283

2019, June 12 Litho. ***Perf. 13¼x13***
810 A283 £2250 multi 2.25 2.25

Traditional Costumes — A284

Designs: No. 811, £2000, 19th century Emir wearing tarboush. No. 812, £2000, 19th century Emira wearing tantour.

2019, July 8 Litho. ***Perf. 13x13¼***
811-812 A284 Set of 2 8.00 8.00

Express Mail Service, 20th Anniv. A285

2019, Sept. 10 Litho. ***Perf. 13¼x13***
813 A285 £2000 multi 2.00 2.00

Mohandas K. Gandhi (1869-1948), Indian Nationalist Leader — A286

2019, Sept. 30 Litho. ***Perf. 13x13¼***
814 A286 £1000 multi 2.00 2.00

Flag of Palestinian Authority, Doves, Dome of the Rock, Jerusalem A287

2019, Oct. 9 Litho. ***Perf. 13x13¼***
815 A287 £2250 multi 2.25 2.25

Jerusalem, capital of Palestinian Authority.

Sacred Heart College, Beirut, 125th Anniv. A288

2019, Oct. 26 Litho. ***Perf. 13¼x13***
816 A288 £1000 multi 1.00 1.00

Evangelical Church, Beirut, 150th Anniv. — A289

2019, Nov. 28 Litho. ***Perf. 13x13¼***
817 A289 £1000 multi 1.00 1.00

Miniature Sheet

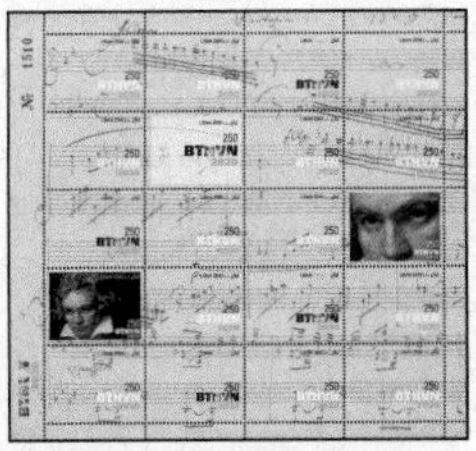

Piano Fantasia in G Minor (Op. 77), by Ludwig Van Beethoven (1770-1827) — A290

No. 818 — Score in Beethoven's handwriting truncated at right: a, Clefs and key signatures, "BTHVN" in white. b, Barred notes in top staff, "BTHVN" in white. c, Note and rest on top staff, "BTHVN" in color. d, Rest on top staff, "BTHVN" in white. e, Start of slur (rising arc above staff), "BTHVN" in white. f, White rectangle and "BTHVN" in color over score. g, Notation above staff, first two notes in series of barred notes, "BTHVN" in white. h, Barred notes in staff, continuation of barred noted from lower staff from above, "BTHVN" in white. i, Two staffs, rest on bottom staff, "BTHVN" in color. j, "Poco" to left of denomination, "BTHVN" in white. k, Four barred notes on lower staff near denomination, "BTHVN" in white. l, Eyes and nose of Beethoven. m, Face and collar of Beethoven. n, Two sets of three barred notes near denomination "BTHVN" in white. o, Two sets of three barred notes, "BTHVN" in color. p, Vertical measure line in center, running through top staff, "BTHVN" in white. q, Lower staff with change of key (four flats), "BTHVN" in white. r, Rest under denomination, "BTHVN" in color. s, Vertical measure line at left, notes similiar to those shown on "r," "BTHVN" in white. t, No measure line at left, notes similar to those on "s," "BTHVN" in white.

2020, Mar. 4 Litho. ***Perf. 13x13¼***
818 A290 £250 Sheet of 20, #a-t *52.50 52.50*

"Thank You to Our Hero Caregivers" A291

2020, July 1 Litho. ***Perf. 13x13¼***
819 A291 £1000 multi *1.00 1.00*

Tribute to coronavirus pandemic caregivers.

Lebanes Red Cross, 75th Anniv. — A292

2020, July 9 Litho. ***Perf. 13x13¼***
820 A292 £1000 multi 1.00 1.00

Traditional Foods — A293

No. 821: a, Hummus. b, Kibbeh. c, Tabbouleh. d, Manousheh.

2020, July 17 Litho. ***Perf. 13x13¼***
821 Horiz. strip of 4 5.75 5.75
a.-d. A293 £1000 Any single 1.40 1.40

Georges Schehadé (1905-89), Writer — A294

2020, Aug. 12 Litho. ***Perf. 13¼x13***
822 A294 £500 multi .80 .80

Ameen Rihani (1876-1940), Writer — A295

2020, Aug. 31 Litho. ***Perf. 13¼x13***
823 A295 £500 multi .80 .80

State of Greater Lebanon, Cent. A296

2020, Sept. 1 Litho. ***Perf. 13¼x13***
824 A296 £1000 met gray brn 1.60 1.60

Michel Eddé (1928-2019), Politician — A297

2020, Sept. 17 Litho. ***Perf. 13¼x13***
825 A297 £500 multi .80 .80

Elias Hoayek (1843-1931), Patriarch of Antioch — A298

2020, Sept. 28 Litho. ***Perf. 13x13¼***
826 A298 £2000 multi 2.00 2.00

Diplomatic Relations Between Lebanon and Mexico, 75th Anniv. — A299

No. 827: a, Templo Mayor Archaeological Site and Metropolitan Cathedral, Mexico City (text in Spanish). b, Temple of Bacchus, Baalbek, Lebanon (text in Arabic).

2020, Sept. 30 Litho. ***Perf. 13¼x13***
827 A299 £5000 Horiz. pair, #a-b 13.50 13.50

See Mexico Nos. 3178-3179.

Beirut Ammonium Nitrate Explosion of Aug. 4, 2020 — A300

2020, Oct. 12 Litho. ***Imperf.***
828 A300 £10,000 multi 10.00 10.00

No. 828 has simulated perforations. Proceeds of the sale of No. 828 go to the Lebanese Civil Defense for the rebuilding of Beirut.

United Nations, 75th Anniv. — A301

2020, Oct. 24 Litho. *Perf. 13¼x13*
829 A301 £2250 multi 2.40 2.40

Arab League, 75th Anniv. — A302

2020, Nov. 13 Litho. *Perf. 13x13¼*
830 A302 £500 multi .80 .80

Fourth Arab Economic and Social Development Summit, Beirut A303

2020, Nov. 25 Litho. *Perf. 13¼x13*
831 A303 £2000 multi 2.00 2.00

Brummana High School, Brummana — A304

2020, Dec. 18 Litho. *Perf. 13½x13*
832 A304 £1000 multi 1.40 1.40

Garden of the Patriarchs, Qannoubine A305

2021, Mar. 25 Litho. *Perf. 13x13¼*
833 A305 £10,000 multi *13.50 13.50*

ESA Business School, Beirut, 25th Anniv. — A306

2021, Apr. 15 Litho. *Perf. 13x13¼*
834 A306 £2000 multi *2.75 2.75*

Earth Day — A307

No. 835: a, Jabal Moussa Reserve. b, Chouf Biosphere Reserve. c, Côtière de Tyr Nature Reserve. d, Aammiq Wetland.

2021, Apr. 21 Litho. *Perf. 13x13¼*
835 Horiz. strip of 4 *11.00 11.00*
a.-d. A307 £2000 Any single *2.75 2.75*

Rhythmical Composition in Red, Painting by Saloua Raouda Choucair (1916-2017) — A308

2021, June 2 Litho. *Perf. 13x13¼*
836 A308 £5000 multi *6.25 6.25*

Miniature Sheet

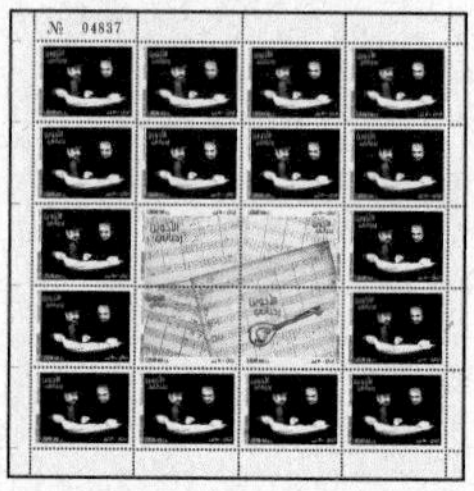

A309

No. 837: a, Sheet music of the Rahbani Brothers, inscriptions in white frame at left and top. b, Sheet music of the Rahbani Brothers, inscriptions in white frame at top and right. c, Sheet music of the Rahbani Brothers, inscriptions in white frame at left and bottom. d, Sheet music of Rahbani Brothers, stringed instrument, inscriptions in white frame at bottom and right. e, Assi (1923-86) and Mansour Rahbani (1925-2009), musicians and composers.

2021, June 21 Litho. *Perf. 13x13¼*
837 A309 Sheet of 20, #837a-837d, 16 #837e *13.50 13.50*
a.-e. £500 Any single *.65 .65*

Traditional Handcrafted Jewelry — A310

2021, Aug. 24 Litho. *Perf. 13¼x13*
838 A310 £2250 multi *3.00 3.00*

Rachid Nakhlé (1873-1939), Lyricist of Lebanese National Anthem A311

Wadia Sabra (1876-1952), Composer of Lebanese National Anthem A312

2021, Nov. Litho. *Perf. 13¼x13*
839 A311 £1750 multi *2.40 2.40*
840 A312 £1750 multi *2.40 2.40*

Salwa and Adib Haddad, Television Actors — A313

2021, Dec. 10 Litho. *Perf. 13x13¼*
841 A313 £1000 multi *1.40 1.40*

SEMI-POSTAL STAMPS

Stamps of 1925 Srchd. in Red or Black

1926 Unwmk. *Perf. 14x13½*
B1 A2 0.25p + 0.25p ol blk 4.25 4.25
B2 A2 0.25p + 0.50p yel grn (B) 4.25 4.25
B3 A2 0.25p + 0.75p brn org (B) 4.25 4.25
B4 A2 0.50p + 1p mag 4.75 4.75
B5 A2 0.50p 1.25p 5.00 5.00
B6 A2 0.50p + 1.50p rose red (B) 5.00 5.00
a. Double surcharge 40.00 30.00
B7 A2 0.75p + 2p dk brn 5.00 5.00
B8 A2 0.75p + 2.50p pck bl 5.50 5.50
B9 A2 1p + 3p org brn 5.50 5.50
B10 A2 1p + 5p vio (B) 5.50 5.50
B11 A3 2p + 10p vio brn (B) 5.50 5.50
B12 A2 5p + 25p ultra 5.50 5.50
Nos. B1-B12 (12) 60.00 60.00

On No. B11 the surcharge is set in six lines to fit the shape of the stamp. All values of this series exist with inverted surcharge. Value each, $17.50.

See Nos. CB1-CB4.

Catalogue values for unused stamps in this section, from this point to the end of the section, are for Never Hinged items.

Boxing SP1

1961, Jan. 12 Litho. *Perf. 13*
B13 SP1 2.50p + 2.50p shown .40 .25
B14 SP1 5p + 5p Wrestling .40 .25
B15 SP1 7.50p + 7.50p Shot put .40 .25
Nos. B13-B15,CB12-CB14 (6) 10.95 4.50

17th Olympic Games, Rome, Aug. 25-Sept. 11, 1960.

Nos. B13-B15 with Arabic and French Overprint in Black, Blue or Green and two Bars through Olympic Inscription: "CHAMPIONNAT D'EUROPE DE TIR, 2 JUIN 1962"

1962, June 2
B16 SP1 2.50p + 2.50p blue & brn (Bk) .40 .25
B17 SP1 5p + 5p org & brn (G) .70 .25
B18 SP1 7.50p + 7.50p vio & brn (Bl) .80 .35
Nos. B16-B18,CB15-CB17 (6) 7.55 3.60

European Marksmanship Championships held in Lebanon.

Red Cross — SP2

No. B20, Stylized profile. No. B21, Globe, emblems, dove.

1988, June 8 Litho. *Perf. 14*
B19 SP2 £10 + £1 shown 1.75
B20 SP2 £20 + £2 multi 2.75
B21 SP2 £30 + £3 multi 3.75
Nos. B19-B21 (3) 8.25

AIR POST STAMPS

Nos. 10-13 with Additional Overprint

1924 Unwmk. *Perf. 14x13½*
C1 A18 2p on 40c 13.00 *13.00*
a. Double surcharge 52.50 52.50
C2 A18 3p on 60c 13.00 *13.00*
a. Invtd. surch. and ovpt. 87.50 87.50
C3 A18 5p on 1fr 13.00 *13.00*
a. Dbl. surch. and ovpt. 72.50 72.50
b. "5" omitted 300.00
C4 A18 10p on 2fr 13.00 *13.00*
a. Invtd. surch. and ovpt. 110.00 110.00
b. Dbl. surch. and ovpt. 60.00 60.00
Nos. C1-C4 (4) 52.00 *52.00*

Nos. 33, 35-37 Overprinted

C5 A18 2p on 40c 13.00 13.00
a. Overprint reversed 45.00
C6 A18 3p on 60c 13.00 13.00
a. Overprint reversed 45.00
C7 A18 5p on 1fr 13.00 13.00
a. Overprint reversed 45.00
C8 A18 10p on 2fr 13.50 13.50
a. Overprint reversed 45.00
b. Double surcharge 45.00
Nos. C5-C8 (4) 52.50 52.50

Nos. 57, 59-61 Overprinted in Green

1925
C9 A2 2p dark brown 4.00 4.00
C10 A2 3p orange brown 4.00 4.00
C11 A2 5p violet 4.00 4.00
a. Inverted overprint
C12 A3 10p violet brown 4.00 4.00
Nos. C9-C12 (4) 16.00 16.00

Nos. 57, 59-61 Ovptd. in Red — c

1926
C13 A2 2p dark brown 5.25 5.25
C14 A2 3p orange brown 5.25 5.25
C15 A2 5p violet 5.25 5.25
C16 A3 10p violet brown 5.25 5.25
Nos. C13-C16 (4) 21.00 21.00

Airplane pointed down on No. C16.
Exist with inverted overprint. Value, each $45.

Issues of Republic under French Mandate

Nos. C13-C16 Overprinted — d

1927
C17 A2 2p dark brown 4.75 4.75
C18 A2 3p orange brown 4.75 4.75
C19 A2 5p violet 4.75 4.75
C20 A3 10p violet brown 4.75 4.75
Nos. C17-C20 (4) 19.00 19.00

On No. C19 "Republique Libanaise" is above the bars. Overprint set in two lines on No. C20.

Nos. C17-C20 with Additional Ovpt. — e

1928 Black Overprint
C21 A2 2p brown 12.50 10.00
a. Double overprint 65.00 65.00
b. Inverted overprint 65.00 65.00
C22 A2 3p orange brown 12.50 10.00
a. Double overprint 65.00 65.00
C23 A2 5p violet 12.50 10.00
a. Double overprint 65.00 65.00
C24 A3 10p violet brown 12.50 10.00
a. Double overprint 65.00 65.00
Nos. C21-C24 (4) 50.00 40.00

On Nos. C21-C24 the airplane is always in red.

Nos. 52, 54, 57, 59-62 Ovptd. in Red or Black — f

1928

C25	A2	2p	dark brown	4.50	4.50
C26	A2	3p	orange brown	3.00	3.00
C27	A2	5p	violet	4.50	4.50
C28	A3	10p	violet brown	4.50	4.50

1929

C33	A2	0.50p	yellow green	1.25	1.25
a.			Inverted overprint	45.00	45.00
C34	A2	1p	magenta (Bk)	1.00	1.00
a.			Inverted overprint	45.00	45.00
C35	A2	25p	ultra	190.00	160.00
a.			Inverted overprint	525.00	525.00
			Nos. C25-C34 (6)	18.75	18.75
			Nos. C25-C35 (7)	208.75	178.75

On Nos. C25-C28 the airplane is always in red.

On No. C28 the overprinted orientation is horizontal. The bars covering the old country names are at the left.

The red overprint of a silhouetted plane and "Republique Libanaise," as on Nos. C25-C27, was also applied to Nos. C9-C12. These are believed to have been essays, and were not regularly issued.

No. 62 with Surcharge Added in Red

Two types of surcharge:

I — The "5" of "15 P." is italic. The "15" is 4mm high. Arabic characters for "Lebanese Republic" and for "15 P." are on same line in that order.

II — The "5" is in Roman type (upright) and smaller; "15" is 3½mm high. Arabic for "Lebanese Republic" is centered on line by itself, with Arabic for "15 P." below right end of line.

C36	A2	15p on 25p ultra (I)	225.00	175.00
a.		Type II (#106)	*800.00*	*800.00*

Nos. 102 Overprinted Type "c" in Blue

C37	A2	0.50p on 0.75p	1.00	1.00
a.		Airplane inverted	45.00	
b.		French and Arabic surch. invtd.		
c.		"P" omitted		
d.		Airplane double	50.00	

No. 55 Surcharged in Red

1930

C38	A2	2p on 1.25p dp green	1.75	1.25
a.		Inverted surcharge	72.50	45.00

Airplane over Racheya — AP2

Designs: 1p, Plane over Broumana. 2p, Baalbek. 3p, Hasroun. 5p, Byblos. 10p, Kadicha River. 15p, Beirut. 25p, Tripoli. 50p, Kabeljas. 100p, Zahle.

1930-31 Photo. *Perf. 13½*

C39	AP2	0.50p	dk violet ('31)	.50	.50
C40	AP2	1p	yellow grn ('31)	.80	.80
C41	AP2	2p	dp orange ('31)	2.50	2.50
C42	AP2	3p	magenta ('31)	2.50	2.50
C43	AP2	5p	indigo	2.50	2.50
C44	AP2	10p	orange red	3.25	3.25
C45	AP2	15p	orange brn	3.25	3.25
C46	AP2	25p	gray vio ('31)	4.75	4.75
C47	AP2	50p	dp claret	9.00	9.00
C48	AP2	100p	olive brown	12.00	12.00
			Nos. C39-C48 (10)	41.05	41.05

Nos. C39-C48 exist imperforate. Value, set $200.

Tourist Publicity Issue

Skiing in Lebanon — AP12

Bay of Jounie — AP13

1936, Oct. 12

C49	AP12	0.50p	slate grn	3.00	3.00
C50	AP13	1p	red orange	3.75	3.75
C51	AP12	2p	black violet	3.75	3.75
C52	AP13	3p	yellow grn	4.00	4.00
C53	AP12	5p	brown car	4.00	4.00
C54	AP13	10p	orange brn	4.00	4.00
C55	AP13	15p	dk carmine	37.50	37.50
C56	AP12	25p	green	125.00	125.00
			Nos. C49-C56 (8)	185.00	185.00

Nos. C49-C56 exist imperforate. Value, set $650.

Lebanese Pavilion at Exposition AP14

1937, July 1 *Perf. 13½*

C57	AP14	0.50p	olive black	1.50	1.50
C58	AP14	1p	yellow green	1.50	1.50
C59	AP14	2p	dk red orange	1.50	1.50
C60	AP14	3p	dk olive grn	1.50	1.50
C61	AP14	5p	deep green	2.00	2.00
C62	AP14	10p	carmine lake	9.00	9.00
C63	AP14	15p	rose lake	10.00	10.00
C64	AP14	25p	orange brn	17.50	17.50
			Nos. C57-C64 (8)	44.50	44.50

Paris International Exposition.

Arcade of Beit-ed-Din Palace — AP15

Ruins of Baalbek — AP16

1937-40 Engr. *Perf. 13*

C65	AP15	0.50p	ultra ('38)	.35	.25
C66	AP15	1p	hen brn ('40)	.35	.25
C67	AP15	2p	sepia ('40)	.35	.25
C68	AP15	3p	rose ('40)	3.25	1.25
C69	AP15	5p	lt green ('40)	.35	.25
C70	AP16	10p	dull violet	.35	.25
C71	AP16	15p	turq bl ('40)	2.75	1.75
C72	AP16	25p	violet ('40)	6.00	5.00
C73	AP16	50p	yel grn ('40)	11.00	7.00
C74	AP16	100p	brown ('40)	6.00	3.50
			Nos. C65-C74 (10)	30.75	19.75

Nos. C65-C74 exist imperforate.

Medical College of Beirut — AP17

1938, May 9 Photo. *Perf. 13*

C75	AP17	2p	green	2.40	*2.75*
C76	AP17	3p	orange	2.40	*2.75*
			Never hinged	4.75	
C77	AP17	5p	lilac gray	4.50	*5.25*
C78	AP17	10p	lake	8.50	*9.75*
			Nos. C75-C78 (4)	17.80	*20.50*

Medical Congress.

Maurice Noguès and View of Beirut AP18

1938, July 15 *Perf. 11*

C79	AP18	10p brown carmine	4.00	1.50
a.		Souv. sheet of 4, perf. 13½	35.00	20.00
b.		Perf. 13½	9.00	4.50

10th anniversary of first Marseille-Beirut flight, by Maurice Noguès.

No. C79a has marginal inscriptions in French and Arabic. Exists imperf.; value $250.

Independent Republic

Plane Over Mt. Lebanon — AP19

1942, Sept. 18 Litho. *Perf. 11½*

C80	AP19	10p	dk brown vio	5.75	*6.50*
C81	AP19	50p	dk gray grn	5.75	*6.50*

1st anniv. of the Proclamation of Independence, Nov. 26, 1941.

Nos. C80 and C81 exist imperforate.

Bechamoun AP20

Rachaya Citadel — AP21

Air View of Beirut — AP22

1943, May 1 *Perf. 11½*

C82	AP20	25p	yellow grn	4.75	4.75
C83	AP20	50p	orange	6.50	5.50
C84	AP21	100p	buff	6.50	5.50
C85	AP21	200p	blue vio	8.00	7.25
C86	AP22	300p	sage green	21.00	17.50
C87	AP22	500p	sepia	42.50	32.50
			Nos. C82-C87 (6)	89.25	73.00

2nd anniv. of the Proclamation of Independence. Nos. C82-C87 exist imperforate.

See Nos. 163-166. For overprints see Nos. C91-C96.

Bhannes Sanatorium AP23

1943, July 8 Photo.

Black Overprint

C88	AP23	20p	orange	3.75	2.75
C89	AP23	50p	steel blue	4.25	3.50
C90	AP23	100p	rose violet	6.00	4.50
			Nos. C88-C90 (3)	14.00	10.75

Arab Medical Congress, Beirut.

Nos. C82 to C87 Overprinted in Red, Blue or Violet

1944, Nov. 23

C91	AP20	25p	yel grn (R)	7.25	7.25
C92	AP20	50p	orange (Bl)	12.00	12.00
C93	AP21	100p	buff (V)	14.00	14.00
C94	AP21	200p	blue vio (R)	25.00	25.00
C95	AP22	300p	sage grn (R)	32.50	30.00
C96	AP22	500p	sepia (Bl)	65.00	60.00
			Nos. C91-C96 (6)	155.75	148.25

Return to office of the President and his ministers, Nov. 22, 1943.

Catalogue values for unused stamps in this section, from this point to the end of the section, are for Never Hinged items.

Falls of Litani AP24

The Cedars AP25

1945, July Unwmk. Litho.

C97	AP24	25p	gray brown	3.50	2.10
C98	AP24	50p	rose violet	5.00	2.75
C99	AP25	200p	violet	15.00	5.25
C100	AP25	300p	brown black	26.50	10.00
			Nos. C97-C100 (4)	50.00	20.10

Lebanese Soldiers at Bir Hacheim — AP26

1946, May 8

C101	AP26	15p	bl blk, org & red org	1.00	.25
C102	AP26	20p	red, lil & bl	1.00	.60
C103	AP26	25p	brt bl, org & red	1.25	.25
C104	AP26	50p	gray blk, bl & red	1.75	.50
C105	AP26	100p	pur, pink & red	5.00	1.25
C106	AP26	150p	brn, pink & red	6.00	3.75
			Nos. C101-C106 (6)	16.00	6.60

Victory of the Allied Nations in WWII, 1st anniv.

Three imperf. souvenir sheets of 14 exist. They contain one each of Nos. C101-C106 and 189-196 in changed colors. One has sepia inscriptions, and one on thin white card has blue inscriptions. Value $30 each. The third, with blue inscriptions, is on thick honeycombed chamois card. Value $110.

Night Herons Type

1946, Sept. 11

C107	A35	10p	orange	5.75	.80
C108	A35	25p	ultra	6.50	.25
C109	A35	50p	blue green	20.00	1.30
C110	A35	100p	dk vio brn	30.00	5.25
			Nos. C107-C110 (4)	62.25	7.60

Symbols of Communications AP28

1946, Nov. 22

C111	AP28	25p	deep blue	1.75	.70
C112	AP28	50p	green	2.50	.80
C113	AP28	75p	orange red	4.25	1.75
C114	AP28	150p	brown black	6.00	2.75
			Nos. C111-C114 (4)	14.50	6.00

Arab Postal Congress, Sofar, 1946.

Stone Tablet, Dog River and Pres. Bechara el-Khoury AP29

1947, Feb. 11

C115	AP29	25p	ultra	7.00	.35
C116	AP29	50p	dull rose	9.00	.60
C117	AP29	75p	gray black	11.00	.65
C118	AP29	150p	blue green	17.50	1.40
			Nos. C115-C118 (4)	44.50	3.00

Evacuation of foreign troops from Lebanon, Dec. 31, 1946.

Bay of Jounie — AP30

Government House, Beirut — AP31

1947, Feb. 11 Grayish Paper

C119	AP30	5p	dp blue grn	.50	.25
C120	AP30	10p	rose vio	.75	.25
C121	AP30	15p	vermilion	1.75	.25
C122	AP30	20p	orange	2.00	.25
a.			20p red orange, white paper	1.75	.25
C123	AP30	25p	deep blue	2.40	.25
C124	AP30	50p	henna brn	4.00	.25
C125	AP30	100p	chocolate	8.50	.25
C126	AP31	150p	dk vio brn	14.50	.40
C127	AP31	200p	slate	22.00	1.90
C128	AP31	300p	black	35.00	5.00
			Nos. C119-C128 (10)	91.40	9.05

See Nos. C145A-C147B.

Post Horn and Letter AP32

Phoenician Galley AP33

1947, June 17 **Litho.**

C129	AP32	10p	brt ultra	1.40	.40
C130	AP32	15p	rose car	1.60	.40
C131	AP32	25p	bright blue	2.00	.65
C132	AP33	50p	dk slate grn	4.75	.75
C133	AP33	75p	purple	5.75	1.55
C134	AP33	100p	dark brown	7.25	2.00
			Nos. C129-C134 (6)	22.75	5.75

Lebanon's participation in the 12th UPU congress, Paris.

Lebanese Village — AP34

1948, Sept. 1 ***Perf. 11½***

C135	AP34	5p	dp orange	.60	.25
C136	AP34	10p	rose lilac	1.40	.25
C137	AP34	15p	orange brn	3.00	.25
C138	AP34	20p	slate	3.75	.25
C139	AP34	25p	Prus blue	8.50	.80
C140	AP34	50p	gray black	14.00	1.15
			Nos. C135-C140 (6)	31.25	2.95

Apollo AP35

Minerva AP36

1948, Nov. 23 **Unwmk.**

C141	AP35	7.50p	blue & lt blue	3.25	.80
C142	AP35	15p	black & gray	4.00	1.00
C143	AP35	20p	rose brn & rose	4.25	1.55
C144	AP36	35p	car rose & rose	6.50	2.00
C145	AP36	75p	bl grn & lt green	12.00	4.00
			Nos. C141-C145 (5)	30.00	9.35

UNESCO. Nos. C141-C145 exist imperforate, and combined with Nos. 220-224 in an imperforate souvenir sheet on thin buff cardboard, with black inscriptions in top margin in Arabic and at bottom in French. Value $250.

Bay Type of 1947 Redrawn

1949 **White Paper**

C145A	AP30	10p	rose lilac	9.00	1.00
C146	AP30	15p	dark green	11.00	1.25
C147	AP30	20p	orange	25.00	9.00
C147A	AP30	25p	dark blue	65.00	3.25
C147B	AP30	50p	brick red	275.00	35.00
			Nos. C145A-C147B (5)	385.00	49.50

In the redrawn designs, Nos. C145A, C147 and C147B have zeros with broader centers than in the 1947 issue (Nos. C120, C122 and C124).

Helicopter Mail Delivery — AP37

1949, Aug. 16 **Unwmk.** ***Perf. 11½***

C148	AP37	25p	deep blue	6.75	3.50
C149	AP37	50p	green	10.00	4.00
a.			Souvenir sheet of 5, #225-227, C148-C149	65.00	30.00

UPU, 75th anniv. No. 149a exists on thin cardboard. Value $250.

Homing Birds — AP38

Pres. Bechara el-Khoury AP39

1950, Aug. 8 **Litho.**

C150	AP38	5p	violet blue	2.75	.65
C151	AP38	15p	rose vio	3.00	.70
C152	AP39	25p	chocolate	2.25	.95
C153	AP39	35p	gray green	3.25	1.40
a.			Souvenir sheet of 6, #243-244, C150-C153, chamois paper	70.00	55.00
			Nos. C150-C153 (4)	11.25	3.70

Conference of Emigrants, 1950.

Crusader Castle, Sidon Harbor — AP40

1950, Sept. 7

C154	AP40	10p	chocolate	1.00	.25
C155	AP40	15p	dark green	2.00	.25
C156	AP40	20p	crimson	4.00	.25
C157	AP40	25p	ultra	7.00	.80
C158	AP40	50p	gray black	10.00	2.25
			Nos. C154-C158 (5)	24.00	3.80

1951, June 9 **Redrawn** **Typo.**

C159	AP40	10p	grnsh black	1.60	.25
C160	AP40	15p	black brown	2.40	.25
C161	AP40	20p	vermilion	2.40	.25
C162	AP40	25p	deep blue	3.25	.25
C163	AP40	35p	lilac rose	6.50	1.90
C164	AP40	50p	indigo	9.00	1.90
			Nos. C159-C164 (6)	25.15	4.80

Nos. C154-C158 are lithographed from a fine-screen halftone; Nos. C159-C164 are typographed and much coarser, with larger plane and many other differences.

Khaldé International Airport, Beirut — AP41

Design: 50p to 300p, Amphitheater, Byblos.

1952 **Litho.** ***Perf. 11½***

C165	AP41	5p	crimson	1.50	.25
C166	AP41	10p	dark gray	1.50	.25
C167	AP41	15p	rose lilac	1.75	.25
C168	AP41	20p	brown org	2.00	.25
C169	AP41	25p	grnsh blue	2.00	.25
C170	AP41	35p	violet bl	2.75	.25
C171	AP41	50p	blue green	14.00	.60
C172	AP41	100p	deep blue	55.00	2.40
C173	AP41	200p	dk blue grn	35.00	3.50
C174	AP41	300p	black brn	52.50	7.50
			Nos. C165-C174 (10)	168.00	15.50

Lockheed Constellation — AP42

1953, Oct. 1

C175	AP42	5p	yellow green	.75	.25
C176	AP42	10p	deep plum	1.00	.25
C177	AP42	15p	scarlet	1.40	.25
C178	AP42	20p	aqua	1.75	.25
C179	AP42	25p	blue	3.25	.25
C180	AP42	35p	orange brn	4.75	.25
C181	AP42	50p	violet blue	9.00	.25
C182	AP42	100p	black brown	13.00	1.90
			Nos. C175-C182 (8)	34.90	3.65

Ruins at Baalbek — AP43

Irrigation Canal, Litani — AP44

1954, Mar.

C183	AP43	5p	yel green	.60	.25
C184	AP43	10p	dull purple	.75	.25
C185	AP43	15p	carmine	1.20	.25
C186	AP43	20p	brown	1.60	.25
C187	AP43	25p	dull blue	2.00	.25
C188	AP43	35p	black brn	2.40	.25
C189	AP44	50p	dk olive grn	8.00	.25
C190	AP44	100p	dp car	15.50	.30
C191	AP44	200p	dark brown	22.00	.60
C192	AP44	300p	dk gray blue	42.50	1.25
			Nos. C183-C192 (10)	96.55	3.90

See Nos. C229-C232.

Khaldé International Airport, Beirut — AP45

1954, Apr. 23 ***Perf. 11½***

C193	AP45	10p	pink & rose red	1.00	.25
C194	AP45	25p	dp bl & gray bl	2.25	.40
C195	AP45	35p	dl brn & yel brn	3.50	.75
C196	AP45	65p	dp grn & grn	5.00	1.30
			Nos. C193-C196 (4)	11.75	2.70

Opening of Beirut's Intl. Airport. Exist imperf.

Arab Postal Union Type of Regular Issue, 1955

1955, Jan. 1 ***Perf. 13½x13***

C197	A52	2.50p	yellow brn	1.25	.25

Rotary Emblem — AP47

1955, Feb. 23 ***Perf. 11½***

C198	AP47	35p	dull green	1.25	.35
C199	AP47	65p	dull blue	2.00	.45

Rotary International, 50th anniversary.

Skiing Among the Cedars — AP48

1955, Feb. 24 **Litho.**

C200	AP48	5p	blue green	1.60	.25
C201	AP48	15p	crimson	1.75	.25
C202	AP48	20p	lilac	2.25	.25
C203	AP48	25p	blue	4.00	.25
C204	AP48	35p	olive brn	5.25	.25
C205	AP48	50p	chocolate	9.00	.60
C206	AP48	65p	deep blue	14.00	1.75
			Nos. C200-C206 (7)	37.85	3.60

See Nos. C233-C235. For surcharge see No. C271.

Tourist — AP49

1955, Sept. 10 **Unwmk.** ***Perf. 13***

C207	AP49	2.50p	brn vio & lt bl	.40	.25
C208	AP49	12.50p	ultra & lt bl	.55	.25
C209	AP49	25p	indigo & lt bl	1.20	.25
C210	AP49	35p	ol grn & lt bl	1.40	.25
a.			Sheet of 4, #C207-C210, imperf.	18.00	6.25
			Nos. C207-C210 (4)	3.55	1.00

Tourist Year. No. C210a is printed on cardboard.

Oranges — AP50

Designs: 25p, 35p, 50p, Grapes, vert. 65p, 100p, 200p, Apples.

1955, Oct. 15

C211	AP50	5p	yel grn & yel	1.00	.25
C212	AP50	10p	dk grn & dp orange	1.10	.25
C213	AP50	15p	yel grn & red orange	1.25	.25
C214	AP50	20p	olive & yel org	1.90	.25
C215	AP50	25p	blue & vio bl	2.60	.25
C216	AP50	35p	green & cl	3.25	.25
C217	AP50	50p	blk brn & dl yel	3.25	.25
C218	AP50	65p	green & lemon	6.25	.25
C219	AP50	100p	yel grn & dp orange	8.00	.70
C220	AP50	200p	green & car	14.00	3.50
			Nos. C211-C220 (10)	42.60	6.20

For surcharge see No. C265.

United Nations Emblem — AP52

1956, Jan. 23 ***Perf. 11½***

C221	AP52	35p	violet blue	4.25	1.50
C222	AP52	65p	green	5.25	1.75

UN, 10th anniv. (in 1955).

An imperf. souvenir sheet contains one each of Nos. C221 and C222. Value $72.50.

Temple of the Sun Colonnade, Masks and Lion's Head — AP53

Temple of Bacchus, Baalbek — AP54

Design: 35p, 65p, Temple of the Sun colonnade, masks and violincello.

1956, Dec. 10 **Litho.** ***Perf. 13***

C223	AP53	2.50p	dark brown	.85	.25
C224	AP53	10p	green	1.10	.25
C225	AP54	12.50p	light blue	1.10	.25
C226	AP54	25p	brt vio bl	1.60	.35
C227	AP53	35p	red lilac	3.00	.45
C228	AP53	65p	slate blue	4.25	.90
			Nos. C223-C228 (6)	11.90	2.45

International Festival at Baalbek.

Skiing Type of 1955 Redrawn and

Irrigation Canal, Litani — AP55

1957 **Litho.** ***Perf. 11½***

C229	AP55	10p	brt violet	.65	.25
C230	AP55	15p	orange	.90	.25
C231	AP55	20p	yel green	1.00	.25
C232	AP55	25p	slate blue	1.10	.25
C233	AP48	35p	gray green	2.50	.25
C234	AP48	65p	dp claret	4.00	.25
C235	AP48	100p	brown	6.00	.65
			Nos. C229-C235 (7)	16.15	2.15

Different Arabic characters used for the country name; letters in "Liban" larger.

For surcharge see No. C271.

Pres. Camille Chamoun and King Saud — AP56

King Saud, Pres. Chamoun, King Hussein, Pres. Kouatly, King Faisal, Pres. Nasser AP57

Pres. Chamoun and: No. C237, King Hussein. No. C238, Pres. Kouatly. No. C239, King Faisal. No. C240, Pres. Nasser. 25p, Map of Lebanon.

1957, July 15 Litho. *Perf. 13*

C236	AP56	15p green	.60	.25
C237	AP56	15p blue	.60	.25
C238	AP56	15p red lilac	.60	.25
C239	AP56	15p red orange	.60	.25
C240	AP56	15p claret	.60	.25
C241	AP56	25p blue	.60	.25
C242	AP57	100p dl red brn	5.00	1.20
		Nos. C236-C242 (7)	8.60	2.70

Congr. of Arab Leaders, Beirut, 11/12-15/56.

Fencing — AP58

50p, Pres. Chamoun and stadium with flags.

1957, Sept. 12 Unwmk. *Perf. 13*

C243	AP58	35p claret	2.75	1.25
C244	AP58	50p lt green	3.50	1.75

2nd Pan-Arab Games, Beirut. See note on souvenir sheet below No. 314.

Symbols of Communications AP59

Power Plant, Chamoun AP60

1957 *Perf. 13x13½, 11½ (AP60)*

C245	AP59	5p brt green	.55	.25
C246	AP59	10p yel orange	.60	.25
C247	AP59	15p brown	.60	.25
C248	AP59	20p maroon	.80	.25
C249	AP59	25p violet blue	1.10	.25
C250	AP60	35p violet brn	1.40	.25
C251	AP60	50p green	1.60	.25
C252	AP60	65p sepia	2.25	.25
C253	AP60	100p dark gray	3.00	.55
		Nos. C245-C253 (9)	11.90	2.55

Plane at Airport — AP61

Cogwheel AP62

1958-59 Unwmk. *Perf. 13*

C254	AP61	5p green	.50	.25
C255	AP61	10p magenta	.65	.25
C256	AP61	15p dull violet	.80	.25
C257	AP61	20p orange ver	.95	.25
C258	AP61	25p dk vio bl	1.20	.25
C259	AP62	35p grnsh gray	1.40	.25
C260	AP62	50p aquamarine	1.90	.25
C261	AP62	65p pale brown	3.25	.25
C262	AP62	100p brt ultra	3.75	.25
		Nos. C254-C262 (9)	14.40	2.25

Nos. C259 and C261 Srchd. in Black or Dark Blue

1959 Unwmk. Litho. *Perf. 13*

C263	AP62	30p on 35p grnsh gray	.80	.25
C264	AP62	40p on 65p pale brn (Bl)	1.25	.40

Arab Engineers Congress.

No. C217 Surcharged

1959, Sept. 1

C265	AP50	40p on 50p blk brn & dull yel	1.25	.40

Arab Lawyers Congress.

Myron's Discobolus AP63

Wreath and Hand Holding Torch AP64

1959, Oct. 11 Litho. *Perf. 11½*

C266	AP63	15p shown	.80	.25
C267	AP63	30p Weight lifter	1.00	.25
C268	AP64	40p shown	1.55	.35
		Nos. C266-C268 (3)	3.35	.85

3rd Mediterranean Games, Beirut.

A souvenir sheet on white cardboard contains one each of Nos. C266-C268, imperf. Sold for 100p. Value *$55*

Soldiers and Flag — AP65

1959, Nov. 25 *Perf. 13½x13*

C269	AP65	40p sep, brick red & sl	1.50	.30
C270	AP65	60p sep, dk grn & brick red	2.00	.35

Lebanon's independence, 1941-1959.

No. C234 Surcharged with New Value and Bars

1959, Dec. 15 *Perf. 11½*

C271	AP48	40p on 65p dp claret	2.60	.30

Hands Planting Tree — AP66

1960, Jan. 18 Litho. *Perf. 11½*

C272	AP66	20p rose vio & grn	.90	.25
C273	AP66	40p dk brn & green	1.10	.35

Friends of the Tree Society, 25th anniv.

Postal Administration Building — AP67

1960, Feb. Unwmk. *Perf. 13*

C274	AP67	20p green	.80	.25

President Fuad Chehab — AP68

1960, Mar. 12 Photo. *Perf. 13½*

C275	AP68	5p green	.40	.25
C276	AP68	10p Prus blue	.40	.25
C277	AP68	15p orange brn	.40	.25
C278	AP68	20p brown	.45	.25
C279	AP68	30p olive	.65	.25
C280	AP68	40p dull red	.75	.25
C281	AP68	50p blue	.80	.25
C282	AP68	70p red lilac	.90	.25
C283	AP68	100p dark green	1.60	.35
		Nos. C275-C283 (9)	6.35	2.35

Uprooted Oak Emblem — AP69

1960, Apr. 7 Litho. *Perf. 13½x13*

Size: 20½x36½mm

C284	AP69	25p yellow brn	.95	.25
C285	AP69	40p green	1.10	.30
a.		Souv. sheet of 2, #C284-C285, imperf.	35.00	15.50

Size: 20x36mm

C284b	AP69	25p yellow brown	1.00	.40
C285b	AP69	40p green	1.75	.65

World Refugee Year, 7/1/59-6/30/60.

No. C285a sold for 150p.

Nos. C284b-C285b appear fuzzy and pale when compared to the bolder, clear-cut printing of Nos. C284-C285. Issue date: July 18.

Nos. C284b-C285b exist with carmine surcharges of "30P.+15P." (on C284b) and "20P.+10P." (on C285b), repeated in Arabic, with ornaments covering original denominations. Value, $17.

Martyrs' Monument — AP70

Martyrs of May 6th: 70p, Statues from Martyrs' monument, vert.

1960, May 6 *Perf. 13x13½, 13½x13*

C286	AP70	20p rose lilac & grn	.65	.25
C287	AP70	40p Prus grn & dk grn	.80	.25
C288	AP70	70p gray olive & blk	1.60	.40
		Nos. C286-C288 (3)	3.05	.90

Pres. Chehab and King of Morocco — AP71

1960, June 1 *Perf. 13x13½*

C289	AP71	30p choc & dk brn	.90	.30
C290	AP71	70p blk, dk brn & buff	1.75	.35

Visit of King Mohammed V of Morocco.

A souvenir sheet of 2 on white cardboard contains Nos. C289-C290, imperf. Value $72.50.

Child Learning to Walk — AP72

1960, Aug. 16 Litho. *Perf. 13½x13*

C291	AP72	20p shown	.80	.25
C292	AP72	60p Mother & child	1.60	.35
		Nos. C291-C292,CB10-CB11 (4)	5.55	1.40

Day of Mother and Child, Mar. 21-22.

Bird, Ribbon of Flags and Map of Beirut — AP73

40p, Cedar & birds. 70p, Globes & cedar, horiz.

Perf. 13½x13, 13x13½

1960, Sept. 20 Unwmk.

C293	AP73	20p multicolored	.50	.25
C294	AP73	40p vio, bl & grn	.75	.25
C295	AP73	70p multicolored	1.00	.25
		Nos. C293-C295 (3)	2.25	.75

Union of Lebanese Emigrants in the World. A souvenir sheet of 3 contains Nos. C293-C295, imperf., printed on cardboard. Sold for 150p. Value $22.50.

Pres. Chehab and Map of Lebanon — AP74

1961, Feb. Litho. *Perf. 13½x13*

C296	AP74	5p bl grn & yel grn	.40	.25
C297	AP74	10p brown & bister	.40	.25
C298	AP74	70p vio & rose lilac	1.00	.30

Casino, Maameltein Lebanon — AP75

1961 *Perf. 13x13½*

C299	AP75	15p rose claret	.55	.25
C300	AP75	30p greenish blue	.90	.25
C301	AP75	40p brown	1.10	.25
C302	AP75	200p bis brn & dl bl	4.25	1.15
		Nos. C296-C302 (7)	8.60	2.70

On Nos. C299-C301, the denomination, inscription and trees differ from No. C302.

UN, 15th Anniv. (in 1960) — AP76

20p, UN Emblem & map of Lebanon, vert. 30p, UN Emblem & symbolic building, vert. 50p, UN Headquarters, New York.

1961, May 5 *Perf. 13½x13, 13x13½*

C306	AP76	20p lake & lt blue	.65	.25
C307	AP76	30p green & beige	.70	.25
C308	AP76	50p vio bl & grnsh bl	1.30	.25
a.		Souvenir sheet of 3	9.00	9.00
		Nos. C306-C308 (3)	2.65	.75

No. C308a contains one each of Nos. C306-C308, imperf., against a light blue background showing UN emblem. Sold for 125p.

Pottery Workers — AP77

1961, July 11 Litho. *Perf. 13x13½*

C309	AP77	30p shown	2.50	.25
C310	AP77	70p Weaver	1.40	.25

Issued for Labor Day, 1961.

Fireworks AP78

Water Skiing AP79

70p, Tourists on boat ride through cave.

1961, Aug. 8 *Perf. 13½x13, 13x13½*

C311	AP78	15p lt pur & dk bl	1.40	.90
C312	AP79	40p blue & pink	2.00	1.10
C313	AP79	70p dull brn & pink	.85	.45
		Nos. C311-C313 (3)	4.25	2.45

Issued to publicize tourist month.

Highway Circle at Dora, Beirut Suburb — AP80

1961, Aug. ***Perf. 11½***

C314 AP80 35p yellow green .95 .25
C315 AP80 50p orange brown 1.15 .40
C316 AP80 100p gray 1.15 .50
Nos. C314-C316 (3) 3.25 1.15

Beach at Tyre — AP81

Afka Falls — AP82

1961, Sept. **Litho.** ***Perf. 13***

C317 AP81 5p carmine rose .50 .25
C318 AP81 10p brt violet .75 .25
C319 AP81 15p bright blue .80 .25
C320 AP81 20p orange 1.00 .25
C321 AP81 30p brt green 1.25 .25
C322 AP82 40p dp claret 1.00 .25
C323 AP82 50p ultramarine 1.10 .25
C324 AP82 70p yellow green 1.50 .25
C325 AP82 100p dark brown 2.00 .35
Nos. C317-C325 (9) 9.90 2.35

See Nos. C341-C342.

Entrance to UNESCO Building AP83

"UNESCO" and Cedar AP84

Design: 50p, UNESCO headquarters, Paris.

1961, Nov. 20 **Unwmk.** ***Perf. 12***

C326 AP83 20p bl, buff & blk .60 .25
C327 AP84 30p lt grn, blk & mag .70 .25
C328 AP83 50p multicolored 1.10 .25
Nos. C326-C328 (3) 2.40 .75

UNESCO, 15th anniv.

Emir Bechir and Fakhr-el-Din El Maani — AP85

1961, Dec. 30 **Litho.**

C329 AP85 25p Cedar emblem .60 .25
C330 AP85 50p shown .90 .25

See note after No. 375.

Scout Types of Regular Issue, 1962

15p, Trefoil & cedar emblem. 20p, Hand making Scout sign. 25p, Lebanese Scout emblem.

1962, Mar. 1 **Unwmk.** ***Perf. 12***

C331 A70 15p grn, blk & red .65 .25
C332 A69 20p lil, blk & yel .75 .25
C333 A70 25p multicolored 1.25 .35
Nos. C331-C333 (3) 2.65 .85

Arab League Building, Cairo — AP86

1962, Mar. 20 ***Perf. 13***

C334 AP86 20p ultra & lt bl .55 .25
C335 AP86 30p red brn & pink .70 .25
C336 AP86 50p grn & grnsh bl .90 .25
Nos. C334-C336 (3) 2.15 .75

Arab League Week, Mar. 22-28. See Nos. C372-C375.

Nos. C334-C336 exist perforated 10½. Only 50 sets known. Value, $180.

Blacksmith AP87

Farm Tractor AP88

Perf. 13½x13, 13x13½

1962, May 1 **Litho.**

C337 AP87 5p green & lt blue .45 .25
C338 AP87 10p blue & pink .45 .25
C339 AP88 25p brt vio & pink .70 .25
C340 AP88 35p car rose & blue .90 .25
Nos. C337-C340 (4) 2.50 1.00

Issued for Labor Day.

Types of 1961 Redrawn with Large Numerals Similar to Redrawn Regular Issue of 1962

1962 ***Perf. 13***

C341 AP81 5p carmine rose 1.10 .25
C342 AP82 40p deep claret 6.25 .40

Hand Reaching for Malaria Eradication Emblem — AP89

Design: 70p, Malaria eradication emblem.

1962, July 2 **Litho.** ***Perf. 13½x13***

C349 AP89 30p tan & brown .80 .25
C350 AP89 70p bluish lil & vio 1.00 .40

WHO drive to eradicate malaria.

Bas-relief of Isis, Kalabsha Temple, Nubia — AP90

1962, Aug. 1 **Unwmk.** ***Perf. 13***

C351 AP90 30p yellow green 1.60 .25
C352 AP90 50p slate 3.25 .50

Campaign to save historic monuments in Nubia.

Spade, Heart, Diamond, Club — AP91

1962, Sept.

C353 AP91 25p car rose, blk & red 3.25 1.25
C354 AP91 40p multicolored 4.50 1.25

European Bridge Championship Tournament.

College Student — AP92

1962, Oct. 1 ***Perf. 12***

C355 AP92 45p multicolored .75 .25

Issued for Students' Day, Oct. 1.

Sword Severing Chain — AP93

1962, Nov. 22 **Litho.** ***Perf. 13***

C356 AP93 25p vio, lt bl & red .90 .25
C357 AP93 25p bl, lt bl & red .90 .25
C358 AP93 25p grn, lt bl & red .90 .25
Nos. C356-C358 (3) 2.70 .75

19th anniversary of independence.

Fruit Type of Regular Issue, 1962

5p, Apricots. 10p, 30p, Plums. 20p, 40p, Apples. 50p, Pears. 70p, Medlar. 100p, Lemons.

1962 **Vignette Multicolored**

C359 A72 5p orange brown .50 .25
C360 A72 10p black .55 .25
C361 A72 20p brown .60 .25
C362 A72 30p gray .75 .25
C363 A72 40p dark gray 1.00 .25
C364 A72 50p light brown 1.25 .25
C365 A72 70p gray olive 1.50 .30
C366 A72 100p blue 3.00 .50
Nos. C359-C366 (8) 9.15 2.30

Harvest — AP94

Design: 15p, 20p, UN Emblem and hand holding Wheat Emblem, horiz.

1963, Mar. 21 **Litho.** ***Perf. 13***

C367 AP94 2.50p ultra & yel .40 .25
C368 AP94 5p gray grn & yel .40 .25
C369 AP94 7.50p rose lil & yel .40 .25
C370 AP94 15p rose brn & pale grn .65 .25
C371 AP94 20p rose & pale grn .80 .25
Nos. C367-C371 (5) 2.65 1.25

FAO "Freedom from Hunger" campaign.

Redrawn Type of 1962, Dated "1963"

Design: Arab League Building, Cairo.

1963, Mar. **Unwmk.** ***Perf. 12***

C372 AP86 5p violet & lt blue .40 .25
C373 AP86 10p green & lt blue .40 .25
C374 AP86 15p claret & lt blue .45 .25
C375 AP86 20p gray & lt blue .60 .25
Nos. C372-C375 (4) 1.85 1.00

Issued for Arab League Week.

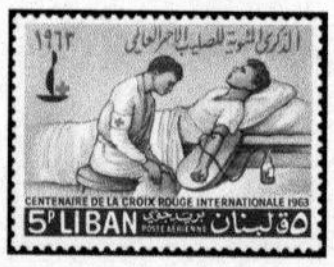

Blood Transfusion AP95

Design: 35p, 40p, Nurse and infant, vert.

1963, Oct. 5 **Unwmk.** ***Perf. 13***

C376 AP95 5p green & red .40 .25
C377 AP95 20p grnsh bl & red .45 .25
C378 AP95 35p org, red & blk .60 .25
C379 AP95 40p purple & red .80 .25
Nos. C376-C379 (4) 2.25 1.00

Centenary of International Red Cross.

Lyre Player and Columns — AP96

1963, Nov. 7 **Unwmk.** ***Perf. 13***

C380 AP96 35p lt bl, org & blk 1.25 .25

International Festival at Baalbek.

Lebanon Flag, Rising Sun — AP97

1964, Jan. 8 **Litho.**

C381 AP97 5p bluish grn, ver & yel .40 .25
C382 AP97 10p yel grn, ver & yel .45 .25
C383 AP97 25p ultra, ver & yel .60 .25
C384 AP97 40p gray, ver & yel .90 .30
Nos. C381-C384 (4) 2.35 1.05

20th anniversary of Independence.

Sports Type of Regular Issue, 1964

1964, Feb. 11 **Unwmk.** ***Perf. 13***

C385 A76 15p Tennis .45 .25
C386 A76 17.50p Swimming, horiz. .55 .25
C387 A76 30p Skiing, horiz. .80 .25
a. Souvenir sheet of 3 13.00 10.00
Nos. C385-C387 (3) 1.80 .75

No. C387a contains three imperf. stamps similar to Nos. C385-C387 with simulated orange brown perforations and green marginal inscription. Sold for 100p.

Anemone — AP98

1964, June 9 **Unwmk.** ***Perf. 13***

C391 AP98 5p Lily .40 .25
C392 AP98 10p Ranunculus .50 .25
C393 AP98 20p shown .60 .25
C394 AP98 40p Tuberose .80 .25
C395 AP98 45p Rhododendron .90 .25
C396 AP98 50p Jasmine 1.00 .25
C397 AP98 70p Yellow broom 1.60 .25
Nos. C391-C397 (7) 5.80 1.75

Girls Jumping Rope — AP99

Children's Day: 20p, 40p, Boy on hobby-horse, vert.

1964, Apr. 8

C398 AP99 5p emer, org & red .40 .25
C399 AP99 10p yel brn, org & red .45 .25
C400 AP99 20p dp ultra, lt bl & org .50 .25
C401 AP99 40p lil, lt bl & yel .80 .25
Nos. C398-C401 (4) 2.15 1.00

Flame and UN Emblem — AP100

40p, Flame, UN emblem and broken chain.

1964, May 15 **Litho.** **Unwmk.**

C402 AP100 20p sal, org & brn .40 .25
C403 AP100 40p lt bl, gray bl & org .60 .25

15th anniv. (in 1963) of the Universal Declaration of Human Rights.

Arab League Conference — AP101

1964, Apr. 20 *Perf. 13x13½*

C404	AP101	5p blk & pale sal	.75	.25
C405	AP101	10p black	.90	.30
C406	AP101	15p green	1.25	.40
C407	AP101	20p dk brn & pink	1.60	.50
		Nos. C404-C407 (4)	4.50	1.45

Arab League meeting.

Child in Crib — AP102

Beit-ed-Din Palace and Children — AP103

1964, July 20 *Perf. 13½x13, 13½*

C408	AP102	2.50p multicolored	.40	.25
C409	AP102	5p multicolored	.40	.25
C410	AP102	15p multicolored	.50	.25
C411	AP103	17.50p multicolored	.65	.25
C412	AP103	20p multicolored	.75	.25
C413	AP103	40p multicolored	.80	.25
		Nos. C408-C413 (6)	3.50	1.50

Ball of the Little White Beds, Beirut, for the benefit of children's hospital beds.

Clasped Hands and Map of Lebanon — AP104

1964, Oct. 16 **Litho.** *Perf. 13½x13*

C414	AP104	20p yel grn, yel & gray	.65	.25
C415	AP104	40p slate, yel & gray	1.10	.40

Congress of the Intl. Lebanese Union.

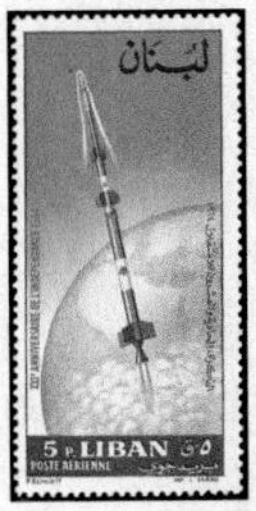

Rocket Leaving Earth — AP105

Battle Scene AP106

1964, Nov. 24 **Unwmk.** *Perf. 13½*

C416	AP105	5p multicolored	.40	.25
C417	AP105	10p multicolored	.40	.25
C418	AP106	40p sl blue & blk	.80	.25
C419	AP106	70p dp claret & blk	1.60	.40
		Nos. C416-C419 (4)	3.20	1.15

21st anniversary of independence.

Woman in Costume — AP107

Design: 10p, 15p, Man in costume.

1965, Jan. 11 **Litho.** *Perf. 13½*

C420	AP107	10p multicolored	.60	.25
C421	AP107	15p multicolored	.75	.25
C422	AP107	25p green & multi	1.00	.30
C423	AP107	40p brown & multi	1.20	.40
		Nos. C420-C423 (4)	3.55	1.20

International Festival at Baalbek.

Equestrian AP108

25p, Target shooting, vert. 40p, Gymnast on rings.

1965, Jan. 23 **Engr.** *Perf. 13*

C424	AP108	15p shown	.40	.25
C425	AP108	25p mutlicolored	.50	.25
C426	AP108	40p multicolored	.60	.25
a.		Souvenir sheet of 3, #C424-C426, imperf.	14.50	7.50
		Nos. C424-C426 (3)	1.50	.75

18th Olympic Games, Tokyo, Oct. 10-25, 1964. No. 426a sold for 100p.

Heliconius Cybria — AP109

30p, Pericallia matronula. 40p, Red admiral. 45p, Satyrus semele. 70p, Machaon. 85p, Aurore. 100p, Morpho cypris. 200p, Erasmia sanguiflua. 300p, Papilio crassus. 500p, Charaxes ameliae.

1965 **Unwmk.** *Perf. 13*

Size: 36x22mm

C427	AP109	30p multi	*3.00*	.25
C428	AP109	35p multi	*4.25*	.35
C429	AP109	40p multi	*5.25*	.35
C430	AP109	45p multi	*6.00*	.50
C431	AP109	70p multi	*7.25*	.75
C432	AP109	85p multi	*8.00*	.90
C433	AP109	100p multi	*12.00*	1.00
C434	AP109	200p multi	*19.00*	1.25
C435	AP109	300p multi	*26.00*	3.50

Engr. and Litho.

Perf. 12

Size: 35x25mm

C436	AP109	500p lt ultra & blk	*52.50*	7.00
		Nos. C427-C436 (10)	*143.25*	15.85

For surcharges see Nos. C654-C656.

Pope Paul VI and Pres. Charles Helou AP110

1965, June 28 **Photo.** *Perf. 12*

C437	AP110	45p gold & brt vio	4.50	.90
a.		Souv. sheet of 1, imperf.	45.00	29.00

Visit of Pope Paul VI to Lebanon. No. C437a sold for 50p.

Cedars of Friendship AP111

1965, Oct. 16 **Photo.** *Perf. 13x12½*

C438	AP111	40p multicolored	1.50	.25

Cocoon, Spindle and Silk — AP112

15p, 30p, 40p, 50p, Silk weaver at loom.

1965, Oct. 16 *Perf. 12½x13*

Design in Buff and Bright Green

C439	AP112	2.50p brown	1.25	.25
C440	AP112	5p dk olive grn	1.25	.25
C441	AP112	7.50p Prus blue	1.25	.25
C442	AP112	15p deep ultra	1.25	.25
C443	AP112	30p deep claret	1.50	.25
C444	AP112	40p brown	2.40	.25
C445	AP112	50p rose brown	3.50	.60
		Nos. C439-C445 (7)	12.40	2.10

Parliament Building — AP113

1965, Oct. 26 *Perf. 13x12½*

C446	AP113	35p red, buff & brn	.65	.25
C447	AP113	40p emer, buff & brn	.80	.25

Centenary of the Lebanese parliament.

UN Headquarters, NYC, UN Emblem and Lebanese Flags — AP114

1965, Nov. 10 **Engr.** *Perf. 12*

C448	AP114	2.50p dull blue	.40	.25
C449	AP114	10p magenta	.40	.25
C450	AP114	17.50p dull violet	.40	.25
C451	AP114	30p green	.50	.25
C452	AP114	40p brown	.70	.25
		Nos. C448-C452 (5)	2.40	1.25

UN, 20th anniv. A souvenir sheet contains one 40p imperf. stamp in bright rose lilac. Sold for 50p. Value $15.

Playing Card King, Laurel and Cedar — AP115

1965, Nov. 15 **Photo.** *Perf. 12½x13*

C453	AP115	2.50p multicolored	.60	.25
C454	AP115	15p multicolored	.90	.25
C455	AP115	17.50p multicolored	1.00	.25
C456	AP115	40p multicolored	1.15	.25
		Nos. C453-C456 (4)	3.65	1.00

Intl. Bridge Championships. A souvenir sheet contains two imperf. stamps similar to Nos. C454 and C456. Sold for 75p. Value $22.50.

Dagger in Map of Palestine — AP116

1965, Dec. 12 *Perf. 12½x11*

C457	AP116	50p multicolored	4.50	.50

Deir Yassin massacre, Apr. 9, 1948.

ITU Emblem, Old and New Communication Equipment and Early Bird Satellite — AP117

1966, Apr. 15 *Perf. 13x12½*

C458	AP117	2.50p multi	.45	.25
C459	AP117	15p multi	.50	.25
C460	AP117	17.50p multi	.55	.25
C461	AP117	25p multi	.90	.25
C462	AP117	40p multi	1.20	.25
		Nos. C458-C462 (5)	3.60	1.25

ITU, centenary (in 1965).

Folk Dancers Before Temple of Bacchus AP118

Designs: 7.50p, 15p, Dancers before Temple of Jupiter, vert. 30p, 40p, Orchestra before Temple of Bacchus.

1966, July 20 **Unwmk.** *Perf. 12*

Gold Frame

C463	AP118	2.50p brn vio, bl & orange	.50	.25
C464	AP118	5p mag, bl & org	.50	.25
C465	AP118	7.50p vio bl, bl & pink	.50	.25
C466	AP118	15p pur, bl & pink	.55	.25
C467	AP118	30p dk grn, org & blue	.60	.25
C468	AP118	40p vio, org & bl	1.00	.25
		Nos. C463-C468 (6)	3.65	1.50

11th International Festival at Baalbek.

Opening of WHO Headquarters, Geneva — AP119

1966, Aug. 25 **Engr.** *Perf. 12*

C469	AP119	7.50p dp yel grn	.35	.25
C470	AP119	17.50p car rose	.45	.25
C471	AP119	25p blue	.70	.25
		Nos. C469-C471 (3)	1.50	.75

Skier — AP120

Designs: 5p, Children on toboggan. 17.50p, Cedar in snow. 25p, Ski lift.

1966, Sept. 15 **Photo.** *Perf. 12x11½*

C472	AP120	2.50p multi	.40	.25
C473	AP120	5p multi	.40	.25
C474	AP120	17.50p multi	.60	.25
C475	AP120	25p multi	.80	.25
		Nos. C472-C475 (4)	2.20	1.00

International Festival of Cedars.

Sarcophagus of King Ahiram with Early Alphabet — AP121

15p, Phoenician ship. 20p, Map of the Mediterranean Sea showing Phoenician travel routes, and ship. 30p, Phoenician with alphabet tablet.

Litho. & Engr.

1966, Sept. 25 *Perf. 12*

C476	AP121	10p dl grn, blk & lt brn	.40	.25
C477	AP121	15p rose lil, brn & ocher	.40	.25
C478	AP121	20p tan, dk brn & bl	.50	.25
C479	AP121	30p org, dk brn & yel	.80	.25
		Nos. C476-C479 (4)	2.10	1.00

Invention of alphabet by Phoenicians.

Child in Bathtub and UNICEF Emblem — AP122

5p, Boy in rowboat. 7.50p, Girl skier. 15p, Girl feeding bird. 20p, Boy doing homework. 50p, Children of various races, horiz.

1966, Oct. 10 Photo. *Perf. 11½x12*

C480 AP122 2.50p multi .40 .25
C481 AP122 5p multi .40 .25
C482 AP122 7.50p multi .50 .25
C483 AP122 15p multi .60 .25
C484 AP122 20p multi .80 .25
Nos. C480-C484 (5) 2.70 1.25

Miniature Sheet

Imperf

C485 AP122 50p dl yellow & multi 6.00 3.00

UNICEF; World Children's Day. No. C485 contains one horizontal stamp 43x33mm.

Scenic Type of Regular Issue, 1966

Designs: 10p, Waterfall, Djezzine. 15p, Castle of the Sea, Saida. 20p, Amphitheater, Jubayl (Byblos). 30p, Temple of the Sun, Baalbek. 50p, Beit-ed-Din Palace. 60p, Church of Christ the King, Nahr-el-Kalb. 75p, Abu Bakr Mosque, Tripoli.

1966, Oct. 12 *Perf. 12x11½*

C486 A82 10p gold & multi .40 .25
C487 A82 15p gold & multi .50 .25
C488 A82 20p gold & multi .60 .25
C489 A82 30p gold & multi .80 .25
C490 A82 50p gold & multi 1.40 .25
C491 A82 60p gold & multi 1.60 .25
C492 A82 75p gold & multi 2.40 .25
Nos. C486-C492 (7) 7.70 1.75

Symbolic Water Cycle — AP123

15p, 20p, Different wave pattern without sun.

1966, Nov. 15 Photo. *Perf. 12½*

C493 AP123 5p red, bl & vio bl .40 .25
C494 AP123 10p org, bl & brn .40 .25
C495 AP123 15p org, emer & dk brn .50 .25
C496 AP123 20p org, emer & grnsh blue .60 .25
Nos. C493-C496 (4) 1.90 1.00

Hydrological Decade (UNESCO), 1965-74.

Daniel Bliss — AP124

Designs: 30p, Chapel, American University, Beirut. 50p, Daniel Bliss, D.D., and American University, horiz.

1966, Dec. 3

C497 AP124 20p grn, yel & brn .50 .25
C498 AP124 30p red brn, grn & blue .60 .25

Souvenir Sheet

Imperf

C499 AP124 50p grn, brn & org brown 3.00 1.50

Cent. of American University, Beirut, founded by the Rev. Daniel Bliss (1823-1916). Nos. C497-C498 are printed each with alternating labels showing University emblem.

No. C499 contains one stamp 59x37mm.

Flags of Arab League Members, Hand Signing Scroll AP125

1967, Aug. 2 Photo. *Perf. 12x11½*

C500 AP125 5p brown & multi .40 .25
C501 AP125 10p multicolored .40 .25
C502 AP125 15p black & multi .45 .25
C503 AP125 20p multicolored .55 .25
Nos. C500-C503 (4) 1.80 1.00

Signing of Arab League Pact in 1945.

Veteran's War Memorial Building, San Francisco AP126

10p, 20p, 30p, Scroll, flags of Lebanon & UN.

1967, Sept. 1 Photo. *Perf. 12x11½*

C504 AP126 2.50p blue & multi .50 .25
C505 AP126 5p multicolored .50 .25
C506 AP126 7.50p multicolored .50 .25
C507 AP126 10p blue & multi .50 .25
C508 AP126 20p multicolored .60 .25
C509 AP126 30p multicolored .75 .25
Nos. C504-C509 (6) 3.35 1.50

San Francisco Pact (UN Charter), 22nd anniv.

Ruins at Baalbek AP127

Intl. Tourist Year: 10p, Ruins at Anjar. 15p, Bridge over Ibrahim River and ruins. 20p, Boat on underground lake, Jaita cave. 50p, St. George's Bay, Beirut.

1967, Sept. 25 *Perf. 12½*

C510 AP127 5p multicolored .50 .25
C511 AP127 10p multicolored .60 .25
C512 AP127 15p violet & multi .80 .25
C513 AP127 20p brn & multi .95 .25
Nos. C510-C513 (4) 2.85 1.00

Souvenir Sheet

Imperf

C514 AP127 50p multicolored *22.00 16.00*

View of Tabarja AP128

Views: 15p, Pigeon Rock and shore, Beirut. 17.50p, Beit-ed-Din Palace. 20p, Ship at Sidon. 25p, Tripoli. 30p, Beach at Byblos. 35p, Ruins, Tyre. 40p, Temple of Bacchus, Baalbek.

1967, Oct. *Perf. 12x11½*

C515 AP128 10p multi *.60* .25
C516 AP128 15p multi *1.15* .25
C517 AP128 17.50p multi *1.60* .25
C518 AP128 20p multi *1.60* .25
C519 AP128 25p multi *1.60* .25
C520 AP128 30p multi *2.25* .25
C521 AP128 35p multi *3.00* .25
C522 AP128 40p multi *4.00* .25
Nos. C515-C522 (8) *15.80* 2.00

Intl. Tourist Year; used as a regular airmail issue.

India Day AP129

1967, Oct. 30 Engr. *Perf. 12*

C523 AP129 2.50p orange .40 .25
C524 AP129 5p magenta .40 .25
C525 AP129 7.50p brown .40 .25
C526 AP129 10p blue .45 .25
C527 AP129 15p green .50 .25
Nos. C523-C527 (5) 2.15 1.25

Globe and Arabic Inscription AP130

Design: 10p, 20p, 30p, UN emblem.

1967, Nov. 25 Engr. *Perf. 12*

C528 AP130 2.50p rose .40 .25
C529 AP130 5p gray blue .40 .25
C530 AP130 7.50p green .40 .25
C531 AP130 10p brt carmine .40 .25
C532 AP130 20p violet blue .50 .25
C533 AP130 30p dark green .65 .25
Nos. C528-C533 (6) 2.75 1.50

Lebanon's admission to the UN. A 100p rose red souvenir sheet in the globe design exists. Value, $5.50.

Basking Shark — AP131

Fish: 30p, Needlefish. 40p, Pollack. 50p, Cuckoo wrasse. 70p, Red mullet. 100p, Rainbow trout.

1968, Feb. Photo. *Perf. 12x11½*

C534 AP131 20p multi 1.40 .25
C535 AP131 30p multi 1.40 .25
C536 AP131 40p multi 2.10 .25
C537 AP131 50p multi 3.00 .25
C538 AP131 70p multi 5.25 .25
C539 AP131 100p multi 6.50 .25
Nos. C534-C539 (6) 19.65 1.50

Ski Jump AP132

5p, 7.50p, 10p, Downhill skiers (various). 25p, Congress emblem (skis and cedar).

1968 *Perf. 12½x11½*

C540 AP132 2.50p multicolored .40 .25
C541 AP132 5p multicolored .40 .25
C542 AP132 7.50p multicolored .40 .25
C543 AP132 10p multicolored .40 .25
C544 AP132 25p multicolored .60 .25
Nos. C540-C544 (5) 2.20 1.25

26th Intl. Ski Congress, Beirut. A 50p imperf. souvenir sheet exists in design of the 25p. Value, $6.50.

Emir Fakhr al-Din II — AP133

2.50p, Emira Khaskiah. 10p, Citadel of Sidon, horiz. 15p, Citadel of Chekif & grazing sheep, horiz. 17.50p, Citadel of Beirut & harbor, horiz.

Perf. 11½x12, 12x11½

1968, Feb. 20 Litho.

C546 AP133 2.50p multicolored .40 .25
C547 AP133 5p multicolored .40 .25
C548 AP133 10p multicolored .40 .25
C549 AP133 15p multicolored .60 .25
C550 AP133 17.50p multicolored .60 .25
Nos. C546-C550 (5) 2.40 1.25

In memory of the Emir Fakhr al-Din II. A 50p imperf. souvenir sheet exists showing the Battle of Anjar. Value $11.50.

Roman Bust — AP134

Ruins of Tyre: 5p, Colonnade, horiz. 7.50p, Arch, horiz. 10p, Banquet, bas-relief.

Litho. & Engr.

1968, Mar. 20 *Perf. 12*

C552 AP134 2.50p pink, brn & buff .40 .25
C553 AP134 5p yel, brn & lt bl .50 .25
C554 AP134 7.50p lt grnsh bl, brn & yel .65 .25
C555 AP134 10p sal, brn & lt bl .80 .25
a. Souvenir sheet 18.00 14.00
Nos. C552-C555 (4) 2.35 1.00

No. C555a contains one dark brown and light blue stamp, perf. 10½x11½. Sold for 50p. Exists imperf. Value $22.50.

For surcharge see No. C657.

Emperor Justinian — AP135

Design: 15p, 20p, Justinian and map of the Mediterranean, horiz.

Perf. 11½x12, 12x11½

1968, May 10 Photo.

C556 AP135 5p blue & multi .45 .25
C557 AP135 10p blue & multi .45 .25
C558 AP135 15p red & multi .50 .25
C559 AP135 20p blue & multi .55 .25
Nos. C556-C559 (4) 1.95 1.00

Beirut, site of one of the greatest law schools in antiquity; Emperor Justinian (483-565), who compiled and preserved the Roman law.

Arab League Emblem — AP136

1968, June 6 Photo. *Perf. 12x11½*

C560 AP136 5p orange & multi .40 .25
C561 AP136 10p multicolored .40 .25
C562 AP136 15p pink & multi .50 .25
C563 AP136 20p multicolored .65 .25
Nos. C560-C563 (4) 1.95 1.00

Issued for Arab League Week.

Cedar and Globe Emblem AP137

1968, July 10

C564 AP137 2.50p sal pink, brn & green .40 .25
C565 AP137 5p gray, brn & grn .45 .25
C566 AP137 7.50p brt bl, brn & grn .50 .25
C567 AP137 10p yel grn, brn & grn .60 .25
Nos. C564-C567 (4) 1.95 1.00

3rd Congress of Lebanese World Union.

Temple of Jupiter, Baalbek AP138

Designs: 10p, Fluted pilasters, cella of Bacchus Temple. 15p, Corniche, south peristyle of Jupiter Temple, horiz. 20p, Gate, Bacchus Temple. 25p, Ceiling detail, south peristyle of Bacchus Temple.

1968, Sept. 25 Photo. *Perf. 12½*

C568	AP138	5p	gold & multi	.40	.25
C569	AP138	10p	gold & multi	.40	.25
C570	AP138	15p	gold & multi	.50	.25
C571	AP138	20p	gold & multi	.60	.25
C572	AP138	25p	gold & multi	.80	.25
	Nos. C568-C572 (5)			2.70	1.25

13th Baalbek International Festival.

Broad Jump and Phoenician Statue AP139

Designs: 10p, High jump and votive stele, Phoenician, 6th century B.C. 15p, Fencing and Olmec jade head, 500-400 B.C. 20p, Weight lifting and axe in shape of human head, Vera Cruz region. 25p, Aztec stone calendar and Phoenician ship.

1968, Oct. 19 Photo. *Perf. 12x11½*

C573	AP139	5p	lt ultra, yel & gray	.45	.25
C574	AP139	10p	mag, lt ultra & blk	.45	.25
C575	AP139	15p	cit, ocher & brn	.45	.25
C576	AP139	20p	dp org, brn & ocher	.55	.25
C577	AP139	25p	light brown	.90	.25
	Nos. C573-C577 (5)			2.80	1.25

19th Olympic Games, Mexico City, 10/12-27.

Human Rights Flame and Tractor — AP140

Human Rights Flame and: 15p, People. 25p, Boys of 3 races placing hands on globe.

1968, Dec. 10 Litho. *Perf. 11½*

C578	AP140	10p	multicolored	.45	.25
C579	AP140	15p	yellow & multi	.55	.25
C580	AP140	25p	lilac & multi	.90	.25
	Nos. C578-C580 (3)			1.90	.75

International Human Rights Year.

Minshiya Stairs, Deir El-Kamar — AP141

Views in Deir El-Kamar: 15p, The Seraglio Kiosk. 25p, Old paved city road.

1968, Dec. 26

C581	AP141	10p	multicolored	.40	.25
C582	AP141	15p	multicolored	.50	.25
C583	AP141	25p	multicolored	.65	.25
	Nos. C581-C583 (3)			1.55	.75

1st Municipal Council in Lebanon, established in Deir El-Kamar by Daoud Pasha, cent.

Nurse Treating Child, and UN Emblem AP142

Designs: 10p, Grain, fish, grapes and jug. 15p, Mother and children. 20p, Reading girl and Phoenician alphabet. 25p, Playing children.

1969, Jan. 20 Litho. *Perf. 12*

C584	AP142	5p	blk, lt bl & sepia	.45	.25
C585	AP142	10p	blk, brt yel & grn	.45	.25
C586	AP142	15p	blk, red lil & ver	.45	.25
C587	AP142	20p	blk, citron & bl	.45	.25
C588	AP142	25p	blk, pink & bis brn	.65	.25
	Nos. C584-C588 (5)			2.45	1.25

UNICEF, 22nd anniversary.

Silver Coin from Byblos, 5th Century B.C. AP143

National Museum, Beirut: 5p, Gold dagger, Byblos, 18th cent. B.C. 7.50p, King Dining in the Land of the Dead, sarcophagus of Ahiram, 13-12th cent. B.C. 30p, Breastplate with cartouche of Amenemhat III (1849-1801 B.C.). 40p, Phoenician bird vase from Khalde, 8th cent. B.C.

Photogravure; Gold Impressed

1969, Feb. 20 *Perf. 12*

C589	AP143	2.50p	grn, yel & lt bl	.45	.25
C590	AP143	5p	vio, brn & yel	.55	.25
C591	AP143	7.50p	dl yel, brn & pink	.70	.25
C592	AP143	30p	blue & multi	.90	.25
C593	AP143	40p	multicolored	1.00	.25
	Nos. C589-C593 (5)			3.60	1.25

Intl. Congress of Museum Councils; 20th anniv. of the Intl. Council of Museums.

Water Skier — AP144

Designs: 5p, Water ballet. 7.50p, Parachutist, vert. 30p, Yachting, vert. 40p, Regatta.

1969, Mar. 3 Litho. *Perf. 11½*

C594	AP144	2.50p	multicolored	.40	.25
C595	AP144	5p	multicolored	.40	.25
C596	AP144	7.50p	multicolored	.40	.25
C597	AP144	30p	multicolored	.80	.25
C598	AP144	40p	multicolored	1.00	.25
	Nos. C594-C598 (5)			3.00	1.25

Tomb of Unknown Soldier at Military School AP145

2.50p, Frontier guard. 7.50p, Soldiers doing forestry work. 15p, Army engineers building road. 30p, Ambulance and helicopter. 40p, Ski patrol.

1969, Aug. 1 Litho. *Perf. 12x11½*

C599	AP145	2.50p	multicolored	.40	.25
C600	AP145	5p	multicolored	.40	.25
C601	AP145	7.50p	multicolored	.40	.25
C602	AP145	15p	multicolored	.40	.25
C603	AP145	30p	multicolored	.50	.25
C604	AP145	40p	multicolored	.60	.25
	Nos. C599-C604 (6)			2.70	1.50

25th anniversary of independence.

Crosses and Circles — AP146

1971, Jan. 6 Photo. *Perf. 11½x12*

C605	AP146	15p	shown	.45	.25
C606	AP146	85p	Crosses, cedar	1.50	.40

Lebanese Red Cross, 25th anniversary.

Foil Fencing AP147

10p, Flags of participating Arab countries. 15p, Flags of participating non-Arab countries. 40p, Sword fencing. 50p, Saber fencing.

1971, Jan. 15 Litho. *Perf. 12*

C607	AP147	10p	yellow & multi	.40	.25
C608	AP147	15p	yellow & multi	.40	.25
C609	AP147	35p	yellow & multi	.50	.25
C610	AP147	40p	yellow & multi	.65	.25
C611	AP147	50p	yellow & multi	.80	.25
	Nos. C607-C611 (5)			2.75	1.25

10th World Fencing Championships, held in Lebanon.

Agricultural Workers, Arab Painting, 12th Century AP148

1971, Feb. 1

C612	AP148	10p	silver & multi	.80	.25
C613	AP148	40p	gold & multi	1.40	.25

International Labor Organization.

UPU Building and Monument, Bern — AP149

1971, Feb. 15 Litho. *Perf. 12*

C614	AP149	15p	yel, blk & dp org	.80	.25
C615	AP149	35p	dp org, yel & blk	1.40	.30

Opening of new UPU Headquarters in Bern, Switzerland.

Ravens Burning Owls — AP150

Children's Day: 85p, Jackal and lion. Designs of the 15p and 85p are after 13th-14th century paintings, illustrations for the "Kalila wa Dumna."

1971, Mar. 1 Photo. *Perf. 11*

Size: 30x30mm

C616	AP150	15p	gold & multi	.25	.25

Perf. 12x11½

Size: 38½x29mm

C617	AP150	85p	gold & multi	2.40	.65

Map and Flag of Arab League AP151

1971, Mar. 20 *Perf. 12x11½*

C618	AP151	30p	orange & multi	.50	.25
C619	AP151	70p	yellow & multi	1.10	.30

Arab League, 25th anniv.

Bechara el Khoury AP152

Famous Lebanese Men: No. C620, Symbolic design for Imam al Ouzai. No. C622, Hassan Kamel al Sabbah. No. C623, Kahlil Gibran.

1971, Apr. 10

C620	AP152	25p	lt grn, gold & brn	.25	.25
C621	AP152	25p	yel, gold & brn	.35	.25
C622	AP152	25p	yel, gold & brn	.35	.25
C623	AP152	25p	lt grn, gold & brn	.35	.25
	Nos. C620-C623 (4)			1.30	1.00

Education Year Emblem, Computer Card — AP153

1971, Apr. 30 Photo. *Perf. 11½x12*

C624	AP153	10p	blk, vio & bl	.35	.25
C625	AP153	40p	blk, org & yel	.70	.25

Intl. Education Year.

Maameltein Bridge AP154

5p, Jamhour Substation. 15p, Hotel Management School. 20p, Litani Dam. 25p, Television set wiring. 35p, Temple of Bziza. 40p, Jounieh Port. 45p, Airport radar. 50p, Flower. 70p, New School of Sciences. 85p, Oranges. 100p, Arbanieh earth satellite station.

1971, May Litho. *Perf. 12*

C626	AP154	5p	multicolored	*.25*	.25
C627	AP154	10p	multicolored	*.25*	.25
C628	AP154	15p	multicolored	*.40*	.25
C629	AP154	20p	multicolored	*.70*	.25
C630	AP154	25p	multicolored	*1.00*	.25
C631	AP154	35p	multicolored	*1.30*	.25
C632	AP154	40p	multicolored	*1.30*	.25
C633	AP154	45p	multicolored	*1.40*	.25
C634	AP154	50p	multicolored	*2.25*	.25
C635	AP154	70p	multicolored	*3.25*	.25
C636	AP154	85p	multicolored	*4.50*	.25
C637	AP154	100p	multicolored	*5.75*	.35
	Nos. C626-C637 (12)			*22.35*	3.10

For overprints and surcharges see Nos. C771, C775, C779, 533.

Dahr-el-Bacheq Sanatorium — AP155

1971, June 1

C638	AP155	50p	shown	1.15	.25
C639	AP155	100p	multi, diff.	1.60	.55

Campaign against tuberculosis.

Solar Wheel (Festival Emblem) — AP156

1971, July 1 Photo. *Perf. 11*

C640	AP156	15p	ultra & org	.25	.25
C641	AP156	85p	Corinthian capital	1.00	.30

16th Baalbek International Festival.

Mirage Fighters Flying Over Baalbek Ruins — AP157

Army Day: 15p, 155mm Cannon. 40p, Army Headquarters. 70p, Naval patrol boat.

1971, Aug. 1 *Perf. 12x11½*
C642 AP157 15p gold & multi *3.00* .25
C643 AP157 25p gold & multi *5.25* .25
C644 AP157 40p gold & multi *7.25* .25
C645 AP157 70p gold & multi *12.00* .25
Nos. C642-C645 (4) *27.50* 1.00

Wooden Console, Al Aqsa Mosque — AP158

1971, Aug. 21 *Perf. 12*
C646 AP158 15p dk brn & ocher .75 .25
C647 AP158 35p dk brn & ocher 1.25 .25

2nd anniversary of the burning of Al Aqsa Mosque in Jerusalem.

Lenin (1870-1924) AP159

1971, Oct. 1 *Perf. 12x11½*
C648 AP159 30p gold & multi .60 .25
C649 AP159 70p multicolored 1.40 .30

UN Emblem, World Map — AP160

1971, Oct. 24 *Perf. 13x12½*
C650 AP160 15p multicolored .35 .25
C651 AP160 85p multicolored 1.15 .35

UN, 25th anniv. (in 1970).

The Rape of Europa, Mosaic from Byblos AP161

1971, Nov 20 **Litho.** *Perf. 12*
C652 AP161 10p slate & multi *.40* .25
C653 AP161 40p gold & multi *2.00* .25

Publicity for World Lebanese Union (ULM).

Nos. C435-C436 Surcharged

Engr.; Engr. & Litho.
1972, May *Perf. 13, 12*
C654 AP109 100p on 300p *16.00* .35
C655 AP109 100p on 500p *16.00* .35
C656 AP109 200p on 300p *28.00* .65
Nos. C654-C656 (3) *60.00* 1.35

The numerals on No. C655 are taller (5mm) and bars spaced 1½mm apart.

No. C554 Surcharged

1972, June **Litho. & Engr.** *Perf. 12*
C657 AP134 5p on 7.50p multi *2.40* .25

Hibiscus — AP162

1973 **Litho.** *Perf. 12*
C658 AP162 2.50p shown *.25* .25
C659 AP162 5p Roses *.25* .25
C660 AP162 15p Tulips *.35* .25
C661 AP162 25p Lilies *.95* .25
C662 AP162 40p Carnations *1.05* .25
C663 AP162 50p Iris *1.50* .25
C664 AP162 70p Apples *1.15* .25
C665 AP162 75p Grapes *1.30* .25
C666 AP162 100p Peaches *1.75* .35
C667 AP162 200p Pears *6.25* .25
C668 AP162 300p Cherries *6.75* .55
C669 AP162 500p Oranges *11.00* .90
Nos. C658-C669 (12) *32.55* 4.05

For overprints see Nos. C758-C759, C763, C766, C769, C772, C776, C778, C782, C785-C787.

Lebanese House — AP163

Designs: Old Lebanese houses.

1973 *Perf. 14*
C670 AP163 35p yel & multi *2.00* .25
C671 AP163 50p lt bl & multi *3.00* .25
C672 AP163 85p buff & multi *4.75* .25
C673 AP163 100p multicolored *6.25* .35
Nos. C670-C673 (4) *16.00* 1.10

For overprints see Nos. C768, C773, C780, C783.

Woman with Rose — AP164

Lebanese Costumes: 10p, Man. 20p, Man on horseback. 25p, Woman playing mandolin.

1973, Sept. 1 **Litho.** *Perf. 14*
C674 AP164 5p yellow & multi *.70* .25
C675 AP164 10p yellow & multi *2.00* .25
C676 AP164 20p yellow & multi *3.25* .25
C677 AP164 25p yellow & multi *4.50* .25
Nos. C674-C677 (4) *10.45* 1.00

For overprints see Nos. C760-C761, C764, C767.

Swimming, Temple at Baalbek AP165

Designs: 10p, Running and portal. 15p, Woman athlete and castle. 20p, Women's volleyball and columns. 25p, Basketball and aqueduct. 50p, Women's table tennis and buildings. 75p, Handball and building. 100p, Soccer and cedar.

1973, Sept. 25 **Photo.** *Perf. 11½x12*
C678 AP165 5p multicolored .25 .25
C679 AP165 10p multicolored .25 .25
C680 AP165 15p grn & multi .30 .25
C681 AP165 20p multicolored .30 .25
C682 AP165 25p ultra & multi .40 .25
C683 AP165 50p org & multi 1.00 .25
C684 AP165 75p vio & multi 1.20 .35
C685 AP165 100p multicolored 2.25 .65
a. Souvenir sheet 3.00 1.40
Nos. C678-C685 (8) 5.95 2.50

5th Pan-Arabic Scholastic Games, Beirut. No. C685a contains one stamp with simulated perforations similar to No. C685; gold inscription and denomination.

View of Brasilia AP166

20p, Old Salvador (Bahia). 25p, Lebanese sailing ship enroute from the Old World to South America. 50p, Dom Pedro I & Emir Fakhr al-Din II.

1973, Nov. 15 **Litho.** *Perf. 12*
C686 AP166 5p gold & multi .35 .25
C687 AP166 20p gold & multi 1.75 .30
C688 AP166 25p gold & multi 1.75 .30
C689 AP166 50p gold & multi 4.00 .55
Nos. C686-C689 (4) 7.85 1.40

Sesquicentennial of Brazil's independence.

Inlay Worker — AP167

1973, Dec. 1
C690 AP167 10p shown *.65* .25
C691 AP167 20p Weaver *1.00* .25
C692 AP167 35p Glass blower *1.60* .30
C693 AP167 40p Potter *2.25* .40
C694 AP167 50p Metal worker *2.40* .40
C695 AP167 70p Cutlery maker *4.00* .55
C696 AP167 85p Lace maker *5.75* .80
C697 AP167 100p Handicraft Museum *6.50* 1.15
Nos. C690-C697 (8) *24.15* 4.10

Lebanese handicrafts.

For overprints see Nos. C762, C765, C770, C774, C777, C781, C784.

Camp Site, Log Fire and Scout Emblem AP168

Designs: 5p, Lebanese Scout emblem and map. 7½p, Lebanese Scout emblem and map of Middle East. 10p, Lord Baden-Powell, ruins of Baalbek. 15p, Girl Guide, camp and emblem. 20p, Lebanese Girl Guide and Scout emblems. 25p, Scouts around camp fire. 30p, Symbolic globe with Lebanese flag and Scout emblem. 35p, Flags of participating nations. 50p, Old man, and Scout chopping wood.

1974, Aug. 24 **Litho.** *Perf. 12*
C698 AP168 2.50p multi *.60* .25
C699 AP168 5p multi *.60* .25
C700 AP168 7.50p multi *1.15* .25
C701 AP168 10p multi *1.15* .25
C702 AP168 15p multi *1.40* .45
a. Vert. strip of 5, #C698-C702 *5.75*
C703 AP168 20p multi *2.00* .55
C704 AP168 25p multi *3.00* .55
C705 AP168 30p multi *4.00* .55
C706 AP168 35p multi *4.75* .75
C707 AP168 50p multi *5.75* 1.15
a. Vert. strip of 5, #C703-C707 *20.00*
Nos. C698-C707 (10) *24.40* 5.00

11th Arab Boy Scout Jamboree, Smar-Jubeil, Aug. 1974. Nos. C702-C703 are for the 5th Girl Guide Jamboree, Deir-el-Kamar.

Mail Train and Postman Loading Mail, UPU Emblem AP169

UPU Emblem and: 20p, Postal container hoisted onto ship. 25p, Postal Union Congress Building, Lausanne, and UPU Headquarters, Bern. 50p, Fork-lift truck loading mail on plane.

1974, Nov. 4 **Photo.** *Perf. 11½x12*
C708 AP169 5p multicolored *.40* .25
C709 AP169 20p multicolored *1.60* .25
C710 AP169 25p multicolored *2.40* .25
C711 AP169 50p ultra & multi *5.00* .60
Nos. C708-C711 (4) *9.40* 1.35

Centenary of Universal Postal Union.

Congress Building, Sofar — AP170

Arab Postal Union Emblem and: 20p, View of Sofar. 25p, APU Headquarters, Cairo. 50p, Ministry of Post, Beirut.

1974, Dec. 4 **Litho.** *Perf. 13x12½*
C712 AP170 5p orange & multi *.30* .25
C713 AP170 20p yellow & multi *.50* .25
C714 AP170 25p blue & multi *.75* .25
C715 AP170 50p multicolored *3.50* .80
Nos. C712-C715 (4) *5.05* 1.55

Arab Postal Union, 25th anniversary.

Mountain Road, by Omar Onsi — AP171

Paintings by Lebanese artists: No. C717, Clouds, by Moustapha Farroukh. No. C718, Woman, by Gebran Kahlil Gebran. No. C719, Embrace, by Cesar Gemayel. No. C720, Self-portrait, by Habib Serour. No. C721, Portrait of a Man, by Daoud Corm.

1974, Dec. 6 **Litho.** *Perf. 13x12½*
C716 AP171 50p lilac & multi *1.60* .40
C717 AP171 50p blue & multi *1.60* .40
C718 AP171 50p green & multi *1.60* .40
C719 AP171 50p lt vio & multi *1.60* .40
C720 AP171 50p brown & multi *1.60* .40
C721 AP171 50p gray brn & multi *1.60* .40
Nos. C716-C721 (6) *9.60* 2.40

Hunter Spearing Lion — AP172

Excavations at Hermel: 10p, Statue of Astarte. 25p, Dogs hunting boar, tiled panel. 35p, Greco-Roman tomb.

1974, Dec. 13
C722 AP172 5p blue & multi *.35* .25
C723 AP172 10p lilac & multi *.80* .25
C724 AP172 25p multicolored *1.90* .25
C725 AP172 35p multicolored *2.40* .35
Nos. C722-C725 (4) *5.45* 1.10

UNESCO Emblems and Globe — AP173

1974, Dec. 16 *Perf. 12½x13*
C726 AP173 5p violet & multi .35 .25
C727 AP173 10p bister & multi .75 .25
C728 AP173 25p blue & multi 1.75 .25
C729 AP173 35p multicolored 2.25 .35
Nos. C726-C729 (4) 5.10 1.10

International Book Year.

Symbolic Stamp under Magnifying Glass — AP174

Designs (Symbolic): 10p, Post horns. 15p, Stamp printing. 20p, Mounted stamp.

1974, Dec. 20 *Perf. 13x12½*
C730 AP174 5p blue & multi .25 .25
C731 AP174 10p olive & multi .35 .25
C732 AP174 15p brown & multi .75 .25
C733 AP174 20p lilac & multi .90 .25
Nos. C730-C733 (4) 2.25 1.00

Georgina Rizk — AP175

5p, 25p, Georgina Rizk in Lebanese costume.

1974, Dec. 21

C734	AP175	5p multicolored		.25	.25
C735	AP175	20p violet & multi		.50	.25
C736	AP175	25p yellow & multi		.70	.25
C737	AP175	50p blue & multi		1.35	.25
a.		Souvenir sheet of 4		7.25	4.00
		Nos. C734-C737 (4)		2.80	1.00

Georgina Rizk, Miss Universe 1971. No. C737a contains 4 stamps similar to Nos. C734-C737 with simulated perforations.

UNICEF Emblem, Helicopter, Camel, Supplies AP176

UNICEF Emblem and: 25p, Child welfare clinic. 35p, Kindergarten class. 70p, Girls in chemistry laboratory.

1974, Dec. 28 Litho. *Perf. 12½x13*

C738	AP176	20p multicolored	.25	.25
C739	AP176	25p multicolored	.25	.25
C740	AP176	35p blue & multi	.70	.25
C741	AP176	70p blue & multi	1.60	.25
a.		Souvenir sheet of 4	5.50	2.90
		Nos. C738-C741 (4)	2.80	1.00

UNICEF, 25th anniv. No. C741a contains 4 stamps similar to Nos. C738-C741 with simulated perforations. Sold for 200p.

Discus and Olympic Rings — AP177

1974, Dec. 30 *Perf. 13x12½*

C742	AP177	5p shown	.25	.25
C743	AP177	10p Shot put	.30	.25
C744	AP177	15p Weight lifting	.40	.25
C745	AP177	35p Running	.80	.25
C746	AP177	50p Wrestling	1.15	.25
C747	AP177	85p Javelin	1.90	.35
a.		Souvenir sheet of 6	7.50	5.00
		Nos. C742-C747 (6)	4.80	1.60

20th Olympic Games, Munich, Aug. 26-Sept. 11, 1972. No. C747a contains 6 stamps similar to Nos. C742-C747 with simulated perforations.

Clouds and Environment Emblem — AP178

1975

C748	AP178	5p shown	.25	.25
C749	AP178	25p Landscape	.50	.25
C750	AP178	30p Flowers and tree	.50	.25
C751	AP178	40p Waves	.75	.25
a.		Souvenir sheet of 4	6.50	4.50
		Nos. C748-C751 (4)	2.00	1.00

UN Conf. on Human Environment, Stockholm, June 5-16, 1972. No. C751a contains four stamps similar to Nos. C748-C751 with simulated perforations. Sold for 150p.

Archaeology AP179

Symbols of: 25p, Science & medicine. 35p, Justice & commerce. 70p, Industry & commerce.

1975, Aug. Litho. *Perf. 12½x13*

C752	AP179	20p multicolored	*.80*	.25
C753	AP179	25p multicolored	*1.15*	.25
C754	AP179	35p blue & multi	*1.60*	.40
C755	AP179	70p buff & multi	*3.50*	.70
		Nos. C752-C755 (4)	*7.05*	1.60

Beirut, University City.

Stamps of 1971-73 Ovptd. with Various Overall Patterns Including Cedars in Blue, Red, Orange, Lilac, Brown or Green

1978 Litho. *Perf. 12, 14*

C758	AP162	2.50p	(#C658;B)	*.30*	.25
C759	AP162	5p	(#C659;R)	*.30*	.25
C760	AP164	5p	(#C674;B)	*.30*	.25
C761	AP164	10p	(#C675;B)	*.30*	.25
C762	AP167	10p	(#C690;O)	*.30*	.25
C763	AP162	15p	(#C660;R)	*1.10*	.25
C764	AP164	20p	(#C676;B)	*.75*	.25
C765	AP167	20p	(#C691;B)	*.75*	.25
C766	AP162	25p	(#C661;L)	*.75*	.25
C767	AP164	25p	(#C677;B)	*1.50*	.25
C768	AP163	35p	(#C670;Br)	*1.75*	.25
C769	AP162	40p	(#C662;L)	*1.75*	.25
C770	AP167	40p	(#C693;G)	*1.75*	.25
C771	AP154	45p	(#C633;L)	*1.75*	.25
C772	AP162	50p	(#C663;L)	*2.60*	.25
C773	AP163	50p	(#C671;L)	*2.60*	.25
C774	AP167	50p	(#C694;Br)	*2.60*	.25
C775	AP154	70p	(#C635;L)	*3.00*	.55
C776	AP162	70p	(#C664;L)	*3.00*	.55
C777	AP167	70p	(#C695;B)	*3.00*	.55
C778	AP162	75p	(#C665;B)	*4.75*	.55
C779	AP154	85p	(#C636;R)	*3.50*	.60
C780	AP163	85p	(#C672;B)	*3.50*	.60
C781	AP167	85p	(#C696;G)	*3.50*	.60
C782	AP162	100p	(#C666;O)	*5.50*	.80
C783	AP163	100p	(#C673;B)	*5.50*	.80
C784	AP167	100p	(#C697;L)	*5.50*	.80
C785	AP162	200p	(#C667;O)	*11.00*	2.75
C786	AP162	300p	(#C668;O)	*15.50*	5.25
C787	AP162	500p	(#C669;O)	*22.00*	7.50
		Nos. C758-C787 (30)		*110.40*	*26.15*

Heart and Arrow — AP180

1978, Apr. 7 Litho. *Perf. 12*

C788	AP180	50p blue, blk & red	1.10	.80

World Health Day; drive against hypertension.

Poet Mikhail Naimy and Sannine Mountains — AP181

Designs: 50p, Naimy and view of Al Chakhroub Baskinta. 75p, Naimy portrait in sunburst, vert.

1978, May 17

C789	AP181	25p gold & multi	*.75*	.25
C790	AP181	50p gold & multi	*1.30*	.45
C791	AP181	75p gold & multi	*2.00*	.65
		Nos. C789-C791 (3)	*4.05*	1.35

Mikhail Naimy Festival.

Army Day Type of 1980

Designs: 50p, Emir Fakhr al-Din statue, vert. 75p, Soldiers and flag.

1980, Dec. 28 Litho. *Perf. 11½*

C792	A86	50p multicolored	*1.20*	.25
C793	A86	75p multicolored	*1.60*	.35

28th UPU Congress, Rio de Janeiro, 1979 — AP182

1981, Feb. 17 Photo. *Perf. 12x11½*

C794	AP182	25p multicolored	.95	.25
C795	AP182	50p multicolored	2.10	.65
C796	AP182	75p multicolored	3.00	.90
		Nos. C794-C796 (3)	6.05	1.80

Intl. Year of the Child (1979) — AP183

1981, Mar. 25 Litho. *Perf. 12x11½*

C797	AP183	100p multicolored	4.00	1.25

1974 Chess Championships AP184

Various chess pieces. Nos. C799-C802 vert.

Perf. 12x11½, 11½x12

1980-81 Photo.

C798	AP184	50p multicolored	1.90	.65
C799	AP184	75p multicolored	2.25	.85
C800	AP184	100p multicolored	2.75	1.25
C801	AP184	150p multicolored	4.50	2.40
C802	AP184	200p multicolored	5.75	3.25
		Nos. C798-C802 (5)	17.15	8.40

Makassed Islamic Institute Centenary (1978) — AP185

1981 Photo. *Perf. 13½x14*

C803	AP185	50p Children	.80	.25
C804	AP185	75p Institute	1.20	.25
C805	AP185	100p Makassed	1.40	.35
		Nos. C803-C805 (3)	3.40	.85

AIR POST SEMI-POSTAL STAMPS

Nos. C13-C16 Surcharged Like Nos. B1-B12

1926 *Perf. 13½*

CB1	A2	1p + 2p dk brn	15.00	8.00
CB2	A2	2p + 3p org brn	15.00	8.00
CB3	A2	3p + 5p violet	15.00	8.00
CB4	A3	5p + 10p vio brn	15.00	8.00
		Nos. CB1-CB4 (4)	60.00	32.00

These stamps were sold for their combined values, original and surcharged. The latter represented their postal franking value and the former was a contribution to the relief of refugees from the Djebel Druze War.

Catalogue values for unused stamps in this section, from this point to the end of the section, are for Never Hinged items.

Independent Republic

Natural Bridge, Faraya — SPAP1

Bay of Jounie — SPAP2

Perf. 11½

1947, June 27 Unwmk. Litho.

Cross in Carmine

CB5	SPAP1	12.50 + 25pi brt bl grn	13.50	3.75
CB6	SPAP1	25 + 50pi blue	17.00	4.50
CB7	SPAP2	50 + 100pi choc	20.00	5.25
CB8	SPAP2	75 + 150pi brt pur	40.00	10.00
CB9	SPAP2	100 + 200pi sl	75.00	14.00
		Nos. CB5-CB9 (5)	165.50	37.50

The surtax was for the Red Cross.

Mother & Child Type of Air Post Stamps, 1960

1960, Aug. 16 *Perf. 13½x13*

CB10	AP72	20p + 10p dk red & buff	.90	.25
CB11	AP72	60p + 15p bl & lt bl	2.25	.55

Olympic Games Type of Semi-Postal Issue, 1961

1961, Jan. 12 Unwmk. *Perf. 13*

CB12	SP1	15p + 15p Fencing	3.25	1.25
CB13	SP1	25p + 25p Bicycling	3.25	1.25
CB14	SP1	35p + 35p Swimming	3.25	1.25
		Nos. CB12-CB14 (3)	9.75	3.75

An imperf. souvenir sheet exists, containing one each of Nos. CB12-CB14. Value $32.50.

Nos. CB12-CB14 with Arabic and French Overprint in Green, Red or Maroon

1962, June 2

CB15	SP1	15p + 15p (G)	1.25	.50
CB16	SP1	25p + 25p (M)	2.00	1.00
CB17	SP1	35p + 35p (R)	2.40	1.25
		Nos. CB15-CB17 (3)	5.65	2.75

European Marksmanship Championships held in Lebanon.

POSTAGE DUE STAMPS

Postage Due Stamps of France, 1893-1920, Surcharged like Regular Issue

1924 Unwmk. *Perf. 14x13½*

J1	D2	50c on 10c choc	6.75	4.25
J2	D2	1p on 20c ol grn	6.75	4.25
J3	D2	2p on 30c red	6.75	4.25
J4	D2	3p on 50c vio brn	6.75	4.25
J5	D2	5p on 1fr red brn, *straw*	6.75	4.25
		Nos. J1-J5 (5)	33.75	21.25

Postage Due Stamps of France, 1893-1920, Surcharged

1924

J6	D2	0.50p on 10c choc	7.25	4.00
J7	D2	1p on 20c ol grn	7.25	4.00
J8	D2	2p on 30c red	7.25	4.00
J9	D2	3p on 50c vio brn	7.25	4.00
J10	D2	5p on 1fr red brn, *straw*	7.25	4.00
		Nos. J6-J10 (5)	36.25	20.00

Ancient Bridge across Dog River — D3

Designs: 1p, Village scene. 2p, Pigeon Rocks, near Beirut. 3p, Belfort Castle. 5p, Venus Temple at Baalbek.

1925 Photo. *Perf. 13½*

J11	D3	0.50p brown, *yellow*	.95	.45
J12	D3	1p violet, *rose*	1.35	.65
J13	D3	2p black, *blue*	2.25	.90
J14	D3	3p black, *red org*	3.50	2.00
J15	D3	5p black, *bl grn*	5.75	3.75
		Nos. J11-J15 (5)	13.80	7.75
		Set, never hinged	42.50	

Nos. J11 to J15 Overprinted

1927

J16 D3 0.50p brown, *yellow* 1.50 .40
J17 D3 1p violet, *rose* 2.50 .85
J18 D3 2p black, *blue* 3.50 1.25
J19 D3 3p black, *red org* 7.25 3.00
J20 D3 5p black, *bl grn* 9.50 4.50
Nos. J16-J20 (5) 24.25 10.00
Set, never hinged 35.00

Nos. J16-J20 with Additional Ovpt.

1928

J21 D3 0.50p brn, *yel* (Bk+R) 1.75 1.25
J22 D3 1p vio, *rose* (Bk) 1.75 1.25
J23 D3 2p blk, *bl* (Bk+R) 3.00 2.00
J24 D3 3p blk, *red org* (Bk) 6.00 3.50
J25 D3 5p blk, *bl grn* (Bk+R) 6.75 4.25
Nos. J21-J25 (5) 19.25 12.25
Set, never hinged 65.00

No. J23 has not the short bars in the upper corners.

Postage Due Stamps of 1925 Overprinted in Red like Nos. J21-J25

1928

J26 D3 0.50p brn, *yel* (R) 1.00 .50
J27 D3 2p blk, *bl* (R) 4.25 3.50
J28 D3 5p blk, *bl grn* (R) 11.50 7.50
Nos. J26-J28 (3) 16.75 11.50
Set, never hinged 32.50

No. J28 has not the short bars in the upper corners.

D4

Bas-relief of a Ship — D5

D6

D7

D8

Bas-relief from Sarcophagus of King Ahiram — D9

D10

1930-40 Photo.; Engr. (No. J35)

J29 D4 0.50p black, *brt rose* .75 .50
J30 D5 1p blk, *gray bl* 1.25 1.00
J31 D6 2p blk, *yellow* 1.75 1.25
J32 D7 3p blk, *bl grn* 1.75 1.25
J33 D8 5p blk, *orange* 7.25 5.50
J34 D9 8p blk, *lt rose* 5.00 3.50
J35 D8 10p dk green ('40) 7.75 4.50
J36 D10 15p black 6.75 2.75
Nos. J29-J36 (8) 32.25 20.25
Set, never hinged 65.00

Nos. J29-J36 exist imperf.

Catalogue values for unused stamps in this section, from this point to the end of the section, are for Never Hinged items.

Independent Republic

National Museum, Beirut — D11

1945 Unwmk. Litho. *Perf. 11½*

J37 D11 2p brn black, *yel* 8.25 2.00
J38 D11 5p ultra, *rose* 10.00 2.50
J39 D11 25p blue, *bl green* 14.00 4.00
J40 D11 50p dark bl, *blue* 17.50 6.00
Nos. J37-J40 (4) 49.75 14.50

D12

1947

J41 D12 5p black, *green* 6.00 1.25
J42 D12 25p blk, *yellow* 62.50 3.50
J43 D12 50p black, *blue* 30.00 6.00
Nos. J41-J43 (3) 98.50 10.75

Hermel Monument — D13

1948

J44 D13 2p blk, *yellow* 4.75 3.75
J45 D13 3p black, *brt rose* 9.00 3.00
J46 D13 10p black, *blue* 22.50 5.50
Nos. J44-J46 (3) 36.25 12.25

D14

1950

J47 D14 1p brt carmine 3.50 .30
J48 D14 5p violet blue 13.00 .60
J49 D14 10p gray green 27.50 1.50
Nos. J47-J49 (3) 44.00 2.40

D15

1952

J50 D15 1p carmine .75 .30
J51 D15 2p bright violet .75 .30
J52 D15 3p dk blue green 1.50 .30
J53 D15 5p blue 2.00 .35
J54 D15 10p chocolate 2.75 .55
J55 D15 25p black 20.00 1.25
Nos. J50-J55 (6) 27.75 3.05

D16

1953

J56 D16 1p carmine red .35 .30
J57 D16 2p blue green .35 .30
J58 D16 3p orange .35 .30
J59 D16 5p lilac rose .60 .30
J60 D16 10p brown .95 .35
J61 D16 15p deep blue 2.00 .75
Nos. J56-J61 (6) 4.60 2.30

D17

1955 Unwmk. *Perf. 13*

J62 D17 1p orange brown .40 .25
J63 D17 2p yellow green .40 .25
J64 D17 3p blue green .40 .25
J65 D17 5p carmine lake .40 .25
J66 D17 10p gray green .60 .25
J67 D17 15p ultramarine .70 .30
J68 D17 25p red lilac 1.50 .80
Nos. J62-J68 (7) 4.40 2.35

Cedar of Lebanon — D18

1966 Photo. *Perf. 11½*

J69 D18 1p bright green .60 .25
J70 D18 5p rose lilac .60 .25
J71 D18 15p ultramarine .75 .55
Nos. J69-J71 (3) 1.95 1.05

Emir Fakhr al-Din II — D19

1968 Litho. *Perf. 11*

J72 D19 1p dk & lt gray .50 .25
J73 D19 2p dk & lt blue grn .50 .25
J74 D19 3p deep org & yel .50 .25
J75 D19 5p brt rose lil & pink .50 .25
J76 D19 10p olive & lemon .50 .25
J77 D19 15p vio & pale violet .75 .40
J78 D19 25p brt & lt blue 1.25 1.00
Nos. J72-J78 (7) 4.50 2.65

POSTAL TAX STAMPS

Fiscal Stamp Surcharged in Violet

Wmk. A T 39 Multiple

1945 *Perf. 13½*

RA1 R1 5pi on 30c red brn 475.00 3.00

The tax was for the Lebanese Army.

No. RA1 Overprinted in Black

1948

RA2 R1 5pi on 30c red brn 20.00 2.50

Fiscal Stamps Surcharged in Various Colors

RA3 R1 5pi on 15pi dk vio bl (R) 22.50 1.60
a. Brown surcharge 52.50 4.50
RA4 R1 5pi on 25c dk blue green (R) 22.50 2.00
RA5 R1 5pi on 30c red brn (Bl) 29.00 4.00
RA6 R1 5pi on 60c lt ultra (Br) 47.50 3.00
RA7 R1 5pi on 3pi salmon rose (Ult) 22.50 3.75

No RA4 exists with watermarks "AT37" or "AT38."

Same With Additional Overprint

RA8 R1 5pi on 10pi red *95.00* 6.50

Fiscal Stamp Surcharged Like Nos. RA3-RA7 with Top Arabic Characters Replaced by

RA9 R1 5pi on 3pi rose (Bk+V) 20.00 2.10

Fiscal Stamp Surcharged in Black and Violet

RA10 R1 5pi on 3pi sal rose *360.00* 25.00

The tax was to aid the war in Palestine.

Catalogue values for unused stamps in this section, from this point to the end of the section, are for Never Hinged items.

Family among Ruins — R2

1956 Unwmk. Litho. *Perf. 13*

RA11 R2 2.50pi brown 5.00 .25

The tax was for earthquake victims. These stamps were obligatory on all inland mail and all mail going to Arab countries.

Building a House — R3

1957-58 *Perf. 13½x13*

RA12 R3 2.50p dk brown 4.25 .25
RA13 R3 2.50p dk blue grn ('58) 2.50 .25

Type of 1957 Redrawn

1959

RA14 R3 2.50p light brown 2.75 .25

On No. RA14 the denomination is on top and the Arabic lines are at the bottom of design.

R4

1961 Unwmk. *Perf. 13½x13*

RA15 R4 2.50p yellow brown 2.50 .25

Building a House — R5

1962 *Perf. 13½x14*

RA16 R5 2.50p blue green 2.50 .25

The tax was for the relief of earthquake victims.

LEEWARD ISLANDS

'lē-wərd 'ī-ləndz

LOCATION — A group of islands in the West Indies, southeast of Puerto Rico
GOVT. — British Colony
AREA — 423 sq. mi.
POP. — 108,847 (1946)
CAPITAL — St. John

While stamps inscribed "Leeward Islands" were in use, 1890-1956, the colony consisted of the presidencies (now colonies) of Antigua, Montserrat, St. Christopher (St. Kitts) with Nevis and Anguilla, the British Virgin Islands and Dominica (which became a separate colony in 1940).

Each presidency issued its own stamps, using them along with the Leeward Islands general issues. The Leeward Islands federation was abolished in 1956.

12 Pence = 1 Shilling
20 Shillings = 1 Pound
100 Cents = 1 Dollar

Catalogue values for unused stamps in this country are for Never Hinged items, beginning with Scott 116.

Queen Victoria — A1

1890 Typo. Wmk. 2 *Perf. 14*

1 A1 ½p lilac & green 3.75 1.40
2 A1 1p lilac & car 8.75 .25
3 A1 2½p lilac & ultra 9.50 .30
4 A1 4p lilac & org 12.00 9.50
5 A1 6p lilac & brown 13.50 15.50
6 A1 7p lilac & slate 12.00 *21.00*
7 A1 1sh green & car 24.00 *62.50*
8 A1 5sh green & ultra 145.00 *330.00*
Nos. 1-8 (8) 228.50 *440.45*

Denomination of Nos. 7-8 are in color on plain tablet: "ONE SHILLING" or "FIVE SHILLINGS."
For overprints and surcharges see Nos. 9-19.

Jubilee Issue

Regular Issue of 1890 Handstamp Overprinted

1897, July 22

9 A1 ½p lilac & green 8.25 *26.00*
10 A1 1p lilac & car 9.25 *26.00*
11 A1 2½p lilac & ultra 9.75 *26.00*
12 A1 4p lilac & org 57.50 *80.00*
13 A1 6p lilac & brown 62.50 *130.00*
14 A1 7p lilac & slate 62.50 *130.00*
15 A1 1sh green & car 130.00 *275.00*
16 A1 5sh green & ultra 525.00 *850.00*
Nos. 9-16 (8) 864.75 *1,543.*

Double Overprints

9a A1 ½p *1,400.*
b. Triple overprint *9,000.*
10a A1 1p *1,150.*
b. Triple overprint *6,250.*
11a A1 2½p *1,350.*
12a A1 4p *1,350.*
13a A1 6p *1,700.* 4,500.
14a A1 7p *1,700.* *2,100.*
15a A1 1sh *2,250.*
16a A1 5sh *6,000.*

60th year of Queen Victoria's reign.
Excellent counterfeits of Nos. 9-16 exist.

Stamps of 1890 Surcharged in Black or Red

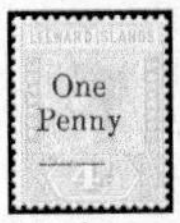
b

c

1902, Aug.

17 A1(b) 1p on 4p lilac & org 7.00 *12.00*
a. Tall narrow "O" in "One" 47.50 *87.50*
b. Double surcharge 6,000.
18 A1(b) 1p on 6p lilac & brn 8.00 *19.00*
a. Tall narrow "O" in "One" 67.50 *150.00*
19 A1(c) 1p on 7p lilac & sl 7.00 *15.00*
Nos. 17-19 (3) 22.00 46.00

King Edward VII — A4

Numerals of ¼p, 2p, 3p and 2sh6p of type A4 are in color on plain tablet. The 1sh and 5sh denominations are expressed as "ONE SHILLING" and "FIVE SHILLINGS" on plain tablet.

1902

20 A4 ½p violet & green 6.00 1.10
21 A4 1p vio & car rose 11.00 .25
22 A4 2p violet & bister 3.00 *4.50*
23 A4 2½p violet & ultra 6.75 2.50
24 A4 3p violet & black 11.50 *8.00*
25 A4 6p violet & brown 3.00 *9.00*
26 A4 1sh grn & car rose 11.50 *30.00*
27 A4 2sh6p green & blk 32.50 *80.00*
28 A4 5sh green & ultra 65.00 *95.00*
Nos. 20-28 (9) 150.25 *230.35*

1905-11 Wmk. 3
Chalky Paper (Ordinary Paper #29, 33)

29 A4 ½p vio & grn ('06) 5.25 2.75
a. Chalky paper ('08) 32.50 23.00
30 A4 1p vio & car rose 11.50 .90
31 A4 2p vio & bis ('08) 14.00 *27.00*
32 A4 2½p vio & ultra 80.00 50.00
33 A4 3p violet & black 25.00 *62.50*
a. Chalky paper ('08) 60.00 100.00
34 A4 3p violet, *yel* ('10) 3.75 *8.00*
35 A4 6p vio & brn ('08) 55.00 *100.00*
36 A4 6p violet & red violet ('11) 10.00 *11.00*
37 A4 1sh grn & car rose ('08) 55.00 *140.00*
38 A4 1sh blk & grn, *grn* ('11) 12.00 *22.50*
39 A4 2sh6p blk & red, *blue* ('11) 45.00 *55.00*
40 A4 5sh grn & red, *yel* ('11) 50.00 *70.00*
Nos. 29-40 (12) 366.50 *549.65*

1907-11 Ordinary Paper

41 A4 ¼p brown ('09) 3.00 1.90
42 A4 ½p green 6.25 1.90
43 A4 1p scarlet 16.50 .85
a. 1p rose carmine 50.00 3.75
44 A4 2p gray ('11) 5.50 *14.50*
45 A4 2½p ultramarine 9.00 4.50
Nos. 41-45 (5) 40.25 *23.65*

King George V — A5

For description of dies I and II, see "Dies of British Colonial Stamps" in Table of Contents.

The ½p, 1p, 2½p and 6p denominations of type A5 show the numeral on horizontally-lined tablet. The 1sh and 5sh denominations are expressed as "ONE SHILLING" and "FIVE SHILLINGS" on plain tablet.

Die I

1912 Ordinary Paper

46 A5 ¼p brown 1.90 1.10
47 A5 ½p green 5.50 2.00
48 A5 1p carmine 5.25 1.10
a. 1p scarlet 15.00 1.10
49 A5 2p gray grn 4.25 *5.75*
50 A5 2½p ultramarine 3.50 *7.25*

1912-22 Chalky Paper

51 A5 3p red brn & vio, *yel* 4.00 *26.00*
52 A5 4p ol & red, *yel* (Die II) ('22) 8.00 *24.00*
53 A5 6p vio & red vio 4.75 *9.25*
54 A5 1sh blk, *bl grn, ol back* 17.50 *8.50*
a. 1sh black, *green* 3.75 *8.50*
55 A5 2sh vio & ultra, *bl* (Die II) ('22) 18.00 *65.00*
56 A5 2sh6p black & red, *blue* ('14) 24.00 *57.50*
57 A5 5sh grn & red, *yel* ('14) 65.00 *120.00*
a. 5sh green & red, *lemon* ('15) 50.00 *85.00*
Nos. 46-57 (12) 161.65 *327.45*

1913, Nov. Surface-colored Paper

58 A5 3p dk vio, *yel* 95.00 *180.00*
59 A5 1sh black, *green* 90.00 40.00
60 A5 5sh green & red, *yel* 55.00 *90.00*
Nos. 58-60 (3) 240.00 310.00

King George V — A6

Die II

1921-32 Wmk. 4 Ordinary Paper

61 A5 ¼p dk brn ('22) 2.50 1.10
a. ¼p dark brown (I) ('32) 16.50 *21.00*
62 A5 ½p green 1.25 .80
a. ½p green (I) ('32) 27.50 *65.00*
63 A5 1p carmine 2.50 .60
a. 1p rose red (I) ('32) 45.00 1.00
b. 1p bright scarlet (II) ('29) 15.00 2.50
64 A5 1p dp violet ('22) 2.50 1.10
65 A5 1½p rose red ('26) 9.25 1.50
66 A5 1½p org brn ('29) 2.25 .25
a. 1½p red brown (I) ('32) 4.50 *3.00*
68 A5 2p gray ('22) 3.25 .85
69 A5 2½p orange ('23) 14.00 *67.50*
70 A5 2½p ultra ('27) 3.75 1.40
a. Die I ('32) 7.50 3.75
71 A5 3p ultra ('23) 17.50 *42.50*
a. 3p deep ultramarine ('25) 65.00 65.00

Chalky Paper

72 A5 3p violet, *yel* *8.50* *6.75*
73 A5 4p blk & red, *yel* ('23) 4.00 *24.00*
74 A5 5p vio & yel ol ('22) 2.75 *4.50*
75 A5 6p vio & red vio ('23) 19.00 *50.00*
a. Die I ('32) 32.50 *100.00*
76 A5 1sh blk, *emer* ('23) 11.00 *8.50*
a. 1sh black, *green* (I) ('32) 60.00 *85.00*
77 A5 2sh vio & ultra, *bl* ('22) 25.00 *45.00*
a. 2sh red purple & blue, *blue* ('26) 14.00 *52.50*
78 A5 2sh6p blk & red, *bl* ('23) 13.00 *27.00*
79 A5 3sh green & vio 12.50 *42.50*
80 A5 4sh black & scar 21.00 *42.50*
81 A5 5sh grn & red, *yel* 50.00 *85.00*
82 A6 10sh red & grn, *emer* ('28) 80.00 *140.00*

Wmk. 3

83 A6 £1 black & vio, *red* ('28) 240.00 325.00
Nos. 61-66,68-83 (22) 545.50 *918.35*

Common Design Types pictured following the introduction.

Silver Jubilee Issue
Common Design Type
Perf. 11x12

1935, May 6 Engr. Wmk. 4

96 CD301 1p car & dk blue 1.75 *3.25*
97 CD301 1½p blk & ultra 2.75 1.60
98 CD301 2½p ultra & brn 4.75 4.75
99 CD301 1sh brn vio & ind 26.50 *40.00*
Nos. 96-99 (4) 35.75 49.60
Set, never hinged 45.00

Coronation Issue
Common Design Type

1937, May 12 *Perf. 13½x14*

100 CD302 1p carmine .50 1.00
101 CD302 1½p org brn .50 1.50
102 CD302 2½p bright ultra .55 1.50
Nos. 100-102 (3) 1.55 4.00
Set, never hinged 3.00

A7

King George VI — A8

1938-51 Typo. *Perf. 14*

103 A7 ¼p brown .40 1.50
a. ¼p deep brown, chalky paper ('49) .25 *1.75*
104 A7 ½p green .75 .75
105 A7 1p carmine 1.25 1.75
a. 1p scarlet ('42) 1.40 12.50
b. 1p red ('48) 3.75 *6.75*
106 A7 1½p red brown .80 .50
107 A7 2p gray 2.00 2.25
a. 2p slate gray ('42) 4.00 3.75
108 A7 2½p ultramarine .60 *4.00*
a. 2½p bright blue 18.00 1.20
109 A7 3p dl org ('42) .40 *.90*
a. 3p brown orange 22.50 2.75
110 A7 6p vio & red vio 6.00 3.50
a. 6p deep dull purple & bright purple 16.00 7.00
b. 6p purple & deep magenta ('47) 9.00 5.50
111 A7 1sh blk & grn, *emer* ('42) 3.50 1.50
a. 1sh black, *emerald*, chalky paper 10.00 5.50
112 A7 2sh vio & ultra, *bl* 7.75 2.25
a. 2sh reddish purple & blue, *blue*, chalky paper 17.00 3.00
113 A7 5sh grn & red, *yel* 21.00 *18.00*
a. 5sh green & red, *yel*, chalky paper 30.00 22.50
114 A8 10sh dp ver & dp grn, *emer*, ordinary paper ('47) 82.50 100.00
a. 10sh dp red & bluish grn, *green*, chalky paper 125.00 *140.00*
b. 10sh dull red & pale grn, *green*, ordinary paper ('44) 475.00 375.00
c. 10sh red & green, *green*, ordinary paper ('45) 100.00 90.00

Two dies were used for the 1p, differing in thickness of shading line at base of "1."

Wmk. 3 *Perf. 13*

115 A8 £1 blk & vio, *scar* ('51) 22.50 *37.50*
a. £1 black & brown purple, *red*, perf. 14 225.00 *375.00*
Never hinged 375.00
b. £1 black & purple, *carmine*, perf. 14 ('41) 55.00 55.00
Never hinged 90.00
c. £1 black & brown purple, *salmon*, perf. 14 ('43) 27.50 29.00
Never hinged 45.00
d. Wmkd. sideways (as #115, perf. 13) *4,000.*
Never hinged 7,000.
Nos. 103-115 (13) 149.45 174.40
Set, never hinged 210.00

The 3p-£1 were issued on chalky paper in 1938 and on ordinary paper in 1942. Values are for the most common varieties.
Issued: #115, 12/13/51; others, 11/25/38.
See Nos. 120-125.

Catalogue values for unused stamps in this section, from this point to the end of the section, are for Never Hinged items.

Peace Issue
Common Design Type
Perf. 13½x14

1946, Nov. 1 Wmk. 4 Engr.

116 CD303 1½p brown .25 .75
117 CD303 3p deep orange .25 .75

Silver Wedding Issue
Common Design Types

1949, Jan. 2 Photo. *Perf. 14x14½*

118 CD304 2½p bright ultra .25 .25

Perf. 11½x11
Engr.; Name Typographed

119 CD305 5sh green 6.75 8.00

George VI Type of 1938

1949, July 1 Typo. *Perf. 13½x14*

120 A7 ½p gray 2.00 1.50
121 A7 1p green .55 .25
122 A7 1½p orange & black 1.75 .40
123 A7 2p crimson rose 1.40 1.25
124 A7 2½p black & plum 1.00 .25
125 A7 3p ultramarine 1.00 .25
Nos. 120-125 (6) 7.70 3.90

UPU Issue
Common Design Types
Engr.; Name Typo. on 3p and 6p

1949, Oct. 10 *Perf. 13½, 11x11½*

126 CD306 2½p slate .25 *2.40*
127 CD307 3p indigo 2.00 2.40
128 CD308 6p red lilac .40 *2.40*
129 CD309 1sh blue green .40 *2.40*
Nos. 126-129 (4) 3.05 *9.60*

University Issue
Common Design Types
Perf. 14x14½

1951, Feb. 16 Engr. Wmk. 4

130 CD310 3c gray black & org .35 *2.00*
131 CD311 12c lilac & rose car 1.00 *2.00*

Coronation Issue
Common Design Type

1953, June 2 *Perf. 13½x13*

132 CD312 3c dk green & black 1.00 *2.25*

A9

Queen Elizabeth II — A10

1954, Feb. 22 **Typo.** ***Perf. 14***

133	A9	½c	brown	.25	.60
134	A9	1c	gray	1.25	1.50
135	A9	2c	green	1.75	.25
136	A9	3c	orange & blk	2.50	1.50
137	A9	4c	rose red	1.75	.25
138	A9	5c	blk & claret	2.25	1.50
139	A9	6c	orange	2.25	.65
140	A9	8c	deep ultra	2.75	.25
141	A9	12c	rose vio & mag	2.00	.25
142	A9	24c	black & green	2.00	.30
143	A9	48c	rose vio & ultra	8.00	4.00
144	A9	60c	brown & green	6.00	3.25
145	A9	$1.20	yel grn & rose red	7.00	4.50

Perf. 13

146	A10	$2.40	red & blue grn	12.00	7.75
147	A10	$4.80	black & claret	16.00	11.00
			Nos. 133-147 (15)	67.75	*37.55*

LESOTHO

lə-'sō-ˌtō

LOCATION — An enclave within the Republic of South Africa
GOVT. — Independent state in British Commonwealth
AREA — 11,720 sq. mi.
POP. — 2,128,950 (1999 est.)
CAPITAL — Maseru

Basutoland, the British Crown Colony, became independent, October 4, 1966, taking the name Lesotho.

100 Cents = 1 Rand
100 Lisente (s) = 1 Maloti (1979)

Catalogue values for all unused stamps in this country are for Never Hinged items.

Watermark

Wmk. 362 — Basotho Hat Multiple

Moshoeshoe I and II — A1

Perf. 12½x13

1966, Oct. 4 Photo. Unwmk.

1	A1	2½c red brn, blk & red	.25	.25
2	A1	5c red brn, blk & brt bl	.25	.25
3	A1	10c red brn, blk & brt green	.25	.25
4	A1	20c red brn, blk & red lilac	.30	.30
		Nos. 1-4 (4)	1.05	1.05

Lesotho's independence, Oct. 4, 1966.

Basutoland Nos. 72-74, 76-82 Overprinted

Perf. 13½

1966, Nov. 1 Wmk. 4 Engr.

5	A7	½c dk brown & gray	.25	.25
6	A7	1c dp grn & gray blk	.25	.25
7	A7	2c orange & dp blue	.90	.25
8	A7	3½c dp blue & indigo	.50	.25
9	A7	5c dk grn & org brn	.30	.25
10	A7	10c rose vio & dk ol	.35	.25
11	A7	12½c aqua & brown	6.00	.35
12	A7	25c lil rose & dp ultra	.70	.25
13	A7	50c dp car & black	1.60	.75

Perf. 11½

14	A8	1r dp claret & blk	2.25	*3.50*
a.		"Lseotho"	85.00	
		Nos. 5-14 (10)	13.10	6.35

Same Overprint on Nos. 87-91 and Type of 1954

Wmk. 314 ***Perf. 13½***

15	A7	1c green & gray blk	.25	.25
16	A7	2½c car & ol green	.65	.25
17	A7	5c dk grn & org brn	.30	.25
18	A7	12½c aqua & brown	.50	.25
19	A7	50c dp car & black	.95	.45

Perf. 11½

20	A8	1r dp claret & blk	.95	.90
a.		"Lseotho"	50.00	*70.00*
		Nos. 15-20 (6)	3.60	2.35

UNESCO Emblem, Microscope, Book, Violin and Retort — A2

Unwmk.

1966, Dec. 1 Litho. *Perf. 14*

21	A2	2½c green & ocher	.25	.25
22	A2	5c olive & brt green	.25	.25
23	A2	12½c ver & lt blue	.30	.25
24	A2	25c dull blue & orange	.50	.60
		Nos. 21-24 (4)	1.30	1.35

20th anniv. of UNESCO.

King Moshoeshoe II and Corn — A3

King Moshoeshoe II — A4

Designs: 1c, Bull. 2c, Aloes. 2½c, Basotho hat. 3½c, Merino sheep. 5c, Basotho pony. 10c, Wheat. 12½c, Angora goat. 25c, Maletsunyane Falls. 50c, Diamonds. 1r, Coat of Arms.

Perf. 13½x14½

1967, Apr. 1 Photo. Unwmk.

25	A3	½c violet & green	.25	.25
26	A3	1c dk red & brown	.25	.25
27	A3	2c green & yellow	.25	*.80*
28	A3	2½c yel bister & blk	.25	.25
29	A3	3½c yellow & black	.25	.25
30	A3	5c brt blue & yel bis	.25	.25
31	A3	10c gray & ocher	.35	.25
32	A3	12½c orange & blk	.30	.30
33	A3	25c ultra & blk	.60	.50
34	A3	50c Prus green & blk	5.00	2.00
35	A3	1r gray & multi	1.00	1.00

Perf. 14½x13½

36	A4	2r mag, blk & gold	1.25	*1.75*
		Nos. 25-36 (12)	10.00	7.85

See Nos. 47-59.

University Buildings and Graduates A4a

1967, Apr. 7 ***Perf. 14x14½***

37	A4a	1c yel, sep & dp blue	.25	.25
38	A4a	2½c blue, sep & dp bl	.25	.25
39	A4a	12½c dl rose, sep & dp bl	.25	.25
40	A4a	25c lt vio, sep & dp bl	.25	.25
		Nos. 37-40 (4)	1.00	1.00

1st conferment of degrees by the Univ. of Botswana, Lesotho and Swaziland at Roma, Lesotho.

Statue of Moshoeshoe I — A5

1st Anniv. of Independence: 12½c, Flag of Lesotho. 25c, Crocodile.

1967, Oct. 4 Photo. *Perf. 14*

41	A5	2½c apple green & black	.25	.25
42	A5	12½c multicolored	.45	.45
43	A5	25c tan, blk & dp green	.80	.80
		Nos. 41-43 (3)	1.50	1.50

Boy Scout and Lord Baden-Powell A6

1967, Nov. 1 Unwmk. *Perf. 14x14½*

44	A6	15c lt ol grn, dk grn & brn	.35	.25

60th anniversary of the Boy Scouts.

World Map and WHO Emblem — A7

20th anniv. of WHO: 25c, Nurse and child, arms of Lesotho and WHO emblem.

1968, Apr. 8 Photo. *Perf. 14x14½*

45	A7	2½c dp bl, car rose & gold	.25	.25
46	A7	25c gold, gray grn & redsh brown	.45	.40

Types of 1967

Design: 3c, Sorghum. Others as before.

Perf. 13½x14½

1968-69 Photo. Wmk. 362

47	A3	½c violet & green	.25	.25
48	A3	1c dk red & brown	.25	.25
49	A3	2c green & yellow	.25	.25
50	A3	2½c yel bister & blk	.25	.25
51	A3	3c lt brn, dk brn & green	.25	.25
52	A3	3½c yellow & black	.25	.25
53	A3	5c brt bl & yel bis	.50	.25
54	A3	10c gray & ocher	.30	.60
55	A3	12½c org & blk ('69)	.80	.90
56	A3	25c ultra & blk ('69)	1.75	1.15
57	A3	50c Prussian grn & black ('69)	12.50	3.00
58	A3	1r gray & multi	2.25	2.25

Perf. 14½x13½

59	A4	2r magenta, blk & gold ('69)	9.00	*11.50*
		Nos. 47-59 (13)	28.60	21.15

Hunters, Rock Painting — A8

Rock Paintings: 3½c, Baboons. 5c, Javelin thrower, vert. 10c, Archers. 15c, Cranes, vert. 20c, Eland. 25c, Hunting scene.

Perf. 14½x14, 14x14½

1968, Nov. 1 Photo. Wmk. 362

60	A8	3c dk & lt green & brn	.35	.25
61	A8	3½c dk brown & yel	.45	.25
62	A8	5c sepia, yel & red brn	.50	.25
63	A8	10c black, brt rose & org	.60	.30
64	A8	15c olive brn & buff	.85	.45
65	A8	20c black, yel & lt grn	1.00	.60
66	A8	25c dk brown, yel & org	1.10	.90
		Nos. 60-66 (7)	4.85	3.00

Protection for Lesotho's rock paintings.

Queen Elizabeth II Hospital — A9

Designs: 10c, Radio Lesotho. 12½c, Leabua Jonathan Airport. 25c, Royal Palace.

1969, Mar. 11 Litho. *Perf. 14x13½*

67	A9	2½c multicolored	.25	.25
68	A9	10c multicolored	.25	.25
69	A9	12½c multicolored	.25	.25
70	A9	25c multicolored	.25	.25
		Nos. 67-70 (4)	1.00	1.00

Centenary of Maseru, capital of Lesotho.

Mosotho Horseman and Car — A10

Designs: 12½c, Car on mountain pass. 15c, View from Sani Pass and signal flags. 20c, Map of Lesotho and Independence Trophy.

1969, Sept. 26 Photo. *Perf. 14½x14*

71	A10	2½c brown & multi	.25	.25
72	A10	12½c multicolored	.25	.25
73	A10	15c multicolored	.30	.30
74	A10	20c yellow & multi	.30	.30
		Nos. 71-74 (4)	1.10	1.10

Roof of Africa Auto Rally, Sept. 19-20.

Gryponyx — A11

Prehistoric Reptile Footprints, Moyeni: 3c, Dinosaur. 10c, Plateosauravus and Footprints. 15c, Tritylodon. 25c, Massospondylus.

Perf. 14½x14

1970, Jan. 5 Wmk. 362

Size: 60x23mm

75	A11	3c brown, yel & black	1.00	.75

Perf. 15x14

Size: 40x23mm

76	A11	5c maroon, blk & pink	1.40	.40
77	A11	10c sepia, blk & yel	1.50	.45
78	A11	15c slate grn, blk & yel	2.00	2.50
79	A11	25c gray blue, blk & bl	3.00	2.50
		Nos. 75-79 (5)	8.90	6.60

Moshoeshoe I — A12

Design: 25c, Moshoeshoe I with top hat.

Perf. 14x13½

1970, Mar. 11 Litho. Wmk. 362

80	A12	2½c brt grn & car rose	.25	.25
81	A12	25c lt blue & org brn	.25	.25

Cent. of the death of Moshoeshoe I, chief of the Bakoena clan of the Basothos.

UN Headquarters, New York — A13

2½c, UN emblem. 12½c, UN emblem, people. 25c, UN emblem, peace dove.

1970, June 26 Litho. *Perf. 14½x14*

82	A13	2½c pink, red brn & bl	.25	.25
83	A13	10c blue & multi	.25	.25
84	A13	12½c olive, ver & lt blue	.25	.25
85	A13	25c tan & multi	.25	.25
		Nos. 82-85 (4)	1.00	1.00

25th anniversary of the United Nations.

Basotho Hat Gift Shop, Maseru — A14

Tourism: 5c, Trout fishing. 10c, Horseback riding. 12½c, Skiing, Maluti Mountains. 20c, Holiday Inn, Maseru.

1970, Oct. 27 ***Perf. 14x14½***

86	A14	2½c multicolored	.25	.25
87	A14	5c multicolored	.25	.25
88	A14	10c multicolored	.30	.30
89	A14	12½c multicolored	.30	.30
90	A14	20c multicolored	.35	.35
		Nos. 86-90 (5)	1.45	1.45

Corn — A15

Designs: 1c, Bull. 2c, Aloes. 2½c, Basotho hat. 3c, Sorghum. 3½c, Merino sheep. 4c, National flag. 5c, Basotho pony. 10c, Wheat. 12½c, Angora goat. 25c, Maletsunyane Falls. 50c, Diamonds. 1r, Coat of Arms. 2r, Statue of King Moshoeshoe I in Maseru, vert.

1971 Litho. Wmk. 362 *Perf. 14*

91	A15	½c lilac & green	.25	.25
92	A15	1c brn red & brn	.25	.25
93	A15	2c yel brn & yel	.25	.25
94	A15	2½c dull yel & blk	.25	.25
95	A15	3c bis, brn & grn	.25	.25
96	A15	3½c yellow & black	.25	.25
97	A15	4c ver & multi	.25	.25
98	A15	5c blue & brown	.25	.25
99	A15	10c gray & ocher	.35	.30
100	A15	12½c orange & brn	.45	.35
101	A15	25c ultra & black	.75	.60
102	A15	50c lt bl grn & blk	6.50	4.00
103	A15	1r gray & multi	1.90	1.75
104	A15	2r ultra & brown	1.40	*2.25*
a.		Unwmkd. ('80)	2.25	*3.50*
		Nos. 91-104 (14)	13.35	11.25

Issue dates: 4c, Apr. 1; others, Jan. 4.
For overprints and surcharges see Nos. 132-135, 245, 312.

Lammergeier — A16

Birds: 5c, Bald ibis. 10c, Rufous rock jumper. 12½c, Blue korhaan (bustard). 15c, Painted snipe. 20c, Golden-breasted bunting. 25c, Ground woodpecker.

1971, Mar. 1 ***Perf. 14***

105	A16	2½c multicolored	2.75	.25
106	A16	5c multicolored	3.75	2.10
107	A16	10c multicolored	4.00	1.60
108	A16	12½c multicolored	4.25	3.25
109	A16	15c multicolored	4.75	4.25
110	A16	20c multicolored	4.75	4.25
111	A16	25c multicolored	5.25	4.25
		Nos. 105-111 (7)	29.50	19.95

Lionel Collett Dam — A17

Designs: 10c, Contour farming. 15c, Earth dams. 25c, Beaver dams.

1971, July 15 **Litho.** **Wmk. 362**

112	A17	4c multicolored	.25	.25
113	A17	10c multicolored	.25	.25
114	A17	15c multicolored	.25	.25
115	A17	25c multicolored	.25	.25
		Nos. 112-115 (4)	1.00	1.00

Soil conservation and erosion control.

Diamond Mining — A18

10c, Potter. 15c, Woman weaver at loom. 20c, Construction worker and new buildings.

1971, Oct. 4

116	A18	4c olive & multi	1.40	.40
117	A18	10c ocher & multi	.55	.25
118	A18	15c red & multi	.85	.60
119	A18	20c dk brown & multi	1.10	1.40
		Nos. 116-119 (4)	3.90	2.65

Mail Cart, 19th Century — A19

Designs: 10c, Postal bus. 15c, Cape of Good Hope No. 17, vert. 20c, Maseru Post Office.

1972, Jan. 3

120	A19	5c pink & black	.25	.25
121	A19	10c lt blue & multi	.25	.25
122	A19	15c gray, black & blue	.25	.25
123	A19	20c yellow & multi	.35	.60
		Nos. 120-123 (4)	1.10	1.35

Centenary of mail service between Maseru and Aliwal North in Cape Colony.

Runner and Olympic Rings — A20

1972, Sept. 1

124	A20	4c shown	.25	.25
125	A20	10c Shot put	.25	.25
126	A20	15c Hurdles	.40	.35
127	A20	25c Broad jump	.60	.60
		Nos. 124-127 (4)	1.50	1.45

20th Olympic Games, Munich, 8/26-9/11.

Adoration of the Shepherds, by Matthias Stomer — A21

1972, Dec. 1 **Litho.** ***Perf. 14***

128	A21	4c blue & multi	.25	.25
129	A21	10c red & multi	.25	.25
130	A21	25c emerald & multi	.25	.25
		Nos. 128-130 (3)	.75	.75

Christmas.

WHO Emblem A22

1973, Apr. 7 **Litho.** ***Perf. 13½***

131	A22	20c blue & yellow	.60	.60

WHO, 25th anniversary.

Nos. 94, 97-99 ovptd. "O.A.U. / 10th Anniversary / Freedom in Unity"

1973, May 25 **Wmk. 362** ***Perf. 14***

132	A15	2½c dull yellow & black	.25	.25
133	A15	4c vermilion & multi	.25	.25
134	A15	5c blue & brown	.25	.25
135	A15	10c gray & ocher	.25	.25
		Nos. 132-135 (4)	1.00	1.00

Basotho Hat, WFP/FAO Emblem A23

Designs: 15c, School lunch. 20c, Child drinking milk and cow. 25c, Map of mountain roads and farm workers.

1973, June 1 ***Perf. 13½***

136	A23	4c ultra & multi	.25	.25
137	A23	15c buff & multi	.25	.25
138	A23	20c yellow & multi	.25	.25
139	A23	25c violet & multi	.25	.25
		Nos. 136-139 (4)	1.00	1.00

World Food Program, 10th anniversary.

Christmas Butterfly — A24

Designs: Butterflies of Lesotho.

1973, Sept. 3 ***Perf. 14x14½***

140	A24	4c Mountain Beauty	1.10	.25
141	A24	5c shown	1.25	.60
142	A24	10c Painted lady	2.00	.60
143	A24	15c Yellow pansy	3.25	2.00
144	A24	20c Blue pansy	3.25	2.10
145	A24	25c African monarch	3.50	2.75
146	A24	30c Orange tip	3.50	3.75
		Nos. 140-146 (7)	17.85	12.05

Map of Northern Lesotho and Location of Diamond Mines — A25

Designs: 15c, Kimberlite (diamond-bearing) rocks. 20c, Diagram of Kimberlite volcano, vert. 30c, Diamond prospector, vert.

Perf. 13½x14, 14x13½

1973, Oct. 1 **Litho.** **Wmk. 362**

147	A25	10c gray & multi	2.25	.50
148	A25	15c multicolored	2.50	2.25
149	A25	20c multicolored	2.50	2.50
150	A25	30c multicolored	3.75	7.00
		Nos. 147-150 (4)	11.00	12.25

International Kimberlite Conference.

Nurses' Training and Medical Care — A26

Designs: 10c, Classroom, student with microscope. 20c, Farmers with tractor and bullock team and crop instruction. 25c, Potter and engineers with lathe. 30c, Boy scouts and young bricklayers.

1974, Feb. 18 **Litho.** ***Perf. 13½x14***

151	A26	4c lt blue & multi	.25	.25
152	A26	10c ocher & multi	.25	.25
153	A26	20c multicolored	.25	.25
154	A26	25c bister & multi	.25	.25
155	A26	30c yellow & multi	.25	.25
		Nos. 151-155 (5)	1.25	1.25

Youth and development.

Open Book and Wreath — A27

Designs: 15c, Flags of Botswana, Lesotho and Swaziland; cap and diploma. 20c, Map of Africa and location of Botswana, Lesotho and Swaziland. 25c, King Moshoeshoe II, Chancellor of UBLS, capping graduate.

1974, Apr. 7 **Litho.** ***Perf. 14***

156	A27	10c multicolored	.25	.25
157	A27	15c multicolored	.25	.25
158	A27	20c multicolored	.25	.25
159	A27	25c multicolored	.25	.50
		Nos. 156-159 (4)	1.00	1.25

10th anniversary of the University of Botswana, Lesotho and Swaziland.

Senqunyane River Bridge, Marakabei A28

5c, Tsoelike River Bridge. 10c, Makhaleng River Bridge. 15c, Seaka Bridge, Orange/Senqu River. 20c, Masianokeng Bridge, Phuthiatsana River. 25c, Mahobong Bridge, Hlotse River.

1974, June 26 **Wmk. 362** ***Perf. 14***

160	A28	4c multicolored	.25	.25
161	A28	5c multicolored	.25	.25
162	A28	10c multicolored	.25	.25
163	A28	15c multicolored	.50	.40
164	A28	20c multicolored	.55	.55
165	A28	25c multicolored	.60	.60
		Nos. 160-165 (6)	2.40	2.30

Bridges and rivers of Lesotho.

UPU Emblem — A29

1974, Sept. 6 **Litho.** ***Perf. 14x13***

166	A29	4c shown	.25	.25
167	A29	10c Map of Lesotho	.25	.25
168	A29	15c GPO, Maseru	.25	.40
169	A29	20c Rural mail delivery	.80	1.00
		Nos. 166-169 (4)	1.55	1.90

Centenary of Universal Postal Union.

Siege of Thaba-Bosiu A30

King Moshoeshoe I A31

5c, King Moshoeshoe II laying wreath at grave of Moshoeshoe I. 20c, Makoanyane, warrior hero.

Perf. 12½x12, 12x12½

1974, Nov. 25

170	A30	4c multicolored	.25	.25
171	A30	5c multicolored	.25	.25
172	A31	10c multicolored	.25	.25
173	A31	20c multicolored	.60	.40
		Nos. 170-173 (4)	1.35	1.15

Sesquicentennial of Thaba-Bosiu becoming the capital of Basutoland and Lesotho.

Mamokhorong A32

Musical Instruments of the Basotho: 10c, Lesiba. 15c, Setolotolo. 20c, Meropa (drums).

Perf. 14x14½

1975, Jan. 25 **Wmk. 362**

174	A32	4c multicolored	.25	.25
175	A32	10c multicolored	.25	.25
176	A32	15c multicolored	.30	.30
177	A32	20c multicolored	.50	.50
	a.	Souvenir sheet of 4, #174-177	1.75	2.00
		Nos. 174-177 (4)	1.30	1.30

View, Sehlabathebe National Park — A33

5c, Natural arch. 15c, Mountain stream. 20c, Lake and mountains. 25c, Waterfall.

1975, Apr. 8 **Litho.** ***Perf. 14***

178	A33	4c multicolored	.35	.25
179	A33	5c multicolored	.35	.25
180	A33	15c multicolored	.70	.70
181	A33	20c multicolored	.70	.70
182	A33	25c multicolored	.90	.90
		Nos. 178-182 (5)	3.00	2.80

Sehlabathebe National Park.

Moshoeshoe I (1824-1870) A34

Mofumahali Mantsebo Seeiso (1940-1960) A35

Leaders of Lesotho: 4c, Moshoeshoe II. 5c, Letsie I (1870-1891). 6c, Lerotholi (1891-1905). 10c, Letsie II (1905-1913). 15c, Griffith (1913-1939). 20c, Seeiso Griffith Lerotholi (1939-1940).

1975, Sept. 10 **Litho.** **Wmk. 362**

183	A34	3c dull blue & black	.25	.25
184	A34	4c lilac rose & black	.25	.25
185	A34	5c pink & black	.25	.25
186	A34	6c brown & black	.25	.25
187	A34	10c rose car & black	.25	.25
188	A34	15c orange & black	.25	.25
189	A34	20c olive & black	.25	.30
190	A35	25c lt blue & black	.25	.40
		Nos. 183-190 (8)	2.00	2.20

No. 190 issued for Intl. Women's Year.

Mokhibo, Women's Dance — A36

Traditional Dances: 10c, Ndlamo, men's dance. 15c, Raleseli, men and women. 20c, Mohobelo, men's dance.

1975, Dec. 17 ***Perf. 14x14½***

191	A36	4c blue & multi	.25	.25
192	A36	10c black & multi	.25	.25
193	A36	15c black & multi	.30	.40

194 A36 20c blue & multi		.40	.70
a. Souvenir sheet of 4, #191-194		5.00	5.00
Nos. 191-194 (4)		1.20	1.60

Enrollment in Junior Red Cross — A37

Designs: 10c, First aid team and truck. 15c, Red Cross nurse on horseback in rural area. 25c, Supplies arriving by plane.

1976, Feb. 20 Litho. *Perf. 14*

195 A37 4c red & multi	.55	.40
196 A37 10c red & multi	.80	.60
197 A37 15c red & multi	1.05	1.00
198 A37 25c red & multi	1.60	2.00
Nos. 195-198 (4)	4.00	4.00

Lesotho Red Cross, 25th anniversary.

Mosotho Horseman A38

King Moshoeshoe II A39

2c, Tapestry (weavers and citation). 4c, Map of Lesotho. 5c, Hand holding Lesotho brown diamond. 10c, Lesotho Bank. 15c, Flags of Lesotho and Organization of African Unity. 25c, Sehlabathebe National Park. 40c, Pottery. 50c, Pre-historic rock painting.

1976, June 2 *Perf. 14*

199 A38 2c multicolored	.25	.35
200 A38 3c multicolored	.25	.30
201 A38 4c multicolored	1.40	.25
202 A38 5c multicolored	.50	.90
203 A38 10c multicolored	.30	.30
204 A38 15c multicolored	1.60	.80
205 A38 25c multicolored	.50	.60
a. Unwmkd. ('80)	1.60	*4.00*
206 A38 40c multicolored	.70	1.25
a. Unwmkd. ('80)	4.25	*11.00*
207 A38 50c multicolored	2.25	2.00
a. Unwmkd. ('80)	6.00	*10.00*
208 A39 1r multicolored	1.00	*1.75*
Nos. 199-208 (10)	8.75	8.50

For surcharges see Nos. 302-311.

Soccer — A40

Olympic Rings and: 10c, Weight lifting. 15c, Boxing. 25c, Discus.

1976, Aug. 9 Litho. Wmk. 362

209 A40 4c citron & multi	.25	.25
210 A40 10c lilac & multi	.25	.25
211 A40 15c salmon & multi	.30	.30
212 A40 25c blue & multi	.65	.65
Nos. 209-212 (4)	1.45	1.45

21st Olympic Games, Montreal, Canada, July 17-Aug. 1.

Rising Sun of Independence — A41

Designs: 10c, Opening gates. 15c, Broken chain. 25c, Plane over Molimo Restaurant.

1976, Oct. 4 *Perf. 14*

213 A41 4c yellow & multi	.25	.25
214 A41 10c pink & multi	.25	.25
215 A41 15c blue & multi	.50	.25
216 A41 25c dull blue & multi	.60	.50
Nos. 213-216 (4)	1.60	1.25

Lesotho's independence, 10th anniversary.

Telephones, 1876 and 1976 — A42

Designs: 10c, Woman using telephone, and 1895 telephone. 15c, Telephone operators and wall telephone. 25c, A.G. Bell and 1905 telephone.

Perf. 13x13½

1976, Dec. 6 Wmk. 362

217 A42 4c multicolored	.25	.25
218 A42 10c multicolored	.25	.25
219 A42 15c multicolored	.35	.35
220 A42 25c multicolored	.50	.50
Nos. 217-220 (4)	1.35	1.35

Centenary of first telephone call by Alexander Graham Bell, Mar. 10, 1876.

Aloe Striatula — A43

Aloes and Succulents: 4c, Aloe aristata. 5c, Kniphofia caulescens. 10c, Euphorbia pulvinata. 15c, Aloe saponaria. 20c, Caralluma lutea. 25c, Aloe polyphylla.

1977, Feb. 14 Litho. *Perf. 14*

221 A43 3c multicolored	.30	.25
222 A43 4c multicolored	.35	.25
223 A43 5c multicolored	.40	.25
224 A43 10c multicolored	.55	.25
225 A43 15c multicolored	1.50	.40
226 A43 20c multicolored	1.50	.60
227 A43 25c multicolored	1.75	.80
Nos. 221-227 (7)	6.35	2.80

Rock Rabbits — A44

Perf. 14x14½

1977, Apr. 25 Wmk. 362

228 A44 4c shown	*6.00*	.55
229 A44 5c Porcupine	*6.00*	.75
230 A44 10c Polecat	*6.00*	.60
231 A44 15c Klipspringers	*18.50*	2.75
232 A44 25c Baboons	*20.00*	3.00
Nos. 228-232 (5)	*56.50*	7.65

Man with Cane, Concentric Circles — A45

Man with Cane: 10c, Surrounded by flames of pain. 15c, Surrounded by chain. 25c, Man and globe.

1977, July 4 Litho. *Perf. 14*

233 A45 4c red & yellow	.25	.25
234 A45 10c dk blue & lt blue	.25	.25
235 A45 15c blue green & yellow	.40	.25
236 A45 25c black & orange	.50	.60
Nos. 233-236 (4)	1.40	1.35

World Rheumatism Year.

Small-mouthed Yellow-fish — A46

Fresh-water Fish: 10c, Orange River mud fish. 15c, Rainbow trout. 25c, Oreodaimon quathlambae.

1977, Sept. 28 Wmk. 362 *Perf. 14*

237 A46 4c multicolored	.40	.25
238 A46 10c multicolored	.75	.25
239 A46 15c multicolored	1.50	.60
240 A46 25c multicolored	1.60	1.25
Nos. 237-240 (4)	4.25	2.35

White and Black Equal — A47

Designs: 10c, Black and white jigsaw puzzle. 15c, White and black cogwheels. 25c, Black and white handshake.

1977, Dec. 12 Litho. *Perf. 14*

241 A47 4c lilac rose & black	.25	.25
242 A47 10c brt blue & black	.25	.25
243 A47 15c orange & black	.25	.25
244 A47 25c lt green & black	.30	.30
Nos. 241-244 (4)	1.05	1.05

Action to Combat Racism Decade.

No. 99 Surcharged

1977, Dec. 7

245 A15 3c on 10c gray & ocher	1.75	1.50

Poppies — A48

Flowers of Lesotho: 3c, Diascia integerrima. 4c, Helichrysum trilineatum. 5c, Zaluzianskya maritima. 10c, Gladioli. 15c, Chironia krebsii. 25c, Wahlenbergia undulata. 40c, Brunsvigia radulosa.

1978, Feb. 13 Litho. Wmk. 362

246 A48 2c multicolored	.25	.30
247 A48 3c multicolored	.25	.30
248 A48 4c multicolored	.25	.25
249 A48 5c multicolored	.25	.25
250 A48 10c multicolored	.25	.30
251 A48 15c multicolored	.25	.45
252 A48 25c multicolored	.80	1.00
253 A48 40c multicolored	1.40	2.00
Nos. 246-253 (8)	3.70	4.85

Edward Jenner Vaccinating Child — A49

Global Eradication of Smallpox: 25c, Child's head and WHO emblem.

1978, May 8 Litho. *Perf. 13½x13*

254 A49 5c multicolored	.40	.25
255 A49 25c multicolored	1.40	1.50

Tsoloane Falls — A50

Lesotho Waterfalls: 10c, Qiloane Falls. 15c, Tsoelikana Falls. 25c, Maletsunyane Falls.

1978, July 28 Litho. *Perf. 14*

256 A50 4c multicolored	.25	.25
257 A50 10c multicolored	.30	.30
258 A50 15c multicolored	.55	.55
259 A50 25c multicolored	.85	.85
Nos. 256-259 (4)	1.95	1.95

Flyer 1 — A51

25c, Orville and Wilbur Wright, Flyer 1.

1978, Oct. 9 Wmk. 362 *Perf. 14½*

260 A51 5c multicolored	.25	.25
261 A51 25c multicolored	1.00	1.00

75th anniversary of 1st powered flight.

Dragonflies — A52

Insects: 10c, Winged grasshopper. 15c, Wasps. 25c, Praying mantis.

1978, Dec. 18 Litho. *Perf. 14*

262 A52 4c multicolored	.25	.25
263 A52 10c multicolored	.30	.30
264 A52 15c multicolored	.45	.45
265 A52 25c multicolored	.75	.75
Nos. 262-265 (4)	1.75	1.75

Trees — A53

1979, Mar. 26 Litho. *Perf. 14*

266 A53 4c Leucosidea Sericea	.25	.25
267 A53 10c Wild olive	.25	.25
268 A53 15c Blinkblaar	.40	.40
269 A53 25c Cape holly	.55	.55
Nos. 266-269 (4)	1.45	1.45

Reptiles — A54

1979, June 4 Wmk. 362 *Perf. 14*

270 A54 4s Agama Lizard	.35	.35
271 A54 10s Berg adder	.45	.40
272 A54 15s Rock lizard	.65	.55
273 A54 25s Spitting snake	1.15	1.00
Nos. 270-273 (4)	2.60	2.30

A55

1979, Oct. 22 Litho. *Perf. 14½*

274 A55 4s Basutoland No. 2	.25	.25
275 A55 15s Basutoland No. 72	.30	.30
276 A55 25s Penny Black	.45	.45
Nos. 274-276 (3)	1.00	1.00

Souvenir Sheet

277 A55 50s Lesotho No. 122	.90	.90

Sir Rowland Hill (1795-1879), originator of penny postage.

Intl. Year of the Child — A56

Children's Games, by Brueghel the Elder, and IYC emblem: 4s, Children Climbing Tree. 10s, Follow the leader. 15s, Three cup montie. 25s, Entire painting.

1979, Dec. 10 Wmk. 362 Perf. 14½

278 A56 4s multicolored .25 .25
279 A56 10s multicolored .25 .25
280 A56 15s multicolored .25 .25
Nos. 278-280 (3) .75 .75

Souvenir Sheet

281 A56 25s multicolored .75 .75

Beer Strainer, Brooms and Mat — A57

1980, Feb. 18 Litho. Perf. 14½

282 A57 4s shown .25 .25
283 A57 10s Winnowing basket .25 .25
284 A57 15s Basotho hat .30 .30
285 A57 25s Grain storage pots .50 .50
Nos. 282-285 (4) 1.30 1.30

Qalabane Ambush — A58

Gun War Centenary: 4s, Praise poet, text. 5s, Basotho army commander Lerotholi. 15s, Snider and Martini-Henry rifles. 25s, Map of Basutoland showing battle sites.

1980, May 6 Litho. Perf. 14

286 A58 4s multicolored .25 .25
287 A58 5s multicolored .25 .25
288 A58 10s multicolored .30 .30
289 A58 15s multicolored .65 .40
290 A58 25s multicolored .80 .65
Nos. 286-290 (5) 2.25 1.85

St. Basil's, Moscow, Olympic Torch — A59

No. 292, Torch and flags. No. 293, Soccer. No. 294, Running. No. 295, Misha and stadium.
No. 296,

1980, Sept. 20 Litho. Perf. 14½

291 A59 25s shown .35 .35
292 A59 25s multicolored .35 .35
293 A59 25s multicolored .35 .35
294 A59 25s multicolored .35 .35
295 A59 25s multicolored .35 .35
a. Strip of 5, #291-295 2.25 2.25

Souvenir Sheet

296 A59 1.40m multicolored 2.00 2.00

22nd Summer Olympic Games, Moscow, July 19-Aug. 3.

Beer Mug and Man Drinking A60

Prince Philip A61

Wmk. 362

1980, Oct. 1 Litho. Perf. 14

297 A60 4s shown .25 .25
298 A60 10s Beer brewing pot .25 .25
299 A60 15s Water pot .25 .25
300 A60 25s Pots and jugs .30 .25
Nos. 297-300 (4) 1.05 1.00

Souvenir Sheet

Perf. 14x14½

301 Sheet of 4 1.25 1.25
a. A61 40s shown .30 .30
b. A61 40s Queen Elizabeth .30 .30
c. A61 40s Prince Charles .30 .30
d. A61 40s Princess Anne .30 .30

Traditional pottery; 250th birth anniversary of Josiah Wedgewood, potter.

Nos. 104, 199-208 Surcharged

Nos. 302-303, 304, 306-308, 310

No. 304a

No. 305

No. 309

Nos. 311-312

Wmk. 362

1980, Oct. 20 Litho. Perf. 14

302 A38 2s on 2c multi .25 .25
303 A38 3s on 3c multi .25 .25
304 A38 5s on 5c multi .25 .25
a. 6s on 5s on 5c multi .25 .25
305 A38 6s on 4c multi .25 .25
306 A38 10s on 10c multi .25 .25
307 A38 25s on 25c multi .35 .35
308 A38 40s on 40c multi .55 .55
309 A38 50s on 50c multi .80 .80
310 A38 75s on 15c multi 2.00 2.00
311 A39 1m on 1r multi 2.40 2.40
312 A15 2m on 2r multi 4.50 4.50
Nos. 302-312 (11) 11.85 11.85

Numerous surcharge errors exist (double triple, inverted, etc.).

Queen Mother Elizabeth and Prince Charles — A62

Basutoland No. 36, Flags of Lesotho and Britain — A63

1980, Dec. 1 Unwmk. Perf. 14½

313 Sheet of 9 3.75 3.75
a. A62 5s shown .25 .25
b. A62 10s Portrait .25 .25
c. A63 1m shown 1.10 1.10

Queen Mother Elizabeth, 80th birthday. No. 313 contains 3 each Nos. 313a-313c.

St. Agnes' Anglican Church, Teyateyaneng A63a

Nativity A64

4s, Lesotho Evangelical Church, Morija. 25s, Our Lady's Victory Cathedral, Maseru. 75s, University Chapel, Roma.

1980, Dec. 8 Perf. 14x14½

314 A63a 4s multicolored .25 .25
315 A63a 15s shown .25 .25
316 A63a 25s multicolored .25 .25
317 A63a 75s multicolored .25 .25
Nos. 314-317 (4) 1.00 1.00

Souvenir Sheet

318 A64 1.50m shown .90 .90

Christmas.

Voyager Satellite and Saturn — A65

1981, Mar. 15 Litho. Perf. 14

319 Strip of 5 2.50 2.50
a. A65 25s Voyager, planet .40 .40
b. A65 25s shown .40 .40
c. A65 25s Voyager, Saturn's rings .40 .40
d. A65 25s Columbia space shuttle .40 .40
e. A65 25s Columbia, diff. .40 .40

Souvenir Sheet

320 A65 1.40m Saturn 2.50 2.50

Voyager expedition to Saturn and flight of Columbia space shuttle.

Rock Pigeons A66

1s, Greater kestrel, vert. 3s, Crowned cranes, vert. 5s, Bokmakierie, vert. 6s, Cape robins, vert. 7s, Yellow canary, vert. 10s, Red-billed teal. 25s, Malachite kingfisher, vert. 40s, Malachite sunbirds. 60s, Orange-throated longclaw. 75s, African hoopoe. 1m, Red bishops. 2m, Egyptian goose. 5m, Lilac-breasted rollers.

1981, Apr. 20 Unwmk. Perf. 14½

321 A66 1s mutlicolored .25 .25
322 A66 2s shown .25 .25
323 A66 3s multicolored .25 .25
324 A66 5s multicolored .25 .25
325 A66 6s multicolored .40 .25
326 A66 7s multicolored .40 .25
327 A66 10s multicolored .40 .25
328 A66 25s multicolored 1.00 .60
329 A66 40s multicolored 1.25 1.00
330 A66 60s multicolored 1.60 1.50
331 A66 75s multicolored 2.00 1.75
332 A66 1m multicolored 2.50 2.50
333 A66 2m multicolored 4.75 4.75
334 A66 5m multicolored 9.00 9.00
Nos. 321-334 (14) 24.30 22.85

For surcharges see Nos. 558A, 561-563, 598A, 599, 600B, 600C.

1981 Perf. 13

321a A66 1s 1.40 .70
322a A66 2s 1.60 .70
324a A66 5s 2.00 .70
327a A66 10s 2.00 .70
Nos. 321a-327a (4) 7.00 2.80

1982, June 14 Wmk. 373 Perf. 14½

321b A66 1s .25 .40
322b A66 2s .25 .40
323a A66 3s .35 .40
324b A66 5s .35 .45
325a A66 6s .35 .25
326a A66 7s .35 .25
327b A66 10s .35 .25
328a A66 25s 1.00 .45
329a A66 40s 1.10 .50
330a A66 60s 1.50 .90
331a A66 75s 2.00 .90
332a A66 1m 2.40 *2.75*
333a A66 2m 3.00 *4.00*
334a A66 5m 6.00 *10.00*
Nos. 321b-334a (14) 19.25 21.90

Common Design Types pictured following the introduction.

Royal Wedding Issue

Common Design Type and

Royal Wedding A66a

Unwmk.

1981, July 22 Litho. Perf. 14

335 CD331 25s Bouquet .25 .25
a. Booklet pane of 3 + label .80
336 CD331 50s Charles .25 .25
a. Booklet pane of 3 + label 1.40
337 CD331 75s Couple .40 .40
b. Booklet pane of 3 + label 1.60
c. Bklt. pane of 3, #335-337 + label 1.25
Nos. 335-337 (3) .90 .90

1981 Litho. Perf. 14½

Souvenir Sheet

337A A66a 1.50m Couple 1.75 1.75

Nos. 335-337A exist imperf. Value, set $8.

Tree Planting — A67

6s, Duke of Edinburgh and flags. 25s, Digging. 40s, Mountain climbing. 75s, Emblem. 1.40m, Duke of Edinburgh.

1981, Oct. 30 Litho. Perf. 14½

338 A67 6s multicolored .25 .25
339 A67 7s shown .25 .25
340 A67 25s multicolored .25 .25
341 A67 40s multicolored .40 .40
342 A67 75s multicolored .65 .65
Nos. 338-342 (5) 1.80 1.80

Souvenir Sheet

343 A67 1.40m multi 1.75 1.75

Duke of Edinburgh's Awards, 25th anniv. No. 343 contains 1 45x29mm stamp, perf. 13½.

Santa Claus at Globe, by Norman Rockwell — A68

The Mystic Nativity, by Botticelli A69

Christmas: Saturday Evening Post covers by Norman Rockwell.

1981, Oct. 5 Perf. 13½x14

344 A68 6s multicolored .25 .25
345 A68 10s multicolored .25 .25
346 A68 15s multicolored .25 .25
347 A68 20s multicolored .30 .30
348 A68 25s multicolored .35 .35
349 A68 60s multicolored .65 .65
Nos. 344-349 (6) 2.05 2.05

Souvenir Sheet

350 A69 1.25m multicolored 2.00 2.00

Chacma Baboons — A70

Perf. 14x13½, 14½ (20s, 40s, 50s)

1982, Jan. 15 — Litho.

351	A70	6s African wild cat	*3.75*	.50
352	A70	20s shown	*4.75*	1.25
353	A70	25s Cape eland	*5.75*	1.90
354	A70	40s Porcupine	*6.75*	2.50
355	A70	50s Oribi	*7.00*	3.25
		Nos. 351-355 (5)	*28.00*	9.40

Souvenir Sheet

Perf. 14

356	A70	1.50m Black-backed jackal	10.50	8.50

6s, 25s; 50x37mm. No. 356 contains one stamp 48x31mm.

Scouting Year — A71

1982, Mar. 5 — Litho. — *Perf. 14x13½*

357	A71	6s Bugle call	.25	.25
358	A71	30s Hiking	.50	.50
359	A71	40s Drawing	.70	.70
360	A71	50s Holding flag	.90	.90
361	A71	75s Salute	1.30	1.30
a.		Booklet pane of 10 + sheet	11.00	
		Nos. 357-361 (5)	3.65	3.65

Souvenir Sheet

362	A71	1.50m Baden-Powell	2.40	2.40

No. 361a contains 2 each Nos. 357-361 with gutter and No. 362.

Nos. 357-361 issued in sheets of 8 with gutter.

1982 World Cup Soccer — A72

Championships, 1930-1978: a, Uruguay, 1930. b, Italy, 1934. c, France, 1938. d, Brazil, 1950. e, Switzerland, 1954. f, Sweden, 1958. g, Chile, 1962. h, England, 1966. i, Mexico, 1970. j, Germany, 1974. k, Argentina, 1978. l, World Cup.

1982, Apr. 14 — *Perf. 14½*

363		Sheet of 12	4.00	4.00
a.-l.	A72	15s any single	.25	.25

Souvenir Sheet

364	A72	1.25m Stadium	2.00	2.00

Nos. 363b, 363c, 363f, 363g, 363j, 363k exist se-tenant in sheets of 72.

George Washington's Birth Bicentenary — A73

Paintings: 6s, Portrait. 7s, With children. 10s, Indian Chief's Prophecy. 25s, With troops. 40s, Arriving at New York. 1m, Entry into New York.

1.25m, Crossing Delaware.

1982, June 7

365	A73	6s multicolored	.25	.25
366	A73	7s multicolored	.25	.25
367	A73	10s multicolored	.25	.25
368	A73	25s multicolored	.35	.35
369	A73	40s multicolored	.45	.45
370	A73	1m multicolored	.90	.90
		Nos. 365-370 (6)	2.45	2.45

Souvenir Sheet

371	A73	1.25m multicolored	1.75	1.75

Princess Diana Issue

Common Design Type

Wmk. 373

1982, July 1 — Litho. — *Perf. 14*

372	CD333	30s Arms	.75	.75
373	CD333	50s Diana	.75	.75
374	CD333	75s Wedding	1.00	1.00
375	CD333	1m Portrait	1.50	1.50
		Nos. 372-375 (4)	4.00	4.00

Sesotho Bible Centenary — A74

6s, Man reading bible. 15s, Angels, bible. 1m, Bible, Maseru Cathedral.

1982, Aug. 20 — Litho. — *Perf. 14½*

376	A74	6s multi	.25	.25
377	A74	15s multi	.25	.25

Size: 59½x40½mm

378	A74	1m multi	.40	.40
		Nos. 376-378 (3)	.90	.90

Issued in sheets of 9 (3 each Nos. 376-378).

Birth of Prince William of Wales, June 21 — A75

1982, Sept. 30

379	A75	6s Congratulation	3.25	3.25
380	A75	60s Diana, William	1.75	1.75

Issued in sheets of 6 (No. 379, 5 No. 380).

Christmas A76

Designs: Scenes from Walt Disney's The Twelve Days of Christmas. Stamps of same denomination se-tenant.

1982, Dec. 1 — Litho. — *Perf. 11*

381	A76	2s multicolored	.25	.25
382	A76	2s multicolored	.25	.25
383	A76	3s multicolored	.25	.25
384	A76	3s multicolored	.25	.25
385	A76	4s multicolored	.25	.25
386	A76	4s multicolored	.25	.25
387	A76	75s multicolored	1.40	2.00
388	A76	75s multicolored	1.40	2.00
		Nos. 381-388 (8)	4.30	5.50

Souvenir Sheet

Perf. 14x13½

389	A76	1.50m multicolored	4.00	4.00

Local Mushrooms A77

10s, Lepista caffrorum. 30s, Broomexia congregate. 50s, Afroboletus luteolus. 75s, Lentinus tuberregium.

1983, Jan. 11 — *Perf. 14½*

390	A77	10s multicolored	.25	.25
391	A77	30s multicolored	.50	.40
a.		Booklet pane of 2, #390, 391	1.05	
392	A77	50s multicolored	.90	.80
393	A77	75s multicolored	1.25	1.10
a.		Booklet pane of 4, #390-393	4.00	
		Nos. 390-393 (4)	2.90	2.55

Commonwealth Day — A78

1983, Mar. 14 — Litho. — *Perf. 14½*

394	A78	5s Ba-Leseli dance	.25	.25
395	A78	30s Tapestry weaving	.25	.25
396	A78	60s Elizabeth II	.35	.35
397	A78	75s Moshoeshoe II	.40	.40
		Nos. 394-397 (4)	1.25	1.25

Trance Dancers — A79

Hunters — A79a

Rock Paintings: 25s, Baboons, Sehonghong Thaba Tseka. 60s, Hunter attacking mountain reedbuck, Makhetha Berera. 75s, Eland, Leribe.

1983, May 20 — Litho. — *Perf. 14½*

398	A79	6s multicolored	.35	.35
399	A79	25s multicolored	.70	.70
400	A79	60s multicolored	.80	.80
401	A79	75s multicolored	.90	.90
		Nos. 398-401 (4)	2.75	2.75

Souvenir Sheet

402		Sheet of 5, #398-401, 402a	3.00	3.00
a.		A79a 10s multicolored	.30	.25

Manned Flight Bicentenary A80

1983, July 11 — Litho. — *Perf. 14½*

403	A80	7s Montgolfier, 1783	.25	.25
404	A80	30s Wright brothers	.45	.35
405	A80	60s 1st airmail plane	.85	.75
406	A80	1m Concorde	2.50	2.50
		Nos. 403-406 (4)	4.05	3.85

Souvenir Sheet

407		Sheet of 5	3.00	3.00
a.		A80 6s Dornier 228	.30	.30

No. 407 contains Nos. 403-406, 407a (60x60mm).

Sesquicentennial of French Missionaries' Arrival — A81

6s, Rev. Eugene Casalis, flags. 25s, Morija, 1833. 40s, Baptism of Libe. 75s, Map of Basutoland, 1834.

1983, Sept. 5 — Litho. — *Perf. 13½x14*

408	A81	6s multicolored	.30	.30
409	A81	25s multicolored	.30	.30
410	A81	40s multicolored	.30	.30
411	A81	75s multicolored	.65	.65
		Nos. 408-411 (4)	1.55	1.55

Christmas A82

Scenes from Disney's Old Christmas, from Washington Irving's Sketch Book: 2s, Christmas Eve, diff. 3s, Christmas Day. 4s, Christmas Day, diff. 5s, Christmas dinner. 6s, Christmas dinner, diff. 75s, Christmas games. 1m, Christmas dancers.

1.75m, Christmas Eve.

1983, Dec. — Litho. — *Perf. 14*

412	A82	1s shown	.25	.25
413	A82	2s multicolored	.25	.25
414	A82	3s multicolored	.25	.25
415	A82	4s multicolored	.25	.25
416	A82	5s multicolored	.25	.25
417	A82	6s multicolored	.25	.25
418	A82	75s multicolored	2.25	2.25
419	A82	1m multicolored	2.50	2.50
		Nos. 412-419 (8)	6.25	6.25

Souvenir Sheet

420	A82	1.75m multicolored	5.00	5.00

African Monarch — A83

Butterflies: 2s, Mountain Beauty. 3s, Orange Tip. 4s, Blue Pansy. 5s, Yellow Pansy. 6s, African Migrant. 7s, African Leopard. 10s, Suffused Acraea. 15s, Painted Lady. 20s, Lemon Traveller. 30s, Foxy Charaxes. 50s, Broad-Bordered Grass Yellow. 60s, Meadow White. 75s, Queen Purple Tip. 1m, Diadem. 5m, Christmas Butterfly.

1984, Jan. 20 — Litho.

421	A83	1s shown	.50	.35
422	A83	2s multicolored	.50	.35
423	A83	3s multicolored	.60	.40
424	A83	4s multicolored	.60	.40
425	A83	5s multicolored	.60	.40
426	A83	6s multicolored	.60	.40
427	A83	7s multicolored	.60	.40
428	A83	10s multicolored	.70	.50
429	A83	15s multicolored	1.10	1.10
430	A83	20s multicolored	1.50	1.25
431	A83	30s multicolored	1.75	1.75
432	A83	50s multicolored	1.75	1.75
433	A83	60s multicolored	1.75	1.75
434	A83	75s multicolored	1.90	2.00
435	A83	1m multicolored	1.90	2.00
436	A83	5m multicolored	3.00	4.50
		Nos. 421-436 (16)	19.35	19.30

For surcharges see Nos. 559-560, 561A, 564-566, 600, 600A, 600D, 617A-617B.

Easter — A84

Designs: Nos. 437a-437j, The Ten Commandments. 1.50m, Moses holding tablets.

1984, Mar. 30 — Litho. — *Perf. 14*

437		Sheet of 10 + 2 labels	6.50	6.50
a.-j.		A84 20s any single	.30	.30

Souvenir Sheet

438	A84	1.50m multicolored	1.75	1.75

No. 438 contains one stamp 45x29mm.

1984 Summer Olympics A85

10s, Torch bearer. 30s, Equestrian. 50s, Swimming. 75s, Basketball. 1m, Running.

1.50m, Flags, flame, stadium.

1984, May 5 — Litho. — *Perf. 13½*

439	A85	10s multicolored	.25	.25
440	A85	30s multicolored	.25	.25
441	A85	50s multicolored	.25	.25
442	A85	75s multicolored	.35	.35
443	A85	1m multicolored	.45	.45
		Nos. 439-443 (5)	1.55	1.55

Souvenir Sheet

444	A85	1.50m multicolored	1.60	1.60

Prehistoric Footprints A86

10s, Sauropodomorph. 30s, Lesothosaurus. 50s, Carnivorous dinosaur.

1984, July 2 — Litho. — *Perf. 13½*

445	A86	10s multicolored	.25	.25
446	A86	30s multicolored	.80	.80
447	A86	50s multicolored	1.45	1.45
		Nos. 445-447 (3)	2.50	2.50

Mail Coach Bicentenary and Ausipex '84 — A87

6s, Wells Fargo, 1852. 7s, Basotho mail cart, 1900. 10s, Bath mail coach, 1784. 30s, Cobb coach, 1853. 50s, Exhibition buildings. 1.75m, Penny Black, Basutoland #O4, Western Australia #3.

1984, Sept. 5 Litho. *Perf. 14*

448	A87	6s multicolored	.25	.25
a.		Sheet of 4 #448, 1 #451A	1.00	1.00
449	A87	7s multicolored	.25	.25
a.		Sheet of 4 #449, 1 #451A	1.00	1.00
450	A87	10s multicolored	.25	.25
a.		Sheet of 4 #450, 1 #451A	1.00	1.00
451	A87	30s multicolored	.25	.25
b.		Sheet of 4 #451, 1 #451A	1.00	1.00

Size: 82x26mm

451A	A87	50s multicolored	.45	.45
		Nos. 448-451A (5)	1.45	1.45

Souvenir Sheet

452	A87	1.75m multicolored	3.25	3.25

No. 452 contains one stamp 82x26mm.

Trains — A88

6s, Orient Express, 1900. 15s, 05.001, Class 5, 1935. 30s, Cardean, Caledonian, 1906. 60s, Santa Fe, Super Chief, 1940. 1m, Flying Scotsman, 1934.
2m, The Blue Train, 1972.

1984, Nov. 5 Litho. *Perf. 13½*

453	A88	6s multicolored	.25	.25
454	A88	15s multicolored	.30	.30
455	A88	30s multicolored	.40	.40
456	A88	60s multicolored	.80	1.25
457	A88	1m multicolored	1.60	2.00
		Nos. 453-457 (5)	3.35	4.20

Souvenir Sheet

Perf. 14x13½

458	A88	2m multicolored	2.10	2.10

Indigenous Young Animals — A89

15s, Cape Eland calf. 20s, Chacma baboons. 30s, Oribo calf. 75s, Red rock hares. 1m, Black-backed jackals.

1984, Dec. 20 *Perf. 14½*

459	A89	15s multicolored	.25	.25
460	A89	20s multicolored	.30	.30
461	A89	30s multicolored	.45	.45
462	A89	75s multicolored	.90	1.25

Size: 47x28mm

Perf. 13½

463	A89	1m multicolored	1.25	1.75
		Nos. 459-463 (5)	3.15	4.00

King Moshoeshoe II — A90

6s, Royal crown, 1974. 30s, Moshoeshoe II, 1966. 75s, In Basotho dress. 1m, In military uniform.

1985, Jan. 30 Litho. *Perf. 15*

464	A90	6s multicolored	.25	.25
465	A90	30s multicolored	.25	.25
466	A90	75s multicolored	.45	.45
467	A90	1m multicolored	.65	.65
		Nos. 464-467 (4)	1.60	1.60

25th anniversary of reign.

Miniature Sheet

Easter — A91

Stations of the Cross: a, Condemned to death. b, Bearing cross. c, Falls the first time. d, Meets his mother. e, Cyrenean helps carry cross. f, Veronica wipes His face. g, Second fall. h, Consoles women of Jerusalem. i, Third fall. j, Stripped. k, Nailed to cross. l, Dies on cross. m, Taken down from cross. n, Laid in sepulchre.

No. 469, The Crucifixion, detail, by Mathias Grunewald (c. 1460-1528).

1985, Mar. 8 *Perf. 11*

468	A91	Sheet of 14 + label	6.50	6.50
a.-n.		20s any single	.25	.25

Souvenir Sheet

Perf. 14

469	A91	2m multicolored	2.25	2.25

Queen Mother, 85th Birthday A92

Photographs: 10s, Queen Mother, Princess Elizabeth, 1931. 30s, 75th birthday portrait. 60s With Queen Elizabeth II and Princess Margaret, 80th birthday. No. 473, With Queen Elizabeth II, Princess Diana, Princes Henry and Charles, christening of Prince Henry.

No. 474, like No. 473, with Prince William.

1985, May 30 *Perf. 13½x14*

470	A92	10s multicolored	.25	.25
471	A92	30s multicolored	.90	.90
472	A92	60s multicolored	1.00	1.00
473	A92	2m multicolored	1.75	1.75
		Nos. 470-473 (4)	3.90	3.90

Souvenir Sheet

474	A92	2m multicolored	2.00	2.00

No. 474 contains one stamp 38x51mm.

Automobile Centenary A93

Luxury cars: 6s, BMW 732i. 10s, Ford LTD Crown Victoria. 30s, Mercedes-Benz 500SE. 90s, Cadillac Eldorado Biarritz. No. 479, Rolls Royce Silver Spirit.

No. 480, 1907 Rolls Royce Silver Ghost Tourer, vert.

1985, June 10 *Perf. 14*

475	A93	6s multicolored	.35	.25
476	A93	10s multicolored	.50	.25
477	A93	30s multicolored	.80	.60
478	A93	90s multicolored	1.50	1.50
479	A93	2m multicolored	3.00	3.00
		Nos. 475-479 (5)	6.15	5.60

Souvenir Sheet

480	A93	2m multicolored	5.50	5.50

No. 480 contains one stamp 38x51mm.

Audubon Birth Bicentenary A94

Illustrations of North American bird species by artist and naturalist John J. Audubon: 5s, Cliff swallow, vert. 6s, Great crested grebe. 10s, Vesper sparrow. 30s, Greenshank. 60s, Stilt sandpiper. 2m, Glossy ibis.

1985, Aug. 5 *Perf. 14½*

481	A94	5s multicolored	.55	.45
482	A94	6s multicolored	.70	.45
483	A94	10s multicolored	1.25	.60
484	A94	30s multicolored	1.75	1.75
485	A94	60s multicolored	2.25	2.25
486	A94	2m multicolored	3.50	3.50
		Nos. 481-486 (6)	10.00	9.00

Nos. 481-486 printed in sheets of 5 with labels picturing various birds.

Intl. Youth Year, Girl Guides 75th Anniv. — A95

10s, Mountain climbing. 30s, Medical research. 75s, Guides on parade. No. 490, 2m, Guide saluting.

No. 491, Lady Baden-Powell, World Chief Guide.

1985, Sept. 26 *Perf. 15*

487	A95	10s multicolored	.25	.25
488	A95	30s multicolored	.60	.60
489	A95	75s multicolored	1.25	1.25
490	A95	2m multicolored	2.50	2.50
		Nos. 487-490 (4)	4.60	4.60

Souvenir Sheet

491	A95	2m multicolored	3.50	3.50

UN, 40th Anniv. — A96

Designs: 10s, UN No. 1, flag, horiz. 30s, Dish satellite, Ha Sofonia Earth Satellite Station, ITU emblem. 50s, Aircraft, Maseru Airport, ICAO emblem, horiz. 2m, Maimonides (1135-1204), medieval Jewish scholar, WHO emblem.

1985, Oct. 15 Litho. *Perf. 15*

492	A96	10s multicolored	.30	.30
493	A96	30s multicolored	.50	.50
494	A96	50s multicolored	.90	.90
495	A96	2m multicolored	4.50	4.50
		Nos. 492-495 (4)	6.20	6.20

Wildflowers — A97

6s, Cosmos. 10s, Small agapanthus. 30s, Pink witchweed. 60s, Small iris. 90s, Wild geranium. 1m, Large spotted orchid.

1985, Nov. 11 *Perf. 11*

496	A97	6s multicolored	.45	.25
497	A97	10s multicolored	.60	.25
498	A97	30s multicolored	1.10	.75
499	A97	60s multicolored	1.75	1.75
500	A97	90s multicolored	2.25	2.25
501	A97	1m multicolored	3.00	3.00
		Nos. 496-501 (6)	9.15	8.25

Mark Twain, Author, Jacob and Wilhelm Grimm, Fabulists — A98

Disney characters acting out Mark Twain quotes or portraying characters from The Wishing Table, by the Grimm Brothers.

1985, Dec. 2 *Perf. 11*

502	A98	6s multicolored	.25	.25
503	A98	10s multicolored	.25	.25
504	A98	50s multicolored	1.40	1.40
505	A98	60s multicolored	1.90	1.90
506	A98	75s multicolored	2.25	2.25
507	A98	90s multicolored	2.75	2.75
508	A98	1m multicolored	3.00	3.00
509	A98	1.50m multicolored	5.00	5.00
		Nos. 502-509 (8)	16.80	16.80

Souvenir Sheets

Perf. 14

510	A98	1.25m multicolored	6.00	6.00
511	A98	1.50m multicolored	6.00	6.00

Christmas. Nos. 505, 507 printed in sheets of 8.

World Wildlife Fund — A99

Lammergeier vulture.

1986, Jan. 20 *Perf. 15*

512	A99	7s Male	*2.00*	*.75*
513	A99	15s Male, female	*3.75*	*1.00*
514	A99	50s Male in flight	*5.50*	*2.00*
515	A99	1m Adult, young	*7.00*	*3.50*
		Nos. 512-515 (4)	18.25	7.25

Flora and Fauna — A100

9s, Prickly pear. 12s, Stapelia. 35s, Pig's ears. No. 519, 2m, Columnar cereus.

No. 520, 2m, Black eagle.

1986, Jan. 20

516	A100	9s multicolored	.50	.25
517	A100	12s multicolored	.50	.25
518	A100	35s multicolored	.75	.50
519	A100	2m multicolored	2.75	2.50
		Nos. 516-519 (4)	4.50	3.50

Souvenir Sheet

520	A100	2m multicolored	9.75	9.75

1986 World Cup Soccer Championships, Mexico — A101

Various soccer plays.

1986, Mar. 17 *Perf. 14*

521	A101	35s multicolored	1.25	1.25
522	A101	50s multicolored	1.75	1.75
523	A101	1m multicolored	3.50	3.50
524	A101	2m multicolored	7.00	7.00
		Nos. 521-524 (4)	13.50	13.50

Souvenir Sheet

525	A101	3m multicolored	10.00	10.00

New Currency, 1st Anniv. (in 1980) A101a

No. 525A — Both sides of: b, 1979 Intl. Year of the Child gold coin. c, Five-maloti banknote. d, 1979 50-lisente coin. e, Ten-maloti banknote. f, 1979 1-sente coin.

1986, Apr. 1 Litho. *Perf. 13¾x14*

525A Horiz. strip of 5 *30.00 32.50*
b.-f. A101a 30s Any single *6.00 6.50*

A102

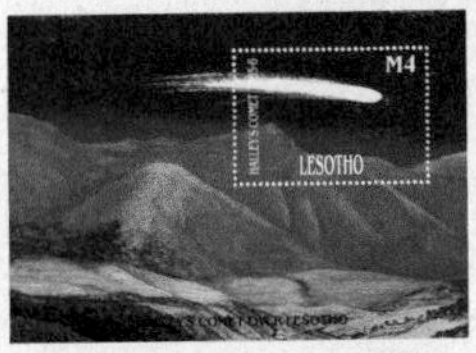

Halley's Comet — A103

Designs: 9s, Hale Telescope, Mt. Palomar, Galileo. 15s, Pioneer Venus 2 probe, 1985 sighting. 70s, 684 sighting illustration, Nuremberg Chronicles. 3m, 1066 sighting, Norman conquest of England. 4m, Comet over Lesotho.

1986, Apr. 5

526 A102 9s multicolored .65 .25
527 A102 15s multicolored .90 .25
528 A102 70s multicolored 2.00 .75
529 A102 3m multicolored 5.50 6.00
Nos. 526-529 (4) 9.05 7.25

Souvenir Sheet

530 A103 4m multicolored 8.50 8.50

Queen Elizabeth II, 60th Birthday
Common Design Type

Designs: 90s, In pantomime during youth. 1m, At Windsor Horse Show, 1971. 2m, At Royal Festival Hall, 1971. 4m, Age 8.

1986, Apr. 21

531 CD339 90s lt yel bis & black .55 .55
532 CD339 1m pale grn & multi .65 .65
533 CD339 2m dull vio & multi 1.30 1.30
Nos. 531-533 (3) 2.50 2.50

Souvenir Sheet

534 CD339 4m tan & black 2.75 2.75

For overprints see Nos. 636-639.

Statue of Liberty, Cent. — A104

Statue and famous emigrants: 15s, Bela Bartok (1881-1945), composer. 35s, Felix Adler (1857-1933), philosopher. 1m, Victor Herbert (1859-1924), composer. No. 538, David Niven (1910-1983), actor. No. 539, Statue, vert.

1986, May 1

535 A104 15s multicolored .90 .25
536 A104 35s multicolored .90 .35
537 A104 1m multicolored 3.25 1.75
538 A104 3m multicolored 5.00 3.00
Nos. 535-538 (4) 10.05 5.35

Souvenir Sheet

539 A104 3m multicolored 6.50 6.50

AMERIPEX '86 — A105

Walt Disney characters: 15s, Goofy, Mickey. 35s, Mickey, Pluto. 1m, Goofy. 2m, Donald, Pete. 4m, Goofy, Chip'n'Dale.

1986, May 22 *Perf. 11*

540 A105 15s multicolored 1.10 .25
541 A105 35s multicolored 1.40 .45
542 A105 1m multicolored 3.00 1.90
543 A105 2m multicolored 3.50 2.50
Nos. 540-543 (4) 9.00 5.10

Souvenir Sheet

Perf. 14

544 A105 4m multicolored 11.00 11.00

Royal Wedding Issue, 1986
Common Design Type

Designs: 50s, Prince Andrew and Sarah Ferguson. 1m, Andrew. 3m, Andrew at helicopter controls. 4m, Couple, diff.

1986, July 23 *Perf. 14*

545 CD340 50s multicolored .50 .50
546 CD340 1m multicolored .95 .95
547 CD340 3m multicolored 2.25 2.25
Nos. 545-547 (3) 3.70 3.70

Souvenir Sheet

548 CD340 4m multicolored 3.75 3.75

Natl. Independence, 20th Anniv. — A106

9s, Basotho pony, rider. 15s, Mohair spinning. 35s, River crossing. 4m, Moshoeshoe I.

1986, Oct. 20 Litho. *Perf. 15*

549 A106 9s multicolored .25 .25
550 A106 15s multicolored .25 .25
551 A106 35s multicolored .35 .35
552 A106 3m Thaba Tseka P.O. 2.25 2.25
Nos. 549-552 (4) 3.10 3.10

Souvenir Sheet

553 A106 4m multicolored 7.00 7.00

Christmas — A107

Walt Disney characters: 15s, Chip'n'Dale. 35s, Mickey, Minnie. 1m, Pluto. 2m, Aunt Matilda. 5m, Huey and Dewey.

1986, Nov. 4 Litho. *Perf. 11*

554 A107 15s multicolored .85 .25
555 A107 35s multicolored 1.25 .40
556 A107 1m multicolored 1.75 1.60
557 A107 2m multicolored 2.50 2.50
Nos. 554-557 (4) 6.35 4.75

Souvenir Sheet

Perf. 14

558 A107 5m multicolored 10.00 10.00

Butterfly and Bird Type of 1981-84 Surcharged

1986 Litho. *Perf. 14, 14½*

558A A66 9s on 10s #327b *6.00 1.75*
b. 9s on 10s #327 *4.00 4.00*
559 A83 9s on 30s No. 431 .25 .25
a. 9s on 30s #431 (surcharge smaller & sans serif) *7.50 5.00*
560 A83 9s on 60s No. 433 .25 .25
561 A66 15s on 1s No. 321 *85.00*
b. 15s on 1s #321a *7.00 8.50*
c. 15s on 1s #321b *10.00 4.50*
561A A83 15s on 1s No. 421 2.50 2.50
562 A66 15s on 2s No. 322 .30 .25
563 A66 15s on 60s No. 330 .30 .25
a. 15s on 60s #330a *4.50 5.00*
564 A83 15s on 2s No. 422 .30 .25
565 A83 15s on 3s No. 423 .30 .25
566 A83 35s on 75s No. 434 *24.00 17.50*
a. 35s on 75s #434, small "s" *50.00 52.50*
Nos. 558A-566 (10) 119.20 23.25

Issued: Nos. 559-560, July 1. Nos. 561-563, Aug. 22. Nos. 561A, 564-566, June 25.
See Nos. 617A-617B.

Roof of Africa Rally — A108

1987, Apr. 28 Litho. *Perf. 14*

567 A108 9s White car .45 .25
568 A108 15s Motorcycle #26 .55 .25
569 A108 35s Motorcycle #25 .75 .35
570 A108 4m Red car 3.25 3.25
Nos. 567-570 (4) 5.00 4.10

1988 Summer Olympics, Seoul — A109

1987, May 29 *Perf. 14*

571 A109 9s Tennis .80 .25
572 A109 15s Judo .80 .25
573 A109 20s Running .90 .25
574 A109 35s Boxing 1.00 .45
575 A109 1m Diving 1.25 1.10
576 A109 3m Bowling 3.00 3.00
Nos. 571-576 (6) 7.75 5.30

Souvenir Sheet

577 A109 2m Tennis, diff. 2.75 2.75
577A A109 4m Soccer 5.25 5.25

See Nos. 606-611.
No. 577A shows green at lower left diagonal half of the flag.

Inventors and Innovators A110

Designs: 5s, Sir Isaac Newton, reflecting telescope. 9s, Alexander Graham Bell, telephone. 75s, Robert H. Goddard, liquid fuel rocket. 4m, Chuck Yeager (b. 1923), test pilot. No. 582, Mariner 10 spacecraft.

1987, June 30 *Perf. 15*

578 A110 5s multicolored .45 .25
579 A110 9s multicolored .45 .25
580 A110 75s multicolored 1.00 .75
581 A110 4m multicolored 3.50 3.50
Nos. 578-581 (4) 5.40 4.75

Souvenir Sheet

582 A110 4m multicolored 4.75 4.75

Fauna and Flora — A111

5s, Gray rhebuck. 9s, Cape clawless otter. 15s, Cape gray mongoose. 20s, Free state daisy. 35s, River bells. 1m, Turkey flower. 2m, Sweet briar. 3m, Mountain reedbuck.
No. 591, Pig-lily. No. 592, Cape wildebeest.

1987, Aug. 14

583 A111 5s multicolored .50 .25
584 A111 9s multicolored .50 .25
585 A111 15s multicolored .70 .25
586 A111 20s multicolored .80 .25
587 A111 35s multicolored .90 .35
588 A111 1m multicolored 2.00 1.00
589 A111 2m multicolored 2.50 2.00
590 A111 3m multicolored 3.00 3.00
Nos. 583-590 (8) 10.90 7.35

Souvenir Sheet

591 A111 2m multicolored 3.00 3.00
592 A111 4m multicolored 5.25 5.25

Nos. 586-589 and 591 vert.

16th World Scout Jamboree, Australia, 1987-88 — A112

1987, Sept. 10 Litho. *Perf. 14*

593 A112 9s Orienteering .25 .25
594 A112 15s Playing soccer .25 .25
595 A112 35s Kangaroos .65 .65
596 A112 75s Salute, flag 1.25 1.25
597 A112 4m Windsurfing 6.25 6.25
Nos. 593-597 (5) 8.65 8.65

Souvenir Sheet

598 A112 4m Map, flag of Australia 5.25 5.25

Nos. 324, 425, 424, 328 and 427 Surcharged

1987 Litho. *Perf. 14½, 14*

598A A66 9s on 5s No. 324 .75 .25
599 A66 15s on 5s No. 324 2.00 .25
600 A83 15s on 5s No. 425 .25 .25
600A A83 20s on 4s No. 424 .25 .25
600B A66 35s on 25s No. 328 1.50 .60
e. 35s on 25s #328, small "s"
f. 35s on 25s #328a
g. 35s on 25s #328a, small "s"
600C A66 35s on 75s #331
h. 35s on 75s #331, small "s"
600D A83 40s on 7s No. 427 .40 .40

Issued: Nos. 599-600, 11/16; No. 600B, 12/15; Nos. 598A, 600A, 600D, 12/30.

A113

A114

Religious paintings (details) by Raphael: 9s, Madonna and Child. 15s, Marriage of the Virgin. 35s, Coronation of the Virgin. 90s, Madonna of the Chair. 3m, Madonna and Child Enthroned with Five Saints.

1987, Dec. 21 *Perf. 14*

601 A113 9s multicolored .25 .25
602 A113 15s multicolored .25 .25
603 A113 35s multicolored 1.25 1.25
604 A113 90s multicolored 3.00 3.00
Nos. 601-604 (4) 4.75 4.75

Souvenir Sheet

605 A114 3m multicolored 4.50 4.50

Christmas.

Summer Olympics Type of 1987

1987, Nov. 30 Litho. *Perf. 14*

606 A109 5s like 9s .25 .25
607 A109 10s like 15s .25 .25
608 A109 25s like 20s .25 .25
609 A109 40s like 35s .35 .35
610 A109 50s like 1m .50 .50
611 A109 3.50m like 3m 3.25 3.25
Nos. 606-611 (6) 4.85 4.85

Souvenir Sheet

612 A109 4m Soccer 4.00 4.00

No. 612 shows green at lower right diagonal half of the flag.

Discovery of America, 500th Anniv. (in 1992) — A115

Columbus's fleet and marine life: 9s, Spotted trunkfish. 15s, Green sea turtle. 35s, Common dolphin. 5m, White-tailed tropicbird. 4m, Ship.

1987, Dec. 14 Litho. *Perf. 14*

613	A115	9s multicolored	.25	.25
614	A115	15s multicolored	.25	.25
615	A115	35s multicolored	.60	.60
616	A115	5m multicolored	8.00	8.00
		Nos. 613-616 (4)	9.10	9.10

Souvenir Sheet

617	A115	4m multicolored	6.50	6.50

Nos. 328, 559 Surcharged

1988

Methods and Perfs as Before

617A	A83	3s on 9s on 30s		
617B	A83	7s on 9s on 30s		
617C	A66	16s on 25s No. 328	—	—

Issued: Nos. 617A, 617B, 2/2/88; No. 617C, 3/88.

Birds — A116

2s, Pied kingfisher. 3s, Three-banded plover. 5s, Spurwing goose. 10s, Clapper lark. 12s, Red-eyed bulbul. 16s, Cape weaver. 20s, Red-headed finch. 30s, Mountain chat. 40s, Stone chat. 55s, Pied barbet. 60s, Cape glossy starling. 75s, Cape sparrow. 1m, Cattle egret. 3m, Giant kingfisher. 10m, Crowned guinea fowl.

1988, Apr. 5 Litho. *Perf. 15*

618	A116	2s multicolored	.25	.25
619	A116	3s multicolored	.25	.25
620	A116	5s multicolored	.25	.25
621	A116	10s multicolored	.25	.25
622	A116	12s multicolored	.25	.25
623	A116	16s multicolored	.25	.25
624	A116	20s multicolored	.25	.25
625	A116	30s multicolored	.30	.30
626	A116	40s multicolored	.40	.40
627	A116	55s multicolored	.55	.55
628	A116	60s multicolored	.60	.60
629	A116	75s multicolored	.75	.75
630	A116	1m multicolored	.85	.85
631	A116	3m multicolored	2.50	2.50
632	A116	10m multicolored	9.00	9.00
		Nos. 618-632 (15)	16.70	16.70

For surcharges see Nos. 755, 805-806.

1989, Sept. 18 *Perf. 14*

620a	A116	5s multicolored	.25	.25
622a	A116	12s multicolored	.25	.25
623a	A116	16s multicolored	.25	.25
624a	A116	20s multicolored	.25	.25
630a	A116	1m multicolored	.80	.80
631a	A116	3m multicolored	2.40	2.40
632a	A116	10m multicolored	8.00	8.00
		Nos. 620a-632a (7)	12.20	12.20

Dated 1989.

1990 *Perf. 12½x12*

620b	A116	5s multicolored	.25	.25
622b	A116	12s multicolored	.25	.25
623b	A116	16s multicolored	.25	.25
624b	A116	20s multicolored	.25	.25
630b	A116	1m multicolored	.80	.80
631b	A116	3m multicolored	2.40	2.40
632b	A116	10m multicolored	8.00	8.00
		Nos. 620b-632b (7)	12.20	12.20

Dated 1989.

1991 (?) *Perf. 11½x13*

620c	A116	5s multicolored	.25	.25
622c	A116	12s multicolored	.25	.25
623c	A116	16s multicolored	.25	.25
624c	A116	20s multicolored	.25	.25
630c	A116	1m multicolored	.80	.80
631c	A116	3m multicolored	2.40	2.40
632c	A116	10m multicolored	8.00	8.00
		Nos. 620c-632c (7)	12.20	12.20

Dated 1989.

Nos. 531-534 Ovptd. "40th WEDDING ANNIVERSARY / H.M. QUEEN ELIZABETH II / H.R.H. THE DUKE OF EDINBURGH" in Silver

1988, May 3 *Perf. 14*

636	CD339	90s lt yel bis & blk	.90	.90
637	CD339	1m pale grn & multi	1.00	1.00
638	CD339	2m dull vio & multi	2.00	2.00
		Nos. 636-638 (3)	3.90	3.90

Souvenir Sheet

639	CD339	4m tan & black	4.00	4.00

FINLANDIA '88, Helsinki, June 1-12 — A117

Disney animated characters and Helsinki sights: 1s, Touring President's Palace. 2s, Sauna. 3s, Lake Country fishing. 4s, Finlandia Hall. 5s, Photographing Sibelius Monument. 10s, Pony trek, youth hostel. 3m, Olympic Stadium. 5m, Santa Claus, Arctic Circle.

No. 648, Market Square. No. 649, Lapp encampment, vert.

1988, June 2 Litho. *Perf. 14x13½*

640	A117	1s multicolored	.25	.25
641	A117	2s multicolored	.25	.25
642	A117	3s multicolored	.25	.25
643	A117	4s multicolored	.25	.25
644	A117	5s multicolored	.25	.25
645	A117	10s multicolored	.30	.30
646	A117	3m multicolored	4.25	3.50
647	A117	5m multicolored	5.25	4.75
		Nos. 640-647 (8)	11.05	9.80

Souvenir Sheets

Perf. 14x13½, 13½x14

648	A117	4m multicolored	4.50	4.50
649	A117	4m multicolored	4.50	4.50

Mickey Mouse, 60th anniv.

A118

55s, Pope giving communion. 2m, Leading procession. 3m, Walking in garden. 4m, Wearing scullcap.

5m, Pope, Archbishop Morapeli of Lesotho, horiz.

1988, Sept. 1 Litho. *Perf. 14*

650	A118	55s multicolored	.50	.50
651	A118	2m multicolored	1.60	1.60
652	A118	3m multicolored	2.50	2.50
653	A118	4m multicolored	3.50	3.50
		Nos. 650-653 (4)	8.10	8.10

Souvenir Sheet

654	A118	5m multicolored	8.00	8.00

Visit of Pope John Paul II, Sept. 14-16.

A119

Small indigenous mammals: 16s, Rock hyrax. 40s, Honey badger. 75s, Genet. 3m, Yellow mongoose.

4m, Meerkat.

1988, Oct. 13 Litho. *Perf. 14*

655	A119	16s multicolored	.25	.25
656	A119	40s multicolored	.85	.85
657	A119	75s multicolored	1.50	1.50
658	A119	3m multicolored	5.75	5.75
		Nos. 655-658 (4)	8.35	8.35

Souvenir Sheet

659	A119	4m multicolored	5.25	5.25

Birth of Venus, 1480, by Botticelli — A120

Paintings: 25s, View of Toledo, 1608, by El Greco. 40s, Maids of Honor, 1656, by Diego Velazquez. 50s, The Fifer, 1866, by Manet. 55s, The Starry Night, 1889, by Van Gogh. 75s, Prima Ballerina, 1876, by Degas. 2m, Bridge over Water Lilies, 1899, by Monet. 3m, Guernica, 1937, by Picasso. No. 668, The Presentation of the Virgin in the Temple, c. 1534, by Titian. No. 669, The Miracle of the Newborn Infant, 1511, by Titian.

1988, Oct. 17 Litho. *Perf. 13½x14*

660	A120	15s multicolored	.40	.25
661	A120	25s multicolored	.55	.25
662	A120	40s multicolored	.65	.40
663	A120	50s multicolored	.75	.50
664	A120	55s multicolored	.80	.55
665	A120	75s multicolored	.90	.90
666	A120	2m multicolored	2.00	2.00
667	A120	3m multicolored	2.50	2.50
		Nos. 660-667 (8)	8.55	7.35

Souvenir Sheets

668	A120	4m multicolored	3.50	3.50
669	A120	4m multicolored	3.50	3.50

1988 Summer Olympics, Seoul — A121

12s, Wrestling, horiz. 16s, Equestrian. 55s, Shooting, horiz.

4m, Olympic flame.

1988, Nov. 11 Litho. *Perf. 14*

670	A121	12s multicolored	.25	.25
671	A121	16s multicolored	.25	.25
672	A121	55s multicolored	.40	.40
673	A121	3.50m like 16s	2.10	2.10
		Nos. 670-673 (4)	3.00	3.00

Souvenir Sheet

674	A121	4m multicolored	4.75	4.75

Intl. Tennis Federation, 75th Anniv. — A122

Tennis champions, views of cities or landmarks: 12s, Yannick Noah, Eiffel Tower, horiz. 20s, Rod Laver, Sydney Opera House and Harbor Bridge, horiz. 30s, Ivan Lendl, Prague, horiz. 65s, Jimmy Connors, Tokyo. 1m, Arthur Ashe, Barcelona. 1.55m, Althea Gibson, NYC. 2m, Chris Evert, Vienna. 2.40m, Boris Becker, London. 3m, Martina Navratilova, Golden Gate Bridge, horiz. 4m, Steffi Graf, Berlin, West Germany.

1988, Nov. 18

675	A122	12s multi	.70	.25
676	A122	20s multi	.90	.25
677	A122	30s multi	.80	.35
678	A122	65s multi	.95	.80
679	A122	1m multi	1.25	1.25
680	A122	1.55m multi	1.50	1.50
681	A122	2m multi	2.25	2.25
682	A122	2.40m multi	2.50	2.50
683	A122	3m multi	3.00	3.00
		Nos. 675-683 (9)	13.85	12.15

Souvenir Sheet

684	A122	4m multi	4.50	4.50

No. 676 has "Sidney" instead of "Sydney." No. 679 has "Ash" instead of "Ashe."

Paintings by Titian — A123

Designs: 12s, The Averoldi Polyptych. 20s, Christ and the Adulteress (Christ). 35s, Christ and the Adulteress (adultress). 45s, Angel of the Annunciation. 65s, Saint Dominic. 1m, The Vendramin Family. 2m, Mary Magdalen. 3m, The Tribute Money. No. 693, Christ and the Woman Taken in Adultery. No. 694, The Mater Dolorosa.

1988, Dec. 1 *Perf. 14x13½*

685	A123	12s multicolored	.40	.25
686	A123	20s multicolored	.50	.25
687	A123	35s multicolored	.60	.35
688	A123	45s multicolored	.70	.45
689	A123	65s multicolored	.70	.65
690	A123	1m multicolored	.90	.90
691	A123	2m multicolored	1.75	1.75
692	A123	3m multicolored	2.50	2.50
		Nos. 685-692 (8)	8.05	7.10

Souvenir Sheets

693	A123	5m multicolored	4.50	4.50
694	A123	5m multicolored	4.50	4.50

Birth of Titian, 500th anniv. Nos. 685-693 inscribed "Christmas 1988."

Intl. Red Cross, 125th Anniv. — A124

Anniv. emblem, supply and ambulance planes: 12s, Pilatus PC-6 Turbo Porter. 20s, Cessna Caravan. 55s, De Havilland DHC-6 Otter. 3m, Douglas DC-3 in thunderstorm. 4m, Douglas DC-3, diff.

1989, Jan. 30 Litho. *Perf. 14*

695	A124	12s multicolored	.25	.25
696	A124	20s multicolored	.25	.25
697	A124	55s multicolored	1.25	1.25
698	A124	3m multicolored	5.25	5.25
		Nos. 695-698 (4)	7.00	7.00

Souvenir Sheet

699	A124	4m multi, vert.	9.00	9.00

Landscapes by Hiroshige A125

Designs: 12s, Dawn Mist at Mishima. 16s, Night Snow at Kambara. 20s, Wayside Inn at Mariko Station. 35s, Shower at Shono. 55s, Snowfall on the Kisokaido Near Oi. 1m, Autumn Moon at Seba. 3.20m, Evening Moon at Ryogaku Bridge. 5m, Cherry Blossoms, Arashiyama. No. 708, Listening to the Singing Insects at Dokanyama. No. 709, Moonlight, Nagakubo.

1989, June 19 Litho. *Perf. 14x13½*

700	A125	12s multi	.40	.25
701	A125	16s multi	.45	.25
702	A125	20s multi	.45	.25
703	A125	35s multi	.45	.30
704	A125	55s multi	.70	.45
705	A125	1m multi	1.00	.80
706	A125	3.20m multi	2.25	2.25
707	A125	5m multi	3.75	3.75
		Nos. 700-707 (8)	9.45	8.30

Souvenir Sheets

708	A125	4m multi	4.25	4.25
709	A125	4m multi	4.25	4.25

Hirohito (1901-1989) and enthronement of Akihito as emperor of Japan.

PHILEXFRANCE '89, French Revolution Bicent. — A126

Disney characters wearing insurgent uniforms: 1s, General. 2s, Infantry. 3s, Grenadier. 4s, Cavalry. 5s, Hussar. 10s, Marine. 3m, Natl. guard. 5m, Admiral.

No. 718, Natl. guard, royal family, horiz. No. 719, La Marseillaise.

1989, July 10 *Perf. 13½x14, 14x13½*

710	A126	1s multicolored	.25	.25
711	A126	2s multicolored	.25	.25
712	A126	3s multicolored	.25	.25
713	A126	4s multicolored	.25	.25
714	A126	5s multicolored	.25	.25
715	A126	10s multicolored	.25	.25
716	A126	3m multicolored	3.00	3.00
717	A126	5m multicolored	4.75	4.75
		Nos. 710-717 (8)	9.25	9.25

Souvenir Sheets

718	A126	4m multicolored	5.00	5.00
719	A126	4m multicolored	5.00	5.00

Maloti Mountains — A127

No. 720: a, Sotho thatched dwellings. b, Two trees, cliff edge. c, Waterfall. d, Tribesman.

1989, Sept. **Litho.** *Perf. 14*

720		Strip of 4	4.00	4.00
a.-d.	A127	1m any single	.75	.75

Souvenir Sheet

721	A127	4m Flora	4.25	4.25

Mushrooms — A128

12s, Paxillus involutus. 16s, Ganoderma applanatum. 55s, Suillus granulatus. 5m, Stereum hirsutum.

4m, Scleroderma flavidum.

1989, Sept. 8 **Litho.** *Perf. 14*

722	A128	12s multicolored	.35	.25
723	A128	16s multicolored	.35	.25
723A	A128	55s multicolored	.65	.55
724	A128	5m multicolored	4.50	4.50
		Nos. 722-724 (4)	5.85	5.55

Souvenir Sheet

725	A128	4m multicolored	6.25	6.25

Birds — A129

12s, Marsh sandpipers. 65s, Little stints. 1m, Ringed plovers. 4m, Curlew sandpipers.

5m, Ruff, vert.

1989, Oct. 23 **Litho.** *Perf. 14*

726	A129	12s multicolored	.25	.25
727	A129	65s multicolored	1.10	1.10
728	A129	1m multicolored	1.75	1.75
729	A129	4m multicolored	6.25	6.25
		Nos. 726-729 (4)	9.35	9.35

Souvenir Sheet

730	A129	5m multicolored	11.00	11.00

1st Moon Landing, 20th Anniv. — A130

Highlights of the Apollo 11 mission: 12s, Liftoff. 16s, Eagle landing. 40s, Astronaut on ladder. 55s, Buzz Aldrin. 1m, Solar wind experiment. 2m, Eagle lifting off. 3m, Columbia in orbit. 4m, Splashdown.

5m, Astronaut, Eagle.

1989, Nov. 6 *Perf. 14*

731	A130	12s multicolored	.25	.25
732	A130	16s multicolored	.25	.25
733	A130	40s multicolored	.40	.40
734	A130	55s multicolored	.60	.60
735	A130	1m multicolored	.90	.90
736	A130	2m multicolored	1.75	1.75
737	A130	3m multicolored	2.40	2.40
738	A130	4m multicolored	3.50	3.50
		Nos. 731-738 (8)	10.05	10.05

Souvenir Sheet

739	A130	5m multicolored	6.75	6.75

Nos. 731, 733, 738-739 vert.

World Stamp Expo '89 — A131

Cathedral Church of Sts. Peter and Paul, Washington, DC — A132

No. 740: a, Postal marking, England, 1680. b, Wax seal and feather, Germany, 1807. c, Crete #1. d, Perot postmaster's provisional, Bermuda, 1848. e, Pony Express handstamp, US, 1860. f, Finland #1. g, Fiji #1. h, Swedish newspaper handstamp, 1823. i, Bhor #1.

1989, Nov. 17 **Litho.** *Perf. 14*

740	A131	Sheet of 9	8.25	8.25
a.-i.		75s any single	.35	.35

Souvenir Sheet

741	A132	4m shown	4.00	4.00

Christmas — A133

Religious paintings by Velazquez: 12s, The Immaculate Conception. 20s, St. Anthony Abbot and St. Paul the Hermit. 35s, St. Thomas the Apostle. 55s, Christ in the House of Martha and Mary. 1m, St. John Writing the Apocalypse on Patmos. 3m, The Virgin Presenting the Chasuble to St. Ildephonsus. 4m, The Adoration of the Magi. 5m, The Coronation of the Virgin.

1989, Dec. 18

742	A133	12s multicolored	.25	.25
743	A133	20s multicolored	.25	.25
744	A133	35s multicolored	.35	.35
745	A133	55s multicolored	.55	.55
746	A133	1m multicolored	.80	.80
747	A133	3m multicolored	2.25	2.25
748	A133	4m multicolored	3.00	3.00
		Nos. 742-748 (7)	7.45	7.45

Souvenir Sheet

749	A133	5m multicolored	9.00	9.00

1990 World Cup Soccer Championships, Italy — A134

Various athletes, emblem and name of previous championship host nations: 12s, England, 1966. 16s, Mexico, 1970. 55s, West Germany, 1974. 5m, Spain, 1982.

4m, Diego Maradona, Argentina.

1989, Dec. 27

750	A134	12s multicolored	.25	.25
751	A134	16s multicolored	.25	.25
752	A134	55s multicolored	1.00	1.00
753	A134	5m multicolored	6.50	6.50
		Nos. 750-753 (4)	8.00	8.00

Souvenir Sheet

754	A134	4m multicolored	7.50	7.50

No. 622a Surcharged

1990 **Litho.** *Perf. 14*

755	A116	16s on 12s multi	—	—

Orchids — A135

Designs: 12s, Satyrium princeps. 16s, Huttonaea pulchra. 55s, Herschelia graminifolia. 1m, Ansellia gigantea. 1.55m, Polystachya pubescens. 2.40m, Penthea filicornis. 3m, Disperis capensis. 4m, Disa uniflora.

5m, Stenoglottis longifolia.

1990, Mar. 12 **Litho.** *Perf. 14*

756	A135	12s multicolored	.25	.25
757	A135	16s multicolored	.25	.25
758	A135	55s multicolored	.90	.90
759	A135	1m multicolored	1.60	1.60
760	A135	1.55m multicolored	2.25	2.25
761	A135	2.40m multicolored	3.50	3.50
762	A135	3m multicolored	4.25	4.25
763	A135	4m multicolored	6.00	6.00
		Nos. 756-763 (8)	19.00	19.00

Souvenir Sheet

764	A135	5m multicolored	10.00	10.00

Expo '90.

Butterflies — A136

12s, Pseudo ergolid. 16s, Painted lady. 55s, Ringed pansy. 65s, False acraea. 1m, Eyed pansy. 2m, Golden pansy. 3m, African monarch. 4m, African giant swallowtail.

5m, Citrus swallowtail.

1990, Feb. 26 **Litho.** *Perf. 14*

765	A136	12s multicolored	.95	.25
766	A136	16s multicolored	1.10	.25
767	A136	55s multicolored	1.60	.55
768	A136	65s multicolored	1.75	.65
769	A136	1m multicolored	2.40	1.10
770	A136	2m multicolored	3.75	2.25
771	A136	3m multicolored	5.25	3.25
772	A136	4m multicolored	6.50	5.50
		Nos. 765-772 (8)	23.30	13.80

Souvenir Sheet

773	A136	5m multicolored	11.00	11.00

Queen Mother, 90th Birthday A137

1990, July 5 **Litho.** *Perf. 14*

774		1.50m In hat	1.25	1.25
775		1.50m Two children	1.25	1.25
776		1.50m Young woman	1.25	1.25
a.	A137	Strip of 3, #774-776	4.50	4.50
		Nos. 774-776 (3)	3.75	3.75

Souvenir Sheet

777	A137	5m Child	5.50	5.50

A139

Designs: 12s, King Moshoeshoe II, Prince Mohato wearing blankets. 16s, Prince Mohato in Seana-Marena blanket. 1m, Pope John Paul II in Seana-Marena blanket. 3m, Basotho men on horses.

5m, Pope with blanket and hat.

1990, Aug. 17 **Litho.** *Perf. 14*

778	A139	12s multicolored	.25	.25
779	A139	16s multicolored	.25	.25
780	A139	1m multicolored	1.40	1.40
781	A139	3m multicolored	3.50	3.50
		Nos. 778-781 (4)	5.40	5.40

Souvenir Sheet

782	A139	5m multi, horiz.	7.50	7.50

Highland Water Project — A140

16s, Moving gravel. 20s, Fuel truck. 55s, Piers for bridge construction. 2m, Road construction.

5m, Drilling blasting holes.

1990, Aug. 24

783	A140	16s multicolored	.25	.25
784	A140	20s multicolored	.25	.25
785	A140	55s multicolored	.90	.90
786	A140	2m multicolored	2.75	2.75
		Nos. 783-786 (4)	4.15	4.15

Souvenir Sheet

787	A140	5m multicolored	7.25	7.25

UNICEF Save the Children Campaign — A141

12s, Breastfeeding. 55s, Oral rehydration. 1m, Baby being weighed.

1990, Sept. 26 **Litho.** *Perf. 14*

788	A141	12s multicolored	.25	.25
789	A141	55s multicolored	1.75	1.75
790	A141	1m multicolored	2.50	2.50
		Nos. 788-790 (3)	4.50	4.50

1992 Summer Olympics, Barcelona — A142

16s, Triple jump. 55s, 200-meter race. 1m, 5000-meter race. 4m, Equestrian show jumping.

5m, Lighting Olympic flame.

1990, Oct. 5

791	A142	16s multicolored	.25	.25
792	A142	55s multicolored	1.00	1.00
793	A142	1m multicolored	1.50	1.50
794	A142	4m multicolored	5.50	5.50
		Nos. 791-794 (4)	8.25	8.25

Souvenir Sheet

795	A142	5m multicolored	8.50	8.50

Christmas — A143

Different details from paintings by Rubens: 12s, 1m, 3m, Virgin and Child. 16s, 80s, 2m, 4m, Adoration of the Magi. 55s, Head of One of the Three Kings, diff. 5m, Assumption of the Virgin.

1990, Dec. 5 Litho. *Perf. 13½x14*

796 A143 12s multicolored	.25	.25
797 A143 16s multicolored	.25	.25
798 A143 55s multicolored	.55	.55
799 A143 80s multicolored	.85	.85
800 A143 1m multicolored	1.00	1.00
801 A143 2m multicolored	2.10	2.10
802 A143 3m multicolored	2.75	2.75
803 A143 4m multicolored	3.75	3.75
Nos. 796-803 (8)	11.50	11.50

Souvenir Sheet

804 A143 5m multicolored 7.25 7.25

Nos. 625-626 Surcharged

1991, Jan. 18 Litho. *Perf. 15*

805 A116 16s on 30s #625 — —
806 A116 16s on 40s #626 — —

Phila Nippon '91 — A144

Walt Disney characters visit Japan: 20s, Mickey at Nagasaki Peace Park. 30s, Mickey at Kamakura Beach. 40s, Mickey, Donald entertain at Bunraku Puppet Theater. 50s, Mickey, Donald eat soba at noodle shop. 75s, Minnie, Mickey at tea house. 1m, Mickey, Bullet Train. 3m, Mickey, deer at Todaiji Temple. 4m, Mickey, Minnie before Imperial Palace. No. 815, Mickey skiing at Happo-One, Nagano. No. 816, Mickey, Minnie at Suizenji Park.

1991, June 10 Litho. *Perf. 14x13½*

807 A144 20s multicolored	.25	.25
808 A144 30s multicolored	.25	.25
809 A144 40s multicolored	.50	.50
810 A144 50s multicolored	.70	.70
811 A144 75s multicolored	1.40	1.40
812 A144 1m multicolored	1.40	1.40
813 A144 3m multicolored	3.75	3.75
814 A144 4m multicolored	5.00	5.00
Nos. 807-814 (8)	13.25	13.25

Souvenir Sheets

815 A144 6m multicolored 5.50 5.50
816 A144 6m multicolored 5.50 5.50

Entertainers in Films About Africa — A145

Designs: 12s, Stewart Granger, King Solomon's Mines. 16s, Johnny Weissmuller, Tarzan, the Ape Man. 30s, Clark Gable, Grace Kelly, Mogambo. 55s, Sigourney Weaver, Gorillas in the Mist. 70s, Humphrey Bogart, Katharine Hepburn, The African Queen. 1m, John Wayne, Hatari. 2m, Meryl Streep, Out of Africa. 4m, Eddie Murphy, Arsenio Hall, Coming to America. 5m, Elsa, Born Free.

1991, June 20 Litho. *Perf. 14*

817 A145 12s multicolored	.65	.25
818 A145 16s multicolored	.65	.25
819 A145 30s multicolored	.80	.25
820 A145 55s multicolored	.95	.70
821 A145 70s multicolored	1.25	.90
822 A145 1m multicolored	1.60	1.25
823 A145 2m multicolored	2.50	2.50
824 A145 4m multicolored	4.25	4.25
Nos. 817-824 (8)	12.65	10.35

Souvenir Sheet

825 A145 5m multicolored 6.75 6.75

Butterflies A146

2s, Satyrus aello. 3s, Erebia medusa. 5s, Melanargia galathea. 10s, Erebia aethiops. 20s, Coenonympha pamphilus. 25s, Pyrameis atalanta. 30s, Charaxes jasius. 40s, Colias palaeno. 50s, Colias cliopatra. 60s, Colias philodice. 70s, Rhumni gonepterix. 1m, Colias caesonia. 2m, Pyrameis cardui. 3m, Danaus chrysippus. 10m, Apatura iris.

No date inscription below design

1991, Aug. 1 Litho. *Perf. 13½*

827 A146 2s multicolored	.25	.25
828 A146 3s multicolored	.25	.25
829 A146 5s multicolored	.25	.25
830 A146 10s multicolored	.25	.25
831 A146 20s multicolored	.30	.25
832 A146 25s multicolored	.30	.25
833 A146 30s multicolored	.45	.30
834 A146 40s multicolored	.45	.35
835 A146 50s multicolored	.50	.45
836 A146 60s multicolored	.60	.55
837 A146 70s multicolored	.60	.60
838 A146 1m multicolored	.90	.90
839 A146 2m multicolored	1.75	1.75
840 A146 3m multicolored	2.50	2.50
840A A146 10m multicolored	8.75	8.75
Nos. 827-840A (15)	18.10	17.65

For surcharge see No. 1062.

1992, Apr. Inscribed "1992"

827a A146 2s multicolored	.25	.25
828a A146 3s multicolored	.25	.25
829a A146 5s multicolored	.25	.25
830a A146 10s multicolored	.25	.25
831a A146 20s multicolored	.30	.25
832a A146 25s multicolored	.30	.25
833a A146 30s multicolored	.45	.30
834a A146 40s multicolored	.50	.35
835a A146 50s multicolored	.65	.45
836a A146 60s multicolored	.70	.70
837a A146 70s multicolored	1.00	1.00
838a A146 1m multicolored	1.25	1.25
839a A146 2m multicolored	2.75	2.75
840a A146 3m multicolored	4.00	4.00
840Aa A146 10m multicolored	8.75	8.75
Nos. 827a-840Aa (15)	21.65	21.05

SADCC, 10th Anniv. — A147

Tourism: 12s, Wattled cranes. 16s, Butterfly, flowers in national parks. 25s, Tourist bus and Mukurub, the Finger of God. 3m, People in traditional dress.

1991, Oct. 10 Litho. *Perf. 14x13½*

841 A147 12s multicolored	1.75	1.75
842 A147 16s multicolored	1.75	1.75
843 A147 25s multicolored	1.75	1.75
Nos. 841-843 (3)	5.25	5.25

Souvenir Sheet

844 A147 3m multicolored 5.50 5.50

Say No to Drugs — A148

1991, Oct. 10

845 A148 16s multicolored 2.25 2.25

Charles de Gaulle, Birth Cent. — A149

DeGaulle: 40s, Wearing brigadier general's kepi. 50s, Facing left. 60s, Facing right. 4m, In later years.

1991, Dec. 6 Litho. *Perf. 14*

846 A149 20s black & brown	.25	.25
847 A149 40s black & violet	.65	.65
848 A149 50s black & olilve	.85	.85
849 A149 60s black & dk blue	1.00	1.00
850 A149 4m black & brn org	6.75	6.75
Nos. 846-850 (5)	9.50	9.50

Christmas — A150

Engravings by Albrecht Durer: 20s, St. Anne with Mary and the Child Jesus. 30s, Mary on the Grass Bench. 50s, Mary with the Crown of Stars. 60s, Mary with Child beside a Tree. 70s, Mary with Child beside the Wall. 1m, Mary in a Halo on the Crescent Moon. 2m, Mary Breastfeeding Her Child. 4m, Mary with the Infant in Swaddling Clothes. No. 859, Holy Family with the Dragonfly. No. 860, The Birth of Christ.

1991, Dec. 13 Litho. *Perf. 12*

851 A150 20s rose & black	.25	.25
852 A150 30s blue & black	.50	.50
853 A150 50s green & black	.80	.80
854 A150 60s red & black	1.00	1.00
855 A150 70s yellow & black	1.10	1.10
856 A150 1m yel org & black	1.60	1.60
857 A150 2m violet & black	2.75	2.75
858 A150 4m dk blue & black	5.75	5.75
Nos. 851-858 (8)	13.75	13.75

Souvenir Sheets

Perf. 14½

859 A150 5m blue & black 5.00 5.00
860 A150 5m pink & black 5.00 5.00

Games — A151

Walt Disney characters playing games: 20s, Mickey, Pluto playing pin the tail on the donkey. 30s, Mickey enjoying board game, Mancala. 40s, Mickey hoop rolling. 50s, Minnie with hula hoops. 70s, Mickey throwing Frisbee to Pluto. 1m, Donald trying to play Diabolo. 2m, Huey, Dewey and Louie playing marbles. 3m, Donald frustrated by Rubik's cube. No. 869, Donald and Mickey's nephews in tug-of-war. No. 870, Mickey, Donald stick fighting.

1991, Dec. 16 *Perf. 13½x14*

861 A151 20s multicolored	.25	.25
862 A151 30s multicolored	.55	.55
863 A151 40s multicolored	.65	.65
864 A151 50s multicolored	.90	.90
865 A151 70s multicolored	1.25	1.25
866 A151 1m multicolored	1.75	1.75
867 A151 2m multicolored	3.25	3.25
868 A151 3m multicolored	5.00	5.00
Nos. 861-868 (8)	13.60	13.60

Souvenir Sheets

869 A151 5m multicolored 6.00 6.00
870 A151 5m multicolored 6.00 6.00

Royal Family Birthday, Anniversary
Common Design Type

1991, Dec. 9 Litho. *Perf. 14*

871 CD347 50s multicolored	.70	.70
872 CD347 70s multicolored	.95	.95
873 CD347 1m multicolored	1.40	1.40
874 CD347 3m multicolored	4.25	4.25
Nos. 871-874 (4)	7.30	7.30

Souvenir Sheet

875 CD347 4m Charles, Diana, sons 6.25 6.25

Charles and Diana, 10th wedding anniversary.

Queen Elizabeth II's Accession to the Throne, 40th Anniv.
Common Design Type

1992, Feb. 6 Litho. *Perf. 14*

881 CD348 20s multicolored	.25	.25
882 CD348 30s multicolored	.40	.40
883 CD348 1m multicolored	1.25	1.25
884 CD348 4m multicolored	4.00	4.00
Nos. 881-884 (4)	5.90	5.90

Souvenir Sheet

885 CD348 5m multicolored 6.00 6.00

Birds — A152

Designs: a, Lanner falcon. b, Bataleur. c, Red-headed finch. d, Lesser-striped swallow. e, Alpine swift. f, Diederik cuckoo. g, Malachite sunbird. h, Crimson-breasted shrike. i, Pin-tailed whydah. j, Lilac-breasted roller. k, Black korhaan. l, Black-collared barbet. m, Secretary bird. n, Red-billed quelea. o, Red bishop. p, Ring-necked dove. q, Yellow canary. r, Orange-throated longclaw. s, Blue waxbill. t, Golden bishop.

1992, Feb. 10 *Perf. 14½*

886 A152 30s Sheet of 20, #a.-t. 17.50 17.50

World Columbian Stamp Expo '92, Chicago — A153

Walt Disney characters depicting native Americans: 30s, Donald Duck making arrowheads. 40s, Goofy playing lacrosse. 1m, Mickey, Donald planting corn. 3m, Minnie Mouse mastering art of beading. No. 891, Mickey as "Blackhawk" hunting for moose.

1992, Apr. Litho. *Perf. 13½x14*

887 A153 30s multicolored	.55	.55
888 A153 40s multicolored	.65	.65
889 A153 1m multicolored	1.75	1.75
890 A153 3m multicolored	4.50	4.50
Nos. 887-890 (4)	7.45	7.45

Souvenir Sheet

891 A153 5m multicolored 7.75 7.75

Granada '92 — A154

Walt Disney characters in Spanish costumes: 20s, Minnie Mouse as Lady of Rank, 1540-1660. 50s, Mickey as conqueror of Lepanto, 1571. 70s, Donald Duck from Galicia, 1880. 2m, Daisy Duck from Aragon, 1880. No. 901, Goofy as bullfighter.

1992, Apr. 13 Litho. *Perf. 13½x14*

897 A154 20s multicolored	.25	.25
898 A154 50s multicolored	1.25	1.25
899 A154 70s multicolored	1.60	1.60
900 A154 2m multicolored	4.00	4.00
Nos. 897-900 (4)	7.10	7.10

Souvenir Sheet

901 A154 5m multicolored 7.75 7.75

Dinosaurs A155

20s, Stegosaurus. 30s, Ceratosaurus. 40s, Procompsognathus. 50s, Lesothosaurus. 70s, Plateosaurus. 1m, Gasosaurus. 2m, Massospondylus. 3m, Archaeopteryx.

No. 915, Archaeopteryx, diff. No. 916, Lesothosaurus, diff.

1992, June 9 *Perf. 14*

907 A155 20s multicolored .25 .25
908 A155 30s multicolored .65 .65
909 A155 40s multicolored .75 .75
910 A155 50s multicolored 1.00 1.00
911 A155 70s multicolored 1.40 1.40
912 A155 1m multicolored 2.00 2.00
913 A155 2m multicolored 3.50 3.50
914 A155 3m multicolored 5.25 5.25
Nos. 907-914 (8) 14.80 14.80

Souvenir Sheet

915 A155 5m multicolored 7.75 7.75
916 A155 5m multicolored 7.75 7.75

No. 915 printed in continuous design.

1992 Olympics, Barcelona and Albertville — A156

Designs: 20s, Discus. 30s, Long jump. 40s, Women's 4x100-meter relay. 70s, Women's 100-meter dash. 1m, Parallel bars. 2m, Two-man luge, horiz. 3m, Women's cross-country skiing, horiz. 4m, Biathlon.
No. 925, Ice hockey, horiz. No. 926, Women's figure skating.

1992, Aug. 5 **Litho.** *Perf. 14*

917 A156 20s multicolored .25 .25
918 A156 30s multicolored .25 .25
919 A156 40s multicolored .30 .30
920 A156 70s multicolored .65 .65
921 A156 1m multicolored .95 .95
922 A156 2m multicolored 1.75 1.75
923 A156 3m multicolored 2.50 2.50
924 A156 4m multicolored 3.50 3.50
Nos. 917-924 (8) 10.15 10.15

Souvenir Sheet

925 A156 5m multicolored 5.25 5.25
926 A156 5m multicolored 5.25 5.25

Christmas — A158

Details or entire paintings: 20s, Virgin and Child, by Sassetta. 30s, Coronation of the Virgin, by Master of Bonastre. 40s, Virgin and Child, by Master of Saints Cosmas and Damian. 70s, The Virgin of Great Panagia, by Russian School, 12th cent. 1m, Madonna and Child, by Vincenzo Foppa. 2m, Madonna and Child, by School of Lippo Memmi. 3m, Virgin and Child, by Barnaba da Modena. 4m, Virgin and Child, by Simone Dei Crocifissi.
No. 935, Virgin & Child Enthroned & Surrounded by Angels, by Cimabue. No. 936, Virgin and Child with Saints (entire triptych), by Dei Crocifissi.

1992, Nov. 2 **Litho.** *Perf. 13½x14*

927 A158 20s multicolored .25 .25
928 A158 30s multicolored .45 .45
929 A158 40s multicolored .55 .55
930 A158 70s multicolored 1.10 1.10
931 A158 1m multicolored 1.50 1.50
932 A158 2m multicolored 2.75 2.75
933 A158 3m multicolored 4.25 4.25
934 A158 4m multicolored 5.75 5.75
Nos. 927-934 (8) 16.60 16.60

Souvenir Sheets

935 A158 5m multicolored 6.50 6.50
936 A158 5m multicolored 6.50 6.50

Souvenir Sheet

World Trade Center, New York City A159

1992, Oct. 28 **Litho.** *Perf. 14*

937 A159 5m multicolored 10.00 10.00

Postage Stamp Mega Event '92, NYC.

Anniversaries and Events — A160

Designs: 20s, Baby harp seal. 30s, Giant panda. 40s, Graf Zeppelin, globe. 70s, Woman grinding corn. 4m, Zeppelin shot down over Cuffley, UK by Lt. Leefe Robinson flying BE 2c, WWI. No. 943, Valentina Tereshkova, first woman in space. No. 944, West African crowned cranes. No. 945, Dr. Ronald McNair.

1993, Jan. **Litho.** *Perf. 14*

938 A160 20s multicolored .25 .25
939 A160 30s multicolored .40 .40
940 A160 40s multicolored .50 .50
941 A160 70s multicolored .90 .90
942 A160 4m multicolored 4.75 4.75
943 A160 5m multicolored 5.75 5.75
Nos. 938-943 (6) 12.55 12.55

Souvenir Sheets

944 A160 5m multicolored 6.50 6.50
945 A160 5m multicolored 6.50 6.50

Earth Summit, Rio de Janeiro (Nos. 938-939, 944). Count Zeppelin, 75th death anniv. (Nos. 940, 942). Intl. Conference on Nutrition, Rome (No. 941). Intl. Space Year (Nos. 943, 945).

Louvre Museum, Bicent. — A161

No. 947 — Details or entire paintings, by Nicolas Poussin: a, Orpheus and Eurydice. b-c, Rape of the Sabine Women (left, right). d-e, The Death of Sapphira (left, right). f-g, Echo and Narcissus (left, right). h, Self-portrait.
No. 948, The Moneychanger and His Wife, by Quentin Metsys.

1993, Mar. 19 **Litho.** *Perf. 12*

947 A161 70s Sheet of 8, #a.-h. + label 8.75 8.75

Souvenir Sheet

Perf. 14½

948 A161 5m multicolored 7.25 7.25

No. 948 contains one 55x88mm stamp.

Flowers — A162

1993, June **Litho.** *Perf. 14*

949 A162 20s Healing plant .25 .25
950 A162 30s Calla lily .25 .25
951 A162 40s Bird of Paradise .30 .30
952 A162 70s Belladonna .75 .75
953 A162 1m African lily 1.00 1.00
954 A162 2m Veldt lily 2.00 2.00
955 A162 4m Watsonia 3.75 3.75
956 A162 5m Gazania 4.50 4.50
Nos. 949-956 (8) 12.80 12.80

Souvenir Sheets

957 A162 7m Leadwort 5.75 5.75
958 A162 7m Desert rose 5.75 5.75

Miniature Sheet

Coronation of Queen Elizabeth II, 40th Anniv. — A163

No. 959: a, 20s, Official coronation photograph. b, 40s, St. Edward's Crown, Scepter with the Cross. c, 1m, Queen Mother. d, 5m, Queen, family.
7m, Conversation Piece at Royal Lodge, Windsor, by Sir James Gunn, 1950.

1993, June 2 **Litho.** *Perf. 13½x14*

959 A163 Sheet, 2 each, #a.-d. 8.00 8.00

Souvenir Sheet

Perf. 14

960 A163 7m multicolored 15.00 15.00

Butterflies A164

20s, Bi-colored pansy. 40s, Golden pansy. 70s, Yellow pansy. 1m, Pseudo ergolid. 2m, African giant swallowtail. 5m, False acraea.
No. 967, 7m, Seasonal pansy. No. 968, 7m, Ringed pansy.

1993, June 30 **Litho.** *Perf. 14*

961 A164 20s multicolored .25 .25
962 A164 40s multicolored .35 .35
963 A164 70s multicolored .55 .55
964 A164 1m multicolored .90 .90
965 A164 2m multicolored 1.75 1.75
966 A164 5m multicolored 3.75 3.75
Nos. 961-966 (6) 7.55 7.55

Souvenir Sheets

967 A164 7m multicolored 5.50 5.50
968 A164 7m multicolored 5.50 5.50

African Trains — A165

Designs: 20s, East African Railways Vulcan 2-8-2, 1929. 30s, Zimbabwe Railways Class 15A, 1952. 40s, South African Railways Class 25 4-8-4, 1953. 70s, East African Railways A58 Class Garratt. 1m, South Africa Class 9E Electric. 2m, East African Railways Class 87, 1971. 3m, East African Railways Class 92, 1971. 5m, South Africa Class 26 2-D-2, 1982.
No. 977, Algeria 231-132BT Class, 1937. No. 978, South African Railway Class 6E Bo-Bo, 1969.

1993, Sept. 24 **Litho.** *Perf. 14*

969 A165 20s multicolored .25 .25
970 A165 30s multicolored .40 .40
971 A165 40s multicolored .45 .45
972 A165 70s multicolored .90 .90
973 A165 1m multicolored 1.25 1.25
974 A165 2m multicolored 2.40 2.40
975 A165 3m multicolored 3.25 3.25
976 A165 5m multicolored 5.25 5.25
Nos. 969-976 (8) 14.15 14.15

Souvenir Sheets

977 A165 7m multicolored 6.75 6.75
978 A165 7m multicolored 6.75 6.75

Taipei '93 — A166

Disney characters in Taiwan: 20s, Chung Cheng Park, Keelung. 30s, Chiao-Tienkung Temple Festival. 40s, Procession. 70s, Temple Festival. 1m, Queen's Head Rock Formation, Yehliu, vert. 1.20m, Natl. Concert Hall, Taiwan, vert. 2m, C.K.S. Memorial Hall, Taiwan, vert. 2.50m, Grand Hotel, Taipei.
No. 987, 5m, Natl. Palace Museum, Taipei. No. 988, 6m, Presidential Palace Museum, Taipei, vert.

1993 **Litho.** *Perf. 14x13½, 13½x14*

979-986 A166 Set of 8 13.00 13.00

Souvenir Sheets

987-988 A166 Set of 2 11.00 11.00

Domestic Cats — A167

Various cats: 20s, 30s, 70s, 5m.
No. 992A, Brown cat eating mouse, vert.

1993, Oct. 29 **Litho.** *Perf. 14*

989-992 A167 Set of 4 6.50 6.50

Souvenir Sheet

992A A167 5m multicolored 5.50 5.50

Traditional Houses — A168

Designs: 20s, Khoaling, Khotla. 30s, Lelapa le seotloana morao ho, 1833. 70s, Thakaneng, Baroetsana. 4m, Mohlongoafatse pele ho, 1833.
No. 996A, Lelapa litema le mekhabiso.

1993, Sept. 24

993-996 A168 Set of 4 7.25 7.25

Souvenir Sheet

996A A168 4m multicolored 5.50 5.50

A169

Players, country: 20s, Khomari, Lesotho. 30s, Mohale, Lesotho. 40s, Davor, Yugoslavia; Rincon, Colombia. 50s, Lekhotla, Lesotho. 70s, Khali, Lesotho. 1m, Milla, Cameroun. 1.20m, Platt, England. 2m, Rummenigge, Germany; Lerby, Denmark.
No. 1005, Stejskal & Hasek, Czechoslovakia; Baresi, Italy, horiz. No. 1006, Lindenberger, Czechoslovakia; Schillaci, Italy.

1993 **Litho.** *Perf. 13½x14*

997-1004 A169 Set of 8 9.50 9.50

Souvenir Sheets

Perf. 13

1005-1006 A169 6m Set of 2 11.00 11.00

1994 World Cup Soccer Championships, US.

A170

New Democratic Government: 20s, King Letsie III signs oath of office under new constitution. 30s, Parliament building. 50s, Dr. Ntsu Mokhehle sworn in as prime minister. 70s, Transfer of power from Major Gen. P. Ramaema to Dr. Mokhehle.
30s, 50s, 70s are horizontal.

1994, Apr. 2 **Litho.** *Perf. 14*

1007 A170 20s multicolored .25 .25
1008 A170 30s multicolored .45 .45
1009 A170 50s multicolored .65 .65
1010 A170 70s multicolored .90 .90
Nos. 1007-1010 (4) 2.25 2.25

A171

PHILAKOREA '94 — A172

Frogs: 35s, Aquatic river. 50s, Bubbling kassina. 1m, Guttural toad. 1.50m, Common river.
No. 1015, 5m, Green frog statue. No. 1016, 5m, Black spotted frog, oriental white-eye bird, vert.

1994, Aug. 16 **Litho.** ***Perf. 14***
1011-1014 A171 Set of 4 3.25 3.25

Souvenir Sheets

1015-1016 A172 Set of 2 11.00 11.00

ICAO, 50th Anniv. — A173

Designs: 35s, Airplane, passengers on ground. 50s, Airplane, control tower. 1m, Airplane banking, terminal, control tower. 1.50m, Airplane ascending.

1994 **Litho.** ***Perf. 14***

1017 A173	35s multicolored	.25	.25
1018 A173	50s multicolored	.65	.65
1019 A173	1m multicolored	1.25	1.25
1020 A173	1.50m multicolored	2.00	2.00
	Nos. 1017-1020 (4)	4.15	4.15

Medicinal Plants — A174

Designs: 35s, Tagetes minuta. 50s, Plantago lanceolata. 1m, Amaranthus spinosus. 1.50m, Taraxacum officinale. 5m, Datura stramonium.

1995, May 22 **Litho.** ***Perf. 14***
1021-1024 A174 Set of 4 2.25 2.25

Souvenir Sheet

1025 A174 5m multicolored 2.75 2.75

Pius XII Natl. University, 50th Anniv. — A175

Designs: 35s, Pius XII College, 1962. 50s, Univ. of Basutoland, Bechuanaland Protectorate & Swaziland, 1965. 70s, Univ. of Botswana, Lesotho & Swaziland, 1970. 1m, Univ. of Bostswana, Lesotho & Swaziland, 1975. 1.50m, Natl. Univ. of Lesotho, 1988. 2m, Natl. Univ. of Lesotho, procession of vice-chancellors at celebration.

1995, July 26 **Litho.** ***Perf. 14***
1026-1031 A175 Set of 6 4.25 4.25

World Tourism Organization, 20th Anniv. — A176

Designs: 35s, Qiloane Pinnacle, Thaba-Bosiu, horiz. 50s, Rock Formation, Ha Mohalenyane, horiz. 1m, Botsoela Falls, Malealea. 1.50m, Backpacking, Makhaleng River Gorge, horiz.
4m, Red hot pokers.

1995, Aug. 28 **Litho.** ***Perf. 14***
1032-1035 A176 Set of 4 2.75 2.75

Souvenir Sheet

1036 A176 4m multicolored 2.50 2.50

No. 1036 contains one 38x58mm stamp.
No. 1036 withdrawn 9/15 because "Pokers" was misspelled "Porkers."

UN, 50th Anniv. — A177

UN emblem and: 35s, Peace dove. 50s, Scales of justice. 1.50m, Handshake of reconciliation, horiz.

1995, Sept. 26
1037-1039 A177 Set of 3 2.25 2.25

Christmas — A178

Roses: 35s, Sutter's Gold. 50s, Michele Meilland. 1m, J. Otto Thilow. 2m, Papa Meilland.

1995, Nov. 1 **Litho.** ***Perf. 14***
1040-1043 A178 Set of 4 2.75 2.75

A179

UNICEF, 50th Anniv.: 35s, Using iodized salt. 50s, Taking care of livestock, horiz. 70s, Children in classroom. horiz. 1.50m, Children learning traditional dance, singing, horiz.

1996, July 30 **Litho.** ***Perf. 14***
1044-1047 A179 Set of 4 2.50 2.50

A180

1996 Summer Olympic Games, Atlanta: 1m, US Basketball team, 1936, horiz. 1.50m, Olympic Stadium, Brandenburg Gate, Berlin, horiz. 2m, Jesse Owens, 1936. 3m, Motor boating, horiz.

Past Olympic medalists: No. 1052a, Glen Morris, long jump, decathlon, 1936. b, Said Aouita, 5000-meters, 1984. c, Arnie Robinson, long jump, 1976. d, Hans Woellke, shot put, 1936. e, Renate Stecher, 100-meters, 1972. f, Evelyn Ashford, 100-meters, 1984. g, Willie Davenport, 110-meter hurdles, 1968. h, Bob Beamon, long jump, 1968. i, Heidi Rosendhal, long jump, 1972.

No. 1053, 8m, Michael Gross, swimming, 1984. No. 1054, 8m, Kornelia Ender, swimming, 1976.

1996, Aug. 1
1048-1051 A180 Set of 4 4.00 4.00
1052 A180 1.50m Sheet of 9, #a.-i. 10.50 10.50

Souvenir Sheets

1053-1054 A180 Set of 2 11.50 11.50

Maps of Lesotho A181

No. 1055 — 1911 map: a, Lephaqlioa. b, Maqaleng. c, Molapo. d, Nkeu. e, No area specified. f, Rafanyane. g, No area specified (7800). h, Madibomatso River. i, Konyani. j, Semena River.

No. 1056 — 1978 map: a, No area specified. b, Lepaqoa. c, Mamoha (name). d, Ha Nkisi. e, Ha Rafanyan, Ha Thoora. f, Ha Mikia, Ha Ntseli. g, Ha Kosetabole, Ha Mpeli. h, Ha Selebeli, Ha Theko. i, Ha Rapooane, Ha Ramabotsa. j, Ha Ramani, Khohlontso (Kolberg).

No. 1057 — Locations on 1994 Map: a, Mafika-Lisiu Pass. b, Rampai's Pass, Ha Lesaoana. c, Ha Masaballa. d, Ha Nkisi, Ha Molotanyan. e, Ha Rafanyane, Kobong. f, Laitsoka Pass. g, Katse Reservoir. h, Seshote. i, Ha Rapoeea, Ha Kennan. j, Katse (i, name), Ha Mense.

1996 **Sheets of 10, #a-j**
1055-1057 A181 35s Set of 3 15.00 15.00

Trains — A182

No. 1058, 1.50m: a, ETR 450, Italy. b, TGV, France. c, XPT, Australia. d, Blue Train, South Africa. e, IC 255, Great Britain. f, Bullet Train, Japan.

No. 1059, 1.50m: a, WP Streamlined 4-6-2, India. b, Canadian Pacific 2471, Canada. c, The Caledonian 4-2-2, Scotland. d, William Mason 4-4-0, US. e, Trans-Siberian Express, Russia. f, Swiss Federal 4-6-0, Switzerland.

No. 1060, 8m, 52 Class, Germany. No. 1061, 8m, ICE, Germany.

1996, Sept. 1 **Litho.** ***Perf. 14***

Sheets of 6, #a-f

1058-1059 A182 Set of 2 11.50 11.50

Souvenir Sheets

1060-1061 A182 Set of 2 9.50 9.50

Nos. 1060-1061 each contain one 56x42mm stamp.

No. 833 Surcharged

1996 **Litho.** ***Perf. 13½***
1062 A146 20s on 30s multi *2.00* 1.00

Christmas — A183

Women from Mother's Unions: 35s, Methodist Church. 50s, Roman Catholic Church. 1m, Lesotho Evangelical Church. 1.50m, Anglican Church.

1996, Dec. 10 **Litho.** ***Perf. 14***
1063-1066 A183 Set of 4 2.75 2.75

Highlands Water Project — A184

Designs: 35s, "Cooperation for Development." 50s, "Nature and Heritage." 1m, "An Engineering Feat." 1.50m, "LHDA 10th Anniv., 1986-1996."

1997, Apr. 21 **Litho.** ***Perf. 14***
1067-1070 A184 Set of 4 3.25 3.25

No. 1070 is 72x25mm.

Environmental Protection — A184a

Emblem of National Environment Secretariat and: 35s, Animals grazing on reclaimed land. 50s, Person throwing trash in can. 1m, Hands holding globe with tree. 1.20m, Trash and recycling emblem. 1.50m, Collection of rainwater.

1997, June 30
1070A-1070E A184a Set of 5 3.00 3.00

1998 World Cup Soccer Championships, France — A185

Players: 1m, Schmeichel, Denmark. 1.50m, Bergkamp, Holland. 2m, Southgate, England. 2.50m, Asprilla, Colombia. 3m, Gascoigne, England. 4m, Giggs, Wales.

No. 1077: Various action scenes of Argentina vs. Holland, 1978.

No. 1078, 8m, Littbarski, W. Germany, horiz. No. 1079, 8m, Shearer, England.

1997, Oct. 31 ***Perf. 13½***
1071-1076 A185 Set of 6 6.50 6.50
1077 A185 1.50m Sheet of 6, #a.-f. 11.00 11.00

Souvenir Sheets

1078-1079 A185 Set of 2 9.00 9.00

Butterflies A186

No. 1080: a, Spialia spio. b, Cyclyrius pirithous. c, Acraea satis. d, Belenois aurota. e, Spindasis natalensis. f, Torynesis orangica. g, Lepidochrysops variabilis. h, Pinacopteryx eriphea. i, Anthene butleri.

No. 1081, 8m, Bematistes aganice. No. 1082, 8m, Papilio demodocus.

1997, Nov. 28 ***Perf. 14***
1080 A186 1.50m Sheet of 9, #a.-i. 7.75 7.75

Souvenir Sheets

1081-1082 A186 Set of 2 11.00 11.00

Morija Museum and Archives, 40th Anniv. — A187

Designs: 35s, Rock paintings, child, vert. 45s, Lower jaw of hippopotamus, hippo walking in water. 50s, Traditional attire, vert. 1m, Traditional musical instruments, vert. 1.50m, Award, Man with ceremonial garb, vert. 2m Boy riding bull.

Perf. 14½ Syncopated Type A

1998, Jan. 30 **Litho.**
1083-1088 A187 Set of 6 3.25 3.25

Diana, Princess of Wales (1961-97) — A188

Designs: No. 1089, Various portaits. No. 1090, Taking flowers from child.

1998, Mar. 16 **Litho.** ***Perf. 13½***
1089 A188 3m Sheet of 6, #a.-f. 9.00 9.00

Souvenir Sheet

1090 A188 9m multicolored 9.00 9.00

A189

A190

Wildlife
A191

No. 1091 — Cape vulture: a, Head. b, Perched on rock with head down. c, Looking left. d, Looking right.

No. 1092: a, Atitlan grebe. b, Cabot's tragopan. c, Spider monkey. d, Dibatag. e, Right whale. f, Imperial parrot. g, Cheetah. h, Brown-eared pheasant. i, Leatherback turtle. j, Imperial woodpecker. k, Andean condor. l, Barbary deer. m, Grey gentle lemur. n, Cuban parrot. o, Numbat. p, Short-tailed albatross. q, Green turtle. r, White rhinoceros. s, Diademed sifaka. t, Galapagos penguin.

No. 1093: a, Impala. b, Black bear. c, Buffalo. d, Elephant. e, Kangaroo. f, Lion. g, Panda. h, Tiger. i, Zebra.

No. 1094, 8m, Nectarinia talatala. No. 1095, 8m, Psephotus chrysopterygius. No. 1096, 8m, Percina tanasi.

No. 1097, 8m, Monkey.

1998, Apr. 27 Litho. *Perf. 14*

1091 A189	1m Strip of 4, #a.-d.	4.50	4.50
1092 A190	1m Sheet of 20, #a.-t.	11.00	11.00
1093 A191	1.50m Sheet of 9, #a.-i.	7.00	7.00

Souvenir Sheets

1094-1096 A190	Set of 3	12.00	12.00
1097 A191	8m multicolored	4.00	4.00

No. 1091 was issued in sheets of 12 stamps. World Wildlife Fund (No. 1091).

Cats — A192

Designs: 70s, Siamese. 1m, Chartreux. 2m, Korat. 3m, Egyptian mau. 4m, Bombay. 5m, Burmese.

No. 1104, 2m: a, Japanese bobtail. b, British white. c, Bengal. d, Abyssinian. e, Snowshoe. f, Scottish fold.

No. 1105, 2m: a, Maine coon. b, Balinese. c, Persian. d, Javanese. e, Turkish angora. f, Tiffany.

No. 1106, 8m, Singapura. No. 1107, 8m, Tonkinese.

1998, May 18

1098-1103 A192	Set of 6	7.75	7.75

Sheets of 6, #a-f

1104-1105 A192	Set of 2	16.00	16.00

Souvenir Sheets

1106-1107 A192	Set of 2	10.00	10.00

Mushrooms
A193

Designs: 70s, Laccaria laccata. 1m, Mutinus caninus. 1.50m, Tricholoma lascivum. 2m, Clitocybe geotrapa. 3m, Amanita excelsa. 4m, Red-capped bolete.

No. 1114: a, Parrot wax cap. b, Cortinarius obtusus. c, Volvariella bombycina. d, Continarius caerylescens. e, Laccaria amethystea. f, Tricholoma aurantium. g, Amanita excelsa. h, Clavaria helvola. i, Cortinarius caerylescens. j, Russula queletii. k, Amanita phalloides. l, Lactarius delicious.

No. 1115, 8m, Amanita pantherina. No. 1116, 8m, Boletus satanus.

1998, June 15 Litho. *Perf. 14*

1108-1113 A193	Set of 6	6.50	6.50
1114 A193	1m Sheet of 12, #a.-l.	6.50	6.50

Souvenir Sheets

1115-1116 A193	Set of 2	9.00	9.00

Japanese Film Stars — A194

No. 1117: a, Takamine Hideko. b, James Shigeta. c, Miyoshi Umeki. d, May Ishimara. e, Sessue Hayakawa. f, Miiko Taka. g, Mori Masayuki. h, Hara Setsuko. i, Kyo Machiko.

10m, Toshiro Mifune.

1998, July 14 Litho. *Perf. 14*

1117 A194	2m Sheet of 9, #a.-i.	7.50	7.50

Souvenir Sheet

1118 A194	10m multicolored	4.00	4.00

Prehistoric Animals — A195

No. 1119, 2m: a, Nyctosaurus (b). b, Volcanoes, wings of nyctosaurus, eudimorphadon. c, Eudimorphodon (b). d, Apatosaurus (g). e, Peteinosaurus (d, f, i). f, Tropeognathus. g, Pteranodon ingens (d). h, Ornithodesmus (g, i). i, Wuerhosaurus.

No. 1120, 2m: a, Ceresiosaurus (b, c, d). b, Rhomaleosaurus (d, e, f). c, Anomalocaris (b, f). d, Mixosaurus (e, g, h). e, Stethacanthus. f, Dunklosteus (c, e, i). g, Tommotia. h, Sanctacaris. i, Ammonites (a, f, h).

No. 1121, 2m: a, Rhamphorhynchus (b, d). b, Brachiosaurus (c, f). c, Mamenchisaurus hochuanensis (a, d, e, f). d, Ceratosaurus nasicornis (e, g, h). e, Archaeopteryx (b). f, Leaellynasaura amicargraphica (e, h, i). g, Chasmosaurus belli (h). h, Deinonychus, Pachyrhinosaurus (g). i, Deinonychus (h).

No. 1122, 10m, Woolly rhinoceros. No. 1123, 10m, Tyrannosaurus. No. 1124, 10m, Coelophysis.

1998, Aug. 10 Sheets of 9, #a-i

1119-1121 A195	Set of 3	24.00	24.00

Souvenir Sheets

1122-1124 A195	Set of 3	14.00	14.00

Intl. Year of the Ocean — A196

Fish: No. 1125, 1m, Treefish. No. 1126, 1m, Tiger barb. No. 1127, 1m, Bandtail puffer. No. 1128, 1m, Cod. No. 1129, 1.50m, Filefish. No. 1130, 1.50m, Clown loach. No. 1131, 1.50m, Sicklefin killie. No. 1132, 1.50m, Christy's lyretail. No. 1133, 2m, Brook trout. No. 1134, 2m, Pacific electric ray. No. 1135, 2m, Bighead searobin. No. 1136, 2m, Emerald betta. 3m, Harlequin tuskfish. 4m, Half-moon angelfish. 5m, Spotted trunkfish. 6m, Wolf-eel. 7m, Cherubfish.

No. 1142, 2m: a, Platy variatus. b, Archerfish. c, Clown knifefish. d, Angelicus. e, Black arowana. f, Spotted scat. g, Kribensis. h, Golden pheasant.

No. 1143, 2m: a, Bluegill. b, Grayling. c, Walleye. d, Brown trout. e, Atlantic salmon. f, Northern pike. g, Large mouth bass. h, Rainbow trout.

No. 1144, 2m: a, Purple firefish. b, Halequin sweetlips. c, Clown wrasse. d, Bicolor angelfish. e, False cleanerfish. f, Mandarinfish. g, Regal tang. h, Clownfish.

No. 1145, 2m: a, Weakfish. b, Red drum. c, Blue marlin. d, Yellowfin tuna. e, Barracuda. f, Striped bass. g, White shark. h, Permit.

No. 1146, 12m, Cyprinus carpio. No. 1147, 12m, Oncorhychus. No. 1148, 12m, Pseudopleuronectes americanus. No. 1149, 12m, Heterodontus francisci.

1998, Oct. 15 Litho. *Perf. 14*

1125-1141 A196	Set of 17	17.50	17.50

Sheets of 8, #a-h

1142-1145 A196	Set of 4	26.00	26.00

Souvenir Sheets

1146-1149 A196	Set of 4	19.00	19.00

Africa in Films — A197

No. 1150: a, "Simba." b, "Call to Freedom." c, "Cry the Beloved Country." d, "King Solomon's Mines." e, "Flame and the Fire." f, "Cry Freedom." g, "Bopha!" h, "Zulu."

10m "Born Free," horiz.

1998, July 14 Litho. *Perf. 14*

1150 A197	2m Sheet of 8, #a.-h.	7.50	7.50

Souvenir Sheet

1151 A197	10m multicolored	4.00	4.00

Flowers — A198

Designs: 10s, Pelargonium sidoides. 15s, Aponogeton ranunculiflorus. 20s, Sebaea leiostyla. 40s, Sebaea grandis. 50s, Satyrium neglectum. 60s, Massonia jasminiflora. 70s, Ajuga ophrydis. 80s, Nemesia fruticans. 1m, Aloe broomii. 2m, Wahlenbergia androsacea. 2.50m, Phygelius capensis. 3m, Dianthus basuticus. 4.50m, Rhodohypoxis baurii. 5m, Turbina oblongata. 6m, Hibiscus microcarpus. 10m, Lobelia erinus, moraea stricta.

1998 Litho. *Perf. 14*

1152	A198	10s multicolored	.25	.25
1153	A198	15s multicolored	.25	.25
1154	A198	20s multicolored	.25	.25
1155	A198	40s multicolored	.25	.25
1156	A198	50s multicolored	.25	.25
1157	A198	60s multicolored	.25	.25
1158	A198	70s multicolored	.25	.25
1159	A198	80s multicolored	.40	.40
1160	A198	1m multicolored	.50	.50
1161	A198	2m multicolored	1.00	1.00
1162	A198	2.50m multicolored	1.25	1.25
1163	A198	3m multicolored	1.50	1.50
1164	A198	4.50m multicolored	2.25	2.25
1165	A198	5m multicolored	2.40	2.40
1166	A198	6m multicolored	3.00	3.00
1167	A198	10m multicolored	4.50	4.50
		Nos. 1152-1167 (16)	18.55	18.55

Nos. 1152-1167 are dated 1997.

Coronation of King Letsie III, 1st Anniv. — A199

No. 1168: a, Receiving crown. b, Waving. c, Facing left.

1998, Oct. 31

1168 A199	1m Strip of 3, #a.-c.	2.25	2.25

Dogs — A200

Designs: 70s, Akita. 1m, Canaan. 2m, Eskimo. 4.50m, Norwegian elkhound.

No. 1173, 2m: a, Cirneco dell'etna. b, Afghan hound. c, Finnish spitz. d, Dalmatian. e, Basset hound. f, Shar-pei.

No. 1174, 2m: a, Boxer. b, Catalan sheepdog. c, English toy spaniel. d, Greyhound. e, Keeshond. f, Bearded collie.

No. 1175, 8m, Rough collie. No. 1176, 8m, Borzoi.

1999, May 18 Litho. *Perf. 14*

1169-1172 A200	Set of 4	4.00	4.00

Sheets of 6, #a-f

1173-1174 A200	Set of 2	11.00	11.00

Souvenir Sheets

1175-1176 A200	Set of 2	10.00	10.00

Birds — A201

Designs: 70s, Belted kingfisher. 1.50m, Palm cockatoo, vert. 2m, Red-tailed hawk. 3m, Tufted puffin. 4m, Reddish egret. 5m, Hoatzin, vert.

No. 1183, 2m: a, Evening grosbeak. b, Lesser blue-winged pitta. c, Altamira oriole. d, Rose-breasted grosbeak. e, Yellow warbler. f, Akiapolaau. g, American goldfinch. h, Northern flicker. i, Western tanager.

No. 1184, 2m, vert: a, Blue jay. b, Northern cardinal. c, Yellow-headed blackbird. d, Red. crossbill. e, Cedar waxwing. f, Vermilion flycatcher. g, Pileated woodpecker. h, Western meadowlark. i, Kingfisher.

No. 1185, 8m, Great egret. No. 1186, 8m, Zosterops erythropleura.

1999, June 28 Litho. *Perf. 14*

1177-1182 A201	Set of 6	8.00	8.00

Sheets of 9, #a-i

1183-1184 A201	Set of 2	19.00	19.00

Souvenir Sheets

1185-1186 A201	Set of 2	10.00	10.00

No. 1183c is incorrectly inscribed "Atlamira."

Orchids — A202

Designs: 1.50m, Cattleya dowiana. 3m, Diurus behri. 4m, Ancistrochilus rothchildianus. 5m, Aerangis curnowiana. 7m, Arachnis flos-aeris. 8m, Aspasia principissa.

No. 1193, 2m: a, Dendrobium bellaudum. b, Dendrobium trigonopus. c, Dimerandra emarginata. d, Dressleria eburnea. e, Dracula tubeana. f, Disa kirstenbosch. g, Encyclia alata. h, Epidendrum pseudepidendrum. i, Eriopsis biloba.

No. 1194, 2m: a, Apasia epidendroides. b, Barkaria lindleyana. c, Bifrenaria terragona. d, Bulbophyllum graveolens. e, Brassavola flagellaris. f, Bollea lawrenceana. g, Caladenia carnea. h, Catasetum macrocarpum. i, Cattleya aurantiaca.

No. 1195, 2m: a, Cochleanthes discolor. b, Cischweinfia dasyandra. c, Ceratostylis retisquama. d, Comparettia speciosa. e, Cryptostylis subulata. f, Cycnoches ventricsum. g, Dactylorhiza maculata. h, Cypripedium calceolus. i, Cymbidium finlaysonianum.

No. 1196, 10m, Paphiopedilum tonsum. No. 1197, 10m, Laelia rubescens. No. 1198, 10m, Ansellium africana. No. 1199, 10m, Ophrys apifera.

1999, July 30 Litho. *Perf. 14*

1187-1192 A202	Set of 6	13.00	13.00

Sheets of 9, #a-i

1193-1195 A202	Set of 3	22.50	22.50

Souvenir Sheets

1196-1199 A202	Set of 4	15.00	15.00

Chinese Art — A203

No. 1200 — Paintings by Pan Tianshou (1897-1971): a, Water Lily at Night. b, Hen and Chicks. c, Plum Blossom and Orchid. d, Plum Blossom and Banana Tree. e, Crane and Pine. f, Swallows. g, Eagle on the Pine (black eagle). h, Palm Tree. i, Eagle on the Pine (gray eagle). j, Orchids.

No. 1201: a, Sponge Gourd. b, Dragonfly.

1999, Aug. 16 ***Perf. 13x13¼***
1200 A203 1.50m Sheet of 10, #a.-j. 8.50 8.50

Souvenir Sheet

1201 A203 6m Sheet of 2, #a.-b. 6.50 6.50

China 1999 World Philatelic Exhibition.
No. 1201 contains two 51x40mm stamps.

Souvenir Sheet

UN Rights of the Child Convention, 10th Anniv. — A204

No. 1202: a, Black boy. b, Asian girl. c, Caucasian boy.

1999, Aug. 16 ***Perf. 14***
1202 A204 2m Sheet of 3, #a.-c. 3.00 3.00

Paintings by Hokusai (1760-1849) — A205

No. 1203, 3m: a, Nakamaro Watching the Moon from a Hill. b, Peonies and Butterfly. c, The Blind (bald man, both eyes open). d, The Blind (bald man, one eye shut). e, People Crossing an Arched Bridge (two at crest). f, People Crossing an Arched Bridge (river).
No. 1204, 3m: a, A View of Sumida River in Snow. b, Two Carp. c, The Blind (man with hair, both eyes shut). d, The Blind (man with hair, one eye open). e, Fishing by Torchlight. f, Whaling off the Goto Islands.
No. 1205, 10m, The Moon Above Yodo River and Osaka Castle, vert. No. 1206, 10m, Bellflower and Dragonfly, vert.

1999, Aug. 16 ***Perf. 13¾***

Sheet of 6, #a-f

1203-1204 A205 Set of 2 14.00 14.00

Souvenir Sheets

1205-1206 A205 Set of 2 8.00 8.00

Queen Mother (b. 1900) — A206

No. 1207: a, Wearing hat, 1938. b, With King George VI, 1948. c, Wearing tiara, 1963. d, Wearing hat, 1989.
15m, Waving at Clarence House.

1999, Aug. 16 ***Perf. 14***
1207 A206 5m Sheet of 4, #a.-d., + label 7.50 7.50

Souvenir Sheet

Perf. 13¾

1208 A206 15m multicolored 6.25 6.25

No. 1208 contains one 38x51mm stamp.

Johann Wolfgang von Goethe (1749-1832) A207

No. 1209: a, Mephistopheles appears as a dog in Faust's study. b, Portraits of Goethe and Friedrich von Schiller. c, Mephistopheles disguised as dog scorching the earth.
12m, Mephistopheles.

1999, Aug. 16 ***Perf. 14***
1209 A207 6m Sheet of 3, #a.-c. 6.25 6.25

Souvenir Sheet

1210 A207 12m multicolored 4.50 4.50

IBRA '99, Nuremberg, Germany — A208

Designs: 7m, Austerity 2-10-10 locomotive, building in Frankfurt am Main. 8m, Adler locomotive, Brandenburg Gate.

1999, Aug. 16 ***Perf. 14x14½***
1211 A208 7m multicolored 2.75 2.75
1212 A208 8m multicolored 3.25 3.25

Ships — A209

No. 1213, 4m: a, James Watt. b, Savannah. c, Amistad. d, Brick. e, Great Briain. f, Sirius.
No. 1214, 4m: a, France. b, Queen Elizabeth II. c, United States. d, Queen Elizabeth I. e, Michelangelo. f, Mauretania.
No. 1215, 4m: a, New Jersey. b, Aquila. c, De Zeven Provincien. d, Formidable. e, Vittorio Veneto. f, Hampshire.
No. 1216, 4m: a, Shearwater. b, British submarine. c, Hovercraft SRN 130. d, Italian submarine. e, Sr. N/3. f, Soucoupe Plongeante.
No. 1217, 15m, E. W. Morrison. No. 1218, 15m, Titanic. No. 1219, 15m, German U-boat. No. 1220, 15m, Enterprise.

1999, Dec. 31 **Litho.** ***Perf. 14***

Sheets of 6, #a.-f.

1213-1216 A209 Set of 4 30.00 30.00

Souvenir Sheets

1217-1220 A209 Set of 4 21.00 21.00

Names of ships are only found on sheet margins.

Millennium — A210

No. 1221 — Highlights of the 12th century: a, Chinese make first rocket. b, Burmese temple guardian. c, Troubador. d, Abbé Suger. e, Pope Adrian IV. f, King Henry II of England. g, Holy Roman Emperor Barbarossa. h, Yoritomo establishes shogunate in Japan. i, Crusader monument. j, Ibn Rushd translates Aristotle. k, Archbishop Thomas Becket. l, Leaning Tower of Pisa. m, Pivot windmill. n, Saladin. o, Richard the Lion-Hearted. p, Easter Island statues (60x40mm) q, Third Crusade begins.

1999, Dec. 31 ***Perf. 12¾x12½***
1221 A210 1.50m Sheet of 17, #a.-q. 11.00 11.00

Wedding of King Letsie III to Karabo Anne Motsoeneng — A211

No. 1222: a, King, bride in Western attire. b, Bride. c, King. d, King, bride in native attire.

2000, Feb. 18 **Litho.** ***Perf. 14***
1222 A211 1m Sheet of 4, #a.-d., + label 3.75 3.75

Prince William, 18th Birthday A212

No. 1223: a, Wearing bow tie. b, Wearing scarf. c, Wearing striped shirt. d, Wearing sweater, holding car door.
15m, Wearing sweater, diff.

2000, June 21 **Litho.** ***Perf. 14***
1223 A212 4m Sheet of 4, #a-d 6.50 6.50

Souvenir Sheet

Perf. 13¾

1224 A212 15m multi 6.50 6.50

No. 1223 contains four 28x42mm stamps.

First Zeppelin Flight, Cent. A213

No. 1225 — Ferdinand von Zeppelin and: a, LZ- 127. b, LZ-130. c, LZ-10.
15m, LZ-130, diff.

2000, July 6 ***Perf. 14***
1225 A213 8m Sheet of 3, #a-c 8.50 8.50

Souvenir Sheet

1226 A213 15m multi 6.50 6.50

No. 1225 contains three 42x28mm stamps.

Berlin Film Festival, 50th Anniv. A214

No. 1227: a, Gena Rowlands. b, Vlastimil Brodsky. c, Carlos Saura. d, La Collectioneuse. e, Le Depart. f, Le Diable Probablement.
15m, Stammheim.

2000, July 6
1227 A214 6m Sheet of 6, #a-f 12.00 12.00

Souvenir Sheet

1228 A214 15m multi 6.50 6.50

Souvenir Sheets

2000 Summer Olympics, Sydney — A215

No. 1229: a, Nedo Nadi. b, Swimming. c, Aztec Stadium, Mexico City and Mexican flag. d, Ancient Greek boxers.

2000, July 6
1229 A215 6m Sheet of 4, #a-d 8.50 8.50

Public Railways, 175th Anniv. — A216

No. 1230: a, George Stephenson. b, Stephenson's patent locomotive engine. c, Stephenson's Britannia Tubular Bridge.

2000, July 6
1230 A216 8m Sheet of 3, #a-c 8.50 8.50

Johann Sebastian Bach (1685-1750) — A217

2000, July 6
1231 A217 15m multi 6.50 6.50

Flowers — A218

Designs: 4m, Moore's crinum. 5m, Flame lily. 6m, Cape clivia. 8m, True sugarbush.
No. 1236, 3m: a, Spotted leaved arum. b, Christmas bells. c, Lady Monson. d, Wild pomegranate. e, Blushing bride. f, Bot River protea.
No. 1237, 3m: a, Starry gardenia. b, Pink hibiscus. c, Dwarf poker. d, Coast kaffirboom. e, Rose cockade. f, Pride of Table Mountain.
No. 1238, 3m: a, Drooping agpanthus. b, Yellow marsh afrikander. c, Weak stemmed painted lady. d, Impala lily. e, Beatrice watsonia. f, Pink arum.
No. 1239, 15m, Green arum. No. 1240, 15m, Red hairy erica, horiz.

2000, July 12
1232-1235 A218 Set of 4 9.00 9.00

Sheets of 6, #a-f

1236-1238 A218 Set of 3 21.00 21.00

Souvenir Sheets

1239-1240 A218 Set of 2 15.00 15.00

Apollo-Soyuz Mission, 25th Anniv. — A219

No. 1241: a, Apollo 18 and Soyuz 19 docked. b, Apollo 18. c, Soyuz 19.

2000, July 6 **Litho.** ***Perf. 14***
1241 A219 8m Sheet of 3, #a-c 9.00 9.00

Souvenir Sheet

1242 A219 15m shown 6.50 6.50

Souvenir Sheet

Albert Einstein (1879-1955) — A220

2000, July 6 ***Perf. 14¼***

1243 A220 15m multi 6.50 6.50

Endangered Wildlife — A221

No. 1244, 4m, horiz.: a, Alethe. b, Temminck's pangolin. c, Cheetah. d, African elephant. e, Chimpanzee. f, Northern white rhinoceros.

No. 1245, 4m, horiz.: a, African black rhinoceros. b, Leopard. c, Roseate tern. d, Mountain gorilla. e, Mountain zebra. f, Zanzibar red colobus monkey.

No. 1246, horiz: a, Wildebeest. b, Tree hyrax. c, Red lechwe. d, Eland.

No. 1247, 15m, Dugong. No. 1248, 15m, West African manatee.

2000, Aug. 10 **Litho.** ***Perf. 14***

Sheets of 6, #a-f

1244-1245 A221 Set of 2 18.00 18.00
1246 A221 5m Sheet of 4, #a-d 7.75 7.75

Souvenir Sheets

1247-1248 A221 Set of 2 16.00 16.00

The Stamp Show 2000, London.

Automobiles — A222

No. 1249, 3m: a, 1960 Cadillac El Dorado Seville. b, 1955-75 Citroen DS. c, 1961 Ford Zephyr Zodiac Mk II. d, 1945-55 MG TF. e, 1949-65 Porsche 356. f, 1955 Ford Thunderbird.

No. 1250, 3m: a, 1948-52 Cisitalia 202 Coupe. b, 1990s Dodge Viper. c, 1968-69, TVR Vixen Sl. d, 1957-70 Lotus 7. e, 1964-68 Ferrari 275 GTB/4. f, 1951 Pegasus Touring Spider.

No. 1251, 4m: a, 1913 Fiat Type O. b, 1914 Stutz Bearcat. c, 1924 French Levat. d, 1888 Benz Motorwagen. e, 1925 Isota Fraschini Type 8A. f, 1887 Markus Motor Carriage.

No. 1252, 4m: a, 1951 Morris Minor. b, 1935 Hispano-Suiza Type 68. c, 1949 MG TC. d, 1955 Morgan 4/4. e, 1950 Jaguar XK120. f, 1946-49 Triumph 1800/2000 Roadster.

No. 1253, 15m, 1896 Bersey Electric Car. No. 1254, 15m, 1948-71 Morris Minor 1000. No. 1255, 15m, 1953-63 AC Ace. No. 1256, 15m, Ferrari F40, vert.

Illustration reduced.

2000, Sept. 1 **Sheets of 6, #a-f**

1249-1252 A222 Set of 4 30.00 30.00

Souvenir Sheets

1253-1256 A222 Set of 4 25.00 25.00

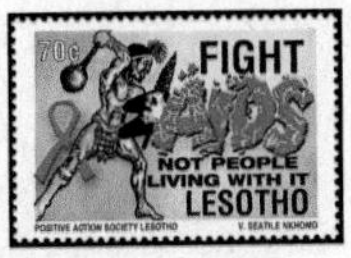

Fight Against AIDS — A223

Designs: 70s, "Fight AIDS, not people living with it." 1m, "Speed kills, so does AIDS. Go Slow!" 1.50m, "People with AIDS need friends, not rejection," vert. 2.10m, "Even when you're off duty, protect the nation."

2001, Jan. 22 **Litho.** ***Perf. 14***

1257-1260 A223 Set of 4 5.00 5.00

Butterflies A224

Designs: 70s, Great orange tip. 1m, Red-banded pereute. 1.50m, Sword grass brown. No. 1264, 2m, Striped blue crow. No. 1265, 3m, Alfalfa. 4m, Doris.

No. 1267, 2m: a, African migrant. b, Large oak blue. c, Wanderer. d, Tiger swallowtail. e, Union jack. f, Saturn. g, Broad-bordered grass yellow. h, Hewitson's uraneis.

No. 1268, 2m: a, Orange-banded sulfur. b, Large wood nymph. c, Postman. d, Palmfly. e, Gulf fritillary. f, Cairns birdwing. g, Common morpho. h, Common dotted border.

No. 1269, 3m: a, Bertoni's antwren (bird). b, Clorinde. c, Iolas blue. d, Mocker swallowtail. e, Common Indian crow. f, Grecian shoemaker. g, Small flambeau. h, Orchid swallowtail.

No. 1270, 15m, Crimson tip. No. 1271, 15m, Forest queen.

2001, Mar. 1 **Litho.** ***Perf. 13¼x13¾***

1261-1266 A224 Set of 6 7.00 7.00

Sheets of 8, #a-h

1267-1269 A224 Set of 3 24.00 24.00

Souvenir Sheets

1270-1271 A224 Set of 2 22.00 22.00

Phila Nippon '01, Japan — A225

Designs: 1.50m, Man in carriage from The Battle of Lepanto and the Map of the World, by unknown artist. 2m, Battle scene from The Battle of Lepanto and the Map of the World. 3m, Crane from Birds and Flowers of the Four Seasons, by Eitoku Kano. 4m, The Four Elegant Pastimes. 7m, Maple Viewing at Mount Takao, by unknown artist. 8m, The Four Accomplishments, by Yusho Kaiho.

No. 1278, 5m: a, Portrait of a Lady, by unknown artist. b, Portrait of Tadakatsu Honda, by unknown artist. c, Portrait of the Wife of Tokujo Goto, by unknown aritst. d, Portrait of Emperor Go-yosei, by Takanobu Kano. e, Portrait of Tenzuiin, Hideyoshi's Mother, by Sochin Hoshuku.

No. 1279, 6m: a, Portrait of Yusai Hosokawa, by Suden Ishin. b, Portrait of Sen No Rikyu, attributed to Tohaku Hasegawa. c, Portrait of Oichi No Kata, by unknown artist. d, Portrait of Ittetsu Inaba, attributed to Hasegawa. e, Portrait of Nobunaga Oda, by Sochin Kokei.

No. 1280, 15m, Portrait of Ieyasu Tokugawa, by unknown artist. No. 1281, 15m, Portrait of Hideyoshi Toyotomi, by unknown artist.

Perf. 13¾, 14 (#1278-1279)

2001, May 31 **Litho.**

1272-1277 A225 Set of 6 6.00 6.00

Sheets of 5, #a-e

1278-1279 A225 Set of 2 30.00 30.00

Souvenir Sheets

1280-1281 A225 Set of 2 14.50 14.50

Size of stamps on Nos. 1278-1279: 85x28mm.

Nos. 1274-1275 are incorrectly inscribed. No. 1274 actually depicts "Landscape with Flowers and Birds." No. 1275 shows a detail from"The Four Elegant Pastimes," by Eitoku Kano.

Mushrooms — A226

Designs: No. 1282, 5m, Bell-shaped panaeolus. No. 1283, 5m, Golden false pholiota. No. 1284, 5m, Shiny cap. No. 1285, 5m, Sooty brown waxy cap.

No. 1286, 3m: a, Violet cortinarius. b, Angel's wings. c, Collybia velutibes. d, Lentinellus. e, Anthurus aseroiformis. f, Caesar's mushroom.

No. 1287, 4m: a, Pungent cortinarius. b, Peziza sarcosphaera. c, Emetic russula. d, Questionable stropharia. e, Apricot jelly mushroom. f, Anise-scented clitocybe.

No. 1288, 15m, Cone-shaped waxy cap, horiz. No. 1289, 15m, Boletus, horiz.

2001, June 29 ***Perf. 14***

1282-1285 A226 Set of 4 9.00 9.00

Sheets of 6, #a-f

1286-1287 A226 Set of 2 19.00 19.00

Souvenir Sheets

1288-1289 A226 Set of 2 14.00 14.00

Belgica 2001 Intl. Stamp Exhibition, Brussels (Nos. 1286-1289).

UN High Commissioner for Refugees, 50th Anniv. — A227

Designs: 70s, Silhouette of woman and child. 1m, Child and animal. 1.50m, Woman, vert. 2.10m, Information technology, vert.

2001, Aug. 20 ***Perf. 14***

1290-1293 A227 Set of 4 4.75 4.75

Birds of Prey — A228

Designs: 70s, Black kite. 1m, Martial eagle. 1.50m, Bateleur. 2.10m, African goshawk. 2.50m, Bearded vulture. 3m, Jackal buzzard.

2001, Oct. 1 **Litho.** ***Perf. 14***

1294-1299 A228 Set of 6 6.00 6.00

Southern African Wildlife — A229

Designs: 1m, Grass owl. 2.10m, Klipspringer. 3m, Saddlebacked jackal. 5m, Black wildebeest.

No. 1304, 4m: a, Damara zebra. b, Bontebok. c, Eland. d, Lion. e, Saddlebacked jackal, diff. f, Yellow-billed kite.

No. 1305, 4m: a, Aardvark. b, Rock kestrel. c, Black-footed cat. d, Springhare. e, Aardwolf. f, Rock hyrax.

No. 1306, 15m, black-shouldered kite. No. 1307, 15m, Caracal, vert.

2001, Oct. 15 **Litho.** ***Perf. 14***

1300-1303 A229 Set of 4 6.00 6.00

Sheets of 6, #a-f

1304-1305 A229 Set of 2 21.00 21.00

Souvenir Sheets

1306-1307 A229 Set of 2 15.00 15.00

Reign of Queen Elizabeth II, 50th Anniv. A230

No. 1308: a, Queen seated. b, Queen with Prince Philip and British flag. c, Queen with man. c, Prince Philip.

20m, Queen wearing black suit.

2002, Feb. 6 **Litho.** ***Perf. 14¼***

1308 A230 8m Sheet of 4, #a-d 13.00 13.00

Souvenir Sheet

1309 A230 20m multi 10.00 10.00

United We Stand — A231

2002, Aug. 13 ***Perf. 14***

1310 A231 7m multi 4.00 4.00

Printed in sheets of 4.

SOS Children's Village, Lithabaneng A232

2002, Aug. 13

1311 A232 10m multi 4.50 4.50

Rotary International in Lesotho, 25th Anniv. — A233

Designs: 8m, Horner Wood. 10m, Paul Harris.

No. 1314, 25m, Stylized globe and clasped hands. No. 1315, 25m, Golden Gate Bridge, horiz.

2002, Aug. 13

1312-1313 A233 Set of 2 7.00 7.00

Souvenir Sheets

1314-1315 A233 Set of 2 18.00 18.00

20th World Scout Jamboree, Thailand — A234

No. 1316: a, Sheet bend knots. b, Pup and forester tents. c, Canoeing. d, Water rescue.

25m, A night under the stars.

2002, Aug. 13

1316 A234 9m Sheet of 4, #a-d 11.50 11.50

Souvenir Sheet

1317 A234 25m multi 11.00 11.00

Intl. Year of Mountains — A235

No. 1318, horiz.: a, Mt. Machache. b, Mt. Thabana Li-Mèle. c, Mt. Qiloane. d, Mt. Thaba Bosiu.
25m, Mt. Rainier, US.

2002, Aug. 13

1318 A235 8m Sheet of 4, #a-d 11.50 11.50

Souvenir Sheet

1319 A235 25m multi 11.50 11.50

Intl. Year of Ecotourism — A236

No. 1320, horiz.: a, Plant. b, Flowers. c, Man and horses. d, Lion. e, Frog. f, House.
20m, Bird.

2002, Aug. 13

1320 A236 6m Sheet of 6, #a-f 13.00 13.00

Souvenir Sheet

1321 A236 20m multi 8.50 8.50

Flowers, Insects and Spiders A237

No. 1322, 6m — Flowers: a, Angel's fishing rod. b, Marigold. c, Joan's blood. d, Mule pink. e, Tiger lily. f, Comtesse de Bouchaud.
No. 1323, 6m — Orchids: a, Phragmipedium besseae. b, Cypripedium calceolus. c, Cattleya Louise Georgiana. d, Brassocattleya binosa. e, Laelia gouldiana. f, Paphiopedilum maudiae.
No. 1324, 6m, horiz. — Insects: a, Leaf grasshopper. b, Golden-ringed dragonfly. c, Weevil-hunting wasp. d, European grasshopper. e, Thread-waisted wasp. f, Mantid.
No. 1325, 20m, Bleeding heart. No. 1326, 20m, Brassavola tuberculata. No. 1327, 20m, Orb web spider.

2002, Aug. 30 ***Perf. 14***

Sheets of 6, #a-f

1322-1324 A237 Set of 3 35.00 35.00

Souvenir Sheets

1325-1327 A237 Set of 3 25.00 25.00

Coronation of Queen Elizabeth II, 50th Anniv. (in 2003) — A238

No. 1328: a, Wearing blue hat. b, Wearing white hat. c, Wearing black hat.
15m, Wearing red hat.

2004, May 17 **Litho.** ***Perf. 14***

1328 A238 8m Sheet of 3, #a-c 7.00 7.00

Souvenir Sheet

1329 A238 15m multi 4.50 4.50

Prince William, 21st Birthday (in 2003) A239

No. 1330: a, Wearing sunglasses. b, Wearing suit and tie c, Wearing sports shirt.
15m, As young boy.

2004, May 17

1330 A239 8m Sheet of 3, #a-c 8.00 8.00

Souvenir Sheet

1331 A239 15m multi 4.75 4.75

Intl. Year of Fresh Water (in 2003) A240

No. 1332: a, Top of Qiloane Falls (gray water at top). b, Middle portion of Qiloane Falls (narrow at top). c, Bottom portion of Qiloane Falls.
15m, Orange River.

2004, May 17 ***Perf. 14¼***

1332 A240 8m Sheet of 3, #a-c 12.00 12.00

Souvenir Sheet

1333 A240 15m multi 7.50 7.50

Powered Flight, Cent. (in 2003) A241

No. 1334: a, Louis Blériot's Canard at Bagatelle, 1906. b, Blériot's Double-winged Libellule, 1907. c, Cross-country flight of Blériot VIII, Toury to Artenay, 1908. d, Blériot XII test flight, 1909.
15m, Blériot XI.

2004, May 17

1334 A241 6m Sheet of 4, #a-d 9.00 9.00

Souvenir Sheet

1335 A241 15m multi 6.75 6.75

Worldwide Fund for Nature (WWF) — A242

No. 1336 — Southern bald ibis: a, On nest, country name in white at LR. b, Flying to right, black denomination. c, Standing on rock, black denomination. d, Facing left.
No. 1337 — Southern bald ibis: a, Standing on rock, red denomination. b, Flying to left, red denomination. c, On nest, country name in black at UR.

2004, May 17 ***Perf. 14***

1336 Horiz. strip of 4 4.00 4.00
a.-d. A242 3m Any single .80 .80
1337 Horiz. strip of 4, #1336d, 1337a-1337c 4.00 4.00
a.-c. A242 3m Any single .80 .80

No. 1336 printed in sheets of 4 strips. No. 1337 printed in sheets of 2 strips.

Mammals A243

Designs: 1m, Cape porcupine. 1.50m, Brown rat. 2.10m, Springhare, vert. No. 1341, 5m, South African galago, vert.
No. 1342, 5m: a, Striped grass mouse. b, Greater galago. c, Ground pangolin. d, Banded mongoose.
15m, Egyptian rousette, vert.

2004, May 17

1338-1341 A243 Set of 4 7.00 7.00
1342 A243 5m Sheet of 4, #a-d 9.50 9.50

Souvenir Sheet

1343 A243 15m multi 8.00 8.00

Birds — A244

Designs: 1.50m, Secretary bird. 2.10m, Gray-crowned crane. 3m, Pied avocet. 5m, Common kestrel.
No. 1348: a, European roller. b, Common cuckoo. c, Great spotted cuckoo. d, Pel's fishing owl.
15m, Kori bustard.

2004, May 17

1344-1347 A244 Set of 4 8.00 8.00
1348 A244 6m Sheet of 4, #a-d 12.00 12.00

Souvenir Sheet

1349 A244 15m multi 9.50 9.50

Butterflies A245

Designs: 1.50m, Acraea rabbaiae. 2.10m, Alaena margaritacea. 4m, Bematistes aganice. No. 1353, 6m, Acraea quirina.
No. 1354, 6m: a, Bematistes excisa male. b, Bematistes excisa female. c, Bematistes epiprotea. d, Bematistes poggei.
15m, Acraea satis.

2004, May 17

1350-1353 A245 Set of 4 8.00 8.00
1354 A245 6m Sheet of 4, #a-d 11.00 11.00

Souvenir Sheet

1355 A245 15m multi 7.50 7.50

Flowers — A246

Designs: 1.50m, Sparaxis grandiflora. 2.10m, Agapanthus africanus. 3m, Protea linearis. No. 1359, 5m, Nerine cultivars.
No. 1360, 5m: a, Kniphofia uvaria. b, Amaryllis belladonna. c, Cazania splendens. d, Erica coronata.
15m, Saintpaulia cultivars.

2004, May 17

1356-1359 A246 Set of 4 6.75 6.75
1360 A246 5m Sheet of 4, #a-d 9.00 9.00

Souvenir Sheet

1361 A246 15m multi 6.00 6.00

Houses — A247

Designs: 70s, Mokhoro. 1m, Heisi. 1.50m, Lesotho. 2.10m, Mohlongoa-Fat'se.

2005, Feb. 21 **Litho.** ***Perf. 14***

1362-1365 A247 Set of 4 4.00 4.00

Girl Guides — A248

Girl Guides: 70s, Dancing. 1m, Marching in parade. 1.50m, Collecting cans, vert. 2.10m, Standing near building.
10m, Leader holding microphone, vert.

2005, May 20 **Litho.** ***Perf. 14***

1366-1369 A248 Set of 4 4.75 4.75

Souvenir Sheet

1370 A248 10m multi 6.25 6.25

Pope John Paul II (1920-2005) — A249

2005, Aug. 22 ***Perf. 12¾***

1371 A249 10m multi 6.25 6.25

Printed in sheets of 4.

Souvenir Sheet

Rotary International, Cent. — A250

No. 1372: a, Alleviating poverty. b, Advancement of literacy. c, Helping at-risk children.

2005, Aug. 22

1372 A250 8m Sheet of 3, #a-c 7.75 7.75

World Cup Soccer Championships, 75th Anniv. — A251

No. 1373, horiz. — Players from final match from: a, 1930. b, 1938. c, 1990.
15m, Bodo Illgner, 1990 goalie for Germany.

2005, Aug. 22 ***Perf. 12***

1373 A251 8m Sheet of 3, #a-c 9.50 9.50

Souvenir Sheet

1374 A251 15m multi 6.50 6.50

Hans Christian Andersen (1805-75), Author — A252

No. 1375: a, Statue of Andersen, Copenhagen. b, Childhood home of Andersen, Odense, Denmark. c, Scene from "The Steadfast Tin Soldier".
15m, Little Mermaid statue, Copenhagen.

2005, Aug. 22 *Perf. 12¾*
1375 A252 8m Sheet of 3, #a-c 9.75 9.75

Souvenir Sheet

1376 A252 15m multi 6.50 6.50

Jules Verne (1828-1905), Writer — A253

No. 1377, horiz.: a, Journey to the Center of the Earth. b, Verne, without hat. c, 20,000 Leagues Under the Sea.
15m, Verne wearing hat.

2005, Aug. 22
1377 A253 8m Sheet of 3, #a-c 10.00 10.00

Souvenir Sheet

1378 A253 15m multi 6.50 6.50

Albert Einstein (1879-1955), Physicist — A254

No. 1379, horiz. — Einstein and: a, Country name in black. b, Nikola Tesla, Charles Steinmetz. c, Country name in red violet.
15m, Time Magazine "Person of the Century" cover.

2005, Aug. 22
1379 A254 8m Sheet of 3, #a-c 10.00 10.00

Souvenir Sheet

1380 A254 15m multi 6.50 6.50

Battle of Trafalgar, Bicent. A255

No. 1381: a, HMS Victory. b, Admiral Horatio Nelson facing left. c, Nelson wounded in battle. d, Ships in battle.
25m, Nelson facing right.

2005, Aug. 22 *Perf. 12¾*
1381 A255 8m Sheet of 4, #a-d 19.00 19.00

Souvenir Sheet

Perf. 12

1382 A255 25m multi 19.00 19.00

No. 1381 contains four 42x28mm stamps.

End of World War II, 60th Anniv. A256

No. 1383, 4m — V-E Day: a, U.S. troops land on Omaha Beach, 1944. b, Gen. George C. Marshall. c, German Field Marshal Wilhelm Keitel signing surrender. d, Generals Dwight D. Eisenhower and George S. Patton. e, Soldiers sifting through war damage.
No. 1384, 4m — V-J Day: a, USS Arizona. b, Bunker, Chula Beach, Tinian Island. c, Bockscar flight crew. d, Newspaper announcing Japanese surrender. e, Historic marker commemorating loading of second atomic bomb on Tinian Island.

2005, Aug. 22 *Perf. 12¾*

Sheets of 5, #a-e

1383-1384 A256 Set of 2 13.00 13.00

A257

People and Livestock A258

Designs: 70 l, Boy riding calf. 1m, Man feeding cattle. 1.50m, Cattle tenders playing game. 2.10m, Shepherd carrying lamb.
10m, Dancers.

2006, Mar. 13 **Litho.** *Perf. 14*
1385-1388 A257 Set of 4 4.00 4.00

Souvenir Sheet

1389 A258 10m multi 6.50 6.50

A259

Women Balancing Items on Heads — A260

Women carrying: 70 l, Sticks. 1m, Cooking pot. 1.50m, Water jar. 2.10m, Bowl of fruit.
10m, Bowl of grain.

2006, June 19
1390-1393 A259 Set of 4 4.00 4.00

Souvenir Sheet

1394 A260 10m multi 5.75 5.75

A261

Handicrafts — A262

Designs: 70 l, Baskets. 1m, Artist and drawing, vert. 1.50m, Painted pottery. 2.10m, Figurines of stork and fish, decorated bull's horn.
10m, Boy, native costume.

2006, Oct. 9 **Litho.** *Perf. 14¼*
1395-1398 A261 Set of 4 4.00 4.00

Souvenir Sheet

1399 A262 10m multi 6.50 6.50

Birds — A263

Designs: 1m, Crested caracara. 1.50m, Wood storks. 2.10m, Tawny-shouldered blackbird. No. 1403, 15m, Jabiru.
No. 1404: a, Great blue heron. b, Anna's hummingbird. c, Gray silky flycatcher. d, Limpkin.
No. 1405, 15m, Western reef heron. No. 1406, 15m, Monk parakeet.

2007, Aug. 20 **Litho.** *Perf. 14*
1400-1403 A263 Set of 4 24.00 24.00
1404 A263 6m Sheet of 4, #a-d 8.00 8.00

Souvenir Sheets

1405-1406 A263 Set of 2 10.00 10.00

Butterflies — A264

Designs: 1m, Mylothris erlangeri. 1.50m, Papilio nireus. 2.10m, Acraea terpiscore. 10m, Salamis temora.
No. 1411: a, Danaus chrysippus. b, Myrina silenus. c, Chrysiridia madagascariensis. d, Hypolimnas dexithea.
No. 1412, 15m, P. demodocus. No. 1413, 15m, Amphicallia tigris.

2007, Aug. 20
1407-1410 A264 Set of 4 9.00 9.00
1411 A264 6m Sheet of 4, #a-d 7.00 7.00

Souvenir Sheets

1412-1413 A264 Set of 2 9.00 9.00

Orchids — A265

Designs: 1.50m, Spiranthes laciniata. 2.10m, Triphora craigheadii. 3m, Arethusa bulbosa. 10m, Calypso bulbosa.
No. 1418: a, Encyclia tampensis. b, Prosthechea cochleata. c, Vanilla pompona. d, Cypripedium acaule.
No. 1419, 15m, Vanilla barbellata. No. 1420, 15m, Epidendrum radicans.

2007, Aug. 20
1414-1417 A265 Set of 4 22.50 22.50
1418 A265 6m Sheet of 4, #a-d 7.50 7.50

Souvenir Sheets

1419-1420 A265 Set of 2 10.00 10.00

A266

A267

Mushrooms — A268

Designs: 1m, Amanita pantherina. 1.50m, Agaricus xanthodermus. 2.10m, Amanita rubescens. No. 1424, 15m, Amanita phalloides.
No. 1425: a, Amanita phalloides, diff. b, Amanita pantherina, diff. c, Panaeolus papilionaceus. d, Amanita rubescens, diff.
No. 1426, 15m, Amanite panther. No. 1427, 15m, Podaxis pistillaris.

2007, Aug. 20
1421-1424 A266 Set of 4 12.00 12.00
1425 A267 6m Sheet of 4, #a-d 12.00 12.00

Souvenir Sheets

1426 A267 15m multi 9.00 9.00
1427 A268 15m multi 9.00 9.00

Miniature Sheet

2008 Summer Olympics, Beijing — A269

No. 1428: a, Rowing. b, Softball. c, Wrestling. d, Volleyball.

2008, Aug. 18 **Litho.** *Perf. 12*
1428 A269 3.50m Sheet of 4, #a-d 6.50 6.50

In 2015 Lesotho postal officials declared as "illegal" a number of souvenir sheets of 1 depicting subjects such as wild mammals, wild cats, dogs, frogs, turtles, insects, penguins, Marie Curie and Brigitte Bardot.

Independence, 50th Anniv. — A270

Designs: 10m, Thaba Bosiu National Monument. 15m, National flags of Lesotho mounted on the Basotho hat. 20m, Lesotho National Parliament Houses.

2016, Oct. 4 **Litho.** *Perf. 13¼*
1429 A270 10m multi — —
1430 A270 15m multi — —
1431 A270 20m multi — —

World Post Day — A271

Inscriptions: 2m, Mail sorting and packaging. 5m, Mail delivery. 10m, Lesotho Central Post Office. 15m, Morija Post Office. 20m, Maseru Main Post Office. 25m, Maseru Central Post Office.

2016, Oct. 9 Litho. *Perf. 13¼*

1432-1437 A271 Set of 6 — —

POSTAGE DUE STAMPS

Basutoland Nos. J9-J10 Overprinted

Wmk. 314

1966, Nov. 1 Typo. *Perf. 14*

J1 D2 1c carmine .30 *.75*
  a. "Lseotho" *35.00*
J2 D2 5c dark purple .30 *.90*
  a. "Lseotho" *55.00*

D1

Perf. 13½

1967, Apr. 1 Unwmk. Litho.

J3 D1 1c dark blue .25 *3.00*
J4 D1 2c dull rose .25 *3.50*
J5 D1 5c emerald .40 *3.50*
  Nos. J3-J5 (3) .90 *10.00*

1976, Nov. 30 Wmk. 362

J7 D1 2c dull rose 3.00 3.00
J8 D1 5c emerald 3.00 3.00

D2

1986 Litho. *Perf. 13x13½*

J9 D2 2s green .55 .55
J10 D2 5s blue .55 .55
J11 D2 25s purple .55 .55
  Nos. J9-J11 (3) 1.65 1.65

LIBERIA

lī-'bir-ē-ə

LOCATION — West coast of Africa, between Ivory Coast and Sierra Leone
GOVT. — Republic
AREA — 43,000 sq. mi.
POP. — 2,602,100 (1997 est.)
CAPITAL — Monrovia

100 Cents = 1 Dollar

Catalogue values for unused stamps in this country are for Never Hinged items, beginning with Scott 330 in the regular postage section, Scott B19 in the semi-postal section, Scott C67 in the airpost section, and Scott CB4 in the airpost semi-postal section.

Values for unused stamps are for examples with original gum as defined in the catalogue introduction. Any exceptions will be noted. Very fine examples of Nos. 1-3, 13-21 and 157-159 will have perforations just clear of the design due to the narrow spacing of the stamps on the plates and/or imperfect perforating methods.

Watermarks

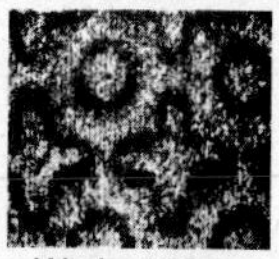

Wmk. 116 — Crosses and Circles

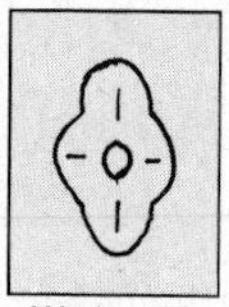

Wmk. 143

For watermarks 373 and 384 see British Watermark page.

"Liberia" — A1

A1a

Thick Paper

1860 Unwmk. Litho. *Perf. 12*

1 A1 6c red 400.00 *300.00*
  a. Imperf, pair 500.00
2 A1 12c deep blue 25.00 *50.00*
  a. Imperf, pair 250.00
3 A1a 24c green 50.00 *50.00*
  a. Imperf, pair 300.00
  Nos. 1-3 (3) 475.00 *400.00*

Stamps set very close together. Examples of the 12c occasionally show traces of a frame line around the design.

Medium to Thin Paper With a single-line frame around each stamp, about 1mm from the border

1864 *Perf. 11, 12*

7 A1 6c red 62.50 *85.00*
  a. Imperf, pair 225.00
8 A1 12c blue 80.00 *95.00*
  a. Imperf, pair 225.00
9 A1a 24c lt green 87.50 *100.00*
  a. Imperf, pair 225.00
  Nos. 7-9 (3) 230.00 *280.00*

Stamps set about 5mm apart. Margins large and perforation usually outside the frame line.

1866-69 Without Frame Line

13 A1 6c lt red 25.00 *40.00*
14 A1 12c lt blue 25.00 *40.00*
15 A1a 24c lt yellow grn 25.00 *40.00*
  Nos. 13-15 (3) 75.00 120.00

Stamps set 2-2½mm apart with small margins. Stamps are usually without frame line but those from one transfer show broken and irregular parts of a frame.

1880 With Frame Line *Perf. 10½*

16 A1 1c ultra 5.00 8.00
17 A1 2c rose 5.00 *5.25*
  a. Imperf, pair 175.00
18 A1 6c violet 5.00 5.25
19 A1 12c yellow 5.00 *5.25*
20 A1a 24c rose red 6.00 5.50
  Nos. 16-20 (5) 26.00 29.25

Unused values for Nos. 16-20 are for stamps without gum.
For surcharges see Nos. 157-159.

Counterfeits

Counterfeits exist of Nos. 1-28, 32 and 64.

From Arms of Liberia — A2

1881

21 A2 3c black 15.00 10.00

Unused value is for a stamp without gum.

A3

A4

Slanting Lines

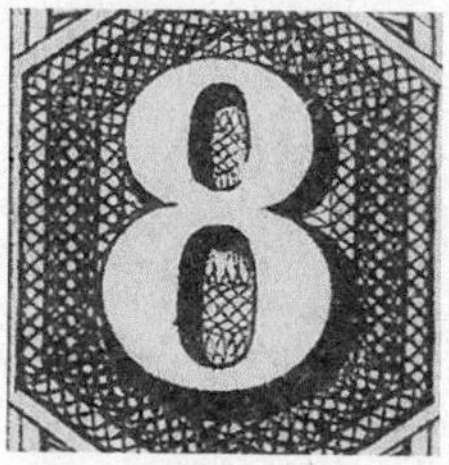

Network Lines

On No. 22 the openings in the figure "8" enclose a pattern of slanting lines. Compare with No. 32.

1882 *Perf. 11½, 12, 14*

22 A3 8c blue 50.00 10.00
23 A4 16c red 8.00 5.00

Canceled to Order

Beginning with the issue of 1885, values in the used column are for "canceled to order" stamps. Postally used examples sell for much more.

A5

A6

From Arms of Liberia — A7

Perf. 10½, 11, 12, 11½x10½, 14, 14½

1885

24 A5 1c carmine 2.00 2.00
  a. 1c rose 2.00 2.00
25 A5 2c green 2.00 2.00
26 A5 3c violet 2.00 2.00
27 A5 4c brown 2.00 2.00
28 A5 6c olive gray 2.00 2.00
29 A6 8c bluish gray 4.00 4.00
  a. 8c lilac 7.00 7.00
30 A6 16c yellow 15.00 12.00
31 A7 32c deep blue 35.00 29.00
  Nos. 24-31 (8) 64.00 55.00

In the 1885 printing, the stamps are spaced 2mm apart and the paper is medium. In the 1892 printing, the stamps are 4½mm apart.
For surcharges see Nos. J1-J2.

Imperf., Pair

24b A5 1c 3.00
25a A5 2c 4.75
26a A5 3c 5.00
27a A5 4c 5.00
28a A5 6c 4.25 4.25
29b A6 8c 12.50
30a A6 16c 30.00
31a A7 32c 50.00

Imperf. pairs with 2mm spacing sell for higher prices.

A8

The openings in the figure "8" are filled with network lines.

1889 *Perf. 12, 14*

32 A8 8c blue 4.25 4.25
  a. Imperf., pair 20.00

See No. 22.

A9

Elephant A10

Oil Palm A11

Pres. Hilary R. W. Johnson A12

Vai Woman in Full Dress A13

Coat of Arms — A14

Liberian Star — A15

Coat of Arms A16

Hippopotamus A17

Liberian Star A18

President Johnson A19

1892-96 Wmk. 143 Engr. *Perf. 15*

33 A9 1c vermilion .50 .40
  a. 1c blue (error) 40.00
34 A9 2c blue .50 .40
  a. 2c vermilion (error) 40.00
35 A10 4c green & blk 2.00 1.25
  a. Center inverted 225.00
36 A11 6c blue green .70 .50
37 A12 8c brown & blk .95 .95
  a. Center inverted 500.00 500.00
  b. Center sideways 750.00
38 A12 10c chrome yel & indigo ('96) .95 .65
39 A13 12c rose red .95 .65
40 A13 15c slate ('96) .95 .65
41 A14 16c lilac 3.50 1.75
  a. 16c deep greenish blue (error) 110.00
42 A14 20c vermilion ('96) 3.50 1.75
43 A15 24c ol grn, *yel* 2.00 1.10
44 A15 25c yel grn ('96) 2.00 1.40
45 A16 30c steel bl ('96) 6.25 4.50
46 A16 32c grnsh blue 3.50 2.75
  a. 32c lilac (error) *110.00*
47 A17 $1 ultra & blk 12.00 9.00
  a. $1 blue & black 13.50 11.00

48	A18	$2 brown, *yel*	9.00	8.00
49	A19	$5 carmine & blk	10.00	10.00
a.		Center inverted	400.00	400.00
		Nos. 33-49 (17)	59.25	45.70

Many imperforates, part-perforated and mis-perforated varieties exist.

The 1c, 2c and 4c were issued in sheets of 60; 6c, sheet of 40; 8c, 10c, sheets of 30; 12c, 15c, 24c, 25c, sheets of 20; 16c, 20c, 30c, sheets of 15; $1, $2, $5, sheets of 10.

For overprints & surcharges see Nos. 50, 64B-64F, 66, 71-77, 79-81, 85-93, 95-100, 160, O1-O13, O15-O25, O37-O41, O44-O45.

No. 36 Surcharged

a

b

1893

50	A11	(a) 5c on 6c blue grn	1.75	1.10
a.		"5" with short flag	6.00	6.00
b.		Both 5's with short flags	5.00	5.00
c.		"i" dot omitted	19.00	19.00
d.		Surcharge "b"	30.00	30.00

"Commerce," Globe and Krumen — A22

1894 Unwmk. Engr. *Imperf.*

52	A22	5c carmine & blk	5.00	5.00
		Rouletted		
53	A22	5c carmine & blk	10.00	7.50

For overprints see Nos. 69, O26-O27.

Oil Palm A23

Hippopotamus A24

Elephant A25

Liberty A26

1897-1905 Wmk. 143 *Perf. 14 to 16*

54	A23	1c lilac rose	1.00	.65
a.		1c violet	1.00	.65
55	A23	1c dp grn ('00)	1.25	.95
56	A23	1c lt green ('05)	3.00	1.60
57	A24	2c bister & blk	3.00	1.60
58	A24	2c org red & blk ('00)	6.00	2.10
59	A24	2c rose & blk ('05)	3.00	1.60
60	A25	5c lake & black	3.00	1.60
a.		5c lilac rose & black	3.00	1.60
61	A25	5c gray bl & blk ('00)	6.00	5.00
62	A25	5c ultra & blk ('05)	4.25	2.75
a.		Center inverted	1,600.	
63	A26	50c red brn & blk	4.00	3.50
		Nos. 54-63 (10)	34.50	21.35

For overprints & surcharges see Nos. 65, 66A-68. 70, 78, 82-84, M1, O28-O36, O42, O92.

A27

Two types:
I — 13 pearls above "Republic Liberia."
II — 10 pearls.

1897 Unwmk. Litho. *Perf. 14*

64	A27	3c red & green (I)	*.25*	*.60*
a.		Type II	*20.00*	*.25*

No. 64a is considered a reprint, unissued. "Used" examples are CTO.

For surcharge see No. 128.

Official Stamps Handstamped in Black

1901-02 Wmk. 143

On Nos. O7-O8, O10-O12

64B	A14	16c lilac	*525.00*	*525.00*
64C	A15	24c ol grn, *yel*	*575.00*	*400.00*
64D	A17	$1 blue & blk	*3,000.*	*2,000.*
64E	A18	$2 brown, *yel*	—	—
64F	A19	$5 car & blk	—	—
		On Stamps with "O S" Printed		
65	A23	1c green	*37.50*	*40.00*
66	A9	2c blue	*100.00*	*100.00*
66A	A24	2c bister & blk	—	*150.00*
67	A24	2c org red & blk	*45.00*	*40.00*
68	A25	5c gray bl & blk	*37.50*	*35.00*
69	A22	5c vio & grn (No. O26)	*300.00*	*300.00*
70	A25	5c lake & blk	*275.00*	*225.00*
71	A12	10c yel & blue blk	*37.50*	*60.00*
a.		"O S" omitted	—	
72	A13	15c slate	*40.00*	*60.00*
73	A14	16c lilac	*550.00*	*350.00*
74	A14	20c vermilion	*42.50*	*50.00*
75	A15	24c ol grn,*yel*	*52.50*	*50.00*
76	A15	25c yellow grn	*42.50*	*50.00*
a.		"O S" omitted	*750.00*	
77	A16	30c steel blue	*42.50*	*40.00*
78	A26	50c red brn & blk	*100.00*	*52.50*
79	A17	$1 ultra & blk	*325.00*	*275.00*
a.		"O S" omitted		
80	A18	$2 brn, *yel*	*2,000.*	*1,800.*
81	A19	$5 car & blk	*2,500.*	*2,000.*
a.		"O S" omitted	*3,000.*	*2,750.*
		On Stamps with "O S" Handstamped		
82	A23	1c deep green	62.50	—
83	A24	2c org red & blk	75.00	—
84	A25	5c lake & blk	200.00	—
85	A12	10c yel & bl blk	125.00	—
86	A14	20c vermilion	140.00	—
87	A15	24c ol grn, *yel*	140.00	—
88	A15	25c yel grn	160.00	—
89	A16	30c steel blue	525.00	—
90	A16	32c grnsh blue	210.00	—

Varieties of Nos. 65-90 include double and inverted overprints.

Nos. 47, O10, O23a Surcharged in Carmine

1902

91	A17	75c on $1 #47	15.00	13.00
a.		Thin "C" and comma	25.00	25.00
b.		Inverted surcharge	62.50	62.50
c.		As "a," inverted		
92	A17	75c on $1 #O10	*2,750.*	
a.		Thin "C" and comma	*4,250.*	
93	A17	75c on $1 #O23a	*4,000.*	
a.		Thin "C" and comma	*5,250.*	

Liberty — A29

1903 Unwmk. Engr. *Perf. 14*

94	A29	3c black	.30	.25
a.		Printed on both sides	50.00	
b.		Perf. 12	20.00	6.00

For overprint see No. O43.

Stamps of 1892 Surcharged in Blue

a

b

1903 Wmk. 143

95	A14	(a) 10c on 16c lilac	3.00	5.00
96	A15	(b) 15c on 24c ol grn, *yel*	4.50	6.00
97	A16	(b) 20c on 32c grnsh bl	6.25	8.50
		Nos. 95-97 (3)	13.75	19.50

Nos. 50, O3 and 45 Surcharged in Black or Red

1904

98	A11	1c on 5c on 6c bl grn	.70	.55
a.		"5" with short flag	4.25	4.25
b.		Both 5's with short flags	8.75	8.75
c.		"i" dot omitted	10.00	10.00
d.		Surcharge on #50d	15.00	15.00
e.		Inverted surcharge	7.50	7.50
99	A10	2c on 4c grn & blk	2.75	4.00
a.		Pair, one without surcharge	35.00	
b.		Double surcharge	*50.00*	
c.		Double surcharge, red and blk	62.50	
d.		Surcharged on back also	25.00	
e.		"Official" overprint missing	35.00	
100	A16	2c on 30c stl bl (R)	9.50	15.00
		Nos. 98-100 (3)	12.95	19.55

African Elephant A33

Mercury A34

Chimpanzee A35

Great Blue Touraco A36

Agama — A37

Egret — A38

Head of Liberty From Coin — A39

A40

Liberian Flag A41

Pygmy Hippopotamus A42

Liberty with Star of Liberia on Cap A43

Mandingos A44

Executive Mansion and Pres. Arthur Barclay — A45

1906 Unwmk. Engr. *Perf. 14*

101	A33	1c green & blk	1.75	.50
102	A34	2c carmine & blk	.35	.25
103	A35	5c ultra & blk	3.00	.85
104	A36	10c red brn & blk	14.00	.85
105	A37	15c pur & dp grn	10.00	3.00
106	A38	20c orange & blk	9.00	2.50
107	A39	25c dull blue & gray	1.00	.25
108	A40	30c deep violet	1.00	.25
109	A41	50c dp grn & blk	1.25	.25
110	A42	75c brown & blk	13.00	2.50
111	A43	$1 rose & gray	3.50	.25
112	A44	$2 dp grn & blk	5.00	.35
113	A45	$5 red brn & blk	10.00	.50
		Nos. 101-113 (13)	72.85	12.30

For surcharges see Nos. 114, 129, 130, 141, 145-149, 161, M2, M5, O72-O73, O82-O85, O96. For overprints see Nos. O46-O58.

Center Inverted

101a	A33	1c	110.00	55.00
102a	A34	2c	120.00	35.00
103a	A35	5c	175.00	175.00
104a	A36	10c	80.00	80.00
105a	A37	15c	175.00	175.00
106b	A38	20c	175.00	175.00
107a	A39	25c	75.00	75.00
109b	A41	50c	75.00	75.00
110b	A42	75c	125.00	125.00
111a	A43	$1	100.00	100.00
112a	A44	$2	95.00	95.00

Imperf., Pairs

101b	A33	1c	13.50	
102b	A34	2c	5.50	
106a	A38	20c	20.00	
107b	A39	25c	55.00	45.00
109a	A41	50c	20.00	
110a	A42	75c	20.00	
113a	A45	$5	27.00	

No. 104 Surcharged in Black

1909

114 A36 3c on 10c red brn & blk 6.00 6.00

Coffee Plantation A46

Pres. Barclay A47

S. S. Pres. Daniel E. Howard, former Gunboat Lark — A48

Commerce with Caduceus — A49

Vai Woman Spinning Cotton A50

Blossom and Fruit of Pepper Plants A51

Circular House A52

President Barclay A53

Men in Canoe — A54

Liberian Village — A55

1909-12 ***Perf. 14***

115 A46 1c yel grn & blk .70 .55
116 A47 2c lake & blk .70 .55
117 A48 5c ultra & blk .70 .55
118 A49 10c plum & blk, perf. 12½ ('12) .70 .55
a. Imperf., pair 19.00
b. Perf 14 ('12) 2.25 2.25
c. As "b," pair, imperf between 27.50
d. Perf 12½x14 2.75 2.25
119 A50 15c indigo & blk 3.50 .60
120 A51 20c rose & grn 4.50 .60
b. Imperf.
121 A52 25c dk brn & blk 1.40 .60
a. Imperf.
122 A53 30c dark brown 4.50 .60
123 A54 50c green & blk 4.50 .60
124 A55 75c red brn & blk 4.50 .60
Nos. 115-124 (10) 25.70 5.80

Roulетted

125 A49 10c plum & blk .75 .45

For surcharges see Nos. 126-127E, 131-133, 136-140, 142-144, 151-156, 162, B1-B2, M3-M4, M6-M7, O70-O71, O74-O81, O86-O91, O97.

For overprints see Nos. O59-O69.

Center Inverted

116a	A47	2c	70.00	60.00
117a	A48	5c	62.50	55.00
119a	A50	15c	100.00	60.00
120a	A51	20c	70.00	55.00
121b	A52	25c	47.50	42.50
123a	A54	50c	95.00	80.00

Stamps and Types of 1909-12 Surcharged in Blue or Red

1910-12 ***Rouletted***

126 A49 3c on 10c plum & blk (Bl) .40 .25
a. "3" inverted
126B A49 3c on 10c blk & ultra (R) 30.00 5.00

No. 126B is roulette 7. It also exists in roulette 13.

Perf. 12½, 14, 12½x14

127 A49 3c on 10c plum & blk (Bl) ('12) .40 .25
a. Imperf., pair 22.50
b. Double surcharge, one invtd. 22.50
c. Double vertical surcharge
127E A49 3c on 10c blk & ultra (R) ('12) 17.00 .55
Nos. 126-127E (4) 47.80 6.05

Nos. 64, 64a Surcharged in Dark Green

1913

128 A27 8c on 3c red & grn (I) .30 .25
a. Surcharge on No. 64a 3.00 .25
b. Double surcharge 6.25
c. Imperf., pair 20.00
d. Inverted surcharge 25.00

Stamps of Preceding Issues Surcharged

a

b

1914 **On Issue of 1906**

129 A39 (a) 2c on 25c dl bl & gray 11.50 3.25
130 A40 (b) 5c on 30c dp vio 11.50 3.25

On Issue of 1909

131 A52 (a) 2c on 25c brn & blk 11.50 3.25
132 A53 (b) 5c on 30c dk brown 11.50 3.25
133 A54 (a) 10c on 50c grn & blk 11.50 3.25
Nos. 129-133 (5) 57.50 16.25

Liberian House — A57

Providence Island, Monrovia Harbor — A58

1915 **Engr.** **Wmk. 116** ***Perf. 14***

134 A57 2c red .25 .25
135 A58 3c dull violet .25 .25

For overprints see Nos. 196-197, O113-O114, O128-O129.

Nos. 109, 111-113, 119-124 Surcharged in Dark Blue, Black or Red

c

d

e

f

g

1915-16 **Unwmk.**

136 A50 (c) 2c on 15c (R) .90 .90
137 A52 (d) 2c on 25c (R) 8.50 8.50
138 A51 (e) 5c on 20c (Bk) 1.10 6.25
139 A53 (f) 5c on 30c (R) 4.50 4.50
a. Double surcharge 15.00 15.00
140 A53 (g) 5c on 30c (R) 40.00 40.00

h

i

141 A41 (h) 10c on 50c (R) 8.00 8.00
a. Double surch., one invtd.
142 A54 (i) 10c on 50c (R) 15.00 15.00
a. Double surcharge red & blk 50.00 35.00
b. Blue surcharge 35.00 35.00
143 A54 (i) 10c on 50c (Bk) 20.00 15.00

j

k

144 A55 (j) 20c on 75c (Bk) 4.00 7.50
145 A43 (k) 25c on $1 (Bk) 42.50 42.50

l

m

146 A44 (l) 50c on $2 (R) 12.00 12.00
a. "Ceuts" 30.00 22.50
147 A44 (m) 50c on $2 (R) 800.00 800.00

n

148 A45 $1 on $5 (Bk) 65.00 65.00
a. Double surcharge 90.00 90.00

o

149 A45 $1 on $5 (R) 52.50 52.50

The color of the red surcharge varies from light dull red to almost brown.

Handstamped Surcharge, Type "i"

150 A54 10c on 50c (Dk Bl) 14.00 14.00

No. 119 Surcharged in Black

151 A50 2c on 15c 650.00 650.00

No. 119 Surcharged in Red

152 A50 2c on 15c 45.00 40.00
a. Double surcharge 92.50

Nos. 116-117 Surcharged in Black or Red

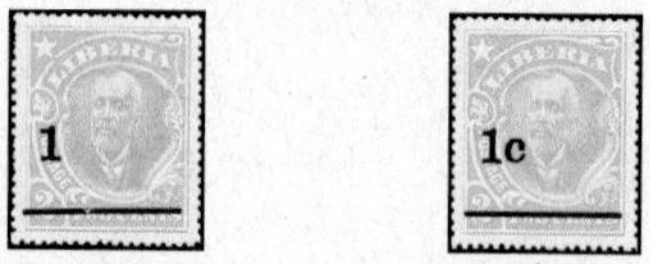

a b

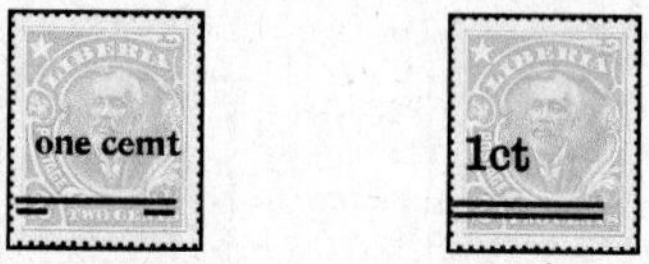

c d

e f

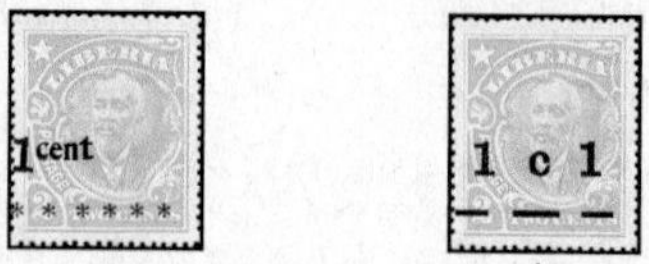

g h

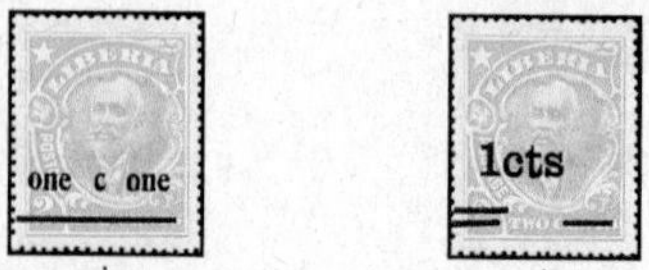

i j

k l

m n

o p

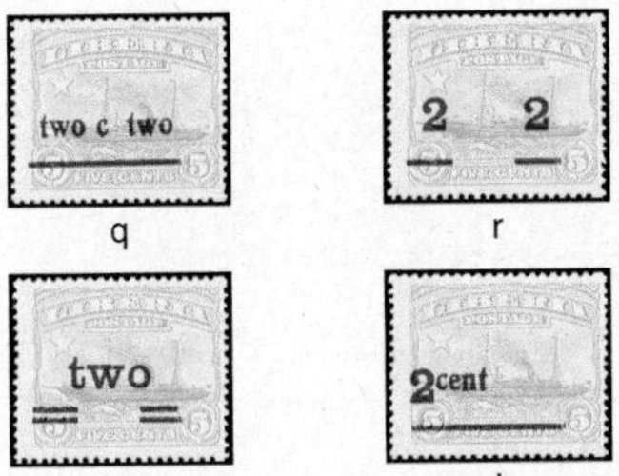

q r s t

Types A-J are for No. 153. Types K-T are for No. 154.

153 A47 1c on 2c lake & blk 2.50 2.50
  a. Strip of 10 types 35.00
154 A48 2c on 5c ultra & blk (R) 3.50 2.50
  a. Black surcharge 14.00 14.00
  b. Strip of 10 types (R) 35.00
  c. Strip of 10 types (Bk) 175.00

The 10 types of surcharge are repeated in illustrated sequence on 1c on 2c in each horiz. row and on 2c on 5c in each vert. row of sheets of 100 (10x10).

No. 116 and Type of 1909 Surcharged

155 A47 1c on 2c lake & blk 190.00 190.00

No. 117 Surcharged

156 A48 2c on 5c turq & blk 140.00 140.00

Nos. 18-20 Surcharged

1916

157 A1 3c on 6c violet 45.00 45.00
  a. Inverted surcharge 100.00 75.00
158 A1 5c on 12c yellow 3.00 3.00
  a. Inverted surcharge 17.50 17.50
  b. Surcharge sideways 17.50
159 A1 10c on 24c rose red 2.75 3.00
  a. Inverted surcharge 15.00 15.00
  b. Surcharge sideways 20.00
  Nos. 157-159 (3) 50.75 51.00

Unused values for Nos. 157-159 are for examples without gum.

Nos. 44 and 108 Surcharged

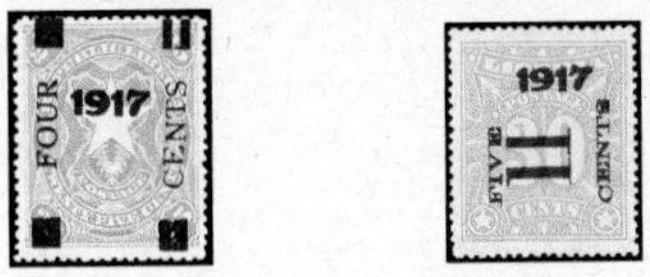

p r

1917 **Wmk. 143**

160 A15 (p) 4c on 25c yel grn 12.00 12.00
  a. "OUR" 27.50 27.50
  b. "FCUR" 27.50 27.50

Unwmk.

161 A40 (r) 5c on 30c dp vio 90.00 90.00

No. 118 Surcharged in Red

1918

162 A49 3c on 10c plum & blk 2.75 4.25
  a. "3" inverted 9.25 9.25

Bongo Antelope A59

Symbols of Liberia A61

Two-spot Palm Civet — A60

A62

Palm-nut Vulture A66

Oil Palm A63

Mercury — A64

Traveler's Tree A65

"Mudskipper" or Bommi Fish — A67

Mandingos A68

"Liberia" A71

Coast Scene — A69

Liberia College — A70

1918 **Engr.** ***Perf. 12½, 14***

163 A59 1c dp grn & blk .75 .25
164 A60 2c rose & blk .90 .25
165 A61 5c gray bl & blk .25 .25
166 A62 10c dark green .30 .25
167 A63 15c blk & dk grn 3.50 .25
168 A64 20c claret & blk .40 .25
169 A65 25c dk grn & grn 3.75 .25
170 A66 30c red vio & blk 17.00 .80
171 A67 50c ultra & blk 30.00 3.50
172 A68 75c ol bis & blk 3.00 .25
173 A69 $1 yel brn & bl 7.50 .25
174 A70 $2 lt vio & blk 8.00 .25
175 A71 $5 dark brown 8.50 .40
  Nos. 163-175 (13) 83.85 7.20

For surcharges see Nos. 176-177, 228-229, 248-270, B3-B15, O111-O112, O155-O157.

For overprints see Nos. O98-O110.

Nos. 163-164, F10-F14 Surcharged

1920

176 A59 3c on 1c grn & blk 1.10 1.10
  a. "CEETS" 17.00 17.00
  b. Double surcharge 10.00 10.00
  c. Triple surcharge 15.00 15.00
177 A60 4c on 2c rose & blk 1.10 1.10
  a. Inverted surcharge 20.00 20.00
  b. Double surcharge 10.00 10.00
  c. Double surcharge, one invtd. 18.00
  d. Triple surcharge, one inverted 25.00 25.00
  e. Quadruple surcharge 30.00 30.00
  f. Typewritten surcharge
  g. Same as "f" but inverted
  h. Printed and typewritten surcharges, both inverted
178 R6 5c on 10c bl & blk 2.50 2.75
  a. Inverted surcharge 10.00 10.00
  b. Double surcharge 10.00 10.00
  c. Double surcharge, one invtd. 15.00 15.00
  d. Typewritten surcharge ("five") 100.00
  e. Printed and typewritten surcharges 100.00
179 R6 5c on 10c org red & blk 2.50 2.75
  a. 5c on 10c orange & black 4.00 2.75
  b. Inverted surcharge 15.00
  c. Double surcharge 15.00
  d. Double surcharge, one invtd. 18.00 15.00
  e. Typewritten surch. in violet 100.00 100.00
  f. Typewritten surch. in black
  g. Printed and typewritten surcharges 100.00
180 R6 5c on 10c grn & blk 2.50 2.75
  a. Double surcharge 10.00 10.00
  b. Double surcharge, one invtd. 18.00 18.00
  c. Inverted surcharge 18.00
  d. Quadruple surcharge 25.00 25.00
  e. Typewritten surcharge 100.00
  f. Printed and typewritten surcharges
181 R6 5c on 10c vio & blk (Monrovia) 4.00 5.00
  a. Double surcharge, one invtd. 25.00 25.00
182 R6 5c on 10c mag & blk (Robertsport) 2.25 2.40
  a. Double surcharge 15.00 15.00
  b. Double surcharge, one invtd. 15.00 15.00
  c. Double surcharge, both invtd. 25.00
  Nos. 176-182 (7) 15.95 17.85

Cape Mesurado A75

Pres. Daniel E. Howard A76

Arms of Liberia A77

Crocodile A78

Pepper Plant — A79

Leopard — A80

Village Scene — A81

Krumen in Dugout — A82

Rapids in St. Paul's River — A83

Bongo Antelope — A84

Hornbill — A85

Elephant — A86

1921 **Wmk. 116** ***Perf. 14***

183 A75 1c green .25 .25
184 A76 5c dp bl & blk .25 .25
185 A77 10c red & dl bl .25 .25
186 A78 15c dl vio & grn 6.50 .55
187 A79 20c rose red & grn 2.75 .25
188 A80 25c org & blk 7.50 .55
189 A81 30c grn & dl vio .40 .25
190 A82 50c org & ultra .45 .25
191 A83 75c red & blk brn .80 .25
  a. Center inverted 70.00
192 A84 $1 red & blk 20.00 1.75
193 A85 $2 yel & blk 16.00 1.25
194 A86 $5 car rose & vio 32.50 1.50
  Nos. 183-194 (12) 87.65 7.35

For overprints see Nos. 195, 198-208, O115-O127, O130-O140.

Nos. 134-135, 183-194 Ovptd.

195 A75 1c green 22.50 .40
196 A57 2c red 22.50 .40
197 A58 3c dull violet 32.50 .40
198 A76 5c dp bl & blk 3.50 .30
199 A77 10c red & dull bl 50.00 .40
200 A78 15c dull vio & grn 22.50 1.40
201 A79 20c rose red & grn, ovpt. invtd. 7.25 .75
202 A80 25c orange & blk 22.50 1.40
203 A81 30c grn & dull vio 2.50 .30
204 A82 50c orange & ultra 3.50 .30
205 A83 75c red & blk brn 4.75 .30
206 A84 $1 red & blk 62.50 2.10
207 A85 $2 yellow & ultra 22.50 2.10
208 A86 $5 car rose & vio 60.00 2.75
  Nos. 195-208 (14) 339.00 13.30

Overprint exists inverted in Nos. 195-208 and normal on No. 201.

First Settlers Landing at Cape Mesurado from U. S. S. Alligator — A87

1923 **Litho.**

209 A87 1c lt blue & blk 18.00 .45
210 A87 2c claret & ol gray 26.00 .45
211 A87 5c ol grn & ind 26.00 .45
212 A87 10c bl grn & vio 1.00 .45
213 A87 $1 rose & brn 3.25 .45
  Nos. 209-213 (5) 74.25 2.25

Centenary of founding of Liberia.

Memorial to J. J. Roberts, 1st Pres. — A88

Hall of Representatives, Monrovia — A89

Liberian Star — A90

A91

Pres. Charles Dunbar Burgess King — A92

Hippopotamus A93

Antelope — A94

West African Buffalo — A95

Grebos Making Dumboy A96

Pineapple A97

Carrying Ivory Tusk — A98

Rubber Planter's House A99

Stockton Lagoon A100

Grebo Houses A101

1923 *Perf. 13½x14½, 14½x13½*

White Paper

214	A88	1c yel grn & dp grn	7.50	1.25
215	A89	2c claret & brn	7.50	.25
216	A90	3c lilac & blk	.35	.25
217	A91	5c bl vio & blk	115.00	.25
218	A92	10c slate & brn	.35	.25
219	A93	15c bister & bl	35.00	.50
220	A94	20c bl grn & vio	2.50	.35
221	A95	25c org red & brn	160.00	.60
222	A96	30c dk brn & vio	.60	.25
223a	A97	50c dull vio & brn, *brnsh*	1.00	.25
224	A98	75c gray & bl	1.90	.40
225a	A99	$1 dp red & dk vio, *brnsh*	4.50	.60
226	A100	$2 orange & blue	7.50	.80
227a	A101	$5 dp grn & brn, *brnsh*	8.00	.90
		Nos. 214-227a (14)	351.70	6.90

No. 163 Surcharged in Black

1926 **Unwmk.** *Perf. 14*

228	A59	2c on 1c dp grn & blk	3.50	3.50
a.		Surcharge with ornamental design as on #O155	17.00	

No. 163 Surcharged in Red

1927

229	A59	2c on 1c dp grn & blk	9.50	9.50
a.		"Ceuts"	14.00	
b.		"Vwo"	14.00	
c.		"Twc"	14.00	
d.		Double surcharge	27.50	
e.		Wavy lines omitted	17.50	

Palms A102

Map of Africa A103

President Burgess King — A104

1928 **Engr.** *Perf. 12*

230	A102	1c green	.75	.50
231	A102	2c violet	.50	.35
232	A102	3c bister brn	.50	.35
a.		Horiz. pair, imperf vert.		—
233	A103	5c ultra	1.00	.55
234	A104	10c olive gray	1.40	.55
235	A103	15c dull violet	6.25	2.25
236	A103	$1 red brown	77.50	26.50
		Nos. 230-236 (7)	87.90	31.05

For surcharges & overprints see Nos. 288A, 289A, 290A-291, 292A, C1-C3, O158-O165.

Nos. 164-168, 170-175 Surcharged in Various Colors and Styles

No. 248

No. 250

1936 *Perf. 12½, 14*

248	A60	1c on 2c (Bl)	.50	*3.50*
249	A61	3c on 5c (Bl)	.45	*2.00*
250	A62	4c on 10c (Br)	.45	*2.00*
251	A63	6c on 15c (Bl)	.50	*3.50*
252	A64	8c on 20c (V)	.45	*2.00*
253	A66	12c on 30c (V)	1.25	*9.75*
254	A67	14c on 50c (Bl)	1.40	*11.00*
255	A68	16c on 75c (Br)	.70	*5.50*
256	A69	18c on $1 (Bk)	.70	*5.50*
a.		22c on $1 yellow brown & blue	*8.00*	
257	A70	22c on $2 (V)	.85	*7.75*
258	A71	24c on $5 (Bk)	1.50	*9.75*
		Nos. 248-258 (11)	8.75	62.25

Official Stamps, Nos. O99-O110, Srchd. or Ovptd. in Various Colors & Styles

1936

259	A60	1c on 2c (Bl)	.45	*4.00*
260	A61	3c on 5c (Bl)	.45	*4.00*
261	A62	4c on 10c (Bl)	.45	*4.00*
262	A63	6c on 15c (Bl)	.45	*4.00*
263	A64	8c on 20c (V)	.45	*4.00*
264	A66	12c on 30c (V)	1.65	*20.00*
a.		"193" instead of "1936"	20.00	
265	A67	14c on 50c (Bl)	2.25	*21.00*
266	A68	16c on 75c (Bk)	1.10	*12.00*
267	A69	18c on $1 (Bk)	1.10	*12.00*
268	A70	22c on $2 (Bl)	1.40	*15.00*
269	A71	24c on $5 (Bk)	1.75	*17.00*
270	A65	25c (Bk)	2.25	*21.00*
		Nos. 259-270 (12)	13.75	138.00

Hornbill A106

Designs: 2c, Bushbuck. 3c, West African dwarf buffalo. 4c, Pygmy hippopotamus. 5c, Lesser egret. 6c, Pres. E. J. Barclay.

Perf. Compound of 11½, 12, 12½, 14

1937, Apr. 10 **Engr.** **Unwmk.**

271	A106	1c yel grn & blk	1.50	.45
272	A106	2c carmine & blk	1.50	.45
273	A106	3c violet & blk	1.50	.45
274	A106	4c orange & blk	2.25	.70
275	A106	5c blue & blk	2.25	.65
276	A106	6c green & blk	.80	.25
		Nos. 271-276 (6)	9.80	2.95

Coast Line of Liberia, 1839 — A107

Seal of Liberia, Map and Farming Scenes A108

Thomas Buchanan and Residence at Bassa Cove — A109

1940, July 29 **Engr.** *Perf. 12*

277	A107	3c dark blue	.35	.35
278	A108	5c dull red brn	.35	.35
279	A109	10c dark green	.35	.35
		Nos. 277-279 (3)	1.05	1.05

100th anniv. of the founding of the Commonwealth of Liberia.

For overprints & surcharges see Nos. 280-282, B16-B18, C14-C16, CB1-CB3, CE1, CF1, E1, F35.

Imperforates

Many stamps of Liberia exist imperforate or with various perforation errors, in issued and trial colors, and also in small presentation sheets in issued colors.

Nos. 277-279 Overprinted in Red or Blue

1941, Feb. 21

280	A107	3c dk blue (R)	2.50	2.50
281	A108	5c dull red brn (Bl)	2.50	2.50
282	A109	10c dark green (R)	2.50	2.50
		Nos. 280-282,C14-C16 (6)	15.75	15.75

Royal Antelope A110

Bay-thighed Diana Monkey A115

2c, Water chevrotain. 3c, White-shouldered duiker. 4c, Bushbuck. 5c, Zebra antelope.

1942 **Engr.**

283	A110	1c violet & fawn	1.10	.25
284	A110	2c brt ultra & yel brn	1.40	.25
285	A110	3c brt grn & yel brn	1.90	.90
286	A110	4c blk & red org	2.40	1.90
287	A110	5c olive & fawn	3.00	1.90
288	A115	10c red & black	5.25	2.40
		Nos. 283-288 (6)	15.05	7.60

Nos. 231, 233-234, 271-276 Srchd. with New Values and Bars or X's in Violet, Black, Red Brown or Blue

No. 288A

No. 289A

No. 292A

No. 295

Perf. 12, 12x12½, 14

1944-46 **Unwmk.**

288A	A102	1c on 2c (Bk)	9.25	6.50
289	A106	1c on 4c (Bk)	60.00	47.50
289A	A104	1c on 10c (R Br)	12.50	9.50
b.		Double surcharge, one red brown, one violet	25.00	19.00
290	A106	2c on 3c	70.00	50.00
290A	A103	2c on 5c (Bk)	2.75	2.75
290B	A103	2c on 5c (Bl)	21.00	9.25
291	A102	3c on 2c	30.00	35.00
292	A106	4c on 5c	11.00	7.25
292A	A104	4c on 10c (Bk)	3.25	3.25
b.		Double surch., one inverted		
293	A106	5c on 1c (Bk)	100.00	50.00
294	A106	6c on 2c (Bk)	11.00	9.50
295	A106	10c on 6c	11.00	9.50
		Nos. 288A-295 (12)	341.75	240.00

Surcharges on Nos. 289, 290, 293, 294 are found double or inverted. Such varieties command a small premium.

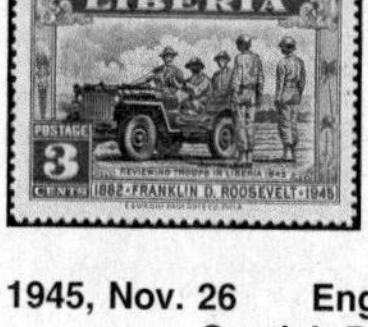

Pres. Franklin D. Roosevelt Reviewing Troops — A116

1945, Nov. 26 **Engr.** *Perf. 12½*

Grayish Paper

296	A116	3c brt violet & blk	.25	.25
297	A116	5c dk blue & blk	.45	.45
		Nos. 296-297,C51 (3)	2.95	2.10

In memory of Pres. Franklin D. Roosevelt (1882-1945).

Monrovia Harbor — A117

1947, Jan. 2

298 A117 5c deep blue		.25	.25

Opening of the Monrovia Harbor Project, Feb. 16, 1946. See No. C52.

Without Inscription at Top

1947, May 16

299 A117 5c violet		.25	.25

See No. C53.

1st US Postage Stamps and Arms of Liberia A118

1947, June 6

300 A118 5c carmine rose	.25	.25
Nos. 300,C54-C56 (4)	1.20	1.00

Cent. of US postage stamps and the 87th anniv. of Liberian postal issues.

Matilda Newport Firing Cannon — A119

1947, Dec. 1 Engr. & Photo.

Center in Gray Black

301 A119 1c brt blue green	.25	.25
302 A119 3c brt red violet	.25	.25
303 A119 5c brt ultra	.60	.25
304 A119 10c yellow	3.25	.80
Nos. 301-304,C57 (5)	5.60	1.85

125th anniv. of Matilda Newport's defense of Monrovia, Dec. 1, 1822.

Liberian Star — A120

Cent. of Independence: 2c, Liberty. 3c, Liberian Arms. 5c, Map of Liberia.

1947, Dec. 22 Engr.

305 A120 1c dark green	.55	.25
306 A120 2c brt red vio	.55	.25
307 A120 3c brt purple	.55	.25
308 A120 5c dark blue	.55	.25
Nos. 305-308,C58-C60 (7)	3.80	1.95

Centenary of independence.

Natives Approaching Village — A124

Rubber Tapping and Planting — A125

Landing of First Colonists A126

Jehudi Ashmun and Defenders A127

1949, Apr. 4 Litho. *Perf. 11½*

309 A124 1c multicolored	.45	.75
310 A125 2c multicolored	.45	.75
311 A126 3c multicolored	.45	.75
312 A127 5c multicolored	.45	.75
Nos. 309-312,C63-C64 (6)	2.50	4.30

Nos. 309-312 exist perf. 12½ and sell at a much lower price. The status of the perf. 12½ set is indefinite.

Stephen Benson — A128

Liberian Presidents: 1c, Pres. Joseph J. Roberts. 3c, Daniel B. Warner. 4c, James S. Payne. 5c, Executive mansion. 6c, Edward J. Roye. 7c, A. W. Gardner and A. F. Russell. 8c, Hilary R. W. Johnson. 9c, Joseph J. Cheeseman. 10c, William D. Coleman. 15c, Garretson W. Gibson. 20c, Arthur Barclay. 25c, Daniel E. Howard. 50c, Charles D. B. King. $1, Edwin J. Barclay.

1948-50 Unwmk. Engr. *Perf. 12½*

Caption and Portrait in Black

313 A128 1c green ('48)	2.75	*7.00*
314 A128 2c salmon pink	.40	*.65*
315 A128 3c rose violet	.40	*.65*
a. "1876-1878" added	16.00	*40.00*
316 A128 4c lt olive grn	.90	.90
317 A128 5c ultra	.50	*.90*
318 A128 6c red orange	.90	*1.75*
319 A128 7c lt blue ('50)	1.10	*2.10*
320 A128 8c carmine	1.10	*2.40*
321 A128 9c red violet	1.25	*2.10*
322 A128 10c yellow ('50)	.85	.55
323 A128 15c yellow orange	1.00	.70
324 A128 20c blue gray	1.40	1.40
325 A128 25c cerise	2.00	2.10
326 A128 50c aqua	3.75	1.40
327 A128 $1 rose lilac	6.25	1.40
Nos. 313-327,C65 (16)	25.15	*26.65*

Issued: 1c, 11/18; 7c, 10c, 1950; others, 7/21/49.

See Nos. 328, 371-378, C65, C118.

Pres. Joseph J. Roberts A129

1950

328 A129 1c green & blk	.25	.25

Hand Holding Book — A130

1950, Feb. 14

329 A130 5c deep blue	.45	.25

National Literacy Campaign. See No. C66.

Catalogue values for unused stamps in this section, from this point to the end of the section, are for Never Hinged items.

UPU Monument A131

First UPU Building, Bern — A132

1950, Apr. 21 Engr. Unwmk.

330 A131 5c green & blk	.25	.25
331 A132 10c red vio & blk	.25	.25
Nos. 330-331,C67 (3)	3.25	3.25

UPU, 75th anniv. (in 1949).

Exist imperf. Value, $6.50.

Jehudi Ashmun and Seal of Liberia A133

John Marshall, Ashmun and Map of Town of Marshall A134

Designs (Map or View and Two Portraits): 2c, Careysburg, Gov. Lott Carey (1780-1828), freed American slave, and Jehudi Ashmun (1794-1828), American missionary credited as founder of Liberia. 3c, Town of Harper, Robert Goodloe Harper (1765-1825), American statesman, and Ashmun. 5c, Upper Buchanan, Gov. Thomas Buchanan and Ashmun. 10c, Robertsport, Pres. Joseph J. Roberts and Ashmun.

1952, Apr. 10 *Perf. 10½*

332 A133 1c deep green	.25	.25
333 A133 2c scarlet & ind	.30	.25
334 A133 3c purple & grn	.30	.25
335 A134 4c brown & grn	.30	.25
336 A133 5c ultra & org red	.30	.25
337 A134 10c org red & dk bl	.30	.25
Nos. 332-337,C68-C69 (8)	2.70	2.45

Nos. 332-337 exist imperf. Value about two and one-half times that of the perf. set.

No. 334 exists with center inverted. Value $50.

See No. C69a.

UN Headquarters Building A135

Scroll and Flags A136

10c, Liberia arms, letters "UN" and emblem.

1952, Dec. 20 Unwmk. *Perf. 12½*

338 A135 1c ultra	.30	.30
339 A136 4c car & ultra	.30	.30
340 A136 10c red brn & yel	.30	.30
a. Souvenir sheet of 3, #338-340	2.00	2.00
Nos. 338-340,C70 (4)	1.80	1.55

Nos. 338-340 and 340a exist imperforate. Values: set $5; souvenir sheet $3.50.

Pepper Bird A137

Roller — A138

Hornbill — A138a

Kingfisher — A138b

Jacana — A138c

Weaver — A138d

1953, Nov. 18 *Perf. 10½*

341 A137 1c shown	1.00	.25
342 A138 3c shown	1.00	.25
343 A138a 4c yellow & brown	1.60	.25
344 A138b 5c mauve & bl grn	1.75	.25
345 A138c 10c grn & dp mag	1.90	.25
346 A138d 12c brn & org	2.50	.25
Nos. 341-346 (6)	9.75	1.50

Exist imperf. Value, set unused $12.

Tennis — A139

1955, Jan. 26 Litho. *Perf. 12½*

347 A139 3c shown	.25	.25
348 A139 5c Soccer	.25	.25
349 A139 25c Boxing	.40	.25
Nos. 347-349,C88-C90 (6)	1.80	1.65

Callichilia Stenosepala — A140

Various Native Flowers: 7c, Gomphia subcordata. 8c, Listrostachys caudata. 9c, Musaenda isertiana.

1955, Sept. 28 Unwmk.

350 A140 6c yel grn, org & yel	.30	.25
351 A140 7c emer, yel & car	.30	.25
352 A140 8c yel grn, buff & bl	.30	.25
353 A140 9c orange & green	.40	.25
Nos. 350-353,C91-C92 (6)	2.10	1.50

Rubber Tapping — A141

1955, Dec. 5 *Perf. 12½*

354 A141 5c emerald & yellow	.25	.25
Nos. 354,C97-C98 (3)	1.20	.75

50th anniv. of Rotary Intl. No. 354 exists printed entirely in emerald.

Statue of Liberty — A142

Coliseum, New York City — A143

Design: 6c, Globe inscribed FIPEX.

1956, Apr. 28 *Perf. 12*

355	A142	3c brt grn & dk red brn	.25	.25
356	A143	4c Prus grn & bis brn	.25	.25
357	A143	6c gray & red lilac	.25	.25
		Nos. 355-357,C100-C102 (6)	2.15	1.50

Fifth International Philatelic Exhibition (FIPEX), NYC, Apr. 28-May 6, 1956.

Kangaroo and Emu — A144

Discus Thrower — A145

Designs: 8c, Goddess of Victory and Olympic symbols. 10c, Classic chariot race.

1956, Nov. 15 **Litho.** **Unwmk.**

358	A144	4c lt ol grn & gldn brn	.25	.25
359	A145	6c emerald & gray	.25	.25
360	A144	8c lt ultra & redsh brn	.25	.25
361	A144	10c rose red & blk	.40	.25
		Nos. 358-361,C104-C105 (6)	2.15	2.00

16th Olympic Games at Melbourne, Nov. 22-Dec. 8, 1956.
Nos. 358-361 exist imperf.

Idlewild Airport, New York — A146

Roberts Field, Liberia, plane & Pres. Tubman — A146a

Lithographed and Engraved

1957, May 4 *Perf. 12*

362	A146	3c orange & dk blue	.25	.25
363	A146a	5c red lilac & blk	.25	.25
		Nos. 362-363,C107-C110 (6)	3.15	1.50

1st anniv. of direct air service between Roberts Field, Liberia, and Idlewild (Kennedy), NY.
See Nos. C107-C110.

Orphanage Playground A147

Orphanage and: 5c, Teacher and pupil. 6c, Singing boys and natl. anthem. 10c, Children and flag.

1957, Nov. 25 **Litho.** *Perf. 12*

364	A147	4c green & red	.25	.25
365	A147	5c bl grn & red brn	.25	.25
366	A147	6c brt vio & bis	.25	.25
367	A147	10c ultra & rose car	.25	.25
		Nos. 364-367,C111-C112 (6)	2.25	1.50

Founding of the Antoinette Tubman Child Welfare Foundation.

Windmill and Dutch Flag — A148

Designs: No. 369, German flag and Brandenburg Gate. No. 370, Swedish flag, palace and crowns.

Engraved and Lithographed

1958, Jan. 10 **Unwmk.** *Perf. 10½*

Flags in Original Colors

368	A148	5c reddish brn	.25	.25
369	A148	5c blue	.25	.25
370	A148	5c lilac rose	.25	.25
		Nos. 368-370,C114-C117 (7)	2.55	2.55

European tour of Pres. Tubman in 1956. Exist imperf.

Presidential Types of 1948-50

Designs as before.

1958-60 **Engr.** *Perf. 12*

Caption and Portrait in Black

371	A129	1c salmon pink	.45	.25
372	A128	2c brt yellow	.45	.25
373	A128	10c blue gray	.55	.55
374	A128	15c brt bl & blk ('59)	.25	.25
375	A128	20c dark red	.65	.65
376	A128	25c blue	.65	.65
377	A128	50c red lil & blk ('59)	.75	.65
378	A128	$1 bister brn ('60)	5.75	.75
		Nos. 371-378,C118 (9)	10.75	4.90

Many shades of 1c.

Open Globe Projection A149

Designs: 5c, UN Emblem and building. 10c, UN Emblem. 12c, UN Emblem and initials of agencies.

1958, Dec. 10 **Litho.** *Perf. 12*

379	A149	3c gray, bl & blk	.30	.25
380	A149	5c blue & choc	.25	.25
381	A149	10c black & org	.40	.25
382	A149	12c black & car	1.10	1.10
		Nos. 379-382 (4)	2.05	1.85

10th anniv. of the Universal Declaration of Human Rights. See No. C119.

People of Africa on the March — A150

1959, Apr. 15

383	A150	20c orange & brown	.45	.45

African Freedom Day, Apr. 15. Exists imperf.
See No. C120.

Symbols of UNESCO — A151

1959, May 11 **Unwmk.**

384	A151	25c dp plum & emer	.55	.55

Opening of UNESCO Headquarters in Paris, Nov. 3, 1958. Exists imperf.
See Nos. C121, C121a.

Abraham Lincoln — A152

1959, Nov. 20 **Engr.** *Perf. 12*

385	A152	10c ultra & blk	.40	.40
386	A152	15c orange & blk	.40	.40
a.		Souv. sheet of 3, Nos. 385-386, C122, imperf.	2.50	4.00
		Nos. 385-386,C122 (3)	1.70	1.70

150th anniv. of the birth of Abraham Lincoln.

Touré, Tubman and Nkrumah — A153

1960, Jan. 27 **Litho.** **Unwmk.**

387	A153	25c crimson & blk	.55	.55

1959 "Big Three" conference of Pres. Sékou Touré of Guinea, Pres. William V. S. Tubman of Liberia and Prime Minister Kwame Nkrumah of Ghana at Saniquellie, Liberia. See No. C123.

World Refugee Year Emblem — A154

1960, Apr. 7 *Perf. 11½*

388	A154	25c emerald & blk	.70	1.00

World Refuge Year, July 1, 1959-June 30, 1960. See No. C124, C124a. Exist imperf.

Map of Africa — A155

1960, May 11 **Litho.** *Perf. 11½*

389	A155	25c green & black	.60	.60

10th anniv. of the Commission for Technical Cooperation in Africa South of the Sahara (C.C.T.A.). See No. C125.

Weight Lifter and Porter — A156

Designs: 10c, Rower and canoeists, horiz. 15c, Walker and porter.

1960, Sept. 6 **Unwmk.**

390	A156	5c dk brn & emer	.25	.25
391	A156	10c brown & red lil	.25	.25
392	A156	15c brown & org	.70	.75
		Nos. 390-392,C126 (4)	2.10	1.95

17th Olympic Games, Rome, 8/25-9/11. Exist imperf.

Liberian Stamps of 1860 — A157

1960, Dec. 1 **Litho.** *Perf. 11½*

393	A157	5c multicolored	.25	.25
394	A157	20c multicolored	.70	.70
		Nos. 393-394,C128 (3)	1.95	1.95

Liberian postage stamps, cent.

Laurel Wreath — A158

1961, May 19 **Unwmk.** *Perf. 11½*

395	A158	25c red & dk blue	.60	.60

Liberia's membership in the UN Security Council. Exists imperf. Value, Nos. 395, C130 $6.
See Nos. C130-C131 and note after No. C131.

Anatomy Class — A159

1961, Sept. 8 *Perf. 11½*

396	A159	25c green & brown	.60	.60

15th anniv. of UNESCO. Nos. 396 and C132 exist imperf. Value, $3.
See Nos. C132-C133.

Joseph J. Roberts Monument, Monrovia — A160

Design: 10c, Pres. Roberts and old and new presidential mansions, horiz.

1961, Oct. 25 **Litho.**

397	A160	5c orange & sepia	.25	.25
398	A160	10c ultra & sepia	.45	.25
		Nos. 397-398,C134 (3)	1.40	1.20

150th anniv. of the birth of Joseph J. Roberts, 1st pres. of Liberia. Exist imperf.

Boy Scout — A161

Design: Insignia and Scouts camping.

1961, Dec. 4 **Unwmk.** *Perf. 11½*

399	A161	5c lilac & sepia	.25	.25
400	A161	10c ultra & bister	.50	.50
		Nos. 399-400,C135 (3)	2.15	2.15

Boy Scouts of Liberia. Exist imperf. Value, $5.50.

Dag Hammarskjold and UN Emblem — A162

1962, Feb. 1 *Perf. 12*

401	A162	20c black & ultra	.45	.45

Dag Hammarskjold, Secretary General of the UN, 1953-61. See Nos. C137-C138.

Malaria Eradication Emblem — A163

1962, Apr. 7 **Litho.** *Perf. 12½*

402	A163	25c dk green & red	.55	.45

WHO drive to eradicate malaria. Nos. 402, C137 exist imperf. Value, $5.
See Nos. C139-C140.

United Nations Emblem — A164

1962, Oct. 22 *Perf. 12x12½*
403 A164 20c green & yel bister .35 .35

Issued to mark the observance of United Nations Day, Oct. 24, as a national holiday.
See Nos. C144-C145.

Executive Mansion, Monrovia — A165

1c, 80c, Executive Mansion, Monrovia. 5c, Treasury Department Building, Monrovia. 10c, Information Service. 15c, Capitol.

1962-64
403A A165 1c vio bl & dp org ('64) .25 .25
404 A165 5c lt blue & pur .25 .25
405 A165 10c bister & brn .25 .25
406 A165 15c salmon & dk bl .40 .30
406A A165 80c brn & yel ('64) 1.75 1.20
Nos. 403A-406A,C146-C148 (9) 8.35 6.30

See Nos. C146-C148.

"FAO" Emblem and Food Bowl — A166

1963, Mar. 21 *Perf. 12½*
407 A166 5c aqua & dk car .40 .25

FAO "Freedom from Hunger" campaign. See Nos. C149-C150.

Rocket in Space — A167

Design: 15c, Space capsule and globe.

1963, May 27 **Litho.** *Perf. 12½*
408 A167 10c dp vio bl & yel .25 .25
409 A167 15c blue & red brn .60 .60
Nos. 408-409,C151 (3) 1.40 1.25

Achievements in space exploration for peaceful purposes. Exist imperf. Value, $8.

Red Cross — A168

10c, Centenary emblem and torch, vert.

1963, Aug. 26 **Unwmk.** *Perf. 11½*
410 A168 5c blue grn & red .25 .25
411 A168 10c gray & red .25 .25
Nos. 410-411,C153-C154 (4) 1.60 1.60

Intl. Red Cross, cent. See Nos. C153-C154.

Palm Tree and Scroll — A169

1963, Oct. 28 *Perf. 12½*
412 A169 20c brown & green .40 .40

Conference of African heads of state for African Unity, Addis Ababa, May, 1963. See No. C156.

Ski Jump — A170

1963, Dec. 11 **Unwmk.** *Perf. 12½*
413 A170 5c rose red & dk vio bl .25 .25
Nos. 413,C157-C158 (3) 1.30 1.30

9th Winter Olympic Games, Innsbruck, Austria, Jan. 29-Feb. 9, 1964. Exist imperf. Value, $6.

John F. Kennedy — A171

1964, Apr. 6 **Litho.**
414 A171 20c blk & brt blue .35 .35

John F. Kennedy (1917-63). Nos. 414, C160 exist imperf. Value, set $5.
See Nos. C160-C161.

Syncom Satellite — A172

Satellites: 15c, Relay I, vert. 25c, Mariner II.

1964, June 22 **Unwmk.** *Perf. 12½*
415 A172 10c orange & emer .30 .25
416 A172 15c brt car rose & vio .40 .25
417 A172 25c blue, org & blk .40 .70
Nos. 415-417 (3) 1.10 1.20

Progress in space communications and the peaceful uses of outer space. See No. C162. Exist imperf. Value, set $9.

Mt. Fuji — A173

Designs: 15c, Torii and Olympic flame. 25c, Cherry blossoms and stadium.

1964, Sept. 15 **Litho.**
418 A173 10c orange yel & emer .25 .25
419 A173 15c lt red & purple .25 .25
420 A173 25c ocher & red .95 .95
Nos. 418-420 (3) 1.45 1.45

Issued for the 18th Olympic Games, Tokyo, Oct. 10-25, 1964. See No. C163. Exist imperf. Value, set $9.

Boy Scout Emblem and Scout Sign — A174

10c, Bugle and Liberian Scout emblem, horiz.

1965, Mar. 8 **Litho.** *Perf. 12½*
421 A174 5c lt blue & brown .30 .25
422 A174 10c dk green & ocher .40 .25
Nos. 421-422,C164 (3) 1.50 1.30

Liberian Boy Scouts. Exist imperf. Value, set $8.

"Emancipation" by Thomas Ball — A175

Designs: 20c, Abraham Lincoln and John F. Kennedy, horiz. 25c, Lincoln by Augustus St. Gaudens, Lincoln Park, Chicago.

1965, May 3 **Unwmk.** *Perf. 12½*
423 A175 5c dk gray & brn org .25 .25
424 A175 20c emer & lt gray .50 .50
425 A175 25c maroon & blue .65 .65
Nos. 423-425 (3) 1.40 1.40

Centenary of the death of Abraham Lincoln. Exist imperf. Value, set $9.
See No. C166.

ICY Emblem — A176

1965, June 21 **Litho.** *Perf. 12½*
426 A176 12c orange & brn .40 .25
427 A176 25c vio blue & brn .75 .40
428 A176 50c emerald & brn 1.50 .85
Nos. 426-428 (3) 2.65 1.50

Intl. Cooperation Year. See No. C167.

ITU Emblem, Old and New Communication Equipment — A177

1965, Sept. 21 **Unwmk.** *Perf. 12½*
429 A177 25c brt grn & red brn .40 .40
430 A177 35c black & car rose .50 .50
Nos. 429-430,C168 (3) 1.70 1.60

Cent. of the ITU.

Pres. Tubman and Liberian Flag — A178

1965, Nov. 29 **Litho.**
431 A178 25c red, ultra & brn .60 .60

Pres. William V. S. Tubman's 70th birthday. See No. C169, C169a.

Churchill in Admiral's Uniform — A179

Designs: 15c, Churchill giving "V" sign, vert.

1966, Jan. 18 **Litho.** *Perf. 12½*
432 A179 15c orange & blk .40 .25
433 A179 20c black & brt grn .90 .90
Nos. 432-433,C170 (3) 2.00 1.70

Issued in memory of Sir Winston Spencer Churchill (1874-1965), statesman and World War II leader. Exist imperf. Value, set $6.

Pres. Joseph J. Roberts — A180

Presidents: 2c, Stephen Benson. 3c, Daniel Bashiel Warner. 4c, James S. Payne. 5c, Edward James Roye. 10c, William D. Coleman. 25c, Daniel Edward Howard. 50c, Charles Dunbar Burgess King. 80c, Hilary R. W. Johnson. $1, Edwin J. Barclay. $2, Joseph James Cheeseman ("Cheesman" on stamp).

1966-69 **Litho.** *Perf. 12½*
434 A180 1c black & brick red .25 .25
435 A180 2c black & yellow .25 .25
436 A180 3c black & lilac .25 .25
437 A180 4c ap grn & blk ('67) .25 .25
438 A180 5c black & dull org .25 .25
439 A180 10c pale grn & blk ('67) .25 .25
440 A180 25c black & lt blue .60 .25
441 A180 50c blk & brt lil rose 1.25 .90
442 A180 80c dp rose & blk ('67) 1.90 1.10
443 A180 $1 black & ocher 2.25 .25

Perf. 11½x11
443A A180 $2 blk & dp red lil ('69) 4.50 3.00
Nos. 434-443A,C182 (12) 12.60 7.30

Soccer Players and Globe — A181

Designs: 25c, World Championships Cup, ball and shoes, vert. 35c, Soccer player dribbling, vert.

1966, May 3 **Litho.** *Perf. 12½*
444 A181 10c brt green & dk brn .40 .25
445 A181 25c brt pink & brn .60 .30
446 A181 35c brown & orange .80 .45
Nos. 444-446 (3) 1.80 1.00

World Cup Soccer Championships, Wembley, England, July 11-30. Exist imperf. Value, $14.
See No. C172.

Pres. Kennedy Taking Oath of Office — A182

20c, 1964 Kennedy stamps, #414, C160.

1966, Aug. 16 **Litho.** *Perf. 12½*
447 A182 15c red & blk .25 .25
448 A182 20c brt bl & red lil .30 .30
Nos. 447-448,C173-C174 (4) 1.45 1.05

3rd anniv. of Pres. Kennedy's death (Nov. 22). Exist imperf. Value, set $12.

Children on Seesaw and UNICEF Emblem — A183

Design: 80c, Boy playing doctor.

1966, Oct. 25 **Unwmk.** *Perf. 12½*
449 A183 5c brt blue & red .35 .25
450 A183 80c org brn & yel grn .90 .90

20th anniv. of UNICEF.

Giraffe — A184

Designs: 3c, Lion. 5c, Slender-nosed crocodile, horiz. 10c, Baby chimpanzees. 15c, Leopard, horiz. 20c, Black rhinoceros, horiz. 25c, Elephant.

1966, Dec. 20
451 A184 2c multicolored 1.00 .25
452 A184 3c multicolored 1.00 .25
453 A184 5c multicolored 1.00 .25
a. Black omitted ("5¢ LIBERIA" and imprint) 50.00
454 A184 10c multicolored 1.00 .25
455 A184 15c multicolored 1.10 .30
456 A184 20c multicolored 1.75 .55
457 A184 25c multicolored 2.40 .65
Nos. 451-457 (7) 9.25 2.50

Jamboree Badge — A185

Designs: 25c, Boy Scout emblem and various sports, horiz. 40c, Scout at campfire and vision of moon landing, horiz.

1967, Mar. 23 **Litho.** *Perf. 12½*
458 A185 10c brt lil rose & grn .25 .25
459 A185 25c brt red & blue .55 .55
460 A185 40c brt grn & brn org 1.00 .85
Nos. 458-460 (3) 1.80 1.65

12th Boy Scout World Jamboree, Farragut State Park, Idaho, Aug. 1-9. Exist imperf. Value, set $9.
See No. C176.

A186

Pre-Hispanic Sculpture of Mexico: 25c, Aztec Calendar and Olympic rings. 40c, Mexican pottery, sombrero and guitar, horiz.

1967, June 20 Litho. *Perf. 12½*

461	A186	10c ocher & violet	.25	.25
462	A186	25c lt bl, org & blk	.50	.25
463	A186	40c yel grn & car	.75	.50
		Nos. 461-463 (3)	1.50	1.00

Issued to publicize the 19th Olympic Games, Mexico City. Exist imperf. Value, set $8.

See No. C177.

A187

Designs: 5c, WHO Office for Africa, horiz. 80c, WHO Office for Africa.

1967, Aug. 28 Litho. *Perf. 12½*

464	A187	5c blue & ol bister	.25	.25
465	A187	80c emer & ol bister	1.50	1.50

Inauguration of the WHO Regional Office for Africa in Brazzaville, Congo.

Boy Playing African Rattle — A188

Africans Playing Native Instruments: 3c, Tom-tom and soko violin, horiz. 5c, Mang harp, horiz. 10c, Alimilim. 15c, Xylophone drums. 25c, Large tom-toms. 35c, Large harp.

1967, Oct. 16 Litho. *Perf. 14*

466	A188	2c violet & multi	.25	.25
467	A188	3c blue & multi	.25	.25
468	A188	5c lilac rose & multi	.25	.25
469	A188	10c yel grn & multi	.25	.25
470	A188	15c violet & multi	.40	.25
471	A188	25c ocher & multi	.80	.40
472	A188	35c dp rose & multi	1.25	.65
		Nos. 466-472 (7)	3.45	2.30

Ice Hockey — A189

Designs: 25c, Ski jump. 40c, Bobsledding.

1967, Nov. 20 Litho. *Perf. 12½*

473	A189	10c emer & vio bl	.25	.25
474	A189	25c grnsh bl & dp plum	.35	.25
475	A189	40c ocher & org brn	.60	.50
		Nos. 473-475 (3)	1.20	1.00

10th Winter Olympic Games, Grenoble, France, Feb. 6-18, 1968. See No. C178.

Pres. William Tubman — A190

1967, Dec. 22 Litho. *Perf. 12½*

476	A190	25c ultra & brown	.75	.30

Souvenir Sheet

Imperf

477	A190	50c ultra & brown	2.00	2.00

Inauguration of President Tubman, Jan. 1, 1968. No. 476 exists imperf. No. 477 contains one stamp with simulated perforations and picture frame.

Human Rights Flame — A191

1968, Apr. 26 Litho. *Perf. 12½*

478	A191	3c ver & dp bl	.25	.25
479	A191	80c brown & emer	1.25	1.25

Intl. Human Rights Year. See No. C179. Exist imperf.

Martin Luther King, Jr. — A192

Designs: 15c, Mule-drawn hearse and Dr. King. 35c, Dr. King and Lincoln monument by Daniel Chester French, horiz.

1968, July 11 Unwmk. *Perf. 12½*

480	A192	15c brt bl & brn	.25	.25
481	A192	25c indigo & brn	.40	.25
482	A192	35c olive & blk	.65	.40
		Nos. 480-482 (3)	1.30	.90

Rev. Dr. Martin Luther King, Jr. (1929-1968), American civil rights leader. Value, set $8.

See No. C180. Exist imperf.

Javelin and Diana Statue, Mexico City — A193

Designs: 25c, Discus, pyramid and serpent god Quetzalcoatl. 35c, Woman diver and Xochicalco from ruins near Cuernavaca.

1968, Aug. 22 Litho. *Perf. 12½*

483	A193	15c dp vio & org brn	.30	.25
484	A193	25c red & brt blue	.50	.25
485	A193	35c brown & emer	.85	.45
		Nos. 483-485 (3)	1.65	.95

19th Olympic Games, Mexico City, Oct. 12-27. Exist imperf. Value, set $7.

See No. C181.

Pres. Wm. V. S. Tubman — A194

1968, Dec. 30 Unwmk. *Perf. 12½*

486	A194	25c silver, blk & brn	1.25	.55

Unification Monument, Voinjama-Lofa County — A195

Souvenir Sheet

Imperf

487	A195	80c silver, ultra & red	2.00	2.00

25th anniv. of Pres. Tubman's administration.

"ILO" with Cogwheel and Wreath — A196

1969, Apr. 16 Litho. *Perf. 12½*

488	A196	25c lt blue & gold	.55	.40

50th anniv. of the ILO. Exists imperf.

See No. C183.

Red Roofs, by Camille Pissarro A197

Paintings: 3c, Prince Balthasar Carlos on Horseback, by Velazquez, vert. 10c, David and Goliath, by Caravaggio. 12c, Still Life, by Jean Baptiste Chardin. 15c, The Last Supper, by Leonardo da Vinci. 20c, Regatta at Argenteuil, by Claude Monet. 25c, Judgment of Solomon, by Giorgione, vert. 35c, Sistine Madonna, by Raphael.

1969, June 26 Litho. *Perf. 11*

489	A197	3c gray & multi	.25	.25
490	A197	5c gray & multi	.25	.25
491	A197	10c lt blue & multi	.25	.25
492	A197	12c gray & multi	.40	.25
493	A197	15c gray & multi	.40	.25
494	A197	20c gray & multi	.55	.25
495	A197	25c gray & multi	.75	.25
496	A197	35c gray & multi	1.10	.35
		Nos. 489-496 (8)	3.95	2.10

See Nos. 502-509.

African Development Bank Emblem — A198

1969, Aug. 12 Litho. *Perf. 12½*

497	A198	25c blue & brown	.55	.35
498	A198	80c yel grn & red	1.40	.65

5th anniversary of the African Development Bank. Exist imperf.

Moon Landing and Liberia No. C174 — A199

15c, Memorial tablet left on moon, rocket, earth & moon, horiz. 35c, Take-off from moon.

1969, Oct. 15 Litho. *Perf. 12½*

499	A199	15c blue & bister	.55	.25
500	A199	25c dk vio bl & org	.80	.25
501	A199	35c gray & red	1.25	.25
		Nos. 499-501 (3)	2.60	.75

Man's 1st landing on the moon, July 20, 1969. US astronauts Neil A. Armstrong and Col. Edwin E. Aldrin, Jr., with Lieut. Col. Michael Collins piloting Apollo 11. Exist imperf. Value, set $10.

See No. C184.

Painting Type of 1969

Paintings: 3c, The Gleaners, by Francois Millet. 5c, View of Toledo, by El Greco, vert. 10c, Heads of Negroes, by Rubens. 12c, The Last Supper, by El Greco. 15c, Dancing Peasants, by Brueghel. 20c, Hunters in the Snow, by Brueghel. 25c, Detail from Descent from the Cross, by Rogier van der Weyden, vert. 35c, The Ascension, by Murillo (inscribed "The Conception"), vert.

1969, Nov. 18 Litho. *Perf. 11*

502	A197	3c lt blue & multi	.25	.25
503	A197	5c lt blue & multi	.25	.25
504	A197	10c lt blue & multi	.25	.25
505	A197	12c gray & multi	.40	.25
506	A197	15c gray & multi	.45	.25
507	A197	20c lt blue & multi	.55	.25
508	A197	25c gray & multi	.80	.30
509	A197	35c lt blue & multi	1.00	.30
		Nos. 502-509 (8)	3.95	2.10

Peace Dove, UN Emblem and Atom — A200

1970, Apr. 16 Litho. *Perf. 12½*

510	A200	5c green & silver	.25	.25

25th anniv. of the UN. Exists imperf.

See No. C185.

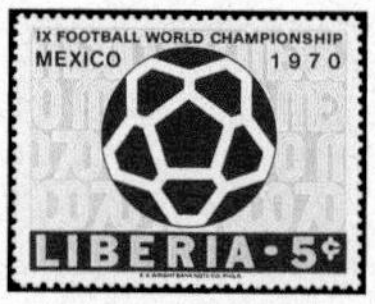

Official Emblem A201

Designs: 10c, Statue of rain god Tlaloc, vert. 25c, Jules Rimet cup and sculptured wall, vert. 35c, Sombrero and soccer ball. 55c, Two soccer players.

1970, June 10 Litho. *Perf. 12½*

511	A201	5c pale blue & brn	.25	.25
512	A201	10c emerald & ocher	.30	.25
513	A201	25c dp rose lil & gold	.55	.25
514	A201	35c ver & ultra	.80	.35
		Nos. 511-514 (4)	1.90	1.10

Souvenir Sheet

Perf. 11½

515	A201	55c brt bl, yel & grn	1.60	1.25

9th World Soccer Championships for the Jules Rimet Cup, Mexico City, May 30-June 21, 1970. Exist imperf.

EXPO '70 Emblem, Japanese Singer and Festival Plaza — A202

Designs (EXPO '70 Emblem and): 3c, Male Japanese singer, EXPO Hall and floating stage. 5c, Tower of the Sun and view of exhibition. 7c, Tanabata Festival. 8c, Awa Dance Festival. 25c, Sado-Okesa Dance Festival. 50c, Ricoh Pavilion with "eye," and Mt. Fuji, vert.

1970, July Litho. *Perf. 11*

516	A202	2c multicolored	.25	.25
517	A202	3c multicolored	.25	.25
518	A202	5c multicolored	.30	.25
519	A202	7c multicolored	.45	.25
520	A202	8c multicolored	.55	.25
521	A202	25c multicolored	1.40	.30
		Nos. 516-521 (6)	3.20	1.55

Souvenir Sheet

522	A202	50c multicolored	2.50	.75

Issued to publicize EXPO '70 International Exhibition, Osaka, Japan, Mar. 15-Sept. 13.

UPU Headquarters and Monument, Bern — A203

Design: 80c, Like 25c, vert.

1970, Aug. 25 *Perf. 12½*

523	A203	25c blue & multi	1.00	.35
524	A203	80c multicolored	1.60	.90

Inauguration of the new UPU Headquarters in Bern. Exist imperf.

Napoleon as Consul, by Joseph Marie Vien, Sr. — A204

Paintings of Napoleon: 5c, Visit to a School, by unknown painter. 10c, Napoleon Bonaparte, by François Pascal Gerard. 12c, The French Campaign, by Ernest Meissonier. 20c, Napoleon Signing Abdication at Fontainebleau, by François Bouchot. 25c, Napoleon Meets Pope Pius VII, by Jean-Louis Demarne. 50c, Napoleon's Coronation, by Jacques Louis David.

1970, Oct. 20 Litho. *Perf. 11*

525	A204	3c blue & multi	.25	.25
526	A204	5c blue & multi	.25	.25
527	A204	10c blue & multi	.45	.25
528	A204	12c blue & multi	.65	.25
529	A204	20c blue & multi	.95	.25
530	A204	25c blue & multi	1.75	.25
		Nos. 525-530 (6)	4.30	1.50

Souvenir Sheet

Imperf

531 A204 50c blue & multi 2.50 .50

200th anniv. of the birth of Napoleon Bonaparte (1769-1821). No. 531 contains one stamp with simulated perforations.

Pres. Tubman — A205

1970, Nov. 20 Litho. *Perf. 13½*

532 A205 25c multicolored 1.00 .35

Souvenir Sheet

Imperf

533 A205 50c multicolored 1.60 1.10

Pres. Tubman's 75th birthday. No. 533 contains one imperf. stamp with simulated perforations.

Adoration of the Kings, by Rogier van der Weyden — A206

Paintings (Adoration of the Kings, by): 5c, Hans Memling. 10c, Stefan Lochner. 12c, Albrecht Altdorfer, vert. 20c, Hugo van der Goes, Adoration of the Shepherds. 25c, Hieronymus Bosch, vert. 50c, Andrea Mantegna (triptych).

Perf. 13½x14, 14x13½

1970, Dec. 21 Litho.

534	A206	3c multicolored	.25	.25
535	A206	5c multicolored	.25	.25
536	A206	10c multicolored	.30	.25
537	A206	12c multicolored	.40	.25
538	A206	20c multicolored	.40	.25
539	A206	25c multicolored	.70	.25
		Nos. 534-539 (6)	2.30	1.50

Souvenir Sheet

Imperf

540 A206 50c multicolored 2.50 .60

Christmas 1970.
No. 540 contains one 60x40mm stamp.

Dogon Tribal Mask — A207

African Tribal Ceremonial Masks: 2c, Bapendé. 5c, Baoulé. 6c, Dédougou. 9c, Dan. 15c, Bamiléké. 20c, Bapendé mask and costume. 25c, Bamiléké mask and costume.

1971, Feb. 24 Litho. *Perf. 11*

541	A207	2c lt green & multi	.25	.25
542	A207	3c pink & multi	.25	.25
543	A207	5c lt blue & multi	.25	.25
544	A207	6c lt green & multi	.25	.25
545	A207	9c lt blue & multi	.25	.25
546	A207	15c pink & multi	.45	.25
547	A207	20c lt green & multi	.55	.35
548	A207	25c pink & multi	.75	.35
		Nos. 541-548 (8)	3.00	2.20

Astronauts on Moon A208

Designs: 5c, Astronaut and lunar transport vehicle. 10c, Astronaut with US flag on moon. 12c, Space capsule in Pacific Ocean. 20c, Astronaut leaving capsule. 25c, Astronauts Alan B. Shepard, Stuart A. Roosa and Edgar D. Mitchell.

1971, May 20 Litho. *Perf. 13½*

549	A208	3c dk blue & multi	.25	.25
550	A208	5c dk blue & multi	.25	.25
551	A208	10c dk blue & multi	.35	.25
552	A208	12c dk blue & multi	.50	.25
553	A208	20c dk blue & multi	.75	.25
554	A208	25c dk blue & multi	.90	.35
		Nos. 549-554 (6)	3.00	1.60

Apollo 14 moon landing, Jan. 31-Feb. 9. Exist imperf.
See No. C186.

Map, Liberian Women and Pres. Tubman — A209

3c, Pres. Tubman & women at ballot box, vert.

1971, May 27 *Perf. 12½*

555	A209	3c ultra & brn	.25	.25
556	A209	80c green & brn	1.75	1.75

25th anniversary of women's suffrage.

Hall of Honor, Munich, and Olympic Flag A210

Munich Views and Olympic Flag: 5c, General view. 10c, National Museum. 12c, Max Joseph's Square. 20c, Propylaeum on King's Square. 25c, Liesel-Karlstadt Fountain.

1971, June 28 Litho. *Perf. 11*

557	A210	3c multicolored	.25	.25
558	A210	5c multicolored	.25	.25
559	A210	10c multicolored	.25	.25
560	A210	12c multicolored	.30	.25
561	A210	20c multicolored	.55	.25
562	A210	25c multicolored	.80	.35
		Nos. 557-562 (6)	2.40	1.60

Publicity for the 20th Summer Olympic Games, Munich, Germany, 1972. Exist imperf. Value, set $7.50.
See No. C187.

Boy Scout, Emblem and US Flag — A211

Boy Scout, Natl. Flag & Boy Scout Emblem of: 5c, German Federal Republic. 10c, Australia. 12c, Great Britain. 20c, Japan. 25c, Liberia.

1971, Aug. 6 Litho. *Perf. 13½*

563	A211	3c multicolored	.25	.25
564	A211	5c multicolored	.25	.25
565	A211	10c multicolored	.25	.25
566	A211	12c multicolored	.30	.25
567	A211	20c multicolored	.50	.25
568	A211	25c multicolored	.75	.25
		Nos. 563-568 (6)	2.30	1.50

13th Boy Scout World Jamboree, Asagiri Plain, Japan, Aug. 2-10. Exist imperf.
See No. C188.

Pres. Tubman (1895-1971) — A212

1971, Aug. 23 *Perf. 12½*

569	A212	3c black, ultra & brn	.25	.25
570	A212	25c blk, brt rose lil & brn	.80	.80

Zebra and UNICEF Emblem A213

Animals (UNICEF Emblem and Animals with their Young): 7c, Koala. 8c, Llama. 10c, Red fox. 20c, Monkey. 25c, Brown bear.

1971, Oct. 1 *Perf. 11*

571	A213	5c multicolored	.25	.25
572	A213	7c multicolored	.40	.25
573	A213	8c multicolored	.40	.25
574	A213	10c multicolored	.55	.25
575	A213	20c multicolored	1.00	.35
576	A213	25c multicolored	1.25	.45
		Nos. 571-576 (6)	3.85	1.80

25th anniv. of UNICEF. See No. C189.

Sapporo 72 Emblem, Long-distance Skiing, Sika Deer — A214

3c, Sledding & black woodpecker. 5c, Ski Jump & brown bear. 10c, Bobsledding & murres. 15c, Figure skating & pikas. 25c, Downhill skiing & Japanese cranes.

1971, Nov. 4 *Perf. 13x13½*

577	A214	2c multicolored	.25	.25
578	A214	3c multicolored	.25	.25
579	A214	5c multicolored	.25	.25
580	A214	10c multicolored	.30	.25
581	A214	15c multicolored	.50	.25
582	A214	25c multicolored	2.10	.25
		Nos. 577-582 (6)	3.65	1.50

11th Winter Olympic Games, Sapporo, Japan, Feb. 3-13, 1972. Exist imperf. Value, set $10.
See No. C190.

Dove Carrying Letter, APU Emblem — A215

1971, Dec. 9 *Perf. 12½*

583	A215	25c ultra & dp org	.60	.55
584	A215	80c gray & dp brn	1.60	1.25

10th anniversary of African Postal Union.

Pioneer Fathers' Monument, Monrovia — A216

Designs: 3c, 25c, Sailing ship "Elizabeth," Providence Island, horiz. 35c, as 20c.

1972, Jan. 1

585	A216	3c lt. blue & yel grn	.25	.25
586	A216	20c orange & blue	.80	.60
587	A216	25c orange & purple	.80	.65
588	A216	35c lil rose & brt grn	1.40	1.00
		Nos. 585-588 (4)	3.25	2.50

Founding of Liberia, sesqui. See No. C191.

Pres. Tolbert and Map of Liberia — A217

Pres. William R. Tolbert, Jr. — A217a

1972, Jan. 1

589	A217	25c brt grn & brown	.65	.40
590	A217a	80c blue & brown	1.75	.70

Inauguration of William R. Tolbert, Jr. as 19th president of Liberia.

Soccer and Swedish Flag A218

Olympic Rings, "Motion" Symbol and: 5c, Swimmers at start, Italian flag. 10c, Equestrian, British flag. 12c, Bicycling, French flag. 20c, Long jump, US flag. 25c, Running and Liberian flag.

1972, May 19 Litho. *Perf. 11*

591	A218	3c lemon & multi	.25	.25
592	A218	5c lt lilac & multi	.25	.25
593	A218	10c multicolored	.55	.25
594	A218	12c gray & multi	.75	.25
595	A218	20c lt blue & multi	1.00	.30
596	A218	25c pink & multi	1.20	.35
		Nos. 591-596 (6)	4.00	1.65

20th Olympic Games, Munich, Aug. 26-Sept. 10. Exist imperf. Value, set $10.
See No. C192.

Y's Men's Club Emblem, Map — A219

Design: 90c, Y's Men's Club emblem and globe; inscribed "fifty and forward."

1972, June 12 *Perf. 13½*

597	A219	15c purple & gold	.40	.25
598	A219	90c vio bl & emer	2.10	1.50

Intl. Y's Men's Club, 50th anniv.

Astronaut and Lunar Rover A220

5c, Moon scene reflected in astronaut's helmet. 10c, Astronauts with cameras. 12c, Astronauts placing scientific equipment on moon. 20c, Apollo 16 badge. 25c, Astronauts riding lunar rover.

1972, June 26

599 A220 3c lt blue & multi .25 .25
600 A220 5c red org & multi .25 .25
601 A220 10c pink & multi .35 .25
602 A220 12c yellow & multi .65 .25
603 A220 20c lt vio & multi .80 .25
604 A220 25c emerald & multi 1.40 .25
Nos. 599-604 (6) 3.70 1.50

Apollo 16 US moon mission, Apr. 15-27, 1972. Exist imperf. Value, set $10.
See No. C193.

Emperor Haile Selassie — A221

1972, July 21 *Perf. 14x14½*

605 A221 20c olive grn & yel .55 .55
606 A221 25c maroon & yel .75 .75
607 A221 35c brown & yel .80 .80
Nos. 605-607 (3) 2.10 2.10

80th birthday of Emperor Haile Selassie of Ethiopia.

Ajax, 1809, and Figurehead — A222

Famous sailing ships and their figureheads: 5c, Hogue, 1811. 7c, Ariadne, 1816. 15c, Royal Adelaide, 1828. 20c, Rinaldo, 1860. 25c, Nymphe, 1888.

1972, Sept. 6 *Perf. 11*

608 A222 3c shown .25 .25
609 A222 5c multicolored .35 .25
610 A222 7c multicolored .55 .25
611 A222 15c multicolored .75 .25
612 A222 20c multicolored .95 .25
613 A222 25c multicolored 1.25 .45
Nos. 608-613 (6) 4.10 1.70

See No. C194.

Pres. Tolbert Taking Oath, Richard A. Henries A223

1972, Oct. 23 **Litho.** *Perf. 13½*

614 A223 15c green & multi .65 .65
615 A223 25c vio blue & multi .95 .95

Pres. William R. Tolbert, Jr. sworn in as 19th President of Liberia, July 23, 1971. See No. C195.

Klaus Dibiasi, Italy, Diving A224

8c, Valery Borzov, USSR, running. 10c, Hideaki Yanagida, Japan, wrestling. 12c, Mark Spitz, US, swimming. 15c, Kipchoge Keino, Kenya, 3000-meter steeplechase. 25c, Richard Meade, Great Britain, equestrian. 55c, Hans Winkler, Germany, grand prix jumping.

1973, Jan. 5 **Litho.** *Perf. 11*

616 A224 5c lt blue & multi .25 .25
617 A224 8c violet & multi .30 .25
618 A224 10c multicolored .40 .25
619 A224 12c green & multi .50 .25
620 A224 15c orange & multi .60 .25
621 A224 25c pale salmon & multi 1.00 .30
Nos. 616-621 (6) 3.05 1.55

Souvenir Sheet

622 A224 55c multicolored 3.25 1.50

Gold medal winners in 20th Olympic Games.
Exist imperf. Values: set $10; souvenir sheet $8.

Astronaut on Moon and Apollo 17 Badge — A225

Designs (Apollo 17 Badge and): 3c, Astronauts on earth in lunar rover. 10c, Astronauts collecting yellow lunar dust. 15c, Astronauts in lunar rover exploring moon crater. 20c, Capt. Eugene A. Cernan, Dr. Harrison H. Schmitt and Comdr. Ronald E. Evans on launching pad. 25c, Astronauts on moon with scientific equipment.

1973, Mar. 28 **Litho.** *Perf. 11*

623 A225 2c blue & multi .30 .25
624 A225 3c blue & multi .30 .25
625 A225 10c blue & multi .30 .25
626 A225 15c blue & multi .50 .25
627 A225 20c blue & multi .90 .30
628 A225 25c blue & multi .90 .40
Nos. 623-628 (6) 3.20 1.70

Apollo 17 US moon mission, Dec. 7-19, 1972. Exist imperf. Value, set $10.
See No. C196.

Locomotive, England — A226

Designs: Locomotives, 1895-1905.

1973, May 4

629 A226 2c shown .25 .25
630 A226 3c Netherlands .35 .25
631 A226 10c France .65 .25
632 A226 15c United States .85 .25
633 A226 20c Japan 1.75 .25
634 A226 25c Germany 2.50 .35
Nos. 629-634 (6) 6.35 1.60

See No. C197.

OAU Emblem and Flags A227

1973, May 24 **Litho.** *Perf. 13½*

635 A227 3c multicolored .25 .25
636 A227 5c multicolored .25 .25
637 A227 10c multicolored .25 .25
638 A227 15c multicolored .30 .25
639 A227 25c multicolored .55 .45
640 A227 50c multicolored 1.25 .95
Nos. 635-640 (6) 2.85 2.40

10th anniv. of the Organization for African Unity.

WHO Emblem, Edward Jenner and Roses A228

Designs (WHO Emblem and): 4c, Sigmund Freud and pansies. 10c, Jonas E. Salk and chrysanthemums. 15c, Louis Pasteur and scabiosa caucasia. 20c, Emil von Behring and rhododendron. 25c, Alexander Fleming and tree mallows.

1973, June 26 **Litho.** *Perf. 11*

641 A228 1c gray & multi .25 .25
642 A228 4c orange & multi .25 .25
643 A228 10c lt blue & multi .25 .25
644 A228 15c rose & multi .35 .25
645 A228 20c blue & multi .50 .25
646 A228 25c yel grn & multi .75 .40
Nos. 641-646 (6) 2.35 1.65

25th anniv. of WHO. See No. C198.

Stanley Steamer, 1910 — A229

Classic automobiles: 3c, Cadillac, 1903. 10c, Clement-Bayard, 1904. 15c, Rolls Royce, 1907. 20c, Maxwell, 1905. 25c, Chadwick, 1907.

1973, Sept. 11 **Litho.** *Perf. 11*

647 A229 2c shown .25 .25
648 A229 3c multicolored .25 .25
649 A229 10c multicolored .30 .25
650 A229 15c multicolored .40 .25
651 A229 20c multicolored .55 .25
652 A229 25c multicolored .65 .35
Nos. 647-652 (6) 2.40 1.60

See No. C199.

Copernicus, Armillary Sphere, Satellite Communication — A230

Portraits of Copernicus and: 4c, Eudoxus solar system. 10c, Aristotle, Ptolemy, Copernicus and satellites. 15c, Saturn and Apollo spacecraft. 20c, Orbiting astronomical observatory. 25c, Satellite tracking station.

1973, Dec. 14 **Litho.** *Perf. 13½*

653 A230 1c yellow & multi .25 .25
654 A230 4c lt violet & multi .25 .25
655 A230 10c lt blue & multi .25 .25
656 A230 15c yel grn & multi .40 .25
657 A230 20c buff & multi .55 .25
658 A230 25c pink & multi .60 .30
Nos. 653-658 (6) 2.30 1.55

Nicolaus Copernicus (1473-1543), Polish astronomer. Exist imperf.
See No. C200.

Radio Tower, Map of Africa — A231

15c, 25c, Map of Liberia, Radio tower and man listening to broadcast. 17c, like 13c.

1974, Jan. 16 **Litho.** *Perf. 13½*

659 A231 13c mag & multi .45 .45
660 A231 15c yellow & multi .45 .45
661 A231 17c lt gray & multi .60 .50
662 A231 25c brt green & multi .75 .50
Nos. 659-662 (4) 2.25 1.90

20th anniv. of Radio ELWA, Monrovia.

Thomas Coutts, 1817; Aureal, 1974; UPU Emblem A232

Designs (UPU Emblem and): 3c, Jet, satellite, Post Office, Monrovia, ship. 10c, US and USSR telecommunication satellites. 15c, Mail runner and jet. 20c, Futuristic mail train and mail truck. 25c, American Pony Express rider.

1974, Mar. 4 **Litho.** *Perf. 13½*

663 A232 2c ocher & multi .25 .25
664 A232 3c lt green & multi .25 .25
665 A232 10c lt blue & multi .25 .25
666 A232 15c pink & multi .35 .25
667 A232 20c gray & multi .80 .25
668 A232 25c lt lilac & multi .75 .40
Nos. 663-668 (6) 2.65 1.65

Cent. of UPU. Exist imperf. Value, set $15.
See No. C201.

Fox Terrier A233

1974, Apr. 16 **Litho.** *Perf. 13½*

669 A233 5c shown .25 .25
670 A233 10c Boxer .25 .25
671 A233 16c Chihuahua .45 .25
672 A233 19c Beagle .55 .25
673 A233 25c Golden retriever .60 .25
674 A233 50c Collie 1.40 .25
Nos. 669-674 (6) 3.50 1.50

Exist imperf. See No. C202.

1974 World Cup Soccer Championships, Munich. — A234

Flags and scenes from games played by: 1c, West Germany and Chile. 2c, Australia and East Germany. 5c, Brazil and Yugoslavia. 10c, Zaire and Scotland. 12c, Netherlands and Uruguay. 15c, Sweden and Bulgaria. 20c, Italy and Haiti. 25c, Poland and Argentina.

1974, June 4 **Litho.** *Perf. 11*

675 A234 1c shown .25 .25
676 A234 2c multicolored .25 .25
677 A234 5c multicolored .25 .25
678 A234 10c multicolored .25 .25
679 A234 12c multicolored .30 .25
680 A234 15c multicolored .45 .25
681 A234 20c multicolored .60 .25
682 A234 25c multicolored .50 .45
Nos. 675-682 (8) 2.85 2.20

Exist imperf. Value, set $20.
See No. C203.

Chrysiridia Madagascariensis — A235

Tropical Butterflies: 2c, Catagramma sorana. 5c, Erasmia pulchella. 17c, Morpho cypris. 25c, Agrias amydon. 40c, Vanessa cardui.

1974, Sept. 11 **Litho.** *Perf. 13½*

683 A235 1c gray & multi .25 .25
684 A235 2c gray & multi .25 .25
685 A235 5c gray & multi .25 .25
686 A235 17c gray & multi .75 .25
687 A235 25c gray & multi 1.00 .30
688 A235 40c gray & multi 1.90 .45
Nos. 683-688 (6) 4.40 1.75

See No. C204.

Pres. Tolbert and Medal A236

$1, Pres. Tolbert, medal & Liberian flag.

1974, Dec. 10 **Litho.** *Perf. 13½*

689 A236 3c multi .25 .25
690 A236 $1 multi, vert. 1.75 1.50

Pres. William R. Tolbert, Jr., recipient of 1974 Family of Man Award.

Winston Churchill, 1940 — A237

Churchill and: 10c, RAF planes in dog fight. 15c, In naval launch on way to Normandy. 17c, In staff car reviewing troops in desert. 20c, Aboard landing craft crossing Rhine. 25c, In conference with Pres. Roosevelt.

1975, Jan. 17 Litho. *Perf. 13½*

691	A237	3c multicolored	.25	.25
692	A237	10c multicolored	.25	.25
693	A237	15c multicolored	.25	.25
694	A237	17c multicolored	.40	.25
695	A237	20c multicolored	.50	.25
696	A237	25c multicolored	.75	.30
		Nos. 691-696 (6)	2.40	1.55

Sir Winston Churchill (1874-1965), birth centenary. Exist imperf. Value, set $10.

See No. C205.

Women's Year Emblem and Marie Curie — A238

3c, Mahalia Jackson with microphone. 5c, Joan of Arc. 10c, Eleanor Roosevelt and children. 25c, Matilda Newport firing cannon. 50c, Valentina Tereshkova in space suit.

1975, Mar. 14 Litho. *Perf. 14½*

697	A238	2c citron & multi	.25	.25
698	A238	3c dull orange & multi	.25	.25
699	A238	5c lilac rose & multi	.25	.25
700	A238	10c yellow & multi	.25	.25
701	A238	25c yellow grn & multi	.55	.25
702	A238	50c lilac & multi	.90	.65
		Nos. 697-702 (6)	2.45	1.90

Intl. Women's Year 1975. Exist imperf. Value, set $10.

See No. C206.

Old State House, Boston, US No. 627 A239

10c, George Washington, US #645. 15c, Town Hall & Court House, Philadelphia, US #798. 20c, Benjamin Franklin, US #835. 25c, Paul Revere's Ride, US #618. 50c, Santa Maria, US #231.

1975, Apr. 25 Litho. *Perf. 13½*

703	A239	5c multicolored	.25	.25
704	A239	10c multicolored	.35	.25
705	A239	15c multicolored	.55	.25
706	A239	20c multicolored	.60	.25
707	A239	25c multicolored	.90	.25
708	A239	50c multicolored	2.00	.50
		Nos. 703-708 (6)	4.65	1.75

American Revolution Bicentennial. Exist imperf. Value, set $10.

See No. C207.

Dr. Schweitzer, Hospital and Baboon Mother A240

Designs (Dr. Schweitzer and): 3c, Elephant, and tribesmen poling boat. 5c, Water buffalo, egret, man and woman paddling canoe. 6c, Antelope and dancer. 25c, Lioness, woman cooking outdoors. 50c, Zebra and colt, doctor's examination at clinic.

1975, June 26 Litho. *Perf. 13½*

709	A240	1c multicolored	.25	.25
710	A240	3c multicolored	.25	.25
711	A240	5c multicolored	.25	.25
712	A240	6c multicolored	.25	.25
713	A240	25c multicolored	.55	.25
714	A240	50c multicolored	1.25	.65
		Nos. 709-714 (6)	2.80	1.90

Dr. Albert Schweitzer (1875-1965), medical missionary, birth centenary. Exist imperf. Value, set $10.

See No. C208.

American-Russian Handshake in Space — A241

Designs (Apollo-Soyuz Emblem and): 5c, Apollo. 10c, Soyuz. 20c, Flags and maps of US and USSR. 25c, A. A. Leonov, and V. N. Kubasov. 50c, D. K. Slayton, V. D. Brand, T. P. Stafford.

1975, Sept. 18 Litho. *Perf. 13½*

715	A241	5c multicolored	.25	.25
716	A241	10c multicolored	.25	.25
717	A241	15c multicolored	.30	.25
718	A241	20c multicolored	.45	.25
719	A241	25c multicolored	.50	.25
720	A241	50c multicolored	1.10	.45
		Nos. 715-720 (6)	2.85	1.70

Apollo Soyuz space test project (Russo-American cooperation), launching July 15; link-up, July 17. Exist imperf. Value, set $10.

See No. C209.

Presidents Tolbert, Siaka Stevens; Treaty Signing; Liberia and Sierra Leone Maps A242

1975, Oct. 3 Litho. *Perf. 13½*

721	A242	2c gray & multi	.25	.25
722	A242	3c gray & multi	.25	.25
723	A242	5c gray & multi	.25	.25
724	A242	10c gray & multi	.25	.25
725	A242	25c gray & multi	.50	.30
726	A242	50c gray & multi	.90	.55
		Nos. 721-726 (6)	2.40	1.85

Mano River Union Agreement between Liberia and Sierra Leone, signed Oct. 3, 1973.

Figure Skating A243

Designs (Winter Olympic Games Emblem and): 4c, Ski jump. 10c, Slalom. 25c, Ice hockey. 35c, Speed skating. 50c, Two-man bobsled.

1976, Jan. 23 Litho. *Perf. 13½*

727	A243	1c lt blue & multi	.25	.25
728	A243	4c lt blue & multi	.25	.25
729	A243	10c lt blue & multi	.35	.25
730	A243	25c lt blue & multi	.75	.25
731	A243	35c lt blue & multi	.90	.25
732	A243	50c lt blue & multi	1.10	.75
		Nos. 727-732 (6)	3.60	2.00

12th Winter Olympic Games, Innsbruck, Austria, Feb. 4-15. Exist imperf. Value, set $11.

See No. C210.

Pres. Tolbert Taking Oath of Office A244

25c, Pres. Tolbert at his desk, vert. $1, Seal & flag of Liberia, $400 commemorative gold coin.

1976, Apr. 5 Litho. *Perf. 13½*

733	A244	3c multicolored	.25	.25
734	A244	25c multicolored	.50	.50
735	A244	$1 multicolored	2.00	1.75
		Nos. 733-735 (3)	2.75	2.50

Inauguration of President William R. Tolbert, Jr., Jan. 5, 1976.

Weight Lifting and Olympic Rings A245

Designs (Olympic Rings and): 3c, Pole vault. 10c, Hammer and shot put. 25c, Yachting. 35c, Women's gymnastics. 50c, Hurdles.

1976, May 4 Litho. *Perf. 13½*

736	A245	2c gray & multi	.25	.25
737	A245	3c orange & multi	.25	.25
738	A245	10c lt violet & multi	.30	.25
739	A245	25c lt green & multi	.60	.25
740	A245	35c yellow & multi	.75	.60
741	A245	50c pink & multi	1.00	.60
		Nos. 736-741 (6)	3.15	2.20

21st Olympic Games, Montreal, Canada, July 17-Aug. 1. Exist imperf. Value, set $11.

See No. C211.

A. G. Bell, Telephone and Receiver, 1876, UPU Emblem A246

UPU Emblem and: 4c, Horsedrawn mail coach and ITU emblem. 5c, Intelsat IV satellite, radar and ITU emblem. 25c, A. G. Bell, ship laying underwater cable, 1976 telephone. 40c, A. G. Bell, futuristic train, telegraph and telephone wires. 50c, Wright brothers' plane, Zeppelin and Concorde.

1976, June 4 Litho. *Perf. 13½*

742	A246	1c green & multi	.25	.25
743	A246	4c ocher & multi	.25	.25
744	A246	5c orange & multi	.25	.25
745	A246	25c green & multi	.90	.25
746	A246	40c lilac & multi	1.10	.25
747	A246	50c blue & multi	1.25	.70
		Nos. 742-747 (6)	4.00	1.95

Cent. of 1st telephone call by Alexander Graham Bell, Mar. 10, 1876. Exist imperf. Value, set $25.

See No. C212.

Gold Nugget on Chain, Gold Panner A247

1c, Mano River Bridge. 5c, "V" ring. 10c, Rubber tire, tree. 15c, Harvesting. 20c, Hydro-electric plant. 25c, Mesurado shrimp. 27c, Woman tie-dying cloth. 55c, Lake Piso, barracuda. $1, Train hauling iron ore.

1976-81 Litho. *Perf. 14½*

749	A247	1c multicolored	.25	.25
750	A247	3c shown	.25	.25
751	A247	5c multicolored	.25	.25
752	A247	7c like 5c ('81)	.75	.25
753	A247	10c multicolored	.30	.25
754	A247	15c multicolored	.55	.45
755	A247	17c like 55c ('81)	1.75	.60
756	A247	20c multicolored	.65	.45
757	A247	25c multicolored	.85	.25
758	A247	27c multicolored	.90	.65
759	A247	55c multicolored	2.75	.75
760	A247	$1 multicolored	3.25	2.50
		Nos. 749-760 (12)	12.50	6.90

See Nos. 945-953.

Rhinoceros A249

African Animals: 3c, Zebra antelope. 5c, Chimpanzee, vert. 15c, Pigmy hippopotamus. 25c, Leopard. $1, Gorilla, vert.

1976, Sept. 1 Litho. *Perf. 13½*

763	A249	2c orange & multi	.25	.25
764	A249	3c gray & multi	.25	.25
765	A249	5c blue & multi	.25	.25
766	A249	15c brt blue & multi	.45	.25
767	A249	25c ultra & multi	1.00	.45
768	A249	$1 multicolored	3.50	1.10
		Nos. 763-768 (6)	5.70	2.55

See No. C213.

Maps of US and Liberia; Statue of Liberty, Unification Monument, Voinjama and Liberty Bell — A250

$1, George Washington, Gerald R. Ford, Joseph J. Roberts (1st Pres. of Liberia), William R. Tolbert, Jr., Bicentennial emblem, US & Liberian flags.

1976, Sept. 21 Litho. *Perf. 13½*

769	A250	25c multicolored	.50	.30
770	A250	$1 multicolored	1.50	.75

American Bicentennial and visit of Pres. William R. Tolbert, Jr. to the US, Sept. 21-30. See No. C214.

Baluba Masks and Festival Emblem — A251

Tribal Masks: 10c, Bateke. 15c, Basshilele. 20c, Igungun. 25c, Masai. 50c, Kifwebe.

1977, Jan. 20 Litho. *Perf. 13½*

771	A251	5c yellow & multi	.25	.25
772	A251	10c green & multi	.30	.25
773	A251	15c salmon & multi	.45	.25
774	A251	20c lt blue & multi	.45	.25
775	A251	25c violet & multi	.60	.25
776	A251	50c lemon & multi	1.20	.30
		Nos. 771-776 (6)	3.25	1.55

FESTAC '77, 2nd World Black and African Festival, Lagos, Nigeria, Jan. 15-Feb. 12. See No. C215.

Latham's Francolin A252

Birds of Liberia: 10c, Narina trogon. 15c, Rufous-crowned roller. 20c, Brown-cheeked hornbill. 25c, Common bulbul. 50c, Fish eagle. 80c, Gold Coast touraco.

1977, Feb. 18 Litho. *Perf. 14*

777	A252	5c multicolored	.30	.25
778	A252	10c multicolored	.45	.25
779	A252	15c multicolored	.65	.25
780	A252	20c multicolored	.95	.25
781	A252	25c multicolored	1.20	.25
782	A252	50c multicolored	2.40	.65
		Nos. 777-782 (6)	5.95	1.90

Souvenir Sheet

783	A252	80c multicolored	3.50	1.75

Edmund Coffin, Combined Training, US — A253

Designs: 15c, Alwin Schockemohle, single jump, Germany, vert. 20c, Christine Stuckelberger, Switzerland, individual dressage. 25c, Prix de Nations (team), France.

1977, Apr. 22 Litho. *Perf. 13½*

784	A253	5c ocher & multi	.35	.25
785	A253	15c ocher & multi	.70	.25
786	A253	20c ocher & multi	.85	.25
787	A253	25c ocher & multi	1.10	.35
		Nos. 784-787,C216 (5)	5.40	1.70

Equestrian gold medal winners in Montreal Olympic Games. Exist imperf. Value, set $10.

See No. C217.

Elizabeth II Wearing Crown A254

Designs: 25c, Elizabeth II Prince Philip, Pres. and Mrs. Tubman. 80c, Elizabeth II, Prince Philip, royal coat of arms.

1977, May 23 Litho. *Perf. 13½*

788 A254 15c silver & multi	.35	.25
789 A254 25c silver & multi	.55	.25
790 A254 80c silver & multi	1.75	.55
Nos. 788-790 (3)	2.65	1.05

25th anniversary of the reign of Queen Elizabeth II. Nos. 788-790 exist imperf. Value, set $8.

See No. C218.

Jesus Blessing Children — A255

Christmas: 25c, The Good Shepherd. $1, Jesus and the Samaritan Woman. Designs after stained-glass windows, Providence Baptist Church, Monrovia.

1977, Nov. 3 Litho. *Perf. 13½*

791 A255 20c lt blue & multi	.30	.25
792 A255 25c lt blue & multi	.45	.35
793 A255 $1 lt blue & multi	1.40	.75
Nos. 791-793 (3)	2.15	1.35

Dornier DOX, 1928 — A256

Progress of Aviation: 3c, Piggyback space shuttle, 1977. 5c, Eddie Rickenbacker and Douglas DC 3. 25c, Charles A. Lindbergh and Spirit of St. Louis. 35c, Louis Bleriot and Bleriot XI. 50c, Orville and Wilbur Wright and flying machine, 1903. 80c, Concorde landing at night at Dulles Airport, Washington, DC.

1978, Jan. 6 Litho. *Perf. 13½*

794 A256 2c multicolored	.25	.25
795 A256 3c multicolored	.25	.25
796 A256 5c multicolored	.25	.25
797 A256 25c multicolored	.55	.25
798 A256 35c multicolored	.90	.55
799 A256 50c multicolored	1.25	.50
Nos. 794-799 (6)	3.45	2.05

Souvenir Sheet

800 A256 80c multicolored	2.75	1.00

Exist imperf. Values, set $10, souvenir sheet $15.

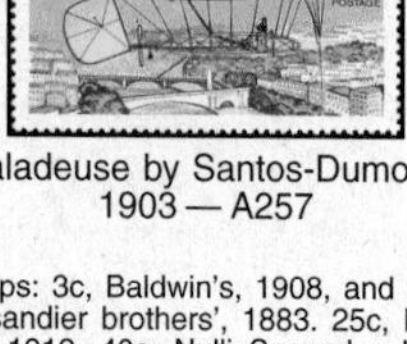

Baladeuse by Santos-Dumont, 1903 — A257

Airships: 3c, Baldwin's, 1908, and US flag. 5c, Tissandier brothers', 1883. 25c, Parseval PL VII, 1912. 40c, Nulli Secundus II, 1908. 50c, R34 rigid airship, 1919.

1978, Mar. 9 Litho. *Perf. 13½*

801 A257 2c multicolored	.25	.25
802 A257 3c multicolored	.25	.25
803 A257 5c multicolored	.25	.25
804 A257 25c multicolored	.50	.25
805 A257 40c multicolored	.70	.25
806 A257 50c multicolored	1.10	.25
Nos. 801-806 (6)	3.05	1.50

75th anniv. of the Zeppelin. Exist imperf. Value, set $12.

See No. C219.

Soccer, East Germany and Brazil A258

Soccer Games: 2c, Poland and Argentina, vert. 10c, West Germany and Netherlands. 25c, Yugoslavia and Brazil. 35c, Poland and Italy, vert. 50c, Netherlands and Uruguay.

1978, May 16 Litho. *Perf. 13½*

807 A258 2c multicolored	.25	.25
808 A258 3c multicolored	.25	.25
809 A258 10c multicolored	.25	.25
810 A258 25c multicolored	.70	.25
811 A258 35c multicolored	.90	.45
812 A258 50c multicolored	1.40	.60
Nos. 807-812 (6)	3.75	2.05

11th World Cup Soccer Championships, Argentina, June 1-25. Exist imperf. Value, set $15.

See No. C220.

Coronation Chair — A259

Designs: 25c, Imperial state crown. $1, Buckingham Palace, horiz.

1978, June 12

813 A259 5c multicolored	.25	.25
814 A259 25c multicolored	.55	.25
815 A259 $1 multicolored	2.10	.75
Nos. 813-815 (3)	2.90	1.25

25th anniversary of coronation of Queen Elizabeth II. Exist imperf. Value, set $9.

See No. C221.

Jinnah, Liberian and Pakistani Flags A260

1978, June Litho. *Perf. 13*

816 A260 30c multicolored	*37.50*	8.25

Mohammed Ali Jinnah (1876-1948), first Governor General of Pakistan.

Carter and Tolbert Families A261

Designs: 25c, Pres. Tolbert, Rosalynn Carter and Pres. Carter at microphone, Robertsfield Airport. $1, Jimmy Carter and William R. Tolbert, Jr. in motorcade from airport.

1978, Oct. 26 Litho. *Perf. 13½*

817 A261 5c multicolored	.25	.25
818 A261 25c multicolored	.65	.65
819 A261 $1 multicolored	2.50	2.50
Nos. 817-819 (3)	3.40	3.40

Pres. Carter's visit to Liberia, Apr. 1978.

Soccer Game: Italy-France A262

Soccer Games: 1c, Brazil-Spain, horiz. 10c, Poland-West Germany, horiz. 27c, Peru-Scotland. 35c, Austria-West Germany. 50c, Argentina the victor.

1978, Dec. 8 Litho. *Perf. 13½*

820 A262 1c multicolored	.25	.25
821 A262 2c multicolored	.25	.25
822 A262 10c multicolored	.30	.25
823 A262 27c multicolored	.70	.50
824 A262 35c multicolored	.90	.60
825 A262 50c multicolored	1.25	.90
Nos. 820-825 (6)	3.65	2.75

1978 World Cup Soccer winners. Exist imperf. Value, set $10.

See No. C222.

Liberian Lumbermen A263

Designs: 10c, Hauling timber by truck, vert. 25c, Felling trees with chain saw. 50c, Moving logs.

1978, Dec. 15 Litho. *Perf. 13½x14*

826 A263 5c multicolored	.25	.25
827 A263 10c multicolored	.30	.25
828 A263 25c multicolored	.65	.40
829 A263 50c multicolored	1.40	.90
Nos. 826-829 (4)	2.60	1.80

8th World Forestry Congress, Djakarta, Indonesia.

"25" and Waves — A264

Design: $1, Radio tower and waves.

1979, Apr. 6 Litho. *Perf. 14x13½*

830 A264 35c multicolored	.65	.65
831 A264 $1 multicolored	1.75	1.75

25th anniversary of Radio ELWA.

Emblems of IYC, African Child's Decade and SOS Village A265

Designs: 25c, $1, like 5c, with UNICEF emblem replacing SOS emblem. 35c, like 5c.

1979, Apr. 6 *Perf. 13½x14*

832 A265 5c multicolored	.25	.25
833 A265 25c multicolored	.25	.25
834 A265 35c multicolored	.60	.60
835 A265 $1 multicolored	1.40	1.40
Nos. 832-835 (4)	2.50	2.50

IYC and Decade of the African Child.

Presidents Gardner and Tolbert, and Post Office, Monrovia A266

Design: 35c, Anthony W. Gardner, William R. Tolbert, Jr. and UPU emblem.

1979, Apr. 2 Litho. *Perf. 13½x14*

836 A266 5c multicolored	.25	.25
837 A266 35c multicolored	.95	.95

Cent. of Liberia's joining UPU.

Unity Problem, Map of Africa, Torches A267

Designs: 27c, Masks. 35c, Elephant, giraffe, lion, antelope, cheetah and map of Africa. 50c, Huts, pepper birds and map of Africa.

1979, July 6 Litho. *Perf. 14x13½*

838 A267 5c multicolored	.30	.25
839 A267 27c multicolored	.50	.35
840 A267 35c multicolored	.75	.45
841 A267 50c multicolored	1.10	1.10
Nos. 838-841 (4)	2.65	2.15

Organization for African Unity, 16th anniversary, and OAU Summit Conference.

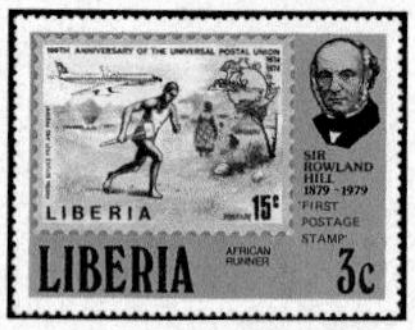

Liberia No. 666, Rowland Hill — A268

10c, Pony Express rider, 1860. 15c, British mail coach, 1800. 25c, Mail steamship John Penn, 1860. 27c, Stanier Pacific train, 1939. 50c, Concorde. $1, Curtiss Jenny, 1916.

1979, July 20

842 A268 3c multicolored	.25	.25
843 A268 10c multicolored	.25	.25
844 A268 15c multicolored	.35	.35
845 A268 25c multicolored	.60	.50
846 A268 27c multicolored	.65	.50
847 A268 50c multicolored	1.10	1.00
Nos. 842-847 (6)	3.20	2.85

Souvenir Sheet

848 A268 $1 multicolored	2.25	1.60

Sir Rowland Hill (1795-1879), originator of penny postage. Exist imperf. Value, set $20.

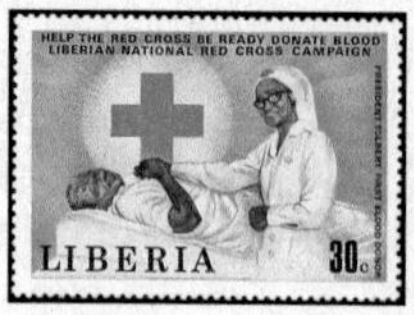

Red Cross, Pres. Tolbert Donating Blood A269

Design: 50c, Red Cross, Pres. Tolbert.

1979, Aug. 15 Litho. *Perf. 13½*

849 A269 30c multicolored	.50	.50
850 A269 50c multicolored	1.25	1.25

National Red Cross, 30th anniversary and blood donation campaign.

M.S. World Peace A270

Design: $1, M.S. World Peace, diff.

1979, Aug. 15

851 A270 5c multicolored	.25	.25
852 A270 $1 multicolored	2.40	2.40

2nd World Maritime Day, March 16; Liberia Maritime Program, 30th anniversary.

A Good Turn, by Norman Rockwell — A271

Paintings — Scouting through the eyes of Norman Rockwell (1925-76): No. 853: a, Stories. b, 3 branches of Scouts. c, camping. d, Church. e, Animal care. f, advancements. g, Scout, Lincoln. h, First aid on puppy. i, Reading with elderly and dog. j, Scout teaching cubs..

No. 854: a, "1910." b, Feeding dog. c, Man, dog, Scout on top of rock. d, Merit badges. e, Hiking in mountains. f, With explorer and eagle. g, Wearing new uniform. h, Indian lore. i, First camping. j, Group saluting.

No. 855: a, Eagle ceremony. b, Hiking with compass. c, The Scouting Trail. d, Phyical fitness. e, Prayer. f, Tales of the sea. g, Foreign and US scouts dancing. h, Building a birdhouse. i, In front of flag. j, Rescueing girl and kitten.

No. 856: a, Painting outdoors. b, Scout saluting in front of flag. c, Scout, Lincoln, Washington, eagle. d, Starting on hike. e, Knot tying. f, Reading instructions. g, Scouts of 6 nations. h, Boy, Girl Scouts and leaders. i, "On my honor..." j, Cooking outdoors.

No. 857: a, Portaging. b, "Spirit of '76." c, Saluting flag with astronaut. d, 5 branches of scouting. e, Planting trees. f, Washington praying. g, First aid on dog. h, Saying grace in mess tent. i, First time in Scout uniform. j, Rock climbing.

1979, Sept. 1 Litho. *Perf. 11*

853 A271 5c #a.-j, any single .40 .25
854 A271 10c #a.-j, any single .40 .25
855 A271 15c #a.-j, any single .65 .35
856 A271 25c #a.-j, any single 1.20 .40
857 A271 35c #a.-j, any single 1.75 .70
Nos. 853-857, Set of 50 in 5 strips of 10 50.00 20.00

Exist imperf. Value, set of 5 strips $55.

Mrs. Tolbert, Children, Children's Village Emblem A272

40c, Mrs. Tolbert, children, emblem, vert.

1979, Nov. 14 Litho. *Perf. 14*

858 A272 25c multicolored .60 .60
859 A272 40c multicolored 1.25 1.00

SOS Children's Village in Monrovia, Liberia.

Rotary International Headquarters, Evanston, Ill., Emblem — A273

Rotary Emblem and: 5c, Vocational services. 17c, Man in wheelchair, nurse, vert. 27c, Flags of several nations. 35c, People of various races holding hands around globe. 50c, Pres. Tolbert, map of Africa, vert. $1, "Gift of Life."

1979, Dec. 28 *Perf. 11*

860 A273 1c multicolored .25 .25
861 A273 5c multicolored .25 .25
862 A273 17c multicolored .40 .40
863 A273 27c multicolored .70 .70
864 A273 35c multicolored .75 .75
865 A273 50c multicolored 1.40 1.40
Nos. 860-865 (6) 3.75 3.75

Souvenir Sheet

866 A273 $1 multicolored 2.75 2.75

Rotary International, 75th anniversary. Exist imperf. Values: set $14; souvenir sheet $11.

Ski Jump, Lake Placid '80 Emblem A274

Lake Placid '80 Emblem and: 5c, Figure skating. 17c, Bobsledding. 27c, Cross-country skiing. 35c, Women's speed skating. 50c, Ice hockey. $1, Slalom.

1980, Jan. 21

867 A274 1c multicolored .30 .25
868 A274 5c multicolored .30 .25
869 A274 17c multicolored .75 .45
870 A274 27c multicolored 1.50 .90
871 A274 35c multicolored 1.50 .90
872 A274 50c multicolored 2.10 1.25
Nos. 867-872 (6) 6.45 4.00

Souvenir Sheet

873 A274 $1 multicolored 2.75 2.00

13th Winter Olympic Games, Lake Placid, NY, Feb. 12-24. Exist imperf. Values: set $12.50; souvenir sheet $25.

Pres. Tolbert, Pres. Stevens, Maps of Liberia and Sierra Leone, Mano River A275

1980, Mar. 6 Litho. *Perf. 14x13½*

874 A275 8c multicolored .25 .25
875 A275 27c multicolored .65 .65
876 A275 35c multicolored .75 .75
877 A275 80c multicolored 1.90 1.90
Nos. 874-877 (4) 3.55 3.55

Mano River Agreement, 5th anniversary; Mano River Postal Union, 1st anniversary.

Redemption Horn — A276

10c, Sgt. Doe and Soldiers, Clenched Hands Angel, horiz. 14c, Citizens, map, Flag, horiz. $2, Sgt. Samuel Doe.

1981, Feb. 6 Litho. *Perf. 14*

878 A276 1c multicolored .25 .25
879 A276 6c like 1c .25 .25
880 A276 10c multicolored .25 .25
881 A276 14c multicolored .30 .25
882 A276 23c like 10c .35 .35
883 A276 31c like 14c .60 .60
884 A276 41c like $2 .75 .75
885 A276 $2 multicolored 4.00 4.00
Nos. 878-885 (8) 6.75 6.70

Establishment of new government under the People's Redemption Council, Apr. 12, 1980.

Soccer Players, World Cup, Flags of 1930 and 1934 Finalists A277

Soccer Players, Cup, Flags of Finalists from: 5c, 1938, 1950. 20c, 1954, 1958. 27c, 1962, 1966. 40c, 1970, 1974. 55c. 1978. $1, Spanish team.

1981, Mar. 4 Litho. *Perf. 14*

886 A277 3c multicolored .25 .25
887 A277 5c multicolored .25 .25
888 A277 20c multicolored .45 .45
889 A277 27c multicolored .65 .65
890 A277 40c multicolored .90 .90
891 A277 55c multicolored 1.25 1.25
Nos. 886-891 (6) 3.75 3.75

Souvenir Sheet

892 A277 $1 multicolored 2.50 1.75

ESPANA '82 World Cup Soccer Championship.

Exists imperf. Values: set, $12; souvenir sheet, $10.

Sgt. Samuel Doe and Citizens A278

27c, Doe, Liberian flag. 30c, Clasped arms. $1, Doe, soldiers, Justice.

1981, Apr. 7 Litho. *Perf. 14*

893 A278 22c shown .50 .50
894 A278 27c multicolored .65 .65
895 A278 30c multicolored .90 .90
896 A278 $1 multicolored 2.50 2.50
Nos. 893-896 (4) 4.55 4.55

People's Redemption Council government, first anniversary.

Royal Wedding — A279

31c, Couple. 41c, Initials, roses. 62c, St. Paul's Cathedral.
$1, Couple, horiz.

1981, Aug. 12 Litho. *Perf. 14x13½*

897 A279 31c multicolored .65 .65
898 A279 41c multicolored .85 .85
899 A279 62c multicolored 1.50 1.50
Nos. 897-899 (3) 3.00 3.00

Souvenir Sheet

900 A279 $1 multicolored 2.50 2.50

Nos. 897-899 exist imperf. Value, set $7.

John Adams, US President, 1797-1801 — A280

Washington Crossing the Delaware — A281

5c, Wm. H. Harrison. 10c, Martin Van Buren. 17c, James Monroe. 20c, John Q. Adams. 22c, James Madison. 27c, Thomas Jefferson. 30c, Andrew Jackson. 40c, John Tyler. 80c, George Washington.

1981, July 4 *Perf. 11*

901 A280 4c shown .25 .25
902 A280 5c multicolored .25 .25
903 A280 10c multicolored .25 .25
904 A280 17c multicolored .40 .30
905 A280 20c multicolored .45 .35
906 A280 22c multicolored .55 .45
907 A280 27c multicolored .60 .55
908 A280 30c multicolored .70 .60
909 A280 40c multicolored .90 .85
910 A280 80c multicolored 1.90 1.60
Nos. 901-910 (10) 6.25 5.45

Souvenir Sheet

911 A281 $1 multicolored 2.75 2.75

1981, Nov. 26 Litho. *Perf. 11*

6c, Rutherford B. Hayes. 12c, Ulysses S. Grant. 14c, Millard Fillmore. 15c, Zachary Taylor. 20c, Abraham Lincoln. 27c, Andrew Johnson. 31c, James Buchanan. 41c, James A. Garfield. 50c, James K. Polk. 55c, Franklin Pierce.
$1, Washington at Valley Forge.

912 A280 6c multicolored .25 .25
913 A280 12c multicolored .25 .25
914 A280 14c multicolored .25 .25
915 A280 15c multicolored .30 .25
916 A280 20c multicolored .45 .30
917 A280 27c multicolored .50 .45
918 A280 31c multicolored .60 .45
919 A280 41c multicolored .90 .75
920 A280 50c multicolored 1.10 .85
921 A280 55c multicolored 1.20 .90
Nos. 912-921 (10) 5.80 4.70

Souvenir Sheet

922 A281 $1 multicolored 4.25 4.25

1982, Apr. 7 Litho. *Perf. 11*

4c, William H. Taft. 5c, Calvin Coolidge. 6c, Benjamin Harrison. 10c, Warren G. Harding. 22c, Grover Cleveland. 27c, Chester Arthur. 31c, Woodrow Wilson. 41c, William McKinley. 80c, Theodore Roosevelt.
$1, Signing Constitution, horiz.

923 A280 4c multicolored .25 .25
924 A280 5c multicolored .25 .25
925 A280 6c multicolored .25 .25
926 A280 10c multicolored .25 .25
927 A280 22c multicolored .60 .50
928 A280 27c multicolored .75 .75
929 A280 31c multicolored .85 .85
930 A280 41c multicolored 1.00 1.00
931 A280 80c multicolored 1.60 1.60
Nos. 923-931 (9) 5.80 5.70

Souvenir Sheet

932 A281 $1 multicolored 2.75 2.75

1982, July 15 Litho. *Perf. 11*

4c, Jimmy Carter. 6c, Gerald Ford. 14c, Harry Truman. 17c, F. D. Roosevelt. 23c, L. B. Johnson. 27c, Richard Nixon. 31c, John F. Kennedy. 35c, Ronald Reagan. 50c, Herbert Hoover. 55c, Dwight D. Eisenhower.
$1, Battle of Yorktown.

933 A280 4c multicolored .25 .25
934 A280 6c multicolored .25 .25
935 A280 14c multicolored .30 .30
936 A280 17c multicolored .40 .40
937 A280 23c multicolored .45 .45
938 A280 27c multicolored .50 .50
939 A280 31c multicolored .60 .60
940 A280 35c multicolored .75 .75
941 A280 50c multicolored 1.00 1.00
942 A280 55c multicolored 1.20 1.20
Nos. 933-942 (10) 5.70 5.70

Souvenir Sheet

Perf. 14x13½

943 A281 $1 multicolored 2.75 2.75

See No. 1113.

Type of 1976

1981-83 Litho. *Perf. 14½x13½*

Size: 34x20mm

945 A247 1c like #749 .25 .25
946 A247 3c like #750 .25 .25
947 A247 6c like #753 .25 .25
948 A247 15c like #754 .60 .60
949 A247 25c like #757 1.00 1.00
950 A247 31c like #756 1.25 1.25
951 A247 41c like #758 1.75 1.75
952 A247 80c like #759 3.50 3.50
953 A247 $1 like #760 5.00 5.00
Nos. 945-953 (9) 13.85 13.85

Issued: Nos. 946-947, 949, 950, 11/27/81; Nos. 945, 953, 10/12/82; Nos. 948, 951, 12/10/82; No. 952, 11/3/83.

Intl. Year of the Disabled (1981) A282

Designs: Various disabled people.

1982, Mar. 24 Litho. *Perf. 14*

954 A282 23c multi, vert. .50 .45
955 A282 62c multicolored 1.10 1.00

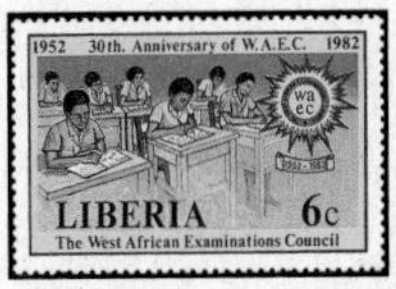

30th Anniv. of West African Examinations Council A283

1982, Mar. 24

956 A283 6c multicolored .25 .25
957 A283 31c multicolored 1.10 1.00

21st Birthday of Princess Diana — A284

31c, 41c, 62c, Diana portraits. $1, Wedding.

1982, July 1 *Perf. 14x13½*

958	A284	31c multicolored	.65	.65
959	A284	41c multicolored	.90	.90
960	A284	62c multicolored	1.50	1.50
		Nos. 958-960 (3)	3.05	3.05

Souvenir Sheet

961	A284	$1 multicolored	2.50	2.50

Nos. 958-961 Overprinted in Silver

1982, Aug. 30 Litho. *Perf. 14x13½*

962	A284	31c multicolored	.65	.65
963	A284	41c multicolored	.90	.90
964	A284	62c multicolored	1.50	1.50
		Nos. 962-964 (3)	3.05	3.05

Souvenir Sheet

965	A284	$1 multicolored	2.50	2.50

Birth of Prince William of Wales, June 21.

3rd Natl. Redemption Day — A285

3c, Fallah Varney. 6c, Samuel Doe. 10c, Jlatoh N. Podier, Jr. 15c, Jeffry S. Gbatu. 31c, Thomas G. Quiwonkpa. 41c, Abraham D. Kollie.

1983, Apr. 5 Litho. *Perf. 13½*

966	A285	3c multicolored	.25	.25
967	A285	6c multicolored	.25	.25
968	A285	10c multicolored	.25	.25
969	A285	15c multicolored	.30	.30
970	A285	31c multicolored	.85	.85
971	A285	41c multicolored	1.40	1.40
		Nos. 966-971 (6)	3.30	3.30

Souvenir Sheet

972	A285	$1 like 6c	2.60	2.60

Natl. Archives Opening A286

Building views.

1983, Apr. 5

973	A286	6c multicolored	*1.25*	*1.25*
974	A286	31c multicolored	*2.25*	*2.25*

Christmas 1983 — A287

Raphael Paintings: 6c, Circumcision of Christ. 15c, Adoration of the Magi. 25c, Announcement to Mary. 31c, Madonna with Baldachin. 41c, Holy Family. 62c, Detail of Madonna with Child Surrounded by Five Saints. $1.25 Madonna of Foligno.

1983, Dec. 14 Litho. *Perf. 13½*

975	A287	6c multicolored	.25	.25
976	A287	15c multicolored	.25	.25
977	A287	25c multicolored	.45	.35
978	A287	31c multicolored	.60	.50
979	A287	41c multicolored	.75	.65
980	A287	62c multicolored	1.00	1.00
		Nos. 975-980 (6)	3.30	3.00

Souvenir Sheet

981	A287	$1.25 multicolored	2.60	1.90

Sheets of 1 showing entire painting exist.

Mano River Union, 10th Anniv. (1983) A288

6c, Training school graduates. 25c, Emblem. 31c, Maps, leaders. 41c, Guinea's accession. 75c, Guinea's accession, diff.

1984, Apr. 6 Litho. *Perf. 14x13½*

982	A288	6c multicolored	.25	.25
983	A288	25c multicolored	.70	.70
984	A288	31c multicolored	.90	.90
985	A288	41c multicolored	1.25	1.25
		Nos. 982-985 (4)	3.10	3.10

Souvenir Sheet

986	A288	75c multicolored	2.60	2.60

4th Natl. Redemption Day — A289

3c, Hospital, New Kru Town. 10c, Ganta-Harper Highway construction. 20c, Constitution Assembly opening. 31c, Doe at highway construction. 41c, Draft Constitution presentation.

1984, Apr. 12 *Perf. 14½*

987	A289	3c multicolored	.25	.25
988	A289	10c multicolored	.25	.25
989	A289	20c multicolored	.45	.45
990	A289	31c multicolored	1.00	1.00
991	A289	41c multicolored	1.40	1.40
		Nos. 987-991 (5)	3.35	3.35

Adoration of the Wise Men, by Rubens (1577-1640) A290

15c, Crowning of Katharina. 25c, Mother and Child Adored by Wise Men. 31c, Madonna and Child with Halo. 41c, Adoration of the Shepherds. 62c, Madonna and Child with Saints.

$1.25, Madonna Adored by Saints.

1984, June 1 Litho. *Perf. 13½*

992	A290	6c shown	.25	.25
993	A290	15c multicolored	.30	.30
994	A290	25c multicolored	.45	.45
995	A290	31c multicolored	.60	.60
996	A290	41c multicolored	.75	.75
997	A290	62c multicolored	1.20	1.20
		Nos. 992-997 (6)	3.55	3.55

Souvenir Sheet

998	A290	$1.25 multicolored	*4.25*	*4.25*

Sheets of 1 showing entire painting exist.

1984 Summer Olympics — A291

3c, Jesse Owens, 1936. 4c, Rafer Johnson, 1960. 25c, Miruts Yifter, 1980. 41c, Kipchoge Keino, 1968, 1972. 62c, Muhammad Ali, 1960. $1.25, Wilma Rudolph, 1960, horiz.

1984, July 2 *Perf. 13½x14*

999	A291	3c multicolored	.25	.25
1000	A291	4c multicolored	.25	.25
1001	A291	25c multicolored	.75	.75
1002	A291	41c multicolored	1.20	1.20
1003	A291	62c multicolored	2.00	2.00
		Nos. 999-1003 (5)	4.45	4.45

Souvenir Sheet

Perf. 14x13½

1004	A291	$1.25 multicolored	4.25	4.25

1984 Louisiana Expo — A292

6c, Water birds. 31c, Ship, Buchanan Harbor. 41c, Fish. 62c, Train carrying iron ore.

1984, July 24 *Perf. 14½*

1005	A292	6c multicolored	.25	.25
1006	A292	31c multicolored	1.00	1.00
1007	A292	41c multicolored	1.25	1.25
1008	A292	62c multicolored	2.00	2.00
		Nos. 1005-1008 (4)	4.50	4.50

Pygmy Hippopotamus, World Wildlife Fund Emblem A293

Various pygmy hippopotomi.

1984, Nov. 22 Litho. *Perf. 14½*

1009	A293	6c multicolored	.75	.75
1010	A293	10c multicolored	1.00	1.00
1011	A293	20c multicolored	2.75	2.75
1012	A293	31c multicolored	4.00	4.00
		Nos. 1009-1012 (4)	8.50	8.50

Exist imperf.

Indigent Children Home, Bensonville A294

First Lady Mrs. Nancy Doe and various children.

1984, Dec. 14

1013	A294	6c multicolored	.25	.25
1014	A294	31c multicolored	1.00	1.00

Natl. Redemption Day, Apr. 12 — A295

6c, Army barracks, Monrovia. 31c, Pan-African Plaza, Monrovia.

1985, Apr. 5 Litho. *Perf. 14½*

1015	A295	6c multicolored	.25	.25
1016	A295	31c multicolored	1.00	1.00

Liberian Revolution, fifth anniv.

Audubon Birth Bicentenary A296

Illustrations by artist/naturalist J. J. Audubon: 1c, Bohemian waxwing. 3c, Bay-breasted warbler. 6c, White-winged crossbill. 31c, Red phalarope. 41c, Eastern bluebird. 62c, Northern cardinal.

1985, Apr. 5

1017	A296	1c multicolored	.25	.25
1018	A296	3c multicolored	.25	.25
1019	A296	6c multicolored	.30	.25
1020	A296	31c multicolored	1.10	1.00
1021	A296	41c multicolored	1.60	.75
1022	A296	62c multicolored	2.25	2.00
		Nos. 1017-1022 (6)	5.75	4.50

Venus and Mirror — A297

Paintings (details) by Rubens: 15c, Adam & Eve in Paradise. 25c, Andromeda. 31c, The Three Graces. 41c, Venus & Adonis. 62c, The Daughters of Leucippus. $1.25, The Judgement of Paris.

1985, Nov. 14 Litho. *Perf. 14*

1023	A297	6c multicolored	.25	.25
1024	A297	15c multicolored	.55	.55
1025	A297	25c multicolored	.85	.85
1026	A297	31c multicolored	1.00	1.00
1027	A297	41c multicolored	1.40	1.40
1028	A297	62c multicolored	2.40	2.40
		Nos. 1023-1028 (6)	6.45	6.45

Souvenir Sheet

1029	A297	$1.25 multicolored	3.25	3.25

Sheets of 1 showing entire painting exist.

1986 World Cup Soccer Championships, Mexico — A298

6c, Germany-Morocco, 1970. 15c, Zaire-Brazil, 1974. 25c, Tunisia-Germany, 1978. 31c, Cameroun-Peru, 1982, vert. 41c, Algeria-Germany, 1982. 62c, 1986 Senegal team.

$1.25, Liberia-Nigeria.

1985, Nov. 14

1030	A298	6c multicolored	.25	.25
1031	A298	15c multicolored	.35	.35
1032	A298	25c multicolored	.60	.60
1033	A298	31c multicolored	.85	.85
1034	A298	41c multicolored	1.10	1.10
1035	A298	62c multicolored	1.60	1.60
		Nos. 1030-1035 (6)	4.75	4.75

Souvenir Sheet

1036	A298	$1.25 multicolored	3.25	3.25

Queen Mother, 85th Birthday — A299

31c, Elizabeth in garter robes. 41c, At the races. 62c, In garden, waving.

$1.25, Wearing diadem.

1985, Dec. 12 Litho. *Perf. 14½*

1037	A299	31c multicolored	.60	.60
1038	A299	41c multicolored	.85	.85
1039	A299	62c multicolored	1.20	1.20
		Nos. 1037-1039 (3)	2.65	2.65

Souvenir Sheet

1040	A299	$1.25 multicolored	2.25	2.25

World Food Day — A300

1985, Dec. 12

1041	A300	25c multicolored	.75	.70
1042	A300	31c multicolored	1.25	1.00

AMERIPEX '86 — A301

25c, The Alamo. 31c, Liberty Bell. 80c, #344, 802, C102.

1986, June 10 Litho. *Perf. 14½*

1043	A301	25c multicolored	1.00	.65
1044	A301	31c multicolored	1.10	.85
1045	A301	80c multicolored	2.90	2.10
		Nos. 1043-1045 (3)	5.00	3.60

Statue of Liberty, Cent. — A302

20c, Unveiling, 1886. 31c, Frederic A. Bartholdi. $1, Statue close-up.

1986, June 10

1046	A302	20c	multicolored	.50	.50
1047	A302	31c	multicolored	.90	.90
1048	A302	$1	multicolored	2.75	2.75
			Nos. 1046-1048 (3)	4.15	4.15

1988 Winter Olympics, Calgary A303

1984 Gold medalists: 3c, Max Julen, Switzerland, men's giant slalom. 6c, Debbie Armstrong, U.S., women's giant slalom. 31c, Peter Angerer, West Germany, biathlon. 60c, Bill Johnson, U.S., men's downhill. 80c, East Germany, 4-man bobsled. $1.25, H. Stangassinger, F. Wembacher, West Germany, 2-man luge.

1987, Aug. 21 Litho. *Perf. 14*

1049	A303	3c	multicolored	.25	.25
1050	A303	6c	multicolored	.25	.25
1051	A303	31c	multicolored	.70	.70
1052	A303	60c	multicolored	1.40	1.40
1053	A303	80c	multicolored	1.60	1.60
			Nos. 1049-1053 (5)	4.20	4.20

Souvenir Sheet

1054	A303	$1.25	multicolored	2.25	2.25

City of Berlin, 750th Anniv. — A304

6c, State (Royal) Theater in the Gendarmenmarkt, c. 1820, architect Schinkel. 31c, Kaiser Friedrich Museum, Museum Is. on River Spree. 60c, Charlottenburg Castle, 17th cent. 80c, Modern church bell tower & Kaiser Wilhelm Gedachtniskirche. $1.50, MIRAK rocket development, Spaceship Society Airfield, Reinickendorf, 1930.

1987, Sept. 4

1055	A304	6c	multicolored	.25	.25
1056	A304	31c	multicolored	.70	.70
1057	A304	60c	multicolored	1.40	1.40
1058	A304	80c	multicolored	1.60	1.60
			Nos. 1055-1058 (4)	3.95	3.95

Souvenir sheet

Perf. 11½

1059	A304	$1.50	buff & dk brown	3.50	3.50

No. 1059 contains one 25x61mm stamp.

Shakespearean Plays — A305

1987, Nov. 6 Litho. *Perf. 14*

1060	A305	Sheet of 8	6.50	6.50
a.		3c Othello	.25	.25
b.		6c Romeo & Juliet	.25	.25
c.		10c The Merry Wives of Windsor	.25	.25
d.		15c Henry IV	.25	.25
e.		31c Hamlet	.45	.45
f.		60c Macbeth	.90	.90
g.		80c King Lear	1.10	1.10
h.		$2 Shakespeare and the Globe Theater, 1598	2.75	2.75

Amateur Radio Association, 25th Anniv. — A306

No. 1061, Emblem. No. 1062, Village. No. 1063, On-the-Air certificate. No. 1064, Globe, flags.

1987, Nov. 23 Litho. *Perf. 14*

1061	A306	10c	multicolored	.35	.35
1062	A306	10c	multicolored	.35	.35
1063	A306	35c	multicolored	1.20	1.20
1064	A306	35c	multicolored	1.20	1.20
			Nos. 1061-1064 (4)	3.10	3.10

Miniature Sheets

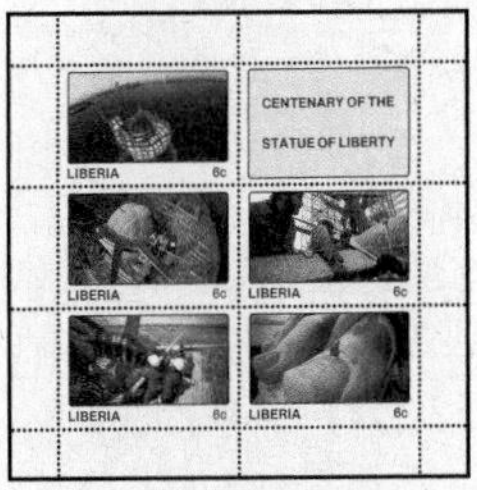

Statue of Liberty, Cent. (in 1986) — A307

No. 1065: a, Torch, southern view of NYC. b, Overhead view of crown and scaffold. c, 4 workmen repairing crown. d, 5 workmen, crown. e, Statue's right foot.

No. 1066: a, Tall ship, statue. b, Bay Queen ferry. c, Statue on poster at a construction site, NYC. d, Tug boat, tall ship. e, Building frieze.

No. 1067: a, Statue flanked by fireworks. b, Lighting of the statue. c, Crown observatory illuminated. d, Statue surrounded by fireworks. e, Crown and torch observatories illuminated.

No. 1068: a, Liberty "Happy Birthday" poster at a construction site. b, Ships in NY Harbor. c, Woman renovating statue nose. d, Man & woman renovating nose. e, Man, nose. #1068a-1068e vert.

1987, Dec. 10 *Perf. 13½*

1065	A307	Sheet of 5 + label	1.10	1.10
a.-e.		6c any single	.25	.25
1066	A307	Sheet of 5 + label	2.25	2.25
a.-e.		15c any single	.40	.40
1067	A307	Sheet of 5 + label	4.25	4.25
a.-e.		31c any single	.80	.80
1068	A307	Sheet of 5 + label	7.50	7.50
a.-e.		60c any single	1.40	1.40
		Nos. 1065-1068 (4)	15.10	

Nos. 1065-1068 contain label inscribed "CENTENARY OF THE STATUE OF LIBERTY" in two or five lines.

Second Republic, 2nd Anniv. — A308

Design: Natl. flag, coat of arms, hand grip, Pres. Doe and Vice Pres. Moniba.

1988, Jan. 6 *Perf. 14½*

1069	A308	10c	multicolored	.45	.45
1070	A308	35c	multicolored	.90	.90

UN Child Survival Campaign A309

3c, Breast-feeding. 6c, Oral rehydration therapy, vert. 31c, Immunization. $1, Growth monitoring, vert.

1988, Jan. 15 *Perf. 13x13½, 13½x13*

1071	A309	3c	multicolored	.25	.25
1072	A309	6c	multicolored	.25	.25
1073	A309	31c	multicolored	1.60	1.60
1074	A309	$1	multicolored	4.50	2.90
			Nos. 1071-1074 (4)	6.60	5.00

Inauguration of the Second Republic — A310

Design: Pres. Doe greeting Chief Justice Emmanuel N. Gbalazeh.

1988, Jan. 15 *Perf. 13x13½*

1075	A310	6c	multicolored	.30	.30

Samuel Kanyon Doe Sports Complex, Opened Apr. 12, 1986 — A311

1988, Jan. 15

1076	A311	31c	multicolored	.90	.90

Green (Agricultural) Revolution A312

1988, Apr. 4 *Perf. 15*

1077	A312	10c	multicolored	.35	.35
1078	A312	35c	multicolored	1.20	1.20

US Peace Corps in Liberia, 25th Anniv. — A313

1988, Apr. 4

1079	A313	10c	multicolored	.35	.35
1080	A313	35c	multicolored	1.20	1.20

Souvenir Sheet

1988 Summer Olympics, Seoul — A314

1988, Apr. 14 *Perf. 14*

1081	A314	$3	multicolored	7.50	7.50

Organization of African Unity, 25th Anniv. — A315

1988, May 25

1082	A315	10c	multicolored	.35	.35
1083	A315	35c	multicolored	1.10	1.10
1084	A315	$1	multicolored	3.50	3.50
			Nos. 1082-1084 (3)	4.95	4.95

Rail Transport — A316

10c, GP10 at Nimba. 35c, Triple-headed iron ore train.

No. 1087, King Edward II, 1930. No. 1088, GWR 57 No. 3697, 1941. No. 1089, GWR 0-4-2T No. 1408, 1932. No. 1090, GWR No. 7034 Ince Castle, 1950.

1988, July 30 Litho. *Perf. 14½*

1085	A316	10c	multicolored	.50	.50
1086	A316	35c	multicolored	1.40	1.40

Souvenir Sheets

Perf. 11

1087	A316	$2	multicolored	*4.25*	*4.25*
1088	A316	$2	multicolored	*4.25*	*4.25*
1089	A316	$2	multicolored	*4.25*	*4.25*
1090	A316	$2	multicolored	*4.25*	*4.25*

Nos. 1087-1090 contain one 64x44mm stamp each.

Nos. 1087-1090 with Added Text

1993, Aug. 3 Souvenir Sheets

1087a	With added text in margin	6.00	6.00
1088a	With added text in margin	6.00	6.00
1089a	With added text in margin	6.00	6.00
1090a	With added text in margin	6.00	6.00

Added text on Nos. 1087a-1090a reads: "25th ANNIVERSARY OF THE LAST STEAM TRAIN TO / RUN ON BRITISH RAIL 1968-1993."

1988 Summer Olympics, Seoul — A317

10c, Baseball. 35c, Hurdles. 45c, Fencing. 80c, Synchronized swimming. $1, Yachting. $1.50, Tennis.

1988, Sept. 13 Litho.

1091	A317	10c	multicolored	.25	.25
1092	A317	35c	multicolored	.65	.65
1093	A317	45c	multicolored	.90	.90
1094	A317	80c	multicolored	1.50	1.50
1095	A317	$1	multicolored	2.00	2.00
			Nos. 1091-1095 (5)	5.30	5.30

Souvenir Sheet

1096	A317	$1.50	multicolored	2.25	2.25

Intl. Tennis Federation, 75th anniv. ($1.50).

St. Joseph's Catholic Hospital, 25th Anniv. — A318

No. 1098, Hospital, 4 staff members. No. 1099, St. John of God. No. 1100, Doctor, nurse, map.

1988, Aug. 26 Litho. *Perf. 14½*

1097	A318	10c	shown	.25	.25
1098	A318	10c	multicolored	.25	.25
1099	A318	35c	multicolored	.70	.70
1100	A318	$1	multicolored	2.00	2.00
			Nos. 1097-1100 (4)	3.20	3.20

Common Design Types pictured following the introduction.

Lloyds of London, 300th Anniv.

Common Design Type

CD341

Designs: 10c, Royal Exchange destroyed by fire, 1838, vert. 35c, Air Liberia BN2A aircraft. 45c, Supertanker Chevron Antwerp. $1, Lakonia on fire off Madeira, 1963, vert.

1988, Oct. 31 Litho. *Perf. 14*

1101	CD341	10c	multicolored	.25	.25
1102	CD341	35c	multicolored	.75	.75
1103	CD341	45c	multicolored	1.00	1.00
1104	CD341	$1	multicolored	2.25	2.25
			Nos. 1101-1104 (4)	4.25	4.25

Sasa Players — A319

10c, Monkey bridge, vert. 45c, Snake dancers, vert.

Perf. 14x14½, 14½x14

1988, Sept. 30 Litho.

1105	A319	10c multicolored	.35	.35
1106	A319	35c shown	1.00	1.00
1107	A319	45c multicolored	1.40	1.40
		Nos. 1105-1107 (3)	2.75	2.75

Intl. Fund for Agricultural Development, 10th Anniv. — A320

10c, Crops. 35c, Spraying crops, livestock.

1988, Oct. 7 Litho. *Perf. 14x14½*

1108	A320	10c multicolored	.40	.40
1109	A320	35c multicolored	1.50	1.50

3rd Anniv. of the 2nd Republic A321

10c, Pres. Doe, officials. 50c, Pres. Doe, doctor.

1989, Jan. 6 Litho. *Perf. 14*

1110	A321	10c multicolored	.35	.35
1111	A321	35c like 10c	1.10	1.10
1112	A321	50c multicolored	1.75	1.75
		Nos. 1110-1112 (3)	3.20	3.20

US Presidents Type of 1981-82

1989, Jan. 20 *Perf. 13½x14*

1113	A280	$1 George Bush	2.60	2.60

Rissho Kosei-Kai Buddhist Assoc., Tokyo, 50th Anniv. — A322

Natl. flags and: No. 1114, "Harmony" in Japanese. No. 1115, Organization headquarters, Tokyo. No. 1116, Nikkyo Niwano, founder. 50c, Statue of Buddha in the Great Sacred Hall.

1989, Feb. 28 Litho. *Perf. 14x14½*

1114	A322	10c multicolored	.45	.45
1115	A322	10c multicolored	.45	.45
1116	A322	10c multicolored	.45	.45
1117	A322	50c multicolored	2.00	2.00
		Nos. 1114-1117 (4)	3.35	3.35

Liberian-Japanese friendship.

Souvenir Sheet

Emperor Hirohito of Japan (1901-1989) — A323

Commemorative coins: a, Silver. b, Gold.

1989, Feb. 28 Unwmk. *Perf. 14½*

1118	A323	Sheet of 2	6.00	6.00
a.-b.		75c any single	2.50	2.50

For overprint see No. 1147.

Mano River Union, 15th Anniv. — A324

Natl. flag, crest and: 10c, Union Glass Factory, Gardnersville, Monrovia. 35c, Pres. Doe, Momoh of Sierra Leone and Conte of Guinea. 45c, Monrovia-Freetown Highway. 50c, Sierra Leone-Guinea land postal services. $1, Communique, 1988 summit.

Unwmk.

1989, May 8 Litho. *Perf. 14*

1119	A324	10c multicolored	.30	.30
1120	A324	35c multicolored	1.00	1.00
1121	A324	45c multicolored	1.25	1.25
1122	A324	50c multicolored	1.40	1.40
1123	A324	$1 multicolored	2.75	2.75
		Nos. 1119-1123 (5)	6.70	6.70

World Telecommunications Day — A325

1989, May 17 Litho. *Perf. 12½*

1124	A325	50c multicolored	1.25	1.25

Common Design Type

Moon Landing, 20th Anniv. — CD342

Apollo 11: 10c, Recovery ship USS Okinawa. 35c, Buzz Aldrin, Neil Armstrong and Michael Collins. 45c, Mission emblem. $1, Aldrin steps on the Moon. $2, Aldrin preparing to conduct experiments on the Moon's surface.

Perf. 14x13½, 14 (35c, 45c)

1989, July 20 Litho. Wmk. 384

Size of Nos. 1126-1127: 29x29mm

1125	CD342	10c multicolored	.25	.25
1126	CD342	35c multicolored	.75	.75
1127	CD342	45c multicolored	1.00	1.00
1128	CD342	$1 multicolored	2.25	2.25
		Nos. 1125-1128 (4)	4.25	4.25

Souvenir Sheet

1129	CD342	$2 multicolored	4.25	4.25

Souvenir Sheet

The Women's March on Versailles — A326

1989, July 7 Wmk. 384 *Perf. 14*

1130	A326	$1.50 multicolored	3.00	3.00

French revolution, bicent., PHILEXFRANCE '89.

Souvenir Sheet

Renovation and Re-dedication of the Statue of Liberty, 1986 — A327

Photographs: a, Workman. b, French dignitary, US flag. c, Dignitaries at ceremony, statue.

Perf. 14x13½

1989, Oct. 2 Litho. Wmk. 373

1131	A327	Sheet of 3	1.75	1.75
a.-c.		25c any single	.55	.55

World Stamp Expo '89 and PHILEXFRANCE '89.

Souvenir Sheet

A328

1989, Nov. 17 Unwmk. *Perf. 14½*

1132	A328	$2 black	4.50	4.50

World Stamp Expo '89, Washington, DC.

Jawaharlal Nehru, 1st Prime Minister of Independent India — A329

45c, Nehru, signature, flag. 50c, Nehru, signature.

1989, Dec. 22 Unwmk. *Perf. 14*

1133	A329	45c multicolored	.75	.75
1134	A329	50c multicolored	1.90	1.90

New Standard-A Earth Satellite Station — A330

1990, Jan. 5

1135	A330	10c shown	.25	.25
1136	A330	35c multi, diff.	1.00	1.00

US Educational & Cultural Foundation in Liberia, 25th Anniv. (in 1989) — A331

1990, Jan. 5

1137	A331	10c multicolored	.25	.25
1138	A331	45c multicolored	1.10	1.10

Pan-African Postal Union, 10th Anniv. — A332

1990, Jan. 18 *Perf. 13x12½*

1139	A332	35c multicolored	.80	.80

Flags of Liberian Counties — A333

Designs: a, Bomi. b, Bong. c, Grand Bassa. d, Grand Cape Mount. e, Grand Gedeh. f, Grand Kru. g, Lofa. h, Margibi. i, Maryland. j, Montserrado. k, Nimba. l, Rivercess. m, Sinoe.

Perf. 14x13½

1990, Mar. 2 Litho. Unwmk.

1140		Strip of 13	5.00	5.00
a.-m.	A333	10c any single	.30	.30
1141		Strip of 13	13.00	13.00
a.-m.	A333	35c any single	1.00	1.00
1142		Strip of 13	15.00	15.00
a.-m.	A333	45c any single	1.10	1.10
1143		Strip of 13	20.00	20.00
a.-m.	A333	50c any single	1.40	1.40
1144		Strip of 13	37.50	37.50
a.-m.	A333	$1 any single	2.75	2.75
		Nos. 1140-1144 (5)	90.50	90.50

Queen Mother, 90th Birthday

Common Design Types

Designs: 10c, At age 6. $2, At age 22.

Perf. 14x15

1991, Oct. 28 Wmk. 384

1145	CD343	10c multicolored	.25	.25

Perf. 14½

1146	CD344	$2 brn & blk	3.00	3.00

For overprints see Nos. 1162-1163.

No. 1118 Overprinted

Perf. 14½

1991, Nov. 16 Litho. Unwmk.

1147	A323	Sheet of 2	3.50	3.50
a.-b.		75c any single	1.50	1.50

National Unity A334

Designs: 35c, Hands clasp over map of Liberia. 45c, Liberian flag, hands, African map. 50c, All Liberia conference, March 1991, conferees, flag, map.

1991, Dec. 30 *Perf. 13½*

1148	A334	35c multicolored	1.00	1.00
1149	A334	45c multicolored	1.25	1.25
1150	A334	50c multicolored	1.40	1.40
		Nos. 1148-1150 (3)	3.65	3.65

1992 Summer Olympics, Barcelona A335

1992, Aug. 7 Litho. *Perf. 14*

1151	A335	45c Boxing	1.50	1.25
1152	A335	50c Soccer	1.60	1.40
1153	A335	$1 Weight lifting	3.25	2.75
1154	A335	$2 Water polo	6.00	5.50
		Nos. 1151-1154 (4)	12.35	10.90

Souvenir Sheet

1155	A335	$1.50 Running	6.00	6.00

Disarmament A336

Designs: 50c, Disarm today. $1, Join your parents & build Liberia. $2, Peace must prevail in Liberia.

1993, Feb. 10 Litho. *Perf. 13½x14*

1156	A336	50c multicolored	1.50	1.50
1157	A336	$1 multicolored	2.90	2.90
1158	A336	$2 multicolored	5.50	5.50
		Nos. 1156-1158 (3)	9.90	9.90

See Nos. 1237-1239.

Miniature Sheets

Flora and Fauna — A337

No. 1159 — Flora: a, Papaya. b, Sausage tree. c, Angraecum eichlerianum. d, Arachnis flos-aeris. e, Screw pine. f, African tulip tree. g, Coffee tree. h, Bolusiella talbotii. i, Bulbophyllum lepidum. j, Oeceoclades maculata. k, Plectrelminthus caudatus. l, Diaphananthe rutila.

No. 1160 — Fauna: a, Diana monkey. b, Flying squirrel. c, Egyptian rousette. d, Serval. e, Potto. f, Chimpanzee. g, African horned chameleon. h, Royal python. i, Golden cat. j, Banded duiker. k, Pygmy hippopotamus. l, Water chevrotain.

No. 1161 — Birds: a, Grey heron. b, Bat hawk. c, Martial eagle. d, Little sparrow hawk. e, Hoopoe. f, Red bishop. g, Purple-throated sunbird. h, African fish eagle. i, African grey parrot. j, Black-crowned night heron. k, Swallow. l, Great white egret.

1993-94 Litho. *Perf. 14*

1159 A337 70c Sheet of 12, #a.-l. 25.00 25.00
1160 A337 90c Sheet of 12, #a.-l. 27.50 27.50
1161 A337 $1 Sheet of 12, #a.-l. 24.00 24.00
Nos. 1159-1161 (3) 76.50 76.50

Issued: 70c, 10/14; 90c, 11/18; $1, 1/14/94.

Nos. 1145-1146 Ovptd. with Hong Kong '94 Emblem

Perf. 14x15

1994, Feb. 18 Litho. Wmk. 384

1162 CD343 10c multicolored .35 .35

Perf. 14½

1163 CD344 $2 multicolored 5.25 5.25

Miniature Sheet

Roberts Field, Monrovia, 50th Anniv. — A338

No. 1164: a, Vickers Supermarine Spitfire Mk IX. b, Boeing B-17G. c, Douglas A-20 Boston. d, North American B-25J Mitchell. e, Beech C-45 Expeditor. f, Douglas C-54. g, Piper L4 Cub. h, Martin PBM-3C.

1994, July 11 Litho. *Perf. 13½x13*

1164 A338 35c Sheet of 8, #a.-h. + label 10.00 10.00

Souvenir Sheets

Locomotives — A339

Designs: No. 1165, $1, Class A3 #60044 Melton, Class A4 #60017 Silver Fox. No. 1166, $1, GWR 2-6-2 Prairie Tank #4561. No. 1167, $1, GWR 2-6-2 Small Prairie. No. 1168, $1, GWR Castle Class 4-6-0 No. Kingswear Castle. No. 1169, $1, GWR 0-6-0 Pannier Tank. No. 1170, $1, Bong Mining Company diesel hauling iron ore.

1994, Aug. 16 Litho. *Perf. 14*

1165-1170 A339 Set of 6 14.00 14.00

See Nos. 1194-1199, 1205.

Liberian Natl. Red Cross, 75th Anniv. — A340

Designs: 70c, No. 1172, Globe. No. 1173, $2, Jean-Henri Dunant.

1994, Oct. 3 Litho. *Perf. 14½x14*

1171 A340 70c multicolored 1.90 1.90
1172 A340 $1 multicolored 2.50 2.50
1173 A340 $1 multicolored 2.50 2.50
1174 A340 $2 multicolored 5.50 5.50
Nos. 1171-1174 (4) 12.40 12.40

End of World War II, 50th Anniv.
Common Design Types

Designs: 70c, Sunderland on U-boat patrol. 90c, US Army Engineer Task Force. $1, MV Abosso sunk off Liberia, 1942. No. 1178, MV Adda sunk off Liberia, 1941.

No. 1179, Obverse of U.S. Victory Medal depicting Liberty.

1995, May 8 Litho. *Perf. 13½*

1175 CD351 70c multicolored 1.75 1.00
1176 CD351 90c multicolored 2.00 1.40
1177 CD351 $1 multicolored 2.50 1.50
1178 CD351 $2 multicolored 4.50 2.75
Nos. 1175-1178 (4) 10.75 6.65

Souvenir Sheet

Perf. 14

1179 CD352 $2 multicolored 4.50 4.50

Wild Animals — A341

1995, June 1 *Perf. 14*

1180 A341 70c Cheetah 2.00 2.00
1181 A341 70c Giraffe 2.00 2.00
1182 A341 90c Rhinoceros 2.00 2.00
1183 A341 $1 Elephant 3.00 3.00
1184 A341 $2 Lion 6.00 6.00
Nos. 1180-1184 (5) 15.00 15.00

Souvenir Sheet

1995 IAAF World Track & Field Championships, Gothenburg — A342

No. 1185: a, Merlene Ottey. b, Heike Drechsler.

1995, Aug. 4 Litho. *Perf. 14*

1185 A342 $1 Sheet of 2, #a.-b. 8.50 8.50

Miniature Sheet

Orchids — A343

No. 1186: a, Ancistrochilus rothschildianus. b, Disa uniflora. c, Polystachya ottoniana. d, Aerangis brachycarpa. e, Plectrelminthus caudatus. f, Polystachya bella. g, Ansellia africana. h, Bulbophyllum cochleatum.

1995, Sept. 1 *Perf. 13*

1186 A343 70c Sheet of 8, #a.-h. + label 17.00 17.00

Singapore '95.

UN, 50th Anniv.
Common Design Type

Designs: 25c, UN Land Rovers. 50c, Delivering food supplies. $1, Ilyushin IL-76 freighter airlifting supplies. $2, MIL MI-8 helicopter.

1995, Oct. 24 Litho. *Perf. 14*

1187 CD353 25c multicolored .90 .90
1188 CD353 50c multicolored 1.50 1.50
1189 CD353 $1 multicolored 3.00 3.00
1190 CD353 $2 multicolored 5.50 5.50
Nos. 1187-1190 (4) 10.90 10.90

Economic Community of West African States, 20th Anniv. — A344

Designs: 25c, Map, Liberian flag, soldiers, civilians. 50c, Soldier carrying child, vert. $1, Logo, vert.

Perf. 13½x13, 13½x13

1995, Nov. 10 Litho.

1191 A344 25c multicolored .75 .75
1192 A344 50c multicolored 1.50 1.50
1193 A344 $1 multicolored 3.00 3.00
Nos. 1191-1193 (3) 5.25 5.25

Train Type of 1994
Souvenir Sheets

Designs: No. 1194, $1, 4-4-0 locomotive 11 "The Reno," galloping horses. No. 1195, $1, Halwill station, Southern Region T9 class locomotive #30719. No. 1196, $1, GWR 0-4-2T "1400" class locomotive #1408, cricket match. No. 1197, $1, LMS Jubilee class 4-6-0, #45684 "Jutland," Kettering station. No. 1198, $1, GWR 2-6-2 "Prairie" locomotive #4547, Lustleigh station. No. 1199, $1, Wainwright "H" class 0-4-4T locomotive, winter countryside.

1996, Feb. 29 Litho. *Perf. 14x15*

1194-1199 A339 Set of 6 15.00 15.00

Modern Olympic Games, Cent. — A345

1996, Apr. 22 Litho. *Perf. 13*

1200 A345 20c Runners .60 .60
1201 A345 35c Boxing 1.00 1.00
1202 A345 50c Javelin 1.40 1.40
1203 A345 $1 Hurdles 2.75 2.75
Nos. 1200-1203 (4) 5.75 5.75

Butterflies — A346

No. 1204: a, Papilio zalmoxis. b, Papilio dardanus. c, Charaxes varanes. d, Acraea natalica. e, Euphaedra neophron. f, Craphium antheus. g, Salamis anacardii. h, Kallima cymodoce. i, Precis hierta.

1996, May 22 Litho. *Perf. 13½*

1204 A346 70c Sheet of 9, #a.-i. 14.00 14.00

Train Type of 1994
Souvenir Sheet

Design: G4a Class Pacific locomotive, Canadian Pacific Railroad.

1996, June 8 Litho. *Perf. 14x15*

1205 A339 $1 multi 2.25 2.25

CAPEX '96.

Fish — A347

No. 1206: a, Atlantic Sailfish. b, Guinean flyingfish. c, Blue marlin. d, Little tunny (e). e, Common dolphinfish (f). f, Guachanche barracuda. g, Guinean parrotfish. h, Cadenat's chromis (g). i, Dusky grouper (h). j, Hoefler's butterflyfish (k). k, African hind (l). l, West African Angelfish.

1996, July 15 Litho. *Perf. 14*

1206 A347 90c Sheet of 12, #a.-l. 20.00 20.00

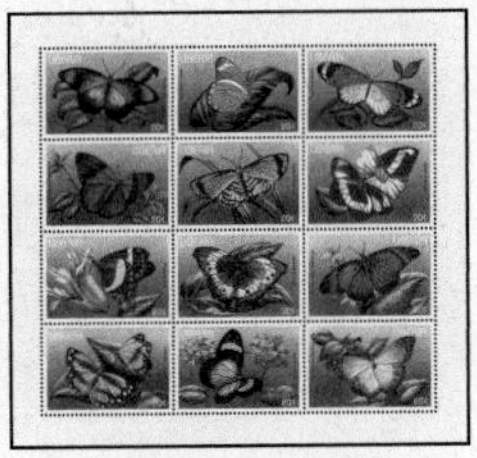

Butterflies — A348

No. 1207: a, Euphaedra judith. b, Euphaedra eleus. c, Acraea encedon. d, Euphaedra neophron. e, Liptena praestans. f, Neptis exalenca. g, Palla decius. h, Salamis cytora. i, Pseudacraea dolomena. j, Anaphaeis eriphia. k, Euphaedra themis. l, Hadrodontes varanes.

No. 1208: a, Papilio mnestheus. b, Papilio nobilis. c, Graphium antheus. d, Asterope benguelae. e, Graphium illyris. f, Emphaedra eupalus. g, Charaxes protoclea. h, Cymothoe beckeri. i, Euphaedra cyparissa. j, Coliades chalybe. k, Mimacraea neokoton. l, Charaxes ethalion.

$2, Charaxes pelias.

1996 Litho. *Perf. 14*

1207 A348 20c Sheet of 12, #a.-l. 7.50 7.50
1208 A348 25c Sheet of 12, #a.-l. 8.00 8.00

Souvenir Sheet

1209 A348 $2 multicolored 4.50 4.50

Birds A349

Designs, horiz: 35c, African jacana. 50c, Pel's fishing owl. $1, Paradise whydah.

No. 1213: a, Turtle dove. b, Bee-eater. c, Golden oriole. d, Pied flycatcher. e, Sardinian warbler. f, Goliath heron. g, Rock thrush. h, Kestrel. i, Cattle egret. j, Woodchat shrike. k, Hoopoe. l, Great egret.

No. 1214, horiz: a, Red faced crimsonwing. b, Egyptian goose. c, African pitta. d, Paradise flycatcher. e, Garganey. f, Southern carmine bee-eater. g, Fulvous whistling duck. h, Village weaver. i, Martial eagle.

$2, Pintail duck, horiz.

1996

1210-1212 A349 Set of 3 4.50 4.50
1213 A349 25c Sheet of 12, #a.-l. 7.25 7.25
1214 A349 35c Sheet of 9, #a.-i. 8.00 8.00

Souvenir Sheet

1215 A349 $2 multicolored 4.75 4.75

Marilyn Monroe (1926-62) — A350

1996

1216 A350 20c multicolored .70 .70

No. 1216 was issued in sheets of 16.

UNICEF, 50th Anniv. — A351

Designs: 35c, Education for all. 70c, Health care. $1, Children first.

1996, Sept. 16 ***Perf. 13½x13***

1217-1219 A351 35c Set of 3 5.50 5.50

1996 Summer Olympic Games, Atlanta — A352

Designs: No. 1220, 20c, Cricket (discontinued sport), vert. No. 1221, 20c, Babe Didrikson, vert. No. 1222, 35c, Vitaly Scherbo, winner of 6 gold medals, 1992, vert. No. 1223, 35c, Betty Robinson, vert. No. 1224, 50c, Cuban baseball team, gold medal, 1992. No. 1225, 50c, Ancient Greek wall painting of boxers, vert. No. 1226, $1, Stadium, Barcelona, 1992. No. 1227, $1, Stadium, Amsterdam, 1928, vert.

No. 1228, 35c, vert. — Olympic events: a, Men's athletics. b, Men's gymnastics. c, Weight lifting. d, Women's volleyball. e, Women's diving. f, Women's gymnastics. g, Women's track. h, Women's tennis. i, Discus.

No. 1229, 35c, vert. — Boxing gold medalists, boxing: a, Tyrell Biggs, U.S. b, Isan Gura, Tanzania (no medal). c, Mark Breland, U.S. d, Teofilo Stevenson, Cuba. e, Ray Leonard, U.S. f, Michael Spinks, U.S. g, Joe Frazier, U.S. h, Floyd Patterson, US. i, George Foreman, US. $2, Evelyn Ashford.

1996 **Litho.** ***Perf. 14***

1220-1227 A352 Set of 8 14.00

Sheets of 9, #a-i

1228-1229 A352 Set of 2 22.50

Souvenir Sheet

1230 A352 $2 multicolored 7.00

Flowers and Flowering Trees — A353

No. 1231: a, Olive tree. b, Olive flower. c, Fig tree. d, Almond tree. e, Almug tree. f, Cedar. g, Pomegranate (b). h, Citron. i, Date palm (d, e, j). j, Date palm (fruit). k, Cedar of Lebanon. l, Rock rose. m, Narcissus. n, Oleander (i). o, Date palm (flower). p, Shittah tree. q, Hyacinth. r, Barley, flax (s). s, Grape vine. t, Lily of the field. u, Mandrake. v, Caper desire. w, Madonna lily. x, Aloe (s). y, Date palm tree.

1996

1231 A353 25c Sheet of 25, #a.-y. 25.00 25.00

History of Rock and Roll A354

No. 1232: a, Wilson Pickett. b, Bill Haley. c, Otis Redding. d, Fats Domino. e, Buddy Holly. f, Chubby Checker. g, Marvin Gaye. h, Jimi Hendrix.

1996 ***Perf. 13½x14***

1232 A354 35c Sheet of 8, #a.-h. + label 8.00 8.00

Kingfisher — A355

No. 1233 — Kingfishers: a, Striped. b, Grey-headed. c, Pied. d, Giant. e, Shining-blue.

1996, Oct. 7 **Litho.** ***Perf. 13½***

1233 A355 75c Strip of 5, #a.-e. 7.50 7.50

See No. 1236.

Mao Zedong, 20th Anniv. of Death — A356

1996, Nov. 1 **Litho.** ***Perf. 14½x14***

1234 A356 $1 shown 2.50 2.50
1235 A356 $1 As older man 2.50 2.50

Kingfisher Type of 1996

Souvenir Sheet

1997, Feb. 3 **Litho.** ***Perf. 14***

1236 A355 $1 Like #1233b 2.00 2.00

Hong Kong '97. No. 1236 contains one 29x43mm stamp.

Disarmament Type of 1993

Inscribed "PEACE TODAY"

1997 **Litho.** **13½x14**

1237 A336 $1 Like #1157 3.00 3.00
1238 A336 $2 Like #1158 5.00 5.00
1239 A336 $3 Like #1156 9.00 9.00
Nos. 1237-1239 (3) 17.00

Nos. 1237-1239 are dated 1996.

Wildlife — A357

No. 1240: a, Olive baboon. b, Leopard. c, African tree pangolin. d, Vervet. e, Aardvark. f, Spotted hyena. g, Hunting dog. h, Thomson's gazelle. i, Warthog. j, African civet. k, Nile crocodile. l, African polecat.

1997, Apr. 2 **Litho.** ***Perf. 14***

1240 A357 50c Sheet of 12, #a.-l. 15.00 15.00

Deng Xiaoping (1904-97), British Transfer of Hong Kong — A358

Different portraits of Deng Xiaoping, "July 1, 1997," Hong Kong: 70c, In daylight, vert. $1, At night.

No. 1243: a, 50c. b, 70c. c, $1.20.

1997 **Litho.** ***Perf. 14***

1241 A358 70c multicolored 2.00
1242 A358 $1 multicolored 3.25
1243 A358 Sheet of 3, #a.-c. 7.75

No. 1241 is 28x44mm, and was issued in sheets of 4. No. 1242 was issued in sheets of 3.

UNESCO, 50th Anniv. A359

No. 1244, 50c, vert.: a, Canals, Venice, Italy. b, Mosque of Badshahi, Gardens of Shalamar, Lahore, Pakistan. c, Palace of Orando, Spain. d, Grounds of Temple of Hera, Greece. e, Church and Monastery of Daphni, Greece. f, Fraser Island, Australia. g, Canadian Rocky Mountains Park, Canada. h, Church of Santo Domingo Puebla, Mexico.

No. 1245, 50c, vert.: a, City of Ohrid and lake, Macedonia. b, Thracian Tomb of Sveshtari, Bulgaria. c, Monastery of Hossios Luckas, Greece. d, Church of Santa Cristina of Lena, Spain. e, Church of Santa Maria Della Salute, Venice, Italy. f, Center of Puebla, Mexico. g, Bagrati Cathedral, Georgia. h, Quebec City, Canada.

No. 1246: a, Ngorongoro Conservation Area, Tanzania. b, Garamba Natl. Park, Zaire. c, Canaima Natl. Park, Venezuela. d, Simien Natl. Park, Ethiopia. e, Mana Pools Natl. Park, Zimbabwe.

No. 1247, $2, Palace of Diocletian, Split, Croatia. No., 1248, $2, Monument of Nubia at Abu Simbel, Egypt. No. 1249, $2, Quedlinberg, Germany.

Perf. 13½x14, 14x13½

1997, June 17 **Litho.**

Sheets of 8, #a-h + Label

1244-1245 A359 Set of 2 27.50
1246 A359 70c Sheet of 5, #a-e, + label 12.50

Souvenir Sheets

1247-1249 A359 Set of 3 21.00

Queen Elizabeth II, Prince Philip, 50th Wedding Anniv. — A360

No. 1250: a, Queen holding umbrella. b, Royal arms. c, Prince in white uniform, Queen. d, Queen waving, Prince. e, Windsor Castle. f, Prince Philip.

No. 1251, $2, Queen seated on sofa. No. 1252, $2, Queen, Prince wearnig robes of Order of the Garter.

1997, June 17 ***Perf. 14***

1250 A360 50c Sheet of 6, #a.-f. 11.00

Souvenir Sheet

1251-1252 A360 $2 Set of 2 14.00

Grimm's Fairy Tales — A361

Mother Goose A362

No. 1253 — Scenes from Rapunzel: a, Girl. b, Wicked person, raven. c, Prince.

No. 1254, Prince rescuing girl.

No. 1255, Little Bo Peep, sheep.

1997, June 17 ***Perf. 13½x14***

1253 A361 $1 Sheet of 3, #a.-c. 10.00

Souvenir Sheets

1254 A361 $2 multicolored 7.00

Perf. 14

1255 A362 $2 multicolored 7.00

1998 Winter Olympics, Nagano — A363

Designs: 50c, Olympic Stadium, Lillehammer, 1994. 70c, Johann Koss, speed skating. $1, Katarina Witt, figure skating. $1.50, Sonia Henie, figure skating.

No. 1260: a, K. Seizinger, Alpine downhill skiing. b, J. Weissflog, 120-m ski jump. c, T. Kono, Nordic combined. d, G. Hackl, luge.

No. 1261: a, E. Bredesen, 90-m ski jump. b, L. Kjus, downhill skiing. c, B. Daehlie, cross-country skiing. d, P. Wiberg, combined Alpine skiing. e, S.L. Hattestad, freestyle skiing. f, G. Weder, D. Acklin, 2-man bobsled. g, Swedish hockey player. h, T. Alsgaard, cross-country skiing.

No. 1262, $2, German biathlete, 1994. No. 1263, $2, M. Wasmeier, giant slalom. No. 1264, $2, J. Koss, speed skating, diff. No. 1265, $2, V. Schneider, slalom.

1997, June 23 ***Perf. 14***

1256-1259 A363 Set of 4 13.00
1260 A363 50c Strip or block of 4, #a.-d. 7.00
1261 A363 50c Sheet of 8, #a.-h. 14.00

Souvenir Sheets

1262-1265 A363 Set of 4 27.50

No. 1260 was issued in sheets of 8 stamps.

Flowers — A364

No. 1266, 50c: a, Sugar cane dahlia. b, Windsor tall phlox. c, Creative art daylily. d, Columbine. e, Infinite Grace bearded iris. f, Fairy lilies mini amaryllis.

No. 1267, 50c: a, White coneflower. b, Peggy Lee hybrid tea rose. c, Daffodil. d, Bowl of Beauty peony. e. Hardy lily. f, Windflower.

No. 1268, $2, Lily-flowered tulip. No. 1269, $2, Chrysanthemum Potomac.

1997, July 1 Litho. *Perf. 14*

Sheets of 6, #a-f

1266-1267 A364 Set of 2 20.00 20.00

Souvenir Sheets

1268-1269 A364 Set of 2 16.00 16.00

Flora and Fauna — A365

No. 1270: a, Lovebirds. b, Genet. c, Leopard, crowned night heron. d, Gorilla. e, Giant wild boar. f, Elephant. g, Sterculia flower, skink. h, Ladybugs, bush baby. i, Cape primroses, ground hornbill.

No. 1271, $2, Rufus-crowned roller. No. 1272, $2, Gray heron.

1997, July 1

1270 A365 50c Sheet of 9, #a.-i. 13.00 13.00

Souvenir Sheets

1271-1272 A365 Set of 2 12.00 12.00

Chernobyl Disaster, 10th Anniv. — A366

1997, June 17 Litho. *Perf. 13½x14*

1273 A366 $1 UNESCO 3.25 3.25

Marcello Mastroianni (1923-96), Actor — A367

No. 1274 — Scenes from motion pictures: a, Casanova, 1970. b, Divorce Italian Style. c, 8½. d, La Dolce Vita.

1997, Sept. 3

1274 A367 75c Sheet of 4, #a.-d. 10.00 10.00

Contemporary Artists and Paintings — A368

No. 1275, 50c: a, Andy Warhol (1927-87). b, "Multicolored Retropective," by Warhol, 1979. c, "The Three Muscians," by Picasso, 1921. d, Pablo Picasso (1881-1973). e, Henri Matisse (1869-1954). f, "The Dance," by Matisse, 1910. g, "Lavender Mist," by Pollock, 1950. h, Jackson Pollock (1912-56).

No. 1276, 50c: a, Piet Mondrian (1872-1944). b, "Broadway Boogie Woogie," by Mondrian, 1942-43. c, "Persistence of Memory," by Dali, 1931. d, Salvador Dali (1904-89). e, Roy Lichtenstein (1923-97). f, "Artist's Studio: The Dance," by Lichtenstein, 1974. g, "Europe After the Rain," by Ernst, 1940-42. h, Max Ernst (1891-1976).

1997, Sept. 3 *Perf. 14*

Sheets of 8, #a-h

1275-1276 A368 Set of 2 27.50 27.50

Nos. 1275b-1275c, 1275f-1275g, 1276b-1276c, 1276f-1276g are 53x38mm.

Owls A369

No. 1277: a, Akun eagle owl. b, Shelley's eagle owl. c, African wood owl. d, Rufous fishing owl. e, Maned owl. f, Sandy scops owl.

1997

1277 A369 50c Sheet of 6, #a.-f. 9.00 9.00

Birds — A370

Designs: 1c, Black bee-eater. 2c, Yellow-billed barbet. 3c, Carmine bee-eater. 4c, Malachite kingfisher. 5c, Emerald cuckoo. 10c, Blue-throated roller. 15c, Blue-headed bee-eater. 20c, Black-collared lovebird. 25c, Broad-billed roller. 50c, Blue-breasted kingfisher. 70c, Little bee-eater. 75c, Yellow spotted barbet. 90c, White-throated bee-eater. $1, Double-toothed barbet. $2, Blue-cheeked bee-eater. $3, Narina's trogon.

1997

1278	A370	1c	multicolored	.25	.25
1279	A370	2c	multicolored	.25	.25
1280	A370	3c	multicolored	.25	.25
1281	A370	4c	multicolored	.25	.25
1282	A370	5c	multicolored	.25	.25
1283	A370	10c	multicolored	.25	.25
1284	A370	15c	multicolored	.40	.40
1285	A370	20c	multicolored	.50	.50
1286	A370	25c	multicolored	.65	.65
1287	A370	50c	multicolored	1.25	1.25
1288	A370	70c	multicolored	1.90	1.90
1289	A370	75c	multicolored	2.00	2.00
1290	A370	90c	multicolored	2.40	2.40
1291	A370	$1	multicolored	2.75	2.75
1292	A370	$2	multicolored	5.25	5.25
1293	A370	$3	multicolored	7.75	7.75
	Nos. 1278-1293 (16)			26.35	26.35

1998 World Cup Soccer A371

Players, country, vert: 50c, Salenko, Russia. 70c, Schillaci, Italy. $1, Lineker, England. $1.50, Pele, Brazil. $2, Fontaine, France. $2, Rahn, W. Germany.

No. 1300, 50c, vert: a, Ardiles, Argentina. b, Romario, Brazil. c, Rummenigge, Germany. d, Charlton, England. e, Villa, Argentina. f, Matthäus, Germany. g, Maradona, Argentina. h, Lineker, England.

No. 1301, 50c: a, Paulo Rossi, Italy. b, Ademir, Brazil. c, Grzegorz Lato, Poland. d, Gary Lineker, England. e, Gerd Muller, W. Germany. f, Johan Cruyff, Holland. g, Karl-Heinz Rummenigge, Germany. h, Mario Kempes, Argentina.

No. 1302, $6, Beckenbauer, W. Germany, vert. No. 1303, $6, Maier, W. Germany, vert.

Perf. 13½x14, 14x13½

1997, Oct. 1 Litho.

1294-1299 A371 Set of 6 18.00 18.00

Sheets of 8, #a-h, + Label

1300-1301 A371 Set of 2 27.50 27.50

Souvenir Sheets

1302-1303 A371 Set of 2 40.00 40.00

Marine Life — A372

No. 1304: a, Flamingoes (beach, palm trees). b, Six flamingoes. c, Sailfish (d). d, Egret. e, Yellow-tail snapper. f, Manatee. g, Clown coris. h, White-collar butterflyfish. i, Royal angelfish. j, Titan triggerfish. k, Three-striped wrasse. l, Pacific blue-eye. m, Wobbegono. n, Jellyfish. o, Sea urchin, red sea triggerfish. p, Harlequin fish.

No. 1305, $2, Seahorses, vert. No. 1306, $2, Anemone fish.

1998, Mar. 9 Litho. *Perf. 14*

1304 A372 20c Sheet of 16, #a.-p. 9.50 9.50

Souvenir Sheets

Perf. 13½x14, 14x13½

1305-1306 A372 Set of 2 12.00 12.00

No. 1305 contains one 38x51mm stamp, No. 1306 contains one 51x38mm stamp.

Butterflies A373

Designs: No. 1307, 50c, Orange tip. No. 1308, 50c, Saturn. No. 1309, 50c, Queen of Spain fritillary. No. 1310, 50c, Plain tiger. No. 1311, 50c, Doris. No. 1312, 50c, Forest queen. No. 1313, 50c, Figure-of-eight. No. 1314, 50c, Orange-barred sulphur.

No. 1315, 50c: a, Alfalfa. b, Orange-barred sulphur, diff. c, Union jack. d, Mocker swallowtail. e, Large green-banded blue. f, Common dotted border.

No. 1316, 50c: a, Cairns birdwing. b, Leafwing. c, Banded kin shoemaker. d, Tiger swallowtail. e, Adonis blue. f, Palmfly.

No. 1317, $2, Great orange tip. No. 1318, $2, Japanese emperor.

1998, Apr. 6 Litho. *Perf. 14*

1307-1314 A373 Set of 8 12.00 12.00

Sheets of 6, #a-f

1315-1316 A373 Set of 2 18.00 18.00

Souvenir Sheets

1317-1318 A373 Set of 2 12.00 12.00

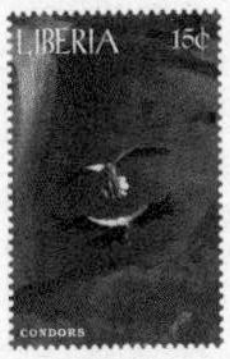

Noah's Ark — A374

No. 1319: a, Condors. b, Giraffes, skunks. c, Mallard ducks. d, Snowy owl. e, Snowy owl (face forward). f, Noah. g, Noah's wife. h, Polar bears. i, Elephants. j, Zebras. k, Rhinoceros. l, Sheep. m. Ruby-throated hummingbird. n, Wives of Noah's sons. o, Bats. p, Ring-necked pheasant. q, Tiger. r, Deer. s, Kangaroos. t, Camels. u, Red-eyed frogs. v, Raccoons. w, Rooster, hen. x, Marmosets. y, Lions.

$2, Black-legged kittiwake gull, ark on top of mountain, horiz.

1998, May 4 Litho. *Perf. 14*

1319 A374 15c Sheet of 25, #a.-y. 11.00 11.00

Souvenir Sheet

1320 A374 $2 multicolored 6.00 6.00

World Wildlife Fund — A375

No. 1321 — Liberian Mongoose: a, Looking straight ahead. b, Holding object between front paws. c, With front legs on branch. d, With mouth wide open.

1998, June 16 Litho. *Perf. 14*

1321 A375 32c Block or strip of 4, #a.-d. 5.50 5.50

Issued in sheets of 12 stamps.

Mushrooms — A376

Designs: 10c, Lepiota cristata. 15c, Russula emetica. 20c, Coprinus comatus. 30c, Russula cyanoxantha. 50c, Cortinarius violaceus. 75c, Amanita cothurnata. $1, Stropharia cyanea. $1.20, Panaeolus semiovatus.

No. 1330, 40c: a, Collybia butryacea. b, Asterophora parasitica. c, Tricholomopsis rutilans. d, Marasmius alliaceus. e, Mycena crocata. f, Mycena polygramma. g, Oudemansiella mucida. h, Entoloma conferendum. i, Entoloma serrulatum.

No. 1331, 40c: a, Cordyceps militaris. b, Xylaria hypoxlon. c, Sarcoscypha austriaca. d, Auriscalpium. e, Fomitopsis pinicola. f, Pleurotus ostreatus. g, Lepista flaccida. h, Clitocybe metachroa. i, Hygrocybe conica.

No. 1332, $2, Gomphidus roseus. No. 1333, $2, Paxillus atrotomentosus. No. 1334, $2, Russula occidentalis. No. 1335, $2, Cantharellus cibarius.

1998, July 1

1322-1329 A376 Set of 8 14.00 14.00

Sheets of 9, #a-i

1330-1331 A376 Set of 2 24.00 24.00

Souvenir Sheets

1332-1335 A376 Set of 4 27.50 27.50

Monarchs — A377

No. 1336, 50c: a, Kaiser Wilhelm II, Germany. b, Qabus Bin Said, Oman. c, King Albert, Belgium. d, Haile Selassie, Ethiopia. e, King Hussein, Jordan. f, Sheik Jaber Al-Ahmad Al-Sabah, Kuwait.

No. 1337, 50c: a, Alexander the Great, Greece. b, Charlemagne, France. c, Cleopatra, Egypt. d, Henry VIII, England. e, Peter the Great, Russia. f, Frederick the Great, Prussia.

No. 1338, 50c: a, Queen Beatrix, Netherlands. b, King Juan Carlos, Spain. c, Queen Elizabeth II, England. d, Franz Joseph I, Austria-Hungary. e, Princess Grace, Monaco. f, King Carl XVI Gustaf, Sweden.

No. 1339, $2, Empress Michiko, Japan. No. 1340, $2, Emperor Akihito, Japan. No. 1341, $2, Kublai Khan, China.

1998, July 27 Litho. *Perf. 14*

Sheets of 6, #a-f

1336-1338 A377 Set of 3 24.00 24.00

Souvenir Sheets

1339-1341 A377 Set of 3 21.00 21.00

Diana, Princess of Wales (1961-97) — A378

Various portraits of Diana in black outfit.

1998 *Imperf.*

1342 A378 50c Sheet of 4, #a.-d. 4.00 4.00

Birds — A379

No. 1343, 32c, Great green macaw. No. 1344, 32c, Crowned pigeon, vert. No. 1345, 32c, Blue-gray tanager. No. 1346, 32c, Roseate spoonbill, vert. No. 1347, 32c, Red-capped manakin. No. 1348, 32c, Groove-billed ani. No. 1349, 32c, South African crowned crane, vert.

No. 1350, vert: a, African sunbird. b, Seven-colored tanager. c, Red-throated bee-eater. d, Blue-crowned motmot. e, Duvaucel's trogon. f, Green bulbul. g, Grass-green tanager. h, Turaco. i, Hammer-head. j, Sarus crane. k, Limpkin. l, Ground hornbill.

No. 1351, $2, Red-crested touraco. No. 1352, $2, Flamingo, vert.

1998, Aug. 31 Litho. *Perf. 14*

1343-1349 A379 Set of 7 7.00 7.00
1350 A379 32c Sheet of 12, #a.-l. 12.00 12.00

Souvenir Sheets

1351-1352 A379 Set of 2 12.00 12.00

Children's Stories — A380

No. 1354: a, Tom Sawyer, by Mark Twain. b, Peter Rabbit, by Beatrix Potter. c, The Nutcracker, by E.T.A. Hoffman. d, Hansel & Gretel, by The Brothers Grimm. e, The Princess and the Pea, by Hans Christian Andersen. f, Oliver Twist, by Charles Dickens. g, Little Red Riding Hood, by The Brothers Grimm. h, Rumpelstiltskin, by The Brothers Grimm. i, The Wind & the Willows, by Kenneth Grahame.

$2, Rapunzel, by Brothers Grimm.

1998, Sept. 16 Litho. *Perf. 14½*

1354 A380 40c Sheet of 9, #a.-i. 12.00 12.00

Souvenir Sheet

Perf. 13½

1355 A380 $2 multicolored 7.00 7.00

No. 1355 contains one 38x51mm stamp.

Island, Marine Life — A381

No. 1356: a, Litoria peronii. b, Volcano, denomination UL. c, Volcano, denomination UR. d, Egretta alba. e, Graphium antiphates itamputi. f, Rhododendron zoelleri. g, Boat. h, Lava flow. i, Cormorants. j, Vaccinium. k, Caranx latus. l, Dugongs. m, Underwater lava flow. n, Cetocarus bicolor. o, Chilomycterus spilostylus. p, Lienardella fasliatus. q, Aerobatus. r, Gray reef shark. s, Acanthurus leucosternon, denomination UR. t, Hippocampus kuda. u, Coral, denomination UR. v, Chelonia. w, Myripristis hexogona. x, Coral, denomination, UL. y, Acanthurus leucosternon, denonination UL.

No. 1357: a, Sperm whale (b, c). b, Lollipop tang. c, Bottlenose dolphin (b, f). d, Jackass penguin (h). e, Harlequin tuskfish. f, Manta ray (a, b, e, j). g, Sealion. h, Grouper (g, l). i, Hammerhead shark (m). j, Butterfly fish. k, Garibaldi (g). l, Marine iguana (p). m, Loggerhead turtle (n). n, Seahorse. o, Horseshow crab (n, p). p, Moray eel.

No. 1358, 32c: a, Walrus. b, Pockfish-harlequin. c, Striped marlin. d, Whale shark. e, Spiny boxfish. f, Porcupine fish. g, Octopus. h, Dragonfish. i, Sea krait.

No. 1359, 32c: a, Snapping turtle. b, Atlantic spadefish. c, Bottlenose dolphin. d, Humpback whale. e, Whitetip shark. f, Twilight and deep seafish. g, Moorish idol. h, American lobster. i, Stingrays.

No. 1360, $2, Great white shark. No. 1361, $2, Banner fish. No. 1362, $2, Killer whale. No. 1363, $2, Surgeon fish.

1998, Oct. 15 *Perf. 14*

1356 A381 15c Sheet of 25, #a.-y. 12.00 12.00
1357 A381 20c Sheet of 16, #a.-p. 10.00 10.00

Sheets of 9, #a-i

1358-1359 A381 Set of 2 18.00 18.00

Souvenir Sheets

1360-1363 A381 Set of 4 22.50 22.50

International Year of the Ocean.

Diana, Princess of Wales (1961-97) — A382

No. 1364: a, Inscription panel at left. b, Panel at right.

1998, Oct. 26 Litho. *Perf. 14½x14*

1364 A382 50c Horiz. pair, #a-b 3.00 3.00

No. 1364 was issued in sheets of 3 pairs.

Pablo Picasso (1881-1973) A383

Entire paintings or details: 50c, Woman Throwing a Stone, 1931. 70c, Man with Sword and Flower, 1969, vert. $1, Large Bather with a Book, 1937, vert.

$2, French Cancan, 1901.

1998, Oct. 26 *Perf. 14½*

1365-1367 A383 Set of 3 7.50 7.50

Souvenir Sheet

1368 A383 $2 multicolored 7.00 7.00

Mahatma Gandhi (1869-1948) — A384

1998, Oct. 26 *Perf. 14*

1369 A384 50c shown 1.75 1.75

Souvenir Sheet

1370 A384 $2 Portrait, diff. 7.00 7.00

No. 1369 was issued in sheets of 4.

1998 World Scout Jamboree, Chile — A385

No. 1371: a, Daniel Carter Beard, Ernest Thompson Seton, award scouts, 1912. b, Robert Baden-Powell in Matabeleland, 1896. c, Scout repairing small girl's wagon.

1998, Oct. 26

1371 A385 $1 Sheet of 3, #a.-c. 10.00 10.00

Enzo Ferrari (1898-1988), Automobile Manufacturer A386

No. 1372: a, King Leopold Cabriolet. b, 195 S. c, 250 GTO 64.

$2, 250MM Cabriolet.

1998, Oct. 26 Litho. *Perf. 14*

1372 A386 $1 Sheet of 3, #a.-c. 9.00 9.00

Souvenir Sheet

1373 A386 $2 multicolored 8.50 8.50

No. 1373 contains one 91x35mm stamp.

Royal Air Force, 80th Anniv. — A387

No. 1374: a, Hawker Hurricane XII. b, Avro Lancaster in flight. c, Avro Lancaster B2. d, Supermarine Spitfire HG Mk 1XB.

No. 1375, $2, Bristol F2B fighter, Eurofighter. No. 1376, $2, Hawk, biplane.

1998, Oct. 26

1374 A387 70c Sheet of 4, #a.-d. 9.50 9.50

Souvenir Sheet

1375-1376 A387 Set of 2 14.00 14.00

Famous People and Events of the Twentieth Cent. — A388

No. 1380, 40c: a, Mao Tse-tung. b, Cultural Revolution begins. c, Promoting Third World unity. d, Zhou Enlai. e, Deng Xiaoping. f, Hong Kong returns to China, 1997. g, Shanghai, an Asian metropolis. h, Jiang Zemin.

No. 1381, 40c: a, Robert E. Peary. b, Expedition to the North Pole. c, Climbing Mt. Everest. d, Sir Edmund Hillary. e, Neil Armstrong. f, Walking on the moon. g, Expedition to the South Pole. h, Roald Amundsen.

$2, Matthew Henson.

1998, Dec. 1 Litho. *Perf. 14*

Sheets of 8, #a-h

1380-1381 A388 Set of 2 22.50 22.50

Souvenir Sheet

1382 A388 $2 multicolored 6.50 6.50

Nos. 1380b-1380c, 1380f-1380g, 1381b-1381c, 1380f-1381g are each 53x38mm.

Classic Cars — A389

Designs: No. 1383, 32c, 1966-72 Lamborghini Miura. No. 1384, 32c, 1966-93 Alfa Romeo Spider. No. 1385, 32c, 1948-61 Jaguar XK140. No. 1386, 32c, 1959-63 Lotus Elite.

No. 1387, 50c: a, 1949-53 Bristol 401. b, 1952-55 Bentley Continental R. c, 1973-75 Lancia stratos. d, 1963-67 Chevrolet Corvette Stingray. e, 1948-52 Austin A90 Atlantic. f, 1969-90 Aston Martin V8.

No. 1388, 50c: a, 1961-75 Jaguar E-Type. b, 1955-57 Ford Thunderbird. c, 1964-73, Ford Mustang GT350. d, 1957-77 Fiat 500. e, 1955-59 BMW 507. f, 1963-65 Buick Riviera.

No. 1389, $2, 1945-55 MG TD. No. 1390, $2, 1959-65 Rolls Royce Silver Cloud.

1998, Dec. 24

1383-1386 A389 Set of 4 4.00 4.00

Sheets of 6, #a-f

1387-1388 A389 Set of 2 20.00 20.00

Souvenir Sheets

1389-1390 A389 Set of 2 13.00 13.00

New Year 1999 (Year of the Rabbit) A390

Paintings, by Liu Jiyou (1918-83): No. 1391, Two rabbits. No. 1392, Three rabbits.

No. 1393, Two rabbits, flowers, vert.

1999, Jan. 5

1391 A390 50c multicolored 1.75 1.75
1392 A390 50c multicolored 1.75 1.75

Souvenir Sheet

1393 A390 $2 multicolored 6.50 6.50

Nos. 1391-1392 were issued in sheets of 2 each. No. 1393 contains one 43x52mm stamp.

US Presidents — A391

No. 1394, 75c, Various portraits of Abraham Lincoln. No. 1395, 75c, Various portraits of Bill Clinton.

1998, Dec. 1 Litho. *Perf. 14*

Sheets of 4, #a-d

1394-1395 A391 Set of 2 20.00 20.00

Zhou Enlai (1898-1976), Chinese Premier — A392

Various portraits.

1999 Litho. *Perf. 14*

1396 A392 50c Sheet of 6, #a.-f. 10.00 10.00

Souvenir Sheet

1397 A392 $2 multicolored 7.00 7.00

Raptors — A393

Designs: 50c, Snowy owl. 70c, Barn owl. $1, American kestrel. $1.50, Golden eagle.

No. 1402, 50c: a, Eurasian eagle owl. b, Osprey. c, Egyptian vulture. d, Lizard buzzard. e, Pale chanting goshawk. f, Bald eagle.

No. 1403, 50c: a, Goshawk. b, Laughing falcon. c, Oriental bay-owl. d, Swallow-tailed kite. e, Secretary bird. f, Brown falcon.

No. 1404, $2, Northern harrier. No. 1405, $2, Peregrine falcon.

1999, Jan. 4

1398-1401 A393 Set of 4 11.00 11.00

Sheets of 6, #a-f

1402-1403 A393 Set of 2 20.00 20.00

Souvenir Sheets

1404-1405 A393 Set of 2 13.00 13.00

Dinosaurs A395

No. 1406, 50c, Pachyrinosaur. No. 1407, 50c, Centrosaurus, vert. No. 1408, 70c, Pentaceratops, vert. No. 1409, 70c, Oviraptor, vert. $1, Corythosaur. $1.50, Stegosaurus, vert.

No. 1412, 40c: a, Baryonyx (e). b, Pachycephalosaur (a, c). c, Homalocephale. d, Pterodustro (c, g). e, Pycnosteroides. f, Giant nautiloid. g, Kronosaur (e, f). h, Giant cephalopod (g).

No. 1413, 40c: a, Camarasaur. b, Albertosaur (c, f, g). c, Eudimorhodon (b, d). d, Dimorphodon (c). e, Compsognathus. f, Torosaurus. g, Nodosaurid (h). h, Probactrosaurus.

No. 1414, $2, Tarbosaurus, vert. No. 1415, $2, Shunosaurus, vert.

1999, Jan. 18

1406-1411 A395 Set of 6 12.00 12.00

Sheets of 8, #a-h

1412-1413 A395 Set of 2 22.50 22.50

Souvenir Sheets

1414-1415 A395 Set of 2 13.00 13.00

Dinosaurs — A396

Designs: 50c, Brachiosaurus, vert. 70c, Tyrannosaurus, vert. $1, Mosasaurus. $1.50, Triceratops.

No. 1420: a, Albertosaurus. b, Parasaurolophus. c, Styracosaurus. d, Struthiomimus. e, Ankylosaurus. f, Chasmosaurus.

No. 1421, $2, Deinonychus. No. 1422, $2, Stegosaurus.

1999

1416-1419 A396 Set of 4 9.00 9.00

1420 A396 50c Sheet of 6, #a.-f. 10.00 10.00

Souvenir Sheets

1421-1422 A396 Set of 2 13.00 13.00

Flowers — A397

Designs: No. 1423, 50c, Tecophilaea cyanocrocus. 70c, Nymphoides peltata. $1, Angraecum scottianum. $1.50, Grevillea dielsiana.

No. 1427, 50c: a, Cyrtopodium parvilforum. b, Catharanthus roseus. c, Acacia acuminata. d, Herbertia lahue. e, Protea venusta. f, Clianthus formosus.

No. 1428, 50c: a, Dendrobium rarum. b, Cyrtorchis arcuata. c, Zygopetalum intermedium. d, Cassia fistula. e, Saintpaulia ionantha. f, Heliconia collinsiana.

No. 1429, $2, Hibiscus tilliaceus. No. 1430, $2, Rhododendron thomsonii.

1999, Feb. 8

1423-1426 A397 Set of 4 11.00 11.00

Sheets of 6, #a-f

1427-1428 A397 Set of 2 20.00 20.00

Souvenir Sheets

1429-1430 A397 Set of 2 13.00 13.00

Orchids — A398

Designs: No. 1431, 50c, Tridactyle bicaudata. No. 1432, 50c, Angraecum infundibulare. No. 1433, 70c, Oeceoclades maculata. No. 1434, 70c, Ophyrs fusca. No. 1435, $1, Sobennikoffia robusta. No. 1436, $1, Stenoglottis fimbriata. No. 1437, $1.50, Plectrelminthus caudatus. No. 1438, $1.50, Satyrium erectum.

No. 1439, 50c: a, Angraecrum eichlerianum. b, Ansellia africana. c, Cymbidiella pardalina. d, Angraecum eburnium. e, Ancistrochilus rothchildianus. f, Aerangis luteoalba.

No. 1440, 50c: a, Dis cardinalis. b, Cytorchus arcuata. c, Cynorkis compacta. d, Disa kewensis. e, Eulophia guineensis. f, Eulophia speciosa.

No. 1441, $2, Angraecum compactum. No. 1442, $2, Calanthe vestita.

1999, Mar. 13

1431-1438 A398 Set of 8 22.50 22.50

Sheets of 6, #a-f

1439-1440 A398 Set of 2 19.00 19.00

Souvenir Sheets

1441-1442 A398 Set of 2 13.00 13.00

Orchids — A399

Designs: No. 1443, 50c, Calypso bulbosa. No. 1444, 50c, Maclellanara pagan lovesong. No. 1445, 70c, Masdevallia chimaera. No. 1446, 70c, Yamadara midnight. $1, Cleistes divaricata. $1.50, Oncidium golden sunset.

No. 1449: a, Trichopilia tortilis. b, Stenoglottis longifolia. c, Telipogon pulcher. d, Esmeralda clarkei. e, Papilionanthe teres. f, Mormodes rolfeanum. g, Cypripedium acaule. h, Serapias lingua.

1999, Mar. 13

1443-1448 A399 Set of 6 15.00 15.00

1449 A399 30c Sheet of 8, #a.-h. 9.00 9.00

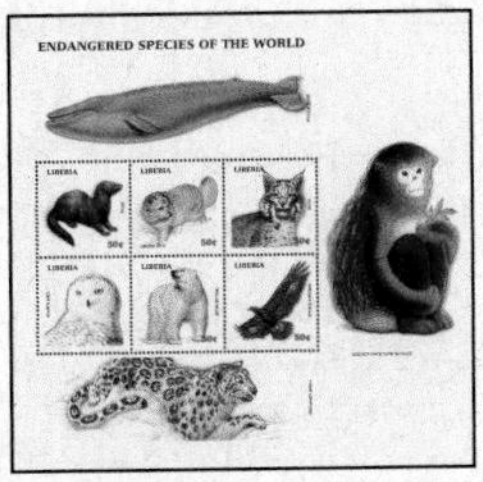

Wildlife A400

No. 1450: a, Mink. b, Arctic fox. c, Lynx. d, Snowy owl. e, Polar bear. f, Golden eagle.

$2, Big horn sheep.

1999, Feb. 24 Litho. ***Perf. 14***

1450 A400 50c Sheet of 6, #a.-f. 7.00 7.00

Souvenir Sheet

1451 A400 $2 multicolored 5.00 5.00

Flora and Fauna A401

No. 1452: a, Madgascan red fody. b, Indri (e). c, Coral-billed nuthatch. d, Sifaka (g, j). e, Golden piper. f, Aye aye (i). g, Broad-bordered grass yellow butterfly. h, Ring-tailed lemur (g, j, k). i, Parson's chameleon. j, Madagascar day gecko. k, Leaf-tailed gecko. l, Orchid.

No. 1453, $2, Wattled false sunbird. No. 1454, $2, Parson's chameleon. No. 1455, $2, Ring-tailed lemur.

1999, Apr. 1

1452 A401 20c Sheet of 12, #a.-l. 7.00 7.00

Souvenir Sheets

1453-1455 A401 Set of 3 15.00 15.00

Seabirds — A402

Designs: No. 1456, 50c, Harlequin duck. No. 1457, 50c, Eleonor's falcon, vert. No. 1458, 70c, Wilson's plover. No. 1459, 70c, Common eider. No. 1460, $1, Little tern. No. 1461, $1, American oystercatcher. No. 1462, $1.50, Herring gull, vert. No. 1463, $1.50, Brown pelican, vert.

No. 1464, 30c, vert: a, Great cormorant. b, Crested cormorant. c, Red faced cormorant. d, Whimbrel. e, Tufted puffin. f, Ivory gull. g, Common murre. h, Shelduck. i, Razorbill.

No. 1465, 30c: a, Common tern. b, Black-legged kittiwake. c, Bernacle goose. d, Black-headed gull. e, Semipalmated plover. f, Northern gannet. g, King eider. h, Iceland gull. i, Ring-billed gull.

No. 1466, $2, Arctic loon. No. 1467, $2, Atlantic puffin. No. 1468, $2, California gull, vert.

1999, Apr. 1 Litho. ***Perf. 14***

1456-1463 A402 Set of 8 17.00 17.00

Sheets of 9, #a-i

1464-1465 A402 Set of 2 13.00 13.00

Souvenir Sheets

1466-1468 A402 Set of 3 15.00 15.00

Queen Mother (b. 1900) — A404

No. 1475: a, With King George VI at wedding, 1923. b, In Nairobi, 1959. c, Wearing tiara, 1953. d, Wearing hat, 1990.

$2, Wearing hat, 1990, diff.

1999, Aug. 4 ***Perf. 14***

1475 A404 $1 Sheet of 4, #a.-d., + label 9.00 9.00

Souvenir Sheet

Perf. 13¾

1476 A404 $2 multicolored 5.00 5.00

No. 1476 contains one 38x51mm stamp.

Trains — A405

Designs: 32c, Nozomi Train, Japan. 40c, 401 Intercity Express, Germany. 50c, C53, Japan Railways. 70c, Beuth 2-2-2, Germany.

No. 1481, 40c: a, "Adler," Germany. b, Suburban EMU, Japan. c, Class 01, 4-6-2, Germany. d, Class 120 Bo-Bo, Germany. e, Class P8, 4-6-0, Germany. f, Fujikawa Express, Japan. g, Class 081, Germany. h, Kodama 8-car train, Japan. i, Class C62, 4-6-4, Japan.

No. 1482, 40c: a, KF Type, 4-8-4, China. b, Minobu Line train, Japan. c, Class S34-40, Germany. d, Class EF81, Bo-Bo, Japan. e, V200, B-B, Germany. f, SVT 877 "Flying Hamburger," Japan. g, C51, 4-6-2 Japan Railways. h, AEO Single rail car, Germany. i, Class D51, Japan.

No. 1483, $2, Yamonote Line train, Japan. No. 1484, $2, Class B8, Germany.

1999, Aug. 25 Litho. ***Perf. 14***

1477-1480 A405 Set of 4 4.50 4.50

Sheets of 9, #a-i

1481-1482 A405 Set of 2 17.00 17.00

Souvenir Sheets

1483-1484 A405 Set of 2 10.00 10.00

Dogs — A406

No. 1485, Lhasa apso. 70c, Samoyed.

No. 1487, vert.: a, Dalmatian. b, Pyrennean Mountain dog. c, Golden retriever. d, Bearded collie. e, Basset hound. f, Bernese Mountain dog.

No. 1488, Beagle, vert.

1999, Aug. 30 ***Perf. 14***

1485 A406 50c multicolored 1.25 1.25

1486 A406 70c multicolored 1.75 1.75

1487 A406 50c Sheet of 6, #a.-f. 7.50 7.50

Souvenir Sheet

1488 A406 $2 multicolored 5.00 5.00

During 1999-2004 Liberia was torn by a brutal and chaotic civil war that reduced the nation to a state of anarchy. Government services, including postal operations, functioned erratically, if at all, for months at a time. During this period, overseas stamp agents continued to produce stamps under pre-war contracts, and a large number of issues appeared to be marketed to overseas collectors. It appears that some of these stamps have been released in Liberia since the end of hostilities. These will be listed when their sale and postal use has been confirmed.

Paintings by Norman Rockwell — A580

Paintings: $15, Playing Party Games. $30, Saturday Night Out. $35, The Portrait. No, 2328, $50, Grandpa's Little Ballerina.

No. 2329, $50: a, The Cave of the Winds. b, Redhead Loves Hatty. c, The Rivals. d, Three's Company.

No. 2330, $50: a, Distortion. b, Summer Vacation. c, Runaway Pants. d, Tumble.

No. 2331, $50: a, Daydreams. b, A Patient Friend. c, Lands of Enchantment. d, The Little Spooners.

No. 2332, $50: a, The Skating Lesson. b, The Fortune Teller. c, God Bless You. d, Knowledge is Power.

2005, Jan. 10 Litho. ***Perf. 14¼***

2325-2328 A580 Set of 4 7.00 7.00

Sheets of 4, #a-d

2329-2332 A580 Set of 4 40.00 40.00

Jules Verne (1828-1905), Writer — A581

No. 2333, $30: a, The Adventures of Captain Hatteras. b, The Mysterious Island (deflated balloon). c, The Mysterious Island (Men looking at ape). d, 20,000 Leagues Under the Sea (spotlights on ship).

No. 2334, $30: a, Around the World in Eighty Days. b, From the Earth to the Moon (people watching man on space capsule ladder). c, Paris in the Twentieth Century. d, Master of the World (ship captain at wheel).

No. 2335, $30: a, The Chase of the Golden Meteor. b, Master of the World (flying machine, country name in white). c, Five Weeks in a Balloon. d, From the Earth to the Moon (rocket in space).

No. 2336, $30: a, The Mysterious Island (People in balloon basket). b, Robur the Conqueror. c, Round the Moon. d, Master of the World (flying machine, country name in black).

No. 2337, $30: Scenes from 20,000 Leagues Under the Sea: a, Ships on water. b, Shark and octopus attacking ship. c, Shark attacking diver. d, Squid attacking ship.

No. 2338, $100, Deep sea divers. No. 2339, $100, Admiral Richard E. Byrd. No. 2340, $100, Radio satellite communication. No. 2341, $100, Long range ballistic missile. No. 2342, $100, Extravehicular satellite repair.

2005, Jan. 11 ***Perf. 13¼x13½***

Sheets of 4, #a-d

2333-2337 A581 Set of 5 32.50 32.50

Souvenir Sheets

2338-2342 A581 Set of 5 27.50 27.50

Marilyn Monroe (1926-62), Actress — A582

2005, Jan. 26 ***Perf. 14***

2343 A582 $12 multi .95 .95

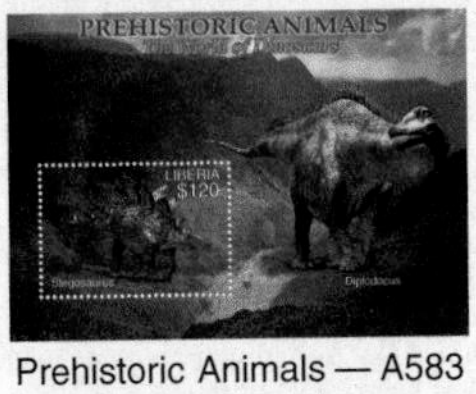

Prehistoric Animals — A583

No. 2344, $50: a, Torosaurus. b, Tyrannosaurus. c, Polacanthus. d, Stegosaurus.

No. 2345, $50: a, Smilodon. b, Brontothere. c, Doedicurus. d, Moeritherium.
No. 2346, $50: a, Cymbospondylus. b, Archelon. c, Xiphactinus. d, Dunkleosteus.
No. 2347, $120, Stegosaurus, diff. No. 2348, $120, Woolly rhinoceros. No. 2349, $120, Odobenocetops.

2005, Jan. 26 ***Perf. 13¼x13½***
Sheets of 4, #a-d
2344-2346 A583 Set of 3 32.50 32.50
Souvenir Sheet
2347-2349 A583 Set of 3 18.00 18.00

Battle of Trafalgar, Bicent. A584

Various ships: $10, $20, $40, $50.
$100, Death of Admiral Horatio Nelson.

2005, May 4 ***Perf. 14¼***
2350-2353 A584 Set of 4 6.00 6.00
Souvenir Sheet
2354 A584 $100 multi 5.50 5.50

Hans Christian Andersen (1805-75), Author — A585

No. 2355: a, Medal. b, Open book. c, Andersen.
$100, Sketch of Little Mermaid.

2005, May 4 ***Perf. 14¼***
2355 A585 $50 Sheet of 3, #a-c 7.50 7.50
Souvenir Sheet
2356 A585 $100 multi 5.50 5.50

Friedrich von Schiller (1759-1805), Writer — A586

No. 2357: a, Bust of Schiller on round pedestal. b, Bust and foliage. c, Bust on monument.
$100, Statue of Schiller, Chicago.

2005, May 4 ***Perf. 14¼***
2357 A586 $50 Sheet of 3, #a-c 7.50 7.50
Size: 48x67mm
Imperf
2358 A586 $100 multi 5.50 7.50

No. 2357 contains three 28x42mm stamps.

Miniature Sheets

Elvis Presley (1935-77) — A587

No. 2359, $35 — Presley in: a, 1956. b, 1969. c, 1969 (country name in yellow). d, 1969 (country name in pink). e, 1970.
No. 2360, $35 — Presley wearing: a, Red suit and white shirt. b, Yellow sweater. c, Red shirt. d, Brown suit. e, Gray suit.

2005, May 19 ***Perf. 13½x13¼***
Sheets of 5, #a-e
2359-2360 A587 Set of 2 19.00 19.00

Pope John Paul II (1920-2005) — A588

2005, Aug. 22 ***Perf. 12¾***
2361 A588 $50 multi 2.50 2.50

Printed in sheets of 4.

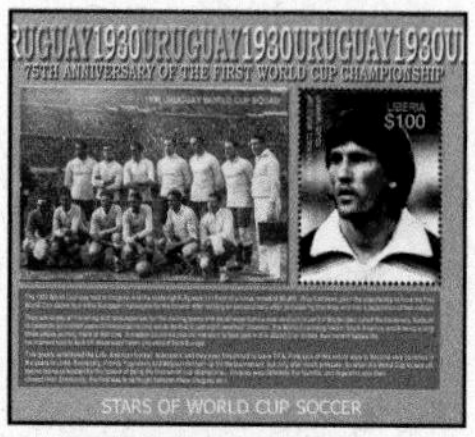

World Cup Soccer Championships, 75th Anniv. — A589

No. 2362: a, Norbert Eder. b, Paul Breitner. c, Thomas Helmer.
$100, Manfred Kaltz.

2005, Aug. 22 ***Perf. 13¼***
2362 A589 $60 Sheet of 3, #a-c 10.00 10.00
Souvenir Sheet
Perf. 12
2363 A589 $100 multi 5.50 5.50

Albert Einstein (1879-1955), Physicist — A590

No. 2364 — Einstein and: a, Charlie Chaplin. b, Max Planck. c, William Allen White.
$100, J. Robert Oppenheimer

2005, Aug. 22 ***Perf. 12¾***
2364 A590 $60 Sheet of 3, #a-c 9.00 9.00
Souvenir Sheet
2365 A590 $100 multi 5.00 5.00

End of World War II, 60th Anniv. A591

No. 2366, $40 — V-E Day: a, Gen. Dwight D. Eisenhower. b, Prime Minister Winston Churchill. c, Gen. George Patton. d, Field Marshal Bernard Montgomery.
No. 2367, $40 — V-E Day: a, Air Marshal Sir Arthur "Bomber" Harris. b, Gen. Douglas MacArthur. c, Field Marshal Alan Brooke. d, Pres. Franklin D. Roosevelt.
No. 2368, $40 — V-J Day: a, RAF Wellington bomber. b, Mitsubishi A6M Zero. c, RAF Hudson bomber. d, B-17 bomber.
No. 2369, $40 — V-J Day: a, P-51 Mustang. b, RAF Hamilcar glider. c, P-38 Lightning. d, RAF Supermarine Spitfire.

2005, Aug. 22 ***Perf. 13¼x13½***
Sheets of 4, #a-d
2366-2369 A591 Set of 4 26.00 26.00

Worldwide Fund for Nature (WWF) — A592

No. 2370: a, Jentink's duiker. b, Head of Ogilby's duiker. c, Ogilby's duiker. d, Head of Jentink's duiker.

2005, Aug. 31 ***Perf. 14***
2370 A592 $20 Block or vert. strip of 4, #a-d 4.00 4.00
e. Miniature sheet, 2 each #2370a-2370d 6.50 6.50

Rotary International, Cent. — A593

Emblem: $10, $25, $35, $50.
$100, Mother Teresa.

2005, Sept. 22 ***Perf. 14***
2371-2374 A593 Set of 4 6.00 6.00
Souvenir Sheet
2375 A593 $100 multi 5.00 5.00

No. 2371-2374 exist imperf. Value, $20.

Christmas — A594

Paintings: $20, Glory to God, by Kim Ki-chang. $25, Flight Into Egypt, by Fra Angelico. $30, Christmas Mom, by Will Hickock Low. $50, The Nativity, by Bernadino Luini.
$100, Adoration of the Magi, by Nicolas Poussin.

2005, Dec. 1
2376-2379 A594 Set of 4 6.00 6.00
Souvenir Sheet
2380 A594 $100 multi 5.00 5.00

Elvis Presley (1935-77) — A595

Variable Serpentine Die Cut
2006, Jan. 17 Litho. & Embossed
Without Gum
2381 A595 $350 gold & multi 20.00 20.00

African Antelopes — A596

No. 2382: a, Gemsbok. b, Kudu. c, Sable antelope. d, Impala.
$100, Springbok.

2006, Jan. 17 Litho. ***Perf. 13½***
2382 A596 $45 Sheet of 4, #a-d 9.00 9.00
Souvenir Sheet
2383 A596 $100 multi 5.00 5.00

Mammals — A597

No. 2384: a, Jackal. b, Fox. c, Wolf. d, Coyote.
$100, Hyena.

2006, Jan. 17
2384 A597 $45 Sheet of 4, #a-d 9.00 9.00
Souvenir Sheet
2385 A597 $100 multi 5.00 5.00

Wild Cats A598

No. 2386: a, Jaguar. b, Lion. c, Puma. d, Cheetah.
$100, Siberian tiger.

2006, Jan. 17
2386 A598 $45 Sheet of 4, #a-d 9.00 9.00
Souvenir Sheet
2387 A598 $100 multi 5.00 5.00

Animals of the Bible A599

No. 2388, $45: a, Lions. b, Camels. c, Doves. d, Donkey.
No. 2389, $45: a, Foxes. b, Vultures. c, Turtles. d, Ducks.
No. 2390, $45: a, Goat. b, Bear. c, Ravens. d, Sheep.
No. 2391, $120, Pig. No. 2392, $120, Whale. No. 2393, $120, Snake.

2006, Jan. 17 Sheets of 4, #a-d
2388-2390 A599 Set of 3 25.00 25.00
Souvenir Sheets
2391-2393 A599 Set of 3 20.00 20.00

Snakes A600

No. 2394: a, Rough green snake. b, Speckled king snake. c, Garter snake. d, Brown snake.
$100, Red milk snake.

2006, Jan. 27
2394 A600 $45 Sheet of 4, #a-d 9.00 9.00
Souvenir Sheet
2395 A600 $100 multi 5.00 5.00

2006 Winter Olympics, Turin — A601

Designs: $20, Austria #B337. $25, Poster for 1976 Innsbruck Winter Olympics, vert. $35, Austria #B338. $50, Austria #B335. $70, US #3555. $100, Poster for 2002 Salt Lake City Winter Olympics, vert.

2006, Apr. 6 ***Perf. 13½***

2396-2399 A601 Set of 4 8.00 8.00
2399A A601 $70 multi 4.00 4.00
2399B A601 $100 multi 6.00 6.00

Nos. 2399A-2399B were not made available until 2007.

Souvenir Sheet

Benjamin Franklin (1706-90), Statesman — A602

2006, May 27 ***Perf. 13½***

2400 A602 $120 multi 7.50 7.50

Washington 2006 World Philatelic Exhibition.

Queen Elizabeth II, 80th Birthday A603

No. 2401 — Hat color: a, Green. b, Blue. c, Beige. d, Black.
$120, Queen wearing tiara.

2006, June 13 ***Perf. 14¼***

2401 A603 $40 Sheet of 4, #a-d 9.00 9.00

Souvenir Sheet

2402 A603 $120 multi 7.00 7.00

Rembrandt (1606-69), Painter — A604

Artwork: $15, Young Man in a Turban. $30, Man Leaning on a Windowsill. $40, Officer with a Gold Chain. $45, The Art Dealer Clement de Jonghe.

No. 2407, $60: a, Self-portrait, 1633. b, Self-portrait, 1634. c, Self-portrait, 1639. d, Self-portrait, 1640.

No. 2408, $60: a, Christ and the Canaanite Woman. b, The Mocking of Christ. c, Head of an Old Man (Three-quarters view). d, Head of an Old Man (profile).

No. 2409, $60: a, David and Jonathan. b, Nude Woman with a Snake. c, The Abduction of Europa. d, Daniel and Cyrus Before the Idol Bel.

No. 2410, $60: a, Shah Jahan and Dara Shikoh. b, Farm Building Surrounded by Trees. c, Two Thatched Cottages with Figures at Window. d, A Sailing Boat on Wide Expanse of Water.

No. 2411, $120, Bearded Old Man with a Gold Chain. No. 2412, $120, A Scholar in His Study. No. 2413, $120, Rembrandt's Mother. No. 2414, $120, Portrait of Jan Six.

2006, June 13 **Litho.**

2403-2406 A604 Set of 4 7.00 7.00

Sheets of 4, #a-d

2407-2410 A604 Set of 4 50.00 50.00

Imperf

Size: 76x103mm

2411-2414 A604 Set of 4 30.00 30.00

Souvenir Sheet

Wolfgang Amadeus Mozart (1756-91), Composer — A605

2006, July 25 ***Perf. 12¾***

2415 A605 $120 multi 7.50 7.50

Miniature Sheet

Chinese Ceramics A606

No. 2416: a, Bowl with red, black and white exterior, brown interior. b, Bowl with blue and white exterior, blue, red and white interior. c, Bowl with green on white exterior, square opening. d, Bowl with red, white and blue exterior, brown interior. e, Bowl with green on white exterior, circular opening. f, Bowl with red, white and green exterior, square opening.

2006, Aug. 16 ***Perf. 12x12¼***

2416 A606 $35 Sheet of 6, #a-f 12.00 12.00

Inauguration of Pres. Ellen Johnson-Sirleaf A607

Designs: $10, Pres. Johnson-Sirleaf and flag. $25, Certification by National Election Commission, horiz. $30, Casting of ballots. $40, Pres. Johnson-Sirleaf holding child, horiz.
$100, Pres. Johnson-Sirleaf at microphone.

2006, Aug. 22 ***Perf. 13¼***

2417-2420 A607 Set of 4 6.00 6.00

Souvenir Sheet

2421 A607 $100 multi 6.00 6.00

Millennium Development Goals A608

Goals: No. 2422, $10, Achieve universal primary education (graduates). No. 2423, $10, Promote gender equality and empower women. No. 2424, $25, Eradicate extreme hunger and poverty. No. 2425, $25, Reduce child mortality. No. 2426, $30, Develop a global partnership for development (map). No. 2427, $30, Develop a global partnership for development (ships and airplane). $40, Improve maternal health. $50, Achieve universal primary education (classroom). No. 2430, $100, Ensure environmental sustainability. No. 2431, $100, Combat HIV/AIDS, malaria and other diseases.

No. 2432, Achieve universal primary education (classroom), vert.

2006, Sept. 22

2422-2431 A608 Set of 10 25.00 25.00

Souvenir Sheet

2432 A608 $100 multi 6.00 6.00

Space Achievements — A609

No. 2433, $40 — Intl. Space Station: a, Country name and denomination in black, at top. b, Country name in black, denomination in white. c, Country name and denomination in white, at top. d, Country name and denomination in black, at bottom. e, Space shuttle (country name and denomination in white, at bottom). f, Astronaut (country name and denomination in white, at bottom.

No. 2434, $40, vert. — Apollo 11: a, Lunar module. b, Rocket on launch pad. c, Nose cone of rocket. d, Astronaut on moon. e, Command module. f, Astronauts and rocket.

No. 2435, $55, vert. — First Flight of Space Shuttle Columbia: a, Astronaut Bob Crippen. b, Front of space shuttle. c, Astronaut John Young. d, Tail of space shuttle.

No. 2436, $55 — Space Shuttle returns to space: a, Wing. b, Fuselage, reflection of sunlight. c, Wing inscribed "Discovery." d, Fuselage and Earth.

No. 2437, $120, Apollo-Soyuz. No. 2438, $120, Mars Reconnaissance Orbiter. No. 2439, $120, Venus Express. No. 2440, $120, Deep Impact Probe.

2006, Oct. 3 **Litho.** ***Perf. 12¾***

Sheets of 6, #a-f

2433-2434 A609 Set of 2 30.00 30.00

Sheets of 4, #a-d

2435-2436 A609 Set of 2 25.00 25.00

Souvenir Sheets

2437-2440 A609 Set of 4 25.00 25.00

Christopher Columbus (1451-1506), Explorer — A610

Designs: $25, Columbus, drawings of ships. $50, Columbus, ships, horiz. $70, Columbus and Santa Maria, horiz. $100, Ship, crew encountering natives, horiz.
$120, Men on shore.

2006, Nov. 15

2441-2444 A610 Set of 4 12.50 12.50

Souvenir Sheet

2445 A610 $120 multi 7.00 7.00

Souvenir Sheet

Christmas — A611

No. 2446 — Details from The Adoration of the Magi, by Peter Paul Rubens: a, Man and boy. b, Mary. c, Man with headcovering. d, Infant Jesus.

2006, Dec. 21 **Litho.** ***Perf. 14***

2446 A611 $40 Sheet of 4, #a-d 9.00 9.00

A612

Concorde — A613

No. 2447, $30 — Concorde: a, G-BOAF. b, G-BOAB.

No. 2448, $35 — Concorde: a, F-BVFA on runway. b, G-BOAA taking off.

2007, Mar. 1 **Litho.** ***Perf. 13½***

Horiz. Pairs, #a-b

2447-2448 A612 Set of 2 7.50 7.50

Litho. & Embossed

Without Gum

Irregular Serpentine Die Cut

2449 A613 $350 gold & multi 20.00 20.00

Souvenir Sheet

Ludwig Durr (1878-1956), Engineer — A614

No. 2450: a, Durr and Zeppelin. b, Interior cabin plan for LZ-127. c, Count Ferdinand von Zeppelin.

2007, Mar. 1 **Litho.** ***Perf. 13¼***

2450 A614 $60 Sheet of 3, #a-c 10.00 10.00

Souvenir Sheet

Marilyn Monroe (1926-62), Actress — A615

Various portraits.

2007, Mar. 1

2451 A615 $50 Sheet of 4, #a-d 12.00 12.00

Pres. John F. Kennedy (1917-62) — A616

No. 2452, $45: a, Signing executive order establishing the Peace Corps. b, With Sargent Shriver. c, Peace Corps volunteers in Tanganyika. d, Jack Hood Vaughn, second director of Peace Corps.

No. 2453, $45 — Kennedy: a, And Eleanor Roosevelt. b, Delivering Alliance for Progress speech. c, With Mrs. Kennedy in Venezuela. d, And Secretary of State Dean Rusk.

2007, Mar. 1 **Litho.**

Sheets of 4, #a-d

2452-2453 A616 Set of 2 20.00 20.00

Mushrooms — A617

Designs: $25, Boletus edulis. $35, Begriipt russula. No. 2456, $45, Lactarius helvus. $50, Amanita pantherina.

No. 2458, $45: a, Russula cyanoxantha. b, Cantharellus subalbidus. c, Leccinum oxydalile. d, Boletus badius.

No. 2459, $45: a, Amanita bingensis. b, Chlorophyllum molybdites. c, Calvatia utriformis. d, Amanita loosii.

No. 2460, $100, Amanita muscaria. No. 2461, $100, Chlorophyllum molybdites, diff. No. 2462, $100, Agaricus silvaticus.

2007, Mar. 1

2454-2457 A617 Set of 4 9.00 9.00

Sheets of 4, #a-d

2458-2459 A617 Set of 2 20.00 20.00

Souvenir Sheets

2460-2462 A617 Set of 3 18.00 18.00

Scouting, Cent. — A618

Designs: $50, Scouts and 2006 World Jamboree emblem. $150, Scouts, horiz.

2007, Mar. 15

2463 A618 $50 multi 3.00 3.00

Souvenir Sheet

2464 A618 $150 multi 9.00 9.00

No. 2463 was printed in sheets of 4.

Pope Benedict XVI — A619

2007, Nov. 30 Litho. ***Perf. 13¼***

2465 A619 $30 multi 1.75 1.75

Miniature Sheet

New Year 2007 (Year of the Boar) A620

No. 2466 — Wild Boar, by Liu Jiyou with text "Year of the Boar" in: a, Red. b, Green. c, Brown. d, Blue.

2007, Nov. 30

2466 A620 $30 Sheet of 4, #a-d 7.00 7.00

Miniature Sheet

Wedding of Queen Elizabeth II and Prince Philip, 60th Anniv. A621

No. 2467: a, Couple, denomination in white. b, Queen, denomination in yellow. c, Couple, denomination in lilac. d, Queen, denomination in white. e, Couple, denomination in yellow. f, Queen, denomination in lilac.

2007, Nov. 30

2467 A621 $35 Sheet of 6, #a-f 12.00 12.00

Princess Diana (1961-97) — A622

No. 2468 — Various depictions of Diana with denomination in: a, Red violet. b, Blue. c, Green. d, Red.
$125, Red denomination.

2007, Nov. 30

2468 A622 $45 Sheet of 4, #a-d 10.00 10.00

Souvenir Sheet

2469 A622 $125 multi 7.50 7.50

Souvenir Sheets

Pres. Ellen Johnson-Sirleaf and Foreign Dignitaries — A623

Pres. Johnson-Sirleaf meeting with: No. 2470, $100, Chinese Pres. Hu Jintao. No. 2471, $100, U.S. Pres. George W. Bush.

2007, Nov. 30

2470-2471 A623 Set of 2 12.00 12.00

Miniature Sheet

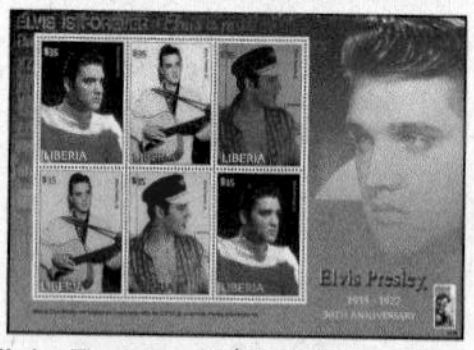

Elvis Presley (1935-77) — A624

No. 2472 — Presley: a, Wearing red and white sweater, country name in white. b, Holding guitar, country name in blue. c, Wearing cap, country name in white. d, Holding guitar, country name in purple. e, Wearing cap, country name in red violet. f, Wearing red and white sweater, country name in yellow.

2007, Nov. 30

2472 A624 $35 Sheet of 6, #a-f 12.00 12.00

Souvenir Sheet

Japanese Prime Minister Junchiro Koizumi, U.S. Pres. George W. Bush and Wife at Graceland — A625

2007, Nov. 30

2473 A625 $100 multi 6.00 6.00

New Year 2008 (Year of the Rat) — A626

2007, Dec. 26 Litho. ***Perf. 11½x12***

2474 A626 $25 multi 1.50 1.50

Printed in sheets of 4.

Birds — A627

Designs: $20, Pin-tailed whydahs. $30, Lesser honeyguides. $40, African jacanas. $50, Malachite sunbirds.

No. 2479, $45, horiz.: a, White-brown sparrow weavers. b, Parasitic weavers. c, Black-winged orioles. d, Crested guineafowl.

No. 2480, $45, horiz.: a, Red-billed francolins. b, Rufous-crowned rollers. c, African golden orioles. d, Black-crowned tchagras.

No. 2481, $100, Kori bustard. No. 2482, $100, Ostrich. No. 2483, $100, Great white pelican, horiz.

2007, Dec. 26 ***Perf. 14***

2475-2478 A627 Set of 4 8.00 8.00

Sheets of 4, #a-d

2479-2480 A627 Set of 2 20.00 20.00

Souvenir Sheets

2481-2483 A627 Set of 3 18.00 18.00

Butterflies — A628

Designs: $20, Appias epaphia. $30, Papilio bromius. $40, Charaxes jasius. $50, Mimacraea marshalli dohertyi.

No. 2488, $45: a, Belenois thysa. b, Papilio pelodorus. c, Cymothoe sangaris. d, Colotis aurigineus.

No. 2489, $45: a, Junonia hierta. b, Myrina silenus. c, Byblia ilithyia. d, Argyrogrammana attsonii.

No. 2490, $100, Iolaus menas. No. 2491, $100, Leptomyrina hirundo. No. 2492, $100, Pinacopteryx eriphia.

2007, Dec. 26

2484-2487 A628 Set of 4 8.00 8.00

Sheets of 4, #a-d

2488-2489 A628 Set of 2 20.00 20.00

Souvenir Sheets

2490-2492 A628 Set of 3 18.00 18.00

Orchids — A629

Designs: $20, Neobenthamia gracilis. $30, Eulophia guineensis. $40, Aerangis curnowiana. $50, Cymbidiella pardalina.

No. 2497, $45: a, Ophrys lutea. b, Ophrys holoserica. c, Ophrys fusca. d, Ophrys scolopax.

No. 2498, $45: a, Disa veitchii. b, Disa racemosa. c, Disa kewensis. d, Disa diores.

No. 2499, $100, Disa crassicornis. No. 2500, $100, Aerangis citrata. No. 2501, $100, Angraecum sororium.

2007, Dec. 26

2493-2496 A629 Set of 4 8.00 8.00

Sheets of 4, #a-d

2497-2498 A629 Set of 2 20.00 20.00

Souvenir Sheets

2499-2501 A629 Set of 3 18.00 18.00

Christmas — A630

Designs: $30, Madonna and Child. $40, Holy Family. $45, Flight into Egypt. $50, The Three Magi, horiz.

2007, Dec. 26 ***Perf. 14x14¾, 14¾x14***

2502-2505 A630 Set of 4 10.00 10.00

Miniature Sheet

2008 Summer Olympics, Beijing — A631

No. 2506: a, Babe Didrikson. b, 1932 Summer Olympics poster. c, Helene Madison. d, Chuhei Nambu.

2008, Apr. 8 ***Perf. 12¾***

2506 A631 $30 Sheet of 4, #a-d 7.00 7.00

National Basketball Association Players — A632

No. 2507 — NBA and Boston Celtics emblems and Kevin Garnett: a, Wearing white uniform, not holding basketball. b, Wearing green uniform. c, Wearing white uniform, holding basketball.

No. 2508 — NBA and Boston Celtics emblems and Paul Pierce: a, Wearing white uniform, hands at side. b, Wearing green uniform. c, Wearing white uniform, pointing.

No. 2509 — NBA and Washington Wizards emblems and Gilbert Arenas: a, Wearing white uniform, hands on hips. b, Wearing blue uniform. c, Wearing white uniform, with basketball.

No. 2510 — NBA and Milwaukee Bucks emblems and Yi Jianlian: a, Wearing white uniform, basketball at left. b, Wearing blue green uniform. c, Wearing white uniform, basketball at right.

2008, Apr. 30 ***Perf. 13½x13¼***

2507 Vert. strip of 3 7.00 7.00
a.-c. A632 $40 Any single 1.25 1.25
2508 Vert. strip of 3 7.00 7.00
a.-c. A632 $40 Any single 1.25 1.25
2509 Vert. strip of 3 7.00 7.00
a.-c. A632 $40 Any single 1.25 1.25
2510 Vert. strip of 3 7.00 7.00
a.-c. A632 $40 Any single 1.25 1.25
Nos. 2507-2510 (4) 28.00 28.00

Nos. 2507-2510 each printed in sheets of 6 containing 2 of each stamp in strip.

Souvenir Sheet

Meeting of Liberian Pres. Ellen Johnson-Sirleaf and US Pres. George W. Bush. — A633

No. 2511: a, Pres. Bush. b, Pres. Johnson-Sirleaf.

2008, June 12 ***Perf. 13¼***

2511 A633 $125 Sheet of 2, #a-b 12.00 12.00

Elvis Presley (1935-77) — A634

No. 2512 — Presley: a, Holding microphone, red background. b, Holding microphone, "Elvis" in lights. c, Holding microphone, blue background. d, Wearing glasses.

2008, June 12 *Perf. 13¼*

2512 A634 $60 Sheet of 4, #a-d 12.00 12.00

Space Achievements — A635

No. 2513, $40 — International Space Station with denomination at: a, UR. b, UL. c, LR.
No. 2514, $40 — Chandra X-ray Observatory: a, Observatory below nebula. b, Interior of Observatory. c, Observatory above nebula.
No. 2515: a, Callisto, Europa, Voyager I, Jupiter and Io. b, Lift-off of Voyager I. c, Voyager I record cover. d, Voyager I, Titan and Saturn.
No. 2516, $150, International Space Station, horiz. No. 2517, $150, Chandra X-ray Observatory, horiz. No. 2518, $150, Voyager I and rings of Saturn, horiz.
Illustration reduced.

2008, June 12 *Perf. 13¼*

Horiz. Strips of 3, #a-c

2513-2514 A635 Set of 2 18.00 18.00

Miniature Sheet

2515 A635 $60 Sheet of 4, #a-d 18.00 18.00

Souvenir Sheets

2516-2518 A635 Set of 3 24.00 24.00

Nos. 2513-2514 were each printed in sheets of 6 containing 2 of each stamp in strip.

Pope Benedict XVI — A636

2008, June 30 **Litho.**

2519 A636 $45 multi 2.00 2.00

Printed in sheets of 4.

County Flags — A637

Flag of: No. 2520, $10, Maryland County. No. 2521, $10, Montserrado County. No. 2522, $25, Gbarpolu County. No. 2523, $25, Grand Bassa County. No. 2524, $30, Grand Cape Mount County. No. 2525, $30, Nimba County. No. 2526, $40, Lofa County. No. 2527, $40, Sinoe County. No. 2528, $50, Bong County. No. 2529, $50, Margibi County. No. 2530, $100, Bomi County. No. 2531, $100, Grand Gedeh County. No. 2532, $100, Grand Kru County. No. 2533, $100, River Cess County. No. 2534, $100, River Gee County.

2008, June 30

2520-2534 A637 Set of 15 26.00 26.00

Miniature Sheet

Ferrari F2008 A638

No. 2535: a, "F" under "E" of "Liberia." b, "F" under "B" of Liberia. c, Side view of car. d, Car straddling yellow line on track.

2008, Sept. 5 **Litho.** *Perf. 13½*

2535 A638 $60 Sheet of 4, #a-d 12.00 12.00

A639

Election of Barack Obama as US President — A640

Inscriptions: No. 2537, Joseph Biden. No. 2539a, Joseph Robinette Biden, Jr.
No. 2539B: c, Barack Obama. d, Joseph Biden.

Perf. 14¼x14¾, 12¼x11¾ (#2538)

2008, Nov. 5

2536 A639 $45 shown 1.50 1.50
2537 A639 $45 multi 1.50 1.50
2538 A640 $65 shown 2.10 2.10
Nos. 2536-2538 (3) 5.10 5.10

Souvenir Sheet

2539 Sheet of 2, #2536, 2539a 3.00 3.00
a. A639 $45 multi 1.50 1.50
2539B Sheet of 2 17.00 17.00
c.-d. A639 $160 Either single 8.50 8.50

No. 2536 was printed in sheets of 9 and in No. 2539. No. 2537 was printed in sheets of 9. No. 2538 was printed in sheets of 4.

A641

Solo Aerial Circumnavigation of the World by Wiley Post, 75th Anniv. — A642

No. 2540: a, Post arriving in Cleveland. b, Harold Gatty, navigator. c, Post wearing pressure suit. d, Post atop plane. e, Post and wife Mae. f, The Winnie Mae.
$100, Post and map of flight.

2008, Nov. 24 *Perf. 13¼*

2540 A641 $40 Sheet of 6, #a-f 12.00 12.00

Souvenir Sheet

2541 A642 $100 multi 6.00 6.00

Christmas — A643

Paintings: $10, The Nativity, by Martin Schongauer. $25, Birth of Christ, by Robert Campin. $30, Adoration of the Magi, by Geertgen tot Sint Jans. $40, The Birth of Christ, by Sandro Botticelli.

2008, Dec. 1 **Litho.** *Perf. 14¼x14¾*

2542-2545 A643 Set of 4 3.50 3.50

New Year 2009 (Year of the Ox) — A644

2009, Jan. 2 *Perf. 12*

2546 A644 $60 multi 1.90 1.90

Printed in sheets of 4.

Blindness — A645

Designs: $10, Blind student reading Braille. $30, Blind man in crosswalk. $45, Blind man, map of Liberia. $100, Sighted man leading blind man.

2009, Jan. 4 *Perf. 14¾x14¼*

2547-2550 A645 Set of 4 5.75 5.75

Miniature Sheets

Star Trek A646

No. 2551: a, Captain Kirk. b, USS Enterprise. c, Scotty. d, Uhura. e, Spock. f, Spock, Rand and Kirk.
No. 2552: a, Scotty. b, Spock and Kirk. c, Dr. McCoy. d, Sulu.

2009, Jan. 14 *Perf. 11½*

2551 A646 $35 Sheet of 6, #a-f 6.75 6.75

Perf. 13½x13¼

2552 A646 $60 Sheet of 4, #a-d 7.50 7.50

No. 2552 contains four 38x51mm stamps.

Miniature Sheet

Abraham Lincoln (1809-65), US President — A647

No. 2553: a, US #1282. b, US #555. c, US #367. d, US #222.

2009, Feb. 2 *Perf. 13¼x13½*

2553 A647 $60 Sheet of 4, #a-d 7.50 7.50

Miniature Sheet

John F. Kennedy (1917-63), US President — A648

No. 2554 — Kennedy: a, Greeting Cuban-exile Bay of Pigs invasion force, with wife Jackie, shaking hand. b, Standing with Jackie. c, In White House. d, With Jackie at stadium.

2009, Feb. 25 *Perf. 11¼x11½*

2554 A648 $50 Sheet of 4, #a-d 6.25 6.25

A649

Peonies A650

No. 2556: a, White peony, tan background. b, Pink peony, white background.

2009, Apr. 10 *Perf. 13¼*

2555 A649 $32 multi 1.00 1.00

Souvenir Sheet

2556 A650 $65 Sheet of 2, #a-b 4.00 4.00

No. 2555 was printed in sheets of 6.

Miniature Sheets

A651

A652

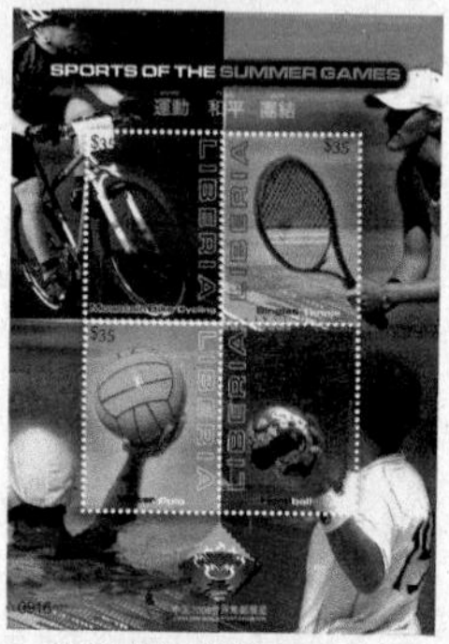

China 2009 World Stamp Exhibition, Luoyang — A653

No. 2557: a, Panda, Chengdu. b, West Lake, Hangzhou. c, Bonsai Garden, Suzhou. d, Fuzi Miao and Qinhuai River, Nanjing.

No. 2558: a, Ornamental plaque (770-476 B.C.). b, Vessel (206 B.C.-A.D. 8). c, Covered jar (1279-1368). d, Head of a Bodhisattva (618-907).

No. 2559: a, Wheel of mountain bike. b, Hand holding tennis racquet. c, Hand holding water polo ball. d, Hand holding handball.

2009, Apr. 10 ***Perf. 12½***

2557	A651	$35	Sheet of 4, #a-d	4.50	4.50
			Perf. 12		
2558	A652	$35	Sheet of 4, #a-d	4.50	4.50
2559	A653	$35	Sheet of 4, #a-d	4.50	4.50
	Nos. 2557-2559 (3)			13.50	13.50

Pope Benedict XVI — A654

2009, May 4 ***Perf. 11¼x11½***

2560 A654 $60 multi 1.75 1.75

Printed in sheets of 4.

Miniature Sheet

Felix Mendelssohn (1809-47), Composer — A655

No. 2561: a, Portrait of young Mendelssohn, by Carl Begas. b, Fanny Mendelssohn, sister of Felix. c, Mendelssohn's sketch of Thomasschule, Leipzig. d, Leipzig Conservatory. e, Portrait of Mendelssohn, by James Warren Childe. f, Mendelssohn drawing made during visit to Scotland.

2009, May 4 ***Perf. 11¼x11½***

2561 A655 $50 Sheet of 6, #a-f 8.75 8.75

A656

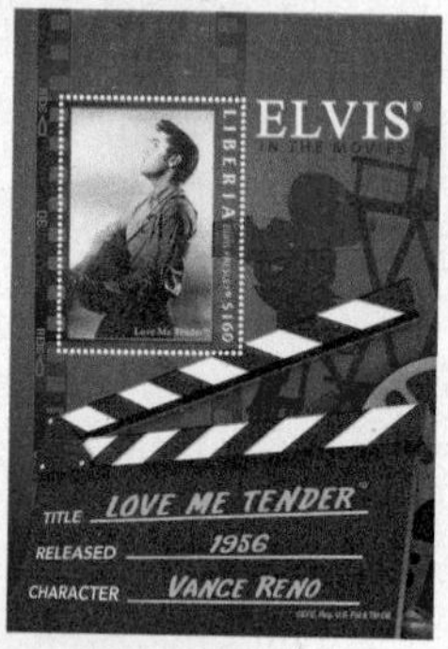

A657

A658

A659

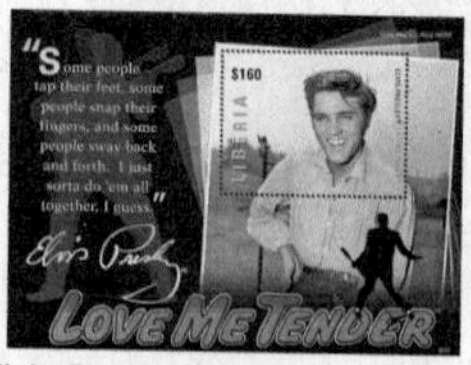

Elvis Presley (1935-77) — A660

No. 2562 — Background color: a, Red brown. b, Tan. c, Gray green. d, Black.

2009, May 4 ***Perf. 13¼***

2562 A656 $65 Sheet of 4, #a-d 7.50 7.50

Souvenir Sheets

Perf. 14¼

2563	A657	$160	multi	4.75	4.75
2564	A658	$160	multi	4.75	4.75
2565	A659	$160	multi	4.75	4.75
2566	A660	$160	multi	4.75	4.75
	Nos. 2563-2566 (4)			19.00	19.00

US Presidents — A661

No. 2567, $20, vert.: a, George Washington. b, John Adams. c, Thomas Jefferson. d, James Madison. e, James Monroe. f, John Quincy Adams. g, Andrew Jackson. h, Martin Van Buren. i, William Henry Harrison. j, John Tyler. k, James K. Polk. l, Zachary Taylor. m, Millard Fillmore. n, Franklin Pierce. o. James Buchanan.

No. 2568, $20, vert.: a, Abraham Lincoln. b, Andrew Johnson. c, Ulysses S. Grant. d, Rutherford B. Hayes. e, James A. Garfield. f, Chester A. Arthur. g, Grover Cleveland (1885-89). h, Benjamin Harrison. i, Grover Cleveland (1893-97). j, William McKinley. k, Theodore Roosevelt. l, William Howard Taft. m, Woodrow Wilson. n, Warren G. Harding. o, Calvin Coolidge.

No. 2569, $20, vert.: a, Herbert Hoover. b, Franklin D. Roosevelt. c, Harry S Truman. d, Dwight D. Eisenhower. e, John F. Kennedy. f, Lyndon B. Johnson. g, Richard M. Nixon. h, Gerald R. Ford. i, Jimmy Carter. j, Ronald Reagan. k, George H. W. Bush (1989-93). l, William J. Clinton. m, George W. Bush (2001-09). n, Barack H. Obama. o, Presidential seal.

$320, Barack Obama.

2009, May 4 ***Perf. 13¼***

Sheets of 15, #a-o

2567-2569	A661	Set of 3	26.00	26.00
2568p		Sheet of 9 #2568a	5.25	5.25
2569p		Miniature sheet, #2569o, 14 #2569n	8.50	8.50

Souvenir Sheet

Perf. 14¼

2570 A661 $320 multi 9.25 9.25

Nos. 2567-2569 each contain fifteen 28x42mm stamps. Issued: No. 2568p, 3/23/10. 2569p, 9/4. See Nos, 3179-3181.

Famous People — A662

Designs: No. 2571, $50, Madame Suakoko (1816-1927), first female paramount chief. No. 2572, $50, Chief Flomo Doughba Barwulor.

2009, Aug. 2 **Litho.** ***Perf. 11¼x11½***

2571-2572 A662 Set of 2 2.75 2.75

Masks — A663

Designs: $10, Korkpor mask. $25, Landa mask. $35, Borwhoo mask. $45, Zoba mask. $100, Kote mask.

2009, Aug. 2 ***Perf. 13¼***

2573-2577 A663 Set of 5 6.00 6.00

Dance — A664

Designs: $30, Traditional dancers. $40, Traditional dancers, diff. $45, Poro dancers.

2009, Aug. 2

2578-2580 A664 Set of 3 3.25 3.25

Souvenir Sheet

Monkey Bridge A665

2009, Aug. 2

2581 A665 $100 multi 2.75 2.75

Miniature Sheets

Players in 2009 National Basketball Association All-Star Game — A666

No. 2582, $30 — Eastern All-stars: a, Ray Allen. b, Kevin Garnett. c, Danny Granger. d, Devin Harris. e, Dwight Howard. f, Allen Iverson. g, LeBron James. h, Joe Johnson. i, Rashard Lewis. j, Paul Pierce. k, Dwayne Wade. l, Mo Williams.

No. 2583, $30 — Western All-stars: a, Chauncey Billups. b, Kobe Bryant. c, Tim Duncan. d, Pau Gasol. e, Yao Ming. f, Dirk Nowitzki. g, Shaquille O'Neal. h, Tony Parker. i, Chris Paul. j, Brandon Roy. k, Amar'e Stoudemire. l, David West.

2009, Aug. 2 ***Perf. 11¼x11½***

Sheets of 12, #a-l

2582-2583 A666 Set of 2 20.00 20.00

Liberian Presidents A667

Designs: $10, Ellen Johnson-Sirleaf. $25, Moses Z. Blah. $35, Charles M.G. Taylor. $45, Samuel K. Doe. $50, William Richard Tolbert. $70, William V.S. Tubman.

Nos. 2590, 2611, Joseph Jenkins Roberts. Nos. 2591, 2612, Stephen Allen Benson. Nos. 2592, 2613, Daniel Bashiel Warner. Nos. 2593, 2614, James Spriggs Payne. Nos. 2594, 2615, Edward James Roye. Nos. 2595, 2616, Anthony Williams Gardiner. Nos. 2596, 2617, Alfred Francis Russell. Nos. 2597, 2618, Hilary R.W. Johnson. Nos. 2598, 2619, Joseph James Cheeseman. Nos. 2599, 2620, William David Coleman. Nos. 2600, 2621, Garretson W. Gibson. Nos. 2601, 2622, Arthur Barclay. Nos. 2602, 2623, Daniel E. Howard. Nos. 2603, 2624, Charles D.B. King. Nos. 2604, 2625, Edwin James Barclay. No. 2605, Tubman. No. 2606, Tolbert. No. 2607, Doe. No. 2608, Taylor. No. 2609, Blah. No. 2610, Johnson-Sirleaf.

2009, Aug. 22 ***Perf. 12¾***

2584	A667	$10	multi	.30	.30
2585	A667	$25	multi	.70	.70
2586	A667	$35	multi	1.00	1.00
2587	A667	$45	multi	1.25	1.25
2588	A667	$50	multi	1.40	1.40
2589	A667	$70	multi	2.00	2.00
2590	A667	$100	multi	2.75	2.75
2591	A667	$100	multi	2.75	2.75
2592	A667	$100	multi	2.75	2.75
2593	A667	$100	multi	2.75	2.75
2594	A667	$100	multi	2.75	2.75
2595	A667	$100	multi	2.75	2.75
2596	A667	$100	multi	2.75	2.75
2597	A667	$100	multi	2.75	2.75
2598	A667	$100	multi	2.75	2.75
2599	A667	$100	multi	2.75	2.75
2600	A667	$100	multi	2.75	2.75
2601	A667	$100	multi	2.75	2.75
2602	A667	$100	multi	2.75	2.75
2603	A667	$100	multi	2.75	2.75
2604	A667	$100	multi	2.75	2.75
2605	A667	$100	multi	2.75	2.75
2606	A667	$100	multi	2.75	2.75
2607	A667	$100	multi	2.75	2.75
2608	A667	$100	multi	2.75	2.75
2609	A667	$100	multi	2.75	2.75
2610	A667	$100	multi	2.75	2.75
2611	A667	$500	multi	14.00	14.00
2612	A667	$500	multi	14.00	14.00
2613	A667	$500	multi	14.00	14.00
2614	A667	$500	multi	14.00	14.00
2615	A667	$500	multi	14.00	14.00
2616	A667	$500	multi	14.00	14.00
2617	A667	$500	multi	14.00	14.00
2618	A667	$500	multi	14.00	14.00
2619	A667	$500	multi	14.00	14.00
2620	A667	$500	multi	14.00	14.00
2621	A667	$500	multi	14.00	14.00
2622	A667	$500	multi	14.00	14.00
2623	A667	$500	multi	14.00	14.00

2624 A667 $500 multi 14.00 14.00
2625 A667 $500 multi 14.00 14.00
Nos. 2584-2625 (42) 274.40 274.40

Chinese Aviation, Cent. A668

No. 2626: a, H-2 missiles. b, H-2B missiles. c, H-12 missiles on trucks. d, H-12 missiles on truck.
$150, H-9 missiles.

2009, Nov. 12 ***Perf. 14***
2626 A668 $50 Sheet of 4, #a-d 6.00 6.00

Souvenir Sheet

Perf. 14¼

2627 A668 $150 multi 4.50 4.50

No. 2626 contains four 42x32mm stamps.

Miniature Sheet

Charles Darwin (1809-82), Naturalist — A669

No. 2628: a, Rhea darwinii. b, Proctotretus fitzingerii. c, Vespertilio chiloensis. d, Geospiza fortis.

2009, Dec. 10 ***Perf. 12x11½***
2628 A669 $60 Sheet of 4, #a-d 7.50 7.50

Miniature Sheet

The Three Stooges A670

No. 2629: a, Stooges with open book. b, Moe sticking drill into Curly's mouth. c, Stooges at table looking at book. d, Curly pointing stick at man.

2009, Dec. 10 ***Perf. 11½x12***
2629 A670 $60 Sheet of 4, #a-d 7.50 7.50

Miniature Sheet

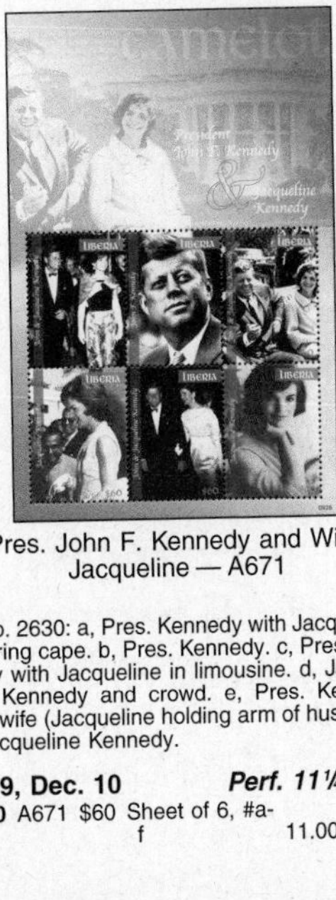

Pres. John F. Kennedy and Wife, Jacqueline — A671

No. 2630: a, Pres. Kennedy with Jacqueline, wearing cape. b, Pres. Kennedy. c, Pres. Kennedy with Jacqueline in limousine. d, Jacqueline Kennedy and crowd. e, Pres. Kennedy and wife (Jacqueline holding arm of husband). f, Jacqueline Kennedy.

2009, Dec. 10 ***Perf. 11¼x11½***
2630 A671 $60 Sheet of 6, #a-f 11.00 11.00

Intl. Year of Astronomy — A672

No. 2631, horiz.: a, Sergei Korolev and Luna 9. b, Luna 9 horizontal on transporter. c, Lift-off of Luna 9. d, Luna 9 over Moon. e, Luna 9 open, with antennae erect. f, Luna 9 open, antennae not erect.
$160, Lift-off of Apollo 11.

2009, Dec. 10 ***Perf. 13½***
2631 A672 $40 Sheet of 6, #a-f 7.50 7.50

Souvenir Sheet

2632 A672 $160 multi 5.00 5.00

Nos. 2631a, 2631b and 2631d have country name misspelled as "Libeira."

Christmas — A673

Paintings: $25, Nativity (Holy Night), by Correggio. $40, Adoration of the Magi, by Bartolomé Esteban Murillo. $50, Adoration of the Magi, by Vicente Gil. $100, Adoration of the Magi, by Peter Paul Rubens.

2009, Dec. 10 ***Perf. 13¼x13***
2633-2636 A673 Set of 4 6.50 6.50

Miniature Sheet

Awarding of Nobel Peace Prize to US Pres. Barack Obama A674

No. 2637 — Pres. Obama wearing: a, Red tie, facing right. b, Red tie, facing forward. c, Blue tie, facing forward. d, Blue tie, facing left.

2009, Dec. 30 **Litho.** ***Perf. 12x11½***
2637 A674 $60 Sheet of 4, #a-d 7.00 7.00

Miniature Sheet

Chinese Zodiac Animals A675

No. 2638: a, Dragon. b, Snake. c, Horse. d, Goat. e, Monkey. f, Rooster. g, Dog. h, Pig. i, Rat. j, Ox. k, Tiger. l, Rabbit.

2010, Jan. 4 ***Perf. 12½***
2638 A675 $15 Sheet of 12, #a-l 6.00 6.00

Souvenir Sheet

New Year 2010 (Year of the Tiger) A676

No. 2639: a, Tiger. b, Tiger and Chinese characters.

2010, Jan. 4 ***Perf. 14¾x14¼***
2639 A676 $130 Sheet of 2, #a-b 7.50 7.50

Miniature Sheets

Dogs A677

No. 2640, $65 — German shorthaired pointer: a, At duckpond. b, With trees and building in background. c, On rocks. d, Sniffing flowers.
No. 2641, $65 — Chihuahua: a, On pink dog bed. b, Standing. c, At pond. d, In small pot.

2010, Jan. 19 ***Perf. 11½x12***

Sheets of 4, #a-d

2640-2641 A677 Set of 2 15.00 15.00

Miniature Sheets

A678

Visit of Pope Benedict XVI to Great Synagogue of Rome — A679

No. 2642: a, Great Synagogue. b, Pope Benedict XVI and Rome's Chief Rabbi Riccardo Di Segni. c, Pope Benedict XVI and Cardinal. d, Rabbi Di Segni and man wearing white yarmulke.
No. 2643: a, Pope Benedict XVI and Rabbi Di Segni seated. b, Rome's former Chief Rabbi Elio Toaff. c, Pope Benedixt XVI, standing and reaching for Toaff. d, Pope Benedict XVI with hands clasped.

2010, Mar. 23 ***Perf. 12x11½***
2642 A678 $110 Sheet of 4, #a-d 12.50 12.50

Perf. 11½

2643 A679 $110 Sheet of 4, #a-d 12.50 12.50

Miniature Sheets

Boy Scouts of America, Cent. A680

No. 2644, $55 — Merit badges: a, Swimming, First Aid. b, Environmental Science, Family Life. c, Citizenship in the Community, Personal Management. d, Camping, Lifesaving. e, Citizenship in the Nation, Communications. f, Personal Fitness, Citizenship in the World.
No. 2645, $55 — Merit badges: a, Aviation, Fishing. b, Engineering, Electronics. c, Medicine, Music. d, Graphic Arts, Soil and Water Conservation. e, Cinematography, Oceanography. f, Animal Science, Art.

2010, Mar. 23 ***Perf. 13¼***

Sheets of 6, #a-f

2644-2645 A680 Set of 2 19.00 19.00

Whales and Dolphins A681

No. 2646: a, Harbor porpoise. b, Killer whale. c, Sowerby's beaked whale. d, Atlantic spotted dolphin. e, Atlantic hump-backed dolphin. f, Clymene dolphin.
$180, Gervais beaked whale.

2010, Apr. 26 ***Perf. 14¾x14¼***
2646 A681 $60 Sheet of 6, #a-f 10.50 10.50

Souvenir Sheet

2647 A681 $180 multi 5.25 5.25

US Pres. Barack Obama and Wife, Michelle A682

No. 2648: a, Pres. Obama. b, Pres Obama with arm around wife's waist. c, Pres. Obama and wife dancing. d, Michelle Obama.
No. 2649, Head of Michelle Obama. No. 2650, Michelle Obama (30x81mm).

2010, Apr. 26 ***Perf. 14¼x14¾***
2648 A682 $60 Sheet of 4, #a-d 7.00 7.00

Souvenir Sheets

2649 A682 $100 multi 3.00 3.00
2650 A682 $100 multi 3.00 3.00

Miniature Sheets

A683

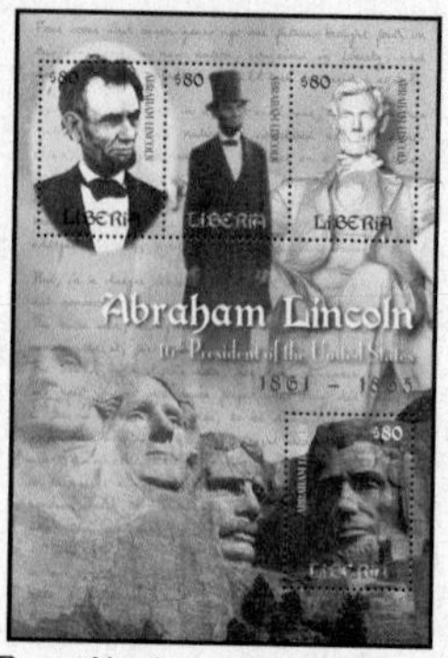

Pres. Abraham Lincoln (1809-65) — A684

No. 2651, $80 — Lincoln: a, Facing right, hand visible at LR. b, Facing left. c, Facing right, no hand visible. d, Facing right, hand visible at center bottom.

No. 2652, $80 — Lincoln: a, Photograph without hat. b, Photograph with hat. c, Lincoln Memorial sculpture. d, Mount Rushmore sculpture.

2010, June 25 *Perf. 12x11½*

2651 A683 $80 Sheet of 4, #a-d 9.00 9.00
2652 A684 $80 Sheet of 4, #a-d 9.00 9.00

Girl Guides, Cent. A685

No. 2653, horiz.: a, Three Girl Guides, one wearing cap. b, Three Girl Guides wearing neckerchiefs. c, Three Girl Guides. d, Five Girl Guides in uniform.

$160, Girl Guide wearing cap.

2010, June 25 *Perf. 13x13¼*

2653 A685 $65 Sheet of 4, #a-d 7.25 7.25

Souvenir Sheet

Perf. 13¼x13

2654 A685 $160 multi 4.50 4.50

Lech Kaczynski (1949-2010), President of Poland — A686

2010, Aug. 27 *Perf. 11½*

2655 A686 $75 multi 2.10 2.10

Printed in sheets of 4.

Paintings by Michelangelo Merisi da Caravaggio (1573-1610) — A687

No. 2656, horiz.: a, The Beheading of St. John the Baptist. b, Judith Beheading Holofernes. c, Abraham's Sacrifice. d, Medusa.

$180, The Penitent Mary Magdalene.

2010, Aug. 27 *Perf. 11½x11¼*

2656 A687 $80 Sheet of 4, #a-d 9.00 9.00

Souvenir Sheet

Perf. 11¼x11½

2657 A687 $180 multi 5.25 5.25

Henri Dunant (1828-1910), Founder of the Red Cross — A688

No. 2658 — Red Cross, Florence Nightingale, depictions of war casualties and nurses, and portrait of Dunant in: a, Gray green. b, Brown. c, Purple. d, Gray blue.

$180, Red Cross, Nightingale, war casualties at Red Cross station, Dunant in purple.

2010, Aug. 27 *Perf. 11½x12*

2658 A688 $80 Sheet of 4, #a-d 9.00 9.00

Souvenir Sheet

Perf. 11½x11¼

2659 A688 $180 multi 5.25 5.25

Miniature Sheets

A689

A690

Princess Diana (1961-97) — A691

No. 2660 — Princess Diana with: a, Bare shoulders and single-stand pearl necklace. b, Pink and white hat. c, White dress, earrings, no hat. d, White hat, dark blue and white dress.

No. 2661 — Princess Diana with: a, Tiara. b, Pink hat and dress. c, Green sweater, white blouse. d, Red and white jacket, white blouse.

No. 2662 — Princess Diana with: a, Red dress and flower bouquet. b, White dress, pendant earrings, no hat. c, Bare shoulders and multi-strand pearl necklace. d, White dress, pearl necklace, no hat.

2010, Aug. 27 *Perf. 13¼*

2660 A689 $75 Sheet of 4, #a-d 8.50 8.50
2661 A690 $75 Sheet of 4, #a-d 8.50 8.50
2662 A691 $75 Sheet of 4, #a-d 8.50 8.50
Nos. 2660-2662 (3) 25.50 25.50

Miniature Sheets

A692

A693

Elvis Presley (1935-77) — A694

No. 2663 — Presley: a, With hands pointing left. b, Holding microphone. c, With guitar, holding microphone.

No. 2664 — Paintings of Presley with backgrounds of: a, Green and black. b, Orange and bister. c, Black and red.

No. 2665: a, Presley's face in orange and yellow. b, Presley's face in light blue and white. c, Presley's face in blue and gray. d, Silhouette of Presley.

2010, Aug. 27 *Perf. 11½x11¼*

2663 A692 $90 Sheet of 3, #a-c 7.75 7.75

Perf. 11¼x11½

2664 A693 $90 Sheet of 3, #a-c 7.75 7.75

Perf. 13

2665 A694 $90 Sheet of 4, #a-d 10.00 10.00
Nos. 2663-2665 (3) 25.50 25.50

Cats A695

No. 2666, vert.: a, Siberian. b, Turkish Angora. c, British shorthair. d, Maine coon. e, Abyssinian. f, Scottish fold.

$180, Bluepoint Himalayan.

2010, Oct. 27 *Perf. 11¼x11½*

2666 A695 $60 Sheet of 6, #a-f 10.50 10.50

Souvenir Sheet

Perf. 11½x11¼

2667 A695 $180 multi 5.25 5.25

Nos. 2666-2667 exist imperf. Value, set $25.

Miniature Sheets

Pres. John F. Kennedy (1917-63) — A696

No. 2668, $80 — Olive bister frames with Kennedy: a, Walking with Vice-president Lyndon B. Johnson. b, On telephone. c, At lectern. d, Looking upwards.

No. 2669, $80 — Blue frames with Kennedy: a, At lectern. b, Walking with McGeorge Bundy. c, Campaigning in New York City. d, With hands clasped.

No. 2670, $80 — Red frames with Kennedy: a, With Dr. Wernher von Braun. b, With wife, Jacqueline, watching space flight on television. c, At lectern. d, Viewing Friendship 7 space capsule.

2010, Oct. 27 *Perf. 12x11½*

Sheets of 4, #a-d

2668-2670 A696 Set of 3 28.00 28.00

Christmas — A697

Paintings: $25, The Annunciation, by Fra Angelico. $40, The Angelic Announcement to the Shepherds, by Taddeo Gaddi. $50, Adoration of the Shepherds, by Guido Reni. $100, Virgin and Child with Angels and Saints, by Felice Torelli.

2010, Oct. 27 **Litho.** *Perf. 11½*

2671-2674 A697 Set of 4 6.25 6.25

Liberian Politicians — A698

Designs: $25, Pres. Ellen Johnson-Sirleaf receiving gift. $45, Pres. Johnson Sirleaf standing with Chinese Pres. Hu Jintao, vert. No. 2677, $50, Pres. Johnson-Sirleaf reading. No. 2678, $50, Vice-president Joseph N. Boakai. No. 2679, $100, Pres. Johnson-Sirleaf sitting with Pres. Hu. No. 2680, $100, Pres. Johnson-Sirleaf shaking hands with Vice-president Boakai. No. 2681, $100, Pres. Johnson-Sirleaf wearing sash of office, vert. No. 2682, $500, Pres. Johnson-Sirleaf meeting with international investors. No. 2683, $500, Pres. Johnson-Sirleaf with Vice-president Boakai and cabinet.

2010, Dec. 16 *Perf. 12*

2675-2683 A698 Set of 9 *5.00 5.00*

Nos. 2675-2683 were sold to the philatelic trade at prices well below that indicated by currency exchange rates at the date of issue.

Mother Teresa (1910-97), Humanitarian — A699

Various photos with frame color of: No. 2684, $80, Olive bister. No. 2685, $80, Blue.

2010, Dec. 16

2684-2685 A699 Set of 2 4.50 4.50

Nos. 2684-2685 each were printed in sheets of 4.

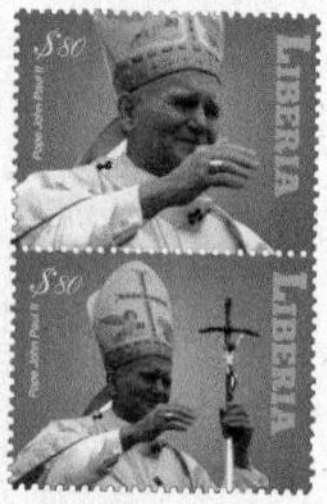

Pope John Paul II (1920-2005) A700

No. 2686 — Red background: a, Without crucifix. b, With crucifix.

No. 2687 — Purple background: a, With crucifix. b, Without crucifix.

2010, Dec. 16

2686 A700 $80 Pair, #a-b 4.50 4.50
2687 A700 $80 Horiz. pair, #a-b 4.50 4.50

Nos. 2686-2687 each were printed in sheets containing two pairs.

Paintings of Sandro Botticelli (1455-1510) — A701

No. 2688 — Details from The Birth of Venus: a, Head of Venus. b, Reversed image of torso of winged zephyrs. c, Reversed image of heads of winged zephyrs. d, Nymph.
$160, Portrait of St. Augustine, vert.

2010, Dec. 16 *Perf. 12*
2688 A701 $80 Sheet of 4, #a-d 9.00 9.00

Souvenir Sheet

Perf. 12½x12¾

2689 A701 $160 multi 4.50 4.50

No. 2689 contains one 38x50mm stamp.

A702

Michael Jackson (1958-2009), Singer — A703

No. 2690 — Jackson: a, With arched back, holding microphone. b, Moving hat to cover face. c, Wearing white glove and hat. d, With arched back, arms stretched outward.
No. 2691 — Jackson: a, Wearing red shirt. b, Holding microphone. c, With arm outstretched. d, With spotlights in background, holding microphone.
$180, Jackson singing.

2010, Dec. 16 *Perf. 12*
2690 A702 $80 Sheet of 4, #a-d 9.00 9.00
2691 A703 $80 Sheet of 4, #a-d 9.00 9.00

Souvenir Sheet

2692 A703 $180 multi 5.00 5.00

Miniature Sheets

Mao Zedong (1893-1976), Chairman of People's Republic of China — A704

Hu Jintao, President of People's Republic of China — A705

No. 2693 — Mao: a, Without cap, no pockets shown on jacket. b, Wearing cap, pockets shown on jacket. c, Without cap, pockets shown on jacket. d, With cap, no pockets shown on jacket.
No. 2694 — Pres. Hu: a, Ear at left visible, tie over jacket. b, Both ears visible. c, Ear at right visible. d, Ear at left visible, tie under jacket.

2010, Nov. 7 **Litho.** *Perf. 12*
2693 A704 $90 Sheet of 4, #a-d 10.50 10.50
2694 A705 $90 Sheet of 4, #a-d 10.50 10.50

Beijing 2010 Intl. Philatelic Exhibition.

Miniature Sheet

Anti-Apartheid Activists of South Africa — A706

No. 2695: a, Helen Suzman (1917-2009). b, Eli Weinberg (1908-81). c, Hymie Barsel (1920-87). d, Esther Barsel (1924-2008), and South African Pres. Nelson Mandela.

2011, Mar. 1
2695 A706 $75 Sheet of 4, #a-d 8.50 8.50

Chinese Zodiac Animals A707

New Year 2011 (Year of the Rabbit) A708

No. 2696: a, Rat. b, Ox. c, Tiger. d, Rabbit. e, Dragon. f, Snake. g, Horse. h, Sheep. i, Monkey. j, Rooster. k, Dog. l, Pig.

2011, Mar. 28
2696 A707 $25 Sheet of 12, #a-l 8.50 8.50

Souvenir Sheet

2697 A708 Sheet of 2 #2697a 5.75 5.75
a. $100 Single stamp 2.75 2.75

British Monarchs — A709

Designs: No. 2698, $80, King George V (1865-1936). No. 2699, $80, King Edward VIII (1894-1972). No. 2700, $80, King George VI (1895-1952). No. 2701, $80, Queen Elizabeth II.

Perf. 13 Syncopated, 12 (#2700)

2011, Mar. 28
2698-2701 A709 Set of 4 9.00 9.00

Nos. 2698-2701 each were printed in sheets of 4.

Princess Diana (1961-97) in India — A710

No. 2702, vert. — Princess Diana: a, Greeting girl with hands together, red background. b, Touching woman on cot, red background. c, Talking with Mother Teresa, red background. d, Shaking hands with seated man, purple background. e, With woman and small boy, purple background. f, At Taj Mahal, purple background.
$360, Princess Diana talking with seated people.

2011, Mar. 28 *Perf. 13 Syncopated*
2702 A710 $60 Sheet of 6, #a-f 10.00 10.00

Souvenir Sheet

2703 A710 $360 multi 10.00 10.00

Indipex 2011 Intl. Philatelic Exhibition, New Delhi.

Engagement of Prince William and Catherine Middleton — A711

Deisgns: No. 2704, $65, Couple, dull green background. No. 2705, $65, Couple, gray background.
No. 2706, $100: a, Catherine Middleton. b, Prince William.
No. 2707, $100, horiz.: a, Couple, Middleton touching hat. b, Couple, Middleton not touching hat.

Perf. 12, 13 Syncopated (#2707)

2011, Mar. 28
2704-2705 A711 Set of 2 3.75 3.75

Sheets of 2, #a-b

2706-2707 A711 Set of 2 11.50 11.50

Pres. John F. Kennedy (1917-63) — A712

No. 2708 — Kennedy: a, Oval portrait. b, Close-up of head. c, Wearing patterned tie. d, Wearing pinstripe suit and solid tie.
$180, Kennedy, diff.

2011, Mar. 28 *Perf. 12*
2708 A712 $80 Sheet of 4, #a-d 9.00 9.00

Souvenir Sheet

2709 A712 $180 multi 5.00 5.00

Miniature Sheets

U.S. Civil War, 150th Anniv. A713

No. 2710, $80 — Lieutenant Colonel John B. Baylor, Major Isaac Lynde and Battle of Mesilla image: a, Town and valley of Mesilla. b, Fort Fillmore. c, Confederates near the Organ Mountains. d, Union soldiers firing at long range.
No. 2711, $80 — Colonel Martin E. Green, Colonel David Moore and Battle of Athens image: a, Confederates near the Fabius River. b, Col. Moore leads Union troops. c, Cavalries clash at Athens encounter. d, Col. Green's Missouri State Guard.
No. 2712, $80 — Major General Sterling Price, Captain Nathaniel Lyon and Battle of Wilson's Creek image: a, Missouri State Guardsmen on Bloody Hill. b, Confederate battery in action. c, Lt. Omar Weaver is wounded. d, 2nd Kansas Infantry on Bloody Hill.
No. 2713, $80 — Brigadier General John B. Floyd, Colonel Erastus Tyler and Battle of Kessler's Cross Lanes image: a, Confederate forces in the Kanawha Valley. b, 7th Ohio Regiment at Kessler's Cross Lanes. c, The Union forces surprised and routed. d, Confederate forces near the Gauley River.
No. 2714, $80 — Captain Samuel Barron, Major General Benjamin F. Butler and Battle of Hatteras Inlet image: a, Capture of Fort Hatteras. b, Union Atlantic blockading squadron. c, USS Harriet Lane. d, USS Cumberland.

2011, Mar. 28 ***Perf. 13 Syncopated***

Sheets of 4, #a-d

2710-2714 A713 Set of 5 45.00 45.00

Mushrooms — A714

No. 2715: a, Penny bun. b, Ola'h. c, The miller. d, False ink cap. e, The blusher. f, Glistening ink cap.
No. 2716: a, Death cap. b, Panther cap.

2011, Mar. 28 *Perf. 12*
2715 A714 $65 Sheet of 6, #a-f 11.00 11.00

Souvenir Sheet

2716 A714 $65 Sheet of 2, #a-b 3.75 3.75

Birds A715

No. 2717: a, Red-faced cisticola. b, Orange-cheeked waxbill. c, Zebra waxbill. d, African firefinch.

No. 2718, $180, Guinea turaco. No. 2719, $180, Lavender waxbill, vert.

Perf. 12, 13 Syncopated (#2718)

2011, Mar. 28

2717 A715 $80 Sheet of 4, #a-d 9.00 9.00

Souvenir Sheets

2718-2719 A715 Set of 2 10.00 10.00

Miniature Sheets

Zodiac Constellations — A716

No. 2720, $100: a, Aries. b, Leo. c, Sagittarius.

No. 2721, $100: a, Gemini. b, Libra. c, Aquarius.

No. 2722, $100: a, Cancer. b, Scorpio. c, Pisces.

No. 2723, $100: a, Virgo. b, Taurus. c, Capricorn.

2011, Mar. 28 ***Perf. 12***

Sheets of 3, #a-c

2720-2723 A716 Set of 4 34.00 34.00

Souvenir Sheets

Pres. Ellen Johnson-Sirleaf — A717

Designs: $45, Pres. Johnson-Sirleaf and Chinese President Hu Jintao. No. 2725, $100, Pres. Johnson-Sirleaf. No. 2726, $100, Pres. Johnson-Sirleaf and Pres. Hu, horiz.

2011, Mar. 28 ***Perf. 13¼x13, 13x13¼***

2724-2726 A717 Set of 3 7.00 7.00

Souvenir Sheets

Popes and Their Arms A718

No. 2727, $250: a, Pope Pius XII (1876-1958). b, Arms of Pope Pius XII.

No. 2728, $250: a, Pope John XXIII (1881-1963). b, Arms of Pope John XXIII.

2011, Mar. 28 ***Imperf.***

Sheets of 2, #a-b
Without Gum

2727-2728 A718 Set of 2 28.00 28.00

Visit of Chinese President Hu Jintao to Washington, D.C. — A719

No. 2729 — Presidents Hu Jintao and Barack Obama: a, Shaking hands. b, Standing near lectern. c, Greeting crowd. d, Walking outside of White House.

$180, Reviewing troops.

2011, Mar. 28 **Litho.** ***Perf. 12***

2729 A719 $75 Sheet of 4, #a-d 8.50 8.50

Souvenir Sheet

2730 A719 $180 multi 5.25 5.25

Back to the Soil — A720

Inscriptions: $25, Invest in the Soil Rubber Farm. $45, Women scratching rice, horiz. $50, Rice nursery in Bong County. $70, The soil is a bank. $100, President Ellen Johnson-Sirleaf harvesting rice, horiz. No. 2736, $500, Fresh fruits and vegetables. No. 2737, $500, Harvesting rice, horiz.

Perf. 12¾x12½, 12½x12¾

2011, Mar. 28

2731-2737 A720 Set of 7 37.50 37.50

Worldwide Fund for Nature (WWF) — A721

No. 2738 — Water chevrotain: a, Standing in foliage. b, In water. c, Eating. d, Pair in foliage.

2011, June 30 ***Perf. 13¼***

2738 Strip of 4 5.75 5.75
a.-d. A721 $50 Any single 1.40 1.40
e. Souvenir sheet of 8, 2 each #2738a-2738d 11.50 11.50

Miniature Sheet

A.C. Milan Soccer Team A722

No. 2739 — Team emblem and photographs of: a, 2003 UEFA Champions League match. b, Centennial emblem, 1999. c, 2001 6-0 A.C. Milan- Milan Inter match. d, Carlo Ancelloti. e, 2010-11 team. f, Paolo Maldini. g, 2007 UEFA Champions League match. h, Team members with 2007 FIFA Club World Cup. i, Team owner Italian Prime Minister Silvio Berlusconi.

2011, June 30 ***Perf. 13½***

2739 A722 $35 Sheet of 9, #a-i 8.75 8.75

Miniature Sheets

A723

Chocolate Candy — A724

No. 2740: a, Cacao pods. b, Sun. c, Ship. d, Fires. e, Mound of cocoa powder. f, Milk and butter. g, Chocolate bar and wrapped candy. h, Cash register and chocolate bar. i, Mouth and chocolate bar.

No. 2741 — Piece of candy with: a, Chocolate coating with white chocolate swirls. b, Dark chocolate coating with walnut. c, White chocolate coating with dark chocolate swirls. d, White chocolate coating with chocolate swirls. e, Chocolate coating with dark chocolate ribbons. f, Dark chocolate coating with chocolate sprinkles. g, Chocolate coating with chocolate rosette. h, Dark chocolate coating with almond. i, White chocolate coating with candy heart.

2011, June 30 ***Perf. 13 Syncopated***

2740 A723 $30 Sheet of 9, #a-i 7.50 7.50
2741 A724 $30 Sheet of 9, #a-i 7.50 7.50

Nos. 2740-2741 each are impregnated with a chocolate aroma.

A725

U.S. Civil War, 150th Anniv. A726

No. 2742: a, Union General Ulysses S. Grant. b, Drum, rifles, Union and Confederate flags. c, Confederate General Robert E. Lee. d, Pres. Abraham Lincoln. e, Cannons.

No. 2743 — Paintings depicting Lincoln: a, Abraham Lincoln, by William F. Cogswell. b, The Peacemakers, by George Healy. c, President Lincoln Writing the Proclamation of Freedom, by David Gilmour Blythe.

2011, June 30 ***Perf. 12¾x13***

2742 A725 $70 Sheet of 5, #a-e 9.75 9.75

Perf. 13¼x13

2743 A726 $100 Sheet of 3, #a-c 8.25 8.25

Jane Goodall's Roots and Shoots, 25th Anniv. A727

No. 2744: a, Adult showing group of children how to plant seedlings. b, Two children planting seedlings. c, Children holding sign. d, Children and teachers in classroom.

$180, Children.

2011, June 30 ***Perf. 13x13¼***

2744 A727 $90 Sheet of 4, #a-d 10.00 10.00

Souvenir Sheet

2745 A727 $180 multi 5.00 5.00

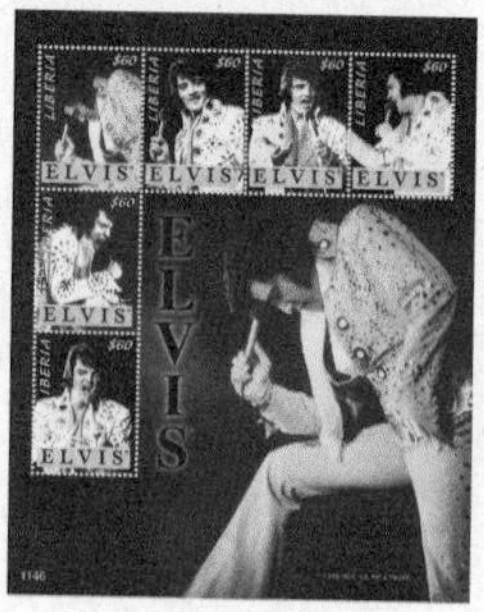

A728

A729

A730

A731

A732

A733

Elvis Presley (1935-77) — A734

No. 2746: a, Face in color. b, Face in black and white, microphone cord above "E." c, As "b," microphone between "I" and "S." d, As "b," microphone cord above "L." e, As "b," microphone cord above "S." f, As "b," microphone cord between "V" and "I."

No. 2747: a, Head of microphone above shoulder. b, Head of microphone even with edge of guitar. c, Head of microphone at right. d, Head of microphone even with tip of chin.

No. 2748 — Presley: a, On motorcycle. b, Wearing white tie. c, Wearing white shirt open at neck. d, Playing guitar.

2011, June 30 ***Perf. 12¾x13***

2746 A728 $60 Sheet of 6, #a-f 10.00 10.00

Perf. 13¼x13

2747 A729 $80 Sheet of 4, #a-d 8.75 8.75

Perf. 13 Syncopated

2748 A730 $90 Sheet of 4, #a-d 10.00 10.00

Nos. 2746-2748 (3) 28.75 28.75

Souvenir Sheets

Perf. 12¾

2749 A731 $180 multi 5.00 5.00
2750 A732 $180 multi 5.00 5.00
2751 A733 $180 multi 5.00 5.00
2752 A734 $180 multi 5.00 5.00

Nos. 2749-2752 (4) 20.00 20.00

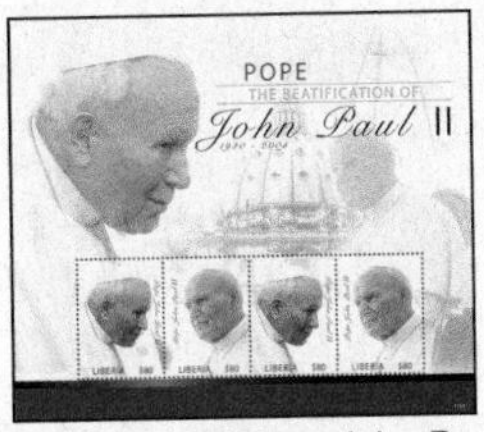

Beatification of Pope John Paul II — A735

No. 2753 — Pope John Paul II facing: a, Right, gray area at LR. b, Left, gray area at top. c, Right, no gray area at LR. d, Left, no gray area at top.

$180, Pope John Paul II wearing miter and green stole.

2011, Aug. 5 **Litho.** ***Perf. 12***

2753 A735 $80 Sheet of 4, #a-d 9.00 9.00

Souvenir Sheet

2754 A735 $180 multi 5.00 5.00

Statue of Liberty, 125th Anniv. A736

No. 2755 — Inscription at right: a, National Monument. b, Lighting the Night Sky. c, Liberty Island, New York Harbor. d, Designed by Frédéric Auguste Bartholdi. e, Enlightening the World, 1886, by Edward Moran. f, Under Construction in Paris, France.

$180, Statue of Liberty and Manhattan buildings, horiz.

2011, Aug. 5 ***Perf. 12***

2755 A736 $60 Sheet of 6, #a-f 10.00 10.00

Souvenir Sheet

Perf. 12½

2756 A736 $180 multi 5.00 5.00

No. 2756 contains one 51x38mm stamp.

Butterflies — A737

No. 2757: a, Gaudy commodore. b, Yellow pansy. c, White lady swallowtail. d, Broad-bordered grass yellow. e, Blue pansy. f, Citrus swallowtail.

No. 2758: a, Mimic female. b, Wandering donkey acaea.

2011, Aug. 5 ***Perf. 12***

2757 A737 $65 Sheet of 6, #a-f 11.00 11.00

Souvenir Sheet

2758 A737 $100 Sheet of 2, #a-b 5.50 5.50

Miniature Sheets

A738

Princess Diana (1961-97) — A739

No. 2759: a, Wearing hat with veil. b, Wearing dark hat and winter jacket. c, Without hat. d, Wearing dark hat and white dress.

No. 2760: a, Wearing blue dress and necklace. b, Wearing blue hat. c, Wearing blue jacket, no necklace. d, Wearing white hat.

2011, Aug. 5 ***Perf. 13 Syncopated***

2759 A738 $75 Sheet of 4, #a-d 8.25 8.25
2760 A739 $75 Sheet of 4, #a-d 8.25 8.25

First Man in Space, 50th Anniv. A740

No. 2761, $80: a, Statue of Yuri Gagarin. b, American astronaut John Glenn. c, Gagarin on medal. d, Vostok spacecraft in orbit.

No. 2762, $80, horiz.: a, Gagarin souvenir medal. b, Mosaic of Gagarin. c, Vostok rocket on train. d, American astronauts Virgil Grissom and John Young.

No. 2763, $180, Gagarin. No. 2764, $180, Vostok spacecraft, horiz.

2011, Aug. 5 ***Perf. 13 Syncopated***

Sheets of 4, #a-d

2761-2762 A740 Set of 2 18.00 18.00

Souvenir Sheets

2763-2764 A740 Set of 2 10.00 10.00

Orchids A741

No. 2765: a, Polystachya longiscapa. b, Vanilla polylepis. c, Ansellia africana. d, Bolusiella maudiae.

No. 2766, $180, Polystachya zambesiaca. No. 2767, $180, Polystachya bella.

2011, Aug. 5 ***Perf. 12***

2765 A741 $80 Sheet of 4, #a-d 9.00 9.00

Souvenir Sheets

2766-2767 A741 Set of 2 10.00 10.00

Sept. 11, 2001 Terrorist Attacks, 10th Anniv. A742

No. 2768: a, World Trade Center. b, September 11 Memorial, New York. c, Tribute in Light. d, The Pentagon.

$200, World Trade Center and Brooklyn Bridge, vert.

2011, Sept. 11 ***Perf. 13 Syncopated***

2768 A742 $75 Sheet of 4, #a-d 8.25 8.25

Souvenir Sheet

2769 A742 $200 multi 5.50 5.50

Chinese Civil Engineering A743

Designs: $40, Qingdao Cross-sea Bridge.

No. 2771 — Qingdao Jiaozhouwan Undersea Tunnel: a, Entrance. b, Cross-sectional diagram.

2011, Oct. 11 **Litho.**

2770 A743 $40 multi 1.10 1.10
2771 A743 $25 Sheet of 6, 3 each #2771a-2771b 4.25 4.25

No. 2770 was printed in sheets of 4.

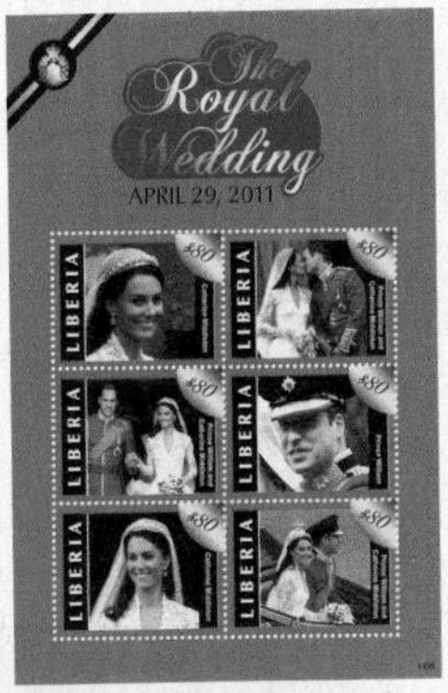

A744

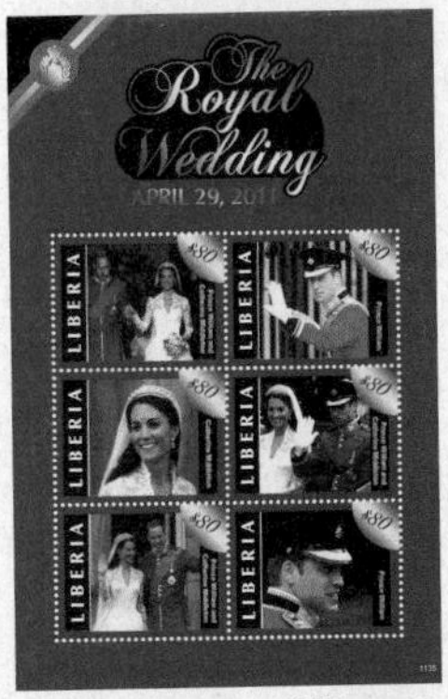

Wedding of Prince William and Catherine Middleton — A745

No. 2772 — Red frames: a, Bride facing right. b, Couple kissing. c, Couple holding hands. d, Groom. e, Bride facing left. f, Couple in coach.

No. 2773 — Blue frames: a, Couple holding hands. b, Groom waving. c, Bride facing left. d, Couple in coach, groom waving. e, Couple standing, bride waving. f, Groom facing right.

$180, Couple in coach, bride waving.

2011, Oct. 11 ***Perf. 12***

2772 A744 $80 Sheet of 6, #a-f 13.50 13.50
2773 A745 $80 Sheet of 6, #a-f 13.50 13.50

Souvenir Sheet

2774 A745 $180 multi 5.00 5.00

Christmas — A746

Paintings: $25, Madonna with Members of the Pesaro Family, by Titian. $40, The Nativity, by Prero della Francesca. $50, The Virgin of the Rocks, by Leonardo da Vinci. $100, Madonna with Child, by Fra Filippo Lippi.

2011, Oct. 11 ***Perf. 13 Syncopated***

2775-2778 A746 Set of 4 6.00 6.00

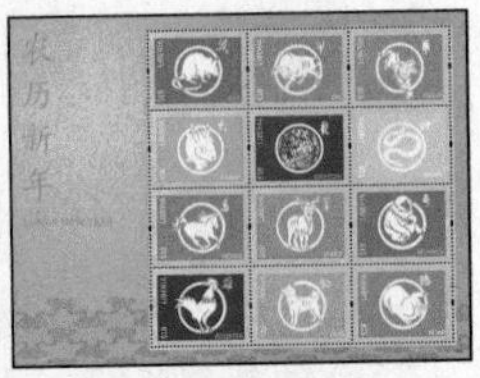

Chinese Zodiac Animals A747

New Year 2012 (Year of the Dragon) A748

No. 2779: a, Rat. b, Ox. c, Tiger. d, Rabbit. e, Dragon. f, Snake. g, Horse. h, Sheep. i, Monkey. j, Rooster. k, Dog. l, Boar.

Litho. With Foil Application

2011, Oct. 11 ***Perf. 13 Syncopated***

2779 A747 $18 Sheet of 12, #a-l 6.00 6.00

Souvenir Sheet

Litho.

Perf. 13¼

2780 A748 $200 multi 5.75 5.75

China 2011 World Philatelic Exhibition, Wuxi (No. 2780).

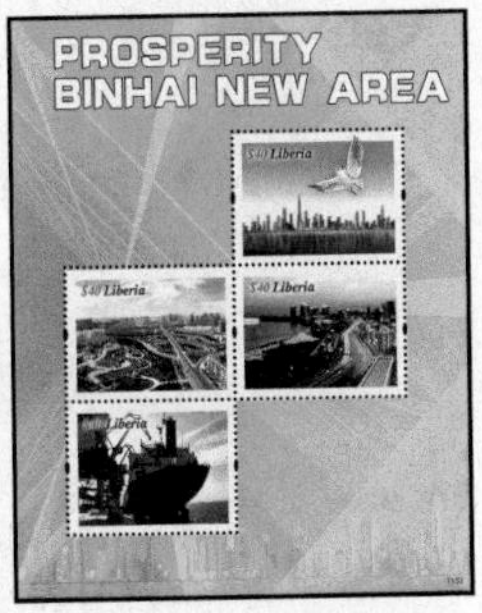

Binhai New Area, People's Republic of China A749

No. 2781: a, Dove, city. b, Highway cloverleaf interchange. c, City at nightfall. d, Ship at dock.

$160, City, ship, airplanes, rocket.

Perf. 13 Syncopated

2011, Oct. 26 **Litho.**

2781 A749 $40 Sheet of 4, #a-d 4.50 4.50

Souvenir Sheet

2782 A749 $160 multi 4.50 4.50

No. 2782 contains one 119x40mm stamp.

Peking Opera A750

No. 2783 — Character with: a, Two sharp teeth, (gray, red and pink face). b, Beard (black and red face). c, Heart-shaped nose (pink, red and black face). d, Ten teeth (red, black and gray face). $180, Character with red, dark red and black face.

2011, Oct. 26 ***Perf. 13¼***

2783 A750 $50 Sheet of 4, #a-d 5.75 5.75

Souvenir Sheet

2784 A750 $180 multi 5.00 5.00

China 2011 Intl. Philatelic Exhibition, Wuxi. No. 2784 contains one 44x44mm stamp.

Pres. Ronald Reagan (1911-2004) — A751

Flags and Pres. Reagan wearing suit: No. 2785, $100, Without handkerchief in suit pocket. No. 2786, $100, With handkerchief in suit pocket.

2011, Dec. 16 ***Perf. 13 Syncopated***
2785-2786 A751 Set of 2 5.50 5.50

Nos. 2785-2786 each were printed in sheets of 3.

Awarding of Nobel Peace Prize to Pres. Ellen Johnson-Sirleaf A752

Designs: $75, Shown. $250, Pres. Johnson-Sirleaf, horiz.

2011, Dec. 5 ***Perf. 12***
2787 A752 $75 multi 2.10 2.10

Souvenir Sheet

2788 A752 $250 multi 7.00 7.00

No. 2787 was printed in sheets of 6. No. 2788 contains one 50x30mm stamp.

Reptiles A753

No. 2789: a, Natal green snake. b, African tree snake. c, African python.

No. 2790: a, African spiny-tailed lizard. b, Western Cape crag lizard. c, Eastern Cape crag lizard. d, Armadillo lizard.

No. 2791: a, African tent tortoise. b, Serrated tortoise.

No. 2792: a, Underside of Nile crocodile. b, Top of Nile crocodile.

2011, Dec. 16 ***Perf. 12***
2789 A753 $90 Sheet of 3, #a-c 7.50 7.50
2790 A753 $90 Sheet of 4, #a-d 10.00 10.00

Souvenir Sheets

2791 A753 $180 Sheet of 2, #a-b 10.00 10.00
2792 A753 $180 Sheet of 2, #a-b 10.00 10.00

No. 2790 contains four 50x30mm stamps. No. 2792 contains two 80x30mm stamps.

Completion of St. Paul's Cathedral, London, 300th Anniv. — A754

No. 2793: a, Plan of Cathedral. b, Building St. Paul's by J. Seymour Lucas. c, Architect Sir Christopher Wren. d, Pope Clement XI. e, St. Paul's Cathedral. f, Pope Benedict XVI.

No. 2794: a, Pope Clement XI, diff. b, Pope Benedict XVI, diff.

2011, Dec. 16 ***Perf. 13 Syncopated***
2793 A754 $50 Sheet of 6, #a-f 8.25 8.25

Souvenir Sheet

2794 A754 $150 Sheet of 2, #a-b 8.25 8.25

St. Paul's Cathedral is an Anglican cathedral and was not visited by Pope Benedict XVI in his travels to the United Kingdom.

Sinking of the Titanic, Cent. A755

No. 2795: a, Titanic Captain Edward J. Smith. b, Cross-section of the Titanic. c, Iceberg. d, Titanic sinking.

$250, Titanic sinking, vert.

2012, Jan. 1 ***Perf. 13¼***
2795 A755 $90 Sheet of 4, #a-d 10.00 10.00

Souvenir Sheet
Perf. 12

2796 A755 $250 multi 7.00 7.00

No. 2796 contains one 38x50mm stamp.

Souvenir Sheet

Pope Benedict XVI, 85th Birthday A756

No. 2797: a, Joseph Ratzinger as young boy (44x25mm). b, Pope Benedict XVI, vert. (30x44mm). c, Birthplace of Pope Benedict XV I(44x25mm)

2012, Feb. 22 ***Imperf.***
2797 A756 $250 Sheet of 3, #a-c 21.00 21.00

Mao Zedong (1893-1976), Chairman of People's Republic of China — A757

Photograph of Mao Zedong: No. 2798, $25, No. 2802a, $90, With blue background. No. 2799, $25, No. 2802b, $90, Reading in library. No. 2800, $25, No. 2802c, $90, Waving. No. 2801, $25, No. 2802d, $90, Seated.

2012, Feb. 22 **Litho.** ***Perf. 14***
2798-2801 A757 Set of 4 2.75 2.75
2802 A757 $90 Sheet of 4, #a-d 9.75 9.75

Premiere of *The Three Stooges* Movie A758

No. 2803: a, Chris Diamantopolous as Moe, denomination in yellow. b, Diamantopolous as Moe, denomination in orange. c, Sean Hayes as Larry, denomination in yellow. d, Hayes as Larry, denomination in orange. e, Will Sasso as Curly, denomination in yellow. f, Sasso as Curly, denomination in orange.

No. 2804: a, Stooges, denomination in blue. b, Stooges, denomination in red violet.

2012, Mar. 13 ***Perf. 13 Syncopated***
2803 A758 $75 Sheet of 6, #a-f 12.50 12.50

Souvenir Sheet

2804 A758 $125 Sheet of 2, #a-b 7.00 7.00

Meeting of U.S. Pres. Barack Obama and Xi Jinping, Vice-President of People's Republic of China — A759

No. 2805: a, Xi Jinping. b, Temple, Beijing. c, Pres. Obama. d, Washington Monument.

No. 2806: a, Xi Jinping, diff. b, Pres. Obama, diff.

2012, Apr. 4 ***Perf. 12***
2805 A759 $90 Sheet of 4, #a-d 10.00 10.00

Souvenir Sheet

2806 A759 $125 Sheet of 2, #a-b 7.00 7.00

African Wildlife A760

No. 2807: a, West African giraffe (30x80mm). b, Dorcas gazelle (30x40mm). c, Blue duiker (30x40mm). d, Red river hog (30x40mm). e, Hartebeest (30x40mm).

No. 2808, horiz.: a, Spotted hyena. b, Side-striped jackal. c, Serval.

No. 2809, African bush elephant. No. 2810, Patas monkey.

2012, May 3 ***Perf. 14***
2807 A760 $75 Sheet of 5, #a-e 10.50 10.50

Perf. 12

2808 A760 $100 Sheet of 3, #a-c 8.25 8.25

Souvenir Sheets

2809 A760 $250 multi 7.00 7.00
2810 A760 $250 multi 7.00 7.00

Miniature Sheet

2012 Summer Olympics, London — A761

No. 2811: a, Track and field. b, Swimming. c, Weight lifting. d, Kayaking.

2012, May 30 ***Perf. 14***
2811 A761 $60 Sheet of 4, #a-d 6.50 6.50

Dinosaurs — A762

No. 2812, horiz.: a, Albertaceratops. b, Zuniceratops. c, Prestosaurus. d, Saurolophus. e, Ampelosaurus. f, Euoplocephalus.

No. 2813: a, Pachyrhinosaurus. b, Hypsilophodon.

2012, June 27 ***Perf. 13 Syncopated***
2812 A762 $75 Sheet of 6, #a-f 12.50 12.50

Souvenir Sheet

2813 A762 $125 Sheet of 2, #a-b 7.00 7.00

Dogs A763

No. 2814, $120: a, Afghan hound. b, Dalmatian. c, Greyhound.

No. 2815, $120: a, English bulldog. b, Bichon Frise. c, Dachshund.

No. 2816, $250, Scottish terrier. No. 2817, $250, Poodle.

2012, June 27 ***Perf. 14, 12 (#2816)***

Sheets of 3, #a-c

2814-2815 A763 Set of 2 20.00 20.00

Souvenir Sheets

2816-2817 A763 Set of 2 14.00 14.00

SOS Children's Village, Liberia, 30th Anniv. (in 2011) — A764

SOS Children's Village emblem, map of Liberia and: $45, Inscription and slogan. $55, Inscription and palm tree.

2012, Feb. 14 ***Perf. 14***
2818-2819 A764 Set of 2 2.75 2.75

Miniature Sheet

Apes A765

No. 2820: a, Barbary macaque. b, Bonobo. c, Silverback gorilla. d, Chacma baboon.

2012, Aug. 9 ***Perf. 12***
2820 A765 $90 Sheet of 4, #a-d 9.75 9.75

Souvenir Sheets

Elvis Presley (1935-77) — A766

Designs: No. 2821, $250, Presley with guitar, light blue frame. No. 2822, $250, Presley behind microphone, light blue frame. No. 2823, $250, Two black-and-white photographs of Presley, dull red frame. No. 2824, $250, Color and black-and-white photographs of Presley, red frame. No. 2825, $250, Presley in army uniform, red frame.

2012, Aug. 9 ***Perf. 12½***
2821-2825 A766 Set of 5 35.00 35.00

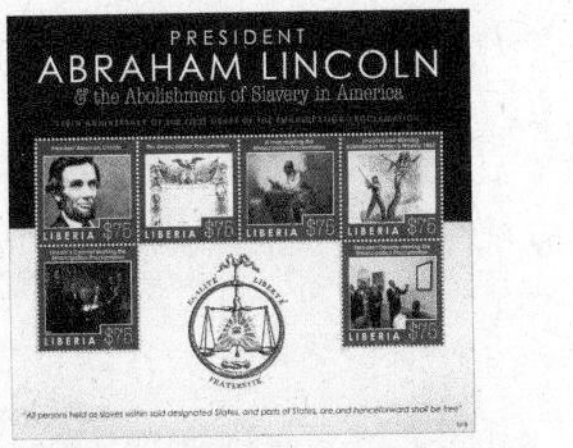

First Draft of the Emancipation Proclamation, 150th Anniv. — A767

No. 2826: a, Pres. Abraham Lincoln. b, Printed copy of Emancipation Proclamation. c, Man reading Emancipation Proclamation. d, Lincoln's Last Warning, political cartoon from Harper's Weekly, 1862. e, First Reading of the Emacipation Proclamation of President Lincoln, by Francis Bicknell Carpenter. f, Pres. Barack Obama viewing Emancipation Proclamation.

$250, President Lincoln Writing the Proclamation of Freedom, by David Gilmour Blythe, horiz.

2012, Sept. 21 ***Perf. 13¾***

2826 A767 $75 Sheet of 6, #a-f 12.50 12.50

Souvenir Sheet

Perf. 12½

2827 A767 $250 multi 7.00 7.00

No. 2827 contains one 51x38mm stamp.

Chinese Zodiac Animals — A768

Designs: No. 2828, $15, Monkeys. No. 2829. $15, Cock.

2012, Sept. 27 ***Perf. 13¼x13***

2828-2829 A768 Set of 2 .85 .85

Christmas — A769

Paintings: $25, Adoration of the Shepherds, by Guido Reni. $35, Adoration of the Shepherds, by Correggio. $40, Holy Family with St. John the Baptist, by Michelangelo. $45, Tempi Madonna (detail), by Raphael. $50, The Annunciation, by Francisco Goya. $100, Virgin and Child Before an Archway, by Albrecht Dürer.

2012, Oct. 1 ***Perf. 12½***

2830-2835 A769 Set of 6 8.25 8.25

Giant Pandas A770

No. 2836 — Giant Panda: a, On tree, facing left. b, Eating. c, Walking, foliage at right. d, With log at right.

$220, Panda on tree, vert.

2012, Nov. 15 ***Perf. 13 Syncopated***

2836 A770 $85 Sheet of 4, #a-d 7.00 7.00

Souvenir Sheet

2837 A770 $220 multi 6.00 6.00

Beijing 2012 Intl. Stamp Exhibition.

Aircraft Carriers A771

No. 2838: a, Admiral Gorshkov, Russia. b, Dédalo, Spain. c, Foch (R99), France. d, USS Philippine Sea. e, USS Intrepid. f, HTMS Chakri Naruebet, Thailand.

$250, USS Ticonderoga, horiz.

2012, Nov. 28 ***Perf. 13¾***

2838 A771 $75 Sheet of 6, #a-f 12.50 12.50

Souvenir Sheet

Perf. 12½

2839 A771 $250 multi 6.75 6.75

No. 2839 contains one 51x38mm stamp.

Flowers A772

No. 2840: a, Nymphaea lotus. b, Papaver somniferum. c, Protea repens. d, Liparia splendens. e, Tulipa florenskyi. f, Gladiolus carmineus.

$280, Zantedeschia aethiopica, vert.

2013, Jan. 8 ***Perf. 13¾***

2840 A772 $70 Sheet of 6, #a-f 11.50 11.50

Souvenir Sheet

Perf. 12½

2841 A772 $280 multi 7.75 7.75

No. 2841 contains one 38x51mm stamp.

World Radio Day A773

No. 2842: a, Hindenburg disaster reporting, 1937. b, Winston Churchill's "We Shall Fight on the Beaches" broadcast, 1940. c, Pres. John F. Kennedy's Cuban Missile Crisis address, 1962. d, Dr. Martin Luther King, Jr.'s "I Have a Dream" speech, 1963.

$250, Orson Welles' "War of the Worlds" broadcast, 1938.

2013, Jan. 8 ***Perf. 12½***

2842 A773 $90 Sheet of 4, #a-d 9.75 9.75

Souvenir Sheet

Perf.

2843 A773 $250 multi 6.75 6.75

No. 2843 contains one 38mm diameter stamp.

Gems and Rocks A774

No. 2844, $100: a, Aquamarine. b, Euclase. c, Rainbow garnet.

No. 2845, $100: a, Rhodochrosite. b, Opal. c, Tanzanite.

Mo. 2846: a, Agate with red inner rings, small hole. b, Agate with white inner rings, large hole.

2013, Jan. 8 ***Perf. 13¾***

Sheets of 3, #a-c

2844-2845 A774 Set of 2 16.50 16.50

Souvenir Sheet

Perf. 12½

2846 A774 $140 Sheet of 2, #a-b 7.75 7.75

Nos. 2844-2845 each contain three 35x35mm stamps.

American Civil Rights Leaders — A775

No. 2847, $85: a, Harriet Tubman (c. 1820-1913), abolitionist (without head covering). b, Frederick Douglass (1818-95), abolitionist. c, John Brown (1800-59), abolitionist. d, Martha Coffin Wright (1806-75), abolitionist.

No. 2848, $85: a, Union Major General David Hunter (1802-86). b, Pres. Abraham Lincoln (1809-65). c, Susan B. Anthony (1820-1906), suffragist. d, Tubman (with head covering).

No. 2849, $280, Tubman and slave capture reward notice. No. 2850, $280, Tubman, daughter Gertie and husband Nelson Davis, horiz.

2013, Mar. 20 ***Perf. 12½***

Sheets of 4, #a-d

2847-2848 A775 Set of 2 18.50 18.50

Souvenir Sheets

Perf. 12

2849-2850 A775 Set of 2 15.50 15.50

No. 2849 contains on 30x40mm stamp. No. 2850 contains one 40x30mm stamp.

African Wildlife A776

No. 2851: a, Acionyx jubatus. b, Aepyceros melampus. c, Diceros bicornis. d, Equus grevyi. e, Panthera leo. f, Phacochoerus africanus.

No. 2852, vert.: a, Giraffa camelopardalis. b, Loxodonta africana. c, Connochaetes taurinus.

$280, Panthera pardus pardus, horiz.

2013, Apr. 3 ***Perf. 13¾***

2851 A776 $70 Sheet of 6, #a-f 11.50 11.50

Perf. 12

2852 A776 $100 Sheet of 3, #a-c 8.25 8.25

Souvenir Sheet

Perf. 12½

2853 A776 $280 multi 7.75 7.75

No. 2852 contains three 30x50mm stamps. No. 2853 contains one 51x38mm stamp.

History of Art A777

No. 2854 — Chamber of Art and Curiosities, by Frans Francken (details) with: a, Fish at UR. b, Seahorse at L. c, Religious painting and tasselled cord. d, Shells, book at LL. e, Shells, bowl at top.

No. 2855, $100, vert.: a, Girl with a Pearl Earring, by Johannes Vermeer. b, A Commander Being Armed for Battle, by Peter Paul Rubens. c, David with the Head of Goliath, by Caravaggio.

No. 2856, $100, vert.: a, Still-life with Flowers, by Rachel Ruysch. b, Maddalena Penitente, by Artemisia Gentileschi. c, The Fruit and Vegetable Costermonger, by Louise Moillon.

$280, La Gamme d'Amour, by Jean-Antoine Watteau.

2013, Apr. 4 **Litho.** ***Perf. 12½***

2854 A777 $75 Sheet of 5, #a-e 10.50 10.50

Sheets of 3, #a-c

2855-2856 A777 Set of 2 16.50 16.50

Souvenir Sheet

2857 A777 $280 multi 7.75 7.75

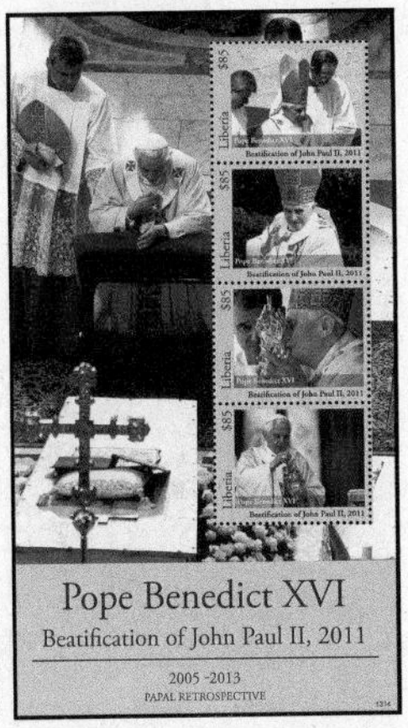

Pope Benedict XVI A778

No. 2858, $85 — Pope Benedict XVI at Beatification Ceremony for Pope John Paul II: a, Wearing miter, with two assistants. b, Wearing miter, waving. c, Kissing glass object. d, Holding censer.

No. 2859, $85 — Pope Benedict XVI visiting Germany: a, Meeting Chancellor Angela Merkel. b, Waving. c, With German President Christian Wulff and wife. d, Facing left.

No. 2860, $280, Pope Benedict XVI seated at beatification ceremony. No. 2861, $280, Pope Benedict XVI with Wulff and Merkel.

2013, Apr. 29 ***Perf. 12***

Sheets of 4, #a-d

2858-2859 A778 Set of 2 18.50 18.50

Souvenir Sheets

2860-2861 A778 Set of 2 15.50 15.50

Lady Margaret Thatcher (1925-2013), British Prime Minister — A779

No. 2862 — Thatcher: a, At microphone. b, Wearing black dress, facing left. c, With Pres. Ronald Reagan. d, With hand on chin.

$280, Thatcher, vert.

2013, June 1 ***Perf. 12***

2862 A779 $85 Sheet of 4, #a-d 9.25 9.25

Souvenir Sheet

Perf. 12½

2863 A779 $280 multi 7.50 7.50

No. 2863 contains one 38x51mm stamp.

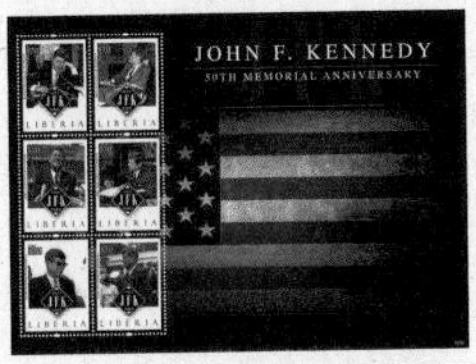

Pres. John F. Kennedy (1917-63) — A780

No. 2864 — Pres Kennedy: a, On telephone. b, Sitting in rocking chair. c, Standing behind microphone. d, Signing document. e, Wearing sunglasses. f, Standing in crowd.
$280, Pres. Kennedy on yacht.

Perf. 13 Syncopated

2013, June 25 Litho.

2864 A780 $70 Sheet of 6, #a-f 11.00 11.00

Souvenir Sheet

2865 A780 $280 multi 7.50 7.50

Medicinal Plants — A781

No. 2866: a, Acacia. b, Rooibos. c, Buchu. d, Caralluma. e, Common myrrh. f, Shea tree.
$280, Aloe, vert.

2013, June 25 Litho. *Perf. 13¾*

2866 A781 $70 Sheet of 6, #a-f 11.00 11.00

Souvenir Sheet

Perf. 12¾

2867 A781 $280 multi 7.50 7.50

No. 2867 contains one 38x51mm stamp.

Birds A782

No. 2868, $85: a, Barnacle geese. b, Brown pelican. c, Long-billed curlew. d, Eurasian griffon.
No. 2869, $85: a, Eastern great egret. b, Red and green macaw. c, Roseate spoonbill. d, Mute swan.
No. 2870, $280, Blue peafowl. No. 2871, $280, Crowned crane, vert.

Perf. 14, 12 (#2871)

2013, July 30 Litho.

Sheets of 4, #a-d

2868-2869 A782 Set of 2 17.50 17.50

Souvenir Sheets

2870-2871 A782 Set of 2 14.50 14.50

Birth of Prince George of Cambridge — A783

No. 2872: a, Duchess of Cambridge handing Prince George to Duke of Cambridge. b, Duke of Cambridge holding Prince George. c, Duchess of Cambridge holding Prince George. d, Duke and Duchess of Cambridge, Prince George.
$280, Duke and Duchess of Cambridge, Prince George.

2013, Sept. 17 Litho. *Perf. 12x12½*

2872 A783 $85 Sheet of 4, #a-d 8.50 8.50

Souvenir Sheet

Perf. 13¼

2873 A783 $280 multi 7.00 7.00

No. 2873 contains one 38x51mm stamp.

Coronation of Queen Elizabeth II, 60th Anniv. — A784

No. 2874 — Queen Elizabeth II wearing: a, Pink jacket and hat. b, Pink jacket, pink and white hat, fur coat. c, Gray hat and dress. d, Black hat and coat.
$280, Queen Elizabeth II wearing black feathered hat.

2013, Oct. 7 Litho. *Perf. 13¾*

2874 A784 $85 Sheet of 4, #a-d 8.50 8.50

Souvenir Sheet

2875 A784 $280 multi 7.00 7.00

Miniature Sheet

2014 Intl. Horiticultural Exposition, Qingdao, People's Republic of China — A785

No. 2876: a, Exposition emblem. b, Mascot waving. c, Mascot with watering can. d, Mascot snorkeling. e, Mascot surfing. f, Mascot teaching.

2013, Jan. 1 Litho. *Perf. 14*

2876 A785 $50 Sheet of 6, #a-f 8.25 8.25

Miniature Sheet

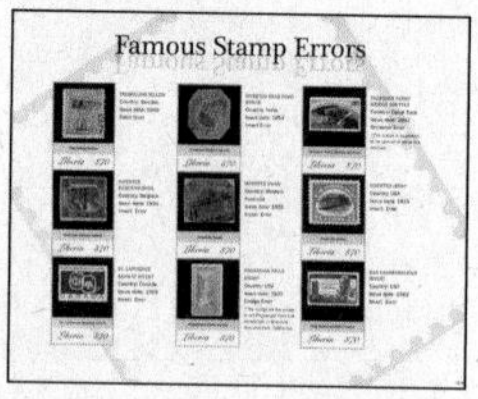

Famous Stamp Errors A786

No. 2877: a, Sweden #1a. b, India #6c. c, Canal Zone #157a. d, Belgium #139a. e, Western Australia #3a. f, United States #C3a. g, Canada #387a. h, Philippines #357. i, United States #1204.

2013, Jan. 1 Litho. *Perf. 14*

2877 A786 $70 Sheet of 9, #a-i 17.50 17.50

New Year 2014 (Year of the Horse) A787

No. 2878 — Six steeds of Zhaoling from the Mausoleum of Tang Emperor Taizong: a, Horse and attendant. b, Horse facing left, galloping. c, Horse facing left, walking. d, Horse facing right, galloping, diagonal crack running from denomination to horse's head. e, Horse facing right, walking. f, Horse facing right, galloping, vertical crack behind horse's head running to bottom.
$280, Horse's head.

2013, Nov. 25 Litho. *Perf. 14*

2878 A787 $70 Sheet of 6, #a-f 10.50 10.50

Souvenir Sheet

Perf. 12

2879 A787 $280 multi 7.00 7.00

Intl. Red Cross, 150th Anniv. A788

No. 2880: a, Horse-drawn ambulances at Red Cross site. b, Red Cross equipment bag. c, Red Cross volunteer tending to prisoners near train. d, Red Cross stenciled on wall.
$280, Jean-Henri Dunant, Red Cross founder.

2013, Dec. 2 Litho. *Perf. 14*

2880 A788 $85 Sheet of 4, #a-d 8.50 8.50

Souvenir Sheet

2881 A788 $280 multi 7.00 7.00

Trains A789

No. 2882: a, 20th Century Limited, United States. b, Ghan, Australia. c, Flying Scotsman, Great Britain. d, Indian Pacific, Australia.
$280, Super Chief, United States, vert.

2013, Dec. 2 Litho. *Perf. 14*

2882 A789 $85 Sheet of 4, #a-d 8.50 8.50

Souvenir Sheet

2883 A789 $280 multi 7.00 7.00

Concorde — A790

No. 2884: a, Concorde in flight. b, Concorde and flight attendants. c, Nose of Concorde. d, Pilot in cockpit window of Concorde.
$280, Concorde in flight in front of clouds.

2013, Dec. 2 Litho. *Perf. 14*

2884 A790 $85 Sheet of 4, #a-d 8.50 8.50

Souvenir Sheet

Perf. 12

2885 A790 $280 multi 7.00 7.00

No. 2885 contains one 50x30mm stamp.

Miniature Sheets

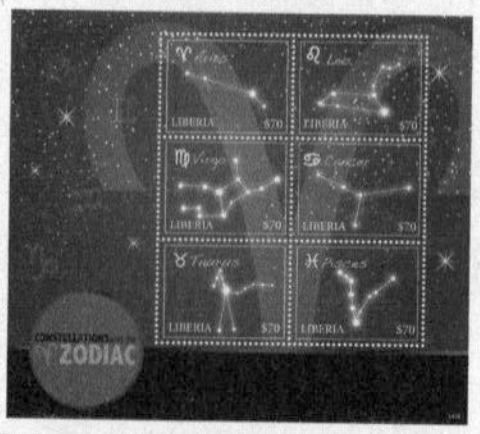

Zodiac Constellations — A791

No. 2886, $70: a, Aries. b, Leo. c, Virgo. d, Cancer. e, Taurus. f, Pisces.
No. 2887, $70: a, Gemini. b, Libra. c, Sagittarius, d, Scorpio. e, Aquarius. f, Capricorn.

2013, Dec. 2 Litho. *Perf. 12*

Sheets of 6, #a-f

2886-2887 A791 Set of 2 21.00 21.00

Military Vehicles A792

No. 2888: a, Light utility vehicle. b, Armored personnel carrier. c, Half-track armored personnel carrier. d, Amphibious vehicle.
$280, Amphibious transport.

2013, Dec. 23 Litho. *Perf. 14*

2888 A792 $85 Sheet of 4, #a-d 8.50 8.50

Souvenir Sheet

Perf. 12

2889 A792 $280 multi 7.00 7.00

Christmas — A793

Paintings: $25, Madonna and Child, by Taddeo di Bartolo. $40, Madonna and Saints, by Giovanni Bellini. $50, Nativity, by Lorenzo Lotto. $175, San Marco Altarpiece, by Fra Angelico.

2013, Dec. 2 Litho. *Perf. 12½*

2890-2893 A793 Set of 4 7.25 7.25

A794

A795

Nelson Mandela (1918-2013), President of South Africa — A796

No. 2894 — Mandela: a, Wearing green and red shirt, denomination in black. b, Close-up of head. c, With clenched fist, two people in background. d, Wearing flowered shirt, brick wall in background. e, With fist raised, crowd in background. f, Sitting in chair, flag in background.
No. 2895 — Mandela: a, Wearing gray blue shirt, pen in breast pocket. b, Wearing suit and tie, curtains in background. c, Wearing shirt with gray squares, black background. d, Wearing blue and white shirt with red AIDS ribbon under collar button. e, Wearing brown and red shirt. f, Wearing suit and tie, with fist raised.

$280, Mandela in suit and tie, diff. $765, Mandela waving.

2013, Dec. 15 Litho. *Perf. 14*

2894 A794 $70 Sheet of 6, #a-f 10.50 10.50
2895 A795 $70 Sheet of 6, #a-f 10.50 10.50

Souvenir Sheets

Perf. 12

2896 A795 $280 multi 7.00 7.00

Litho., Margin Embossed With Foil Application

Without Gum

Imperf

2897 A796 $765 multi 19.00 19.00

Christening of Prince George of Cambridge — A797

No. 2898: a, Prince George. b, Duchess of Cambridge holding Prince George. c, Duke of Cambridge holding Prince George. d, Duke and Duchess of Cambridge, Prince George.
$280, Prince George, diff.

2013, Dec. 31 Litho. *Perf. 14*

2898 A797 $85 Sheet of 4, #a-d 8.50 8.50

Souvenir Sheet

Perf. 12

2899 A797 $280 multi 7.00 7.00

Poems by Mao Zedong — A798

A799

Mao Zedong (1893-1976), Chinese Communist Leader — A800

No. 2900 — Poem with: a, 13 vertical columns of characters. b, 12 vertical columns of characters. c, 11 vertical columns of characters.
No. 2901 — Mao Zedong: a, With other people, building's roof visible. b, With Jawaharlal Nehru. c, With Kwame Nkrumah at dinner table. d, Surrounded by people from different countries.
No. 2902: a, Painting of Mao Zedong carrying scroll. b, Black-and-white photograph of Mao Zedong without hat. c, Painting of Mao Zedong with cap. d, Black-and-white photograph of Mao Zedong with cap. e, Painting of Mao Zedong without cap. f, Great Wall of China.

2013, Mar. 7 Litho. *Perf. 14*

2900 Horiz. strip of 3 1.25 1.25
a.-c. A798 $15 Any single .40 .40
2901 A799 $15 Sheet of 4, #a-d 1.60 1.60
2902 A800 $15 Sheet of 6, #a-f 2.50 2.50

No, 2900 was printed in sheets of 6, containing two of each stamp.

World Leaders — A800a

Designs: No. 2902A, $100, Liberian Pres. Ellen Johnson Sirleaf, People's Republic of China Premier Xi Jinping, U.S. Pres. Barack Obama. No. 2902B, $100, Former leaders of People' Republic of China Hu Jintao and Mao Zedong. $125, Mao Zedong and first Liberian Pres. Joseph Jenkins Roberts. $150, Xi Jinping and Ellen Johnson Sirleaf.

2013, Dec. 6 Litho. *Perf. 12*

2902A-2902D A800a Set of 4 12.00 12.00

Souvenir Sheet

Elvis Presley (1935-77) — A801

Litho., Sheet Margin Embossed

2014, Jan. 1 *Imperf.*

2903 A801 $740 multi 18.50 18.50

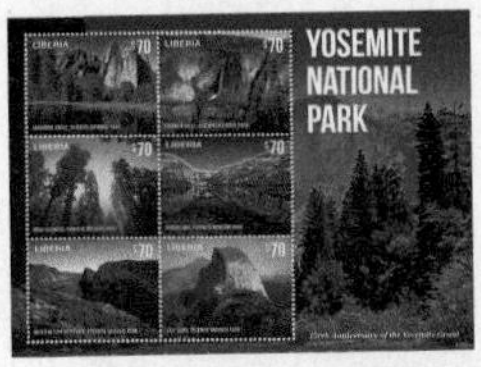

Yosemite National Park A802

No. 2904: a, Cathedral Rocks. b, Yosemite Falls. c, Giant sequoias. d, Tenaya Lake. e, Hetch Hetchy Reservoir. f, Half Dome.
$280, El Capitan.

2014, Jan. 2 Litho. *Perf. 14*

2904 A802 $70 Sheet of 6, #a-f 10.50 10.50

Souvenir Sheet

Perf. 12¾

2905 A802 $280 multi 7.00 7.00

Yosemite Grant, 150th anniv. No. 2905 contains one 51x38mm stamp.

Miniature Sheets

Winter Games A803

No. 2906, $85: a, Snowboarding. b, Alpine skiing. c, Curling. d, Freestyle skiing. e, Figure skating.
No. 2907, $85: a, Ski jumping. b, Ice hockey. c, Bobsled. d, Cross-country skiing. e, Speed skating.

2014, Mar. 5 Litho. *Perf. 13¾*

Sheets of 5, #a-e

2906-2907 A803 Set of 2 20.00 20.00

Paintings A804

No. 2908, $125: a, Portrait of a Man Aged 32, by Frans Pourbus the Younger. b, Apricot Branch, by Georg Flegel. c, Meu Taporo, by Paul Gauguin.
No. 2909, $125: a, Portrait of a Woman, by Antonio del Pollaiuolo. b, A World, by Maximilian Lenz. c, Woman Carrying a Pitcher on Her Head, by Camille Pissarro.
No. 2910, $350, The Piano Lesson, by Pierre-Auguste Renoir. No. 2911, $350, The Japanese Bridge, by Claude Monet.

2014, Mar. 10 Litho. *Perf. 12¾*

Sheets of 3, #a-c

2908-2909 A804 Set of 2 17.50 17.50

Size: 100x100mm

Imperf

2910-2911 A804 Set of 2 16.50 16.50

A805

A806

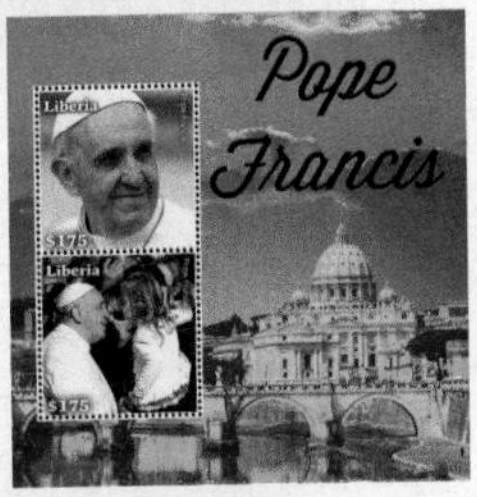

A807

Pope Francis A808

No. 2912 — Pope Francis: a, Waving. b, Looking up. c, Hugging boy. d, Smiling.
No. 2913 — Pope Francis: a, Looking left. b, Waving, diff. c, Waving, with other hand over heart. d, Waving in front of building.
No. 2914 — Pope Francis, denominations with large numerals: a, Looking right. b, Talking to young girl.
No. 2915 — Pope Francis, denominations with small numerals: a, Smiling, diff. b, With arm extended.

2014, Mar. 24 Litho. *Perf. 13¾*

2912 A805 $100 Sheet of 4, #a-d 9.50 9.50
2913 A806 $100 Sheet of 4, #a-d 9.50 9.50

Souvenir Sheets

2914 A807 $175 Sheet of 2, #a-b 8.25 8.25
2915 A808 $175 Sheet of 2, #a-b 8.25 8.25

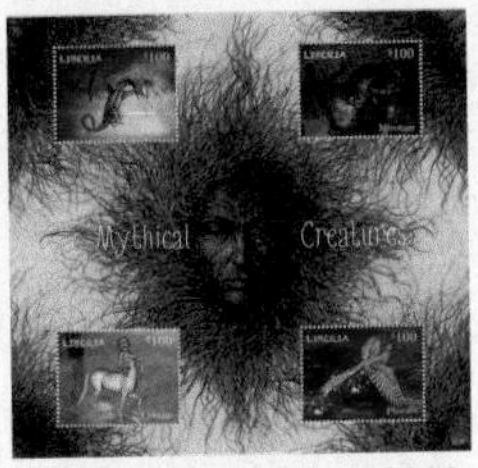

Mythical Creatures — A809

No. 2916, $100: a, Dragon. b, Minotaur. c, Centaur. d, Phoenix.
No. 2917, $100, vert.: a, Vampire. b, Leprechaun. c, Mermaid. d, Angel.
No. 2918, $175, vert.: a, Werewolf. b, Unicorn.
No. 2919, $175, vert.: a, Mermaid, with arms above head. b, Mermaid, swimming.

Perf. 14 (#2916), 12¾

2014, Apr. 2 Litho.

Sheets of 4, #a-d

2916-2917 A809 Set of 2 19.00 19.00

Souvenir Sheets of 2, #a-b

2918-2919 A809 Set of 2 16.50 16.50

No. 2917 contains four 38x51mm stamps. Nos. 2918-2919 each contain two 38x51mm stamps.

A810

World War I, Cent. A811

No. 2920: a, Battle of Vimy Ridge, 1915. b, Battle of Gallipoli, 1915. c, Battle of the Somme, 1916. d, Battle of St. Mihiel, 1918.
No. 2921 — Battleships: a, Voltaire. b, Slava. c, Kaiser Barbarossa. d, Asahi.
No. 2922: a, Battle of Verdun, 1916. b, Third Battle of Ypres, 1917.
No. 2923 — Battleships: a, USS Alabama. b, SMS Helgoland.

2014, May 19 Litho. *Perf. 12*

2920 A810 $100 Sheet of 4, #a-d 9.50 9.50
2921 A811 $100 Sheet of 4, #a-d 9.50 9.50

Souvenir Sheets

2922 A810 $175 Sheet of 2, #a-b 8.25 8.25

Perf. 14

2923 A811 $175 Sheet of 2, #a-b 8.25 8.25

Korean Food A812

No. 2924: a, Boneless ribs and Kimchi. b, Cucumber kimchi and Gyeongdan. c, Seafood pancake and Japchae.
$350, Soft tofu stew.

2014, June 17 Litho. *Perf. 13*

2924 A812 $125 Sheet of 3, #a-c, + central label 8.25 8.25

Souvenir Sheet

Perf.

2925 A812 $350 multi 7.75 7.75

Philakorea 2014 World Stamp Exhibition, Seoul

2014 World Cup Soccer Championships, Brazil — A813

Team photographs: No. 2926, $30, Algeria. No. 2927, $30, Argentina. No. 2928, $30, Australia. No. 2929, $30, Belgium. No. 2930, $30, Bosnia & Herzegovina. No. 2931, $30, Brazil. No. 2932, $30, Cameroun. No. 2933, $30, Chile. No. 2934, $30, Colombia. No. 2935, $30, Costa Rica. No. 2936, $30, Cote d'Ivoire (Ivory Coast). No. 2937, $30, Croatia. No. 2938, $30, Ecuador. No. 2939, $30, England. No. 2940, $30, France. No. 2941, $30, Germany. No. 2942, $30, Ghana. No. 2943, $30, Greece. No. 2944, $30, Honduras. No. 2945, $30, Iran. No. 2946, $30, Italy. No. 2947, $30, Japan. No. 2948, $30, South Korea. No. 2949, $30, Mexico. No. 2950, $30, Netherlands. No. 2951, $30, Nigeria. No. 2952, $30, Portugal. No. 2953, $30, Russia. No. 2954, $30, Spain. No. 2955, $30, Switzerland. No. 2956, $30, United States. No. 2957, $30, Uruguay.

2014, June 17 Litho. *Perf. 14*

2926-2957 A813 Set of 32 21.50 21.50

Nos. 2926-2957 each were printed in sheets of 6. See No. 2980.

Orchids A814

No. 2958, $100: a, Disa racemosa. b, Eulophia nutans. c, Eulophia hians. d, Eulophia ensata.

No. 2959, $100: a, Satyrium erectum. b, Satyrium coriifolium. c, Eulophia buchanani. d, Disa gladioflora.

No. 2960, $175: a, Habenaria bonatea. b, Polystachya pubescens.

No. 2961, $175: a, Eulophia reichenbachiana. b, Disa uniflora.

2014, June 23 Litho. *Perf. 14*

Sheets of 4, #a-d

2958-2959 A814 Set of 2 18.00 18.00

Souvenir Sheets of 2, #a-b

2960-2961 A814 Set of 2 15.50 15.50

Bats A815

No. 2962, $100: a, Lissonycteris angolensis. b, Epomophorus gambianus. c, Nanonycteris veldkampii. d, Epomops buettikoferi.

No. 2963, $100: a, Coleura afrea. b, Epomophorus wahlbergi. c, Miniopterus africanus. d, Rhinolophus ferrumequinum.

No. 2964, $175: a, Miniopterus inflatus. b, Taphozous mauritianus.

No. 2965, $175: a, Micropteropus pusillus. b, Rousettus aegyptiacus.

2014, Aug. 14 Litho. *Perf. 12x12½*

Sheets of 4, #a-d

2962-2963 A815 Set of 2 17.50 17.50

Souvenir Sheets of 2, #a-b

2964-2965 A815 Set of 2 15.50 15.50

Mongooses — A816

No. 2966, $100: a, Dwarf mongoose. b, Selous's mongoose. c, Kusimanse. d, Long-nosed mongoose.

No. 2967, $100: a, Angolan slender mongoose. b, Yellow mongoose. c, Ethiopian dwarf mongoose. d, Banded mongoose.

No. 2968, $175: a, Meerkat. b, Alexander's kusimanse.

No. 2969, $175: a, Slender mongoose. b, Somalian slender mongoose.

2014, Aug. 27 Litho. *Perf. 14*

Sheets of 4, #a-d

2966-2967 A816 Set of 2 17.50 17.50

Souvenir Sheets of 2, #a-b

2968-2969 A816 Set of 2 15.50 15.50

Paintings by Henri de Toulouse-Lautrec (1864-1901) — A817

No. 2970, $100: a, Party in the Moulin Rouge. b, Count Alphonse de Toulouse-Lautrec Driving a Four-Horse Hitch. c, Equestrienne. d, Two Girls in Bed.

No. 2971, $100, vert.: a, Moulin Rouge La Goulue. b, Babylone d'Allemagne. c, Portrait of Madame la Comtesse de Toulouse-Lautrec. d, Portait of Vincent van Gogh.

No. 2972, $200, vert.: a, La Clownesse Assise. b, La Clownesse.

No. 2973, $200, vert.: a, The Stage Manager Behind the Scenes. b, Portrait of Louis Pascal.

2014, Aug. 27 Litho. *Perf. 14*

Sheets of 4, #a-d

2970-2971 A817 Set of 2 17.50 17.50

Souvenir Sheets of 2, #a-b

2972-2973 A817 Set of 2 17.50 17.50

National Parks of Africa A818

No. 2974: a, Serengeti National Park, Tanzania (single tree). b, Victoria Falls, Zambia. c, Mt. Kilimanjaro, Kenya (view from mountain). d, Drakensberg Mountains, South Africa. e, Matopos National Park, Zimbabwe. f, Serengeti National Park (trees and vehicle path). g, Mt. Kilimanjaro (view of mountain). h, Sapo National Park, Liberia. i, Golden Gate Highlands National Park, South Africa.

$350, Namib-Naukluft National Park, Namibia.

2014, Sept. 3 Litho. *Perf. 13¾*

2974 A818 $85 Sheet of 9, #a-i 16.50 16.50

Souvenir Sheet

2975 A818 $350 multi 7.50 7.50

Race Horses A819

No. 2976, $100: a, Flying Childers. b, Highflyer. c, Regulus. d, Sceptre.

No. 2977, $100: a, Cherimoya. b, American Eclipse. c, Bay Middleton. d, Crucifix.

No. 2978, $175: a, Kincsem. b, Eclipse.

$350, Goldfinder.

2014, Sept. 3 Litho. *Perf. 14*

Sheets of 4, #a-d

2976-2977 A819 Set of 2 17.50 17.50

Perf. 12½

2978 A819 $175 Sheet of 2, #a-b 7.50 7.50

Souvenir Sheet

2979 A819 $350 multi 7.50 7.50

No. 2978 contains two 51x38mm stamps; No. 2979 contains one 51x38 stamp.

No. 2941 With Inscription Added in Yellow

and

German Soccer Team, 2014 World Cup Champions — A820

2014, Sept. 4 Litho. *Perf. 14*

2980 A813 $30 multi .65 .65

Souvenir Sheet

Perf. 12½

2981 A820 $350 multi 7.50 7.50

Maps and Flags of Liberian Counties — A821

County: $35, Gbarpolu. $45, Lofa. $55, Grand Cape Mount. $70, Bomi. $90, Montserrado. No. 2987, Bong. No. 2988, Margibi. $150, Grand Bassa. $175, Rivercess. $250, Nimba. $350, Sinoe. No. 2993, Grand Gedeh. No. 2994, Grand Kru. No. 2995, Maryland. No. 2996, Rivergee.

2014, July 1 Litho. *Perf. 14*

2982	A821	$35 multi	.80	.80
2983	A821	$45 multi	1.00	1.00
2984	A821	$55 multi	1.25	1.25
2985	A821	$70 multi	1.60	1.60
2986	A821	$90 multi	2.00	2.00
2987	A821	$100 multi	2.25	2.25
2988	A821	$100 multi	2.25	2.25
2989	A821	$150 multi	3.50	3.50
2990	A821	$175 multi	4.00	4.00
2991	A821	$250 multi	5.50	5.50
2992	A821	$350 multi	7.75	7.75
2993	A821	$500 multi	11.00	11.00
2994	A821	$500 multi	11.00	11.00
2995	A821	$500 multi	11.00	11.00
2996	A821	$500 multi	11.00	11.00
		Nos. 2982-2996 (15)	75.90	75.90

Mei Lanfang (1894-1961), Peking Opera Performer — A822

No. 2997 — Mei Lanfang in various costumes, as shown.

$350, Mei Lanfang, diff.

2014, Sept. 4 Litho. *Perf. 12*

2997 A822 $100 Sheet of 4, #a-d 8.75 8.75

Souvenir Sheet

2998 A822 $350 multi 7.75 7.75

Gold Medalists at 2014 Winter Olympics, Sochi, Russia — A823

No. 2999: a, Vic Wild, snowboarding, Russia (40x30mm). b, Canadian ice hockey player (40x30mm). c, Jorgen Graabak, Nordic combined skiing, Norway (40x60mm).

No. 3000: a, Kamil Stoch, ski jumping, Poland (30x40mm). b, Anton Kushnir, freestyle skiing, Belarus (30x40mm).

2014, Sept. 15 Litho. *Perf. 14*

2999 A823 $125 Sheet of 3, #a-c 8.25 8.25

Souvenir Sheet

3000 A823 $175 Sheet of 2, #a-b 7.75 7.75

Endangered African Animals — A824

No. 3001, $100: a, Okapi. b, Barbary macaque. c, African wild dog. d, Abbott's duiker.

No. 3002, $100: a, Aldabra flying fox. b, Black and rufous elephant shrew. c, Mandrill. d, Sun-tailed monkey.

No. 3003, $350, Alaotran gentle lemur. No. 3004, $350, Mountain gorilla.

2014, Oct. 20 Litho. *Perf. 14*

Sheets of 4, #a-d

3001-3002 A824 Set of 2 17.50 17.50

Souvenir Sheets

Perf. 12½

3003-3004 A824 Set of 2 15.00 15.00

Nos. 3003-3004 each contain one 38x51mm stamp.

Garden Flowers A825

No. 3005, $125: a, Coneflowers. b, Calendulas. c, Purple asters.

No. 3006, $125: a, French marigolds. b, Tickseeds. c, Cosmos.

No. 3007, $350, Black-eyed Susans. No. 3008, $350, Forget-me-nots.

2014, Oct. 20 Litho. *Perf. 12*

Sheets of 3, #a-c

3005-3006 A825 Set of 2 16.50 16.50

Souvenir Sheets

3007-3008 A825 Set of 2 15.00 15.00

A826

New Year 2015 (Year of the Ram) A827

No. 3010 — Ram facing: a, Forward. b, Left.

2014, Nov. 3 Litho. *Perf. 14*

3009 A826 $100 multi 2.25 2.25

Perf. 12½

3010 A827 $100 Horiz. pair, #a-b 4.50 4.50

No. 3009 was printed in sheets of 6. No. 3010 was printed in sheets containing two pairs.

Campaign Against Ebola Virus — A828

No. 3011: a, Medical worker wearing protective gear. b, Child. b, Mother holding child. c, Woman and medical device.

2014, Nov. 11 Litho. *Perf. 14*

3011 A828 $50 Block or horiz. strip of 4, #a-d 4.50 4.50

Printed in sheets of 16, containing 3 #3011c, 4 each #3011a, 3011b, 3011d, + label.

Christmas — A829

Paintings by Peter Paul Rubens (1577-1640): $100, The Education of the Virgin. $125, Saint Francis Receiving the Infant Jesus from the Hands of the Virgin. No. 3014, $175, Teresa of Avila's Vision of the Dove. No. 3015, $175, The Assumption of the Virgin Mary.

2014, Nov. 24 Litho. *Perf. 12½*

3012-3015 A829 Set of 4 12.50 12.50

A830

Domestic Cats A831

No. 3016 — British shorthair cat with background color of: a, Gray. b, Pink. c, Blue. d, Green blue.

No. 3017 — Various photographs of Maine Coon cats, as shown.

No. 3018, $350, Siberian cat. No. 3019, $350, Ragdoll cat.

2014, Dec. 16 Litho. *Perf. 14*

3016 A830 $100 Sheet of 4, #a-d 8.75 8.75

3017 A831 $100 Sheet of 6, #a-f 13.00 13.00

Souvenir Sheets

3018 A831 $350 multi 7.50 7.50

Perf. 13¼

3019 A831 $350 multi 7.50 7.50

No. 3019 contains one 35x35mm stamp.

A832

Wild Cats A833

No. 3020 — Various photographs of lions, as shown.

No. 3021 — Various photographs of cheetahs, as shown.

No. 3022, $350, Serval. No. 3023, $350, Caracal.

Perf. 13 Syncopated

2014, Dec. 16 Litho.

3020 A832 $100 Sheet of 4, #a-d 8.75 8.75

3021 A833 $100 Sheet of 4, #a-d 8.75 8.75

Souvenir Sheets

3022 A833 $350 multi 7.50 7.50

3023 A833 $350 multi 7.50 7.50

Economic Community of West African States, 40th Anniv. — A834

2015 Litho. *Perf. 13x13¼*

3024 A834 $50 multi — —

Birds of Prey A835

No. 3025, $125: a, Jackal buzzard (64x32mm). b, Spotted eagle owl (32x32mm). c, Cape vulture (32x32mm).

No. 3026, $125: a, African goshawk (32x64mm). b, Bateleur (32x32mm). c, Eurasian eagle owl (32x32mm).

No. 3027, $350, Golden eagle, vert. No. 3028, $350, Martial eagle, vert.

2015, Jan. 5 Litho. *Perf. 12½*

Sheets of 3, #a-c

3025-3026 A835 Set of 2 16.50 16.50

Souvenir Sheets

Perf. 13¼

3027-3028 A835 Set of 2 15.00 15.00

Nos. 3027-3028 each contain one 38x51mm stamp.

Photographs of Earth Taken from Space — A836

No. 3029: a, Kizimen Volcano, Russia. b, Issaouane Erg, Algeria. c, Fringing Coral Reef, Red Sea. d, Ice on Lake Michigan, United States. e, Paris, France. f, Zambezi River Delta, Mozambique.

$350, Mr. Everest and nearby Himalayan peaks.

2015, Jan. 21 Litho. *Perf. 11½x12*

3029 A836 $100 Sheet of 6, #a-f 13.00 13.00

Souvenir Sheet

3030 A836 $350 multi 7.75 7.75

A837

Spheniscus Demersus — A838

No. 3031: a, One penguin in water. b, Three penguins under water. c, Penguin out of water. d, Three penguins with heads above water.

No. 3032: a, One penguin facing right on beach, yellow sky. b, One penguin facing left on beach, light blue sky. c, One penguin facing right on beach, pale green water in background. d, One penguin, foliage in foreground. e, Two penguins. f, Three penguins.

No. 3033, $350, One penguin, diff. No. 3034, $350, Two penguins, diff.

2015, Feb. 2 Litho. *Perf. 14*

3031 A837 $100 Sheet of 4, #a-d 8.75 8.75

3032 A838 $100 Sheet of 6, #a-f 13.00 13.00

Souvenir Sheets

3033-3034 A838 Set of 2 15.00 15.00

Fennec Fox A839

No. 3035: a, Fox facing left. b, Fox facing forward. c, Fox asleep.

$350, Fox facing forward, diff.

2015, Feb. 2 Litho. *Perf. 12½*

3035 A839 $125 Sheet of 3, #a-c 8.25 8.25

Souvenir Sheet

3036 A839 $350 multi 7.75 7.75

World War I Alpine Troops of Italy A840

No. 3037: a, Regiment members carrying bicycle. b, Regiment members on mountaintop. c, Regiment members climbing mountain. d, Soldier with camera on tripod.

$350, Regiment members near mountain barracks.

2015, Feb. 2 Litho. *Perf. 14*

3037 A840 $100 Sheet of 4, #a-d 8.75 8.75

Souvenir Sheet

Perf. 12

3038 A840 $350 multi 7.75 7.75

World War I, cent.

Evacuation of Dunkirk, 75th Anniv. — A841

No. 3039: a, Soldier on beach. b, Troops gathered for evacuation. c, Troops on ship. d, Little boats returning from evacuation.

$350, Troops on little boats.

2015, Mar. 2 Litho. *Perf. 14*

3039 A841 $100 Sheet of 4, #a-d 8.75 8.75

Souvenir Sheet

Perf. 12½

3040 A841 $350 multi 7.75 7.75

No. 3040 contains one 51x38mm stamp.

Mammals — A842

No. 3041, $100: a, African bush elephant. b, Common warthog. c, Four-toed hedgehog. d, Common chimpanzee.

No. 3042, $100: a, Gambian epauletted fruit bat. b, Bushbuck. c, Leopard. d, Hippopotamus.

No. 3043, $350, Campbell's mona monkey, vert. No. 3044, $350, Giant pangolin, vert.

2015, Mar. 2 Litho. *Perf. 14¾x14*
Sheets of 4, #a-d

3041-3042 A842 Set of 2 17.50 17.50

Souvenir Sheets
Perf. 14x14¾

3043-3044 A842 Set of 2 15.00 15.00

Stonehenge — A843

No. 3045: Various photographs of stone pillars at Stonehenge, as shown.
$350, Stonehenge, diff.

2015, Mar. 3 Litho. *Perf. 11½x12*

3045 A843 $100 Sheet of 4, #a-d 8.75 8.75

Souvenir Sheet
Perf. 13½x13¼

3046 A843 $350 multi 7.75 7.75

2015 Europhilex Stamp Exhibition, London. No. 3046 contains one 50x30mm stamp.

Popes
A844

No. 3047: a, St. John Paul II. b, Pope Francis. c, St. John XXIII. d, Pope Benedict XVI.
$350, Pope Benedict XVI, diff.

2015, Mar. 24 Litho. *Perf. 14*

3047 A844 $100 Sheet of 4, #a-d 8.75 8.75

Souvenir Sheet
Perf. 12

3048 A844 $350 multi 7.75 7.75

Canonization of St. John Paul II and St. John XXIII.

Western
Bongo
A845

No. 3049 — Western bongo: a, Blue green background, four legs visible. b, Red background, adult and juvenile. c, Red background, bongo facing right. d, Blue green background, no legs visible. e, Blue green background, head of bongo. f, Red background, bongo facing left.
$350, Head of bongo, vert.

2015, Mar. 24 Litho. *Perf. 14*

3049 A845 $100 Sheet of 6, #a-f 13.00 13.00

Souvenir Sheet
Perf. 12

3050 A845 $350 multi 7.75 7.75

Visit of
Prince
William
to Japan
A846

No. 3051 — Prince William and: a, Tokyo Governor Yoichi Masuzoe holding umbrellas. b, Crown Prince Naruhito shaking hands. c, Japanese Prime Minister Shinzo Abe with children at Koriyama park. d, Masuzoe at tea ceremony. e, Abe, Prince William waving. f, Dinner guests at Ryokan, Koriyama.
$350, Prince William visiting British Commonwealth war graves, Yokohama.

2015, May 4 Litho. *Perf. 13x13¼*

3051 A846 $100 Sheet of 6, #a-f 13.00 13.00

Souvenir Sheet
Perf. 12x12½

3052 A846 $350 multi 7.75 7.75

Queen Elizabeth II, Longest-Reigning British Monarch — A847

No. 3051 — Photographs of Queen Elizabeth II with dogs taken in: a, 1974. b, 1972. c, 1936. d, 1976. e, 1971.
$350, Queen Elizabeth II and dog, 1971, diff.

2015, May 25 Litho. *Perf. 14*

3053 A847 $100 Sheet of 5, #a-e 11.00 11.00

Souvenir Sheet
Perf. 12

3054 A847 $350 multi 7.75 7.75

Lee Kuan Yew (1923-2015), Prime Minister of Singapore — A848

No. 3055 — Lee with: a, Queen Elizabeth II, 1989. b, Pres. Barack Obama, 2009. c, Pres. George H. W. Bush, 1989. d, Chinese General Secretary Xi Jinping, 2010.
No. 3056: a, Lee Kuan Yew, 2009. b, Pres. Obama, 2009.

2015, May 25 Litho. *Perf. 14*

3055 A848 $100 Sheet of 4, #a-d 8.75 8.75

Souvenir Sheet

3056 A848 $175 Sheet of 2, #a-b 7.75 7.75

Birth of Princess Charlotte of Cambridge — A849

No. 3057: a, Duke and Duchess of Cambridge holding Princess Charlotte, window behind Duke. b, As "a," window behind Duchess. c, Duchess of Cambridge holding Princess Charlotte. d, As "a," steps in background.
$350, Princess Charlotte.

2015, July 13 Litho. *Perf. 14*

3057 A849 $100 Sheet of 4, #a-d 8.75 8.75

Souvenir Sheet

3058 A849 $350 multi 7.75 7.75

African
Wildlife
A850

No. 3059: a, African buffalo. b, Side-striped jackal. c, African bush elephant. d, Patas monkey. e, Common kusimanse. f, African pygmy hedgehog.
$350, African leopard.

2015, July 13 Litho. *Perf. 14*

3059 A850 $100 Sheet of 6, #a-f 13.00 13.00

Souvenir Sheet
Perf. 12

3060 A850 $350 multi 7.75 7.75

Sir Rowland Hill (1795-1879), Postal Reformer — A851

No. 3061: a, Hill as older man. b, Hill as younger man, hand on neck.
$3.50, Hill and Great Britain #1.

2015, July 13 Litho. *Perf. 12*

3061 A851 $100 Pair, #a-b 4.50 4.50

Souvenir Sheet
Perf. 13¾

3062 A851 $350 multi 7.75 7.75

No. 3061 is printed in sheets containing two pairs. No. 3062 contains one 35x70mm stamp.

Miniature Sheets

Stamps of United Nations Member Countries — A852

No. 3063, $100: a, Lesotho #1. b, Liberia #1. c, Libya #1. d, Liechtenstein #1. e, Lithuania #1. f, Luxembourg #1.
No. 3064, $100: a, Macedonia #1. b, Malagasy Republic (Madagascar) #8. c, Malawi #1. d, Malaysia #1. e, Maldive Islands #1. f, Mali #1.
No. 3065, $100: a, Malta #1. b, Marshall Islands #1. c, Mauritania #1. d, Mauritius #1. e, Mexico #1. f, Micronesia #1.
No. 3066, $100: a, Moldova #1. b, Monaco #1. c, Mongolia #1. d, Montenegro #123. e, Morocco #A1. f, Mozambique #1.
No. 3067, $100: a, Switzerland #41. b, Syria #11. c, Tajikistan #1. d, Tanzania #5. e, Thailand #1. f, Timor #1.
No. 3068, $100: a, Togo #1. b, Tonga #1. c, Trinidad & Tobago #1. d, Tunisia #1. e, Turkey #1. f, Turkmenistan #1.
No. 3069, $100: a, Tuvalu #1. b, Uganda #1. c, Ukraine #100. d, United Arab Emirates #1. e, Uruguay #1. f, Uzbekistan #1.
No. 3070, $100: a, Vanuatu #280a. b, Venezuela #4. c, Viet Nam #1. d, Yemen #2. e, Zambia #1. f, Zimbabwe #414.

2015, July 13 Litho. *Perf. 12¾x12½*
Sheets of 6, #a-f

3063-3070 A852 Set of 8 105.00 105.00

Magna
Carta,
800th
Anniv.
A853

No. 3071: a, King John. b, Dark brown image of riginal Magna Carta manuscript, 1215. c, King John on throne. d, As "b," beige image.
$350, Signing of the Magna Carta.

2015, Aug. 3 Litho. *Perf. 14*

3071 A853 $100 Sheet of 4, #a-d 8.75 8.75

Souvenir Sheet

3072 A853 $350 multi 7.75 7.75

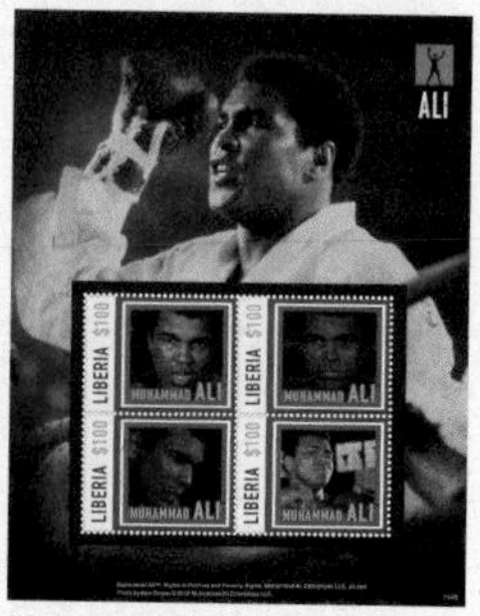

Muhammad Ali (1942-2016), Boxer — A854

No. 3073: Various photographs of Ali, as shown.
$350, Ali, diff.

2015, Aug. 10 Litho. *Perf. 12½x12*

3073 A854 $100 Sheet of 4, #a-d 8.75 8.75

Souvenir Sheet

3074 A854 $350 multi 7.75 7.75

Pres. Abraham Lincoln (1809-65) — A855

No. 3073: Various photographs of Lincoln, as shown.
$350, Lincoln, diff.

2015, Sept. 2 Litho. *Perf. 12*

3075 A855 $100 Sheet of 4, #a-d 8.75 8.75

Souvenir Sheet
Perf. 12¾

3076 A855 $350 multi 7.75 7.75

No. 3076 contains one 38x51mm stamp.

Sir Winston Churchill (1874-1965), Prime Minister of Great Britain — A856

No. 3077 — Churchill: a, Sitting with dog. b, Sitting with wife, Clementine. c, Aiming gun. d, Shielding his eyes. e, Painting. f, With kangaroo.
$350, Churchill with wife on ship.

2015, Sept. 30 Litho. *Perf. 13¾*

3077 A856 $100 Sheet of 6, #a-f 13.00 13.00

Souvenir Sheet

3078 A856 $350 multi 7.75 7.75

Details of Paintings of Flowers by Vincent van Gogh (1853-90) — A857

No. 3078: a, Three Sunflowers in a Vase, 1888. b, Still Life: Japanese Vase with Roses and Anemones, 1890. c, Vase with Red Poppies, 1886. d, Vase with Oleanders and Books, 1888. e, Vase with Red Gladioli, 1886. f, Blossoming Almond Branch in a Glass with a Book, 1888.
$350, Still Life: Vase with Pink Roses, 1890, horiz.

2015, Nov. 2 Litho. *Perf. 13¼x12½*

3079 A857 $100 Sheet of 6, #a-f 13.00 13.00

Souvenir Sheet

Perf. 12

3080 A857 $350 multi 7.75 7.75

No. 3080 contains one 50x30mm stamp.

Christmas — A858

Paintings by Filippo Lippi (c. 1406-69): $100, Martelli Annunciation. $150, Adoration in the Forest. $175, Annunciation. $200, Madonna and Child.

2015, Nov. 2 Litho. *Perf. 12½*

3081-3084 A858 Set of 4 13.50 13.50

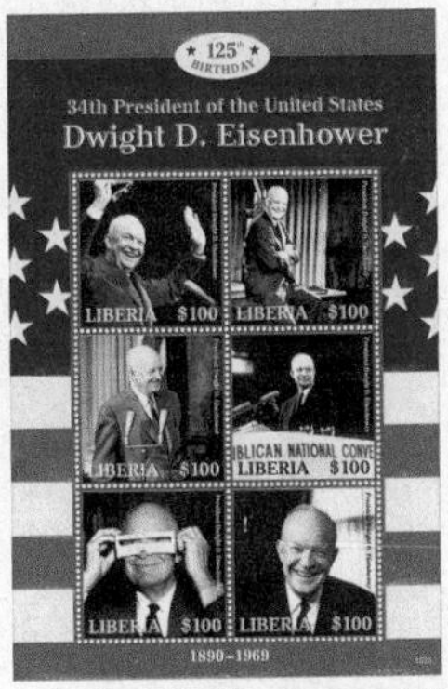

Pres. Dwight D. Eisenhower (1890-1969) — A859

No. 3085 — Eisenhower: a, With arms raised. b, Sitting on desk. c, Standing behind microphones, flag in background. d, At rostrum with microphones and water glasses. e, Looking through blinker glasses. f, Smiling, window in background.
$350, Eisenhower and Richard M. Nixon, horiz.

2015, Nov. 25 Litho. *Perf. 13¾*

3085 A859 $100 Sheet of 6, #a-f 13.00 13.00

Souvenir Sheet

Perf. 14

3086 A859 $350 multi 7.75 7.75

No. 3086 contains one 80x30mm stamp.

New Year 2016 (Year of the Monkey) — A860

Nos. 3087 and 3088: a, Monkey holding fruit near mouth. b, Moneky standing in tree above fruit.

2015, Nov. 25 Litho. *Perf. 13¾*

3087 A860 $32 Vert. pair, #a-b 1.40 1.40

Souvenir Sheet

Perf. 13¾x13½

3088 A860 $90 Sheet of 2, #a-b 4.00 4.00

No. 3087 was printed in sheets containing four pairs.

Pope Francis in New York City A861

No. 3089 — Various photographs of Pope Francis at World Trade Center, as shown.
$350, Pope Francis waving, New York City skyline in background.

2015, Nov. 25 Litho. *Perf. 14*

3089 A861 $100 Sheet of 6, #a-f 13.00 13.00

Souvenir Sheet

Perf. 12

3090 A861 $350 multi 7.75 7.75

Reunification of Germany, 25th Anniv. — A862

No. 3091: a, Person hammering at Berlin Wall. b, Piece of Berlin Wall on street corner. c, Border marker with emblem of German Democratic Republic.
$350, Wall with graffiti, horiz.

2015, Dec. 7 Litho. *Perf. 12*

3091 A862 $125 Sheet of 3, #a-c 9.00 9.00

Souvenir Sheet

3092 A862 $350 multi 8.25 8.25

No. 3092 contains one 80x30mm stamp.

Miniature Sheets

Ships of World War I — A863

No. 3093, $30: a, HMS Algerine. b, HMS Amethyst. c, HMS Cardiff. d, HMS Dartmouth. e, HMS Fantome. f, HMS Goliath. g, HMS Hildebrand. h, HMS Laburnum. i, HMS Malaya. j, SS Kinsfauns Castle. k, SS Orcoma. l, HMS Renown. m, HMS Adventuress. n, SS Himalaya. o, SS Patuca. p, RFA Bacchus. q, SS Alsatian. r, SS Arlanza. s, SS Caronia. t, SS Empress of Britain.

No. 3094, $30: a, HMS Amazon. b, HMS Antrim. c, HMS Astraea. d, HMS Birmingham. e, HMS Bristol. f, HMS Cicala. g, HMS Euryalus. h, HMS Galatea. i, HMS Hampshire. j, SS City of London. k, SS Laconia. l, HMS Humber. m, HMS Kent. n, SS Orvieto. o, SS Wonganella. p, HMS Nighthawk. q, HMS Rinaldo. r, HMS Valerian. s, MS Jupiter. t, SS Armadale.

2015, Dec. 7 Litho. *Perf. 14*

Sheets of 20, #a-t

3093-3094 A863 Set of 2 28.50 28.50

Aliens in *Star Trek: Enterprise* Television Series — A864

No. 3095: a, Silik, a Suliban. b, Shran, a Andorian. c, Antaak, a Klingon. d, T'Pol, a Vulcan. e, Soval, a Vulcan. f, Dr. Phlox, a Denobulan.
$350, Dr. Phlox, diff.

Perf. 13¼x12½

2015, Dec. 21 Litho.

3095 A864 $100 Sheet of 6, #a-f 14.50 13.00

Souvenir Sheet

Perf. 13¼

3096 A864 $350 multi 8.25 8.25

No. 3096 contains one 38x51mm stamp.

Miniature Sheets

A865

Declaration of the Roman Catholic Church With Non-Christian Religions, 50th Anniv. — A866

No. 3097: a, Pope John Paul II at Western Wall, Jerusalem. b, Pope Benedict XVI at Western Wall. c, Pope Francis at Western Wall. d, Pope John Paul II, Chief Rabbis of Israel Yisrael Meir Lau and Eliyahu Bakshi-Doron. e, Pope Benedict XVI , Chief Rabbis of Israel Yona Metzger and Shlomo Amar. f, Pope Francis, Chief Rabbis David Lau and Shlomo Amar.
No. 3098: a, Pope John Paul II, Bernard-Henri Lévy. b, Pope Benedict XVI, Rabbi Riccardo DiSegni. c, Pope Benedict XVI, Rabbi David Rosen, Chief Rabbi Amar. d, Pope Benedict XVI, Chief Rabbi Lord Jonathan Sacks. e, Pope Francis, Martin Budd, Chair of International Jewish Committee for Interreligious Consultations. f, Pope Francis, Chief Rabbi David Lau, Vatican Secretary of State Pietro Parolin. g, Pope Francis at Yad Vashem, Israel.

2015, Dec. 21 Litho. *Perf. 14*

3097 A865 $100 Sheet of 6, #a-f 14.50 14.50

3098 A866 $100 Sheet of 7, #a-g 16.50 16.50

Seashells and Marine Life — A867

No. 3099: a, Horse conch. b, Mushroom coral. c, Nautilus. d, Green sea urchin.
No. 3100: a, Sea snail shell. b, Triton's trumpet. c, Tiger cowrie. d, Giant African snail shell. e, Pearlized nautilus shell. f, Banded bonnet.
$350, Scallops.

Perf. 12, 14 (#3100)

2015, Dec. 31 Litho.

3099 A867 $100 Sheet of 4, #a-d 9.50 9.50

3100 A867 $100 Sheet of 6, #a-f 14.50 14.50

Souvenir Sheet

3101 A867 $350 multi 8.25 8.25

Souvenir Sheets

Elvis Presley (1935-77) — A868

Inscriptions: No. 3102, $350, Joining the fight against cancer. No. 3103, $350, Donates wallaby to Memphis Zoo. No. 3104, $350, First Las Vegas concert. No. 3105, $350, Promoting polio awareness.

Perf. 12, 14 (#3104-3105)

2016, Jan. 28 Litho.

3102-3105 A868 Set of 4 34.00 34.00

Reptiles A869

No. 3106: a, Leopard tortoise. b, Eyelash bush viper. c, Gaboon viper. d, Mossy leaf-tailed gecko.
No. 3107: a, Madagascar day gecko. b, Radiated turtle. c, Red-headed rock agama. d, Nile crocodile. e, Pancake tortoise. f, Nile monitor.
$350, Parson's chameleon.

2016, Jan. 28 Litho. *Perf. 12*

3106 A869 $100 Sheet of 4, #a-d 9.75 9.75

3107 A869 $100 Sheet of 6, #a-f 14.50 14.50

Souvenir Sheet

3108 A869 $350 multi 8.50 8.50

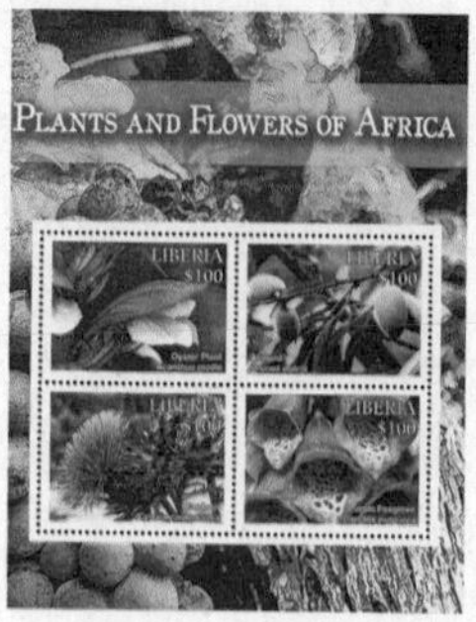

Flora
A870

No. 3109: a, Oyster plant. b, Almond. c, Cardoon. d, Purple foxglove.
No. 3110: a, Burning bush. b, Bay laurel. c, African oil palm. d, Poppy. e, Bird cherry. f, Blessed Mary's thistle.
$350, Maidenhair ferns, vert.

2016, Feb. 20 Litho. *Perf. 14*

3109 A870 $100 Sheet of 4, #a-d 9.50 9.50
3110 A870 $100 Sheet of 6, #a-f 14.50 14.50

Souvenir Sheet

3111 A870 $350 multi 8.25 8.25

Birds
A871

No. 3112: a, African broadbill. b, Buff-spotted woodpecker. c, Rufous-naped lark. d, Eurasian wryneck.
No. 3113: a, African pied hornbill. b, Black-and-white-casqued hornbill. c, Black-casqued hornbill. d, African gray hornbill. e, White-crested hornbill. f, Yellow-casqued hornbill.
$350, Flamingos.

2016, Feb. 20 Litho. *Perf. 14*

3112 A871 $100 Sheet of 4, #a-d 9.50 9.50
3113 A871 $100 Sheet of 6, #a-f 14.50 14.50

Souvenir Sheet

Perf. 12

3114 A871 $350 multi 8.25 8.25

Turacos
A872

No. 3115: a, Fischer's turaco. b, Purple-crested turaco. c, Great blue turaco. d, Guinea turaco.
No. 3116, vert.: a, Green turaco. b, Turaco unicolor. c, Violet turaco. d, White-cheeked turaco. e, Livingstone's turaco. f, White-crested turaco.
$350, Red-crested turaco.

2016, Feb. 20 Litho. *Perf. 14*

3115 A872 $100 Sheet of 4, #a-d 9.50 9.50
3116 A872 $100 Sheet of 6, #a-f 14.50 14.50

Souvenir Sheet

Perf. 12

3117 A872 $350 multi 8.25 8.25

Jimi Hendrix (1942-70), Rock Musician — A873

No. 3118 — Various photographs of Hendrix, as shown.
$350, Hendrix, horiz.

2016, Mar. 8 Litho. *Perf. 14*

3118 A873 $100 Sheet of 6, #a-f 13.50 13.50

Souvenir Sheet

Perf. 12½

3119 A873 $350 multi 7.75 7.75

No. 3119 contains one 51x38mm stamp.

Ancient Egypt A874

No. 3120: a, Great Sphinx of Giza. b, Ramesseum. c, Papyrus. d, Pyramids of Giza. e, Ram-headed Sphinxes. f, Giant Temple of Ramesses II.
$350, Wall painting.

2016, Mar. 18 Litho. *Perf. 14*

3120 A874 $100 Sheet of 6, #a-f 13.50 13.50

Souvenir Sheet

Perf. 12

3121 A874 $350 multi 7.75 7.75

90th Birthday of Queen Elizabeth II A875

No. 3122 — Queen Elizabeth II: a, In 1927. b, In 1953, wearing George IV State diamond diadem. c, In 1953, wearing Imperial State Crown. d, In 1928.
$415, Queen Elizabeth II wearing diadem, 1953, diff.

2016, Apr. 1 Litho. *Perf. 13¾*

3122 A875 $100 Sheet of 4, #a-d 9.00 9.00

Souvenir Sheet

3123 A875 $415 multi 9.25 9.25

New York City Landmarks — A876

No. 3124: a, Chrysler Building. b, Empire State Building. c, Rockefeller Center. d, St. Patrick's Cathedral.
$415, Brooklyn Bridge, horiz.

2016, Apr. 1 Litho. *Perf. 12½*

3124 A876 $100 Sheet of 4, #a-d 9.00 9.00

Souvenir Sheet

Perf. 14

3125 A876 $415 multi 9.25 9.25

2016 World Stamp Show, New York City. No. 3125 contains one 80x30mm stamp.

William Shakespeare (1564-1616), Writer — A877

No. 3126 — Various scenes from *Julius Caesar*, as shown.
$500, Shakespeare, vert.

2016, May 30 Litho. *Perf. 12½*

3126 A877 $100 Sheet of 4, #a-d 9.00 9.00

Souvenir Sheet

Perf. 12

3127 A877 $500 multi 11.00 11.00

No. 3127 contains one 50x60mm stamp.

Souvenir Sheet

2016 World Stamp Show, New York City A878

2016, May 30 Litho. *Perf. 12½x12*

3128 A878 $925 multi 20.50 20.50

Statue of Liberty, 130th Anniv. A879

No. 3129 — Various photographs of Statue of Liberty, as shown.
No. 3130: a, Statue of Liberty, diff. b, Statue of Liberty and Manhattan buildings.
$415, Statue of Liberty, diff.

2016, June 30 Litho. *Perf. 14*

3129 A879 $100 Sheet of 6, #a-f 13.00 13.00

Souvenir Sheets

Perf. 12

3130 A879 $200 Sheet of 2, #a-b 8.75 8.75

Perf. 12½

3131 A879 $415 multi 9.00 9.00

No. 3131 contains one 38x51mm stamp.

Souvenir Sheets

Elvis Presley (1935-77) — A880

Inscriptions: No. 3132, $415, Visits memorial he helped build. No. 3133, $415, Plays Cotton Pickin' Jamboree. No. 3134, $415, Tupelo Youth Center fundraiser. No. 3135, $415, Sponsors football team, horiz.

Perf. 13¼x13, 13x13¼

2016, June 30 Litho.

3132-3135 A880 Set of 4 36.50 36.50

2016 Summer Olympics, Rio de Janeiro — A881

No. 3136, $140: a, BMX cycling. b, Field hockey. c, Marathon swimming. d, Shooting.
No. 3137, $140: a, Judo. b, Canoe slalom. c, Triathlon. d, Equestrian jumping.
No. 3138, $200: a, Running. b, Karoline Radke (1903-83), 1928 gold medalist in 800-meter race.

2016, July 7 Litho. *Perf. 14*

Sheets of 4, #a-d

3136-3137 A881 Set of 2 24.50 24.50

Souvenir Sheet

Perf. 12½

3138 A881 $200 Sheet of 2, #a-b 8.75 8.75

No. 3138 contains two 38x51mm stamps.

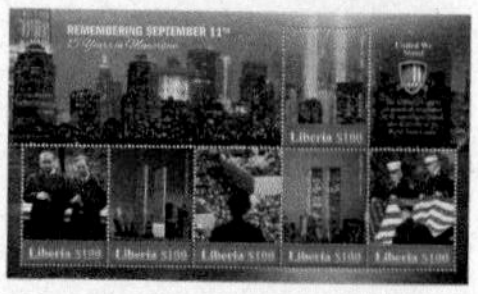
Sept. 11, 2001 Terrorist Attacks, 15th Anniv. A882

No. 3139: a, Tribute in Light. b, Firefighters with caps removed. c, World Trade Center during day. d, Firefighter and flowers. e, World Trade Center at night. f, Firefighters with flags.
$400, Tribute in Light, diff.

2016, July 19 Litho. *Perf. 14*

3139 A882 $100 Sheet of 6, #a-f 13.50 13.50

Souvenir Sheet

Perf. 12½

3140 A882 $400 multi 8.75 8.75

No. 3140 contains one 38x51mm stamp.

A883

A884

Hillary Clinton, 2016 Democratic Candidate for U.S. President — A885

A886

A887

Donald Trump, 2016 Republican Candidate for U.S. President — A888

A889

A890

A891

No. 3157: a, Hillary Clinton and her husband, Pres. Bill Clinton. b, Hillary Clinton.
No. 3158: a, Hillary Clinton, diff. b, Donald Trump, diff.
No. 3159: a, Trump and his wife, Melania. b, Donald Trump, diff.

2016, July 19 Litho. *Perf. 12½*

3141	A883 $20.16 multi		.45	.45
3142	A884 $20.16 multi		.45	.45
3143	A885 $20.16 multi		.45	.45
3144	A886 $20.16 multi		.45	.45
3145	A887 $20.16 multi		.45	.45
3146	A888 $20.16 multi		.45	.45

Size: 35x35mm

Perf. 13¾

3147	A883 $100 multi	2.25	2.25
3148	A884 $100 multi	2.25	2.25
3149	A885 $100 multi	2.25	2.25
3150	A886 $100 multi	2.25	2.25
3151	A887 $100 multi	2.25	2.25
3152	A888 $100 multi	2.25	2.25
3153	Horiz. pair	6.50	6.50
a.	A883 $140 multi	3.25	3.25
b.	A884 $140 multi	3.25	3.25
3154	A885 $140 multi	3.25	3.25
3155	A886 $100 multi	3.25	3.25
3156	Horiz. pair	6.50	6.50
a.	A887 $140 multi	3.25	3.25
b.	A888 $140 multi	3.25	3.25
	Nos. 3141-3156 (16)	35.70	35.70

Souvenir Sheets

Perf. 13¼

3157	A889 $200 Sheet of 2, #a-b	8.75	8.75
3158	A890 $200 Sheet of 2, #a-b	8.75	8.75
3159	A891 $200 Sheet of 2, #a-b	8.75	8.75
	Nos. 3157-3159 (3)	26.25	26.25

Nos. 3141 and 3142 were printed in sheets of 20 containing ten of each stamp. Nos. 3143 and 3144 were printed in sheets of 20 containing ten of each stamp. Nos. 3145 and 3146 were printed in sheets of 20 containing ten of each stamp. Nos. 3147 and 3148 were printed in sheets of six containing three of each stamp. Nos. 3149 and 3150 were printed in sheets of six containing three of each stamp. Nos. 3151 and 3152 were printed in sheets of six containing three of each stamp. Nos. 3153 and 3156 were each printed in sheets containing two pairs. Nos. 3154 and 3155 were printed in sheets of four containing two of each stamp.

Captains From *Star Trek* Television Series — A892

No. 3160: a, Capt. Jonathan Archer. b, Capt. Jean-Luc Picard. c, Capt. James T. Kirk. d, Capt. Benjamin Sisko. e, Capt. Kathryn Janeway.
$400, Captains Archer, Picard, Kirk, Sisko and Janeway, horiz.

2016, Aug. 29 Litho. *Perf. 12*

3160	A892 $150 Sheet of 5, #a-e	17.00	17.00

Souvenir Sheet

3161	A892 $400 multi	9.00	9.00

No. 3161 contains one 90x50mm stamp.

European Space Agency, 50th Anniv. — A893

No. 3162: a, European Space Agency Headquarters, Paris. b, French Guyana Space Center. c, Giotto Probe and Halley's Comet. d, Ariane N'Koltang Tracking Station, Gabon.
$400, Ariane 1 rocket, vert.

2016, Sept. 9 Litho. *Perf. 14*

3162	A893 $150 Sheet of 4, #a-d	13.50	13.50

Souvenir Sheet

Perf. 12

3163	A893 $400 multi	9.00	9.00

Visit to Argentina of Pres. Barack Obama — A894

No. 3164: a, Pres. Obama and Argentina Pres. Mauricio Macri, denomination at LR (60x40mm). b, Pres. Obama (30x40mm). c, Presidents Obama and Macri, denomination at LL (60x40mm). d, Pres. Macri (30x40mm).
$400, Presidents Obama and Macri shaking hands, horiz.

2016, Sept. 26 Litho. *Perf. 14*

3164	A894 $150 Sheet of 4, #a-d	13.50	13.50

Souvenir Sheet

Perf. 12½

3165	A894 $400 multi	9.00	9.00

No. 3165 contains one 51x38mm stamp.

A895

A896

Diplomatic Relations Between Liberia and People's Republic of China, 40th Anniv. — A897

2016, Nov. 3 Litho. *Perf. 12*

3166	Sheet of 25, #3166c, 12 each #3166a-3166b	58.50	58.50
a.	A895 $100 multi	2.25	2.25
b.	A896 $100 multi	2.25	2.25
c.	A897 $200 multi	4.50	4.50

A898

A899

A900

Worldwide Fund for Nature (WWF) — A901

2016, Nov. 3 Litho. *Perf. 14*

3167	Horiz. strip of 4	9.00	9.00
a.	A898 $100 multi	2.25	2.25
b.	A899 $100 multi	2.25	2.25
c.	A900 $100 multi	2.25	2.25
d.	A901 $100 multi	2.25	2.25
e.	Souvenir sheet of 8, 2 each #3167a-3167d	18.00	18.00

Paintings by Hieronymus Bosch (c. 1450-1516) — A902

No. 3168 — Details fom *The Haywain Triptych*: a, Adam and Eve. b, Lute player, woman and angels. c, Creatures with tails. d, Creatures with animal's heads.
No. 3169 — Details from *The Last Judgment* with denomination at: a, LL. b, LR.

2016, Nov. 14 Litho. *Perf. 14*

3168	A902 $180 Sheet of 4, #a-d	16.00	16.00

Souvenir Sheet

Perf. 12

3169	A902 $250 Sheet of 2, #a-b	11.00	11.00

No. 3169 contains two 30x50mm stamps.

New Year 2017 (Year of the Rooster) A903

No. 3170 — Rooster facing: a, Right. b, Left.

2016, Nov. 17 Litho. *Perf. 13¾*

3170	A903 $180 Horiz. pair, #a-b	8.00	8.00

No. 3170 was printed in sheets containing two pairs.

A904

Christmas — A905

2016, Dec. 1 Litho. *Perf. 12½*

Ribbon Color

3171	A904 $180 red	4.00	4.00
3172	A905 $180 red	4.00	4.00
3173	A904 $360 green	8.00	8.00
3174	A905 $360 green	8.00	8.00
	Nos. 3171-3174 (4)	24.00	24.00

A906

A907

The Monkey King A908

No. 3175 — Scenes from *The Monkey King*, as shown.

2016, Dec. 1 Litho. *Perf. 12½*

3175	A906 $180 Sheet of 4, #a-d	16.00	16.00

Souvenir Sheets

Perf. 12

3176	A907 $360 multi	8.00	8.00
3177	A908 $360 multi	8.00	8.00

Miniature Sheet

New Year 2017 (Year of the Rooster) A909

No. 3178 — Color of square behind rooster: a, Pink. b, Peach. c, Pale yellow. d, Dull blue green. e, Light green. f, Light blue. g, Gray blue. h, Reddish lilac.

2016, Dec. 15 Litho. *Perf. 13¾*

3178	A909 $90 Sheet of 8, #a-h, + central label	16.00	16.00

U.S. Presidents Type of 2009

No. 3179, vert: a, Herbert Hoover. b, Franklin D. Roosevelt. c, Harry S. Truman. d, Dwight D. Eisenhower. e, John F. Kennedy. f, Lyndon B. Johnson. g, Richard M. Nixon. h, Gerald R.

Ford. i, Jimmy Carter. j, Ronald Reagan. k, George H.W. Bush. l, William J. Clinton. m, George W. Bush. n, Barack H. Obama. o, Donald J. Trump.
No. 3180: a, Presidential seal.
$450, Donald J. Trump.

2016-17 Litho. *Perf. 13¼*

3179 A669 $45 Sheet of 15, #a-o 14.50 14.50
3180 A661 $45 Sheet of 15, #3180a, 14 #3179o 14.50 14.50

Souvenir Sheet

Perf. 12½

3181 A661 $450 multi 10.00 10.00

Issued: No. 3179, 2/28/17; No. 3180, 4/28/17; No. 3181, 12/26/16. Nos. 3179 and 3180 each contain fifteen 28x42mm stamps. A souvenir sheet similar to No. 3181 depicting Hillary Clinton exists.

A910

Wolverine Frogs — A911

No. 3182: a, Top of frog's leg under "1." b, Head of frog at bottom. c, Top of frog's leg under "A." d, White background.
No. 3183: a, Head of frog. b, Head of frog and body of other frog.

2017, Feb. 28 Litho. *Perf. 12*

3182 A910 $180 Sheet of 4, #a-d 15.50 15.50

Souvenir Sheet

Perf. 12x12½

3183 A911 $250 Sheet of 2, #a-b 11.00 11.00

Chinese People's Liberation Army, 90th Anniv. — A912

Designs: No. 3184, $30, Soldiers, flag, Great Wall of China. No. 3185, $30, Soldiers, flag, tank, ship and airplanes.

Perf. 13¼x13¾

2017, Mar. 14 Litho.

3184-3185 A912 Set of 2 1.40 1.40

Return of Hong Kong to People's Republic of China, 20th Anniv. — A913

Golden Bauhinia sculpture, Hong Kong, and No. 3186, $20, Aerial view of Hong Kong. No. 3187, $20, Lion sculpture, Hong Kong skyline.

Perf. 13¼x13¾

2017, Mar. 14 Litho.

3186-3187 A913 Set of 2 .85 .85

Wildlife — A914

Designs: $4000, Nile crocodile. $6000, Red river hog. $10,000, Leopard.

Perf. 12½x13¼

2017, Mar. 14 Litho.

3188 A914 $4000 multi 85.00 85.00
3189 A914 $6000 multi 130.00 130.00
3190 A914 $10,000 multi 215.00 215.00
Nos. 3188-3190 (3) 430.00 430.00

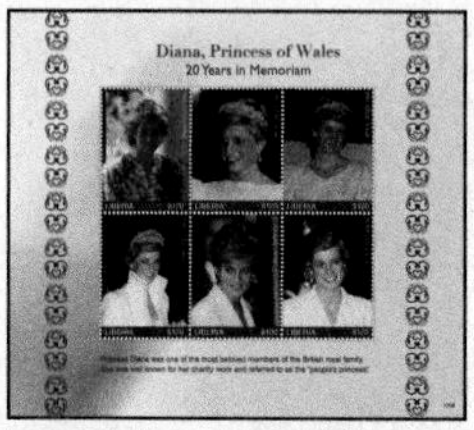

Princess Diana (1961-97) — A915

No. 3191 — Princess Diana wearing: a, Blue and white tunic. b, White dress and tiara. c, Pale blue dress and tiara. d, White jacket with high collar and tiara. e, White jacket, man in background. f, White jacket and pearl earrings.
No. 3192 — Princess Diana wearing: a, White jacket and cap. b, Blue green dress and white hat.

2017, Mar. 31 Litho. *Perf. 14*

3191 A915 $120 Sheet of 6, #a-f 15.50 15.50

Souvenir Sheet

3192 A915 $180 Sheet of 2, #a-b 7.75 7.75

Miniature Sheets

Pres. John F. Kennedy (1917-63) — A916

No. 3193, $180 — Pres. Kennedy: a, In official presidential portrait (30x80mm). b, Looking at Friendship 7 space capsule (30x40mm). c, Pointing at announcement of creation of Committee on Equal Opportunity in Housing (30x80mm). d, Signing document during Cuban Missile Crisis (30x40mm).
No. 3194, $180 — Pres. Kennedy: a, With photographer in background (40x30mm). b, In car shaking hands (40x30mm). c, Standing behind microphone (40x30mm). d, On campaign poster (80x30mm).
No. 3195, $180 — Pres. Kennedy with: a, Brothers, Robert and Edward (35x35mm). b, Son, John, Jr. (35x35mm). c, Daughter, Caroline (35x35mm). d, Wife, Jacqueline (35x35mm)

Perf. 14, 13¾ (#3195)

2017, Mar. 31 Litho.

Sheets of 4, #a-d

3193-3195 A916 Set of 3 46.00 46.00

Animals of the World A917

No. 3196: a, Malaysian golden gliding frog. b, Honeybee. c, African wild dog. d, Monarch butterflies.
$360, Matschie's tree kangaroo, vert.

2017, Apr. 14 Litho. *Perf. 12½*

3196 A917 $180 Sheet of 4, #a-d 15.50 15.50

Souvenir Sheet

3197 A917 $360 multi 7.75 7.75

Flag of People's Republic of China, Golden Bauhinia Statue, Hong Kong and Deng Xiaoping (1904-97), Leader of People's Republic of China — A918

2017, Apr. 14 Litho. *Perf. 13½*

3198 A918 $20 multi .45 .45

Hong Kong Special Administrative Region, 20th anniv.

Hong Kong Special Administrative Region, 20th Anniv. — A919

Scenes of Hong Kong and years: No. 3199, $20, "1997-1998." No. 3200, $20, "1999." No. 3201, $20, "2000." No. 3202, $20, "2001." No. 3203, $20, "2002." No. 3204, $20, "2003." No. 3205, $20, "2004." No. 3206, $20, "2005." No. 3207, $20, "2006." No. 3208, $20, "2007." No. 3209, $20, "2008." No. 3210, $20, "2009." No. 3211, $20, "2010." No. 3212, $20, "2011." No. 3213, $20, "2012." No. 3214, $20, "2013." No. 3215, $20, "2014." No. 3216, $20, "2015." No. 3217, $20, "2016." No. 3218, $20, "2017."

2017, Apr. 14 Litho. *Perf. 14½x14*

3199-3218 A919 Set of 20 8.75 8.75

Fennec Foxes A920

No. 3219: a, Head of fox facing forward. b, Head of fox facing right. c, Fox sleeping. d, Fox standing on rock.
No. 3220; a, Fox sitting. b, Fox standing.

2017, July 24 Litho. *Perf. 14*

3219 A920 $180 Sheet of 4, #a-d 16.00 16.00

Souvenir Sheet

3220 A920 $250 Sheet of 2, #a-b 11.00 11.00

Diana Monkeys A921

No. 3221: a, Monkey holding food in paw. b, Monkey, front tooth visible. c, Monkey, diff.
No. 3222, horiz.: a, Monkey and wooden pole. b, Monkey and tree leaves.

2017, July 24 Litho. *Perf. 14*

3221 A921 $200 Sheet of 3, #a-c 13.50 13.50

Souvenir Sheet

3222 A921 $200 Sheet of 2, #a-b 9.00 9.00

A922

Elephants — A923

No. 3223: a, Two adults and one juvenile elephants. b, One adult elephant in jungle. b, Four elephants. c, Elephant in grassland.
No. 3224 — Adult and juvenile elephants: a, Adult facing left. b, Adult's trunk touching juvenile. c, Juvenile's trunk touching adult's trunk.

2017, July 24 Litho. *Perf. 14*

3223 A922 $180 Sheet of 4, #a-d 16.00 16.00

Souvenir Sheet

3224 A923 $180 Sheet of 3, #a-c 12.00 12.00

A924

African Penguins A925

No. 3225: a, Two penguins on beach. b, One penguin, feet not visible. c, Two penguins grooming. d, One penguin, feet visible.
No. 3226 — Various photographs of penguins, as shown.

2017, July 24 Litho. *Perf. 14*

3225 A924 $180 Sheet of 4, #a-d 16.00 16.00

Souvenir Sheet

3226 A925 $180 Sheet of 3, #a-c 12.00 12.00

New Year 2018 (Year of the Dog) A926

No. 3227: a, Laika, first dog to orbit Earth. b, Morris Frank and Buddy, first seeing-eye dog in the U.S. c, Hachiko, dog that waited for dead owner for nine years. d, Balto, lead sled dog in 1925 Nome serum run.
$360, Owney, the mail dog.

2017, July 24 Litho. *Perf. 14*

3227 A926 $180 Sheet of 4, #a-d 16.00 16.00

Souvenir Sheet

Perf. 12¾

3228 A926 $360 multi 8.00 8.00

No. 3228 contains one 38x51mm stamp.

Souvenir Sheets

Elvis Presley (1935-77) — A927

Inscription: No. 3229, $360, First National #1 Best Seller. No. 3230, $360, Elvis' First RCA Recording Session. No. 3231, $360,

Appears in First Movie. No. 3232, $360, Elvis Decides to Record "Hound Dog."

2017, Oct. 26 Litho. *Perf. 12¾*
3229-3232 A927 Set of 4 24.00 24.00

A928

Lions Clubs International, Cent. — A929

No. 3233: a, Helen Keller. b, Lions Club Youth with earphones. c, Lions Club Youth near tents. d, 1918 emblem.e, 1920 emblem. f, Current emblem.

No. 3234 — Centenary emblem and: a, Members and statue of lion. b, Confetti. c, Slogan. d, Melvin Jones (1879-1961), founder.

2017, Oct. 26 Litho. *Perf. 14*
3233 A928 $100 Sheet of 6, #a-f 10.00 10.00

Souvenir Sheet
Perf. 12¾

3234 A929 $100 Sheet of 4, #a-d 6.75 6.75

Miniature Sheet

World War I, Cent. A930

No. 3235 — Poster inscribed: a, "Fight or Buy Bonds." b, "U.S. Marines First to Fight in France For Freedom." c, "For Action Enlist in the Air Service." d, "Men Wanted for the Army." e, "Pull Together Men the Navy Needs Us." f, "The Veteran's Farewell."

2017, Nov. 17 Litho. *Perf. 14*
3235 A930 $120 Sheet of 6, #a-f 11.50 11.50

A931

2018 World Cup Soccer Championships, Russia — A932

2018, Jan. 1 Litho. *Perf. 14*
3236 A931 $150 multi 2.40 2.40
3237 A932 $150 multi 2.40 2.40
a. Sheet of 8, 4 each #3236-3237 19.50 19.50

Miniature Sheet

Visit of Pres. Donald Trump to Asia-Pacific Economic Cooperation Economic Leaders Meeting, Viet Nam — A933

No. 3238: a, Vietnamese Prime Minister Nguyen Xuân Phúc wearing blue tie. b, Pres. Trump wearing red tie. c, Prime Minister Nguyen wearing red tie. d, Pres. Trump wearing blue striped tie.

2018, Jan. 24 Litho. *Perf. 13x12½*
3238 A933 $180 Sheet of 4, #a-d 12.00 12.00

Hyenas A934

No. 3239: a, $90, Two Spotted hyenas. b, $90, Brown hyena. c, $100, Striped hyena. d, $100, Spotted hyena. e, $150, Spotted hyena, diff. f, $150, Aardwolf.

No. 3240 — Various photographs of Spotted hyenas: a, $175. b, $185. c, $195.

2018, Jan. 24 Litho. *Perf. 14*
3239 A934 Sheet of 6, #a-f 11.00 11.00

Souvenir Sheet
Perf. 12

3240 A934 Sheet of 3, #a-c 9.00 9.00

Presidents and Vice-Presidents of the United States — A935

No. 3241, $100: a, George Washington, John Adams and flag. b, Adams. c, Washington, Adams and their signatures. d, Adams, Thomas Jefferson and flag. e, Jefferson. f, Adams, Jefferson and their signatures.

No. 3242, $100: a, Jefferson, Aaron Burr and flag. b, Burr. c, Jefferson, Burr and their signatures. d, Jefferson, George Clinton and flag. e, Clinton. f, Jefferson, Clinton and their signatures.

No. 3243, $100: a, James Madison, Elbridge Gerry and flag. b, Gerry. c, Madison, Gerry and their signatures. d, James Monroe, Daniel D. Tompkins and flag. e, Tompkins. f, Monroe, Tompkins and their signatures.

2018, Feb. 1 Litho. *Perf. 14*
Blocks of 6, #a-f
3241-3243 A935 Set of 3 30.00 30.00

Monkeys A936

No. 3244: a, Collared mangabey. b, Mona monkey. c, Green monkey. d, Patas monkey.

No. 3245, horiz.: a, Diana monkey. b, Sooty mangabey,

2018, Feb. 8 Litho. *Perf. 13¾*
3244 A936 $180 Sheet of 4, #a-d 11.00 11.00

Souvenir Sheet
Perf. 14

3245 A936 $250 Sheet of 2, #a-b 7.75 7.75

No. 3245 contains two 40x30mm stamps.

A937

Wild Horses A938

No. 3246: a, $150, Brown horse on beach. b, $200, Two horses in field. c, $250, Herd of horses. d, $300, Gray horse in water.

No. 3247: a, $200, Horse and colt. b, $250, Two horses, diff. c, $300, Black horse with white blaze.

2018, Feb. 8 Litho. *Perf. 14*
3246 A937 Sheet of 4, #a-d 14.00 14.00

Souvenir Sheet

3247 A938 Sheet of 3, #a-c 11.50 11.50

Puyang, People's Republic of China A939

No. 3248: a, $150, Qicheng Ruins. b, $350, Dragon statue. c, $550, Dragon statue and building.

$850, Red Dragon statue, vert.

2018, Mar. 14 Litho. *Perf. 14*
3248 A939 Sheet of 3, #a-c 16.00 16.00

Souvenir Sheet

3249 A939 $850 multi 13.00 13.00

No. 3249 contains one 40x60mm stamp.

Planets A940

No. 3250: a, Mercury, Venus, Earth, Mars and Jupiter. b, Jupiter, Saturn, Uranus and Neptune.

$550, Sun and the planets.

2018, Apr. 23 Litho. *Perf. 14*
3250 A940 $390 Sheet of 2, #a-b 12.00 12.00

Souvenir Sheet

3251 A940 $550 multi 8.50 8.50

No. 3251 contains one 80x30mm stamp.

Pres. Theodore Roosevelt (1858-1919) — A941

No. 3252 — Roosevelt: a, In 1885. b, In 1898. c, In 1903. d, In 1904. e, Circa 1909-10. f, On Mount Rushmore.

$360, Official White House portrait of Roosevelt, by John Singer Sargent.

2018, Apr. 23 Litho. *Perf. 14*
3252 A941 $120 Sheet of 6, #a-f 11.00 11.00

Souvenir Sheet
Perf. 12

3253 A941 $360 multi 5.50 5.50

Miniature Sheet

Billy Graham (1918-2018), Evangelist — A942

No. 3254 — Graham with: a, His wife, Ruth, Queen Elizabeth II, Queen Mother and Prince Philip (80x30mm). b, Pres. Barack Obama (40x30mm). c, Pres. John F. Kennedy (40x30mm). d, Pres. George W. Bush (40x30mm). e, Pres. Richard Nixon (40x30mm).

2018, Apr. 26 Litho. *Perf. 14*
3254 A942 $200 Sheet of 5, #a-e 15.00 15.00

Souvenir Sheet

Pres. Donald Trump at World Economic Forum — A943

No. 3255 — Pres. Trump and: a, Swiss Pres. Alain Berset. b, British Prime Minister Theresa May. c, Israeli Prime Minister Benjamin Netanyahu.

2018, Apr. 26 Litho. *Perf. 14*
3255 A943 $260 Sheet of 3, #a-c 12.00 12.00

United States Air Mail, Cent. A944

No. 3256: a, 1930 Graf Zeppelin cover with handwritten address. b, United States #C14. c, United States #C15. d, 1930 Graf Zeppelin cover with typewritten address.

$500, United States #C13.

2018, Apr. 26 Litho. *Perf. 14*
3256 A944 $250 Sheet of 4, #a-d 15.00 15.00

Souvenir Sheet
Perf. 12¾

3257 A944 $500 multi 7.50 7.50

No. 3257 contains one 51x38mm stamp.

Miniature Sheets

2018 Winter Olympics, Pyeongchang, South Korea — A945

No. 3258, $175: a, Speed skiing. b, Bobsledding. c, Figure skating. d, Ice hockey. e, Nordic combined skiing.
No. 3259, $175: a, Short track speed skating. b, Ski jumping. c, Skeleton. d, Snowboarding. e, Speed skating.
No. 3260, $175: a, Biathlon. b, Cross-country skiing. c, Curling. d, Freestyle skiing. e, Luge.

2018, Apr. 26 Litho. *Perf. 13¾*
Sheets of 5, #a-e

3258-3260 A945 Set of 3 40.00 40.00

Liberian President George Weah — A946

Various photographs of Weah and Liberian flag: $100, $200, $250.
No. 3264, $500, Weah wearing suit and tie. No. 3265, $500, Weah wearing green presidential sash.

2018 Litho. *Perf. 13¼x12½*
3261-3263 A946 Set of 3 8.00 8.00

Souvenir Sheets
Perf. 13¾

3264-3265 A946 Set of 2 13.50 13.50

Issued: Nos. 3261-3263, 5/12; Nos. 3264-3265, 6/30. Nos. 3264-3265 each contain one 70x70mm stamp.

Miniature Sheet

Wild Cats A947

No. 3266: a, $100, Lion. b, $100, Snow leopard. c, $200, Cheetah. d, $200, Black panther. e, $300, Leopard. f, $300, Tiger.

Die Cut Perf. 13
2018, May 22 Litho.
Self-Adhesive

3266 A947 Sheet of 6, #a-f 17.50 17.50

Miniature Sheet

Mushrooms — A948

No. 3267: a, $100, Penny buns. b, $100, Crab brittlegills. c, $200, Chanterelles. d, $200, Field mushrooms. e, $300, Honey fungus. f, $300, Sponge morels.

2018, May 22 Litho. *Perf. 14*
3267 A948 Sheet of 6, #a-f 17.50 17.50

Duikers A949

No. 3268: a, $200, Common duiker. b, $250, Red forest duiker. c, $300, Two Red forest duikers. d, $350, Common duiker, diff.
$500, Common duiker, diff.

2018, May 22 Litho. *Perf. 14*
3268 A949 Sheet of 4, #a-d 16.00 16.00

Souvenir Sheet
Perf. 12¾

3269 A949 $500 multi 7.25 7.25

No. 3269 contains one 51x38mm stamp.

Coronation of Queen Elizabeth II, 65th Anniv. — A950

No. 3270 — Queen Elizabeth II: a, $250, Waving (30x40mm). b, $250, Sitting in coach (30x40mm). c, $390, Wearing coronation robes (30x80mm).
$500, Queen Elizabeth II holding orb and scepter.

2018, May 22 Litho. *Perf. 14*
3270 A950 Sheet of 3, #a-c 13.00 13.00

Souvenir Sheet
Perf. 12¾

3271 A950 $500 multi 7.25 7.25

No. 3271 contains one 38x51mm stamp.

Miniature Sheet

Birth of Prince Louis of Cambridge — A951

No. 3272 — Duke and Duchess of Cambridge: a, At their wedding. b, With Prince George. c, With Princess Charlotte. d, With Prince Louis.

2018, July 13 Litho. *Perf. 13¾*
3272 A951 $250 Sheet of 4, #a-d 13.00 13.00

Miniature Sheet

Engagement of Prince Harry and Meghan Markle — A952

No. 3273: a, Prince Harry, arms not visible. b, Markle, crowd in background. c, Prince Harry, arms visible. d, Markle, and woman standing behind her.

2018, July 13 Litho. *Perf. 14*
3273 A952 $250 Sheet of 4, #a-d 13.00 13.00

Wedding of Prince Harry and Meghan Markle A953

No. 3274: a, Couple holding hands. b, Arms of the Duchess of Sussex. c, Arms of the Duke of Sussex. d, Couple kissing.
$500, Couple holding hands, diff.

2018, July 13 Litho. *Perf. 13¾*
3274 A953 $250 Sheet of 4, #a-d 13.00 13.00

Souvenir Sheet

3275 A953 $500 multi 6.50 6.50

Souvenir Sheets

Elvis Presley (1935-77) — A954

Inscriptions: No. 3276, $500, *Girls! Girls! Girls!* No. 3277, $500, Mexico City bans Elvis's movie *G.I. Blues*. No. 3278, $500, Public karate demonstration. No. 3279, $500, Documentary *That's the Way It Is*, horiz.

2018, July 13 Litho. *Perf. 14*
3276-3279 A954 Set of 4 26.00 26.00

Souvenir Sheets

Praga 2018 World Stamp Exhibition, Prague — A955

Illustrations by Alfons Mucha (1860-1939): No. 3280, $500, Epopea Slava. No. 3281, $500, 8th Sokol Festival, Prague.

2018, July 15 Litho. *Perf. 12*
3280-3281 A955 Set of 2 13.00 13.00

Souvenir Sheet

Nelson Mandela (1918-2013), President of South Africa — A956

2018, July 18 Litho. *Perf. 13¾*
3282 A956 $550 multi 7.25 7.25

African Guineafowl — A957

No. 3283: a, $170, Helmeted Guineafowl. b, $170, Crested Guineafowl. c, $170, Vulturine Guineafowl. d, $180, Helmeted Guineafowl, diff. e, $180, Crested Guineafowl, diff. f, $180m Vulturine Guineafowl, diff.
$500, White-breasted Guineafowl.

2018, Aug. 8 Litho. *Perf. 14*
3283 A957 Sheet of 6, #a-f 14.00 14.00

Souvenir Sheet
Perf. 13¾

3284 A957 $500 multi 6.50 6.50

No. 3284 contains one 35x35mm stamp.

Souvenir Sheets

Comet Moth Caterpillars — A958

Comet Moths A959

No. 3285: a, One caterpillar. b, Two caterpillars. No. 3286: a, Moth above green foliage. b, Moth on tree.

2018, Aug. 8 Litho. *Perf.*
3285 A958 $390 Sheet of 2, #a-b 10.00 10.00
3286 A959 $390 Sheet of 2, #a-b 10.00 10.00

Wild Cats
A960

No. 3287: a, African wildcat. b, Black-footed cat. c, Jungle cat. d, Caracal.
$500, Sand cat, horiz.

2018, Sept. 14 Litho. *Perf. 14*

3287 A960 $250 Sheet of 4, #a-d 13.00 13.00

Souvenir Sheet

Perf. 12¾

3288 A960 $500 multi 6.50 6.50

No. 3288 contains one 51x38mm stamp.

A961

New Year 2019 (Year of the Pig)
A962

No. 3289: a, Red pig facing right. b, Yellow pig facing left and flowers. c, Red pig facing left.

2018, Sept. 14 Litho. *Perf. 14*

3289 A961 $210 Sheet of 3, #a-c 8.25 8.25

Souvenir Sheet

Perf. 13¾

3290 A962 $300 multi 4.00 4.00

Souvenir Sheet

Butterflies — A963

No. 3291: a, $100, Giant blue swallowtail. b, $200, Blue mother-of-pearl. c, $300, Blue diadem.

2018, Oct. 25 Litho. *Perf.*

3291 A963 Sheet of 3, #a-c 7.75 7.75

Souvenir Sheet

Donkeys and Zebras
A964

No. 3292: a, $200, Two donkeys. b, $250, Zedonk. c, $300, Five zebras.

2018, Oct. 25 Litho. *Perf. 12*

3292 A964 Sheet of 3, #a-c 9.75 9.75

Great Zebra Migration
A965

No. 3293 — Various photographs of Burchell's zebras: a, $150. b, $250. c, $350. d, $450.
$600, Burchell's zebras, diff.

2018, Oct. 25 Litho. *Perf. 12*

3293 A965 Sheet of 4, #a-d 15.50 15.50

Souvenir Sheet

3294 A965 $600 multi 7.25 7.25

No. 3294 contains one 40x30mm stamp.

Oxpeckers — A966

No. 3295: a, $80, Red-billed oxpecker on giraffe. b, $90, Red-billed oxpecker. c, $100, Yellow-billed oxpecker on hippopotamus. d, $200, Red-billed oxpecker on Plains zebra. e, $300, Yellow-billed oxpecker. f, $400, Red-billed oxpecker on impala.
$600, Five Red-billed oxpeckers on African buffalo, horiz.

2018, Oct. 25 Litho. *Perf. 12*

3295 A966 Sheet of 6, #a-f 15.00 15.00

Souvenir Sheet

Perf. 12¾

3296 A966 $600 multi 7.75 7.75

No. 3296 contains one 51x38mm stamp.

Flight of Apollo 11, 50th Anniv. (in 2019)
A967

No. 3297: a, $150, Crew members Edwin "Buzz" Aldrin, Neil Armstrong and Michael Collins in suits and ties. b, $250, Crew members in space suits. c, $350, Pres. Nixon addressing quarantined crew members after flight.
$500, Crew members in space capsule.

2018, Oct. 25 Litho. *Perf. 12*

3297 A967 Sheet of 3, #a-c 9.75 9.75

Souvenir Sheet

Perf. 12¾

3298 A967 $500 multi 6.50 6.50

No. 3298 contains one 51x38mm stamp.

Souvenir Sheet

Mohandas K. Gandhi (1869-1948), Indian Nationalist Leader — A968

No. 3299 — Various photographs of Gandhi: a, $350. b, $500.

2018, Dec. 5 Litho. *Perf. 14*

3299 A968 Sheet of 2, #a-b 11.00 11.00

African Waterfalls — A969

No. 3300: a, $160, Boti Falls. b, $260, Boti Falls, diff. c, $360, Kintampo Waterfalls.
No. 3301: a, $160, Wli Waterfalls. b, $260, Ouzoud Falls. c, $360, Murchison Falls.
$500, Kpatawee Waterfall, horiz.

2018, Dec. 17 Litho. *Perf. 12*

Sheets of 3, #a-c

3300-3301 A969 Set of 2 20.00 20.00

Souvenir Sheet

Perf. 12¾x12½

3302 A969 $500 multi 6.50 6.50

No. 3302 contains one 51x38mm stamp.

New Year 2019 (Year of the Pig)
A970

No. 3303 — Stamps with red frames and heads of various pigs: a, $150. b, $200. c, $250. d, $300.
No. 3304, $300: a, Panda. b, Pig (green panels).

2018, Dec. 17 Litho. *Perf. 12*

3303 A970 Sheet of 4, #a-d 11.50 11.50

Souvenir Sheet

3304 A970 $300 Sheet of 2, #a-b 7.75 7.75

Lizards
A971

No. 3305: a, $170, Red-headed rock agama. b, $170, Mwanza flat-headed rock agama. c, $170, Ground agama. d, $180, Mwanza flat-headed rock agama, diff. e, $180, Ground agama, diff. f, $180, Red-headed rock agama, diff.

2018, Dec. 25 Litho. *Perf. 14*

3305 A971 Sheet of 6, #a-f 13.50 13.50

Meleguetta Peppers — A972

No. 3306: a, $100, Seeds. b, $200, Flower bud. c, $300, Flower. d, $400, Fruits.
$500, Flower, vert.

2018, Dec. 31 Litho. *Perf. 12½*

3306 A972 Sheet of 4, #a-d 13.00 13.00

Souvenir Sheet

Perf. 12

3307 A972 $500 multi 6.50 6.50

No. 3307 contains one 30x50mm stamp.

Miniature Sheet

Garden Bulbul, National Bird of Liberia
A973

No. 3308 — Arms of Liberia and: a, $100, Bird on perch. b, $200, Head of bird. c, $300, Bird on branch. d, $400, Two birds.

2018, Dec. 31 Litho. *Perf. 14*

3308 A973 Sheet of 4, #a-d 13.00 13.00

White Rhinoceros — A974

No. 3309: a, $100, Adult and juvenile rhinoceros. b, $300, Adult rhinoceros. c, $500, Rhinoceros and lion.
$800, Head of rhinoceros

2019, Feb. 25 Litho. *Perf. 12*

3309 A974 Sheet of 3, #a-c 11.00 11.00

Souvenir Sheet

Perf.

3310 A974 $800 multi 10.00 10.00

No. 3310 contains one 38mm diameter stamp.

Miniature Sheet

Marabou Stork
A975

No. 3311 — Various photographs of stork: a, $250. b, $300. c, $350. d, $400.

2019, Mar. 11 Litho. *Perf. 12*

3311 A975 Sheet of 4, #a-d 16.00 16.00

Souvenir Sheet

African Openbill Stork
A976

No. 3312 — Various photographs of stork: a, $200. b, $300. c, $400.

2019, Mar. 11 Litho. *Perf. 14*
3312 A976 Sheet of 3, #a-c 11.00 11.00

Souvenir Sheet

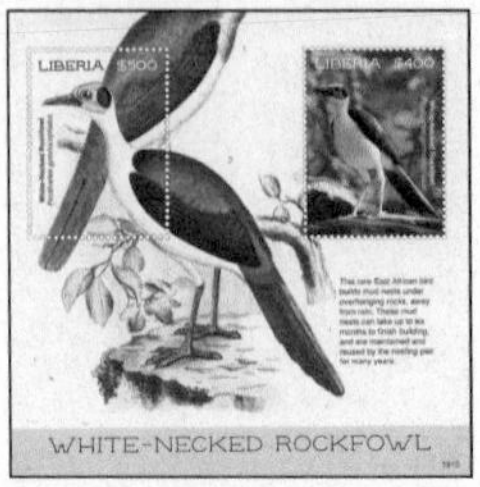

White-necked Rockfowl — A977

No. 3313: a, $400, Photograph. b, $500, Drawing.

2019, Mar. 11 Litho. *Perf. 14*
3313 A977 Sheet of 2, #a-b 11.00 11.00

Miniature Sheet

Cuckooshrikes — A978

No. 3314: a, Blue cuckooshrike. b, Ghana cuckooshrike. c, Female red-shouldered cuckooshrike. d, Male red-shouldered cuckooshrike.

2019, Mar. 13 Litho. *Perf. 14*
3314 A978 $300 Sheet of 4, #a-d 15.00 15.00

Souvenir Sheets

Spiders A979

Insects A980

No. 3315 — Various photographs of Wasp spider: a, $100. b, $300. c, $500.
No. 3316 — Various photographs of Dung beetle, as shown.
No. 3317 — Various photographs of Giant African mantis: a, $200. b, $300. c, $400.
No. 3318: a, $250, Rainbow bush locust. b, $300, Migratory locust. c, $350, Milkweed grasshopper.
No. 3319, $300: a, African fruit beetle. b, Derby's flower beetle. c, Goliath beetle.

2019, Mar. 29 Litho. *Perf. 12*
3315 A979 Sheet of 3, #a-c 11.00 11.00
3316 A980 $300 Sheet of 3, #a-c 11.00 11.00
3317 A979 Sheet of 3, #a-c 11.00 11.00
3318 A980 Sheet of 3, #a-c 11.00 11.00
3319 A980 $300 Sheet of 3, #a-c 11.00 11.00
Nos. 3315-3319 (5) 55.00 55.00

Long-beaked Common Dolphin — A981

No. 3320: a, $100, Dolphin and fish. b, $100, Two dolphins. c, $200, Dolphin at water's surface. d, $200, Dolphin and fish, diff. e, $300, Dolphin and tail fin of other dolphin. f, $300, Dolphin, diff.
$800, Dolphin and Pomarine jaeger, horiz.

2019, Apr. 8 Litho. *Perf. 14*
3320 A981 Sheet of 6, #a-f 14.00 14.00

Souvenir Sheet

3321 A981 $800 multi 9.50 9.50

No. 3321 contains one 80x30mm stamp.

Piapiacs A982

No. 3322: a, $250, Piapiac on branch. b, $300, Two piapiacs. c, $350, Piapiac on ground.
$800, Piapiac on animal's back.

2019, Apr. 18 Litho. *Perf. 12*
3322 A982 Sheet of 3, #a-c 10.50 10.50

Souvenir Sheet

Perf.

3323 A982 $800 multi 9.50 9.50

No. 3323 contains one 33x43mm stamp.

African Buffalo A983

No. 3324: a, $150, Head of buffalo. b, $250, Buffalo and cattle egrets. c, $350, Herd. d, $450, Buffalo, diff.
$800, Buffalo, diff.

2019, Apr. 19 Litho. *Perf. 12*
3324 A983 Sheet of 4, #a-d 14.00 14.00

Souvenir Sheet

Perf. 12½

3325 A983 $800 multi 9.50 9.50

No. 3325 contains one 51x38mm stamp.

Reptiles A984

No. 3326: a, $150, Nile monitor. b, $200, African spurred tortoise. c, $250, Dwarf crocodile. d, $300, African rock python. e, $350, Namaqua chameleon.
$800, Nile crocodile.

2019, Apr. 24 Litho. *Perf. 14*
3326 A984 Sheet of 5, #a-e 15.00 15.00

Souvenir Sheet

3327 A984 $800 multi 9.50 9.50

No. 3327 contains one 80x30mm stamp.

Chimpanzees — A985

No. 3328: a, $150, Head of Common chimpanzee. b, $250, Adult and juvenile Eastern chimpanzees. c, $350, Three Common chimpanzees. d, $450, Head of Eastern chimpanzee.
No. 3329, $500: a, Common chimpanzee. b, Head of Eastern chimpanzee, diff.

2019, May 1 Litho. *Perf. 12*
3228 A985 Sheet of 4, #a-d 14.00 14.00

Souvenir Sheet

Perf. 14

3329 A985 $500 Sheet of 2, #a-b 12.00 12.00

D-Day, 75th Anniv. A986

No. 3330: a, $150, U.S. troops on Omaha Beach. b, $250, U.S. troops in landing craft. c, $350, U.S. troops debark from their landing craft. d, $450, Loading bombs onto U.S. vessel.
$750, The Tough Beach, by Dwight Shepler.

2019, May 29 Litho. *Perf. 12*
3330 A986 Sheet of 4, #a-d 12.50 12.50

Souvenir Sheet

Perf. 14

3331 A986 $750 multi 8.00 8.00

Guinea Turaco A987

No. 3332: a, $200, One Guinea turaco. b, $300, Two Guinea turacos. c, $400, One Guinea turaco, diff.
$800, Head of Gunea turaco, vert.

2019, June 8 Litho. *Perf. 12*
3332 A987 Sheet of 3, #a-c 9.25 9.25

Souvenir Sheet

Perf.

3333 A987 $800 multi 8.25 8.25

No. 3333 contains one 33x43mm oval stamp.

Slender Mongoose — A988

No. 3334 — Various photographs of mongooses: a, $150. b, $250. c, $350. d, $450.
No. 3335 — Mongoose: a, To left of dirt mound. b, To right of dirt mound.

2019, June 8 Litho. *Perf. 14*
3334 A988 Sheet of 4, #a-d 12.50 12.50

Souvenir Sheet

Perf. 12

3335 A988 $500 Sheet of 2, #a-b 10.50 10.50

China 2019 World Stamp Exhibition, Wuhan — A989

No. 3336 — Various photographs of Wuhan: a, $100. b, $200. c, $300. d, $400.
$500, Pagoda, vert.

2019, June 10 Litho. *Perf. 14*
3336 A989 Sheet of 4, #a-d 10.50 10.50

Souvenir Sheet

Perf. 12½

3337 A989 $500 multi 5.25 5.25

No. 3337 contains one 38x51mm stamp.

Miniature Sheet

Birth of Archie Mountbatten-Windsor — A990

No. 3338: a, $200, King George VI, Queen Mary and infant Princess Elizabeth. b, $200, Prince Charles, Princess Diana and infant Prince Harry. c, $400, Duke and Duchess of Cambridge with infant Prince George. d, $400, Duke and Duchess of Sussex with infant Archie Mountbatten-Windsor.

2019, June 29 Litho. *Perf. 14*
3338 A990 Sheet of 4, #a-d 12.50 12.50

Flowers A991

No. 3339: a, $80, Tiger lily. b, $90, Pink flamingo. c, $100, Magenta orchid. d, $200, Buttercup. e, $300, White lotus. f, $400, Red hibiscus.
No. 3340: a, $100, Pink daisy. b, $200, White tulip. c, $300, Morning glory. d, $400, Orange rose.

2019, Sept. 29 Litho. *Perf. 12*
3339 A991 Sheet of 6, #a-f 11.50 11.50

Souvenir Sheet
Perf. 14

3340 A991 Sheet of 4, #a-d 9.75 9.75

Hornbills
A992

No. 3341: a, $200, Black-casqued hornbill. b, $300, Grey-checkered hornbill. c, $400, White-crested hornbill.
No. 3342: $800, African grey hornbill, vert.

2019, Sept. 29 Litho. *Perf. 14*
3341 A992 Sheet of 3, #a-c 8.75 8.75

Souvenir Sheet
Perf. 14

3342 A992 $800 multi 7.75 7.75

No. 3342 contains one 38x51mm stamp.

A993

No. 3343, $200 — Minerals: a, Galena ore. b, Ruby. c, Quarts on pyrite. d, Petalite. e, Malachite. f, Sapphire.
No. 3344, $200 — Monkeys: a, Mandrillus sphinx. b, Nasalis larvatus. c, Macac silenus. d, Macaca fuscata. e, Saguinus oedipus. f, Saimiri sciureus.
No. 3345, $200 — Birds of Liberia: a, Coracias cyanogaster. b, Corythornis cristatus. c, Otus sengalensis. d, Numida meleagris. e, Corythaeola cristata. f, Psittacula krameri.
No. 3346, $200 — Cats: a, Persian. b, American shorthair. c, Sphynx. d, Turkish angora. e, Bengal. f, Somali.
No. 3347, $200 — Mushrooms and Owls: a, Boletus edulis and Strix varia. b, Athene cunicularia and Cantharellus cibarius. c, Lentinula edodes and Tyto alba. d, Amanita virosa and Asio otus. e, Strix aluco and Hypsizygus tessellatus. f, Morchella esculenta and Asio flammeus.
No. 3348, $200 — Orchids: a, Dendrobium speciosum. b, Cymbidium Enzan Knuckle "Pink Puma". c, Calypso bulbosa. d, Serapias lingua. e, Rhyncholaeliocattleya Vasin "Yen Jitt". f, Platanthera chlorantha.
No. 3349, $1200, Fluorite. No. 3350, $1200, Macaca mulatta. No. 3351, $1200, Haliaeetus vocifer. No. 3352, $1200, Selkirk Rex. No. 3353, $1200, Lactarius deliciosus and Strix varia. No. 3354, $1200, Cypripedium calceolus.

2020, Jan. 6 Litho. *Perf. 13x13¼*
Sheets of 6 # a-f

3343-3348 A993 Set of 6 75.00 75.00

Souvenir Sheets

3349-3354 A993 Set of 6 75.00 75.00

A994

No. 3355, $200 — Dogs: a, Bernese mountain dog. b, Pug. c, Weimaraner. d, Rhodesian ridgeback. e, English bulldog. f, Beagle.
No. 3356, $200 — Marine life of Liberia: a, Aetobatus narinari. b, Orcinus orca. c, Megaptera novaeangliae. d, Physeter macrocephalus. e, Stenella longirostris. f, Chelonia mydas.
No. 3357, $200 — Crocodiles: a, Crocodylus siamensis. b, Melanosuchus niger. c, Gavialis gangeticus; d, Crocodylus niloticus. e, Crocodylus palustris. f, Crocodylus acutus.
No. 3358, $200 — Leopards: a, Panthera pardus in tree. b, Adult with cub. c, Standing to left. d, Standing to right. e, Facing forward. f, Laying down.
No. 3359, $200 — Elephants: a, Loxodonta Africana adult and baby. b, Spraying water. c, Facing right. d, Facing left. e, Facing forward. f, Two adults.
No. 3360, $200 — Dinosaurs: a, Einiosaurus procurvicornis. b, Parasaurolophus walker. c, Apatosaurus ajax. d, Stegosaurus stenops. e, Coelurus bauri. f, Pachycephalosaurus wyomingensis.
No. 3361, $200 — Butterflies: a, Gonepteryx rhamni. b, Nymphalis antiopa. c, Polyommatus bellargus. d, Melanargia galathea. e, Pieris napi. f, Anthocharis cardamines.
No. 3362, $1200, Golden retriever. No. 3363, $1200, Makaira nigricans. No. 3364, $1200, Crocodylus niloticus. No. 3365, $1200, Panthera pardus. No. 3366, $1200, Loxodonta Africana. No. 3367, $1200, Tyrannosaurus rex. No. 3368, $1200, Apatura iris.

2020, Jan. 6 Litho. *Perf. 13x13¼*
Sheets of 6 # a-f

3355-3361 A994 Set of 7 90.00 90.00

Souvenir Sheets

3362-3368 A994 Set of 7 90.00 90.00

A995

No. 3369: Year of the Rat with rat in 50 different poses.

2020, Jan. 6 Litho. *Perf. 13x13½*
3369 A995 $100 Sheet of 50, #a-ax 55.00 55.00

A996

A997

A998

Personalized Stamps — A999

2020, Jan. 6 Litho. *Perf. 13x13¼*
Liberian Flag

3370 A996 $210 red & dk bl 2.25 2.25

"Republique of Liberia"

3371 A997 $210 red & dk bl 2.25 2.25

Green Panel with White Star

3372 A998 $210 grn 2.25 2.25

"Liberia" with Red Star

3373 A999 $210 dk bl & red 2.25 2.25

Nos. 3370-3373 were each printed in sheets of 24 that could be personalized. A generic image showing Pope John Paul II was made available. Values are for stamps with or without printed vignette.

Penny Black, 180th Anniv. — A1000

Litho. With Foil Application

2020, Mar 26 *Perf. 13½x13*
3374 A1000 $250 gold & multi 2.50 2.50

Souvenir Sheet
Perf. 13x13½

3375 A1000 $1300 gold & multi 13.00 13.00

No. 3374 was printed in sheets of 6.

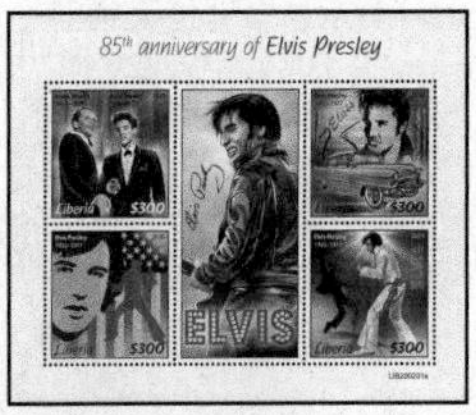

A1001

A1002

No. 3376, $300 — Elvis Presley (1935-77): a, With Frank Sinatra. b, With pink 1955 Cadillac. c, With American flag. d, Under spotlight.
No. 3377, $300 — Queen (musical group), 50th anniv.: a, Freddie Mercury. b, Brian May. c, John Deacon. d, Roger Taylor.
No. 3378, $300 — Nelson Mandela's release from prison, 30th anniv.: a, Facing left. b, At Nobel prize ceremony. c, Waving flag. d, Facing right.
No. 3379, $300 — Rabindranath Tagore (1861-1941), writer: a, With Mahatma Gandhi. b, And Nobel Prize in Literature. c, Holding book. d, With Albert Einstein.
No. 3380, $300 — Albert Einstein (1878-1955), physicist: a, Smoking pipe. b, Equation on paper. c, With medal for Nobel Prize in Physics. d, With signature.
No. 3381, $300 — Jules Verne (1828-1905), writer of: a, In Search of the Castaways. b, Around the Moon. c, The Archipelago on Fire. d, Twenty Thousand Leagues Under the Sea.
No. 3382, $300 — Boris Pasternak (1890-1960), writer: a, Portrait with pen nib. b, With medal for Nobel Prize in Literature, holding book. c, With Nobel medal, notepad and pen. d, As young man.
No. 3383, $300 — High-speed trains: a, E6 Series Shinkansen. b, British Rail Class 801. c, ICE 4. d, RENFE Class 490.
No. 3384, $300 — African trains: a, Locomotive CDD3B1. b, South African Class 5 4-6-2. c, Class 15A (4-6-4+4-6-4). d, EMD G22C series.
No. 3385, $300 — Concorde: a, Concorde Air France. b, Beatrice Vialle, the first French female pilot on a supersonic airliner. c, Mike Bannister, the chief pilot of British Airways Concorde fleet. d, Barbara Harmer, the first qualified female Concorde pilot.
No. 3386, $300 — Airbus A380: a, A380 over Dubai. b, British Airways A380. c, A380 plus. d, Gray livery A380 (no markings on airplane).
No. 3387, $300 — Fire engines: a, Yankee-Walter PLF 6000. b, IFA G5 TLF 15 fire truck. c, Scania R480 CB. d, Mercedes-Benz L 1113.
No. 3388, $300 — Special transport: a, HMMWV M997. b, Renault Midlum security and public order vehicle. c, Ford F150 Raptor police vehicle. d, Ford E-450 ambulance.
No. 3389, $300 — Extinct species: a, Purgatorius unio. b, Equus scotti. c, Entelodon magnus. d, Deinotherium giganteum.
No. 3390, $600 — Presley: a, With American flag, diff. b, At microphone.
No. 3391, $600 — Queen: a, Entire band. b, Mercury, diff.
No. 3392, $600 — Mandela: a, Like #3378a. b, Africa map and child.
No. 3393, $600 — Tagore: a, With medal for Nobel Prize in Literature, diff. b, Like #3379a.
No. 3394, $600 — Einstein: a, In front of chalkboard. b, And Relativity equation.
No. 3395, $600 — Verne: a, Portrait and signature. b, The Chase of the Golden Meteor.
No. 3396, $600 — Pasternak: a, With Nobel medal and books. b, Like #3382a.
No. 3397, $600 — High-speed trains: a, ED250. b, H5 Series Shinkansen.
No. 3398, $600 — African trains: a, South African Class 25NC 4-8-4. b, South African Class B 0-6-4T.
No. 3399, $600 — Concorde: a, Like #3385d. b, British Airways Concorde.
No. 3400, $600 — Airbus A380: a, Lufthansa A380. b, A380, diff.
No. 3401, $600 — Fire engines: a, Ford C Tanker. b, KAMAZ 43502 Fire Truck.
No. 3402, $600 — Special transport: a, Eurocopter AS 365 N2 Dauphin. b, KATMERCILER riot control vehicle.
No. 3403, $600 — Extinct species: a, Kaprosuchus saharicus. b, Carcharocles megalodon.

2020, Mar. 26 Litho. *Perf. 13x13½*
Sheets of 4 # a-d, + Central Label

3376-3389 A1001 Set of 14 170.00 170.00

Souvenir Sheets

3390-3403 A1002 Set of 14 170.00 170.00

A1003

No. 3404, $300 — Carassius auratus goldfish: a, With blue in background. b, Swimming up. c, White and orange fish. d, Swimming down.
No. 3405, $300 — Tulips and Windmill at: a, Zaanse Schans, Netherlands. b, Bremen, Germany. c, Valensole, France. d, Sanok, Poland.
No. 3406, $300 — Critically endangered species: a, Panthera pardus orientalis. b, Eretmochelys imbricata. c, Elephas maximus sumatranus. d, Propithecus diadema.
No. 3407, $300 — Dolphins: a, Lagenorhynchus obscurus. b, Cephalorhynchus commersonii. c, Grampus griseus. d, Stenella longirostris.
No. 3408, $300 — Lighthouses: a, Lindesnes Lighthouse, Norway. b, Brockton Point Lighthouse, Canada. c, Chroicocephalus ridibundus and Cape Horn Lighthouse, Chile. d, Alnes Lighthouse, Norway.
No. 3409, $300 — Turtles: a, Chelonoidis carbonaria. b, Chelonia mydas. c, Centrochelys sulcate. d, Stigmochelys pardalis.
No. 3410, $300 — Snakes: a, Protobothrops jerdonii. b, Vipera seoanei. c, Vipera berus. d, Eryx johni.
No. 3411, $300 — Parrots: a, Ara macao. b, Ara militaris. c, Aratinga solstitialis. d, Myiopsitta monachus.
No. 3412, $300 — Rare birds: a, Amazilia luciae and Neophema chrysogaster. b, Leucopsar Rothschildi. c, Mergus squamatus. d, Strigops habroptilus.
No. 3413, $300 — Rare birds: a, Pharomachrus mocinno. b, Crax rubra. c, Batrachostomus moniliger. d, Aix galericulata.
No. 3414, $300 — Bees: a, Apis mellifera. b, Bombus affinis. c, Bombus terrestris. d, Xylocopa virginica.
No. 3415, $300 — Beetles: a, Leptinotarsa decemlineata. b, Lygistopterus sanguineus. c, Anoplotrupes stercorosus. d, Cetonia aurata.
No. 3416, $300 — Big cats: a, Panthera uncia. b, Panthera onca. c, Panthera tigris. d, Panthera pardus.
No. 3417, $300 — Giraffes: a, Giraffa camelopardalis giraffa. b, Giraffa camelopardalis peralta. c, Giraffa camelopardalis camelopardalis. d, Giraffa camelopardalis tippelskirchi.
No. 3418, $300 — Arctic Ocean animals: a, Sterna paradisaea. b, Pusa hispida. c, Vulpes lagopus. d, Monodon monoceros.
No. 3419, $600 — Goldfish: a, Orange and white fish, diff. b, Orange, white and black fish.
No. 3420, $600 — Tulips and Windmill at: a, Keukenhof, Lisse, South Holland. b, Sibiu, Transylvania, Romania.
No. 3421, $600 — Critically Endangered Species: a, Diceros bicornis. b, Alcedo euryzona.
No. 3422, $600 — Dolphins: a, Stenella frontalis. b, Tursiops truncatus.
No. 3423, $600 — Lighthouses: a, Sterna paradisaea and Tranoy Lighthouse, Norway. b, Stercorarius parasiticus and Kermorvan Lighthouse, France.
No. 3424, $600 — Turtles: a, Chelonia mydas, diff. b, Testudo horsfieldii.
No. 3425, $600 — Snakes: a, Boa constrictor. b, Python bivittatus.
No. 3426, $600 — Parrots: a, Melopsittacus undulatus. b, Eolophus roseicapilla.
No. 3427, $600 — Rare birds: a, Geronticus eremita. b, Porphyrio hochstetteri.
No. 3428, $600 — Rare birds: a, Rupicola peruvianus peruvianus. b, Eumomota superciliosa.
No. 3429, $600 — Bees: a, Thyreus nitidulus. b, Andrena cineraria.
No. 3430, $600 — Beetles: a, Eupatorus gracilicornis. b, Coccinella septempunctata.
No. 3431, $600 — Big cats: a, Panthera leo. b, Panthera tigris altaica.
No. 3432, $600 — Giraffes: a, Giraffa camelopardalis reticulata. b, Giraffa camelopardalis angolensis.
No. 3433, $600 — Arctic Ocean animals: a, Fratercula arctica. b, Odobenus rosmarus.

2020, Mar. 26 Litho. *Perf. 13x13½*
Sheets of 4 # a-d, + Central Label

3404-3418 A1003 Set of 15 180.00 180.00

Souvenir Sheets

3419-3433 A1003 Set of 15 180.00 180.00

Ludwig van Beethoven (1770-1827), Composer — A1004

2020, June 28 Litho. *Perf. 13x13½*

3434 A1004 $300 multi + label 2.50 2.50

H.H. Dorje Chang Buddha III, Religious Leader — A1005

2020, June 28 Litho. *Perf. 13x13½*

3435 A1005 $100 multi 1.00 1.00

No. 3435 was printed in sheets of 6.

Fighting the Coronavirus Pandemic — A1006

No. 3436 — Various healthcare workers, patients and family members, as shown.

2020, June 28 Litho. *Perf. 13x13½*

3436 A1006 $120 Sheet of 16, #a-p 19.50 19.50

The Penny Black Against COVID-19 — A1007

No. 3437 — Penny Black stamp with various protective face masks, as shown.

2020, June 28 Litho. *Perf. 13½x13*

3437 A1007 $200 Sheet of 6, #a-f 12.00 12.00

Stop COVID-19 Novel Coronavirus — A1008

No. 3438 — Various depictions of coronavirus, as shown.
$1200, Coronavirus, diff.

2020, June 28 Litho. *Perf.*

3438 A1008 $300 Sheet of 4, #a-d 12.00 12.00

Souvenir Sheet

3439 A1008 $1200 multi 12.00 12.00

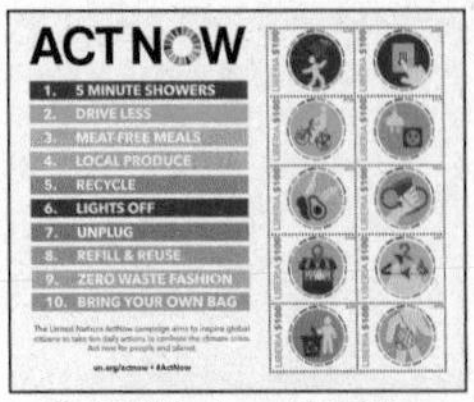

United Nations Act Now Campaign — A1009

No. 3440: a, Five-minute showers. b, Lights off. c, Drive less. d, Unplug. e, Meat-free meals. f, Refill and reuse. g, Local produce. h, Zero-waste fashion. i, Recycle. j, Bring your own bag.

Perf. 13¼x13½

2020, June 28 Litho.

3440 A1009 $100 Sheet of 10, #a-j 10.00 10.00

Great Britain's Withdrawal From the European Union — A1010

Nos. 3441a-3441-bx: Great Britain Penny Black with different letters. Nos. 3441by-3441cv, Great Britain Penny Red with different letters.

2020, June 28 Litho. *Perf. 13½x13*

3441 Sheet of 100, #a-cv 1.20 1.20
a.-cv. A1010 $1.20 Any single .25 .25

A1011

No. 3442, $200 — Towards the Year of the Ox: a-f, Ox in various poses, as shown.

No. 3443, $200 — Butterflies: a, Nymphalis antiopa. b, Aglais io. c, Eurema nicippe. d, Argynnis pandora. e, Parnassius apollo. f, Castalius rosimon.

No. 3444, $200 — Paintings by Peter Paul Rubens (1577-1640): a, Old Woman and Boy with Candles. b, The Battle of the Amazons. c, Self-portrait. d, The Tiger Hunt. e, Portrait of Alatheia Talbot, Countess of Arundel. f, Daniel in the Lion's Den.

No. 3445, $200 — Mushrooms: a, Flammulina velutipes. b, Morchella esculenta. c, Melolontha melolontha and Fistulina hepatica. d, Arion vulgaris and Cerioporus squamosus. e, Flammulina velutipes. f, Omocestus viridulus and Lentinula edodes.

No. 3446, $1200, Ox, diff. No. 3447, $1200, Siproeta stelenes. No. 3448, $1200, The Virgin and Child in a Painting Surrounded by Fruit and Flowers, by Rubens. No. 3449, $1200, Coccinella septempunctata and Boletus edulis.

2020, June 28 Litho. *Perf. 13x13½*
Sheets of 6 # a-f

3442-3445 A1011 Set of 4 48.00 48.00

Souvenir Sheets

3446-3449 A1011 Set of 4 48.00 48.00

A1012

No. 3450, $300 — Marilyn Monroe (1926-62), actress: a, With spotlight in background. b, Photos looking forward and to left. c, With bedroom in background. d, With camera, clapboard and stage.

No. 3451, $300 — Neil Armstrong (1930-2012), first man on Moon: a, Apollo 11 Command and Service Module. b, Armstrong and Apollo 11 patch. c, Armstrong in space suits. d, Gemini 8 spacecraft and patch.

No. 3452, $300 — St. John Paul II (1920-2005): a, Holding crucifix, wearing miter. b, With Pope Francis. c, With Mother Teresa. d, Wearing miter, giving blessing.

No. 3453, $300 — Fire engines: a, Isuzu FTR 900. b, Scania P320 4x2 Pumper. c, Scania 94D 260. d, Hino 500.

No. 3454, $300 — Steam trains: a, Ja 1271. b, VSM 50 3654-6. c, C17 Class No. 974. d, E&P 4.

No. 3455, $300 — The Launch of SpaceX Demo-2: a, Dragon 2. b, Astronauts Robert L. Behnken and Douglas G. Hurley and Falcon 9 rocket, May 30, 2020. c, Elon Musk and Falcon 9 over Scripps Pier at La Jolla shores. d, Falcon 9 rocket with SpaceX Demo-2.

No. 3456, $300 — Princess Diana: a, With crowd in background. b, Wearing glasses. c, Wearing bridal veil. d, Holding Prince William.

No. 3457, $1200, Monroe, clapboard and film reel. No. 3458, $1200, Armstrong and footprint on Moon. No. 3459, $1200, St. John Paul II, diff. No. 3460, $1200, Isuzu FVZ. No. 3461, $1200, LNER Class A3 4472 Flying Scotsman. No. 3462, $1200, Falcon 9 rocket. No. 3463, $1200, Princess Diana wearing hat.

2020, June 28 Litho. *Perf. 13½*
Sheets of 4 # a-d

3450-3456 A1012 Set of 7 42.00 42.00

Souvenir Sheets

3457-3463 A1012 Set of 7 42.00 42.00

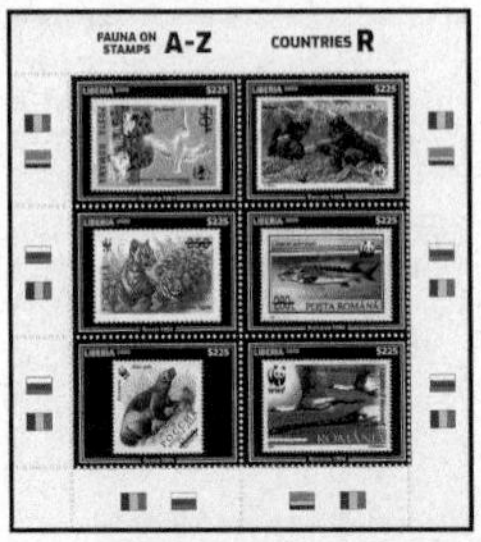

A1013

Worldwide Fund for Nature Stamps From Countries Beginning With "R" — A1014

No. 3464 — Stamp from: a, Romania, from 1984. b, Rwanda, from 1985. c, Russia, from 1993. d, Romania, from 1994. e, Russia, from 2004. f, Romania, from 2006.

No. 3465, $330, Romania, from 2006. No. 3466, $330, Romania, from 1994. No. 3467, $330, Russia, from 1993. No. 3468, $330, Rwanda, from 1985. No. 3469, $330, Russia, from 2004, vert. No. 3470, $330, Romania, from 1984, vert.

Perf. 13¼x13½

2020, June 28 Litho.

3464 A1013 $225 Sheet of 6, # a-f 13.50 13.50

Souvenir Sheets

Perf. 13x13½, 13½x13 (#3469, 3470)

3465-3470 A1014 Set of 6 19.50 19.50

A1015

A1016

A1017

A1018

Oxen From "Five Oxen," Painting by Han Huang (723-87) — A1019

Entire "Five Oxen" Painting A1020

No. 3476: a, Three oxen. b, Two oxen.

2020, Oct. 26 Litho. *Perf. 13x13¼*

3471	A1015 $3 multi		.25	.25
3472	A1016 $3 multi		.25	.25
3473	A1017 $3 multi		.25	.25
3474	A1018 $3 multi		.25	.25
3475	A1019 $3 multi		.25	.25
a.	Horiz. strip of 5, #3471-3475		.25	.25
3476	A1020 $3 Horiz. pair, #a-b		.25	.25

No. 3475a was printed in a sheet containing four strips. Nos. 3471-3476 were printed in a sheet containing four each of Nos. 3471-3475 and two No. 3476.

Liquid Natural Gas Tanker Ship Maria Energy A1021

2020, Oct. 26 Litho. *Perf. 13x13¼*

3477 A1021 $500 multi 5.50 5.50

International Day of Family Remittances A1022

2020, Oct. 26 Litho. *Perf. 13x13¼*

3478 A1022 $300 multi 3.25 3.25

Souvenir Sheet

3479 A1022 $1200 multi 13.00 13.00

No. 3478 was printed in sheets of 8 + central label.

Souvenir Sheet

2020 United States Presidential Candidates — A1023

No. 3480: a, Donald J. Trump. b, Joseph R. Biden Jr.

2020, Oct. 26 Litho. *Perf. 13¼x13*

3480 A1023 $600 Sheet of 2, #a-b 13.00 13.00

A1024

A1025

Liberian National COVID-19 Response — A1026

No. 3481 — Map of Liberia and: a, Stylized people around globe. b, Ministry of Health emblem. c, Ebola virus.

No. 3482: a, Ministry of Health emblem (39x39mm). b, Ebola virus (39x39mm). c, Stylized people around globe (39x50mm).

$2000, Stylized people around globe, diff.

Perf. 13x13¼ (#3481), 13¼ (#3482a-3482b), 13¼x13 (#3482c, 3483)

2020, Oct. 26 Litho.

3481	A1024	$300 Vert. strip of 3, #a-c		10.00	10.00

Souvenir Sheets

3482	A1025	$1200 Sheet of 3, #a-c		40.00	40.00
3483	A1026	$2000 multi		22.00	22.00

COVID-19 Virus and Soccer Field A1027

2020, Oct. 26 Litho. *Perf. 13x13¼*

3484	A1027 $2000 multi		22.00	22.00
a.	Souvenir sheet of 1		22.00	22.00

Suspension of sporting events due to COVID-19 pandemic.

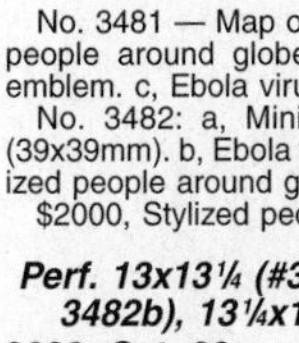

Tropical Forest Animal Conservation A1028

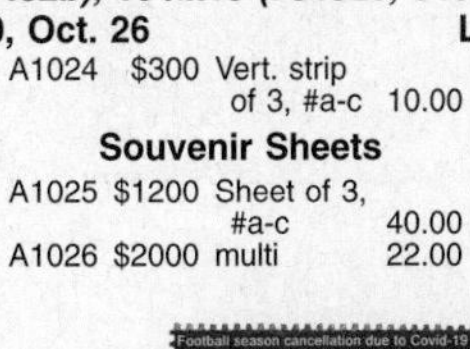

Monitoring of Illegal Logging During COVID-19 Pandemic — A1029

Designs: No. 3485, $400, Chimpanzee. No. 3486, $400, Timneh parrot. No. 3487, $400, Slender-snouted crocodile. No. 3488, $400, Diana monkey. No. 3489, $400, White-bellied pangolin. No. 3490, $400, Pygmy hippopotamus.

2020, Oct. 26 Litho. *Perf. 13x13¼*

3485-3490	A1028	Set of 6	26.50	26.50
3490a		Souvenir sheet of 6, #3485-3490	26.50	26.50

Souvenir Sheet

Perf. 13¼

3491	A1029	$2500 multi	27.50	27.50

Nos. 3485-3490 were each printed in sheets of 8 + central label.

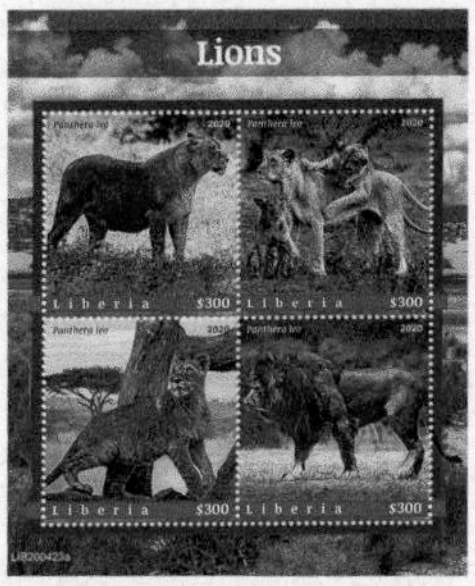

A1030

No. 3492, $300 — Panthera leo: a, Lioness facing right. b, Lioness and cubs. c, Lion and tree. d, Male lion facing left.

No. 3493, $300 — Cats: a, American shorthair cat. b, Maine coon cat. c, Ragdoll cat. d, British shorthair cat.

No. 3494, $300 — Owls: a, Tyto alba. b, Strix varia and Amanita muscaria. c, Bubo scandiacus and Morchella esculenta. d, Athene cunicularia.

No. 3495, $300 — Bee-eaters: a, Merops pusillus. b, Merops albicollis. c, Merops viridis. d, Merops apiaster.

No. 3496, $300 — Bees: a, Andrena fulva. b, Apis dorsata. c, Andrena cineraria. d, Xylocopa virginica.

No. 3497, $300 — Shells: a, Spondylus gaederopus. b, Cypraecassis rufa. c, Turbo petholatus. d, Phyllonotus pomum.

No. 3498, $300 — Orchids: a, Paphiopedilum lawrenceanum. b, Cymbidium aloifolium. c, Dendrobium kingianum. d, Cattleya labiata.

No. 3499, $300 — Prehistoric humans: a, Neanderthals hunting a bison. b, Skulls of Neanderthal and modern human. c, Tools used by prehistoric humans. d, Homo neanderthalensis.

No. 3500, $300 — Egyptian monuments: a, Temple of Edfu. b, Pyramid of Djoser. c, Bent Pyramid. d, Great Temple of Abu Simbel.

No. 3501, $300 — Fight against malaria: a, Hand holding blood vial testing positive for malaria, mosquito. b, Mosquito on arm, blood cells. c, Man spraying field with insecticide. d, Red Cross worker carrying sick person, mosquito.

No. 3502, $300 — Paintings by Vincent van Gogh (1853-90) (detail): a, Ward in the Hospital in Arles, 1889. b, The Sower, 1888. c, Memory of the Garden at Etten, 1888. d, The Red Vineyard, 1888.

No. 3503, $300 — Art by Alphonse Mucha (1860-1939) (detail): a, Lefevre Utile, 1903. b, The Slav Epic No. 4: Tsar Simeon I of Bulgaria, 1923. c, The Slav Epic No. 19: The Abolition of Serfdom in Russia, 1914. d, Flirt Lefevre Utile, 1899.

No. 3504, $300 — Chess in paintings: a, The Chess Game, by Ludwig Deutsch (1855-1935) (detail). b, A Game of Chess, by Henry Siddons Mowbray (1858-1928). c, The Chess Players, by Honoré Daumier (1808-79) (detail). d, Faust and Mephistopheles Playing Chess, by Friedrich August Moritz Retzsch (1779-1857).

No. 3505, $300 — Lighthouses: a, Lindesnes Lighthouse, Norway. b, Grótta Lighthouse, Iceland. c, Portofino Lighthouse, Italy. d, Lista Lighthouse, Norway.

No. 3506, $1200, Panthera leo with its kill. No. 3507, $1200, Russian blue cat. No. 3508, $1200, Bubo virginianus. No. 3509, $1200, Merops apiaster, diff. No. 3510, $1200, Osmia bicornis. No. 3511, $1200, Nautilus pompilius. No. 3512, $1200, Rhynchostylis gigantea. No. 3513, $1200, Homo neanderthalensis making fire. No. 3514, $1200, Karnak Temple Complex. No. 3515, $1200, Doctor treating child with malaria. No. 3516, $1200, The Night Café, by van Gogh, 1888. No. 3517, $1200, Reverie, by Mucha, 1897. No. 3518, $1200, The Chess Players, by Jacques-Clément Bernard Wagrez (1850-1908). No. 3519, $1200, Cape Blanco Lighthouse, Oregon.

2020, Oct. 26 Litho. *Perf. 13¼*

Sheets of 4, #a-d

3492-3505	A1030	Set of 14	185.00	185.00

Souvenir Sheets

Perf. 13¼x13

3506-3519	A1030	Set of 14	185.00	185.00

Nos. 3506-3519 each contain one 39x60mm stamp.

A1031

No. 3520, $300 — Princess Diana (1961-97): a, With roses and Kensington Palace in background. b, Holding Prince William. c, With children, holding flowers. d, With Launceston Place, London in background.

No. 3521, $300 — Meghan, Duchess of Sussex: a, Standing with Prince Harry, and scene from television movie *When Sparks Fly.* b, Wearing hat. c, Walking with Prince Harry, scene from movie *Horrible Bosses.* d, With Prince Harry at their wedding, scene from television movie *Dater's Handbook.*

No. 3522, $300 — Battle of France, 80th anniv.: a, French soldiers in World War II, coin and battle map. b, Soldiers, Arc de Triomphe, German Sd. Kfz 231 armored car. c, French SOMUA S35 tank, soldier and battle map. d, German Panzer IV tank ans soldiers.

No. 3523, $1200, Princess Diana wearing gown. No. 3524, $1200, Duke and Duchess of Sussex. No. 3625, $1200, French SOMUA S35 tank, Gen. Charles de Gaulle 1890-1970), Eiffel Tower and flag of France.

2020, Oct. 26 Litho. *Perf. 13¼x13*

Sheets of 4, #a-d

3520-3522	A1031	Set of 3	40.00	40.00

Souvenir Sheets

3523-3525	A1031	Set of 3	40.00	40.00

A1032

No. 3526, $300 — 80th birthday of Pelé: a, Pelé and soccer player Ivan Vutsov (1939-2019). b, Pelé dribbling soccer ball, and holding soccer ball. c, Pelé holding soccer ball. d, Pelé and soccer player Gustavo Peña (1955-2004).

No. 3527, $300 — Battle of Okinawa, 75th anniv.: a, Lieutenant General Simon Bolivar Buckner, Jr. (1886-1945), flag of the United States, Stinson L-5 Sentinel. b, Map of Okinawa, flag of Japan and Mitsuru Ushijima (1887-1945), Japanese general. c, Marines on beach and USS Idaho. d, Mitsubishi Ki-67.

No. 3528, $300 — Flying dinosaurs: a, Anhanguera blittersdorffi. b, Anurognathus ammoni. c, Pteranodon longiceps. d, Microraptor zhaoianus.

No. 3529, $300 — Tall ships: a, Christian Radich, Norway. b, Juan Sebastián de Elcano, Spain. c, Royal Clipper, Sweden. d, Amerigo Vespucci, Italy.

No. 3530, $300 — Steam locomotives: a, London and South Western Railway N15 Class "King Arthur." b, Metropolitan Railway E Class O-4-4T No. 1. c, London, Brighton and South Coast Railway B1 Class 0-4-2. d, London, Brighton and South Coast Railway Terrier Class No. 672 "Fenchurch."

No. 3531, $300 — Trains of Norway: a, NSB Di 4. b, NSB Class 69. c, NSB Class 73. d, CargoNet CD 312.

No. 3532, $300 — Audi automobiles, 110th anniv.: a, DKW Junior. b, Audi Quattro B2. c, Audi 100 LS. d, Auto Union 1000.

No. 3533, $300 — Fire engines: a, 1994 Mercedes-Benz Unimog U1550 L. b, 1995 Montauk, New York Fire Department 9-3-1 Pierce Lance. c, 2013 Ferrara Intruder II. d, 1989 Mercedes-Benz 1222 AF.

No. 3534, $1200, Pelé, soccer stadium flag of Brazil. No. 3535, $1200, Japanese battleship Yamato. No. 3536, $1200, Pteranodon longiceps, diff. No. 3537, $1200, Statsraad Lehmkuhl, Norway. No. 3538, $1200, Fairburn Class 4 2-6-4T locomotive. No. 3539, $1200, NSB Class 72. No. 3540, $1200, Auto Union 1000 Sp. No. 3541, $1200, 2005 American LaFrance1500/750/F fire truck.

2020, Oct. 26 Litho. *Perf. 13x13¼*

Sheets of 4, #a-d

3526-3533	A1032	Set of 8	105.00	105.00

Souvenir Sheets

3534-3541	A1032	Set of 8	105.00	105.00

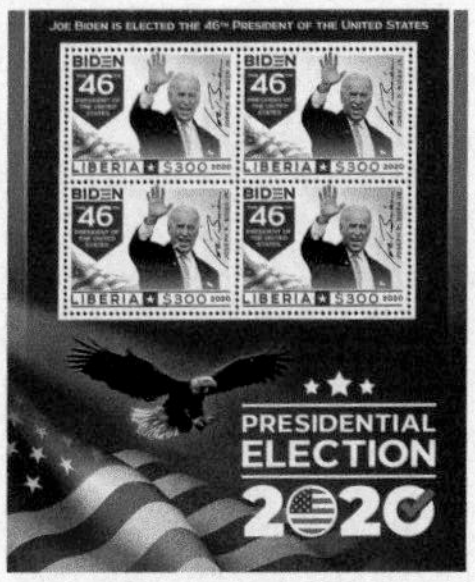

Joseph R. Biden Jr., 2020 President-Elect of the Untied States — A1033

No. 3542 — Background color: a, Blue. b, Org brown. c, Purple. d, Green.

$1200, President-elect Biden and Pres. Donald J. Trump.

2020, Nov. 30 Litho. *Perf. 13x13¼*

3542	A1033	$300 Sheet of 4, #a-d	15.50	15.50

Souvenir Sheet

3543	A1033	$1200 multi	15.50	15.50

No. 3543 contains one 50x39mm stamp.

A1034

No. 3544, $300 — Bruce Lee (1940-1973), movie actor: a, With leg raised at right. b, Wearing suit and tie at right. c, Wearing white t-shirt at left. d, With dragon at left.

No. 3545, $300 — James Dean (1931-55), movie actor: a, Standing and wearing cowboy hat at right. b, Sitting on steps at left. c, Wearing blue shirt at left and cowboy hat at right. d, On motorcycle at right.

No. 3546, $300 — Freemasons: a, Sugar Ray Robinson (1921-89), boxer. b, Henry Ford (1863-1947), automobile manufacturer. c, Alexander Fleming (1881-1955), discoverer of penicillin. d, Wolfgang Amadeus Mozart (1756-91), composer.

No. 3547, $300 — Salvation Army, 155th anniv.: a, Musicians. b, Bell ringer. c, People at food pantry. d, Salvation Army hat and cornet.

No. 3548, $300 — Discovery of Lascaux, France cave paintings, 80th anniv.: a, Cave painting and discoverers Marcel Ravidat (1922-95), Georges Agniel (1924-2012), Jacques Marsal (1926-89), and Simon Coencas (1927-2020). b, Cave painting and Ravidat holding lantern. c, Cave painting and iron oxide rock. d, People viewing cave painting.

No. 3549, $300 — Sinking of the RMS Titanic: a, Titanic under construction. b, Titanic and its captain, Edward Smith (1850-1912). c, Titanic sinking. d, Titanic and front pages of newspapers reporting on the sinking.

No. 3550, $300 — Submarines: a, Jin-class submarine. b, Seawolf-class submarine. c, Song-class submarine. d, Collins-class submarine.

No. 3551, $300 — First Zeppelin flight, 120th anniv.: a, Ferdinand von Zeppelin (1838-1917), manufacture, Graf Zeppelin in flight, map of world. b, Signature of Zeppelin, medal depicting Zeppelin, Zeppelin in flight. c, LZ127 Graf Zeppelinand airplanes in flight, medal depicting Zeppelin, ferry boat. d, Zeppelin, Graf Zeppelin at mooring site, automobile.

No. 3552, $300 — Max Immelmann (1890-1916), German World War I flying ace: a, Immelman, flag and German airplane. b, Airplane and diagram showing Immelmann turn. c, MG 08 machine gun and Iron Cross. d, Immelman, medal depicting him, and Fokker E.III airplane.

No. 3553, $300 — Launch of Lunokhod I lunar probe, 50th anniv.: a, Lunokhod 1 on Moon, mission pin. b, Lunokhod 1 control panel, Russia #3834. c, Lunokhod 1 control panel, sectional view of wheel hub, Luna 17. d,

Luna, 17, Lunokhod 1 and Lunokhod 1 wristwatch.

No. 3554, $300 — Neil Armstrong (1930-2012), first man on Moon: a, Armstrong in space suit, medals. b, Apollo 11 spacecraft and mission patch. c, Gemini 8 spacecraft and mission patch. d, Armstrong and jet plane.

No. 3555, $300 — 1980 Summer Olympics, Moscow, 40th anniv.: a, Russia #6576l and memorabilia. b, Russia #B104 and shotputter. c, Russia #B66 and weight lifter. d, Romania #2868 and Olympic torch.

No. 3556, $300 — Dinosaurs: a, Ankylosaurus magniventris. b, Spinosaurus aegyptiacus. c, Triceratops prorsus. d, Heterodontosaurus tucki.

No. 3557, $1200, Lee, dragon and film reel. No. 3558, $1200, Dean and his signature. No. 3559, $1200, George Washington (1732-99), first president of United States, and Masonic square and compass. No. 3560, $1200, Salvation Army member and child. No. 3561, $1200, Ravidat and Lascaux cave painting. No. 3562, $1200, Titanic, newspaper front page reporting on the sinking, paperboy selling newspapers. No. 3563, $1200, Vanguard-class submarine. No. 3564, $1200, Map of Europe, North and South America showing path of Zeppelin flight, Zeppelin wearing hat, Zeppelin in flight. No. 3565, $1200, Immelmann, Fokker E.III, Prussian Order of Merit. No. 3566, $1200, Lunokhod 1 crew training, and Lunokhod 1 mission pin. No. 3567, $1200, Armstrong, Apollo 11 crewmembers Edwin "Buzz" Aldrin, Jr. and Michael Collins and flag of the United States. No. 3568, $1200, Russia #B99, hurdler. No. 3569, $1200, Tarbosaurus bataar, Stegosaurus stenops.

2020, Nov. 30 Litho. *Perf. 13¼*

Sheets of 4, #a-d

3544-3556 A1034 Set of 13 200.00 200.00

Souvenir Sheets

3557-3569 A1034 Set of 13 200.00 200.00

A1035

No. 3570, $300 — Pandas: a, Ailurus fulgens with head at left. b, Ailuropoda melanoleuca with arm wrapped around tree. c, Ailuropoda melanoleuca facing left. d, Ailurus fulgens with head at right.

No. 3571, $300 — Tigers: a, Panthera tigris tigris, head at right. b, Panthera tigris tigris drinking at water hole. c, Panthera tigris sondaica. d, Panthera tigris tigris in water.

No. 3572, $300 — Sled dogs: a, Four Siberian huskies. b, Two Kugsha dogs. c, Two Siberian huskies leading dog team, musher in background. d, Alaskan huskies.

No. 3573, $300 — Service dogs: a, Newfoundland. b, St. Bernard. c, Golden retriever. d, Labrador retriever.

No. 3574, $300 — Dugong dugon: a, With four striped fish. b, With fish's tail at right. c, With two striped fish. d, With one striped fish.

No. 3575, $300 — Dolphins: a, Stenella longirostris jumping out of water. b, Stenella longirostris above water and arcing toward water. c, Three Tursiops truncatus. d, Two Tursiops truncatus and fish.

No. 3576, $300 — Hummingbirds: a, Calypte costae. b, Calypte anna. c, Archilochus colubris. d, Colibri thalassinus.

No. 3577, $300 — Water birds: a, Gavia arctica. b, Platalea leucorodia. c, Calidris pusilla. d, Fratercula cirrhata.

No. 3578, $300 — Butterflies: a, Pontia protodice. b, Colias philodice. c, Dryas iulia. d, Phyciodes tharos.

No. 3579, $300 — Mushrooms: a, Pholiota flammans and Calliphora vomitoria. b, Entoloma hochstetteri. c, Clitocybe nuda and Apantesis phalerata. d, Gyromitra esculenta.

No. 3580, $300 — Fossils: a, Asteroceras obtusum. b, Carcharocles megalodon tooth. c, Seirocrinus subangularis. d, Athleta spinosa.

No. 3581, $300 — Johann Sebasstian Bach (1685-1750), composer: a, Drawing depicting Bach and his signature. b, Statue of Bach, Leipzig, Germany. c, Bach playing organ. d, Bust of Bach.

No. 3582, $300 — Gustav Mahler (1860-1911), composer: a, Mahler looking right, orchestra in background. b, Mahler seated, piano in background. c, Mahler standing, choir in background. d, Mahler looking right, orchestra in background.

No. 3583, $300 — Detail of paintings by Ilya Repin (1844-1930): a, Leo Tolstoy in the Forest, 1891. b, Ivan the Terrible and His Son Ivan on November 16, 1581. c, Sadko, 1876. d, What a Freedom!, 1903.

No. 3584, $300 — Detail of paintings by Claude Monet (1840-1926): a, The Studio Boat, 1874. b, Madame Monet in a Japanese Kimono, 1876. c, Woman with a Parasol — Madame Monet and Her Son, 1875. d, Garden at Sainte-Adresse, 1867.

No. 3585, $300 — Campaign against COVID-19: a, Health worker holding vial. b, Sign for personal distancing. c, People touching glass partition. d, Workers spraying disinfectant.

No. 3586, $300 — International Year of Plant Health: a, Hand watering sprout in test tube. b, Hand touching grain stalk. c, Sprouting plant in ground. d, Hypodermic needle in tomato.

No. 3587, $300 — Lighthouses decorated with Christmas decorations: a, Fort Gratiot Lighthouse, Michigan. b, Nobska Lighthouse, Massachusetts. c, Kleiner Preusse, Germany. d, Sanibel Island light, Florida.

No. 3588, $1200, Ailurus fulgens, horiz. No. 3589, $1200, Ailuropoda melanoleuca, horiz. No. 3590, $1200, Panthera tigris tigris leaping, horiz. No. 3591, $1200, Panthera tigris sondaica, horiz. No. 3592, $1200, Team of Siberian huskies pulling sled, horiz. No. 3593, $1200, Alaskan huskies pulling sled, horiz. No. 3594, $1200, Labrador retriever guide dog, horiz. No. 3595, $1200, German shepherd police dog, horiz. No. 3596, $1200, Dugong dugon an striped fish, horiz. No. 3597, $1200, Dugong dugon alone, horiz. No. 3598, $1200, Delphinus capensis, horiz. No. 3599, $1200, Two Tursiops truncatus, horiz. No. 3600, $1200, Anthracothorax prevostii, horiz. No. 3601, $1200, Calliphlox amethystina, horiz. No. 3602, $1200, Pelecanus erythrorhynchos, horiz. No. 3603, $1200, Actophilornis africanus, horiz. No. 3604, $1200, Plebejus argyrognomon, horiz. No. 3605, Lycaena hylus, horiz. No. 3606, $1200, Mycena crocata, horiz. No. 3607, $1200, Laccaria amethystina, horiz. No. 3608, $1200, Latimeria chalumnae fossil, horiz. No. 3609, $1200, Eusthenopteron foordi, horiz. No. 3610, Sculpture of Bach, horiz. No. 3611, $1200, Drawing of Bach, musicians, horiz. No. 3612, $1200, Mahler, silhouettes of musicians, horiz. No. 3613, $1200, Mahler, person writing musical notes, horiz. No. 3614, $1200, Demonstration On October 17, 1905, painting by Repin, 1906-10, horiz. No. 3615, $1200, Self-portrait with Natalia Nordman, painting by Repin, 1903, horiz. No. 3616, $1200, Grand Canal, Venice, painting by Monet, 1908, horiz. No. 3617, $1200, Springtime, painting by Monet, 1872, horiz. No. 3618, $1200, Doctor with stethoscope holding housing symbol, horiz. No. 3619, $1200, Health workers in laboratory, horiz. No. 3620, $1200, Seedling in earth, symbols, horiz. No. 3621, $1200, Technician holding seedling in Petri dish, horiz. No. 3622, $1200, Nubble Lighthouse, Maine, with Christmas lights, horiz. No. 3623, $1200, Roanoke Marshes Lighthouse, North Carolina, and boats with Christmas lights, horiz.

2020, Nov. 30 Litho. *Perf. 13¼*

Sheets of 4, #a-d

3570-3587 A1035 Set of 18 275.00 275.00

Souvenir Sheets

3588-3623 A1035 Set of 36 550.00 550.00

Nos. 3588-3623 each contain one 48x33mm stamp.

New Year 2021 (Year of the Ox) — A1036

Designs: $300, Two cows. $600, Two oxen.

2020, Nov. 30 Litho. *Perf. 13¼*

3624-3625 A1036 Set of 2 11.50 11.50

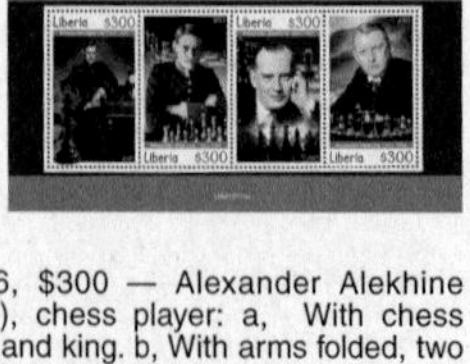

A1037

No. 3626, $300 — Alexander Alekhine (1892-1946), chess player: a, With chess table, clock and king. b, With arms folded, two chess boards. c, With hand touching his head. d, With arms folded behind chess board.

No. 3627, $300 — Wolfgang Amadeus Mozart (1756-91), composer and: a, His signature. b, 2008 Austrian 1-euro coin, 1988 Austrian 5000-schilling banknote. c, Musical score. d, Medal depicting him.

No. 3628, $300 — Antonio Vivaldi (1678-1741), composer: a, Violin and San Giovanni Church, Bragora, Italy, site of Vivaldi's baptism. b, Vivaldi and title page of his oratorio, Juditha Triumphans Devicta Holofernis Barbarie. c, Musical score, piano, violin and medal depicting Vivaldi. d, Musical score and monument to Vivaldi, Vienna.

No. 3629, $300 — First smallpox vaccination by Edward Jenner (1749-1823), 225th anniv.: a, Vial of smallpox vaccine, vaccinated and unvaccinated boys. b, Jenner and smallpox virus. c, Edward Jenner Vaccinating a Boy, painting by Eugène-Ernest Hillemacher (1818-87). d, Child with smallpox, smallpox viuses.

No. 3630, $300 — Heinrich Barth (1821-65), explorer of Africa, and: a, Map of his 1850-55 journeys, Barth's arrival in Timbuktu. b, His signature, map of Africa, people outside of walled town. c, Map of Africa, map of Lac region of Chad, compass. d, His signature, compass, map of his 1850-55 journeys.

No. 3631, $300 — Richard Francis Burton (1821-90), explorer of Africa, and: a, Map of Africa and Lake Tanganyika. b, His signature and map of Africa. c, Map of his journey in central Africa, canoe. d, Map of Africa and Masonic square and compass.

No. 3632, $300 — Fridtjof Nansen (1861-1930), 1922 Nobel peace laureate and explorer, and: a, Nobel medal, map of his 1888 Greenland expedition. b, His whaling ship, the Jason. c, His invention, the Nansen bottle. d, Ship.

No. 3633, $300 — Fire engines: a, E-One Custom Pumper. b, Scania 113H. c, HME 4x4 Custom Pumper. d, HME Custom Rescue Pumper.

No. 3634, $300 — Boeing airplanes: a, Boeing-Stearman Model 75 over Boeing Plant 1. b, Boeing Model 40C and William E. Boeing (1881-1956), airplane manufacturer. c, Boeing 247D and Boeing. d, Boeing P-26 Peashooter over manufacturing plant.

No. 3635, $300 — Commercial air service of the Concorde: a, British Airways Concorde, flag of Great Britain at UL. b, Air France Concorde, Eiffel Tower, flag of France at top. c, British Airways Concorde, Big Ben, flag of Great Britain at UR. d, Air France Concorde, flag of France at bottom.

No. 3636, $300 — Sergei P. Korolev (1907-66), spacecraft designer, and: a, R-7 Semyorka rocket and medal depicting Korolev. b, Yuri Gagarin (1934-68), first man in space. c, Sputnik 2. d, Sputnik 1.

No. 3637, $300 — Launch of Shenzhou 2, 20th anniv: a, Shenzhou 2, flag of People's Republic of China on flagpole, lower star on flag partially visible. b, Shenzhou 2, Jiuquan Satellite Launch Center, flag of People's Republic of China. c, Shenzhou 2, flag of People's Republic of China on flagpole, all stars on flag complete. d, Shenzhou 2, flag of People's Republic of China, no flagpole.

No. 3638, $1200, Alekhine and chess pieces. No. 3639, $1200, Mozart playing harpsichord and musical score. No. 3640, $1200, Vivaldi and musical score. No. 3641, $1200, Edward Jenner Vaccinating His Own Son Against Smallpox, sculpture by Giulio Monteverde (1837-1917). No. 3642, $1200, Barth, his signature, compass, map of Africa, and expedition members and animals. No. 3643, $1200, Burton, maps of Africa and the African Great Lakes region. No. 3644, $1200, Nansen and his wife, Eva (1858-1907), opera singer. No. 3645, $1200, Isuzu FTR fire truck. No. 3646, $1200, Boeing B-1, Frederick Rentschler (1887-1956), aircraft engine designer, and Boeing. No. 3647, $1200, British Airways Concorde and flag of Great Britain made into paper airplane. No. 3648, $1200, Korolev and medal. No. 3649, $1200, Shenzhou 2, flag of People's Republic of China on flagpole, diff.

2021, Feb. 1 Litho. *Perf. 13¼*

Sheets of 4, #a-d

3626-3637 A1037 Set of 12 170.00 170.00

Souvenir Sheets

3638-3649 A1037 Set of 12 170.00 170.00

Garnets A1038

No. 3650 — Garnet from: a, Little Three Mine, California. b, Outokumpu, Finland. c, Vesper Peak, Washington. d, Merelani Hills, Tanzania. e, Asbestos, Quebec, Canada.

No. 3651 — Garnet from: a, Val Malenco, Italy. b, Wrangell Island, Alaska.

2021, Feb. 1 Litho. *Perf. 13x13¼*

3650 A1038 $200 Sheet of 5, #a-e, + label 12.00 12.00

Souvenir Sheet

3651 A1038 $600 Sheet of 2, #a-b 14.00 14.00

A1039

No. 3652, $300 — John le Carré (1931-2020), writer of spy novels: a, Le Carré holding umbrella and handwriting manuscript. b, Scene from 1990 film, The Russia House. c, Rover P6 3500 S RHD automobile. d, Le Carré and Brandenburg Gate Quadriga.

No. 3653, $300 — Princess Diana (1961-97): a, Wearing yellow dress. b, Wearing red jacket. c, Wearing white hat. d, Wearing purple blouse.

No. 3654, $300 — Marilyn Monroe (1926-62), actress: a, At seashore. b, Looking out of window. c, With Hollywood sign. d, Sitting on chair with leg raised.

No. 3655, $300 — Clark Gable (1901-60), actor, Masonic square and compass, and movie poster for: a, The Misfits. b, Gone With the Wind. c, Honky Tonk. d, Boom Town.

No. 3656, $300 — African trains: a, South African Class Afro 4000. b, TER Dakar-AIBD. c, South African Class 37-076. d, AML ES44AC.

No. 3657, $300 — Chinese high-speed trains: a, CRH380A. b, China Star DJJ2. c, CRH3. d, CRH2B.

No. 3658, $1200, Le Carré, buildings and palm trees. No. 3659, $1200, Princess Diana wearing blue hat and jacket. No. 3660, $1200, Monroe and Tom Ewell (1909-94), actor. No. 3661, $1200, Gable, movie projector reel, Masonic square and compass. No. 3662, $1200, Lamco 79094 train. No. 3663, $1200, CRH2A-2260.

2021, Feb. 1 Litho. *Perf. 13x13¼*

Sheets of 4, #a-d

3652-3657 A1039 Set of 6 85.00 85.00

Souvenir Sheets

3658-3663 A1039 Set of 6 85.00 85.00

A1040

No. 3664, $300 — Cats: a, Scottish Fold cat. b, Don Sphynx cat. c, Abyssinian cat. d, American Shorthair cat.

No. 3665, $300 — Cuckoos: a, Cacomantis pallidus. b, Carpococcyx renauldi. c, Guira guira. d, Cuculus saturatus.

No. 3666, $300 — Warblers: a, Setophaga ruticilla. b, Protonotaria citrea. c, Cardellina pusilla. d, Setophaga pensylvanica.

No. 3667, $300 — Butterflies: a, Tirumala septentrionis. b, Pararge aegeria. c, Phengaris arion. d, Gonepteryx rhamni.

No. 3668, $300 — Fish: a, Balistoides conspicillum. b, Cheilinus fasciatus. c, Haplochromis ahli. d, Zebrasoma flavescens.

No. 3669, $300 — Turtles: a, Trachemys scripta elegans. b, Chelonia mydas. c, Pelodiscus sinensis. d, Chrysemys picta.

No. 3670, $300 — Prehistoric water animals: a, Eurhinosaurus longirostris. b, Ceresiosaurus lanzi. c, Tylosaurus proriger. d, Ichthyosaurus communis.

No. 3671, $300 — Extinct species: a, Thylacinus cynocephalus. b, Gomphotherium angustidens. c, Coelodonta antiquitatis. d, Thylacoleo carnifex.

No. 3672, $300 — Orchids: a, Epidendrum radicans. b, Calena major. c, Habenaria medusa. d, Habenaria rhodocheila.

No. 3673, $300 — Lighthouses: a, Cape Neddick Light, Maine. b, Rokkozaki Lighthouse, Japan. c, Tokarev Lighthouse, Russia. d, Race Point Lighthouse, Massachusetts.

No. 3674, $1200, Scottish Straight cat. No. 3675, $1200, Clamator jacobinus. No. 3676, $1200, Phylloscopus sibilatrix. No. 3677, $1200, Papilio machaon. No. 3678, $1200, Arothron nigropunctatus. No. 3679, $1200, Chelonia mydas, diff. No. 3680, $1200, Hybodus hauffianus. No. 3681, $1200, Smilodon fatalis. No. 3682, $1200, Pecteilis radiata. No. 3683, $1200, Highland Lighthouse, Massachusetts.

2021, Feb. 1 Litho. *Perf. 13x13¼*

Sheets of 4, #a-d

3664-3673 A1040 Set of 10 140.00 140.00

Souvenir Sheets

3674-3683 A1040 Set of 10 140.00 140.00

New England Wildflowers — A1041

No. 3684, $200: a, Bittersweet nightshade. b, Creeping buttercup. c, Swamp azalea. d, Orange jewelweed. e, Japanese rose. f, American white waterlily.

No. 3685, $200, vert.: a, Black-eyed Susan. b, English plantain. c, Spotted St. John's wort. d, Indian pipe. e, Spotted knapweed. f, Common soapwort.

No. 3686, $1200, Bittersweet nightshade, diff. No. 3687, $1200, Wood sorrel.

2021, Feb. 1 Litho. *Perf. 13¼*

Sheets of 4, #a-d

3684-3685 A1041 Set of 2 28.00 28.00

Souvenir Sheets

3686-3687 A1041 Set of 2 28.00 28.00

No. 3686 contains one 75x51mm stamp. No. 3687 contains one 51x51mm stamp.

Paintings A1042

No. 3688, $300 — Paintings by Pierre-Auguste Renoir (1841-1919): a, Dance at Le Moulin de la Galette, 1876. b, The Large Bathers, 1884-87. c, The Bathers, 1918-19. d, Luncheon of the Boating Party, 1880-81.

No. 3689, $300 — Paintings by Rembrandt van Rijn (1606-69): a, The Anatomy Lesson of Dr. Nicolaes Tulp, 1632. b, Danae, 1636-43. c, The Blinding of Samson, 1636. d, The Night Watch (detail), 1642.

No. 3690, $1200, Dance in the City, by Renoir, 1883, vert. No. 3691, $1200, The Prodigal Son in the Tavern, by Rembrandt, c. 1637, vert.

2021, Feb. 1 Litho. *Perf. 13x13¼*

Sheets of 4, #a-d

3688-3689 A1042 Set of 2 28.00 28.00

Souvenir Sheets

Perf. 13¼x13

3690-3691 A1042 Set of 2 28.00 28.00

COVID-19 Pandemic A1043

COVID-19 virus, world leaders infected with virus, flags and Red Cross emblems: No. 3692, $125, Valery Giscard d'Estaing (1926-2020), ex-President of France, flag of France, French Red Cross emblem. No. 3693, $125, Donald Trump, United States President, flag of United States, American Red Cross emblem. No. 3694, $125, Jair Bolsonaro, President of Brazil, flag of Brazil, Brazilian Red Cross emblem. No. 3695, $125, Silvio Berlusconi, Prime Minister of Italy, flag of Italy, Italian Red Cross emblem. No. 3696, $125, Emmanuel Macron, President of France, flag of France, French Red Cross emblem. No. 3697, $125, Prince Albert II of Monaco, flag of Monaco, Monegasque Red Cross emblem. No. 3698, $125, Boris Johnson, Prime Minister of Great Britain, flag of Great Britain, British Red Cross emblem. No. 3699, $125, Michel Barnier, European Union Brexit negotiator, Baron David Frost, British Brexit negotiator, flags of Great Britain and European Union, emblem of the European Union Red Cross office. No. 3700, $125, Mikhail Mishustin, Prime Minister of Russia, flag of Russia, Russian Red Cross emblem.

2021, Feb. 1 Litho. *Perf. 12¾x13¼*

3692-3700 A1043 Set of 9 13.50 13.50
3700a Souvenir sheet of 9, #3692-3700 13.50 13.50

Nos. 3692-3700 were each printed in sheets of 8 + central label.

SEMI-POSTAL STAMPS

No. 127 Surcharged in Red

1915 Unwmk. *Perf. 14*

B1 A49 2c + 3c on 10c 2.00 *3.50*
a. Double red surcharge
b. Double blue surcharge
c. Both surcharges double
d. Pair, one without "2c"

Same Surcharge On Official Stamp of 1912

B2 A49 2c + 3c on 10c blk & ultra 2.00 *3.50*
a. Double surcharge

Regular Issue of 1918 Surcharged in Black and Red

1918 *Perf. 12½, 14*

B3 A59 1c + 2c dp grn & blk 1.40 *10.50*
B4 A60 2c + 2c rose & blk 1.40 *10.50*
a. Double surch., one inverted
b. Invtd. surch., cross double
c. Invtd. surch., cross omitted 17.00
B5 A61 5c + 2c gray bl & blk .65 *3.00*
a. Imperf., pair 19.00
B6 A62 10c + 2c dk green 1.25 *3.00*
a. Inverted surcharge 5.75 *27.50*
B7 A63 15c + 2c blk & dk grn 5.25 10.50
B8 A64 20c + 2c claret & blk 2.10 *8.50*
B9 A65 25c + 2c dk grn & grn 4.25 *15.00*
B10 A66 30c + 2c red vio & blk 10.00 *10.50*
B11 A67 50c + 2c ultra & blk 8.50 *16.00*
B12 A68 75c + 2c ol bis & blk 3.75 *30.00*
B13 A69 $1 + 2c yel brn & bl 6.25 *57.50*
B14 A70 $2 + 2c lt vio & blk 8.50 *80.00*
B15 A71 $5 + 2c dk brown 20.00 *200.00*
Nos. B3-B15 (13) 73.30 455.00

Used values are for postally canceled stamps.

Nos. 277-279 Surcharged in Red or Blue

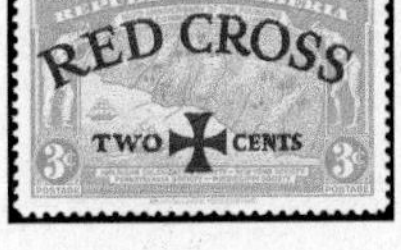

1941 Unwmk. *Perf. 12*

B16 A107 3c + 2c dk blue (R) 2.25 2.25
B17 A108 5c + 2c dull red brn 2.25 2.25
B18 A109 10c + 2c dk grn (R) 2.25 2.25
Nos. B16-B18 (3) 6.75 6.75

Catalogue values for unused stamps in this section, from this point to the end of the section, are for Never Hinged items.

Research SP1

Lithographed and Engraved

1954 Unwmk. *Perf. 12½*

B19 SP1 5c + 5c rose lilac & blk .25 .25
Nos. B19,CB4-CB6 (4) 1.40 1.00

The surtax was for the Liberian Government Hospital. No. B19 exists imperforate.

Remember the African Child — SP2

Designs: 25c + 10c, Village life. 70c + 20c, Mr. Sean feeding children. 75c + 15c, Fleeing conflict. 80c + 20c, Nuns teaching children. No. B24, Nuns killed in Oct. 1992, vert. No. B25, Sean Devereux (1964-93), vert.

Perf. 13½x14

1994, Jan. 6 Unwmk. Litho.

B20 SP2 25c +10c multi 1.00 1.00
B21 SP2 70c +20c multi 2.75 2.75
B22 SP2 75c +15c multi 2.75 2.75
B23 SP2 80c +20c multi 3.00 3.00
Nos. B20-B23 (4) 9.50 9.50

Souvenir Sheets

B24 SP2 $1.50 +50c multi 6.00 6.00
B25 SP2 $1.50 +50c multi 6.00 6.00

Surtax for Sean Devereux Liberian Children's Fund.

Charities SP3

Designs: 25c+10c, No. B30, Natl. map in flag colors, blind man with cane. No. B27, Logo depicting children. No. B28, Blind man crossing street. No. B29, Dr. Herman Gmeiner, children.

1995 Litho. *Perf. 14*

B26 SP3 25c +10c multi .80 .80
B27 SP3 80c +20c multi 2.40 2.40
B28 SP3 80c +20c multi 2.40 2.40
B29 SP3 $1.50 +50c multi 5.50 5.50
B30 SP3 $1.50 +50c multi 5.50 5.50
Nos. B26-B30 (5) 16.60 16.60

Christian Assoc. of the Blind, 10th anniv. (Nos. B26, B28, B30). SOS Children's Village (Nos. B27, B29).

Issued: Nos. B27, B29, 4/26; others, 4/28.

George Weah, Soccer Player — SP4

Designs: 50c+20c, In AC Milan strip. 75c+25c, In Liberia Natl. strip. 80c+20c, With 1989 Golden Ball Award. $1.50+50c, Two-time Golden Ball Winner.

1995, Oct. 6 Litho. *Perf. 13x13½*

B31 SP4 50c +20c multi 2.00 2.00
B32 SP4 75c +25c multi 2.75 2.75
B33 SP4 80c +20c multi 2.75 2.75
B34 SP4 $1.50 +50c multi 5.25 5.25
a. Souvenir sheet of 1, perf. 13 5.25 5.25
Nos. B31-B34 (4) 12.75 12.75

Issued: No. B34a, 6/24/96. Surcharge for Liberian charities supported by George Weah.

AIR POST STAMPS

Regular Issue of 1928 Srchd. in Black

1936, Feb. 28 Unwmk. *Perf. 12*

C1 A102 6c on 2c violet 250.00 *275.00*
C2 A102 6c on 3c bis brn 250.00 *275.00*

Same Srch. on Official Stamp of 1928

C3 A102 6c on 1c green 250.00 *275.00*
m. On No. 230 (error) *750.00*
Nos. C1-C3 (3) 750.00 825.00

Values are for stamps with disturbed gum. Many counterfeits exist.

Waco Plane AP1

1936, Sept. 30 Engr. *Perf. 14*

C3A AP1 1c yellow grn & blk .30 .30
C3B AP1 2c carmine & blk .30 .30
C3C AP1 3c purple & blk .30 .30
C3D AP1 4c orange & blk .30 .30
C3E AP1 5c blue & blk .30 .30
C3F AP1 6c green & blk .30 .30
Nos. C3A-C3F (6) 1.80 1.80

Liberia's 1st air mail service of Feb. 28, 1936.

Nos. C3A-C3F exist in pairs imperf. between (value, $50 each) and in pairs imperf. (value $15 each).

Eagle in Flight — AP2

Trimotor Plane — AP3

Egrets — AP4

Sikorsky Amphibian — AP5

Designs: 3c, 30c, Albatross.

1938, Sept. 12 Photo. *Perf. 12½*

C4 AP2 1c green .25 .25
C5 AP3 2c red orange .40 .25
C6 AP3 3c olive green .50 .25
C7 AP4 4c orange .60 .25
C8 AP4 5c brt blue grn 1.00 .25
C9 AP3 10c violet 1.00 .25
C10 AP5 20c magenta 1.25 .25
C11 AP3 30c gray black 2.25 .25
C12 AP2 50c brown 3.00 .25
C13 AP5 $1 blue 5.25 .25
Nos. C4-C13 (10) 15.50 2.50

For surcharges see Nos. C17-C36, C45-C46, C47-C48, C49-C50.

Nos. 280-282 Overprinted in Red or Dark Blue

1941, Feb. 25 *Perf. 12*
C14 A107 3c dark blue (R) 2.75 2.75
C15 A108 5c dull red brn (DB) 2.75 2.75
C16 A109 10c dark green (R) 2.75 2.75
Nos. C14-C16 (3) 8.25 8.25

Nos. C4-C13 Surcharged in Black

1941 *Perf. 12½*
C17 AP2 50c on 1c green *3,250.* 325.00
C18 AP3 50c on 2c red org 200.00 105.00
C19 AP3 50c on 3c ol grn 200.00 105.00
C20 AP4 50c on 4c org 90.00 60.00
C21 AP4 50c on 5c brt bl grn 90.00 60.00
C22 AP3 50c on 10c vio 90.00 50.00
C23 AP5 50c on 20c mag *2,750.* 70.00
C24 AP3 50c on 30c gray blk 75.00 40.00
C25 AP2 50c brown 75.00 40.00
C26 AP5 $1 blue 90.00 40.00

Nos. C18, C19, C22, C24, and C26 exist with inverted overprints. Values C18 and C19, $225 each; others, $100 each.

Nos. C17 to C26 with Additional Overprint

1942
C27 AP2 50c on 1c green 6.75 6.75
C28 AP3 50c on 2c red org 6.75 5.75
C29 AP3 50c on 3c ol grn 6.00 5.75
C30 AP4 50c on 4c orange 4.75 6.00
C31 AP4 50c on 5c brt bl grn 3.00 3.00
C32 AP3 50c on 10c violet 4.25 4.25
C33 AP5 50c on 20c mag 4.25 4.25
C34 AP3 50c on 30c gray blk 4.75 4.75
C35 AP2 50c brown 4.75 4.75
C36 AP5 $1 blue 4.25 4.25
Nos. C27-C36 (10) 49.50 49.50

Plane and Air Route from United States to South America and Africa — AP6

Plane over House — AP7

1942-44 **Engr.** *Perf. 12*
C37 AP6 10c rose .25 .25
C38 AP7 12c brt ultra ('44) .25 .25
C39 AP7 24c turq grn ('44) .25 .25
C40 AP6 30c brt green .25 .25
C41 AP6 35c red lilac ('44) .25 .25
C42 AP6 50c violet .25 .25
C43 AP6 70c olive gray ('44) .35 .25
C44 AP6 $1.40 scarlet ('44) 1.00 .45
Nos. C37-C44 (8) 2.85 2.20

No. C3A-C3C, C5-C8, C12 Srchd. with New Values and Large Dot, Bar or Diagonal Line in Violet, Blue, Black or Violet and Black

No. C45

No. C46

No. C46A

No. C48

No. C48B

No. C49

No. C50

1944-45 *Perf. 12½*
C45 AP3 10c on 2c (V+Bk) 40.00 25.00
C46 AP4 10c on 5c (V+Bk) ('45) 14.00 12.00
C46A AP1 30c on 1c (Bk) 150.00 70.00
C47 AP3 30c on 3c (V) 165.00 65.00
C48 AP4 30c on 4c (V+Bk) 14.00 12.00
C48A AP1 50c on 3c (Bk) 37.50 32.50
C48B AP1 70c on 2c (Bk) 70.00 60.00
C49 AP3 $1 on 3c (Bl) 27.50 22.50
C50 AP2 $1 on 50c (V) 42.50 26.50
Nos. C45-C50 (9) 560.50 325.50

These surcharges were handstamped with the possible exception of the large "10 CTS." of No. C46 and the "30 CTS." of No. C48. On No. C47, the new value was created by handstamping a small, violet, broken "O" beside the large "3" of the basic stamp.

Surcharges on Nos. C46A, C48A, C48B are found inverted. Values same as normal.

Roosevelt Type of Regular Issue

1945, Nov. 26 **Engr.**
C51 A116 70c brn & blk, *grysh* 2.25 1.40

Examples on thick white paper appeared later on the stamp market. Value, $1 unused or used.

Monrovia Harbor Type

1947, Jan. 2
C52 A117 24c brt bluish grn 1.50 1.25

Without Inscription at Top

1947, May 16
C53 A117 25c dark carmine .90 .45

1st US Postage Stamps Type

1947, June 6
C54 A118 12c green .25 .25
C55 A118 25c brt red violet .30 .25
C56 A118 50c brt blue .40 .25
a. Souv. sheet of 4, #300, C54-C56 50.00
Never hinged 100.00
Nos. C54-C56 (3) .60 .60
Set, never hinged 2.10

No. C56a exists imperf. Values: hinged $65; never hinged $160.

Matilda Newport Firing Cannon AP11

1947, Dec. 1 **Engr. & Photo.**
C57 AP11 25c scar & gray blk 1.25 .30

See note after No. 304.

Monument to Joseph J. Roberts AP12

Centenary Monument AP14

Design: 25c, Flag of Liberia.

1947, Dec. 22 **Engr.**
C58 AP12 12c brick red .30 .25
C59 AP12 25c carmine .50 .25
C60 AP14 50c red brown .80 .45
Nos. C58-C60 (3) 1.60 .85
Set, never hinged 6.00

Centenary of independence.

L. I. A. Plane in Flight — AP15

1948, Aug. 17 *Perf. 11½*
C61 AP15 25c red 1.50 1.50
C62 AP15 50c deep blue 1.00 1.00
Set, never hinged 5.00

1st flight of Liberian Intl. Airways, Aug. 17, 1948. Exist imperf.

Map and Citizens AP16

Farm Couple, Arms and Agricultural Products AP17

1949, Apr. 12 **Litho.** *Perf. 11½*
C63 AP16 25c multicolored .35 .65
C64 AP17 50c multicolored .35 .65
Set, never hinged 2.00

Nos. C63-C64 exist perf. 12½. Definite information concerning the status of the perf. 12½ set has not reached the editors. The set also exists imperf.

Type of Regular Issue of 1948-50

Design: William V. S. Tubman.

1949, July 21 **Engr.** *Perf. 12½*
C65 A128 25c blue & black .60 .65
Never hinged 1.60

See No. C118.

Sun and Open Book — AP18

1950, Feb. 14 **Engr.** *Perf. 12½*
C66 AP18 25c rose carmine 1.00 .50
Never hinged 2.75
a. Souv. sheet of 2, #329, C66, imperf. 1.75 1.75
Never hinged 4.75

Campaign for National Literacy.

Catalogue values for unused stamps in this section, from this point to the end of the section, are for Never Hinged items.

UPU Monument — AP19

1950, Apr. 21
C67 AP19 25c orange & vio 2.75 2.75
a. Souv. sheet of 3, #330-331, C67, imperf. 24.00 24.00

UPU, 75th anniv. (in 1949).
No. C67 exists imperf.

Map of Monrovia, James Monroe and Ashmun AP20

50c, Jehudi Ashmun, President Tubman & map.

1952, Apr. 1 *Perf. 10½*
C68 AP20 25c lilac rose & blk .25 .25
C69 AP20 50c dk blue & car .70 .70
a. Souvenir sheet of 8 24.00

Nos. C68-C69 exist imperf. Value about two and one half times that of the perf. set.

Nos. C68-C69 exist with center inverted. Value $50 each.

No. C69a contains one each of Nos. 332 and C68, and types of Nos. 333-337 and C69 with centers in black; imperf.

The 25c exists in colors of the 50c and vice versa. Value, each $8.

Flags of Five Nations AP21

1952, Dec. 10 *Perf. 12½*
C70 AP21 25c ultra & carmine .90 .65
a. Souvenir sheet 2.25 2.25

Nos. C70 and C70a exist imperforate. Value, No. C70a, imperf., $4.50.

Road Building AP22

Designs: 25c, Ships in Monrovia harbor. 35c, Diesel locomotive. 50c, Free port, Monrovia. 70c, Roberts Field. $1, Wm. V. S. Tubman bridge.

1953, Aug. 3 **Litho.**
C71 AP22 12c orange brown .25 .25
C72 AP22 25c lilac rose .25 .25
C73 AP22 35c purple 1.00 .25
C74 AP22 50c orange 1.00 .25
C75 AP22 70c dull green 1.75 .25
C76 AP22 $1 blue 2.25 1.00
Nos. C71-C76 (6) 6.50 2.25

Exist imperf. See Nos. C82-C87.

Flags, Emblem and Children
AP23

1954, Sept. 27 Size: 51x39mm
C77 AP23 $5 bl, red, vio bl & blk 40.00 40.00

A reproduction of No. C77, size 63x49mm, was prepared for presentation purposes. Value $35.
Half the proceeds from the sale of No. C77 was given to the UNICEF.

UN Technical Assistance Agencies AP24

Designs: 15c, Printing instruction. 20c, Sawmill maintenance. 25c, Geography class.

1954, Oct. 25
C78 AP24 12c black & blue .25 .25
C79 AP24 15c dk brown & yel .25 .25
C80 AP24 20c black & yel grn .25 .25
C81 AP24 25c vio blue & red .80 .25
Nos. C78-C81 (4) 1.55 1.00

UN Technical Assistance program.
Nos. C78-C81 exist imperf.

Type of 1953 Inscribed: "Commemorating Presidential Visit U. S. A.-1954"

Designs as before.

1954, Nov. 19
C82 AP22 12c vermilion .25 .25
C83 AP22 25c blue .80 .25
C84 AP22 35c carmine rose 3.50 2.00
C85 AP22 50c rose violet .95 .30
C86 AP22 70c orange brown 1.25 .55
C87 AP22 $1 dull green 1.90 .80
Nos. C82-C87 (6) 8.65 4.15

Visit of Pres. William V.S. Tubman to the US. Exist imperforate.

Baseball — AP25

1955, Jan. 26 Litho. *Perf. 12½*
C88 AP25 10c shown .30 .30
C89 AP25 12c Swimming .30 .30
C90 AP25 25c Running .30 .30
a. Souvenir sheet 18.00 18.00
Nos. C88-C90 (3) .90 .90

No. C90a contains 1 each of Nos. 349, C90 with colors transposed. Exists imperf.; same value.

Costus — AP26

Design: 25c, Barteria nigritiana.

1955, Sept. 28 Unwmk. *Perf. 12½*
C91 AP26 20c violet, grn & yel .40 .25
C92 AP26 25c green, red & yel .40 .25

UN Emblem AP27 UN Charter AP28

15c, General Assembly. 25c, Gabriel L. Dennis signing UN Charter for Liberia.

1955, Oct. 24 Unwmk. *Perf. 12*
C93 AP27 10c ultra & red .25 .25
C94 AP27 15c violet & blk .25 .25
C95 AP27 25c green & red brn .60 .25
C96 AP28 50c brick red & grn 1.50 .25
Nos. C93-C96 (4) 2.60 1.00

10th anniv. of the UN, Oct. 24, 1955.

Rotary International Headquarters, Evanston, Ill. — AP29

Design: 15c, View of Monrovia.

1955, Dec. 5 Litho. *Perf. 12½*
C97 AP29 10c deep ultra & red .25 .25
C98 AP29 15c redsh brn, red & bis .70 .25

Souvenir Sheet

C99 AP29 50c deep ultra & red 1.75 1.75
Nos. C97-C99 (3) 2.70 2.25

No. C99 design as No. C97, but redrawn and with leaves omitted.
50th anniversary of Rotary International.
Nos. C97-C99 exist without Rotary emblem; No. C97 printed entirely in deep ultramarine; No. C98 with bister impression omitted.

FIPEX Type of Regular Issue

10c, New York Coliseum. 12c, Globe inscribed FIPEX. 15c, 50c, Statue of Liberty.

1956, Apr. 28 Unwmk. *Perf. 12*
C100 A143 10c rose red & ultra .25 .25
C101 A143 12c orange & purple .25 .25
C102 A142 15c aqua & red lilac .90 .25
Nos. C100-C102 (3) 1.40 .75

Souvenir Sheet

C103 A142 50c lt green & brn 1.75 1.75

Olympic Park, Melbourne AP32

20c, 40c, Map of Australia & Olympic torch.

1956, Nov. 15 Unwmk. *Perf. 12*
C104 AP32 12c emerald & vio .50 .50
C105 AP32 20c multicolored .50 .50

Souvenir Sheet

C106 AP32 40c multicolored 7.50 7.50
Nos. C104-C106 (3) 8.50 8.50

16th Olympic Games, Melbourne, 11/22-12/8.
Nos. C104-C105 exist imperf.

Type of Regular Issue, 1957

12c, 25c, Idlewild airport, NYC. 15c, 50c, Roberts Field, Liberia, plane & Pres. Tubman.

Lithographed and Engraved

1957, May 4 *Perf. 12*
C107 A146 12c brt grn & dk bl .25 .25
C108 A146 15c red brn & blk .25 .25
C109 A146 25c carmine & dk bl .75 .25
C110 A146 50c lt ultra & blk 1.40 .25
Nos. C107-C110 (4) 2.65 1.00

Type of Regular Issue, 1957

Orphanage and: 15c, Nurse inoculating boy. 35c, The Kamara triplets. 70c, Children and flag.

1957, Nov. 25 Litho. *Perf. 12*
C111 A147 15c lt blue & brn .25 .25
C112 A147 35c maroon & lt gray 1.00 .25

Souvenir Sheet

C113 A147 70c ultra & rose car 1.50 1.25
Nos. C111-C113 (3) 2.75 1.75

Type of Regular Issue, 1958

10c, Italian flag & Colosseum. #C115, French flag & Arc de Triomphe. #C116, Swiss flag & chalet. #C117, Vatican flag & St. Peter's.

Engr. and Litho.

1958, Jan. 10 *Perf. 10½*

Flags in Original Colors

C114 A148 10c dark gray .45 .45
C115 A148 15c dp yellow grn .45 .45
C116 A148 15c ultra .45 .45
C117 A148 15c purple .45 .45
Nos. C114-C117 (4) 1.80 1.80

Type of Regular Issue, 1948-50

Design: William V. S. Tubman.

1958 Engr. *Perf. 12*
C118 A128 25c lt green & blk 1.25 .90

Souvenir Sheet

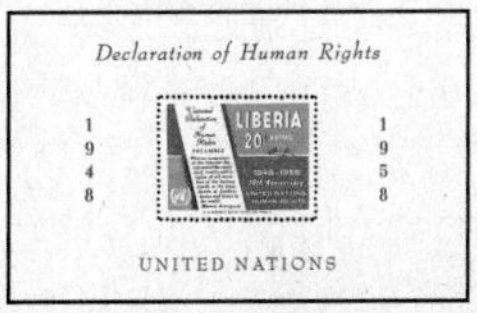

Preamble to Declaration of Human Rights — AP33

1958, Dec. 17 Litho. *Perf. 12*
C119 AP33 20c blue & red 2.75 2.75

10th anniv. of the signing of the Universal Declaration of Human Rights. Exists imperf.

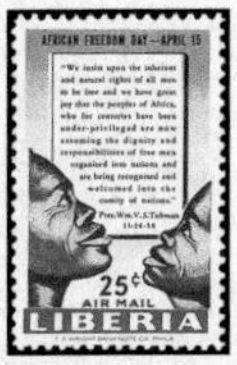

Liberians Reading Proclamation — AP34

1959, Apr. 15 Unwmk.
C120 AP34 25c blue & brown .60 .60

African Freedom Day, Apr. 15.

UNESCO Building, Paris — AP35

1959, May 1
C121 AP35 25c ultra & red .60 .50
a. Souvenir sheet 1.75 1.75

Opening of UNESCO Headquarters in Paris, Nov. 3, 1958.

Lincoln Type of Regular Issue

1959, Nov. 20 Engr. *Perf. 12*
C122 A152 25c emerald & black .90 .90

For souvenir sheet see No. 386a.

Touré, Tubman and Nkrumah — AP36

1960, Jan. 27 Litho. Unwmk.
C123 AP36 25c beige, vio bl & blk .60 .80

See note after No. 387.

WRY Type of Regular Issue, 1960

1960, Apr. 7 *Perf. 11½*
C124 A154 25c ultra & black .80 .70
a. Souv. sheet of 2, #388, C124, imperf. 3.50 2.75

Map of Africa — AP37

1960, May 11 *Perf. 11½*
C125 AP37 25c ultra & brown .80 .80

See note after No. 389.

Olympic Games Type of 1960

Designs: 25c, Javelin thrower and hunter, horiz. 50c, Runner and stadium, horiz.

1960, Sept. 6 *Perf. 11½*
C126 A156 25c brown & brt ultra .90 .70

Souvenir Sheet

Imperf

C127 A156 50c lilac & brown 3.50 3.50

Stamp Centenary Type of 1960

1960, Dec. 1 Litho. *Perf. 11½*
C128 A157 25c multicolored 1.00 1.00

Souvenir Sheet

C129 A157 50c multicolored 1.75 1.75

No. C129 exists imperf.

Globe, Dove and UN Emblem — AP38

Design: 50c, Globe and dove.

1961, May 19 Unwmk. *Perf. 11½*
C130 AP38 25c indigo & red .50 .50

Souvenir Sheet

C131 AP38 50c red brn & emerald 2.25 2.25

Liberia's membership in the UN Security Council.
A second souvenir sheet contains one each of Nos. 395, C130 and the 50c from No. C131, imperf. Size: 133x83mm. Value $8.
No. C130 exists imperf.

Science Class — AP39

Design: 50c, Science class, different design.

1961, Sept. 8 Litho.
C132 AP39 25c purple & brown .50 .25

Souvenir Sheet

C133 AP39 50c blue & brown 1.75 1.75

15th anniv. of UNESCO.

Joseph J. Roberts and Providence Island — AP40

1961, Oct. 25 Litho. *Perf. 11½*
C134 AP40 25c emerald & sepia .70 .70
a. Souvenir sheet of 3 1.75 1.75

150th anniv. of the birth of Joseph J. Roberts, 1st pres. of Liberia.
No. C134a contains three imperf. stamps similar to Nos. 397-398 and C134, but printed in different colors; 5c, emerald & sepia. 10c, orange & sepia. 25c, ultramarine & sepia.

Scout Type of Regular Issue and

Boy Scout — AP41

1961, Dec. 4 Unwmk. *Perf. 11½*
C135 AP41 25c emerald & sepia 1.40 1.40

Souvenir Sheet

Design: Like No. 399.

C136 A161 35c dull blue & sepia 3.50 3.50

No. C136 exists imperf. Value, $10.

Dag Hammarskjold Type of 1962

1962, Feb. 1 Unwmk. *Perf. 12*
C137 A162 25c black & red lilac .60 .60

Souvenir Sheet

Imperf

C138 A162 50c black & ultra 1.75 1.75

Malaria Eradication Emblem — AP42

1962, Apr. 7 *Perf. 12½*
C139 AP42 25c purple & orange .60 .50

Souvenir Sheet

Imperf

C140 AP42 50c dark red & ultra 2.00 1.50

AP43

Design: 12c, 25c, 50c, Pres. Tubman, Statue of Liberty, New York Skyline and Flags of US and Liberia.

1962, Sept. 17 Litho. *Perf. 11½x12*
C141 AP43 12c multicolored .25 .25
C142 AP43 25c multicolored .60 .50
C143 AP43 50c multicolored 1.25 .85
Nos. C141-C143 (3) 2.10 1.60

Pres. Tubman's visit to the US in 1961.

United Nations Emblem and Flags — AP44

Design: 50c, UN emblem.

1962, Oct. 22 *Perf. 12x12½*
C144 AP44 25c lt ultra & dk bl .50 .50

Souvenir Sheet

Imperf

C145 AP44 50c brt grnsh bl & blk 2.00 1.25

Observance of UN Day, Oct. 24, as a national holiday.

Building Type of Regular Issue

12c, 70c, Capitol. 50c, Information Service. $1, Treasury Department Building, Monrovia.

1962-63 *Perf. 12x12½, 12 (70c)*
C146 A165 12c brt yel grn & mar .25 .25
C147 A165 50c orange & ultra 1.20 1.20
C147A A165 70c brt pink & dk bl ('63) 1.60 1.20
C148 A165 $1 sal & blk ('63) 2.40 1.40
Nos. C146-C148 (4) 5.45 4.05

"FAO" Emblem and Globe — AP45

Design: 50c, "FAO" and UN Emblems.

1963, Mar. 21 Unwmk. *Perf. 12½*
C149 AP45 25c dk green & yel .65 .50

Souvenir Sheet

Perf. 12

C150 AP45 50c emerald & ultra 2.00 1.75

FAO "Freedom from Hunger" campaign.

Type of Regular Issue, 1963

Designs: 25c, Telstar satellite, vert. 50c, Telstar and rocket, vert.

1963, May 27 Litho. *Perf. 12½*
C151 A167 25c Prus blue & org .55 .40

Souvenir Sheet

Perf. 12

C152 A167 50c dp violet & yel 2.50 1.50

No. C152 exists imperf. Value $12.50.

Red Cross — AP45a

Design: 25c, Red Cross and globe. 50c, Centenary emblem and globe.

1963, Aug. 26 Unwmk. *Perf. 12*
C153 AP45a 25c purple & red .40 .40
C154 AP45a 50c deep ultra & red .70 .70

Map of Africa — AP46

1963, Oct. 28 *Perf. 12½*
C156 AP46 25c red orange & grn .30 .30

See note after No. 412.

Olympic Type of Regular Issue

10c, Torch and mountains. 25c, Mountains, horiz. 50c, Torch, background like No. 413.

1963, Dec. 11 Litho. *Perf. 12½*
C157 A170 10c vio blue & red .25 .25
C158 A170 25c green & orange .80 .80

Souvenir Sheet

Perf. 12

C159 A170 50c gray & red 1.75 1.75

No. C159 exists imperf. Value $12.

Kennedy Type of Regular Issue, 1964

Designs: 25c, John F. Kennedy, vert. 50c, John F. Kennedy (like No. 414).

1964, Apr. 6 Unwmk. *Perf. 12½*
C160 A171 25c blk & red lil .60 .50

Souvenir Sheet

Perf. 12

C161 A171 50c blk & red lil 1.75 1.40

An imperf. miniature sheet containing one of No. C160 exists. No marginal inscription. Value $10.

Satellite Type of Regular Issue

Souvenir Sheet

Design: Launching rocket separating from booster in space, vert.

1964, June 22 Litho.
C162 A172 50c vio bl & red 3.00 3.00

Exists imperf. Value $9.

Olympic Type of Regular Issue

Souvenir Sheet

Design: 50c, Runner and Olympic rings.

1964, Sept. 15 Unwmk. *Perf. 12*
C163 A173 50c grnsh bl & red 3.00 1.25

Exists imperf. Value $6.

Scout Type of Regular Issue, 1965

Designs: 25c, Liberian flag and fleur-delis. 50c, Globe and Scout emblem.

1965, Mar. 8 Litho. *Perf. 12½*
C164 A174 25c crimson & ultra .80 .80

Souvenir Sheet

Perf. 12

C165 A174 50c yellow & lilac 3.00 3.00

No. C165 exists imperf. Value $7.

Lincoln Type of Regular Issue

Souvenir Sheet

50c, Lincoln and John F. Kennedy, horiz.

1965, May 3 Unwmk. *Perf. 12*
C166 A175 50c dp plum & lt gray 1.75 1.75

Exists imperf. Value $5.50.

ICY Type of Regular Issue, 1965

Souvenir Sheet

1965, June 21 Litho.
C167 A176 50c car rose & brn 1.75 1.75

ITU Type of Regular Issue, 1965

1965, Sept. 21 Unwmk. *Perf. 12½*
C168 A177 50c red org & vio bl .80 .70

Tubman Type of Regular Issue

25c, Pres. Tubman and coat of arms.

1965, Nov. 29 Litho. *Perf. 12½*
C169 A178 25c ultra, red & brn .70 .70
a. Souv. sheet of 2, #431, C169, imperf. 1.75 1.75

Churchill Type of Regular Issue

25c, "Angry Lion" portrait by Karsh & Parliament, London. 50c, "Williamsburg Award Dinner" portrait by Karsh & map of Europe.

1966, Jan. 18 Litho. *Perf. 12½*
C170 A179 25c blk & vio bl .70 .55

Souvenir Sheet

Perf. 12

C171 A179 50c blk & red lil 1.75 1.75

No. C171 exists imperf.

Soccer Type of Regular Issue

Souvenir Sheet

Design: 50c, Soccer match in stadium.

1966, May 3 Litho. *Perf. 11½*
C172 A181 50c ultra & red brn 2.50 2.50

Exists imperf. Value $15.

Kennedy Type of Regular Issue

25c, UN General Assembly & Pres. Kennedy. 35c, Pres. Kennedy & rocket on launching pad, Cape Kennedy. 40c, Flame on grave at Arlington.

1966, Aug. 16 Litho. *Perf. 12½*
C173 A182 25c ultra, blk & ocher .40 .25
C174 A182 35c dk vio bl & pink .50 .25

Souvenir Sheet

Perf. 11½

C175 A182 40c dk vio bl & multi 2.00 2.00

No. C175 exists imperf. Value $20.

Boy Scout Type of Regular Issue

Souvenir Sheet

50c, Scout at campfire & vision of moon landing.

1967, Mar. 23 Litho. *Perf. 12½*
C176 A185 50c brt red lil & scar 4.00 4.00

Exists imperf. Value $8.

Olympic Type of Regular Issue

Souvenir Sheet

Design: 50c, Pre-Hispanic sculpture, serape and Olympic rings, horiz.

1967, June 20 Litho. *Perf. 12½*
C177 A186 50c vio & car 3.75 1.60

Exists imperf. Value $15.

Winter Olympic Games Type of Regular Issue

Souvenir Sheet

Design: 50c, Woman skater.

1967, Nov. 20 Litho. *Perf. 11½*
C178 A189 50c ver & blk 2.25 .70

Exists imperf. Value $15.

Human Rights Type of Regular Issue

Souvenir Sheet

1968, Apr. 26 Litho. *Perf. 11½*
C179 A191 80c bl & red 2.50 1.10

No. C179 exists imperf.

M. L. King Type of Regular Issue

Souvenir Sheet

55c, Pres. Kennedy congratulating Dr. King.

1968, July 11 Litho. *Perf. 11½*
C180 A192 55c brn & blk 3.00 1.00

Exist imperf. Value, $9.

Olympic Type of Regular Issue

Souvenir Sheet

Design: 50c, Steeplechase and ancient sculpture.

1968, Aug. 22 Litho. *Perf. 11½*
C181 A193 50c brt bl & org brn 2.25 1.10

Exists imperf. Value $15.

President Type of Regular Issue 1966-69

Design: 25c, Pres. William V. S. Tubman.

1969, Feb. 18 Litho. *Perf. 11½x11*
C182 A180 25c blk & emer .60 .30

ILO Type of Regular Issue

Design: 80c, "ILO" surrounded by cogwheel and wreath, vert.

1969, Apr. 16 Litho. *Perf. 12½*
C183 A196 80c emer & gold 2.00 1.10

No. C183 exists imperf.

Apollo 11 Type of Regular Issue

Souvenir Sheet

65c, Astronauts Neil A. Armstrong, Col. Edwin E. Aldrin, Jr., & Lieut. Col. Michael Collins, horiz.

1969, Oct. 15 Litho. *Perf. 11½*
C184 A199 65c dk vio bl & brt red 2.00 1.10

Exists imperf. Value $20.

UN Type of 1970

Design: $1, UN emblem, olive branch and plane as symbols of peace and progress, vert.

1970, Apr. 16 Litho. *Perf. 12½*
C185 A200 $1 ultra & sil 2.00 1.00

Exists imperf.

Apollo 14 Type of Regular Issue

Souvenir Sheet

Design: 50c, Moon, earth and star.

1971, May 20 Litho. *Imperf.*
C186 A208 50c multi 2.75 2.75

Souvenir Sheet

Olympic Yachting Village, Kiel, and Yachting AP47

1971, June 28 Litho. *Perf. 14½x14*
C187 AP47 Sheet of 2 2.75 2.75
a. 25c multi .65 .65
b. 30c multi .80 .80

Publicity for the 20th Summer Olympic Games, and the yachting races in Kiel, Germany, 1972. Exists imperf. Value, $9.

Boy Scout Type of Regular Issue

Souvenir Sheet

Boy Scouts of various nations cooking, horiz.

1971, Aug. 6 Litho. ***Perf. 15***
C188 A211 50c multi 3.50 3.50

Exists imperf.

UNICEF Type of Regular Issue

Souvenir Sheet

UNICEF emblem & Bengal tigress with cubs.

1971, Oct. 1 ***Imperf.***
C189 A213 50c multi 3.00 3.00

Souvenir Sheet

Japanese Royal Family — AP48

1971, Nov. 4 ***Perf. 15***
C190 AP48 50c multi 3.25 3.25

11th Winter Olympic Games, Sapporo, Japan, Feb. 3-13, 1972. Exists imperf. Value $15.

Sesquicentennial Type of Regular Issue

Souvenir Sheet

Design: 50c, Sailing ship "Elizabeth" between maps of America and Africa, horiz.

1972, Jan. 1 Litho. ***Imperf.***
C191 A216 50c car & vio bl 2.40 2.40

Olympic Type of Regular Issue

Souvenir Sheet

Design: 55c, View of Olympic Stadium and symbol of "Motion."

1972, May 19 Litho. ***Perf. 15***
C192 A218 55c multi 4.00 4.00

Exists imperf. Value, $8.

Apollo 16 Type of Regular Issue

Souvenir Sheet

Lt. Comdr. Thomas K. Mattingly, 2nd, Capt. John W. Young & Lt. Col. Charles M. Duke, Jr.

1972, June 26 Litho. ***Perf. 15***
C193 A220 55c pink & multi 2.00 2.00

Exists imperf. Value $10.

Ship Type of 1972

Souvenir Sheet

Design: Lord Nelson's flagship Victory, and her figurehead (1765).

1972, Sept. 6 Litho. ***Perf. 15***
C194 A222 50c multi 2.50 2.50

Pres. Tolbert Type of 1972.

Souvenir Sheet

1972, Oct. 23 Litho. ***Perf. 15***
C195 A223 55c multi 1.60 1.60

Apollo 17 Type of Regular Issue

Souvenir Sheet

55c, Apollo 17 badge, moon and earth.

1973, Mar. 28 Litho. ***Perf. 11***
C196 A225 55c bl & multi 1.90 1.90

Exists imperf. Value $10.

Locomotive Type of Regular Issue

Souvenir Sheet

Design: 55c, Swiss locomotive.

1973, May 4 Litho. ***Perf. 11***
C197 A226 55c multi 2.75 2.75

WHO Type of Regular Issue 1973

Souvenir Sheet

Design: 55c, WHO emblem, Paul Ehrlich and poppy anemones.

1973, June 26 Litho. ***Perf. 11***
C198 A228 55c lt vio & multi 2.00 2.00

Automobile Type of Regular Issue

Souvenir Sheet

Franklin 10 HP cross-engined 1904-05 models.

1973, Sept. 11 Litho. ***Perf. 11***
C199 A229 55c multi 2.00 2.00

Copernicus Type of Regular Issue

Souvenir Sheet

Design: 55c, Copernicus and concept of orbiting station around Mars.

1973, Dec. 14 Litho. ***Perf. 13½***
C200 A230 55c gray & multi 2.00 2.00

Exists imperf. Value $15.

UPU Type of Regular Issue

Souvenir Sheet

55c, UPU emblem and English coach, 1784.

1974, Mar. 4 Litho. ***Perf. 13½***
C201 A232 55c multi 2.50 2.25

Exists imperf. Value $15.

Dog Type of Regular Issue

Souvenir Sheet

Design: Hungarian sheepdog (kuvasz).

1974, Apr. 16 Litho. ***Perf. 13½***
C202 A233 75c multi 3.25 2.25

Exists imperf.

Soccer Type of Regular Issue

Souvenir Sheet

Design: 60c, World Soccer Championship Cup and Munich Stadium.

1974, June 4 Litho. ***Perf. 11***
C203 A234 60c multi 2.00 2.00

Exists imperf. Value $12.

Butterfly Type of Regular Issue

Souvenir Sheet

Tropical butterfly: 60c, Pierella nereis.

1974, Sept. 11 Litho. ***Perf. 13½***
C204 A235 60c gray & multi *3.50 2.50*

Churchill Type of 1974

Souvenir Sheet

60c, Churchill at easel painting landscape.

1975, Jan. 17 Litho. ***Perf. 13½***
C205 A237 60c multi 1.50 1.50

Exists imperf. Value $10.

Women's Year Type of 1975

Souvenir Sheet

Design: 75c, Vijaya Lakshmi Pandit, Women's Year emblem and dais of UN General Assembly.

1975, Mar. 14 Litho. ***Perf. 13***
C206 A238 75c gray & multi 1.25 1.25

Exists imperf. Value $10.

American Bicentennial Type

Souvenir Sheet

Design: 75c, Mayflower and US No. 548.

1975, Apr. 25 Litho. ***Perf. 13½***
C207 A239 75c multi 2.50 2.50

Exists imperf. Value $11.

Dr. Schweitzer Type, 1975

Souvenir Sheet

Schweitzer as surgeon in Lambarene Hospital.

1975, June 26 Litho. ***Perf. 13½***
C208 A240 60c multi 2.25 2.25

Exists imperf. Value $11.

Apollo-Soyuz Type, 1975

Souvenir Sheet

75c, Apollo-Soyuz link-up and emblem.

1975, Sept. 18 Litho. ***Perf. 13½***
C209 A241 75c multi 2.00 1.90

Winter Olympic Games Type, 1976

Souvenir Sheet

Downhill skiing & Olympic Games emblem.

1976, Jan. 23 Litho. ***Perf. 13½***
C210 A243 75c multi 1.60 1.50

Exists imperf. Value $9.

Olympic Games Type, 1976

Souvenir Sheet

Design: 75c, Dressage and jumping.

1976, May 4 Litho. ***Perf. 13½***
C211 A245 75c multi 1.90 1.90

Exists imperf. Value $9.

Bell Type

Souvenir Sheet

Design: 75c, A. G. Bell making telephone call, UPU and ITU emblems.

1976, June 4 Litho. ***Perf. 13½***
C212 A246 75c ocher & multi 2.50 2.25

Exists imperf. Value $11.

Animal Type of 1976

Souvenir Sheet

Design: 50c, Elephant, vert.

1976, Sept. 1 Litho. ***Perf. 13½***
C213 A249 50c org & multi 3.25 2.00

Bicentennial Type of 1976

Souvenir Sheet

Design: 75c, Like No. 770.

1976, Sept. 21 Litho. ***Perf. 13½***
C214 A250 75c multi 2.40 2.40

Exist imperf. Value, $12.

Mask Type of 1977

Souvenir Sheet

75c, Ibo mask and Festival emblem.

1977, Jan. 20 Litho. ***Perf. 13½***
C215 A251 75c lil & multi 1.75 1.75

Equestrian Type of 1977

Designs: 55c, Military dressage (team), US. 80c, Winners receiving medals, vert.

1977, Apr. 22 Litho. ***Perf. 13½***
C216 A253 55c ocher & multi 2.40 .60

Souvenir Sheet

C217 A253 80c ocher & multi 2.10 2.10

No. C217 exists imperf. Value $9.

Elizabeth II Type of 1977

Souvenir Sheet

75c, Elizabeth II, laurel and crowns.

1977, May 23 Litho. ***Perf. 13½***
C218 A254 75c sil & multi 1.25 1.25

Exists imperf. Value $9.

Zeppelin Type of 1978

Souvenir Sheet

75c, Futuristic Goodyear aerospace airship.

1978, Mar. 9 Litho. ***Perf. 13½***
C219 A257 75c multi 1.75 1.40

Exists imperf. Value $10.

Soccer Type of 1978

Souvenir Sheet

Soccer game Netherlands & Uruguay, vert.

1978, May 16 Litho. ***Perf. 13½***
C220 A258 75c multi 2.00 1.25

Exists imperf. Value $20.

Coronation Type of 1978

Souvenir Sheet

Design: 75c, Coronation coach, horiz.

1978, June 12
C221 A259 75c multi 2.25 1.75

Exists imperf. Value $14.

Soccer Winners' Type of 1978

Souvenir Sheet

Design: 75c, Argentine team, horiz.

1978, Dec. 8 Litho. ***Perf. 13½***
C222 A262 75c multi 2.50 1.20

Exists imperf. Value $12.50.

AIR POST SEMI-POSTAL STAMPS

Nos. C14-C16 Overprinted in Red or Blue Like Nos. B16-B18

1941 Unwmk. ***Perf. 12***

CB1	A107	3c +2c dk bl (R)	4.00	4.00
CB2	A108	5c +2c dl red brn (Bl)	4.00	4.00
CB3	A109	10c +2c dk grn (R)	4.00	4.00
		Nos. CB1-CB3 (3)	12.00	12.00

Catalogue values for unused stamps in this section, from this point to the end of the section, are for Never Hinged items.

Nurses Taking Oath SPAP1

Designs: 20c+5c, Liberian Government Hospital. 25c+5c, Medical examination.

1954, June 21 Litho. & Engr.

Size: 39½x28½mm

CB4	SPAP1	10c +5c car & blk	.30	.25
CB5	SPAP1	20c +5c emer & blk	.40	.25

Size: 45x34mm

CB6	SPAP1	25c +5c ultra, car & blk	.45	.25
		Nos. CB4-CB6 (3)	1.15	.75

Surtax for the Liberian Government Hospital. Nos. CB4-CB6 exist imperf. No. CB6 exists with carmine omitted.

AIR POST SPECIAL DELIVERY STAMP

No. C15 Overprinted in Dark Blue Like No. E1

1941 Unwmk. ***Perf. 12***
CE1 A108 10c on 5c dl red brn 2.00 2.00

AIR POST REGISTRATION STAMP

No. 278 Overprinted in Dark Blue

1941 Unwmk. ***Perf. 12***
CF1 A108 10c on 5c dl red brn 2.00 2.00

SPECIAL DELIVERY STAMP

No. 278 Surcharged in Dark Blue

1941	Unwmk.	*Perf. 12*	
E1 A108 10c on 5c dl red brn		2.00	2.00

REGISTRATION STAMPS

R1

1893 Unwmk. Litho. *Perf. 14, 15*
Without Value Surcharged

F1 R1 (10c) blk (Buchanan)	250.	250.
F2 R1 (10c) blk (Greenville)	*2,500.*	—
F3 R1 (10c) blk (Harper)	*2,500.*	—
F4 R1 (10c) blk (Monrovia)	30.	30.
F5 R1 (10c) blk (Robertsport)	1,000.	1,000.

Types of 1893 Surcharged in Black

1894	*Perf. 14*	
F6 R1 10c bl, *pink* (Buchanan)	5.50	5.50
F7 R1 10c grn, *buff* (Harper)	5.50	5.50
F8 R1 10c red, *yel* (Monrovia)	5.50	5.50
F9 R1 10c rose, *blue* (Robertsport)	5.50	5.50
Nos. F6-F9 (4)	22.00	22.00

Exist imperf or missing one 10. Value, each $10.

President Garretson W. Gibson — R6

1903 Engr.	*Perf. 14*	
F10 R6 10c bl & blk (Buchanan)	1.75	.25
a. Center inverted	100.00	
F11 R6 10c org red & blk ("Grenville")	1.75	
a. Center inverted	100.00	
b. 10c orange & black	1.90	.25
F12 R6 10c grn & blk (Harper)	1.75	.25
a. Center inverted	100.00	
F13 R6 10c vio & blk (Monrovia)	1.75	.25
a. Center inverted	100.00	
b. 10c lilac & black	1.90	
F14 R6 10c magenta & blk (Robertsport)	1.75	.25
a. Center inverted	100.00	
Nos. F10-F14 (5)	8.75	
Nos. F10, F11b, F12-F14		.75

For surcharges see Nos. 178-182.

S.S. Quail on Patrol R7

1919 Litho.	*Serrate Roulette 12*	
F15 R7 10c blk & bl (Buchanan)	1.40	2.75

Serrate Roulette 12, Perf. 14

F16 R7 10c ocher & blk ("Grenville")	1.40	2.75
F17 R7 10c grn & blk (Harper)	1.40	2.75
F18 R7 10c vio & bl (Monrovia)	1.40	2.75
F19 R7 10c rose & blk (Robertsport)	1.40	2.75
Nos. F15-F19 (5)	7.00	13.75

Gabon Viper R8

Wmk. Crosses and Circles (116)

1921 Engr.	*Perf. 13x14*	
F20 R8 10c cl & blk (Buchanan)	80.00	3.50
F21 R8 10c red & blk (Greenville)	30.00	3.50
F22 R8 10c ultra & blk (Harper)	40.00	3.50
F23 R8 10c org & blk (Monrovia)	30.00	3.50
a. Imperf., pair	225.00	
F24 R8 10c grn & blk (Robertsport)	30.00	3.50
a. Imperf., pair	225.00	
Nos. F20-F24 (5)	210.00	17.50

Nos. F-20-F24 Overprinted in Black

F25 R8 10c (Buchanan)	37.50	6.25
F26 R8 10c (Greenville)	37.50	6.25
F27 R8 10c (Harper)	37.50	6.25
F28 R8 10c (Monrovia)	37.50	6.25
F29 R8 10c (Robertsport)	37.50	6.25
Nos. F25-F29 (5)	187.50	31.25

Nos. F20-F24 are printed tete-beche. Thus, the "1921" overprint appears upright on half the stamps in a sheet and inverted on the other half. Values are the same for either variety.

Passengers Going Ashore from Ship — R9

Designs: No. F31, Transporting merchandise, shore to ship (Greenville). No. F32, Sailing ship (Harper). No. F33, Ocean liner (Monrovia). No. F34, Canoe in surf (Robertsport).

1924 Litho.	*Perf. 14*	
F30 R9 10c gray & carmine	7.00	.60
F31 R9 10c gray & blue grn	7.00	.60
F32 R9 10c gray & orange	7.00	.60
F33 R9 10c gray & blue	7.00	.60
F34 R9 10c gray & violet	7.00	.60
Nos. F30-F34 (5)	35.00	3.00

No. 278 Surcharged in Dark Blue

1941 Unwmk.	*Perf. 12*	
F35 A108 10c on 5c dull red brn	2.00	2.00

POSTAGE DUE STAMPS

Nos. 26, 28 Surcharged

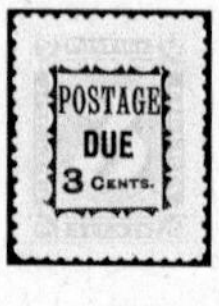

1892 Unwmk.	*Perf. 11*	
J1 A5 3c on 3c violet	6.50	4.25
a. Imperf., pair	30.00	
b. Inverted surcharge	45.00	45.00
c. As "a," inverted surcharge	110.00	

Perf. 12

J2 A5 6c on 6c olive gray	15.00	13.50
a. Imperf., pair	40.00	
b. Inverted surcharge	52.50	35.00

D2

Engr.; Figures of Value Typographed in Black

1893 Wmk. 143	*Perf. 14, 15*	
J3 D2 2c org, *yel*	2.00	1.00
J4 D2 4c rose, *rose*	2.00	1.00
J5 D2 6c brown, *buff*	2.00	1.25
J6 D2 8c blue, *blue*	2.00	1.25
J7 D2 10c grn, *lil rose*	2.25	1.50
J8 D2 20c vio, *gray*	2.25	1.50
a. Center inverted	110.00	110.00
J9 D2 40c ol brn, *grnsh*	4.50	3.00
Nos. J3-J9 (7)	17.00	10.50

All values of the above set exist imperforate. Each value also exists with center inverted.

MILITARY STAMPS

"LFF" are the initials of "Liberian Frontier Force." Nos. M1-M7 were issued for the use of troops sent to guard the frontier.

Issues of 1905, 1906 and 1909 Surcharged

1916	Wmk. 143	
M1 A23 1c on 1c lt grn	190.00	190.00
a. 2nd "F" inverted	250.00	250.00
b. "FLF"	250.00	250.00
c. Inverted surcharge	250.00	250.00

Unwmk.

M2 A33 1c on 1c grn & blk	600.00	550.00
a. 2nd "F" inverted	700.00	600.00
b. "FLF"	700.00	600.00
M3 A46 1c on 1c yel grn & blk	4.00	4.75
a. 2nd "F" inverted	7.50	7.50
b. "FLF"	7.50	7.50
M4 A47 1c on 2c lake & blk	4.00	4.75
a. 2nd "F" inverted	7.50	7.50
b. "FLF"	7.50	7.50

Surcharge exists sideways on Nos. M2, M5; double on Nos. M1-M4; inverted on Nos. M2-M4.

Nos. O46, O59-O60 Surcharged

M5 A33 1c on 1c	500.00	475.00
a. 2nd "F" inverted	700.00	650.00
b. "FLF"	700.00	650.00
M6 A46 1c on 1c	4.75	5.50
a. 2nd "F" inverted	9.00	9.00
b. "FLF"	9.00	9.00
c. "LFF 1c" inverted	12.50	12.50
d. As "a" and "1c" inverted		15.00
e. "FLF 1c" inverted		15.00
M7 A47 1c on 2c	3.25	4.00
a. 2nd "F" inverted	6.50	6.50
b. "FLF"	6.50	6.50
c. Pair, one without "LFF 1c"		

OFFICIAL STAMPS

Types of Regular Issues Overprinted in Various Colors

Perf. 12½ to 15 and Compound

1892	Wmk. 143	
O1 A9 1c vermilion	.80	.80
O2 A9 2c blue	.80	.80
O3 A10 4c grn & blk	.80	.80
O4 A11 6c bl grn	.80	.80
O5 A12 8c brn & blk	.80	.80
O6 A13 12c rose red	2.00	2.00
O7 A14 16c red lilac	2.00	2.00
O8 A15 24c ol grn, *yel*	2.00	2.00
O9 A16 32c grnsh bl	2.00	2.00
O10 A17 $1 bl & blk	40.00	16.00
O11 A18 $2 brn, *yel*	16.00	11.50
O12 A19 $5 car & blk	24.00	9.00
Nos. O1-O12 (12)	92.00	48.50

a

"5" With Short Flag

1893		
O13 A11 5c on 6c bl grn (a) (No. 50)	1.20	1.20
a. "5" with short flag	6.00	6.00
b. Both 5's with short flags	6.00	6.00
c. "i" dot omitted	20.00	20.00
d. Overprinted on #50d	45.00	45.00

Overprinted in Various Colors

1894		
O15 A9 1c vermilion	.70	.35
O16 A9 2c blue	.85	.40
a. Imperf.		
O17 A10 4c grn & blk	1.00	.55
O18 A12 8c brn & blk	1.00	.55
O19 A13 12c rose red	1.40	.60
O20 A14 16c red lilac	1.40	.60
O21 A15 24c ol grn, *yel*	1.40	.70
O22 A16 32c grnsh bl	2.75	.80
O23 A17 $1 bl & blk	27.50	21.00
a. $1 ultra & black	27.50	21.00
O24 A18 $2 brn, *yel*	27.50	21.00
O25 A19 $5 car & blk	125.00	87.50
Nos. O15-O25 (11)	190.50	134.05

Unwmk.

Imperf

O26 A22 5c vio & grn	3.50	2.25

Rouletted

O27 A22 5c vio & grn	3.50	2.25

Regular Issue of 1896-1905 Overprinted in Black or Red

1898-1905 Wmk. 143	*Perf. 14, 15*	
O28 A23 1c lil rose	1.10	.90
O29 A23 1c dp grn ('00)	1.10	.90
O30 A23 1c lt grn (R) ('05)	1.10	.90
O31 A24 2c bis & blk	2.25	.60
a. Pair, one without overprint	900.00	
O32 A24 2c org red & blk ('00)	3.25	1.50
O33 A24 2c rose & blk ('05)	5.50	2.75
O34 A25 5c lake & blk	3.75	1.50
O35 A25 5c gray bl & blk ('00)	4.25	1.50
O36 A25 5c ultra & blk (R) ('05)	7.25	3.75
O37 A12 10c chr yel & ind	2.25	1.75
O38 A13 15c slate	2.25	1.75
O39 A14 20c vermilion	3.75	2.10
O40 A15 25c yel grn	2.25	1.75
O41 A16 30c steel blue	5.50	2.75
O42 A26 50c red brn & blk	5.50	2.75
Nos. O28-O42 (15)	51.05	27.15

For surcharge see No. O92.

Official stamps overprinted "ORDINARY" or with a bar with an additional surcharge are listed as Nos. 64B-90, 92-93, 99.

Red Overprint

1903 **Unwmk.** ***Perf. 14***

O43 A29 3c green .25 .25
a. Overprint omitted 5.00
b. Inverted overprint

Two overprint types: I — Thin, sharp, dark red. II — Thick, heavier, orange red. Same value.

No. 50 Surcharged in Black

No. 45 Surcharged in Red

1904 **Wmk. 143**

O44 A11 1c on 5c on 6c bl grn 1.60 2.00
a. "5" with short flag 4.25
b. Both "5s" with straight flag 8.00 8.00
O45 A16 2c on 30c steel blue 9.50 9.50
a. Double surcharge, red and black
b. Surcharge also on back

Types of Regular Issue Overprinted in Various Colors a

1906 **Unwmk.**

O46 A33 1c grn & blk (R) .65 .40
O47 A34 2c car & blk (Bl) .25 .25
a. Center and overprint inverted 30.00 3.00
b. Inverted overprint 6.00
O48 A35 5c ultra & blk (Bk) .65 .40
a. Inverted overprint 15.00 15.00
b. Center and overprint invtd. 50.00
O49 A36 10c dl vio & blk (R) .75 .55
a. Inverted overprint 10.00 10.00
b. Center and overprint invtd. 50.00
O50 A37 15c brn & blk (Bk) 3.00 .55
a. Inverted overprint 4.50
b. Overprint omitted 12.00 6.00
c. Center and overprint invtd. 60.00
O51 A38 20c dp grn & blk (R) .75 .55
a. Overprint omitted 15.00
O52 A39 25c plum & gray (Bl) .50 .25
a. With 2nd ovpt. in blue, invtd. 15.00
O53 A40 30c dk brn (Bk) .55 .25
O54 A41 50c org brn & dp grn (G) .75 .25
a. Inverted overprint 5.00 4.00
O55 A42 75c ultra & blk (Bk) 1.40 .95
a. Inverted overprint 9.50 5.75
b. Overprint omitted 22.50
O56 A43 $1 dp grn & gray (R) .90 .25
a. Inverted overprint
O57 A44 $2 plum & blk (Bl) 2.75 .25
a. Overprint omitted 22.50 15.00
O58 A45 $5 org & blk (Bk) 5.50 .25
a. Overprint omitted 11.00
b. Inverted overprint 12.00 8.00
Nos. O46-O58 (13) 18.40 5.15

Nos. O52, O54, O55, O56 and O58 are known with center inverted.

For surcharges see Nos. O72, O82-O85, O96.

b

1909-12

O59 A46 1c emer & blk (R) .40 .25
O60 A47 2c car rose & brn (Bl) .40 .25
a. Overprint omitted
O61 A48 5c turq & blk (Bk) .45 .25
a. Double overprint, one inverted 7.50
O62 A49 10c blk & ultra (R) ('12) .60 .25
O63 A50 15c cl & blk (Bl) .60 .45
O64 A51 20c bis & grn (Bk) 1.10 .55
O65 A52 25c ultra & grn (Bk) 1.10 .55
a. Double overprint 4.75 4.75
O66 A53 30c dk bl (R) .85 .25
O67 A54 50c brn & grn (Bk) 1.40 .40
a. Center inverted 27.50
b. Inverted overprint 4.00 2.75
O68 A55 75c pur & blk (R) 1.50 .25
Nos. O59-O68 (10) 8.40 3.45

Nos. O63, O64, O67 and O68 are known without overprint and with center inverted.

For surcharges see Nos. O74-O81, O86-O90, O97.

Rouletted

O69 A49 10c blk & ultra (R) 1.00 .95

Nos. 126B and 127E Overprinted type "a" ("OS") in Red

1910-12 ***Rouletted***

O70 A49 3c on 10c blk & ultra .70 1.25

Perf. 12½, 14, 12½x14

O71 A49 3c on 10c blk & ultra ('12) .70 .40
a. Pair, one without srch., the other with dbl. srch., one invtd.
b. Double surcharge, one inverted 4.00

Stamps of Preceding Issues Srchd. with New Values like Regular Issue and — c

1914 **On Nos. O52 and 110**

O72 A39 (a) 2c on 25c plum & gray 30.00 10.50
O73 A42 (c) 20c on 75c brn & blk 8.75 5.25

On Nos. O66 and O68

O74 A53 (b) 5c on 30c dk bl 8.75 5.25
O75 A55 (c) 20c on 75c pur & blk (R) 13.00 5.25
Nos. O72-O75 (4) 60.50 26.25

Official Stamps of 1906-09 Surcharged Like Regular Issues of Same Date

1915-16

O76 A50 (c) 2c on 15c (Bk) .95 .50
O77 A52 (d) 2c on 25c (Bk) 5.25 5.25
O78 A51 (e) 5c on 20c (Bk) .95 .65
O79 A53 (g) 5c on 30c (R) 10.00 8.50
O80 A54 (i) 10c on 50c (Bk) 5.50 3.25
O81 A55 (j) 20c on 75c (R) 2.75 2.75
O82 A43 (k) 25c on $1 (R) 20.00 20.00
a. "25" double 25.00
b. "OS" inverted 25.00
O83 A44 (l) 50c on $2 (Bk) 50.00 50.00
a. "Ceuts" 70.00 70.00
O84 A44 (m) 50c on $2 (Br) 22.50 22.50
O85 A45 (n) $1 on $5 (Bk) 21.00 21.00

Handstamped Surcharge

O86 A54 (i) 10c on 50c (Bk) 11.00 11.00

Nos. O60-O61 Surcharged like Nos. 153-154 in Black or Red

a1, b1

c1, d1

e1, f1

g1, h1

i1, j1

O87 A47 1c on 2c 2.75 2.75
Strip of 10 types 30.00
O88 A48 2c on 5c (R) 2.75 2.75
Strip of 10 types (R) 30.00
a. Black surcharge 10.00 10.00
Strip of 10 types (Bk) 140.00

See note following Nos. 153-154.

Nos. O60-O61 Surcharged

O90 A47 1c on 2c 125.00 125.00
O91 A48 2c on 5c 100.00 100.00

No. O42 Surcharged

O92 A26 10c on 50c (Bk) 11.00 11.00

No. O53 Surcharged

1917

O96 A40 5c on 30c dk brn 21.00 21.00
a. "FIV" 35.00 35.00

The editors consider the 1915-17 issues unnecessary and speculative.

No. O62 Surcharged in Red like No. 162

1918

O97 A49 3c on 10c blk & ultra 2.40 2.40

Types of Regular Issue of 1918 Ovptd. Type "a" in Black, Blue or Red

1918 **Unwmk.** ***Perf. 12½, 14***

O98 A59 1c dp grn & red brn (Bk) .60 .25
O99 A60 2c red & blk (Bl) .60 .25
O100 A61 5c ultra & blk (R) 1.10 .25
O101 A62 10c ultra (R) .60 .25
O102 A63 15c choc & dk grn (Bl) 2.75 .60
O103 A64 20c gray lil & blk (R) .85 .25
O104 A65 25c choc & grn (Bk) 5.25 .65
O105 A66 30c brt vio & blk (R) 6.50 .65
O106 A67 50c mar & blk (Bl) 7.75 .65
a. Overprint omitted 11.00
O107 A68 75c car brn & blk (Bl) 3.00 .25
O108 A69 $1 ol bis & turq bl (Bk) 6.00 .25
O109 A70 $2 ol bis & blk (R) 9.25 .25
O110 A71 $5 yel grn (Bk) 12.00 .40
Nos. O98-O110 (13) 56.25 4.95

For surcharges see Nos. 259-269, O111-O112, O155-O157. For overprint see No. 270.

Official Stamps of 1918 Surcharged like Regular Issue

1920

O111 A59 3c on 1c grn & red brn 1.10 .70
a. "CEETS" 15.00 15.00
b. Double surcharge 8.00 8.00
c. Double srch., one invtd. 15.00 15.00
d. Triple surcharge 20.00 20.00
O112 A60 4c on 2c red & blk .70 .70
a. Inverted surcharge 12.00 12.00
b. Double surcharge 12.00 12.00
c. Double srch., one invtd. 10.00 10.00
d. Triple surcharge 15.00 15.00

Types of Regular Issues of 1915-21 Overprinted

1921 **Wmk. 116** ***Perf. 14***

O113 A57 2c rose red 8.25 .25
O114 A58 3c brown 1.75 .25
O115 A79 20c brn & ultra 2.25 .40

Regular Issues of 1921 Overprinted

O116 A75 1c dp grn 1.75 .25
O117 A76 5c dp bl & brn 1.75 .25
O118 A77 10c red vio & blk .85 .25
O119 A78 15c blk & grn 4.75 .60
a. Double overprint
O120 A80 25c org & grn 6.50 .60
O121 A81 30c brn & red 1.75 .25
O122 A82 50c grn & blk 1.75 .25
a. Overprinted "S" only
O123 A83 75c bl & vio 3.25 .25
O124 A84 $1 bl & blk 22.50 .65
O125 A85 $2 grn & org 12.00 .95
O126 A86 $5 grn & bl 13.50 2.10
Nos. O113-O126 (14) 82.60 7.30

Preceding Issues Overprinted

1921

O127 A75 1c dp grn 7.50 .25
O128 A57 2c rose red 7.50 .25
O129 A58 3c brown 7.50 .25
O130 A76 5c dp bl & brn 4.50 .25
O131 A77 10c red vio & blk 7.50 .25
O132 A78 15c blk & grn 8.50 .25
O133 A79 20c brn & ultra 8.50 .40
O134 A80 25c org & grn 8.25 .80
O135 A81 30c brn & red 7.50 .25
O136 A82 50c grn & blk 8.75 .25
O137 A83 75c bl & vio 5.50 .25
O138 A84 $1 bl & blk 15.00 2.00
O139 A85 $2 org & grn 19.00 2.25
O140 A86 $5 grn & bl 15.00 3.25
Nos. O127-O140 (14) 130.50 10.95

Types of Regular Issue of 1923 Ovptd.

1923 ***Perf. 13½x14½, 14½x13½***

White Paper

O141 A88 1c bl grn & blk 8.75 .25
O142 A89 2c dl red & yel brn 8.75 .25
O143 A90 3c gray bl & blk 8.75 .25
O144 A91 5c org & dk grn 8.75 .25
O145 A92 10c ol bis & dk vio 8.75 .25
O146 A93 15c yel grn & bl 1.10 .40
O147 A94 20c vio & ind 1.10 .40
O148 A95 25c brn & red brn 32.50 .40

White, Buff or Brownish Paper

O149a A96 30c dp ultra & brn 1.10 .30
b. Overprint omitted 2.00
O150a A97 50c dl bis & red brn 2.25 .45
O151 A98 75c gray & grn 2.25 .25
O152a A99 $1 red org & grn 2.25 .65
b. Overprint omitted 11.00
O153 A100 $2 red lil & ver 6.00 .25
O154a A101 $5 bl & brn vio 4.50 2.25
Nos. O141-O154a (14) 96.80 6.25

No. O98 Surcharged in Red Brown

1926 **Unwmk.** ***Perf. 14***

O155 A59 2c on 1c 2.25 2.25
a. "Gents" 15.00
b. Surcharged in black 5.75
c. As "b," "Gents" 15.00

No. O98 Surcharged in Black

1926
O156 A59 2c on 1c 1.00 1.00
a. Inverted surcharge 20.00
b. "Gents" 10.00

No. O98 Surcharged in Red

1927
O157 A59 2c on 1c 35.00 35.00
a. "Ceuts" 55.00
b. "Vwo" 55.00
c. "Twc" 55.00

Regular Issue of 1928 Overprinted in Red or Black

1928 ***Perf. 12***
O158 A102 1c grn (R) 1.10 .55
O159 A102 2c gray vio (R) 3.50 2.10
O160 A102 3c bis brn (Bk) 3.75 4.25
O161 A103 5c ultra (R) 1.10 .55
O162 A104 10c ol gray (R) 3.50 1.75
O163 A103 15c dl vio (R) 3.50 1.00
O164 A103 $1 red brn (Bk) 77.50 22.50
Nos. O158-O164 (7) 93.95 32.70

For surcharges see Nos. C3, O165.

No. O162 Surcharged with New Value and Bar in Black

1945 **Unwmk.** ***Perf. 12***
O165 A104 4c on 10c (Bk) 12.00 12.00

LIBYA

'li-bē-ə

(Libia)

LOCATION — North Africa, bordering on the Mediterranean Sea
GOVT. — Republic
AREA — 679,358 sq. mi.
POP. — 4,992,838 (1999 est.)
CAPITAL — Tripoli

In 1939, the four northern provinces of Libya, a former Italian colony, were incorporated in the Italian national territory. Included in the territory is the former Turkish Vilayet of Tripoli, annexed in 1912. Libya became a kingdom on Dec. 24, 1951. The Libyan Arab Republic was established Sept. 1, 1969. "People's Socialist . . ." was added to its name in 1977. See Cyrenaica and Tripolitania.

100 Centesimi = 1 Lira
Military Authority Lira (1951)
Franc (1951)
1,000 Milliemes = 1 Pound (1952)
1,000 Dirhams = 1 Dinar (1972)

Watermarks

Wmk. 140 — Crown

Wmk. 195 — Multiple Crown and Arabic F

Wmk. 310 — Multiple Crescent and Star

Catalogue values for unused stamps in this country are for Never Hinged items, beginning with Scott 102 in the regular postage section, Scott C51 in the airpost section, Scott E13 in the special delivery section, Scott J25 in the postage due section, Scott O1 in the official section, Scott N1 in the Fezzan-Ghadames section, Scott 2N1 in the Fezzan section, Scott 2NB1 in the Fezzan semi-postal section, Scott 2NC1 in the Fezzan airpost section, Scott 2NJ1 in the Fezzan postage due section, Scott 3N1 in the Ghadames section, and Scott 3NC1 in the Ghadames airpost section.

Used values in italics are for postally used stamps. CTO's sell for about the same as unused, hinged stamps.

Stamps of Italy Overprinted in Black

1912-22 **Wmk. 140** ***Perf. 14***
1 A42 1c brown ('15) 1.40 .85
a. Double overprint 250.00 250.00
2 A43 2c orange brn 1.40 .50
3 A48 5c green 1.50 .35
a. Double overprint 90.00 90.00
b. Imperf., pair 300.00
c. Inverted overprint —
d. Pair, one without overprint 450.00 450.00
4 A48 10c claret 14.00 .35
a. Pair, one without overprint 475.00 475.00
b. Double overprint 160.00 160.00
5 A48 15c slate ('22) 5.50 *8.50*
6 A45 20c orange ('15) 5.50 .35
a. Double overprint 175.00 *175.00*
b. Pair, one without overprint 800.00 800.00
7 A50 20c brn org ('18) 4.25 *5.50*
a. Double overprint 175.00 —
8 A49 25c blue 5.50 .35
b. Double overprint 175.00 —
9 A49 40c brown 14.00 1.00
10 A45 45c ol grn ('17) 37.50 30.00
a. Inverted overprint 675.00
11 A49 50c violet 35.00 1.40
12 A49 60c brn car ('18) 19.00 *25.00*
13 A46 1 l brn & grn ('15) 62.50 1.75
14 A46 5 l bl & rose ('15) 425.00 500.00
15 A51 10 l gray grn & red ('15) 35.00 *190.00*
Nos. 1-15 (15) 667.05 *765.90*

Two types of overprint were applied to this issue. Type I has bold letters, with dots close within "i"; type II has thinner letters, with dots further away within "i." All values, along with Nos. E1 and E2, received the type I overprint, and values shown are for this type. Nos. 1, 3-4, 6, 8, 11, 13-15 and E1-E2 also received the type II overprint. For detailed listings, see the *Scott Classic Specialized Catalogue of Stamps and Covers.*

For surcharges see Nos. 37-38.

Overprinted in Violet

1912 **Unwmk.**
16 A58 15c slate 275.00 3.00
a. Blue black overprint *21,000.* 42.50

No. 16 Surcharged

1916, Mar. **Unwmk.**
19 A58 20c on 15c slate 60.00 12.50

Roman Legionary A1

Diana of Ephesus A2

Ancient Galley Leaving Tripoli A3

"Victory" A4

1921 **Engr.** **Wmk. 140** ***Perf. 14***
20 A1 1c blk & gray brn 2.75 *7.00*
21 A1 2c blk & red brn 2.75 *7.00*
22 A1 5c blk & grn 3.50 .70
a. 5c black & red brown (error) 1,900.
b. Center inverted 60.00 90.00
c. Imperf., pair 550.00 550.00
23 A2 10c blk & rose 3.50 .70
a. Center inverted 60.00 90.00
24 A2 15c blk brn & brn org 85.00 2.75
a. Center inverted 150.00 *275.00*
25 A2 25c dk bl & bl 3.50 .25
a. Center inverted 20.00 30.00
b. Imperf., pair 775.00 775.00
26 A3 30c blk & blk brn 35.00 .70
a. Center inverted 2,750. 3,000.
27 A3 50c blk & ol grn 16.00 .25
a. 50c black & brown (error) 625.00
b. Center inverted *4,750.*
28 A3 55c black & vio 16.00 *24.00*
29 A4 1 l dk brn & brn 47.50 .25
30 A4 5 l blk & dk blue 27.50 21.00
31 A4 10 l dk bl & ol grn 300.00 160.00
Nos. 20-31 (12) 543.00 224.60

See No. 47-61. For surcharges see No. 102-121.

Perf. 14x13¼
20d A1 1c blk & gray brn 5.50 11.00
21d A1 2c blk & red brn 5.50 11.00
22d A1 5c blk & red green 7.00 1.40
23d A2 10c blk & rose 7.00 1.40
24d A2 15c blk & brn org 160.00 5.50
25d A2 25c dk bl & bl 7.00 .35
26d A3 30c blk & blk brn 70.00 1.40
27d A3 50c blk & ol grn 32.50 .35
28d A3 55c blk & vio 32.50 55.00
29d A4 1 l dk brn & brn 95.00 .35
30d A4 5 l blk & dk blue 55.00 30.00
31d A4 10 l blk & ol grn 625.00 190.00

Italy Nos. 136-139 Overprinted

1922, Apr.
33 A64 5c olive green 1.75 *6.25*
a. Double overprint 475.00 475.00
34 A64 10c red 1.75 *6.25*
a. Double overprint 475.00 475.00
b. Inverted overprint 950.00 950.00
35 A64 15c slate green 2.00 *11.00*
36 A64 25c ultramarine 2.00 *11.00*
Nos. 33-36 (4) 7.50 *34.50*

3rd anniv. of the victory of the Piave.

Nos. 11, 8 Surcharged

1922, June 1
37 A49 40c on 50c violet 3.50 2.10
38 A49 80c on 25c blue 3.50 *8.50*

Libyan Sibyl — A6

1924-31 **Unwmk.** ***Perf. 14½x14***
39 A6 20c deep green .70 .25
c. Vert. pair, imperf between and top 1,400.
d. Horiz. pair, imperf between and at right 1,400.
e. Horiz. pair, imperf between and at left 1,400.
40 A6 40c brown 2.10 .70
b. Imperf single 275.00 *425.00*
41 A6 60c deep blue .70 .25
b. Imperf single 275.00
42 A6 1.75 l orange ('31) 1.40 .25
43 A6 2 l carmine 4.25 1.00
b. Imperf single 275.00 *425.00*
44 A6 2.55 l violet ('31) 8.50 17.50
Nos. 39-44 (6) 17.65 19.95

1926-29 ***Perf. 11***
39a A6 20c 45.00 .30
40a A6 40c 32.50 2.40
41a A6 60c 32.50 .45
43a A6 2 l ('29) 15.00 5.00
Nos. 39a-43a (4) 125.00 8.15

Type of 1921

1924-40 **Unwmk.** ***Perf. 13½ to 14***
47 A1 1c blk & gray brown 2.75 5.50
48 A1 2c blk & red brn 2.75 5.50
49 A1 5c blk & green 3.50 .70
50 A1 7½c blk & brn ('31) 1.40 14.00
51 A2 10c blk & dl red 2.75 .30
b. 10c blk & carmine 2.75 .30
c. As "b," center inverted 175.00
52 A2 15c blk brn & org 8.50 1.00
b. Center inverted, perf. 11 *4,500.* *6,500.*
53 A2 25c dk bl & bl 42.50 .50
a. Center inverted 240.00 350.00
54 A3 30c blk & blk brn 2.75 .50
55 A3 50c blk & ol grn 2.75 .30
b. Center inverted 4,500.
56 A3 55c black & vio 625.00 825.00
57 A4 75c vio & red ('31) 6.50 .25
58 A4 1 l dk brn & brn 10.00 .35
59 A3 1.25 l indigo & ultra ('31) 1.40 .25
60 A4 5 l blk & dk bl ('40) 150.00 *175.00*
Nos. 47-60 (14) 862.55 1,029.

Perf. 11
47a A1 1c 375.00
48a A1 2c 375.00
49a A1 5c 70.00 17.50
51a A2 10c 35.00 7.00
52a A2 15c 475.00 45.00
54a A3 30c 140.00 2.10
55a A3 50c 775.00 .25
58a A4 1 l 350.00 .35
60a A4 5 l ('37) *2,400.* 450.00
61 A4 10 l dk bl & ol grn ('37) 625.00 500.00

Nos. 47a and 48a were not sent to the colony. A few philatelically inspired covers exist.

Italy Nos. 197 and 88 Overprinted Like Nos. 1-15

1929 **Wmk. 140** ***Perf. 14***
62 A86 7½c light brown 10.00 *55.00*
a. Double overprint — —
63 A46 1.25 l blue & ultra 60.00 21.00
a. Inverted overprint 3,750.

Italy No. 193 Overprinted Like Nos. 33-36

1929 **Unwmk.** ***Perf. 11***
64 A85 1.75 l deep brown 75.00 2.10
h. Perf 13¾ *12,000.*

Water Carriers — A7

Man of Tripoli — A8

Designs: 25c, Minaret. 30c, 1.25 l, Tomb of Holy Man near Tagiura. 50c, Statue of Emperor Claudius at Leptis. 75c, Ruins of gardens.

1934, Feb. 17 **Photo.** ***Perf. 14***
64A A7 10c brown 4.25 *17.50*
64B A8 20c car rose 4.25 *15.00*
64C A8 25c green 4.25 *15.00*

64D	A7	30c	dark brown	4.25	*15.00*
64E	A8	50c	purple	4.25	*15.00*
64F	A7	75c	rose	4.25	*27.50*
64G	A7	1.25 l	blue	55.00	*95.00*
			Nos. 64A-64G (7)	80.50	*200.00*
			Nos. 64A-64G,C14-C18 (12)	508.50	*980.00*

8th Sample Fair, Tripoli.

Bedouin Woman — A15

1936, May 11 Wmk. 140 *Perf. 14*

65	A15	50c	violet	1.75	*2.75*
66	A15	1.25 l	deep blue	1.75	*7.75*

10th Sample Fair, Tripoli.

Highway Memorial Arch — A16

1937, Mar. 15

67	A16	50c	copper red	2.75	*5.50*
68	A16	1.25 l	sapphire	2.75	*12.50*
			Nos. 67-68,C28-C29 (4)	11.00	*36.00*

Coastal road to the Egyptian frontier, opening.

Nos. 67-68 Overprinted in Black

1937, Apr. 24

69	A16	50c	copper red	14.00	*35.00*
70	A16	1.25 l	sapphire	14.00	*35.00*
			Nos. 69-70,C30-C31 (4)	56.00	*140.00*

11th Sample Fair, Tripoli.

Roman Wolf and Lion of St. Mark — A17

View of Fair Buildings — A18

1938, Feb. 20

71	A17	5c	brown	.30	1.00
72	A18	10c	olive brown	.30	.70
73	A17	25c	green	.55	1.25
74	A18	50c	purple	.55	.55
75	A17	75c	rose red	1.40	*2.75*
76	A18	1.25 l	dark blue	1.40	*7.00*
			Nos. 71-76,C32-C33 (8)	7.30	*21.50*

12th Sample Fair, Tripoli.

Augustus Caesar (Octavianus) A19

Goddess Abundantia A20

1938, Apr. 25

77	A19	5c	olive brown	.25	1.40
78	A20	10c	brown red	.25	1.40
79	A19	25c	dk yel green	.50	.70
80	A20	50c	dk violet	.50	.45
81	A19	75c	orange red	1.40	*1.75*
82	A20	1.25 l	dull blue	1.40	*2.75*
			Nos. 77-82,C34-C35 (8)	5.65	*13.95*

Birth bimillenary of Augustus Caesar (Octavianus), first Roman emperor.

Desert City — A21

View of Ghadames — A22

1939, Apr. 12 Photo.

83	A21	5c	olive brown	.70	1.00
84	A22	20c	red brown	.70	1.00
85	A21	50c	rose violet	.70	1.00
86	A22	75c	scarlet	.70	*3.50*
87	A21	1.25 l	gray blue	1.40	*4.25*
			Nos. 83-87,C36-C38 (8)	6.60	*17.70*

13th Sample Fair, Tripoli.

Modern City — A23

Oxen and Plow A24

Mosque A25

1940, June 3 Wmk. 140 *Perf. 14*

88	A23	5c	brown	.70	1.00
89	A24	10c	red orange	.70	.70
90	A25	25c	dull green	.70	*1.00*
91	A23	50c	dark violet	.70	.70
92	A24	75c	crimson	.70	*3.50*
93	A25	1.25 l	ultramarine	1.40	*5.50*
94	A24	2 l + 75c	rose lake	1.40	*16.00*
			Nos. 88-94,C39-C42 (11)	9.70	*50.50*

Triennial Overseas Exposition, Naples.

"Two Peoples, One War," Hitler and Mussolini — A26

1941, May 16

95	A26	5c	orange	2.10	*8.00*
96	A26	10c	brown	2.10	*8.00*
97	A26	20c	dull violet	3.50	*8.00*
98	A26	25c	green	3.50	*8.00*
99	A26	50c	purple	3.50	*8.00*
100	A26	75c	scarlet	3.50	*21.00*
101	A26	1.25 l	sapphire	3.50	*21.00*
			Nos. 95-101,C43 (8)	24.45	*124.50*
			Set, never hinged	42.50	

The Rome-Berlin Axis.

Catalogue values for unused stamps in this section, from this point to the end of the section, are for Never Hinged items.

United Kingdom of Libya

Stamps of Cyrenaica 1950 Surcharged in Black

For Use in Tripolitania

1951, Dec. 24 Unwmk. *Perf. 12½*

102	A2	1mal	on 2m rose car	.30	.30
103	A2	2mal	on 4m dk grn	.30	.30
104	A2	4mal	on 8m red org	.30	.30
105	A2	5mal	on 10m pur	.50	.50
106	A2	6mal	on 12m red	.50	.50
a.			Inverted surcharge	30.00	30.00
107	A2	10mal	on 20m dp bl	.90	.90
a.			Arabic "20" for "10"	25.00	25.00
108	A3	24mal	on 50m choc & ultra	3.50	3.50
109	A3	48mal	on 100m bl blk & car rose	14.00	14.00
110	A3	96mal	on 200m vio & pur	30.00	30.00
111	A3	240mal	on 500m dk grn & org	75.00	75.00
			Nos. 102-111 (10)	125.30	*125.30*

The surcharge is larger on Nos. 108 to 111.

For Use in Fezzan

Same Surcharge in Francs

112	A2	2fr	on 2m rose car	.30	.70
113	A2	4fr	on 4m dk grn	.30	.70
114	A2	8fr	on 8m red org	.40	.90
115	A2	10fr	on 10m pur	.55	1.40
116	A2	12fr	on 12m red	1.00	2.25
117	A2	20fr	on 20m dp bl	2.00	*5.00*
118	A3	48fr	on 50m choc & ultra	42.50	*47.50*
119	A3	96fr	on 100m bl blk & car rose	42.50	*260.00*
120	A3	192fr	on 200m vio & pur	120.00	*275.00*
121	A3	480fr	on 500m dk grn & org	225.00	*300.00*
			Nos. 112-121 (10)	434.55	*893.45*

The surcharge is larger on Nos. 118-121.

A second printing of Nos. 118-121 has an elongated first character in second line of Arabic surcharge.

Cyrenaica Nos. 65-77 Overprinted in Black

For Use in Cyrenaica

122	A2	1m	dark brown	.25	.45
123	A2	2m	rose carmine	.30	.45
124	A2	3m	orange	.30	.55
125	A2	4m	dark green	35.00	55.00
126	A2	5m	gray	.30	*.55*
127	A2	8m	red orange	.75	*1.50*
128	A2	10m	purple	1.25	*2.15*
129	A2	12m	red	1.40	*2.50*
130	A2	20m	deep blue	2.00	*4.00*
131	A3	50m	choc & ultra	9.50	*19.00*
132	A3	100m	bl blk & car rose	17.50	*24.00*
133	A3	200m	violet & pur	55.00	*70.00*
134	A3	500m	dk grn & org	180.00	*190.00*
			Nos. 122-134 (13)	303.55	*370.15*

Wider spacing between the two lines on Nos. 131-134.

King Idris

A27 A28

1952, Apr. 15 Engr. *Perf. 11½*

135	A27	2m	yellow brown	.30	.25
136	A27	4m	gray	.30	.25
137	A27	5m	blue green	20.00	.65
138	A27	8m	vermilion	.90	.55
139	A27	10m	purple	20.00	.40
140	A27	12m	lilac rose	1.75	.40
141	A27	20m	deep blue	22.50	.90
142	A27	25m	chocolate	22.50	.90
143	A28	50m	brown & blue	3.00	1.40
144	A28	100m	gray blk & car rose	5.25	3.00
145	A28	200m	dk blue & pur	11.00	6.00
146	A28	500m	dk grn & brn orange	37.50	21.00
			Nos. 135-146 (12)	145.00	35.70

For surcharge and overprints see Nos. 168, O1-O8.

Globe — A29

Perf. 13½x13

1955, Jan. 1 Photo. Wmk. 195

147	A29	5m	yellow brown	2.00	1.30
148	A29	10m	green	3.00	2.00
149	A29	30m	violet	5.50	3.50
			Nos. 147-149 (3)	10.50	6.80

Arab Postal Union founding, July 1, 1954.

Nos. 147-149 Overprinted

1955, Aug. 1

150	A29	5m	yellow brn	1.00	.65
151	A29	10m	green	2.00	1.10
152	A29	30m	violet	3.75	2.00
			Nos. 150-152 (3)	6.75	3.75

Arab Postal Congress, Cairo, Mar. 15.

Emblems of Tripolitania, Cyrenaica and Fezzan with Royal Crown — A30

1955 Engr. Wmk. 310 *Perf. 11½*

153	A30	2m	lemon	2.00	.70
154	A30	3m	slate blue	.25	.25
155	A30	4m	gray green	2.75	1.25
156	A30	5m	light blue grn	.85	.25
157	A30	10m	violet	1.50	.25
158	A30	18m	crimson	.25	.25
159	A30	20m	orange	.50	.25
160	A30	30m	blue	.85	.25
161	A30	35m	brown	1.25	.25
162	A30	40m	rose carmine	2.00	.60
163	A30	50m	olive	1.25	.60

Size: 27½x32½mm

164	A30	100m	dk green & pur	2.75	1.20
165	A30	200m	ultra & rose car	13.00	2.50
166	A30	500m	grn & orange	20.00	12.00

Size: 26½x32mm

167	A30	£1	ocher, brn & grn, *yel*	30.00	18.00
			Nos. 153-167 (15)	79.20	38.60

See Nos. 177-179, 192-206A.

No. 136 Surcharged

1955, Aug. 25 Unwmk.

168	A27	5m	on 4m gray	2.00	.90

Tomb of El Senussi, Jagbub — A31

Perf. 13x13½

1956, Sept. 14 Photo. Wmk. 195

169	A31	5m	green	.50	.50
170	A31	10m	bright violet	.60	.50
171	A31	15m	rose carmine	1.40	1.25
172	A31	30m	sapphire	2.25	1.40
			Nos. 169-172 (4)	4.75	3.65

Death centenary of the Imam Seyyid Mohammed Aly El Senussi (in 1859).

Map, Flags and UN Headquarters — A32

1956, Dec. 14 Litho. *Perf. 13½x13*

173	A32	15m	bl, ocher & ol bis	.75	.35
174	A32	35m	bl, ocher & vio brn	1.60	.75

Libya's admission to the UN, 1st anniv.

Globe and Postal Emblems — A33

1957 Wmk. 195 *Perf. 13½x13*
175 A33 15m blue 1.50 1.50
176 A33 500m yellow brown 22.00 12.00

Arab Postal Congress, Tripoli, Feb. 9.

Emblems Type of 1955

1957 Wmk. 310 Engr. *Perf. 11½*
177 A30 1m black, *yellow* .25 .25
178 A30 2m bister brown .25 .25
179 A30 4m brown carmine .35 .35
Nos. 177-179 (3) .85 .85

UN Emblem and Broken Chain — A34

Unwmk.

1958, Dec. 10 Photo. *Perf. 14*
180 A34 10m bluish violet .35 .25
181 A34 15m green .60 .35
182 A34 30m ultramarine 1.50 .85
Nos. 180-182 (3) 2.45 1.45

Universal Declaration of Human Rights, 10th anniv.

Date Palms and FAO Emblem — A35

1959, Dec. 5 Unwmk. *Perf. 14*
183 A35 10m pale vio & black .40 .25
184 A35 15m bluish grn & blk .60 .45
185 A35 45m light blue & blk 1.50 1.20
Nos. 183-185 (3) 2.50 1.90

1st Intl. Dates Conf., Tripoli, Dec. 5-11.

Arab League Center, Cairo, and Arms of Libya — A36

Perf. 13x13½

1960, Mar. 22 Wmk. 328
186 A36 10m dull grn & blk .60 .35

Opening of the Arab League Center and the Arab Postal Museum in Cairo.

Emblems of WRY and UN, Arms of Libya — A37

1960, Apr. 7 Unwmk. *Perf. 14*
187 A37 10m violet & black .60 .35
188 A37 45m blue & black 1.75 1.25

World Refugee Year, 7/1/59-6/30/60.

Palm Tree and Radio Mast — A38

1960, Aug. 4 Engr. *Perf. 13x13½*
189 A38 10m violet .35 .25
190 A38 15m blue green .50 .25
191 A38 45m dk carmine rose 1.80 1.25
Nos. 189-191 (3) 2.65 1.75

3rd Arab Telecommunications Conf., Tripoli, Aug. 4.

Emblems Type of 1955

1960 Wmk. 310 Engr. *Perf. 11½*

Size: 18x21½mm
192 A30 1m black, *gray* .25 .25
193 A30 2m bis brn, *buff* .25 .25
194 A30 3m blue, *bluish* .25 .25
195 A30 4m brn car, *rose* .25 .25
196 A30 5m grn, *greenish* .25 .25
197 A30 10m vio, *pale vio* .25 .25
198 A30 15m brown, *buff* .25 .25
199 A30 20m orange, *buff* .50 .25
200 A30 30m red, *pink* .50 .25
201 A30 40m rose car, *rose* .75 .25
202 A30 45m blue, *bluish* .85 .25
203 A30 50m olive, *buff* .85 .25

Size: 27½x32½mm
204 A30 100m dk grn & pur, *gray* 1.50 .70
205 A30 200m bl & rose car, *bluish* 4.25 1.40
206 A30 500m green & org, *greenish* 30.00 9.00

Size: 26½x32mm
206A A30 £1 ocher, brn & grn, *brn* 35.00 18.00
Nos. 192-206A (16) 75.95 32.10

Watchtower and Broken Chain — A39

1961, Aug. 9 Photo. Unwmk.
207 A39 5m lt yel grn & brn .50 .25
208 A39 15m light blue & brn .85 .35

Issued for Army Day, Aug. 9, 1961.

Map of Zelten Oil Field and Tanker at Marsa Brega — A40

1961, Oct. 25 *Perf. 11½*
209 A40 15m ol grn & buff .50 .25
210 A40 50m red brn & pale vio 1.50 1.00
211 A40 100m ultra & blue 3.50 1.25
Nos. 209-211 (3) 5.50 2.50

Opening of first oil pipe line in Libya.

Hands Breaking Chain, Tractor and Cows — A41

Designs: 50m, Modern highways and buildings. 100m, Machinery.

1961, Dec. 24 *Perf. 11½*

Granite Paper
212 A41 15m pale grn, grn & brown .25 .25
213 A41 50m buff & brown .90 .60
214 A41 100m sal, vio & brn 3.25 1.25
Nos. 212-214 (3) 4.40 2.10

10th anniversary of independence.

Camel Riders A42

15m, Well. 50m, Oil installations in desert.

1962, Feb. 20 Photo. *Perf. 12*
215 A42 10m choc & org brn .85 .25
216 A42 15m plum & yel grn 1.00 .60
217 A42 50m emer & ultra 2.75 2.10
a. Souv. sheet of 3, #215-217, imperf. 65.00 30.00
Nos. 215-217 (3) 4.60 2.95

Intl. Fair, Tripoli, Feb. 20-Mar. 20.
Nos. 215-217 exist imperf. Value about twice that of perf.

Malaria Eradication Emblem and Palm — A43

1962, Apr. 7 Unwmk. *Perf. 11½*
218 A43 15m multicolored .60 .50
219 A43 50m grn, yel & brn 1.50 1.20

WHO drive to eradicate malaria.

Exist imperf. Value $10.
Two imperf. souvenir sheets exist, one containing the 15m, the other the 50m. Sold for 20m and 70m respectively. Value for both, $34.

Ahmed Rafik El Mehdawi (1898-1961), Poet — A44

1962, July 6 Engr. *Perf. 13x14*
220 A44 15m green .40 .25
221 A44 20m brown .85 .50

El Mehdawi, 1st death anniv.

Clasped Hands and Scout Emblem — A45

Designs: 10m, 30m, Boy Scouts. 15m, 50m, Scout emblem and tents.

1962, July 13 Photo. *Perf. 12*
222 A45 5m yel, blk & red .25 .25
223 A45 10m bl, blk & yel .50 .25
224 A45 15m multicolored .60 .50
Nos. 222-224 (3) 1.35 1.00

Souvenir Sheet

Imperf
225 Sheet of 3 20.00 20.00
a. A45 20m yellow, black & red 5.00 5.00
b. A45 30m blue, black & yellow 5.00 5.00
c. A45 50m blue gray, yel, blk & grn 5.00 5.00

Third Libyan Scout meeting (Philia).
Nos. 222-224 exist imperf. Value for set, $3.

Drop of Oil with New City, Desert, Oil Wells and Map of Coast Line — A46

1962, Nov. 25 *Perf. 11x11½*
226 A46 15m grn & vio blk .50 .25
227 A46 50m brn org & ol 1.40 .75

Opening of the Essider Terminal Sidrah pipeline system.

Centenary Emblem — A47

Litho. & Photo.

1963, Jan. 1 *Perf. 11½*
228 A47 10m rose, blk, red & bl .75 .40
229 A47 15m citron, blk, red & bl .85 .60
230 A47 20m gray, blk, red & bl 1.60 .85
Nos. 228-230 (3) 3.20 1.85

Centenary of the International Red Cross.

Rainbow and Arches over Map of Africa and Libya A48

1963, Feb. 28 Litho. *Perf. 13½*
231 A48 15m multicolored .50 .35
232 A48 30m multicolored .85 .35
233 A48 50m multicolored 1.80 1.00
Nos. 231-233 (3) 3.15 1.70

Tripoli Intl. Fair "Gateway of Africa," Feb. 28-Mar. 28. Every other horizontal row inverted in sheet of 50 (25 tête bêche pairs). Value, set of tête bêche pairs, $6.50.

Date Palm and Well — A49

Designs: 15m, Camel and flock of sheep. 45m, Sower and tractor.

1963, Mar. 21 Photo. *Perf. 11½*
234 A49 10m green, lt bl & bis .50 .25
235 A49 15m pur, lt grn & bis .60 .50
236 A49 45m dk bl, sal & sep 1.60 1.00
Nos. 234-236 (3) 2.70 1.75

FAO "Freedom from Hunger" campaign.

Man with Whip and Slave Reaching for UN Emblem — A50

1963, Dec. 10 Unwmk. *Perf. 11½*
237 A50 5m red brown & bl .25 .25
238 A50 15m deep claret & bl .50 .25
239 A50 50m green & blue 1.25 .75
Nos. 237-239 (3) 2.00 1.25

Universal Declaration of Human Rights, 15th anniv.

Exhibition Hall and Finger Pointing to Libya — A51

1964, Feb. 28 Photo. *Perf. 11½*
240 A51 10m red brn, gray grn & brn 1.00 .25
241 A51 15m pur, gray grn & brn 1.40 .60
242 A51 30m dk bl, gray grn & brn 2.00 1.40
Nos. 240-242 (3) 4.40 2.25

3rd Intl. Fair, Tripoli, Feb. 28-Mar. 20.

Child Playing with Blocks — A52

Design: 15m, Child in bird's nest.

1964, Mar. 22 *Perf. 11½*
243 A52 5m multicolored .25 .25
244 A52 15m multicolored .60 .25
245 A52 45m multicolored 1.75 .85
a. Souvenir sheet of 3, #243-245, imperf. 5.00 5.00
Nos. 243-245 (3) 2.60 1.35

Children's Day. Exist imperf. Value about 1½ times that of perf.
No. 245a sold for 100m.

Lungs and Stethoscope — A53

1964, Apr. 7 Photo. *Perf. 13½x14*
246 A53 20m deep purple 1.25 .60

Campaign against tuberculosis.

Map of Libya — A54

1964, Apr. 27 Unwmk. *Perf. 11½*

247 A54 5m emerald & org .25 .25
248 A54 50m blue & yellow 1.50 .60

First anniversary of Libyan union.

Moth Emerging from Cocoon, Veiled and Modern Women — A55

1964, June 15 Litho. & Engraved

249 A55 10m vio bl & lt grn .35 .25
250 A55 20m vio blue & yel .75 .60
251 A55 35m vio bl & pink 1.25 1.10
a. Souv. sheet of 3, #249-251 5.50 5.50
Nos. 249-251 (3) 2.35 1.95

To honor Libyan women in a new epoch. No. 251a sold for 100m.

Hand Giving Scout Sign, Scout and Libyan Flags — A56

Design: 20m, Libyan Scout emblem and hands.

1964, July 24 Photo. *Perf. 12x11½*

252 A56 10m lt bl & multi .85 .35
253 A56 20m multicolored 1.75 .85
a. Souvenir sheet of 2, #252-253, imperf. 11.50 11.50

Opening of new Boy Scout headquarters; installation of Crown Prince Hassan al-Rida el Senussi as Chief Scout. No. 253a sold for 50m.

Nos. 252-253 exist imperf. Value about 1½ times that of perf.

Bayonet, Wreath and Map — A57

1964, Aug. 9 Litho. *Perf. 14x13½*

254 A57 10m yel grn & brn .25 .25
255 A57 20m org & blk .75 .35

Founding of the Senussi Army.

Ahmed Bahloul el-Sharef — A58

1964, Aug. 11 Engr. *Perf. 11½*

256 A58 15m lilac .50 .25
257 A58 20m greenish blue .85 .50

Poet Ahmed Bahloul el-Sharef, died 1953.

Soccer — A59

1964, Oct. 1 Litho. *Perf. 14*

Black Inscriptions and Gold Olympic Rings

258 A59 5m shown .75 .50
259 A59 10m Bicycling .75 .50
260 A59 20m Boxing .75 .50
261 A59 30m Sprinter .75 .60
262 A59 35m Woman diver .75 .60
263 A59 50m Hurdling .75 .60
a. Block of 6, #258-263 5.00 5.00

18th Olympic Games, Tokyo, Oct. 10-25. No. 263a printed in sheet of 48. The two blocks in each double row are inverted in relation to the two blocks in the next row, providing various tete beche and se-tenant arrangements.

Nos. 258-263 exist imperf. Value for set, $27.50.

Perf. and imperf. souvenir sheets exist containing six 15m stamps in the designs and colors of Nos. 258-263. Sheets sold for 100m. Value for both, $32.50.

Arab Postal Union Emblem — A59a

1964, Dec. 1 Photo. *Perf. 11x11½*

264 A59a 10m yellow & blue .25 .25
265 A59a 15m pale vio & org brn .50 .25
266 A59a 30m lt yel grn & brn 1.40 .85
Nos. 264-266 (3) 2.15 1.35

Permanent Office of the APU, 10th anniv.

International Cooperation Year Emblem — A60

1965, Jan. 1 Litho. *Perf. 14½x14*

267 A60 5m vio bl & gold .50 .25
268 A60 15m rose car & gold 1.50 .70

Imperfs. exist. Value about twice that of perfs.

See Nos. C51-C51a.

European Bee Eater — A61

Birds: 5m, Long-legged buzzard, vert. 15m, Chestnut-bellied sandgrouse. 20m, Houbara bustard. 30m, Spotted sandgrouse. 40m, Libyan Barbary partridge, vert.

1965, Feb. 10 Photo. *Perf. 11½*

Granite Paper

Birds in Natural Colors

269 A61 5m gray & black 1.25 .50
270 A61 10m lt bl & org brn 2.00 .55
271 A61 15m lt green & blk 2.25 .60
272 A61 20m pale lil & blk 3.75 .85
273 A61 30m tan & dark brn 4.75 1.50
274 A61 40m dull yel & blk 5.50 1.90
Nos. 269-274 (6) 19.50 5.90

Map of Africa with Libya — A62

1965, Feb. 28 Photo. *Perf. 11½*

Granite Paper

275 A62 50m multicolored 1.00 .55

4th Intl. Tripoli Fair, Feb. 28-Mar. 20.

Compass Rose, Rockets, Balloons and Stars — A63

1965, Mar. 23 Litho.

276 A63 10m multicolored .25 .25
277 A63 15m multicolored .50 .35
278 A63 50m multicolored 1.50 1.00
Nos. 276-278 (3) 2.25 1.60

Fifth World Meteorological Day.

ITU Emblem, Old and New Communication Equipment — A64

1965, May 17 Unwmk.

279 A64 10m sepia .25 .25
280 A64 20m red lilac .35 .25
281 A64 50m lilac rose 1.25 .90
Nos. 279-281 (3) 1.85 1.40

ITU, centenary.

Library Aflame and Lamp — A65

1965, June Litho. *Perf. 11½*

282 A65 15m multicolored .50 .25
283 A65 50m multicolored 1.25 .55

Burning of the Library of Algiers, June 7, 1962.

Rose — A66

1965, Aug. Litho. *Perf. 14*

284 A66 1m shown .25 .25
285 A66 2m Iris .25 .25
286 A66 3m Opuntia .35 .25
287 A66 4m Sunflower .75 .25
Nos. 284-287 (4) 1.60 1.00

Jet Plane and Globe — A67

1965, Oct. Photo. *Perf. 11½*

288 A67 5m multicolored .25 .25
289 A67 10m multicolored .50 .25
290 A67 15m multicolored 1.00 .25
Nos. 288-290 (3) 1.75 .75

Issued to publicize Libyan Airlines.

Forum, Cyrene — A68

Designs: 100m, Arch of Trajan. 200m, Temple of Apollo, Cyrene. 500m, Antonine Temple of Jupiter, Sabratha, horiz. £1, Theater, Sabratha.

Perf. 12x11½, 11½x12

1965, Dec. 24 Engr. Wmk. 310

291 A68 50m vio blue & olive 2.00 .60
292 A68 100m Prus bl & dp org 2.75 .85
293 A68 200m pur & Prus bl 6.50 1.50
294 A68 500m car rose & grn 15.00 4.00
295 A68 £1 grn & dp org 32.50 10.00
Nos. 291-295 (5) 58.75 16.95

Nos. 293-295 with "Kingdom of Libia" in both Arabic and English blocked out with a blue felt-tipped pen were issued June 21, 1970, by the Republic.

Mausoleum at Germa — A69

Perf. 11½

1966, Feb. 10 Unwmk. Litho.

296 A69 70m purple & salmon 3.00 1.00

"POLIGRAFICA & CARTEVALORI-NAPLES" and Libyan Coat of Arms printed on back in yellow green. See No. E13.

Booklet pane containing 4 No. 296 and 4 No. E13 exists. Value $30.

Globe in Space, Satellites A70

1966, Feb. 28 *Perf. 12*

297 A70 15m multi & gold .50 .25
298 A70 45m multi & gold 1.00 .45
299 A70 55m multi & gold 1.25 .65
Nos. 297-299 (3) 2.75 1.35

5th Intl. Fair at Tripoli, Feb. 28-Mar. 20.

Arab League Center, Cairo, and Emblem — A71

Litho. & Photo.

1966, Mar. 22 *Perf. 11*

300 A71 20m car, emer & blk .35 .35
301 A71 55m brt bl, ver & blk 1.50 .65

Issued to publicize the Arab League.

Souvenir Sheet

WHO Headquarters, Geneva, and Emblem — A72

1966, May 3 Litho. *Imperf.*

302 A72 50m multicolored 9.50 *15.00*

Inauguration of the WHO headquarters. See Nos. C55-C57.

Tuareg and Camel — A73

A74

Three Tuareg Riders A75

Design: 20m, like 10m, facing left.

1966, June 20 Unwmk. *Perf. 10*

303 A73 10m bright red 1.25 .80
304 A73 20m ultramarine 2.75 1.50
305 A74 50m multicolored 6.00 4.00
a. Strip of 3, Nos. 303-305 11.00 8.50

Imperf

306 A75 100m multicolored 16.00 16.00

Gazelle
A76

Emblem
A77

Perf. 13x11, 11x13

1966, Aug. 12 **Litho.**

307 A76 5m lt grn, blk & red .50 .25
308 A77 25m multicolored .90 .35
309 A77 65m multicolored 2.50 .65
Nos. 307-309 (3) 3.90 1.25

1st Arab Girl Scout Camp (5m); 7th Arab Boy Scout Camp, Good Daim, Libya, Aug. 12 (25m, 60m).

UNESCO Emblem — A78

1967, Jan. **Litho.** ***Perf. 10x10½***

310 A78 15m multicolored .50 .25
311 A78 25m multicolored 1.10 .45

UNESCO, 20th anniv. (in 1966).

Castle of Columns, Tolemaide — A79

Design: 55m, Sebha Fort, horiz.

Perf. 13x13½, 13½x13

1966, Dec. 24 **Engr.**

312 A79 25m lil, red brn & blk .65 .35
313 A79 55m blk, lil & red brn 1.25 .65

Fair Emblem — A80

1967, Feb. 28 **Photo.** ***Perf. 11½***

314 A80 15m multicolored .65 .25
315 A80 55m multicolored 1.00 .55

6th Intl. Fair, Tripoli, Feb. 28-Mar. 20.

Oil Tanker, Marsa Al Hariga Terminal
A81

1967, Feb. 14 **Litho.** ***Perf. 10***

316 A81 60m multicolored 2.25 .75

Opening of Marsa Al Hariga oil terminal.

Tourist Year Emblem — A82

1967, May 1 **Litho.** ***Perf. 10½x10***

317 A82 5m gray, blk & brt bl .25 .25
318 A82 10m lt bl, blk & brt bl .25 .25
319 A82 45m pink, blk & brt bl .75 .35
Nos. 317-319 (3) 1.25 .85

International Tourist Year.

Map of Mediterranean and Runners — A83

1967, Sept. 8 **Litho.** ***Perf. 10½***

320 A83 5m shown .25 .25
321 A83 10m Javelin .25 .25
322 A83 15m Bicyling .25 .25
323 A83 45m Soccer .75 .55
324 A83 75m Boxing 1.10 .75
Nos. 320-324 (5) 2.60 2.05

5th Mediterranean Games, Tunis, Sept. 8-17.

A84

Arab League emblem and hands reaching for knowledge.

1967, Oct. 1 **Litho.** ***Perf. 12½x13***

325 A84 5m orange & dk pur .25 .25
326 A84 10m brt grn & dk pur .25 .25
327 A84 15m lilac & dk pur .25 .25
328 A84 25m blue & dk pur .50 .25
Nos. 325-328 (4) 1.25 1.00

Literacy campaign.

Human Rights Flame — A85

1968, Jan. 15 **Litho.** ***Perf. 13½x14***

329 A85 15m grn & vermilion .35 .25
330 A85 60m org & vio bl .90 .55

International Human Rights Year.

Map, Derrick, Plane and Camel Riders — A86

1968, Feb. 28 **Photo.** ***Perf. 11½***

331 A86 55m car rose, brn & yel 1.25 .75

7th Intl. Fair, Tripoli, Feb. 28-Mar. 20.

Arab League Emblem — A87

1968, Mar. 22 **Engr.** ***Perf. 13½***

332 A87 10m blue gray & car .25 .25
333 A87 45m fawn & green .90 .65

Issued for Arab League Week.

Children, Statuary Group — A88

Children's Day: 55m, Mother and children.

1968, Mar. 21 **Litho.** ***Perf. 11***

334 A88 25m gray, blk & mag .65 .35
335 A88 55m gray & multi 1.25 .65

Hands Reaching for WHO Emblem — A89

1968, Apr. 7 **Photo.** ***Perf. 13½x14½***

336 A89 25m rose cl, dk bl & gray bl .60 .25
337 A89 55m bl, blk & gray .90 .55

WHO, 20th anniversary.

From Oil Field to Tanker — A90

1968, Apr. 23 **Litho.** ***Perf. 11***

338 A90 10m multicolored .50 .25
339 A90 60m multicolored 1.50 .80

Opening of the Zueitina oil terminal.

Teacher and Crowd — A91

1968, Sept. 8 **Litho.** ***Perf. 13½***

340 A91 5m bright pink .25 .25
341 A91 10m orange .25 .25
342 A91 15m blue .25 .25
343 A91 20m emerald .50 .50
Nos. 340-343 (4) 1.25 1.25

Literacy campaign.

Arab Labor Emblem — A92

1968, Nov. 3 **Photo.** ***Perf. 14x13½***

344 A92 10m multicolored .25 .25
345 A92 15m multicolored .50 .25

4th session of the Arab Labor Ministers' Conf., Tripoli, Nov. 3-10.

Wadi el Kuf Bridge and Road Sign — A93

1968, Dec. 25 **Litho.** ***Perf. 11x11½***

346 A93 25m ultra & multi .40 .35
347 A93 60m emer & multi 1.00 .90

Opening of the Wadi el Kuf Bridge.

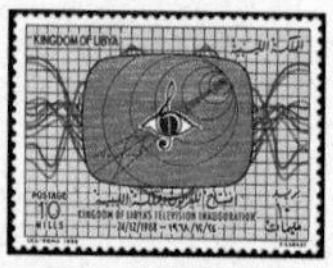

Television Screen and Chart — A94

1968, Dec. 25 **Photo.** ***Perf. 14x13½***

348 A94 10m yellow & multi .25 .25
349 A94 30m lilac & multi .90 .45

Inauguration of television service, Dec. 24.

Melons — A95

1969, Jan. **Photo.** ***Perf. 11½***

Granite Paper

350 A95 5m shown .25 .25
351 A95 10m Peanuts .25 .25
352 A95 15m Lemons .25 .25
353 A95 20m Oranges .40 .25
354 A95 25m Peaches .65 .35
355 A95 35m Pears 1.25 .55
Nos. 350-355 (6) 3.05 1.90

Nos. 350-355 with "Kingdom of Libya" in both English and Arabic blocked out with a blue felt-tipped pen were issued in December, 1971, by the Republic.

Tripoli Fair Emblem — A96

1969, Apr. 8 **Granite Paper**

356 A96 25m silver & multi .40 .25
357 A96 35m bronze & multi .65 .35
358 A96 40m gold & multi .75 .45
Nos. 356-358 (3) 1.80 1.05

8th Intl. Fair, Tripoli, Mar. 6-26.

Weather Balloon and Observer — A97

1969, Mar. 23 **Photo.** ***Perf. 14x13***

359 A97 60m gray & multi 1.50 .80

World Meteorological Day, Mar. 23.

Cogwheel and Workers — A98

1969, Mar. 29 **Litho.** ***Perf. 13½***

360 A98 15m blue & multi .25 .25
361 A98 55m salmon & multi .75 .55

10th anniversary of Social Insurance.

ILO Emblem — A99

1969, June 1 **Photo.** ***Perf. 14***

362 A99 10m bl grn, blk & lt ol .25 .25
363 A99 60m car rose, blk & lt ol .90 .65

ILO, 50th anniversary.

African Tourist Year Emblem
A100

1969, July ***Perf. 11½***

Emblem in Emerald, Light Blue & Red

364 A100 15m emer & silver .45 .25
365 A100 30m blk & gold .90 .65

Issued to publicize African Tourist Year.

Libyan Arab Republic

Soldiers, Tanks and Planes — A101

1969, Dec. 7 **Photo.** ***Perf. 12x12½***

366 A101 5m org & multi .45 .25
367 A101 10m ultra & multi .70 .40
368 A101 15m multicolored 1.00 .50
369 A101 25m multicolored 1.50 .70

370 A101 45m brt bl & multi 1.75 1.10
371 A101 60m multicolored 3.00 1.50
Nos. 366-371 (6) 8.40 4.45

Establishment of the Libyan Arab Republic, Sept. 1, 1969. See Nos. 379-384.

Dish Antenna, Flags and Carrier Pigeon — A102

1970, Mar. 1 Photo. *Perf. 11½*
Granite Paper

372 A102 15m multicolored .70 .25
373 A102 20m multicolored 1.10 .40
374 A102 25m multicolored 1.50 .50
375 A102 40m multicolored 2.10 1.10
Nos. 372-375 (4) 5.40 2.25

Map of Arab League Countries, Flag and Emblem A102a

1970, Mar. 22

376 A102a 10m lt bl, brn & grn .35 .25
377 A102a 15m org, brn & grn .60 .25
378 A102a 20m ol, brn & grn 1.00 .45
Nos. 376-378 (3) 1.95 .95

25th anniversary of the Arab League.

Type A101 Redrawn — A103

1970, May 2 Photo. *Perf. 12x12½*

379 A103 5m org & multi .40 .25
380 A103 10m ultra & multi .70 .60
381 A103 15m multicolored 1.00 .50
382 A103 25m multicolored 1.50 1.40
383 A103 45m brt bl & multi 1.75 1.10
384 A103 60m multicolored 3.00 1.50
Nos. 379-384 (6) 8.35 5.35

On Nos. 379-384 the numerals are in black, the bottom inscription is in 2 lines and several other changes.

Inauguration of UPU Headquarters, Bern — A104

1970, May 20 Photo. *Perf. 11½x11*

385 A104 10m multicolored .25 .25
386 A104 25m multicolored .60 .25
387 A104 60m multicolored 1.25 .65
Nos. 385-387 (3) 2.10 1.15

Arms of Libyan Arab Republic — A105

1970, June 20 Photo. *Perf. 11*

388 A105 15m black & brt rose .25 .25
389 A105 25m vio bl, yel & brt rose .50 .25
390 A105 45m emer, yel & brt rose 1.75 .45
Nos. 388-390 (3) 2.50 .95

Evacuation of US military base in Libya.

Flags, Soldiers and Tank — A106

1970, Sept. 1 Photo. *Perf. 11x11½*

391 A106 20m multicolored .75 .25
392 A106 25m multicolored 1.00 .55
393 A106 30m blue & multi 1.60 .75
Nos. 391-393 (3) 3.35 1.55

Libyan Arab Republic, 1st anniv.

UN Emblem, Dove and Scales — A107

1970, Oct. 24 Photo. *Perf. 11x11½*

394 A107 5m org & multi .60 .35
395 A107 10m olive & multi .90 .45
396 A107 60m multicolored 2.50 .90
Nos. 394-396 (3) 4.00 1.70

25th anniversary of the United Nations.

Map and Flags of UAR, Libya, Sudan — A107a

1970, Dec. 27 Photo. *Perf. 11½*

397 A107a 15m lt grn, car & blk 7.00 2.25

Signing of the Charter of Tripoli affirming the unity of UAR, Libya and the Sudan, Dec. 27, 1970.

UN Emblem, Dove and Globe — A108

1971, Jan. 10 Litho. *Perf. 12x11½*

398 A108 15m multicolored .60 .25
399 A108 20m multicolored .90 .45
400 A108 60m lt vio & multi 2.50 .90
Nos. 398-400 (3) 4.00 1.60

UN declaration on granting of independence to colonial countries and peoples, 10th anniv.

Education Year Emblem — A109

1971, Jan. 16

401 A109 5m red, blk & ocher .25 .25
402 A109 10m red, blk & emer .60 .55
403 A109 20m red, blk & vio bl 1.60 .80
Nos. 401-403 (3) 2.45 1.60

International Education Year.

Al Fatah Fighter — A110

1971, Mar. 14 Photo. *Perf. 11*

404 A110 5m ol & multi .50 .25
405 A110 10m yel & multi .80 .25
406 A110 100m multicolored 1.90 .25
Nos. 404-406 (3) 3.20 .75

Fight for the liberation of Palestine.

Tripoli Fair Emblem — A111

1971, Mar. 18 Litho. *Perf. 14*

407 A111 15m multicolored .35 .25
408 A111 30m org & multi .90 .45

9th International Fair at Tripoli.

10th Anniv. of OPEC — A112

1971, May 29 Litho. *Perf. 12*

409 A112 10m yellow & brown .25 .25
410 A112 70m pink & vio bl 1.60 .65

Globe and Waves — A113

1971, June 10 *Perf. 14½x13½*

411 A113 25m brt grn, blk & vio bl .50 .25
412 A113 35m gray & multi 1.25 1.00

3rd World Telecommunications Day, May 17, 1971.

Map of Africa and Telecommunications Network — A114

1971, June 10

413 A114 5m yel, blk & grn .25 .25
414 A114 15m dl bl, blk & grn .40 .25

Pan-African telecommunications system.

Torchbearer and Banner — A115

1971, June 15 Photo. *Perf. 11½x12*

415 A115 5m yel & multi .25 .25
416 A115 10m org & multi .35 .35
417 A115 15m multicolored .50 .45
Nos. 415-417 (3) 1.10 1.05

Evacuation of US military base, 1st anniv.

Ramadan Suehli — A116

1971, Aug. 24 *Perf. 14x14½*

418 A116 15m multicolored .25 .25
419 A116 55m bl & multi 1.00 .55

Ramadan Suehli (1879-1920), freedom fighter.

See Nos. 422-423, 426-427, 439-440, 479-480.

Date Palm — A117

1971, Sept. 1

420 A117 5m multicolored .25 .25
421 A117 15m multicolored 1.25 1.25

Sept. 1, 1969 Revolution, 2nd anniv.

Portrait Type of 1971

Portrait: Omar el Mukhtar (1858-1931), leader of the Martyrs.

1971, Sept. 16 *Perf. 14x14½*

422 A116 5m lt grn & multi .25 .25
423 A116 100m multicolored 2.50 1.50

Gamal Abdel Nasser (1918-1970), President of Egypt — A118

1971, Sept. 28 Photo. *Perf. 11x11½*

424 A118 5m lil, grn & blk .35 .25
425 A118 15m grn, lil & blk 1.25 .25

Portrait Type of 1971

Ibrahim Usta Omar (1908-50), patriotic poet.

1971, Oct. 8 Litho. *Perf. 14x14½*

426 A116 25m vio bl & multi .60 .60
427 A116 30m multicolored 1.10 .45

Racial Equality Emblem — A119

1971, Oct. 24 *Perf. 13½x14½*

428 A119 25m multicolored .60 .25
429 A119 35m multicolored 1.10 .45

Intl. Year Against Racial Discrimination.

Arab Postal Union Emblem — A120

1971, Nov. 6 Litho. *Perf. 14½*
Emblem in Black, Yellow and Blue

430 A120 5m red .25 .25
431 A120 10m violet .40 .25
432 A120 15m bright rose lilac .40 .25
Nos. 430-432 (3) 1.05 .75

Conference of Sofar, Lebanon, establishing Arab Postal Union, 25th anniv.

Postal Union Emblem and Letter — A121

25m, 55m, APU emblem, letter and dove.

1971, Dec. Photo. *Perf. 11½x11*

433 A121 10m org brn, bl & blk .35 .25
434 A121 15m org, lt bl & blk .50 .35
435 A121 25m lt grn, org & blk .75 .55
436 A121 55m lt brn, yel & blk 1.60 .70
Nos. 433-436 (4) 3.20 1.85

10th anniversary of African Postal Union. Issued: 25m, 55m, 12/2; 10m, 15m, 12/12.

Despite the change from milliemes to dirhams in 1972, both currencies appear on stamps until August.

Book Year Emblem — A122

1972, Jan. 1 Litho. *Perf. 12½x13*

437 A122 15m ultra, brn, gold & blk .35 .35
438 A122 20m gold, brn, ultra & blk .60 .60

International Book Year.

Portrait Type of 1971

Ahmed Gnaba (1898-1968), poet of unity.

1972, Jan. 12 *Perf. 14x14½*

439 A116 20m red & multi .60 .25
440 A116 35m olive & multi .85 .45

Coat of Arms — A123

1972, Feb. 10 Photo. *Perf. 14½*
Size: 19x23mm

441 A123 5m gray & multi .25 .25
442 A123 10m lt ol & multi .25 .25
443 A123 15d lilac & multi .25 .25
445 A123 25m lt bl & multi .25 .25
446 A123 30m rose & multi .35 .25
447 A123 35m lt ol & multi .45 .25
448 A123 40m dl yel & multi .60 .25
449 A123 45m lt grn & multi .75 .35
451 A123 55m multicolored 1.00 .50
452 A123 60m bister & multi 1.90 .65
453 A123 65d multicolored .75 .55
454 A123 70d lt vio & multi 1.00 .65
455 A123 80d ocher & multi 1.50 .80
456 A123 90m bl & multi 1.90 .90

Size: 27x32mm
Perf. 14x14½

457 A123 100d multicolored 2.25 1.20
458 A123 200d multicolored 3.75 2.25
459 A123 500d multicolored 9.50 6.50
460 A123 £1 multicolored 17.50 11.00
Nos. 441-460 (18) 44.20 27.10

During the transition from millimemes and pounds to dirhams and dinars, stamps were issued in both currencies.

A124

A124a

A124b

Coil Stamps

1972, July 27 Photo. *Perf. 14½x14*

461 A124 5m sl bl, ocher & black 2.75 2.25
462 A124a 20m bl, lil & blk 12.00 2.25
463 A124b 50m bl, ol & blk 27.50 5.50
Nos. 461-463 (3) 42.25 10.00

See Nos. 496-498, 575-577.

Tombs at Ghirza — A125

Designs: 10m, Kufic inscription, Agedabia, horiz. 15m, Marcus Aurelius Arch, Tripoli. 25m, Exchange of weapons, mural from Wan Amil Cave. 55m, Garamanthian (Berber) chariot, petroglyph, Wadi Zigza. 70m, Nymph Cyrene strangling a lion, bas-relief, Cyrene.

1972, Feb. 15 Litho. *Perf. 14*

464 A125 5m lilac & multi .50 .50
465 A125 10m multicolored .50 .50
466 A125 15m dp org & multi 1.00 .35
467 A125 25m emer & multi 1.50 .90
468 A125 55m scar & multi 3.50 .90
469 A125 70m ultra & multi 7.00 1.25
Nos. 464-469 (6) 14.00 4.40

Fair Emblem — A126

1972, Mar. 1

470 A126 25d gray & multi .60 .25
471 A126 35d multicolored .65 .25
472 A126 50d multicolored 1.40 .35
473 A126 70d multicolored 1.60 .60
Nos. 470-473 (4) 4.25 1.45

10th International Fair at Tripoli.

Dissected Arm, and Heart — A127

1972, Apr. 7 *Perf. 14½*

474 A127 15d multicolored 1.50 .45
475 A127 25d multicolored 3.25 1.00

"Your heart is your health," World Health Day.

"Arab Unity" — A128

Litho. & Engr.

1972, Apr. 17 *Perf. 13½x13*

476 A128 15d bl, yel & blk .25 .25
477 A128 20d lt grn, yel & blk .60 .25
478 A128 25d lt ver, yel & blk 1.25 .80
Nos. 476-478 (3) 2.10 1.30

Fed. of Arab Republics Foundation, 1st anniv.

Portrait Type of 1971

Suleiman el Baruni (1870-1940), patriotic writer.

1972, May 1 Litho. *Perf. 14x14½*

479 A116 10m yellow & multi 1.25 .80
480 A116 70m dp org & multi 2.00 1.00

Environment Emblem — A129

1972, Aug. 15 Litho. *Perf. 14½*

481 A129 15m red & multi .60 .25
482 A129 55m green & multi 1.40 .40

UN Conference on Human Environment, Stockholm, June 5-16.

Olympic Emblems — A130

1972, Aug. 26

483 A130 25d brt bl & multi 2.00 .60
484 A130 35d red & multi 3.00 1.25

20th Olympic Games, Munich, 8/26-9/11.

Emblem and Broken Chain — A131

1972, Oct. 1 Litho. *Perf. 14x13½*

485 A131 15d blue & multi .40 .25
486 A131 25d yellow & multi .90 .35

Libyan Arab Republic, 3rd anniv.

Dome of the Rock, Jerusalem — A132

1972 *Perf. 12½x13*

487 A132 10d multicolored .40 .25
488 A132 25d multicolored .60 .25

Nicolaus Copernicus (1473-1543), Polish Astronomer — A133

Design: 25d, Copernicus in Observatory, by Jan Matejko, horiz.

Perf. 14½x13½, 13½x14½

1973, Feb. 26

489 A133 15d yellow & multi .40 .25
490 A133 25d blue & multi .60 .35

Eagle and Fair Buildings — A134

1973, Mar. 1 *Perf. 13½x14½*

491 A134 5d dull red & multi .40 .25
492 A134 10d blue grn & multi .60 .25
493 A134 15d vio blue & multi 1.25 .25
Nos. 491-493 (3) 2.25 .75

11th International Fair at Tripoli.

Blind Person, Books, Loom and Basket — A135

1973, Apr. 18 Photo. *Perf. 12x11½*

494 A135 20d gray & multi 8.25 1.60
495 A135 25d dull yel & multi 12.00 5.25

Role of the blind in society.

Numeral Type of 1972
Denominations in Dirhams

A135a

A135b

A135c

Coil Stamps

1973, Apr. 26 Photo. *Perf. 14½x14*

496 A135a 5d sl bl, ocher & blk 1.00 1.00
497 A135b 20d blue, lilac & blk 1.50 1.50
498 A135c 50d blue, olive & blk 5.50 5.50
Nos. 496-498 (3) 8.00 8.00

Map of Africa — A136

1973, May 25 Photo. *Perf. 11x11½*

499 A136 15d yel, green & brown .50 .25
500 A136 25d lt yel grn, grn & blk 1.00 .50

"Freedom in Unity" (Org. for African Unity).

INTERPOL Emblem and General Secretariat, Paris — A138

Perf. 13½x14½

1973, June 30 Litho.

501 A138 10d lilac & multi .25 .25
502 A138 15d ocher & multi .50 .25
503 A138 25d lt grn & multi .75 .25
Nos. 501-503 (3) 1.50 .75

50th anniv. of Intl. Criminal Police Org.

Map of Libya, Houses, People, Factories, Tractor — A139

1973, July 15 Photo. *Perf. 11½*

504 A139 10d rose red, black & ultra 4.25 .85
505 A139 25d ultra, blk & grn 6.00 1.90
506 A139 35d grn, blk & org 11.50 3.75
Nos. 504-506 (3) 21.75 6.50

General census.

World Meteorological Organization Emblem — A140

1973, Aug. 1 *Perf. 12½x11*

507 A140 5d ver, blk & bl .25 .25
508 A140 10d yel grn, blk & bl .50 .50

Intl. meteorological cooperation, cent.

Soccer A141

1973, Aug. 10 Photo. *Perf. 11½*

509 A141 5d yel grn & dk brn .50 .25
510 A141 25d orange & dk brn 1.10 .70

2nd Palestinian Cup Soccer Tournament.

Torch and Grain — A142

1973, Sept. 1 Litho. *Perf. 14*

511 A142 15d brown & multi .50 .25
512 A142 25d emer & multi 1.40 .25

4th anniv. of Sept. 1 Revolution.

Writing Hand, Lamp and Globe — A143

1973, Sept. 8

513 A143 25d multicolored .60 .60

Literacy campaign.

Gate of First City Hall — A144

1973, Sept. 18 *Perf. 13*

514 A144 10d shown .50 .50
515 A144 25d Khondok fountain .60 .60
516 A144 35d Clock tower .90 .35
Nos. 514-516 (3) 2.00 1.45

Centenary of Tripoli as a municipality.

Militia, Flag and Factories — A145

1973, Oct. 7 Photo. *Perf. 11½x11*

517 A145 15d yel, blk & red .50 .25
518 A145 25d green & multi .75 .35

Libyan Militia.

Revolutionary Proclamation by Khadafy — A146

70d, as 25d, with English inscription.

1973, Oct. 15 Litho. *Perf. 12½*

519 A146 25d orange & multi .50 .50
520 A146 70d green & multi 1.50 .75

Proclamation of People's Revolution by Pres. Muammar Khadafy.

FAO Emblem, Camel Pulling Plow — A147

1973, Nov. 1 Photo. *Perf. 11*

521 A147 10d ocher & multi .25 .25
522 A147 25d dk brn & multi .50 .50
523 A147 35d black & multi .75 .35
Nos. 521-523 (3) 1.50 1.10

World Food Org., 10th anniv.

Human Rights Flame — A148

1973, Dec. 20 Photo. *Perf. 11x11½*

524 A148 25d pur, car & dk bl .35 .35
525 A148 70d lt grn, car & dk bl 1.50 .65

Universal Declaration of Human Rights, 25th anniv.

Fish — A149

Designs: Various fish from Libyan waters.

1973, Dec. 31 Photo. *Perf. 14x13½*

526 A149 5d light blue & multi .65 .50
527 A149 10d light blue & multi 1.25 .45
528 A149 15d light blue & multi 1.90 .55
529 A149 20d light blue & multi 2.75 .60
530 A149 25d light blue & multi 5.25 1.50
Nos. 526-530 (5) 11.80 3.60

1975, Jan. 5

526a A149 5d greenish blue & multi 2.25 1.50
527a A149 10d greenish blue & multi 4.50 1.50
528a A149 15d greenish blue & multi 4.50 1.50
529a A149 20d greenish blue & multi 6.50 .75
530a A149 25d greenish blue & multi 8.50 2.75
Nos. 526a-530a (5) 26.25 8.00

Scout, Sun and Scout Signs — A150

1974, Feb. 1 Litho. *Perf. 11½*

531 A150 5d lt blue & multi 1.25 .40
532 A150 20d rose lil & multi 3.50 .65
533 A150 25d turq grn & multi 5.75 2.60
Nos. 531-533 (3) 10.50 3.65

Libyan Boy Scouts.

Fair Emblem, Flags of Participants — A151

1974, Mar. 1 Litho. *Perf. 12x11½*

534 A151 10d lt ultra & multi .65 .40
535 A151 25d tan & multi 1.00 .55
536 A151 35d lt green & multi 1.90 .25
Nos. 534-536 (3) 3.55 1.20

12th Tripoli International Fair.

Protected Family, WHO Emblem — A152

1974, Apr. 7 Litho. *Perf. 12½*

537 A152 5d lt green & multi .35 .25
538 A152 25d red & multi .60 .60

World Health Day.

Minaret and Star — A153

1974, Apr. 16 *Perf. 11½x11*

539 A153 10d pink & multi .50 .50
540 A153 25d yellow & multi 1.00 .60
541 A153 35d orange & multi 1.40 .50
Nos. 539-541 (3) 2.90 1.60

City University of Bengazi, inauguration.

UPU Emblem and Star — A154

1974, May 22 Litho. *Perf. 13½x14½*

542 A154 25d multicolored 7.50 1.10
543 A154 70d multicolored 14.00 2.25

Centenary of Universal Postal Union.

Traffic Signs — A156

1974, June 8 Photo. *Perf. 11*

547 A156 5d gold & multi .25 .25
548 A156 10d gold & multi .40 .25
549 A156 25d gold & multi .50 .25
Nos. 547-549 (3) 1.15 .75

Automobile and Touring Club of Libya.

Tank, Oil Refinery, Book — A157

Symbolic "5" A158

1974, Sept. 1 Litho. *Perf. 14*

550 A157 5d red & multi .25 .25
551 A157 20d violet & multi .40 .40
552 A157 25d vio bl & multi .40 .40
553 A157 35d green & multi .50 .50
Nos. 550-553 (4) 1.55 1.55

Souvenir Sheet

Perf. 13

554 A158 55d yel & maroon 9.50 9.50

Revolution of Sept. 1, 5th anniv. English inscription on No. 554.

WPY Emblem and Crowd — A159

1974, Oct. 19 *Perf. 14*

555 A159 25d multicolored .35 .25
556 A159 35d lt brn & multi .75 .60

World Population Year.

Libyan Woman — A160

Libyan Costumes: 10d, 15d, Women. 20d, Old man. 25d, Man riding camel. 50d, Man on horseback.

1975, Mar. 1 Litho. *Perf. 13x12½*

557 A160 5d org yel & multi .25 .25
558 A160 10d org yel & multi .25 .25
559 A160 15d org yel & multi .50 .25
560 A160 20d org yel & multi .75 .25
561 A160 25d org yel & multi 1.50 .75
562 A160 50d org yel & multi 2.75 .75
Nos. 557-562 (6) 6.00 2.50

Congress Emblem — A161

1975, Mar. 4 Litho. *Perf. 12x12½*

563 A161 10d brown & multi .25 .25
564 A161 25d vio & multi .40 .40
565 A161 35d gray & multi .75 .25
Nos. 563-565 (3) 1.40 .90

Arab Labor Congress.

Teacher Pointing to Blackboard A162

1975, Mar. 10 *Perf. 11½*

566 A162 10d gold & multi .25 .25
567 A162 25d gold & multi .50 .25

Teacher's Day.

Bodies, Globe, Proclamation — A163

1975, Apr. 7 Litho. *Perf. 12½*

568 A163 20d lilac & multi .40 .40
569 A163 25d emer & multi .50 .25

World Health Day.

Woman and Man in Library — A164

1975, May 25 Litho. *Perf. 12½*

570 A164 10d bl grn & multi .25 .25
571 A164 25d olive & multi .50 .50
572 A164 35d lt vio & multi .60 .60
Nos. 570-572 (3) 1.35 1.35

Libyan Arab Book Exhibition.

Festival Emblem — A165

1975, July 5 Litho. *Perf. 13x12½*

573 A165 20d lt bl & multi .40 .40
574 A165 25d orange & multi .50 .50

2nd Arab Youth Festival.

Redrawn Type of 1973 Without "LAR"

Coil Stamps

1975, Aug. 15 Photo. *Perf. 14½x14*

575 A124 5d blue, org & blk .50 .50
576 A124 20d blue, yel & blk 1.00 1.00
577 A124 50d blue, grn & blk 2.00 2.00
Nos. 575-577 (3) 3.50 3.50

Games Emblem and Arms — A166

1975, Aug. 23 *Perf. 13x12½*

578 A166 10d salmon & multi .25 .25
579 A166 25d lilac & multi .50 .50
580 A166 50d yellow & multi 1.40 .40
Nos. 578-580 (3) 2.15 1.15

7th Mediterranean Games, Algiers, 8/23-9/6.

Peace Dove, Symbols of Agriculture and Industry — A167

Khadafy's Head Over Desert — A168

Design: 70d, Peace dove, diff.

1975, Sept. Litho. *Perf. 13x12½*

581 A167 25d multicolored .40 .25
582 A167 70d multicolored 1.40 .50

Souvenir Sheet

Imperf

Litho. & Embossed

583 A168 100d multicolored 6.00 6.00

6th anniversary of Sept. 1 revolution. No. 583 contains one stamp with simulated perforations.

Khalil Basha Mosque A169

Al Kharruba Mosque A170

Mosques: 10d, Sidi Abdulla El Shaab. 15d, Sidi Ali El Fergani. 25d, Katikhtha. 30d, Murad Agha. 35d, Maulai Mohammed.

1975, Dec. 13 Litho. *Perf. 12½*

584 A169 5d gray & multi .25 .25
585 A169 10d purple & multi .25 .25
586 A169 15d green & multi .25 .25
587 A170 20d ocher & multi .40 .25
588 A170 25d multicolored .40 .25
589 A170 30d multicolored .50 .25
590 A170 35d lilac & multi .75 .60
Nos. 584-590 (7) 2.80 2.10

Mohammed's 1405th birthday.

Arms of Libya and People — A171

1976, Jan. 15 Photo. *Perf. 13*

591 A171 35d blue & multi .50 .25
592 A171 40d multicolored .60 .25

General National (People's) Congress.

Islamic - Christian Dialogue Emblem — A172

1976, Feb. 5 Litho. *Perf. 13x12½*

593 A172 40d gold & multi .60 .25
594 A172 115d gold & multi 1.90 .90

Seminar of Islamic-Christian Dialogue, Tripoli, Feb. 1-5.

Woman Blowing Horn — A173

National Costumes: 20d, Lancer. 30d, Drummer. 40d, Bagpiper. 100d, Woman carrying jug on head.

1976, Mar. 1 Litho. *Perf. 13x12½*

595 A173 10d multicolored .25 .25
596 A173 20d multicolored .50 .40
597 A173 30d pink & multi 1.00 .25
598 A173 40d multicolored 1.25 .25
599 A173 100d yel & multi 3.00 .50
Nos. 595-599 (5) 6.00 1.65

14th Tripoli International Fair.

Telephones, 1876 and 1976, ITU and UPU Emblems — A174

70d, Alexander Graham Bell, telephone, satellites, radar, ITU & UPU emblems.

1976, Mar. 10 Photo. *Perf. 13*

600 A174 40d multicolored 2.50 .80
  a. Souvenir sheet of 4 10.00 10.00
601 A174 70d multicolored 4.00 .80
  a. Souvenir sheet of 4 16.50 16.50

Centenary of first telephone call by Alexander Graham Bell, Mar. 10, 1876.

Nos. 600a and 601a exist imperf. Value, both sheets $100.

Mother and Child — A175

1976, Mar. 21 *Perf. 12*

602 A175 85d gray & multi 1.50 1.25
603 A175 110d pink & multi 1.60 1.50

International Children's Day.

Hands, Eye and Head — A176

1976, Apr. 7 Photo. *Perf. 13½x13*

604 A176 30d multicolored .35 .35
605 A176 35d multicolored .50 .50
606 A176 40d multicolored .60 .60
Nos. 604-606 (3) 1.45 1.45

"Foresight prevents blindness;" World Health Day.

Little Bittern — A177

Birds of Libya: 10d, Great gray shrike. 15d, Songbird. 20d, European bee-eater, vert. 25d, Hoopoe.

Perf. 13x13½, 13½x13

1976, May 1 Litho.

607 A177 5d orange & multi .65 .50
608 A177 10d ultra & multi 1.40 1.10
609 A177 15d rose & multi 2.75 1.40
610 A177 20d yellow & multi 4.75 1.50
611 A177 25d blue & multi 9.50 2.75
Nos. 607-611 (5) 19.05 7.25

Al Barambekh — A178

Designs: 15d, Whale, horiz. 30d, Lizard (alwaral), horiz. 40d, Mastodon skull, horiz. 70d, Hawk. 115d, Wild mountain sheep.

1976, June 20 Litho. *Perf. 12½*

612 A178 10d multicolored 1.40 1.10
613 A178 15d multicolored 2.50 1.90
614 A178 30d multicolored 3.00 2.40
615 A178 40d multicolored 5.00 4.25
616 A178 70d multicolored 8.75 7.25
617 A178 115d multicolored 14.50 12.25
Nos. 612-617 (6) 35.15 29.15

Museum of Natural History.

Bicycling — A179

1976, July 17 Litho. *Perf. 12x11½*

Granite Paper

618 A179 15d shown .25 .25
619 A179 25d Boxing .50 .50
620 A179 70d Soccer 1.50 1.50
Nos. 618-620 (3) 2.25 2.25

Souvenir Sheet

621 A179 150d Symbolic of various sports 16.00 16.00

21st Olympic Games, Montreal, Canada, July 17-Aug. 1.

Tree Growing from Globe — A180

1976, Aug. 9 *Perf. 13*

622 A180 115d multicolored 1.25 .90

5th Conference of Non-Aligned Countries, Colombo, Sri Lanka, Aug. 9-19.

Beginning with No. 622 numerous issues are printed with multiple coats of arms in pale green on back of stamps.

Symbols of Agriculture and Industry — A181

Drummer and Pipeline A182

1976, Sept. 1 *Perf. 14½x14*

623 A181 30d yel & multi .40 .25
624 A181 40d multicolored .50 .25
625 A181 100d multicolored 1.25 .90
Nos. 623-625 (3) 2.15 1.40

Souvenir Sheet

Perf. 13

626 A182 200d multicolored 6.00 6.00

Sept. 1 Revolution, 7th anniv.

Sports, Torch and Emblems — A183

145d, Symbolic wrestlers and various emblems.

1976, Oct. 6 Litho. *Perf. 13*

627 A183 15d multicolored .25 .25
628 A183 30d multicolored .35 .35
629 A183 100d multicolored 1.60 .90
Nos. 627-629 (3) 2.20 1.50

Souvenir Sheet

630 A183 145d multi, horiz. 4.50 4.50

5th Arab Games, Damascus, Syria.

Chess Board, Rook, Knight, Emblem — A184

1976, Oct. 24 Photo. *Perf. 11½*

631 A184 15d pink & multi 2.10 .45
632 A184 30d buff & multi 3.50 1.00
633 A184 100d multicolored 10.50 2.00
Nos. 631-633 (3) 16.10 3.45

The "Against" (protest) Chess Olympiad, Tripoli, Oct. 24-Nov. 15.

A185

Designs: Various local flowers.

1976, Nov. 1 Photo. *Perf. 11½*

Granite Paper

634 A185 15d lilac & multi .35 .35
635 A185 20d multicolored .35 .35
636 A185 35d yellow & multi .80 .25
637 A185 40d salmon & multi 1.25 .35
638 A185 70d multicolored 3.00 .50
Nos. 634-638 (5) 5.75 1.80

International Archives Council Emblem and Document — A186

1976, Nov. 10 Litho. *Perf. 13x13½*

639 A186 15d brown, org & buff .25 .25
640 A186 35d brn, brt grn & buff .35 .35
641 A186 70d brown, blue & buff .75 .75
Nos. 639-641 (3) 1.35 1.35

Arab Regional Branch of International Council on Archives, Baghdad.

Holy Ka'aba and Pilgrims — A187

1976, Dec. 12 Litho. *Perf. 14*

642 A187 15d multicolored .25 .25
643 A187 30d multicolored .25 .25
644 A187 70d multicolored .80 .80
645 A187 100d multicolored 1.00 1.00
Nos. 642-645 (4) 2.30 2.30

Pilgrimage to Mecca.

Numeral — A188

Coil Stamps

1977, Jan. 15 Photo. *Perf. 14½x14*

646 A188 5d multicolored .25 .25
647 A188 20d multicolored .35 .35
648 A188 50d multicolored .90 .90
Nos. 646-648 (3) 1.50 1.50

Covered Basket — A189

Designs: 20d, Leather bag. 30d, Vase. 40d, Embroidered slippers. 50d, Ornate saddle. 100d, Horse with saddle and harness.

1977, Mar. 1 Litho. ***Perf. 12½x12***

649	A189	10d	multicolored	.25	.25
650	A189	20d	multicolored	.25	.25
651	A189	30d	multicolored	.35	.25
652	A189	40d	multicolored	.60	.35
653	A189	50d	multicolored	1.00	.35
			Nos. 649-653 (5)	2.45	1.45

Souvenir Sheet

Imperf

654	A189	100d	multicolored	4.50	4.50

15th Tripoli International Fair. No. 654 contains one stamp 49x53mm with simulated perforations.

Girl and Flowers, UNICEF Emblem — A190

Children's drawings, UNICEF Emblem and: 30d, Clothing store. 40d, Farm yard.

1977, Mar. 28 Litho. ***Perf. 13x13½***

655	A190	10d	multicolored	.35	.25
656	A190	30d	multicolored	.60	.35
657	A190	40d	multicolored	.75	.50
			Nos. 655-657 (3)	1.70	1.10

Children's Day.

Gun, Fighters, UN Headquarters A191

1977, Mar. 13 ***Perf. 13½***

658	A191	15d	multicolored	*.25*	.25
659	A191	25d	multicolored	*.25*	.25
660	A191	70d	multicolored	*1.25*	1.25
			Nos. 658-660 (3)	*1.75*	1.75

Battle of Al-Karamah, 9th anniversary.

Child, Raindrop, WHO Emblem — A192

1977, Apr. 7 Litho. ***Perf. 13x12½***

661	A192	15d	multicolored	.25	.25
662	A192	30d	multicolored	.50	.50

World Health Day.

Arab Postal Union, 25th Anniv. — A193

1977, Apr. 12 ***Perf. 13½***

663	A193	15d	multicolored	.25	.25
664	A193	30d	multicolored	.35	.35
665	A193	40d	multicolored	.50	.50
			Nos. 663-665 (3)	1.10	1.10

Maps of Africa and Libya — A194

1977, May 8 Litho. ***Perf. 14x13½***

666	A194	40d	multicolored	1.50	1.25
667	A194	70d	multicolored	2.25	1.90

African Labor Day.

Map of Libya and Heart — A195

1977, May 10 ***Perf. 14½x14***

668	A195	5d	multicolored	.35	.25
669	A195	10d	multicolored	.50	.35
670	A195	30d	multicolored	1.40	.60
			Nos. 668-670 (3)	2.25	1.20

Libyan Red Crescent Society.

Electronic Tree, ITU Emblem, Satellite and Radar — A196

Electronic Tree, ITU Emblem and: 115d, Communications satellite, Montreal Olympics emblem, boxer on TV screen. 200d, Spacecraft over earth. 300d, Solar system.

1977, May 17 Litho. ***Perf. 13½x13***

671	A196	60d	multicolored	.80	.80
672	A196	115d	multicolored	2.00	2.00
673	A196	200d	multicolored	3.75	3.75
			Nos. 671-673 (3)	6.55	6.55

Souvenir Sheet

674	A196	300d	multicolored	*8.50*	*6.50*

9th World Telecommunications Day. No. 674 contains one stamp 52x35mm.

Nos. 671-673 exist imperf. Value, set $45. They also exist in miniature sheets of 4, perf and imperf. Values: set perf, $100; set imperf, $135.

Plane over Tripoli, Messenger A197

UPU Emblem and: 25d, Concorde, messenger on horseback. 150d, Loading transport plane and messenger riding camel. 300d, Graf Zeppelin LZ127 over Tripoli.

1977, May 17 Litho. ***Perf. 13½***

675	A197	20d	multicolored	.80	.80
676	A197	25d	multicolored	1.75	1.75
677	A197	150d	multicolored	3.50	3.50
			Nos. 675-677 (3)	6.05	6.05

Souvenir Sheet

678	A197	300d	multicolored	*8.50*	*6.50*

UPU centenary (in 1974). No. 678 contains one stamp 52x35mm.

Nos. 675-678 exist imperf. Values: set $45; souvenir sheet, $50. Nos. 675-677 also exist in miniature sheets of 4, perf and imperf. Values: set perf, $60; set imperf, $125.

Mosque — A198

Various Mosques. 50d, 100d, vertical.

1977, June 1 Photo. ***Perf. 14***

679	A198	40d	multicolored	.55	.55
680	A198	50d	multicolored	.80	.80
681	A198	70d	multicolored	1.10	1.10
682	A198	90d	multicolored	1.40	1.40
683	A198	100d	multicolored	1.60	1.60
684	A198	115d	multicolored	2.10	2.10
			Nos. 679-684 (6)	7.55	7.55

Palestinian Archbishop Hilarion Capucci, Jailed by Israel in 1974, Map of Palestine — A199

1977, Aug. 18 Litho. ***Perf. 13½***

687	A199	30d	multicolored	.40	.40
688	A199	40d	multicolored	.55	.55
689	A199	115d	multicolored	2.10	1.00
			Nos. 687-689 (3)	3.05	1.95

Raised Hands, Pylons, Wheel, Buildings — A200

Star and Ornament — A201

1977, Sept. 1 Litho. ***Perf. 13½x12½***

690	A200	15d	multicolored	.25	.25
691	A200	30d	multicolored	.35	.35
692	A200	85d	multicolored	1.25	.60
			Nos. 690-692 (3)	1.85	1.20

Souvenir Sheet

Perf. 12½

693	A201	100d	gold & multi	5.00	3.50

8th anniversary of Sept. 1 Revolution.

Team Handball A202

1977, Oct. 8 ***Perf. 13½***

694	A202	5d	Swimmers, vert.	.25	.25
695	A202	10d	shown	.25	.25
696	A202	15d	Soccer, vert.	.25	.25
697	A202	25d	Table tennis	.75	.75
698	A202	40d	Basketball, vert.	1.60	.90
			Nos. 694-698 (5)	3.10	2.40

7th Arab School Games.

Steeplechase A203

Show Emblem and: 10d, Bedouin on horseback. 15d, Show emblem (Horse and "7"), vert. 45d, Steeplechase. 100d, Hurdles. 115d, Bedouins on horseback.

1977, Oct. 10 ***Perf. 14½***

699	A203	5d	multicolored	.25	.25
700	A203	10d	multicolored	.25	.25
701	A203	15d	multicolored	.35	.35
702	A203	45d	multicolored	.90	.90
703	A203	115d	multicolored	2.00	2.00
			Nos. 699-703 (5)	3.75	3.75

Souvenir Sheet

704	A203	100d	multicolored	4.50	4.50

7th Intl. Turf Championships, Tripoli, Oct. 1977.

Dome of the Rock, Jerusalem — A204

1977, Oct. 14 ***Perf. 14½x14***

705	A204	5d	multicolored	.30	.25
706	A204	10d	multicolored	.45	.25

Palestinian fighters and their families.

"The Green Book" A205

35d, Hands with broken chain holding hook over citadel. 40d, Hands above chaos. 115d, Dove and Green Book rising from Africa, world map.

1977 Litho. ***Perf. 14***

707	A205		Strip of 3	2.75	2.75
a.		35d	multicolored	.35	.35
b.		40d	multicolored	.50	.50
c.		115d	multicolored	1.75	1.75

The Green Book, by Khadafy outlines Libyan democracy. Green descriptive inscription on back beneath gum, in English on 35d, French on 40d, Arabic on 115d.

Emblems A206

1977 ***Perf. 12½x13***

708	A206	5d	multicolored	.60	.25
709	A206	15d	multicolored	.80	.25
710	A206	30d	multicolored	1.10	.35
			Nos. 708-710 (3)	2.50	.85

Standardization Day.

Elephant hunt. — A207

Rock Carvings, Wadi Mathendous, c. 8000 B.C.: 10d, Crocodile and Young. 20d, Giraffe, vert. 30d, Antelope. 40d, Trumpeting elephant.

1978, Jan. 1 ***Perf. 12½x13, 13x12½***

711	A207	10d	multicolored	.25	.25
712	A207	15d	multicolored	.25	.25
713	A207	20d	multicolored	.35	.35
714	A207	30d	multicolored	.60	.60
715	A207	40d	multicolored	1.00	1.00
			Nos. 711-715 (5)	2.45	2.45

Silver Pendant — A208

Silver Jewelry: 10d, Ornamental plate. 20d, Necklace with pendants. 25d, Crescent-shaped brooch. 115d, Armband.

1978, Mar. 1 Litho. ***Perf. 13x12½***

716	A208	5d	multicolored	.25	.25
717	A208	10d	multicolored	.25	.25
718	A208	20d	multicolored	.25	.25
719	A208	25d	multicolored	.25	.25
720	A208	115d	multicolored	1.50	1.50
			Nos. 716-720 (5)	2.50	2.50

Tripoli International Fair.

Emblem, Compass and Lightning — A209

1978, Mar. 10 ***Perf. 13½***

721	A209	30d	multicolored	.50	.50
722	A209	115d	multicolored	2.00	2.00

Arab Cultural Education Organization.

Children's Drawings and UNICEF Emblem — A210

a, Dancing. b, Children with posters. c, Shopping street. d, Playground. e, Bride and attendants.

1978, Mar. 21

723 A210 40d Strip of 5, #a.-e. 7.25 7.25

Children's Day.

Clenched Fist, Made of Bricks — A211

1978, Mar. 22

728 A211 30d multicolored .65 .40
729 A211 115d multicolored 1.50 .70

Determination of Arab people.

Blood Pressure Gauge, WHO Emblem — A212

1978, Apr. 7 ***Perf. 13x12½***

730 A212 30d multicolored .35 .35
731 A212 115d multicolored 1.75 .90

World Health Day, drive against hypertension.

Antenna and ITU Emblem — A213

1978, May 17 Photo. ***Perf. 13½***

732 A213 30d silver & multi .35 .25
733 A213 115d gold & multi 1.50 .65

10th World Telecommunications Day.

Games Emblem — A214

1978, July 13 Litho. ***Perf. 12½***

734 A214 15d multicolored .25 .25
735 A214 30d multicolored .35 .35
736 A214 115d multicolored 1.50 1.50
Nos. 734-736 (3) 2.10 2.10

3rd African Games, Algiers, 1978.

Inauguration of Tripoli International Airport — A215

1978, Aug. 10 Litho. ***Perf. 13½***

737 A215 40d shown .50 .50
738 A215 115d Terminal 2.00 .90

View of Ankara — A216

1978, Aug. 17

739 A216 30d multicolored .50 .25
740 A216 35d multicolored .60 .35
741 A216 115d multicolored 1.60 1.60
Nos. 739-741 (3) 2.70 2.20

Turkish-Libyan friendship.

Soldiers, Jet, Ship — A217

35d, Tower, Green Book, oil derrick. 100d, View of Tripoli with mosque and modern buildings. 115d, View of Tripoli within cogwheel.

1978, Sept. 1 ***Perf. 14½***

742 A217 30d multicolored .50 .50
743 A217 35d org & multi .35 .35
744 A217 115d blue & multi 1.50 1.25
Nos. 742-744 (3) 2.35 2.10

Souvenir Sheet

745 A217 100d multicolored 2.75 2.75

9th anniversary of Sept. 1 Revolution. No. 745 contains one 50x41mm stamp.

Quarry and Symposium Emblem — A218

Designs: 40d, Oasis lake. 115d, Crater.

1978, Sept. 16 ***Perf. 13½***

746 A218 30d multicolored .50 .50
747 A218 40d multicolored .60 .60
748 A218 115d multicolored 2.00 2.00
Nos. 746-748 (3) 3.10 3.10

2nd Symposium on Libyan Geology.

Green Book and Three Races — A219

1978, Oct. 18 ***Perf. 12½***

749 A219 30d multicolored .25 .25
750 A219 40d multicolored .50 .50
751 A219 115d multicolored 1.25 1.25
Nos. 749-751 (3) 2.00 2.00

International Anti-Apartheid Year.

Pilgrims, Minarets, Holy Kaaba — A220

1978, Nov. 9 Photo. ***Perf. 12***

752 A220 5d multicolored .25 .25
753 A220 10d multicolored .25 .25
754 A220 15d multicolored .25 .25
755 A220 20d multicolored .25 .25
Nos. 752-755 (4) 1.00 1.00

Pilgrimage to Mecca.

Handclasp over Globe — A221

1978, Nov. 10 Litho. ***Perf. 13½***

756 A221 30d multicolored .40 .30
757 A221 40d multicolored .50 .40
758 A221 115d multicolored 1.50 1.25
Nos. 756-758 (3) 2.40 1.95

Technical Cooperation Among Developing Countries Conf., Buenos Aires, Argentina, Sept. 1978.

Fists, Guns, Map of Israel — A222

40d, 115d, Map of Arab countries and Israel, eagle and crowd. 145d, like 30d.

1978, Dec. 5 Litho. ***Perf. 13½***

759 A222 30d multi .35 .35
760 A222 40d multi, horiz. .50 .50
761 A222 115d multi, horiz. 1.25 1.25
762 A222 145d multi 1.50 .90
Nos. 759-762 (4) 3.60 3.00

Anti-Israel Summit Conf., Baghdad, Dec. 2-8.

Scales, Globe and Human Rights Flame — A223

1978, Dec. 10

763 A223 15d multicolored .25 .25
764 A223 30d multicolored .50 .50
765 A223 115d multicolored 1.25 1.25
Nos. 763-765 (3) 2.00 2.00

Universal Declaration of Human Rights, 30th anniv.

Libyan Fort and Horse Racing — A224

1978, Dec. 11

766 A224 20d multicolored .40 .25
767 A224 40d multicolored .50 .50
768 A224 115d multicolored 1.50 1.50
Nos. 766-768 (3) 2.40 2.25

Libyan Study Center.

Lilienthal's Glider, 1896 — A225

25d, Spirit of St. Louis, 1927. 30d, Adm. Byrd's Polar flight, 1929. 50d, Graf Zeppelin, 1934, hydroplane and storks. 115d, Wilbur and Orville Wright and Flyer A. No. 774, Icarus falling. No. 775, Eagle and Boeing 727.

1978, Dec. 26 Litho. ***Perf. 14***

769 A225 20d multicolored .25 .25
770 A225 25d multicolored .45 .45
771 A225 30d multicolored 1.40 1.40
772 A225 50d multicolored 1.60 1.60
773 A225 115d multicolored 1.40 1.40
Nos. 769-773 (5) 5.10 5.10

Souvenir Sheets

774 A225 100d multicolored 3.00 3.00
775 A225 100d multicolored 3.00 3.00

75th anniversary of 1st powered flight.
Nos. 769-773 issued also in sheets of 4. Value, set perf. $45. Also exists imperf.
Nos. 774-775 exist imperf. Value, pair $50.

Mounted Stag's Head — A226

Coil Stamps

1979, Jan. 15 Photo. ***Perf. 14½x14***

776 A226 5d multicolored .35 .35
777 A226 20d multicolored .75 .75
778 A226 50d multicolored 1.50 1.50
Nos. 776-778 (3) 2.60 2.60

Carpobrotus Acinaciformis A227

Flora of Libya: 15d, Caralluma europaea. 20d, Arum cirenaicum. 35d, Lavatera arborea. 40d, Capparis spinosa. 50d, Ranunculus asiaticus.

1979, May 15 Litho. ***Perf. 14***

779 A227 10d multicolored .25 .25
780 A227 15d multicolored .25 .25
781 A227 20d multicolored .25 .25
782 A227 35d multicolored .60 .60
783 A227 40d multicolored .60 .60
784 A227 50d multicolored .75 .75
Nos. 779-784 (6) 2.70 2.70

People, Torch, Olive Branches — A228

1979 Litho. ***Perf. 13x12½***

Size: 18x23mm

785 A228 5d multi .25 .25
786 A228 10d multi .25 .25
787 A228 15d multi .25 .25
788 A228 30d multi .35 .25
789 A228 50d multi .50 .25
790 A228 60d multi .60 .35
791 A228 70d multi .75 .35
792 A228 100d multi 1.25 .60
793 A228 115d multi 1.25 .60

Perf. 13½

Size: 26½x32mm

794 A228 200d multi 1.90 1.25
795 A228 500d multi 4.75 2.50
796 A228 1000d multi 10.00 6.25
Nos. 785-796 (12) 22.10 13.15

See Nos. 1053-1055.

Tortoise — A229

Animals: 10d, Antelope. 15d, Hedgehog. 20d, Porcupine. 30d, Arabian camel. 35d, African wildcat. 45d, Gazelle. 115d, Cheetah. 10d, 30d, 35d, 45d, vert.

1979, Feb. 1 Litho. ***Perf. 14½***

797 A229 5d multicolored .25 .25
798 A229 10d multicolored .25 .25
799 A229 15d multicolored .65 .65
800 A229 20d multicolored .65 .65
801 A229 30d multicolored 1.10 .65
802 A229 35d multicolored 1.50 .65
803 A229 45d multicolored 1.75 .80
804 A229 115d multicolored 3.50 1.25
Nos. 797-804 (8) 9.65 5.15

Rug and Tripoli Fair Emblem A230

Tripoli Fair emblem and various rugs.

1979, Mar. 1 Litho. ***Perf. 11***

805 A230 10d multicolored .25 .25
806 A230 15d multicolored .25 .25
807 A230 30d multicolored .35 .35
808 A230 45d multicolored .50 .50
809 A230 115d multicolored 1.25 1.25
Nos. 805-809 (5) 2.60 2.60

17th Tripoli Fair.
Exist imperf. Value, set $30.

Children's Drawings and IYC Emblem — A231

a, Families and planes. b, Shepherd, sheep and dog. c, Beach umbrellas. d, Boat in storm. e, Traffic policeman.

1979, Mar. 20 ***Perf. 13½***

810 A231 20d Strip of 5, #a.-e. 5.00 3.50

Intl. Year of the Child.
Exists imperf. Value $30.

Book, World Map, Arab Achievements A232

1979, Mar. 22 ***Perf. 13***

815 A232 45d multicolored .50 .50
816 A232 70d multicolored .75 .75

WMO Emblem, Weather Map and Tower — A233

1979, Mar. 23

817 A233 15d multicolored .25 .25
818 A233 30d multicolored .35 .35
819 A233 50d multicolored .60 .60
Nos. 817-819 (3) 1.20 1.20

World Meteorological Day.

Medical Services, WHO Emblem A234

1979, Apr. 7

820 A234 40d multicolored .60 .60

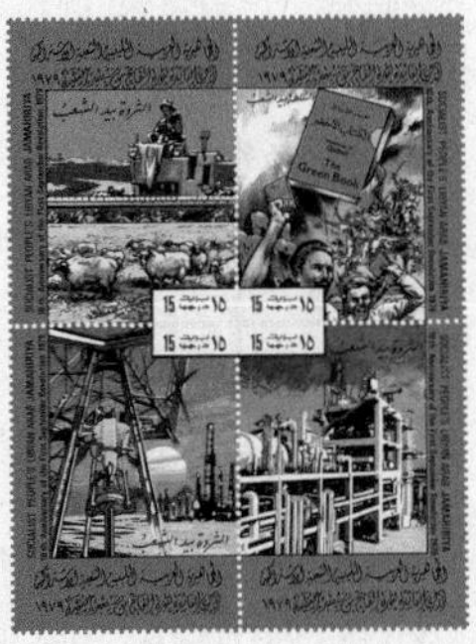

Farmer Plowing and Sheep A235

1979, Sept. 1 **Litho.** ***Perf. 14½***

821 A235 Block of 4 1.00 1.00
a. 15d Harvester, sheep .25 .25
b. 15d Men holding Green Book .25 .25
c. 15d Oil field .25 .25
d. 15d Oil refinery .25 .25
822 A235 Block of 4 2.00 2.00
a. 30d Dish antenna .40 .40
b. 30d Hospital .40 .40
c. 30d Doctor examining patient .40 .40
d. 30d Surgery .40 .40
823 A235 Block of 4 3.00 3.00
a. 40d Street, Tripoli .50 .50
b. 40d Steel mill .50 .50
c. 40d Tanks .50 .50
d. 40d Tuareg horsemen .50 .50
824 A235 Block of 4 4.00 4.00
a. 70d Revolutionaries, Green Book .90 .90
b. 70d Crowd, map of Libya .90 .90
c. 70d Mullah .90 .90
d. 70d Student .90 .90
Nos. 821-824 (4) 10.00 10.00

Souvenir Sheets

Imperf

825 A235 50d Revolution symbols, Green Book 2.50 2.50
826 A235 50d Monument 2.50 2.50

Sept. 1st revolution, 10th anniversary.

Volleyball — A236

1979, Sept. 10

827 A236 45d shown .50 .50
828 A236 115d Soccer 1.25 1.25

Universiade '79 World University Games, Mexico City, Sept.
Exists imperf. Value, set $17.50.

Mediterranean Games, Split, Yugoslavia A237

1979, Sept. 15 **Litho.** ***Perf. 12x11½***

829 A237 15d multicolored .50 .50
830 A237 30d multicolored 1.40 .50
831 A237 70d multicolored 3.50 1.00
Nos. 829-831 (3) 5.40 2.00

Exhibition Emblem — A238

1979, Sept. 25 **Photo.** ***Perf. 11½x11***

832 A238 45d multicolored .50 .50
833 A238 115d multicolored 1.50 1.50

TELECOM '79, 3rd World Telecommunications Exhibition, Geneva, Sept. 20-26.

A239

No. 834: a, 10d, Seminar emblem, Green Book, crowd. b, 35d, Meeting hall (Size: 67x43½mm). c, 100d, Col. Khadafy.
No. 835, Central portion of #834c.

1979, Oct. 1

834 A239 Strip of 3, #a.-c. 2.50 2.50

Size: 87x114mm

Imperf

835 A239 100d multicolored 3.50 3.50

Intl. Seminar of the Green Book, Benghazi, Oct. 1-3. No. 834 has continuous design.

Evacuation of Foreign Forces A240

1979, Oct. 7

837 A240 30d shown .60 .40
838 A240 40d Tuareg horsemen .90 .50

Souvenir Sheet

Imperf

839 A240 100d Vignettes 3.00 3.00

Cyclist, Championship Emblem A241

15d, Cyclist, emblem on left side. 30d, Two cyclists, emblem on right side.

1979, Nov. 21

840 A241 15d shown .25 .25
841 A241 30d multicolored .50 .50

Junior Cycling Championships, Tripoli, Nov. 21-23. Issued in sheetlets of 4.

Hurdles, Olympic Rings, Moscow '80 Emblem A242

1979, Nov. 21

842 A242 45d Equestrian .50 .50
843 A242 60d Javelin .75 .75
844 A242 115d Hurdles 1.50 1.50
845 A242 160d Soccer 1.75 1.75
Nos. 842-845 (4) 4.50 4.50

Souvenir Sheets

846 A242 150d shown 3.75 3.75
847 A242 150d like #845 3.75 3.75

Pre-Olympics (Moscow '80 Olympic Games). Nos. 842-845 issued in sheetlets of 4 and sheets of 20 (4x5) with silver Moscow '80 Emblem covering background of every 20 stamps. Value, set of sheetlets of 4, $45.
Nos. 842-847 exist imperf. Values: set $55; souvenir sheets, $90.

Intl. Day of Cooperation with Palestinian People — A242a

1979, Nov. 29 **Photo.** ***Perf. 12***

847A A242a 30d multicolored .25 .25
847B A242a 115d multicolored 1.75 1.75

Tug of War, Jumping A243

National Games: No. 848, Polo, leap frog. No. 849, Racing, ball game, No. 850, Wrestling, log rolling. No. 852, Horsemen.

1980, Feb. 15 ***Perf. 14½***

848 A243 Block of 4, #a.-d. 1.00 1.00
849 A243 Block of 4, #a.-d. 1.00 1.00
850 A243 Block of 4, #a.-d. 1.00 1.00
851 A243 Block of 4, #a.-d. 2.00 2.00
852 A243 Block of 4, #a.-d. 3.50 3.50
Nos. 848-852 (5) 8.50 8.50

Battles A244

No. 853: a, 20d, Gardabia, 1915. b, 35d, same. No. 854: a, 20d, Shoghab, 1913. b, 35d, same. No. 855: a, 20d, Fundugh Al-Shibani, 1922. b, 35d, same. No. 856: a, 20d, Ghira. b, 35d, same.

Pairs have continuous design.

1980 **Litho.** ***Perf. 14½***

853 A244 Pair, #a.-b. *1.25 1.25*
854 A244 Pair, #a.-b. *1.25 1.25*
855 A244 Pair, #a.-b. *1.25 1.25*
856 A244 Pair, #a.-b. *1.25 1.25*
Nos. 853-856 (4) *5.00 5.00*

Issued: No. 853, 4/28; No. 854, 5/25; No. 855, 6/1; No. 856, 8/15.
See Nos. 893-896, 921-932, 980-991, 1059-1070.

Girl Guides Examining Plant — A245

30d, Guides cooking. 50d, Scouts at campfire. 115d, Scouts reading map.

1980, Aug. 22 ***Perf. 13½***

861 A245 15d shown .25 .25
862 A245 30d multicolored .35 .35
863 A245 50d multicolored .60 .60
864 A245 115d multicolored 1.50 1.50
Nos. 861-864 (4) 2.70 2.70

Souvenir Sheets

865 A245 100d like #861 2.25 2.25
866 A245 100d like #863 2.25 2.25

8th Pan Arab Girl Guide and 14th Pan Arab Scout Jamborees, Aug.

Men Holding OPEC Emblem — A246

1980, Sept. 15 ***Perf. 14½***

867 A246 45d Emblem, globe .50 .50
868 A246 115d shown 1.50 1.50

20th anniversary of OPEC.

Martyrdom of Omar Muktar, 1931 — A247

1980, Sept. 16

869 A247 20d multicolored .25 .25
870 A247 35d multicolored .50 .50

Souvenir Sheet

870A A247 100d multicolored 2.50 2.50

UNESCO Emblem and Avicenna — A248

1980, Sept. 20

871 A248 45d Scientific symbols .50 .50
872 A248 115d shown 1.50 1.50

School Scientific Exhibition, Sept. 20-24 and birth millenium of Arab physician Avicenna (115d).

18th Tripoli Fair — A249

Various musical instruments. 15d vert.

1980 Litho. Perf. 13½

873	A249	5d multicolored	.25	.25
874	A249	10d multicolored	.25	.25
875	A249	15d multicolored	.25	.25
876	A249	20d multicolored	.25	.25
877	A249	25d multicolored	.40	.40
		Nos. 873-877 (5)	1.40	1.40

Souvenir Sheet

878 A249 100d Musicians 2.50 2.50

World Olive Oil Year — A250

1980, Jan. 15 Litho. Perf. 13½

879	A250	15d multicolored	.25	.25
880	A250	30d multicolored	.35	.35
881	A250	45d multicolored	.50	.50
		Nos. 879-881 (3)	1.10	1.10

Intl. Year of the Child (1979) — A251

Children's drawings: a, Riding horses. b, water sports. c, Fish. d, Gift sale. e, Preparing feast.

1980, Mar. 21

882 Strip of 5 5.00 5.00
a.-e. A251 20d any single .50 .40

The Hegira, 1500th Anniv. — A252

1980, Apr. 1

883	A252	50d multicolored	.60	.60
884	A252	115d multicolored	1.50	1.50

Operating Room, Hospital A253

1980, Apr. 7 Litho. Perf. 13½

885	A253	20d multicolored	.40	.40
886	A253	50d multicolored	.75	.75

World Health Day.

Sheik Zarruq Festival, Misurata, June 16-20 — A254

1980, June 16

887	A254	40d multicolored	.50	.50
888	A254	115d multicolored	1.50	1.50

Souvenir Sheet

889 A254 100d multicolored 2.75 2.75

Arabian Towns Organization — A255

1980, July 1 Perf. 11½x12

890	A255	15d Ghadames	.25	.25
891	A255	30d Derna	.35	.35
892	A255	50d Tripoli	.60	.60
		Nos. 890-892 (3)	1.20	1.20

Battles Type of 1980

No. 893: a, 20d, Yefren, 1915, b, 35d, same. No. 894: a, 20d, El Hani, 1911, b, 35d, same. No. 895: a, 20d, Sebha, 1914, b, 35d, same. No. 896: a, 20d, Sirt, 1912, b, 35d, same.
Pairs have continuous design.

1980 Perf. 13½

893	A244	Pair, #a.-b.	1.25	1.25
894	A244	Pair, #a.-b.	1.25	1.25
895	A244	Pair, #a.-b.	1.25	1.25
896	A244	Pair, #a.-b.	1.25	1.25
		Nos. 893-896 (4)	5.00	5.00

Issued: No. 893, 7/16; No. 894, 10/23; No. 895, 11/27; No. 896, 12/31.

Sept. 1 Revolution, 11th Anniv. — A256

Achievements of the Revolution: 5d, Oil industry. 10d, Youth festival. 15d, Agriculture. 25d, Transportation. 40d, Education. 115d, Housing.
100d, Montage of achievements.

1980, Sept. 1

901	A256	5d multicolored	.25	.25
902	A256	10d multicolored	.25	.25
903	A256	15d multicolored	.50	.50
904	A256	25d multicolored	1.25	.50
905	A256	40d multicolored	1.25	.50
906	A256	115d multicolored	3.00	1.25
		Nos. 901-906 (6)	6.50	3.25

Souvenir Sheet

907 A256 100d multicolored 2.75 2.75

No. 907 contains one stamp 30x50mm.

World Tourism Conference — A257

1980, Sept. 10

908	A257	45d multicolored	.50	.50
909	A257	115d multicolored	1.50	1.50

Intl. Year of the Disabled — A258

Intl. Year of the Disabled emblem and: 20d, Eye, man on crutches. 45d, Stylized globe. 115d, Eye, man on crutch, hands.

1981, Jan. 1 Perf. 15

910	A258	20d lt. green, blue & blk	.25	.25
911	A258	45d blue, blk & grn	.35	.25
912	A258	115d lt. grn, blue & grn	1.50	.50
		Nos. 910-912 (3)	2.10	1.00

Nos. 911-912 Redrawn with Arabic Writing and "Arab League" Above Emblem

1981, Nov. 21 Litho. Perf. 15

913	A258	45d blue & multi	.35	.25
914	A258	115d rose & multi	1.10	1.10

UPA Disabled Persons Campaign. Design redrawn to include Arab League Emblem.

Mosaics A259

1981, Jan. 15 Perf. 13½

915	A259	10d Horse	1.00	.25
916	A259	20d Sailing ship	1.00	.50
917	A259	30d Peacocks	2.00	.50
918	A259	40d Panther	2.00	.50
919	A259	50d Musician	2.50	.50
920	A259	115d Fish	6.50	1.00
		Nos. 915-920 (6)	15.00	3.25

Battles Type of 1980

No. 921: a, 20d, Dernah, 1912, b, 35d, same. No. 922: a, 20d, Bir Tagreft, 1928. b, 35d, same. No. 923: a, 20d, Tawargha, 1923. b, 35d, same. No. 924: a, 20d, .Funduk El-Jamel Misurata, 1915 b, 35d, same. No. 925: a, 20d, Zuara, 1912. b, 35d, same. No. 926: a, 20d, Sidi El-Khemri, 1915. b, 35d, same. No. 927: a, 20d, El-Khoms, 1913. b, 35d, same. No. 928: a, 20d, Roghdalin, 1912. b, 35d, same. No. 929: a, 20d, Rughbat El-Naga, 1925. b, 35d, same. No. 930: a, 20d, Tobruk. 1911. 1922, b, 35d, same. No. 931: a, 20d, Bir Ikshadia, 1924. b, 35d, same. No. 932: a, 20d, Ain Zara, 1924. b, 35d, same.
Pairs have continuous design.

1981 Perf. 13½, 14½ (#926, 932)

921	A244	Pair, #a.-b.	1.25	1.25
922	A244	Pair, #a.-b.	1.25	1.25
923	A244	Pair, #a.-b.	1.25	1.25
924	A244	Pair, #a.-b.	1.25	1.25
925	A244	Pair, #a.-b.	1.25	1.25
926	A244	Pair, #a.-b.	1.25	1.25
927	A244	Pair, #a.-b.	1.25	1.25
928	A244	Pair, #a.-b.	1.25	1.25
929	A244	Pair, #a.-b.	1.25	1.25
930	A244	Pair, #a.-b.	1.25	1.25
931	A244	Pair, #a.-b.	1.25	1.25
932	A244	Pair, #a.-b.	1.25	1.25
		Nos. 921-932 (12)	15.00	15.00

Issued: No. 921, 1/17; No. 922, 2/25; No. 923, 3/20; No. 924, 4/13; No. 925, 5/26; No. 926, 6/4; No. 927, 7/27; No. 928, 8/15; No. 929, 9/16; No. 930, 10/27; No. 931, 11/19; No. 932, 12/4.

Tripoli Intl. Fair — A260

Ceramicware.

1981, Mar. 1 Perf. 13½

945	A260	5d Bowls, horiz.	.25	.25
946	A260	10d Lamp	.25	.25
947	A260	15d Vase	.25	.25
948	A260	45d Water jar, horiz.	.60	.25
949	A260	115d Spouted water jar, horiz.	1.75	.60
		Nos. 945-949 (5)	3.10	1.60

No. 707b, Crowd — A261

1981, Mar. 2 Perf. 15

950	A261	50d multicolored	.35	.35
951	A261	115d multicolored	1.50	.50

People's Authority Declaration, The Green Book.

Children's Day, IYC — A262

Children's illustrations: a, Desert camp. b, Women doing chores. c, Village scene. d, Airplane over playground. e, Minaret, camel, man.

1981, Mar. 21 Litho. Perf. 13½

952 Strip of 5 5.00 5.00
a.-e. A262 20d any single .50 .40

Bank of Libya, 25th Anniv. — A263

1981, Apr. 1 Litho. Perf. 13½

953	A263	45d multicolored	.50	.35
954	A263	115d multicolored	1.75	1.10

Souvenir Sheet

955 A263 50d multicolored 1.50 1.50

World Health Day — A264

1981, Apr. 7 Perf. 14

956	A264	45d multicolored	.50	.50
957	A264	115d multicolored	1.50	.75

Intl. Year for Combating Racial Discrimination — A265

1981, July 1 Perf. 15

958	A265	45d multicolored	1.10	.65
959	A265	50d multicolored	1.50	.75

September 1 Revolution, 12th Anniv. — A266

No. 960: a-b, Helicopter and jets; c-d, Paratroopers. No. 961: a-b, Tanks; c-d, Frogman parade. No. 962: a-b, Twelve-barrel rocket launchers; c-d, Trucks with rockets. No. 963: a-b, Sailor parade; c-d, Jeep and trucks with twelve-barrel rocket launchers. No. 964: a-b, Wheeled tanks and jeeps; c-d, Tank parade. Nos. 960-962 vert. Pairs have continuous designs.

1981, Sept. 1 Perf. 14½

960	A266	5d Block of 4, #a.-d.	1.40	1.40
961	A266	10d Block of 4, #a.-d.	1.40	1.40
962	A266	15d Block of 4, #a.-d.	1.40	1.40
963	A266	20d Block of 4, #a.-d.	1.40	1.40
964	A266	25d Block of 4, #a.-d.	2.75	2.75
		Nos. 960-964 (5)	8.35	8.35

Souvenir Sheet

Perf. 11

965 A266 50d Naval troop marching 7.00 7.00

No. 965 contains one 63x38mm stamp.

Miniature Sheet

Butterflies — A267

1981, Oct. 1 *Perf. 14½*

966	A267	Sheet of 16	11.00	
a.-d.		5d, any single	.25	.25
e.-h.		10d, any single	.45	.25
i.-l.		15d, any single	.50	.40
m.-p.		25d, any single	1.00	.60

No. 966 printed in a continuous design, stamps of same denomination in blocks of 4. Sheetlets exist containing blocks of 4 for each denomination. Value, set of 4 sheets, $20.

World Food Day — A268

1981, Oct. 16 *Perf. 15*

967	A268	45d multicolored	.50	.50
968	A268	200d multicolored	2.50	2.50

Fruit — A269

1981, Nov. 17 *Perf. 13½*

969	A269	5d Grapes	.25	.25
970	A269	10d Dates	.25	.25
971	A269	15d Lemons	.25	.25
972	A269	20d Oranges	.40	.25
973	A269	35d Cactus fruit	.80	.35
974	A269	55d Pomegranates	1.50	.60
		Nos. 969-974 (6)	3.45	1.95

Miniature Sheet

A270

Mosaics: a, Animals facing right. b, Orpheus playing music. c, Animals facing left. d, Fish. e, Fishermen. f, Fish in basket. g, Farm yard. h, Birds eating fruit. i, Milking a goat.

1982, Jan. 1 *Perf. 13½*

975	A270	Sheet of 9	9.00	9.00
a.-i.		45d any single	.75	.75

Nos. 975a-975c, shown in illustration, printed in continuous design.

3rd Intl. Koran Reading Contest — A271

Designs: 10d, Stone tablets, Holy Ka'aba, Mecca. 35d, Open Koran, creation of the world. 115d, Scholar, students.

1982, Jan. 7

976	A271	10d multicolored	.25	.25
977	A271	35d multicolored	.50	.25
978	A271	115d multicolored	1.50	.75
		Nos. 976-978 (3)	2.25	1.25

Souvenir Sheet

979	A271	100d like 115d	3.50	3.50

Battles Type of 1980

No. 980: a, 20d, Hun Gioffra, 1915; b, 35d, same. No. 981: a, 20d, Gedabia, 1914; b, 35d, same. No. 982: a, 20d, El-Asaba, 1913; b, 35d, same. No. 983: a, 20d, El-Habela, 1917; b, 35d, same. No. 984: a, 20d, Suk El-Ahad, 1915; b, 35d, same. No. 985: a, 20d, El-Tangi, 1913; b, 35d, same. No. 986: a, 20d, Sokna, 1913; b, 35d, same. No. 987: a, 20d, Wadi Smalus, 1925; b, 35d, same. No. 988: a, 20d, Sidi Abuagela, 1917; b, 35d, same. No. 989: a, 20d, Sidi Surur, 1914; b, 35d, same. No. 990: a, 20d, Kuefia, 1911; b, 35d, same. No. 991: a, 20d, Abunjeim, 1940; b, 35d, same.

Pairs have continuous design.

1982 *Perf. 13½, 14½ (#985-988)*

980	A244	Pair, #a.-b.	1.25	1.25
981	A244	Pair, #a.-b.	1.25	1.25
982	A244	Pair, #a.-b.	1.25	1.25
983	A244	Pair, #a.-b.	1.25	1.25
984	A244	Pair, #a.-b.	1.25	1.25
985	A244	Pair, #a.-b.	1.25	1.25
986	A244	Pair, #a.-b.	1.25	1.25
987	A244	Pair, #a.-b.	1.25	1.25
988	A244	Pair, #a.-b.	1.25	1.25
989	A244	Pair, #a.-b.	1.25	1.25
990	A244	Pair, #a.-b.	1.25	1.25
991	A244	Pair, #a.-b.	1.25	1.25
		Nos. 980-991 (12)	15.00	15.00

Issued: No. 980, 1/26; No. 981, 3/8; No. 982, 3/23; No. 983, 4/24; No. 984, 5/15; No. 985, 6/19; No. 986, 7/23; No. 987, 8/11; No. 988, 9/4; No. 989, 10/14; No. 990, 11/28; No. 991, 12/13.

Tripoli Intl. Fair — A272

5d, Grinding stone. 10d, Ox-drawn plow. 25d, Pitching hay. 35d, Tapestry weaving. 45d, Traditional cooking. 100d, Grain harvest.

1982, Mar. 1 *Perf. 13x12½*

1004	A272	5d multicolored	.25	.25
1005	A272	10d multicolored	.25	.25
1006	A272	25d multicolored	.25	.25
1007	A272	35d multicolored	.50	.25
1008	A272	45d multicolored	.75	.35
1009	A272	100d multicolored	1.50	.75
		Nos. 1004-1009 (6)	3.50	2.10

People's Authority Declaration, The Green Book — A273

1982, Mar. 2 *Perf. 13½*

1010		Strip of 3	8.00	8.00
a.		A273 100d Harvester combine	1.25	.60
b.		A273 200d Khadafy, scholar, rifles	2.50	2.25
c.		A273 300d Govt. building, citizens	3.25	2.25

Scouting Movement, 75th Anniv. — A274

1982, Mar. 2

1011		Strip of 4	22.50	22.50
a.		A274 100d Cub scout, blimp	1.75	.80
b.		A274 200d Scouts, dog	3.25	1.60
c.		A274 300d Scholar, scout	4.75	2.00
d.		A274 400d Boy scout, rocket	7.25	3.75

Souvenir Sheets

1012	A274	500d Green Book	8.00	8.00
1013	A274	500d Khadafy, scouts	8.00	8.00

Nos. 1012-1013 each contain one stamp 39x42mm.

Nos. 1011-1013 exist imperf.

13th African Soccer Cup Championships A275

1982, Mar. 5

1014	A275	100d multi	1.50	.75
1015	A275	200d multi	3.00	1.50

1982 World Cup Soccer Championships, Spain — A276

World Cup trophy and various soccer plays.

1982, Mar. 15 *Perf. 14½*

1016	A276	45d multi	.60	.60
1017	A276	100d multi	1.50	1.50
1018	A276	200d multi	2.75	2.75
1019	A276	300d multi	3.25	3.25
		Nos. 1016-1019 (4)	8.10	8.10

Souvenir Sheets

1020	A276	500d like 45d	7.50	7.50
1021	A276	500d like 100d	7.50	7.50

Nos. 1016-1019 issued in sheets of 8 overprinted in silver with soccer ball in motion. Value $75. Sheetlets of 4 in each denomination exist without overprint.

Nos. 1020-1021 have Arabic text in green on reverse. Value $35.

Nos. 1016-1019 exist imperf. Value $15. Nos. 1020-1021 also exist imperf.

Palestinian Children's Day — A277

Designs: a, Two children. b, Girl with bowl. c, Girl with kaffiyeh. d, Girl hiding. e, Boy.

1982, Mar. 7 *Perf. 13½*

1022		Strip of 5	2.75	2.75
a.-e.		A277 20d, any single	.40	.40

Miniature Sheet

Birds A278

1982, Apr. 1 *Perf. 14½*

1023	A278	Sheet of 16	20.00	20.00
a.-d.		15d, any single	.50	.45
e.-h.		25d, any single	.75	.60
i.-l.		45d, any single	1.10	1.00
m.-p.		95d, any single	2.40	1.80

No. 1023a-1023p printed se-tenant in a continuous design; stamps of same denomination in blocks of 4.

Each denomination was also printed in a sheet of 16, each sheet containing four se-tenant blocks of the same denomination. Value, set of four sheets, $75.

Teaching Hospitals Anniv. — A279

1982, Apr. 7 *Perf. 13x12½*

1024	A279	95d multi	1.25	1.25
1025	A279	100d multi	1.25	1.25
1026	A279	205d multi	2.75	2.75
		Nos. 1024-1026 (3)	5.25	5.25

Arab Postal Union, 30th — A280

1982, Apr. 12 *Perf. 13½*

1027	A280	100d multi	1.50	.75
1028	A280	200d multi	2.75	1.50

1982 World Chess Championships — A281

Board positions and chessmen: a, Chinese piece. b, African piece. c, Modern piece. d, European piece.

500d, Overhead view of chessboard.

1982, May 1

1029	A281	Block of 4	10.00	10.00
a.-d.		100d, any single	2.25	1.10

Souvenir Sheet

1030	A281	500d multicolored	10.00	10.00

No. 1030 contains one stamp 39x42mm.

Nos. 1029 and 1030 exist imperf.

World Telecommunications Day — A282

1982, May 17

1031	A282	100d multi	1.25	1.25
1032	A282	200d multi	2.50	2.50

Map of Libya, Green Book — A283

1982, June 11

1033	A283	200d multi	2.50	1.50

Souvenir Sheet

1034	A283	300d multi	5.00	5.00

Post Day, FIP 51st anniv.

Organization of African Unity, 19th Summit — A284

50d, OAU flag, Arab family. 100d, Map of Africa, emblem. 200d, Khadafy, Green Book. 300d, Fist, map.

1982, Aug. 5 *Perf. 14*

1035	A284	50d multicolored	.75	.75
1036	A284	100d multicolored	1.25	1.25

Size: 69x40mm

1037	A284	200d multicolored	2.50	2.50
		Nos. 1035-1037 (3)	4.50	4.50

Souvenir Sheet

Perf. 13x13½

1038	A284	300d multicolored	5.00	5.00

No. 1038 contains one stamp 29x42mm.

September 1 Revolution, 13th Anniv. — A285

Khadafy in uniforms and various armed forces' exercises.

1982, Sept. 1 *Perf. 11½*

1039	A285	15d multi	.25	.25
1040	A285	20d multi	.25	.25
1041	A285	30d multi	1.00	1.00
1042	A285	45d multi	.60	.60
1043	A285	70d multi	1.00	1.00
1044	A285	100d multi	1.50	1.50
		Nos. 1039-1044 (6)	4.60	4.60

Souvenir Sheet

Imperf

1045	A285	200d multi	4.00	4.00

Libyan Red Crescent, 25th Anniv. — A286

1982, Oct. 5 *Perf. 13½*

1046	A286	100d Palm tree	1.75	1.25
1047	A286	200d "25," crescents	3.50	2.50

Intl. Day of Cooperation with Palestinian People — A287

1982, Nov. 29

1048	A287	100d gray grn & blk	1.50	.75
1049	A287	200d brt bl, gray grn & blk	2.75	1.50

Al-Fateh University Symposium on Khadafy's Green Book — A288

100d, Khadafy in uniform. 200d, Khadafy, map, Green Book.

1982, Dec. 1 *Perf. 12*

1050	A288	100d multicolored	1.25	1.10
1051	A288	200d multicolored	2.50	2.50

Miniature Sheet

Flowers — A289

Designs: a, Philadelphus. b, Hypericum. c, Antinhinum. d, Lily. e, Capparis. f, Tropaeolum. g, Rose. h, Chrysanthemum. i, Nigella damascena. j, Gaillardia lanceolata. k, Dahlia. l, Dianthus carophyllus. m, Notobasis syriaca. n, Nerium oleander. o, Iris histriodes. p, Scolymus hispanicus.

1983, Jan. 1 *Perf. 14½*

1052	A289	Sheet of 16	10.00	10.00
a.-p.		25d, any single	.50	.40

Torch Type of 1979

1983, Jan. 2 *Perf. 13½*

Size: 26½x32mm

1053	A228	250d multi	3.25	2.00
1054	A228	1500d multi	20.00	12.50
1055	A228	2500d multi	37.50	25.00
		Nos. 1053-1055 (3)	60.75	39.50

Customs Cooperation Council, 30th Anniv. — A290

1983, Jan. 15 *Perf. 14½x14*

1056	A290	25d Arab riding horse	.25	.25
1057	A290	50d Riding camel	.60	.60
1058	A290	100d Drawing sword	1.50	1.50
		Nos. 1056-1058 (3)	2.35	2.35

Battles Type of 1980

No. 1059, Ghaser Ahmed, 1922. No. 1060, Sidi Abuarghub, 1923. No. 1061, Ghar Yunes, 1913. No. 1062, Bir Otman, 1926. No. 1063, Sidi Sajeh, 1922. No. 1064, Ras El-Hamam, 1915. No. 1065, Zawiet Ishghefa, 1913. No. 1066, Wadi Essania, 1930. No. 1067, El-Meshiashta, 1917. No. 1068, Gharara, 1925. No. 1069, Abughelan, 1922. No. 1070, Mahruka, 1913.

Pairs have continuous design.

1983 *Perf. 13½*

1059	A244	50d Pair, #a.-b.	2.00	2.00
1060	A244	50d Pair, #a.-b.	2.00	2.00
1061	A244	50d Pair, #a.-b.	2.00	2.00
1062	A244	50d Pair, #a.-b.	2.00	2.00
1063	A244	50d Pair, #a.-b.	2.00	2.00
1064	A244	50d Pair, #a.-b.	2.00	2.00
1065	A244	50d Pair, #a.-b.	2.00	2.00
1066	A244	50d Pair, #a.-b.	2.00	2.00
1067	A244	50d Pair, #a.-b.	2.00	2.00
1068	A244	50d Pair, #a.-b.	2.00	2.00
1069	A244	50d Pair, #a.-b.	2.00	2.00
1070	A244	50d Pair, #a.-b.	2.00	2.00
		Nos. 1059-1070 (12)	24.00	24.00

Issued: No. 1059, 1/26; No. 1060, 2/2; No. 1061, 3/26; No. 1062, 4/9; No. 1063, 5/2; No. 1064, 6/24; No. 1065, 7/13; No. 1066, 8/8; No. 1067, 9/9; No. 1068, 10/22; No. 1069, 11/17; No. 1070, 12/24.

Miniature Sheet

Farm Animals — A291

Designs: a, Camel. b, Cow. c, Horse. d, Bull. e, Goat. f, Dog. g, Sheep. h, Ram. i, Goose. j, Turkey hen. k, Rabbit. l, Pigeon. m, Turkey. n, Rooster. o, Hen. p, Duck.

1983, Feb. 15 *Perf. 14½*

1083	A291	Sheet of 16	10.00	10.00
a.-p.		25d any single	.50	.40

Tripoli Intl. Fair — A292

Libyans playing traditional instruments.

1983, Mar. 5 *Perf. 14½x14, 14x14½*

1084	A292	40d multi, vert.	.60	.40
1085	A292	45d multicolored	.75	.50
1086	A292	50d multi, vert.	.75	.50
1087	A292	55d multicolored	1.00	.60
1088	A292	75d multi, vert.	1.25	.90
1089	A292	100d multi, vert.	1.60	1.10
		Nos. 1084-1089 (6)	5.95	4.00

Intl. Maritime Organization, 25th Anniv. — A293

Early sailing ships.

1983, Mar. 17 *Perf. 14½*

1090	A293	100d Phoenician	2.00	.75
1091	A293	100d Viking	2.00	.75
1092	A293	100d Greek	2.00	.75
1093	A293	100d Roman	2.00	.75
1094	A293	100d Libyan	2.00	.75
1095	A293	100d Pharoah's ship	2.00	.75
		Nos. 1090-1095 (6)	12.00	4.50

Children's Day (1983) — A294

Children's illustrations: a, Car. b, Tractor towing trailer. c, Children, dove. d, Boy Scouts. e, Dinosaur.

1983, Mar. 21 *Perf. 14x14½*

1096		Strip of 5	2.75	2.75
a.-e.	A294	20d, any single	.40	.30

1st Intl. Symposium on Khadafy's Green Book — A295

50d, Khadafy, Green Book, map. 70d, Lecture hall, emblem. 80d, Khadafy, Green Book, emblem.

100d, Khadafy, Green Books.

1983, Apr. 1 *Perf. 13½*

1097	A295	50d multicolored	.60	.40
1098	A295	70d multicolored	1.00	.50
1099	A295	80d multicolored	1.10	.75
		Nos. 1097-1099 (3)	2.70	1.65

Souvenir Sheet

Perf. 12½

1100	A295	100d multicolored	3.00	3.00

No. 1100 contains one stamp 57x48mm.

World Health Day — A296

25d, Healthy children, vert. 50d, Man in wheelchair, vert. 100d, Girl in hospital bed.

1983, Apr. 7 *Perf. 12½*

1101	A296	25d multicolored	.25	.25
1102	A296	50d multicolored	.60	.40
1103	A296	100d multicolored	1.25	.75
		Nos. 1101-1103 (3)	2.10	1.40

Pan-African Economic Committee, 25th Anniv. — A297

1983, Apr. 20 *Perf. 13½*

1104	A297	50d multi	.60	.40
1105	A297	100d multi	1.25	.75
1106	A297	250d multi	3.00	2.00
		Nos. 1104-1106 (3)	4.85	3.15

Miniature Sheet

Fish — A298

Designs: a, Labrus bimaculatus. b, Trigloporus lastoviza. c, Thalassoma pavo. d, Apogon imberbis. e, Scomber scombrus. f, Spondyliosoma cantharus. g, Trachinus draco. h, Blennius pavo. i, Scorpaena notata. j, Serranus scriba. k, Lophius piscatorius. l, Uranoscopus scaber. m, Auxis thazard. n, Zeus faber. o, Dactylopterus volitans. p, Umbrina cirrosa.

1983, May 15 *Perf. 14½*

1107	A298	Sheet of 16	10.00	10.00
a.-p.		25d any single	.40	.30

Still-life by Gauguin (1848-1903) — A299

Paintings: No. 1108b, Abstract, unattributed. c, The Conquest of Tunis by Charles V, by Rubens. d, Arab Musicians in a Carriage, unattributed.

No. 1109a, Khadafy Glorified on Horseback, unattributed, vert. b, Triumph of David over the Syrians, by Raphael, vert. c, Laborers, unattributed, vert. d, Flower Vase, by van Gogh, vert.

1983, June 1 *Perf. 11*

1108		Strip of 4	3.00	3.00
a.-d.	A299	50d, any single	.50	.35
1109		Strip of 4	3.00	3.00
a.-d.	A299	50d, any single	.50	.35

Souvenir Sheet

Ali Siala A300

Scientists: No. 1110b, Ali El-Najar.

1983, June 1

1110	A300	Sheet of 2	3.50	3.50
a.-b.		100d, any single	1.50	1.50

1984 Summer Olympic Games, Los Angeles — A301

1983, June 15 *Perf. 13½*

1111	A301	10d Basketball	.25	.25
1112	A301	15d High jump	.25	.25
1113	A301	25d Running	.25	.25
1114	A301	50d Gymnastics	.50	.40
1115	A301	100d Wind surfing	1.25	.75
1116	A301	200d Shot put	2.50	1.60
		Nos. 1111-1116 (6)	5.00	3.50

Souvenir Sheets

1117	A301	100d Equestrian	*3.00*	*3.00*
1118	A301	100d Soccer	*3.00*	*3.00*

Nos. 1111-1116 exist imperf. Value, set $22.50. Nos. 1117-1118 also exist imperf.

Nos. 1111-1116 exist printed together in a miniature sheet of 6. Values: perf $35; imperf $50. Each value was also printed in a miniature sheet of 4. Value, set of 6 sheets, $45.

World Communications Year — A302

1983, July 1 *Perf. 13*

1119 A302 10d multicolored .40 .30
1120 A302 50d multicolored .90 .60
1121 A302 100d multicolored 2.00 1.25
Nos. 1119-1121 (3) 3.30 2.15

The Green Book, by Khadafy — A303

Ideologies: 10d, The House is to be served by its residents. 15d, Power, wealth and arms are in the hands of the people. 20d, Masters in their own castles, vert. 35d, No democracy without popular congress. 100d, The authority of the people, vert. 140d, The Green Book is the guide of humanity for final release.
200d, Khadafy in uniform.

1983, Aug. 1 *Perf. 13½*

1122 A303 10d multi .25 .25
1123 A303 15d multi .25 .25
1124 A303 20d multi .25 .25
1125 A303 35d multi .40 .25
1126 A303 100d multi 1.25 .75
1127 A303 140d multi 1.75 1.25
Nos. 1122-1127 (6) 4.15 3.00

Souvenir Sheet

Litho. & Embossed

1128 A303 200d multi 4.50 4.50

No. 1128 contains one gold embossed stamp 36x51mm.

2nd African Youth Sports Festival — A304

Designs: a, Team Handball. b, Basketball. c, Javelin. d, Running. e, Soccer.

1983, Aug. 22 **Litho.**

1129 Strip of 5 7.50 4.00
a.-e. A304 100d, any single 1.25 .75

September 1 Revolution, 14th Anniv. — A305

Women in the Armed Forces.

1983, Sept. 1 *Perf. 11½*

1130 A305 65d multi .75 .75
1131 A305 75d multi .90 .90
1132 A305 90d multi 1.00 1.00
1133 A305 100d multi 1.25 1.25
1134 A305 150d multi 1.75 1.75
1135 A305 250d multi 3.25 3.25
Nos. 1130-1135 (6) 8.90 8.90

Souvenir Sheet

Perf. 11

1136 A305 200d multi 4.50 4.50

No. 1136 contains one stamp 63x38mm.

2nd Islamic Scout Jamboree A306

1983, Sept. 2 *Perf. 12½*

1137 A306 50d Saluting .75 .75
1138 A306 100d Camping 2.00 2.00

Souvenir Sheet

1139 Sheet of 2 4.50 4.50
a. A306 100d like 50d 2.00 2.00

No. 1139 contains Nos. 1138 and 1139a.

Traffic Day — A307

30d, Youth traffic monitors. 70d, Traffic officer. 200d, Motorcycle police.

1983, Oct. 1 *Perf. 14½x14*

1140 A307 30d multicolored 1.25 .75
1141 A307 70d multicolored 2.50 1.00
1142 A307 200d multicolored 8.00 3.50
Nos. 1140-1142 (3) 11.75 5.25

Saadun (1893-1923) — A308

1983, Oct. 11 *Perf. 13½*

1143 A308 100d multicolored 1.50 .75

1st Manned Flight, Bicent. A309

Early aircraft and historic flights: a, Americana, 1910. b, Nulli Secundus, 1907. c, J. B. Meusnier, 1785. d, Blanchard and Jeffries, 1785, vert. e, Pilatre de Rozier, 1784, vert. f, Montgolfiere, Oct. 19, 1783, vert.

1983, Nov. 1

1144 Strip of 6 11.00 11.00
a.-f. A309 100d, any single 1.60 .85

Intl. Day of Cooperation with Palestinian People — A310

1983, Nov. 29 *Perf. 14½x14*

1145 A310 30d pale vio & lt bl grn .50 .30
1146 A310 70d lil & lt yel grn 1.40 .55
1147 A310 200d lt ultra & grn 3.75 2.00
Nos. 1145-1147 (3) 5.65 2.85

Miniature Sheet

Roman Mosaic A311

Designs: Nos. 1148a-1148c, Gladiators. Nos. 1148d-1148f, Musicians, Nos. 1148g-1148i, Hunters.

1983, Dec. 1 *Perf. 12*

1148 A311 Sheet of 9 7.00 7.00
a.-i. 50d, any single .75 .35

Nos. 1148a-1148c, 1148d-1148f and 1148g-1148i se-tenant in a continuous design.

Achievements of the Sept. 1 Revolution A312

1983, Dec. 15 *Perf. 13½*

1149 A312 10d Mosque .25 .25
1150 A312 15d Agriculture .25 .25
1151 A312 20d Industry .40 .25
1152 A312 35d Office building .50 .25
1153 A312 100d Health care 1.50 .60
1154 A312 140d Airport 2.25 1.10
Nos. 1149-1154 (6) 5.15 2.70

Souvenir Sheet

Litho. & Embossed

1155 A312 200d Khadafy 4.50 4.50

No. 1155 contains one gold embossed stamp 36x51mm.

Khadafy, Irrigation Project Survey Map — A313

1983, Dec. 15

1156 A313 150d multicolored 2.25 1.25

A314

A315

Famous men: No. 1157a, Mahmud Burkis. No. 1157b, Ahmed El-Bakbak. No. 1157c, Mohamed El-Misurati. No. 1157d, Mahmud Ben Musa. No. 1157e, Abdulhamid Ben Ashiur. No. 1158a, Hosni Fauzi El-Amir. No. 1158b, Ali Haidar El-Saati. No. 1159, Mahmud Mustafa Dreza. No. 1160, Mehdi El-Sherif. No. 1161a, Ali El-Gariani. No. 1161b, Muktar Shakshuki. No. 1161c, Abdurrahman El-Busayri. No. 1161d, Ibbrahim Bakir. No. 1161e, Mahmud El-Janzuri. No. 1162a, Ahmed El-Feghi Hasan. No. 1162b, Bashir El Jawab.

1984 **Litho.** *Perf. 13½*

1157 Strip of 5 6.00 6.00
a.-e. A314 100d any single 1.10 1.10
1158 Pair 3.50 1.50
a.-b. A314 100d any single 1.50 .60
1159 A314 100d multi 1.75 .60
1160 A315 100d multi 1.75 .60
1161 Strip of 5 15.00 15.00
a.-e. A314 200d any single 2.50 2.50
1162 Pair 6.00 6.00
a.-b. A315 200d any single 2.50 2.50
Nos. 1157-1162 (6) 34.00 29.70

Issued: Nos. 1157, 1161-1162, 1/1; No. 1158-1160, 2/20.

Miniature Sheet

Water Sports — A316

Designs: a, Two windsurfers. b, Two-man craft. c, Two-man craft, birds. d, Wind sailing, skis. e, Water skier facing front. f, Fisherman in boat. g, Power boating. h, Water skier facing right. i, Fisherman in surf. j, Kayaking. k, Surfing. l, Water skier wearing life jacket. m, Scuba diver sketching underwater. n, Diver. o, Snorkel diver removing fish from harpoon. p, Scuba diver surfacing.

1984, Jan. 10 *Perf. 14½*

1164 A316 Sheet of 16 8.50 8.50
a.-p. 25d any single .50 .50

African Children's Day — A317

Designs: a, Khadafy, girl scouts. b, Khadafy, children. c, Map, Khadafy, children (size: 63x44mm).

1984, Jan. 15 **Litho.** *Perf. 14½*

1165 A317 Strip of 3 3.50 3.50
a.-b. 50d, any single .80 .80
c. 100d multi 2.00 2.00

Women's Emancipation A318

70d, Women, diff., vert. 100d, Soldiers, Khadafy.

1984, Jan. 20 *Perf. 12*

1166 A318 55d multicolored .75 .40
1167 A318 70d multicolored 1.25 .45
1168 A318 100d multicolored 1.50 .75
Nos. 1166-1168 (3) 3.50 1.60

Irrigation — A319

No. 1169: a, Desert, water. b, Produce, sheep grazing. c, Khadafy, irrigation of desert (size: 63x44mm). Nos. 1170-1171, Khadafy, map.

1984, Feb. 1 *Perf. 14½*

1169 A319 Strip of 3 2.50 2.50
a.-b. 50d any single .50 .25
c. 100d multicolored 1.50 .60

Size: 72x36mm

Perf. 13½

1170 A319 100d multicolored 1.50 .60

Souvenir Sheet

1171 A319 300d multicolored *7.00 7.00*

World Heritage A320

Architectural ruins: 50d, Theater, Sabratha. 60d, Temple, Cyrene. 70d, Monument, Sabratha, vert. 100d, Arena, Leptis Magna. 150d, Temple, Cyrene, diff. 200d, Basilica, Leptis Magna.

1984, Feb. 10 *Perf. 12*

1172 A320 50d multicolored .60 .25
1173 A320 60d multicolored .75 .30
1174 A320 70d multicolored .90 .35
1175 A320 100d multicolored 1.50 .60
1176 A320 150d multicolored 2.00 .90
1177 A320 200d multicolored 2.75 1.40
Nos. 1172-1177 (6) 8.50 3.80

Silver Dirhams Minted A.D. 671-757 — A321

Designs: a, Hegira 115. b, Hegira 93. c, Hegira 121. d, Hegira 49. e, Hegira 135.

Litho. & Embossed

1984, Feb. 15 *Perf. 13½*

1178 Strip of 5 15.00 15.00
a.-e. A321 200d, any single 2.75 1.25

Tripoli Intl. Fair — A322

Tea served in various settings.

1984, Mar. 5 Litho. *Perf. 12½*

1179 A322 25d multicolored .25 .25
1180 A322 35d multicolored .40 .25
1181 A322 45d multicolored .75 .25
1182 A322 55d multicolored .90 .40
1183 A322 75d multicolored 1.10 .40
1184 A322 100d multicolored 1.75 .95
Nos. 1179-1184 (6) 5.15 2.50

Musicians — A323

Designs: a, Muktar Shiaker Murabet. b, El-Aref El-Jamal. c, Ali Shiaalia. d, Bashir Fehmi.

1984, Mar. 15 *Perf. 14½*

1185 Strip of 4 + label 9.00 9.00
a.-d. A323 100d, any single 1.90 1.00

Children's Day, IYC — A324

Children's drawings: a, Recreation. b, Rainy day. c, Military strength. d, Playground. e, Porch swing, children, motorcycle.

1984, Mar. 21 *Perf. 14*

1186 Strip of 5 2.75 2.75
a.-e. A324 20d, any single .45 .25

Arab League Constitution, 39th Anniv. — A325

1984, Mar. 22 *Perf. 13½*

1187 A325 30d multicolored .60 .60
1188 A325 40d multicolored .70 .70
1189 A325 50d multicolored 1.00 1.00
Nos. 1187-1189 (3) 2.30 2.30

Miniature Sheet

Automobiles, Locomotives — A326

1984, Apr. 1

1190 A326 Sheet of 16 30.00 30.00
a.-h. 100d, Car, any single 1.75 .90
i.-p. 100d, Locomotive, any single 1.75 .90

No. 1190 pictures outline of two camels in gold. Size: 214x135mm.

World Health Day — A327

1984, Apr. 7 *Perf. 14½*

1191 A327 20d Stop Polio .25 .25
1192 A327 30d No. 910 .40 .25
1193 A327 40d Arabic text .90 .40
Nos. 1191-1193 (3) 1.55 .90

Crafts — A328

Designs: a, Shoemaker. b, Saddler. c, Women, wool. d, Spinner. e, Weaver. f, Tapestry weavers.

1984, May 1 *Perf. 12½*

1194 Strip of 6 15.00 15.00
a.-f. A328 150d, any single 2.25 1.25

Postal and Telecommunications Union Congress — A329

Designs: a, Telephones, mail. b, Computer operators. c, Emblem.

1984, May 15 *Perf. 14½*

1195 A329 Strip of 3 3.50 3.50
a.-b. 50d, any single .75 .40
c. 100d multicolored 1.50 .75

Armed Crowd — A330

A331

No. 1197a, Map, Fire, Military. No. 1197b, Soldiers. No. 1197c, Khadafy. No. 1198, Khadafy giving speech.

1984, May 17 *Perf. 12, 14½ (#1197)*

1196 A330 50d multi .90 .40
1197 A331 Strip of 3 3.00 3.00
a.-b. 50d, any single .75 .25
c. 100d multi 1.75 .90
1198 A330 100d multi 1.50 .75
Nos. 1196-1198 (3) 5.40 4.15

Abrogation of the May 17 Treaty. Size of No. 1197c: 63x45mm.

Youth War Casualties A332

70d, Damaged flag. 100d, Children imprisoned.

1984, June 4 *Perf. 10*

1199 A332 70d multi 1.00 .40
1200 A332 100d multi 1.50 .75

Miniature Sheet

Green Book Quotations — A333

Designs: a, The Party System Aborts Democracy. b, Khadafy. c, Partners Not Wage-Workers. d, No Representation in Lieu of the People . . . e, Green Book. f, Committees Everywhere. g, Forming Parties Splits Societies. h, Party building, text on track. i, No Democracy without Popular Congresses.

1984, June 20 *Perf. 14*

1201 A333 Sheet of 9 14.00 14.00
a.-i. 100d, any single 1.50 .75

See No. 1270.

Folk Costumes — A334

Background colors: a, Green. b, Beige. c, Violet. d, Pale greenish blue. e, Salmon rose. f, Blue.

1984, July 1 *Perf. 14½x14*

1202 Strip of 6 12.50 12.50
a.-f. A334 100d, any single 1.75 1.00

Miniature Sheet

Natl. Soccer Championships — A335

Stadium, star, world cup and various action scenes.

1984, July 15 *Perf. 13½*

1203 A335 Sheet of 16 20.00 20.00
a.-p. 70d, any single 1.10 .60

1984 Los Angeles Olympics — A336

1984, July 28

1204 A336 100d Soccer 2.00 1.10
1205 A336 100d Basketball 2.00 1.10
1206 A336 100d Swimming 2.00 1.10
1207 A336 100d Sprinting 2.00 1.10
1208 A336 100d Windsurfing 2.00 1.10
1209 A336 100d Discus 2.00 1.10
Nos. 1204-1209 (6) 12.00 6.60

Souvenir Sheets

1210 A336 250d Equestrian 6.25 6.25
1211 A336 250d Arab equestrian 6.25 6.25

World Food Day — A337

1212, Forest scenes. 1213, Men riding camels, oasis.

1984, Aug. 1 *Perf. 12*

1212 A337 100d multicolored 1.75 .75
1213 A337 200d multicolored 3.50 1.25

Miniature Sheet

Sept. 1 Revolution, 15th Anniv. — A338

Designs: a, Green books, building at right angle. b, Green book, building, minaret. c, Minaret, party building and grounds. d, Revolution leader. e, Eight-story building. f, Construction, dome. g, Highway, bridge. h, Green book, building at left angle. i, Shepherd, sheep. j, Harvester. k, Tractors. l, Industry. m, Khadafy. n, Irrigation pipe, man drinking. o, Silos, factory. p, Shipping.

1984, Sept. 15 *Perf. 14½*

1214 A338 Sheet of 16 9.00 9.00
a.-p. 25d any single .50 .25

A339

Evacuation Day — A340

No. 1215: b, Warrior facing left; c, Khadafy leading battle (size: 63x45mm). No. 1216, Female rider. No. 1217, Battle scene. No. 1218, Italian whipping Libyan.

1984, Oct. 7

1215 A339 Strip of 3 3.50 3.50
a.-b. 50d, any single .75 .40
c. 100d multi 1.50 .60

Perf. 11½

1216 A340 100d multicolored 1.50 .60
1217 A340 100d multicolored 1.50 .60
1218 A340 100d multicolored 1.50 .60
Nos. 1215-1218 (4) 8.00 5.30

Miniature Sheet

Equestrians — A341

Various jumping, racing and dressage exercises printed in a continuous design.

1984, Oct. 15 *Perf. 13½*

1219 A341 Sheet of 16 9.00 9.00
a.-p. 25d any single .50 .50

PHILAKOREA '84.

Agricultural Traditions — A342

Designs: a, Farmer. b, Well, man, ox. c, Basket weaver. d, Shepherd, ram. e, Tanning hide. f, Coconut picker.

1984, Nov. 1 ***Perf. 13½***
1220 Strip of 6 12.50 12.50
a.-f. A342 100d, any single 1.75 1.00

Union of Arab Pharmacists, 9th Congress — A343

1984, Nov. 6 ***Perf. 12***
1221 A343 100d multicolored 1.75 1.75
1222 A343 200d multicolored 3.50 3.50

Arab-African Union — A344

No. 1223, Map, banner, crowd. No. 1224, Men, flags.

1984, Nov. 15 ***Perf. 12***
1223 A344 100d multicolored 1.75 1.75
1224 A344 100d multicolored 1.75 1.75

Nos. 1046, 1147 — A345

1984, Nov. 29 ***Perf. 12½***
1225 A345 100d pink & multi 3.75 3.75
1226 A345 150d brt yel grn & multi 4.75 4.75

Intl. Day of Cooperation with the Palestinian People.

Miniature Sheet

Intl. Civil Aviation Organization, 40th Anniv. — A346

Aircraft: a, Boeing 747 SP, 1975. b, Concorde, 1969. c, Lockheed L1011-500 Tristar, 1978. d, Airbus A310, 1982. e, Tupolev TU-134A, 1962. f, Shorts 360, 1981. g, Boeing 727, 1963. h, Caravelle 10, 1965. i, Fokker F27, 1955. j, Lockheed 749A Constellation, 1946. k, Martin 130, 1955. l, Douglas DC-3, 1936. m, Junkers JU-52, 1932. n, Lindbergh's Spirit of St. Louis, 1927 Ryan. o, De Havilland Moth, 1925. p, Wright Flyer, 1903.

1984, Dec. 7 ***Perf. 13½***
1227 A346 Sheet of 16 27.50 27.50
a.-p. 70d any single 1.50 .75

African Development Bank, 20th Anniv. — A347

"20" in different configurations and: 70d, Map, symbols of industry, education and agriculture. 100d, Symbols of research and development.

1984, Dec. 15
1228 A347 50d multicolored .90 .90
1229 A347 70d multicolored 1.25 1.25
1230 A347 100d multicolored 1.75 1.75
Nos. 1228-1230 (3) 3.90 3.90

UN Child Survival Campaign — A348

No. 1231, Mother, child. No. 1232, Children. No. 1233, Boys at military school. No. 1234, Khadafy, children.

1985, Jan. 1 ***Perf. 12***
1231 A348 70d multicolored 1.50 .75
1232 A348 70d multicolored 1.50 .75
1233 A348 70d multicolored 1.50 .75
1234 A348 70d multicolored 1.50 .75
Nos. 1231-1234 (4) 6.00 3.00

Irrigation — A349

Drop of Water, Map A350

1985, Jan. 15 ***Perf. 14½x14***
1235 A349 100d shown 2.00 1.00
1236 A349 100d Flowers 2.00 1.00
1237 A349 100d Map, water 2.00 1.00
Nos. 1235-1237 (3) 6.00 3.00

Souvenir Sheet

Perf. 14x14½

1238 A350 200d shown 4.00 4.00

Musicians A351

No 1239: a, Kamel El-Ghadi; b, Lute. No. 1240: a, Ahmed El-Khogia; b, Violin. No. 1241: a, Mustafa El-Fallah; b, Zither. No. 1242: a, Mohamed Hamdi; b, Mask.

1985, Feb. 1 ***Perf. 14½***
1239 A351 Pair 5.00 3.75
a.-b. 100d, any single 2.25 1.75
1240 A351 Pair 5.00 3.75
a.-b. 100d, any single 2.25 1.75
1241 A351 Pair 5.00 3.75
a.-b. 100d, any single 2.25 1.75
1242 A351 Pair 5.00 3.75
a.-b. 100d, any single 2.25 1.75
Nos. 1239-1242 (4) 20.00 15.00

Nos. 1239-1242 printed in sheets of 20, four strips of 5 consisting of two pairs each musician flanking center stamps picturing instruments.

Gold Dinars Minted A.D. 699-727 A352

No. 1243: a, Hegira 105. b, Hegira 91. c, Hegira 77. No. 1244, Dinar from Zuela.

Litho. and Embossed

1985, Feb. 15 ***Perf. 13½***
1243 Strip of 3 12.50 12.50
a.-c. A352 200d, any single 4.00 2.50

Souvenir Sheet

1244 A352 300d multi 7.50 7.50

Fossils — A353

1985, Mar. 1 **Litho.** ***Perf. 13½***
1245 A353 150d Frog 6.00 3.00
1246 A353 150d Fish 6.00 3.00
1247 A353 150d Mammal 6.00 3.00
Nos. 1245-1247 (3) 18.00 9.00

People's Authority Declaration — A354

Khadafy wearing: a, Folk costume. b, Academic robe. c, Khaki uniform. d, Black uniform. e, White uniform.

1985, Mar. 2 **Litho.** ***Perf. 14½***
1248 Strip of 5 10.00 10.00
a.-e. A354 100d, any single 2.00 1.50

Tripoli Intl. Fair — A355

Musicians playing: a, Cymbals. b, Double flute, bongo. c, Wind instrument, drum. d, Drum. e, Tambourine.

1985, Mar. 5 ***Perf. 14***
1249 Strip of 5 10.00 10.00
a.-e. A355 100d, any single 1.90 1.75

Children's Day, IYC — A356

Children's drawings, various soccer plays: a, Goalie and player. b, Four players. c, Players as letters of the alphabet. d, Goalie save. e, Player heading the ball.

1985, Mar. 21 ***Perf. 12***
1250 Strip of 5 7.50 7.50
a.-e. A356 20d, any single .40 .25

Intl. Program for Development of Telecommunications — A357

1985, Apr. 1
1251 A357 30d multicolored .40 .40
1252 A357 70d multicolored 1.00 1.00
1253 A357 100d multicolored 2.00 2.00
Nos. 1251-1253 (3) 3.40 3.40

World Health Day — A358

1985, Apr. 7
1254 A358 40d Invalid, nurses 1.00 .60
1255 A358 60d Nurse, surgery 1.50 1.00
1256 A358 100d Nurse, child 2.50 1.60
Nos. 1254-1256 (3) 5.00 3.20

Miniature Sheet

Sea Shells — A359

Designs: a, Mytilidae. b, Muricidae (white). c, Cardiidae. d, Corallophiliidae. e, Muricidae. f, Muricacea. g, Turridae. h, Argonautidae. i, Tonnidae. j, Aporrhaidae. k, Trochidae. l, Cancellariidae. m, Epitoniidae. n, Turbnidae. o, Mitridae. p, Pectinidae.

1985, Apr. 20
1257 A359 Sheet of 16 13.00 13.00
a.-p. 25d, any single .60 .25

Tripoli Intl. Book Fair — A360

1985, Apr. 28 ***Perf. 13½***
1258 A360 100d multi 2.00 1.50
1259 A360 200d multi 4.00 3.00

Intl. Youth Year — A361

Games: No. 1260a, Jump rope. No. 1260b, Board game. No. 1260c, Hopscotch. No. 1260d, Stickgame. No. 1260e, Tops. No. 1261a, Soccer. No. 1261b, Basketball.

1985, May 1
1260 Strip of 5 6.00 6.00
a.-e. A361 20d, any single .40 .25

Souvenir Sheet

1261 Sheet of 2 9.00 9.00
a.-b. A361 100d, any single 3.00 1.00

No. 1261 contains 2 stamps 30x42mm.

Miniature Sheet

Mosque Minarets and Towers — A362

Mosques: a, Abdussalam Lasmar. b, Zaoviat Kadria. c, Zaoviat Amura. d, Gurgi. e, Mizran. f, Salem. g, Ghat. h, Ahmed Karamanli. i, Atya. j, El Kettani. k, Benghazi. l, Derna. m, El Derug. n, Ben Moussa. o, Ghadames. p, Abdulwahab.

1985, May 15 *Perf. 12*
1262 A362 Sheet of 16 15.00 15.00
a.-p. 50d, any single .75 .60

Hamida El-Anezi — A363

1985, June 1 Litho. *Perf. 13½*
1263 A363 100d multicolored 2.00 1.50
1264 A363 100d Jamila Zemerli 2.00 1.50

Teachers' Day.

A364

Battle of the Philadelphia: a, Ship sinking. b, Militia. c, Hand-to-hand combat.

1985 June 12
1265 A364 Strip of 3 4.00 4.00
a.-b. 50d, any single 1.00 1.00
c. 100d multicolored 1.75 1.75

Size of No. 1265c: 60x48mm. Continuous design with No. 1265c in middle.

A365

Khadafy's Islamic Pilgrimage — A366

"The Holy Koran is the Law of Society" and Khadafy: a, Writing. b, Kneeling. c, With Holy Kaaba. d, Looking in window. e, Praying at pilgrimage ceremony.

1985, June 16
1266 Strip of 5 22.50 22.50
a.-e. A365 200d, any single 4.00 2.50

Souvenir Sheet

1267 A366 300d multicolored 6.50 6.50

Miniature Sheet

Mushrooms — A367

Designs: a, Leucopaxillus lepistoides. b, Amanita caesarea. c, Coriolus hirsutus. d, Cortinarius subfulgens. e, Dermocybe pratensis. f, Macrolepiota excoriata. g, Amanita curtipes. h, Trametes ljubarskyi. i, Pholiota aurivella. j, Boletus edulis. k, Geastrum sessile. l, Russula sanguinea. m, Cortinarius herculeus. n, Pholiota lenta. o, Amanita rubenscens. p, Scleroderma polyrhizum.

1985, July 15
1268 A367 Sheet of 16 17.50 17.50
a.-p. 50d, any single 1.00 .40

No. 1268 exists imperf. Value $50.

Women's Folk Costumes — A368

Designs: a, Woman in violet. b, In white. c, In brown and blue. d, In blue. e, In red.

1985, Aug. 1 *Perf. 14½x14*
1269 Strip of 5 10.00 10.00
a.-e. A368 100d, any single 1.75 1.50

Green Book Quotations Type of 1984

Miniature Sheet

Designs: a, In Need Freedom Is Latent. b, Khadafy reading. c, To Make A Party You Split Society. d, Public Sport Is for All the Masses. e, Green Books, doves. f, Wage-Workers Are a Type of Slave . . . g, People Are Only Harmonious with Their Own Arts and Heritages. h, Khadafy orating. i, Democracy Means Popular Rule Not Popular Expression.

1985, Aug. 15 *Perf. 14*
1270 Sheet of 9 17.50 17.50
a.-i. A333 100d, any single 1.75 1.50

A369

September 1 Revolution, 16th Anniv. — A370

Designs: a, Food. b, Oil pipeline, refinery. c, Capital, olive branch. d, Mosque, modern buildings. e, Flag, mountains. f, Telecommunications apparatus.

1985, Sept. 1 *Perf. 12½*
1271 Strip of 6 12.50 12.50
a.-f. A369 100d, any single 2.00 1.50

Souvenir Sheet

1272 A370 200d multi 4.50 4.50

Mosque Entrances — A371

Designs: a, Zauiet Amoura, Janzour. b, Shiaieb El-ain, Tripoli. c, Zauiet Abdussalam El-asmar, Zliten. d, Karamanli, Tripoli. e, Gurgi, Tripoli.

1985, Sept. 15 *Perf. 14*
1273 Strip of 5 10.00 10.00
a.-e. A371 100d, any single 2.00 1.50

Miniature Sheet

Basketball — A372

Various players in action.

1985, Oct. 1 Litho. *Perf. 13x12½*
1274 Sheet of 16 9.00 9.00
a.-p. A372 25d any single .50 .40

Evacuation — A373

Designs: a, Man on crutches, web, tree. b, Man caught in web held by disembodied hands. c, Three men basking in light.

1985, Oct. 7 *Perf. 15*
1275 A373 Strip of 3 7.00 7.00
a.-c. 100d any single 1.75 1.50

Stamp Day — A374

Italia 85: a, Man sitting at desk, Type A228, Earth. b, Magnifying glass, open stock book, Type A228. c, Stamps escaping envelope.

1985, Oct. 25 *Perf. 12*
1276 A374 Strip of 3 4.00 4.00
a.-c. 50d, any single 1.00 .60

1986 World Cup Soccer Championships A375

No. 1277, Block, heading the ball. No. 1278, Kick, goalie catching ball. No. 1279, Goalie, block, dribble. No. 1280, Goalie, dribble, sliding block. No. 1281, Goalie catching the ball. No. 1282, Block.
No. 1283, Four players.

1985, Nov. 1 *Perf. 13½*
1277 A375 100d multicolored 2.00 1.50
1278 A375 100d multicolored 2.00 1.50
1279 A375 100d multicolored 2.00 1.50
1280 A375 100d multicolored 2.00 1.50
1281 A375 100d multicolored 2.00 1.50
1282 A375 100d multicolored 2.00 1.50
Nos. 1277-1282 (6) 12.00 9.00

Souvenir Sheet

1283 A375 200d multicolored 8.50 8.50

Intl. Day of Cooperation with the Palestinian People — A376

1985, Nov. 29 Litho. *Perf. 12½*
1284 A376 100d multi 1.75 1.50
1285 A376 150d multi 3.25 2.25

Khadafy

A377

A377a

Perf. 12½x13, 13¼x13

1986, Jan. 1 **Engr.**
1286 A377 50d vermilion *40.00 70.00*
1287 A377 60d blue *40.00 70.00*
1288 A377 70d carmine *40.00 70.00*
1289 A377 80d violet *40.00 70.00*
1290 A377 90d brown *40.00 70.00*
1291 A377 100d dk grn *50.00 80.00*
1292 A377 200d dk rose *50.00 80.00*
1293 A377 250d brt grn *50.00 80.00*
1294 A377a 300d grysh blue *50.00 80.00*
1295 A377a 500d redsh brn *50.00 80.00*
1296 A377a 1500d grysh grn *55.00 85.00*
1297 A377a 2500d purple *65.00 95.00*
Nos. 1286-1297 (12) *570.00 930.00*

Supposedly Nos. 1286-1297 were on sale for two hours. Value on first day cover, $400.

Importation Prohibited
Importation of the stamps of Libya was prohibited as of Jan. 7, 1986.

General Post and Telecommunications Co. — A378

1986, Jan. 15 *Perf. 12*
1298 A378 100d yel & multi 2.25 1.50
1299 A378 150d yel grn & multi 2.75 2.00

Peoples Authority Declaration — A379

Designs: b, Hand holding globe and paper. c, Dove, Khadafy's Green Book (size: 53x37mm).

1986, Mar. 2 *Perf. 12½x13*
1300 A379 Strip of 3 4.50 4.50
a.-b. 50d, any single 1.00 .60
c. 100d multicolored 2.00 1.25

Musical Instruments A380

Designs: a, Flute. b, Drums. c, Horn. d, Cymbals. e, Hand drum.

1986, Mar. 5
1301 Strip of 5 10.00 10.00
a.-e. A380 100d any single 2.00 1.50

Tripoli International Fair.

Intl. Children's Day — A381

Designs: a, Boy Scout fishing. b, Riding camel. c, Chasing butterflies. d, Beating drum. e, Soccer game.

1986, Mar. 21 *Perf. 13½*
1302 Strip of 5 8.50 8.50
a.-e. A381 50d any single 1.25 .75

World Health Day — A382

1986, Apr. 7
1303 A382 250d sil & multi 5.00 3.00
1304 A382 250d gold & multi 5.00 3.00

Government Programs — A383

Designs: a, Medical examinations. b, Education. c, Farming (size: 63x42mm).

1986, May 1 — *Perf. 14½*

1305 A383 Strip of 3 — 3.75 3.75
a.-b. 50d any single — .85 .60
c. 100d multicolored — 1.75 1.25

Miniature Sheet

World Cup Soccer Championships, Mexico — A384

Designs: No. 1306a, 2 players. No. 1306b, 3 players in red and white shirts, one in green. No. 1306c, 2 players, referee. No. 1306d, Shot at goal. No. 1306e, 2 players with striped shirts. No. 1306f, 2 players with blue shirts, one with red.

No. 1307, 7 players. No. 1308, 1st Libyan team, 1931.

1986, May 31 — *Perf. 13½*

1306 A384 Sheet of 6 — 7.50 7.50
a.-f. 50d any single — 1.10 .75

Souvenir Sheets

1307 A384 200d multicolored — 6.50 6.50
1308 A384 200d multicolored — 6.50 6.50

Nos. 1307-1308 each contain one 52x37mm stamp.

Miniature Sheet

Vegetables — A385

Designs: a, Peas. b, Zucchini. c, Beans. d, Eggplant. e, Corn. f, Tomato. g, Red pepper. h, Cucumbers. i, Garlic. j, Cabbage. k, Cauliflower. l, Celery. m, Onions. n, Carrots. o, Potato. p, Radishes.

1986, June 1 — *Perf. 13x12½*

1309 Sheet of 16 — 15.00 15.00
a.-p. A385 50d any single — .85 .75

No. 1309 has a continuous design.

Miniature Sheet

Khadafy and Irrigation Project — A386

Khadafy and: a, Engineer reviewing plans, drill rig. b, Map. c, Well. d, Drought conditions. e, Water pipe. f, Pipes, pulleys, equipment. g, Lowering water pipe. h, Construction workers, trailer. i, Hands holding water. j, Opening water valve. k, Laying pipeline. l, Trucks hauling pipes. m, Khadafy holding green book, city. n, Giving vegetables to people. o, Boy drinking, man cultivating field. p, Men in prayer, irrigation. (Khadafy not shown on Nos. 1310h, 1310i, 1310k, 1310 l, 1310o.)

1986, July 1 — *Perf. 13½*

1310 Sheet of 16 — 35.00 35.00
a.-p. A386 100d any single — 2.00 1.40

A387

A388

American Attack on Libya, Apr. 15 — A389

Designs: Nos. 1311a-1311p, Various scenes in Tripoli during and after air raid. No. 1312a. F14 aircraft. No. 1312b, Aircraft carrier, people. No. 1312c, Sinking of USS *Philadelphia,* 1801.

1986, July 13

1311 A387 Sheet of 16, #a.-p. — 26.00 26.00
1312 A388 Strip of 3 — 3.50 3.50
a.-b. 50d multicolored — .85 .65
c. 100d multicolored — 1.75 1.25
1313 A389 100d multicolored — 2.10 1.50

No. 1312 has a continuous design. Size of No. 1312b: 60x38mm.

Khadafy's Peace Methods — A390

Khadafy: b, Reading Green Book. c, With old woman. d, Praying with children. e, Visiting sick. f, Driving tractor.

1986, July 13

1314 Sheet of 6 — 12.50 12.50
a.-f. A390 100d any single — 2.00 1.40

Miniature Sheet

Green Book Quotations A391

Designs: a, The House Must be Served by its Own Tenant. b, Khadafy. c, The Child is Raised by His Mother. d, Democracy is the Supervision of the People by the People. e, Green Books. f, Representation is a Falsification of Democracy. g, The Recognition of Profit is an Acknowledgement of Exploitation. h, Flowers. i, Knowledge is a Natural Right of Every Human Being...

1986, Aug. 1 — *Perf. 14*

1315 Sheet of 9 — 19.00 19.00
a.-i. A391 100d any single — 2.00 1.40

Sept. 1st Revolution, 17th Anniv. — A392

a, Public health. b, Agriculture. c, Sunflowers by Vincent Van Gogh. d, Defense. e. Oil industry.

1986, Sept. 1

1316 Strip of 5 — 22.50 22.50
a.-e. A392 200d any single — 4.00 2.75

A393

Arab-African Union, 1st Anniv. — A394

No. 1317, Libyan, Arab horsemen. No. 1318, Women in native dress.

1986, Sept. 15 — *Perf. 12*

1317 A393 250d multicolored — 5.00 4.00
1318 A394 250d multicolored — 5.00 4.00

Evacuation Day — A395

Designs: a, Mounted warrior. b, Two horsemen, infantry. c, Cavalry charge.

1986, Oct. 7 — *Perf. 13½*

1319 A395 Strip of 3 — 6.00 6.00
a. 50d multicolored — 1.00 .60
b. 100d multicolored — 2.00 1.10
c. 150d multicolored — 2.75 2.40

Intl. Peace Year — A396

1986, Oct. 24 — *Perf. 14½*

1320 A396 200d bl & multi — 4.00 3.00
1321 A396 200d grn & multi — 4.00 3.00

Solidarity with the Palestinians A397

1986, Nov. 29 — *Perf. 12½*

1322 A397 250d pink & multi — 5.00 4.00
1323 A397 250d blue & multi — 5.00 4.00

Music and Dance — A398

Designs: a, Man beating drum. b, Masked dancer. c, Woman dancing with jugs on her head. d, Man playing bagpipe. e, Man beating hand drum.

1986, Dec. 1 — *Perf. 12*

1324 Strip of 5 — 8.00 8.00
a.-e. A398 70d any single — 1.50 1.25

Gazella Leptoceros A399

1987, Mar. 2 — *Perf. 13½*

1325 A399 100d Two adults — 3.00 2.00
1326 A399 100d Fawn nursing — 3.00 2.00
1327 A399 100d Adult sleeping — 3.00 2.00
1328 A399 100d Adult drinking — 3.00 2.00
Nos. 1325-1328 (4) — 12.00 8.00

World Wildlife Fund.

Nos. 1325-1328 exist imperf. Value, set $27.50.

A400

Crowd of People and: a, Oilfields. b, Buildings. c, Khadafy, buildings, globe.

1987, Mar. 2 — *Perf. 13½*

1329 A400 Strip of 3 — 40.00 40.00
a.-b. 500d multicolored — 10.00 8.00
c. 1000d multicolored — 20.00 15.00

People's Authority declaration.

No. 1329 has a continuous design. Size of No. 1329c: 42x37mm.

Miniature Sheet

A401

Sept. 1st Revolution, 18th Anniv.: a, Shepherd, sheep. b, Khadafy. c, Mosque. d, Irrigation pipeline. e, Combine in field. f, Khadafy at microphones. g, Harvesting grain. h, Irrigation. i, Soldier. j, Militiaman. k, Fountain. l, Skyscrapers. m, House, women. n, Children. o, Assembly hall. p, Two girls.

1987, Sept. 1 — *Perf. 13½*

1330 A401 Sheet of 16 — 70.00 70.00
a.-p. 150d any single — 3.00 2.25

No. 1330 has a continuous design.

Libyan Freedom Fighters — A402

No. 1331: a, Omer Abed Anabi Al Mansuri. b, Ahmed Ali Al Emrayd. c, Khalifa Said Ben Asker. d, Mohamed Ben Farhat Azawi. e, Mohamed Souf Al Lafi Al Marmori.

1988, Feb. 15

1331 Strip of 5 — 29.00 29.00
a. A402 100d multicolored — 2.00 1.25
b. A402 200d multicolored — 5.75 4.25
c. A402 300d multicolored — 8.00 4.50
d. A402 400d multicolored
e. A402 500d multicolored — 9.00 6.50

Freedom Festival Day — A403

1988, June 1

1332 A403 100d yel & multi — 1.75 1.25
1333 A403 150d grn & multi — 3.00 2.00
1334 A403 250d brn org & multi — 5.00 3.50
Nos. 1332-1334 (3) — 9.75 6.75

Miniature Sheet

American Attack on Libya, 2nd Anniv. — A404

Khadafy: a, With woman and children. b, Playing chess. c, Fleeing from bombing with children. d, Praying in desert. e, Praying with children. f, Visiting wounded child. g, With infants and children, horiz. h, Delivering speech, horiz. i, With family, horiz.

No. 1336, In desert, vert. No. 1337, Making speech.

1988, July 13

1335 A404 Sheet of 9 — 25.00 25.00
a.-i. 150d any single — 2.75 2.00

Souvenir Sheets
Litho. & Embossed

1336 A404 500d gold & multi 10.00 10.00
1337 A404 500d gold & multi 10.00 10.00

No. 1335 exists imperf.

September 1st Revolution, 19th Anniv. — A405

1988, Sept. 19 **Litho.**

1338 A405 100d brt bl & multi 1.75 1.25
1339 A405 250d gray & multi 4.50 3.00
1340 A405 300d cit & multi 5.00 4.25
1341 A405 500d bl grn & multi 10.00 7.00
Nos. 1338-1341 (4) 21.25 15.50

1988 Summer Olympics, Seoul — A406

1988, Sept. 17

1342 A406 150d Tennis 2.75 2.00
1343 A406 150d Equestrian 2.75 2.00
1344 A406 150d Relay race 2.75 2.00
1345 A406 150d Soccer 2.75 2.00
1346 A406 150d Distance race 2.75 2.00
1347 A406 150d Cycling 2.75 2.00
Nos. 1342-1347 (6) 16.50 12.00

Souvenir Sheet

1348 A406 750d Soccer, diff. 13.00 13.00

No. 1348 contains one 30x42mm stamp. Exists imperf. Nos. 1342-1347 exist in miniature sheets of 1. Value, set $37.50.

Miniature Sheet

1988 Summer Olympics, Seoul — A407

1988, Sept 17

1350 A407 Sheet of 3 8.50 8.50
a. 100d Bedouin rider 2.00 2.00
b. 200d shown 3.00 3.00
c. 200d Show jumping, diff. 3.00 3.00

Olymphilex '88, Seoul.

A408

Design: Libyan Palm Tree.

1988, Nov. 1

1351 A408 500d Fruit 10.00 6.50
1352 A408 1000d Palm tree 18.00 12.00

A409

1988

1353 A409 Strip of 3 11.50 11.50
a. 100d shown 2.00 1.40
b. 200d Boy with rocks 3.50 2.75
c. 300d Flag, map 5.75 4.25

Palestinian uprising. No. 1353b, size: 45x39mm.

People's Authority Declaration A410

1989

1354 A410 260d dk grn & multi 5.00 3.00
1355 A410 500d gold & multi 10.00 6.00

Miniature Sheet

September 1 Revolution, 20th Anniv. — A411

Designs: a, Crowd, Green Books, emblem. b, Soldiers, Khadafy, irrigation pipeline. c, Military equipment, Khadafy, communication and transportation. d, Mounted warriors. e, Battle scenes.

1989 ***Perf. 13½***

1356 A411 Sheet of 5 14.00 14.00
a.-e. 150d any single 2.75 2.00
f. Bklt. pane of 5, perf. 13½ horiz. 14.00 14.00

Souvenir Sheet

1357 A411 250d Khadafy 4.00 4.00

No. 1357 contains one 36x51mm stamp. Stamps from No. 1356f have gold border at right.

Libyans Deported to Italy A412

No. 1359, Libyans in boats. No. 1360, Khadafy, crescent moon. No. 1361, Khadafy at left, in desert. No.1362, Khadafy at right, soldiers. No. 1363, Khadafy in center, Libyans.

1989

1358 A412 100d shown 1.75 1.25
1359 A412 100d multicolored 1.75 1.25
1360 A412 100d multicolored 1.75 1.25
1361 A412 100d multicolored 1.75 1.25
1362 A412 100d multicolored 1.75 1.25
Nos. 1358-1362 (5) 8.75 6.25

Souvenir Sheet

1363 A412 150d multicolored 3.00 3.00

No. 1363 contains one 72x38mm stamp.

A413

1989 ***Perf. 12***

1364 A413 150d multicolored 2.75 2.75
1365 A413 200d multicolored 4.25 4.25

Demolition of Libyan-Tunisian border fortifications.

Solidarity with the Palestinians — A414

300d, Man, flag, crowd. 500d, Emblem.

1989 ***Perf. 12x11½***

1366 A414 100d shown 2.25 2.25
1367 A414 300d multicolored 6.50 6.50
1368 A414 500d multicolored 10.00 10.00
Nos. 1366-1368 (3) 18.75 18.75

Ibn Annafis, Physician — A415

1989 ***Perf. 12***

1369 A415 100d multicolored 2.75 2.75
1370 A415 150d multicolored 4.00 4.00

Intl. Literacy Year — A416

1990, Oct. 18 **Litho.** ***Perf. 14***

Granite Paper

1371 A416 100d multicolored 1.75 1.75
1372 A416 300d multicolored 8.00 8.00

A417

1990, Oct. 18 **Granite Paper**

1373 A417 100d multicolored 1.75 1.75
1374 A417 400d multicolored 5.25 5.25

Organization of Petroleum Exporting Countries (OPEC), 30th anniv.

A418

1990, June 28 ***Perf. 11½x12***

1375 A418 100d brt org & multi 1.75 1.75
1376 A418 400d grn & multi 8.00 8.00

Evacuation of US military base, 20th anniv.

People's Authority Declaration — A419

1990, Apr. 24

1377 A419 300d bl & multi 5.00 5.00
1378 A419 500d vio & multi 10.00 10.00

A420

Plowing Season in Libya: 2000d, Man on tractor plowing field.

1990, Dec. 4 ***Perf. 14***

Granite Paper

1379 A420 500d multicolored 11.00 11.00
1380 A420 2000d multicolored 37.50 37.50

A421

1990, Nov. 5 ***Perf. 14***

Granite Paper

1381 A421 100d grn & multi 1.75 1.75
1382 A421 400d vio & multi 8.00 8.00
1383 A421 500d bl & multi 9.25 9.25
Nos. 1381-1383 (3) 19.00 19.00

Souvenir Sheet
Perf. 11½

1384 A421 500d Trophy, map, horiz. 11.00 11.00

World Cup Soccer Championships, Italy. No. 1384 contains one 38x33mm stamp.

Sept. 1st Revolution, 21st Anniv. — A422

1990, Sept. 3 ***Perf. 14***

Granite Paper

1385 A422 100d multicolored 2.00 2.00
1386 A422 400d multicolored 8.50 8.50
1387 A422 1000d multicolored 21.00 21.00
Nos. 1385-1387 (3) 31.50 31.50

Imperf
Size: 120x90mm

1388 A422 200d multi, diff. 8.50 8.50

Maghreb Arab Union, 2nd Anniv. — A423

1991, Mar. 10 **Litho.** ***Perf. 13½***

1389 A423 100d multicolored 2.00 2.00
1390 A423 300d gold & multi 5.75 5.75

People's Authority Declaration A424

1991, Mar. 10

1391 A424 300d multicolored 5.00 5.00
1392 A424 400d silver & multi 10.00 10.00

Children's Day — A425

100d, Butterflies, girl. 400d, Bird, boy.

1991, Mar. 22

1393	A425	100d multicolored		2.75	2.75
1394	A425	400d multicolored		10.00	10.00

World Health Day — A426

1991, Apr. 7

1395	A426	100d blue & multi	1.75	1.75
1396	A426	200d green & multi	3.50	3.50

Scenes from Libya — A427

100d, Wadi el Hayat, vert. 250d, Mourzuk. 500d, Ghadames.

1991, June 20

1397	A427	100d multicolored	1.75	1.75
1398	A427	250d multicolored	5.00	5.00
1399	A427	500d multicolored	10.00	10.00
		Nos. 1397-1399 (3)	16.75	16.75

Irrigation Project — A428

a, Laborers, heavy equipment. b, Khadafy, heavy equipment. c, Livestock, fruit & vegetables.

1991, Aug. 28 ***Perf. 12***

1400	A428	50d Strip of 3, #a.-c.	3.50	3.50

No. 1400 has a continuous design. Size of No. 1400b: 60x36mm.

Sept. 1st Revolution, 22nd Anniv. — A429

300d, Chains, roses & "22". 400d, Chains, "22".

1991, Sept. 1 ***Perf. 13½***

1401	A429	300d multicolored	5.75	5.75
1402	A429	400d multicolored	7.25	7.25
a.		Souv. sheet of 2, #1401-1402	16.00	16.00

Telecom '91 — A430

100d, Emblems, vert. 500d, Buildings, satillite dish.

1991, Oct. 7 **Litho.** ***Perf. 13½***

1403	A430	100d multicolored	1.75	1.75
1404	A430	500d multicolored	9.25	9.25

Libyans Deported to Italy — A431

100d, Monument, soldier. 400d, Ship, refugees, soldiers.

1991, Oct. 26 **Litho.** ***Perf. 13½***

1405	A431	100d multicolored	1.75	1.75
1406	A431	400d multicolored	7.25	7.25
a.		Souv. sheet of 2, #1405-1406	10.00	10.00

Arab Unity — A432

1991, Nov. 15 ***Perf. 12***

1407	A432	50d tan & multi	1.00	1.00
1408	A432	100d blue & multi	2.00	2.00

Miniature Sheet

Trucks, Automobiles and Motorcycles — A433

Designs: a-d, Various trucks. e-h, Various off-road race cars. i-p, Various motorcycles.

1991, Dec. 28 ***Perf. 14***

1409	A433	50d Sheet of 16, #a.-p.	17.50	17.50

Eagle A434

Col. Khadafy A434a

1992 ***Perf. 11½***

Granite Paper (#1412-1419)

Background Colors

1412	A434	100d	yellow	1.40	.85
1413	A434	150d	blue gray	2.25	1.25
1414	A434	200d	brt blue	2.75	1.75
1415	A434	250d	orange	3.75	2.00
1416	A434	300d	purple	4.25	2.50
1418	A434	400d	brt pink	5.75	3.50
1419	A434	450d	brt grn	7.25	3.75

Perf. 13½

1420	A434a	500d	yel grn	6.50	3.50
1421	A434a	1000d	rose	13.00	7.00
1422	A434a	2000d	blue	26.00	14.00
1423	A434a	5000d	violet	65.00	37.50
1424	A434a	6000d	yel brn	80.00	45.00
		Nos. 1412-1424 (12)		217.90	122.60

Issued: No 1412-1416, 1418-1419, 1/1; Nos. 1420-1424, 9/1.

People's Authority Declaration — A435

1992, Mar. **Litho.** ***Perf. 12***

1425	A435	100d yellow & multi	1.50	1.50
1426	A435	150d blue & multi	2.25	2.25

African Tourism Year (in 1991) — A436

1992, Apr. 5 ***Perf. 14½***

Granite Paper

1427	A436	50d purple & multi	.75	.75
1428	A436	100d pink & multi	1.40	1.40

1992 Summer Olympics, Barcelona — A437

1992, June 15 ***Perf. 12***

1429	A437	50d Tennis	.75	.75
1430	A437	50d Long jump	.75	.75
1431	A437	50d Discus	.75	.75
		Nos. 1429-1431 (3)	2.25	2.25

Size: 106x82mm

Imperf

1432	A437	100d Olympic torch, rings	1.50	1.50

Revolutionary Achievements A438

Designs: 100d, Palm trees. 150d, Steel mill. 250d, Cargo ship. 300d, Libyan Airlines. 400d, Natl. Assembly, Green Books. 500d, Irrigation pipeline, Khadafy.

1992, June 30 ***Perf. 14***

Granite Paper

1433	A438	100d multicolored	1.40	1.40
1434	A438	150d multicolored	2.25	2.25
1435	A438	250d multicolored	3.75	3.75
1436	A438	300d multicolored	4.25	4.25
1437	A438	400d multicolored	5.75	5.75
1438	A438	500d multicolored	7.25	7.25
		Nos. 1433-1438 (6)	24.65	24.65

Tripoli Intl. Fair — A439

50d, Horse & buggy. 100d, Horse & sulky.

1992, Mar. ***Perf. 12***

1439	A439	50d multicolored		
1440	A439	100d multicolored		

Maghreb Arab Union Philatelic Exhibition A440

1992, Feb. 17 ***Perf. 14½***

1441	A440	75d blue green & multi	2.50	1.75
1442	A440	80d blue & multi	2.50	1.75

Miniature Sheet

Fish — A441

Designs: a, Fish with spots near eye. b, Thin fish. d, Brown fish, currents. e, Fish, plants at LR. f, Fish, plants at LL.

1992, Apr. 15 ***Perf. 14***

1443	A441	100d Sheet of 6, #a.-f.	14.00	14.00

Miniature Sheet

Horsemanship — A442

Designs: a, Woman rider with gun. b, Man on white horse. c, Mongol rider. d, Roman officer. e, Cossack rider. f, Arab rider. 250d, Two Arab riders.

1992, Apr. 25 ***Perf. 13½x14***

1444	A442	100d Sheet of 6, #a.-f.	9.50	9.50

Souvenir Sheet

1445	A442	250d multicolored	5.00	5.00

Khadafy A443

Designs: No. 1450a, like No. 1446. b, like No. 1447. c, like No. 1448. d, like No. 1449.

1992, Jan. 1 ***Perf. 14x13½***

1446	A443	100d blue grn & multi	2.00	2.00
1447	A443	100d gray & multi	2.00	2.00
1448	A443	100d rose lake & multi	2.00	2.00
1449	A443	100d yellow & multi	2.00	2.00
		Nos. 1446-1449 (4)	8.00	8.00

Souvenir Sheet

1450	A443	150d Sheet of 4, #a.-d.	11.00	11.00

Evacuation of Foreign Forces — A444

75d, Horse, broken chain. 80d, Flag, broken chain.

1992, Oct. 7 **Litho.** ***Perf. 14***

1451	A444	75d multicolored	1.00	1.00
1452	A444	80d multicolored	1.00	1.00

Costumes — A445

Women wearing various traditional costumes.

Denomination color: a, green. b, black. c, violet blue. d, sky blue. e, yellow brown.

1992, Dec. 15 **Litho.** ***Perf. 12***

1453	A445	50d Strip of 5, #a.-e.	4.00	4.00

Sept. 1st Revolution, 23rd Anniv. — A446

50d, Torch, "23". 100d, Flag, "23". 250d, Eagle, "23".

1992, Sept. 1

1454	A446	50d multicolored	.75	.75
1455	A446	100d multicolored	1.40	1.40

Souvenir Sheet

1456	A446	250d multicolored	3.50	3.50

No. 1456 contains one 50x40mm stamp.

Libyans Deported to Italy — A447

1992, Oct. 26

1457	A447	100d tan & multi	1.40	1.40
1458	A447	250d blue & multi	3.00	3.00

Oasis — A448

Designs: 100d, Gazelle drinking. 200d, Camels, palm trees, vert. 300d, Palm trees, camel and rider.

1992, Oct. 1 ***Perf. 14***

1459	A448	100d multicolored		1.50	1.50
1460	A448	200d multicolored		3.00	3.00
1461	A448	300d multicolored		5.00	5.00
		Nos. 1459-1461 (3)		9.50	9.50

Palestinian Intifada A449

Designs: 100d, Palestinian holding rock and flag. 300d, Map of Israel and Palestine, Dome of the Rock, Palestinian flag, olives, hand holding rock, vert.

1992, Nov. 26 **Litho.** ***Perf. 12***
1462-1463 A449 Set of 2 4.50 4.50

Doctors — A450

Designs: 40d, Dr. Mohamed Ali Imsek (1883-1945). 60d, Dr. Aref Adhani Arif (1884-1935).

1993, Feb. 1
1464-1465 A450 Set of 2 1.25 1.25

Intl. Conference on Nutrition, Rome — A451

Background colors: 70d, Blue. 80d, Green.

1993, Feb. 15
1466-1467 A451 Set of 2 1.75 1.75

People's Authority Declaration A452

Col. Khadafy, map of Libya, crowd, eagle, oil rig, pipeline and tanker: 60d, 65d, 75d.

1993, Mar. 2 ***Perf. 14¾***
1468-1470 A452 Set of 3 2.25 2.25

Tripoli Intl. Fair — A453

Various Fair participants, Fair emblem and panel color of: No. 1471, 60d, Pink. No. 1472, 60d, Yellow green. No. 1473, 60d, Blue, vert. No. 1474, 60d, Orange, vert.
100d, People on horses.

1993, Mar. 15 ***Perf. 14***
1471-1474 A453 Set of 4 2.50 2.50

Souvenir Sheet

Perf. 11¾

1475 A453 100d multi 1.50 1.50

No. 1475 contains one 38x32mm stamp.

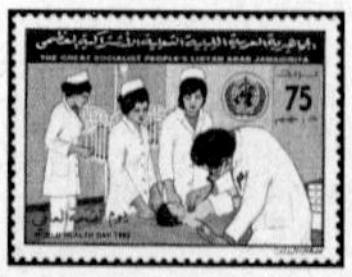

World Health Day — A454

Designs: 75d, Doctor and three nurses examining child. 85d, Doctor and two nurses examining woman.

1993, Apr. 7 ***Perf. 13¼***
1476-1477 A454 Set of 2 1.60 1.60

Children's Day — A455

No. 1478 — Various girls with background of: a, Gray green (red headdress). b, Red curtains. c, Gray. d, Home furnishings. e, Beige.

1993, May 1 ***Perf. 13¾***

1478	Horiz. strip of 5		4.25	4.25
a.-e.	A455 75d Any single		.80	.80

Miniature Sheet

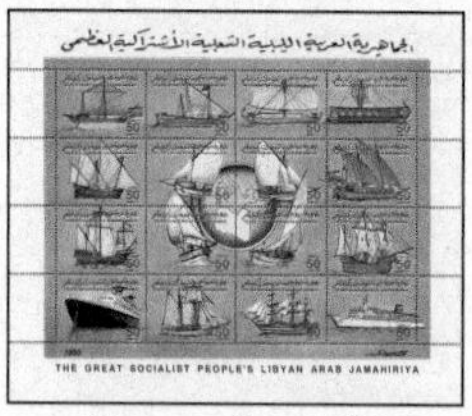

Watercraft — A456

No. 1479: a, Ship with swan's head figurehead. b, Ship with triangular sail and oars. c, Ship with one large white sail. d, Ship with rectangular sail and oars. e, Ship with three triangular sails. f, Sailboat, map of Western Mediterranean area. g, Sailboat, map of Eastern Mediterranean area. h, Ship with two red triangular sails. i, Ship with four sails, red flag. j, Sailboat, map of Western Libya. k, Sailboat, map of Eastern Libya. l, Ship with three sails on main mast. m, Ocean liner with black hull. n, Ship with six tan sails. o, Ship with furled sails. p, Ocean liner with white hull.

1993, July 15 ***Perf. 13¼***
1479 A456 50d Sheet of 16, #a-p 10.00 10.00

Miniature Sheet

Sept. 1 Revolution, 24th Anniv. — A457

No. 1480: a, Grain combine. b, Col. Khadafy. c, Cows, man with feed bucket. d, Shepherd and sheep. e, Oil platform, map of Western Libya. f, Eagle, man on camel, map of Eastern Libya. g, Cranes lifting large tanks. h, Water pipeline. i, Man picking dates. j, Man in field, crates of vegetables. k, Crates of vegetables. l, Man picking vegetables. m, Three children. n, Building, women at typewriter and microscope. o, Man in field, tractor. p, Tractors in field.

1993, Dec. 10 ***Perf. 14***
1480 A457 50d Sheet of 16, #a-p 12.00 12.00

Miniature Sheet

Libyans Deported to Italy A458

No. 1481: a, Guard tower, soldier with gun, woman tending to sick man. b, Soldier with gun and bayonet guarding Libyans. c, Col. Khadafy with headdress. d, Man holding box and walking stick. e, Soldiers whipping man. f, Man on horse. g, Four men. h, Soldier guarding people looking at hanged man. i, Soldier standing near wooden post, soldier guarding Libyans. j, Woman on camel, soldiers. k, Soldiers on horses among Libyans. l, Boat with deportees. m, Col. Khadafy without headdress. n, Libyan with arm raised, hand of Col. Khadafy. o, Soldier pointing gun at horseman with sword. p, Horseman carrying gun.

1993, Dec. 15 ***Perf. 14½***
1481 A458 50d Sheet of 16, #a-p 12.00 12.00

Miniature Sheet

Items Made of Silver A459

No. 1482: a, Medallion with five-pointed star and tassels. b, Wristband. c, Medallion with star with ten rays and tassels. d, Rod with tassels. e, Necklace. f, Slippers.

Litho. & Embossed With Foil Application

1994, Aug. 10 ***Perf. 13¼***
1482 A459 55d Sheet of 6, #a-f 4.25 4.25

A460

Sept. 1 Revolution, 25th Anniv. — A461

No. 1483: a, Jet, Col. Khadafy in robe (40x40mm). b, Warriors on horseback, mother and child, Col. Khadafy in military uniform (60x40mm). c, Ship, shepherd, man and woman, man on camel (40x40mm).

1994, Sept. 1 **Litho.** ***Perf. 12***
1483 A460 100d Horiz. strip of 3, #a-c 4.25 4.25

Souvenir Sheet

1484 A461 1000d multi 13.50 13.50

1994 World Cup Soccer Championships, United States — A462

World Cup, and various soccer players with horizontal stripes in: No. 1485, 100d, Red and brown. No. 1486, 100d, Red violet, purple, and green. No. 1487, 100d, Green and purple. No. 1488, 100d, Green, black and yellow. No. 1489, 100d, Orange, brown and red. No. 1490, 100d, Yellow orange, brown and orange.
No. 1491, 500d, Soccer players, World Cup, red violet background. No. 1492, 500d, Soccer player, ball, "1990," horiz.

1994, Oct. 15 ***Perf. 13¼***
1485-1490 A462 Set of 6 8.50 8.50

Souvenir Sheets

1491-1492 A462 Set of 2 14.00 14.00

No. 1491 contains one 42x51mm stamp; No. 1492 contains one 51x42mm stamp.

Miniature Sheet

Libyans Deported to Italy A463

No. 1493: a, Col. Khadafy. b, Airplane, man with rifle. c, Two men, one with rifle, nose of airplane. d, Tail of airplane, man with rifle. e, Soldier with bayoneted rifle, Libyans looking at dead animal. f, Libyans with rifles, camel. g, Nose of camel, horsemen and soldiers. h, Man carrrying child, drawn swords, horsemen. i, Soldier with whip. j, Man with open mouth. k, Tank and soldiers. l, Soldiers on horseback, women. m, Woman tending to injured man, man with bound hands, rifles. n, Soldier bayoneting man. o, Building, women, soldiers on horseback. p, Deportees in boats.

1994, Oct. 26 ***Perf. 12***
1493 A463 95d Sheet of 16, #a-p 22.50 22.50

Mosques — A464

No. 1494 — Mosques in: a, Darghut. b, Benghazi. c, Kabao. d, Gouzgu. e, Siala. f, El Kettani.

1994, Nov. 15 **Litho.**

1494	Horiz. strip of 6		11.50	11.50
a.-f.	A464 70d Any single		1.50	1.50

Miniature Sheet

People's Authority Declaration — A465

No. 1495: a, Navy ship, jet, women soldiers. b, Wheat, hand holding Green Book, tractor trailer cab. c, Family, water pipeline, tractor trailers. d, Fruit, vegetables, people holding Green Book. e, Col. Khadafy, butterfly, flowers. f, Young men, fruit and vegetables.

1994, Dec. 1 ***Perf. 14¾***
1495 A465 80d Sheet of 6, #a-f 12.00 12.00

Evacuation of Foreign Forces — A466

Denomination in: 65d, Blue. 95f, Green.

1994, Dec. 15 *Perf. 14*
1496-1497 A466 Set of 2 2.75 2.75

Miniature Sheet

Khadafy Prize for Human Rights A467

No. 1498: a, Helmeted soldiers, men with sticks, South African flag. b, Men with sticks, South African flag. c, South African Pres. Nelson Mandela. d, Col. Khadafy. e, Indian at fire, crescent moon. f, Armed Indians on horses. g, Indian chief. h, Indian dancer. i, Men with rifles, jets. j, Women, jet, open book. k, Open book. l, Surgeons. m, Palestinians with flag, denomination at left. n, Palestinians with flag, denomination at right. o, Palestinians throwing rocks. p, Palestinians, soldiers.

1994, Dec. 31 *Perf. 13¼*
1498 A467 95d Sheet of 16, #a-p *20.00 40.00*

No. 1498 was first issued with marginal inscription with incorrect spelling of "Prize" as "Price." Value is for sheet with corrected spelling. Value, sheet with incorrect spelling $300.

People's Authority Declaration — A468

Background color: No. 1499, 100d, Green. No. 1500, 100d, Blue. No. 1501, 100d, Yellow.

1995, July 1 *Perf. 12*
1499-1501 A468 Set of 3 2.25 2.25

Arab League, 50th Anniv. — A469

Background color: No. 1502, 200d, Green. No. 1503, 200d, Blue.

No. 1504: a, Emblem in silver. b, Emblem in gold.

1995, July 20 **Litho.** *Perf. 13¼*
1502-1503 A469 Set of 2 7.50 7.50

Litho. & Embossed With Foil Application

1504 A469 1000d Sheet of 2, #a-b 13.00 13.00

Miniature Sheet

Libyan Soccer Players A470

No. 1505: a, Messaud Zentuti. b, Salem Shermit. c, Ottoman Marfua. d, Ghaleb Siala. e, 1935 Libyan Team. f, Senussi Mresila.

1995, Aug. 1 **Litho.**
1505 A470 100d Sheet of 6, #a-f 9.50 9.50

Miniature Sheet

Zoo Animals A471

No. 1506: a, Camel. b, Secretary bird. c, African wild dog. d, Oryx. e, Baboon. f, Golden jackal. g, Crowned eagle. h, Eagle owl. i, Desert hedgehog. j, Sand gerbil. k, Addax. l, Fennec. m, Lanner falcon. n, Desert wheatear. o, Pintailed sandgrouse. p, Jerboa.

1995, Aug. 15 *Perf. 13¾x14*
1506 A471 100d Sheet of 16, #a-p 25.00 25.00

Miniature Sheet

Fruit A472

No. 1507: a, Grapefruit. b, Wild cherries. c, Mulberries. d, Strawberry tree fruit (arbutus). e, Plums. f, Pears. g, Apricots. h, Almonds. i, Prickly pears. j, Lemons. k, Peaches. l, Dates. m, Olives. n, Oranges. o, Figs. p, Grapes.

1995, Aug. 20
1507 A472 100d Sheet of 16, #a-p 24.00 24.00

Miniature Sheet

Sept. 1 Revolution, 26th Anniv. — A473

No. 1508: a, Students and chemist. b, Minaret, fist of Col. Khadafy, men. c, Col. Khadafy. d, Scientists and buildings. e, Nurses, doctor and patients. f, Surgeons. g, Woman at keyboard, shoemakers. h, Audio technicians, musician. i, Crane, bulldozer and buildings. j, Grain elevator. k, Offshore oil rig, nose of airplane. l, Tail of airplane, ship. m, Goats and sheep. n, Water pipeline. o, Camels, vegetables, water. p, Fruit, grain combine.

1995, Sept. 1
1508 A473 100d Sheet of 16, #a-p 22.50 22.50

Scouts A474

No. 1509 — Scouting emblem and: a, Antelope, Scout and butterflies (40x40mm). b, Scouts, butterflies, antelope and cat (60x40mm). c, Scouts, wheat, butterfly, flower.

1995, Sept. 10 *Perf. 12*
1509 A474 250d Horiz. strip of 3, #a-c 17.00 17.00

American Attack on Libya, 9th Anniv. — A475

No. 1510: a, Ships and people (40x50mm). b, Airplanes, helicopters and people, hand holding Green Book (60x50mm). c, Airplane, mother and child (40x50mm).

1995, Sept. 15
1510 A475 100d Horiz. strip of 3, #a-c 4.50 4.50

Tripoli Intl. Fair — A476

Horsemen with background colors of: No. 1511, 100d, Light blue. No. 1512, 100d, Blue. No. 1513, 100d, Violet. No. 1514, 100d, Blue green, vert. No. 1515, 100d, Blue green with black stripes, vert. No. 1516, 100d, Orange, vert.

1000d, Col. Khadafy on horse.

1995, Sept. 20
1511-1516 A476 Set of 6 9.00 9.00

Souvenir Sheet

1517 A476 1000d multi 14.00 14.00

No. 1517 contains one 80x50mm stamp.

Miniature Sheet

City of Ghadames — A477

No. 1518: a, Camel, woman with water jugs. b, Woman with bread on wooden board. c, Seated woman with vase. d, Woman feeding chickens. e, Woman at spinning wheel. f, Woman standing. g, Woman cooking. h, Woman milking goat. i, Shoemaker. j, Man at loom. k, Metalworker with hammer. l, Date picker. m, Men at religious school. n, Potter. o, Tanner. p, Man picking tomatoes.

Perf. 14½x14¼

1995, Sept. 30 **Litho.**
1518 A477 100d Sheet of 16, #a-p 21.00 21.00

Evacuation of Foreign Forces — A478

Panel color: 50d, Pink. 100d, Green. 200d, Lilac.

1995, Oct. 7 **Litho.** *Perf. 14¾x14¼*
1519-1521 A478 Set of 3 5.00 5.00

Bees and Flowers — A479

Panel color: No. 1522, 100d, Green. No. 1523, 100d, Pink. No. 1524, 100d, Purple.

1995, Oct. 10 *Perf. 14¼x14¾*
1522-1524 A479 Set of 3 4.50 4.50

Dr. Mohamed Feituri — A480

1995, Oct. 20 *Perf. 14¾x14¼*
1525 A480 200d multi 2.75 2.75

Campaign Against Smoking — A481

Color of central stripe: No. 1526, 100d, Orange. No. 1527, 100d, Yellow.

1995, Oct. 20
1526-1527 A481 Set of 2 3.25 3.25

Miniature Sheet

Libyans Deported to Italy A482

No. 1528: a, Col. Khadafy. b, Horsemen. c, Battle scene with blue sky, denomination at LR. d, Battle scene with blue sky, airplane, denomination at LL. e, Battle scene, arch. f, Battle scene, red building at UR. g, Battle scene with red sky, soldier holding pistol. h, Battle scene with red sky, building at UR. i, Three Libyans in foreground. j, Battle scene with running soldiers. k, Battle scene of horsemen and riflemen facing right. l, Soldiers, Libyan man in foreground at LR. m, Two horesemen with arms raised. n, Man in foreground shooting at horsemen. o, Children. p, Child, deportees in boats.

1995, Oct. 26 *Perf. 12*
1528 A482 100d Sheet of 16, #a-p 22.00 22.00

Miniature Sheet

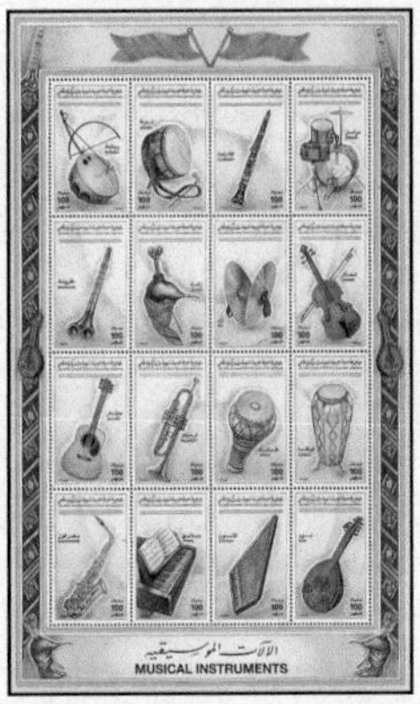

Musical Instruments — A483

No. 1529: a, Rababa. b, Nouba (drum). c, Clarinet. d, Drums. e, Magruna. f, Zukra. g, Zil (cymbals). h, Kaman (violin). i, Guitar. j, Trumpet. k, Tapla (drum). l, Gonga (drum). m, Saxophone. n, Piano. o, Gandon (zither). p, Ood.

1995, Nov. 1 ***Perf. 13¾x14***
1529 A483 100d Sheet of 16, #a-p 21.00 21.00

Doors of Mizda — A484

No. 1530: a, Blue door. b, Door with arched design in rectangular doorway. c, Log door. d, Door with rounded top in archway. e, Door of planks in rectangular doorway.

1995, Nov. 10 ***Perf. 13¼***
1530 Horiz. strip of 5 3.50 3.50
a.-e. A484 100d Any single .65 .65

Intl. Olympic Committee, Cent. — A485

Denomination color: No. 1531, 100d, Red. No. 1532, 100d, Black.

1995, Nov. 15 ***Perf. 13½***
1531-1532 A485 Set of 2 1.40 1.40

Prehistoric Animals — A486

No. 1533: a, Baryonyx. b, Oviraptor. c, Stenonychosaurus. d, Tenontosaurus. e, Yangchuanosaurus. f, Stegotetrabelodon, denomination at LR. g, Stegotetrabelodon, denomination at LL. h, Psittacosaurus. i, Heterodontosaurus. j, Loxodonta atlantica. k, Mammuthus. l, Erlikosaurus. m, Cynognathus. n, Plateosaurus. o, Staurikosaurus. p, Lystrosaurus.
500d, Stegotetrabelodon, horiz.

1995, Nov. 20 ***Perf. 13½***
1533 A486 Miniature sheet of 16 12.50 12.50
a.-p. 100d Any single .75 .70

Souvenir Sheet
Perf. 13¼

1534 A486 500d multi 4.25 4.25

No. 1534 contains one 53x49mm stamp.

Children's Day — A487

No. 1535: a, Boy, dinosaur with cane. b, Boy on elephant. c, Boy, Scout emblem, turtle and mushroom. d, Dinosaur and soccer ball. e, Boy with gun, pteranodon.

1995, Nov. 25 ***Perf. 13½***
1535 Horiz. strip of 5 15.00 15.00
a.-e. A487 100d Any single 2.75 2.75

Palestinian Intifada — A488

No. 1536: a, Boy throwing object at helicopter. b, Dome of the Rock, Palestinian with flag. c, People, Palestinian flag.

1995, Nov. 29 ***Perf. 14***
1536 A488 100d Horiz. strip of 3, #a-c 4.50 4.50

Intl. Civil Aviation Organization, 50th Anniv. — A489

Denomination color: No. 1537, 100d, Black. No. 1538, 100d, Blue.

1995, Dec. 7 ***Perf. 13½x13¼***
1537-1538 A489 Set of 2 1.40 1.40

United Nations, 50th Anniv. — A490

Background color: No. 1539, 100d, Dark red lilac. No. 1540, 100d, Light red lilac.

1995, Dec. 20 ***Perf. 13½***
1539-1540 A490 Set of 2 1.40 1.40

Miniature Sheet

Flowers A491

No. 1541: a, Iris germanica. b, Canna edulis. c, Nerium oleander. d, Papaver rhoeas. e, Strelitzia reginae. f, Amygdalus communis.

1995, Dec. 31 ***Perf. 14¾***
1541 A491 200d Sheet of 6, #a-f 11.00 11.00

People's Authority Declaration — A492

Panel color: 100d, Pink. 150d, Light blue. 200d, Light green.

1996, Mar. 2 ***Perf. 13¼***
1542-1544 A492 Set of 3 5.00 5.00

1996 Summer Olympics, Atlanta — A493

No. 1545: a, Soccer. b, Long jump. c, Tennis. d, Cycling. e, Boxing. f, Equestrian.
No. 1546, 500d, Runner. No. 1547, 500d, Equestrian, diff.

1996, Aug. 15 ***Perf. 14½***
1545 A493 100d Sheet of 6, #a-f 6.75 6.75

Souvenir Sheets

1546-1547 A493 Set of 2 11.00 11.00

Miniature Sheet

Sept. 1 Revolution, 27th Anniv. — A494

No. 1548: a, Camel, man, fruits, water. b, Water pipeline, fruit. c, Tractor, water, women. d, Oil worker. e, Tailor. f, Seamstress, Col. Khadafy's fist. g, Col. Khadafy. h, Building, women with microscope. i, Nurses at anatomy lesson, man with microscope. j, School child. k, Woman with open book. l, Man playing zither. m, Airplanes. n, Dish antenna, ship, man on camel. o, Ship, television camera. p, Television actress, woman at microphone.

1996, Sept. 1 ***Perf. 13¾x14***
1548 A494 100d Sheet of 16, #a-p 20.00 20.00

Miniature Sheet

American Attack on Libya, 10th Anniv. — A495

No. 1549: a, Left side of missile, explosion. b, Right side of missile, man with raised arms. c, Casualties, airplanes. d, Airplane at left, man on ground. e, Firefighter spraying burning car. f, Damaged vehicles. g, Col. Khadafy. h, Casualties, airplane at top. i, Rescuers assisting casualties. j, Man with extended hand. k, Woman with hands to face. l, Stretcher bearers. m, Three men and casualty. n, Man with bloody hand. o, Woman and child casualties. p, Burning car, rescuers attending to bleeding casualty.

1996, Sept. 15 ***Perf. 13¾***
1549 A495 100d Sheet of 16, #a-p 20.00 20.00

Miniature Sheet

Crustaceans — A496

No. 1550: a, Necora puber. b, Lissa chiragra. c, Palinurus elephas. d, Scyllarus arctus. e, Carcinus maenas. f, Calappa granulata. g, Parapenaeus longirostris. h, Nephrops norvegicus. i, Eriphia verrucosa. j, Cancer pagurus. k, Penaeus kerathurus. l, Squilla mantis. m, Maja squinado. n, Pilumnus hirtellus. o, Pagurus alatus. p, Macropodia tenuirostris.

1996, Oct. 1 ***Perf. 14x13¾***
1550 A496 100d Sheet of 16, #a-p 20.00 20.00

Miniature Sheet

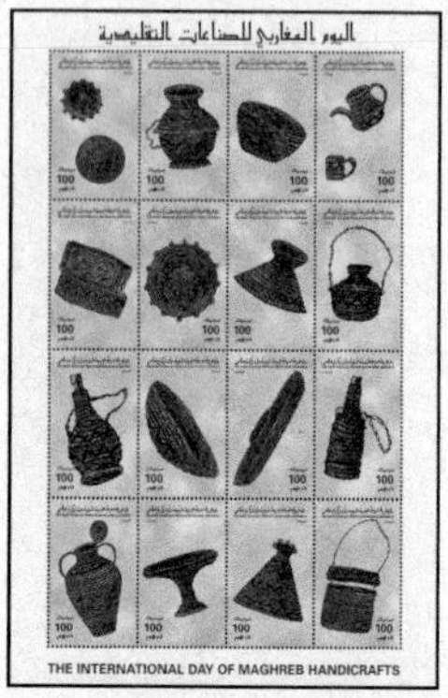

Intl. Day of Maghreb Handicrafts — A497

Various handicrafts.

1996, Oct. 15 ***Perf. 13¾x14***
1551 A497 100d Sheet of 16, #a-p 20.00 20.00

Miniature Sheet

Libyans Deported to Italy A498

No. 1552: a, Guard tower, soldier with gun, woman tending to sick man. b, Soldier with gun and bayonet, soldier on horseback. c, Col. Khadafy with headdress. d, Man holding box and walking stick. e, Soldiers whipping man. f, Man on horse. g, Four men. h, Soldier guarding people looking at hanged man. i, Soldier standing near wooden post, soldier guarding Libyans. j, Woman on camel, soldiers. k, Soldiers on horses among Libyans. l, Boat with deportees. m, Col. Khadafy without headdress. n, Libyan with arm raised, hand of Col. Khadafy. o, Soldier pointing gun at horseman with sword. p, Horseman carrying gun.

1996, Oct. 26 **Litho.**
1552 A498 100d Sheet of 16, #a-p 20.00 20.00

Miniature Sheet

Horses A499

No. 1553: a, Brown horse, lake at right. b, Brown horse in front of lake, tree at right. c, Brown horse in front of lake, tree at right. d, Dark brown horse, trees in background. e, Dark brown horse with raised leg. f, Horse at base of tree. g, Gray horse galloping. h, Piebald horse. i, Gray horse, palm tree at left. j, Head of black horse and tail of brown horse. k, Brown horse, palm fronds at upper right. l, Brown horse with gray mane, palm tree at right. m, Head of black horse, body of gray horse, tail of brown horse. n, Head of brown horse, body of black horse, hindquarters of two brown horses. o, Head of brown horse, parts of three other brown horses. p, Head of brown horse, chest of another brown horse, palm tree at right.

1996, Oct. 30 ***Perf. 14x13¾***
1553 A499 100d Sheet of 16, #a-p 20.00 20.00

Miniature Sheet

Camels A500

No. 1554: a, Camelus dromedarius with head at right. b, Head of Camelus dromedarius. c, Camelus dromedarius with head at left. d, Camelus ferus bactrianus with head at right. e, Camelus ferus ferus. f, Camelus ferus bactrianus with head at left.

1996, Nov. 15 ***Perf. 12***
1554 A500 200d Sheet of 6, #a-f 13.50 13.50

Press and Information — A501

Designs: 100d, Photographer, newspapers, computer. 200d, Musicians, video technician, computer, dish antenna.

1996, Nov. 20
1555-1556 A501 Set of 2 3.25 3.25

Miniature Sheet

Fossils and Prehistoric Animals — A502

No. 1557: a, Mene rhombea fossil. b, Mesodon macrocephalus fossil. c, Eyron arctiformis fossil. d, Stegosaurus. e, Pteranodon. f, Allosaurus.

1996, Nov. 25
1557 A502 200d Sheet of 6, #a-f 16.00 16.00

Palestinian Intifada — A503

Frame color: 100d, Yellow. 150d, Green. 200d, Blue.

1996, Nov. 29
1558-1560 A503 Set of 3 5.00 5.00

African Children's Day — A504

Designs: 50d, Child, beige frame. 150d, Child, blue frame. 200d, Mother, child, dove.

1996, Dec. 5 ***Perf. 13¼***
1561-1563 A504 Set of 3 2.50 2.50

Children's Day — A505

No. 1564 — Various cats with background colors of: a, Rose. b, Blue green. c, Blue. d, Yellow green. e, Gray green.

1996, Dec. 5
1564 Horiz. strip of 5 5.50 5.50
a.-e. A505 100d Any single 1.00 1.00

Intl. Family Day A506

No. 1565 — Family and: a, 150d, Building (21x27mm). b, 150d, Automobile (21x27mm). c, 200d, Stylized globe (46x27mm).

1996, Dec. 10 ***Perf. 13x13¼***
1565 A506 Horiz. strip of 3, #a-c 3.00 3.00

Miniature Sheet

Teachers A507

No. 1566: a, Mohamed Kamel El-Hammali. b, Mustafa Abdulla Ben-Amer. c, Mohamed Messaud Fesheka. d, Kairi Mustafa Serraj. e, Muftah El-Majri. f, Mohamed Hadi Arafa.

1996, Dec. 15 ***Perf. 13¼***
1566 A507 100d Sheet of 6, #a-f 3.75 3.75

Miniature Sheet

Singers A508

No. 1567: a, Mohamed Salim and zither. b, Mohamed M. Sayed Bumedyen and flute. c, Otman Najim and ood. d, Mahmud Sherif and tapla. e, Mohamed Ferjani Marghani and piano. f, Mohamed Kabazi and violin.

1996, Dec. 15
1567 A508 100d Sheet of 6, #a-f 3.75 3.75

Miniature Sheet

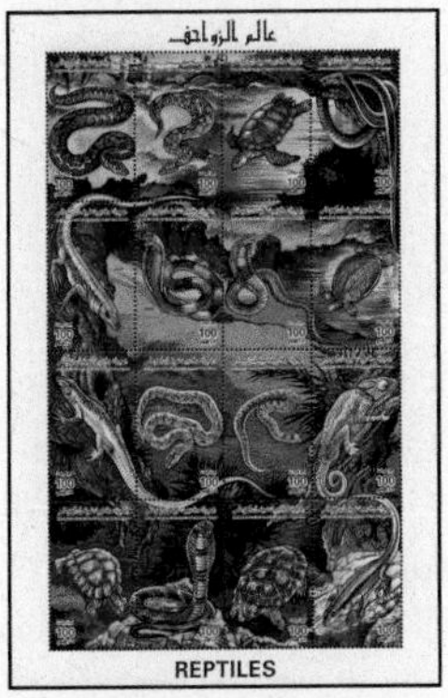

Reptiles A509

No. 1568: a, Snake, leaves and building at top. b, Snake, building at top. c, Turtle, water and part of snake. d, Snake on tree branch. e, Brown lizard on rock. f, Cobra with head at left. g, Cobra and water. h, Turtle, water, tail of cobra. i, Green lizard on rock. j, Snake, foliage at bottom. k, Snake, foliage at bottom and right. l, Lizard with curled tail. m, Turtle on rock. n, Cobra with head at right. o, Turtle on grass. p, Gray lizard on rock.

1996, Dec. 20 ***Perf. 13¾x14***
1568 A509 100d Sheet of 16, #a-p 18.50 18.50

Miniature Sheet

Tripoli Intl. Fair A510

No. 1569: a, Mirror and brush. b, Container and plate. c, Two containers with rounded bases. d, Two containers on pedestals. e, Oval ornament. f, Brushes.

Litho. & Embossed with Foil Application

1996, Dec. 30 ***Perf. 13¾***
1569 A510 100d Sheet of 6, #a-f 6.75 6.75

A511

People's Authority Declaration, 20th Anniv. — A512

Frame color: 100d, Yellow. 200d, Blue. 300d, Green.

1997, Mar. 2 **Litho.** ***Perf. 12***
1570-1572 A511 Set of 3 7.75 7.75

Souvenir Sheet

Imperf

1573 A512 10,000d multi 90.00 90.00

No. 1573 has a perforated label that bears the denomination but lacks the country name.

Scouts and Philately A513

No. 1574: a, 50d, Group of scouts, open album, wheat, flag. b, 50d, Two scouts, two albums, wheat. c, 100d, Butterflies, books, scouts and flags.

1997, Mar. 15 ***Perf. 14***
1574 A513 Horiz. strip of 3, #a-c 2.75 2.75

Health Care A514

No. 1575: a, 50d, Doctor looking at test tube. b, 50d, Doctor, microscope. c, 100d, Doctor and nurse examining baby.

1997, Apr. 7
1575 A514 Horiz. strip of 3, #a-c 2.25 2.25

Buildings — A515

Designs: 50d, Shown. 100d, Building with attached tower, vert. 200d, Tower, vert.

Perf. 14¼x14¾, 14¾x14¼

1997, Apr. 15
1576-1578 A515 Set of 3 5.00 5.00

Campaign Against Smoking — A516

Frame color: 100d, Blue. 150d, Green. 200d, Pink.

1997, Apr. 30 ***Perf. 14¾x14¼***
1579-1581 A516 Set of 3 2.75 2.75

Arab National Central Library — A517

Building, map, open book, and olive branches with background in: 100d, Blue. 200d, Green.

1000d, Building, map, books, computer and Col. Khadafy, horiz.

1997, Aug. 10 ***Perf. 13¼***
1582-1583 A517 Set of 2 1.75 1.75

Souvenir Sheet

1584 A517 1000d multi 6.00 6.00

No. 1584 contains one 116x49mm stamp.

Arab Tourism Year — A518

Perf. 13¼x13½

1997, Aug. 20 **Litho.**
1585 A518 Horiz. strip of 3 10.50 10.50
a. 100d Black denomination 2.00 2.00
b. 200d Red denomination 3.75 3.75
c. 250d Blue denomination 4.75 4.75

Miniature Sheet

A519

Sept. 1 Revolution, 28th Anniv. — A520

No. 1586: a, 100d, Mother and child. b, 100d, Col. Khadafy as student. c, 100d, Khadafy at microphone. d, 100d, People on tank. e, 100d, Khadafy and man in suit. f, 100d, Khadafy with fist raised. g, 100d, Woman, child, corner of Green Book. h, 100d, Three people, corner of Green Book. i, 100d, Khadafy with pen. j, 100d, Man and child. k, 100d, Government buildings, helicopters. l, 100d, Khadafy in military uniform. m, 500d, Khadafy on horse. Size of Nos. 1586a-1586l: 28x43mm. Size of No. 1586m: 56x86mm.

Litho., Litho with Foil Application (#1586m)

1997, Sept. 1 *Perf. 14*

1586 A519 Sheet of 13, #a-m 17.50 17.50

Souvenir Sheet

Perf. 13¾

1587 A520 500d multi 6.00 6.00

Miniature Sheet

Intl. Day of Maghreb Handicrafts — A521

No. 1588 — Various shoes with toes pointing to: a, LR corner. b, Bottom. c, LL corner. d, UR corner. e, Top. f, UL corner.

Litho. With Foil Application

1997, Sept. 20 *Perf. 13¾*

1588 A521 300d Sheet of 6, #a-f 18.00 18.00

Miniature Sheet

Tripoli Intl. Fair A522

No. 1589 — Items made of silver: a, Medallion with tassels. b, Round medallion. c, Diamond-shaped medallion with tassels. d, Curved medallion. e, Necklace. f, Ring.

Litho. & Embossed With Foil Application

1997, Sept. 20

1589 A522 500d Sheet of 6, #a-f 19.00 19.00

Evacuation of Foreign Forces — A523

Denominations: 100d, 150d, 250d.

1997, Oct. 7 Litho. *Perf. 14¾x14¼*

1590-1592 A523 Set of 3 2.75 2.75

Miniature Sheet

Libyans Deported to Italy A524

No. 1593: a, Person carrying water jug. b, Col. Khadafy with headdress. c, Man, soldier on horse. d, Soldier and Libyans. e, Soldier whipping man. f, Soldier, man on horse. g, Libyan man and man in uniform. h, People at hanging. i, Man with purple fez, woman with red headdress. j, People, horse and camel. k, Col. Khadafy without headdress. l, Deportees on boats. m, Hand of Khadafy above pillars. n, Horsemen and pillars. o, Horsemen. p, Horsemen and hand of Khadafy.

1997, Oct. 26 *Perf. 14*

1593 A524 200d Sheet of 16, #a-p 32.50 32.50

Worldwide Fund for Nature (WWF) — A525

No. 1594 — Felis lybica: a, With prey at water. b, Adult and kittens. c, Under tree. d, Two adults.

1997, Nov. 1 *Perf. 13¼*

1594 Horiz. strip of 4 7.50 7.50
a.-d. A525 200d Any single 1.75 1.75

Printed in sheets containing two strips.

Souvenir Sheet

Natl. Society for Wildlife Conservation — A526

No. 1595: a, Antelope facing forward. b, Ram. c, Antelope facing left.

1997, Nov. 1 *Perf. 13¼*

1595 A526 100d Sheet of 3, #a-c 14.00 14.00

Miniature Sheet

American Attack on Libya, 11th Anniv. — A527

No. 1596: a, Explosion. b, Green Book, Libyan airplanes. c, Minarets, hand of Col. Khadafy. d, Col. Khadafy without headdress. e, Wing of American airplane. f, Nose of American airplane. g, Libyan airplanes. h, People looking at tail of American airplane. i, Rockets hitting American airplane. j, Arm of Col. Khadafy. k, Col. Khadafy with headdress. l, Man, fist of Col. Khadafy. m, Rockets and people. n, Col. Khadafy visiting injured person. o, Col. Khadafy kissing girl's hand. p, People with fists raised.

1997, Nov. 15 *Perf. 14*

1596 A527 200d Sheet of 16, #a-p 34.00 34.00

Miniature Sheet

Great Man-Made River — A528

No. 1597: a, Fist, outline map of Libya. b, Col. Khadafy pointing to pipeline. c, Technicians reading paper, equipment. d, Col. Khadafy pointing to map. e, Col. Khadafy. f, Pipe, crane lifting cylinders. g, Col. Khadafy, pipe, vertical cylinder. h, Col. Khadafy, vertical cylinder. i, Col. Khadafy, construction trailer. j, Technician and equipment. k, Col. Khadafy, pipes lifted by crane. l, Col. Khadafy, line of trucks carrying pipe. m, Man with hand on spigot. n, Col. Khadafy with clasped hands. o, Hands under faucet, crops. p, Woman, child, flowers and fruit.

1997, Dec. 1 *Perf. 14*

1597 A528 200d Sheet of 16, #a-p 34.00 34.00

People's Authority Declaration A529

Panel color: 150d, Blue green. 250d, Purple. 300d, Blue.

1998, Mar. 2 *Perf. 13¼*

1598-1600 A529 Set of 3 10.50 10.50

Miniature Sheet

Tripoli Intl. Fair A530

No. 1601 — Items made of silver: a, Container with two spouts. b, Bowl on pedestal. c, Amphora. d, Container on tray. e, Lidded bowl. f, Three-legged container.

Litho. & Embossed With Foil Application

1998, Mar. 5 *Perf. 13¾*

1601 A530 400d Sheet of 6, #a-f 24.00 24.00

Children's Day — A531

No. 1602 — Various girls in native dress with background colors of: a, Light blue. b, Yellow green. c, Red orange. d, Lilac. e, Yellow brown.

1998, Mar. 21 Litho. *Perf. 13¼*

1602 Horiz. strip of 5 5.50 5.50
a.-e. A531 100d Any single 1.00 1.00

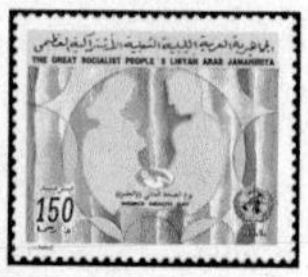

World Health Day — A532

Panel color: 150d, Buff. 250d, Light blue. 300d, Lilac.

1998, Apr. 7

1603-1605 A532 Set of 3 7.75 7.75

American Attack on Libya, 12th Anniv. — A533

No. 1606 — Airplanes, ships and: a, Helicopters, people with raised fists (28x48mm). b, Mother and child, Col. Khadafy (60x48mm). c, Man, boy and birds (28x48mm).

1998, Apr. 15

1606 A533 100d Horiz. strip of 3, #a-c 3.50 3.50

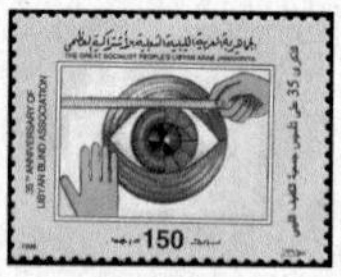

Libyan Blind Association, 35th Anniv. — A534

Designs: 150d, Eye, hand with cane, raised hand. 250d, Blind people, stringed instrument, books.

1998, May 1 *Perf. 12*

1607-1608 A534 Set of 2 4.75 4.75

Arab Bee Union — A535

Frame color: 250d, Blue. 300d, Yellow. 400d, Light green.

1998, June 1

1609-1611 A535 Set of 3 13.50 13.50

1998 World Cup Soccer Championships, France — A536

No. 1612 — Soccer player with: a, Ball at LR, orange and white lines at bottom. b, Top of World Cup. c, Ball at left, orange and white lines at bottom. d, No visible uniform number, left part of stadium at bottom. e, Bottom of World Cup, stadium. f, Uniform No. 5, right part of stadium at bottom.

No. 1613, 1000d, Player, World Cup, denomination at LL. No. 1614, 1000d, Player, World Cup, denomination at LR.

1998, June 10 *Perf. 13¼*

1612 A536 200d Sheet of 6, #a-f *15.00 15.00*

Souvenir Sheets

1613-1614 A536 Set of 2 *24.00 24.00*

Nos. 1613-1614 each contain one 42x51mm stamp.

Miniature Sheet

World Book Day
A537

No. 1615: a, Man, boy, mosque. b, Gymnasts. c, Science teacher at blackboard, student, ear. d, Men picking vegetables. e, Men at blackboard, man with machinery. f, Man with headset microphone, world map. g, Teacher with compass, student. h, Scientists with microscope. i, Girl writing, horseman. j, Teacher, student, map of Libya, globe. k, Music teacher at blackboard, student. l, Woman at sewing machine. m, Chemistry teacher and student. n, Teacher and women at typewriters. o, Cooks. p, Woman at computer keyboard, computer technician.

1998, June 23
1615 A537 100d Sheet of 16, #a-p 17.50 17.50

Map of the Great Man-Made River — A538

Denomination color: 300d, Green. 400d, Blue.
2000d, Bister.

Litho. & Embossed With Foil Application

1998, July 1
1616-1617 A538 Set of 2 8.50 8.50

Souvenir Sheet

1618 A538 2000d gold & multi 22.00 22.00

Miniature Sheet

Great Man-Made River and Vegetables — A539

No. 1619: a, Garlic. b, Peas. c, Potatoes. d, Corn. e, Leeks. f, Tomatoes. g, Carrots. h, Radishes. i, Beans. j, Peppers. k, Eggplant. l, Lettuce. m, Squash. n, Cucumbers. o, Onions, p, Cauliflower.

1998, Sept. 1 **Litho.** ***Perf. 14***
1619 A539 100d Sheet of 16, #a-p 21.00 21.00

Miniature Sheet

Children's Day — A540

No. 1620 — Scouting trefoil and: a, Scouts, dog. b, Scouts saluting, birds. c, Scouts saluting, flags, tents. d, Scouts, sheep. e, Scouts playing musical instruments, tying down tent. f, Scouts at campfire, bird, boat.

1998, Aug. 1 ***Perf. 14¼***
1620 A540 400d Sheet of 6, #a-f *55.00 55.00*

A541

Sept. 1 Revolution, 29th Anniv. — A542

No. 1621: a, Col. Khadafy. b, Horseman, pipeline, vegetables. c, Fruit, pipeline, head of eagle. d, Tail of eagle, minaret. e, Surgeons, students. f, Book, map of Northwestern Africa. g, Book, men, map of Northeastern Africa and Arabian Peninsula. h, Mosque. i, People with flags, grain combine. j, Ship. k, Apartment buildings, l, Boy. m, People, irrigation rig, building. n, Building with flagpole at right. o, Building with flagpole at right, irrigation rig. p, Building, irrigation rig.

1998, Sept. 1 **Litho.** ***Perf. 14¼***
1621 A541 200d Sheet of 16, #a-p *37.50 37.50*

Souvenir Sheet

Litho. & Embossed

Perf. 13½x13¾

1622 A542 200d shown 2.50 2.50

Evacuation of Foreign Forces — A543

Panel color: 100d, Pink. 150d, Light green. 200d, Light blue.

1998, Oct. 7 **Litho.** ***Perf. 13¼***
1623-1625 A543 Set of 3 5.00 5.00

Stamp Day — A544

Panel color: 300d, Buff. 400d, Blue.

1998, Oct. 9 ***Perf. 12***
1626-1627 A544 Set of 2 10.00 10.00

Miniature Sheet

Libyans Deported to Italy
A545

No. 1628: a, Ship, trucks. b, Bound woman, barbed wire. c, Man, barbed wire. d, Soldiers marching Libyans at gunpoint. e, Airplane, battle scene. f, Barbed wire, line of Libyans. g, Barbed wire, soldier and Libyan. h, Soldiers aiming rifles at Libyans, man with camel. i, Horseman, man ladling water. j, Soldier in boat. k, Boats with deportees. l, Boats with deportees, ships. m, Horsemen, man carrying woman. n, Horsemen raising rifles. o, Horseman and flag. p, Mother and child.

1998, Oct. 26 ***Perf. 13¼***
1628 A545 150d Sheet of 16, #a-p 26.00 26.00

Miniature Sheet

Leadership of Islam — A546

No. 1629: a, 100d, White mosque, minaret at left. b, 100d, White mosque, minaret at right. c, 100d, Modern mosque. d, 100d, Mosque seen through arch. e, 100d, Mosque and palm tree, minaret at left. f, 100d, Mosque with blue dome. g, 100d, Mosque with brown dome, six minarets. h, 100d, Mosque, five minarets. i, 500d, Koran, Holy Kaaba. j, 500d, Col. Khadafy on horse. Sizes: 100d stamps, 28x42mm; 500d stamps, 56x84mm.

Litho., Litho. With Foil Application (#1629j)

1998, Nov. 1 ***Perf. 14***
1629 A546 Sheet of 10, #a-j 22.00 22.00

Miniature Sheet

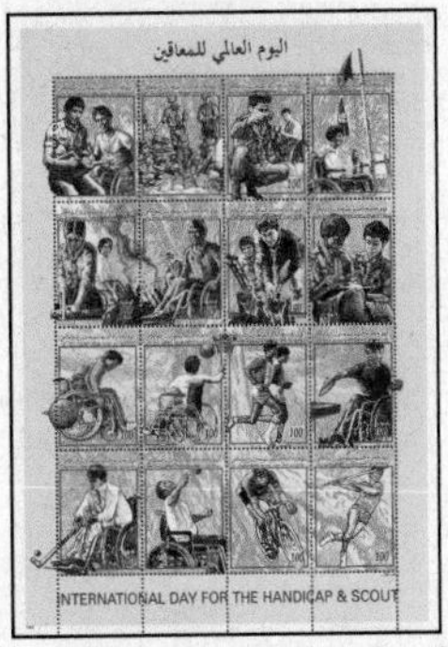

Scouts and the Handicapped — A547

No. 1630: a, Scout reading to boy in wheelchair, butterfly. b, Scout leader instructing group of Scouts. c, Scout photographing bird, boy in wheelchair. d, Scout raising flag, boy in wheelchair. e, Scout sawing log, boy in wheelchair. f, Scout near campfire, boy in wheelchair. g, Scouts with pots in fire, crutches. h, Scouts with pad of paper and pencil. i, Wheelchair basketball player in purple uniform. j, Wheelchair basketball player making shot. k, Handicapped runners. l, Man in wheelchair playing table tennis. m, Man in wheelchair playing hockey. n, Man in wheelchair throwing shot put. o, Handicapped cyclist. p, Handicapped javelin thrower.

1998, Nov. 15 **Litho.** ***Perf. 13¼***
1630 A547 100d Sheet of 16, #a-p 27.50 27.50

Miniature Sheet

A548

Sept. 1 Revolution, 30th Anniv. — A549

No. 1631: a, 100d, Antelopes and "30." b, 100d, Mosque. c, 100d, Woman playing stringed instrument. d, 100d, Horsemen in desert. e, 100d, Grain combine. f, 100d, Ship. g, 100d, Ship, horsemen, flag. h, 100d, Horsemen, flag. i, 100d, Water pipeline, fruit. j, 100d, Butterflies, shepherd and sheep. k, 100d, Building, ship, horse's legs. l, 100d, Dates. m, 200d, Col. Khadafy on horse. Sizes: 100d stamps; 28x42mm, 200d, 56x84mm.

Litho., Litho. With Foil Application (#1631m, 1632)

1999, Sept. 1 ***Perf. 14***
1631 A548 Sheet of 13, #a-m 12.00 12.00

Souvenir Sheet

Perf. 13¾

1632 A549 200d shown 2.00 2.00

A550

Organization of African Unity Assembly of Heads of State and Government, Tripoli — A551

No. 1633: a, Pipeline worker, musicians, minarets. b, Surgeons, woman carrying jug. c, Artisan, camel rider, satellite. d, Col. Khadafy, butterflies. e, Pipeline worker, fruit picker. f, Fruit picker, grain combine.

1999, Sept. 8 **Litho.** ***Perf. 14¼x14½***
1633 A550 300d Sheet of 6, #a-f 13.50 13.50

Souvenir Sheet

Perf. 13¾x14

1634 A551 500d shown 4.00 4.00

Evacuation of Foreign Forces — A552

Frame color: 150d, Pink. 250d, Beige. 300d, Light blue.

1999, Oct. 7 ***Perf. 12***
1635-1637 A552 Set of 3 8.25 8.25

A553

People's Authority Declaration — A554

No. 1638: a, Col. Khadafy with fist raised, man on camel. b, People looking at book. c, Airplane, building, dish antenna. d, Antelope, weaver, tractor. e, Open faucet, pipeline. f, Pipleine, fruit pickers.
No. 1639, 300d, Map of Libya, Col. Khadafy with raised fist, building. No. 1640, 300d, Dove, people, Col. Khadafy.

2000, Mar. 2 Litho. ***Perf. 14½x14¼***
1638 A553 100d Sheet of 6, #a-f 4.75 4.75

Souvenir Sheets

Perf. 13¾

Litho. & Embossed with Foil Application

1639-1640 A554 Set of 2 5.00 5.00

A555

Sept. 1 Revolution, 31st Anniv. — A556

No. 1641: a, Man walking, camel rider. b, Tea drinkers, camels. c, Col. Khadafy. d, Men with raised fists. e, Machinist with torch. f, Boy reading. g, Classroom. h, Scientist. i, Mother and child. j, People attending speech. k, Man and palm tree. l, Patient in X-ray machine. m, Mosque, n, Bulldozer, crane and building. o, Oil workers. p, Bulldozer.
No. 1642, 300d, Col. Khadafy, minaret. No. 1643, 300d, Col. Khadafy, boy and palm tree.

2000, Sept. 1 Litho. ***Perf. 14***
1641 A555 100d Sheet of 16, #a-p 12.50 12.50

Souvenir Sheets

Litho. With Foil Application

Perf. 13¾

1642-1643 A556 Set of 2 5.00 5.00

El-Mujahed Mohamed Abdussalam Ahmeda Abouminiar El-Gaddafi — A557

No. 1644: a, Man holding box. b, Palm tree and horsemen. c, Horsemen and soldiers on horseback. d, Soldiers and armed horsemen. e, Horseman raising rifle above head. f, Men raising rifles, Col. Khadafy.
300d, Man reading book.

2000, Sept. 9 Litho. ***Perf. 13¼***
1644 A557 200d Sheet of 6, #a-f 9.50 9.50

Souvenir Sheet

Litho. & Embossed With Foil Application

1645 A557 300d multi 2.50 2.50

Souvenir Sheet

España 2000 Intl. Philatelic Exhibition — A558

No. 1646: a, A. Castellano (1926-97). b, M. B. Karamanli (1922-95).

2000, Oct. 6 Litho. ***Imperf.***
1646 A558 250d Sheet of 2, #a-b 4.00 4.00

People's Authority Declaration — A559

Denomination color: 150d, Pink. 200d, Blue.

2001, Mar. 2 ***Perf. 14***
1647-1648 A559 Set of 2 2.75 2.75

Miniature Sheet

Organization of African Unity Assemby of Heads of State and Government — A560

No. 1649: a, Heads of various states. b, Heads of state, horsemen. c, Men on camels. d, People with hands raised. e, Man holding picture of Col. Khadafy. f, Col. Khadafy at microphone.

2001, Mar. 2 Litho. ***Perf. 13½x13¼***
1649 A560 200d Sheet of 6, #a-f 9.50 9.50

Souvenir Sheets

Organization of African Unity Assembly of Heads of State and Government — A561

Background colors: No. 1650, 500d, Gold. No. 1651, 500d, Silver.

Litho. & Embossed With Foil Application

2001, Mar. 2 ***Perf. 13¼***
1650-1651 A561 Set of 2 8.50 8.50

Miniature Sheet

Tripoli Intl. Fair A562

No. 1652: a, Rear view of saddle. b, Side view of saddle. c, Front view of saddle. d, Stirrup. e, Four pieces of tack. f, Two pieces of tack.

Litho. & Embossed with Foil Application

2001, Apr. 2 ***Perf. 13¾***
1652 A562 300d Sheet of 6, #a-f 22.00 22.00

Miniature Sheet

Fight Against American Aggression — A563

No. 1653: a, Exploding jet. b, American jet. c, Pilot. d, American plane shooting missile. e, Parachute. f, Airplanes. g, Child crying. h, Palm tree, explosion. i, Missiles. j, Broken egg. k, Teddy bear. l, Clock. m, Explosion in city. n, Man rescuing casualty. o, Man holding child casualty. p, Family fleeing.

2001, Apr. 15 Litho. ***Perf. 13¼***
1653 A563 100d Sheet of 16, #a-p *13.00 13.00*

Desertification Project — A564

No. 1654: a, Man with hoe (30x39mm). b, Men near stream (60x39mm). c, Camels (30x39mm).

2001, June 26 Litho. ***Perf. 13¼***
1654 A564 250d Horiz. strip of 3, #a-c 12.00 12.00

Miniature Sheet

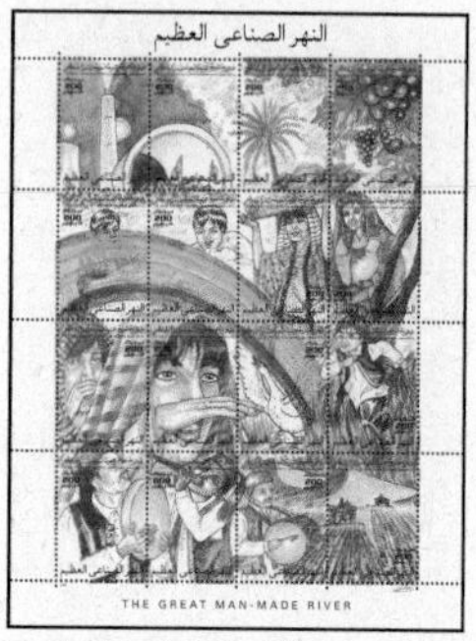

Great Man-Made River — A565

No. 1655: a, Smokestack. b, Pipeline and flags. c, Palm tree, fruit. d, Grapes. e, Clothed boy, rainbow. f, Bathing boy, rainbow. g, Woman carrying fruit. h, Woman holding jug. i, Woman with red and black headdress. j, Woman with green striped headdress. k, Duck, rainbow. l, Boy running. m, Drummer hitting drum with hand. n, Horn player. o, Drummer hitting drum with stick. p, Tractors in field.

2001, Sept. 15 Litho. ***Perf. 11¾***
1655 A565 200d Sheet of 16, #a-p *29.00 29.00*

A566

Sept. 1 Revolution, 32nd Anniv. — A567

No. 1656: a, Col. Khadafy in headdress. b, Buildings, water pipeline, helicopters, tank, horsemen. c, Ship, airplane, camel rider. d, Tea drinkers. e, Children. f, Pillars, antelopes, woman. g, Man walking, camel rider. h, Camels, birds. i, Woman with container. j, Sword fight. k, Man and camel rider. l, Camels, pipeline worker, fruit. m, Potter. n, Musicians and weaver. o, Artisan. p, Col. Khadafy with clasped hands.
No. 1657, 300d, Col. Khadafy, pipeline and fruit (gold background). No. 1658, 300d, Col. Khadafy, pipeline and fruit (silver background).

Litho. and Hologram

2001, Sept. 1 ***Perf. 13¼***
1656 A566 100d Sheet of 16, #a-p *27.50 27.50*
q. Booklet pane, #a-p, litho. *27.50* —
Complete booklet, #1656q *27.50*

Souvenir Sheets

Litho. & Embossed With Foil Application

1657-1658 A567 Set of 2 *5.50 5.50*

Intl. Day of the Orphan — A568

Panel color: 100d, Blue. 200d, Red violet. 300d, Olive green.

2001, Oct. 1 Litho. *Perf. 14¾x14½*
1659-1661 A568 Set of 3 9.00 9.00

Health Care — A569

Arabic inscription color: 200d, Green. 300d, Yellow orange.

2001, Dec. 1 Litho. *Perf. 14*
1662-1663 A569 Set of 2 6.50 6.50

Miniature Sheet

Tourism A570

Various tourist attractions.

2002, May 1 *Perf. 11¾*
1664 A570 200d Sheet of 16, #a-p 52.50 52.50

Intl. Customs Day — A571

Designs: 200d, 400d.

2002, July 1 *Perf. 14*
1665-1666 A571 Set of 2 8.25 8.25

A572

Sept. 1 Revolution, 33rd Anniv. — A573

No. 1667: a, Col. Khadafy. b, Airplanes. c, Camel rider, woman pouring tea. d, Artisans. e, Bulldozer, building. f, Chemist, oil rig. g, Ships. h, Doctors and patients. i, Technician at industrial plant. j, Man at computer, k, Man, spigot, water pipeline, crane. l, Chemist, man at microscope. m, Television camera and technician. n, Fruit, vegetables, grain combine. o, Spear carriers, musician. p, Map of Africa, musicians.

No. 1668, 300d, Col. Khadafy, map of Africa (gold background). No. 1669, 300d, Col. Khadafy, map of Africa (silver background).

Litho. & Hologram

2002, Sept. 1 *Perf. 13¼*
1667 A572 100d Sheet of 16, #a-p 22.50 22.50
q. Booklet pane, #a-p, litho. 40.00 —
Complete booklet, #1667q 50.00

Souvenir Sheets

Litho. & Embossed With Foil Application

1668-1669 A573 Set of 2 8.00 8.00

Universal Declaration of Human Rights, 50th Anniv. — A576

Panel color: 250d, Red orange. 500d, Blue green.

2002, Nov. 1 Litho. *Perf. 14*
1672-1673 A576 Set of 2 9.50 9.50

Universal Postal Union, 125th Anniv. — A577

Panel color: 200d, Blue. 250d, Red violet.

2002, Dec. 1
1674-1675 A577 Set of 2 5.50 5.50

A580

September 1 Revolution, 34th Anniv. — A581

No. 1679: a, 300d, Doctors and microscope (30x40mm). b, 300d, Nurses studying anatomy (30x40mm). c, 300d, Mother and child (30x40mm). d, 300d, Soldiers, white flag (30x40mm). e, 500d, Teachers, students, building (60x40mm). f, 500d, Helicopter, pilot, women, nurse and patients (60x40mm). g, 500d, Marching band, soldiers in vehicle (60x40mm). h, 1000d, Col. Khadafy, airplane, satellite dish.

2003, May 20 Litho. *Perf. 12*
1679 A580 Sheet of 8, #a-h 22.50 22.50

Souvenir Sheet

Litho. & Embossed With Foil Application

1680 A581 2000d multi 17.00 17.00

September 1 Revolution, 35th Anniv. — A582

Background color: 750d, Gray green. 1000d, Yellow green.

2004 Litho. *Perf. 13*
1681-1682 A582 Set of 2 4.50 4.50

Khairi Khaled Nuri (1943-2004), Philatelist — A583

2004 Litho. & Hologram *Perf. 13¼*
1683 A583 500d multi 2.00 2.00

People's Authority Declaration, 27th Anniv. — A584

Color of rays: 400d, Yellow brown. 1000d, Blue green.

2004 Litho. *Perf. 13*
1684-1685 A584 Set of 2 12.00 12.00

1st Communication and Information Technology Exhibition — A585

2005, July 29 *Perf. 13*
1686 A585 750d multi 5.00 5.00

Souvenir Sheet

Imperf

1687 A585 1000d multi 6.00 6.00

People's Authority Declaration, 28th Anniv. — A586

Delegates: 300d, Seated. 1000d, Voting.

2005 *Perf. 13*
1688-1689 A586 Set of 2 12.00 12.00

September 1 Revolution, 36th Anniv. — A587

Background color: 750d, Yellow orange. 1000d, Blue.

2005
1690-1691 A587 Set of 2 15.00 15.00

Miniature Sheet

Total Solar Eclipse of March 29, 2006 A588

No. 1692 — Eclipse and: a, Band of totality over map of Libya. b, Buildings, map of Libya. c, Altitude and duration figures. d, Stylized fish, camel, cactus, palm tree and Libyan. e, Saddled camel. f, Camels and riders.

2006, Mar. 29
1692 A588 250d Sheet of 6, #a-f 12.50 12.50

People's Authority Declaration, 29th Anniv. — A589

Wheat ear, flag, fist and torch with background color of: 400d, Yellow. 1000d, Blue.

2006, Nov. 1
1693-1694 A589 Set of 2 11.00 11.00

September 1 Revolution, 37th Anniv. A590

2006
1695 A590 1000d multi 8.00 8.00

Famous African Leaders — A591

Map of Africa and: No. 1696, 500d, Gamal Abdel Nasser (1918-70), Egyptian President. No. 1697, 500d, Kwame Nkrumah (1909-72), President of Ghana. No. 1698, 500d, Ahmed Ben Bella, President of Algeria. No. 1699, 500d, Patrice Lumumba (1925-61), Congolese Prime Minister. No. 1700, 500d, Kenneth Kaunda, President of Zambia. No. 1701, 500d, Julius Nyerere (1922-99), President of Tanzania. No. 1702, 500d, Modibo Keita (1915-77), President of Mali.

1000d, Map of Africa, Nasser, Nkrumah, Ben Bella, Lumumba, Kaunda, Nyerere and Keita, horiz.

2007, Mar. 6 *Perf. 12¾*
1696-1702 A591 Set of 7 32.50 32.50
1702a Miniature sheet of 7, #1696-1702 32.50 32.50

Size: 98x75mm

Imperf

1703 A591 1000d multi 8.00 8.00

Third Communication and Information Technology Exhibition — A592

2007, May 27 *Perf. 13*
1704 A592 750d multi 6.50 6.50

Tripoli, Capital of Islamic Culture — A593

2007, June 16 **Litho.**
1705 A593 500d multi *4.50 4.50*

Intl. Day Against Drug Abuse and Illicit Trafficking — A594

2007, June 26
1706 A594 750d multi *6.50 6.50*

People's Authority Declaration, 30th Anniv. — A595

2007, July 4
1707 A595 750d multi *6.50 6.50*

36th Tripoli Intl. Fair A596

No. 1708: a, Ring (orange background). b, Pendant (green background). c, Ring (purple background).
Illustration reduced.

2007, July 4 ***Perf. 13x13x13¼***
1708 Strip of 3 *16.00 16.00*
a.-c. A596 500d Any single 3.50 3.00

Printed in sheets containing 2 strips + 2 labels. Value, $32.50.

Mosque — A597

2007, Aug. 24 **Litho.** ***Perf. 13***
1709 A597 500d multi *5.00 5.00*
a. Souvenir sheet of 1 *5.00 5.00*

African Soccer Federation, 50th Anniv. — A598

2007, Aug. 25
1710 A598 750d multi *6.50 6.50*

Values are for stamps with surrounding selvage.

September 1 Revolution, 38th Anniv. A599

2007, Sept. 1 **Litho.** ***Perf. 13***
1711 A599 1000d multi *8.00 8.00*
a. Souvenir sheet of 1 *8.00 8.00*

Khadafy Project for African Women, Children and Youth — A600

2007, Sept. 9
1712 A600 500d multi *4.25 4.25*

Libyan Red Crescent Society, 50th Anniv. — A601

Red Crescent emblem and: 500d, Red Crescent volunteers. 1000d, 50th anniversary emblem.

2007 ***Perf. 13***
1713-1714 A601 Set of 2 *12.50 12.50*

People's Authority Declaration, 31st Anniv. A602

Type I — Two dots and vertical line in Arabic inscription directly above second "A" in "Jamahiriya."
Type II — No dots or vertical line in Arabic inscription directly above second "A" in "Jamahiriya."

2008, Mar. 2 **Litho.** ***Perf. 13***
1715 A602 500d multi, type I *50.00 50.00*
a. Type II *4.50 4.50*

37th Tripoli International Fair — A603

No. 1716: a, Emblems, colored rectangles. b, Emblems. c, Emblems, buildings, displays.
Illustration reduced.

2008, Apr. 2 ***Perf. 13x12¾***
1716 A603 500d Horiz. strip of 3, #a-c *13.00 13.00*

Printed in sheets of 6 containing two of each stamp.

Worldwide Fund for Nature (WWF) — A604

Rueppell's fox: No. 1717, Head. No. 1718, Walking. No. 1719, Curled up. No. 1720, Sitting.

2008, May 1 ***Perf. 12***
1717 A604 750f multi 1.50 1.50
a. Imperf. 6.00 6.00
1718 A604 750f multi 1.50 1.50
a. Imperf. 6.00 6.00
1719 A604 750f multi 1.50 1.50
a. Imperf. 6.00 6.00
1720 A604 750f multi 1.50 1.50
a. Imperf. 6.00 6.00
b. Horiz. strip of 4, #1717-1720 8.00 8.00
c. Horiz. strip of 4, #1717a-1720a 35.00 35.00

Fourth Telecommunications and Information Technology Exhibition — A605

2008, May 25 ***Perf. 13***
1721 A605 1000d multi 6.75 6.75

Gamal Abdel Nasser (1918-70), Egyptian President — A606

2008, July 23
1722 A606 500d multi 5.00 5.00

Egyptian Revolution, 56th anniv.

Khadafy 6+6 Mediterranean Project — A607

2008, July 27
1723 A607 750d multi *5.00 5.00*

Tenth Meeting of Leaders and Heads of State of Community of Sahel-Sahara Countries — A608

2008, Aug. 3
1724 A608 1000d multi *6.00 6.00*

Libyan Participation in 2008 Summer Olympics, Beijing — A609

2008, Aug. 18
1725 A609 1000d multi 8.00 8.00

September 1 Revolution, 39th Anniv. — A610

Col. Khadafy with denomination in: No. 1726, White. No. 1727, Green.

2008, Sept. 1 ***Perf. 13x12¾***
1726 A610 1000d multi *8.00 8.00*

Souvenir Sheet

1727 A610 1000d multi *8.00 8.00*

Total Mobile Phone Penetration in Libya — A611

2008, Sept. 11 ***Perf. 13***
1728 A611 750d multi 6.00 6.00

Fourth Intl. Waatasemu Women's Competition for Koran Memorization A612

2008, Sept. 23
1729 A612 750d multi 5.00 5.00

Koran Exhibition — A613

2008, Sept. 26
1730 A613 500d multi 3.50 3.50

People's Authority Declaration, 32nd Anniv. A614

2009, Mar. 9
1731 A614 500d multi 3.00 3.00

Support for Gaza Palestinians A615

2009, May 7
1732 A615 1000d multi *5.00 5.00*

American Aggression Against Libya A616

2009, May 14 Litho. ***Perf. 13***
1733 A616 500d multi 4.00 4.00

Fifth Telecommunications and Information Technology Exhibition — A617

2009, May 30
1734 A617 500d multi 3.00 3.00

Omar Bongo (1935-2009), President of Gabon — A618

2009, June 20 Litho. ***Perf. 13***
1735 A618 750d multi 3.00 3.00

16th Mediterranean Games, Pescara, Italy — A619

2009, June 26
1736 A619 500d multi 3.00 3.00

Jerusalem, Capital of Arab Culture A620

2009, Aug. 3
1737 A620 1000d multi 4.50 4.50

25th African Men's Basketball Championships, Libya — A621

2009
1738 A621 500d multi 3.00 3.00

Souvenir Sheet

September 1 Revolution, 40th Anniv. — A622

No. 1739 — Col. Khadafy and background color of: a, 400d, Yellow. b, 600d, White. c, 750d, Green.

2009
1739 A622 Sheet of 3, #a-c 7.50 7.50

Col. Khadafy, Map of Africa and African Union Emblem A623

Litho. & Embossed With Foil Application
2009 ***Serpentine Die Cut 11***
Self-Adhesive
1740 A623 1000d multi 4.50 4.50

Souvenir Sheet
1741 A623 2000d multi 9.00 9.00

First Al Fateh Futsal (Indoor Soccer) Contintental Cup Tournament A624

2009, Oct. 12 Litho. ***Perf. 13***
1742 A624 500d multi 1.50 1.50

Another 500d stamp depicting the camel mascot of the tournament, the emblem of the tournament (pictured on No, 1742) and flags of Libya, Guatemala, Solomon Islands, Iran, Uruguay and Spain, was printed se-tenant with No. 1742, but this additional stamp was not issued.

Pan-African Postal Union, 30th Anniv. A625

2010, Jan. 18
1743 A625 500d multi 1.50 1.50

People's Authority Declaration, 33rd Anniv. — A626

Litho. With Foil Application
2010, Mar. 2 ***Serpentine Die Cut 10***
Self-Adhesive
1744 A626 500d multi 1.50 1.50

22nd Session of the Council of the League of Arab States, Sirt — A627

Serpentine Die Cut 10
2010, Mar. 27 Self-Adhesive
1745 A627 500d multi 1.50 1.50

Organization of Petroleum Exporting Countries, 50th Anniv. — A628

2010, June 1 Litho. ***Perf. 13***
1746 A628 1000d multi 2.75 2.75

Evacuation of US Forces From Bases in Libya, 40th Anniv. — A629

2010, June 9
1747 A629 1000d multi 3.00 3.00

Libyan Revolution After 40 Years — A630

No. 1748: a, Nationalization of banks and insurance companies. b, Nationalization of the oil sector. c, Declaration of the People's Revolution, 1973 d, Arab Republics Union. e, Italian evacuation from Libyan soil. f, Evacuation of American troops from Libyan soil. g, Evacuation of British troops from Libyan soil. h, Dawn of Great A-Fatah, 1969. i, Al-Fatah, an industrial revolution. j, Huge residential projects. k, Al-Fatah, an agricultural revolution. l, Establishment of the largest electricity networks. m, Establishment of roads network in Great Jamahiriya. n, Al-Fatah scientific revolution. o, Comprehensive health welfare. p, Al-Fatah, an Islamic revolution. q, Defining death line. r, The great Man-made River builder. s, Wajda City Agreement, 1984. t, Producer's revolution, 1978. u, The Green Book. v, The birth of first Jamahiriya in history, 1977. w, Student's revolution, 1976. x, Tunisia-Libya Jerba Unity Agreement. y, The African Arab Union, Sept. 9, 1999. z, By the Community of Sahel and Saharan States. aa, Break of the injustice embargo against Great Jamahiriya. ab, Demolition of borders. ac, The Arab Magreb Union, 1989. ad, Great Green Charter for Human Rights. ae, Demolition of jails. af, Courageous response to the failed NATO aggression. ag, The 40th anniversary of the 1st September Revolution. ah, Moammar Khadafy, heart of the world. ai, The return of the political hostage A. B. Almagrahi. aj, Italian apology to Libya about the Colonial period. ak, Moammar Khadafy, the king of Africa kings. al, Revolution of telecommunication and technology. am, The establishment of huge fleet maritime transports. an, Emancipation of women lost by the Great Al-Fatah Revolution.

Litho. With Foil Application
Serpentine Die Cut 10
2010, Aug. 23 Self-Adhesive
1748 Sheet of 40 57.50
a.-an. A630 400d Any single 1.40 1.40

Great Green Document of Human Rights, 22nd Anniv. — A631

Dr. Martin Luther King, Jr., civil rights marchers, and scroll with: 1500d, Arabic text. 2000d, English text.

2010, Aug, 28 Litho. ***Perf. 13***
1749-1750 A631 Set of 2 15.00 15.00

Miniature Sheets

Sept. 23, 2009 Speech of Col. Khadafy to United Nations Security Council, 1st Anniv. A633

No. 1753, 1000d — Map of world, Col. Khadafy, U.N. emblem, text of speech in Arabic with: a, First line of text 53mm, second line of text 47mm. b, First line of text 68mm. c, First line of text 53mm, second line of text 52mm. d, First line of text 44mm, second line of text 42mm. e, First line of text 61mm. f, First line of text 45mm, second line of text 58mm.

No. 1754, 1000d — Map of world, Col. Khadafy, U.N. emblem, text of speech in English starting with: a, "Brothers, you can in our political life . . ." b, "In order that colonization is not repeated . . ." c, "The solution to achieve democracy . . ." d, "The International Court of Justice . . ." e, "Africa as of now . . ." f, "The International Atomic Energy Agency . . ."

No. 1755, 1000d — Map of world, Col. Khadafy, U.N. emblem, text of speech in French starting with: a, "Vous voyez, mes frères . . ." b, "Pour eviter une nouvelle colonisation . . ." c, "Donc la solution . . ." d, "La Cour Internationale de Justice . . ." e, "L'Afrique a besoin . . ." f, "L'Agence Internationale de l'Energie . . ."

2010, Sept. 23 Litho. ***Perf. 13***
Sheets of 6, #a-f
1753-1755 A633 Set of 3 60.00 60.00

February 17, 2011 Revolution — A635

Denominations: 250d, 500d, 750d, 1000d, 5000d.

2011 Litho. ***Perf. 13¼***
1757-1761 A635 Set of 5 22.50 22.50

February 17 Revolution, 1st Anniv. — A636

No. 1762: a, Woman in burqa, man waving flag. b, Crowd with flag. c, Flowers and emblem. No. 1763, Map of Libya, flag in circle.

2012, Feb. 17 ***Perf. 13***
1762 Horiz. strip of 3 6.00 6.00
a.-b. A636 500d Either single 1.50 1.50
c. A636 1000d multi 3.00 3.00

Souvenir Sheet
1763 A636 1000d multi 3.00 3.00

Children's Drawings — A637

No. 1764: a, Tree with colors of Libyan flag, flowers. b, Flowers and trees. c, People and various animals. d, Child with flag, house. e, Boat with flag, palm tree.

2012, Sept. 12 *Perf. 12¾*

1764	Horiz. strip of 5	8.25	8.25
a.	A637 100d multi	.40	.40
b.	A637 200d multi	.80	.80
c.	A637 250d multi	1.00	1.00
d.	A637 500d multi	2.00	2.00
e.	A637 1000d multi	4.00	4.00

Independence, 61st Anniv. — A638

National colors, "61," and: 500d, Crescent and star. 1000d, Olive branch, crescent and star.

2012, Dec. 24 *Perf. 13¼*

1765-1766 A638 Set of 2 16.50 16.50

Monument to the Foundation of the Libyan Army — A639

2013, Feb. 17

1767 A639 500d multi 6.50 6.50

A640

A641

February 17 Revolution, 2nd Anniv. — A642

2013, Feb. 17 *Perf. 13*

1768	Horiz. strip of 3	19.50	19.50
a.	A640 250d multi	2.75	2.75
b.	A641 500d multi	5.50	5.50
c.	A642 1000d multi	11.00	11.00

Miniature Sheet

Tripoli International Fair — A643

No. 1769: a, Necklace and pendants. b, Fair emblem. c, Triangular pendant. d, Semi-circular pendant. e, Pin. f, Earrings.

2013, Apr. 2

1769 A643 500d Sheet of 6, #a-f 19.50 19.50

Intl. Letter Writing Competition for Young People — A644

2013, May 4 **Litho.** *Perf. 13*

1770 A644 1000d multi 6.75 6.75

February 17 Revolution, 2nd Anniv. — A645

Libyan flag with background color of: 5000d, Light blue. 10,000d, Light orange.

Litho. & Embossed With Foil Application

2013, May 27 ***Serpentine Die Cut 10***

Self-Adhesive

1771	A645 5000d multi	24.00	24.00
1772	A645 10,000d multi	47.50	47.50

Campaign Against Desertification A646

2013, June 17 **Litho.** *Perf. 13¼*

1773 A646 500d multi 10.00 10.00

Libyan Parliament Building, Al Bayda, 50th Anniv. (in 2014) — A647

2013, Aug. 20 **Litho.** *Perf. 13¼*

1774 A647 500d multi 4.25 4.25

Benghazi Lighthouse — A648

2013, Aug. 20 **Litho.** *Perf. 13*

1775 A648 1000d multi 11.00 11.00

Miniature Sheet

Dinosaurs — A651

No. 1779: a, Triceratops. b, Head of dinosaur, building ruins. c, Tyrannosaurus, sky in background. d, Tyrannosaurus, head upright, building ruins in background, no sky. e, Dinosaurs and flowers. f, Tyrannosaurus, head lowered, building ruins in background, no sky.

2013, Dec. 11 **Litho.** *Perf. 12¾*

1779 A651 250d Sheet of 6, #a-f 19.00 19.00

Independence, 62nd Anniv. — A652

No. 1780: a, King Idris, Libyan flag. b, Emblem. c, Horseman carrying flag, King Idris, Omar Mukhtar, map of Libya.

2013, Dec. 24 **Litho.** *Perf. 13*

1780	Horiz. strip of 3	13.00	13.00
a.	A652 250d multi	1.75	1.75
b.	A652 750d multi	5.00	5.00
c.	A652 1000d multi	6.50	6.50

National Post Day — A653

2013, Dec. 24 **Litho.** *Perf. 13¼*

1781 A653 100d multi 7.75 7.75

2013 National Stamp Exhibition — A654

2013, Dec. 25 **Litho.** *Perf. 13*

1782 A654 100d multi 4.25 4.25

February 17th Revolution, 3rd Anniv. — A655

No. 1783: a, Stylized people and emblem. b, Libyan people and flags. c, Torch and map of Libya.

2014, Feb. 17 **Litho.** *Perf. 13*

1783	Horiz. strip of 3	16.50	16.50
a.	A655 500d multi	3.75	3.75
b.	A655 750d multi	5.50	5.50
c.	A655 1000d multi	7.25	7.25

Libya, Champions of 2014 African Nations Soccer Championships — A656

No. 1784: a, 500d, Libyan team, trophy. b, 750d, Trophy, Libyan Soccer Federation emblem, map of Libya.

2014, Feb. 17 **Litho.** *Perf. 13*

1784 A656 Horiz. pair, #a-b 7.75 7.75

Miniature Sheet

Vegetables — A657

No. 1786: a, Garlic. b, Onions. c, Tomatoes. d, Peppers. e, Eggplants. f, Potatoes.

2014, Feb. 24 **Litho.** *Perf. 12¾*

1786 A657 500d Sheet of 6, #a-f 19.00 19.00

Scouting in Libya, 60th Anniv. A658

No. 1787: a, 500d, Scouts. b, 1000d, Ali Khalefa Zaidi (1909-66), scouting leader.

2014, Feb. 27 **Litho.** *Perf. 13*

1787 A658 Horiz. pair, #a-b 19.00 19.00

Miniature Sheet

2014 Tripoli International Fair — A659

No. 1788: a, Bazin with meat. b, Fair emblem, map of Libya. c, Couscous with meat. d, Bazin with fish. e, Fair emblems. f, Couscous with fish.

2014, Apr. 2 **Litho.** *Perf. 13*

1788 A659 500d Sheet of 6, #a-f 19.00 19.00

Castles A660

Designs: 100d, Sebha Castle. 1000d, Murzuq Castle.

2014, June 26 **Litho.** *Perf. 13*

1789-1790 A660 Set of 2 9.00 9.00

A661

A662

Mosques — A663

2014, July 20 **Litho.** *Perf. 13*

1791	Horiz. strip of 3	11.50	11.50
a.	A661 500d multi	3.75	3.75
b.	A662 500d multi	3.75	3.75
c.	A663 500d multi	3.75	3.75

Euromed Postal Emblem and Mediterranean Sea — A664

2014, July 28 **Litho.** *Perf. 13*

1792 A664 500d multi 9.00 9.00

Libyan Army, 63rd Anniv. — A665

2014, Aug. 9 **Litho.** ***Perf. 13***
1793 A665 500d multi 7.75 7.75

Liberation of Tripoli, 3rd Anniv. A666

2014, Aug. 20 **Litho.** ***Perf. 13***
1794 A666 500d multi 10.00 10.00

Martyr's Day — A667

2014, Sept. 16 **Litho.** ***Perf. 13***
1795 A667 500d multi 7.75 7.75

Libya Insurance Company, 50th Anniv. — A668

2014, Dec. 24 **Litho.** ***Perf. 13***
1796 A668 1000d multi 10.00 10.00

Independence, 63rd Anniv. — A669

2014, Dec. 24 **Litho.** ***Perf. 13***
1797 A669 1000d multi 7.75 7.75

Intl. Children's Day — A670

No. 1798 — UNICEF emblem and: a, Scout, tent, butterflies, Libyan flag. b, Hands. c, Scout, butterflies, mushrooms.

2014 **Litho.** ***Perf. 13***
1798 Horiz. strip of 3 14.00 14.00
a. A670 250d multi 1.75 1.75
b. A670 750d multi 5.25 5.25
c. A670 1000d multi 7.00 7.00

A671

A672

February 17 Revolution, 4th Anniv. — A673

2015, Feb. 17 **Litho.** ***Perf. 13***
1799 Horiz. strip of 3 15.00 15.00
a. A671 1000d multi 5.00 5.00
b. A672 1000d multi 5.00 5.00
c. A673 1000d multi 5.00 5.00

Boats in Harbor — A674

2015, July 9 **Litho.** ***Perf. 13***
1800 A674 750d multi 7.75 7.75

Miniature Sheet

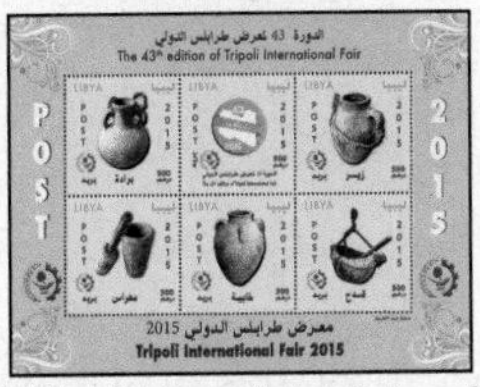

2015 Tripoli International Fair — A675

No. 1801: a, Pot with handles, rope and wide bottom. b, Map of Libya. c, Pot with narrow bottom and two handles connected by rope. d, Mortar and pestle. e, Pot with three handles. f, Pot suspended from rope.

2015, Apr. 2 **Litho.** ***Perf. 13***
1801 A675 500d Sheet of 6, #a-f 15.50 15.50

Martyr's Day A676

Omar Mukhtar (1858-1931), resistance leader, and: 500d, Horsemen, eagle, flowers. 1000d, Libyan flag.

2015, Sept. 16 **Litho.** ***Perf. 13***
1802 A676 500d multi 6.50 6.50

Size: 120x80mm

Imperf

1803 A676 1000d multi 9.00 9.00

Miniature Sheet

Flowers A677

No. 1804: a, Narcissi. b, Ophrys fuciflora. c, Calla lily. d, Cestrum nocturnum. e, Bird of paradise. f, Jasmine.

2015, Nov. 1 **Litho.** ***Perf. 13***
1804 A677 500d Sheet of 6, #a-f 17.00 17.00

UNESCO, 70th Anniv. A678

2015, Nov. 16 **Litho.** ***Perf. 13***
1805 A678 500d multi 6.50 6.50

International Children's Day — A679

2015, Nov. 20 **Litho.** ***Perf. 13***
1806 A679 500d multi 6.50 6.50

Architecture A680

Designs: No. 1807, 750d, Nalut Archaeological Site. No. 1808, 750d, Building in Ghadames.

2015, Dec. 10 **Litho.** ***Perf. 13***
1807-1808 A680 Set of 2 12.00 12.00

Independence Day — A681

2015, Dec. 24 **Litho.** ***Perf. 13***
1809 A681 500d multi 6.50 6.50

Stamp Day — A682

2015, Dec. 24 **Litho.** ***Perf. 13***
1810 A682 500d multi 6.50 6.50

Dates — A683

2015, Dec. 31 **Litho.** ***Perf. 13½***

Background Color

1811 A683 500d yel grn 2.00 2.00
1812 A683 1000d lilac 4.00 4.00
1813 A683 2000d bistre yellow 8.00 8.00
1814 A683 5000d turq blue 20.00 20.00
1815 A683 10,000d brt green 40.00 40.00
Nos. 1811-1815 (5) 74.00 74.00

Second National Stamp Exhibition — A684

2016, Jan. 30 **Litho.** ***Perf. 13***
1816 A684 1000d multi 9.00 9.00

February 17 Revolution, 5th Anniv. — A685

No. 1817 — Laurel branches and: a, Flag and map of Libya. b, Handshake. c, Map of Libya.

2016, Feb. 17 **Litho.** ***Perf. 13***
1817 Horiz. strip of 3 12.00 12.00
a.-c. A685 500d Any single 4.00 4.00

Martyr's Day — A686

Omar Mukhtar (1858-1931), resistance leader, and: 500d, Building. 1000d, Map of Libya, building, Mukhtar on horse.

2016, Sept. 16 **Litho.** ***Perf. 13***
1818 A686 500d multi 7.75 7.75

Size: 110x76mm

Imperf

1819 A686 1000d multi 13.00 13.00

International Children's Day — A687

No. 1820 — UNICEF emblem and: a, Two children with sign. b, Three children holding pictures. c, Child reading book.

2016, Nov. 20 **Litho.** ***Perf. 13***
1820 Horiz. strip of 3 10.50 10.50
a.-c. A687 500d Any single 3.50 3.50

Independence Day — A688

2016, Dec. 24 **Litho.** ***Perf. 13***
1821 A688 1000d multi 7.75 7.75

February 17 Revolution, 6th Anniv. — A689

No. 1822: a, 500d, Map and flag of Libya. b, 1000d, Map of Libya in circle.

2017, Feb. 17 **Litho.** ***Perf. 13***
1822 A689 Horiz. pair, #a-b 10.00 10.00

Children's Day — A690

No. 1823: a, Map of Libya, children, flag, butterflies, flowers. b, Map of Libya, flowers, children with balloons. c, Boy with kites and camel.

2017, Mar. 21 Litho. *Perf. 13¼x13*
1823 A690 500d Horiz. strip of 3, #a-c 11.50 11.50

Miniature Sheet

2017 Tripoli International Fair — A691

No. 1824: a, Bowl with lid. b, Emblem. c, Lidded bowl with handles. d, Stirrups. e, Coffee pot. f, Candleholder.

2017, Apr. 2 Litho. *Perf. 13*
1824 A691 500d Sheet of 6, #a-f 14.50 14.50

Month of Ramadan — A692

2017, June 23 Litho. *Perf. 13¼x13*
1825 A692 1000d multi — —

Olives and Olive Tree — A693

2017, Aug. 6 Litho. *Perf. 13*
1826 A693 5000d yel & multi 14.50 14.50
1827 A693 10,000d rose lil & multi 29.00 29.00

Souvenir Sheet

Omar Mukhtar (1858-1931), National Hero — A694

2017, Nov. 1 Litho. *Perf. 13*
1828 A694 1000d multi 10.00 10.00

Martyr's Day.

International Children's Day — A695

2017, Nov. 20 Litho. *Perf. 13*
1829 A695 1000d multi 10.00 10.00

International Day of Solidarity With the Palestinian People — A696

2017, Nov. 29 Litho. *Perf. 13*
1830 A696 2000d multi 16.00 16.00

Libyan postal officials have declared as "illegal" miniature sheets and souvenir sheets depicting high-speed trains and Renaissance paintings of Jacopo Pontormo that are inscribed "State of Libya."

Independence, 66th Anniv. — A697

2017, Dec. 24 Litho. *Perf. 13*
1831 A697 500d multi 7.25 7.25

Amazigh Year (Year of the Berber People) — A698

2018, Jan. 13 Litho. *Perf. 13*
1832 A698 2000d multi 8.75 8.75

February 17th Revolution, 7th Anniv. — A699

2018, Feb. 23 Litho. *Perf. 13*
1833 A699 1000d multi 5.75 5.75

Miniature Sheet

Tripoli International Fair — A700

No. 1834: a, Picture with circle in square frame depicting two men in boat. b, Fair emblem. c, Mosaic depicting woman. d, Hexagonal picture depicting man. e, Main gate of fair. f, Mosaic depicting ship.

2018, Apr. 2 Litho. *Perf. 13*
1834 A700 500d Sheet of 6, #a-f 8.75 8.75

A701

A702

A703

A704

Koran Competition A705

2018, May 10 Litho. *Perf. 13½*
1835 Horiz. strip of 5 1.75 1.75
a. A701 50d multi .35 .35
b. A702 50d multi .35 .35
c. A703 50d multi .35 .35
d. A704 50d multi .35 .35
e. A705 50d multi .35 .35

Souvenir Sheet

Nelson Mandela (1918-2013), President of South Africa — A706

2018, July 18 Litho. *Perf. 13½*
1836 A706 1000d multi 4.50 4.50

Miniature Sheet

International Migrants Day — A707

No. 1837: a, Migrants and truck convoy. b, Migrants in truck. c, Migrant man and baby near truck. d, Woman carrying infant, man carrying suitcase, child. e, Boat and map of Mediterranean area. f, Women carrying two children. g, Migrant in water wearing life vest, head at top center. h, Migrant in water wearing life vest, head at upper right. i, Woman holding a child with pacifier in mouth. j, Migrants in water wearing life vest near life boat. k, Migrants in life boat. l, Migrants in water near sinking ship.

2018, Dec. 18 Litho. *Perf. 13¼*
1837 A707 100d Sheet of 12, #a-l 10.00 10.00

Independence, 67th Anniv. — A708

2018, Dec. 24 Litho. *Perf. 13¼x13*
1838 A708 1000d multi 5.75 5.75

Third National Stamp Exhibition — A709

2018, Dec. 25 Litho. *Perf. 13*
1839 A709 1000d multi 5.75 5.75

Berber (Amazigh) New Year — A710

2019, Jan. 13 Litho. *Perf. 13*
1840 A710 500d multi — —

February 17 Revolution, 8th Anniv. — A711

2019, Feb. 17 Litho. *Perf. 13*
1841 A711 500d multi — —

A712

A713

A714

A715

A716

Textiles — A717

2019, Apr. 2 Litho. *Perf. 13*

1842	Sheet of 6	10.00	10.00
a.	A712 500d multi	1.60	1.60
b.	A713 500d multi	1.60	1.60
c.	A714 500d multi	1.60	1.60
d.	A715 500d multi	1.60	1.60
e.	A716 500d multi	1.60	1.60
f.	A717 500d multi	1.60	1.60

2019 Tripoli International Fair.

February 17 Revolution, 9th Anniv. — A718

2020, Feb. 17 Litho. *Perf. 14¼x14*

1843	A718 500d multi	—	—

SEMI-POSTAL STAMPS

Many issues of Italy and Italian Colonies include one or more semipostal denominations. To avoid splitting sets, these issues are generally listed as regular postage, semipostals or airmails, etc.

Semi-Postal Stamps of Italy Overprinted

1915-16 Wmk. 140 *Perf. 14*

B1	SP1 10c + 5c rose	3.50	14.00
a.	Double overprint	825.00	
B2	SP2 15c + 5c slate	30.00	24.00
B3	SP2 20c + 5c org ('16)	4.25	30.00
	Nos. B1-B3 (3)	37.75	68.00

No. B2 with Additional Surcharge

1916, Mar.

B4	SP2 20c on 15c + 5c slate	30.00	30.00
a.	Double surcharge	850.00	

View of Port, Tripoli — SP1

Designs: B5, B6, View of port, Tripoli. B7, B8, Arch of Marcus Aurelius. B9, B10, View of Tripoli.

1927, Feb. 15 Litho.

B5	SP1 20c + 5c brn vio & black	3.50	15.00
B6	SP1 25c + 5c bl grn & black	3.50	15.00
B7	SP1 40c + 10c blk brn & black	3.50	15.00
B8	SP1 60c + 10c org brn & black	3.50	15.00
B9	SP1 75c + 20c red & black	3.50	15.00
B10	SP1 1.25 l + 20c bl & blk	24.00	42.50
	Nos. B5-B10 (6)	41.50	117.50

First Sample Fair, Tripoli. Surtax aided fair. See Nos. EB1-EB2.

View of Tripoli SP2

Knights of Malta Castle SP3

Designs: 50c+20c, Date palm. 1.25 l+20c, Camel riders. 2.55 l+50c, View of Tripoli. 5 l+1 l, Traction well.

1928, Feb. 20 Wmk. 140 *Perf. 14*

B11	SP2 30c + 20c mar & blk	3.50	15.00
B12	SP2 50c + 20c bl grn & blk	3.50	15.00
B13	SP2 1.25 l + 20c red & blk	3.50	15.00
B14	SP3 1.75 l + 20c bl & blk	3.50	15.00
B15	SP3 2.55 l + 50c brn & blk	7.00	22.50
B16	SP3 5 l + 1 l pur & blk	9.50	35.00
	Nos. B11-B16 (6)	30.50	117.50

2nd Sample Fair, Tripoli, 1928. The surtax was for the aid of the Fair.

Olive Tree — SP4

Herding — SP5

Designs: 50c+20c, Dorcas gazelle. 1.25 l+20c, Peach blossoms. 2.55 l+50c, Camel caravan. 5 l+1 l, Oasis with date palms.

1929, Apr. 7

B17	SP4 30c + 20c mar & blk	14.00	27.50
B18	SP4 50c + 20c bl grn & blk	14.00	27.50
B19	SP4 1.25 l + 20c scar & blk	14.00	27.50
B20	SP5 1.75 l + 20c bl & blk	14.00	27.50
B21	SP5 2.55 l + 50c yel brn & blk	14.00	27.50
B22	SP5 5 l + 1 l pur & blk	125.00	300.00
	Nos. B17-B22 (6)	195.00	437.50

3rd Sample Fair, Tripoli, 1929. The surtax was for the aid of the Fair.

Harvesting Bananas SP6

Water Carriers SP7

Designs: 50c, Tobacco plant. 1.25 l, Venus of Cyrene. 2.55 l+45c, Black bucks. 5 l+1 l, Motor and camel transportation. 10 l+2 l, Rome pavilion.

1930, Feb. 20 Photo.

B23	SP6 30c dark brown	4.25	17.50
B24	SP6 50c violet	4.25	17.50
B25	SP6 1.25 l deep blue	4.25	17.50
B26	SP7 1.75 l + 20c scar	7.00	26.00
B27	SP7 2.55 l + 45c dp grn	16.00	37.50
B28	SP7 5 l + 1 l dp org	16.00	50.00
B29	SP7 10 l + 2 l dk vio	16.00	62.50
	Nos. B23-B29 (7)	67.75	228.50

4th Sample Fair at Tripoli, 1930. The surtax was for the aid of the Fair.

Statue of Ephebus SP8

Exhibition Pavilion SP9

Designs: 25c, Arab musician. 50c, View of Zeughet. 1.25 l, Snake charmer. 1.75 l+25c, Windmill. 2.75 l+45c, "Zaptie." 5 l+1 l, Mounted Arab.

1931, Mar. 8

B30	SP8 10c black brown	5.50	9.75
B31	SP8 25c green	5.50	9.75
B32	SP8 50c purple	5.50	9.75
B33	SP8 1.25 l blue	5.50	14.00
B34	SP8 1.75 l + 25c car rose	5.50	16.00
B35	SP8 2.75 l + 45c org	5.50	24.00
B36	SP8 5 l + 1 l dl vio	15.00	35.00
B37	SP9 10 l + 2 l brn	50.00	70.00
	Nos. B30-B37 (8)	98.00	188.25
	Nos. B30-B37,C3,EB3 (10)	104.90	229.75

Fifth Sample Fair, Tripoli. Surtax aided fair.

Papaya Tree SP10

Dorcas Gazelle SP12

Ar Tower, Mogadiscio SP11

Designs: 10c, 50c, Papaya tree. 20c, 30c, Euphorbia abyssinica. 25c, Fig cactus. 75c, Mausoleum, Ghirza. 1.75 l+25c, Lioness. 5 l+1 l, Bedouin with camel.

1932, Mar. 8

B38	SP10 10c olive brn	7.00	16.00
B39	SP10 20c brown red	7.00	16.00
B40	SP10 25c green	7.00	16.00
B41	SP10 30c olive blk	7.00	16.00
B42	SP10 50c dk violet	7.00	16.00
B43	SP10 75c carmine	8.50	16.00
B44	SP11 1.25 l dk blue	8.50	24.00
B45	SP11 1.75 l + 25c ol brn	27.50	77.50
B46	SP11 5 l + 1 l dp bl	27.50	190.00
B47	SP12 10 l + 2 l brn violet	125.00	350.00
	Nos. B38-B47 (10)	232.00	737.50
	Nos. B38-B47,C4-C7 (14)	416.00	1,168.

Sixth Sample Fair, Tripoli. Surtax aided fair.

Ostrich SP13

Arab Musician SP14

Designs: 25c, Incense plant. 30c, Arab musician. 50c, Arch of Marcus Aurelius. 1.25 l, African eagle. 5 l+1 l, Leopard. 10 l+2.50 l, Tripoli skyline and fasces.

1933, Mar. 2 Photo. Wmk. 140

B48	SP13 10c dp violet	37.50	42.50
B49	SP13 25c dp green	21.00	42.50
B50	SP14 30c org brn	21.00	42.50
B51	SP13 50c purple	21.00	42.50
B52	SP13 1.25 l dk blue	50.00	77.50
B53	SP14 5 l + 1 l ol brn	110.00	175.00
B54	SP13 10 l + 2.50 l car	110.00	300.00
	Nos. B48-B54 (7)	370.50	722.50
	Nos. B48-B54,C8-C13 (13)	481.50	1,103.

Seventh Sample Fair, Tripoli. Surtax aided fair.

Pomegranate Tree — SP15

Designs: 50c+10c, 2 l+50c, Musician. 75c+15c, 1.25 l+25c, Tribesman.

1935, Feb. 16

B55	SP15 10c + 10c brn	1.75	5.00
B56	SP15 20c + 10c rose red	1.75	5.00
B57	SP15 50c + 10c pur	1.75	5.00
B58	SP15 75c + 15c car	1.75	5.00
B59	SP15 1.25 l + 25c dl blue	1.75	5.00
B60	SP15 2 l + 50c ol grn	1.75	12.50
	Nos. B55-B60 (6)	10.50	37.50
	Nos. B55-B60,C19-C24 (12)	27.00	108.00

Ninth Sample Fair, Tripoli. Surtax aided fair.

AIR POST STAMPS

Italy Nos. C3 and C5 Overprinted

1928-29 Wmk. 140 *Perf. 14*

C1	AP2 50c rose red	14.00	27.50
C2	AP2 80c brn vio & brn ('29)	55.00	77.50

Airplane — AP1

1931, Mar. 8 Photo. Wmk. 140

C3	AP1 50c blue	1.40	14.00

See note after No. B37.

Seaplane over Bedouin Camp — AP2

Designs: 50c, 1 l, Seaplane over Bedouin camp. 2 l+1 l, 5 l+2 l, Seaplane over Tripoli.

1932, Mar. 1 *Perf. 14*

C4	AP2 50c dark blue	15.00	42.50
C5	AP2 1 l org brown	15.00	42.50
C6	AP2 2 l + 1 l dk gray	29.00	120.00
C7	AP2 5 l + 2 l car	125.00	225.00
	Nos. C4-C7 (4)	207.50	495.00

See note after No. B47.

Seaplane Arriving at Tripoli — AP3

Designs: 50c, 2 l+50c, Seaplane arriving at Tripoli. 75c, 10 l+2.50 l, Plane over Tagiura. 1 l, 5 l+1 l, Seaplane leaving Tripoli.

1933, Mar. 1

C8	AP3 50c dp green	11.00	22.50
C9	AP3 75c carmine	11.00	22.50
C10	AP3 1 l dk blue	11.00	22.50
C11	AP3 2 l + 50c pur	18.00	52.50
C12	AP3 5 l + 1 l org brn	30.00	85.00
C13	AP3 10 l + 2.50 l gray blk	30.00	175.00
	Nos. C8-C13 (6)	125.00	390.00

See note after No. B54.

Seaplane over Tripoli Harbor AP4

Airplane and Camel AP5

Designs: 50c, 5 l+1 l, Seaplane over Tripoli harbor. 75c, 10 l+2 l, Plane and minaret.

1934, Feb. 17 Photo. Wmk. 140

C14	AP4 50c slate bl	14.00	30.00
C15	AP4 75c red org	14.00	30.00
C16	AP4 5 l + 1 l dp grn	125.00	210.00

C17 AP4 10 l + 2 l dl vio 125.00 *210.00*
C18 AP5 25 l + 3 l org brn 150.00 *300.00*
Nos. C14-C18 (5) 487.00 *900.00*

Eighth Sample Fair, Tripoli. Surtax aided fair. See Nos. CE1-CE2.

Plane and Ancient Tower AP6

Camel Train AP7

Designs: 25c+10c, 3 l+1.50 l, Plane and ancient tower. 50c+10c, 2 l+30c, Camel train. 1 l+25c, 10 l+5 l, Arab watching plane.

1935, Apr. 12

C19 AP6 25c + 10c green 1.40 *5.50*
C20 AP7 50c + 10c slate bl 1.40 *5.50*
C21 AP7 1 l + 25c blue 1.40 *5.50*
C22 AP7 2 l + 30c rose red 1.40 *9.50*
C23 AP6 3 l + 1.50 l brn 1.40 *9.50*
C24 AP7 10 l + 5 l dl vio 9.50 *35.00*
Nos. C19-C24 (6) 19.00 *81.50*

See note after No. B60.

Cyrenaica No. C6 Overprinted in Black

1936, Oct.

C25 AP2 50c purple 24.00 .35

Same on Tripolitania Nos. C8 and C12

1937

C26 AP1 50c rose carmine .70 .25
C27 AP2 1 l deep blue 2.10 .85
Set, never hinged 7.00

See Nos. C45-C50.

Ruins of Odeon Theater, Sabrata — AP8

1937, Mar. 15 **Photo.**

C28 AP8 50c dark violet 2.75 *7.00*
C29 AP8 1 l vio black 2.75 *11.00*
Set, never hinged 13.50

Opening of a coastal road to the Egyptian frontier.

Nos. C28-C29 Overprinted "XI FIERA DI TRIPOLI"

1937, Mar. 15

C30 AP8 50c dark violet 14.00 *35.00*
C31 AP8 1 l violet blk 14.00 *35.00*
Set, never hinged 70.00

11th Sample Fair, Tripoli.

View of Tripoli — AP9

1938, Mar. 12 ***Perf. 14***

C32 AP9 50c dk olive grn 1.40 *2.75*
C33 AP9 1 l slate blue 1.40 *5.50*
Set, never hinged 7.00

12th Sample Fair, Tripoli.

Eagle Attacking Serpent — AP10

1938, Apr. 25 **Wmk. 140**

C34 AP10 50c olive brown .35 *1.75*
C35 AP10 1 l brn violet 1.00 *3.75*
Set, never hinged 3.25

Birth bimillenary Augustus Caesar (Octavianus), first Roman emperor.

Arab and Camel — AP11

Design: 50c, Fair entrance.

1939, Apr. 12 **Photo.**

C36 AP11 25c green .70 *2.10*
C37 AP11 50c olive brown .70 *2.10*
C38 AP11 1 l rose violet 1.00 *2.75*
Nos. C36-C38 (3) 1.90 *6.70*
Set, never hinged 6.00

13th Sample Fair, Tripoli.

Plane Over Modern City — AP12

Design: 1 l, 5 l+2.50 l, Plane over oasis.

1940, June 3

C39 AP12 50c brn blk .70 *.85*
C40 AP12 1 l brn vio .70 *1.75*
C41 AP12 2 l + 75c indigo 1.00 *7.00*
C42 AP12 5 l + 2.50 l copper brn 1.00 *12.50*
Nos. C39-C42 (4) 4.10 *25.50*
Set, never hinged 8.50

Triennial Overseas Exposition, Naples.

AP13

Design: 50c, Hitler, Mussolini and Inscription "Two Peoples, One War".

1941, Apr. 24

C43 AP13 50c slate green 2.75 *42.50*
Never hinged 7.00

Rome-Berlin Axis.

Cyrenaica No. C9 Overprinted in Black Like No. C25

1941

C44 AP3 1 l black 12.50 *70.00*
Never hinged 30.00

Same Overprint on Tripolitania Nos. C9-C11, C13-C15

C45 AP1 60c red orange .75
C46 AP1 75c deep blue .75 47.50
C47 AP1 80c dull violet .75 100.00
C48 AP2 1.20 l dark brown .75 140.00
C49 AP2 1.50 l orange red .75 175.00
C50 AP2 5 l green .75
Nos. C45-C50 (6) 4.50
Set, never hinged 10.00

Catalogue values for unused stamps in this section, from this point to the end of the section, are for Never Hinged items.

United Kingdom of Libya

ICY Type of Regular Issue

Perf. 14½x14

1965, Jan. 1 **Litho.** **Unwmk.**

C51 A60 50m reddish lil & gold 1.90 .90
a. Souvenir sheet 5.00 5.00

No. C51a exists with simulated perfs.; same value.

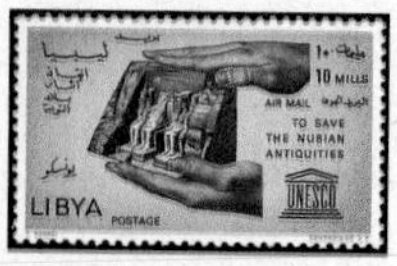

Hands Holding Facade of Abu Simbel AP14

1966, Jan. 1 **Photo.** ***Perf. 11½***

Granite Paper

C52 AP14 10m bis & dk brn .40 .25
a. Souvenir sheet of 4 2.00 3.75
C53 AP14 15m gray grn & dk grn .50 .25
a. Souvenir sheet of 4 2.50 5.00
C54 AP14 40m dl sal & dk brn 1.60 .65
a. Souvenir sheet of 4 6.50 13.00
Nos. C52-C54 (3) 2.50 1.15

UNESCO world campaign to save historic monuments in Nubia.

Inauguration of WHO Headquarters, Geneva — AP15

Perf. 10x10½

1966, May 3 **Litho.** **Unwmk.**

C55 AP15 20m blk, yel & bl .25 .25
C56 AP15 50m blk, yel grn & red .90 .65
C57 AP15 65m blk, sal & brn red 1.40 1.40
Nos. C55-C57 (3) 2.55 2.30

Flag and Globe — AP16

1966, Oct. 1 **Photo.** ***Perf. 11½***

Granite Paper

C58 AP16 25m multicolored .50 .40
C59 AP16 60m multicolored 1.40 1.00
C60 AP16 85m gray & multi 1.90 1.40
Nos. C58-C60 (3) 3.80 2.80

Inauguration of Kingdom of Libya Airlines, 1st anniv.

AIR POST SPECIAL DELIVERY STAMPS

APSD1

Wmk. 140

1934, Feb. 17 **Photo.** ***Perf. 14***

CE1 APSD1 2.25 l olive blk 55.00 *70.00*
CE2 APSD1 4.50 l + 1 l gray blk 55.00 *70.00*
Set, never hinged 280.00

8th Sample Fair at Tripoli. The surtax was for the aid of the Fair.

SPECIAL DELIVERY STAMPS

Special Delivery Stamps of Italy Overprinted

Two types of overprint. See note preceding No. 1 for descriptions.

1915-16. **Wmk. 140** ***Perf. 14***

E1 SD1 25c rose red, ovpt. type I 80.00 32.50
E2 SD2 30c blue & rose, ovpt. type I 8.00 *32.50*
Set, never hinged 217.50

Issued: Nos. E1, E2, Nov. 1915.

For surcharges see Nos. E7-E8.

"Italia" — SD3

No. E3

No. E4

No. E5

No. E6

Nos. E5-E6 bottom-corner denominations and words are reversed from Nos. E3-E4.

1921-23 **Engr.** ***Perf. 13½***

E3 SD3 30c blue & rose 2.25 *8.00*
E4 SD3 50c rose red & brn 4.75 *11.00*
E5 SD3 60c dk red & brn ('23) 8.00 *17.00*
E6 SD3 2 l dk bl & red ('23) 15.00 *30.00*
Nos. E3-E6 (4) 30.00 *66.00*
Set, never hinged 65.00

30c, 2 l inscribed "EXPRES."

For surcharges see Nos. E9-E12.

Nos. E1-E2 Surcharged

1922, June 1

E7 SD1 60c on 25c rose red 12.50 *17.50*
E8 SD2 1.60 l on 30c bl & rose 15.00 *35.00*
Set, never hinged 67.50

Nos. E5-E6 Surcharged in Blue or Red

No. E9

Nos. E10, E12

No. E11

1926-36

E9 SD3 70c on 60c 7.50 *15.00*
E10 SD3 2.50 l on 2 l (R) 14.00 *27.50*

Perf. 11

E11	SD3	1.25 l on 60c	5.50	1.75
a.		Perf. 14 ('36)	21.00	3.50
		Never hinged	52.50	
b.		Black surcharge	105,000.	18,000.
E12	SD3	2.50 l on 2 l (R)	240.00	850.00
		Nos. E9-E12 (4)	267.00	894.25
		Set, never hinged	625.00	

Issued: Nos. E9-E10, July 1926; Nos. E11-E12, 1927.

Catalogue values for unused stamps in this section, from this point to the end of the section, are for Never Hinged items.

United Kingdom of Libya

Zuela Saracen Castle — SD4

Perf. 11½

1966, Feb. 10 Unwmk. Litho.

E13	SD4	90m car rose & lt grn	3.00	1.60

Coat of Arms of Libya and "POLIGRAFICA & CARTEVALORI — NAPLES" printed on back in yellow green.

SEMI-POSTAL SPECIAL DELIVERY STAMPS

Camel Caravan SPSD1

Wmk. 140

1927, Feb. 15 Litho. *Perf. 14*

EB1	SPSD1	1.25 l + 30c pur & blk	8.50	42.50
EB2	SPSD1	2.50 l + 1 l yel & blk	8.50	42.50
		Set, never hinged	42.00	

See note after No. B10.

No. EB2 is inscribed "EXPRES."

War Memorial SPSD2

1931, Mar. 8 Photo.

EB3	SPSD2	1.25 l + 20c car rose	5.50	*27.50*
		Never hinged	14.00	

See note after No. B37.

AUTHORIZED DELIVERY STAMPS

Italy No. EY1 Overprinted in Black

1929, May 11 Wmk. 140 *Perf. 14*

EY1	AD1	10c dull blue	30.00	*70.00*
		Never hinged	77.50	
a.		Perf. 11	125.00	275.00
		Never hinged	300.00	

Italy No. EY2 Overprinted in Black

1941, May *Perf. 14*

EY2	AD2	10c dark brown	11.00	47.50
		Never hinged	27.50	

A variety of No. EY2, with larger "LIBIA" and yellow gum, was prepared in 1942, but not issued. Value 85 cents, never hinged $2.10.

AD1

1942 Litho. Wmk. 140

EY3	AD1	10c sepia	.85
		Never hinged	2.10

No. EY3 was not issued.

POSTAGE DUE STAMPS

Italian Postage Due Stamps, 1870-1903 Overprinted in Black

1915, Nov. Wmk. 140 *Perf. 14*

J1	D3	5c buff & mag	2.10	*10.00*
J2	D3	10c buff & mag	2.10	*5.50*
J3	D3	20c buff & mag	2.75	*8.50*
a.		Double overprint	500.00	500.00
b.		Inverted overprint	500.00	
J4	D3	30c buff & mag	7.00	*10.00*
J5	D3	40c buff & mag	10.00	*12.50*
a.		"40" in black	4,500.	
J6	D3	50c buff & mag	7.00	*8.50*
J7	D3	60c buff & mag	10.00	*19.00*
J8	D3	1 l blue & mag	7.00	*19.00*
a.		Double overprint	*10,500.*	*16,000.*
J9	D3	2 l blue & mag	55.00	*110.00*
J10	D3	5 l blue & mag	77.50	*190.00*
		Nos. J1-J10 (10)	180.45	*393.00*

1926

J11	D3	60c buff & brown	175.00	*325.00*

Postage Due Stamps of Italy, 1934, Overprinted in Black

1934

J12	D6	5c brown	.35	*2.75*
J13	D6	10c blue	.35	*2.75*
J14	D6	20c rose red	1.40	1.40
J15	D6	25c green	1.40	1.40
J16	D6	30c red orange	1.40	*5.50*
J17	D6	40c black brn	1.40	*3.50*
J18	D6	50c violet	1.75	.35
J19	D6	60c black	1.75	*17.50*
J20	D7	1 l red orange	1.40	.35
J21	D7	2 l green	42.50	17.50
J22	D7	5 l violet	95.00	37.50
J23	D7	10 l blue	12.50	*52.50*
J24	D7	20 l carmine	12.50	*70.00*
		Nos. J12-J24 (13)	173.70	*213.00*

In 1942 a set of 11 "Segnatasse" stamps, picturing a camel and rider and inscribed "LIBIA," was prepared but not issued. Values for set: hinged $12; never hinged $30.

Catalogue values for unused stamps in this section, from this point to the end of the section, are for Never Hinged items.

United Kingdom of Libya

Postage Due Stamps of Cyrenaica, 1950 Surcharged in Black

For Use in Tripolitania

1951 Unwmk. *Perf. 12½*

J25	D1	1mal on 2m dk brown	9.00	18.00
J26	D1	2mal on 4m dp grn	15.00	*30.00*
J27	D1	4mal on 8m scar	25.00	*50.00*
J28	D1	10mal on 20m org yel	50.00	*100.00*
a.		Arabic "20" for "10"	—	
J29	D1	20mal on 40m dp bl	80.00	*160.00*
		Nos. J25-J29 (5)	179.00	*358.00*

Cyrenaica Nos. J1-J7 Overprinted in Black

For Use in Cyrenaica

Overprint 13mm High

1952 Unwmk. *Perf. 12½*

J30	D1	2m dark brown	10.00	*20.00*
J31	D1	4m deep green	10.00	*20.00*
J32	D1	8m scarlet	15.00	*30.00*
J33	D1	10m vermilion	20.00	*4.00*
J34	D1	20m orange yel	30.00	*60.00*
J35	D1	40m deep blue	42.50	*85.00*
J36	D1	100m dk gray	92.50	*180.00*
		Nos. J30-J36 (7)	220.00	*399.00*

D1

1952 Litho. *Perf. 11½*

J37	D1	2m chocolate	1.00	.35
J38	D1	5m blue green	1.60	.90
J39	D1	10m carmine	3.00	1.50
J40	D1	50m violet blue	11.00	4.00
		Nos. J37-J40 (4)	16.60	6.75

Castle at Tripoli — D2

1964, Feb. 1 Photo. *Perf. 14*

J41	D2	2m red brown	.25	.25
J42	D2	6m Prus green	.50	.50
J43	D2	10m rose red	1.00	1.00
J44	D2	50m brt blue	2.00	2.00
		Nos. J41-J44 (4)	3.75	3.75

Men in Boat, Birds, Mosaic — D3

Ancient Mosaics: 10d, Head of Medusa. 20d, Peacock. 50d, Fish.

1976, Nov. 15 Litho. *Perf. 14*

J45	D3	5d bister & multi	.25	.25
J46	D3	10d orange & multi	.25	.25
J47	D3	20d blue & multi	.35	.35
J48	D3	50d emerald & multi	.80	.80
		Nos. J45-J48 (4)	1.65	1.65

Nos. J45-J48 have multiple coat of arms printed on back in pale green beneath gum.

OFFICIAL STAMPS

Catalogue values for unused stamps in this section are for Never Hinged items.

United Kingdom of Libya

Nos. 135-142 Overprinted in Black

1952 Unwmk. *Perf. 11½*

O1	A27	2m yel brn	.90	.60
O2	A27	4m gray	1.50	.90
O3	A27	5m bl grn	7.50	3.00
O4	A27	8m vermilion	5.50	2.50
O5	A27	10m purple	7.00	3.00
O6	A27	12m lil rose	11.00	6.25
O7	A27	20m dp bl	19.00	9.50
O8	A27	25m chocolate	25.00	12.50
		Nos. O1-O8 (8)	77.40	38.25

PARCEL POST STAMPS

These stamps were used by affixing them to the way bill so that one half remained on it following the parcel, the other half staying on the receipt given the sender. Most used halves are right halves. Complete stamps were obtainable canceled, probably to order. Both unused and used values are for complete stamps.

Italian Parcel Post Stamps, 1914-22, Overprinted

1915-24 Wmk. 140 *Perf. 13½*

Q1	PP2	5c brown	7.00	*14.00*
a.		Double overprint	375.00	
Q2	PP2	10c deep blue	7.00	*14.00*
Q3	PP2	20c blk ('18)	8.50	*14.00*
Q4	PP2	25c red	8.50	*14.00*
Q5	PP2	50c orange	10.00	*14.00*
Q6	PP2	1 l violet	10.00	*21.00*
Q7	PP2	2 l green	14.00	*21.00*
Q8	PP2	3 l bister	21.00	*21.00*
Q9	PP2	4 l slate	21.00	*21.00*
Q10	PP2	10 l rose lil ('24)	70.00	*125.00*
Q11	PP2	12 l red brn ('24)	140.00	*260.00*
Q12	PP2	15 l ol grn ('24)	140.00	*425.00*
Q13	PP2	20 l brn vio ('24)	210.00	*510.00*
		Nos. Q1-Q13 (13)	667.00	*1,474.*

Halves Used

Q1	1.25
Q2	1.75
Q3	1.75
Q4	1.75
Q5	1.75
Q6	1.75
Q7	1.75
Q8	1.75
Q9	1.75
Q10	11.00
Q11	12.00
Q12	27.50
Q13	67.50

Same Overprint on Parcel Post Stamps of Italy, 1927-36

1927-38

Q14	PP3	10c dp bl ('36)	7.00	*10.00*
Q15	PP3	25c red ('36)	7.00	*10.00*
Q16	PP3	30c ultra ('29)	3.50	*7.00*
Q17	PP3	50c orange	50.00	*350.00*
a.		Overprint 8¾x2mm ('31)	87.50	*450.00*
Q18	PP3	60c red ('29)	3.50	*7.00*
Q19	PP3	1 l lilac ('36)	37.50	*140.00*
Q20	PP3	2 l grn ('38)	45.00	*140.00*
Q21	PP3	3 l bister	4.25	*14.00*
Q22	PP3	4 l gray	4.25	*21.00*
Q23	PP3	10 l rose lil ('36)	275.00	625.00
Q24	PP3	20 l brn vio ('36)	300.00	*850.00*
		Nos. Q14-Q24 (11)	737.00	*2,174.*

Halves Used

Q14	.50
Q15	.50
Q16	.50
Q17	12.50
Q17a	22.50
Q18	.50
Q19	7.50
Q20	7.50
Q21	1.50
Q22	2.50
Q23	30.00
Q24	35.00

The overprint measures 10x1½mm on No. Q17.

Same Overprint on Italy No. Q24

1939

Q25	PP3	5c brown	*15,000.*
		Never hinged	*22,500.*

The overprint was applied to the 5c in error. Few examples exist.

OCCUPATION STAMPS

Catalogue values for unused stamps in this section are for Never Hinged items.

Issued under French Occupation

Stamps of Italy and Libya were overprinted in 1943: "FEZZAN Occupation Française" and "R. F. FEZZAN" for use in this region when General Leclerc's forces 1st occupied it.

Fezzan-Ghadames

Sebha Fort — OS1

Mosque and Fort Turc Murzuch — OS2

Map of Fezzan-Ghadames, Soldier and Camel — OS3

1946 Unwmk. Engr. *Perf. 13*

1N1	OS1	10c black	.35	.35
1N2	OS1	50c rose	.35	.35
1N3	OS1	1fr brown	.45	.45
1N4	OS1	1.50fr green	.55	.55
1N5	OS1	2fr ultramarine	.70	.70
1N6	OS2	2.50fr violet	.90	.90
1N7	OS2	3fr rose carmine	1.20	1.20
1N8	OS2	5fr chocolate	1.20	1.20
1N9	OS2	6fr dark green	1.10	1.10
1N10	OS2	10fr blue	1.20	1.20
1N11	OS3	15fr violet	1.50	1.50
1N12	OS3	20fr red	1.75	1.75
1N13	OS3	25fr sepia	1.75	1.75
1N14	OS3	40fr dark green	2.25	2.25
1N15	OS3	50fr deep blue	2.50	2.50
		Nos. 1N1-1N15 (15)	17.75	17.75

FEZZAN

Catalogue values for unused stamps in this section are for Never Hinged items.

Monument, Djerma Oasis OS1

Tombs of the Beni-Khettab OS2

Well at Gorda — OS3

Col. Colonna d'Ornano and Fort at Murzuch — OS4

Philippe F. M. de Hautecloque (Gen. Jacques Leclerc) — OS5

1949 Unwmk. Engr. *Perf. 13*

2N1	OS1	1fr black	1.20	1.20
2N2	OS1	2fr lil pink	1.25	1.25
2N3	OS2	4fr red brn	2.10	2.10
2N4	OS2	5fr emerald	2.10	2.10
2N5	OS3	8fr blue	2.75	2.75
2N6	OS3	10fr brown	4.50	4.50
2N7	OS3	12fr dk grn	7.00	7.00
2N8	OS4	15fr sal red	10.00	10.00
2N9	OS4	20fr brn blk	5.00	5.00
2N10	OS5	25fr dk bl	5.50	5.50
2N11	OS5	50fr cop red	10.00	10.00
		Nos. 2N1-2N11 (11)	51.40	51.40

Camel Raising — OS6

Agriculture OS7

Well Drilling OS8

Ahmed Bey — OS9

1951

2N12	OS6	30c brown	1.40	1.40
2N13	OS6	1fr dp bl	1.40	1.40
2N14	OS6	2fr rose car	1.40	1.40
2N15	OS7	4fr red	2.10	2.10
2N16	OS7	5fr green	2.10	2.10
2N17	OS7	8fr dp bl	2.10	2.10
2N18	OS8	10fr sepia	5.50	5.50
2N19	OS8	12fr dp grn	6.25	6.25
2N20	OS8	15fr brt red	7.00	7.00
2N21	OS9	20fr blk brn & vio brn	7.00	7.00
2N22	OS9	25fr dk bl & bl	7.75	7.75
2N23	OS9	50fr ind & brn org	8.50	8.50
		Nos. 2N12-2N23 (12)	52.50	52.50

OCCUPATION SEMI-POSTAL STAMPS

Catalogue values for unused stamps in this section are for Never Hinged items.

"The Unhappy Ones" OSP1 OSP2

1950 Unwmk. Engr. *Perf. 13*

2NB1	OSP1	15fr + 5fr red brn	3.25	3.25
2NB2	OSP2	25fr + 5fr blue	3.25	3.25

The surtax was for charitable works.

OCCUPATION AIR POST STAMPS

Catalogue values for unused stamps in this section are for Never Hinged items.

Airport in Fezzan OAP1

Plane over Fezzan OAP2

1948 Unwmk. Engr. *Perf. 13*

2NC1	OAP1	100fr red	7.00	7.00
2NC2	OAP2	200fr indigo	10.00	10.00

Oasis — OAP3

Murzuch — OAP4

1951

2NC3	OAP3	100fr dark blue	9.75	9.75
2NC4	OAP4	200fr vermilion	14.00	14.00

OCCUPATION POSTAGE DUE STAMPS

Catalogue values for unused stamps in this section are for Never Hinged items.

Oasis of Brak — D1

1950 Unwmk. Engr. *Perf. 13*

2NJ1	D1	1fr brown black	1.40	1.40
2NJ2	D1	2fr deep green	1.40	1.40
2NJ3	D1	3fr red brown	2.10	2.10
2NJ4	D1	5fr purple	2.10	2.10
2NJ5	D1	10fr red	4.25	4.25
2NJ6	D1	20fr deep blue	6.25	6.25
		Nos. 2NJ1-2NJ6 (6)	17.50	17.50

GHADAMES

Catalogue values for unused stamps in this section are for Never Hinged items.

Cross of Agadem — OS1

1949 Unwmk. Engr. *Perf. 13*

3N1	OS1	4fr sep & red brn	1.75	1.75
3N2	OS1	5fr pck bl & dk grn	1.75	1.75
3N3	OS1	8fr sep & org brn	4.50	4.50
3N4	OS1	10fr blk & dk ultra	4.50	4.50
3N5	OS1	12fr vio & red vio	12.00	12.00
3N6	OS1	15fr brn & red brn	8.50	8.50
3N7	OS1	20fr sep & emer	10.00	10.00
3N8	OS1	25fr sepia & blue	12.50	12.50
		Nos. 3N1-3N8 (8)	55.50	55.50

OCCUPATION AIR POST STAMPS

Catalogue values for unused stamps in this section are for Never Hinged items.

Cross of Agadem — OAP1

1949 Unwmk. Engr. *Perf. 13*

3NC1	OAP1	50fr pur & rose	16.00	16.00
3NC2	OAP1	100fr sep & pur brn	19.00	19.00

LIECHTENSTEIN

'lik-tən-,shtin

LOCATION — Central Europe southeast of Lake Constance, between Austria and Switzerland
GOVT. — Principality
AREA — 61.8 sq. mi.
POP. — 31,320 (1997)
CAPITAL — Vaduz

The Principality of Liechtenstein is a sovereign state consisting of the two counties of Schellenberg and Vaduz. Since 1921 the post office has been administered by Switzerland.

100 Heller = 1 Krone
100 Rappen = 1 Franc (1921)

Catalogue values for unused stamps in this country are for Never Hinged items, beginning with Scott 368 in the regular postage section, Scott B22 in the semi-postal section, Scott C24 in the air post section, and Scott O30 in the offical section.

Watermarks

Greek Cross — Wmk. 183

Crown and Initials — Wmk. 296

Austrian Administration of the Post Office

Prince Johann II — A1

Perf. 12½x13

1912, Feb. 1 Unwmk. Typo.

Thick Chalky Paper

1	A1	5h yellow green	42.50	17.50
2	A1	10h rose	85.00	17.50
3	A1	25h dark blue	85.00	55.00
		Nos. 1-3 (3)	212.50	90.00
		Set, never hinged	900.00	

1915 Thin Unsurfaced Paper

1a	A1	5h yellow green	14.00	21.00
2a	A1	10h rose	85.00	32.50
3a	A1	25h dark blue	600.00	200.00
b.		25h ultramarine	350.00	425.00
		Never hinged	1,550.	
		#1a-3a, never hinged	2,500.	

Coat of Arms — A2

Prince Johann II — A3

1917-18

4	A2	3h violet	2.00	2.00
5	A2	5h yellow green	2.00	2.00
6	A3	10h claret	2.00	2.00
7	A3	15h dull red	2.00	2.00
8	A3	20h dark green	2.00	2.00
9	A3	25h deep blue	2.00	2.00
		Nos. 4-9 (6)	12.00	12.00
		Set, never hinged	51.00	

Exist imperf. Value set unused original gum, $525; never hinged, $1,150.

For surcharges see Nos. 11-16.

Prince Johann II — A4

Dates in Upper Corners

1918, Nov. 12

10	A4	20h dark green	.70	2.75
		Never hinged	5.50	

Accession of Prince Johann II, 60th anniv.

Exists imperf. Value, unused original gum, $225; never hinged, $560.

National Administration of the Post Office

Stamps of 1917-18 Overprinted or Surcharged

a

b

c

1920

11	A2(a)	5h yellow green	2.75	8.75
a.		Inverted overprint	70.00	175.00
		Never hinged	140.00	
b.		Double overprint	14.00	85.00
		Never hinged	35.00	
12	A3(a)	10h claret	2.75	9.50
a.		Inverted overprint	70.00	175.00
		Never hinged	140.00	
b.		Double overprint	14.00	105.00
		Never hinged	35.00	
c.		Overprint type "c"	14.00	105.00
		Never hinged	27.50	
13	A3(a)	25h deep blue	2.75	9.50
a.		Inverted overprint	70.00	175.00
		Never hinged	140.00	
b.		Double overprint	14.00	105.00
		Never hinged	27.50	
14	A2(b)	40h on 3h violet	2.75	9.50
a.		Inverted surcharge	70.00	175.00
		Never hinged	140.00	
15	A3(c)	1k on 15h dull red	2.75	9.50
a.		Inverted surcharge	70.00	175.00
b.		Overprint type "a"	87.50	350.00
		Never hinged	315.00	
16	A3(c)	2½k on 20h dk grn	2.75	9.50
a.		Inverted surcharge	70.00	175.00
		Nos. 11-16 (6)	16.50	56.25
		Set, never hinged	71.00	

Coat of Arms A5

Chapel of St. Mamertus A6

Coat of Arms with Supporters — A15

Designs: 40h, Gutenberg Castle. 50h, Courtyard, Vaduz Castle. 60h, Red Tower, Vaduz. 80h, Old Roman Tower, Schaan. 1k, Castle at Vaduz. 2k, View of Bendern. 5k, Prince Johann I. 7½k, Prince Johann II.

1920 Engr. *Imperf.*

18	A5	5h olive bister	.35	5.75
19	A5	10h deep orange	.35	5.75
20	A5	15h dark blue	.35	5.75
21	A5	20h deep brown	.35	5.75
22	A5	25h dark green	.35	5.75
23	A5	30h gray black	.35	5.75
24	A5	40h dark red	.35	5.75
25	A6	1k blue	.35	5.75

Perf. 12½

32	A5	5h olive bister	.35	.70
33	A5	10h deep orange	.35	.70
34	A5	15h deep blue	.35	.70
35	A5	20h red brown	.35	.70
36	A6	25h olive green	.35	.70
37	A5	30h dark gray	.35	.70
38	A6	40h claret	.35	.70
39	A6	50h yellow green	.35	.70
40	A6	60h red brown	.35	.70
41	A6	80h rose	.35	.70
42	A6	1k dull violet	.70	1.00
43	A6	2k light blue	.70	1.25
44	A6	5k black	.70	1.50
45	A6	7½k slate	.70	1.75
46	A15	10k ocher	.70	3.00
		Nos. 18-46 (23)	9.80	61.50
		Set, never hinged	41.00	

No. 25 perf. 12½ was not officially issued. It is known mint, used and on cover.

Used values for Nos. 18-46 are for canceled to order stamps. Value with postal cancels approximately $95.

Many denominations of Nos. 32-46 are found imperforate, imperforate vertically and imperforate horizontally.

For surcharges see Nos. 51-52.

Madonna and Child — A16

1920, Oct. 5

47	A16	50h olive green	1.00	2.10
48	A16	80h brown red	1.00	2.10
49	A16	2k dark blue	1.00	2.75
		Nos. 47-49 (3)	3.00	6.95
		Set, never hinged	10.50	

80th birthday of Prince Johann II.

Imperf., Singles

47a	A16	50h	7.00	1,400.
48a	A16	80h	7.00	1,400.
49a	A16	2k	7.00	1,400.
		Set, never hinged	63.00	

On 1/31/21 the Swiss took over the Post Office administration. Previous issues were demonetized and remainders of Nos. 4-49 were sold.

Swiss Administration of the Post Office

No. 19 Surcharged

No. 51

No. 52

1921 Unwmk. Engr. *Imperf.*

51	A5	2rp on 10h dp org	1.40	50.00
a.		Double surcharge	105.00	140.00
b.		Inverted surcharge	105.00	160.00
c.		Double surch., one inverted	105.00	175.00
52	A5	2rp on 10h dp org	.70	50.00
		First day cover (2/27/21)		875.00
a.		Double surcharge	72.50	160.00
b.		Inverted surcharge	72.50	160.00
c.		Double surch., one inverted	87.50	190.00

Arms with Supporters A19

Chapel of St. Mamertus A20

View of Vaduz — A21

Designs: 25rp, Castle at Vaduz. 30rp, View of Bendern. 35rp, Prince Johann II. 40rp, Old Roman Tower at Schaan. 50rp, Gutenberg Castle. 80rp, Red Tower at Vaduz.

1921 *Perf. 12½, 9½ (2rp, 10rp, 15rp)*

Surface Tinted Paper (#54-61)

54	A19	2rp lemon	1.40	14.00
55	A19	2½rp black	2.10	17.50
a.		Perf. 9½	1.40	70.00
56	A19	3rp orange	2.10	17.50
a.		Perf. 9½	140.00	5,000.
57	A19	5rp olive green	14.00	2.10
a.		Perf. 9½	70.00	27.50
		Never hinged	225.00	
58	A19	7½rp dark blue	7.00	42.50
a.		Perf. 9½	275.00	1,050.
59	A19	10rp yellow green	27.50	17.50
a.		Perf. 12½	27.50	14.00
60	A19	13rp brown	10.50	90.00
a.		Perf. 9½	100.00	2,450.
		Never hinged	250.00	
b.		Perf. 12½x9½	210.00	—
		Never hinged	425.00	
61	A19	15rp dark violet	25.00	70.00
a.		Perf. 12½	27.50	27.50
		Never hinged	50.00	
62	A20	20rp dull vio & blk	70.00	2.10
63	A20	25rp rose red & blk	3.50	5.00
64	A20	30rp dp grn & blk	85.00	21.00
65	A20	35rp brn & blk, *straw*	7.00	17.50
66	A20	40rp dk blue & blk	10.50	7.00
67	A20	50rp dk grn & blk	17.50	10.50
68	A20	80rp gray & blk	32.00	85.00
69	A21	1fr dp claret & blk	55.00	55.00
		Nos. 54-69 (16)	370.10	474.20
		Set, never hinged	1,039.	

Nos. 54-69 exist imperforate; Nos. 54-61, partly perforated. See Nos. 73, 81. For surcharges see Nos. 70-71.

Nos. 58, 60a Surcharged in Red

1924 *Perf. 12½, 9½*

70	A19	5rp on 7½rp	1.40	3.50
a.		Perf. 9½	19.00	17.50
		Never hinged	50.00	
71	A19	10rp on 13rp	1.75	3.50
		Never hinged	5.25	
a.		Perf. 12½	20.00	52.50

Type of 1921
Granite Paper

1924 Wmk. 183 *Perf. 11½*

73 A19 10rp green 21.00 3.50

Peasant A28

Government Palace and Church at Vaduz A30

10rp, 20rp, Courtyard, Vaduz Castle.

1924-28 Typo. *Perf. 11½*

74	A28	2½rp ol grn & red vio ('28)	1.40	*5.50*
75	A28	5rp brown & blue	2.75	.75
76	A28	7½rp bl grn & brn ('28)	2.10	*5.50*
77	A28	15rp red brn & bl grn ('28)	10.50	*35.00*

Engr.

78	A28	10rp yellow grn	11.25	.70
79	A28	20rp deep red	42.50	.70
80	A30	1½fr blue	85.00	*110.00*
		Nos. 74-80 (7)	155.50	*158.15*
		Set, never hinged	503.00	

Bendern Type of 1921

1925

81 A20 30rp blue & blk 17.50 3.50

Prince Johann II — A31

Prince Johann II as Boy and Man — A32

1928, Nov. 12 Typo. Wmk. 183

82	A31	10rp lt brn & ol grn	7.00	7.00
83	A31	20rp org red & ol grn	10.50	14.00
84	A31	30rp sl bl & ol grn	35.00	25.00
85	A31	60rp red vio & ol grn	70.00	*70.00*

Engr.
Unwmk.

86	A32	1.20fr ultra	50.00	*87.50*
87	A32	1.50fr blk brn	87.50	*210.00*
88	A32	2fr deep car	87.50	*210.00*
89	A32	5fr dark green	87.50	*245.00*
		Nos. 82-89 (8)	435.00	*868.50*
		Set, never hinged	1,040.	

70th year of the reign of Prince Johann II.

Prince Francis I, as a Child — A33

Prince Francis I as a Man — A34

Princess Elsa — A35

Prince Francis and Princess Elsa — A36

1929, Dec. 2 Photo.

90	A33	10rp olive green	.55	*4.25*
91	A34	20rp carmine	.85	*7.00*
92	A35	30rp ultra	1.40	*17.50*
93	A36	70rp brown	25.00	*110.00*
		Nos. 90-93 (4)	27.80	*138.75*
		Set, never hinged	77.00	

Accession of Prince Francis I, Feb. 11, 1929.

Grape Girl — A37

Chamois Hunter — A38

Mountain Cattle — A39

Courtyard, Vaduz Castle — A40

Mt. Naafkopf A41

Chapel at Steg A42

Rofenberg Chapel A43

Chapel of St. Mamertus A44

Alpine Hotel, Malbun A45

Gutenberg Castle A46

Schellenberg Monastery A47

Castle at Vaduz A48

Mountain Cottage A49

Prince Francis and Princess Elsa A50

1930 *Perf. 10½, 11½, 11½x10½*

94	A37	3rp brown lake	1.10	2.80
95	A38	5rp deep green	2.80	7.00
96	A39	10rp dark violet	2.50	7.00
a.		Perf. 11½x10½	11.00	*120.00*
		Never hinged	28.00	
97	A40	20rp dp rose red	42.50	7.00
98	A41	25rp black	8.50	*45.00*
a.		Perf. 11½	105.00	*350.00*
		Never hinged	350.00	
99	A42	30rp dp ultra	8.50	10.50
a.		Perf. 11½x10½	1,050.	*2,500.*
		Never hinged	2,175.	
100	A43	35rp dark green	11.00	*21.00*
a.		Perf. 11½	*8,750.*	*14,000.*
		Never hinged	*13,500.*	
101	A44	40rp lt brown	11.00	11.00
102	A45	50rp blk brn	105.00	21.00
a.		Perf. 11½	165.00	*245.00*
		Never hinged	600.00	
103	A46	60rp olive blk	105.00	42.50
104	A47	90rp violet brn	105.00	*350.00*
105	A48	1.20fr olive brn	125.00	*375.00*
a.		Perf. 11½x10½	*8,750.*	*14,000.*
		Never hinged	*13,500.*	
106	A49	1.50fr black violet	70.00	77.50
107	A50	2fr gray grn & red brn	85.00	*140.00*
a.		Perf. 11½x10½	*3,850.*	*7,750.*
		Never hinged	*6,750.*	
		Nos. 94-107 (14)	681.90	*1,117.*
		Set, never hinged	1,600.	

For overprints see Nos. O1-O8.

Mt. Naafkopf A51

Gutenberg Castle A52

Vaduz Castle — A53

1933, Jan. 23 *Perf. 14½*

108	A51	25rp red orange	200.00	87.50
109	A52	90rp dark green	10.50	*105.00*
110	A53	1.20fr red brown	85.00	*300.00*
		Nos. 108-110 (3)	295.50	*492.50*
		Set, never hinged	840.00	

For overprints see Nos. O9-O10.

80th Birthday of Prince Francis I — A54

1933, Aug. 28 *Perf. 11*

111	A54	10rp purple	21.00	*42.50*
112	A54	20rp brn car	21.00	*42.50*
113	A54	30rp dark blue	21.00	*42.50*
		Nos. 111-113 (3)	63.00	*127.50*
		Set, never hinged	180.00	

Prince Francis I — A55

1933, Dec. 15 Engr. *Perf. 12½*

114	A55	3fr violet blue	125.00	*250.00*
		Never hinged	250.00	

See No. 152.

Agricultural Exhibition Issue
Souvenir Sheet

Arms of Liechtenstein — A56

1934, Sept. 29 *Perf. 12*
Granite Paper

115	A56	5fr brown	*1,400.*	*2,500.*
		Never hinged	*2,250.*	
		Single stamp	*1,000.*	*1,750.*
		Never hinged	*1,400.*	

See No. 131.

Coat of Arms A57

"Three Sisters" (Landmark) A58

Church of Schaan A59

Bendern A60

Rathaus, Vaduz A61

Samina Valley A62

Samina Valley in Winter — A63

Ruin at Schellenberg A64

Government Palace — A65

Vaduz Castle — A66

Gutenberg Castle — A68

Alpine Hut — A69

Princess Elsa — A70

Coat of Arms — A71

60rp, Vaduz castle, diff. 1.50fr, Valuna.

1934-35 Photo. *Perf. 11½*

116	A57	3rp copper red	.35	.70
117	A58	5rp emerald	5.50	2.10
118	A59	10rp deep violet	2.75	1.40
119	A60	15rp red org	.35	1.40
120	A61	20rp red	.70	1.40
121	A62	25rp brown	28.00	*65.00*
122	A63	30rp dk blue	5.50	2.10
123	A64	35rp gray grn	2.75	*8.50*
124	A65	40rp brown	1.75	*7.00*
125	A66	50rp lt brown	25.00	21.00
126	A66	60rp claret	2.10	*9.00*
127	A68	90rp deep green	8.50	*32.00*
128	A69	1.20fr deep blue	3.50	*32.00*
129	A69	1.50fr brn car	4.25	*35.00*
		Nos. 116-129 (14)	91.00	*218.60*
		Set, never hinged	275.00	

Engr.
Perf. 12½

130	A70	2fr hen brn ('35)	85.00	*250.00*
		Never hinged	140.00	
131	A71	5fr dk vio ('35)	425.00	*1,050.*
		Never hinged	700.00	

No. 131 has the same design as the 5fr in the souvenir sheet, No. 115. See No. 226, B14. For overprints see Nos. O11-O20.

Bridge at Malbun — A72

Labor: 20rp, Constructing Road to Triesenberg. 30rp, Binnen Canal. 50rp, Bridge near Planken.

1937, June 30 **Photo.**

132	A72	10rp brt violet	1.75	2.10
133	A72	20rp red	1.75	*2.75*
134	A72	30rp brt blue	1.75	*3.50*
135	A72	50rp yellow brown	1.75	*4.25*
		Nos. 132-135 (4)	7.00	12.60
		Set, never hinged	21.00	

Ruin at Schalun A76

Peasant in Rhine Valley A77

Ruin at Schellenberg A78

Knight and Gutenberg Castle — A79

Baron von Brandis and Vaduz Castle — A80

Designs: 5rp, Chapel at Masescha. 10rp, Knight and Vaduz Castle. 15rp, Upper Valüna Valley. 20rp, Wooden Bridge over Rhine, Bendern. 25rp, Chapel at Steg. 90rp, "The Three Sisters". 1fr, Frontier stone. 1.20fr, Gutenberg Castle and Harpist. 1.50fr, Alpine View of Lawena and Schwartzhorn.

1937-38

136	A76	3rp yellow brown	.35	*.70*
		Pale Buff Shading		
137	A76	5rp emerald	.35	.35
138	A76	10rp violet	.35	.35
139	A76	15rp dk slate grn	.35	*.70*
140	A76	20rp brn org	.35	*.70*
141	A76	25rp chestnut	.70	*3.50*
142	A77	30rp blue & gray	3.50	1.40
144	A78	40rp dark green	2.10	2.75
145	A79	50rp dark brown	1.40	*7.00*
146	A80	60rp dp claret ('38)	2.75	*3.50*
147	A80	90rp gray vio ('38)	7.00	*42.50*
148	A80	1fr red brown	2.10	*17.50*
149	A80	1.20fr dp brn ('38)	7.00	*32.00*
150	A80	1.50fr slate bl ('38)	4.25	*32.50*
		Nos. 136-150 (14)	32.55	*145.45*
		Set, never hinged	97.00	

For overprints see Nos. O21-O29.

Souvenir Sheet

Josef Rheinberger — A91

1938, July 30 **Engr.** ***Perf. 12***

151	A91	Sheet of 4	27.50	27.50
		Never hinged	70.00	
a.		50rp slate gray	3.50	5.25
		Never hinged	7.00	

Third Philatelic Exhibition of Liechtenstein. Sheet size: 99¾x135mm.
See No. 153.

Francis Type of 1933
Thick Wove Paper

1938, Aug. 15 ***Perf. 12½***

152	A55	3fr black, *buff*	10.50	*100.00*
		Never hinged	21.00	

Issued in memory of Prince Francis I, who died July 25, 1938. Sheets of 20.

Josef Gabriel Rheinberger (1839-1901), German Composer and Organist — A92

1939, Mar. 31

153	A92	50rp slate green	1.10	*6.25*
		Never hinged	2.40	

Issued in sheets of 20. See No. 151.

Scene of Homage, 1718 — A93

1939, May 29

154	A93	20rp brown lake	1.40	2.75
155	A93	30rp slate blue	1.40	2.75
156	A93	50rp gray green	1.40	2.75
		Nos. 154-156 (3)	4.20	8.25
		Set, never hinged	14.00	

Honoring Prince Franz Joseph II. Sheets of 20.

Cantonal Coats of Arms — A94

Prince Franz Joseph II — A96

Design: 3fr, Arms of Principality.

1939

157	A94	2fr dk green, *buff*	7.00	*42.50*
158	A94	3fr indigo, *buff*	4.50	*42.50*
159	A96	5fr brown, *buff*	14.00	*27.50*
a.		Sheet of 4	90.00	*140.00*
		Never hinged	175.00	
		Nos. 157-159 (3)	25.50	*112.50*
		Set, never hinged	63.00	

2fr, 3fr issued in sheets of 12; 5fr in sheets of 4.

Prince Johann as a Child — A100

Memorial Tablet — A101

Prince Johann II — A102

30rp, Prince Johann and Tower at Vaduz. 50rp, Prince Johann and Gutenberg Castle. 1fr, Prince Johann in 1920 and Vaduz Castle.

1940 **Photo.** ***Perf. 11½.***

160	A100	20rp henna brown	.60	*2.25*
161	A100	30rp indigo	.60	*3.25*
162	A100	50rp dk slate grn	1.10	*10.50*
163	A100	1fr brown vio	8.25	*70.00*
164	A101	1.50fr violet blk	10.50	*67.50*
165	A102	3fr brown	4.25	*22.50*
		Nos. 160-165 (6)	25.30	*176.00*
		Set, never hinged	52.50	

Birth centenary of Prince Johann II.
Nos. 160-164 issued in sheets of 25; No. 165 in sheets of 12.
Issue dates: 3fr, Oct. 5; others Aug. 10.

Gathering Corn — A103

Wine Press — A104

Sharpening Scythe — A105

Milkmaid and Cow — A106

Native Costume — A107

1941, Apr. 7

166	A103	10rp dull red brown	.75	.45
167	A104	20rp lake	.75	1.10
168	A105	30rp royal blue	.75	*2.50*
169	A106	50rp myrtle green	2.40	*14.00*
170	A107	90rp deep claret	2.40	*14.00*
		Nos. 166-170 (5)	7.05	*32.05*
		Set, never hinged	16.00	

Madonna and Child — A108

1941, July 7 **Engr.**

171	A108	10fr brown car	37.50	*97.50*
		Never hinged	75.00	

Issued in sheets of 4.

Johann Adam Andreas — A109

Designs: 30rp, Wenzel. 100rp, Anton Florian. 150rp, Joseph Adam.

1941, Dec. 18 **Photo.**

172	A109	20rp brown car	.50	*1.25*
173	A109	30rp royal blue	.70	*2.50*
174	A109	100rp violet blk	1.90	*13.00*
175	A109	150rp slate green	1.90	*13.00*
		Nos. 172-175 (4)	5.00	*29.75*
		Set, never hinged	11.00	

Saint Lucius A113

Designs: 30rp, Reconstruction of Vaduz Castle. 50rp, Signing the Treaty of May 3, 1342. 1fr, Battle of Gutenberg. 2fr, Scene of Homage, 1718.

1942, Apr. 22 **Engr.** ***Perf. 11½***

176	A113	20rp brn org, *buff*	1.40	.95
177	A113	30rp steel bl, *buff*	1.40	1.40
178	A113	50rp dk ol grn, *buff*	1.90	*5.50*
179	A113	1fr dull brn, *buff*	2.50	*13.50*
180	A113	2fr vio blk, *buff*	2.75	*14.00*
		Nos. 176-180 (5)	9.95	*35.35*
		Set, never hinged	20.00	

600th anniversary of the separation of Liechtenstein from the House of Monfort.

Johann Karl — A118

30rp, Franz Joseph I. 1fr, Alois I. 1.50fr, Johann I.

1942, Oct. 5 **Photo.**

181	A118	20rp rose	.50	1.25
182	A118	30rp brt blue	.50	*3.00*
183	A118	1fr rose lilac	1.75	*16.00*
184	A118	1.50fr deep brown	2.00	*16.00*
		Nos. 181-184 (4)	4.75	*36.25*
		Set, never hinged	11.00	

Prince Franz Joseph II A122

Countess Georgina von Wilczek A123

Prince and Princess A124

1943, Mar. 5

185	A122	10rp dp rose violet	.55	*1.10*
186	A123	20rp henna brown	.55	*1.10*
187	A124	30rp slate blue	.55	*1.10*
		Nos. 185-187 (3)	1.65	3.30
		Set, never hinged	3.50	

Marriage of Prince Franz Joseph II and Countess Georgina von Wilczek.

Prince Johann II — A126

Princes: 20rp, Alois II. 100rp, Franz Joseph I. 150rp, Franz Joseph II.

Perf. 11½
1943, July 5 **Unwmk.** **Photo.**

188	A126	20rp copper brown	.35	*.60*
189	A126	30rp deep ultra	.60	*1.10*
190	A126	100rp olive gray	1.10	*7.00*
191	A126	150rp slate green	1.25	*7.00*
		Nos. 188-191 (4)	3.30	*15.70*
		Set, never hinged	8.00	

Sheets of 20.

Terrain before Reclaiming — A129

30rp, Draining the Canal. 50rp, Plowing Reclaimed Land. 2fr, Harvesting Crops.

1943, Sept. 6

192	A129	10rp violet black	.30	*.55*
193	A129	30rp deep blue	.85	*2.00*
194	A129	50rp slate green	1.10	*8.50*
195	A129	2fr olive brown	2.00	*12.50*
		Nos. 192-195 (4)	4.25	*23.55*
		Set, never hinged	8.75	

Vaduz A133

Gutenberg A134

1943, Dec. 27

196	A133	10rp dark gray	.45	.45
197	A134	20rp chestnut brown	.50	1.00
		Set, never hinged	2.40	

Planken A135

Bendern A136

Designs: 10rp, Triesen. 15rp, Ruggell. 20rp, Vaduz. 25rp, Triesenberg. 30rp, Schaan. 40rp, Balzers. 50rp, Mauren. 60rp, Schellenberg. 90rp, Eschen. 1fr, Vaduz Castle. 120rp, Valuna Valley. 150rp, Lawena.

1944-45

198	A135	3rp dk brn & buff	.25	.25
199	A136	5rp sl grn & buff	.25	.25
200	A136	10rp gray & buff	.25	.25
201	A136	15rp bl gray & buff	.30	.60
202	A136	20rp org red & buff	.30	.40
203	A136	25rp dk rose vio & buff	.30	.80
204	A136	30rp blue & buff	.35	.40
205	A136	40rp brown & buff	.55	1.00
206	A136	50rp bluish blk & pale gray	.70	1.60
207	A136	60rp green & buff	3.75	5.00
208	A136	90rp ol grn & buff	3.75	5.00
209	A136	1fr dp cl & buff	2.25	5.00
210	A136	120rp red brown	2.25	5.75
211	A136	150rp royal blue	2.25	5.75
		Nos. 198-211 (14)	17.50	32.05
		Set, never hinged	40.00	

Issue years: 10rp, 15rp, 40rp-1fr, 1945; others, 1944. See No. 239. For surcharge and overprints see No. 236, O30-O36.

Crown and Rose — A149

1945, Apr. 9

212	A149	20rp multicolored	.85	.55
213	A149	30rp multicolored	.85	1.40
214	A149	1fr multicolored	1.00	4.50
		Nos. 212-214 (3)	2.70	6.45
		Set, never hinged	4.50	

Birth of Prince Johann Adam Pius, Feb. 14, 1945. Sheets of 20.

Prince Franz Joseph II — A150

Arms of Liechtenstein and Vaduz Castle — A152

Design: 3fr, Princess Georgina.

1944-45 Photo.

215	A150	2fr brown, *buff*	6.00	16.00
216	A150	3fr dark green	3.50	11.50

Engr.

217	A152	5fr bl gray, *cr* ('45)	10.50	32.50
		Nos. 215-217 (3)	20.00	60.00
		Set, never hinged	40.00	

Nos. 215-217 were issued in sheets of 8. See Nos. 222, 259-260.

Saint Lucius — A153

1946, Mar. 14 Unwmk. *Perf. 11½*

218	A153	10fr gray blk, *cr*	16.00	30.00
		Never hinged	45.00	
		Sheet of 4	150.00	200.00
		Never hinged	190.00	

Issued in sheets measuring 105x130mm.

Red Deer — A154

Varying Hare — A155

Capercaillie — A156

1946, Dec. 10 Photo.

219	A154	20rp henna brown	1.50	2.50
220	A155	30rp grnsh blue	1.50	3.25
221	A156	150rp olive brown	3.00	11.50
		Nos. 219-221 (3)	6.00	17.25
		Set, never hinged	12.00	

Arms Type of 1945

1947, Mar. 20 Engr.

222	A152	5fr henna brn, *cream*	11.00	37.50
		Never hinged	25.00	

Issued in sheets of 8.

Chamois A157

Alpine Marmot A158

Golden Eagle — A159

1947, Oct. 15 Photo. Unwmk.

223	A157	20rp henna brown	1.60	1.90
224	A158	30rp grnsh blue	2.25	3.25
225	A159	150rp dark brown	4.25	19.00
		Nos. 223-225 (3)	8.10	24.15
		Set, never hinged	17.00	

Elsa Type of 1935

1947, Dec. 10 Engr. *Perf. 14½*

226	A70	2fr black, *yelsh*	2.25	12.50
		Never hinged	5.00	

Issued in memory of Princess Elsa, who died Sept. 28, 1947. Sheets of 20.

Portrait of Ginevra dei Benci by Leonardo da Vinci — A160

Designs: 20rp, Girl, Rubens. 30rp, Self-portrait, Rembrandt. 40rp, Canon, Massys. 50rp, Madonna, Memling. 60rp, French Painter, 1456, Fouquet. 80rp, Lute Player, Gentileschi. 90rp, Man, Strigel. 120rp, Man, Raphael.

1949, Mar. 15 Photo. *Perf. 11½*

227	A160	10rp dark green	.25	.35
228	A160	20rp henna brown	.60	.80
229	A160	30rp sepia	1.25	.90
230	A160	40rp blue	3.00	.90
231	A160	50rp violet	2.50	6.75
232	A160	60rp grnsh gray	5.50	6.25
233	A160	80rp brown orange	1.25	4.25
234	A160	90rp olive bister	5.50	5.75
235	A160	120rp claret	1.25	5.25
		Nos. 227-235 (9)	21.10	31.20
		Set, never hinged	47.50	

Issued in sheets of 12. See No. 238.

No. 198 Surcharged with New Value and Bars in Dark Brown

1949, Apr. 14

236	A135	5rp on 3rp dk brn & buff	.35	.55
		Never hinged	.85	

Map, Post Horn and Crown — A161

1949, May 23

237	A161	40rp blue & indigo	2.00	4.00
		Never hinged	3.75	

75th anniversary of the UPU. For surcharge see No. 246.

Portrait Type of 1949

Souvenir Sheet

Unwmk.

1949, Aug. 6 Photo. *Imperf.*

238		Sheet of 3	55.00	95.00
		Never hinged	110.00	
a.	A160	10rp dull green	4.75	10.00
b.	A160	20rp lilac rose	30.00	60.00
c.	A160	40rp blue	4.75	10.00

5th Philatelic Exhibition. Sheet size: 121½x69½mm. Sold for 3fr.

Scenic Type of 1944

1949, Dec. 1 *Perf. 11½*

239	A136	5rp dk brown & buff	12.00	1.20
		Never hinged	26.00	

Rossauer Castle, Vienna — A163

Church at Bendern — A164

Prince Johann Adam Andreas — A165

1949, Nov. 15 Engr. *Perf. 14½*

240	A163	20rp dark violet	.90	2.00
241	A164	40rp blue	2.25	6.25
242	A165	150rp brown red	5.00	9.25
		Nos. 240-242 (3)	8.15	17.50
		Set, never hinged	20.00	

250th anniv. of the purchase of the former dukedom of Schellenberg. Sheets of 20. For surcharge see No. 265.

Roe Deer A166

Black Grouse A167

Badger — A168

1950, Mar. 7 Photo. *Perf. 11½*

243	A166	20rp red brown	6.00	6.00
244	A167	30rp Prus green	6.25	9.00
245	A168	80rp dark brown	13.50	45.00
		Nos. 243-245 (3)	25.75	60.00
		Set, never hinged	50.00	

Issued in sheets of 20.

No. 237 Surcharged with New Value and Bars Obliterating Commemorative Inscriptions

1950, Nov. 7

246	A161	1fr on 40rp bl & ind	10.00	45.00

Boy Cutting Bread — A169

Designs: 10rp, Laborer. 15rp, Cutting hay. 20rp, Harvesting corn. 25rp, Load of hay. 30rp, Wine grower. 40rp, Farmer and scythe. 50rp, Cattle raising. 60rp, Plowing. 80rp, Woman with potatoes. 90rp, Potato cultivation. 1fr, Tractor with potatoes.

Perf. 11½

1951, May 3 Unwmk. Photo.

247	A169	5rp claret	.25	.25
248	A169	10rp green	.25	.45
249	A169	15rp yellow brown	1.75	5.00
250	A169	20rp olive brown	.50	.65
251	A169	25rp rose brown	2.25	5.00
252	A169	30rp grnsh gray	1.25	.55
253	A169	40rp deep blue	3.75	6.50
254	A169	50rp violet brown	3.00	4.00
255	A169	60rp brown	3.00	4.00
256	A169	80rp henna brown	3.75	6.75
257	A169	90rp olive green	7.00	7.50
258	A169	1fr indigo	18.00	9.00
		Nos. 247-258 (12)	44.75	49.65
		Set, never hinged	110.00	

Types of 1944, Redrawn

Perf. 12½x12

1951, Nov. 20 Engr. Wmk. 296

259	A150	2fr dark blue	9.00	37.50
a.		Perf. 14½	450.00	160.00
260	A150	3fr dk red brown	80.00	110.00
a.		Perf. 14½	50.00	210.00
		Set, never hinged	175.00	
		Set, perf. 14½, never hinged	900.00	

Issued in sheets of 20.

Portrait, Savolodo
A170

Madonna, Botticelli
A171

Design: 40rp St. John, Del Sarto.

Perf. 11½

1952, Mar. 27 Unwmk. Photo.

261 A170 20rp violet brown 15.00 2.75
262 A171 30rp brown olive 10.50 7.00
263 A170 40rp violet blue 5.25 5.75
Nos. 261-263 (3) 30.75 15.50
Set, never hinged 80.00

Issued in sheets of 12.

Vaduz Castle — A172

Wmk. 296

1952, Sept. 25 Engr. *Perf. 14½*

264 A172 5fr deep green 85.00 150.00
Never hinged 140.00

Issued in sheets of 9.

No. 241 Surcharged with New Value and Wavy Lines in Red

1952, Sept. 25 Unwmk.

265 A164 1.20fr on 40rp blue 12.00 *50.00*
Never hinged 24.00

Portrait of a Young Man
A173

St. Nicholas by Zeitblom
A174

Designs: 30rp, St. Christopher by Cranach. 40rp, Leonhard, Duke of Hag, by Kulmbach.

Perf. 11½

1953, Feb. 5 Unwmk. Photo.

266 A173 10rp dk olive green 1.25 1.25
267 A174 20rp olive brown 5.25 3.00
268 A174 30rp violet brown 13.00 10.00
269 A173 40rp slate blue 18.00 *40.00*
Nos. 266-269 (4) 37.50 *54.25*
Set, never hinged 75.00

Issued in sheets of 12.

Lord Baden-Powell
A175

1953, Aug. 4 Engr. *Perf. 13x13½*

270 A175 10rp deep green .70 .90
271 A175 20rp dark brown 6.75 2.25
272 A175 25rp red 5.75 18.00
273 A175 40rp deep blue 5.50 6.00
Nos. 270-273 (4) 18.70 27.15
Set, never hinged 37.50

Intl. Scout Conf. Sheets of 20.

Alemannic Disc, 600 A. D. — A176

Prehistoric Settlement of Borscht — A177

Design: 1.20fr, Rössen jug.

1953, Nov. 26 *Perf. 11½*

274 A176 10rp orange brown 4.00 *11.50*
275 A177 20rp deep gray green 4.75 *11.50*
276 A176 1.20fr dark blue gray 17.50 *32.50*
Nos. 274-276 (3) 26.25 *55.50*
Set, never hinged 65.00

Opening of National Museum, Vaduz.

Soccer Players — A178

Designs: 20rp, Player kicking ball. 25rp, Goalkeeper. 40rp, Two opposing players.

1954, May 18 Photo.

277 A178 10rp dull rose & brn 1.25 .90
278 A178 20rp olive green 3.75 1.40
279 A178 25rp orange brown 7.50 *30.00*
280 A178 40rp lilac gray 7.50 9.00
Nos. 277-280 (4) 20.00 *41.30*
Set, never hinged 42.50

See Nos. 289-292, 297-300, 308-311, 320-323.

Nos. B19-B21 Surcharged with New Value and Bars in Color of Stamp

1954, Sept. 28 Unwmk. *Perf. 11½*

281 SP15 35rp on 10rp+10rp 2.50 2.25
282 SP16 60rp on 20rp+10rp 11.00 10.50
283 SP15 65rp on 40rp+10rp 3.50 7.25
Nos. 281-283 (3) 17.00 20.00
Set, never hinged 30.00

Madonna in Wood, 14th Century — A179

1954, Dec. 16 Engr.

284 A179 20rp henna brown 1.50 1.90
285 A179 40rp gray 8.50 17.50
286 A179 1fr dark brown 8.50 17.00
Nos. 284-286 (3) 18.50 36.40
Set, never hinged 37.50

Prince Franz Joseph II
A180

Princess Georgina
A181

1955, Apr. 5 *Perf. 14½*

Cream Paper

287 A180 2fr dark brown 32.50 37.50
288 A181 3fr dark green 32.50 37.50
Set, never hinged 140.00

Issued in sheets of 9.

Sports Type of 1954

Designs: 10rp, Slalom. 20rp, Mountain climbing. 25rp, Skiing. 40rp, Resting on summit.

1955, June 14 Photo. *Perf. 11½*

289 A178 10rp aqua & brn vio .45 .80
290 A178 20rp green & ol bis 2.50 .80
291 A178 25rp lt ultra & sep 7.50 16.00
292 A178 40rp olive & pink 7.50 6.00
Nos. 289-292 (4) 17.95 23.60
Set, never hinged 37.50

Prince Johann Adam — A183

Portraits: 20rp, Prince Philipp. 40rp, Prince Nikolaus. 60rp, Princess Nora.

Granite Paper

1955, Dec. 14 Cross in Red

293 A183 10rp dull violet .75 .70
294 A183 20rp slate green 3.00 1.60
295 A183 40rp olive brown 3.00 7.25
296 A183 60rp rose brown 3.25 4.00
Nos. 293-296 (4) 10.00 13.55
Set, never hinged 20.00

Liechtenstein Red Cross, 10th anniversary.

Sports Type of 1954

Designs: 10rp, Javelin thrower. 20rp, Hurdling. 40rp, Pole vaulting. 1fr, Sprinters.

Perf. 11½

1956, June 21 Unwmk. Photo.

Granite Paper

297 A178 10rp lt red brn & ol grn .45 .60
298 A178 20rp lt ol grn & pur 1.90 .60
299 A178 40rp blue & vio brn 2.75 3.25
300 A178 1fr org ver & ol brn 6.50 12.00
Nos. 297-300 (4) 11.60 16.45
Set, never hinged 22.50

Eagle, Crown and Oak Leaves — A184

1956, Aug. 21 Granite Paper

301 A184 10rp dk brown & gold 1.10 1.00
302 A184 120rp slate blk & gold 4.25 4.25
Set, never hinged 12.50

150th anniversary of independence.

Prince Franz Joseph II — A185

1956, Aug. 21

303 A185 10rp dark green .95 .45
304 A185 15rp bright ultra 1.40 2.75
305 A185 25rp purple 1.40 2.75
306 A185 60rp dark brown 4.75 2.25
Nos. 303-306 (4) 8.50 8.20
Set, never hinged 17.50

50th birthday of Prince Franz Joseph II.

Prince Johann Adam — A186

1956, Aug. 21 Granite Paper

307 A186 20rp olive green 1.75 .70
Never hinged 3.50

Issued to publicize the 6th Philatelic Exhibition, Vaduz, Aug. 25-Sept. 2. Sheets of 9.

Sports Type of 1954

Designs: 10rp, Somersault on bar. 15rp, Exercise on pommel horse. 25rp, Exercise on rings. 1.50fr, Somersault on parallel bars.

1957, May 14 Photo. *Perf. 11½*

308 A178 10rp pale rose & ol grn .95 .95
309 A178 15rp pale grn & dl pur 2.75 *7.00*
310 A178 25rp ol bis & Prus grn 3.75 *8.25*
311 A178 1.50fr lemon & sepia 11.00 *19.00*
Nos. 308-311 (4) 18.45 35.20
Set, never hinged 32.50

Pine — A187

Designs: 20rp, Wild roses. 1fr, Birches.

1957, Sept. 10 *Perf. 11½*

Granite Paper

312 A187 10rp dark violet 1.90 2.25
313 A187 20rp brown carmine 1.90 .95
314 A187 1fr green 3.25 8.00
Nos. 312-314 (3) 7.05 11.20
Set, never hinged 16.00

See Nos. 326-328, 332-334, 353-355.

Lord Baden-Powell — A188

Design: 10rp, Symbolical torchlight parade.

1957, Sept. 10 Unwmk.

315 A188 10rp blue black .75 1.50
316 A188 20rp dark brown .75 1.50
a. Sheet, 6 each #315-316 12.00 21.00
Never hinged 21.00
Set, never hinged 3.00

Cent. of the birth of Lord Baden-Powell and the 60th anniv. of the Boy Scout movement.

Chapel of St. Mamertus — A189

40rp, Madonna and saints. 1.50fr, Pieta.

1957, Dec. 16 *Perf. 11½*

317 A189 10rp dark brown .35 .35
318 A189 40rp dark blue 1.10 *5.50*
319 A189 1.50fr brown lake 6.50 9.50
Nos. 317-319 (3) 7.95 15.35
Set, never hinged 15.00

Issued in sheets of 20. Sheet inscribed: "Furstentum Liechtenstein" and "Weihnacht 1957" (Christmas 1957).

Sports Type of 1954

Designs: 15rp, Girl swimmer. 30rp, Fencers. 40rp, Tennis. 90rp, Bicyclists.

1958, Mar. 18 Photo.

Granite Paper

320 A178 15rp lt blue & pur .65 1.00
321 A178 30rp pale rose lil & ol gray 1.50 6.00
322 A178 40rp sal pink & sl bl 2.50 6.00
323 A178 90rp lt ol grn & vio brn .80 4.00
Nos. 320-323 (4) 5.45 17.00
Set, never hinged 21.00

Relief Map of Liechtenstein
A190

1958, Mar. 18

324 A190 25rp bister, vio & red .35 .75
325 A190 40rp blue, vio & red .75 .75
Set, never hinged 2.25

World's Fair, Brussels, Apr. 17-Oct. 19. Sheets of 25. For surcharges see Nos. B22-B23.

Tree-Bush Type of 1957

Designs: 20rp, Maples at Lawena. 50rp, Holly at Schellenberg. 90rp, Yew at Maurerberg.

1958, Aug. 12 *Perf. 11½*

Granite Paper

326 A187 20rp chocolate 1.75 .75
327 A187 50rp olive green 7.00 4.50
328 A187 90rp violet blue 1.75 2.75
Nos. 326-328 (3) 10.50 8.00
Set, never hinged 19.00

Sts. Moritz and Agatha — A191

Christmas: 35rp, St. Peter. 80rp, Chapel of St. Peter, Mals-Balzers.

1958, Dec. 4 Photo. Unwmk.
Granite Paper

329	A191 20rp dk slate green	1.90	2.50
330	A191 35rp dk blue violet	1.90	2.50
331	A191 80rp dark brown	1.90	2.50
	Nos. 329-331 (3)	5.70	7.50
	Set, never hinged	9.50	

Issued in sheets of 20.

Tree-Bush Type of 1957

Designs: 20rp, Larch in Lawena. 50rp, Holly on Alpila. 90rp, Linden in Schaan.

1959, Apr. 15 *Perf. 11½*

332	A187 20rp dark violet	2.50	2.40
333	A187 50rp henna brown	2.50	2.40
334	A187 90rp dark green	2.50	2.40
	Nos. 332-334 (3)	7.50	7.20
	Set, never hinged	14.00	

"The Good Shepherd" — A192

1959, Apr. 15 Unwmk.

335	A192 30rp rose violet & gold	.50	.85
	Never hinged	.90	

Issued in memory of Pope Pius XII.

Flags and Rhine Valley — A193

Man Carrying Hay — A194

Apple Harvest — A195

Designs: 5rp, Church at Bendern and sheaves. 20rp, Rhine embankment. 30rp, Gutenberg Castle. 40rp, View from Schellenberg. 50rp, Vaduz Castle. 60rp, Naafkopf, Falknis Range. 75rp, Woman gathering sheaves. 90rp, Woman in vineyard. 1fr, Woman in kitchen. 1.30fr, Return from the field. 1.50fr, Family saying grace.

1959-64 Granite Paper

336	A193 5rp gray olive ('61)	.25	.25
337	A193 10rp dull violet	.25	.25
338	A193 20rp lilac rose	.25	.25
339	A193 30rp dark red	.25	.25
340	A193 40rp olive grn ('61)	1.10	.55
341	A193 50rp deep blue	.30	.35
342	A193 60rp brt grnsh bl	.45	.55
343	A194 75rp deep ocher ('60)	1.10	1.00
344	A194 80rp olive grn ('61)	.90	.90
345	A194 90rp red lilac ('61)	.90	.90
346	A194 1fr chestnut ('61)	.90	.90
347	A195 1.20fr orange ver ('60)	1.40	1.10
348	A195 1.30fr brt green ('64)	1.10	.90
349	A195 1.50fr brt blue ('60)	1.40	1.40
	Nos. 336-349 (14)	10.55	9.55
	Set, never hinged	12.50	

Belfry, Bendern Church — A196

Christmas: 60rp, Sculpture, bell, St. Theodul's church. 1fr, Sculpture, tower of St. Lucius' church.

1959, Dec. 2 Unwmk. *Perf. 11½*

350	A196 5rp dk slate green	.55	.25
351	A196 60rp olive	3.50	4.25
352	A196 1fr deep claret	2.75	2.50
	Nos. 350-352 (3)	6.80	7.00
	Set, never hinged	11.00	

Issued in sheets of 20.

Tree-Bush Type of 1957

Designs: 20rp, Beech tree on Gafadura. 30rp, Juniper on Alpila. 50rp, Pine on Sass.

1960, Sept. 19

353	A187 20rp brown	3.75	5.25
354	A187 30rp deep plum	3.75	5.25
355	A187 50rp Prus green	12.00	15.00
	Nos. 353-355 (3)	19.50	25.50
	Set, never hinged	32.50	

Europa Issue

Honeycomb A197

1960, Sept. 19 *Perf. 14*

356	A197 50rp multicolored	*30.00*	*30.00*
	Never hinged	*55.00*	

Issued to promote the idea of a united Europe. Sheets of 20.

Princess Gina — A198

Portraits: 1.70fr, Prince Johann Adam Pius. 3fr, Prince Franz Joseph II.

1960-64 Engr. *Perf. 14*

356A	A198 1.70fr violet ('64)	1.00	1.50
b.	Imperf., pair	*1,750.*	*1,750.*
357	A198 2fr dark blue	2.25	2.00
a.	Imperf., pair	*1,750.*	*1,750.*
358	A198 3fr deep brown	2.25	2.00
	Nos. 356A-358 (3)	5.50	5.50
	Set, never hinged	7.00	

Issued in sheets of 16.

Heinrich von Frauenberg — A199

Minnesingers: 20rp, King Konradin. 25rp, Ulrich von Liechtenstein. 30rp, Kraft von Toggenburg. 35rp, Ulrich von Gutenberg. 40rp, Heinrich von Veldig. 1fr, Konrad von Alstetten. 1.50fr, Walther von der Vogelweide. 2fr, Tannhäuser. (Designs from 14th century Manesse manuscript.)

1961-62 Photo. *Perf. 11½*

359	A199 15rp multi	.60	.75
360	A199 20rp multi ('62)	.30	.30
361	A199 25rp multi	1.25	1.65
362	A199 30rp multi ('62)	.40	.40
363	A199 35rp multi	1.50	2.00
364	A199 40rp multi ('62)	.65	.65
365	A199 1fr multi	2.50	2.00
366	A199 1.50fr multi	9.25	15.00
367	A199 2fr multi ('62)	1.65	1.65
	Nos. 359-367 (9)	18.10	24.40
	Set, never hinged	22.50	

Issued in sheets of 20. See Nos. 381-384, 471.

Catalogue values for unused stamps in this section, from this point to the end of the section, are for Never Hinged items.

Europa Issue, 1961

Cogwheels — A200

1961, Oct. 3 Unwmk. *Perf. 13½*

368	A200 50rp multicolored	*.35*	.25

Printed in sheets of 20.

Souvenir Sheet

Prince Johann II — A201

Portraits: 10rp, Francis I. 25rp, Franz Joseph II.

1962, Aug. 2 Photo. *Perf. 11½*

369	A201 Sheet of 3	7.00	5.00
a.	5rp gray green	2.00	1.25
b.	10rp deep rose	2.00	1.25
c.	25rp blue	2.00	1.25

50th anniv. of Liechtenstein's postage stamps and in connection with the Anniv. Stamp Exhib., Vaduz, Aug. 4-12. No. 369 sold for 3fr.

Hands — A202

1962, Aug. 2

370	A202 50rp indigo & red	*.45*	*.45*

Europa. Issued in sheets of 20.

Malaria Eradication Emblem — A203

1962, Aug. 2 Engr.

371	A203 50rp turquoise blue	.60	.45

WHO drive to eradicate malaria. Sheets of 20.

Pietà — A204

Designs: 50rp, Angel with harp, fresco. 1.20fr, View of Mauren.

1962, Dec. 6 Photo.

372	A204 30rp magenta	.60	.60
373	A204 50rp deep orange	.85	.85
374	A204 1.20fr deep blue	1.10	1.10
	Nos. 372-374 (3)	2.55	2.55

Issued in sheets of 20.

Prince Franz Joseph II — A205

1963, Apr. 3 Engr. *Perf. 13½x14*

375	A205 5fr dull green	4.00	3.00

Accession of Prince Franz Joseph II, 25th anniv.
Sheets of 8. Exists imperf. Value $1,500.

Angel of the Annunciation — A206

Perf. 11½

1963, Aug. 26 Unwmk. Photo.

376	A206 20rp shown	.60	.40
377	A206 80rp Three Kings	.60	.40
378	A206 1fr Family	1.00	.80
	Nos. 376-378 (3)	2.20	1.60

Centenary of the International Red Cross.

Europa Issue

Greek Architectural Elements — A207

1963, Aug. 26

379	A207 50rp multicolored	*1.00*	*1.00*

Bread and Milk — A208

1963, Aug. 26

380	A208 50rp dk red pur & brn	.70	.50

FAO "Freedom from Hunger" campaign.

Minnesinger Type of 1961-62

Minnesingers: 25rp, Heinrich von Sax. 30rp, Kristan von Hamle. 75rp, Werner von Teufen. 1.70fr, Hartmann von Aue.

Perf. 11½

1963, Dec. 5 Unwmk. Photo.

381	A199 25rp multicolored	.45	.45
382	A199 30rp multicolored	.45	.45
383	A199 75rp multicolored	.75	.75
384	A199 1.70fr multicolored	1.50	1.50
	Nos. 381-384 (4)	3.15	3.15

Issued in sheets of 20.

Olympic Rings, Flags of Austria and Japan — A209

1964, Apr. 15 *Perf. 11½*

385	A209 50rp Prus bl, red & blk	.60	.60

Olympic Games 1964. Sheets of 20.

Arms of Counts of Werdenberg-Vaduz A210

Coats of Arms: 30rp, Barons of Brandis. 80rp, Counts of Sulz. 1.50fr, Counts of Hohenems.

1964, Sept. 1 Photo.

386	A210 20rp multicolored	.40	.40
387	A210 30rp multicolored	.40	.40
388	A210 80rp multicolored	.40	.40
389	A210 1.50fr multicolored	.80	.80
	Nos. 386-389 (4)	2.00	2.00

See Nos. 396-399.

Europa Issue

Roman Castle, Schaan — A211

1964, Sept. 1 *Perf. 13x14*

390	A211 50rp multicolored	*.75*	*.75*

Masescha Chapel — A212

40rp, Mary Magdalene, altarpiece. 1.30fr, Madonna with Sts. Sebastian & Roch, altarpiece.

1964, Dec. 9 Photo. *Perf. 11½*

391 A212 10rp violet black .40 .40
392 A212 40rp dark blue .40 .40
393 A212 1.30fr deep claret 1.00 1.00
Nos. 391-393 (3) 1.80 1.80

Issued in sheets of 20.

Peter Kaiser — A213

1964, Dec. 9 Engr.

394 A213 1fr dk grn, *buff* .95 .95

Kaiser (1793-1864), historian. Sheets of 20.

Madonna, Wood Sculpture, 18th Century — A214

Perf. 11½

1965, Apr. 22 Unwmk. Engr.

395 A214 10fr orange red 7.00 4.00

Issued in sheets of 4.

Arms Type of 1965

Lords of: 20rp, Schellenberg. 30rp, Gutenberg. 80rp, Frauenberg. 1fr, Ramschwag.

Perf. 11½

1965, Aug. 31 Unwmk. Photo.

396 A210 20rp multicolored .45 .45
397 A210 30rp multicolored .45 .45
398 A210 80rp multicolored .65 .65
399 A210 1fr multicolored .65 .65
Nos. 396-399 (4) 2.20 2.20

Alemannic Ornament — A215

Europa: The design is from a belt buckle, about 600 A.D., found in a man's tomb near Eschen.

1965, Aug. 31

400 A215 50rp vio bl, gray & brn *.45 .35*

The Annunciation by Ferdinand Nigg — A216

Paintings by Nigg: 30rp, The Three Kings. 1.20fr, Jesus in the Temple, horiz.

1965, Dec. 7 Photo. *Perf. 11½*

401 A216 10rp yel grn & dk grn .40 .40
402 A216 30rp orange & red brn .40 .40
403 A216 1.20fr ultra & grnsh bl .60 .60
Nos. 401-403 (3) 1.40 1.40

Ferdinand Nigg (1865-1949), painter.

Princess Gina and Prince Franz Josef Wenzel — A217

1965, Dec. 7

404 A217 75rp gray, buff & gold .60 .50

Communication Symbols — A218

1965, Dec. 7

405 A218 25rp multicolored .60 .45

Centenary of the ITU.

Soil Conservation, Tree — A219

20rp, Clean air, bird. 30rp, Unpolluted water, fish. 1.50fr, Nature preservation, sun.

1966, Apr. 26 Photo. *Perf. 11½*

406 A219 10rp brt yellow & grn .40 .40
407 A219 20rp blue & dk blue .40 .40
408 A219 30rp brt green & ultra .40 .40
409 A219 1.50fr yellow & red .70 .70
Nos. 406-409 (4) 1.90 1.90

Issued to publicize nature conservation.

Prince Franz Joseph II — A220

1966, Apr. 26

410 A220 1fr gray, gold, buff & dk brn .75 .75

60th birthday of Prince Franz Joseph II.

Arms of Barons of Richenstein — A221

Coats of Arms: 30rp, Vaistli knights. 60rp, Lords of Trisun. 1.20fr, von Schiel.

Light Gray Background

1966, Sept. 6 Photo. *Perf. 11½*

411 A221 20rp multicolored .30 .30
412 A221 30rp multicolored .30 .30
413 A221 60rp multicolored .30 .30
414 A221 1.20fr multicolored .60 .60
Nos. 411-414 (4) 1.50 1.50

Common Design Types pictured following the introduction.

Europa Issue, 1966

Common Design Type

1966, Sept. 6 Photo. *Perf. 14x13*

Size: 25x32mm

415 CD9 50rp ultra, dp org & lt grn *.40 .35*

Vaduz Parish Church A222

St. Florin A223

30rp, Madonna. 1.70fr, God the Father.

1966, Dec. 6 Photo. *Perf. 11½*

416 A222 5rp orange red & cit .30 .25
417 A223 20rp lemon & magenta .30 .25
418 A223 30rp dull rose & dp bl .30 .25
419 A223 1.70fr gray & red brown .85 .65
Nos. 416-419 (4) 1.75 1.40

Restoration of the Vaduz Parish Church.

Europa Issue, 1967

Common Design Type

1967, Apr. 20 Photo. *Perf. 11½*

420 CD10 50rp multicolored .45 *.40*

The Man from Malans and his White Horse — A225

Fairy Tales of Liechtenstein: 30rp, The Treasure of Gutenberg. 1.20fr, The Giant of Guflina slaying the Dragon.

1967, Apr. 20

421 A225 20rp multicolored .30 .25
422 A225 30rp multicolored .30 .25
423 A225 1.20fr green & multi .85 .65
Nos. 421-423 (3) 1.45 1.15

See Nos. 443-445, 458-460.

Souvenir Sheet

Prince Hans Adam and Countess Kinsky — A226

1967, June 26 Engr. *Perf. 14x13½*

424 A226 Sheet of 2 2.40 2.00
a. 1.50fr slate blue (Prince) 1.00 1.00
b. 1.50fr red brown (Countess) 1.00 1.00

Wedding of Prince Hans Adam of Liechtenstein and Marie Aglae Countess Kinsky of Wichnitz and Tettau, July 30, 1967.

EFTA Emblem — A227

1967, Sept. 28 Photo. *Perf. 11½*

425 A227 50rp multicolored .55 .45

European Free Trade Association. See note after Norway No. 501.

A228

Christian Symbols: 20rp, Alpha and Omega. 30rp, Trophaeum (The Victorious Cross). 70rp, Chrismon.

1967, Sept. 28

426 A228 20rp rose cl, blk, & gold .25 .25
427 A228 30rp multicolored .25 .25
428 A228 70rp dp ultra, blk & gold .60 .45
Nos. 426-428 (3) 1.10 .95

A229

1967, Sept. 28 Engr. & Litho.

429 A229 1fr rose claret & pale grn .75 .55

Johann Baptist Büchel (1853-1927), priest, educator, historian and poet. Printed on fluorescent paper.

Peter and Paul, Patron Saints of Mauren — A230

Patron Saints: 5rp, St. Joseph, Planken. 10rp, St. Laurentius, Schaan. 30rp, St. Nicholas, Balzers. 40rp, St. Sebastian, Nendeln. 50rp, St. George, Schellenberg Chapel. 60rp, St. Martin, Eschen. 70rp, St. Fridolin, Ruggell. 80rp, St. Gallus, Triesen. 1fr, St. Theodul, Triesenberg. 1.20fr, St. Ann, Vaduz Castle. 1.50fr, St. Mary, Bendern-Gamprin. 2fr, St. Lucius, patron saint of the Principality.

1967-71 Photo. *Perf. 11½*

430 A230 5rp multi ('68) .25 .25
431 A230 10rp multi ('68) .25 .25
432 A230 20rp blue & multi .25 .25
433 A230 30rp dark red & multi .25 .25
433A A230 40rp multi ('71) .45 .35
434 A230 50rp multi ('68) .40 .30
435 A230 60rp multi ('68) .45 .35
436 A230 70rp multi .50 .40
437 A230 80rp multi ('68) .55 .50
438 A230 1fr multi ('68) .75 .55
439 A230 1.20fr violet bl & multi .80 .90
440 A230 1.50fr multi ('68) 1.10 .95
441 A230 2fr multi ('68) 1.25 1.25
Nos. 430-441 (13) 7.25 6.55

Issued: 20rp, 30rp, 70rp, 1.20fr, 12/7/67; 5rp, 1.50fr, 8/29/68; 40rp, 6/11/71; 2fr, 12/5/68; others 4/25/68.

Europa Issue, 1968

Common Design Type

1968, Apr. 25

Size: 32½x23mm

442 CD11 50rp crimson, gold & ultra *.45 .40*

Fairy Tale Type of 1967

30rp, The Treasure of St. Mamerten. 50rp, The Goblin from the Bergerwald. 80rp, The Three Sisters. (Denominations at right.)

1968, Aug. 29

443 A225 30rp Prus blue, yel & red .25 .25
444 A225 50rp green, yel & bl .40 .30
445 A225 80rp brt bl, yel & lt bl .65 .55
Nos. 443-445 (3) 1.30 1.10

Arms of Liechtenstein and Wilczek — A231

1968, Aug. 29

446 A231 75rp multicolored .65 .65

Silver wedding anniversary of Prince Franz Joseph II and Princess Gina.

Sir Rowland Hill — A232

Portraits: 30rp, Count Philippe de Ferrari. 80rp, Carl Lindenberg. 1fr, Maurice Burrus. 1.20fr, Théodore Champion.

1968-69 Engr. *Perf. 14x13½*

447 A232 20rp green .25 .25
448 A232 30rp red brown .25 .25
449 A232 80rp dark brown .55 .45
450 A232 1fr black .70 .65
451 A232 1.20fr dark blue .90 .70
Nos. 447-451 (5) 2.65 2.30

Issued to honor "Pioneers of Philately."
Issued: 80rp, 1.20fr, 8/28/69; others, 12/5/68.
See Nos. 509-511.

Coat of Arms — A233

1969, Apr. 24 Engr. *Perf. 14x13½*

452 A233 3.50fr dark brown 2.50 1.60

Sheets of 16.

Europa Issue, 1969
Common Design Type

1969, Apr. 24 Photo. *Perf. 14*
Size: 33x23mm

453 CD12 50rp brn red, yel & grn *.45 .45*

"Biology" (Man and DNA Molecule) — A234

30rp, "Physics" (man and magnetic field). 50rp, "Astronomy" (man and planets). 80rp, "Art" (artist and Prince Franz Joseph II and Princess Gina).

1969, Aug. 28 Photo. *Perf. 11½*

454 A234 10rp grn, dk bl & dp cl .25 .25
455 A234 30rp brown & multi .25 .25
456 A234 50rp ultra & green .50 .30
457 A234 80rp brn, dk brn & yel .75 .50
Nos. 454-457 (4) 1.75 1.30

250th anniv. of the Duchy of Liechtenstein.

Fairy Tale Type of 1967

20rp, The Cheated Devil. 50rp, The Fiery Red Goat. 60rp, The Grafenberg Treasure (toad). (Denominations at right.)

1969, Dec. 4 Photo. *Perf. 11½*

458 A225 20rp multicolored .25 .25
459 A225 50rp yellow & multi .40 .35
460 A225 60rp red & multi .55 .45
Nos. 458-460 (3) 1.20 1.05

"T" and Arms of Austria-Hungary, Liechtenstein and Switzerland — A235

1969, Dec. 4 *Perf. 13½*

461 A235 30rp gold & multi .45 .30

Cent. of the Liechtenstein telegraph system.

Arms of St. Lucius Monastery, Chur — A236

Arms of Ecclesiastic Patrons: 50rp, Pfäfers Abbey (dove). 1.50fr, Chur Bishopric (stag).

1969, Dec. 4 *Perf. 11½*

462 A236 30rp multicolored .45 .25
463 A236 50rp multicolored .45 .35
464 A236 1.50fr multicolored 1.25 1.00
Nos. 462-464 (3) 2.15 1.60

See Nos. 475-477, 486-488.

Prince Wenzel — A237

1970, Apr. 30 Photo. *Perf. 11½*

465 A237 1fr sepia & multi .80 .80

25th anniv. of the Liechtenstein Red Cross.

Orange Lily — A238

Native Flowers: 30rp, Bumblebee orchid. 50rp, Glacier crowfoot. 1.20fr, Buck bean.

1970, Apr. 30

466 A238 20rp multicolored .25 .25
467 A238 30rp green & multi .25 .25
468 A238 50rp olive & multi .55 .55
469 A238 1.20fr multicolored 1.10 .75
Nos. 466-469 (4) 2.15 1.80

Issued to publicize the European Conservation Year 1970. See Nos. 481-484, 500-503.

Europa Issue, 1970
Common Design Type

1970, Apr. 30 Litho. *Perf. 14*
Size: 31½x20½mm

470 CD13 50rp emerald, dk bl & yel *.45 .45*

Minnesinger Type of 1961-62
Souvenir Sheet

Minnesingers: 30rp, Wolfram von Eschenbach. 50rp, Reinmar der Fiedler. 80rp, Hartmann von Starkenberg. 1.20fr, Friedrich von Hausen.

1970, Aug. 27 Photo. *Perf. 11½*

471 Sheet of 4 2.50 2.25
a. A199 30rp multicolored .25 .25
b. A199 50rp multicolored .30 .30
c. A199 80rp multicolored .50 .50
d. A199 1.20fr multicolored .65 .65

Wolfram von Eschenbach (1170-1220), German minnesinger (poet). Sold for 3fr.

Prince Franz Joseph II — A239

Portrait: 2.50fr, Princess Gina.

1970-71 Engr. *Perf. 14x13½*

472 A239 2.50fr violet blue ('71) 1.90 1.40
473 A239 3fr black 2.25 1.25

Issued: 2.50fr, 6/11; 3fr, 12/3. Sheets of 16.

Mother & Child, Sculpture by Rudolf Schädler — A240

1970, Dec. 3 Photo. *Perf. 11½*

474 A240 30rp dark red & multi .45 .35

Christmas.

Ecclesiastic Arms Type of 1969

Arms of Ecclesiastic Patrons: 20rp, Abbey of St. John in Thur Valley (Lamb of God). 30rp, Ladies' Abbey, Schänis (crown). 75rp, Abbey of St. Gallen (bear rampant).

1970, Dec. 3

475 A236 20rp lt blue & multi .25 .25
476 A236 30rp gray, red & gold .25 .25
477 A236 75rp multicolored .60 .50
Nos. 475-477 (3) 1.10 1.00

Bronze Boar, La Tène Period — A241

30rp, Peacock, Roman, 2nd cent. 75rp, Decorated copper bowl, 13th cent.

1971, Mar. 11 Photo. *Perf. 11½*

478 A241 25rp dp ultra & bluish blk .25 .25
479 A241 30rp dk brown & green .25 .25
480 A241 75rp green, yel & brn .60 .45
Nos. 478-480 (3) 1.10 .95

Opening of the National Museum, Vaduz.

Flower Type of 1970

Flowers: 10rp, Cyclamen. 20rp, Moonwort. 50rp, Superb pink. 1.50fr, Alpine columbine.

1971, Mar. 11

481 A238 10rp multicolored .25 .25
482 A238 20rp multicolored .25 .25
483 A238 50rp multicolored .45 .35
484 A238 1.50fr multicolored 1.25 .85
Nos. 481-484 (4) 2.20 1.70

Europa Issue, 1971
Common Design Type

1971, June 11 Photo. *Perf. 13½*
Size: 31x21mm

485 CD14 50rp grnsh bl, yel & blk *.45 .45*

Ecclesiastic Arms Type of 1969

Arms of Ecclesiastic Patrons: 30rp, Knights of St. John, Feldkirch (Latin and moline crosses). 50rp, Weingarten Abbey (grapes). 1.20fr, Ottobeuren Abbey (eagle and cross).

1971, Sept. 2 Photo. *Perf. 11½*

486 A236 30rp bister & multi .25 .25
487 A236 50rp multicolored .40 .30
488 A236 1.20fr gray & multi 1.00 .75
Nos. 486-488 (3) 1.65 1.30

Princely Crown — A242

Design: 70rp, Page from constitution.

1971, Sept. 2

489 A242 70rp grn, gold, blk & cop .55 .55
490 A242 80rp dk bl, gold, red & plum .65 .65

50th anniversary of the constitution.

Madonna, by Andrea della Robbia — A243

1971, Dec. 9

491 A243 30rp multicolored .45 .35

Christmas 1971.

Long-distance Skiing — A244

Olympic Rings and: 40rp, Ice hockey. 65rp, Downhill skiing, women's. 1.50fr, Figure skating, women's.

1971, Dec. 9

492 A244 15rp lemon & dk brn .25 .25
493 A244 40rp multicolored .35 .30
494 A244 65rp multicolored .55 .45
495 A244 1.50fr multicolored 1.25 .90
Nos. 492-495 (4) 2.40 1.90

11th Winter Olympic Games, Sapporo, Japan, Feb. 3-13, 1972.

1972, Mar. 16 Photo. *Perf. 11*

10rp, Gymnast. 20rp, High jump. 40rp, Running, women's. 60rp, Discus. All horiz.

496 A244 10rp claret, brn & gray .25 .25
497 A244 20rp olive, brn & yel .25 .25
498 A244 40rp red, brn & gray .30 .30
499 A244 60rp brn, dk brn & bl .65 .50
Nos. 496-499 (4) 1.45 1.30

20th Olympic Games, Munich, Aug. 26-Sept. 10.

Flower Type of 1970

Flowers: 20rp, Anemone. 30rp, Turk's cap. 60rp, Alpine centaury. 1.20fr, Reed mace.

1972, Mar. 16

500 A238 20rp dk blue & multi .25 .25
501 A238 30rp olive & multi .25 .25
502 A238 60rp multicolored .45 .40
503 A238 1.20fr multicolored .85 .75
Nos. 500-503 (4) 1.80 1.65

Europa Issue, 1972
Common Design Type

1972, Mar. 16

504 CD15 40rp dk ol, bl grn & rose red *.45 .45*

Souvenir Sheet

Bendern and Vaduz Castle A246

1972, June 8 Engr. *Perf. 13½*

505 A246 Sheet of 2 2.40 1.75
a. 1fr violet blue .75 .65
b. 2fr carmine 1.50 1.10

8th Liechtenstein Philatelic Exhibition, LIBA 1972, Vaduz, Aug. 18-27.

Faun, by Rudolf Schädler — A247

1972, Sept. 7 Photo. *Perf. 11½*

506 A247 20rp shown .25 .25
507 A247 30rp Dancer .25 .25
508 A247 1.10fr Owl .85 .60
Nos. 506-508 (3) 1.35 1.10

Sculptures made of roots and branches by Rudolf Schädler.

Portrait Type of 1968-69

Portraits: 30rp, Emilio Diena. 40rp, André de Cock. 1.30fr, Theodore E. Steinway.

1972, Sept. 7 Engr. *Perf. 14x13½*

509 A232 30rp Prus green .25 .25
510 A232 40rp dk violet brn .30 .25
511 A232 1.30fr violet blue 1.00 .80
Nos. 509-511 (3) 1.55 1.30

Pioneers of Philately.

Madonna with Angels, by Ferdinand Nigg — A248

1972, Dec. 7 Photo. *Perf. 11½*

512 A248 30rp black & multi .50 .40

Christmas 1972.

Silum — A249

Landscapes: 10rp, Lawena Springs. 15rp, Ruggell Marsh. 25rp, Steg, Kirchlispitz. 30rp, Fields, Schellenberg. 40rp, Rennhof, Mauren. 50rp, Tidrüfe Vaduz. 60rp, Eschner Riet. 70rp,

Mittagspitz. 80rp, Three Sisters, Schaan Forest. 1fr, St. Peter's and Tower House, Mäls. 1.30fr, Road, Frommenhaus. 1.50fr, Ox Head Mountain. 1.80fr, Hehlawangspitz. 2fr, Saminaschlucht.

1972-73 Engr. & Litho. *Perf. 11½*

513	A249	5rp	brn, yel & mag	.25	.25
514	A249	10rp	slate grn & cit	.25	.25
515	A249	15rp	red brn & cit	.25	.25
516	A249	25rp	dk vio & pale grn	.25	.25
517	A249	30rp	purple & buff	.25	.25
518	A249	40rp	vio & pale salmon	.30	.25
519	A249	50rp	vio bl & rose	.40	.35
520	A249	60rp	grn & yel	.50	.45
521	A249	70rp	dk & lt blue	.60	.50
522	A249	80rp	Prus grn & cit	.65	.55
523	A249	1fr	red brn & lt grn	.85	.65
524	A249	1.30fr	ultra & lt grn	1.10	1.00
525	A249	1.50fr	brn & lt blue	1.25	1.00
526	A249	1.80fr	brown & buff	1.50	1.25
527	A249	2fr	sepia & pale grn	1.65	1.40
			Nos. 513-527 (15)	10.05	8.65

Issued: 10rp, 15rp, 80rp, 1fr, 1.50fr, 12/7; 30rp, 1.30fr, 1.80fr, 3/8/73; 50rp, 60rp, 70rp, 6/7/73; 5rp, 25rp, 40rp, 2fr, 12/6/73.

Europa Issue, 1973

Common Design Type

1973, Mar. 8 Photo. *Perf. 11½*

Size: 33x23mm

528	CD16	30rp	purple & multi	*.25*	*.25*
529	CD16	40rp	blue & multi	*.35*	*.35*

Nautilus Cup — A250

70rp, Ivory tankard. 1.10fr, Silver goblet.

1973, June 7 Photo. *Perf. 11½*

530	A250	30rp	gray & multi	.25	.25
531	A250	70rp	multicolored	.50	.40
532	A250	1.10fr	dk blue & multi	.90	.60
			Nos. 530-532 (3)	1.65	1.25

Drinking vessels from the Princely Treasury.

Arms of Liechtenstein and Municipalities A251

Engraved & Photogravure

1973, Sept. 6 *Perf. 14x13½*

533	A251	5fr	black & multi	4.00	2.50

Coenonympha Oedippus — A252

Designs: 15rp, Alpine newt. 25rp, European viper (adder). 40rp, Common curlew. 60rp, Edible frog. 70rp, Dappled butterfly. 80rp, Grass snake. 1.10fr, Three-toed woodpecker.

1973-74 Photo. *Perf. 11½*

534	A252	15rp	bl grn & multi	.25	.25
535	A252	25rp	yellow & multi	.30	.25
536	A252	30rp	orange & multi	.25	.25
537	A252	40rp	brown & multi	.35	.35
538	A252	60rp	bl grn & multi	.60	.60
539	A252	70rp	brt blue & multi	.65	.60
540	A252	80rp	blue & multi	.70	.70
541	A252	1.10fr	org red & multi	1.00	1.00
			Nos. 534-541 (8)	4.10	4.00

Issue dates: 30rp, 40rp, 60rp, 80rp, Dec. 6. 15rp, 25rp, 70rp, 1.10fr, June 6, 1974.

Virgin and Child, by Bartolomeo di Tommaso — A253

Engraved & Lithographed

1973, Dec. 6 *Perf. 13½*

542	A253	30rp	gold & multi	.50	.30

Christmas 1973.

The Vociferant Horseman, by Andrea Riccio — A254

Europa: 40rp, Kneeling Venus, by Antonio Susini.

1974, Mar. 21 Photo. *Perf. 11½*

543	A254	30rp	tan & multi	*.35*	*.30*
544	A254	40rp	ultra & multi	*.50*	*.45*

Chinese Vase, 19th Century — A255

Chinese vases from Princely Treasury.

1974, Mar. 21

545	A255	30rp	shown	.30	.25
546	A255	50rp	from 1740	.45	.35
547	A255	60rp	from 1830	.55	.40
548	A255	1fr	circa 1700	.95	.60
			Nos. 545-548 (4)	2.25	1.60

Soccer — A256

1974, Mar. 21

549	A256	80rp	lemon & multi	.80	.75

World Soccer Championships, Munich June 13-July 7.

Post Horn and UPU Emblem — A257

1974, June 6 *Perf. 13½*

550	A257	40rp	gold, green & blk	.35	.30
551	A257	60rp	gold, red & blk	.55	.40

Centenary of Universal Postal Union.

Bishop F. A. Marxer — A258

Photogravure and Engraved

1974, June 6 *Perf. 14x13½*

552	A258	1fr	multicolored	.95	.75

Bicentenary of the death of Bishop Franz Anton Marxer (1703-1775).

Prince Constantin — A259

Prince Hans Adam — A260

Princess Gina and Prince Franz Joseph II — A261

80rp, Prince Maximilian. 1.20fr, Prince Alois.

1974-75 Photo. *Perf. 11½*

553	A259	70rp	dk green & gold	.70	.55
554	A259	80rp	dp claret & gold	.75	.65
555	A259	1.20fr	bluish blk & gold	1.10	1.00

Engr.

Perf. 14x13½

556	A260	1.70fr	slate green	1.40	1.00

Photogravure and Engraved

Perf. 13½x14

557	A261	10fr	gold & choc	6.50	4.50
			Nos. 553-557 (5)	10.45	7.70

No. 557 printed in sheets of 4.

Issued: 1.70fr, 12/5; 10fr, 9/5/74; others, 3/13/75.

St. Florian — A262

50rp, St. Wendelin. 60rp, Virgin Mary with Sts. Anna and Joachim. 70rp, Nativity.

1974, Dec. 5 Photo. *Perf. 12*

560	A262	30rp	multicolored	.30	.25
561	A262	50rp	multicolored	.40	.35
562	A262	60rp	multicolored	.50	.40
563	A262	70rp	multicolored	.65	.50
			Nos. 560-563 (4)	1.85	1.50

Designs are from 19th century devotional glass paintings. Christmas 1974.

"Cold Sun," by Martin Frommelt — A263

Europa: 60rp, "Village," by Louis Jaeger.

1975, Mar. 13 *Perf. 11½*

564	A263	30rp	multicolored	*.25*	*.25*
565	A263	60rp	multicolored	*.50*	*.45*

Red Cross Activities — A264

1975, June 5 Photo. *Perf. 11½*

566	A264	60rp	dk blue & multi	.55	.55

30th anniv. of the Liechtenstein Red Cross.

Coronation Robe A265

Imperial Crown — A266

1975 Engr. & Photo. *Perf. 14*

567	A266	30rp	Imperial cross	.30	.25
568	A266	60rp	Imperial sword	.45	.40
569	A266	1fr	Orb	.90	.75
570	A265	1.30fr	shown	1.75	1.60
571	A266	2fr	shown	3.50	2.75
			Nos. 567-571 (5)	6.90	5.75

Treasures of the Holy Roman Empire from the Treasury of the Hofburg in Vienna, Austria.

Issue dates: 1.30fr, Sept. 4; others, June 5.

See Nos. 617-620.

St. Mamerten, Triesen — A267

Designs: 50rp, Red House, Vaduz, 14th century. 70rp, Prebendary House, Eschen, 14th century. 1fr, Gutenberg Castle.

1975, Sept. 4 Photo. *Perf. 11½*

572	A267	40rp	multicolored	.40	.30
573	A267	50rp	multicolored	.45	.30
574	A267	70rp	plum & multi	.85	.60
575	A267	1fr	dk blue & multi	1.10	.75
			Nos. 572-575 (4)	2.80	1.95

European Architectural Heritage Year 1975.

Speed Skating — A268

Designs (Olympic Rings and): 25rp, Ice hockey. 70rp, Downhill skiing. 1.20fr, Slalom.

1975, Dec. 4 Photo. *Perf. 11½*

576	A268	20rp	multicolored	.25	.25
577	A268	25rp	multicolored	.25	.25
578	A268	70rp	multicolored	.65	.50
579	A268	1.20fr	yellow & multi	1.25	.95
			Nos. 576-579 (4)	2.40	1.95

12th Winter Olympic Games, Innsbruck, Austria, Feb. 4-15, 1976.

Daniel in the Lions' Den — A269

Designs: 60rp, Virgin and Child. 90rp, St. Peter. All designs are from Romanesque sculptured capitals in Chur Cathedral, c. 1208.

Photogravure and Engraved

1975, Dec. 4 *Perf. 14*

580	A269	30rp	gold & purple	.25	.25
581	A269	60rp	gold & green	.45	.40
582	A269	90rp	gold & claret	.80	.75
			Nos. 580-582 (3)	1.50	1.40

Christmas and Holy Year 1975.

River Crayfish — A270

World Wildlife Fund: 40rp, European pond turtle. 70rp, Old-world otter. 80rp, Lapwing.

1976, Mar. 11 Photo. *Perf. 11½*

583	A270	25rp	multicolored	.50	.25
584	A270	40rp	multicolored	.75	.35
585	A270	70rp	multicolored	1.10	.55
586	A270	80rp	multicolored	1.75	1.00
			Nos. 583-586 (4)	4.10	2.15

Mouflon — A271

Europa: 80rp, Pheasant family. Ceramics by Prince Hans von Liechtenstein.

1976, Mar. 11

587	A271	40rp multicolored	*.40*	*.35*
588	A271	80rp violet & multi	*.80*	*.75*

Roman Fibula, 3rd Century — A272

1976, Mar. 11

589	A272	90rp vio bl, grn & gold	1.00	.80

Historical Association of Liechtenstein, 75th anniversary.

Souvenir Sheet

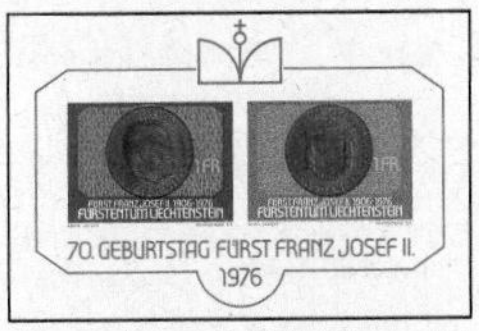
Franz Josef II 50fr-Memorial Coin — A273

1976, June 10 Photo. *Imperf.*

590	A273	Sheet of 2	1.75	1.75
a.		1fr blue & multi	.85	.85
b.		1fr red & multi	.85	.85

70th birthday of Prince Franz Joseph II of Liechtenstein.

Judo and Olympic Rings — A274

Designs (Olympic Rings and): 50rp, volleyball. 80rp, Relay race. 1.10fr, Long jump, women's.

1976, June 10 *Perf. 11½*

591	A274	35rp multicolored	.25	.25
592	A274	50rp multicolored	.45	.40
593	A274	80rp multicolored	.65	.60
594	A274	1.10fr multicolored	1.00	.75
		Nos. 591-594 (4)	2.35	2.00

21st Olympic Games, Montreal, Canada, July 17-Aug. 1.

Rubens' Sons, Albrecht and Nikolas — A275

Rubens Paintings: 50rp, Singing Angels. 1fr, The Daughters of Cecrops, horiz. (from Collection of Prince of Liechtenstein).

Size: 24x38mm

1976, Sept. 9 Engr. *Perf. 13½x14*

595	A275	50rp gold & multi	.70	.70
596	A275	70rp gold & multi	1.00	1.00

Size: 48x38mm

597	A275	1fr gold & multi	2.75	2.75
		Nos. 595-597 (3)	4.45	4.45

400th anniversary of the birth of Peter Paul Rubens (1577-1640), Flemish painter. Sheets of 8 (2x4).

Zodiac Signs — A276

1976-78 Photo. *Perf. 11½*

598	A276	20rp Pisces	.25	.25
599	A276	40rp Aries	.35	.35
600	A276	40rp Cancer ('77)	.40	.35
601	A276	40rp Scorpio ('78)	.45	.45
602	A276	50rp Sagittarius ('78)	.50	.45
603	A276	70rp Leo ('77)	.65	.65
604	A276	80rp Taurus	.75	.70
605	A276	80rp Virgo ('77)	.75	.75
606	A276	80rp Capricorn ('78)	.75	.70
607	A276	90rp Gemini	1.00	.75
608	A276	1.10fr Libra ('77)	1.10	1.10
609	A276	1.50fr Aquarius ('78)	1.25	1.25
		Nos. 598-609 (12)	8.20	7.75

Flight into Egypt — A277

Monastic Wax Works: 20rp, Holy Infant of Prague, horiz. 80rp, Holy Family and Trinity. 1.50fr, Holy Family, horiz.

1976, Dec. 9 Photo. *Perf. 11½*

610	A277	20rp multicolored	.25	.25
611	A277	50rp multicolored	.45	.35
612	A277	80rp multicolored	.60	.50
613	A277	1.50fr multicolored	1.40	1.10
		Nos. 610-613 (4)	2.70	2.20

Christmas 1976.

Ortlieb von Brandis, Sarcophagus — A278

Photogravure and Engraved

1976, Dec. 9 *Perf. 13½x14*

614	A278	1.10fr gold & dk brown	1.00	.70

Ortlieb von Brandis, Bishop of Chur (1458-1491).

Map of Liechtenstein, by J. J. Heber, 1721 — A279

Europa: 80rp, View of Vaduz, by Ferdinand Bachmann, 1815.

1977, Mar. 10 Photo. *Perf. 12½*

615	A279	40rp multicolored	*.40*	*.40*
616	A279	80rp multicolored	*.80*	*.80*

Treasure Type of 1975

40rp, Holy Lance and Particle of the Cross. 50rp, Imperial Evangel of St. Matthew. 80rp, St. Stephen's Purse. 90rp, Tabard of Imperial Herald.

Engraved and Photogravure

1977, June 8 *Perf. 14*

617	A266	40rp gold & multi	.40	.25
618	A266	50rp gold & multi	.50	.40
619	A266	80rp gold & multi	.70	.55
620	A266	90rp gold & multi	1.00	.80
		Nos. 617-620 (4)	2.60	2.00

Treasures of the Holy Roman Empire from the Treasury of the Hofburg in Vienna.

Emperor Constantius II Coin — A280

Coins: 70rp, Lindau bracteate, c. 1300. 80rp, Ortlieb von Brandis, 1458-1491.

1977, June 8 Photo. *Perf. 11½*

Granite Paper

621	A280	35rp gold & multi	.35	.25
622	A280	70rp silver & multi	.60	.50
623	A280	80rp silver & multi	.80	.55
		Nos. 621-623 (3)	1.75	1.30

Frauenthal Castle — A281

Castles: 50rp, Gross Ullersdorf. 80rp, Liechtenstein Castle near Mödling, Austria. 90rp, Liechtenstein Palace, Vienna.

Engraved and Photogravure

1977, Sept. 8 *Perf. 13½x14*

624	A281	20rp slate grn & gold	.25	.25
625	A281	50rp magenta & gold	.50	.40
626	A281	80rp dk violet & gold	.80	.65
627	A281	90rp dk blue & gold	.90	.75
		Nos. 624-627 (4)	2.45	2.05

Children — A282

Traditional Costumes: 70rp, Two girls. 1fr, Woman in festival dress.

1977, Sept. 8 Photo. *Perf. 11½*

Granite Paper

628	A282	40rp multicolored	.50	.35
629	A282	70rp multicolored	.75	.60
630	A282	1fr multicolored	1.25	.75
		Nos. 628-630 (3)	2.50	1.70

Princess Tatjana — A283

1977, Dec. 7 Photo. *Perf. 11½*

631	A283	1.10fr brown & gold	1.20	.75

Angel — A284

Sculptures by Erasmus Kern: 50rp, St. Rochus. 80rp, Virgin and Child. 1.50fr, God the Father.

1977, Dec. 7

632	A284	20rp multicolored	.25	.25
633	A284	50rp multicolored	.45	.35
634	A284	80rp multicolored	.75	.50
635	A284	1.50fr multicolored	1.50	1.00
		Nos. 632-635 (4)	2.95	2.10

Christmas 1977.

Liechtenstein Palace, Vienna — A285

Europa: 80rp, Feldsberg Castle.

Photogravure and Engraved

1978, Mar. 2 *Perf. 14*

636	A285	40rp gold & slate blue	*.35*	*.30*
637	A285	80rp gold & claret	*.75*	*.70*

Farmhouse, Triesen — A286

Designs: 20rp, Houses, Upper Village, Triesen. 35rp, Barns, Balzers. 40rp, Monastery, Bendern. 50rp, Residential Tower, Balzers-Mäls. 70rp, Parish house. 80rp, Farmhouse, Schellenberg. 90rp, Parish house, Balzers. 1fr, Rheinberger House, Music School, Vaduz. 1.10fr, Street, Mitteldorf, Vaduz. 1.50fr, Town Hall, Triesenberg. 2fr, National Museum and Administrator's Residence, Vaduz.

1978 Photo. *Perf. 11½*

638	A286	10rp multicolored	.25	.25
639	A286	20rp multicolored	.25	.25
640	A286	35rp multicolored	.30	.25
641	A286	40rp multicolored	.30	.25
642	A286	50rp multicolored	.45	.30
643	A286	70rp multicolored	.60	.40
644	A286	80rp multicolored	.65	.45
645	A286	90rp multicolored	.80	.50
646	A286	1fr multicolored	.85	.55
647	A286	1.10fr multicolored	1.00	.65
648	A286	1.50fr multicolored	1.20	.80
649	A286	2fr multicolored	1.75	1.10
		Nos. 638-649 (12)	8.40	5.75

Vaduz Castle — A287

Vaduz Castle: 50rp, Courtyard. 70rp, Staircase. 80rp, Triptych from High Altar, Castle Chapel.

Engraved and Photogravure

1978, June 1 *Perf. 13½x14*

650	A287	40rp gold & multi	.40	.30
651	A287	50rp gold & multi	.50	.40
652	A287	70rp gold & multi	.70	.60
653	A287	80rp gold & multi	.95	.70
		Nos. 650-653 (4)	2.55	2.00

40th anniversary of reign of Prince Franz Joseph II. Sheet of 8.

Prince Karl I, Coin, 1614 — A288

Designs: 50rp, Prince Johann Adam, medal, 1694. 80rp, Prince Josef Wenzel, medal, 1773.

1978, Sept. 7 Photo. *Perf. 11½*

654	A288	40rp multicolored	.35	.30
655	A288	50rp multicolored	.50	.40
656	A288	80rp multicolored	.95	.70
		Nos. 654-656 (3)	1.80	1.40

Adoration of the Shepherds — A289

Stained-glass Windows, Triesenberg: 50rp, Holy Family. 80rp, Adoration of the Kings.

1978, Dec. 7 Photo. *Perf. 11½*

657	A289	20rp multicolored	.25	.25
658	A289	50rp multicolored	.50	.40
659	A289	80rp multicolored	.80	.70
		Nos. 657-659 (3)	1.55	1.35

Christmas 1978.

Piebald, by Hamilton and Faistenberger A290

Golden Carriage of Prince Joseph Wenzel, by Martin von Meytens A291

Design: 80rp, Black stallion, by Johann Georg von Hamilton.

Photo. & Engr.

1978, Dec. 7 ***Perf. 13½x14***

660	A290	70rp multicolored	.60	.50
661	A290	80rp multicolored	.70	.60

Perf. 12

662	A291	1.10fr multicolored	.95	.70
		Nos. 660-662 (3)	2.25	1.80

Sheets of 8.

Mail Plane over Schaan — A292

Europa: 80rp, Zeppelin over Vaduz Castle.

1979, Mar. 8 **Photo.** ***Perf. 11½***

663	A292	40rp multicolored	*.50*	*.45*
664	A292	80rp multicolored	*.65*	*.60*

First airmail service, St. Gallen to Schaan, Aug. 31, 1930, and first Zeppelin flight to Liechtenstein, June 10, 1931.

Child Drinking — A293

90rp, Child eating. 1.10fr, Child reading.

1979, Mar. 8

665	A293	80rp silver & multi	.75	.70
666	A293	90rp silver & multi	.85	.85
667	A293	1.10fr silver & multi	.95	.95
		Nos. 665-667 (3)	2.55	2.50

International Year of the Child.

Ordered Wave Fields A294

Sun over Continents A296

Council of Europe — A295

1979, June 7 **Litho.** ***Perf. 11½***

668	A294	50rp multicolored	.50	.40

Photo.

669	A295	80rp multicolored	.65	.55
670	A296	100rp multicolored	.80	.65
		Nos. 668-670 (3)	1.95	1.60

Intl. Radio Consultative Committee (CCIR) of the Intl. Telecommunications Union, 50th anniv. (50rp); Entry into Council of Europe (80rp); aid to developing countries (100rp).

Heraldic Panel of Carl Ludwig von Sulz — A297

Heraldic Panels of: 70rp, Barbara von Sulz, née zu Staufen. 1.10fr, Ulrich von Ramschwag and Barbara von Hallwil.

Photogravure and Engraved

1979, June 1 ***Perf. 13½***

671	A297	40rp multicolored	.55	.30
672	A297	70rp multicolored	.65	.50
673	A297	1.10fr multicolored	1.10	.95
		Nos. 671-673 (3)	2.30	1.75

Sts. Lucius and Florin, Fresco in Waltensburg-Vuorz Church — A298

Photogravure and Engraved

1979, Sept. 6 ***Perf. 13½***

674	A298	20fr multicolored	14.00	7.50

Patron saints of Liechtenstein. Printed in sheets of 4.

Annunciation, Embroidery A299

Christmas (Ferdnand Nigg Embroideries): 50rp, Christmas. 80rp, Blessed Are the Peacemakers.

1979, Dec. 6 **Engr.** ***Perf. 13½***

675	A299	20rp multicolored	.50	.25
676	A299	50rp multicolored	.50	.35
677	A299	80rp multicolored	.80	.50
		Nos. 675-677 (3)	1.80	1.10

Cross-Country Skiing — A300

Olympic Rings and: 70rp, Oxhead Mountain. 1.50fr, Ski lift.

1979, Dec. 6 **Photo.** ***Perf. 12***

678	A300	40rp multicolored	.45	.25
679	A300	70rp multicolored	.65	.45
680	A300	1.50fr multicolored	1.25	1.00
		Nos. 678-680 (3)	2.35	1.70

13th Winter Olympic Games, Lake Placid, NY, Feb. 12-24, 1980.

Arms of Bailiff Andreas Buchel, 1690 — A301

Various arms: 70rp, Georg Marxer, 1745. 80rp, Luzius Frick, 1503. 1.10rp, Adam Oehri, 1634.

1980, Mar. 10 **Photo.** ***Perf. 11½***

Granite Paper

681	A301	40rp shown	.30	.30
682	A301	70rp multicolored	.50	.45
683	A301	80rp multicolored	.85	.70
684	A301	1.10fr multicolored	.75	.70
		Nos. 681-684 (4)	2.40	2.15

See Nos. 704-707, 729-732.

Princess Maria Leopoldine Esterhazy, by Antonio Canova — A302

Europa: 80rp, Maria Theresa, Duchess of Savoy, by Martin van Meytens.

1980, Mar. 10

685	A302	40rp multicolored	*.40*	*.35*
686	A302	80rp multicolored	*.60*	*.50*

Milking Pail — A303

Old Alpine Farm Tools: 50rp, Wooden heart, ceremonial cattle decoration. 80rp, Butter churn.

1980, Sept. 8

687	A303	20rp multicolored	.25	.25
688	A303	50rp multicolored	.45	.35
689	A303	80rp multicolored	.75	.55
		Nos. 687-689 (3)	1.45	1.15

Liechtenstein No. 94 — A304

1980, Sept 8

690	A304	80rp multicolored	.80	.60

Postal Museum, 50th anniversary.

Crossbow with Spanning Device — A305

90rp, Spear, knife. 1.10fr, Rifle, powderhorn.

1980, Sept. 8 **Engr.** ***Perf. 13½x14***

691	A305	80rp shown	.60	.55
692	A305	90rp multicolored	.75	.60
693	A305	1.10fr multicolored	.90	.65
		Nos. 691-693 (3)	2.25	1.80

Triesenberg Family In Traditional Costumes — A306

70rp, Folk dancers, Schellenberg. 80rp, Brass band, Mauren.

1980, Sept. 8 **Photo.** ***Perf. 12***

Granite Paper

694	A306	40rp shown	.45	.25
695	A306	70rp multicolored	.70	.50
696	A306	80rp multicolored	.75	.60
		Nos. 694-696 (3)	1.90	1.35

Green Beeches, Matrula Forest — A307

50rp, White firs, Valorsch Valley. 80rp, Beech forest, Schaan. 1.50fr, Forest, Oberplanken.

Photogravure and Engraved

1980, Dec. 9 ***Perf. 14***

697	A307	40rp shown	.35	.25
698	A307	50rp multicolored	.45	.40
699	A307	80rp multicolored	.75	.55
700	A307	1.50fr multicolored	1.40	1.00
		Nos. 697-700 (4)	2.95	2.20

Glad Tidings — A308

1980, Dec. 9 **Photo.** ***Perf. 11½***

Granite Paper

701	A308	20rp shown	.25	.25
702	A308	50rp Creche	.45	.35
703	A308	80rp Epiphany	.70	.60
		Nos. 701-703 (3)	1.40	1.20

Christmas 1980.

Bailiff Arms Type of 1980

40rp, Anton Meier, 1748. 70rp, Kaspar Kindle, 1534. 80rp, Hans Adam Negele, 1600. 1.10fr, Peter Matt, 1693.

1981, Mar. 9 **Photo.** ***Perf. 11½***

Granite Paper

704	A301	40rp multicolored	.45	.30
705	A301	70rp multicolored	.75	.50
706	A301	80rp multicolored	.80	.60
707	A301	1.10fr multicolored	1.10	.90
		Nos. 704-707 (4)	3.10	2.30

Fireworks at Vaduz Castle — A309

Europa: 80rp, National Day procession.

1981, Mar. 9 ***Perf. 12½***

Granite Paper

708	A309	40rp multicolored	*.35*	*.30*
709	A309	80rp multicolored	*.65*	*.60*

Souvenir Sheet

Prince Alois, Princess Elisabeth and Prince Franz Joseph II A310

1981, June 9 **Photo.** ***Perf. 13***

Granite Paper

710	A310	Sheet of 3	2.75	2.50
a.		70rp shown	.50	.50
b.		80rp Princes Alois and Franz Joseph II	.55	.55
c.		150rp Prince Franz Joseph II	1.00	1.00

75th birthday of Prince Franz Joseph II.

Scout Emblems — A311

1981, June 9

711	A311	20rp multicolored	.50	.40

50th anniversary of Boy Scouts and Girl Guides.

Man in Wheelchair — A312

1981, June 9
712 A312 40rp multicolored .50 .40

International Year of the Disabled.

St. Theodul, 1600th Birth Anniv. — A313

1981, June 9
713 A313 80rp multicolored .80 .55

Mosses and Lichens — A314

40rp, Xanthoria parietina. 50rp, Parmelia physodes. 70rp, Sphagnum palustre. 80rp, Amblystegium.

Photogravure and Engraved
1981, Sept. 7 *Perf. 13½*
714 A314 40rp multicolored .45 .30
715 A314 50rp multicolored .45 .35
716 A314 70rp multicolored .60 .50
717 A314 80rp multicolored .70 .60
Nos. 714-717 (4) 2.20 1.75

Gutenberg Castle — A315

1981, Sept. 7
718 A315 20rp shown .45 .25
719 A315 40rp Castle yard .45 .30
720 A315 50rp Parlor .45 .35
721 A315 1.10fr Great Hall .95 .85
Nos. 718-721 (4) 2.30 1.75

St. Charles Borromeo (1538-1584) — A316

Famous Visitors to Liechtenstein (Paintings): 70rp, Goethe (1749-1832), by Angelica Kauffmann. 80rp, Alexander Dumas (1824-1895). 1fr, Hermann Hesse (1877-1962), by Cuno Amiet.

Lithographed and Engraved
1981, Dec. 7 *Perf. 14*
722 A316 40rp multicolored .35 .30
723 A316 70rp multicolored .60 .50
724 A316 80rp multicolored .70 .60
725 A316 1fr multicolored .80 .70
Nos. 722-725 (4) 2.45 2.10

See Nos. 747-750.

St. Nicholas — A317

50rp, Adoration of the Kings. 80rp, Holy Family.

1981, Dec. 7 Photo. *Perf. 11½*
Granite Paper
726 A317 20rp shown .25 .25
727 A317 50rp multicolored .45 .40
728 A317 80rp multicolored .70 .60
Nos. 726-728 (3) 1.40 1.25

Christmas 1981.

Bailiff Arms Type of 1980

40rp, Johann Kaiser, 1664. 70rp, Joseph Anton Kaufmann, 1748. 80rp, Christoph Walser, 1690. 1.10fr, Stephan Banzer, 1658.

1982, Mar. 8 Photo.
Granite Paper
729 A301 40rp multicolored .35 .35
730 A301 70rp multicolored .55 .50
731 A301 80rp multicolored .70 .60
732 A301 1.10fr multicolored 1.00 .80
Nos. 729-732 (4) 2.60 2.25

Europa 1982 — A318

40rp, Peasants' Uprising, 1525. 80rp, Imperial Direct Rule, 1396.

1982, Mar. 8 Granite Paper
733 A318 40rp multicolored *.35 .30*
734 A318 80rp multicolored *.65 .60*

Hereditary Prince Hans Adam — A319

No. 736, Princess Marie Aglae.

1982, June 7 Granite Paper
735 A319 1fr shown .75 .75
736 A319 1fr multicolored .75 .75

LIBA '82, 10th Liechtenstein Philatelic Exhibition, Vaduz, July 31-Aug. 8.

1982 World Cup — A320

Designs: Sports arenas.

1982, June 7 Granite Paper
737 A320 15rp Triesenberg .40 .25
738 A320 25rp Mauren .40 .25
739 A320 1.80fr Balzers 1.40 1.25
Nos. 737-739 (3) 2.20 1.75

Farming — A321

1982, Sept. 20 Photo. *Perf. 11½*
Granite Paper
740 A321 30rp shown .40 .25
741 A321 50rp Horticulture .40 .40
742 A321 70rp Forestry .60 .50
743 A321 150rp Dairy farming 1.25 1.10
Nos. 740-743 (4) 2.65 2.25

View of Neu-Schellenberg, 1861, by Moriz Menzinger (1832-1914) A322

Photogravure and Engraved
1982, Sept. 20 *Perf. 13½x14*
744 A322 40rp shown .50 .30
745 A322 50rp Vaduz, 1860 .60 .35
746 A322 100rp Bendern, 1868 1.00 .85
Nos. 744-746 (3) 2.10 1.50

Visitor Type of 1981

Paintings: 40rp, Emperor Maximilian I (1459-1519), by Bernhard Strigel. 70rp, Georg Jenatsch (1596-1639). 80rp, Angelika Kaufmann (1741-1807), self portrait. 1fr, Fidelis von Sigmaringen (1577-1622).

1982, Dec. 6 *Perf. 14*
747 A316 40rp multicolored .45 .30
748 A316 70rp multicolored .70 .45
749 A316 80rp multicolored .80 .45
750 A316 1fr multicolored 1.00 .65
Nos. 747-750 (4) 2.95 1.85

Christmas 1982 — A323

Chur Cathedral sculptures: 20rp, Angel playing lute. 50rp, Virgin and Child. 80rp, Angel playing organ.

1982, Dec. 6 Photo. *Perf. 11½*
Granite Paper
751 A323 20rp multicolored .25 .25
752 A323 50rp multicolored .50 .35
753 A323 80rp multicolored .75 .55
Nos. 751-753 (3) 1.50 1.15

Europa 1983 — A324

Designs: 40rp, Notker Balbulus of St. Gall (840-912), Benedictine monk, poet and liturgical composer. 80rp, St. Hildegard of Bingen (1098-1179).

1983, Mar. 7 Photo.
754 A324 40rp multicolored *.40 .30*
755 A324 80rp multicolored *.65 .55*

A325

Shrovetide and Lenten customs: 40rp, Last Thursday before Lent. 70rp, Begging for eggs on Shrove Tuesday. 180fr, Bonfire, first Sunday in Lent.

Photogravure and Engraved
1983, Mar. 7 *Perf. 14*
756 A325 40rp multicolored .35 .30
757 A325 70rp multicolored .60 .45
758 A325 1.80fr multicolored 1.50 1.25
Nos. 756-758 (3) 2.45 2.00

See Nos. 844-846, 915-917, 952-954.

A326

Landscapes by Anton Ender (b. 1898): 40rp, Schaan, on the Zollstrasse. 50rp, Balzers with Gutenberg Castle. 2fr, Stag by the Reservoir.

1983, June 6 Photo. *Perf. 12*
759 A326 40rp multicolored .35 .30
760 A326 50rp multicolored .50 .35
761 A326 2fr multicolored 2.00 1.50
Nos. 759-761 (3) 2.85 2.15

Protection of Shores and Coasts — A327

40rp, Manned flight bicentenary. 50rp, World communications year. 80rp, Humanitarian aid.

1983, June 6
762 A327 20rp shown .25 .25
763 A327 40rp multicolored .35 .35
764 A327 50rp multicolored .45 .45
765 A327 80rp multicolored .70 .70
Nos. 762-765 (4) 1.75 1.75

Pope John Paul II — A328

1983, Sept. 5 Photo.
766 A328 80rp multicolored .90 .75

Princess Gina — A329

3fr, Prince Franz Joseph II.

1983, Sept. 5 *Perf. 12x11½*
767 A329 2.50fr shown 2.25 1.25
768 A329 3fr multicolored 2.75 1.75

Christmas 1983 — A330

1983, Dec. 5 Photo. *Perf. 12*
Granite Paper
769 A330 20rp Seeking shelter .25 .25
770 A330 50rp Child Jesus .40 .30
771 A330 80rp The Three Magi .70 .55
Nos. 769-771 (3) 1.35 1.10

1984 Winter Olympics, Sarajevo — A331

Snowflakes.

1983, Dec. 5 Photo. *Perf. 11½x12*
Granite Paper
772 A331 40rp multicolored .40 .30
773 A331 80rp multicolored .80 .60
774 A331 1.80fr multicolored 1.65 1.10
Nos. 772-774 (3) 2.85 2.00

Famous Visitors to Liechtenstein — A332

Paintings: 40rp, Count Alexander Wassiljewitsch Suworow-Rimnikski (1730-1800), Austro-Russian Army general. 70rp, Karl Rudolf Count von Buol-Schauenstein (1760-1833). 80rp, Carl Zuckmayer (1896-1977), playwright. 1fr, Curt Goetz (1888-1960), actor and playwright.

Photogravure and Engraved
1984, Mar. 12 *Perf. 14*
775 A332 40rp multicolored .40 .30
776 A332 70rp multicolored .70 .55
777 A332 80rp multicolored .80 .60
778 A332 1fr multicolored 1.00 .75
Nos. 775-778 (4) 2.90 2.20

Europa (1959-1984) — A333

1984, Mar. 12 Photo. *Perf. 12*
Granite Paper
779 A333 50rp multicolored *.45 .40*
780 A333 80rp multicolored *.65 .60*

A334

The Destruction of Trisona Fairy Tale Illustrations: Root Carvings by Beni Gassner — 35rp, Warning messenger. 50rp, Buried town. 80rp, Spared family.

Photogravure and Engraved

1984, June 12 *Perf. 14*

781 A334 35rp multicolored .35 .30
782 A334 50rp multicolored .50 .40
783 A334 80rp multicolored .80 .70
Nos. 781-783 (3) 1.65 1.40

1984 Summer Olympics — A335

1984, June 12 Photo. *Perf. 11½*
Granite Paper

784 A335 70rp Pole vault .65 .50
785 A335 80rp Discus .75 .55
786 A335 1fr Shot put 1.00 .75
Nos. 784-786 (3) 2.40 1.80

Industries and Occupations A336

5rp, Banking & trading. 10rp, Construction, plumbing. 20rp, Production, factory worker. 35rp, Contracting, draftswoman. 45rp, Manufacturing, sales rep. 50rp, Catering. 60rp, Carpentry. 70rp, Public health. 80rp, Industrial research. 1fr, Masonry. 1.20fr, Industrial management. 1.50fr, Post & communications.

1984, Sept. 10 Photo. *Perf. 11½*

787 A336 5rp multicolored .25 .25
788 A336 10rp multicolored .25 .25
789 A336 20rp multicolored .25 .25
790 A336 35rp multicolored .35 .30
791 A336 45rp multicolored .45 .35
792 A336 50rp multicolored .50 .40
793 A336 60rp multicolored .60 .50
794 A336 70rp multicolored .70 .55
795 A336 80rp multicolored .80 .65
796 A336 1fr multicolored 1.00 .80
797 A336 1.20fr multicolored 1.25 1.00
798 A336 1.50fr multicolored 1.50 1.20
Nos. 787-798 (12) 7.90 6.50

Princess Marie Aglae — A337

2fr, Prince Hans Adam.

Photogravure and Engraved

1984, Dec. 10 *Perf. 14x13½*

799 A337 1.70fr shown 1.50 1.25
800 A337 2fr multicolored 1.90 1.40

Christmas 1984 — A338

1984, Dec. 10 Photo. *Perf. 11*

801 A338 35rp Annunciation .35 .30
802 A338 50rp Holy Family .55 .40
803 A338 80rp Three Kings .80 .70
Nos. 801-803 (3) 1.70 1.40

Europa 1985 — A339

1985, Mar. 11 Photo. *Perf. 11½*

804 A339 50rp Three Muses *.45 .40*
805 A339 80rp Pan and Muses *.70 .65*

Orders and Monestaries A340

50rp, St. Elisabeth. 1fr, Schellenberg Convent. 1.70fr, Gutenberg Mission.

Photogravure and Engraved

1985, Mar. 11 *Perf. 13½x14*

806 A340 50rp multicolored .55 .45
807 A340 1fr multicolored 1.10 .90
808 A340 1.70fr multicolored 1.90 1.60
Nos. 806-808 (3) 3.55 2.95

Cardinal Virtues — A341

1985, June 10 Photo. *Perf. 11½x12*

809 A341 35rp Justice .35 .30
810 A341 50rp Temperance .50 .40
811 A341 70rp Prudence .70 .55
812 A341 1fr Fortitude 1.00 .80
Nos. 809-812 (4) 2.55 2.05

Princess Gina, President of Natl. Red Cross, 40th Anniv. — A342

Portrait and: 20rp, Helping refugees, 1945. 50rp, Rescue service. 1.20fr, Child refugees, 1979.

1985, June 10 *Perf. 12x11½*

813 A342 20rp multicolored .25 .25
814 A342 50rp multicolored .65 .40
815 A342 1.20fr multicolored 1.50 1.10
Nos. 813-815 (3) 2.40 1.75

Souvenir Sheet

State Visit of Pope John Paul II A343

Designs: 50rp, Papal coat of arms. 80rp, Chapel of St. Maria zum Trost, Dux, Schaan. 1.70fr, Our Lady of Liechtenstein, St. Mary the Comforter.

1985, Feb. 2 *Perf. 11½*

816 A343 Sheet of 3 3.25 2.75
a. 50rp multi 1.00 .90
b. 80rp multi 1.00 .90
c. 1.70fr multi 1.00 .90

Paintings from the Princely Collections — A344

50rp, Portrait of a Canon, by Quintin Massys (1466-1530). 1fr, Portrait of Clara Serena Rubens, by Peter Paul Rubens (1577-1640). 1.20fr, Portrait of the Duke of Urbino, by Raphael (1483-1520).

Photogravure and Engraved

1985, Sept. 2 *Perf. 14*

817 A344 50rp multicolored .55 .50
818 A344 1fr multicolored 1.25 1.10
819 A344 1.20fr multicolored 1.50 1.40
Nos. 817-819 (3) 3.30 3.00

Christmas 1985 — A345

1985, Dec. 9 Photo. *Perf. 11½x12*

820 A345 35rp Frankincense .45 .35
821 A345 50rp Gold .65 .50
822 A345 80rp Myrrh 1.10 .85
Nos. 820-822 (3) 2.20 1.70

Kirchplatz Theater, 15th Anniv. — A346

50rp, Tragedy. 80rp, Commedia dell'arte. 1.50rp, Opera buffa.

Photogravure and Engraved

1985, Dec. 9 *Perf. 14*

823 A346 50rp multicolored .40 .35
824 A346 80rp multicolored .55 .45
825 A346 1.50rp multicolored 1.75 1.40
Nos. 823-825 (3) 2.70 2.20

Weapons from the Prince's Armory — A347

Designs: 35rp, Halberd, bodyguard of Prince Charles I. 50rp, German morion, 16th cent. 80rp, Halberd, bodyguard of Prince Carl Eusebius.

1985, Dec. 9 *Perf. 13½x14½*

826 A347 35rp multicolored .35 .35
827 A347 50rp multicolored .45 .40
828 A347 80rp multicolored .75 .65
Nos. 826-828 (3) 1.55 1.40

Europa 1986 — A348

1986, Mar. 10 Photo. *Perf. 12*

829 A348 50rp Swallows *.45 .40*
830 A348 90rp Robin *.95 .90*

A349

Views of Vaduz Castle: 20rp, Outer courtyard. 25rp, View from the south ('89). 50rp, Castle, mountains. 90rp, Inner gate ('87). 1.10fr, Back view. 1.40fr, Inner courtyard ('87).

Granite Paper

1986-89 Photo. *Perf. 11½x12*

832 A349 20rp multicolored .25 .25
833 A349 25rp multicolored .35 .35
835 A349 50rp multicolored .40 .35
838 A349 90rp multicolored 1.10 .70
840 A349 1.10fr multicolored .90 .75
841 A349 1.40fr multicolored 1.75 1.20
Nos. 832-841 (6) 4.75 3.60

Fasting Sacrifice — A350

1986, Mar. 10 Photo. *Perf. 12*

843 A350 1.40fr multicolored 1.50 1.25

Customs Type of 1983

35rp, Palm Sunday procession. 50rp, Wedding. 70rp, Rogation Day procession.

Photogravure and Engraved

1986, June 9 *Perf. 13½*

844 A325 35rp multicolored .40 .35
845 A325 50rp multicolored .60 .40
846 A325 70rp multicolored .80 .60
Nos. 844-846 (3) 1.80 1.35

A352

Karl Freiherr Haus von Hausen (1823-89), founder.

1986, June 9 Photo. *Perf. 11½*

847 A352 50rp multicolored .65 .50

Natl. Savings Bank, Vaduz, 125th anniv.

A353

Photogravure and Engraved

1986, June 9 *Perf. 13½*

848 A353 3.50fr multicolored 3.50 2.50

Prince Franz Joseph II, 80th birthday.

Hunting — A354

35rp, Roebuck, Ruggeller Riet. 50rp, Chamois in winter, Rappenstein. 1.70fr, Rutting stag, Lawena.

1986, Sept. 9 *Perf. 13x13½*

849 A354 35rp multicolored .35 .25
850 A354 50rp multicolored .50 .40
851 A354 1.70fr multicolored 1.90 1.50
Nos. 849-851 (3) 2.75 2.15

Crops — A355

50rp, White cabbage, beets. 80rp, Red cabbage. 90rp, Potatoes, onions, garlic.

1986, Sept. 9 Photo. *Perf. 12x11½*

852 A355 50rp multicolored .55 .45
853 A355 80rp multicolored .90 .70
854 A355 90rp multicolored 1.00 .80
Nos. 852-854 (3) 2.45 1.95

Christmas — A356

Archangels.

1986, Dec. 9 *Perf. 11½*

855 A356 35rp Michael .45 .30
856 A356 50rp Gabriel .65 .50
857 A356 90rp Raphael 1.25 1.00
Nos. 855-857 (3) 2.35 1.80

Trees — A357

1986, Dec. 9

858	A357	25rp Silver fir	.30	.25
859	A357	90rp Spruce	1.10	.85
860	A357	1.40fr Oak	1.65	1.25
		Nos. 858-860 (3)	3.05	2.35

Europa 1987 — A358

Modern architecture: 50rp, Primary school, 1980, Gamprin. 90rp, Parish church, c. 1960, Schellenburg.

1987, Mar. 9 Photo. *Perf. 11½x12*

Granite Paper

861	A358	50rp multicolored	*.60*	*.55*
862	A358	90rp multicolored	*1.25*	*1.00*

Nicholas Among the Thorns — A359

1987, Mar. 9 *Perf. 11½*

Granite Paper

863	A359	1.10fr multicolored	1.40	1.00

Nicholas von der Flue (1417-1487), canonized in 1947.

Hereditary Prince Alois — A360

Photo. & Engr.

1987, June 9 *Perf. 14*

864	A360	2fr multicolored	2.50	2.00

No. 864 printed in sheets of 8.

Fish — A361

50rp, Cottus gobio. 90rp, Salmo trutta fario. 1.10fr, Thymallus thymallus.

1987, June 9 Photo. *Perf. 11½*

865	A361	50rp multicolored	.60	.50
866	A361	90rp multicolored	1.10	.85
867	A361	1.10fr multicolored	1.40	1.10
		Nos. 865-867 (3)	3.10	2.45

A362

Liechtenstein City Palace, Vienna.

1987, Sept. 7 Photo. *Perf. 11½*

Granite Paper

868	A362	35rp Arch	.45	.35
869	A362	50rp Entrance	.60	.50
870	A362	90rp Staircase	1.10	.90
		Nos. 868-870 (3)	2.15	1.75

House of Liechtenstein Coat of Arms — A363

1987, Sept. 7 *Perf. 11½*

871	A363	1.40fr multicolored	1.60	1.25

Purchase of County of Vaduz, 275th anniv.

Diet, 125th Anniv. — A364

1987, Sept. 7 *Perf. 11½*

872	A364	1.70fr Constitution of 1862	2.00	1.50

Christmas — A365

The Evangelists, illuminated codices from the Golden Book, c. 1100, Abbey of Pfafers, purportedly made under the direction of monks from Reichenau Is.

Photo. & Engr.

1987, Dec. 7 *Perf. 14*

873	A365	35rp St. Matthew	.50	.30
874	A365	50rp St. Mark	.65	.40
875	A365	60rp St. Luke	.80	.50
876	A365	90rp St. John	1.25	.75
		Nos. 873-876 (4)	3.20	1.95

1988 Winter Olympics, Calgary — A366

Humorous drawings by illustrator Paul Flora of Austria: 25rp, The Toil of the Cross-country Skier. 90rp, Courageous Pioneer of Skiing. 1.10fr, As Grandfather Used to Ride on a Bobsled.

1987, Dec. 7 *Perf. 14x13½*

877	A366	25rp multicolored	.30	.30
878	A366	90rp multicolored	1.10	1.00
879	A366	1.10fr multicolored	1.40	1.25
		Nos. 877-879 (3)	2.80	2.55

See Nos. 888-891.

Europa 1988 — A367

Modern communication & transportation: 50rp, Satellite dish. 90rp, High-speed monorail.

1988, Mar. 7 Photo. *Perf. 11½x12*

Granite Paper

880	A367	50rp multicolored	*.60*	*.55*
881	A367	90rp multicolored	*1.00*	*.90*

European Campaign to Protect Undeveloped and Developing Lands — A368

80rp, Forest preservation. 90rp, Layout for village development. 1.70rp, Traffic planning.

1988, Mar. 7 *Perf. 12*

Granite Paper

882	A368	80rp multicolored	.85	.75
883	A368	90rp multicolored	.90	.85
884	A368	1.70rp multicolored	1.75	1.50
		Nos. 882-884 (3)	3.50	3.10

Balancing nature conservation with natl. development.

Souvenir Sheet

Succession to the Throne — A369

Portraits: a, Crown Prince Hans Adam. b, Prince Alois, successor to the crown prince. c, Prince Franz Josef II, ruler.

Photo. & Engr.

1988, June 6 *Perf. 14½x13½*

885	A369	Sheet of 3	4.50	3.50
a.		50rp black, gold & bright blue	.70	.55
b.		50rp black, gold & sage green	.70	.55
c.		2fr black, gold & deep rose	3.00	2.25

North and South Campaign — A370

1988, June 6 Photo. *Perf. 12x11½*

Granite Paper

886	A370	50rp Public radio	.85	.55
887	A370	1.40fr Adult education	2.40	1.50

Cultural cooperation with Costa Rica. See Costa Rica Nos. 401-402.

Olympics Type of 1988

Humorous drawings by illustrator Paul Flora of Austria: 50rp, Cycling. 80rp, Gymnastics. 90rp, Running. 1.40fr, Equestrian.

Photo. & Engr.

1988, Sept. 5 *Perf. 14x13½*

888	A366	50rp multicolored	.70	.50
889	A366	80rp multicolored	1.10	.75
890	A366	90rp multicolored	1.20	.80
891	A366	1.40fr multicolored	1.90	1.40
		Nos. 888-891 (4)	4.90	3.45

Roadside Shrines — A371

25rp, Kaltweh Chapel, Balzers. 35rp, Oberdorf, Vaduz, c. 1870. 50rp, Bangstrasse, Ruggell.

1988, Sept. 5 Photo. *Perf. 11½x12*

Granite Paper

892	A371	25rp multicolored	.35	.30
893	A371	35rp multicolored	.45	.40
894	A371	50rp multicolored	.65	.55
		Nos. 892-894 (3)	1.45	1.25

Christmas — A372

35rp, Joseph, Mary. 50rp, Christ child. 90rp, Adoration of the Magi.

1988, Dec. 5 Photo. *Perf. 11½x12*

Granite Paper

895	A372	35rp multicolored	.40	.30
896	A372	50rp multicolored	.55	.40
897	A372	90rp multicolored	1.00	.70
		Nos. 895-897 (3)	1.95	1.40

The Letter — A373

Details of Portrait of Marie-Therese de Lamballe (The Letter), by Anton Hickel (1745-1798): 90rp, Handkerchief and writing materials in open desk. 2fr, Entire painting.

Photo. & Engr.

1988, Dec. 5 *Perf. 13x13½*

898	A373	50rp shown	.65	.50
899	A373	90rp multicolored	1.10	.80
900	A373	2fr multicolored	2.50	1.90
		Nos. 898-900 (3)	4.25	3.20

Europa 1989 — A374

Traditional children's games: 50rp, Cat and Mouse. 90rp,

Granite Paper

1989, Mar. 6 Photo. *Perf. 11½x12*

901	A374	50rp multicolored	*.70*	*.65*
902	A374	90rp multicolored	*1.40*	*1.25*

Josef Gabriel Rheinberger (1839-1901), Composer, and Score — A375

Photo. & Engr.

1989, Mar. 6 *Perf. 14x13½*

903	A375	2.90fr multicolored	3.25	2.50

Fish — A376

50rp, Esox lucius. 1.10fr, Salmo trutta lacustris. 1.40fr, Noemacheilus barbatulus.

1989, June 5 Photo. *Perf. 12x11½*

Granite Paper

904	A376	50rp multicolored	.65	.50
905	A376	1.10fr multicolored	1.40	1.00
906	A376	1.40fr multicolored	1.75	1.25
		Nos. 904-906 (3)	3.80	2.75

World Wildlife Fund — A377

25rp, Charadrius dubius. 35rp, Hyla arborea. 50rp, Libelloides coccajus. 90rp, Putorius putorius.

1989, June 5 *Perf. 12*

Granite Paper

907	A377	25rp multicolored	.55	.35
908	A377	35rp multicolored	.90	.55
909	A377	50rp multicolored	1.20	.75
910	A377	90rp multicolored	2.25	1.40
		Nos. 907-910 (4)	4.90	3.05

Mountains — A378

1989, Sept. 4 Photo. *Perf. 11½*
Granite Paper

911	A378	50rp Falknis	.50	.45
912	A378	75rp Plassteikopf	.75	.65
913	A378	80rp Naafkopf	.80	.70
914	A378	1.50fr Garselliturm	1.50	1.25
		Nos. 911-914 (4)	3.55	3.05

See Nos. 930-939.

Customs Type of 1983

Autumn activities: 35rp, Alpine herdsman and flock return from pasture. 50rp, Shucking corn. 80rp, Cattle market.

Photo. & Engr.
1989, Sept. 4 *Perf. 14*

915	A325	35rp multicolored	.40	.30
916	A325	50rp multicolored	.60	.45
917	A325	80rp multicolored	.95	.75
		Nos. 915-917 (3)	1.95	1.50

Christmas — A379

Details of the triptych *Adoration of the Magi,* by Hugo van der Goes (50rp) and student (35rp, 90rp), late 15th cent.: 35rp, Melchior and Balthazar. 50rp, Caspar and holy family. 90rp, Donor with St. Stephen.

1989, Dec. 4 *Perf. 13½*
Size of 35rp and 90rp: 23x41mm

918	A379	35rp multicolored	.45	.35
919	A379	50rp shown	.60	.45
920	A379	90rp multicolored	1.10	.80
		Nos. 918-920 (3)	2.15	1.60

Minerals — A380

1989, Dec. 4 *Perf. 13½x13*

921	A380	50rp Scepter quartz	.60	.50
922	A380	1.10fr Pyrite ball	1.40	1.00
923	A380	1.50fr Calcite	1.75	1.25
		Nos. 921-923 (3)	3.75	2.75

Europa 1990 — A381

Post offices.

1990, Mar. 5 Photo. *Perf. 11½x12*
Granite Paper

924	A381	50rp shown	*.70*	*.60*
925	A381	90rp Modern p.o.	*1.25*	*1.10*

Postage Stamps, 150th Anniv. — A382

1990, Mar. 5 *Perf. 11½*
Granite Paper

926	A382	1.50fr Penny Black	2.25	1.65

1990 World Cup Soccer Championships, Italy — A383

1990, Mar. 5 Granite Paper *Perf. 12*

927	A383	2fr multicolored	2.75	1.75

1st Anniv. of Death — A384

2fr, Princess Gina, (1921-1989). 3fr, Prince Franz Joseph II, (1906-1989).

1990, June 5 Litho. *Perf. 11½*
Granite Paper

928	A384	2fr shown	2.25	1.40
929	A384	3fr multi	3.25	2.25

Mountains Type of 1989

5rp, Augstenberg. 10rp, Hahnenspiel. 35rp, Nospitz. 40rp, Ochsenkopf. 45rp, Drei Schwestern. 60rp, Kuhgrat. 70rp, Galinakopf. 1fr, Schonberg. 1.20fr, Bleikaturm. 1.60fr, Schwarzhorn. 2fr, Scheienkopf.

1990-93 Granite Paper

930	A378	5rp multicolored	.25	.25
931	A378	10rp multicolored	.25	.25
933	A378	35rp multicolored	.45	.30
933A	A378	40rp multicolored	.50	.45
934	A378	45rp multicolored	.45	.35
935	A378	60rp multicolored	.70	.55
936	A378	70rp multicolored	.75	.60
938	A378	1fr multicolored	.95	.75
939	A378	1.20fr multicolored	1.40	1.10
940	A378	1.60fr multicolored	2.00	1.40
941	A378	2fr multicolored	2.50	1.75
		Nos. 930-941 (11)	10.20	7.75

Issued: 5, 45, 70rp, 1fr, 6/5; 10, 35, 60rp, 1.20fr, 9/3; 40rp, 6/3/91; 1.60fr, 3/2/92; 2fr, 3/1/93.

A385

Paintings by Benjamin Steck (1902-1981): 80rp, Fruit, dish. 1.50fr, Basket, fruit, stein.

Photo. & Engr.
1990, June 5 *Perf. 14*

942	A385	50rp shown	.70	.55
943	A385	80rp multicolored	1.10	.80
944	A385	1.50fr multicolored	2.25	1.60
		Nos. 942-944 (3)	4.05	2.95

A386

Game birds.

Photo. & Engr.
1990, Sept. 3 *Perf. 13x13½*

945	A386	25rp Pheasant	.35	.25
946	A386	50rp Blackcock	.70	.45
947	A386	2fr Mallard duck	2.75	1.90
		Nos. 945-947 (3)	3.80	2.60

European Postal Communications, 500th Anniv. — A387

1990, Dec. 3 *Perf. 13½x14*

948	A387	90rp multicolored	1.50	1.00

A388

Christmas (Lenten Cloth of Bendern): 35rp, The Annunciation. 50rp, Birth of Christ. 90rp, Adoration of the Magi.

1990, Dec. 3 Photo. *Perf. 12*
Granite Paper

949	A388	35rp multicolored	.50	.35
950	A388	50rp multicolored	.70	.50
951	A388	90rp multicolored	1.25	.90
		Nos. 949-951 (3)	2.45	1.75

A389

Holiday Customs: 35rp, St. Nicholas Visiting Children on Feast of St. Nicholas. 50rp, Waking "sleepyheads" on New Year's Day. 1.50fr, Good wishes on New Year's Day.

Photo. & Engr.
1990, Dec. 3 *Perf. 14*

952	A389	35rp multicolored	.45	.30
953	A389	50rp multicolored	.65	.45
954	A389	1.50fr multicolored	2.00	1.40
		Nos. 952-954 (3)	3.10	2.15

Europa — A390

Designs: 50rp, Telecommunications satellite, Olympus I. 90rp, Weather satellite, Meteosat.

1991, Mar. 4 Photo. *Perf. 11½*
Granite Paper

955	A390	50rp multicolored	*.80*	*.60*
956	A390	90rp multicolored	*1.25*	*1.10*

St. Ignatius of Loyola (1491-1556), Founder of Jesuit Order — A391

90rp, Wolfgang Amadeus Mozart.

1991, Mar. 4 *Perf. 11½*
Granite Paper

957	A391	80rp multicolored	1.10	.80
958	A391	90rp multicolored	1.25	.90

UN Membership, 1990 — A392

1991, Mar. 4 *Perf. 11½*
Granite Paper

959	A392	2.50fr multicolored	3.00	2.00

A393

Paintings: 50rp, Maloja, by Giovanni Giacometti. 80rp, Rheintal, by Ferdinand Gehr. 90rp, Bergell, by Augusto Giacometti. 1.10fr, Hoher Kasten, by Hedwig Scherrer.

Granite Paper
1991, June 3 Photo. *Perf. 11½*

960	A393	50rp multicolored	.60	.40
961	A393	80rp multicolored	.95	.65
962	A393	90rp multicolored	1.00	.65
963	A393	1.10fr multicolored	1.40	.95
		Nos. 960-963 (4)	3.95	2.65

Swiss Confederation, 700th anniv.

Military Uniforms — A394

Designs: 50rp, Non-commissioned officer, private. 70rp, Uniform tunic, trunk. 1fr, Sharpshooters, officer and private.

Photo. & Engr.
1991, June 3 *Perf. 13½x14*

964	A394	50rp multicolored	.75	.55
965	A394	70rp multicolored	1.10	.75
966	A394	1fr multicolored	1.20	.85
		Nos. 964-966 (3)	3.05	2.15

Last action of Liechtenstein's military, 1866 (70rp).

Princess Marie — A395

3.40fr, Prince Hans Adam II.

Photo. & Engr.
1991, Sept. 2 *Perf. 13x13½*

967	A395	3fr shown	2.90	2.25
968	A395	3.40fr multicolored	3.25	2.60

LIBA 92, Natl. Philatelic Exhibition — A396

1991, Sept. 2 Photo. *Perf. 11½*
Granite Paper

969	A396	90rp multicolored	1.10	.95

A397

Christmas (Altar of St. Mamertus Chapel, Triesen): 50rp, Mary. 80rp, Madonna and Child. 90rp, Angel Gabriel.

Photo. & Engr.
1991, Dec. 2 *Perf. 13½x14*

970	A397	50rp multicolored	.70	.50
971	A397	80rp multicolored	1.10	.80
972	A397	90rp multicolored	1.25	.90
		Nos. 970-972 (3)	3.05	2.20

A398

1992 Winter Olympics, Albertville: 70rp, Cross-country skiers, doping check. 80rp, Hockey players, good sportsmanship. 1.60rp, Downhill skier, safety precautions.

Granite Paper
1991, Dec. 2 Photo. *Perf. 11½x12*

973	A398	70rp multicolored	.95	.70
974	A398	80rp multicolored	1.10	.85
975	A398	1.60fr multicolored	2.25	1.75
		Nos. 973-975 (3)	4.30	3.30

1992, Mar. 2 Photo. *Perf. 11½*

1992 Summer Olympics, Barcelona: 50rp, Women's relay, drugs, broken medal. 70rp, Cycling, safety precautions. 2.50fr, Judo, good sportsmanship.

Granite Paper

976	A398	50rp multicolored	.65	.50
977	A398	70rp multicolored	.90	.70
978	A398	2.50fr multicolored	3.25	2.50
		Nos. 976-978 (3)	4.80	3.70

Discovery of America, 500th Anniv. — A400

1992, Mar. 2 **Granite Paper**

979 A400 80rp shown *1.10 1.00*
980 A400 90rp New York skyline *1.40 1.25*

Europa.

Postillion Blowing Horn A401

Clown in Envelope A402

Designs: No. 982, Postillion delivering valentine. No. 984, Wedding violinist.

Photo. & Engr.

1992, June 1 ***Perf. 14x13½***

981 A401 50rp multicolored .65 .55
982 A401 50rp multicolored .65 .55

Photo.

Perf. 12½

Granite Paper

983 A402 50rp multicolored .65 .55
984 A402 50rp multicolored .65 .55
Nos. 981-984 (4) 2.60 2.20

Souvenir Sheet

Prince Hans-Adam and Princess Marie, 25th Wedding Anniv. — A403

Designs: a, 2fr, Coat of Arms of Liechtenstein-Kinsky Alliance. b, 2.50fr, Prince Hans-Adam and Princess Marie.

1992, June 1 ***Perf. 11½***

Granite Paper

985 A403 Sheet of 2, #a.-b. 5.75 4.00

Ferns — A404

40rp, Blechnum spicant. 50rp, Asplenium trichomanes. 70rp, Phyllitis scolopendrium. 2.50fr, Asplenium ruta-muraria.

Photo. & Engr.

1992, Sept. 7 ***Perf. 14***

986 A404 40rp multicolored .50 .35
987 A404 50rp multicolored .55 .40
988 A404 70rp multicolored .85 .60
989 A404 2.50fr multicolored 3.00 2.25
Nos. 986-989 (4) 4.90 3.60

Creation of Vaduz County, 650th Anniv. — A405

1992, Sept. 7 ***Perf. 13½x14***

990 A405 1.60fr multicolored 2.50 1.60

Christmas — A406

Scenes in Triesen: 50rp, Chapel, St. Mamertus. 90rp, Nativity scene, St. Gallus Church. 1.60rp, St. Mary's Chapel.

1992, Dec. 7 **Photo.** ***Perf. 11½***

Granite Paper

991 A406 50rp multicolored .60 .45
992 A406 90rp multicolored 1.10 .80
993 A406 1.60fr multicolored 2.00 1.40
Nos. 991-993 (3) 3.70 2.65

Hereditary Prince Alois — A407

Photo. & Engr.

1992, Dec. 7 ***Perf. 13x13½***

994 A407 2.50fr multicolored 3.50 3.50

A408

Europa (Contemporary paintings): 80rp, 910805, by Bruno Kaufmann. 1fr, The Little Blue, by Evi Kliemand.

1993, Mar. 1 **Photo.** ***Perf. 11½x12***

Granite Paper

995 A408 80rp multicolored *.90 .75*
996 A408 1fr multicolored *1.10 .90*

A409

Paintings by Hans Gantner (1853-1914): 50rp, Chalets in Steg and Naafkopf. 60rp, Sass Mountain with Hunting Lodge. 1.80fr, Red House in Vaduz.

1993, Mar. 1 ***Perf. 11½***

Granite Paper

997 A409 50rp multicolored .65 .45
998 A409 60rp multicolored .75 .50
999 A409 1.80fr multicolored 2.25 1.50
Nos. 997-999 (3) 3.65 2.45

Tibetan Art — A410

60rp, Detail from Thangka painting, Tale of the Ferryman. 80rp, Religious dance mask. 1fr, Detail from Thangka painting, The Tale of the Fish.

1993, June 7 **Photo.** ***Perf. 11½***

Granite Paper

1000 A410 60rp multicolored .75 .55
1001 A410 80rp multicolored 1.00 .75
1002 A410 1fr multicolored 1.25 .95
Nos. 1000-1002 (3) 3.00 2.25

Church Missionary Work — A411

1993, June 7 ***Perf. 11½x12***

Granite Paper

1003 A411 1.80fr Tree of life 2.10 1.60

A412

Contemporary painting: Black Hatter, by Friedensreich Hundertwasser.

Photo. & Engr.

1993, June 7 ***Perf. 14x13½***

1004 A412 2.80fr multicolored 4.00 2.40

Souvenir Sheet

Marriage of Hereditary Prince Alois and Duchess Sophie of Bavaria, July 3 — A413

1993, June 7 **Photo.** ***Perf. 11½***

Granite Paper

1005 A413 4fr multicolored 5.25 3.50

Wild Animals — A414

Photo. & Engr.

1993, Sept. 6 ***Perf. 13x13½***

1006 A414 60rp Badger .85 .60
1007 A414 80rp Marten 1.10 .75
1008 A414 1fr Fox 1.40 .95
Nos. 1006-1008 (3) 3.35 2.30

Meadow Plants — A415

50rp, Origanum vulgare. 60rp, Salvia pratensis. 1fr, Seseli annuum. 2.50fr, Prunella grandiflora.

1993, Sept. 6

1009 A415 50rp multicolored .65 .45
1010 A415 60rp multicolored .80 .55
1011 A415 1fr multicolored 1.25 .85
1012 A415 2.50fr multicolored 3.25 2.25
Nos. 1009-1012 (4) 5.95 4.10

See Nos. 1056-1059.

Christmas — A416

Calligraphic Christmas texts by: 60rp, Rainer Maria Rilke. 80rp, Th. Friedrich. 1fr, Rudolph Alexander Schroder.

1993, Dec. 6 **Photo.** ***Perf. 11½x12***

Granite Paper

1013 A416 60rp multicolored .80 .55
1014 A416 80rp multicolored 1.00 .70
1015 A416 1fr multicolored 1.25 .90
Nos. 1013-1015 (3) 3.05 2.15

A417

1993, Dec. 6 **Granite Paper**

1016 A417 60rp Ski jump .80 .65
1017 A417 80rp Slalom skiing 1.00 .80
1018 A417 2.40fr Bobsled 3.00 2.40
Nos. 1016-1018 (3) 4.80 3.85

1994 Winter Olympics, Lillehammer.

Anniversaries and Events — A418

A419

A420

1994, Mar. 7 **Photo.** ***Perf. 11½***

Granite Paper

1019 A418 60rp multicolored .70 .70
1020 A419 1.80fr multicolored 2.00 2.00
1021 A420 2.80fr multicolored 3.00 3.00
Nos. 1019-1021 (3) 5.70 5.70

Principality of Liechtenstein, 275th anniv. (No. 1019). Intl. Olympic Committee, cent. (No. 1020). 1994 World Cup Soccer Championships, US (No. 1021).

Alexander von Humboldt (1769-1859) — A421

Europa: 80rp, Vultur gryphus. 1fr, Rhexia cardinalis.

Photo. & Engr.

1994, Mar. 7 ***Perf. 13x13½***

1022 A421 80rp multicolored *1.10 .90*
1023 A421 1fr multicolored *1.40 1.00*

Mobile, by Jean Tinguely (1925-91) — A422

Photo. & Engr.

1994, June 6 ***Perf. 13½x14***

1024 A422 4fr multicolored 4.50 4.50

Letter Writing — A423

1994, June 6 **Photo.** ***Perf. 12½***

Granite Paper

1025 A423 60rp Elephant .90 .80
1026 A423 60rp Cherub .90 .80
1027 A423 60rp Pig .90 .80
1028 A423 60rp Dog .90 .80
Nos. 1025-1028 (4) 3.60 3.20

Life Cycle of Grape Vine — A424

Designs: No. 1029, Spring, vine beginning to flower. No. 1030, Summer, green grapes on vine. No. 1031, Autumn, ripe grapes ready for harvest. No. 1032, Winter, bare vine in snow.

1994, Sept 5 **Photo.** ***Perf. 11½***

Granite Paper

1029 A424 60rp multicolored .90 .80
1030 A424 60rp multicolored .90 .80
1031 A424 60rp multicolored .90 .80
1032 A424 60rp multicolored .90 .80
a Block of 4, #1029-1032 4.00 4.00

No. 1032a is continuous design.

Minerals — A425

60rp, Strontianite. 80rp, Faden quartz. 3.50fr, Ferrous dolomite.

Photo. & Engr.

1994, Sept. 5 ***Perf. 13½x12½***

1033 A425 60rp multicolored .80 .80
1034 A425 80rp multicolored 1.10 1.10
1035 A425 3.50fr multicolored 4.75 4.75
Nos. 1033-1035 (3) 6.65 6.65

A426

Christmas contemporary art, by Anne Frommelt: 60rp, The True Light. 80rp, Peace on Earth. 1fr, See the House of God.

1994, Dec. 5 **Photo.** ***Perf. 11½***
Granite Paper

1036 A426 60rp multicolored .80 .60
1037 A426 80rp multicolored 1.10 .80
1038 A426 1fr multicolored 1.40 .90
Nos. 1036-1038 (3) 3.30 2.30

A427

The Four Elements, by Ernst Steiner.

Photo. & Engr.

1994, Dec. 5 ***Perf. 14***

1039 A427 60rp Earth .75 .60
1040 A427 80rp Water 1.10 .80
1041 A427 1fr Fire 1.25 .90
1042 A427 2.50fr Air 3.50 2.60
Nos. 1039-1042 (4) 6.60 4.90

Peace and Freedom — A428

Europa: 80rp, 1fr, Excerpts from speeches of Prince Franz Josef II.

1995, Mar. 6 **Photo.** ***Perf. 11½***
Granite Paper

1043 A428 80rp multicolored *1.10 .90*
1044 A428 1fr multicolored *1.40 1.10*

A429

Anniversaries and Events
A430 A431

60rp, Princess Marie, Bosnian children.

1995, Mar. 6 **Granite Paper**

1045 A429 60rp multicolored .80 .60
1046 A430 1.80fr multicolored 2.50 2.00
1047 A431 3.50fr multicolored 4.75 3.50
Nos. 1045-1047 (3) 8.05 6.10

Liechtenstein Red Cross, 50th anniv. (No. 1045). UN, 50th anniv. (No. 1046). The Alps, European Landscape of the Year 1995-96 (No. 1047).

Falknis Group, by Anton Frommelt (1895-1975) — A432

Paintings: 80rp, Three Oaks. 4.10fr, Rhine below Triesen.

1995, June 6 **Photo.** ***Perf. 12***
Granite Paper

1048 A432 60rp multicolored .85 .65
1049 A432 80rp multicolored 1.20 .90
1050 A432 4.10fr multicolored 6.00 4.75
Nos. 1048-1050 (3) 8.05 6.30

Letter Writing — A433

No. 1051, Girl, boy building heart with bricks. No. 1052, Boy, girl bandaging sunflower. No. 1053, Girl, boy & rainbow. No. 1054, Boy in hot air balloon delivering letter to girl.

1995, June 6 ***Perf. 12½***
Granite Paper

1051 A433 60rp multicolored .85 .65
1052 A433 60rp multicolored .85 .65
1053 A433 60rp multicolored .85 .65
1054 A433 60rp multicolored .85 .65
a. Vert. strip of 4, #1051-1054 + label 3.50 3.50

Liechtenstein-Switzerland Postal Relationship — A434

Litho. & Engr.

1995, Sept. 5 ***Perf. 13½***

1055 A434 60rp multicolored 1.00 .65

See Switzerland No. 960.

No. 1055 and Switzerland No. 960 are identical. This issue was valid for postage in both countries.

Plant Type of 1993

60rp, Arnica montana. 80rp, Urtica dioica. 1.80fr, Valeriana officinalis. 3.50rp, Ranunculus ficaria.

Photo. & Engr.

1995, Sept. 5 ***Perf. 13x13½***

1056 A415 60rp multicolored .75 .65
1057 A415 80rp multicolored 1.00 .90
1058 A415 1.80fr multicolored 2.25 2.00
1059 A415 3.50fr multicolored 4.50 4.00
Nos. 1056-1059 (4) 8.50 7.55

Christmas — A435

Paintings by Lorenzo Monaco: 60rp, Angel kneeling, facing right. 80rp, Madonna and Child, two angels at her feet. 1fr, Angel kneeling, facing left.

Photo. & Engr.

1995, Dec. 4 ***Perf. 14½x13½***

1060 A435 60rp multicolored .80 .65
1061 A435 80rp multicolored 1.10 .90
1062 A435 1fr multicolored 1.40 1.10
Nos. 1060-1062 (3) 3.30 2.65

A436

Painting: 4fr, Lady with Lap Dog, by Paul Wunderlich.

1995, Dec. 4

1063 A436 4fr multicolored 5.50 4.50

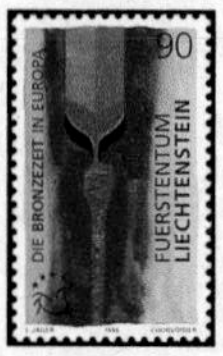

Bronze Age in Europe — A437

1996, Mar. 4 **Photo.** ***Perf. 11½***
Granite Paper

1064 A437 90rp Crucible, pin 1.50 1.25

Countess Nora Kinsky (1888-1923), Nurse, Mother of Princess Gina — A438

Profile and: 90rp, Mar. 7, 1917 diary entry. 1.10fr, Feb. 28, 1917 diary entry.

1996, Mar. 4 **Granite Paper**

1065 A438 90rp multicolored *1.75 1.00*
1066 A438 1.10fr multicolored *2.25 1.25*

Paintings of Village Views, by Marianne Siegl, Based on Sketches by Otto Zeiller — A439

10rp, Eschen. 20rp, Farmhouse, St. Joseph's Chapel, Planken. 80rp, Farmhouse, Ruggell. 1fr, Postal auxiliary office, Nendeln. 1.20fr, Buildings, Triesen. 1.30fr, Upper Village, Triesen. 1.70fr, St. Theresa's Church, Schaanwald. 2fr, Rural houses, barns, Gamprin. 4fr, Parish Church, center of village, Triesenberg. 5fr, Vaduz Castle.

1996-99 **Photo.** ***Perf. 12***
Granite Paper

1068 A439 10rp multicolored .25 .25
1069 A439 20rp multicolored .35 .25
1070 A439 80rp multicolored 1.25 .90
1071 A439 1fr multicolored 1.75 .90
1072 A439 1.20fr multicolored 2.00 1.10
1073 A439 1.30fr multicolored 2.25 1.10
1074 A439 1.70fr multicolored 2.75 1.50
1075 A439 2fr multicolored 2.75 1.75
1076 A439 4fr multicolored 6.75 3.50
1077 A439 5fr multicolored 8.50 5.50
Nos. 1068-1077 (10) 28.60 16.75

Issued: 10rp, 5fr, 3/4/96; 20rp, 1.30fr, 1.70fr, 3/3/97; 2fr, 4fr, 6/2/98; 80rp, 1fr, 1.20fr, 3/1/99.

See Nos. 1167-1175A

Modern Olympic Games, Cent. — A440

1996, June 3 **Photo.** ***Perf. 11½***
Granite Paper

1079 A440 70rp Gymnastics 1.10 .90
1080 A440 90rp Hurdles 1.40 1.00
1081 A440 1.10fr Cycling 2.00 1.10
Nos. 1079-1081 (3) 4.50 3.00

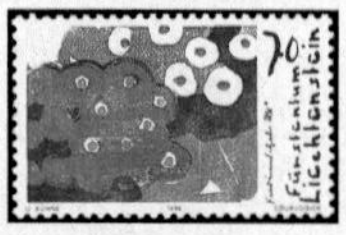

Ferdinand Gehr, 100th Birthday — A441

Various paintings of flowers.

1996, June 3 **Granite Paper**

1083 A441 70rp multicolored 1.10 .90
1084 A441 90rp multicolored 1.40 1.00
1085 A441 1.10fr multicolored 2.00 1.10

Size: 33x23mm

1086 A441 1.80fr multicolored 2.75 2.00
Nos. 1083-1086 (4) 7.25 5.00

Austria, Millennium
A442

Photo. & Engr.

1996, Sept. 2 ***Perf. 13½***

1087 A442 90rp multicolored 1.50 1.10

New Constitution, 75th Anniv.
A443

Litho., Engr. & Embossed

1996, Sept. 2 ***Perf. 14***

1088 A443 10fr Natl. arms 14.00 13.00

A444

Paintings by Russian Artist, Eugen Zotow (1881-1953): 70rp, "Country Estate in Poltava." 1.10fr, "Three Bathers in a Park in Berlin." 1.40fr, "View of Vaduz."

Photo. & Engr.

1996, Dec. 2 ***Perf. 14***

1089 A444 70rp multicolored 1.10 .75
1090 A444 1.10fr multicolored 2.00 1.10
1091 A444 1.40fr multicolored 2.25 1.50
Nos. 1089-1091 (3) 5.35 3.35

A445

Christmas: Illuminated manuscripts, symbols of the Evangelists.

1996, Dec. 2

1092 A445 70rp Matthew 1.10 .75
1093 A445 90rp Mark 1.40 .90
1094 A445 1.10fr Luke 1.75 1.10
1095 A445 1.80fr John 2.75 2.00
Nos. 1092-1095 (4) 7.00 4.75

A446

Photo. & Engr.

1997, Mar. 3 ***Perf. 13½***

1096 A446 70rp multicolored 1.10 .65

Franz Schubert (1797-1828), composer.

A447

Europa, Liechtenstein Myths: 90rp, Wild Gnomes. 1.10fr, Foal of Planken.

1997, Mar. 3 **Photo.** ***Perf. 12***
Granite Paper

1097 A447 90rp multicolored *1.75 1.00*
1098 A447 1.10fr multicolored *2.25 1.10*

St. Lucius, Virgin Mary Holding Infant Jesus, St. Florin, by Gabriel Dreher — A448

Photo. & Engr.

1997, June 2 *Perf. 13½x13*

1099 A448 20fr multicolored 24.00 17.00

A449

Painting, "Jeune Fille en Fleur," by Enrico Baj.

1997, Aug. 22 Photo. *Perf. 11½*
Granite Paper

1100 A449 70rp multicolored 1.40 1.00

Mushrooms — A450

70rp, Phaeolepiota aurea. 90rp, Helvella silvicola. 1.10fr, Aleuria aurantia.

Photo. & Engr.

1997, Aug. 22 *Perf. 14*

1101 A450 70rp multicolored 1.20 .60
1102 A450 90rp multicolored 1.50 .80
1103 A450 1.10fr multicolored 1.90 1.00
Nos. 1101-1103 (3) 4.60 2.40

Railway in Liechtenstein, 125th Anniv. — A451

Train stations: 70rp, Schaanwald. 90rp, Nendeln. 1.80fr, Schaan-Vaduz.

1997, Aug. 22 Photo. *Perf. 11½*
Granite Paper

1104 A451 70rp multicolored 1.20 .60
1105 A451 90rp multicolored 1.50 .80
1106 A451 1.80fr multicolored 2.90 1.60
Nos. 1104-1106 (3) 5.60 3.00

Christmas Tree Decorations — A452

90rp, Bell. 1.10fr, Oval with pointed ends.

Photo. & Engr.

1997, Dec. 1 *Perf. 14*

1107 A452 70rp shown 1.20 .60
1108 A452 90rp multicolored 1.50 .80
1109 A452 1.10fr multicolored 1.90 1.60
Nos. 1107-1109 (3) 4.60 3.00

A453

Skiing, 1998 Winter Olympic Games, Nagano.

1997, Dec. 1 Photo. *Perf. 12½*
Granite Paper

1110 A453 70rp Cross-country 1.40 1.00
1111 A453 90rp Slalom 1.75 1.25
1112 A453 1.80fr Downhill 3.50 2.50
Nos. 1110-1112 (3) 6.65 4.75

A454

Contemporary Art, Paintings by Heinz Mack: No. 1113, Verano (Der Sommer). No. 1114, Hommage An Liechtenstein. No. 1115, Zwischen Tag Und Traum. No. 1116, Salute Chirico!.

1998, Mar. 2 *Perf. 12*
Granite Paper

1113 A454 70rp multicolored 1.20 .85
1114 A454 70rp multicolored 1.20 .85
1115 A454 70rp multicolored 1.20 .85
1116 A454 70rp multicolored 1.20 .85
a. Block or strip of 4, #1113-1116 5.00 3.50

Festivals — A455

Europa: 90rp, National holiday. 1.10fr, Festival of the Musical Societies.

1998, Mar. 2 Granite Paper

1117 A455 90rp multicolored *1.75 1.00*
1118 A455 1.10fr multicolored *2.25 1.10*

Customs Treaty with Switzerland, 75th Anniv. — A456

1998, Mar. 2 Granite Paper

1119 A456 1.70fr multicolored 2.75 2.00

1998 World Cup Soccer Championships, France — A457

1998, Mar. 2 Granite Paper

1120 A457 1.80fr multicolored 2.75 2.00

Letter Writing — A458

Clown: No. 1121, With woman. No. 1122, Holding four leaf clovers. No. 1123, Tipping hat. No. 1124, Holding paper with heart.

Photo. & Engr.

1998, June 2 *Perf. 14*

1121 A458 70rp multicolored 1.20 .60
1122 A458 70rp multicolored 1.20 .60
1123 A458 70rp multicolored 1.20 .60
1124 A458 70rp multicolored 1.20 .60
a. Strip of 4, #1121-1124 5.00 3.50

1848 Protest March — A459

1998, Sept. 7 Photo. *Perf. 12*
Granite Paper

1125 A459 1.80fr multicolored 3.00 1.75

A460

Traditional Crafts: 90rp, Cooper's tools, tub. 2.20fr, Wooden shoemaker's tools, clog. 3.50fr, Cartwright's tools, wheel.

1998, Sept. 7 Granite Paper

1126 A460 90rp multicolored 1.40 1.00
1127 A460 2.20fr multicolored 3.50 2.40
1128 A460 3.50fr multicolored 5.50 3.75
Nos. 1126-1128 (3) 10.40 7.15

See Nos. 1215-1217.

A461

Christmas (Nativity Scene in high relief): 70rp, Soldier, Virgin Mary. 90rp, Entire nativity scene. 1.10fr, Joseph, donkey.

Photo. & Engr.

1998, Dec. 7 *Perf. 14*

1129 A461 70rp multicolored 1.20 .75
1130 A461 90rp multicolored 1.40 1.00
1131 A461 1.10fr multicolored 1.75 1.25
Nos. 1129-1131 (3) 4.35 3.00

No. 1130 is 34x26mm.

Preservation of Historic Sites — A462

Older buildings, Hinterschellengerg: 90rp, Guest house. 1.70fr, St. George's Chapel, vert. 1.80fr, Farmhouse.

1998, Dec. 7 Photo. *Perf. 11½*
Granite Paper

1132 A462 90rp multicolored 1.40 1.00
1133 A462 1.70fr multicolored 2.75 2.00
1134 A462 1.80fr multicolored 2.75 2.00
Nos. 1132-1134 (3) 6.90 5.00

Telephone in Liechtenstein, Cent. — A463

1998, Dec. 7 Granite Paper

1135 A463 2.80fr multicolored 5.00 3.25

A464

Europa (Conservation Areas): 90rp, Snake, Schwabbrünnen-Aescher marshland. 1.10fr, Bird, Ruggell marsh.

Granite Paper

1999, Mar. 1 Photo. *Perf. 11½x12*

1136 A464 90rp multicolored *1.75 1.00*
1137 A464 1.10fr multicolored *2.25 1.25*

Unterland, 300th Anniv. — A465

Continuous scene of villages: a, Schellenberg, buildings, fortress. b, Mauren, domed steeple on church. c, Eschen,, church, houses. d, Ruggell, road leading into village. e, Gamprin, gray-roofed buildings, church.

1999, Mar. 1 *Perf. 12*
Granite Paper

1138 A465 Sheet of 5 + label 9.00 6.25
a.-e. 90rp any single 1.75 1.25

Anniversaries — A466

Stylized designs: No. 1139, Council of Europe 50th anniv. emblem. No. 1140, Bird holding letter. No. 1141, Hand holding heart.

1999, May 25 Photo. *Perf. 11½x12*
Granite Paper

1139 A466 70rp multicolored .90 .60
1140 A466 70rp multicolored .90 .60
1141 A466 70rp multicolored .90 .60
Nos. 1139-1141 (3) 2.70 1.80

No. 1140, UPU, 125th anniv. No. 1141, Caritas Liechtenstein, 75th anniv.

8th Games of the Small European States — A467

1999, May 25 Granite Paper

1142 A467 70rp Judo .90 .60
1143 A467 70rp Swimming .90 .60
1144 A467 70rp Javelin .90 .60
1145 A467 90rp Volleyball 1.25 .75
1146 A467 90rp Squash 1.25 .75
1147 A467 90rp Tennis 1.25 .75
1148 A467 90rp Table tennis 1.25 .75
1149 A467 90rp Cycling 1.25 .75
1150 A467 90rp Shooting 1.25 .75
Nos. 1142-1150 (9) 10.20 6.30

Johann Wolfgang von Goethe (1749-1832), Poet — A468

Quotations and scenes from Faust: 1.40fr, "Grey, dear friend, is all theory and green the golden tree of life." 1.70fr, "I'll take the wager!...Done! And again, and again!"

Photo. & Engr.

1999, Sept. 9 *Perf. 14*

1151 A468 1.40fr multicolored 1.50 1.10
1152 A468 1.70fr multicolored 2.50 1.50

Paintings by Eugen Verling (1891-1968) — A469

Designs: 70rp, Herrengasse. 2fr, Old Vaduz with Castle. 4fr, House in Fürst-Franz-Josef-Strasse, Vaduz.

1999, Sept. 9

1153 A469 70rp multicolored .90 .60
1154 A469 2fr multicolored 2.60 1.50
1155 A469 4fr multicolored 5.25 3.25
Nos. 1153-1155 (3) 8.75 5.35

A470

Walser house identification marks.

1999, Dec. 6 Photo. *Perf. 11¾*
Granite Paper

1156 A470 70rp Door mark .90 .60
1157 A470 90rp Picture mark 1.10 .75
1158 A470 1.80fr Axe mark 2.10 1.75
Nos. 1156-1158 (3) 4.10 3.10

A471

3.60fr, Johann Gutenberg, inventor of letter-press printing.

Photo. & Engr.

1999, Dec. 6 *Perf. 13½*
1159 A471 3.60fr multicolored 4.50 3.25

Christmas Paintings by Joseph Walser — A472

70rp, The Annunciation. 90rp, Nativity. 1.10fr, Presentation of Jesus.

1999, Dec. 6 *Perf. 13½x14¼*

1160	A472	70rp multicolored	.90	.60
1161	A472	90rp multicolored	1.10	.75
1162	A472	1.10fr multicolored	1.40	.95
		Nos. 1160-1162 (3)	3.40	2.30

Souvenir Sheet

Millennium — A473

Designs: 70rp, The Adoration of the Shepherds, by Matthias Stomer. 1.10fr, The Magi, by Ferdinand Gehr.

2000, Jan. 1 **Photo.** *Perf. 12*
Granite Paper

1163	A473	Sheet of 2	4.00	2.25
a.		70rp multi	1.40	.85
b.		1.10fr multi	2.25	1.40

Christianity, 2000th anniv.

Creation of Liechtenstein Post, Ltd. — A474

2000, Jan. 1 *Perf. 11¾*
Granite Paper
1164 A474 90rp multi 2.00 1.10

Village Views Type of 1996

Designs: 50rp, Church and vicarage, Ruggell. 60rp, Chapel of St. Peter, Balzers. 70rp, Parish church, Schellenberg. 1.10fr, Holy Cross Chapel, Eschen. 1.40fr, Farmhouse, parish church, Mauren. 1.80fr, Chapel of Peace, Malbun. 1.90fr, Tower of Church of St. Lawrence, Schaan. 2.20fr, Höfle District, Balzers. 4.50fr, Church mound, Bendern.

2000-01 **Photo.** *Perf. 11¾*
Granite Paper

1167	A439	50rp multi	.75	.45
1168	A439	60rp multi	.95	.50
1169	A439	70rp multi	1.10	.65
1171	A439	1.10fr multi	1.75	1.10
1172	A439	1.40fr multi	2.10	1.40
1173	A439	1.80fr multi	2.75	1.75
1174	A439	1.90fr multi	2.75	1.75
1175	A439	2.20fr multi	3.50	2.00
1175A	A439	4.50fr multi	7.00	4.25
		Nos. 1167-1175A (9)	22.65	13.85

Issued: 70rp, 1.80fr, 2.20fr, 4.50fr, 6/5/01.

"Gods Once Walked" Exhibition at Vaduz Museum of Art — A475

Designs: 70rp, Mars and Rhea Silvia, by Peter Paul Rubens. 1.80fr, Cupid With Soap Bubble, by Rembrandt.

Photo. & Engr.

2000, Mar. 6 *Perf. 13½x12¾*

1176	A475	70rp multi	1.10	.65
1177	A475	1.80fr multi	2.60	1.75

Europa, 2000
Common Design Type

2000, May 9 **Photo.** *Perf. 11½x11¾*
Granite Paper
1178 CD17 1.10fr multi *2.25 1.75*

Expo 2000, Hanover — A476

Art by Friedensreich Hundertwasser: 70rp, Fragrance of Humus. 90rp, Do Not Wait Houses — Move. 1.10fr, The Car: A Drive Towards Nature and Creation.

Photo. & Engr.

2000, May 9 *Perf. 14¼x13½*

1179	A476	70rp multi	1.40	.80
1180	A476	90rp multi	1.75	1.00
1181	A476	1.10fr multi	2.25	1.25
		Nos. 1179-1181 (3)	5.40	3.05

Images of Peace — A477

Art by mouth and foot painters: 1.40fr, Dove of Peace, by Antonio Martini. 1.70fr, Universal Peace, by Alberto Alvarez. 2.20fr, Rainbow, by Eiichi Minami.

2000, May 9 **Photo.** *Perf. 11¾x11½*

1182	A477	1.40fr multi	2.25	1.25
1183	A477	1.70fr multi	2.60	1.50
1184	A477	2.20fr multi	3.50	2.00
		Nos. 1182-1184 (3)	8.35	4.75

2000 Summer Olympics, Sydney — A478

Designs: 80rp, Koalas on rings. 1fr, High jump by kangaroo joey. 1.30fr, Emus racing. 1.80fr, Platypuses swimming.

2000, Sept. 4 **Photo.** *Perf. 11¾*
Granite Paper

1185	A478	80rp multi	1.10	.65
1186	A478	1fr multi	1.25	.75
1187	A478	1.30fr multi	1.60	1.00
1188	A478	1.80fr multi	2.25	1.40
		Nos. 1185-1188 (4)	6.20	3.80

Organization for Security and Co-operation In Europe, 25th Anniv. — A479

2000, Sept. 4 **Granite Paper**
1189 A479 1.30fr multi 2.50 1.50

Issued in sheets of 20 stamps and 5 labels.

Opening Of Liechtenstein Art Museum — A480

Designs: 80rp, The Dreaming Bee, by Joan Miró. 1.20fr, Cube by Sol LeWitt. 2fr, A Bouquet of Flowers, by Roelant Savery.

2000, Sept. 4 **Photo.** *Perf. 11¾*
Granite Paper (#1190-1191)

1190	A480	80rp multi	1.60	.95
1191	A480	1.20fr multi	2.40	1.40

Size: 31x46mm
Photo. & Engr.
Perf. 13¾

1192	A480	2fr multi	4.00	2.40
		Nos. 1190-1192 (3)	8.00	4.75

Mushrooms — A481

90rp, Mycena adonis. 1.10fr, Chalciporus amarellus. 2fr, Hygrocybe caylptriformis.

Photo. & Engr.

2000, Dec. 4 *Perf. 14¼*
1193-1195 A481 Set of 3 8.00 4.50

Christmas — A482

Various creches: 80rp, 1.30fr, 1.80fr.

2000, Dec. 4 *Perf. 13¾x14*
1196-1198 A482 Set of 3 6.50 4.00

Europa — A483

2001, Mar. 5 **Photo.** *Perf. 11½x11¾*
Granite Paper
1199 A483 1.30fr multi *2.25 1.50*

Liechtenstein's Presidency of Council of Europe — A484

2001, Mar. 5 *Perf. 11¾*
Granite Paper
1200 A484 1.80fr multi 2.90 1.75

Scratch-off Greetings — A485

Postman in: No. 1201, 70rp, Red uniform (hidden flower bouquet). No. 1202, 70rp, Blue uniform (hidden envelope).

2001, Mar. 5 **Granite Paper**

1201-1202 A485	Set of 2 un-scratched	2.50	1.25
	Set, scratched		1.50

Easter Eggs of the Russian Czars — A486

Designs: 1.20fr, Silver egg. 1.80fr, Cloisonné egg. 2fr, Porcelain egg.

Photo. & Engr.

2001, Mar. 5 *Perf. 13¾*
1203-1205 A486 Set of 3 10.00 6.00

Liechtenstein Historical Association, Cent. — A487

Designs: No. 1206, 70rp, Mars of Gutenberg. No. 1207, Carolignian cruciform fibula.

2001, June 5 **Photo.** *Perf. 11¾*
Granite Paper
1206-1207 A487 Set of 2 2.75 1.75

Josef Gabriel Rheinberger (1839-1901), Musician — A488

Photo. & Engr.

2001, Sept. 3 *Perf. 14*
1208 A488 3.50fr multi 5.75 3.50

Votive Pictures — A489

Designs: 70rp, 1733 picture, Chapel of Our Lady, Dux. 1.20fr, 1802 picture, St. George's Chapel, Schellenberg. 1.30fr, 1718 picture, Chapel of Our Lady, Dux.

2001, Sept. 3 *Perf. 13½*
1209-1211 A489 Set of 3 6.50 4.00

Building Preservation — A490

Designs: 70rp, St. Theresa's Chapel, Schaanwald. 90rp, St. Johann's winery, Mauren. 1.10fr, Pirsch transformer station, Schaanwald.

2001, Sept. 3 **Photo.** *Perf. 11¾*
Granite Paper
1212-1214 A490 Set of 3 5.25 3.25

See Nos. 1232-1233, 1251-1252, 1295-1296, 1323-1324, 1361-1362, 1394-1395, 1424.

Traditional Crafts Type of 1998

Designs: 70rp, Blacksmith's tools, horseshoe, yoke bars. 90rp, Rakemaker's tools, rake. 1.20fr, Saddler's tools, horse collar.

2001, Dec. 3 **Photo.** *Perf. 11¾*
Granite Paper
1215-1217 A460 Set of 3 4.50 3.00

Abstract Art by Gottfried Honegger — A491

Untitled works: 1.80fr, 2.20fr.

2001, Dec. 3 *Perf. 11½*
Granite Paper
1218-1219 A491 Set of 2 6.50 4.00

Christmas — A492

Medallions: 70rp, Annunciation. 90rp, Nativity. 1.30fr, The Presentation of the Lord.

2001, Dec. 3 *Perf. 12x11¾*
Granite Paper
1220-1222 A492 Set of 3 4.00 3.50

Liechtenstein Students' Spice Bees Experiment on Space Shuttle — A493

2002, Mar. 4 Photo. ***Perf. 13½x14¼***
1223 A493 90rp multi 1.75 1.10

LIBA.02 Stamp Exhibition, Vaduz — A494

2002, Mar. 4 ***Perf. 13¾***
1224 A494 1.20fr multi 2.10 1.10

Europa — A495

Designs: 90rp, Tightrope walker. 1.30fr, Juggler.

Photo. & Engr.

2002, Mar. 4 ***Perf. 14¼x14***
1225-1226 A495 Set of 2 *4.25 3.75*

Intl. Year of Mountains A496

Intl. Commision for Protection of the Alps A497

2002, Mar. 4 Photo. ***Perf. 13¾x13½***
1227 A496 70rp multi 1.40 .85
1228 A497 1.20fr multi 2.40 1.40

Paintings by Friedrich Kaufmann (1892-1972) A498

Views of: 70rp, Schellenberg. 1.30fr, Schaan. 1.80fr, Steg.

2002, Mar. 4 ***Perf. 13½x13¾***
1229-1231 A498 Set of 3 6.50 4.00

Building Preservation Type of 2001

Designs: 70rp, House, Popers, horiz. 1.20fr, House, Weiherring, horiz.

Perf. 13¾x13½
2002, June 3 Photo.
1232-1233 A490 Set of 2 3.25 2.00

2002 World Cup Soccer Championships, Japan and Korea — A499

2002, June 3 ***Perf. 13½x14¼***
1234 A499 1.80fr multi 3.25 2.00

Royalty — A500

Designs: 3fr, Princess Marie. 3.50fr, Prince Hans Adam II.

2002, June 3 ***Perf. 13¾x13½***
1235-1236 A500 Set of 2 10.00 7.00

Liba.02 Stamp Exhibition, Vaduz — A501

Liechtenstein stamps depicting: 90rp, Various topics. 1.30fr, Royalty.

2002, Aug. 8 Photo. ***Perf. 13½***
1237-1238 A501 Set of 2 3.50 2.50

Royalty Type of 2002

Designs: 2fr, Hereditary Princess Sophie. 2.50fr, Hereditary Prince Alois.

2002, Aug. 8 ***Perf. 13¾x13½***
1239-1240 A500 Set of 2 7.00 4.00

Orchids — A502

Designs: 70rp, Epipogium aphyllum. 1.20fr, Ophrys insectifera. 1.30fr, Nigritella nigra.

2002, Aug. 8 ***Perf. 13½x13¾***
1241-1243 A502 Set of 3 5.25 3.75

See Nos. 1288-1290.

Inn Sign Art — A503

Designs: 1.20fr, Eagle, Vaduz. 1.80fr, Angel, Balzers. 3fr, Eagle, Bendern.

Photo. & Engr.

2002, Nov. 25 ***Perf. 13½x14¼***
1244-1246 A503 Set of 3 10.00 5.25

Christmas — A504

Batik art by Sister Regina Hassler: 70rp, Search for Shelter. 1.20fr, Nativity. 1.80fr, Flight to Egypt.

Perf. 14¼x13½
2002, Nov. 25 Photo.
1247-1249 A504 Set of 3 6.25 4.50

Europa — A505

2003, Mar. 3 Photo. ***Perf. 13½x12¾***
1250 A505 1.20fr multi *2.25 2.00*

Building Preservation Type of 2001

Designs: 70rp, St. Fridolin Church, Ruggell. 2.50fr, House, Spidach, horiz..

Perf. 13½x13¾, 13¾x13½
2003, Mar. 3
1251-1252 A490 Set of 2 5.50 4.25

Viticulture Throughout the Year — A506

Designs: 1.30fr, Pruning (February). 1.80fr, Tying vines to arbor (March). 2.20fr, Hoeing soil (April).

2003 ***Perf. 14¼***
1253-1255 A506 Set of 3 9.00 6.50

Designs: 1.20fr, Looping vines (May). 1.80fr, Leaf work (June). 3.50fr, Removing high growth (July).

1256-1258 A506 Set of 3 11.00 8.25

Designs: 70rp, Thinning out of vines (August). 90rp, Harvesting grapes (September). 1.10fr, Pressing grapes (October).

1259-1261 A506 Set of 3 5.00 3.75

Designs: 70rp, First tasting of wine (November). 90rp, Harvest of frozen grapes (December). 1.20fr, Bottling wine (January).

1262-1264 A506 Set of 3 5.00 3.75

Issued: Nos. 1253-1255, 3/3; Nos. 1256-1258, 6/2; Nos. 1259-1261, 9/1; Nos. 1262-1264, 11/24.

Liechtenstein Association for the Disabled, 50th Anniv. — A507

2003, June 2 Photo. ***Perf. 14¼***
1265 A507 70rp multi 1.40 1.10

Reopening of National Museum — A508

Museum building and: 1.20fr, Ammonite fossil. 1.30fr, Shield of bailiff of Vaduz.

2003, June 2 ***Perf. 14***
1266-1267 A508 Set of 2 5.00 3.75

White Storks and Nest — A509

Photo. & Engr.

2003, Sept. 1 ***Perf. 12¾x13½***
1268 A509 2.20fr multi 3.75 2.75

Saints — A510

Designs: No. 1269, 1.20fr, St. Blasius. No. 1270, 1.20fr, St. George. No. 1271, 1.30fr, St. Erasmus. No. 1272, 1.30fr, St. Vitus.

2003, Sept. 1 ***Perf. 13½***
1269-1272 A510 Set of 4 8.00 6.00

Stamps of the same denomination were printed in sheets of 20 arranged in blocks of 10 of each stamp separated by a horizontal gutter.

See Nos. 1280-1285, 1308-1311.

Children's Drawings — A511

Designs: 70rp, Cow, by Laura Beck. No. 1274, 1.80fr, Apple Tree, by Patrick Marxer, vert. No. 1275, 1.80fr, Bee, by Laura Lingg.

Perf. 13½x14¼, 14¼x13½
2003, Nov. 24 Photo.
1273-1275 A511 Set of 3 7.00 5.00

Christmas — A512

Reverse glass paintings: 70rp, Archangel Gabriel. 90rp, Nativity. 1.30fr, Three Magi.

2003, Nov. 24 ***Perf. 14¼x13½***
1276-1278 A512 Set of 3 5.75 4.25

AHV Old Age and Survivor's Insurance, 50th Anniv. — A513

2004, Jan. 3 Photo. ***Perf. 14***
1279 A513 85rp multi 1.40 1.00

Saints Type of 2003

Designs: No. 1280, 1fr, St. Achatius. No. 1281, 1fr, St. Margareta. No. 1282, 1.20fr, St. Christophorus. No. 1283, 1.20fr, St. Pantaleon. No. 1284, 2.50fr, St. Aegidius. No. 1285, 2.50fr, St. Cyriakus.

Photo. & Engr.

2004, Mar. 1 ***Perf. 13½***
1280-1285 A510 Set of 6 15.00 13.00

Stamps of the same denomination were printed in sheets of 20 arranged in blocks of 10 of each stamp separated by a horizontal gutter.

Europa — A514

2004, Mar. 1 Photo. ***Perf. 13¾x13½***
1286 A514 1.30fr multi *2.50 2.25*

2004 Summer Olympics, Athens — A515

2004, June 1 Photo. ***Perf. 14¼***
1287 A515 85rp multi 1.50 1.25

Orchid Type of 2002

Designs: 85rp, Ophrys apifera. 1fr, Orchis ustulata. 1.20fr, Epipactis purpurata.

2004, June 1 ***Perf. 13½x13¾***
1288-1290 A502 Set of 3 6.00 4.75

Aerial Views — A516

2004, June 1 ***Perf. 13½***
1291 A516 15rp Bendern .30 .25
1292 A516 85rp Gross-Steg 1.50 1.20
1293 A516 1fr Tuass 1.75 1.40
1294 A516 6fr Gutenberg 10.00 7.75
Nos. 1291-1294 (4) 13.55 10.60

See No. 1312, 1331-1333, 1340-1341, 1375-1377.

Building Preservation Type of 2001

Designs: 2.20fr, House on Unterdorfstrasse, horiz. 2.50fr, Row of houses, Dorfstrasse, horiz.

Perf. 13¾x13½
2004, Sept. 6 Photo.
1295-1296 A490 Set of 2 7.50 6.00

Sciences — A517

Designs: 85rp, Mathematics. 1fr, Physics. 1.30fr, Chemistry. 1.80fr, Astronomy.

2004, Sept. 6 *Perf. 13¾x14*
1297-1300 A517 Set of 4 7.50 6.00

Digital Palimpsest Research — A518

Photo. & Engr.

2004, Nov. 22 *Perf. 14¼*
1301 A518 2.50fr multi 4.25 3.50

Fossils — A519

Designs: 1.20fr, Ammonite. 1.30fr, Sea urchin. 2.20fr, Shark tooth.

2004, Nov. 22
1302-1304 A519 Set of 3 7.50 6.50

Christmas — A520

Designs: 85rp, Annunciation. 1fr, Holy Family. 1.80fr, Adoration of the Magi.

2004, Nov. 22 Photo. ***Rouletted 6¾***
1305-1307 A520 Set of 3 6.00 5.00

Punched holes are in stamp frames to give stamps a lace-like appearance.

Saints Type of 2003

Designs: No. 1308, 85rp, St. Eustachius. No. 1309, 85rp, St. Dionysius. No. 1310, 1.80fr, St. Catharine. No. 1311, 1.80fr, St. Barbara.

Photo. & Engr.

2005, Mar. 7 *Perf. 13½*
1308-1311 A510 Set of 4 9.00 7.50

Aerial Views Type of 2004

2005, Mar. 7 **Photo.**
1312 A516 3.60fr Triesenberg 5.50 4.50

Europa — A521

2005, Mar. 7
1313 A521 1.30fr multi *2.10 1.90*

Venus at a Mirror, by Peter Paul Rubens — A522

2005, Mar. 7 **Photo. & Engr.**
1314 A522 2.20fr multi 4.50 4.00

See Austria No. 1980.

Paintings of Flower Arrangements — A523

Designs: No. 1315, 85rp, Magnolia Flowers, by Chen Hongshou (shown). No. 1316, 85rp, Flower Vase in a Windoe Niche, by Ambrosius Bosschaert the Elder.

2005, May 18 **Photo.** *Perf. 14*
1315-1316 A523 Set of 2 3.50 3.00

See People's Republic of China Nos. 3433-3434.

Inn Signs — A524

Designs: 1fr, Stallion, Rössle Inn, Schaan. 1.40fr, Edelweiss Inn, Triesenberg. 2.50fr, Lion, Löwen Inn, Bendern.

Photo. & Engr.

2005, June 6 *Perf. 14¼x13½*
1317-1319 A524 Set of 3 7.50 6.25

Postal Museum, 75th Anniv. — A525

Designs: 1.10fr, Hermann E. Sieger, museum founder. 1.30fr, Liechtenstein stamps on stock page. 1.80fr, 1930 Zeppelin cover.

Perf. 13½x14¼

2005, June 6 **Photo.**
1320-1322 A525 Set of 3 6.50 5.25

Building Preservation Type of 2001

Designs: 85rp, Oberbendern. 2.20fr, Church Hill, Bendern.

Perf. 13¾x13½

2005, Sept. 5 **Photo.**
1323-1324 A490 Set of 2 5.00 4.00

Bats — A526

Designs: 1.80fr, Plecotus auritus. 2fr, Myotis myotis.

2005, Sept. 5 *Perf. 14¼*
1325-1326 A526 Set of 2 6.00 5.00

Pastures — A527

Designs: 85rp, Bargälla. 1fr, Pradamee. 1.30fr, Gritsch. 1.80fr, Valüna.

2005, Sept. 5 *Perf. 13½x14¼*
1327-1330 A527 Set of 4 7.50 6.00

See nos. 1356-1358, 1384-1386, 1403-1404.

Aerial Views Type of 2004

2005, Nov. 21 **Photo.** *Perf. 13½*
1331 A516 1.50fr Oberland 2.25 1.75
1332 A516 1.60fr Ruggeller Riet 2.50 1.90
1333 A516 3fr Naafkopf 4.50 3.50
Nos. 1331-1333 (3) 9.25 7.15

2006 Winter Olympics, Turin, Italy — A528

Designs: 1.20fr, Ski jumping. 1.30fr, Biathlon. 1.40fr, Slalom skiing.

2005, Nov. 21 *Perf. 14¼x14*
1334-1336 A528 Set of 3 7.00 5.50

Christmas — A529

Wood sculptures by Toni Gstöhl: 85rp, The Annunciation. 1fr, Holy Family. 1.30fr, Adoration of the Shepherds.

Photo. & Engr.

2005, Nov. 21 *Perf. 14¼x13½*
1337-1339 A529 Set of 3 5.00 4.00

Aerial Views Type of 2004

2006, Mar. 6 **Photo.** *Perf. 13½*
1340 A516 2.50fr Rhine Canal 3.75 3.00
1341 A516 3.50fr Rhine Valley 5.25 4.75

Lost in Her Dreams, by Friedrich von Amerling — A530

2006, Mar. 6 **Photo. & Engr.**
1342 A530 2.20fr multi 3.50 2.75

See Austria No. 2041.

Paintings by Eugen Wilhelm Schüepp (1915-74) — A531

Designs: 1fr, Peat Cutters, Ruggell Marsh. 1.80fr, Neugut, Schaan.

2006, Mar. 6 **Photo.** *Perf. 13½x14¼*
1343-1344 A531 Set of 2 4.50 3.75

Europa — A532

Winning designs from stamp design contest: 1.20fr, Bridge, by Nadja Beck. 1.30fr, Face of Integration, by Elisabeth Müssner.

2006, Mar. 6
1345-1346 A532 Set of 2 *5.00 4.00*

2006 World Cup Soccer Championships, Germany — A533

Perf. 13½x14¼

2006, June 6 **Photo.**
1347 A533 3.30fr multi 5.00 5.00

Tourism Promotion — A534

Designs: 85rp, Woman holding G clef. 1fr, Backpacker. 1.20fr, Restaurant patron. 1.80fr, Skier.

2006, June 6 *Perf. 13¾*
1348-1351 A534 Set of 4 8.50 7.00

Prince Johann I — A535

National Flag — A535a

Flag of the Princely House of Liechtenstein — A535b

National Arms — A535c

2006, June 6 **Litho. & Engr.**
1352 A535 85rp multi 1.70 1.30
1353 A535a 1fr gold & multi 1.85 1.50
1354 A535b 1.30fr gold & multi 2.05 1.70
1355 A535c 1.80fr multi 2.90 2.50
Nos. 1352-1355 (4) 8.50 7.00

Full Sovereignty, Bicent.

Pastures Type of 2005

Designs: 85rp, Lawena. 1.30fr, Gapfahl. 2.40fr, Gafadura.

Perf. 13½x14¼

2006, Sept. 4 **Photo.**
1356-1358 A527 Set of 3 7.50 6.00

Wolfgang Amadeus Mozart (1756-91), Composer — A536

2006, Sept. 4 *Perf. 13¾x14¼*
1359 A536 1.20fr multi 2.50 2.00

Miniature Sheet

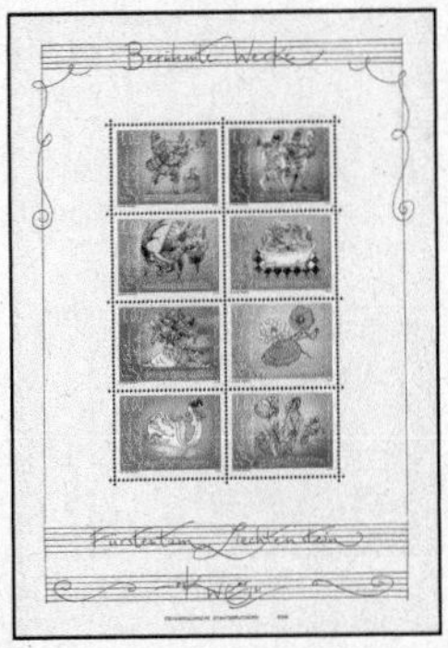

Classical Music A537

No. 1360: a, The Magic Flute, by Wolfgang Amadeus Mozart. b, Radetzky March, by Johann Strauss. c, Rhapsody in Blue, by George Gershwin. d, Water Music, by George Frideric Handel. e, Pastoral Symphony, by Ludwig van Beethoven. f, Waltz of the Flowers, by Peter Ilich Tchaikovsky. g, The Swan, by Camille Saint-Saens. h, A Midsummer Night's Dream, by Felix Mendelssohn.

2006, Sept. 4 *Perf. 13½x14¼*
1360 A537 Sheet of 8 14.00 14.00
a.-h. 1fr Any single 1.75 1.50

Building Preservation Type of 2001

Designs: 1.80fr, Governor's residence and Liechtenstein Institute, Bendern. 3.50fr, Bühl House, Gamprin, horiz.

Perf. 13½x13¾, 13¾x13½

2006, Nov. 20 **Photo.**
1361-1362 A490 Set of 2 8.00 6.50

Inventions — A538

Designs: 1.30fr, Curta calculator. 1.40fr, Carena film camera. 2.40fr, PAV sliding caliper.

2006, Nov. 20 *Perf. 14¼x14*
1363-1365 A538 Set of 3 8.00 6.50

Christmas — A539

Frescos from Chapel of St. Mary, Dux: 85rp, The Annunciation. 1fr, Nativity. 1.30fr, Presentation at the Temple.

Photo. & Engr.

2006, Nov. 20 *Perf. 13½*
1366-1368 A539 Set of 3 6.25 5.00

Scouting, Cent. — A540

2007, Mar. 5 **Photo.** *Perf. 14¼*
1369 A540 1.30fr multi 2.00 1.75

Portrait of a Lady, by Bernardino Zaganelli da Cotignola — A541

Litho. & Engr.

2007, Mar. 5 *Perf. 13¾*
1370 A541 2.40fr multi 4.00 3.50

See Austria No. 2086.

Musical Terms — A542

Designs: 85rp, Allegro. 1.80fr, Capriccio. 2fr, Crescendo. 3.50fr, Con fuoco.

2007, Mar. 5 **Photo.** *Perf. 13½*
1371-1374 A542 Set of 4 14.00 12.00

Aerial Views Type of 2004

2007, June 4 **Photo.** *Perf. 13½*
1375 A516 1.10fr Nendeln 1.75 1.40
1376 A516 1.80fr Malbun 2.75 2.10
1377 A516 2.60fr Ackerland 4.00 3.00
Nos. 1375-1377 (3) 8.50 6.50

Greeting Card Art — A543

Designs: 85rp, Boy delivering flower and letter to girl. 1fr, Two children carrying litter with cake, flowers and letter. 1.30fr, Bird carrying letter.

2007, June 4 *Rouletted 6¾*
1378-1380 A543 Set of 3 6.00 6.00

Punched holes are in stamp frames to give stamps a lacelike appearance.

Paintings of Rhine Landscapes by Johann Ludwig Bleuler (1792-1850) A544

Designs: 1fr, Castle and Village of Vaduz. 1.30fr, Rätikon Mountain. 2.40fr, Confluence of the Ill and Rhine.

Perf. 13½x14¼

2007, June 4 **Photo. & Engr**
1381-1383 A544 Set of 3 7.00 7.00

Pastures Type of 2005

Designs: 1fr, Hintervalorsch. 1.40fr, Sücka. 2.20fr, Guschgfiel.

Perf. 13½x14¼

2007, Sept. 3 **Photo.**
1384-1386 A527 Set of 3 7.00 7.00

Technical Innovations From Liechtenstein — A545

Designs: 1.30fr, Hilti hammer and drill. 1.80fr, Kaiser mobile walking excavator. 2.40fr, Hoval AluFer composite heating tube.

2007, Sept. 3 *Perf. 14¼*
1387-1389 A545 Set of 3 8.00 6.00

See Nos. 1425-1427.

Beetles — A546

Designs: 85rp, Trichodes apiarius. 100rp, Cetania aurata. 130rp, Dytiscus marginalis.

2007, Sept. 3 **Litho.** *Perf. 13¾x14*
1390-1392 A546 Set of 3 5.75 4.00

Panoramic View of Liechtenstein — A547

2007, Oct. 1 **Litho.** *Perf. 14*
1393 A547 130rp multi 2.50 2.00

Building Preservation Type of 2001

Designs: 2fr, St. Martin's Church, Eschen. 2.70fr, Mill, Eschen, horiz.

Perf. 13½x13¾, 13¾x13½

2007, Nov. 19 **Photo.**
1394-1395 A490 Set of 2 7.00 5.00

New Parliament Building — A548

2007, Nov. 19 *Perf. 13¾*
1396 A548 130rp multi 2.00 1.50

Natural Phenomena — A549

Designs: 85rp, Rainbow above Three Sisters Massif. 100rp, Lightning over Bendern. 180rp, Ice crystal halo around Moon over Malbun.

2007, Nov. 19 **Litho.** *Perf. 14¼*
1397-1399 A549 Set of 3 5.00 4.00

Christmas — A550

Designs: 85rp, Chapel of St. Mary, Gamprin-Oberbühl. 1fr, Büel Chapel, Eschen. 1.30fr, Chapel of St. Wolfgang, Triesen.

Perf. 13½x14¼

2007, Nov. 19 **Photo.**
1400-1402 A550 Set of 3 5.25 4.00

Pastures Type of 2005

Designs: 2.60fr, Guschg. 3fr, Güschgle.

2008, Mar. 3 **Photo.** *Perf. 13½x14¼*
1403-1404 A527 Set of 2 9.50 7.50

Europa — A551

2008, Mar. 3 **Litho.** *Perf. 13½x13¾*
1405 A551 130rp multi 2.00 1.50

Volunteer Fire Fighters — A552

2008, Mar. 3 *Perf. 13½*
1406 A552 1fr multi 2.00 1.50

Sleeping Princess Marie Franziska, by Friedrich von Amerling — A553

2008, Mar. 3 **Photo. & Engr.**
1407 A553 2.40fr multi 4.00 3.50

See Austria No. 2144.

Spoerry-Areal, Vaduz — A554

Chapel of St. Mamertus, Triesen — A555

Vaduz Castle — A556

2008, Mar. 3 **Litho.** *Perf. 14*
1408 A554 85rp multi 1.50 1.10
1409 A555 1fr multi 1.75 1.25
1410 A556 1.30fr multi 2.25 1.60
Nos. 1408-1410 (3) 5.50 3.95

Mother and Queen of the Precious Blood with Child, by Unknown Artist — A557

2008, June 2 **Litho.** *Perf. 12¾x13½*
1411 A557 220rp multi 4.25 3.50

Schellenberg Convent, 150th anniv.

2008 Summer Olympics, Beijing — A558

Mascots involved in: 85rp, Martial arts. 100rp, Soccer.

2008, June 2 *Perf. 14¼x13½*
1412-1413 A558 Set of 2 3.50 2.75

2008 Paralympics, Beijing — A559

Designs: 130rp, Marathon. 180rp, Table tennis.

2008, June 2 *Perf. 13½x14¼*
1414-1415 A559 Set of 2 5.00 4.00

2008 European Soccer Championships, Austria and Switzerland — A560

Designs: No. 1416, 130rp, St. Stephen's Cathedral, Vienna, soccer player waltzing, violinist. No. 1417, 130rp, Soccer fans holding Liechtenstein flag, wearing Swiss hat, and

Austrian scarf. No. 1418, 130rp, Alphorn player, Matterhorn, soccer player.

2008, June 2 ***Perf. 14***
1416-1418 A560 Set of 3 7.50 6.50

Nos. 1416-1418 printed in sheets containing 4 No. 1417 and 6 each Nos. 1416 and 1418.

Hymenopterans A561

Designs: 85rp, Osmia brevicornis. 1fr, Epeoloides coecutiens. 1.30fr, Odynerus spinipes.

2008, June 2 ***Perf. 14¼***
1419-1421 A561 Set of 3 6.00 5.00

Souvenir Sheet

Prince Karl I (1569-1627) — A562

Photo. & Engr.

2008, Sept. 1 ***Perf. 13¾x13½***
1422 A562 5fr multi 9.00 9.00

Princely house of Liechtenstein, 400th anniv.

Miniature Sheet

Drawings by Wilhelm Busch (1832-1908) — A563

No. 1423: a, Schoolmaster Lampel. b, Hans Huckebein. c, Max and Moritz. d, Widow Bolte. e, Pious Helene. f, Fipps the Monkey. g, Tailor Böck. h, Balduin Bählamm.

2008, Sept. 1 Photo. ***Perf. 14x13¾***
1423 A563 Sheet of 8 20.00 20.00
a.-h. 1.30fr Any single 2.50 2.00

Building Preservation Type of 2001

Design: Schädler Ceramics Building, Nendeln, horiz.

Perf. 13¾x13½

2008, Nov. 17 **Photo.**
1424 A490 3.80fr multi 7.50 6.50

Technical Innovations Type of 2007

Designs: 1.20fr, Neutrik NC3MX audio cable connectors. 1.40fr, Ivoclar Vivadent bluephase polymerization unit. 2.20fr, Presta DeltaValveControl variable valve-lift system.

2008, Nov. 17 ***Perf. 14¼***
1425-1427 A545 Set of 3 7.50 6.50

Christmas — A564

Designs: 85rp, Candles, flowers and evergreen branches. 100rp, Children carrying holly, horiz. 130rp, Christmas tree and gifts.

Perf. 14¼x14½, 14½x14¼

2008, Nov. 17 **Litho.**
1428-1430 A564 Set of 3 6.00 5.00

Civil Protection Volunteers A565

2009, Mar. 2 Litho. ***Perf. 13¾x13½***
1431 A565 1fr multi 1.75 1.40

See Nos. 1471-1472, 1566-1567.

Europa — A566

Litho. With Hologram Affixed

2009, Mar. 2 ***Perf. 14¼***
1432 A566 1.30fr multi 2.50 2.00

Land Registry, 200th Anniv. — A567

2009, Mar. 2 **Litho.** ***Perf. 13¾***
1433 A567 330rp multi 6.25 5.00

Liechtenstein Post AG, 10th Anniv. — A568

Designs: 85rp, Counter clerk handling package. 100rp, Mail deliverer. 130rp, Mail sorter.

2009, Mar. 2 ***Perf. 13¾x13½***
1434-1436 A568 Set of 3 6.00 5.00

Linoleum Prints by Stephan Sude — A569

Designs: 1fr, Unfolding. 1.30fr, Awareness. 2.70fr, Fulfillment.

2009, Mar. 2 ***Perf. 14x13¼***
1437-1439 A569 Set of 3 9.50 7.50

Alpine Association, Cent. — A570

Crosses on summits of: 100rp, Kuegrat. 130rp, Langspitz, vert. 220rp, Rappastein, vert. 240rp, Jahn-Turm and Wolan.

Perf. 13¾x13½, 13½x13¾

2009, June 8 **Litho.**
1440-1443 A570 Set of 4 12.00 8.00

Forests — A571

Designs: 85rp, Ants in forest. 1fr, Path in forest. 1.40fr, Boulder against tree on hillside. 1.60fr, Cut timber.

2009, June 8 ***Perf. 13½***
1444-1447 A571 Set of 4 9.00 7.00

Vaduz Castle — A572

Castle in: 130rp, Spring. 180rp, Summer.

2009, June 8 **Photo.** ***Perf. 13¾***
1448-1449 A572 Set of 2 5.50 4.50

See Nos. 1488-1489.

Liechtenstein Philatelic Society, 75th Anniv. — A573

2009, Sept. 7 **Litho.** ***Perf. 13x13¼***
1450 A573 130rp multi 2.25 1.50

Holes are drilled along the map border.

Badminton Cabinet Ornamentation A574

Panels with bird and flower designs: 1.30fr, Bird with blue head. 2fr, Three birds, vert. (35x50mm). 4fr, Bird with red head.

Perf. 14, 13¾ (2fr)

2009, Sept. 7 **Photo. & Engr.**
1451-1453 A574 Set of 3 12.50 9.00

Butterflies — A575

Designs: 85rp, Pieris rapae. 100rp, Parnassius apollo. 130rp, Melanargia galathea. 200rp, Vanessa atalanta.

2009, Sept. 7 **Litho.** ***Perf. 12x12½***
Self-Adhesive
1454-1457 A575 Set of 4 9.00 7.00

See Nos. 1480-1482, 1515-1516.

Chapel of St. Mamerta, Triesen — A576

2009, Sept. 16 ***Perf. 14***
1458 A576 130rp multi 2.25 1.50

Contemporary Architecture A577

Designs: 85rp, University of Applied Sciences, Vaduz. 260rp, Art Museum, Vaduz. 350rp, Border crossing, Rugell.

Perf. 13½x13¾

2009, Nov. 16 **Litho.**
1459-1461 A577 Set of 3 12.50 9.00

See Nos. 1473-1474.

Lifestyle Museum, Schellenberg A578

Former Customs House, Vaduz A579

Parish House, Bendern — A580

2009, Nov. 16 ***Perf. 12¼***
Self-Adhesive

1462 A578 20rp multi .35 .25
1463 A579 50rp multi .85 .65
1464 A580 60rp multi 1.10 .75
Nos. 1462-1464 (3) 2.30 1.65

Christmas — A581

Advent windows by children: 85rp, Annunciation. 100rp, Journey to Bethlehem. 130rp, Nativity. 180rp, Magi and Star of Bethlehem.

2009, Nov. 16 ***Perf. 13½x13¾***
1465-1468 A581 Set of 4 8.00 6.00

2010 Winter Olympics, Vancouver — A582

Designs: 1fr, Downhill skier. 1.80fr, Cross-country skier, horiz.

2010, Feb. 12 **Litho.** ***Perf. 13¾***
1469-1470 A582 Set of 2 4.50 3.50

Civil Protection Volunteers Type of 2009

Designs: 85rp, Mountain rescuers. 1.30fr, Water rescuers.

2010, Mar. 1 ***Perf. 13¾x13½***
1471-1472 A565 Set of 2 3.50 2.75

Contemporary Architecture Type of 2009

Designs: 260rp, Natural gas filling station, Vaduz. 360rp, Liechtenstein Electric Power Authority transformer station, Schaan.

2010, Mar. 1 ***Perf. 13½x13¾***
1473-1474 A577 Set of 2 9.50 7.00

Agriculture — A583

Designs: 85rp, Fields. 1fr, Flowers, hillside farmers. 1.10fr, Combine in field. 1.30fr, Cattle.

2010, Mar. 1 **Photo.** ***Perf. 13½x13¼***
1475-1478 A583 Set of 4 7.00 5.00

Souvenir Sheet

Expo 2010, Shanghai — A584

No. 1479: a, Atmospheric View of Vaduz, by Johann Jakob Schmidt (40x36mm). b, Tidal Bore on the Qiantang River, by Xu Gu (32x60mm).

Photo. & Engr.

2010, May 1 *Perf. 14*
1479 A584 Sheet of 2 6.50 6.50
a. 1.60fr multi 3.00 3.00
b. 1.90fr multi 3.50 3.50
c. As #1479, imperf. 6.50 6.50
d. As "a," imperf. 3.00 3.00
e. As "b," imperf. 3.50 3.50

Butterflies Type of 2009

Designs: 140rp, Coenonympha oedippus. 160rp, Gonepteryx rhamni. 260rp, Papilio machaon.

2010, June 7 Litho. *Perf. 12x12½*
Self-Adhesive
1480-1482 A575 Set of 3 9.75 8.00

Liechtenstein Disability Insurance, 50th Anniv. — A585

2010, June 7 *Perf. 14x13¼*
1483 A585 1fr multi 1.75 1.40

European Free Trade Association, 50th Anniv. — A586

2010, June 7 *Perf. 12x12½*
1484 A586 140rp multi 2.50 2.00

Interpol Vaduz, 50th Anniv. — A587

2010, June 7 *Perf. 12¼*
1485 A587 1.90fr multi 3.50 2.75

Ceiling Frescoes in Liechtenstein Museum, Vienna — A588

Frescoes by Johann Michael Rottmayr: 1fr, Ariadne Giving Theseus the Thread. 1.40fr, Surrender of the Golden Fleece to Jason.

Photo. & Engr.

2010, June 7 *Perf. 14*
1486-1487 A588 Set of 2 4.25 3.50

Values are for stamps with surrounding selvage.

Vaduz Castle Type of 2009

Castle in: 140rp, Autumn, vert. 190rp, Winter, vert.

2010, Sept. 6 Photo. *Perf. 13¾*
1488-1489 A572 Set of 2 6.50 5.00

Europa — A589

2010, Sept. 6 Litho. *Perf. 14*
1490 A589 140rp multi 2.75 2.25

Renewable Energy — A590

Designs: 100rp, Water. 140rp, Wood. 280rp, Geothermal.

Litho. & Photo.

2010, Sept. 6 *Perf. 14x13¾*
1491-1493 A590 Set of 3 10.50 8.00

Parts of the designs of Nos. 1491-1493 were printed with thermochromic ink that changes color when warmed. See Nos. 1509-1511.

Rhine Valley Landscape — A591

No. 1494: a, Eschnerberg and Dreischwestern Mountains, cart path, denomination at LL. b, Alvier Mountains, denomination at LR.

2010, Sept. 6 Litho. *Perf. 14x13¼*
1494 Horiz. pair 4.00 4.00
a.-b. A591 1fr Either single 2.00 1.75

Schaan-Vaduz Railroad Station — A592

Red House, Vaduz — A593

St. Joseph Church, Triesenberg — A594

2010, Nov. 15 Litho. *Perf. 12¼*
Self-Adhesive
1495 A592 1.10fr multi 1.90 1.50
1496 A593 1.80fr multi 3.25 2.50
1497 A594 1.90fr multi 3.50 2.75
Nos. 1495-1497 (3) 8.65 6.75

Works From Liechtenstein Museum of Art — A595

Designs: 100rp, Normale e Anormale, embroidery by Alighiero Boetti. 220rp, Testa, sculpture by Marisa Merz. 360rp, Untitled sculpture by Jannis Kounellis.

2010, Nov. 15 *Perf. 13¾x13½*
1498-1500 A595 Set of 3 12.00 9.00

Christmas — A596

Ceiling frescoes from Maria-Hilf Chapel, Mäls: 85rp, Annunciation. 1fr, Visitation of Mary. 1.40fr, Presentation of Jesus in the Temple.

2010, Nov. 15 Photo. *Perf. 14*
1501-1503 A596 Set of 3 6.25 5.00

National Library, 50th Anniv — A597

Litho. With Foil Application

2011, Mar. 14 *Perf. 12½x12*
Self-Adhesive
1504 A597 1fr black & gold 2.25 2.25

Liechtensteinische Landesbank, 150th Anniv. — A598

2011, Mar. 14 Litho. *Perf. 12¼*
Self-Adhesive
1505 A598 1fr multi 2.25 2.25

2011 Games of the Small States, Liechtenstein A599

Designs: 85rp, Track, volleyball, cycling. 1fr, Judo, shooting, squash. 1.40fr, Table tennis, tennis, swimming.

2011, Mar. 14 Litho. *Perf. 13½*
1506-1508 A599 Set of 3 6.25 4.50

Renewable Energy Type of 2010

Designs: 100rp, Photovoltaics. 110rp, Solar energy. 290rp, Wind energy.

Litho. & Photo.

2011, Mar. 14 *Perf. 14x13¾*
1509-1511 A590 Set of 3 9.50 7.50

Parts of the designs of Nos. 1509-1511 were printed with thermochromic ink that changes color when warmed.

Decorative Eggs Collected by Adulf Peter Goop — A600

Designs: 1fr, Moscow Workshop Easter egg. 1.40fr, Apple Blossom Egg, by Karl Fabergé, horiz. (47x33mm). 2.60fr, Easter egg, by Pavel Akimovich Ovchinnikov.

Litho. & Engr.

2011, Mar. 14 *Perf. 13¾*
1512-1514 A600 Set of 3 9.50 7.50

Butterflies Type of 2009

Designs: 220rp, Inachis io. 500rp, Anthocharis cardamines.

2011, June 6 Litho. *Perf. 12x12½*
Self-Adhesive
1515-1516 A575 Set of 2 15.00 15.00

For surcharges, see Nos. 1556, 1856.

Europa — A601

2011, June 6 *Perf. 12½x12*
1517 A601 1.40fr multi 3.00 2.50

Intl. Year of Forests.

Children of Hereditary Prince Alois and Duchess Sophie — A602

Designs: 1fr, Prince Nikolaus. 1.80fr, Prince Georg. 2fr, Princess Marie Caroline. 2.60fr, Prince Joseph Wenzel.

Photo. & Engr.

2011, June 6 *Perf. 13½*
1518-1521 A602 Set of 4 15.00 12.00
1521a Souvenir sheet of 4, #1518-1521 15.00 15.00

Fruit, by Shirana Shahbazi — A603

2011, Sept. 9 Litho. *Perf. 13¼x13½*
1522 A603 100rp multi 2.00 1.50

See Switzerland No. 1423.

Photographs of Liechtenstein by Xiao Hui Wang — A604

Designs: 1.30fr, Alpine Rhine. 3.70fr, Water Reflections.

2011, Sept. 9 *Perf. 13¼x14*
1523-1524 A604 Set of 2 9.50 7.50

Miniature Sheet

Worldwide Fund for Nature (WWF), 50th Anniv. — A605

No. 1525 — Endangered birds in Liechtenstein: a, Falco subbuteo. b, Glaucidium passerinum. c, Oriolus oriolus. d, Jynx torquilla. e, Luscinia megarhynchos. f, Phoenicurus phoenicurus. g, Lanius collurio. h, Saxicola rubetra.

2011, Sept. 9 *Perf. 12½*
Self-Adhesive
1525 A605 Sheet of 8 16.00 16.00
a.-h. 100rp Any single 2.00 2.00

Ruggell Marsh A606

2011, Sept. 28 *Perf. 14*
1526 A606 140rp multi 2.75 2.25

Castles — A607

Designs: 100rp, Gutenberg Castle. 140rp, Schellenberg Castle. 200rp, Schalun Castle. 260rp, Vaduz Castle.

Photo. & Engr.
2011, Nov. 14 *Perf. 13½x14¼*
1527-1530 A607 Set of 4 13.00 10.00

Christmas — A608

Creche figures from: 85rp, St. Gallus Church, Triesen. 100rp, St. Florin Church, Vaduz (38x32mm). 140rp, Church of the Assumption, Bendern (32x38mm).

Perf. 12¼, 12x12½ (100rp), 12½x12 (140rp)
2011, Nov. 14 **Litho.**
Self-Adhesive
1531-1533 A608 Set of 3 6.00 4.50

New Year 2012 (Year of the Dragon) A609

Litho. With Foil Application
2011, Nov. 14 *Perf. 12½*
Self-Adhesive
1534 A609 190rp red & gold 4.25 4.25

The dragon vignette was laser cut. Printed in sheets of 4.

Liechtenstein Postage Stamps, Cent. — A610

Princes of Liechtenstein: 1fr, Johann II. 1.40fr, Franz I. 2.20fr, Franz Josef II. 2.80fr, Hans Adam II.

2012, Feb. 1 **Litho.** *Perf. 13½x13¾*
1535-1538 A610 Set of 4 14.00 11.00
1538a Souvenir sheet of 4, #1535-1538, imperf. 14.00 14.00

A booklet containing four panes each containing eight examples of each stamp, No. 1538a, a designer-signed and numbered example of No. 1538a in changed colors, examples of Nos. 1535-1538 and their imperforates with first day cancels, and reproductions of Nos. 1-3 was printed in limited quantities and sold for 100fr.

Cattle Moving Past Parliament Building — A611

2012, Mar. 5 *Perf. 13¾*
1539 A611 140rp multi 2.75 2.25

Europa.

Liechtenstein Parilament and Constitution, 150th Anniv. — A612

Designs: 1fr, Reverse of 1862 Vereinsthaler, excerpt from first page of Constitutional Charter. 1.40fr, Obverse of 1862 Vereinsthaler, letter authorizing the opening of Parliament.

Litho. & Embossed
2012, Mar. 5 *Perf. 13½x13¾*
1540-1541 A612 Set of 2 4.50 3.50

Pfälzer Hutte Mountain Lodge — A613

2012, June 14 **Litho.** *Perf. 13¾*
1542 A613 140rp multi 3.00 3.00

See Germany No. 2677.

2012 Summer Olympics, London — A614

Designs: 100rp, Swimming. 140rp, Tennis.

2012, June 14 *Perf. 13¼*
1543-1544 A614 Set of 2 4.50 3.50

Flowers — A615

Designs: 85rp, Dahlie (dahlia). 140pr, Pfingstrose (peony). 500rp, Zinnie (zinnia).

2012, June 14 *Perf. 12½x12*
Self-Adhesive
1545-1547 A615 Set of 3 15.00 15.00

See Nos. 1573-1575, 1643-1645.

Mountain Valleys A616

No. 1548: a, Lawenatal Valley (denomination at LL). b, Valünatal Valley (denomination at LR).

2012, June 14 *Perf. 14x13¼*
1548 Horiz. pair 4.25 4.25
a.-b. A616 1fr Either single 2.10 2.10

Souvenir Sheet

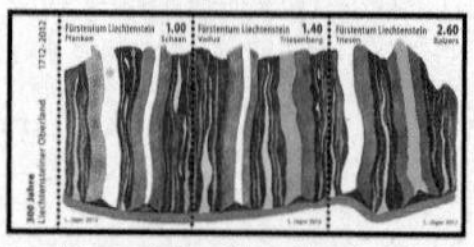
Liechtenstein Oberland, 300th Anniv. — A617

No. 1549 — Stylized flags of: a, Planken and Schaan. b, Vaduz and Tresenberg. c, Triesen and Balzers.

Perf. 14 Vert. on 1 or 2 Sides
2012, June 14
1549 A617 Sheet of 3 9.50 9.50
a. 1fr multi 1.75 1.75
b. 1.40fr multi 2.50 2.50
c. 2.60fr multi 4.50 4.50

Souvenir Sheet

Winning Art in Stamp Design Contest A618

No. 1550 — Art by: a, N. Schwarz. b, R. Graf. c, G. Rodrigues-Margreiter.

2012, Aug. 16 *Perf. 13¾x13½*
1550 A618 Sheet of 3 13.00 13.00
a. 100rp multi 2.25 2.25
b. 140rp multi 3.00 3.00
c. 360rp multi 7.75 7.75

LIBA 2012 Stamp Exhibition, Schaan.

Antique Automobiles A619

Designs: 85rp, 1908 Brasier. 100rp, 1911 Stanley Steamer. 140rp, 1915 Ford Model T Speedster. 190rp, 1920 Hinstin.

Litho. with Foil Application
2012, Sept. 3
1551-1554 A619 Set of 4 11.00 11.00

Miniature Sheet

Characters From Literature — A620

No. 1555: a, Till Eulenspiegel. b, Sherlock Holmes. c, Don Quixote. d, Hamlet. e, Robin Hood. f, Robinson Crusoe. g, Baron Münchhausen. h, Quasimodo.

2012, Sept. 3 **Litho.** *Perf. 13¾*
1555 A620 Sheet of 8 18.00 18.00
a.-h. 1fr Any single 2.25 2.25

No. 1516 Surcharged in Purple

Self-Adhesive
2012, Oct. 4 *Perf. 12x12½*
1556 A575 600rp on 500rp #1516 13.00 13.00

Reliefs by Massimiliano Soldani-Benzi (1656-1740) — A621

Designs: 1fr, Christ's Descent from the Cross. 1.40fr, Christ on the Mount of Olives.

Litho. & Engr.
2012, Nov. 12 *Perf. 13¾x14*
1557-1558 A621 Set of 2 5.25 5.25

Art by Hanna Roeckle — A622

Designs: 100rp, Crystal B. 140rp, Crystal G.

2012, Nov. 12 **Litho.** *Perf. 13¾*
1559-1560 A622 Set of 2 5.25 5.25

Christmas — A623

Archangels: 85rp, Raphael. 100rp, Michael. 140rp, Gabriel. 190rp, Uriel.

Self-Adhesive
Litho. With Foil Application
2012, Nov. 12 *Perf. 12¼x12½*
1561-1564 A623 Set of 4 11.00 11.00

New Year 2013 (Year of the Snake) — A624

Self-Adhesive
Litho. With Foil Application
2012, Nov. 12 *Perf. 12½*
1565 A624 190rp red & gold 4.25 4.25

The snake vignette was laser cut. Printed in sheets of 4.

Civil Protection Volunteers Type of 2009

Designs: 1fr, Avalanche rescue squad. 1.40fr, Civil protection and emergency management workers.

2013, Mar. 4 **Litho.** *Perf. 13¾x13½*
1566-1567 A565 Set of 2 5.25 5.25

Europa — A625

2013, Mar. 4 *Perf. 14¼x14½*
1568 A625 1.40fr multi 3.00 3.00

Mathematics and Nature — A626

Various leaves and: 100rp, Fibonacci sequence. 260rp, Sum of adjacent Fibonacci numbers. 400rp, Golden ratio.

Litho. With Foil Application
2013, Mar. 4 *Perf. 13¼x13½*
1569-1571 A626 Set of 3 16.50 16.50

Switzerland-Liechtenstein Customs Treaty, 90th Anniv. — A627

No. 1572: a, Rhine Valley, Gonzen, Swiss flag, denomination at UL. b, Liechtenstein Valley, Ellhorn and Liechtenstein flag, denomination at UR.

2013, Mar. 4 Litho. *Perf. 13¼*

1572 Horiz. pair 8.75 8.75
a.-b. A627 2fr Either single 4.25 4.25

Flowers Type of 2012

Designs: 100rp, Gentiana rhaetica. 190rp, Myosotis alpestris. 400rp, Rhododendrum hirsutum.

2013, June 3 *Perf. 12½x12*
Self-Adhesive

1573-1575 A615 Set of 3 15.00 15.00

Landscapes by Hans Kliemand (1922-76) A628

Designs: 100rp, View of Vaduz. 190rp, View Into the Rhine Valley.

Litho. & Engr.

2013, June 3 *Perf. 12¾x13*

1576-1577 A628 Set of 2 6.50 6.50

Baby Animals — A629

Designs: 85rp, Ibex. 100rp, Chamois.140rp, Marmot. 190rp, Alpine hare.

2013, June 3 Litho. *Perf. 12x12½*
Self-Adhesive

1578-1581 A629 Set of 4 11.50 11.50

Bridges A630

No. 1582: a, End of Vaduz-Sevelen Bridge over Rhine River (27x27mm). b, Entire Vaduz-Sevelen Bridge (57x27mm).

No. 1583: a, End of Schaan-Buchs Railway Bridge (27x27mm). b, Entire Schaan-Buchs Bridge (57x27mm).

2013, June 3 *Perf. 14x13¼*

1582 A630 Horiz. pair 4.25 4.25
a. 85rp multi 1.90 1.90
b. 100rp multi 2.25 2.25
1583 A630 Horiz. pair 7.25 7.25
a. 140rp multi 3.00 3.00
b. 190rp multi 4.25 4.25

See Nos. 1600-1601.

Performing Arts — A631

Designs: 100rp, Ballet dancer. 140rp, Actors in theater production. 200rp, Actors in musical theater production. 400rp, Magician.

2013, Sept. 2 *Perf. 12x12½*
Self-Adhesive

1584-1587 A631 Set of 4 18.00 18.00

Automobiles A632

Designs: 85rp, 1954 Aston Martin DB 2/4. 100rp, 1958 Ferrari 250 GT PF. 140rp, 1955 Jaguar XK 140. 190rp, 1956 Mercedes-Benz 300 SL.

Litho. & Embossed With Foil Application

2013, Sept. 2 *Perf. 13¼x13*

1588-1591 A632 Set of 4 11.00 11.00

Paintings by Ivan Myasoyedov (Eugen Zotow) (1881-1953) A633

No. 1592: a, Voyage of the Argonauts, 1909. b, Silum, 1945.

2013, Sept. 2 Litho. *Perf. 14*

1592 Pair 8.75 8.75
a. A633 140rp multi 3.00 3.00
b. A633 260rp multi 5.75 5.75

Printed in sheets of 10 containing 5 each #1592a-1592b, + 2 labels. See Russia No. 7473.

2014 Winter Olympics, Sochi, Russia — A634

Litho. & Thermographed With Foil Application

2013, Nov. 11 *Perf. 13¼x13½*

1593 A634 2.60fr multi 5.75 5.75

Portions of the design contain grit from a stone from Sochi.

Souvenir Sheet

Floral-Patterned Silk Wall Covering in Small Courbaril Room of Liechtenstein Palace, Vienna — A635

Litho. & Embossed With Foil Application

2013, Nov. 11 *Perf. 14¼x14½*
Silk-Faced Paper

1594 A635 Sheet of 3 13.00 13.00
a. 1fr multi 2.25 2.25
b. 1.40fr multi 3.00 3.00
c. 3.60fr multi 7.75 7.75

Christmas — A636

Designs: 85rp, Annunciation. 1fr, Nativity. 1.40fr, Angel announcing birth of Christ to shepherds and sheep. 1.90fr, Three Kings.

Litho. With Foil Application

2013, Nov. 11 *Perf. 12½x12*
Self-Adhesive

1595-1598 A636 Set of 4 11.50 11.50

New Year 2013 (Year of the Horse) — A637

Litho. With Foil Application

2013, Nov. 11 *Perf. 12½*
Self-Adhesive

1599 A637 190rp red & gold 4.25 4.25

The horse vignette was laser cut. Printed in sheets of 4.

In 2014, Liechtenstein began issuing personalizable stamps bearing the inscription "Liechtensteinsche Post AG." Stamps in three different orientations (square, landscape and portrait) could be created for two different frame types, each of which were made available initially in denominations of 55c, 85c, €1, €1.40, €1.90, and €2. These were sold in sheets of 20 stamps. Sheets containing 10 stamps with various non-personalizable images were to be produced and sold for special events.

Bridges Type of 2013

No. 1582: a, End of Buchs-Schaan Footbridge (27x27mm). b, Entire Buchs-Schaan Bridge (57x27mm).

No. 1583: a, End of Bendern-Haag Bridge over the Rhine River (27x27mm). b, Entire Bendern-Haag Bridge (57x27mm).

2014, Mar. 10 Litho. *Perf. 14x13¼*

1600 A630 Horiz. pair 4.25 4.25
a. 85rp multi 1.90 1.90
b. 100rp multi 2.25 2.25
1601 A630 Horiz. pair 7.50 7.50
a. 140rp multi 3.25 3.25
b. 190rp multi 4.25 4.25

Josef Gabriel Rheinberger (1839-1901), Composer — A638

Perf. 13¾x13¼

2014, Mar. 10 Litho.

1602 A638 1.40fr multi 3.25 3.25

Europa — A639

2014, Mar. 10 Litho. *Perf. 12½x12*

1603 A639 140rp multi 3.25 3.25

Souvenir Sheet

Winged Altarpiece Bequeathed to National Museum — A640

No. 1604 — Details of altarpiece: a, St. Christopher Carrying the Christ Child (33x45mm). b, St. Sebastian (33x45mm). c, St. Anne and St. Mary with the Christ Child (84x44mm).

Perf. 14x13¾, 13½ (600rp)

2014, Mar. 10 Litho.

1604 A640 Sheet of 3 20.50 20.50
a. 100rp multi 2.25 2.25
b. 200rp multi 4.50 4.50
c. 600rp multi 13.50 13.50

No. 1640 is sold folded in half, with stamps appearing through the die cut holes in the sheet margin. The top part of the sheet margin, with the holes, is printed on both sides.

Souvenir Sheet

Canonization of Pope John Paul II — A641

Litho. With Foil Application

2014, Apr. 28 *Perf. 14¼x14*

1605 A641 1.40fr multi 3.25 3.25

Ancient Coins Found in Liechtenstein A642

Map of Liechtenstein and: 85rp, Roman silver denarius of Julius Caesar, c. 49-48 B.C. 100rp, Florentine golden florin, c. 1360. 130rp, Silver penny, c. 1360.

Litho. & Embossed With Foil Application

2014, June 2 *Perf. 13½x13¾*

1606-1608 A642 Set of 3 7.00 7.00

Amphibians — A643

Designs: 85rp, Yellow-bellied toad. 2.90fr, Great crested newt. 3.70fr, Alpine salamander.

2014, June 2 Litho. *Perf. 12¼*
Self-Adhesive

1609-1611 A643 Set of 3 17.00 17.00

Flowers — A644

Designs: 100rp, Iris sibirica. 280rp, Parnassia palustris. 360rp, Menyanthes trifoliata.

2014, June 2 Litho. *Perf. 12½x12*
Self-Adhesive

1612-1614 A644 Set of 3 16.50 16.50

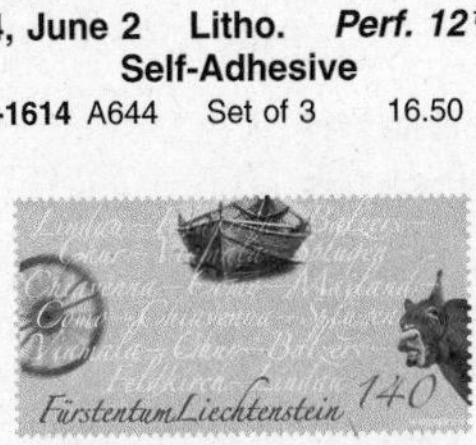

Lindau Messenger Courier Service — A645

2014, Sept. 1 Litho. *Perf. 14x13¼*

1615 A645 140rp multi 3.00 3.00

No. 1615 was printed in sheets of 8 + 4 labels.

Etchings by Brigitte Hasler — A646

Designs: 100rp, Dust Image A. 140rp, Dust Image B.

Litho. With Foil Application

2014, Sept. 1 ***Perf. 13¼***

1616-1617 A646 Set of 2 5.25 5.25

Intl. Year of Crystallography — A647

Designs: 100rp, Initial crystal metamorphosis sequence. 200rp, Final crystal metamorphosis sequence.

Litho. & Embossed

2014, Sept. 1 ***Perf. 13½x13¼***

1618-1619 A647 Set of 2 6.50 6.50

Sedans — A648

Designs: 85rp, 1933 Rolls-Royce Phantom II. 100rp, 1929 Pierce-Arrow Type 133. 140rp, 1935 Studebaker Big Six. 190rp, 1948 Jaguar Mark IV.

Litho. With Foil Application

2014, Sept. 1 ***Perf. 13¼x13***

1620-1623 A648 Set of 4 11.50 11.50

1620a Inscribed "Rolls-Royce" (with hyphen) 1.75 1.75

Issued: No. 1620a, 11/10. No. 1620 is inscribed "Rolls Royce" (without hyphen).

Reign of Prince Hans Adam II, 25th Anniv. — A649

Perf. 13¼x13¾

2014, Nov. 10 **Litho. & Engr.**

1624 A649 2fr multi 4.25 4.25

Painting by Jens W. Beyrich — A650

Painting by Hong Sek-Chern A651

2014, Nov. 10 **Litho.** ***Perf. 13x13¼***

1625 A650 190rp multi 4.00 4.00

1626 A651 190rp multi 4.00 4.00

See Singapore Nos. 1706-1707.

Chinese Porcelain in Princely Collection — A652

Designs: 1fr, Famille Rose plate, c. 1722-35. 1.90fr, Kraak kendi, c. 1572-1620 (27x43mm). 2.80fr, Imari baluster vase with lid, c. 1736-95 (27x43mm). 3.60fr, Imari plate with lotus blossoms, c. 1736-95.

Perf. 13¾x13¼, 12x11¼ (#1628-1629)

Litho. & Engr. With Foil Application

2014, Nov. 10

1627-1630 A652 Set of 4 19.00 19.00

Christmas — A653

Chapels: 85rp, Freedom Chapel, Malbun. 100rp, St. Wendelin's Chapel, Steg. 140rp, St. Theodul's Chapel, Masescha.

Litho. With Foil Application

2014, Nov. 10 ***Perf. 12¼x12½***

Self-Adhesive

1631-1633 A653 Set of 3 6.75 6.75

New Year 2015 (Year of the Ram) — A654

Litho. With Foil Application

2014, Nov. 10 ***Perf. 12½***

Self-Adhesive

1634 A654 190rp red & gold 4.00 4.00

The ram vignette was laser cut. Printed in sheets of 4.

Prince Hans Adam II, 70th Birthday — A655

Perf. 13¼x13¾

2015, Feb. 14 **Litho. & Engr.**

1635 Pair 6.50 6.50

a. A655 1fr green & multi 2.10 2.10

b. A655 2fr red & multi 4.25 4.25

No. 1635 was printed in sheets containing two pairs.

Liechtenstein Traditional Costume Association, 50th Anniv. — A656

2015, Mar. 2 **Litho.** ***Perf. 12x12½***

Self-Adhesive

1636 A656 85rp multi 1.75 1.75

Liechtenstein Development Service, 50th Anniv. — A657

2015, Mar. 2 **Litho.** ***Perf. 12x12½***

Self-Adhesive

1637 A657 100rp multi 2.10 2.10

Postage Stamps, 175th Anniv. — A658

2015, Mar. 2 **Litho.** ***Perf. 12½x12***

Self-Adhesive

1638 A658 1.40fr multi 3.00 3.00

Liechtenstein's Admission to United Nations, 25th Anniv. — A659

2015, Mar. 2 **Litho.** ***Perf. 13½x13***

1639 A659 190rp multi 4.00 4.00

International Year of Light — A660

2015, Mar. 2 **Litho.** ***Perf. 13¾x13¼***

1640 A660 1.90fr multi 4.00 4.00

Microperforations are incorporated in the vignette.

Europa — A661

Toys: No. 1641, 1.40fr, Polar bear in freezer. No. 1642, 1.40fr, Goat on lemon.

2015, Mar. 2 **Litho.** ***Perf. 13½x13¼***

1641-1642 A661 Set of 2 6.00 6.00

Flowers Type of 2012

Designs: 85rp, Succisa pratensis. 100rp, Astrantia major. 130rp, Leucanthemum vulgare.

2015, June 1 **Litho.** ***Perf. 12½x12***

Self-Adhesive

1643-1645 A615 Set of 3 6.75 6.75

Reptiles — A662

Designs: 1.80fr, Zauneidechse (sand lizard). 2fr, Schlingnatter (smooth snake). 5fr, Bergeidechse (common lizard).

2015, June 1 **Litho.** ***Perf. 12¼***

Self-Adhesive

1646-1648 A662 Set of 3 19.00 19.00

Keystone Decorations From Cathedral of St. Florin, Vaduz — A663

Designs: 100rp, Pelican. 140rp, Lamb of God. 190rp, Eagle. 200rp, Lion.

2015, June 1 **Litho.** ***Perf. 13***

1649-1652 A663 Set of 4 13.50 13.50

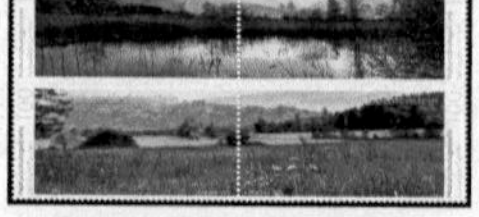

Schwabbrünnen Nature Reserve — A664

No. 1653: a, Pond, denomination at UL. b, Pond, denomination at UR. c, Meadow, denomination at UL. d, Meadow, denomination at UR.

2015, June 1 **Litho.** ***Perf. 13¼***

1653 A664 Block of 4 8.50 8.50

a.-d. 100rp Any single 2.10 2.10

Alpine Landscapes — A665

No. 1654: a, Malbuntal, Liechtenstein. b, Herder's dwellings, Velika Planina, Slovenia.

2015, Sept. 7 **Litho.** ***Perf. 14x13½***

1654 A665 Pair 6.00 6.00

a.-b. 140rp Either single 3.00 3.00

See Slovenia No. 1141.

Commercial Vehicles — A666

Designs: 85rp, 1945 Kaiser Auto tractor. 100rp, 1967 Raimündle tractor. 140rp, Unimog. 190rp, 1921 Fordson tractor.

Litho. With Foil Application

2015, Sept. 7 ***Perf. 13¼x13***

1655-1658 A666 Set of 4 10.50 10.50

Miniature Sheet

Apple Varieties A667

No. 1659: a, Treisenberger Weinapfel. b, Damason Reinette. c, Leuser. d, Grosser Rheinischer Bohnapfel. e, Freiherr von Berlepsch. f, Rollapfel. g, Goldparmäne. h, Rösli Marie.

2015, Sept. 7 **Litho.** ***Perf. 12½***

Self-Adhesive

1659 A667 Sheet of 8 24.00 24.00

a.-h. 140rp Any single 3.00 3.00

Jewelry Found at Archaeological Sites — A668

Map of Liechtenstein and: 85rp, Red jasper brooch, 1st-2nd cent. 100rp, Gold ring with chalcedony cameo, 3rd cent. 130rp, Glass cameo, 1st cent.

Litho. & Embossed With Foil Application

2015, Nov. 16 ***Perf. 13¼x13½***

1660-1662 A668 Set of 3 6.25 6.25

Paintings by Jacques Jordaens (1593-1678) A669

Designs: 100rp, Adoration of the Shepherds. 140rp, As the Old Sing, So the Young Ones Pipe (47x38mm). 190rp, Meleager and Atalante (44x38mm).

2015, Nov. 16 **Litho.** ***Perf. 13¼***

1663-1665 A669 Set of 3 8.50 8.50

Christmas — A670

Designs (from Christmas carols): 85p, Rose (Lo, How a Rose E'er Blooming). 100rp, Nativity (Silent Night). 140rp, Angels (Oh, How Joyfully). 190rp, Shepherds and Star of Bethlehem (Come, All Ye Shepherds).

Perf. 12¼x12½

2015, Nov. 16 **Litho.**

Self-Adhesive

1666-1669 A670 Set of 4 10.00 10.00

New Year 2016 (Year of the Monkey) A671

Litho. With Foil Application

2015, Nov. 16 ***Perf. 12½***

Self-Adhesive

1670 A671 190rp red & gold 3.75 3.75

The monkey vignette was laser cut. Printed in sheets of 4.

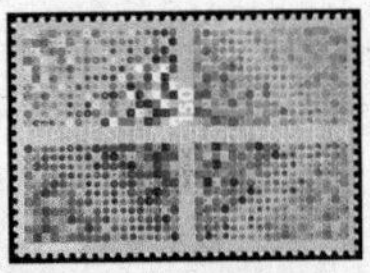

Four Seasons A672

2016, Mar. 7 **Litho.** ***Perf. 13¼x14***

1671 A672 150rp multi 3.00 3.00

A673

Europa — A674

2016, Mar. 7 **Litho.** ***Perf. 14x13½***

1672 A673 150rp multi 3.00 3.00

Self-Adhesive

Perf. 12x12½

1673 A674 150rp multi 3.00 3.00

Paintings by Alois Ritter (1910-86) A675

Designs: 100rp, Ruggeller Riet, 1951. 200rp, Im Bofel, 1986.

2016, Mar. 7 **Litho.** ***Perf. 13½x13¾***

1674-1675 A675 Set of 2 6.00 6.00

Tools Found at Archaeological Sites — A676

Map of Liechtenstein and: 100rp, Flint dagger, 4th cent. B.C. 150rp, Razor, 12th cent. B.C. 200rp, Winged axe, 5th cent. B.C.

Litho. & Embossed With Foil Application

2016, Mar. 7 ***Perf. 13¼x13½***

1676-1678 A676 Set of 3 9.00 9.00

Trees — A677

2016, Mar. 7 **Litho.** ***Perf. 13x13¼***

Self-Adhesive

1679 A677 85rp Oak 1.75 1.75
1680 A677 100rp Weeping willow 2.00 2.00
1681 A677 150rp Walnut 3.00 3.00
1682 A677 170rp Aspen 3.50 3.50
1683 A677 200rp Birch 4.00 4.00
Nos. 1679-1683 (5) 14.25 14.25

2016 Summer Olympics, Rio de Janeiro — A678

Designs: 100rp, Archery. 200rp, Judo.

Litho. With Foil Application

2016, June 6 ***Perf. 12½x12***

Self-Adhesive

1684-1685 A678 Set of 2 6.25 6.25

17th Century Gold and Silver Items — A679

Designs: 1fr, Sailing boat drinking vessel. 1.50fr, Diana on a stag drinking vessel. 2fr, Turbo shell cup.

Litho. With Foil Application

2016, June 6 ***Perf. 13¾x13½***

1686-1688 A679 Set of 3 9.25 9.25

Ruggeller Riet Nature Reserve — A680

No. 1689: a, Pond, denomination at UL. b, Pond, denomination at UR. c, Meadow in fog, denomination at UL. d, Meadow in fog, denomination at UR.

2016, June 6 **Litho.** ***Perf. 13¼***

1689 A680 Block of 4 8.50 8.50
a.-d. 100rp Any single 2.10 2.10

Miniature Sheet

Pear Varieties A681

No. 1690: a, Herbstlängler. b, Kugeläugstler. c, Hermannsbirne. d, Rote Holzbirne. e, Sulse Längler. f, Sülibirne. g, Wolfsbirne. h, Tollbirne.

2016, June 6 **Litho.** ***Perf. 12½***

Self-Adhesive

1690 A681 Sheet of 8 17.00 17.00
a.-h. 100rp Any single 2.10 2.10

Young Woman on a Balcony, by Gerrit Dou — A682

2016, Sept. 5 **Engr.** ***Perf. 11¾***

1691 A682 150rp multi 3.25 3.25

See Czech Republic No. 3680.

Religious Fraternities A683

Map of Liechtenstein and religious art: 100rp, Maria Hilf Fraternity (Madonna and Child altarpeice, Maria Hilf Chapel, Balzers). 150rp, St. Anne Fraternity (statue of St. Anne, Vaduz Castle) (42x35mm). 200rp, St. Sebastian Fraternity (St. Sebastian and angels, St. Sebastain Chapel, Nendeln).

2016, Sept. 5 **Litho.** ***Perf. 14½***

1692-1694 A683 Set of 3 9.25 9.25

Photographs of Tree Bark, by Erich Allgäuer — A684

Designs: 100rp, Woman. 150rp, Man. 200rp, Woman with Hat.

2016, Sept. 5 **Litho.** ***Perf. 13½***

1695-1697 A684 Set of 3 9.25 9.25

Motorcycles A685

Designs: 85rp, 1928 M. Thun. 100rp, 1920 Harley-Davidson. 150rp, 1948 Norton with Type Stolz sidecar. 200rp, 1933 Rudge.

Litho. With Foil Application

2016, Sept. 5 ***Perf. 13¼***

1698-1701 A685 Set of 4 11.00 11.00

Souvenir Sheet

Liechtenstein Without People — A686

No. 1702: a, Border marker, rusted sign, badger (20 years after people). b, Eagle (100 years after people). c, Parrots and rainbow (500 years after people).

Litho. With Foil Application

2016, Nov. 14 ***Perf. 14x13½***

1702 A686 Sheet of 3 12.00 12.00
a.-c. 200rp Any single 4.00 4.00

No. 1702 was sold folded into thirds.

Christmas — A687

Christmas card illustrations: 85rp, Child with lantern. 100rp, Family exchanges Christmas presents, vert. 150rp, City scene with snow, vert. 200rp, Children walking in forest.

Litho. With Foil Application

Perf. 12x12½, 12½x12

2016, Nov. 14

Self-Adhesive

1703-1706 A687 Set of 4 11.00 11.00

New Year 2017 (Year of the Rooster) A688

Litho. With Foil Application

2016, Nov. 14 ***Perf. 12½***

Self-Adhesive

1707 A688 200rp red & gold 4.00 4.00

The rooster vignette was laser cut. Printed in sheets of 4.

Europa A689

Designs: No. 1708, 150rp, Vaduz Castle. No. 1709, 150rp, Gutenberg Castle, Balzers.

2017, Mar. 6 **Litho.** ***Perf. 14¼***

1708-1709 A689 Set of 2 6.00 6.00

Outdoor Sports — A690

Winning photographs in youth photography contest: 85rp, Smooth Powder Turn, by Julius Tiefenthaler. 100rp, Winter Storm Windsurfing, by Yannick Oberhofer. 200rp, Sunset Backflip, by Tiefenthaler.

2017, Mar. 6 **Litho.** ***Perf. 13½***

1710-1712 A690 Set of 3 7.75 7.75

Tools of Tradesmen — A691

Hand and tools of: 130rp, Mason. 180rp, Tailor. 200rp, Goldsmith.

2017, Mar. 6 **Litho.** ***Perf. 12½x12¼***

Dated "2017"

1713-1715 A691 Set of 3 10.00 10.00

See Nos. 1741-1743.

Grain Crops — A692

Designs: 85rp, Oats. 100rp, Barley. 150rp, Corn. 200rp, Millet.

2017, Mar. 6 Litho. *Perf. 12¼*
Self-Adhesive

1716-1719 A692 Set of 4 10.50 10.50

HPZ Remedial Education Center, Schaan, 50th Anniv. — A693

2017, June 6 Litho. *Perf. 12x12½*
Self-Adhesive

1720 A693 1fr multi 2.10 2.10

Paintings by Peter Fendi (1796-1842) — A694

Designs: 85rp, Request for Admission. 1fr, Sneaking a Peek. 1.50fr, A Child's Prayer.

Litho. With Foil Application
2017, June 6 *Perf. 13½x13¼*

1721-1723 A694 Set of 3 7.00 7.00

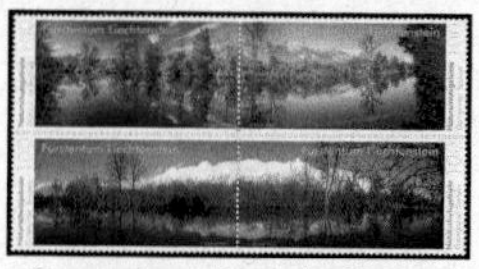

Gampriner Seelein Nature Reserve — A695

No. 1724 — Lake Gampriner Seelein in: a, Autumn, denomination at UL. b, Autumn, denomination at UR. c, Winter, denomination at UL. d, Winter, denomination at UR.

2017, June 6 Litho. *Perf. 13¼*

1724 A695 Block of 4 8.50 8.50
a.-d. 100rp Any single 2.10 2.10

Souvenir Sheet

50th Wedding Anniversary of Prince Hans-Adam II and Princess Marie — A696

No. 1725: a, Vaduz Castle and flower (18x60mm). b, Prince and Princess (46x60mm). c, Crown and joined wedding rings (41x60mm).

Litho. With Foil Application, Litho. & Embossed With Foil Application (2.80fr)
2017, June 6 *Perf. 14¼x14½*

1725 A696 Sheet of 3 13.00 13.00
a. 1.30fr multi 2.75 2.75
b. 2.20fr multi 4.50 4.50
c. 2.80fr multi 5.75 5.75

Settlement Area of Liechtenstein A697

2017, Sept. 4 Litho. *Perf. 14x13¼*

1726 A697 150rp multi 3.25 3.25

Rappastein, Painting by Helmut Ditsch — A698

2017, Sept. 4 Litho. *Perf. 14x13½*

1727 A698 380rp multi 8.00 8.00

Souvenir Sheet

Balzers Mail Collection Station, 200th Anniv. — A699

No. 1728: a, Postman and girl. b, Posthorn. c, Horse-drawn mail coach.

Litho. & Engr. With Foil Application
2017, Sept. 4 *Perf. 13¾x14¼*

1728 A699 Sheet of 3 13.50 13.50
a. 1.30fr multi 2.75 2.75
b. 2.20fr multi 4.75 4.75
c. 2.80fr multi 6.00 6.00

Miniature Sheet

Stone Fruit Varieties A700

No. 1729: a, Mombacher Frühaprikose apricots. b, Kirkespflaume plums. c, Grüne Reineclaude plums. d, Hauszwetschge plums. e, Ungarische Beste apricots. f, Schauenburger cherries. g, Mirabelle von Nancy plums. h, Gelbe Denise cherries.

2017, Sept. 4 Litho. *Perf. 12½*
Self-Adhesive

1729 A700 Sheet of 8 17.00 17.00
a.-h. 100rp Any single 2.10 2.10

2018 Winter Olympics, Pyeongchang, South Korea — A701

Designs: 170rp, Nordic skiing. 200rp, Alpine skiing.

2017, Nov. 13 Litho. *Perf. 12x12½*

1730-1731 A701 Set of 2 7.75 7.75

Worldwide Fund for Nature (WWF) — A702

Designs: 85rp, Castor fiber. 100rp, Lynx lynx. 130rp, Canis lupus. 150rp, Ciconia ciconia.

2017, Nov. 13 Litho. *Perf. 12x12½*
Self-Adhesive

1732-1735 A702 Set of 4 9.50 9.50

Christmas — A703

Designs: 85rp, Star of Bethlehem, trees and house. 100rp, Star, forest and house. 150rp, Moon, forest and house. 200rp, Moon over church.

2017, Nov. 13 Litho. *Perf. 12½x12*
Self-Adhesive

1736-1739 A703 Set of 4 11.00 11.00

New Year 2018 (Year of the Dog) — A704

Litho. With Foil Application
2017, Nov. 13 *Perf. 12½*
Self-Adhesive

1740 A704 200rp red & gold 4.25 4.25

The dog vignette was laser cut. Printed in sheets of 4.

Tools of Tradesmen Type of 2017

Hand and tools of: 100rp, Bookbinder. 130rp, Instrument maker. 180rp, Shoemaker.

2018, Mar. 5 Litho. *Perf. 12½x12¼*
Dated "2018"

1741-1743 A691 Set of 3 8.75 8.75

Balzers Footbridge — A705

Old Rhine Bridge, Vaduz A706

Litho. With Foil Application
2018, Mar. 5 *Perf. 14x13¼*

1744 A705 150rp sil & multi 3.25 3.25
1745 A706 150rp sil & multi 3.25 3.25

Europa.

Paintings by Gustav Klimt (1862-1918) — A707

Designs: 2.60fr, The Kiss. 3.70fr, Death and Life.

Litho. With Foil Application
2018, Mar. 5 *Perf. 14½*

1746-1747 A707 Set of 2 13.50 13.50

Vegetables — A708

Designs: 85rp, Eggplant. 100rp, Radishes. 150rp, Zucchinis. 200rp, Peperoni peppers.

2018, Mar. 5 Litho. *Perf. 12¼*
Self-Adhesive

1748-1751 A708 Set of 4 11.50 11.50

Direct Suffrage, Cent. — A709

2018, June 4 Litho. *Perf. 13¾x13¼*

1752 A709 100rp multi 2.00 2.00

Mountain Summit Crosses — A710

Cross on: 100rp, Kelchle. 150rp, Kläusli. 200rp, Mittlerspitz. 260rp, Hubel.

2018, June 4 Litho. *Perf. 13x13¼*

1753-1756 A710 Set of 4 14.50 14.50

Hälos Nature Reserve A711

No. 1757 — Reserve in: a, Spring (blue skies, denomination at UL). b, Spring (blue skies, denomination at UR). c, Summer (cloudy skies, denomination at UL). d, Summer (cloudy skies, denomination at UR).

2018, June 4 Litho. *Perf. 13¼*

1757 A711 Block of 4 8.00 8.00
a.-d. 100rp Any single 2.00 2.00

Souvenir Sheet

50th Birthday of Hereditary Prince Alois — A712

No. 1758: a, Green princely hat (30x30mm). b, Hereditary Prince Alois (30x36mm). c, Red princely hat (30x30mm).

Litho. & Engr.
2018, June 11 *Perf. 14x13¼*

1758 A712 Sheet of 3 6.75 6.75
a. 1.30fr multi 1.40 1.40
b. 2.20fr multi 2.25 2.25
c. 2.80fr multi 3.00 3.00

Biedermann House, Schellenberg, 500th Anniv. — A713

Litho. & Embossed
2018, Sept. 3 *Perf. 13¼x14*

1759 A713 2fr multi 4.25 4.25

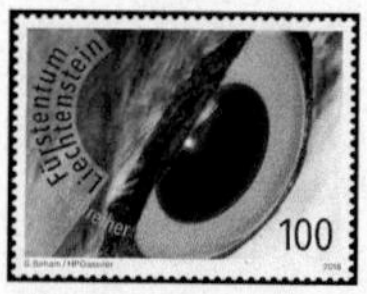

Bird's Eyes — A714

Eye of: 100rp, Gray heron. 130rp, Great crested grebe. 150rp, Cormorant.

Litho. & Embossed

2018, Sept. 3 *Perf. 14*
1760-1762 A714 Set of 3 7.75 7.75

18th Century Tapestries by the Firm of Jean Barraband II — A715

Designs: 100rp, The Tea Ceremony. 150rp, Audience with the Emperor of China (60x42mm). 180rp, The Scholar Before the Great Mogul (33x36mm).

2018, Sept. 3 Litho. *Perf. 13¼*
1763-1765 A715 Set of 3 9.00 9.00

Miniature Sheet

Music for Dancing A716

No. 1766: a, Saxophone player. b, Dancer with castanets. c, Roller skater with boom box. d, Keytar player. e, Concertina player. f, Banjo player. g, Dancer with maracas. h, Cello player.

2018, Sept. 3 Litho. *Perf. 14*
1766 A716 Sheet of 8 17.00 17.00
a.-h. 100rp Any single 2.10 2.10

Immigrants — A717

Map of Liechtenstein and: 85rp, Arab man. 100rp, African man. 130rp, Asian woman.

2018, Nov. 12 Litho. *Perf. 14x13¾*
1767-1769 A717 Set of 3 6.50 6.50

Christmas — A718

Star of Bethlehem and: 85rp, Three Magi. 100rp, Magi and shepherds. 150rp, People and dog. 200rp, Nativity.

2018, Nov. 12 Litho. *Perf. 12x12½*
Self-Adhesive
1770-1773 A718 Set of 4 11.00 11.00

New Year 2019 (Year of the Boar) — A719

Litho. With Foil Application
2018, Nov. 12 *Perf. 12½*
Self-Adhesive
1774 A719 200rp red & gold 4.00 4.00

The boar vignette was laser cut. Printed in sheets of 4.

Principality of Liechtenstein, 300th Anniv. — A720

2019, Jan. 23 Embroidered *Imperf.*
Self-Adhesive
1775 A720 630rp gold & red 13.00 13.00

An item similar to No. 1775 with gold threads and eight Swarovski crystals was produced in limited quantities and sold for 300fr.

Emil Beck (1888-1973), Envoy to Switzerland and Prince Eduard (1872-1951), Envoy to Austria A721

2019, Mar. 4 Litho. *Perf. 13¼x13*
1776 A721 220rp multi 4.50 4.50

Representation of Liechtenstein in foreign countries, cent.

A722

Golden Eagle (National Bird) — A723

2019, Mar. 4 Litho. *Perf. 13¾x14*
1777 Vert. pair 6.00 6.00
a. A722 1.50fr multi 3.00 3.00
b. A723 1.50fr multi 3.00 3.00

Europa.

Dragonflies A724

Designs: 85rp, Calopteryx virgo. 100rp, Anax imperator. 180rp, Phyrrhosoma nymphula. 260rp, Calopteryx splendens.

2019, Mar. 4 Litho. *Perf. 12x12½*
Self-Adhesive
1778-1781 A724 Set of 4 12.50 12.50

See Nos. 1804-1807.

First Man on the Moon, 50th Anniv. — A725

Designs: 180rp, Astronaut on Moon. 200rp, Lunar Module on Moon.

Litho. With Foil Application
2019, June 3 *Perf. 12*
1782-1783 A725 Set of 2 7.75 7.75

Mountains — A726

No. 1784: a, Falkniskette, denomination at UL. b, Falkniskette, denomination at UR. c, Schönberg, denomination at UL. d, Schönberg, denomination at UR.

2019, June 3 Litho. *Perf. 13¼*
1784 A726 Block of 4 8.00 8.00
a.-d. 100rp Any single 2.00 2.00

Souvenir Sheet

Leonardo da Vinci (1452-1519), Sculptor and Painter — A727

No. 1785: a, Sketch of flying machine. b, Self-portrait. c, Anatomical sketches.

2019, June 3 Litho. *Perf. 13½x13¼*
1785 A727 Sheet of 3 13.00 13.00
a. 1.30fr multi 2.60 2.60
b. 2.20fr multi 4.50 4.50
c. 2.60fr multi 5.75 5.75

Souvenir Sheet

Coat of Arms of Liechtenstein — A728

Litho. & Embossed With Foil Application
2019, June 3 *Perf. 14x13¾*
1786 A728 630rp multi 13.00 13.00

Principality of Liechtenstein, 300th Anniv.

Red House, Vaduz — A729

Litho. & Engr. With Foil Application
2019, Sept. 2 *Perf. 13*
1787 A729 150rp gold & multi 3.00 3.00

Triesen A730

Designs: 130rp, Lady Chapel. 200rp, Old Village Center.

Litho. & Embossed
2019, Sept. 2 *Perf. 13½x13¾*
1788-1789 A730 Set of 2 6.75 6.75

Sculptures by Pier Jacopo Alari-Bonacolsi (c. 1455-1528) — A731

Designs: 1.40fr, Bust of a Young Man. 1.70fr, Hercules with a Lion's Skin. 2.20fr, Equestrian Statue of Marcus Aurelius.

Litho. With Foil Application
2019, Sept. 2 *Perf. 12x11¼*
1790-1792 A731 Set of 3 10.00 10.00

Souvenir Sheet

Circumnavigation by Crew of Ferdinand Magellan, 500th Anniv. — A732

No. 1793: a, Magellan's ship, Victoria. b, Death of Magellan in the Philippines. c, Magellan (c. 1480-1521).

Litho. Sheet Margin Litho. With Foil Application
Perf. 12 on 3 or 4 Sides
2019, Sept. 2
1793 A732 Sheet of 3 13.00 13.00
a. 130rp multi 2.75 2.75
b. 220rp multi 4.50 4.50
c. 280rp multi 5.75 5.75

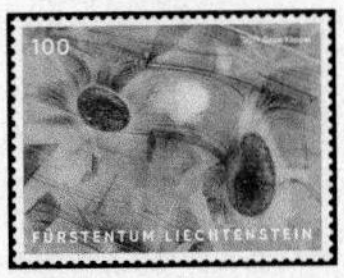

Photographs of Ice, by Sepp Köppel — A733

Designs: 100rp, Ice Flow. 110rp, Stone Islands. 130rp, Streamlines.

Litho. & Embossed With Thermography
2019, Nov. 11 *Perf. 13¼x13½*
1794-1796 A733 Set of 3 7.00 7.00

Grit is embedded in the thermographic ink used on parts of the vignette.

Christmas — A734

Designs: 85rp, Snowman. 100rp, Nutcracker. 150rp, Rocking horse. 200rp, Angel.

Litho. With Foil Application
2019, Nov. 11 *Perf. 12½*
Self-Adhesive
1797-1800 A734 Set of 4 11.00 11.00

New Year 2020 (Year of the Rat) — A735

Litho. With Foil Application
2019, Nov. 11 *Perf. 12½*
Self-Adhesive
1801 A735 200rp red & gold 4.00 4.00

The rat vignette was laser cut. Printed in sheets of 4.

A736

Diversity — A737

Perf. 13¼x13½
2019, Nov. 14 Litho.
1802 A736 85rp multi 1.75 1.75
1803 A737 100rp multi 2.00 2.00

See Switzerland Nos. 1743-1744.

Dragonflies Type of 2019

Designs: 85rp, Platycnemis latipes. 130rp, Sympetrum fonscolombii. 180rp, Crocothemis erythraea. 200rp, Sympetrum depressiusculum.

2020, Mar. 2 Litho. *Perf. 12x12½*
Self-Adhesive

1804-1807 A724 Set of 4 12.50 12.50

Liechtenstein's Membership in European Economic Area, 25th Anniv. — A738

2020, Mar. 2 Litho. *Perf. 13¼x13*

1808 A738 220rp multi 4.75 4.75

Europa A739

No. 1809 — Lindau Messenger Courier Service: a, Mounted postrider. b, Stagecoach.

2020, Mar. 2 Litho. *Perf. 14*

1809 A739 Pair 6.50 6.50
a.-b. 150rp Either single 3.25 3.25

Printed in sheets containing 2 each Nos. 1809a-1809b.

Souvenir Sheet

Royal Birthdays A740

No. 1810: a, Princess Marie, 80th birthday. b, Prince Hans-Adam II, 75th birthday.

Litho. With Foil Application
2020, Mar. 2 *Perf. 13¼x13*

1810 A740 Sheet of 2 13.50 13.50
a. 2fr gold & multi 4.25 4.25
b. 4.30fr gold & multi 9.00 9.00

Untitled (Indian Banner: World), Printed Banner by Matt Mullican — A741

2020, June 2 Litho. *Perf. 12*

1811 A741 150rp black & red 3.25 3.25

2020 Summer Olympics, Tokyo — A742

Designs: 170rp, Synchronized swimming. 280rp, Judo.

Litho. With Foil Application
2020, June 2 *Perf. 12*

1812-1813 A742 Set of 2 9.50 9.50

The 2020 Summer Olympics were postponed until 2021 because of the coronavirus pandemic.

Waters of Liechtenstein — A743

No. 1814: a, Valunerbach, denomination at UL. b, Valunerbach, denomination at UR. c, Schwabbrünnen, denomination at UL. d, Schwabbrünnen, denomination at UR.

2020, June 2 Litho. *Perf. 13¼*

1814 A743 Block of 4 8.50 8.50
a.-d. 100rp Any single 2.10 2.10

Souvenir Sheet

Egon Rheinberger (1870-1936), Artist and Architect — A744

No. 1815: a, Sketch of the Maultasch Ruins Near Appiano. b, Wall painting of unicorn in Gutenberg Castle. c, Rheinberger.

Litho., Sheet Margin Litho. With Foil Application
2020, June 2 *Perf. 12*

1815 A744 Sheet of 3 13.50 13.50
a. 130rp multi 2.75 2.75
b. 220rp multi 4.75 4.75
c. 280rp multi 6.00 6.00

Recycling A745

2020, Sept. 7 Embroidered *Imperf.*
Self-Adhesive

1816 A745 630rp green & blue 14.00 14.00

Balzers A746

Designs: 100rp, Mill buildings. 180rp, Mäls District buildings.

Litho. & Embossed
2020, Sept. 7 *Perf. 13¼*

1817-1818 A746 Set of 2 6.25 6.25

Paintings by Peter Paul Rubens (1577-1640) — A747

Designs: 1.50fr, The Hunt of Diana. 2.20fr, The Hunt of Meleager and Atalanta.

Litho. With Foil Application
2020, Sept. 7 *Perf. 12*

1819-1820 A747 Set of 2 8.00 8.00

Souvenir Sheet

Self-portrait, by Raphael (1483-1520) — A748

Litho. With Foil Application
2020, Sept. 7 *Perf. 12*

1821 A748 630rp multi 14.00 14.00

Souvenir Sheet

Ludwig van Beethoven (1770-1827), Composer — A749

Litho. & Engr.
2020, Nov. 16 *Perf. 13¼*

1822 A749 6.30fr multi 14.00 14.00

Christmas — A750

Numerals in denominations hanging like Christmas ornaments: 85rp, 100rp, 150rp, 200rp.

Litho. With Holographic Foil
2020, Nov. 16 *Perf. 12½x12*
Self-Adhesive

1823-1826 A750 Set of 4 12.00 12.00

New Year 2021 (Year of the Ox) — A751

Litho. With Foil Application
2020, Nov. 16 *Perf. 12½*
Self-Adhesive

1827 A751 200rp red & gold 4.50 4.50

The ox vignette was laser cut. Printed in sheets of 4.

Operette Balzers, 75th Anniv. — A752

Litho. With Foil Application
2021, Mar. 1 *Perf. 12*

1828 A752 85rp gold & multi 1.90 1.90

First Session of United Nations General Assembly, 75th Anniv. A753

2021, Mar. 1 Litho. *Perf. 11¼x11½*

1829 A753 5.20fr multi 11.50 11.50

Songbirds — A754

Designs: 85rp, Fichtenkreuzschnabel (crossbill). 100rp, Zitronenzeisig (lemon siskin). 150rp, Mauerläufer (wall creeper). 200rp, Neuntöter (red-backed shrike).

2021, Mar. 1 Litho. *Perf. 12½x12*
Self-Adhesive

1830-1833 A754 Set of 4 12.00 12.00

For surcharge, see No. 1855.

Europa A755

No. 1834 — Endangered species: a, Astacus astacus. b, Mustela nivalis.

2021, Mar. 1 Litho. *Perf. 14¼x14*

1834 A755 Pair 6.50 6.50
a.-b. 150rp Either single 3.25 3.25

1620 Map of Upper Rhine Valley by Hans Conrad Gyger (1599-1674) — A756

Litho. & Embossed
2021, June 7 *Perf. 13¾x13½*

1835 A756 150rp multi 3.25 3.25

Art by Prince Hans (1910-75) A757

Designs: 260rp, Elephant. 430rp, Zebra Herd.

Litho. & Embossed
2021, June 7 *Perf. 13½*

1836-1837 A757 Set of 2 15.00 15.00

Trails A758

No. 1838: a, Upper Silum Trail, denomination at UL. b, Upper Silum Trail, denomination at UR. c, Trail to Gapfahl, denomination at UL. d, Trail to Gapfahl, denomination at UR.

2021, June 7 Litho. *Perf. 13¼*

1838 A758 Block of 4 9.00 9.00
a.-d. 100rp Any single 2.25 2.25

Souvenir Sheet

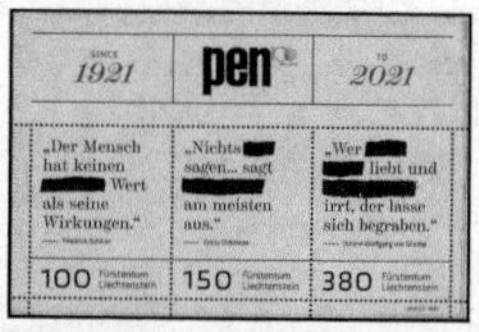

PEN International, Cent. — A759

No. 1839 — Quotations (in German) with words covered by scratch-off panel from: a, Friedrich Schiller (1759-1805). b, Emily Dickinson (1830-86). c, Johann Wolfgang von Goethe (1749-1832).

Litho. With Scratch-off Coating
2021, June 7 *Perf. 13x13¼*

1839 A759 Sheet of 3 14.00 14.00
a. 100rp multi 2.25 2.25
b. 150rp multi 3.25 3.25
c. 380rp multi 8.25 8.25

Values are for unscrached stamps.

First E-Mail Message, 50th Anniv. — A760

2021, Sept. 6 Litho. *Perf. 12*

1840 A760 100rp multi 2.25 2.25

Constitution of the Principality of Liechtenstein, Cent. — A761

Designs: 85rp, Freedom. 100rp, Peace. 150rp, Democracy.

2021, Sept. 6 Litho. *Perf. 14x13½*

1841-1843 A761 Set of 3 7.25 7.25

Souvenir Sheet

Paintings by Eugen Zotow (1881-1953) — A762

No. 1844: a, View of Vaduz Castle (47x32mm). b, Self-portrait (32x32mm).

2021, Sept. 6 Litho. *Perf. 12*

1844 A762 Sheet of 2 7.75 7.75
a. 140rp multi 3.00 3.00
b. 220rp multi 4.75 4.75

See Ukraine No. 1314.

Souvenir Sheet

Dante Alighieri (c. 1265-1321), Writer — A763

No. 1845: a, Portrait of Alighieri. b, Writing hand with quill.

Litho. & Engr.

2021, Sept. 6 *Perf. 13¾x14*

1845 A763 Sheet of 2 17.00 17.00
a. 3.70fr gray & black 8.00 8.00
b. 4fr gray & black 8.75 8.75

Souvenir Sheet

Blockchain Technology — A764

2021, Sept. 6 Litho. *Perf. 12½x12¼*

1846 A764 520rp multi 11.50 11.50

Doctors Without Borders, 50th Anniv. — A765

2021, Nov. 15 Litho. *Perf. 13½*

1847 A765 370rp multi 8.00 8.00

Liechtenstein Chess Federation, 50th Anniv. — A766

Chess board and pieces: 85rp, Knight. 180rp, King.

Litho. & Embossed With Foil Application

2021, Nov. 15 *Perf. 13½*

1848-1849 A766 Set of 2 5.75 5.75

Christmas — A767

Designs: 85rp, Star of Bethlehem. 100rp, Sheep and flowers. 150rp, Dove with olive branch. 200rp, Candle.

Litho. With Foil Application

2021, Nov. 15 *Perf. 12¼*

Self-Adhesive

1850-1853 A767 Set of 4 12.00 12.00

New Year 2022 (Year of the Tiger) — A768

Litho. With Foil Application

2021, Nov. 15 *Perf. 12½*

Self-Adhesive

1854 A768 200rp red & gold 4.50 4.50

The tiger vignette was laser cut. Printed in sheets of 4.

No. 1831 Surcharged

No. 1515 Surcharged

Methods and Perfs As Before

2022, Jan. 3

Self-Adhesive

1855 A754 90rp on 100rp #1831 2.00 2.00
1856 A575 110rp on 220rp #1515 2.40 2.40

Wild Bees — A769

Designs: 90rp, Large scabious mining bee. 1.10fr, Carpenter bee. 1.80fr, Mountain bumblebee. 2.30fr, Cuckoo bee.

2022, Jan. 3 Litho. *Perf. 12¼*

Self-Adhesive

1857-1860 A769 Set of 4 13.50 13.50

2022 Winter Olympics, Beijing — A770

Designs: 1.10fr, Skiing. 2.10fr, Two-man bobsledding.

Litho. & Embossed With Foil Application

2022, Feb. 4 *Perf. 13½*

1861-1862 A770 Set of 2 7.00 7.00

Chimney Sweeps and Good Luck Symbols — A771

Designs: 90rp, Male chimney sweep and horseshoes. 110rp, Female chimney sweep and four-leaf clovers.

Litho. With Foil Application

2022, Mar. 7 *Perf. 13½*

1863-1864 A771 Set of 2 4.50 4.50

Europa A772

No. 1865: a, Legend of the Tälibudel. b, Legend of the White Woman.

2022, Mar. 7 Litho. *Perf. 12¼x12*

1865 A772 Pair 8.00 8.00
a.-b. 1.80fr Either single 4.00 4.00

Souvenir Sheet

Molière (1622-73), Playwright and Actor — A773

No. 1866: a. Molière's acting group, Troupe du Roi. b, L'Ecole des Femmes, play by Molière. c, Portrait of Molière, by Pierre Mignard.

2022, Mar. 7 Litho. *Perf. 12*

1866 A773 Sheet of 3 11.50 11.50
a.-b. 110rp Either single 2.00 2.00
c. 410rp multi 7.25 7.25

Glass of Water — A774

2022, June 7 Litho. *Perf. 12*

1867 A774 180rp multi 3.75 3.75

Mountains — A775

No. 1868: a, Alpspitz, denomination at UL. b, Alpspitz, denomination at UR. c, Drei Kapuziner, denomination at UL. d, Drei Kapuziner, denomination at UR.

2022, June 7 Litho. *Perf. 13¼*

1868 A775 Block of 4 9.00 9.00
a.-d. 110rp Any single 2.25 2.25

Souvenir Sheet

Princess Marie of Liechtenstein (1940-2021) — A776

2022, June 7 Litho. *Perf. 12*

1869 A776 6.30fr multi 13.50 13.50

Souvenir Sheet

Oskar Werner (1922-84), Actor — A777

No. 1870 — Werner: a, Looking left, as young man. b, Wearing sunglasses. c, Looking right, holding drink.

Litho. With Foil Application

2022, June 7 *Perf. 12*

1870 A777 Sheet of 3 6.25 6.25
a.-b. 90rp Either single 1.90 1.90
c. 110rp multi 2.25 2.25

Planken A778

Designs: 90rp, Village center. 110rp, Schuhmacher-Nägele House.

Litho. & Embossed

2022, Sept. 9 *Perf. 13¼*

1871-1872 A778 Set of 2 4.00 4.00

Paintings by Ferdinand Runk (1764-1834) A779

Paintings: 90rp, Eisgrub Castle Park. 1.10fr, Lundenburg Castle. 1.80fr, Schlössen am Schüttel in the Prater.

Litho. With Foil Application

2022, Sept. 9 *Perf. 12*

1873-1875 A779 Set of 3 7.75 7.75

Souvenir Sheet

Austrian Federal Railways Reihe 4024 Railcar A780

2022, Sept. 9 Litho. *Perf. 12*

1876 A780 180rp multi 3.75 3.75
a. Souvenir sheet of 3, Austria #3010, Liechtenstein #1876, Switzerland #1891 9.50 —

Feldkirch-Schaan-Buchs railway line, 150th anniv. No. 1876a sold for 4.65fr. See Austria No. 3010, Switzerland No. 1891.

Souvenir Sheet

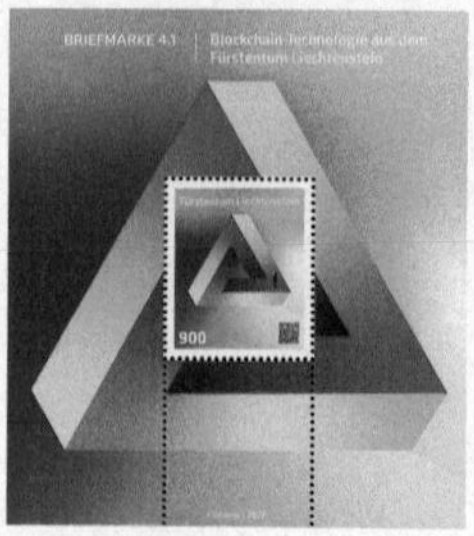

Optical Illusion and QR Code
A781

2022, Sept. 9 Litho. *Perf. 12½x12¼*
1877 A781 900rp multi 18.50 18.50

Blockchain technology.

SEMI-POSTAL STAMPS

Prince Johann II — SP1

Wmk. 183

1925, Oct. 5 Engr. *Perf. 11½*

B1	SP1 10rp yellow green	42.50	22.50
B2	SP1 20rp deep red	21.00	22.50
B3	SP1 30rp deep blue	7.00	7.00
	Nos. B1-B3 (3)	70.50	52.00
	Set, never hinged	210.00	

85th birthday of the Prince Regent. Sold at a premium of 5rp each, the excess being devoted to charities.

Coat of Arms — SP2

1927, Oct. 5 Typo.

B4	SP2 10rp multicolored	10.50	*25.00*
B5	SP2 20rp multicolored	10.50	*25.00*
B6	SP2 30rp multicolored	5.00	*21.00*
	Nos. B4-B6 (3)	26.00	*71.00*
	Set, never hinged	62.00	

87th birthday of Prince Johann II.
These stamps were sold at premiums of 5, 10 and 20rp respectively. The money thus obtained was devoted to charity.

Railroad Bridge Demolished by Flood — SP3

Designs: 10rp+10rp, Inundated Village of Ruggel. 20rp+10rp, Austrian soldiers rescuing refugees. 30rp+10rp, Swiss soldiers salvaging personal effects.

1928, Feb. 6 Litho. Unwmk.

B7	SP3 5rp + 5rp brn vio & brn	17.50	26.00
B8	SP3 10rp + 10rp bl grn & brn	25.00	26.00
B9	SP3 20rp + 10rp dl red & brn	25.00	26.00
B10	SP3 30rp + 10rp dp bl & brn	21.00	26.00
	Nos. B7-B10 (4)	88.50	104.00
	Set, never hinged	220.00	

The surtax on these stamps was used to aid the sufferers from the Rhine floods.

Coat of Arms — SP7

Princess Elsa — SP8

Design: 30rp, Prince Francis I.

1932, Dec. 21 Photo.

B11	SP7 10rp (+ 5rp) olive grn	17.50	*25.00*
B12	SP8 20rp (+ 5rp) rose red	17.50	*22.50*
B13	SP8 30rp (+ 10rp) ultra	22.50	*32.50*
	Nos. B11-B13 (3)	57.50	*80.00*
	Set, never hinged	160.00	

The surtax was for the Child Welfare Fund.

Postal Museum Issue
Souvenir Sheet

SP10

1936, Oct. 24 Litho. *Imperf.*

B14	SP10 Sheet of 4	15.00	*35.00*
	Never hinged	60.00	

Sheet contains 2 each, Nos. 120, 122. Sold for 2fr.

"Protect the Child" — SP11

Designs: No. B16, "Take Care of the Sick." No. B17, "Help the Aged."

Perf. 11½

1945, Nov. 27 Photo. Unwmk.

B15	SP11 10rp + 10rp multi	.65	*1.75*
B16	SP11 20rp + 20rp multi	.65	*2.25*
B17	SP11 1fr + 1.40fr multi	4.75	*20.00*
	Nos. B15-B17 (3)	6.05	*24.00*
	Set, never hinged	11.00	

Souvenir Sheet

Post Coach
SP14

1946, Aug. 10

B18	SP14 Sheet of 2	21.00	*32.50*
	Never hinged	35.00	
a.	10rp dark violet brown & buff	5.00	*15.00*
	Never hinged	12.50	

25th anniv. of the Swiss-Liechtenstein Postal Agreement. Sheet, size: 82x60½mm, sold for 3fr.

Canal by Albert Cuyp
SP15

Willem van Huythuysen by Frans Hals
SP16

40rp+10rp, Landscape by Jacob van Ruysdael.

1951, July 24 *Perf. 11½*

B19	SP15 10rp + 10rp ol grn	5.00	7.00
B20	SP16 20rp + 10rp dk vio brn	5.00	*7.00*
B21	SP15 40rp + 10rp blue	5.00	7.00
	Nos. B19-B21 (3)	15.00	*21.00*
	Set, never hinged	30.00	

Issued in sheets of 12. For surcharges see Nos. 281-283.

Catalogue values for unused stamps in this section, from this point to the end of the section, are for Never Hinged items.

Nos. 324-325 Surcharged with New Value and Uprooted Oak Emblem

1960, Apr. 7

B22	A190 30rp + 10rp on 40rp	.55	*1.00*
B23	A190 50rp + 10rp on 25rp	.90	*2.00*

World Refugee Year, July 1, 1959-June 30, 1960. The surtax was for aid to refugees.

Growth Symbol — SP17

1967, Dec. 7 Photo. *Perf. 11½*

B24	SP17 50rp + 20rp multi	.50	.60

Surtax was for development assistance.

AIR POST STAMPS

Airplane over Snow-capped Mountain Peaks — AP1

Airplane above Vaduz Castle — AP2

Airplane over Rhine Valley — AP3

Perf. 10½, 10½x11½

1930, Aug. 12 Photo. Unwmk.

Gray Wavy Lines in Background

C1	AP1 15rp dark brown	10.50	*17.50*
C2	AP1 20rp slate	25.00	*25.00*
C3	AP2 25rp olive brown	14.00	*45.00*
C4	AP2 35rp slate blue	21.00	*42.50*
C5	AP3 45rp olive green	50.00	*87.50*
C6	AP3 1fr lake	55.00	*62.50*
	Nos. C1-C6 (6)	175.50	*280.00*
	Set, never hinged	518.00	

For surcharge see No. C14.

Zeppelin over Naafkopf, Falknis Range — AP4

Design: 2fr, Zeppelin over Valüna Valley.

1931, June 1 *Perf. 11½*

C7	AP4 1fr olive black	70.00	*125.00*
C8	AP4 2fr blue black	140.00	*400.00*
	Set, never hinged	565.00	

Golden Eagle — AP6

15rp, Golden Eagle in flight, diff. 20rp, Golden Eagle in flight, diff. 30rp, Osprey. 50rp, Eagle.

1934-35

C9	AP6 10rp brt vio ('35)	9.00	*32.50*
C10	AP6 15rp red org ('35)	22.50	*30.00*
C11	AP6 20rp red ('35)	82.50	*30.00*
C12	AP6 30rp brt bl ('35)	22.50	*30.00*
C13	AP6 50rp emerald	15.00	*35.00*
	Nos. C9-C13 (5)	151.50	157.50
	Set, never hinged	300.00	

No. C6 Surcharged

1935, June 24 *Perf. 10½x11½*

C14	AP3 60rp on 1fr lake	40.00	42.50
	Never hinged	130.00	

Airship "Hindenburg" AP11

Design: 2fr, Airship "Graf Zeppelin."

1936, May 1 *Perf. 11½*

C15	AP11 1fr rose carmine	40.00	75.00
C16	AP11 2fr violet	30.00	75.00
	Set, never hinged	160.00	

AP13

10rp, Barn swallows. 15rp, Black-headed Gulls. 20rp, Gulls. 30rp, Eagle. 50rp, Northern Goshawk. 1fr, Lammergeier. 2fr, Lammergeier.

1939, Apr. 3 Photo.

C17	AP13 10rp violet	.60	.70
C18	AP13 15rp red orange	.60	2.00
C19	AP13 20rp dark red	2.75	.80
C20	AP13 30rp dull blue	1.20	1.50
C21	AP13 50rp brt green	3.00	3.25
C22	AP13 1fr rose car	2.25	*12.00*
C23	AP13 2fr violet	2.25	*12.00*
	Nos. C17-C23 (7)	12.65	*32.25*
	Set, never hinged	40.00	

Catalogue values for unused stamps in this section, from this point to the end of the section, are for Never Hinged items.

AP20

Designs: 10rp, Leonardo da Vinci. 15rp, Joseph Montgolfier. 20rp, Jacob Degen. 25rp, Wilhelm Kress. 40rp, E. G. Robertson. 50rp, W. S. Henson. 1fr, Otto Lilienthal. 2fr, S. A. Andrée. 5fr, Wilbur Wright. 10fr, Icarus.

1948

C24	AP20 10rp dark green	.75	.25
C25	AP20 15rp dark violet	.75	.80
C26	AP20 20rp brown	1.00	.25
a.	20rp reddish brown	95.00	3.25
C27	AP20 25rp dark red	1.50	1.25
C28	AP20 40rp violet blue	1.75	1.25
C29	AP20 50rp Prus blue	2.00	1.25
C30	AP20 1fr chocolate	3.50	2.75
C31	AP20 2fr rose lake	5.25	3.50
C32	AP20 5fr olive green	6.50	4.75
C33	AP20 10fr slate black	42.50	14.00
	Nos. C24-C33 (10)	65.50	30.05

Issued in sheets of 9.
Exist imperf. Value, set $6,500.

Helicopter, Bell 47-J — AP21

Planes: 40rp, Boeing 707 jet. 50rp, Convair 600 jet. 75rp, Douglas DC-8.

1960, Apr. 7 Unwmk. *Perf. 11½*

C34	AP21 30rp red orange	2.25	2.25
C35	AP21 40rp blue black	3.75	2.25
C36	AP21 50rp deep claret	9.50	4.00
C37	AP21 75rp olive green	2.00	2.25
	Nos. C34-C37 (4)	17.50	10.75

30th anniv. of Liechtenstein's air post stamps.

POSTAGE DUE STAMPS

National Administration of the Post Office

D1

1920 Unwmk. Engr. *Perf. 12½*

J1	D1	5h rose red	.35	.40
J2	D1	10h rose red	.35	.40
J3	D1	15h rose red	.35	.40
J4	D1	20h rose red	.35	.55
J5	D1	25h rose red	.35	.55
J6	D1	30h rose red	.35	.55
J7	D1	40h rose red	.35	.55
J8	D1	50h rose red	.35	.55
J9	D1	80h rose red	.35	.55
J10	D1	1k dull blue	.40	1.40
J11	D1	2k dull blue	.40	1.40
J12	D1	5k dull blue	.40	1.75
		Nos. J1-J12 (12)	4.35	9.05
		Set, never hinged	12.50	

Nos. J1-J12 exist imperf. (value, unused, set $260) and part perf. (value, each: unused $2; never hinged $7; used $7).

J3 lacks the outside frame lines.

Swiss Administration of the Post Office

D2

1928 Litho. Wmk. 183 *Perf. 11½*

Granite Paper

J13	D2	5rp pur & org	1.20	*3.00*
J14	D2	10rp pur & org	1.20	*3.00*
J15	D2	15rp pur & org	1.75	*13.50*
J16	D2	20rp pur & org	1.75	*3.00*
J17	D2	25rp pur & org	1.75	*9.00*
J18	D2	30rp pur & org	6.00	*13.50*
J19	D2	40rp pur & org	7.00	*14.00*
J20	D2	50rp pur & org	9.00	*17.50*
		Nos. J13-J20 (8)	29.65	*76.50*
		Set, never hinged	65.00	

Post Horn — D3

Engraved; Value Typographed in Dark Red

1940 Unwmk. *Perf. 11½*

J21	D3	5rp gray blue	1.25	*2.75*
J22	D3	10rp gray blue	.60	*1.40*
J23	D3	15rp gray blue	1.25	*5.00*
J24	D3	20rp gray blue	.60	*2.00*
J25	D3	25rp gray blue	1.25	*3.50*
J26	D3	30rp gray blue	2.00	*5.50*
J27	D3	40rp gray blue	2.00	*5.50*
J28	D3	50rp gray blue	3.00	*5.50*
		Nos. J21-J28 (8)	11.95	*31.15*
		Set, never hinged	35.00	

OFFICIAL STAMPS

Regular Issue of 1930 Overprinted in Various Colors

Perf. 10½, 11½, 11½x10½

1932 Unwmk.

O1	A38	5rp dk grn (Bk)	10.50	15.50
O2	A39	10rp dark vio (R)	75.00	15.50
O3	A40	20rp dp rose red (Bl)	90.00	15.50
O4	A42	30rp ultra (R)	17.50	21.00
O5	A43	35rp dp grn (Bk)	14.00	*35.00*
O6	A45	50rp blk brn (Bl)	77.50	*21.00*
O7	A46	60rp olive blk (R)	14.00	*50.00*
O8	A48	1.20fr olive brn (G)	150.00	425.00
		Nos. O1-O8 (8)	448.50	598.50
		Set, never hinged	1,763.	

Values are for the most common perf. variety. See Scott Classic Specialized catalogue for detailed listings.

Nos. 108, 110 Overprinted in Black

1933 *Perf. 14½*

O9	A51	25rp red orange	42.50	45.00
O10	A53	1.20fr red brown	85.00	*275.00*
		Set, never hinged	360.00	

Regular Issue of 1934-35 Ovptd. in Various Colors

1934-36 *Perf. 11½*

O11	A58	5rp emerald (R)	2.10	*3.50*
O12	A59	10rp dp vio (Bk)	4.25	*3.50*
O13	A60	15rp red org (V)	.90	*3.50*
O14	A61	20rp red (Bk)	.70	*3.50*
O15	A62	25rp brown (R)	35.00	*115.00*
O16	A62	25rp brown (Bk)	3.50	*15.00*
O17	A63	30rp dark bl (R)	5.00	*10.50*
O18	A66	50rp lt brown (V)	1.40	*17.50*
O19	A68	90rp dp grn (Bk)	7.50	*10.50*
O20	A69	1.50fr brn car (Bl)	42.50	*280.00*
		Nos. O11-O20 (10)	102.85	*462.50*
		Set, never hinged	358.00	

Regular Issue of 1937-38 Overprinted in Black, Red or Blue

1937-41

O21	A76	5rp emerald (Bk)	.40	.75
O22	A76	10rp vio & buff (R)	.80	2.00
O23	A76	20rp brn org (Bl)	1.60	2.00
O24	A76	20rp brn org (Bk) ('41)	1.60	2.75
O25	A76	25rp chestnut (Bk)	.80	2.75
O26	A77	30rp blue & gray (Bk)	2.75	2.75
O27	A79	50rp dk brn & buff (R)	1.25	2.10
O28	A80	1fr red brown (Bk)	1.25	*12.00*
O29	A80	1.50fr slate bl (Bk) ('38)	5.00	*17.50*
		Nos. O21-O29 (9)	15.45	*44.60*
		Set, never hinged	49.50	

Catalogue values for unused stamps in this section, from this point to the end of the section, are for Never Hinged items.

Stamps of 1944-45 Overprinted in Black

1947

O30	A136	5rp slate grn & buff	1.60	1.10
O31	A136	10rp gray & buff	1.60	1.10
O32	A136	20rp org red & buff	2.10	1.10
O33	A136	30rp blue & buff	2.75	1.75
O34	A136	50rp bluish blk & pale gray	2.75	3.50
O35	A136	1fr dp cl & buff	11.00	11.00
O36	A136	150rp royal blue	11.00	14.00
		Nos. O30-O36 (7)	32.80	33.55

Crown — O1

Engr.; Value Typo.

1950-68 Unwmk. *Perf. 11½*

Buff Granite Paper

Narrow Gothic Numerals

O37	O1	5rp red vio & gray	.25	.25
O38	O1	10rp ol grn & mag	.25	.25
O39	O1	20rp org brn & bl	.25	.25
O40	O1	30rp dk red brn & org red	.25	.25
O41	O1	40rp blue & hn brn	.35	.35
O42	O1	55rp dk gray grn & red	.70	1.10
a.		White paper ('68)	45.00	*125.00*
O43	O1	60rp slate & mag	.70	1.10
a.		White paper ('68)	6.00	*22.50*
O44	O1	80rp red org & gray	.70	.90
O45	O1	90rp choc & blue	.90	1.25
O46	O1	1.20fr grnsh bl & org	1.10	1.25
		Nos. O37-O46 (10)	5.45	6.95

1968-69 *Perf. 11½*

White Granite Paper

Broad Numerals, Varying Thickness

O47	O1	5rp olive brn & org	.25	.25
O48	O1	10rp violet & car	.25	.25
O49	O1	20rp ver & emer	.25	.25
O50	O1	30rp green & red	.25	.25
O51	O1	50rp ultra & red	.35	.35
O52	O1	60rp orange & ultra	.40	.40
O53	O1	70rp maroon & emer	.50	.50
O54	O1	80rp bl grn & car	.55	.55
O55	O1	95rp slate & red ('69)	.65	.65
O56	O1	1fr rose cl & grn	.70	.70
O57	O1	1.20fr lt red brn & grn	.80	.80
O58	O1	2fr brn & org ('69)	1.25	1.25
		Nos. O47-O58 (12)	6.20	6.20

Government Building, Vaduz — O2

Engr., Value Typo.

1976-89 *Perf. 14*

O59	O2	10rp yel brn & vio	.25	.25
O60	O2	20rp car lake & bl	.25	.25
O61	O2	35rp blue & red	.25	.25
O62	O2	40rp dull pur & grn	.30	.30
O63	O2	50rp slate & mag	.40	.40
O64	O2	70rp vio brn & bl grn	.55	.55
O65	O2	80rp green & mag	.60	.60
O66	O2	90rp vio & bl grn	.70	.70
O67	O2	1fr olive & mag	.80	.80
O68	O2	1.10fr brown & ultra	.85	.85
O69	O2	1.50fr dull grn & red	1.25	1.25
O70	O2	2fr orange & blue	1.60	1.60
O75	O2	5fr rose vio & brn org	5.75	5.75
		Nos. O59-O75 (13)	13.55	13.55

Issued: 5fr, 9/4/89; others, 12/9/76.

LITHUANIA

ˌli-thə-ˈwā-nē-ə

(Lietuva)

LOCATION — Northern Europe bordering on the Baltic Sea
GOVT. — Independent republic
AREA — 25,170 sq. mi.
POP. — 3,584,966 (1999 est.)
CAPITAL — Vilnius

Lithuania was under Russian rule when it declared its independence in 1918. The League of Nations recognized it in 1922. In 1940 it became a republic in the Union of Soviet Socialist Republics.

Lithuania declared its independence on March 11, 1990. Lithuanian independence was recognized by the Soviet Union on Sept. 6, 1991.

100 Skatiku = 1 Auksinas
100 Centai = 1 Litas (1922, 1993)
100 Kopecks = 1 Ruble (1991)
100 Cents = 1 Euro (2015)

Catalogue values for unused stamps in this country are for Never Hinged items, beginning with Scott 371 in the regular postage section and Scott B55 in the semi-postal section.

Nos. 1-26 were printed in sheets of 20 (5x4) which were imperf. at the outer sides, so that only 6 stamps in each sheet were fully perforated. Values are for the stamps partly imperf. The stamps fully perforated sell for at least double these values. There was also a printing of Nos. 19-26 in a sheet of 160, composed of blocks of 20 of each stamp. Pairs or blocks with different values se-tenant sell for considerably more than the values for the stamps singly.

Nos. 1-26 are without gum.

Watermarks

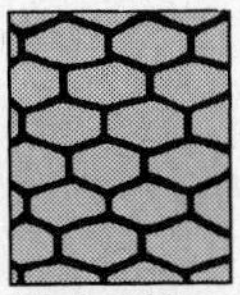
Wmk. 109 — Webbing

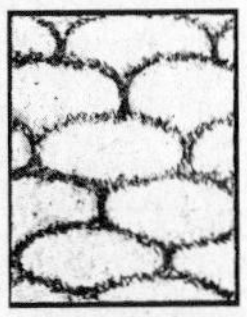
Wmk. 144 — Network

Wmk. 145 — Wavy Lines

Wmk. 146 — Zigzag Lines Forming Rectangles

Wmk. 147 — Parquetry

Wmk. 198 — Intersecting Diamonds

Wmk. 209 — Multiple Ovals

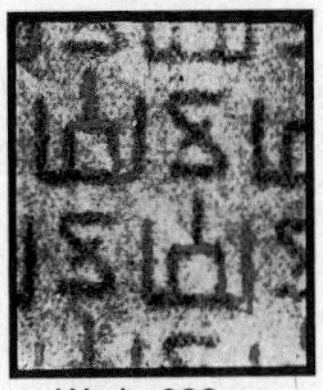
Wmk. 238 — Multiple Letters

First Vilnius Printing

A1

Thin Figures

Perf. 11½

1918, Dec. 27 Unwmk. Typeset

1	A1	10sk black	150.00	125.00
2	A1	15sk black	150.00	100.00

Second Vilnius Printing

1918, Dec. 31 **Thick Figures**

3	A1	10sk black	70.00	55.00
4	A1	15sk black	70.00	55.00
5	A1	20sk black	30.00	16.00
6	A1	30sk black	35.00	17.50
7	A1	40sk black	50.00	25.00
8	A1	50sk black	40.00	17.50
		Nos. 3-8 (6)	295.00	186.00

First Kaunas Issue

A2

1919, Jan. 29

9	A2	10sk black	7.50	3.75
10	A2	15sk black	7.50	3.75
a.		"5" for "15"	95.00	72.50
11	A2	20sk black	7.50	3.75
12	A2	30sk black	7.50	3.75
		Nos. 9-12 (4)	30.00	15.00

Second Kaunas Issue

A3

1919, Feb. 18

13	A3	10sk black	4.25	2.50
14	A3	15sk black	4.25	2.50
15	A3	20sk black	4.25	2.50
a.		"astas" for "pastas"	80.00	75.00
16	A3	30sk black	4.25	2.50
17	A3	40sk black	4.25	2.50
18	A3	50sk black	4.25	2.50
19	A3	60sk black	4.25	2.50
		Nos. 13-19 (7)	29.75	17.50

Third Kaunas Issue

A4

1919, Mar. 1

20	A4	10sk black	4.25	1.75
21	A4	15sk black	4.25	1.75
22	A4	20sk black	4.25	1.75
23	A4	30sk black	4.25	1.75
24	A4	40sk black	4.25	1.75
25	A4	50sk black	4.25	1.75
26	A4	60sk black	4.25	1.75
		Nos. 20-26 (7)	29.75	12.25

The White Knight "Vytis"

A5 A6

A7

Perf. 10½ to 14 & Compound

1919 **Litho.** **Wmk. 144**

Gray Granite Paper

30	A5	10sk deep rose	1.25	.40
a.		Wmk. vert.	17.50	15.00
31	A5	15sk violet	1.25	.40
a.		Wmk. vert.	17.50	15.00
32	A5	20sk dark blue	1.60	.40
33	A5	30sk deep orange	1.60	.40
a.		Wmk. vert.	17.50	15.00
34	A5	40sk dark brown	1.60	.40
35	A6	50sk blue green	1.60	.50
36	A6	75sk org & dp rose	1.60	.50
37	A7	1auk gray & rose	3.25	.50
38	A7	3auk bis brn & rose	3.25	.50
39	A7	5auk blue grn & rose	3.25	.80
		Nos. 30-39 (10)	20.25	4.80

Nos. 30a, 31a and 33a are from the first printing with watermark vertical showing points to left; various perforations.

Nos. 30-39 exist imperf. Value in pairs, $100.

Issued: Nos. 30a, 31a, 33a, 2/17/19; Nos. 30-36, 3/20/19.

Thick White Paper

1919 **Wmk. 145**

40	A5	10sk dull rose	.35	.25
41	A5	15sk violet	.35	.25
42	A5	20sk dark blue	.35	.25
43	A5	30sk orange	.35	.25
44	A5	40sk red brown	.35	.25
45	A6	50sk pale grayish green	.35	.25
46	A6	75sk yel & dp rose	.35	.25
47	A7	1auk gray & rose	.95	.35
48	A7	3auk yel brn & rose, perf. 12½	.60	.40
49	A7	5auk bl grn & rose	1.00	.40
		Nos. 40-49 (10)	5.00	2.90

Nos. 40-49 exist imperf. Value in pairs, $90.

A8

Perf. 10½ to 14 & Compound

1919, May 8 **Thin White Paper**

50	A5	10sk red	.45	.25
51	A5	15sk lilac	.45	.25
52	A5	20sk dull blue	.45	.25
53	A5	30sk buff	.45	.25
54	A5	40sk gray brn	.45	.25
55	A6	50sk lt green	.45	.25
56	A6	60sk violet & red	.45	.25
57	A6	75sk bister & red	.45	.25
58	A8	1auk gray & red	.45	.25
59	A8	3auk lt brown & red	.45	.30
60	A8	5auk blue grn & red	.45	.45
		Nos. 50-60 (11)	4.95	3.00

Nos. 50-60 exist imperf. Value, pairs $150.

See Nos. 93-96. For surcharges see Nos. 114-115, 120-139, 149-150.

"Lithuania" Receiving Benediction
A9

The Spirit of Lithuania Rises
A10

"Lithuania" with Chains Broken
A11

White Knight
A12

1920, Feb. 16 **Wmk. 146** ***Perf. 11½***

70	A9	10sk dp rose	3.75	*5.25*
71	A9	15sk lt violet	3.75	*5.25*
72	A9	20sk gray blue	3.75	*5.25*
73	A10	30sk yellow brn	3.75	*5.25*
74	A11	40sk brown & grn	3.75	*5.25*
75	A10	50sk deep rose	3.75	*5.25*
76	A10	60sk lt violet	3.75	*5.25*
77	A11	80sk purple & red	3.75	*5.25*
78	A11	1auk green & red	3.75	*5.25*
79	A12	3auk brown & red	3.75	*5.25*
80	A12	5auk green & red	3.75	*5.25*
a.		Right "5" dbl., grn and red	90.00	90.00
		Nos. 70-80 (11)	41.25	*57.75*

Anniv. of natl. independence. The stamps were on sale only 3 days in Kaunas. The stamps were available in other cities after that. Only a limited number of stamps was sold at post offices but 40,000 sets were delivered to the bank of Kaunas.

All values exist imperforate.

White Knight
A13

Grand Duke Vytautas
A14

Grand Duke Gediminas
A15

Sacred Oak and Altar
A16

1920, Aug. 25

81	A13	10sk rose	.80	1.60
a.		Imperf., pair	40.00	
82	A13	15sk dark violet	.80	1.60
83	A14	20sk grn & lt grn	.80	1.60
84	A13	30sk brown	.80	1.60
a.		Pair, #82, 84	40.00	
85	A15	40sk gray grn & vio	.80	1.60
86	A14	50sk brn & brn org	2.00	2.00
87	A14	60sk red & org	.80	1.60
88	A15	80sk blk, db & red	.80	1.60
89	A16	1auk orange & blk	1.25	1.60
90	A16	3auk green & blk	1.25	1.60
91	A16	5auk gray vio & blk	3.25	2.40
		Nos. 81-91 (11)	13.35	18.80

Opening of Lithuanian National Assembly. On sale for three days.

1920

92	A14	20sk green & lilac	125.00
92A	A15	40sk gray grn, buff & vio	125.00
92B	A14	50sk brown & gray lil	125.00
92C	A14	60sk red & green	125.00
92D	A15	80sk black, grn & red	125.00
		Nos. 92-92D (5)	625.00

Nos. 92 to 92D were trial printings. By order of the Ministry of Posts, 2,000 examples of each were placed on sale at post offices.

Type of 1919 Issue

1920 **Unwmk.** ***Perf. 11½***

93	A5	15sk lilac	6.00	4.50
94	A5	20sk deep blue	6.00	4.50

Wmk. 109

95	A5	20sk deep blue	5.00	5.00
96	A5	40sk gray brown	9.75	8.50
		Nos. 93-96 (4)	26.75	22.50
		Set, never hinged	40.00	

Watermark vertical or horizontal on Nos. 95-96.

No. 96 exists perf. 10½x11½.

Imperf., Pairs

93a	A5	15sk	32.00	32.00
94a	A5	20sk	32.00	32.00
95a	A5	20sk	17.00	17.00
96a	A5	40sk	48.00	48.00

Sower
A17

Peasant Sharpening Scythe
A18

Prince Kestutis
A19

Black Horseman
A20

Perf. 11, 11½ and Compound

1921-22

97	A17	10sk brt rose	.85	.55
98	A17	15sk violet	.35	*.70*
99	A17	20sk ultra	.25	.25
100	A18	30sk brown	2.50	*1.10*
101	A19	40sk red	.25	.25
102	A18	50sk olive	.35	.25
103	A18	60sk grn & vio	2.50	*1.65*
104	A19	80sk brn org & car	.35	.25
105	A19	1auk brown & grn	.35	.25
106	A19	2auk gray bl & red	.35	.25
107	A20	3auk yel brn & dk bl	1.00	.40
108	A17	4auk yel & dk bl ('22)	.45	.25
109	A20	5auk gray blk & rose	1.00	*1.50*
110	A17	8auk grn & blk ('22)	.45	.25
111	A20	10auk rose & vio	1.00	.55
112	A20	25auk bis brn & grn	1.25	*2.75*
113	A20	100auk dl red & gray blk	12.50	8.00
		Nos. 97-113 (17)	25.75	19.20
		Set, never hinged	85.00	

Imperf., Pairs

97a	A17	10sk	—	
98a	A17	15sk	—	
99a	A17	20sk	—	
100a	A18	30sk	—	
101a	A19	40sk	25.00	
102a	A18	50sk	25.00	
103a	A18	60sk	—	
104a	A19	80sk	—	
105a	A19	1auk	—	
106a	A19	2auk	120.00	
107a	A20	3auk	120.00	
109a	A20	5auk	120.00	
110a	A17	8auk	10.00	10.00
111a	A20	10auk	50.00	
112a	A20	25auk	50.00	
113a	A20	100auk	50.00	

For surcharges see Nos. 140-148, 151-160.

No. 57 Surcharged

Perf. 12½x11½

1922, May **Wmk. 145**

114	A6	4auk on 75sk bis & red	.90	.25
a.		Inverted surcharge	35.00	35.00

Same with Bars over Original Value

115	A6	4auk on 75sk bis & red	4.00	*8.00*
a.		Double surcharge	30.00	30.00

Povilas Luksis — A20a

Justinas Staugaitis, Antanas Smetona, Stasys Silingas — A20b

Portraits: 40s, Lt. Juozapavicius. 50s, Dr. Basanavicius. 60s, Mrs. Petkeviciute. 1auk, Prof. Voldemaras. 2auk, Pranas Dovidaitis. 3auk, Dr. Slezevicius. 4auk, Dr. Galvanauskas. 5auk, Kazys Grinius. 6auk, Dr. Stulginskis. 8auk, Pres. Smetona.

1922 **Litho.** **Unwmk.**

116	A20a	20s blk & car rose	1.25	*2.10*
116A	A20a	40s bl grn & vio	1.25	*2.10*
116B	A20a	50s plum & grnsh bl	1.25	*2.10*
117	A20a	60s pur & org	1.25	*2.10*
117A	A20a	1auk car & lt bl	1.25	*2.10*
117B	A20a	2auk dp bl & yel brn	1.25	*2.10*
c.		Center inverted	100.00	100.00
118	A20a	3auk mar & ultra	1.25	*2.10*
118A	A20a	4auk dk grn & red vio	1.25	*2.10*
118B	A20a	5auk blk brn & dp rose	1.25	*2.10*
119	A20a	6auk dk bl & grnsh bl	1.25	*2.10*
a.		Cliché of 8auk in sheet of 6auk	175.00	*175.00*
119B	A20a	8auk ultra & bis	1.25	*2.10*
119C	A20b	10auk dk vio & bl grn	1.25	*2.10*
		Nos. 116-119C (12)	15.00	25.20
		Set, never hinged	45.00	

League of Nations' recognition of Lithuania. Sold only on Oct. 1, 1922.

Forty sheets of the 6auk each included eight examples of the 8auk.

Stamps of 1919-22 Surcharged in Black, Carmine or Green On Nos. 37-39

1922 **Wmk. 144** ***Perf. 11½x12***

Gray Granite Paper

120	A7	3c on 1auk	100.00	*100.00*
121	A7	3c on 3auk	100.00	*100.00*
122	A7	3c on 5auk	150.00	*150.00*
		Nos. 120-122 (3)	350.00	350.00
		Set, never hinged	750.00	

White Paper

Perf. 14, 11½, 12½x11½

Wmk. 145

123	A5	1c on 10sk red	.55	1.50
124	A5	1c on 15sk lilac	.80	1.50
125	A5	1c on 20sk dull bl	.50	1.50
126	A5	1c on 30sk org	*250.00*	*110.00*
127	A5	1c on 30sk buff	.25	.40
128	A5	1c on 40sk gray brn	1.60	1.50

129 A6 2c on 50sk green .70 1.50
130 A6 2c on 60sk vio & red .25 .25
131 A6 2c on 75sk bis & red .40 1.50
132 A8 3c on 1auk gray & red .25 .25
133 A8 3c on 3auk brn & red .25 .25
134 A8 3c on 5auk bl grn & red .25 .25
Nos. 123-125,127-134 (11) 5.80 10.40
Set, never hinged, *Nos. 123-125, 127-134)* 24.00

On Stamps of 1920

1922 Unwmk. *Perf. 11*
136 A5 1c on 20sk dp bl (C) 3.75 2.00

Wmk. Webbing (109)
Perf. 11, 11½
138 A5 1c on 20sk dp bl (C) 3.50 2.00
139 A5 1c on 40sk gray brn (C) 7.50 1.25

Stamps of 1921-22 Surcharged

140 A18 1c on 50sk ol (C) .25 .25
a. Imperf., pair 45.00
b. Inverted surcharge 40.00
c. Double surch., one invtd.
141 A17 3c on 10sk 11.00 8.00
142 A17 3c on 15sk .25 .25
143 A17 3c on 20sk .40 1.50
144 A18 3c on 30sk 18.50 12.00
145 A19 3c on 40sk .40 .40
a. Imperf., pair
146 A18 5c on 50sk .25 .25
147 A18 5c on 60sk 18.50 18.50
148 A19 5c on 80sk .55 .55
a. Imperf., pair 35.00 15.00

Wmk. Wavy Lines (145)
Perf. 12½x11½
149 A6 5c on 4auk on 75sk (No. 114) (G) 1.60 10.00
150 A6 5c on 4auk on 75sk (No. 115) (G) 16.00 17.50

Wmk. Webbing (109)
Perf. 11, 11½
151 A19 10c on 1auk .80 .25
a. Inverted surcharge 55.00
152 A19 10c on 2auk .25 .25
a. Inverted surcharge 50.00
b. Imperf., pair 45.00
153 A17 15c on 4auk .25 .25
a. Inverted surcharge 45.00
154 A20 25c on 3auk 18.50 18.50
155 A20 25c on 5auk 11.00 5.00
156 A20 25c on 10auk 2.25 1.50
a. Imperf., pair 45.00
157 A17 30c on 8auk (C) 1.15 .35
a. Inverted surcharge 45.00 25.00
158 A20 50c on 25auk 3.75 2.50
160 A20 1 l on 100auk 4.00 2.50
Nos. 136-160 (23) 124.40 105.55
Set, never hinged 140.00

A21

Ruin — A22

Seminary Church, Kaunas — A23

1923 Litho. Wmk. 109 *Perf. 11*
165 A21 10c violet 7.00 .25
166 A21 15c scarlet 2.50 .25
167 A21 20c olive brown 2.50 .25
168 A21 25c dark blue 2.50 .25
169 A22 50c yellow green 2.50 .25
170 A22 60c red 2.50 .25
171 A23 1 l orange & grn 10.50 .25
172 A23 3 l red & gray 15.00 .45
173 A23 5 l brown & blue 21.00 1.00
Nos. 165-173 (9) 66.00 3.20
Set, never hinged 125.00

See Nos. 189-209, 281-282. For surcharges see Nos. B1-B42.

Memel Coat of Arms — A24

Lithuanian Coat of Arms — A25

Biruta Chapel A26

Kaunas, War Memorial A27

Trakai Ruins — A28

Memel Lighthouse A29

Memel Harbor — A30

Perf. 11, 11½, 12
1923, Aug. Unwmk.
176 A24 1c rose, grn & blk 1.25 1.60
177 A25 2c dull vio & blk 1.25 1.60
178 A26 3c yellow & blk 1.25 1.60
179 A24 5c bl, buff & blk 2.50 4.50
180 A27 10c orange & blk 1.90 3.00
181 A27 15c green & blk 1.90 3.00
182 A28 25c brt vio & blk 1.90 3.00
183 A25 30c red vio & blk 4.00 *7.50*
184 A29 60c ol grn & blk 2.25 *3.00*
185 A30 1 l bl grn & blk 2.25 *3.00*
186 A26 2 l red & black 8.25 15.00
187 A28 3 l blue & black 8.25 15.00
188 A29 5 l ultra & black 8.25 15.00
Nos. 176-188 (13) 45.20 76.80
Set, never hinged 100.00

This series was issued ostensibly to commemorate the incorporation of Memel with Lithuania.

Type of 1923

1923 Unwmk. *Perf. 11*
189 A21 5c pale green 3.75 .75
190 A21 10c violet 5.00 .75
a. Imperf., pair 50.00
191 A21 15c scarlet 6.00 .75
a. Imperf., pair 50.00
193 A21 25c blue 10.00 .75
Nos. 189-193 (4) 24.75 3.00
Set, never hinged 60.00

1923 Wmk. 147
196 A21 2c pale brown 1.50 .45
197 A21 3c olive bister 2.25 .45
198 A21 5c pale green 2.25 .45
199 A21 10c violet 4.50 .45
202 A21 25c deep blue 11.00 .45
a. Imperf., pair 40.00
204 A21 36c orange brown 17.50 1.50
Nos. 196-204 (6) 39.00 3.75
Set, never hinged 70.00

Perf. 11½, 14½, 11½x14½
1923-25 Wmk. 198
207 A21 25c deep blue 750.00 450.00
208 A22 50c deep green ('25) *25.00* 1.00
209 A22 60c carmine ('25) *25.00* .50

Double-barred Cross — A31

1927, Jan. *Perf. 11½, 14½*
210 A31 2c orange 1.50 .35
211 A31 3c deep brown 1.50 .35
212 A31 5c green 2.25 .35
a. Imperf., pair 25.00
213 A31 10c violet 3.25 .35
214 A31 15c red 3.25 .35
a. Imperf., pair 25.00
215 A31 25c blue 3.25 .30
Nos. 210-215 (6) 15.00 2.05
Set, never hinged 45.00

1926-30 Wmk. 147 *Perf. 14½*
216 A31 5c green 35.00 *150.00*
217 A31 30c blue ('30) 30.00 10.00

See Nos. 233-240, 278-280.

Dr. Jonas Basanavicius — A32

1927 Unwmk. *Perf. 11½, 14½x11½*
219 A32 15c claret & blk 3.00 1.50
220 A32 25c dull blue & blk 3.00 1.50
221 A32 50c dk green & blk 3.00 1.50
222 A32 60c dk violet & blk 9.00 3.00
Nos. 219-222 (4) 18.00 7.50
Set, never hinged 35.00

Dr. Jonas Basanavicius (1851-1927), patriot and folklorist.

National Arms — A33

1927, Dec. 23 Wmk. 109 *Perf. 14½*
223 A33 1 l blue grn & gray 6.50 .80
224 A33 3 l vio & pale grn 5.00 .80
225 A33 5 l brown & gray 6.00 1.40
Nos. 223-225 (3) 17.50 3.00
Set, never hinged 25.00

Pres. Antanas Smetona A34

Decade of Independence A35

Dawn of Peace — A36

1928, Feb. Wmk. 109
226 A34 5c org brn & grn 1.00 .75
227 A34 10c violet & blk 1.25 .75
228 A34 15c orange & brn 1.25 .75
229 A34 25c blue & indigo 1.25 .75
230 A35 50c ultra & dl vio 1.50 .75
231 A35 60c carmine & blk 1.75 .75
232 A36 1 l blk brn & drab 2.00 2.25
Nos. 226-232 (7) 10.00 6.75
Set, never hinged 15.00

10th anniv. of Lithuanian independence.

Type of 1926

1929-31
233 A31 2c orange ('31) 12.00 1.60
234 A31 5c green 4.00 .35
235 A31 10c violet ('31) 10.00 2.00
237 A31 15c red 4.50 .45
a. Tête bêche pair 45.00 35.00
239 A31 30c dark blue 6.00 .45

Unwmk.
240 A31 15c red ('30) 10.00 .75
Nos. 233-240 (6) 46.50 5.60
Set, never hinged 85.00

Grand Duke Vytautas A37

Grand Duke, Mounted A38

1930, Feb. 16 *Perf. 14*
242 A37 2c yel brn & dk brn .30 .25
243 A37 3c dk brn & vio .30 .25
244 A37 5c yel grn & dp org .30 .25
245 A37 10c vio & emer .30 .25
246 A37 15c dp rose & vio .30 .25
247 A37 30c dk bl & brn vio .50 .25
248 A37 36c brn vio & ol blk .75 .30
249 A37 50c dull grn & ultra .50 .35
250 A37 60c dk blue & rose .50 .40
251 A38 1 l bl grn, db & red brn 2.10 1.00
252 A38 3 l dk brn, sal & dk vio 3.25 1.75
253 A38 5 l ol brn, gray & red 7.50 2.75
254 A38 10 l multicolored 20.00 16.00
255 A38 25 l multicolored 42.50 55.00
Nos. 242-255 (14) 79.10 79.05
Set, never hinged 200.00

5th cent. of the death of the Grand Duke Vytautas.

Kaunas, Railroad Station — A39

Cathedral at Vilnius — A39a

Designs: 15c, 25c, Landscape on the Neman River. 50c, Main Post Office, Kaunas.

1932, July 21 Wmk. 238 *Perf. 14*
256 A39 10c dk red brn & ocher .40 *.40*
257 A39 15c dk brown & ol .40 *.40*
258 A39 25c dk blue & ol 1.25 *1.25*
259 A39 50c gray blk & ol 2.50 2.50
260 A39a 1 l blue & gray 6.50 6.50
261 A39a 3 l red brn & gray grn 6.50 6.50

Wmk. 198
262 A39 5c vio bl & ocher .40 *.40*
263 A39a 60c grnsh blk & lil 6.50 6.50
Nos. 256-263 (8) 24.45 24.45
Set, never hinged 60.00

Imperf.
256a A39 10c dk red brn & ocher .35 .35
257a A39 15c dk brown & ol .65 .65
258a A39 25c dk blue & ol 1.00 1.00
259a A39 50c gray blk & ol 2.00 2.00
260a A39a 1 l dk blue & ol 5.25 5.25
261a A39a 3 l red brn & gray grn 5.25 5.25
262a A39 5c violet bl & ocher .35 .35
263a A39a 60c grnsh blk & lil 5.25 5.25
Set, never hinged 35.00

Issued for the benefit of Lithuanian orphans.

In September, 1935, a red overprint was applied to No. 259: "ORO PASTAS / LITUANICA II / 1935 / NEW YORK-KAUNAS." Value, $400.

Vytautas Fleeing from Prison, 1382 — A40

Designs: 15c, 25c, Conversion of Ladislas II Jagello and Vytautas (1386). 50c, 60c, Battle at Tannenberg (1410). 1 l, 3 l, Meeting of the Nobles (1429).

1932 Wmk. 209 *Perf. 14*
264 A40 5c red & rose lake .35 *.35*
265 A40 10c ol bis & org brn .35 *.35*
266 A40 15c rose lil & ol grn .35 *.35*
267 A40 25c dk vio brn & ocher 1.00 *1.00*

268 A40 50c dp grn & bis brn 1.00 *1.00*
269 A40 60c ol grn & brn car 2.40 *2.40*
270 A40 1 l ultra & ol grn 2.40 *2.40*
271 A40 3 l dk brn & dk grn 2.40 *2.40*
Nos. 264-271 (8) 10.25 *10.25*
Set, never hinged 25.00

Imperf.

264a A40 5c red & rose lake .65 .65
265a A40 10c ol bis & org brn .65 .65
266a A40 15c rose lil & ol grn .65 .65
267a A40 25c dk vio brn & ocher 2.00 2.00
268a A40 50c dp grn & bis brn 4.50 4.50
269a A40 60c ol grn & brn car 4.50 4.50
270a A40 1 l ultra & ol grn 4.50 4.50
271a A40 3 l dk brn & dk grn 4.50 4.50
Set, never hinged 35.00

15th anniversary of independence.

A. Visteliauskas — A41

Designs: 15c, 25c, Petras Vileisis. 50c, 60c, Dr. John Sliupas. 1 l, 3 l, Jonas Basanavicius.

1933 ***Perf. 14***
272 A41 5c yel grn & car .40 .40
273 A41 10c ultra & car .40 .40
274 A41 15c orange & red .40 .40
275 A41 25c dk bl & blk brn 1.25 *1.25*
276 A41 50c ol gray & dk bl 1.25 *1.25*
277 A41 60c org brn & chnt 5.50 5.50
277A A41 1 l red & vio brn 5.50 5.50
277B A41 3 l turq grn & vio brn 5.50 5.50
Nos. 272-277B (8) 20.20 20.20
Set, never hinged 35.00

Imperf.

272a A41 5c yel grn & car .40 .40
273a A41 10c ultra & car .40 .40
274a A41 15c orange & red .40 .40
275a A41 25c dk bl & blk brn 1.25 1.25
276a A41 50c ol gray & dk bl 1.25 1.25
277a A41 60c org brn & chnt 5.50 5.50
277Aa A41 1 l red & vio brn 5.50 5.50
277Ba A41 3 l turq grn & vio brn 5.50 5.50
Set, never hinged 35.00

50th anniv. of the 1st newspaper, "Ausra," in lithuanian language.

Mother and Child — A42

Boy Reading — A42a

Boy Playing With Blocks A42b

Woman and Boy at the Spinning Wheel — A42c

Designs: 25c, Boy reading. 60c, Boy playing with blocks. 3 l, Woman and boy at the spinning wheel.

1933, Sept. ***Perf. 14***
277C A42 5c dp yel grn & org brn .35 .35
277D A42 10c rose brn & ultra .35 *.35*
277E A42a 15c ol grn & plum .35 *.35*
277F A42a 25c org & gray blk 1.40 *1.40*
277G A42b 50c ol grn & car 1.40 *1.40*
277H A42b 60c blk & yel org 5.75 5.75
277I A42c 1 l dk brn & ultra 5.75 5.75
277K A42c 3 l rose lil & ol grn 5.75 *5.75*
Nos. 277C-277K (8) 21.10 *21.10*
Set, never hinged 35.00

Imperf.

277Ca A42 5c dp yel grn & org brn .25 .25
277Da A42 10c rose brn & ultra .25 .25
277Ea A42a 15c ol grn & plum .25 .25
277Fa A42a 25c org & gray blk 1.00 1.00
277Ga A42b 50c ol gray & dk bl 1.00 1.00
277Ha A42b 60c org brn & chnt 4.25 4.25
277Ia A42c 1 l dk brn & ultra 4.25 4.25
277Ka A42c 3 l rose lil & ol grn 4.25 4.25
Set, never hinged 25.00

Issued for the benefit of Lithuanian orphans.

Types of 1923-26

1933-34 **Wmk. 238** ***Perf. 14***
278 A31 2c orange 42.50 6.50
279 A31 10c dark violet 60.00 9.50
280 A31 15c red 42.50 4.50
281 A22 50c green 42.50 9.50
282 A22 60c red 42.50 9.50
Nos. 278-282 (5) 230.00 39.50
Set, never hinged 400.00

Pres. Antanas Smetona, 60th Birthday — A43

1934 **Engr.** **Unwmk.** ***Perf. 11½***
283 A43 15c red 6.50 1.50
284 A43 30c green 8.25 1.50
285 A43 60c blue 10.00 2.00
Nos. 283-285 (3) 24.75 5.00
Set, never hinged 42.50

A44

Arms A45

Girl with Wheat A46

A47

Knight — A48

Wmk. 198; Wmk. 209 (35c, 10 l)

1934-35 **Litho.** ***Perf. 14***
286 A44 2c rose & dull org 1.50 .25
287 A44 5c bl grn & grn 1.50 .25
288 A45 10c chocolate 3.50 .25
289 A46 25c dk brn & emer 5.50 .25
290 A45 35c carmine 5.50 .25
291 A46 50c dk blue & blue 10.00 .25
292 A47 1 l salmon & mar 92.50 .25
293 A47 3 l grn & gray grn .45 .25
294 A48 5 l maroon & gray bl .65 .45
295 A48 10 l choc & yel 4.50 3.75
Nos. 286-295 (10) 125.60 6.20
Set, never hinged 275.00

No. 290 exists imperf. Value, pair $65.
For overprint see No. 2N9.

1936-37 **Wmk. 238** ***Perf. 14***
Size: 17½x23mm
296 A44 2c orange ('37) .40 .30
297 A44 5c green .40 .30

Pres. Smetona — A49

1936-37 **Unwmk.**
298 A49 15c carmine 5.50 .35
299 A49 30c green ('37) 9.00 .35
300 A49 60c ultra ('37) 10.00 .35
Nos. 298-300 (3) 24.50 1.05
Set, never hinged 40.00

Arms — A50

No. 304 exists in two types:
I — "50" is fat and broad, with "0" leaning to right.
II — "50" is thinner and narrower, with "0" straight.

Paper with Gray Network

1937-39 **Wmk. 238** ***Perf. 14***
301 A50 10c green .85 .25
302 A50 25c magenta .25 .25
303 A50 35c red .50 .25
304 A50 50c brown .30 .25
305 A50 1 l dp vio bl ('39) .35 .45
Nos. 301-305 (5) 2.25 1.45
Set, never hinged 10.00

For overprint see No. 2N10.

Jonas Basanavicius Reading Act of Independence A51

President Antanas Smetona A52

Perf. 13x13½

1939, Jan. 15 **Engr.** **Unwmk.**
306 A51 15c dark red .25 *.30*
307 A52 30c deep green .50 .30
308 A51 35c red lilac .60 .45
309 A52 60c dark blue .75 .60
a. Souvenir sheet of 2, #308-309 5.00 10.00
b. As "a," imperf. 35.00 45.00
Nos. 306-309 (4) 2.10 1.65
Set, never hinged 5.00

20th anniv. of Independence.
Nos. 309a, 309b sold for 2 l.

Same Overprinted in Blue

1939
310 A51 15c dark red .50 *.90*
311 A52 30c deep green .50 *.90*
312 A51 35c red lilac 1.25 1.00
313 A52 60c dark blue 1.25 1.00
Nos. 310-313 (4) 3.50 3.80
Set, never hinged 7.00

Recovery of Vilnius.

View of Vilnius A53

Gediminas A54

Trakai Ruins — A55

Unwmk.

1940, May 6 **Photo.** ***Perf. 14***
314 A53 15c brn & pale brn .40 .25
315 A54 30c dk grn & lt grn .90 .50
316 A55 60c dk bl & lt bl 2.00 .70
a. Souv. sheet of 3, #314-316, imperf. 8.00 *16.00*
Nos. 314-316 (3) 3.30 1.45
Set, never hinged 5.00

Return of Vilnius to Lithuania, Oct. 10, 1939. Exist imperf.
No. 316a has simulated perforations in gold. Sold for 2 l.

White Knight A56

Angel A57

Woman Releasing Dove A58

Mother and Children A59

Liberty Bell A60

Mythical Animal A61

1940
317 A56 5c brown carmine .40 *.30*
318 A57 10c green .40 *.45*
319 A58 15c dull orange .40 *.30*
320 A59 25c light brown .40 *.40*
321 A60 30c Prussian green .40 *.30*
322 A61 35c red orange .40 *.35*
Nos. 317-322 (6) 2.40 *2.10*
Set, never hinged 4.50

Nos. 317-322 exist imperf.
For overprints see Nos. 2N11-2N16.

Catalogue values for unused stamps in this section, from this point to the end of the section, are for Never Hinged items.

Nos. 371-399 were issued before the Soviet Union recognized the independence of Lithuania on Sept. 6, 1991, but were available and valid for use after that date.

Angel and Map — A66

Colors: 5k, Green. 10k, Brown violet. 20k, Blue. 50k, Red.

1990, Oct. 7 **Litho.** ***Imperf.***
Without Gum
371-374 A66 Set of 4 1.75 1.75

Simulated Perforations and Denomination in Brownish Gray

Colors as before.

1990, Dec. 22 **Without Gum**
375-378 A66 Set of 4 1.60 1.60

White Knight "Vytis" A67

Hill With Crosses, Siauliai A68

Design: 200k, Liberty Bell.

1991 **Photo.** ***Perf. 14***
379 A67 10k multi .30 .25
380 A67 15k multi .30 .25
381 A67 20k multi .30 .25
382 A67 30k multi .30 .25
383 A68 50k multi .30 .25
384 A68 200k multi .40 .25

Litho.
Imperf
Without Gum

385 A67 15k dl grn & blk .30 .25
386 A67 25k brn & blk .30 .25
387 A67 30k plum & blk .30 .25
Nos. 379-387 (9) 2.80 2.25

Issued: 10k, 20k, No. 382, 50k, 200k, 1/10; No. 380, 3/15; No. 385, 3/13; 25k, No 387, 7/23.

No. 385 has a simulated outline of a perforated stamp.

See Nos. 411-418.

Liberty Statue — A69

1991, Feb. 16 Photo. ***Perf. 13¾x14***
388 A69 20k multi .50 .25

Declaration of Independence from Soviet Union, 1st Anniv. — A70

1991, Mar. 11 Litho. ***Perf. 13¼x13***
389 A70 20k multi .50 .25

Religious Symbols — A71

Designs: 40k, Crosses. 70k, Madonna. 100k, Spires, St. Anne's Church, Vilnius.

1991, Mar. 15 Photo. ***Perf. 13¾x14***
390-392 A71 Set of 3 1.25 .75

Resistance to Soviet and German Occupation, 50th Anniv. — A72

Designs: 20k, Candle, barbed wire. 50k, Heart, daggers. 70k, Sword, wreath.

1991, June 14 Litho. ***Perf. 13¼***
393-395 A72 Set of 3 1.25 .75

Fourth World Lithuanian Games — A73

Emblem and: 20k, Map. 50k+25k, Head.

1991, July 27 Photo. ***Perf. 13¼x13***
396-397 A73 Set of 2 1.00 .50

Expedition to Mt. Everest — A74

Denominations: 20k, 70k.

1991. Aug. 20 Litho. ***Perf. 12½x13***
398-399 A74 Set of 2 1.00 .75

A75

1991, Sept. 28 Litho. ***Perf. 13x13½***
400 A75 30k Castle .50 .30
401 A75 50k Grand Duke .50 .50
402 A75 70k Early view of Vilnius 1.00 1.00
Nos. 400-402 (3) 2.00 1.80

Grand Duke Gediminas, 650th death anniv.

Ciconia Nigra — A76

Design: 50k, Grus grus.

1991, Nov. 21 Litho. ***Perf. 14***
403 A76 30k +15k multi .90 .55
404 A76 50k multicolored 1.00 .65

White Knight Type of 1991

1991, Dec. 20 Photo. ***Perf. 14***
Background Colors

411 A67 40k black .25 .25
412 A67 50k purple .25 .25
415 A67 100k dark green .25 .25
418 A67 500k blue 1.25 .55
Nos. 411-418 (4) 2.00 1.30

For surcharges see Nos. 450-452.

Lithuanian Admission to UN — A78

1992, Mar. 15 Litho. ***Perf. 13x13½***
421 A78 100k multicolored .50 .30

Lithuanian Olympic Participation — A79

Emblems: No. 422, Olympic Committee. No. 423, Albertville. No. 424, Barcelona.

1992, Mar. 22
422 A79 50k +25k multi .30 .30
423 A79 130k multi .45 .45
424 A79 280k multi 1.25 1.25
Nos. 422-424 (3) 2.00 2.00

Surtax for Lithuanian Olympic Committee.

A80

200k, Cypripedium. 300k, Eringium maritimum.

1992, July 11 ***Perf. 12½x13***
425 A80 200k multicolored .40 .30
426 A80 300k multicolored .60 .50

A81

Birds of the Baltic Shores: No. 427, Pandion haliaetus. No. 428, Limosa limosa. No. 429, Mergus merganser. No. 430, Tadorna tadorna.

Litho. & Engr.

1992, Oct. 3 ***Perf. 12½x13***
Booklet Stamps

427 A81 B grn & grnsh blk .70 .50
428 A81 B grn & red brn .70 .50
429 A81 B grn, red brn & brn .70 .50
430 A81 B grn & red brn .70 .50
a. Booklet pane of 4, #427-430 3.50

Sold for 15r on day of issue.

See Estonia Nos. 231-234a, Latvia Nos. 332-335a and Sweden Nos. 1975-1978a.

Coats of Arms — A82

1992, Oct. 11 Litho. ***Perf. 14***
431 A82 2r Kedainiai .25 .25
432 A82 3r Vilnius .25 .25
433 A82 10r National .55 .55
Nos. 431-433 (3) 1.05 1.05

See Nos. 454-456, 497-499, 521-522, 554-556, 586-588, 607-609, 642-644, 677-679, 704-706, 716-718, 736-740, 762-764, 788-789, 813-815, 833-835, 879-881, 887-889, 910-912, 945-947, 958-960.

19th Cent. Costumes — A83

Couples in different traditional costumes of the Suwalki region.

1992, Oct. 18 ***Perf. 13x13½***
434 A83 2r multicolored .25 .25
435 A83 5r multicolored .25 .25
436 A83 7r multicolored .50 .35
Nos. 434-436 (3) 1.00 .85

See Nos. 465-467, 493-495, 511-513, 539-541.

Churches — A84

300k, Zapishkis Church, 16th cent. 1000k, Saints Peter & Paul Church, Vilnius, 17th cent. 1500k, Christ Church of the Resurrection, Kaunas, 1934.

1993, Jan. 15 Litho. ***Perf. 12***
437 A84 300k bister & blk .30 .25
438 A84 1000k blue green & blk .70 .25
439 A84 1500k gray & blk 1.00 .30
Nos. 437-439 (3) 2.00 .80

See Nos. 502-504

Independence A85

Designs: A, Jonas Basanavicius (1851-1927), journalist and politician. B, Jonas Vileisis (1872-1942), lawyer and politician.

1993, Feb. 16
440 A85 (A) red & multi .25 .25
441 A85 (B) green & multi .95 .65

No. 440 sold for 3r and No. 441 sold for 15r on day of issue.

See Nos. 479-480, 506-507, 536-537, 563-564, 592-593, 622-623, 660-661, 686-687, 711-712.

A86

Grand Duke Vytautas, 600th Birth Anniv. — A87

Designs: 500k, Royal Seal. 1000k, 5000k, Portrait. 1500k, Vytautas in Battle of Grunwald, by Jan Matejko.

1993, Feb. 27
442 A86 500k bister, red & blk .30 .25
443 A87 1000k citron, blk & red .70 .30
444 A87 1500k lem, blk & red 1.00 .50
Nos. 442-444 (3) 2.00 1.05

Souvenir Sheet

445 A87 5000k citron, black & red 2.00 2.00

Famous Lithuanians — A88

Designs: 1000k, Simonas Daukantas (1793-1864), educator and historian. 2000k, Vydunas (1868-1953), preserver of Lithuanian traditional culture. 4500k, Vincas Mykolaitis Putinas (1893-1967), philosopher and psychologist.

1993, Mar. 13
446 A88 1000k multicolored .25 .25
447 A88 2000k multicolored .50 .50
448 A88 4500k multicolored 1.25 .90
Nos. 446-448 (3) 2.00 1.65

See Nos. 475-477, 514-516, 533-535, 560-562, 599-601, 624-626.

No. 382, 387 and 411 Surcharged

1993 Photo, Litho. (#451) ***Perf. 14***
450 A67 100k on 30k magenta .25 .25
451 A67 100k on 30k magenta, imperf, without gum .50 .25
452 A67 300k on 40k #411 .25 .25
Nos. 450-452 (3) 1.00 .75

Issued: 300k, 1/19; No. 450, 1/26; No. 451, 3/10.

Coat of Arms Type of 1992
Size: 24x31mm

1993, July 3 Litho. ***Perf. 11***
454 A82 5c Skuodas .25 .25
a. Tete-beche pair .40 .40
455 A82 30c Telsiai .35 .30
a. Tete-beche pair 1.20 .60
456 A82 50c Klaipeda .55 .45
a. Tete-beche pair 1.70 .90
Nos. 454-456 (3) 1.15 1.00

World Lithuanian Unity Day — A89

5c, The Spring, by M. K. Ciurlionis. 80c, Capts. Steponas Darius and Stasys Girenas.

1993, July 17 ***Perf. 13***
457 A89 5c multicolored .25 .25
a. Tete-beche pair .30
458 A89 80c multicolored .75 .75
a. Tete-beche pair 2.40

Deaths of Darius and Girenas, 60th anniv. (No. 458).

Natl. Arms — A90

1993, July 21 Litho. *Perf. 13x12½*

459	A90	(A) bister & multi	.30	.25
460	A90	(B) green & multi	.80	.25

No. 459 sold for 5c, No. 460 for 80c on day of issue.
Dated 1992.

Visit of Pope John Paul II — A91

1993, Sept. 3 Litho. *Perf. 13½x13*

461	A91	60c Kryziu Kalnas	.50	.30
462	A91	60c Siluva	.50	.30
463	A91	80c Vilnius	.70	.35
464	A91	80c Kaunas	.70	.35
		Nos. 461-464 (4)	2.40	1.30

Natl. Costumes Type of 1992

Couples in different traditional costumes of the Dzukai.

1993, Oct. 30 Litho. *Perf. 12*
Size: 23x36mm

465	A83	60c multicolored	.40	.25
466	A83	80c multicolored	.60	.35
467	A83	1 l multicolored	1.00	.45
		Nos. 465-467 (3)	2.00	1.05

Lithuanian Postal System, 75th Anniv. — A92

Post offices: No. 468, Klaipeda. No. 469, Kaunas. 80c, Vilnius. 1 l, No. 1.

1993, Nov. 16

468	A92	60c multicolored	.40	.25
469	A92	60c multicolored	.40	.25
470	A92	80c multicolored	.60	.30
471	A92	1 l multicolored	.90	.40
		Nos. 468-471 (4)	2.30	1.20

Europa — A93

80c, The Old Master, by A. Gudaitis, 1939.

1993, Dec. 24 Litho. *Perf. 12*

472	A93	80c multicolored	2.00	1.40
a.		Tete-beche pair	4.00	4.00

Endangered Species — A94

1993, Dec. 30 Litho. *Perf. 12*

473	A94	80c Emys orbicularis	.60	.30
474	A94	1 l Bufo calamita	1.00	.40

See Nos. 500-501, 519-520.

Famous Lithuanians Type of 1993

Designs: 60c, Kristijonas Donelaitis (1714-80), poet. 80c, Vincas Kudirka (1858-99), physician, writer. 1 l, Maironis (1862-1932), poet.

1994, Mar. 26 Litho. *Perf. 12*

475	A88	60c multicolored	.40	.25
476	A88	80c multicolored	.65	.30
477	A88	1 l multicolored	1.00	.40
		Nos. 475-477 (3)	2.05	.95

1994 Winter Olympics, Lillehammer — A95

1994, Feb. 11

478	A95	1.10 l multicolored	1.00	.40

Independence Type of 1993

No. 479, Pres. Antanas Smetona (1874-1944). No. 480, Aleksandras Stulginskis.

1994, Feb. 16

479	A85	1 l red brown & multi	.80	.35
480	A85	1 l brown & multi	.80	.35

A96

Natl. Arms — A96a

Perf. 12, 13½ (40c), 13½x13 (50c)
1994-97 Litho.

481	A96	5c dark brown	.25	.25
482	A96	10c deep violet	.25	.25
483	A96	20c dark green	.25	.25
484	A96	40c deep rose mag	.25	.25
485	A96	50c green blue	.30	.25
486	A96a	1 l gray & multi	.50	.25
a.		Souvenir sheet of 4	3.00	3.00
487	A96a	2 l buff & multi	1.90	.50
488	A96a	3 l green & multi	2.50	.75
		Nos. 481-488 (8)	6.20	2.75

Independence, 5th anniv. (No. 486a).
Issued: 5c, 10c, 4/9/94; 20c, 11/19/94; 2 l, 3 l, 7/23/94; 1 l, 3/11/95; 40c, 5/4/96; 50c, 4/5/97.

Europa — A97

80c, Artillery rockets, 17th cent.

1994, May 7 Litho. *Perf. 12*

491	A97	80c multicolored	.50	.40

Souvenir Sheet

100th Postage Stamp A98

1994, May 21 Litho. *Perf. 12*

492	A98	10 l multicolored	10.00	10.00

No. 492 sold for 12 l.

Natl. Costumes Type of 1992

Couples in different traditional costumes of Samogitia.

1994, June 25 Litho. *Perf. 12*

493	A83	5c multicolored	.30	.25
494	A83	80c multicolored	.60	.25
495	A83	1 l multicolored	.70	.30
		Nos. 493-495 (3)	1.60	.80

Lithuanian World Song Festival — A99

1994, July 6

496	A99	10c multicolored	.50	.25

Coat of Arms Type of 1992

1994, Sept. 10 Litho. *Perf. 12*
Size: 25x32mm

497	A82	10c Punia	.25	.25
498	A82	60c Alytus	.45	.25
499	A82	80c Perloja	.60	.30
		Nos. 497-499 (3)	1.30	.80

Endangered Species Type of 1993

1994, Oct. 22 Litho. *Perf. 12*

500	A94	20c Nyctalus noctula	.35	.25
501	A94	20c Glis glis	.35	.25

Church Type of 1993

1994, Nov. 12

502	A84	10c Kaunus, 16th cent.	.25	.25
503	A84	60c Kedainiu, 17th cent.	.45	.25
504	A84	80c Vilnius, 18th cent.	.60	.35
		Nos. 502-504 (3)	1.30	.85

Christmas A101

1994, Dec. 3 Litho. *Perf. 12*

505	A101	20c multicolored	.25	.25

Independence Type of 1993

No. 506, Pranas Dovydaitis. No. 507, Steponas Kairys.

1995, Feb. 16 Litho. *Perf. 12*

506	A85	20c multicolored	.25	.25
507	A85	20c multicolored	.25	.25

A102

Via Baltica Highway Project: Nos. 508, 509c, Kaunas, Lithuania: No. 509a, Beach Hotel, Parnu, Estonia. No. 509b, Castle, Bauska, Latvia.

1995, Apr. 20 Litho. *Perf. 14*

508	A102	20c multicolored	.25	.25

Souvenir Sheet

509	A102	1 l Sheet of 3, #a.-c.	2.50	2.50

See Estonia Nos. 288-289, Latvia Nos. 394-395.

Sculpture, Mother's School — A103

1995, Apr. 29 Litho. *Perf. 12*

510	A103	1 l multicolored	1.00	1.00

Europa.

Natl. Costumes Type of 1992

Couples in traditional costumes of Aukstaiciai.

1995, May 20 Litho. *Perf. 12*

511	A83	20c multicolored	.25	.25
512	A83	70c multicolored	.60	.25
513	A83	1 l multicolored	.75	.30
		Nos. 511-513 (3)	1.60	.80

Famous People Type of 1993

Writers: 30c, Motiejus Valancius (1801-75). 40c, Zemaite (1845-1921). 70c, Kipras Petrauskas (1885-1968).

1995, May 27 Litho. *Perf. 12*

514	A88	30c multicolored	.25	.25
515	A88	40c multicolored	.40	.25
516	A88	70c multicolored	.60	.25
		Nos. 514-516 (3)	1.25	.75

Day of Mourning & Hope — A104

1995, June 14 Litho. *Perf. 12*

517	A104	20c multicolored	.25	.25

5th World Sports Games — A105

1995, July 30 Litho. *Perf. 12*

518	A105	30c multicolored	.25	.25

Endangered Species Type of 1993

1995, Aug. 26 Litho. *Perf. 12*

519	A94	30c Arctia villica	.40	.25
520	A94	30c Baptria tibiale	.40	.25

Coat of Arms Type of 1992
Size: 25x32mm

Arms of villages in Suvalkija: 40c, Virbalis. 1 l, Kudirkos Naumiestis, horiz.

1995, Sept. 16 Litho. *Perf. 12*

521	A82	40c multicolored	.30	.25
522	A82	1 l multicolored	.75	.30

Valerie Mesalina, by Pranciskus Smuglevicius A106

1995, Oct. 6 Litho. *Perf. 12½*

523	A106	40c multicolored	.50	.25

Castles A107

1995, Nov. 18 *Perf. 11½x12*

524	A107	40c Vilnius	.30	.25
525	A107	70c Trakai	.60	.30
526	A107	1 l Birzai	.90	.45
		Nos. 524-526 (3)	1.80	1.00

Christmas — A108

Designs: 40c, People celebrating Christmas in outdoor snow scene. 1 l, People with lanterns walking toward church.

1995, Dec. 2 Litho. *Perf. 13*

527	A108	40c multicolored	.30	.25
528	A108	1 l multicolored	.75	.45

Bison Bonasus — A109

1996, Jan. 20 *Perf. 13x13½*

529	A109	30c shown	.25	.25
530	A109	40c Two adults	.40	.25
531	A109	70c Adult, calf	.60	.40
532	A109	1 l Two adults, calf	.80	.80
a.		Miniature sheet, 2 each #529-532	4.50	4.50
		Nos. 529-532 (4)	2.05	1.70

World Wildlife Fund.

Famous Lithuanians Type of 1993

Designs: 40c, Kazys Grinius (1866-1950). No. 534, Antanas Zmudzinavicius (1876-1966). No. 535, Balys Sruoga (1896-1947).

1996, Feb. 2 Litho. *Perf. 13x13½*

533 A88	40c multicolored	.30	.25
534 A88	1 l multicolored	.60	.40
535 A88	1 l multicolored	.60	.40
	Nos. 533-535 (3)	1.50	1.05

Independence Type of 1993

No. 536, Vladas Mironas. No. 537, Jurgis Saulys.

1996, Feb. 16 Litho. *Perf. 13½x13*

536 A85	40c gray, blk & buff	.30	.25
537 A85	40c olive, blk & buff	.30	.25

Barbora Radvilaite (1520-51) — A110

1996, Apr. 27 Litho. *Perf. 13½x13*

538 A110	1 l multicolored	1.00	1.00

Europa.

19th Cent. Costumes Type of 1992

Couples in different traditional costumes of the Klaipeda region: No. 540, Man in blue coat. No. 541, Man wearing wooden shoes.

1996, May 25 Litho. *Perf. 13½*

539 A83	40c multicolored	.35	.25
540 A83	1 l multicolored	.75	.35
541 A83	1 l multicolored	.75	.35
	Nos. 539-541 (3)	1.85	.95

Day of Mourning and Hope — A116

1996, June 14 Litho. *Perf. 13½*

547 A116	40c Christ	.40	.25
548 A116	40c Angel	.40	.25

A117

Designs: No. 549, Greek discus thrower. No. 550, Basketball players.

1996, July 19 *Perf. 13½x13*

549 A117	1 l multicolored	1.00	.50
550 A117	1 l multicolored	1.00	.50

1996 Summer Olympic Games, Atlanta.

Paintings, by M.K. Ciurlionis — A118

No. 551, Kapines, 1909. No. 552, Auka, 1909.
No. 553: a, Andante, 1908. b, Allegro, 1908.

1996, Sept. 21 Litho. *Perf. 13½x13*

551 A118	40c multicolored	.35	.25
552 A118	40c multicolored	.35	.25

Souvenir Sheet
Perf. 12½x11½

553 A118	3 l Sheet of 2, #a.-b.	5.00	5.00

No. 553 contains 26x53mm stamps.

Coat of Arms Type of 1992
Size: 25x33mm

1996, Oct. 19 Litho. *Perf. 13½x13*

554 A82	50c Seduva	.45	.25
555 A82	90c Panevezys	.65	.35
556 A82	1.20 l Zarasai	.90	.50
	Nos. 554-556 (3)	2.00	1.10

Souvenir Sheet

Lithuanian Basketball Team, Bronze Medalists, 1996 Summer Olympic Games, Atlanta A119

1996, Nov. 16 *Perf. 12½*

557 A119	4.20 l multicolored	3.50	3.50

Christmas — A120

1996, Nov. 30 *Perf. 13½x13*

558 A120	50c Angels	.35	.25
559 A120	1.20 l Santa on horse	1.00	.50

Famous Lithuanians Type of 1993

Designs: 50c, Ieva Simonaityte (1897-1978). 90c, Jonas Sliupas (1861-1944). 1.20 l, Vladas Jurgutis (1885-1966).

1997, Jan. 23 Litho. *Perf. 13x13½*

560 A88	50c brown & greem	.40	.25
561 A88	90c gray & yellow	.70	.35
562 A88	1.20 l blue green & orange	.90	.45
	Nos. 560-562 (3)	2.00	1.05

Independence Type of 1993

No. 563, Mykolas Birziska. No. 564, Kazimieras Saulys.

1997, Feb. 16 Litho. *Perf. 13½x13*

563 A85	50c multicolored	.35	.25
564 A85	50c multicolored	.35	.25

First Lithuanian Book, 450th Anniv. — A121

1997, Feb. 15 Litho. *Perf. 13½x13*

565 A121	50c gray & red	.45	.25

Souvenir Sheet

566 A121	4.80 l like #565	3.50	3.50

No. 566 contains one 29x38mm stamp.

Souvenir Sheet

Flag on Mountain Top A122

1997, Feb. 25 *Perf. 11½x12½*

567 A122	4.80 l multicolored	4.00	4.00

Expeditions to highest peaks on each continent.

Stories and Legends — A123

Children's drawings: No. 568, Girl, horse. No. 569, King, moon, stars, bird, vert.

1997, Apr. 12 Litho. *Perf. 13*

568 A123	1.20 l multicolored	1.00	1.00
569 A123	1.20 l multicolored	1.00	1.00

Europa.

A124

1997, May 9 Litho. *Perf. 13*

570 A124	50c multicolored	.45	.25

First Lithuanian School, 600th Anniv.

A125

Old Ships of the Baltic Sea: 50c, Kurenas, 16th cent.
No. 572: a, Kurenas, 16th cent., diff. b, Maasilinn ship, 16th cent. c, Linijkugis, 17th cent.

1997, May 10 *Perf. 14x14½*

571 A125	50c multicolored	.45	.25
572 A125	1.20 l Sheet of 3, #a.-c.	3.00	3.00

See Estonia Nos. 322-323, Latvia Nos. 443-444.

Palanga Botanical Park, Cent. — A126

1997, June 1 Litho. *Perf. 13½x13*

573 A126	50c multicolored	.45	.25
a.	Tete-beche pair	.90	.90

Numbers 574-577 are unassigned.

2nd Baltic Sea Games — A127

1997, June 25 Litho. *Perf. 13½*

578 A127	90c multicolored	.75	.35

Museum Art — A128

Designs: 90c, Animal face carved on ritual staff. 1.20 l, Coins, 15th cent.

1997, July 12 *Perf. 13½x13*

579 A128	90c multicolored	.75	.35
580 A128	1.20 l multicolored	1.00	.50

Double Barred Crosses — A129

1997, Aug. 2 Litho. *Perf. 13½*

581 A129	20c olive	.30	.25
582 A129	50c brown	.50	.25
a.	Inscribed "1998"	.50	.25

Nos. 581 and 582 are inscribed "1997." See Nos. 602, 604, 617-619.

Mushrooms — A130

Designs: No. 583, Morchella elata. No. 584, Boletus aereus.

1997, Sept. 20 Litho. *Perf. 13½x13*

583 A130	1.20 l multicolored	1.00	.50
a.	Tete-beche pair	2.00	2.00
584 A130	1.20 l multicolored	1.00	.50
a.	Tete-beche pair	2.00	2.00

Letters of Grand Duke Gediminas — A131

1997, Oct. 4 *Perf. 14*

585 A131	50c multicolored	.50	.25

Coat of Arms Type of 1992
Size: 25x33mm

1997, Oct. 18 Litho. *Perf. 13½x13*

586 A82	50c Neringa	.45	.25
587 A82	90c Vilkaviskis	.80	.35
588 A82	1.20 l Pasvalys	1.00	.45
	Nos. 586-588 (3)	2.25	1.05

Christmas and New Year — A132

1997, Nov. 22 Litho. *Perf. 13*

589 A132	50c shown	.40	.25
590 A132	1.20 l Snow on trees	1.00	.50

1998 Winter Olympic Games, Nagano — A133

1998, Jan. 17 Litho. *Perf. 14*

591 A133	1.20 l multicolored	1.00	.45
a.	Tete-beche pair	2.00	2.00

Independence Type of 1993 and

Declaration of Independence — A134

Designs: 50c, Alfonsas Petrulis. 90c, Jokubas Sernas.

Perf. 13½x12½

1998, Feb. 16 Litho.

592 A85	50c olive and black	.35	.25
593 A85	90c brown and black	.65	.40

Souvenir Sheet
Perf. 12½x11½

594 A134	6.60 l multicolored	5.00	5.00

Independence, 80th anniv.

Souvenir Sheet

National Anthem, Cent. A135

1998, Feb. 16 *Perf. 12½*

595 A135	5.20 l multicolored	4.00	4.00

Antanas Gustaitis, Aviator, Birth Cent. — A136

Designs: 2 l, Portrait of Gustaitis, ANBO 41. 3 l, Design drawings, ANBO-VIII.

1998, Mar. 27 Litho. *Perf. 14*

596 A136 2 l multicolored 1.50 .85
597 A136 3 l multicolored 2.50 1.10

Natl. Song Festival — A137

1998, Apr. 18 *Perf. 13½*

598 A137 1.20 l multicolored 1.25 1.25
a. Tete-beche pair 3.25 3.25

Europa.

Famous Lithuanians Type of 1993

50c, Tadas Ivanauskas (1882-1971), scientist. No. 600, Jurgis Baltrusaitis (1873-1944), writer, Jurgis Baltrusaitis (1903-88), historian. No. 601, Stasys Lozoraitis (1898-1983), Stasys Lozoraitis (1924-94), politicians.

1998, Apr. 25 *Perf. 13x13½*

599 A88 50c multicolored .40 .25

Size: 45x26mm

600 A88 90c multicolored .70 .35
601 A88 90c multicolored .70 .35
Nos. 599-601 (3) 1.80 .95

Double-Barred Crosses Type of 1997

1998, June 1 Litho. *Perf. 13½*

602 A129 70c yellow bister .65 .30
a. Inscribed "1999" .90 .30

No. 602 is inscribed "1998."

2nd Lithuanian Olympic Games, 6th World Lithuanian Games — A138

1998, June 23 *Perf. 14*

603 A138 1.35 l multicolored 1.00 .55
a. Tete beche pair 2.00 2.00

Double-Barred Crosses Type of 1997

1998, July 4 Litho. *Perf. 13½*

604 A129 35c plum & pink .30 .25

Red Book of Lithuania — A139

Fish: No. 605, Coregonus lavaretus holsatus. No. 606, Salmo salar.

1998, July 11 *Perf. 13x13½*

605 A139 1.40 l multicolored 1.10 .55
606 A139 1.40 l multicolored 1.10 .55

Coat of Arms Type of 1992
Size: 25x33mm

1998, Sept. 12 Litho. *Perf. 13*

607 A82 70c Kernave .50 .25
608 A82 70c Trakai .50 .25
609 A82 1.35 l Kaunas 1.00 .55
Nos. 607-609 (3) 2.00 1.05

Vilnius-Cracow Post Route Established, 1562 — A141

1998, Oct. 9 Litho. *Perf. 14*

611 A141 70c multicolored .60 .30

Souvenir Sheet

Lithuanian Post, 80th Anniv. A142

1998, Oct. 9 Litho. *Perf. 12*

612 A142 13 l multicolored 10.00 10.00

No. 612 contains a holographic image. Soaking in water may affect the hologram.

Museum Paintings A143

70c, "Through the Night," by Antanas Zmuidzinavicius (1876-1966). 1.35 l, "The Garden of Bernardines, Vilnius," by Juozapas Marsevskis (1825-83).

1998, Oct. 17 Litho. *Perf. 13½x13*

613 A143 70c multicolored .60 .30
614 A143 1.35 l multicolored 1.00 .50

New Year — A144

Christmas: 1.35 l, Winter scene, people walking through giant tree, village.

1998, Nov. 14 Litho. *Perf. 12½*

615 A144 70c multicolored .50 .25
616 A144 1.35 l multicolored 1.10 .55

Double-Barred Crosses Type of 1997

1998, Nov. 14 Litho. *Perf. 13½*

617 A129 5c lt & dk citron .25 .25
a. Inscribed "1999" .25 .25
618 A129 10c tan & brown .25 .25
a. Inscribed "1999" .25 .25
619 A129 20c lt & dk olive green .25 .25
a. Inscribed "1999" .25 .25
Nos. 617-619 (3) .75 .75

Nos. 617-619 inscribed "1998."

Adam Mickiewicz (1798-1855), Poet — A145

1998, Dec. 24 *Perf. 14*

620 A145 70c multicolored .60 .30
a. Tete beche pair 1.25 1.25

Souvenir Sheet

Publication of "Postile," by M. Dauksa (1527-1613), 400th Anniv. — A146

1999, Jan. 23 Litho. *Perf. 12½*

621 A146 5.90 l brown & gray 5.00 5.00

Independence Type of 1993

Designs: No. 622, Petras Klimas. No. 623, Donatas Malinauskas.

Perf. 13½x12½

1999, Feb. 16 Litho.

622 A85 70c red & black .50 .30
623 A85 70c blue & black .50 .30

Famous Lithuanians Type of 1993

Designs: No. 624, Juozas Matulis (1899-1993). No. 625, Augustinas Gricius (1899-1972). 1.35 l, Pranas Skardzius (1899-1975).

1999, Mar. 19 Litho. *Perf. 13*

624 A88 70c multicolored .50 .30
625 A88 70c multicolored .50 .30
626 A88 1.35 l multicolored 1.00 .55
Nos. 624-626 (3) 2.00 1.15

NATO, 50th Anniv. — A147

1999, Mar. 27 Litho. *Perf. 13¾x14*

627 A147 70c multicolored .60 .30

National Parks — A148

Europa: No. 628, Traditional homes, lake, islands, Aukotaitija Natl. Park. No. 629, Sand dunes, amber, Curonian Spit Natl. Park.

1999, Apr. 10 Litho. *Perf. 13x13¼*

628 A148 1.35 l multicolored 1.25 1.25
629 A148 1.35 l multicolored 1.25 1.25

Council of Europe, 50th Anniv. — A149

1999, May 1 Litho. *Perf. 14*

630 A149 70c multicolored .60 .30

Melniai Windmill — A150

1999, May 8 Litho. *Perf. 14*

631 A150 70c shown 1.00 .35
632 A150 70c Pumpenai Windmill 1.00 .35

Bees — A151

Designs: 70c, Dasypoda argentata. 2 l, Bombus pomorum.

1999, June 12 *Perf. 13¼x13*

633 A151 70c multicolored .70 .35
634 A151 2 l multicolored 1.60 .80

UPU, 125th Anniv. — A152

1999, July 3 Litho. *Perf. 14*

635 A152 70c multicolored .60 .30

Lithuanian Philatelic Society Emblems, No. 1, Pre-independence Stamp — A153

1999, July 31 Litho. *Perf. 14*

636 A153 1 l multicolored 1.00 .50
Complete booklet, 10 #636 11.00

Lithuanian Philatelic Society, 75th Anniv.

Souvenir Sheet

Centenary of First Performance of Play, "America in the Baths" — A154

Designs: a, Producers. b, Theater poster.

1999, Aug. 20 Litho. *Perf. 12½*

637 A154 4 l Sheet of 2, #a.-b. 5.00 5.00

A155

Baltic Chain, 10th Anniv. — Family and flags: 1 l, No. 640a, Lithuanian.
No. 640: b, Estonian. c, Latvian.

1999, Aug. 23 Litho. *Perf. 12¾*

639 A155 1 l multicolored .85 .40

Souvenir Sheet

640 A155 2 l Sheet of 3, #a.-c. 5.00 5.00

See Estonia Nos. 366-367, Latvia Nos. 493-494.

A156

1999, Aug. 28 Litho. *Perf. 14*

641 A156 70c multicolored .60 .25

Freedom fight movement, 50th anniv.

Coat of Arms Type of 1992
Size: 25x33mm

1999, Sept. 18 *Perf. 13½x13*

642 A82 70c Marijampole .50 .25
643 A82 1 l Siaulai 1.00 .35
644 A82 1.40 l Rokiskis 1.25 .45
Nos. 642-644 (3) 2.75 1.05

Museum Pieces — A157

Designs: 70c, Sword of Gen. S. Zukauskas. 3 l, Hussar armor.

1999, Oct. 9 ***Perf. 13¼x13½***

645 A157 70c multicolored .40 .25
646 A157 3 l multicolored 1.00 1.00

A158

1999, Oct. 23 **Litho.** ***Perf. 14***

647 A158 70c multicolored .60 .25

Simonas Stanevicius (1799-1848), writer.

A159

Christmas and New Year's Day: 1.35 l, Buildings, candles.

Perf. 12½x13½

1999, Nov. 13 **Litho.**

648 A159 70c shown .40 .25
649 A159 1.35 l multicolored .75 .50

Forged Monument Tops — A160

Designs: 10c, Rietavas. 20c, Andriunal. 1 l, Veivirzenai. 1.30 l, Vaizgakiemis. 1.70 l, Baukai.

2000-06 **Litho.** ***Perf. 13½x13¼***

Vignettes in Blue

Designs 22mm High

650 A160 10c tan .30 .25
a. Perf. 11¼, inscr. "2002" .30 .25
b. As "a," inscr. "2003" .30 .25
c. As "a," inscr. "2004" .30 .25
651 A160 20c yellow .35 .25
a. Perf. 11¼, inscr. "2002" .35 .25
b. As "a," inscr. "2003" .35 .25
c. As "a," inscr. "2004" .35 .25
652 A160 1 l pale rose .90 .45
a. Perf. 11¼, inscr. "2002" 1.00 .50
653 A160 1.30 l lt green 1.10 .55
654 A160 1.70 l lt blue 1.40 .70
Nos. 651-654 (4) 3.75 1.95

Perf. 13x12½

Designs 20mm High

655 A160 10c tan .25 .25
a. Inscr. "2006" .25 .25
656 A160 20c yellow .25 .25
a. Inscr. "2006" .25 .25

Designs 21mm High

657 A160 1 l pale rose .75 .35
658 A160 1.30 l lt green 1.00 .50
Nos. 655-658 (4) 2.25 1.35

Issued: Nos. 650-654, 1/3/00; Nos. 650a, 651a, 652a, 5/4/02; Nos. 655-656, 10/8/05; Nos. 657-658, 5/27/06.

Independence Type of 1993

Designs: 1.30 l, Jonas Vailokaitis (1886-1994), banker. 1.70 l, Jonas Smilgevicius (1870-1942), banker.

Perf. 13¼x12¾

2000, Feb. 16 **Litho.**

660 A85 1.30 l multi .75 .50
661 A85 1.70 l multi 1.25 .75

Souvenir Sheet

Declaration of Independence From Soviet Union, 10th Anniv. — A161

Perf. 12¼x11½

2000, Mar. 11 **Litho.**

662 A161 7.40 l multi 5.00 5.00

Famous Lithuanians — A162

Designs: 1 l, Vincas Pietaris (1850-1902), writer. 1.30 l, Kanutas Ruseckas (1800-60), artist. 1.70 l, Povilas Visinskis (1875-1906), writer.

2000, Mar. 25 ***Perf. 13x13¼***

663 A162 1 l multi .80 .40
664 A162 1.30 l multi .90 .50
665 A162 1.70 l multi 1.25 .70
Nos. 663-665 (3) 2.95 1.60

See Nos. 688-690.

Items From Klaipeda Clock Museum — A163

1 l, Sundial. 2 l, Renaissance-style clock.

2000, Apr. 15 ***Perf. 12***

666 A163 1 l multi 1.00 .50
667 A163 2 l multi 1.25 .75

Europa, 2000

Common Design Type

2000, May 9 ***Perf. 13¼x13***

668 CD17 1.70 l multi 1.50 1.50

Birds of Prey From Red Book of Lithuania — A164

1 l, Pandion haliaetus. 2 l, Milvus migrans.

2000, June 2 ***Perf. 13¼x13***

669 A164 1 l multi .75 .45
670 A164 2 l multi 1.60 .80

Sea Museum of Lithuania — A165

No. 671, Spheniscus magellanicus. No. 672, Halichoerus grypus.

2000, Aug. 26 **Litho.** ***Perf. 12***

671-672 A165 1 l Set of 2 1.50 1.00
671a Tete beche pair 2.25 2.25
672a Tete beche pair 2.25 2.25

2000 Summer Olympics, Sydney — A166

Designs: 1 l, Cycling. 3 l, Swimming.

2000, Sept. 2

673-674 A166 Set of 2 3.00 1.75

Souvenir Sheet

Mikalojus Konstantinas Ciurlionis (1875-1911), Artist — A167

2000, Sept. 22 **Litho.** ***Perf. 12***

675 A167 4 l multi 3.00 3.00

Reappearance of Lithuanian Postage Stamps, 10th Anniv. — A168

2000, Oct. 7 **Litho.** ***Perf. 12***

676 A168 1 l multi .80 .40

Arms Type of 1992

Designs: No. 677, 1 l, Raseiniai. No. 678, 1 l, Taurage. 1.30 l, Utena.

2000, Oct. 21 **Litho.** ***Perf. 12***

Size: 25x33mm

677-679 A82 Set of 3 2.50 1.40

Christmas and New Year's Day — A169

Roadside shrines: 1 l, 1.70 l.

2000, Nov. 11

680-681 A169 Set of 2 2.00 1.00

Souvenir Sheet

Holy Year 2000 A170

No. 682: a, Nativity. b, Jesus and disciples. c, Crucifixion. d, Resurrection.

2000, Nov. 25

682 A170 2 l Sheet of 4, #a-d 6.25 6.25

Advent of New Millennium — A171

2000, Dec. 2

683 A171 1 l multi .80 .40

Souvenir Sheet

Medals Won at 2000 Summer Olympics, Sydney — A172

2000, Dec. 9 **Litho.** ***Perf.***

684 A172 4 l multi 3.25 3.25

Storming of TV Station by Soviet Troops, 10th Anniv. A173

2001, Jan. 13 ***Perf. 12***

685 A173 1 l multi + label .85 .40

Independence Type of 1993

Designs: 1 l, Saliamonas Banaitis (1866-1933), newspaper publisher and politician. 2 l, Justinas Staugaitis (1863-1943), bishop and politician.

2001, Feb. 16 **Litho.** ***Perf. 12***

686-687 A85 Set of 2 2.50 1.25

Famous Lithuanians Type of 2000

Designs: No. 688, 1 l, Juozas Mikenas (1901-64), artist. No. 689, 1 l, Pranas Vaicaitis (1876-1901), poet. 1.70 l, Petras Vileisis (1851-1926), civil engineer.

2001, Mar. 24 **Litho.** ***Perf. 12***

688-690 A162 Set of 3 3.00 1.50

Europa — A174

Designs: No. 691, 1.70 l, Neman River. No. 692, 1.70 l, Lake Galve.

2001, Apr. 14 ***Perf. 13x13¼***

691-692 A174 Set of 2 3.00 3.00

Flowers From Red Book of Lithuania — A175

Designs: 2 l, Nymphoide peltata. 3 l, Erica tetralix.

2001, May 12 ***Perf. 13¼x13***

693-694 A175 Set of 2 4.00 2.00

Bridges — A176

Designs: 1 l, Papalauja Bridge. 1.30 l, Pakurojis Dam Bridge.

2001, June 9 ***Perf. 12***
695-696 A176 Set of 2 1.80 .95

Souvenir Sheet

Lithuania, 1000th Anniv. (in 2009) — A177

Designs: a, Flag. b, Arms. c, Map of country. d, Map of Europe.

2001, June 23 ***Perf. 11***
697 A177 2 l Sheet of 4, #a-d + 2 labels 6.25 6.25

Baltic Coast Landscapes — A178

Designs: 1 l, No. 699a, Palanga. No. 699b, Lahemaa. No. 699c, Vidzeme.

2001, Sept. 15 **Litho.** ***Perf. 13½***
698 A178 1 l multi .85 .40

Souvenir Sheet

699 Sheet of 3 4.75 4.75
a.-c. A178 2 l Any single 1.40 1.10

See Estonia Nos. 423-424, Latvia Nos. 534-535.

Ethnographic Open Air Museum Exhibits — A179

19th cent. dwellings from: 1 l, Kirdeikiai. 2 l, Darbenai.

2001, Sept. 22 ***Perf. 12***
700-701 A179 Set of 2 2.40 1.25

Sculpture by Juozas Zikaras (1881-1944) — A180

2001, Oct. 4
702 A180 3 l multi 2.40 1.25

Postal Regulations Enacted by Stefan Bathory, 1583 — A181

2001, Oct. 6
703 A181 1 l multi .85 .40

Coat of Arms Type of 1992

Size: 25x33mm

Designs: 1 l, Lazdijai. 1.30 l, Birzai. 1.70 l, Veliuona.

2001, Oct. 27 **Litho.** ***Perf. 12***
704-706 A82 Set of 3 3.00 1.60

Christmas and New Year — A182

Birds on: 1 l, Covered tree. 1.70 l, Christ's cradle.

2001, Nov. 10 **Litho.** ***Perf. 12***
707-708 A182 Set of 2 2.00 1.00

Souvenir Sheet

Dr. Jonas Basanavicius (1851-1927), Patriot, Folklorist — A183

2001, Nov. 17 ***Perf. 12x11½***
709 A183 5 l multi 4.00 4.00

2002 Winter Olympics, Salt Lake City — A184

2002, Jan. 26 **Litho.** ***Perf. 12***
710 A184 1.70 l multi 1.40 .70

Independence Type of 1993

Designs: No. 711, 1 l, Kazys Bizauskas (1892-1941), statesman. No. 712, 1 l, Stanislovas Narutavicius (1862-1932), politician.

2002, Feb. 16
711-712 A85 Set of 2 1.50 .80

Famous Lithuanians — A185

Designs: 1 l, Antanas Salys (1902-72), linguist. 1.30 l, Satrijos Ragana (1877-1930), writer. 1.70 l, Oskaras Milasius (1877-1939), poet.

2002, Mar. 2 **Litho.** ***Perf. 12***
713-715 A185 Set of 3 3.00 1.50

See Nos. 734-735, 759-761, 782-784, 805-807, 830-832, 858-860, 884-886, 906-908, 934-936, 967-969.

Coat of Arms Type of 1992

Size: 25x33mm

Designs: No. 716, 1 l, Anyksciai. No. 717, 1 l, Birstonas. 1.70 l, Prienai.

2002, Mar. 23
716-718 A82 Set of 3 3.00 1.50

State Historical Archives, 150th Anniv. — A186

2002, Apr. 6
719 A186 1 l multi .85 .40

Mammals From Red Book of Lithuania — A187

Designs: 1 l, Mustela erminea. 3 l, Lynx lynx.

2002, Apr. 13 ***Perf. 13x13¼***
720-721 A187 Set of 2 3.00 1.60

Europa — A188

2002, May 4 **Litho.** ***Perf. 13¼x13***
722 A188 1.70 l multi 1.50 1.50

Vilnius Fire ad Rescue Brigade, Bicent. — A189

2002, May 25 ***Perf. 12***
723 A189 1 l multi .85 .40

Narrow-gauge Railways — A190

Designs: 1.30 l, TU2 diesel locomotive. 2 l, PT4 steam engine.

2002, June 8
724-725 A190 Set of 2 2.75 1.40

Souvenir Sheet

Lithuania, 1000th Anniv. (in 2009) — A191

Designs: a, Artifact of first people in Lithuania, 10,000 B.C. b, Roman historian Tacitus mentions Aestii people, 98. c, Vikings attack Apuole Castle, 853. d, First mention of Lithuania in Quedlinburg Annals, 1009.

2002, June 22 ***Perf. 11***
726 A191 2 l Sheet of 4, #a-d, + 2 labels 6.25 6.25

Souvenir Sheet

Klaipeda, 750th Anniv. A192

2002, Aug. 1 ***Perf. 11½x12¼***
727 A192 5 l multi 4.00 4.00

Maironis Lithuanian Literature Museum, Kaunas — A193

Designs: 1 l, Exhibits. 3 l, Museum exterior.

2002, Sept. 7 ***Perf. 12***
728-729 A193 Set of 2 3.00 1.50

Establishment of Postal Service by King Sigismund III Vasa, 1620 — A194

2002, Oct. 5
730 A194 1 l multi .85 .40

Christmas and New Year's Day — A195

Cross and: 1 l, Clock, candles and holly. 1.70 l, Christmas tree and angels.

2002, Nov. 9
731-732 A195 Set of 2 2.10 1.00

European Children's Day — A196

2002, Nov. 16
733 A196 1 l multi .85 .40

Famous Lithuanians Type of 2002

Designs: 1 l, Laurynas Stuoka-Gucevicius (1753-98), architect. 1.30 l, Juozas Eretas (1896-1984), author and politician.

2003, Jan. 25 ***Perf. 12***
734-735 A185 Set of 2 1.80 .85

Coat of Arms Type of 1992

Designs: No. 736, 1 l, Gargzdai. No. 737, 1 l, Kretinga. No. 738, 1 l, Palanga. No. 739, 1 l, Papile. No. 740, 1 l, Rietavas.

2003, Feb. 15 **Litho.** ***Perf. 12***
Size: 25x33mm
736-740 A82 Set of 5 4.00 2.00

Lighthouses — A198

Designs: 1 l, Pervalka. 3 l, Uostodvaris.

2003, Mar. 15
741-742 A198 Set of 2 3.25 1.50

Europa — A199

2003, Apr. 19 **Litho.** ***Perf. 13½x13***
743 A199 1.70 l multi 1.50 1.50
a. Tete beche pair 3.25 3.25

Rebuilding of Palace of Lithuania's Rulers — A200

2003, Apr. 26 ***Perf. 12***
744 A200 1 l multi .85 .40

Vilnius University Astronomical Observatory, 250th Anniv. — A201

2003, May 10 *Perf. 12*
745 A201 1 l multi .85 .40

Insects From Red Book of Lithuania — A202

Designs: No. 746, 3 l, Lucanus cervus. No. 747, 3 l, Cerambyx cerdo.

2003, May 24 *Perf. 13x13½*
746-747 A202 Set of 2 5.00 2.50

Souvenir Sheet

Lithuania, 1000th Anniv. (in 2009) — A203

No. 748: a, Rise of Lithuania, 1183. b, Battle of Siauliai, 1236. c, Coronation of Mindaugas, 1253. d, Selection of Vilnius as capital of Lithuania, 1323.

2003, June 21 *Perf. 11*
748 A203 2 l Sheet of 4, #a-d, + 2 labels 6.25 3.25

Souvenir Sheet

Coronation of Mindaugas, 750th Anniv. — A204

2003, July 5 *Perf. 11½x12¼*
749 A204 5 l multi 4.00 2.00

13th European Hot Air Balloon Championships A205

2003, Aug. 8 *Perf. 12*
750 A205 1.30 l multi 1.00 .55

Vincentas Cardinal Sladkevicius (1920-2000) — A206

2003, Aug. 20
751 A206 1 l multi .85 .40

Panevezys, 500th Anniv. — A207

2003, Sept. 7
752 A207 1 l multi .85 .40

Map of Kaunas-Vilnius-Grodno Postal Route, 1664 — A208

2003, Oct. 4
753 A208 1 l multi .85 .40

Christmas and New Year's Day — A209

Villages at: 1 l, Christmas. 1.70 l, New Year's Eve.

2003, Nov. 8
754-755 A209 Set of 2 2.10 1.00

Souvenir Sheet

Lithuania, 2003 European Men's Basketball Champions — A210

2003, Dec. 6 **Litho.** *Perf. 12x11½*
756 A210 5 l multi 4.00 2.00

Gliders in Lithuanian Aviation Museum — A211

Designs: No. 757, 1 l, BK-7. No. 758, 1 l, BRO-12.

2003, Dec. 17 *Perf. 12*
757-758 A211 Set of 2 1.75 .80

Famous Lithuanians Type of 2002

Designs: No. 759, 1 l, Jonas Aistis (1904-73), poet. No. 760, 1 l, Kazimieras Buga (1879-1924), philologist. No. 761, 1 l, Adolfas Jucys (1904-74), physicist.

2004, Jan. 24 **Litho.** *Perf. 12*
759-761 A185 Set of 3 2.25 1.25

Coat of Arms Type of 1992

Designs: 1 l, Mazeikiai. 1.30 l, Radviliskis. 1.40 l, Ukmerge.

2004, Feb. 14 **Size: 25x33mm**
762-764 A82 Set of 3 2.75 1.50

Vilnius University, 425th Anniv. — A213

2004, Mar. 20
765 A213 1 l multi .85 .40

Europa — A214

Designs: No. 766, 1.70 l, Sailboat. No. 767, 1.70 l, Beach umbrella.

2004, Apr. 10 **Litho.** *Perf. 12*
766-767 A214 Set of 2 3.00 3.00

Return to Printing Lithuanian in Latin Letters, Cent. — A215

2004, May 1 **Litho.** *Perf. 12*
768 A215 1.30 l multi 1.00 .50

Admission to European Union — A216

No. 769: a, Stars, flags of newly-added countries, map of Europe. b, Stars and Lithuanian flag, map and arms.

2004, May 1
769 A216 1.70 l Horiz. pair, #a-b 2.75 1.25

FIFA (Fédération Internationale de Football Association), Cent. — A217

2004, May 15
770 A217 3 l multi 2.25 1.10

Chiune Sugihara (1900-86), Japanese Diplomat Who Issued Transit Visas to Jews in World War II — A218

2004, June 19 **Litho.** *Perf. 12*
771 A218 1 l multi .85 .40

Souvenir Sheet

Lithuania, 1000th Anniv. — A219

No. 772: a, Defense of Pilenai Castle, 1336. b, Battle at the Blue Waters, 1362. c, Christening of Lithuania, 1387. d, Battle of Zalgiris, 1410.

2004, July 3 *Perf. 11*
772 A219 2 l Sheet of 4, #a-d, + 2 labels 6.00 4.00

Exhibits in Tadas Ivanauskas Zoology Museum, Kaunas — A220

No. 773: a, Aquila chrysaetos. b, Iguana iguana.

2004, July 10 *Perf. 12*
773 A220 1 l Horiz. pair, #a-b 1.50 .80

2004 Summer Olympics, Athens — A221

2004 Olympic emblem and: 2 l, Pentathlon equestrian event. 3 l, Canoeing.

2004, July 31
774-775 A221 Set of 2 4.00 2.00

Owls From Red Book of Lithuania — A222

Designs: 1.30 l, Bubo bubo. 3 l, Asio flammeus.

2004, Oct. 2 **Litho.** *Perf. 12*
776-777 A222 Set of 2 3.25 1.75

Kaunas Funiculars — A223

Designs: 1 l, Aleksotas Funicular. 1.30 l, Zaliakalnis Funicular.

2004, Oct. 16
778-779 A223 Set of 2 1.75 .95

Christmas A224

Stars and: 1 l, Christmas tree. 1.70 l, Bird.

2004, Nov. 6
780-781 A224 Set of 2 2.00 1.50

Famous Lithuanians Type of 2002

Designs: No. 782, 1 l, Kazys Boruta (1905-65), writer. No. 783, 1 l, Petras Kalpokas (1880-1945), painter. No. 784, 1 l, Jonas Puzinas (1905-78), archaeologist.

2005, Jan. 8 **Litho.** *Perf. 12*
782-784 A185 Set of 3 2.00 1.50

Congratulations A225

Designs: No. 785, 1 l, Gerbera daisies, freesias and scroll. No. 786, 1 l, Lilies, freesias and box.

Serpentine Die Cut 6¾
2005, Jan. 29 **Litho.**
Booklet Stamps
Self-Adhesive
785-786 A225 Set of 2 1.40 1.10
786a Booklet pane, 4 each #785-786 5.50

Sartai Horse Race, Cent. — A226

2005, Feb. 5 *Perf. 12*
787 A226 1 l multi .65 .40

Coat of Arms Type of 1992

Designs: No. 788, 1 l, Druskininkai. No. 789, 1 l, Vabalninkas.

2005, Mar. 5 **Size: 25x33mm**
788-789 A82 Set of 2 1.40 1.10

Europa — A227

Designs: No. 790, 1.70 l, Cow, cheese. No. 791, 1.70 l, Loaf of black bread.

2005, Apr. 9 **Litho.** ***Perf. 12***
790-791 A227 Set of 2 3.00 3.00

National Museum, 150th Anniv. A228

No. 792: a, Brass jewelry, 1st-2nd cent. b, Illustration of first exhibition in Aula Hall, Vilnius University.

2005, May 7
792 A228 1 l Pair, #a-b 1.40 1.40

Train and Kaunas Railway Tunnel — A229

2005, June 11
793 A229 3 l multi 2.00 1.50

Souvenir Sheet

Lithuania, 1000th Anniv. — A230

No. 794: a, Battle of Pabaiskas, 1435. b, Valakai Reform, 1557. c, First Lithuanian statute, 1529. d, Union of Lublin, 1569.

2005, July 2 ***Perf. 11***
794 A230 2 l Sheet of 4, #a-d, + 2 labels 5.50 5.50

90th World Esperanto Congress, Vilnius — A231

2005, July 23 **Litho.** ***Perf. 12***
795 A231 1 l multi .70 .50

Churches — A232

Designs: 1 l, Vilnius Evangelical Lutheran Church. 1.30 l, St. Casimir Church, Vilnius.

2005, Sept. 3 ***Perf. 13½***
796-797 A232 Set of 2 1.50 1.00

Flora and Fauna from Red Book of Lithuania A233

No. 798: a, Gavia arctica. b, Trapa natans.

2005, Sept. 10
798 A233 1 l Horiz. pair, #a-b 1.40 1.40

Souvenir Sheet

Mikolajus Konstantinas Ciurlionis (1875-1911), Painter and Composer — A234

No. 799 — Details from Sonata of the Sea triptych: a, Allegro. b, Andante. c, Finale.

2005, Sept. 24 ***Perf. 14***
799 A234 2 l Sheet of 3, #a-c, + label 4.00 4.00

Map of St. Petersburg-Warsaw Post Road, 1830-36 — A235

2005, Oct. 8 **Litho.** ***Perf. 14¼x14***
800 A235 1 l multi .65 .45

Christmas A236

Designs: 1 l, Candle and snow-covered evergreen branch. 1.70 l, Santa Claus in sleigh.

2005, Nov. 5 ***Perf. 12¾x13***
801-802 A236 Set of 2 1.75 1.25

Dr. Jonas Basanavicius, Vilnius City Hall and Commemorative Medal — A237

2005, Dec. 3 ***Perf. 14¼x14***
803 A237 1 l multi .65 .45

Congress of Lithuanians, cent.

2006 Winter Olympics, Turin — A238

2006, Jan. 28 **Litho.** ***Perf. 14x14¼***
804 A238 1.70 l multi 1.25 .75

Famous Lithuanians Type of 2002

Designs: No. 805, 1 l, Adolfas Sapoka (1906-61), historian. No. 806, 1 l, Petras Rimsa (1881-1961), sculptor. No. 807, 1 l, Antanas Vaiciulaitis (1906-92), writer.

2006, Feb. 11 ***Perf. 13½***
805-807 A185 Set of 3 2.00 1.50

Vilnius Album, by Jonas K. Vilcinskis, 160th Anniv. of Publication — A239

2006, Feb. 25 ***Perf. 13x12¾***
808 A239 1 l multi .65 .45

Social Insurance System, 80th Anniv. — A240

2006, Mar. 18 ***Perf. 14¼x14***
809 A240 1 l multi .65 .45

Lithuanian Theater, Music and Cinema Museum, 80th Anniv. — A241

No. 810: a, Parvo camera, 1930s. b, Music box, 1900.

2006, Mar. 18 ***Perf. 13½***
810 A241 1 l Pair, #a-b 1.25 1.25

Printed in sheets containing 10 of each stamp + 5 labels. Each sheet contains se-tenant pairs of the same stamp.

Europa — A242

Designs: No. 811, 1.70 l, Woman dancing with man in wheelchair. No. 812, 1.70 l, People in wheelchairs being pushed around track.

2006, Apr. 15
811-812 A242 Set of 2 3.00 3.00

Coat of Arms Type of 1992

Designs: No. 813, 1 l, Kupiskis. No. 814, 1 l, Sakiai. No. 815, 1 l, Silute.

2006, May 13 ***Perf. 14x14¼***
Size: 25x33mm
813-815 A82 Set of 3 2.00 1.50

Souvenir Sheet

Lithuania, 1000th Anniv. — A243

No. 816: a, Establishment of Vilnius University, 1579. b, Truce of Andrusov, 1667. c, Four-year Sejm, 1788. d, Uprising of 1794.

2006, July 1 ***Perf. 11***
816 A243 2 l Sheet of 4, #a-d, + 2 labels 5.25 5.25

Basilicas — A244

Designs: 1 l, Vilnius Basilica. 1.70 l, Kaunas Basilica.

2006, Aug. 5 ***Perf. 12¾x13***
817-818 A244 Set of 2 1.75 1.25

Birds and Fish From Red Book of Lithuania — A245

No. 819: a, Polysticta stelleri. b, Acipenser sturio.

2006, Sept. 16 ***Perf. 13½***
819 A245 1 l Vert. pair, #a-b 1.40 1.40

Establishment of Lithuania Post and First Postage Stamps, 1918 — A246

2006, Oct. 7 ***Perf. 14¼x14***
820 A246 1 l multi .65 .45

Premiere of Opera "Birute," Cent. — A247

2006, Nov. 4 **Litho.** ***Perf. 13¼x12¾***
821 A247 2 l multi 1.25 .85

Christmas A248

Designs: 1 l, Birds, triangular window. 1.70 l, Trees, star, berries, straw.

2006, Nov. 18 ***Perf. 12¾x13¼***
822-823 A248 Set of 2 1.75 1.40

18th Century Wooden Church Belfries — A249

Belfries from churches in: 10c, Pasvalys. 20c, Rozalimas. 50c, Tryskiai. 1 l, Saukenai. 1.30 l, Vaiguva. 1.70 l, Vajasiskis.

Die Cut Perf. 12½

2007, Jan. 1 **Litho.**
Self-Adhesive

824	A249	10c blue & blk	.25	.25
825	A249	20c org & blk	.25	.25
826	A249	50c bl grn & blk	.40	.40
a.		Dated 2009	.40	.40
b.		Dated 2011	.40	.40
827	A249	1 l brn & blk	.80	.80
a.		Dated 2009	.80	.80
b.		Dated 2011	.80	.80
828	A249	1.30 l lil & blk	1.00	1.00
829	A249	1.70 l ol brn & blk	1.40	1.40
		Nos. 824-829 (6)	4.10	4.10

Issued: Nos. 826a, 827a, 2/21/09. Nos. 826b, 827b, 1/8/11.

See Nos. 842-846, 1034.

Famous Lithuanians Type of 2002

Designs: No. 830, 1 l, Bernardas Brazdzionis (1907-2002), writer. No. 831, 1 l, Vytautas Kazimieras Jonynas (1907-97), artist. 3 l, Leonas Sapiega (1557-1633), state chancellor of the Grand Duchy of Lithuania.

2007, Jan. 27 ***Perf. 13½***
830-832 A185 Set of 3 3.75 3.00

Coat of Arms Type of 1992

Designs: 1 l, Svencionys. 1.30 l, Kelme. 2 l, Moletai.

2007, Mar. 3 ***Perf. 14x14¼***
Size: 25x33mm
833-835 A82 Set of 3 3.25 2.50

Europa — A250

Designs: No. 836, 1.70 l, Scouting flag, musical score. No. 837, 1.70 l, Symbols of Lithuanian Scouts.

2007, Apr. 14 Litho. *Perf. 13½*
836-837 A250 Set of 2 2.25 1.60

Scouting, cent.

Churches A251

Designs: 1 l, St. Anne's and Bernardine Churches, Vilnius. 1.30 l, Church buildings, Pazaislis.

2007, May 12 *Perf. 12¾x13*
838-839 A251 Set of 2 2.00 1.50

Souvenir Sheet

Lithuania, 1000th Anniv. — A252

No. 840: a, Publication of first Lithuanian newspaper, "Ausra," 1883. b, Abolition of the prohibition on printing in Latin characters, 1904. c, Great Seimas of Vilnius, 1905. d, Lithuanian Declaration of Independence, 1918.

2007, June 23 Litho. *Perf. 11*
840 A252 3 l Sheet of 4, #a-d, + 2 labels 9.00 9.00

Trakai History Museum A253

No. 841: a, Map of New Trakai in 1600, by J. Kamarauskas. b, Chess pieces, 15th cent.

2007, July 28 Litho. *Perf. 13½*
841 A253 2 l Pair, #a-b 3.00 3.00

Printed in sheets containing 10 of each stamp + 5 labels.

Wooden Church Belfries Type of 2007

Belfries from churches in: 5c, Vabalininkas, 19th cent. 35c, Varputenai, 18th cent. 1.35 l, Deguciai, 19th cent. 1.55 l, Geidziai, 19th cent. 2.15 l, Pavandenes, 17th cent.

Die Cut Perf. 12½
2007, Sept. 1 Litho.
Self-Adhesive

842 A249 5c yel grn & blk .25 .25
843 A249 35c gray & blk .30 .30
844 A249 1.35 l yel & blk 1.00 .75
845 A249 1.55 l brn org & blk 1.10 .80
846 A249 2.15 l rose lake & blk 1.25 1.75
Nos. 842-846 (5) 3.90 3.85

Juozas Miltinis (1907-94), Actor and Theater Founder — A254

2007, Sept. 1 Litho. *Perf. 12¾x13*
847 A254 2.45 l multi 1.75 1.25

Birds — A255

No. 848 — Birds of the Cepkeliai Nature Reserve, Lithuania and Katra Sanctuary, Belarus: a, Gallinago media. b, Crex crex.

2007, Oct. 3 *Perf. 14*
848 Horiz. pair + central label 5.00 5.00
a.-b. A255 2.90 l Either single 2.25 2.25

See Belarus No. 625.

Stamps and Covers From Establishment of Lithuania Post in 1992 — A256

2007, Oct. 6
849 A256 1.35 l multi 1.25 1.25

Christmas — A257

Conifer sprigs and: 1.35 l, Snowflake, Christmas ornaments. 2.45 l, Stars, globe.

2007, Nov. 10 *Perf. 13x12¾*
850-851 A257 Set of 2 3.25 3.25

Wooden Churches — A258

Churches in: 5c, Antazave, 1794. 10c, Deguciai, 1757. 20c, Inturke, 1855. 35c, Prienai, 1750. 1.35 l, Siaudine, 1775. 1.55 l, Uzventis, 1703.

Die Cut Perf. 12½
2008, Jan. 5 Litho.
Self-Adhesive

852 A258 5c multi .25 .25
a. Dated 2011 .25 .25
853 A258 10c multi .25 .25
a. Dated 2009 .25 .25
b. Dated 2011 .25 .25
854 A258 20c multi .25 .25
a. Dated 2009 .25 .25
b. Dated 2011 .25 .25
855 A258 35c multi .30 .30
a. Dated 2011 .30 .30
856 A258 1.35 l multi 1.00 1.00
a. Dated 2009 1.00 1.00
b. Dated 2011 1.10 1.10
857 A258 1.55 l multi 1.10 1.10
Nos. 852-857 (6) 3.15 3.15

Issued: Nos. 853a, 854a, 856a, 2/21/09; Nos. 853b, 856b, 1/8/11. Nos. 852a, 854b, 855a, 10/8/11.

Famous Lithuanians Type of 2002

Designs: 2 l, Martynas Jankus (1858-1946), publisher. 2.15 l, Zenonas Ivinskis (1908-71), historian. 2.90 l, Antanas Maceina (1908-87), philosopher.

2008, Jan. 19 Litho. *Perf. 13½*
858-860 A185 Set of 3 5.25 4.00

Restoration of Independence, 90th Anniv. — A259

2008, Feb. 16
861 A259 1.35 l multi 1.10 .80

State Awards of the Baltic Countries — A260

Designs: Nos. 862, 863a, Order of Vytautas the Great, Lithuania. No. 863b, Order of the National Coat of Arms, Estonia. No. 863c, Order of Three Stars, Latvia.

Perf. 13½x13¾
2008, Mar. 15 Litho.
862 A260 7 l multi 5.00 3.50

Souvenir Sheet

863 A260 5 l Sheet of 3, #a-c, + label 13.00 13.00

See Estonia Nos. 592-593, Latvia Nos. 701-702.

Items From Rokiskis Regional Museum A261

No. 864: a, Wood carving, by Lionginas Sepka. b, 19th cent. women's clothing.

2008, Apr. 19 Litho. *Perf. 14*
864 A261 1.55 l Horiz. pair, #a-b 2.25 2.25

Europa — A262

Designs: No. 865, 2.45 l, Grand Duke Gediminas and his letters of 1323. No. 866, 2.45 l, Vilnius, 2009 European Cultural Capital.

2008, May 3
865-866 A262 Set of 2 3.50 2.75

Sajudis Party, 20th Anniv. — A263

2008, May 31
867 A263 1.35 l multi 1.00 .75

Expo Zaragoza 2008 — A264

2008, June 7 *Die Cut Perf. 12½*
Self-Adhesive
868 A264 2.45 l multi 1.75 1.25

Miniature Sheet

Lithuania, 1000th Anniv. — A265

No. 869: a, First Lithuanian Cabinet of Ministers, 1918. b, Consitituent Assembly, 1920. c, Opening of Kaunas University, 1922. d, Occupation of Memel (Klaipeda) by Lithuania, 1923. e, Opening of Zemaiciai Road (man signing document, 1939). f, Return of Vilnius to Lithuania from Poland, 1939.

2008, June 28 *Perf. 14*
869 A265 3 l Sheet of 6, #a-f 13.00 13.00

Crashed Transatlantic Flight of Captains Steponas Darius and Stasys Girenas, 75th Anniv. — A266

2008, July 12
870 A266 2.90 l multi 2.25 1.60

2008 Summer Olympics, Beijing — A267

Designs: 2.15 l, Women's marathon. 2.45 l, Yachting.

2008, July 26
871-872 A267 Set of 2 3.50 2.75

Apparitions of the Virgin Mary at Siluva, 400th Anniv. — A268

2008, Aug. 30 Litho. *Perf. 14*
873 A268 1.55 l multi 1.25 1.00

Worldwide Fund for Nature (WWF) — A269

Coracias garrulus: Nos. 874, 878a, 1.35 l, On branch with beak closed, denomination at LR. Nos. 875, 878b, 1.35 l, In flight. Nos. 876, 878c, 1.35 l, On branch with beak open, denomination at LL. Nos. 877, 878d, 1.35 l, On branch with beak closed, denomination at LL.

2008, Sept. 6 *Perf. 14*
Stamps With White Frames
874-877 A269 Set of 4 4.00 3.00

Souvenir Sheet
Stamps Without White Frames
878 A269 1.35 l Sheet of 4, #a-d 4.00 4.00

Arms Type of 1992

Designs: No. 879, 1.35 l, Jurbarkas. No. 880, 1.35 l, Joniskis. 3 l, Sirvintos.

2008, Oct. 4 Litho.
Size: 26x31mm
879-881 A82 Set of 3 4.25 3.50

Christmas and New Year's Day — A270

Designs: 1.35 l, Holiday lights. 2.45 l, Snow-covered evergreen branch.

2008, Nov. 8 *Perf. 14*
882-883 A270 Set of 2 2.75 2.10

Famous Lithuanians Type of 2002

Designs: 1.35 l, Jonas Zemaitas (1909-54), military officer. 2 l, Vaclovas Birziska (1884-1956), educator and library founder. 2.15 l, Mecislovas Reinys (1884-1953), archbishop.

2009, Jan. 17 Litho. *Perf. 14*
884-886 A185 Set of 3 4.00 3.00

Arms Type of 1992

Designs: No. 887, 1.35 l, Krekenava. No. 888, 1.35 l, Pakruojis. 3 l, Salcininkai.

2009, Feb. 21 Litho. *Perf. 14*
Size: 26x31mm
887-889 A82 Set of 3 4.50 3.25

Souvenir Sheet

Protection of Polar Regions and Glaciers — A271

No. 890 — Glacier with sky in: a, Dark blue. b, Light blue.

2009, Mar. 27
890 A271 2.90 l Sheet of 2, #a-b 4.50 4.50

Vilnius, 2009 European Cultural Capital — A272

2009, Apr. 11
891 A272 2.15 l multi 1.75 1.25

Europa — A273

Telescope and: No. 892, Galileo Galilei, Moon. No. 893, Vilnius University Observatory, Sun.

2009, Apr. 25 Litho. *Perf. 14*
892 A273 2.45 l multi 2.00 1.50
893 A273 2.45 l multi 2.00 1.50

Intl. Year of Astronomy.

Great Synagogue of Vilnius — A274

2009, May 23
894 A274 1.35 l multi 1.00 .75

Palanga Amber Museum A275

No. 895: a, "Sun Stone" (large piece of amber). b, Museum building.

2009, June 13
895 A275 1.55 l Pair, #a-b 2.50 2.50

Spindle — A276

2009, June 27 Litho. *Perf. 14*
896 A276 3.35 l multi 2.75 1.75

Millennium Song Festival, Vilnius.

Miniature Sheet

Lithuania, 1000th Anniv. — A277

No. 897: a, Acceptance of declaration of the Council of the Movement for the Freedom of Lithuania, 1949. b, Illegal production of "Chronicle of the Catholic Church in Lithuania," 1972. c, Lithuanian Reform Movement, 1988. d, Signing of declaration of Lithuanian independence, 1990. e, Entry into European Union, 2004. f, Acceptance into Schengen Area, 2007.

2009, July 4 Litho. *Perf. 14*
897 A277 3 l Sheet of 6, #a-f 14.00 14.00

Tall Ships Regatta A278

Perf. 13½x13¾
2009, Sept. 25 Litho.
898 A278 3 l multi + label 2.50 1.75

Railways in Lithuania, 150th Anniv. — A279

2009, Aug. 8 Litho. *Perf. 14*
899 A279 2.90 l multi 2.40 1.75

Order of the Cross of Vytis — A280

2009, Sept. 19 *Perf. 13½x13¾*
900 A280 7 l multi 6.00 4.50

Flora and Fauna From Red Book of Lithuania A281

No. 901: a, Papilio machaon. b, Gentiana pneumonanthe.

2009, Oct. 10 *Perf. 14*
901 A281 1.55 l Horiz. pair, #a-b 2.75 2.75

Struve Geodetic Arc UNESCO World Heritage Site — A282

Designs: No. 902, 2 l, Friedrich Georg Wilhelm von Struve and map of Europe. No. 903, 2 l, Arc post in Meskonys, map of triangulation points.

2009, Oct. 24
902-903 A282 Set of 2 3.50 2.75

Christmas and New Year's Day — A283

Designs: 1.35 l, Village church. 2.45 l, Houses.

2009, Nov. 7
904-905 A283 Set of 2 3.25 2.50

Famous Lithuanians Type of 2002

Designs: No. 906, 1.35 l, Jonas Karolis Chodkevicius (Jan Karol Chodkiewicz, 1560-1621), hetman and military leader. No. 907, 1.35 l, Jonas Jablonskis (1860-1930), linguist. 3 l, Mykolas Krupavicius (1885-1970), Minister of Agriculture.

2010, Jan. 16 Litho. *Perf. 14*
906-908 A185 Set of 3 4.50 3.25

2010 Winter Olympics, Vancouver — A284

2010, Jan. 30
909 A284 2.45 l multi 2.00 1.50

Arms Type of 1992

Designs: 1.35 l, Silale. 2 l, Jonava. 2.15 l, Varena.

2010, Feb. 20 *Perf. 14*
Size: 26x31mm
910-912 A82 Set of 3 4.25 3.25

Independence, 20th Anniv. — A285

2010, Mar. 6 Litho.
913 A285 1.35 l multi 1.00 .75

Easter — A286

2010, Mar. 20 *Perf. 14*
914 A286 1.35 l multi 1.00 .75

Expo 2010, Shanghai — A287

2010, Apr. 10
915 A287 2.90 l multi 2.25 1.60

Vladas Mikenas (1910-92), Chess Grand Master — A288

2010, Apr. 17
916 A288 2 l multi 1.60 1.25

Europa — A289

Half of book and: No. 917, 2.45 l, Rabbit, girl, numerals. No. 918, 2.45 l, Letters, bird, boy.

2010, May 8
917-918 A289 Set of 2 3.50 3.50

Souvenir Sheet

Oak of Stelmuze A290

2010, June 5
919 A290 8 l multi 5.75 5.75

Battle of Grunwald, 600th Anniv. — A291

2010, July 3
920 A291 2.45 l multi 1.90 1.50

Kretinga Museum, 75th Anniv. A292

No. 921 — Items in Kretinga Museum: a, Fastener fron 2nd-3rd cent., monument b, St. George slaying the dragon, musuem.

2010, July 10 Litho.
921 A292 1.35 l Pair, #a-b 2.10 1.60

Printed in sheets containing 10 pairs and 5 labels.

2010 Youth Olympics, Singapore — A293

2010, July 31 *Perf. 14*
922 A293 2.90 l multi 2.25 1.60

Kernave Archaeological UNESCO World Heritage Site — A294

Designs: No. 923, 3 l, View of town and burial mounds. No. 924, 3 l, Road and burial mound.

2010, Aug. 7
923-924 A294 Set of 2 4.50 3.50

Flora and Fauna from Red Book of Lithuania A295

No. 925: a, Columba oenas. b, Anax parthenope and flowers.

2010, Sept. 11
925 A295 1.35 l Horiz. pair, #a-b 2.00 1.50

Cathedrals — A296

Designs: No. 926, 1.35 l, Transfiguration Cathedral, Kaisiadorys. No. 927, 1.35 l, St. Anthony of Padua Cathedral, Telsiai.

2010, Oct. 16 ***Perf. 14***
926-927 A296 Set of 2 2.00 1.50

See Nos. 949-950.

Christmas A297

New Year 2011 — A298

2010, Nov. 6 **Litho.**
928 A297 1.35 l multi 1.00 .75
929 A298 2.45 l multi 2.00 1.50

Grand Cross of the Order of the Lithuanian Grand Duke Gediminas — A299

2010, Nov. 20 ***Perf. 13½x13¾***
930 A299 7 l multi 5.25 3.75

Defenders of Freedom Day — A300

2011, Jan. 8 **Litho.** ***Perf. 14***
931 A300 1.35 l multi 1.10 .80

37th European Basketball Championships, Lithuania — A301

2011, Jan. 22 ***Perf. 14¼x14***
932 A301 2.45 l multi 1.90 1.50

2011 Census — A302

2011, Feb. 26 ***Perf. 14***
933 A302 1.35 l multi 1.10 .80

Famous Lithuanians Type of 2002

Designs: 1.35 l, Gabriele Petkevicaite-Bite (1861-1943), writer. 2.15 l, Justinas Vienozinskis (1886-1960), artist. 2.90 l, Stasys Salkauskis (1886-1941), philosopher.

2011, Mar. 5
934-936 A185 Set of 3 5.00 3.75

Souvenir Sheet

Kaunas, 650th Anniv. A303

No. 937 — Buildings in Kaunas: a, Kauno Rotuse (City Hall). b, Kauno Centrinis Pastas (Main Post Office). c, Perkuno Namas Kaune (Perkunas House).

2011, Mar. 19
937 A303 3 l Sheet of 3, #a-c 7.00 7.00

Europa — A304

Tree in foreground, forest and: No. 938, 2.45 l, Field (denomination at LR). No. 939, 2.45 l, River (denomination at LL).

2011, Apr. 23
938-939 A304 Set of 2 3.50 2.75

Intl. Year of Forests.

Pilgrim Route of Pope John Paul II — A305

2011, May 7
940 A305 2.15 l multi 1.75 1.25

Miniature Sheet

Zoo Animals A306

No. 941: a, Giraffa camelopardalis. b, Pelecanus. c, Cichlasoma octofasciatum. d, Ursus maritimus.

2011, May 21 ***Perf. 14¼x13½***
941 A306 4 l Sheet of 4, #a-d 12.50 12.50

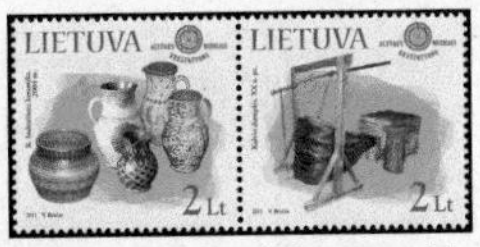

Items in Alytus Ethnographic Museum — A307

No. 942: a, Pot and pitchers. b, Blacksmith's bellows.

2011, June 4 ***Perf. 14***
942 A307 2 l Pair, #a-b 3.00 3.00

Czeslaw Milosz (1911-2004), 1980 Nobel Laureate in Literature — A308

2011, June 18 **Litho.**
943 A308 3.35 l multi 2.75 1.75

Water Measuring Station, Smalininkai, 200th Anniv. — A309

2011, July 16
944 A309 1.35 l multi 1.10 .80

Printed in sheets of 4.

Arms Type of 1992

Designs: 1.35 l, Plunge. 2.15 l, Kasiadorys. 2.90 l, Ignalina.

2011, July 30 ***Perf. 14***
945-947 A82 Set of 3 5.00 3.75

Souvenir Sheet

Stone of Puntukas A310

2011, Aug. 20
948 A310 8 l multi 6.25 6.25

Churches — A311

Designs: No. 949, 1.55 l, Church, Trakai. No. 950, 1.55 l, Cathedral, Siaulai.

2011, Sept. 3
949-950 A311 Set of 2 2.50 1.75

Battle of Saule, 775th Anniv. — A312

2011, Sept. 17
951 A312 2.45 l multi 2.00 1.50

Vilnius Historic Center UNESCO World Heritage Site — A313

Designs: No. 952, 3 l, Gate of Dawn (Ausros Vartai). No. 953, 3 l, St. John's Church.

2011, Sept. 29 **Litho.**
952-953 A313 Set of 2 4.50 3.75

Haliaeetus Albicilla — A314

2011, Oct. 8 ***Perf. 13½***
954 A314 2.15 l multi 1.75 1.25

Endangered fauna from Red Book of Lithuania.

Christmas — A315

Designs: 1.35 l, Snowman. 2.45 l, Snowflake.

2011, Nov. 5 ***Perf. 14***
955-956 A315 Set of 2 3.00 2.25

Grand Cross of the Order for Merits to Lithuania — A316

2011, Nov. 26 ***Perf. 13½x13¾***
957 A316 7 l multi 5.50 3.75

Arms Type of 1992

Designs: No. 958, 1.35 l, Kalvarija. No. 959, 1.35 l, Kavarskas. 2.45 l, Naujoji Akmene.

2012, Jan. 7 ***Perf. 14***
Size: 26x31mm
958-960 A82 Set of 3 4.00 2.75

Traditional Musical Instruments — A317

Designs: 10c, Wooden panpipes. 20c, Clay pipes. 35c, Bladderbow bass. 1 l, Alder bark trumpet. 1.35 l, Zither. 2.15 l, Cowhorn reed pipes.

2012, Jan. 7 ***Die Cut Perf. 12½***
Self-Adhesive

961	A317	10c multi	.25	.25
a.		Dated "2013"	.25	.25
962	A317	20c multi	.25	.25
a.		Dated "2013"	.25	.25
963	A317	35c multi	.25	.25
a.		Dated "2013"	.25	.25
964	A317	1 l multi	.75	.75
a.		Dated "2013"	.80	.80
965	A317	1.35 l multi	1.00	1.00
a.		Dated "2013"	1.10	1.10
966	A317	2.15 l multi	1.75	1.75
		Nos. 961-966 (6)	4.25	4.25

Issued: Nos. 964a, 965a, 5/11/13.

Famous Lithuanians Type of 2002

Designs: 1.55 l, Mikalojus Radvila Rudasis (Mikolaj Radziwill) (1512-84), Grand Chancellor of Lithuania. 2 l, Domicele Tarabildiene (1912-85), artist. 2.90 l, Stasys Simkus (1887-1943), composer.

2012, Feb. 4 ***Perf. 14***
967-969 A185 Set of 3 4.75 3.50

Maironis (1862-1932), Poet — A318

2012, Feb. 25
970 A318 3.35 l multi 2.60 1.75

Spiders From Red Book of Lithuania A319

No. 971: a, Dolomedes plantarius. b, Eresus cinnaberinus.

2012, Mar. 17
971 A319 2.90 l Horiz. pair, #a-b 4.25 4.25

Christianization of Lithuania, 625th Anniv. — A320

2012, Mar. 24 ***Perf. 14***
972 A320 1.35 l multi 1.00 1.00

Europa — A321

Designs: No. 973, Hills, trees and river. No. 974, Buildings.

2012, Apr. 28
973 A321 2.45 l multi 1.75 1.75
974 A321 2.45 l multi 1.75 1.75

Souvenir Sheet

Year of Museums — A322

2012, May 12
975 A322 7 l multi 5.25 5.25

Curonian Spit UNESCO World Heritage Site — A323

Designs: No. 976, 3 l, Fisherman's boat and house. No. 977, 3 l, Sand dunes.

2012, May 26
976-977 A323 Set of 2 4.50 4.50

2012 Summer Olympics, London — A324

2012, June 9
978 A324 3.35 l Boxing 2.40 2.40
979 A324 3.55 l Rowing 2.60 2.60

Klaipeda, 760th Anniv. — A325

2012, July 14
980 A325 2 l multi 1.50 1.50

Battle of Blue Waters, 650th Anniv. — A326

2012, Aug. 25
981 A326 2.45 l multi 1.90 1.90

Pres. Algirdas Brazauskas (1932-2010) A327

2012, Sept. 22
982 A327 1.35 l multi 1.00 1.00

Establishment of Provisional Lithuanian Currency, 20th Anniv. — A328

2012, Sept. 29
983 A328 2 l multi 1.50 1.50

Oskar Minkowski (1858-1931), Diabetes Researcher — A329

2012, Oct. 20
984 A329 1.35 l multi 1.00 1.00

Railway Bridges — A330

Train and: Nos. 985, 986a, Lyduvenai Bridge, Lithuania. No. 986b, Narva Bridge, Estonia. No. 986c, Carnikava Bridge, Latvia.

2012, Oct. 25
985 A330 8 l multi 6.00 6.00

Souvenir Sheet

Perf. 13½

986 A330 4 l Sheet of 3, #a-c 9.00 9.00

See Estonia Nos. 713-714, Latvia Nos. 815-816.

Christmas — A331

Designs: 1.35 l, Body of water. 2.45 l, Snow-covered house.

2012, Nov. 10 ***Perf. 14***
987-988 A331 Set of 2 2.75 2.75

Christianization of Samogitia, 600th Anniv. — A332

2013, Jan. 5 ***Perf. 13x13¼***
989 A332 2.45 l multi 2.00 2.00

Souvenir Sheet

Flora and Fauna of Zuvintas Biosphere Reserve — A333

No. 990: a, Vulpes vulpes. b, Panurus biarmicus. c, Dactylorhiza maculata.

2013, Jan. 19 ***Perf. 14¼x14½***
990 A333 3 l Sheet of 3, #a-c 7.25 7.25

New Year 2013 (Year of the Snake) — A334

2013, Feb. 9 ***Perf. 13x13¼***
991 A334 2.90 l multi 2.25 2.25

Lithuanian Laser Industry — A335

2013, Feb. 23 ***Perf. 13¼x13***
992 A335 1.35 l multi 1.00 1.00

Famous Lithuanians — A336

Designs: 1.35 l, Antanas Strazdas (1763-1833), poet. 2 l, Pranas Masiotas (1863-1940), writer.

2013, Mar. 9 ***Perf. 13¼x13***
993-994 A336 Set of 2 2.50 2.50

Uprising of 1863, 150th Anniv. — A337

2013, Mar. 23 ***Perf. 13x13¼***
995 A337 1.35 l multi 1.00 1.00

Ciconia Ciconia — A338

2013, Apr. 6 ***Perf. 11***
996 A338 7 l multi 5.50 5.50

No. 996 was printed in sheets of 2.

Europa — A339

Postal vehicles: No. 997, 2.45 l, Tazzari Zero (yellow vehicle). No. 998, 2.45 l, Moskvitch 401 (blue vehicle).

2013, Apr. 27 ***Perf. 13x13¼***
997-998 A339 Set of 2 3.75 3.75

Mother's Day — A340

2013, May 4 ***Perf. 13¼x13***
999 A340 1.35 l multi 1.10 1.10

International Red Cross, 150th Anniv. — A341

2013, May 11
1000 A341 2.15 l multi 1.75 1.75

Father's Day — A342

2013, June 1
1001 A342 1.35 l multi 1.10 1.10

Kaunas Cathedral Basilica, 600th Anniv. — A343

2013, June 8 ***Perf. 13x13¼***
1002 A343 1.35 l multi 1.10 1.10

Lithuanian Presidency of the European Union — A344

2013, June 15 ***Perf. 14½x14***
1003 A344 2.45 l multi 1.90 1.90

Souvenir Sheet

Transfer of Klaipeda (Memel) to Lithuanian Control, 90th Anniv. — A345

2013, June 29 ***Perf. 14¼x14½***
1004 A345 7 l multi 5.25 5.25

First Lithuanian National Olympics, 75th Anniv. — A346

2013, July 13 ***Perf. 13x13¼***
1005 A346 1.35 l multi 1.10 1.10

A347

2.90 l, Death of Captains Steponas Darius and Stasys Girenas on New York-Kaunas Transatlantic Flight, 80th Anniv.

2013, July 20
1006 A347 2.90 l multi 2.25 2.25

Lighthouses — A348

Designs: No. 1007, 2.45 l, Cape Vente Lighthouse. No. 1008, 2.45 l, Kaunas Lighthouse.

2013, July 27 ***Perf. 13¼x13***
1007-1008 A348 Set of 2 3.75 3.75

Military Uniforms — A349

2013, Aug. 24 Litho. ***Perf. 13¼x13***
1009 A349 1.35 l multi 1.10 1.10

Birds From Red Book of Lithuania — A350

Designs: 2.15 l, Acrocephalus paludicola. 2.90 l, Anthus campsetris.

2013, Sept. 7 Litho. ***Perf. 13¼x13***
1010 A350 2.15 l multi 1.75 1.75
1011 A350 2.90 l multi 2.25 2.25

Postcrossing Post Cards — A351

2013, Oct. 5 Litho. ***Perf. 13¼x13***
1012 A351 2.45 l multi 2.00 2.00

Christmas and New Year's Day — A352

Bear and fox: 1.35 l, Exchanging gifts. 2.45 l, Watching fireworks display.

2013, Nov. 9 Litho. ***Perf. 13x13¼***
1013-1014 A352 Set of 2 3.00 3.00

Kristijonas Donelaitis (1714-80), Poet — A353

2014, Jan. 4 Litho. ***Perf. 13x13¼***
1015 A353 1.55 l multi 1.25 1.25

2014 Winter Olympics, Sochi, Russia — A354

Designs: 2.15 l, Two-man bobsled. 2.90 l, Ice hockey.

2014, Jan. 18
1016-1017 A354 Set of 2 4.00 4.00

Souvenir Sheet

New Year 2014 (Year of the Horse) A355

2014, Feb. 1 Litho. ***Perf. 14¼x14½***
1018 A355 7 l multi 5.50 5.50

Shrove Tuesday Masks — A356

2014. Feb. 15 Litho. ***Perf. 13x13¼***
1019 A356 2 l multi 1.60 1.60

Re-establishment of Vytautas Magnus University, 25th Anniv. — A357

2014, Mar. 8 Litho. ***Perf. 13¼x13***
1020 A357 1.55 l multi 1.25 1.25

Admission to NATO, 10th Anniv. — A358

2014, Mar. 29 Litho. ***Perf. 13x13¼***
1021 A358 2.15 l multi 1.75 1.75

Owls From Red Book of Lithuania — A359

Designs: 2 l, Tyto alba. 3 l, Glaucidium passerinum.

2014, Apr. 5 Litho. ***Perf. 13¼x13***
1022-1023 A359 Set of 2 4.00 4.00
1023a Booklet pane of 6, 3 each #1022-1023 12.00 —
Complete booklet, #1023a 12.00

Admission to the European Union, 10th Anniv. — A360

2014, Apr. 26 Litho. ***Perf. 13c13¼***
1024 A360 2.15 l multi 1.75 1.75

Europa — A361

Designs: No. 1025, 2.45 l, Goat horn (ozragis), wooden bells (skrabalai). No. 1026, 2.45 l, Reed pipe (birbyne), zither (kankles).

2014, May 3 Litho. ***Perf. 13x13¼***
1025-1026 A361 Set of 2 4.00 4.00

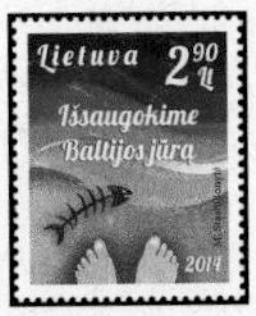

Protection of the Baltic Sea — A362

2014, May 24 Litho. ***Perf. 13¼x13***
1027 A362 2.90 l multi 2.40 2.40
a. Tête-bêche pair 4.80 4.80
b. Souvenir sheet of 3 #1027a 14.50 —

No. 1027 was printed in sheets of 9, with the central stamp inverted in relation to the others. No. 1027b was sold with, but not attached to, a booklet cover.

Karaite Judaism A363

No. 1028: a, Seraya Szapszal (1873-1961), leader of Lithuanian Karaite community. b, Kenesa (synagogue), Vilnius.

2014, June 7 Litho. ***Perf. 13x13¼***
1028 A363 2.15 l Pair, #a-b 3.50 3.50

Lithuanian Song Festival, 90th Anniv. — A364

2014, June 28 Litho. ***Perf. 13¼x13***
1029 A364 1.35 l multi 1.10 1.10

Lithuanian Term as Non-Permanent Member of United Nations Security Council — A365

2014, July 12 Litho. ***Perf. 13¼x13***
1030 A365 1.35 l multi 1.10 1.10

In anticipation of Lithuania's official change to Euro currency in January 2015, No. 1030 and stamps issued through the end of 2014 are denominated in litas and the equivalent value in the not-yet-accepted euro currency.

Souvenir Sheet

Baltic Chain Demonstration, 25th Anniv. — A366

No. 1031: a, Five adults and one child. b, Three women. c, Man and child.

2014, Aug. 23 Litho. ***Perf. 13¼***
1031 A366 7 l Sheet of 3, #a-c 16.00 16.00

See Estonia Nos. 764-765, Latvia Nos. 883-884.

Battle of Orsha, 500th Anniv. — A367

2014, Sept. 6 Litho. ***Perf. 13x13¼***
1032 A367 2.60 l multi 1.90 1.90

Earth, LituanicaSAT-1 and Litsat-1 — A368

2014, Sept. 20 Litho. ***Perf. 13x13¼***
1033 A368 2.90 l multi 2.25 2.25
a. Tete-beche pair 4.50 4.50
b. Miniature sheet of 6 + 2 labels 13.50

No. 1033 was printed in sheets of 16 + 4 labels. No. 1033b was sold with, but unattached to, a booklet cover.

Wooden Church Belfries Type of 2007 With Added Euro Denomination

Design: 5c, Belfry from church in Vabalininkas, 19th cent.

Die Cut Perf. 12½

2014, Oct. 11 Litho.

Self-Adhesive

1034 A249 5c multi .25 .25

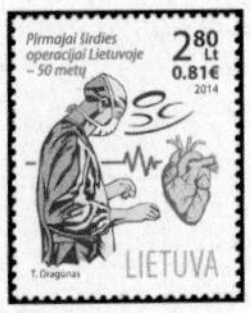

Open Heart Surgery, 50th Anniv. — A369

2014, Oct. 11 Litho. ***Perf. 13¼x13***
1035 A369 2.80 l multi 2.10 2.10

Christmas — A370

Designs: 1.35 l, Man holding letter and umbrella. 2.80 l, Santa Claus in balloon.

2014, Nov. 8 Litho. ***Perf. 13¼x13***
1036-1037 A370 Set of 2 3.00 3.00

100 Cents = 1 Euro

Introduction of Euro Currency — A371

2015, Jan. 2 Litho. ***Perf. 13x13¼***
1038 A371 75c multi 1.90 1.90

Coins Depicting White Knight "Vytis" — A372

Coin from: 1c, 1388-90. 3c, 1440-92. 10c, 1562. 29c, 1660. 39c, 1754. 62c, 1925.

Die Cut Perf. 12½

2015, Jan. 2 Litho.

Self-Adhesive

1039 A372 1c ol bis & blk .25 .25
1040 A372 3c ol bis & blk .25 .25
1041 A372 10c ol bis & blk .25 .25
1042 A372 29c ol bis & blk .70 .70
1043 A372 39c ol bis & blk .95 .95
1044 A372 62c ol bis & blk 1.50 1.50
Nos. 1039-1044 (6) 3.90 3.90

Endangered Animals — A373

Designs: 71c, Lutra lutra. 87c, Mustela lutreola.

2015, Jan. 17 Litho. ***Perf. 13¼x13***
1045-1046 A373 Set of 2 3.75 3.75

Mikolaj Radziwill (the Black) (1515-65), Grand Hetman — A374

2015, Feb. 7 Litho. ***Perf. 13x13¼***
1047 A374 45c multi 1.00 1.00

Declaration of Independence from Soviet Union, 25th Anniv. — A375

2015, Mar. 7 Litho. ***Perf. 13x13¼***
1048 A375 84c multi 1.90 1.90

Kaunas Fortress — A376

2015, Apr. 11 Litho. ***Perf. 13x13¼***
1049 A376 €2.03 multi 4.75 4.75

A377

Wooden Toys — A378

2015, May 9 Litho. ***Perf. 13¼x13***
1050 A377 71c multi 1.60 1.60
1051 A378 71c multi 1.60 1.60

Europa.

Jonas Juska (1815-86), Linguist — A379

2015, June 6 Litho. ***Perf. 13x13¼***
1052 A379 58c multi 1.25 1.25

Pervalka Nature Preserve — A380

2015, June 20 Litho. ***Perf. 13x13¼***
1053 A380 97c multi 2.25 2.25

Kretinga Railway Bridge — A381

2015, July 4 Litho. ***Perf. 13x13¼***
1054 A381 87c multi 1.90 1.90

Miniature Sheet

Embroidery Designs — A382

No. 1055 — Embroidery designs of various ethnographic groups: a, Mazoji Lietuva. b, Zemaitija. c, Aukstaitija. d, Suvalkija. e, Dzukija.

2015, July 18 Litho. ***Perf. 13x13½***
1055 A382 75c Sheet of 5, #a-e 8.25 8.25

Year of Ethnography.

Gown Designed by Juozas Statkevicius A383

2015, Aug. 8 Litho. ***Perf. 13½x13¾***
1056 A383 €2.03 multi 4.75 4.75
a. Sheet of 4 34.00 34.00

No. 1056 was printed in sheets of 2. No. 1056a was sold for €15 with a booklet cover, but unattached to it.

Education and Knowledge Day — A384

2015, Aug. 29 Litho. ***Perf. 13¼x13***
1057 A384 45c multi 1.00 1.00

Michal Kleofas Oginski (1765-1833), Composer and Politician — A385

2015, Sept. 26 Litho. ***Perf. 13x13¼***
1058 A385 81c multi 1.90 1.90

Information Technologies A386

2015, Oct. 24 Litho. ***Perf. 13x13¼***
1059 A386 84c multi 1.90 1.90

Traditional Handicrafts — A387

2015, Nov. 7 Litho. ***Perf. 13x13¼***
1060 A387 75c multi 1.60 1.60

Christmas and New Year's Day — A388

Christmas tree, people and: 39c, House. 81c, Snowman.

2015, Nov. 14 Litho. ***Perf. 13x13¼***
1061-1062 A388 Set of 2 2.60 2.60

White Knight "Vytis" and Flag — A389

Various depictions of Vytis on horseback and flags from: 1c, 1410. 3c, 1553. 10c, 1863. 29c, 1929. 39c, 1989. 62c, 1993.

Die Cut Perf. 12½
2016, Jan. 2 Litho.
Self-Adhesive

1063	A389	1c red & black	.25	.25
1064	A389	3c red & black	.25	.25
1065	A389	10c red & black	.25	.25
1066	A389	29c red & black	.65	.65
1067	A389	39c red & black	.85	.85
1068	A389	62c red & black	1.40	1.40
		Nos. 1063-1068 (6)	3.65	3.65

Soviet Military Actions Against Lithuania, 25th Anniv. — A390

2016, Jan. 12 Litho. ***Perf. 13¼x13***
1069 A390 45c multi 1.00 1.00

Mushrooms — A391

Designs: No. 1070, 84c, Boletus radicans. No. 1071, 84c, Gomphus clavatus.

2016, Feb. 13 Litho. ***Perf. 13¼x13***
1070-1071 A391 Set of 2 3.75 3.75
1071a Booklet pane of 6, 3 each #1070-1071 11.50 —
Complete booklet, #1071a 11.50

No. 1071a contains one example of No. 1070 that is tete-beche in relation to the three adjacent stamps.

Julius Juzeliunas (1916-2001), Composer — A392

2016, Feb. 20 Litho. ***Perf. 13x13¼***
1072 A392 39c multi .85 .85

New Verkiai Paper Factory, Vilnius — A393

2016, Mar. 5 Litho. ***Perf. 13x13¼***
1073 A393 58c multi 1.40 1.40

Oak Trees, Azuolynas Park, Kaunas — A395

2016, Apr. 2 Litho. ***Perf. 13x13¼***
1075 A395 87c multi 2.00 2.00
a. Booklet pane of 4 8.00 —
Complete booklet, #1075a 8.00

No. 1075a contains two tete-beche pairs.

Diplomatic Relations Between Lithuania and Japan, 25th Anniv. — A396

2016, Apr. 16 Litho. ***Perf. 13x13¼***
1076 A396 €1 multi 2.40 2.40

George Maciunas (1931-78), Co-Founder of Fluxus Art Community — A397

2016, Apr. 16 Litho. ***Perf. 13¼x13***
1077 A397 75c multi 1.75 1.75

A398

Europa — A399

2016, May 7 Litho. ***Perf. 13x13¼***
1078 A398 71c multi 1.60 1.60
1079 A399 71c multi 1.60 1.60
a. Tete-beche pair 3.20 3.20
b. Booklet pane of 6 #1079 9.75 9.75
Complete booklet, #1079b 9.75

Think Green Issue.
No. 1079a is found only in No. 1079b.

Cucumbers and Honey — A400

2016, July 9 Litho. ***Perf. 13x13¼***
1080 A400 39c multi .90 .90

Souvenir Sheet

Zemaitukas Horses — A401

2016, July 9 Litho. ***Perf. 13x13½***
1081 A401 €1.56 multi 3.50 3.50

2016 Summer Olympics, Rio de Janeiro — A402

Christ the Redeemer Statue, Rio de Janeiro, and: 81c, Swimming. 84c, Equestrian.

2016, Aug. 6 Litho. ***Perf. 13x13¼***
1082-1083 A402 Set of 2 3.75 3.75

Lithuanian Admission to United Nations, 25th Anniv. — A403

2016, Sept. 17 Litho. ***Perf. 13¼x13***
1084 A403 75c multi 1.75 1.75

Seated, by Petras Repsys — A404

2016, Oct. 9 Litho. ***Perf. 13¾***
1085 A404 48c multi 1.10 1.10

Pres. Kazys Grinius (1866-1950) — A405

2016, Oct. 29 Litho. ***Perf. 13¼x13***
1086 A405 45c multi 1.00 1.00

Souvenir Sheet

Revival of the Lithuanian State, Cent. — A406

No. 1087: a, Auszra Newspaper. b, Dr. Jonas Basanavicius (1851-1927), founder of Auszra. c, Varpas Newspaper.

2016, Nov. 5 Litho. ***Perf. 14***
1087 A406 €1.16 Sheet of 3, #a-c 7.50 7.50

Baltic Assembly, 25th Anniv. — A407

2016, Nov. 8 Litho. *Perf. 13½x13¼*

Stamp With White Frame

1088 A407 45c multi .95 .95

Souvenir Sheet

Stamp With Multicolored Frame

1089 A407 97c multi 2.10 2.10

See Estonia Nos. 827-828, Latvia Nos. 948-949.

Christmas and New Year's Day — A408

Designs: 39c, Adult and child with sled, snow-covered houses. 81c, People on city street in winter.

2016, Nov. 12 Litho. *Perf. 13x12¾*

1090-1091 A408 Set of 2 2.60 2.60

Protestant Reformation, 500th Anniv. — A409

2017, Jan. 7 Litho. *Perf. 14*

1092 A409 39c multi .85 .85

Diplomatic Relations Between Lithuania and Israel, 25th Anniv. — A410

2017, Jan. 7 Litho. *Perf. 14*

1093 A410 97c multi 2.10 2.10

White Knight "Vytis" on Horseback — A411

Depiction of Vytis from: 3c, 14th-15th cent. 10c, 15th cent. 39c, 15th cent., diff. 42c, 16th cent. 94c, 17th-18th cent. €1, 20th cent.

Die Cut Perf. 12½

2017, Jan. 14 Litho.

Self-Adhesive

1094 A411 3c black .25 .25
1095 A411 10c black .25 .25
1096 A411 39c black .85 .85
1097 A411 42c black .90 .90
1098 A411 94c black 2.00 2.00
1099 A411 €1 black 2.25 2.25
Nos. 1094-1099 (6) 6.50 6.50

Establishment of Samogitian Diocese, 600th Anniv. — A412

2017, Feb. 10 Litho. *Perf. 14*

1100 A412 €1 multi 2.10 2.10

See Vatican City No. 1641.

Kazys Bradunas (1917-2009), Writer — A413

2017, Feb. 11 Litho. *Perf. 14*

1101 A413 39c multi .85 .85

Souvenir Sheet

Revival of the Lithuanian State, Cent. — A414

No. 1102: a, Return of Lithuanian press, 1904. b, Great Seimas of Vilnius, 1905. c, Vilnius Conference, 1917.

2017, Feb. 11 Litho. *Perf. 14*

1102 A414 €1.16 Sheet of 3, #a-c 7.50 7.50

Algirdas Julien Greimas (1917-92), Semiotician A415

2017, Mar. 4 Litho. *Perf. 14*

1103 A415 39c multi .85 .85

Mammals From Red Book of Lithuania — A416

Designs: No. 1104, 42c, Sicista betulina. No. 1105, 42c, Eliomys quercinus.

2017, Apr. 8 Litho. *Perf. 14*

1104-1105 A416 Set of 2 1.90 1.90

Klaipeda Castle — A417

Birzai Castle — A418

2017, Apr. 29 Litho. *Perf. 14*

1106 A417 81c multi 1.75 1.75
1107 A418 81c multi 1.75 1.75

Europa.

Caraway Seed Cheese — A419

2017, May 20 Litho. *Perf. 14*

1108 A419 52c multi 1.25 1.25

King Wilhelm's Canal Lock — A420

2017, June 10 Litho. *Perf. 14*

1109 A420 94c multi 2.25 2.25

Seimyniskiai Hillfort — A421

2017, July 8 Litho. *Perf. 14*

1110 A421 39c multi .95 .95

Lazarus Arise, by Stanislovas Kuzma — A422

2017, Aug. 26 Litho. *Perf. 14*

1111 A422 94c multi 2.25 2.25

Souvenir Sheet

Animals A423

No. 1112: a, Lepus europaeus (European hare). b, Meles meles (European badger). c, Cervus elaphus (red deer).

2017, Sept. 7 Litho. *Perf. 14*

1112 A423 84c Sheet of 3, #a-c 6.00 6.00

Menorah — A424

2017, Sept. 23 Litho. *Perf. 14*

1113 A424 94c multi 2.25 2.25

Jewish minority in Lithuania.

Souvenir Sheet

Lithuanian Constitutions — A425

No. 1114 — Scroll and year: a, 1791. b, 1922. c, 1992.

2017, Oct. 28 Litho. *Perf. 14*

1114 A425 84c Sheet of 3, #a-c 6.00 6.00

Constitution of the Republic of Lithuania, 25th anniv.

Christmas A426

New Year 2018 A427

2017, Nov. 25 Litho. *Perf. 12½x12*

1115 A426 39c blue & red org .95 .95
1116 A427 81c blue & red org 2.00 2.00

Columns of Gediminas — A428

Columns of Gediminas depictions from: 3c, 15th cent. 10c, 16th cent. 39c, 20th cent. 42c, 19th cent.

Die Cut Perf. 12½

2018, Jan. 5 Litho.

Self-Adhesive

1117 A428 3c black .25 .25
1118 A428 10c black .25 .25
1119 A428 39c black 1.00 1.00
1120 A428 42c black 1.10 1.10
Nos. 1117-1120 (4) 2.60 2.60

2018 Winter Olympics, PyeongChang, South Korea — A429

Designs: 84c, Curling. 94c, Speed skating.

2018, Jan. 26 Litho. *Perf. 14*

1121-1122 A429 Set of 2 4.50 4.50

Souvenir Sheet

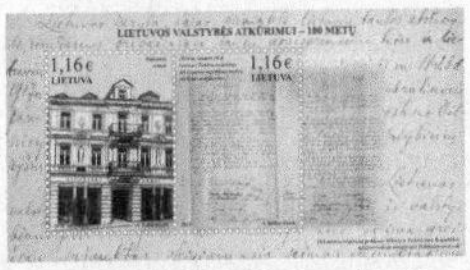

Restoration of the State of Lithuania, Cent. — A430

No. 1123: a, House of the Signatories, Vilnius. b, Act of Independence.

2018, Feb. 9 Litho. *Perf. 13¾*

1123 A430 €1.16 Sheet of 2, #a-b 5.75 5.75

Illustration From *The Eternal Flame*, by Vydunas — A431

2018, Mar. 16 Litho. *Perf. 13¾*

1124 A431 94c multi 2.40 2.40

Vydunas (1863-1953), writer.

Scouting in Lithuania, Cent. — A432

2018, Mar. 30 Litho. *Perf. 14*

1125 A432 52c multi 1.40 1.40

Bridge, Klaipeda — A433

Bridge, Trakai — A434

2018, Apr. 20 Litho. *Perf. 14*

1126 A433 75c multi 1.90 1.90
1127 A434 75c multi 1.90 1.90

Europa.

Jedrzej Sniadecki (1768-1838), Chemist — A435

2018, May 18 **Litho.** ***Perf. 13¾***
1128 A435 97c multi 2.25 2.25

Tatars — A436

2018, June 8 **Litho.** ***Perf. 14***
1129 A436 €1 multi 2.40 2.40

Miniature Sheet

Lithuanians Abroad — A437

No. 1130 — Faces of Lithuanians on stylized maps of continents: a, 24 people on North America (58x36mm). b, 18 people on Europe (45x31mm). c, 21 people on East Asia (35x48mm). d. 14 people on South America (37x46mm). e, 13 people on Africa (35x47mm). f, 10 people on Australia (45x29mm).

Serpentine Die Cut 9¾x9½ (#1130a), 10¼x10 (#1130b, 1130f), 10x9¾ (#1130c), 9½ (#1130d), 10 (#1130e)
2018, June 29 **Litho.**
Self-Adhesive
1130 A437 Sheet of 6 14.00
a.-f. €1 Any single 2.25 2.25

Coronation of Mother of God of Trakai, 300th Anniv. — A438

2018, July 27 **Litho.** ***Perf. 13¾***
1131 A438 €1.56 multi 3.75 3.75

No. 1131 was printed in sheets of 4 + 2 labels.

Vanellus Vanellus A439

No. 1132: a, Two lapwings flying to right. b, Two lapwings flying to left. c, Two lapwings, one with worm in beak. d, Lapwing and chick at nest.

2018, Aug. 17 **Litho.** ***Perf. 14***
1132 A439 49c Block of 4, #a-d 4.50 4.50

Souvenir Sheet

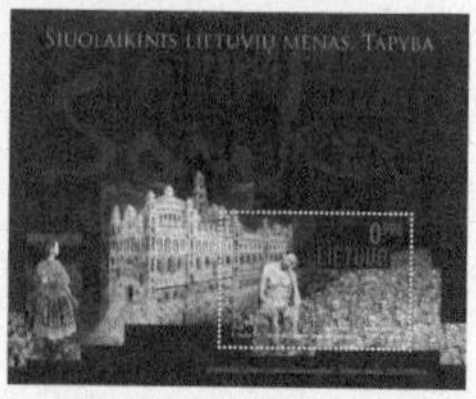

Painting for the Millennium of Lithuania, by Sarunas Sauka — A440

2018, Sept. 14 **Litho.** ***Perf. 14***
1133 A440 99c multi 2.40 2.40

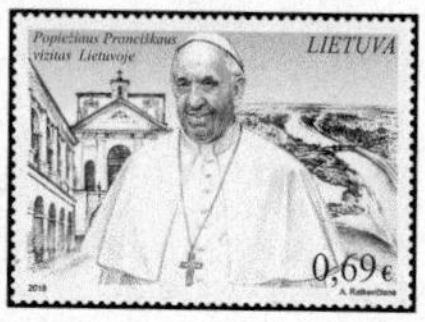

Visit to Lithuania of Pope Francis A441

2018, Sept. 22 **Litho.** ***Perf. 14***
1134 A441 69c multi 1.60 1.60

Souvenir Sheet

Lithuanian Authorities, Cent. — A442

No. 1135: a, Army (tank). b, Jurgis Saulys (1879-1948), diplomat. c, Elena Jackevicaite (1891-1977), first female judge. d, Augustinas Voldemaras (1883-1942), first Prime Minister, and members of his Cabinet.

2018, Oct. 12 **Litho.** ***Perf. 14***
1135 A442 85c Sheet of 4, #a-d 7.75 7.75

Woman Suffrage in Lithuania, Cent. — A443

2018, Oct. 26 **Litho.** ***Perf. 14***
1136 A443 55c multi 1.25 1.25

Christmas and New Year's Day — A444

Christmas tree branch and: 10c, Star-shaped cookie ornament. 40c, Orange slice ornament.

2018, Nov. 23 **Litho.** ***Perf. 14***
1137-1138 A444 Set of 2 1.25 1.25

Lithuania Nos. 1 and 2 — A445

2018, Nov. 30 **Litho.** ***Perf. 14***
1139 A445 84c multi 1.90 1.90

First Lithuanian postage stamps, cent.

Presidential Flag A446

Historical State Flag A447

National Flag — A448

Die Cut Perf. 12½
2019, Jan. 4 **Litho.**
Self-Adhesive
1140 A446 3c multi .25 .25
1141 A447 10c multi .25 .25
1142 A448 49c multi 1.10 1.10
a. Die cut perf. 9¼, dated "2021" 1.10 1.10
Nos. 1140-1142 (3) 1.60 1.60

Issued: No. 1142a, 9/2/21.

Souvenir Sheet

Lithuanian Institutions, Cent. — A449

No. 1143: a, State control (valstybes kontrolei). b, Rifleman's Union (sauliu sajungos ikurimui). c, Customs office (muitinei).

2019, Jan. 11 **Litho.** ***Perf. 14***
1143 A449 79c Sheet of 3, #a-c, + label 5.50 5.50

First Mention of Samogitia in Historical Documents, 800th Anniv. — A450

2019, Jan. 18 **Litho.** ***Perf. 14***
1144 A450 €1.05 multi 2.40 2.40

Medal for 1919 Battle of Kedainiai — A451

2019, Feb. 1 **Litho.** ***Perf. 14***
1145 A451 81c multi 1.90 1.90

Souvenir Sheet

Lithuanian Partisans — A452

No. 1146: a, Partisan's bunker. b, Council of the Union of Lithuanian Freedom Fighters declaration of 1949.

2019, Feb. 15 **Litho.** ***Perf. 14***
1146 A452 99c Sheet of 2, #a-b 4.50 4.50

Europa — A453

Ciconia ciconia: No. 1147, 75c, Two adult birds in tree. No. 1148, 75c, Two adults, nest and three chicks.

2019, Apr. 5 **Litho.** ***Perf. 14***
1147-1148 A453 Set of 2 3.50 3.50

Allium Ursinum — A454

2019, Apr. 26 **Litho.** ***Perf. 14***
1149 A454 84c multi 1.90 1.90

Lithuanian Red Cross, Cent. — A455

2019, May 3 **Litho.** ***Perf. 14***
1150 A455 84c multi 1.90 1.90

Family Day A456

2019, May 10 **Litho.** ***Perf. 14***
1151 A456 84c multi + label 1.90 1.90

Stanislaw Moniuszko (1819-72), Composer — A457

2019, Aug. 9 **Litho.** ***Perf. 14***
1152 A457 49c multi 1.10 1.10

Juozas Tumas (Vaizgantas) (1869-1933), Priest and Writer, and His Dog — A458

2019, Sept. 20 **Litho.** ***Perf. 14***
1153 A458 49c multi 1.10 1.10

Scene From *Boris Godunov,* Play Directed by Eimuntas Nekrosius (1952-2018) A459

2019, Oct. 25 **Litho.** ***Perf. 13¾***
1154 A459 49c multi 1.10 1.10

Poppy Milk A460

Sheep A461

2019, Nov. 22 **Litho.** ***Perf. 14***
1155 A460 49c multi 1.10 1.10
1156 A461 81c multi 1.75 1.75

Christmas.

Banknotes — A462

Designs: 10c, September 1922 1-litas banknote. 49c, November 1922 1-litas banknote. 59c, 1928 100-litas banknote.

Die Cut Perf. 9¼

2020, Jan. 17 **Litho.**

Self-Adhesive

1157 A462 10c multi .25 .25
1158 A462 49c multi 1.10 1.10
1159 A462 59c multi 1.40 1.40
Nos. 1157-1159 (3) 2.75 2.75

Aegolius Funereus — A463

2020, Jan. 31 **Litho.** ***Perf. 13¼***
1160 A463 75c multi 1.75 1.75

Souvenir Sheet

Partisans A464

No. 1161: a, Jonas Zemaitis-Vytautas (1909-54), Juozas Sibaila-Merainis (1905-53). b, Vytautas Guzas-Kardas (1920-49), Aleksandras Grybinas-Faustas (1920-49).

2020, Feb. 15 **Litho.** ***Perf. 13¼***
1161 A464 Sheet of 2 3.75 3.75
a. 81c multi 1.75 1.75
b. 84c multi 1.90 1.90

Souvenir Sheet

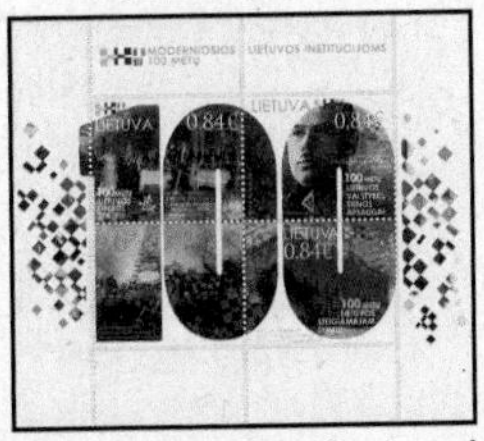

Lithuanian Institutions, Cent. — A465

No. 1162: a, Lithuanian Opera House (operos teatrui). b, Lithuanian border guards (valstybes sienos apsaugai). c, Constituent Seimas (steigiamajam seimui).

2020, Mar. 6 **Litho.** ***Perf. 13¼***
1162 A465 84c Sheet of 3, #a-c, + label 5.50 5.50

Restoration of Independence, 30th Anniv. — A466

2020, Mar. 6 **Litho.** ***Perf. 13¼***
1163 A466 49c multi 1.10 1.10

Elijah of Vilnius (1720-97), Talmudic Scholar — A467

2020, June 5 **Litho.** ***Perf. 13¼***
1164 A467 81c multi 1.90 1.90

1841 Letter From Svencionys to Moscow — A468

Taurage Post Office — A469

2020, June 12 **Litho.** ***Perf. 13¼***
1165 A468 75c multi 1.75 1.75
1166 A469 75c multi 1.75 1.75

Europa.

Cold Borscht — A470

2020, June 19 **Litho.** ***Perf. 13¼***
1167 A470 49c multi 1.10 1.10

Sigismund II Augustus and Barbara at the Radziwill Court in Vilnius, by Jan Matejko A471

2020, Aug. 1 **Litho.** ***Perf. 13¾x14***
1168 A471 81c gold & multi 1.90 1.90

Sigismund II Augustus (1520-72), King of Poland and Grand Duke of Lithuania. See Poland No. 4493.

Medal for 1920 Battle of Sirvintos-Giedraiciai — A472

2020, Sept. 11 **Litho.** ***Perf. 13¼***
1169 A472 81c multi 1.90 1.90

Wars of Independence, Cent.

Photograph by Vitas Luckus (1943-87) — A473

2020, Sept. 25 **Litho.** ***Perf. 13¼***
1170 A473 84c multi 2.00 2.00

Autumn Wind, by Ferdinand Ruscic (1870-1936) A474

Lithuanian Peasants, by Franciskus Smuglevicius (1745-1807) A475

2020, Oct. 2 **Litho.** ***Perf. 13¼***
1171 A474 €1.98 multi 4.75 4.75
1172 A475 €2.09 multi 5.00 5.00

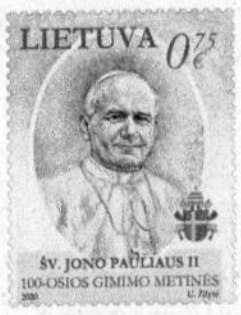

St. John Paul II (1920-2005) — A476

2020, Oct. 16 **Litho.** ***Perf. 13¼***
1173 A476 75c multi 1.75 1.75

Belarussian Woman in Traditional Clothing — A477

2020, Oct. 30 **Litho.** ***Perf. 13¼***
1174 A477 55c multi 1.30 1.30

Christmas — A478

Designs: 49c, Boy and girl decorating Christmas tree. 81c, Girl decorating Christmas tree.

2020, Nov. 27 **Litho.** ***Perf. 13¼***
1175-1176 A478 Set of 2 3.25 3.25

National Archives, Cent. — A479

2021, Jan. 8 **Litho.** ***Perf. 13¼***
1177 A479 49c multi 1.25 1.25

Birute Marija Alseikaite-Gimbutiene (1921-94), Archaeologist, and Artifacts — A480

2021, Jan. 22 **Litho.** ***Perf. 13¼***
1178 A480 49c multi 1.25 1.25

Souvenir Sheet

Partisans A481

No. 1179: a, 81c, Petras Bartkus-Zadgaila (1925-49), Adolfas Ramanauskas-Vanagas (1918-57). b, 84c, Bronius Liesys-Naktis (1922-49), Leonardas Vilhelmas Grigonis-Uzpalis (1905-50).

2021, Feb. 17 **Litho.** ***Perf. 13¼***
1179 A481 Sheet of 2, #a-b 4.00 4.00

Grand Dukes of Lithuania — A482

Designs: 10c, Gediminas (c. 1275-1341). 49c, Mindaugas (c. 1203-63).

Die Cut Perf. 9¼

2021, Mar. 12 **Litho.**

Self-Adhesive

1180 A482 10c multi .25 .25
1181 A482 49c multi 1.25 1.25

See Nos. 1193-1194.

Pier, Palanga — A483

2021, Mar. 26 **Litho.** ***Perf. 13¼***
1182 A483 81c multi 1.90 1.90

Europa — A484

Endangered animals: No. 1183, 75c, Halichoerus grypus. No. 1184, 75c, Lynx lynx.

2021, Apr. 23 **Litho.** ***Perf. 13¼***
1183-1184 A484 Set of 2 3.75 3.75

Vincas Cepinskis (1871-1940), Physicist and Politician — A485

2021, Apr. 30 **Litho.** ***Perf. 13¼***
1185 A485 84c multi 2.10 2.10

Assumption Cathedral, Vilnius — A486

2021, June 11 **Litho.** ***Perf. 13¼***
1186 A486 81c multi 2.00 2.00

Sailboat Jurate — A487

2021, June 25 **Litho.** ***Perf. 13¼***
1187 A487 84c multi 2.00 2.00

Jonas Kubilius (1921-2011), Mathematician A488

2021, July 9 **Litho.** ***Perf. 13¼***
1188 A488 55c multi 1.30 1.30

2020 Summer Olympics, Tokyo — A489

2021, July 23 **Litho.** ***Perf. 13¼***
1189 A489 84c multi 2.00 2.00

The 2020 Summer Olympics were postponed until 2021 because of the COVID-19 pandemic.

Battle of Chocim, by Józef Brandt (1841-1915) — A490

Perf. 11x11½ Syncopated

2021, Sept. 2 Litho.

1190 A490 €1.29 multi 3.00 3.00

Battle of Chocim, 400th anniv. See Poland No. 4567; Ukraine No. 1313.

Christmas — A491

Designs: 49c, Reindeer. 81c, Gift box with ribbon.

2021, Nov. 27 Litho. *Perf. 13¼*

1191-1192 A491 Set of 2 3.00 3.00

Grand Dukes of Lithuania Type of 2021

Designs: 10c, Jogaila (c. 1352-1434). 55c, Vytautas Didysis (Vytautas the Great) (c. 1350-1430).

Die Cut Perf. 9¼

2022, Jan. 14 Litho.

Self-Adhesive

1193 A482 10c multi .30 .30
1194 A482 55c multi 1.25 1.25

Miniature Sheet

Events of 1922, Cent. A492

No. 1195: a, Vladas Jurgutis (1885-1966), chairman of Bank of Lithuania, and 1922 litas banknote. b, Enactment of Lithuanian Constitution by Constituent Seimas. c, First Lithuanian men's and women's basketball teams. d, Mykolas Krupavicius (1885-1970), Minister of Agriculture and land reformer.

2022, Jan. 28 Litho. *Perf. 13¼*

1195 A492 60c Sheet of 4, #a-d 5.50 5.50

Vytautas Magnus University, Kaunas, Cent. — A493

2022, Feb. 11 Litho. *Perf. 13¼*

1196 A493 95c multi 2.25 2.25

Resistance to Soviet Rule — A494

No. 1197: a, Romas Kalanta (1953-72), student who set himself on fire in protest of Soviet rule. b, Chronicles of the Lithuanian Catholic Church, 50th anniv.

2022, Mar. 18 Litho. *Perf. 13¼*

1197 A494 70c Horiz. pair, #a-b 3.25 3.25

Kazimieras Vasiliauskas (1922-2001), Priest Exiled to Siberia by Soviets — A495

2022, Apr. 8 Litho. *Perf. 13¼*

1198 A495 75c multi 1.60 1.60

Egle, the Queen of Serpents A496

Fern Flower A497

2022, Apr. 29 Litho. *Perf. 13¼*

1199 A496 95c multi 2.00 2.00
1200 A497 95c multi 2.00 2.00

Europa. Lithuanian myths and legends.

Souvenir Sheet

Selection of Esch-sur-Alzette, Luxembourg and Kaunas, Lithuania as 2022 European Capitals of Culture — A498

No. 1598: a, The Bath, by Stasys Usinskas (1905-74). b, Nemrod, by Foni Thyssen (1909-75).

2022, May 13 Litho. *Perf. 11½*

1201 A498 Sheet of 2 5.25 5.25
a.-b. (€1.20) Either single 2.60 2.60

Joint issue between Lithuania and Luxembourg. See Luxembourg No. 1598.

Publication of Little Travel Book, by Pranciscus Skorina, First Book Published in Lithuania, 500th Anniv. — A499

2022, May 20 Litho. *Perf. 13¼*

1202 A499 60c multi 1.30 1.30

World Environment Day — A500

2022, June 3 Litho. *Perf. 13¼*

1203 A500 70c multi 1.50 1.50

Minesweeper Suduvis — A501

2022, July 22 Litho. *Perf. 13¼*

1204 A501 65c multi 1.40 1.40

Tree Cake — A502

2022, Aug. 13 Litho. *Perf. 13¼*

1205 A502 55c multi 1.10 1.10

Lithuanian Membership in the Universal Postal Union, Cent. — A504

2022, Oct. 7 Litho. *Perf. 13¼*

1207 A504 60c multi 1.25 1.25

A505

Christmas — A506

2022, Nov. 25 Litho. *Perf. 13¼*

1208 A505 55c multi 1.25 1.25
1209 A506 95c multi 2.00 2.00

Jonas Mekas (1922-2019), Film Director — A507

2022, Dec. 21 Litho. *Perf. 13¼*

1210 A507 70c multi 1.50 1.50

SEMI-POSTAL STAMPS

Regular Issue of 1923-24 Surcharged in Blue, Violet or Black

On A21

On A22

On A23

1924, Feb. Wmk. 147 *Perf. 11*

B1 A21 2c + 2c pale brn (Bl) .90 *2.25*
B2 A21 3c + 3c ol bis (Bl) .90 *2.25*
B3 A21 5c + 5c pale grn (V) .90 *2.25*
B4 A21 10c + 10c vio (Bk) 2.25 *3.25*
B5 A21 36c + 34c org brn (V) 4.75 *12.00*

Wmk. Webbing (109)

B6 A21 10c + 10c vio (Bk) 7.50 *20.00*
B7 A21 15c + 15c scar (V) 1.10 *2.50*
B8 A21 20c + 20c ol brn (Bl) 2.25 *4.00*
B9 A21 25c + 25c bl (Bk) 21.00 *55.00*
B10 A22 50c + 50c yel grn (V) 5.25 *12.00*
B11 A22 60c + 60c red (V) 5.25 *12.00*
B12 A23 1 l + 1 l org & grn (V) 6.00 *16.00*
B13 A23 3 l + 2 l red & gray (V) 9.00 *32.50*
B14 A23 5 l + 3 l brn & bl (V) 15.00 *40.00*

Unwmk.

B15 A21 25c + 25c dp bl (Bk) 4.75 *12.00*
Nos. B1-B15 (15) 86.80 228.00
Set, never hinged 225.00

For War Invalids

Semi-Postal Stamps of 1924 Surcharged in Gold or Copper

1926, Dec. 3 Wmk. 147

B16 A21 1 + 1c on #B1 1.00 1.25
a. Inverted surcharge 40.00
B17 A21 2 + 2c on #B2 (C) 1.00 1.25
B19 A21 2 + 2c on #B3 1.00 1.25
a. Double surch., one inverted 40.00
B20 A21 5 + 5c on #B4 2.00 2.00
B21 A21 14 + 14c on #B5 6.00 7.00

Wmk. Webbing (109)

B22 A21 5 + 5c on #B6 10.00 10.00
B23 A21 5 + 5c on #B7 2.00 2.00
B24 A21 10 + 10c on #B8 2.00 2.00
B25 A21 10 + 10c on #B9 65.00 65.00

Unwmk.

B26 A21 10 + 10c on #B15 4.00 5.00

Surcharged in Copper or Silver

On A22

On A23

Wmk. Webbing (109)

B27 A22 20 + 20c on #B10 4.00 5.00
B28 A22 25 + 25c on #B11 (S) 6.00 7.00
B29 A23 30 + 30c on #B12 (S) 9.00 11.00
Nos. B16-B29 (13) 113.00 119.75
Set, never hinged 225.00

For War Orphans

Surcharged in Gold

1926, Dec. 3 Wmk. 147

B30 A21 1 + 1c on #B1 .90 .90
B31 A21 2 + 2c on #B2 .90 .90
a. Inverted surcharge 260.00
B32 A21 2 + 2c on #B3 .90 .90
a. Inverted surcharge 30.00
B33 A21 5 + 5c on #B4 2.00 2.25
B34 A21 19 + 19c on #B5 4.00 5.00

Wmk. Webbing (109)

B35 A21 5 + 5c on #B6 10.00 10.00
B36 A21 10 + 10c on #B7 1.75 2.00
B37 A21 15 + 15c on #B8 2.00 2.25
B38 A21 15 + 15c on #B9 65.00 65.00

Unwmk.

B39 A21 15 + 15c on #B15 3.00 3.00

Surcharged in Gold

On A22

On A23

Wmk. 109

B40 A22 25c on #B10 5.00 6.00
B41 A22 30c on #B11 8.00 7.00
B42 A23 50c on #B12 10.00 11.00
Nos. B30-B42 (13) 113.45 116.20
Set, never hinged 225.00

Javelin throwing — SP1

Natl. Olympiad, July 15-20: 5c+5c, Archery. 30c+10c, Diving. 60c+15c, Running.

Unwmk.

1938, July 13 Photo. *Perf. 14*

B43 SP1 5c + 5c grn & dk grn 2.50 2.50
B44 SP1 15c + 5c org & red org 2.50 2.50

B45 SP1 30c + 10c bl & dk bl 4.50 4.50
B46 SP1 60c + 15c tan & brn 5.75 5.75
Nos. B43-B46 (4) 15.25 15.25
Set, never hinged 45.00

Same Overprinted in Red, Blue or Black

Nos. B47, B50

Nos. B48-B49

1938, July 13
B47 SP1 5c + 5c (R) 5.00 5.00
B48 SP1 15c + 5c (Bl) 5.00 5.00
B49 SP1 30c + 10c (R) 5.00 5.00
B50 SP1 60c + 15c (Bk) 10.00 10.00
Nos. B47-B50 (4) 25.00 25.00
Set, never hinged 50.00

National Scout Jamboree, July 12-14. Forged cancellations exist.

Basketball Players
SP6 SP7

Flags of Competing Nations and Basketball
SP8

1939 **Photo.** ***Perf. 14***
B52 SP6 15c + 10c copper brn & brn 3.25 *6.50*
B53 SP7 30c + 15c myrtle grn & grn 3.25 *6.50*
B54 SP8 60c + 40c blue vio & gray vio 6.00 *12.00*
Nos. B52-B54 (3) 12.50 *25.00*
Set, never hinged 25.00

3rd European Basketball Championships held at Kaunas. The surtax was used for athletic equipment. Nos. B52-B54 exist imperf. Value, set pairs, $500.

Catalogue values for unused stamps in this section, from this point to the end of the section, are for Never Hinged items.

People Hugging — SP9

2022, May 6 **Litho.** ***Perf. 13¼***
B55 SP9 €1+€1 multi 4.25 4.25

No. B55 was printed in sheets of 4 + 2 labels. Surtax for Blue/Yellow, an organization supporting the defense of Ukraine against its Russian invaders.

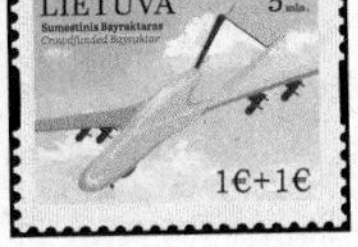

Bayraktar Drone for Ukraine Purchased With Donations From Lithuanians
SP10

Die Cut Perf. 8¾ Syncopated
2022, June 9 **Litho.**
Self-Adhesive
B56 SP10 €1+€1 multi 4.25 4.25

Surtax for Blue/Yellow, an organization supporting the defense of Ukraine against its Russian invaders.

AIR POST STAMPS

Winged Posthorn
AP1

Airplane over Neman River
AP2

Air Squadron
AP3

Plane over Gediminas Castle
AP4

1921 **Litho.** **Wmk. 109** ***Perf. 11½***
C1 AP1 20sk ultra 1.25 .75
C2 AP1 40sk red orange 1.00 .75
C3 AP1 60sk green *1.10* .75
a. Imperf., pair *45.00*
C4 AP1 80sk lt rose 1.50 .75
a. Horiz. pair, imperf. vert. *50.00* *40.00*
C5 AP2 1auk green & red *1.50* .75
a. Imperf., pair 90.00 *175.00*
C6 AP3 2auk brown & blue 1.60 .75
C7 AP4 5auk ol blk & yel 2.00 1.75
Nos. C1-C7 (7) 9.95 6.25
Set, never hinged 30.00

For surcharges see Nos. C21-C26, C29.

Allegory of Flight — AP5

1921, Nov. 6
C8 AP5 20sk org & gray bl 1.40 *2.00*
C9 AP5 40sk dl bl & lake 1.40 *2.00*
C10 AP5 60sk vio bl & ol grn 1.40 *2.00*
C11 AP5 80sk ocher & dp grn 1.40 *2.00*
a. Vert. pair, imperf. btwn. 35.00 35.00
C12 AP5 1auk bl grn & bl 1.40 *2.00*
C13 AP5 2auk gray & brn org 1.40 *2.00*
C14 AP5 5auk dl lil & Prus bl 1.40 *2.00*
Nos. C8-C14 (7) 9.80 *14.00*
Set, never hinged 17.50

Opening of airmail service.

Plane over Kaunas
AP6

Black Overprint

1922, July 16 ***Perf. 11, 11½***
C15 AP6 1auk ol brn & red 1.00 *2.75*
a. Imperf., pair 60.00
C16 AP6 3auk violet & grn 1.00 *2.75*
C17 AP6 5auk dp blue & yel 1.00 *4.00*
Nos. C15-C17 (3) 3.00 *9.50*
Set, never hinged 9.75

Nos. C15-C17, without overprint, were to be for the founding of the Air Post service but they were not put in use at that time. Subsequently the word "ZENKLAS" (stamp) was overprinted over "ISTEIGIMAS" (founding) and the date "1921, VI, 25" was obliterated by short vertical lines.

For surcharge see No. C31.

Plane over Gediminas Castle — AP7

1922, July 22
C18 AP7 2auk blue & rose 1.10 .85
C19 AP7 4auk brown & rose 1.10 .85
C20 AP7 10auk black & gray bl 1.25 1.40
Nos. C18-C20 (3) 3.45 3.10
Set, never hinged 11.00

For surcharges see Nos. C27-C28, C30.

Nos. C1-C7, C17-C20 Surcharged like Regular Issues in Black or Carmine

1922
C21 AP1 10c on 20sk 3.25 2.50
C22 AP1 10c on 40sk 1.75 1.50
C23 AP1 10c on 60sk 1.75 1.50
a. Inverted surcharge 45.00
C24 AP1 10c on 80sk 1.75 1.50
C25 AP2 20c on 1auk 11.00 6.00
C26 AP3 20c on 2auk 11.00 7.50
a. Without "CENT" 200.00 140.00
C27 AP7 25c on 2auk 1.00 *1.00*
a. Inverted surcharge 45.00 40.00
C28 AP7 30c on 4auk (C) 1.00 *1.00*
a. Double surcharge 50.00 45.00
C29 AP4 50c on 5auk 2.00 1.50
C30 AP7 50c on 10auk 1.00 *1.00*
a. Inverted surcharge 50.00 45.00
C31 AP6 1 l on 5auk 16.00 15.00
a. Double surcharge 50.00
Nos. C21-C31 (11) 51.50 40.00
Set, never hinged 92.50

Airplane and Carrier Pigeons — AP8

"Flight" — AP9

1924, Jan. 28 **Wmk. 147** ***Perf. 11***
C32 AP8 20c yellow 1.15 .75
C33 AP8 40c emerald 1.15 .75
a. Horiz. or vert. pair, imperf. between 60.00
C34 AP8 60c rose 1.15 .75
a. Imperf., pair 75.00
C35 AP9 1 l dk brown 2.50 .75
Nos. C32-C35 (4) 5.95 3.00
Set, never hinged 25.00

Most stamps, if not all, of the "unwatermarked" varieties show faint traces of watermark, according to experts.

For surcharges see Nos. CB1-CB4.

Swallow — AP10

1926, June 17 **Wmk. 198** ***Perf. 14½***
C37 AP10 20c carmine rose 1.10 .50
a. Horiz. or vert. pair, imperf. between 55.00
C38 AP10 40c violet & red org 1.10 .50
a. Horiz. or vert. pair, imperf. between 55.00
C39 AP10 60c blue & black 2.25 .50
a. Horiz. or vert. pair, imperf. between 55.00
c. Center inverted 250.00 160.00
Nos. C37-C39 (3) 4.45 1.50
Set, never hinged 6.00

Juozas Tubelis
AP11

Vytautas and Airplane over Kaunas
AP12

Vytautas and Antanas Smetona — AP13

1930, Feb. 16 **Wmk. 109** ***Perf. 14***
C40 AP11 5c blk, bis & brn 1.50 .35
C41 AP11 10c dk bl, db & blk 1.50 .35
C42 AP11 15c mar, gray & bl 1.50 .35
C43 AP12 20c dk brn, org & dl red 1.50 .80
C44 AP12 40c dk bl, lt bl & vio 4.00 .80
C45 AP13 60c bl grn, lil & blk 5.00 .85
C46 AP13 1 l dl red, lil & blk 9.00 1.60
Nos. C40-C46 (7) 24.00 5.10
Set, never hinged 100.00

5th cent. of the death of the Grand Duke Vytautas.

Map of Lithuania, Klaipeda and Vilnius — AP14

15c, 20c, Airplane over Neman. 40c, 60c, City Hall, Kaunas. 1 l, 2 l, Church of Vytautas, Kaunas.

Wmk. Multiple Letters (238)

1932, July 21 ***Perf. 14***
C47 AP14 5c ver & ol grn .35 *.70*
C48 AP14 10c dk red brn & ocher .35 *.70*
C49 AP14 15c dk bl & org yel .35 *.70*
C50 AP14 20c sl blk & org 1.75 *5.50*
C51 AP14 60c ultra & ocher 2.50 *7.00*
C52 AP14 2 l dk bl & yel 2.75 *7.00*

Wmk. 198
C53 AP14 40c vio brn & yel 2.00 *5.50*
C54 AP14 1 l vio brn & grn 3.00 *7.00*
Nos. C47-C54 (8) 13.05 *34.10*
Set, never hinged 50.00

Imperf.
C47a AP14 5c ver & ol grn .35 *.70*
C48a AP14 10c dk red brn & ocher .35 *.70*
C49a AP14 15c dk bl & org yel .35 *.70*
C50a AP14 20c sl blk & org 1.75 *5.50*
C51a AP14 60c ultra & ocher 2.50 *5.50*
C52a AP14 2 l dk bl & yel 2.75 *7.00*
C53a AP14 40c vio brn & yel 2.00 *7.00*
C54a AP14 1 l vio brn & grn 3.00 *7.00*
Set, never hinged 50.00

Issued for the benefit of Lithuanian orphans.

Mindaugas in the Battle of Shauyai, 1236 — AP15

15c, 20c, Coronation of Mindaugas (1253). 40c, Grand Duke Gediminas and his followers. 60c, Founding of Vilnius by Gediminas (1332). 1 l, Gediminas capturing the Russian Fortifications. 2 l, Grand Duke Algirdas before Moscow (1368).

1932, Nov. 28 **Wmk. 209** ***Perf. 14***
C55 AP15 5c grn & red lil .45 *.70*
C56 AP15 10c emer & rose .45 *.70*
C57 AP15 15c rose vio & bis brn .45 *.70*
C58 AP15 20c rose red & blk brn 2.25 *3.50*
C59 AP15 40c choc & dk gray 3.25 *4.75*
C60 AP15 60c org & gray blk 4.50 *7.00*
C61 AP15 1 l rose vio & grn 4.50 *7.00*
C62 AP15 2 l dp bl & brn 4.50 *7.00*
Nos. C55-C62 (8) 20.35 *31.35*
Set, never hinged 45.00

Imperf.
C55a AP15 5c grn & red lil .45 .70
C56a AP15 10c emer & rose .45 .70
C57a AP15 15c rose vio & bis brn .45 .70
C58a AP15 20c rose red & blk brn 2.25 3.50
C59a AP15 40c choc & dk gray 3.25 4.75
C60a AP15 60c org & gray blk 4.50 7.00
C61a AP15 1 l rose vio & grn 4.50 7.00
C62a AP15 2 l dp bl & brn 4.50 7.00
Set, never hinged 45.00

Anniv. of independence.

Nos. C58-C62 exist with overprint "DARIUS-GIRENAS / NEW YORK-1933- KAUNAS" below small plane. The overprint was applied in New York with the approval of the Lithuanian consul general. The Lithuanian postal authorities seem not to have been involved in the creation or release of these overprints.

Trakai Castle, Home of the Grand Duke Kestutis
AP16

Designs: 15c, 20c, Meeting of Kestutís and the Hermit Birute. 40c, 60c, Hermit Birute. 1 l, 2 l, Kestutis and his Brother Algirdas.

1933, May 6 — *Perf. 14, 11*

C63 AP16 5c ol gray & dp bl	.40	.70
b. Perf. 11	.40	.70
C64 AP16 10c gray vio & org brn	.40	.70
C65 AP16 15c dp blue & lilac	.40	.70
C66 AP16 20c org brn & lilac	2.00	4.00
C67 AP16 40c lt ultra & lilac	2.00	4.00
C68 AP16 60c brown & lt ultra	5.25	9.75
C69 AP16 1 l ol gray & dp bl	5.25	9.75
C70 AP16 2 l vio gray & yel grn	5.25	9.75
Nos. C63-C70 (8)	20.95	39.35
Set, never hinged	35.00	

Imperf.

C63a AP16 5c ol gray & dp bl	.40	.70
C64a AP16 10c gray vio & org brn	.40	.70
C65a AP16 15c dp blue & lilac	.70	.70
C66a AP16 20c org brn & lilac	2.00	4.00
C67a AP16 40c lt ultra & lilac	2.00	4.00
C68a AP16 60c brown & lt ultra	5.25	9.75
C69a AP16 1 l ol gray & dp bl	5.25	9.75
C70a AP16 2 l vio gray & yel grn	5.25	9.75
Set, never hinged	35.00	

Reopening of air service to Berlin-Kaunas-Moscow, and 550th anniv. of the death of Kestutis.

Joseph Maironis
AP17

Joseph Tumas-Vaizgantas — AP17a

Designs: 40c, 60c, Vincas Kudirka. 1 l, 2 l, Julia A. Zemaite.

1933, Sept. 15 — *Perf. 14*

C71 AP17 5c crim & dp bl	.25	.30
C72 AP17 10c bl vio & grn	.25	.30
C73 AP17a 15c dk grn & choc	.25	.30
C74 AP17a 20c brn car & ultra	.50	.60
C75 AP17 40c red brn & ol grn	1.50	2.50
C76 AP17 60c dk bl & choc	1.50	6.00
C77 AP17 1 l citron & indigo	2.50	6.25
C78 AP17 2 l dp grn & red brn	3.50	10.00
Nos. C71-C78 (8)	10.25	26.25
Set, never hinged	25.00	

Imperf.

C71a AP17 5c crim & dp bl	.25	.30
C72a AP17 10c bl vio & grn	.25	.30
C73a AP17a 15c dk grn & choc	.25	.30
C74a AP17a 20c brn car & ol grn	.50	.60
C75a AP17 40c red brn & ol grn	1.50	2.50
C76a AP17 60c dk bl & choc	1.50	6.00
C77a AP17 1 l citron & indigo	2.50	6.25
C78a AP17 2 l dp grn & red brn	3.50	10.00
Set, never hinged	25.00	

Issued for the benefit of Lithuanian orphans.

Capts. Steponas Darius and Stasys Girenas
AP18

Ill-Fated Plane "Lituanica"
AP19

The Dark Angel of Death
AP20

"Lituanica" over Globe
AP21

"Lituanica" and White Knight — AP22

Perf. 11½

1934, May 18 — **Unwmk.** — **Engr.**

C79 AP18 20c scarlet & blk	.25	.25
C80 AP19 40c dp rose & bl	.25	.25
C81 AP18 60c dk vio & blk	.25	.25
C82 AP20 1 l black & rose	.35	.25
C83 AP21 3 l gray grn & org	.45	.50
C84 AP22 5 l dk brn & bl	1.75	3.25
Nos. C79-C84 (6)	3.30	4.75
Set, never hinged	5.50	

Death of Capts. Steponas Darius and Stasys Girenas on their New York-Kaunas flight of 1933.

No. C80 exists with diagonal overprint: "F. VAITKUS / nugalejo Atlanta / 21-22-IX-1935." Value $400.

Felix Waitkus and Map of Transatlantic Flight — AP23

Wmk. 238

1936, Mar. 24 — **Litho.** — *Perf. 14*

C85 AP23 15c brown lake	2.25	.85
C86 AP23 30c dark green	3.25	.85
C87 AP23 60c blue	4.50	2.50
Nos. C85-C87 (3)	10.00	4.20
Set, never hinged	13.75	

Transatlantic Flight of the Lituanica II, Sept. 21-22, 1935.

AIR POST SEMI-POSTAL STAMPS

Nos. C32-C35 Surcharged like Nos. B1-B9 (No. CB1), Nos. B10-B11 (Nos. CB2-CB3), and Nos. B12-B14 (No. CB4) in Red, Violet or Black

1924 — **Wmk. 147** — *Perf. 11*

CB1 AP8 20c + 20c yellow (R)	12.00	12.00
CB2 AP8 40c + 40c emerald (V)	12.00	12.00
CB3 AP8 60c + 60c rose (V)	12.00	12.00
CB4 AP9 1 l + 1 l dk brown	12.00	12.00
Nos. CB1-CB4 (4)	48.00	48.00
Set, never hinged	80.00	

Surtax for the Red Cross. See note following No. C35.

SOUTH LITHUANIA

GRODNO DISTRICT

Russian Stamps of 1909-12 Surcharged in Black or Red

1919 — **Unwmk.** — *Perf. 14, 14½x15*

L1 A14 50sk on 3k red	60.00	57.50
a. Double surcharge	250.00	250.00
L2 A14 50sk on 5k claret	60.00	57.50
a. Imperf., pair	550.00	475.00
L3 A15 50sk on 10k dk bl (R)	60.00	57.50
L4 A11 50sk on 15k red brn & bl	60.00	57.50
a. Imperf., pair	650.00	550.00
L5 A11 50sk on 25k grn & gray vio (R)	60.00	57.50
L6 A11 50sk on 35k red brn & grn	60.00	57.50
L7 A8 50sk on 50k vio & grn	60.00	57.50
L8 A11 50sk on 70k brn & org	60.00	57.50
Nos. L1-L8 (8)	480.00	460.00

Excellent counterfeits are plentiful.

This surcharge exists on Russia No. 119, the imperf. 1k orange of 1917. Value, unused $90, used $60.

OCCUPATION STAMPS

The issue formerly listed as Lithuania 1N1-1N12 is now listed as Russia N1-N12.

Issued under Russian Occupation

Lithuanian Stamps of 1937-40 Overprinted in Red or Blue

1940 — **Wmk. 238** — *Perf. 14*

2N9 A44 2c orange (Bl)	.25	.25
Never hinged	.30	
2N10 A50 50c brown (Bl)	.25	.25
Never hinged	.75	

Unwmk.

2N11 A56 5c brown car (Bl)	.25	.40
Never hinged	.30	
2N12 A57 10c green (R)	3.75	8.00
Never hinged	10.00	
2N13 A58 15c dull orange (Bl)	.25	.35
Never hinged	.30	
2N14 A59 25c lt brown (R)	.25	.35
Never hinged	.65	
2N15 A60 30c Prus green (R)	.25	.50
Never hinged	.65	
2N16 A61 35c red orange (Bl)	.35	.50
Never hinged	.90	
Nos. 2N9-2N16 (8)	5.60	10.60
Set, never hinged	10.00	

Values for used stamps are for CTOs. Postally used examples are worth considerably more.

The Lithuanian Soviet Socialist Republic was proclaimed July 21, 1940.

LOURENCO MARQUES

lə-'ren‚t‚-‚sō-‚mär-'kes

LOCATION — In the southern part of Mozambique in Southeast Africa
GOVT. — Part of Portuguese East Africa Colony
AREA — 28,800 sq. mi. (approx.)
POP. — 474,000 (approx.)
CAPITAL — Lourenço Marques

Stamps of Mozambique replaced those of Lourenço Marques in 1920. See Mozambique No. 360.

1000 Reis = 1 Milreis
100 Centavos = 1 Escudo (1913)

King Carlos — A1

Perf. 11½, 12½, 13½

1895 — **Typo.** — **Unwmk.**

1 A1 5r yellow	.80	.50
2 A1 10r redsh violet	.80	.55
3 A1 15r chocolate	1.50	1.00
4 A1 20r lavender	1.50	1.00
5 A1 25r blue green	1.50	.50
a. Perf. 11½	4.75	1.50
6 A1 50r light blue	2.90	2.00
a. Perf. 13½	22.50	11.00
b. Perf. 11½	4.75	1.50
7 A1 75r rose	2.25	1.80
8 A1 80r yellow grn	6.75	4.50
9 A1 100r brn, *yel*	4.00	1.60
a. Perf. 12½	7.25	4.75
10 A1 150r car, *rose*	6.50	4.25
11 A1 200r dk bl, *bl*	6.50	4.00
12 A1 300r dk bl, *sal*	7.25	4.75
Nos. 1-12 (12)	42.25	26.45

For surcharges and overprints see Nos. 29, 58-69, 132-137, 140-143, 156-157, 160.

Saint Anthony of Padua Issue

Regular Issues of Mozambique, 1886 and 1894, Overprinted in Black

On 1886 Issue

1895 — **Without Gum** — *Perf. 12½*

13 A2 5r black	26.00	17.50
14 A2 10r green	32.00	17.50
15 A2 20r rose	35.00	19.00
16 A2 25r lilac	40.00	20.00
17 A2 40r chocolate	37.50	19.00
18 A2 50r bl, perf. 13½	30.00	22.00
a. Perf. 12½	67.50	50.00
19 A2 100r yellow brn	115.00	100.00
20 A2 200r gray vio	62.50	43.00
21 A2 300r orange	70.00	57.50

On 1894 Issue

Perf. 11½

22 A3 5r yellow	29.00	17.00
23 A3 10r redsh vio	42.00	22.00
24 A3 50r light blue	67.50	45.00
a. Perf. 12½	325.00	325.00
25 A3 75r rose, perf. 12½	77.50	57.50
26 A3 80r yellow grn	97.50	77.50
27 A3 100r brown, *buff*	240.00	190.00
28 A3 150r car, *rose*, perf. 12½	67.50	45.00
Nos. 13-28 (16)	1,069.	769.50

No. 12 Surcharged in Black

1897, Jan. 2

29 A1 50r on 300r	275.00	220.00

Most examples of No. 29 were issued without gum.

King Carlos — A2

Name, Value in Black except 500r

1898-1903 — *Perf. 11½*

30 A2 2½r gray	.50	.45
31 A2 5r orange	.50	.45
32 A2 10r lt green	.50	.45
33 A2 15r brown	1.70	1.20
34 A2 15r gray green ('03)	1.10	.85
a. Imperf.		
35 A2 20r gray violet	1.00	.60
a. Imperf.		
36 A2 25r sea green	1.10	.60
a. Perf. 13½	50.00	12.00
b. 25r light green (error)	30.00	30.00
c. Perf. 12½	160.00	140.00
37 A2 25r car ('03)	.75	.50
a. Imperf.		
38 A2 50r blue	2.25	1.20
39 A2 50r brown ('03)	1.40	1.10
40 A2 65r dull bl ('03)	9.00	6.75
41 A2 75r rose	2.90	2.00
42 A2 75r lilac ('03)	2.00	1.60
a. Imperf.		
43 A2 80r violet	3.50	1.90
44 A2 100r dk blue, *blue*	2.50	1.00
a. Perf. 13½	25.00	7.50
45 A2 115r org brn, *pink* ('03)	7.75	7.00
46 A2 130r brn, *straw* ('03)	7.75	7.00
47 A2 150r brn, *straw*	3.75	1.90
48 A2 200r red lil, *pnksh*	4.75	2.50
49 A2 300r dk bl, *rose*	4.25	2.50
50 A2 400r dl bl, *straw* ('03)	10.00	7.50
51 A2 500r blk & red, *bl* ('01)	9.00	4.75
52 A2 700r vio, *yelsh* ('01)	30.00	12.50
Nos. 30-52 (23)	107.95	66.30

For surcharges and overprints see Nos. 57, 71-74, 76-91, 138, 144-155.

Coat of Arms — A3

Surcharged On Upper and Lower Halves of Stamp

1899 ***Imperf.***

53 A3 5r on 10r grn & brn 20.00 7.00
54 A3 25r on 10r grn & brn 20.00 7.00
55 A3 50r on 30r grn & brn 30.00 11.00
a. Inverted surcharge 42.50 50.00
56 A3 50r on 800r grn & brn 40.00 20.00
Nos. 53-56 (4) 110.00 45.00

The lower half of No. 55 can be distinguished from that of No. 56 by the background of the label containing the word "REIS." The former is plain, while the latter is formed of white intersecting curved horizontal lines over vertical shading of violet brown.

Values are for undivided stamps. Halves sell for ¼ as much.

Most examples of Nos. 53-56 were issued without gum. Values are for stamps without gum. Values for stamps with gum are two times the values shown.

No. 41 Surcharged in Black

1899 ***Perf. 11½***

57 A2 50r on 75r rose 7.75 4.50

Most examples of No. 57 were issued without gum. Values are for stamp without gum.

Surcharged in Black

On Issue of 1895

1902 ***Perf. 11½, 12½***

58 A1 65r on 5r yellow 4.25 3.50
59 A1 65r on 15r choc 4.25 3.50
60 A1 65r on 20r lav 4.25 3.50
a. Perf. 12½ 75.00 62.50
61 A1 115r on 10r red vio 4.75 4.00
62 A1 115r on 200r bl, *bl* 4.75 3.75
63 A1 115r on 300r bl, *sal* 4.75 3.75
64 A1 130r on 25r grn, perf. 12½ 4.00 3.25
a. Perf. 11½ 40.00 30.00
65 A1 130r on 80r yel grn 4.75 4.00
66 A1 130r on 150r car, *rose* 5.00 4.00
67 A1 400r on 50r lt bl 11.75 6.50
68 A1 400r on 75r rose 11.00 6.50
69 A1 400r on 100r brn, *buff* 7.75 6.00

On Newspaper Stamp of 1893

70 N1 65r on 2½ brn 4.25 3.00
Nos. 58-70 (13) 75.50 55.25

Surcharge exists inverted on Nos. 61, 70.

Nos. 64, 67 and 68 have been reprinted on thin white paper with shiny white gum and clean-cut perforation 13½. Value $6 each.

For overprints see Nos. 132-137, 140-143, 156-157, 160.

Issue of 1898-1903 Overprinted in Black

1903 ***Perf. 11½***

71 A2 15r brown 3.00 1.60
72 A2 25r sea green 2.25 1.40
73 A2 50r blue 3.75 1.75
74 A2 75r rose 4.75 2.75
a. Inverted overprint 50.00 50.00
Nos. 71-74 (4) 13.75 7.50

Surcharged in Black

1905

76 A2 50r on 65r dull blue 4.75 3.50

Regular Issues Overprinted in Carmine or Green

1911

77 A2 2½r gray .50 .45
78 A2 5r orange .50 .45
a. Double overprint 10.00 10.00
b. Inverted overprint 10.00 10.00
79 A2 10r lt grn .70 .60
80 A2 15r gray grn .70 .60
a. Inverted overprint 10.00 10.00
81 A2 20r dl vio .70 .60
82 A2 25r car (G) 1.40 .75
83 A2 50r brown 1.20 .90
84 A2 75r lilac 1.90 .90
85 A2 100r dk bl, *bl* 1.20 .90
86 A2 115r org brn, *pink* 15.00 6.00
87 A2 130r brn, *straw* 1.40 .90
88 A2 200r red lil, *pnksh* 1.50 .90
89 A2 400r dl bl, *straw* 2.75 1.75
90 A2 500r blk & red, *bl* 3.00 1.75
91 A2 700r vio, *yelsh* 4.00 1.90
Nos. 77-91 (15) 36.45 19.35

Vasco da Gama Issue of Various Portuguese Colonies Common Design Types Surcharged

On Stamps of Macao

1913 ***Perf. 12½-16***

92 CD20 ¼c on ½a bl grn 2.50 2.25
93 CD21 ½c on 1a red 2.50 2.25
94 CD22 1c on 2a red vio 2.50 2.25
95 CD23 2½c on 4a yel grn 2.50 2.25
96 CD24 5c on 8a dk bl 2.50 2.25
97 CD25 7½c on 12a vio brn 4.75 3.50
98 CD26 10c on 16a bis brn 3.50 2.50
a. Inverted surcharge 40.00 32.50
99 CD27 15c on 24a bister 3.75 2.50
Nos. 92-99 (8) 24.50 19.75

On Stamps of Portuguese Africa

100 CD20 ¼c on 2½r bl grn 2.40 2.20
101 CD21 ½c on 5r red 2.40 2.20
102 CD22 1c on 10r red vio 2.40 2.20
103 CD23 2½c on 25r yel grn 2.40 2.20
104 CD24 5c on 50r dk bl 2.40 2.20
105 CD25 7½c on 75r vio brn 5.75 4.75
106 CD26 10c on 100r bis brn 3.75 2.75
107 CD27 15c on 150r bis 3.75 2.75
Nos. 100-107 (8) 25.25 21.25

On Stamps of Timor

108 CD20 ¼c on ½a bl grn 2.40 1.90
109 CD21 ½c on 1a red 2.40 1.90
110 CD22 1c on 2a red vio 2.40 1.90
111 CD23 2½c on 4a yel grn 2.40 1.90
112 CD24 5c on 8a dk bl 2.50 2.30
113 CD25 7½c on 12a vio brn 4.75 3.50
114 CD26 10c on 16a bis brn 3.25 2.50
115 CD27 15c on 24a bister 3.25 2.50
Nos. 108-115 (8) 23.35 18.40
Nos. 92-115 (24) 73.10 59.40

Ceres — A4

Chalky Paper
Name and Value in Black

1914 **Typo.** ***Perf. 15x14***

116 A4 ¼c olive brn .70 .55
117 A4 ½c black .70 .55
118 A4 1c blue grn .65 .50
119 A4 1½c lilac brn 1.15 1.00
120 A4 2c carmine 1.90 1.00
121 A4 2½c lt vio 1.90 1.00
122 A4 5c dp blue 1.50 1.00
123 A4 7½c yellow brn 1.90 1.50
124 A4 8c slate 1.90 1.50
125 A4 10c orange brn 2.20 1.40
126 A4 15c plum 2.00 1.50
127 A4 20c yellow grn 2.90 1.90
128 A4 30c brown, *green* 3.50 1.80
129 A4 40c brown, *pink* 10.00 6.00
130 A4 50c orange, *sal* 6.50 4.00
131 A4 1e green, *blue* 8.50 4.00
Nos. 116-131 (16) 39.25 16.00

Glazed Paper

131A A4 1c blue grn 1.75 1.45
131B A4 2½c lt vio 1.75 1.45

1918 **Ordinary Paper**

131C A4 ¼c olive brn .45 .40
131D A4 ½c black .45 .40
a. Value omitted 20.00
131E A4 1c blue grn .45 .40
131F A4 1½c lilac brn .45 .40
a. Imperf.
131G A4 2c carmine .45 .40
131H A4 2½c lt vio .45 .40
131I A4 5c dp blue 1.20 1.00
131J A4 7½c yellow brn 1.40 1.00
131K A4 8c slate 1.40 1.00
131L A4 10c orange brn 32.50 24.00
131M A4 15c plum 2.00 1.75
Nos. 131C-131M (11) 41.20 31.15

For surcharges see Nos. 139, 159, 161-162, B1-B12.

In 1921 Nos. 131D and 131F were surcharged 10c and 30c respectively, for use in Mozambique as Nos. 230 and 231. These same values, surcharged 5c and 10c respectively, with the addition of the word "PORTEADO," were used in Mozambique as postage dues, Nos. J44 and J45.

Provisional Issue of 1902 Overprinted Locally in Carmine

1914 ***Perf. 11½, 12½***

132 A1 115r on 10r red vio 1.70 1.70
a. "Republica" inverted 20.00
133 A1 115r on 200r bl, *bl* 1.70 1.40
134 A1 115r on 300r bl, *sal* 1.70 1.70
a. Double overprint 40.00 40.00
135 A1 130r on 25r grn 2.00 1.70
a. Perf. 12½ 2.90 2.20
136 A1 130r on 80r yel grn 2.00 1.70
137 A1 130r on 150r car, *rose* 2.00 1.70
Nos. 132-137 (6) 11.10 9.90

No. 135a was issued without gum.

Nos. 78 and 117 Perforated Diagonally and Surcharged in Carmine

1915 ***Perf. 11½***

138 A2 ¼c on half of 5r org, pair 6.00 5.50
a. Pair without dividing perfs. 20.00 20.00

Perf. 15x14

139 A4 ¼c on half of ½c blk, pair 8.50 8.00

The added perforation on Nos. 138-139 runs from lower left to upper right corners, dividing the stamp in two. Values are for pairs, both halves of the stamp.

Provisional Issue of 1902 Overprinted in Carmine

1915 ***Perf. 11½, 12½***

140 A1 115r on 10r red vio 1.00 .80
141 A1 115r on 200r bl, *bl* 1.10 .80
142 A1 115r on 300r bl, *sal* 1.10 .80
143 A1 130r on 150r car, *rose* 1.20 .80
Nos. 140-143 (4) 4.40 3.20

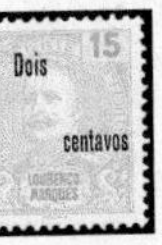

Nos. 34 and 80 Surcharged

1915 **On Issue of 1903**

144 A2 2c on 15r gray grn 1.70 1.20

On Issue of 1911

145 A2 2c on 15r gray grn 1.70 1.20
a. New value inverted 22.50

Regular Issues of 1898-1903 Overprinted Locally in Carmine

1916

146 A2 15r gray grn 2.00 1.50
147 A2 50r brown 4.00 2.60
a. Inverted overprint
148 A2 75r lilac 4.00 2.75
149 A2 100r blue, *bl* 3.50 1.90
150 A2 115r org brn, *pink* 3.50 1.90
151 A2 130r brown, *straw* 12.50 8.75
152 A2 200r red lil, *pnksh* 5.25 2.75
153 A2 400r dull bl, *straw* 8.00 5.50
154 A2 500r blk & red, *bl* 5.25 4.00
155 A2 700r vio, *yelsh* 8.50 6.00
Nos. 146-155 (10) 56.50 37.65

Same Overprint on Nos. 67-68

1917

156 A1 400r on 50r lt blue 2.00 1.70
a. Perf. 13½ 11.50 9.00
157 A1 400r on 75r rose 3.50 2.50

No. 69 exists with this overprint. It was not officially issued.

Type of 1914 Surcharged in Red

1920 ***Perf. 15x14***

159 A4 4c on 2½c violet 1.40 .60

Stamps of 1914 Surcharged in Green or Black

a

b

1921

160 A1(a) ¼c on 115r on 10r red vio (G) 1.40 1.20
161 A4(b) 1c on 2½c vio (Bk) 1.00 .70
a. Inverted surcharge 40.00
162 A4(b) 1½c on 2½c vio (Bk) 1.20 .80
Nos. 160-162 (3) 3.60 2.70

Nos. 159-162 were postally valid throughout Mozambique. No. 162 exists on glazed paper. Value the same as No. 162.

SEMI-POSTAL STAMPS

Regular Issue of 1914 Overprinted or Surcharged

a

b

c

1918 ***Perf. 15x14½***

B1 A4(a) ¼c olive brn 3.75 4.00
B2 A4(a) ½c black 3.75 4.00
B3 A4(a) 1c bl grn 3.75 4.00
B4 A4(a) 2½c violet 4.00 4.00
B5 A4(a) 5c blue 4.00 4.75

Chalky Paper

B5A A4(a) 5c blue 4.00 4.75
B6 A4(a) 10c org brn 5.00 5.25
B7 A4(b) 20c on 1½c lil brn 5.00 6.00
B8 A4(a) 30c brn, *grn* 6.00 6.50
B9 A4(b) 40c on 2c car, ord. paper 6.00 7.50
B10 A4(b) 50c on 7½c bis 8.00 8.00
B11 A4(b) 70c on 8c slate 10.00 10.00
B12 A4(c) $1 on 15c mag 10.00 10.00
Nos. B1-B12 (13) 73.25 78.75

Nos. B1-B12 were used in place of ordinary postage stamps on Mar. 9, 1918. Nos. B3 and B4 also exist on glazed paper. The unsurfaced paper on which Nos. B1-B5 were printed show a diamond pattern when held to the light. This pattern is used to determine genuine stamps.

NEWSPAPER STAMPS

Numeral of Value — N1

Perf. 11½

1893, July 28 **Typo.** **Unwmk.**

P1 N1 2½r brown .60 .65
a. Perf. 12½ 30.00 27.50

For surcharge see No. 70.

Saint Anthony of Padua Issue

Mozambique No. P6 Overprinted

1895, July 1 *Perf. 11½, 13½*
P2 N3 2½r brown 12.50 8.50
a. Inverted overprint 30.00 30.00

LUXEMBOURG

'lək-səm-ˌbərg

LOCATION — Western Europe between southern Belgium, Germany and France
GOVT. — Grand Duchy
AREA — 999 sq. mi.
POP. — 476,200 (2007)
CAPITAL — Luxembourg

12½ Centimes = 1 Silbergroschen
100 Centimes = 1 Franc
100 Cents = 1 Euro (2002)

Catalogue values for unused stamps in this country are for Never Hinged items, beginning with Scott 321 in the regular postage section, Scott B216 in the semi-postal section.

Watermarks

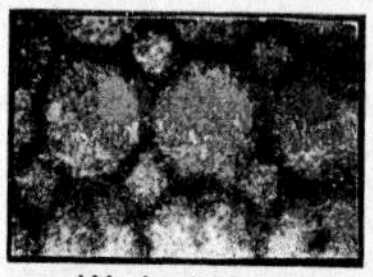
Wmk. 110 — Octagons

Wmk. 149 — W

Wmk. 213 — Double Wavy Lines

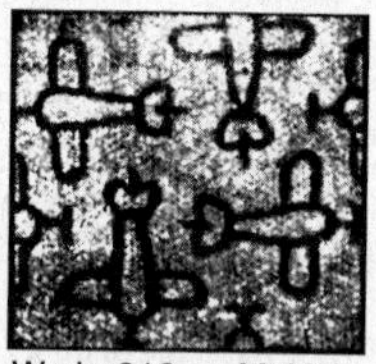
Wmk. 216 — Multiple Airplanes

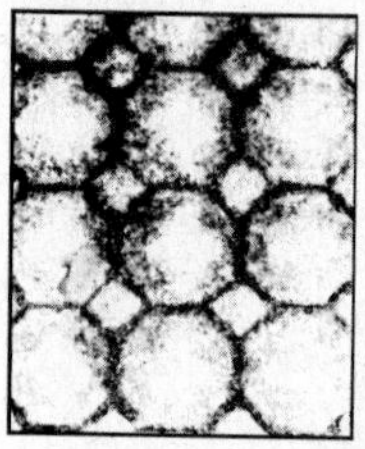
Wmk. 246 — Multiple Cross Enclosed in Octagons

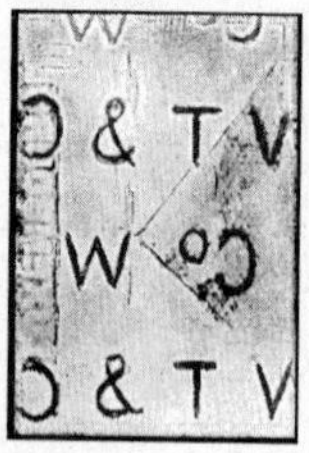
Wmk. 247 — Multiple Letters

Unused values of Nos. 1-47 are for stamps without gum. Though these stamps were issued with gum, most examples offered are without gum. Stamps with original gum sell for more.

Grand Duke William III — A1

Luxembourg Print

Wmk. 149

1852, Sept. 15 **Engr.** *Imperf.*
1 A1 10c gray black *2,100.* 55.00
a. 10c greenish black ('53) *2,250.* 55.00
b. 10c intense black ('54) *2,400.* 120.00
2 A1 1sg brown red ('53) 1,500. 75.00
a. 1sg brick red 1,500. 80.00
b. 1sg orange red ('54) 1,300. 87.50
c. 1sg blood red 2,750. 475.00
3 A1 1sg rose ('55) 1,350. 87.50
a. 1sg carmine rose ('56) 1,250. 80.00
b. 1sg dark carmine rose, thin paper ('59) *1,400.* *240.00*
Nos. 1-3 (3) 217.50

Reprints of both values exist on watermarked paper. Some of the reprints show traces of lines cancelling the plates, but others can be distinguished only by an expert.
See Nos. 278-279, 603.

Coat of Arms
A2 A3

Frankfurt Print

1859-64 **Typo.** **Unwmk.**
4 A2 1c buff ('63) 130.00 *450.00*
5 A2 2c black ('60) 95.00 *550.00*
6 A2 4c yellow ('64) 175.00 175.00
a. 4c orange ('64) 190.00 190.00
7 A3 10c blue 175.00 20.00
8 A3 12½c rose 275.00 160.00
9 A3 25c brown 350.00 275.00
10 A3 30c rose lilac 290.00 225.00
11 A3 37½c green 325.00 200.00
12 A3 40c red orange 875.00 240.00

Counterfeits of Nos. 1-12 exist.
See Nos. 13-25, 27-38, 40-47. For surcharges and overprints see Nos. 26, 39, O1-O51.

1865-71 *Rouletted*
13 A2 1c red brown 200.00 240.00
14 A2 2c black ('67) 20.00 13.50
15 A2 4c yellow ('67) 600.00 175.00
16 A2 4c green ('71) 40.00 24.00
Nos. 13-16 (4) 860.00 452.50

1865-74 *Rouletted in Color*
17 A2 1c red brn ('72) 35.00 8.00
18 A2 1c orange ('69) 40.00 8.00
a. 1c brown orange ('67) 120.00 35.00
b. 1c red orange ('69) 1,350. 325.00
19 A3 10c rose lilac 120.00 4.00
a. 10c lilac 100.00 4.00
b. 10c gray lilac 100.00 4.00
20 A3 12½c car ('71) 175.00 8.00
a. 12½c rose 175.00 8.00
21 A3 20c gray brn ('72) 120.00 8.00
a. 20c yellow brown ('69) 125.00 8.00
22 A3 25c blue ('72) 1,100. 11.00
22A A3 25c ultra ('65) 1,100. 11.00
23 A3 30c lilac rose 1,200. 80.00
24 A3 37½c bister ('66) 750.00 240.00
25 A3 40c pale org ('74) 40.00 80.00
a. 40c orange red ('66) 1,050. 60.00

No. 24 Surcharged in Black

1873
26 A3 1fr on 37½c bis 875.00 80.00
a. Surcharge inverted *3,600.*

Luxembourg Print

1874 **Typo.** *Imperf.*
27 A2 4c green 110.00 110.00

A5

1875-79 **Narrow Margins** *Perf. 13*
29 A2 1c red brn ('78) 35.00 8.00
30 A2 2c black 125.00 27.50
31 A2 4c green 2.40 *9.50*
32 A2 5c yellow ('76) 175.00 24.00
a. 5c orange yellow 600.00 125.00
b. Imperf. 925.00 1,100.
33 A3 10c gray lilac 475.00 2.40
b. 10c lilac 1,350. 29.00
c. Imperf. 2,700. *3,250.*
34 A3 12½c lil rose ('77) 600.00 20.00
35 A3 12½c car rose ('76) 400.00 27.50
36 A3 25c blue ('77) 800.00 14.00
37 A3 30c dull rose ('78) 750.00 450.00
38 A3 40c orange ('79) 1.60 *9.50*
39 A5 1fr on 37½c bis ('79) 8.00 *27.50*
a. "Pranc" *5,250.* *6,400.*
b. Without surcharge 475.00
c. As "b," imperf. 700.00
As "c," pair *1,400.*

In the Luxembourg print the perforation is close to the border of the stamp. Excellent forgeries of No. 39a are plentiful, as well as faked cancellations on Nos. 31, 38 and 39.
Nos. 32b and 33c are said to be essays; Nos. 39b and 39c printer's waste.

Haarlem Print

Perf. 11½x12, 12½x12, 13½

1880-81 **Wide Margins**
40 A2 1c yel brn ('81) 8.75 6.00
41 A2 2c black 7.25 1.60
42 A2 5c yellow ('81) 200.00 95.00
43 A3 10c gray lilac 160.00 1.60
44 A3 12½c rose ('81) 190.00 190.00
45 A3 20c gray brn ('81) 45.00 20.00
46 A3 25c blue 240.00 4.75
47 A3 30c dull rose ('81) 8.00 *24.00*

Gray Yellowish Paper

Perf. 12½
42a A2 5c 7.25
43a A3 10c 4.00
44a A3 12½c 9.50
46a A3 25c 5.50
Nos. 42a-46a (4) 26.25

Nos. 42a-46a were not regularly issued.

"Industry" and "Commerce" — A6

Perf. 11½x12, 12½x12, 12½, 13½

1882, Dec. 1 **Typo.**
48 A6 1c gray lilac .25 *.40*
49 A6 2c olive gray .25 *.40*
50 A6 4c olive bister .25 *2.00*
51 A6 5c lt green .80 .40
52 A6 10c rose 8.00 .40
53 A6 12½c slate 1.25 *24.00*
54 A6 20c orange 3.25 1.60
55 A6 25c ultra 175.00 1.60
56 A6 30c gray green 24.00 12.00
57 A6 50c bister brown 1.20 *12.00*
58 A6 1fr pale violet 1.60 *24.00*
59 A6 5fr brown orange 37.50 *160.00*
Nos. 48-59 (12) 253.35 *238.80*

For overprints see Nos. O52-O64.

Grand Duke Adolphe — A7

Perf. 11, 11½, 11½x11, 12½

1891-93 **Engr.**
60 A7 10c carmine .35 *.30*
a. Sheet of 25, perf. 11½ 125.00
61 A7 12½c slate grn ('93) 1.00 *.70*
62 A7 20c orange ('93) 13.00 1.00
a. 20c brown, perf. 11½ *160.00* 240.00
63 A7 25c blue 1.00 1.00
a. Sheet of 25, perf. 11½ *1,000.*
64 A7 30c olive grn ('93) 1.00 1.00
65 A7 37½c green ('93) 2.60 3.00
66 A7 50c brown ('93) 10.50 4.00
67 A7 1fr dp violet ('93) 16.00 9.00
68 A7 2½fr black ('93) 1.60 *10.00*
69 A7 5fr lake ('93) 35.00 70.00
Nos. 60-69 (10) 82.05 100.00

No. 62a was never on sale at any post office, but exists postally used.
Perf. 11½ stamps are from the sheets of 25.
For overprints see Nos. O65-O74.

Grand Duke Adolphe — A8

1895, May 4 **Typo.** *Perf. 12½*
70 A8 1c pearl gray 3.25 .40
71 A8 2c gray brown .30 *.25*
72 A8 4c olive bister .30 *.75*
73 A8 5c green 4.25 .25
74 A8 10c carmine 11.00 .25
Nos. 70-74 (5) 19.10 1.90

For overprints see Nos. O75-O79.

Coat of Arms
A9

Grand Duke William IV
A10

1906-26 **Typo.** *Perf. 12½*
75 A9 1c gray ('07) .25 .25
76 A9 2c ol brn ('07) .25 .25
77 A9 4c bister ('07) .25 .25
78 A9 5c green ('07) .25 .25
79 A9 5c lilac ('26) .25 .25
80 A9 6c violet ('07) .25 .25
81 A9 7½c orange ('19) .25 *1.50*

Engr.

Perf. 11, 11½x11
82 A10 10c scarlet 2.00 .25
a. Souvenir sheet of 10 450.00 *1,200.*
83 A10 12½c sl grn ('07) 2.00 .45
84 A10 15c org brn ('07) 2.60 .75
85 A10 20c orange ('07) 3.25 .75
86 A10 25c ultra ('07) 65.00 .45
87 A10 30c ol grn ('08) .65 .75
88 A10 37½c green ('07) .65 1.00
a. Perf. 12½ 16.00 12.00
89 A10 50c brown ('07) 5.25 1.25
90 A10 87½c dk blue ('08) 2.00 12.50
91 A10 1fr violet ('08) 8.00 2.00
92 A10 2½fr ver ('08) 52.50 *95.00*
93 A10 5fr claret ('08) 6.50 45.00
Nos. 75-93 (19) 152.15 *163.15*

No. 82a for accession of Grand Duke William IV to the throne.
For surcharges and overprints see Nos. 94-96, 112-117, O80-O98.

Nos. 90, 92-93 Surcharged in Red or Black

1912-15
94 A10 62½c on 87½c (R) 2.75 2.50
95 A10 62½c on 2½fr (Bk) ('15) 2.75 *4.50*
96 A10 62½c on 5fr (Bk) ('15) 2.00 *3.00*
Nos. 94-96 (3) 7.50 *10.00*

Grand Duchess Marie Adelaide — A11

1914-17 **Engr.** *Perf. 11½, 11½x11*
97 A11 10c lake .25 .25
98 A11 12½c dull green .25 .25
99 A11 15c sepia .25 *.25*
100 A11 17½c dp brown ('17) .25 *.40*
101 A11 25c ultra .25 .25
102 A11 30c bister .25 *.50*
103 A11 35c dark blue .25 *.30*
104 A11 37½c black brn .25 *.30*
105 A11 40c orange .25 *.30*
106 A11 50c dark gray .25 *.60*
107 A11 62½c blue green .40 *2.00*
108 A11 87½c orange ('17) .40 *2.00*
109 A11 1fr orange brown 2.00 1.50
110 A11 2½fr red .40 *1.50*
111 A11 5fr dark violet 9.50 *35.00*
Nos. 97-111 (15) 15.20 *45.40*
Set, never hinged 65.00

For surcharges and overprints see Nos. 118-124, B7-B10, O99-O113. Nos. 97, 98, 101, 107, 109 and 111 overprinted "Droits de statistique" are revenue stamps.

Stamps of 1906-19 Surcharged with New Value and Bars in Black or Red

1916-24
112 A9 2½c on 5c ('18) .25 .25
a. Double surcharge 75.00
113 A9 3c on 2c ('21) .25 *.25*
114 A9 5c on 1c ('23) .25 *.25*
115 A9 5c on 4c ('23) .25 *.40*
116 A9 5c on 7½c ('24) .25 *.25*
117 A9 6c on 2c (R) ('22) .25 *.25*
118 A11 7½c on 10c ('18) .25 .25
119 A11 17½c on 30c .25 *.40*
120 A11 20c on 17½c ('21) .25 *.25*
121 A11 25c on 37½c ('23) .25 *.25*
a. Double surcharge 90.00
122 A11 75c on 62½c (R) ('22) .25 *.25*

123	A11	80c on 87½c ('22)	.25	*.25*
124	A11	87½c on 1fr	.55	*5.50*
		Nos. 112-124 (13)	3.55	*8.80*

Grand Duchess Charlotte — A12

1921, Jan. 6 Engr. *Perf. 11½*

125	A12	15c rose	.25	.25
	a.	Sheet of 5, perf 11	400.00	*250.00*
		Never hinged	925.00	
	b.	Sheet of 25, perf. 11½, 11x11½, 12x11½	8.00	*17.00*

Birth of Prince Jean, first son of Grand Duchess Charlotte, Jan. 5 (No. 125a). No. 125 was printed in sheets of 100.

See Nos. 131-150. For surcharges and overprints see Nos. 154-158, O114-O131, O136.

Vianden Castle — A13

Foundries at Esch — A14

Adolphe Bridge — A15

1921-34 *Perf. 11, 11½, 11x11½*

126	A13	1fr carmine	.25	*.40*
127	A13	1fr dk blue ('26)	.25	*.45*

Perf. 11½x11; 11½ (#129, 130)

128	A14	2fr indigo	.30	*.80*
129	A14	2fr dk brown ('26)	7.00	2.00
130	A15	5fr dk violet	20.00	9.50
		Nos. 126-130 (5)	27.80	13.15

For overprints see Nos. O132-O135, O137-138, O140.

See No. B85.

Charlotte Type of 1921

1921-26 *Perf. 11½*

131	A12	2c brown	.25	.25
132	A12	3c olive green	.25	.25
	a.	Sheet of 25	10.00	25.00
133	A12	6c violet	.25	.25
	a.	Sheet of 25	10.00	25.00
134	A12	10c yellow grn	.25	.25
135	A12	10c olive brn ('24)	.25	.25
136	A12	15c brown olive	.25	.25
137	A12	15c pale grn ('24)	.25	.25
138	A12	15c dp orange ('26)	.25	.25
139	A12	20c dp orange	.25	.25
	a.	Sheet of 25	60.00	*110.00*
140	A12	20c yellow grn ('26)	.25	.25
141	A12	25c dk green	.25	.25
142	A12	30c carmine rose	.25	.25
143	A12	40c brown orange	.25	.25
144	A12	50c deep blue	.25	.25
145	A12	50c red ('24)	.25	.25
146	A12	75c red	.25	1.00
	a.	Sheet of 25	325.00	
147	A12	75c deep blue ('24)	.25	.25
148	A12	80c black	.25	.70
	a.	Sheet of 25	325.00	
		Nos. 131-148 (18)	4.50	5.70

For surcharges and overprints see Nos. 154-158, O114-O131, O136.

Philatelic Exhibition Issue

1922, Aug. 27 *Imperf.*

Laid Paper

149	A12	25c dark green	1.75	*6.00*
150	A12	30c carmine rose	1.75	*6.00*

Nos. 149 and 150 were sold exclusively at the Luxembourg Phil. Exhib., Aug. 1922.

Souvenir Sheet

View of Luxembourg — A16

1923, Jan. 3 *Perf. 11*

151	A16	10fr dp grn, sheet	1,500.	*2,400.*
		Never hinged	3,000.	

Birth of Princess Elisabeth. See No. 1606.

1923, Mar. *Perf. 11½*

152	A16	10fr black	4.50	*12.00*
	a.	Perf. 12½ ('34)	4.50	*12.00*

For overprint see No. O141.

The Wolfsschlucht near Echternach — A17

1923-34 *Perf. 11½*

153	A17	3fr dk blue & blue	1.50	.80
	a.	Perf. 12½ ('34)	1.50	.80

For overprint see No. O139.

Stamps of 1921-26 Surcharged with New Values and Bars

1925-28

154	A12	5c on 10c yel grn	.25	.30
155	A12	15c on 20c yel grn ('28)	.25	.25
	a.	Bars omitted		
156	A12	35c on 40c brn org ('27)	.25	.25
157	A12	60c on 75c dp bl ('27)	.25	.25
158	A12	60c on 80c blk ('28)	.40	.35
		Nos. 154-158 (5)	1.40	1.40

Grand Duchess Charlotte — A18

1926-35 Engr. *Perf. 12*

159	A18	5c dk violet	.25	.25
160	A18	10c olive grn	.25	.25
161	A18	15c black ('30)	.25	.25
162	A18	20c orange	.25	.30
163	A18	25c yellow grn	.25	.30
164	A18	25c vio brn ('27)	.25	.30
165	A18	30c yel grn ('27)	.25	.30
166	A18	30c gray vio ('30)	.55	.25
167	A18	35c gray vio ('28)	3.25	.25
168	A18	35c yel grn ('30)	.25	.25
169	A18	40c olive gray	.25	.25
170	A18	50c red brown	.25	.25
171	A18	60c blue grn ('28)	3.25	.25
172	A18	65c black brn	.25	.90
173	A18	70c blue vio ('35)	.25	.25
174	A18	75c rose	.25	.30
175	A18	75c bis brn ('27)	.25	.25
176	A18	80c bister brn	.25	1.25
177	A18	90c rose ('27)	1.25	1.40
178	A18	1fr black	1.25	.30
179	A18	1fr rose ('30)	.55	.25
180	A18	1¼fr dk blue	.25	.55
181	A18	1¼fr yellow ('30)	9.50	1.75
182	A18	1¼fr blue grn ('31)	.45	.45
183	A18	1¼fr rose car ('34)	15.00	2.00
184	A18	1½fr dp blue ('27)	1.75	1.50
185	A18	1¾fr dk blue ('30)	.90	.40
		Nos. 159-185 (27)	41.70	15.00
		Set, never hinged	135.00	

For surcharges and overprints see Nos. 186-193, N17-N29, O142-O178.

Stamps of 1926-35, Surcharged with New Values and Bars

1928-39

186	A18	10(c) on 30c yel grn ('29)	.40	.40
187	A18	15c on 25c yel grn	.30	.65
187A	A18	30c on 60c bl grn ('39)	.25	1.40
188	A18	60c on 65c blk brn	.25	.30
189	A18	60c on 75c rose	.25	.30
190	A18	60c on 80c bis brn	.30	.60
191	A18	70(c) on 75c bis brn ('35)	6.00	.40
192	A18	75(c) on 90c rose ('29)	2.00	.40
193	A18	1¾(fr) on 1½fr dp bl ('29)	4.50	1.60
		Nos. 186-193 (9)	14.25	6.05
		Set, never hinged	45.00	

The surcharge on No. 187A has no bars.

View of Clervaux — A19

1928-34 *Perf. 12½*

194	A19	2fr black ('34)	1.50	.80
		Never hinged	4.00	
	a.	Perf. 11½ ('28)	2.75	.80
		Never hinged	6.00	—

See No. B66. For overprint see No. O179.

Coat of Arms — A20

1930, Dec. 20 Typo. *Perf. 12½*

195	A20	5c claret	.85	.40
196	A20	10c olive green	1.10	.25
		Set, never hinged	5.50	

View of the Lower City of Luxembourg — A21

1931, June 20 Engr.

197	A21	20fr deep green	3.50	*12.00*
		Never hinged	8.00	

For overprint see No. O180.

Gate of "Three Towers" — A22

1934, Aug. 30 *Perf. 14x13½*

198	A22	5fr blue green	2.50	*10.00*
		Never hinged	7.50	

For surcharge and overprint see Nos. N31, O181.

Castle From Our Valley — A23

1935, Nov. 15 *Perf. 12½x12*

199	A23	10fr green	3.00	*12.00*
		Never hinged	6.50	

For surcharge and overprint see Nos. N32, O182.

Municipal Palace — A24

1936, Aug. 26 Photo. *Perf. 11½*

Granite Paper

200	A24	10c brown	.25	.30
201	A24	35c green	.30	.30
202	A24	70c red orange	.40	*.75*
203	A24	1fr carmine rose	1.10	*1.50*
204	A24	1.25fr violet	2.00	*9.00*
205	A24	1.75fr brt ultra	1.25	*6.00*
		Nos. 200-205 (6)	5.30	*17.85*
		Set, never hinged	16.00	

11th Cong. of Intl. Federation of Philately. See No. 859.

Arms of Luxembourg A25

William I A26

Designs: 70c, William II. 75c, William III. 1fr, Prince Henry. 1.25fr, Grand Duke Adolphe. 1.75fr, William IV. 3fr, Regent Marie Anne. 5fr, Grand Duchess Marie Adelaide. 10fr, Grand Duchess Charlotte.

1939, May 27 Engr. *Perf. 12½x12*

206	A25	35c brt green	.25	.25
207	A26	50c orange	.25	.25
208	A26	70c slate green	.25	.25
209	A26	75c sepia	.65	*1.25*
210	A26	1fr red	1.75	*2.50*
211	A26	1.25fr brown violet	.25	.25
212	A26	1.75fr dark blue	.25	.25
213	A26	3fr lt brown	.25	.70
214	A26	5fr gray black	.50	*3.00*
215	A26	10fr copper red	1.00	*6.50*
		Nos. 206-215 (10)	5.40	*15.20*
		Set, never hinged	11.00	

Centenary of Independence.

Allegory of Medicinal Baths — A35

1939, Sept. 18 Photo. *Perf. 11½*

216	A35	2fr brown rose	.50	2.50
		Never hinged	1.25	

Elevation of Mondorf-les-Bains to town status.

See No. B104. For surcharge see No. N30.

Souvenir Sheet

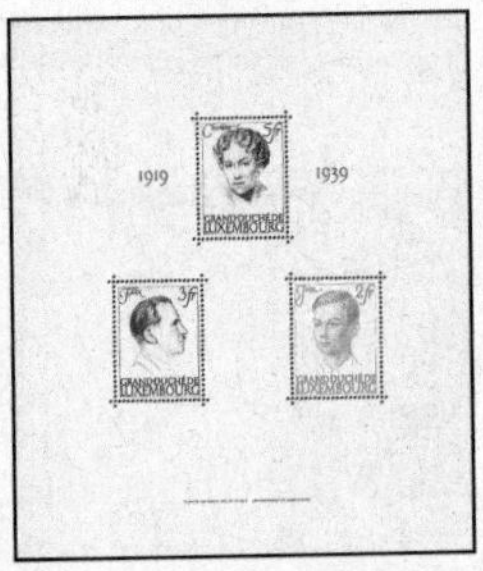

A36

1939, Dec. 20 Engr. *Perf. 14x13*

217	A36	Sheet of 3	45.00	*100.00*
		Sheet, never hinged	100.00	
	a.	*2fr vermilion, buff*	12.00	*22.50*
	b.	*3fr dark green, buff*	12.00	*22.50*
	c.	*5fr blue, buff*	12.00	*22.50*

20th anniv. of the reign of Grand Duchess Charlotte (Jan. 15, 1919) and her marriage to Prince Felix (Nov. 6, 1919).

See Nos. B98-B103.

Grand Duchess Charlotte — A37

1944-46 Unwmk. *Perf. 12*

218	A37	5c brown red	.25	.25
219	A37	10c black	.25	.25
219A	A37	20c orange ('46)	.25	.25
220	A37	25c sepia	.25	.25
220A	A37	30c carmine ('46)	.25	.40
221	A37	35c green	.25	.40
221A	A37	40c dk blue ('46)	.25	.40
222	A37	50c dk violet	.25	.25
222A	A37	60c orange ('46)	.80	.25
223	A37	70c rose pink	.25	.25
223A	A37	70c dp green ('46)	.35	*.65*
223B	A37	75c sepia ('46)	.25	.25
224	A37	1fr olive	.25	.25
225	A37	1¼fr red orange	.25	*.25*
226	A37	1½fr red orange ('46)	.25	.25
227	A37	1¾fr blue	.25	.25
228	A37	2fr rose car ('46)	1.40	.25
229	A37	2½fr dp violet ('46)	2.50	*4.50*
230	A37	3fr dp yel grn ('46)	.35	.50
231	A37	3½fr brt blue ('46)	.35	*.75*
232	A37	5fr dk blue grn	.25	.25
233	A37	10fr carmine	.25	1.20
234	A37	20fr deep blue	.45	*8.00*
		Nos. 218-234 (23)	10.20	*20.30*
		Set, never hinged	16.00	

Lion from Duchy Arms — A38

1945 **Engr.** ***Perf. 14x13***

235 A38 20c black .25 .25
236 A38 30c brt green .25 .40
237 A38 60c deep violet .25 .25
238 A38 75c brown red .25 .25
239 A38 1.20fr red .25 .25
240 A38 1.50fr rose lilac .25 .25
241 A38 2.50fr lt blue .25 .40
Set, never hinged 1.60

Issued: 1.20fr, 5/15/45; 30c, 1.50fr, 2.50fr, 7/19; 20c, 75c, 10/1; 60c, 12/13.

Patton's Grave, US Military Cemetery, Hamm — A39

Gen. Patton, Broken Chain and Advancing Tanks — A40

1947, Oct. 24 **Photo.** ***Perf. 11½***

242 A39 1.50fr dk carmine .25 *.25*
243 A40 3.50fr dull blue 1.00 *2.00*
244 A39 5fr dk slate grn 1.00 *2.90*
245 A40 10fr chocolate 5.25 *40.00*
Nos. 242-245 (4) 7.50 *45.15*
Set, never hinged 15.00

George S. Patton, Jr. (1885-1945), American general.

Esch-sur-Sûre Fortifications A41

Luxembourg A44

Moselle River — A42

Steel Mills — A43

Perf. 11½x11, 11x11½

1948, Aug. 5 **Engr.** **Unwmk.**

246 A41 7fr dark brown 6.00 .80
247 A42 10fr dark green 1.00 .25
248 A43 15fr carmine 1.00 .80
249 A44 20fr dark blue 1.00 .80
Nos. 246-249 (4) 9.00 2.65
Set, never hinged 29.00

Grand Duchess Charlotte — A45

1948-49 ***Perf. 11½***

250 A45 15c olive brn ('49) .25 .25
251 A45 25c slate .25 .25
252 A45 60c brown ('49) .25 .25
253 A45 80c green ('49) .25 .25
254 A45 1fr red lilac .70 .25
255 A45 1.50fr grnsh bl .70 .25
256 A45 1.60fr slate gray ('49) .70 *1.40*
257 A45 2fr dk vio brn .70 .25
258 A45 4fr violet blue 1.40 .40
259 A45 6fr brt red vio ('49) 2.25 .40
260 A45 8fr dull green ('49) 2.25 1.20
Nos. 250-260 (11) 9.70 5.15
Set, never hinged 26.00

See Nos. 265-271, 292, 337-340, B151.

Self-Inking Canceller — A46

1949, Oct. 6 **Photo.**

261 A46 80c blk, Prus grn & pale grn .25 .55
262 A46 2.50fr dk brn, brn red & sal rose 1.00 *2.00*
263 A46 4fr blk, bl & pale bl 2.75 *6.00*
264 A46 8fr dk brn, brn & buff 9.00 *20.00*
Nos. 261-264 (4) 13.00 *28.55*
Set, never hinged 25.00

UPU, 75th anniv.

Charlotte Type of 1948-49

1951, Mar. 15 **Engr.** **Unwmk.**

265 A45 5c red orange .25 .25
266 A45 10c ultra .25 .25
267 A45 40c crimson .25 .25
268 A45 1.25fr dk brown .70 .35
269 A45 2.50fr red .70 .25
270 A45 3fr blue 4.50 .35
271 A45 3.50fr rose lake 1.90 .40
Nos. 265-271 (7) 8.55 2.10
Set, never hinged 22.50

Agriculture and Industry — A47

Globe and Scales — A48

1fr, 3fr, People of Europe & Charter of Freedom.

1951, Oct. 25 **Photo.** ***Perf. 11½***

272 A47 80c deep green *4.00* *9.50*
273 A47 1fr purple *1.75* *.55*
274 A48 2fr black brown *12.00* *.55*
275 A47 2.50fr dk carmine *12.00* *20.00*
276 A47 3fr orange brn *22.50* *30.00*
277 A48 4fr blue *32.50* *40.00*
Nos. 272-277 (6) *84.75* *100.60*
Set, never hinged *175.00*

Issued to promote a united Europe.

Grand Duke William III — A49

Perf. 13½x13

1952, May 24 **Engr.** **Unwmk.**
Dates, Ornaments in Olive Green

278 A49 2fr black 21.00 *30.00*
Never hinged 30.00
279 A49 4fr red brown 21.00 *30.00*
Never hinged 30.00
a. Se-tenant pair, #278-279 47.50 *75.00*
Never hinged 75.00

Printed in sheets containing two panes of eight stamps each, alternating the two denominations. Centenary of Luxembourg's postage stamps. Price per set, 26fr, which included admission to the CENTILUX exhibition.

See Nos. C16-C20.

Hurdle Race — A50

Designs: 2fr, Football. 2.50fr, Boxing. 3fr, Water polo. 4fr, Bicycle racing. 8fr, Fencing.

1952, Aug. 20 **Photo.** ***Perf. 11½***
Designs in Black

280 A50 1fr pale green .25 .25
281 A50 2fr brown buff 1.00 .25
282 A50 2.50fr salmon pink 1.50 .35
283 A50 3fr buff 1.75 .80
284 A50 4fr lt blue 10.50 6.00
285 A50 8fr lilac 6.00 3.50
Nos. 280-285 (6) 21.00 11.15
Set, never hinged 50.00

15th Olympic Games, Helsinki; World Bicycling Championships of 1952.

Wedding of Princess Josephine-Charlotte of Belgium and Hereditary Grand Duke Jean — A51

1953, Apr. 1

286 A51 80c dull violet .25 .25
287 A51 1.20fr lt brown .25 .25
288 A51 2fr green .25 .25
289 A51 3fr red lilac .25 .30
290 A51 4fr brt blue 2.50 1.00
291 A51 9fr brown red 3.50 1.00
Nos. 286-291 (6) 7.00 3.05
Set, never hinged 17.50

Charlotte Type of 1948-49

1953, May 18 **Engr.**

292 A45 1.20fr gray .40 .25
Never hinged .90

Radio Luxembourg A52

Victor Hugo's Home, Vianden — A53

1953, May 18 ***Perf. 11½x11***

293 A52 3fr purple 2.75 1.50
294 A53 4fr Prussian blue 1.75 1.50
Set, never hinged 9.50

150th birth anniv. of Victor Hugo (No. 294).

St. Willibrord Basilica Restored — A54

Design: 2.50fr, Interior view.

1953, Sept. 18 ***Perf. 13x13½***

295 A54 2fr red 1.60 .40
296 A54 2.50fr dk gray grn 2.75 5.60
Set, never hinged 8.50

Consecration of St. Willibrord Basilica at Echternach.

Pierre d'Aspelt — A55

1953, Sept. 25

297 A55 4fr black 4.00 4.00
Never hinged 7.00

Pierre d'Aspelt (1250-1320), chancellor of the Holy Roman Empire and Archbishop of Mainz.

Fencing Swords, Mask and Glove — A56

1954, May 6 ***Perf. 13½x13***

298 A56 2fr red brn & blk brn, *gray* 1.75 .75
Never hinged 3.75

World Fencing Championship Matches, Luxembourg, June 10-22.

Winged "L" Over Map — A57

1954, May 6 **Photo.** ***Perf. 11½***

299 A57 4fr dp bl, yel & red 6.00 3.50
Never hinged 9.00

6th Intl. Fair, Luxembourg, July 10-25.

Flowers — A58

Designs: 80c, Tulips. 2fr, Daffodils. 3fr, Hyacinths. 4fr, Parrot tulips.

1955, Apr. 1

300 A58 80c multi .25 .25
301 A58 2fr multi .25 .25
302 A58 3fr multi 1.75 3.25
303 A58 4fr multi 2.25 5.00
Nos. 300-303 (4) 4.50 8.75
Set, never hinged 8.50

Flower festival at Mondorf-les-Bains.
See Nos. 351-353.

Artisan, Wheel and Tools — A59

1955, Sept. 1 **Engr.** ***Perf. 13***

304 A59 2fr dk gray & blk brn .70 .35
Never hinged 1.25

Natl. Handicraft Exposition at Luxembourg — Limpertsburg, Sept. 3-12.

Dudelange Television Station — A60

1955, Sept. 1 **Unwmk.**

305 A60 2.50fr dk brn & redsh brn .65 .55
Never hinged 1.75

Installation of the Tele-Luxembourg station at Dudelange.

United Nations Emblem and Children Playing — A61

UN, 10th anniv.: 80c, "Charter." 4fr, "Justice" (Sword and Scales). 9fr, "Assistance" (Workers).

1955, Oct. 24 ***Perf. 11x11½***

306 A61 80c black & dk bl .25 .30
307 A61 2fr red & brown 1.75 .25
308 A61 4fr dk blue & red 2.00 3.25
309 A61 9fr dk brn & sl grn .65 .80
Nos. 306-309 (4) 4.65 4.60
Set, never hinged 11.00

A62

2fr, Anemones. 2.50fr, 4fr, Roses. 3fr, Crocuses.

1956 Photo. *Perf. 11½*
Flowers in Natural Colors

310	A62	2fr gray violet	.25	.25
311	A62	2.50fr brt blue	2.50	3.75
312	A62	3fr red brown	1.00	2.00
313	A62	4fr purple	1.25	1.60
		Nos. 310-313 (4)	5.00	7.60
		Set, never hinged	10.00	

Flower Festival at Mondorf-les-Bains (Nos. 310, 312). Nos. 311 and 313 are inscribed: "Luxembourg-Ville des Roses."

Issued: Nos. 310, 312, 4/27; Nos. 311, 313, 5/30.

A63

Steel beam and city emblem.

1956, May 30

314	A63 2fr brt grnsh bl, red & blk	.95	.50
	Never hinged	2.25	

50th anniversary of Esch-sur-Alzette.

Bessemer Converter and Blast Furnaces A64

Steel Beam and Model of City of Luxembourg A65

Design: 4fr, 6-link chain, miner's lamp.

Perf. 11x11½, 11½x11
1956, Aug. 10 Engr.

315	A64 2fr dull red	11.00	.30
316	A65 3fr dark blue	11.00	*17.00*
317	A64 4fr green	2.00	*2.75*
	Nos. 315-317 (3)	*24.00*	*20.05*
	Set, never hinged	45.00	

4th anniv. of the establishment in Luxembourg of the headquarters of the European Coal and Steel Community.

"Rebuilding Europe" — A66

1956, Sept. 15 *Perf. 13*

318	A66 2fr brown & black	*37.50*	*.50*
319	A66 3fr brick red & car	*25.00*	*37.50*
320	A66 4fr brt bl & dp bl	*3.00*	*4.00*
	Nos. 318-320 (3)	65.50	42.00
	Set, never hinged	*155.00*	

Cooperation among the six countries comprising the Coal and Steel Community.

Catalogue values for unused stamps in this section, from this point to the end of the section, are for Never Hinged items.

Central Station from Train Window — A67

1956, Sept. 29 *Perf. 13x12½*

321	A67 2fr black & sepia	2.50	.55

Electrification of Luxembourg railways.

Ignace de la Fontaine — A68

Design: 7fr, Grand Duchess Charlotte.

1956, Nov. 7 *Perf. 11½*

322	A68 2fr gray brown	1.00	.25
323	A68 7fr dull purple	2.75	.90

Centenary of the Council of State.

Lord Baden-Powell and Luxembourg Scout Emblems — A69

Designs: 2.50fr, Lord Baden-Powell and Luxembourg Girl Scout emblems.

1957, June 17 *Perf. 11½x11*

324	A69 2fr ol grn & red brn	1.00	.50
325	A69 2.50fr dk vio & claret	2.50	2.50

Birth centenary of Robert Baden-Powell and 50th anniv. of the founding of the Scout movement.

Prince Henry — A70

Children's Clinic — A71

Design: 4fr, Princess Marie-Astrid.

1957, June 17 Photo. *Perf. 11½*

326	A70 2fr brown	.60	.25
327	A71 3fr bluish grn	3.00	*1.75*
328	A70 4fr ultra	2.00	*2.10*
	Nos. 326-328 (3)	5.60	*4.10*

Children's Clinic of the Prince Jean-Princess Josephine-Charlotte Foundation.

"United Europe" — A72

1957, Sept. 16 Engr. *Perf. 12½x12*

329	A72 2fr reddish brn	*3.00*	*.35*
330	A72 3fr red	*23.00*	*10.00*
331	A72 4fr rose lilac	*23.00*	*10.00*
	Nos. 329-331 (3)	49.00	*20.35*
	Set, hinged	19.00	

A united Europe for peace and prosperity.

Fair Building and Flags — A73

1958, Apr. 16 *Perf. 12x11½*

332	A73 2fr ultra & multi	.40	.25

10th International Luxembourg Fair.

Luxembourg Pavilion, Brussels — A74

1958, Apr. 16 Unwmk.

333	A74 2.50fr car & ultra	.30	.25

International Exposition at Brussels.

St. Willibrord — A75

1fr, Sts. Willibrord & Irmina from "Liber Aureus." 5fr, St. Willibrord, young man & wine cask.

1958, May 23 Engr. *Perf. 13x13½*

334	A75 1fr red	.25	.25
335	A75 2.50fr olive brn	.45	.25
336	A75 5fr blue	1.00	*.90*
	Nos. 334-336 (3)	1.70	*1.40*

1300th birth anniv. of St. Willibrord, apostle of the Low Countries and founder of Echternach Abbey.

Charlotte Type of 1948-49

1958 Unwmk. *Perf. 11½*

337	A45 20c dull claret	.25	.25
338	A45 30c olive	.25	.25
339	A45 50c dp org	.35	.25
340	A45 5fr violet	8.25	.40
	Nos. 337-340 (4)	9.10	1.15

Issued: No. 337, 8/1; Nos. 338-340, 7/1.

Common Design Types pictured following the introduction.

Europa Issue, 1958
Common Design Type

1958, Sept. 13 Litho. *Perf. 12½x13*
Size: 21x34mm

341	CD1 2.50fr car & bl	*.25*	*.25*
342	CD1 3.50fr green & org	*.35*	*.25*
343	CD1 5fr blue & red	*.75*	*.40*
	Nos. 341-343 (3)	1.35	.90

Wiltz Open-Air Theater — A76

Vintage, Moselle — A77

1958, Sept. 13 Engr. *Perf. 11x11½*

344	A76 2.50fr slate & sepia	.60	.25
345	A77 2.50fr lt grn & sepia	.60	.25

No. 345 issued to publicize 2,000 years of grape growing in Luxembourg region.

Grand Duchess Charlotte — A78

1959, Jan. 15 Photo. *Perf. 11½*

346	A78 1.50fr pale grn & dk grn	.65	.25
347	A78 2.50fr pink & dk brn	.65	.25
348	A78 5fr lt bl & dk bl	1.25	*.90*
	Nos. 346-348 (3)	2.55	*1.40*

40th anniv. of the accession to the throne of the Grand Duchess Charlotte.

NATO Emblem — A79

1959, Apr. 3 *Perf. 12½x12*

349	A79 2.50fr brt ol & bl	.25	.25
350	A79 8.50fr red brn & bl	.40	.35

NATO, 10th anniversary.

Flower Type of 1955, Inscribed "1959"

1fr, Iris. 2.50fr, Peonies. 3fr, Hydrangea.

1959, Apr. 3 *Perf. 11½*
Flowers in Natural Colors

351	A58 1fr dk bl grn	.25	.25
352	A58 2.50fr deep blue	.40	.25
353	A58 3fr deep red lilac	.65	.65
	Nos. 351-353 (3)	1.30	1.15

Flower festival, Mondorf-les-Bains.

Europa Issue, 1959
Common Design Type

Perf. 12½x13½
1959, Sept. 19 Litho.
Size: 22x33mm

354	CD2 2.50fr olive	*.90*	*.35*
355	CD2 5fr dk blue	*1.75*	*.65*

Locomotive of 1859 and Hymn — A80

1959, Sept. 19 Engr. *Perf. 13½*

356	A80 2.50fr red & ultra	2.00	.40

Centenary of Luxembourg's railroads.

Man and Child Knocking at Door — A81

Holy Family, Flight into Egypt — A82

Perf. 11½x11, 11x11½
1960, Apr. 7 Unwmk.

357	A81 2.50fr org & slate	.25	.25
358	A82 5fr pur & slate	.40	.40

World Refugee Year, July 1, 1959-June 30, 1960.

Steel Worker Drawing CECA Initials and Map of Member Countries — A83

1960, May 9 *Perf. 11x11½*

359	A83 2.50fr dk car rose	.50	.25

10th anniv. of the Schumann Plan for a European Steel and Coal Community.

European School and Children — A84

1960, May 9

360	A84 5fr bl & gray blk	1.00	.85

Establishment of the first European school in Luxembourg.

Heraldic Lion and Tools — A85

1960, June 14 Photo. *Perf. 11½*

361	A85 2.50fr gray, red, bl & blk	1.40	.30

Natl. Exhibition of Craftsmanship, Luxembourg-Limpertsberg, July 9-18.

Grand Duchess Charlotte — A86

1960-64 Engr. Unwmk.

362	A86	10c claret ('61)	.25	.25
363	A86	20c rose red ('61)	.25	.25
363A	A86	25c org ('64)	.25	.25
364	A86	30c gray olive	.25	.25
365	A86	50c dull grn	.60	.25
366	A86	1fr vio blue	.75	.25
367	A86	1.50fr rose lilac	.75	.25
368	A86	2fr blue ('61)	.80	.25
369	A86	2.50fr rose vio	1.40	.25
370	A86	3fr vio brn ('61)	1.60	.25
371	A86	3.50fr aqua ('64)	2.25	1.90
372	A86	5fr lt red brn	2.25	.25
373	A86	6fr slate ('64)	2.75	.25
		Nos. 362-373 (13)	14.15	4.90

The 50c, 1fr and 3fr were issued in sheets and in coils. Every fifth coil stamp has control number on back.

Europa Issue, 1960

Common Design Type

1960, Sept. 19 *Perf. 11x11½*

Size: 37x27mm

374	CD3	2.50fr indigo & emer	*.50*	*.40*
375	CD3	5fr maroon & blk	*.50*	*.40*

Great Spotted Woodpecker — A87

Designs: 1.50fr, Cat, horiz. 3fr, Filly, horiz. 8.50fr, Dachshund.

1961, May 15 Photo. *Perf. 11½*

376	A87	1fr multicolored	.25	.25
377	A87	1.50fr multicolored	.30	.25
378	A87	3fr gray, buff & red brn	.55	.30
379	A87	8.50fr lt grn, blk & ocher	.90	.40
		Nos. 376-379 (4)	2.00	1.20

Issued to publicize animal protection.

Clervaux and Abbey of St. Maurice and St. Maur — A88

1961, June 8 Engr. *Perf. 11½x11*

380	A88	2.50fr green	.50	.25

General Patton Monument, Ettelbruck — A89

1961, June 8 *Perf. 11x11½*

381	A89	2.50fr dark blue & gray	.50	.25

The monument commemorates the American victory of the 3rd Army under Gen. George S. Patton, Jr., Battle of the Ardennes Bulge, 1944-45.

Europa Issue, 1961

Common Design Type

1961, Sept. 18 *Perf. 13x12½*

Size: 29½x27mm

382	CD4	2.50fr red	*.25*	*.25*
383	CD4	5fr blue	*.30*	*.30*

Cyclist Carrying Bicycle — A90

Design: 5fr, Emblem of 1962 championship.

1962, Jan. 22 Photo. *Perf. 11½*

384	A90	2.50fr lt ultra, crim & blk	.25	.25
385	A90	5fr multicolored	.30	.30

Intl. Cross-country Bicycle Race, Esch-sur-Alzette, Feb. 18.

Europa Issue, 1962

Common Design Type

1962, Sept. 17 Unwmk. *Perf. 11½*

Size: 32½x23mm

386	CD5	2.50fr ol bis, yel grn & brn blk	*.30*	*.25*
387	CD5	5fr rose lil, lt grn & brn blk	*.45*	*.30*

St. Laurent's Church, Diekirch — A91

1962, Sept. 17 Engr. *Perf. 11½x11*

388	A91	2.50fr brown & blk	.50	.25

Bock Rock Castle, 10th Century A92

Gate of Three Towers, 11th Century A93

Designs (each stamp represents a different century): No. 391, Benedictine Abbey, Munster. No. 392, Great Seal of Luxembourg, 1237. No. 393, Rham Towers. No. 394, Black Virgin, Grund. No. 395, Grand Ducal Palace. No. 396, The Citadel of the Holy Ghost. No. 397, Castle Bridge. No. 398, Town Hall. No. 399, Municipal theater, bridge and European Community Center.

Perf. 14x13 (A92), 11½ (A93)

Engr. (A92), Photo. (A93)

1963, Apr. 13

389	A92	1fr slate blue	.25	.25
390	A93	1fr multicolored	.25	.25
391	A92	1.50fr dl red brn	.25	.25
392	A93	1.50fr multicolored	.25	.25
393	A92	2.50fr gray grn	.25	.25
394	A93	2.50fr multicolored	.25	.25
395	A92	3fr brown	.25	.25
396	A93	3fr multicolored	.25	.25
397	A92	5fr brt violet	.25	.25
398	A93	5fr multicolored	.50	.50
399	A92	11fr multicolored	1.00	.65
		Nos. 389-399 (11)	3.75	3.40

Millennium of the city of Luxembourg; MELUSINA Intl. Phil. Exhib., Luxembourg, Apr. 13-21. Set sold only at exhibition. Value of 62fr included entrance ticket. Nos. 390, 392, 394 and 396 however were sold without restriction.

Blackboard Showing European School Buildings — A94

1963, Apr. 13 Photo. *Perf. 11½*

400	A94	2.50fr gray, grn & mag	.35	.25

10th anniv. of the European Schools in Luxembourg, Brussels, Varese, Mol and Karlsruhe.

Colpach Castle and Centenary Emblem — A95

1963, May 8 Engr. *Perf. 13*

401	A95	2.50fr hn brn, gray & red	.35	.25

Centenary of the Intl. Red Cross. Colpach Castle, home of Emile Mayrisch, was donated to the Luxembourg League of the Red Cross for a rest home.

Twelve Stars of Council of Europe — A96

1963, June 25 *Perf. 13x14*

402	A96	2.50fr dp ultra, *gold*	.30	.25

10th anniv. of the European Convention of Human Rights.

Europa Issue, 1963

Common Design Type

1963, Sept. 16 Photo. *Perf. 11½*

Size: 32½x23mm

403	CD6	3fr bl grn, lt grn & org	*.30*	*.25*
404	CD6	6fr red brn, org red & org	*.45*	*.30*

Brown Trout Taking Bait — A97

1963, Sept. 16 Engr. *Perf. 13*

405	A97	3fr indigo	.30	.25

World Fly-Fishing Championship, Wormeldange, Sept. 22.

Map of Luxembourg, Telephone Dial and Stars — A98

1963, Sept. 16 Photo. *Perf. 11½*

406	A98	3fr ultra, brt grn & blk	.30	.25

Completion of telephone automation.

Power House — A99

3fr, Upper reservoir, horiz. 6fr, Lohmuhle dam.

1964, Apr. 17 Engr. *Perf. 13*

407	A99	2fr red brn & sl	.25	.25
408	A99	3fr red, sl grn & lt bl	.25	.25
409	A99	6fr choc, grn & bl	.25	.25
		Nos. 407-409 (3)	.75	.75

Inauguration of the Vianden hydroelectric station.

Barge Entering Lock at Grevenmacher Dam — A100

1964, May 26 Unwmk.

410	A100	3fr indigo & brt bl	.30	.25

Opening of Moselle River canal system.

Europa Issue, 1964

Common Design Type

1964, Sept. 14 Photo. *Perf. 11½*

Size: 22x38mm

411	CD7	3fr org brn, yel & dk bl	*.30*	*.25*
412	CD7	6fr yel grn, yel & dk brn	*.45*	*.30*

New Atheneum Educational Center and Students — A101

1964, Sept. 14 Unwmk.

413	A101	3fr dk bl grn & blk	.30	.25

Benelux Issue

King Baudouin, Queen Juliana and Grand Duchess Charlotte A101a

1964, Oct. 12 Size: 45x26mm

414	A101a	3fr dull bl, yel & brn	.30	.25

20th anniv. of the customs union of Belgium, Netherlands and Luxembourg.

Grand Duke Jean and Grand Duchess Josephine Charlotte — A102

1964, Nov. 11 Photo. *Perf. 11½*

415	A102	3fr indigo	.30	.25
416	A102	6fr dk brown	.40	.30

Grand Duke Jean's accession to throne.

Rotary Emblem and Cogwheels — A103

1965, Apr. 5 Photo. *Perf. 11½*

417	A103	3fr gold, car, gray & ultra	.30	.25

Rotary International, 60th anniversary.

Grand Duke Jean — A104

1965-71 Engr. Unwmk.

418	A104	25c olive bister ('66)	.25	.25
419	A104	50c rose red	.25	.25
420	A104	1fr ultra	.25	.25
421	A104	1.50fr dk vio brn ('66)	.25	.25
422	A104	2fr magenta ('66)	.25	.25
423	A104	2.50fr orange ('71)	.35	.25
424	A104	3fr gray	.50	.25
425	A104	3.50fr brn org ('66)	.35	.40
426	A104	4fr vio brn ('71)	.30	.25
427	A104	5fr green ('71)	.35	.25
428	A104	6fr purple	.75	.25
429	A104	8fr bl grn ('71)	.65	.25
		Nos. 418-429 (12)	4.50	3.15

The 50c, 1fr, 2fr, 3fr, 4fr, 5fr and 6fr were issued in sheets and in coils. Every fifth coil stamp has control number on back.

See Nos. 570-576.

ITU Emblem, Old and New Communication Equipment A105

1965, May 17 Litho. *Perf. 13½*

431	A105	3fr dk pur, claret & blk	.35	.25

ITU, centenary.

Europa Issue, 1965

Common Design Type

Perf. 13x12½

1965, Sept. 27 Photo. Unwmk.

Size: 30x23½mm

432	CD8	3fr grn, maroon & blk	.35	*.25*
433	CD8	6fr tan, dk bl & grn	.40	*.30*

Inauguration of WHO Headquarters, Geneva — A106

1966, Mar. 7 Engr. *Perf. 11x11½*
434 A106 3fr green .30 .25

Torch and Banner — A107

1966, Mar. 7 Photo. *Perf. 11½*
435 A107 3fr gray & brt red .30 .25

50th anniversary of the Workers' Federation in Luxembourg.

Key and Arms of City of Luxembourg, and Arms of Prince of Chimay — A108

Designs: 2fr, Interior of Cathedral of Luxembourg, painting by Juan Martin. 3fr, Our Lady of Luxembourg, engraving by Richard Collin. 6fr, Column and spandrel with sculptured angels from Cathedral.

1966, Apr. 28 Engr. *Perf. 13x14*
436 A108 1.50fr green .25 .25
437 A108 2fr dull red .25 .25
438 A108 3fr dk blue .25 .25
439 A108 6fr red brown .25 .25
Nos. 436-439 (4) 1.00 1.00

300th anniv. of the Votum Solemne (Solemn Promise) which made the Virgin Mary Patron Saint of the City of Luxembourg.

Europa Issue, 1966
Common Design Type
Perf. 13½x12½
1966, Sept. 26 Litho.
Size: 25x37mm
440 CD9 3fr gray & vio bl .30 *.25*
441 CD9 6fr olive & dk grn .40 *.30*

Diesel Locomotive — A109

Design: 3fr, Electric locomotive.

1966, Sept. 26 Photo. *Perf. 11½*
442 A109 1.50fr multicolored *.75* .25
443 A109 3fr multicolored *.75* .30

5th Intl. Philatelic Exhibition of Luxembourg Railroad Men, Sept. 30-Oct. 3.

Grand Duchess Charlotte Bridge — A110

1966, Sept. 26 Engr. *Perf. 13*
444 A110 3fr dk car rose .30 .25

Tower Building, Kirchberg, Seat of European Community — A111

Design: 13fr, Design for Robert Schuman monument, Luxembourg.

1966, Sept. 26
445 A111 1.50fr dk green .25 .25
446 A111 13fr deep blue .60 .25

"Luxembourg, Center of Europe."

View of Luxembourg, 1850, by Nicolas Liez — A112

Map of Luxembourg Fortress, 1850, by Theodore de Cederstolpe — A113

1967, Mar. 6 Engr. *Perf. 13*
447 A112 3fr bl, vio brn & grn .25 .25
448 A113 6fr blue, brn & red .25 .25

Centenary of the Treaty of London, which guaranteed the country's neutrality after the dismantling of the Fortress of Luxembourg.

Europa Issue, 1967
Common Design Type
1967, May 2 Photo. *Perf. 11½*
Size: 33x22mm
449 CD10 3fr cl brn, gray & buff *.50 .35*
450 CD10 6fr dk brn, vio gray & lt bl *.50 .35*

Lion, Globe and Lions Emblem — A115

1967, May 2 Photo. *Perf. 11½*
451 A115 3fr multicolored .30 .25

Lions International, 50th anniversary.

> Canceled to Order
> Luxembourg's Office des Timbres, Direction des Postes, was offering, at least as early as 1967, to sell commemorative issues canceled to order.

NATO Emblem and European Community Administration Building — A116

1967, June 13 Litho. *Perf. 13x12½*
452 A116 3fr lt grn & dk grn .25 .25
453 A116 6fr dp rose & dk car .40 .40

NATO Council meeting, Luxembourg, June 13-14.

Youth Hostel, Ettelbruck — A117

1967, Sept. 14 Photo. *Perf. 11½*
454 A117 1.50fr multicolored .25 .25

Luxembourg youth hostels.

Home Gardener — A118

1967, Sept. 14
455 A118 1.50fr brt grn & org .25 .25

16th Congress of the Intl. Assoc. of Home Gardeners.

Shaving Basin with Wedding Scene, 1819 — A119

Design: 3fr, Ornamental vase, 1820, vert.

1967, Sept. 14
456 A119 1.50fr ol grn & multi .25 .25
457 A119 3fr ultra & lt gray .25 .25

Faience industry in Luxembourg, 200th anniv.

Wormeldange - Moselle River — A120

Mertert, Moselle River Port — A121

1967, Sept. 14 Engr. *Perf. 13*
458 A120 3fr dp bl, claret & ol .40 .25
459 A121 3fr violet bl & slate .25 .25

Swimming — A122

Sport: 1.50fr, Soccer. 2fr, Bicycling. 3fr, Running. 6fr, Walking. 13fr, Fencing.

1968, Feb. 22 Photo. *Perf. 11½*
460 A122 50c bl & grnsh bl .25 .25
461 A122 1.50fr brt grn & emer .25 .25
462 A122 2fr yel grn & lt yel grn .25 .25
463 A122 3fr dp org & dl org .25 .25
464 A122 6fr grnsh bl & pale grn .55 .25
465 A122 13fr rose cl & rose .60 .25
Nos. 460-465 (6) 2.15 1.50

Issued to publicize the 19th Olympic Games, Mexico City, Oct. 12-27.

Europa Issue, 1968
Common Design Type
1968, Apr. 29 Photo. *Perf. 11½*
Size: 32½x23mm
466 CD11 3fr ap grn, blk & org brn *.40 .35*
467 CD11 6fr brn org, blk & ap grn *.40 .35*

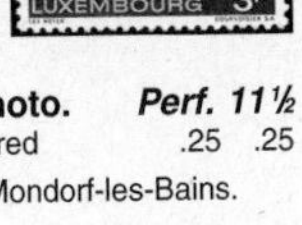

Kind Spring Pavilion — A123

1968, Apr. 29 Photo. *Perf. 11½*
468 A123 3fr multicolored .25 .25

Issued to publicize Mondorf-les-Bains.

Fair Emblem — A124

1968, Apr. 29
469 A124 3fr dp vio, dl bl gold & red .25 .25

20th Intl. Fair, Luxembourg City, May 23-June 2.

Children's Village of Mersch A125

Orphan and Foster Mother A126

1968, Sept. 18 Engr. *Perf. 13*
470 A125 3fr slate grn & dk red brn .25 .25
471 A126 6fr slate bl, blk & brn .40 .25

Mersch children's village. (Modeled after Austrian SOS villages for homeless children.)

Red Cross and Symbolic Blood Transfusion — A127

1968, Sept. 18 Photo. *Perf. 11½*
472 A127 3fr lt blue & car .40 .25

Voluntary Red Cross blood donors.

Luxair Plane over Luxembourg A128

1968, Sept. 18 Engr. *Perf. 13*
473 A128 50fr olive, bl & dk bl 3.25 .25

Issued for tourist publicity.

Souvenir Sheet

"Youth and Leisure" A129

Designs, a, 3fr, Doll. b, 6fr, Ballplayers. c, 13fr, Book, compass rose and ball.

1969, Apr. 3 Photo. *Perf. 11½*
Granite Paper
474 A129 Sheet of 3 3.25 3.50
a.-c. any single 1.00 1.00

1st Intl. Youth Phil. Exhib., JUVENTUS 1969, Luxembourg, Apr. 3-8.
No. 474 was on sale only at the exhibition. Sold only with entrance ticket for 40fr.

Europa Issue, 1969
Common Design Type
1969, May 19 Photo. *Perf. 11½*
Size: 32½x23mm
475 CD12 3fr gray, brn & org *.45 .25*
476 CD12 6fr vio gray, blk & yel *.50 .25*

Boy on Hobbyhorse, by Joseph Kutter (1894-1941) A130

Design: 6fr, View of Luxembourg, by Kutter.

1969, May 19 Engr. *Perf. 12x13*

477 A130 3fr multicolored .45 .25
a. Green omitted *150.00 150.00*
478 A130 6fr multicolored .45 .35

ILO, 50th Anniv. — A131

Photo.; Gold Impressed (Emblem)

1969, May 19 *Perf. 14x14½*

479 A131 3fr brt grn, vio & gold .25 .25

Mobius Strip in Benelux Colors — A131a

1969, Sept. 8 Litho. *Perf. 12½x13½*

480 A131a 3fr multicolored .30 .25

25th anniv. of the signing of the customs union of Belgium, Netherlands and Luxembourg.

NATO, 20th Anniv. — A132

1969, Sept. 8 *Perf. 13½x12½*

481 A132 3fr org brn & dk brn .35 .25

Grain and Mersch Agricultural Center — A133

1969, Sept. 8 Photo. *Perf. 11½*

482 A133 3fr bl grn, gray & blk .25 .25

Issued to publicize agricultural progress.

St. Willibrord's Basilica and Abbey, Echternach A134

No. 484, Castle and open-air theater, Wiltz.

1969, Sept. 8 Engr. *Perf. 13*

483 A134 3fr dark blue & indigo .30 .25
484 A134 3fr slate green & indigo .30 .25

Pasqueflower — A135

Design: 6fr, Hedgehog and 3 young.

1970, Mar. 9 Photo. *Perf. 11½*

485 A135 3fr multicolored .25 .25
486 A135 6fr green & multi .40 .30

European Conservation Year.

Goldcrest — A136

1970, Mar. 9 Engr. *Perf. 13*

487 A136 1.50fr org, grn & blk brn .30 .25

Luxembourg Society for the protection and study of birds, 50th anniv.

Traffic Sign and Street Scene — A137

1970, May 4 Photo. *Perf. 11½*

488 A137 3fr rose mag, red & blk .30 .25

The importance of traffic safety.

Europa Issue, 1970

Common Design Type

1970, May 4 Size: 32½x23mm

489 CD13 3fr brown & multi *.40 .25*
490 CD13 6fr green & multi *.40 .30*

Empress Kunigunde and Emperor Henry II, Window, Luxembourg Cathedral A138

1970, Sept. 14 Photo. *Perf. 12*

491 A138 3fr multicolored .25 .25

Centenary of the Diocese of Luxembourg.

Census Symbol — A139

1970, Sept. 14 *Perf. 11½*

492 A139 3fr dk grn, grnsh bl & red .25 .25

Census of Dec. 31, 1970.

Lion, Luxembourg City Hall — A140

1970, Sept. 14

493 A140 3fr bister, lt bl & dk brn .25 .25

50th anniversary of the City of Luxembourg through the union of 5 municipalities.

UN Emblem — A141

Perf. 12½x13½

1970, Sept. 14 Litho.

494 A141 1.50fr bl & vio bl .25 .25

25th anniversary of the United Nations.

Monks in Abbey Workshop — A142

Miniatures Painted at Echternach, about 1040: 3fr, Laborers going to the vineyard (Matthew 20:1-6). 6fr, Laborers toiling in vineyard. 13fr, Workers searching for graves of the saints.

1971, Mar. 15 Photo. *Perf. 12*

495 A142 1.50fr gold & multi .25 .25
496 A142 3fr gold & multi .25 .25
497 A142 6fr gold & multi .30 .25
498 A142 13fr gold & multi 1.20 .45
Nos. 495-498 (4) 2.00 1.20

Olympic Rings, Arms of Luxembourg — A143

1971, May 3 Photo. *Perf. 12½*

499 A143 3fr ultra & multi .35 .25

Intl. Olympic Committee, 71st session.

Europa Issue, 1971

Common Design Type

1971, May 3 *Perf. 12½x13*

Size: 34x25mm

500 CD14 3fr ver, brn & blk *.50 .25*
501 CD14 6fr brt grn, brn & blk *.50 .40*

A145

1971, May 3 Litho. *Perf. 13x13½*

502 A145 3fr org, dk brn & yel .25 .25

Christian Workers Union, 50th anniv.

Artificial Lake, Upper Sure — A146

Designs: No. 504, Water treatment plant, Esch-sur-Sure. 15fr, ARBED Steel Corporation Headquarters, Luxembourg.

1971, Sept. 13 Engr. *Perf. 13*

503 A146 3fr ol, grnsh bl & indigo .40 .25
504 A146 3fr brn, sl grn & grnsh bl .45 .25
505 A146 15fr indigo & blk brn 1.00 .25
Nos. 503-505 (3) 1.85 .75

School Girl with Coin — A147

1971, Sept. 13 Photo. *Perf. 11½*

506 A147 3fr violet & multi .30 .25

School children's savings campaign.

Coins of Luxembourg and Belgium — A148

1972, Mar. 6

507 A148 1.50fr lt grn, sil & blk .25 .25

Economic Union of Luxembourg and Belgium, 50th anniversary.

Bronze Mask — A149

Archaeological Objects, 4th to 1st centuries, B.C.: 1fr, Earthenware bowl, horiz. 8fr, Limestone head. 15fr, Glass jug in shape of head.

1972, Mar. 6

508 A149 1fr lemon & multi .25 .25
509 A149 3fr multicolored .35 .25
510 A149 8fr multicolored .75 .60
511 A149 15fr multicolored .90 .45
Nos. 508-511 (4) 2.25 1.55

Europa Issue 1972

Common Design Type

1972, May 2 Photo. *Perf. 11½*

Size: 22x33mm

512 CD15 3fr rose vio & multi .45 *.25*
513 CD15 8fr gray blue & multi .50 *.40*

Archer — A150

1972, May 2

514 A150 3fr crimson, blk & olive .45 .25

3rd European Archery Championships.

Robert Schuman Medal — A151

1972, May 2 Engr. *Perf. 13*

515 A151 3fr gray & slate green .60 .25

Establishment in Luxembourg of the European Coal and Steel Community, 20th anniv.

The Fox Wearing Tails — A152

1972, Sept. 11 Photo. *Perf. 11½*

516 A152 3fr scarlet & multi .30 .25

Centenary of the publication of "Renert," satirical poem by Michel Rodange.

National Monument A153

Court of Justice of European Communities, Kirchberg — A154

1972, Sept. 11 Engr. *Perf. 13*

517 A153 3fr sl grn, olive & vio .45 .25
518 A154 3fr brn, bl & slate grn .75 .25

Epona on Horseback — A155

Archaeological Objects: 4fr, Panther killing swan, horiz. 8fr, Celtic gold stater inscribed Pottina. 15fr, Bronze boar, horiz.

1973, Mar. 14 Photo. *Perf. 11½*

519 A155 1fr salmon & multi .25 .25
520 A155 4fr beige & multi .30 .25
521 A155 8fr multicolored 1.75 .60
522 A155 15fr multicolored .75 .60
Nos. 519-522 (4) 3.05 1.70

Europa Issue 1973

Common Design Type

1973, Apr. 30 Photo. *Perf. 11½*

Size: 32x22mm

523 CD16 4fr org, dk vio & lt bl *.45 .25*
524 CD16 8fr ol, vio blk & yel *.45 .50*

Bee on Honeycomb — A156

1973, Apr. 30 Photo. *Perf. 11½*
525 A156 4fr ocher & multi .45 .25

Publicizing importance of beekeeping.

Nurse Holding Child — A157

1973, Apr. 30
526 A157 4fr multicolored .40 .25

Publicizing importance of day nurseries.

Laurel Branch — A158

1973, Sept. 10 Photo. *Perf. 11½*
527 A158 3fr violet bl & multi .25 .25

50th anniv. of Luxembourg Board of Labor.

Jerome de Busleyden — A159

1973, Sept. 10 Engr. *Perf. 13*
528 A159 4fr black, brn & pur .30 .25

Council of Mechelen, 500th anniv.

National Strike Memorial, Wiltz — A160

1973, Sept. 10
529 A160 4fr ol bis, sl & sl grn .50 .25

In memory of the Luxembourg resistance heroes who died during the great strike of 1942.

Capital, Byzantine Hall, Vianden A161

St. Gregory the Great A161a

Designs: No. 534, Sts. Cecilia and Valerian crowned by angel, Hollenfels Church. No. 535, Interior, Septfontaines Church. 8fr, Madonna and Child, St. Irmina's Chapel, Rosport. 12fr, St. Augustine Sculptures by Jean-Georges Scholtus from pulpit in Feulen parish church, c. 1734.

1973-77 *Perf. 13x12½, 14 (6fr, 12fr)*
533 A161 4fr green & rose vio .30 .25
534 A161 4fr red brn, grn & lil .40 .25
535 A161 4fr gray, brn & dk vio .40 .25
536 A161a 6fr maroon .50 .25
537 A161 8fr sepia & vio bl 1.00 .60
538 A161a 12fr slate blue 1.00 .65
Nos. 533-538 (6) 3.60 2.25

Architecture of Luxembourg: Romanesque, Gothic, Baroque.
Issued: No. 533, 8fr, 9/10/73; Nos. 534-535, 9/9/74; 6fr, 12fr, 9/16/77.

Princess Marie Astrid — A162

1974, Mar. 14 Photo. *Perf. 11½*
540 A162 4fr blue & multi 1.50 .30

Princess Marie-Astrid, president of the Luxembourg Red Cross Youth Section.

Torch — A163

1974, Mar. 14
541 A163 4fr ultra & multi .50 .20

50th anniversary of Luxembourg Mutual Insurance Federation.

Royal Seal of Henri VII — A164

Seals from 13th-14th Centuries: 3fr, Equestrian, seal of Jean, King of Bohemia. 4fr, Seal of Town of Diekirch. 19fr, Virgin and Child, seal of Convent of Marienthal.

1974, Mar. 14
542 A164 1fr purple & multi .25 .25
543 A164 3fr green & multi .30 .25
544 A164 4fr multicolored .35 .25
545 A164 19fr multicolored 1.00 .75
Nos. 542-545 (4) 1.90 1.50

Hind, by Auguste Trémont — A165

Europa: 8fr, "Growth," abstract sculpture, by Lucien Wercollier.

1974, Apr. 29 Photo. *Perf. 11½*
546 A165 4fr ocher & multi *.50* .30
547 A165 8fr brt blue & multi *1.50* *1.20*

Winston Churchill, by Oscar Nemon — A166

1974, Apr. 29
548 A166 4fr lilac & multi .40 .25

Sir Winston Churchill (1874-1965), statesman.

Fairground, Aerial View — A167

1974, Apr. 29
549 A167 4fr silver & multi .40 .25

Publicity for New International Fairground, Luxembourg-Kirchberg.

Theis, the Blind — A168

1974, Apr. 29
550 A168 3fr multicolored .40 .25

Mathias Schou, Theis the Blind (1747-1824), wandering minstrel.

UPU Emblem and "100" — A169

1974, Sept. 9 Photo. *Perf. 11½*
551 A169 4fr multicolored .30 .25
552 A169 8fr multicolored .90 .55

Centenary of Universal Postal Union.

"BENELUX" A170

1974, Sept. 9
553 A170 4fr bl grn, dk grn & lt bl .90 .25

30th anniversary of the signing of the customs union of Belgium, Netherlands and Luxembourg.

View of Differdange A171

1974, Sept. 9 Engr. *Perf. 13*
554 A171 4fr rose claret 1.00 .25

Bourglinster A172

Designs: 1fr, Fish Market, Old Luxembourg, vert. 4fr, Market Square, Echternach. 19fr, St. Michael's Square, Mersch, vert.

Perf. 14x13½, 13½x14
1975, Mar. 10 Engr.
555 A172 1fr olive green .60 .25
556 A172 3fr deep brown .90 .30
557 A172 4fr dark purple .90 .25
558 A172 19fr copper red 1.25 .65
Nos. 555-558 (4) 3.65 1.45

European Architectural Heritage Year.

Joseph Kutter, Self-portrait A173

Moselle Bridge, Remich, by Nico Klopp A174

Paintings: 8fr, Still Life, by Joseph Kutter. 20fr, The Dam, by Dominique Lang.

1975, Apr. 28 Photo. *Perf. 11½*
559 A173 1fr multicolored .30 .25
560 A174 4fr multicolored *1.20* *.25*
561 A174 8fr multicolored 1.75 1.25
562 A173 20fr multicolored 1.50 .50
Nos. 559-562 (4) 4.75 2.25

Cultural series. Nos. 560-561 are Europa Issue.

Robert Schuman, Gaetano Martino, Paul-Henri Spaak Medals — A175

1975, Apr. 28
563 A175 4fr yel grn, gold & brn .70 .25

Robert Schuman's declaration establishing European Coal and Steel Community, 25th anniv.

Albert Schweitzer (1875-1965), Medical Missionary — A176

1975, Apr. 28 Engr. *Perf. 13*
564 A176 4fr bright blue .70 .25

Civil Defense Emblem — A177

1975, Sept. 8 Photo. *Perf. 11½*
565 A177 4fr multicolored .60 .25

Civil Defense Org. for protection and rescue.

Figure Skating — A178

4fr, Water skiing, horiz. 15fr, Mountain climbing.

1975, Sept. 8 Engr. *Perf. 13*
566 A178 3fr green, bl & lilac .30 .25
567 A178 4fr dk brn, grn & lt brn .45 .25
568 A178 15fr brown, indigo & grn 1.40 .55
Nos. 566-568 (3) 2.15 1.05

Grand Duke Type of 1965-71

1975-91 Engr. *Perf. 11½*
Granite Paper (14fr, 22fr)
570 A104 7fr orange .45 .25
571 A104 9fr yellow green .90 .25
572 A104 10fr black .50 .25
573 A104 12fr brick red 1.20 .25
573A A104 14fr dark blue .65 .30
574 A104 16fr green 1.00 .25
574A A104 18fr brown olive .80 .40
575 A104 20fr blue 1.20 .25
576 A104 22fr orange brown 1.10 .80
Nos. 570-576 (9) 7.80 3.00

Issued: 10fr, 1/9; 9fr, 12fr, 20fr, 12/23; 16fr, 2/25/82; 7fr, 7/1/83; 18fr, 3/3/86; 14fr, 1/2/90; 22fr, 9/23/91.

Grand Duchess Charlotte — A179

Design: No. 580, Prince Henri.

1976, Mar. 8 Litho. *Perf. 14x13½*
579 A179 6fr green & multi 1.60 .30
580 A179 6fr dull blue & multi 1.60 .30

80th birthday of Grand Duchess Charlotte and 21st birthday of Prince Henri, heir to the throne.

Gold Brooch — A180

5fr, Footless beaker, horiz. 6fr, Decorated vessel, horiz. 12fr, Gold coin. All designs show excavated items of Franco-Merovingian period.

Perf. 13½x12½, 12½x13½

1976, Mar. 8

581	A180	2fr blue & multi	.25	.25
582	A180	5fr black & multi	.25	.25
583	A180	6fr lilac & multi	.45	.25
584	A180	12fr multicolored	.75	.75
		Nos. 581-584 (4)	1.70	1.50

Soup Tureen — A181

Europa: 12fr, Deep bowl. Tureen and bowl after pottery from Nospelt, 19th century.

1976, May 3 Photo. *Perf. 11½*

585	A181	6fr lt violet & multi	*.90*	*.25*
586	A181	12fr yel grn & multi	*1.00*	*1.00*

Independence Hall, Philadelphia — A182

1976, May 3

587	A182	6fr lt blue & multi	.50	.25

American Bicentennial.

Boomerang — A183

1976, May 3

588	A183	6fr brt rose lil & gold	.50	.25

21st Olympic Games, Montreal, Canada, July 17-Aug. 1.

"Vibrations of Sound" — A184

1976, May 3

589	A184	6fr red & multi	.50	.25

Jeunesses Musicales (Young Music Friends), association to foster interest in music and art.

Alexander Graham Bell — A185

1976, Sept. 9 Engr. *Perf. 13*

590	A185	6fr slate green	.50	.25

Centenary of first telephone call by Alexander Graham Bell, Mar. 10, 1876.

Virgin and Child with St. Anne — A186

Renaissance sculptures: 12fr, Grave of Bernard de Velbruck, Lord of Beaufort.

1976, Sept. 9 Photo. *Perf. 11½*

591	A186	6fr gold & multi	.30	.25
592	A186	12fr gold, gray & blk	1.20	.70

Johann Wolfgang von Goethe — A187

Portraits: 5fr, J. M. William Turner. 6fr, Victor Hugo. 12fr, Franz Liszt.

1977, Mar. 14 Engr. *Perf. 13*

593	A187	2fr lake	.25	.25
594	A187	5fr purple	.30	.25
595	A187	6fr slate green	.75	.25
596	A187	12fr violet blue	.75	.45
		Nos. 593-596 (4)	2.05	1.20

Famous visitors to Luxembourg.

Old Luxembourg — A188

Europa: 12fr, Adolphe Bridge and European Investment Bank headquarters.

1977, May 3 Photo. *Perf. 11½*

597	A188	6fr multicolored	*.90*	*.25*
598	A188	12fr multicolored	*1.00*	*.80*

Esch-sur-Sure — A189

Design: 6fr, View of Ehnen.

1977, May 3 Engr. *Perf. 13*

599	A189	5fr Prus blue	.50	.25
600	A189	6fr deep brown	.50	.25

Marguerite de Busbach — A190

No. 602, Louis Braille, by Lucienne Filippi.

1977, May 3 Photo. *Perf. 11½*

601	A190	6fr multicolored	.50	.25
602	A190	6fr multicolored	.50	.25

Notre Dame Congregation, founded by Marguerite de Busbach, 350th anniversary; Louis Braille (1809-1852), inventor of the Braille system of writing for the blind.

Souvenir Sheet

Luxembourg Nos. 1-2 — A191

Engr. & Photo.

1977, Sept. 15 *Perf. 13½*

603	A191	40fr gray & red brown	4.50	5.25

125th anniv. of Luxembourg's stamps.

Head of Medusa, Roman Mosaic, Diekirch, 3rd Century A.D. — A192

1977, Sept. 15 Photo. *Perf. 11½*

604	A192	6fr multicolored	1.00	.25

Orpheus and Eurydice, by C. W. Gluck — A193

1977, Sept. 15 *Perf. 11½x12*

605	A193	6fr multicolored	.70	.25

Intl. Wiltz Festival, 25th anniv.

Europa Tamed, by R. Zilli, and Map of Europe — A194

1977, Dec. 5 Photo. *Perf. 11½*

606	A194	6fr multicolored	.70	.25

20th anniversary of the Treaties of Rome, setting up the European Economic Community and the European Atomic Energy Commission.

Souvenir Sheet

Grand Duke and Grand Duchess of Luxembourg — A195

Photogravure and Engraved

1978, Apr. 3 *Perf. 13½x14*

607	A195	Sheet of 2	1.75	1.75
a.		6fr dark blue & multi	.60	.75
b.		12fr dark red & multi	.60	.75

Silver wedding anniversary of Grand Duke Jean and Grand Duchess Josephine Charlotte.

Souvenir Sheet

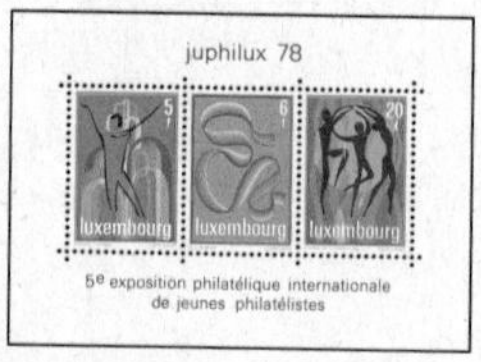

Youth Fountain, Streamer and Dancers A196

1978, Apr. 3 Photo. *Perf. 11½*

608	A196	Sheet of 3	3.75	3.75
a.		5fr ultra & multi	1.00	1.20
b.		6fr orange & multi	1.00	1.20
c.		20fr yellow green & multi	1.00	1.20

Juphilux 78, 5th International Young Philatelists' Exhibition, Luxembourg, Apr. 6-10.

Charles IV, Statue, Charles Bridge, Prague — A197

Europa: 12fr, Pierre d'Aspelt, tomb, Mainz Cathedral.

1978, May 18 Engr. *Perf. 13½*

609	A197	6fr dark violet blue	*.60*	*.25*
610	A197	12fr dull rose lilac	*1.00*	*.80*

Charles IV (1316-78), Count of Luxembourg, Holy Roman Emperor. Pierre d'Aspelt (c. 1250-1320), Archbishop of Mainz and Prince-Elector.

Emile Mayrisch, by Theo Van Rysselberghe — A198

1978, May 18 *Perf. 11½*

611	A198	6fr multicolored	1.00	.25

Emile Mayrisch (1862-1928), president of International Steel Cartel and promoter of United Europe.

Our Lady of Luxembourg A199

Trumpeters and Old Luxembourg A200

1978, May 18 Photo. *Perf. 11½*

612	A199	6fr multicolored	.50	.25
613	A200	6fr multicolored	.50	.25

Our Lady of Luxembourg, patroness, 300th anniv.; 135th anniv. of Grand Ducal Military Band.

Starving Child, Helping Hand, Millet A201

League Emblem, Lungs, Open Window A202

Open Prison Door — A203

1978, Sept. 11 Photo. *Perf. 11½*

614	A201	2fr multicolored	.25	.25
615	A202	5fr multicolored	.25	.25
616	A203	6fr multicolored	.50	.25
		Nos. 614-616 (3)	1.00	.75

"Terre des Hommes," an association to help underprivileged children; Luxembourg Anti-Tuberculosis League, 70th anniv.; Amnesty Intl. and 30th anniv. of Universal Declaration of Human Rights.

Squared Stone Emerging from Rock, City of Luxembourg A204

1978, Sept. 11 Engr. *Perf. 13½x13*

617	A204	6fr violet blue	.60	.25

Masonic Grand Lodge of Luxembourg, 175th anniversary.

Julius Caesar on Denarius, c. 44 B.C. — A205

Roman Coins, Found in Luxembourg: 6fr, Empress Faustina I on Sestertius, 141 A.D. 9fr, Empress Helena on Follis, c. 324-330. 26fr, Emperor Valens on Solidus, c. 367-375.

1979, Mar. 5 **Photo.** ***Perf. 11½***

618 A205	5fr multicolored	.35	.25
619 A205	6fr multicolored	.40	.25
620 A205	9fr multicolored	.60	.40
621 A205	26fr multicolored	1.40	.90
	Nos. 618-621 (4)	2.75	1.80

St. Michael's Church, Mondorf-les-Bains A206

Design: 6fr, Luxembourg Central Station.

1979, Mar. 5 **Engr.** ***Perf. 13***

622 A206	5fr multicolored	.45	.25
623 A206	6fr rose claret	.90	.25

Troisvierges Stagecoach A207

Europa: 12fr, Early wall telephone, vert.

1979, Apr. 30 **Photo.** ***Perf. 11½***

624 A207	6fr multicolored	*1.90*	.25
625 A207	12fr multicolored	*1.90*	*1.50*

Michel Pintz Facing Jury — A208

1979, Apr. 30 **Engr.** ***Perf. 13***

626 A208	2fr rose lilac	.45	.25

180th anniversary of peasant uprising against French occupation.

Antoine Meyer A209

Abundance Crowning Work and Thrift, by Auguste Vinet A210

Design: 6fr, Sidney Gilchrist Thomas.

1979, Apr. 30

627 A209	5fr carmine	.40	.25
628 A209	6fr light blue	.40	.25
629 A210	9fr black	.40	.25
	Nos. 627-629 (3)	1.20	.75

Antoine Meyer (1801-1857), mathematician and first national poet; centenary of acquisition of Thomas process for production of high-quality steel; 50th anniversary of Luxembourg Stock Exchange.

European Parliament — A211

1979, June 7 **Photo.** ***Perf. 11½***

630 A211	6fr multi	1.40	.45

European Parliament, first direct elections, June 7-10.

Angel with Chalice, by Barthelemy Namur — A212

Rococo Art: 12fr, Angel with anchor, by Namur, from High Altar, St. Michael's Church, Luxembourg.

Engraved and Photogravure

1979, Sept. 10 ***Perf. 13½***

631 A212	6fr multi	.30	.25
632 A212	12fr multi	.60	.50

Road Safety for Children — A213

1979, Sept. 10 **Photo.** ***Perf. 11½***

633 A213	2fr multi	.25	.25

International Year of the Child.

Radio Tele-Luxembourg Emblem — A214

1979, Sept. 10

634 A214	6fr ultra, blue & red	.50	.25

50 years of broadcasting in Luxembourg.

John the Blind, Silver Coin, 1331 — A215

14th Century Coins: 2fr, Sts. Gervase and Protais, silver grosso. 6fr, Easter lamb, gold coin. 20fr, Crown and arms, silver grosso.

1980, Mar. 5 **Photo.** ***Perf. 11½***

635 A215	2fr multi	.25	.25
636 A215	5fr multi	.25	.25
637 A215	6fr multi	.75	.25
638 A215	20fr multi	1.50	.60
	Nos. 635-638 (4)	2.75	1.35

See Nos. 651-654.

Ettelbruck Town Hall — A216

No. 640, State Archives Building, horiz.

1980, Mar. 5 **Engr.** ***Perf. 13***

639 A216	6fr brn & dk red	.75	.25
640 A216	6fr multi	.75	.25

Jean Monnet — A217

Europa: 12fr, St. Benedict of Nursia.

1980, Apr. 28 ***Perf. 13½***

641 A217	6fr dark blue	*.85*	*.30*
642 A217	12fr olive green	*.85*	*.45*

Sports for All — A218

1980, Apr. 28 **Photo.** ***Perf. 11½***

Granite Paper

643 A218	6fr multi	1.00	.30

Worker Pouring Molten Iron — A219

Design: 6fr, Man, hand, gears, horiz.

1980, Apr. 28

644 A219	2fr multi	.25	.25
645 A219	6fr multi	.40	.25

9th World Congress on Prevention of Occupational Accidents & Diseases, Amsterdam, May 6-9.

Mercury by Jean Mich — A220

Art Nouveau Sculpture by Jean Mich.

1980, Sept. 10 **Engr.** ***Perf. 14***

646 A220	8fr shown	.45	.30
647 A220	12fr Ceres	.75	.45

Introduction of Postal Code — A221

1980, Sept. 10 **Photo.** ***Perf. 11½***

648 A221	4fr multi	.70	.25

Police Car and Officers — A222

1980, Sept. 10

649 A222	8fr multi	.70	.25

State control of police force, 50th anniv.

Grand Duke Jean, Personal Arms A223

Photo. & Engr.

1981, Jan. 5 ***Perf. 13½***

650 A223	Sheet of 3	2.10	2.10
a.	8fr multi	.35	.35
b.	12fr multi	.55	.55
c.	30fr multi	1.00	1.00

Grand Duke Jean, 60th birthday.

Coin type of 1980

Silver Coins: 4fr, Philip IV patagon, 1635. 6fr, Empress Maria Theresa 12 sol, 1775. 8fr, Emperor Joseph II 12 sol, 1789. 30fr, Emperor Francois II 72 sol, 1795.

1981, Mar. 5 **Photo.** ***Perf. 11½***

651 A215	4fr multi	.25	.25
652 A215	6fr multi	.30	.25
653 A215	8fr multi	.45	.25
654 A215	30fr multi	1.40	.90
	Nos. 651-654 (4)	2.40	1.65

National Library — A225

No. 656, European Hemicycle, Kirchberg.

1981, Mar. 5 **Engr.** ***Perf. 13***

655 A225	8fr shown	.50	.25
656 A225	8fr multicolored	.50	.25

Hammelsmarsch (Sheep Procession) — A226

Europa: 12fr, Bird-shaped whistle, Eimaischen market.

1981, May 4 **Photo.** ***Perf. 13½***

657 A226	8fr multi	*.60*	*.25*
658 A226	12fr multi	*.85*	*.45*

Knight on Chessboard A227

Savings Account Book, State Bank A228

First Bank Note, 1856 — A229

1981, May 4 ***Perf. 11½***

Granite Paper

659 A227	4fr multi	.50	.30
660 A228	8fr multi	.45	.25
661 A229	8fr multi	.45	.30

Luxembourg Chess Federation, 50th anniv.; State Savings Bank, 125th anniv.; Intl. Bank of Luxembourg, 125th anniv. of issuing rights.

Wedding of Prince Henri and Maria Teresa Mestre, Feb. 14 — A230

Photo. & Engr.

1981, June 22 ***Perf. 13½***

662 A230	8fr multi	.55	.35

Sheets of 12.

Single-seater Gliders — A231

16fr, Propeller planes, horiz. 35fr, Jet, Luxembourg Airport, horiz.

1981, Sept. 28 **Photo.** ***Perf. 11½***

Granite Paper

663 A231	8fr shown	.40	.30
664 A231	16fr multicolored	1.00	.60
665 A231	35fr multicolored	1.50	.75
	Nos. 663-665 (3)	2.90	1.65

Energy Conservation — A232

1981, Sept. 28 **Granite Paper**

666	A232	8fr multi	.50	.25

Apple Trees in Blossom, by Frantz Seimetz (1858-1914) A233

Landscape Paintings: 6fr, Summer Landscape, by Pierre Blanc (1872-1946). 8fr, The Larger Hallerbach, by Guido Oppenheim (1862-1942). 16fr, Winter Evening, by Eugene Mousset (1877-1941).

1982, Feb. 25 **Engr.** ***Perf. 11½***

667	A233	4fr multi	.25	.25
668	A233	6fr multi	.35	.25
669	A233	8fr multi	.75	.25
670	A233	16fr multi	.75	.55
		Nos. 667-670 (4)	2.10	1.30

World War II Resistance — A234

Design: Cross of Hinzert (Natl. Monument of the Resistance and Deportation) and Political Prisoner, by Lucien Wercollier.

1982, Feb. 25

671	A234	8fr multi	.50	.25

Europa — A235

8fr, Treaty of London, 1867. 16fr, Treaty of Paris, 1951.

1982, May 4 **Photo.**
Granite Paper

672	A235	8fr multicolored	*.75*	.25
673	A235	16fr multicolored	*.90*	.65

St. Theresa of Avila (1515-1582) — A236

Design: 8fr, Raoul Follereau (1903-1977), "Apostle of the Lepers."

1982, May 4 **Granite Paper**

674	A236	4fr multi	.25	.25
675	A236	8fr multi	.45	.25

State Museum — A237

No. 677, Synagogue of Luxembourg.

1982, May 4 **Photo. & Engr.**

676	A237	8fr shown	.35	.25
677	A237	8fr multicolored	.35	.25

Bourscheid Castle — A238

Designs: Restored castles.

1982, Sept. 9 **Engr.** ***Perf. 11½***
Granite Paper

678	A238	6fr shown	.45	.25
679	A238	8fr Vianden, horiz.	.75	.25

Intl. Youth Hostel Federation, 50th Anniv. — A239

1982, Sept. 9 **Photo.**

680	A239	4fr shown	.45	.25
681	A239	8fr Scouting year, vert.	.45	.30

Civilian and Military Deportation Monument — A240

1982, Sept. 9

682	A240	8fr multi	.55	.25

Mercury, Sculpture by Auguste Tremont — A241

1983, Mar. 7 **Photo.** ***Perf. 11½***
Granite Paper

683	A241	4fr multi	.25	.25

FOREX '83, 25th Intl. Assoc. of Foreign Exchange Dealers' Congress, June 2-5.

NATO Emblem, Flags — A242

1983, Mar. 7 **Granite Paper**

684	A242	6fr multi	.30	.25

25th anniv. of NAMSA (NATO Maintenance and Supply Agency).

Echternach Cross of Justice, 1236 — A243

1983, Mar. 7 **Granite Paper**

685	A243	8fr multi	.35	.25

30th Cong. of Intl. Union of Barristers, July 3-9.

Globe, CCC Emblem — A244

1983, Mar. 7 **Granite Paper**

686	A244	8fr multi	.35	.25

30th anniv. of Council of Customs Cooperation.

Natl. Federation of Fire Brigades Centenary — A245

1983, Mar. 7 **Granite Paper**

687	A245	8fr Fire engine, 1983	.60	.20
688	A245	16fr Hand pump, 1740	1.20	.60

Europa 1983 — A246

The Good Samaritan, Codex Aureus Escorialensis Miniatures, 11th Cent., Echternach.

1983, May 3 **Photo.**

689	A246	8fr Highway robbers	*1.00*	*.45*
690	A246	16fr Good Samaritan	*1.75*	*.45*

Giant Bible, 11th Cent. — A247

Illuminated Letters. 8fr, "h," Book of Baruch. 35fr, "B," letter of St. Jerome.

Photo. & Engr.
1983, May 3 ***Perf. 14***

691	A247	8fr multicolored	.45	.25
692	A247	35fr multicolored	1.40	1.00

World Com- munications Year — A248

No. 693, Post code. No. 694, Satellite relay, horiz.

1983, May 3 **Photo.** ***Perf. 11½***

693	A248	8fr multicolored	.90	.30
694	A248	8fr multicolored	1.75	.30

Town Hall, Dudelange — A249

7fr, St. Lawrence Church, Diekirch, vert.

1983, Sept. 7 **Photo. & Engr.**

695	A249	7fr multi	.35	.30
696	A249	10fr multi	.55	.30

Basketball Fed., 50th Anniv. A250

European Working Dog Championship A251

Tourism — A252

No. 698, Alsatian sheepdog. No. 699, View of Luxembourg.

1983, Sept. 7 **Photo.**
Granite Paper

697	A250	7fr multicolored	.45	.25
698	A251	10fr multicolored	.75	.35
699	A252	10fr multicolored	1.20	.30
		Nos. 697-699 (3)	2.40	.90

Environment Protection — A253

1984, Mar. 6 **Photo.** ***Perf. 11½***
Granite Paper

700	A253	7fr Pedestrian zoning	.60	.25
701	A253	10fr Water purification	.75	.35

2nd European Parliament Election — A254

1984, Mar. 6 **Granite Paper**

702	A254	10fr Hands holding emblem	.70	.30

A255

1984, Mar. 6 **Engr.** ***Perf. 12½x13***

703	A255	10fr No. 1	.75	.30
704	A255	10fr Union meeting	.75	.30
705	A255	10fr Mail bag	.75	.30
706	A255	10fr Train	.75	.30
		Nos. 703-706 (4)	3.00	1.20

Philatelic Federation (1934); Civil Service Trade Union (1909); Postal Workers' Union (1909); Railroad (1859).

1984 Summer Olympics — A256

10fr, The Race, by Jean Jacoby (1891-1936).

1984, May 7 **Photo.** ***Perf. 11½x12***

707	A256	10fr multicolored	.70	.25

Europa (1959-84) — A257

1984, May 7 ***Perf. 11½***
Granite Paper

708	A257	10fr green	*1.50*	*.30*
709	A257	16fr orange	*1.60*	*.80*

Young Turk Caressing His Horse, by Delacroix — A258

Paintings: 4fr, The Smoker, by David Teniers the Younger (1610-90). 10fr, Epiphany, by Jan Steen (1626-79). 50fr, The Lacemaker, by Pieter van Slingelandt (1640-91). 4fr, 50fr vert.

Photo. & Engr.
1984, May 7 ***Perf. 14***

710	A258	4fr multi	.35	.30
711	A258	7fr multi	.55	.30
712	A258	10fr multi	.90	.30
713	A258	50fr multi	3.75	1.75
		Nos. 710-713 (4)	5.55	2.65

Marine Life Fossils — A259

4fr, Pecten sp. 7fr, Gryphaea arcuata. 10fr, Coeloceras raqyinianum. 16fr, Daildius.

1984, Sept. 10 Photo. *Perf. 11½*

714 A259 4fr multicolored .30 .25
715 A259 7fr multicolored .50 .25
716 A259 10fr multicolored .80 .25
717 A259 16fr multicolored 1.40 .90
Nos. 714-717 (4) 3.00 1.65

Restored Castles — A260

1984, Sept. 10 Engr.

718 A260 7fr Hollenfels .35 .25
719 A260 10fr Larochette .55 .35

A261

1984, Sept. 10 *Perf. 12x12½*

720 A261 10fr Soldier, US flag 1.75 .30

40th Anniv. of D Day (June 6).

A262

Portrait medals in the state museum: 4fr, Jean Bertels (1544-1607), Historian, Abbott of Echternach. 7fr, Emperor Charles V (1500-1558). 10fr, King Philip II of Spain (1527-1598). 30fr, Prince Maurice of Orange-Nassau, Count of Vianden (1567-1625).

Granite Paper

1985, Mar. 4 Photo. *Perf. 11½*

721 A262 4fr multi .25 .25
722 A262 7fr multi .35 .25
723 A262 10fr multi .60 .25
724 A262 30fr multi 2.10 .90
Nos. 721-724 (4) 3.30 1.65

See Nos. 739-742.

Anniversaries A263

No. 725, Benz Velo, First automobile in Luxembourg, 1895. No. 726, Push-button telephone, sound waves. No. 727, Fencers.

1985, Mar. 4 *Perf. 12x11½*
Granite Paper

725 A263 10fr multi .90 .30
726 A263 10fr multi .60 .25
727 A263 10fr multi .75 .25
Nos. 725-727 (3) 2.25 .80

Centenary of the first automobile; Luxembourg Telephone Service, cent.; Luxembourg Fencing Federation, 50th anniv.

Visit of Pope John Paul II — A264

1985, Mar. 4 *Perf. 11½x12*
Granite Paper

728 A264 10fr Papal arms .70 .25

Europa 1985 — A265

Designs: 10fr, Grand-Duke Adolphe Music Federation. 16fr, Luxembourg Music School.

1985, May 8 *Perf. 11½*

729 A265 10fr multi *1.60 .45*
730 A265 16fr multi *2.40 1.10*

Souvenir Sheet

End of World War II, 40th Anniv. A266

Designs: a, Luxembourg resistance fighters, Wounded Fighters medal. b, Luxembourg War Cross. c, Badge of the Union of Luxembourg Resistance Movements. d, Liberation of the concentration camps.

1985, May 8 *Perf. 11½x12*
Granite Paper

731 A266 Sheet of 4 4.00 4.00
a.-d. 10fr, any single .75 .60

Endangered Wildlife — A267

4fr, Athene nocturna, vert. 7fr, Felis silvestris. 10fr, Vanessa atalantica. 50fr, Hyla arborea, vert.

1985, Sept. 23 Photo. *Perf. 12x11½*

732 A267 4fr multicolored .90 .30
733 A267 7fr multicolored 1.50 .30
734 A267 10fr multicolored 2.40 .30
735 A267 50fr multicolored 5.25 1.75
Nos. 732-735 (4) 10.05 2.65

Historic Monuments — A268

7fr, Echternach Orangery, 1750. 10fr, Mohr de Waldt House, 17th cent., vert.

1985, Sept. 23 Engr. *Perf. 11½*

736 A268 7fr multicolored .45 .25
737 A268 10fr multicolored .50 .25

Natl. Art Collection — A269

10fr, 18th cent. book cover, Natl. Library.

Photo. & Engr.

1985, Sept. 23 *Perf. 14*

738 A269 10fr multicolored .70 .25

Portrait Medals Type of 1985

10fr, Count of Monterey, 1675. 12fr, Louis XIV, 1684. 18fr, Pierre de Weyms, c. 1700. 20fr, Duke of Marlborough, 1706.

1986, Mar. 3 Photo. *Perf. 11½*
Granite Paper

739 A262 10fr multicolored .45 .30
740 A262 12fr multicolored .60 .25
741 A262 18fr multicolored .75 .45
742 A262 20fr multicolored 1.25 .60
Nos. 739-742 (4) 3.05 1.60

Federation of Luxembourg Beekeepers' Associations, Cent. — A270

Mondorf State Spa, Cent. — A271

Natl. Table Tennis Federation, 50th Anniv. — A272

No. 743, Bee collecting pollen. No. 744, Mosaic. No. 745, Boy playing table tennis.

1986, Mar. 3 *Perf. 11½*

743 A270 12fr multicolored .85 .30
744 A271 12fr multicolored .85 .30
745 A272 12fr multicolored .85 .30
Nos. 743-745 (3) 2.55 .90

Europa 1986 — A273

12fr, Polluted forest, city. 20fr, Man, pollution sources.

1986, May 5 Photo. *Perf. 12*
Granite Paper

751 A273 12fr multicolored *1.25 .25*
752 A273 20fr multicolored *1.75 1.00*

Fortifications — A274

15fr, Ft. Thungen, horiz. 18fr, Invalid's Gate. 50fr, Malakoff Tower.

1986, May 5 Granite Paper

753 A274 15fr multicolored 1.40 .35
754 A274 18fr multicolored 1.40 .45
755 A274 50fr multicolored 3.00 .75
Nos. 753-755 (3) 5.80 1.55

Robert Schuman (1886-1963), European Cooperation Promulgator — A275

1986, June 26 *Perf. 12 on 3 Sides*
Granite Paper

756 A275 2fr pink & blk .25 .25
a. Bklt. pane of 4 .30
757 A275 10fr lt bl & blk .45 .30
a. Bklt. pane of 4 2.75
b. Bklt. pane of 2, #756-757 + 2 labels 1.40

Nos. 756-757 issued in booklets only.

European Road Safety Year — A276

1986, Sept. 15 Photo. *Perf. 11½*

758 A276 10fr multi .60 .25

Bas-relief, Town Hall, Esch-Sur-Alzette A277

Design: No. 760, Stairs to the Chapel of the Cross, Grevenmacher.

Photogravure & Engraved

1986, Sept. 15 *Perf. 14x13½*

759 A277 12fr shown 1.00 .30
760 A277 12fr multi 1.00 .30

Countess Ermesinde (1186-1247), Ruler of Luxembourg — A278

Designs: No. 761, Presentation of the letter of freedom to Echternach inhabitants, 1236, engraving (detail) by P.H. Witkamp, c. 1873. 30fr, Charter seal, Marienthal Convent, 1238.

1986, Sept. 15 *Perf. 13½x14*

761 A278 12fr multi .60 .25
762 A278 30fr multi 1.50 .75

Wildlife Conservation — A279

6fr, Eliomys quercinus, horiz. 10fr, Calopteryx splendens. 12fr, Cinclus cinclus. 25fr, Salamandra salamandra terrestris, horiz.

1987, Mar. 9 Photo. *Perf. 11½*

763 A279 6fr multicolored .45 .30
764 A279 10fr multicolored .90 .45
765 A279 12fr multicolored 1.40 .30
766 A279 25fr multicolored 2.50 1.10
Nos. 763-766 (4) 5.25 2.15

A280

1987, Mar. 9

767 A280 12fr multi .70 .30

Natl. Home Amateur Radio Operators Network, 50th anniv.

A281

1987, Mar. 9

768 A281 12fr multi .70 .25

Luxembourg Intl. Fair, 50th anniv.

Europa 1987 — A282

12fr, Aquatic Sports Center. 20fr, European Communities Court of Justice and abstract sculpture by Henry Moore (1898-1986).

1987, May 4 Photo. *Perf. 11½*

769 A282 12fr multi *1.50 .30*
770 A282 20fr multi *1.75 .90*

St. Michael's Church Millenary — A283

Designs: 12fr, Consecration of the church by Archbishop Egbert of Trier, 987, stained glass window by Gustav Zanter. 20fr, Baroque organ-chest, 17th century.

Photogravure & Engraved

1987, May 4		**Perf. 14**	
771 A283 12fr multi		1.00	.30
772 A283 20fr multi		1.40	.60

15th Century Paintings by Giovanni Ambrogio Bevilacqua — A284

Polyptych panels in the State Museum: 10fr, St. Bernard of Sienna and St. John the Baptist. 18fr, St. Jerome and St. Francis of Assisi.

1987, May 4	**Perf. 11½**	
773 A284 10fr multi	.60	.30
774 A284 18fr multi	1.25	.60

Rural Architecture — A285

10fr, Hennesbau Bark Mill, 1826, Niederfeulen. 12fr, Health Center, 18th cent., Mersch. 100fr, Post Office, 18th cent., Bertrange.

Photo. & Engr.

1987, Sept. 14	**Perf. 13½**	
775 A285 10fr multicolored	.60	.30
776 A285 12fr multicolored	.60	.25
777 A285 100fr multicolored	5.00	1.10
Nos. 775-777 (3)	6.20	1.65

Chamber of Deputies (Parliament) 139th Anniv. — A286

Designs: 6fr, Charles Metz (1799-1853), first President. 12fr, Parliament, 1860, designed by Antoine Hartmann (1817-1891).

1987, Sept. 14 **Engr.**	**Perf. 14**	
778 A286 6fr violet brn	.30	.25
779 A286 12fr blue black	.75	.35

Flowers by Botanical Illustrator Pierre-Joseph Redoute (1759-1840) — A287

6fr, Orange lily, water lily. 10fr, Primula, double narcissus. 12fr, Tulip. 50fr, Iris, gorteria.

1988, Feb. 8 **Photo.**	**Perf. 11½x12**	
780 A287 6fr multicolored	.80	.30
781 A287 10fr multicolored	.80	.30
782 A287 12fr multicolored	1.60	.45
783 A287 50fr multicolored	4.00	1.60
Nos. 780-783 (4)	7.20	2.65

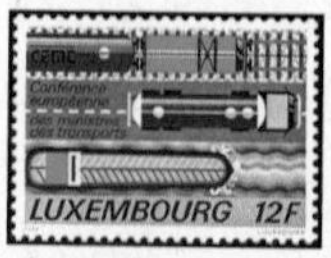

European Conf. of Ministers of Transport — A288

Eurocontrol, 25th Anniv. — A289

1988, Feb. 8	**Perf. 12**	
784 A288 12fr multi	.75	.30
785 A289 20fr multi	1.40	.75

Souvenir Sheet

Family of Prince Henri A290

1988, Mar. 29 **Photo.**	**Perf. 12**	
786 A290 Sheet of 3	5.50	5.50
a. 12fr Maria Theresa	.60	.60
b. 18fr Guillaume, Felix and Louis	.90	.90
c. 50fr Prince Henri	2.75	2.75

JUVALUX '88, 9th intl. youth philatelic exhibition, Mar. 29-Apr. 4.

Europa 1988 — A291

Communication: 12fr, Automatic mail handling. 20fr, Electronic mail.

1988, June 6 **Photo.**	**Perf. 11½**	
787 A291 12fr multicolored	*1.75*	*.40*
788 A291 20fr multicolored	*1.75*	*1.75*

Tourism — A292

Designs: 10fr, Wiltz town hall and Cross of Justice Monument, c. 1502. 12fr, Castle, Differdange, 16th cent., vert.

Photo. & Engr.

1988, June 6	**Perf. 13½**	
789 A292 10fr multi	.90	.30
790 A292 12fr multi	.90	.30

See Nos. 824-825, 841-842.

League of Luxembourg Student Sports Associations (LASEL), 50th Anniv. — A293

1988, June 6 **Photo.**	**Perf. 11½**	
791 A293 12fr multi	.80	.35

Doorways — A294

Architectural drawings by Joseph Wegener (1895-1980) and his students, 1949-1951: 12fr, Septfontaines Castle main entrance, 1785. 25fr, National Library regency northwing entrance, c. 1720. 50fr, Holy Trinity Church baroque entrance, c. 1740.

Litho. & Engr.

1988, Sept. 12	**Perf. 14**	
792 A294 12fr black & buff	.65	.30
793 A294 25fr blk & citron	1.25	.60
794 A294 50fr blk & yel bister	2.60	1.25
Nos. 792-794 (3)	4.50	2.15

Jean Monnet (1888-1979), French Economist A295

1988, Sept. 12	**Engr.**	
795 A295 12fr multi	1.00	.35

European Investment Bank, 30th Anniv. — A296

1988, Sept. 12	**Litho. & Engr.**	
796 A296 12fr yel grn & blk	.90	.30

1988 Summer Olympics, Seoul — A297

1988, Sept. 12 **Photo.**	**Perf. 11½**	
797 A297 12fr multi	.85	.30

A298

Design: 12fr, Portrait and excerpt from his speech to the Chamber of Deputies, 1896.

1989, Mar. 6 **Photo.**	**Perf. 11½x12**	
798 A298 12fr multi	.65	.35

C.M. Spoo (1837-1914), advocate of Luxembourgish as the natl. language.

Book Workers' Fed., 125th Anniv. — A299

1989, Mar. 6		
799 A299 18fr multi	.95	.50

Natl. Red Cross, 75th Anniv. — A300

1989, Mar. 6		
800 A300 20fr Henri Dunant	1.60	.90

Independence of the Grand Duchy, 150th Anniv. — A301

Design: 12fr, Lion, bronze sculpture by Auguste Tremont (1892-1980) guarding the grand ducal family vault, Cathedral of Luxembourg.

Photo. & Engr.

1989, Mar. 6	**Perf. 14**	
801 A301 12fr multi	1.00	.35

Astra Telecommunications Satellite — A302

1989, Mar. 6 **Photo.**	**Perf. 11½**	
802 A302 12fr multi	1.00	.35

Europa 1989 — A303

Paintings (children at play): 12fr, *Three Children in a Park,* 19th cent., anonymous. 20fr, *Child with Drum,* 17th cent., anonymous.

1989, May 8 **Photo.**	**Perf. 11½x12**	
803 A303 12fr multi	*.90*	*.90*
804 A303 20fr multi	*.90*	*.90*

Tour de France — A304

1989, May 8	**Perf. 11½**	
805 A304 9fr multi	.90	.45

Start of the bicycle race in Luxembourg City.

Interparliamentary Union, Cent. — A305

1989, May 8	**Perf. 11½x12**	
806 A305 12fr multi	.75	.40

A306

1989, May 8		
807 A306 12fr multi	.85	.45

European Parliament 3rd elections.

Council of Europe, 40th Anniv. — A307

1989, May 8	**Perf. 12x11½**	
808 A307 12fr multi	.85	.45

Reign of Grand Duke Jean, 25th Anniv. — A308

1989, Sept. 18 **Photo.** ***Perf. 12x11½***

Booklet Stamps

810 A308 3fr black & orange	1.50	1.40
a. Bklt. pane of 4	6.00	
811 A308 9fr black & blue green	1.25	1.25
a. Bklt. pane of 4	5.00	
b. Bklt. pane, 1 each #810, 811 + 2 labels	2.50	
Booklet, 1 each #810a, 811a, 811b	16.00	

Charles IV (1316-1378) — A309

Stained-glass windows by Joseph Oberberger in the Grand Ducal Loggia, Cathedral of Luxembourg: 20fr, John the Blind (1296-1346). 25fr, Wenceslas II (1361-1419).

Photo. & Engr.

1989, Sept. 18 *Perf. 13½x14*

821 A309 12fr shown .70 .25
822 A309 20fr multi 1.10 .85
823 A309 25fr multi 1.40 1.00
Nos. 821-823 (3) 3.20 2.10

Independence of the Grand Duchy, 150th anniv.

Tourism Type of 1988

Designs: 12fr, Clervaux Castle interior courtyard, circa 12th cent. 18fr, Bronzed wild boar of Titelberg, 1st cent., vert.

Litho. & Engr.

1989, Sept. 18 *Perf. 13½*

824 A292 12fr multi .70 .35
825 A292 18fr multi 1.40 .55

Views of the Former Fortress of Luxembourg, 1814-1815, Engravings by Christoph Wilhelm Selig (1791-1837) A310

1990, Mar. 5 **Photo.** *Perf. 12x11½*

826 A310 9fr shown .55 .35
827 A310 12fr multi, diff. .70 .35
828 A310 20fr multi, diff. 1.50 .90
829 A310 25fr multi, diff. 2.00 1.00
Nos. 826-829 (4) 4.75 2.60

Congress of Vienna, 1815, during which the Duchy of Luxembourg was elevated to the Grand Duchy of Luxembourg.

Schueberfouer Carnival, 650th Anniv. — A311

1990, Mar. 15 *Perf. 11½x12*

830 A311 9fr Carnival ride .75 .30

Batty Weber (1860-1940), Writer — A312

1990, Mar. 15

831 A312 12fr multi .75 .30

ITU, 125th Anniv. — A313

1990, Mar. 15

832 A313 18fr multicolored 1.10 .60

A314

Europa (Post Offices): 12fr, Luxembourg City. 20fr, Esch-Sur-Alzette, vert.

Litho. & Engr.

1990, May 28 *Perf. 13½*

833 A314 12fr buff & blk *1.75 .30*
834 A314 20fr lt bl & blk *1.75 1.20*

A315

Prime Ministers: 9fr, Paul Eyschen (1841-1915). 12fr, Emmanuel Servais (1811-1890).

Photo. & Engr.

1990, May 28 *Perf. 14x13½*

835 A315 9fr multicolored .55 .35
836 A315 12fr multicolored .75 .35

Psallus Pseudoplatani — A316

1990, May 28 **Photo.** *Perf. 11½*

837 A316 12fr multicolored .75 .35

Luxembourg Naturalists' Society, cent.

A317

Fountains: 12fr, Sheep's march by Will Lofy. 25fr, Fountain of Doves. 50fr, "Maus Ketty" by Lofy.

Litho. & Engr.

1990, Sept. 24 *Perf. 14*

838 A317 12fr multicolored .75 .25
839 A317 25fr multicolored 1.50 .90
840 A317 50fr multicolored 3.25 1.60
Nos. 838-840 (3) 5.50 2.75

Tourism Type of 1988

1990, Sept. 24 *Perf. 13½*

841 A292 12fr Mondercange 1.00 .35
842 A292 12fr Schifflange 1.00 .35

Souvenir Sheet

Nassau-Weilburg Dynasty, Cent. — A318

Designs: a, Grand Duke Adolphe. b, Grand Duchess Marie-Adelaide. c, Grand Ducal House arms. d, Grand Duchess Charlotte. e, Grand Duke Guillaume. f, Grand Duke Jean.

Photo. & Engr.

1990, Nov. 26 *Perf. 14x13½*

843 A318 Sheet of 6 8.50 8.50
a.-b. 12fr multicolored 1.25 1.25
c.-d. 18fr multicolored 1.40 1.40
e.-f. 20fr multicolored 1.60 1.60

View From the Trier Road by Sosthene Weis (1872-1941) A319

Paintings: 18fr, Vauban Street and the Viaduct. 25fr, St. Ulric Street.

Perf. 12x11½, 11½x12

1991, Mar. 4 **Photo.**

844 A319 14fr multicolored .90 .50
845 A319 18fr multicolored 1.25 .75
846 A319 25fr multi, vert. 1.50 .90
Nos. 844-846 (3) 3.65 2.15

Fungi — A320

No. 847, Geastrum varians. No. 848, Agaricus (Gymnopus) thiebautii. No. 849, Agaricus (lepiota) lepidocephalus. No. 850, Morchella favosa.

1991, Mar. 4 *Perf. 11½*

847 A320 14fr multicolored .90 .45
848 A320 14fr multicolored .90 .45
849 A320 18fr multicolored 1.25 .90
850 A320 25fr multicolored 2.25 1.10
Nos. 847-850 (4) 5.30 2.90

Europa — A321

No. 851, Astra 1A, 1B satellites. No. 852, Betzdorf ground station.

1991, May 13 **Photo.** *Perf. 12x11½*

851 A321 14fr multicolored *1.50 .35*
852 A321 18fr multicolored *1.75 1.40*

Natl. Miners' Monument, Kayl — A322

Designs: No. 854, Magistrates' Court, Redange-Sur-Attert, horiz.

1991, May 23 *Perf. 11½x12, 12x11½*

853 A322 14fr multicolored 1.00 .40
854 A322 14fr multicolored 1.00 .40

Art by Emile Kirscht — A323

No. 856, Edmund de la Fontaine (1823-91), poet.

1991, May 23 *Perf. 11½*

855 A323 14fr multicolored 1.00 .40
856 A323 14fr multicolored 1.00 .40

Labor Unions, 75th anniv. (No. 855).

Post and Telecommunications Museum — A324

Perf. 11½ on 3 sides

1991, Sept. 23 **Photo.**

Booklet Stamps

857 A324 4fr Old telephone 2.50 1.40
a. Bklt. pane of 1 + 3 labels 3.50
858 A324 14fr Old postbox .75 .35
a. Bklt. pane of 4 3.00

Stamp Day, 50th Anniv. — A325

1991, Sept. 23 *Perf. 11½*

859 A325 14fr Stamp of Type A24 1.00 .50

A326

Gargoyles: 14fr, Young girl's head. 25fr, Woman's head. 50fr, Man's head.

Photo. & Engr.

1991, Sept. 23 *Perf. 14*

860 A326 14fr multicolored .75 .40
861 A326 25fr multicolored 1.50 .65
862 A326 50fr multicolored 2.50 1.40
Nos. 860-862 (3) 4.75 2.45

See Nos. 874-876.

Jean-Pierre Pescatore Foundation, Cent. — A327

Buildings: No. 864, High Technology Institute. No. 865, New Fair and Congress Centre.

1992, Mar. 16 **Photo.** *Perf. 11½*

863 A327 14fr lil rose & multi .85 .45
864 A327 14fr grn & multi .85 .45
865 A327 14fr brt bl & multi .85 .45
Nos. 863-865 (3) 2.55 1.35

Bettembourg Castle — A328

25fr, Walferdange station.

1992, Mar. 16

866 A328 18fr shown 1.00 .35
867 A328 25fr multicolored 1.50 .75

Europa — A329

Emigrants to US: 14fr, Nicholas Gonner (1835-1892), newspaper editor. 22fr, N. E. Becker (1842-1920), journalist.

Photo. & Engr.

1992, May 18 *Perf. 13½x14½*

868 A329 14fr multicolored *1.75 .50*
869 A329 22fr multicolored *1.75 1.25*

Lions Clubs Intl., 75th Anniv. A330

General Strike, 50th Anniv. A331

1992, May 18 **Photo.** *Perf. 11½*

870 A330 14fr multicolored 1.00 .35
871 A331 18fr sepia & lake 1.10 .55

1992 Summer Olympics, Barcelona — A332

1992, May 18 ***Perf. 12x11½***
872 A332 14fr multicolored 1.50 .45

Expo '92, Seville — A333

1992, May 18 ***Perf. 11½***
873 A333 14fr Luxembourg pavilion .85 .50

Gargoyle Type of 1991

Photo. & Engr.

1992, Oct. 5 ***Perf. 14***
874 A326 14fr Ram's head .75 .35
875 A326 22fr Lion's head 1.25 .90
876 A326 50fr Satyr's head 2.50 1.50
Nos. 874-876 (3) 4.50 2.75

Stained Glass Windows, by Auguste Tremont — A334

1992, Oct. 5 **Photo.** ***Perf. 11½x12***
877 A334 14fr Post horn, letters .75 .50
878 A334 22fr Post rider 1.25 1.00
879 A334 50fr Insulators 2.60 1.40
Nos. 877-879 (3) 4.60 2.90

Luxembourg Post and Telecommunications, 150th anniv.

Single European Market — A335

1992, Oct. 5 ***Perf. 11½x12***
880 A335 14fr multicolored .85 .40

Fountain of the Children with Grapes, Schwebsingen — A336

Design: No. 882, Old Ironworks Cultural Center, Steinfort.

1993, Mar. 8 **Photo.** ***Perf. 12x11½***
881 A336 14fr multicolored .85 .35
882 A336 14fr multicolored .85 .35

Grand Duke Jean — A337

Litho. & Engr.

1993-95 ***Perf. 13½x13***

Background Color

883 A337 1fr yellow brown .25 .25
883A A337 2fr olive gray .25 .25
884 A337 5fr yellow green .25 .25
885 A337 7fr brick red .25 .25
886 A337 10fr blue .55 .25
887 A337 14fr pink 1.40 .30
888 A337 15fr green .85 .25
889 A337 16fr orange 1.00 .50
890 A337 18fr orange .70 .35
891 A337 20fr red 1.00 .45
892 A337 22fr dark green .90 .75
893 A337 25fr gray blue 1.00 .65
894 A337 100fr brown 5.00 2.75
Nos. 883-894 (13) 13.40 7.25

Issued: 5, 7, 14, 18, 22, 25fr, 3/8/93; 1, 15, 20, 100fr, 3/7/94; 2, 10, 16fr, 1/30/95.
See Nos. 957, 1026.

New Technologies in Surgery — A338

1993, May 10 **Photo.** ***Perf. 11½***
895 A338 14fr multicolored .85 .45

Contemporary Paintings — A339

Europa: 14fr, Rezlop, by Fernand Roda. 22fr, So Close, by Sonja Roef.

1993, May 10
896 A339 14fr multicolored *1.25 .40*
897 A339 22fr multicolored *1.75 .80*

A340

Designs: 14fr, Burgundy Residence. 20fr, Simons House. 50fr, Cassal House.

Photo. & Engr.

1993, May 10 ***Perf. 14***
898 A340 14fr multicolored .75 .35
899 A340 20fr multicolored 1.50 .45
900 A340 50fr multicolored 3.50 1.90
Nos. 898-900 (3) 5.75 2.70

A341

1993, Sept. 20 **Photo.** ***Perf. 11½***
901 A341 14fr multicolored .90 .45

Environmental protection.

A342

A343

1993, Sept. 20
902 A342 14fr multicolored .90 .45
903 A343 14fr multicolored .90 .45

Jean Schortgen (1880-1918), 1st worker elected to Parliament (No. 902); Artistic Circle of Luxembourg, cent.

Museum Exhibits — A344

14fr, Electric tram, Tram & Bus Museum, City of Luxembourg. 22fr, Iron ore tipper wagon, Natl. Mining Museum, Rumelange. 60fr, Horse-drawn carriage, Wiltz Museum of Ancient Crafts.

Photo. & Engr.

1993, Sept. 20 ***Perf. 14***
904 A344 14fr multicolored .90 .35
905 A344 22fr multicolored 1.25 .70
906 A344 60fr multicolored 3.25 2.00
Nos. 904-906 (3) 5.40 3.05

See Nos. 933-935.

Snow-Covered Landscape, by Joseph Kutter (1894-1941) — A345

Design: No. 908, The Moselle, by Nico Klopp (1894-1930).

1994, Mar. 7 **Photo.** ***Perf. 11½x12***
907 A345 14fr multicolored .90 .45
908 A345 14fr multicolored .90 .45

4th General Elections to European Parliament — A346

1994, May 16 **Photo.** ***Perf. 11½***
909 A346 14fr multicolored .85 .70

European Inventions, Discoveries — A347

1994, May 16
910 A347 14fr Armillary sphere *1.00 .40*
911 A347 22fr Sail boats, map *1.25 1.00*

Europa.

21st Intl. Congress of Genealogy & Heraldry A348

14th World Congress of Intl. Police Assoc. A349

Intl. Year of the Family — A350

1994, May 16 ***Perf. 11½***
912 A348 14fr multicolored 1.25 .35
913 A349 18fr multicolored 1.25 .45
914 A350 25fr multicolored 1.75 1.25
Nos. 912-914 (3) 4.25 2.05

Europe — A351

1994, Sept. 19 ***Perf. 11½***
915 A351 14fr Dove, stars 1.25 .45
916 A351 14fr Circle of stars 1.25 .45
917 A351 14fr Bronze Age bowl 2.50 2.75
Nos. 915-917 (3) 5.00 3.65

Western European Union, 40th anniv. (No. 915). Office for Official Publications of European Communities, 25th anniv. (No. 916). European Bronze Age Research Campaign (No. 917).

Liberation, 50th Anniv. — A352

1994, Sept. 19 **Photo.** ***Perf. 12x11½***
918 A352 14fr multicolored .75 .50

Former Refuges in Luxembourg A353

Designs: 15fr, Munster Abbey. 25fr, Holy Spirit Convent. 60fr, St. Maximine Abbey of Trier.

Photo. & Engr.

1994, Sept. 19 ***Perf. 14***
919 A353 15fr multicolored .85 .35
920 A353 25fr multicolored 1.25 1.00
921 A353 60fr multicolored 3.25 1.75
Nos. 919-921 (3) 5.35 3.10

A354

City of Luxembourg, 1995 European City of Culture — A355

A356

Paintings by Hundertwasser A357

Panoramic view of city showing buildings and: No. 923a, Steeples, trees. b, Gateway through fortress wall. c, Angles in fortress wall. d, Roof of church.

Designs: No. 924, The King of the Antipodes. No. 925, The House with the Arcades and the Yellow Tower. No. 926, Small Path.

Perf. 12x11½, 11½x12

1995, Mar. 6 **Photo.**
922 A354 16fr multicolored 1.60 .90
923 A355 Strip of 4 4.25 3.50
a.-d. 16fr any single .90 .45

Photo. & Engr.

Perf. 14

924 A356 16fr gold, silver & multi 1.60 .90
925 A357 16fr black & multi 1.60 .90
926 A357 16fr yellow & multi 1.60 .90
Nos. 922-926 (5) 10.65 7.10

No. 923 is a continuous design.

Liberation of the Concentration Camps, 50th Anniv. — A358

Europa: 25fr, Barbed wire, cracked plaster.

1995, May 15 **Photo.** ***Perf. 11½x12***
927 A358 16fr multicolored *1.25 .50*
928 A358 25fr multicolored *2.00 .80*

European Nature Conservation Year — A359

1995, May 15 **Litho.** ***Perf. 13½***
929 A359 16fr multicolored .85 .55

A360

1995, May 15 Photo. *Perf. 11½x12*
930 A360 16fr multicolored .90 .40

Small States of Europe Games, Luxembourg.

European Geodynamics and Seismology Center — A361

1995, May 15 *Perf. 11½*
931 A361 32fr multicolored 2.00 1.00

UN, 50th Anniv. — A362

1995, May 15 *Perf. 11½x12*
932 A362 80fr multicolored 4.00 2.50

Museum Exhibits Type of 1993

Designs, vert: 16fr, Churn, Country Art Museum, Vianden. 32fr, Wine press, Wine Museum, Ehnen. 80fr, Sculpture of a Potter, by Leon Nosbusch, Pottery Museum, Nospelt.

Photo. & Engr.

1995, Sept. 18 *Perf. 14*
933 A344 16fr multicolored .85 .40
934 A344 32fr multicolored 1.75 1.00
935 A344 80fr multicolored 4.00 2.50
Nos. 933-935 (3) 6.60 3.90

Luxembourg-Reykjavik, Iceland Air Route, 40th Anniv. — A363

1995, Sept. 18 Litho. *Perf. 13*
936 A363 16fr multicolored 1.00 .55

See Iceland No. 807.

Tourism — A364

1995, Sept. 18 Photo. *Perf. 11½*
937 A364 16fr Erpeldange 1.00 .55
938 A364 16fr Schengen 1.00 .55

Portrait of Emile Mayrisch (1862-1928), by Théo Van Rysselberghe (1862-1926) A365

1996, Mar. 2 Photo. *Perf. 11½*
939 A365 (A) multicolored 1.00 .55

On day of issue No. 939 was valued at 16fr.
See Belgium No. 1602.

National Railway, 50th Anniv. A366

Passenger train: a, Cab facing left. b, Hooked together. c, Cab facing right.

1996, Mar. 4 Photo. *Perf. 11½*
940 Strip of 3 4.25 2.50
a.-c. A366 16fr Any single 1.25 .55

No. 940 is a continuous design.

Grand Duchess Charlotte (1896-1985) — A367

Design: Statue, Luxembourg City.

1996, Mar. 4 Booklet Stamp
941 A367 16fr multicolored 1.25 .55
a. Booklet pane of 8 10.00
Complete booklet, #941a 10.00

Mihály Munkácsy (1844-1900), Hungarian Painter A368

Designs: No. 942, Portrait of Munkácsy, by Edouard Charlemont, 1884. No. 943, Portrait of Marie Munchen, by Munkácsy, 1885, vert.

1996, May 20 Photo. *Perf. 11½*
942 A368 16fr multicolored 1.00 .55
943 A368 16fr multicolored 1.00 .55

Famous Women — A369

Europa: 16fr, Marie de Bourgogne (1457-82), duchess of Luxembourg. 25fr, Empress Maria-Theresa of Austria (1717-80), duchess of Luxembourg.

Photo. & Engr.

1996, May 20 *Perf. 14x13½*
944 A369 16fr multicolored *1.00* *.70*
945 A369 25fr multicolored *1.50* *.90*

Luxembourg Confederation of Christian Trade Unions, 75th Anniv. — A370

Radio, Cent. — A371

Modern Olympic Games, Cent. — A372

Motion Pictures, Cent. — A373

Perf. 12x11½, 11½x12

1996, May 20 Photo.
946 A370 16fr multicolored .90 .30
947 A371 20fr multicolored 1.10 .45
948 A372 25fr multicolored 1.25 1.10
949 A373 32fr multicolored 2.10 1.40
Nos. 946-949 (4) 5.35 3.25

Registration and Property Administration, Bicent. — A374

1996, Sept. 23 Photo. *Perf. 11½*
950 A374 16fr multicolored 1.00 .55

Let Us Live Together — A375

No. 951, Four children. No. 952, "L'Abbraccio," bronze statue by M.J. Kerschen, vert.

1996, Sept. 23
951 A375 16fr multicolored .90 .50
952 A375 16fr multicolored .90 .50

Mustelidae A376

Litho. & Engr.

1996, Sept. 23 *Perf. 13½*
953 A376 16fr Meles meles .85 .35
954 A376 20fr Mustela putorius 1.10 .55
955 A376 80fr Lutra lutra 4.00 2.75
Nos. 953-955 (3) 5.95 3.65

John the Blind (1296-1346), King of Bohemia, Count of Luxembourg — A377

Litho. & Engr.

1996, Dec. 9 *Perf. 13½*
956 A377 32fr multicolored 1.75 1.00

Grand Duke Jean Type of 1993

Litho. & Engr.

1997, Jan. 2 *Perf. 13½x13*
957 A337 8fr green & black .70 .30

Treaties of Rome, 40th Anniv. — A378

Belgian-Luxembourg Economic Union, 75th Anniv. — A379

1997, Mar. 3 Photo. *Perf. 11½*
958 A378 16fr multicolored 1.00 .60
959 A379 20fr multicolored 1.25 .60

Tourism — A380

Designs: No. 960, Servais House, Mersch. No. 961, Baroque Church, Koerich, vert.

1997, Mar. 3
960 A380 16fr multicolored .85 .50
961 A380 16fr multicolored .85 .50

11th World Congress of Rose Societies A381

Roses: 16fr, Grand Duchess Charlotte. 20fr, Beautiful Sultana. 80fr, In Memory of Jean Soupert.

1997, Mar. 3 *Perf. 11½*
962 A381 16fr multicolored 1.10 .55

Size: 33x25mm

963 A381 20fr multicolored 1.40 .75
964 A381 80fr multicolored 4.50 2.50
Nos. 962-964 (3) 7.00 3.80

Stories and Legends — A382

Europa: 16fr, Melusina of Luxembourg. 25fr, Hunter of Hollenfels.

1997, May 12
965 A382 16fr multicolored *1.25* *.60*
966 A382 25fr multicolored *2.25* *.80*

A383

A384

Mondorf Spa, 150th Anniv. — A385

1997, May 12
967 A383 16fr multicolored 1.00 .55
968 A384 16fr multicolored 1.00 .55
969 A385 16fr multicolored 1.00 .55
Nos. 967-969 (3) 3.00 1.65

Grand-Ducal Gendarmerie, bicent. (No. 967). Union of Small Domestic Animals Farming Societies, 75th anniv. (No. 968).

JUVALUX 98 — A386

1997, May 12
970 A386 16fr Emblem 1.10 .55
971 A386 80fr Postal history 4.50 2.75

Saar-Lorraine-Luxembourg Summit — A387

1997, Oct. 16 Photo. *Perf. 11½*
972 A387 16fr multicolored 1.00 .50

See Germany No. 1982 & France No. 2613.

Mills — A388

Litho. & Engr.

1997, Oct. 16 ***Perf. 13½***

973	A388	16fr Kalborn Mill, horiz.	1.25	.55
974	A388	50fr Ramelli Mill	2.60	1.60

Clocks — A389

Designs: 16fr, Oak wall clock, 1816. 32fr, Astronomic clock with walnut case, mid 19th cent. 80fr, Pear tree wood wall clock, 1815.

Photo. & Engr.

1997, Oct. 16 ***Perf. 13x13½***

975	A389	16fr multicolored	1.10	.50
976	A389	32fr multicolored	1.75	.90
977	A389	80fr multicolored	4.25	2.50
		Nos. 975-977 (3)	7.10	3.90

Henry V, the Blonde (1247-81), Count of Luxembourg — A390

1997, Dec. 8 Photo. ***Perf. 11½***

978	A390	32fr multicolored	1.75	.90

Tourism — A391

No. 979, Hesperange. No. 980, Rodange Church, vert.

1998, Mar. 23 Photo. ***Perf. 11½***

979	A391	16fr multicolored	1.00	.55
980	A391	16fr multicolored	1.00	.55

See Nos. 1023-1024, 1048-1049.

Freshwater Fish — A392

Designs: 16fr, Salmo trutta. 25fr, Cottus gobio. 50fr, Alburnoides bipunctatus.

Litho. & Engr.

1998, Mar. 23 ***Perf. 13½x13***

981	A392	16fr multicolored	1.40	.55
982	A392	25fr multicolored	2.00	1.25
983	A392	50fr multicolored	3.50	2.00
		Nos. 981-983 (3)	6.90	3.80

NGL (Independent Luxembourg Trade Union), 50th Anniv. A393

Broom Festival, Wiltz, 50th Anniv. A394

Jean Antoine Zinnen (1827-98), Composer A395

Abolition of Censorship, 150th Anniv. A396

1998, Mar. 23 Photo. ***Perf. 11½***

984	A393	16fr multicolored	1.00	.45
985	A394	16fr multicolored	1.00	.45
986	A395	20fr multicolored	1.40	.55
987	A396	50fr multicolored	3.50	2.00
		Nos. 984-987 (4)	6.90	3.45

King Henri VII (1275?-1313) of Luxembourg, King of Germany, Holy Roman Emperor — A397

1998, June 18 Photo. ***Perf. 11½***

988	A397	(A) multicolored	1.00	.50

Granting of the Right to hold a Luxembourg Fair, 700th anniv.

No. 988 was valued at 16fr on the day of issue.

Natl. Holidays and Festivals — A398

Europa: 16fr, Fireworks over bridge, National Day. 25fr, Flame, stained glass window, National Remembrance Day.

1998, June 18

989	A398	16fr multicolored	*1.40*	*.50*
990	A398	25fr multicolored	*1.60*	*.65*

Juvalux 98 — A399

A400

16fr, Town postman, 1880. 25fr, Letter, 1590, horiz. 50fr, Country postman, 1880.

No. 994, Engraving showing 1861 view of Luxembourg.

1998, June 18 Photo. & Engr.

991	A399	16fr multicolored	1.25	.55
992	A399	25fr multicolored	1.60	1.25
993	A399	50fr multicolored	2.75	1.40
		Nos. 991-993 (3)	5.60	3.20

Souvenir Sheet

994	A400	Sheet of 2	6.00	6.00
a.		16fr multicolored	.90	.90
b.		80fr multicolored	4.00	4.00

St. Jean de L'Esperance, Grand Lodge of Luxembourg, 150th Anniv. — A401

1998, Sept. 21 Litho. ***Perf. 13½***

995	A401	16fr multicolored	1.00	.55

Abbey of Echternach, 1300th Anniv. — A402

Various architectural drawings.

1998, Sept 21 Photo. ***Perf. 11½***

996	A402	16fr multicolored	1.25	.55
997	A402	48fr multicolored	2.50	1.75
998	A402	60fr multicolored	3.25	1.75
		Nos. 996-998 (3)	7.00	4.05

Museum Exhibits — A403

City of Luxembourg History Museum: 16fr, Spanish army helmet, 16th cent. 80fr, Wayside Cross, Hollerich, 1718.

Litho. & Engr.

1998, Sept. 21 ***Perf. 13½***

999	A403	16fr multicolored	.90	.55
1000	A403	80fr multicolored	4.50	2.75

NAMSA (NATO Maintenance and Supply Organization), 40th Anniv. — A404

1998, Dec. 7 Photo. ***Perf. 11½***

1001	A404	36fr multicolored	2.25	1.25

Introduction of the Euro — A405

1999, Mar. 8 Photo. ***Perf. 11½***

1002	A405	(A) multicolored	1.25	.70

No. 1002 was valued at 16fr on the day of issue.

Council of Europe, 50th Anniv. A406

1999, Mar. 8

1003	A406	16fr multicolored	1.25	.85

Owls — A407

1999, Mar. 8 ***Perf. 12***

1004	A407	(A) Strix aluco, vert.	.90	.65
1005	A407	32fr Bubo bubo	1.60	1.10
1006	A407	60fr Tyto alba	3.50	2.50
		Nos. 1004-1006 (3)	6.00	4.25

No. 1004 was valued at 16fr on the day of issue.

NATO, 50th Anniv. A408

1999, Mar. 8 ***Perf. 11½***

1007	A408	80fr multicolored	5.50	3.50

Europa A409

National Parks: 16fr, Haute-Sûre. 25fr, Ardennes-Eifel.

1999, May 17 Photo. ***Perf. 11½x12***

1008	A409	16fr multicolored	*1.25*	*.45*
1009	A409	25fr multicolored	*1.75*	*.80*

Natl. Federation of Mutuality, 75th Anniv. A410

Intl. Year of Older Persons A411

UPU, 125th Anniv. — A412

A413

A414

1999, May 17 ***Perf. 11½***

1010	A410	16fr multicolored	.85	.65
1011	A411	16fr multicolored	.90	.55
1012	A412	16fr multicolored	.90	.55
1013	A413	32fr multicolored	1.60	1.40
1014	A414	80fr multicolored	4.50	2.75
		Nos. 1010-1014 (5)	8.75	5.90

Luxembourg Federation of Amateur Photographers, 50th anniv. (No. 1013). Luxembourg Gymnastics Federation, cent. (No. 1014).

18th Birthday of Prince Guillaume — A415

Photo. & Engr.

1999, Sept. 21 ***Perf. 13½***

1015	A415	16fr multicolored	.85	.55

Aline Mayrisch-de Saint-Hubert (1874-1947), President of Luxembourg Red Cross — A416

1999, Sept. 21 Litho. & Engr.

1016	A416	20fr multicolored	1.60	.55

Travelling Into the Future — A417

16fr, Communication by road. 20fr, Information age. 80fr, Conquering space.

1999, Sept. 21 Photo. ***Perf. 11¾***

1017	A417	16fr multicolored	.85	.55
1018	A417	20fr multicolored	1.00	.85
1019	A417	80fr multicolored	4.25	1.75
		Nos. 1017-1019 (3)	6.10	3.15

See Nos. 1063-1065.

Johann Wolfgang von Goethe (1749-1832), German Poet — A418

1999, Nov. 30 Photo. ***Perf. 11¾***

1020	A418	20fr henna & dk brn	1.25	.70

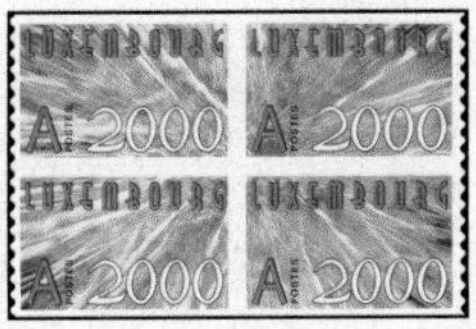

Year 2000 A419

No. 1021: a, Large white area under A and 2000. b, Large blue area under A. c, Large blue area under A and URG. d, Large blue area under LUX.

Serpentine Die Cut 8 Vert.

2000, Jan. 3 **Photo.**

Self-Adhesive

Booklet Stamps

1021	A419 Booklet pane of 4	4.25	
a.-d.	(A) Any single	1.00	.70
	Booklet, 2 #1021	8.50	

Nos. 1021a-1021d sold for 16fr on day of issue.

Holy Roman Emperor Charles V (1500-58) — A420

Litho. & Engr.

2000, Mar. 7 *Perf. 13½*

1022	A420 A multi	.90	.50

Sold for 16fr on day of issue.

Tourism Type of 1998

Designs: No. 1023, Walferdange Castle. No. 1024, Wasserbillig railway station, vert.

Perf. 11¾x11½, 11½x11¾

2000, Mar. 7 **Photo.**

Granite Paper

1023	A391 A multi	1.00	.50
1024	A391 A multi	1.00	.50

Sold for 16fr on day of issue.

World Mathematics Year — A421

2000, Mar. 7 *Perf. 11½x11¾*

1025	A421 80fr multi	4.50	2.75

Grand Duke Jean Type of 1993

Litho. & Engr.

2000, Mar. 31 *Perf. 13¼x13*

Background Color

1026	A337 9fr pink	.60	.30

Musical Instruments — A422

Perf. 11½x11¾

2000, Mar. 31 **Photo.**

Granite Paper

1027	A422 3fr French horn	.25	.25
1028	A422 12fr Saxophone	.60	.35
1029	A422 21fr Violin	1.25	.55
1030	A422 30fr Piano	1.50	1.10
	Nos. 1027-1030 (4)	3.60	2.25

See Nos. 1045-1046.

Ducks — A423

Designs: 18fr, Anas platyrhynchos. 24fr, Aythya ferina, vert. 30fr, Aythya fuligula.

2000, May 9 *Perf. 11¾x11½*

Granite Paper

1031	A423 18fr multi	1.25	.70

Perf. 11½x11¾

1032	A423 24fr multi	1.60	.90
1033	A423 30fr multi	1.75	1.25
	Nos. 1031-1033 (3)	4.60	2.85

Esch-sur-Alzette Gas Works, Cent. (in 1999) — A424

2000, May 9 *Perf. 11¾x11½*

Granite Paper

1034	A424 18fr multi	1.25	.65

Europa, 2000

Common Design Type

2000, May 9 *Perf. 11½x11¾*

Granite Paper

1035	CD17 21fr multi	*1.40*	*.85*

Robert Schuman's European Unity Plan, 50th Anniv. — A425

2000, May 9 *Perf. 11½x11¾*

1036	A425 21fr multi	1.40	.85

Art Collection of Luxembourg Posts & Telecommunications — A426

Art by: 21fr, Will Kesseler. 24fr, Joseph Probst, vert. 36fr, Mett Hoffmann.

Perf. 11¾x11½, 11½x11¾

2000, Sept. 27 **Photo.**

Granite Paper

1037	A426 21fr multi	1.10	.60
1038	A426 24fr multi	1.50	1.00
1039	A426 36fr multi	2.25	1.40
	Nos. 1037-1039 (3)	4.85	3.00

Towers on Historic Walking Trails — A427

Designs: 18fr, Tower of Jacob, Wenzel trail. 42fr, Bons Malades Gate, Vauban trail.

Photo. & Engr.

2000, Sept. 27 *Perf. 13½x14¼*

1040	A427 18fr multi	1.25	.55
1041	A427 42fr multi	2.75	1.60

Blast Furnace "B," Esch-Belval — A428

2000, Sept. 27 *Perf. 11¾x11½*

1042	A428 A multi	1.25	.55

No. 1042 sold for 18fr on day of issue.

Accession of Grand Duke Henri — A429

Designs: 18fr, Prince Henri in uniform, Princess Maria Teresa in pink suit. 100fr, Prince in suit, Princess in red blouse.

2000, Sept. 27 **Photo.** *Perf. 11¾*

Granite Paper (18fr)

1043	A429 18fr multi	1.00	.55

Souvenir Sheet

Photo. (margin Photo. & Engr.)

Perf. 11½

1044	A429 100fr multi	6.50	6.50

No. 1043 issued in sheets of 12, five of which (positions 6, 8, 9, 10 and 11) have a red and blue "ribbon" running diagonally through stamp margin. No. 1044 contains one 46x35mm stamp.

Musical Instruments Type of 2000

2000, Dec. 5 **Photo.** *Perf. 11½x11¾*

Granite Paper

1045	A422 9fr Electric guitar	.90	.35
1046	A422 24fr Accordion	1.60	1.00

Treaty Establishing European Coal and Steel Community, 50th Anniv. — A430

Perf. 11¼x11½

2001, Mar. 20 **Photo.**

1047	A430 21fr multi	1.25	.85

Tourism Type of 1998

Designs: No. 1048, 18fr, Bestgen Mill, Schifflange. No. 1049, 18fr, Chapel, Wormeldange, and millstone, Ahn, vert.

Perf. 11¾x11½, 11½x11¾

2001, Mar. 20

Granite Paper

1048-1049	A391 Set of 2	2.00	1.10

Writers — A431

Designs: 18fr, Nik Welter (1871-1951). 24fr, André Gide (1869-1951). 30fr, Michel Rodange (1827-76).

Perf. 13½x13¼

2001, Mar. 20 **Litho. & Engr.**

1050-1052	A431 Set of 3	4.50	3.00

Europa — A432

Designs: A (18fr), Stream, Mullerthal region. 21fr, Pond and Kaltreis water tower, Luxembourg-Bonnevoie.

Perf. 11¾x11½, 11½x11¾

2001, May 22 **Photo.**

Granite Paper

1053-1054	A432 Set of 2	2.25	1.60

Rescue Workers — A433

Designs: 18fr, Air rescue. 30fr, Rescue divers. 45fr, Fire fighters.

2001, May 22 *Perf. 11½x11¾*

Granite Paper

1055-1057	A433 Set of 3	6.00	4.00

Humanitarian Services — A434

Designs: 18fr, Humanitarian aid. 24fr, Intl. Organization for Migration, 50th anniv.

2001, May 22 *Perf. 11½*

1058-1059	A434 Set of 2	2.75	1.75

Old Postal Vehicles — A435

Designs: 3fr, Citroen 2CV Mini-van, 1960s. 18fr, Volkswagen Beetle, 1970s.

Granite Paper

Serpentine Die Cut 8¼ Vert.

2001, May 22 **Booklet Stamps**

1060	A435 3fr multi	.25	.25
1061	A435 18fr multi	1.10	.75
a.	Booklet, 6 each #1060-1061	8.50	

European Year of Languages — A436

2001, Oct. 1 **Photo.** *Perf. 11¾x11½*

Granite Paper

1062	A436 A multi	1.25	.70

Luxembourg postal officials state that No. 1062 sold for 45 eurocents on the day of issue, though euro currency was not in circulation on the day of issue. On the day of issue, 45 eurocents was the equivalent of approximately 18fr.

Nos. 1063-1071, 1074, 1076, 1078, 1080, 1084, and B425-B429 are denominated solely in euro currency though euro currency would not circulate until Jan. 1, 2002. From their date of issue until Dec. 31, 2001, these stamps could be purchased for Luxembourg francs. The official pegged rate of 40.3399 francs to the euro made rounding the franc purchase price a necessity for such purchases. The approximate franc equivalent of the euro denominations is shown in parentheses in the listings.

Traveling Into the Future Type of 1999

Designs: 45c (18fr), Renewable energy. 59c (24fr), Waste recycling. 74c (30fr), Biological research.

2001, Oct. 1 *Perf. 11¾*

Granite Paper

1063-1065	A417 Set of 3	5.50	4.00

Euro Coinage — A437

Designs: Coin obverses with values of stamp denominations.

2001, Oct. 1 *Perf. 11½*

1066	A437 5c (2fr) multi	.25	.25
1067	A437 10c (4fr) multi	.25	.25
1068	A437 20c (8fr) multi	.60	.40
1069	A437 50c (20fr) multi	1.40	1.00
1070	A437 €1 (40fr) multi	3.00	1.75
1071	A437 €2 (80fr) multi	6.00	4.50
	Nos. 1066-1071 (6)	11.50	8.15

Grand Duke Henri — A438

Photo. & Engr.

2001-03 *Perf. 11¾x11½*

Vignette Color

1072	A438 1c blue	.25	.25
1073	A438 3c green	.25	.25
1074	A438 7c (3fr) blue	.25	.25
1075	A438 22c (9fr) brown	.50	.40
1076	A438 30c (12fr) green	.90	.45
1077	A438 45c (18fr) violet	1.40	.65
1078	A438 52c brown	1.25	.75

1079 A438 59c blue 1.50 1.00
1080 A438 74c brown 2.00 1.00
1081 A438 89c red violet 2.50 1.25
Nos. 1072-1081 (10) 10.80 6.25

Issued: 7c, 22c, 30c, 45c, 10/1/01. 52c, 59c, 74c, 89c, 3/5/02. 1c, 3c, 10/1/03.

See Nos. 1124-1133A

Kiwanis International A439

2001, Dec. 6 Photo. *Perf. 11½*
1084 A439 52c (21fr) multi 1.75 1.25

100 Cents = 1 Euro (€)

Art Collection of Luxembourg Posts & Telecommunications — A440

Art by: 22c, Moritz Ney, vert. 45c, Dany Prüm. 59c, Christiane Schmit, vert.

Perf. 14¼x14, 14x14¼
2002, Mar. 5 Photo.
1085-1087 A440 Set of 3 4.00 3.00

European Court Anniversaries A441

Designs: 45c, European Court of Auditors, 25th anniv. 52c, Court of Justice of the European communities, 50th anniv.

2002, Mar. 5 Litho. *Perf. 13½*
1088-1089 A441 Set of 2 3.00 2.00

Sports — A442

No. 1090: a, Snowboarding. b, Skateboarding. c, Rollerblading. d, Bicycling. e, Volleyball. f, Basketball.

Booklet Stamps

Die Cut Perf. 10 on 3 Sides
2002, Mar. 5 Self-Adhesive
1090 Booklet pane of 6 4.50
a.-c. A442 7c Any single .25 .25
d.-f. A442 45c Any single 1.25 1.00
Booklet, 2 #1090 9.00

Europa — A443

Designs: 45c, Tightrope walker. 52c, Clown.

2002, May 14 Litho. *Perf. 13½*
1091-1092 A443 Set of 2 *3.00 1.75*

Cultural Anniversaries A444

Designs: A, 50th Wiltz Festival. €1.12, Victor Hugo (1802-85), writer.

2002, May 14 *Perf. 13¼*
1093-1094 A444 Set of 2 5.00 3.50

No. 1093 sold for 45c on day of issue.

Start of Tour de France in Luxembourg — A445

Designs: 45c, Stylized bicycle. 52c, François Faber (1887-1915), 1909 champion, vert. €2.45, The Champion, by Joseph Kutter, vert.

Litho. (45c), Litho. & Engr.
Perf. 13¼x13½, 13½x13¼
2002, May 14
1095-1097 A445 Set of 3 9.00 6.25

Grevenmacher Charter of Freedom, 750th Anniv. — A446

2002, Sept. 14 Litho. *Perf. 13¼x13*
1098 A446 74c multi 1.90 1.50

Nature Museum, Museum of Natural History — A447

No. 1099: a, Water drop on spruce needle. b, Butterfly. c, Leaf rosette of *Echeveria* plant. d, Berries.

Serpentine Die Cut 8 Vert.
2002, Sept. 14 Photo.
Self-Adhesive
1099 Booklet pane of 4 4.50
a.-d. A447 A Any single 1.10 .80
Booklet, 2 #1099 9.00

Nos. 1099a-1099d had franking value of 45c on day of issue, but booklet sold for discounted price of €3.35.

Souvenir Sheet

Luxembourg Stamps, 150th Anniv. — A448

No. 1100: a, Grand Duke William II, man and woman, 1852 (47x27mm). b, Grand Duke Adolphe, woman, 1902 (47x27mm). c, Grand Duchess Charlotte, street scene, 1952 (47x27mm). d, Grand Duke Henri, hot air balloons in street, 2002 (71x27mm).

Photo. & Engr.
2002, Sept. 14 *Perf. 11¾*
1100 A448 45c Sheet of 4, #a-d 4.75 4.75

The Post in 50 Years — A449

Designs: 22c, Postmen in spacecraft, buildings, vert. A, Spacecraft in flight, cell phone, letter and "@" in orbit around planet.

Perf. 14x14½, 14½x14
2002, Oct. 19 Litho.
1101-1102 A449 Set of 2 1.75 1.40

No. 1102 sold for 45c on day of issue.

Grand Duke Jean and Princess Joséphine-Charlotte, 50th Wedding Anniv. — A450

Perf. 14¼x14½
2003, Mar. 18 Litho.
1103 A450 45c multi 1.10 .95

Official Journal of the European Communities, 50th Anniv. — A451

2003, Mar. 18 *Perf. 14½x14*
1104 A451 52c multi 1.40 1.10

Famous Women — A452

Designs: No. 1105, 45c, Catherine Schleimer-Kill (1884-1973), feminist leader. No. 1106, 45c, Lou Koster (1889-1973), composer.

2003, Mar. 18 Photo. *Perf. 11½*
1105-1106 A452 Set of 2 2.40 1.90

Tourism — A453

Designs: 50c, Fontaine Marie Convent, Differdange. €1, Castle, Mamer. €2.50, St. Joseph Church, Esch-sur-Alzette, vert.

Perf. 14½x14, 14x14½
2003, Mar. 18 Litho.
1107-1109 A453 Set of 3 9.50 9.50

Luxembourg Athénée, 400th Anniv. — A454

2003, May 20 Litho. *Perf. 14¼x14½*
1110 A454 45c multi 1.10 1.00

Europa — A455

Poster art: 45c, 1952 poster for National Lottery, by Roger Gerson. 52c, 1924 poster for Third Commercial Fair, by Auguste Trémont.

2003, May 20 *Perf. 13¼x13*
1111-1112 A455 Set of 2 *2.25* 1.75

Bridges A456

Designs: 45c, Adolphe Bridge, 1903. 59c, Stierchen Bridge, 14th cent. (36x26mm). 89c, Victor Bodson Bridge, 1994 (36x26mm).

Photo. & Engr.
2003, May 20 *Perf. 11½*
1113-1115 A456 Set of 3 5.00 4.25

Electrification of Luxembourg, 75th Anniv. — A457

Litho. & Embossed
2003, Sept. 23 *Perf. 13¼x13*
1116 A457 A multi 1.25 1.25

Sold for 50c on day of issue.

Breastfeeding A458

2003, Sept. 23 Litho. *Perf. 13½*
1117 A458 A multi 1.25 1.25

Sold for 50c on day of issue.

Gaart an Heem Agricultural Cooperatives, 75th Anniv. — A459

Gardeners with: 25c, Spade. A, Basket and rake. €2, Watering can.

2003, Sept. 23 *Perf. 14½x14*
1118-1120 A459 Set of 3 7.00 6.50

No. 1119 sold for 50c on day of issue.

Industrial Products Made in Luxembourg A460

Designs: 60c, Steel. 70c, Industrial valve. 80c, Polyester film.

2003, Oct. 1 Photo. *Perf. 11½*
1121-1123 A460 Set of 3 5.00 5.00

Grand Duke Henri Type of 2001-03

Photo. & Engr.
2004-2010 *Perf. 11¾x11½*
Vignette Color

1124	A438	5c violet brn	.25	.25
1125	A438	10c black	.30	.30
1126	A438	25c claret	.65	.65
1129	A438	50c black	1.25	1.25
1130	A438	60c blue	1.50	1.50
1131	A438	70c purple	1.75	1.75
1132	A438	80c olive black	2.10	2.00
1133	A438	90c brown	2.25	2.25
1133A	A438	€1 blue	2.60	2.60
		Nos. 1126-1133A (7)	12.10	12.00

Issued: 25c, 50c, 60c, 80c, 3/16/04; 70c, 90c, €1, 9/26/06; 5c, 10c, 12/7/10.

Emigrants to the United States — A461

Designs: 50c, Edward Steichen (1879-1973), photographer. 70c, Hugo Gernsbach (1884-1967), science fiction writer.

Photo. & Engr.
2004, Mar. 16 *Perf. 11½*
1134-1135 A461 Set of 2 3.25 3.00

Anniversaries of Commercial Events — A462

Designs: No. 1136, 50c, Commercial Union of Esch-sur-Alzette, cent. No. 1137, 50c, Luxembourg City Annual Street Market, 75th anniv.

2004, Mar. 16 **Litho.** ***Perf. 14¼***
1136-1137 A462 Set of 2 2.60 2.60

Mushrooms — A463

No. 1138: a, Cantharellus tubaeformis. b, Ramaria flava. c, Stropharia cyanea. d, Helvella lacunosa. e, Anthurus archeri. f, Clitopilus prunulus.

Die Cut Perf. 10

2004, Mar. 16 **Litho.**

Self-Adhesive

1138 Booklet pane of 6 4.50
a.-c. A463 10c Any single .25 .25
d.-f. A463 50c Any single 1.25 1.25
Complete booklet, 2 #1138 9.00

European Parliament Elections — A464

2004, May 9 **Litho.** ***Perf. 13¼x13***
1139 A464 50c multi 1.25 1.25

2004 Summer Olympics, Athens — A465

European Sports Education Year — A466

2004, May 9 **Photo.** ***Perf. 11½x11¾***
1140 A465 50c multi 1.25 1.25
1141 A466 60c multi 1.40 1.40

European School, 50th Anniv. — A467

2004, May 9 **Litho.** ***Perf. 14¼x14½***
1142 A467 70c multi 1.75 1.75

Europa — A468

Designs: 50c, Stone bridge over Schiessentuempel. 60c, Bourscheid Beach, Bourscheid Castle.

2004, May 9 ***Perf. 13¼x13***
1143-1144 A468 Set of 2 *3.00 3.00*

Luxembourg Stock Exchange, 75th Anniv. — A469

Perf. 11¼x11½

2004, Sept. 28 **Litho. & Engr.**
1145 A469 50c multi 1.25 1.25

Food Products Made in Luxembourg A470

Designs: 35c, Baked goods, beer. 60c, Meats, wine. 70c, Dairy products.

Perf. 13½x13¾

2004, Sept. 28 **Litho.**
1146-1148 A470 Set of 3 4.00 4.00

National Museum of History and Art — A471

Designs: 50c, Museum building. €1.10, Young Woman with a Fan, by Luigi Rubio. €3, Charity, by Lucas Cranach the Elder or Lucas Cranach the Younger.

2004, Sept. 28 **Photo.** ***Perf. 11¾***
1149-1151 A471 Set of 3 11.50 11.50

World War II Liberation, 60th Anniv. — A472

2004, Dec. 7 **Litho.** ***Perf. 14x13½***
1152 A472 70c multi 1.90 1.90

Luxembourg's Presidency of European Union — A473

No. 1153: a, Building with glass facade. b, Arch, Echternach Basilica. c, Vineyard along Moselle River. d, Rusted iron girder.

Serpentine Die Cut 8¼ Vert.

2005, Jan. 25 **Photo.**

Self-Adhesive

1153 Booklet pane of 4 5.00
a.-d. A473 A any single 1.25 1.25
Complete booklet, 2 #1153 10.00

On the day of issue, Nos. 1153a-1153d each had a franking value of 50c, but complete booklet sold for €3.80.

Rotary International, Cent. — A474

2005, Mar. 15 **Litho.** ***Perf. 13½x13***
1154 A474 50c multi 1.40 1.40

Ettelbrück Neuro-psychiatric Medical Center, 150th Anniv. — A475

2005, Mar. 15 ***Perf. 13½***
1155 A475 50c multi 1.40 1.40

76th Intl. Congress of Applied Mathematics and Mechanics — A476

2005, Mar. 15
1156 A476 60c multi 1.60 1.60

Benelux Parliament, 50th Anniv. — A477

2005, Mar. 15 ***Perf. 13¼x12¾***
1157 A477 60c multi 1.60 1.60

Tourism — A478

Designs: 50c, Shoe factory, Kayl-Tétange. 60c, Village scene and website address of National Tourist Office (44x31mm). €1, Statue of St. Eloi, Rodange, and foundry worker.

Perf. 14x13¼, 12¾ (60c)

2005, Mar. 15
1158-1160 A478 Set of 3 5.50 5.50

Opening of Grand Duchess Joséphine-Charlotte Concert Hall — A479

2005, May 24 ***Perf. 13¼x13¾***
1161 A479 50c multi 1.25 1.25

Europa — A480

Designs: 50c, Judd mat Gaardebounen (pork and beans). 60c, Feirstengszalot (beef, egg and pickle salad).

2005, May 24 ***Perf. 13½***
1162-1163 A480 Set of 2 *2.75 2.75*

Railways — A481

Designs: 50c, Niederpallen Station, CVE 357 car of De Jhangeli narrow-gauge railway. 60c, AL-T3 locomotive. €2.50, PH 408 passenger car.

2005, May 24 **Photo.** ***Perf. 11½***
1164-1166 A481 Set of 3 9.00 9.00

Hand Lifting Self-Adhesive Paper From Backing — A482

Coil Stamps

Serpentine Die Cut 11x11¼

2005, May 24 **Self-Adhesive**

1167 Vert. strip of 4 2.50
a. A482 25c dark red & multi .60 .60
b. A482 25c red orange & multi .60 .60
c. A482 25c orange & multi .60 .60
d. A482 25c yellow & multi .60 .60
1168 Vert. strip of 4 5.00
a. A482 50c dark green & multi 1.25 1.25
b. A482 50c green & multi 1.25 1.25
c. A482 50c emerald & multi 1.25 1.25
d. A482 50c yellow green & multi 1.25 1.25

Rolls of 100 of the 25c stamps sold for €24, and rolls of 100 of the 50c stamps sold for €48.

Famous People — A483

Designs: 50c, Jean-Pierre Pescatore (1793-1855), philanthropist. 90c, Marcel Reuland (1905-56), writer. €1, Marie-Henriette Steil (1898-1930), writer, vert.

Photo. & Engr.

2005, Sept. 27 ***Perf. 11½***
1169-1171 A483 Set of 3 6.00 6.00

Butterflies — A484

Designs: 35c, Papilio machaon. 70c, Argynnis paphia, vert. €1.80, Lysandra coridon.

2005, Sept. 27 **Litho.**
1172-1174 A484 Set of 3 7.25 7.25

Rocks — A485

No. 1175: a, Schist. b, Rocks with iron (minerai de fer). c, Luxembourg sandstone. d, Conglomerate rocks.

Serpentine Die Cut 12¾ Vert.

2005, Sept. 27 **Self-Adhesive**

1175 Booklet pane of 4 4.75
a.-d. A485 A Any single 1.10 1.10
Complete booklet, 2 #1175 9.50

The complete booklet sold for €3.80, but each stamp had a franking value of 50c on the day of issue.

Seeing Eye Dog — A486

Litho. & Embossed

2005, Dec. 6 ***Perf. 13x13¼***
1176 A486 70c dk blue & lemon 1.75 1.75

25th Wedding Anniversary of Grand Duke Henri and Grand Duchess Maria Teresa — A487

2006, Feb. 7 **Litho.** ***Perf. 13¼x13¾***
1177 A487 50c multi 1.25 1.25

Souvenir Sheet

Perf. 13¼x13

1178 A487 €2.50 multi 6.25 6.25

No. 1178 contains one 26x37mm stamp.

Blood Donation — A488

2006, Mar. 14 **Litho.** ***Perf. 13¼***
1179 A488 50c multi 1.25 1.25

Tourism — A489

Designs: No. 1180, 50c, Parc Merveilleux, Bettembourg. No. 1181, 50c, Birelerhaff Pigeon Tower, Sandweiler, vert.

2006, Mar. 14 ***Perf. 11½***
1180-1181 A489 Set of 2 2.40 1.25

Electrification of Railway Network, 50th Anniv. — A490

Designs: 50c, Train passing station. 70c, Train on bridge. €1, Railway workers repairing electrical wires, vert.

2006, Mar. 14 ***Perf. 13¼x13, 13x13¼***
1182-1184 A490 Set of 3 5.25 5.25

Personalized Stamp Website "meng.post.lu" — A491

2006, May 16 **Litho.** ***Perf. 11½***
1185 A491 A multi + label 1.40 1.40

No. 1185 sold for 50c on day of issue. Labels could be personalized for a fee.

Esch-sur-Alzette, Cent. — A492

2006, May 16 ***Perf. 13½***
1186 A492 50c multi 1.40 1.40

Soccer Teams in Luxembourg, Cent. — A493

2006 World Cup Soccer Championships, Germany — A494

2006, May 16 ***Perf. 13x13¼***
1187 A493 50c multi 1.40 1.40
1188 A494 90c multi 2.40 2.40

Europa — A495

Contest-winning cell phone photos: 50c, Hands making heart. 70c, People holding globe.

2006, May 16 ***Perf. 12½***
1189-1190 A495 Set of 2 3.25 3.25

State Council, 150th Anniv. — A496

Litho. & Embossed

2006, Sept. 26 ***Perf. 13½***
1191 A496 50c multi 1.25 1.25

Luxembourg Chess Federation, 75th Anniv. — A497

2006, Sept. 26
1192 A497 90c multi 2.25 2.25

Bank Sesquicentenaries A498

Designs: No. 1193, 50c, State Savings Bank (Spuerkeess). No. 1194, 50c, Dexia-BIL Bank.

2006, Sept. 26 **Litho.** ***Perf. 13¼x13***
1193-1194 A498 Set of 2 2.60 2.60

Fight Against Drug Addiction — A499

Designs: 50c, Children's drawing of man and "No Drugs" sign. €1, Ashtray with vegetables and cheese, vert.

2006, Sept. 26 ***Perf. 11½***
1195-1196 A499 Set of 2 3.75 3.75

Luxembourg Horticultural Federation, 75th Anniv. — A500

No. 1197: a, Flowers. b, Fruits and vegetables.

2006, Dec. 5 **Litho.** ***Perf. 13¼x13¾***
1197 A500 Horiz. pair 3.75 3.75
a.-b. 70c Either single 1.75 1.75

Luxembourg, 2007 European Cultural Capital — A501

No. 1198 — Silhouettes of deer and men with deer heads with background color of: a, Blue. b, Orange. c, Bright yellow green. d, Red violet.

Serpentine Die Cut 8½ Vert.

2007, Jan. 30 **Litho.**
1198 Booklet pane of 4 5.25
a.-d. A501 A Any single 1.25 1.25
Complete booklet, 2 #1198 10.50

Nos. 1198a-1198d each sold for 50c on day of issue.

Luxembourg Caritas, 75th Anniv. — A502

2007, Mar. 20 **Litho.** ***Perf. 11½***
1199 A502 50c multi 1.40 1.40

Luxembourg Automobile Club, 75th Anniv. — A503

2007, Mar. 20
1200 A503 50c multi 1.40 1.40

Treaty of Rome, 50th Anniv. — A504

Designs: 70c, Delegates. €1, Text and stars.

2007, Mar. 20 ***Perf. 13x13¼***
1201-1202 A504 Set of 2 4.75 4.75

"Postes" A505

Denomination A506

Serpentine Die Cut 11x11¼

2007, Mar. 20 **Photo.**

Self-Adhesive

Coil Stamps

1203	A505 25c pur & multi	.70	.70
1204	A506 25c brn & multi	.70	.70
1205	A505 25c dk bl & multi	.70	.70
1206	A506 25c dk grn & multi	.70	.70
a.	Vert. strip of 4, #1203-1206	2.80	
1207	A505 50c red vio & multi	1.40	1.40
1208	A506 50c red & multi	1.40	1.40
1209	A505 50c bl & multi	1.40	1.40
1210	A506 50c grn & multi	1.40	1.40
a.	Vert. strip of 4, #1207-1210	5.60	
	Nos. 1203-1210 (8)	8.40	8.40

Europa — A507

Designs: 50c, Scout campground. 70c, Scouts, globe, knot.

2007, May 22 **Litho.** ***Perf. 13x13¼***
1211-1212 A507 Set of 2 3.25 3.25

Scouting, cent.

Town Centenaries A508

Designs: No. 1213, 50c, Differdange. No. 1214, 50c, Dudelenge. No. 1215, 50c, Ettelbruck. No. 1216, 50c, Rumelange.

2007, May 22 **Photo.** ***Perf. 11½***
1213-1216 A508 Set of 4 5.50 5.50

Places of Culture — A509

Designs: 50c, Rockhal. 70c, Grand Duke Jean Museum of Modern Art. €1, Neumünster Abbey.

2007, May 22 ***Perf. 12½***
1217-1219 A509 Set of 3 6.00 6.00

"Transborderism" A510

2007, Sept. 3 **Photo.** ***Perf. 11½***
1220 A510 50c multi 1.40 1.40

Rotunda of Luxembourg Train Station — A511

2007, Sept. 3 **Photo. & Engr.**
1221 A511 70c multi 1.90 1.90

See Belgium No. 2253.

Casa Luxemburg, Sibiu, Romania — A512

2007, Sept. 3 **Litho.** ***Perf. 13x13¼***
1222 A512 70c multi 1.90 1.90

See Romania Nos. 4993-4994.

Luxembourg Army Peace-keeping Missions — A513

2007, Sept. 3 **Photo.** ***Perf. 11½***
1223 A513 70c multi 1.90 1.90

Souvenir Sheet

Roman Mosaic, Vichten A514

No. 1224: a, Thalia and Euterpe. b, Terpsichore and Melpomene. c, Clio and Urania. d, Polymnia and Erato. e, Calliope and Homer. Nos. 1224a-1224d are 58x29mm octagonal stamps, No. 1224e is a 55x55mm diamond-shaped stamp.

2007, Sept. 3 **Litho.** ***Perf. 14¼***
1224 A514 Sheet of 5 8.25 8.25
a.-d. 50c Any single 1.40 1.40
e. €1 multi 2.60 2.60

Esch-sur-Sure Dam — A515

Uewersauer Stauséi — A516

Serpentine Die Cut 12½x13½

2007, Dec. 4 **Litho.** **Self-Adhesive**
1225 Horiz. pair 4.25
a. A515 70c multi 2.10 2.10
b. A516 70c multi 2.10 2.10

St. Willibrord (658-739) — A517

2008, Mar. 18 **Litho.** ***Perf. 13***
1226 A517 50c multi 1.60 1.60

European Investment Bank, 50th Anniv. — A518

2008, Mar. 18 *Perf. 13x13¼*
1227 A518 70c purple & silver 2.25 2.25

Eurosystem, 10th Anniv. — A519

2008, Mar. 18 *Perf. 13½x13¾*
1228 A519 €1 multi 3.25 3.25

Luxembourg Philharmonic Orchestra, 75th Anniv. — A520

Henri Pensis (1900-58), Conductor A521

2008, Mar. 18
1229 A520 50c multi 1.60 1.60
1230 A521 70c multi 2.25 2.25

2008 Summer Olympics, Beijing — A522

2008, May 20 Litho. *Perf. 14x13½*
1231 A522 70c multi 2.25 2.25

Luxembourg Basketball Federation, 75th Anniv. — A523

Luxembourg Soccer Federation, Cent. — A524

2008, May 20 *Perf. 12½*
1232 A523 A multi 1.60 1.60
1233 A524 A multi 1.60 1.60

Nos. 1232 and 1233 each sold for 50c on day of issue.

Europa — A525

Smiling letter with wings: 50c, Standing on hand. 70c, Flying.

2008, May 20
1234-1235 A525 Set of 2 4.00 4.00

Tourism — A526

Designs: No. 1236, A, Bridge, Diekirch, and city arms. No. 1237, A, Building, Leudelange, and city arms. No. 1238, A, Rindschleiden Church, Wahl, vert.

2008, May 20 *Perf. 11½*
1236-1238 A526 Set of 3 4.75 4.75

Diekirch, 125th anniv., Leudelange, 150th anniv. Nos. 1236-1238 each sold for 50c on day of issue.

Medico-social League, Cent. — A527

2008, Sept. 30 Litho. *Perf. 13¾*
1239 A527 A multi 1.40 1.40

Sold for 50c on day of issue.

Agricultural Technical School, Ettelbruck, 125th Anniv. — A528

2008, Sept. 30
1240 A528 A multi 1.40 1.40

Sold for 50c on day of issue.

Federation of Popular Education Associations, Cent. — A529

2008, Sept. 30 *Perf. 13x13¼*
1241 A529 A multi 1.40 1.40

Sold for 50c on day of issue.

Natl. League for the Protection of Animals, Cent. — A530

2008, Sept. 30
1242 A530 A multi 1.40 1.40

Sold for 50c on day of issue.

NATO Maintenance and Supply Agency, 50th Anniv. — A531

2008, Sept. 30
1243 A531 70c multi 2.00 2.00

Greetings — A532

Winning art from children's stamp design contest by: 70c, A. Wainer. €1, S. Rauschenberger.

2008, Sept. 30 *Perf. 11½*
1244-1245 A532 Set of 2 4.75 4.75

A533

A534

Different shapes of colored background lines with "ATR" at: No. 1246, LR. No. 1247, UL. No. 1248, LL. No. 1249, UR.

Different shapes of colored background lines with "A" at: No. 1250, LL. No. 1251, UL. No. 1252, LR. No. 1253, UR.

Coil Stamps

Serpentine Die Cut 11

2008, Sept. 30 Self-Adhesive
1246 A533 ATR blue .70 .70
1247 A533 ATR purple .70 .70
1248 A533 ATR green .70 .70
1249 A533 ATR red .70 .70
a. Vert. strip of 4, #1246-1249 2.80
1250 A534 A multi 1.40 1.40
1251 A534 A multi 1.40 1.40
1252 A534 A multi 1.40 1.40
1253 A534 A multi 1.40 1.40
a. Vert. strip of 4, #1250-1253 5.60
Nos. 1246-1253 (8) 8.40 8.40

On day of issue, Nos. 1246-1249 each sold for 25c, Nos. 1250-1253, for 50c.

Happiness — A535

No. 1254: a, Bowling pins, denomination over red violet. b, Gift, denomination over yellow green. c, Wrapped candies, denomination over green. d, Wrapped candies, denomination over blue. e, Gift, denomination over green. f, Bowling pins, denomination over yellow green. g, Dice, "A" over red violet. h, Drum and sticks, "A" over yellow green. i, Four-leaf clovers, "A" over green. j, Four-leaf clovers, "A" over blue. k, Drum and sticks, "A" over green. l, Dice, "A" over yellow green.

Die Cut Perf. 10 on 3 Sides

2008, Sept. 30 Self-Adhesive
1254 Booklet pane of 12 12.00
a.-f. A535 20c Any single .55 .55
g.-l. A535 A Any single 1.40 1.40

Nos. 1254g-1254l each sold for 50c on day of issue.

New Courthouse of Court of Justice of the European Communities A536

2008, Dec. 2 Litho. *Perf. 14x13¼*
1255 A536 70c multi 1.90 1.90

Election of Holy Roman Emperor Henry VII (c. 1269-1313), 700th Anniv. — A537

2008, Dec. 2 *Perf. 13¼x13*
1256 A537 €1 multi 2.60 2.60

Introduction of the Euro, 10th Anniv. — A538

2009, Mar. 17 Litho. *Perf. 12½*
1257 A538 A multi 1.25 1.25

No. 1257 sold for 50c on day of issue.

Luxembourg Aero Club, Cent. — A539

New Airport Terminal — A540

No. 1258: a, Satellite, airplane, hang glider, left half of balloon. b, Right half of balloon, glider, parachutist, jet plane.

2009, Mar. 17 *Perf. 11½*
1258 A539 50c Horiz. pair, #a-b 2.60 2.60
1259 A540 90c multi 2.25 2.25

Natl. Federation of Fire Fighters, 125th Anniv. — A541

Designs: 20c, Modern fire truck. A, Fire fighter rescuing child. €2, Antique fire truck.

2008, Mar. 17 *Perf. 13x13¼*
1260-1262 A541 Set of 3 7.00 7.00

No. 1261 sold for 50c on day of issue.

Postmen's Federation, Cent. — A542

General Confederation of the Civil Service, Cent. — A543

Natl. Federation of Railroad and Transportation Workers, Cent. — A544

2009, Mar. 17 *Perf. 14x13¼*
1263 A542 50c multi 1.25 1.25
1264 A543 A multi 1.25 1.25
1265 A544 A multi 1.25 1.25
Nos. 1263-1265 (3) 3.75 3.75

On day of issue, Nos. 1264-1265 each sold for 50c.

June 7 European Elections — A545

2009, May 12 Litho. *Perf. 13*
1266 A545 50c multi 1.40 1.40

National Research Fund, 10th Anniv. — A546

2009, May 12 *Perf. 13½*
1267 A546 A multi 1.40 1.40

No. 1267 sold for 50c on day of issue.

Children's Houses, 125th Anniv. — A547

2009, May 12 *Perf. 12½*
1268 A547 A multi 1.40 1.40

No. 1268 sold for 50c on day of issue.

Europa — A548

Designs: 50c, Father and child watching comet. 70c, Galileo, telescope, planets.

2009, May 12 ***Perf. 13½***
1269-1270 A548 Set of 2 3.25 3.25

Intl. Year of Astronomy.

Personalized Stamps — A549

Stripe color: A, Red. A Europe, Blue.

2009, May 12 ***Perf. 11¾x11½***
Stamp + Label
1271-1272 A549 Set of 2 3.25 3.25

On day of issue, No. 1271 sold for 50c; No. 1272, 70c. Labels bearing text "PostMusée" and pictures are generic and sold for these prices. Labels could be personalized for an additional fee.

Famous People — A550

Designs: 70c, Foni Tissen (1909-75), painter. 90c, Charles Bernhoeft (1859-1933), photographer. €1, Henri Tudor (1859-1928), electrical engineer.

Litho. & Engr.
2009, May 12 ***Perf. 13½***
1273-1275 A550 Set of 3 7.00 7.00

Vianden Castle — A551

Perf. 13¼x12¾
2009, Sept. 16 **Litho.**
1276 A551 70c multi 2.00 2.00

Louis Braille (1809-52), Educator of the Blind — A552

Litho. & Embossed
2009, Sept. 16 ***Perf. 13¼x13***
1277 A552 90c multi 2.60 2.60

Railroads in Luxembourg, 150th Anniv. — A553

Designs: 50c, Modern electric train. €1, Older electric train. €3, Steam locomotive.

2009, Sept. 16 **Litho.** ***Perf. 12½***
1278-1280 A553 Set of 3 13.00 13.00

Souvenir Sheet

Luxembourg Federation of Philatelic Societies, 75th Anniv. — A554

No. 1281: a, Luxembourg #198. b, Gate of Three Towers.

Litho. & Embossed
2009, Sept. 16 ***Perf. 13¾x14***
1281 A554 Sheet of 2 3.50 3.50
a. 50c multi 1.50 1.50
b. 70c multi 2.00 2.00

Johannes Gutenberg (c. 1390-1468), Inventor of Movable Type Presses A555

Website Addresses and Movable Type A556

2009, Dec. 1 **Litho.** ***Perf. 13¼x13½***
1282 A555 50c multi 1.50 1.50
1283 A556 70c multi 2.10 2.10

See Switzerland No. 1344.

Schengen Convention, 25th Anniv. — A557

2010, Mar. 16 **Litho.** ***Perf. 13½x13***
1284 A557 70c multi 1.90 1.90

Luxembourg Pavilion, Expo 2010, Shanghai A558

2010, Mar. 16 ***Perf. 14x13½***
1285 A558 90c multi 2.50 2.50

Eisch Valley Castles A559

No. 1286 — Various castles with country name at: a, UL. b, LR.

Serpentine Die Cut 12¼x13¼
2010, Mar. 16 **Self-Adhesive**
1286 Horiz. pair 4.00
a.-b. A559 A Either single 1.90 1.90

On day of issue, Nos. 1286a-1287a each sold for 70c.

Countdown 2010 — A560

Designs: 70c, Arnica montana. €1, Mussels.

2010, Mar. 16 ***Perf. 11½***
1287-1288 A560 Set of 2 4.75 4.75

A561

Royalty A562

Designs: 50c, Grand Duke Henri. €1, Grand Duchess Charlotte (1896-1985).

€3, Grand Duke Henri and Grand Duchess Maria Teresa.

2010, Mar. 16 ***Perf. 11½***
1289-1290 A561 Set of 2 4.25 4.25
Souvenir Sheet
1291 A562 €3 multi 8.25 8.25

Grand Duke Henri's accession to the throne, 10th anniv. (No. 1289).

Marriage of John of Luxembourg and Elizabeth of Bohemia, 700th Anniv. — A563

Photo. & Engr.
2010, June 16 ***Perf. 11¾x11¼***
1292 A563 70c multi 1.75 1.75

Accession to the throne of Bohemia by the House of Luxembourg. See Czech Republic No. 3457.

Europa — A564

Designs: 50c, Child and dragon reading book. 70c, Girl with lasso riding book.

2010, June 16 **Litho.** ***Perf. 13½***
1293-1294 A564 Set of 2 3.00 3.00

Outdoor Activities — A565

Designs: No. 1295, A, Motorcycling. No. 1296, A Europe, Camping.

2010, June 16 ***Perf. 13½x13***
1295-1296 A565 Set of 2 3.00 3.00

On day of issue, No. 1295 sold for 50c, and No. 1296 sold for 70c. See Nos. 1337-1338.

Souvenir Sheet

Philalux 2011 Intl. Philatelic Exhibition, Luxembourg — A566

No. 1297 — Various sites in Luxembourg: a, 50c (38x38mm). b, 70c, (38x38mm). c, €3, (60x38mm).

Perf. 13¾, 13¼x13¾ (#1297c)
2010, June 16
1297 A566 Sheet of 3 10.50 10.50
a. 50c multi 1.25 1.25
b. 70c multi 1.75 1.75
c. €3 multi 7.50 7.50

Souvenir Sheet

Superjhemp, Comic Strip by Lucien Czuga — A567

No. 1298: a, Bernie the Dog. b, Man smoking pipe. c, Woman, vert. d, Superjhemp. e, Man with glasses, vert.

Serpentine Die Cut 12¼
2010, June 16 **Self-Adhesive**
1298 A567 Sheet of 5 6.25 6.25
a.-e. A Any single 1.25 1.25

On day of issue, Nos. 1298a-1298e each sold for 50c.

A568

Winning Art in Children's "Fight Against Poverty" Stamp Design Contest — A569

2010, Sept. 27 **Litho.** ***Perf. 11½***
1299 A568 A multi 1.25 1.25
1300 A569 A Europe multi 1.75 1.75

On day of issue No. 1299 sold for 50c and No. 1300 sold for 70c.

Famous People — A570

Designs: 70c, Anne Beffort (1880-1966), educator and writer. 90c, Jean Soupert (1834-1910), rose cultivator. €1, Nicolas Frantz (1899-1985), cyclist.

Litho. & Engr.
2010, Sept. 27 ***Perf. 13½***
1301-1303 A570 Set of 3 6.75 6.75

Bagatelle Rose — A571

Bona Rose — A572

Bordeaux Rose — A573

Reine Marguerite d'Italie Rose — A574

Souvenir de Maria de Zayas Rose — A575

Clotilde Rose — A576

Prince Jean de Luxembourg Rose — A577

Pierre Watine Rose — A578

Ivan Misson Rose — A579

William Notting Rose — A580

Serpentine Die Cut 9¾

2010, Sept. 27 Litho.

Self-Adhesive

1304	Booklet pane of 10	12.50	
a.	A571 A multi	1.25	1.25
b.	A572 A multi	1.25	1.25
c.	A573 A multi	1.25	1.25
d.	A574 A multi	1.25	1.25
e.	A575 A multi	1.25	1.25
f.	A576 A multi	1.25	1.25
g.	A577 A multi	1.25	1.25
h.	A578 A multi	1.25	1.25
i.	A579 A multi	1.25	1.25
j.	A580 A multi	1.25	1.25

Nos. 1304a-1304j each sold for 50c on day of issue.

Luxembourg Maritime Cluster — A581

No. 1305 — Ships with lion emblem at: a, Left. b, Right.

2010, Dec. 7 Litho. *Perf. 11½*
1305 A581 A Horiz. pair, #a-b 4.75 4.75

Nos. 1305a and 1305b each sold for 85c on day of issue.

European Year of Volunteering A582

2011, Mar. 15 *Perf. 13¼x13*
1306 A582 A multi 1.75 1.75

No. 1306 sold for 60c on day of issue.

Royalty — A583

Designs: 85c, Prince Guillaume, 30th birthday. €1.10, Grand Duke Jean, 90th birthday.

2011, Mar. 15 *Perf. 11½*
1307-1308 A583 Set of 2 5.50 5.50

Anniversaries — A584

Designs: No. 1309, 60c, Luxembourg Federation of Quilleurs (nine-pin bowling), 50th anniv. No. 1310, 60c, Amnesty International, 50th anniv. No. 1311, 60c, Stamp Day, 75th anniv.

2011, Mar. 15
1309-1311 A584 Set of 3 5.00 5.00

Europa — A585

Designs: 60c, Forest. 80c, Hills.

2011, May 17 Litho. *Perf. 13½*
1312-1313 A585 Set of 2 4.25 4.25

Intl. Year of Forests.

Viticulture — A586

Designs: 60c, Sun with grapes, wine glass and bottle. 85c, Cork of Crémant de Luxembourg sparkling wine bottle.

2011, May 17 *Perf. 11½*
1314-1315 A586 Set of 2 4.25 4.25

Federation of Viticulture Associations of Luxembourg, cent. (No. 1314), Crémant de Luxembourg, 20th anniv. (No. 1315).

Personalized Stamps A587

Denominations: 60c, 85c, vert.

Perf. 11¼x11½, 11½x11¼

2011, May 17 Self-Adhesive
1316-1317 A587 Set of 2 4.25 4.25

Vignettes showing picture and "Mäi Moment / Meng Photo / Meng Post" text are generic and sold at their face values. Vignettes could be personalized for an additional fee.

Miniature Sheet

The Last Knight, Comic Strip by Lucien Czuga and Andy Genen A588

No. 1318: a, Dragon. b, Knight wearing sunglasses, horiz. c, Man, horiz. d, Cat.

Serpentine Die Cut 12¼

2011, May 17 Self-Adhesive
1318 A588 Sheet of 4 7.00
a.-d. A Any single 1.75 1.75

On day of issue, Nos. 1318a-1318d each sold for 60c.

Luxembourg Consumers Union, 50th Anniv. — A589

2011, Sept. 27 *Perf. 11½*
1319 A589 60c multi 1.75 1.75

Campaign Against AIDS, 30th Anniv. — A590

2011, Sept. 27
1320 A590 60c multi 1.75 1.75

Cercle Cité, Luxembourg — A591

2011, Sept. 27
1321 A591 A multi 1.75 1.75

No. 1321 sold for 60c on day of issue.

Franz Liszt (1811-86), Composer — A592

2011, Sept. 27 *Perf. 14¼x14¾*
1322 A592 85c multi 2.40 2.40

Chemin de la Corniche, Luxembourg — A593

2011, Sept. 27 *Perf. 11½*
1323 A593 85c multi 2.40 2.40

Post Checks, Cent. — A594

2011, Dec. 6 Litho. *Perf. 11½x11¾*
1324 A594 60c multi 1.60 1.60

Souvenir Sheet

Echternach Hopping Procession (UNESCO Intangible Heritage) — A595

No. 1325 — Procession participants and: a, Left side of scarf. b, Right side of scarf.

2011, Dec. 6 *Perf. 14*
1325 A595 Sheet of 2 4.00 4.00
a. 60c multi 1.60 1.60
b. 85c multi 2.40 2.40

Architecture — A596

No. 1326 — Designs: a, Eislek. b, Réidener Streech. c, Iechternacher Streech. d, Minett.

Serpentine Die Cut 12½

2011, Dec. 6 Self-Adhesive
1326 Booklet pane of 4 6.50
a.-d. A596 A Any single 1.60 1.60
Complete booklet, 2 #1326 13.00

Nos. 1326a-1326d each sold for 60c on day of issue.

Luxembourg Amateur Radio Society, 75th Anniv. — A597

2012, Mar. 13 *Perf. 11½*
1327 A597 60c multi 1.60 1.60

Grand Ducal Institute Arts and Letters Section, 50th Anniv. — A598

2012, Mar. 13
1328 A598 60c multi 1.60 1.60

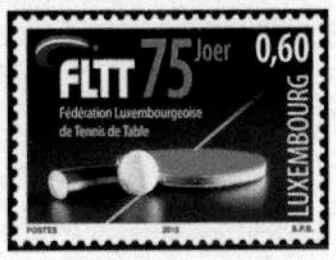

Luxembourg Table Tennis Federation, 75th Anniv. — A599

2012, Mar. 13
1329 A599 60c multi 1.60 1.60

Introduction of Euro Currency, 10th Anniv. — A600

Litho. & Embossed

2012, Mar. 13 *Perf. 13*
1330 A600 85c multi 2.25 2.25

Natl. Institute of Statistics and Economic Studies, 50th Anniv. — A601

2012, May 15 Litho. *Perf. 12½*
1331 A601 60c multi 1.60 1.60

Luxembourg Olympic Committee, Cent. — A602

2012 Summer Olympics, London — A603

2012, May 15 *Perf. 14¼x14¾*
1332 A602 60c multi 1.60 1.60
1333 A603 €1.10 multi 3.00 3.00

Europa — A604

Luxembourg tourism website address and various Luxembourg buildings and monuments: 60c, 85c.

2012, May 15 *Perf. 13½*
1334-1335 A604 Set of 2 4.00 4.00

Miniature Sheet

Characters from Mil's Adventures, Comic Strip by Gab Weis — A605

No. 1336 — Various unnamed characters with country name in: a, Red violet (Mil). b, Green. c, Orange. d, Lilac, vert. e, Red violet (2 characters), vert.

Serpentine Die Cut 12¼

2012, May 15 **Self-Adhesive**

1336 A605 Sheet of 5 8.00
a.-e. A Any single 1.60 1.60

On day of issue, Nos. 1336a-1336e each sold for 60c.

Outdoor Activities Type of 2010

Designs: 60c, Paragliding. 85c, Diving.

2012, Sept. 25 ***Perf. 13¼x13***
1337-1338 A565 Set of 2 3.75 3.75

A606

Potable Water — A607

2012, Sept. 25 ***Perf. 11½***
1339 A606 60c multi 1.50 1.50
1340 A607 85c multi 2.25 2.25

Architecture — A608

Paintings by Christian Frantzen of: €1.20, Footbridge, Esch-sur-Alzette. €2.20, Belval-Université Station, Esch-sur-Alzette. €4, Pfaffenthal-Upper Town Link, Luxembourg.

2012, Sept. 25
1341-1343 A608 Set of 3 19.00 19.00

Wedding of Prince Guillaume and Countess Stéphanie de Lannoy — A609

Designs: 60c, Couple. 85c, Couple, diff.

2012, Sept. 25 ***Perf. 13½***
1344 A609 60c multi 1.50 1.50

Souvenir Sheet

1345 Sheet of 2, #1344, 1345a 3.75 3.75
a. A609 85c multi 2.25 2.25

Souvenir Sheet

Wedding of Prince Guillaume and Countess Stéphanie de Lannoy — A610

2012, Oct. 20 ***Perf. 13¼***
1346 A610 €4 multi 10.50 10.50

European Court of Justice, 60th Anniv. — A611

2012, Dec. 4 ***Perf. 12½***
1347 A611 85c maroon & lt blue 2.25 2.25

European Year of Citizens — A612

2013, Mar. 12 ***Perf. 13¼x13***
1348 A612 60c multi 1.60 1.60

Grand Duke Adolphe Union, 150th Anniv. — A613

2013, Mar. 12 ***Perf. 11½***
1349 A613 60c multi 1.60 1.60

Emile Metz Private Technical High School, Cent. — A614

2013, Mar. 12
1350 A614 60c multi 1.60 1.60

Round Table Luxembourg, 50th Anniv. — A615

2013, Mar. 12
1351 A615 60c multi 1.60 1.60

Holy Roman Emperor Henry VII (c.1275-1313) A616

2013, Mar. 12
1352 A616 €1.10 multi 3.00 3.00

Famous Men — A617

Designs: No. 1353, 60c, Nicolas Adames (1813-87), theologian. No. 1354, 60c, Putty Stein (1888-1955), composer.

2013, May 2
1353-1354 A617 Set of 2 3.25 3.25

Europa — A618

Postal vehicles: 60c, Citroen 2 CV AZU. 85c, Renault Kangoo.

2013, May 2 ***Perf. 13x13¼***
1355-1356 A618 Set of 2 3.75 3.75

15th Games of the Small States of Europe, Luxembourg — A619

2013, May 2 ***Perf. 11½***
1357 A619 Horiz. pair 3.25 3.25
a.-b. 60c Either single 1.60 1.60

Souvenir Sheet

100th Tour de France Bicycle Race A620

2013, May 2 ***Perf. 12***
1358 A620 €4 multi 10.50 10.50

Completion of 11th Turbine for Société Electrique de l'Our — A621

2013, Sept. 24 ***Perf. 11½***
1359 A621 60c multi 1.60 1.60

Wild Cats — A622

Designs: 20c, Panthera tigris sumatrae. 30c, Lynx lynx. 60c, Felis silvestris.

2013, Sept. 24
1360-1362 A622 Set of 3 3.00 3.00

Souvenir Sheet

Selection of "The Family of Man" Photographic Exhibition to UNESCO Memory of the World Register — A623

No. 1363: a, Photograph of crowd. b, Self-portrait of Edward Steichen.

2013, Sept. 24 ***Perf. 13¾x14***
1363 A623 Sheet of 2 4.00 4.00
a. 60c blue & black 1.60 1.60
b. 85c blue & black 2.25 2.25

A624

A625

A626

A627

Serpentine Die Cut 11

2013, Sept. 24 **Self-Adhesive**

Coil Stamps

1364 Vert. strip of 4 6.50
a. A624 (60c) multi 1.60 1.60
b. A625 (60c) multi 1.60 1.60
c. A626 (60c) multi 1.60 1.60
d. A627 (60c) multi 1.60 1.60

Moselle Valley A628

No. 1365 — Various buildings and: a, Bridge over river in foreground. b, Moselle River running through town.

Serpentine Die Cut 12½x13½

2013, Sept. 24 **Self-Adhesive**

1365 A628 Horiz. pair 4.50
a.-b. (85c) Either single 2.25 2.25

Pierre Werner (1913-2002), Prime Minister — A629

2013, Dec. 3 **Litho.** ***Perf. 11½***
1366 A629 60c multi 1.75 1.75

Mushrooms — A630

Designs: No. 1367, Pezize orangée. No. 1368, Bolet bai. No. 1369, Polypore versicolore. No. 1370, Amanite "tue-mouche." No. 1371, Vesse de loup perlée.

Serpentine Die Cut 12¼

2013, Dec. 3 **Litho.**

Booklet Stamps
Self-Adhesive

1367 A630 (60c) multi 1.75 1.75
1368 A630 (60c) multi 1.75 1.75
1369 A630 (60c) multi 1.75 1.75
1370 A630 (60c) multi 1.75 1.75
1371 A630 (60c) multi 1.75 1.75
a. Booklet pane of 10, 2 each #1367-1371 17.50
Nos. 1367-1371 (5) 8.75 8.75

Scouting in Luxembourg, Cent. — A631

2014, Mar. 11 **Litho.** ***Perf. 11½***
1372 A631 60c multi 1.75 1.75

Primary Schools Sports League, 50th Anniv. — A632

2014, Mar. 11 **Litho.** ***Perf. 11½***
1373 A632 60c multi 1.75 1.75

Ligue HMC, 50th Anniv. — A633

2014, Mar. 11 **Litho.** ***Perf. 11½***
1374 A633 60c multi 1.75 1.75

Luxembourg Red Cross, Cent. — A634

2014, Mar. 11 Litho. *Perf. 11½*

1375 A634 60c multi 1.75 1.75

Souvenir Sheet

Luxembourg Federation of Philatelic Societies, 80th Anniv. — A635

No. 1376: a, Magnifying glass, hand holding stamp tongs, children looking at stamps on stock page. b, Bridge, buildings.

2014, Mar. 11 Litho. *Perf. 13¾x14*

Silk-Faced Paper

1376	A635	Sheet of 2	4.00	4.00
a.		60c multi	1.75	1.75
b.		85c multi	2.25	2.25

May 25, 2014 European Elections — A636

2014, May 8 Litho. *Perf. 13¼x13*

1377 A636 60c multi 1.75 1.75

First Public Recital of Lyrics to National Anthem, 150th Anniv. — A637

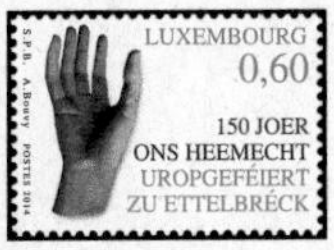

Independence, 175th Anniv. — A638

2014, May 8 Litho. *Perf. 11½*

1378 A637 60c multi 1.75 1.75

1379 A638 60c multi 1.75 1.75

Moselle Commission, 50th Anniv. — A639

2014, May 8 Litho. *Perf. 13x13¼*

1380 A639 85c multi 2.40 2.40

Europa — A640

Various musicians: 60c, 85c.

2014, May 8 Litho. *Perf. 12½*

1381-1382 A640 Set of 2 4.25 4.25

Souvenir Sheet

City of Luxembourg as UNESCO World Heritage Site, 20th Anniv. — A641

No. 1383 — Buildings and fortifications of Old City: a, 60c. b, 85c.

2014, May 8 Litho. *Perf. 13¾x14*

1383	A641	Sheet of 2	4.25	4.25
a.		60c multi	1.75	1.75
b.		85c multi	2.40	2.40

German Invasion of Luxembourg, Cent. — A642

2014, Sept. 23 Litho. *Perf. 11½*

1384 A642 60c multi 1.50 1.50

World War I, cent.

A643

Winning Designs in Children's Art Contest on Soil and the Environment — A644

2014, Sept. 23 Litho. *Perf. 11½*

1385 A643 60c multi 1.50 1.50

1386 A644 85c multi 2.25 2.25

Famous People — A645

Designs: No. 1387, 60c, Samuel Hirsch (1809-89), rabbi. No. 1388, 60c, Nikolaus Hein (1889-1969), writer. No. 1389, 60c, Marie Speyer (1880-1914), educator.

2014, Sept. 23 Litho. *Perf. 11½*

1387-1389 A645 Set of 3 4.50 4.50

Vegetables — A646

Designs: 85c, Tragopogon porrifolius. €1, Pisum sativum. €1.10, Cichorium intybus.

2014, Sept. 23 Litho. *Perf. 11½*

1390-1392 A646 Set of 3 7.50 7.50

See Nos. 1410-1412, 1437-1439.

Accession to Throne of Grand Duke Jean, 50th Anniv. — A647

2014, Dec. 2 Litho. *Perf. 13¼x13*

1393 A647 (60c) multi 1.50 1.50

Grand Duke Henri — A648

Litho. & Engr.

2015, Mar. 3 *Perf. 13½x13*

Panel Color

1394	A648	L	green	1.40	1.40
1395	A648	E	blue	1.90	1.90
1396	A648	M	rose carmine	2.50	2.50
		Nos. 1394-1396 (3)		5.80	5.80

On day of issue, Nos. 1394-1396 each sold for 60c, 85c and €1.10 respectively.

Organized Philately in Luxembourg, 125th Anniv. — A649

2015, Mar. 3 Litho. *Perf. 11½*

1397 A649 60c multi 1.40 1.40

Order of Architects and Consulting Engineers, 25th Anniv. — A650

2015, Mar. 3 Litho. *Perf. 11½*

1398 A650 60c multi 1.40 1.40

Omega 90, 25th Anniv. — A651

2015, Mar. 3 Litho. *Perf. 11½*

1399 A651 60c multi 1.40 1.40

Creation of Grand Duchy of Luxembourg, 200th Anniv. — A652

2015, Mar. 3 Litho. *Perf. 11½*

1400 A652 60c multi 1.40 1.40

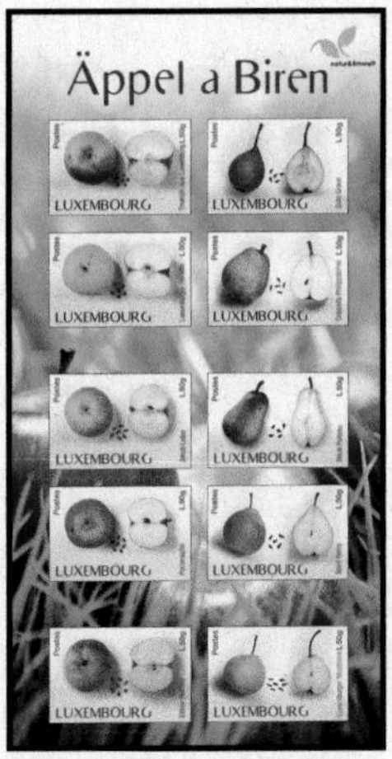

Fruit — A653

No. 1401 — Apple and pear varieties: a, Triumph aus Luxemburg apples. b, Gute Graue pears. c, Luxemburger Renette apples. d, Doppelte Philippsbirne pears. e, Jakob Lebel apples. f, Neue Poiteau pears. g, Porzenapfel apples. h, Saint Remy pears. i, Eifeler Rambur apples. j, Luxemburger Mostbirne pears.

Serpentine Die Cut 9¾

2015, Mar. 3 Litho.

Self-Adhesive

1401	A653	Booklet pane of 10	14.00	
a.-j.		L Any single	1.40	1.40

On day of issue, Nos. 1401a-1401j each sold for 60c.

Europa — A654

Designs: 60c, Building blocks. 85c, Doll and doll house furniture.

2015, May 5 Litho. *Perf. 13½*

1402-1403 A654 Set of 2 3.25 3.25

Famous Men — A655

Designs: No. 1404, 60c, Claus Cito (1882-1965), sculptor. No. 1405, 60c, Robert Krieps (1922-90), politician. No. 1406, 60c, René Engelmann (1880-1915), writer.

2015, May 5 Litho. *Perf. 11½*

1404-1406 A655 Set of 3 4.25 4.25

Miniature Sheet

End of World War II, 70th Anniv. A656

No. 1407: a, Railroad car and concentration camp gate (40x30mm). b, Star of David, triangles and "70" (40x30mm). c, Luxembourger in German uniform holding Luxembourg flag (30x30mm). d, Civil courage (30x30mm). e, Blindfolded person behind barbed wire (40x30mm). f, Resistance (40x30mm).

2015, May 5 Litho. *Perf. 12*

1407	A656	Sheet of 6	8.50	8.50
a.-f.		60c Any single	1.40	1.40

A657

Luxembourg Presidency of the Council of the European Union — A658

2015, July 1 Litho. *Perf. 12½x12*
Self-Adhesive

1408 A657 (60c) multi 1.40 1.40
1409 A658 (85c) multi 1.90 1.90

Vegetables Type of 2014

Root vegetables: 20c, Pastinaca sativa. 25c, Apium graveolens. 35c, Beta vulgaris.

2015, Sept. 22 Litho. *Perf. 11½*
1410-1412 A646 Set of 3 1.90 1.90

Luxembourg No. 1 — A659

2015, Sept. 22 Litho. *Perf. 15x14½*
1413 A659 70c blk & gold 1.60 1.60

Penny Black, 175th anniv.

Grand Duke Henri and Grand Duchess Maria Teresa A660

Litho. & Engr.

2015, Sept. 22 *Perf. 13*
1414 A660 70c multi 1.60 1.60

Opening of Wiltheim Wing of National Museum of History and Art — A661

Designs: 70c, Museum. 95c, Silver tea caddy made by Johann Michael Kutzer (1700-60). €1.30, Helios, ceramic sculpture by Villeroy & Boch.

Litho., Litho. & Embossed (95c, €1.30)

2015, Sept. 22 *Perf. 13x13¼*
1415-1417 A661 Set of 3 6.75 6.75

Nature Reserves — A662

Designs: No. 1418, (70c), Mellerdall Nature Reserve. No. 1419, (70c), Oewersauer Nature Reserve. No. 1420, (70c), Our Nature Reserve.

2015, Sept. 22 Litho. *Perf. 12¾*
1418-1420 A662 Set of 3 4.75 4.75

Nos. 1418-1420 are each inscribed "L50g."

Flowers — A663

No. 1421: a, Maargréitchen (daisy). b, Karblumm (cornflower). c, Deschtel (thistle). d, Feierblumm (red poppy).

Die Cut Perf. 13x12¾

2015, Dec. 1 Coil Stamps Litho.
Self-Adhesive

1421 Vert. strip of 4 3.00
a.-d. A663 (35c) Any single .75 .75

Nos. 1421a-1421d are each inscribed "ATR 50g."

Opening of Belval Campus Headquarters of University of Luxembourg — A664

2016, Mar. 3 Litho. *Perf. 14*
Foil-faced Paper

1422 A664 70c multi 1.50 1.50

Port of Mertert, 50th Anniv. — A665

Luxembourg Maritime Register, 25th Anniv. — A666

Center for Equal Treatment, 10th Anniv. — A667

2016, Mar. 3 Litho. *Perf. 11½*
1423 A665 70c multi 1.50 1.50
1424 A666 70c multi 1.50 1.50
1425 A667 70c multi 1.50 1.50
Nos. 1423-1425 (3) 4.50 4.50

Royalty A668

No. 1426: a, Grand Duchess Maria Teresa. b, Grand Duchess Maria Teresa, Prince Sébastien, Princess Alexandra.

2016, Mar. 3 Litho. *Perf. 13¼x13*
1426 A668 Horiz. pair 3.00 3.00
a.-b. 70c Either single 1.50 1.50

2016 Summer Olympics, Rio de Janeiro — A669

Litho. & Embossed

2016, May 10 *Perf. 13¾x13½*
1427 A669 70c multi 1.60 1.60

A670

Europa — A671

2016, May 10 Litho. *Perf. 11½*
1428 A670 70c multi 1.60 1.60
1429 A671 95c multi 2.10 2.10

Think Green Issue.

Famous Men — A672

Designs: No. 1430, 70c, Marcel Noppeney (1877-1966), President of Society of Francophone Luxembourgian Writers. No. 1431, 70c, Joseph Hackin (1886-1941), archaeologist. No. 1432, 70c, Jean Jacoby (1891-1936), artist.

2016, May 10 Litho. *Perf. 11½*
1430-1432 A672 Set of 3 4.75 4.75

Meng.post.lu Website for Personalized Stamps, 10th Anniv. A673

Pets: 70c, Cat named Margot. 95c, Dog named Goethe. €1.30, Cat named Mäischen.

2016, May 10 Litho. *Perf. 11¼*
Self-Adhesive

1433-1435 A673 Set of 3 6.75 6.75

Stamp vignettes could be personalized by customers, presumably for an extra fee. Printed stamps having customer-provided personalized images may not show the green and yellow Luxembourg Post emblem found in the lower right corner of illustration A673, based on mockup images shown when ordering these sheets on the meng.post.lu website.

Nos. 1433-1435 were later printed with various other images by Luxembourg Post and offered for sale in full panes at a premium over face value. Only Nos. 1433-1435 were offered at face value. Stamps with other denominations bearing images chosen by Luxembourg Post were produced later, all of which were sold at a premium over face value.

Souvenir Sheet

Passage Through Luxembourg of Thurn and Taxis Postal Route, 500th Anniv. — A674

Litho. & Embossed

2016, May 10 *Perf. 11½*
1436 A674 €4 multi + label 9.00 9.00

Vegetables Type of 2014

Designs: 95c, Cucumis sativus. €1.30, Phaseolus vulgaris. €2, Allium cepa var. proliferum.

2016, Sept. 13 Litho. *Perf. 11½*
1437-1439 A646 Set of 3 9.50 9.50

Jesus Christ and Virgin Mary, by Albrecht Bouts (c. 1451-1549) A675

2016, Sept. 13 Litho. *Perf. 11½*
1440 A675 70c multi 1.60 1.60

Luxembourg National Museum of History and Art exhibition of paintings by Bouts.

Election of the Virgin Mary as Patroness of Luxembourg, 350th Anniv. — A676

2016, Sept. 13 Engr. *Perf. 13*
1441 A676 70c multi 1.60 1.60

No. 1441 was printed in sheets of 4. See Vatican City No. 1631.

Grand Duchess Charlotte Bridge (Red Bridge), 50th Anniv. A677

2016, Sept. 13 Litho. *Perf. 12*
1442 A677 70c multi 1.60 1.60

Spring in the Ostling — A678

2016, Sept. 13 Litho. *Perf. 11½*
1443 A678 95c multi 2.25 2.25

Biodiversity — A679

Winning designs in children's stamp design contest: 70c, Woodpecker, by Yann Klees. 95c, Wolf, by Christine Guirsch, horiz.

Perf. 14x14¾, 14¾x14

2016, Sept. 13 Litho.
1444-1445 A679 Set of 2 3.75 3.75

A680

A681

New Emblem for Luxembourg — A682

2016, Oct. 10 Litho. *Perf. 12½x12*
Self-Adhesive

1446 A680 70c multi 1.60 1.60
1447 A681 95c multi 2.10 2.10
1448 A682 €1.30 multi 3.00 3.00
Nos. 1446-1448 (3) 6.70 6.70

Museums — A683

Designs: No. 1449, Steam locomotive, Minett Park, Differdange. No. 1450, Playing cards, Kulturhuef Printing Museum, Grevenmacher. No. 1451, Carriage, Rural and Artisanal Museum, Peppange. No. 1452,

Slate, hammer and pick, Slate Museum, Haut-Martelange. No. 1453, Airplane, Luxembourg Aviation Museum, Mondorf-les-Bains.

Die Cut Perf. 11½

2016, Dec. 6 Litho.

Booklet Stamps
Self-Adhesive

1449 A683 70c multi	1.50	1.50
1450 A683 70c multi	1.50	1.50
1451 A683 70c multi	1.50	1.50
1452 A683 70c multi	1.50	1.50
1453 A683 70c multi	1.50	1.50
a. Booklet pane of 10, 2 each #1449-1453	15.00	
Nos. 1449-1453 (5)	7.50	7.50

Josy Barthel (1927-92), Olympic Gold Medalist Runner — A684

2017, Mar. 7 Litho. *Perf. 11½*
1454 A684 70c multi 1.50 1.50

Fieldgen Private School, 125th Anniv. — A685

Fifty-One International, 51st Anniv. — A686

Luxembourg Alzheimer Association, 30th Anniv. — A687

2017, Mar. 7 Litho. *Perf. 11½*

1455 A685 70c multi	1.50	1.50
1456 A686 70c multi	1.50	1.50
1457 A687 70c multi	1.50	1.50
Nos. 1455-1457 (3)	4.50	4.50

Famous Men — A688

Designs: No. 1458, 70c, Jean Jules Linden (1817-98), botanist. No. 1459, 70c, Pierre Frieden (1892-1959), politician. No. 1460, 70c, Tony Bourg (1912-91), literature professor.

2017, Mar. 7 Litho. *Perf. 11½*
1458-1460 A688 Set of 3 4.50 4.50

Souvenir Sheet

Apparition of the Virgin Mary at Fatima, Portugal, Cent. — A689

2017, Mar. 7 Litho. *Perf. 11¾x12*
1461 A689 95c multi 2.00 2.00

See Poland No. 4277, Portugal No. 3888, Slovakia No. 759.

Treaty of London, 150th Anniv. A690

Litho. With Foil Application

2017, May 9 *Perf. 13*
1462 A690 70c multi 1.60 1.60

Count Peter-Ernst von Mansfeld (1517-1604), Governor of Luxembourg A691

2017, May 9 Litho. *Perf. 11½*
1463 A691 95c multi 2.10 2.10

Military Anniversaries A692

Designs: 70c, Military musicians. 95c, Soldiers in fatigues.

2017, May 9 Litho. *Perf. 12x12½*
Self-Adhesive
1464-1465 A692 Set of 2 3.75 3.75

Luxembourg Military Band, 175th anniv. (No. 1464); voluntary military service, 50th anniv. (No. 1465).

Europa — A693

Designs: 70c, Beggen Castle. 95c, Dommeldange Castle.

2017, May 9 Litho. ***Perf. 11½***
1466-1467 A693 Set of 2 *25.00 25.00*

Nos. 1466-1467 were withdrawn from sale on July 1, 2017, because of missing country name.

Luxembourgish Cycling Federation, Cent. — A694

2017, July 4 Litho. *Perf. 11½*
1468 A694 70c multi 1.75 1.75

Start of Fourth Stage of 2017 Tour de France Bicycle Race in Mondorf-les-Bains A695

2017, July 4 Litho. *Perf. 11½*
1469 A695 70c multi 1.75 1.75

Souvenir Sheet

Multilateral Philatelic Exhibition, s'Hertogenbosch, Netherlands — A696

No. 1470: a, Zoete Lieve Gerritje Statue, St. John's Cathedral, s'Hertogenbosch. b, Grand Duke's Palace, Remembrance Monument, Luxembourg Philharmonic, Luxembourg, Church of the Assumption, Ljubljana, Slovenia.

2017, Aug. 25 Litho. *Perf. 14½*

1470 A696 Sheet of 2	4.00	4.00
a. 70c multi	1.75	1.75
b. 95c multi	2.25	2.25

A souvenir sheet containing No. 1470a and Netherlands No. 1553b was given free to standing order subscribers of Luxembourg Post, but was available for sale from the Dutch Post in a package that sold for €15 that contained this sheet, Luxembourg No. 1470 and Netherlands No. 1553. See Netherlands No. 1553.

Parish Church of Simmer (Septfontaines), 700th Anniv. — A697

2017, Sept. 19 Litho. *Perf. 11½*
1471 A697 70c multi 1.75 1.75

Green Fingers, Ceramic Sculpture by Ellen van der Woude — A698

2017, Sept. 19 Litho. *Perf. 13½*
1472 A698 95c multi 2.25 2.25

Souvenir Sheet

Luxembourg Postal Service, 175th Anniv. — A699

No. 1473: a, Letter, post card, building, postal van, credit cards. b, Telephone, telephone booth, computer, cell phone, satellite dish.

2017, Sept. 19 Litho. *Perf. 13¾x14*

1473 A699 Sheet of 2	4.00	4.00
a. 70c multi	1.75	1.75
b. 95c multi	2.25	2.25

Rose Varieties — A700

No. 1474: a, Grand-Duc Adolphe de Luxembourg, 1891. b, Princesse Marie-Adélaide, 1893. c, Grande-Duchesse Charlotte, 1939. d, Grand-Duc Jean, 2010. e, Grand-Duc Henri, 2001. f, Indépendence du Luxembourg, 1990.

Serpentine Die Cut 11¼

2017, Dec. 5 Litho.

Coil Stamps
Self-Adhesive

1474 Vert. strip of 6	10.50	
a.-f. A700 (70c) Any single	1.75	1.75

New Luxembourg City Tram — A701

Pfaffenthal-Kirchberg Funicular — A702

2017, Dec. 5 Litho. *Perf. 12*
1475 A701 70c multi 1.75 1.75

Perf. 11½
1476 A702 70c multi 1.75 1.75

National Orders of Merit — A703

Designs: No. 1477, 70c, Order of Merit of the Grand Duchy of Luxembourg (carmine red panel at right). No. 1478, 70c, Civil and Military Order of Merit of Adolphe of Nassau (royal blue panel at right). No. 1479, 70c, Order of the Oak Crown (green panel at right).

Photo. & Embossed

2017, Dec. 5 *Perf. 13¼x13*
1477-1479 A703 Set of 3 5.25 5.25

SOS Children's Village in Luxembourg, 50th Anniv. — A704

2018, Mar. 6 Litho. *Perf. 11½x11¾*
1480 A704 70c multi 1.75 1.75

Association of Parents of Mentally Handicapped Children, 50th Anniv. — A705

2018, Mar. 6 Litho. *Perf. 11½x11¾*
1481 A705 70c multi 1.75 1.75

Lycée de Garçons (Boys High School), Luxembourg, 125th Anniv. — A706

2018, Mar. 6 Litho. *Perf. 11¾x11½*
1482 A706 70c multi 1.75 1.75

NATO Support and Procurement Agency, 50th Anniv. in Luxembourg A707

2018, Mar. 6 Litho. *Perf. 12½*
1483 A707 70c multi 1.75 1.75

European Year of Cultural Heritage — A708

2018, Mar. 6 Litho. *Perf. 12½*
1484 A708 70c multi 1.75 1.75

Grand Ducal Institute, 150th Anniv. — A709

2018, May 15 Litho. *Perf. 11½*
1485 A709 70c multi 1.75 1.75

Comic Book Festival, Contern, 25th Anniv. — A710

2018, May 15 Litho. *Perf. 12x12½*
Self-Adhesive
1486 A710 70c multi 1.75 1.75

Beaufort Castle — A711

2018, May 15 Litho. *Perf. 12x12½*
Self-Adhesive
1487 A711 95c multi 2.25 2.25

Europa — A712

Winning children's art in contest with theme of bridges by: 70c, Lola Kirsch. 95c, Gaia Vetere.

2018, May 15 Litho. *Perf. 11½*
1488-1489 A712 Set of 2 4.00 4.00

Birds — A713

Designs: 25c, Rousserolle effarvatte (reed warbler). 70c, Hirondelle rustique (barn swallow). 95c, Gorgebleue à miroir (bluethroat).

2018, May 15 Litho. *Perf. 13¾*
1490-1492 A713 Set of 3 4.50 4.50

Famous People — A714

Designs: No. 1493, 70c, Jean Schortgen (1880-1918), coal miner and trade union leader. No. 1494, 70c, Hélène Palgen (1902-93), linguist. No. 1495, 70c, Antoine Hirsch (1868-1934), architect and artist.

2018, May 15 Litho. *Perf. 11½*
1493-1495 A714 Set of 3 5.00 5.00

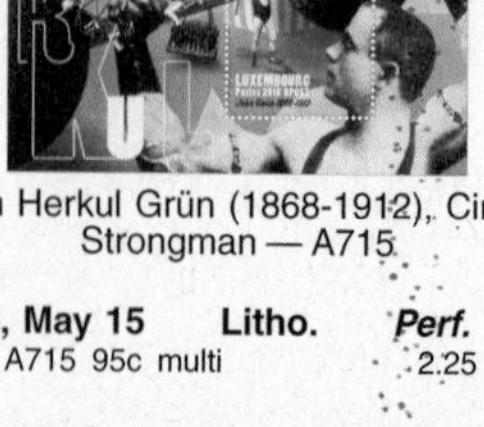

John Herkul Grün (1868-1912), Circus Strongman — A715

2018, May 15 Litho. *Perf. 11½*
1496 A715 95c multi 2.25 2.25

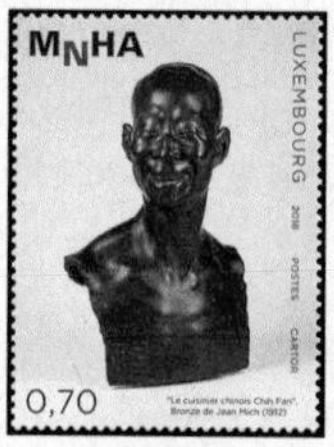

The Chinese Cook, Chih Fan, Sculpture by Jean Mich (1871-1932) A716

Litho. & Embossed With Foil Application

2018, Sept. 18 *Perf. 13*
1497 A716 70c multi 1.75 1.75

National Museum of History and Art Exhibition of works by Mich.

Breast Cancer Prevention A717

2018, Sept. 18 Litho. *Perf. 11½*
1498 A717 70c multi 1.75 1.75

Railway for Iron Ore Cars, Tétange A718

2018, Sept. 18 Litho. *Perf. 11½*
1499 A718 70c multi 1.75 1.75

Stamp Day.

Artistic Circle of Luxembourg, 125th Anniv. — A719

2018, Sept. 18 Litho. *Perf. 12½*
1500 A719 70c multi 1.75 1.75

Ecological Movement, 50th Anniv. — A720

2018, Sept. 18 Litho. *Perf. 12½*
1501 A720 70c multi 1.75 1.75

Miami University of Ohio in Luxembourg, 50th Anniv. — A721

2018, Sept. 18 Litho. *Perf. 11½*
1502 A721 €1.30 multi 3.00 3.00

Souvenir Sheet

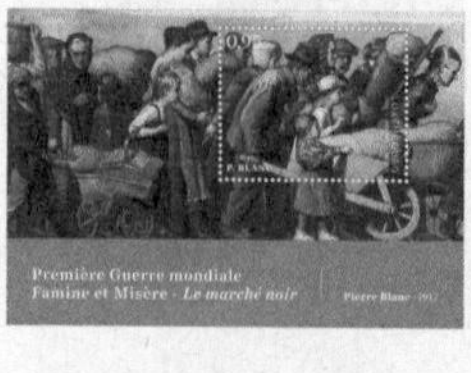

Famine and Misery, by Pierre Blanc A722

2018, Sept. 18 Litho. *Perf. 11½*
1503 A722 95c multi 2.25 2.25

End of World War I, cent.

Plum Varieties — A723

Designs: No. 1504, Wénkelcher. No. 1505, Koupanz. No. 1506, Duederer. No. 1507, Prenzenpromm. No. 1508, Karschnatzpromm.

Serpentine Die Cut 11
2018, Dec. 4 Litho.
Booklet Stamps
Self-Adhesive

1504	A723 (95c) multi	2.25	2.25
1505	A723 (95c) multi	2.25	2.25
1506	A723 (95c) multi	2.25	2.25
1507	A723 (95c) multi	2.25	2.25
1508	A723 (95c) multi	2.25	2.25
a.	Booklet pane of 10, 2 each #1504-1508	22.50	
	Nos. 1504-1508 (5)	11.25	11.25

Luxembourg Guides and Scouts, Cent. — A724

2019, Apr. 1 Litho. *Perf. 11½*
1509 A724 70c multi 1.60 1.60

Luxembourg Cancer Foundation, 25th Anniv. — A725

2019, Apr. 1 Litho. *Perf. 12½*
1510 A725 70c multi 1.60 1.60

Self-portrait, by Dominique Lang (1874-1919) — A726

2019, Apr. 1 Litho. *Perf. 11½*
1511 A726 70c multi 1.60 1.60

Trinity Church, Luxembourg — A727

2019, Apr. 1 Litho. *Perf. 11½*
1512 A727 70c multi 1.60 1.60

Protestant Church in Luxembourg, 200th anniv.

Publications Office of the European Union, 50th Anniv. — A728

2019, Apr. 1 Litho. *Perf. 11½*
1513 A728 95c multi 2.25 2.25

New National Library A729

2019, May 7 Litho. *Perf. 11½*
1514 A729 80c multi 1.90 1.90

2019 European Elections — A730

2019, May 7 Litho. *Perf. 12½*
1515 A730 80c multi 1.90 1.90

Saint Cecile Choir of Notre Dame Cathedral of Luxembourg, 175th Anniv. — A731

2019, May 7 Litho. *Perf. 13*
1516 A731 80c multi 1.90 1.90

Villa Clivio, Luxembourg A732

2019, May 7 Litho. *Perf. 11½*
1517 A732 €1.05 multi 2.40 2.40

Rural Tourism — A733

Tourists and: 80c, Horses. €1.05, Sheep.

2019, May 7 Litho. *Perf. 12x12½*
Self-Adhesive
1518-1519 A733 Set of 2 4.25 4.25

Europa — A734

Birds: 80c, Bruant jaune (yellowhammer). €1.05, Linotte mélodieuse (common linnet).

2019, May 7 Litho. *Perf. 13½*
1520-1521 A734 Set of 2 4.25 4.25

Laval-Tudor Cultural Center, Steinsel — A735

2019, Sept. 17 Litho. *Perf. 11½*
1522 A735 80c multi 1.75 1.75

Stamp Day.

Liberation of Luxembourg, 75th Anniv. A736

2019, Sept. 17 Litho. *Perf. 11½*
1523 A736 80c multi 1.75 1.75

Grand Duchess Charlotte (1896-1985) and 1919 Referendum Ballot — A737

2019, Sept. 17 Litho. *Perf. 11½*
1524 A737 80c multi 1.75 1.75

Referendum of 1919, cent.

Universal Suffrage in Luxembourg, Cent. — A738

2019, Sept. 17 Litho. *Perf. 12½*
1525 A738 80c multi 1.75 1.75

Luxembourg Midwives Association, Cent. — A739

2019, Sept. 17 Litho. *Perf. 12½*
1526 A739 80c multi 1.75 1.75

Souvenir Sheet

Federation of Luxembourg Philatelic Societies, 85th Anniv. — A740

Litho. & Engr.
2019, Sept. 17 *Perf. 14x13¼*
1527 A740 80c multi 1.75 1.75

Casemates Defensive Tunnel, Luxembourg — A741

2019, Nov. 8 Litho. *Perf. 12½*
1528 A741 80c multi 1.75 1.75

See Gibraltar No. 1739.

Space Resources A742

2019, Nov. 8 Litho. *Perf. 13¼*
On Mirrored Foil
1529 A742 €1.40 multi 3.25 3.25

Souvenir Sheet

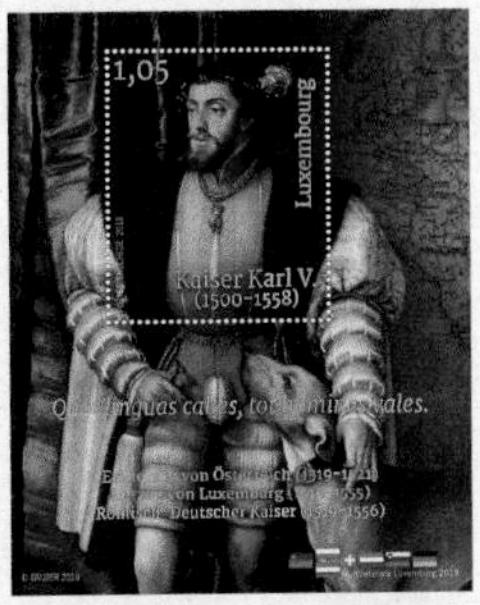

Reign of Charles V (1500-58) as Archduke of Austria and His Selection as Holy Roman Emperor, 500th Anniv. — A743

Litho. With Foil Application
2019, Nov. 8 *Perf. 13x13¼*
1530 A743 €1.05 gold & multi 2.40 2.40

See Austria No. 2829.

Battle of the Ardennes, 75th Anniv. A744

2019, Dec. 3 Litho. *Perf. 11½*
1531 A744 80c multi 1.75 1.75

Souvenir Sheet

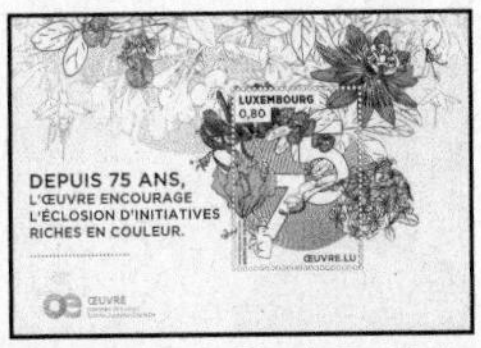

Grand Duchess Charlotte National Relief Institution, 75th Anniv. — A745

2019, Dec. 3 Litho. *Perf. 13¾*
1532 A745 80c multi 1.75 1.75

Selection of Old City of Luxembourg as UNESCO World Heritage Site, 25th Anniv. — A746

2020, Mar. 10 Litho. *Perf. 12½*
1533 A746 80c multi 1.75 1.75

Gabriel Lippmann (1845-1921), 1908 Nobel Laureate in Physics A747

2020, Mar. 10 Litho. *Perf. 11½*
1534 A747 80c multi 1.75 1.75

International Year of Plant Health A748

2020, Mar. 10 Litho. *Perf. 11½*
1535 A748 €1.05 multi 2.25 2.25

Birds — A749

Designs: 40c, Alouette des champs (skylark). 80c, Roitelet huppé (goldcrest). €1.40, Moineau domestique (house sparrow). €5, Rouge-gorge (robin).

2020, Mar. 10 Litho. *Perf. 13¼*
1536-1539 A749 Set of 4 16.50 16.50

Luxembourg Nature and Bird Protection Society, cent. (No. 1537).

Art Education in Secondary Schools, 40th Anniv. — A750

2020, June 9 Litho. *Perf. 11½*
1540 A750 80c multi 1.90 1.90

Diocese of Luxembourg, 150th Anniv. — A751

2020, June 9 Litho. *Perf. 11½*
1541 A751 80c multi 1.90 1.90

Europa — A752

Map of old postal route and post rider facing: 80c, Right. €1.05, Left.

2020, June 9 Litho. *Perf. 13¼*
1542-1543 A752 Set of 2 4.25 4.25

Rural Tourism — A753

Designs: 80c, Cyclists near tower. €1.05, Children feeding chickens.

2020, June 9 Litho. *Perf. 12x12½*
Self-Adhesive
1544-1545 A753 Set of 2 4.25 4.25

Railway Bridge, Ettelbruck A754

2020, Sept. 15 Litho. *Perf. 11½*
1546 A754 80c multi 1.90 1.90

Stamp Day.

Peter of Aspelt (c. 1240-1320), Archbishop of Mainz — A755

2020, Sept. 15 Litho. *Perf. 11½*
1547 A755 80c multi 1.90 1.90

Many Spoken Words, Fountain by Su-Mei Tse — A756

2020, Sept. 15 Litho. *Perf. 11½*
1548 A756 80c multi 1.90 1.90

SEPAC Issue.

Non-Violence, Sculpture by Carl Fredrik Reutersward A757

2020, Sept. 15 Litho. *Perf. 11½*
1549 A757 €1.40 multi 3.25 3.25

United Nations, 75th anniv.

Accession to the Throne of Grand Duke Henri, 20th Anniv. — A758

2020, Dec. 8 Litho. *Perf. 12*
1550 A758 80c multi 2.00 2.00

Bees — A759

No. 1551: a, Bombus pratorum. b, Osmia cornuta. c, Trachusa byssina. d, Anthophora bimaculata. e, Eucera nigrescens.

Serpentine Die Cut 11¼
2020, Dec. 8 Litho.
Coil Stamps
Self-Adhesive
1551 Vert. strip of 5 13.00
a.-e. A759 (€1.05) Any single 2.60 2.60

Items in Luxembourg Museums — A760

Designs: No. 1552, Miner's equipment and identity tags, National Iron Mining Museum, Rumelange. No. 1553, Brewery tools, National Brewing Museum, Wiltz. No. 1554, Pitcher, Museum of Pottery, Nospelt. No. 1555, Mortar, pestle, and mustard seeds, Muerbelsmillen Mustard Factory Museum, Luxembourg. No. 1556, Spools of yarn and loom shuttle, Duchfabrik, Esch-sur-Sûre.

Serpentine Die Cut 12¼

2020, Dec. 8 **Litho.**

Booklet Stamps Self-Adhesive

1552 A760 (80c) multi 2.00 2.00
1553 A760 (80c) multi 2.00 2.00
1554 A760 (80c) multi 2.00 2.00
1555 A760 (80c) multi 2.00 2.00
1556 A760 (80c) multi 2.00 2.00
a. Booklet pane of 10, 2 each #1552-1556 20.00
Nos. 1552-1556 (5) 10.00 10.00

40th Wedding Anniversary of Grand Duke Henri and Grand Duchess Maria Teresa A761

2021, Mar. 9 **Litho.** ***Perf. 11½***
1557 A761 80c multi 1.90 1.90

Luxembourg National Fruit Growing Association, 125th Anniv. — A762

2021, Mar. 9 **Litho.** ***Perf. 12***
1558 A762 80c multi 1.90 1.90

House of the Open Door Foundation, 50th Anniv. — A763

2021, Mar. 9 **Litho.** ***Perf. 11½***
1559 A763 80c multi 1.90 1.90

Luxembourg Handball Federation, 75th Anniv. — A764

2021, Mar. 9 **Litho.** ***Perf. 11½***
1560 A764 80c multi 1.90 1.90

Soroptomist International, Cent. — A765

2021, Mar. 9 **Litho.** ***Perf. 11½***
1561 A765 80c multi 1.90 1.90

Luxembourg Hiking Federation, 50th Anniv. — A766

2021, Mar. 9 **Litho.** ***Perf. 11½***
1562 A766 80c multi 1.90 1.90

High School of Arts and Crafts, 125th Anniv. — A767

Litho. With Foil Application

2021, May 11 ***Perf. 13¼***
1563 A767 80c gold & multi 2.00 2.00

2020 Summer Olympics, Tokyo — A768

2021, May 11 **Litho.** ***Perf. 11½***
1564 A768 80c multi 2.00 2.00

The 2020 Summer Olympics were postponed until 2021 because of the COVID-19 pandemic.

Luxembourg Autism Foundation, 25th Anniv. — A769

2021, May 11 **Litho.** ***Perf. 12¾***
1565 A769 80c multi 2.00 2.00

Luxembourg City Museum, 25th Anniv. A770

2021, May 11 **Litho.** ***Perf. 11½***
1566 A770 80c multi 2.00 2.00

Europa — A771

Endangered animals: 80c, Grand murin (greater mouse-eared bat). €1.05, Putois d'Europe (European polecat).

2021, May 11 **Litho.** ***Perf. 13¼***
1567-1568 A771 Set of 2 4.50 4.50

Villa Bourg, Capellen A772

Perf. 12½x11¾

2021, Sept. 14 **Litho.**
1569 A772 80c multi 1.90 1.90

Stamp Day.

Luxembourg Pavilion at Expo 2020, Dubai — A773

Perf. 13¾x12½

2021, Sept. 14 **Litho.**

Self-Adhesive

1570 A773 80c multi 1.90 1.90

Opening of New Headquarters of Grand Ducal Fire and Rescue Corps — A774

2021, Sept. 14 **Litho.** ***Perf. 12¾***
1571 A774 80c multi 1.90 1.90

Opening of Luxembourg Stadium A775

2021, Sept. 14 **Litho.** ***Perf. 12***
1572 A775 80c multi 1.90 1.90

Family Picnicking Near Vianden Castle — A776

Rural Tourism Emblems — A777

2021, Sept. 14 **Litho.** ***Perf. 12x12½***

Self-Adhesive

1573 A776 80c multi 1.90 1.90
1574 A777 €1.05 multi 2.50 2.50

Luxembourg Rural Tourism Promotion Association, 30th anniv. (No. 1574).

16th Century Map of Luxembourg by Jacob van Deventer (c. 1500-75) A778

2021, Sept. 14 **Litho.** ***Perf. 11½***
1575 A778 €1.05 multi 2.50 2.50

Forget-me-nots A779

Bird's Foot Trefoils A780

Common Whitlow Grass A781

Bladder Campions A782

Serpentine Die Cut 11

2021, Nov. 16 **Litho.**

Coil Stamps Self-Adhesive

1576 Vert. strip of 4 3.75
a. A779 (40c) blue & multi .90 .90
b. A780 (40c) org yellow & multi .90 .90
c. A781 (40c) yel green & multi .90 .90
d. A782 (40c) purple & multi .90 .90

Numismatics A783

Placomusophilia (Collecting of Wine Bottle Cap and Coverings) A784

Tegestology (Collecting of Beer Coasters) A785

Litho. & Embossed

2021, Nov. 16 ***Perf. 13¾***
1577 A783 80c multi 1.90 1.90
1578 A784 80c multi 1.90 1.90

Litho.

On Thick Cardboard Without Gum

1579 A785 80c multi 1.90 1.90
Nos. 1577-1579 (3) 5.70 5.70

Values are for stamps with surrounding selvage.

Doctors Without Borders, 50th Anniv. — A786

2021, Nov. 16 **Litho.** ***Perf. 12½***
1580 A786 80c multi 1.90 1.90

A787

Esch-sur-Alzette, 2022 European Capital of Culture — A788

Inscriptions: No. 1582, Remix Culture. No. 1583, Remix Nature. No. 1584, Remix art. No. 1585, Remix Europe. No. 1586, Remix Yourself.

2022, Feb. 22 **Litho.** ***Perf. 11½***
1581 A787 80c multi 1.75 1.75

Booklet Stamps Self-Adhesive

Serpentine Die Cut 12¼

1582 A788 (80c) multi 1.75 1.75
1583 A788 (80c) multi 1.75 1.75
1584 A788 (80c) multi 1.75 1.75
1585 A788 (80c) multi 1.75 1.75
1586 A788 (80c) multi 1.75 1.75
a. Booklet pane of 10, 2 each #1582-1586 17.50
Nos. 1582-1586 (5) 8.75 8.75

Motor-Union Luxembourg (Motorcyclists' Association), Cent. — A789

2022, Mar. 18 **Litho.** ***Perf. 12¼x12***
1587 A789 80c multi 1.75 1.75

Engineers and Scientists of Luxembourg, 125th Anniv. — A790

2022, Mar. 18 **Litho.** ***Perf. 12¾***
1588 A790 80c multi 1.75 1.75

Sosthène Weis (1872-1941), Architect
A791

2022, Mar. 18 Litho. *Perf. 11½*
1589 A791 80c multi 1.75 1.75

Wilhalm Voigt (1849-1922), Petty Thief and Military Officer Impostor Called "Captain of Kopenick" — A792

2022, Mar. 18 Litho. *Perf. 11½*
1590 A792 €1.05 multi 2.40 2.40

Campaign for Greener Urban Areas — A793

2022, May 17 Litho. *Perf. 11½*
1591 A793 (80c) multi 1.75 1.75

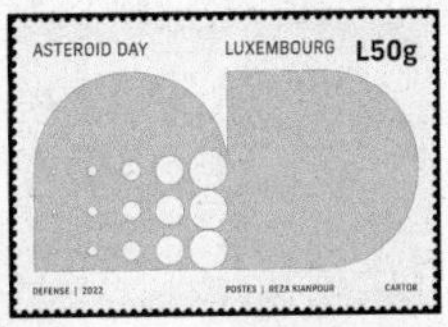

Asteroid Day
A794

Litho. With Foil Application

2022, May 17 *Perf. 14*
1592 A794 (80c) black & silver 1.75 1.75

Legend of the Kropermann
A795

Legend of Melusina
A796

2022, May 17 Litho. *Perf. 12½x12*
Self-Adhesive

1593 A795 (80c) multi 1.75 1.75
1594 A796 (€1.05) multi 2.25 2.25

Europa.

Mammals
A797

Designs: 10c, Muscardin (Common dormouse). 25c, Hérisson commun (Western hedgehog). (€1.40), Lievre d'Europe (Brown hare).

2022, May 17 Litho. *Perf. 13¾x14*
1595 A797 10c multi .30 .30
1596 A797 25c multi .55 .55
1597 A797 (€1.40) multi 3.00 3.00
Nos. 1595-1597 (3) 3.85 3.85

No. 1597 is inscribed "M50g." See No. F1.

Souvenir Sheet

Selection of Esch-sur-Alzette, Luxembourg and Kaunas, Lithuania as 2022 European Capitals of Culture — A798

No. 1598: a, The Bath, by Stasys Usinskas (1905-74). b, Nemrod, by Foni Thyssen (1909-75).

2022, May 17 Litho. *Perf. 11½*
1598 A798 Sheet of 2 3.50 3.50
a.-b. (80c) Either single 1.75 1.75

Joint issue between Luxembourg and Lithuania. See Lithuania No. 1201.

10th Wedding Anniversary of Hereditary Grand Duke Guillaume and Countess Stéphanie
A799

2022, Sept. 13 Litho. *Perf. 12*
1599 A799 €1 multi 2.00 2.00

Painted Cooling Towers, Differdange — A800

2022, Sept. 13 Litho. *Perf. 12*
1600 A800 (€1) multi 2.00 2.00

Stamp Day.

Postcrossing
A801

2022, Sept. 13 Litho. *Perf. 11½*
1601 A801 (€1.40) multi 3.00 3.00

Moselle Wine — A802

2022, Sept. 13 Litho. *Perf. 11½*
On Wine Label Paper

1602 A802 (€1.40) multi 3.00 3.00

Souvenir Sheet

Jean-Gaspard de Cicignon (c. 1625-96), Soldier and Rebuilder or Trondheim, Norway — A803

No. 1603: a, Cicignon's coat of arms. b, Cicignon.

Litho. & Engr.

2022, Sept. 13 *Perf. 13¼x14*
1603 A803 Sheet of 2 4.00 4.00
a.-b. (€1) Either single 2.00 2.00

New Headquarters for Luxembourg Postal Service
A804

2022, Nov. 15 Litho. *Perf. 11½*
1604 A804 €1 multi 2.10 2.10

European Union Court of Justice, Luxembourg, 70th Anniv. — A805

2022, Nov. 15 Litho. *Perf. 12*
1605 A805 €1.40 multi 3.00 3.00

View of Luxembourg Type of 1923
With Euro Denomination
Souvenir Sheet

2023, Mar. 14 Engr. *Perf. 11*
1606 A16 €5 dk green 11.00 11.00

Mammals
A806

Designs: 20c, Musaraigne d'eau (water shrew). 40c, Oreillard gris (gray long-eared bat). €1.40, Castor d'Europe (European beaver). €1.75, Renard roux (red fox).

2023, Mar. 14 Litho. *Perf. 14*
1607-1610 A806 Set of 4 8.00 8.00

National Library of Luxembourg, 225th Anniv. — A807

2023, Mar. 14 Litho. *Perf. 12*
1611 A807 €1 multi 2.25 2.25

Souvenir Sheet

Diplomatic Relations Between Luxembourg and India, 75th Anniv. — A808

No. 1612 — Amar Nath Sehgal (1922-2007) and his sculptures: a, Joueur de Flûte (Flute Player). b, Amis (Friends).

2023, Mar. 14 Litho. *Perf. 12*
1612 A808 Sheet of 2 4.25 4.25
a.-b. €1 Either single 2.10 2.10

See India No.

SEMI-POSTAL STAMPS

Clervaux Monastery
SP1

Designs: 15c+10c, View of Pfaffenthal. 25c+10c, View of Luxembourg.

Engr.; Surcharge Typo. in Red

1921, Aug. 2 Unwmk. *Perf. 11½*
B1 SP1 10c + 5c green .25 *2.00*
B2 SP1 15c + 10c org red .40 *3.00*
B3 SP1 25c + 10c dp grn .25 *2.00*
Nos. B1-B3 (3) .90 *7.00*
Set, never hinged 2.00

The amount received from the surtax on these stamps was added to a fund for the erection of a monument to the soldiers from Luxembourg who died in World War I.

Nos. B1-B3 with Additional Surcharge in Red or Black

1923, May 27
B4 SP1 25c on #B1 (R) 1.00 *11.00*
B5 SP1 25c on #B2 1.00 *16.00*
B6 SP1 25c on #B3 1.00 *11.00*
Nos. B4-B6 (3) 3.00 *38.00*
Set, never hinged 10.00

Unveiling of the monument to the soldiers who died in World War I.

Regular Issue of 1914-15 Surcharged in Black or Red

1924, Apr. 17 *Perf. 11½x11*
B7 A11 12½c + 7½c grn .25 *1.00*
B8 A11 35c + 10c dk bl (R) .25 *1.00*
B9 A11 2½fr + 1fr red .65 *10.00*
B10 A11 5fr + 2fr dk vio .45 *8.00*
Nos. B7-B10 (4) 1.60 *20.00*
Set, never hinged 4.00

Nurse and Patient — SP4

1925, Dec. 21 Litho. *Perf. 13*
B11 SP4 5c (+ 5c) dl vio .25 .30
B12 SP4 30c (+ 5c) org .25 .50
B13 SP4 50c (+ 5c) red brn .25 *1.25*
B14 SP4 1fr (+ 10c) dp bl .40 *5.00*
Nos. B11-B14 (4) 1.15 *7.05*
Set, never hinged 1.75

Prince Jean — SP5

1926, Dec. 15 Photo. *Perf. 12½x12*
B15 SP5 5c (+ 5c) vio & blk .25 .25
B16 SP5 40c (+ 10) grn & blk .25 .40
B17 SP5 50c (+ 15c) lem & blk .25 .40
B18 SP5 75c (+ 20c) lt red & blk .25 *3.50*
B19 SP5 1.50fr (+ 30c) gray bl & blk .35 *3.50*
Nos. B15-B19 (5) 1.35 *8.05*
Set, never hinged 2.50

Grand Duchess Charlotte and Prince Felix — SP6

1927, Sept. 4 Engr. *Perf. 11½*
B20 SP6 25c dp vio 1.10 *6.00*
B21 SP6 50c green 1.50 *8.00*
B22 SP6 75c rose lake 1.10 *7.00*
B23 SP6 1fr gray blk 1.10 *7.00*
B24 SP6 1½fr dp bl 1.10 *7.00*
Nos. B20-B24 (5) 5.90 *35.00*
Set, never hinged 16.00

Introduction of postage stamps in Luxembourg, 75th anniv. These stamps were sold exclusively at the Luxembourg Philatelic Exhibition, September 4-8, 1927, at a premium of 3 francs per set, which was donated to the exhibition funds.

Princess Elisabeth — SP7

1927, Dec. 1 Photo. *Perf. 12½*

B25 SP7	10c (+ 5c) turq bl & blk	.25	*.25*
B26 SP7	50c (+ 10c) dk brn & blk	.25	*.30*
B27 SP7	75c (+ 20c) org & blk	.25	*.65*
B28 SP7	1fr (+ 30c) brn lake & blk	.25	*3.50*
B29 SP7	1½fr (+ 50c) ultra & blk	.25	*3.50*
	Nos. B25-B29 (5)	1.25	*8.20*
	Set, never hinged	3.50	

The surtax was for Child Welfare societies.

Princess Marie Adelaide — SP8

1928, Dec. 12 *Perf. 12½x12*

B30 SP8	10c (+ 5c) ol grn & brn vio	.30	*.25*
B31 SP8	60c (+ 10c) brn & ol grn	.50	*2.00*
B32 SP8	75c (+ 15c) vio rose & bl grn	.75	*1.50*
B33 SP8	1fr (+ 25c) dk grn & brn	1.25	*4.50*
B34 SP8	1½fr (+ 50c) cit & bl	1.25	*5.00*
	Nos. B30-B34 (5)	4.05	*13.25*
	Set, never hinged	11.00	

Princess Marie Gabrielle — SP9

1929, Dec. 14 *Perf. 13*

B35 SP9	10c (+ 10c) brn & grn	.25	*.75*
B36 SP9	35c (+ 15c) dk grn & red brn	1.50	*2.25*
B37 SP9	75c (+ 30c) ver & blk	1.75	*3.00*
B38 SP9	1¼fr (+ 50c) claret & bl grn	2.25	*10.00*
B39 SP9	1¾fr (+ 75c) Prus bl & sl	2.75	*14.00*
	Nos. B35-B39 (5)	8.50	*30.00*
	Set, never hinged	20.00	

The surtax was for Child Welfare societies.

Prince Charles — SP10

1930, Dec. 10 *Perf. 12½*

B40 SP10	10c (+ 5c) bl grn & ol brn	.25	.50
B41 SP10	75c (+ 10c) vio brn & bl grn	1.10	*2.00*
B42 SP10	1fr (+ 25c) car rose & vio	2.50	*6.50*
B43 SP10	1¼fr (+ 75c) ol bis & dk brn	4.00	*10.50*
B44 SP10	1¾fr (+ 1.50fr) ultra & red brn	4.50	*13.00*
	Nos. B40-B44 (5)	12.35	*32.50*
	Set, never hinged	36.00	

The surtax was for Child Welfare societies.

Princess Alix — SP11

1931, Dec. 10

B45 SP11	10c (+ 5c) brn org & gray	.30	.65
B46 SP11	75c (+ 10c) clar & bl grn	3.00	*6.00*
B47 SP11	1fr (+ 25c) dp grn & gray	8.00	*16.00*
B48 SP11	1¼fr (+ 75c) dk vio & bl grn	6.50	*16.00*
B49 SP11	1¾fr (+ 1.50fr) bl & gray	13.00	*40.00*
	Nos. B45-B49 (5)	30.80	*78.65*
	Set, never hinged	85.00	

The surtax was for Child Welfare societies.

Countess Ermesinde — SP12

1932, Dec. 8

B50 SP12	10c (+ 5c) ol bis	.25	.35
B51 SP12	75c (+ 10c) dp vio	1.40	*5.00*
B52 SP12	1fr (+ 25c) scar	9.00	*21.00*
B53 SP12	1¼fr (+ 75c) red brn	9.00	*25.00*
B54 SP12	1¾fr (+ 1.50fr) dp bl	9.00	*26.00*
	Nos. B50-B54 (5)	28.65	*77.35*
	Set, never hinged	85.00	

The surtax was for Child Welfare societies.

Count Henry VII — SP13

1933, Dec. 12

B55 SP13	10c (+ 5c) yel brn	.35	.75
B56 SP13	75c (+ 10c) dp vio	5.00	*7.00*
B57 SP13	1fr (+ 25c) car rose	10.00	*26.00*
B58 SP13	1¼fr (+ 75c) org brn	12.00	*30.00*
B59 SP13	1¾fr (+ 1.50fr) brt bl	12.00	*37.50*
	Nos. B55-B59 (5)	39.35	*101.25*
	Set, never hinged	115.00	

John the Blind — SP14

1934, Dec. 5

B60 SP14	10c (+ 5c) dk vio	.25	1.00
B61 SP14	35c (+ 10c) dp grn	2.50	*7.00*
B62 SP14	75c (+ 15c) rose lake	2.50	*7.00*
B63 SP14	1fr (+ 25c) dp rose	14.50	*45.00*
B64 SP14	1¼fr (+ 75c) org	14.50	*45.00*
B65 SP14	1¾fr (+ 1.50fr) brt bl	14.50	*45.00*
	Nos. B60-B65 (6)	48.75	*150.00*
	Set, never hinged	125.00	

Teacher SP15

Sculptor and Painter SP16

Journalist SP17

Engineer — SP18

Scientist SP19

Lawyer SP20

Savings Bank and Adolphe Bridge SP21

Surgeon SP22

1935, May 1 Unwmk. *Perf. 12½*

B65A SP15	5c	violet	.30	*.25*
B65B SP16	10c	brn red	.30	*.45*
B65C SP17	15c	olive	.60	*.70*
B65D SP18	20c	orange	.60	*.90*
B65E SP19	35c	yel grn	.60	*1.10*
B65F SP20	50c	gray blk	1.25	*1.50*
B65G SP21	70c	dk green	1.75	*3.50*
B65H SP22	1fr	car red	1.75	*5.00*
B65J SP19	1.25fr	turq	8.00	*17.00*
B65K SP18	1.75fr	blue	9.00	*22.50*
B65L SP16	2fr	lt brown	25.00	*67.50*
B65M SP17	3fr	dk brown	30.00	*95.00*
B65N SP20	5fr	lt blue	60.00	*160.00*
B65P SP15	10fr	red vio	150.00	*350.00*
B65Q SP22	20fr	dk green	160.00	*400.0*
	Nos. B65A-B65Q (15)		449.15	*1,125.*
	Set, never hinged		1,100.	

Sold at double face, surtax going to intl. fund to aid professional people.

Philatelic Exhibition Issue

Type of Regular Issue of 1928

Wmk. 246

1935, Aug. 15 Engr. *Imperf.*

B66 A19	2fr (+ 50c) blk	6.00	*13.00*
	Never hinged	13.00	

Philatelic exhibition held at Esch-sur-Alzette.

Charles I — SP23

Perf. 11½

1935, Dec. 2 Photo. Unwmk.

B67 SP23	10c (+ 5c) vio	.25	.30
B68 SP23	35c (+ 10c) grn	.30	*.55*
B69 SP23	70c (+ 20c) dk brn	.55	*1.50*
B70 SP23	1fr (+ 25c) rose lake	11.00	*21.00*
B71 SP23	1.25fr (+ 75c) org brn	12.00	*22.00*
B72 SP23	1.75fr (+ 1.50fr) bl	12.00	*27.00*
	Nos. B67-B72 (6)	36.10	*72.35*
	Set, never hinged	110.00	

Wenceslas I, Duke of Luxembourg — SP24

1936, Dec. 1 *Perf. 11½x13*

B73 SP24	10c + 5(c) blk brn	.25	.25
B74 SP24	35c + 10(c) bl grn	.25	*.50*
B75 SP24	70c + 20(c) blk	.35	*.75*
B76 SP24	1fr + 25(c) rose car	2.00	*6.50*
B77 SP24	1.25fr + 75(c) vio	4.50	*10.00*
B78 SP24	1.75fr + 1.50(fr) saph	4.50	*12.00*
	Nos. B73-B78 (6)	11.85	*30.00*
	Set, never hinged	32.50	

Wenceslas II — SP25

1937, Dec. 1 *Perf. 11½x12½*

B79 SP25	10c + 5c car & blk	.25	.25
B80 SP25	35c + 10c red vio & grn	.25	.35
B81 SP25	70c + 20c ultra & red brn	.35	.35
B82 SP25	1fr + 25c dk grn & scar	1.25	*5.00*
B83 SP25	1.25fr + 75c dk brn & vio	2.25	*7.00*
B84 SP25	1.75fr + 1.50fr blk & ultra	2.25	*8.50*
	Nos. B79-B84 (6)	6.60	*21.45*
	Set, never hinged	20.00	

Souvenir Sheet

SP26

Wmk. 110

1937, July 25 Engr. *Perf. 13*

B85 SP26	Sheet of 2	5.00	*11.50*
	Never hinged	11.00	
a.	2fr red brown, single stamp	1.50	*5.50*

National Philatelic Exposition at Dudelange on July 25-26.

Sold for 5fr per sheet, of which 1fr was for the aid of the exposition.

Portrait of St. Willibrord SP28

St. Willibrord, after a Miniature SP29

Abbey at Echternach SP30

Designs: No, B87, The Rathaus at Echternach. No. B88, Pavilion in Abbey Park, Echternach. No. B91, Dancing Procession in Honor of St. Willibrord.

Perf. 14x13, 13x14

1938, June 5 Engr. Unwmk.

B86 SP28	35c + 10c dk bl grn	.40	*.55*
B87 SP28	70c + 10c ol gray	.70	*.55*
B88 SP28	1.25fr + 25c brn car	1.50	*2.50*
B89 SP29	1.75fr + 50c sl bl	2.50	*2.75*
B90 SP30	3fr + 2fr vio brn	5.50	*9.00*
B91 SP30	5fr + 5fr dk vio	6.50	*7.25*
	Nos. B86-B91 (6)	17.10	22.60
	Set, never hinged	50.00	

12th centenary of the death of St. Willibrord. The surtax was used for the restoration of the ancient Abbey at Echternach.

Duke Sigismond — SP32

1938, Dec. 1 Photo. *Perf. 11½*

B92 SP32	10c + 5c lil & blk	.25	.25
B93 SP32	35c + 10c grn & blk	.25	.50
B94 SP32	70c + 20c buff & blk	.25	*.50*

B95 SP32 1fr + 25c red org & blk 2.40 *7.50*
B96 SP32 1.25fr + 75c gray bl & blk 2.40 *9.00*
B97 SP32 1.75fr + 1.50fr bl & blk 3.50 *12.00*
Nos. B92-B97 (6) 9.05 *29.75*
Set, never hinged 22.00

Prince Jean — SP33

Designs: Nos. B99, B102, Prince Felix. Nos. B100, B103, Grand Duchess Charlotte.

1939, Dec. 1 Litho. *Perf. 14x13*

B98 SP33 10c + 5c red brn, *buff* .25 .25
B99 SP33 35c + 10c sl grn, *buff* .25 .30
B100 SP33 70c + 20c blk, *buff* .95 *1.50*
B101 SP33 1fr + 25c red org, *buff* 4.00 *13.00*
B102 SP33 1.25fr + 75c vio brn, *buff* 4.75 *13.00*
B103 SP33 1.75fr + 1.50fr lt bl, *buff* 5.50 *26.00*
Nos. B98-B103 (6) 15.70 *54.05*
Set, never hinged 36.00

See No. 217 (souvenir sheet).

Allegory of Medicinal Baths — SP36

1940, Mar. 1 Photo. *Perf. 11½*

B104 SP36 2fr + 50c gray, blk & slate grn 1.25 *10.00*
Never hinged 4.00

For similar stamp see No. 216.

Stamps of 1944, type A37, surcharged "+50C," "+5F" or "+15F" in black, were sold only in canceled condition, affixed to numbered folders. The surtax was for the benefit of Luxembourg evacuees. Value for folder, $15.

Homage to France — SP37

Thanks to: No. B118, USSR. No. B119, Britannia. No. B120, America.

1945, Mar. 1 Engr. *Perf. 13*

B117 SP37 60c + 1.40fr dp grn .25 .25
B118 SP37 1.20fr + 1.80fr red .25 .25
B119 SP37 2.50fr + 3.50fr dp bl .25 .25
B120 SP37 4.20fr + 4.80fr dp vio .25 .25
Nos. B117-B120 (4) 1.00 1.00
Set, never hinged 1.25

Issued to honor the Allied Nations. Exist imperf. Value, set $175.

Statue Carried in Procession SP41

Statue of Our Lady "Patrona Civitatis" SP42

"Our Lady of Luxembourg" SP43

Cathedral Façade SP44

Altar with Statue of Madonna SP45

1945, June 4

B121 SP41 60c + 40c grn .25 .50
B122 SP42 1.20fr + 80c red .25 .50
B123 SP43 2.50fr + 2.50fr dp bl .25 *3.00*
B124 SP44 5.50fr + 6.50fr dk vio .55 *11.00*
B125 SP45 20fr + 20fr choc .55 *12.50*
Nos. B121-B125 (5) 1.85 *27.50*
Set, never hinged 3.50

Exist imperf. Value, set $250.

Souvenir Sheet

"Our Lady of Luxembourg" — SP46

1945, Sept. 30 Engr. *Imperf.*

B126 SP46 50fr + 50fr blk 1.00 *42.50*
Never hinged 2.25

Young Fighters SP47

Refugee Mother and Children SP48

Political Prisoner SP49

Executed Civilian SP50

1945, Dec. 20 Photo. *Perf. 11½*

B127 SP47 20c + 30c sl grn & buff .25 *1.00*
B128 SP48 1.50fr + 1fr brn red & buff .25 *1.00*
B129 SP49 3.50fr + 3.50fr bl, dp bl & buff .25 *8.50*
B130 SP50 5fr + 10fr brn, dk brn & buff .25 *8.50*
Nos. B127-B130 (4) 1.00 *19.00*
Set, never hinged 1.25

Souvenir Sheet

1946, Jan. 30 Unwmk. *Perf. 11½*

B131 Sheet of 4 12.00 *350.00*
Never hinged 25.00
a. SP47 2.50fr + 2.50fr sl grn & buff 3.00 *50.00*
b. SP48 3.50fr + 6.50fr brown red & buff 3.00 *50.00*
c. SP49 5fr + 15fr bl, dp bl & buff 3.00 *50.00*
d. SP50 20fr + 20fr brown, dark brown & buff 3.00 *50.00*

Tribute to Luxembourg's heroes and martyrs. The surtax was for the National Welfare Fund.

Souvenir Sheet

Old Rolling Mill, Dudelange — SP52

1946, July 28 Engr. & Typo.

B132 SP52 50fr brn & dk bl, *buff* 7.00 *30.00*
Never hinged 14.00

National Postage Stamp Exhibition, Dudelange, July 28-29, 1946. The sheets sold for 55fr.

Jean l'Aveugle — SP53

1946, Dec. 5 Photo.

B133 SP53 60c + 40c dk grn .25 *1.00*
B134 SP53 1.50fr + 50c brn red .25 *2.00*
B135 SP53 3.50fr + 3.50fr dp bl .60 *7.00*
B136 SP53 5fr + 10fr sepia .30 *10.00*
Nos. B133-B136 (4) 1.40 *20.00*
Set, never hinged 3.50

600th anniv. of the death of Jean l'Aveugle (John the Blind), Count of Luxembourg.

Ruins of St. Willibrord Basilica SP54

Twelfth Century Miniature of St. Willibrord SP59

Designs: No. B138, Statue of Abbot Jean Bertels. No. B139, Emblem of Echternach Abbey. No. B140, Ruins of the Basilica's Interior. No. B141, St. Irmine and Pepin of Hersta Holding Model of the Abbey.

Perf. 13x14, 14x13

1947, May 25 Engr.

B137 SP54 20c + 10c blk .25 .25
B138 SP54 60c + 10c dk grn .40 .55
B139 SP54 75c + 25c dk car .55 .75
B140 SP54 1.50fr + 50c dk brn .70 .75
B141 SP54 3.50fr + 2.50fr dk bl 2.25 *4.75*
B142 SP59 25fr + 25fr dk pur 15.00 *25.00*
Nos. B137-B142 (6) 19.15 *32.05*
Set, never hinged 40.00

The surtax was to aid in restoring the Basilica of Saint Willibrord at Echternach.

Michel Lentz — SP60

1947, Dec. 4 Photo. *Perf. 11½*

B143 SP60 60c + 40c sep & buff .25 1.10
B144 SP60 1.50fr + 50c dp plum & buff .25 1.10
B145 SP60 3.50fr + 3.50fr dp bl & gray 2.75 *16.00*
B146 SP60 10fr + 5fr dk grn & gray 2.40 *16.00*
Nos. B143-B146 (4) 5.65 *34.20*
Set, never hinged 14.00

Edmond de La Fontaine (Dicks) — SP61

1948, Nov. 18

B147 SP61 60c + 40c brn & pale bis .25 .65
B148 SP61 1.50fr + 50c brn car & buff .35 .65
B149 SP61 3.50fr + 3.50fr dp bl & gray 4.50 *9.00*
B150 SP61 10fr + 5fr dk grn & gray 3.50 *9.00*
Nos. B147-B150 (4) 8.60 *19.30*
Set, never hinged 19.00

125th anniversary of the birth of Edmond de La Fontaine, poet and composer.

Type of Regular Issue of 1948

Souvenir Sheet

1949, Jan. 8 Unwmk. *Perf. 11½*

B151 Sheet of 3 45.00 45.00
Never hinged 90.00
a. A45 8fr + 3fr blue gray 13.00 15.00
b. A45 12fr + 5fr green 13.00 15.00
c. A45 15fr + 7fr brown 13.00 15.00

30th anniversary of Grand Duchess Charlotte's ascension to the throne. Border and dates "1919-1949" in gray.

Michel Rodange — SP62

1949, Dec. 5

B152 SP62 60c + 40c ol grn & gray .40 .50
B153 SP62 2fr + 1fr dk vio & rose 2.75 *5.00*
B154 SP62 4fr + 2fr sl blk & gray 4.50 *7.50*
B155 SP62 10fr + 5fr brn & buff 4.50 *12.00*
Nos. B152-B155 (4) 12.15 *25.00*
Set, never hinged 22.50

Wards of the Nation
SP63 SP64

1950, June 24 Engr. *Perf. 12½x12*

B156 SP63 60c + 15c dk sl bl .50 .65
B157 SP64 1fr + 20c dk car rose .80 1.00
B158 SP63 2fr + 30c red brn 1.00 1.00
B159 SP64 4fr + 75c dk bl 6.50 *10.50*
B160 SP63 8fr + 3fr blk 18.00 *32.50*
B161 SP64 10fr + 5fr lil rose 19.00 *32.50*
Nos. B156-B161 (6) 45.80 *78.15*
Set, never hinged 90.00

The surtax was for child welfare.

Jean A. Zinnen — SP65

1950, Dec. 5 Photo. *Perf. 11½*

B162 SP65 60c + 10c ind & gray .35 .25
B163 SP65 2fr + 15c cer & buff .35 .40
B164 SP65 4fr + 15c vio bl & bl gray 3.25 *6.50*
B165 SP65 8fr + 5fr dk brn & buff 9.25 *25.00*
Nos. B162-B165 (4) 13.20 *32.15*
Set, never hinged 27.50

Laurent Menager — SP66

1951, Dec. 5 **Gray Background**

B166 SP66 60c + 10c sepia .25 .40
B167 SP66 2fr + 15c dl ol grn .25 .40
B168 SP66 4fr + 15c blue 2.50 *4.00*
B169 SP66 8fr + 5fr vio brn 10.50 *30.00*
Nos. B166-B169 (4) 13.50 *34.80*
Set, never hinged 29.00

50th anniversary of the death of Laurent Menager, composer.

J. B. Fresez — SP67

1952, Dec. 3

B170 SP67 60c + 15c dk bl grn & pale bl .25 .35
B171 SP67 2fr + 25c chnt brn & buff .25 .35
B172 SP67 4fr + 25c dk vio bl & gray 1.50 *2.75*
B173 SP67 8fr + 4.75fr dp plum & lil gray 12.50 *29.00*
Nos. B170-B173 (4) 14.50 *32.45*
Set, never hinged 32.50

Traditions — SP68

Designs: Nos. B174, B177, Candlemas Singing. Nos. B175, B178, Procession with ratchets. Nos. B176, B179, Breaking Easter eggs.

1953, Dec. 3

B174 SP68 25c + 15c red org & dp car .25 .25
B175 SP68 80c + 20c vio brn & bl gray .25 .25
B176 SP68 1.20fr + 30c bl grn & ol grn .50 1.00
B177 SP68 2fr + 25c brn car & brn .25 .60
B178 SP68 4fr + 50c grnsh bl & vio bl 4.00 *8.00*
B179 SP68 7fr + 3.35fr vio & pur 6.00 *16.00*
Nos. B174-B179 (6) 11.25 *26.10*
Set, never hinged 24.00

The surtax was for the National Welfare Fund of Grand Duchess Charlotte.

Clay Censer and Whistle — SP69

Designs: 80c+20c, 4fr+50c, Sheep and bass drum. 1.20fr+30c, 7fr+3.45fr, Merry-go-round horses. 2fr+25c, As No. B180.

1954, Dec. 3

B180 SP69 25c + 5c car lake & cop brn .25 .40
B181 SP69 80c + 20c dk gray .25 .40
B182 SP69 1.20fr + 30c dk bl grn & cr .65 1.25
B183 SP69 2fr + 25c brn & ocher .35 .70
B184 SP69 4fr + 50c brt bl 3.50 *5.00*
B185 SP69 7fr + 3.45fr pur 9.00 *18.00*
Nos. B180-B185 (6) 14.00 *25.75*
Set, never hinged 29.00

Toys for St. Nicholas Day — SP70

Designs: 80c+20c, 4fr+50c, Christ child and lamb (Christmas). 1.20fr+30c, 7fr+3.45fr, Star, crown and cake (Epiphany).

1955, Dec. 5 **Unwmk.** ***Perf. 11½***

B186 SP70 25c + 5c sal & dk car .25 .25
B187 SP70 80c + 20c gray & gray blk .25 .25
B188 SP70 1.20fr + 30c ol grn & sl grn .25 .50
B189 SP70 2fr + 25c buff & dk brn .35 .25
B190 SP70 4fr + 50c lt bl & brt bl 2.50 *7.00*
B191 SP70 7fr + 3.45fr rose vio & claret 6.50 *13.00*
Nos. B186-B191 (6) 10.10 *21.25*
Set, never hinged 20.00

Coats of Arms — SP71

Arms: 25c+5c, 2fr+25c, Echternach. 80c+20c, 4fr+50c, Esch-sur-Alzette. 1.20fr+30c, 7fr+3.45fr, Grevenmacher.

1956, Dec. 5 **Photo.**

Arms in Original Colors

B192 SP71 25c + 5c blk & sal pink .25 .25
B193 SP71 80c + 20c ultra & yel .25 .25
B194 SP71 1.20fr + 30c ultra & gray .25 .45
B195 SP71 2fr + 25c blk & buff .25 .25
B196 SP71 4fr + 50c ultra & lt bl 1.90 *3.25*
B197 SP71 7fr + 3.45fr ultra & pale vio 4.00 *8.50*
Nos. B192-B197 (6) 6.90 *12.95*
Set, never hinged 12.50

1957, Dec. 4 **Unwmk.** ***Perf. 11½***

25c+5c, 2fr+25c, Luxembourg. 80c+20c, 4fr+50c, Mersch. 1.20fr+30c, 7fr+3.45fr, Vianden.

Arms in Original Colors

B198 SP71 25c + 5c ultra & org .25 *.25*
B199 SP71 80c + 20c blk & lem .25 *.25*
B200 SP71 1.20fr + 30c ultra & lt bl grn .25 *.35*
B201 SP71 2fr + 25c ultra & pale brn .25 *.30*
B202 SP71 4fr + 50c blk & pale vio bl .50 *4.00*
B203 SP71 7fr + 3.45fr ultra & rose lil 3.00 *7.00*
Nos. B198-B203 (6) 4.50 12.15
Set, never hinged 11.50

1958, Dec. 3 ***Perf. 11½***

30c+10c, 2.50fr+50c, Capellen. 1fr+25c, 5fr+50c, Diekirch. 1.50fr+25c, 8.50fr+4.60fr, Redange.

Arms in Original Colors

B204 SP71 30c + 10c blk & pink .25 *.25*
B205 SP71 1fr + 25c ultra & buff .25 *.25*
B206 SP71 1.50fr + 25c ultra & pale grn .25 *.40*
B207 SP71 2.50fr + 50c blk & gray .25 *.25*
B208 SP71 5fr + 50c ultra 1.75 *3.00*
B209 SP71 8.50fr + 4.60fr ultra & lil 2.00 *7.00*
Nos. B204-B209 (6) 4.75 *11.15*
Set, never hinged 9.00

1959, Dec. 2

30c+10c, 2.50fr+50c, Clervaux. 1fr+25c, 5fr+50c, Remich. 1.50fr+25c, 8.50fr+4.60fr, Wiltz.

Arms in Original Colors

B210 SP71 30c + 10c ultra & pink .25 .25
B211 SP71 1fr + 25c ultra & pale lem .25 .25
B212 SP71 1.50fr + 25c blk & pale grn .25 .45
B213 SP71 2.50fr + 50c ultra & pale fawn .25 .25
B214 SP71 5fr + 50c ultra & lt bl .65 *1.60*
B215 SP71 8.50fr + 4.60fr blk & pale vio 2.75 *8.00*
Nos. B210-B215 (6) 4.40 *10.80*
Set, never hinged 8.00

Catalogue values for unused stamps in this section, from this point to the end of the section, are for Never Hinged items.

Princess Marie-Astrid — SP72

1fr+25c, 5fr+50c, Princess in party dress. 1.50fr+25c, 8.50fr+4.60fr, Princess with book.

1960, Dec. 5 **Photo.** ***Perf. 11½***

B216 SP72 30c + 10c brn & lt bl .25 .25
B217 SP72 1fr + 25c brn & pink .25 .25
B218 SP72 1.50fr + 25c brn & lt bl .55 .40
B219 SP72 2.50fr + 50c brn & yel .40 .30
B220 SP72 5fr + 50c brn & pale lil 1.25 *1.00*
B221 SP72 8.50fr + 4.60fr brn & pale ol 8.00 *6.00*
Nos. B216-B221 (6) 10.70 8.20

Type of 1960

Prince Henri: 30c+10c, 2.50fr+50c, Infant in long dress. 1fr+25c, 5fr+50c, Informal portrait. 1.50fr+25c, 8.50fr+ 4.60fr, In dress suit.

1961, Dec. 4 **Unwmk.** ***Perf. 11½***

B222 SP72 30c + 10c brn & brt pink .25 .25
B223 SP72 1fr + 25c brn & lt vio .30 .25
B224 SP72 1.50fr + 25c brn & sal .35 .30
B225 SP72 2.50fr + 50c brn & pale grn .40 .40
B226 SP72 5fr + 50c brn & cit 2.00 1.40
B227 SP72 8.50fr + 4.60fr brn & gray 3.75 *4.50*
Nos. B222-B227 (6) 7.05 7.10

Prince Jean — SP73

Designs: Different portraits of the twins Prince Jean and Princess Margaretha. Nos. B228 and B233 are horizontal.

Inscriptions and Portraits in Dark Brown

1962, Dec. 3 **Photo.** ***Perf. 11½***

B228 SP73 30c + 10c org yel .25 .25
B229 SP73 1fr + 25c lt bl .25 .25
B230 SP73 1.50fr + 25c pale ol .35 .35
B231 SP73 2.50fr + 50c rose .35 .25
B232 SP73 5fr + 50c lt yel grn 1.00 *1.25*
B233 SP73 8.50fr + 4.60fr lil gray 3.25 *3.50*
Nos. B228-B233 (6) 5.45 5.85

St. Roch, Patron of Bakers — SP74

Patron Saints: 1fr+25c, St. Anne, tailors. 2fr+25c, St. Eloi, smiths. 3fr+50c, St. Michael, shopkeepers. 6fr+50c, St. Bartholomew, butchers. St. Theobald, seven crafts.

1963, Dec. 2 **Unwmk.** ***Perf. 11½***

Background Color

B234 SP74 50c + 10c pale lil .25 .25
B235 SP74 1fr + 25c tan .25 .25
B236 SP74 2fr + 25c lt grnsh bl .25 .25
B237 SP74 3fr + 50c lt bl .25 .25
B238 SP74 6fr + 50c buff .90 *.90*
B239 SP74 10fr + 5.90fr pale yel grn 1.50 *2.00*
Nos. B234-B239 (6) 3.40 3.90

Three Towers — SP75

Children's paintings: 1fr+25c, 6fr+50c, Grand Duke Adolphe Bridge, horiz. 2fr+25c, 10fr+5.90fr, The Lower City.

1964, Dec. 7 **Photo.** ***Perf. 11½***

B240 SP75 50c + 10c multi .25 .25
B241 SP75 1fr + 25c multi .25 .25
B242 SP75 2fr + 25c multi .25 .25
a. Value omitted *300.00*
B243 SP75 3fr + 50c multi .25 .25
B244 SP75 6fr + 50c multi .90 1.00
B245 SP75 10fr + 5.90fr multi 1.10 *1.75*
Nos. B240-B245 (6) 3.00 3.75

The Roman Lady of Titelberg — SP76

Fairy Tales of Luxembourg: 1fr+25c, Schäppchen, the Huntsman. 2fr+25c, The Witch of Koerich. 3fr+50c, The Gnomes of Schoenfels. 6fr+50c, Tollchen, Watchman of Hesperange. 10fr+5.90fr, The Old Spinster of Heispelt.

1965, Dec. 6 **Photo.** ***Perf. 11½***

B246 SP76 50c + 10c multi .25 .25
B247 SP76 1fr + 25c multi .25 .25
B248 SP76 2fr + 25c multi .25 .25
B249 SP76 3fr + 50c multi .25 .25
B250 SP76 6fr + 50c multi .40 *.40*
B251 SP76 10fr + 5.90fr multi 1.00 *1.25*
Nos. B246-B251 (6) 2.40 2.65

Fairy Tale Type of 1965

Fairy Tales of Luxembourg: 50c+10c, The Veiled Matron of Wormeldange. 1.50fr+25c, Jekel, Warden of the Wark. 2fr+25c, The Black Man of Vianden. 3fr+50c, The Gracious Fairy of Rosport. 6fr+1fr, The Friendly Shepherd of Donkolz. 13fr+6.90fr, The Little Sisters of Trois-Vièrges.

1966, Dec. 6 **Photo.** ***Perf. 11½***

B252 SP76 50c + 10c multi .25 .25
B253 SP76 1.50fr + 25c multi .25 .25
B254 SP76 2fr + 25c multi .25 .25
B255 SP76 3fr + 50c multi .25 .25
B256 SP76 6fr + 1fr multi .35 *.40*
B257 SP76 13fr + 6.90fr multi .85 *1.00*
Nos. B252-B257 (6) 2.20 2.40

Prince Guillaume SP77

Castle of Berg SP78

Portraits: 1.50fr+25c, Princess Margaretha. 2fr+25c, Prince Jean. 3fr+50c, Prince Henri as Boy Scout. 6fr+1fr, Princess Marie-Astrid.

1967, Dec. 6 **Photo.** ***Perf. 11½***

B258 SP77 50c + 10c yel & brn .25 .25
B259 SP77 1.50fr + 25c gray bl & brn .25 .25
B260 SP77 2fr + 25c pale rose & brn .25 .25
B261 SP77 3fr + 50c lt ol & brn .50 .25
B262 SP77 6fr + 1fr lt vio & brn .35 *.50*
B263 SP78 13fr + 6.90fr multi .50 *1.00*
Nos. B258-B263 (6) 2.10 2.50

Medico-professional Institute at Cap SP79

Deaf-mute Child Imitating Bird SP80

Handicapped Children: 2fr+25c, Blind child holding candle. 3fr+50c, Nurse supporting physically handicapped child. 6fr+1fr, Cerebral palsy victim. 13fr+6.90fr, Mentally disturbed child.

1968, Dec. 5 **Photo.** ***Perf. 11½***

Designs and Inscriptions in Dark Brown

B264 SP79 50c + 10c lt bl .25 .25
B265 SP80 1.50fr + 25c lt grn .25 .25
B266 SP80 2fr + 25c yel .25 .25

B267	SP80	3fr + 50c bl	.25	.25
B268	SP80	6fr + 1fr buff	.40	.55
B269	SP80	13fr + 6.90fr pink	1.00	*1.50*
		Nos. B264-B269 (6)	2.40	3.05

Vianden Castle — SP81

Luxembourg Castles: 1.50fr+25c, Lucilinburhuc. 2fr+25c, Bourglinster. 3fr+50c, Hollenfels. 6fr+1fr, Ansembourg. 13fr+6.90fr, Beaufort.

1969, Dec. 8 Photo. *Perf. 11½*

B270	SP81	50c + 10c multi	.25	.25
B271	SP81	1.50fr + 25c multi	.25	.25
B272	SP81	2fr + 25c multi	.25	.25
B273	SP81	3fr + 50c multi	.25	.25
B274	SP81	6fr + 1fr multi	.45	*.75*
B275	SP81	13fr + 6.90fr multi	.60	*1.25*
		Nos. B270-B275 (6)	2.05	3.00

1970, Dec. 7 Photo. *Perf. 11½*

Luxembourg Castles: 50c+10c, Clervaux. 1.50fr+25c, Septfontaines. 2fr+25c, Bourscheid. 3fr+50c, Esch-sur-Sure. 6fr+1fr, Larochette. 13fr+6.90fr, Brandenbourg.

B276	SP81	50c + 10c multi	.25	.25
B277	SP81	1.50fr + 25c multi	.25	.25
B278	SP81	2fr + 25c multi	.25	.25
B279	SP81	3fr + 50c multi	.25	.25
B280	SP81	6fr + 1fr multi	.40	*.55*
B281	SP81	13fr + 6.90fr multi	.75	*1.25*
		Nos. B276-B281 (6)	2.15	2.80

The surtax on Nos. B180-B281 was for charitable purposes.

Children of Bethlehem — SP82

Wooden Statues from Crèche of Beaufort Church: 1.50fr+25c, Shepherds. 3fr+50c, Nativity. 8fr+1fr, Herdsmen. 18fr+6.50fr, King offering gift.

1971, Dec. 6 Photo. *Perf. 11½*

Sculptures in Shades of Brown

B282	SP82	1fr + 25c lilac	.25	.25
B283	SP82	1.50fr + 25c olive	.25	.25
B284	SP82	3fr + 50c gray	.25	.25
B285	SP82	8fr + 1fr lt ultra	.50	*.75*
B286	SP82	18fr + 6.50fr grn	1.75	*2.50*
		Nos. B282-B286 (5)	3.00	4.00

The surtax was for various charitable organizations.

Angel — SP83

Stained Glass Windows, Luxembourg Cathedral: 1.50fr+25c, St. Joseph. 3fr+50c, Virgin and Child. 8fr+1fr, People of Bethlehem. 18fr+6.50fr, Angel facing left.

1972, Dec. 4

B287	SP83	1fr + 25c multi	.25	.25
B288	SP83	1.50fr + 25c multi	.25	.25
B289	SP83	3fr + 50c multi	.25	.25
B290	SP83	8fr + 1fr multi	.75	*1.40*
B291	SP83	18fr + 6.50fr multi	2.40	*3.50*
		Nos. B287-B291 (5)	3.90	5.65

Surtax was for charitable purposes.

Sts. Anne and Joachim — SP84

Sculptures: 3fr+25c, Mary meeting Elizabeth. 4fr+50c, Virgin and Child and a King. 8fr+1fr, Shepherds. 15fr+7fr, St. Joseph holding candle. Designs from 16th century reredos, Hermitage of Hachiville.

1973, Dec. 5 Photo. *Perf. 11½*

B292	SP84	1fr + 25c multi	.25	.25
B293	SP84	3fr + 25c multi	.25	.25
B294	SP84	4fr + 50c multi	.25	.25
B295	SP84	8fr + 1fr multi	.90	*1.50*
B296	SP84	15fr + 7fr multi	2.00	*3.25*
		Nos. B292-B296 (5)	3.65	5.50

Annunciation — SP85

Crucifixion — SP86

Designs: 3fr+25c, Visitation. 4fr+50c, Nativity. 8fr+1fr, Adoration of the King. 15fr+7fr, Presentation at the Temple. Designs of Nos. B297-B301 are from miniatures in the "Codex Aureus Epternacensis" (Gospel from Echternach Abbey). The Crucifixion is from the carved ivory cover of the Codex, by the Master of Echternach, c. 983-991.

1974, Dec. 5 Photo. *Perf. 11½*

B297	SP85	1fr + 25c multi	.25	.25
B298	SP85	3fr + 25c multi	.25	.25
B299	SP85	4fr + 50c multi	.25	.25
B300	SP85	8fr + 1fr multi	.85	*1.25*
B301	SP85	15fr + 7fr multi	2.00	*3.00*
		Nos. B297-B301 (5)	3.60	5.00

Souvenir Sheet

Photogravure & Engraved

Perf. 13½

B302	SP86	20fr + 10fr multi	3.50	6.00

50th anniversary of Caritas issues. No. B302 contains one 34x42mm stamp.

Fly Orchid — SP87

Flowers: 3fr+25c, Pyramidal orchid. 4fr+50c, Marsh hellebore. 8fr+1fr, Pasqueflower. 15fr+7fr, Bee orchid.

1975, Dec. 4 Photo. *Perf. 11½*

B303	SP87	1fr + 25c multi	.25	.25
B304	SP87	3fr + 25c multi	.30	.25
B305	SP87	4fr + 50c multi	.40	.40
B306	SP87	8fr + 1fr multi	.90	*1.50*
B307	SP87	15fr + 7fr multi	2.75	*3.00*
		Nos. B303-B307 (5)	4.60	5.40

The surtax on Nos. B303-B317 was for various charitable organizations.

1976, Dec. 6

Flowers: 2fr+25c, Gentian. 5fr+25c, Narcissus. 6fr+50c, Red hellebore. 12fr+1fr, Late spider orchid. 20fr+8fr, Two-leafed squill.

B308	SP87	2fr + 25c multi	.25	.25
B309	SP87	5fr + 25c multi	.25	.25
B310	SP87	6fr + 50c multi	.30	.30
B311	SP87	12fr + 1fr multi	.90	*1.25*
B312	SP87	20fr + 8fr multi	2.40	*3.50*
		Nos. B308-B312 (5)	4.10	5.55

Lilies of the Valley — SP88

Flowers: 5fr+25c, Columbine. 6fr+50c, Mezereon. 12fr+1fr, Early spider orchid. 20fr+8fr, Spotted orchid.

1977, Dec. 5 Photo. *Perf. 11½*

B313	SP88	2fr + 25c multi	.25	.25
B314	SP88	5fr + 25c multi	.30	.30
B315	SP88	6fr + 50c multi	.45	.45
B316	SP88	12fr + 1fr multi	1.25	*2.00*
B317	SP88	20fr + 8fr multi	2.40	*3.25*
		Nos. B313-B317 (5)	4.65	6.25

St. Matthew — SP89

Behind-glass Paintings, 19th Century: 5fr+25c, St. Mark. 6fr+50c, Nativity. 12fr+1fr, St. Luke. 20fr+8fr, St. John.

1978, Dec. 5 Photo. *Perf. 11½*

B318	SP89	2fr + 25c multi	.25	.25
B319	SP89	5fr + 25c multi	.30	.30
B320	SP89	6fr + 50c multi	.45	.45
B321	SP89	12fr + 1fr multi	1.10	1.40
B322	SP89	20fr + 8fr multi	1.60	*2.00*
		Nos. B318-B322 (5)	3.70	4.40

Surtax was for charitable organizations.

Spring — SP90

Behind-glass Paintings, 19th Century: 5fr+25c, Summer. 6fr+50c, Charity. 12fr+1fr, Autumn. 20fr+8fr, Winter.

1979, Dec. 5 Photo. *Perf. 12*

B323	SP90	2fr + 25c multi	.25	.25
B324	SP90	5fr + 25c multi	.25	.25
B325	SP90	6fr + 50c multi	.30	.25
B326	SP90	12fr + 1fr multi	.65	*1.10*
B327	SP90	20fr + 8fr multi	1.50	*2.75*
		Nos. B323-B327 (5)	2.95	4.60

St. Martin — SP91

Behind-glass Paintings, 19th Century: 6fr+50c, St. Nicholas. 8fr+1fr, Madonna and Child. 30fr+1fr, St. George the Martyr.

1980, Dec. 5 Photo. *Perf. 11½*

B328	SP91	4fr + 50c multi	.25	.25
B329	SP91	6fr + 50c multi	.30	.30
B330	SP91	8fr + 1fr multi	.60	.60
B331	SP91	30fr + 10fr multi	1.60	2.25
		Nos. B328-B331 (4)	2.75	3.40

Surtax was for charitable organizations.

Arms of Petange SP92

Nativity, by Otto van Veen (1556-1629) SP93

1981, Dec. 4 Photo.

Granite Paper

B332	SP92	4fr + 50c shown	.25	.25
B333	SP92	6fr + 50c Larochette	.25	.25
B334	SP93	8fr + 1fr shown	.35	.35
B335	SP92	16fr + 2fr Stadtbredimus	.75	1.00
B336	SP92	35fr + 12fr Weiswampach	2.00	2.50
		Nos. B332-B336 (5)	3.60	4.35

Surtax was for charitable organizations.

1982, Dec. 6 Photo. *Perf. 11½*

Design: 8fr+1fr, Adoration of the Shepherds, stained-glass window, by Gust Zanter, Hoscheid Parish Church.

Granite Paper

B337	SP92	4fr + 50c Bettembourg	.25	.25
B338	SP92	6fr + 50c Frisange	.30	.30
B339	SP93	8fr + 1fr multi	.35	.30
B340	SP92	16fr + 2fr Mamer	1.00	1.40
B341	SP92	35fr + 12fr Heinerscheid	2.25	2.25
		Nos. B337-B341 (5)	4.15	4.50

Surtax was for charitable organizations.

1983, Dec. 5 Photo.

B342	SP92	4fr + 1fr Winseler	.25	.25
B343	SP92	7fr + 1fr Beckerich	.35	.35
B344	SP93	10fr + 1fr Nativity	.60	.55
B345	SP92	16fr + 2fr Feulen	.75	.85
B346	SP92	40fr + 13fr Mertert	2.25	2.75
		Nos. B342-B346 (5)	4.20	4.75

Surtax was for charitable organizations.

Inquisitive Child — SP94

Children Exhibiting Various Moods.

1984, Dec. 5 Photo.

B347	SP94	4fr + 1fr shown	.45	.45
B348	SP94	7fr + 1fr Daydreaming	.75	.75
B349	SP94	10fr + 1fr Nativity	.80	1.00
B350	SP94	16fr + 2fr Sulking	2.00	2.25
B351	SP94	40fr + 13fr Admiring	5.00	5.00
		Nos. B347-B351 (5)	9.00	9.45

Surtax was for charitable organizations.

1985, Dec. 5 Photo.

B352	SP94	4fr + 1fr Girl drawing	.50	.50
B353	SP94	7fr + 1fr Two boys	.60	.60
B354	SP94	10fr + 1fr Adoration of the Magi	.90	.90
B355	SP94	16fr + 2fr Fairy tale characters	2.00	2.00
B356	SP94	40fr + 13fr Embarrassed girl	6.50	6.50
		Nos. B352-B356 (5)	10.50	10.50

Surtax was for charitable organizations.

SP95

Christmas: Illuminated text — No. B357, Annunciation. No. B358, Angel appears to the Shepherds. No. B359, Nativity. No. B360, Adoration of the Magi. No. B361, Flight into Egypt.

1986, Dec. 8 Photo. *Perf. 11½*

B357	SP95	6fr + 1fr multi	.90	.90
B358	SP95	10fr + 1fr multi	.60	.60
B359	SP95	12fr + 2fr multi	.90	.90
B360	SP95	18fr + 2fr multi	1.75	1.75
B361	SP95	20fr + 8fr multi	4.25	4.25
		Nos. B357-B361 (5)	8.40	8.40

SP96

No. B362, Annunciation. No. B363, Visitation. No. B364, Adoration of the Magi. No. B365, Presentation in the Temple. No. B366, Flight into Egypt.

1987, Dec. 1 *Perf. 12*

B362	SP96	6fr + 1fr multi	.60	.60
B363	SP96	10fr + 1fr multi	.90	.90
B364	SP96	12fr + 2fr multi	1.50	1.50
B365	SP96	18fr + 2fr multi	2.40	2.40
B366	SP96	20fr + 8fr multi	4.75	4.75
		Nos. B362-B366 (5)	10.15	10.15

Book of Hours, France, c. 1550, Natl. Library — SP97

No. B367, Annunciation to the Shepherds. No. B368, Adoration of the Magi. No. B369, Virgin and Child. No. B370, Pentecost.

1988, Dec. 5 **Perf. 11½**

B367 SP97 9fr +1fr multi .60 .60
B368 SP97 12fr +2fr multi .60 .60
B369 SP97 18fr +2fr multi 2.00 2.00
B370 SP97 20fr +8fr multi 2.75 2.75
Nos. B367-B370 (4) 5.95 5.95

Surtax for charitable organizations.

Christmas — SP98

Chapels: No. B371, St. Lambert and St. Blase, Fennange, vert. No. B372, St. Quirinus, Luxembourg. No. B373, St. Anthony the Hermit, Reisdorf, vert. No. B374, The Hermitage, Hachiville.

1989, Dec. 11 Photo. **Perf. 12x11½**

B371 SP98 9fr +1fr multi .45 .45
B372 SP98 12fr +2fr multi .60 .60
B373 SP98 18fr +3fr multi 1.75 1.75
B374 SP98 25fr +8fr multi 2.75 2.75
Nos. B371-B374 (4) 5.55 5.55

Surtax for social work.

1990, Nov. 26 Photo. **Perf. 11½**

Chapels: No. B375, Congregation of the Blessed Virgin Mary, Vianden, vert. No. B376, Our Lady, Echternach. No. B377, Our Lady, Consoler of the Afflicted, Grentzingen. B378, St. Pirmin, Kaundorf, vert.

B375 SP98 9fr +1fr multi .50 .50
B376 SP98 12fr +2fr multi 1.00 1.00
B377 SP98 18fr +3fr multi 2.00 1.50
B378 SP98 25fr +8fr multi 3.50 3.50
Nos. B375-B378 (4) 7.00 6.50

Surtax for charitable organizations.

1991, Dec. 9 Photo. **Perf. 11½**

Chapels: No. B379, St. Donatus, Arsdorf, vert. No. B380, Our Lady of Sorrows, Brandenbourg. No. B381, Our Lady, Luxembourg. No. B382, The Hermitage, Wolwelange, vert.

B379 SP98 14fr +2fr multi .90 .90
B380 SP98 14fr +2fr multi .90 .90
B381 SP98 18fr +3fr multi 1.75 1.75
B382 SP98 22fr +7fr multi 3.00 3.00
Nos. B379-B382 (4) 6.55 6.55

Surtax used for philanthropic work.

Endangered Birds — SP99

Designs: No. B383, Hazel grouse. No. B384, Golden oriole, vert. 18fr+3fr, Black stork. 22fr+7fr, Red kite, vert.

1992, Dec. 7 Photo. **Perf. 11½**

B383 SP99 14fr +2fr multi .90 .90
B384 SP99 14fr +2fr multi .90 .90
B385 SP99 18fr +3fr multi 2.75 2.25
B386 SP99 22fr +7fr multi 3.75 3.25
Nos. B383-B386 (4) 8.30 7.30

Surtax for Luxembourg charitable organizations.

1993, Dec. 6 Photo. **Perf. 11½**

Designs: No. B387, Snipe. No. B388, Kingfisher, vert. 18fr+3fr, Little ringed plover. 22fr+7fr, Sand martin, vert.

B387 SP99 14fr +2fr multi .90 .90
B388 SP99 14fr +2fr multi .90 .90
B389 SP99 18fr +3fr multi 2.75 1.75
B390 SP99 22fr +7fr multi 4.00 2.75
Nos. B387-B390 (4) 8.55 6.30

Surtax for Luxembourg charitable organizations.

1994, Sept. 19 Photo. **Perf. 11½**

Designs: No. B391, Partridge. No. B392, Stonechat, vert. 18fr+3fr, Blue-headed wagtail. 22fr+7fr, Great grey shrike, vert.

B391 SP99 14fr +2fr multi 1.00 .90
B392 SP99 14fr +2fr multi 1.00 .90
B393 SP99 18fr +3fr multi 2.75 2.25
B394 SP99 22fr +7fr multi 3.50 2.50
Nos. B391-B394 (4) 8.25 6.55

Christmas — SP100

Design: 16fr + 2fr, Stained glass window, parish church of Alzingen.

1995, Dec. 4 Photo. **Perf. 11½**

B395 SP100 16fr +2fr multi 2.50 1.75

Surtax for Luxembourg charitable organizations.

Trees — SP101

Designs: No. B396, Tilia platyphyllos. No. B397, Aesculus hippocastanum, horiz. 20fr+3fr, Quercus pedunculata, horiz. 32fr+7fr, Betula pendula.

1995, Dec. 4

B396 SP101 16fr +2fr multi .90 .90
B397 SP101 16fr +2fr multi .90 .90
B398 SP101 20fr +3fr multi 1.75 1.75
B399 SP101 32fr +7fr multi 2.75 2.75
Nos. B396-B399 (4) 6.30 6.30

Surtax for Luxembourg charitable organizations.
See Nos. B400-B403, B405-B408.

1996, Dec. 9

Designs: No. B400, Fraxinus excelsior. No. B401, Salix SSP, horiz. 20fr+3fr, Sorbus domestica, horiz. 32fr+7fr, Fagus silvatica.

B400 SP101 16fr +2fr multi .90 .90
B401 SP101 16fr +2fr multi .90 .90
B402 SP101 20fr +3fr multi 1.75 1.75
B403 SP101 32fr +7fr multi 3.00 3.00
Nos. B400-B403 (4) 6.55 6.55

Surtax for Luxembourg charitable organizations.

Christmas — SP102

1996, Dec. 9

B404 SP102 16fr +2fr multi 1.50 1.50

Surtax for Luxembourg charitable organizations.

Tree Type of 1995

Designs: No. B405, Ulmus glabra. No. B406, Acer platanoides. 20fr+3fr, Prunus avium. 32fr+7fr, Juglans regia, horiz.

1997, Dec. 8 Photo. **Perf. 11½**

B405 SP101 16fr +2fr multi .90 .90
B406 SP101 16fr +2fr multi .90 .90
B407 SP101 20fr +3fr multi 2.00 2.00
B408 SP101 32fr +7fr multi 2.75 2.50
Nos. B405-B408 (4) 6.55 6.30

Christmas — SP103

1997, Dec. 8

B409 SP103 16fr +2fr multi 1.50 1.50

Christmas — SP104

1998, Dec. 7 Photo. **Perf. 11½**

B410 SP104 16fr +2fr multi 1.50 1.50

Charity Stamps — SP105

Drawings of villages by Abbot Jean Bertels, 16th cent.: No. B411, Bech. No. B412, Ermesturf (Ermsdorf). 20fr+3fr, Itsich (Itzig). 32fr+7fr, Steinhem (Steinheim).

1998, Dec. 7

B411 SP105 16fr +2fr grn & multi 1.00 1.00
B412 SP105 16fr +2fr brn & multi 1.00 1.00
B413 SP105 20fr +3fr red & multi 1.25 1.25
B414 SP105 32fr +7fr blue & multi 2.25 2.25
Nos. B411-B414 (4) 5.50 5.50

See Nos. B415-B418, B420-B423.

Perf. 11¾x11½

1999, Nov. 30 **Photo.**

Drawings of villages by Abbot Jean Bertels, 16th cent.: No. B415, Oswiler (Osweiler). No. B416, Bettemburch (Bettembourg). 20fr+3fr, Cruchte auf der Alset (Cruchten). 32fr+7fr, Berchem.

B415 SP105 16fr +2fr red vio & multi 1.25 1.25
B416 SP105 16fr +2fr blue & multi 1.25 1.25
B417 SP105 20fr +3fr bl grn & multi 1.25 1.25
B418 SP105 32fr +7fr brown & multi 2.25 2.25
Nos. B415-B418 (4) 6.00 6.00

Surtax for Luxembourg charitable organizations.

Christmas — SP106

1999, Nov. 30 **Perf. 11¾**

B419 SP106 16fr +2fr multi 1.25 1.25

Surtax for Luxembourg charitable organizations.

Village Drawings Type of 1998

By Abbot Jean Bertels, 16th cent.: 18fr+2fr, Lorentzwiler (Lorentzweiler). 21fr+3fr, Costurf (Consdorf). 24fr+3fr, Elfingen (Elvange). 36fr+7fr, Sprenckigen (Sprinkange).

2000, Dec. 5 Photo. **Perf. 11¾x11½**
Granite Paper

B420 SP105 18fr +2fr grn & multi .90 .90
B421 SP105 21fr +3fr brn & multi 1.25 1.25
B422 SP105 24fr +3fr red & multi 1.25 1.25
B423 SP105 36fr +7fr bl & multi 2.25 2.25
Nos. B420-B423 (4) 5.65 5.65

Surtax for Luxembourg charitable organizations.

Christmas — SP107

2000, Dec. 5 **Perf. 11¾**
Granite Paper

B424 SP107 18fr +2fr multi 2.00 2.00

Surtax for Luxembourg charitable organizations.

Christmas — SP108

2001, Dec. 6 Photo. **Perf. 14**

B425 SP108 45c +5c (18fr+2fr) multi 1.25 1.25

See note before No. 1063. A star-shaped hole is found at the UL portion of the design.

Fauna — SP109

Designs: 45c+5c (18fr+2fr), Squirrel. 52c+8c (21fr+3fr), Wild boar. 59c+11c (24fr+4fr), Hare, vert. 89c+21c (36fr+8fr), Wood pigeon, vert.

Perf. 11¾x11½, 11½x11¾
2001, Dec. 6 **Granite Paper**

B426-B429 SP109 Set of 4 7.00 7.00

Christmas — SP110

2002, Dec. 10 Photo. **Perf. 13¾**

B430 SP110 45c +5c multi 1.25 1.25

Surtax for Grand Duchess Charlotte charities.

Fauna — SP111

Designs: 45c+5c, Red fox. 52c+8c, Hedgehog and snail, vert. 59c+11c, Pheasant. 89c+21c, Deer, vert.

2002, Dec. 10 **Perf. 11½**

B431-B434 SP111 Set of 4 7.00 7.00

Christmas — SP112

No. B435: a, Round Church of Ehnen, Christmas tree. b, Wormer Koeppchen Chapel.

2003, Dec. 9 Litho. **Perf. 14¼**

B435 SP112 50c +5c Pair, #a-b 2.75 2.75

Surtax for Luxembourg charitable organizations.

Fauna — SP113

Designs: 50c+5c, Roe deer, vert. 60c+10c, Raccoons. 70c+10c, Weasel, vert. €1+25c, Goshawk.

2003, Dec. 9 Photo. **Perf. 11½**

B436-B439 SP113 Set of 4 8.00 8.00

Surtax for Luxembourg charitable organizations.

Christmas
SP114

Litho. & Embossed

2004, Dec. 7 *Perf. 13*
B440 SP114 50c +5c multi 1.50 1.50

Sports — SP115

Designs: 50c+5c, Skiing. 60c+10c, Running, vert. 70c+10c, Swimming. €1+25c, Soccer, vert.

Perf. 13x13½, 13½x13

2004, Dec. 7 **Litho.**
B441-B444 SP115 Set of 4 8.75 8.75

See Nos. B446-B449.

Christmas
SP116

2005, Dec. 6 **Litho.** *Perf. 13¼*
B445 SP116 50c +5c multi 1.40 1.40

Sports Type of 2004

Designs: 50c+5c, Figure skating, vert. 70c+10c, Basketball, vert. 90c+10c, Judo, vert. €1+25c, Tennis, vert.

2005, Dec. 6 *Perf. 13½x13*
B446-B449 SP115 Set of 4 8.50 8.50

Christmas — SP117

2006, Dec. 5 **Litho.** *Perf. 12½*
B450 SP117 50c +5c multi 1.40 1.40

Modern Pipe
Organs — SP118

Organ from: 50c+5c, Grand Auditorium of the Luxembourg Music Conservatory. 70c+10c, Bridel. 90c+10c, Mondercange Parish Church. €1+25c, Luxembourg-Grund.

2006, Dec. 5 *Perf. 13¼x13*
B451-B454 SP118 Set of 4 9.25 9.25

See Nos. B456-B459, B461-B464, B466-B469.

Christmas — SP119

2007, Dec. 4 **Litho.** *Perf. 12½*
B455 SP119 50c +5c multi 1.60 1.60

Modern Pipe Organs Type of 2006

Organ from: 50c+5c, Church of Niederwiltz. 70c+10c, Sandweiler, horiz. 90c+10c, Echternacht Basilica, horiz. €1+25c, St. Joseph's Church, Esch-sur-Alzette.

2007, Dec. 4 *Perf. 13½x13, 13x13½*
B456-B459 SP118 Set of 4 10.50 10.50

Christmas — SP120

2008, Dec. 2 **Litho.** *Perf. 12½*
B460 SP120 50c +5c multi 1.40 1.40

Modern Pipe Organs Type of 2006

Organ from: 50c+5c, Junglinster. 70c+10c, Church, Mondorf-les-Bains, horiz. 90c+10c, Church, Vianden. €1+25c, Notre Dame Cathedral, Luxembourg.

2008, Dec. 2 *Perf. 13½x13, 13x13½*
B461-B464 SP118 Set of 4 9.25 9.25

Christmas — SP121

2009, Dec. 1 **Litho.** *Perf. 12½*
B465 SP121 50c + 5c multi 1.75 1.75

Modern Pipe Organs Type of 2006

Organ from: 50c+5c, Luxembourg Philharmonic. 70c+10c, St. Martin's Church, Dudelange. 90c+10c, Church, Nommern. 1fr+25c, Saint-Pierre aux Liens Church, Heiderscheid.

2009, Dec. 1 *Perf. 13½x13*
B466-B469 SP118 Set of 4 11.00 11.00

Christmas — SP122

2010, Dec. 7 **Litho.** *Perf. 12½*
B470 SP122 60c + 5c multi 1.90 1.90

Occupations of the
Past — SP123

Designs: 60c+5c, Blacksmith. 85c+10c, Basketmaker. €1.10+10c, Grinder, horiz. €1.20+25c, Cooper, horiz.

Litho. & Embossed With Foil Application

2010, Dec. 7 *Perf. 13¼x13, 13x13¼*
B471-B474 SP123 Set of 4 12.00 12.00

See Nos. B476-B479, B482-B485, B488-B491.

Christmas — SP124

2011, Dec. 6 **Litho.** *Perf. 12½*
B475 SP124 60c+5c multi 1.75 1.75

No. B475 is impregnated with a pine scent.

Occupations of the Past Type of 2010

Designs: 60c+5c, Wood joiner (schräiner). 85c+10c, Potter (aulebacker). €1.10+10c, Stonemason (steemetzer), horiz. €1.20+25c, Printer (buchdréker), horiz.

Litho. & Embossed With Foil Application

2011, Dec. 6 *Perf. 13¼x13, 13x13¼*
B476-B479 SP123 Set of 4 11.50 11.50

Christmas
SP125

Stars, Christmas tree and: 60c+5c, Open mailbox. 85c+10c, Open envelope.

Litho. With Foil Application

2012, Dec. 4 *Perf. 13¼*
B480-B481 SP125 Set of 2 4.25 4.25

Occupations of the Past Type of 2010

Designs: 60c+5c, Washerwomen, horiz. 85c+10c, Hatter. €1.10+10c, Farmer. €1.20+25c, Vegetable sellers, horiz.

Litho. & Embossed With Foil Application

2012, Dec. 4 *Perf. 13x13¼, 13¼x13*
B482-B485 SP123 Set of 4 11.00 11.00

Christmas
SP126

Designs: 60c+5c, One Christmas ornament. 85c+10c, Two Christmas ornaments.

2013, Dec. 3 **Litho.** *Perf. 13*
B486-B487 SP126 Set of 2 4.50 4.50

Nos. B486 and B487 have laser-cut holes as part of the design.

Occupations of the Past Type of 2010

Designs: 60c+5c, Miller. 85c+10c, Distiller, horiz. €1.10+10c, Wheelwright. €1.20+25c, Cobbler, horiz.

Litho. & Embossed With Foil Application

2013, Dec. 3 *Perf. 13¼x13, 13x13¼*
B488-B491 SP123 Set of 4 12.00 12.00

Christmas
SP127

Designs: 60c+5c, Fox and rabbit. 85c+10c, Owl and mouse.

2014, Dec. 2 **Litho.** *Perf. 14¼*
Flocked Granite Paper
B492-B493 SP127 Set of 2 4.00 4.00

Automobiles
SP128

Designs: 60c+5c, 1899 De Dion-Bouton Vis-à-vis Type D. 85c+10c, 1904 Peugeot Bébé. €1.10+10c, 1909 Opel 10/20. €1.20+25c, 1910 Renault AX.

Litho. & Embossed With Foil Application

2014, Dec. 2 *Perf. 13x13¼*
B494-B497 SP128 Set of 4 10.50 10.50

See Nos. B500-B503, B506-B509.

Christmas — SP129

Trees in winter with denomination in: 70c+5c, Blue. 95c+10c, Orange.

Litho. & Thermography

2015, Dec. 1 *Perf. 13¼*
B498-B499 SP129 Set of 2 4.00 4.00

Automobiles Type of 2014

Designs: 70c+5c, 1913 Philos A 4M. 95c+10c, 1914 Morris Oxford Bullnose. €1.30+10c, 1918 Delaunay Belleville. €1.40+25c, 1919 Berliet V8.

Litho. & Embossed

2015, Dec. 1 *Perf. 13x13¼*
B500-B503 SP128 Set of 4 10.50 10.50

Christmas — SP130

St. Nicholas with: 70c+5c, Boy. 95c+10c, Girl and crowd.

2016, Dec. 6 **Litho.** *Perf. 13*
B504-B505 SP130 Set of 2 3.75 3.75

Automobiles Type of 2014

Designs: 70c+5c, 1924 Ford Model T. 95c+10c, 1924 Donnet Zedel Cl-6. €1.30+10c, 1927 Paige 6-45 sedan. €1.40+25c, 1928 Chenard Walcker Z5.

Litho. & Embossed

2016, Dec. 6 *Perf. 13x13¼*
B506-B509 SP128 Set of 4 10.00 10.00

Christmas — SP131

Designs: 70c+5c, Boy kissing girl. 95c+10c, Children putting star on top of Christmas tree.

2017, Dec. 5 **Litho.** *Perf. 13*
B510-B511 SP131 Set of 2 4.50 4.50

Automobiles Type of 2014

Designs: 70c+5c, 1931 Packard Standard Eight 833. 95c+10c, 1934 Rolls-Royce 20/25. €1.30+10c, 1936 Panhard & Levassor Panoramique 6DS X71. €1.40+25c, 1940 Buick 56C.

Litho. & Embossed

2017, Dec. 5 *Perf. 13x13¼*
B512-B515 SP128 Set of 4 12.00 12.00

Christmas — SP132

Decorated head of: 70c+5c, Man. 95c+10c, Woman.

Die Cut Perf. 13¼

2018, Dec. 4 **Litho.**
On Translucent Plastic Foil
Self-Adhesive
B516-B517 SP132 Set of 2 4.25 4.25

Grape Varieties of Moselle Region — SP133

Designs: 70c+5c, Riesling. 95c+10c, Pinot gris. €1.30+10c, Rivaner. €1.40+25c, Auxerrois.

2018, Dec. 4 Litho. *Perf. 13x13¼*

B518-B521	SP133	Set of 4	11.00	11.00

Mosselle Region Buildings SP134

Designs: 80c+10c, Zéintscheier, Grevenmacher. €1.05+15c, Vintner's house, Ahn. €1.40+15c, Winery, Remich. €1.60+30c, Vintner's house, Wellenstein.

Litho. & Engr.

2019, Dec. 3 *Perf. 11½*

B522-B525	SP134	Set of 4	12.50	12.50

Christmas — SP135

Collage depicting Christmas tree with background color of: 80c+10c, Magenta. €1.05+15c, Dark Ultramarine.

2019, Dec. 3 Litho. *Perf. 13¼*

B526-B527	SP135	Set of 2	4.75	4.75

Customs of the Moselle Region — SP136

Designs: 80c+10c, Schwebsingen Wine Festival. €1.05+15c, Coronation of the Wine Queen, Grevenmacher. €1.40+15c, Burning of the straw figure, Remich. €1.60+30c, Members of Brotherhood of St. Cunibert, Ehnen.

2020, Dec. 8 Litho. *Perf. 11½*

B528-B531	SP136	Set of 4	14.00	14.00

Christmas — SP137

Designs: 80c+10c, People at ice rink. €1.05+15c, Children building snowman and people walking in snow.

Litho. With Glitter Affixed

2020, Dec. 8 *Perf. 13¼*

B532-B533	SP137	Set of 2	5.25	5.25

Moselle Valley Towns SP138

Designs: 80c+10c, Schengen. €1.05+15c, Reimech. €1.40+15c, Meechtem. €1.60+30c, Greiwemaacher.

Digital Printing

2021, Nov. 16 *Perf. 12½*

B534-B537	SP138	Set of 4	12.50	12.50

Christmas — SP139

Stars with background color of: 80c+10c, Deep blue green. €1.05+15c, Red.

2021, Nov. 16 Litho. *Perf. 13¼*

B538-B539	SP139	Set of 2	4.75	4.75

Wild Orchids — SP140

Designs: €1+10c, Orchis purpurea. €1.40+15c, Dactylorhiza majalis. €1.75+15c, Cephalanthera damasonium. €2+30c, Ophrys apifera.

2022, Nov. 15 Litho. *Perf. 12*

B540-B543	SP140	Set of 4	14.50	14.50

Christmas — SP141

Designs: €1+10c, Forest animals decorating Christmas tree. €1.40+15c, Forest animals making snowman.

2022, Nov. 15 Litho. *Perf. 13*

B544-B545	SP141	Set of 2	5.50	5.50

AIR POST STAMPS

Airplane over Luxembourg AP1

1931-33 Unwmk. Engr. *Perf. 12½*

C1	AP1	50c green ('33)	.55	*1.10*
C2	AP1	75c dark brown	.55	*1.50*
C3	AP1	1fr red	.55	*1.50*
C4	AP1	1¼fr dark violet	.55	*1.50*
C5	AP1	1¾fr dark blue	.55	*1.50*
C6	AP1	3fr gray black ('33)	1.10	*5.00*
		Nos. C1-C6 (6)	3.85	*12.10*
		Set, never hinged	9.50	

Aerial View of Moselle River AP2

Wing and View of Luxembourg AP3

Vianden Castle — AP4

1946, June 7 Photo. *Perf. 11½*

C7	AP2	1fr dk ol grn & gray	.25	.25
C8	AP3	2fr chnt brn & buff	.25	*.25*
C9	AP4	3fr sepia & brown	.25	*.25*
C10	AP2	4fr dp vio & gray vio	.25	*.40*
C11	AP3	5fr dp mag & buff	.25	*.40*
C12	AP4	6fr dk brown & gray	.25	*.55*
C13	AP2	10fr henna brn & buff	.40	*.55*
C14	AP3	20fr dk blue & cream	.80	*2.00*
C15	AP4	50fr dk green & gray	1.25	2.50
		Nos. C7-C15 (9)	3.95	7.15
		Set, never hinged	8.00	

1852 and 1952 — AP5

Stamps in Gray and Dark Violet Brown

1952, May 24

C16	AP5	80c olive grn	.25	.45
C17	AP5	2.50fr brt car	.50	1.00
C18	AP5	4fr brt blue	1.60	2.50
C19	AP5	8fr brown red	17.50	*40.00*
C20	AP5	10fr dull brown	15.00	*30.00*
		Nos. C16-C20 (5)	34.85	*73.95*
		Set, never hinged	75.00	

Centenary of Luxembourg's postage stamps. Nos. C16-C18 were available at face, but complete sets sold for 45.30fr, which included admission to the CENTILUX exhibition.

POSTAGE DUE STAMPS

Coat of Arms — D1

1907 Unwmk. Typo. *Perf. 12½*

J1	D1	5c green & black	.25	*.25*
J2	D1	10c green & black	.95	.25
J3	D1	12½c green & black	.25	*.80*
J4	D1	20c green & black	.55	*.80*
J5	D1	25c green & black	16.00	1.20
J6	D1	50c green & black	.45	*3.50*
J7	D1	1fr green & black	.25	*3.50*
		Nos. J1-J7 (7)	18.70	10.30

See Nos. J10-J22.

Nos. J3, J5 Surcharged

1920

J8	D1	15c on 12½c	.50	*7.25*
J9	D1	30c on 25c	.60	*9.00*
		Set, never hinged	3.50	

Arms Type of 1907

1921-35

J10	D1	5c green & red	.25	*.40*
J11	D1	10c green & red	.25	*.35*
J12	D1	20c green & red	.25	*.35*
J13	D1	25c green & red	.25	*.35*
J14	D1	30c green & red	.55	*.60*
J15	D1	35c green & red ('35)	.55	.35
J16	D1	50c green & red	.55	*.60*
J17	D1	60c green & red ('28)	.45	*.50*
J18	D1	70c green & red ('35)	.55	.35
J19	D1	75c green & red ('30)	.55	.25
J20	D1	1fr green & red	.55	*1.10*
J21	D1	2fr green & red ('30)	.55	*6.50*
J22	D1	3fr green & red ('30)	1.60	*18.00*
		Nos. J10-J22 (13)	6.90	29.70
		Set, never hinged	27.50	

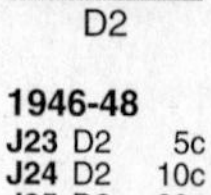

D2

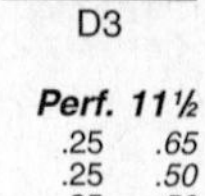

D3

1946-48 Photo. *Perf. 11½*

J23	D2	5c bright green	.25	*.65*
J24	D2	10c bright green	.25	*.50*
J25	D2	20c bright green	.25	*.50*
J26	D2	30c bright green	.25	*.50*
J27	D2	50c bright green	.25	*.70*
J28	D2	70c bright green	.25	*.70*
J29	D3	75c brt green ('48)	.70	.25
J30	D3	1fr carmine	.25	*.25*
J31	D3	1.50fr carmine	.25	*.25*
J32	D3	2fr carmine	.25	*.25*
J33	D3	3fr carmine	.25	*.35*
J34	D3	5fr carmine	.55	.45
J35	D3	10fr carmine	.95	*4.00*
J36	D3	20fr carmine	2.75	*22.50*
		Nos. J23-J36 (14)	7.45	31.85
		Set, never hinged	22.50	

REGISTRATION STAMPS

Roe Deer — R1

2022, May 17 Litho. *Perf. 13¾x14*

F1	R1	(€5) multi	11.00	11.00

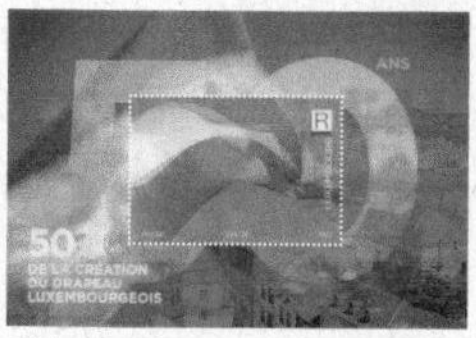

Flag of Luxembourg, 50th Anniv. — R2

Lenticular Printing

2022, May 17 *Perf. 14¼x14*

F2	R2	(€5) multi	11.00	11.00

OFFICIAL STAMPS

Forged overprints on Nos. O1-O64 abound.

Unused values of Nos. O1-O51 are for stamps without gum. Though these stamps were issued with gum, most examples offered are without gum. Stamps with original gum sell for somewhat more.

Regular Issues Overprinted Reading Diagonally Up or Down

Frankfurt Print

Rouletted in Color except 2c

1875 Unwmk.

O1	A2	1c red brown	27.50	37.50
O2	A2	2c black	27.50	37.50
O3	A3	10c lilac	2,400.	2,400.
O4	A3	12½c rose	475.00	600.00
O5	A3	20c gray brn	37.50	57.50
O6	A3	25c blue	250.00	140.00
O7	A3	25c ultra	2,100.	1,400.
O8	A3	30c lilac rose	32.50	*75.00*
O9	A3	40c pale org	160.00	240.00
a.		40c org red, thick paper	250.00	325.00
c.		As "a," thin paper	1,650.	1,400.
O10	A3	1fr on 37½c bis	150.00	22.50

Double overprints exist on Nos. O1-O6, O8-O10.

Overprints reading diagonally down sell for more.

Inverted Overprint

O1a	A2	1c	190.00	225.00
O2a	A2	2c	190.00	225.00
O3a	A3	10c	2,500.	2,500.
O4a	A3	12½c	650.00	925.00
O5a	A3	20c	55.00	75.00
O6a	A3	25c	1,100.	1,300.
O7a	A3	25c	2,100.	1,500.
O8a	A3	30c	650.00	925.00
O9b	A3	40c pale orange	325.00	450.00
O10a	A3	1fr on 37½c	175.00	75.00

Luxembourg Print

1875-76 *Perf. 13*

O11	A2	1c red brown	9.50	27.50
O12	A2	2c black	12.00	32.50
O13	A2	4c green	90.00	160.00
O14	A2	5c yellow	65.00	80.00
a.		5c orange yellow	75.00	110.00
O15	A3	10c gray lilac	92.50	120.00
O16	A3	12½c rose	85.00	120.00
O17	A3	12½c lilac rose	225.00	275.00
O18	A3	25c blue	11.00	*32.50*
O19	A3	1fr on 37½c bis	35.00	60.00
		Nos. O11-O19 (9)	625.00	907.50

Double overprints exist on Nos. O11-O15.

Inverted Overprint

O11a	A2	1c	92.50	*110.00*
O12a	A2	2c	150.00	190.00
O13a	A2	4c	160.00	190.00
O14b	A2	5c	500.00	650.00
O15a	A3	10c	500.00	190.00

O16a	A3	12½c	400.00	550.00
O17a	A3	12½c	450.00	525.00
O18a	A3	25c	125.00	175.00
O19a	A5	1fr on 37½c	190.00	250.00
		Nos. O11a-O19a (9)	2,568.	2,830.

Haarlem Print

1880 *Perf. 11½x12, 12½x12, 13½*

O22	A3	25c blue	2.25	2.75

Overprinted

Frankfurt Print

1878 *Rouletted in Color*

O23	A2	1c red brown	140.00	160.00
O25	A3	20c gray brn	190.00	225.00
O26	A3	30c lilac rose	750.00	575.00
O27	A3	40c orange	325.00	450.00
O28	A3	1fr on 37½c bis	550.00	110.00
		Nos. O23-O28 (5)	1,955.	1,520.

Inverted Overprint

O23a	A2	1c	225.00	300.00
O25a	A3	20c	325.00	400.00
O26a	A3	30c	925.00	700.00
O27a	A3	40c	875.00	925.00
O28a	A3	1fr on 37½c	650.00	200.00

Luxembourg Print

1878-80 *Perf. 13*

O29	A2	1c red brown	750.00	925.00
O30	A2	2c black	190.00	225.00
O31	A2	4c green	190.00	225.00
O32	A2	5c yellow	375.00	450.00
O33	A3	10c gray lilac	375.00	400.00
O34	A3	12½c rose	65.00	110.00
O35	A3	25c blue	525.00	550.00
		Nos. O29-O35 (7)	2,470.	2,885.

Inverted Overprint

O29a	A2	1c	140.00	160.00
O30a	A2	2c	14.50	27.50
O31a	A2	4c	150.00	190.00
O32a	A2	5c	1,500.	1,500.
O33a	A3	10c	92.50	110.00
O34a	A3	12½c	525.00	600.00
O35a	A3	25c	850.00	1,000.

Overprinted

Frankfurt Print

1881 *Rouletted in Color*

O39	A3	40c orange	37.50	75.00
a.		Inverted overprint	210.00	275.00

"S.P." are initials of "Service Public."

Luxembourg Print
Perf. 13

O40	A2	1c red brown	125.00	160.00
O41	A2	4c green	175.00	200.00
a.		Inverted overprint	250.00	
O42	A2	5c yellow	600.00	750.00
O43	A3	1fr on 37½c bis	32.50	47.50
		Nos. O40-O43 (4)	932.50	1,158.

Haarlem Print
Perf. 11½x12, 12½x12, 13½

O44	A2	1c yellow brn	8.50	9.25
O45	A2	2c black	9.25	9.25
O46	A2	5c yellow	160.00	200.00
a.		Inverted overprint	225.00	
O47	A3	10c gray lilac	160.00	200.00
O48	A3	12½c rose	175.00	240.00
O49	A3	20c gray brown	72.50	92.50
O50	A3	25c blue	72.50	92.50
O51	A3	30c dull rose	75.00	120.00
		Nos. O44-O51 (8)	732.75	963.50

Stamps of the 1881 issue with the overprint of the 1882 issue shown below were never issued.

Overprinted

Perf. 11½x12, 12½x12, 12½, 13½

1882

O52	A6	1c gray lilac	.25	.40
O53	A6	2c ol gray	.25	.40
a.		"S" omitted	110.00	
O54	A6	4c ol bister	.25	.45
O55	A6	5c lt green	.25	.55
O56	A6	10c rose	12.00	16.00
O57	A6	12½c slate	1.60	4.75
O58	A6	20c orange	1.60	4.00
O59	A6	25c ultra	19.00	24.00
O60	A6	30c gray grn	4.00	8.75
O61	A6	50c bis brown	.95	2.75
O62	A6	1fr pale vio	.95	4.00
O63	A6	5fr brown org	16.00	40.00
		Nos. O52-O63 (12)	57.10	106.05

Nos. O52-O63 exist without one or both periods, also with varying space between "S" and "P." Nine denominations exist with double overprint, six with inverted overprint.

Overprinted

1883 *Perf. 13½*

O64	A6	5fr brown org	2,200.	2,200.

Overprinted

1891-93 *Perf. 11, 11½, 11½x11, 12½*

O65	A7	10c carmine	.25	.50
a.		Sheet of 25	55.00	
O66	A7	12½c slate grn	8.00	7.25
O67	A7	20c orange	13.00	8.50
O68	A7	25c blue	.25	.45
a.		Sheet of 25	65.00	
O69	A7	30c olive grn	8.00	8.00
O70	A7	37½c green	8.00	8.00
O71	A7	50c brown	6.00	8.75
O72	A7	1fr dp vio	8.00	9.50
O73	A7	2½fr black	45.00	72.50
O74	A7	5fr lake	40.00	55.00
		Nos. O65-O74 (10)	136.50	178.45

1895 *Perf. 12½*

O75	A8	1c pearl gray	1.90	2.50
O76	A8	2c gray brn	.75	2.00
O77	A8	4c olive bis	.75	2.00
O78	A8	5c green	2.25	3.50
O79	A8	10c carmine	40.00	40.00
		Nos. O75-O79 (5)	45.65	50.00

Nos. O66-O79 exist without overprint and perforated "OFFICIEL" through the stamp. Values for set: unused, $12; used, $45.

Nos. O65a and O68a were issued to commemorate the coronation of Grand Duke Adolphe.

Regular Issue of 1906-26 Overprinted

1908-26 *Perf. 11x11½, 12½*

O80	A9	1c gray	.25	.40
a.		Inverted overprint	125.00	
O81	A9	2c olive brn	.25	.40
O82	A9	4c bister	.25	.40
a.		Double overprint	140.00	
O83	A9	5c green	.25	.40
O84	A9	5c lilac ('26)	.25	.40
O85	A9	6c violet	.25	.40
O86	A9	7½c org ('19)	.25	.40
O87	A10	10c scarlet	.25	.40
O88	A10	12½c slate grn	.25	.55
O89	A10	15c orange brn	.25	.55
O90	A10	20c orange	.25	.75
O91	A10	25c ultra	.25	.75
O92	A10	30c olive grn	2.75	6.50
O93	A10	37½c green	.45	.75
O94	A10	50c brown	.75	1.50
O95	A10	87½c dk blue	2.00	3.50
O96	A10	1fr violet	2.75	4.00
O97	A10	2½fr vermilion	75.00	65.00
O98	A10	5fr claret	55.00	45.00
		Nos. O80-O98 (19)	141.70	132.05

On Regular Issue of 1914-17

1915-17

O99	A11	10c lake	.25	.75
O100	A11	12½c dull grn	.25	.75
O101	A11	15c olive blk	.25	.75
O102	A11	17½c dp brn ('17)	.25	.75
O103	A11	25c ultra	.25	.75
O104	A11	30c bister	1.40	5.00
O105	A11	35c dk blue	.25	1.20
O106	A11	37½c blk brn	.25	1.60
O107	A11	40c orange	.30	1.20
O108	A11	50c dk gray	.30	.95
O109	A11	62½c blue grn	.30	1.60
O110	A11	87½c org ('17)	.30	1.60
O111	A11	1fr orange brn	.30	1.60
O112	A11	2½fr red	.30	2.50
O113	A11	5fr dk violet	.30	2.75
		Nos. O99-O113 (15)	5.25	23.75

On Regular Issues of 1921-26 in Black

1922-26 *Perf. 11½, 11½x11, 12½*

O114	A12	2c brown	.25	.25
O115	A12	3c olive grn	.25	.25
O116	A12	6c violet	.25	.40
O117	A12	10c yellow grn	.25	.40
O118	A12	10c ol grn ('24)	.25	.40
O119	A12	15c brown ol	.25	.40
O120	A12	15c pale grn ('24)	.25	.40
O121	A12	15c dp org ('26)	.25	.40
O122	A12	20c dp orange	.25	.40
O123	A12	20c yel grn ('26)	.25	.40
O124	A12	25c dk green	.25	.40
O125	A12	30c car rose	.25	.40
O126	A12	40c brown org	.25	.40
O127	A12	50c dp blue	.25	.45
O128	A12	50c red ('24)	.25	.55
O129	A12	75c red	.25	.55
O130	A12	75c dp bl ('24)	.25	.45
O131	A12	80c black	4.75	8.00
O132	A13	1fr carmine	.40	2.00
O133	A14	2fr indigo	3.00	6.00
O134	A14	2fr dk brn ('26)	1.75	5.00
O135	A15	5fr dk vio	17.50	40.00
		Nos. O114-O135 (22)	31.65	67.90

On Regular Issues of 1921-26 in Red

1922-34 *Perf. 11, 11½, 11½x11, 12½*

O136	A12	80c blk, perf. 11½	.25	.45
O137	A13	1fr dk bl, perf. 11½ ('26)	.25	1.20
O138	A14	2fr ind, perf. 11½x11	.55	2.00
O139	A17	3fr dk bl & bl, perf. 11	2.75	2.75
a.		Perf. 11½	.60	1.40
b.		Perf. 12½	.50	1.40
O140	A15	5fr dk vio, perf. 11½x11	4.00	9.00
a.		Perf. 12½ ('34)	12.00	20.00
O141	A16	10fr blk, perf. 11½	12.00	24.00
a.		Perf. 12½	12.00	27.50
		Nos. O136-O141 (6)	19.80	39.40

On Regular Issue of 1926-35

1926-27 *Perf. 12*

O142	A18	5c dk violet	.25	.25
O143	A18	10c olive grn	.25	.25
O144	A18	20c orange	.25	.25
O145	A18	25c yellow grn	.25	.25
O146	A18	25c blk brn ('27)	.35	.55
O147	A18	30c yel grn ('27)	.65	1.20
O148	A18	40c olive gray	.25	.25
O149	A18	50c red brown	.25	.25
O150	A18	65c black brn	.25	.25
O151	A18	75c rose	.25	.25
O152	A18	75c bis brn ('27)	.35	.55
O153	A18	80c bister brn	.25	.40
O154	A18	90c rose ('27)	.35	.55
O155	A18	1fr black	.25	.45
O156	A18	1¼fr dk blue	.25	.45
O157	A18	1½fr dp blue ('27)	.55	1.20
		Nos. O142-O157 (16)	5.00	7.35

Type of Regular Issue, 1926-35, Overprinted

1928-35 Wmk. 213

O158	A18	5c dk violet	.25	.40
O159	A18	10c olive grn	.25	.40
O160	A18	15c black ('30)	.25	1.20
O161	A18	20c orange	.45	.75
O162	A18	25c violet brn	.45	.75
O163	A18	30c yellow grn	.50	1.40
O164	A18	30c gray vio ('30)	.25	1.20
O165	A18	35c yel grn ('30)	.25	1.20
O166	A18	35c gray vio	.35	.90
O167	A18	40c olive gray	.35	.75
O168	A18	50c red brown	.35	.75
O169	A18	60c blue grn	.35	.75
O170	A18	70c blue vio ('35)	3.50	7.25
O171	A18	75c bister brn	.35	.75
O172	A18	90c rose	.35	1.20
O173	A18	1fr black	.35	1.20
O174	A18	1fr rose ('30)	.45	2.40
O175	A18	1¼fr yel ('30)	4.00	6.50
O176	A18	1¼fr bl grn ('31)	1.50	4.00
O177	A18	1½fr deep blue	.35	1.40
O178	A18	1¾fr dk blue ('30)	.45	1.60
		Nos. O158-O178 (21)	15.35	36.75

Type of Regular Issues of 1928-31 Overprinted Like Nos. O80-O98

1928-31 Wmk. 216 *Perf. 11½*

O179	A19	2fr black	.50	1.60

Wmk. 110 *Perf. 12½*

O180	A21	20fr dp green ('31)	2.25	8.00

No. 198 Overprinted Like Nos. O80-O98

1934 Unwmk. *Perf. 14x13½*

O181	A22	5fr blue green	2.10	6.00

Type of Regular Issue of 1935 Overprinted Like Nos. O158-O178 in Red

1935 Wmk. 247 *Perf. 12½x12*

O182	A23	10fr green	1.75	7.00

OCCUPATION STAMPS

Issued under German Occupation

Stamps of Germany, 1933-36, Overprinted in Black

1940, Oct. 1 Wmk. 237 *Perf. 14*

N1	A64	3pf olive bis	.25	.25
N2	A64	4pf dull blue	.25	.25
N3	A64	5pf brt grn	.25	.25
N4	A64	6pf dark green	.25	.25
N5	A64	8pf vermilion	.25	.25
N6	A64	10pf chocolate	.25	.25
N7	A64	12pf deep car	.25	.25
N8	A64	15pf maroon	.35	.45
a.		Inverted overprint	450.00	1,300.
N9	A64	20pf bright blue	.50	.45
N10	A64	25pf ultra	.50	.60
N11	A64	30pf olive green	.50	.60
N12	A64	40pf red violet	.50	.75
N13	A64	50pf dk grn & blk	.60	.75
N14	A64	60pf claret & blk	.90	3.00
N15	A64	80pf dk blue & blk	2.25	9.00
N16	A64	100pf org & blk	1.60	4.50
		Nos. N1-N16 (16)	9.45	21.85
		Set, never hinged	24.00	

Nos. 159-162, 164, 168-171, 173, 175, 179, 182, 216, 198-199 Surcharged in Black

a

b

c

d

Perf. 12, 14x13½, 12½x12, 11½

1940, Dec. 5 Unwmk.

N17	A18(a)	3rpf on 15c	.25	.35
N18	A18(a)	4rpf on 20c	.25	.35
N19	A18(a)	5rpf on 35c	.25	.35
N20	A18(a)	6rpf on 10c	.25	.35
N21	A18(a)	8rpf on 25c	.25	.35
N22	A18(a)	10rpf on 40c	.25	.35
N23	A18(a)	12rpf on 60c	.25	.35
N24	A18(a)	15rpf on 1fr rose	.25	.35
N25	A18(a)	20rpf on 50c	.25	.60
N26	A18(a)	25rpf on 5c	.25	1.20
N27	A18(a)	30rpf on 70c	.25	.60
N28	A18(a)	40rpf on 75c	.30	1.20
N29	A18(a)	50rpf on 1¼fr	.25	.60
N30	A35(b)	60rpf on 2fr	1.40	9.50
N31	A22(c)	80rpf on 5fr	.40	2.00
N32	A23(d)	100rpf on 10fr	.65	2.75
		Nos. N17-N32 (16)	5.75	21.25
		Set, never hinged	9.00	

OCCUPATION SEMI-POSTAL STAMPS

Semi-Postal Stamps of Germany, 1940 Overprinted in Black

1941, Jan. 12 Unwmk. *Perf. 14*

NB1	SP153	3pf + 2pf dk brn	.25	.45
NB2	SP153	4pf + 3pf bluish blk	.25	.45

NB3	SP153	5pf + 3pf yel grn	.25	*.45*
NB4	SP153	6pf + 4pf dk grn	.25	*.45*
NB5	SP153	8pf + 4pf dp org	.25	*.45*
NB6	SP153	12pf + 6pf carmine	.25	*.45*
NB7	SP153	15pf + 10pf dk vio brn	1.25	*1.60*
NB8	SP153	25pf + 15pf dp ultra	1.25	*3.50*
NB9	SP153	40pf + 35pf red lil	2.25	*6.00*
		Nos. NB1-NB9 (9)	6.25	*13.80*
		Set, never hinged	10.00	

Vols. 4A-4B number additions, deletions and changes

Number in 2023 Catalogue	Number in 2024 Catalogue

No changes

INDEX AND IDENTIFIER

All page numbers shown are those in this Volume 4A.

Postage stamps that do not have English words on them are shown in the Scott *Stamp Illustrated Identifier*. To purchase it visit AmosAdvantage.com or call Amos Media at 800-572-6885.

INDEX TO ADVERTISERS 2024 VOLUME 4A

2024
VOLUME 4A
DEALER DIRECTORY
YELLOW PAGE LISTINGS

This section of your Scott Catalogue contains advertisements to help you conveniently find what you need, when you need it...!

Appraisals

DR. ROBERT FRIEDMAN & SONS STAMP & COIN BUYING CENTER
2029 W. 75th St.
Woodridge, IL 60517
PH: 800-588-8100
FAX: 630-985-1588
stampcollections@drbobstamps.com
www.drbobfriedmanstamps.com

Auctions

DUTCH COUNTRY AUCTIONS
The Stamp Center
4115 Concord Pike
Wilmington, DE 19803
PH: 302-478-8740
FAX: 302-478-8779
auctions@dutchcountryauctions.com
www.dutchcountryauctions.com

KELLEHER & ROGERS LTD.
4 Finance Drive, Ste. 200
Danbury, CT 06810
PH: 203-297-6056
FAX: 203-297-6059
info@kelleherauctions.com
www.kelleherauctions.com

British Asia

THE STAMP ACT
PO Box 1136
Belmont, CA 94002
PH: 650-703-2342
thestampact@sbcglobal.net

British Commonwealth

ARON R. HALBERSTAM PHILATELISTS, LTD.
PO Box 150168
Van Brunt Station
Brooklyn, NY 11215-0168
PH: 718-788-3978
arh@arhstamps.com
www.arhstamps.com

ROY'S STAMPS
PO Box 28001
600 Ontario Street
St. Catharines, ON
CANADA L2N 7P8
Phone: 905-934-8377
Email: roystamp@cogeco.ca
www.roysstamps.com

THE STAMP ACT
PO Box 1136
Belmont, CA 94002
PH: 650-703-2342
thestampact@sbcglobal.net

Buying

DR. ROBERT FRIEDMAN & SONS STAMP & COIN BUYING CENTER
2029 W. 75th St.
Woodridge, IL 60517
PH: 800-588-8100
FAX: 630-985-1588
stampcollections@drbobstamps.com
www.drbobfriedmanstamps.com

Canada

CANADA STAMP FINDER LLC
2800 N 6th Street, Unit 1-708
St. Augustine, FL 32084
PH: 904-217-2166
Canadian Address:
PO Box 92591
Brampton, ON L6W 4R1
PH: 514-238-5751
Toll Free in North America:
877-412-3106
FAX: 323-315-2635
canadastampfinder@gmail.com
www.canadastampfinder.com

ROY'S STAMPS
PO Box 28001
600 Ontario Street
St. Catharines, ON
CANADA L2N 7P8
Phone: 905-934-8377
Email: roystamp@cogeco.ca
www.roysstamps.com

Collections

DR. ROBERT FRIEDMAN & SONS STAMP & COIN BUYING CENTER
2029 W. 75th St.
Woodridge, IL 60517
PH: 800-588-8100
FAX: 630-985-1588
stampcollections@drbobstamps.com
www.drbobfriedmanstamps.com

Ducks

MICHAEL JAFFE
PO Box 61484
Vancouver, WA 98666
PH: 360-695-6161
PH: 800-782-6770
FAX: 360-695-1616
mjaffe@brookmanstamps.com
www.brookmanstamps.com

German Colonies

COLONIAL STAMP COMPANY
5757 Wilshire Blvd. PH #8
Los Angeles, CA 90036
PH: 323-933-9435
FAX: 323-939-9930
info@colonialstamps.com
www.colonialstamps.com

Great Britain

COLONIAL STAMP COMPANY
5757 Wilshire Blvd. PH #8
Los Angeles, CA 90036
PH: 323-933-9435
FAX: 323-939-9930
info@colonialstamps.com
www.colonialstamps.com

Japan

ASIA PHILATELICS
3276 Andora Drive
San Jose, CA 95148
PH: 408-238-0893
Richard@asiaphilatelics.com

THE STAMP ACT
PO Box 1136
Belmont, CA 94002
PH: 650-703-2342
thestampact@sbcglobal.net

Kenya, Uganda, Tanzania

COLONIAL STAMP COMPANY
5757 Wilshire Blvd. PH #8
Los Angeles, CA 90036
PH: 323-933-9435
FAX: 323-939-9930
info@colonialstamps.com
www.colonialstamps.com

Kiauchau (German)

COLONIAL STAMP COMPANY
5757 Wilshire Blvd. PH #8
Los Angeles, CA 90036
PH: 323-933-9435
FAX: 323-939-9930
info@colonialstamps.com
www.colonialstamps.com

Leeward Islands

COLONIAL STAMP COMPANY
5757 Wilshire Blvd. PH #8
Los Angeles, CA 90036
PH: 323-933-9435
FAX: 323-939-9930
info@colonialstamps.com
www.colonialstamps.com

Liechtenstein

HENRY GITNER PHILATELISTS, INC.
PO Box 3077-S
Middletown, NY 10940
PH: 845-343-5151
PH: 800-947-8267
FAX: 845-343-0068
hgitner@hgitner.com
www.hgitner.com

Luxembourg

HENRY GITNER PHILATELISTS, INC.
PO Box 3077-S
Middletown, NY 10940
PH: 845-343-5151
PH: 800-947-8267
FAX: 845-343-0068
hgitner@hgitner.com
www.hgitner.com

Madagascar (British Issues)

COLONIAL STAMP COMPANY
5757 Wilshire Blvd. PH #8
Los Angeles, CA 90036
PH: 323-933-9435
FAX: 323-939-9930
info@colonialstamps.com
www.colonialstamps.com

Malaya

COLONIAL STAMP COMPANY
5757 Wilshire Blvd. PH #8
Los Angeles, CA 90036
PH: 323-933-9435
FAX: 323-939-9930
info@colonialstamps.com
www.colonialstamps.com

THE STAMP ACT
PO Box 1136
Belmont, CA 94002
PH: 650-703-2342
thestampact@sbcglobal.net

Mariana Islands (Ger & Sp)

COLONIAL STAMP COMPANY
5757 Wilshire Blvd. PH #8
Los Angeles, CA 90036
PH: 323-933-9435
FAX: 323-939-9930
info@colonialstamps.com
www.colonialstamps.com

British Commonwealth

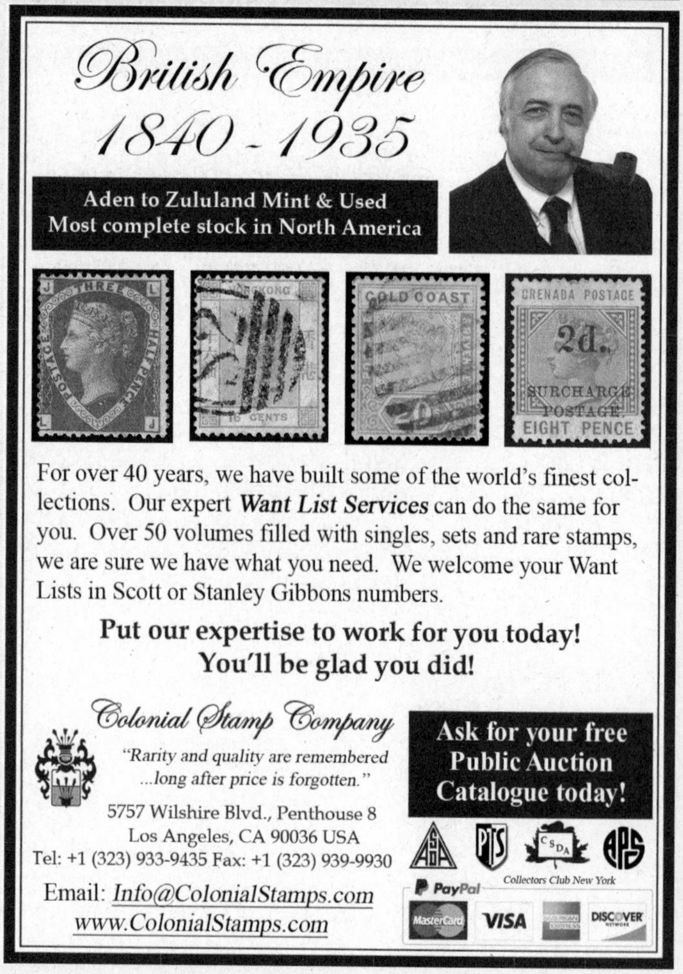

Marshall Islands

COLONIAL STAMP COMPANY
5757 Wilshire Blvd. PH #8
Los Angeles, CA 90036
PH: 323-933-9435
FAX: 323-939-9930
info@colonialstamps.com
www.colonialstamps.com

Mauritius

COLONIAL STAMP COMPANY
5757 Wilshire Blvd. PH #8
Los Angeles, CA 90036
PH: 323-933-9435
FAX: 323-939-9930
info@colonialstamps.com
www.colonialstamps.com

Mesopotamia

COLONIAL STAMP COMPANY
5757 Wilshire Blvd. PH #8
Los Angeles, CA 90036
PH: 323-933-9435
FAX: 323-939-9930
info@colonialstamps.com
www.colonialstamps.com

Natal

COLONIAL STAMP COMPANY
5757 Wilshire Blvd. PH #8
Los Angeles, CA 90036
PH: 323-933-9435
FAX: 323-939-9930
info@colonialstamps.com
www.colonialstamps.com

New Britain

COLONIAL STAMP COMPANY
5757 Wilshire Blvd. PH #8
Los Angeles, CA 90036
PH: 323-933-9435
FAX: 323-939-9930
info@colonialstamps.com
www.colonialstamps.com

New Issues

DAVIDSON'S STAMP SERVICE
Personalized Service since 1970
PO Box 36355
Indianapolis, IN 46236-0355
PH: 317-826-2620
ed-davidson@earthlink.net
www.newstampissues.com

New Zealand

COLONIAL STAMP COMPANY
5757 Wilshire Blvd. PH #8
Los Angeles, CA 90036
PH: 323-933-9435
FAX: 323-939-9930
info@colonialstamps.com
www.colonialstamps.com

Niger Coast Protectorate

COLONIAL STAMP COMPANY
5757 Wilshire Blvd. PH #8
Los Angeles, CA 90036
PH: 323-933-9435
FAX: 323-939-9930
info@colonialstamps.com
www.colonialstamps.com

Orange River Colony

COLONIAL STAMP COMPANY
5757 Wilshire Blvd. PH #8
Los Angeles, CA 90036
PH: 323-933-9435
FAX: 323-939-9930
info@colonialstamps.com
www.colonialstamps.com

Proofs & Essays

HENRY GITNER PHILATELISTS, INC.
PO Box 3077-S
Middletown, NY 10940
PH: 845-343-5151
PH: 800-947-8267
FAX: 845-343-0068
hgitner@hgitner.com
www.hgitner.com

Rhodesia

COLONIAL STAMP COMPANY
5757 Wilshire Blvd. PH #8
Los Angeles, CA 90036
PH: 323-933-9435
FAX: 323-939-9930
info@colonialstamps.com
www.colonialstamps.com

Stamp Stores

California

COLONIAL STAMP COMPANY
5757 Wilshire Blvd. PH #8
Los Angeles, CA 90036
PH: 323-933-9435
FAX: 323-939-9930
info@colonialstamps.com
www.colonialstamps.com

Delaware

DUTCH COUNTRY AUCTIONS
The Stamp Center
4115 Concord Pike
Wilmington, DE 19803
PH: 302-478-8740
FAX: 302-478-8779
auctions@dutchcountryauctions.com
www.dutchcountryauctions.com

Florida

DR. ROBERT FRIEDMAN & SONS STAMP & COIN BUYING CENTER
PH: 800-588-8100
FAX: 630-985-1588
stampcollections@drbobstamps.com
www.drbobfriedmanstamps.com

Illinois

DR. ROBERT FRIEDMAN & SONS STAMP & COIN BUYING CENTER
2029 W. 75th St.
Woodridge, IL 60517
PH: 800-588-8100
FAX: 630-985-1588
stampcollections@drbobstamps.com
www.drbobfriedmanstamps.com

Indiana

KNIGHT STAMP & COIN CO.
237 Main St.
Hobart, IN 46342
PH: 219-942-4341
PH: 800-634-2646
knight@knightcoin.com
www.knightcoin.com

New Jersey

BERGEN STAMPS & COLLECTIBLES
306 Queen Anne Rd.
Teaneck, NJ 07666
PH: 201-836-8987
bergenstamps@gmail.com

Stamp Stores

New Jersey

TRENTON STAMP & COIN
Thomas DeLuca
Store: Forest Glen Plaza
1800 Highway #33, Suite 103
Hamilton Square, NJ 08690
Mail: PO Box 8574
Trenton, NJ 08650
PH: 609-584-8100
FAX: 609-587-8664
TOMD4TSC@aol.com
www.trentonstampandcoin.com

New York

CHAMPION STAMP CO., INC.
432 West 54th St.
New York, NY 10019
PH: 212-489-8130
FAX: 212-581-8130
championstamp@aol.com
www.championstamp.com

Ohio

HILLTOP STAMP SERVICE
Richard A. Peterson
PO Box 626
Wooster, OH 44691
PH: 330-262-8907 (0)
PH: 330-201-1377 (H)
hilltop@bright.net
hilltopstamps@sssnet.com
www.hilltopstamps.com

Supplies

BROOKLYN GALLERY COIN & STAMP, INC.
8725 4th Ave.
Brooklyn, NY 11209
PH: 718-745-5701
FAX: 718-745-2775
info@brooklyngallery.com
www.brooklyngallery.com

Topicals

E. JOSEPH MCCONNELL, INC.
PO Box 683
Monroe, NY 10949
PH: 845-783-9791
ejstamps@gmail.com
www.EJMcConnell.com

Topicals - Columbus

MR. COLUMBUS
PO Box 1492
Fennville, MI 49408
PH: 269-543-4755
David@MrColumbus1492.com
www.MrColumbus1492.com

United States

ACS STAMP COMPANY
2914 W 135th Ave
Broomfield, Colorado 80020
303-841-8666
www.ACSStamp.com

BROOKMAN STAMP CO.
PO Box 90
Vancouver, WA 98666
PH: 360-695-1391
PH: 800-545-4871
FAX: 360-695-1616
info@brookmanstamps.com
www.brookmanstamps.com

U.S. Classics/Moderns

BARDO STAMPS
PO Box 7437
Buffalo Grove, IL 60089
PH: 847-634-2676
jfb7437@aol.com
www.bardostamps.com

U.S.-Collections Wanted

DUTCH COUNTRY AUCTIONS
The Stamp Center
4115 Concord Pike
Wilmington, DE 19803
PH: 302-478-8740
FAX: 302-478-8779
auctions@dutchcountryauctions.com
www.dutchcountryauctions.com

DR. ROBERT FRIEDMAN & SONS STAMP & COIN BUYING CENTER
2029 W. 75th St.
Woodridge, IL 60517
PH: 800-588-8100
FAX: 630-985-1588
stampcollections@drbobstamps.com
www.drbobfriedmanstamps.com

Want Lists - British Empire 1840-1935 German Cols./Offices

COLONIAL STAMP COMPANY
5757 Wilshire Blvd. PH #8
Los Angeles, CA 90036
PH: 323-933-9435
FAX: 323-939-9930
info@colonialstamps.com
www.colonialstamps.com

Wanted - Worldwide Collections

DUTCH COUNTRY AUCTIONS
The Stamp Center
4115 Concord Pike
Wilmington, DE 19803
PH: 302-478-8740
FAX: 302-478-8779
auctions@dutchcountryauctions.com
www.dutchcountryauctions.com

KELLEHER & ROGERS LTD.
4 Finance Drive, Ste. 200
Danbury, CT 06810
PH: 203-297-6056
FAX: 203-297-6059
info@kelleherauctions.com
www.kelleherauctions.com

Websites

ACS STAMP COMPANY
2914 W 135th Ave
Broomfield, Colorado 80020
303-841-8666
www.ACSStamp.com

Worldwide

GUILLERMO JALIL
Maipu 466, local 4
1006 Buenos Aires
Argentina
guillermo@jalilstamps.com
philatino@philatino.com
www.philatino.com (worldwide stamp auctions)
www.jalilstamps.com (direct sale, worldwide stamps)

Worldwide-Collections

DR. ROBERT FRIEDMAN & SONS STAMP & COIN BUYING CENTER
2029 W. 75th St.
Woodridge, IL 60517
PH: 800-588-8100
FAX: 630-985-1588
stampcollections@drbobstamps.com
www.drbobfriedmanstamps.com